# FOOTBALL
# YEARBOOK
# 2013-2014

**Compiled by**
**John Anderson**

**Front cover photographs:** (left and background) Robin van Persie (Manchester United) – *Action Images/Carl Recine*; (centre) Rickie Lambert (Southampton) – *Offside/Rex Features*; (right) Theo Walcott (Arsenal) – *Action Images/Alan Walter*

**Spine photograph:** Sir Alex Ferguson with the Barclays Premier League trophy – *Martin Rickett/PA Wire/Press Association Images*

**Back cover photographs:** (above) Chelsea v Benfica, Europa League final – *Reuters/Michael Kooren/Action Images*; (below) Mihael Kovacevic (Ross County) and Emilio Izaguirre (Celtic) – *Action Images/Graham Stuart Livepic*

Cataloguing in Publication Data is available from the British Library

ISBN 978 0 7553 6412 1 (Hardback)
ISBN 978 0 7553 6413 8 (Trade paperback)

Typeset by Wearset Ltd, Boldon, Tyne and Wear

Printed and bound in the UK by
CPI Mackays, Chatham ME5 8TD

Headline's policy is to use papers that are natural, renewable and recyclable products and made from wood grown in sustainable forests. The logging and manufacturing processes are expected to conform to the environmental regulations of the country of origin.

HEADLINE PUBLISHING GROUP
An Hachette UK Company
338 Euston Road
London NW1 3BH

www.headline.co.uk
www.hachette.co.uk

# CONTENTS

## INTERNATIONAL FOOTBALL

## NON-LEAGUE FOOTBALL

## INFORMATION AND RECORDS

# WELCOME

Welcome to the 2013–14 edition of the *Sky Sports Football Yearbook*.

I can't wait for the new season to begin. As well as promising all the thrills and spills we've come to expect, it's also the biggest ever season of football on Sky Sports with 116 live Barclays Premier League games and unrivalled Football League coverage as part of a schedule of over 500 live matches from the domestic, European and international game.

And as football fans through and through, we can't wait to get started.

We aim to provide our viewers with the best seat in the house if they aren't at the game. We've invested in our football coverage over the years, providing enhanced viewing with technologies such as HD and 3D, and Sky Go plus our portfolio of apps have brought live football on the move. Our on-air touchscreen technology, interactive coverage and multi-match choice all immerse the viewer in even greater depth.

This season we're pleased to welcome new people, studios, technology and programming to our line-up. We're honoured that Jamie Carragher has chosen to join us following his retirement from the pitch, bringing with him current insight, experience and incredible knowledge of the game. On air, we've launched new programming to augment our football coverage as well as bringing fresh ideas to enhance the stalwart favourites.

Sky Sports News remains an integral part of our coverage of the game, delivering breaking exclusive stories to Sky Sports viewers first and fast alongside reliable round-the-clock news. The bi-annual Transfer Deadline Day on Sky Sports News has flourished into one of the highlights of the season.

Sky Sports has been a supporter, investor, partner and fan of football for over 22 years now. Our commitment to the game is evident not only from this long-standing and successful partnership but also from our passion for and investment in the game at all levels. Most recently, David Beckham has joined the Sky family, and will be a fantastic ambassador alongside Jessica Ennis supporting our secondary schools sport initiative Sky Sports Living For Sport.

As always you can be sure we'll strive to deliver the best coverage and programming, and to ensure that Sky Sports continues to be the benchmark for sports broadcasting.

To those teams enjoying a hard-earned promotion – congratulations. And to every team across the leagues – good luck. We can't wait to get underway.

**Barney Francis**
**Sky Sports Managing Director**

Barney Francis

# FOREWORD

The 2013–2014 season will kick off in August and, as always, we are enthralled by the next campaign before it has even begun.

Truth is, this intense focus on next season started before the old one had even finished. In the Premier League, we witnessed the end of an era when Sir Alex called it a day at United, then a changing of the guard when Mancini parted ways with trophy-less City. Who could have predicted both Manchester giants would face such early upheaval? The questions that arise from this series of events set the tone for further excitement and discussion.

For starters, how will both clubs fare under the new leadership of Moyes and Pellegrini? Will United be business as usual? How well will City's new boss answer the same queries as he grapples with his paymaster's hurried desire to rule the football world?

And does all this uncertainty in Manchester mean there is new hope for the London pretenders to the throne: Arsenal, Spurs and Chelsea?

Can Chelsea's re-appointment of 'The Chosen One' trump the strange success of 'Rafa the Misfit', who lifted silverware but still left Stamford Bridge friendless? Mourinho's efforts to disprove the old saying 'never go back' will surely make for compelling viewing.

And what of Arsenal next season? Will Arsene Wenger strengthen his squad wisely, sensationally or both? Will his players build on their tremendous finish to last season? Are the board as hungry and as driven for success as the paying faithful? Time will tell.

Whatever your team or league, and whatever questions lie unanswered, the football season is coming around once more. Again it is sure to create high drama, showcase incredible skill and athleticism, huge passion, sheer joy and – for some – utter heartbreak. We will see punishing levels of commitment from great players, great coaches and great referees and we'll wonder at what goes wrong as well as at success. From top to bottom we will be entertained week in, week out, as all manner of stories unfold. Throw in the best TV coverage and the most passionate fans in world sport, then we really do have something special to look forward to. It has the makings of a truly vintage year and I have the great privilege of watching the action play out from the best seat in the house. I look forward to your company.

**Niall Quinn**

Niall Quinn

# INTRODUCTION

The 44th edition of the Yearbook, our eleventh with sponsors Sky Sports, is our first in the modern era without the magnificent Jack and Glenda Rollin. They have moved on to ventures new – not retired, or out to pasture – but continuing life's great adventure with new and equally rewarding projects. We were all deeply sorry to lose them.

It would be difficult to fully encapsulate the extraordinary contributions Jack and Glenda have made to the Yearbook over the years. Jack's involvement stretches back to the very beginning and he has been editor since the 19th edition for the 1988–89 season. He was then joined by his daughter Glenda as assistant editor for the 26th edition and as joint editor from the 27th edition. Their dedication, good humour, humility, work ethic, not to mention extraordinary attention to detail, will be greatly missed. Everyone associated with this publication owes them both a huge debt of gratitude. We can only hope to live up to them.

With Sir Alex Ferguson announcing his retirement at the end of last season, career statistics for this icon of the modern domestic game have been included.

The concise feature entitled Cups and Ups and Downs is again included with dates of those events affecting cup finals, plus promotion and relegation issues.

This new edition gives full coverage of the World Cup 2014 qualifying competition for Europe and South America including full line-ups for each qualifying match. Results and league tables are included for all of the qualifying matches throughout the rest of the world. Other international football at various levels is also well catered for in this edition.

At European level, both the Champions League and Europa League have their usual comprehensive details included, with results, goalscorers, attendances, full line-ups and formations from the qualifying rounds onwards and also including all the league tables from the respective group stages onwards.

The 2012–13 season, whilst not as exciting as the previous chase for the Premier League title, had plenty of highlights. Two Premier League games with more than 10 goals and the first 5-5 draw in Premier League history. All these statistics are reproduced in the pages devoted to not only the Premier League, but the three Football League competitions too, as well as all major allied cup competitions.

While transfer fees are invariably those reported at the time and rarely given as official figures, the edition reflects those listed at the time.

In the club-by-club pages that contain the line-ups of all league matches, appearances are split into starting and substitute appearances. In the Players Directory the totals show figures combined.

Barnet move not only ground but division, their respective new homes being The Hive and the Football Conference.

The Players Directory and its accompanying A to Z index enables the reader to quickly find the club of any specific player.

Throughout the book players sent off are designated thus *, substitutes in the club pages are 12, 13 and 14. Included for the first time in main competitions are the formations for each team.

In addition to competitions already mentioned there is full coverage of Scottish Premier League and Scottish League and cup competitions. There are also sections devoted to Welsh, Irish, Women's football, the Under-21s and various other UEFA youth levels, schools, reserve team, academies, referees and the leading non-league competitions as well as the work of the chaplains at clubs. The chief tournaments outside the UK at club and national level are not forgotten. The International Directory itself features Europe in some depth as well as every FIFA country's international records for the previous year.

Naturally there are international appearances and goals scored by players for England, Scotland, Northern Ireland, Wales and the Republic. For easy reference, those players making appearances and scoring goals in the season covered are picked out in bold type.

The Yearbook would like to extend its appreciation to the publishers Headline for excellent support in the preparation of this edition, particularly Jonathan Taylor for photographic selection throughout the book and to Graham Green for his continued support.

Special thanks to Niall Quinn, Barney Francis and Peter Fraser from Sky Sports for their pieces, and to Paul McCarthy for the Editorial.

Thanks are also due to Ian Nannestad for the Obituaries and Did You Know and Fact File features in the club section. Many thanks also to John English for his conscientious proof reading and compilation of the International Directory.

# ACKNOWLEDGEMENTS

In addition the Yearbook is also keen to thank the following individuals and organisations for their co-operation.

David Barber at the Football Association, David C. Thompson (Scottish League), Rev. Nigel Sands for his contribution to the Chaplain's page, Bob Bannister, and Holly Harris at Headline.

Sincere thanks to George Schley and Simon Dunnington for their excellent work on the database, and to Andy Cordiner, Geoff Turner, Brian Tait, Mick Carruthers and the staff at Wearset for their much appreciated efforts in the production of the book throughout the year.

Finally, the Yearbook would like to extend particularly warm thanks to Wearset's John Anderson for this year taking on even more responsibility than usual for ensuring that the publication emerges in the very best possible shape. John's passion for, and dedication to, the Yearbook are remarkable.

# EDITORIAL

All hail the cult of the manager!

Despite its most esteemed exponent having ridden off into the sunset, managers have never been more scrutinised, lionised and thrust into the spotlight than they will be this season.

In fact, the retirement of Sir Alex Ferguson has served only to heighten the hysteria surrounding the profession. Where once the player was king, managers have now stolen the mantle, such is the anticipation of a post-Fergie era Barclays Premier League.

Think about it. Jose Mourinho swaggering back to the Bridge, Manuel Pellegrini overseeing the fresh, holistic approach at Manchester City, David Moyes stepping into the most daunting of shoes while Roberto Martinez seeks a new challenge at Goodison Park, shrugging off the twin imposters of an FA Cup triumph and the disaster of relegation with Wigan.

Throw Mark Hughes into the mix at Stoke, Ian Holloway's return to the grandest stage and the continual pantomime/farce/saga which surrounds Paolo Di Canio at Sunderland and it's not difficult to see why the headlines will be about men in suits rather than mud on boots.

These are the big signings and arrivals of the summer. Clubs will have spent countless millions by the time the transfer window closes in September but no mere player will ever attract the same level of interest as Mourinho.

He is *the* box office attraction, the superstar, the stellar performer whose every move and word will be dissected across the full range of newspapers, television, radio and Twitter. Not a shrug or grimace will go unnoticed or judged.

The same goes for Pellegrini, Moyes, Martinez, Hughes and every one of the 20 brave souls whose rewards are massive but who are emotionally stripped bare on the touchline and in post-match press conferences twice a week between August and May.

There is, of course, a price to pay for this adulation and hoopla. The pressure these men are under is both frightening and ridiculous. When Moyes quit Everton, every club out of the 92 throughout the league save for Arsenal had changed manager since Arsenal last won a trophy.

That is a statistic to chill the blood of the League Managers' Association who have made such strides in protecting their members but who still seem to fight a losing battle when the boardroom ignores the need for stability in favour of the quick-fix phenomenon.

Roy Hodgson is the president of the LMA, a post handed to every England manager. And to be fair to Hodgson, while the job is largely titular, he plays a far more active role in the association than did, say, Fabio Capello or Sven-Goran Eriksson.

Yet the irony cannot be lost on Hodgson that it is his colleagues in the Barclays Premier League who are the ones making his job virtually impossible.

The demand for immediate results causes short-term thinking and planning. Manchester City chief executive Ferran Soriano made great play of underlining the need to incorporate a youth ethos into the first team structure at the Etihad. But in the next breath he said the new manager needed to win five trophies in five seasons, a fact further emphasised by chairman Khaldoon Al Mubarak who expects to win *every* competition City enter.

With that kind of scrutiny on Pellegrini, is it likely City fans will see home-grown English youngsters playing a major role in any title or Champions League push? Or will City lose faith in Soriano's vision and resort to the cheque book come January if they are off the pace?

City are hardly alone. Chelsea under Mourinho are less likely to recall the likes of Josh McEachran than to take the plunge in the transfer market to satisfy the new manager's wishes. In his decade at the Bridge, Roman Abramovich has spent millions on an academy structure but has barely anything to show for it since the arrival of John Terry into the first team.

Only Moyes at Manchester United, with the security of a six-year contract behind him, *may* be willing to give youth its head in the shape of Nick Powell and Wilfried Zaha. That, at least, is part of the remit at Old Trafford.

And so it goes on, an ever-dwindling pool of English talent – down to a little over 30 per cent of players for Hodgson to select from last season – as managers and boards sacrifice any thoughts of long-term planning for instant results. Or the sack.

So should England qualify for a Brazilian World Cup next summer and live down to expectations, who should we be blaming? Hodgson, or his club colleagues who've dealt him such a shockingly poor hand?

**Paul McCarthy, Football Writers' Association**

# SKY SPORTS FOOTBALL YEARBOOK HONOURS

## GARY NEVILLE'S PREMIER LEAGUE TEAM OF THE SEASON 2012–13

David De Gea
*(Manchester U)*

| Pablo Zabaleta | Rio Ferdinand | Jan Vertonghen | Leighton Baines |
|---|---|---|---|
| *(Manchester C)* | *(Manchester U)* | *(Tottenham H)* | *(Everton)* |

| Juan Mata | Steven Gerrard | Michael Carrick | Gareth Bale |
|---|---|---|---|
| *(Chelsea)* | *(Liverpool)* | *(Manchester U)* | *(Tottenham H)* |

Luis Suarez       Robin van Persie
*(Liverpool)*      *(Manchester U)*

**Manager:**
Sir Alex Ferguson *(Manchester U)*

## GARY NEVILLE'S TOP THREE PREMIER LEAGUE GOALS 2012–13

Robin van Persie *(Manchester U v Aston V)*
Luis Suarez *(Liverpool v Newcastle U)*
Matt Lowton *(Aston V v Stoke C)*

## EUROPEAN GOLDEN SHOE

The European Golden Shoe award is presented to the leading goalscorer in European League football. However, the determination of the winner comes from a points system which depends on the status of the country involved. The goals total is multiplied by a factor of either two, one and a half or just by one.

Lionel Messi became the only player to win the award three times, 2010, 2012 and 2013. The top 20 places were as follows:

|    | Scorer | Team | Country | Goals | Factor | Points |
|----|--------|------|---------|-------|--------|--------|
| 1  | L. Messi | Barcelona | Spain | 46 | 2.0 | 92.0 |
| 2  | C. Ronaldo | Real Madrid | Spain | 34 | 2.0 | 68.0 |
| 3  | E. Cavani | Napoli | Italy | 29 | 2.0 | 58.0 |
| 4  | R. Falcao | Atletico Madrid | Spain | 28 | 2.0 | 56.0 |
| 5  | R. van Persie | Manchester U | England | 26 | 2.0 | 52.0 |
| 6  | J. Martinez | Porto | Portugal | 26 | 2.0 | 52.0 |
| 7  | A. Negredo | Sevilla | Spain | 25 | 2.0 | 50.0 |
| 8  | S. Kiessling | Bayer Leverkusen | Germany | 25 | 2.0 | 50.0 |
| 9  | R. Lewandowski | Borussia Dortmund | Germany | 24 | 2.0 | 48.0 |
| 10 | P. Hosiner | Austria Wien | Austria | 32 | 1.5 | 48.0 |
| 11 | R. Soldado | Valencia | Spain | 24 | 2.0 | 48.0 |
| 12 | B. Wilfried | Vitesse Arnhem | Holland | 31 | 1.5 | 46.5 |
| 13 | A. Di Natale | Udinese | Italy | 23 | 2.0 | 46.0 |
| 14 | L. Suarez | Liverpool | England | 23 | 2.0 | 46.0 |
| 15 | Z. Ibrahimovic | Paris Saint Germain | France | 30 | 1.5 | 45.0 |
| 16 | G. Bale | Tottenham H | England | 21 | 2.0 | 42.0 |
| 17 | R. Lima | Benfica | Portugal | 20 | 2.0 | 40.0 |
| 18 | M. Higdon | Motherwell | Scotland | 26 | 1.5 | 39.0 |
| 19 | G. Pelle | Feyenoord | Holland | 26 | 1.5 | 39.0 |
| 20 | J. Soriano | Salzburg | Austria | 26 | 1.5 | 39.0 |

# FOOTBALL AWARDS 2013

### FOOTBALLER OF THE YEAR

The Football Writers' Association Sir Stanley Matthews Trophy for the Footballer of the Year was awarded to Gareth Bale of Tottenham H and Wales. Luis Suarez (Liverpool) was runner-up and Robin van Persie (Manchester U) came third.

**Past Winners**

1947–48 Stanley Matthews (Blackpool), 1948–49 Johnny Carey (Manchester U), 1949–50 Joe Mercer (Arsenal), 1950–51 Harry Johnston (Blackpool), 1951–52 Billy Wright (Wolverhampton W), 1952–53 Nat Lofthouse (Bolton W), 1953–54 Tom Finney (Preston NE), 1954–55 Don Revie (Manchester C), 1955–56 Bert Trautmann (Manchester C), 1956–57 Tom Finney (Preston NE), 1957–58 Danny Blanchflower (Tottenham H), 1958–59 Syd Owen (Luton T), 1959–60 Bill Slater (Wolverhampton W), 1960–61 Danny Blanchflower (Tottenham H), 1961–62 Jimmy Adamson (Burnley), 1962–63 Stanley Matthews (Stoke C), 1963–64 Bobby Moore (West Ham U), 1964–65 Bobby Collins (Leeds U), 1965–66 Bobby Charlton (Manchester U), 1966–67 Jackie Charlton (Leeds U), 1967–68 George Best (Manchester U), 1968–69 Dave Mackay (Derby Co) shared with Tony Book (Manchester C), 1969–70 Billy Bremner (Leeds U), 1970–71 Frank McLintock (Arsenal), 1971–72 Gordon Banks (Stoke C), 1972–73 Pat Jennings (Tottenham H), 1973–74 Ian Callaghan (Liverpool), 1974–75 Alan Mullery (Fulham), 1975–76 Kevin Keegan (Liverpool), 1976–77 Emlyn Hughes (Liverpool), 1977–78 Kenny Burns (Nottingham F), 1978–79 Kenny Dalglish (Liverpool), 1979–80 Terry McDermott (Liverpool), 1980–81 Frans Thijssen (Ipswich T), 1981–82 Steve Perryman (Tottenham H), 1982–83 Kenny Dalglish (Liverpool), 1983–84 Ian Rush (Liverpool), 1984–85 Neville Southall (Everton), 1985–86 Gary Lineker (Everton), 1986–87 Clive Allen (Tottenham H), 1987–88 John Barnes (Liverpool), 1988–89 Steve Nicol (Liverpool), 1989–90 John Barnes (Liverpool), 1990–91 Gordon Strachan (Leeds U), 1991–92 Gary Lineker (Tottenham H), 1992–93 Chris Waddle (Sheffield W), 1993–94 Alan Shearer (Blackburn R), 1994–95 Jurgen Klinsmann (Tottenham H), 1995–96 Eric Cantona (Manchester U), 1996–97 Gianfranco Zola (Chelsea), 1997–98 Dennis Bergkamp (Arsenal), 1998–99 David Ginola (Tottenham H), 1999–2000 Roy Keane (Manchester U), 2000–01 Teddy Sheringham (Manchester U), 2001–02 Robert Pires (Arsenal), 2002–03 Thierry Henry (Arsenal), 2003–04 Thierry Henry (Arsenal), 2004–05 Frank Lampard (Chelsea), 2005–06 Thierry Henry (Arsenal), 2006–07 Cristiano Ronaldo (Manchester U), 2007–08 Cristiano Ronaldo (Manchester U), 2008–09 Ryan Giggs (Manchester U), 2009–10 Wayne Rooney (Manchester U), 2010–11 Scott Parker (West Ham U), 2011–12 Robin van Persie (Arsenal), 2012–13 Gareth Bale (Tottenham H).

### THE PFA AWARDS 2013

Player of the Year: Gareth Bale, Tottenham H and Wales.
Young Player of the Year: Gareth Bale, Tottenham H and Wales.
Women's Player of the Year: Kim Little, Arsenal and Scotland.

## OTHER AWARDS

### EUROPEAN FOOTBALLER OF THE YEAR 2012

Andres Iniesta, Barcelona and Spain

### WORLD PLAYER OF THE YEAR 2012

Lionel Messi, Barcelona and Argentina

### WOMEN'S PLAYER OF THE YEAR 2012

Abby Wambach, Western New York Flash and USA

### SCOTTISH PFA PLAYER OF THE YEAR AWARDS 2013

Player of the Year: Michael Higdon, Motherwell.
Young Player of the Year: Leigh Griffiths, Hibernian.
First Division Player of the Year: Lyle Taylor, Falkirk.
Second Division Player of the Year: Nicky Clark, Queen of the S.
Third Division Player of the Year: Lee Wallace, Rangers.
Manager of the Year: Allan Johnston, Queen of the S.

### SCOTTISH FOOTBALL WRITERS' ASSOCIATION 2013

Player of the Year: Leigh Griffiths, Hibernian and Scotland.
Young Player of the Year: Stuart Armstrong, Dundee U and Scotland.
Manager of the Year: Neil Lennon, Celtic.

# SIR ALEX FERGUSON

Born Alexander Chapman Ferguson on New Year's Eve 1941 in Govan, Glasgow. His playing career began as an amateur with Queen's Park in 1957, while he was an apprentice toolmaker. He moved to St Johnstone as a part-time professional in 1960 and then as a full-time professional joined Dunfermline Athletic in 1964. In 1967 he was transferred to Rangers for £65,000 and after two seasons with the Glasgow giants he moved to Falkirk in 1969 for £20,000. In 1973, he joined the part-timers Ayr United while he ran a Glasgow pub. His playing career ended in 1974 after he had made 317 league appearances scoring 170 goals. He appeared for the Scottish League but although he was never selected to play for Scotland at national level, represented his country in a Scotland XI tour of Asia and Oceania in 1967, appearing 7 times and scoring 9 goals.

His first managerial appointment was at East Stirlingshire in 1974 and the great career began. He announced his retirement from management in early May 2013, after 1500 games in charge, winning a staggering 48 major trophies.

His remarkable managerial career is outlined below.

## EAST STIRLINGSHIRE – 1 June 1974
First game – Forfar Ath 3 East Stirlingshire 3
 Scottish League Cup, 10 August 1974.
*East Stirling:* Gourlay; Stirling, McGregor, Donnelly, Simpson (Meakin), Dunne, Robertson, McCulley, Hulston, Mullen (2), Browning (1 pen).

| | P | W | D | L | F | A | Pts | Pos |
|---|---|---|---|---|---|---|---|---|
| 1974–75 Division 2* | 12 | 7 | 2 | 3 | 24 | 19 | 16 | |

*Left for St Mirren in October

## ST MIRREN – 21 October 1974
First game – Clydebank 0 St Mirren 0
 Scottish League Division 2, 26 October 1974.
*St Mirren:* McLachlan, Beckett, Young, Brown, Provan, Laurie (Walker), Fitzpatrick, Third, Biggar, Borthwick.

| | P | W | D | L | F | A | Pts |
|---|---|---|---|---|---|---|---|
| 1974–75 Division 2* | 27 | 13 | 6 | 8 | 47 | 31 | 28 |

*Arrived in October

| | | | | | | | | |
|---|---|---|---|---|---|---|---|---|
| 1975–76 Division 1 | 26 | 9 | 8 | 9 | 37 | 37 | 26 | 6 |
| 1976–77 Division 1 | 39 | 25 | 12 | 2 | 91 | 38 | 62 | 1 |
| 1977–78 Premier | 36 | 11 | 8 | 17 | 52 | 63 | 30 | 8 |

## ABERDEEN – 1 August 1978
First game – Aberdeen 4 Hearts 1
 Scottish Premier Division, 12 August 1978.
*Aberdeen:* Leighton; Kennedy, McLelland, McMaster, Garner, Miller, Sullivan, Archibald (2), Harper (1), Jarvie, Davidson (1) (Scanlon).

| | | | | | | | | |
|---|---|---|---|---|---|---|---|---|
| 1978–79 Premier | 36 | 13 | 14 | 9 | 59 | 36 | 40 | 4 |
| 1979–80 Premier | 46 | 19 | 10 | 71 | 61 | 38 | 48 | 1 |
| 1980–81 Premier | 36 | 19 | 11 | 6 | 61 | 26 | 49 | 2 |
| 1981–82 Premier | 36 | 23 | 7 | 6 | 71 | 29 | 53 | 2 |

*FA:* Winners v Rangers 4-1 *aet* (Hampden, 22.5.82)

| | | | | | | | | |
|---|---|---|---|---|---|---|---|---|
| 1982–83 Premier | 36 | 25 | 5 | 6 | 76 | 24 | 55 | 3 |

*FA:* Winners v Rangers 1-0 *aet* (Hampden, 21.5.83)
*CWC:* Winners v Real Madrid 2-1 *aet* (Gothenburg, 11.5.83)

| | | | | | | | | |
|---|---|---|---|---|---|---|---|---|
| 1983–84 Premier | 36 | 25 | 7 | 4 | 78 | 21 | 57 | 1 |

*FA:* Winners v Celtic 2-1 *aet* (Hampden, 9.5.84) 2-1

| | | | | | | | | |
|---|---|---|---|---|---|---|---|---|
| 1984–85 Premier | 36 | 27 | 5 | 4 | 89 | 26 | 59 | 1 |
| 1985–86 Premier | 36 | 16 | 12 | 8 | 62 | 31 | 44 | 4 |

*LC:* Winners v Hibernian 3-0 (Hampden, 27.10.85)
*FA:* Winners v Hearts 3-0 (Hampden, 10.5.86)

| | | | | | | | | |
|---|---|---|---|---|---|---|---|---|
| 1986–87 Premier* | 15 | 7 | 5 | 3 | 25 | 14 | 19 | |

*Left for Manchester U in November

## SCOTLAND – October 1985 – June 1986

| | | | | | | |
|---|---|---|---|---|---|---|
| Full Internationals | 10 | 3 | 4 | 3 | 8 | 5 |

*Includes 3 games in 1986 Mexico World Cup*

## MANCHESTER U – 6 NOVEMBER 1986
First game – Oxford U 2 Manchester U 0
 Football League Division 1, 8 November 1986.
*Manchester U:* Turner; Duxbury, Albiston, Moran, McGrath (Olsen), Hogg, Blackmore, Moses, Stapleton, Davenport, Barnes.

| | | | | | | | | |
|---|---|---|---|---|---|---|---|---|
| 1986–87 Division 1* | 29 | 11 | 10 | 8 | 36 | 29 | 32 | |

*Replaced Ron Atkinson in November

| | | | | | | | | |
|---|---|---|---|---|---|---|---|---|
| 1987–88 Division 1 | 40 | 23 | 12 | 5 | 71 | 38 | 81 | 2 |
| 1988–89 Division 1 | 38 | 13 | 12 | 13 | 45 | 35 | 51 | 11 |
| 1989–90 Division 1 | 38 | 13 | 9 | 16 | 46 | 47 | 48 | 13 |

*FA:* Winners v Crystal Palace 3-3 (Wembley, 12.5.90)
 *Replay* Crystal Palace 1-0 (Wembley, 17.5.90)

| | | | | | | | | |
|---|---|---|---|---|---|---|---|---|
| 1990–91 Division 1 | 38 | 16 | 12 | 10 | 58 | 45 | 62 | 6 |

*LC:* Runners-up v Sheffield W 0-1 (Wembley, 21.4.91)
*CS:* Shared v Liverpool 1-1 (Wembley, 18.8.90)
*CWC:* Winners v Barcelona 2-1 (Feyenoord, 15.5.91)

| | | | | | | | | |
|---|---|---|---|---|---|---|---|---|
| 1991–92 Division 1 | 42 | 21 | 15 | 6 | 63 | 33 | 78 | 2 |

*LC:* Winners v Nottingham F 1-0 (Wembley, 12.4.92)
*SC:* Winners v Red Star Belgrade 1-0 (Old Trafford, 19.11.91)

| | | | | | | | | |
|---|---|---|---|---|---|---|---|---|
| 1992–93 Premier | 42 | 24 | 12 | 6 | 67 | 31 | 84 | 1 |
| 1993–94 Premier | 42 | 27 | 11 | 4 | 80 | 38 | 92 | 1 |

*LC:* Runners-up v Aston Villa 1-3 (Wembley, 27.3.94)
*FA:* Winners v Chelsea 4-0 (Wembley, 14.5.94)
*CS:* Winners v Arsenal 1-1 (Wembley, 7.8.93)
 *aet.* Manchester U won 5-4 on penalties

| | | | | | | | | |
|---|---|---|---|---|---|---|---|---|
| 1994–95 Premier | 42 | 26 | 10 | 6 | 77 | 28 | 88 | 2 |

*FA:* Runners-up v Everton 0-1 (Wembley, 20.5.95)
*CS:* Winners v Blackburn R 2-0 (Wembley, 14.8.94)

| | | | | | | | | |
|---|---|---|---|---|---|---|---|---|
| 1995–96 Premier | 38 | 25 | 7 | 6 | 73 | 35 | 82 | 1 |

*FA:* Winners v Liverpool 1-0 (Wembley, 11.5.96)

| | | | | | | | | |
|---|---|---|---|---|---|---|---|---|
| 1996–97 Premier | 38 | 21 | 12 | 5 | 76 | 44 | 75 | 1 |

*CS:* Winners v Newcastle U 4-0 (Wembley, 11.8.96)

| | | | | | | | | |
|---|---|---|---|---|---|---|---|---|
| 1997–98 Premier | 38 | 23 | 8 | 7 | 73 | 26 | 77 | 2 |

*CS:* Winners v Chelsea 1-1 (Wembley, 3.8.97)
 *aet.* Manchester U won 4-2 on penalties

| | | | | | | | | |
|---|---|---|---|---|---|---|---|---|
| 1998–99 Premier | 38 | 22 | 13 | 3 | 80 | 37 | 79 | 1 |

*FA:* Winners v Newcastle U 2-0 (Wembley, 22.5.99)
*CL:* Winners v Bayern Munich 2-1 (Barcelona, 26.5.99)

| | | | | | | | | |
|---|---|---|---|---|---|---|---|---|
| 1999–2000 Premier | 38 | 28 | 7 | 3 | 97 | 45 | 91 | 1 |

*IC:* Winners v Palmeiras 1-0 (Tokyo, 30.11.99)

| | | | | | | | | |
|---|---|---|---|---|---|---|---|---|
| 2000–01 Premier | 38 | 24 | 8 | 6 | 79 | 31 | 80 | 1 |
| 2001–02 Premier | 38 | 24 | 5 | 9 | 87 | 45 | 77 | 3 |
| 2002–03 Premier | 38 | 25 | 8 | 5 | 74 | 34 | 83 | 1 |

*LC:* Runners-up v Liverpool 0-2 (Cardiff, 2.3.03)

| | | | | | | | | |
|---|---|---|---|---|---|---|---|---|
| 2003–04 Premier | 38 | 23 | 6 | 9 | 73 | 26 | 75 | 3 |

*FA:* Winners v Millwall 3-0 (Cardiff, 22.5.04)
*CS:* Winners v Arsenal 1-1 (Cardiff, 10.8.03)
 Manchester U won 4-3 on penalties

| | | | | | | | | |
|---|---|---|---|---|---|---|---|---|
| 2004–05 Premier | 38 | 22 | 11 | 5 | 58 | 26 | 77 | 3 |
| 2005–06 Premier | 38 | 25 | 8 | 5 | 72 | 34 | 83 | 2 |

*LC:* Winners v Wigan Ath 4-0 (Cardiff, 26.2.06)

| | | | | | | | | |
|---|---|---|---|---|---|---|---|---|
| 2006–07 Premier | 38 | 28 | 5 | 5 | 83 | 27 | 89 | 1 |

*FA:* Runners-up v Chelsea 0-1 (Wembley, 19.5.07)

| | | | | | | | | |
|---|---|---|---|---|---|---|---|---|
| 2007–08 Premier | 38 | 27 | 6 | 5 | 80 | 22 | 87 | 1 |

*CS:* Winners v Chelsea 1-1 (Wembley, 5.8.07)
 *aet.* Manchester U won 3-0 on penalties
*CL:* Winners v Chelsea 1-1 (Moscow, 21.5.08)
 *aet.* Manchester U won 6-5 on penalties

| | | | | | | | | |
|---|---|---|---|---|---|---|---|---|
| 2008–09 Premier | 38 | 28 | 6 | 4 | 68 | 24 | 90 | 1 |

*LC:* Winners v Tottenham H 0-0 (Wembley, 1.3.09)
 *aet.* Manchester U won 4-1 on penalties
*CS:* Winners v Portsmouth 0-0 (Wembley, 10.8.08)
 Manchester U won 3-1 on penalties
*CL:* Runners-up v Barcelona 0-2 (Rome, 27.5.09)
*WC:* Winners v LDU Quito 1-0 (Yokohama, 21.12.08)

| | | | | | | | | |
|---|---|---|---|---|---|---|---|---|
| 2009–10 Premier | 38 | 27 | 4 | 7 | 86 | 28 | 86 | 2 |

*LC:* Winners v Aston Villa 2-1 (Wembley, 28.2.10)

| | | | | | | | | |
|---|---|---|---|---|---|---|---|---|
| 2010–11 Premier | 38 | 23 | 11 | 4 | 78 | 37 | 80 | 1 |

*CL:* Runners-up v Barcelona 1-3 (Wembley, 28.5.11)
*CS:* Winners v Chelsea 3-1 (Wembley, 8.8.10)

| | | | | | | | | |
|---|---|---|---|---|---|---|---|---|
| 2011–12 Premier | 38 | 28 | 5 | 5 | 89 | 33 | 89 | 2 |

*CS:* Winners v Manchester C 3-2 (Wembley, 7.8.11)

| | | | | | | | | |
|---|---|---|---|---|---|---|---|---|
| 2012–13 Premier | 38 | 28 | 5 | 5 | 86 | 43 | 89 | 1 |

Key: *FA:* FA Cup, *LC:* League Cup, *CS:* Charity/Community Shield, *EC:* European Cup, *CL:* Champions League, *CWC:* Cup Winners' Cup, *UC:* UEFA Cup, *SC:* Super Cup, *IC:* Inter-Continental Cup, *WC:* World Club Championship.

# BARCLAYS PREMIER LEAGUE 2012–13

(P) *Promoted into division at end of 2011–12 season.*

| | | | | | | | Total | | | | | Home | | | | | Away | | | | | |
|---|---|---|---|---|---|---|---|---|---|---|---|---|---|---|---|---|---|---|---|---|---|---|---|
| | | P | W | D | L | F | A | W | D | L | F | A | W | D | L | F | A | GD | Pts |
| 1 | Manchester U | 38 | 28 | 5 | 5 | 86 | 43 | 16 | 0 | 3 | 45 | 19 | 12 | 5 | 2 | 41 | 24 | 43 | 89 |
| 2 | Manchester C | 38 | 23 | 9 | 6 | 66 | 34 | 14 | 3 | 2 | 41 | 15 | 9 | 6 | 4 | 25 | 19 | 32 | 78 |
| 3 | Chelsea | 38 | 22 | 9 | 7 | 75 | 39 | 12 | 5 | 2 | 41 | 16 | 10 | 4 | 5 | 34 | 23 | 36 | 75 |
| 4 | Arsenal | 38 | 21 | 10 | 7 | 72 | 37 | 11 | 5 | 3 | 47 | 23 | 10 | 5 | 4 | 25 | 14 | 35 | 73 |
| 5 | Tottenham H | 38 | 21 | 9 | 8 | 66 | 46 | 11 | 5 | 3 | 29 | 18 | 10 | 4 | 5 | 37 | 28 | 20 | 72 |
| 6 | Everton | 38 | 16 | 15 | 7 | 55 | 40 | 12 | 6 | 1 | 33 | 17 | 4 | 9 | 6 | 22 | 23 | 15 | 63 |
| 7 | Liverpool | 38 | 16 | 13 | 9 | 71 | 43 | 9 | 6 | 4 | 33 | 16 | 7 | 7 | 5 | 38 | 27 | 28 | 61 |
| 8 | WBA | 38 | 14 | 7 | 17 | 53 | 57 | 9 | 4 | 6 | 32 | 25 | 5 | 3 | 11 | 21 | 32 | –4 | 49 |
| 9 | Swansea C | 38 | 11 | 13 | 14 | 47 | 51 | 6 | 8 | 5 | 28 | 26 | 5 | 5 | 9 | 19 | 25 | –4 | 46 |
| 10 | West Ham U (P) | 38 | 12 | 10 | 16 | 45 | 53 | 9 | 6 | 4 | 34 | 22 | 3 | 4 | 12 | 11 | 31 | –8 | 46 |
| 11 | Norwich C | 38 | 10 | 14 | 14 | 41 | 58 | 8 | 7 | 4 | 25 | 20 | 2 | 7 | 10 | 16 | 38 | –17 | 44 |
| 12 | Fulham | 38 | 11 | 10 | 17 | 50 | 60 | 7 | 3 | 9 | 28 | 30 | 4 | 7 | 8 | 22 | 30 | –10 | 43 |
| 13 | Stoke C | 38 | 9 | 15 | 14 | 34 | 45 | 7 | 7 | 5 | 21 | 22 | 2 | 8 | 9 | 13 | 23 | –11 | 42 |
| 14 | Southampton (P) | 38 | 9 | 14 | 15 | 49 | 60 | 6 | 7 | 6 | 26 | 24 | 3 | 7 | 9 | 23 | 36 | –11 | 41 |
| 15 | Aston Villa | 38 | 10 | 11 | 17 | 47 | 69 | 5 | 5 | 9 | 23 | 28 | 5 | 6 | 8 | 24 | 41 | –22 | 41 |
| 16 | Newcastle U | 38 | 11 | 8 | 19 | 45 | 68 | 9 | 1 | 9 | 24 | 31 | 2 | 7 | 10 | 21 | 37 | –23 | 41 |
| 17 | Sunderland | 38 | 9 | 12 | 17 | 41 | 54 | 5 | 8 | 6 | 20 | 19 | 4 | 4 | 11 | 21 | 35 | –13 | 39 |
| 18 | Wigan Ath | 38 | 9 | 9 | 20 | 47 | 73 | 4 | 6 | 9 | 26 | 39 | 5 | 3 | 11 | 21 | 34 | –26 | 36 |
| 19 | Reading (P) | 38 | 6 | 10 | 22 | 43 | 73 | 4 | 8 | 7 | 23 | 33 | 2 | 2 | 15 | 20 | 40 | –30 | 28 |
| 20 | QPR | 38 | 4 | 13 | 21 | 30 | 60 | 2 | 8 | 9 | 13 | 28 | 2 | 5 | 12 | 17 | 32 | –30 | 25 |

## LEADING GOALSCORERS 2012–13

| | League | FA Cup | Capital One Cup | Other | Total |
|---|---|---|---|---|---|
| Robin van Persie *(Manchester U)* | 26 | 1 | 0 | 3 | 30 |
| Luis Suarez *(Liverpool)* | 23 | 2 | 1 | 4 | 30 |
| Gareth Bale *(Tottenham H)* | 21 | 1 | 1 | 3 | 26 |
| Christian Benteke *(Aston Villa)* | 19 | 0 | 4 | 0 | 23 |
| Michu *(Swansea C)* | 18 | 1 | 3 | 0 | 22 |
| Romelu Lukaku *(WBA)* | 17 | 0 | 0 | 0 | 17 |
| Demba Ba *(Chelsea)* | 15 | 4 | 0 | 0 | 19 |
| *(Includes 13 League goals for Newcastle U)* | | | | | |
| Frank Lampard *(Chelsea)* | 15 | 2 | 0 | 0 | 17 |
| Dimitar Berbatov *(Fulham)* | 15 | 0 | 0 | 0 | 15 |
| Rickie Lambert *(Southampton)* | 15 | 0 | 0 | 0 | 15 |
| Theo Walcott *(Arsenal)* | 14 | 1 | 5 | 1 | 21 |
| Edin Dzeko *(Manchester C)* | 14 | 0 | 0 | 1 | 15 |
| Juan Mata *(Chelsea)* | 12 | 1 | 2 | 5 | 20 |
| Sergio Aguero *(Manchester C)* | 12 | 3 | 0 | 2 | 17 |
| Wayne Rooney *(Manchester U)* | 12 | 3 | 0 | 1 | 16 |
| Adam Le Fondre *(Reading)* | 12 | 2 | 0 | 0 | 14 |
| Santi Cazorla *(Arsenal)* | 12 | 0 | 0 | 0 | 12 |
| Carlos Tevez *(Manchester C)* | 11 | 5 | 0 | 1 | 17 |
| Olivier Giroud *(Arsenal)* | 11 | 2 | 2 | 2 | 17 |
| Lukas Podolski *(Arsenal)* | 11 | 1 | 0 | 4 | 16 |
| Jermain Defoe *(Tottenham H)* | 11 | 0 | 0 | 4 | 15 |
| Arouna Kone *(Wigan Ath)* | 11 | 2 | 0 | 0 | 13 |
| Daniel Sturridge *(Liverpool)* | 11 | 1 | 1 | 0 | 13 |
| *(Includes 1 League goal and 1 Capital One Cup goal for Chelsea)* | | | | | |
| Marouane Fellaini *(Everton)* | 11 | 1 | 0 | 0 | 12 |
| Steven Fletcher *(Sunderland)* | 11 | 0 | 0 | 0 | 11 |

*Other matches consist of European games, World Club Cup, Community Shield. Players listed in order of League goals total.*

## BARCLAYS PREMIER LEAGUE – RESULTS 2012-13

| | Arsenal | Aston Villa | Chelsea | Everton | Fulham | Liverpool | Manchester C | Manchester U | Newcastle U | Norwich C | QPR | Reading | Southampton | Stoke C | Sunderland | Swansea C | Tottenham H | WBA | West Ham U | Wigan Ath |
|---|---|---|---|---|---|---|---|---|---|---|---|---|---|---|---|---|---|---|---|---|
| Arsenal | — | 2-1 | 1-2 | 0-0 | 3-3 | 2-2 | 0-2 | 1-1 | 7-3 | 3-1 | 1-0 | 4-1 | 6-1 | 1-0 | 0-0 | 0-2 | 5-2 | 2-0 | 5-1 | 4-1 |
| Aston Villa | 0-0 | — | 1-2 | 1-3 | 1-1 | 2-2 | 0-2 | 2-3 | 1-2 | 1-1 | 3-2 | 1-0 | 0-1 | 1-0 | 6-1 | 2-0 | 0-4 | 1-0 | 2-1 | 0-3 |
| Chelsea | 2-1 | 8-0 | — | 2-1 | 0-0 | 1-1 | 0-0 | 2-3 | 2-0 | 4-1 | 0-1 | 4-2 | 2-2 | 1-0 | 2-1 | 2-0 | 2-1 | 2-1 | 2-0 | 4-1 |
| Everton | 1-1 | 3-3 | 1-2 | — | 1-0 | 2-2 | 2-0 | 1-0 | 2-2 | 1-1 | 2-0 | 3-1 | 3-1 | 1-0 | 2-1 | 1-2 | 2-1 | 3-0 | 2-0 | 2-1 |
| Fulham | 0-1 | 1-0 | 0-3 | 2-2 | — | 1-3 | 1-2 | 0-1 | 2-1 | 5-0 | 3-2 | 2-4 | 1-1 | 1-0 | 1-3 | 1-2 | 0-3 | 3-0 | 3-1 | 1-1 |
| Liverpool | 0-2 | 1-3 | 2-2 | 0-0 | 4-0 | — | 2-2 | 1-2 | 1-1 | 5-0 | 1-0 | 1-0 | 1-0 | 0-0 | 3-0 | 5-0 | 3-2 | 0-2 | 0-0 | 3-0 |
| Manchester C | 1-1 | 5-0 | 2-0 | 1-1 | 2-0 | 2-2 | — | 2-3 | 4-0 | 2-3 | 3-1 | 1-0 | 3-2 | 3-0 | 3-0 | 1-0 | 2-1 | 1-0 | 2-1 | 1-0 |
| Manchester U | 2-1 | 3-0 | 0-1 | 2-0 | 3-2 | 2-1 | 1-2 | — | 4-3 | 4-0 | 3-1 | 1-0 | 2-1 | 4-2 | 3-1 | 2-1 | 2-3 | 2-0 | 1-0 | 4-0 |
| Newcastle U | 0-1 | 1-1 | 3-2 | 1-2 | 1-0 | 0-6 | 1-3 | 0-3 | — | 1-0 | 1-0 | 1-2 | 4-2 | 2-1 | 0-3 | 1-2 | 2-1 | 2-1 | 0-1 | 3-0 |
| Norwich C | 1-0 | 1-1 | 0-1 | 2-1 | 0-0 | 2-5 | 3-4 | 1-0 | 0-0 | — | 1-1 | 2-1 | 1-3 | 1-0 | 2-1 | 2-2 | 1-1 | 4-0 | 0-0 | 2-1 |
| QPR | 0-1 | 1-1 | 0-0 | 1-1 | 2-1 | 0-3 | 0-2 | 0-2 | 1-2 | 0-0 | — | 1-1 | 0-2 | 0-2 | 3-1 | 0-5 | 1-3 | 1-2 | 1-2 | 1-1 |
| Reading | 2-5 | 1-2 | 2-2 | 2-1 | 3-3 | 0-0 | 0-2 | 3-4 | 2-2 | 0-0 | 0-0 | — | 0-2 | 1-1 | 2-1 | 0-0 | 1-3 | 3-2 | 1-0 | 0-3 |
| Southampton | 1-1 | 4-1 | 2-1 | 0-0 | 2-2 | 3-1 | 2-3 | 2-3 | 2-0 | 1-1 | 1-2 | 1-0 | — | 1-1 | 0-1 | 1-1 | 1-2 | 0-3 | 1-1 | 0-2 |
| Stoke C | 0-0 | 1-3 | 0-4 | 1-1 | 1-0 | 3-1 | 1-1 | 0-2 | 2-1 | 1-0 | 1-0 | 2-1 | 3-3 | — | 0-0 | 2-0 | 1-2 | 0-0 | 0-1 | 2-2 |
| Sunderland | 0-1 | 0-1 | 1-3 | 1-0 | 2-2 | 1-1 | 0-1 | 0-1 | 1-1 | 1-1 | 0-0 | 3-0 | 1-1 | 1-1 | — | 0-0 | 1-2 | 2-4 | 3-0 | 1-0 |
| Swansea C | 0-2 | 2-2 | 1-1 | 0-3 | 0-3 | 0-0 | 0-0 | 1-1 | 1-0 | 3-4 | 4-1 | 2-2 | 0-0 | 3-1 | 2-2 | — | 1-2 | 3-1 | 3-0 | 2-1 |
| Tottenham H | 2-1 | 2-0 | 2-4 | 2-2 | 0-1 | 2-1 | 3-1 | 1-1 | 2-1 | 1-1 | 2-1 | 3-1 | 1-0 | 0-0 | 2-1 | 1-0 | — | 1-1 | 3-1 | 0-1 |
| WBA | 1-2 | 2-2 | 2-1 | 2-0 | 1-2 | 3-0 | 1-2 | 5-5 | 2-1 | 2-1 | 3-2 | 1-0 | 3-0 | 0-1 | 2-1 | 2-1 | 0-1 | — | 0-0 | 2-3 |
| West Ham U | 1-3 | 1-0 | 3-1 | 1-2 | 3-0 | 2-3 | 2-1 | 2-1 | 0-0 | 2-1 | 1-1 | 4-2 | 4-1 | 1-1 | 1-1 | 1-0 | 2-3 | 3-1 | — | 2-0 |
| Wigan Ath | 0-1 | 2-2 | 0-2 | 2-2 | 1-2 | 0-4 | 0-2 | 0-4 | 2-1 | 1-0 | 2-2 | 3-2 | 2-2 | 2-2 | 2-3 | 2-3 | 2-2 | 1-2 | 2-1 | — |

# NPOWER FOOTBALL LEAGUE CHAMPIONSHIP
## 2012–13

(P) *Promoted into division at end of 2011–12 season.*  (R) *Relegated into division at end of 2011–12 season.*

| | | | Total | | | | Home | | | | | Away | | | | | | |
|---|---|---|---|---|---|---|---|---|---|---|---|---|---|---|---|---|---|---|
| | | P | W | D | L | F | A | W | D | L | F | A | W | D | L | F | A | GD | Pts |
| 1 | Cardiff C | 46 | 25 | 12 | 9 | 72 | 45 | 15 | 6 | 2 | 37 | 15 | 10 | 6 | 7 | 35 | 30 | 27 | 87 |
| 2 | Hull C | 46 | 24 | 7 | 15 | 61 | 52 | 13 | 4 | 6 | 35 | 22 | 11 | 3 | 9 | 26 | 30 | 9 | 79 |
| 3 | Watford | 46 | 23 | 8 | 15 | 85 | 58 | 11 | 5 | 7 | 41 | 27 | 12 | 3 | 8 | 44 | 31 | 27 | 77 |
| 4 | Brighton & HA | 46 | 19 | 18 | 9 | 69 | 43 | 11 | 9 | 3 | 39 | 17 | 8 | 9 | 6 | 30 | 26 | 26 | 75 |
| 5 | Crystal Palace¶ | 46 | 19 | 15 | 12 | 73 | 62 | 13 | 8 | 2 | 52 | 31 | 6 | 7 | 10 | 21 | 31 | 11 | 72 |
| 6 | Leicester C | 46 | 19 | 11 | 16 | 71 | 48 | 13 | 4 | 6 | 46 | 23 | 6 | 7 | 10 | 25 | 25 | 23 | 68 |
| 7 | Bolton W (R) | 46 | 18 | 14 | 14 | 69 | 61 | 14 | 6 | 3 | 37 | 20 | 4 | 8 | 11 | 32 | 41 | 8 | 68 |
| 8 | Nottingham F | 46 | 17 | 16 | 13 | 63 | 59 | 10 | 8 | 5 | 37 | 28 | 7 | 8 | 8 | 26 | 31 | 4 | 67 |
| 9 | Charlton Ath (P) | 46 | 17 | 14 | 15 | 65 | 59 | 8 | 6 | 9 | 32 | 34 | 9 | 8 | 6 | 33 | 25 | 6 | 65 |
| 10 | Derby Co | 46 | 16 | 13 | 17 | 65 | 62 | 12 | 7 | 4 | 43 | 22 | 4 | 6 | 13 | 22 | 40 | 3 | 61 |
| 11 | Burnley | 46 | 16 | 13 | 17 | 62 | 60 | 9 | 8 | 6 | 31 | 22 | 7 | 5 | 11 | 31 | 38 | 2 | 61 |
| 12 | Birmingham C | 46 | 15 | 16 | 15 | 63 | 69 | 7 | 9 | 7 | 29 | 34 | 8 | 7 | 8 | 34 | 35 | -6 | 61 |
| 13 | Leeds U | 46 | 17 | 10 | 19 | 57 | 66 | 13 | 3 | 7 | 30 | 26 | 4 | 7 | 12 | 27 | 40 | -9 | 61 |
| 14 | Ipswich T | 46 | 16 | 12 | 18 | 48 | 61 | 10 | 5 | 8 | 34 | 27 | 6 | 7 | 10 | 14 | 34 | -13 | 60 |
| 15 | Blackpool | 46 | 14 | 17 | 15 | 62 | 63 | 8 | 9 | 6 | 32 | 24 | 6 | 8 | 9 | 30 | 39 | -1 | 59 |
| 16 | Middlesbrough | 46 | 18 | 5 | 23 | 61 | 70 | 13 | 3 | 7 | 38 | 27 | 5 | 2 | 16 | 23 | 43 | -9 | 59 |
| 17 | Blackburn R (R) | 46 | 14 | 16 | 16 | 55 | 62 | 10 | 6 | 7 | 27 | 23 | 4 | 10 | 9 | 28 | 39 | -7 | 58 |
| 18 | Sheffield W (P) | 46 | 16 | 10 | 20 | 53 | 61 | 9 | 4 | 10 | 30 | 35 | 7 | 6 | 10 | 23 | 26 | -8 | 58 |
| 19 | Huddersfield T (P) | 46 | 15 | 13 | 18 | 53 | 73 | 7 | 10 | 6 | 28 | 26 | 8 | 3 | 12 | 25 | 47 | -20 | 58 |
| 20 | Millwall | 46 | 15 | 11 | 20 | 51 | 62 | 8 | 4 | 11 | 24 | 30 | 7 | 7 | 9 | 27 | 32 | -11 | 56 |
| 21 | Barnsley | 46 | 14 | 13 | 19 | 56 | 70 | 9 | 5 | 9 | 26 | 31 | 5 | 8 | 10 | 30 | 39 | -14 | 55 |
| 22 | Peterborough U | 46 | 15 | 9 | 22 | 66 | 75 | 8 | 5 | 10 | 34 | 39 | 7 | 4 | 12 | 32 | 36 | -9 | 54 |
| 23 | Wolverhampton W (R) | 46 | 14 | 9 | 23 | 55 | 69 | 7 | 7 | 9 | 30 | 35 | 7 | 2 | 14 | 25 | 34 | -14 | 51 |
| 24 | Bristol C | 46 | 11 | 8 | 27 | 59 | 84 | 8 | 4 | 11 | 40 | 44 | 3 | 4 | 16 | 19 | 40 | -25 | 41 |

¶*Crystal Palace promoted via play-offs.*

## LEADING GOALSCORERS 2012–13

| | League | FA Cup | Capital One Cup | Play-Offs | Total |
|---|---|---|---|---|---|
| Glenn Murray *(Crystal Palace)* | 30 | 1 | 0 | 0 | 31 |
| Jordan Rhodes *(Blackburn R)* | 29 | 1 | 0 | | 30 |
| *(Includes 2 League goals for Huddersfield T)* | | | | | |
| Charlie Austin *(Burnley)* | 24 | 0 | 3 | | 27 |
| Matej Vydra *(Watford)* | 22 | 0 | 0 | 2 | 24 |
| Chris Wood *(Leicester C)* | 20 | 2 | 0 | 0 | 22 |
| *(Includes 11 League goals for Millwall)* | | | | | |
| Troy Deeney *(Watford)* | 20 | 0 | 0 | 1 | 21 |
| Thomas Ince *(Blackpool)* | 18 | 0 | 0 | | 18 |
| Luciano Becchio *(Leeds U)* | 15 | 1 | 3 | | 18 |
| David Nugent *(Leicester C)* | 14 | 0 | 0 | 2 | 16 |
| Sylvan Ebanks-Blake *(Wolverhampton W)* | 14 | 0 | 1 | | 15 |
| James Vaughan *(Huddersfield T)* | 14 | 0 | 0 | | 14 |
| Marlon King *(Birmingham C)* | 13 | 0 | 1 | | 14 |
| Steve Davies *(Bristol C)* | 13 | 0 | 0 | | 13 |
| Dwight Gayle *(Peterborough U)* | 13 | 0 | 0 | | 13 |
| Scott McDonald *(Middlesbrough)* | 12 | 0 | 1 | | 13 |
| Craig Davies *(Bolton W)* | 12 | 0 | 1 | | 13 |
| *(Includes 8 League goals and 1 Capital One Cup goal for Barnsley)* | | | | | |
| Almen Abdi *(Watford)* | 12 | 0 | 0 | 0 | 12 |
| Chris Eagles *(Bolton W)* | 12 | 0 | 0 | | 12 |
| Jamie Ward *(Derby Co)* | 12 | 0 | 0 | | 12 |
| Johnnie Jackson *(Charlton Ath)* | 12 | 0 | 0 | | 12 |
| Yann Kermorgant *(Charlton Ath)* | 12 | 0 | 0 | | 12 |
| Lee Tomlin *(Peterborough U)* | 11 | 0 | 2 | | 13 |
| Craig Mackail-Smith *(Brighton & HA)* | 11 | 0 | 0 | 0 | 11 |
| Billy Sharp *(Nottingham F)* | 10 | 1 | 0 | | 11 |
| Sam Baldock *(Bristol C)* | 10 | 0 | 0 | | 10 |
| George Boyd *(Hull C)* | 10 | 0 | 0 | | 10 |
| DJ Campbell *(Blackburn R)* | 10 | 0 | 0 | | 10 |
| Chris O'Grady *(Barnsley)* | 10 | 0 | 0 | | 10 |

## NPOWER FOOTBALL LEAGUE CHAMPIONSHIP – RESULTS 2012-13

| | Wolverhampton W | Watford | Sheffield W | Peterborough U | Nottingham F | Millwall | Middlesbrough | Leicester C | Leeds U | Ipswich T | Hull C | Huddersfield T | Derby Co | Crystal Palace | Charlton Ath | Cardiff C | Burnley | Bristol C | Brighton & HA | Bolton W | Blackpool | Blackburn R | Birmingham C | Barnsley |
|---|---|---|---|---|---|---|---|---|---|---|---|---|---|---|---|---|---|---|---|---|---|---|---|---|
| Barnsley | 2-1 | 1-0 | 0-1 | 0-2 | 1-4 | 2-0 | 1-0 | 2-0 | 2-0 | 1-1 | 2-0 | 0-1 | 1-1 | 1-1 | 0-6 | 1-2 | 1-1 | 1-0 | 2-1 | 2-3 | 1-1 | 1-3 | 1-2 | — |
| Birmingham C | 2-3 | 0-4 | 1-0 | 1-0 | 2-1 | 1-1 | 3-2 | 1-1 | 1-0 | 0-1 | 2-3 | 1-0 | 3-1 | 2-2 | 0-0 | 0-1 | 2-2 | 2-0 | 2-2 | 2-1 | 1-1 | 1-1 | — | 0-5 |
| Blackburn R | 0-1 | 1-0 | 1-0 | 2-3 | 3-0 | 0-2 | 1-2 | 2-1 | 3-3 | 3-0 | 3-3 | 1-0 | 2-0 | 1-0 | 0-1 | 1-1 | 1-1 | 2-0 | 2-2 | 2-1 | 1-1 | — | 1-1 | 2-1 |
| Blackpool | 1-2 | 2-2 | 0-0 | 0-1 | 2-2 | 4-1 | 0-0 | 0-0 | 2-0 | 6-1 | 0-0 | 1-3 | 2-2 | 1-0 | 0-2 | 1-2 | 1-0 | 0-0 | 1-1 | 2-2 | — | 1-1 | 2-2 | 1-2 |
| Bolton W | 2-0 | 2-1 | 0-1 | 1-0 | 2-2 | 2-0 | 3-2 | 0-0 | 2-2 | 4-1 | 1-0 | 1-0 | 2-0 | 3-0 | 2-0 | 2-1 | 2-1 | 3-2 | 1-0 | — | 2-2 | 1-0 | 3-1 | 1-1 |
| Brighton & HA | 2-0 | 1-3 | 3-0 | 1-0 | 0-0 | 1-1 | 2-0 | 1-1 | 1-1 | 1-2 | 1-0 | 4-1 | 1-2 | 4-1 | 0-0 | 0-0 | 1-0 | 2-0 | — | 1-1 | 1-1 | 1-1 | 0-1 | 5-1 |
| Bristol C | 1-4 | 2-0 | 1-1 | 4-2 | 2-0 | 1-1 | 0-1 | 0-1 | 1-1 | 0-1 | 0-1 | 1-3 | 0-4 | 0-1 | 0-2 | 4-2 | 3-4 | — | 0-0 | 1-2 | 1-0 | 3-5 | 0-1 | 5-3 |
| Burnley | 2-0 | 2-0 | 3-3 | 5-2 | 1-1 | 1-0 | 0-0 | 1-1 | 1-0 | 1-2 | 1-2 | 1-3 | 2-0 | 4-1 | 0-2 | 1-1 | — | 3-1 | 0-0 | 2-0 | 1-0 | 1-1 | 1-2 | 1-1 |
| Cardiff C | 3-1 | 1-1 | 1-0 | 1-2 | 3-0 | 1-0 | 0-0 | 1-1 | 0-1 | 2-1 | 2-1 | 0-1 | 1-1 | 2-1 | 0-1 | — | 4-0 | 2-1 | 0-2 | 1-1 | 3-0 | 3-0 | 2-1 | 1-1 |
| Charlton Ath | 2-1 | 2-1 | 1-0 | 2-0 | 0-2 | 0-2 | 1-4 | 1-1 | 2-1 | 1-1 | 2-1 | 0-1 | 1-1 | 0-1 | — | 5-4 | 0-1 | 4-1 | 3-0 | 0-0 | 2-1 | 1-1 | 0-4 | 0-1 |
| Crystal Palace | 2-1 | 1-2 | 1-2 | 3-2 | 1-1 | 2-2 | 4-1 | 2-2 | 2-2 | 5-0 | 4-2 | 3-0 | 3-0 | — | 2-1 | 3-2 | 4-3 | 3-0 | 3-0 | 0-0 | 2-2 | 2-0 | 3-2 | 0-0 |
| Derby Co | 1-0 | 2-3 | 2-2 | 3-1 | 1-1 | 3-0 | 3-1 | 2-1 | 3-1 | 0-0 | 1-2 | 3-0 | — | 0-1 | 3-2 | 1-1 | 1-2 | 1-0 | 2-1 | 1-1 | 4-1 | 1-1 | 3-2 | 2-0 |
| Huddersfield T | 1-3 | 1-0 | 1-2 | 6-1 | 2-1 | 1-0 | 1-0 | 1-2 | 4-0 | 3-0 | 3-0 | — | 1-0 | 1-2 | 1-2 | 2-2 | 4-3 | 1-0 | 0-0 | 2-2 | 1-0 | 1-1 | 0-1 | 1-0 |
| Hull C | 2-0 | 2-3 | 1-0 | 0-1 | 1-0 | 0-1 | 1-2 | 0-1 | 2-3 | 0-1 | — | 0-1 | 1-0 | 1-2 | 0-1 | 1-2 | 1-1 | 1-0 | 1-0 | 1-2 | 2-0 | 1-0 | 1-1 | 1-0 |
| Ipswich T | 2-1 | 0-1 | 1-0 | 1-0 | 3-1 | 3-0 | 4-0 | 1-0 | 3-0 | — | 1-2 | 2-2 | 1-2 | 3-0 | 1-2 | 0-1 | 2-1 | 1-1 | 0-3 | 1-0 | 2-3 | 1-1 | 3-1 | 1-1 |
| Leeds U | 1-0 | 1-6 | 2-1 | 2-0 | 2-1 | 1-0 | 2-1 | 1-0 | — | 2-0 | 2-3 | 2-2 | 1-2 | 0-0 | 1-2 | 2-1 | 1-0 | 1-1 | 1-2 | 1-0 | 2-0 | 3-3 | 0-1 | 3-3 |
| Leicester C | 2-1 | 1-2 | 0-1 | 2-0 | 2-2 | 0-1 | 1-0 | — | 1-0 | 6-0 | 3-1 | 6-1 | 4-1 | 1-2 | 1-2 | 2-1 | 2-1 | 2-0 | 3-1 | 3-2 | 1-0 | 3-0 | 0-1 | 2-2 |
| Middlesbrough | 2-0 | 1-2 | 3-1 | 0-0 | 1-0 | 1-2 | — | 1-2 | 1-0 | 2-0 | 2-0 | 4-0 | 3-0 | 2-1 | 1-2 | 2-1 | 3-2 | 2-1 | 0-2 | 2-1 | 4-2 | 1-0 | 0-1 | 2-3 |
| Millwall | 0-2 | 1-0 | 1-2 | 1-5 | 0-1 | — | 3-1 | 1-0 | 4-2 | 2-0 | 1-0 | 4-0 | 3-0 | 2-2 | 0-0 | 3-1 | 0-2 | 2-1 | 1-2 | 1-1 | 0-2 | 1-2 | 3-3 | 1-2 |
| Nottingham F | 3-1 | 0-3 | 1-0 | 2-1 | — | 1-4 | 0-0 | 2-3 | 4-2 | 1-0 | 1-2 | 3-1 | 0-0 | 2-2 | 2-1 | 3-1 | 2-0 | 3-1 | 2-2 | 1-1 | 1-2 | 0-0 | 0-1 | 0-0 |
| Peterborough U | 0-2 | 3-2 | 1-0 | — | 0-1 | 1-2 | 2-3 | 2-1 | 1-1 | 1-1 | 1-1 | 3-1 | 1-2 | 1-2 | 2-2 | 3-1 | 2-2 | 3-1 | 2-2 | 1-1 | 0-2 | 1-4 | 0-2 | 2-1 |
| Sheffield W | 0-2 | 1-4 | — | 2-1 | 0-1 | 3-2 | 2-0 | 0-2 | 1-1 | 1-1 | 0-1 | 4-0 | 2-2 | 1-0 | 2-0 | 0-0 | 3-3 | 2-2 | 0-1 | 2-1 | 0-2 | 3-2 | 3-2 | 2-1 |
| Watford | 0-0 | — | 2-1 | 1-0 | 2-0 | 0-0 | 1-2 | 2-1 | 1-2 | 0-1 | 1-2 | 4-0 | 1-1 | 2-2 | 3-4 | 0-0 | 3-3 | 2-1 | 0-1 | 2-1 | 1-2 | 4-0 | 2-0 | 4-1 |
| Wolverhampton W | — | 1-1 | 1-0 | 0-3 | 0-1 | 0-1 | 3-2 | 2-1 | 2-2 | 0-2 | 1-0 | 1-3 | 1-1 | 1-2 | 1-1 | 1-2 | 1-2 | 2-1 | 3-3 | 2-2 | 1-2 | 1-1 | 1-0 | 3-1 |

# NPOWER FOOTBALL LEAGUE 1 2012–13

(P) *Promoted into division at end of 2011–12 season.* (R) *Relegated into division at end of 2011–12 season.*

|  |  |  | Total | | | | | Home | | | | | Away | | | | | | |
|---|---|---|---|---|---|---|---|---|---|---|---|---|---|---|---|---|---|---|---|---|
|  |  | P | W | D | L | F | A | W | D | L | F | A | W | D | L | F | A | GD | Pts |
| 1 | Doncaster R (R) | 46 | 25 | 9 | 12 | 62 | 44 | 10 | 5 | 8 | 26 | 23 | 15 | 4 | 4 | 36 | 21 | 18 | 84 |
| 2 | Bournemouth | 46 | 24 | 11 | 11 | 76 | 53 | 13 | 6 | 4 | 43 | 21 | 11 | 5 | 7 | 33 | 32 | 23 | 83 |
| 3 | Brentford | 46 | 21 | 16 | 9 | 62 | 47 | 14 | 6 | 3 | 37 | 22 | 7 | 10 | 6 | 25 | 25 | 15 | 79 |
| 4 | Yeovil T¶ | 46 | 23 | 8 | 15 | 71 | 56 | 13 | 4 | 6 | 36 | 22 | 10 | 4 | 9 | 35 | 34 | 15 | 77 |
| 5 | Sheffield U | 46 | 19 | 18 | 9 | 56 | 42 | 8 | 11 | 4 | 31 | 21 | 11 | 7 | 5 | 25 | 21 | 14 | 75 |
| 6 | Swindon T (P) | 46 | 20 | 14 | 12 | 72 | 39 | 10 | 9 | 4 | 44 | 15 | 10 | 5 | 8 | 28 | 24 | 33 | 74 |
| 7 | Leyton Orient | 46 | 21 | 8 | 17 | 55 | 48 | 13 | 3 | 7 | 31 | 20 | 8 | 5 | 10 | 24 | 28 | 7 | 71 |
| 8 | Milton Keynes D | 46 | 19 | 13 | 14 | 62 | 45 | 12 | 5 | 6 | 35 | 21 | 7 | 8 | 8 | 27 | 24 | 17 | 70 |
| 9 | Walsall | 46 | 17 | 17 | 12 | 65 | 58 | 10 | 8 | 5 | 38 | 29 | 7 | 9 | 7 | 27 | 29 | 7 | 68 |
| 10 | Crawley T (P) | 46 | 18 | 14 | 14 | 59 | 58 | 9 | 9 | 5 | 34 | 27 | 9 | 5 | 9 | 25 | 31 | 1 | 68 |
| 11 | Tranmere R | 46 | 19 | 10 | 17 | 58 | 48 | 10 | 6 | 7 | 31 | 21 | 9 | 4 | 10 | 27 | 27 | 10 | 67 |
| 12 | Notts Co | 46 | 16 | 17 | 13 | 61 | 49 | 9 | 6 | 8 | 32 | 26 | 7 | 11 | 5 | 29 | 23 | 12 | 65 |
| 13 | Crewe Alex (P) | 46 | 18 | 10 | 18 | 54 | 62 | 12 | 3 | 8 | 26 | 22 | 6 | 7 | 10 | 28 | 40 | -8 | 64 |
| 14 | Preston NE | 46 | 14 | 17 | 15 | 54 | 49 | 8 | 9 | 6 | 31 | 22 | 6 | 8 | 9 | 23 | 27 | 5 | 59 |
| 15 | Coventry C* (R) | 46 | 18 | 11 | 17 | 66 | 59 | 7 | 7 | 9 | 29 | 27 | 11 | 4 | 8 | 37 | 32 | 7 | 55 |
| 16 | Shrewsbury T (P) | 46 | 13 | 16 | 17 | 54 | 60 | 9 | 7 | 7 | 29 | 27 | 4 | 9 | 10 | 25 | 33 | -6 | 55 |
| 17 | Carlisle U | 46 | 14 | 13 | 19 | 56 | 77 | 7 | 7 | 9 | 32 | 43 | 7 | 6 | 10 | 24 | 34 | -21 | 55 |
| 18 | Stevenage | 46 | 15 | 9 | 22 | 47 | 64 | 7 | 5 | 11 | 26 | 34 | 8 | 4 | 11 | 21 | 30 | -17 | 54 |
| 19 | Oldham Ath | 46 | 14 | 9 | 23 | 46 | 59 | 8 | 4 | 11 | 25 | 26 | 6 | 5 | 12 | 21 | 33 | -13 | 51 |
| 20 | Colchester U | 46 | 14 | 9 | 23 | 47 | 68 | 8 | 4 | 11 | 25 | 31 | 6 | 5 | 12 | 22 | 37 | -21 | 51 |
| 21 | Scunthorpe U | 46 | 13 | 9 | 24 | 49 | 73 | 7 | 6 | 10 | 31 | 38 | 6 | 3 | 14 | 18 | 35 | -24 | 48 |
| 22 | Bury | 46 | 9 | 14 | 23 | 45 | 73 | 6 | 6 | 11 | 24 | 33 | 3 | 8 | 12 | 21 | 40 | -28 | 41 |
| 23 | Hartlepool U | 46 | 9 | 14 | 23 | 39 | 67 | 5 | 8 | 10 | 19 | 27 | 4 | 6 | 13 | 20 | 40 | -28 | 41 |
| 24 | Portsmouth† (R) | 46 | 10 | 12 | 24 | 51 | 69 | 7 | 5 | 11 | 27 | 27 | 3 | 7 | 13 | 24 | 42 | -18 | 32 |

*Coventry C deducted 10 points. †Portsmouth deducted 10 points. ¶Yeovil T promoted via play-offs.*

## LEADING GOALSCORERS 2012–13

|  | League | FA Cup | Capital One Cup | J Paint Trophy | Play-Offs | Total |
|---|---|---|---|---|---|---|
| Patrick Madden *(Yeovil T)* | 23 | 0 | 0 | 0 | 1 | 24 |
| Leon Clarke *(Coventry C)* | 19 | 0 | 0 | 2 |  | 21 |
| *(Includes 11 League goals for Scunthorpe U)* | | | | | | |
| William Grigg *(Walsall)* | 19 | 0 | 0 | 1 |  | 20 |
| Brett Pitman *(Bournemouth)* | 19 | 0 | 0 | 0 |  | 19 |
| Clayton Donaldson *(Brentford)* | 18 | 4 | 0 | 0 | 2 | 24 |
| David McGoldrick *(Coventry C)* | 16 | 0 | 0 | 1 |  | 17 |
| Kevin Lisbie *(Leyton Orient)* | 16 | 0 | 0 | 0 |  | 16 |
| James Hayter *(Yeovil T)* | 14 | 0 | 0 | 2 | 0 | 16 |
| Jose Baxter *(Oldham Ath)* | 13 | 2 | 0 | 0 |  | 15 |
| Lewis Grabban *(Bournemouth)* | 13 | 0 | 0 | 0 |  | 13 |
| Billy Paynter *(Doncaster R)* | 13 | 0 | 0 | 0 | 0 | 13 |
| Mathias Pogba *(Crewe Alex)* | 12 | 1 | 2 | 1 |  | 16 |
| Carl Baker *(Coventry C)* | 12 | 1 | 1 | 1 |  | 15 |
| Jamie Paterson *(Walsall)* | 12 | 1 | 0 | 0 |  | 13 |
| Matt Ritchie *(Bournemouth)* | 12 | 0 | 0 | 0 |  | 12 |
| Nick Blackman *(Sheffield U)* | 11 | 2 | 1 | 0 | 0 | 14 |
| Dave Kitson *(Sheffield U)* | 11 | 1 | 0 | 0 | 0 | 12 |
| Ryan Lowe *(Milton Keynes D)* | 11 | 1 | 0 | 0 |  | 12 |
| Andrew Williams *(Swindon T)* | 11 | 0 | 1 | 0 | 0 | 12 |
| Jake Cassidy *(Tranmere R)* | 11 | 0 | 0 | 0 |  | 11 |
| Karl Hawley *(Scunthorpe U)* | 11 | 0 | 0 | 0 |  | 11 |
| Izale McLeod *(Milton Keynes D)* | 11 | 0 | 0 | 0 |  | 11 |
| Billy Clarke *(Crawley T)* | 10 | 2 | 1 | 1 |  | 14 |
| Adam Rooney *(Swindon T)* | 10 | 0 | 0 | 0 | 1 | 11 |
| Lucas Akins *(Stevenage)* | 10 | 0 | 0 | 0 |  | 10 |
| David Cotterill *(Doncaster R)* | 10 | 0 | 0 | 0 |  | 10 |
| Andy Robinson *(Tranmere R)* | 10 | 0 | 0 | 0 |  | 10 |
| Akpo Sodje *(Scunthorpe U)* | 10 | 0 | 0 | 0 |  | 10 |

## NPOWER FOOTBALL LEAGUE 1 – RESULTS 2012-13

| | Bournemouth | Brentford | Bury | Carlisle U | Colchester U | Coventry C | Crawley T | Crewe Alex | Doncaster R | Hartlepool U | Leyton O | Milton Keynes D | Notts Co | Oldham Ath | Portsmouth | Preston NE | Scunthorpe U | Sheffield U | Shrewsbury T | Stevenage | Swindon T | Tranmere R | Walsall | Yeovil T |
|---|---|---|---|---|---|---|---|---|---|---|---|---|---|---|---|---|---|---|---|---|---|---|---|---|
| Bournemouth | — | 2-2 | 4-1 | 3-1 | 1-0 | 0-2 | 3-0 | 3-1 | 1-2 | 1-1 | 2-0 | 1-1 | 3-1 | 4-1 | 2-0 | 1-1 | 1-0 | 0-1 | 2-1 | 1-1 | 1-1 | 3-1 | 1-2 | 3-0 |
| Brentford | 0-0 | — | 2-2 | 2-1 | 1-0 | 2-1 | 2-1 | 5-1 | 0-1 | 2-2 | 2-2 | 3-2 | 2-0 | 1-0 | 3-2 | 1-0 | 1-0 | 2-0 | 0-0 | 2-0 | 2-1 | 1-2 | 0-0 | 1-3 |
| Bury | 2-2 | 0-0 | — | 1-1 | 1-2 | 0-2 | 0-2 | 2-2 | 2-0 | 2-1 | 0-2 | 1-4 | 0-2 | 0-1 | 2-0 | 1-2 | 2-1 | 0-2 | 2-2 | 2-0 | 0-1 | 0-1 | 1-1 | 3-2 |
| Carlisle U | 2-4 | 2-1 | 2-1 | — | 0-2 | 0-2 | 0-2 | 2-2 | 1-3 | 3-0 | 1-4 | 1-1 | 0-4 | 3-1 | 4-2 | 1-1 | 1-1 | 1-3 | 2-2 | 2-1 | 2-2 | 0-3 | 0-3 | 3-3 |
| Colchester U | 0-1 | 1-3 | 2-0 | 2-0 | — | 1-3 | 1-1 | 2-0 | 1-2 | 3-1 | 1-4 | 0-2 | 2-2 | 3-1 | 2-2 | 1-1 | 1-1 | 1-1 | 0-0 | 1-0 | 2-2 | 1-5 | 2-0 | 2-0 |
| Coventry C | 1-0 | 1-1 | 2-2 | 1-2 | 1-3 | — | 1-1 | 1-2 | 1-0 | 3-1 | 2-1 | 2-3 | 1-2 | 2-1 | 2-2 | 1-1 | 1-2 | 1-1 | 2-2 | 1-0 | 0-1 | 1-0 | 2-0 | 1-1 |
| Crawley T | 3-1 | 1-2 | 3-2 | 1-1 | 0-0 | 2-1 | — | 2-0 | 1-0 | 2-2 | 1-1 | 2-0 | 0-0 | 1-1 | 0-3 | 1-0 | 3-0 | 0-2 | 1-1 | 1-2 | 1-1 | 2-5 | 5-1 | 0-1 |
| Crewe Alex | 1-2 | 0-2 | 3-2 | 1-0 | 2-2 | 1-0 | 2-0 | — | 1-2 | 3-0 | 1-0 | 2-0 | 0-0 | 0-2 | 1-1 | 1-0 | 3-0 | 1-0 | 1-0 | 1-2 | 2-1 | 2-1 | 2-2 | 0-1 |
| Doncaster R | 0-1 | 2-1 | 1-0 | 0-2 | 1-2 | 1-4 | 0-1 | 1-2 | — | 2-3 | 2-0 | 0-1 | 3-0 | 0-2 | 0-3 | 1-3 | 2-3 | 0-2 | 2-2 | 1-1 | 1-2 | 0-3 | 2-0 | 0-1 |
| Hartlepool U | 1-2 | 1-1 | 2-1 | 1-2 | 0-0 | 0-5 | 0-1 | 0-2 | 2-3 | — | 2-1 | 1-0 | 3-0 | 0-1 | 1-3 | 0-1 | 5-0 | 1-2 | 1-0 | 1-1 | 0-1 | 1-0 | 1-2 | 1-1 |
| Leyton O | 3-1 | 1-0 | 2-0 | 4-1 | 0-2 | 0-1 | 0-1 | 3-0 | 0-2 | 2-1 | — | 2-0 | 1-1 | 1-2 | 0-0 | 2-0 | 0-0 | 1-2 | 2-2 | 1-1 | 1-0 | 3-1 | 0-0 | 0-0 |
| Milton Keynes D | 0-3 | 2-0 | 1-1 | 2-0 | 5-1 | 2-3 | 0-0 | 1-1 | 0-1 | 1-0 | 2-0 | — | 1-2 | 3-1 | 1-0 | 0-1 | 2-1 | 1-0 | 2-1 | 4-1 | 1-2 | 1-0 | 2-1 | 1-0 |
| Notts Co | 3-3 | 2-0 | 4-1 | 1-0 | 2-2 | 2-2 | 1-1 | 1-1 | 3-0 | 3-0 | 1-1 | 1-2 | — | 2-0 | 0-2 | 3-1 | 2-2 | 1-1 | 2-2 | 1-0 | 1-1 | 1-1 | 0-1 | 1-0 |
| Oldham Ath | 0-1 | 0-2 | 1-2 | 1-2 | 2-0 | 0-1 | 2-1 | 1-2 | 0-2 | 0-1 | 2-0 | 3-1 | 2-0 | — | 0-1 | 3-1 | 2-2 | 0-2 | 2-2 | 2-1 | 1-0 | 3-1 | 1-1 | 1-2 |
| Portsmouth | 1-1 | 0-1 | 2-0 | 1-1 | 2-3 | 1-0 | 1-2 | 2-0 | 0-3 | 1-3 | 2-1 | 1-0 | 2-2 | 0-1 | — | 1-1 | 2-1 | 3-0 | 2-1 | 2-1 | 5-0 | 2-2 | 1-2 | 3-2 |
| Preston NE | 2-0 | 1-1 | 0-0 | 1-1 | 0-0 | 1-2 | 0-0 | 1-3 | 1-3 | 0-1 | 1-0 | 0-1 | 1-1 | 3-1 | 1-0 | — | 2-3 | 0-1 | 0-0 | 2-1 | 1-1 | 3-1 | 1-3 | 1-0 |
| Scunthorpe U | 1-2 | 1-1 | 1-2 | 3-1 | 1-0 | 1-2 | 2-1 | 1-2 | 2-3 | 5-0 | 0-0 | 2-1 | 2-2 | 2-2 | 2-1 | 2-3 | — | 1-1 | 1-0 | 1-1 | 1-1 | 1-0 | 1-4 | 1-2 |
| Sheffield U | 5-3 | 2-2 | 1-1 | 0-0 | 3-0 | 1-2 | 0-2 | 3-3 | 0-2 | 1-2 | 1-2 | 1-0 | 1-1 | 0-2 | 3-0 | 0-1 | 3-0 | — | 1-2 | 4-1 | 1-1 | 1-3 | 1-0 | 0-4 |
| Shrewsbury T | 0-3 | 0-0 | 0-0 | 2-1 | 2-2 | 4-1 | 3-0 | 1-0 | 2-2 | 1-0 | 2-2 | 2-1 | 2-2 | 2-2 | 3-2 | 1-4 | 1-0 | 1-2 | — | 2-1 | 1-1 | 1-1 | 3-1 | 0-2 |
| Stevenage | 0-1 | 2-0 | 0-1 | 1-1 | 0-2 | 3-0 | 1-2 | 2-2 | 1-1 | 1-1 | 1-1 | 4-1 | 1-0 | 2-1 | 2-1 | 2-1 | 1-1 | 4-1 | 2-1 | — | 3-0 | 1-0 | 3-0 | 0-2 |
| Swindon T | 4-0 | 2-1 | 1-0 | 4-0 | 1-3 | 1-3 | 3-0 | 4-1 | 1-2 | 0-1 | 1-0 | 1-2 | 1-1 | 1-0 | 5-0 | 1-1 | 1-1 | 1-1 | 1-1 | 0-4 | — | 5-0 | 2-2 | 1-3 |
| Tranmere R | 0-0 | 1-1 | 3-0 | 0-1 | 4-0 | 2-0 | 2-0 | 2-1 | 0-3 | 1-0 | 3-1 | 1-0 | 1-1 | 3-1 | 2-2 | 3-1 | 1-0 | 1-1 | 3-1 | 3-0 | 2-0 | — | 0-0 | 2-0 |
| Walsall | 3-1 | 2-2 | 1-1 | 1-2 | 1-0 | 4-0 | 2-2 | 2-2 | 2-0 | 1-1 | 1-2 | 2-1 | 1-1 | 3-1 | 1-2 | 1-3 | 1-4 | 1-0 | 3-1 | 3-0 | 2-2 | 0-0 | — | 2-2 |
| Yeovil T | 0-1 | 3-0 | 2-1 | 1-3 | 3-1 | 1-1 | 2-2 | 1-0 | 0-1 | 1-0 | 3-0 | 1-0 | 0-0 | 4-1 | 1-2 | 3-1 | 3-0 | 0-1 | 2-1 | 1-3 | 1-3 | 2-0 | 2-2 | — |

# NPOWER FOOTBALL LEAGUE 2 2012–13

(P) *Promoted into division at end of 2011–12 season.*     (R) *Relegated into division at end of 2011–12 season.*

| | | | Total | | | | | Home | | | | | Away | | | | | | |
|---|---|---|---|---|---|---|---|---|---|---|---|---|---|---|---|---|---|---|---|
| | | P | W | D | L | F | A | W | D | L | F | A | W | D | L | F | A | GD | Pts |
| 1 | Gillingham | 46 | 23 | 14 | 9 | 66 | 39 | 12 | 5 | 6 | 37 | 21 | 11 | 9 | 3 | 29 | 18 | 27 | 83 |
| 2 | Rotherham U | 46 | 24 | 7 | 15 | 74 | 59 | 14 | 1 | 8 | 44 | 29 | 10 | 6 | 7 | 30 | 30 | 15 | 79 |
| 3 | Port Vale | 46 | 21 | 15 | 10 | 87 | 52 | 10 | 7 | 6 | 50 | 26 | 11 | 8 | 4 | 37 | 26 | 35 | 78 |
| 4 | Burton Alb | 46 | 22 | 10 | 14 | 71 | 65 | 17 | 3 | 3 | 49 | 23 | 5 | 7 | 11 | 22 | 42 | 6 | 76 |
| 5 | Cheltenham T | 46 | 20 | 15 | 11 | 58 | 51 | 14 | 7 | 2 | 34 | 16 | 6 | 8 | 9 | 24 | 35 | 7 | 75 |
| 6 | Northampton T | 46 | 21 | 10 | 15 | 64 | 55 | 17 | 2 | 4 | 41 | 16 | 4 | 8 | 11 | 23 | 39 | 9 | 73 |
| 7 | Bradford C¶ | 46 | 18 | 15 | 13 | 63 | 52 | 12 | 5 | 6 | 34 | 21 | 6 | 10 | 7 | 29 | 31 | 11 | 69 |
| 8 | Chesterfield (R) | 46 | 18 | 13 | 15 | 60 | 45 | 9 | 8 | 6 | 39 | 24 | 9 | 5 | 9 | 21 | 21 | 15 | 67 |
| 9 | Oxford U | 46 | 19 | 8 | 19 | 60 | 61 | 9 | 6 | 8 | 29 | 27 | 10 | 2 | 11 | 31 | 34 | -1 | 65 |
| 10 | Exeter C (R) | 46 | 18 | 10 | 18 | 63 | 62 | 7 | 6 | 10 | 29 | 26 | 11 | 4 | 8 | 34 | 36 | 1 | 64 |
| 11 | Southend U | 46 | 16 | 13 | 17 | 61 | 55 | 6 | 8 | 9 | 24 | 25 | 10 | 5 | 8 | 37 | 30 | 6 | 61 |
| 12 | Rochdale (R) | 46 | 16 | 13 | 17 | 68 | 70 | 8 | 8 | 7 | 33 | 27 | 8 | 5 | 10 | 35 | 43 | -2 | 61 |
| 13 | Fleetwood T (P) | 46 | 15 | 15 | 16 | 55 | 57 | 7 | 9 | 7 | 27 | 32 | 8 | 6 | 9 | 28 | 25 | -2 | 60 |
| 14 | Bristol R | 46 | 16 | 12 | 18 | 60 | 69 | 11 | 4 | 8 | 32 | 28 | 5 | 8 | 10 | 28 | 41 | -9 | 60 |
| 15 | Wycombe W (R) | 46 | 17 | 9 | 20 | 50 | 60 | 8 | 7 | 8 | 27 | 24 | 9 | 2 | 12 | 23 | 36 | -10 | 60 |
| 16 | Morecambe | 46 | 15 | 13 | 18 | 55 | 61 | 8 | 9 | 6 | 28 | 27 | 7 | 4 | 12 | 27 | 34 | -6 | 58 |
| 17 | York C (P) | 46 | 12 | 19 | 15 | 50 | 60 | 6 | 8 | 9 | 25 | 31 | 6 | 11 | 6 | 25 | 29 | -10 | 55 |
| 18 | Accrington S | 46 | 14 | 12 | 20 | 51 | 68 | 7 | 7 | 9 | 28 | 34 | 7 | 5 | 11 | 23 | 34 | -17 | 54 |
| 19 | Torquay U | 46 | 13 | 14 | 19 | 55 | 62 | 9 | 6 | 8 | 38 | 40 | 4 | 8 | 11 | 17 | 22 | -7 | 53 |
| 20 | AFC Wimbledon | 46 | 14 | 11 | 21 | 54 | 76 | 6 | 8 | 9 | 28 | 34 | 8 | 3 | 12 | 26 | 42 | -22 | 53 |
| 21 | Plymouth Arg | 46 | 13 | 13 | 20 | 46 | 55 | 8 | 7 | 8 | 25 | 24 | 5 | 6 | 12 | 21 | 31 | -9 | 52 |
| 22 | Dagenham & R | 46 | 13 | 12 | 21 | 55 | 62 | 7 | 6 | 10 | 28 | 28 | 6 | 6 | 11 | 27 | 34 | -7 | 51 |
| 23 | Barnet | 46 | 13 | 12 | 21 | 47 | 59 | 8 | 9 | 6 | 28 | 23 | 5 | 3 | 15 | 19 | 36 | -12 | 51 |
| 24 | Aldershot T | 46 | 11 | 15 | 20 | 42 | 60 | 7 | 4 | 12 | 22 | 30 | 4 | 11 | 8 | 20 | 30 | -18 | 48 |

¶*Bradford C promoted via play-offs.*

## LEADING GOALSCORERS 2012–13

| | League | FA Cup | Capital One Cup | J Paint Trophy | Play-Offs | Total |
|---|---|---|---|---|---|---|
| Tom Pope *(Port Vale)* | 31 | 1 | 0 | 1 | | 33 |
| Jamie Cureton *(Exeter C)* | 21 | 0 | 0 | 0 | | 21 |
| Nahki Wells *(Bradford C)* | 18 | 1 | 3 | 0 | 4 | 26 |
| Daniel Nardiello *(Rotherham U)* | 18 | 1 | 0 | 0 | | 19 |
| Adebayo Akinfenwa *(Northampton T)* | 16 | 0 | 0 | 1 | 0 | 17 |
| Rene Howe *(Torquay U)* | 16 | 0 | 0 | 0 | | 16 |
| Jacques Maghoma *(Burton Alb)* | 15 | 1 | 1 | 0 | 1 | 18 |
| Britt Assombalonga *(Southend U)* | 15 | 0 | 0 | 1 | | 16 |
| Robert Grant *(Rochdale)* | 15 | 0 | 0 | 1 | | 16 |
| Jack Redshaw *(Morecambe)* | 15 | 0 | 0 | 1 | | 16 |
| Danny Kedwell *(Gillingham)* | 14 | 1 | 1 | 0 | | 16 |
| Jake Hyde *(Barnet)* | 14 | 0 | 0 | 0 | | 14 |
| Gavin Tomlin *(Southend U)* | 13 | 2 | 0 | 1 | | 16 |
| Jack Midson *(AFC Wimbledon)* | 13 | 2 | 0 | 0 | | 15 |
| Billy Kee *(Burton Alb)* | 13 | 1 | 0 | 0 | | 14 |
| Deon Burton *(Gillingham)* | 12 | 1 | 0 | 0 | | 13 |
| Marc Richards *(Chesterfield)* | 12 | 0 | 0 | 0 | | 12 |
| James Hanson *(Bradford C)* | 11 | 1 | 2 | 0 | 2 | 16 |
| Calvin Makongo Zola *(Burton Alb)* | 11 | 3 | 0 | 0 | 2 | 16 |
| Kevin Ellison *(Morecambe)* | 11 | 1 | 0 | 1 | | 13 |
| John O'Flynn *(Exeter C)* | 11 | 0 | 1 | 0 | | 12 |
| Craig Reid *(Aldershot T)* | 11 | 0 | 0 | 1 | | 12 |
| Matt McClure *(Wycombe W)* | 11 | 0 | 0 | 0 | | 11 |
| Junior Brown *(Fleetwood T)* | 10 | 2 | 0 | 0 | | 12 |
| Tom Craddock *(Oxford U)* | 10 | 0 | 0 | 2 | | 12 |
| Jon Parkin *(Fleetwood T)* | 10 | 2 | 0 | 0 | | 12 |
| Ashley Grimes *(Rochdale)* | 10 | 0 | 0 | 1 | | 11 |
| Joel Grant *(Wycombe W)* | 10 | 0 | 0 | 1 | | 11 |
| Alfie Potter *(Oxford U)* | 10 | 0 | 0 | 1 | | 11 |
| Romuald Boco *(Accrington S)* | 10 | 0 | 0 | 0 | | 10 |
| Ashley Chambers *(York C)* | 10 | 0 | 0 | 0 | | 10 |
| Lee Hughes *(Port Vale)* | 10 | 0 | 0 | 0 | | 10 |

## NPOWER FOOTBALL LEAGUE 2 – RESULTS 2012–13

| | Accrington S | AFC Wimbledon | Aldershot T | Barnet | Bradford C | Bristol R | Burton Alb | Cheltenham T | Chesterfield | Dagenham & R | Exeter C | Fleetwood T | Gillingham | Morecambe | Northampton T | Oxford U | Plymouth Arg | Port Vale | Rochdale | Rotherham U | Southend U | Torquay U | Wycombe W | York C |
|---|---|---|---|---|---|---|---|---|---|---|---|---|---|---|---|---|---|---|---|---|---|---|---|---|
| Accrington S | — | 4-0 | 1-0 | 3-2 | 1-1 | 1-0 | 3-3 | 2-2 | 1-0 | 0-2 | 0-3 | 0-3 | 1-1 | 2-0 | 2-4 | 0-3 | 1-1 | 2-0 | 2-3 | 1-2 | 1-1 | 0-0 | 0-2 | 0-1 |
| AFC Wimbledon | 1-2 | — | 1-1 | 0-1 | 1-1 | 3-1 | 1-1 | 1-2 | 1-0 | 2-2 | 2-2 | 2-1 | 0-1 | 2-0 | 1-1 | 0-3 | 1-1 | 2-2 | 1-2 | 0-1 | 0-4 | 0-1 | 2-2 | 3-2 |
| Aldershot T | 2-0 | 0-1 | — | 1-0 | 0-2 | 2-2 | 1-2 | 0-1 | 0-1 | 1-0 | 1-2 | 2-0 | 0-1 | 0-0 | 1-2 | 3-2 | 1-2 | 1-3 | 4-2 | 0-3 | 0-2 | 1-0 | 0-0 | 0-2 |
| Barnet | 1-1 | 1-1 | 0-1 | — | 2-0 | 2-2 | 3-2 | 0-0 | 0-2 | 1-0 | 1-2 | 2-0 | 1-3 | 4-1 | 4-0 | 2-2 | 1-4 | 1-3 | 0-0 | 0-3 | 2-0 | 1-0 | 1-0 | 1-3 |
| Bradford C | 2-1 | 5-1 | 1-1 | 3-0 | — | 4-1 | 1-0 | 3-1 | 0-0 | 1-1 | 0-1 | 1-0 | 3-1 | 3-1 | 1-0 | 1-2 | 1-0 | 0-1 | 2-4 | 0-2 | 2-2 | 1-0 | 1-0 | 1-1 |
| Bristol R | 0-1 | 1-0 | 2-2 | 2-1 | 3-3 | — | 3-0 | 0-1 | 3-2 | 0-1 | 2-0 | 0-0 | 0-2 | 0-3 | 3-1 | 0-2 | 2-1 | 1-1 | 2-1 | 1-2 | 2-3 | 3-2 | 1-0 | 0-0 |
| Burton Alb | 1-0 | 6-2 | 0-1 | 1-0 | 1-0 | 1-1 | — | 3-1 | 0-1 | 3-2 | 4-2 | 0-1 | 0-2 | 0-3 | 3-3 | 4-0 | 1-0 | 1-1 | 3-2 | 2-0 | 2-0 | 3-2 | 2-0 | 3-1 |
| Cheltenham T | 0-3 | 2-1 | 1-1 | 1-0 | 0-0 | 1-1 | 3-1 | — | 4-1 | 1-2 | 3-0 | 1-2 | 3-2 | 2-0 | 1-0 | 2-1 | 2-1 | 1-1 | 0-0 | 3-0 | 1-3 | 2-1 | 4-0 | 1-1 |
| Chesterfield | 4-3 | 2-0 | 0-0 | 0-1 | 0-0 | 2-0 | 1-1 | 4-1 | — | 1-2 | 4-0 | 1-2 | 1-0 | 1-1 | 3-0 | 2-1 | 2-1 | 2-2 | 1-1 | 1-1 | 0-1 | 1-1 | 3-1 | 3-0 |
| Dagenham & R | 1-1 | 0-1 | 0-0 | 1-0 | 0-1 | 2-4 | 1-1 | 1-0 | 0-1 | — | 1-1 | 1-0 | 0-1 | 1-2 | 0-1 | 0-1 | 0-0 | 2-3 | 2-1 | 5-0 | 0-3 | 2-2 | 3-0 | 0-1 |
| Exeter C | 2-0 | 0-0 | 0-0 | 2-2 | 3-0 | 1-2 | 1-1 | 0-1 | 0-1 | 0-1 | — | 2-2 | 0-0 | 0-3 | 3-0 | 1-3 | 1-1 | 0-2 | 1-2 | 0-1 | 3-0 | 0-1 | 3-2 | 1-1 |
| Fleetwood T | 1-3 | 1-1 | 0-0 | 2-1 | 0-4 | 1-2 | 0-4 | 1-1 | 1-3 | 0-1 | 0-0 | — | 2-2 | 1-0 | 1-0 | 3-0 | 3-0 | 2-5 | 0-3 | 1-1 | 0-0 | 0-0 | 3-2 | 1-1 |
| Gillingham | 1-0 | 2-2 | 4-0 | 2-1 | 3-1 | 4-0 | 4-1 | 0-0 | 1-1 | 2-1 | 2-3 | 2-2 | — | 2-1 | 2-0 | 0-1 | 2-1 | 1-2 | 1-2 | 1-0 | 0-0 | 1-0 | 0-1 | 1-1 |
| Morecambe | 0-0 | 3-1 | 2-1 | 4-1 | 1-0 | 1-1 | 0-3 | 0-0 | 2-0 | 2-1 | 0-3 | 0-4 | 1-1 | — | 1-1 | 1-1 | 2-3 | 1-3 | 3-0 | 2-1 | 1-0 | 0-2 | 0-1 | 2-2 |
| Northampton T | 2-0 | 2-0 | 2-0 | 2-0 | 0-1 | 1-0 | 1-0 | 2-3 | 0-0 | 3-1 | 3-0 | 3-1 | 1-2 | 3-0 | — | 1-0 | 1-0 | 2-0 | 3-1 | 2-1 | 3-3 | 1-0 | 3-1 | 0-0 |
| Oxford U | 5-0 | 3-2 | 1-1 | 1-0 | 0-2 | 0-2 | 1-1 | 1-0 | 0-1 | 2-3 | 2-4 | 1-2 | 0-0 | 1-1 | 2-1 | — | 2-1 | 2-1 | 3-1 | 0-4 | 2-0 | 0-0 | 0-1 | 0-0 |
| Plymouth Arg | 0-0 | 1-2 | 0-2 | 2-1 | 0-2 | 1-1 | 1-2 | 2-0 | 0-2 | 0-0 | 1-0 | 2-1 | 2-2 | 2-1 | 3-2 | 0-1 | — | 1-3 | 3-1 | 0-1 | 1-1 | 1-1 | 0-1 | 2-0 |
| Port Vale | 3-0 | 3-0 | 1-1 | 3-0 | 3-2 | 4-0 | 1-1 | 3-2 | 1-1 | 1-1 | 2-3 | 2-1 | 0-2 | 2-1 | 2-2 | 3-0 | 4-0 | — | 2-2 | 6-2 | 1-2 | 1-1 | 4-1 | 2-3 |
| Rochdale | 0-3 | 1-1 | 2-0 | 0-0 | 4-1 | 2-1 | 0-1 | 4-1 | 2-3 | 1-1 | 2-3 | 0-0 | 1-2 | 1-2 | 0-0 | 2-0 | 1-0 | 2-2 | — | 1-2 | 4-2 | 1-0 | 4-1 | 2-3 |
| Rotherham U | 4-1 | 1-0 | 1-1 | 0-2 | 1-3 | 3-0 | 0-1 | 4-2 | 1-0 | 3-1 | 4-1 | 2-1 | 1-2 | 2-1 | 3-1 | 3-1 | 1-0 | 1-0 | 2-3 | — | 0-3 | 1-0 | 2-3 | 1-1 |
| Southend U | 0-1 | 1-3 | 1-2 | 0-2 | 2-2 | 0-0 | 0-1 | 1-2 | 3-0 | 3-1 | 2-1 | 1-1 | 0-1 | 0-1 | 1-2 | 1-0 | 0-2 | 0-0 | 3-1 | 1-1 | — | 1-1 | 1-0 | 0-0 |
| Torquay U | 3-1 | 2-3 | 4-3 | 3-2 | 1-3 | 3-3 | 1-1 | 2-2 | 2-1 | 2-1 | 1-1 | 1-0 | 2-1 | 1-0 | 1-1 | 1-3 | 0-0 | 0-1 | 4-2 | 2-2 | 1-4 | — | 1-2 | 2-1 |
| Wycombe W | 0-1 | 0-1 | 2-1 | 0-0 | 3-2 | 2-0 | 3-0 | 1-1 | 2-1 | 1-0 | 0-1 | 1-0 | 0-1 | 2-2 | 0-0 | 1-3 | 1-1 | 1-1 | 1-2 | 2-2 | 1-2 | 2-1 | — | 4-0 |
| York C | 1-1 | 0-3 | 0-0 | 1-2 | 3-0 | 4-1 | 3-0 | 0-0 | 3-0 | 0-1 | 1-2 | 0-2 | 0-0 | 1-4 | 1-1 | 3-1 | 2-0 | 0-2 | 0-0 | 0-0 | 2-1 | 0-2 | 1-3 | — |

# FOOTBALL LEAGUE PLAY-OFFS 2012–13

■ *Denotes player sent off.*

## CHAMPIONSHIP SEMI-FINAL FIRST LEG

Thursday, 9 May 2013
**Leicester C (0) 1** *(Nugent 82)*
**Watford (0) 0**                                   29,560
*Leicester C:* (442) Schmeichel; De Laet, Morgan, Keane, Schlupp; Knockaert (Drinkwater 90), James, King, Dyer; Wood (Kane 63), Nugent.
*Watford:* (352) Almunia; Doyley (Hall 85), Ekstrand, Cassetti, Anya, Abdi, Chalobah, Hogg, Pudil (Briggs 73); Geijo, Vydra (Forestieri 90).

Friday, 10 May 2013
**Crystal Palace (0) 0**
**Brighton & HA (0) 0**                              23,294
*Crystal Palace:* (433) Speroni; Ward, Delaney, Gabbidon, Moxey; Dikgacoi, Jedinak, Garvan (Phillips 86); Williams (Bolasie 76), Murray (Wilbraham 67), Zaha.
*Brighton & HA:* (433) Kuszczak; Calderon, Greer, Upson, Bridge; Bridcutt, Lopez, Hammond; Buckley (LuaLua 73), Ulloa, Orlandi (Barnes 86).

## CHAMPIONSHIP SEMI-FINAL SECOND LEG

Sunday, 12 May 2013
**Watford (1) 3** *(Vydra 15, 65, Deeney 90)*
**Leicester C (1) 1** *(Nugent 19)*                  16,142
*Watford:* (352) Almunia; Doyley (Forestieri 64), Cassetti, Ekstrand; Briggs, Anya, Abdi, Battocchio (Hogg 79), Chalobah; Deeney, Vydra.
*Leicester C:* (442) Schmeichel; De Laet, Morgan, Keane, Schlupp; King, Dyer (Drinkwater 66), James, Knockaert; Nugent, Wood (Kane 61).

Monday, 13 May 2013
**Brighton & HA (0) 0**
**Crystal Palace (0) 2** *(Zaha 69, 88)*             29,518
*Brighton & HA:* (433) Kuszczak; Calderon (LuaLua 72), Greer, Upson, Bridge; Bridcutt, Lopez, Hammond; Buckley, Ulloa, Orlandi (Barnes 64).

*Crystal Palace:* (451) Speroni; Ward, Delaney, Gabbidon, Moxey; Dikgacoi, Garvan (Moritz 62), Jedinak, Zaha (O'Keefe 90), Williams (Bolasie 62); Wilbraham.

## CHAMPIONSHIP FINAL (at Wembley)

Monday, 27 May 2013
**Crystal Palace (0) 1** *(Phillips 105 (pen))*
**Watford (0) 0**                                    82,025
*Crystal Palace:* (451) Speroni; Ward, Gabbidon, Delaney, Moxey; Zaha, Jedinak, Garvan (Moritz 84), Dikgacoi (O'Keefe 17), Williams (Phillips 65); Wilbraham.
*Watford:* (3412) Almunia; Doyley, Ekstrand, Cassetti; Anya (Forestieri 86), Chalobah (Battocchio 74), Hogg, Pudil; Abdi; Deeney, Vydra (Geijo 45).
*aet.*
*Referee:* Martin Atkinson.

## LEAGUE ONE SEMI-FINAL FIRST LEG

Friday, 3 May 2013
**Sheffield U (0) 1** *(McFadzean 45)*
**Yeovil T (0) 0**                                   15,262
*Sheffield U:* (442) Long; Westlake, Maguire, Collins, Hill; Murphy, McDonald, Doyle, Robson (McFadzean 31); Porter (Whitehouse 90), Kitson (Ironside 74).
*Yeovil T:* (442) Stech; Ayling, Webster, Burn, McAllister; Dawson, Upson, Edwards, Foley, Madden, Hayter (Balanta 73).

Saturday, 4 May 2013
**Swindon T (0) 1** *(Luongo 70)*
**Brentford (0) 1** *(O'Connor 90 (pen))*            10,595
*Swindon T:* (451) Foderingham; Devera, Flint, Ward, Byrne; Rooney A, Ferry (Collins 82), McCormack, Luongo, Roberts; Williams.
*Brentford:* (442) Moore; Logan, O'Connor, Dean, Bidwell; Hodson (Forrester 77), Douglas, Adeyemi, Forshaw (Saunders 82); Donaldson, Wright-Phillips (El Alagui 68).

Patrick Madden (right) celebrates scoring Yeovil Town's first goal in their 2-1 triumph over Brentford in the League One Play-Off Final. Yeovil are entering the second tier for the first time in their history. (Action Images)

Bradford City's Nahki Wells pounces to score his side's third and final goal as the Yorkshire club eased into League One with a convincing 3-0 victory over Northampton Town in the League Two Play-Off Final. All three of City's goals came in the opening 28 minutes. (PA)

## LEAGUE ONE SEMI-FINAL SECOND LEG

Monday, 6 May 2013

**Brentford (2) 3** *(Rooney A 24 (og), Donaldson 40, 47)*
**Swindon T (1) 3** *(Rooney A 44, Devera 57, Flint 90)*  9109
*Brentford:* (442) Moore; Logan, Dean, Craig, Forshaw; Trotta (Hayes 82), Adeyemi (Douglas 56), Diagouraga, Bidwell; Donaldson, Forrester (Saunders 70).
*Swindon T:* (442) Foderingham; Flint, Devera, McCormack, Ward; Roberts, Williams (Collins 51), Byrne▪, Luongo; Rooney A (De Vita 51), Ferry (Storey 78).
*aet; Brentford won 5-4 on penalties.*

**Yeovil T (1) 2** *(Dawson 6, Upson 85)*
**Sheffield U (0) 0**  8152
*Yeovil T:* (442) Stech; Ayling, Burn, Webster, McAllister; Dawson, Upson, Edwards, Foley; Hayter (Hinds 90), Madden.
*Sheffield U:* (442) Long; Westlake (Higginbotham 55), Maguire, Collins, Hill; McFadzean (Flynn 87), Doyle, McDonald, Murphy; Ironside (Kitson 64), Porter.

## LEAGUE ONE FINAL (at Wembley)

Sunday, 19 May 2013

**Brentford (0) 1** *(Dean 51)*
**Yeovil T (2) 2** *(Madden 6, Burn 42)*  41,955
*Brentford:* (433) Moore; Logan, Craig, Dean, Bidwell; Forshaw, Adeyemi, Diagouraga (Hayes 82); Donaldson, Forrester (Saunders 68), Trotta (Wright-Phillips 62).
*Yeovil T:* (442) Stech; Ayling, Burn, Webster, McAllister (Maksimenko 77); Dawson, Edwards, Upson, Foley; Hayter (Dolan 88), Madden.
*Referee:* Andy D'Urso.

## LEAGUE TWO SEMI-FINAL FIRST LEG

Thursday, 2 May 2013

**Bradford C (1) 2** *(Wells 38 (pen), Thompson 74)*
**Burton Alb (3) 3** *(Zola 22, 28, Weir 44)*  14,657
*Bradford C:* (442) McLaughlin; Darby, McArdle, Nelson, Meredith; Jones, Thompson, Ravenhill (Doyle 57), Atkinson (Reid 57); Wells (Connell 89), Hanson.
*Burton Alb:* (4141) Tomlinson; O'Connor, Holness, Sharps, McCrory; Diamond; MacDonald (Drury 89), McGrath, Weir, Maghoma; Zola (Kee 67).

**Northampton T (1) 1** *(O'Donovan 27)*
**Cheltenham T (0) 0**  6563
*Northampton T:* (442) Nicholls G; Tozer, Cameron, Carlisle, Collins; Hackett, Guttridge, Harding, Demontagnac (Johnson 76); Akinfenwa, O'Donovan.
*Cheltenham T:* (442) Brown; Lowe, Hector (Jones 53), Elliott, Jombati; McGlashan (Deering 90), Pack, Penn, Mohamed; Harrison (Taylor 71), Benson.

## LEAGUE TWO SEMI-FINAL SECOND LEG

Sunday, 5 May 2013

**Burton Alb (0) 1** *(Maghoma 55 (pen))*
**Bradford C (1) 3** *(Wells 27, 57, Hanson 50)*  6148
*Burton Alb:* (4141) Tomlinson; O'Connor, Sharps, Holness (Kee 56), McCrory; Diamond; MacDonald, McGrath (Phillips 80), Weir, Maghoma; Zola (Symes 73).
*Bradford C:* (442) McLaughlin; Darby, McArdle, Davies, Meredith; Thompson, Jones, Doyle, Reid (Atkinson 73); Wells, Hanson.

**Cheltenham T (0) 0**
**Northampton T (1) 1** *(Guttridge 28)*  5955
*Cheltenham T:* (442) Brown; Lowe, Hector, Elliott, Jombati; McGlashan (Mohamed 73), Pack, Penn (Harrison 88), Deering; Duffy, Benson.
*Northampton T:* (451) Nicholls G; Johnson, Carlisle, Cameron, Collins; Hackett, Tozer, Harding, Guttridge (Hornby 75), O'Donovan; Akinfenwa (Langmead 71).

## LEAGUE TWO FINAL (at Wembley)

Saturday, 18 May 2013

**Bradford C (3) 3** *(Hanson 15, McArdle 19, Wells 28)*
**Northampton T (0) 0**  47,127
*Bradford C:* (442) McLaughlin; Darby, McArdle, Davies, Meredith; Thompson, Jones, Doyle (Ravenhill 87), Reid (Atkinson 78); Hanson, Wells (Connell 85).
*Northampton T:* (442) Nicholls G; Tozer, Carlisle, Cameron, Collins (Widdowson 53); Hackett, Harding, Guttridge, Demontagnac (Hornby 70); O'Donovan, Platt (Akinfenwa 55).
*Referee:* Keith Stroud.

# CUPS AND UPS AND DOWNS DIARY

**JANUARY**
12   Welsh Premier League Cup Final: Carmarthen T 3 The New Saints 3.
     *(Carmarthen T won 3-1 on penalties).*

**FEBRUARY**
24   Carling Cup Final: Swansea C 5 Bradford C 0.

**MARCH**
17   Scottish Communities League Cup Final: St Mirren 3 Hearts 2.
24   FA Trophy Final: Grimsby T 1 Wrexham 1.
     *(Wrexham won 4-1 on penalties).*
27   Queen of the S champions of Scottish League Division 2.
30   Rangers champions of Scottish League Division 3.
     AFC Telford relegated from Blue Square Premier League.

**APRIL**
 1   The New Saints Welsh Premier League Champions.
 6   Gillingham promoted to Football League One.
     Chester promoted to Blue Square Premier.
 7   Johnstone's Paint Trophy Final: Crewe Alex 2 Southend U 0.
     Ramsdens Cup Final: Queen of the S 1 Partick Th 1.
     *(Queen of the S won 6-5 on penalties).*
13   Bury relegated to Football League Two.
     Ebbsfleet U and Barrow relegated from Blue Square Premier League.
     Airdrie U relegated from Scottish First Division.
16   Cardiff C promoted to Premier League.
     Bristol City relegated to Football League One.
     Hartlepool U and Portsmouth relegated to Football League Two.
20   Cardiff C champions of Football League Championship.
     Bournemouth promoted to Football League Championship.
     Gillingham champions of Football League Two.
     Mansfield T promoted to Football League Two as champions of Blue Square Premier League.
     Stockport Co relegated from Blue Square Premier League.
21   Celtic Scottish Premier League Champions.
22   Manchester U Premier League Champions.
27   Doncaster R champions of Football League One.
     Port Vale and Rotherham U promoted to Football League One.
     Scunthorpe U relegated to Football League Two.
     Aldershot T and Barnet relegated to Blue Square Premier League.
28   QPR and Reading relegated to Football League Championship.

**MAY**
 4   FA Vase Final: Spennymoor U 2 Tunbridge Wells 1.
 5   Hull C promoted to Premier League.
     Wolverhampton W and Peterborough U relegated to Football League One.
     Blue Square Play-off Final: Newport Co 2 Wrexham 0.
     *(Newport Co promoted to Football League Two).*
 6   Welsh Cup Final: Prestatyn T 3 Bangor C 1 *aet.*
11   FA Cup Final: Wigan Ath 1 Manchester C 0.
14   Wigan Ath relegated to Football League Championship.
15   Europa League Final: Chelsea 2 Benfica 1.
16   Scottish First Division Play-off First Leg Alloa Ath 3 Dunfermline Ath 0.
     Scottish Second Division Play-off First Leg East Fife 0 Peterhead 0.
18   Football League One Play-off Final: Yeovil T 2 Brenford 1.
     *(Yeovil T promoted to Football League Championship).*
19   Football League Two Play-off Final: Bradford C 3 Northampton T 0.
     *(Bradford C promoted to Football League Championship).*
     Scottish First Division Play-off Second Leg Dunfermline Ath 1 Alloa Ath 0 (1-3 on aggregate).
     *(Dunfermline Ath relegated from Scottish First Division, Alloa Ath promoted from Scottish Second Division).*
     Scottish Second Division Play-off Second Leg Peterhead 0 East Fife 1 (0-1 on aggregate).
     *(East Fife remain in Scottish Second Division, Peterhead remain in Scottish Third Division).*
25   Champions League Final: Bayern Munich 2 Borussia Dortmund 1.
26   William Hill Scottish Cup Final: Celtic 3 Hibernian 0.
26   Women's FA Cup Final: Arsenal Ladies 3 Bristol Academy 0.
27   Football League Championship Play-off Final: Crystal Palace 1 Watford 0 *aet.*
     *(Crystal Palace promoted to Premier League).*

# REVIEW OF THE SEASON

The abiding memory of the 2012–13 season will be that of saying goodbye to the retiring Sir Alex Ferguson. To the backdrop of the iconic image of thousands of Manchester United fans waving flags aloft at Old Trafford in May, football said farewell to arguably the greatest manager in its history. But so much had also gone before that emotional send-off in a campaign which, although not necessarily considered a classic, was full of drama.

United were the eventual Premier League champions by an 11-point margin after what had, in truth, been a parade towards the title, while Queens Park Rangers, Reading and FA Cup winners Wigan Athletic were relegated.

But reigning European champions Chelsea were the top flight's August pacesetters with three wins from three. Swansea City, likewise, made a good start to an excellent first season under Michael Laudrup, which included winning the League Cup. The Welsh club's star signing, Michu, arguably the buy of the season in a £2m deal from Rayo Vallecano, gave an early indication of what was to come in scoring twice on his debut in the 5-0 thrashing of a QPR side who looked doomed from the off.

Everton made a nonsense of their perennial tag of slow starters as September arrived. David Moyes would go on and earn the Manager of the Month award and justifiably so after several Marouane Fellaini-inspired results helped the Goodison Park club to second in the early standings. Chelsea, under the management of Roberto Di Matteo – whose caretaker role from the previous season had been made permanent over the summer following 2012's famous UEFA Champions League and FA Cup double – continued to lead the way after an unbeaten six games. In contrast, Manchester United experienced an inconsistent start. Robin van Persie would finish as the league's 26-goal top scorer and the £24m summer signing from Arsenal scored three of those in a comeback win at Southampton. But United would also suffer a first home league loss to Tottenham Hotspur since 1989 in an engrossing 3-2 encounter. Gareth Bale was on the score-sheet at Old Trafford and it would be a campaign to remember for the Welshman, which ended in the double PFA and FWA Player of the Year awards. Luis Suarez, who would go on to finish second in the Premier League scoring charts despite causing more controversy, also scored a hat-trick as Brendan Rodgers recorded his first league win as Liverpool manager in a 5-2 thrashing of Norwich City.

Dimitar Berbatov enjoyed a good start to life at Fulham and the classy Bulgarian helped his new club to a surprising seventh place in the table in October. But it was their West London rivals Chelsea who continued to top the table, despite losing a seesaw 3-2 game to Manchester United at Stamford Bridge. Everton maintained their form by fighting back from two goals down to draw 2-2 with Liverpool in the first Merseyside derby of the season at Goodison Park, where Suarez grabbed the headlines by responding to play-acting accusations with a swan-dive celebration in front of Moyes.

November brought the first sackings in the Premier League. Mark Hughes was fired at winless QPR after a loss to Southampton, who were finding some momentum and went unbeaten in the month. Hughes would be replaced by Harry Redknapp. Controversially, Di Matteo was also fired by Chelsea after failing to win in the league in November. Rafa Benitez was subsequently brought in for the start of a rollercoaster interim spell until the end of the season. Manchester United took advantage of Chelsea's problems to ominously move to the top of the table for the first time. But they also lost at Norwich, who, after a difficult opening under new boss Chris Hughton, were picking up points that would prove vital in the long run. Defending champions Manchester City climbed to second. Meanwhile, Suarez scored one of the goals of the season as Liverpool drew with Newcastle United at Anfield, Arsenal won a classic North London derby 5-2 against Tottenham and West Bromwich Albion continued to cause surprises by sitting fourth as Steve Clarke took to life as a manager with ease.

The end of 2012 saw Benitez begin to settle at Chelsea, despite the majority of the club's fans making it clear the former Liverpool boss was not popular. An 8-0 December demolition of Aston Villa two days before Christmas was a fine response to losing the Club World Cup final in Japan. At the same time, the Premier League as a whole finished with 41 goals being scored on the final weekend of 2012. Stoke City would sit eighth in the table after Cameron Jerome's outrageous, long-range strike earned a late 3-3 draw with Southampton. It would, however, be downhill from there for Tony Pulis's side, who again failed to reach such an impressive position for the remainder of the campaign.

December also served up some of the games of the season. In the Manchester derby, Van Persie's injury-time free-kick earned United a 3-2 win at City to ensure they went the month unbeaten and sat seven points clear at the top of the table. City would remain second for the rest of the term. But Van Persie's former club, Arsenal, were not to be outdone as they also went goal crazy in a 7-3 win over struggling Newcastle courtesy of Theo Walcott's hat-trick, having already hammered Reading 5-2.

January saw Nigel Adkins lose his job as manager of Southampton despite guiding them out of the relegation zone – a feat which, in the same month, earned Brian McDermott the Manager of the Month award at Reading. Mauricio Pochettino was immediately brought in as a replacement at Southampton. Manchester United enjoyed another unbeaten month, including a 2-1 win over old rivals Liverpool.

Newcastle boosted their survival hopes in February with their only back-to-back league wins, including an electrifying 3-2 win over Chelsea in which January signing Moussa Sissoko scored twice. Manchester United made it three wins from three in the month to continue to lead the way at the top,

although their victory at Fulham descended into chaos with a 10-minute delay due to a floodlight failure. A 3-0 win at Reading moved Wigan out of the relegation zone. Rodgers' Liverpool – who would lose club legend Jamie Carragher to retirement at the end of the season – hammered his former club, Swansea, 5-0 at Anfield. But Swansea had selected a much-changed team in preparation for the League Cup final, which they won at Wembley by the same scoreline against League Two Bradford City.

February ended in style as Bale further underlined his star status with a sensational, last-gasp winner to add to an earlier strike in Tottenham's 3-2 victory at 2011–12 Championship play-off winners West Ham United, who were on their way to a respectable 10th-placed finish. It was Bale's ninth goal in seven games for club and country.

Two managers lost their jobs amid relegation fears in March. McDermott was sacked by Reading after a 2-1 defeat by fellow strugglers Aston Villa left them second from bottom of the table. He was replaced by Adkins. Four days later, Sunderland called time on Martin O'Neill after an eight-game winless run in which they picked up just three points. Meanwhile, Bale continued his seemingly relentless top form by scoring in Tottenham's 2-1 home win over Arsenal, which put Andre Villas-Boas' side in pole position to finish ahead of their local rivals in the top four. Pochettino was also doing well at Southampton after wins over Liverpool, Chelsea and Reading moved the South Coast club up to a season's high position of 11th.

The inevitable became reality at the end of April, when Manchester United ensured they would be champions following a 3-0 win over relegation-threatened Aston Villa at Old Trafford. Van Persie smashed a wonderful volley in a first-half hat-trick to secure the title. At the other end of the table, Reading and QPR were both relegated after a miserable goalless draw at the Madejski Stadium, which summed up their respective seasons. At the same time, one of the lowlights of the campaign saw Liverpool striker Suarez banned for 10 games as a result of his shocking bite on Chelsea defender Branislav Ivanovic. Elsewhere, Paolo Di Canio had been appointed as Sunderland's new head coach and the controversial Italian lost his first game in charge at Chelsea. But he then inspired a famous 3-0 win in the Tyne–Wear derby at Newcastle. Tottenham won 3-1 against Manchester City but still fell out of the top four for the first time since before Christmas. Aston Villa had spent the campaign in serious relegation danger but back-to-back wins, including a 6-1 hammering of Di Canio's Sunderland, would help Paul Lambert's young squad to eventual survival.

Much had already been decided by the time May arrived but Wigan Athletic were relegated in their penultimate game of the season. A 4-1 loss at Arsenal, just three days after shocking heavy favourites Manchester City to win the FA Cup, sent Roberto Martinez's men down. Benitez ensured his interim tenure at Chelsea was a success as they won the Europa League against Benfica and finished third in the Premier League. Manchester United famously said their farewells to Ferguson, along with Paul Scholes, in their final home game, with Rio Ferdinand's late goal defeating Swansea. Arsenal were also celebrating as they pipped a devastated Tottenham to fourth place and the Champions League as both teams won against the already-safe Newcastle and Sunderland respectively on the final day. In true Ferguson style, Manchester United signed off with a piece of history in the Premier League's first 5-5 draw, when West Brom were the opponents at The Hawthorns.

It was another typically frantic season in the Championship, where Cardiff City won the league by eight points and were followed in the automatic promotion places by Hull City. Ian Holloway's Crystal Palace defeated Watford in an anxiety-riddled play-off final at Wembley.

For Cardiff's Malaysian owners, topping the table was justification for a contentious rebranding of the club's colours. Malky Mackay's side had always looked like promotion favourites and never surrendered top spot from the end of November before wrapping up the title with a 1-1 draw at Burnley towards the end of April.

Having been painfully sacked by Premier League Sunderland in the previous season, Steve Bruce secured a sweet return to the top flight with Hull City. After a slow start, the Humberside club discovered some consistency around Christmas, which would ultimately prove enough. But it was not without drama as the nerve-shredding 2-2 draw with Cardiff on the final day of the league season was just enough to guarantee second place.

That topsy-turvy conclusion to the campaign will also live long in the memory for other clubs. Watford missed out on second place after losing to Leeds United. But Gianfranco Zola's team could have overtaken Hull had they found a winner in a lengthy period of injury time, which meant their game finished almost 15 minutes after the Hull–Cardiff match.

Also on the last day, Peterborough United and Wolverhampton Wanderers were the sides to join already-relegated Bristol City in dropping down to League One. Huddersfield Town, Blackburn Rovers, Millwall – who said goodbye to Kenny Jackett after six years at the end of the season – Barnsley and Sheffield Wednesday narrowly dodged demotion. Wolves' demise was particularly shocking given they had been a Premier League club just 12 months previously. Relegation cost Dean Saunders his job at Molineux only four months after he had succeeded Stale Solbakken.

Palace were the side to secure the final promotion place after the tense play-off final win over Watford, who had been criticised throughout the season for taking advantage of a loophole in the loan transfer rules. Despite losing the Championship's 30-goal top scorer, Glenn Murray, to injury, Palace had beaten Brighton & Hove Albion in a semi-final grudge tie. Watford, meanwhile, overcame Leicester City in a ludicrously eventful second leg, where Troy Deeney's injury-time decider came just 20 seconds after Anthony Knockaert had seen a penalty saved at the other end.

Kevin Phillips drives home the penalty that clinches a Premier League place for Crystal Palace, who beat Watford 1-0 in the Championship Playoff Final at Wembley on 27th May. (Action Images)

Having sat at the top of the table in autumn, Leicester were left to rue a poor second half of the season. Bolton Wanderers missed out on the play-offs on goal difference while Middlesbrough started the season with promotion hopes but finished just five points above the bottom three.

Nottingham Forest, Blackburn and Blackpool could not be ignored for the wrong reasons off the field during the course of the season after they all hired and fired several managers. Forest employed Sean O'Driscoll, Alex McLeish and Billy Davies while Blackpool also used three men in Ian Holloway, Michael Appleton and Paul Ince. Blackburn employed Steve Kean, Henning Berg, Michael Appleton and Gary Bowyer.

Charlton Athletic took advantage of the tight nature of the Championship to impressively finish ninth, four points ahead of Derby County, after finishing the season with an eight-game unbeaten run. Former Premier League clubs Burnley, Birmingham City, Leeds United (whose manager, Neil Warnock, resigned in the final weeks of the season to be replaced by Brian McDermott), and Ipswich Town all had to settle for disappointing mid-table finishes.

Doncaster Rovers won League One to go straight back to the Championship at the first time of asking but Bournemouth and Yeovil Town followed after securing surprise promotions.

Following a positive but slightly inconsistent start to the season, Saunders' January move to Wolves proved to have little impact on Doncaster. Brian Flynn succeeded his fellow Welshman until the end of the season at the Keepmoat Stadium and would go on to lose just six games as the title was secured by one point.

However, it would not be football if there was not an element of theatre and, like the Championship, it came on the final day of the season. Doncaster defeated Brentford as James Coppinger's winner in the fifth minute of added time settled the promotion shoot-out seconds after on-loan Fulham striker Marcello Trotta had hit the crossbar with a penalty for the opposition.

Brentford, as a result, had to settle for third position and a place in the play-offs, where, after beating Swindon Town on penalties in the semi-finals, they would lose the final in a dream promotion story for Sheffield United's conquerors, Gary Johnson's Yeovil.

Bournemouth turned their fortunes around after finishing in the mediocrity of 11th in 2011–12. With Eddie Howe back in charge from October, the South Coast club earned automatic promotion with a second-place finish, having only been denied the title on the final day following a costly draw at Tranmere Rovers.

Coventry City had been hoping to gate-crash the play-off places when they sat 10th in the table and just five points off the top six at the end of March. But a 10-point deduction for going into administration ended any such optimism.

Leyton Orient began with three straight defeats but a late surge saw them almost reach the play-offs. However, they joined MK Dons, Walsall and 10th-placed Crawley in finishing agonisingly short.

Tranmere Rovers had topped the table going into February but just three more wins from then until the end of the season saw them finish 11th, only two points ahead of Notts County and three points clear of 13th-placed Crewe Alexandra. Preston North End peaked in fifth in the opening weeks but finished in 14th, narrowly above Shrewsbury Town, Carlisle United and Stevenage.

The legendary Sir Alex Ferguson acknowledges the Manchester United fans after the club's final game of the season at The Hawthorns, bringing to an end a 26-year spell as manager at Old Trafford. (PA)

As was widely expected, off-field problems cost Portsmouth. The 2008 FA Cup winners and 2010 finalists were relegated to the lowest tier of the Football League and finished a huge 19 points from safety. A 10-point deduction for coming out of administration, when the Pompey Supporters' Trust completed their takeover in April, was critical. But Portsmouth had also gone on a 22-game winless run between the end of October and February.

Cash-strapped Bury, though, had been the first to be confirmed as relegated and they were soon followed by Hartlepool, who were condemned when Lee Johnson's Oldham Athletic defeated his father, Gary's, Yeovil in mid-April. Scunthorpe went down in 21st position on the final day of the season, despite a win over Swindon. Colchester United survived by three points.

Gillingham were crowned League Two champions, winning their first piece of silverware since 1964 in the process, and they were joined in promotion by Rotherham United, Port Vale and play-off winners Bradford City.

Martin Allen, at Gillingham, and Port Vale's Micky Adams were among the pick of the league's best managers. Allen guided Gillingham to the title with one game to spare and they lost just nine all season in an extremely competitive division. Adams had to overcome talk of Vale going out of business to produce results on the pitch, including a 6-2 thrashing of promotion rivals Rotherham and a 7-1 embarrassment of eventual play-off semi-finalists Burton Albion. Vale, helped by the league's runaway leading scorer, Tom Pope with 31 goals, finished third. Rotherham took second position having hit form at the right time with five successive wins in their final games.

Bradford were one of the stories of the season after Phil Parkinson's men reached the League Cup final, including penalty shoot-out wins over Premier League Wigan and Arsenal before beating Aston Villa over two legs in the semi-finals, only to suffer the heavy loss to Swansea. Parkinson's men eased their Wembley heartbreak at the end of the season when they defeated Northampton Town 3-0 in a dominant play-off final performance following a dramatic 5-4 aggregate victory over Burton in the semi-finals. Cheltenham Town had fallen to Northampton Town in the semis.

Chesterfield spent the season flirting with the play-off places but could never force their way into the top seven. An eight-game unbeaten run in mid-season was the best Oxford United achieved and they finished in the top half along with Exeter City, Southend United and Rochdale.

At the wrong end of League Two, there was the usual drama. Aldershot Town and Edgar Davids' Barnet both fell out of the Football League after final-day defeats by Rotherham and Northampton respectively. Dagenham & Redbridge survived on goal difference after limping over the finish line with three successive losses. Plymouth Argyle, AFC Wimbledon and Torquay United had all looked in trouble but narrowly managed to stay up.

York City climbed clear of trouble on their return to the Football League with an unbeaten run in their final six matches. Accrington Stanley, who suffered a mere two defeats in their last nine games, were also safe. Fleetwood Town, Bristol Rovers and Wycombe Wanderers all finished on 60 points in mid-table with 16th-placed Morecambe two points behind.

**Peter Fraser, Sky Sports**

# THE FA CHARITY SHIELD WINNERS 1908–2012

| Year | Match | Score | Year | Match | Score |
|---|---|---|---|---|---|
| 1908 | Manchester U v QPR | 4-0 after 1-1 draw | 1968 | Manchester C v WBA | 6-1 |
| 1909 | Newcastle U v Northampton T | 2-0 | 1969 | Leeds U v Manchester C | 2-1 |
| 1910 | Brighton v Aston Villa | 1-0 | 1970 | Everton v Chelsea | 2-1 |
| 1911 | Manchester U v Swindon T | 8-4 | 1971 | Leicester C v Liverpool | 1-0 |
| 1912 | Blackburn R v QPR | 2-1 | 1972 | Manchester C v Aston Villa | 1-0 |
| 1913 | Professionals v Amateurs | 7-2 | 1973 | Burnley v Manchester C | 1-0 |
| 1920 | WBA v Tottenham H | 2-0 | 1974 | Liverpool† v Leeds U | 1-1 |
| 1921 | Tottenham H v Burnley | 2-0 | 1975 | Derby Co v West Ham U | 2-0 |
| 1922 | Huddersfield T v Liverpool | 1-0 | 1976 | Liverpool v Southampton | 1-0 |
| 1923 | Professionals v Amateurs | 2-0 | 1977 | Liverpool v Manchester U | 0-0* |
| 1924 | Professionals v Amateurs | 3-1 | 1978 | Nottingham F v Ipswich T | 5-0 |
| 1925 | Amateurs v Professionals | 6-1 | 1979 | Liverpool v Arsenal | 3-1 |
| 1926 | Amateurs v Professionals | 6-3 | 1980 | Liverpool v West Ham U | 1-0 |
| 1927 | Cardiff C v Corinthians | 2-1 | 1981 | Aston Villa v Tottenham H | 2-2* |
| 1928 | Everton v Blackburn R | 2-1 | 1982 | Liverpool v Tottenham H | 1-0 |
| 1929 | Professionals v Amateurs | 3-0 | 1983 | Manchester U v Liverpool | 2-0 |
| 1930 | Arsenal v Sheffield W | 2-1 | 1984 | Everton v Liverpool | 1-0 |
| 1931 | Arsenal v WBA | 1-0 | 1985 | Everton v Manchester U | 2-0 |
| 1932 | Everton v Newcastle U | 5-3 | 1986 | Everton v Liverpool | 1-1* |
| 1933 | Arsenal v Everton | 3-0 | 1987 | Everton v Coventry C | 1-0 |
| 1934 | Arsenal v Manchester C | 4-0 | 1988 | Liverpool v Wimbledon | 2-1 |
| 1935 | Sheffield W v Arsenal | 1-0 | 1989 | Liverpool v Arsenal | 1-0 |
| 1936 | Sunderland v Arsenal | 2-1 | 1990 | Liverpool v Manchester U | 1-1* |
| 1937 | Manchester C v Sunderland | 2-0 | 1991 | Arsenal v Tottenham H | 0-0* |
| 1938 | Arsenal v Preston NE | 2-1 | 1992 | Leeds U v Liverpool | 4-3 |
| 1948 | Arsenal v Manchester U | 4-3 | 1993 | Manchester U† v Arsenal | 1-1 |
| 1949 | Portsmouth v Wolverhampton W | 1-1* | 1994 | Manchester U v Blackburn R | 2-0 |
| 1950 | World Cup Team v Canadian Touring Team | 4-2 | 1995 | Everton v Blackburn R | 1-0 |
| 1951 | Tottenham H v Newcastle U | 2-1 | 1996 | Manchester U v Newcastle U | 4-0 |
| 1952 | Manchester U v Newcastle U | 4-2 | 1997 | Manchester U† v Chelsea | 1-1 |
| 1953 | Arsenal v Blackpool | 3-1 | 1998 | Arsenal v Manchester U | 3-0 |
| 1954 | Wolverhampton W v WBA | 4-4* | 1999 | Arsenal v Manchester U | 2-1 |
| 1955 | Chelsea v Newcastle U | 3-0 | 2000 | Chelsea v Manchester U | 2-0 |
| 1956 | Manchester U v Manchester C | 1-0 | 2001 | Liverpool v Manchester U | 2-1 |
| 1957 | Manchester U v Aston Villa | 4-0 | 2002 | Arsenal v Liverpool | 1-0 |
| 1958 | Bolton W v Wolverhampton W | 4-1 | 2003 | Manchester U† v Arsenal | 1-1 |
| 1959 | Wolverhampton W v Nottingham F | 3-1 | 2004 | Arsenal v Manchester U | 3-1 |
| 1960 | Burnley v Wolverhampton W | 2-2* | 2005 | Chelsea v Arsenal | 2-1 |
| 1961 | Tottenham H v FA XI | 3-2 | 2006 | Liverpool v Chelsea | 2-1 |
| 1962 | Tottenham H v Ipswich T | 5-1 | 2007 | Manchester U† v Chelsea | 1-1 |
| 1963 | Everton v Manchester U | 4-0 | 2008 | Manchester U† v Portsmouth | 0-0 |
| 1964 | Liverpool v West Ham U | 2-2* | 2009 | Chelsea† v Manchester U | 2-2 |
| 1965 | Manchester U v Liverpool | 2-2* | 2010 | Manchester U v Chelsea | 3-1 |
| 1966 | Liverpool v Everton | 1-0 | 2011 | Manchester U v Manchester C | 3-2 |
| 1967 | Manchester U v Tottenham H | 3-3* | 2012 | Manchester C v Chelsea | 3-2 |

*\* Each club retained shield for six months.   † Won on penalties.*

## THE FA COMMUNITY SHIELD 2012

### Manchester C (0) 3, Chelsea (1) 2

At Villa Park, 12 August 2012, attendance 36,394

*Manchester C:* Pantilimon; Zabaleta, Kolarov, Kompany, Savic (Clichy 46), De Jong, Toure Y, Milner, Nasri (Silva 77), Aguero, Tevez (Dzeko 89).
*Scorers:* Toure Y 53, Tevez 59, Nasri 65.

*Chelsea:* Cech; Ivanovic■, Cole, David Luiz, Terry, Ramires, Lampard, Mikel, Mata (Sturridge 75), Hazard (Bertrand 71), Torres.
*Scorers:* Torres 40, Bertrand 80.

*Referee:* Kevin Friend (Leicestershire).

# ACCRINGTON STANLEY

## FOUNDATION

Accrington Football Club, founder members of the Football League in 1888, were not connected with Accrington Stanley. In fact both clubs ran concurrently between 1891 when Stanley were formed and 1895 when Accrington FC folded. Actually Stanley Villa was the original name, those responsible for forming the club living in Stanley Street and using the Stanley Arms as their meeting place. They became Accrington Stanley in 1893. In 1894–95 they joined the Accrington & District League, playing at Moorhead Park. Subsequently they played in the North-East Lancashire Combination and the Lancashire Combination before becoming founder members of the Third Division (North) in 1921, two years after moving to Peel Park. In 1962 they resigned from the Football League, were wound up, re-formed in 1963, disbanded in 1966 only to restart as Accrington Stanley (1968), returning to the Lancashire Combination in 1970.

*The Crown Ground, Livingstone Road, Accrington, Lancashire BB5 5BX.*
*Telephone:* (0871) 434 1968.
*Fax:* (01254) 356 951.
*Ticket Office:* (0871) 434 1968.
*Website:* www.accringtonstanley.co.uk
*Email:* info@accringtonstanley.co.uk
*Ground Capacity:* 5,057.
*Record Attendance:* 13,181 v Hull C, Division 3 (N), 28 September 1948 (at Peel Park); 4,368 v Colchester U, FA Cup 1st rd, 3 January 2004 (at Fraser Eagle Stadium – Crown Inn).
*Pitch Measurements:* 101m × 65m (111yd × 72yd)
*Chairman:* Peter Marsden.
*Managing Director:* Robert Heys.
*Manager:* James Beattie.
*Assistant Manager:* Paul Stephenson.
*Physio:* Paul Morgan.
*Colours:* Red shirts, red shorts, red socks.
*Year Formed:* 1891, reformed 1968.
*Turned Professional:* 1919.
*Club Nickname:* 'The Reds'.
*Previous Names:* 1891, Stanley Villa; 1893, Accrington Stanley.
*Grounds:* 1891, Moorhead Park; 1897, Bell's Ground; 1919, Peel Park; 1970, Crown Inn.
*First Football League Game:* 27 August 1921, Division 3 (N), v Rochdale (a) L 3-6 – Tattersall; Newton, Baines, Crawshaw, Popplewell, Burkinshaw, Oxley, Makin, Green (1), Hosker (2), Hartles.

## HONOURS

**Football League – Division 3 (N):** *Runners-up* 1954–55, 1957–58.
**Conference:** *Champions* 2005–06.
**FA Cup:** 4th rd 1927, 1937, 1959, 2010.
**Football League Cup:** never past 2nd rd.
**Northern Premier League:** *Champions* 2002–03.
**Northern League – Division 1:** *Champions* 1999–2000.
**North-West Counties:** *Runners-up* 1986–87.
**Cheshire County League – Division 2:** *Champions* 1980–81; *Runners-up* 1979–80.
**Lancashire Combination:** *Champions* 1973–74, 1977–78; *Runners-up* 1971–72, 1975–76.
**Lancashire Combination Cup:** *Winners* 1971–72, 1972–73, 1973–74, 1976–77.

## sky SPORTS FACT FILE

Accrington Stanley returned to the Football League in 2006 after winning the Conference finishing 11 points ahead of their nearest rivals. The campaign included an incredible run of 16 wins out of 18 games and they led the table from early December through to the end of the season.

*Record League Victory:* 8–0 v New Brighton, Division 3 (N), 17 March 1934 – Maidment; Armstrong (pen), Price, Dodds, Crawshaw, McCulloch, Wyper, Lennox (2), Cheetham (4), Leedham (1), Watson.

*Record Cup Victory:* 7–0 v Spennymoor U, FA Cup 2nd rd, 8 December 1938 – Tootill; Armstrong, Whittaker, Latham, Curran, Lee, Parry (2), Chadwick, Jepson (3), McLoughlin (2), Barclay.

*Record Defeat:* 1–9 v Lincoln C, Division 3 (N), 3 March 1951.

*Most League Points (2 for a win):* 61, Division 3 (N), 1954–55.

*Most League Points (3 for a win):* 73, FL 2, 2010–11.

*Most League Goals:* 96, Division 3 (N), 1954–55.

*Highest League Scorer in Season:* George Stewart, 35, Division 3 (N), 1955–56; George Hudson, 35, Division 4, 1960–61.

*Most League Goals in Total Aggregate:* George Stewart, 136, 1954–58.

*Most League Goals in One Match:* 5, Billy Harker v Gateshead, Division 3 (N), 16 November 1935; George Stewart v Gateshead, Division 3 (N), 27 November 1954.

*Most Capped Player:* Romuald Boco, 19 (42), Benin.

*Most League Appearances:* Jim Armstrong, 260, 1927–34.

*Youngest League Player:* Ian Gibson, 15 years 358 days, v Norwich C, 23 March 1959.

*Record Transfer Fee Received:* £250,000 (including sell-on from Blackpool 2001) for Brett Ormerod, March 1997.

*Record Transfer Fee Paid:* £85,000 to Swansea C for Ian Craney, January 2008.

*Football League Record:* 1921 Original Member of Division 3 (N); 1958–60 Division 3; 1960–62 Division 4; 2006– FL 2.

## MANAGERS

William Cronshaw *c.*1894
John Haworth 1897–1910
Johnson Haworth *c.*1916
Sam Pilkingson 1919–24
  (*Tommy Booth p-m 1923–24*)
Ernie Blackburn 1924–32
Amos Wade 1932–35
John Hacking 1935–49
Jimmy Porter 1949–51
Walter Crook 1951–53
Walter Galbraith 1953–58
George Eastham snr 1958–59
Harold Bodle 1959–60
James Harrower 1960–61
Harold Mather 1962–63
Jimmy Hinksman 1963–64
Terry Neville 1964–65
Ian Bryson 1965
Danny Parker 1965–66
Gerry Keenan
Gary Pierce
Dave Thornley
Phil Staley
Eric Whalley
Stan Allen 1995–96
Tony Greenwood 1996–98
Billy Rodaway 1998
Wayne Harrison 1998–99
John Coleman 1999–2012
Paul Cook 2012
Leam Richardson 2012–13
James Beattie May 2013–

## LATEST SEQUENCES

*Longest Sequence of League Wins:* 7, 27.12.1954 – 5.2.1955.

*Longest Sequence of League Defeats:* 9, 8.3.1930 – 21.4.1930.

*Longest Sequence of League Draws:* 4, 10.9.1927 – 27.9.1927.

*Longest Sequence of Unbeaten League Matches:* 14, 15.3.2011 – 6.8.2011.

*Longest Sequence Without a League Win:* 18, 17.9.1938 – 31.12.1938.

*Successive Scoring Runs:* 22 from 14.11.1936.

*Successive Non-scoring Runs:* 5 from 15.3.1930.

## TEN YEAR LEAGUE RECORD

|         |      | P  | W  | D  | L  | F  | A  | Pts | Pos |
|---------|------|----|----|----|----|----|----|-----|-----|
| 2003-04 | Conf | 42 | 15 | 13 | 14 | 68 | 61 | 58  | 10  |
| 2004-05 | Conf | 42 | 18 | 11 | 13 | 72 | 58 | 65  | 10  |
| 2005-06 | Conf | 42 | 28 | 7  | 7  | 76 | 45 | 91  | 1   |
| 2006-07 | FL 2 | 46 | 13 | 11 | 22 | 70 | 81 | 50  | 20  |
| 2007-08 | FL 2 | 46 | 16 | 3  | 27 | 49 | 83 | 51  | 17  |
| 2008-09 | FL 2 | 46 | 13 | 11 | 22 | 42 | 59 | 50  | 16  |
| 2009-10 | FL 2 | 46 | 18 | 7  | 21 | 62 | 74 | 61  | 15  |
| 2010-11 | FL 2 | 46 | 18 | 19 | 9  | 73 | 55 | 73  | 5   |
| 2011-12 | FL 2 | 46 | 14 | 15 | 17 | 54 | 66 | 57  | 14  |
| 2012-13 | FL 2 | 46 | 14 | 12 | 20 | 51 | 68 | 54  | 18  |

## DID YOU KNOW ?

Defender Phil Edwards finished as Accrington Stanley's joint-top scorer in the 2010–11 season with 13 goals, 11 of which came from penalties including two spot kicks in each of the home games against Gillingham and Stockport County.

## ACCRINGTON STANLEY – FOOTBALL LEAGUE TWO 2012–13 LEAGUE RECORD

| Match No. | Date | | Venue | Opponents | Result | | H/T Score | Lg Pos. | Goalscorers | Attendance |
|---|---|---|---|---|---|---|---|---|---|---|
| 1 | Aug | 18 | A | Southend U | W | 1-0 | 0-0 | 9 | Sheppard [61] | 4673 |
| 2 | | 21 | H | Port Vale | W | 2-0 | 1-0 | 3 | Amond (pen) [43], Gray [90] | 1946 |
| 3 | | 25 | H | Exeter C | L | 0-3 | 0-1 | 7 | | 1149 |
| 4 | Sept | 1 | A | Cheltenham T | W | 3-0 | 2-0 | 4 | Amond [4], Miller [33], Boco [47] | 2708 |
| 5 | | 8 | H | Bradford C | D | 1-1 | 0-0 | 5 | Amond [73] | 3010 |
| 6 | | 15 | A | Dagenham & R | D | 1-1 | 0-0 | 5 | Murphy [85] | 1529 |
| 7 | | 18 | A | Chesterfield | L | 3-4 | 1-2 | 6 | Boco 2 [28, 76], Murphy [58] | 4359 |
| 8 | | 22 | H | Aldershot T | W | 1-0 | 0-0 | 6 | Amond [90] | 1379 |
| 9 | | 29 | A | AFC Wimbledon | W | 2-1 | 1-0 | 4 | Amond [25], Murphy [78] | 3405 |
| 10 | Oct | 6 | H | Rochdale | L | 2-3 | 1-2 | 9 | Mingoia [37], Boco [47] | 2678 |
| 11 | | 13 | A | Torquay U | L | 1-3 | 0-1 | 11 | Amond [65] | 2474 |
| 12 | | 20 | A | Oxford U | L | 0-5 | 0-3 | 16 | | 5403 |
| 13 | | 23 | H | York C | L | 0-1 | 0-0 | 16 | | 1506 |
| 14 | | 27 | H | Bristol R | W | 1-0 | 0-0 | 12 | Amond [79] | 1462 |
| 15 | Nov | 6 | A | Morecambe | D | 0-0 | 0-0 | 13 | | 1410 |
| 16 | | 10 | H | Northampton T | L | 2-4 | 1-1 | 16 | Miller [37], Boco [57] | 1441 |
| 17 | | 16 | A | Barnet | D | 1-1 | 0-0 | 16 | Boco [53] | 2238 |
| 18 | | 20 | A | Fleetwood T | W | 3-1 | 2-0 | 14 | Beattie (pen) [9], Miller [17], Boco [62] | 2472 |
| 19 | | 24 | H | Gillingham | D | 1-1 | 0-1 | 14 | Beattie (pen) [72] | 1624 |
| 20 | | 27 | H | Rotherham U | L | 1-2 | 1-1 | 14 | Winnard [2] | 1424 |
| 21 | Dec | 9 | A | Burton Alb | L | 0-1 | 0-1 | 17 | | 2530 |
| 22 | | 15 | H | Wycombe W | L | 0-2 | 0-2 | 19 | | 1050 |
| 23 | | 22 | H | Plymouth Arg | D | 1-1 | 0-1 | 17 | Beattie [52] | 2012 |
| 24 | | 26 | A | Bradford C | L | 1-2 | 0-1 | 18 | Boco [80] | 11,181 |
| 25 | | 29 | A | Rotherham U | L | 1-4 | 1-1 | 19 | Lindfield [40] | 7304 |
| 26 | Jan | 1 | H | Chesterfield | W | 1-0 | 0-0 | 17 | Boco [66] | 1586 |
| 27 | | 5 | H | Dagenham & R | L | 0-2 | 0-1 | 18 | | 1031 |
| 28 | | 12 | A | Aldershot T | L | 0-2 | 0-1 | 19 | | 1912 |
| 29 | | 26 | A | Plymouth Arg | D | 0-0 | 0-0 | 19 | | 6509 |
| 30 | Feb | 2 | A | Port Vale | L | 0-3 | 0-0 | 20 | | 5172 |
| 31 | | 9 | H | Southend U | D | 1-1 | 0-0 | 21 | Gray [58] | 1589 |
| 32 | | 15 | A | Exeter C | L | 0-2 | 0-0 | 21 | | 3924 |
| 33 | | 23 | H | Cheltenham T | D | 2-2 | 1-1 | 23 | Beattie 2 [40, 64] | 1216 |
| 34 | | 26 | A | Rochdale | W | 3-0 | 0-0 | 22 | Molyneux 2 [76, 80], Boco [86] | 1780 |
| 35 | Mar | 2 | H | Torquay U | D | 0-0 | 0-0 | 22 | | 1197 |
| 36 | | 9 | A | Northampton T | L | 0-2 | 0-2 | 23 | | 4746 |
| 37 | | 12 | H | Fleetwood T | L | 0-3 | 0-1 | 24 | | 1388 |
| 38 | | 16 | H | Barnet | W | 3-2 | 3-1 | 24 | Molyneux 3 (1 pen) [8, 25, 34 (p)] | 1559 |
| 39 | | 19 | H | AFC Wimbledon | W | 4-0 | 3-0 | 22 | Jeffers 2 [5, 19], Hatfield [32], Molyneux [64] | 2149 |
| 40 | | 23 | A | Gillingham | L | 0-1 | 0-1 | 22 | | 10,097 |
| 41 | | 29 | A | Wycombe W | W | 1-0 | 0-0 | 20 | Molyneux [90] | 4577 |
| 42 | Apr | 1 | H | Burton Alb | D | 3-3 | 1-1 | 20 | Hatfield [7], Amond [60], Beattie [90] | 1619 |
| 43 | | 6 | A | York C | D | 1-1 | 0-1 | 20 | Murphy [90] | 4446 |
| 44 | | 12 | H | Morecambe | W | 2-0 | 1-0 | 18 | Murphy [28], Amond [58] | 2473 |
| 45 | | 20 | A | Bristol R | W | 1-0 | 1-0 | 17 | Molyneux [2] | 7673 |
| 46 | | 27 | H | Oxford U | L | 0-3 | 0-0 | 18 | | 2028 |

**Final League Position: 18**

### GOALSCORERS

*League (51):* Boco 10, Amond 9 (1 pen), Molyneux 8 (1 pen), Beattie 6 (2 pens), Murphy 5, Miller 3, Gray 2, Hatfield 2, Jeffers 2, Lindfield 1, Mingoia 1, Sheppard 1, Winnard 1.
*FA Cup (7):* Hatfield 4, Beattie 1, Lindfield 1, Molyneux 1.
*Capital One Cup (0).*
*Johnstone's Paint Trophy (0).*

| Dunbavin J 20 | Lindfield C 18 + 11 | Nsiala A 15 + 2 | Murphy P 42 + 3 | Liddle M 27 + 5 | Hatfield W 23 + 9 | Joyce L 44 | Clark L 2 + 4 | Miller G 22 + 3 | Chippendale A 2 + 4 | Sheppard K 5 + 5 | Winnard D 39 + 1 | Barnett C 6 + 8 | Amond P 24 + 12 | Eckersley T 1 + 1 | Gray J 8 + 8 | Boco R 42 | Molyneux L 33 + 6 | Schofield D 6 + 2 | Whichelow M 2 + 2 | Mingoia P 4 + 3 | Atkinson R 12 | Sampson J 2 + 3 | Dixon B 1 + 5 | Osawe O — + 2 | Beattie J 18 + 7 | Rachubka P 21 | Carver M 1 + 10 | Dawber A — + 2 | Belford C 5 | Hunt N 11 | Wilson L 19 | Hughes M 5 | Linganzi A 10 + 3 | Aldred T 12 + 1 | Jeffers F 4 + 3 | Match No. |
|---|---|---|---|---|---|---|---|---|---|---|---|---|---|---|---|---|---|---|---|---|---|---|---|---|---|---|---|---|---|---|---|---|---|---|---|---|
| 1 | 2 | 3 | 4 | 5 | 6 | 7 | $8^2$ | 9 | $10^1$ | $11^3$ | 12 | 13 | 14 | | | | | | | | | | | | | | | | | | | | | | | 1 |
| 1 | 8 | $3^2$ | 4 | 5 | 10 | 6 | | 7 | | $11^1$ | 2 | 12 | $9^3$ | 13 | 14 | | | | | | | | | | | | | | | | | | | | | 2 |
| 1 | $6^1$ | 3 | 4 | 5 | 9 | 7 | 14 | $8^2$ | 13 | $11^3$ | 2 | 12 | 10 | | | | | | | | | | | | | | | | | | | | | | | 3 |
| 1 | 14 | 3 | 4 | 5 | 9 | 6 | | 7 | | 13 | $2^3$ | 12 | $11^2$ | | | 8 | $10^1$ | | | | | | | | | | | | | | | | | | | 4 |
| 1 | 13 | 4 | 3 | 5 | $9^2$ | 6 | | 7 | | 14 | 2 | 12 | $11^3$ | | | 8 | $10^1$ | | | | | | | | | | | | | | | | | | | 5 |
| 1 | 13 | 3 | 4 | 5 | $7^3$ | 8 | | $6^1$ | | 14 | $2^2$ | 10 | 9 | | | 11 | 12 | | | | | | | | | | | | | | | | | | | 6 |
| 1 | 2 | 4 | 3 | $5^4$ | | 6 | 14 | $9^2$ | | $11^3$ | 8 | $10^1$ | 7 | | | 12 | 13 | | | | | | | | | | | | | | | | | | | 7 |
| 1 | 2 | 3 | | | $9^2$ | 8 | | | 13 | $11^3$ | | | 14 | | 10 | 5 | 7 | $6^1$ | 12 | 4 | | | | | | | | | | | | | | | | 8 |
| 1 | $2^2$ | 12 | 4 | | 10 | 6 | 14 | | | $11^3$ | 8 | | | | | 3 | 7 | $9^1$ | 13 | 5 | | | | | | | | | | | | | | | | 9 |
| 1 | 2 | 4 | | 14 | | 6 | | 12 | | $8^1$ | 11 | 10 | 5 | | | $7^2$ | 13 | $9^3$ | 3 | | | | | | | | | | | | | | | | | 10 |
| 1 | | 3 | | 5 | 14 | 11 | | | | $10^1$ | 2 | | 12 | | | 9 | | $6^2$ | | 8 | 4 | $7^3$ | 13 | | | | | | | | | | | | | 11 |
| 1 | $2^2$ | 12 | | 14 | | 6 | | | | 3 | | | 11 | | | 8 | $5^3$ | $7^1$ | | 9 | 4 | 10 | 13 | | | | | | | | | | | | | 12 |
| 1 | 14 | 3 | | $5^2$ | $9^1$ | 6 | | 7 | 13 | | $2^3$ | | 11 | | | 8 | 10 | | | 4 | 13 | 14 | 12 | | | | | | | | | | | | | 13 |
| 1 | | 3 | | 5 | $9^1$ | 6 | | 7 | | | 2 | | $11^2$ | | | 8 | $10^3$ | | | 4 | 13 | 14 | 12 | | | | | | | | | | | | | 14 |
| 1 | | 3 | | $5^2$ | $11^1$ | 7 | | 6 | | | 2 | 12 | 9 | | | 8 | 10 | | | 4 | 13 | | | | | | | | | | | | | | | 15 |
| 1 | | 3 | | $6^1$ | 7 | 8 | | | | | 2 | 12 | 10 | | $11^2$ | 9 | 5 | | | 4 | 13 | | | | | | | | | | | | | | | 16 |
| 1 | | 3 | | $6^1$ | 7 | 8 | | | | | 2 | | 10 | | 11 | 9 | 5 | | | 4 | | 12 | | | | | | | | | | | | | | 17 |
| 1 | $8^3$ | 4 | 3 | 5 | | 6 | | 7 | | | 2 | 13 | 12 | | | 9 | $10^1$ | 14 | $11^2$ | | | | | | | | | | | | | | | | | 18 |
| 1 | $8$ | 3 | | 5 | | 6 | | 7 | | | 2 | | 12 | | | 9 | $10^1$ | 4 | 11 | | | | | | | | | | | | | | | | | 19 |
| 1 | 8 | 3 | 14 | 5 | | 7 | | $6^3$ | | 13 | 2 | | | | | $10^2$ | $11^1$ | 12 | 9 | 4 | | | | | | | | | | | | | | | | 20 |
| | 2 | 3 | 4 | 5 | 14 | 8 | | 7 | | 13 | | | $11^2$ | | | 12 | 10 | $9^3$ | | $6^1$ | | | | | | 1 | | | | | | | | | | 21 |
| | 13 | 3 | 4 | $5^2$ | 14 | 6 | | $7^1$ | | 11 | 2 | | | | | 8 | 10 | $9^3$ | | | | | | | $9^3$ | 1 | 12 | | | | | | | | | 22 |
| | $8^3$ | 2 | 3 | 5 | | 6 | | 7 | | 4 | | 12 | 9 | | | $10^1$ | $11^2$ | | | | | | | | | 1 | | 13 | 14 | | | | | | | 23 |
| | 6 | 2 | 3 | 5 | | 7 | | 8 | | | | $4^4$ | 13 | | | 11 | $9^1$ | | | | | | | | | 1 | | 12 | | | | | | | | 24 |
| | 2 | | 3 | 5 | 13 | 7 | $8^3$ | | | | | $6^1$ | 14 | 4 | | 9 | 12 | | | | | | | | | 1 | | 11 | | 1 | | | | | | 25 |
| | $6^2$ | | 4 | 14 | 13 | 8 | | 7 | | | | 3 | $11^1$ | | | $9^3$ | 5 | | | | | | | | | 1 | | 12 | | 1 | 2 | | | | | 26 |
| | 6 | | 4 | 12 | | 7 | 14 | $8^3$ | | 3 | | | $11^1$ | | | 9 | 5 | | | | 13 | | 10 | | | 1 | | | | 1 | | $2^2$ | | | | 27 |
| | 2 | | | $9^1$ | 7 | 13 | $8^2$ | 4 | | | | | 10 | | | $5^3$ | | | | 12 | | 11 | 14 | | 1 | 6 | 3 | | | | | | | | | 28 |
| | $6^2$ | | 4 | 9 | | 7 | 13 | | | | 3 | 8 | | | | 10 | | | | | | 11 | 12 | | 1 | $2^1$ | 5 | | | | | | | | | 29 |
| | 2 | | $5^1$ | 7 | 8 | | | 4 | | | $9^4$ | | | | | 10 | 13 | | | | | $11^2$ | 1 | 12 | | 6 | 3 | | | | | | | | | 30 |
| | 6 | | $5^1$ | 13 | 7 | 3 | | 14 | | | | | $11^3$ | 8 | 12 | $9^2$ | 1 | | | | | | | | 2 | 10 | 4 | | | | | | | | 31 |
| | 8 | | 5 | 7 | 4 | | | 14 | | | | | $10^3$ | 8 | 12 | $11^2$ | 1 | 13 | | | | | | | 2 | $9^1$ | 3 | | | | | | | | 32 |
| | 7 | | 5 | 6 | 3 | | | 13 | | | | | $9^2$ | 8 | | $11^1$ | 1 | | | | | | | | 2 | 10 | 4 | 12 | | | | | | | 33 |
| | 7 | | 5 | 6 | 4 | | | $11^3$ | | | | | 8 | 13 | 9 | $9^1$ | | | | | | | | | | | 2 | $10^2$ | $3^1$ | 14 | 12 | | | | | 34 |
| | 7 | | | 13 | $8^1$ | 3 | | | | | | | 11 | 6 | 9 | $10^2$ | 1 | | | | | | | | | | 2 | 5 | | 12 | 4 | 12 | | | | 35 |
| | $6^1$ | | 8 | 14 | | 3 | | | | | | | $11^2$ | $10^3$ | 9 | 1 | | 13 | | | | | | | | | 2 | $9^1$ | 3 | | | | | | | 36 |
| | 8 | | $5^2$ | 14 | | 3 | | | | | | | 12 | 6 | 13 | $10^1$ | 1 | | | | | | | | | | 2 | 9 | 7 | 4 | $11^3$ | | | | | 37 |
| | 13 | | 12 | $10^2$ | 7 | 3 | | | | | | | 14 | 6 | 9 | 1 | | | | | | | | | | | $2^1$ | 5 | 8 | 4 | $11^3$ | | | | | 38 |
| | 12 | | 2 | $10^2$ | 7 | 3 | | | | | | | 13 | $6^1$ | 9 | 14 | 1 | | | | | | | | | | 5 | 8 | 4 | $11^3$ | | | | | 39 |
| | 12 | | 2 | 10 | 7 | 3 | | | | | $6^1$ | | 9 | 13 | 1 | | | | | | | | | | | 5 | 8 | 4 | $11^2$ | | | | | | 40 |
| | 12 | | 4 | 8 | 7 | 3 | | | | 13 | | | $10^1$ | 9 | $11^2$ | 1 | | | | | | | | | | 2 | 6 | 5 | | | | | | | 41 |
| | 12 | | 2 | $10^1$ | 8 | 3 | | | | 11 | | 14 | 6 | 9 | 13 | 1 | | | | | | | | | | 5 | $5^3$ | $7^2$ | 4 | | | | | | 42 |
| | 13 | | 2 | $7^3$ | 8 | 12 | | | | 4 | | | $11^1$ | $5^2$ | 9 | 10 | 1 | 14 | | | | | | | | | 6 | | 3 | | | | | | | 43 |
| | 12 | | 2 | 14 | $9^1$ | 6 | | | | 3 | | | $11^2$ | 8 | $10^3$ | 13 | 1 | | | | | | | | | | 5 | 7 | 4 | | | | | | | 44 |
| | | | 2 | 14 | $9^1$ | 7 | | | | 3 | | | $11^2$ | 10 | 8 | 13 | 1 | | | | | | | | | | $5^3$ | 6 | 4 | 12 | | | | | | 45 |
| | | | 2 | $5^3$ | $10^2$ | 6 | | | | 3 | | | 11 | 8 | $9^4$ | 14 | $11^1$ | | | 12 | | | | | | | 7 | 4 | 13 | | | | | | | 46 |

# AFC WIMBLEDON

## FOUNDATION

While the history of AFC Wimbledon is straightforward since it was a new club formed in 2002, there were in effect two clubs operating for two years with Wimbledon connections. The other club was MK Dons, of course. In August 2001, the Football League had rejected the existing Wimbledon's application to move to Milton Keynes. In May 2002, they rejected local sites and were given permission to move by an independent commission set up by the Football League. AFC Wimbledon was founded in the summer of 2002 and held its first trials on Wimbledon Common. In subsequent years, there was considerable debate over the rightful home of the trophies obtained by the former Wimbledon football club. In October 2006, an agreement was reached between Milton Keynes Dons FC, its Supporters Association, the Wimbledon Independent Supporters Association and the Football Supporters Federation to transfer such trophies and honours to the London Borough of Merton.

*The Cherry Red Records Fans' Stadium, Kingsmeadow, Jack Goodchild Way, 422a Kingston Road, Kingston-upon-Thames, Surrey KT1 3PB.*

*Telephone:* (0208) 547 3528.

*Fax:* (0808) 2800 816.

*Website:* www.afcwimbledon.co.uk

*Email:* info@afcwimbledon.co.uk

*Ground Capacity:* 5,339.

*Record Attendance:* 4,738 v Fleetwood T, FL 2, 27 April 2013.

*Pitch Measurements:* 100m × 68m (110yd × 75yd)

*Chief Executive:* Erik Samuelson.

*Manager:* Neal Ardley.

*Assistant Manager:* Neil Cox.

*First Team Coach:* Simon Bassey.

*Physio:* Mike Rayner.

*Club Nickname:* 'The Dons'.

*Colours:* All blue with yellow trim.

*Year Formed:* 2002.

*Turned Professional:* 2002.

## MANAGERS

**Terry Eames** 2002–04
**Nicky English** *(Caretaker)* 2004
**Dave Anderson** 2004–07
**Terry Brown** 2007–12
**Neal Ardley** October 2012–

## sky SPORTS FACT FILE

AFC Wimbledon played their first-ever competitive game away to Sandhurst Town on 17 August 2002. The Dons won the Combined Counties League fixture by a 2-1 margin in front of a crowd of 2,449 but it was not until the following season that they secured promotion to the Isthmian League.

*First Football League Game:* 6 August 2011, FL 2 v Bristol R (h) L 2–3 – Brown; Hatton, Gwillim (Bush), Porter (Minshull), Stuart (1), Johnson B, Moore L, Wellard, Jolley (Ademeno (1)), Midson, Yussuff.

*Record League Victory:* 4–0 v Burton Alb, FL 2, 24 March 2012 – Brown; Hatton, Gwillim, Moncur (1), Mitchel-King, Balkestein, Moore S (1), Knott (Wellard), Jolley, Midson, Moore L (1) (Harrison (1)).

*Record Cup Victory:* 4–3 v York City, FA Cup 1st rd replay, 12 November 2012 – Brown; Fenlon (Osano), Mambo, Mitchel-King, Cummings, Jolley, Gregory, Johnson (Harrison (1)), Yussuff (Long), Midson (1), Strutton (2).

*Record Defeat:* 2–6 v Burton Alb, FL 2, 25 August 2012.

*Most League Points (3 for a win):* 54, FL 2, 2011–12.

*Most League Goals:* 62, FL 2, 2011–12.

*Highest League Scorer in Season:* Jack Midson, 18, 2011–12.

*Most League Goals in Total Aggregate:* Kevin Cooper, 107, 2002–04.

*Most Capped Player:* Shane Smeltz, 5 (48), New Zealand.

*Most League Appearances:* Jack Midson, 89, 2011–13.

*Youngest League Player:* George Moncur, 18 years 148 days v Port Vale, 14 January 2012.

*Record Transfer Fee Received:* £120,000 from Coventry C for Chris Hussey, January 2010.

*Record Transfer Fee Paid:* Undisclosed to Stevenage for Byron Harrison, January 2012.

*Football League Record:* Promoted to Football League 2011– FL 2.

## HONOURS

**Blue Square Conference:** *Runners-up* 2010–11.

**Blue Square South:** *Champions* 2008–09.

**Isthmian League – Premier Division:** *Play-off Winners* 2007–08. **Division 1:** *Champions* 2004–05.

**Combined Counties League:** *Champions* 2003–04.

**Combined Counties League:** *Challenge Cup Winners* 2004.

**Surrey Senior Cup:** *Winners* 2005; *Runners-up* 2006.

**Supporters Direct Cup:** *Winners* 2003, 2006, 2010; *Runners-up* 2005, 2007.

**Phil Ledger Memorial Cup:** *Winners* 2011.

## LATEST SEQUENCES

*Longest Sequence of League Wins:* 4, 17.9.2011 – 8.10.2011.

*Longest Sequence of League Defeats:* 6, 26.2.2012 – 20.4.2013.

*Longest Sequence of League Draws:* 5, 29.3.2013 – 20.4.2013.

*Longest Sequence of Unbeaten League Matches:* 5, 29.3.2013 – 20.4.2013.

*Longest Sequence Without a League Win:* 12, 15.10.2011 – 2.1.2012.

*Successive Scoring Runs:* 8 from 1.9.2012.

*Successive Non-scoring Runs:* 4 from 5.1.2013.

## TEN YEAR LEAGUE RECORD

|         |         | P  | W  | D  | L  | F   | A  | Pts | Pos |
|---------|---------|----|----|----|----|-----|----|-----|-----|
| 2003-04 | CC      | 46 | 42 | 4  | 0  | 180 | 32 | 130 | 1   |
| 2004-05 | Isth DI | 42 | 29 | 10 | 3  | 91  | 33 | 97  | 1   |
| 2005-06 | Isth PR | 42 | 22 | 11 | 9  | 67  | 36 | 77  | 4   |
| 2006-07 | Isth PR | 42 | 21 | 15 | 6  | 76  | 37 | 75  | 5   |
| 2007-08 | Isth PR | 42 | 22 | 9  | 11 | 81  | 47 | 75  | 3   |
| 2008-09 | Conf S  | 42 | 26 | 10 | 6  | 86  | 36 | 88  | 1   |
| 2009-10 | BSP     | 44 | 18 | 10 | 16 | 61  | 47 | 64  | 8   |
| 2010-11 | BSP     | 46 | 27 | 9  | 10 | 83  | 47 | 90  | 2   |
| 2011-12 | FL 2    | 46 | 15 | 9  | 22 | 62  | 78 | 54  | 16  |
| 2012-13 | FL 2    | 46 | 14 | 11 | 21 | 54  | 76 | 53  | 20  |

## DID YOU KNOW ?

The first player to win a full international cap while on the books of AFC Wimbledon was striker Shane Smeltz who was capped by New Zealand in the 2005–06 season. At the time the Dons were playing in the Premier Division of the Isthmian League.

## AFC WIMBLEDON – FOOTBALL LEAGUE TWO 2012–13 LEAGUE RECORD

| Match No. | Date | Venue | Opponents | Result | H/T Score | Lg Pos. | Goalscorers | Attendance |
|---|---|---|---|---|---|---|---|---|
| 1 | Aug 18 | H | Chesterfield | W 1-0 | 1-0 | 10 | Midson [35] | 3780 |
| 2 | 21 | A | Burton Alb | L 2-6 | 0-4 | 14 | Harrison [79], Balkestein [80] | 1948 |
| 3 | 25 | A | Bradford C | L 1-5 | 1-5 | 17 | Harrison [35] | 9436 |
| 4 | Sept 1 | H | Dagenham & R | D 2-2 | 2-1 | 17 | Midson [30], Harrison [35] | 3507 |
| 5 | 8 | A | Northampton T | L 0-2 | 0-0 | 21 | | 4235 |
| 6 | 15 | H | Rochdale | L 1-2 | 0-2 | 21 | Moore, L [81] | 3529 |
| 7 | 18 | H | Torquay U | L 0-1 | 0-1 | 21 | | 3350 |
| 8 | 22 | A | Wycombe W | W 1-0 | 1-0 | 20 | Moore, S [40] | 4260 |
| 9 | 29 | H | Accrington S | L 1-2 | 0-1 | 22 | Moore, S [90] | 3405 |
| 10 | Oct 2 | A | Oxford U | L 2-3 | 2-1 | 22 | Harrison [20], Fenlon [36] | 5206 |
| 11 | 6 | A | Plymouth Arg | W 2-1 | 1-0 | 21 | Harrison [13], Yussuff [90] | 6271 |
| 12 | 13 | H | Cheltenham T | L 1-2 | 0-1 | 22 | Harrison [90] | 4409 |
| 13 | 20 | A | Fleetwood T | D 1-1 | 0-1 | 22 | Harrison [62] | 2547 |
| 14 | 23 | H | Bristol R | W 3-1 | 3-0 | 21 | Kenneth (og) [20], Yussuff 2 [29, 33] | 3714 |
| 15 | 27 | H | Gillingham | L 0-1 | 0-1 | 21 | | 4546 |
| 16 | Nov 6 | A | Exeter C | L 0-2 | 0-1 | 21 | | 3249 |
| 17 | 10 | A | York C | W 3-0 | 0-0 | 21 | Harrison [54], Long [80], Midson (pen) [85] | 3585 |
| 18 | 17 | H | Aldershot T | D 1-1 | 0-1 | 20 | Long [77] | 4321 |
| 19 | 20 | H | Southend U | L 0-4 | 0-1 | 20 | | 3753 |
| 20 | 24 | A | Morecambe | L 1-3 | 0-2 | 22 | Midson (pen) [67] | 1616 |
| 21 | Dec 8 | A | Barnet | D 1-1 | 0-0 | 19 | Midson [84] | 3217 |
| 22 | 15 | H | Rotherham U | L 0-1 | 0-0 | 20 | | 3718 |
| 23 | 29 | H | Oxford U | L 0-3 | 0-2 | 24 | | 4401 |
| 24 | Jan 1 | A | Torquay U | W 3-2 | 2-1 | 24 | McCallum [5], Mitchel-King [33], Long (pen) [90] | 2618 |
| 25 | 5 | A | Rochdale | W 1-0 | 0-0 | 22 | McCallum [56] | 2071 |
| 26 | 12 | H | Wycombe W | D 2-2 | 2-1 | 23 | McCallum 2 [16, 41] | 4507 |
| 27 | 24 | H | Port Vale | D 2-2 | 2-1 | 23 | Midson 2 (1 pen) [8, 42 (p)] | 3395 |
| 28 | Feb 2 | H | Burton Alb | D 1-1 | 1-1 | 24 | Alexander [27] | 3684 |
| 29 | 5 | A | Port Vale | L 0-3 | 0-2 | 24 | | 5567 |
| 30 | 9 | A | Chesterfield | L 0-2 | 0-0 | 24 | | 5235 |
| 31 | 16 | H | Bradford C | W 2-1 | 0-0 | 24 | Midson [83], Alexander [90] | 4320 |
| 32 | 19 | H | Northampton T | D 1-1 | 1-0 | 24 | Bennett, A [28] | 4129 |
| 33 | 23 | A | Dagenham & R | W 1-0 | 0-0 | 21 | Sainte-Luce [80] | 2265 |
| 34 | 26 | H | Plymouth Arg | D 1-1 | 1-1 | 23 | Pell [28] | 4480 |
| 35 | Mar 2 | A | Cheltenham T | L 1-2 | 0-1 | 24 | Dickenson [63] | 3177 |
| 36 | 9 | H | York C | W 3-2 | 1-1 | 21 | Mitchel-King [21], Dickenson [60], Pell [79] | 4349 |
| 37 | 12 | H | Southend U | W 3-1 | 1-1 | 18 | Balkestein [32], Midson [47], Moore, L [69] | 4236 |
| 38 | 16 | A | Aldershot T | W 1-0 | 0-0 | 18 | Midson [72] | 3699 |
| 39 | 19 | A | Accrington S | L 0-4 | 0-3 | 18 | | 2149 |
| 40 | 23 | H | Morecambe | W 2-0 | 2-0 | 16 | Sainte-Luce [38], Midson (pen) [45] | 3902 |
| 41 | 29 | A | Rotherham U | L 0-1 | 0-0 | 18 | | 7594 |
| 42 | Apr 1 | H | Barnet | L 0-1 | 0-0 | 19 | | 4696 |
| 43 | 6 | A | Bristol R | L 0-1 | 0-0 | 21 | | 6881 |
| 44 | 13 | H | Exeter C | D 2-2 | 0-1 | 21 | Moore, L 2 [58, 63] | 4749 |
| 45 | 20 | A | Gillingham | D 2-2 | 0-2 | 23 | Midson [65], Meades [82] | 11,172 |
| 46 | 27 | H | Fleetwood T | W 2-1 | 0-0 | 20 | Alexander [61], Midson (pen) [72] | 4738 |

**Final League Position: 20**

### GOALSCORERS

*League (54):* Midson 13 (5 pens), Harrison 8, McCallum 4, Moore, L 4, Alexander 3, Long 3 (1 pen), Yussuff 3, Balkestein 2, Dickenson 2, Mitchel-King 2, Moore, S 2, Pell 2, Sainte-Luce 2, Bennett, A 1, Fenlon 1, Meades 1, own goal 1.
*FA Cup (6):* Strutton 3, Midson 2, Harrison 1.
*Capital One Cup (1):* Kiernan 1.
*Johnstone's Paint Trophy (1):* Merrifield 1.

| Brown S 16 | MacDonald A 2 + 2 | Balkestein P 22 + 2 | Mitchel-King M 22 + 1 | Cummings W 7 + 2 | Long S 23 + 5 | Moore S 25 + 3 | Harris L 6 + 1 | Kiernan B 2 + 4 | Moore L 27 + 8 | Midson J 38 + 5 | Jolley C 6 + 9 | Yussuff R 16 + 7 | Fenlon J 16 + 1 | Harrison B 16 + 5 / Alexander G 16 + 2 | Haynes-Brown C 3 + 3 | Merrifield F 1 + 4 / Bennett A 18 | Francomb G 14 + 1 | Bennett D 5 / Dickenson B 5 + 2 | Johnson H 1 + 7 | Jaimez-Ruiz M 1 / Sainte-Luce K 5 + 9 | Antwi W 22 + 1 | Gregory S 15 | Strutton C 2 + 12 / Darko J 2 + 10 | Osano C 15 + 2 | Mambo Y 13 | Meades J 26 | Reeves J 5 | Sullivan N 18 | Djilali K — + 5 / Sullivan J 11 | McNaughton C 1 | McCallum P 6 + 3 | Ajala T 11 + 1 | Prior J 1 + 5 / Youga K 3 | Sweeney D 1 | Hussey C 18 + 1 | Sweeney P 6 | Pell H 17 | Match No. |
|---|---|---|---|---|---|---|---|---|---|---|---|---|---|---|---|---|---|---|---|---|---|---|---|---|---|---|---|---|---|---|---|---|---|---|---|---|---|---|
| 1 | 2 | 3 | 4 | 5 | 6² | 7 | 8 | 9¹ | 10 | 11 | 12 | 13 | | | | | | | | | | | | | | | | | | | | | | | | | | 1 |
| 1 | 2 | 3 | 4 | 5¹ | 7 | 6 | 8² | 9³ | 10 | 11 | | 13 | 12 | 14 | | | | | | | | | | | | | | | | | | | | | | | | 2 |
| 1 | 13 | 3 | 4 | 12 | 6 | 8 | 7 | | 10 | 11³ | | | | 2² | 9 | 5¹ | 14 | | | | | | | | | | | | | | | | | | | | | 3 |
| 1 | 4 | | | | 9¹ | 7 | 8² | 14 | | 10 | 6 | | | 2 | 11³ | | 12 | 3 | 5 | 13 | | | | | | | | | | | | | | | | | | 4 |
| | 12 | 3 | | | 5 | 6² | 8 | 14 | 11 | 13 | | 10 | | 9 | 2 | 4¹ | 7² | | | 1 | | | | | | | | | | | | | | | | | | 5 |
| 1 | 4 | | | | 6¹ | 7 | 14 | | 10 | 11* | 9² | 12 | | 13 | 5³ | | 2 | | 3 | 8 | | | | | | | | | | | | | | | | | | 6 |
| 1 | 3² | | 5³ | | 6 | 8¹ | | 9 | 11* | 13 | | 10 | | 12 | 2 | | 4 | 7 | 14 | | | | | | | | | | | | | | | | | | | 7 |
| 1 | | | | | 9¹ | 8 | | | 11³ | | 6² | 5 | 10 | 12 | 2 | 3 | 13 | | 4 | 7 | 14 | | | | | | | | | | | | | | | | | 8 |
| 1 | | | 12 | | 9 | | 8 | | 6³ | 10 | 5¹ | 11 | | | 2 | 4² | | 3 | 7 | 14 | 13 | | | | | | | | | | | | | | | | | 9 |
| 1 | | | | | 7 | | 9¹ | 11 | 6² | 12 | 5 | 10² | | | 2 | | 13 | | 4 | 8 | 14 | | 3 | | | | | | | | | | | | | | | 10 |
| 1 | | | | | 7 | | 9² | 11 | 12 | 6³ | 5 | 10¹ | 14 | | 2 | | 13 | | 3 | 8 | | 4 | | | | | | | | | | | | | | | | 11 |
| 1 | | | 13 | | 7¹ | | 9 | 11 | 12 | 6² | 5 | 10 | | | 2 | | | | 4 | 8 | | 3 | | | | | | | | | | | | | | | | 12 |
| 1 | | | 6 | 7¹ | | 10 | | 12 | 5² | 11 | 13 | | 9 | | | 4 | 8 | | 2 | 3 | | | | | | | | | | | | | | | | | | 13 |
| 1 | | | 8 | | 12 | 11 | 14 | 9 | 5¹ | 10² | 13 | | 6³ | | | 4 | 7 | | 2 | 3 | | | | | | | | | | | | | | | | | | 14 |
| 1 | | | 8¹ | | 12 | 10 | 13 | 9 | 11 | 5² | | | 6 | | | 3 | 7 | | 2 | 4 | | | | | | | | | | | | | | | | | | 15 |
| 1 | | | 12 | | 14 | 11 | 13 | 9¹ | 10 | | | | 6³ | | | 3 | 8 | | 2 | 4 | 5 | 7² | | | | | | | | | | | | | | | | 16 |
| 1 | | | 8² | | | 11 | 13 | | 10¹ | | | | 6 | | 14 | 3 | 9³ | 12 | 2 | 4 | 5 | 7 | | | | | | | | | | | | | | | | 17 |
| 1 | | | 9 | | | 11 | | 10 | | | 13 | | | 4 | 7² | 6¹ | 2 | 3 | 5 | 8 | 1 | 12 | | | | | | | | | | | | | | | | 18 |
| | | | 6² | | | 10 | 7³ | 11¹ | | 9 | | 14 | 4 | | 12 | 2 | 3 | 5 | 8 | 1 | 13 | | | | | | | | | | | | | | | | | 19 |
| | | | 8¹ | | | 10 | | 3 | | 4 | 7 | 12 | 2² | | 9 | 6 | 1 | 13 | 5 | 11* | | | | | | | | | | | | | | | | | | 20 |
| | | | 7 | | | 8³ | 10 | | 5 | 13 | | | 12 | | 4 | 11² | 2 | 3 | 6¹ | 1 | 14 | | 9 | | | | | | | | | | | | | | | 21 |
| | 12 | | 9² | | | 8¹ | 10 | 5 | | 4 | 7 | | 2 | 3 | 11 | 1 | 13 | | 6 | | | | | | | | | | | | | | | | | | | 22 |
| | | 5 | 7 | | 14 | 10 | 13 | 9² | | 4 | | 2 | 3 | 8 | 1 | 11¹ | 6³ | 12 | | | | | | | | | | | | | | | | | | | | 23 |
| | 4 | 5 | 3 | 7 | 14 | 12 | 10² | 8 | | 2 | 9 | 1 | 11¹ | 6³ | 13 | | | | | | | | | | | | | | | | | | | | | | | 24 |
| | 3 | 5¹ | 7 | 14 | 10 | 12 | 8 | | 4 | 2 | 9 | 1 | 11² | 6³ | 13 | | | | | | | | | | | | | | | | | | | | | | | 25 |
| | 3 | 6 | | 7 | 11³ | | | 13 | | 5 | 2¹ | 4 | 1 | 10² | 9 | 14 | 8 | 12 | | | | | | | | | | | | | | | | | | | | 26 |
| | 4 | 3 | 14 | 12 | 9 | 11 | | 2 | 13 | | 7³ | | 1 | 10² | 6¹ | | | 5 | 8 | | | | | | | | | | | | | | | | | | | 27 |
| | 2 | 3 | | 4² | 11¹ | 13 | 10 | | 11 | | | | 5 | 1 | 12 | 7 | | 6 | 8 | 9 | | | | | | | | | | | | | | | | | | 28 |
| | 3³ | 5 | 14 | 9 | 13 | | 7 | 2 | 11² | 4 | | | 1 | 12 | 6 | | 10 | 8¹ | | | | | | | | | | | | | | | | | | | | 29 |
| | 4 | 7² | 14 | | 9 | 10¹ | | 2 | 11 | 3 | | | 8 | 1 | 13 | 12 | | 5 | 6³ | | | | | | | | | | | | | | | | | | | 30 |
| 13 | 4³ | | 8¹ | | 12 | | 11 | 3 | | 14 | | 2 | 1 | 6 | | | 5 | 7 | 9 | | | | | | | | | | | | | | | | | | | 31 |
| 4 | | | 12 | | 9² | 11 | | 10 | 3 | | 13 | 2 | 1 | 6 | | | 5 | 8¹ | 7 | | | | | | | | | | | | | | | | | | | 32 |
| 4 | 12 | | 7 | | 8 | 9 | 10³ | 3 | 11² | 13 | 14 | 2¹ | | 5 | | 6 | | | | | | | | | | | | | | | | | | | | | | 33 |
| 4 | 3 | | 7 | | 6² | 9 | 11 | 2 | 10¹ | 13 | 12 | | 1 | 5 | | 8 | | | | | | | | | | | | | | | | | | | | | | 34 |
| 4 | 3 | | 7 | | 6¹ | 10³ | 11 | 2 | 12 | 13 | 9² | 14 | 1 | 5 | | 8 | | | | | | | | | | | | | | | | | | | | | | 35 |
| 4 | 2 | | 7 | | 9 | | | 6² | 11 | 3 | 10¹ | 12 | 13 | 5 | | 1 | | 8 | | | | | | | | | | | | | | | | | | | | 36 |
| 3¹ | 2 | | 7 | 13 | 12 | | | 11 | 4 | 10³ | 6³ | | 14 | 9 | | 1 | | 5 | | 8 | | | | | | | | | | | | | | | | | | 37 |
| | 4 | | 7 | 14 | 11 | 6³ | | 10³ | 3 | 9¹ | | 12 | 13 | 5 | | 1 | | 2 | | 8 | | | | | | | | | | | | | | | | | | 38 |
| | 3 | 8 | 7¹ | | 6² | 13 | | 10 | 4 | 11³ | 14 | | 1 | 2 | | 5 | | 9 | | | | | | | | | | | | | | | | | | | | 39 |
| | 2 | 12 | | | 8 | 11 | 9 | 10³ | 3 | | 6¹ | 4 | 13 | 1 | | 5 | | 7 | | | | | | | | | | | | | | | | | | | | 40 |
| 4 | 2 | | | | 9 | 11 | 8² | 10¹ | 3 | | | 12 | 13 | 6 | | 1 | | 5 | | 7 | | | | | | | | | | | | | | | | | | 41 |
| | 2 | 8² | | | 13 | 10 | | 12 | 4 | | 6³ | 3 | 11¹ | 14 | 9 | 1 | | 5 | | 7 | | | | | | | | | | | | | | | | | | 42 |
| 3 | | 6 | | | 11² | 10 | | 9¹ | 4 | | | 13 | 12 | 8 | | 1 | | 2 | | 5 | | 7 | | | | | | | | | | | | | | | | 43 |
| 3 | 2² | | 10 | | 6 | 11 | | | 4 | 9¹ | 12 | 13 | 8 | | | 1 | | 5 | | 7 | | | | | | | | | | | | | | | | | | 44 |
| 3 | 2² | | 9³ | | 6 | 11 | | 14 | 4 | | | 13 | 12 | 8 | | 1 | | 10¹ | | 5 | | 7 | | | | | | | | | | | | | | | | 45 |
| | 4 | | 8¹ | | 11² | 9 | | 10³ | 3 | | | 13 | 12 | 2 | | 6 | 1 | 14 | | 5 | | 7 | | | | | | | | | | | | | | | | 46 |

**FA Cup**

| First Round | York C | (a) | 1-1 |
|---|---|---|---|
| *Replay* | York C | (h) | 4-3 |
| Second Round | Milton Keynes D | (a) | 1-2 |

**Capital One Cup**

| First Round | Stevenage | (a) | 1-3 |
|---|---|---|---|

**Johnstone's Paint Trophy**

| First Round | Southend U | (a) | 1-2 |
|---|---|---|---|

# ALDERSHOT TOWN

## FOUNDATION

It was through the initiative of Councillor Jack White, a local newsagent, who immediately captured the interest of the Town Clerk D. Llewellyn Griffiths, that Aldershot Town was formed in 1926. Having established a limited liability company under the chairmanship of Norman Clinton, an Aldershot resident and chairman of the Hampshire County FA, they rented the Recreation Ground from the Aldershot Borough Council. Admitted to the Southern League for 1927–28, they were elected to the Football League in 1932 but were removed from the competition in March 1992 and their record expunged. Re-formed almost immediately as Aldershot Town Football Club.

*The EBB Stadium at the Recreation Ground, High Street, Aldershot, Hampshire GU11 1TW.*

*Telephone:* (01252) 320211.

*Fax:* (01252) 324347.

*Ticket Office:* (01252) 320211.

*Website:* www.theshots.co.uk

*Email:* admin@theshots.co.uk

*Ground Capacity:* 6,785.

*Record Attendance:* 19,138 v Carlisle U, FA Cup 4th rd (replay), 28 January 1970.

*Pitch Measurements:* 106m × 68m (117yd × 75yd)

*Chairman:* Shahid Azeem.

*Chief Executive:* Andrew Mills.

*Manager:* Andy Scott.

*Assistant Manager:* Terry Bullivant.

*Physio:* Mick Preston.

*Colours:* All red shirts, blue shorts with white trim, white socks.

*Year Formed:* 1926.

*Turned Professional:* 1927.

*Previous Names:* 1926, Aldershot Town; c.1937 Aldershot; 1992, Aldershot Town.

*Club Nickname:* 'The Shots'.

*Ground:* 1927, Recreation Ground.

## HONOURS

**Football League:** Best season: 8th, Division 3, 1973–74.

**FA Cup:** Best season: 5th rd, 1932–33, 5th rd replay, 1978–79.

**Football League Cup:** Best season: 4th rd, 2011–12.

**Blue Square Premier League:** *Champions* 2007–08.

**Conference:** *Runners-up* 2003–04.

**Southern League:** *Champions* 1929–30; *Runners-up* 1930–31.

**Football Combination Division 2:** *Champions* 1930–31.

**Isthmian League Division 3:** *Champions* 1992–93.

**Isthmian First Division Champions:** 1997–98.

**Isthmian League Premier Division:** *Champions* 2002–03.

**Hampshire Senior Cup:** *Winners* 1928, 1999, 2000, 2002, 2003, 2007.

**Setanta Shield:** *Winners* 2008.

*First Football League Game:* 27 August 1932, Division 3 (S), v Southend U (h) L 1–2 – Robb; Wade, McDougall, Lawson, Spence, Middleton, Proud, White, Gamble, Douglas, Fishlock (1).

## sky SPORTS FACT FILE

The reformed Aldershot Town FC entered the Isthmian League Division Three for their first season, 1992–93. They began the campaign with a 4-2 home win over Clapton and went on to walk away with the title, finishing with 92 points, 18 clear of their nearest rivals.

**Record League Victory:** 8–1 v Gateshead, Division 4, 13 September 1958 – Marshall; Henry, Jackson, Mundy, Price, Gough, Walters, Stepney (3), Lacey (3), Matthews (2), Tyrer.

**Record Cup Victory:** 7–0 v Chelmsford, FA Cup, 1st rd, 28 November 1931 – Robb; Twine, McDougall (1), Norman Wilson, Gardiner, Middleton (1), Blackbourne, Stevenson (1), Thom (3), Hopkins (1), Edgar. 7–0 v Newport (IW), FA Cup, 2nd rd, 8 December 1945 – Reynolds; Horton, Sheppard, Ray, White, Summerbee, Sinclair, Hold (1), Brooks (5), Fitzgerald, Hobbs (1). *N.B.* 11–1 v Kingstonian, FA Cup, 4th qual rd, 16 November 1929 – Mobbs; Thomas, McDougall, Norman Wilson, Gardiner, Middleton (2), Young (1), Common (1), Horton (2), Hopkins (3), Edgar (2).

**Record Defeat:** 1–10 v Southend U, Leyland DAF Cup, Pr rd, 6 November 1990.

**Most League Points: (2 for a win):** 57, Division 4, 1978–79.

**Most League Points (3 for a win):** 75, Division 4, 1983–84.

**Most League Goals:** 83, Division 4, 1963–64.

**Highest League Scorer in Season:** John Dungworth, 26, Division 4, 1978–79.

**Most League Goals in Total Aggregate:** Jack Howarth, 171, 1965–71 and 1972–77.

**Most League Goals in One Match:** 5, Charlie Mortimore v Leyton Orient, Division 3 (S), 25 February 1950.

**Most Capped Player:** Anthony Straker, 5, Grenada.

**Most League Appearances:** Murray Brodie, 461, 1970–83.

**Youngest League Player:** Clive Jackman, 16 years 135 days v Leyton Orient, 16 April 1953.

**Record Transfer Fee Received:** Reported £200,000 from Swansea C for Scott Donnelly, July 2010.

**Record Transfer Fee Paid:** £54,000 to Portsmouth for Colin Garwood, February 1980.

**Football League Record:** 1932 Elected to Division 3 (S); 1958–73 Division 4; 1973–76 Division 3; 1976–87 Division 4; 1987–89 Division 3; 1989–92 Division 4; 1992–93 Isthmian League Division 3; 1993–94 Isthmian League Division 2; 1994–98 Isthmian League Division 1; 1998–2003 Isthmian League Premier Division; 2003–08 Conference; 2008–13 FL 2; 2013– Conference.

## MANAGERS

**Angus Seed** 1927–37
**Bill McCracken** 1937–49
**Gordon Clark** 1950–55
**Harry Evans** 1955–59
**Dave Smith** 1959–71
 (*General Manager from 1967*)
**Tommy McAnearney** 1967–68
**Jimmy Melia** 1968–72
**Tommy McAnearney** 1972–81
**Len Walker** 1981–84
**Ron Harris** (*General Manager*) 1984–85
**Len Walker** 1985–91
**Brian Talbot** 1991
**Ian McDonald** 1991–92
**Steve Wignall** 1992–95
**Steve Wigley** 1995–97
**George Borg** 1997–2002
**Terry Brown** 2002–07
**Gary Waddock** 2007–09
**Kevin Dillon** 2009–11
**Dean Holdsworth** 2011–13
**Andy Scott** February 2013–

## LATEST SEQUENCES

*Longest Sequence of League Wins:* 6, 28.1.2012 – 3.3.2012.
*Longest Sequence of League Defeats:* 9, 20.11.1965 – 5.2.1966.
*Longest Sequence of League Draws:* 6, 6.10.1962 – 27.10.1962.
*Longest Sequence of Unbeaten League Matches:* 13, 30.9.1978 – 26.12.1978.
*Longest Sequence Without a League Win:* 17, 10.10.1936 – 30.1.1937.
*Successive Scoring Runs:* 29 from 1.4.1961.
*Successive Non-scoring Runs:* 6 from 22.3.1988.

## TEN YEAR LEAGUE RECORD

| | | P | W | D | L | F | A | Pts | Pos |
|---|---|---|---|---|---|---|---|---|---|
| 2003-04 | Conf | 42 | 20 | 10 | 12 | 80 | 67 | 70 | 5 |
| 2004-05 | Conf | 42 | 21 | 10 | 11 | 68 | 52 | 73 | 4 |
| 2005-06 | Conf | 42 | 16 | 6 | 20 | 61 | 74 | 54 | 13 |
| 2006-07 | Conf | 46 | 18 | 11 | 17 | 64 | 62 | 65 | 9 |
| 2007-08 | BSP | 46 | 31 | 8 | 7 | 82 | 48 | 101 | 1 |
| 2008-09 | FL 2 | 46 | 14 | 12 | 20 | 59 | 80 | 54 | 15 |
| 2009-10 | FL 2 | 46 | 20 | 12 | 14 | 69 | 56 | 72 | 6 |
| 2010-11 | FL 2 | 46 | 14 | 19 | 13 | 54 | 54 | 61 | 14 |
| 2011-12 | FL 2 | 46 | 19 | 9 | 18 | 54 | 52 | 66 | 11 |
| 2012-13 | FL 2 | 46 | 11 | 15 | 20 | 42 | 60 | 48 | 24 |

## DID YOU KNOW ?

When Aldershot Town won the Conference title in 2007–08 they created new records for total wins (31) and points (101) for the competition. Two teams have since achieved more points, but no team has exceeded the number of wins, although Crawley Town equalled the total in 2010–11.

## ALDERSHOT TOWN – FOOTBALL LEAGUE TWO 2012–13 LEAGUE RECORD

| Match No. | Date | Venue | Opponents | Result | H/T Score | Lg Pos. | Goalscorers | Attendance |
|---|---|---|---|---|---|---|---|---|
| 1 | Aug 18 | A | Plymouth Arg | W 2-0 | 1-0 | 6 | Brown 5, Payne (pen) 54 | 7020 |
| 2 | 21 | H | Exeter C | L 1-2 | 1-1 | 9 | Reid 17 | 2678 |
| 3 | 25 | H | Cheltenham T | L 0-1 | 0-0 | 16 | | 2166 |
| 4 | Sept 1 | A | Fleetwood T | L 1-4 | 1-1 | 21 | Davies (og) 37 | 2510 |
| 5 | 8 | A | Bristol R | D 2-2 | 1-1 | 20 | Reid 18, Rodman 57 | 5117 |
| 6 | 15 | H | Morecambe | D 0-0 | 0-0 | 18 | | 1960 |
| 7 | 18 | H | Barnet | W 1-0 | 0-0 | 18 | Reid 68 | 1760 |
| 8 | 22 | A | Accrington S | L 0-1 | 0-0 | 19 | | 1379 |
| 9 | 29 | H | York C | L 0-2 | 0-0 | 19 | | 2176 |
| 10 | Oct 2 | A | Torquay U | L 3-4 | 2-0 | 20 | Reid 3 (1 pen) 28, 37 (p), 47 | 2358 |
| 11 | 6 | H | Chesterfield | L 0-1 | 0-0 | 23 | | 2006 |
| 12 | 13 | A | Gillingham | L 0-4 | 0-3 | 23 | | 5039 |
| 13 | 20 | H | Rotherham U | L 0-3 | 0-1 | 23 | | 1953 |
| 14 | 23 | A | Southend U | L 2-1 | 1-0 | 23 | Hylton 1, Bradley 87 | 4225 |
| 15 | 27 | A | Dagenham & R | D 0-0 | 0-0 | 23 | | 1771 |
| 16 | Nov 6 | H | Wycombe W | D 0-0 | 0-0 | 24 | | 2042 |
| 17 | 10 | H | Bradford C | L 0-2 | 0-2 | 24 | | 2143 |
| 18 | 17 | A | AFC Wimbledon | D 1-1 | 1-1 | 23 | Lopez 45 | 4321 |
| 19 | 20 | A | Burton Alb | W 1-0 | 1-0 | 22 | Lopez 4 | 1712 |
| 20 | 24 | H | Port Vale | L 1-3 | 1-1 | 23 | Lopez 29 | 1992 |
| 21 | Dec 8 | A | Oxford U | D 1-1 | 0-1 | 22 | Mekki 84 | 5721 |
| 22 | 15 | H | Rochdale | W 4-2 | 3-1 | 21 | Lopez 8, Vincenti 39, Rose (pen) 45, Reid 90 | 1910 |
| 23 | 22 | A | Northampton T | L 0-2 | 0-0 | 21 | | 4574 |
| 24 | 26 | H | Bristol R | D 2-2 | 1-0 | 22 | Hector 33, Reid (pen) 76 | 2862 |
| 25 | Jan 1 | A | Barnet | W 1-0 | 0-0 | 20 | Reid (pen) 48 | 2772 |
| 26 | 12 | H | Accrington S | W 2-0 | 1-0 | 21 | Brown 12, Lopez 81 | 1912 |
| 27 | 19 | A | York C | D 0-0 | 0-0 | 21 | | 2757 |
| 28 | 22 | H | Northampton T | L 1-2 | 1-2 | 21 | Lopez 2 | 1191 |
| 29 | Feb 2 | A | Exeter C | D 0-0 | 0-0 | 21 | | 3755 |
| 30 | 9 | H | Plymouth Arg | L 1-2 | 1-2 | 23 | Vincenti 11 | 3241 |
| 31 | 12 | A | Morecambe | L 1-2 | 0-0 | 23 | Hylton 90 | 1226 |
| 32 | 16 | A | Cheltenham T | D 1-1 | 1-0 | 23 | Rose 23 | 3119 |
| 33 | 19 | H | Torquay U | W 1-0 | 0-0 | 20 | Brown 83 | 2095 |
| 34 | 23 | A | Fleetwood T | W 2-0 | 1-0 | 20 | Hylton 2 38, 84 | 2032 |
| 35 | 26 | A | Chesterfield | D 0-0 | 0-0 | 19 | | 3968 |
| 36 | Mar 2 | H | Gillingham | D 1-1 | 0-0 | 19 | Reid 47 | 3267 |
| 37 | 9 | A | Bradford C | D 1-1 | 1-0 | 20 | Cadogan 45 | 10,397 |
| 38 | 12 | H | Burton Alb | L 1-2 | 1-1 | 21 | McCallum 3 | 1568 |
| 39 | 16 | H | AFC Wimbledon | L 0-1 | 0-0 | 23 | | 3699 |
| 40 | 29 | A | Rochdale | D 1-1 | 0-0 | 23 | Mekki 73 | 2280 |
| 41 | Apr 1 | H | Oxford U | W 3-2 | 1-0 | 24 | McCallum 13, Reid (pen) 49, Goulding 87 | 2927 |
| 42 | 9 | A | Port Vale | D 1-1 | 0-1 | 24 | McCallum 74 | 6197 |
| 43 | 13 | A | Wycombe W | L 1-2 | 0-0 | 24 | Stanley 89 | 4290 |
| 44 | 16 | H | Southend U | L 0-2 | 0-0 | 24 | | 2568 |
| 45 | 20 | H | Dagenham & R | W 1-0 | 0-0 | 24 | Rankine 56 | 2861 |
| 46 | 27 | A | Rotherham U | L 0-2 | 0-0 | 24 | | 11,300 |

**Final League Position: 24**

### GOALSCORERS

*League (42):* Reid 11 (4 pens), Lopez 6, Hylton 4, Brown 3, McCallum 3, Mekki 2, Rose 2 (1 pen), Vincenti 2, Bradley 1, Cadogan 1, Goulding 1, Hector 1, Payne 1 (1 pen), Rankine 1, Rodman 1, Stanley 1, own goal 1.
*FA Cup (9):* Hylton 8, Vincenti 1.
*Capital One Cup (1):* Rankine 1.
*Johnstone's Paint Trophy (1):* Reid 1.

| Young J 44 | Herd B 43 | Brown T 34 | Bradley S 42 | Tonkin A 36+1 | Mekki A 14+15 | Morris A 29+8 | Payne J 9+6 | Stanley C 5 | Rodman A 9+2 | Rankine M 10+14 | Reid C 29+10 | Bergqvist D 1+3 | Anderson M —+5 | Cooksley H —+1 | Madjo G —+3 | Connolly R —+1 | Roberts J 1+4 | Vincenti P 35+4 | Lancashire O 10+2 | Appiah K —+2 | Hylton D 25+2 | Donnelly S 4 | Branston G 3 | Rose D 34 | Cadogan K 20+3 | Sinclair R 1+5 | Seidi A —+1 | Lopez D 11+1 | Hector M 8 | Risser O 11+3 | Ainsworth L 3+4 | McNamee A —+1 | Hall A 12+4 | Goulding J 5+5 | Forbes T 10 | McCallum P 6+3 | Morris G 1+1 | Worner R 1 | Match No. |
|---|---|---|---|---|---|---|---|---|---|---|---|---|---|---|---|---|---|---|---|---|---|---|---|---|---|---|---|---|---|---|---|---|---|---|---|---|---|---|---|
| 1 | 2 | 3 | 4 | 5 | 6[1] | 7 | 8[3] | 9 | 10 | 11[2] | 12 | 13 | 14 | | | | | | | | | | | | | | | | | | | | | | | | | | 1 |
| 1 | 2 | 3 | 4 | 5 | 9 | 7 | 8 | | 6[2] | 11[3] | 10[1] | | 13 | | 12 | 14 | | | | | | | | | | | | | | | | | | | | | | | 2 |
| 1 | 2 | 3 | 4 | 5 | 6 | 7 | 8 | | | | 10 | | 13 | | | 12 | | 9[1] | 11[2] | | | | | | | | | | | | | | | | | | | | 3 |
| 1 | 2 | 8[1] | 4 | 5 | | 7 | 6[5] | 12 | 10[2] | 11 | | | | | 13 | | | 9 | 3 | | | | | | | | | | | | | | | | | | | | 4 |
| 1 | 2 | 4 | 10 | 5 | 8 | 3 | 12 | 9[1] | 13 | 11 | | | | | | | | 7[2] | 6 | | | | | | | | | | | | | | | | | | | | 5 |
| 1 | 2 | 3 | 4 | 5 | 9[3] | 7 | | | 6[2] | 12 | 11 | | | | | | | 14 | 10[1] | 8 | 13 | | | | | | | | | | | | | | | | | | 6 |
| 1 | 2 | 3 | 4 | 5 | 6[3] | 14 | 7 | 9[1] | 10 | | | | 13 | | | | | 12 | 8 | | 11[2] | | | | | | | | | | | | | | | | | | 7 |
| 1 | 2 | 7 | 4 | 5 | 6[1] | 14 | 8 | 9[3] | 12 | 11 | | | | | | | | 13[8] | 3 | | 10[2] | | | | | | | | | | | | | | | | | | 8 |
| 1 | 2 | 8[1] | 4 | 5 | 6[2] | 7 | 12 | 13 | 14 | 11 | | | | | | | | | 3 | 10 | 9[3] | | | | | | | | | | | | | | | | | | 9 |
| 1 | 2 | 8[3] | | 5 | 6 | 9 | 12 | | 10[2] | | | | 13 | | | | | | 3 | 14 | 11[1] | 7 | 4 | | | | | | | | | | | | | | | | 10 |
| 1 | 2 | 8 | | 5 | 12 | 7[3] | 13 | 6[2] | 14 | 10 | | | | | | | | | 3 | | 9 | 11[1] | 4 | | | | | | | | | | | | | | | | 11 |
| 1 | 2 | 3 | | 5 | 6[1] | 8 | 12 | | | | | | 13 | | 11[2] | | | 7 | | | | | | 10 | 4 | 9 | | | | | | | | | | | | | 12 |
| 1 | 2 | 3 | 14 | 13 | 5 | 7[1] | 6[2] | 10[3] | 9 | | | | | | | | | 12 | 4 | | 11 | | | 8 | | | | | | | | | | | | | | | 13 |
| 1 | 2 | 3 | 4 | 5 | 12 | 7 | | | | | 10 | | 11[1] | | | | | 6 | | | 9 | | | 8 | | | | | | | | | | | | | | | 14 |
| 1 | 2 | 3 | 4 | 5 | 11 | 6 | | | | | 10 | | | | | | | 7 | | | 9 | | | 8 | | | | | | | | | | | | | | | 15 |
| 1 | 2 | 7 | 4 | 5[4] | 12 | 8 | | | 10[2] | | | | | | | | | 9 | | | 11 | | | 3 | 6[1] | 13 | | | | | | | | | | | | | 16 |
| 1 | 2 | 3 | 4 | 5 | 7 | 14 | | | | | | | | | | | | 9[3] | | | 11 | | | 10[1] | 8 | 6[2] | | 12 | 13 | | | | | | | | | | 17 |
| 1 | 2 | 4 | 9 | 5 | 3 | 12 | | | | | | | | | | | | 7 | | | 11 | | | | 8 | 6 | | 10[1] | | | | | | | | | | | 18 |
| 1 | 2 | 3 | 4 | 5 | 8 | 14 | | | | | | 13 | | | | | | 9 | | | 10[2] | | | | 7 | 6[1] | | 12 | 11[2] | | | | | | | | | | 19 |
| 1 | 2 | 3 | 4 | 5 | 12 | 7[3] | | | | | | | 14 | | | | | 9 | | | 11 | | | | 8[2] | 6[1] | | 13 | | 10 | | | | | | | | | 20 |
| 1 | 2 | 4 | 3 | 5 | 12 | | | | | | | | 13 | | | | | 9[1] | | | 10 | | | | 7 | 6 | | 11[2] | 8 | | | | | | | | | | 21 |
| 1 | 2[8] | 3 | | 5 | 7 | | | | | 12 | | | 14 | | | | | 9[1] | | | 10[3] | | | | 8 | 6 | | 13 | 11[2] | 4 | | | | | | | | | 22 |
| 1 | | 4 | 12 | 5 | | | | | | 11[1] | 2 | | | | | 13 | | 6 | | | | | | | 9 | 8[2] | 7 | 10 | 3 | | | | | | | | | | 23 |
| | | 3 | 8 | 5 | 13 | 2 | | | | | 12 | | 14 | | | | | 9[3] | | | 10[1] | | | | 7 | 6[2] | | 11 | 4 | | | | | | | | | | 24 |
| | | 3 | 4 | 5 | 12 | 2 | | | 10[3] | | | | | | | | | 9 | | | 14 | | | | 8 | 6[2] | | 13 | 11[1] | 7 | | | | | | | | | 25 |
| 1 | 2 | 3 | 8 | 5 | | | | | | | 13 | | | | | | | 12 | 10[1] | | 9 | | | | 7[2] | 6 | | 11[3] | 4 | 14 | | | | | | | | | 26 |
| 1 | 2 | 3 | 4 | 5 | | 14 | | | | | 12 | | 11[2] | | | | | 9 | | | | | | | 7 | 6[1] | | 10[1] | 8 | 13 | | | | | | | | | 27 |
| 1 | 2 | 3 | 4 | | 6[1] | 8 | | | 10[3] | | | | | | | | | 9 | | | | | | | 7[2] | | | 11 | 5 | 14 | 12 | 13 | | | | | | | 28 |
| 1 | 2 | 3 | 4 | 5 | | | | | | | 13 | | | | | | | 10 | | | 11[2] | | | | 7 | 8[1] | | | | | | | 6 | 12 | | 9 | | | 29 |
| 1 | 2 | 3 | 4 | 5 | 12 | | | | | | 11 | | | | | | | 9 | | | 7 | | | | 8[3] | 6[1] | | | | | | | 10[2] | 13 | | 14 | | | 30 |
| 1 | 2 | 3 | 4 | 5 | 13 | | | | | | | | | | | | | 12 | | | 10 | | | | 11 | 6 | | | | | | | 8[2] | 7[3] | 14 | 9[1] | | | 31 |
| 1 | 2 | 3 | 4 | 5[8] | | 14 | | | | | | | | | | | | 9 | | | 10[2] | | | | 7 | 12[3] | | | | | | | 8 | 6[1] | | 13 | 11 | | 32 |
| 1 | 2 | 3 | 4 | | 6[3] | 5 | | | | | | | 13 | | | | | 14 | | | 12 | | | | 11 | 8 | | | | | | | 7 | | | 9[1] | 10[1] | | 33 |
| 1 | 2 | 4 | 7[1] | 5 | 12 | | | | | | | | | | | | | 10 | | | 11 | | | | 9 | | | | | | | | 8 | 6 | 3 | | | | 34 |
| 1 | 2 | 4 | 5 | 12 | | | | | | | 11 | | | | | | | 9 | | | 10 | | | | 8 | 6[1] | | | | | | | 7 | | 3 | | | | 35 |
| 1 | 2 | 3 | 5 | 13 | | | | | | | 11 | | | | | | | 9[1] | | | 10 | | | | 7 | 6[2] | | | | | | | 8 | | 12 | 4 | | | 36 |
| 1[1] | 2[2] | 4 | | 5 | | | | | | | 11[3] | | | | | | | 9 | 13 | | | | | | 7 | 6 | | | | | | | 8 | 14 | 3 | 10 | 12 | | 37 |
| | 2 | 4 | 12 | 7 | | | | | | | 10 | | | | | | | 9[2] | | | | | | | 6 | | | | | | | | 8[1] | 5 | 13 | 14 | 3[3] | 11 | 38 |
| 1 | 2 | 4 | 13 | 5 | | | | | | | 11 | | | | | | | 12 | | | | | | | 7 | 14 | | | | | | | 8[3] | 6[2] | 9 | 12 | 3 | 10[1] | 39 |
| 1 | 2 | 3 | 5 | 12 | 6 | | | | | | 10 | | | | | | | 7 | | | 9[2] | | | | 6 | | | | | | | | 8 | 11[1] | 4 | 13 | | | 40 |
| | 2 | 4 | 5 | 12 | 7[1] | | | | | | 11[3] | | | | | | | 14 | 9 | | | | | | 6 | | | | | | | | 8 | 13 | 3 | 10[2] | | 1 | 41 |
| 1 | 2 | 4 | 5 | | | | | 9 | | 13 | 10[1] | | | | | | | 6 | | | | | | | 8 | | | | | | | | 7 | 11[2] | 3 | 12 | | | 42 |
| 1 | 2 | 4 | 5 | | | | | 8 | | 12 | 14 | | | | | 13 | | 6[1] | | | | | | | 9[2] | | | | | | | | 7 | 11[3] | 3 | 10 | | | 43 |
| 1 | 2 | 3[4] | 4 | 5 | 13 | | 7 | 10 | | 12 | | | | | | | | 6[2] | | | | | | | 9 | | | | | | | | 8 | 14 | 11[1] | | | | 44 |
| 1 | 2 | 4[2] | 9 | 3 | | 7 | 5 | 8[3] | | | | | | | | | | 6[1] | 12 | | | | | | 11 | 13 | | | | | | | | 10 | | 14 | | | 45 |
| 1 | 2 | 5 | 3 | 7 | | | 8 | 10 | | 12 | | | | | | | | 6[1] | 4 | | | | | | 11 | | | | | | | | | 9 | | | | | 46 |

**FA Cup**

| | | | |
|---|---|---|---|
| First Round | Hendon FC | (h) | 2-1 |
| Second Round | Fleetwood T | (a) | 3-2 |
| Third Round | Rotherham U | (h) | 3-1 |
| Fourth Round | Middlesbrough | (a) | 1-2 |

**Capital One Cup**

| | | | |
|---|---|---|---|
| First Round | Wolverhampton W | (a) | 1-1 |

(aet; lost 6-7 on pens)

**Johnstone's Paint Trophy**

| | | | |
|---|---|---|---|
| First Round | Exeter C | (a) | 0-0 |

(aet; won 4-3 on pens)

| | | | |
|---|---|---|---|
| Second Round | Plymouth Arg | (a) | 1-2 |

# ARSENAL

## FOUNDATION

Formed by workers at the Royal Arsenal, Woolwich in 1886, they began as Dial Square (name of one of the workshops), and included two former Nottingham Forest players, Fred Beardsley and Morris Bates. Beardsley wrote to his old club seeking help and they provided the new club with a full set of red jerseys and a ball. The club became known as the 'Woolwich Reds' although their official title soon after formation was Woolwich Arsenal.

*Emirates Stadium, Highbury House, 75 Drayton Park, Islington, London N5 1BU.*

*Telephone:* (020) 7619 5003.

*Fax:* (020) 7704 4001.

*Ticket Office:* (020) 7619 5003.

*Website:* www.arsenal.com

*Email:* ask@arsenal.com

*Ground Capacity:* 60,362.

*Record Attendance:* 73,295 v Sunderland, Div 1, 9 March 1935 (at Highbury); 73,707 v RC Lens, UEFA Champions League, 25 November 1998 (at Wembley); 60,162 v Manchester U, FA Premier League, 3 November 2007 (at Emirates).

*Pitch Measurements:* 105m × 68m (114yd × 74yd)

*Chairman:* Sir John 'Chips' Keswick.

*Chief Executive:* Ivan Gazidis.

*Manager:* Arsène Wenger.

*Assistant Manager:* Steve Bould.

*Physio:* Colin Lewin.

*Colours:* Red shirts with white sleeves with blue and red trim, white shorts, white socks with blue and red hoops.

*Year Formed:* 1886.

*Turned Professional:* 1891.

*Previous Names:* 1886, Dial Square; 1886, Royal Arsenal; 1891, Woolwich Arsenal; 1914, Arsenal.

*Club Nickname:* 'The Gunners'.

*Grounds:* 1886, Plumstead Common; 1887, Sportsman Ground; 1888, Manor Ground; 1890, Invicta Ground; 1893, Manor Ground; 1913, Highbury; 2006, Emirates Stadium.

## HONOURS

**FA Premier League:**
*Champions* 1997–98, 2001–02, 2003–04. *Runners-up* 1998–99, 1999–2000, 2000–01, 2002–03, 2004–05.

**Football League – Division 1:**
*Champions* 1930–31, 1932–33, 1933–34, 1934–35, 1937–38, 1947–48, 1952–53, 1970–71, 1988–89, 1990–91;
*Runners-up* 1925–26, 1931–32, 1972–73;
**Division 2:** *Runners-up* 1903–04.

**FA Cup:** *Winners* 1930, 1936, 1950, 1971, 1979, 1993, 1998, 2002, 2003, 2005; *Runners-up* 1927, 1932, 1952, 1972, 1978, 1980, 2001.

**Double performed:** 1970–71, 1997–98, 2001–02.

**Football League Cup:** *Winners* 1987, 1993; *Runners-up* 1968, 1969, 1988, 2007, 2011.

**European Competitions**
**European Cup:** 1971–72, 1991–92.
**UEFA Champions League:** 1998–99, 1999–2000, 2000–01, 2001–02, 2002–03, 2003–04, 2004–05, 2005–06 (*runners-up*), 2006–07, 2007–08 (*q-f*), 2008–09 (*s-f*), 2009–10, 2010–11, 2011–12, 2012–13.
**Fairs Cup:** 1963–64, 1969–70 (*winners*), 1970–71. **UEFA Cup:** 1978–79, 1981–82, 1982–83, 1996–97, 1997–98, 1999–2000 (*runners-up*).
**European Cup-Winners' Cup:** 1979–80 (*runners-up*), 1993–94 (*winners*), 1994–95 (*runners-up*). **Super Cup:** 1994 (*runners-up*).

## sky SPORTS FACT FILE

Arsenal completed the double over neighbours Tottenham Hotspur when they won the Football League championship in 1934–35. The Gunners won 5-1 at Highbury and followed up with a 6-0 win at White Hart Lane. Tottenham finished bottom of the division and were relegated.

*First Football League Game:* 2 September 1893, Division 2, v Newcastle U (h) D 2–2 – Williams; Powell, Jeffrey; Devine, Buist, Howat; Gemmell, Henderson, Shaw (1), Elliott (1), Booth.

*Record League Victory:* 12–0 v Loughborough T, Division 2, 12 March 1900 – Orr; McNichol, Jackson; Moir, Dick (2), Anderson (1); Hunt, Cottrell (2), Main (2), Gaudie (3), Tennant (2).

*Record Cup Victory:* 11–1 v Darwen, FA Cup 3rd rd, 9 January 1932 – Moss; Parker, Hapgood; Jones, Roberts, John; Hulme (2), Jack (3), Lambert (2), James, Bastin (4).

*Record Defeat:* 0–8 v Loughborough T, Division 2, 12 December 1896.

*Most League Points (2 for a win):* 66, Division 1, 1930–31.

*Most League Points (3 for a win):* 90, FA Premier League, 2003–04.

*Most League Goals:* 127, Division 1, 1930–31.

*Highest League Scorer in Season:* Ted Drake, 42, 1934–35.

*Most League Goals in Total Aggregate:* Thierry Henry, 175, 1999–2007; 2011–12.

*Most League Goals in One Match:* 7, Ted Drake v Aston Villa, Division 1, 14 December 1935.

*Most Capped Player:* Thierry Henry, 81 (123), France.

*Most League Appearances:* David O'Leary, 558, 1975–93.

*Youngest League Player:* Jack Wilshere, 16 years 256 days v Blackburn R, 13 September 2008.

*Record Transfer Fee Received:* £29,000,000 from Barcelona for Cesc Fabregas, August 2011.

*Record Transfer Fee Paid:* £15,000,000 to Zenit for Andrei Arshavin, February 2009.

*Football League Record:* 1893 Elected to Division 2; 1904–13 Division 1; 1913–19 Division 2; 1919–92 Division 1; 1992– FA Premier League.

| MANAGERS |
| --- |
| Sam Hollis 1894–97 |
| Tom Mitchell 1897–98 |
| George Elcoat 1898–99 |
| Harry Bradshaw 1899–1904 |
| Phil Kelso 1904–08 |
| George Morrell 1908–15 |
| Leslie Knighton 1919–25 |
| Herbert Chapman 1925–34 |
| George Allison 1934–47 |
| Tom Whittaker 1947–56 |
| Jack Crayston 1956–58 |
| George Swindin 1958–62 |
| Billy Wright 1962–66 |
| Bertie Mee 1966–76 |
| Terry Neill 1976–83 |
| Don Howe 1984–86 |
| George Graham 1986–95 |
| Bruce Rioch 1995–96 |
| Arsène Wenger September 1996– |

## LATEST SEQUENCES

*Longest Sequence of League Wins:* 14, 10.2.2002 – 18.8.2002.

*Longest Sequence of League Defeats:* 7, 12.2.1977 – 12.3.1977.

*Longest Sequence of League Draws:* 6, 4.3.1961 – 1.4.1961.

*Longest Sequence of Unbeaten League Matches:* 49, 7.5.2003 – 24.10.2004.

*Longest Sequence Without a League Win:* 23, 28.9.1912 – 1.3.1913.

*Successive Scoring Runs:* 55 from 19.5.2001.

*Successive Non-scoring Runs:* 6 from 25.2.1987.

## TEN YEAR LEAGUE RECORD

| | | P | W | D | L | F | A | Pts | Pos |
| --- | --- | --- | --- | --- | --- | --- | --- | --- | --- |
| 2003-04 | PR Lge | 38 | 26 | 12 | 0 | 73 | 26 | 90 | 1 |
| 2004-05 | PR Lge | 38 | 25 | 8 | 5 | 87 | 36 | 83 | 2 |
| 2005-06 | PR Lge | 38 | 20 | 7 | 11 | 68 | 31 | 67 | 4 |
| 2006-07 | PR Lge | 38 | 19 | 11 | 8 | 63 | 35 | 68 | 4 |
| 2007-08 | PR Lge | 38 | 24 | 11 | 3 | 74 | 31 | 83 | 3 |
| 2008-09 | PR Lge | 38 | 20 | 12 | 6 | 68 | 37 | 72 | 4 |
| 2009-10 | PR Lge | 38 | 23 | 6 | 9 | 83 | 41 | 75 | 3 |
| 2010-11 | PR Lge | 38 | 19 | 11 | 8 | 72 | 43 | 68 | 4 |
| 2011-12 | PR Lge | 38 | 21 | 7 | 10 | 74 | 49 | 70 | 3 |
| 2012-13 | PR Lge | 38 | 21 | 10 | 7 | 72 | 37 | 73 | 4 |

### DID YOU KNOW ?

Andy Ducat, who made 175 Football League games for Arsenal between 1907 and 1912, was a dual international who was capped six times by England at football and won a single cap for the England cricket team when he played against Australia at Lords in 1921.

## ARSENAL – FA PREMIERSHIP 2012–13 LEAGUE RECORD

| Match No. | Date | Venue | Opponents | Result | H/T Score | Lg Pos. | Goalscorers | Atten- dance |
|---|---|---|---|---|---|---|---|---|
| 1 | Aug 18 | H | Sunderland | D 0-0 | 0-0 | 8 | | 60,078 |
| 2 | 26 | A | Stoke C | D 0-0 | 0-0 | 12 | | 27,072 |
| 3 | Sept 2 | A | Liverpool | W 2-0 | 1-0 | 8 | Podolski [31], Cazorla [68] | 44,932 |
| 4 | 15 | H | Southampton | W 6-1 | 4-1 | 3 | Hooiveld (og) [11], Podolski [31], Gervinho 2 [35, 71], Clyne (og) [37], Walcott [88] | 60,097 |
| 5 | 23 | A | Manchester C | D 1-1 | 0-1 | 5 | Koscielny [82] | 47,318 |
| 6 | 29 | H | Chelsea | L 1-2 | 1-1 | 7 | Gervinho [42] | 60,101 |
| 7 | Oct 6 | A | West Ham U | W 3-1 | 1-1 | 5 | Giroud [41], Walcott [77], Cazorla [83] | 34,974 |
| 8 | 20 | A | Norwich C | L 0-1 | 0-1 | 9 | | 26,825 |
| 9 | 27 | H | QPR | W 1-0 | 0-0 | 4 | Arteta [84] | 60,103 |
| 10 | Nov 3 | A | Manchester U | L 1-2 | 0-1 | 6 | Cazorla [90] | 75,492 |
| 11 | 10 | H | Fulham | D 3-3 | 2-2 | 7 | Giroud 2 [11, 69], Podolski [23] | 60,093 |
| 12 | 17 | H | Tottenham H | W 5-2 | 3-1 | 6 | Mertesacker [24], Podolski [42], Giroud [46], Cazorla [60], Walcott [90] | 60,111 |
| 13 | 24 | A | Aston Villa | D 0-0 | 0-0 | 6 | | 34,607 |
| 14 | 28 | A | Everton | D 1-1 | 1-1 | 7 | Walcott [1] | 37,141 |
| 15 | Dec 1 | H | Swansea C | L 0-2 | 0-0 | 10 | | 60,098 |
| 16 | 8 | H | WBA | W 2-0 | 1-0 | 6 | Arteta 2 (2 pens) [26, 64] | 60,083 |
| 17 | 17 | A | Reading | W 5-2 | 3-0 | 5 | Podolski [14], Cazorla 3 [32, 34, 60], Walcott [80] | 24,125 |
| 18 | 22 | A | Wigan Ath | W 1-0 | 0-0 | 3 | Arteta (pen) [60] | 21,754 |
| 19 | 29 | H | Newcastle U | W 7-3 | 1-1 | 5 | Walcott 3 [20, 73, 90], Oxlade-Chamberlain [50], Podolski [64], Giroud 2 [85, 87] | 60,087 |
| 20 | Jan 1 | A | Southampton | D 1-1 | 1-1 | 5 | Do Prado (og) [41] | 31,743 |
| 21 | 13 | H | Manchester C | L 0-2 | 0-2 | 6 | | 60,107 |
| 22 | 20 | A | Chelsea | L 1-2 | 0-2 | 6 | Walcott [58] | 41,784 |
| 23 | 23 | H | West Ham U | W 5-1 | 1-1 | 6 | Podolski [22], Giroud 2 [47, 57], Cazorla [53], Walcott [54] | 60,081 |
| 24 | 30 | H | Liverpool | D 2-2 | 0-1 | 6 | Giroud [64], Walcott [67] | 60,089 |
| 25 | Feb 2 | H | Stoke C | W 1-0 | 0-0 | 6 | Podolski [78] | 59,872 |
| 26 | 9 | A | Sunderland | W 1-0 | 1-0 | 5 | Cazorla [35] | 46,402 |
| 27 | 23 | A | Aston Villa | W 2-1 | 1-0 | 5 | Cazorla 2 [6, 85] | 60,079 |
| 28 | Mar 3 | A | Tottenham H | L 1-2 | 0-2 | 5 | Mertesacker [51] | 36,170 |
| 29 | 16 | A | Swansea C | W 2-0 | 0-0 | 5 | Monreal [74], Gervinho [90] | 20,583 |
| 30 | 30 | H | Reading | W 4-1 | 1-0 | 5 | Gervinho [11], Cazorla [48], Giroud [67], Arteta (pen) [77] | 60,082 |
| 31 | Apr 6 | A | WBA | W 2-1 | 1-0 | 4 | Rosicky 2 [20, 50] | 26,144 |
| 32 | 13 | H | Norwich C | W 3-1 | 0-0 | 3 | Arteta (pen) [85], Giroud [88], Podolski [90] | 60,095 |
| 33 | 16 | H | Everton | D 0-0 | 0-0 | 3 | | 60,071 |
| 34 | 20 | A | Fulham | W 1-0 | 1-0 | 3 | Mertesacker [43] | 25,700 |
| 35 | 28 | H | Manchester U | D 1-1 | 1-1 | 4 | Walcott [2] | 60,112 |
| 36 | May 4 | A | QPR | W 1-0 | 1-0 | 3 | Walcott [1] | 18,178 |
| 37 | 14 | H | Wigan Ath | W 4-1 | 1-1 | 4 | Podolski 2 [11, 68], Walcott [63], Ramsey [71] | 60,068 |
| 38 | 19 | A | Newcastle U | W 1-0 | 0-0 | 4 | Koscielny [52] | 52,354 |

**Final League Position: 4**

### GOALSCORERS

*League (72):* Walcott 14, Cazorla 12, Giroud 11, Podolski 11, Arteta 6 (5 pens), Gervinho 5, Mertesacker 3, Koscielny 2, Rosicky 2, Monreal 1, Oxlade-Chamberlain 1, Ramsey 1, own goals 3.
*FA Cup (6):* Giroud 2, Gibbs 1, Podolski 1, Walcott 1, Wilshere 1.
*Capital One Cup (14):* Walcott 5, Chamakh 2, Giroud 2, Arshavin 1, Koscielny 1, Miquel 1, Oxlade-Chamberlain 1, Vermaelen 1.
*UEFA Champions League (13):* Podolski 4, Gervinho 2, Giroud 2, Koscielny 1, Ramsey 1, Rosicky 1, Walcott 1, Wilshere 1.

| Szczesny W 25 | Jenkinson C 14 | Mertesacker P 33+1 | Vermaelen T 25+4 | Gibbs K 23+4 | Diaby A 10+1 | Arteta M 34 | Cazorla S 37+1 | Walcott T 24+8 | Gervinho 12+6 | Podolski L 25+8 | Giroud O 24+10 | Ramsey A 21+15 | Arshavin A —+7 | Mannone V 9 | Oxlade-Chamberlain A 11+14 | Andre Santos C 3+5 | Koscielny L 20+5 | Coquelin F 3+8 | Gnabry S —+1 | Sagna B 25 | Wilshere J 20+5 | Rosicky T 7+3 | Monreal N 9+1 | Miquel I —+1 | Fabianski L 4 | Match No. |
|---|---|---|---|---|---|---|---|---|---|---|---|---|---|---|---|---|---|---|---|---|---|---|---|---|---|---|
| 1 | 2 | 3 | 4 | 5 | $6^{2}$ | 7 | 8 | $9^{3}$ | 10 | $11^{1}$ | 12 | 13 | 14 | | | | | | | | | | | | | 1 |
| | 2 | 3 | 4 | 5 | 7 | 6 | $8^{3}$ | 12 | $11^{2}$ | $9^{1}$ | 10 | 14 | | 1 | 13 | | | | | | | | | | | 2 |
| | 2 | 3 | $4^{3}$ | 5 | 6 | 7 | 9 | | | $10^{2}$ | 11 | 12 | | 1 | | | $8^{1}$ | 13 | 14 | | | | | | | 3 |
| 1 | 2 | 3 | 4 | 5 | | 7 | 9 | 14 | $11^{3}$ | $10^{2}$ | 13 | 12 | | | 8 | | | $6^{1}$ | | | | | | | | 4 |
| | 2 | 4 | | 5 | $7^{1}$ | 8 | 9 | 13 | $10^{3}$ | $11^{2}$ | 12 | 6 | | 1 | | 3 | 14 | | | | | | | | | 5 |
| | 2 | | 4 | 5 | $6^{1}$ | 7 | 9 | 13 | 11 | $10^{3}$ | 14 | $8^{2}$ | | 1 | 12 | 3 | | | | | | | | | | 6 |
| | 2 | 3 | 4 | $5^{1}$ | | 8 | 7 | 13 | $9^{2}$ | $11^{3}$ | 10 | 6 | | 1 | | 12 | 14 | | | | | | | | | 7 |
| | 2 | 3 | 4 | | | 7 | 8 | | 9 | $11^{1}$ | 10 | $6^{3}$ | 13 | 1 | $12^{2}$ | 5 | | 14 | | | | | | | | 8 |
| | | 3 | 4 | | | 6 | 8 | 12 | $13^{3}$ | $10^{2}$ | 11 | 9 | 14 | 1 | | 5 | | | | 2 | $7^{1}$ | | | | | 9 |
| | | 3 | 4 | | | 6 | 9 | 12 | | $10^{2}$ | 11 | $7^{1}$ | 13 | 1 | | 5 | | | | 2 | $8^{8}$ | | | | | 10 |
| | | 4 | 5 | | | 7 | 8 | $9^{3}$ | | $10^{2}$ | 11 | 12 | 14 | 1 | 13 | | 3 | $6^{1}$ | | 2 | | | | | | 11 |
| 1 | | 3 | 5 | | | 7 | 8 | 9 | | $11^{2}$ | $10^{3}$ | 12 | | | 14 | 13 | 4 | | | 2 | $6^{1}$ | | | | | 12 |
| 1 | 2 | 3 | | 5 | | 6 | 9 | | 12 | $10^{1}$ | $11^{3}$ | 7 | 13 | | $8^{2}$ | | 4 | 14 | | | | | | | | 13 |
| 1 | | 3 | 5 | 12 | | 8 | $10^{3}$ | 6 | 13 | | 11 | $7^{2}$ | | | | | $4^{1}$ | 14 | | 2 | 9 | | | | | 14 |
| 1 | 2 | 3 | 4 | 5 | | 7 | 6 | 9 | 10 | $11^{2}$ | 13 | | | | 12 | | | | | $8^{3}$ | 14 | | | | | 15 |
| 1 | | 3 | 4 | 5 | | 7 | $8^{3}$ | | $10^{2}$ | 14 | 11 | | | | $9^{1}$ | | 12 | | | 2 | 6 | 13 | | | | 16 |
| 1 | | 3 | 4 | 5 | | 6 | $8^{2}$ | $10^{3}$ | | 11 | 14 | 12 | | | $9^{1}$ | | 13 | | | 2 | 7 | | | | | 17 |
| 1 | | 3 | 4 | 5 | | 6 | $9^{3}$ | 11 | | $10^{2}$ | | 12 | | | $8^{1}$ | 14 | 13 | | | 2 | 7 | | | | | 18 |
| 1 | | | 4 | 5 | | 6 | $8^{3}$ | 11 | | $10^{2}$ | 12 | 13 | | | $9^{1}$ | 3 | 14 | | | 2 | 7 | | | | | 19 |
| 1 | | | 4 | 5 | | 6 | $9^{3}$ | 11 | 14 | $10^{1}$ | 12 | 13 | | | $8^{2}$ | | 3 | | | 2 | 7 | | | | | 20 |
| 1 | 12 | | 4 | 5 | $6^{3}$ | | 8 | 11 | | $10^{2}$ | 13 | 14 | | | $9^{1}$ | | $3^{8}$ | | | 2 | 7 | | | | | 21 |
| 1 | | 3 | 4 | 5 | $7^{2}$ | | 10 | 8 | | 11 | 12 | 13 | | | | | $6^{1}$ | | | 2 | 9 | | | | | 22 |
| 1 | | 3 | $4^{1}$ | 5 | | | 8 | 9 | | $11^{2}$ | $10^{3}$ | 6 | | | 14 | 13 | 12 | | | 2 | 7 | | | | | 23 |
| 1 | | 3 | 4 | $5^{1}$ | | | 8 | 9 | | 10 | 11 | 6 | | | | 12 | | | | 2 | 7 | | | | | 24 |
| 1 | | 3 | | | $6^{2}$ | 7 | 12 | $10^{3}$ | | 13 | 11 | 14 | | | $9^{1}$ | | 4 | | | 2 | 8 | | 5 | | | 25 |
| 1 | $4^{8}$ | 3 | | | 12 | 6 | 11 | $9^{2}$ | | | 10 | 8 | | | | | | | | 2 | $7^{1}$ | | 5 | 13 | | 26 |
| 1 | $2^{2}$ | 3 | 4 | | $6^{1}$ | 7 | 8 | $10^{3}$ | | 13 | 11 | 12 | | | | 14 | | | | | 9 | 12 | 5 | | | 27 |
| 1 | $2^{1}$ | 3 | 4 | | | $7^{2}$ | 10 | 8 | | 13 | 11 | 6 | | | | | | | | | 9 | 12 | 5 | | | 28 |
| | 2 | 3 | | 14 | $7^{2}$ | 6 | 9 | $8^{3}$ | 13 | | 11 | 12 | | $10^{1}$ | 4 | | | | | | | | 5 | 1 | | 29 |
| | | 3 | | 12 | | 6 | 10 | | $9^{2}$ | 13 | $11^{3}$ | 8 | | 14 | 4 | | 2 | | | | 7 | $5^{1}$ | | 1 | | 30 |
| | | $3^{8}$ | 12 | 13 | | 10 | $9^{3}$ | | $8^{1}$ | | 11 | 7 | | | 4 | 14 | 2 | | | | $6^{2}$ | 5 | | 1 | | 31 |
| | | | 4 | 5 | | 6 | 9 | 13 | $10^{2}$ | 12 | 11 | 8 | | 14 | 3 | | $2^{3}$ | $7^{1}$ | | | | 1 | | | | 32 |
| 1 | | 3 | | $5^{1}$ | | 7 | 11 | $9^{2}$ | | 13 | 10 | 6 | | 12 | 4 | | | | | 2 | $8^{1}$ | | 14 | | | 33 |
| 1 | | 3 | 14 | | | 7 | $11^{3}$ | $9^{1}$ | | 12 | $10^{8}$ | 8 | | | 4 | | 2 | 13 | | | $6^{2}$ | 5 | | | | 34 |
| 1 | | 3 | | 5 | | 6 | 9 | 10 | 13 | $11^{2}$ | | $7^{2}$ | | 14 | 4 | | 2 | 12 | | | $8^{1}$ | | | | | 35 |
| 1 | | 3 | 14 | | | 7 | $10^{2}$ | 9 | | $11^{1}$ | 6 | | | 12 | 4 | | 2 | 13 | | | $8^{3}$ | 5 | | | | 36 |
| 1 | | 3 | 14 | 5 | | $7^{3}$ | 10 | 9 | | $11^{1}$ | 6 | | | 13 | 4 | | 2 | 12 | | | $8^{2}$ | | | | | 37 |
| 1 | | 3 | | 5 | | $7^{1}$ | $10^{3}$ | 8 | | $11^{2}$ | 13 | 6 | | 12 | 4 | | 2 | 14 | | | 9 | | | | | 38 |

**FA Cup**

|  |  | |  |
|---|---|---|---|
| Third Round | Swansea C | (a) | 2-2 |
| *Replay* | Swansea C | (h) | 1-0 |
| Fourth Round | Brighton & HA | (a) | 3-2 |
| Fifth Round | Blackburn R | (h) | 0-1 |

**Capital One Cup**

|  |  | |  |
|---|---|---|---|
| Third Round | Coventry C | (h) | 6-1 |
| Fourth Round | Reading | (a) | 7-5 |
| Quarter-Finals | Bradford C | (a) | 1-1 |
| *(aet; lost 2-3 on pens)* | | | |

**UEFA Champions League**

| |  | |  |
|---|---|---|---|
| Group B | Montpellier | (a) | 2-1 |
| | Olympiakos | (h) | 3-1 |
| | Schalke 04 | (h) | 0-2 |
| | Schalke 04 | (a) | 2-2 |
| | Montpellier | (h) | 2-0 |
| | Olympiakos | (a) | 1-2 |
| Knock-out Round | Bayern Munich | (h) | 1-3 |
| | Bayern Munich | (a) | 2-0 |

# ASTON VILLA

## FOUNDATION

Cricketing enthusiasts of Villa Cross Wesleyan Chapel, Aston, Birmingham decided to form a football club during the winter of 1874–75. Football clubs were few and far between in the Birmingham area and in their first game against Aston Brook St Mary's rugby team they played one half rugby and the other soccer. In 1876 they were joined by Scottish soccer enthusiast George Ramsay who was immediately appointed captain and went on to lead Aston Villa from obscurity to one of the country's top clubs in a period of less than ten years.

*Villa Park, Birmingham B6 6HE.*

*Telephone:* (0121) 327 2299.

*Fax:* (0121) 322 2107.

*Ticket Office/Consumer Sales:* (0800) 612 0970.

*Website:* www.avfc.co.uk

*Email:* (via website)

*Ground Capacity:* 42,785.

*Record Attendance:* 76,588 v Derby Co, FA Cup 6th rd, 2 March 1946.

*Pitch Measurements:* 105m × 68m (114yd × 74yd)

*Chairman:* Randolph Lerner.

*Manager:* Paul Lambert.

*Assistant Manager:* Ian Culverhouse.

*Physio:* Alan Smith.

*Colours:* Claret shirts, sky blue sleeves with claret trim, white shorts with sky blue and claret trim, sky blue socks with claret hoops.

*Year Formed:* 1874.

*Turned Professional:* 1885.

*Club Nickname:* 'The Villans'.

*Grounds:* 1874, Wilson Road and Aston Park (also used Aston Lower Grounds for some matches); 1876, Wellington Road, Perry Barr; 1897, Villa Park.

*First Football League Game:* 8 September 1888, Football League, v Wolverhampton W (a) D 1–1 – Warner; Cox, Coulton; Yates, Harry Devey, Dawson; Albert Brown, Green (1), Allen, Garvey, Hodgetts.

*Record League Victory:* 12–2 v Accrington S, Division 1, 12 March 1892 – Warner; Evans, Cox; Harry Devey, Jimmy Cowan, Baird; Athersmith (1), Dickson (2), John Devey (4), Lewis Campbell (4), Hodgetts (1).

## HONOURS

**FA Premier League:**
*Runners-up* 1992–93.

**Football League – Division 1:**
*Champions* 1893–94, 1895–96, 1896–97, 1898–99, 1899–1900, 1909–10, 1980–81;
*Runners-up* 1888–89, 1902–03, 1907–08, 1910–11, 1912–13, 1913–14, 1930–31, 1932–33, 1989–90;
**Division 2:** *Champions* 1937–38, 1959–60; *Runners-up* 1974–75, 1987–88;
**Division 3:** *Champions* 1971–72.

**FA Cup:** *Winners* 1887, 1895, 1897, 1905, 1913, 1920, 1957;
*Runners-up* 1892, 1924, 2000.

**Double Performed:** 1896–97.

**Football League Cup:** *Winners* 1961, 1975, 1977, 1994, 1996;
*Runners-up* 1963, 1971, 2010.

**European Competitions**
**European Cup:** 1981–82 (*winners*), 1982–83. **UEFA Cup:** 1975–76, 1977–78, 1983–84, 1990–91, 1993–94, 1994–95, 1996–97, 1997–98, 1998–99, 2001–02, 2008–09.
**Europa League:** 2009–10, 2010–11.
**World Club Championship:** 1982.
**Super Cup:** 1982 (*winners*). **Intertoto Cup:** 2000, 2001 (*winners*), 2002, 2008 (*winners*).

## sky SPORTS FACT FILE

In 1930–31 Aston Villa scored a record 128 League goals but could still only finish as runners-up to First Division champions Arsenal. Centre forward Pongo Waring finished as leading scorer with 49 goals from his 39 appearances including three occasions when he netted four goals in a game.

*Record Cup Victory:* 13–0 v Wednesbury Old Ath, FA Cup 1st rd, 30 October 1886 – Warner; Coulton, Simmonds; Yates, Robertson, Burton (2); Richard Davis (1), Albert Brown (3), Hunter (3), Loach (2), Hodgetts (2).

*Record Defeat:* 0–8 v Chelsea, FA Premier League, 23 December 2012.

*Most League Points (2 for a win):* 70, Division 3, 1971–72.

*Most League Points (3 for a win):* 78, Division 2, 1987–88.

*Most League Goals:* 128, Division 1, 1930–31.

*Highest League Scorer in Season:* 'Pongo' Waring, 49, Division 1, 1930–31.

*Most League Goals in Total Aggregate:* Harry Hampton, 215, 1904–15.

*Most League Goals in One Match:* 5, Harry Hampton v Sheffield W, Division 1, 5 October 1912; 5, Harold Halse v Derby Co, Division 1, 19 October 1912; 5, Len Capewell v Burnley, Division 1, 29 August 1925; 5, George Brown v Leicester C, Division 1, 2 January 1932; 5, Gerry Hitchens v Charlton Ath, Division 2, 18 November 1959.

*Most Capped Player:* Steve Staunton 64 (102), Republic of Ireland.

*Most League Appearances:* Charlie Aitken, 561, 1961–76.

*Youngest League Player:* Jimmy Brown, 15 years 349 days v Bolton W, 17 September 1969.

*Record Transfer Fee Received:* £24,000,000 from Manchester C for James Milner, August 2010.

*Record Transfer Fee Paid:* £19,000,000 (rising to 24,000,000) to Sunderland for Darren Bent, January 2011.

*Football League Record:* 1888 Founder Member of the League; 1936–38 Division 2; 1938–59 Division 1; 1959–60 Division 2; 1960–67 Division 1; 1967–70 Division 2; 1970–72 Division 3; 1972–75 Division 2; 1975–87 Division 1; 1987–88 Division 2; 1988–92 Division 1; 1992– FA Premier League.

## MANAGERS

George Ramsay 1884–1926
*(Secretary-Manager)*
W. J. Smith 1926–34
*(Secretary-Manager)*
Jimmy McMullan 1934–35
Jimmy Hogan 1936–44
Alex Massie 1945–50
George Martin 1950–53
Eric Houghton 1953–58
Joe Mercer 1958–64
Dick Taylor 1964–67
Tommy Cummings 1967–68
Tommy Docherty 1968–70
Vic Crowe 1970–74
Ron Saunders 1974–82
Tony Barton 1982–84
Graham Turner 1984–86
Billy McNeill 1986–87
Graham Taylor 1987–90
Dr Jozef Venglos 1990–91
Ron Atkinson 1991–94
Brian Little 1994–98
John Gregory 1998–2002
Graham Taylor OBE 2002–03
David O'Leary 2003–06
Martin O'Neill 2006–10
Gerard Houllier 2010–11
Alex McLeish 2011–12
Paul Lambert June 2012–

## LATEST SEQUENCES

*Longest Sequence of League Wins:* 9, 15.10.1910 – 10.12.1910.

*Longest Sequence of League Defeats:* 11, 23.3.1963 – 4.5.1963.

*Longest Sequence of League Draws:* 6, 12.9.1981 – 10.10.1981.

*Longest Sequence of Unbeaten League Matches:* 15, 12.3.1949 – 27.8.1949.

*Longest Sequence Without a League Win:* 13, 24.3.2012 – 15.9.2012.

*Successive Scoring Runs:* 35 from 10.11.1895.

*Successive Non-scoring Runs:* 5 from 29.2.1992.

## TEN YEAR LEAGUE RECORD

| | | P | W | D | L | F | A | Pts | Pos |
|---|---|---|---|---|---|---|---|---|---|
| 2003-04 | PR Lge | 38 | 15 | 11 | 12 | 48 | 44 | 56 | 6 |
| 2004-05 | PR Lge | 38 | 12 | 11 | 15 | 45 | 52 | 47 | 10 |
| 2005-06 | PR Lge | 38 | 10 | 12 | 16 | 42 | 55 | 42 | 16 |
| 2006-07 | PR Lge | 38 | 11 | 17 | 10 | 43 | 41 | 50 | 11 |
| 2007-08 | PR Lge | 38 | 16 | 12 | 10 | 71 | 51 | 60 | 6 |
| 2008-09 | PR Lge | 38 | 17 | 11 | 10 | 54 | 48 | 62 | 6 |
| 2009-10 | PR Lge | 38 | 17 | 13 | 8 | 52 | 39 | 64 | 6 |
| 2010-11 | PR Lge | 38 | 12 | 12 | 14 | 48 | 59 | 48 | 9 |
| 2011-12 | PR Lge | 38 | 7 | 17 | 14 | 37 | 53 | 38 | 16 |
| 2012-13 | PR Lge | 38 | 10 | 11 | 17 | 47 | 69 | 41 | 15 |

## DID YOU KNOW ?

Former Aston Villa player Eric Houghton returned to manage the club and led the team to victory in the 1956–57 FA Cup final. Eric, who later became a director at Villa Park, was also an accomplished cricketer appearing for Warwickshire in the County Championship in the late 1940s.

## ASTON VILLA – FA PREMIERSHIP 2012–13 LEAGUE RECORD

| Match No. | Date | Venue | Opponents | Result | H/T Score | Lg Pos. | Goalscorers | Attendance |
|---|---|---|---|---|---|---|---|---|
| 1 | Aug 18 | A | West Ham U | L 0-1 | 0-1 | 17 | | 34,172 |
| 2 | 25 | H | Everton | L 1-3 | 0-3 | 19 | El Ahmadi [74] | 36,565 |
| 3 | Sept 2 | A | Newcastle U | D 1-1 | 1-0 | 17 | Clark [22] | 48,245 |
| 4 | 15 | H | Swansea C | W 2-0 | 1-0 | 11 | Lowton [16], Benteke [88] | 34,005 |
| 5 | 22 | A | Southampton | L 1-4 | 1-0 | 14 | Bent [36] | 30,713 |
| 6 | 30 | H | WBA | D 1-1 | 0-0 | 15 | Bent [80] | 34,489 |
| 7 | Oct 7 | A | Tottenham H | L 0-2 | 0-0 | 16 | | 35,802 |
| 8 | 20 | A | Fulham | L 0-1 | 0-0 | 17 | | 25,693 |
| 9 | 27 | H | Norwich C | D 1-1 | 1-0 | 17 | Benteke [27] | 33,184 |
| 10 | Nov 3 | A | Sunderland | W 1-0 | 0-0 | 17 | Agbonlahor [57] | 41,515 |
| 11 | 10 | H | Manchester U | L 2-3 | 1-0 | 17 | Weimann 2 [45, 50] | 40,538 |
| 12 | 17 | A | Manchester C | L 0-5 | 0-1 | 18 | | 47,072 |
| 13 | 24 | H | Arsenal | D 0-0 | 0-0 | 17 | | 34,607 |
| 14 | 27 | H | Reading | W 1-0 | 0-0 | 17 | Benteke [80] | 28,692 |
| 15 | Dec 1 | A | QPR | D 1-1 | 1-1 | 16 | Holman [8] | 17,387 |
| 16 | 8 | H | Stoke C | D 0-0 | 0-0 | 16 | | 30,110 |
| 17 | 15 | A | Liverpool | W 3-1 | 2-0 | 14 | Benteke 2 [29, 51], Weimann [40] | 44,607 |
| 18 | 23 | A | Chelsea | L 0-8 | 0-3 | 16 | | 41,363 |
| 19 | 26 | H | Tottenham H | L 0-4 | 0-0 | 16 | | 36,863 |
| 20 | 29 | H | Wigan Ath | L 0-3 | 0-1 | 17 | | 33,374 |
| 21 | Jan 1 | A | Swansea C | D 2-2 | 1-1 | 16 | Weimann [44], Benteke (pen) [84] | 20,406 |
| 22 | 12 | H | Southampton | L 0-1 | 0-1 | 18 | | 32,500 |
| 23 | 19 | A | WBA | D 2-2 | 2-0 | 17 | Benteke [12], Agbonlahor [31] | 25,583 |
| 24 | 29 | H | Newcastle U | L 1-2 | 0-2 | 18 | Benteke (pen) [49] | 30,334 |
| 25 | Feb 2 | A | Everton | D 3-3 | 2-1 | 19 | Benteke 2 [2, 61], Agbonlahor [24] | 38,121 |
| 26 | 10 | H | West Ham U | W 2-1 | 0-0 | 17 | Benteke (pen) [74], N'Zogbia [79] | 30,503 |
| 27 | 23 | A | Arsenal | L 1-2 | 0-1 | 18 | Weimann [68] | 60,079 |
| 28 | Mar 4 | H | Manchester C | L 0-1 | 0-1 | 18 | | 33,217 |
| 29 | 9 | A | Reading | W 2-1 | 2-1 | 17 | Benteke [33], Agbonlahor [45] | 24,102 |
| 30 | 16 | H | QPR | W 3-2 | 1-1 | 17 | Agbonlahor [45], Weimann [59], Benteke [81] | 38,594 |
| 31 | 31 | H | Liverpool | L 1-2 | 1-0 | 18 | Benteke [31] | 42,037 |
| 32 | Apr 6 | A | Stoke C | W 3-1 | 1-0 | 16 | Agbonlahor [9], Lowton [87], Benteke [90] | 27,544 |
| 33 | 13 | H | Fulham | D 1-1 | 0-0 | 16 | N'Zogbia [55] | 37,011 |
| 34 | 22 | A | Manchester U | L 0-3 | 0-3 | 17 | | 75,591 |
| 35 | 29 | H | Sunderland | W 6-1 | 2-1 | 16 | Vlaar [31], Weimann [38], Benteke 3 [55, 59, 72], Agbonlahor [88] | 37,428 |
| 36 | May 4 | A | Norwich C | W 2-1 | 0-0 | 13 | Agbonlahor 2 [55, 89] | 26,842 |
| 37 | 11 | H | Chelsea | L 1-2 | 1-0 | 13 | Benteke [15] | 42,084 |
| 38 | 19 | A | Wigan Ath | D 2-2 | 1-2 | 15 | Bent [5], Vlaar [61] | 23,001 |

**Final League Position: 15**

### GOALSCORERS

*League (47):* Benteke 19 (3 pens), Agbonlahor 9, Weimann 7, Bent 3, Lowton 2, N'Zogbia 2, Vlaar 2, Clark 1, El Ahmadi 1, Holman 1.
*FA Cup (3):* Bent 2, Weimann 1.
*Capital One Cup (17):* Benteke 4, Weimann 4, Agbonlahor 3, Bent 1, Delph 1, Herd 1, Holman 1, N'Zogbia 1, own goal 1.

| Given S 2 | Lowton M 37 | Vlaar R 27 | Clark C 28+1 | Baker N 25+1 | Holman B 16+11 | El Ahmadi K 12+8 | Delph F 19+5 | N'Zogbia C 11+10 | Ireland S 9+4 | Bent D 8+8 | Weimann A 26+4 | Gardner G —+2 | Bannan B 18+6 | Herd C 9 | Delfouneso N 1 | Lichaj E 9+8 | Guzan B 36 | Agbonlahor G 24+4 | Westwood A 28+2 | Benteke C 32+2 | Bennett J 21+4 | Albrighton M 4+5 | Stevens E 6+1 | Bowery J 3+7 | Williams D —+1 | Sylla Y 7+4 | Dawkins S —+4 | Match No. |
|---|---|---|---|---|---|---|---|---|---|---|---|---|---|---|---|---|---|---|---|---|---|---|---|---|---|---|---|---|
| 1 | 2 | 3 | 4 | 5 | 6¹ | 7 | 8³ | 9² | 10 | 11 | 12 | 13 | 14 | | | | | | | | | | | | | | | 1 |
| 1 | 2 | 3 | 5⁴ | 4 | 12 | 8 | 6 | | | 11 | 14 | | | 9³ | 7² | 10¹ | 13 | | | | | | | | | | | 2 |
| | 2 | 3 | 4 | | 10 | 7² | | 13 | 8 | 11 | 9¹ | | 6 | | | 5 | 1 | 12 | | | | | | | | | | 3 |
| | 2 | 4 | 3 | | 6³ | 7 | | 14 | 8¹ | 11 | 10² | | 9 | | | 5 | 1 | | 12 | 13 | | | | | | | | 4 |
| | 2 | 3 | 4 | | 6 | 8 | | | 7¹ | 10 | | | 9² | | | 5³ | 1 | 13 | 12 | 11 | 14 | | | | | | | 5 |
| | 2 | 3 | 4 | | 7 | 8 | 9³ | 12 | | 13 | | | 14 | | | 1 | 10 | | | 11² | 5 | 6¹ | | | | | | 6 |
| 5 | 3 | 4 | | | 6³ | 7 | | 8² | 13 | | 12 | | 14 | | | 1 | 11 | | 10 | 2 | 9¹ | | | | | | | 7 |
| | 2 | 3 | 4¹ | | 9 | 7 | 8 | 13 | | 6² | 10³ | | | | | 12 | 1 | 11 | | 14 | 5 | | | | | | | 8 |
| | 4 | 3 | | | 8³ | 7 | 9 | | | 13 | 14 | | | 2 | | 12 | 1 | 10¹ | | 11² | 5⁴ | 6 | | | | | | 9 |
| | 2 | 3 | 4 | | 14 | | | 7 | | 6³ | 9 | | 12⁷ | | | 1 | 10 | 8 | 11 | 5¹ | 13 | | | | | | | 10 |
| | 2 | 3 | 4 | | 13 | 12 | 14 | 8¹ | | 6² | 9³ | | | | | 1 | 10 | 7 | 11 | 5 | | | | | | | | 11 |
| 5 | 3 | 4 | | | 13 | | | 9¹ | | 10² | 6 | | | | | 1 | 8 | 7 | 11³ | 12 | 2 | 14 | | | | | | 12 |
| | 2 | 3¹ | 4 | | 13 | 6² | | | | 8³ | 9 | | | 12 | | 1 | 10 | 7 | 11 | 14 | 5 | | | | | | | 13 |
| | 2 | | 4 | 3 | 6² | | | 13 | | | 9³ | 8 | | 12 | | 1 | 10 | 7 | 11 | 14 | 5¹ | | | | | | | 14 |
| | 2 | | 3 | 4 | 6³ | 14 | 13 | | | 9² | 7¹ | | 5 | | | 1 | 11 | 8 | 10 | | | 12 | | | | | | 15 |
| | 2 | | 4 | 3 | 7¹ | | 14 | 13 | 12 | 9³ | 6 | | 5 | | | 1 | 11² | 8 | 10 | | | | | | | | | 16 |
| | 2 | | 4 | 3 | 8¹ | 13 | 12 | 14 | | 11³ | 9² | 7 | 5 | | | 1 | | 6 | 10 | | | | | | | | | 17 |
| 5 | 3 | 4 | 10³ | | | | | 13 | | 9 | 6 | 2 | 8¹ | | | 1 | | 7² | 11 | 12 | | 14 | | | | | | 18 |
| | 2 | | 4 | 5¹ | 10 | | 8 | 9 | | 12 | | | 3 | | | 1 | | 7² | 11 | 6 | 13 | | | | | | | 19 |
| 5 | 3 | | | | 7² | 13 | | 6¹ | | 10 | 8 | 2 | 4³ | | | 1 | | 11 | 9 | 14 | 12 | | | | | | | 20 |
| | 2 | 4 | | 12 | | | 8 | | | 10 | 13 | 3 | | | | 1 | | 7² | 11 | 9 | 6³ | 5¹ | 14 | | | | | 21 |
| | 2 | 3 | 4 | 6¹ | | 8 | 9² | | | 11 | 12 | | | | | 1 | 13 | 7³ | 10 | | | 5 | 14 | | | | | 22 |
| 5 | 2 | 3 | 4¹ | 14 | | 7² | 8³ | | | 13 | | 12 | | | | 1 | 10 | 6 | 11 | 9 | | | | | | | | 23 |
| 5 | 3 | 2 | 4 | | | 8 | | 11¹ | 13 | | 7 | | | | | 1 | 12 | 6 | 10 | 9² | | | | | | | | 24 |
| | 2 | 3 | 4 | 14 | 13 | 7² | | 9¹ | | 10 | | | | | | 1 | 8³ | 6 | 11 | 5 | | | | 12 | | | | 25 |
| | 2 | 3 | 4 | 5 | | 8 | 10³ | | 12 | 6² | | | | | | 1 | | 7 | 11 | | | | | 9¹ | | 14 | 13 | 26 |
| | 2 | | 3 | 4 | 12 | 6 | 8² | | | 9 | | | | | | 1 | 11 | 7¹ | 10 | 5 | | | | | | 13 | | 27 |
| | 2 | | 3 | 4 | 12 | 14 | 8 | 10¹ | | 6² | | | | | | 1 | 9 | 7³ | 11 | 5 | | | | | | 13 | | 28 |
| | 2 | 4 | 3 | 5² | | | 12 | | | 6 | 7¹ | | | | | 1 | 10 | 8 | 11 | 13 | | | 9 | | | | | 29 |
| | 2 | 3 | 4 | 5¹ | | 13 | | 9³ | 8 | | | | | | | 1 | 11 | 7 | 10 | 12 | | 14 | 6² | | | | | 30 |
| | 2 | 3 | | 4 | 14 | 12 | 13 | 9² | 8¹ | | | | | | | 1 | 11 | 7 | 10 | 5 | | | 6³ | | | | | 31 |
| | 2 | 3 | 4 | | 7 | 13 | 14 | 9³ | | | | | | | | 1 | 10¹ | 8 | 11 | 5 | | | 6² | 12 | | | | 32 |
| | 2 | 3 | 4 | 13 | | 7 | 10¹ | 14 | | 9³ | | | | | | 1 | 6 | 11 | 5 | | | | 8² | 12 | | | | 33 |
| | 2 | 3 | 13 | 4 | 12 | 7 | 9¹ | | 8 | | | | | | | 1 | 10 | 6 | 11 | 5² | | | | | | | | 34 |
| | 2 | 3 | 4 | | 7 | | 12 | 9 | | | | | | | | 1 | 11 | 6 | 10¹ | 5 | | | 8 | | | | | 35 |
| 2¹ | 3 | 4 | 13 | | 7 | | | 11 | | 12 | | | | | | 1 | 9 | 6 | 10 | 5 | | | 8² | | | | | 36 |
| | 3 | 4 | | | 7 | | | 9 | | | | | 2 | | | 1 | 11 | 6 | 10⁸ | 5 | | | 8 | | | | | 37 |
| | 2 | 3 | 4 | | 8 | | | 10 | 9 | 14 | | | | | | 1 | 11² | 7³ | 5 | | | 13 | 6¹ | 12 | | | | 38 |

**FA Cup**

|  |  | |  |
|---|---|---|---|
| Third Round | Ipswich T | (h) | 2-1 |
| Fourth Round | Millwall | (a) | 1-2 |

**Capital One Cup**

|  |  | |  |
|---|---|---|---|
| Second Round | Tranmere R | (h) | 3-0 |
| Third Round | Manchester C | (a) | 4-2 |
| Fourth Round | Swindon T | (a) | 3-2 |
| Quarter-Finals | Norwich C | (a) | 4-1 |
| Semi-Finals | Bradford C | (a) | 1-3 |
| | Bradford C | (h) | 2-1 |

# BARNET

## FOUNDATION

Barnet Football Club was formed in 1888 as an amateur organisation and they played at a ground in Queen's Road until they disbanded in 1901. A club known as Alston Works FC was then formed and they played at Totteridge Lane until changing to Barnet Alston FC in 1906. They moved to their present ground a year later, combining with The Avenue to form Barnet and Alston in 1912. The club progressed to senior amateur football by way of the Athenian and Isthmian Leagues, turning professional in 1965. It was as a Southern League and Conference club that they made their name.

*The Hive Stadium, Camrose Avenue, Edgware HA8 6AG.*

*Telephone:* (020) 831 3800.

*Fax:* (020) 8447 0655.

*Ticket Office:* (020) 8449 6325.

*Website:* www.barnetfc.com

*Email:* info@barnetfc.com

*Ground Capacity:* 6,023.

*Record Attendance:* 11,026 v Wycombe Wanderers, FA Amateur Cup 4th rd, 1951–52.

*Pitch Measurements:* 105m × 68m (115yd × 75yd)

*Chairman:* Anthony Kleanthous.

*Group Finance Director:* Andrew Adie.

*Head Coach:* Edgar Davids.

*Assistant Head Coach:* Ulrich Landvreugd.

*Head of Sports Medicine:* Stuart Ayles.

*Colours:* Black and amber striped shirts, black shorts, black and amber socks.

*Year Formed:* 1888.

*Turned Professional:* 1965.

*Previous Name:* 1906, Barnet Alston FC; 1919, Barnet.

*Club Nickname:* 'The Bees'.

*Grounds:* 1888, Queen's Road; 1901, Totteridge Lane; 1907, Barnet Lane; 2013, The Hive.

*First Football League Game:* 17 August 1991, Division 4, v Crewe Alex (h) L 4–7 – Phillips; Blackford, Cooper (Murphy), Horton, Bodley (Stein), Johnson, Showler, Carter (2), Bull (2), Lowe, Evans.

*Record League Victory:* 7–0 v Blackpool, Division 3, 11 November 2000 – Naisbitt; Stockley, Sawyers, Niven (Brown), Heald, Arber (1), Currie (3), Doolan, Richards (2) (McGleish), Cottee (1) (Riza), Toms.

## HONOURS

**Football League – Division 2:** Best season: 24th, 1993–94.

**FA Amateur Cup:** *Winners* 1946.

**FA Trophy:** *Runners-up* 1972.

**GM Vauxhall Conference:** *Winners* 1990–91.

**Conference:** *Winners* 2004–05.

**FA Cup:** 4th rd, 2007, 2008.

**League Cup:** Best season: 3rd rd, 2006.

## sky SPORTS FACT FILE

The BBC experimented by televising a number of live games in the 1946–47 season. The first of these was Barnet's Athenian League fixture with Wealdstone played at Underhill on 19 October 1946. The game attracted a bumper gate of 5,000 with the Bees winning 3-2.

**Record Cup Victory:** 6–1 v Newport Co, FA Cup 1st rd, 21 November 1970 – McClelland; Lye, Jenkins, Ward, Embery, King, Powell (1), Ferry, Adams (1), Gray, George (3), (1 og).

**Record Defeat:** 1–9 v Peterborough U, Division 3, 5 September 1998.

**Most League Points (3 for a win):** 79, Division 3, 1992–93.

**Most League Goals:** 81, Division 4, 1991–92.

**Highest League Scorer in Season:** Dougie Freedman, 24, Division 3, 1994–95.

**Most League Goals in Total Aggregate:** Sean Devine, 47, 1995–99.

**Most League Goals in One Match:** 4, Dougie Freedman v Rochdale, Division 3, 13 September 1994; 4, Lee Hodges v Rochdale, Division 3, 8 April 1996.

**Most Capped Player:** Ken Charlery, 4, St Lucia.

**Most League Appearances:** Lee Harrison, 270, 1996–2002, 2006–09.

**Youngest League Player:** Kieran Adams, 17 years 71 days v Mansfield T, 31 December 1994.

**Record Transfer Fee Received:** £800,000 from Crystal Palace for Dougie Freedman, September 1995.

**Record Transfer Fee Paid:** £130,000 to Peterborough U for Greg Heald, August 1997.

**Football League Record:** 1991 Promoted to Division 4 from GMVC; 1991–92 Division 4; 1992–93 Division 3; 1993–94 Division 2; 1994–2001 Division 3; 2001–05 Conference; 2005–13 FL 2; 2013– Conference.

## MANAGERS

Lester Finch
George Wheeler
Dexter Adams
Tommy Coleman
Gerry Ward
Gordon Ferry
Brian Kelly
Bill Meadows 1976–79
Barry Fry 1979–85
Roger Thompson 1985
Don McAllister 1985–86
Barry Fry 1986–93
Edwin Stein 1993
Gary Phillips (*Player-Manager*) 1993–94
Ray Clemence 1994–96
Alan Mullery (*Director of Football*) 1996–97
Terry Bullivant 1997
John Still 1997–2000
Tony Cottee 2000–01
John Still 2001–02
Peter Shreeves 2002–03
Martin Allen 2003–04
Paul Fairclough 2004–08
Ian Hendon 2008–10
Mark Stimson 2010–11
Martin Allen 2011
Lawrie Sanchez 2011–12
Mark Robson 2012
Edgar Davids December 2012–

## LATEST SEQUENCES

**Longest Sequence of League Wins:** 6, 28.8.1993 – 25.9.1999.

**Longest Sequence of League Defeats:** 11, 8.5.1993 – 2.10.1993.

**Longest Sequence of League Draws:** 4, 22.1.1994 – 12.2.1994.

**Longest Sequence of Unbeaten League Matches:** 12, 5.12.1992 – 2.3.1993.

**Longest Sequence Without a League Win:** 14, 24.4.1993 – 10.10.1993.

**Successive Scoring Runs:** 12 from 19.3.1995.

**Successive Non-scoring Runs:** 5 from 12.2.2000.

## TEN YEAR LEAGUE RECORD

|         |        | P  | W  | D  | L  | F  | A  | Pts | Pos |
|---------|--------|----|----|----|----|----|----|-----|-----|
| 2003-04 | Conf   | 42 | 19 | 14 | 9  | 60 | 48 | 71  | 4   |
| 2004-05 | Conf   | 42 | 26 | 8  | 8  | 90 | 44 | 86  | 1   |
| 2005-06 | FL 2   | 46 | 12 | 18 | 16 | 44 | 57 | 54  | 18  |
| 2006-07 | FL 2   | 46 | 16 | 11 | 19 | 55 | 70 | 59  | 14  |
| 2007-08 | FL 2   | 46 | 16 | 12 | 18 | 56 | 63 | 60  | 12  |
| 2008-09 | FL 2   | 46 | 11 | 15 | 20 | 56 | 74 | 48  | 17  |
| 2009-10 | FL 2   | 46 | 12 | 12 | 22 | 47 | 63 | 48  | 21  |
| 2010-11 | FL 2   | 46 | 12 | 12 | 22 | 58 | 77 | 48  | 22  |
| 2011-12 | FL 2   | 46 | 12 | 10 | 24 | 52 | 79 | 46  | 22  |
| 2012-13 | FL 2   | 46 | 13 | 12 | 21 | 47 | 59 | 51  | 23  |

## DID YOU KNOW ?

Outside left Lester Finch was one of Barnet's greatest-ever players. He won 16 amateur caps for England, represented Great Britain at the 1936 Olympic Games and lined up for the full England team in the wartime international with Wales at Cardiff on 7 June 1941.

## BARNET – FOOTBALL LEAGUE TWO 2012–13 LEAGUE RECORD

| Match No. | Date | Venue | Opponents | Result | H/T Score | Lg Pos. | Goalscorers | Attendance |
|---|---|---|---|---|---|---|---|---|
| 1 | Aug 18 | A | Port Vale | L | 0-3 | 0-2 | 22 | | 4608 |
| 2 | 21 | H | Bristol R | D | 1-1 | 1-0 | 23 | Holmes [9] | 1794 |
| 3 | 25 | H | York C | L | 1-3 | 1-3 | 24 | Nurse [30] | 1889 |
| 4 | Sept 1 | A | Rochdale | L | 0-2 | 0-2 | 24 | | 2021 |
| 5 | 8 | H | Gillingham | L | 1-3 | 1-3 | 24 | Saville [23] | 2835 |
| 6 | 15 | A | Bradford C | L | 0-3 | 0-0 | 24 | | 9566 |
| 7 | 18 | A | Aldershot T | L | 0-1 | 0-0 | 24 | | 1760 |
| 8 | 22 | H | Rotherham U | D | 0-0 | 0-0 | 24 | | 1821 |
| 9 | 29 | A | Fleetwood T | L | 1-2 | 1-1 | 24 | Hyde [5] | 3615 |
| 10 | Oct 2 | H | Exeter C | L | 1-2 | 0-1 | 24 | Hyde [81] | 1483 |
| 11 | 6 | A | Southend U | D | 2-2 | 0-0 | 24 | Holmes [54], Hyde [65] | 5025 |
| 12 | 13 | H | Plymouth Arg | L | 1-4 | 1-2 | 24 | Stephens [16] | 3229 |
| 13 | 19 | H | Northampton T | W | 4-0 | 0-0 | 24 | Pearce [56], Yiadom [65], Edgar [90], Oster [90] | 2721 |
| 14 | 23 | A | Wycombe W | D | 0-0 | 0-0 | 24 | | 3244 |
| 15 | 27 | A | Chesterfield | W | 1-0 | 0-0 | 24 | Byrne (pen) [90] | 5611 |
| 16 | Nov 6 | H | Torquay U | W | 1-0 | 0-0 | 23 | Kamdjo [79] | 1544 |
| 17 | 10 | A | Morecambe | L | 1-4 | 0-2 | 23 | Nurse [90] | 1653 |
| 18 | 16 | H | Accrington S | D | 1-1 | 0-0 | 22 | Byrne (pen) [71] | 2238 |
| 19 | 20 | H | Oxford U | D | 2-2 | 1-1 | 24 | Hyde 2 [5, 70] | 1626 |
| 20 | 24 | A | Cheltenham T | L | 0-1 | 0-0 | 24 | | 2591 |
| 21 | Dec 8 | H | AFC Wimbledon | D | 1-1 | 0-0 | 24 | Hyde [64] | 3217 |
| 22 | 15 | A | Dagenham & R | L | 0-1 | 0-1 | 24 | | 2020 |
| 23 | 21 | H | Burton Alb | W | 3-2 | 1-1 | 22 | Holmes 3 (1 pen) [42, 53 (p), 66] | 1751 |
| 24 | 26 | A | Gillingham | W | 1-0 | 1-0 | 21 | Hyde [19] | 7448 |
| 25 | 29 | A | Exeter C | D | 2-2 | 0-2 | 21 | Nurse [76], Iro [90] | 4085 |
| 26 | Jan 1 | H | Aldershot T | L | 0-1 | 0-0 | 22 | | 2772 |
| 27 | 5 | H | Bradford C | W | 2-0 | 1-0 | 20 | Atieno [41], Oster [48] | 2317 |
| 28 | 12 | A | Rotherham U | W | 2-0 | 1-0 | 20 | Hyde [21], Yiadom [82] | 7434 |
| 29 | 26 | A | Burton Alb | L | 0-1 | 0-1 | 20 | | 2050 |
| 30 | Feb 1 | A | Bristol R | L | 1-2 | 0-0 | 21 | Crawford [90] | 8527 |
| 31 | 9 | H | Port Vale | D | 0-0 | 0-0 | 22 | | 2398 |
| 32 | 16 | A | York C | W | 2-1 | 1-1 | 20 | Yiadom [25], Hyde [73] | 3594 |
| 33 | 23 | H | Rochdale | D | 0-0 | 0-0 | 22 | | 1870 |
| 34 | 26 | H | Southend U | W | 2-0 | 1-0 | 21 | Hyde [33], Davids [84] | 2211 |
| 35 | Mar 2 | A | Plymouth Arg | L | 1-2 | 1-1 | 21 | Hyde [21] | 8210 |
| 36 | 9 | H | Morecambe | W | 4-1 | 0-1 | 18 | Gambin [52], Lopez 3 (1 pen) [65, 70 (p), 87] | 2012 |
| 37 | 12 | A | Oxford U | L | 0-1 | 0-0 | 20 | | 5027 |
| 38 | 16 | H | Accrington S | L | 2-3 | 1-3 | 22 | Johnson [45], Jenkins [63] | 1559 |
| 39 | 19 | H | Fleetwood T | W | 2-0 | 1-0 | 21 | Byrne [23], Gambin [60] | 1731 |
| 40 | 23 | H | Cheltenham T | D | 0-0 | 0-0 | 20 | | 2400 |
| 41 | 29 | H | Dagenham & R | D | 0-0 | 0-0 | 21 | | 3680 |
| 42 | Apr 1 | A | AFC Wimbledon | W | 1-0 | 0-0 | 18 | Marsh-Brown [85] | 4696 |
| 43 | 6 | H | Chesterfield | L | 0-2 | 0-0 | 19 | | 2574 |
| 44 | 16 | A | Torquay U | L | 2-3 | 0-1 | 23 | Hyde 2 [58, 77] | 2722 |
| 45 | 20 | H | Wycombe W | W | 1-0 | 0-0 | 22 | Hyde [81] | 6001 |
| 46 | 27 | A | Northampton T | L | 0-2 | 0-0 | 23 | | 7471 |

**Final League Position: 23**

### GOALSCORERS

*League (47):* Hyde 14, Holmes 5 (1 pen), Byrne 3 (2 pens), Lopez 3 (1 pen), Nurse 3, Yiadom 3, Gambin 2, Oster 2, Atieno 1, Crawford 1, Davids 1, Edgar 1, Iro 1, Jenkins 1, Johnson 1, Kamdjo 1, Marsh-Brown 1, Pearce 1, Saville 1, Stephens 1.
*FA Cup (0).*
*Capital One Cup (1):* Nurse 1.
*Johnstone's Paint Trophy (0).*

| O'Brien L 3 | Warren F 1+1 | Fortune J 4+2 | Kamdjo C 21+5 | N'Gala B 5+1 | Brown J 21 | Edgar A 7+4 | Lopez D 5 | Abdulla A 4+2 | Lee O 6+5 | Yiadom A 31+8 | Nurse J 18+8 | Holmes R 25 | Vilhete M 4+1 | Weston C 19+10 | Byrne M 36+4 | Saville J 4+2 | Fuller B 39 | Hyde J 31+9 | Sykes G —+3 | Jenkins R 3+2 | Lowe J 3+5 | Stack G 42 | Stephens D 42 | Oster J 23+5 | Pearce K 17 | Gambin L 5+5 | Cowler S 1+1 | Kamara I —+1 | Flanagan T 8+1 | John C 1 | Davids E 28 | Johnson E 25+1 | Vose D —+2 | Barker G 1 | Holwijn M —+1 | De Silva K 1+2 | Iro A 9 | Atieno T 1+3 | Thompson A —+1 | Sekajja I 3+1 | Crawford H 3+7 | Allen I —+2 | NToko C 2 | Marsh-Brown K 3+2 | Beattie C 1+4 | Match No. |
|---|---|---|---|---|---|---|---|---|---|---|---|---|---|---|---|---|---|---|---|---|---|---|---|---|---|---|---|---|---|---|---|---|---|---|---|---|---|---|---|---|---|---|---|---|---|---|
| 1 | 2 | $3^3$ | 4 | $5^3$ | 6 | $7^1$ | 8 | | 9 | 10 | $11^2$ | 12 | | 13 | 14 | | | | | | | | | | | | | | | | | | | | | | | | | | | | | | | 1 |
| 1 | | 4 | | 3 | 8 | | 13 | | $7^2$ | 10 | $11^1$ | 9 | | $6^3$ | 5 | | 2 | 12 | 14 | | | | | | | | | | | | | | | | | | | | | | | | | | | 2 |
| 1 | | 4 | | 3 | $8^1$ | | 13 | | 7 | $10^2$ | 11 | $9^3$ | | 6 | 5 | | 2 | 12 | | 14 | | | | | | | | | | | | | | | | | | | | | | | | | | 3 |
| 13 | 4 | | 3 | 14 | 12 | $6^1$ | | $9^2$ | | 8 | 10 | $7^3$ | | 5 | 2 | 11 | | | | | | 1 | | | | | | | | | | | | | | | | | | | | | | | | 4 |
| | | 11 | 5 | | | | | | $6^3$ | 10 | 9 | 8 | | $7^1$ | $4^2$ | 2 | 13 | | | 14 | 1 | 3 | 12 | | | | | | | | | | | | | | | | | | | | | | | 5 |
| | | 8 | 5 | 13 | | | | | | 11 | 10 | 9 | | 2 | | | | $6^2$ | 1 | 3 | $7^1$ | 4 | 12 | | | | | | | | | | | | | | | | | | | | | | | 6 |
| | | 7 | 5 | | 12 | | | | | $11^2$ | 9 | 8 | | $2^1$ | 14 | 13 | $10^3$ | | 1 | 3 | 6 | 4 | | | | | | | | | | | | | | | | | | | | | | | | 7 |
| | 13 | 7 | 5 | | $8^1$ | $6^2$ | | | | 10 | 12 | | | 2 | 11 | | | 1 | 3 | 9 | 4 | | | | | | | | | | | | | | | | | | | | | | | | | 8 |
| | | 7 | $5^2$ | | $6^1$ | $8^3$ | | | | 10 | | | 13 | 2 | 11 | | | $1^1$ | 3 | 9 | 4 | 12 | 14 | | | | | | | | | | | | | | | | | | | | | | | 9 |
| | | 6 | 5 | | $8^2$ | $7^1$ | 12 | | | 11 | | | 13 | 2 | 9 | | 14 | | 4 | $10^3$ | 3 | 1 | | | | | | | | | | | | | | | | | | | | | | | | 10 |
| | | 7 | 5 | | | | 6 | 13 | $10^1$ | | 8 | | | 2 | $11^2$ | | 9 | 1 | 3 | 12 | 4 | | | | | | | | | | | | | | | | | | | | | | | | | 11 |
| | | 7 | 5 | 13 | | | $9^2$ | | $6^3$ | | 8 | | | 2 | 10 | 14 | | 1 | 3 | 12 | 4 | | | $11^1$ | | | | | | | | | | | | | | | | | | | | | | 12 |
| | | 7 | 5 | 9 | | | 6 | | | | | | | 2 | 11 | | | 1 | 4 | 10 | 3 | | | 8 | | | | | | | | | | | | | | | | | | | | | | 13 |
| | | 8 | 5 | $9^1$ | | | 6 | | | | | | | 12 | | | | 2 | 11 | 1 | 3 | 7 | 4 | 10 | | | | | | | | | | | | | | | | | | | | | | 14 |
| | | 8 | 5 | $12^2$ | | | 13 | 10 | 14 | | | | | 6 | | | 2 | $11^3$ | 1 | 3 | $7^1$ | 4 | 9 | | | | | | | | | | | | | | | | | | | | | | | 15 |
| | | 8 | | | $9^1$ | | 12 | 10 | | | | | | 6 | | | | 2 | 11 | 1 | 3 | 4 | | 7 | 5 | | | | | | | | | | | | | | | | | | | | | 16 |
| | | 6 | | $8^1$ | | | | 10 | 12 | | | | | 7 | | | 2 | 11 | 13 | 1 | 4 | 3 | | 9 | $5^2$ | | | | | | | | | | | | | | | | | | | | | 17 |
| | 13 | $6^2$ | 5 | | | | | 14 | 8 | $10^3$ | 12 | 7 | | 2 | 11 | | | 1 | $4^1$ | 3 | | | | $9^*$ | | | | | | | | | | | | | | | | | | | | | | 18 |
| | | 7 | 5 | | | 12 | | 6 | 10 | $9^1$ | | 8 | | 2 | 11 | | | 1 | 3 | 4 | | | | 9 | | | | | | | | | | | | | | | | | | | | | | 19 |
| | | 8 | 5 | | | | 6 | 12 | 10 | | | $7^1$ | | 2 | 11 | | | 1 | 4 | 3 | | | | 9 | | | | | | | | | | | | | | | | | | | | | | 20 |
| | | 14 | | | | | $6^3$ | 12 | | 9 | | 7 | | 2 | 11 | | | 1 | 3 | 4 | | | | $8^1$ | 5 | $10^2$ | 13 | | | | | | | | | | | | | | | | | | | 21 |
| | | 7 | | | | | | 6 | 11 | 9 | 12 | | | $2^1$ | 10 | | | 1 | 3 | 4 | | | | 8 | 5 | | | | | | | | | | | | | | | | | | | | | 22 |
| | | $7^1$ | | | | | | 8 | 14 | $10^3$ | 13 | 6 | | 2 | 11 | | | 1 | 4 | 12 | | | | $9^2$ | 5 | | 3 | | | | | | | | | | | | | | | | | | | 23 |
| | | | | | | | | 8 | | $10^1$ | 12 | 6 | | 2 | 11 | | | 1 | 4 | 7 | | | | 9 | 5 | | 3 | | | | | | | | | | | | | | | | | | | 24 |
| | | | | | | | | $6^1$ | 13 | 10 | 12 | $8^3$ | | 2 | 11 | | | 1 | 4 | 7 | | | | $9^2$ | 5 | | 3 | 14 | | | | | | | | | | | | | | | | | 25 |
| | | | 5 | | | | | 9 | $10^*$ | 6 | 8 | 12 | | 2 | 11 | | | 1 | 3 | $7^1$ | | | | $4^2$ | 13 | | | | | | | | | | | | | | | | | | | | | 26 |
| | | | | | | | | 6 | | $10^1$ | 7 | 9 | | 2 | 13 | | | 1 | 4 | 8 | | | | | 5 | | 3 | $11^{12}$ | 12 | | | | | | | | | | | | | | | | | 27 |
| | | 12 | | | | | | 13 | | 9 | 7 | 6 | | 2 | $10^3$ | | | 1 | 3 | | | | | $8^2$ | 5 | | $4^1$ | 14 | 11 | | | | | | | | | | | | | | | | | 28 |
| | | 13 | | | | | | $6^2$ | | 9 | $10^1$ | 7 | | 2 | | | | 1 | 3 | 8 | | | | | 5 | | 4 | | 11 | 12 | | | | | | | | | | | | | | | | 29 |
| | | 13 | | | | | | 2 | 10 | $9^1$ | 6 | | | 1 | 4 | $7^2$ | | | | | | | | 8 | 3 | | 5 | | $11^3$ | 12 | 14 | | | | | | | | | | | | | | | 30 |
| | | | | | | | | 9 | $10^1$ | | 13 | 7 | | 2 | $11^3$ | | | 1 | 4 | 6 | | | | $8^2$ | 3 | | 5 | | 12 | 14 | | | | | | | | | | | | | | | | 31 |
| | 14 | | $5^1$ | | | | | 6 | 10 | | | 7 | | 2 | 13 | | | 1 | 3 | 8 | | | | 9 | 12 | | | | | | | | | | | | | | | | | | $4^3$ | $11^2$ | | 32 |
| | 4 | 13 | | | | 11 | | $9^3$ | | 14 | $7^2$ | 6 | | 2 | $10^1$ | | | 1 | 3 | | | | | 8 | 5 | | | | | | | | | | | | | | | | | | | 12 | | 33 |
| | 3 | 7 | | | | 11 | | 12 | | $6^1$ | 13 | 9 | | 2 | $10^2$ | | | 1 | 4 | | | | | 8 | 5 | | | | | | | | | | | | | | | | | | | | | 34 |
| | 3 | $6^2$ | | | | 10 | | $9^3$ | | 13 | 7 | | | 2 | $11^1$ | | | 1 | 4 | | | 12 | | 8 | 5 | | | | | | | | | | | | 14 | | | | | | | | | 35 |
| | 4 | | | | | $10^2$ | | 12 | $11^1$ | 7 | | | | 2 | 13 | 6 | | 1 | 3 | | | 9 | | 8 | 5 | | | | | | | | | | | | | | | | | | | | | 36 |
| | 3 | | | | | $11^2$ | 12 | $6^1$ | | 8 | | | | 2 | 13 | 9 | | 1 | 4 | | | 10 | | 7 | 5 | | | | | | | | | | | | | | | | | | | | | 37 |
| | | | | | | | | $11^2$ | | 9 | 2 | 10 | | 8 | | | 1 | 4 | $6^3$ | | 12 | | 14 | $7^*$ | 5 | | | | | | | | | | | | | | | | | | $3^1$ | 13 | | 38 |
| | | 5 | | | | | | $9^1$ | | 6 | 8 | 2 | | | | | 1 | 3 | 7 | | 11 | | 4 | | | 12 | | | | | | | 10 | | | | | | | | | | | | | 39 |
| | | | | | | | | 9 | | 8 | 6 | 2 | | 13 | | | 1 | $4^1$ | $7^3$ | | $11^1$ | | 3 | | 5 | | | 12 | | 12 | | | $10^2$ | | | | | | | | | | | | | 40 |
| | | | | | | | 13 | 10 | | 6 | 7 | 2 | | $11^3$ | | | 1 | 4 | $8^1$ | | | | 3 | $9^2$ | 5 | | $12^*$ | | | | | | | | | | | | | | | | | | | 41 |
| | | | | | | | 2 | $10^1$ | | 6 | 7 | $11^2$ | 14 | | | | 1 | 3 | $8^3$ | | 4 | | 9 | 5 | | | | | | | | 13 | 12 | | | | | | | | | | | | | 42 |
| | | | | | | | 2 | $10^2$ | | 6 | $8^3$ | $11^1$ | | | | | 1 | 4 | 7 | | 3 | | 9 | 5 | | | | | | | | 14 | 13 | 12 | | | | | | | | | | | | 43 |
| | | | | | | | 2 | 14 | | 7 | 8 | 12 | | | | | 1 | 3 | $9^1$ | | 13 | | 4 | $10^2$ | 5 | | | | | | | 11 | $6^4$ | | | | | | | | | | | | | 44 |
| | | | | | | | 2 | | | 6 | 8 | 10 | | $11^1$ | | | 1 | 4 | 14 | | 10 | | 3 | $7^3$ | 5 | $11^1$ | | | | | | 13 | $9^2$ | | | | | | | | | | | | | 45 |
| | | | | | | | 2 | 12 | | 7 | $9^2$ | $11^3$ | | | | | 1 | 3 | | | 10 | | 4 | 8 | 5 | 14 | | | | | | 13 | $6^1$ | | | | | | | | | | | | | 46 |

**FA Cup**
First Round     Oxford U     (h)   0-2

**Capital One Cup**
First Round     Birmingham C     (a)   1-5

**Johnstone's Paint Trophy**
Second Round     Leyton Orient     (a)   0-1

# BARNSLEY

## FOUNDATION

Many clubs owe their inception to the Church and Barnsley are among them, for they were formed in 1887 by the Rev. T. T. Preedy, curate of Barnsley St Peter's, and went under that name until it was dropped in 1897 a year before being admitted to the Second Division of the Football League.

*Oakwell Stadium, Grove Street, Barnsley, South Yorkshire S71 1ET.*

*Telephone:* (01226) 211 211.

*Fax:* (01226) 211 444.

*Ticket Office:* (0871) 22 66 777.

*Website:* www.barnsleyfc.co.uk

*Email:* thereds@barnsleyfc.co.uk

*Ground Capacity:* 23,287.

*Record Attendance:* 40,255 v Stoke C, FA Cup 5th rd, 15 February 1936.

*Pitch Measurements:* 100m × 68m (110yd × 75yd)

*Owner:* Patrick Cryne.

*Director:* Barry Taylor.

*General Manager:* Albert Donald Rowing.

*Manager:* David Flitcroft.

*First Team Coach:* Martin Scott.

*Head Physio:* Craig Sedgwick.

*Colours:* Red shirts with white trim, white shorts, red socks.

*Year Formed:* 1887.

*Turned Professional:* 1888.

*Previous Name:* 1887, Barnsley St Peter's; 1897, Barnsley.

*Club Nickname:* 'The Tykes', 'The Reds', 'The Colliers'.

*Ground:* 1887, Oakwell.

### HONOURS

**Football League – Division 1:**
*Runners-up* 1996–97;
**Division 3 (N):** *Champions* 1933–34, 1938–39, 1954–55; *Runners-up* 1953–54;
**Division 3:** *Runners-up* 1980–81;
**Division 4:** *Runners-up* 1967–68.
**FA Cup:** *Winners* 1912;
*Runners-up* 1910.
**Football League Cup:** Best season: 5th rd, 1982.

*First Football League Game:* 1 September 1898, Division 2, v Lincoln C (a) L 0–1 – Fawcett; McArtney, Nixon; King, Burleigh, Porteous; Davis, Lees, Murray, McCullough, McGee.

*Record League Victory:* 9–0 v Loughborough T, Division 2, 28 January 1899 – Greaves; McArtney, Nixon; Porteous, Burleigh, Howard; Davis (4), Hepworth (1), Lees (1), McCullough (1), Jones (2). 9–0 v Accrington S, Division 3 (N), 3 February 1934 – Ellis; Cookson, Shotton; Harper, Henderson, Whitworth; Spence (2), Smith (1), Blight (4), Andrews (1), Ashton (1).

*Record Cup Victory:* 6–0 v Blackpool, FA Cup 1st rd replay, 20 January 1910 – Mearns; Downs, Ness; Glendinning, Boyle (1), Utley; Bartrop, Gadsby (1), Lillycrop (2), Tufnell (2), Forman. 6–0 v Peterborough U, League Cup 1st rd 2nd leg, 15 September 1981 – Horn; Joyce, Chambers, Glavin (2), Banks, McCarthy, Evans, Parker (2), Aylott (1), McHale, Barrowclough (1).

*Record Defeat:* 0–9 v Notts Co, Division 2, 19 November 1927.

## sky SPORTS FACT FILE

When Barnsley reached the FA Cup final in 1910 the team was accompanied by a live mascot: a donkey named Amos ridden by a diminutive jockey. On that occasion Barnsley lost out to Newcastle United in a replay at Goodison Park after drawing the first tie 1-1 at Crystal Palace.

*Most League Points (2 for a win):* 67, Division 3 (N), 1938–39.

*Most League Points (3 for a win):* 82, Division 1, 1999–2000.

*Most League Goals:* 118, Division 3 (N), 1933–34.

*Highest League Scorer in Season:* Cecil McCormack, 33, Division 2, 1950–51.

*Most League Goals in Total Aggregate:* Ernest Hine, 123, 1921–26 and 1934–38.

*Most League Goals in One Match:* 5, Frank Eaton v South Shields, Division 3 (N), 9 April 1927; 5, Peter Cunningham v Darlington, Division 3 (N), 4 February 1933; 5, Beau Asquith v Darlington, Division 3 (N), 12 November 1938; 5, Cecil McCormack v Luton T, Division 2, 9 September 1950.

*Most Capped Player:* Gerry Taggart, 35 (50), Northern Ireland.

*Most League Appearances:* Barry Murphy, 514, 1962–78.

*Youngest League Player:* Reuben Noble-Lazarus, 15 years 45 days v Ipswich T, 30 September 2008.

*Record Transfer Fee Received:* £4,500,000 from Blackburn R for Ashley Ward, December 1998.

*Record Transfer Fee Paid:* £1,500,000 to Partizan Belgrade for Georgi Hristov, July 1997.

*Football League Record:* 1898 Elected to Division 2; 1932–34 Division 3 (N); 1934–38 Division 2; 1938–39 Division 3 (N); 1946–53 Division 2; 1953–55 Division 3 (N); 1955–59 Division 2; 1959–65 Division 3; 1965–68 Division 4; 1968–72 Division 3; 1972–79 Division 4; 1979–81 Division 3; 1981–92 Division 2; 1992–97 Division 1; 1997–98 FA Premier League; 1998–2002 Division 1; 2002–04 Division 2; 2004–06 FL 1; 2006– FL C.

## LATEST SEQUENCES

*Longest Sequence of League Wins:* 10, 5.3.1955 – 23.4.1955.

*Longest Sequence of League Defeats:* 9, 14.3.1953 – 25.4.1953.

*Longest Sequence of League Draws:* 7, 28.3.1911 – 22.4.1911.

*Longest Sequence of Unbeaten League Matches:* 21, 1.1.1934 – 5.5.1934.

*Longest Sequence Without a League Win:* 26, 13.12.1952 – 26.8.1953.

*Successive Scoring Runs:* 44 from 2.10.1926.

*Successive Non-scoring Runs:* 6 from 7.10.1899.

## MANAGERS

**Arthur Fairclough** 1898–1901 (*Secretary-Manager*)
**John McCartney** 1901–04 (*Secretary-Manager*)
**Arthur Fairclough** 1904–12
**John Hastie** 1912–14
**Percy Lewis** 1914–19
**Peter Sant** 1919–26
**John Commins** 1926–29
**Arthur Fairclough** 1929–30
**Brough Fletcher** 1930–37
**Angus Seed** 1937–53
**Tim Ward** 1953–60
**Johnny Steele** 1960–71 (*continued as General Manager*)
**John McSeveney** 1971–72
**Johnny Steele** (*General Manager*) 1972–73
**Jim Iley** 1973–78
**Allan Clarke** 1978–80
**Norman Hunter** 1980–84
**Bobby Collins** 1984–85
**Allan Clarke** 1985–89
**Mel Machin** 1989–93
**Viv Anderson** 1993–94
**Danny Wilson** 1994–98
**John Hendrie** 1998–99
**Dave Bassett** 1999–2000
**Nigel Spackman** 2001
**Steve Parkin** 2001–02
**Glyn Hodges** 2002–03
**Gudjon Thordarson** 2003–04
**Paul Hart** 2004–05
**Andy Ritchie** 2005–06
**Simon Davey** 2007–10 (*caretaker from November 2006*)
**Mark Robins** 2009–11
**Keith Hill** 2011–12
**David Flitcroft** January 2013–

## TEN YEAR LEAGUE RECORD

|         |       | P  | W  | D  | L  | F  | A  | Pts | Pos |
|---------|-------|----|----|----|----|----|----|-----|-----|
| 2003-04 | Div 2 | 46 | 15 | 17 | 14 | 54 | 58 | 62  | 12  |
| 2004-05 | FL 1  | 46 | 14 | 19 | 13 | 69 | 64 | 61  | 13  |
| 2005-06 | FL 1  | 46 | 18 | 18 | 10 | 62 | 44 | 72  | 5   |
| 2006-07 | FL C  | 46 | 15 | 5  | 26 | 53 | 85 | 50  | 20  |
| 2007-08 | FL C  | 46 | 14 | 13 | 19 | 52 | 65 | 55  | 18  |
| 2008-09 | FL C  | 46 | 13 | 13 | 20 | 45 | 58 | 52  | 20  |
| 2009-10 | FL C  | 46 | 14 | 12 | 20 | 53 | 69 | 54  | 18  |
| 2010-11 | FL C  | 46 | 14 | 14 | 18 | 55 | 66 | 56  | 17  |
| 2011-12 | FL C  | 46 | 13 | 9  | 24 | 49 | 74 | 48  | 21  |
| 2012-13 | FL C  | 46 | 14 | 13 | 19 | 56 | 70 | 55  | 21  |

## DID YOU KNOW ?

Barnsley won the Division Three North title by a four-point margin from Accrington Stanley in 1954–55. They won 10 consecutive games between 5 March and 23 April. The first eight of these wins were achieved without conceding a goal.

## BARNSLEY – FL CHAMPIONSHIP 2012–13 LEAGUE RECORD

| Match No. | Date | Venue | Opponents | Result | H/T Score | Lg Pos. | Goalscorers | Attendance |
|---|---|---|---|---|---|---|---|---|
| 1 | Aug 18 | H | Middlesbrough | W 1-0 | 1-0 | 5 | Davies [45] | 12,203 |
| 2 | 21 | A | Wolverhampton W | L 1-3 | 0-1 | 16 | Cywka [79] | 24,400 |
| 3 | 25 | A | Brighton & HA | L 1-5 | 1-3 | 20 | Davies (pen) [35] | 24,594 |
| 4 | Sept 1 | H | Bristol C | W 1-0 | 0-0 | 13 | Mellis [50] | 8088 |
| 5 | 15 | H | Blackpool | D 1-1 | 1-1 | 12 | Davies [14] | 14,134 |
| 6 | 18 | A | Blackburn R | L 1-2 | 1-1 | 17 | Mellis [32] | 12,772 |
| 7 | 22 | A | Birmingham C | W 5-0 | 0-0 | 12 | Foster [50], Davies 4 [54, 60, 65, 73] | 13,893 |
| 8 | 29 | H | Ipswich T | D 1-1 | 0-1 | 12 | Dawson [73] | 8571 |
| 9 | Oct 2 | H | Peterborough U | L 0-2 | 0-2 | 16 | | 8319 |
| 10 | 6 | A | Leeds U | L 0-1 | 0-1 | 19 | | 22,569 |
| 11 | 20 | A | Charlton Ath | W 1-0 | 0-0 | 17 | Cywka [64] | 26,185 |
| 12 | 23 | H | Crystal Palace | D 1-1 | 0-1 | 17 | Perkins [86] | 8195 |
| 13 | 27 | H | Nottingham F | L 1-4 | 1-3 | 19 | Harewood [24] | 10,186 |
| 14 | Nov 3 | A | Hull C | L 0-1 | 0-1 | 20 | | 15,598 |
| 15 | 6 | A | Derby Co | L 0-2 | 0-0 | 21 | | 20,808 |
| 16 | 10 | H | Huddersfield T | L 0-1 | 0-1 | 21 | | 12,130 |
| 17 | 17 | A | Bolton W | D 1-1 | 0-1 | 20 | Davies [65] | 16,965 |
| 18 | 24 | H | Cardiff C | L 1-2 | 0-1 | 20 | Mellis [76] | 8227 |
| 19 | 27 | H | Burnley | D 1-1 | 1-1 | 20 | Tudgay [37] | 8610 |
| 20 | Dec 1 | A | Watford | L 1-4 | 0-1 | 21 | Tudgay [90] | 11,335 |
| 21 | 8 | A | Leicester C | D 2-2 | 2-1 | 22 | Dawson [27], Noble-Lazarus [39] | 23,579 |
| 22 | 15 | H | Sheffield W | L 0-1 | 0-1 | 22 | | 12,484 |
| 23 | 22 | A | Millwall | W 2-1 | 1-0 | 22 | Dawson [31], Tudgay [90] | 10,118 |
| 24 | 26 | H | Birmingham C | L 1-2 | 1-1 | 23 | Greening [38] | 9191 |
| 25 | 29 | H | Blackburn R | L 1-3 | 0-2 | 24 | Mellis [73] | 9153 |
| 26 | Jan 1 | A | Peterborough U | L 1-2 | 0-1 | 24 | Harewood [79] | 7339 |
| 27 | 12 | H | Leeds U | W 2-0 | 0-0 | 23 | Dagnall 2 (1 pen) [63 (p), 66] | 13,999 |
| 28 | 19 | A | Ipswich T | D 1-1 | 0-0 | 23 | Rose [89] | 15,913 |
| 29 | 29 | H | Millwall | W 2-0 | 0-0 | 22 | Dagnall [56], Scotland [67] | 7844 |
| 30 | Feb 2 | A | Blackpool | W 2-1 | 1-0 | 22 | O'Brien [25], Scotland [88] | 13,695 |
| 31 | 9 | A | Middlesbrough | W 3-2 | 1-0 | 22 | O'Brien [6], Golbourne [70], Scotland [76] | 15,034 |
| 32 | 19 | H | Wolverhampton W | W 2-1 | 0-1 | 20 | Dagnall [49], Mellis [73] | 10,972 |
| 33 | 23 | A | Bristol C | L 3-5 | 0-2 | 21 | Fontaine (og) [58], Cywka [82], Scotland [90] | 13,008 |
| 34 | Mar 2 | H | Bolton W | L 2-3 | 0-2 | 21 | Cywka [47], O'Grady [53] | 10,862 |
| 35 | 5 | A | Burnley | D 1-1 | 0-1 | 22 | Cywka [84] | 10,584 |
| 36 | 12 | H | Brighton & HA | W 2-1 | 1-0 | 21 | Scotland [15], Dagnall (pen) [64] | 7869 |
| 37 | 16 | H | Watford | W 1-0 | 1-0 | 20 | Hassell [35] | 9076 |
| 38 | 30 | A | Sheffield W | L 1-2 | 0-0 | 23 | Mellis [90] | 29,697 |
| 39 | Apr 1 | H | Leicester C | W 2-0 | 2-0 | 20 | Keane (og) [4], O'Grady [40] | 10,429 |
| 40 | 6 | A | Crystal Palace | D 0-0 | 0-0 | 20 | | 21,281 |
| 41 | 9 | A | Cardiff C | D 1-1 | 0-0 | 19 | Foster [90] | 22,584 |
| 42 | 13 | H | Charlton Ath | L 0-6 | 0-2 | 22 | | 9469 |
| 43 | 16 | H | Derby Co | D 1-1 | 0-0 | 23 | O'Grady [47] | 9007 |
| 44 | 20 | A | Nottingham F | D 0-0 | 0-0 | 23 | | 22,230 |
| 45 | 27 | H | Hull C | W 2-0 | 1-0 | 22 | Mellis [4], O'Grady [51] | 15,744 |
| 46 | May 4 | A | Huddersfield T | D 2-2 | 1-0 | 21 | O'Grady [14], Scotland [74] | 21,614 |

**Final League Position: 21**

### GOALSCORERS

*League (56):* Davies 8 (1 pen), Mellis 6, Scotland 6, Cywka 5, Dagnall 5 (2 pens), O'Grady 5, Dawson 4, Tudgay 3, Foster 2, Harewood 2, O'Brien 2, Golbourne 1, Greening 1, Hassell 1, Noble-Lazarus 1, Perkins 1, Rose 1, own goals 2.
*FA Cup (5):* Dagnall 3, Harewood 1, Rose 1.
*Capital One Cup (5):* Dagnall 2, Davies 1, Hassell 1, Stones 1.

| Gonzalez D 3 | Wiseman S 34+2 | Foster S 29+2 | Stones J 19+3 | Golbourne S 31 | Cywka T 20+9 | Mellis J 32+4 | Perkins D 31+4 | Done M 6+7 | Davies C 19+1 | Harewood M 17+15 | Etuhu K 17+9 | Dawson S 29+3 | Hassell B 11+6 | Dagnall C 25+11 | Cranie M 34+2 | Alnwick B 10 | Kennedy T 23+1 | Rose D —+8 | Steele L 33 | Silva T —+1 | McNulty J 10+2 | O'Brien J 21+9 | Mido —+1 | Noble-Lazarus R 5+9 | Tudgay M 8+1 | Greening J 6 | Buzsaky A 4+1 | Sinclair E 1+3 | Scotland J 6+12 | Delap R 6 | O'Grady C 13+3 | Tunnicliffe R 2 | Jones A 1+1 | Match No. |
|---|---|---|---|---|---|---|---|---|---|---|---|---|---|---|---|---|---|---|---|---|---|---|---|---|---|---|---|---|---|---|---|---|---|---|
| 1 | 2 | 3 | 4 | 5 | 6 | 7² | 8 | 9¹ | 10 | 11 | 12 | 13 |  |  |  |  |  |  |  |  |  |  |  |  |  |  |  |  |  |  |  |  |  | 1 |
| 1 | 4 | 3 |  | 5 | 9 | 8 | 7¹ |  | 11 | 10² | 6 | 12 | 2³ | 13 | 14 |  |  |  |  |  |  |  |  |  |  |  |  |  |  |  |  |  |  | 2 |
| 1 | 3 | 2 | 4² | 5 | 8 | 9 |  |  | 11 | 10 | 7 | 6 | 13 | 12 |  |  |  |  |  |  |  |  |  |  |  |  |  |  |  |  |  |  |  | 3 |
|  | 4 | 3 | 12 | 5 | 6 | 9¹ |  |  |  | 11² | 13 |  | 7 | 8 | 10 | 2 | 1 |  |  |  |  |  |  |  |  |  |  |  |  |  |  |  |  | 4 |
|  | 4 | 3 | 2 | 5 | 6 | 9³ |  | 13 | 11¹ | 12 | 14 | 7 |  | 10² | 8 | 1 |  |  |  |  |  |  |  |  |  |  |  |  |  |  |  |  |  | 5 |
|  | 3 | 4 | 2³ | 5 | 6 | 9 | 14 |  | 11¹ | 12 | 13 | 7 |  | 10² | 8 | 1 |  |  |  |  |  |  |  |  |  |  |  |  |  |  |  |  |  | 6 |
|  | 4 | 3 |  | 5 | 9 | 8 |  |  | 10¹ | 12 |  | 6 |  | 11² | 7 | 1 | 2 | 13 |  |  |  |  |  |  |  |  |  |  |  |  |  |  |  | 7 |
|  | 4 | 3 | 12 | 5 | 8 | 9 |  |  | 10 |  |  | 6 |  | 11² | 7 | 1 | 2¹ | 13 |  |  |  |  |  |  |  |  |  |  |  |  |  |  |  | 8 |
|  | 4 |  | 2 | 5 | 8 | 9³ | 13 | 14 | 11 | 12 |  | 6 |  | 7² | 10¹ | 3 | 1 |  |  |  |  |  |  |  |  |  |  |  |  |  |  |  |  | 9 |
|  | 4 | 3¹ | 2 | 5 | 9³ | 8 | 7 |  | 10 | 11² | 14 | 6 | 12 | 13 |  | 1 |  |  |  |  |  |  |  |  |  |  |  |  |  |  |  |  |  | 10 |
|  | 4 | 3 | 2 | 5 | 9² | 6¹ | 8 |  | 11³ | 14 | 12 | 7 | 13 | 10 |  | 1 |  |  |  |  |  |  |  |  |  |  |  |  |  |  |  |  |  | 11 |
|  | 4 | 3 | 2 | 5 | 9² | 6 | 8 | 12 |  | 10 | 13 | 7³ |  | 11¹ |  | 1 |  |  |  |  | 14 |  |  |  |  |  |  |  |  |  |  |  |  | 12 |
|  | 4 | 3 | 2 | 5 | 9² | 6 | 8 | 11¹ |  | 10 | 12 | 7³ |  | 14 |  | 1 | 13 |  |  |  |  |  |  |  |  |  |  |  |  |  |  |  |  | 13 |
|  | 4 | 3 | 5 | 2 | 8³ |  | 7¹ | 10² |  | 14 | 11 | 6 |  | 12 | 9 |  | 1 | 13 |  |  |  |  |  |  |  |  |  |  |  |  |  |  |  | 14 |
|  | 3 |  | 5 | 9¹ | 10³ |  | 12 |  | 14 | 6² | 7 |  | 11 | 8 |  | 2 | 1 |  | 4 | 13 |  |  |  |  |  |  |  |  |  |  |  |  |  | 15 |
|  | 3 | 4 | 2 | 5 | 10² | 9 |  | 11 | 7¹ | 8³ |  | 6 |  |  |  | 1 |  |  | 13 | 12 | 14 |  |  |  |  |  |  |  |  |  |  |  |  | 16 |
|  | 3 | 14 |  | 5 | 13 | 7³ |  | 9² | 10 |  | 8 |  |  | 2 |  | 1 |  |  | 4 | 6¹ |  | 12 | 11 |  |  |  |  |  |  |  |  |  |  | 17 |
|  | 3 |  |  | 5 |  | 6 |  | 9² | 10 |  | 8¹ |  |  | 2 |  | 1 |  |  | 4 |  | 13 | 11³ | 7 | 12 | 14 |  |  |  |  |  |  |  |  | 18 |
|  |  | 3 |  | 5 |  | 9² |  | 10¹ |  |  |  | 12 |  | 2 |  | 1 |  |  | 4 | 13 | 11 | 7³ | 8 | 10² |  |  |  |  |  |  |  |  |  | 19 |
|  |  | 3 |  | 5 |  | 6¹ |  | 9 |  | 12 |  |  |  | 2 |  | 1 |  |  | 4 | 14 | 13 | 11 | 7³ | 8 | 10² |  |  |  |  |  |  |  |  | 20 |
|  | 4 |  | 2² | 5 |  |  | 14 |  | 11 |  | 13 | 6 |  | 3 |  | 1 |  |  |  | 9 | 10³ | 12 | 8 | 7¹ |  |  |  |  |  |  |  |  |  | 21 |
|  | 3 | 2 | 5 | 9² |  | 12 |  | 10 | 14 |  | 8 |  |  | 4 |  | 1 |  |  |  | 13 | 11¹ | 7³ | 6¹ |  |  |  |  |  |  |  |  |  |  | 22 |
| 12 | 3 | 2 | 5 |  |  | 9³ | 14 |  | 13 |  |  | 6 | 7 | 11 | 4¹ |  | 1 |  |  | 8² |  | 10 |  |  |  |  |  |  |  |  |  |  |  | 23 |
|  | 2 | 5 |  |  |  | 8² | 13 | 12 |  |  | 9 | 3 | 11¹ |  |  | 1 |  |  |  | 4 | 6 |  | 10 | 7 |  |  |  |  |  |  |  |  |  | 24 |
| 2¹ | 3 | 12 | 5 |  |  | 8 | 9² | 11³ |  |  | 7 |  |  |  |  | 1 |  |  |  | 4 | 6 | 13 | 10 |  | 14 |  |  |  |  |  |  |  |  | 25 |
|  | 2 | 9 |  |  |  |  | 7 |  | 10¹ | 12 |  | 8 |  | 11 | 4 |  | 5 | 1 |  | 3 | 6² | 13 |  |  |  |  |  |  |  |  |  |  |  | 26 |
|  | 2 | 9 |  |  |  | 12² | 8 |  | 11 |  |  | 7 |  | 10³ | 3 |  | 5 | 13 | 1 |  | 4 | 6¹ | 14 |  |  |  |  |  |  |  |  |  |  | 27 |
|  | 4 | 2 | 6² |  |  | 8 | 9 | 13 | 11 | 12 | 7¹ |  | 10 | 3 |  |  | 5 | 14 | 1 |  |  |  |  |  |  |  |  |  |  |  |  |  |  | 28 |
|  | 2 | 5 | 9 |  |  | 13 | 8 |  | 10¹ | 6 |  | 11³ |  | 3 |  | 4 | 14 | 1 |  | 7² |  |  |  |  | 12 |  |  |  |  |  |  |  |  | 29 |
| 12 | 3 | 5 |  |  |  | 8 |  |  | 10³ | 9 |  | 11 |  | 2 | 4 |  |  | 7² |  |  |  | 14 | 6¹ | 13 |  |  |  |  |  |  |  |  |  | 30 |
|  | 2 | 8 |  |  |  |  | 6 |  | 11¹ | 7 |  | 14 | 10³ | 3 | 4 |  | 5² |  |  |  |  | 13 | 9 | 12 |  |  |  |  |  |  |  |  |  | 31 |
| 2 | 3 |  |  |  |  | 13 | 8 |  | 9¹ |  |  | 10 | 4 |  | 5 |  | 14 | 6 |  |  |  | 12 | 7 | 11³ |  |  |  |  |  |  |  |  |  | 32 |
|  | 4¹ |  |  | 14 |  | 7 |  |  | 11³ |  |  | 10 | 2 | 9 |  | 3 | 8² |  |  |  |  | 13 | 5 | 12 | 6 |  |  |  |  |  |  |  |  | 33 |
| 2 |  |  |  | 9 | 13 | 8 |  |  | 12 | 7 |  | 10 | 3 |  | 5 |  | 6² |  |  |  | 14 |  |  | 11¹ | 4³ |  |  |  |  |  |  |  |  | 34 |
| 2 | 3 |  |  | 12 | 8 | 7 |  |  | 11¹ | 6³ |  | 9² | 4 |  | 5 |  | 14 |  |  |  | 13 |  |  | 10 |  |  |  |  |  |  |  |  |  | 35 |
| 3 |  |  |  | 13 | 9 | 8 |  |  | 7 |  | 14 | 12 | 4 |  | 5 |  | 6² |  |  |  | 10¹ | 2³ | 11 |  |  |  |  |  |  |  |  |  | 36 |
| 4 |  |  |  | 14 | 9³ | 8 |  |  | 6 |  | 12 | 13 | 3 |  | 5 |  | 7 |  |  |  | 10¹ | 2² | 11 |  |  |  |  |  |  |  |  |  | 37 |
| 3 |  |  |  | 9 | 7 |  | 11 | 8³ |  | 2 | 10² | 4 |  | 5 | 14 | 1 | 6¹ |  | 12 |  |  | 13 |  |  |  |  |  |  |  |  |  |  |  | 38 |
| 2 | 13 |  |  | 6³ | 9 |  | 7 | 8 | 3 | 12 | 4² |  | 5 |  | 1 | 14 |  |  |  |  | 11¹ |  | 10 |  |  |  |  |  |  |  |  |  |  | 39 |
| 3 | 4 |  | 14 | 7³ | 6 |  | 8¹ | 9 | 2 | 13 |  |  | 5 |  | 1 | 12 |  |  |  |  | 11² |  | 10 |  |  |  |  |  |  |  |  |  |  | 40 |
| 2 | 4 |  | 12 | 6³ | 9 |  | 10² | 7 | 3 | 14 |  |  | 5 |  | 1 | 8¹ |  |  |  |  | 13 | 11 |  |  |  |  |  |  |  |  |  |  | 41 |
| 2 | 3 |  | 6¹ | 9³ | 8 |  | 13 |  | 7⁴ | 4 | 11 |  | 5⁸ |  | 1 | 14 |  |  |  |  | 12 | 10² |  |  |  |  |  |  |  |  |  |  | 42 |
| 2 |  |  | 6³ | 8 | 7 |  | 14 |  | 4¹ | 13 | 3 |  | 1 | 5 | 9 |  |  |  |  |  | 11² | 10 | 12 |  |  |  |  |  |  |  |  |  | 43 |
| 5 |  |  | 13 | 8 | 7 |  | 14 |  | 12 | 4 | 3 |  | 1 | 6³ | 10² |  |  |  |  |  | 9¹ | 11 | 2 |  |  |  |  |  |  |  |  |  | 44 |
| 3 |  |  | 6¹ | 8 |  |  | 5 |  | 11² | 2 | 4 | 14 | 1 | 13 | 7 | 9 |  |  |  |  | 12 | 10³ |  |  |  |  |  |  |  |  |  |  | 45 |
| 2 |  |  | 14 | 8¹ | 6 |  | 7 | 9³ |  | 11² | 3 | 4 | 1 |  | 5 | 12 |  |  |  |  | 13 | 10 |  |  |  |  |  |  |  |  |  |  | 46 |

**FA Cup**

| | | | |
|---|---|---|---|
| Third Round | Burnley | (h) | 1-0 |
| Fourth Round | Hull C | (a) | 1-0 |
| Fifth Round | Milton Keynes D | (a) | 3-0 |
| Sixth Round | Manchester C | (a) | 0-5 |

**Capital One Cup**

| | | | |
|---|---|---|---|
| First Round | Rochdale | (a) | 4-3 |
| Second Round | Swansea C | (a) | 1-3 |

# BIRMINGHAM CITY

## FOUNDATION

In 1875, cricketing enthusiasts who were largely members of Trinity Church, Bordesley, determined to continue their sporting relationships throughout the year by forming a football club which they called Small Heath Alliance. For their earliest games played on waste land in Arthur Street, the team included three Edden brothers and two James brothers.

*St Andrews Stadium, Birmingham B9 4RL.*
*Telephone:* (0844) 557 1875.
*Fax:* (0844) 557 1975.
*Ticket Office:* (0844) 557 1875 (then option 2).
*Website:* www.bcfc.com
*Email:* reception@bcfc.com
*Ground Capacity:* 29,409.
*Record Attendance:* 66,844 v Everton, FA Cup 5th rd, 11 February 1939.
*Pitch Measurements:* 105m × 68m (115yd × 75yd)
*President:* Carson Yeung.
*Vice-chairman:* Peter Pannu.
*Manager:* Lee Clark.
*Assistant Manager:* Terry McDermott.
*Head of Sports Science:* Nick Davies.
*Colours:* Blue shirts with black trim, white shorts, blue socks.
*Year Formed:* 1875.
*Turned Professional:* 1885.

## HONOURS

**Football League – FL C:**
*Runners-up* 2006–07, 2008–09;
**Division 2:** *Champions* 1892–93, 1920–21, 1947–48, 1954–55, 1994–95; *Runners-up* 1893–94, 1900–01, 1902–03, 1971–72, 1984–85;
**Division 3:** *Runners-up* 1991–92.
**FA Cup:** *Runners-up* 1931, 1956.
**Football League Cup:** *Winners* 1963, 2011; *Runners-up* 2001.
**Leyland DAF Cup:** *Winners* 1991.
**Auto Windscreens Shield:** *Winners* 1995.
**European Competitions**
**European Fairs Cup:** 1955–58, 1958–60 (*runners-up*), 1960–61 (*runners-up*), 1961–62.
**Europa League:** 2011–12.

*Previous Names:* 1875, Small Heath Alliance; 1888, dropped 'Alliance'; 1905, Birmingham; 1945, Birmingham City.
*Club Nickname:* 'Blues'.
*Grounds:* 1875, waste ground near Arthur St; 1877, Muntz St, Small Heath; 1906, St Andrews.
*First Football League Game:* 3 September 1892, Division 2, v Burslem Port Vale (h) W 5–1 – Charsley; Bayley, Speller; Ollis, Jenkyns, Devey; Hallam (1), Edwards (1), Short (1), Wheldon (2), Hands.
*Record League Victory:* 12–0 v Walsall T Swifts, Division 2, 17 December 1892 – Charsley; Bayley, Jones; Ollis, Jenkyns, Devey; Hallam (2), Walton (3), Mobley (3), Wheldon (2), Hands (2). 12–0 v Doncaster R, Division 2, 11 April 1903 – Dorrington; Goldie, Wassell; Beer, Dougherty (1), Howard; Athersmith, Leonard (4), McRoberts (1), Wilcox (4), Field (1), (1 og).
*Record Cup Victory:* 9–2 v Burton W, FA Cup 1st rd, 31 October 1885 – Hedges; Jones, Evetts (1); Fred James, Felton, Arthur James (1); Davenport (2), Stanley (4), Simms, Figures, Morris (1).

## sky SPORTS FACT FILE

Birmingham City were the first English club side to appear in a major European competition. On 16 May 1956 they drew 0-0 with Internazionale in Milan in an Inter Cities Fairs Cup match. The Blues reached the semi-final stage before going down 2-1 to Barcelona in a replay.

**Record Defeat:** 1–9 v Sheffield W, Division 1, 13 December 1930. 1–9 v Blackburn R, Division 1, 5 January 1895.

**Most League Points (2 for a win):** 59, Division 2, 1947–48.

**Most League Points (3 for a win):** 89, Division 2, 1994–95.

**Most League Goals:** 103, Division 2, 1893–94 (only 28 games).

**Highest League Scorer in Season:** Joe Bradford, 29, Division 1, 1927–28.

**Most League Goals in Total Aggregate:** Joe Bradford, 249, 1920–35.

**Most League Goals in One Match:** 5, Walter Abbott v Darwen, Division 2, 26 November, 1898; 5, John McMillan v Blackpool, Division 2, 2 March 1901; 5, James Windridge v Glossop, Division 2, 23 January 1915.

**Most Capped Player:** Maik Taylor, 50 (88), Northern Ireland.

**Most League Appearances:** Frank Womack, 491, 1908–28.

**Youngest League Player:** Trevor Francis, 16 years 7 months v Cardiff C, 5 September 1970.

**Record Transfer Fee Received:** £6,800,000 from Liverpool for Jermaine Pennant, July 2006.

**Record Transfer Fee Paid:** £8,500,000 to Santos Laguna for Christian Benitez, July 2009.

**Football League Record:** 1892 Elected to Division 2; 1894–96 Division 1; 1896–1901 Division 2; 1901–02 Division 1; 1902–03 Division 2; 1903–08 Division 1; 1908–21 Division 2; 1921–39 Division 1; 1946–48 Division 2; 1948–50 Division 1; 1950–55 Division 2; 1955–65 Division 1; 1965–72 Division 2; 1972–79 Division 1; 1979–80 Division 2; 1980–84 Division 1; 1984–85 Division 2; 1985–86 Division 1; 1986–89 Division 2; 1989–92 Division 3; 1992–94 Division 1; 1994–95 Division 2; 1995–2002 Division 1; 2002–06 FA Premier League; 2006–07 FL C; 2007–08 FA Premier League; 2008–09 FL C; 2009–11 FA Premier League; 2011– FL C.

## LATEST SEQUENCES

**Longest Sequence of League Wins:** 13, 17.12.1892 – 16.9.1893.

**Longest Sequence of League Defeats:** 8, 28.9.1985 – 23.11.1985.

**Longest Sequence of League Draws:** 8, 18.9.1990 – 23.10.1990.

**Longest Sequence of Unbeaten League Matches:** 20, 3.9.1994 – 2.1.1995.

**Longest Sequence Without a League Win:** 17, 28.9.1985 – 18.1.1986.

**Successive Scoring Runs:** 24 from 24.9.1892.

**Successive Non-scoring Runs:** 6 from 1.10.1949.

## MANAGERS

**Alfred Jones** 1892–1908
  (*Secretary-Manager*)
**Alec Watson** 1908–10
**Bob McRoberts** 1910–15
**Frank Richards** 1915–23
**Billy Beer** 1923–27
**William Harvey** 1927–28
**Leslie Knighton** 1928–33
**George Liddell** 1933–39
**William Camkin and Ted Goodier**
  were in charge during 1939–45
**Harry Storer** 1945–48
**Bob Brocklebank** 1949–54
**Arthur Turner** 1954–58
**Pat Beasley** 1959–60
**Gil Merrick** 1960–64
**Joe Mallett** 1964–65
**Stan Cullis** 1965–70
**Fred Goodwin** 1970–75
**Willie Bell** 1975–77
**Sir Alf Ramsay** 1977–78
**Jim Smith** 1978–82
**Ron Saunders** 1982–86
**John Bond** 1986–87
**Garry Pendrey** 1987–89
**Dave Mackay** 1989–91
**Lou Macari** 1991
**Terry Cooper** 1991–93
**Barry Fry** 1993–96
**Trevor Francis** 1996–2001
**Steve Bruce** 2001–07
**Alex McLeish** 2007–11
**Chris Hughton** 2011–12
**Lee Clark** June 2012–

## TEN YEAR LEAGUE RECORD

|         |        | P  | W  | D  | L  | F  | A  | Pts | Pos |
|---------|--------|----|----|----|----|----|----|-----|-----|
| 2003-04 | PR Lge | 38 | 12 | 14 | 12 | 43 | 48 | 50  | 10  |
| 2004-05 | PR Lge | 38 | 11 | 12 | 15 | 40 | 46 | 45  | 12  |
| 2005-06 | PR Lge | 38 | 8  | 10 | 20 | 28 | 50 | 34  | 18  |
| 2006-07 | FL C   | 46 | 26 | 8  | 12 | 67 | 42 | 86  | 2   |
| 2007-08 | PR Lge | 38 | 8  | 11 | 19 | 46 | 62 | 35  | 19  |
| 2008-09 | FL C   | 46 | 23 | 14 | 9  | 54 | 37 | 83  | 2   |
| 2009-10 | PR Lge | 38 | 13 | 11 | 14 | 38 | 47 | 50  | 9   |
| 2010-11 | PR Lge | 38 | 8  | 15 | 15 | 37 | 58 | 39  | 18  |
| 2011-12 | FL C   | 46 | 20 | 16 | 10 | 78 | 51 | 76  | 4   |
| 2012-13 | FL C   | 46 | 15 | 16 | 15 | 63 | 69 | 61  | 12  |

## DID YOU KNOW ?

Full back Jeff Hall was a regular for Birmingham City from the 1953–54 season and won 17 caps for England. After falling ill towards the end of March 1959 he was diagnosed with polio and never recovered, passing away on 4 April 1959 at the age of 27.

## BIRMINGHAM CITY – FL CHAMPIONSHIP 2012–13 LEAGUE RECORD

| Match No. | Date | Venue | Opponents | Result | H/T Score | Lg Pos. | Goalscorers | Attendance |
|---|---|---|---|---|---|---|---|---|
| 1 | Aug 18 | H | Charlton Ath | D | 1-1 | 0-0 | 12 | Zigic [90] | 18,210 |
| 2 | 21 | A | Sheffield W | L | 2-3 | 0-2 | 19 | Zigic [78], King (pen) [90] | 25,379 |
| 3 | 25 | A | Watford | L | 0-2 | 0-2 | 22 | | 11,022 |
| 4 | Sept 1 | H | Peterborough U | W | 1-0 | 1-0 | 21 | Elliott [29] | 14,929 |
| 5 | 15 | A | Nottingham F | D | 2-2 | 0-0 | 21 | Mullins [69], King [71] | 22,738 |
| 6 | 18 | H | Bolton W | W | 2-1 | 1-1 | 11 | Lita [16], King (pen) [48] | 14,693 |
| 7 | 22 | H | Barnsley | L | 0-5 | 0-0 | 19 | | 13,893 |
| 8 | 29 | A | Brighton & HA | W | 1-0 | 1-0 | 13 | Burke [27] | 26,121 |
| 9 | Oct 2 | A | Cardiff C | L | 1-2 | 0-1 | 18 | Lita [54] | 20,278 |
| 10 | 6 | H | Huddersfield T | L | 0-1 | 0-1 | 21 | | 18,437 |
| 11 | 20 | H | Leicester C | D | 1-1 | 1-0 | 20 | Lovenkrands [45] | 18,271 |
| 12 | 23 | A | Millwall | D | 3-3 | 1-3 | 20 | King 3 [45, 49, 63] | 9258 |
| 13 | 27 | A | Leeds U | W | 1-0 | 0-0 | 17 | Lita [76] | 22,152 |
| 14 | Nov 3 | H | Ipswich T | L | 0-1 | 0-1 | 18 | | 18,063 |
| 15 | 6 | H | Bristol C | W | 2-0 | 0-0 | 18 | Burke [59], King [73] | 14,380 |
| 16 | 10 | A | Blackburn R | D | 1-1 | 1-1 | 18 | King [17] | 14,919 |
| 17 | 17 | H | Hull C | L | 2-3 | 1-3 | 19 | Morrison [38], King [46] | 17,363 |
| 18 | 24 | A | Derby Co | L | 2-3 | 0-1 | 19 | King (pen) [73], Lovenkrands [82] | 21,505 |
| 19 | 27 | A | Blackpool | D | 1-1 | 0-1 | 19 | Davies [48] | 13,111 |
| 20 | 30 | H | Middlesbrough | W | 3-2 | 1-1 | 18 | King 2 (1 pen) [45 (p), 81], Elliott [66] | 15,322 |
| 21 | Dec 8 | A | Wolverhampton W | L | 0-1 | 0-1 | 19 | | 21,339 |
| 22 | 15 | H | Crystal Palace | D | 2-2 | 0-1 | 19 | Zigic [66], Diop [82] | 17,158 |
| 23 | 22 | H | Burnley | D | 2-2 | 1-0 | 19 | Davies [30], Zigic [89] | 17,284 |
| 24 | 26 | A | Barnsley | W | 2-1 | 1-1 | 19 | Davies 2 [35, 77] | 9191 |
| 25 | 29 | A | Bolton W | L | 1-3 | 1-2 | 20 | Zigic [11] | 17,068 |
| 26 | Jan 1 | H | Cardiff C | L | 0-1 | 0-1 | 20 | | 17,493 |
| 27 | 12 | A | Huddersfield T | D | 1-1 | 1-0 | 20 | Reilly [45] | 14,214 |
| 28 | 19 | H | Brighton & HA | D | 2-2 | 1-2 | 20 | Caldwell [18], Zigic [90] | 15,299 |
| 29 | 26 | A | Burnley | W | 2-1 | 1-0 | 17 | Davies [21], King [90] | 11,576 |
| 30 | Feb 2 | H | Nottingham F | W | 2-1 | 1-0 | 16 | Burke 2 [45, 80] | 17,738 |
| 31 | 9 | A | Charlton Ath | D | 1-1 | 0-0 | 16 | Elliott [90] | 17,269 |
| 32 | 16 | H | Watford | L | 0-4 | 0-2 | 17 | | 18,933 |
| 33 | 19 | H | Sheffield W | D | 0-0 | 0-0 | 17 | | 15,738 |
| 34 | 23 | A | Peterborough U | W | 2-0 | 1-0 | 16 | Zigic [34], Burke [80] | 8350 |
| 35 | Mar 2 | A | Hull C | L | 2-5 | 0-3 | 17 | Lovenkrands [83], Burke [87] | 17,146 |
| 36 | 5 | H | Blackpool | D | 1-1 | 1-0 | 18 | Davies [45] | 13,532 |
| 37 | 9 | H | Derby Co | W | 3-1 | 0-1 | 14 | Thomas 2 [68, 90], Redmond [75] | 15,850 |
| 38 | 16 | A | Middlesbrough | W | 1-0 | 0-0 | 11 | Zigic [81] | 14,348 |
| 39 | 29 | A | Crystal Palace | W | 4-0 | 2-0 | 10 | Redmond [24], Delaney (og) [32], Morrison [64], Ferguson [69] | 17,189 |
| 40 | Apr 1 | H | Wolverhampton W | L | 2-3 | 0-3 | 11 | Elliott 2 (1 pen) [55 (p), 90] | 19,630 |
| 41 | 6 | H | Millwall | D | 1-1 | 0-0 | 13 | Thomas [49] | 15,302 |
| 42 | 12 | A | Leicester C | D | 2-2 | 0-1 | 13 | Zigic [61], Burke (pen) [90] | 25,554 |
| 43 | 16 | A | Bristol C | W | 1-0 | 1-0 | 12 | Elliott [16] | 12,093 |
| 44 | 20 | H | Leeds U | W | 1-0 | 0-0 | 11 | Mullins [72] | 17,666 |
| 45 | 27 | A | Ipswich T | L | 1-3 | 0-2 | 11 | Burke [90] | 21,921 |
| 46 | May 4 | H | Blackburn R | D | 1-1 | 1-0 | 12 | Morrison [42] | 18,979 |

**Final League Position: 12**

### GOALSCORERS
*League (63):* King 13 (4 pens), Zigic 9, Burke 8 (1 pen), Davies 6, Elliott 6 (1 pen), Lita 3, Lovenkrands 3, Morrison 3, Thomas 3, Mullins 2, Redmond 2, Caldwell 1, Diop 1, Ferguson 1, Reilly 1, own goal 1.
*FA Cup (2):* Elliott 2.
*Capital One Cup (7):* Lovenkrands 2, Ambrose 1, Caldwell 1, Elliott 1, King 1 (1 pen), Spector 1.

| Butland J 46 | Packwood W 5 | Caldwell S 33+1 | Davies C 40+1 | Murphy D 13 | Burke C 29+12 | Mullins H 22+6 | Ambrose D 3+3 | Morrison R 23+4 | King M 23+4 | Lovenkrands P 13+9 | Spector J 25+4 | Redmond N 22+16 | Zigic N 23+12 | Elliott W 38+6 | Gordon B 1 | Gomis M 9+6 | Caddis P 27 | Ibanez P 6 | Lita L 9+1 | Fahey K 5+4 | Robinson P 34+1 | Hurst J 2+1 | Hancox M 14+5 | Hall R 11+2 | Diop P 1+1 | Reilly C 14+4 | Jervis J —+2 | Thomas W 5+6 | Ferguson S 10+1 | Arthur K —+2 | Match No. |
|---|---|---|---|---|---|---|---|---|---|---|---|---|---|---|---|---|---|---|---|---|---|---|---|---|---|---|---|---|---|---|---|
| 1 | 2² | 3 | 4 | 5 | 6 | 7 | 8 | 9¹ | 10 | 11³ | 12 | 13 | 14 |  |  |  |  |  |  |  |  |  |  |  |  |  |  |  |  |  | 1 |
| 1 |  | 3 | 4 |  | 6 | 7 | 8 | 10 |  | 11 | 9 | 2 | 12 | 5¹ |  |  |  |  |  |  |  |  |  |  |  |  |  |  |  |  | 2 |
| 1 |  | 3 | 4 |  | 6 | 8 | 7¹ | 14 | 11 | 13 | 2 | 9 | 10² | 5³ | 12 |  |  |  |  |  |  |  |  |  |  |  |  |  |  |  | 3 |
| 1 |  | 3 |  | 5 | 6 | 8 |  | 10 | 11² | 7 | 12 |  | 9¹ | 13 | 2 | 4 |  |  |  |  |  |  |  |  |  |  |  |  |  |  | 4 |
| 1 |  | 3 |  | 5 | 6² | 7 |  | 10 | 9¹ | 8 | 13 | 12 |  | 2 | 4 | 11³ | 14 |  |  |  |  |  |  |  |  |  |  |  |  |  | 5 |
| 1 |  | 3 | 13 | 5 | 6³ | 7¹ |  | 11 | 8 | 14 | 9 | 2² | 4 | 10 | 12 |  |  |  |  |  |  |  |  |  |  |  |  |  |  |  | 6 |
| 1 |  | 3 |  | 5¹ | 6 | 7² | 12 | 10 | 2 | 13 | 14 | 8 | 4 | 11³ | 9 |  |  |  |  |  |  |  |  |  |  |  |  |  |  |  | 7 |
| 1 | 7² | 3 | 4 | 6 | 13 |  |  | 14 | 10¹ | 2 | 12 | 8 |  | 11³ | 9 | 5 |  |  |  |  |  |  |  |  |  |  |  |  |  |  | 8 |
| 1 | 9¹ | 2 | 3 | 6 |  |  |  | 13 | 10³ | 4 | 14 | 7 |  | 11² | 8 | 5 | 12 |  |  |  |  |  |  |  |  |  |  |  |  |  | 9 |
| 1 |  | 3 | 4³ | 6 | 13 |  |  | 7 | 9 | 12⁸ | 10 |  | 11 | 8¹ | 5 | 2² | 14 |  |  |  |  |  |  |  |  |  |  |  |  |  | 10 |
| 1 |  | 3 | 4 | 5 | 6¹ | 8 | 10 | 11² | 7⁸ | 9 | 12 | 13 | 14 | 2³ |  |  |  |  |  |  |  |  |  |  |  |  |  |  |  |  | 11 |
| 1 |  | 3 | 4 | 5 | 12 | 8 | 7 | 11 |  | 9¹ | 6 | 10 |  | 2 |  |  |  |  |  |  |  |  |  |  |  |  |  |  |  |  | 12 |
| 1 |  | 4 | 3 | 5 | 12 | 8 | 7 | 11² | 13 | 6¹ | 9 | 10 |  | 2 |  |  |  |  |  |  |  |  |  |  |  |  |  |  |  |  | 13 |
| 1 |  | 3 | 4 | 5 | 12 | 8 | 7 | 10 | 14 | 6¹ | 13 | 9³ | 11² | 2 |  |  |  |  |  |  |  |  |  |  |  |  |  |  |  |  | 14 |
| 1 |  | 4 | 3¹ | 5 | 6 | 7 | 8 | 11² | 13 | 12 | 10 | 9 |  | 2 |  |  |  |  |  |  |  |  |  |  |  |  |  |  |  |  | 15 |
| 1 |  | 3 | 5 | 6² | 8 | 13 | 7 | 11 | 2 | 12 | 10¹ | 9 |  | 4 |  |  |  |  |  |  |  |  |  |  |  |  |  |  |  |  | 16 |
| 1 |  | 3 | 5² | 6 | 8 | 7 | 10 | 2 | 12 | 11 | 9¹ | 4 |  | 13 |  |  |  |  |  |  |  |  |  |  |  |  |  |  |  |  | 17 |
| 1 |  | 3 | 4 | 6¹ | 7 | 8 | 11 | 13 | 2 | 10 | 9² | 5 | 12 |  |  |  |  |  |  |  |  |  |  |  |  |  |  |  |  |  | 18 |
| 1 |  | 3 | 12 | 8² | 7 | 11³ | 6¹ | 9 | 14 | 10 | 2 | 4 | 5 | 13 |  |  |  |  |  |  |  |  |  |  |  |  |  |  |  |  | 19 |
| 1 | 4 | 13 | 7 | 6¹ | 10 | 14 | 8 | 11³ | 12 | 2 | 3 | 5 | 9² |  |  |  |  |  |  |  |  |  |  |  |  |  |  |  |  |  | 20 |
| 1 | 4 | 3 | 14 | 8 | 12 | 11 | 13 | 7¹ | 10² | 6 | 2 | 5 | 9³ |  |  |  |  |  |  |  |  |  |  |  |  |  |  |  |  |  | 21 |
| 1 |  | 3 | 4 | 6³ | 10 | 11 | 14 | 9¹ | 2² | 5 | 13 | 12 | 8 | 7 |  |  |  |  |  |  |  |  |  |  |  |  |  |  |  |  | 22 |
| 1 | 2 | 3 | 4 | 12 | 7 | 9¹ |  | 10 | 11 | 13 | 5 | 6² | 8 |  |  |  |  |  |  |  |  |  |  |  |  |  |  |  |  |  | 23 |
| 1 |  | 3 | 4 | 12 | 7 | 11¹ | 10 | 9 | 13 | 2 | 5 | 6² | 8 |  |  |  |  |  |  |  |  |  |  |  |  |  |  |  |  |  | 24 |
| 1 |  | 3 | 4 | 11² | 7 | 8¹ | 13 | 10⁸ | 12 | 5 | 2 | 9 | 6³ | 14 |  |  |  |  |  |  |  |  |  |  |  |  |  |  |  |  | 25 |
| 1 | 2³ | 3 | 4 | 11 | 8 | 10 | 9² | 12 | 5 | 14 | 7 | 6¹ | 13 |  |  |  |  |  |  |  |  |  |  |  |  |  |  |  |  |  | 26 |
| 1 |  | 3 | 4 | 6 | 10³ | 13 | 12 | 9² | 14 | 7 | 8 | 2 | 5 | 11¹ |  |  |  |  |  |  |  |  |  |  |  |  |  |  |  |  | 27 |
| 1 |  | 3 | 4 | 6 | 14 | 13 | 10² | 12 | 9¹ | 8 | 2 | 5 | 11 | 7³ |  |  |  |  |  |  |  |  |  |  |  |  |  |  |  |  | 28 |
| 1 |  | 3 | 4 | 6 | 10 | 12 | 13 | 11 | 7 | 2 | 5 | 9¹ | 8² |  |  |  |  |  |  |  |  |  |  |  |  |  |  |  |  |  | 29 |
| 1 |  | 3 | 4 | 6 | 10 | 12 | 14 | 7 | 8² | 2 | 5 | 9¹ | 13 | 11³ |  |  |  |  |  |  |  |  |  |  |  |  |  |  |  |  | 30 |
| 1 |  | 3 | 4 | 6 | 11 | 13 | 14 | 7 | 9¹ | 2 | 5 | 10² | 8³ | 12 |  |  |  |  |  |  |  |  |  |  |  |  |  |  |  |  | 31 |
| 1 |  | 3 | 4 | 6 | 10 | 12 | 8 | 7 | 2 | 5² | 13 | 9¹ | 11 |  |  |  |  |  |  |  |  |  |  |  |  |  |  |  |  |  | 32 |
| 1 |  | 3 | 4 | 6 | 10¹ | 12 | 7 | 11 | 9 | 2 | 5 | 8 |  |  |  |  |  |  |  |  |  |  |  |  |  |  |  |  |  |  | 33 |
| 1 | 4 | 3 | 6 | 14 | 10² | 8 | 11³ | 9 | 12 | 2 | 5 | 7¹ | 13 |  |  |  |  |  |  |  |  |  |  |  |  |  |  |  |  |  | 34 |
| 1 | 3¹ | 4 | 6 | 10 | 7 | 14 | 11 | 9 | 2 | 12 | 5³ | 8² | 13 |  |  |  |  |  |  |  |  |  |  |  |  |  |  |  |  |  | 35 |
| 1 |  | 3 | 6 | 10² | 7 | 11 | 12 | 2 | 4 | 5¹ | 8 | 13 | 9 |  |  |  |  |  |  |  |  |  |  |  |  |  |  |  |  |  | 36 |
| 1 |  | 4 | 6¹ | 14 | 10² | 7 | 12 | 11 | 9 | 2 | 3 | 8³ | 13 | 5 |  |  |  |  |  |  |  |  |  |  |  |  |  |  |  |  | 37 |
| 1 | 13 | 3 | 14 | 6 | 8¹ | 9 | 10 | 7 | 2 | 12 | 4 | 11³ | 5² |  |  |  |  |  |  |  |  |  |  |  |  |  |  |  |  |  | 38 |
| 1 | 4 | 12 | 14 | 10² | 6 | 11 | 7 | 2 | 8¹ | 3 | 9 | 13 | 5³ |  |  |  |  |  |  |  |  |  |  |  |  |  |  |  |  |  | 39 |
| 1 | 4 | 8 | 13 | 6² | 10 | 7 | 2 | 3 | 9¹ | 11 | 5 | 12 |  |  |  |  |  |  |  |  |  |  |  |  |  |  |  |  |  |  | 40 |
| 1 | 3 | 8 | 14 | 7¹ | 6 | 10³ | 9² | 2 | 4 | 5 | 12 | 11 | 13 |  |  |  |  |  |  |  |  |  |  |  |  |  |  |  |  |  | 41 |
| 1 | 2 | 13 | 7 | 10 | 11 | 9¹ | 8 | 4 | 5 | 3 | 12 | 6² |  |  |  |  |  |  |  |  |  |  |  |  |  |  |  |  |  |  | 42 |
| 1 | 3 | 13 | 12 | 8 | 9 | 11³ | 7 | 6¹ | 2 | 4 | 5 | 14 | 10² |  |  |  |  |  |  |  |  |  |  |  |  |  |  |  |  |  | 43 |
| 1 | 3 | 12 | 10 | 7 | 6 | 11 | 8 | 2 | 4 | 5 | 9¹ |  |  |  |  |  |  |  |  |  |  |  |  |  |  |  |  |  |  |  | 44 |
| 1 | 3 | 12 | 7¹ | 8 | 6 | 11 | 9² | 13 | 2 | 4 | 5 | 10 |  |  |  |  |  |  |  |  |  |  |  |  |  |  |  |  |  |  |  | 45 |
| 1 | 3 | 6 | 9 | 11 | 10 | 7 | 8¹ | 2 | 4 | 12 | 5 |  |  |  |  |  |  |  |  |  |  |  |  |  |  |  |  |  |  |  |  | 46 |

| **FA Cup** | | | | |
|---|---|---|---|---|
| Third Round | Leeds U | (a) | 1-1 | |
| *Replay* | Leeds U | (h) | 1-2 | |

| **Capital One Cup** | | | | |
|---|---|---|---|---|
| First Round | Barnet | (h) | 5-1 | |
| Second Round | Coventry C | (a) | 2-3 | |

# BLACKBURN ROVERS

## FOUNDATION

It was in 1875 that some public school old boys called a meeting at which the Blackburn Rovers club was formed and the colours blue and white adopted. The leading light was John Lewis, later to become a founder of the Lancashire FA, a famous referee who was in charge of two FA Cup finals, and a vice-president of both the FA and the Football League.

*Ewood Park, Blackburn, Lancashire BB2 4JF.*

*Telephone:* (0871) 702 1875.

*Fax:* (01254) 671 042.

*Ticket Office:* (0871) 222 1444.

*Website:* www.rovers.co.uk

*Email:* (via website)

*Ground Capacity:* 31,154.

*Record Attendance:* 62,522 v Bolton W, FA Cup 6th rd, 2 March 1929.

*Pitch Measurements:* 105m × 69m (115yd × 76yd)

*Managing Director:* Derek Shaw.

*Directors:* Robert Coar, Gandhi Babu.

*Manager:* Gary Bowyer.

*Assistant Manager:* Terry McPhillips.

*Head of Sports Medicine:* Dave Fevre.

*Colours:* Blue and white halved shirts, white shorts, blue socks with blue hoops.

*Year Formed:* 1875.

*Turned Professional:* 1880.

*Club Nickname:* 'Rovers'.

### HONOURS

**FA Premier League:**
*Champions* 1994–95;
*Runners-up* 1993–94.

**Football League: Division 1:**
*Champions* 1911–12, 1913–14;
*Runners-up* 2000–01;
**Division 2:** *Champions* 1938–39;
*Runners-up* 1957–58;
**Division 3:** *Champions* 1974–75;
*Runners-up* 1979–80.

**FA Cup:** *Winners* 1884, 1885, 1886, 1890, 1891, 1928; *Runners-up* 1882, 1960.

**Football League Cup:** *Winners* 2002.

**Full Members' Cup:** *Winners* 1987.

**European Competitions**
**European Cup:** 1995–96.
**UEFA Cup:** 1994–95, 1998–99, 2002–03, 2003–04, 2006–07, 2007–08.
**Intertoto Cup:** 2007.

*Grounds:* 1875, all matches played away; 1876, Oozehead Ground; 1877, Pleasington Cricket Ground; 1878, Alexandra Meadows; 1881, Leamington Road; 1890, Ewood Park.

*First Football League Game:* 15 September 1888, Football League, v Accrington (h) D 5–5 – Arthur; Beverley, James Southworth; Douglas, Almond, Forrest; Beresford (1), Walton, John Southworth (1), Fecitt (1), Townley (2).

*Record League Victory:* 9–0 v Middlesbrough, Division 2, 6 November 1954 – Elvy; Suart, Eckersley; Clayton, Kelly, Bell; Mooney (3), Crossan (2), Briggs, Quigley (3), Langton (1).

*Record Cup Victory:* 11–0 v Rossendale, FA Cup 1st rd, 13 October 1884 – Arthur; Hopwood, McIntyre; Forrest, Blenkhorn, Lofthouse; Sowerbutts (2), Jimmy Brown (1), Fecitt (4), Barton (3), Birtwistle (1).

## sky SPORTS FACT FILE

Alan Shearer has scored the highest number of Premier League hat-tricks. He managed a total of 11 during his career including nine for Blackburn Rovers. His best season was 1995–96 when he scored five trebles, four of which came at Ewood Park and one at White Hart Lane.

*Record Defeat:* 0–8 v Arsenal, Division 1, 25 February 1933.

*Most League Points (2 for a win):* 60, Division 3, 1974–75.

*Most League Points (3 for a win):* 91, Division 1, 2000–01.

*Most League Goals:* 114, Division 2, 1954–55.

*Highest League Scorer in Season:* Ted Harper, 43, Division 1, 1925–26.

*Most League Goals in Total Aggregate:* Simon Garner, 168, 1978–92.

*Most League Goals in One Match:* 7, Tommy Briggs v Bristol R, Division 2, 5 February 1955.

*Most Capped Player:* Morten Gamst Pederson, 70 (74), Norway.

*Most League Appearances:* Derek Fazackerley, 596, 1970–86.

*Youngest League Player:* Harry Dennison, 16 years 155 days v Bristol C, 8 April 1911.

*Record Transfer Fee Received:* £18,000,000 from Manchester C for Roque Santa Cruz, June 2009.

*Record Transfer Fee Paid:* £8,000,000 to Huddersfield T for Jordan Rhodes, August 2012.

*Football League Record:* 1888 Founder Member of the League; 1936–39 Division 2; 1946–48 Division 1; 1948–58 Division 2; 1958–66 Division 1; 1966–71 Division 2; 1971–75 Division 3; 1975–79 Division 2; 1979–80 Division 3; 1980–92 Division 2; 1992–99 FA Premier League; 1999–2001 Division 1; 2001–12 FA Premier League; 2012– FL C.

## LATEST SEQUENCES

*Longest Sequence of League Wins:* 8, 1.3.1980 – 7.4.1980.

*Longest Sequence of League Defeats:* 7, 12.3.1966 – 16.4.1966.

*Longest Sequence of League Draws:* 5, 11.10.1975 – 1.11.1975.

*Longest Sequence of Unbeaten League Matches:* 23, 30.9.1987 – 27.3.1988.

*Longest Sequence Without a League Win:* 16, 11.11.1978 – 24.3.1979.

*Successive Scoring Runs:* 32 from 24.4.1954.

*Successive Non-scoring Runs:* 4 from 12.12.1908.

## MANAGERS

**Thomas Mitchell** 1884–96
  (*Secretary-Manager*)
**J. Walmsley** 1896–1903
  ((*Secretary-Manager*)
**R. B. Middleton** 1903–25
**Jack Carr** 1922–26
  (*Team Manager under*
  *Middleton to 1925*)
**Bob Crompton** 1926–31
  (*Hon. Team Manager*)
**Arthur Barritt** 1931–36
  (*had been Secretary from 1927*)
**Reg Taylor** 1936–38
**Bob Crompton** 1938–41
**Eddie Hapgood** 1944–47
**Will Scott** 1947
**Jack Bruton** 1947–49
**Jackie Bestall** 1949–53
**Johnny Carey** 1953–58
**Dally Duncan** 1958–60
**Jack Marshall** 1960–67
**Eddie Quigley** 1967–70
**Johnny Carey** 1970–71
**Ken Furphy** 1971–73
**Gordon Lee** 1974–75
**Jim Smith** 1975–78
**Jim Iley** 1978
**John Pickering** 1978–79
**Howard Kendall** 1979–81
**Bobby Saxton** 1981–86
**Don Mackay** 1987–91
**Kenny Dalglish** 1991–95
**Ray Harford** 1995–96
**Roy Hodgson** 1997–98
**Brian Kidd** 1998–99
**Graeme Souness** 2000–04
**Mark Hughes** 2004–08
**Paul Ince** 2008
**Sam Allardyce** 2008–10
**Steve Kean** 2010–12
**Henning Berg** 2012
**Michael Appleton** 2013
**Gary Bowyer** March 2013–

## TEN YEAR LEAGUE RECORD

|  |  | P | W | D | L | F | A | Pts | Pos |
|---|---|---|---|---|---|---|---|---|---|
| 2003-04 | PR Lge | 38 | 12 | 8 | 18 | 51 | 59 | 44 | 15 |
| 2004-05 | PR Lge | 38 | 9 | 15 | 14 | 32 | 43 | 42 | 15 |
| 2005-06 | PR Lge | 38 | 19 | 6 | 13 | 51 | 42 | 63 | 6 |
| 2006-07 | PR Lge | 38 | 15 | 7 | 16 | 52 | 54 | 52 | 10 |
| 2007-08 | PR Lge | 38 | 15 | 13 | 10 | 50 | 48 | 58 | 7 |
| 2008-09 | PR Lge | 38 | 10 | 11 | 17 | 40 | 60 | 41 | 15 |
| 2009-10 | PR Lge | 38 | 13 | 11 | 14 | 41 | 55 | 50 | 10 |
| 2010-11 | PR Lge | 38 | 11 | 10 | 17 | 46 | 59 | 43 | 15 |
| 2011-12 | PR Lge | 38 | 8 | 7 | 23 | 48 | 78 | 31 | 19 |
| 2012-13 | FL C | 46 | 14 | 16 | 16 | 55 | 62 | 58 | 17 |

## DID YOU KNOW ?

Blackburn Rovers used just 18 players in the 1954–55 season, six of whom played two or fewer games. In the first 19 games Rovers fielded the same line-up on 17 occasions, while four players (Ronnie Clayton, Eric Bell, Frank Mooney and Bobby Langton) were ever-present during the campaign.

## BLACKBURN ROVERS – FL CHAMPIONSHIP 2012–13 LEAGUE RECORD

| Match No. | Date | Venue | Opponents | Result | H/T Score | Lg Pos. | Goalscorers | Attendance |
|---|---|---|---|---|---|---|---|---|
| 1 | Aug 18 | A | Ipswich T | D 1-1 | 1-0 | 13 | Kazim-Richards [21] | 19,117 |
| 2 | 22 | H | Hull C | W 1-0 | 0-0 | 4 | Kazim-Richards [77] | 13,562 |
| 3 | 25 | H | Leicester C | W 2-1 | 1-0 | 3 | Nuno Gomes [33], Pedersen [79] | 13,935 |
| 4 | Sept 1 | A | Leeds U | D 3-3 | 2-1 | 2 | Olsson, Marcus [19], Nuno Gomes [27], Rochina [84] | 24,411 |
| 5 | 15 | A | Bristol C | W 5-3 | 1-1 | 1 | Rhodes 2 [28, 90], Nuno Gomes [55], Rochina [82], Dann [90] | 14,657 |
| 6 | 18 | A | Barnsley | W 2-1 | 1-1 | 1 | Rhodes [45], Nuno Gomes [85] | 12,772 |
| 7 | 21 | H | Middlesbrough | L 1-2 | 0-1 | 1 | Hanley, G [89] | 13,405 |
| 8 | 29 | A | Charlton Ath | D 1-1 | 1-1 | 4 | Etuhu [16] | 17,169 |
| 9 | Oct 3 | A | Nottingham F | D 0-0 | 0-0 | 5 | | 18,748 |
| 10 | 6 | H | Wolverhampton W | L 0-1 | 0-0 | 9 | | 17,034 |
| 11 | 20 | A | Derby Co | D 1-1 | 1-0 | 10 | Rhodes [34] | 22,958 |
| 12 | 24 | H | Sheffield W | W 1-0 | 1-0 | 5 | Hanley, G [5] | 13,782 |
| 13 | 27 | H | Watford | W 1-0 | 0-0 | 5 | Rhodes [90] | 13,233 |
| 14 | Nov 3 | A | Crystal Palace | L 0-2 | 0-1 | 6 | | 16,744 |
| 15 | 6 | H | Huddersfield T | D 2-2 | 1-1 | 6 | Rhodes [43], Murphy (pen) [55] | 14,597 |
| 16 | 10 | H | Birmingham C | D 1-1 | 1-1 | 7 | Rochina (pen) [13] | 14,919 |
| 17 | 17 | A | Peterborough U | W 4-1 | 3-0 | 6 | Formica [3], Rhodes 3 [20, 39, 79] | 5997 |
| 18 | 24 | H | Millwall | L 0-2 | 0-0 | 9 | | 13,898 |
| 19 | 28 | H | Bolton W | L 1-2 | 0-1 | 10 | Rhodes [82] | 18,010 |
| 20 | Dec 2 | A | Burnley | D 1-1 | 0-0 | 9 | Rhodes [68] | 21,341 |
| 21 | 7 | H | Cardiff C | L 1-4 | 0-1 | 10 | King [51] | 12,460 |
| 22 | 15 | A | Blackpool | L 0-2 | 0-1 | 15 | | 15,907 |
| 23 | 26 | A | Middlesbrough | L 0-1 | 0-0 | 17 | | 22,882 |
| 24 | 29 | A | Barnsley | W 3-1 | 2-0 | 15 | King [29], Rochina [44], Rhodes [90] | 9153 |
| 25 | Jan 1 | H | Nottingham F | W 3-0 | 0-0 | 13 | Rochina [48], Rhodes [75], Kazim-Richards [78] | 15,490 |
| 26 | 11 | A | Wolverhampton W | D 1-1 | 1-0 | 12 | Rhodes (pen) [26] | 20,264 |
| 27 | 19 | H | Charlton Ath | L 1-2 | 0-1 | 14 | Rhodes [48] | 13,647 |
| 28 | 22 | H | Brighton & HA | D 1-1 | 1-0 | 14 | Rhodes (pen) [45] | 12,230 |
| 29 | Feb 2 | H | Bristol C | W 2-0 | 1-0 | 13 | Rhodes 2 [28, 65] | 13,539 |
| 30 | 9 | H | Ipswich T | W 1-0 | 0-0 | 8 | Rhodes [61] | 14,342 |
| 31 | 12 | A | Brighton & HA | D 1-1 | 1-0 | 8 | Dann [24] | 24,759 |
| 32 | 19 | A | Hull C | L 0-2 | 0-0 | 10 | | 15,981 |
| 33 | 23 | H | Leeds U | D 0-0 | 0-0 | 10 | | 18,467 |
| 34 | 26 | A | Leicester C | L 0-3 | 0-2 | 11 | | 19,561 |
| 35 | Mar 2 | H | Peterborough U | L 2-3 | 0-3 | 12 | Rhodes [73], Jones [90] | 13,192 |
| 36 | 5 | A | Bolton W | L 0-1 | 0-0 | 13 | | 19,063 |
| 37 | 17 | A | Burnley | D 1-1 | 0-1 | 18 | Dunn [90] | 20,735 |
| 38 | 29 | H | Blackpool | D 1-1 | 0-0 | 16 | Rhodes [79] | 17,764 |
| 39 | Apr 1 | A | Cardiff C | L 0-3 | 0-1 | 19 | | 24,327 |
| 40 | 6 | A | Sheffield W | L 2-3 | 1-2 | 22 | Rhodes (pen) [12], Dann [71] | 24,660 |
| 41 | 13 | H | Derby Co | W 2-0 | 2-0 | 20 | Rhodes (pen) [9], Dann [45] | 13,391 |
| 42 | 16 | H | Huddersfield T | W 1-0 | 1-0 | 19 | Rhodes [37] | 15,317 |
| 43 | 20 | A | Watford | L 0-4 | 0-0 | 20 | | 13,775 |
| 44 | 23 | A | Millwall | W 2-1 | 0-1 | 15 | Jones [56], Rhodes (pen) [78] | 8607 |
| 45 | 27 | H | Crystal Palace | D 1-1 | 1-1 | 17 | Rhodes [42] | 19,796 |
| 46 | May 4 | A | Birmingham C | D 1-1 | 0-1 | 17 | Rhodes [66] | 18,979 |

**Final League Position: 17**

### GOALSCORERS

*League (55):* Rhodes 27 (5 pens), Rochina 5 (1 pen), Dann 4, Nuno Gomes 4, Kazim-Richards 3, Hanley, G 2, Jones 2, King 2, Dunn 1, Etuhu 1, Formica 1, Murphy 1 (1 pen), Olsson, Marcus 1, Pedersen 1.
*FA Cup (6):* Kazim-Richards 2, Dann 1, Hanley G 1, Murphy 1, Rhodes 1.
*Capital One Cup (1):* Goodwillie 1.

| Robinson P 21 | Lowe J 31 + 5 | Givet G 15 + 1 | Dann S 46 | Orr B 18 + 1 | Formica M 12 + 3 | Murphy D 31 + 2 | Etuhu D 19 + 1 | Pedersen M 17 + 11 | Nuno Gomes M 8 + 10 | Kazim-Richards C 22 + 6 | Olsson Marcus 19 + 4 | Dunn D 9 + 6 | Jorge P — +1 | Nunes F 2 + 4 | Ribeiro B 4 + 1 | Junior E 1 | Goodwillie D 2 + 6 | Rochina R 11 + 8 | Rhodes J 42 + 1 | Hanley G 35 + 4 | Olsson Martin 27 + 2 | Henley A 13 + 2 | Vukcevic S 4 + 5 | Rosado D 1 + 1 | King J 11 + 5 | Kean J 18 | Kane T 13 + 1 | Morris J 7 + 3 | Campbell D 5 + 2 | Williamson L 9 | Rekik K 4 + 1 | Bentley D 4 + 1 | Stewart C 3 + 4 | Jones D 11 + 1 | Best L 4 + 2 | Sandomierski G 7 + 1 | O'Sullivan J — +1 | Match No. |
|---|---|---|---|---|---|---|---|---|---|---|---|---|---|---|---|---|---|---|---|---|---|---|---|---|---|---|---|---|---|---|---|---|---|---|---|---|---|---|
| 1 | 2 | 3 | 4 | 5 | 6[1] | 7[3] | 8 | 9 | 10[2] | 11 | 12 | 13 | 14 |  |  |  |  |  |  |  |  |  |  |  |  |  |  |  |  |  |  |  |  |  |  |  |  | 1 |
| 1 | 5 | 4 | 3 | 2 |  | 6 | 7 | 14 | 13 | 11[3] | 10 | 9[1] |  |  | 8[2] | 12 |  |  |  |  |  |  |  |  |  |  |  |  |  |  |  |  |  |  |  |  |  | 2 |
| 1 | 2 | 3 | 4 |  |  | 7 | 8 | 9 | 11[2] |  | 5 |  |  |  |  | 6 | 10[1] | 12 | 13 |  |  |  |  |  |  |  |  |  |  |  |  |  |  |  |  |  |  | 3 |
| 1 | 13 | 3 | 4[3] |  | 6[1] | 8 | 7 | 9 | 10[2] |  | 5 |  |  |  | 2 |  |  |  | 14 | 11 | 12 |  |  |  |  |  |  |  |  |  |  |  |  |  |  |  |  | 4 |
| 1 |  | 3[2] | 4 | 2 |  | 8 | 7 | 9 | 10[3] |  | 5[1] |  |  |  | 6 |  |  |  | 14 | 11 | 13 | 12 |  |  |  |  |  |  |  |  |  |  |  |  |  |  |  | 5 |
| 1 | 14 |  | 3 | 2 | 6[3] | 7 | 8 | 9[2] | 12 |  |  | 13 |  |  |  |  |  |  | 10[1] | 11 | 4 | 5 |  |  |  |  |  |  |  |  |  |  |  |  |  |  |  | 6 |
| 1 |  | 4 | 3 | 2 | 12 | 7 | 8 |  |  | 10 |  |  |  | 9 | 6[1] |  |  |  |  | 11 | 13 | 5[2] |  |  |  |  |  |  |  |  |  |  |  |  |  |  |  | 7 |
| 1 | 6 | 3[1] | 4 | 2 |  | 7 | 8 | 9 | 10[2] |  |  | 13 |  |  |  |  |  |  |  | 11 | 12 | 5 |  |  |  |  |  |  |  |  |  |  |  |  |  |  |  | 8 |
| 1 | 6 | 5 | 4 | 2 | 7 | 8 |  |  | 10[1] | 12 |  | 13 |  |  |  |  |  |  |  | 11[2] | 3 | 9 |  |  |  |  |  |  |  |  |  |  |  |  |  |  |  | 9 |
| 1 | 9[2] | 4 | 3 | 2 | 6[1] | 8 | 13 |  | 10 |  |  |  |  |  |  |  | 12 |  |  | 11 | 7 | 5 |  |  |  |  |  |  |  |  |  |  |  |  |  |  |  | 10 |
| 1 | 6 | 4 | 3 | 2 | 12 |  | 8 | 9 |  |  | 11 |  | 7[1] |  |  |  |  |  |  | 10 |  | 5 |  |  |  |  |  |  |  |  |  |  |  |  |  |  |  | 11 |
| 1 | 6 | 4 | 3 | 2 | 14 | 8 | 13 |  | 11[3] |  |  |  | 7[1] |  |  |  |  | 12 | 10 | 9 | 5[2] |  |  |  |  |  |  |  |  |  |  |  |  |  |  |  |  | 12 |
| 1 | 7[3] | 5[1] | 3 | 2 |  | 14 | 8 | 9[2] | 13 | 6 |  |  |  |  |  |  |  |  | 10 | 11 | 4 | 12 |  |  |  |  |  |  |  |  |  |  |  |  |  |  |  | 13 |
| 1 |  |  | 3 |  | 13 | 8 | 7 | 6[2] |  | 10[1] | 9[3] |  |  |  |  |  |  |  | 12 | 11 | 4 | 5 | 2 | 14 |  |  |  |  |  |  |  |  |  |  |  |  |  | 14 |
| 1 |  |  | 4 |  | 6[2] | 7 | 8 |  | 9 |  |  |  |  |  |  |  |  | 11[1] | 10 | 3 | 5 | 2 | 12 | 13 |  |  |  |  |  |  |  |  |  |  |  |  |  | 15 |
| 1 | 14 |  | 3 |  | 6 | 8[3] | 7 |  | 9[2] |  |  | 13 |  |  |  |  |  | 10[1] | 11 | 4 | 5 | 2 | 12 |  |  |  |  |  |  |  |  |  |  |  |  |  |  | 16 |
| 1 | 12 |  | 4 |  | 6 | 7[1] | 8 | 14 | 13 |  |  |  |  |  |  |  |  | 9[2] | 11 | 10[3] | 3 | 5 | 2 |  |  |  |  |  |  |  |  |  |  |  |  |  |  | 17 |
| 1 |  |  | 3 |  | 6[2] | 7[3] | 8 |  | 13 |  |  |  |  |  |  |  |  | 9[1] | 11 | 10 | 4 | 5 | 2 | 14 |  | 12 |  |  |  |  |  |  |  |  |  |  |  | 18 |
| 1 | 12 |  | 4 |  | 6 | 7 | 8[1] | 13 | 14 |  |  |  |  |  |  |  |  | 10[2] | 11 | 3 | 5 | 2 |  |  | 9[3] |  |  |  |  |  |  |  |  |  |  |  |  | 19 |
| 1 | 8 |  | 4 |  | 6[2] | 7 |  | 9[1] | 10 |  |  |  |  |  |  |  |  |  | 11 | 3 | 5 | 2 | 13 | 12 |  |  |  |  |  |  |  |  |  |  |  |  |  | 20 |
| 1 | 8 |  | 4 |  | 6[2] |  | 7[3] |  | 12 | 9[1] |  | 13 |  |  |  |  | 14 | 11 | 3 | 5 | 2 |  |  | 10 |  |  |  |  |  |  |  |  |  |  |  |  |  | 21 |
|  | 7 | 4 | 3 |  |  | 8 |  |  | 11 |  |  |  |  |  |  |  |  | 12 | 10 |  | 5 | 2 | 6[1] |  | 9 | 1 |  |  |  |  |  |  |  |  |  |  |  | 22 |
|  | 8 | 4 |  |  | 7 |  |  | 11[2] | 12 |  |  |  |  |  |  |  |  | 13 | 10 | 3 | 5 | 2 | 6[1] | 9 | 1 |  |  |  |  |  |  |  |  |  |  |  | 23 |
|  | 8 | 4 |  |  | 7 |  | 14 | 12 | 13 |  |  |  |  |  |  |  |  | 6[2] | 10 | 3 | 5 | 2 | 9[1] | 11[3] | 1 |  |  |  |  |  |  |  |  |  |  |  |  | 24 |
|  | 8 | 4 |  |  | 7 | 12 |  | 9 | 13 |  |  |  | 14 |  |  |  |  | 6[1] | 11[3] | 3 | 5 | 2 |  | 10[2] | 1 |  |  |  |  |  |  |  |  |  |  |  |  | 25 |
|  | 8 | 14 | 3 |  |  | 7 | 12 | 10 |  |  |  |  |  |  |  |  |  | 6[2] | 11 | 4[3] | 5 |  | 9[1] |  | 1 | 2 | 13 |  |  |  |  |  |  |  |  |  |  | 26 |
|  | 7 | 4 |  |  | 6 | 12 | 13 | 8 |  |  |  |  |  |  |  |  |  | 10[2] | 11 | 3 | 5 |  | 9[1] |  | 1 | 2 |  |  |  |  |  |  |  |  |  |  |  | 27 |
|  | 8 | 3 |  |  | 7 |  | 6 | 10 | 9[1] |  |  |  | 12 |  |  |  |  | 11 | 4 | 5 |  |  |  |  | 1 | 2 |  |  |  |  |  |  |  |  |  |  |  | 28 |
|  | 8 | 4 | 2 |  | 7 |  | 6 | 10 | 9[1] |  |  |  |  |  |  |  |  | 11 | 3 | 5 |  |  |  |  | 1 | 12 |  |  |  |  |  |  |  |  |  |  |  | 29 |
|  | 8 | 3 | 2 |  | 7 | 6[1] |  | 10 | 9 |  |  |  |  |  |  |  |  | 11 | 4 | 5 |  |  |  |  | 1 |  |  | 12 |  |  |  |  |  |  |  |  |  | 30 |
|  | 7 | 3 | 2 |  | 8 |  |  | 6 | 9 |  |  |  |  |  |  |  |  | 11 | 4 | 5 |  |  |  |  | 1 |  |  | 10 |  |  |  |  |  |  |  |  |  | 31 |
|  | 7 | 3 | 2 |  | 8 |  |  | 11 |  |  |  |  |  |  |  |  |  | 10 | 4 | 5 |  |  |  |  | 1 |  |  | 12 | 6[2] | 9[1] | 13 |  |  |  |  |  |  | 32 |
|  | 8 | 3 | 2 |  | 7 | 12 |  | 9[1] |  |  |  |  |  |  |  |  |  | 11 | 4 |  |  |  |  |  | 1 |  |  | 10 |  | 5 | 6 |  |  |  |  |  |  | 33 |
|  | 6 | 3 | 2 |  | 8 | 7[1] | 14 | 12 |  |  |  |  |  |  |  |  |  | 11[3] | 5 |  | 13 |  |  |  | 1 |  |  | 10 |  | 4[2] | 9 |  |  |  |  |  |  | 34 |
|  | 7 | 3 | 2[2] |  | 8[1] |  |  | 9 |  |  |  |  |  |  |  |  |  | 10 | 4 |  | 14 |  |  |  | 1 |  |  | 11 |  | 5 | 6[3] | 12 | 13 |  |  |  |  | 35 |
|  | 7 | 3 |  |  |  | 6 |  | 5 |  |  |  |  |  |  |  |  |  | 11 | 4 | 2 |  |  |  |  | 1 |  |  | 10[1] |  |  | 9 | 8 | 12 |  |  |  |  | 36 |
|  | 6 | 4 |  |  |  | 13 |  |  | 7 |  |  |  |  |  |  |  |  | 11 | 3 | 5[2] |  |  |  |  |  | 1 | 2 | 12 |  |  | 9 | 8 | 10[1] |  |  |  |  | 37 |
|  | 7 | 4 |  |  |  |  | 12 | 8[3] |  |  |  |  |  |  |  |  |  | 11 | 3 |  |  |  | 10[1] |  | 1 | 2 | 5 | 6 |  | 14 | 9[1] | 13 |  |  |  |  | 38 |
|  |  | 2 |  |  | 7[3] | 6 | 11 | 13 |  |  |  |  |  |  |  |  |  | 14 | 5 |  |  |  | 11 | 3 | 4 |  |  | 8[2] |  | 9 | 10 | 12 |  |  |  |  |  | 39 |
|  | 7 | 3 |  |  |  |  | 12 | 10 |  |  |  |  |  |  |  |  |  | 11 | 4 |  |  |  | 13 | 2 | 5 | 8[2] |  | 6[1] | 9 |  | 1 |  |  |  |  |  |  | 40 |
|  | 7[2] | 3 |  |  |  | 13 | 10 | 6[1] |  |  |  | 14 |  |  |  |  |  | 11[3] | 4 |  |  |  | 12 | 2 | 5 | 9 |  |  | 8 |  | 1 |  |  |  |  |  |  | 41 |
|  | 6[2] | 4 | 3 |  |  | 13 |  | 5 | 14 |  |  | 12 |  |  |  |  |  | 10 |  |  |  |  | 9[3] | 2 |  | 7 |  |  |  |  | 8 | 11[1] | 1 |  |  |  |  | 42 |
|  | 4[1] | 3 |  |  |  | 13 |  | 5 | 6 |  |  |  |  |  |  |  |  | 11[3] |  |  |  |  | 7[2] | 2 | 14 | 8 | 12 |  |  | 9 | 10[8] | 1 |  |  |  |  |  | 43 |
|  |  | 3 | 14 |  |  |  | 11[1] | 5[2] | 7[3] |  |  | 12 |  |  |  |  |  | 10 | 4 |  |  |  | 13 | 2 | 9 | 6 |  |  | 8 |  | 1 |  |  |  |  |  |  | 44 |
|  |  | 3 |  |  |  | 12 | 9[1] |  |  |  |  | 10 |  |  |  |  |  | 11 | 4 |  |  |  | 6[2] | 2 | 5 | 7 |  | 13 | 8 |  | 1 |  |  |  |  |  |  | 45 |
|  |  | 3 |  |  |  | 8 |  |  | 9[2] |  |  |  |  |  |  |  |  | 11 | 4 |  |  |  | 10 | 2 | 5 | 6[1] |  |  | 12 | 7 |  | 1 | 13 |  |  |  |  | 46 |

**FA Cup**

| | | | | |
|---|---|---|---|---|
| Third Round | Bristol C | (h) | 2-0 |
| Fourth Round | Derby Co | (a) | 3-0 |
| Fifth Round | Arsenal | (a) | 1-0 |
| Sixth Round | Millwall | (a) | 0-0 |
| *Replay* | Millwall | (h) | 0-1 |

**Capital One Cup**

| | | | |
|---|---|---|---|
| Second Round | Milton Keynes D | (a) | 1-2 |

# BLACKPOOL

## FOUNDATION

Old boys of St John's School, who had formed themselves into a football club, decided to establish a club bearing the name of their town and Blackpool FC came into being at a meeting at the Stanley Arms Hotel in the summer of 1887. In their first season playing at Raikes Hall Gardens, the club won both the Lancashire Junior Cup and the Fylde Cup.

*Bloomfield Road, Seasiders Way, Blackpool, Lancashire FY1 6JJ.*

*Telephone:* (0871) 6221 953.

*Fax:* (01253) 405 011.

*Ticket Office:* (0844) 847 1953.

*Website:* www.blackpoolfc.co.uk

*Email:* secretary@blackpoolfc.co.uk

*Ground Capacity:* 16,007.

*Record Attendance:* 38,098 v Wolverhampton W, Division 1, 17 September 1955.

*Pitch Measurements:* 102m × 67m (112yd × 74yd)

*Chairman:* Karl Oyston.

*Manager:* Paul Ince.

*Assistant Manager:* Steve Thompson.

*Physio:* Phil Horner.

## HONOURS

**Football League – Division 1:**
*Runners-up* 1955–56;
**Division 2:** *Champions* 1929–30;
*Runners-up* 1936–37, 1969–70;
**Division 4:** *Runners-up* 1984–85.

**FA Cup:** *Winners* 1953;
*Runners-up* 1948, 1951.

**Football League Cup:** Semi-final 1962.

**Anglo-Italian Cup:** *Winners* 1971;
*Runners-up* 1972.

**LDV Vans Trophy:** *Winners* 2002, 2004.

*Colours:* Tangerine shirts, white shorts, tangerine socks with white tops.

*Year Formed:* 1887.

*Turned Professional:* 1887.

*Previous Name:* 'South Shore' combined with Blackpool in 1899, twelve years after the latter had been formed on the breaking up of the old 'Blackpool St John's' club.

*Club Nickname:* 'The Seasiders'.

*Grounds:* 1887, Raikes Hall Gardens; 1897, Athletic Grounds; 1899, Raikes Hall Gardens; 1899, Bloomfield Road.

*First Football League Game:* 5 September 1896, Division 2, v Lincoln C (a) L 1–3 – Douglas; Parr, Bowman; Stuart, Stirzaker, Norris; Clarkin, Donnelly, Robert Parkinson, Mount (1), Jack Parkinson.

*Record League Victory:* 7–0 v Reading, Division 2, 10 November 1928 – Mercer; Gibson, Hamilton, Watson, Wilson, Grant, Ritchie, Oxberry (2), Hampson (5), Tufnell, Neal. 7–0 v Preston NE (away), Division 1, 1 May 1948 – Robinson; Shimwell, Crosland; Buchan, Hayward, Kelly; Hobson, Munro (1), McIntosh (5), McCall, Rickett (1). 7–0 v Sunderland, Division 1, 5 October 1957 – Farm; Armfield, Garrett, Kelly J, Gratrix, Kelly H, Matthews, Taylor (2), Charnley (2), Durie (2), Perry (1).

*Record Cup Victory:* 7–1 v Charlton Ath, League Cup 2nd rd, 25 September 1963 – Harvey; Armfield, Martin; Crawford, Gratrix, Cranston; Lea, Ball (1), Charnley (4), Durie (1), Oates (1).

## sky SPORTS FACT FILE

Centre forward Adam Wolanin had a spell on Blackpool's books in the 1946–47 season, turning out for the reserve and A teams. A Polish airman, he later emigrated to the United States and was a member of his adopted country's squad for the 1950 World Cup finals.

**Record Defeat:** 1–10 v Small Heath, Division 2, 2 March 1901 and v Huddersfield T, Division 1, 13 December 1930.

**Most League Points (2 for a win):** 58, Division 2, 1929–30 and Division 2, 1967–68.

**Most League Points (3 for a win):** 86, Division 4, 1984–85.

**Most League Goals:** 98, Division 2, 1929–30.

**Highest League Scorer in Season:** Jimmy Hampson, 45, Division 2, 1929–30.

**Most League Goals in Total Aggregate:** Jimmy Hampson, 248, 1927–38.

**Most League Goals in One Match:** 5, Jimmy Hampson v Reading, Division 2, 10 November 1928; 5, Jimmy McIntosh v Preston NE, Division 1, 1 May 1948.

**Most Capped Player:** Jimmy Armfield, 43, England.

**Most League Appearances:** Jimmy Armfield, 568, 1952–71.

**Youngest League Player:** Matty Kay, 16 years 32 days v Scunthorpe U, 13 November 2005.

**Record Transfer Fee Received:** £6,750,000 from Liverpool for Charlie Adam, July 2011.

**Record Transfer Fee Paid:** £1,500,000 to Leicester C for D.J. Campbell, August 2010.

**Football League Record:** 1896 Elected to Division 2; 1899 Failed re-election; 1900 Re-elected; 1900–30 Division 2; 1930–33 Division 1; 1933–37 Division 2; 1937–67 Division 1; 1967–70 Division 2; 1970–71 Division 1; 1971–78 Division 2; 1978–81 Division 3; 1981–85 Division 4; 1985–90 Division 3; 1990–92 Division 4; 1992–2000 Division 2; 2000–01 Division 3; 2001–04 Division 2; 2004–07 FL 1; 2007–10 FL C; 2010–11 FA Premier League; 2011– FL C.

## LATEST SEQUENCES

**Longest Sequence of League Wins:** 9, 21.11.1936 – 1.1.1937.

**Longest Sequence of League Defeats:** 8, 26.11.1898 – 7.1.1899.

**Longest Sequence of League Draws:** 5, 4.12.1976 – 1.1.1977.

**Longest Sequence of Unbeaten League Matches:** 17, 6.4.1968 – 21.9.1968.

**Longest Sequence Without a League Win:** 19, 19.12.1970 – 24.4.1971.

**Successive Scoring Runs:** 33 from 23.2.1929.

**Successive Non-scoring Runs:** 5 from 12.4.1975.

## MANAGERS

**Tom Barcroft** 1903–33
    (*Secretary-Manager*)
**John Cox** 1909–11
**Bill Norman** 1919–23
**Maj. Frank Buckley** 1923–27
**Sid Beaumont** 1927–28
**Harry Evans** 1928–33
    (*Hon. Team Manager*)
**Alex 'Sandy' Macfarlane** 1933–35
**Joe Smith** 1935–58
**Ronnie Suart** 1958–67
**Stan Mortensen** 1967–69
**Les Shannon** 1969–70
**Bob Stokoe** 1970–72
**Harry Potts** 1972–76
**Allan Brown** 1976–78
**Bob Stokoe** 1978–79
**Stan Ternent** 1979–80
**Alan Ball** 1980–81
**Allan Brown** 1981–82
**Sam Ellis** 1982–89
**Jimmy Mullen** 1989–90
**Graham Carr** 1990
**Bill Ayre** 1990–94
**Sam Allardyce** 1994–96
**Gary Megson** 1996–97
**Nigel Worthington** 1997–99
**Steve McMahon** 2000–04
**Colin Hendry** 2004–05
**Simon Grayson** 2005–08
**Ian Holloway** 2009–12
**Michael Appleton** 2012–13
**Paul Ince** February 2013–

## TEN YEAR LEAGUE RECORD

|         |        | P  | W  | D  | L  | F  | A  | Pts | Pos |
|---------|--------|----|----|----|----|----|----|-----|-----|
| 2003-04 | Div 2  | 46 | 16 | 11 | 19 | 58 | 65 | 59  | 14  |
| 2004-05 | FL 1   | 46 | 15 | 12 | 19 | 54 | 59 | 57  | 16  |
| 2005-06 | FL 1   | 46 | 12 | 17 | 17 | 56 | 64 | 53  | 19  |
| 2006-07 | FL 1   | 46 | 24 | 11 | 11 | 76 | 49 | 83  | 3   |
| 2007-08 | FL C   | 46 | 12 | 18 | 16 | 59 | 64 | 54  | 19  |
| 2008-09 | FL C   | 46 | 13 | 17 | 16 | 47 | 58 | 56  | 16  |
| 2009-10 | FL C   | 46 | 19 | 13 | 14 | 74 | 58 | 70  | 6   |
| 2010-11 | PR Lge | 38 | 10 | 9  | 19 | 55 | 78 | 39  | 19  |
| 2011-12 | FL C   | 46 | 20 | 15 | 11 | 79 | 59 | 75  | 5   |
| 2012-13 | FL C   | 46 | 14 | 17 | 15 | 62 | 63 | 59  | 15  |

## DID YOU KNOW ?

Blackpool visited New Zealand in May and June 1964 where they played 11 fixtures. All the games were against Sheffield United, with the Tangerines winning four and losing six, Ray Charnley topped the scoring charts for the club with five goals. The winners received the BOAC Trophy.

## BLACKPOOL – FL CHAMPIONSHIP 2012–13 LEAGUE RECORD

| Match No. | Date | Venue | Opponents | Result | H/T Score | Lg Pos. | Goalscorers | Attendance |
|---|---|---|---|---|---|---|---|---|
| 1 | Aug 18 | A | Millwall | W | 2-0 | 1-0 | 1 | Ince 2 [32, 60] | 11,010 |
| 2 | 21 | H | Leeds U | W | 2-1 | 0-1 | 1 | Dicko [75], Phillips, M [80] | 14,315 |
| 3 | 25 | H | Ipswich T | W | 6-0 | 2-0 | 1 | Cresswell (og) [13], Taylor-Fletcher [45], Ince 2 [49, 58], Cathcart [62], Dicko [90] | 14,266 |
| 4 | Sept 1 | A | Leicester C | L | 0-1 | 0-0 | 1 | | 18,655 |
| 5 | 15 | A | Barnsley | D | 1-1 | 1-1 | 2 | Ince [30] | 14,134 |
| 6 | 18 | H | Middlesbrough | W | 4-1 | 2-1 | 2 | Delfouneso 2 [10, 36], Ince [56], Grandin (pen) [86] | 12,746 |
| 7 | 24 | H | Huddersfield T | L | 1-3 | 1-2 | 4 | Taylor-Fletcher [27] | 13,886 |
| 8 | 29 | A | Cardiff C | L | 0-3 | 0-2 | 7 | | 21,216 |
| 9 | Oct 2 | A | Hull C | W | 3-2 | 1-1 | 4 | Phillips, M [11], Phillips, K [71], Dicko [83] | 14,919 |
| 10 | 6 | H | Charlton Ath | L | 0-2 | 0-0 | 8 | | 13,482 |
| 11 | 20 | A | Burnley | L | 0-1 | 0-1 | 12 | | 12,925 |
| 12 | 23 | H | Nottingham F | D | 2-2 | 0-1 | 11 | Grandin [70], Taylor-Fletcher [75] | 13,228 |
| 13 | 27 | H | Brighton & HA | D | 1-1 | 0-0 | 12 | Grandin [72] | 14,038 |
| 14 | Nov 3 | A | Derby Co | L | 1-4 | 0-2 | 16 | Ince (pen) [49] | 22,272 |
| 15 | 6 | A | Sheffield W | W | 2-0 | 1-0 | 12 | Ince [18], Sylvestre [83] | 19,978 |
| 16 | 10 | H | Bolton W | D | 2-2 | 1-1 | 14 | Ince [19], Delfouneso [81] | 15,525 |
| 17 | 17 | A | Bristol C | D | 1-1 | 0-0 | 12 | Ince (pen) [90] | 12,009 |
| 18 | 24 | H | Watford | D | 2-2 | 0-2 | 14 | Phillips, K [52], Osbourne [90] | 13,076 |
| 19 | 27 | H | Birmingham C | D | 1-1 | 1-0 | 16 | Ince [17] | 13,111 |
| 20 | Dec 1 | A | Peterborough U | W | 4-1 | 0-0 | 11 | Thomas [51], Ince 2 (1 pen) [58 (p), 88], Dicko [83] | 5633 |
| 21 | 8 | A | Crystal Palace | D | 2-2 | 1-0 | 11 | Delfouneso [37], Dicko [89] | 15,594 |
| 22 | 15 | H | Blackburn R | W | 2-0 | 1-0 | 11 | Thomas [22], Broadfoot [81] | 15,907 |
| 23 | 21 | H | Wolverhampton W | L | 1-2 | 0-1 | 11 | Baptiste [89] | 14,556 |
| 24 | 26 | A | Huddersfield T | D | 1-1 | 0-0 | 11 | Delfouneso [90] | 16,832 |
| 25 | 29 | A | Middlesbrough | L | 2-4 | 0-2 | 12 | Thomas [59], Basham [76] | 18,164 |
| 26 | Jan 1 | H | Hull C | D | 0-0 | 0-0 | 14 | | 13,691 |
| 27 | 12 | A | Charlton Ath | L | 1-2 | 0-2 | 15 | Eccleston [90] | 16,846 |
| 28 | 19 | H | Cardiff C | L | 1-2 | 0-0 | 15 | Taylor-Fletcher [60] | 13,998 |
| 29 | 26 | A | Wolverhampton W | W | 2-1 | 1-1 | 14 | Ince 2 [45, 78] | 20,100 |
| 30 | Feb 2 | H | Barnsley | L | 1-2 | 0-1 | 15 | Ince [55] | 13,695 |
| 31 | 9 | H | Millwall | W | 2-1 | 0-1 | 14 | Ince [61], Delfouneso [90] | 12,653 |
| 32 | 16 | A | Ipswich T | L | 0-1 | 0-0 | 14 | | 16,673 |
| 33 | 20 | A | Leeds U | L | 0-2 | 0-0 | 15 | | 25,532 |
| 34 | 23 | H | Leicester C | D | 0-0 | 0-0 | 17 | | 14,509 |
| 35 | Mar 2 | H | Bristol C | D | 0-0 | 0-0 | 16 | | 12,934 |
| 36 | 5 | A | Birmingham C | D | 1-1 | 0-1 | 17 | Broadfoot [74] | 13,532 |
| 37 | 9 | A | Watford | W | 2-1 | 0-1 | 13 | Ince [76], MacKenzie [88] | 13,857 |
| 38 | 16 | H | Peterborough U | L | 0-1 | 0-1 | 17 | | 13,037 |
| 39 | 29 | A | Blackburn R | D | 1-1 | 0-0 | 15 | MacKenzie [65] | 17,764 |
| 40 | Apr 1 | H | Crystal Palace | W | 1-0 | 0-0 | 15 | Phillips, M [85] | 14,373 |
| 41 | 6 | A | Nottingham F | D | 1-1 | 1-0 | 17 | Sylvestre [27] | 22,814 |
| 42 | 13 | A | Burnley | W | 1-0 | 0-0 | 12 | Sylvestre [58] | 14,437 |
| 43 | 16 | H | Sheffield W | D | 0-0 | 0-0 | 14 | | 13,845 |
| 44 | 20 | A | Brighton & HA | L | 1-6 | 0-3 | 16 | Hammond (og) [53] | 28,499 |
| 45 | 27 | H | Derby Co | W | 2-1 | 1-0 | 15 | Taylor-Fletcher [18], Sylvestre [90] | 14,775 |
| 46 | May 4 | A | Bolton W | D | 2-2 | 2-2 | 15 | Phillips, M [21], Sylvestre [35] | 24,844 |

**Final League Position: 15**

### GOALSCORERS

*League (62):* Ince 18 (3 pens), Delfouneso 6, Dicko 5, Sylvestre 5, Taylor-Fletcher 5, Phillips, M 4, Grandin 3 (1 pen), Thomas 3, Broadfoot 2, MacKenzie 2, Phillips, K 2, Baptiste 1, Basham 1, Cathcart 1, Eccleston 1, Osbourne 1, own goals 2.
*FA Cup (2):* Delfouneso 1, Sylvestre 1.
*Capital One Cup (1):* Baptiste 1.

| Gilks M 45 | Eardley N 20 + 3 | Baptiste A 43 | Evatt I 11 | Crainey S 43 | Ferguson B 19 | Osbourne I 23 + 5 | Taylor-Fletcher G 28 + 7 | Gomes T 21 + 4 | Ince T 42 + 2 | Phillips K 9 + 9 | Dicko N 2 + 20 | Grandin E 6 + 6 | Cathcart C 22 + 3 | Martinez A 17 + 4 | Phillips M 28 + 6 | Sylvestre L 21 + 8 | Noguera A — + 1 | Eccleston N — + 6 | Harris R 3 + 1 | Delfouneso N 22 + 18 | Broadfoot K 32 | Robertson S 1 | Bruna G — + 1 | Basham C 24 + 2 | Thomas W 7 + 2 | Derbyshire M 4 + 8 | Halstead M 1 + 1 | Wabara R — + 1 | MacKenzie G 12 | Futacs M — + 4 | Match No. |
|---|---|---|---|---|---|---|---|---|---|---|---|---|---|---|---|---|---|---|---|---|---|---|---|---|---|---|---|---|---|---|---|
| 1 | 2 | 3 | 4 | 5 | 6 | 7 | $8^2$ | $9^1$ | 10 | $11^3$ | 12 | 13 | 14 | | | | | | | | | | | | | | | | | | 1 |
| 1 | 2 | | 4 | 5 | 6 | 9 | $7^1$ | 11 | $10^3$ | 13 | | | 3 | $8^2$ | 12 | 14 | | | | | | | | | | | | | | | 2 |
| 1 | 2 | | 4 | 5 | 6 | $9^3$ | 8 | 11 | $10^1$ | 12 | | | 3 | $7^2$ | 14 | | 13 | | | | | | | | | | | | | | 3 |
| 1 | 3 | 2 | | 5 | $7^3$ | 8 | 10 | $6^1$ | 9 | 14 | $11^2$ | | 4 | | 12 | | 13 | | | | | | | | | | | | | | 4 |
| 1 | 3 | 2 | 4 | | | 12 | $11^2$ | 13 | 9 | $10^3$ | | | | $8^1$ | 6 | 7 | | | 5 | 14 | | | | | | | | | | | 5 |
| 1 | 2 | 8 | | 5 | 7 | 4 | $10^1$ | $9^2$ | $6^3$ | 13 | 12 | | 3 | | 14 | | | | | 11 | | | | | | | | | | | 6 |
| 1 | $2^3$ | 3 | 4 | 5 | $8^1$ | 7 | 9 | $6^2$ | 11 | 13 | 14 | | | | 12 | | | | | 10 | | | | | | | | | | | 7 |
| 1 | 4 | 3 | 2 | | 13 | | | | | 11 | | $10^3$ | | 9 | 7 | $8^1$ | | | 14 | 12 | 5 | | $6^2$ | | | | | | | | 8 |
| 1 | 3 | 2 | 4 | 5 | 8 | 9 | 10 | $7^1$ | | 12 | 13 | | | $6^2$ | 14 | | | | | $11^3$ | | | | | | | | | | | 9 |
| 1 | 2 | 3 | 4 | 5 | 6 | $7^3$ | 9 | $8^1$ | | 12 | 13 | | 14 | | 11 | | | | | $10^2$ | | | | | | | | | | | 10 |
| 1 | 2 | 4 | 3 | 5 | | 7 | 9 | $10^2$ | | 13 | | | | 6 | $8^3$ | 12 | | | | $11^1$ | | | | | 14 | | | | | | 11 |
| 1 | $2^3$ | 4 | 3 | 5 | | 7 | 11 | $8^1$ | 10 | 13 | | 12 | | 9 | $6^2$ | | | | | 14 | | | | | | | | | | | 12 |
| 1 | | 3 | 4 | 5 | | $7^1$ | $10^3$ | 11 | | 14 | 8 | | | 6 | 9 | 12 | | | | 13 | | | $2^2$ | | | | | | | | 13 |
| 1 | | 4 | 3 | 5 | | | 10 | 11 | | 12 | $7^2$ | | | $8^1$ | 9 | 6 | | | | 2 | | | 13 | | | | | | | | 14 |
| 1 | 2 | | 3 | 5 | | | $9^1$ | 13 | 11 | 14 | | 6 | 4 | | $10^3$ | $7^2$ | | | | 12 | | | | 8 | | | | | | | 15 |
| 1 | 2 | 4 | | 5 | | | $10^1$ | | 11 | 13 | | $6^2$ | 3 | | 9 | 8 | | | | 12 | | | | 7 | | | | | | | 16 |
| 1 | 2 | | 4 | 5 | | | | 9 | $10^1$ | 12 | | 8 | 3 | | 6 | | | | | 11 | | | | 7 | | | | | | | 17 |
| 1 | 4 | 3 | | 5 | | 12 | 11 | $7^1$ | $10^3$ | | | | 13 | $8^2$ | | | | | | 9 | 2 | | | 6 | 14 | | | | | | 18 |
| 1 | | 3 | | 5 | | $8^1$ | 7 | | 9 | $10^2$ | | | 13 | | 4 | | | | | 11 | 2 | | | 6 | 12 | | | | | | 19 |
| 1 | | 4 | | 5 | | $7^1$ | 8 | 9 | 14 | 12 | | | 3 | 13 | | | | | | $11^2$ | 2 | | | 6 | $10^3$ | | | | | | 20 |
| 1 | | 3 | | 5 | | 8 | $7^2$ | 9 | 14 | 13 | | | 4 | $6^1$ | 12 | | | | | $11^3$ | 2 | | | 10 | | | | | | | 21 |
| 1 | 2 | | | | 6 | 12 | 7 | $11^2$ | | 13 | | | 4 | 8 | | | | | 5 | 9 | 3 | | | $10^1$ | | | | | | | 22 |
| 1 | | 3 | | 5 | | 7 | 12 | 8 | 11 | 13 | 14 | | | $6^2$ | | | | | | $9^1$ | 3 | | | 2 | $10^1$ | | | | | | 23 |
| 1 | 2 | | | 5 | | 8 | $10^2$ | $7^3$ | 9 | 14 | 13 | | 4 | | | | | | | 12 | 3 | | | 6 | $11^1$ | | | | | | 24 |
| 1 | 5 | | | 2 | | 8 | $7^2$ | 11 | | 4 | 12 | | 13 | | | | | | | $9^1$ | 3 | | | 6 | 10 | | | | | | 25 |
| 1 | 2 | 4 | | 5 | | 6 | $10^2$ | 9 | 13 | | | | | 7 | | | | | | 12 | 3 | | | 8 | $11^1$ | | | | | | 26 |
| 1 | 2 | 3 | | 5 | | $7^1$ | 12 | 14 | 9 | $10^3$ | | | | 8 | | | | | 13 | $11^2$ | 4 | | | 6 | | | | | | | 27 |
| 1 | | | | | | $7^2$ | 10 | $6^1$ | 9 | | | | 4 | 13 | 12 | 8 | | | 13 | 5 | 11 | | | 2 | | | | | | | 28 |
| 1 | 2 | | | 5 | | | 10 | 7 | 11 | | | | 3 | 6 | $9^1$ | | | | | 4 | | | | 6 | 12 | | | | | | 29 |
| $1$ | 2 | | | 5 | | | $10^2$ | $6^3$ | 9 | | | | 4 | 8 | $11^1$ | | | | | 14 | 3 | | | 7 | 13 | 12 | | | | | 30 |
| | 2 | | | 5 | | | 10 | $6^1$ | 11 | | | | 3 | 7 | $9^2$ | | | | | 13 | 4 | | | 8 | 12 | 1 | | | | | 31 |
| 1 | | 3 | | 5 | | | $9^3$ | $7^2$ | 13 | | | | 4 | 8 | 11 | | | | | 14 | $2^1$ | | | 6 | 10 | 12 | | | | | 32 |
| 1 | | 2 | | 5 | 6 | 8 | $10^1$ | | 11 | | | | 4 | | 9 | $7^2$ | | | | 12 | 3 | | | | 13 | | | | | | 33 |
| 1 | 6 | 2 | | 5 | 7 | | $10^1$ | | 9 | | | | 3 | | $11^2$ | | | | | 12 | 4 | | | 8 | 13 | | | | | | 34 |
| 1 | $6^1$ | 2 | | 5 | 7 | | 13 | | 10 | | | | 8 | | $9^2$ | | | | | 12 | 3 | | | | 11 | | | 4 | | | 35 |
| 1 | $6^2$ | 2 | | 5 | 7 | | $10^1$ | | 11 | | | | $8^2$ | $9^3$ | 13 | | | | | 14 | 3 | | | | | | | 4 | | 12 | 36 |
| 1 | $6^1$ | 2 | | 5 | 7 | | | | 10 | | | | $8^3$ | 9 | 12 | | | | | 13 | 4 | | | | | $11^2$ | | 3 | | 14 | 37 |
| 1 | | 2 | | 5 | $6^1$ | $7^2$ | | 9 | | 13 | | | 12 | 11 | 8 | | | | | $10^3$ | 3 | | | | | | | 4 | | 14 | 38 |
| 1 | | 2 | | 5 | 6 | | | 11 | | 13 | | | $9^2$ | 8 | 12 | | | | | 12 | 3 | | | $7^3$ | $10^1$ | | | 4 | | 14 | 39 |
| 1 | 13 | 2 | | 5 | $6^4$ | 12 | | $11^2$ | | | | | $9^2$ | 7 | 8 | | | | | $10^3$ | 3 | | | 8 | 14 | | | 4 | | | 40 |
| 1 | | 2 | | 5 | | $6^4$ | | $11^3$ | | | | | $9^2$ | 7 | 14 | 13 | 10 | | | 10 | 3 | | | 8 | | | | $4^1$ | | | 41 |
| 1 | 12 | 2 | | 5 | 6 | | 14 | 11 | | 13 | | | $9^2$ | $7^1$ | | | | | | $10^3$ | 3 | | | 8 | | | | 4 | | | 42 |
| 1 | | 2 | | 5 | 6 | | 12 | 11 | | 13 | | | $9^1$ | 8 | | | | | | $10^3$ | 4 | | | $7^2$ | 14 | | | 3 | | | 43 |
| 1 | | 3 | | 2 | 7 | $12^2$ | 10 | | | | | | $9^3$ | 6 | | | 14 | | | 11 | 5 | | | $4^1$ | 13 | | | 8 | | | 44 |
| 1 | 13 | | | 5 | 7 | | $10^1$ | $11^2$ | | | | | 6 | 8 | | | | | | 9 | 4 | | | 12 | | | | 2 | | | 45 |
| 1 | 7 | | | 5 | 8 | 12 | $10^1$ | | 11 | | | | $9^3$ | 4 | | | 14 | | | 13 | 2 | | | $6^2$ | | | | 3 | | | 46 |

**FA Cup**
Third Round    Fulham    (a)    1-1
*Replay*    Fulham    (h)    1-2

**Capital One Cup**
First Round    Morecambe    (h)    1-2

# BOLTON WANDERERS

## FOUNDATION

In 1874 boys of Christ Church Sunday School, Blackburn Street, led by their master Thomas Ogden, established a football club which went under the name of the school and whose president was vicar of Christ Church. Membership was 6d (two and a half pence). When their president began to lay down too many rules about the use of church premises, the club broke away and formed Bolton Wanderers in 1877, holding their earliest meetings at the Gladstone Hotel.

*The Reebok Stadium, Burnden Way, Lostock, Bolton BL6 6JW.*

*Telephone:* (0844) 871 2932. *Fax:* (0844) 871 2931.

*Ticket Office:* (0844) 871 2932.

*Website:* www.bwfc.co.uk

*Email:* reception@bwfc.co.uk

*Ground Capacity:* 28,100.

*Record Attendance:* 69,912 v Manchester C, FA Cup 5th rd, 18 February 1933 (at Burnden Park); 28,353 v Leicester C, FA Premier League, 23 December 2003 (at The Reebok Stadium).

*Pitch Measurements:* 105m × 68m (114yd × 74yd)

*Chairman:* Phil A. Gartside.

*Chief Operating Officer:* Bradley Cooper.

*Manager:* Dougie Freedman.

*Assistant Manager:* Lennie Lawrence.

*Fitness Coaches:* James Barrow and Mike Rawson.

*Colours:* White shirts with blue body trim, blue shorts, white socks.

*Year Formed:* 1874.

*Turned Professional:* 1880.

*Previous Name:* 1874, Christ Church FC; 1877, Bolton Wanderers.

*Club Nickname:* 'The Trotters'.

*Grounds:* Park Recreation Ground and Cockle's Field before moving to Pike's Lane ground 1881; 1895, Burnden Park; 1997, Reebok Stadium.

*First Football League Game:* 8 September 1888, Football League, v Derby Co (h) L 3–6 – Harrison; Robinson, Mitchell; Roberts, Weir, Bullough, Davenport (2), Milne, Coupar, Barbour, Brogan (1).

*Record League Victory:* 8–0 v Barnsley, Division 2, 6 October 1934 – Jones; Smith, Finney; Goslin, Atkinson, George Taylor; George T. Taylor (2), Eastham, Milsom (1), Westwood (4), Cook, (1 og).

*Record Cup Victory:* 13–0 v Sheffield U, FA Cup 2nd rd, 1 February 1890 – Parkinson; Robinson (1), Jones; Bullough, Davenport, Roberts; Rushton, Brogan (3), Cassidy (5), McNee, Weir (4).

## HONOURS

**Football League – Division 1:** *Champions* 1996–97;

**Division 2:** *Champions* 1908–09, 1977–78; *Runners-up* 1899–1900, 1904–05, 1910–11, 1934–35, 1992–93;

**Division 3:** *Champions* 1972–73.

**FA Cup:** *Winners* 1923, 1926, 1929, 1958; *Runners-up* 1894, 1904, 1953.

**Football League Cup:** *Runners-up* 1995, 2004.

**Freight Rover Trophy:** *Runners-up* 1986.

**Sherpa Van Trophy:** *Winners* 1989.

**European Competitions UEFA Cup:** 2005–06, 2007–08.

## sky SPORTS FACT FILE

When ITV agreed a deal to televise live matches in 1960, the first game broadcast was between Blackpool and Bolton Wanderers on 10 September. Wanderers won 1-0 with a goal from Freddie Hill, but the attendance at the ground was so poor that the deal was scrapped.

**Record Defeat:** 1–9 v Preston NE, FA Cup 2nd rd, 10 December 1887.

**Most League Points (2 for a win):** 61, Division 3, 1972–73.

**Most League Points (3 for a win):** 98, Division 1, 1996–97.

**Most League Goals:** 100, Division 1, 1996–97.

**Highest League Scorer in Season:** Joe Smith, 38, Division 1, 1920–21.

**Most League Goals in Total Aggregate:** Nat Lofthouse, 255, 1946–61.

**Most League Goals in One Match:** 5, Tony Caldwell v Walsall, Division 3, 10 September 1983.

**Most Capped Player:** Ricardo Gardner, 63 (109), Jamaica.

**Most League Appearances:** Eddie Hopkinson, 519, 1956–70.

**Youngest League Player:** Ray Parry, 15 years 267 days v Wolverhampton W, 13 October 1951.

**Record Transfer Fee Received:** £15,000,000 from Chelsea for Nicolas Anelka, January 2008.

**Record Transfer Fee Paid:** £8,200,000 to Toulouse for Johan Elmander, July 2008.

**Football League Record:** 1888 Founder Member of the League; 1899–1900 Division 2; 1900–03 Division 1; 1903–05 Division 2; 1905–08 Division 1; 1908–09 Division 2; 1909–10 Division 1; 1910–11 Division 2; 1911–33 Division 1; 1933–35 Division 2; 1935–64 Division 1; 1964–71 Division 2; 1971–73 Division 3; 1973–78 Division 2; 1978–80 Division 1; 1980–83 Division 2; 1983–87 Division 3; 1987–88 Division 4; 1988–92 Division 3; 1992–93 Division 2; 1993–95 Division 1; 1995–96 FA Premier League; 1996–97 Division 1; 1997–98 FA Premier League; 1998–2001 Division 1; 2001–12 FA Premier League; 2012– FL C.

## LATEST SEQUENCES

**Longest Sequence of League Wins:** 11, 5.11.1904 – 2.1.1905.

**Longest Sequence of League Defeats:** 11, 7.4.1902 – 18.10.1902.

**Longest Sequence of League Draws:** 6, 25.1.1913 – 8.3.1913.

**Longest Sequence of Unbeaten League Matches:** 23, 13.10.1990 – 9.3.1991.

**Longest Sequence Without a League Win:** 26, 7.4.1902 – 10.1.1903.

**Successive Scoring Runs:** 24 from 22.11.1996.

**Successive Non-scoring Runs:** 5 from 3.1.1898.

## MANAGERS

Tom Rawthorne 1874–85
  *(Secretary)*
J. J. Bentley 1885–86
  *(Secretary)*
W. G. Struthers 1886–87
  *(Secretary)*
Fitzroy Norris 1887
  *(Secretary)*
J. J. Bentley 1887–95
  *(Secretary)*
Harry Downs 1895–96
  *(Secretary)*
Frank Brettell 1896–98
  *(Secretary)*
John Somerville 1898–1910
Will Settle 1910–15
Tom Mather 1915–19
Charles Foweraker 1919–44
Walter Rowley 1944–50
Bill Ridding 1951–68
Nat Lofthouse 1968–70
Jimmy McIlroy 1970
Jimmy Meadows 1971
Nat Lofthouse 1971
  *(then Admin. Manager to 1972)*
Jimmy Armfield 1971–74
Ian Greaves 1974–80
Stan Anderson 1980–81
George Mulhall 1981–82
John McGovern 1982–85
Charlie Wright 1985
Phil Neal 1985–92
Bruce Rioch 1992–95
Roy McFarland 1995–96
Colin Todd 1996–99
McFarland and Todd joint
  managers 1995–96
Sam Allardyce 1999–2007
Sammy Lee 2007
Gary Megson 2007–09
Owen Coyle 2010–12
Dougie Freedman October 2012–

## TEN YEAR LEAGUE RECORD

|         |        | P  | W  | D  | L  | F  | A  | Pts | Pos |
|---------|--------|----|----|----|----|----|----|-----|-----|
| 2003-04 | PR Lge | 38 | 14 | 11 | 13 | 48 | 56 | 53  | 8   |
| 2004-05 | PR Lge | 38 | 16 | 10 | 12 | 49 | 44 | 58  | 6   |
| 2005-06 | PR Lge | 38 | 15 | 11 | 12 | 49 | 41 | 56  | 8   |
| 2006-07 | PR Lge | 38 | 16 | 8  | 14 | 47 | 52 | 56  | 7   |
| 2007-08 | PR Lge | 38 | 9  | 10 | 19 | 36 | 54 | 37  | 16  |
| 2008-09 | PR Lge | 38 | 11 | 8  | 19 | 41 | 53 | 41  | 13  |
| 2009-10 | PR Lge | 38 | 10 | 9  | 19 | 42 | 67 | 39  | 14  |
| 2010-11 | PR Lge | 38 | 12 | 10 | 16 | 52 | 56 | 46  | 14  |
| 2011-12 | PR Lge | 38 | 10 | 6  | 22 | 46 | 77 | 36  | 18  |
| 2012-13 | FL C   | 46 | 18 | 14 | 14 | 69 | 61 | 68  | 7   |

## DID YOU KNOW ?

Bolton Wanderers drew their first away game of the 1979–80 season at Anfield then lost the next 11 away fixtures to establish a new club record. They did not win a single League game away from Burnden Park all season and were relegated to Division Two.

## BOLTON WANDERERS – FL CHAMPIONSHIP 2012–13 LEAGUE RECORD

| Match No. | Date | Venue | Opponents | Result | H/T Score | Lg Pos. | Goalscorers | Attendance |
|---|---|---|---|---|---|---|---|---|
| 1 | Aug 18 | A | Burnley | L 0-2 | 0-1 | 22 | | 18,407 |
| 2 | 21 | H | Derby Co | W 2-0 | 0-0 | 14 | Davies, K [77], Eagles [90] | 17,050 |
| 3 | 24 | H | Nottingham F | D 2-2 | 1-1 | 8 | Eagles [39], Sordell [49] | 17,361 |
| 4 | Sept 1 | A | Hull C | L 1-3 | 1-1 | 20 | Eagles [17] | 15,304 |
| 5 | 15 | H | Watford | W 2-1 | 2-0 | 10 | Mills [3], Davies, K [42] | 16,608 |
| 6 | 18 | A | Birmingham C | L 1-2 | 1-1 | 15 | Eagles [44] | 14,693 |
| 7 | 22 | A | Sheffield W | W 2-1 | 1-0 | 13 | Alonso [44], Davies, M [65] | 26,598 |
| 8 | 29 | H | Crystal Palace | L 0-1 | 0-0 | 17 | | 16,727 |
| 9 | Oct 2 | H | Leeds U | D 2-2 | 1-1 | 17 | Davies, K 2 [14, 79] | 21,255 |
| 10 | 6 | A | Millwall | L 1-2 | 0-1 | 18 | Eagles [50] | 10,116 |
| 11 | 20 | H | Bristol C | W 3-2 | 1-2 | 16 | Eagles [31], Spearing [62], Petrov [82] | 17,259 |
| 12 | 23 | A | Wolverhampton W | D 2-2 | 1-2 | 16 | Afobe [21], Davies, M [90] | 20,915 |
| 13 | 27 | A | Middlesbrough | L 1-2 | 1-0 | 18 | Lee [42] | 16,200 |
| 14 | Nov 3 | H | Cardiff C | W 2-1 | 0-1 | 17 | Petrov (pen) [69], Ngog [74] | 17,304 |
| 15 | 6 | H | Leicester C | D 0-0 | 0-0 | 17 | | 16,754 |
| 16 | 10 | A | Blackpool | D 2-2 | 1-1 | 16 | Davies, M [16], Lee [71] | 15,525 |
| 17 | 17 | H | Barnsley | D 1-1 | 1-0 | 17 | Davies, K [24] | 16,965 |
| 18 | 24 | A | Brighton & HA | D 1-1 | 0-0 | 18 | Ngog [90] | 26,455 |
| 19 | 28 | A | Blackburn R | W 2-1 | 1-0 | 17 | Davies, K [2], Lee [61] | 18,010 |
| 20 | Dec 1 | H | Ipswich T | L 1-2 | 1-0 | 18 | Davies, M [6] | 17,208 |
| 21 | 8 | A | Huddersfield T | D 2-2 | 0-1 | 18 | Davies, M [70], Eagles [80] | 16,372 |
| 22 | 15 | H | Charlton Ath | W 2-0 | 0-0 | 13 | Ngog 2 [74, 80] | 15,991 |
| 23 | 22 | A | Peterborough U | L 4-5 | 1-2 | 16 | Andrews 2 (2 pens) [45, 56], Afobe [85], Petrov [87] | 6600 |
| 24 | 26 | H | Sheffield W | L 0-1 | 0-1 | 16 | | 22,292 |
| 25 | 29 | H | Birmingham C | W 3-1 | 2-1 | 14 | Alonso [27], Lee [33], Andrews (pen) [79] | 17,068 |
| 26 | Jan 1 | A | Leeds U | L 0-1 | 0-0 | 16 | | 22,386 |
| 27 | 12 | A | Millwall | D 1-1 | 1-1 | 16 | Andrews (pen) [34] | 16,985 |
| 28 | 19 | A | Crystal Palace | D 0-0 | 0-0 | 16 | | 17,033 |
| 29 | Feb 2 | A | Watford | L 1-2 | 1-1 | 20 | Sordell (pen) [32] | 13,223 |
| 30 | 9 | H | Burnley | W 2-1 | 0-0 | 17 | Davies, C [66], Ngog [81] | 19,767 |
| 31 | 16 | A | Nottingham F | D 1-1 | 0-0 | 16 | Davies, C [77] | 24,409 |
| 32 | 19 | A | Derby Co | D 1-1 | 1-0 | 16 | Keogh (og) [45] | 22,145 |
| 33 | 23 | H | Hull C | W 4-1 | 3-0 | 15 | Pratley [2], Davies, M [5], Dawson 2 [8, 70] | 17,655 |
| 34 | 26 | H | Peterborough U | W 1-0 | 1-0 | 10 | Dawson [5] | 15,675 |
| 35 | Mar 2 | A | Barnsley | W 3-2 | 2-0 | 10 | Ngog [15], Spearing [38], Dawson [59] | 10,862 |
| 36 | 5 | H | Blackburn R | W 1-0 | 0-0 | 9 | Eagles [90] | 19,063 |
| 37 | 9 | H | Brighton & HA | W 1-0 | 1-0 | 8 | Alonso [20] | 17,599 |
| 38 | 16 | A | Ipswich T | L 0-1 | 0-0 | 8 | | 17,034 |
| 39 | 30 | A | Charlton Ath | L 2-3 | 2-1 | 8 | Sordell [4], Medo [20] | 17,322 |
| 40 | Apr 2 | H | Huddersfield T | W 1-0 | 0-0 | 8 | Eagles [58] | 17,891 |
| 41 | 6 | H | Wolverhampton W | W 2-0 | 2-0 | 8 | Ngog [3], Alonso [10] | 18,432 |
| 42 | 13 | A | Bristol C | W 2-1 | 1-0 | 6 | Fontaine (og) [2], Davies, C (pen) [79] | 12,935 |
| 43 | 16 | A | Leicester C | L 2-3 | 1-2 | 7 | Ngog (pen) [3], Pratley [71] | 22,442 |
| 44 | 20 | H | Middlesbrough | W 2-1 | 0-0 | 6 | Eagles [50], Sordell (pen) [59] | 18,420 |
| 45 | 27 | A | Cardiff C | D 1-1 | 1-0 | 6 | Eagles [18] | 26,418 |
| 46 | May 4 | H | Blackpool | D 2-2 | 2-2 | 7 | Eagles [45], Davies, C [45] | 24,844 |

**Final League Position: 7**

### GOALSCORERS

*League (69):* Eagles 12, Ngog 8 (1 pen), Davies, K 6, Davies, M 6, Alonso 4, Andrews 4 (4 pens), Davies, C 4 (1 pen), Dawson 4, Lee 4, Sordell 4 (2 pens), Petrov 3 (1 pen), Afobe 2, Pratley 2, Spearing 2, Medo 1, Mills 1, own goals 2.
*FA Cup (5):* Sordell 4 (1 pen), Lee 1.
*Capital One Cup (1):* Afobe 1.

| Bogdan A 41 | Mears T 25+1 | Ream T 13+2 | Knight Z 43 | Ricketts S 30+2 | Lee C 34+7 | Davies M 23+1 | Andrews K 22+3 | Petrov M 6+8 | Sordell M 13+9 | Davies K 28+7 | Eagles C 40+3 | Alobe B 5+15 | Pratley D 23+8 | Mills M 16+2 | Spearing J 36+1 | Alonso M 25+1 | Ngog D 23+8 | Warnock S 15 | Butterfield J 4+4 | Vela J 3+1 | Davies C 5+13 | De Ridder S 2+1 | Dawson C 16 | Medo M 7+5 | Wheater D —+4 | Holden S —+2 | Lonergan A 5 | Butterfield D 2+4 | Odelusi S —+1 | Eaves T —+3 | Hall R 1 | Match No. |
|---|---|---|---|---|---|---|---|---|---|---|---|---|---|---|---|---|---|---|---|---|---|---|---|---|---|---|---|---|---|---|---|---|
| 1 | 2 | 3 | 4 | 5 | 6 | 7³ | 8 | 9² | 10 | 11¹ | 12 | 13 | 14 | | | | | | | | | | | | | | | | | | | 1 |
| 1 | 2 | 3 | | 5 | 6 | 7 | 8 | | | 10¹ | 11 | 9 | 12 | 4 | | | | | | | | | | | | | | | | | | 2 |
| 1 | 2 | | 4 | 5 | 6 | 7 | 8 | | | 11¹ | 10 | 9 | 12 | 3 | | | | | | | | | | | | | | | | | | 3 |
| 1 | 2 | 3 | 4 | 5 | 6 | 9 | 8¹ | | | 13 | 11² | 10 | 12 | | | 7 | | | | | | | | | | | | | | | | 4 |
| 1 | 2 | | 4 | | 6 | 7² | | | 10 | 9 | 12 | 13 | | | 3 | 8 | 5 | 11¹ | | | | | | | | | | | | | | 5 |
| 1 | 2 | | 4 | | 6³ | 7 | 12 | 14 | 11 | 9 | 13 | | | 3 | 8¹ | 5 | 10² | | | | | | | | | | | | | | 6 |
| 1 | 2 | | 4 | | | 8 | 7² | | | 11 | 6 | 12 | 13 | | 3 | 9 | 5 | 10¹ | | | | | | | | | | | | | | 7 |
| 1 | 2 | | 4 | | 14 | 6 | 7¹ | 12 | 13 | 10 | 9³ | | | 3 | 8 | 11² | 5 | | | | | | | | | | | | | | 8 |
| 1 | 2 | | 4 | | | 6 | 7 | 12 | 13 | 10 | 9 | 11² | | 3 | 8¹ | 5 | | | | | | | | | | | | | | | | 9 |
| 1 | 2 | | 4 | | 14 | 9 | 7² | | | 10 | 6 | 12 | 13 | 3 | 8³ | 11¹ | 5 | | | | | | | | | | | | | | | 10 |
| 1 | 2 | 4 | | | 12 | 7 | 9² | | | 10 | 6 | 11¹ | 13 | 3 | 8 | 5 | | | | | | | | | | | | | | | | 11 |
| 1 | 2 | 4 | | 13 | | 8 | 14 | 9 | | 10 | 6 | 11¹ | | 3² | 7 | 12 | 5³ | | | | | | | | | | | | | | | 12 |
| 1 | 2³ | 4 | 3 | 8 | 7² | | | 10¹ | | 11 | 6 | 12 | 13 | | 9 | 14 | 5 | | | | | | | | | | | | | | | 13 |
| 1 | 14 | 3 | 2 | 6³ | 10 | 7 | 12 | | | 11² | 9 | | 8¹ | 4 | | 13⁴ | 5 | | | | | | | | | | | | | | | 14 |
| 1 | | 4 | 2 | 6¹ | 10 | 8 | 12 | | | 11 | 9² | 7 | 3 | | | | 5 | | | | | | | | | | | | | | | 15 |
| 1 | | 4 | 2 | 12 | 9 | 6 | 10¹ | | | 14 | 8² | 13 | 3 | 7 | | 11³ | 5 | | | | | | | | | | | | | | | 16 |
| 1 | 12 | 4 | 2 | 14 | 7 | 13 | | | | 11 | 9 | | | 3 | 8 | 10³ | 5¹ | 6² | | | | | | | | | | | | | | 17 |
| 1 | 2 | 7³ | 4 | | 10 | | | | | 13 | 9 | 6¹ | 8² | 3 | 14 | 11 | 5 | 12 | | | | | | | | | | | | | | 18 |
| 1 | 2 | | 3 | 4 | 10³ | | | | 8 | 12 | | 11 | 6² | 13 | 14 | | 9 | 5 | 7¹ | | | | | | | | | | | | | 19 |
| 1 | 2 | | 3 | 4 | 12 | 8 | 7³ | | | 11² | 10¹ | 13 | | | 6 | 5 | 9 | 14 | | | | | | | | | | | | | | 20 |
| 1 | | 12 | 3 | 4 | 10 | 9 | 7 | | | 11 | 8 | | | 2¹ | 6 | | 5 | | | | | | | | | | | | | | | 21 |
| 1 | 2 | | 4 | 3 | 8² | | | | | 6 | 13 | 11 | 10 | | 7 | 12 | 5 | 9¹ | | | | | | | | | | | | | | 22 |
| 1 | 2 | | 4 | 3 | 8² | | | | | 7³ | 14 | 13 | 11 | 10 | 12 | 6 | 5 | 9¹ | | | | | | | | | | | | | | 23 |
| 1 | 2 | 3 | 4 | 5² | 12 | | | | | 7 | 9 | 14 | | | 6³ | 11 | 8 | 13 | 10 | | | | | | | | | | | | | 24 |
| 1 | 2 | 4 | 3 | | 8 | | | | | 6 | | | | | 11 | 10² | 13 | 9 | 7¹ | | 5 | | 12 | | | | | | | | | 25 |
| 1 | 2 | 4 | 3 | | 8² | | | | | 6 | | | | | 11 | 10 | 13 | 9¹ | 7³ | | 5 | 12 | 14 | | | | | | | | | 26 |
| 1 | | 4 | 3 | 2 | 6¹ | | 7 | | | 13 | 10 | 9² | 12 | | 8 | 5 | 11 | | | | | | | | | | | | | | | 27 |
| 1 | 2 | 3 | 4 | | 6 | | 8¹ | | | 11³ | 9 | 10² | | | 8 | 5 | 13 | | | | 12 | 14 | | | | | | | | | | 28 |
| 1 | | 3 | 4 | 2 | 10 | | | | | 11³ | 13 | 6¹ | | 8 | 7 | 5 | | | 9¹ | 14 | 12 | | | | | | | | | | | 29 |
| 1 | 2 | 3 | | 9 | | 11² | 14 | | | 6³ | | 7 | | 8 | 5 | 12 | | | | | 13 | 10¹ | 4 | | | | | | | | | 30 |
| 1 | 2 | 3 | | 6² | 10 | 11³ | | | | 12 | | 8 | | 7 | 5⁴ | 14 | | | | | 13 | 9¹ | 4 | | | | | | | | | 31 |
| 1 | 2 | 3 | 5 | | 8 | 14 | 13 | | | 12 | 6³ | 9 | | 7 | 10¹ | | | | | | 11² | | 4 | | | | | | | | | 32 |
| 1 | | 3 | 2 | 9 | 6³ | | | | | 10¹ | 8 | 7 | | 5 | 11² | | | | | | 12 | | 4 | 13 | 14 | | | | | | | 33 |
| 1 | | 3 | 2 | 9 | 6¹ | | | | | 10² | 14 | 8 | | 7 | 5 | 11³ | | | | | 13 | | 4 | 12 | | | | | | | | 34 |
| | | 4 | 3 | 9 | | | | | | 6¹ | 8 | | | 7 | 5 | 10 | 11² | | | | 2 | 12 | 13 | | | | 1 | | | | | 35 |
| | | 3 | 2 | 9 | | | | | | 10² | 12 | 8¹ | | 7 | 5 | 11 | | | | | 13 | 4 | 6 | | | | 1 | | | | | 36 |
| | | 3 | 2 | 9 | | | | | | 11² | 6¹ | 8 | | 7 | 5 | 10³ | | | | | 13 | 4 | 12 | 14 | | | 1 | | | | | 37 |
| | | 4 | 2 | 6 | | | | | | 13 | 12 | 9 | | 8 | 7 | 5 | 10 | | | | 11¹ | 3² | | | | | 1 | | | | | 38 |
| | | 3 | 2⁸ | 11² | | | | | | 10¹ | | 8³ | | 7 | 5 | 9 | | | | | 13⁸ | 4 | 6 | | | | 1 | 12 | 14 | | | 39 |
| | | 3 | | 6 | | | | | | 11¹ | | 9² | | 8 | 13 | 7 | 5 | 10 | | | | 4 | 12 | | | | 1 | 2 | | | | 40 |
| 1 | | 3 | 2 | 6 | | | | | | 11¹ | | 8 | | | 5 | 10² | | | | | 12 | 4 | 7 | | | | | 13 | | | | 41 |
| 1 | | 3 | 2 | 9 | | | | | | 11² | 6³ | 7 | | 8¹ | 5 | 10 | | | | | 13 | 4 | 12 | | | | | 14 | | | | 42 |
| 1 | | 3 | 13 | 10 | | | | | | | 9 | 8 | | 5 | 11³ | | | 7¹ | 12 | | 4 | 6 | | | | 2² | | | 14 | | | 43 |
| 1 | | 3 | 2 | 6 | | | | | | 11² | | 9 | | 7 | 5 | 10¹ | | | | | 4 | 8 | | | | 13 | | 12 | | | | 44 |
| 1 | | 4 | 2 | 10 | | | | | | 11¹ | | 9 | | 8 | 5 | 7² | | | | | 12 | 3 | 6 | | | | 13 | | | | | 45 |
| 1 | 4³ | 3 | 2 | 9 | | | | | | 12 | | 6 | | 8 | 5 | 11² | | | | | 7 | 14 | | | | | | | 13 | 10¹ | | 46 |

**FA Cup**

| | | | |
|---|---|---|---|
| Third Round | Sunderland | (h) | 2-2 |
| *Replay* | Sunderland | (a) | 2-0 |
| Fourth Round | Everton | (h) | 1-2 |

**Capital One Cup**

| | | | |
|---|---|---|---|
| Second Round | Crawley T | (a) | 1-2 |

# AFC BOURNEMOUTH

## FOUNDATION

There was a Bournemouth FC as early as 1875, but the present club arose out of the remnants of the Boscombe St John's club (formed 1890). The meeting at which Boscombe FC came into being was held at a house in Gladstone Road in 1899. They began by playing in the Boscombe and District Junior League.

*Goldsands Stadium, Dean Court, Kings Park, Bournemouth, Dorset BH7 7AF.*

*Telephone:* (0844) 576 1910.

*Fax:* (01202) 726 373.

*Ticket Office:* (0844) 576 1910.

*Website:* www.afcb.co.uk

*Email:* enquiries@afcb.co.uk

*Ground Capacity:* 9,287.

*Record Attendance:* 28,799 v Manchester U, FA Cup 6th rd, 2 March 1957.

*Pitch Measurements:* 105m × 64m (115yd × 71yd)

*Chairmen:* Eddie Mitchell and Maxim Demin.

*Chief Executive:* Neill Blake.

*Manager:* Eddie Howe.

*Assistant Manager:* Jason Tindall.

*Physio:* Steve Hard.

*Colours:* Red and black striped shirts, black shorts with red side panels, black socks with red hoops.

*Year Formed:* 1899.

*Turned Professional:* 1910.

*Previous Names:* 1890, Boscombe St John's; 1899, Boscombe FC; 1923, Bournemouth & Boscombe Ath FC; 1971, AFC Bournemouth.

*Club Nickname:* 'Cherries'.

*Grounds:* 1899, Castlemain Road, Pokesdown; 1910, Dean Court.

*First Football League Game:* 25 August 1923, Division 3 (S); v Swindon T (a) L 1–3 – Heron; Wingham, Lamb; Butt, Charles Smith, Voisey; Miller, Lister (1), Davey, Simpson, Robinson.

*Record League Victory:* 7–0 v Swindon T, Division 3 (S), 22 September 1956 – Godwin; Cunningham, Keetley; Clayton, Crosland, Rushworth; Siddall (1), Norris (2), Arnott (1), Newsham (2), Cutler (1). 10–0 win v Northampton T at start of 1939–40 expunged from the records on outbreak of war.

*Record Cup Victory:* 11–0 v Margate, FA Cup 1st rd, 20 November 1971 – Davies; Machin (1), Kitchener, Benson, Jones, Powell, Cave (1), Boyer, MacDougall (9 incl. 1p), Miller, Scott (De Garis).

*Record Defeat:* 0–9 v Lincoln C, Division 3, 18 December 1982.

## HONOURS

**Football League:**
**Division 3:** *Champions* 1986–87;
**FL 1:** *Runners-up* 2012–13;
**Division 3 (S):** *Runners-up* 1947–48;
**Division 4:** *Runners-up* 1970–71.
**FL 2:** *Runners-up* 2009–10.
**FA Cup:** Best season: 6th rd, 1957.
**Football League Cup:** Best season: 4th rd, 1962, 1964.
**Associate Members' Cup:** *Winners* 1984.
**Auto Windscreens Shield:** *Runners-up* 1998.

## sky SPORTS FACT FILE

Striker Ted MacDougall was the Football League's top goalscorer in both 1970–71 and 1971–72. He hit a total of 77 League and 19 Cup goals over the two seasons including nine in an 11-0 FA Cup win over Margate in November 1971.

*Most League Points (2 for a win):* 62, Division 3, 1971–72.

*Most League Points (3 for a win):* 97, Division 3, 1986–87.

*Most League Goals:* 88, Division 3 (S), 1956–57.

*Highest League Scorer in Season:* Ted MacDougall, 42, 1970–71.

*Most League Goals in Total Aggregate:* Ron Eyre, 202, 1924–33.

*Most League Goals in One Match:* 4, Jack Russell v Clapton Orient, Division 3 (S), 7 January 1933; 4, Jack Russell v Bristol C, Division 3 (S), 28 January 1933; 4, Harry Mardon v Southend U, Division 3 (S), 1 January 1938; 4, Jack McDonald v Torquay U, Division 3 (S), 8 November 1947; 4, Ted MacDougall v Colchester U, 18 September 1970; 4, Brian Clark v Rotherham U, 10 October 1972; 4, Luther Blissett v Hull C, 29 November 1988; 4, James Hayter v Bury, Division 2, 21 October 2000.

*Most Capped Player:* Gerry Peyton, 7 (33), Republic of Ireland.

*Most League Appearances:* Steve Fletcher, 628, 1992–2007; 2008–13.

*Youngest League Player:* Jimmy White, 15 years 321 days v Brentford, 30 April 1958.

*Record Transfer Fee Received:* £1,000,000 from Burnley for Danny Ings, August 2011.

*Record Transfer Fee Paid:* £800,000 to Crawley T for Matt Tubbs, January 2012.

*Football League Record:* 1923 Elected to Division 3 (S) and remained a Third Division club for record number of years until 1970; 1970–71 Division 4; 1971–75 Division 3; 1975–82 Division 4; 1982–87 Division 3; 1987–90 Division 2; 1990–92 Division 3; 1992–2002 Division 2; 2002–03 Division 3; 2003–04 Division 2; 2004–08 FL 1; 2008–10 FL 2; 2010–13 FL 1; 2013– FL C.

## MANAGERS

Vincent Kitcher 1914–23
*(Secretary-Manager)*
Harry Kinghorn 1923–25
Leslie Knighton 1925–28
Frank Richards 1928–30
Billy Birrell 1930–35
Bob Crompton 1935–36
Charlie Bell 1936–39
Harry Kinghorn 1939–47
Harry Lowe 1947–50
Jack Bruton 1950–56
Fred Cox 1956–58
Don Welsh 1958–61
Bill McGarry 1961–63
Reg Flewin 1963–65
Fred Cox 1965–70
John Bond 1970–73
Trevor Hartley 1974–75
John Benson 1975–78
Alec Stock 1979–80
David Webb 1980–82
Don Megson 1983
Harry Redknapp 1983–92
Tony Pulis 1992–94
Mel Machin 1994–2000
Sean O'Driscoll 2000–06
Kevin Bond 2006–08
Jimmy Quinn 2008
Eddie Howe 2008–11
Lee Bradbury 2011–12
Paul Groves 2012
Eddie Howe October 2012–

## LATEST SEQUENCES

*Longest Sequence of League Wins:* 8, 12.3.2013 – 20.4.2013.

*Longest Sequence of League Defeats:* 7, 13.8.1994 – 13.9.1994.

*Longest Sequence of League Draws:* 5, 25.4.2000 – 12.8.2000.

*Longest Sequence of Unbeaten League Matches:* 18, 6.3.1982 – 28.8.1982.

*Longest Sequence Without a League Win:* 14, 6.3.1974 – 27.4.1974.

*Successive Scoring Runs:* 31 from 28.10.2000.

*Successive Non-scoring Runs:* 6 from 1.2.1975.

## TEN YEAR LEAGUE RECORD

|  |  | P | W | D | L | F | A | Pts | Pos |
|---|---|---|---|---|---|---|---|---|---|
| 2003-04 | Div 2 | 46 | 17 | 15 | 14 | 56 | 51 | 66 | 9 |
| 2004-05 | FL 1 | 46 | 20 | 10 | 16 | 77 | 64 | 70 | 8 |
| 2005-06 | FL 1 | 46 | 12 | 19 | 15 | 49 | 53 | 55 | 17 |
| 2006-07 | FL 1 | 46 | 13 | 13 | 20 | 50 | 64 | 52 | 19 |
| 2007-08 | FL 1 | 46 | 17 | 7 | 22 | 62 | 72 | 48* | 21 |
| 2008-09 | FL 2 | 46 | 17 | 12 | 17 | 59 | 51 | 46† | 21 |
| 2009-10 | FL 2 | 46 | 25 | 8 | 13 | 61 | 44 | 83 | 2 |
| 2010-11 | FL 1 | 46 | 19 | 14 | 13 | 75 | 54 | 71 | 6 |
| 2011-12 | FL 1 | 46 | 15 | 13 | 18 | 48 | 52 | 58 | 11 |
| 2012-13 | FL 1 | 46 | 24 | 11 | 11 | 76 | 53 | 83 | 2 |

*\*10 pts deducted; †17 pts deducted.*

## DID YOU KNOW ?

Harry Redknapp was appointed caretaker-manager of Bournemouth in December 1982 and in his first game in charge the Cherries lost 9-0 at Lincoln City. Nevertheless he was appointed to the position on a permanent basis in October 1983 and went on to achieve great success as a manager.

## AFC BOURNEMOUTH – FOOTBALL LEAGUE ONE 2012–13 LEAGUE RECORD

| Match No. | Date | Venue | Opponents | Result | H/T Score | Lg Pos. | Goalscorers | Atten-dance |
|---|---|---|---|---|---|---|---|---|
| 1 | Aug 18 | A | Portsmouth | D 1-1 | 0-1 | 7 | Barnard [78] | 17,703 |
| 2 | 21 | H | Milton Keynes D | D 1-1 | 1-0 | 13 | Grabban [17] | 5407 |
| 3 | 25 | H | Preston NE | D 1-1 | 0-0 | 15 | Elphick [52] | 5329 |
| 4 | Sept 1 | A | Sheffield U | L 3-5 | 1-3 | 18 | Elphick [20], Barnard [48], Pugh [87] | 18,790 |
| 5 | 8 | A | Yeovil T | W 1-0 | 1-0 | 15 | Hughes [35] | 5238 |
| 6 | 15 | H | Hartlepool U | D 1-1 | 0-0 | 15 | Tubbs [90] | 5308 |
| 7 | 18 | H | Brentford | D 2-2 | 2-1 | 17 | Tubbs [17], Daniels (pen) [25] | 5117 |
| 8 | 22 | A | Swindon T | L 0-4 | 0-2 | 17 | | 8533 |
| 9 | 29 | H | Walsall | L 1-2 | 0-1 | 18 | Daniels [82] | 4951 |
| 10 | Oct 2 | A | Crawley T | L 1-3 | 0-2 | 20 | Barnard [52] | 2928 |
| 11 | 6 | A | Coventry C | L 0-1 | 0-0 | 21 | | 10,458 |
| 12 | 13 | H | Leyton Orient | W 2-0 | 0-0 | 20 | Grabban [65], Pugh [67] | 5715 |
| 13 | 20 | H | Tranmere R | W 3-1 | 0-1 | 18 | Gibson (og) [53], Arter [58], Francis [72] | 6233 |
| 14 | 23 | A | Notts Co | D 3-3 | 0-2 | 19 | McQuoid [51], Arter (pen) [60], Tubbs [85] | 4584 |
| 15 | 27 | A | Carlisle U | W 4-2 | 2-1 | 16 | Pugh 2 [8, 31], Grabban [51], Barnard [61] | 4050 |
| 16 | Nov 6 | H | Shrewsbury T | W 2-1 | 2-1 | 12 | Daniels [3], McQuoid [6] | 5022 |
| 17 | 10 | A | Doncaster R | W 1-0 | 1-0 | 12 | Arter [38] | 5951 |
| 18 | 17 | H | Oldham Ath | W 4-1 | 0-0 | 11 | Grabban 3 [53, 55, 72], Daniels [81] | 6118 |
| 19 | 20 | H | Stevenage | D 1-1 | 0-1 | 11 | Tubbs [74] | 5504 |
| 20 | 24 | A | Bury | D 2-2 | 0-1 | 10 | Grabban [59], Pitman [90] | 2541 |
| 21 | Dec 8 | A | Scunthorpe U | W 2-1 | 2-0 | 9 | Grabban [27], Fogden [30] | 2875 |
| 22 | 15 | H | Colchester U | W 1-0 | 1-0 | 9 | Grabban [41] | 6145 |
| 23 | 26 | H | Yeovil T | W 3-0 | 1-0 | 7 | Grabban [32], Arter [73], Pitman (pen) [86] | 8016 |
| 24 | 29 | H | Crawley T | W 3-0 | 2-0 | 5 | Alexander (og) [16], Pitman [40], O'Kane [84] | 7855 |
| 25 | Jan 1 | A | Brentford | D 0-0 | 0-0 | 7 | | 8059 |
| 26 | 12 | H | Swindon T | D 1-1 | 1-0 | 7 | Arter [26] | 8777 |
| 27 | 19 | A | Walsall | L 1-3 | 0-2 | 8 | Pitman [49] | 3173 |
| 28 | 22 | H | Hartlepool U | W 2-1 | 1-0 | 6 | McQuoid [28], Grabban (pen) [63] | 2502 |
| 29 | 26 | H | Crewe Alex | W 3-1 | 1-0 | 5 | Pitman 3 (2 pens) [8 (p), 67, 82 (p)] | 8628 |
| 30 | Feb 2 | A | Milton Keynes D | W 3-0 | 2-0 | 3 | Grabban [9], Pugh [45], Arter [84] | 9233 |
| 31 | 9 | H | Portsmouth | W 2-0 | 0-0 | 4 | Grabban [63], Pugh [77] | 9135 |
| 32 | 12 | A | Crewe Alex | W 2-1 | 0-0 | 1 | Pitman 2 (1 pen) [59 (p), 84] | 4005 |
| 33 | 16 | A | Preston NE | L 0-2 | 0-2 | 1 | | 8899 |
| 34 | 23 | H | Sheffield U | L 0-1 | 0-1 | 6 | | 8497 |
| 35 | 26 | H | Coventry C | L 0-2 | 0-1 | 7 | | 7411 |
| 36 | Mar 2 | A | Leyton Orient | L 1-3 | 0-1 | 7 | Pitman [66] | 5136 |
| 37 | 9 | H | Doncaster R | L 1-2 | 0-0 | 7 | Tubbs [86] | 7178 |
| 38 | 12 | A | Stevenage | W 1-0 | 1-0 | 7 | Pitman (pen) [38] | 2418 |
| 39 | 16 | H | Oldham Ath | W 1-0 | 1-0 | 4 | Pitman [22] | 3540 |
| 40 | 23 | H | Bury | W 4-1 | 1-1 | 3 | Pitman [8], Ritchie [55], Arter [80], Tubbs [89] | 7229 |
| 41 | 29 | A | Colchester U | W 1-0 | 1-0 | 2 | Pitman [19] | 4727 |
| 42 | Apr 1 | H | Scunthorpe U | W 1-0 | 1-0 | 2 | Pitman [11] | 7465 |
| 43 | 6 | A | Notts Co | W 3-1 | 2-1 | 2 | Ritchie 2 [17, 85], Pitman [26] | 7551 |
| 44 | 13 | A | Shrewsbury T | W 3-0 | 1-0 | 2 | Pitman 2 (1 pen) [5 (p), 53], Grandison (og) [62] | 6047 |
| 45 | 20 | H | Carlisle U | W 3-1 | 1-0 | 1 | Cook [25], Arter [56], Pitman [90] | 9014 |
| 46 | 27 | A | Tranmere R | D 0-0 | 0-0 | 2 | | 6745 |

**Final League Position: 2**

### GOALSCORERS
*League (76):* Pitman 19 (6 pens), Grabban 13 (1 pen), Arter 8 (1 pen), Pugh 6, Tubbs 6, Barnard 4, Daniels 4 (1 pen), McQuoid 3, Ritchie 3, Elphick 2, Cook 1, Fogden 1, Francis 1, Hughes 1, O'Kane 1, own goals 3.
*FA Cup (8):* Fogden 2, McQuoid 2, O'Kane 2, Pugh 2.
*Capital One Cup (0).*
*Johnstone's Paint Trophy (2):* MacDonald 2.

| Jalal S 17 | Francis S 42 | Addison M 20 | Elphick T 34 | Daniels C 33 + 1 | O'Kane E 33 + 4 | MacDonald S 19 + 9 | Partington J 8 + 6 | Pugh M 38 + 2 | Barnard L 15 | Thomas W 3 + 3 | Grabban L 39 + 3 | Arter H 35 + 2 | Tubbs M 6 + 25 | Cook S 32 + 1 | Fletcher S — + 11 | Hughes R 7 + 14 | McQuoid J 21 + 13 | Fogden W 12 + 14 | McDermott D 2 + 4 | Wakefield J — + 1 | James D 19 | Zubar S 2 | Davids L 2 + 1 | Demouge F 2 | Carmichael J 2 + 1 | Pitman B 23 + 3 | Seaborne D 13 | Ritchie M 15 + 2 | Painter M 2 | Fraser R — + 5 | Allsop R 10 | Match No. |
|---|---|---|---|---|---|---|---|---|---|---|---|---|---|---|---|---|---|---|---|---|---|---|---|---|---|---|---|---|---|---|---|---|
| 1 | 2 | 3 | 4 | 5 | 6 | $7^1$ | $8^2$ | 9 | 10 | $11^3$ | 12 | 13 | 14 | | | | | | | | | | | | | | | | | | | 1 |
| 1 | 2 | 5 | 3 | | 9 | 8 | 6 | 11 | $10^2$ | $7^1$ | 13 | 4 | 12 | | | | | | | | | | | | | | | | | | | 2 |
| 1 | 2 | 5 | 4 | 3 | $9^1$ | 12 | $8^3$ | 6 | $11^2$ | 10 | 13 | 7 | 14 | | | | | | | | | | | | | | | | | | | 3 |
| 1 | 2 | 4 | 3 | 5 | $6^3$ | $7^1$ | $8^2$ | 9 | 10 | 11 | | | | | | 12 | 13 | 14 | | | | | | | | | | | | | | 4 |
| 1 | 2 | 3 | 4 | | | 7 | 12 | 14 | | | 13 | 10 | 6 | | 5 | $8^1$ | $11^2$ | $9^3$ | | | | | | | | | | | | | | 5 |
| 1 | 2 | 5 | 4 | 13 | | 9 | 8 | 12 | | | 11 | $6^1$ | 14 | $3^2$ | | $10^3$ | 7 | | | | | | | | | | | | | | | 6 |
| 1 | 2 | 5 | 4 | 3 | | | 8 | 7 | 6 | | $11^2$ | $9^1$ | 10 | | | 13 | 12 | | | | | | | | | | | | | | | 7 |
| 1 | | 4 | 3 | 5 | 7 | | | 9 | | | 11 | 10 | 2 | | | 13 | $6^1$ | $8^2$ | 12 | | | | | | | | | | | | | 8 |
| | 4 | | 6 | $7^3$ | $8^2$ | | | 11 | | | | 14 | 2 | | $5^1$ | 13 | | | | | 1 | 3 | 9 | 10 | 12 | | | | | | | 9 |
| | | 3 | 5 | 4 | $9^3$ | | | | | 13 | 10 | | 12 | | 14 | 6 | | | | | 1 | 2 | $8^2$ | $11^1$ | 7 | | | | | | | 10 |
| | 2 | 4 | 3 | 5 | | $7^2$ | 12 | 10 | $11^3$ | | | 6 | | 13 | | 14 | | 8 | | | 1 | | | | $9^1$ | | | | | | | 11 |
| | 2 | 4 | 3 | 5 | 6 | | 8 | | 11 | 10 | | 9 | | | | $7^1$ | | | | | 1 | | 12 | | | | | | | | | 12 |
| | 2 | 3 | 4 | 5 | | 7 | 13 | 9 | 10 | | $11^1$ | $8^2$ | 12 | | | $6^3$ | 14 | | | | 1 | | | | | | | | | | | 13 |
| | 2 | 4 | 3 | | 8 | | | 6 | | | $11^2$ | 7 | 12 | 5 | 13 | 10 | $9^1$ | | | | 1 | | | | | | | | | | | 14 |
| | 2 | 4 | 3 | 5 | 12 | | 8 | 9 | | | $10^1$ | $6^3$ | 7 | | 13 | $11^2$ | | | | | 1 | | | | | | | | | | | 15 |
| | 2 | 3 | 4 | 5 | | | 8 | 9 | | | $11^1$ | 10 | 7 | | 13 | $6^2$ | 12 | | | | 1 | | | | | | | | | | | 16 |
| | | 3 | 4 | 5 | 7 | | | 9 | | | $11^2$ | 12 | $10^3$ | 8 | 2 | 14 | $6^1$ | 13 | | | 1 | | | | | | | | | | | 17 |
| | 2 | 4 | 3 | 5 | 13 | 7 | | $9^3$ | | | 11 | $10^1$ | $8^2$ | | | 6 | 12 | 14 | | | 1 | | | | | | | | | | | 18 |
| | 2 | 4 | 3 | 5 | | | 8 | 9 | | | $11^1$ | 10 | 7 | | | 12 | 13 | $6^2$ | | | 1 | | | | | | | | | | | 19 |
| | 2 | 4 | 3 | 5 | 14 | | 8 | | | | 10 | $7^3$ | $11^1$ | | | $6^2$ | 13 | | | | 1 | | | | | 12 | | | | | | 20 |
| | 2 | | 4 | 5 | 8 | 7 | 13 | $9^1$ | | | 11 | | | 3 | | 12 | $6^2$ | | | | 1 | | | | | 10 | | | | | | 21 |
| | 2 | 3 | | 5 | 7 | $8^1$ | 14 | 9 | | | 10 | 12 | | 4 | | 13 | $6^3$ | | | | 1 | | | | | $11^2$ | | | | | | 22 |
| | 2 | 3 | | 5 | 8 | | | 9 | | | $10^2$ | 7 | | 4 | | 13 | 12 | $6^1$ | 14 | | 1 | | | | | $11^3$ | | | | | | 23 |
| | 2 | 3 | | 5 | 7 | | | 9 | | | 10 | $8^3$ | 14 | 4 | | 13 | $6^1$ | 12 | | | 1 | | | | | $11^2$ | | | | | | 24 |
| | 2 | | 4 | 5 | 7 | | | 9 | | | $10^2$ | 8 | 13 | 3 | | 12 | 6 | | | | 1 | | | | | $11^1$ | | | | | | 25 |
| | 2 | 3 | | 5 | 7 | | | 9 | | 13 | 10 | $8^3$ | | 4 | | 14 | $6^1$ | 12 | | | 1 | | | | | $11^2$ | | | | | | 26 |
| | 2 | | 4 | 5 | 8 | | | | | | $10^2$ | 9 | $7^1$ | 13 | 3 | 14 | 12 | $6^3$ | | | 1 | | | | | 11 | | | | | | 27 |
| 1 | 2 | 3 | $5^2$ | | 8 | | | 9 | | | $10^1$ | 7 | | | | 12 | 11 | 6 | 13 | | | | | | | 4 | | | | | | 28 |
| 1 | 2 | 3 | | | 8 | | | 9 | | | $11^3$ | 7 | 14 | 4 | | 13 | $6^1$ | 12 | | | | | | | | $10^2$ | 5 | | | | | 29 |
| 1 | 2 | $4^1$ | | | 8 | | | 9 | | | $10^3$ | 7 | 14 | 3 | | 13 | $6^2$ | | | | | | | | | 11 | 5 | 12 | | | | 30 |
| 1 | 2 | | | | 8 | 14 | | 9 | | | $10^1$ | $7^2$ | 12 | 3 | | 13 | 6 | | | | | | | | | $11^3$ | 4 | 5 | | | | 31 |
| 1 | 2 | | | | $9^2$ | 13 | | 7 | | | 8 | 14 | | 4 | | 6 | $10^1$ | 12 | | | | | | | | $11^3$ | 3 | 5 | | | | 32 |
| 1 | 2 | | | | 12 | 8 | | $6^1$ | | | 10 | $7^3$ | 14 | 4 | | | 13 | | | | | | | | | 11 | | 5 | 9 | $3^2$ | | 33 |
| 1 | 2 | | | | 8 | | | 9 | | | $11^3$ | 7 | 14 | 3 | | | 12 | | | | | | | | | $10^2$ | 4 | 6 | $5^1$ | 13 | | 34 |
| 1 | 2 | | | | 7 | | | 11 | | | 8 | $10^1$ | 14 | 3 | | | $9^3$ | $6^2$ | | | | | | | | 12 | 4 | 5 | 13 | | | 35 |
| 1 | 2 | | | | 7 | | | $9^3$ | | | $11^2$ | 13 | | 4 | | 8 | 10 | $6^1$ | | | | | | | | 12 | 3 | 5 | 14 | | | 36 |
| | 2 | | | | 7 | | | $8^3$ | | | 9 | $10^2$ | 13 | 3 | | 14 | | $6^1$ | | | | | | | | 11 | 4 | 5 | 12 | 1 | | 37 |
| | 2 | | | | 8 | 14 | | 5 | | | 11 | $6^3$ | | 3 | | 13 | 7 | 9 | | | | | | | | 4 | $10^1$ | $12^2$ | 1 | | | 38 |
| | 2 | | $5^2$ | | 7 | | | 9 | | | $11^1$ | 8 | | 4 | | 12 | 6 | | | | | | | | | 10 | 3 | 13 | | 1 | | 39 |
| | 2 | | 5 | | 8 | | | $9^2$ | | | $10^1$ | 7 | | 3 | | 13 | 14 | | | | | | | | | 11 | 4 | $6^3$ | | 1 | | 40 |
| | 2 | | 4 | 5 | $8^1$ | 12 | | $9^3$ | | | $10^2$ | 7 | | 3 | | 13 | 14 | | | | | | | | | 11 | | 6 | | 1 | | 41 |
| | 2 | | 4 | 5 | 7 | 13 | | $9^2$ | | | 8 | $10^1$ | | 3 | | 12 | 14 | | | | | | | | | 11 | | $6^3$ | | 1 | | 42 |
| | 2 | | 4 | 5 | $7^2$ | 13 | | $9^3$ | | | 12 | 8 | $10^1$ | 3 | | 14 | | | | | | | | | | 11 | | 6 | | 1 | | 43 |
| | 2 | | 4 | 5 | $8^3$ | 14 | | $9^2$ | | | $11^1$ | 7 | | 3 | | 12 | 13 | | | | | | | | | 10 | | 6 | | 1 | | 44 |
| | 2 | 3 | | 5 | $8^1$ | 13 | | 9 | | | $11^2$ | 7 | | 4 | | 12 | | | | | | | | | | 10 | | 6 | | 1 | | 45 |
| | | 5 | 4 | 2 | $8^1$ | | | 6 | | | $10^2$ | 7 | | 3 | | 14 | 12 | 13 | | | | | | | | 11 | | $9^3$ | | 1 | | 46 |

**FA Cup**

|  |  | |  |
|---|---|---|---|
| First Round | Dagenham & R | (h) | 4-0 |
| Second Round | Carlisle U | (a) | 3-1 |
| Third Round | Wigan Ath | (a) | 1-1 |
| *Replay* | Wigan Ath | (h) | 0-1 |

**Capital One Cup**

| First Round | Oxford U | (a) | 0-0 |
|---|---|---|---|

*(aet; lost 3-5 on pens)*

**Johnstone's Paint Trophy**

| First Round | Portsmouth | (a) | 2-2 |
|---|---|---|---|

*(aet; lost 3-4 on pens)*

# BRADFORD CITY

## FOUNDATION

Bradford was a rugby stronghold around the turn of the 20th century but after Manningham RFC held an archery contest to help them out of financial difficulties in 1903, they were persuaded to give up the handling code and turn to soccer. So they formed Bradford City and continued at Valley Parade. Recognising this as an opportunity to spread the dribbling code in this part of Yorkshire, the Football League immediately accepted the new club's first application for membership of the Second Division.

*Coral Windows Stadium, Valley Parade, Bradford, West Yorkshire BD8 7DY.*

*Telephone:* (0871) 978 1911.

*Fax:* (01274) 773 356.

*Ticket Office:* (0871) 978 8000.

*Website:* www.bradfordcityfc.co.uk

*Email:* bradfordcityfc@compuserve.com

*Ground Capacity:* 25,136.

*Record Attendance:* 39,146 v Burnley, FA Cup 4th rd, 11 March 1911.

*Pitch Measurements:* 103m × 64m (113yd × 70yd)

*Joint Chairmen:* Julian Rhodes and Mark Lawn.

*Manager:* Phil Parkinson.

*Assistant Manager:* Steve Parkin.

*Head Physio:* Matt Barrass.

*Colours:* Claret and amber striped shirts, white shorts, white socks.

*Year Formed:* 1903.

*Turned Professional:* 1903.

*Club Nickname:* 'The Bantams'.

*Ground:* 1903, Valley Parade.

## HONOURS

**Football League –**
Division 1: *Runners-up* 1998–99;
Division 2: *Champions* 1907–08;
Division 3: *Champions* 1984–85;
Division 3 (N): *Champions* 1928–29;
Division 4: *Runners-up* 1981–82.

**FA Cup:** *Winners* 1911.

**Football League Cup:** *Runners-up* 2012–13.

**European Competitions:**
**Intertoto Cup:** 2000.

*First Football League Game:* 1 September 1903, Division 2, v Grimsby T (a) L 0–2 – Seymour; Wilson, Halliday; Robinson, Millar, Farnall; Guy, Beckram, Forrest, McMillan, Graham.

*Record League Victory:* 11–1 v Rotherham U, Division 3 (N), 25 August 1928 – Sherlaw; Russell, Watson; Burkinshaw (1), Summers, Bauld; Harvey (2), Edmunds (3), White (3), Cairns, Scriven (2).

*Record Cup Victory:* 11–3 v Walker Celtic, FA Cup 1st rd (replay), 1 December 1937 – Parker; Rookes, McDermott; Murphy, Mackie, Moore; Bagley (1), Whittingham (1), Deakin (4 incl. 1p), Cooke (1), Bartholomew (4).

## sky SPORTS FACT FILE

Bradford City won the short-lived Division Three North Cup in 1938–39. They knocked out Rotherham United, Hull City and Hartlepools United before defeating Accrington Stanley 3-0 in the final with goals from Archie Hastie, George Hinsley and Jimmy Smailes.

*Record Defeat:* 1–9 v Colchester U, Division 4,
30 December 1961.

*Most League Points (2 for a win):* 63, Division 3 (N),
1928–29.

*Most League Points (3 for a win):* 94, Division 3, 1984–85.

*Most League Goals:* 128, Division 3 (N), 1928–29.

*Highest League Scorer in Season:* David Layne, 34,
Division 4, 1961–62.

*Most League Goals in Total Aggregate:* Bobby Campbell,
121, 1981–84, 1984–86.

*Most League Goals in One Match:* 7, Albert Whitehurst v
Tranmere R, Division 3 (N), 6 March 1929.

*Most Capped Player:* Jamie Lawrence, 19 (24), Jamaica.

*Most League Appearances:* Cec Podd, 502, 1970–84.

*Youngest League Player:* Robert Cullingford, 16 years
141 days v Mansfield T, 22 April 1970.

*Record Transfer Fee Received:* £2,000,000 from
Newcastle U for Des Hamilton, March 1997; £2,000,000
from Newcastle U for Andrew O'Brien, March 2001.

*Record Transfer Fee Paid:* £2,500,000 to Leeds U for
David Hopkin, July 2000.

*Football League Record:* 1903 Elected to Division 2;
1908–22 Division 1; 1922–27 Division 2; 1927–29
Division 3 (N); 1929–37 Division 2; 1937–61 Division 3;
1961–69 Division 4; 1969–72 Division 3; 1972–77 Division 4;
1977–78 Division 3; 1978–82 Division 4; 1982–85 Division 3;
1985–90 Division 2; 1990–92 Division 3; 1992–96 Division 2;
1996–99 Division 1; 1999–2001 FA Premier League;
2001–04 Division 1; 2004–07 FL 1; 2007–13 FL 2; 2013– FL 1.

## LATEST SEQUENCES

*Longest Sequence of League Wins:* 10, 26.11.1983 – 3.2.1984.

*Longest Sequence of League Defeats:* 8, 21.1.1933 –
11.3.1933.

*Longest Sequence of League Draws:* 6, 30.1.1976 –
13.3.1976.

*Longest Sequence of Unbeaten League Matches:* 21,
11.1.1969 – 2.5.1969.

*Longest Sequence Without a League Win:* 16, 28.8.1948 –
20.11.1948.

*Successive Scoring Runs:* 30 from 26.12.1961.

*Successive Non-scoring Runs:* 7 from 18.4.1925.

## MANAGERS

Robert Campbell 1903–05
Peter O'Rourke 1905–21
David Menzies 1921–26
Colin Veitch 1926–28
Peter O'Rourke 1928–30
Jack Peart 1930–35
Dick Ray 1935–37
Fred Westgarth 1938–43
Bob Sharp 1943–46
Jack Barker 1946–47
John Milburn 1947–48
David Steele 1948–52
Albert Harris 1952
Ivor Powell 1952–55
Peter Jackson 1955–61
Bob Brocklebank 1961–64
Bill Harris 1965–66
Willie Watson 1966–69
Grenville Hair 1967–68
Jimmy Wheeler 1968–71
Bryan Edwards 1971–75
Bobby Kennedy 1975–78
John Napier 1978
George Mulhall 1978–81
Roy McFarland 1981–82
Trevor Cherry 1982–87
Terry Dolan 1987–89
Terry Yorath 1989–90
John Docherty 1990–91
Frank Stapleton 1991–94
Lennie Lawrence 1994–95
Chris Kamara 1995–98
Paul Jewell 1998–2000
Chris Hutchings 2000
Jim Jefferies 2000–01
Nicky Law 2001–03
Bryan Robson 2003–04
Colin Todd 2004–07
Stuart McCall 2007–10
Peter Taylor 2010–11
Peter Jackson 2011
Phil Parkinson August 2011–

## TEN YEAR LEAGUE RECORD

| | | P | W | D | L | F | A | Pts | Pos |
|---|---|---|---|---|---|---|---|---|---|
| 2003-04 | Div 1 | 46 | 10 | 6 | 30 | 38 | 69 | 36 | 23 |
| 2004-05 | FL 1 | 46 | 17 | 14 | 15 | 64 | 62 | 65 | 11 |
| 2005-06 | FL 1 | 46 | 14 | 19 | 13 | 51 | 49 | 61 | 11 |
| 2006-07 | FL 1 | 46 | 11 | 14 | 21 | 47 | 65 | 47 | 22 |
| 2007-08 | FL 2 | 46 | 17 | 11 | 18 | 63 | 61 | 62 | 10 |
| 2008-09 | FL 2 | 46 | 18 | 13 | 15 | 66 | 55 | 67 | 9 |
| 2009-10 | FL 2 | 46 | 16 | 14 | 16 | 59 | 62 | 62 | 14 |
| 2010-11 | FL 2 | 46 | 15 | 7 | 24 | 43 | 68 | 52 | 18 |
| 2011-12 | FL 2 | 46 | 12 | 14 | 20 | 54 | 59 | 50 | 18 |
| 2012-13 | FL 2 | 46 | 18 | 15 | 13 | 63 | 52 | 69 | 7 |

## DID YOU KNOW

Outside right Dickie Bond
made over 300 appearances
for Bradford City between
1909 and 1922, winning three
England caps during his time
at Valley Parade. He enlisted
in the Army in April 1915 and
spent two years as a prisoner
of war before resuming his
career with the Bantams.

## BRADFORD CITY – FOOTBALL LEAGUE TWO 2012–13 LEAGUE RECORD

| Match No. | Date | Venue | Opponents | Result | H/T Score | Lg Pos. | Goalscorers | Attendance |
|---|---|---|---|---|---|---|---|---|
| 1 | Aug 18 | A | Gillingham | L | 1-3 | 0-1 | 17 | Wells (pen) [62] | 5127 |
| 2 | 21 | H | Fleetwood T | W | 1-0 | 0-0 | 12 | Hanson [59] | 9224 |
| 3 | 25 | H | AFC Wimbledon | W | 5-1 | 5-1 | 4 | Wells [3], Haynes-Brown (og) [13], Davies [31], McArdle [37], Hanson [45] | 9436 |
| 4 | Sept 1 | A | Rotherham U | L | 0-4 | 0-3 | 12 | | 11,199 |
| 5 | 8 | A | Accrington S | D | 1-1 | 0-0 | 14 | Connell [83] | 3010 |
| 6 | 15 | H | Barnet | W | 3-0 | 0-0 | 7 | Hanson [47], Connell [55], Davies [57] | 9566 |
| 7 | 18 | H | Morecambe | W | 3-1 | 1-0 | 5 | Hanson [45], Reid [80], Jones, G [87] | 9054 |
| 8 | 22 | A | Oxford U | W | 2-0 | 0-0 | 4 | Davies [53], Wells [68] | 6032 |
| 9 | 29 | H | Port Vale | L | 0-1 | 0-1 | 6 | | 11,030 |
| 10 | Oct 2 | A | Rochdale | D | 0-0 | 0-0 | 6 | | 3461 |
| 11 | 6 | A | Dagenham & R | L | 3-4 | 0-2 | 8 | Wells 2 (1 pen) [55, 61 (p)], Connell [84] | 1768 |
| 12 | 13 | H | York C | D | 1-1 | 0-1 | 8 | Hines [59] | 11,883 |
| 13 | 20 | H | Cheltenham T | W | 3-1 | 1-1 | 5 | Wells 2 (1 pen) [45 (p), 68], Meredith [83] | 9648 |
| 14 | 23 | A | Northampton T | W | 1-0 | 0-0 | 5 | Wells [53] | 3541 |
| 15 | 27 | A | Burton Alb | L | 0-1 | 0-0 | 5 | | 2791 |
| 16 | Nov 6 | H | Chesterfield | D | 0-0 | 0-0 | 5 | | 8841 |
| 17 | 10 | A | Aldershot T | W | 2-0 | 2-0 | 4 | Wells 2 [28, 39] | 2143 |
| 18 | 17 | H | Exeter C | L | 0-1 | 0-1 | 7 | | 10,434 |
| 19 | 20 | H | Plymouth Arg | W | 1-0 | 1-0 | 5 | Jones, G [21] | 8843 |
| 20 | 24 | A | Bristol R | D | 3-3 | 1-2 | 5 | Wells [28], McHugh [55], Hanson [68] | 5092 |
| 21 | Dec 8 | H | Torquay U | W | 1-0 | 0-0 | 4 | Connell [85] | 9347 |
| 22 | 15 | A | Southend U | D | 2-2 | 1-0 | 5 | Wells [28], Prosser (og) [64] | 5142 |
| 23 | 26 | H | Accrington S | W | 2-1 | 1-0 | 5 | Thompson [24], Connell [86] | 11,181 |
| 24 | 29 | H | Rochdale | L | 2-4 | 2-4 | 6 | Connell 2 (2 pens) [19, 36] | 11,198 |
| 25 | Jan 1 | A | Morecambe | D | 0-0 | 0-0 | 7 | | 3635 |
| 26 | 5 | A | Barnet | L | 0-2 | 0-1 | 8 | | 2317 |
| 27 | 12 | H | Oxford U | L | 1-2 | 1-1 | 9 | Wells [14] | 10,087 |
| 28 | Feb 2 | A | Fleetwood T | D | 2-2 | 1-1 | 10 | Wells [45], Dickson [52] | 3577 |
| 29 | 9 | H | Gillingham | L | 0-1 | 0-0 | 12 | | 10,887 |
| 30 | 12 | A | Wycombe W | W | 3-0 | 1-0 | 10 | Doyle 2 (1 pen) [1, 83 (p)], Atkinson [81] | 3068 |
| 31 | 16 | A | AFC Wimbledon | L | 1-2 | 0-0 | 11 | Thompson [59] | 4320 |
| 32 | 27 | A | Dagenham & R | D | 1-1 | 0-0 | 12 | Hanson [90] | 10,006 |
| 33 | Mar 2 | H | York C | W | 2-0 | 0-0 | 12 | Hanson [77], Thompson [86] | 5678 |
| 34 | 5 | A | Port Vale | D | 0-0 | 0-0 | 10 | | 4281 |
| 35 | 9 | H | Aldershot T | D | 1-1 | 0-1 | 11 | Connell (pen) [90] | 10,397 |
| 36 | 12 | A | Plymouth Arg | D | 0-0 | 0-0 | 11 | | 5609 |
| 37 | 16 | A | Exeter C | L | 1-4 | 0-2 | 12 | Reid [79] | 4199 |
| 38 | 19 | H | Wycombe W | W | 1-0 | 1-0 | 11 | Thompson [7] | 8047 |
| 39 | 29 | H | Southend U | D | 2-2 | 0-2 | 11 | Hines [53], Hanson [83] | 10,598 |
| 40 | Apr 1 | A | Torquay U | W | 3-1 | 2-1 | 9 | McArdle [7], Thompson [18], Hanson [48] | 2569 |
| 41 | 6 | H | Northampton T | W | 1-0 | 1-0 | 8 | Wells [23] | 10,389 |
| 42 | 9 | H | Bristol R | W | 4-1 | 3-0 | 7 | Wells 2 (1 pen) [6, 22 (p)], Davies [45], Thompson [57] | 10,621 |
| 43 | 13 | A | Chesterfield | D | 2-2 | 1-0 | 7 | Wells [36], Ravenhill [79] | 7290 |
| 44 | 16 | H | Rotherham U | L | 0-2 | 0-0 | 7 | | 13,461 |
| 45 | 20 | A | Burton Alb | W | 1-0 | 1-0 | 7 | Hanson [44] | 13,235 |
| 46 | 27 | A | Cheltenham T | D | 0-0 | 0-0 | 7 | | 5888 |

**Final League Position: 7**

### GOALSCORERS

*League (63):* Wells 18 (4 pens), Hanson 10, Connell 8 (3 pens), Thompson 6, Davies 4, Doyle 2 (1 pen), Hines 2, Jones, G 2, McArdle 2, Reid 2, Atkinson 1, Dickson 1, McHugh 1, Meredith 1, Ravenhill 1, own goals 2.
*FA Cup (7):* Atkinson 2, Connell 1 (1 pen), Hanson 1, McHugh 1, Reid 1, Wells 1 (1 pen).
*Capital One Cup (11):* Wells 3, Hanson 2, Thompson 2, Darby 1, McArdle 1, McHugh 1, Reid 1.
*Johnstone's Paint Trophy (3):* Forsyth 1, Jones R 1, Reid 1.
*League Two Play-Offs (8):* Wells 4 (1 pen), Hanson 2, McArdle 1, Thompson 1.

| Duke M 23+1 | Oliver L 15 | Meredith J 32 | Darby S 33+2 | Reid K 25+8 | Thompson G 26+15 | Atkinson W 26+16 | Jones G 38+1 | McArdle R 38+2 | Connell A 8+22 | Hanson J 39+4 | Hines Z 19+13 | Wells N 29+10 | Davies A 27+1 | Doyle N 34+3 | McLaughlin J 23 | Ravenhill R 21+1 | Forsyth C 5+2 | McHugh C 12+4 | Egan J 4 | Naylor T 4+1 | Jones R 2+2 | Turgott B —+4 | Hannah R —+1 | Good C 2+1 | Dickson R 3+2 | Gray A 6+1 | Nelson M 12+1 | Match No |
|---|---|---|---|---|---|---|---|---|---|---|---|---|---|---|---|---|---|---|---|---|---|---|---|---|---|---|---|---|
| 1 | 2 | 3 | $4^3$ | 5 | $6^2$ | 7 | 8 | 9 | $10^1$ | 11 | 12 | 13 | 14 | | | | | | | | | | | | | | | 1 |
| 1 | 4 | 5 | 14 | 9 | 12 | 13 | 7 | 2 | | 11 | $6^1$ | $10^3$ | 3 | $8^2$ | | | | | | | | | | | | | | 2 |
| 1 | 4 | 5 | | 9 | 12 | 13 | 7 | 2 | 14 | 11 | $6^1$ | $10^2$ | 3 | $8^2$ | | | | | | | | | | | | | | 3 |
| 1 | 4 | 5 | | 9 | 13 | 12 | 7 | 2 | 14 | 10 | $6^1$ | $11^3$ | 3 | $8^2$ | | | | | | | | | | | | | | 4 |
| | 4 | 5 | $2^2$ | 11 | 12 | 8 | 7 | 13 | 14 | 10 | $9^1$ | | 3 | $6^3$ | 1 | | | | | | | | | | | | | 5 |
| | 3 | 5 | $9^2$ | 13 | 14 | 8 | 2 | $11^1$ | 10 | 6 | 12 | 4 | $7^3$ | | 1 | | | | | | | | | | | | | 6 |
| 14 | 3 | 5 | 9 | | 13 | 7 | 2 | $10^1$ | 11 | $6^2$ | 12 | 4 | 8 | | $1^3$ | | | | | | | | | | | | | 7 |
| | 3 | 5 | $6^2$ | 12 | 9 | 7 | 2 | 10 | 13 | $11^1$ | | 4 | 8 | 1 | | | | | | | | | | | | | | 8 |
| | $4^2$ | 5 | $9^1$ | 14 | $6^1$ | 7 | 2 | 13 | 11 | 12 | 10 | | 3 | 8 | 1 | | | | | | | | | | | | | 9 |
| | 4 | 5 | $9^1$ | 13 | 6 | | 2 | 14 | 10 | 12 | $11^3$ | | 3 | 8 | 1 | $7^2$ | | | | | | | | | | | | 10 |
| | 3 | 5 | | 13 | $6^2$ | | 2 | 12 | 11 | $9^1$ | 10 | | 4 | 8 | 1 | 7 | | | | | | | | | | | | 11 |
| | 4 | 5 | 2 | 12 | 6 | | | $8^1$ | 10 | 13 | 11 | | 3 | 9 | 1 | $7^2$ | | | | | | | | | | | | 12 |
| | 4 | 5 | $9^2$ | 13 | 6 | | | | 11 | 12 | 10 | | 3 | 8 | 1 | 7 | $2^1$ | | | | | | | | | | | 13 |
| | 4 | 5 | | 12 | 6 | | 2 | | 10 | 11 | | | 3 | 8 | 1 | 7 | $9^1$ | | | | | | | | | | | 14 |
| | $4^1$ | 5 | | 12 | 6 | | 2 | 13 | 11$^2$ | 10 | | | $3^3$ | | 1 | 7 | $8^4$ | 9 | 14 | | | | | | | | | 15 |
| 1 | | 5 | 2 | $11^1$ | 6 | 8 | 4 | 12 | $9^2$ | 10 | | | 7 | 13 | 3 | | | | | | | | | | | | | 16 |
| 1 | | 5 | 2 | | 3 | 8 | 4 | 10 | 12 | $11^1$ | | | | 7 | 9 | 6 | | | | | | | | | | | | 17 |
| 1 | | | 13 | 6 | 7 | 3 | 12 | 10 | | 11 | | | | 8 | | $9^1$ | 5 | 4 | $2^2$ | | | | | | | | | 18 |
| 1 | | 5 | 2 | $9^3$ | 6 | 7 | 4 | 13 | 10 | $11^1$ | | | | 8 | | 12 | $3^1$ | 14 | | | | | | | | | | 19 |
| 1 | | 3 | 2 | | $6^1$ | 7 | 8 | 5 | 13 | 10 | | | | $11^2$ | | $9^4$ | | 4 | 12 | | | | | | | | | 20 |
| 1 | | 5 | 2 | | $6^1$ | 9 | 7 | 4 | 13 | 10 | | | | $11^3$ | | 8 | | $3^2$ | 14 | 12 | | | | | | | | 21 |
| 1 | | 5 | 2 | | $6^1$ | 9 | 7 | 3 | | 11 | 13 | $10^2$ | | $8^3$ | | 14 | 12 | 4 | | | | | | | | | | 22 |
| 1 | | 5 | 2 | 14 | 6 | $9^3$ | 7 | 4 | 13 | 10 | $11^1$ | $12^2$ | | 8 | | | 3 | | | | | | | | | | | 23 |
| 1 | | 5 | 2 | 9 | $6^1$ | 12 | 7 | 8 | 11 | 10 | | | | $3^2$ | | | $4^3$ | | 14 | 13 | | | | | | | | 24 |
| 1 | | $5^1$ | 2 | 14 | | 8 | $9^3$ | 3 | | 10 | $11^2$ | 13 | | 4 | | 7 | | 6 | | 12 | | | | | | | | 25 |
| 1 | | | $2^3$ | 12 | | 9 | 8 | 3 | 13 | 10 | | 11 | | 4 | | $7^2$ | | $6^1$ | 14 | 5 | | | | | | | | 26 |
| 1 | | | 2 | 12 | | $9^1$ | 7 | 4 | 14 | | $6^2$ | $11^3$ | | 8 | | | 3 | | | | 13 | | | | 5 | 10 | | 27 |
| 1 | | | 2 | 13 | $6^2$ | 9 | 7 | $3^1$ | | 11 | | $10^3$ | | 8 | | | 5 | | | | | 12 | 14 | | 4 | | | 28 |
| 1 | | | 2 | 9 | 12 | | | 8 | | 14 | 10 | $6^2$ | 11 | 7 | | | | $3^2$ | | | | $5^1$ | 13 | | 4 | | | 29 |
| 1 | | | 2 | 10 | 6 | 9 | 7 | | | | 12 | | | $3^2$ | 8 | | 13 | | | | | | | 5 | $11^1$ | 4 | | 30 |
| 1 | | | 2 | $9^2$ | 11 | 6 | 7 | | | 12 | | | | 13 | 3 | 8 | | | | | | | | 5 | $10^1$ | 4 | | 31 |
| | | $5^3$ | 9 | $11^2$ | | 7 | 2 | 14 | 13 | 6 | 12 | 4 | 8 | 1 | | | | | | | | | | | $10^1$ | 3 | | 32 |
| | | | 2 | 9 | 12 | | $6^2$ | 7 | | 11 | 13 | $10^1$ | 3 | 1 | 8 | | 5 | | | | | | | | | 4 | | 33 |
| | | | 2 | 13 | $11^1$ | 6 | $7^3$ | 3 | | 10 | $9^2$ | 12 | | 14 | 1 | 8 | 5 | | | | | | | | | 4 | | 34 |
| | | | 2 | 13 | 12 | 9 | 8 | 3 | 14 | 10 | 6 | $11^2$ | | | 1 | $7^1$ | 5 | | | | | | | | $4^3$ | | | 35 |
| 1 | | | 2 | 9 | $10^3$ | 13 | | 3 | 14 | 12 | $6^2$ | | 4 | 7 | | 8 | 5 | | | | | | | | $11^1$ | | | 36 |
| 1 | | | 2 | 12 | $10^1$ | 8 | 6 | | 9 | 11 | 13 | | 3 | $7^2$ | | 8 | 5 | | | | | | | | | 4 | | 37 |
| | | 5 | 2 | 9 | $11^3$ | 12 | 8 | 3 | 10 | $6^2$ | 14 | 4 | 13 | 1 | $7^1$ | | | | | | | | | | | | | 38 |
| | | 5 | $2^3$ | 9 | 11 | 12 | 8 | 4 | 13 | 10 | $6^1$ | 14 | 3 | 1 | $7^2$ | | | | | | | | | | | | | 39 |
| | | 5 | 2 | 9 | 11 | 12 | 8 | 4 | | 10 | | $6^1$ | 3 | 1 | 7 | | | | | | | | | | | | | 40 |
| | | 5 | 2 | 9 | $6^1$ | 13 | 8 | 3 | | 11 | 12 | $10^2$ | 4 | 1 | 7 | | | | | | | | | | | | | 41 |
| | | 5 | 2 | 9 | $6^2$ | 13 | $8^1$ | 3 | 14 | 11 | | $10^3$ | 4 | 12 | 1 | 7 | | | | | | | | | | | | 42 |
| | | 5 | 2 | $9^1$ | $6^2$ | 12 | 8 | 4 | | 10 | 13 | 11 | | 1 | 7 | | | | | | | | | | | 3 | | 43 |
| | | $5^2$ | $2^3$ | 6 | 9 | | 7 | 4 | 14 | 11 | | 10 | $3^1$ | 1 | 8 | 13 | | | | | | | | | 12 | | | 44 |
| | | 5 | 2 | $9^1$ | $6^3$ | 14 | 8 | 4 | 13 | 11 | 12 | $10^2$ | | 1 | 7 | | | | | | | | | | | 3 | | 45 |
| 1 | | | 2 | 13 | 9 | | 12 | $11^1$ | | 6 | | $3^4$ | 7 | | 8 | 5 | | | | | | | | | $10^2$ | 4 | | 46 |

**FA Cup**

| | | | | |
|---|---|---|---|---|
| First Round | Northampton T | (a) 1-1 *Replay* (h) | | 3-3 |
| (*aet; won 4-2 on pens*) | | | | |
| Second Round | Brentford | (h) 1-1 *Replay* (a) | | 2-4 |

**Johnstone's Paint Trophy**

| | | | |
|---|---|---|---|
| Second Round | Hartlepool U | (a) | 0-0 |
| (*aet; won 3-2 on pens*) | | | |
| Northern Quarter-Finals | Port Vale | (a) | 2-0 |
| Northern Semi-Finals | Crewe Alex | (a) | 1-4 |

**Capital One Cup**

| | | | | |
|---|---|---|---|---|
| First Round | Notts Co | | (a) | 1-0 |
| Second Round | Watford | | (a) | 2-1 |
| Third Round | Burton | | (h) | 3-2 |
| Fourth Round | Wigan Ath (*aet; won 4-2 on pens*) | | (a) | 0-0 |
| Quarter-Finals | Arsenal (*aet; won 3-2 on pens*) | | (h) | 1-1 |
| Semi-Finals | Aston Villa | (h) 3-1 | (a) | 1-2 |
| Final (*at Wembley*) | Swansea C | | | 0-5 |

**League Two Play-Offs**

| | | | | |
|---|---|---|---|---|
| Semi-Finals | Burton Alb | (h) 2-3 | (a) | 3-1 |
| Final (*at Wembley*) | Northampton T | | | 3-0 |

# BRENTFORD

## FOUNDATION

Formed as a small amateur concern in 1889 they were very successful in local circles. They won the championship of the West London Alliance in 1893 and a year later the West Middlesex Junior Cup before carrying off the Senior Cup in 1895. After winning both the London Senior Amateur Cup and the Middlesex Senior Cup in 1898 they were admitted to the Second Division of the Southern League.

*Griffin Park, Braemar Road, Brentford, Middlesex TW8 0NT.*

*Telephone:* (0845) 3456 442.

*Fax:* (020) 8380 9937.

*Ticket Office:* (0845) 3456 442 (option 4).

*Website:* www.brentfordfc.co.uk

*Email:* enquiries@brentfordfc.co.uk

*Ground Capacity:* 12,763.

*Record Attendance:* 38,678 v Leicester C, FA Cup 6th rd, 26 February 1949.

*Pitch Measurements:* 100m × 66m (110yd × 73yd)

*Chairman:* Greg Dyke.

*Chief Executive:* Mark Devlin.

*Manager:* Uwe Rosler.

*Assistant Manager:* Alan Kernaghan.

*Physio:* Ben Wood.

*Colours:* Red and white striped shirts, black shorts, black socks with red hoops.

*Year Formed:* 1889.

*Turned Professional:* 1899.

*Club Nickname:* 'The Bees'.

## HONOURS

**Football League – Division 1:** Best season: 5th, 1935–36;
**Division 2:** *Champions* 1934–35, 1994–95; **Division 3:** *Champions* 1991–92, 1998–99;
**Division 3 (S):** *Champions* 1932–33, *Runners-up* 1929–30, 1957–58;
**Division 4:** *Champions* 1962–63; **FL 2:** *Champions* 2008–09.
**FA Cup:** Best season: 6th rd, 1938, 1946, 1949, 1989.
**Football League Cup:** Best season: 4th rd, 1983, 2011.
**Freight Rover Trophy:** *Runners-up* 1985.
**LDV Vans Trophy:** *Runners-up* 2001.
**Johnstone's Paint Trophy:** *Runners-up* 2011.

*Grounds:* 1889, Clifden Road; 1891, Benns Fields, Little Ealing; 1895, Shotters Field; 1898, Cross Road, S. Ealing; 1900, Boston Park; 1904, Griffin Park.

*First Football League Game:* 28 August 1920, Division 3, v Exeter C (a) L 0–3 – Young; Hodson, Rosier, Jimmy Elliott, Levitt, Amos, Smith, Thompson, Spreadbury, Morley, Henery.

*Record League Victory:* 9–0 v Wrexham, Division 3, 15 October 1963 – Cakebread; Coote, Jones; Slater, Scott, Higginson; Summers (1), Brooks (2), McAdams (2), Ward (2), Hales (1), (1 og).

*Record Cup Victory:* 7–0 v Windsor & Eton (away), FA Cup 1st rd, 20 November 1982 – Roche; Rowe, Harris (Booker), McNichol (1), Whitehead, Hurlock (2), Kamara, Joseph (1), Mahoney (3), Bowles, Roberts. *N.B.* 8–0 v Uxbridge: Frail, Jock Watson, Caie, Bellingham, Parsonage (1), Jay, Atherton, Leigh (1), Bell (2), Buchanan (2), Underwood (2), FA Cup, 3rd Qual rd, 31 October 1903.

## sky SPORTS FACT FILE

Goalkeeper Joe Crozier made 200 peacetime League appearances for Brentford between 1937 and 1948. He spent much of the war as a guest player north of the border and won three wartime caps for Scotland, making his debut in the 8-0 defeat by England in October 1943.

*Record Defeat:* 0–7 v Swansea T, Division 3 (S), 8 November 1924; v Walsall, Division 3 (S), 19 January 1957; v Peterborough U, 24 November 2007.

*Most League Points (2 for a win):* 62, Division 3 (S), 1932–33 and Division 4, 1962–63.

*Most League Points (3 for a win):* 85, Division 2, 1994–95, Division 3, 1998–99 and FL 2, 2008–09.

*Most League Goals:* 98, Division 4, 1962–63.

*Highest League Scorer in Season:* Jack Holliday, 38, Division 3 (S), 1932–33.

*Most League Goals in Total Aggregate:* Jim Towers, 153, 1954–61.

*Most League Goals in One Match:* 5, Jack Holliday v Luton T, Division 3 (S), 28 January 1933; 5, Billy Scott v Barnsley, Division 2, 15 December 1934; 5, Peter McKennan v Bury, Division 2, 18 February 1949.

*Most Capped Player:* John Buttigieg, 22 (98), Malta.

*Most League Appearances:* Ken Coote, 514, 1949–64.

*Youngest League Player:* Danis Salman, 15 years 248 days v Watford, 15 November 1975.

*Record Transfer Fee Received:* £2,500,000 from Wimbledon for Hermann Hreidarsson, October 1999.

*Record Transfer Fee Paid:* £750,000 to Crystal Palace for Hermann Hreidarsson, September 1998.

*Football League Record:* 1920 Original Member of Division 3; 1921–33 Division 3 (S); 1933–35 Division 2; 1935–47 Division 1; 1947–54 Division 2; 1954–62 Division 3 (S); 1962–63 Division 4; 1963–66 Division 3; 1966–72 Division 4; 1972–73 Division 3; 1973–78 Division 4; 1978–92 Division 3; 1992–93 Division 1; 1993–98 Division 2; 1998–99 Division 3; 1999–04 Division 2; 2004–07 FL 1; 2007–09 FL 2; 2009– FL 1.

## LATEST SEQUENCES

*Longest Sequence of League Wins:* 9, 30.4.1932 – 24.9.1932.

*Longest Sequence of League Defeats:* 9, 20.10.1928 – 25.12.1928.

*Longest Sequence of League Draws:* 5, 16.3.1957 – 6.4.1957.

*Longest Sequence of Unbeaten League Matches:* 26, 20.2.1999 – 16.10.1999.

*Longest Sequence Without a League Win:* 18, 9.9.2006 – 26.12.2006.

*Successive Scoring Runs:* 26 from 4.3.1963.

*Successive Non-scoring Runs:* 7 from 7.3.2000.

### MANAGERS

Will Lewis 1900–03
  *(Secretary-Manager)*
Dick Molyneux 1902–06
W. G. Brown 1906–08
Fred Halliday 1908–12, 1915–21, 1924–26
  *(only Secretary to 1922)*
Ephraim Rhodes 1912–15
Archie Mitchell 1921–24
Harry Curtis 1926–49
Jackie Gibbons 1949–52
Jimmy Bain 1952–53
Tommy Lawton 1953
Bill Dodgin Snr 1953–57
Malcolm Macdonald 1957–65
Tommy Cavanagh 1965–66
Billy Gray 1966–67
Jimmy Sirrel 1967–69
Frank Blunstone 1969–73
Mike Everitt 1973–75
John Docherty 1975–76
Bill Dodgin Jnr 1976–80
Fred Callaghan 1980–84
Frank McLintock 1984–87
Steve Perryman 1987–90
Phil Holder 1990–93
David Webb 1993–97
Eddie May 1997
Micky Adams 1997–98
Ron Noades 1998–2000
Ray Lewington 2000–01
Steve Coppell 2001–02
Wally Downes 2002–04
Martin Allen 2004–06
Leroy Rosenior 2006
Scott Fitzgerald 2006–07
Terry Butcher 2007
Andy Scott 2007–11
Nicky Forster 2011
Uwe Rosler June 2011–

### TEN YEAR LEAGUE RECORD

| | | P | W | D | L | F | A | Pts | Pos |
|---|---|---|---|---|---|---|---|---|---|
| 2003-04 | Div 2 | 46 | 14 | 11 | 21 | 52 | 69 | 53 | 17 |
| 2004-05 | FL 1 | 46 | 22 | 9 | 15 | 57 | 60 | 75 | 4 |
| 2005-06 | FL 1 | 46 | 20 | 16 | 10 | 72 | 52 | 76 | 3 |
| 2006-07 | FL 1 | 46 | 8 | 13 | 25 | 40 | 79 | 37 | 24 |
| 2007-08 | FL 2 | 46 | 17 | 8 | 21 | 52 | 70 | 59 | 14 |
| 2008-09 | FL 2 | 46 | 23 | 16 | 7 | 65 | 36 | 85 | 1 |
| 2009-10 | FL 1 | 46 | 14 | 20 | 12 | 55 | 52 | 62 | 9 |
| 2010-11 | FL 1 | 46 | 17 | 10 | 19 | 55 | 62 | 61 | 11 |
| 2011-12 | FL 1 | 46 | 18 | 13 | 15 | 63 | 52 | 67 | 9 |
| 2012-13 | FL 1 | 46 | 21 | 16 | 9 | 62 | 47 | 79 | 3 |

### DID YOU KNOW ?

Bill Dodgin was manager of Brentford from October 1953 to May 1957. His son, also Bill Dodgin, was in charge of the Bees from September 1976 to March 1980, winning promotion from the old Fourth Division in 1977–78.

## BRENTFORD – FOOTBALL LEAGUE ONE 2012–13 LEAGUE RECORD

| Match No. | Date | Venue | Opponents | Result | H/T Score | Lg Pos. | Goalscorers | Attendance |
|---|---|---|---|---|---|---|---|---|
| 1 | Aug 18 | A | Bury | D 0-0 | 0-0 | 13 | | 2659 |
| 2 | 21 | H | Yeovil T | L 1-3 | 0-1 | 18 | Donaldson [55] | 5269 |
| 3 | 25 | H | Crewe Alex | W 5-1 | 3-0 | 9 | Donaldson 2 [13, 89], El Alagui 2 [20, 45], Dean [84] | 4858 |
| 4 | Sept 1 | A | Walsall | D 2-2 | 0-2 | 11 | Douglas [86], Donaldson [90] | 3434 |
| 5 | 8 | H | Colchester U | W 1-0 | 0-0 | 6 | El Alagui [88] | 5499 |
| 6 | 13 | A | Leyton Orient | L 0-1 | 0-0 | 8 | | 3333 |
| 7 | 18 | A | Bournemouth | D 2-2 | 1-2 | 12 | Francis (og) [10], Forrester [68] | 5117 |
| 8 | 22 | H | Oldham Ath | W 1-0 | 1-0 | 9 | Forshaw [17] | 5251 |
| 9 | 29 | A | Tranmere R | D 1-1 | 0-0 | 11 | Douglas [90] | 5720 |
| 10 | Oct 2 | H | Shrewsbury T | D 0-0 | 0-0 | 10 | | 4384 |
| 11 | 6 | H | Crawley T | W 2-1 | 1-0 | 9 | Donaldson 2 [23, 76] | 5607 |
| 12 | 13 | A | Scunthorpe U | D 1-1 | 1-0 | 8 | Forrester [43] | 3008 |
| 13 | 20 | A | Doncaster R | L 1-2 | 1-0 | 10 | Douglas [45] | 6555 |
| 14 | 23 | H | Coventry C | W 2-1 | 1-1 | 9 | Forrester 2 (1 pen) [41, 90 (p)] | 5415 |
| 15 | 27 | H | Hartlepool U | D 2-2 | 1-1 | 11 | Hayes 2 [11, 58] | 5213 |
| 16 | Nov 6 | A | Portsmouth | W 1-0 | 1-0 | 8 | Donaldson [9] | 11,328 |
| 17 | 10 | H | Carlisle U | W 2-1 | 1-1 | 8 | Douglas [20], Hayes [61] | 6763 |
| 18 | 17 | A | Preston NE | D 1-1 | 0-0 | 9 | German [89] | 8804 |
| 19 | 20 | A | Swindon T | W 1-0 | 0-0 | 7 | Donaldson [59] | 7431 |
| 20 | 24 | H | Sheffield U | W 2-0 | 2-0 | 5 | Donaldson [3], Forrester [29] | 7763 |
| 21 | Dec 8 | H | Milton Keynes D | W 3-2 | 1-1 | 4 | Donaldson 2 [43, 89], Forrester [72] | 5833 |
| 22 | 15 | A | Notts Co | W 2-1 | 1-1 | 2 | Forshaw [36], Donaldson [88] | 5307 |
| 23 | 26 | A | Colchester U | W 3-1 | 2-1 | 3 | Trotta [4], Forshaw [12], Dean [85] | 4200 |
| 24 | 29 | A | Shrewsbury T | D 0-0 | 0-0 | 4 | | 5715 |
| 25 | Jan 1 | H | Bournemouth | D 0-0 | 0-0 | 4 | | 8059 |
| 26 | 12 | A | Oldham Ath | W 2-0 | 1-0 | 3 | Donaldson 2 [5, 82] | 4615 |
| 27 | 19 | H | Tranmere R | L 1-2 | 0-1 | 4 | Dean [50] | 6948 |
| 28 | 22 | H | Leyton Orient | D 2-2 | 2-1 | 3 | Hayes [16], Donaldson [39] | 4523 |
| 29 | Feb 2 | A | Yeovil T | L 0-3 | 0-2 | 5 | | 4106 |
| 30 | 9 | H | Bury | D 2-2 | 0-0 | 6 | Forrester [52], Trotta [68] | 5137 |
| 31 | 12 | H | Stevenage | W 2-0 | 1-0 | 6 | Adeyemi [44], Trotta [86] | 7022 |
| 32 | 23 | H | Walsall | D 0-0 | 0-0 | 7 | | 4781 |
| 33 | 26 | A | Crawley T | W 2-1 | 2-0 | 5 | Saunders [16], Donaldson [32] | 2544 |
| 34 | Mar 2 | H | Scunthorpe U | W 1-0 | 0-0 | 4 | Adeyemi [70] | 5400 |
| 35 | 5 | A | Stevenage | L 0-1 | 0-0 | 5 | | 2794 |
| 36 | 9 | A | Carlisle U | L 0-2 | 0-1 | 6 | | 3858 |
| 37 | 12 | H | Swindon T | W 2-1 | 1-0 | 3 | Saunders (pen) [72], Donaldson [76] | 5867 |
| 38 | 16 | H | Preston NE | W 1-0 | 0-0 | 4 | Saunders (pen) [90] | 6512 |
| 39 | 29 | H | Notts Co | W 2-1 | 1-0 | 3 | Diagouraga [21], Wright-Phillips [70] | 7412 |
| 40 | Apr 1 | A | Milton Keynes D | L 0-2 | 0-1 | 3 | | 10,455 |
| 41 | 6 | A | Coventry C | D 1-1 | 0-1 | 4 | Forrester [47] | 10,642 |
| 42 | 10 | A | Crewe Alex | W 2-0 | 1-0 | 3 | Wright-Phillips [12], Trotta [83] | 4594 |
| 43 | 13 | H | Portsmouth | W 3-2 | 1-1 | 3 | Wright-Phillips 2 [21, 85], Donaldson [86] | 9149 |
| 44 | 16 | A | Sheffield U | D 2-2 | 1-0 | 2 | Trotta (pen) [24], Wright-Phillips [89] | 23,431 |
| 45 | 20 | A | Hartlepool U | D 1-1 | 1-1 | 3 | Trotta [39] | 3541 |
| 46 | 27 | H | Doncaster R | L 0-1 | 0-0 | 3 | | 12,300 |

**Final League Position: 3**

## GOALSCORERS

*League (62):* Donaldson 18, Forrester 8 (1 pen), Trotta 6 (1 pen), Wright-Phillips 5, Douglas 4, Hayes 4, Dean 3, El Alagui 3, Forshaw 3, Saunders 3 (2 pens), Adeyemi 2, Diagouraga 1, German 1, own goal 1.
*FA Cup (13):* Donaldson 4, Forrester 3 (1 pen), Trotta 3 (1 pen), Adeyemi 1, Hayes 1, own goal 1.
*Capital One Cup (0).*
*Johnstone's Paint Trophy (2):* Hayes 1, Saunders 1.
*League One Play-Offs (5):* Donaldson 2, Dean 1, O'Connor 1, own goal 1.

| Moore S 43 | Legge L 3+4 | Dean H 44 | Craig T 44 | Logan S 41+4 | Forshaw A 37+6 | Douglas J 44 | Diagouraga T 28+11 | Barron S 5+7 | Saunders S 13+18 | Donaldson C 43+1 | El Alagui F 7+4 | O'Connor K 6+6 | Fredericks R 1+3 | Hayes P 10+13 | Forrester H 25+11 | Bidwell J 37+3 | Adeyemi T 21+9 | Dallas S 3+4 | Spencer J —+2 | Lee R 3 | German A —+2 | Kiernan R 5+3 | Trotta M 16+6 | Hodson L 7+6 | Reeves J 4+2 | Wright-Phillips B 10+5 | Moore L 6+1 | Adams C —+1 | Match No. |
|---|---|---|---|---|---|---|---|---|---|---|---|---|---|---|---|---|---|---|---|---|---|---|---|---|---|---|---|---|---|
| 1 | 2 | 3 | 4 | 5 | 6[2] | 7 | 8 | 9[3] | 10[1] | 11 | 12 | 13 | 14 | | | | | | | | | | | | | | | | 1 |
| 1 | 4 | | 3 | 2 | 9 | 7 | 8[2] | 5 | 6[1] | 10 | 11 | | | 12 | 13 | | | | | | | | | | | | | | 2 |
| 1 | 13 | 3 | 4 | 2 | | 8 | 6 | 5[2] | 9[3] | 11 | 10[1] | 7 | | 12 | 14 | | | | | | | | | | | | | | 3 |
| 1 | | 4 | 3 | 2 | 12 | 8 | 6[1] | 5[3] | 9 | 10 | 11 | | 7[2] | | 13 | | 14 | | | | | | | | | | | | 4 |
| 1 | | 4 | 3 | 2 | 7[3] | 8 | 9 | | 6[1] | 11[2] | 10 | | | | 13 | 12 | 5 | 14 | | | | | | | | | | | 5 |
| 1 | | 3 | 4 | 2 | 7[1] | 6 | 8 | | 14 | 10 | 13 | | | | 11[2] | 9[3] | 5 | 12 | | | | | | | | | | | 6 |
| 1 | 5 | 4 | 2 | | 7 | 6 | 8[1] | | | 10 | 11[2] | 14 | | | 13 | 12 | 3 | 9[3] | | | | | | | | | | | 7 |
| 1 | 14 | 4 | 3 | 2[3] | 7[1] | 8 | 12 | | 11[2] | 10 | | 13 | | | 9 | 5 | 6 | | | | | | | | | | | | 8 |
| 1 | | 4 | 3 | 2[3] | 14 | 9 | | | | | 13 | 12 | | 7 | 10[2] | 11 | 6[1] | 5 | 8 | | | | | | | | | | 9 |
| 1 | 3 | | 4 | 2 | 9 | 8 | | | | 11 | 10[2] | 6[1] | 14 | 13 | 12 | 5 | 7 | | | | | | | | | | | | 10 |
| 1 | | 3 | 4 | 2 | 6[3] | 7 | 8[1] | | | 10 | | 13 | 14 | | 11[2] | 9 | 5 | 12 | | | | | | | | | | | 11 |
| 1 | 4 | 3 | 2 | | 6[2] | 7 | 8 | | 12 | 11 | | | | 10[1] | 9[3] | 5 | 13 | 14 | | | | | | | | | | | 12 |
| 1 | 12 | 4 | 3 | 2 | 7[2] | 6 | 9 | | | 11 | | 13 | | | 10 | 5[1] | 8[3] | 14 | | | | | | | | | | | 13 |
| 1 | | 4 | 3 | 2 | 9 | 7 | 6[2] | | | 10 | | | | 11[1] | 8 | 5 | 13 | 12 | | | | | | | | | | | 14 |
| 1 | 12 | 4[1] | 3 | 2 | 6[3] | 8 | 7 | | | 10 | | | | 11[2] | 9 | 5 | 14 | 13 | | | | | | | | | | | 15 |
| | 4 | 3 | 2 | 9 | 7 | 8 | 13 | 14 | 10 | | 12[2] | | | | 11[3] | 5 | 6[1] | | 1 | | | | | | | | | | 16 |
| 1 | 4 | 3 | 2 | 10[2] | 7 | 8 | 12 | 13 | 11 | | | | | 9 | 6[1] | 5 | | | | | | | | | | | | | 17 |
| 1 | 4 | 3 | 2 | 7[3] | 8 | 9 | 12 | 10[2] | 11 | | | | | 13 | 6[1] | 5 | | | | | 14 | | | | | | | | 18 |
| 1 | 4 | 3 | 2 | 6[3] | 7 | 8 | 9[1] | 13 | 10 | | 11[2] | 12 | 5 | | | | | | | | 14 | | | | | | | | 19 |
| 1 | 4 | 3 | 2 | 10 | | 7 | | 12 | 11 | 13 | 6[1] | 5 | | | 8[2] | 9[3] | 14 | | | | | | | | | | | | 20 |
| 1 | 3 | 4 | 2 | 6[2] | 8 | 7[1] | | 11 | | 9 | 5 | | | 12 | 10[3] | 14 | 13 | | | | | | | | | | | | 21 |
| 1 | 4 | 3 | 2 | 7 | 8 | | 11 | | 13 | 9 | 5 | 12 | | 6[1] | 10[2] | | | | | | | | | | | | | | 22 |
| | 4 | 3 | 12 | 9[2] | 6 | 13 | | 8 | | 10[3] | 7• | | | | 14 | 11[1] | 2 | | | 1 | | | | | | | | | 23 |
| | 3 | 4 | 2 | 13 | 7 | 8 | | 10 | | 14 | 12 | 5 | | 9[2] | 6[3] | 11[1] | | | | 1 | | | | | | | | | 24 |
| 1 | 4 | 3 | 2[1] | 7[2] | 6 | 13 | | 10 | | 14 | 11 | 5 | 8 | | 9[3] | 12 | | | | | | | | | | | | | 25 |
| 1 | 5 | 4 | 2 | 10 | 9 | 12 | 13 | 14 | 7 | | 8[2] | 3 | | | 6[1] | 11[3] | | | | | | | | | | | | | 26 |
| 1 | 4 | 3 | 2 | 6 | 8 | 7[2] | | 13 | 10 | | 14 | 9[3] | 5 | | 11 | 12 | | | | | | | | | | | | | 27 |
| 1 | 4 | 3 | 13 | 8 | 7 | 14 | 12 | 11[3] | 9 | 10[2] | | | | | 5• | 6[1] | | 2 | | | | | | | | | | | 28 |
| 1 | 4 | 3 | 2 | 9[1] | 7 | | 13 | 10 | | 14 | 11[3] | 5 | 8 | | 6[2] | 12 | | | | | | | | | | | | | 29 |
| 1 | 3 | 4 | 2[1] | 7 | 8 | | 13 | 12 | 11 | 10[2] | 5 | 6 | | | 9 | | | | | | | | | | | | | | 30 |
| 1 | 4 | 3 | | 8[3] | 6 | 14 | | 13 | 9 | 10[1] | 11[2] | 5 | 7 | | 12 | | | | | | | | | | | | | | 31 |
| 1 | 4 | 3 | 2 | 9[3] | 7 | 13 | 14 | 8 | | 12 | 5 | 6[2] | | 11 | 10[1] | | | | | | | | | | | | | | 32 |
| 1 | 4 | 5 | 14 | 6• | 7 | 13 | 12 | 9[1] | 10 | | 8[3] | | | | | | | | 2 | | | | | | | 11[2] | 3 | | 33 |
| 1 | 3 | 4 | 2 | | 7 | 10[1] | | | | 6[3] | 14 | 13 | 12 | | 9 | | | | | | | 8[2] | 11 | 5 | | | | | 34 |
| 1 | 4 | 3 | 13 | 6 | 7 | | 10 | | | 12 | 2[2] | 8[3] | 14 | | | | 6 | | | | | 9[1] | 11 | 5 | | | | | 35 |
| 1 | 4 | 5 | 2 | 9[2] | 8 | 7 | | 10[1] | | | | 6 | | | 11 | | | | | | | 9[2] | 12 | 3 | 13 | | | | 36 |
| 1 | 3 | 5 | 2 | 7 | 8 | 14 | 12 | 10 | | | | 6[3] | 11[1] | | 9[2] | | | | | | | 13 | 4 | | | | | | 37 |
| 1 | 3 | 5[1] | 2 | 13 | 7 | 8 | | 6 | 11 | | 12 | 9[2] | | 14 | | | | | | | | 10[3] | 4 | | | | | | 38 |
| 1 | 3 | 4 | 2 | 12 | 7 | 8 | | 6[1] | 11 | | 14 | 5 | 9[2] | | | | | | | | | 10[3] | 13 | | | | | | 39 |
| 1 | 4 | 5 | 2 | 6 | 7 | 8 | 14 | 10[2] | | | 9[3] | 3 | | 13 | 11[1] | | | | | | 12 | | | | | | | | 40 |
| 1 | 4 | 3 | 2 | 6 | 7[1] | 12 | 14 | 11 | | 10[3] | 5 | 8 | | | 9[2] | | 13 | | | | | | | | | | | | 41 |
| 1 | 3 | 4 | 2 | 9[2] | 7 | 12 | | 6[1] | 10 | | 5 | 8 | | | 14 | 13 | 11[3] | | | | | | | | | | | | 42 |
| 1 | 4 | 3 | 2 | 9[3] | 8[1] | 5 | 7[2] | 10 | | 6 | | | | | 14 | 13 | 12 | 11 | | | | | | | | | | | 43 |
| 1 | 4 | 3• | 2 | 9[2] | | 7 | 13 | 10• | 12 | | 5 | | | | 11[3] | 6[1] | 8 | 14 | | | | | | | | | | | 44 |
| 1 | 4 | | 2 | 9 | 7 | | | 14 | 3 | | 12 | 5 | 13 | | 11[3] | 6[1] | 8[2] | 10 | | | | | | | | | | | 45 |
| 1 | 4 | | 2[1] | 12 | 7[3] | 6 | | 13 | 10 | 3 | | 9[2] | 5 | 8 | 14 | | 11 | | | | | | | | | | | | 46 |

## FA Cup

| | | | |
|---|---|---|---|
| First Round | Boreham Wood | (a) | 2-0 |
| Second Round | Bradford C | (a) | 1-1 |
| *Replay* | Bradford C | (h) | 4-2 |
| Third Round | Southend U | (a) | 2-2 |
| *Replay* | Southend U | (h) | 2-1 |
| Fourth Round | Chelsea | (h) | 2-2 |
| *Replay* | Chelsea | (a) | 0-4 |

## Capital One Cup

| | | | |
|---|---|---|---|
| First Round | Walsall | (a) | 0-1 |

## Johnstone's Paint Trophy

| | | | |
|---|---|---|---|
| Second Round | Crawley T | (h) | 1-0 |
| Southern Quarter-Finals | Southend U | (a) | 1-2 |

## League One Play-Offs

| | | | |
|---|---|---|---|
| Semi-Finals | Swindon T | (a) | 1-1 |
| | Swindon T | (h) | 3-3 |
| *(aet; won 5-4 on pens)* | | | |
| Final *(at Wembley)* | Yeovil T | | 1-2 |

# BRIGHTON & HOVE ALBION

## FOUNDATION

A professional club Brighton United was formed in November 1897 at the Imperial Hotel, Queen's Road, but folded in March 1900 after less than two seasons in the Southern League at the County Ground. An amateur team Brighton & Hove Rangers was then formed by some prominent United supporters and after one season at Withdean, decided to turn semi-professional and play at the County Ground. Rangers were accepted into the Southern League but folded in June 1901. John Jackson, the former United manager, organised a meeting at the Seven Stars public house, Ship Street on 24 June 1901 at which a new third club Brighton & Hove United was formed. They took over Rangers' place in the Southern League and pitch at County Ground. The name was changed to Brighton & Hove Albion before a match was played because of objections by Hove FC.

*American Express Community Stadium, Village Way, Falmer, Brighton BN1 9BL.*
*Telephone:* (0845) 873 0251.
*Fax:* (01273) 878 238.
*Ticket Office:* (0844) 327 1901.
*Website:* www.seagulls.co.uk
*Email:* customerservices@bhafc.co.uk
*Ground Capacity:* 30,250.
*Record Attendance:* 36,747 v Fulham, Division 2, 27 December 1958 (at Goldstone Ground); 8,691 v Leeds U, FL 1, 20 October 2007 (at Withdean); 30,003 v Wolverhampton W, 4 May 2013 (at Amex).
*Pitch Measurements:* 105m × 68m (115yd × 75yd)
*Chairman:* Tony Bloom.
*Chief Executive:* Paul Barber.
*Head Coach:* Óscar Garcia.
*Head of Sports Medicine and Science:* Nathan Ring.
*Colours:* Blue and white striped shirts with white sleeves and yellow trim, blue shorts, white socks with thin yellow stripes.
*Year Formed:* 1901.
*Turned Professional:* 1901.
*Club Nickname:* 'The Seagulls'.
*Grounds:* 1901, County Ground; 1902, Goldstone Ground; 1997, groundshare at Gillingham FC; 1999, Withdean Stadium; 2011, American Express Community Stadium.
*First Football League Game:* 28 August 1920, Division 3, v Southend U (a) L 0–2 – Hayes; Woodhouse, Little; Hall, Comber, Bentley; Longstaff, Ritchie, Doran, Rodgerson, March.
*Record League Victory:* 9–1 v Newport Co, Division 3 (S), 18 April 1951 – Ball; Tennant (1p); Mansell (1p); Willard, McCoy, Wilson; Reed, McNichol (4), Garbutt, Bennett (2), Keene (1). 9–1 v Southend U, Division 3, 27 November 1965 – Powney; Magill, Baxter; Leck, Gall, Turner; Gould (1), Collins (1), Livesey (2), Smith (3), Goodchild (2).

## HONOURS

**Football League – Division 1:** Best season: 13th, 1981–82;
**Division 2:** *Champions* 2001–02;
*Runners-up* 1978–79;
**FL 1:** *Champions* 2010–11.
**Division 3 (S):** *Champions* 1957–58;
*Runners-up* 1953–54, 1955–56;
**Division 3:** *Champions* 2000–01;
*Runners-up* 1971–72, 1976–77, 1987–88;
**Division 4:** *Champions* 1964–65.
**FA Cup:** *Runners-up* 1983.
**Football League Cup:** Best season: 5th rd, 1979.
**Charity Shield:** *Winners* 1910.

## sky SPORTS FACT FILE

Brighton were only saved from relegation to the Conference on the final day of the 1996–97 season when a second-half equaliser from Robbie Reinelt earned them a draw at Hereford. The point meant that Albion stayed above Hereford on goal difference with the Bulls dropping out of the League.

**Record Cup Victory:** 10–1 v Wisbech, FA Cup 1st rd, 13 November 1965 – Powney; Magill, Baxter; Collins (1), Gall, Turner; Gould, Smith (2), Livesey (3), Cassidy (2), Goodchild (1), (1 og).

**Record Defeat:** 0–9 v Middlesbrough, Division 2, 23 August 1958.

**Most League Points (2 for a win):** 65, Division 3 (S), 1955–56 and Division 3, 1971–72.

**Most League Points (3 for a win):** 95, FL 1, 2010–11.

**Most League Goals:** 112, Division 3 (S), 1955–56.

**Highest League Scorer in Season:** Peter Ward, 32, Division 3, 1976–77.

**Most League Goals in Total Aggregate:** Tommy Cook, 114, 1922–29.

**Most League Goals in One Match:** 5, Jack Doran v Northampton T, Division 3 (S), 5 November 1921; 5, Adrian Thorne v Watford, Division 3 (S), 30 April 1958.

**Most Capped Player:** Steve Penney, 17, Northern Ireland.

**Most League Appearances:** 'Tug' Wilson, 509, 1922–36.

**Youngest League Player:** Ian Chapman, 16 years 259 days v Birmingham C, 14 February 1987.

**Record Transfer Fee Received:** £1,500,000 from Tottenham H for Bobby Zamora, July 2003; £1,500,000 from Celtic for Adam Virgo, July 2005; £1,500,000 from Norwich C for Elliott Bennett, June 2011.

**Record Transfer Fee Paid:** £2,500,000 to Peterborough U for Craig Mackail-Smith, July 2011.

**Football League Record:** 1920 Original Member of Division 3; 1921–58 Division 3 (S); 1958–62 Division 2; 1962–63 Division 3; 1963–65 Division 4; 1965–72 Division 3; 1972–73 Division 2; 1973–77 Division 3; 1977–79 Division 2; 1979–83 Division 1; 1983–87 Division 2; 1987–88 Division 3; 1988–96 Division 2; 1996–2001 Division 3; 2001–02 Division 2; 2002–03 Division 1; 2003–04 Division 2; 2004–06 FL C; 2006–11 FL 1; 2011– FL C.

## MANAGERS

John Jackson 1901–05
Frank Scott-Walford 1905–08
John Robson 1908–14
Charles Webb 1919–47
Tommy Cook 1947
Don Welsh 1947–51
Billy Lane 1951–61
George Curtis 1961–63
Archie Macaulay 1963–68
Fred Goodwin 1968–70
Pat Saward 1970–73
Brian Clough 1973–74
Peter Taylor 1974–76
Alan Mullery 1976–81
Mike Bailey 1981–82
Jimmy Melia 1982–83
Chris Cattlin 1983–86
Alan Mullery 1986–87
Barry Lloyd 1987–93
Liam Brady 1993–95
Jimmy Case 1995–96
Steve Gritt 1996–98
Brian Horton 1998–99
Jeff Wood 1999
Micky Adams 1999–2001
Peter Taylor 2001–02
Martin Hinshelwood 2002
Steve Coppell 2002–03
Mark McGhee 2003–06
Dean Wilkins 2006–08
Micky Adams 2008–09
Russell Slade 2009
Gus Poyet 2009–13
Óscar Garcia June 2013–

## LATEST SEQUENCES

**Longest Sequence of League Wins:** 9, 2.10.1926 – 20.11.1926.

**Longest Sequence of League Defeats:** 12, 17.8.2002 – 26.10.2002.

**Longest Sequence of League Draws:** 6, 16.2.1980 – 15.3.1980.

**Longest Sequence of Unbeaten League Matches:** 16, 8.10.1930 – 28.1.1931.

**Longest Sequence Without a League Win:** 15, 21.10.1972 – 27.1.1973

**Successive Scoring Runs:** 31 from 4.2.1956.

**Successive Non-scoring Runs:** 6 from 8.11.1924.

## TEN YEAR LEAGUE RECORD

| | | P | W | D | L | F | A | Pts | Pos |
|---|---|---|---|---|---|---|---|---|---|
| 2003-04 | Div 2 | 46 | 22 | 11 | 13 | 64 | 43 | 77 | 4 |
| 2004-05 | FL C | 46 | 13 | 12 | 21 | 40 | 65 | 51 | 20 |
| 2005-06 | FL C | 46 | 7 | 17 | 22 | 39 | 71 | 38 | 24 |
| 2006-07 | FL 1 | 46 | 14 | 11 | 21 | 49 | 58 | 53 | 18 |
| 2007-08 | FL 1 | 46 | 19 | 12 | 15 | 58 | 50 | 69 | 7 |
| 2008-09 | FL 1 | 46 | 13 | 13 | 20 | 55 | 70 | 52 | 16 |
| 2009-10 | FL 1 | 46 | 15 | 14 | 17 | 56 | 60 | 59 | 13 |
| 2010-11 | FL 1 | 46 | 28 | 11 | 7 | 85 | 40 | 95 | 1 |
| 2011-12 | FL C | 46 | 17 | 15 | 14 | 52 | 52 | 66 | 10 |
| 2012-13 | FL C | 46 | 19 | 18 | 9 | 69 | 43 | 75 | 4 |

## DID YOU KNOW ?

Centre forward Arthur Attwood scored in eight consecutive League and FA Cup games for Brighton in 1931–32 and then repeated the feat the following season. Arthur, who was signed from Bristol Rovers in November 1931, finished as leading scorer for Albion in each of the two campaigns.

## BRIGHTON & HOVE ALBION – FL CHAMPIONSHIP 2012–13 LEAGUE RECORD

| Match No. | Date | Venue | Opponents | Result | H/T Score | Lg Pos. | Goalscorers | Attendance |
|---|---|---|---|---|---|---|---|---|
| 1 | Aug 18 | A | Hull C | L 0-1 | 0-0 | 17 | | 15,794 |
| 2 | 21 | H | Cardiff C | D 0-0 | 0-0 | 21 | | 25,518 |
| 3 | 25 | H | Barnsley | W 5-1 | 3-1 | 10 | Barnes 2 [4, 81], Bridge [14], Mackail-Smith 2 [38, 50] | 24,594 |
| 4 | Sept 1 | A | Burnley | W 3-1 | 1-0 | 4 | Mackail-Smith 2 [18, 77], Greer [88] | 11,413 |
| 5 | 14 | H | Sheffield W | W 3-0 | 1-0 | 1 | Bridge [24], Mackail-Smith [54], Buckley [58] | 26,594 |
| 6 | 18 | A | Watford | W 1-0 | 0-0 | 3 | Mackail-Smith (pen) [50] | 11,894 |
| 7 | 22 | H | Millwall | W 2-1 | 1-0 | 1 | Barnes [17], El-Abd [50] | 12,191 |
| 8 | 29 | H | Birmingham C | L 0-1 | 0-1 | 1 | | 26,121 |
| 9 | Oct 2 | H | Ipswich T | D 1-1 | 0-1 | 3 | Buckley [80] | 24,736 |
| 10 | 6 | A | Derby Co | D 0-0 | 0-0 | 5 | | 22,059 |
| 11 | 20 | H | Middlesbrough | L 0-1 | 0-1 | 8 | | 26,293 |
| 12 | 23 | A | Leicester C | L 0-1 | 0-1 | 9 | | 25,726 |
| 13 | 27 | A | Blackpool | D 1-1 | 0-0 | 10 | Barnes [56] | 14,038 |
| 14 | Nov 2 | H | Leeds U | D 2-2 | 1-1 | 9 | Mackail-Smith 2 (1 pen) [16 (p), 48] | 26,402 |
| 15 | 6 | H | Peterborough U | W 1-0 | 0-0 | 8 | Dobbie [90] | 23,703 |
| 16 | 10 | A | Wolverhampton W | D 3-3 | 1-1 | 8 | Mackail-Smith [43], Buckley [72], Dobbie (pen) [89] | 21,583 |
| 17 | 17 | A | Huddersfield T | W 2-1 | 2-0 | 7 | Buckley 2 [5, 40] | 13,299 |
| 18 | 24 | H | Bolton W | D 1-1 | 0-0 | 8 | Saltor [54] | 26,455 |
| 19 | 27 | H | Bristol C | W 2-0 | 2-0 | 7 | Hammond [6], Orlandi [26] | 24,044 |
| 20 | Dec 1 | A | Crystal Palace | L 0-3 | 0-1 | 8 | | 20,114 |
| 21 | 8 | A | Charlton Ath | D 2-2 | 1-1 | 8 | Mackail-Smith [28], LuaLua [75] | 19,018 |
| 22 | 15 | H | Nottingham F | D 0-0 | 0-0 | 8 | | 26,684 |
| 23 | 18 | H | Millwall | D 2-2 | 1-1 | 8 | LuaLua [61], Lopez (pen) [88] | 24,773 |
| 24 | 29 | H | Watford | L 1-3 | 0-0 | 10 | Lopez (pen) [65] | 26,727 |
| 25 | Jan 1 | A | Ipswich T | W 3-0 | 2-0 | 9 | Hammond [15], Mackail-Smith [34], Bridge [67] | 19,018 |
| 26 | 12 | H | Derby Co | W 2-1 | 2-0 | 8 | Barnes [2], Orlandi [25] | 25,464 |
| 27 | 19 | A | Birmingham C | D 2-2 | 2-1 | 8 | Barnes [24], Lopez [43] | 15,299 |
| 28 | 22 | A | Blackburn R | D 1-1 | 0-1 | 7 | Lopez (pen) [90] | 12,230 |
| 29 | Feb 2 | A | Sheffield W | L 1-3 | 0-2 | 8 | Orlandi [54] | 22,044 |
| 30 | 9 | H | Hull C | W 1-0 | 0-0 | 7 | Vicente [83] | 25,367 |
| 31 | 12 | H | Blackburn R | D 1-1 | 0-1 | 7 | Vicente (pen) [57] | 24,759 |
| 32 | 19 | A | Cardiff C | W 2-0 | 1-0 | 7 | Orlandi [43], Ulloa [90] | 23,782 |
| 33 | 23 | H | Burnley | W 1-0 | 1-0 | 6 | Lopez [20] | 25,836 |
| 34 | Mar 2 | H | Huddersfield T | W 4-1 | 1-1 | 6 | Ulloa 3 [20, 76, 78], Lopez (pen) [81] | 25,831 |
| 35 | 5 | A | Bristol C | D 0-0 | 0-0 | 6 | | 12,267 |
| 36 | 9 | A | Bolton W | L 0-1 | 0-1 | 7 | | 17,599 |
| 37 | 12 | A | Barnsley | L 1-2 | 0-1 | 7 | Ulloa [59] | 7869 |
| 38 | 17 | H | Crystal Palace | W 3-0 | 2-0 | 7 | Ulloa 2 [43, 50], Lopez [45] | 28,499 |
| 39 | 30 | A | Nottingham F | D 2-2 | 0-0 | 6 | Ulloa [57], Buckley [85] | 28,124 |
| 40 | Apr 2 | H | Charlton Ath | D 0-0 | 0-0 | 6 | | 28,043 |
| 41 | 6 | A | Leicester C | D 1-1 | 0-0 | 6 | LuaLua [88] | 28,493 |
| 42 | 13 | A | Middlesbrough | W 2-0 | 0-0 | 5 | Orlandi [60], Lopez [76] | 14,925 |
| 43 | 16 | A | Peterborough U | D 0-0 | 0-0 | 4 | | 8780 |
| 44 | 20 | H | Blackpool | W 6-1 | 3-0 | 4 | Buckley [9], Upson [23], Orlandi [45], Lopez [46], Barnes 2 [76, 90] | 28,499 |
| 45 | 27 | A | Leeds U | W 2-1 | 1-0 | 4 | Buckley [10], Ulloa [88] | 24,904 |
| 46 | May 4 | H | Wolverhampton W | W 2-0 | 2-0 | 4 | LuaLua 2 [5, 39] | 30,003 |

**Final League Position: 4**

## GOALSCORERS

*League (69):* Barnes 8, Buckley 8, Orlandi 6, LuaLua 5, Bridge 3, Mackail-Smith 11 (2 pens), Lopez 9 (4 pens), Ulloa 9, Dobbie 2 (1 pen), Hammond 2, Vicente 2 (1 pen), El-Abd 1, Greer 1, Saltor 1, Upson 1.
*FA Cup (4):* Barnes 1, Hoskins 1, Orlandi 1, Ulloa 1.
*Capital One Cup (0).*
Championship Play-Offs (0).

| Kuszczak T 43 | Saltor B 29+1 | Greer G 37+1 | El-Abd A 31+1 | Bridge W 37 | Crofts A 17+7 | Dicker G 12+11 | Bridcutt L 41 | Barnes A 26+8 | Mackail-Smith C 24+5 | Noone C 3 | LuaLua K 8+14 | Agdestein T —+2 | Harley R —+2 | Vicente R 6+6 | Buckley W 28+8 | Orlandi A 30+5 | Hammond D 31+6 | Dobbie S 5+10 | Lopez D 27+4 | Calderon I 18+10 | Dunk L 7+1 | Hoskins W 4+7 | Brezovan P 1 | Painter M 5 | Upson M 18 | Ulloa J 16+1 | Forster-Caskey J —+3 | Barker G —+3 | Ankergren C 2+1 | Match No. |
|---|---|---|---|---|---|---|---|---|---|---|---|---|---|---|---|---|---|---|---|---|---|---|---|---|---|---|---|---|---|---|
| 1 | 2 | 3 | 4 | 5 | 6 | $7^2$ | 8 | 9 | 10 | $11^1$ | 12 | 13 | | | | | | | | | | | | | | | | | | 1 |
| 1 | 2 | 3 | 4 | 5 | 6 | $7^3$ | 8 | $9^1$ | 11 | $10^2$ | 12 | | 13 | 14 | | | | | | | | | | | | | | | | 2 |
| 1 | 2 | 3 | 4 | 5 | $6^1$ | 7 | 8 | $11^3$ | 10 | $9^2$ | | 13 | 14 | 12 | | | | | | | | | | | | | | | | 3 |
| 1 | 2 | 3 | 4 | 5 | $7^1$ | 8 | 6 | 11 | 10 | | | | | $9^2$ | 12 | 13 | | | | | | | | | | | | | | 4 |
| 1 | 2 | 3 | 4 | 5 | | 8 | 7 | $11^3$ | $10^1$ | | | | | $9^2$ | 12 | 13 | | | | | | | | | | | | | | 5 |
| 1 | $2^2$ | 3 | 4 | 5 | | 8 | 9 | 12 | $11^2$ | | | | | 10 | $7^1$ | 6 | 13 | 14 | | | | | | | | | | | | 6 |
| 1 | $2^2$ | 3 | 4 | 5 | | 12 | 6 | 10 | $11^1$ | | 14 | | | 7 | $8^3$ | 9 | 13 | | | | | | | | | | | | | 7 |
| 1 | | 3 | $4^1$ | 5 | | 7 | 8 | 9 | 13 | | $11^2$ | | | 6 | 10 | 12 | 2 | | | | | | | | | | | | | 8 |
| 1 | | 3 | 4 | 5 | 13 | 7 | 9 | $11^1$ | 12 | | $8^3$ | | | $6^2$ | 10 | 14 | 2 | | | | | | | | | | | | | 9 |
| 1 | 2 | 3 | 4 | 5 | 9 | 6 | 11 | $7^1$ | $10^3$ | | | | | 13 | 12 | 8 | | | | | | | | | | | | | | 10 |
| 1 | 2 | 3 | $4^2$ | 5 | $8^1$ | 7 | 9 | 11 | 14 | | 12 | | | 6 | 13 | $10^3$ | | | | | | | | | | | | | | 11 |
| 1 | 2 | 3 | 4 | 5 | $8^2$ | $7^1$ | 6 | 10 | 11 | | | | | 9 | 13 | 12 | | | | | | | | | | | | | | 12 |
| 1 | 2 | 3 | 4 | 5 | 7 | $9^1$ | 10 | $11^2$ | | | | | | 6 | 12 | 8 | 13 | | | | | | | | | | | | | 13 |
| 1 | 2 | 3 | 4 | 5 | 13 | 12 | 8 | $9^1$ | 10 | | | | | 11 | $7^1$ | $6^2$ | 14 | | | | | | | | | | | | | 14 |
| 1 | 2 | 3 | | 5 | $7^1$ | | 11 | $10^2$ | | | | | | 9 | $8^3$ | 6 | 12 | 14 | | 4 | 13 | | | | | | | | | 15 |
| 1 | 2 | 3 | | $5^1$ | $6^3$ | | 7 | 13 | 11 | | | | | 14 | 9 | | 8 | $10^2$ | 12 | 4 | | | | | | | | | | 16 |
| | 2 | 3 | | | | | 12 | 9 | $8^1$ | $11^2$ | | | | | 6 | 7 | 10 | | 14 | 4 | 13 | 1 | $5^3$ | | | | | | | 17 |
| 1 | 2 | 3 | | | | | 12 | 8 | $9^1$ | $10^3$ | | | | | 11 | 7 | 6 | | 13 | 4 | 14 | | | $5^2$ | | | | | | 18 |
| 1 | 2 | 3 | | | | | 13 | 6 | 12 | | | | | | 9 | 8 | 7 | $10^1$ | | 14 | 4 | $11^2$ | | $5^3$ | | | | | | 19 |
| 1 | 2 | 3 | | | | | 12 | 13 | 8 | 10 | 11 | | | | $6^2$ | $9^1$ | 7 | | | 5 | $4$■ | | | | | | | | | 20 |
| 1 | $2^3$ | 3 | 4 | 5 | | | 8 | 12 | 11 | | 13 | | | | 9 | | 7 | $6^1$ | | 14 | | $10^2$ | | | | | | | | 21 |
| 1 | | 4 | 5 | 3 | 6 | | $8^3$ | 13 | 10 | | 12 | | | 11 | | 14 | | | $7^2$ | 2 | | $9^1$ | | | | | | | | 22 |
| 1 | | 3 | 2 | 6 | $9^2$ | | $7^3$ | 13 | 10 | | 12 | | | 8 | | 5 | | | 11 | $4$■ | 14 | | | | | | | | | 23 |
| 1 | 2 | 3 | 4 | 5 | $6^3$ | | 8 | 12 | 9 | | 11 | | | $7^1$ | | 14 | $10^2$ | | 13 | | | | | | | | | | | 24 |
| 1 | | 4 | 3 | 5 | | | 12 | 6 | 9 | $10^3$ | $11^1$ | | | $8^2$ | 7 | 14 | 2 | | 13 | | | | | | | | | | | 25 |
| 1 | | 3 | 4 | 5 | 14 | | 12 | 8 | 11 | | 13 | | | $9^2$ | $6^1$ | 7 | $10^3$ | | 2 | | | | | | | | | | | 26 |
| 1 | | 3 | 4 | 5 | 13 | | 8 | 6 | $10^3$ | | 14 | | | 12 | $9^2$ | 7 | $11^1$ | | 2 | | | | | | | | | | | 27 |
| 1 | | 3 | 4 | 5 | | | 8 | 6 | $9^1$ | 13 | | | | $11^1$ | 12 | $7^2$ | | | 10 | 2 | | 14 | | | | | | | | 28 |
| 1 | | 3 | 5 | | | | $6^1$ | $8$■ | 12 | | | | | 13 | | 7 | 9 | | 10 | 2 | | | | | | 4 | $11^2$ | | | 29 |
| 1 | $2^2$ | 3 | 5 | | | | 8 | | $10^3$ | | | | | 12 | 13 | 9 | $6^1$ | | 7 | 14 | | | | | | 4 | 11 | | | 30 |
| 1 | 2 | 3 | 5 | | | | 8 | | | 13 | | | | 7 | $11^2$ | 12 | 6 | | | $9^1$ | | | | | | 4 | 10 | | | 31 |
| 1 | 2 | 3 | 5 | | 12 | | 9 | | | | | | | $6^3$ | $10^1$ | $7^2$ | | | 8 | 13 | | | | | | 4 | 11 | 14 | | 32 |
| 1 | 2 | 14 | 3 | 5 | | | 8 | 13 | 12 | | | | | $7^3$ | | $9^1$ | 6 | | 11 | | | | | | | 4 | $10^2$ | | | 33 |
| 1 | 2 | 3 | | | $7^1$ | | 12 | 13 | | | | | | $11^2$ | 9 | 6 | | | 8 | 5 | | | | | | 4 | $10^3$ | 14 | | 34 |
| 1 | 2 | 3 | | | | 6 | | 10$^1$ | | | | | | 9 | 11 | 7 | | | 8 | 5 | | | | | | 4 | 12 | | | 35 |
| 1 | 2 | 3 | $5^2$ | $6^1$ | | 7 | $8$■ | | | | | | | 9 | 12 | 13 | | | 10 | | | | | | | 4 | 11 | | | 36 |
| 1 | $2^2$ | 3 | 13 | | 7 | | | 12 | | | | | | 9 | 11 | $8^3$ | | | $6^1$ | 5 | | | | | | 4 | 10 | 14 | | 37 |
| | | 3 | 5 | 12 | | 8 | | 11 | | | | | | 9 | $6^1$ | 13 | | | $7^2$ | 2 | | | | | | 4 | 10 | | | 38 |
| | | 3 | 5 | 7 | | | | $11^1$ | | | | | | 9 | $8^2$ | 12 | 6 | | 2 | 13 | | | | | | 4 | 10 | | 1 | 39 |
| 1 | | 3 | 5 | | 7 | | | 10 | | | | | | 9 | 6 | 8 | | | 2 | | | | | | | 4 | 11 | | | 40 |
| 1 | | 3 | 5 | 6 | | | 12 | 13 | | | | | | $9^1$ | $11^3$ | 7 | | | $8^2$ | 2 | | | | | | 4 | 10 | 14 | | 41 |
| | 4 | | 2 | 7 | 12 | 8 | | | | | | | | $10^2$ | 6 | $9^1$ | 3 | | | 5 | 11 | 13 | | | | | | 1 | 42 |
| 1 | | 3 | 5 | 10 | 6 | | | 9 | | | | | | 8 | 7 | 2 | | | | | | | | | | 4 | 11 | | | 43 |
| $1^1$ | 13 | 3 | $5^2$ | | 6 | 9 | | 14 | | | | | | $11^3$ | $10$ | 7 | 8 | | 2 | | | | | | 4 | | | 12 | | 44 |
| 1 | $2^3$ | 4 | | 12 | | 11 | | 13 | | | | | | $9^2$ | 8 | 7 | 6 | $14$■ | | | | | | | $5^1$ | 3 | 10 | | | 45 |
| 1 | | 3 | 12 | | 7 | | 6 | 9 | | $11^1$ | | | | $8^3$ | | 13 | 2 | | | | | | | | $5^2$ | 4 | 10 | 14 | | 46 |

**FA Cup**

| Third Round | Newcastle U | (h) | 2-0 |
|---|---|---|---|
| Fourth Round | Arsenal | (h) | 2-3 |

**Capital One Cup**

| First Round | Swindon T | (a) | 0-3 |
|---|---|---|---|

**Championship Play-Offs**

| Semi-Finals | Crystal Palace | (a) | 0-0 |
|---|---|---|---|
| | Crystal Palace | (h) | 0-2 |

# BRISTOL CITY

## FOUNDATION

The name Bristol City came into being in 1897 when the Bristol South End club, formed three years earlier, decided to adopt professionalism and apply for admission to the Southern League after competing in the Western League. The historic meeting was held at the Albert Hall, Bedminster. Bristol City employed Sam Hollis from Woolwich Arsenal as manager and gave him £40 to buy players. In 1900 they merged with Bedminster, another leading Bristol club.

*Ashton Gate Stadium, Bristol BS3 2EJ.*

*Telephone:* (0117) 963 0600.

*Fax:* (0117) 9630 700.

*Ticket Office:* (0117) 963 0600.

*Website:* www.bcfc.co.uk

*Email:* enquiries@bcfc.co.uk

*Ground Capacity:* 21,804.

*Record Attendance:* 43,335 v Preston NE, FA Cup 5th rd, 16 February 1935.

*Pitch Measurements:* 105m × 68m (115yd × 75yd)

*Chairman:* Keith Dawe.

*Managing Director, Football:* Jon Lansdown.

*Head Coach:* Sean O'Driscoll.

*Assistant Head Coach:* John Pemberton.

*Physio:* Michael McBride.

*Colours:* Red shirts with white trim, red shorts, red socks.

*Year Formed:* 1894.

*Turned Professional:* 1897.

*Previous Name:* 1894, Bristol South End; 1897, Bristol City.

*Club Nickname:* 'Robins'.

*Grounds:* 1894, St John's Lane; 1904, Ashton Gate.

*First Football League Game:* 7 September 1901, Division 2, v Blackpool (a) W 2–0 – Moles; Tuft, Davies; Jones, McLean, Chambers; Bradbury, Connor, Boucher, O'Brien (2), Flynn.

*Record League Victory:* 9–0 v Aldershot, Division 3 (S), 28 December 1946 – Eddols; Morgan, Fox; Peacock, Roberts, Jones (1); Chilcott, Thomas, Clark (4 incl. 1p), Cyril Williams (1), Hargreaves (3).

*Record Cup Victory:* 11–0 v Chichester C, FA Cup 1st rd, 5 November 1960 – Cook; Collinson, Thresher; Connor, Alan Williams, Etheridge; Tait (1), Bobby Williams (1), Atyeo (5), Adrian Williams (3), Derrick, (1 og).

## HONOURS

**Football League –**
**Division 1:** *Runners-up* 1906–07;
**Division 2:** *Champions* 1905–06;
*Runners-up* 1975–76, 1997–98;
**FL 1:** *Runners-up* 2006–07;
**Division 3 (S):** *Champions* 1922–23, 1926–27, 1954–55;
*Runners-up* 1937–38;
**Division 3:** *Runners-up* 1964–65, 1989–90.

**FA Cup:** *Runners-up* 1909.

**Football League Cup:** Semi-final 1971, 1989.

**Welsh Cup:** *Winners* 1934.

**Anglo-Scottish Cup:** *Winners* 1978.

**Freight Rover Trophy:** *Winners* 1986; *Runners-up* 1987.

**Auto Windscreens Shield:** *Runners-up* 2000.

**LDV Vans Trophy:** *Winners* 2003.

## sky SPORTS FACT FILE

Bristol City began the 1905–06 season with a 5-1 defeat away to Manchester United. The team only suffered one further loss all season. They won the next 14 games and went on to secure the Second Division title by four clear points from United.

*Record Defeat:* 0–9 v Coventry C, Division 3 (S), 28 April 1934.

*Most League Points (2 for a win):* 70, Division 3 (S), 1954–55.

*Most League Points (3 for a win):* 91, Division 3, 1989–90.

*Most League Goals:* 104, Division 3 (S), 1926–27.

*Highest League Scorer in Season:* Don Clark, 36, Division 3 (S), 1946–47.

*Most League Goals in Total Aggregate:* John Atyeo, 314, 1951–66.

*Most League Goals in One Match:* 6, Tommy 'Tot' Walsh v Gillingham, Division 3 (S), 15 January 1927.

*Most Capped Player:* Billy Wedlock, 26, England.

*Most League Appearances:* John Atyeo, 597, 1951–66.

*Youngest League Player:* Marvin Brown, 16 years 105 days v Bristol R, 17 October 1999.

*Record Transfer Fee Received:* £3,500,000 from Wolverhampton W for Ade Akinbiyi, September 1999.

*Record Transfer Fee Paid:* £2,250,000 to Crewe Alex for Nicky Maynard, August 2008.

*Football League Record:* 1901 Elected to Division 2; 1906–11 Division 1; 1911–22 Division 2; 1922–23 Division 3 (S); 1923–24 Division 2; 1924–27 Division 3 (S); 1927–32 Division 2; 1932–55 Division 3 (S); 1955–60 Division 2; 1960–65 Division 3; 1965–76 Division 2; 1976–80 Division 1; 1980–81 Division 2; 1981–82 Division 3; 1982–84 Division 4; 1984–90 Division 3; 1990–92 Division 2; 1992–95 Division 1; 1995–98 Division 2; 1998–99 Division 1; 1999–04 Division 2; 2004–07 FL 1; 2007–13 FL C; 2013– FL 1.

### LATEST SEQUENCES

*Longest Sequence of League Wins:* 14, 9.9.1905 – 2.12.1905.

*Longest Sequence of League Defeats:* 7, 3.10.1970 – 7.11.1970; 7, 6.10.2012 – 11.11.2012.

*Longest Sequence of League Draws:* 4, 6.11.1999 – 27.11.1999.

*Longest Sequence of Unbeaten League Matches:* 24, 9.9.1905 – 10.2.1906.

*Longest Sequence Without a League Win:* 15, 29.4.1933 – 4.11.1933.

*Successive Scoring Runs:* 25 from 26.12.1905.

*Successive Non-scoring Runs:* 6 from 10.9.1910.

## MANAGERS

Sam Hollis 1897–99
Bob Campbell 1899–1901
Sam Hollis 1901–05
Harry Thickett 1905–10
Frank Bacon 1910–11
Sam Hollis 1911–13
George Hedley 1913–17
Jack Hamilton 1917–19
Joe Palmer 1919–21
Alex Raisbeck 1921–29
Joe Bradshaw 1929–32
Bob Hewison 1932–49
  (*under suspension 1938–39*)
Bob Wright 1949–50
Pat Beasley 1950–58
Peter Doherty 1958–60
Fred Ford 1960–67
Alan Dicks 1967–80
Bobby Houghton 1980–82
Roy Hodgson 1982
Terry Cooper 1982–88
  (*Director from 1983*)
Joe Jordan 1988–90
Jimmy Lumsden 1990–92
Denis Smith 1992–93
Russell Osman 1993–94
Joe Jordan 1994–97
John Ward 1997–98
Benny Lennartsson 1998–99
Tony Pulis 1999–2000
Tony Fawthrop 2000
Danny Wilson 2000–04
Brian Tinnion 2004–05
Gary Johnson 2005–10
Steve Coppell 2010
Keith Millen 2010–11
Derek McInnes 2011–13
Sean O'Driscoll January 2013–

## TEN YEAR LEAGUE RECORD

| | | P | W | D | L | F | A | Pts | Pos |
|---|---|---|---|---|---|---|---|---|---|
| 2003-04 | Div 2 | 46 | 23 | 13 | 10 | 58 | 37 | 82 | 3 |
| 2004-05 | FL 1 | 46 | 18 | 16 | 12 | 74 | 57 | 70 | 7 |
| 2005-06 | FL 1 | 46 | 18 | 11 | 17 | 66 | 62 | 65 | 9 |
| 2006-07 | FL 1 | 46 | 25 | 10 | 11 | 63 | 39 | 85 | 2 |
| 2007-08 | FL C | 46 | 20 | 14 | 12 | 54 | 53 | 74 | 4 |
| 2008-09 | FL C | 46 | 15 | 16 | 15 | 54 | 54 | 61 | 10 |
| 2009-10 | FL C | 46 | 15 | 18 | 13 | 56 | 65 | 63 | 10 |
| 2010-11 | FL C | 46 | 17 | 9 | 20 | 62 | 65 | 60 | 15 |
| 2011-12 | FL C | 46 | 12 | 13 | 21 | 44 | 68 | 49 | 20 |
| 2012-13 | FL C | 46 | 11 | 8 | 27 | 59 | 84 | 41 | 24 |

## DID YOU KNOW ?

Between 1933 and 1940 no Welsh-based club won the Welsh Cup! Bristol City were the winners in May 1934 when they defeated another English club, Tranmere Rovers. The first game, played at Chester, resulted in a 1-1 draw, but City won the replay 3-0 at Wrexham.

## BRISTOL CITY – FL CHAMPIONSHIP 2012–13 LEAGUE RECORD

| Match No. | Date | Venue | Opponents | Result | H/T Score | Lg Pos. | Goalscorers | Attendance |
|---|---|---|---|---|---|---|---|---|
| 1 | Aug 18 | A | Nottingham F | L | 0-1 | 0-0 | 18 | | 21,575 |
| 2 | 21 | H | Crystal Palace | W | 4-1 | 2-0 | 7 | Taylor [9], Woolford [12], Stead (pen) [59], Adomah [82] | 12,221 |
| 3 | 25 | H | Cardiff C | W | 4-2 | 2-0 | 4 | Pearson [32], Woolford 2 [45, 70], Baldock [87] | 14,368 |
| 4 | Sept 1 | A | Barnsley | L | 0-1 | 0-0 | 8 | | 8088 |
| 5 | 15 | H | Blackburn R | L | 3-5 | 1-1 | 13 | Adomah [1], Pearson [69], Baldock [83] | 14,657 |
| 6 | 18 | A | Peterborough U | W | 2-1 | 0-0 | 7 | Baldock 2 [56, 62] | 5435 |
| 7 | 22 | A | Watford | D | 2-2 | 0-0 | 9 | Elliott [63], Davies [83] | 11,886 |
| 8 | 29 | H | Leeds U | L | 2-3 | 0-0 | 14 | Adomah [70], Austin (og) [90] | 15,692 |
| 9 | Oct 2 | H | Millwall | D | 1-1 | 1-1 | 14 | Davies [28] | 12,010 |
| 10 | 6 | A | Leicester C | L | 0-2 | 0-1 | 17 | | 22,529 |
| 11 | 20 | A | Bolton W | L | 2-3 | 2-1 | 21 | Davies 2 (1 pen) [3, 21 (p)] | 17,259 |
| 12 | 23 | H | Burnley | L | 3-4 | 1-1 | 21 | Davies [17], Baldock (pen) [77], Anderson [90] | 11,836 |
| 13 | 27 | H | Hull C | L | 1-2 | 1-1 | 23 | Davies [25] | 12,354 |
| 14 | Nov 3 | A | Huddersfield T | L | 0-1 | 0-1 | 23 | | 12,561 |
| 15 | 6 | A | Birmingham C | L | 0-2 | 0-0 | 23 | | 14,380 |
| 16 | 11 | H | Charlton Ath | L | 0-2 | 0-1 | 24 | | 13,009 |
| 17 | 17 | H | Blackpool | D | 1-1 | 0-0 | 23 | Davies (pen) [81] | 12,009 |
| 18 | 24 | A | Middlesbrough | W | 3-1 | 1-1 | 21 | Adomah [13], Pearson [63], Davies [89] | 20,585 |
| 19 | 27 | A | Brighton & HA | L | 0-2 | 0-2 | 22 | | 24,044 |
| 20 | Dec 1 | H | Wolverhampton W | L | 1-4 | 0-4 | 22 | Danns [85] | 13,892 |
| 21 | 8 | A | Sheffield W | W | 3-2 | 1-1 | 21 | Baldock 2 (2 pens) [18, 86], Adomah [88] | 20,449 |
| 22 | 15 | H | Derby Co | L | 0-2 | 0-2 | 21 | | 12,526 |
| 23 | 22 | A | Ipswich T | D | 1-1 | 1-1 | 23 | Danns [11] | 17,290 |
| 24 | 29 | H | Peterborough U | W | 4-2 | 2-1 | 22 | Anderson [5], Baldock 2 (1 pen) [37, 64 (p)], McManus [59] | 12,991 |
| 25 | Jan 1 | A | Millwall | L | 1-2 | 0-1 | 23 | Stead [63] | 9784 |
| 26 | 12 | H | Leicester C | L | 0-4 | 0-3 | 24 | | 13,078 |
| 27 | 19 | A | Leeds U | L | 0-1 | 0-0 | 24 | | 18,156 |
| 28 | 26 | A | Ipswich T | W | 2-1 | 0-1 | 24 | Davies [47], Stead [90] | 12,662 |
| 29 | 29 | H | Watford | W | 2-0 | 1-0 | 23 | Cunningham [43], Anderson [65] | 13,586 |
| 30 | Feb 2 | A | Blackburn R | L | 0-2 | 0-1 | 23 | | 13,539 |
| 31 | 9 | H | Nottingham F | W | 2-0 | 0-0 | 23 | Davies [50], Elliott [62] | 13,768 |
| 32 | 16 | A | Cardiff C | L | 1-2 | 0-1 | 23 | Nugent (og) [90] | 25,586 |
| 33 | 19 | A | Crystal Palace | L | 1-2 | 0-1 | 24 | Parr (og) [90] | 16,191 |
| 34 | 23 | H | Barnsley | W | 5-3 | 2-0 | 23 | Stead 2 [16, 52], Fontaine [35], Nyatanga [55], Davies [67] | 13,008 |
| 35 | Mar 2 | A | Blackpool | D | 0-0 | 0-0 | 24 | | 12,934 |
| 36 | 5 | H | Brighton & HA | D | 0-0 | 0-0 | 24 | | 12,267 |
| 37 | 9 | H | Middlesbrough | W | 2-0 | 1-0 | 22 | Adomah [32], Davies [52] | 13,524 |
| 38 | 16 | A | Wolverhampton W | L | 1-2 | 1-0 | 24 | Davis (og) [25] | 21,711 |
| 39 | 29 | A | Derby Co | L | 0-3 | 0-1 | 24 | | 23,483 |
| 40 | Apr 1 | H | Sheffield W | D | 1-1 | 0-1 | 24 | Baldock [90] | 19,148 |
| 41 | 6 | A | Burnley | L | 1-3 | 1-0 | 24 | Adomah [35] | 11,539 |
| 42 | 13 | A | Bolton W | L | 1-2 | 0-1 | 24 | Davies [49] | 12,935 |
| 43 | 16 | H | Birmingham C | L | 0-1 | 0-1 | 24 | | 12,093 |
| 44 | 19 | H | Hull C | D | 0-0 | 0-0 | 24 | | 18,595 |
| 45 | 27 | H | Huddersfield T | L | 1-3 | 0-2 | 24 | Nyatanga [90] | 13,376 |
| 46 | May 4 | A | Charlton Ath | L | 1-4 | 0-0 | 24 | Reid [59] | 18,981 |

**Final League Position: 24**

## GOALSCORERS

*League (59):* Davies 13 (2 pens), Baldock 10 (4 pens), Adomah 7, Stead 5 (1 pen), Anderson 3, Pearson 3, Woolford 3, Danns 2, Elliott 2, Nyatanga 2, Cunningham 1, Fontaine 1, McManus 1, Reid 1, Taylor 1, own goals 4.
*FA Cup (0).*
*Capital One Cup (1):* Elliott 1.

| Heaton T 43 | Wilson M 7 + 1 | Fontaine L 41 | Carey Louis 13 + 3 | Cunningham G 29 + 1 | Foster R 27 + 3 | Skuse C 24 + 1 | Pearson S 33 + 3 | Woolford M 10 + 5 | Stead J 21 + 7 | Adomah A 29 + 11 | Elliott M 25 + 7 | Anderson P 18 + 11 | Pitman B — + 3 | Taylor R 16 + 9 | Davies S 21 + 16 | Morris J 2 + 2 | Baldock S 23 + 11 | Wilson J 5 + 1 | Bryan J 9 + 4 | Kilkenny N 15 + 9 | Elokobi G 1 | Nyatanga L 18 + 1 | McManus S 11 | Briggs M 4 | Gerken D 3 | Bates M 12 + 1 | Danns N 9 | Reid B 1 + 3 | Wilson D — + 1 | Kelly L 19 | Moloney B 17 | Burns W — + 6 | Howard B — + 6 | Ajala T — + 2 | Match No. |
|---|---|---|---|---|---|---|---|---|---|---|---|---|---|---|---|---|---|---|---|---|---|---|---|---|---|---|---|---|---|---|---|---|---|---|---|
| 1 | 2 | 3 | 4 | 5 | $6^1$ | 7 | $8^3$ | $9^2$ | 10 | 11 | 12 | 13 | 14 | | | | | | | | | | | | | | | | | | | | | | 1 |
| 1 | | 4 | 3 | 5 | 2 | 7 | $8^3$ | 9 | $11^1$ | 6 | 12 | | | $10^2$ | 13 | 14 | | | | | | | | | | | | | | | | | | | 2 |
| 1 | 2 | 4 | 3 | 5 | | 7 | 8 | 9 | $11^1$ | $6^3$ | 13 | | | $10^2$ | 14 | | $11^2$ | | | | | | | | | | | | | | | | | | 3 |
| 1 | 2 | 7 | 3 | 5 | | 4 | $9^3$ | 8 | 10 | $6^1$ | 12 | | | 13 | 14 | | $11^2$ | | | | | | | | | | | | | | | | | | 4 |
| 1 | | 4 | 3 | 5 | 2 | 7 | 8 | $9^1$ | $11^1$ | 6 | | | 14 | $10^2$ | 13 | | 12 | | | | | | | | | | | | | | | | | | 5 |
| 1 | | 4 | $5^2$ | 2 | $6^1$ | | 8 | 9 | 12 | 7 | | | | $11^3$ | 14 | | 10 | 3 | | | | 13 | | | | | | | | | | | | | 6 |
| 1 | | 3 | 2 | | | 7 | $6^1$ | 9 | $8^2$ | 11 | 13 | 14 | | $10^3$ | 4 | 5 | 12 | | | | | | | | | | | | | | | | | | 7 |
| 1 | | 4 | 13 | | 2 | | 8 | 9 | $10^3$ | 6 | | | | 11 | 14 | 3 | $12^2$ | 7 | $5^1$ | | | | | | | | | | | | | | | | 8 |
| 1 | 2 | 3 | | | 5 | 7 | 9 | 13 | | 6 | | | 14 | 12 | $11^1$ | | $10^3$ | | | $8^2$ | | 4 | | | | | | | | | | | | | 9 |
| 1 | 13 | 3 | $5^2$ | 2 | 6 | 7 | | 9 | | | | | 14 | 10 | 12 | | $8^3$ | $11^1$ | | | | 4 | | | | | | | | | | | | | 10 |
| 1 | | 5 | 3 | 2 | 7 | 8 | $9^2$ | | 6 | | | | 13 | 12 | $11^1$ | | 10 | | | | | 4 | | | | | | | | | | | | | 11 |
| 1 | 2 | $3^1$ | 12 | 5 | 8 | | | | 6 | | | | 14 | 13 | $11^3$ | 7 | 10 | $9^2$ | | | | 4 | | | | | | | | | | | | | 12 |
| 1 | $2^2$ | | | 6 | 7 | 8 | $10^3$ | 13 | | | | 14 | 11 | $9^1$ | 12 | | | | | 4 | 3 | 5 | | | | | | | | | | | | | 13 |
| | | 4 | | 2 | 6 | $8^3$ | 14 | $10^2$ | 9 | $7^1$ | 13 | | | 11 | 12 | | | | | 3 | 5 | 1 | | | | | | | | | | | | | 14 |
| | | 4 | | 2 | $8^1$ | 9 | 13 | $11^2$ | 6 | $7^3$ | 14 | | | 10 | 12 | | | | | 3 | 5 | 1 | | | | | | | | | | | | | 15 |
| 1 | | 4 | | 2 | 14 | 9 | 13 | 6 | 7 | $10^2$ | 12 | | | $11^1$ | 3 | | $8^3$ | | | | 5 | | | | | | | | | | | | | | 16 |
| 1 | | 4 | | 2 | 11 | $10^2$ | 9 | 8 | 12 | | | | 13 | | | 5 | $7^3$ | | | | | | 3 | $6^1$ | 14 | | | | | | | | | | 17 |
| 1 | 2 | 3 | | 5 | 11 | 12 | | 6 | 8 | | | | $10^2$ | 13 | | $4^3$ | $7^1$ | | | | | | | 9 | | 14 | | | | | | | | | 18 |
| 1 | 3 | | 2 | 11 | | | $9^2$ | $7^2$ | 12 | | | 10¹ | 13 | 5 | $8^3$ | | | | | | | | 4 | 6 | 14 | | | | | | | | | | 19 |
| 1 | 4 | | 2 | 10 | | | 6 | 7 | $11^2$ | 13 | | | 12 | 5 | $8^1$ | | | | | | | | 3 | 9 | | | | | | | | | | | 20 |
| 1 | 5 | | 2 | 13 | | | 6 | 7 | 12 | 11 | | | $10^2$ | $9^1$ | | 3 | | | | | | | 4 | 8 | | | | | | | | | | | 21 |
| 1 | 5 | 12 | 2 | | 14 | 6 | 8 | | $11^2$ | 13 | | | 10 | $9^3$ | | 4 | | | | | | | $3^1$ | 7 | | | | | | | | | | | 22 |
| 1 | 3 | 6 | 2 | $8^2$ | 11 | 7 | 12 | 10¹ | 13 | | | | | | 4 | | 5 | 9 | | | | | | | | | | | | | | | | | 23 |
| 1 | | 4 | $9^1$ | 7 | | | $11^3$ | 5 | | $8^2$ | 14 | 10 | 12 | 13 | | 3 | | 2 | 6 | | | | | | | | | | | | | | | | 24 |
| 1 | $2^3$ | $3^2$ | 6 | 8 | 12 | 11 | 7 | 10¹ | 14 | 13 | | | 5 | | | 4 | 9 | | | | | | | | | | | | | | | | | | 25 |
| | 2 | 6 | 5 | 7 | 9 | $11^2$ | 12 | 10 | $3^1$ | 13 | | | | 4 | 1 | 14 | $8^3$ | | | | | | | | | | | | | | | | | | 26 |
| 1 | 4 | 3 | 5 | 2 | 7 | $9^3$ | 12 | 10¹ | 11 | 13 | | | | $8^2$ | | 6 | | | | | | | | | | | | | | | | | | | 27 |
| 1 | 3 | 4 | 5 | | 8 | 13 | 14 | 9 | 10¹ | 12 | | | $11^2$ | $6^3$ | | 7 | 2 | | | | | | | | | | | | | | | | | | 28 |
| 1 | 4 | 3 | $5^3$ | | $7^1$ | 9 | 13 | 12 | 6 | | | | $10^2$ | 11 | | 14 | 8 | 2 | | | | | | | | | | | | | | | | | 29 |
| 1 | 3 | $4^1$ | 5 | | 9 | 13 | 7 | $6^3$ | | | | | $10^2$ | 11 | 12 | 8 | 2 | 14 | | | | | | | | | | | | | | | | | 30 |
| 1 | 3 | 5 | 13 | | 9 | 11 | 7 | $6^2$ | | | | | 10¹ | | 4 | 8 | 2 | 12 | | | | | | | | | | | | | | | | | 31 |
| 1 | 2 | 5 | | $7^3$ | 10 | 12 | 9 | $8^1$ | 11 | | | 13 | 3 | | | $6^4$ | 4 | 14 | | | | | | | | | | | | | | | | | 32 |
| 1 | 3 | 2 | 12 | $6^2$ | 11 | $10^3$ | 8 | 7 | 13 | | | | 4 | | 9 | $5^1$ | 14 | | | | | | | | | | | | | | | | | | 33 |
| 1 | 3 | 5 | | $9^3$ | 10 | 12 | 7 | $6^1$ | 11 | | 13 | | 4 | | | $8^2$ | 2 | 14 | | | | | | | | | | | | | | | | | 34 |
| 1 | 3 | 5 | 13 | $9^2$ | 11 | 12 | 8 | 6 | 10¹ | | | | 4 | | | 7 | 2 | | | | | | | | | | | | | | | | | | 35 |
| 1 | 4 | 10 | 7 | $5^1$ | 11 | 12 | 8 | $6^2$ | 13 | | | | 3 | | | 9 | 2 | | | | | | | | | | | | | | | | | | 36 |
| 1 | 4 | 5 | 9 | 10¹ | $12^3$ | 8 | $11^2$ | 13 | | 7 | | | 3 | | | 6 | 2 | 14 | | | | | | | | | | | | | | | | | 37 |
| 1 | 3 | 5 | 8 | $11^2$ | 12 | 6 | $9^1$ | 10 | 13 | | 14 | | 4 | | | $7^3$ | 2 | | | | | | | | | | | | | | | | | | 38 |
| 1 | 4 | $5^2$ | 7 | 13 | 12 | $6^1$ | 9 | 11 | 10 | | 8 | | 3 | | | 2 | | | | | | | | | | | | | | | | | | | 39 |
| 1 | 4 | 5 | $7^3$ | $9^1$ | 12 | 8 | 14 | 11 | 10 | 13 | | | 3 | | | $6^2$ | 2 | | | | | | | | | | | | | | | | | | 40 |
| 1 | 4 | 5 | $9^2$ | | 6 | 7 | 10 | 11 | 12 | | | 3 | | | | $8^1$ | 2 | 13 | | | | | | | | | | | | | | | | | 41 |
| 1 | $4^2$ | 5 | $9^1$ | | 6 | 7 | 12 | 14 | 11 | 10 | | 3 | | | 13 | 8 | $2^3$ | | | | | | | | | | | | | | | | | | 42 |
| 1 | | 5 | 13 | | 9 | | $6^1$ | 11 | 10 | $7^3$ | 4 | | $3^2$ | | | 8 | 2 | 12 | 14 | | | | | | | | | | | | | | | | 43 |
| 1 | | 5 | 2 | | $6^1$ | 12 | | $11^2$ | $10^3$ | 7 | 3 | | 9 | | | 8 | 4 | 13 | 14 | | | | | | | | | | | | | | | | 44 |
| 1 | 13 | 5 | 2 | | 12 | 9 | $8^1$ | $10^2$ | 11 | 6 | 4 | | $3^3$ | | | 7 | | | 14 | | | | | | | | | | | | | | | | 45 |
| 1 | 3 | 4 | 5 | | 12 | 6 | $11^2$ | 10¹ | 8 | $7^3$ | 2 | | 9 | | | | 13 | 14 | | | | | | | | | | | | | | | | | 46 |

**FA Cup**
Third Round    Blackburn R    (a)  0-2

**Capital One Cup**
First Round    Gillingham    (h)  1-2

# BRISTOL ROVERS

## FOUNDATION

Bristol Rovers were formed at a meeting in Stapleton Road, Eastville, in 1883. However, they first went under the name of the Black Arabs (wearing black shirts). Changing their name to Eastville Rovers in their second season in 1888–89, they won the Gloucestershire Senior Cup. Original members of the Bristol & District League in 1892, this eventually became the Western League and Eastville Rovers adopted professionalism in 1897.

*The Memorial Stadium, Filton Avenue, Horfield, Bristol BS7 0BF.*

*Telephone:* (0117) 909 6648.

*Fax:* (0117) 907 4312.

*Ticket Office:* (0117) 909 8848.

*Website:* www.bristolrovers.co.uk

*Email:* rodwesson@bristolrovers.co.uk; dave@bristolrovers.co.uk

*Ground Capacity:* 11,626.

*Record Attendance:* 38,472 v Preston NE, FA Cup 4th rd, 30 January 1960 (at Eastville); 9,464 v Liverpool, FA Cup 4th rd, 8 February 1992 (at Twerton Park); 12,011 v WBA, FA Cup 6th rd, 9 March 2008 (at Memorial Stadium).

*Pitch Measurements:* 100m × 66m (110yd × 73yd)

*Chairman:* Nick Higgs.

*Manager:* John Ward.

*Assistant Manager:* Darrell Clarke.

*Physio:* Phil Kite.

*Colours:* Blue and white quarters, blue shorts with white trim, blue socks with white trim.

*Year Formed:* 1883.

*Turned Professional:* 1897.

*Previous Names:* 1883, Black Arabs; 1884, Eastville Rovers; 1897, Bristol Eastville Rovers; 1898, Bristol Rovers. *Club Nicknames:* 'The Pirates', 'The Gas'.

*Grounds:* 1883, Purdown; Three Acres, Ashley Hill; Rudgeway, Fishponds; 1897, Eastville; 1986, Twerton Park; 1996, The Memorial Stadium.

*First Football League Game:* 28 August 1920, Division 3, v Millwall (a) L 0–2 – Stansfield; Bethune, Panes; Boxley, Kenny, Steele; Chance, Bird, Sims, Bell, Palmer.

*Record League Victory:* 7–0 v Brighton & HA, Division 3 (S), 29 November 1952 – Hoyle; Bamford, Fox; Pitt, Warren, Sampson; McIlvenny, Roost (2), Lambden (1), Bradford (1), Petherbridge (2), (1 og). 7–0 v Swansea T, Division 2, 2 October 1954 – Radford; Bamford, Watkins; Pitt, Muir, Anderson; Petherbridge, Bradford (2), Meyer, Roost (1), Hooper (2), (2 og). 7–0 v Shrewsbury T, Division 3, 21 March 1964 – Hall; Hillard, Gwyn Jones; Oldfield, Stone (1), Mabbutt; Jarman (2), Brown (1), Biggs (1p), Hamilton, Bobby Jones (2).

## HONOURS

**Football League – Division 2:** Best season: 4th, 1994–95; **Division 3 (S):** *Champions* 1952–53; **Division 3:** *Champions* 1989–90; *Runners-up* 1973–74.

**FA Cup:** Best season: 6th rd, 1951, 1958, 2008.

**Football League Cup:** Best season: 5th rd, 1971, 1972.

**Leyland DAF:** *Runners-up* 1990.

**Johnstone's Paint Trophy:** *Runners-up* 2007.

## sky SPORTS FACT FILE

Bristol Rovers won the Watney Cup in August 1972, defeating Sheffield United 7-6 in a penalty shoot-out after the teams had produced a 0-0 draw after extra time. The game attracted an attendance of 19,768 to Eastville.

**Record Cup Victory:** 6–0 v Merthyr Tydfil, FA Cup 1st rd, 14 November 1987 – Martyn; Alexander (Dryden), Tanner, Hibbitt, Twentyman, Vaughan Jones, Holloway, Meacham (1), White (2), Penrice (3) (Reece), Purnell.

**Record Defeat:** 0–12 v Luton T, Division 3 (S), 13 April 1936.

**Most League Points (2 for a win):** 64, Division 3 (S), 1952–53.

**Most League Points (3 for a win):** 93, Division 3, 1989–90.

**Most League Goals:** 92, Division 3 (S), 1952–53.

**Highest League Scorer in Season:** Geoff Bradford, 33, Division 3 (S), 1952–53.

**Most League Goals in Total Aggregate:** Geoff Bradford, 242, 1949–64.

**Most League Goals in One Match:** 4, Sidney Leigh v Exeter C, Division 3 (S), 2 May 1921; 4, Jonah Wilcox v Bournemouth, Division 3 (S), 12 December 1925; 4, Bill Culley v QPR, Division 3 (S), 5 March 1927; 4, Frank Curran v Swindon T, Division 3 (S), 25 March 1939; 4, Vic Lambden v Aldershot, Division 3 (S), 29 March 1947; 4, George Petherbridge v Torquay U, Division 3 (S), 1 December 1951; 4, Vic Lambden v Colchester U, Division 3 (S), 14 May 1952; 4, Geoff Bradford v Rotherham U, Division 2, 14 March 1959; 4, Robin Stubbs v Gillingham, Division 2, 10 October 1970; 4, Alan Warboys v Brighton & HA, Division 3, 1 December 1973; 4, Jamie Cureton v Reading, Division 2, 16 January 1999.

**Most Capped Player:** Vitalijs Astafjevs, 31 (167), Latvia.

**Most League Appearances:** Stuart Taylor, 546, 1966–80.

**Youngest League Player:** Ronnie Dix, 15 years 173 days v Charlton Ath, 25 February 1928.

**Record Transfer Fee Received:** £2,100,000 from Fulham for Barry Hayles, November 1998; £2,100,000 from WBA for Jason Roberts, July 2000.

**Record Transfer Fee Paid:** £375,000 to QPR for Andy Tillson, November 1992.

**Football League Record:** 1920 Original Member of Division 3; 1921–53 Division 3 (S); 1953–62 Division 2; 1962–74 Division 3; 1974–81 Division 2; 1981–90 Division 3; 1990–92 Division 2. 1992–93 Division 1; 1993–2001 Division 2; 2001–04 Division 3; 2004–07 FL 2; 2007–11 FL 1; 2011– FL 2.

## MANAGERS

Alfred Homer 1899–1920
  (*continued as Secretary to 1928*)
Ben Hall 1920–21
Andy Wilson 1921–26
Joe Palmer 1926–29
Dave McLean 1929–30
Albert Prince-Cox 1930–36
Percy Smith 1936–37
Brough Fletcher 1938–49
Bert Tann 1950–68 (*continued as General Manager to 1972*)
Fred Ford 1968–69
Bill Dodgin Snr 1969–72
Don Megson 1972–77
Bobby Campbell 1978–79
Harold Jarman 1979–80
Terry Cooper 1980–81
Bobby Gould 1981–83
David Williams 1983–85
Bobby Gould 1985–87
Gerry Francis 1987–91
Martin Dobson 1991
Dennis Rofe 1992
Malcolm Allison 1992–93
John Ward 1993–96
Ian Holloway 1996–2001
Garry Thompson 2001
Gerry Francis 2001
Garry Thompson 2001–02
Ray Graydon 2002–04
Ian Atkins 2004–05
Paul Trollope 2005–10
Dave Penney 2011
Paul Buckle 2011
Mark McGhee 2012
John Ward December 2012–

## LATEST SEQUENCES

**Longest Sequence of League Wins:** 12, 18.10.1952 – 17.1.1953.

**Longest Sequence of League Defeats:** 8, 26.10.2002 – 21.12.2002.

**Longest Sequence of League Draws:** 5, 1.11.1975 – 22.11.1975.

**Longest Sequence of Unbeaten League Matches:** 32, 7.4.1973 – 27.1.1974.

**Longest Sequence Without a League Win:** 20, 5.4.1980 – 1.11.1980.

**Successive Scoring Runs:** 26 from 26.3.1927.

**Successive Non-scoring Runs:** 6 from 14.10.1922.

## TEN YEAR LEAGUE RECORD

| | | P | W | D | L | F | A | Pts | Pos |
|---|---|---|---|---|---|---|---|---|---|
| 2003-04 | Div 3 | 46 | 14 | 13 | 19 | 50 | 61 | 55 | 15 |
| 2004-05 | FL 2 | 46 | 13 | 21 | 12 | 60 | 57 | 60 | 12 |
| 2005-06 | FL 2 | 46 | 17 | 9 | 20 | 59 | 67 | 60 | 12 |
| 2006-07 | FL 2 | 46 | 20 | 12 | 14 | 49 | 42 | 72 | 6 |
| 2007-08 | FL 1 | 46 | 12 | 17 | 17 | 45 | 53 | 53 | 16 |
| 2008-09 | FL 1 | 46 | 17 | 12 | 17 | 79 | 61 | 63 | 11 |
| 2009-10 | FL 1 | 46 | 19 | 5 | 22 | 59 | 70 | 62 | 11 |
| 2010-11 | FL 1 | 46 | 11 | 12 | 23 | 48 | 82 | 45 | 22 |
| 2011-12 | FL 2 | 46 | 15 | 12 | 19 | 60 | 70 | 57 | 13 |
| 2012-13 | FL 2 | 46 | 16 | 12 | 18 | 60 | 69 | 60 | 14 |

## DID YOU KNOW

Goalkeeper Jesse Whatley conceded five goals on his debut for Bristol Rovers in a Southern League match against Norwich City in November 1919, but went on to play over 400 games for the Pirates. He set a club record of 246 consecutive Football League appearances in the 1920s.

## BRISTOL ROVERS – FOOTBALL LEAGUE TWO 2012–13 LEAGUE RECORD

| Match No. | Date | Venue | Opponents | Result | H/T Score | Lg Pos. | Goalscorers | Attendance |
|---|---|---|---|---|---|---|---|---|
| 1 | Aug 18 | H | Oxford U | L | 0-2 | 0-2 | 19 | | 7451 |
| 2 | 21 | A | Barnet | D | 1-1 | 0-1 | 20 | Harrold [55] | 1794 |
| 3 | Sept 1 | H | Morecambe | L | 0-3 | 0-0 | 23 | | 5207 |
| 4 | 8 | H | Aldershot T | D | 2-2 | 1-1 | 23 | Clarkson [11], Broghammer [90] | 5117 |
| 5 | 15 | A | Gillingham | L | 0-4 | 0-3 | 23 | | 4768 |
| 6 | 18 | A | Plymouth Arg | D | 1-1 | 0-1 | 23 | Parkes [70] | 6303 |
| 7 | 22 | H | Fleetwood T | D | 0-0 | 0-0 | 23 | | 5079 |
| 8 | 29 | A | Exeter C | W | 2-1 | 1-0 | 21 | Clarkson [5], Richards [69] | 5054 |
| 9 | Oct 3 | H | Cheltenham T | L | 0-1 | 0-1 | 21 | | 5747 |
| 10 | 6 | H | Northampton T | W | 3-1 | 0-0 | 20 | Eaves [53], Kenneth [57], Norburn [84] | 5166 |
| 11 | 13 | A | Burton Alb | D | 1-1 | 1-0 | 21 | Clarkson [30] | 2961 |
| 12 | 20 | H | Torquay U | W | 3-2 | 2-0 | 20 | Eaves 2 [15, 76], Lund [17] | 6331 |
| 13 | 23 | A | AFC Wimbledon | L | 1-3 | 0-3 | 20 | Eaves [73] | 3714 |
| 14 | 27 | A | Accrington S | L | 0-1 | 0-0 | 20 | | 1462 |
| 15 | Nov 6 | H | Southend U | L | 2-3 | 1-2 | 20 | Broghammer [10], Clarkson (pen) [85] | 4721 |
| 16 | 10 | H | Chesterfield | W | 3-2 | 1-1 | 20 | Togwell (og) [5], Anyinsah [59], Eaves [90] | 5491 |
| 17 | 17 | A | Rochdale | L | 1-2 | 1-1 | 21 | Clarkson (pen) [14] | 2204 |
| 18 | 20 | A | Port Vale | L | 0-4 | 0-3 | 21 | | 4177 |
| 19 | 24 | H | Bradford C | D | 3-3 | 2-1 | 21 | Branston [2], Eaves [33], Smith [62] | 5092 |
| 20 | Dec 1 | A | Wycombe W | L | 0-2 | 0-1 | 21 | | 3740 |
| 21 | 8 | H | Dagenham & R | L | 0-1 | 0-1 | 23 | | 4874 |
| 22 | 15 | A | York C | L | 1-4 | 1-4 | 23 | Eaves [15] | 3109 |
| 23 | 26 | A | Aldershot T | D | 2-2 | 0-1 | 24 | Clarkson (pen) [54], Richards [87] | 2862 |
| 24 | Jan 1 | H | Plymouth Arg | W | 2-1 | 2-0 | 23 | Anyinsah [19], Lund [25] | 7332 |
| 25 | 5 | H | Gillingham | L | 0-2 | 0-2 | 24 | | 6088 |
| 26 | 12 | A | Fleetwood T | W | 3-0 | 2-0 | 24 | Woodards [5], Richards [27], O'Toole [49] | 2811 |
| 27 | 26 | A | Rotherham U | W | 3-1 | 1-0 | 23 | Brown, L (pen) [43], Harrison [52], Anyinsah [61] | 6582 |
| 28 | Feb 1 | H | Barnet | W | 2-1 | 0-0 | 19 | Broghammer [78], Brunt [90] | 8527 |
| 29 | 5 | A | Cheltenham T | D | 1-1 | 0-1 | 19 | Norburn [90] | 4436 |
| 30 | 9 | A | Oxford U | W | 2-0 | 0-0 | 19 | Brown, L (pen) [55], Richards [90] | 7608 |
| 31 | 16 | H | Wycombe W | W | 1-0 | 1-0 | 18 | Brunt [35] | 7324 |
| 32 | 19 | H | Rotherham U | L | 1-2 | 0-0 | 18 | Anyinsah [81] | 8646 |
| 33 | 23 | A | Morecambe | D | 1-1 | 0-1 | 18 | Richards [48] | 1736 |
| 34 | 26 | A | Northampton T | L | 0-1 | 0-0 | 18 | | 4077 |
| 35 | Mar 2 | H | Burton Alb | W | 3-0 | 1-0 | 17 | Brunt [5], O'Toole [62], Richards [70] | 6065 |
| 36 | 6 | H | Exeter C | W | 2-0 | 1-0 | 15 | Norburn [23], Brown, L [82] | 7107 |
| 37 | 9 | A | Chesterfield | L | 0-2 | 0-0 | 17 | | 4814 |
| 38 | 12 | H | Port Vale | W | 2-0 | 2-0 | 15 | Brunt 2 [7, 38] | 5111 |
| 39 | 16 | H | Rochdale | W | 2-1 | 0-0 | 14 | Harrison 2 [62, 84] | 6691 |
| 40 | 30 | H | York C | D | 0-0 | 0-0 | 14 | | 7378 |
| 41 | Apr 1 | A | Dagenham & R | W | 4-2 | 3-1 | 13 | O'Toole [4], Tounkara 2 [6, 70], Woodards [20] | 2082 |
| 42 | 6 | A | AFC Wimbledon | W | 1-0 | 0-0 | 11 | Hitchcock [82] | 6881 |
| 43 | 9 | A | Bradford C | L | 1-4 | 0-3 | 11 | Hitchcock [50] | 10,621 |
| 44 | 13 | A | Southend U | D | 0-0 | 0-0 | 12 | | 4612 |
| 45 | 20 | H | Accrington S | L | 0-1 | 0-1 | 13 | | 7673 |
| 46 | 27 | A | Torquay U | D | 3-3 | 1-0 | 14 | Hitchcock [31], Jarvis (og) [55], Harrold [90] | 5666 |

**Final League Position: 14**

### GOALSCORERS

*League (60):* Eaves 7, Clarkson 6 (3 pens), Richards 6, Brunt 5, Anyinsah 4, Broghammer 3, Brown, L 3 (2 pens), Harrison 3, Hitchcock 3, Norburn 3, O'Toole 3, Harrold 2, Lund 2, Tounkara 2, Woodards 2, Branston 1, Kenneth 1, Parkes 1, Smith 1, own goals 2.
*FA Cup (1):* Clarkson 1.
*Capital One Cup (1):* Smith 1.
*Johnstone's Paint Trophy (0).*

| Walker S 11 | Smith M 33+5 | Paterson J 23+3 | Virgo A 9+1 | Brown L 33+6 | Brown W 12+6 | Gill M 10+1 | Lund M 14+4 | Anyinsah J 24+7 | Clarkson D 21+5 | Harrold M 5+1 | Richards E 21+19 | Broghammer F 25+11 | Norbum O 25+10 | Parkes T 40 | Clucas S 14+5 | Bolger C 3 | Kenneth G 18 | Etheridge N 12 | Riordan D 7+4 | Eaves T 16 | Clarke O 2+3 | Woodards D 20+2 | Santos A —+1 | Branston G 4 | Mildenhall S 22 | O'Toole J 18 | Hitchcock T 7+10 | Harding M —+5 | McChrystal M 21 | Harrison E 10+3 | Lockyer T —+4 | Brunt R 17+1 | McDonald C 4+2 | Tounkara O 4+5 | Gough C 1 | Match No. |
|---|---|---|---|---|---|---|---|---|---|---|---|---|---|---|---|---|---|---|---|---|---|---|---|---|---|---|---|---|---|---|---|---|---|---|---|---|
| 1 | 2 | 3 | 4 | 5 | 6[3] | 7 | 8[1] | 9[2] | 10 | 11 | 12 | 13 | 14 | | | | | | | | | | | | | | | | | | | | | | | 1 |
| 1 | 2 | 6 | 5 | 4 | 12 | 7 | | 9 | 10 | 11[2] | 13 | | | 3 | 8[1] | | | | | | | | | | | | | | | | | | | | | 2 |
| 1 | 2 | 5 | 4 | 8[2] | 7[1] | 6 | 12 | 14 | 9 | 11 | 10[3] | 13 | | 3 | | | | | | | | | | | | | | | | | | | | | | 3 |
| 1 | 12 | 5[2] | 2[1] | 8 | 7[3] | 6 | | | 10 | 11 | 9 | 13 | 14 | 3 | | | 4 | | | | | | | | | | | | | | | | | | | 4 |
| 1 | 2 | 5[2] | 4 | 8 | 7 | 9[3] | 14 | | 10 | 11[1] | 6 | 12 | 13 | 3 | | | | | | | | | | | | | | | | | | | | | | 5 |
| 1 | 13 | | 2[2] | 5 | 9[3] | 8 | 6[1] | 14 | 11 | | 12 | 10 | 7 | 4 | | 3 | | | | | | | | | | | | | | | | | | | | 6 |
| | 2 | | | 5 | 7[1] | 6 | 13 | 9[2] | 11 | | 12 | 10 | 8 | 3 | | 4 | 1 | | | | | | | | | | | | | | | | | | | 7 |
| | 5 | 2 | 13 | | 7 | 14 | | 6 | | | 12 | 9[2] | 8 | 4 | | 3 | 1 | 10[3] | 11[1] | | | | | | | | | | | | | | | | | 8 |
| | 5[2] | 3 | 14 | 13 | 6 | 2 | | 8 | | | 12 | 9[1] | 7[3] | | | 4 | 1 | 11 | 10 | | | | | | | | | | | | | | | | | 9 |
| | 13 | 5 | | 14 | 12 | | 2 | | 8[1] | | 6 | 9[3] | 7[3] | | | 4 | 1 | 11[2] | 10 | | | | | | | | | | | | | | | | | 10 |
| | 5[1] | 14 | 12 | 13 | | 2 | 6[3] | 7 | | | 10 | 9[2] | 8 | 4 | | 3 | 1 | | 11 | | | | | | | | | | | | | | | | | 11 |
| | 5 | | 12 | 13 | | 2 | 8[2] | 7 | | | 11 | 9[1] | 6 | 3 | | 4 | 1 | | 10 | | | | | | | | | | | | | | | | | 12 |
| | 5 | 4[1] | | 6 | | 8 | 12 | 11 | | | 10[2] | | 7 | 2[8] | | 3 | 1 | | 9 | 13 | | | | | | | | | | | | | | | | 13 |
| | 4 | | 5 | 6 | | 2 | 13 | 7 | | | 10 | 9[2] | 8[1] | 3 | | | 1 | 12 | 11 | | | | | | | | | | | | | | | | | 14 |
| | 5[2] | | 6 | 12 | | 2 | | 7 | | | 14 | 9 | 13[8] | 3 | 8[1] | 4 | 1 | 11 | 10[3] | | | | | | | | | | | | | | | | | 15 |
| | 13 | 5 | | 6 | | 2 | 8 | 7 | | | 12 | 9[1] | | 3 | | 4 | 1 | 11[2] | 10 | | | | | | | | | | | | | | | | | 16 |
| | 2 | 5 | | 8 | | 10 | 7[1] | 14[8] | 12 | | | 4 | 13 | 3[8] | 1 | | 9[3] | 11 | | 6[2] | | | | | | | | | | | | | | | | 17 |
| | 2 | 8 | | 4 | 10 | 12 | 9 | | | | 6[3] | | 3 | 7[2] | | 1 | 13 | 11 | | 5[1] | 14 | | | | | | | | | | | | | | | 18 |
| 1 | 6 | 5 | | 7[8] | | 10 | | | | | 8 | | 4 | 9 | 11 | | 2 | 3 | | | | | | | | | | | | | | | | | | 19 |
| 1 | 8[2] | 3 | | 9[1] | 7[8] | 10 | | | 12 | 6 | 14 | | 4 | 13 | 11 | | 2[3] | 5 | | | | | | | | | | | | | | | | | | 20 |
| 1 | | 5 | | 10[3] | 8 | | 12 | 9 | 6[1] | 7 | 13 | | 4[2] | 14 | 11 | | 2 | 3 | | | | | | | | | | | | | | | | | | 21 |
| 1 | 13 | 5 | | 7[2] | 10 | 6 | 14 | 9 | | 8 | 12 | | 4 | | 11 | | 2[1] | 3[3] | | | | | | | | | | | | | | | | | | 22 |
| 1 | 2 | 9[1] | 12 | | 10 | 6[2] | 14 | 7 | 13 | 4 | 8[3] | 5 | 3 | | 11 | | | | | | | | | | | | | | | | | | | | | 23 |
| | 2 | | | 5 | | 6 | 8[3] | 13 | 9[2] | 7[1] | 3 | 12 | 4 | | | | | | | | | | | | 1 | 10 | 11 | 14 | | | | | | | | 24 |
| | 2 | | | 5 | | 10[2] | | 11 | 9[3] | 12 | 6 | 7 | | 3[1] | | | | | | | | | | | 1 | 8 | 13 | 14 | 4 | | | | | | | 25 |
| | 2 | | | 5 | | 11 | | | 4 | 7 | | | 6[1] | | | | | | | | | | | | 1 | 8 | 10 | 12 | 3 | 9[2] | 13 | | | | | 26 |
| | 2 | | | 5 | | 11[2] | 13 | 10[1] | | 6 | 3 | 7 | | 14 | | | | | | | | | | | 1 | 8 | | 4 | 12 | | 9[3] | | | | | 27 |
| | 2 | | | 5 | | 10[1] | 12 | 13 | 9[3] | 7[2] | 3 | 6 | | 14 | | | | | | | | | | | 1 | 8 | | 4 | | | 11 | | | | | 28 |
| | 5 | | | 2 | | 9[3] | | 13 | 12 | 7 | 4 | 8[2] | | 6[1] | | | | | | | | | | | 1 | 10 | 14 | 3 | | 11 | | | | | | 29 |
| | 2 | | | 5 | | 6[1] | 12 | 14 | 13 | 7[3] | 4 | 9 | | 10[2] | | | | | | | | | | | 1 | 8 | | 3 | | 11 | | | | | | 30 |
| | 2 | | | 5 | | 9[2] | 12 | 13 | 10[3] | 7[1] | 3 | 6 | | | | | | | | | | | | | 1 | 8 | | 4 | | 11 | 14 | | | | | 31 |
| | 2 | | | 5 | | 9 | 13 | | 12 | 10[1] | 7[3] | 3 | 6 | | | | | | | | | | | | 1 | 8 | 14 | 4 | | 11[2] | | | | | | 32 |
| | 2 | 14 | | 5 | | 9 | | 10 | | 12 | 4 | 7[2] | | 6[1] | | | | | | | | | | | 1 | 8 | 11[3] | 3 | 13 | | | | | | | 33 |
| | 2 | | | 5 | | 9[1] | | 11 | | 7 | 3 | | 6 | | | | | | | | | | | | 1 | 8 | 10[1] | 4 | 12 | | | | | | | 34 |
| | 2 | 14 | | 5 | | 9[1] | | 10 | | 12 | 3 | | 7 | | | | | | | | | | | | 1 | 8 | | 4 | 6[3] | 11[2] | 13 | | | | | 35 |
| | 2 | | | 5 | | 10[2] | 12 | 9 | 3 | | 7[3] | | | | | | | | | | | | | | 1 | 8 | 13 | 4 | 6[1] | 11 | 14 | | | | | 36 |
| | 2 | | | 5 | | 9[1] | | 11 | 12 | 6 | 3 | | 7[2] | | | | | | | | | | | | 1 | 8 | 13 | 4 | 10[3] | 14 | | | | | | 37 |
| | 2 | 6 | | 5 | | 10[1] | 7[2] | 3 | | 4 | | | | | | | | | | | | | | | 1 | 8 | 12 | 14 | 9[3] | 13 | 11 | | | | | 38 |
| | 2 | 6[1] | | 5 | | 10 | | 3 | | 7 | | | | | | | | | | | | | | | 1 | 8 | 12 | 4 | 9[2] | 11 | 13 | | | | | 39 |
| | 2 | | | 5 | | 6 | 10[3] | 12 | 3 | | 7 | | | | | | | | | | | | | | 1 | 8 | 14 | 4 | 9[1] | 11[2] | 13 | | | | | 40 |
| | 2[2] | 12 | | 5[1] | | 9[3] | 3 | | 8 | | 7 | 14 | 4 | 6 | 13 | 11 | 10 | | | | | | | | | | | | | | | | | | 1 | 41 |
| | 2 | | | 5 | | 12 | 8[3] | 6 | 3 | | 7 | | | | | | | | | | | | | | 1 | 13 | | 4 | 9[1] | 14 | 11[2] | 3 | 10 | | | 42 |
| | 2 | | | 5 | | 6[2] | 13 | 9 | 7 | | | 12 | 8[1] | | | | | | | | | 1 | | 11 | 3 | | 10 | 4 | | | | | | | 43 |
| | 2 | | | 5 | | 13 | 14 | 9[3] | 7 | 8 | | 12 | 6[2] | | | | | | | | | 1 | | 6[2] | | | 4 | | 10[1] | 3 | 11 | | | | 44 |
| | 2 | | | 5 | | 14 | 11 | 6 | 12 | 7 | | 8 | | 1 | | | | | | | | | 4 | 9[2] | | | 13 | 3[1] | 10[3] | | | | | | 45 |
| | 2 | | | 5 | | 13 | | 9 | 7 | 3 | | 8 | | 1 | | | | | | | | | 11[3] | 12 | 4 | 6[1] | | 10[2] | 14 | | | | | | 46 |

**FA Cup**
First Round　　Sheffield U　　(h)　　1-2

**Capital One Cup**
First Round　　Ipswich T　　(a)　　1-3

**Johnstone's Paint Trophy**
First Round　　Yeovil T　　(h)　　0-3

# BURNLEY

## FOUNDATION

On 18 May 1882 Burnley (Association) Football Club was still known as Burnley Rovers as members of that rugby club had decided on that date to play Association Football in the future. It was only a matter of days later that the members met again and decided to drop Rovers from the club's name.

*Turf Moor, Harry Potts Way, Burnley, Lancashire BB10 4BX.*

*Telephone:* (0871) 221 1882.

*Fax:* (01282) 700 014.

*Ticket Office:* (0871) 221 1914.

*Website:* www.burnleyfootballclub.com

*Email:* info@burnleyfc.com

*Ground Capacity:* 21,940.

*Record Attendance:* 54,775 v Huddersfield T, FA Cup 3rd rd, 23 February 1924.

*Pitch Measurements:* 105m × 66m (115yd × 73yd)

*Chairmen:* Mike Garlick and John Banaszkiewicz.

*Chief Executive:* Lee Hoos.

*Manager:* Sean Dyche.

*Assistant Manager:* Ian Woan.

*Head Physio:* Ally Beattie.

*Colours:* Claret shirts with blue sleeves, blue shorts with claret trim, blue socks with claret hoop.

*Year Formed:* 1882.

*Turned Professional:* 1883.

*Previous Name:* 1882, Burnley Rovers; 1882, Burnley.

*Club Nickname:* 'The Clarets'.

*Grounds:* 1882, Calder Vale; 1883, Turf Moor.

*First Football League Game:* 8 September 1888, Football League, v Preston NE (a) L 2–5 – Smith; Lang, Bury, Abrahams, Friel, Keenan, Brady, Tait, Poland (1), Gallocher (1), Yates.

*Record League Victory:* 9–0 v Darwen, Division 1, 9 January 1892 – Hillman; Walker, McFettridge, Lang, Matthews, Keenan, Nicol (3), Bowes, Espie (1), McLardie (3), Hill (2).

*Record Cup Victory:* 9–0 v Crystal Palace, FA Cup 2nd rd (replay), 10 February 1909 – Dawson; Barron, McLean; Cretney (2), Leake, Moffat; Morley, Ogden, Smith (3), Abbott (2), Smethams (1). 9–0 v New Brighton, FA Cup 4th rd, 26 January 1957 – Blacklaw; Angus, Winton; Seith, Adamson, Miller; Newlands (1), McIlroy (3), Lawson (3), Cheesebrough (1), Pilkington (1). 9–0 v Penrith, FA Cup 1st rd, 17 November 1984 – Hansbury; Miller, Hampton, Phelan, Overson (Kennedy), Hird (3 incl. 1p), Grewcock (1), Powell (2), Taylor (3), Biggins, Hutchison.

*Record Defeat:* 0–10 v Aston Villa, Division 1, 29 August 1925 and v Sheffield U, Division 1, 19 January 1929.

## HONOURS

**Football League – Division 1:** *Champions* 1920–21, 1959–60; *Runners-up* 1919–20, 1961–62; **Division 2:** *Champions* 1897–98, 1972–73; *Runners-up* 1912–13, 1946–47, 1999–2000; **Division 3:** *Champions* 1981–82; **Division 4:** *Champions* 1991–92. Record 30 consecutive Division 1 games without defeat 1920–21.

**FA Cup:** *Winners* 1914; *Runners-up* 1947, 1962.

**Football League Cup:** Semi-final 1961, 1969, 1983, 2009.

**Anglo–Scottish Cup:** *Winners* 1979.

**Sherpa Van Trophy:** *Runners-up* 1988.

**European Competitions European Cup:** 1960–61. **European Fairs Cup:** 1966–67.

## sky SPORTS FACT FILE

Burnley were third in the table with one First Division fixture of the 1959–60 season remaining. One point behind Wolverhampton Wanderers and with inferior goal average, only victory would secure the title. Goals from Brian Pilkington and Trevor Meredith gave them a 2-1 win over Manchester City and the championship.

*Most League Points (2 for a win):* 62, Division 2, 1972–73.

*Most League Points (3 for a win):* 88, Division 2, 1999–2000.

*Most League Goals:* 102, Division 1, 1960–61.

*Highest League Scorer in Season:* George Beel, 35, Division 1, 1927–28.

*Most League Goals in Total Aggregate:* George Beel, 179, 1923–32.

*Most League Goals in One Match:* 6, Louis Page v Birmingham C, Division 1, 10 April 1926.

*Most Capped Player:* Jimmy McIlroy, 51 (55), Northern Ireland.

*Most League Appearances:* Jerry Dawson, 522, 1907–28.

*Youngest League Player:* Tommy Lawton, 16 years 174 days v Doncaster R, 28 March 1936.

*Record Transfer Fee Received:* £7,000,000 from Southampton for Jay Rodriguez, June 2012.

*Record Transfer Fee Paid:* £3,000,000 to Hibernian for Steven Fletcher, June 2009.

*Football League Record:* 1888 Original Member of the Football League; 1897–98 Division 2; 1898–1900 Division 1; 1900–13 Division 2; 1913–30 Division 1; 1930–47 Division 2; 1947–71 Division 1; 1971–73 Division 2; 1973–76 Division 1; 1976–80 Division 2; 1980–82 Division 3; 1982–83 Division 2; 1983–85 Division 3; 1985–92 Division 4; 1992–94 Division 2; 1994–95 Division 1; 1995–2000 Division 2; 2000–04 Division 1; 2004–09 FL C; 2009–10 FA Premier League; 2010– FL C.

## LATEST SEQUENCES

*Longest Sequence of League Wins:* 10, 16.11.1912 – 18.1.1913.

*Longest Sequence of League Defeats:* 8, 2.1.1995 – 25.2.1995.

*Longest Sequence of League Draws:* 6, 21.2.1931 – 28.3.1931.

*Longest Sequence of Unbeaten League Matches:* 30, 6.9.1920 – 25.3.1921.

*Longest Sequence Without a League Win:* 24, 16.4.1979 – 17.11.1979.

*Successive Scoring Runs:* 27 from 13.2.1926.

*Successive Non-scoring Runs:* 6 from 9.8.1997.

## MANAGERS

**Harry Bradshaw** 1894–99
(*Secretary-Manager from 1897*)
**Club Directors** 1899–1900
**J. Ernest Mangnall** 1900–03
(*Secretary-Manager*)
**Spen Whittaker** 1903–10
(*Secretary-Manager*)
**John Haworth** 1910–24
(*Secretary-Manager*)
**Albert Pickles** 1925–31
(*Secretary-Manager*)
**Tom Bromilow** 1932–35
**Selection Committee** 1935–45
**Cliff Britton** 1945–48
**Frank Hill** 1948–54
**Alan Brown** 1954–57
**Billy Dougall** 1957–58
**Harry Potts** 1958–70
(*General Manager to 1972*)
**Jimmy Adamson** 1970–76
**Joe Brown** 1976–77
**Harry Potts** 1977–79
**Brian Miller** 1979–83
**John Bond** 1983–84
**John Benson** 1984–85
**Martin Buchan** 1985
**Tommy Cavanagh** 1985–86
**Brian Miller** 1986–89
**Frank Casper** 1989–91
**Jimmy Mullen** 1991–96
**Adrian Heath** 1996–97
**Chris Waddle** 1997–98
**Stan Ternent** 1998–2004
**Steve Cotterill** 2004–07
**Owen Coyle** 2007–10
**Brian Laws** 2010
**Eddie Howe** 2011–12
**Sean Dyche** October 2012–

## TEN YEAR LEAGUE RECORD

| | | P | W | D | L | F | A | Pts | Pos |
|---|---|---|---|---|---|---|---|---|---|
| 2003-04 | Div 1 | 46 | 13 | 14 | 19 | 60 | 77 | 53 | 19 |
| 2004-05 | FL C | 46 | 15 | 15 | 16 | 38 | 39 | 60 | 13 |
| 2005-06 | FL C | 46 | 14 | 12 | 20 | 46 | 54 | 54 | 17 |
| 2006-07 | FL C | 46 | 15 | 12 | 19 | 52 | 49 | 57 | 15 |
| 2007-08 | FL C | 46 | 16 | 14 | 16 | 60 | 67 | 62 | 13 |
| 2008-09 | FL C | 46 | 21 | 13 | 12 | 72 | 60 | 76 | 5 |
| 2009-10 | PR Lge | 38 | 8 | 6 | 24 | 42 | 82 | 30 | 18 |
| 2010-11 | FL C | 46 | 18 | 14 | 14 | 65 | 61 | 68 | 8 |
| 2011-12 | FL C | 46 | 17 | 11 | 18 | 61 | 58 | 62 | 13 |
| 2012-13 | FL C | 46 | 16 | 13 | 17 | 62 | 60 | 61 | 11 |

## DID YOU KNOW ?

Goalkeeper Jimmy Strong signed for Burnley in January 1946 and played in the Clarets' first post-war fixture, against Coventry City in August 1946. He did not miss a game until 24 March 1951, establishing a club record of 220 consecutive League and Cup appearances.

## BURNLEY – FL CHAMPIONSHIP 2012–13 LEAGUE RECORD

| Match No. | Date | Venue | Opponents | Result | H/T Score | Lg Pos. | Goalscorers | Attendance |
|---|---|---|---|---|---|---|---|---|
| 1 | Aug 18 | H | Bolton W | W 2-0 | 1-0 | 2 | Paterson [39], Austin [57] | 18,407 |
| 2 | 21 | A | Middlesbrough | L 2-3 | 1-1 | 8 | Austin [41], Stanislas [86] | 15,559 |
| 3 | 25 | A | Huddersfield T | L 0-2 | 0-1 | 18 | | 15,483 |
| 4 | Sept 1 | H | Brighton & HA | L 1-3 | 0-1 | 22 | Greer (og) [60] | 11,413 |
| 5 | 15 | H | Peterborough U | W 5-2 | 2-2 | 15 | McCann [7], Austin 3 (1 pen) [39, 74, 81 (p)], Stanislas [86] | 10,979 |
| 6 | 19 | A | Leicester C | L 1-2 | 1-0 | 19 | Marney [10] | 18,480 |
| 7 | 22 | A | Derby Co | W 2-1 | 1-1 | 16 | Austin 2 [32, 89] | 21,347 |
| 8 | 29 | H | Millwall | D 2-2 | 2-1 | 16 | Mee [19], Austin [43] | 11,192 |
| 9 | Oct 2 | H | Sheffield W | D 3-3 | 2-1 | 15 | Austin 3 [22, 38, 84] | 12,122 |
| 10 | 6 | A | Crystal Palace | L 3-4 | 2-1 | 16 | McCann [26], Paterson [29], Austin [81] | 20,863 |
| 11 | 20 | H | Blackpool | W 1-0 | 1-0 | 15 | Austin [19] | 12,925 |
| 12 | 23 | A | Bristol C | W 4-3 | 1-1 | 14 | Austin 2 (1 pen) [9, 59 (p)], Paterson [60], McCann [90] | 11,836 |
| 13 | 27 | A | Cardiff C | L 0-4 | 0-2 | 14 | | 21,191 |
| 14 | Nov 3 | H | Wolverhampton W | W 2-0 | 1-0 | 13 | Paterson [18], Austin [53] | 12,295 |
| 15 | 6 | H | Leeds U | W 1-0 | 0-0 | 10 | Austin [63] | 14,470 |
| 16 | 10 | A | Ipswich T | L 1-2 | 0-0 | 13 | Vokes [80] | 16,297 |
| 17 | 17 | H | Charlton Ath | L 0-1 | 0-0 | 15 | | 11,405 |
| 18 | 24 | A | Hull C | W 1-0 | 1-0 | 13 | Marney [40] | 17,782 |
| 19 | 27 | A | Barnsley | D 1-1 | 1-1 | 14 | Austin [5] | 8610 |
| 20 | Dec 2 | H | Blackburn R | D 1-1 | 0-0 | 14 | Vokes [89] | 21,341 |
| 21 | 8 | A | Nottingham F | L 0-2 | 0-0 | 17 | | 19,672 |
| 22 | 15 | H | Watford | D 1-1 | 1-1 | 16 | Austin (pen) [28] | 14,896 |
| 23 | 22 | A | Birmingham C | D 2-2 | 0-1 | 14 | Ings [66], Wallace [68] | 17,284 |
| 24 | 26 | H | Derby Co | W 2-0 | 1-0 | 13 | Austin [40], Duff [74] | 13,779 |
| 25 | 29 | H | Leicester C | L 0-1 | 0-1 | 13 | | 13,050 |
| 26 | Jan 1 | A | Sheffield W | W 2-0 | 0-0 | 12 | Treacy [63], Wallace (pen) [76] | 23,677 |
| 27 | 12 | H | Crystal Palace | W 1-0 | 0-0 | 10 | Stanislas [81] | 11,564 |
| 28 | 19 | A | Millwall | W 2-0 | 1-0 | 7 | Vokes [19], Ings [59] | 9384 |
| 29 | 26 | H | Birmingham C | L 1-2 | 0-1 | 8 | Wallace (pen) [56] | 11,576 |
| 30 | Feb 2 | A | Peterborough U | D 2-2 | 1-0 | 7 | Austin [1], Paterson [85] | 6648 |
| 31 | 9 | A | Bolton W | L 1-2 | 0-0 | 9 | Edgar [55] | 19,767 |
| 32 | 19 | H | Middlesbrough | D 0-0 | 0-0 | 11 | | 12,394 |
| 33 | 23 | A | Brighton & HA | L 0-1 | 0-1 | 12 | | 25,836 |
| 34 | 26 | H | Huddersfield T | L 0-1 | 0-0 | 13 | | 11,266 |
| 35 | Mar 2 | A | Charlton Ath | W 1-0 | 1-0 | 11 | Austin [43] | 20,065 |
| 36 | 5 | H | Barnsley | D 1-1 | 1-0 | 11 | Austin [9] | 10,584 |
| 37 | 11 | H | Hull C | L 0-1 | 0-0 | 11 | | 10,450 |
| 38 | 17 | A | Blackburn R | D 1-1 | 1-0 | 11 | Shackell [32] | 20,735 |
| 39 | 29 | A | Watford | D 3-3 | 2-2 | 13 | Austin 2 (1 pen) [1, 24 (p)], Vokes [90] | 15,435 |
| 40 | Apr 1 | H | Nottingham F | D 1-1 | 0-0 | 13 | Stanislas [68] | 13,618 |
| 41 | 6 | H | Bristol C | W 3-1 | 0-1 | 11 | Shackell [52], McCann [61], Paterson [90] | 11,539 |
| 42 | 13 | A | Blackpool | L 0-1 | 0-0 | 14 | | 14,437 |
| 43 | 16 | A | Leeds U | L 0-1 | 0-0 | 17 | | 16,788 |
| 44 | 20 | H | Cardiff C | D 1-1 | 0-1 | 15 | Edgar [90] | 13,264 |
| 45 | 27 | A | Wolverhampton W | W 2-1 | 1-0 | 14 | Ings [8], Paterson [53] | 24,199 |
| 46 | May 4 | H | Ipswich T | W 2-0 | 0-0 | 11 | Stanislas [60], Paterson [87] | 12,820 |

**Final League Position: 11**

### GOALSCORERS

*League (62):* Austin 25 (4 pens), Paterson 8, Stanislas 5, McCann 4, Vokes 4, Ings 3, Wallace 3 (2 pens), Edgar 2, Marney 2, Shackell 2, Duff 1, Mee 1, Treacy 1, own goal 1.
*FA Cup (0).*
*Capital One Cup (5):* Austin 3, Marney 1, McCann 1.

| Grant L 46 | Trippier K 45 | Shackell J 44 | Edgar D 20 + 7 | Mills J 9 + 1 | Wallace R 33 + 3 | Marney D 38 | McCann C 40 + 1 | Stanislas J 27 + 8 | Austin C 37 | Paterson M 28 + 11 | Vokes S 13 + 33 | Mee B 16 + 3 | Stock B 18 + 7 | Bartley M 8 + 13 | Duff M 23 + 1 | Treacy K 4 + 11 | MacDonald A — + 1 | Stewart C 2 + 7 | Long K 13 + 1 | Ings D 15 + 17 | Lafferty D 21 + 3 | Richards D — + 1 | Kacaniklic A 6 | O'Neill L — + 1 | Jensen B — + 1 | Match No. |
|---|---|---|---|---|---|---|---|---|---|---|---|---|---|---|---|---|---|---|---|---|---|---|---|---|---|---|
| 1 | 2 | 3 | 4 | 5 | 6 | 7 | 8 | 9[2] | 10[3] | 11[1] | 12 | 13 | 14 | | | | | | | | | | | | | 1 |
| 1 | 2 | 3 | 4 | 5 | 7[2] | 8 | 6 | 9 | 10 | 11[1] | | 13 | | | 12 | | | | | | | | | | | 2 |
| 1 | 2 | 3 | 5 | 4[2] | 6 | 8 | 7 | 9[3] | 11 | 10[1] | | | | | 12 | 13 | 14 | | | | | | | | | 3 |
| 1 | 2 | 3 | 4 | 5 | 13 | 8[3] | 6 | 9 | 10 | 12 | 14 | | | | | 7[1] | | | 11[2] | | | | | | | 4 |
| 1 | 2 | | 4 | 5 | 6[2] | 7 | 8 | 9 | 10[3] | 11[1] | 12 | | | | 14 | | 3 | | 13 | | | | | | | 5 |
| 1 | 2 | 3 | 4 | 5[3] | 14 | 8 | 7 | 9 | | 11[2] | 13 | | 12 | | 6[1] | | | | 10 | | | | | | | 6 |
| 1 | 2 | 4 | 3 | | 6 | 8 | 7 | 9[1] | 11[3] | 10[2] | 13 | | 5 | | 14 | | | | 12 | | | | | | | 7 |
| 1 | 2 | 4 | | | 6[3] | 7 | 8[1] | 9 | 11 | 10[2] | 13 | | 5 | | 12 | 3 | | | 14 | | | | | | | 8 |
| 1 | 2 | 4 | | | 6 | 7 | | 9[1] | 11 | 10[1] | 14 | | 5 | 8 | | 3[2] | | 12 | 13 | | | | | | | 9 |
| 1 | 2 | 3 | 4 | | 14 | 7 | 8[2] | 9[1] | 11 | 10[1] | 13 | | 5 | | 6 | | | | 12 | | | | | | | 10 |
| 1 | 2 | 4 | | | 9 | 6 | 8 | 11[2] | 10[3] | 13 | 14 | | 5 | | 7[1] | | | 12 | 3 | | | | | | | 11 |
| 1 | 2 | 4 | | | 9 | 8 | 10[2] | 11[3] | 7[1] | 14 | 5 | | 6 | | 3 | | | | 13 | 12 | | | | | | 12 |
| 1 | 2 | 4 | 5 | | 7 | 6 | 10[1] | 11 | 9[2] | 12 | 8[3] | | 3 | | | | | | 14 | 13 | | | | | | 13 |
| 1 | 2 | 4 | 6 | | 9[1] | 8[2] | | 13 | 10 | 11[3] | 14 | 5 | 7 | | 3 | | | | | 12 | | | | | | 14 |
| 1 | 2 | 4 | | | 9 | 6 | 8 | 10 | 11 | 13 | 5[1] | | 7[2] | | 3 | | | | | | 12 | | | | | 15 |
| 1 | 2 | 4 | | | 6[1] | 8[3] | 9 | 12 | 11 | 10 | 14 | | 7[2] | 13 | 3 | | | | | | 5 | | | | | 16 |
| 1 | 2[4] | 4 | 13 | | 6 | 8 | 11[1] | 10 | 9[3] | 14 | 7 | | 3 | | | | | | 12 | | 5[2] | | | | | 17 |
| 1 | | 4 | 2 | | 6[2] | 9 | 7 | 11[3] | 10 | 12 | 5 | | 8[1] | 14 | 3 | | | | 13 | | | | | | | 18 |
| 1 | 2 | 4 | 13 | | 9[3] | 7 | | 10 | 11 | 14 | 5 | | 8[2] | 6[1] | 3 | | | | 12 | | | | | | | 19 |
| 1 | 2 | 4 | | | 9 | 6 | 8[3] | 12 | 10 | 11[1] | 14 | 5 | 7[2] | | 3 | | | | 13 | | | | | | | 20 |
| 1 | 2 | 4 | | | 10[3] | 9 | 8 | 13 | 11 | 6[2] | 12 | | 7[1] | | 3 | | | | 14 | 5 | | | | | | 21 |
| 1 | 2 | 4 | 8 | | 6[3] | 7 | | 12 | 11 | 9[1] | 14 | | | | | | 13 | 3 | | 10[2] | 5 | | | | | 22 |
| 1 | 2 | 4 | | 5 | 6 | 7[3] | 8 | | 11 | 9[1] | 14 | | | | | 13 | | 3 | 12 | 10[2] | | | | | | 23 |
| 1 | 2 | 4 | | | 6 | 7 | 8 | | 11[2] | 9[1] | 13 | | | | | 14 | | 3 | 12 | 10[1] | 5 | | | | | 24 |
| 1 | 2 | 4 | | | 6[1] | 7 | 8 | | 11[2] | 12 | 13 | | | | | 14 | | 3 | | 10 | 5 | 9[3] | | | | 25 |
| 1 | 2 | 4 | 13 | | 9 | | 6[2] | | 11[1] | 10 | | | 8[3] | 14 | | | | 3 | | 7 | 5 | 9 | | | | 26 |
| 1 | 2 | 4 | | | 6 | 8[2] | 7 | | 10[1] | 11 | | | | | | 13 | | 3 | | 9 | 5 | | | | | 27 |
| 1 | 2 | 3 | 4 | | 10 | 7 | 8 | 6[1] | | 13 | 11 | | | | | | | 3 | | 9[2] | 5 | | | | | 28 |
| 1 | 2 | 3 | 4 | | 6[1] | 8[3] | 9 | 10[2] | | 13 | 11 | 12 | | | 14 | | | | | 7[3] | 5 | | | | | 29 |
| 1 | 2 | 3 | 12 | | 6[2] | 7 | 8 | 9 | 10[3] | 14 | 13 | | | | 4[1] | | | | | 11 | 5 | | | | | 30 |
| 1 | 2 | 4 | 3 | | 6[1] | 8 | 7 | 10[3] | 11 | 12 | 13 | | | | 14 | | | | | 9[2] | 5 | | | | | 31 |
| 1 | 2 | 4 | | | 6 | 8 | 11 | 10 | 9[3] | 13 | | | | 7[1] | | | | 3 | | 12 | 5 | | | | | 32 |
| 1 | 2 | 4 | | | 9[2] | 7 | 6[1] | 11 | | 14 | | | 8[3] | 13 | | | | 10 | | 3 | 12 | 5 | | | | 33 |
| 1 | 2 | 4 | | | 7[1] | 8[3] | | 11 | | 13 | | 6 | 14 | | | | 10 | | 3 | 9 | 5 | 12[2] | | | | 34 |
| 1 | 2 | 3 | 7 | | | 6[1] | 10[2] | 11 | 13 | 14 | 8 | | | | | | | 4 | | 12 | 5 | | 9[3] | | | 35 |
| 1 | 2 | 4 | 7[2] | | | 12 | 11[1] | 10 | 9[3] | 14 | 6 | | | | | | | 3 | | 13 | 5 | | 8 | | | 36 |
| 1 | 2 | 4 | 7[2] | 9[3] | | 8 | 10 | | 12 | 5 | 13 | | | | | 3 | | | | 11[1] | | 14 | 6 | | | 37 |
| 1 | 2 | 4 | 9[1] | | | 8 | 10[2] | 11[3] | 14 | 5[4] | 7 | 3 | | | | | | | 13 | 12 | | | 6 | | | 38 |
| 1 | 2 | 4 | 6[2] | | | 7 | 11 | 14 | 13 | 12 | 8[1] | 3 | | | | 10 | | | | | 5 | | 9[3] | | | 39 |
| 1 | 2 | 4 | 14 | 12 | 6[2] | 8 | 9[3] | 11 | 10 | 5[1] | 7 | | | | | | | 3 | | 13 | | | | | | 40 |
| 1 | 2 | 4 | 5 | 6[2] | 7 | 8 | 11 | 9 | 12 | 10[1] | | | | | | | | 3 | | 13 | | | | | | 41 |
| 1 | 2 | 4 | 12 | 6[1] | 7[3] | 8 | 9[2] | 10 | 13 | 11 | 5 | | | | | | | 3 | | 14 | | | | | | 42 |
| 1 | 2 | 3 | 9[3] | 8 | 7 | 13 | 11[2] | 10 | 5[1] | | 4 | | | | | | | 14 | 12 | | | 6 | | | | 43 |
| 1 | 2 | 4 | 12 | 8[2] | 6[3] | 7 | 10[1] | 13 | 11 | 14 | | 3 | | | | | | | | 9 | 5 | | | | | 44 |
| 1 | 2 | 4 | 6 | 8 | 7 | 12 | 11[1] | 10[2] | 13 | 3[4] | | | | | | | | | | 9 | 5 | | | | | 45 |
| 1[3] | 2[2] | 4 | 6 | 8 | 12 | 11 | 10 | 7[1] | 3 | | | | | | | | | | | 9 | 5 | | | 13 | 14 | 46 |

**FA Cup**

| Third Round | Barnsley | (a) | 0-1 |
|---|---|---|---|

**Capital One Cup**

| First Round | Port Vale | (a) | 3-1 |
|---|---|---|---|
| Second Round | Plymouth Arg | (h) | 1-1 |
| *(aet; won 3-2 on pens)* | | | |
| Third Round | Swindon T | (a) | 1-3 |

# BURTON ALBION

## FOUNDATION

Once upon a time there were three Football League clubs bearing the name Burton. Then there was none. In reality it had been two. Originally Burton Swifts and Burton Wanderers competed in it until 1901 when they amalgamated to form Burton United. This club disbanded in 1910. There was no senior club representing the town until 1924 when Burton Town, formerly known as Burton All Saints, played in the Birmingham & District League, subsequently joining the Midland League in 1935–36. When the Second World War broke out the club fielded a team in a truncated version of the Birmingham & District League taking over from the club's reserves. But it was not revived in peacetime. So it was not until a further decade that a club bearing the name of Burton reappeared. Founded in 1950 Burton Albion made progress from the Birmingham & District League, too, then into the Southern League and because of its geographical situation later had spells in the Northern Premier League. In April 2009 Burton Albion restored the name of the town to the Football League competition as champions of the Blue Square Premier League.

*Pirelli Stadium, Princess Way, Burton-on-Trent, Staffordshire DE13 0AR.*

*Telephone:* (01283) 565 938.

*Fax:* (01283) 523 199.

*Ticket Office:* (01283) 565 938.

*Website:* www.burtonalbionfc.co.uk

*Email:* bafc@burtonalbionfc.co.uk

*Ground Capactiy:* 6,912.

*Record Attendance:* 5,806 v Weymouth, Southern League Cup final 2nd leg 1964 (at Eton Park); 6,192 v Oxford U, Blue Square Premier, 17 April 2009 (at Pirelli Stadium).

*Pitch Measurements:* 100m × 65m (110yd × 72yd)

*Chairman:* Ben Robinson.

*Manager:* Gary Rowett.

*Assistant Manager:* Kevin Summerfield.

*Physio:* James Rowland.

*Colours:* Black and yellow striped shirts, black shorts, black socks with yellow trim.

*Year Formed:* 1950.

*Turned Professional:* 1950.

## HONOURS

**Conference:** *Champions* 2008–09.
**FA Cup:** Best season: 4th rd, 2011.
**Football League Cup:** Best season: 3rd rd, 2013.
**FA Trophy:** *Runners-up* 1986–87.
**Southern League – Premier Division:** *Runners-up* 1999–2000, 2000–01; **Division 1 (N):** *Runners-up* 1971–72, 1973–74. **Shared Cup:** 2000.
**Southern League Cup:** *Winners* 1964, 1997, 2000; *Runners-up* 1989.
**Northern Premier League:** *Champions* 2001–02.
**Northern Premier League Shield:** 1983. **Challenge Cup:** *Winners* 1983; *Runners-up* 1987.
**President's Cup:** *Runners-up* 1983, 1986.
**Birmingham Senior Cup:** *Winners* 1954, 1997; *Runners-up* 1970, 1971, 1987.
**Staffordshire Senior Cup:** *Winners* 1956; *Runners-up* 1977.
**Midland Floodlit Cup:** *Winners* 1976; *Runners-up* 1973.

## sky SPORTS FACT FILE

Burton Albion's FA Cup third round tie against Leicester City in January 1985 was ordered to be replayed after being interrupted by crowd disturbances. The second meeting took place at Coventry City's Highfield Road ground behind closed doors with Leicester winning 1-0.

**Club Nickname:** 'The Brewers'.

**Grounds:** 1950, Eton Park; 2005, Pirelli Stadium.

**First Football League Game:** 8 August 2009, FL 2, v Shrewsbury T (a) L 1–3 – Redmond; Edworthy, Boertien, Austin, Branston, McGrath, Maghoma, Penn, Phillips (Stride), Walker, Shroot (Pearson) (1).

**Record League Victory:** 6-1 v Aldershot T, FL 2, 12 December 2009 – Krysiak; James, Boertien, Stride, Webster, McGrath, Jackson, Penn, Kabba (2), Pearson (3) (Harrad) (1), Gilroy (Maghoma).

**Record Cup Victory:** 12–1 v Coalville T, Birmingham Senior Cup, 6 September 1954.

**Record Defeat:** 0–10 v Barnet, Southern League, 7 February 1970.

**Most League Points (3 for a win):** 76, FL 2, 2012–13.

**Most League Goals:** 71, FL 2, 2009–10; 2012–13.

**Highest League Scorer in Season:** Shaun Harrad, 21, 2009–10.

**Most League Goals in Total Aggregate:** Shaun Harrad, 31, 2009–11.

**Most League Goals in One Match:** 3, Greg Pearson v Aldershot T, FL 2, 12 December 2009; 3, Shaun Harrad v Rotherham U, FL 2, 11 September 2010.

**Most Capped Player:** Jacques Maghoma, 3, DR Congo.

**Most League Appearances:** Jacques Maghoma, 155, 2009–13.

**Youngest League Player:** Tom Parkes, 18 years 8 days v Torquay U, 23 January 2010.

**Record Transfer Fee Received:** £130,000 from Crewe Alex for John Brayford, September 2008; £130,000 from Derby Co for Adam Legzdins, June 2011.

**Record Transfer Fee Paid:** £20,000 to Kidderminster H for Russell Penn, July 2009; £20,000 to Torquay U for Billy Kee, August 2011.

**Football League Record:** Promoted from Blue Square Premier 2008–09; 2009– FL 2.

## MANAGERS

Reg Weston
Sammy Crooks 1957
Eddie Shimwell 1958
Bill Townsend 1959–62
Peter Taylor 1962–65
Richie Norman
Reg Gutteridge
Harold Bodle 1974–76
Ian Storey-Moore 1978–81
Neil Warnock 1981–86
Brian Fidler 1986–88
Vic Halom 1988
Bobby Hope 1988
Chris Wright 1988–89
Ken Blair 1989–90
Steve Powell 1990–91
Brian Fidler 1991–92
Brian Kenning 1992–94
John Barton 1994–98
Nigel Clough 1998–2009
Roy McFarland 2009
Paul Peschisolido 2009–12
Gary Rowett March 2012–

## LATEST SEQUENCES

**Longest Sequence of League Wins:** 4, 9.2.2013 – 26.2.2013.

**Longest Sequence of League Defeats:** 8, 25.2.2012 – 24.3.2012.

**Longest Sequence of League Draws:** 6, 25.4.2011 – 16.8.2011.

**Longest Sequence of Unbeaten League Matches:** 10, 16.4.2011 – 20.8.2012.

**Longest Sequence Without a League Win:** 16, 31.12.2011 – 24.3.2012.

**Successive Scoring Runs:** 18 from 16.4.2011 – 8.10.2011.

**Successive Non-scoring Runs:** 5 from 25.2.2012 – 10.3.2012.

## TEN YEAR LEAGUE RECORD

| | | P | W | D | L | F | A | Pts | Pos |
|---|---|---|---|---|---|---|---|---|---|
| 2003-04 | Conf | 42 | 15 | 7 | 20 | 57 | 59 | 51* | 14 |
| 2004-05 | Conf | 42 | 13 | 11 | 18 | 50 | 66 | 50 | 16 |
| 2005-06 | Conf | 42 | 16 | 12 | 14 | 50 | 52 | 60 | 9 |
| 2006-07 | Conf | 46 | 22 | 9 | 15 | 52 | 47 | 75 | 6 |
| 2007-08 | BSP | 46 | 23 | 12 | 11 | 79 | 56 | 81 | 5 |
| 2008-09 | BSP | 46 | 27 | 7 | 12 | 81 | 52 | 88 | 1 |
| 2009-10 | FL 2 | 46 | 17 | 11 | 18 | 71 | 71 | 62 | 13 |
| 2010-11 | FL 2 | 46 | 12 | 15 | 19 | 56 | 70 | 51 | 19 |
| 2011-12 | FL 2 | 46 | 14 | 12 | 20 | 54 | 81 | 54 | 17 |
| 2012-13 | FL 2 | 46 | 22 | 10 | 14 | 71 | 65 | 76 | 4 |

*1 pt deducted.

## DID YOU KNOW ?

On 9 May 1987 Burton Albion made their Wembley debut, drawing 0-0 with Kidderminster Harriers in the FA Trophy final in front of a crowd of 23,617. The replay was held the following Tuesday at The Hawthorns, with Albion going down 2-1.

## BURTON ALBION – FOOTBALL LEAGUE TWO 2012–13 LEAGUE RECORD

| Match No. | Date | Venue | Opponents | Result | H/T Score | Lg Pos. | Goalscorers | Attendance |
|---|---|---|---|---|---|---|---|---|
| 1 | Aug 18 | A | Rotherham U | L 0-3 | 0-2 | 23 | | 11,441 |
| 2 | 21 | H | AFC Wimbledon | W 6-2 | 4-0 | 8 | Taylor [8], Kee [13], Maghoma [15], Richards [28], Weir [53], Diamond [68] | 1948 |
| 3 | 25 | H | Fleetwood T | L 0-1 | 0-0 | 15 | | 2349 |
| 4 | Sept 1 | A | Exeter C | L 0-3 | 0-2 | 20 | | 3707 |
| 5 | 8 | A | Rochdale | W 1-0 | 0-0 | 15 | Paterson [52] | 2199 |
| 6 | 15 | H | Oxford U | W 4-0 | 2-0 | 10 | Zola 2 [25, 66], Maghoma 2 [45, 65] | 2389 |
| 7 | 19 | H | York C | W 3-1 | 1-1 | 6 | Bell [23], Zola [65], Paterson [90] | 2368 |
| 8 | 22 | A | Torquay U | D 1-1 | 0-1 | 7 | Zola [89] | 2438 |
| 9 | 29 | H | Northampton T | D 3-3 | 1-0 | 9 | Zola [9], Langmead (og) [60], Diamond [80] | 2857 |
| 10 | Oct 2 | A | Southend U | W 1-0 | 0-0 | 5 | Maghoma [90] | 4150 |
| 11 | 6 | A | Morecambe | D 0-0 | 0-0 | 7 | | 1585 |
| 12 | 13 | H | Bristol R | D 1-1 | 0-1 | 5 | Kee [50] | 2961 |
| 13 | 20 | A | Gillingham | L 1-4 | 0-2 | 6 | Diamond [54] | 7268 |
| 14 | 23 | H | Port Vale | D 1-1 | 0-0 | 10 | Chapell [73] | 3975 |
| 15 | 27 | H | Bradford C | W 1-0 | 0-0 | 8 | Zola [80] | 2791 |
| 16 | Nov 7 | A | Plymouth Arg | W 2-1 | 0-0 | 5 | Stanton [74], Weir [79] | 5219 |
| 17 | 10 | A | Cheltenham T | L 0-1 | 0-0 | 7 | | 2804 |
| 18 | 17 | H | Dagenham & R | W 3-2 | 0-1 | 6 | McCrory [51], Paterson [53], Kee [79] | 2369 |
| 19 | 20 | H | Aldershot T | L 0-1 | 0-1 | 10 | | 1712 |
| 20 | 24 | A | Wycombe W | L 0-3 | 0-1 | 11 | | 3191 |
| 21 | Dec 9 | H | Accrington S | W 1-0 | 1-0 | 9 | Kee [10] | 2530 |
| 22 | 15 | A | Chesterfield | D 1-1 | 1-0 | 9 | Maghoma [34] | 5741 |
| 23 | 21 | A | Barnet | L 2-3 | 1-1 | 10 | Kee (pen) [16], Maghoma (pen) [90] | 1751 |
| 24 | 26 | H | Rochdale | W 3-2 | 2-1 | 8 | Kee 2 [15, 57], Zola [25] | 2994 |
| 25 | 29 | H | Southend U | W 2-0 | 2-0 | 7 | Zola [16], Bell [36] | 2636 |
| 26 | Jan 1 | A | York C | L 0-3 | 0-2 | 8 | | 3863 |
| 27 | 12 | H | Torquay U | W 2-1 | 0-1 | 6 | Zola [59], Paterson [84] | 2356 |
| 28 | 19 | A | Northampton T | L 0-1 | 0-0 | 7 | | 4090 |
| 29 | 26 | H | Barnet | W 1-0 | 1-0 | 6 | Maghoma (pen) [4] | 2050 |
| 30 | 29 | A | Oxford U | D 1-1 | 0-0 | 3 | Maghoma [70] | 4906 |
| 31 | Feb 2 | A | AFC Wimbledon | D 1-1 | 1-1 | 4 | Symes [36] | 3684 |
| 32 | 9 | H | Rotherham U | W 2-0 | 1-0 | 3 | Kee 2 [36, 55] | 3967 |
| 33 | 16 | A | Fleetwood T | W 4-0 | 0-0 | 3 | Maghoma 2 (1 pen) [59 (p), 87], Kee [76], Zola [90] | 2698 |
| 34 | 23 | H | Exeter C | W 4-2 | 3-0 | 3 | Symes [11], Holness [27], Maghoma [34], Bell [60] | 2823 |
| 35 | 26 | H | Morecambe | W 3-2 | 2-0 | 3 | Maghoma [18], Kee 2 [45, 49] | 2170 |
| 36 | Mar 2 | A | Bristol R | L 0-3 | 0-1 | 3 | | 6065 |
| 37 | 9 | H | Cheltenham T | W 3-1 | 2-0 | 3 | MacDonald [22], Weir 2 [26, 48] | 2680 |
| 38 | 12 | A | Aldershot T | W 2-1 | 1-1 | 2 | Weir [44], Symes [65] | 1568 |
| 39 | 16 | A | Dagenham & R | D 1-1 | 1-0 | 3 | Bell [34] | 1364 |
| 40 | 30 | H | Chesterfield | L 0-1 | 0-0 | 4 | | 3823 |
| 41 | Apr 1 | A | Accrington S | D 3-3 | 1-1 | 5 | Paterson [36], Diamond [67], Maghoma [73] | 1619 |
| 42 | 5 | A | Port Vale | L 1-7 | 0-3 | 5 | Paterson [70] | 10,978 |
| 43 | 9 | H | Wycombe W | W 2-0 | 0-0 | 3 | Maghoma 2 [49, 68] | 2202 |
| 44 | 13 | H | Plymouth Arg | W 1-0 | 0-0 | 3 | Paterson [90] | 4392 |
| 45 | 20 | A | Bradford C | L 0-1 | 0-1 | 5 | | 13,235 |
| 46 | 27 | H | Gillingham | W 3-2 | 2-1 | 4 | Kee [33], Symes [39], Zola [63] | 5426 |

**Final League Position: 4**

### GOALSCORERS

*League (71):* Maghoma 15 (3 pens), Kee 13 (1 pen), Zola 11, Paterson 7, Weir 5, Bell 4, Diamond 4, Symes 4, Chapell 1, Holness 1, MacDonald 1, McCrory 1, Richards 1, Stanton 1, Taylor 1, own goal 1.
*FA Cup (6):* Zola 3, Diamond 1, Maghoma 1, Palmer C 1.
*Capital One Cup (8):* Taylor 2, Kee 1, Maghoma 1, Palmer C 1, Webster 1, Weir 1 (1 pen), Yussuf 1.
*Johnstone's Paint Trophy (0).*
*League Two Play-Offs (4):* Zola 2, Maghoma 1 (1 pen), Weir 1.

| Atkins R 4 | Stanton N 15+3 | Diamond Z 37 | O'Connor A 46 | McCrory D 42 | Taylor C 11+7 | Weir R 42 | Bell L 42+1 | Maghoma J 43 | Kee B 27+13 | Yussuf A 1+7 | Dyer J 15+13 | Richards J 4+9 | Paterson M 15+16 | Palmer C 7+2 | Zola C 26+5 | Holness M 18+4 | Tomlinson S 25 | Corbett A —+5 | Kiernan R 6 | Rooney L 3 | Webster A 5+4 | Chapell J —+2 | Lyness D 14+1 | Oxley M 3 | McGrath J 1+5 | Blyth J —+2 | Phillips J 1+6 | Drury A 6+6 | Sharps I 16 | MacDonald A 15 | Symes M 14+1 | Fowler L 2+1 | Palmer M —+2 | Match No. |
|---|---|---|---|---|---|---|---|---|---|---|---|---|---|---|---|---|---|---|---|---|---|---|---|---|---|---|---|---|---|---|---|---|---|---|
| 1 | 2 | 3 | 4 | 5 | 6² | 7 | 8⁴ | 9 | 10³ | 11¹ | 12 | 13 | 14 | | | | | | | | | | | | | | | | | | | | | 1 |
| 1 | 4 | 3 | 2¹ | 5 | 6² | 7 | | 9 | 11³ | 12 | 8 | 10¹ | 14 | 13 | | | | | | | | | | | | | | | | | | | | 2 |
| 1 | 4 | 3 | 2 | 5 | 6³ | 7 | 13 | 9 | 10 | 12 | 8² | 11¹ | | 14 | | | | | | | | | | | | | | | | | | | | 3 |
| 1 | | 3 | 2 | 5 | 7² | 8 | 6³ | 9 | 12 | 14 | | 13 | | | 10¹ | 11 | 4 | | | | | | | | | | | | | | | | | 4 |
| | 3 | 2 | 5 | 13 | 7 | 8 | 9 | | 12 | 14 | 11¹ | | | 6² | 10³ | 4 | 1 | | | | | | | | | | | | | | | | | 5 |
| | 3 | 2 | 5 | 6¹ | 7 | 8 | 9 | | 12 | 14 | 10² | | | 11³ | 4 | 1 | 13 | | | | | | | | | | | | | | | | | 6 |
| 12 | 3 | 2 | 5 | | 7 | 8 | 9 | | | 6 | | 11 | | | 10 | 4¹ | 1 | | | | | | | | | | | | | | | | | 7 |
| | 3 | 4 | 2 | 5 | 13 | 8 | 7 | 9³ | 12 | 14 | 6² | | | 10¹ | 11 | 1 | | | | | | | | | | | | | | | | | 8 |
| 13 | 3 | 2 | 5 | | 7 | 8 | 9 | 12 | | | 11² | | | 10¹ | | 1 | | 4 | 6³ | 14 | | | | | | | | | | | | | | 9 |
| | 3 | 2 | 5 | 14 | 7 | 8 | 9 | 10² | 12 | | 13 | 11¹ | | | | 1 | | 4 | 6³ | | | | | | | | | | | | | | | 10 |
| 14 | 3 | 2³ | 5 | | 7 | 8 | 9 | | 12 | 13 | 10 | 11¹ | | | | 1 | | 4 | 6² | | | | | | | | | | | | | | | 11 |
| | 4 | 2 | 5 | 6 | | 8 | 9 | 11² | 12 | 7 | 10¹ | 13 | | | | 1 | | 3 | | | | | | | | | | | | | | | | 12 |
| | 4 | 2 | 5 | 14 | 6 | 8 | 9² | 12 | | 7 | 13 | 10¹ | | 11² | | 1 | | 3 | | | | | | | | | | | | | | | | 13 |
| | 3 | 2 | 5 | 6² | 8 | 7 | 9 | 12 | | | 10¹ | | | 11 | 1³ | | 4 | | | 13 | 14 | | | | | | | | | | | | | 14 |
| 3 | 4 | 2 | 5 | 6¹ | 7 | 8 | 9 | 11² | | | 13 | | 10 | | 1 | | | | 12 | 1 | | | | | | | | | | | | | | 15 |
| 4 | 3 | 2 | 5 | 6¹ | 10 | 7 | 9² | 12 | | 8 | | | 13 | 11 | | 1 | | | | | 1 | | | | | | | | | | | | | 16 |
| 5 | 3 | 2 | | 13 | 7 | 8 | | 12 | | 6² | | 11¹ | 9 | 10 | 4 | | | | | | 1 | | | | | | | | | | | | | 17 |
| 3 | 4 | 2 | 5 | | 7 | 8 | 9 | 11 | 13 | | 12³ | 6² | 10¹ | 14 | | | | | | | 1 | | | | | | | | | | | | | 18 |
| 4 | 3 | 2 | 5 | | 7² | 8 | 9³ | 10 | | 12 | 11¹ | 6 | | | | | | | | | 1 | | 13 | 14 | | | | | | | | | | 19 |
| 3 | 4¹ | 2 | 5 | | 7 | 8 | 9 | 11¹ | | | 6 | 10³ | 12 | 13 | | | | | | | 1 | | 14 | | | | | | | | | | | 20 |
| | 3 | 2 | 5 | 12 | 8³ | 7 | 9 | 11² | 14 | | 6¹ | 10 | 4 | | | | | | | | 1 | | 13 | | | | | | | | | | | 21 |
| | 3 | 2 | 5 | 7¹ | 8 | 6 | 10 | 12 | 9 | 13 | 11² | 4 | | | | | | | | | 1 | | | | | | | | | | | | | 22 |
| | 3 | 2 | 8 | 7 | 5 | | 6 | 11¹ | 9 | 12 | 10 | 4 | | | | | | | | | 1 | | | | | | | | | | | | | 23 |
| 4 | 3 | 2 | 5 | | 8 | 7 | 9 | 11¹ | 6² | | | 10 | | | 13 | | | | | | 1 | | 12 | | | | | | | | | | | 24 |
| 4¹ | 3 | 2 | 5 | | 8 | 7 | 9 | 10¹ | 6 | | | 11 | | | | 12 | | | | | 1 | | | | | | | | | | | | | 25 |
| | 2¹ | 5 | 12 | 8² | 7 | 9 | 10 | 6 | | | 11 | 3 | | | | 4 | | | | 1 | 14 | 13 | | | | | | | | | | | | 26 |
| 4 | 3 | 2 | 5 | | 7 | 8³ | 9 | 11 | 12 | | 13 | 10² | | | | | | 14 | | 1 | | | | | | | 6¹ | | | | | | | 27 |
| 3 | 4 | 2 | 5 | | 9 | 8¹ | 10² | 12 | | | 14 | 11³ | | | | | | 6 | | 1 | | | 13 | 7 | | | | | | | | | | 28 |
| | 3 | 2 | 5 | | 7 | 8 | 9 | 10¹ | 13 | | 12 | 11² | | 1 | | | | | | 14 | | | | | | | 6 | 4 | | | | | | 29 |
| | 3 | 2 | 5 | | 8 | 7 | 9 | 12 | 14 | | 11² | | | 10¹ | 13 | 1 | | | | | | | | | | | 6³ | 4 | | | | | | 30 |
| | | 3⁴ | 2 | | 7 | 6 | 8 | 13 | | | | 11² | | | 14 | | 1 | | 5 | | | | | | | 12 | 4 | 9¹ | 10³ | | | | | 31 |
| 3 | | 2 | | | 8 | 7 | 9³ | 10² | 12 | | 13 | | | 4 | 1 | | | 5 | | | 14 | | | | | | | 6¹ | 11 | | | | | 32 |
| | | 2 | 5 | | 7 | 8 | 9 | 10³ | | | | 14 | | 13 | 3 | 1 | | | | | | | | | | 12 | 4 | 6¹ | 11² | | | | | 33 |
| | | 2 | 5 | | 7 | 8 | 9 | 11² | | | | | | 13 | 3 | 1 | | | | | | | | | | 12 | 4 | 6¹ | 10 | | | | | 34 |
| | | 2 | 5 | | 8 | 7 | 9¹ | 10 | 13 | | | | | | 3 | 1 | | | | | | | | | | 12 | 4 | 6² | 11 | | | | | 35 |
| | | 2 | 5 | | 6³ | 7 | 9¹ | 10² | 14 | | | | | | 13 | 3 | 1 | | | | | | | | | 12 | 4 | 8 | 11 | | | | | 36 |
| 3 | | 2 | 5 | | 8 | 7 | 9 | 10 | | | | | | | | 1 | | | | | | | | | | | 4 | 6 | 11 | | | | | 37 |
| | 4 | 2 | 6 | | 7 | 9 | | | | | 12 | | 10¹ | | 1 | | | | | | | | 11 | 3 | 5 | 8 | | | | | | | | 38 |
| | 3 | 2 | 5 | | 8 | 7 | 9 | 11¹ | | | 12 | | 10 | | 1 | | | | | | | | 13 | 4 | 6² | | | | | | | | | 39 |
| | 3 | 2 | 5 | | 8 | 7 | 9² | 10 | | | 12 | | | | 1 | | | | | | | | 13 | 14 | 4 | 6³ | 11¹ | | | | | | | 40 |
| | 3 | 2 | 5 | | 7 | 9 | 12 | | 8 | | 10¹ | | | | 1 | | | | | | | | 4 | 6 | 11² | 13 | | | | | | | | 41 |
| | 4 | 2 | 5 | | | 9³ | 6 | | 8 | | 12 | | | 1 | 13 | | | | | | | | 3 | 10² | 11 | 7¹ | 14 | | | | | | | 42 |
| | | 2 | 5 | | 8 | 7 | 9¹ | 10 | | | 13 | | | 3 | | | | | 1 | | | | | | 12 | 4 | 6 | 11² | | | | | | 43 |
| | | 2 | 5 | | 7 | 8 | 9 | 10³ | | | 12 | | | 4 | | 14 | 1 | | | | | | | 13 | 3 | 6¹ | 11² | | | | | | | 44 |
| | | 2 | 5 | | 8 | 7⁸ | 9 | 13 | 12³ | | 11¹ | | | 10² | 3 | | | 1 | | | | | | 4 | 6 | 14 | | | | | | | | 45 |
| | 3 | 2 | | | | | | 10¹ | | | | | | 12 | 4 | 1 | 14 | | 5 | | | 7 | 9⁵ | 6 | | 11 | 8² | 13 | | | | | | 46 |

**FA Cup**

|  |  | |  |
|---|---|---|---|
| First Round | Altrincham | (h) | 3-3 |
| *Replay* | Altrincham | (a) | 2-0 |
| Second Round | Crewe Alex | (a) | 1-0 |
| Third Round | Leicester C | (a) | 0-2 |

**Capital One Cup**

|  |  | |  |
|---|---|---|---|
| First Round | Sheffield U | (a) | 2-2 |
| *(aet; won 5-4 on pens)* | | | |
| Second Round | Leicester C | (a) | 4-2 |
| Third Round | Bradford C | (a) | 2-3 |

**Johnstone's Paint Trophy**

|  |  | |  |
|---|---|---|---|
| First Round | Coventry C | (a) | 0-0 |
| *(aet; lost 9-10 on pens)* | | | |

**League Two Play-Offs**

|  |  | |  |
|---|---|---|---|
| Semi-Finals | Bradford C | (a) | 3-2 |
| | Bradford C | (h) | 1-3 |

# BURY

## FOUNDATION

A meeting at the Waggon & Horses Hotel, attended largely by members of Bury Wesleyans and Bury Unitarians football clubs, decided to form a new Bury club. This was officially formed at a subsequent gathering at the Old White Horse Hotel, Fleet Street, Bury on 24 April 1885.

*Gigg Lane, Bury, Lancashire BL9 9HR.*

*Telephone:* (08445) 790009.

*Fax:* (0161) 764 5521.

*Ticket Office:* (08445) 790009.

*Website:* www.buryfc.co.uk

*Email:* info@buryfc.co.uk

*Ground Capacity:* 11,313.

*Record Attendance:* 35,000 v Bolton W, FA Cup 3rd rd, 9 January 1960.

*Pitch Measurements:* 102m × 66m (112yd × 73yd)

*Chairman:* Stewart Day.

*Directors:* Mark Catlin, Jeremy Rothwell, Margaret Ladkin, David Manchester.

*Manager:* Kevin Blackwell.

*Assistant Manager:* Ronnie Jepson.

*Physio:* Tom Walsh.

*Colours:* White shirts, blue shorts, blue socks.

*Year Formed:* 1885.

*Turned Professional:* 1885.

*Club Nickname:* 'The Shakers'.

*Ground:* 1885, Gigg Lane.

### HONOURS

**Football League – Division 1:**
Best season: 4th, 1925–26;
**Division 2:** *Champions* 1894–95, 1996–97; *Runners-up* 1923–24;
**Division 3:** *Champions* 1960–61;
*Runners-up* 1967–68;
**FL 2:** *Runners-up* 2010–11.

**FA Cup:** *Winners* 1900, 1903.

**Football League Cup:** Semi-final 1963.

*First Football League Game:* 1 September 1894, Division 2, v Manchester C (h) W 4–2 – Lowe; Gillespie, Davies; White, Clegg, Ross; Wylie, Barbour (2), Millar (1), Ostler (1), Plant.

*Record League Victory:* 8–0 v Tranmere R, Division 3, 10 January 1970 – Forrest; Tinney, Saile; Anderson, Turner, McDermott; Hince (1), Arrowsmith (1), Jones (4), Kerr (1), Grundy, (1 og).

*Record Cup Victory:* 12–1 v Stockton, FA Cup 1st rd (replay), 2 February 1897 – Montgomery; Darroch, Barbour; Hendry (1), Clegg, Ross (1); Wylie (3), Pangbourn, Millar (4), Henderson (2), Plant, (1 og).

*Record Defeat:* 0–10 v Blackburn R, FA Cup pr rd, 1 October 1887. 0–10 v West Ham U, Milk Cup 2nd rd 2nd leg, 25 October 1983.

*Most League Points (2 for a win):* 68, Division 3, 1960–61.

*Most League Points (3 for a win):* 84, Division 4, 1984–85 and Division 2, 1996–97.

## sky SPORTS FACT FILE

Bury were one of the pioneers of floodlit football. Gigg Lane was the first senior ground in the north-west to install lights and these were opened with a friendly match against Wolverhampton Wanderers in October 1953. The match attracted a crowd of 17,272.

*Most League Goals:* 108, Division 3, 1960–61.

*Highest League Scorer in Season:* Craig Madden, 35, Division 4, 1981–82.

*Most League Goals in Total Aggregate:* Craig Madden, 129, 1978–86.

*Most League Goals in One Match:* 5, Eddie Quigley v Millwall, Division 2, 15 February 1947; 5, Ray Pointer v Rotherham U, Division 2, 2 October 1965.

*Most Capped Player:* Bill Gorman, 11 (13), Republic of Ireland and (4), Northern Ireland.

*Most League Appearances:* Norman Bullock, 506, 1920–35.

*Youngest League Player:* Brian Williams, 16 years 133 days v Stockport Co, 18 March 1972.

*Record Transfer Fee Received:* £1,100,000 from Ipswich T for David Johnson, November 1997.

*Record Transfer Fee Paid:* £200,000 to Ipswich T for Chris Swailes, November 1997; £200,000 to Swindon T for Darren Bullock, February 1999.

*Football League Record:* 1894 Elected to Division 2; 1895–1912 Division 1; 1912–24 Division 2; 1924–29 Division 1; 1929–57 Division 2; 1957–61 Division 3; 1961–67 Division 2; 1967–68 Division 3; 1968–69 Division 2; 1969–71 Division 3; 1971–74 Division 4; 1974–80 Division 3; 1980–85 Division 4; 1985–96 Division 3; 1996–97 Division 2; 1997–99 Division 1; 1999–2002 Division 2; 2002–04 Division 3; 2004–11 FL 2; 2011–13 FL 1; 2013– FL 2.

## LATEST SEQUENCES

*Longest Sequence of League Wins:* 9, 26.9.1960 – 19.11.1960.

*Longest Sequence of League Defeats:* 8, 18.8.2001 – 25.9.2001.

*Longest Sequence of League Draws:* 6, 6.3.1999 – 3.4.1999.

*Longest Sequence of Unbeaten League Matches:* 18, 4.2.1961 – 29.4.1961.

*Longest Sequence Without a League Win:* 19, 1.4.1911 – 2.12.1911.

*Successive Scoring Runs:* 24 from 1.9.1894.

*Successive Non-scoring Runs:* 6 from 11.1.1969.

## MANAGERS

**T. Hargreaves** 1887
(*Secretary-Manager*)
**H. S. Hamer** 1887–1907
(*Secretary-Manager*)
**Archie Montgomery** 1907–15
**William Cameron** 1919–23
**James Hunter Thompson** 1923–27
**Percy Smith** 1927–30
**Arthur Paine** 1930–34
**Norman Bullock** 1934–38
**Charlie Dean** 1938–44
**Jim Porter** 1944–45
**Norman Bullock** 1945–49
**John McNeil** 1950–53
**Dave Russell** 1953–61
**Bob Stokoe** 1961–65
**Bert Head** 1965–66
**Les Shannon** 1966–69
**Jack Marshall** 1969
**Colin McDonald** 1970
**Les Hart** 1970
**Tommy McAnearney** 1970–72
**Alan Brown** 1972–73
**Bobby Smith** 1973–77
**Bob Stokoe** 1977–78
**David Hatton** 1978–79
**Dave Connor** 1979–80
**Jim Iley** 1980–84
**Martin Dobson** 1984–89
**Sam Ellis** 1989–90
**Mike Walsh** 1990–95
**Stan Ternent** 1995–98
**Neil Warnock** 1998–99
**Andy Preece** 1999–2003
**Graham Barrow** 2003–05
**Chris Casper** 2005–08
**Alan Knill** 2008–11
**Richie Barker** 2011–12
**Kevin Blackwell** September 2012–

## TEN YEAR LEAGUE RECORD

|         |       | P  | W  | D  | L  | F  | A  | Pts | Pos |
|---------|-------|----|----|----|----|----|----|-----|-----|
| 2003-04 | Div 3 | 46 | 15 | 11 | 20 | 54 | 64 | 56  | 12  |
| 2004-05 | FL 2  | 46 | 14 | 16 | 16 | 54 | 54 | 58  | 17  |
| 2005-06 | FL 2  | 46 | 12 | 17 | 17 | 45 | 57 | 52* | 19  |
| 2006-07 | FL 2  | 46 | 13 | 11 | 22 | 46 | 61 | 50  | 21  |
| 2007-08 | FL 2  | 46 | 16 | 11 | 19 | 58 | 61 | 59  | 13  |
| 2008-09 | FL 2  | 46 | 21 | 15 | 10 | 63 | 43 | 78  | 4   |
| 2009-10 | FL 2  | 46 | 19 | 12 | 15 | 54 | 59 | 69  | 9   |
| 2010-11 | FL 2  | 46 | 23 | 12 | 11 | 82 | 50 | 81  | 2   |
| 2011-12 | FL 1  | 46 | 15 | 11 | 20 | 60 | 79 | 56  | 14  |
| 2012-13 | FL 1  | 46 | 9  | 14 | 23 | 45 | 73 | 41  | 22  |

*1 pt deducted.

## DID YOU KNOW ?

The FA Cup third round tie between Bury and Stoke City went to five matches before the teams could be separated. An extra-time goal gave Stoke a 3-2 victory in the fourth replay at Old Trafford. The teams had played for a total of 9 hours and 22 minutes.

## BURY – FOOTBALL LEAGUE ONE 2012–13 LEAGUE RECORD

| Match No. | Date | Venue | Opponents | Result | H/T Score | Lg Pos. | Goalscorers | Atten- dance |
|---|---|---|---|---|---|---|---|---|
| 1 | Aug 18 | H | Brentford | D | 0-0 | 0-0 | 14 | | 2659 |
| 2 | 21 | A | Doncaster R | L | 1-2 | 1-1 | 16 | Skarz [5] | 6380 |
| 3 | 25 | A | Coventry C | D | 2-2 | 0-2 | 18 | Healy (pen) [55], John-Lewis [69] | 10,285 |
| 4 | Sept 1 | H | Notts Co | L | 0-2 | 0-1 | 22 | | 2725 |
| 5 | 8 | H | Preston NE | L | 1-2 | 0-1 | 23 | Skarz [90] | 5213 |
| 6 | 15 | A | Sheffield U | D | 1-1 | 1-1 | 22 | Sweeney [12] | 16,866 |
| 7 | 18 | A | Tranmere R | L | 0-3 | 0-1 | 24 | | 4976 |
| 8 | 22 | H | Milton Keynes D | L | 1-4 | 0-1 | 24 | John-Lewis [81] | 2321 |
| 9 | 29 | A | Stevenage | D | 2-2 | 1-0 | 24 | Hopper [26], Cullen [85] | 2660 |
| 10 | Oct 6 | H | Swindon T | L | 0-1 | 0-1 | 24 | | 2683 |
| 11 | 13 | A | Crawley T | L | 2-3 | 0-1 | 24 | Hopper [66], Bishop [69] | 3300 |
| 12 | 16 | H | Carlisle U | D | 1-1 | 1-0 | 24 | Thompson [36] | 1913 |
| 13 | 20 | A | Yeovil T | L | 1-2 | 0-1 | 24 | Poleon [74] | 3386 |
| 14 | 23 | H | Hartlepool U | W | 2-1 | 1-0 | 23 | Hopper [37], Worrall [55] | 1877 |
| 15 | 27 | A | Walsall | D | 1-1 | 1-1 | 23 | Poleon [11] | 2514 |
| 16 | Nov 6 | A | Oldham Ath | W | 2-1 | 1-0 | 23 | Tarkowski (og) [34], Schumacher (pen) [86] | 4120 |
| 17 | 10 | H | Portsmouth | W | 2-0 | 1-0 | 22 | Lockwood [19], Schumacher (pen) [56] | 3280 |
| 18 | 17 | A | Colchester U | L | 0-2 | 0-0 | 23 | | 3214 |
| 19 | 20 | A | Scunthorpe U | W | 2-1 | 1-0 | 22 | Schumacher [12], Hewitt [54] | 3027 |
| 20 | 24 | H | Bournemouth | D | 2-2 | 1-0 | 21 | Hewitt [14], Worrall [78] | 2541 |
| 21 | Dec 8 | H | Leyton Orient | L | 0-2 | 0-1 | 22 | | 2121 |
| 22 | 15 | A | Crewe Alex | L | 0-1 | 0-0 | 23 | | 4648 |
| 23 | 21 | H | Shrewsbury T | D | 2-2 | 1-1 | 22 | Doherty [10], Schumacher [90] | 2536 |
| 24 | 26 | A | Preston NE | D | 0-0 | 0-0 | 22 | | 12,014 |
| 25 | 29 | A | Carlisle U | L | 1-2 | 0-2 | 22 | Schumacher [53] | 4435 |
| 26 | Jan 1 | H | Tranmere R | L | 0-1 | 0-0 | 22 | | 3208 |
| 27 | 12 | A | Milton Keynes D | D | 1-1 | 0-1 | 22 | Schumacher [66] | 7384 |
| 28 | 26 | A | Shrewsbury T | D | 0-0 | 0-0 | 22 | | 4795 |
| 29 | Feb 2 | H | Doncaster R | W | 2-0 | 2-0 | 21 | Bishop [25], Ajose [36] | 3618 |
| 30 | 9 | A | Brentford | D | 2-2 | 0-0 | 22 | Soares [65], Ajose [76] | 5137 |
| 31 | 12 | H | Sheffield U | L | 0-2 | 0-1 | 22 | | 3064 |
| 32 | 16 | H | Coventry C | L | 0-2 | 0-1 | 22 | | 3745 |
| 33 | 22 | A | Notts Co | L | 1-4 | 1-0 | 22 | Schumacher [24] | 5795 |
| 34 | 26 | A | Swindon T | W | 1-0 | 1-0 | 22 | Schumacher [21] | 7508 |
| 35 | Mar 2 | H | Crawley T | L | 0-2 | 0-1 | 22 | | 2491 |
| 36 | 9 | A | Portsmouth | L | 0-2 | 0-0 | 24 | | 11,493 |
| 37 | 16 | H | Colchester U | L | 1-2 | 1-2 | 24 | Fagan [26] | 2018 |
| 38 | 19 | H | Stevenage | W | 2-0 | 0-0 | 22 | Jones, C [82], Clarke-Harris [90] | 1396 |
| 39 | 23 | A | Bournemouth | L | 1-4 | 1-1 | 23 | Bishop [24] | 7229 |
| 40 | 29 | H | Crewe Alex | D | 2-2 | 0-1 | 23 | Soares [59], Bishop (pen) [90] | 2749 |
| 41 | Apr 1 | A | Leyton Orient | L | 0-2 | 0-2 | 23 | | 3713 |
| 42 | 6 | A | Hartlepool U | L | 0-2 | 0-1 | 24 | | 2939 |
| 43 | 13 | H | Oldham Ath | L | 0-1 | 0-0 | 24 | | 4558 |
| 44 | 16 | H | Scunthorpe U | W | 2-1 | 0-1 | 24 | Clarke-Harris [68], Ajose [70] | 1567 |
| 45 | 20 | A | Walsall | D | 1-1 | 0-1 | 23 | Sodje [90] | 4745 |
| 46 | 27 | H | Yeovil T | W | 3-2 | 3-0 | 22 | Clarke-Harris 2 [5, 25], Ajose [32] | 2440 |

**Final League Position: 22**

### GOALSCORERS

*League (45):* Schumacher 8 (2 pens), Ajose 4, Bishop 4 (1 pen), Clarke-Harris 4, Hopper 3, Hewitt 2, John-Lewis 2, Poleon 2, Skarz 2, Soares 2, Worrall 2, Cullen 1, Doherty 1, Fagan 1, Healy 1 (1 pen), Jones, C 1, Lockwood 1, Sodje 1, Sweeney 1, Thompson 1, own goal 1.
*FA Cup (3):* Doherty 1 (1 pen), Sodje 1, Thompson 1.
*Capital One Cup (1):* Hughes 1.
*Johnstone's Paint Trophy (4):* Schumacher 2, Doherty 1, Skarz 1.

| Carson T 39 | Jones A 8+2 | Lockwood A 17 | Hughes M 25+2 | Skarz J 39 | Carrington M 20+7 | Schumacher S 38+1 | Sweeney P 13+3 | Worrall D 37+4 | Bishop A 19+5 | Elford-Alliyu L 1+4 | Cullen M 7+3 | John-Lewis L 5+11 | Jones C 7+18 | Marshall M 4+5 | Byrne S 1+2 | Healy D 8+8 | Picken P 2 | Sodje E 17+2 | Hopper T 22 | Doherty M 17 | Thompson Z 29 | Poleon D 7 | Hewitt T 5+3 | Ebanks-Landell E 24 | Soares T 20+3 | Wylde G 4 | Carole S —+4 | Eastham A 18+1 | Zubar S 6 | Ajose N 15+4 | Regan C 9+1 | Fagan C 9+2 | Clarke-Harris J 4+8 | Mezague V 2+5 | Belford C 7 | Pratt T —+2 | Holden E 1 | Match No. |
|---|---|---|---|---|---|---|---|---|---|---|---|---|---|---|---|---|---|---|---|---|---|---|---|---|---|---|---|---|---|---|---|---|---|---|---|---|---|---|
| 1 | 2 | 3 | 4 | 5 | 6 | 7 | 8 | 9 | $10^2$ | $11^1$ | 12 | 13 | | | | | | | | | | | | | | | | | | | | | | | | | | 1 |
| 1 | 5 | 4 | 3 | 2 | 6 | $7^8$ | 8 | $9^1$ | $10^2$ | | | $11^3$ | 13 | 12 | 14 | | | | | | | | | | | | | | | | | | | | | | | 2 |
| 1 | 2 | 3 | 4 | 5 | | 7 | | 9 | | | | 12 | 10 | 14 | $6^1$ | 13 | $8^2$ | $11^3$ | | | | | | | | | | | | | | | | | | | | 3 |
| 1 | | 3 | 4 | 5 | $9^2$ | 7 | 8 | $6^3$ | | | | 12 | $10^1$ | 11 | 14 | 13 | | 2 | | | | | | | | | | | | | | | | | | | | 4 |
| 1 | 14 | 3 | 4 | 5 | $9^1$ | 7 | 8 | 6 | | | | $10^2$ | 11 | 13 | | 12 | | $2^3$ | | | | | | | | | | | | | | | | | | | | 5 |
| 1 | 2 | 3 | 13 | 5 | | 7 | 8 | | | | | $10^3$ | 12 | 6 | 9 | 14 | | $4^2$ | $11^1$ | | | | | | | | | | | | | | | | | | | 6 |
| 1 | 2 | 4 | | 5 | | 7 | 8 | | | | | 13 | $10^1$ | 12 | 6 | 9 | | 3 | $11^2$ | | | | | | | | | | | | | | | | | | | 7 |
| 1 | 5 | $4^1$ | 3 | 9 | 7 | 6 | $8^2$ | 13 | | | | | 14 | | 12 | 10 | | 2 | $11^3$ | | | | | | | | | | | | | | | | | | | 8 |
| 1 | 2 | 3 | 4 | 5 | $8^3$ | 7 | 13 | 6 | | | | 14 | $9^1$ | 12 | | | | $10^2$ | 11 | | | | | | | | | | | | | | | | | | | 9 |
| 1 | | 3 | 4 | 5 | $6^2$ | 8 | 7 | | | | | 14 | 12 | 13 | 9 | $11^1$ | | $10^3$ | 2 | | | | | | | | | | | | | | | | | | | 10 |
| 1 | | 3 | 4 | 2 | 8 | 6 | | | | | | 12 | 11 | $9^1$ | 13 | $7^2$ | | 10 | 5 | | | | | | | | | | | | | | | | | | | 11 |
| 1 | | 4 | 3 | 5 | | 7 | | 6 | 10 | | | 12 | | | | 11 | | 2 | 8 | $9^1$ | | | | | | | | | | | | | | | | | | 12 |
| 1 | | 3 | $4^3$ | 5 | $9^2$ | 13 | | 6 | 10 | | | 14 | | | | $11^1$ | | 2 | $7^8$ | 8 | | | | | | | | | | | | | | | | | | 13 |
| 1 | | 3 | 13 | 5 | | 7 | 8 | 6 | $10^1$ | | | | 12 | | | | | 4 | 11 | 2 | $9^2$ | | | | | | | | | | | | | | | | | 14 |
| 1 | | 4 | | 5 | 14 | 7 | $8^3$ | 6 | | | | 13 | | | | $10^1$ | | 3 | 11 | 2 | $9^2$ | 12 | | | | | | | | | | | | | | | | 15 |
| 1 | | 3 | 4 | 5 | | 8 | | 9 | 13 | | | | | | | $10^1$ | | $11^2$ | 2 | 7 | 6 | 12 | | | | | | | | | | | | | | | | 16 |
| 1 | 13 | $3^2$ | 4 | 5 | | 7 | | 6 | 12 | | | 14 | | | | | | 11 | 2 | 8 | $9^3$ | $10^1$ | | | | | | | | | | | | | | | | 17 |
| 1 | | $4^2$ | 5 | 14 | $7^3$ | 12 | 6 | | | | | 13 | | | | | | 11 | 2 | 8 | 9 | | | | 3 | $10^1$ | | | | | | | | | | | | 18 |
| 1 | | 4 | 5 | | 8 | | | | | | | 12 | | | | | | 13 | $11^1$ | 2 | 7 | | $10^2$ | | 3 | 6 | | | | | | | | | | | | 19 |
| 1 | | 4 | 5 | | 8 | | 6 | | | | | 12 | | | | | | | $11^1$ | 3 | 9 | | 7 | 2 | 10 | | | | | | | | | | | | | 20 |
| 1 | | | 5 | | 12 | $8^1$ | 9 | 10 | | | | | | | | | | 3 | $11^2$ | 2 | 7 | | | 4 | 13 | $6^3$ | 14 | | | | | | | | | | | 21 |
| 1 | | 4 | 5 | 12 | 8 | 7 | | | | | | 13 | | | | | | 14 | $3$ | $11^3$ | 2 | 9 | | $10^2$ | $6^1$ | | | | | | | | | | | | | 22 |
| 1 | | $4^3$ | 5 | | 7 | | 6 | | | | | 14 | | | | | | $10^1$ | 3 | $11^2$ | 2 | 8 | 12 | 13 | 9 | | | | | | | | | | | | | 23 |
| 1 | | 4 | 5 | | 7 | | 6 | | | | | 12 | 13 | | | | | $10^1$ | 3 | 11 | 2 | 8 | | $9^2$ | | | | | | | | | | | | | | 24 |
| 1 | | 4 | 5 | | 7 | | 6 | | | | | 13 | | | | | | 3 | 11 | 2 | 8 | $10^1$ | | | $9^2$ | 12 | | | | | | | | | | | | 25 |
| 1 | 3 | | 5 | | 7 | | $6^2$ | | | | | 14 | | | | 13 | | 11 | 2 | 8 | 4 | $10^1$ | | | $9^3$ | 12 | | | | | | | | | | | | 26 |
| 1 | | 4 | 3 | 13 | 8 | | 2 | | | | | 11 | 12 | | | | | 5 | $10^1$ | 6 | | 9 | $7^2$ | | | | | | | | | | | | | | | 27 |
| 1 | | | 5 | 14 | 7 | | 2 | 12 | | | | $11^1$ | 13 | | | | | | $9^3$ | | 8 | $10^2$ | | | | | | 3 | 4 | 6 | | | | | | | | 28 |
| 1 | | | 5 | | 9 | | | 11 | | | | | | | | | | 7 | | | | | | | 6 | 10 | | 3 | 4 | 8 | 2 | | | | | | | 29 |
| 1 | | | 5 | | 7 | | | 12 | 11 | | | | | | | | | | 9 | | | | | | $8^1$ | 6 | | 3 | 4 | 10 | 2 | | | | | | | 30 |
| 1 | | | 5 | | $8^1$ | | | 12 | $10^2$ | | | 13 | | | | | | | 9 | | | | | | 6 | 9 | | 3 | 4 | 11 | 2 | | | | | | | 31 |
| 1 | | | 5 | | 8 | | | 6 | 10 | | | 12 | | | | | | | 7 | | | | | | $9^2$ | | 13 | 4 | 3 | $11^3$ | $2^1$ | 14 | | | | | | 32 |
| 1 | | | 5 | | 14 | | | 8 | 10 | | | 11 | | | | | | | $7^3$ | | | | | | 9 | 12 | | 4 | $3^1$ | $6^2$ | 2 | 13 | | | | | | 33 |
| 1 | | | 5 | | 8 | | | 7 | 2 | | | 13 | | | | | | | 9 | | | | | | 4 | $6^1$ | | 3 | | 10 | | $11^2$ | 12 | | | | | 34 |
| 1 | | | 5 | | 6 | | | 9 | 2 | | | 13 | | | | | | 12 | 14 | | | | | | $7^2$ | 4 | | $10^1$ | 3 | | $8^3$ | 11 | | | | | | 35 |
| 1 | | | 5 | | 6 | | | 8 | 2 | | | 12 | | | | | | $10^1$ | $9^2$ | | | | | | | 4 | | 3 | | 14 | 7 | $11^3$ | 13 | | | | | 36 |
| 1 | | | 5 | | 8 | | | 7 | 6 | | | 10 | | | | | | $9^3$ | | | 14 | | | | 4 | | | 3 | | 12 | $2^1$ | $11^2$ | 13 | | | | | 37 |
| 1 | | | 5 | | 4 | | | 7 | 6 | | | $10^1$ | | | | | | 9 | | $3^2$ | | | | | 8 | | | 2 | | 14 | | $11^3$ | 12 | 13 | | | | 38 |
| 1 | | | 5 | | $9^3$ | | | 8 | 10 | | | 11 | | | | | | $6^1$ | | 3 | $7^2$ | | | | 2 | | | 4 | | 12 | | | 13 | 14 | | | | 39 |
| | | | | | | | | 7 | 8 | | | 5 | 10 | | | | | 13 | | | 13 | | | | 3 | | | 2 | | $9^2$ | 4 | $6^1$ | 11 | 12 | 1 | | | 40 |
| | | | | | | | | 8 | 7 | | | 5 | 10 | | | | | $4^1$ | | | 2 | | | | 9 | | | 3 | | $6^2$ | 11 | 13 | 12 | 1 | | | | 41 |
| | | | | | | | | | 6 | | | 5 | 11 | | | | | 3 | | | $7^2$ | | | | 2 | | $8^3$ | 4 | | $9^1$ | 14 | $10^4$ | 12 | 13 | 1 | | | 42 |
| | 3 | | | | | | | 7 | | | | 2 | $11^3$ | | | | | 13 | | | 8 | | | | $5^1$ | 6 | | 4 | | 9 | | $10^2$ | 12 | 1 | | | 14 | 43 |
| | 3 | | | | | | | 7 | | | | 5 | | | | | | | | | 9 | | | | 10 | | | 4 | | 6 | 2 | 11 | 8 | 1 | | | 44 |
| | 3 | | | | | | | 5 | | | | | | | | | | 13 | | | 7 | | | | $9$ | $6^1$ | | 4 | | 11 | $2^2$ | 10 | 8 | 1 | 12 | | 45 |
| | 4 | | | | | | | 2 | | | | | | | | | | 3 | | | 8 | | | | 5 | 6 | | 12 | | 9 | | 11 | 10 | 1 | $7^1$ | | 46 |

**FA Cup**

| First Round | Exeter C | (h) | 1-0 |
|---|---|---|---|
| Second Round | Southend U | (h) | 1-1 |
| Replay | Southend U | (a) | 1-1 |

*(aet; lost 2-3 on pens)*

**Capital One Cup**

| First Round | Middlesbrough | (h) | 1-2 |
|---|---|---|---|

**Johnstone's Paint Trophy**

| Second Round | Rochdale | (a) | 1-1 |
|---|---|---|---|
| *(aet; won 5-4 on pens)* | | | |
| Northern Quarter-Finals | Preston NE | (h) | 3-3 |

*(aet; lost 4-5 on pens)*

# CARDIFF CITY

## FOUNDATION

Credit for the establishment of a first class professional football club in such a rugby stronghold as Cardiff is due to members of the Riverside club formed in 1899 out of a cricket club of that name. Cardiff became a city in 1905 and in 1908 the South Wales and Monmouthshire FA granted Riverside permission to call themselves Cardiff City. The club turned professional under that name in 1910.

*Cardiff City Stadium, Leckwith Road, Cardiff CF11 8AZ.*

*Telephone:* (0845) 365 1115. *Fax:* (0845) 365 1116.

*Ticket Office:* (0845) 345 1400.

*Website:* www.cardiffcityfc.co.uk

*Email:* club@cardiffcityfc.co.uk

*Ground Capacity:* 26,847.

*Record Attendance:* 57,893 v Arsenal, Division 1, 22 April 1953 (at Ninian Park); 26,588 v Nottingham F, FL C, 13 April 2013 (at Cardiff City Stadium).

*Ground Record Attendance:* 62,634, Wales v England, 17 October 1959 (at Ninian Park).

*Pitch Measurements:* 100m × 68m (110yd × 75yd)

*Chairman/Chief Executive:* Simon Lim.

*Manager:* Malky Mackay.

*Assistant Manager:* David Kerslake.

*Physio:* Sean Connelly.

*Colours:* Red shirts, black shorts, red socks.

*Year Formed:* 1899.

*Turned Professional:* 1910.

*Previous Names:* 1899, Riverside; 1902, Riverside Albion; 1908, Cardiff City.

*Club Nickname:* 'The Bluebirds'.

*Grounds:* Riverside, Sophia Gardens, Old Park and Fir Gardens; 1910, Ninian Park; 2009, Cardiff City Stadium.

## HONOURS

**Football League Division 1:**
*Runners-up* 1923–24;
**Division 2:** *Runners-up* 1920–21, 1951–52, 1959–60;
**FL C:** *Champions* 2012–13;
**Division 3 (S):** *Champions* 1946–47;
**Division 3:** *Champions* 1992–93.
*Runners-up* 1975–76, 1982–83, 2000–01;
**Division 4:** *Runners-up* 1987–88.

**FA Cup:** *Winners* 1927 (only occasion the Cup has been won by a club outside England); *Runners-up* 1925, 2008.

**Football League Cup:** *Runners-up* 2012.

**Welsh Cup:** *Winners* 22 times (joint record).

**Charity Shield:** Winners 1927.

**European Competitions**
**European Cup-Winners' Cup:**
1964–65, 1965–66, 1967–68 (*s-f*), 1968–69, 1969–70, 1970–71, 1971–72, 1973–74, 1974–75, 1976–77, 1977–78, 1988–89, 1992–93, 1993–94.

*First Football League Game:* 28 August 1920, Division 2, v Stockport Co (a) W 5–2 – Kneeshaw; Brittan, Leyton; Keenor (1), Smith, Hardy; Grimshaw (1), Gill (2), Cashmore, West, Evans (1).

*Record League Victory:* 9–2 v Thames, Division 3 (S), 6 February 1932 – Farquharson; Eric Morris, Roberts; Galbraith, Harris, Ronan; Emmerson (1), Keating (1), Jones (1), McCambridge (1), Robbins (5).

## sky SPORTS FACT FILE

Cardiff City reached the quarter-final stage of the European Cup Winners' Cup in 1970–71 where they faced Real Madrid. The Bluebirds won the home leg with a goal from Brian Clark, only to lose the away tie 2-0 and exit the competition.

*Record Cup Victory:* 8–0 v Enfield, FA Cup 1st rd, 28 November 1931 – Farquharson; Smith, Roberts; Harris (1), Galbraith, Ronan; Emmerson (2), Keating (3); O'Neill (2), Robbins, McCambridge.

*Record Defeat:* 2–11 v Sheffield U, Division 1, 1 January 1926.

*Most League Points (2 for a win):* 66, Division 3 (S), 1946–47.

*Most League Points (3 for a win):* 87, FL C, 2012–13.

*Most League Goals:* 95, Division 3, 2000–01.

*Highest League Scorer in Season:* Robert Earnshaw, 31, Division 2, 2002–03.

*Most League Goals in Total Aggregate:* Len Davies, 128, 1920–31.

*Most League Goals in One Match:* 5, Hugh Ferguson v Burnley, Division 1, 1 September 1928; 5, Walter Robbins v Thames, Division 3 (S), 6 February 1932; 5, William Henderson v Northampton T, Division 3 (S), 22 April 1933.

*Most Capped Player:* Alf Sherwood, 39 (41), Wales.

*Most League Appearances:* Phil Dwyer, 471, 1972–85.

*Youngest League Player:* Bob Adams, 15 years 355 days v Southend U, 18 February 1933.

*Record Transfer Fee Received:* £5,000,000 from Sunderland for Michael Chopra, August 2006; £5,000,000 from Arsenal for Aaron Ramsey, June 2008; £5,000,000 from Birmingham C for Roger Johnson, June 2009.

*Record Transfer Fee Paid:* £7,500,000 to FC Copenhagen for Andreas Cornelius, July 2013.

*Football League Record:* 1920 Elected to Division 2; 1921–29 Division 1; 1929–31 Division 2; 1931–47 Division 3 (S); 1947–52 Division 2; 1952–57 Division 1; 1957–60 Division 2; 1960–62 Division 1; 1962–75 Division 2; 1975–76 Division 3; 1976–82 Division 2; 1982–83 Division 3; 1983–85 Division 2; 1985–86 Division 3; 1986–88 Division 4; 1988–90 Division 3; 1990–92 Division 4; 1992–93 Division 3; 1993–95 Division 2; 1995–99 Division 3; 1999–2000 Division 2; 2000–01 Division 3; 2001–03 Division 2; 2003–04 Division 1; 2004–13 FL C; 2013– FA Premier League.

## MANAGERS

Davy McDougall 1910–11
Fred Stewart 1911–33
Bartley Wilson 1933–34
B. Watts-Jones 1934–37
Bill Jennings 1937–39
Cyril Spiers 1939–46
Billy McCandless 1946–48
Cyril Spiers 1948–54
Trevor Morris 1954–58
Bill Jones 1958–62
George Swindin 1962–64
Jimmy Scoular 1964–73
Frank O'Farrell 1973–74
Jimmy Andrews 1974–78
Richie Morgan 1978–81
Graham Williams 1981–82
Len Ashurst 1982–84
Jimmy Goodfellow 1984
Alan Durban 1984–86
Frank Burrows 1986–89
Len Ashurst 1989–91
Eddie May 1991–94
Terry Yorath 1994–95
Eddie May 1995
Kenny Hibbitt (*Chief Coach*) 1995
Phil Neal 1996
Russell Osman 1996–97
Kenny Hibbitt 1997–98
Frank Burrows 1998–2000
Billy Ayre 2000
Bobby Gould 2000
Alan Cork 2000–02
Lennie Lawrence 2002–05
Dave Jones 2005–11
Malky Mackay June 2011–

## LATEST SEQUENCES

*Longest Sequence of League Wins:* 9, 26.10.1946 – 28.12.1946.

*Longest Sequence of League Defeats:* 7, 4.11.1933 – 25.12.1933.

*Longest Sequence of League Draws:* 6, 29.11.1980 – 17.1.1981.

*Longest Sequence of Unbeaten League Matches:* 21, 21.9.1946 – 1.3.1947.

*Longest Sequence Without a League Win:* 15, 21.11.1936 – 6.3.1937.

*Successive Scoring Runs:* 24 from 25.8.2012.

*Successive Non-scoring Runs:* 8 from 20.12.1952.

## TEN YEAR LEAGUE RECORD

|         |       | P  | W  | D  | L  | F  | A  | Pts | Pos |
|---------|-------|----|----|----|----|----|----|-----|-----|
| 2003-04 | Div 1 | 46 | 17 | 14 | 15 | 68 | 58 | 65  | 13  |
| 2004-05 | FL C  | 46 | 13 | 15 | 18 | 48 | 51 | 54  | 16  |
| 2005-06 | FL C  | 46 | 16 | 12 | 18 | 58 | 59 | 60  | 11  |
| 2006-07 | FL C  | 46 | 17 | 13 | 16 | 57 | 53 | 64  | 13  |
| 2007-08 | FL C  | 46 | 16 | 16 | 14 | 59 | 55 | 64  | 12  |
| 2008-09 | FL C  | 46 | 19 | 17 | 10 | 65 | 53 | 74  | 7   |
| 2009-10 | FL C  | 46 | 22 | 10 | 14 | 73 | 54 | 76  | 4   |
| 2010-11 | FL C  | 46 | 23 | 11 | 12 | 76 | 54 | 80  | 4   |
| 2011-12 | FL C  | 46 | 19 | 18 | 9  | 66 | 53 | 75  | 6   |
| 2012-13 | FL C  | 46 | 25 | 12 | 9  | 72 | 45 | 87  | 1   |

## DID YOU KNOW ?

Fred Keenor made his debut for Cardiff City in December 1913 then enlisted in the Footballers' Battalion during the First World War when he suffered a leg wound. He recovered to take his place in the Bluebirds' line-up and captained the side to victory over Arsenal in the 1927 Cup final.

## CARDIFF CITY – FL CHAMPIONSHIP 2012–13 LEAGUE RECORD

| Match No. | Date | Venue | Opponents | Result | H/T Score | Lg Pos. | Goalscorers | Atten-dance |
|---|---|---|---|---|---|---|---|---|
| 1 | Aug 17 | H | Huddersfield T | W 1-0 | 0-0 | 1 | Hudson [90] | 21,127 |
| 2 | 21 | A | Brighton & HA | D 0-0 | 0-0 | 6 | | 25,518 |
| 3 | 25 | A | Bristol C | L 2-4 | 0-2 | 15 | Mason [57], Helguson [82] | 14,368 |
| 4 | Sept 2 | H | Wolverhampton W | W 3-1 | 2-1 | 8 | Whittingham 3 (1 pen) [11 (p), 14, 65] | 22,020 |
| 5 | 15 | H | Leeds U | W 2-1 | 0-0 | 5 | Bellamy [67], Whittingham (pen) [73] | 23,836 |
| 6 | 18 | A | Millwall | W 2-0 | 0-0 | 5 | Whittingham [53], Noone [55] | 9295 |
| 7 | 22 | A | Crystal Palace | L 2-3 | 2-0 | 6 | Gunnarsson [13], Cowie [15] | 12,757 |
| 8 | 29 | H | Blackpool | W 3-0 | 2-0 | 2 | Connolly 2 [17, 57], Whittingham [27] | 21,216 |
| 9 | Oct 2 | H | Birmingham C | W 2-1 | 1-0 | 1 | Bellamy [39], Hudson [57] | 20,278 |
| 10 | 6 | A | Ipswich T | W 2-1 | 0-1 | 1 | Helguson 2 [63, 88] | 16,434 |
| 11 | 20 | A | Nottingham F | L 1-3 | 0-2 | 2 | Helguson [74] | 21,491 |
| 12 | 23 | H | Watford | W 2-1 | 0-1 | 2 | Whittingham (pen) [71], Gunnarsson [90] | 20,077 |
| 13 | 27 | H | Burnley | W 4-0 | 2-0 | 1 | Mason [3], Noone [41], Connolly [82], Gunnarsson [85] | 21,191 |
| 14 | Nov 3 | A | Bolton W | L 1-2 | 1-0 | 1 | Noone [40] | 17,304 |
| 15 | 6 | A | Charlton Ath | L 4-5 | 2-2 | 3 | Helguson [4], Mason [24], Noone [90], Gunnarsson [90] | 15,778 |
| 16 | 10 | H | Hull C | W 2-1 | 1-0 | 3 | Helguson [3], Hudson [82] | 20,058 |
| 17 | 17 | H | Middlesbrough | W 1-0 | 1-0 | 2 | Connolly [19] | 21,578 |
| 18 | 24 | A | Barnsley | W 2-1 | 1-0 | 1 | Nugent [22], Gunnarsson [51] | 8227 |
| 19 | 27 | A | Derby Co | D 1-1 | 1-0 | 1 | Helguson [11] | 20,911 |
| 20 | Dec 2 | H | Sheffield W | W 1-0 | 0-0 | 1 | Conway [80] | 22,034 |
| 21 | 7 | A | Blackburn R | W 4-1 | 1-0 | 1 | Hudson [30], Bellamy [56], Mason [84], Kim [85] | 12,460 |
| 22 | 15 | H | Peterborough U | L 1-2 | 0-1 | 1 | Gestede [89] | 22,073 |
| 23 | 22 | A | Leicester C | W 1-0 | 1-0 | 1 | Bellamy [25] | 25,055 |
| 24 | 26 | H | Crystal Palace | W 2-1 | 1-1 | 1 | Noone [44], Gunnarsson [73] | 26,098 |
| 25 | 29 | H | Millwall | W 1-0 | 1-0 | 1 | Gestede [8] | 24,263 |
| 26 | Jan 1 | A | Birmingham C | W 1-0 | 1-0 | 1 | Mason [41] | 17,493 |
| 27 | 12 | H | Ipswich T | D 0-0 | 0-0 | 1 | | 22,724 |
| 28 | 19 | A | Blackpool | W 2-1 | 0-0 | 1 | Kim [54], Smith [64] | 13,998 |
| 29 | Feb 2 | A | Leeds U | W 1-0 | 0-0 | 1 | Campbell [64] | 19,236 |
| 30 | 9 | A | Huddersfield T | D 0-0 | 0-0 | 1 | | 15,265 |
| 31 | 16 | H | Bristol C | W 2-1 | 1-0 | 1 | Campbell 2 [45, 58] | 25,586 |
| 32 | 19 | H | Brighton & HA | L 0-2 | 0-1 | 1 | | 23,782 |
| 33 | 24 | A | Wolverhampton W | W 2-1 | 1-0 | 1 | Campbell 2 [20, 67] | 20,930 |
| 34 | Mar 2 | A | Middlesbrough | L 1-2 | 0-2 | 1 | Gunnarsson [67] | 15,440 |
| 35 | 5 | H | Derby Co | D 1-1 | 0-0 | 1 | Noone [82] | 21,544 |
| 36 | 12 | H | Leicester C | D 1-1 | 0-0 | 1 | Gestede [90] | 23,231 |
| 37 | 16 | A | Sheffield W | W 2-0 | 1-0 | 1 | Cowie [45], Connolly [65] | 24,191 |
| 38 | 30 | A | Peterborough U | L 1-2 | 1-0 | 1 | Gunnarsson [23] | 9236 |
| 39 | Apr 1 | H | Blackburn R | W 3-0 | 1-0 | 1 | Campbell [40], Mason [86], Whittingham (pen) [90] | 24,327 |
| 40 | 6 | A | Watford | D 0-0 | 0-0 | 1 | | 15,550 |
| 41 | 9 | A | Barnsley | D 1-1 | 0-0 | 1 | Turner [59] | 22,584 |
| 42 | 13 | H | Nottingham F | W 3-0 | 1-0 | 1 | Helguson [26], Gestede 2 [60, 66] | 26,588 |
| 43 | 16 | H | Charlton Ath | D 0-0 | 0-0 | 1 | | 26,338 |
| 44 | 20 | A | Burnley | D 1-1 | 1-0 | 1 | Conway [27] | 13,264 |
| 45 | 27 | A | Bolton W | D 1-1 | 0-1 | 1 | Noone [68] | 26,418 |
| 46 | May 4 | A | Hull C | D 2-2 | 0-0 | 1 | Campbell [49], Maynard (pen) [90] | 23,812 |

**Final League Position: 1**

## GOALSCORERS

*League (72):* Gunnarsson 8, Helguson 8, Whittingham 8 (4 pens), Campbell 7, Noone 7, Mason 6, Connolly 5, Gestede 5, Bellamy 4, Hudson 4, Conway 2, Cowie 2, Kim 2, Maynard 1 (1 pen), Nugent 1, Smith 1, Turner 1.
*FA Cup (1):* Jarvis 1.
*Capital One Cup (1):* Helguson 1 (1 pen).

| Marshall D 46 | McNaughton K 24 + 3 | Taylor A 43 | Hudson M 33 | Turner B 30 + 1 | Whittingham P 37 + 3 | Cowie D 15 + 10 | Gunnarsson A 35 + 10 | Mutch J 18 + 4 | Bellamy C 28 + 5 | Helguson H 27 + 11 | Mason J 12 + 16 | Kiss F — + 2 | Conway C 21 + 6 | Velikonja E 1 + 2 | Connolly M 36 | Smith T 19 + 5 | Ralls J 1 + 3 | Noone C 25 + 7 | Maynard N 3 + 1 | Kim B 20 + 8 | Gestede R 5 + 22 | Frei K 1 + 2 | Nugent B 7 + 5 | Lappin S 2 | Campbell F 9 + 3 | Barnett L 8 | Match No. |
|---|---|---|---|---|---|---|---|---|---|---|---|---|---|---|---|---|---|---|---|---|---|---|---|---|---|---|---|
| 1 | 2 | 3 | 4 | 5 | 6 | $7^1$ | 8 | $9^2$ | 10 | 11 | 12 | 13 | | | | | | | | | | | | | | | 1 |
| 1 | 2 | 3 | 4 | 5 | 6 | 7 | 8 | $9^1$ | $11^2$ | $10^3$ | 12 | 13 | 14 | | | | | | | | | | | | | | 2 |
| 1 | 2 | 5 | 3 | | 9 | 6 | $7^1$ | $8^3$ | | 11 | 12 | | | 13 | 4 | $10^2$ | 14 | | | | | | | | | | 3 |
| 1 | 2 | 3 | 4 | | 6 | 14 | 12 | $9^1$ | | 10 | 13 | | | | 5 | 7 | | $8^3$ | $11^2$ | | | | | | | | 4 |
| 1 | 2 | 5 | 3 | | 6 | 14 | 13 | $9^2$ | 12 | 10 | | | | | 4 | 7 | | $8^1$ | $11^3$ | | | | | | | | 5 |
| 1 | 2 | 3 | 4 | | 6 | 8 | 7 | | 12 | | | | | | 5 | 10 | | $9^2$ | $11^1$ | 13 | | | | | | | 6 |
| 1 | 2 | 5 | 3 | | 8 | $6^1$ | 7 | | $11^2$ | 10 | 13 | | | | 4 | | | $9^3$ | 12 | 14 | | | | | | | 7 |
| 1 | 2 | 3 | 4 | | 6 | 14 | 8 | | $11^2$ | $10^3$ | 12 | | | | 5 | | | $9^1$ | 7 | 13 | | | | | | | 8 |
| 1 | 2 | 3 | 4 | | 6 | 12 | 7 | | $9^1$ | 11 | 10 | | | | 5 | | | $8^2$ | | 13 | | | | | | | 9 |
| 1 | $2^3$ | 5 | 3 | 14 | 8 | 9 | 7 | | | 11 | $10^2$ | | 12 | | 4 | | | $6^1$ | | 13 | | | | | | | 10 |
| 1 | $2^3$ | 5 | 3 | | 7 | 8 | $9^2$ | | | 11 | 14 | | $6^1$ | | 4 | 10 | | 12 | | 13 | | | | | | | 11 |
| 1 | | 5 | 3 | $4^2$ | 7 | 8 | 14 | | $10^1$ | 11 | 12 | | 2 | | $9^3$ | | | 6 | | 13 | | | | | | | 12 |
| 1 | 2 | 3 | 4 | | 6 | 7 | 13 | | $11^1$ | 10 | | | | | 5 | | | $9^3$ | | $8^2$ | 12 | 14 | | | | | 13 |
| 1 | | 5 | 3 | 4 | 7 | 6 | 13 | | $11^1$ | $10^3$ | | | | | 2 | | | 9 | | $8^2$ | 12 | 14 | | | | | 14 |
| 1 | | 5 | 3 | 4 | 9 | $7^2$ | 13 | | $11^3$ | 8 | | | | | 2 | 10 | | 12 | | 14 | $6^1$ | | | | | | 15 |
| 1 | $2^1$ | 5 | 3 | 4 | 7 | | 9 | | $11^3$ | 10 | $12^2$ | | | 13 | 6 | | | 8 | 14 | | | | | | | | 16 |
| 1 | $2^2$ | 3 | $4^1$ | 6 | $9^3$ | | 14 | 11 | 10 | | | | 5 | | 13 | | | 8 | | 7 | | | 12 | | | | 17 |
| 1 | | 3 | | 10 | $7^2$ | 13 | 14 | $11^1$ | $9^3$ | | | | 2 | | 6 | | | 5 | 12 | | 4 | $8^■$ | | | | | 18 |
| 1 | | 3 | | 7 | $8^2$ | 12 | $11^1$ | $10^3$ | 14 | | | 13 | | | 2 | | 5 | $6^■$ | | 9 | | 4 | | | | | 19 |
| 1 | | 5 | 3 | 4 | 10 | | 14 | | $9^3$ | 6 | $11^2$ | 12 | | | 7 | | | 2 | | $8^1$ | 13 | | | | | | 20 |
| 1 | | 5 | 3 | 4 | 9 | 8 | | | $10^2$ | $11^3$ | 13 | | | | 7 | | | 2 | | $6^1$ | 12 | 14 | | | | | 21 |
| 1 | $2^1$ | 5 | | 3 | 6 | $7^2$ | 12 | 13 | 11 | 10 | | | | | $8^3$ | | | 4 | | 9 | | | 14 | | | | 22 |
| 1 | | 2 | 3 | 4 | 7 | 13 | 14 | $8^3$ | 10 | $11^1$ | | | | | 9 | 5 | | | | $6^2$ | 12 | | | | | | 23 |
| 1 | 2 | 3 | 4 | 5 | 6 | | 12 | $9^1$ | 10 | $11^2$ | 14 | | | | 7 | | | | | $8^3$ | 13 | | | | | | 24 |
| 1 | 2 | 5 | 3 | 4 | 7 | 13 | | $8^1$ | 12 | 10 | 14 | | | | 6 | | | | | $9^2$ | $11^3$ | | | | | | 25 |
| 1 | | 3 | 4 | | 12 | 7 | $8^1$ | 11 | | | $10^3$ | | 6 | | 2 | | | 13 | | $9^2$ | 14 | | 5 | | | | 26 |
| 1 | 2 | 3 | 4 | 6 | | 9 | | | 10 | 14 | 12 | | $7^3$ | | 5 | 13 | | $8^2$ | | | $11^1$ | | | | | | 27 |
| 1 | 2 | 5 | $4^1$ | | 9 | 14 | 7 | | | 13 | 11 | 10 | | | 3 | $8^2$ | | | | $6^3$ | | | 12 | | | | 28 |
| 1 | | 5 | 3 | 4 | | 8 | 7 | | 11 | 13 | | | $6^2$ | | 2 | 10 | | $9^1$ | | | | | 12 | | | | 29 |
| 1 | $2^1$ | 5 | 3 | | 7 | | 8 | 6 | 12 | 9 | | | 4 | | $11^3$ | | | $10^2$ | | 13 | | | 14 | | | | 30 |
| 1 | | 2 | 3 | | 6 | 12 | 9 | | 10 | 13 | | | 4 | | $7^1$ | | | $8^3$ | | 14 | | | 5 | | $11^2$ | | 31 |
| 1 | | 5 | 3 | 4 | 7 | | 9 | | 10 | 13 | | | 12 | | 2 | 8 | | $6^1$ | | | | | | | $11^2$ | | 32 |
| 1 | 12 | 5 | $3^1$ | 4 | 7 | $8^2$ | 9 | | 10 | 14 | | | 6 | | 2 | | | | | 13 | | | | | $11^3$ | | 33 |
| 1 | $5^1$ | 2 | | 4 | 8 | 7 | | | $10^3$ | 13 | | | 9 | | 3 | $6^2$ | | 14 | | | | | 12 | | 11 | | 34 |
| 1 | | 2 | | 3 | 6 | | 9 | | | $10^2$ | 13 | | $7^3$ | | 5 | $8^1$ | | 12 | | 14 | | | 4 | | 11 | | 35 |
| 1 | 13 | 5 | $3^1$ | | 7 | | 9 | | 12 | | | | $6^3$ | | 2 | 8 | | $10^2$ | | 14 | | | 4 | | 11 | | 36 |
| 1 | | 5 | | | 8 | 6 | 7 | | $9^1$ | $10^2$ | | | | | 2 | 12 | | | | 13 | | | 4 | | 11 | 3 | 37 |
| 1 | | 5 | | 4 | $9^2$ | 7 | 8 | | | $10^3$ | 14 | | 13 | | 2 | 6 | | | | 12 | | | | | $11^1$ | 3 | 38 |
| 1 | | 2 | | 3 | 13 | | 8 | $10^2$ | $9^3$ | | 12 | | 6 | | 4 | | | 7 | 14 | | | | | | $11^1$ | 5 | 39 |
| 1 | 12 | 5 | | 3 | | 7 | 8 | 11 | | | $10^1$ | | $9^2$ | | $2^3$ | 14 | | 6 | | 13 | | | | | | 4 | 40 |
| 1 | 2 | 5 | | 3 | 13 | | 8 | 9 | 10 | 12 | $11^1$ | | 14 | | | $6^3$ | | $7^2$ | | | | | | | | 4 | 41 |
| 1 | 2 | 3 | | 4 | 14 | | 8 | $9^3$ | 11 | $10^1$ | | | | | $7^2$ | | 13 | | | $6^1$ | 12 | | | | | 5 | 42 |
| 1 | 2 | 5 | | 3 | | | 8 | | 9 | 10 | | | | | 12 | | | $6^1$ | | 7 | 11 | | | | | 4 | 43 |
| 1 | 2 | 5 | | 4 | | 13 | 7 | $6^2$ | 12 | | | | 10 | | | | | $8^1$ | | 9 | 11 | | | | | 3 | 44 |
| 1 | $2^3$ | 3 | | 5 | | | 8 | $9^2$ | 10 | | | | $6^1$ | | 4 | 13 | | 12 | | $7^1$ | 11 | 14 | | | | | 45 |
| 1 | 2 | $5^■$ | | 3 | | | 7 | 11 | | | | | 9 | $10^1$ | | | | $6^3$ | 14 | $8^2$ | 13 | | 4 | | 12 | | 46 |

# CARLISLE UNITED

## FOUNDATION

Carlisle United came into being when members of Shaddongate United voted to change its name on 17 May 1904. The new club was admitted to the Second Division of the Lancashire Combination in 1905–06, winning promotion the following season. Devonshire Park was officially opened on 2 September 1905, when St Helens Town were the visitors. Despite defeat in a disappointing 3–2 start, a respectable mid-table position was achieved.

*Brunton Park, Warwick Road, Carlisle, Cumbria*
*CA1 1LL.*

*Telephone:* (01228) 526 237.

*Fax:* (01228) 554 141.

*Ticket Office:* (0844) 371 1921.

*Website:* www.carlisleunited.co.uk

*Email:* enquiries@carlisleunited.co.uk

*Ground Capacity:* 16,683.

*Record Attendance:* 27,500 v Birmingham C, FA Cup 3rd rd, 5 January 1957 and v Middlesbrough, FA Cup 5th rd, 7 February 1970.

*Pitch Measurements:* 102m × 67m (112yd × 74yd)

*Chairman:* Andrew Jenkins.

*Manager:* Greg Abbott.

*Assistant Manager:* Graham Kavanagh.

*Physio:* Neil Dalton.

*Colours:* Blue shirts with white and red trim, white shorts, white socks with red trim.

*Year Formed:* 1904.

*Turned Professional:* 1921.

*Previous Name:* 1904, Shaddongate United; 1904, Carlisle United.

*Club Nicknames:* 'The Cumbrians', 'The Blues'.

*Grounds:* 1904, Milholme Bank; 1905, Devonshire Park; 1909, Brunton Park.

*First Football League Game:* 25 August 1928, Division 3 (N), v Accrington S (a) W 3–2 – Prout; Coulthard, Cook; Harrison, Ross, Pigg; Agar (1), Hutchison, McConnell (1), Ward (1), Watson.

*Record League Victory:* 8–0 v Hartlepool U, Division 3 (N), 1 September 1928 – Prout; Smiles, Cook; Robinson (1) Ross, Pigg; Agar (1), Hutchison (1), McConnell (4), Ward (1), Watson. 8–0 v Scunthorpe U, Division 3 (N), 25 December 1952 – MacLaren; Hill, Scott; Stokoe, Twentyman, Waters; Harrison (1), Whitehouse (5), Ashman (2), Duffett, Bond.

*Record Cup Victory:* 6–0 v Shepshed Dynamo, FA Cup 1st rd, 16 November 1996 – Caig; Hopper, Archdeacon (pen), Walling, Robinson, Pounewatchy, Peacock (1), Conway (1) (Jansen), Smart (McAlindon (1)), Hayward, Aspinall (Thorpe), (2 og).

## HONOURS

**Football League – Division 1:** 22nd, 1974–75;

**Division 3:** *Champions* 1964–65, 1994–95; *Runners-up* 1981–82;

**Division 4:** *Runners-up* 1963–64;

**FL 2:** *Champions* 2005–06.

**FA Cup:** 6th rd 1975.

**Football League Cup:** Semi-final 1970.

**Auto Windscreens Shield:** *Winners* 1997; *Runners-up* 1995.

**LDV Vans Trophy:** *Runners-up* 2003, 2006.

**Johnstone's Paint Trophy:** *Winners* 2011; *Runners-up* 2010.

## sky SPORTS FACT FILE

Carlisle United, needing to win their final match of the 1998–99 season against Plymouth Argyle to stay in the Football League, were drawing 1-1 as the game entered injury time. Goalkeeper Jimmy Glass moved up to join the attack and scored to ensure the Cumbrians retained their senior status.

*Record Defeat:* 1–11 v Hull C, Division 3 (N), 14 January 1939.

*Most League Points (2 for a win):* 62, Division 3 (N), 1950–51.

*Most League Points (3 for a win):* 91, Division 3, 1994–95.

*Most League Goals:* 113, Division 4, 1963–64.

*Highest League Scorer in Season:* Jimmy McConnell, 42, Division 3 (N), 1928–29.

*Most League Goals in Total Aggregate:* Jimmy McConnell, 126, 1928–32.

*Most League Goals in One Match:* 5, Hugh Mills v Halifax T, Division 3 (N), 11 September 1937; 5, Jim Whitehouse v Scunthorpe U, Division 3 (N), 25 December 1952.

*Most Capped Player:* Eric Welsh, 4, Northern Ireland.

*Most League Appearances:* Allan Ross, 466, 1963–79.

*Youngest League Player:* John Slaven, 16 years 162 days v Scunthorpe U, 16 March 2002.

*Record Transfer Fee Received:* £1,500,000 from Crystal Palace for Matt Jansen, February 1998.

*Record Transfer Fee Paid:* £140,000 to Blackburn R for Joe Garner, August 2007.

*Football League Record:* 1928 Elected to Division 3 (N); 1958–62 Division 4; 1962–63 Division 3; 1963–64 Division 4; 1964–65 Division 3; 1965–74 Division 2; 1974–75 Division 1; 1975–77 Division 2; 1977–82 Division 3; 1982–86 Division 2; 1986–87 Division 3; 1987–92 Division 4; 1992–95 Division 3; 1995–96 Division 2; 1996–97 Division 3; 1997–98 Division 2; 1998–04 Division 3; 2004–05 Conference; 2005–06 FL 2; 2006– FL 1.

## LATEST SEQUENCES

*Longest Sequence of League Wins:* 7, 18.2.06 – 8.4.06.

*Longest Sequence of League Defeats:* 12, 27.9.2003 – 13.12.2003.

*Longest Sequence of League Draws:* 6, 11.2.1978 – 11.3.1978.

*Longest Sequence of Unbeaten League Matches:* 19, 1.10.1994 – 11.2.1995.

*Longest Sequence Without a League Win:* 14, 19.1.1935 – 19.4.1935.

*Successive Scoring Runs:* 26 from 23.8.1947.

*Successive Non-scoring Runs:* 5 from 24.8.1968.

## MANAGERS

Harry Kirkbride 1904–05 (*Secretary-Manager*)
McCumiskey 1905–06 (*Secretary-Manager*)
Jack Houston 1906–08 (*Secretary-Manager*)
Bert Stansfield 1908–10
Jack Houston 1910–12
Davie Graham 1912–13
George Bristow 1913–30
Billy Hampson 1930–33
Bill Clarke 1933–35
Robert Kelly 1935–36
Fred Westgarth 1936–38
David Taylor 1938–40
Howard Harkness 1940–45
Bill Clark 1945–46 (*Secretary-Manager*)
Ivor Broadis 1946–49
Bill Shankly 1949–51
Fred Emery 1951–58
Andy Beattie 1958–60
Ivor Powell 1960–63
Alan Ashman 1963–67
Tim Ward 1967–68
Bob Stokoe 1968–70
Ian MacFarlane 1970–72
Alan Ashman 1972–75
Dick Young 1975–76
Bobby Moncur 1976–80
Martin Harvey 1980
Bob Stokoe 1980–85
Bryan 'Pop' Robson 1985
Bob Stokoe 1985–86
Harry Gregg 1986–87
Cliff Middlemass 1987–91
Aidan McCaffery 1991–92
David McCreery 1992–93
Mick Wadsworth (*Director of Coaching*) 1993–96
Mervyn Day 1996–97
David Wilkes and John Halpin (*Directors of Coaching*), and Michael Knighton 1997–99
Nigel Pearson 1998–99
Keith Mincher 1999
Martin Wilkinson 1999–2000
Ian Atkins 2000–01
Roddy Collins 2001–02; 2002–03
Paul Simpson 2003–06
Neil McDonald 2006–07
John Ward 2007–08
Greg Abbott December 2008–

## TEN YEAR LEAGUE RECORD

|         |        | P  | W  | D  | L  | F  | A  | Pts | Pos |
|---------|--------|----|----|----|----|----|----|-----|-----|
| 2003-04 | Div 3  | 46 | 12 | 9  | 25 | 46 | 69 | 45  | 23  |
| 2004-05 | Conf   | 42 | 20 | 13 | 9  | 74 | 37 | 73  | 3   |
| 2005-06 | FL 2   | 46 | 25 | 11 | 10 | 84 | 42 | 86  | 1   |
| 2006-07 | FL 1   | 46 | 19 | 11 | 16 | 54 | 55 | 68  | 8   |
| 2007-08 | FL 1   | 46 | 23 | 11 | 12 | 64 | 46 | 80  | 4   |
| 2008-09 | FL 1   | 46 | 12 | 14 | 20 | 56 | 69 | 50  | 20  |
| 2009-10 | FL 1   | 46 | 15 | 13 | 18 | 63 | 66 | 58  | 14  |
| 2010-11 | FL 1   | 46 | 16 | 11 | 19 | 60 | 62 | 59  | 12  |
| 2011-12 | FL 1   | 46 | 18 | 15 | 13 | 65 | 66 | 69  | 8   |
| 2012-13 | FL 1   | 46 | 14 | 13 | 19 | 56 | 77 | 55  | 17  |

## DID YOU KNOW

Inside forward Ivor Broadis was appointed as player-manager for Carlisle United in August 1946 at the age of 23. In January 1949 he became the first manager to transfer himself when he signed for Sunderland for a fee of £18,000.

## CARLISLE UNITED – FOOTBALL LEAGUE ONE 2012–13 LEAGUE RECORD

| Match No. | Date | Venue | Opponents | Result | H/T Score | Lg Pos. | Goalscorers | Attendance |
|---|---|---|---|---|---|---|---|---|
| 1 | Aug 18 | A | Stevenage | D 1-1 | 0-0 | 8 | Robson [73] | 2736 |
| 2 | 21 | H | Tranmere R | L 0-3 | 0-2 | 21 | | 4192 |
| 3 | 25 | H | Portsmouth | W 4-2 | 1-0 | 12 | Jervis [13], Livesey [48], Berrett [90], Madden [90] | 5120 |
| 4 | Sept 1 | A | Milton Keynes D | L 0-2 | 0-1 | 16 | | 7227 |
| 5 | 8 | A | Hartlepool U | W 2-1 | 0-1 | 12 | Cadamarteri [76], Robson [85] | 4474 |
| 6 | 15 | H | Swindon T | D 2-2 | 2-2 | 13 | Jervis 2 [14, 30] | 4987 |
| 7 | 18 | H | Crewe Alex | D 0-0 | 0-0 | 14 | | 3519 |
| 8 | 22 | A | Coventry C | W 2-1 | 1-1 | 10 | Cadamarteri (pen) [25], Livesey [57] | 10,674 |
| 9 | 29 | H | Crawley T | L 0-2 | 0-0 | 12 | | 4221 |
| 10 | Oct 6 | A | Walsall | W 2-1 | 1-1 | 12 | Garner [29], Noble [90] | 3964 |
| 11 | 13 | H | Notts Co | L 0-4 | 0-2 | 13 | | 4731 |
| 12 | 16 | A | Bury | D 1-1 | 0-1 | 13 | Garner [91] | 1913 |
| 13 | 20 | A | Colchester U | L 0-2 | 0-2 | 17 | | 3335 |
| 14 | 23 | H | Oldham Ath | W 3-1 | 0-0 | 13 | Garner 2 [57, 74], Robson [82] | 3310 |
| 15 | 27 | H | Bournemouth | L 2-4 | 1-2 | 14 | Noble [18], Symington [76] | 4050 |
| 16 | Nov 6 | A | Preston NE | D 1-1 | 1-0 | 15 | Garner (pen) [31] | 9249 |
| 17 | 10 | A | Brentford | L 1-2 | 1-1 | 15 | Garner [26] | 6763 |
| 18 | 17 | H | Leyton Orient | L 1-4 | 1-4 | 18 | Murphy [25] | 3964 |
| 19 | 20 | H | Doncaster R | L 1-3 | 0-2 | 19 | Symington [66] | 3229 |
| 20 | 24 | A | Yeovil T | W 3-1 | 1-0 | 18 | Beck 2 [21, 46], Garner [70] | 3394 |
| 21 | Dec 8 | H | Sheffield U | L 1-3 | 0-2 | 18 | Livesey [71] | 4892 |
| 22 | 15 | A | Shrewsbury T | L 1-2 | 1-1 | 19 | Noble [33] | 5260 |
| 23 | 26 | H | Hartlepool U | W 3-0 | 2-0 | 18 | Collins (og) [21], Robson [27], Miller [73] | 5380 |
| 24 | 29 | H | Bury | W 2-1 | 2-0 | 17 | Miller (pen) [2], Robson [10] | 4435 |
| 25 | Jan 1 | A | Crewe Alex | L 0-1 | 0-1 | 17 | | 4802 |
| 26 | 5 | A | Swindon T | L 0-4 | 0-2 | 18 | | 9162 |
| 27 | 13 | H | Coventry C | W 1-0 | 1-0 | 17 | Robson [2] | 4071 |
| 28 | 26 | H | Scunthorpe U | D 1-1 | 0-0 | 17 | Symington [76] | 3829 |
| 29 | Feb 2 | A | Tranmere R | W 1-0 | 1-0 | 16 | Loy [44] | 5713 |
| 30 | 9 | H | Stevenage | W 2-1 | 2-1 | 16 | Loy [9], Miller (pen) [14] | 3944 |
| 31 | 12 | A | Scunthorpe U | L 1-3 | 1-2 | 16 | Berrett [45] | 3112 |
| 32 | 16 | A | Portsmouth | D 1-1 | 0-0 | 16 | Loy [51] | 11,466 |
| 33 | 23 | H | Milton Keynes D | D 1-1 | 0-1 | 16 | Beck [85] | 4283 |
| 34 | 26 | H | Walsall | L 0-3 | 0-1 | 16 | | 3266 |
| 35 | Mar 2 | A | Notts Co | L 0-1 | 0-1 | 16 | | 5553 |
| 36 | 5 | A | Crawley T | D 1-1 | 1-0 | 16 | McGovern [23] | 2654 |
| 37 | 9 | H | Brentford | W 2-0 | 1-0 | 16 | O'Hanlon [23], Beck [54] | 3858 |
| 38 | 16 | A | Leyton Orient | L 1-4 | 0-2 | 17 | Robson [78] | 4387 |
| 39 | 23 | H | Yeovil T | D 3-3 | 1-1 | 17 | Miller 2 [39, 90], Ayling (og) [90] | 3809 |
| 40 | 29 | H | Shrewsbury T | D 2-2 | 0-0 | 17 | Miller 2 (2 pens) [65, 82] | 4472 |
| 41 | Apr 1 | A | Sheffield U | D 0-0 | 0-0 | 18 | | 19,005 |
| 42 | 6 | A | Oldham Ath | W 2-1 | 2-0 | 17 | Noble [9], Mustoe [33] | 4271 |
| 43 | 9 | A | Doncaster R | W 2-0 | 1-0 | 17 | Noble 2 [35, 86] | 7884 |
| 44 | 13 | H | Preston NE | D 1-1 | 1-1 | 15 | Miller [38] | 5965 |
| 45 | 20 | A | Bournemouth | L 1-3 | 0-1 | 15 | Miller [50] | 9014 |
| 46 | 27 | H | Colchester U | L 0-2 | 0-0 | 17 | | 5427 |

**Final League Position: 17**

### GOALSCORERS

*League (56):* Miller 9 (4 pens), Garner 7 (1 pen), Robson 7, Noble 6, Beck 4, Jervis 3, Livesey 3, Loy 3, Symington 3, Berrett 2, Cadamarteri 2 (1 pen), Madden 1, McGovern 1, Murphy 1, Mustoe 1, O'Hanlon 1, own goals 2.
*FA Cup (5):* Beck 1, Berrett 1, Garner 1, Noble 1, Symington 1.
*Capital One Cup (3):* Beck 1, Robson 1, Symington 1.
*Johnstone's Paint Trophy (1):* McGovern 1.

| Collin A 11 +1 | Robson M 35 +1 | McGovern J 37 +1 | Livesey D 35 +4 | Noble L 29 +6 | Thirlwell P 30 +2 | Miller L 23 | Edwards M 22 +1 | Potts B 25 +2 | Berrett J 42 | Bugno A 2 | Cadamarteri D 14 +11 | Simek F 36 +2 | Beck M 7 +20 | Symington D 3 +28 | Chantler C 24 +1 | Murphy P 16 +5 | Jervis J 5 | Madden P — +1 | O'Halloran M — +1 | Gillespie M 35 | Garner J 15 +1 | Higginbotham K 7 +3 | Welsh A 8 +4 | Todd J — +1 | McGinty S — +1 | Loy R 12 +1 | O'Hanlon S 19 | Mustoe J 14 | Manset M — +7 | Salmon A — +2 | Match No. |
|---|---|---|---|---|---|---|---|---|---|---|---|---|---|---|---|---|---|---|---|---|---|---|---|---|---|---|---|---|---|---|---|
| 1 | 2 | 3 | 4 | 5 | 6 | 7¹ | 8 |  | 9² | 10 | 11 | 12 | 13 |  |  |  |  |  |  |  |  |  |  |  |  |  |  |  |  |  | 1 |
| 1 | 11 | 9² | 3 | 6¹ | 7 |  | 4 |  | 8 | 5³ | 10 |  |  | 12 | 13 | 14 |  |  |  |  |  |  |  |  |  |  |  |  |  |  | 2 |
| 1 | 9 | 6 | 3 | 7 |  |  | 8 |  | 10¹ |  | 2 |  |  | 5 | 4 | 11 | 12 |  |  |  |  |  |  |  |  |  |  |  |  |  | 3 |
| 1 | 3² | 6³ |  | 7 | 12 |  | 4 | 2 | 8¹ |  | 11 |  | 14 | 9 | 5 | 10 |  | 13 |  |  |  |  |  |  |  |  |  |  |  |  | 4 |
|  | 9 | 6² | 14 |  | 8 |  | 3 |  | 7 |  | 10 | 2 | 12 | 13 | 5 | 4³ | 11¹ |  |  | 1 |  |  |  |  |  |  |  |  |  |  | 5 |
|  | 9 | 6³ | 13 |  | 7 |  | 3² |  | 8 |  | 10¹ | 2 | 12 | 14 | 5 | 4 | 11 |  |  | 1 |  |  |  |  |  |  |  |  |  |  | 6 |
|  | 9 | 6² | 3 |  | 8 |  | 7 |  | 10 |  | 2 |  |  | 13 | 5 | 4 | 11¹ |  |  | 1 | 12 |  |  |  |  |  |  |  |  |  | 7 |
|  | 9 | 6 | 3³ |  | 8¹ | 14 | 12 | 7 | 10 |  | 2 |  |  | 5 | 4 |  |  |  |  | 1 | 11² | 13 |  |  |  |  |  |  |  |  | 8 |
|  | 9 | 6² | 3 | 12 | 8¹ |  | 7 |  | 11³ |  | 2 | 14 |  | 5 | 4 |  |  |  |  | 1 | 10 | 13 |  |  |  |  |  |  |  |  | 9 |
|  | 9 |  | 4 | 12 | 7 |  | 3¹ | 2 | 8 |  | 11² |  | 14 | 5 | 13 |  |  |  |  | 1 | 10 | 6³ |  |  |  |  |  |  |  |  | 10 |
|  | 2 |  | 3 | 12 | 6¹ |  | 4 | 8² | 7 |  | 10³ | 14 | 13 | 5 |  |  |  |  |  | 1 | 11 | 9 |  |  |  |  |  |  |  |  | 11 |
| 11³ |  | 6² | 7 |  | 3 |  | 8 |  | 2 |  | 13 | 12 | 5 | 4 |  |  |  |  |  | 1 | 10 | 9¹ | 14 |  |  |  |  |  |  |  | 12 |
|  | 9 |  | 8³ |  | 4 | 13 | 7 |  | 10¹ |  | 2 | 14 | 12 | 5 | 3 |  |  |  |  | 1 | 11 | 6² |  |  |  |  |  |  |  |  | 13 |
|  | 11 | 12 | 6 | 7 | 3 |  | 8 |  | 9 | 2 |  |  |  | 5 | 4¹ |  |  |  |  | 1 | 10 |  |  |  |  |  |  |  |  |  | 14 |
|  | 11 | 13 | 6 | 7¹ | 3² |  | 8 |  | 9³ | 2 | 14 | 12 | 5 | 4 |  |  |  |  |  | 1 | 10 |  |  |  |  |  |  |  |  |  | 15 |
| 1 |  | 9 |  | 7 | 3 | 6 | 8 |  | 2 |  |  |  |  | 5 | 4 |  |  |  |  | 10 | 11 |  |  |  |  |  |  |  |  |  | 16 |
| 1 |  | 7¹ |  | 8³ | 4 | 5 | 6 |  | 2 |  | 14 | 12 | 9 | 3 |  |  |  |  | 11 | 10¹ | 13 |  |  |  |  |  |  |  |  |  | 17 |
| 1 | 12 | 11¹ |  | 6³ | 4 | 7 | 8 |  | 2 | 14 | 13 | 5 | 3 |  |  |  |  |  | 10 | 9² |  |  |  |  |  |  |  |  |  |  | 18 |
| 1 | 9 |  | 3 |  | 4 | 7 | 8 |  | 2 |  | 10 | 6 | 5 |  |  |  |  |  | 11¹ | 12 |  |  |  |  |  |  |  |  |  |  | 19 |
| 1 | 9 | 12 | 4 |  | 3 | 8 | 7 |  | 2 |  | 10 | 6¹ | 5 |  |  |  |  |  |  | 11 |  |  |  |  |  |  |  |  |  |  | 20 |
| 1 | 6 | 9 | 3 | 8 | 7 |  | 4 | 5 |  | 10² |  | 13 | 12 | 2¹ |  |  |  |  | 11 |  |  |  |  |  |  |  |  |  |  |  | 21 |
|  | 9 | 6¹ | 3 | 7 | 8 | 10³ | 4 |  | 14 | 2 | 13 | 12 | 5 |  |  |  |  |  | 1 | 11² |  |  |  |  |  |  |  |  |  |  | 22 |
| 11 | 9 | 3 | 6 | 7¹ | 10² | 4 | 8 |  | 2 | 12 |  | 5³ |  |  |  |  |  |  | 1 |  | 13 | 14 |  |  |  |  |  |  |  |  | 23 |
| 11 | 9² | 3 | 6 |  | 10 | 4 | 7 | 8¹ | 2 | 12 | 13 | 5 |  |  |  |  |  |  | 1 |  |  |  |  |  |  |  |  |  |  |  | 24 |
| 11 | 9² | 3 | 7 |  | 10 | 4 | 6¹ | 8 | 2 |  | 13 | 5 |  |  |  |  |  |  | 1 |  |  | 12 |  |  |  |  |  |  |  |  | 25 |
| 5 | 9 | 3 | 7 |  | 11 | 4² | 6¹ | 8 | 2 |  | 13 |  | 12 |  |  |  |  |  | 1 |  |  | 10 |  |  |  |  |  |  |  |  | 26 |
| 11 | 9³ | 3 | 7² | 12 | 10 |  | 6¹ | 8 | 13 | 2 | 14 | 5 |  |  |  |  |  |  | 1 |  |  |  | 4 |  |  |  |  |  |  |  | 27 |
| 3 | 7² | 6 | 8¹ |  | 11 |  | 10 | 9 | 2 | 12 | 13 |  |  |  |  |  |  |  | 1 | 4 |  | 5 |  |  |  |  |  |  |  |  | 28 |
| 5 | 6 | 3 | 12 | 7 | 11 |  | 8 |  | 2 | 13 |  |  |  |  |  |  |  |  | 1 | 9¹ |  | 10² | 4 |  |  |  |  |  |  |  | 29 |
| 5 | 9 | 4 | 13 | 7² | 10 |  | 8 |  | 14 | 2 | 12 |  |  |  |  |  |  |  | 1 | 6¹ |  | 11³ | 3 |  |  |  |  |  |  |  | 30 |
| 5 | 9 | 3² |  | 7 | 11 |  | 8 |  | 14 | 2 | 13 | 12 |  |  |  |  |  |  | 1 | 6¹ |  | 10² | 4 |  |  |  |  |  |  |  | 31 |
| 5 | 6 | 3 | 9¹ | 8 | 11 |  | 7 |  | 2 |  | 12 |  |  |  |  |  |  |  | 1 | 10 |  |  | 4 |  |  |  |  |  |  |  | 32 |
|  | 9 | 3² | 6 | 7¹ | 10 |  | 8 |  | 2 | 14 | 12 | 13 |  |  |  |  |  |  | 1 | 11³ |  |  | 4 | 5 |  |  |  |  |  |  | 33 |
|  | 6² | 3 | 7 |  | 10³ |  | 8 |  | 14 | 2 | 12 | 9 |  |  |  |  |  |  | 1 | 13 |  |  | 11¹ | 4 | 5 |  |  |  |  |  | 34 |
|  | 11 | 4 | 6¹ | 7 | 10⁴ |  | 8 |  | 13 | 2 | 14 | 12 |  |  |  |  |  |  | 1 | 9² |  | 3 | 5³ |  |  |  |  |  |  |  | 35 |
|  | 8 | 3 | 7 |  | 6² | 9 | 13 | 2 | 10 | 12 |  |  |  |  |  |  |  |  | 1 | 11¹ |  | 4 | 5 |  |  |  |  |  |  |  | 36 |
| 10¹ | 6 | 3 |  | 8 | 7 | 9 |  | 2 | 11 |  |  |  |  |  |  |  |  |  | 1 | 12 |  | 4 | 5 |  |  |  |  |  |  |  | 37 |
| 14 | 11 | 9² | 3¹ | 6 |  | 7 | 8³ | 2 | 10 | 13 | 12 |  |  |  |  |  |  |  | 1 |  |  | 5 | 4 |  |  |  |  |  |  |  | 38 |
| 1 | 9 | 6 |  | 7 | 10 |  | 8 |  | 2 | 11¹ | 13 | 4 |  |  |  |  |  |  | 3 |  |  |  | 5² | 12 |  |  |  |  |  |  | 39 |
| 9² | 6 | 4 | 14 | 7³ | 10 |  | 8 |  | 2 | 11¹ | 12 |  |  |  |  |  |  |  | 1 |  |  | 3 | 5 | 13 |  |  |  |  |  |  | 40 |
|  | 6² | 3 | 9 | 8 | 11 |  | 7 |  | 2 | 12 |  |  |  |  |  |  |  |  | 1 | 10¹ |  | 4⁴ | 5 | 13 |  |  |  |  |  |  | 41 |
|  | 9¹ | 3 | 8 | 6 | 10 | 2 | 7 | 13 |  | 4 |  |  |  |  |  |  |  |  | 1 | 11² |  |  | 5 | 12 |  |  |  |  |  |  | 42 |
|  | 5 | 3 | 6 | 7¹ | 11 | 10 | 8 |  | 12 |  |  |  |  |  |  |  |  |  | 1 | 4 |  |  | 2 | 9 |  |  |  |  |  |  | 43 |
|  | 6 | 3 | 8 |  | 11 | 2 | 7 | 13 |  |  |  |  |  |  |  |  |  |  | 1 | 9¹ |  | 10² | 4 | 5 | 12 |  |  |  |  |  | 44 |
|  | 5 | 7² | 3 | 8 | 11 | 2 | 9 |  | 14 |  |  |  |  |  |  |  |  |  | 1 | 10¹ |  | 4 | 6² | 12 | 13 |  |  |  |  |  | 45 |
|  | 11 |  | 3 | 6 | 8¹ | 10 | 2 | 7 |  |  |  |  |  |  |  |  |  |  | 1 | 9⁴ |  | 4 | 5 | 12 | 13 |  |  |  |  |  | 46 |

**FA Cup**

| | | | |
|---|---|---|---|
| First Round | Ebbsfleet U | (h) | 4-2 |
| Second Round | Bournemouth | (h) | 1-3 |

**Capital One Cup**

| | | | |
|---|---|---|---|
| First Round | Accrington S | (h) | 1-0 |
| Second Round | Ipswich T | (h) | 2-1 |
| Third Round | Tottenham H | (h) | 0-3 |

**Johnstone's Paint Trophy**

| | | | |
|---|---|---|---|
| First Round | Preston NE | (h) | 1-1 |
| *(aet; lost 1-3 on pens)* | | | |

# CHARLTON ATHLETIC

## FOUNDATION

The club was formed on 9 June 1905, by a group of 14- and 15-year-old youths living in streets by the Thames in the area which now borders the Thames Barrier. The club's progress through local leagues was so rapid that after the First World War they joined the Kent League where they spent a season before turning professional and joining the Southern League in 1920. A year later they were elected to the Football League's Division 3 (South).

*The Valley, Floyd Road, Charlton, London SE7 8BL.*

*Telephone:* (020) 8333 4000.

*Fax:* (020) 8333 4001.

*Ticket Office:* (0871) 226 1905.

*Website:* www.cafc.co.uk

*Email:* customerservices@cafc.co.uk

*Ground Capacity:* 27,111.

*Record Attendance:* 75,031 v Aston Villa, FA Cup 5th rd, 12 February 1938 (at The Valley).

*Pitch Measurements:* 102m × 66m (112yd × 73yd)

*Chairman:* Michael Slater.

*Executive Vice-chairman:* Martin Prothero.

*Manager:* Chris Powell.

*Assistant Manager:* Alex Dyer.

*Head Physio:* Erol Umut.

*Colours:* Red shirts, white shorts, red socks with white tops.

*Year Formed:* 1905.

*Turned Professional:* 1920.

*Club Nickname:* 'The Addicks'.

## HONOURS

**Football League – FL 1** *Champions* 2011–12; **Division 1:** *Champions* 1999–2000; *Runners-up* 1936–37; **Division 2:** *Runners-up* 1935–36, 1985–86;

**Division 3 (S):** *Champions* 1928–29, 1934–35.

**FA Cup:** *Winners* 1947; *Runners-up* 1946.

**Football League Cup:** Quarter-final 2007.

**Full Members' Cup:** *Runners-up* 1987.

*Grounds:* 1906, Siemen's Meadow; 1907, Woolwich Common; 1909, Pound Park; 1913, Horn Lane; 1920, The Valley; 1923, Catford (The Mount); 1924, The Valley; 1985, Selhurst Park; 1991, Upton Park; 1992, The Valley.

*First Football League Game:* 27 August 1921, Division 3 (S), v Exeter C (h) W 1–0 – Hughes; Johnny Mitchell, Goodman; Dowling (1), Hampson, Dunn; Castle, Bailey, Halse, Green, Wilson.

*Record League Victory:* 8–1 v Middlesbrough, Division 1, 12 September 1953 – Bartram; Campbell, Ellis; Fenton, Ufton, Hammond; Hurst (2), O'Linn (2), Leary (1), Firmani (3), Kiernan.

*Record Cup Victory:* 7–0 v Burton A, FA Cup 3rd rd, 7 January 1956 – Bartram; Campbell, Townsend; Hewie, Ufton, Hammond; Hurst (1), Gauld (1), Leary (3), White, Kiernan (2).

*Record Defeat:* 1–11 v Aston Villa, Division 2, 14 November 1959.

## sky SPORTS FACT FILE

When Charlton Athletic played Huddersfield Town at The Valley in 21 December 1957 they found themselves 5-1 down with less than 30 minutes to play. In a remarkable comeback they won the match 7-6 with Johnny Summers scoring five, including four in a 17-minute spell.

*Most League Points (2 for a win):* 61, Division 3 (S), 1934–35.

*Most League Points (3 for a win):* 101, FL 1, 2011–12.

*Most League Goals:* 107, Division 2, 1957–58.

*Highest League Scorer in Season:* Ralph Allen, 32, Division 3 (S), 1934–35.

*Most League Goals in Total Aggregate:* Stuart Leary, 153, 1953–62.

*Most League Goals in One Match:* 5, Wilson Lennox v Exeter C, Division 3 (S), 2 February 1929; 5, Eddie Firmani v Aston Villa, Division 1, 5 February 1955; 5, John Summers v Huddersfield T, Division 2, 21 December 1957; 5, John Summers v Portsmouth, Division 2, 1 October 1960.

*Most Capped Player:* Jonatan Johansson, 42 (105), Finland.

*Most League Appearances:* Sam Bartram, 579, 1934–56.

*Youngest League Player:* Jonjo Shelvey, 16 years 59 days v Burnley, 26 April 2008.

*Record Transfer Fee Received:* £16,500,000 from Tottenham H for Darren Bent, May 2007

*Record Transfer Fee Paid:* £4,750,000 to Wimbledon for Jason Euell, January 2001.

*Football League Record:* 1921 Elected to Division 3 (S); 1929–33 Division 2; 1933–35 Division 3 (S); 1935–36 Division 2; 1936–57 Division 1; 1957–72 Division 2; 1972–75 Division 3; 1975–80 Division 2; 1980–81 Division 3; 1981–86 Division 2; 1986–90 Division 1; 1990–92 Division 2; 1992–98 Division 1; 1998–99 FA Premier League; 1999–2000 Division 1; 2000–07 FA Premier League; 2007–09 FL C; 2009–12 FL 1; 2012– FL C.

### MANAGERS

Walter Rayner 1920–25
Alex Macfarlane 1925–27
Albert Lindon 1928
Alex Macfarlane 1928–32
Albert Lindon 1932–33
Jimmy Seed 1933–56
Jimmy Trotter 1956–61
Frank Hill 1961–65
Bob Stokoe 1965–67
Eddie Firmani 1967–70
Theo Foley 1970–74
Andy Nelson 1974–79
Mike Bailey 1979–81
Alan Mullery 1981–82
Ken Craggs 1982
Lennie Lawrence 1982–91
Steve Gritt/Alan Curbishley 1991–95
Alan Curbishley 1995–2006
Iain Dowie 2006
Les Reed 2006
Alan Pardew 2006–08
Phil Parkinson 2008–10
Chris Powell January 2011–

## LATEST SEQUENCES

*Longest Sequence of League Wins:* 12, 26.12.1999 – 7.3.2000.

*Longest Sequence of League Defeats:* 10, 11.4.1990 – 15.9.1990.

*Longest Sequence of League Draws:* 6, 13.12.1992 – 16.1.1993.

*Longest Sequence of Unbeaten League Matches:* 15, 4.10.1980 – 20.12.1980.

*Longest Sequence Without a League Win:* 18, 18.10.2008 – 17.1.2009.

*Successive Scoring Runs:* 25 from 26.12.1935.

*Successive Non-scoring Runs:* 5 from 6.9.1922.

## TEN YEAR LEAGUE RECORD

| | | P | W | D | L | F | A | Pts | Pos |
|---|---|---|---|---|---|---|---|---|---|
| 2003-04 | PR Lge | 38 | 14 | 11 | 13 | 51 | 51 | 53 | 7 |
| 2004-05 | PR Lge | 38 | 12 | 10 | 16 | 42 | 58 | 46 | 11 |
| 2005-06 | PR Lge | 38 | 13 | 8 | 17 | 41 | 55 | 47 | 13 |
| 2006-07 | PR Lge | 38 | 8 | 10 | 20 | 34 | 60 | 34 | 19 |
| 2007-08 | FL C | 46 | 17 | 13 | 16 | 63 | 58 | 64 | 11 |
| 2008-09 | FL C | 46 | 8 | 15 | 23 | 52 | 74 | 39 | 24 |
| 2009-10 | FL 1 | 46 | 23 | 15 | 8 | 71 | 48 | 84 | 4 |
| 2010-11 | FL 1 | 46 | 15 | 14 | 17 | 62 | 66 | 59 | 13 |
| 2011-12 | FL 1 | 46 | 30 | 11 | 5 | 82 | 36 | 101 | 1 |
| 2012-13 | FL C | 46 | 17 | 14 | 15 | 65 | 59 | 65 | 9 |

### DID YOU KNOW ?

In May 1968 Charlton Athletic achieved a unique double in five-a-side football. They defeated Crystal Palace 2-1 to win the London *Evening Standard* competition and a week later beat Gillingham 1-0 to win the national *Daily Express* tournament.

## CHARLTON ATHLETIC – FL CHAMPIONSHIP 2012–13 LEAGUE RECORD

| Match No. | Date | Venue | Opponents | Result | H/T Score | Lg Pos. | Goalscorers | Attendance |
|---|---|---|---|---|---|---|---|---|
| 1 | Aug 18 | A | Birmingham C | D 1-1 | 0-0 | 14 | Cort [82] | 18,210 |
| 2 | 21 | H | Leicester C | W 2-1 | 2-0 | 3 | Wright-Phillips [18], Kermorgant [32] | 16,658 |
| 3 | 25 | H | Hull C | D 0-0 | 0-0 | 9 | | 16,202 |
| 4 | Sept 1 | A | Nottingham F | L 1-2 | 0-1 | 16 | Camp (og) [88] | 19,745 |
| 5 | 14 | H | Crystal Palace | L 0-1 | 0-0 | 17 | | 21,730 |
| 6 | 18 | A | Derby Co | L 2-3 | 0-1 | 22 | Green [70], Kermorgant [72] | 20,063 |
| 7 | 22 | A | Ipswich T | W 2-1 | 0-0 | 18 | Jackson [48], Fuller [50] | 16,587 |
| 8 | 29 | H | Blackburn R | D 1-1 | 1-1 | 19 | Jackson [27] | 17,169 |
| 9 | Oct 2 | H | Watford | L 1-2 | 1-1 | 20 | Fuller [35] | 15,585 |
| 10 | 6 | A | Blackpool | W 2-0 | 0-0 | 15 | Cort [49], Solly [73] | 13,482 |
| 11 | 20 | H | Barnsley | L 0-1 | 0-0 | 18 | | 26,185 |
| 12 | 23 | A | Leeds U | D 1-1 | 0-1 | 18 | Dervite [50] | 17,484 |
| 13 | 27 | A | Wolverhampton W | D 1-1 | 0-1 | 20 | Wilson [58] | 22,198 |
| 14 | Nov 3 | H | Middlesbrough | L 1-4 | 1-1 | 21 | Hulse [12] | 17,744 |
| 15 | 6 | H | Cardiff C | W 5-4 | 2-2 | 19 | Jackson 2 [39, 45], Stephens [54], Haynes [59], Hulse [65] | 15,778 |
| 16 | 11 | A | Bristol C | W 2-0 | 1-0 | 16 | Haynes [20], Morrison [56] | 13,009 |
| 17 | 17 | A | Burnley | W 1-0 | 0-0 | 14 | Haynes [69] | 11,405 |
| 18 | 24 | H | Huddersfield T | D 1-1 | 0-0 | 15 | Hulse [60] | 20,012 |
| 19 | 27 | H | Peterborough U | W 2-0 | 0-0 | 13 | Fuller [77], Kermorgant [85] | 17,377 |
| 20 | Dec 1 | A | Millwall | D 0-0 | 0-0 | 13 | | 18,013 |
| 21 | 8 | H | Brighton & HA | D 2-2 | 1-1 | 12 | Wilson [9], Pritchard [70] | 19,018 |
| 22 | 15 | A | Bolton W | L 0-2 | 0-0 | 14 | | 15,991 |
| 23 | 22 | A | Sheffield W | L 0-2 | 0-1 | 17 | | 20,517 |
| 24 | 26 | H | Ipswich T | L 1-2 | 0-2 | 17 | Haynes (pen) [73] | 18,380 |
| 25 | 29 | H | Derby Co | D 1-1 | 1-0 | 17 | Haynes [19] | 17,761 |
| 26 | Jan 1 | A | Watford | W 4-3 | 2-1 | 15 | Hoban (og) [34], Kermorgant 2 [37, 70], Jackson [78] | 14,221 |
| 27 | 12 | H | Blackpool | W 2-1 | 2-0 | 14 | Jackson [23], Wagstaff [45] | 16,846 |
| 28 | 19 | A | Blackburn R | W 2-1 | 1-0 | 12 | Stephens [26], Kermorgant [64] | 13,647 |
| 29 | 26 | H | Sheffield W | L 1-2 | 0-0 | 12 | Jackson [47] | 20,292 |
| 30 | Feb 2 | A | Crystal Palace | L 1-2 | 1-0 | 14 | Fuller [15] | 17,945 |
| 31 | 9 | H | Birmingham C | D 1-1 | 0-0 | 15 | Kermorgant [88] | 17,269 |
| 32 | 16 | A | Hull C | L 0-1 | 0-1 | 15 | | 16,849 |
| 33 | 19 | A | Leicester C | W 2-1 | 1-0 | 12 | Kermorgant [19], Haynes [78] | 19,920 |
| 34 | 23 | H | Nottingham F | L 0-2 | 0-0 | 14 | | 18,697 |
| 35 | Mar 2 | H | Burnley | L 0-1 | 0-1 | 15 | | 20,065 |
| 36 | 5 | A | Peterborough U | D 2-2 | 0-1 | 14 | Jackson [55], Haynes [59] | 6050 |
| 37 | 9 | A | Huddersfield T | W 1-0 | 1-0 | 12 | Harriott [4] | 13,591 |
| 38 | 16 | H | Millwall | L 0-2 | 0-0 | 14 | | 18,514 |
| 39 | 30 | H | Bolton W | W 3-2 | 1-2 | 14 | Jackson [25], Dervite [60], Kermorgant (pen) [63] | 17,322 |
| 40 | Apr 2 | A | Brighton & HA | D 0-0 | 0-0 | 14 | | 28,043 |
| 41 | 6 | H | Leeds U | W 2-1 | 0-0 | 12 | Jackson [47], Obika [90] | 18,900 |
| 42 | 13 | A | Barnsley | W 6-0 | 2-0 | 9 | Pritchard [4], Jackson [19], Kermorgant [48], Harriott [59], Kerkar [80], Fuller [90] | 9469 |
| 43 | 16 | A | Cardiff C | D 0-0 | 0-0 | 9 | | 26,338 |
| 44 | 20 | H | Wolverhampton W | W 2-1 | 0-0 | 9 | Dervite [63], Obika [90] | 19,023 |
| 45 | 27 | A | Middlesbrough | D 2-2 | 2-0 | 9 | Pritchard [1], Williams, R (og) [17] | 15,011 |
| 46 | May 4 | H | Bristol C | W 4-1 | 0-0 | 9 | Kermorgant 2 [47, 51], Obika [80], Jackson [85] | 18,981 |

**Final League Position: 9**

### GOALSCORERS

*League (65):* Jackson 12, Kermorgant 12 (1 pen), Haynes 7 (1 pen), Fuller 5, Dervite 3, Hulse 3, Obika 3, Pritchard 3, Cort 2, Harriott 2, Stephens 2, Wilson 2, Green 1, Kerkar 1, Morrison 1, Solly 1, Wagstaff 1, Wright-Phillips 1, own goals 3.
*FA Cup (0).*
*Capital One Cup (1):* Wagstaff 1.

| Hamer B 41 | Solly C 45 | Morrison M 44 | Cort L 30 | Wiggins R 19+1 | Pritchard B 36+6 | Stephens D 26+2 | Hollands D 11+3 | Jackson J 41+2 | Kermorgant Y 28+4 | Wright-Phillips B 10+9 | Cook J 1+6 | Taylor M 6+6 | Wilson L 25+5 | Kerkar S 15+7 | Haynes D 12+8 | Fuller R 20+11 | Green D 7+10 | Dervite D 20+10 | Evina C 10+2 | Hulse R 10+5 | Razak A 2 | Seaborne D 7 | Jonsson E 1+1 | Frimpong E 6 | Wagstaff S 7+2 | Harriott C 11+3 | Obika J 2+8 | Button D 5 | Hughes A 6 | Gower M 2+4 | Pope N —+1 | Match No. |
|---|---|---|---|---|---|---|---|---|---|---|---|---|---|---|---|---|---|---|---|---|---|---|---|---|---|---|---|---|---|---|---|---|
| 1 | 2 | 3 | 4 | 5 | 6 | 7 | 8 | 9² | 10 | 11¹ | 12 | 13 | | | | | | | | | | | | | | | | | | | | 1 |
| 1 | 2 | 3 | 4 | 5 | 6 | 7¹ | 8 | 9² | 10 | 11³ | 14 | | 12 | 13 | | | | | | | | | | | | | | | | | | 2 |
| 1 | 2 | 3 | 4 | 5 | 6 | 7 | 8 | 9 | 10 | 11 | | | | | | | | | | | | | | | | | | | | | | 3 |
| 1 | 2 | 4 | 3 | 5 | 8 | 7³ | 6 | 10 | 11² | 9¹ | | | | | 13 | 12 | 14 | | | | | | | | | | | | | | | 4 |
| 1 | 2 | 4 | 3 | 5¹ | 6³ | 7 | 8 | 9² | 11 | 10 | | | 12 | | 13 | 14 | | | | | | | | | | | | | | | | 5 |
| 1 | 5 | 4 | 3 | | 6 | 8 | 7² | 9 | 11 | 10¹ | | | 2 | 12 | 13 | 6 | | | | | | | | | | | | | | | | 6 |
| 1 | 5 | 3 | 4 | | 12 | 7 | | 8 | 11² | | | | 2 | 9¹ | 13 | 10³ | 6 | 14 | | | | | | | | | | | | | | 7 |
| 1 | 3 | 5 | 4 | | 12 | 7 | 9 | 8¹ | 10 | | | | 2 | 11² | | 6 | | 13 | | | | | | | | | | | | | | 8 |
| 1 | 5 | 4 | 3 | | 12 | 7 | 8¹ | | 11 | | | | 2 | 9 | | 10 | 6² | | 13 | | | | | | | | | | | | | 9 |
| 1 | 5 | 4 | 3 | | 12 | 7 | 9 | | | | | | 2 | 10 | | 11³ | 6¹ | 13 | 14 | 8² | | | | | | | | | | | | 10 |
| 1 | 5 | 3 | 4 | | 14 | 7 | | 8¹ | 13 | | | | 2 | 9 | | 10 | 6³ | | 11² | | | | | | | | | | | | | 11 |
| 1 | 2 | 4 | 3 | | 9 | | 13 | 8 | | 12 | | | 7 | 10² | | | 6 | 5 | 11¹ | | | | | | | | | | | | | 12 |
| 1 | 2 | 3 | 4 | | 9² | | 13 | 7 | | 12 | | | 6 | 10¹ | | | 8 | 5 | 11 | | | | | | | | | | | | | 13 |
| 1 | 5 | 3 | 4³ | | 6 | 12 | | 9 | 11² | 13 | | | 2¹ | 7 | 14 | | 8 | | 10 | | | | | | | | | | | | | 14 |
| 1 | 2 | 4 | 3 | | 9 | 7² | 13 | 10 | | 12 | | | 5 | 6¹ | | | 8 | | 11 | | | | | | | | | | | | | 15 |
| 1 | 2 | 4 | 3 | | 6 | 7 | | 9 | | | | 14 | 8³ | 11¹ | 13 | 12 | | 10² | | 5 | | | | | | | | | | | | 16 |
| 1 | 2 | 3 | 4 | | 6 | | 7 | | | | | 14 | 9 | 10² | 12 | 13 | | 11³ | 5 | 8¹ | | | | | | | | | | | | 17 |
| 1 | 2 | 4 | 3 | | 6 | 7 | | 9 | 13 | | | | 5 | 10² | 12 | | 11 | | | 8¹ | | | | | | | | | | | | 18 |
| 1 | 2 | 4 | 3 | | 6 | | 8 | 11³ | | | | | 9 | 10² | 12 | | 13 | 5 | 14 | 7¹ | | | | | | | | | | | | 19 |
| 1 | 2 | | 4 | | 8 | 7 | | 6 | 10² | 13 | | | 9¹ | | | 12 | 3 | 11 | 5 | | | | | | | | | | | | | 20 |
| 1 | 5 | 3 | | | 6 | 7 | | 9² | 12 | | | | 2 | 13 | 10¹ | 4 | | 11 | | 8 | | | | | | | | | | | | 21 |
| 1 | 4 | 3 | | | | 6 | | 8 | 10 | 12 | 13 | | 5 | | 11¹ | 2 | | 9 | 7² | | | | | | | | | | | | | 22 |
| 1 | 2 | 3 | 4 | | | 7 | 11 | | 6 | 9¹ | 10² | 12 | 13 | | 14 | | 5 | 8³ | | | | | | | | | | | | | | 23 |
| 1 | 5 | 3 | 2 | | 12 | 6 | | 13 | 14 | | | | 10 | 11³ | 8¹ | | 9 | 4 | 7² | | | | | | | | | | | | | 24 |
| 1 | 2 | 3⁴ | 4 | | 8 | 7² | | 9 | 10³ | 12 | | | 6 | 11¹ | 14 | 13 | 5 | | | | | | | | | | | | | | | 25 |
| 1 | 5 | | 4² | | 8 | 7 | | 3 | 10 | | 12 | 13 | 9¹ | | 11³ | | 6 | 2 | 14 | | | | | | | | | | | | | 26 |
| 1 | 2 | 4 | | | 8 | 7² | | 9 | 11 | | 3 | 6 | 13 | | | | 5 | | | | | | | 10¹ | 12 | | | | | | | 27 |
| 1 | 2 | 4 | | | 8 | 9 | | 7 | 11 | | 3 | 6² | | | | 12 | 5 | | | | | | | 10¹ | 13 | | | | | | | 28 |
| 1 | 2 | 4 | | | 7 | 8³ | | 9 | 11 | 12 | 3 | 6² | | | 13 | 14 | 5¹ | | | | | | | 10 | | | | | | | | 29 |
| 1 | 3 | 4 | 9 | 12 | 7 | | | 6³ | 14 | | | 8² | 13 | 11 | | 5 | 2 | | | | | | | 10¹ | | | | | | | | 30 |
| 1 | 2 | 4 | 3 | | | 7 | | 8 | 11 | 13 | | | 6¹ | | 10³ | 12 | 14 | 5 | | | | | | 9² | | | | | | | | 31 |
| 1 | 2 | 3 | 4 | | 8 | 7 | | 9 | 10 | 13 | | | 6² | | 12 | 11¹ | | 14 | 5³ | | | | | | | | | | | | | 32 |
| 1 | 2 | 5 | 4 | 3 | 7 | 6² | | 9 | 11 | | 14 | 13 | | 12 | | | 8¹ | | | | | | | | 10³ | | | | | | | 33 |
| 1 | 2 | 5 | 3 | 6 | 7³ | 8¹ | | 9 | 11■ | | | | 13 | 12 | | 4 | | | | | | | | | 10² | 14 | | | | | | 34 |
| | 4 | 3 | 5 | 7 | | 9 | | | 2 | | | | 6 | 11 | 12 | 8² | | | | | | | | | 13 | 10¹ | 1 | | | | | 35 |
| | 2 | 3 | | 5 | 7 | | 8 | | | 4 | 6 | | 10² | 11¹ | | 13 | | | | | | | | | | 9 | 12 | 1 | | | | 36 |
| | 2 | 3 | | 5 | 7 | | 8 | | | 4 | 6 | | 11³ | 10¹ | | 12 | 13 | | | | | | | | | 9² | 14 | 1 | | | | 37 |
| | 2 | 4 | | 5 | 7 | | 8 | 11 | | 3 | 6¹ | | 10² | 12 | | 13 | 9 | | | | | | | | | | | 1 | | | | 38 |
| 1 | 2 | 3 | | 5 | 6 | | 8 | 10 | | | | 13 | 14 | 11³ | | 4 | | | | | | | | | 9² | | | | 7¹ | 12 | | 39 |
| 1 | 2 | 3 | | 5 | 7 | 12 | | 9 | 10 | | 13 | 6¹ | | | 4 | | | | | | | | | | 11 | | | | 8² | | | 40 |
| 1 | 2 | 4 | | 5 | 6 | | 8 | 10 | | 12 | | | 11¹ | | 3 | | | | | | | | | | 9² | 13 | 7 | | | | | 41 |
| 1 | 2 | 3 | | 6 | 8 | | 7² | 11¹ | | 14 | | | 10 | | 9 | | | | | | | | | | 5³ | 12 | 4 | 13 | | | | 42 |
| 1 | 2 | 3 | | 5 | 9³ | | 8 | 10 | | 11² | 14 | | | | 4 | | | | | | | | | | 6 | 12 | 7¹ | 13 | | | | 43 |
| 1 | 2 | 4 | | 3 | 6 | | 9² | 10 | | 11³ | 13 | | | | 5 | | | | | | | | | | 7 | 14 | 8¹ | 12 | | | | 44 |
| 1 | 2 | 3 | | 5 | 6 | | 8 | | 11 | | | 13 | | 10¹ | | 4 | | | | | | | | | 9² | 12 | 7 | | | | | 45 |
| | 2 | 5 | | 3¹ | 6 | | 8 | 11 | | 12 | | | | | 4 | | | | | | | | | | 14 | 9³ | 10 | 1² | | 7 | 13 | 46 |

**FA Cup**
Third Round        Huddersfield T        (h)    0-1

**Capital One Cup**
First Round        Leyton Orient        (h)    1-1
(aet; lost 3-4 on pens)

# CHELSEA

## FOUNDATION

Chelsea may never have existed but for the fact that Fulham rejected an offer to rent the Stamford Bridge ground from Mr H. A. Mears who had owned it since 1904. Fortunately he was determined to develop it as a football stadium rather than sell it to the Great Western Railway and got together with Frederick Parker, who persuaded Mears of the financial advantages of developing a major sporting venue. Chelsea FC was formed in 1905 and applications made to join both the Southern League and Football League. The latter competition was decided upon because of its comparatively meagre representation in the south of England.

*Stamford Bridge, Fulham Road, London SW6 1HS.*
*Telephone:* (0871) 984 1955. *Fax:* (020) 7381 4831.
*Ticket Office:* (0871) 984 1905.
*Website:* www.chelseafc.com
*Email:* (via website).
*Ground Capacity:* 41,798.
*Record Attendance:* 82,905 v Arsenal, Division 1, 12 October 1935.
*Pitch Measurements:* 103m × 67m (112yd × 73yd)
*Chairman:* Bruce Buck. *Chief Executive:* Ron Gourlay.
*Manager:* Jose Mourinho.
*Technical Director:* Michael Emenalo.
*Assistant First Team Coaches:* Rui Faria, Steve Holland, Silvino Louro, Jose Morais.
*Medical Director:* Paco Biosca.
*Colours:* Reflex blue shirt with gold trim, reflex blue shorts with gold trim, white socks with reflex blue and gold trim.
*Year Formed:* 1905. *Turned Professional:* 1905.
*Club Nickname:* 'The Blues'.
*Ground:* 1905, Stamford Bridge.
*First Football League Game:* 2 September 1905, Division 2, v Stockport Co (a) L 0–1 – Foulke; Mackie, McEwan; Key, Harris, Miller; Moran, Jack Robertson, Copeland, Windridge, Kirwan.
*Record League Victory:* 8–0 v Wigan Ath, FA Premier League, 9 May 2010 – Cech; Ivanovic (Belletti), Ashley Cole (1), Ballack (Matic), Terry, Alex, Kalou (1) (Joe Cole), Lampard (pen), Anelka (2), Drogba (3, 1 pen), Malouda; 8–0 v Aston Villa, FA Premier League, 23 December 2012 – Cech; Azpilicueta, Ivanovic (1), Cahill, Cole, Luiz (1), Lampard (1) (Ramirez (2)), Moses, Mata (Piazon), Hazard (1), Torres (1) (Oscar (1)).

## HONOURS

**FA Premier League:**
*Champions* 2004–05, 2005–06, 2009–10.
*Runners-up* 2003–04, 2006–07, 2007–08, 2010–11.
**Football League – Division 1:**
*Champions* 1954–55; **Division 2:**
*Champions* 1983–84, 1988–89;
*Runners-up* 1906–07, 1911–12, 1929–30, 1962–63, 1976–77.
**FA Cup:** *Winners* 1970, 1997, 2000, 2007, 2009, 2010, 2012. *Runners-up* 1915, 1967, 1994, 2002.
**Football League Cup:** *Winners* 1965, 1998, 2005, 2007; *Runners-up* 1972, 2008.
**Full Members' Cup:** *Winners* 1986.
**Zenith Data Systems Cup:**
*Winners* 1990.
**European Competitions**
**Champions League:** 1999–2000, 2003–04 (*s-f*), 2004–05 (*s-f*), 2005–06, 2006–07 (*s-f*), 2007–08 (*runners-up*), 2008–09 (*s-f*), 2009–10, 2010–11, 2011–12 (*winners*), 2012–13.
**European Fairs Cup:** 1958–60, 1965–66, 1968–69. **European Cup-Winners' Cup:** 1970–71 (*winners*), 1971–72, 1994–95, 1997–98 (*winners*), 1998–99 (*s-f*).
**UEFA Cup:** 2000–01, 2001–02, *2002–03,* 2012. **Super Cup:** 1998–99 (*winners*), **Europa League:** 2012–13 (*winners*). **Club World Cup:** 2012 (*runners-up*).

## sky SPORTS FACT FILE

Chelsea reached three consecutive FA Cup semi-finals in the 1960s. They were defeated 2-0 by Liverpool in 1964–65 and lost by the same score to Sheffield Wednesday the following season. The Blues were more successful in 1966–67 defeating Leeds 1-0, only to lose to Tottenham Hotspur in an all-London final.

*Record Cup Victory:* 13–0 v Jeunesse Hautcharage, ECWC, 1st rd 2nd leg, 29 September 1971 – Bonetti; Boyle, Harris (1), Hollins (1p), Webb (1), Hinton, Cooke, Baldwin (3), Osgood (5), Hudson (1), Houseman (1).

*Record Defeat:* 1–8 v Wolverhampton W, Division 1, 26 September 1953.

*Most League Points (2 for a win):* 57, Division 2, 1906–07.

*Most League Points (3 for a win):* 99, Division 2, 1988–89.

*Most League Goals:* 103, FA Premier League, 2009–10.

*Highest League Scorer in Season:* Jimmy Greaves, 41, 1960–61.

*Most League Goals in Total Aggregate:* Bobby Tambling, 164, 1958–70.

*Most League Goals in One Match:* 5, George Hilsdon v Glossop, Division 2, 1 September 1906; 5, Jimmy Greaves v Wolverhampton W, Division 1, 30 August 1958; 5, Jimmy Greaves v Preston NE, Division 1, 19 December 1959; 5, Jimmy Greaves v WBA, Division 1, 3 December 1960; 5, Bobby Tambling v Aston Villa, Division 1, 17 September 1966; 5, Gordon Durie v Walsall, Division 2, 4 February 1989.

*Most Capped Player:* Frank Lampard, 95 (97), England.

*Most League Appearances:* Ron Harris, 655, 1962–80.

*Youngest League Player:* Ian Hamilton, 16 years 138 days v Tottenham H, 18 March 1967.

*Record Transfer Fee Received:* £24,000,000 from Real Madrid for Arjen Robben, August 2007.

*Record Transfer Fee Paid:* £50,000,000 to Liverpool for Fernando Torres, January 2011.

*Football League Record:* 1905 Elected to Division 2; 1907–10 Division 1; 1910–12 Division 2; 1912–24 Division 1; 1924–30 Division 2; 1930–62 Division 1; 1962–63 Division 2; 1963–75 Division 1; 1975–77 Division 2; 1977–79 Division 1; 1979–84 Division 2; 1984–88 Division 1; 1988–89 Division 2; 1989–92 Division 1; 1992– FA Premier League.

## MANAGERS

**John Tait Robertson** 1905–07
**David Calderhead** 1907–33
**Leslie Knighton** 1933–39
**Billy Birrell** 1939–52
**Ted Drake** 1952–61
**Tommy Docherty** 1961–67
**Dave Sexton** 1967–74
**Ron Suart** 1974–75
**Eddie McCreadie** 1975–77
**Ken Shellito** 1977–78
**Danny Blanchflower** 1978–79
**Geoff Hurst** 1979–81
**John Neal** 1981–85 (*Director to 1986*)
**John Hollins** 1985–88
**Bobby Campbell** 1988–91
**Ian Porterfield** 1991–93
**David Webb** 1993
**Glenn Hoddle** 1993–96
**Ruud Gullit** 1996–98
**Gianluca Vialli** 1998–2000
**Claudio Ranieri** 2000–04
**Jose Mourinho** 2004–07
**Avram Grant** 2007–08
**Luiz Felipe Scolari** 2008–09
**Guus Hiddink** 2009
**Carlo Ancelotti** 2009–11
**Andre Villas-Boas** 2011–12
**Roberto Di Matteo** 2012
**Rafael Benitez** 2012–13
**Jose Mourinho** June 2013–

## LATEST SEQUENCES

*Longest Sequence of League Wins:* 11, 25.4.2009 – 20.9.2009.
*Longest Sequence of League Defeats:* 7, 1.11.1952 – 20.12.1952.
*Longest Sequence of League Draws:* 6, 20.8.1969 – 13.9.1969.
*Longest Sequence of Unbeaten League Matches:* 40, 23.10.2004 – 29.10.2005.
*Longest Sequence Without a League Win:* 21, 3.11.1987 – 2.4.1988.
*Successive Scoring Runs:* 27 from 29.10.1988.
*Successive Non-scoring Runs:* 9 from 14.3.1981.

## TEN YEAR LEAGUE RECORD

|         |        | P  | W  | D  | L  | F   | A  | Pts | Pos |
|---------|--------|----|----|----|----|-----|----|-----|-----|
| 2003-04 | PR Lge | 38 | 24 | 7  | 7  | 67  | 30 | 79  | 2   |
| 2004-05 | PR Lge | 38 | 29 | 8  | 1  | 72  | 15 | 95  | 1   |
| 2005-06 | PR Lge | 38 | 29 | 4  | 5  | 72  | 22 | 91  | 1   |
| 2006-07 | PR Lge | 38 | 24 | 11 | 3  | 64  | 24 | 83  | 2   |
| 2007-08 | PR Lge | 38 | 25 | 10 | 3  | 65  | 26 | 85  | 2   |
| 2008-09 | PR Lge | 38 | 25 | 8  | 5  | 68  | 24 | 83  | 3   |
| 2009-10 | PR Lge | 38 | 27 | 5  | 6  | 103 | 32 | 86  | 1   |
| 2010-11 | PR Lge | 38 | 21 | 8  | 9  | 69  | 33 | 71  | 2   |
| 2011-12 | PR Lge | 38 | 18 | 10 | 10 | 65  | 46 | 64  | 6   |
| 2012-13 | PR Lge | 38 | 22 | 9  | 7  | 75  | 39 | 75  | 3   |

## DID YOU KNOW ?

Amateur players made significant contributions to Chelsea's first Football League title win in 1954–55. Jim Lewis scored 6 goals from 17 appearances while Seamus O'Connell netted 7 from 10. A third member of the squad, Derek Saunders, had represented Great Britain at the 1952 Olympic Games before turning professional.

## CHELSEA – FA PREMIERSHIP 2012–13 LEAGUE RECORD

| Match No. | Date | Venue | Opponents | Result | H/T Score | Lg Pos. | Goalscorers | Attendance |
|---|---|---|---|---|---|---|---|---|
| 1 | Aug 19 | A | Wigan Ath | W 2-0 | 2-0 | 4 | Ivanovic 2, Lampard (pen) 7 | 19,738 |
| 2 | 22 | H | Reading | W 4-2 | 1-2 | 1 | Lampard (pen) 18, Cahill 69, Torres 81, Ivanovic 90 | 41,733 |
| 3 | 25 | H | Newcastle U | W 2-0 | 2-0 | 1 | Hazard (pen) 22, Torres 45 | 41,718 |
| 4 | Sept15 | A | QPR | D 0-0 | 0-0 | 1 | | 18,271 |
| 5 | 22 | H | Stoke C | W 1-0 | 0-0 | 1 | Cole 85 | 41,112 |
| 6 | 29 | A | Arsenal | W 2-1 | 1-1 | 1 | Torres 20, Mata 53 | 60,101 |
| 7 | Oct 6 | H | Norwich C | W 4-1 | 3-1 | 1 | Torres 14, Lampard 22, Hazard 31, Ivanovic 76 | 41,784 |
| 8 | 20 | A | Tottenham H | W 4-2 | 1-0 | 1 | Cahill 17, Mata 2 66.69, Sturridge 90 | 36,060 |
| 9 | 28 | H | Manchester U | L 2-3 | 1-2 | 1 | Mata 44, Ramires 53 | 41,644 |
| 10 | Nov 3 | A | Swansea C | D 1-1 | 0-0 | 2 | Moses 61 | 20,527 |
| 11 | 11 | H | Liverpool | D 1-1 | 1-0 | 3 | Terry 20 | 41,627 |
| 12 | 17 | A | WBA | L 1-2 | 1-1 | 3 | Hazard 39 | 25,933 |
| 13 | 25 | H | Manchester C | D 0-0 | 0-0 | 4 | | 41,792 |
| 14 | 28 | H | Fulham | D 0-0 | 0-0 | 3 | | 41,707 |
| 15 | Dec 1 | A | West Ham U | L 1-3 | 1-0 | 3 | Mata 13 | 35,005 |
| 16 | 8 | A | Sunderland | W 3-1 | 2-0 | 3 | Torres 2 (1 pen) 11, 45 (p), Mata 49 | 39,273 |
| 17 | 23 | H | Aston Villa | W 8-0 | 3-0 | 3 | Torres 3, Luiz 29, Ivanovic 34, Lampard 58, Ramires 2 75.90, Oscar (pen) 79, Hazard 83 | 41,363 |
| 18 | 26 | A | Norwich C | W 1-0 | 1-0 | 3 | Mata 38 | 26,831 |
| 19 | 30 | A | Everton | W 2-1 | 1-1 | 3 | Lampard 2 42.72 | 39,485 |
| 20 | Jan 2 | H | QPR | L 0-1 | 0-0 | 4 | | 41,634 |
| 21 | 12 | A | Stoke C | W 4-0 | 1-0 | 3 | Walters (2 ogs) 45, 62, Lampard (pen) 65, Hazard, E 73 | 27,348 |
| 22 | 16 | H | Southampton | D 2-2 | 2-0 | 3 | Ba 25, Hazard 45 | 38,484 |
| 23 | 20 | H | Arsenal | W 2-1 | 2-0 | 3 | Mata 6, Lampard (pen) 16 | 41,784 |
| 24 | 30 | A | Reading | D 2-2 | 1-0 | 3 | Mata 45, Lampard 66 | 24,097 |
| 25 | Feb 2 | A | Newcastle U | L 2-3 | 0-1 | 3 | Lampard 55, Mata 61 | 52,314 |
| 26 | 9 | H | Wigan Ath | W 4-1 | 1-0 | 3 | Ramires 23, Hazard 56, Lampard 86, Marin 90 | 41,562 |
| 27 | 24 | A | Manchester C | L 0-2 | 0-0 | 3 | | 47,256 |
| 28 | Mar 2 | H | WBA | W. 1-0 | 1-0 | 3 | Ba 28 | 41,548 |
| 29 | 17 | H | West Ham U | W 2-0 | 1-0 | 3 | Lampard 19, Hazard 50 | 41,639 |
| 30 | 30 | A | Southampton | L 1-2 | 1-2 | 4 | Terry 33 | 31,779 |
| 31 | Apr 7 | H | Sunderland | W 2-1 | 0-1 | 3 | Kilgallon (og) 47, Ivanovic 55 | 41,500 |
| 32 | 17 | A | Fulham | W 3-0 | 2-0 | 3 | Luiz 30, Terry 2 43.71 | 25,002 |
| 33 | 21 | A | Liverpool | D 2-2 | 1-0 | 4 | Oscar 26, Hazard (pen) 57 | 45,009 |
| 34 | 28 | H | Swansea C | W 2-0 | 2-0 | 3 | Oscar 43, Lampard (pen) 45 | 41,780 |
| 35 | May 5 | A | Manchester U | W 1-0 | 0-0 | 3 | Mata 87 | 75,500 |
| 36 | 8 | H | Tottenham H | D 2-2 | 2-1 | 3 | Oscar 11, Ramires 39 | 41,581 |
| 37 | 11 | A | Aston Villa | W 2-1 | 0-1 | 3 | Lampard 2 61.88 | 42,084 |
| 38 | 19 | H | Everton | W 2-1 | 1-1 | 3 | Mata 7, Torres 76 | 41,794 |

**Final League Position: 3**

### GOALSCORERS

*League (75):* Lampard 15 (5 pens), Mata 12, Hazard 9 (2 pens), Torres 8 (1 pen), Ivanovic 5, Ramires 5, Oscar 4 (1 pen), Terry 4, Ba 2, Cahill 2, Luiz 2, Cole 1, Marin 1, Moses 1, Sturridge 1, own goals 3.
*FA Cup (17):* Ba 4, Lampard 2 (1 pen), Moses 2, Oscar 2, Ramires 2, Hazard 1, Ivanovic 1, Mata 1, Terry 1, Torres 1.
*Capital One Cup (16):* Cahill 2, Hazard 2 (1 pen), Mata 2, Moses 2, Torres 2, Bertrand 1, Ivanovic 1, Luiz 1 (1 pen), Ramires 1, Romeu 1 (1 pen), Sturridge 1.
*Community Shield (2):* Bertrand 1, Torres 1.
*Europa League (17):* Torres 6, Moses 4, Luiz 2, Hazard 1, Ivanovic 1, Mata 1, Oscar 1, Terry 1.
*UEFA Super Cup (1):* Cahill 1.
*FIFA World Club Cup (3):* Mata 1, Torres 1, own goal 1.
*UEFA Champions League (16):* Oscar 5, Mata 3, Torres 3, Luiz 2 (1 pen), Cahill 1, Moses 1, Ramires 1.

| Cech P 36 | Ivanovic B 33+1 | Luiz D 29+1 | Terry J 11+3 | Cole A 31 | Lampard F 21+8 | Mikel J 19+3 | Hazard E 31+3 | Mata J 31+4 | Bertrand R 14+5 | Torres F 28+8 | Oscar E 24+10 | Meireles R 1+2 | Cahill G 24+2 | Ramires 28+7 | Sturridge D 1+6 | Moses V 12+11 | Azpilicueta C 24+3 | Romeu O 4+2 | Marin M 2+4 | Piazon L —+1 | Ake N 1+2 | Turnbull R 2+1 | Ba D 11+3 | Ferreira P —+2 | Benayoun Y —+6 | Match No. |
|---|---|---|---|---|---|---|---|---|---|---|---|---|---|---|---|---|---|---|---|---|---|---|---|---|---|---|
| 1 | 2 | 3 | 4 | 5 | 6 | 7 | 8¹ | 9² | 10 | 11 | 12 | 13 | | | | | | | | | | | | | | 1 |
| 1 | 2 | | 4 | 5 | 7 | 6² | 9 | 10³ | | 11 | 12 | 14 | 3 | 8¹ | 13 | | | | | | | | | | | 2 |
| 1 | 2 | 3 | | 5 | 13 | 6 | 9 | 10¹ | 8 | 11 | | 7² | 4 | 12 | | | | | | | | | | | | 3 |
| 1 | 2 | 3 | 4 | 5 | 7 | 6 | 9 | | 10¹ | 11² | | 8 | 13 | 12 | | | | | | | | | | | | 4 |
| 1 | 2 | 3 | 14 | 5 | 13 | 6² | 10¹ | 9³ | | 11 | 7 | | 4 | 8 | 12 | | | | | | | | | | | 5 |
| 1 | 2 | 3² | 4 | 5 | | 6 | 9 | 10³ | 14 | 11 | 8¹ | 13 | 7 | 12 | | | | | | | | | | | | 6 |
| 1 | 2² | 3 | 4 | 5 | 7¹ | 6³ | 10 | 8 | | 11 | 9 | | 12 | | | | 13 | 14 | | | | | | | | 7 |
| 1 | 2 | 3 | | 5 | 13 | 7 | 9² | 10 | | 11 | 8¹ | | 4 | 6 | 12 | | | | | | | | | | | 8 |
| 1 | 2¹ | 3 | | 5 | | 6 | 8³ | 10² | 13 | 11⁴ | 9¹ | | 4 | 7 | 14 | | 12 | | | | | | | | | 9 |
| 1 | 4 | | 5 | | 7 | 10 | | 14 | 11 | 9³ | | 3 | 12 | 13 | 8² | 2 | 6¹ | | | | | | | | | 10 |
| 1 | 4 | 3¹ | | | 6 | 8 | 10 | 5 | 11³ | 9² | | 12 | 7 | 14 | 13 | 2 | | | | | | | | | | 11 |
| 1 | | 4 | | | 7³ | 8 | 13 | 5 | 10¹ | 12 | | 3 | 14 | 9 | 11 | 2 | 6² | | | | | | | | | 12 |
| 1 | 3 | 4 | | 5 | 7² | 10¹ | 9 | | 11 | 8 | | 6 | | 12 | 2 | 13 | | | | | | | | | | 13 |
| 1 | 3 | 4 | | 5 | | 8² | 12 | 10¹ | 11 | 9 | | 7 | | | 2 | 6 | 13 | | | | | | | | | 14 |
| 1 | 3 | | 5 | | 6 | 9¹ | 10 | | 11 | 12 | | 4 | 7 | | 8² | 2 | 13 | | | | | | | | | 15 |
| 1 | 2 | 3 | | 5 | 14 | | 10³ | 8 | 13 | 11 | 12 | | 4 | 6 | | 9² | | 7¹ | | | | | | | | 16 |
| 1 | 3 | 6 | | 5 | 7¹ | | 10 | 9³ | | 11² | 13 | | 4 | 12 | | 8 | 2 | | 14 | | | | | | | 17 |
| 1 | 3 | 7 | | 5 | 12 | 6¹ | 13 | 10³ | | 11 | 9 | | 4 | | | 8² | 2 | | 14 | | | | | | | 18 |
| 1¹ | 3 | 7 | | 5 | 8 | | 11² | 9³ | | 10 | 14 | | 4 | 6 | | 13 | 2 | | | 12 | | | | | | 19 |
| | 3 | 6 | | | 7³ | | 12 | 13 | 5 | 11 | 9 | | 4 | 14 | | 10² | 2 | 8¹ | | 1 | | | | | | 20 |
| 1 | 3 | 4 | 13 | 5 | 7 | | 6 | 10² | 9 | 12 | | | 8 | | | 2³ | | | | | | 11¹ | 14 | | | 21 |
| 1 | | 4 | | 5 | 7¹ | | 10 | 9 | | 12 | 8 | | 3 | 6 | | 2 | | | | | | 11 | | | | 22 |
| 1 | 4 | | | | 9 | 9 | 10 | 12 | 11² | 8¹ | | 3 | 6 | | 2 | 14 | | | | | | 13 | | | | 23 |
| | 3 | | | 5 | 8 | | 6¹ | 10 | 11² | 9 | | 4 | 7 | | | 2 | | | | | 1 | 13 | 12 | | | 24 |
| 1 | 2 | | 4 | 5 | 7 | | 9 | 10 | 12 | 8 | | 3 | 6 | | | 2 | | | | | | 11¹ | | | | 25 |
| 1 | 3 | 6 | | 5 | 9 | | 10³ | 12 | | 11 | 8¹ | | 4² | 7 | | 2 | 14 | | | | | | 13 | | | 26 |
| 1 | 2 | 3 | | 5 | 7 | 6³ | 9¹ | 10 | | 4 | 12 | | 4 | 8 | 13 | | | | | | | 11 | | | | 27 |
| 1 | 3 | 4 | | 5 | 7 | 14 | 8¹ | 9³ | | 13 | 10 | | 6 | 12 | 2 | | | | | | | 11² | | | | 28 |
| 1 | 4² | 13 | 5 | 6 | 14 | 10 | 9³ | | | 12 | | 3 | 7 | 8¹ | 2 | | | | | | | 11 | | | | 29 |
| 1 | 3 | | 4 | | 7 | 6² | 12 | | 5 | 11 | 9³ | | 13 | 8 | 2 | 10¹ | | | | | | 14 | | | | 30 |
| 1 | 3 | 4 | | 14 | 7 | 10² | 9³ | 5 | 12 | 8 | | 6 | | 2 | | | | | | | 11¹ | 13 | | | | 31 |
| 1 | 2 | 4 | 3 | | 7 | 13 | 10¹ | 9³ | 5 | 11 | 12 | | 6² | | | | | | | | | 14 | | | | 32 |
| 1 | 3 | 4 | | 14 | 7 | 10¹ | 8³ | 5 | 11 | 9² | | 6 | 13 | 2 | | | | | | | | 12 | | | | 33 |
| 1 | 6 | 4 | 5 | 12 | 10 | 9 | | 8 | | 3 | 7¹ | | 2 | | | | | | | | 11 | | | | | 34 |
| 1 | 3 | 4 | | 5 | 7 | 9² | 12 | 8 | | 6 | 10¹ | | 2 | | 13 | 11 | | | | | | | | | | 35 |
| 1 | 4 | 7 | 5 | | 10¹ | 9 | 11 | 8² | | 3 | 6 | 12 | 2 | | | | | | | | | 13 | | | | 36 |
| 1 | 13 | 12 | 4² | 5 | 7 | 10 | 9 | 14 | | 3 | 6⁴ | | 8¹ | 2 | | | | | | | | 11³ | | | | 37 |
| 1 | 2 | 4 | | 5 | 6 | 9² | 8 | 10³ | | 3 | 12 | 13 | | | | | 7 | | 11¹ | 14 | | | | | | 38 |

**FA Cup**

| | | | |
|---|---|---|---|
| Third Round | Southampton | (a) | 5-1 |
| Fourth Round | Brentford | (a) | 2-2 |
| *Replay* | Brentford | (h) | 4-0 |
| Fifth Round | Middlesbrough | (a) | 2-0 |
| Sixth Round | Manchester U | (a) | 2-2 |
| *Replay* | Manchester U | (h) | 1-0 |
| Semi-Finals | Manchester C (*at Wembley*) | | 1-2 |

**Capital One Cup**

| | | | |
|---|---|---|---|
| Third Round | Wolverhampton W | (h) | 6-0 |
| Fourth Round | Manchester U | (h) | 5-4 |
| Quarter-Finals | Leeds U | (a) | 5-1 |
| Semi-Finals | Swansea C | (h) | 0-2 |
| | Swansea C | (a) | 0-0 |

**Community Shield**

| | | |
|---|---|---|
| (*at Villa Park*) | Manchester C | 2-3 |

**UEFA Super Cup**

| | | |
|---|---|---|
| Final (Monaco) | Atletico Madrid | 1-4 |

**FIFA World Club Cup**

| | | |
|---|---|---|
| Semi-Finals | CF Monterrey | 3-1 |
| Final (Yokohama) | Corinthians | 0-1 |

**UEFA Champions League**

| | | | |
|---|---|---|---|
| Group E | Juventus | (h) | 2-2 |
| | Nordsjaelland | (a) | 4-0 |
| | Shakhtar Donetsk | (a) | 1-2 |
| | Shakhtar Donetsk | (h) | 3-2 |
| | Juventus | (a) | 0-3 |
| | Nordsjaelland | (h) | 6-1 |

**Europa League**

| | | | |
|---|---|---|---|
| Second Round | Sparta Prague | (a) | 1-0 |
| | Sparta Prague | (h) | 1-1 |
| Third Round | Steaua Bucharest | (a) | 0-1 |
| | Steaua Bucharest | (h) | 3-1 |
| Quarter-Finals | Rubin Kazan | (h) | 3-1 |
| | Rubin Kazan | (a) | 2-3 |
| Semi-Finals | FC Basel | (a) | 2-1 |
| | FC Basel | (h) | 3-1 |
| Final (Amsterdam) | Benfica | | 2-1 |

# CHELTENHAM TOWN

## FOUNDATION

Although a scratch team representing Cheltenham played a match against Gloucester in 1884, the earliest recorded match for Cheltenham Town FC was a friendly against Dean Close School on 12 March 1892. The School won 4–3 and the match was played at Prestbury (half a mile from Whaddon Road). Cheltenham Town played Wednesday afternoon friendlies at a local cricket ground until entering the Mid Gloucester League. In those days the club played in deep red coloured shirts and were nicknamed 'the Rubies'. The club moved to Whaddon Lane for season 1901–02 and changed to red and white colours two years later.

*The Abbey Business Stadium, Whaddon Road, Cheltenham, Gloucestershire GL52 5NA.*

*Telephone:* (01242) 573 558.

*Fax:* (01242) 224 675.

*Ticket Office:* (01242) 588 117.

*Website:* www.ctfc.com

*Email:* info@ctfc.com

*Ground Capacity:* 7,133.

*Record Attendance:* 10,389 v Blackpool, FA Cup 3rd rd, 13 January 1934 (at Cheltenham Athletic Ground); 8,326 v Reading, FA Cup 1st rd, 17 November 1956 (at Whaddon Road).

*Pitch Measurements:* 101m × 65m (111yd × 72yd)

*Chairman:* Paul Baker.

*Vice-chairman:* Colin Farmer.

*Manager:* Mark Yates.

*Assistant Manager:* Neil Howarth.

*Senior Sports Therapist:* Ian Weston.

*Colours:* Red and white striped shirts, red shorts, red socks.

*Year Formed:* 1892.

*Turned Professional:* 1932.

*Club Nickname:* 'The Robins'.

*Grounds:* Pre-1932, Agg-Gardner's Recreation Ground; Whaddon Lane; Carter's Lane; 1932, Whaddon Road.

*First Football League Game:* 7 August 1999, Division 3, v Rochdale (h) L 0–2 – Book; Griffin, Victory, Banks, Freeman, Brough (Howarth), Howells, Bloomer (Devaney), Grayson, Watkins (McAuley), Yates.

## HONOURS

**Football League:** Best season: Division 3 2001–02 (4th).

**FA Cup:** Best season: 5th rd, 2002.

**Football League Cup:** never past 2nd rd.

**Football Conference:** *Champions* 1998–99, *Runners-up* 1997–98.

**Trophy:** *Winners* 1997–98.

**Southern League:** *Champions* 1984–85; **Southern League Cup:** *Winners* 1957–58, *runners-up* 1968–69, 1984–85; **Southern League Merit Cup:** *Winners* 1984–85; **Southern League Championship Shield:** *Winners* 1985.

**Gloucestershire Senior Cup:** *Winners* 1998–99; **Gloucestershire Northern Senior Professional Cup:** *Winners* 30 times; **Midland Floodlit Cup:** *Winners* 1985–86, 1986–87, 1987–88; **Mid Gloucester League:** *Champions* 1896–97; **Gloucester and District League:** *Champions* 1902–03, 1905–06; **Cheltenham League:** *Champions* 1910–11, 1913–14; **North Gloucestershire League:** *Champions* 1913–14; **Gloucestershire Northern Senior League:** *Champions* 1928–29, **1932–33;** **Gloucestershire Northern Senior Amateur Cup:** *Winners* 1929–30, 1930–31, 1932–33, 1933–34, 1934–35; **Leamington Hospital Cup:** *Winners* 1934–35.

## sky SPORTS FACT FILE

Wing half Tim Ward was one of Cheltenham Town's greatest-ever products. Signed by the Robins in the summer of 1935, he was sold to Derby County in April 1937 for a fee of £100. He went on to captain the Rams and win two full England caps.

*Record League Victory:* 5–0 v Manfield T, FL 2, 6 May 2006 – Higgs; Gallinagh, Bell, McCann (1) (Connolly), Caines, Duff, Wilson, Bird (1p), Gillespie (1) (Spencer), Guinan (Odejayi (1)), Vincent (1).

*Record Cup Victory:* 12–0 v Chippenham R, FA Cup 3rd qual. rd, 2 November 1935 – Bowles; Whitehouse, Williams; Lang, Devonport (1), Partridge (2); Perkins, Hackett, Jones (4), Black (4), Griffiths (1).

*Record Defeat:* 1–8 v Crewe Alex, FL 2, 2 April 2011. *N.B.* 1–10 v Merthyr T, Southern League, 8 March 1952.

*Most League Points (2 for a win):* 60, Southern League Division 1, 1963–64.

*Most League Points (3 for a win):* 78, Division 3, 2001–02.

*Most League Goals:* 66, Division 3, 2001–02; 66, FL 2, 2011–12.

*Highest League Scorer in Season:* Julian Alsop, 20, Division 3, 2001–02.

*Most League Goals in Total Aggregate:* Julian Alsop, 39, 2000–03; 2009–10.

*Most League Goals in One Match:* 3, Martin Devaney v Plymouth Arg, Division 3, 23 September 2000; 3, Neil Grayson v Cardiff C, Division 3, 1 April 2001; 3, Damien Spencer v Hull C, Division 3, 23 August 2003; 3, Damien Spencer v Milton Keynes D, FL 1, 31 January 2009; 3, Michael Pook v Burton Alb, FL 2, 13 March 2010.

*Most Capped Player:* Grant McCann, 7 (39), Northern Ireland.

*Most League Appearances:* David Bird, 288, 2001–11.

*Youngest League Player:* Kyle Haynes, 17 years, 2 months, 26 days v Oldham Ath, FL 1, 24 March 2009.

*Record Transfer Fee Received:* £400,000 from Colchester U for Steve Gillespie, July 2008.

*Record Transfer Fee Paid:* £60,000 to Aldershot T for Jermaire McGlashan, January 2012.

*Football League Record:* 1999 Promoted to Division 3; 2002 Division 2; 2003–04 Division 3; 2004–06 FL 2; 2006–09 FL 1; 2009– FL 2.

### MANAGERS

George Blackburn 1932–34
George Carr 1934–37
Jimmy Brain 1937–48
Cyril Dean 1948–50
George Summerbee 1950–52
William Raeside 1952–53
Arch Anderson 1953–58
Ron Lewin 1958–60
Peter Donnelly 1960–61
Tommy Cavanagh 1961
Arch Anderson 1961–65
Harold Fletcher 1965–66
Bob Etheridge 1966–73
Willie Penman 1973–74
Dennis Allen 1974–79
Terry Paine 1979
Alan Grundy 1979–82
Alan Wood 1982–83
John Murphy 1983–88
Jim Barron 1988–90
John Murphy 1990
Dave Lewis 1990–91
Ally Robertson 1991–92
Lindsay Parsons 1992–95
Chris Robinson 1995–97
Steve Cotterill 1997–2002
Graham Allner 2002–03
Bobby Gould 2003
John Ward 2003–07
Keith Downing 2007–08
Martin Allen 2008–09
Mark Yates December 2009–

## LATEST SEQUENCES

*Longest Sequence of League Wins:* 5, 29.10.2011 – 10.12.2011.
*Longest Sequence of League Defeats:* 7, 27.1.2009 – 28.2.2009
*Longest Sequence of League Draws:* 5, 5.4.2003 – 21.4.2003.
*Longest Sequence of Unbeaten League Matches:* 16, 1.12.2001 – 12.3.2002.
*Longest Sequence Without a League Win:* 14, 20.12.2008 – 7.3.2009
*Successive Scoring Runs:* 17 from 16.2.2008.
*Successive Non-scoring Runs:* 5 from 10.3.2012 – 30.3.2012.

### TEN YEAR LEAGUE RECORD

|         |       | P  | W  | D  | L  | F  | A  | Pts | Pos |
|---------|-------|----|----|----|----|----|----|-----|-----|
| 2003-04 | Div 3 | 46 | 14 | 14 | 18 | 57 | 71 | 56  | 14  |
| 2004-05 | FL 2  | 46 | 16 | 12 | 18 | 51 | 54 | 60  | 14  |
| 2005-06 | FL 2  | 46 | 19 | 15 | 12 | 65 | 53 | 72  | 5   |
| 2006-07 | FL 1  | 46 | 15 | 9  | 22 | 49 | 61 | 54  | 17  |
| 2007-08 | FL 1  | 46 | 13 | 12 | 21 | 42 | 64 | 51  | 19  |
| 2008-09 | FL 1  | 46 | 9  | 12 | 25 | 51 | 91 | 39  | 23  |
| 2009-10 | FL 2  | 46 | 10 | 18 | 18 | 54 | 71 | 48  | 22  |
| 2010-11 | FL 2  | 46 | 13 | 13 | 20 | 56 | 77 | 52  | 17  |
| 2011-12 | FL 2  | 46 | 23 | 8  | 15 | 66 | 50 | 77  | 6   |
| 2012-13 | FL 2  | 46 | 20 | 15 | 11 | 58 | 51 | 75  | 5   |

### DID YOU KNOW ?

Roger Thorndale holds Cheltenham Town's all-time appearance record. A local-born right back he played over 700 times for the Robins between 1958 and 1976 when the club were members of the Southern League.

## CHELTENHAM TOWN – FOOTBALL LEAGUE TWO 2012–13 LEAGUE RECORD

| Match No. | Date | Venue | Opponents | Result | H/T Score | Lg Pos. | Goalscorers | Attendance |
|---|---|---|---|---|---|---|---|---|
| 1 | Aug 18 | H | Dagenham & R | W 2-0 | 1-0 | 7 | Harrad [45], McGlashan [49] | 2655 |
| 2 | 21 | A | Torquay U | D 2-2 | 1-2 | 5 | Harrad [15], Zebroski [80] | 2517 |
| 3 | 25 | A | Aldershot T | W 1-0 | 0-0 | 3 | Harrad [73] | 2166 |
| 4 | Sept 1 | H | Accrington S | L 0-3 | 0-2 | 10 | | 2708 |
| 5 | 8 | A | Wycombe W | D 1-1 | 1-1 | 9 | Harrad (pen) [38] | 3667 |
| 6 | 15 | H | Southend U | L 1-3 | 1-1 | 15 | McGlashan [15] | 2751 |
| 7 | 18 | H | Oxford U | W 2-1 | 1-0 | 9 | Carter [30], Harrad [60] | 3037 |
| 8 | 22 | A | York C | D 0-0 | 0-0 | 11 | | 3477 |
| 9 | 28 | H | Morecambe | W 2-0 | 1-0 | 5 | Carter 2 [2, 90] | 2563 |
| 10 | Oct 3 | A | Bristol R | W 1-0 | 1-0 | 5 | Zebroski [39] | 5747 |
| 11 | 6 | H | Fleetwood T | D 2-2 | 0-1 | 6 | Goulding [64], Jombati [75] | 2702 |
| 12 | 13 | A | AFC Wimbledon | W 2-1 | 1-0 | 3 | Pack [25], Mohamed [56] | 4409 |
| 13 | 20 | H | Bradford C | L 1-3 | 1-1 | 4 | Pack (pen) [29] | 9648 |
| 14 | 23 | H | Plymouth Arg | W 2-1 | 1-1 | 4 | Elliott [37], Mohamed [78] | 3058 |
| 15 | 27 | H | Exeter C | W 3-0 | 0-0 | 3 | D'Ath [55], Lowe 2 [62, 87] | 3545 |
| 16 | Nov 6 | A | Gillingham | D 0-0 | 0-0 | 3 | | 6096 |
| 17 | 10 | H | Burton Alb | W 1-0 | 0-0 | 3 | Zebroski [86] | 2804 |
| 18 | 17 | A | Rotherham U | L 2-4 | 2-3 | 3 | Lowe [1], Zebroski [31] | 6705 |
| 19 | 20 | A | Chesterfield | L 1-4 | 0-2 | 3 | Mohamed [57] | 4333 |
| 20 | 24 | H | Barnet | W 1-0 | 0-0 | 3 | Goulding [80] | 2591 |
| 21 | Dec 8 | A | Northampton T | W 3-2 | 2-2 | 3 | Carter [25], Zebroski [28], Duffy [80] | 4625 |
| 22 | 15 | H | Port Vale | D 1-1 | 0-0 | 3 | Carter [61] | 3670 |
| 23 | 21 | A | Rochdale | L 1-4 | 0-2 | 3 | Edwards, P (og) [48] | 1605 |
| 24 | 26 | H | Wycombe W | W 4-0 | 2-0 | 3 | Taylor, Jake [29], Goulding [32], Duffy [54], McGlashan [69] | 3501 |
| 25 | Jan 1 | A | Oxford U | L 0-1 | 0-1 | 4 | | 6951 |
| 26 | 12 | H | York C | D 1-1 | 0-0 | 5 | Harrad [67] | 2881 |
| 27 | 18 | A | Morecambe | D 0-0 | 0-0 | 4 | | 1586 |
| 28 | 25 | H | Rochdale | D 0-0 | 0-0 | 5 | | 2348 |
| 29 | Feb 2 | H | Torquay U | W 2-1 | 1-0 | 3 | Lowe [33], Harrad [51] | 2961 |
| 30 | 5 | A | Bristol R | D 1-1 | 1-0 | 3 | Harrad [45] | 4436 |
| 31 | 9 | A | Dagenham & R | L 0-1 | 0-0 | 5 | | 1526 |
| 32 | 12 | A | Southend U | W 2-1 | 2-0 | 3 | Pack (pen) [13], Benson [38] | 3908 |
| 33 | 16 | H | Aldershot T | D 1-1 | 0-1 | 4 | Benson [67] | 3119 |
| 34 | 23 | A | Accrington S | D 2-2 | 1-1 | 6 | Pack 2 (1 pen) [32 (p), 70] | 1216 |
| 35 | 26 | A | Fleetwood T | D 1-1 | 1-0 | 7 | Pack [24] | 2031 |
| 36 | Mar 2 | H | AFC Wimbledon | W 2-1 | 1-0 | 6 | Elliott [10], Carter [56] | 3177 |
| 37 | 5 | H | Chesterfield | W 1-0 | 0-0 | 3 | Benson [90] | 2195 |
| 38 | 9 | A | Burton Alb | L 1-3 | 0-2 | 5 | Harrison [90] | 2680 |
| 39 | 16 | H | Rotherham U | W 3-0 | 2-0 | 4 | McGlashan [32], Pack [41], Elliott [84] | 3241 |
| 40 | 23 | A | Barnet | D 0-0 | 0-0 | 5 | | 2400 |
| 41 | 29 | A | Port Vale | L 2-3 | 0-1 | 5 | Mohamed [47], Benson [54] | 5867 |
| 42 | Apr 1 | H | Northampton T | W 1-0 | 1-0 | 4 | Elliott [44] | 4042 |
| 43 | 6 | A | Plymouth Arg | L 0-2 | 0-1 | 4 | | 7941 |
| 44 | 13 | H | Gillingham | W 1-0 | 0-0 | 4 | Hector [67] | 4939 |
| 45 | 20 | A | Exeter C | W 1-0 | 1-0 | 4 | Penn [5] | 5247 |
| 46 | 27 | H | Bradford C | D 0-0 | 0-0 | 5 | | 5888 |

**Final League Position: 5**

### GOALSCORERS

*League (58):* Harrad 8 (1 pen), Pack 7 (3 pens), Carter 6, Zebroski 5, Benson 4, Elliott 4, Lowe 4, McGlashan 4, Mohamed 4, Goulding 3, Duffy 2, D'Ath 1, Harrison 1, Hector 1, Jombati 1, Penn 1, Taylor, Jake 1, own goal 1.
*FA Cup (7):* Harrad 2 (1 pen), Mohamed 2, Penn 1, Zebroski 1, own goal 1.
*Capital One Cup (1):* Mohamed 1.
*Johnstone's Paint Trophy (2):* Duffy 1, Lowe 1.
*League Two Play-Offs (0).*

| Brown S 46 | Jombati S 37 | Hooman H 4 | Elliott S 46 | Jones B 39 | McGlashan J 37+8 | Pack M 40+3 | Penn R 37+6 | Zebroski C 20+1 | Deering S 17+15 | Harrad S 20+11 | Goulding J 5+14 | Graham B —+1 | Duffy D 3+21 | Carter D 27+7 | Lowe K 24+7 | Mohamed K 24+15 | Bennett A 17 | D'Ath L 1+1 | Hanks J —+1 | Andrew D —+1 | Taylor Jake 7+1 | Hector M 18 | Taylor Jason 14+2 | Benson P 15+1 | Harrison B 8+9 | McCullough L —+1 | Match No. |
|---|---|---|---|---|---|---|---|---|---|---|---|---|---|---|---|---|---|---|---|---|---|---|---|---|---|---|---|
| 1 | 2 | 3 | 4 | 5 | 6 | 7 | 8 | 9² | 10¹ | 11³ | 12 | 13 | 14 | | | | | | | | | | | | | | 1 |
| 1 | 2 | | 4 | 5 | 3 | 8 | 6 | 9 | 10 | 7¹ | 11² | | 12 | 13 | | | | | | | | | | | | | 2 |
| 1 | 2 | | 4 | 3 | 5 | 9 | 6 | 8¹ | 10 | 11² | 7³ | | | 13 | 12 | 14 | | | | | | | | | | | 3 |
| 1 | 2 | 3 | 4 | 5 | 6 | 7 | 8³ | 11 | 13 | 10² | | | | 12 | 14 | 9¹ | | | | | | | | | | | 4 |
| 1 | 2 | | 3 | 5 | 10¹ | 7 | 12 | 9² | 11³ | 13 | | | | 14 | 6 | 4 | 8 | | | | | | | | | | 5 |
| 1 | 2 | | 4 | 5 | 8³ | 6 | 13 | 9² | 11 | 14 | | | | 12 | 7 | 3 | 10¹ | | | | | | | | | | 6 |
| 1 | 2 | | 4 | 5 | 8³ | 6 | 12 | 10² | 9¹ | 11 | | | | 7 | 14 | 13 | 3 | | | | | | | | | | 7 |
| 1 | 2 | | 4 | 5 | 9³ | 8 | 6 | 11 | 13 | 10¹ | | | 14 | 7² | 12 | | 3 | | | | | | | | | | 8 |
| 1 | 2 | | 4 | 5 | 8 | 6 | 12 | 10³ | 9¹ | 11² | | | | 14 | 7 | 10 | 3 | | | | | | | | | | 9 |
| 1 | 5 | 3 | 2 | | 9¹ | 7 | 8³ | 11 | 14 | 12 | | | | 6 | 13 | 10² | 4 | | | | | | | | | | 10 |
| 1 | 2 | | 4 | 5 | 8 | 6¹ | 9³ | 11 | 12 | 13 | | | | 7 | 14 | 10² | 3⁸ | | | | | | | | | | 11 |
| 1 | 2 | | 4 | 5 | 8 | 7 | 9 | 11 | | | | | | 12 | 6 | 3 | 10¹ | | | | | | | | | | 12 |
| 1 | 6 | 3 | | 5 | 9 | 7 | 8¹ | 11³ | 13 | 12 | | | | 14 | 4 | 2 | 10² | | | | | | | | | | 13 |
| 1 | 2 | | 4 | 5 | 8³ | 6 | 9 | 10 | 14 | 11² | | | | 12 | 7¹ | 13 | 3 | | | | | | | | | | 14 |
| 1 | | | 4 | 5 | 6³ | 7 | | | 10² | | 12 | | | 11¹ | 2 | 9 | 3 | 8 | 13 | 14 | | | | | | | 15 |
| 1 | 2 | | 4 | 5 | 8 | 6 | 9² | 11 | 13 | 12 | | | | 7 | | 10¹ | 3 | | | | | | | | | | 16 |
| 1 | 2 | | 4 | 5 | 8³ | 6 | 9² | 11 | 13 | 12 | | | | 7 | 14 | 10¹ | 3 | | | | | | | | | | 17 |
| 1 | | | 4 | 5 | 9³ | 8 | 6¹ | 10 | 14 | 12 | 13 | | | 7 | 2 | 11² | 3 | | | | | | | | | | 18 |
| 1 | | 3 | 5 | 12 | 7 | 9 | 8³ | 13 | 11² | 14 | | | | 6¹ | 2 | 10 | 4 | | | | | | | | | | 19 |
| 1 | | | 4 | 5 | 8¹ | 6 | 13 | 10 | 12 | 11 | 14 | | | 7³ | 2 | | 3 | | | | 9² | | | | | | 20 |
| 1 | 6 | 3 | | 5 | | 14 | 7 | 9¹ | | 11² | | | | 12 | 8 | 2 | 13 | 4 | | | 10³ | | | | | | 21 |
| 1 | 2 | | 4 | 5 | 13 | 7 | 6² | 11 | 10¹ | 14 | | | | 12 | 8 | | 3 | | | | 9³ | | | | | | 22 |
| 1 | 2 | | 4 | 5 | 12 | 7¹ | 6 | 10 | 11² | 13 | | | | 14 | 8 | | 3 | | | | 9³ | | | | | | 23 |
| 1 | 2¹ | | 4 | 5 | 6³ | 7² | | 10 | 11 | | | | | 8 | 12 | 14 | 3 | 13 | | | 9 | | | | | | 24 |
| 1 | 2 | | 4 | 5 | 6 | 12 | 7 | | 14 | 11 | | | | 10³ | 8¹ | 13 | 3 | | | | 9² | | | | | | 25 |
| 1 | 2 | | 4 | 5 | 13 | 6 | 8 | | 14 | 10 | 11¹ | | | 9² | 3 | 12 | | | | | 7³ | | | | | | 26 |
| 1 | 2 | | 4 | 5 | 6 | 7 | 8 | 9 | 10¹ | | | | | 12 | 3 | 11 | | | | | | | | | | | 27 |
| 1 | 2 | | 4 | 5 | 6² | 7 | 8 | 9¹ | 10³ | 14 | | | | 12 | 3 | 11 | | | | | | 13 | | | | | 28 |
| 1 | 5 | | 4 | | 6 | 7 | | | 10² | | | | 13 | 14 | 2 | 9³ | | | | | | | 3 | 8 | 11¹ | 12 | 29 |
| 1 | 5 | | 4 | | 6 | 8 | | | 14 | 10¹ | | | | 12 | 2 | 9³ | | | | | | | 3 | 7 | 11² | 13 | 30 |
| 1 | | 3 | 5 | | 6² | 14 | 7³ | | 10¹ | | | | | 12 | 2 | 9 | | | | | | | 4 | 8 | 11 | 13 | 31 |
| 1 | 5 | | 4 | | 6 | 7 | 8³ | | 14 | | | | 13 | | 2 | 12 | | | | | | | 3 | 9 | 10¹ | 11² | 32 |
| 1 | 5 | | 4¹ | | 6 | 8 | 9² | | 14 | | | | | | 2 | 13 | | | | | | | 3 | 7 | 11 | 10³ 12 | 33 |
| 1 | 5 | | 4 | | 6¹ | 7 | | | 12 | 14 | | | 13 | | 2 | 9² | | | | | | | 3 | 8 | 10 | 11³ | 34 |
| 1 | | 3 | 5 | 12 | 6 | 8 | | 9 | | | | | | 10¹ | 2 | | | | | | | | 4 | 7 | 11 | | 35 |
| 1 | | | 4 | 5 | 14 | 6 | 8³ | 9 | | | | | | 10¹ | 2 | 12 | | | | | | | 3 | 7 | 11² 13 | | 36 |
| 1 | | | 4 | 5 | 12 | 6 | 8² | 9³ | | | | | | 10¹ | 2 | 14 | | | | | | | 3 | 7 | 11 13 | | 37 |
| 1 | | 3 | 5 | 12 | 6 | 8² | | 9 | | | | | | 10³ | 2 | 14 | | | | | | | 4 | 7¹ | 11 13 | | 38 |
| 1 | 2 | | 4 | 5 | 6³ | 7 | 8 | 10 | | 14 | 13 | | | | | 9² | | | | | | | 3 | | 11¹ 12 | | 39 |
| 1 | 2 | | 3 | 5 | 10¹ | 7 | 9² | 8 | | 14 | | | | 6 | | | | | | | | | 4 | 13 | 11³ 12 | | 40 |
| 1 | 2 | | 4 | 5¹ | 9 | 8 | 7 | | 14 | | | | | | 12 | 6³ | | | | | | | 3 | 10² | 11 13 | | 41 |
| 1 | 5 | | 4 | | 6³ | 7 | 14 | 9¹ | | | | | | 8 | 2 | 12 | | | | | | | 3 | 13 | 10 11² | | 42 |
| 1 | 5 | | 4 | | 6 | 7 | 14 | 9² | | 12 | | | | 8³ | 2 | 13 | | | | | | | 3 | 10¹ | 11 | | 43 |
| 1 | 2 | | 4 | 5 | 6 | 7 | 10 | | | | | | | | | 9 | | | | | | | 3 | 8 | 11 | | 44 |
| 1 | 2 | | 3 | 5 | 9 | 6 | 7 | 12 | | | | | 13 | | | 11 | | | | | | | 4 | 8¹ | 10² | | 45 |
| 1 | 2 | | 4 | 5 | 6 | 7 | 10³ | 14 | 13 | | | | | | | 9 | | | | | | | 3 | 8¹ | 12 11² | | 46 |

**FA Cup**

| | | | |
|---|---|---|---|
| First Round | Yate T | (h) | 3-0 |
| Second Round | Hereford U | (h) | 1-1 |
| *Replay* | Hereford U | (a) | 2-1 |
| Third Round | Everton | (h) | 1-5 |

**Capital One Cup**

| | | | |
|---|---|---|---|
| First Round | Milton Keynes D | (h) | 1-1 |

*(aet; lost 3-5 on pens)*

**Johnstone's Paint Trophy**

| | | | |
|---|---|---|---|
| Second Round | Oxford U | (h) | 2-4 |

**League Two Play-Offs**

| | | | |
|---|---|---|---|
| Semi-Finals | Northampton T | (a) | 0-1 |
| | Northampton T | (h) | 0-1 |

# CHESTERFIELD

## FOUNDATION

Chesterfield are fourth only to Stoke, Notts County and Nottingham Forest in age for they can trace their existence as far back as 1866, although it is fair to say that they were somewhat casual in the first few years of their history, playing only a few friendlies a year. However, their rules of 1871 are still in existence, showing an annual membership of 2s (10p), but it was not until 1891 that they won a trophy (the Barnes Cup) and followed this a year later by winning the Sheffield Cup, Barnes Cup and the Derbyshire Junior Cup.

*The Proact Stadium, 1866 Sheffield Road, Whittington Moor, Chesterfield S41 8NZ.*

*Telephone:* (01246) 209 765.

*Fax:* (01246) 556 799.

*Ticket Office:* (01246) 488 232.

*Website:* www.chesterfield-fc.co.uk

*Email:* reception@chesterfield-fc.co.uk

*Ground Capacity:* 10,300.

*Record Attendance:* 30,968 v Newcastle U, Division 2, 7 April 1939 (at Saltergate); 10,089 v Rotherham U, FL 2, 18 March 2011 (at b2net Stadium (now called the Proact Stadium)).

*Pitch Measurements:* 101m × 64m (111yd × 71yd)

*Chairman:* Dave Allen.

*Vice-chairman:* David C. Jones.

*Manager:* Paul Cook.

*Assistant Manager:* Leam Richardson.

*Sports Therapist:* Jamie Hewitt.

*Colours:* Blue shirts with white trim, white shorts with blue trim, white socks with blue trim.

*Year Formed:* 1866.

*Turned Professional:* 1891.

*Previous Name:* 1867, Chesterfield Town; 1919, Chesterfield.

*Club Nicknames:* 'The Blues', 'The Spireites'.

*Grounds:* 1867, Drill Field; 1871, Recreation Ground, Saltergate; 2010, b2net Stadium (renamed The Proact Stadium).

*First Football League Game:* 2 September 1899, Division 2, v Sheffield W (a) L 1–5 – Hancock; Pilgrim, Fletcher; Ballantyne, Bell, Downie; Morley, Thacker, Gooing, Munday (1), Geary.

*Record League Victory:* 10–0 v Glossop NE, Division 2, 17 January 1903 – Clutterbuck; Thorpe, Lerper; Haig, Banner, Thacker; Tomlinson (2), Newton (1), Milward (3), Munday (2), Steel (2).

*Record Cup Victory:* 6–1 v Hartlepool U (h), FA Cup 1st rd, 3 November 2012 – O'Donnell; Talbot, Forbes (1), Cooper (Westcarr (1)), Smith, Whitaker, Clay (1), Togwell, Randall (1) (Broadhead), Darika, Boden (1) (Lester (1)).

## HONOURS

**Football League – Division 2:**
Best season: 4th, 1946–47;
**Division 3 (N):** *Champions* 1930–31, 1935–36; *Runners-up* 1933–34;
**FL 2:** *Champions* 2010–11;
**Division 4:** *Champions* 1969–70, 1984–85.

**FA Cup:** Semi-final 1997.

**Football League Cup:** Best season: 4th rd, 1965, 2007.

**Johnstone's Paint Trophy:** *Winners* 2012.

**Anglo-Scottish Cup:** *Winners* 1981.

## sky SPORTS FACT FILE

Chesterfield travelled to Luton Town on Boxing Day 1899 and won their Division Two fixture 3-0 before an estimated attendance of 2,000. Exactly 100 years later, on Boxing Day 1999, the two clubs met again at Luton when they drew 1-1 in front of a crowd of 5,870.

**Record Defeat:** 0–10 v Gillingham, Division 3, 5 September 1987.

**Most League Points (2 for a win):** 64, Division 4, 1969–70.

**Most League Points (3 for a win):** 91, Division 4, 1984–85.

**Most League Goals:** 102, Division 3 (N), 1930–31.

**Highest League Scorer in Season:** Jimmy Cookson, 44, Division 3 (N), 1925–26.

**Most League Goals in Total Aggregate:** Ernie Moss, 161, 1969–76, 1979–81 and 1984–86.

**Most League Goals in One Match:** 4, Jimmy Cookson v Accrington S, Division 3 (N), 16 January 1926; 4, Jimmy Cookson v Ashington, Division 3 (N), 1 May 1926; 4, Jimmy Cookson v Wigan Borough, Division 3 (N), 4 September 1926; 4, Tommy Lyon v Southampton, Division 2, 3 December 1938.

**Most Capped Player:** Walter McMillen, 4 (7), Northern Ireland; Mark Williams, 4 (30), Northern Ireland.

**Most League Appearances:** Dave Blakey, 613, 1948–67.

**Youngest League Player:** Dennis Thompson, 16 years 160 days v Notts Co, 26 December 1950.

**Record Transfer Fee Received:** £750,000 from Southampton for Kevin Davies, May 1997.

**Record Transfer Fee Paid:** £250,000 to Watford for Jason Lee, August 1998.

**Football League Record:** 1899 Elected to Division 2; 1909 failed re-election; 1921–31 Division 3 (N); 1931–33 Division 2; 1933–36 Division 3 (N); 1936–51 Division 2; 1951–58 Division 3 (N); 1958–61 Division 3; 1961–70 Division 4; 1970–83 Division 3; 1983–85 Division 4; 1985–89 Division 3; 1989–92 Division 4; 1992–95 Division 3; 1995–2000 Division 2; 2000–01 Division 3; 2001–04 Division 2; 2004–07 FL 1; 2007–11 FL 2; 2011–12 FL 1; 2012– FL 2.

## LATEST SEQUENCES

**Longest Sequence of League Wins:** 10, 6.9.1933 – 4.11.1933.

**Longest Sequence of League Defeats:** 9, 22.10.1960 – 27.12.1960.

**Longest Sequence of League Draws:** 8, 26.11.2005 – 2.1.2006.

**Longest Sequence of Unbeaten League Matches:** 21, 26.12.1994 – 29.4.1995.

**Longest Sequence Without a League Win:** 18, 11.9.1999 – 3.1.2000.

**Successive Scoring Runs:** 46 from 25.12.1929.

**Successive Non-scoring Runs:** 7 from 23.9.1977.

## MANAGERS

E. Russell Timmeus 1891–95
(*Secretary-Manager*)
Gilbert Gillies 1895–1901
E. F. Hind 1901–02
Jack Hoskin 1902–06
W. Furness 1906–07
George Swift 1907–10
G. H. Jones 1911–13
R. L. Weston 1913–17
T. Callaghan 1919
J. J. Caffrey 1920–22
Harry Hadley 1922
Harry Parkes 1922–27
Alec Campbell 1927
Ted Davison 1927–32
Bill Harvey 1932–38
Norman Bullock 1938–45
Bob Brocklebank 1945–48
Bobby Marshall 1948–52
Ted Davison 1952–58
Duggie Livingstone 1958–62
Tony McShane 1962–67
Jimmy McGuigan 1967–73
Joe Shaw 1973–76
Arthur Cox 1976–80
Frank Barlow 1980–83
John Duncan 1983–87
Kevin Randall 1987–88
Paul Hart 1988–91
Chris McMenemy 1991–93
John Duncan 1993–2000
Nicky Law 2000–01
Dave Rushbury 2002–03
Roy McFarland 2003–07
Lee Richardson 2007–09
John Sheridan 2009–12
Paul Cook October 2012–

## TEN YEAR LEAGUE RECORD

|         |       | P  | W  | D  | L  | F  | A  | Pts | Pos |
|---------|-------|----|----|----|----|----|----|-----|-----|
| 2003-04 | Div 2 | 46 | 12 | 15 | 19 | 49 | 71 | 51  | 20  |
| 2004-05 | FL 1  | 46 | 14 | 15 | 17 | 55 | 62 | 57  | 17  |
| 2005-06 | FL 1  | 46 | 14 | 14 | 18 | 63 | 73 | 56  | 16  |
| 2006-07 | FL 1  | 46 | 12 | 11 | 23 | 45 | 53 | 47  | 21  |
| 2007-08 | FL 2  | 46 | 19 | 12 | 15 | 76 | 56 | 69  | 8   |
| 2008-09 | FL 2  | 46 | 16 | 15 | 15 | 62 | 57 | 63  | 10  |
| 2009-10 | FL 2  | 46 | 21 | 7  | 18 | 61 | 62 | 70  | 8   |
| 2010-11 | FL 2  | 46 | 24 | 14 | 8  | 85 | 51 | 86  | 1   |
| 2011-12 | FL 1  | 46 | 10 | 12 | 24 | 56 | 81 | 42  | 22  |
| 2012-13 | FL 2  | 46 | 18 | 13 | 15 | 60 | 45 | 67  | 8   |

## DID YOU KNOW ?

Gordon Banks, a World Cup winner with England in 1966, began his career with Chesterfield. He was a member of the team defeated by Manchester United in the 1955–56 FA Youth Cup final and went on to make 26 first-team appearances for the Spireites before being sold to Leicester City.

## CHESTERFIELD – FOOTBALL LEAGUE TWO 2012–13 LEAGUE RECORD

| Match No. | Date | Venue | Opponents | Result | H/T Score | Lg Pos. | Goalscorers | Attendance |
|---|---|---|---|---|---|---|---|---|
| 1 | Aug 18 | A | AFC Wimbledon | L | 0-1 | 0-1 | 15 | | 3780 |
| 2 | 21 | H | Rochdale | D | 1-1 | 0-0 | 17 | Lester [90] | 4595 |
| 3 | 25 | H | Rotherham U | D | 1-1 | 1-0 | 18 | Bowery [3] | 7232 |
| 4 | Sept 1 | A | Gillingham | D | 1-1 | 1-1 | 19 | Westcarr [13] | 4380 |
| 5 | 8 | A | York C | D | 2-2 | 2-1 | 19 | Hird [36], Westcarr [41] | 5119 |
| 6 | 15 | H | Wycombe W | W | 3-1 | 2-0 | 16 | Atkinson [14], Lester [20], Hird [85] | 5113 |
| 7 | 18 | H | Accrington S | W | 4-3 | 2-1 | 11 | Lester 2 [8, 66], Richards [11], Forbes [84] | 4359 |
| 8 | 22 | A | Northampton T | D | 0-0 | 0-0 | 13 | | 4709 |
| 9 | 29 | H | Torquay U | D | 1-1 | 0-0 | 14 | Darikwa [49] | 5117 |
| 10 | Oct 2 | A | Morecambe | L | 0-2 | 0-1 | 15 | | 1285 |
| 11 | 6 | A | Aldershot T | W | 1-0 | 0-0 | 13 | Atkinson [76] | 2006 |
| 12 | 13 | H | Dagenham & R | L | 1-2 | 0-1 | 15 | Lester [55] | 5082 |
| 13 | 20 | A | Exeter C | W | 1-0 | 1-0 | 13 | Atkinson [32] | 3668 |
| 14 | 23 | H | Fleetwood T | L | 1-2 | 1-1 | 13 | Darikwa [44] | 4372 |
| 15 | 27 | H | Barnet | L | 0-1 | 0-0 | 16 | | 5611 |
| 16 | Nov 6 | A | Bradford C | D | 0-0 | 0-0 | 16 | | 8841 |
| 17 | 10 | A | Bristol R | L | 2-3 | 1-1 | 18 | Randall [20], Dickenson [65] | 5491 |
| 18 | 17 | H | Oxford U | W | 2-1 | 1-1 | 16 | Cooper [45], Atkinson [90] | 5433 |
| 19 | 20 | H | Cheltenham T | W | 4-1 | 2-0 | 12 | Atkinson [16], Togwell [45], Richards [59], Lester [75] | 4333 |
| 20 | 24 | A | Plymouth Arg | W | 1-0 | 0-0 | 12 | Richards [66] | 5711 |
| 21 | Dec 8 | A | Port Vale | W | 2-0 | 1-0 | 9 | O'Shea [37], Darikwa [64] | 5298 |
| 22 | 15 | H | Burton Alb | D | 1-1 | 0-1 | 10 | Richards [74] | 5741 |
| 23 | 21 | A | Southend U | L | 0-3 | 0-0 | 12 | | 5273 |
| 24 | 26 | H | York C | W | 3-0 | 0-0 | 9 | Talbot [46], Whitaker [75], Darikwa [77] | 7322 |
| 25 | 29 | H | Morecambe | D | 1-1 | 1-1 | 9 | Townsend [40] | 6358 |
| 26 | Jan 1 | A | Accrington S | L | 0-1 | 0-0 | 11 | | 1586 |
| 27 | 5 | A | Wycombe W | L | 1-2 | 1-1 | 11 | O'Shea [29] | 3492 |
| 28 | 12 | H | Northampton T | W | 3-0 | 3-0 | 11 | O'Shea [18], Richards 2 [19, 25] | 5467 |
| 29 | 26 | H | Southend U | L | 0-1 | 0-0 | 11 | | 4817 |
| 30 | Feb 2 | A | Rochdale | D | 1-1 | 0-0 | 11 | O'Shea [55] | 2746 |
| 31 | 9 | H | AFC Wimbledon | W | 2-0 | 0-0 | 10 | Gnanduillet [59], Lester [83] | 5235 |
| 32 | 16 | A | Rotherham U | L | 0-1 | 0-0 | 12 | | 11,143 |
| 33 | 23 | H | Gillingham | L | 0-1 | 0-0 | 12 | | 5235 |
| 34 | 26 | H | Aldershot T | D | 0-0 | 0-0 | 14 | | 3968 |
| 35 | Mar 2 | A | Dagenham & R | W | 1-0 | 1-0 | 14 | Ogogo (og) [19] | 1675 |
| 36 | 5 | A | Cheltenham T | L | 0-1 | 0-0 | 14 | | 2195 |
| 37 | 9 | H | Bristol R | W | 2-0 | 0-0 | 12 | O'Shea [53], Gnanduillet [73] | 4814 |
| 38 | 16 | A | Oxford U | W | 1-0 | 1-0 | 11 | Richards [5] | 6003 |
| 39 | 19 | A | Torquay U | L | 1-2 | 0-2 | 12 | Cooper [77] | 2047 |
| 40 | 30 | A | Burton Alb | W | 1-0 | 0-0 | 10 | Talbot [52] | 3823 |
| 41 | Apr 1 | H | Port Vale | D | 2-2 | 2-1 | 11 | Richards 2 [14, 19] | 6669 |
| 42 | 6 | A | Barnet | W | 2-0 | 0-0 | 9 | O'Shea [57], Togwell [78] | 2574 |
| 43 | 13 | H | Bradford C | D | 2-2 | 0-1 | 9 | Darikwa [70], Togwell [90] | 7290 |
| 44 | 16 | H | Plymouth Arg | L | 1-2 | 0-2 | 9 | Branston (og) [57] | 4988 |
| 45 | 20 | A | Fleetwood T | W | 3-1 | 2-0 | 8 | Gnanduillet [44], Richards 2 [45, 64] | 3705 |
| 46 | 27 | H | Exeter C | W | 4-0 | 3-0 | 8 | O'Shea [22], Richards [30], Lester 2 (1 pen) [34 (p), 59] | 5762 |

**Final League Position: 8**

### GOALSCORERS

*League (60):* Richards 12, Lester 9 (1 pen), O'Shea 7, Atkinson 5, Darikwa 5, Gnanduillet 3, Togwell 3, Cooper 2, Hird 2, Talbot 2, Westcarr 2, Bowery 1, Dickenson 1, Forbes 1, Randall 1, Townsend 1, Whitaker 1, own goals 2.
*FA Cup (7):* Boden 1, Clay 1, Cooper 1, Forbes 1, Lester 1, Randall 1, Westcarr 1.
*Capital One Cup (1):* Lester 1.
*Johnstone's Paint Trophy (2):* Whitaker 1, own goal 1.

| Lee T 32 | Forbes T 17 | Trotman N 31 | Hird S 36 + 5 | Smith N 27 + 2 | Talbot D 41 + 1 | Togwell S 45 | Randall M 18 + 11 | Whitaker D 19 + 11 | Richards M 30 + 4 | Bowery J 3 | Boden S 4 + 5 | Westcarr C 10 + 5 | Lester J 11 + 23 | Clay C 7 + 12 | Allott M 4 + 4 | Ridehalgh L 12 + 2 | O'Donnell R 14 | Hazel J 1 + 1 | Atkinson C 13 + 2 | Darikwa T 31 + 5 | Evans M 1 + 3 | Boa Morte L 8 + 4 | Dickenson B 5 + 6 | Cooper L 29 | O'Shea J 25 + 1 | Townsend C 16 + 4 | Wafula J — + 1 | Gnanduillet A 4 + 9 | Brindley R 10 + 2 | Henshall A 1 + 6 | Clark J 1 + 1 | Match No. |
|---|---|---|---|---|---|---|---|---|---|---|---|---|---|---|---|---|---|---|---|---|---|---|---|---|---|---|---|---|---|---|---|---|
| 1 | 2 | $3^2$ | 4 | 5 | 6 | 7 | 8 | 9 | $10^3$ | $11^1$ | 12 | 13 | 14 | | | | | | | | | | | | | | | | | | | 1 |
| 1 | 2 | 3 | 4 | 5 | 6 | 7 | $8^2$ | $9^3$ | $10^1$ | 11 | | 13 | 12 | 14 | | | | | | | | | | | | | | | | | | 2 |
| 1 | 2 | 4 | 3 | 5 | 6 | 8 | | $9^2$ | $10^1$ | 11 | | 12 | | | | 7 | 13 | | | | | | | | | | | | | | | 3 |
| 1 | 2 | 4 | 3 | | 6 | 8 | 13 | 9 | $10^3$ | | | $11^8$ | 14 | $12^2$ | | $7^1$ | 5 | | | | | | | | | | | | | | | 4 |
| | 2 | 3 | 4 | | 8 | 7 | | | $10^9$ | | | 12 | 11 | 14 | 13 | $6^2$ | 5 | 1 | $9^1$ | | | | | | | | | | | | | 5 |
| | 2 | 3 | 4 | | 6 | 8 | 14 | 11 | | | | $9^2$ | $10^1$ | | 13 | 5 | 1 | | $7^3$ | 12 | | | | | | | | | | | | 6 |
| | 2 | 3 | 4 | | 6 | 7 | 13 | 10 | | | | $9^1$ | $11^3$ | | 14 | 5 | 1 | | $8^2$ | 12 | | | | | | | | | | | | 7 |
| | 2 | 3 | 4 | | 9 | 7 | | 12 | | | | 10 | $11^1$ | | 13 | 5 | 1 | | $8^2$ | 6 | | | | | | | | | | | | 8 |
| | 2 | $4^2$ | 3 | | $6^1$ | 7 | | 13 | | | | $8^3$ | 10 | | | 5 | 1 | 14 | 11 | 9 | 12 | | | | | | | | | | | 9 |
| | 2 | 3 | 4 | | 10 | 8 | | $9^1$ | | | | $11^3$ | 14 | | 13 | 5 | 1 | | $7^2$ | 6 | 12 | | | | | | | | | | | 10 |
| | 2 | 3 | | | 10 | 8 | | | | | | 11 | 13 | 12 | $7^1$ | 5 | 1 | | 9 | 4 | $6^2$ | | | | | | | | | | | 11 |
| | 2 | $3^1$ | 4 | | 6 | $8^2$ | 13 | | | | | 14 | $10^3$ | 11 | | 5 | 1 | | 7 | 12 | | 9 | | | | | | | | | | 12 |
| | 3 | | 4 | 13 | 2 | 7 | 12 | | | | | $11^3$ | 14 | $8^1$ | | 5 | 1 | | $9^2$ | 6 | | 10 | | | | | | | | | | 13 |
| | 2 | | 3 | 12 | 6 | 7 | | $8^2$ | $13^3$ | | | 14 | 10 | | | $5^1$ | | | 4 | 9 | | 11 | | | | | | | | | | 14 |
| | 3 | | 4 | $8^1$ | 2 | $7^2$ | 12 | 9 | | | | 13 | 11 | | | 5 | 1 | | 10 | $6^3$ | 14 | | | | | | | | | | | 15 |
| | 4 | | 3 | 5 | 2 | 7 | $10^1$ | $8^2$ | | | | $11^3$ | 14 | | 6 | 13 | 1 | | 12 | 9 | | | | | | | | | | | | 16 |
| | 3 | | 4 | 2 | 5 | 6 | $10^1$ | 8 | | | | $11^2$ | | 13 | $7^3$ | | 1 | | 14 | 9 | | 12 | | | | | | | | | | 17 |
| 1 | | 3 | 5 | 2 | 6 | | | $9^2$ | 12 | | | $11^1$ | 13 | | | 7 | 8 | | 14 | $10^2$ | 4 | | | | | | | | | | | 18 |
| 1 | | 3 | 5 | 2 | 7 | | | $9^1$ | $11^3$ | | | | 14 | 12 | | 6 | 8 | | 13 | $10^2$ | 4 | | | | | | | | | | | 19 |
| 1 | | 3 | 5 | 2 | 7 | | | $9^2$ | $11^3$ | | | | 13 | 14 | | 6 | 8 | | 12 | $10^1$ | 4 | | | | | | | | | | | 20 |
| 1 | | 4 | 5 | 9 | 8 | $2^2$ | 14 | 11 | | | | | 13 | | | 7 | | | | $6^1$ | 12 | 3 | $10^3$ | | | | | | | | | 21 |
| 1 | | 4 | 5 | 2 | 6 | $7^3$ | | 11 | | | | $12^8$ | 14 | | | 8 | | | $10^1$ | 3 | $9^2$ | 13 | | | | | | | | | | 22 |
| 1 | | 4 | 5 | 2 | 7 | $6^3$ | | $11^1$ | 12 | | | | 14 | | | 8 | | | $10^2$ | 13 | 3 | 9 | | | | | | | | | | 23 |
| 1 | | 3 | 5 | 2 | 6 | $7^1$ | 13 | | | | | | 12 | | | 8 | | | $11^3$ | 14 | 4 | 9 | $10^2$ | | | | | | | | | 24 |
| 1 | | 4 | 5 | $2^3$ | 7 | | 10 | | | | | 12 | | | | 13 | | | 8 | 14 | $9^1$ | 3 | $11^2$ | $6^8$ | | | | | | | | 25 |
| 1 | | 3 | 5 | 2 | 6 | 7 | $8^3$ | 12 | 10 | | | | $11^2$ | | | | | | 6 | | | $9^1$ | 14 | 4 | 13 | | | | | | | 26 |
| 1 | | 5 | 3 | $2^1$ | 7 | | $6^3$ | 14 | 11 | | | 12 | | | | 8 | | | | | | $9^2$ | 13 | 4 | 10 | | - | | | | | 27 |
| 1 | | 3 | 2 | 5 | | | 6 | 12 | 10 | $11^2$ | | | 13 | $7^1$ | | | | | | | 8 | | | | | 4 | $9^3$ | 14 | | | | | 28 |
| 1 | | $3^2$ | 2 | 5 | | | 6 | | $10^2$ | 11 | | | 12 | 7 | | | | | | | $9^1$ | | | | | 4 | 9 | 13 | 14 | | | | 29 |
| 1 | | 3 | 2 | 5 | | | 8 | 12 | $10^3$ | 11 | | | | $7^2$ | | | | | | | $6^1$ | | | | | 4 | 9 | 13 | 14 | | | | 30 |
| 1 | | 3 | 7 | 5 | 2 | 6 | | $9^2$ | $8^3$ | $11^1$ | | | 12 | | | | | | | | 9 | | | | | 4 | 10 | | | 13 | 14 | | 31 |
| 1 | | 3 | 7 | 5 | 2 | 8 | | $6^3$ | 10 | | | | $11^1$ | | | | | | | | 9 | | | | | 4 | $9^2$ | 12 | | 13 | 14 | | 32 |
| 1 | | $3^3$ | | 5 | 6 | 7 | | | 11 | | | | 13 | $8^2$ | | | | | | | 9 | | | | | 4 | $10^1$ | 9 | | 2 | 12 | 14 | 33 |
| 1 | | 3 | | 5 | 6 | | | 14 | 12 | 11 | | | 13 | | | | | | | | 9 | | | | | 4 | $10^3$ | 9 | | $2^1$ | $8^2$ | 7 | 34 |
| 1 | | 4 | 7 | 5 | 2 | 8 | | | | 11 | | | | | | | | | | | | | | | | 3 | 6 | 9 | 10 | | | | 35 |
| 1 | | 4 | 8 | 5 | 2 | 7 | | | $11^1$ | | | | | | | | | | | | 13 | | | | | 3 | 6 | 9 | $10^2$ | | | | 36 |
| 1 | | 3 | 8 | 5 | | 7 | | 14 | 13 | | | | $10^1$ | | | | | | | | 12 | | | | | 4 | 6 | $9^3$ | $11^2$ | 2 | | | 37 |
| 1 | | 4 | 6 | $7^1$ | 13 | 8 | 14 | 12 | 11 | | | | | | | | | | | | $5^2$ | | | | | 3 | 10 | 9 | $2^3$ | | | | 38 |
| 1 | | 3 | 6 | | 10 | $7^2$ | 13 | 14 | 11 | | | | 12 | | | | | | | | $8^1$ | | | | | 4 | 9 | $5^3$ | 2 | | | | 39 |
| 1 | | 3 | 13 | | 6 | 8 | 7 | | $11^1$ | | | | | | | | | | | | 9 | | | | | 4 | $10^2$ | 5 | 12 | 2 | | | 40 |
| 1 | | 3 | 12 | | 9 | 7 | 8 | | $11^3$ | | | | 14 | | | | | | | | 6 | | | | | $4^1$ | $10^2$ | 5 | 13 | 2 | | | 41 |
| 1 | | 3 | 12 | | 2 | 7 | $8^2$ | $6^1$ | | 10 | | | 14 | | | | | | | | 9 | | | | | 4 | $11^3$ | 5 | | | 13 | | 42 |
| 1 | | 4 | | | 9 | 7 | 11 | | 12 | | | | 13 | | | | | | | | 6 | | | | | 3 | $8^3$ | $5^1$ | $10^2$ | 2 | 14 | | 43 |
| 1 | | $5^3$ | 14 | | 9 | 7 | 8 | | | | | | 6 | | | | | | | | 4 | | | | | 10 | 3 | $2^2$ | 12 | | | | 44 |
| 1 | | 3 | 13 | | 9 | 7 | $8^2$ | | 10 | | | | 6 | | | | | | | | 4 | | | | | $11^3$ | 5 | 12 | $2^1$ | 14 | | | 45 |
| | 3 | | | | 2 | 7 | 8 | 12 | $10^2$ | | | | $11^3$ | | | | | 1 | | | 6 | | | | | 4 | $9^1$ | 5 | 13 | | 14 | | 46 |

**FA Cup**

| | | | | |
|---|---|---|---|---|
| First Round | Hartlepool U | (h) | 6-1 | |
| Second Round | Tranmere R | (a) | 1-2 | |

**Capital One Cup**

| | | | |
|---|---|---|---|
| First Round | Tranmere R | (h) | 1-2 |

**Johnstone's Paint Trophy**

| | | | |
|---|---|---|---|
| First Round | Oldham Ath | (h) | 2-1 |
| Second Round | Doncaster R | (a) | 0-1 |

# COLCHESTER UNITED

## FOUNDATION

Colchester United was formed in 1937 when a number of enthusiasts of the much older Colchester Town club decided to establish a professional concern as a limited liability company. The new club continued at Layer Road which had been the amateur club's home since 1909.

*Weston Homes Community Stadium, United Way, Colchester, Essex CO4 5UP.*

*Telephone:* (01206) 755 100.

*Fax:* (01206) 715 327.

*Ticket Office:* (0845) 437 9089.

*Website:* www.cu-fc.com

*Email:* media@colchesterunited.net

*Ground Capacity:* 10,105.

*Record Attendance:* 19,072 v Reading, FA Cup 1st rd, 27 November 1948 (at Layer Road); 10,064 v Norwich C, FL 1, 16 January 2010 (at Community Stadium).

*Pitch Measurements:* 100m × 64m (110yd × 70yd)

*Executive Chairman:* Robbie Cowling.

*Vice-chairman:* Richard Cowling.

*Manager:* Joe Dunne.

*Assistant Manager:* Mark Kinsella.

*Physio:* Tony Flynn.

*Colours:* Royal blue and white striped shirts, royal blue shorts, white socks with blue trim.

*Year Formed:* 1937.

*Turned Professional:* 1937.

*Club Nickname:* 'The U's'.

*Grounds:* 1937, Layer Road; 2008, Weston Homes Community Stadium.

*First Football League Game:* 19 August 1950, Division 3 (S), v Gillingham (a) D 0–0 – Wright; Kettle, Allen; Bearryman, Stewart, Elder; Jones, Curry, Turner, McKim, Church.

*Record League Victory:* 9–1 v Bradford C, Division 4, 30 December 1961 – Ames; Millar, Fowler; Harris, Abrey, Ron Hunt; Foster, Bobby Hunt (4), King (4), Hill (1), Wright.

*Record Cup Victory:* 9-1 v Leamington, FA Cup 1st rd, 5 November 2005 – Davison; Stockley (Garcia), Duguid, Brown (1), Chilvers, Watson (1), Halford (1), Izzet (Danns) (2), Iwelumo (1) (Williams), Cureton (2), Yeates (1).

## HONOURS

**Football League – FL 1:**
*Runners-up* 2005–06;
**Division 4:** *Runners-up* 1961–62.
**FA Cup:** Best season: 6th rd, 1971.
**Football League Cup:** Best season: 5th rd, 1975.
**Auto Windscreens Shield:** *Runners-up* 1997.
**GM Vauxhall Conference:** *Winners* 1991–92.
**FA Trophy:** *Winners* 1992.

## sky SPORTS FACT FILE

Colchester United won the Watney Cup in August 1971 when they defeated West Bromwich Albion on penalties at Layer Road after the teams had fought out a 4-4 draw. This was the first time that a trophy in English senior football had been decided by a penalty shoot-out.

*Record Defeat:* 0–8 v Leyton Orient, Division 4, 15 October 1988.

*Most League Points (2 for a win):* 60, Division 4, 1973–74.

*Most League Points (3 for a win):* 81, Division 4, 1982–83.

*Most League Goals:* 104, Division 4, 1961–62.

*Highest League Scorer in Season:* Bobby Hunt, 38, Division 4, 1961–62.

*Most League Goals in Total Aggregate:* Martyn King, 130, 1956–64.

*Most League Goals in One Match:* 4, Bobby Hunt v Bradford C, Division 4, 30 December 1961; 4, Martyn King v Bradford C, Division 4, 30 December 1961; 4, Bobby Hunt v Doncaster R, Division 4, 30 April 1962.

*Most Capped Player:* Bela Balogh, 2 (9), Hungary.

*Most League Appearances:* Micky Cook, 613, 1969–84.

*Youngest League Player:* Lindsay Smith, 16 years 218 days v Grimsby T, 24 April 1971.

*Record Transfer Fee Received:* £2,500,000 from Reading for Greg Halford, January 2007.

*Record Transfer Fee Paid:* £400,000 to Cheltenham T for Steve Gillespie, July 2008.

*Football League Record:* 1950 Elected to Division 3 (S); 1958–61 Division 3; 1961–62 Division 4; 1962–65 Division 3; 1965–66 Division 4; 1966–68 Division 3; 1968–74 Division 4; 1974–76 Division 3, 1976–77 Division 4; 1977–81 Division 3; 1981–90 Division 4; 1990–92 GM Vauxhall Conference; 1992–98 Division 3; 1998–04 Division 2; 2004–06 FL 1; 2006–08 FL C; 2008– FL 1.

## MANAGERS

Ted Fenton 1946–48
Jimmy Allen 1948–53
Jack Butler 1953–55
Benny Fenton 1955–63
Neil Franklin 1963–68
Dick Graham 1968–72
Jim Smith 1972–75
Bobby Roberts 1975–82
Allan Hunter 1982–83
Cyril Lea 1983–86
Mike Walker 1986–87
Roger Brown 1987–88
Jock Wallace 1989
Mick Mills 1990
Ian Atkins 1990–91
Roy McDonough 1991–94
George Burley 1994
Steve Wignall 1995–99
Mick Wadsworth 1999
Steve Whitton 1999–2003
Phil Parkinson 2003–06
Geraint Williams 2006–08
Paul Lambert 2008–09
Aidy Boothroyd 2009–10
John Ward 2010–12
Joe Dunne September 2012–

## LATEST SEQUENCES

*Longest Sequence of League Wins:* 7, 29.11.1968 – 1.2.1969.

*Longest Sequence of League Defeats:* 9, 20.11.2012 – 12.1.2013.

*Longest Sequence of League Draws:* 6, 21.3.1977 – 11.4.1977.

*Longest Sequence of Unbeaten League Matches:* 20, 22.12.1956 – 19.4.1957.

*Longest Sequence Without a League Win:* 20, 2.3.1968 – 31.8.1968.

*Successive Scoring Runs:* 24 from 15.9.1962.

*Successive Non-scoring Runs:* 5 from 7.4.1981.

## TEN YEAR LEAGUE RECORD

|         |       | P  | W  | D  | L  | F  | A  | Pts | Pos |
|---------|-------|----|----|----|----|----|----|-----|-----|
| 2003-04 | Div 2 | 46 | 17 | 13 | 16 | 52 | 56 | 64  | 11  |
| 2004-05 | FL 1  | 46 | 14 | 17 | 15 | 60 | 50 | 59  | 15  |
| 2005-06 | FL 1  | 46 | 22 | 13 | 11 | 58 | 40 | 79  | 2   |
| 2006-07 | FL C  | 46 | 20 | 9  | 17 | 70 | 56 | 69  | 10  |
| 2007-08 | FL C  | 46 | 7  | 17 | 22 | 62 | 86 | 38  | 24  |
| 2008-09 | FL 1  | 46 | 18 | 9  | 19 | 58 | 58 | 63  | 12  |
| 2009-10 | FL 1  | 46 | 20 | 12 | 14 | 64 | 52 | 72  | 8   |
| 2010-11 | FL 1  | 46 | 16 | 14 | 16 | 57 | 63 | 62  | 10  |
| 2011-12 | FL 1  | 46 | 13 | 20 | 13 | 61 | 66 | 59  | 10  |
| 2012-13 | FL 1  | 46 | 14 | 9  | 23 | 47 | 68 | 51  | 20  |

## DID YOU KNOW ?

Colchester United spent their inaugural season as members of the Southern League. The U's drew 3-3 with Ipswich Town in their first-ever home fixture in the competition but lost the return game between the clubs 3-2 in front of a crowd of 23,890.

## COLCHESTER UNITED – FOOTBALL LEAGUE ONE 2012–13 LEAGUE RECORD

| Match No. | Date | Venue | Opponents | Result | H/T Score | Lg Pos. | Goalscorers | Attendance |
|---|---|---|---|---|---|---|---|---|
| 1 | Aug 18 | A | Preston NE | D 0-0 | 0-0 | 15 | | 10,034 |
| 2 | 21 | H | Portsmouth | D 2-2 | 1-1 | 14 | Rose [45], Okuonghae [83] | 4335 |
| 3 | 25 | H | Sheffield U | D 1-1 | 0-1 | 16 | Morrison [72] | 4017 |
| 4 | Sept 1 | A | Tranmere R | L 0-4 | 0-1 | 19 | | 4711 |
| 5 | 8 | A | Brentford | L 0-1 | 0-0 | 21 | | 5499 |
| 6 | 15 | H | Doncaster R | L 1-2 | 1-1 | 4 | Okuonghae [30] | 3262 |
| 7 | 18 | H | Crawley T | D 1-1 | 0-0 | 22 | Wordsworth (pen) [87] | 2484 |
| 8 | 22 | A | Scunthorpe U | L 0-1 | 0-0 | 22 | | 3133 |
| 9 | 29 | H | Hartlepool U | W 3-1 | 2-1 | 19 | Massey [39], Ibehre 2 [43, 62] | 3471 |
| 10 | Oct 2 | A | Swindon T | W 1-0 | 0-0 | 17 | Rose [70] | 7443 |
| 11 | 6 | A | Yeovil T | L 1-3 | 1-2 | 19 | Ibehre [25] | 3002 |
| 12 | 13 | H | Stevenage | W 1-0 | 0-0 | 17 | Watt [55] | 4045 |
| 13 | 20 | H | Carlisle U | W 2-0 | 2-0 | 15 | Eastmond [25], Ibehre [31] | 3335 |
| 14 | 23 | A | Leyton Orient | W 2-0 | 1-0 | 12 | Wordsworth [33], Henderson [51] | 3378 |
| 15 | 27 | A | Shrewsbury T | D 2-2 | 1-0 | 12 | Eastmond [3], Watt [62] | 5066 |
| 16 | Nov 6 | H | Notts Co | L 0-2 | 0-2 | 13 | | 3051 |
| 17 | 10 | A | Crewe Alex | L 2-3 | 2-0 | 14 | Sears [3], Henderson [30] | 4292 |
| 18 | 17 | H | Bury | W 2-0 | 0-0 | 13 | Wordsworth [56], Sears [61] | 3214 |
| 19 | 20 | H | Coventry C | L 1-3 | 0-2 | 16 | Eastman [71] | 3229 |
| 20 | 24 | A | Milton Keynes D | L 1-5 | 0-2 | 17 | Henderson [63] | 7443 |
| 21 | Dec 8 | H | Oldham Ath | L 0-2 | 0-1 | 17 | | 2987 |
| 22 | 15 | A | Bournemouth | L 0-1 | 0-1 | 17 | | 6145 |
| 23 | 22 | A | Walsall | L 0-1 | 0-0 | 19 | | 3006 |
| 24 | 26 | H | Brentford | L 1-3 | 1-2 | 20 | Wright, Drey [23] | 4200 |
| 25 | Jan 1 | A | Crawley T | L 0-3 | 0-1 | 20 | | 3160 |
| 26 | 5 | A | Doncaster R | L 0-1 | 0-0 | 20 | | 6373 |
| 27 | 12 | H | Scunthorpe U | L 1-2 | 0-1 | 21 | Sears [59] | 3258 |
| 28 | 26 | H | Walsall | W 2-0 | 0-0 | 20 | Ibehre [79], Sears [89] | 2865 |
| 29 | Feb 2 | A | Portsmouth | W 3-2 | 3-1 | 19 | Massey 2 [2, 20], Sears (pen) [16] | 11,132 |
| 30 | 5 | H | Swindon T | L 0-1 | 0-0 | 19 | | 3214 |
| 31 | 9 | H | Preston NE | W 1-0 | 0-0 | 19 | Sears [55] | 3215 |
| 32 | 16 | A | Sheffield U | L 0-3 | 0-1 | 20 | | 16,860 |
| 33 | 23 | H | Tranmere R | L 1-5 | 1-2 | 21 | Okuonghae [29] | 3077 |
| 34 | 26 | H | Yeovil T | W 2-0 | 1-0 | 21 | Clifford [45], Sears [62] | 2367 |
| 35 | Mar 2 | A | Stevenage | W 2-0 | 0-0 | 19 | Ibehre 2 [62, 73] | 3144 |
| 36 | 5 | A | Hartlepool U | D 0-0 | 0-0 | 19 | | 3148 |
| 37 | 9 | H | Crewe Alex | L 1-2 | 1-1 | 19 | Porter [42] | 3085 |
| 38 | 12 | A | Coventry C | D 2-2 | 1-0 | 19 | Massey [39], Smith [72] | 9431 |
| 39 | 16 | A | Bury | W 2-1 | 2-1 | 19 | Thompson [30], Morrison [31] | 2018 |
| 40 | 29 | H | Bournemouth | L 0-1 | 0-1 | 19 | | 4727 |
| 41 | Apr 1 | A | Oldham Ath | D 1-1 | 1-0 | 19 | Wright, Drey [20] | 4244 |
| 42 | 6 | H | Leyton Orient | W 2-1 | 2-1 | 19 | Massey [20], Wright, Drey [24] | 4704 |
| 43 | 13 | A | Notts Co | L 1-3 | 1-1 | 19 | Ibehre [37] | 4306 |
| 44 | 16 | H | Milton Keynes D | L 0-2 | 0-1 | 20 | | 3175 |
| 45 | 20 | H | Shrewsbury T | D 0-0 | 0-0 | 20 | | 5862 |
| 46 | 27 | A | Carlisle U | W 2-0 | 0-0 | 20 | Massey [65], Eastman [80] | 5427 |

**Final League Position: 20**

### GOALSCORERS

*League (47):* Ibehre 8, Sears 7 (1 pen), Massey 6, Henderson 3, Okuonghae 3, Wordsworth 3 (1 pen), Wright, Drey 3, Eastman 2, Eastmond 2, Morrison 2, Rose 2, Watt 2, Clifford 1, Porter 1, Smith 1, Thompson 1.
*FA Cup (1):* Rose 1.
*Capital One Cup (0).*
*Johnstone's Paint Trophy (1):* Sears 1.

| Cousins M 23 | Rose M 22 | Okuonghae M 42 + 1 | Heath M 6 | Wilson B 41 | Sears F 22 + 13 | Bean M 26 + 5 | O'Toole J 4 + 11 | Wordsworth A 23 + 1 | Henderson I 14 + 8 | Morrison C 17 + 15 | Eastman T 26 + 3 | Bond A 16 + 11 | White J 16 + 6 | Wright Drey 9 + 12 | Massey G 34 + 6 | Duguid K 3 + 2 | Coker B 1 | Izzet K 9 + 2 | Eastmond C 12 | Ibehre J 30 | Watt S 5 + 1 | Sullivan J 4 | Thompson J 16 + 6 | Potts D 5 | Gilbey A 2 + 1 | Ladapo F —+ 4 | Compton J 1 + 6 | Porter G 13 + 6 | Samuel D 2 | Clifford B 18 | Walker S 19 | Wright David 12 | Garmston B 10 + 3 | Smith M 3 + 5 | Hewitt T —+ 1 | Olufemi T —+ 1 | Match No. |
|---|---|---|---|---|---|---|---|---|---|---|---|---|---|---|---|---|---|---|---|---|---|---|---|---|---|---|---|---|---|---|---|---|---|---|---|---|---|
| 1 | 2 | 3 | $4^1$ | 5 | 6 | 7 | $8^2$ | 9 | 10 | $11^3$ | 12 | 13 | 14 | | | | | | | | | | | | | | | | | | | | | | | | 1 |
| 1 | 5 | 4 | 3 | 2 | 10 | 7 | $8^2$ | 9 | 6 | $11^1$ | | 13 | 12 | | | | | | | | | | | | | | | | | | | | | | | | 2 |
| 1 | 5 | 3 | 4 | 2 | $8^2$ | 7 | $6^1$ | 9 | 10 | 11 | 12 | 13 | | | | | | | | | | | | | | | | | | | | | | | | | 3 |
| 1 | 5 | 3 | 4 | 2 | $10^3$ | 8 | 14 | $9^1$ | 13 | 11 | | | 7 | | 12 | $6^2$ | | | | | | | | | | | | | | | | | | | | | 4 |
| 1 | 2 | 3 | | | 10 | 6 | | $9^1$ | | 11 | 12 | 4 | 7 | | | | | 5 | 8 | | | | | | | | | | | | | | | | | | 5 |
| 1 | 5 | 3 | | 2 | 10 | 6 | 13 | 9 | 12 | 4 | | $8^1$ | | | 11 | | | $7^2$ | | | | | | | | | | | | | | | | | | | 6 |
| 1 | 5 | 3 | | 2 | 12 | 8 | 13 | 7 | $9^1$ | 10 | 4 | | | | 11 | | | $6^2$ | | | | | | | | | | | | | | | | | | | 7 |
| 1 | 5 | | 3 | 2 | 14 | 8 | 7 | 12 | 10 | 4 | | 13 | | | $11^2$ | $9^3$ | | $6^1$ | | | | | | | | | | | | | | | | | | | 8 |
| 1 | 5 | 4 | | 2 | 12 | 6 | 8 | 13 | 3 | $9^1$ | 14 | | | | 7 | | | $10^2$ | $11^2$ | | | | | | | | | | | | | | | | | | 9 |
| 1 | 5 | 4 | | 2 | 12 | 8 | 9 | 13 | 14 | 3 | | | | | $6^3$ | | | 7 | $11^2$ | $10^1$ | | | | | | | | | | | | | | | | | 10 |
| 1 | 5 | 4 | | 2 | 12 | $6^2$ | 8 | 14 | 3 | | $10^1$ | | | | 13 | | | 7 | 11 | $9^3$ | | | | | | | | | | | | | | | | | 11 |
| 1 | 5 | 3 | | 2 | 13 | 6 | 8 | 12 | 4 | | $11^1$ | | | | 7 | | | 10 | $9^2$ | | | | | | | | | | | | | | | | | | 12 |
| 1 | 5 | 3 | | $2^1$ | 13 | 6 | 8 | 14 | 4 | | 11 | | | | 7 | | | $10^3$ | $9^2$ | | | | | | | | | | | | | | | | | | 13 |
| 1 | 5 | 3 | | 2 | 12 | $8^3$ | 13 | 7 | 9 | 4 | $11^1$ | 14 | | | $6^2$ | 10 | | | | | | | | | | | | | | | | | | | | | 14 |
| 1 | 5 | 3 | | 2 | 14 | $6^2$ | 13 | $9^3$ | 4 | | $11^1$ | 8 | | | 7 | 10 | 12 | | | | | | | | | | | | | | | | | | | | 15 |
| 1 | 5 | 3 | | 2 | 12 | $6^2$ | 8 | 11 | 14 | 4 | 13 | | | | $9^1$ | $7^3$ | 10 | | | | | | | | | | | | | | | | | | | | 16 |
| | 5 | 3 | | 2 | $10^2$ | 6 | $8^3$ | 11 | 12 | 4 | 14 | | | | 13 | $7^1$ | 9 | | | | | 1 | | | | | | | | | | | | | | | 17 |
| | 5 | 3 | | 2 | 9 | 6 | 8 | $11^2$ | 12 | 4 | 13 | | | | $7^3$ | $10^1$ | | | | | 1 | 1 | 14 | | | | | | | | | | | | | | 18 |
| | 5 | 3 | | 2 | 11 | $6^1$ | 8 | $9^2$ | 13 | 4 | 14 | | | | 12 | $7^3$ | 10 | 1 | | | | | | | | | | | | | | | | | | | 19 |
| | | 3 | | 2 | 11 | 13 | 8 | 9 | 10 | $4^2$ | $6^1$ | | | | $12^4$ | $7^3$ | | 1 | | | | 14 | 5 | | | | | | | | | | | | | | 20 |
| 1 | | 3 | | 2 | 9 | $6^1$ | 8 | $11^3$ | 14 | 4 | $7^2$ | 12 | | | 10 | | | | | | | | | 5 | 13 | | | | | | | | | | | | 21 |
| 1 | 10 | | | | 6 | | $7^2$ | 9 | | 13 | 3 | 14 | 2 | 12 | $8^3$ | | | 11 | | | | | 4 | $5^1$ | | | | | | | | | | | | | 22 |
| 1 | $5^1$ | | | | 6 | $9^3$ | | 14 | 7 | 13 | 11 | 3 | 2 | 12 | 8 | | | 10 | | | | | 4 | | | | | | | | | | | | | | 23 |
| 1 | 12 | | | | 9 | 14 | | 11 | 4 | 2 | 10 | $6^2$ | | | $8^3$ | | | | | | | | $3^4$ | 5 | | $7^1$ | 13 | | | | | | | | | | 24 |
| 1 | | 3 | 4 | 5 | 7 | 8 | | 11 | | | 9 | $10^1$ | | | $6^2$ | | | | | | | | 2 | | | 12 | 13 | | | | | | | | | | 25 |
| 1 | 5 | 3 | | 2 | 9 | 8 | | | 13 | | $10^1$ | 6 | | | $7^2$ | | | | | | | | 4 | | | 12 | 14 | $11^3$ | | | | | | | | | 26 |
| 1 | 5 | 3 | | 2 | 12 | $7^1$ | | 13 | | | $11^3$ | 9 | | | | | | | | | | | 4 | | 8 | | 14 | $10^2$ | 6 | | | | | | | | 27 |
| | | 3 | | 2 | 14 | $6^3$ | | | 12 | | 5 | $11^2$ | 9 | | 10 | | | | | | | | $4^1$ | | | | 13 | | 8 | 1 | 7 | | | | | | 28 |
| | | 3 | | 2 | $11^1$ | 12 | | | | | 14 | 5 | 13 | 6 | | | | | | | | | 10 | | | | | 4 | | $9^2$ | 1 | 7 | | | | | 29 |
| | | 3 | | 2 | 10 | | | | 13 | | | 5 | 12 | $9^1$ | | | | | | | | | 11 | | | | 14 | $6^2$ | | $8^3$ | 1 | 7 | | | | | 30 |
| | | 4 | | $2^1$ | 10 | 14 | | | | | 12 | | 5 | | 6 | | | | | | | | 11 | | | | 13 | $9^2$ | | $7^3$ | 1 | 8 | | | | | 31 |
| | | 3 | | | 10 | | | | | | 14 | 2 | 13 | $6^2$ | 11 | | | | | | | | 4 | | | | 12 | $9^1$ | | 8 | 1 | $7^3$ | 5 | | | | 32 |
| | | 3 | | | 10 | | | | 14 | | 13 | 2 | 12 | $9^1$ | 11 | | | | | | | | 4 | | | | | $6^1$ | | $8^3$ | 1 | $7^2$ | 5 | | | | 33 |
| | | 3 | | 2 | 10 | | | | 13 | 4 | 14 | 6 | | | $11^2$ | | | | | | | | 12 | | | | | $9^3$ | | 8 | 1 | | $5^1$ | | | | 34 |
| | | 3 | | 7 | $10^1$ | | | | 12 | 8 | 9 | 13 | | | $6^2$ | | | | | | | | 11 | | | | 14 | $4^3$ | | 5 | 1 | | 2 | | | | 35 |
| | | 4 | | 2 | | | | | $11^1$ | 3 | 6 | 14 | | 10 | | | | | | | | | $9^4$ | | | | 13 | | 12 | $8^2$ | $7^3$ | 1 | | 5 | | | 36 |
| | | 3 | | 2 | | | | | $10^3$ | $4^1$ | 7 | 5 | | 9 | | | | | | | | | 12 | | | | 11 | 6 | | 8 | 1 | $6^2$ | | | 13 | 14 | 37 |
| | | 4 | | 2 | | | | | $10^2$ | | 8 | 14 | | 9 | | | | | | | | | 3 | | | | 12 | 13 | 6 | 7 | 1 | | $5^3$ | $11^1$ | | | 38 |
| | | 3 | | | 13 | | | | $11^1$ | 7 | | | | 6 | | | | | | | | | 4 | | | 14 | $9^4$ | | $8^2$ | 1 | 2 | 5 | $10^3$ | | 12 | 39 |
| | | 3 | | 2 | | | | | $9^3$ | | 6 | 12 | 13 | 8 | | | | | | | | | 11 | | | | $10^2$ | | | 7 | 1 | | $5^1$ | 14 | | | 40 |
| | | 3 | | 2 | | 12 | | | 14 | | 6 | 5 | | $10^3$ | $8^2$ | | | | | | | | 11 | | | | 4 | | | 1 | 7 | 13 | $9^1$ | | | | 41 |
| | | 3 | | 2 | | 13 | | | $11^3$ | | 5 | 9 | | 6 | 10 | | | | | | | | $4^1$ | | | | | | | $7^2$ | 1 | 8 | 12 | 14 | | | 42 |
| | | 3 | | 2 | 13 | | | | 12 | | $10^2$ | 8 | 5 | $9^3$ | 6 | | | | | | | | 11 | | | | | 14 | | 1 | $7^1$ | 4 | | | | 43 |
| | | 3 | | 2 | $11^3$ | | | | 14 | $7^2$ | 4 | $9^1$ | 6 | 10 | | | | | | | | | 12 | | | | | 8 | 1 | 5 | 13 | | | | | 44 |
| | | 3 | | 2 | $11^2$ | | | | 14 | 4 | 7 | 5 | 12 | $9^1$ | 10 | | | | | | | | 6 | | | | | $8^3$ | 1 | | 13 | | | | | 45 |
| | | 3 | | 5 | $7^3$ | 13 | | | 4 | 2 | 11 | 14 | 10 | $9^1$ | $8^2$ | | | | | | | | 1 | | | | | $9^1$ | $8^2$ | 1 | 6 | 12 | | | | 46 |

**FA Cup**
First Round    Chelmsford    (a)  1-3

**Capital One Cup**
First Round    Yeovil T    (a)  0-3

**Johnstone's Paint Trophy**
Second Round    Northampton T    (a)  1-2

# COVENTRY CITY

## FOUNDATION

Workers at Singers' cycle factory formed a club in 1883. The first success of Singers' FC was to win the Birmingham Junior Cup in 1891 and this led in 1894 to their election to the Birmingham & District League. Four years later they changed their name to Coventry City and joined the Southern League in 1908 at which time they were playing in blue and white quarters.

*The Ricoh Arena, Phoenix Way, Foleshill, Coventry CV6 6GE.*

*Telephone:* (0844) 873 1883.

*Fax:* (0247) 623 4099.

*Ticket Office:* (0844) 873 1883 (option 1).

*Website:* www.ccfc.co.uk

*Email:* info@ccfc.co.uk

*Ground Capacity:* 32,604.

*Record Attendance:* 51,455 v Wolverhampton W, Division 2, 29 April 1967 (at Highfield Road); 31,407 v Chelsea, FA Cup 6th rd, 7 March 2009 (at Ricoh Arena).

*Pitch Measurements:* 105m × 67m (115yd × 74yd)

*Managing Director:* Tim Fisher.

*Manager:* Steven Pressley.

*Assistant Manager:* Neil MacFarlane.

*Physio:* David Hart.

*Colours:* Sky blue shirts with grey horizontal stripes, sky blue shorts, sky blue socks.

*Year Formed:* 1883.

*Turned Professional:* 1893.

*Previous Name:* 1883, Singers' FC; 1898, Coventry City.

*Club Nickname:* 'Sky Blues'.

*Grounds:* 1883, Binley Road; 1887, Stoke Road; 1899, Highfield Road; 2005, Ricoh Arena.

*First Football League Game:* 30 August 1919, Division 2, v Tottenham H (h) L 0–5 – Lindon; Roberts, Chaplin, Allan, Hawley, Clarke, Sheldon, Mercer, Sambrooke, Lowes, Gibson.

*Record League Victory:* 9–0 v Bristol C, Division 3 (S), 28 April 1934 – Pearson; Brown, Bisby; Perry, Davidson, Frith; White (2), Lauderdale, Bourton (5), Jones (2), Lake.

*Record Cup Victory:* 8–0 v Rushden & D, League Cup 2nd rd, 2 October 2002 – Debec; Caldwell, Quinn, Betts (1p), Konjic (Shaw), Davenport, Pipe, Safri (Stanford), Mills (2) (Bothroyd (2)), McSheffery (3), Partridge.

*Record Defeat:* 2–10 v Norwich C, Division 3 (S), 15 March 1930.

*Most League Points (2 for a win):* 60, Division 4, 1958–59 and Division 3, 1963–64.

## HONOURS

**Football League – Division 1:**
Best season: 6th, 1969–70;
**Division 2:** *Champions* 1966–67;
**Division 3:** *Champions* 1963–64;
**Division 3 (S):** *Champions* 1935–36;
*Runners-up* 1933–34;
**Division 4:** *Runners-up* 1958–59.

**FA Cup:** *Winners* 1987.

**Football League Cup:** Semi-final 1981, 1990.

**European Competitions**
**European Fairs Cup:** 1970–71.

## sky SPORTS FACT FILE

Patsy Hendren, a winger with Coventry City in 1909–10 and 1910–11, was also a top-class cricketer who played in 51 Test matches for England between 1920 and 1935. Patsy was a double international, winning his football cap in the Victory international with Wales at Cardiff in October 1919.

*Most League Points (3 for a win):* 66, Division 1, 2001–02.

*Most League Goals:* 108, Division 3 (S), 1931–32.

*Highest League Scorer in Season:* Clarrie Bourton, 49, Division 3 (S), 1931–32.

*Most League Goals in Total Aggregate:* Clarrie Bourton, 171, 1931–37.

*Most League Goals in One Match:* 5, Clarrie Bourton v Bournemouth, Division 3 (S), 17 October 1931; 5, Arthur Bacon v Gillingham, Division 3 (S), 30 December 1933.

*Most Capped Player:* Magnus Hedman, 44 (58), Sweden.

*Most League Appearances:* Steve Ogrizovic, 507, 1984–2000.

*Youngest League Player:* Ben Mackey, 16 years 167 days v Ipswich T, 12 April 2003.

*Record Transfer Fee Received:* £13,000,000 from Internazionale for Robbie Keane, July 2000.

*Record Transfer Fee Paid:* £6,500,000 to Norwich C for Craig Bellamy, August 2000.

*Football League Record:* 1919 Elected to Division 2; 1925–26 Division 3 (N); 1926–36 Division 3 (S); 1936–52 Division 2; 1952–58 Division 3 (S); 1958–59 Division 4; 1959–64 Division 3; 1964–67 Division 2; 1967–92 Division 1; 1992–2001 FA Premier League; 2001–04 Division 1; 2004–12 FL C; 2012– FL 1.

## LATEST SEQUENCES

*Longest Sequence of League Wins:* 6, 25.4.1964 – 5.9.1964.

*Longest Sequence of League Defeats:* 9, 30.8.1919 – 11.10.1919.

*Longest Sequence of League Draws:* 6, 1.11.2003 – 29.11.2003.

*Longest Sequence of Unbeaten League Matches:* 25, 26.11.1966 – 13.5.1967.

*Longest Sequence Without a League Win:* 19, 30.8.1919 – 20.12.1919.

*Successive Scoring Runs:* 25 from 10.9.1966.

*Successive Non-scoring Runs:* 11 from 11.10.1919.

## MANAGERS

**H. R. Buckle** 1909–10
**Robert Wallace** 1910–13
  (*Secretary-Manager*)
**Frank Scott-Walford** 1913–15
**William Clayton** 1917–19
**H. Pollitt** 1919–20
**Albert Evans** 1920–24
**Jimmy Kerr** 1924–28
**James McIntyre** 1928–31
**Harry Storer** 1931–45
**Dick Bayliss** 1945–47
**Billy Frith** 1947–48
**Harry Storer** 1948–53
**Jack Fairbrother** 1953–54
**Charlie Elliott** 1954–55
**Jesse Carver** 1955–56
**George Raynor** 1956
**Harry Warren** 1956–57
**Billy Frith** 1957–61
**Jimmy Hill** 1961–67
**Noel Cantwell** 1967–72
**Bob Dennison** 1972
**Joe Mercer** 1972–75
**Gordon Milne** 1972–81
**Dave Sexton** 1981–83
**Bobby Gould** 1983–84
**Don Mackay** 1985–86
**George Curtis** 1986–87
  (*became Managing Director*)
**John Sillett** 1987–90
**Terry Butcher** 1990–92
**Don Howe** 1992
**Bobby Gould** 1992–93
  (*Bobby Gould and Don Howe joint managers June 1992*)
**Phil Neal** 1993–95
**Ron Atkinson** 1995–96
  (*became Director of Football*)
**Gordon Strachan** 1996–2001
**Roland Nilsson** 2001–02
**Gary McAllister** 2002–04
**Eric Black** 2004
**Peter Reid** 2004–05
**Micky Adams** 2005–07
**Iain Dowie** 2007–08
**Chris Coleman** 2008–10
**Aidy Boothroyd** 2010–11
**Andy Thorn** 2011–12
**Mark Robins** 2012–13
**Steven Pressley** March 2013–

## TEN YEAR LEAGUE RECORD

|  |  | P | W | D | L | F | A | Pts | Pos |
|---|---|---|---|---|---|---|---|---|---|
| 2003-04 | Div 1 | 46 | 17 | 14 | 15 | 67 | 54 | 65 | 12 |
| 2004-05 | FL C | 46 | 13 | 13 | 20 | 61 | 73 | 52 | 19 |
| 2005-06 | FL C | 46 | 16 | 15 | 15 | 62 | 65 | 63 | 8 |
| 2006-07 | FL C | 46 | 16 | 8 | 22 | 47 | 62 | 56 | 17 |
| 2007-08 | FL C | 46 | 14 | 11 | 21 | 52 | 64 | 53 | 21 |
| 2008-09 | FL C | 46 | 13 | 15 | 18 | 47 | 58 | 54 | 17 |
| 2009-10 | FL C | 46 | 13 | 15 | 18 | 47 | 64 | 54 | 19 |
| 2010-11 | FL C | 46 | 14 | 13 | 19 | 54 | 58 | 55 | 18 |
| 2011-12 | FL C | 46 | 9 | 13 | 24 | 41 | 65 | 40 | 23 |
| 2012-13 | FL 1 | 46 | 18 | 11 | 17 | 66 | 59 | 55* | 15 |

*\* 10 pts deducted.*

## DID YOU KNOW ?

George Raynor, manager of Coventry City from January to June 1956, was one of the most successful international coaches of the post-war period. He led Sweden to Gold at the 1948 Olympics and 10 years later to a place in the World Cup final when they were defeated by Brazil.

## COVENTRY CITY – FOOTBALL LEAGUE ONE 2012–13 LEAGUE RECORD

| Match No. | Date | Venue | Opponents | Result | H/T Score | Lg Pos. | Goalscorers | Attendance |
|---|---|---|---|---|---|---|---|---|
| 1 | Aug 18 | A | Yeovil T | D | 1-1 | 1-1 | 9 | McDonald [10] | 6006 |
| 2 | 21 | H | Sheffield U | D | 1-1 | 0-0 | 15 | Elliott [62] | 12,621 |
| 3 | 25 | H | Bury | D | 2-2 | 2-0 | 14 | Barton [18], Baker [28] | 10,285 |
| 4 | Sept 1 | A | Crewe Alex | L | 0-1 | 0-1 | 17 | | 5738 |
| 5 | 9 | H | Stevenage | L | 1-2 | 1-1 | 20 | McGoldrick [11] | 9458 |
| 6 | 15 | A | Tranmere R | L | 0-2 | 0-0 | 23 | | 6087 |
| 7 | 18 | A | Shrewsbury T | L | 1-4 | 0-2 | 23 | Fleck (pen) [75] | 5960 |
| 8 | 22 | H | Carlisle U | L | 1-2 | 1-1 | 23 | McGoldrick [38] | 10,674 |
| 9 | 29 | A | Oldham Ath | W | 1-0 | 0-0 | 22 | McDonald [89] | 4022 |
| 10 | Oct 2 | H | Milton Keynes D | D | 1-1 | 1-1 | 22 | Wood [34] | 9848 |
| 11 | 6 | H | Bournemouth | W | 1-0 | 0-0 | 20 | McGoldrick [61] | 10,458 |
| 12 | 13 | A | Swindon T | D | 2-2 | 2-0 | 19 | McGoldrick 2 [13, 37] | 9808 |
| 13 | 20 | H | Notts Co | L | 1-2 | 0-1 | 21 | Wood [87] | 11,882 |
| 14 | 23 | A | Brentford | L | 1-2 | 1-1 | 21 | McGoldrick [7] | 5415 |
| 15 | 27 | A | Leyton Orient | W | 1-0 | 1-0 | 21 | McGoldrick [7] | 4741 |
| 16 | Nov 6 | H | Crawley T | W | 3-1 | 2-0 | 19 | Fleck [9], McGoldrick 2 [45, 65] | 8862 |
| 17 | 10 | H | Scunthorpe U | L | 1-2 | 1-1 | 20 | Baker [35]    – | 9892 |
| 18 | 17 | A | Hartlepool U | W | 5-0 | 0-0 | 16 | Baker 2 [51, 59], McGoldrick (pen) [58], Moussa [75], Barton [78] | 4404 |
| 19 | 20 | A | Colchester U | W | 3-1 | 2-0 | 15 | Moussa [34], Edjenguele [37], McGoldrick [87] | 3229 |
| 20 | 24 | H | Portsmouth | D | 1-1 | 1-0 | 15 | McSheffrey [41] | 11,295 |
| 21 | Dec 8 | H | Walsall | W | 5-1 | 3-1 | 15 | Baker 2 [29, 84], McGoldrick 2 [39, 41], Christie [61] | 10,986 |
| 22 | 15 | A | Doncaster R | W | 4-1 | 2-0 | 13 | Moussa [3], McGoldrick 2 [26, 58], Barton [89] | 6623 |
| 23 | 22 | H | Preston NE | D | 1-1 | 1-0 | 13 | Bailey [22] | 12,230 |
| 24 | 26 | A | Stevenage | W | 3-1 | 0-1 | 11 | Wood [79], Baker [90], McGoldrick [90] | 4102 |
| 25 | 29 | A | Milton Keynes D | W | 3-2 | 1-2 | 9 | Moussa [27], Elliott 2 [49, 51] | 13,620 |
| 26 | Jan 1 | H | Shrewsbury T | L | 0-1 | 0-0 | 11 | | 15,185 |
| 27 | 13 | A | Carlisle U | L | 0-1 | 0-1 | 13 | | 4071 |
| 28 | 16 | H | Tranmere R | W | 1-0 | 1-0 | 10 | Clarke, L [20] | 9668 |
| 29 | 19 | A | Oldham Ath | W | 2-1 | 0-0 | 7 | Elliott [61], Bailey [90] | 10,108 |
| 30 | 26 | A | Preston NE | D | 2-2 | 1-1 | 7 | Clarke, L [38], Robertson (og) [53] | 8474 |
| 31 | Feb 1 | A | Sheffield U | W | 2-1 | 1-0 | 7 | Clarke, L 2 [14, 87] | 17,511 |
| 32 | 9 | H | Yeovil T | L | 0-1 | 0-1 | 8 | | 11,277 |
| 33 | 16 | A | Bury | W | 2-0 | 1-0 | 8 | Clarke, L [3], Baker [73] | 3745 |
| 34 | 23 | H | Crewe Alex | L | 1-2 | 1-1 | 8 | Clarke, L [12] | 10,139 |
| 35 | 26 | H | Bournemouth | W | 2-0 | 1-0 | 8 | Clarke, L [45], Baker (pen) [84] | 7411 |
| 36 | Mar 2 | H | Swindon T | L | 1-2 | 1-2 | 9 | Moussa [2] | 14,280 |
| 37 | 9 | A | Scunthorpe U | W | 2-1 | 1-1 | 8 | Baker [46], Clarke, L [77] | 3676 |
| 38 | 12 | A | Colchester U | D | 2-2 | 0-1 | 9 | Wilson [77], Baker [90] | 9431 |
| 39 | 16 | H | Hartlepool U | W | 1-0 | 1-0 | 8 | McDonald [33] | 10,412 |
| 40 | 23 | A | Portsmouth | L | 0-2 | 0-1 | 10 | | 12,601 |
| 41 | 29 | H | Doncaster R | W | 1-0 | 1-0 | 14 | Christie [13] | 9000 |
| 42 | Apr 1 | A | Walsall | L | 0-4 | 0-1 | 14 | | 7504 |
| 43 | 6 | H | Brentford | D | 1-1 | 1-0 | 14 | Baker (pen) [45] | 10,642 |
| 44 | 13 | A | Crawley T | L | 0-2 | 0-1 | 16 | | 3900 |
| 45 | 20 | H | Leyton Orient | L | 0-1 | 0-1 | 16 | | 11,234 |
| 46 | 27 | A | Notts Co | D | 2-2 | 0-1 | 15 | Fleck [50], Moussa [86] | 7608 |

**Final League Position: 15**

### GOALSCORERS

*League (66):* McGoldrick 16 (1 pen), Baker 12 (2 pens), Clarke, L 8, Moussa 6, Elliott 4, Barton 3, Fleck 3 (1 pen), McDonald 3, Wood 3, Bailey 2, Christie 2, Edjenguele 1, McSheffrey 1, Wilson 1, own goal 1.
*FA Cup (5):* Baker 1, Ball 1, Christie 1, Jennings 1, McSheffrey 1 (1 pen).
*Capital One Cup (5):* Kilbane 1 (pen), Baker 1, Ball 1, McDonald 1.
*Johnstone's Paint Trophy (10):* Clarke L 2, Baker 1, Ball 1, Hussey 1, Jennings 1, McGoldrick 1, own goals 3.

| Murphy J 45 | Clarke J 15 + 5 | Brown R 6 | Wood R 36 | Hussey C 8 + 2 | Fleck J 22 + 13 | Daniels B 3 + 1 | Kilbane K 8 + 1 | Barton A 14 + 8 | McDonald C 9 + 11 | Ball C 6 + 9 | McSheffrey G 26 + 6 | Elliott S 10 + 8 | Jennings S 36 + 3 | Malaga K 2 | Baker C 41 + 2 | Edjenguele W 30 + 3 | McGoldrick D 21 + 1 | Thomas C 2 + 9 | O'Donovan R — + 4 | Henderson C 1 + 1 | Reckord J 7 + 2 | Bailey J 29 + 1 | Moussa F 31 + 7 | Christie C 31 | Cameron N 8 + 1 | Adams B 16 | Clarke L 11 + 1 | Wilson C 3 + 8 | Dickinson C 6 | Martin A 12 | Bell D 2 + 5 | Willis J — + 1 | Stewart J 6 | Haynes R 1 | Philliskirk D 1 | Dunn C 1 | Match No. |
|---|---|---|---|---|---|---|---|---|---|---|---|---|---|---|---|---|---|---|---|---|---|---|---|---|---|---|---|---|---|---|---|---|---|---|---|---|---|
| 1 | 2 | 3 | 4 | 5 | 6¹ | 7³ | 8 | 9 | 10 | 11² | 12 | 13 | 14 | | | | | | | | | | | | | | | | | | | | | | | | 1 |
| 1 | | 3 | 4 | 5 | | | 8 | 7 | 10 | 12 | 13 | 11¹ | 6 | 2 | 9² | | | | | | | | | | | | | | | | | | | | | | 2 |
| 1 | 2 | | 4 | 5 | | | 8 | 7 | 10² | 13 | 12 | 11 | 6 | 3 | 9¹ | | | | | | | | | | | | | | | | | | | | | | 3 |
| 1 | 2 | 3 | | 5 | | | 9 | 7 | 11¹ | 14 | 13 | 10³ | 6² | | 8 | 4 | 12 | | | | | | | | | | | | | | | | | | | | 4 |
| 1 | 2 | | 4 | 5² | | | 8 | 7¹ | 13 | 14 | | 10³ | 6 | | 9 | 3 | 11 | 12 | | | | | | | | | | | | | | | | | | | 5 |
| 1 | 2 | 3 | | 5 | 14 | | 7 | 9 | | | 12 | 10³ | 8³ | | 6¹ | 4 | 11 | | | | 13 | | | | | | | | | | | | | | | | 6 |
| 1 | 2 | 3 | | 5 | 12 | 13 | 9³ | 7² | | | 14 | 11 | 8 | | 6¹ | 4 | 10 | | | | | | | | | | | | | | | | | | | | 7 |
| 1 | 2 | 3 | 4 | | 10 | 8³ | 5 | | | 14 | | 9³ | 7¹ | | 6 | | 11 | | | 12 | 13 | | | | | | | | | | | | | | | | 8 |
| 1 | 2³ | 4 | 3 | | 13 | | | 12 | | 10² | | | | | 6 | 14 | 11 | | | 7¹ | 5 | 8 | 9 | | | | | | | | | | | | | | 9 |
| 1 | | 4 | | | 13 | | | | 7³ | 14 | 10¹ | | | | 6 | 3² | 11 | | | | 5 | 8 | 9 | 2 | 12 | | | | | | | | | | | | 10 |
| 1 | 2 | | 4 | | 10 | | | | 7¹ | 12 | | 13 | | | 6 | | 11² | | | | 5 | 8 | 9 | 3 | | | | | | | | | | | | | 11 |
| 1 | 2 | | 4¹ | 13 | 9² | | | | | 11 | | | | | 8 | 12 | 10 | | | | 5 | 6 | 7 | 3 | | | | | | | | | | | | | 12 |
| 1 | 2 | | 4 | 14 | 9 | | | | 13 | 10 | | | 12 | | 6¹ | | 11 | | | | 5³ | 7² | 8 | 3 | | | | | | | | | | | | | 13 |
| 1 | 2 | | 9 | 5¹ | 6 | | 13 | | 14 | 10³ | | | 7 | | 12 | | 11 | | | | 4² | 8 | 3 | | | | | | | | | | | | | | 14 |
| 1 | | 5 | 7 | | | | | 9¹ | 13 | 8 | | 6 | 3 | 11² | | | | | 4 | 10 | 12 | 2 | | | | | | | | | | | | | | | 15 |
| 1 | 5² | 4 | 9 | | | | | 10¹ | | 7 | | 6 | 3 | 11 | | | | | 13 | 8 | 12 | 2 | | | | | | | | | | | | | | | 16 |
| 1 | 5 | 4 | 9² | | | | | 10¹ | 12 | 7 | | 6 | 3 | 11 | 14 | | | | 8³ | 13 | 2 | | | | | | | | | | | | | | | | 17 |
| 1 | 14 | 3 | | | 12 | | | 10 | | 9 | | | 6 | 4 | 11² | 13 | | | | 8¹ | 7 | 2³ | 5 | | | | | | | | | | | | | | 18 |
| 1 | | 3 | | | 12 | | | 10¹ | | 8 | | 6 | 4 | 11 | | | | | 7 | 9 | 2 | 5 | | | | | | | | | | | | | | | 19 |
| 1 | | 3 | | | 12 | | | 10¹ | | 6 | | 8 | 4 | 11 | | | | | 7 | 9 | 2 | 5 | | | | | | | | | | | | | | | 20 |
| 1 | | 3 | 13 | | 14 | 12 | | 10² | | 7 | | 6 | 4 | 11 | | | | | 8³ | 9¹ | 2 | 5 | | | | | | | | | | | | | | | 21 |
| 1 | 12 | 3 | | | 6² | | | 10 | | 8 | | 4 | 11 | 13 | | | | | 9 | 7¹ | 2 | 5 | | | | | | | | | | | | | | | 22 |
| 1 | | 3 | 13 | | | | | 9² | | 10 | | 13 | 8 | 12 | 4 | 11 | | | | 7 | 6¹ | 2 | 5 | | | | | | | | | | | | | | 23 |
| 1 | | 3 | 13 | | 12 | | | 10² | | 7¹ | | 6 | 4 | 11 | | | | | 9 | 8 | 2 | 5 | | | | | | | | | | | | | | | 24 |
| 1 | | 3 | 9 | | 13 | | | 11² | 10¹ | 7 | | 6 | 4 | | | 12 | | | | 8 | 2 | 5 | | | | | | | | | | | | | | | 25 |
| 1 | | 3 | 9¹ | | 14 | | | 10 | | 7² | | 6 | 4 | 11 | | | | | 13 | 8³ | 2 | 5 | 12 | | | | | | | | | | | | | | 26 |
| 1 | 2 | 3 | 7¹ | | | | | 10² | 12 | 8 | | 6³ | 4 | 13 | | | | | 9 | | 5 | 11 | 14 | | | | | | | | | | | | | | 27 |
| 1 | | 3 | 10¹ | | | | | 9 | 12 | 7 | | 6 | 4 | 13 | | | | | 8² | 2 | 5 | 11 | | | | | | | | | | | | | | | 28 |
| 1 | | 3 | 10² | | | | | 9³ | 12 | 7¹ | | 6 | 4 | 14 | | | | | 8 | 13 | 2 | 5 | 11 | | | | | | | | | | | | | | 29 |
| 1 | | 3 | 10¹ | | 12 | | | | | 9 | | 6 | 4 | | | | | | 8 | 7 | 2 | 5 | 11 | | | | | | | | | | | | | | 30 |
| 1 | | 3 | 13 | | | | | 9² | 8¹ | 7 | | 6 | 4 | 12 | | | | | 10 | 2 | 5 | 11 | | | | | | | | | | | | | | | 31 |
| 1 | 12 | 3 | 14 | | | | | 10² | 13 | 7³ | | 6 | 4 | | | | | | 8 | 9 | 2 | 5¹ | 11 | | | | | | | | | | | | | | 32 |
| 1 | | 4 | 13 | | | | | 9² | 11¹ | 7³ | | 6 | | | 14 | | | | 8 | 12 | 2 | 3 | 10 | 5 | | | | | | | | | | | | | 33 |
| 1 | | | 13 | | | | | 9² | 10¹ | 7³ | | 6 | 4 | | | | | | 8 | 12 | 2 | 3 | 11 | 14 | 5 | | | | | | | | | | | | 34 |
| 1 | | | | | | | 14 | | 10¹ | 7 | | 6 | 13 | | | | | | 8 | 9² | 2 | 3 | 11³ | | 5 | 4 | 12 | | | | | | | | | | 35 |
| 1 | | | | | | | 13 | | 10¹ | 8 | | 6 | | | | | | | 7 | 9² | 2 | 3 | 11 | | 5 | 4 | 12 | | | | | | | | | | 36 |
| 1 | | | 12 | | | | | | 9¹ | 7 | | 6² | 4 | | | | | | 8 | 10 | 2 | | 11 | | 5 | 3 | | 13 | | | | | | | | | 37 |
| 1 | | | 13 | | | | | 11 | 10¹ | 8 | | 6 | 4 | | | | | | 7 | 9² | 2 | | 12 | 5 | 3 | | | | | | | | | | | | 38 |
| 1 | | | 13 | | | | | 11¹ | 10³ | 7 | | 6 | 4 | | | | | | 8 | 9² | 2 | | 12 | | 3 | 14 | | 5 | | | | | | | | | 39 |
| 1 | | | 6 | | | | | 11 | 14 | 10² | | 7¹ | | | 3 | | 13 | | 8 | 9 | 4 | | 12 | | 2 | | | | 5³ | | | | | | | | 40 |
| 1 | | | 9³ | | 6 | | | 11¹ | | 7² | | 4 | | | 14 | | 8 | | 10 | 2 | | 12 | | 3 | | 13 | | 5 | | | | | | | | | 41 |
| 1 | 14 | | 9 | | 6² | | | 11¹ | | 13 | | 7 | 4 | | | | 8 | | 10³ | 2 | | 12 | | 3 | | | | 5⁸ | | | | | | | | | 42 |
| 1 | | 4 | 10 | | | | | 13 | | 8 | | 6 | | | | | 7¹ | | 9² | 2 | | 11 | | 3 | 12 | | 5 | | | | | | | | | | 43 |
| 1 | 2 | 3 | 10 | 6¹ | | | | 12 | | | | 8 | | | 7 | | | | 9 | | | 11 | 4 | | 5 | | | | | | | | | | | | 44 |
| 1 | 12 | 4 | 10 | | | | | 13 | | 8³ | | 6 | | | 9 | | | | 2 | | 14 | 3 | 7 | 5¹ | 11² | | | | | | | | | | | | 45 |
| | | 4 | 10 | | | | | 9² | 12 | | | 6 | | | 7 | | 13 | 2 | | 5 | | 11¹ | 3 | 8 | | | | | | | | | | | | 1 | 46 |

**FA Cup**

| | | | |
|---|---|---|---|
| First Round | Arlesey T | (h) | 3-0 |
| Second Round | Morecambe | (h) | 2-1 |
| Third Round | Tottenham H | (a) | 0-3 |

**Capital One Cup**

| | | | |
|---|---|---|---|
| First Round | Dagenham & R | (a) | 1-0 |
| Second Round | Birmingham C | (h) | 3-2 |
| Third Round | Arsenal | (a) | 1-6 |

**Johnstone's Paint Trophy**

| | | | |
|---|---|---|---|
| First Round | Burton | (h) | 0-0 |
| *(aet; won 10-9 on pens)* | | | |
| Second Round | York C | (a) | 4-0 |
| Northern Quarter-Finals | Sheffield U | (h) | 1-1 |
| *(aet; won 4-1 on pens)* | | | |
| Northern Semi-Finals | Preston NE | (h) | 3-2 |
| Northern Final | Crewe Alex | (h) | 0-3 |
| | Crewe Alex | (a) | 2-0 |

# CRAWLEY TOWN

## FOUNDATION

Formed in 1896, Crawley Town initially entered the West Sussex League before switching to the mid-Sussex League in 1901, winning the Second Division in its second season. The club remained at such level until 1951 when it became members of the Sussex County League and five years later moved to the Metropolitan League while remaining as an amateur club. It was not until 1962 that the club turned semi-professional and a year later, joined the Southern League. Many honours came the club's way, but the most successful run was achieved in 2010–11 when they reached the fifith round of the FA Cup and played before a crowd of 74,778 spectators at Old Trafford against Manchester United. Crawley Town spent 48 years at the Town Mead ground before a new site was occupied at Broadfield in 1997, ideally suited to access from the neighbouring motorway. History was also made on 9 April when the team won promotion to the Football League after beating Tamworth 3-0 to stretch their unbeaten League record to 26 games. They finished the season with a Conference record points total of 105 and at the same time, established another milestone for the longest unbeaten run, having extended it to 30 matches by the end of the season.

*Broadfield Stadium, Winfield Way, Crawley, Sussex RH11 9RX.*

*Telephone:* (01293) 410 000.

*Fax:* (01293) 410 002.

*Website:* www.crawleytownfc.com

*Email:* feedback@crawleytownfc.com

*Ground Capacity:* 5,973.

*Record Attendance:* 5,058 v Portsmouth, FL 1, 9 September 2012.

*Pitch Measurements:* 100m × 65m (110yd × 72yd)

*Chairman:* Victor Marley.

*Chief Executive:* Richard Low.

*Manager:* Richie Barker.

*Assistant Manager:* Anthony Williams.

*Physio:* James Barker.

*Club Nickname:* 'The Red Devils'.

*Colours:* Red and white striped shirts, white shorts with red trim, red socks with white trim.

*Year Formed:* 1896.

## MANAGERS

Managers have included:
**Tom Jarvie**
**John Hollins**
**Colin Pates**
**Francis Vines**
**Simon Wormull**
**David Woozley**
**Steve Evans** 2007–12
**Sean O'Driscoll** 2012
**Richie Barker** August 2012–

## sky SPORTS FACT FILE

Tom Jarvie made over 200 appearances for Hamilton Academical between 1936 and 1944, and later served Crawley Town as player-manager in the 1950s. He held a degree in veterinary medicine and was the vet for the *Blue Peter* television programme for many years from the 1960s onwards.

*Turned Professional:* 1962.

*Grounds:* Town Mead to 1997; Broadfield Stadium 1997.

*First Football League Game:* 6 August 2011, FL 2 v Port Vale (a) D 2-2 – Shearer; Hunt, Howell, Bulman, McFadzean (1), Dempster (Thomas), Simpson, Torres, Tubbs (Neilson), Barnett (1) (Wassmer), Smith.

*Record League Victory:* 5-2 v AFC Wimbledon, FL 2, 22 October 2011.

*Record League Defeat:* 6-0 v Morecambe, FL 2, 10 September 2011.

*Most League Points (3 for a win):* 84, FL 2, 2011–12.

*Most League Goals:* 76, FL 2, 2011–12.

*Highest League Scorer in Season:* Tyrone Barnett, 14, 2011–12.

*Most League Appearances:* Dannie Bulman, 77, 2011–13.

*Most League Goals in Total Aggregate:* Tyrone Barnett, 14, 2011–12.

*Youngest League Player:* Jonte Smith, 18 years 162 days v Bournemouth, 29 December 2012.

*Record Transfer Fee Received:* £1,100,000 from Peterborough U for Tyrone Barnett, July 2012.

*Record Transfer Fee Paid:* £100,000 to Peterborough U for Sergio Raul Torres, July 2010.

*Football League Record:* 2011–12 FL 2; 2012– FL 1.

## LATEST SEQUENCES

*Longest Sequence of League Wins:* 7, 17.9.2011 – 25.10.2011.

*Longest Sequence of League Defeats:* 2, 10.9.2011 – 13.9.2011; 27.2.2012 – 3.3.2012; 20.11.2012 – 24.11.2012.

*Longest Sequence of League Draws:* 4, 5.3.2013 – 16.3.2013.

*Longest Sequence of Unbeaten League Matches:* 13, 17.9.2011 – 17.12.2011

*Longest Sequence Without a League Win:* 7, 14.2.2012 – 13.3.2012; 27.10.2012 – 8.12.2012.

*Successive Scoring Runs:* 16 from 17.9.2011 – 2.1.2012.

*Successive Non-scoring Runs:* 2 from 10.9.2011 – 13.9.2011; 20.11.2012 – 24.11.2012; 1.4.2013 – 6.4.2013.

## HONOURS

**Football League – FL 2:** Best season: 3rd (promoted) 2011–12.

**FA Cup:** Best season: 5th rd 2011, 2012.

**Football League Cup:** Best season: 3rd rd 2013.

**Blue Square Premier:** *Champions* 2010–11.

**Southern League:** *Champions* 2003–04.

**Southern League Cup:** *Winners* 2003, 2004.

**Southern League Championship Trophy:** *Winners* 2004, 2005.

**Southern League Merit Cup:** *Winners* 1971.

**Sussex Professional Cup:** *Winners* 1970.

**Sussex Senior Cup:** *Winners* 1990, 1991, 2003, 2005.

**Sussex Intermediate Cup:** *Winners* 1928.

**Sussex Floodlit Cup:** *Winners* 1991, 1992, 1993, 1999.

**Southern Counties Floodlit League:** *Champions* 1985–86.

**Mid-Sussex Senior League:** *Champions* 1902–03.

**Montgomery Cup:** *Winners* 1926.

**Gilbert Rice Floodlit Cup:** *Winners* 1980, 1984.

**Roy Hayden Trophy:** *Winners* 1991, 1992.

**William Hill Senior Cup:** *Winners* 1993.

**Metropolitan League Challenge Cup:** *Winners* 1959.

**Highest Placed Amateur Award:** 1961–62.

**FA Ronnie Radford Award:** 2011.

## TEN YEAR LEAGUE RECORD

|         |       | P  | W  | D  | L  | F  | A  | Pts | Pos |
|---------|-------|----|----|----|----|----|----|-----|-----|
| 2003-04 | S PR  | 42 | 25 | 9  | 8  | 77 | 43 | 84  | 1   |
| 2004-05 | Conf  | 42 | 16 | 9  | 17 | 50 | 50 | 57  | 12  |
| 2005-06 | Conf  | 42 | 12 | 11 | 19 | 48 | 55 | 44  | 17  |
| 2006-07 | Conf  | 46 | 17 | 12 | 17 | 52 | 52 | 53  | 18  |
| 2007-08 | BSP   | 46 | 19 | 9  | 18 | 73 | 67 | 60  | 15  |
| 2008-09 | BSP   | 46 | 19 | 14 | 13 | 77 | 55 | 70  | 9   |
| 2009-10 | BSP   | 44 | 19 | 9  | 16 | 50 | 57 | 66  | 7   |
| 2010-11 | BSP   | 46 | 31 | 12 | 3  | 93 | 50 | 105 | 1   |
| 2011-12 | FL 2  | 46 | 23 | 15 | 8  | 76 | 54 | 84  | 3   |
| 2012-13 | FL 1  | 46 | 18 | 14 | 14 | 59 | 58 | 68  | 10  |

## DID YOU KNOW ?

Crawley Town reached the third round of the FA Cup for the first time in the 1991–92 season. They defeated Molesey, Sheppey United, Erith & Belvedere, Horsham, Northampton Town and Hayes before going down 5-0 to near neighbours Brighton & Hove Albion in front of 18,031 fans.

## CRAWLEY TOWN – FOOTBALL LEAGUE ONE 2012–13 LEAGUE RECORD

| Match No. | Date | Venue | Opponents | Result | H/T Score | Lg Pos. | Goalscorers | Attendance |
|---|---|---|---|---|---|---|---|---|
| 1 | Aug 18 | H | Scunthorpe U | W | 3-0 | 1-0 | 1 | Alexander 2 (1 pen) [33, 64 (p)], Forte [80] | 3172 |
| 2 | 21 | A | Swindon T | L | 0-3 | 0-2 | 9 | | 7658 |
| 3 | 25 | A | Doncaster R | W | 1-0 | 0-0 | 7 | Ajose [87] | 6403 |
| 4 | Sept 1 | H | Leyton Orient | W | 1-0 | 0-0 | 4 | Ajose [72] | 4287 |
| 5 | 9 | H | Portsmouth | L | 0-3 | 0-0 | 6 | | 5058 |
| 6 | 15 | A | Preston NE | W | 2-1 | 0-0 | 4 | Alexander 2 [54, 58] | 9812 |
| 7 | 18 | A | Colchester U | D | 1-1 | 0-0 | 4 | McFadzean [71] | 2484 |
| 8 | 22 | H | Tranmere R | L | 2-5 | 2-2 | 8 | Simpson [12], McFadzean [16] | 3099 |
| 9 | 29 | A | Carlisle U | W | 2-0 | 0-0 | 7 | Byrne [64], Adams [73] | 4221 |
| 10 | Oct 2 | H | Bournemouth | W | 3-1 | 2-0 | 3 | Akpan [31], Walsh [45], Adams [62] | 2928 |
| 11 | 6 | A | Brentford | L | 1-2 | 0-1 | 6 | Adams [59] | 5607 |
| 12 | 13 | H | Bury | W | 3-2 | 1-0 | 4 | Adams 2 [43, 90], Akpan [53] | 3300 |
| 13 | 20 | A | Hartlepool U | W | 1-0 | 1-0 | 4 | Akpan [15] | 3852 |
| 14 | 23 | H | Milton Keynes D | W | 2-0 | 1-0 | 4 | Clarke 2 [21, 90] | 2853 |
| 15 | 27 | H | Oldham Ath | D | 1-1 | 0-0 | 2 | McFadzean [79] | 3375 |
| 16 | Nov 6 | A | Coventry C | L | 1-3 | 0-2 | 4 | Clarke [56] | 8862 |
| 17 | 10 | A | Notts Co | D | 1-1 | 1-1 | 4 | Forte [45] | 5685 |
| 18 | 17 | H | Walsall | D | 2-2 | 1-1 | 6 | Clarke [22], Forte [81] | 3039 |
| 19 | 20 | H | Yeovil T | L | 0-1 | 0-0 | 9 | | 2912 |
| 20 | 24 | A | Crewe Alex | L | 0-2 | 0-0 | 9 | | 5236 |
| 21 | Dec 8 | H | Shrewsbury T | D | 2-2 | 1-2 | 10 | Simpson 2 [1, 81] | 2770 |
| 22 | 15 | A | Stevenage | W | 2-1 | 0-0 | 10 | Akpan [65], Bulman [69] | 3066 |
| 23 | 22 | H | Sheffield U | L | 0-2 | 0-1 | 10 | | 4604 |
| 24 | 26 | A | Portsmouth | W | 2-1 | 1-1 | 8 | Adams [28], Clarke [73] | 13,169 |
| 25 | 29 | A | Bournemouth | L | 0-3 | 0-2 | 8 | | 7855 |
| 26 | Jan 1 | H | Colchester U | W | 3-0 | 1-0 | 8 | Connolly [5], Clarke [71], Adams [87] | 3160 |
| 27 | 12 | A | Tranmere R | L | 0-2 | 0-2 | 9 | | 5011 |
| 28 | Feb 2 | H | Swindon T | D | 1-1 | 1-0 | 14 | Clarke (pen) [23] | 3558 |
| 29 | 9 | A | Scunthorpe U | L | 1-2 | 0-0 | 15 | Sparrow [48] | 3124 |
| 30 | 18 | H | Doncaster R | D | 1-1 | 1-1 | 14 | Simpson [25] | 3267 |
| 31 | 23 | A | Leyton Orient | W | 1-0 | 1-0 | 12 | Clarke [11] | 3463 |
| 32 | 26 | H | Brentford | L | 1-2 | 0-2 | 14 | Adams [66] | 2544 |
| 33 | Mar 2 | A | Bury | W | 2-0 | 1-0 | 12 | Proctor 2 [17, 48] | 2491 |
| 34 | 5 | H | Carlisle U | D | 1-1 | 0-1 | 12 | Sadler [56] | 2654 |
| 35 | 9 | H | Notts Co | D | 0-0 | 0-0 | 13 | | 3689 |
| 36 | 12 | A | Yeovil T | D | 2-2 | 0-2 | 12 | Walsh [46], Sparrow [62] | 3338 |
| 37 | 16 | A | Walsall | D | 2-2 | 0-0 | 13 | Proctor [52], Hayes [71] | 5003 |
| 38 | 26 | H | Crewe Alex | W | 2-0 | 0-0 | 12 | Proctor 2 [77, 78] | 2544 |
| 39 | 29 | H | Stevenage | D | 1-1 | 0-1 | 12 | Sparrow [55] | 3395 |
| 40 | Apr 1 | A | Shrewsbury T | L | 0-3 | 0-0 | 13 | | 5196 |
| 41 | 6 | A | Milton Keynes D | D | 0-0 | 0-0 | 12 | | 7746 |
| 42 | 9 | A | Sheffield U | W | 2-0 | 0-0 | 11 | Clarke [77], Hayes [84] | 18,680 |
| 43 | 13 | H | Coventry C | W | 2-0 | 1-0 | 11 | Clarke [15], Essam [60] | 3900 |
| 44 | 20 | A | Oldham Ath | L | 1-2 | 0-0 | 12 | Connolly [77] | 4794 |
| 45 | 23 | H | Preston NE | W | 1-0 | 1-0 | 10 | Jones, M [6] | 3026 |
| 46 | 27 | H | Hartlepool U | D | 2-2 | 0-0 | 10 | Proctor 2 [70, 89] | 4100 |

**Final League Position: 10**

### GOALSCORERS

*League (59):* Clarke 10 (1 pen), Adams 8, Proctor 7, Akpan 4, Alexander 4 (1 pen), Simpson 4, Forte 3, McFadzean 3, Sparrow 3, Ajose 2, Connolly 2, Hayes 2, Walsh 2, Bulman 1, Byrne 1, Essam 1, Jones, M 1, Sadler 1.
*FA Cup (6):* Adams 2, Clarke 2, Alexander 1 (1 pen), Simpson 1.
*Capital One Cup (6):* Akpan 2, Adams 1, Ajose 1, Clarke 1, Simpson 1.
*Johnstone's Paint Trophy (3):* Clarke 1, Neilson 1, Walsh 1.

| Jones P 46 | Connolly M 25+8 | McFadzean K 17 | Davis C 16 | Sadler M 46 | Simpson J 30+6 | Akpan H 21 | Bulman D 26+10 | Adams N 45+1 | Alexander G 25+2 | Clarke B 28+8 | Forte J 4+8 | Torres S 7+16 | Ajose N 10+9 | Cooper S 5+3 | Hunt D 19+4 | Jones M 35+5 | Walsh J 27+3 | Byrne N 11+1 | Akinde J —+6 | Clifford C —+1 | Smith J —+4 | Sparrow M 13+4 | Elford-Alliyu L —+6 | Dumbuya M 14+1 | Proctor J 15+3 | O'Brien A —+9 | Essam C 8+1 | Taylor J 4 | Hayes P 9+2 | Match No. |
|---|---|---|---|---|---|---|---|---|---|---|---|---|---|---|---|---|---|---|---|---|---|---|---|---|---|---|---|---|---|---|
| 1 | 2 | 3 | 4 | 5 | 6 | 7 | $8^2$ | $9^3$ | 10 | $11^1$ | 12 | 13 | 14 | | | | | | | | | | | | | | | | | 1 |
| 1 | 2 | 3 | $4^3$ | 5 | 7 | 6 | $8^1$ | 9 | 11 | $10^2$ | 12 | | | 13 | 14 | | | | | | | | | | | | | | | 2 |
| 1 | | | 4 | $3^1$ | 5 | 12 | 8 | 13 | 6 | 11 | | | | | 9 | $10^2$ | 7 | 2 | | | | | | | | | | | | 3 |
| 1 | | 3 | $4^1$ | 2 | 8 | 7 | | 6 | 11 | $10^2$ | 14 | | | | $9^3$ | 12 | 5 | 13 | | | | | | | | | | | | 4 |
| 1 | 13 | 4 | | 5 | $8^2$ | $7^8$ | 12 | 6 | 11 | | | | | | $10^2$ | 3 | 2 | $9^1$ | | | | | | | | | | | | 5 |
| 1 | 8 | 4 | | 5 | | 7 | | 6 | 10 | 12 | | | | | $11^1$ | 3 | 2 | $9^2$ | 13 | | | | | | | | | | | 6 |
| 1 | 4 | 3 | | 5 | 12 | 7 | | 6 | 10 | 13 | | | | | $11^2$ | $8^1$ | 2 | 9 | | | | | | | | | | | | 7 |
| 1 | 3 | 4 | | 2 | 8 | 7 | 13 | $6^3$ | 11 | 12 | 14 | | | | 10 | | $5^1$ | $9^2$ | | | | | | | | | | | | 8 |
| 1 | | 3 | 5 | 8 | | 7 | 12 | 9 | 11 | | | 13 | | | $10^2$ | | | $6^1$ | 4 | 2 | | | | | | | | | | 9 |
| 1 | 12 | | $4^1$ | 2 | 9 | 7 | 14 | 6 | 11 | | | 13 | | | $10^2$ | | | $8^3$ | 3 | 5 | | | | | | | | | | 10 |
| 1 | | 3 | | 5 | $6^2$ | 7 | | 9 | 10 | 12 | 11 | | 13 | | | | | $8^1$ | 4 | 2 | | | | | | | | | | 11 |
| 1 | | 4 | | 2 | 9 | 8 | | 6 | 10 | 13 | 12 | $11^2$ | | | | | | $7^1$ | 3 | 5 | | | | | | | | | | 12 |
| 1 | 13 | $3^2$ | 4 | 2 | 9 | $7^3$ | 14 | 6 | 10 | 12 | $11^1$ | | | | | 8 | | 5 | | | | | | | | | | | | 13 |
| 1 | 13 | 3 | 4 | 2 | 9 | $8^2$ | $7^1$ | 6 | 11 | $10^3$ | 12 | | | | | 14 | | 5 | | | | | | | | | | | | 14 |
| 1 | | 3 | 4 | 2 | 8 | $7^8$ | | 6 | 11 | $10^1$ | 13 | 12 | 14 | | | $9^2$ | | $5^3$ | | | | | | | | | | | | 15 |
| 1 | | 3 | 4 | 5 | 8 | | $7^1$ | 9 | $11^2$ | 10 | | 12 | | | 2 | 6 | | | 13 | | | | | | | | | | | 16 |
| 1 | | 3 | 4 | 5 | 8 | | 7 | 9 | 12 | $10^2$ | $11^1$ | 13 | | | 6 | | | 2 | | | | | | | | | | | | 17 |
| 1 | 14 | | 3 | 2 | 7 | | 8 | 9 | 13 | $11^1$ | $10^3$ | | 12 | | | $6^2$ | $4^8$ | 5 | | | | | | | | | | | | 18 |
| 1 | 4 | $3^1$ | | 2 | 7 | 8 | | 6 | 11 | 10 | | 13 | | | 12 | $9^2$ | | 5 | | | | | | | | | | | | 19 |
| 1 | 3 | $4^1$ | | 2 | 7 | | 9 | 11 | 10 | | 13 | | | | $6^2$ | 12 | $2^2$ | 14 | | | | | | | | | | | | 20 |
| 1 | 3 | | 4 | 2 | 7 | 8 | 12 | $9^3$ | 11 | | $6^2$ | $10^1$ | | | 5 | 14 | | 13 | | | | | | | | | | | | 21 |
| 1 | 4 | | $3^1$ | 2 | 10 | 9 | 6 | $7^2$ | 11 | | 5 | 8 | 12 | | | | | 13 | | | | | | | | | | | | 22 |
| 1 | 4 | | 2 | 8 | 9 | $7^1$ | 6 | $11^2$ | 12 | | 14 | | | | $5^3$ | 10 | 3 | 13 | | | | | | | | | | | | 23 |
| 1 | 4 | 3 | 5 | 9 | 6 | 12 | $10^2$ | $11^3$ | $7^1$ | | 13 | 2 | 8 | | | | | 14 | | | | | | | | | | | | 24 |
| 1 | 4 | 3 | 5 | 8 | | 7 | $6^2$ | 11 | 12 | | | $9^1$ | 2 | $10^3$ | | | | 14 | 13 | | | | | | | | | | | 25 |
| 1 | 4 | | 2 | 7 | 8 | 13 | 6 | $11^3$ | $10^2$ | | 5 | $9^1$ | 3 | 12 | | | | 14 | | | | | | | | | | | | 26 |
| 1 | 5 | | 3 | 7 | | $8^1$ | $6^2$ | 10 | 11 | | 2 | $9^3$ | 4 | | | | | 14 | 12 | 13 | | | | | | | | | | 27 |
| 1 | 3 | | 5 | 8 | | | 6 | $10^1$ | 13 | | $9^2$ | 4 | | | | | | 7 | 12 | | 2 | 11 | | | | | | | | 28 |
| 1 | 3 | | $5^3$ | 8 | | | 6 | 10 | 12 | | $9^4$ | 4 | | | | | | 14 | 7 | 13 | $2$ | $11^2$ | | | | | | | | 29 |
| 1 | 3 | | 5 | $6^1$ | | 7 | 9 | 10 | 12 | | 4 | | | | | | | 8 | | | 2 | 11 | | | | | | | | 30 |
| 1 | 3 | | 5 | | | 8 | $9^2$ | $10^1$ | 12 | | 6 | 4 | | | | | | 7 | | | 2 | 11 | 13 | | | | | | | 31 |
| 1 | $3^8$ | | $5^1$ | | | 7 | 9 | $10^2$ | | | $6^1$ | 4 | | | | | | 8 | 14 | | 2 | 11 | 13 | 12 | | | | | | 32 |
| 1 | | | 5 | | | 6 | $10^9$ | | 12 | | 14 | $8^1$ | 3 | | | | | 7 | | | 2 | $11^2$ | 13 | 4 | 9 | | | | | 33 |
| 1 | | | 5 | | | 8 | 9 | | 13 | | $6^2$ | 4 | | | | | | 7 | | | 2 | 10 | 12 | 3 | $11^1$ | | | | | 34 |
| 1 | | | 5 | | | $7^2$ | $8^3$ | | 13 | | $6^1$ | 4 | | | | | | 10 | 14 | | 2 | 11 | 12 | 3 | 9 | | | | | 35 |
| 1 | | | 5 | | | 8 | 12 | $9^3$ | $6^1$ | | 14 | 3 | | | | | | 7 | | | 2 | $10^3$ | 13 | 4 | | 11 | | | | 36 |
| 1 | | | 5 | | | 12 | 6 | $9^2$ | | | 13 | 4 | | | | | | 7 | | | 2 | $10^3$ | 14 | 3 | $8^1$ | 11 | | | | 37 |
| 1 | 3 | | 5 | 12 | $8^1$ | 9 | $6^3$ | 14 | | | 13 | 4 | | | | | | 7 | | | $2^2$ | 11 | | | 10 | | | | 38 |
| 1 | 3 | | $5^3$ | $7^2$ | 9 | 12 | 13 | | | | $6^1$ | 4 | | | | | | 8 | 14 | | 2 | 10 | | | 11 | | | | 39 |
| 1 | 4 | | 5 | 12 | 8 | 9 | 6 | 13 | | | 3 | | | | | | | $7^1$ | | | $2^2$ | $10^3$ | 14 | | 11 | | | | 40 |
| 1 | 14 | | 3 | | | 8 | $9^2$ | 11 | 6 | | 13 | $7^3$ | 4 | | | | | | | | 2 | 12 | | 5 | | $10^1$ | | | 41 |
| 1 | 13 | | 5 | | | 8 | 6 | $10^2$ | $7^3$ | | 2 | 9 | 3 | | | | | $11^1$ | 14 | 4 | | 12 | | | | | | | | 42 |
| 1 | 12 | | 5 | 13 | | 7 | $6^3$ | $10^2$ | 8 | | 2 | 9 | 4 | | | | | 14 | | | | $3^1$ | | | 11 | | | | 43 |
| 1 | 3 | | 5 | 13 | $7^2$ | 9 | 11 | $8^1$ | | | 2 | $6^3$ | 4 | | | | | 14 | | | | 12 | | | 10 | | | | 44 |
| 1 | 3 | | 5 | 8 | 7 | $9^3$ | $10^2$ | 14 | | | 2 | 6 | 4 | | | | | 13 | | | | 12 | | | $11^1$ | | | | 45 |
| 1 | 4 | | 2 | 7 | $8^2$ | $6^1$ | 10 | | | | 5 | 9 | 3 | | | | | 13 | | | | 11 | | | 12 | | | | 46 |

**FA Cup**

| | | | | |
|---|---|---|---|---|
| First Round | Metropolitan Police | (a) | 2-1 | |
| Second Round | Chelmsford | (h) | 3-0 | |
| Third Round | Reading | (h) | 1-3 | |

**Capital One Cup**

| | | | | |
|---|---|---|---|---|
| First Round | Millwall | (a) | 2-2 | |
| *(aet; won 4-1 on pens)* | | | | |
| Second Round | Bolton W | (h) | 2-1 | |
| Third Round | Swansea C | (h) | 2-3 | |

**Johnstone's Paint Trophy**

| | | | |
|---|---|---|---|
| First Round | Gillingham | (h) | 3-2 |
| Second Round | Brentford | (a) | 0-1 |

# CREWE ALEXANDRA

## FOUNDATION

The first match played at Crewe was on 1 December 1877 against Basford, the leading North Staffordshire team of that time. During the club's history they have also played in a number of other leagues including the Football Alliance, Football Combination, Lancashire League, Manchester League, Central League and Lancashire Combination. Two former players, Aaron Scragg in 1899 and Jackie Pearson in 1911, had the distinction of refereeing FA Cup finals. Pearson was also capped for England against Ireland in 1892.

*The Alexandra Stadium, Gresty Road, Crewe, Cheshire CW2 6EB.*

*Telephone:* (01270) 213 014.

*Fax:* (01270) 216 320.

*Ticket Office:* (01270) 252 610.

*Website:* www.crewealex.net

*Email:* info@crewealex.net

*Ground Capacity:* 10,109.

*Record Attendance:* 20,000 v Tottenham H, FA Cup 4th rd, 30 January 1960.

*Pitch Measurements:* 91m × 60m (100yd × 66yd)

*Chairman:* John Bowler.

*Vice-chairman:* David Rowlinson.

*Manager:* Steve Davis.

*Assistant Manager:* Neil Baker.

*Physio:* Rob Sharp.

*Colours:* Red shirts, white shorts, red socks.

*Year Formed:* 1877. *Turned Professional:* 1893.

*Club Nickname:* 'The Railwaymen'.

*Ground:* 1898, Gresty Road.

## HONOURS

**Football League – Division 2:** *Runners-up* 2002–03.

**FA Cup:** Semi-final 1888.

**Football League Cup:** never past 3rd round.

**Welsh Cup:** *Winners* 1936, 1937.

**Johnstone's Paint Trophy:** *Winners* 2013.

*First Football League Game:* 3 September 1892, Division 2, v Burton Swifts (a) L 1–7 – Hickton; Moore, Cope; Linnell, Johnson, Osborne; Bennett, Pearson (1), Bailey, Barnett, Roberts.

*Record League Victory:* 8–0 v Rotherham U, Division 3 (N), 1 October 1932 – Foster; Pringle, Dawson; Ward, Keenor (1), Turner (1); Gillespie, Swindells (1), McConnell (2), Deacon (2), Weale (1).

*Record Cup Victory:* 8–0 v Hartlepool U, Auto Windscreens Shield 1st rd, 17 October 1995 – Gayle; Collins (1), Booty, Westwood (Unsworth), Macauley (1), Whalley (1), Garvey (1), Murphy (1), Savage (1) (Rivers (1p)), Lennon, Edwards, (1 og). 8–0 v Doncaster R, LDV Vans Trophy 3rd rd, 10 November 2002 – Bankole; Wright, Walker, Foster, Tierney; Lunt (1), Brammer, Sorvel, Vaughan (1) (Bell); Ashton (3) (Miles), Jack (2) (Jones (1)).

## sky SPORTS FACT FILE

Crewe Alexandra had to seek re-election to the Football League on a total of 13 occasions before automatic promotion and relegation was introduced in 1986–87. The Railwaymen were successful on all but one occasion, 1895–96.

*Record Defeat:* 2–13 v Tottenham H, FA Cup 4th rd replay, 3 February 1960.

*Most League Points (2 for a win):* 59, Division 4, 1962–63.

*Most League Points (3 for a win):* 86, Division 2, 2002–03.

*Most League Goals:* 95, Division 3 (N), 1931–32.

*Highest League Scorer in Season:* Terry Harkin, 35, Division 4, 1964–65.

*Most League Goals in Total Aggregate:* Bert Swindells, 126, 1928–37.

*Most League Goals in One Match:* 5, Tony Naylor v Colchester U, Division 3, 24 April 1993.

*Most Capped Player:* Clayton Ince, 38 (79), Trinidad & Tobago.

*Most League Appearances:* Tommy Lowry, 436, 1966–78.

*Youngest League Player:* Steve Walters, 16 years 119 days v Peterborough U, 6 May 1988.

*Record Transfer Fee Received:* £4,000,000 from Derby Co for Seth Johnson, May 1999 (including sell-on).

*Record Transfer Fee Paid:* £650,000 to Torquay U for Rodney Jack, June 1998.

*Football League Record:* 1892 Original Member of Division 2; 1896 Failed re-election; 1921 Re-entered Division (N); 1958–63 Division 4; 1963–64 Division 3; 1964–68 Division 4; 1968–69 Division 3; 1969–89 Division 4; 1989–91 Division 3; 1991–92 Division 4; 1992–94 Division 3; 1994–97 Division 2; 1997–2002 Division 1; 2002–03 Division 2; 2003–04 Division 1; 2004–06 FL C; 2006–09 FL 1; 2009–12 FL 2; 2012– FL 1.

## LATEST SEQUENCES

*Longest Sequence of League Wins:* 7, 30.4.1994 – 3.9.1994.

*Longest Sequence of League Defeats:* 10, 16.4.1979 – 22.8.1979.

*Longest Sequence of League Draws:* 5, 31.8.1987 – 18.9.1987; 1.9.2012 – 22.9.2012.

*Longest Sequence of Unbeaten League Matches:* 17, 25.3.1995 – 16.9.1995.

*Longest Sequence Without a League Win:* 30, 22.9.1956 – 6.4.1957.

*Successive Scoring Runs:* 26 from 7.4.1934.

*Successive Non-scoring Runs:* 9 from 6.11.1974.

## MANAGERS

**W. C. McNeill** 1892–94
 (*Secretary-Manager*)
**J. G. Hall** 1895–96
 (*Secretary-Manager*)
**R. Roberts** (*1st team Secretary-Manager*) 1897
**J. B. Blomerley** 1898–1911
 (*Secretary-Manager, continued as Hon. Secretary to 1925*)
**Tom Bailey** (*Secretary only*) 1925–38
**George Lillycrop** (*Trainer*) 1938–44
**Frank Hill** 1944–48
**Arthur Turner** 1948–51
**Harry Catterick** 1951–53
**Ralph Ward** 1953–55
**Maurice Lindley** 1956–57
**Willie Cook** 1957–58
**Harry Ware** 1958–60
**Jimmy McGuigan** 1960–64
**Ernie Tagg** 1964–71
 (*continued as Secretary to 1972*)
**Dennis Viollet** 1971
**Jimmy Melia** 1972–74
**Ernie Tagg** 1974
**Harry Gregg** 1975–78
**Warwick Rimmer** 1978–79
**Tony Waddington** 1979–81
**Arfon Griffiths** 1981–82
**Peter Morris** 1982–83
**Dario Gradi** 1983–2007
**Steve Holland** 2007–08
**Gudjon Thordarson** 2008–09
**Dario Gradi** 2009–11
**Steve Davis** October 2011–

## TEN YEAR LEAGUE RECORD

| | | P | W | D | L | F | A | Pts | Pos |
|---|---|---|---|---|---|---|---|---|---|
| 2003-04 | Div 1 | 46 | 14 | 11 | 21 | 57 | 66 | 53 | 18 |
| 2004-05 | FL C | 46 | 12 | 14 | 20 | 66 | 86 | 50 | 21 |
| 2005-06 | FL C | 46 | 9 | 15 | 22 | 57 | 86 | 42 | 22 |
| 2006-07 | FL 1 | 46 | 17 | 9 | 20 | 66 | 72 | 60 | 13 |
| 2007-08 | FL 1 | 46 | 12 | 14 | 20 | 47 | 65 | 50 | 20 |
| 2008-09 | FL 1 | 46 | 12 | 10 | 24 | 59 | 82 | 46 | 22 |
| 2009-10 | FL 2 | 46 | 15 | 10 | 21 | 68 | 73 | 55 | 18 |
| 2010-11 | FL 2 | 46 | 18 | 11 | 17 | 87 | 65 | 65 | 10 |
| 2011-12 | FL 2 | 46 | 20 | 12 | 14 | 67 | 59 | 72 | 7 |
| 2012-13 | FL 1 | 46 | 18 | 10 | 18 | 54 | 62 | 64 | 13 |

## DID YOU KNOW

Crewe Alexandra's first-ever FA Cup tie took place against Queen's Park on 6 October 1883. The Glasgow club won a very uneven affair 10-0 in front of an estimated attendance of 2,000. Scottish clubs regularly entered the competition before the Scottish FA issued a ban in 1887.

## CREWE ALEXANDRA – FOOTBALL LEAGUE ONE 2012–13 LEAGUE RECORD

| Match No. | Date | Venue | Opponents | Result | H/T Score | Lg Pos. | Goalscorers | Atten- dance |
|---|---|---|---|---|---|---|---|---|
| 1 | Aug 18 | H | Notts Co | L 1-2 | 0-1 | 19 | Pogba [73] | 5718 |
| 2 | 21 | A | Scunthorpe U | W 2-1 | 1-1 | 10 | Leitch-Smith [1], Murphy [73] | 3215 |
| 3 | 25 | A | Brentford | L 1-5 | 0-3 | 17 | Pogba [48] | 4858 |
| 4 | Sept 1 | H | Coventry C | W 1-0 | 1-0 | 10 | Clayton, M [24] | 5738 |
| 5 | 8 | H | Tranmere R | D 0-0 | 0-0 | 13 | | 5740 |
| 6 | 15 | A | Stevenage | D 2-2 | 2-1 | 14 | Leitch-Smith 2 [6, 8] | 2826 |
| 7 | 18 | A | Carlisle U | D 0-0 | 0-0 | 15 | | 3519 |
| 8 | 22 | H | Leyton Orient | D 1-1 | 1-1 | 15 | Tootle [2] | 5183 |
| 9 | 29 | A | Milton Keynes D | L 0-1 | 0-1 | 15 | | 11,037 |
| 10 | Oct 2 | H | Oldham Ath | L 0-2 | 0-0 | 18 | | 3935 |
| 11 | 6 | H | Hartlepool U | W 2-1 | 1-1 | 15 | Aneke [45], Ellis [70] | 4375 |
| 12 | 13 | A | Portsmouth | L 0-2 | 0-2 | 18 | | 11,829 |
| 13 | 20 | A | Walsall | D 2-2 | 1-2 | 19 | Ellis [44], Aneke [90] | 3836 |
| 14 | 23 | H | Swindon T | W 2-1 | 2-1 | 16 | Moore 2 [29, 41] | 4010 |
| 15 | 27 | H | Yeovil T | L 0-1 | 0-1 | 18 | | 4176 |
| 16 | Nov 6 | A | Doncaster R | W 2-0 | 1-0 | 14 | Dalla Valle [5], Pogba [71] | 5411 |
| 17 | 10 | H | Colchester U | W 3-2 | 0-2 | 13 | Dalla Valle [51], Murphy (pen) [64], Pogba [74] | 4292 |
| 18 | 17 | A | Shrewsbury T | L 0-1 | 0-1 | 14 | | 6169 |
| 19 | 20 | A | Sheffield U | D 3-3 | 2-2 | 14 | Ellis [42], Pogba [45], Aneke [47] | 16,000 |
| 20 | 24 | H | Crawley T | W 2-0 | 0-0 | 14 | Dalla Valle 2 [62, 65] | 5236 |
| 21 | Dec 8 | A | Preston NE | W 3-1 | 1-0 | 12 | Murphy [32], Inman [49], Pogba [52] | 8542 |
| 22 | 15 | H | Bury | W 1-0 | 0-0 | 11 | Inman [88] | 4648 |
| 23 | 26 | A | Tranmere R | L 1-2 | 1-0 | 13 | Inman [12] | 7252 |
| 24 | 29 | A | Oldham Ath | W 2-1 | 0-0 | 13 | Pogba [61], Ellis [84] | 3451 |
| 25 | Jan 1 | H | Carlisle U | W 1-0 | 1-0 | 10 | Dalla Valle [44] | 4802 |
| 26 | 5 | H | Stevenage | L 1-2 | 1-0 | 11 | Aneke [32] | 4262 |
| 27 | 12 | A | Leyton Orient | D 1-1 | 1-1 | 10 | Moore [39] | 3755 |
| 28 | 26 | A | Bournemouth | L 1-3 | 0-1 | 13 | Colclough [76] | 8628 |
| 29 | Feb 2 | H | Scunthorpe U | W 1-0 | 0-0 | 12 | Leitch-Smith [75] | 4302 |
| 30 | 9 | A | Notts Co | D 1-1 | 1-0 | 12 | Murphy (pen) [45] | 5450 |
| 31 | 12 | H | Bournemouth | L 1-2 | 0-0 | 13 | Pogba [79] | 4005 |
| 32 | 23 | A | Coventry C | W 2-1 | 1-1 | 11 | Ellis [16], Clayton, M [78] | 10,139 |
| 33 | 26 | A | Hartlepool U | L 0-3 | 0-2 | 11 | | 3509 |
| 34 | Mar 2 | H | Portsmouth | L 1-2 | 0-2 | 14 | Pogba [63] | 5120 |
| 35 | 9 | A | Colchester U | W 2-1 | 1-1 | 14 | Murphy (pen) [25], Pogba [72] | 3085 |
| 36 | 16 | H | Shrewsbury T | D 1-1 | 1-1 | 14 | Moore [10] | 5106 |
| 37 | 19 | H | Milton Keynes D | W 2-1 | 1-1 | 13 | Pogba 2 [40, 84] | 3770 |
| 38 | 26 | A | Crawley T | L 0-2 | 0-0 | 14 | | 2544 |
| 39 | 29 | A | Bury | D 2-2 | 1-0 | 13 | Clayton, M [28], Inman [83] | 2749 |
| 40 | Apr 1 | H | Preston NE | W 1-0 | 1-0 | 12 | Inman [32] | 6366 |
| 41 | 10 | H | Brentford | L 0-2 | 0-1 | 13 | | 4594 |
| 42 | 13 | H | Doncaster R | L 1-2 | 0-0 | 13 | Clayton, M [54] | 5465 |
| 43 | 16 | A | Swindon T | L 1-4 | 0-3 | 13 | Davis (pen) [65] | 7169 |
| 44 | 20 | A | Yeovil T | L 0-1 | 0-1 | 14 | | 5293 |
| 45 | 23 | H | Sheffield U | W 1-0 | 0-0 | 13 | Aneke [49] | 5379 |
| 46 | 27 | H | Walsall | W 2-0 | 0-0 | 13 | Murphy (pen) [78], Aneke [85] | 6547 |

**Final League Position: 13**

### GOALSCORERS

*League (54):* Pogba 12, Aneke 6, Murphy 6 (4 pens), Dalla Valle 5, Ellis 5, Inman 5, Clayton, M 4, Leitch-Smith 4, Moore 4, Colclough 1, Davis 1 (1 pen), Tootle 1.
*FA Cup (4):* Aneke 1, Ellis 1, Murphy 1, Pogba 1.
*Capital One Cup (5):* Clayton M 2, Pogba 2, Leitch-Smith 1.
*Johnstone's Paint Trophy (12):* Clayton M 3, Inman 3, Murphy 2, Aneke 1, Leitch-Smith 1, Pogba 1, own goal 1.

| Martin A 25+1 | Davis H 42 | Ellis M 43+1 | Dugdale A 14+4 | Robertson G 25+4 | Pogba M 31+3 | Westwood A 3 | Osman A 37+1 | Moore B 35+6 | Leitch-Smith A 25+3 | Clayton M 22+13 | Murphy L 38+1 | Mellor K 33+2 | Bunn H 2+2 | Tootle M 30+7 | Aneke C 21+9 | Daniels B 2+5 | Turton O 7+13 | Colclough R 5+13 | Bond A 4 | West M 5+3 | Guthrie J 1+1 | Dalla Valle L 10 | Inman B 17+4 | Phillips S 20 | Ellington N 2+6 | Stewart K 4 | Ray G 2+2 | Garratt B 1 | Match No. |
|---|---|---|---|---|---|---|---|---|---|---|---|---|---|---|---|---|---|---|---|---|---|---|---|---|---|---|---|---|---|
| 1 | 2² | 3 | 4 | 5 | 6 | 7 | 8¹ | 9 | 10 | 11 | 12 | 13 | | | | | | | | | | | | | | | | | 1 |
| 1 | 2 | 3 | 4 | 5 | 11² | 7 | 8 | 9 | 10¹ | 12 | 6 | 13 | | | | | | | | | | | | | | | | | 2 |
| 1 | 2 | 3 | 4 | 5¹ | 11 | 7 | 6 | 9 | 10² | 13 | 8 | 12 | | | | | | | | | | | | | | | | | 3 |
| 1 | 3 | 4 | | 5 | | | 7 | 6 | 10 | 11 | 8 | 2 | 9¹ | 12 | | | | | | | | | | | | | | | 4 |
| 1 | 2 | 4 | | 5 | | | 8 | 6 | 11³ | 10² | 7 | 3 | 9¹ | 13 | 12 | 14 | | | | | | | | | | | | | 5 |
| 1 | 2 | 3 | | 5 | | | 9 | 6 | 11¹ | 10 | 4 | 7 | | 12 | 8■ | | | | | | | | | | | | | | 6 |
| 1 | 4 | 3 | | 5 | | | 8 | 9 | 11 | 10 | 7 | 2 | 6¹ | | 12 | | | | | | | | | | | | | | 7 |
| 1 | 2 | 3 | | 5 | | | 8¹ | | 11 | 10 | 7 | 4 | 6 | | 9² | 12 | 13 | | | | | | | | | | | | 8 |
| 1 | 5 | 4 | | 3 | 12 | | 9 | 11¹ | 10² | 7 | 2 | 6³ | | | 14 | 13 | 8 | | | | | | | | | | | | 9 |
| 1 | 4 | 3 | | 5 | | | 9 | 10 | | 12 | 7 | 2 | 6¹ | 11² | 13 | | 8 | | | | | | | | | | | | 10 |
| 1 | 4 | 3 | 14 | 9 | | | 10³ | 11² | 7 | 2 | 5 | 6¹ | 12 | 13 | | | 8 | | | | | | | | | | | | 11 |
| 1 | 3 | 4 | | 9 | | | 12 | 10¹ | 6 | 8 | 2 | 5 | 11 | | 7 | | | | | | | | | | | | | | 12 |
| 1 | 3 | 4 | 14 | 11 | | | 8 | 6 | 10² | 7 | 2 | 5³ | 13 | 9¹ | 12 | | | | | | | | | | | | | | 13 |
| 1 | 3 | 4 | 13 | 11 | | | 8¹ | 9 | 7 | 2 | 5 | 10² | 12 | | | 6³ | 14 | | | | | | | | | | | | 14 |
| 1 | 3 | 4 | | 11 | | | 9 | 7 | 2 | 5 | 10 | 12 | 8 | 6¹ | | | | | | | | | | | | | | | 15 |
| 1 | 3 | 4 | | 13 | 6 | | 7 | 9¹ | | 8 | 2 | 5 | 10² | | 12 | 11 | | | | | | | | | | | | | 16 |
| 1 | 3 | 4 | | 5 | 6 | | 8 | 9 | | 7 | 2 | 10 | | | | 11 | | | | | | | | | | | | | 17 |
| 1 | 3 | 4 | | 5 | 6² | | 8¹ | 9 | 12 | 7 | 2 | 10 | | | 13 | 11 | | | | | | | | | | | | | 18 |
| 1 | 3 | 4 | 14 | 5 | 7 | | 8 | 10³ | 12 | 6 | 2 | 9¹ | | | 13 | 11² | | | | | | | | | | | | | 19 |
| 1 | 3 | 4 | | 5 | 9 | | 8 | 6 | | 7 | 2 | 10 | | | | 11 | | | | | | | | | | | | | 20 |
| 1 | 4 | 2 | 3 | 9 | 10 | | 7 | 11¹ | | 6 | | | | 12 | | | | 5 | | 8 | | | | | | | | | 21 |
| 1 | 4 | 3 | 2 | 9 | 10 | | 12 | | 13 | 7 | | 5 | | | 6¹ | | | | | 8 | | | 11² | | | | | | 22 |
| | 2 | 3 | 4 | 9 | 10¹ | | 7³ | 12 | 13 | 6 | | 5 | | | | | | 14 | | 8¹ | | | 11² | | | | | | 23 |
| | 2 | 4 | 3 | 14 | 10³ | | 6 | 13 | 12 | 7 | 9 | 5 | | | | | | | | 8² | | | 11¹ | 1 | | | | | 24 |
| | 4 | 3 | | 14 | 11³ | | 6 | 9 | | 12 | 7 | 2 | | | 13 | | | | | 8² | | | 10¹ | 1 | | | | | 25 |
| | 3 | 4 | | 10³ | | | 6 | 9 | | 12 | 7 | 2 | | | 5 | | | 14 | | 8² | | | 11¹ | 1 | 13 | | | | 26 |
| | 4 | 3 | | 4 | 11 | | 8 | 9 | 11¹ | 7 | 2 | 5 | | | | | | | | 10 | | | 12 | 1 | | | | | 27 |
| 2 | 4 | | | 11 | | | 7 | 9 | 12 | 10² | 8 | 5 | | | 13 | | | | | | 3 | | 6¹ | 1 | | | | | 28 |
| 4¹ | 12 | 3 | | 10³ | | | 9 | 11 | 13 | 6² | 7 | 5 | 2 | | | | 14 | | | 8 | | | | 1 | | | | | 29 |
| | 3 | 4 | | 12 | | | 8 | 6¹ | 11 | 7 | 5 | 2 | | | 10² | | 13 | | | 9 | | | | 1 | | | | | 30 |
| | 4 | 3 | 5 | 9 | | | 8 | 13 | 11² | 14 | 6 | 2 | | | | | 10¹ | | | 12 | | | 7³ | 1 | | | | | 31 |
| 10¹ | 4 | 3 | 5 | 11² | | | 8 | 6 | 13 | 7 | 2 | | | | 12 | | 14 | | | | | | 9³ | 1 | | | | | 32 |
| | 3 | 4 | 5 | 12 | | | 8 | 9 | 10³ | 13 | 7 | 2 | | | 11² | | 14 | | | | | | 6¹ | 1 | | | | | 33 |
| | 4 | 3 | 5 | 6 | | | 8 | 9 | 11 | 12 | 7 | | | | 13 | | 2² | 10¹ | | | | | | 1 | | | | | 34 |
| | 3 | 4 | 13 | 5 | 6² | | 7 | 9 | 10 | 11¹ | 8 | | | | 2 | | | | | | 12 | | | 1 | | | | | 35 |
| | 3 | 4 | | 5 | 11 | | 8 | 9 | 10 | 6¹ | 7 | 2² | | | 13 | | | | | | | | 1 | 12 | | | | | 36 |
| | 4 | 3 | | 5 | 11 | | 8 | 9³ | | 7¹ | 2 | 14 | 13 | | 12 | 6 | | | | | | | 1 | 10² | | | | | 37 |
| | 4 | 3 | 2² | | 6 | | 9³ | 10 | | 5 | | 13 | 12 | | | 8 | 7 | 14 | | | | | | 1 | 11¹ | | | | 38 |
| | 4 | 3 | | 6 | | | 7 | 11¹ | 10 | 2 | 5 | 14 | | 13 | 9³ | 8² | | | | | | | 12 | 1 | | | | | 39 |
| 1 | 3 | 4 | | 11² | | | 7 | 12 | 10³ | 2 | | 14 | | 8 | 6 | | | | | | | | 9¹ | | 13 | | 5 | | 40 |
| 12 | 3 | 4 | | | | | 8 | 9 | 10 | 11 | 6² | 2 | | | 13 | | 14 | | | | | | 7³ | 1¹ | | | 5 | | 41 |
| 1 | 4 | 2 | 3 | | 11 | | 10 | 9 | | 5 | 7³ | | | 12 | 13 | | 6¹ | | | 8² | | | | | 14 | | | | 42 |
| 1 | 3 | 4¹ | | 6 | | | 11 | | | 2 | 5 | 10 | | 7 | 8³ | | | | | | | | 13 | | 14 | | 9² | 12 | 43 |
| | 4 | 3 | | | | 7 | 8 | 9² | 10³ | 2 | 5 | 11¹ | | | 14 | | 12 | | | | | | 6 | 1 | | | 13 | | 44 |
| | 4 | 3 | | | | 7 | 6 | | 11² | 2 | | 10¹ | | 8 | | | | | | | | | 9 | 1 | 12 | 5 | 13 | | 45 |
| | 3 | | | | | | 14 | 9 | 11² | 10¹ | 8 | 2 | | | 5 | | 12 | | | 7³ | 6 | | 13 | | | | 4 | 1 | 46 |

**FA Cup**

| | | | |
|---|---|---|---|
| First Round | Wycombe W | (h) | 4-1 |
| Second Round | Burton | (h) | 0-1 |

**Capital One Cup**

| | | | |
|---|---|---|---|
| First Round | Hartlepool U | (h) | 5-0 |
| Second Round | West Ham U | (a) | 0-2 |

**Johnstone's Paint Trophy**

| | | | |
|---|---|---|---|
| Second Round | Shrewsbury T | (a) | 2-1 |
| Northern Quarter-Finals | Doncaster R | (h) | 1-1 |
| *(aet; won 5-3 on pens)* | | | |
| Northern Semi-Finals | Bradford C | (h) | 4-1 |
| Northern Final | Coventry C | (a) | 3-0 |
| Northern Final | Coventry C | (h) | 0-2 |
| Final *(at Wembley)* | Southend U | | 2-0 |

# CRYSTAL PALACE

## FOUNDATION

There was a Crystal Palace club as early as 1861 but the present organisation was born in 1905 after the formation of a club by the company that controlled the Crystal Palace (building) had been rejected by the FA, who did not like the idea of the Cup Final hosts running their own club. A separate company had to be formed and they had their home on the old Cup Final ground until 1915.

*Selhurst Park Stadium, Whitehorse Lane, London SE25 6PU.*

*Telephone:* (020) 8768 6000.

*Fax:* (020) 8771 5311.

*Ticket Office:* (0871) 200 0071.

*Website:* www.cpfc.co.uk

*Email:* info@cpfc.co.uk

*Ground Capacity:* 26,225.

*Record Attendance:* 51,482 v Burnley, Division 2, 11 May 1979 (at Selhurst Park).

*Pitch Measurements:* 100m × 67m (110yd × 74yd)

*Co-Chairmen:* Steve Parish, Martin Long, Jeremy Hosking and Steve Browett.

*Chief Executive:* Phil Alexander.

*Manager:* Ian Holloway.

*Assistant Manager:* Keith Millen.

*Physio:* Alex Manos.

## HONOURS

**Football League –**
**Division 1:** *Champions* 1993–94;
**Division 2:** *Champions* 1978–79;
*Runners-up* 1968–69;
**Division 3:** *Runners-up* 1963–64;
**Division 3 (S):** *Champions* 1920–21;
*Runners-up* 1928–29, 1930–31, 1938–39;
**Division 4:** *Runners-up* 1960–61.
**FA Cup:** *Runners-up* 1990.
**Football League Cup:** Semi-final 1993, 1995, 2001.
**Zenith Data Systems Cup:** *Winners* 1991.
**European Competition**
**Intertoto Cup:** 1998.

*Colours:* Red and blue striped shirts, blue shorts, blue socks.

*Year Formed:* 1905.

*Turned Professional:* 1905.

*Club Nickname:* 'The Eagles'.

*Grounds:* 1905, Crystal Palace; 1915, Herne Hill; 1918, The Nest; 1924, Selhurst Park.

*First Football League Game:* 28 August 1920, Division 3, v Merthyr T (a) L 1–2 – Alderson; Little, Rhodes; McCracken, Jones, Feebury; Bateman, Conner, Smith, Milligan (1), Whibley.

*Record League Victory:* 9–0 v Barrow, Division 4, 10 October 1959 – Rouse; Long, Noakes; Truett, Evans, McNichol; Gavin (1), Summersby (4 incl. 1p), Sexton, Byrne (2), Colfar (2).

*Record Cup Victory:* 8–0 v Southend U, Rumbelows League Cup 2nd rd (1st leg), 25 September 1990 – Martyn; Humphrey (Thompson (1)), Shaw, Pardew, Young, Thorn, McGoldrick, Thomas, Bright (3), Wright (3), Barber (Hodges (1)).

*Record Defeat:* 0–9 v Burnley, FA Cup 2nd rd replay, 10 February 1909; 0–9 v Liverpool, Division 1, 12 September 1990.

## sky SPORTS FACT FILE

Crystal Palace opened their floodlights with a match against the mighty Real Madrid on 18 April 1962. A memorable occasion attracted an attendance of 24,470 with the visitors winning 4-3, their goalscorers including Alfredo Di Stefano, Francisco Gento and Ferenc Puskas.

*Most League Points (2 for a win):* 64, Division 4, 1960–61.

*Most League Points (3 for a win):* 90, Division 1, 1993–94.

*Most League Goals:* 110, Division 4, 1960–61.

*Highest League Scorer in Season:* Peter Simpson, 46, Division 3 (S), 1930–31.

*Most League Goals in Total Aggregate:* Peter Simpson, 153, 1930–36.

*Most League Goals in One Match:* 6, Peter Simpson v Exeter C, Division 3 (S), 4 October 1930.

*Most Capped Player:* Aleksandrs Kolinko, 23 (86), Latvia.

*Most League Appearances:* Jim Cannon, 571, 1973–88.

*Youngest League Player:* John Bostock, 15 years 287 days v Watford, 29 October 2007.

*Record Transfer Fee Received:* £15,000,000 from Manchester U for Wilfried Zaha, January 2013.

*Record Transfer Fee Paid:* £2,750,000 to RC Strasbourg for Valerien Ismael, January 1998.

*Football League Record:* 1920 Original Members of Division 3; 1921–25 Division 2; 1925–58 Division 3 (S); 1958–61 Division 4; 1961–64 Division 3; 1964–69 Division 2; 1969–73 Division 1; 1973–74 Division 2; 1974–77 Division 3; 1977–79 Division 2; 1979–81 Division 1; 1981–89 Division 2; 1989–92 Division 1; 1992–93 FA Premier League; 1993–94 Division 1; 1994–95 FA Premier League; 1995–97 Division 1; 1997–98 FA Premier League; 1998–2004 Division 1; 2004–05 FA Premier League; 2005–13 FL C; 2013– FA Premier League.

## LATEST SEQUENCES

*Longest Sequence of League Wins:* 8, 9.2.1921 – 26.3.1921.

*Longest Sequence of League Defeats:* 8, 10.1.1998 – 14.3.1998.

*Longest Sequence of League Draws:* 5, 21.9.2002 – 19.10.2002.

*Longest Sequence of Unbeaten League Matches:* 18, 22.2.1969 – 13.8.1969.

*Longest Sequence Without a League Win:* 20, 3.3.1962 – 8.9.1962.

*Successive Scoring Runs:* 24 from 27.4.1929.

*Successive Non-scoring Runs:* 9 from 19.11.1994.

## MANAGERS

**John T. Robson** 1905–07
**Edmund Goodman** 1907–25
 (*Secretary 1905–33*)
**Alex Maley** 1925–27
**Fred Mavin** 1927–30
**Jack Tresadern** 1930–35
**Tom Bromilow** 1935–36
**R. S. Moyes** 1936
**Tom Bromilow** 1936–39
**George Irwin** 1939–47
**Jack Butler** 1947–49
**Ronnie Rooke** 1949–50
**Charlie Slade and Fred Dawes**
 (*Joint Managers*) 1950–51
**Laurie Scott** 1951–54
**Cyril Spiers** 1954–58
**George Smith** 1958–60
**Arthur Rowe** 1960–62
**Dick Graham** 1962–66
**Bert Head** 1966–72 (*continued as General Manager to 1973*)
**Malcolm Allison** 1973–76
**Terry Venables** 1976–80
**Ernie Walley** 1980
**Malcolm Allison** 1980–81
**Dario Gradi** 1981
**Steve Kember** 1981–82
**Alan Mullery** 1982–84
**Steve Coppell** 1984–93
**Alan Smith** 1993–95
**Steve Coppell** (*Technical Director*) 1995–96
**Dave Bassett** 1996–97
**Steve Coppell** 1997–98
**Attilio Lombardo** 1998
**Terry Venables** (*Head Coach*) 1998–99
**Steve Coppell** 1999–2000
**Alan Smith** 2000–01
**Steve Bruce** 2001
**Trevor Francis** 2001–03
**Steve Kember** 2003
**Iain Dowie** 2003–06
**Peter Taylor** 2006–07
**Neil Warnock** 2007–10
**Paul Hart** 2010
**George Burley** 2010–11
**Dougie Freedman** 2011–12
**Ian Holloway** November 2012–

## TEN YEAR LEAGUE RECORD

|  |  | P | W | D | L | F | A | Pts | Pos |
|---|---|---|---|---|---|---|---|---|---|
| 2003-04 | Div 1 | 46 | 21 | 10 | 15 | 72 | 61 | 73 | 6 |
| 2004-05 | PR Lge | 38 | 7 | 12 | 19 | 41 | 62 | 33 | 18 |
| 2005-06 | FL C | 46 | 21 | 12 | 13 | 67 | 48 | 75 | 6 |
| 2006-07 | FL C | 46 | 18 | 11 | 17 | 59 | 51 | 65 | 12 |
| 2007-08 | FL C | 46 | 18 | 17 | 11 | 58 | 42 | 71 | 5 |
| 2008-09 | FL C | 46 | 15 | 12 | 19 | 52 | 55 | 57 | 15 |
| 2009-10 | FL C | 46 | 14 | 17 | 15 | 50 | 53 | 49* | 21 |
| 2010-11 | FL C | 46 | 12 | 12 | 22 | 44 | 69 | 48 | 20 |
| 2011-12 | FL C | 46 | 13 | 17 | 16 | 46 | 51 | 56 | 17 |
| 2012-13 | FL C | 46 | 19 | 15 | 12 | 73 | 62 | 72 | 5 |

* 10 pts deducted.

## DID YOU KNOW ?

Goalkeeper Vic Rouse made 257 appearances for Crystal Palace between 1957 and 1963. On 22 April 1959 he became the first player from Division Four to win an international cap when he lined up for Wales against Northern Ireland.

## CRYSTAL PALACE – FL CHAMPIONSHIP 2012–13 LEAGUE RECORD

| Match No. | Date | Venue | Opponents | Result | H/T Score | Lg Pos. | Goalscorers | Attendance |
|---|---|---|---|---|---|---|---|---|
| 1 | Aug 18 | H | Watford | L | 2-3 | 2-1 | 16 | Garvan 2 (1 pen) [13 (p), 29] | 17,109 |
| 2 | 21 | A | Bristol C | L | 1-4 | 0-2 | 24 | Dikgacoi [74] | 12,221 |
| 3 | 25 | A | Middlesbrough | L | 1-2 | 0-1 | 24 | Easter (pen) [56] | 15,494 |
| 4 | Sept 1 | H | Sheffield W | W | 2-1 | 1-0 | 23 | Murray 2 [1, 83] | 14,043 |
| 5 | 14 | A | Charlton Ath | W | 1-0 | 0-0 | 14 | Dikgacoi [51] | 21,730 |
| 6 | 18 | A | Nottingham F | D | 1-1 | 0-0 | 16 | Dikgacoi [50] | 13,153 |
| 7 | 22 | H | Cardiff C | W | 3-2 | 0-2 | 14 | Murray 3 (2 pens) [52 (p), 62, 72 (p)] | 12,757 |
| 8 | 29 | A | Bolton W | W | 1-0 | 0-0 | 10 | Murray (pen) [80] | 16,727 |
| 9 | Oct 2 | A | Wolverhampton W | W | 2-1 | 0-0 | 6 | Zaha 2 [67, 73] | 19,561 |
| 10 | 6 | H | Burnley | W | 4-3 | 1-2 | 5 | Zaha 2 [41, 53], Delaney [66], Murray [75] | 20,863 |
| 11 | 20 | H | Millwall | D | 2-2 | 2-1 | 5 | Jedinak [35], Delaney [39] | 16,124 |
| 12 | 23 | A | Barnsley | D | 1-1 | 1-0 | 5 | Murray [11] | 8195 |
| 13 | 27 | A | Leicester C | W | 2-1 | 2-0 | 5 | Delaney [23], Ramage [28] | 23,646 |
| 14 | Nov 3 | H | Blackburn R | W | 2-0 | 1-0 | 4 | Murray 2 (1 pen) [45, 65 (p)] | 16,744 |
| 15 | 6 | H | Ipswich T | W | 5-0 | 1-0 | 1 | Bolasie [24], Murray 3 (2 pens) [50 (p), 55 (p), 63], Moritz [90] | 15,517 |
| 16 | 10 | A | Peterborough U | W | 2-1 | 0-1 | 1 | Moritz [80], Dikgacoi [82] | 9691 |
| 17 | 17 | A | Derby Co | W | 3-0 | 1-0 | 1 | Murray 2 [12, 82], Moritz [58] | 16,211 |
| 18 | 24 | A | Leeds U | L | 1-2 | 0-0 | 2 | Ramage [86] | 20,964 |
| 19 | 27 | H | Hull C | D | 0-0 | 0-0 | 2 | | 16,656 |
| 20 | Dec 1 | H | Brighton & HA | W | 3-0 | 1-0 | 1 | Murray 2 (1 pen) [38, 54 (p)], Garvan (pen) [71] | 20,114 |
| 21 | 8 | H | Blackpool | D | 2-2 | 0-1 | 2 | Garvan [52], Murray [64] | 15,594 |
| 22 | 15 | A | Birmingham C | D | 2-2 | 1-0 | 2 | Murray 2 [39, 60] | 17,158 |
| 23 | 22 | H | Huddersfield T | D | 1-1 | 1-0 | 3 | Zaha [39] | 17,993 |
| 24 | 26 | A | Cardiff C | L | 1-2 | 1-1 | 4 | Jedinak [4] | 26,098 |
| 25 | 29 | A | Nottingham F | D | 2-2 | 1-1 | 4 | Murray 2 [9, 81] | 23,703 |
| 26 | Jan 1 | H | Wolverhampton W | W | 3-1 | 2-0 | 3 | Moritz 2 [31, 52], Bolasie [40] | 17,453 |
| 27 | 12 | A | Burnley | L | 0-1 | 0-0 | 4 | | 11,564 |
| 28 | 19 | H | Bolton W | D | 0-0 | 0-0 | 4 | | 17,033 |
| 29 | 30 | A | Huddersfield T | L | 0-1 | 0-0 | 5 | | 13,471 |
| 30 | Feb 2 | H | Charlton Ath | W | 2-1 | 0-1 | 5 | Murray 2 [75, 79] | 17,945 |
| 31 | 8 | A | Watford | D | 2-2 | 0-2 | 5 | Ramage [66], Phillips [70] | 15,079 |
| 32 | 16 | H | Middlesbrough | W | 4-1 | 1-0 | 4 | Murray 2 [9, 57], Ramage [48], Phillips [84] | 17,213 |
| 33 | 19 | H | Bristol C | W | 2-1 | 1-0 | 4 | Murray [35], Dobbie [65] | 16,191 |
| 34 | 23 | A | Sheffield W | L | 0-1 | 0-0 | 4 | | 23,475 |
| 35 | Mar 1 | A | Derby Co | W | 1-0 | 1-0 | 4 | Bolasie [13] | 23,065 |
| 36 | 5 | H | Hull C | W | 4-2 | 1-0 | 4 | Phillips 3 (1 pen) [45 (p), 52, 53], Zaha [77] | 16,230 |
| 37 | 9 | H | Leeds U | D | 2-2 | 1-0 | 3 | Murray 2 [27, 84] | 19,976 |
| 38 | 17 | A | Brighton & HA | L | 0-3 | 0-2 | 4 | | 28,499 |
| 39 | 29 | H | Birmingham C | L | 0-4 | 0-2 | 4 | | 17,189 |
| 40 | Apr 1 | A | Blackpool | L | 0-1 | 0-0 | 4 | | 14,373 |
| 41 | 6 | H | Barnsley | D | 0-0 | 0-0 | 4 | | 21,281 |
| 42 | 16 | A | Ipswich T | L | 0-3 | 0-3 | 5 | | 17,656 |
| 43 | 20 | H | Leicester C | D | 2-2 | 1-1 | 5 | Gabbidon [26], Dobbie [67] | 18,563 |
| 44 | 27 | A | Blackburn R | D | 1-1 | 1-1 | 5 | Dobbie [28] | 19,796 |
| 45 | 30 | A | Millwall | D | 0-0 | 0-0 | 5 | | 12,745 |
| 46 | May 4 | H | Peterborough U | W | 3-2 | 1-1 | 5 | Murray (pen) [45], Phillips [83], Jedinak [89] | 22,154 |

**Final League Position: 5**

### GOALSCORERS

*League (73):* Murray 30 (8 pens), Phillips 6 (1 pen), Zaha 6, Moritz 5, Dikgacoi 4, Garvan 4 (2 pens), Ramage 4, Bolasie 3, Delaney 3, Dobbie 3, Jedinak 3, Easter 1 (1 pen), Gabbidon 1.
*FA Cup (1):* Murray 1 (1 pen).
*Capital One Cup (3):* Dikgacoi 1, Easter 1, Wilbraham 1.
*Championship Play-Offs (3):* Zaha 2, Phillips 1.

| Speroni J 46 | Ward J 22+3 | Martin A 3+1 | Ramage P 39+1 | Moxey D 20+10 | Parr J 33+5 | Dikgacoi K 39 | Jedinak M 41 | Garvan O 23+4 | Zaha W 43 | Wilbraham A 4+17 | Wright D —+1 | Appiah K —+2 | De Silva K —+1 | Blake D 9+1 | Bolasie Y 39+4 | Easter J 2+6 | Moritz A 12+15 | Delaney D 40 | Murray G 42 | Goodwillie D —+1 | Williams J 11+18 | O'Keefe S 2+3 | Gabbidon D 8+2 | Nimely A 1+1 | Butterfield J 4+5 | Marrow A 3+1 | Richards J 10+1 | Phillips K 2+12 | Dobbie S 8+7 | Match No. |
|---|---|---|---|---|---|---|---|---|---|---|---|---|---|---|---|---|---|---|---|---|---|---|---|---|---|---|---|---|---|---|
| 1 | 2 | 3 | 4 | 5 | 6¹ | 7 | 8 | 9 | 10 | 11 | 12 | | | | | | | | | | | | | | | | | | | 1 |
| 1 | 2 | 3 | 4 | 5¹ | 6 | 7² | 8 | 9 | 10 | 11 | | 12 | 13 | | | | | | | | | | | | | | | | | 2 |
| 1 | | 3 | 2 | 14 | 5 | 6¹ | 8 | 7 | 10 | | | | 13 | 4 | 9³ | 11² | 12 | | | | | | | | | | | | | 3 |
| 1 | | | 5 | 12 | 3 | | 8 | 6 | 9 | | | | | 7¹ | 4³ | | 11² | 2 | 10 | 13 | 14 | | | | | | | | | 4 |
| 1 | 14 | | 3 | | 5 | 6 | 8 | 7 | 10³ | 13 | | | 2 | 9¹ | 4 | 11² | 12 | | | | | | | | | | | | | 5 |
| 1 | 2 | | 3 | 5³ | 13 | 8² | 6 | 7 | 9 | | | | 12 | 14 | 4 | 10 | 11¹ | | | | | | | | | | | | | 6 |
| 1 | 12 | | 3¹ | 14 | 5 | 7 | 6 | | 8 | | | | 2 | 10³ | 9² | 4 | 11 | 13 | | | | | | | | | | | | 7 |
| 1 | 2 | | | 12 | 3¹ | 7 | 8 | 6 | 11 | | | | 4 | 10² | 5 | 9 | 13 | | | | | | | | | | | | | 8 |
| 1 | 2 | | 14 | 5 | 13 | | 8 | 7 | 9³ | | | | 4 | 11¹ | 12 | 3 | 10 | 6² | | | | | | | | | | | | 9 |
| 1 | | | 3 | 5 | 13 | 6 | 7 | 14 | 9 | | | | 2 | 11¹ | 8³ | 4 | 10 | 12² | | | | | | | | | | | | 10 |
| 1 | 13 | | 3 | 5⁴ | 12 | 8 | 9 | 7¹ | 11 | | | | 2² | 6³ | 4 | 10 | 14 | | | | | | | | | | | | | 11 |
| 1 | 2 | | 3 | | 5 | 6 | 7 | 9 | | | | | 10 | 8¹ | 4 | 11 | 12 | | | | | | | | | | | | | 12 |
| 1 | 4 | | 2 | 13 | 5 | 7 | 9 | 8 | 10² | 12 | | | 6 | 3 | 11¹ | | | | | | | | | | | | | | | 13 |
| 1 | 2 | | 3 | 12 | 5 | 7 | 6 | 8 | 10¹ | | | | 9 | 4 | 11 | | | | | | | | | | | | | | | 14 |
| 1 | 2 | | 4 | 14 | 5 | 8 | 6 | 7¹ | 9³ | | | | 11 | 12 | 13 | 3 | 10² | | | | | | | | | | | | | 15 |
| 1 | 2² | | 4 | | 5 | 6 | 7 | 8¹ | 9 | 13 | | | 14 | 11³ | | 12 | 3 | 10 | | | | | | | | | | | | 16 |
| 1 | 2 | | 4 | | 5 | 6 | 8 | 12 | 11 | 14 | | | | 9³ | 13 | 7¹ | 3 | 10² | | | | | | | | | | | | 17 |
| 1 | 2³ | | 3 | | 5 | 8 | 7 | 9¹ | 6 | 14 | | | | 10² | 13 | 12 | 4 | 11 | | | | | | | | | | | | 18 |
| 1 | 2 | | 3 | | 5 | 7 | 9 | 8 | 6 | 12 | | | | 10 | 11¹ | | 4 | | | | | | | | | | | | | 19 |
| 1 | 2¹ | | 3 | 14 | 5 | 6 | 8³ | 7 | 9 | 13 | | | | 11 | | 12 | 4 | 10² | | | | | | | | | | | | 20 |
| 1 | | | 3 | 13 | 5 | 7 | 10 | 8 | 6 | | | | 2¹ | 9² | | 12 | 4 | 11 | | | | | | | | | | | | 21 |
| 1 | 2 | | 3 | | 5 | 8 | | | 7 | 9 | 13 | | | 6 | | 11¹ | 4 | 10² | | | 12 | | | | | | | | | 22 |
| 1 | 2² | | 3 | 13 | 5 | 9 | 8 | 7¹ | 6 | | | | | 10³ | | 14 | 4⁴ | 11 | | | 12 | | | | | | | | | 23 |
| 1 | | | 4 | 3 | 2² | 6 | 8 | 7 | 9 | | | | | 11¹ | 13 | 12 | | 10 | | | | 5 | | | | | | | | 24 |
| 1 | | | 4 | 2 | 5 | 7 | 8 | 14 | 9¹ | | | | | 6³ | 12 | 11² | | 10 | 13 | 3 | | | | | | | | | | 25 |
| 1 | 12 | | 4 | 5 | 2 | 8 | 7 | | 6 | | | | | 9³ | | 10² | | 11 | 13 | 14 | 3¹ | | | | | | | | | 26 |
| 1 | | | 4 | 5 | 2 | | 7 | | 8 | 14 | | | | 10³ | | 9¹ | 3 | 11 | 12 | 6² | | 13 | | | | | | | | 27 |
| 1 | | | 4² | 5 | 2 | | 7 | | 10 | | | | | 9 | | 12 | 3 | 11 | 14 | | | 6¹ | | 8³ | 13 | | | | | 28 |
| 1 | | | 4 | | 5³ | | 7 | | 9 | 14 | | | | 6 | 13 | 10¹ | 3 | 11 | 12 | | | 8 | | 2² | | | | | | 29 |
| 1 | | | 3 | 4 | | | | 11 | | | | | | 9² | | | 2 | 10 | 13 | 8³ | | | 6¹ | 7 | 5 | 12 | 14 | | | 30 |
| 1 | | | 4 | 5 | | 6 | | | 11 | | | | | 9² | | | 3 | 12 | | | | 14 | 7¹ | 2 | 13 | 8³ | | | | 31 |
| 1 | | | 4 | | 5 | 8² | 7 | | 6 | | | | | 14 | | | 3 | 11 | 9¹ | | | 13 | | 14 | 2 | 12 | 10³ | | | 32 |
| 1 | | | 4 | | 5 | 8 | 7 | | 6² | | | | | 9³ | | | 3 | 11 | 10¹ | | | 14 | | 2 | 12 | 13 | | | | 33 |
| 1 | | | 4 | | 5³ | 7 | 8 | | | 14 | | | | 6 | | | 3 | 11 | 9¹ | | | 13 | | 2 | 12 | 10² | | | | 34 |
| 1 | | | 2 | 5 | | 4 | 6 | | 8 | | | | | 10³ | | | 3 | 11 | 13 | | | 12 | | 7² | 14 | 9¹ | | | | 35 |
| 1 | | | 4 | 5 | 12 | 2 | 7 | | 6 | | | | | 13 | | | 3 | 11 | 9¹ | | | 8³ | | 10² | 14 | | | | | 36 |
| 1 | | | 3 | | 5 | 6 | 7 | | 10 | 14 | | | | 8¹ | 13 | 4 | 11 | 2³ | | | | | 12 | 9² | | | | | 37 |
| 1 | | | 4³ | | 5 | 9 | 7 | | 10 | 14 | | | | 6² | 13 | 3 | 11 | 8¹ | | | | | 2 | 12 | | | | | | 38 |
| 1 | | | 5 | | 7 | 8 | | | 14 | | | | | 6 | 13 | 4 | 11 | 9³ | | 3 | | | 2¹ | 10² | 12 | | | | | 39 |
| 1 | | | 3 | | 5 | 7² | 6 | | 11 | 14 | | | | 9 | 13 | 4 | 10 | 12 | | | | | 2³ | | 8¹ | | | | | 40 |
| 1 | 2 | | 3 | | 5 | | 7 | | 6 | 14 | | | | 9² | 10¹ | 4 | 11³ | 8 | | | | | 12 | 13 | | | | | 41 |
| 1 | 2³ | | 3 | | 5¹ | 7 | | | 9 | 14 | | | | 10 | 8 | 4 | 11 | 6² | | | | | 12 | 13 | | | | | 42 |
| 1 | 2 | | | 5 | | 7 | | | 6 | 11³ | | | | 12 | | | 4 | 10 | | | 13 | 3 | | 8² | | 14 | 9¹ | | 43 |
| 1 | 2 | | | 5 | | 8 | 7 | 13 | 6 | 11¹ | | | | | | | 3 | 10 | 12 | | 4 | | | | | | 9² | | 44 |
| 1 | 2 | | | 5 | | 7 | 9 | 8¹ | 10 | | | | | 6² | | | 3 | 11 | 12 | | 4 | | | | | | 13 | | 45 |
| 1 | 2 | | | 5 | | 7³ | 9 | 8² | 10 | | | | | 6¹ | | | 3 | 11 | 12 | | 4 | | | | | 13 | 14 | | 46 |

**FA Cup**

| | | | |
|---|---|---|---|
| Third Round | Stoke C | (h) | 0-0 |
| *Replay* | Stoke C | (a) | 1-4 |

**Capital One Cup**

| | | | |
|---|---|---|---|
| First Round | Exeter C | (a) | 2-1 |
| Second Round | Preston NE | (a) | 1-4 |

**Championship Play-Offs**

| | | | |
|---|---|---|---|
| Semi-Finals | Brighton & HA | (h) | 0-0 |
| | Brighton & HA | (a) | 2-0 |
| Final (*at Wembley*) | Watford | | 1-0 |

# DAGENHAM & REDBRIDGE

## FOUNDATION

The roots of Dagenham & Redbridge lie firmly in the Essex side of the Greater London area. Though formed only in 1992 their complex origins date back to the 19th century involving Ilford (founded 1881) and Leytonstone (1886) who merged in 1979 to form Leytonstone-Ilford. They and Walthamstow Avenue (1900) joined together in 1988 to become Redbridge Forest who in turn merged with Dagenham FC (1949) in 1992. Victoria Road has existed as a football ground since 1917. Initially used by Sterling Works, in the summer of 1955 Briggs Sports vacated the premises and Dagenham FC moved in and the pitch was enclosed.

*The London Borough of Barking and Dagenham Stadium, Victoria Road, Dagenham, Essex RM10 7XL.*

*Telephone:* (020) 8592 1549.

*Fax:* (020) 8593 7227.

*Ticket Office:* (020) 8592 1549 (extension 21).

*Website:* www.daggers.co.uk

*Email:* info@daggers.co.uk

*Ground Capacity:* 6,070.

*Record Attendance:* 4,791 v Shrewsbury T, FL 2, 2 May 2009.

*Pitch Measurements:* 102m × 65m (112yd × 72yd)

*Chairman:* David J. Andrews.

*Managing Director:* Stephen Thompson.

*Manager:* Wayne Burnett.

*Assistant Manager:* Warren Hackett.

*First Team Coach:* Darren Currie.

*Physio:* John Gowens.

*Colours:* Red shirts with blue trim, blue shorts with red trim, blue socks.

*Year Formed:* 1992.

*Turned Professional:* 1992.

*Club Nickname:* 'The Daggers'.

*Ground:* 1992, Victoria Road.

*First Football League Game:* 11 August 2007, FL 2 v Stockport Co (a) L 0–1 – Roberts; Foster, Griffiths, Rainford, Uddin, Boardman, Saunders (Strevens), Southam, Benson (Moore), Nurse, Sloma (Huke).

*Record League Victory:* 6–0 v Chester C, FL 2, 9 August 2008 – Roberts; Okuonghae, Griffiths, Arber, Uddin, Taiwo, Saunders (2), Green (1) (Southam), Benson (1) (Nurse), Strevens (1p) (Nwokeji (1)), Gain.

## MANAGERS

**John Still** 1992–94
**Dave Cusack** 1994–95
**Graham Carr** 1995–96
**Ted Hardy** 1996–99
**Garry Hill** 1999–2004
**John Still** 2004–13
**Wayne Burnett** February 2013–

## sky SPORTS FACT FILE

Dagenham & Redbridge had to wait until their fourth game in the Football League before they achieved their maiden victory. This came courtesy of a Paul Benson goal which ensured a 1-0 win over Lincoln City on 1 September 2007.

*Record Cup Victory:* 6–1 v Stowmarket T, FA Cup 2nd qual rd, 28 September 1992; 6–1 v Wealdstone (a), FA Cup 3rd qual rd, 12 October 1992.

*Record Defeat:* 0–9 v Hereford U, Conference, 27 February 2004.

*Most League Points (3 for a win):* 72, FL 2, 2009–10.

*Most League Goals:* 77, FL 2, 2008–09.

*Highest League Scorer in Season:* Paul Benson, 28, Conference, 2006–07.

*Most League Goals in Total Aggregate:* 40, Paul Benson, 2007–11.

*Most League Goals in One Match:* 4, Paul Benson v Shrewsbury T, FL 2, 18 August 2009.

*Most Capped Player:* Jon Nurse, 6, Barbados.

*Most League Appearances:* Jon Nurse, 179, 2007–12.

*Youngest League Player:* Dominic Green, 18 years 93 days v Brentford, 2 October 2007.

*Record Transfer Fee Received:* £700,000 from Peterborough U for Dwight Gayle, January 2013.

*Record Transfer Fee Paid:* £20,000 to Plymouth Arg for Damien McCrory, February 2010.

*Football League Record:* 2006–07 Promoted from Conference; 2007–10 FL 2; 2010–11 FL 1; 2011– FL 2.

## LATEST SEQUENCES

*Longest Sequence of League Wins:* 5, 12.2.2008 – 1.3.2008.

*Longest Sequence of League Defeats:* 9, 8.10.2011 – 10.12.2011.

*Longest Sequence of League Draws:* 3, 21.9.2010 – 28.9.2010.

*Longest Sequence of Unbeaten League Matches:* 8, 17.3.2012 – 21.4.2012.

*Longest Sequence Without a League Win:* 10, 8.10.2011 – 17.12.2011.

*Successive Scoring Runs:* 16 from 12.4.2008.

*Successive Non-scoring Runs:* 3 from 12.1.2008; 3 from 16.2.2013.

## HONOURS

**Football League – FL 2:** Best season: 7th (promoted via play-offs) 2009–10.

**FA Cup:** Best season: 3rd rd, 2008, 2012.

**Football League Cup:** Best season: never beyond 1st rd.

**Conference:** *Champions* 2006–07. *Runners-up* 2001–02.

**Isthmian League (Premier):** *Champions* 1999–2000.

**Essex Senior Cup:** *Winners* 1997–98, 2000–01; *Runners-up* 2001–02.

### AS DAGENHAM FC
**FA Trophy:** *Winners* 1979–80; *Runners-up* 1976–77.
**Amateur Cup:** *Runners-up* 1969–70, 1970–71.

### AS ILFORD
**FA Amateur Cup:** *Winners* 1929, 1930. **Isthmian League:** *Champions* 1906–07, 1920–21, 1921–22.

### AS LEYTONSTONE
**FA Amateur Cup:** *Winners* 1947, 1948, 1968.
**Isthmian League:** *Champions* 1918–19, 1937–38, 1938–39, 1946–47, 1947–48, 1949–50, 1950–51, 1951–52, 1965–66.

### AS LEYTONSTONE/ILFORD
**Isthmian League:** *Champions* 1981–82, 1988–89.

### AS WALTHAMSTOW AVENUE
**FA Amateur Cup:** *Winners* 1952, 1961. **Isthmian League:** *Champions* 1945–46, 1948–49, 1952–53, 1954–55.
**Athenian League:** *Champions* 1929–30, 1932–33, 1933–34, 1937–38, 1938–39.

### AS REDBRIDGE FOREST
**Isthmian League:** *Winners* 1990–91.

## TEN YEAR LEAGUE RECORD

|         |      | P  | W  | D  | L  | F  | A  | Pts | Pos |
|---------|------|----|----|----|----|----|----|-----|-----|
| 2003-04 | Conf | 42 | 15 | 9  | 18 | 59 | 64 | 54  | 13  |
| 2004-05 | Conf | 42 | 19 | 8  | 15 | 68 | 60 | 65  | 11  |
| 2005-06 | Conf | 42 | 16 | 19 | 16 | 63 | 59 | 58  | 10  |
| 2006-07 | Conf | 46 | 28 | 11 | 7  | 93 | 48 | 95  | 1   |
| 2007-08 | FL 2 | 46 | 13 | 10 | 23 | 49 | 70 | 49  | 20  |
| 2008-09 | FL 2 | 46 | 19 | 11 | 16 | 77 | 53 | 68  | 8   |
| 2009-10 | FL 2 | 46 | 20 | 12 | 14 | 69 | 58 | 72  | 7   |
| 2010-11 | FL 1 | 46 | 12 | 11 | 23 | 52 | 70 | 47  | 21  |
| 2011-12 | FL 2 | 46 | 14 | 8  | 24 | 50 | 72 | 50  | 19  |
| 2012-13 | FL 2 | 46 | 13 | 12 | 21 | 55 | 62 | 51  | 22  |

## DID YOU KNOW ?

Dagenham & Redbridge achieved their only Football League promotion to date in May 2010 when they defeated Rotherham United in the League Two play-off final at Wembley Stadium. The match attracted an attendance of 32,054.

## DAGENHAM & REDBRIDGE – FOOTBALL LEAGUE TWO 2012–13 LEAGUE RECORD

| Match No. | Date | Venue | Opponents | Result | | H/T Score | Lg Pos. | Goalscorers | Attendance |
|---|---|---|---|---|---|---|---|---|---|
| 1 | Aug 18 | A | Cheltenham T | L | 0-2 | 0-1 | 20 | | 2655 |
| 2 | 21 | H | Plymouth Arg | D | 0-0 | 0-0 | 21 | | 1878 |
| 3 | 25 | H | Gillingham | L | 1-2 | 1-1 | 22 | Gayle (pen) [34] | 2251 |
| 4 | Sept 1 | A | AFC Wimbledon | D | 2-2 | 1-2 | 22 | Spillane [28], Howell [56] | 3507 |
| 5 | 8 | A | Southend U | L | 1-3 | 1-2 | 22 | Gayle [45] | 5348 |
| 6 | 15 | H | Accrington S | D | 1-1 | 0-0 | 22 | Howell [61] | 1529 |
| 7 | 18 | H | Northampton T | L | 0-1 | 0-0 | 22 | | 1429 |
| 8 | 22 | A | Rochdale | D | 2-2 | 0-2 | 22 | Spillane (pen) [61], Williams [68] | 2120 |
| 9 | 29 | H | Wycombe W | W | 3-0 | 1-0 | 20 | Gayle [26], Spillane (pen) [57], Bingham [89] | 1680 |
| 10 | Oct 2 | A | Port Vale | D | 1-1 | 0-0 | 19 | Howell [72] | 4355 |
| 11 | 6 | H | Bradford C | W | 4-3 | 2-0 | 18 | Bingham [6], Spillane [30], Wilkinson [51], Gayle [76] | 1768 |
| 12 | 13 | A | Chesterfield | W | 2-1 | 1-0 | 17 | Williams 2 [42, 57] | 5082 |
| 13 | 20 | H | York C | L | 2-3 | 1-2 | 19 | Wilkinson 2 [23, 90] | 3391 |
| 14 | 23 | H | Exeter C | D | 1-1 | 1-0 | 19 | Elito [37] | 1487 |
| 15 | 27 | H | Aldershot T | D | 0-0 | 0-0 | 19 | | 1771 |
| 16 | Nov 6 | A | Oxford U | W | 3-2 | 1-0 | 15 | Williams [36], Howell [54], Wilkinson [62] | 5074 |
| 17 | 10 | H | Rotherham U | W | 5-0 | 2-0 | 14 | Gayle 2 [5, 90], Howell 2 [35, 75], Elito [81] | 1720 |
| 18 | 17 | A | Burton Alb | L | 2-3 | 1-0 | 14 | Gayle [29], Williams [78] | 2369 |
| 19 | 24 | H | Fleetwood T | W | 1-0 | 0-0 | 15 | Williams (pen) [90] | 1618 |
| 20 | Dec 1 | A | Torquay U | L | 1-2 | 0-1 | 16 | Saunders [73] | 2069 |
| 21 | 8 | A | Bristol R | W | 1-0 | 1-0 | 14 | Williams [19] | 4874 |
| 22 | 15 | H | Barnet | W | 1-0 | 1-0 | 12 | Saunders [17] | 2020 |
| 23 | 26 | H | Southend U | L | 0-3 | 0-2 | 14 | | 3555 |
| 24 | 29 | H | Port Vale | L | 2-3 | 1-3 | 15 | Williams (pen) [18], Doe [84] | 1697 |
| 25 | Jan 1 | A | Northampton T | L | 1-3 | 0-2 | 16 | Doe [71] | 4368 |
| 26 | 5 | A | Accrington S | W | 2-0 | 1-0 | 14 | Saunders [21], Howell [52] | 1031 |
| 27 | 8 | A | Morecambe | L | 1-2 | 1-0 | 14 | Woodall [7] | 4029 |
| 28 | 12 | H | Rochdale | W | 2-1 | 0-0 | 13 | Ogogo [75], Elito [90] | 2289 |
| 29 | 19 | A | Wycombe W | L | 0-1 | 0-1 | 13 | | 2365 |
| 30 | 26 | H | Morecambe | L | 1-2 | 0-0 | 14 | Wilkinson [61] | 1370 |
| 31 | Feb 2 | A | Plymouth Arg | D | 0-0 | 0-0 | 15 | | 6234 |
| 32 | 9 | H | Cheltenham T | W | 1-0 | 0-0 | 13 | Howell [58] | 1526 |
| 33 | 16 | A | Gillingham | L | 1-2 | 0-1 | 15 | Ilesanmi [52] | 5611 |
| 34 | 23 | H | AFC Wimbledon | L | 0-1 | 0-0 | 16 | | 2265 |
| 35 | 27 | A | Bradford C | D | 1-1 | 0-0 | 15 | Howell [69] | 10,006 |
| 36 | Mar 2 | H | Chesterfield | L | 0-1 | 0-1 | 15 | | 1675 |
| 37 | 9 | A | Rotherham U | W | 2-1 | 0-0 | 15 | Elito (pen) [59], Wilkinson [82] | 7309 |
| 38 | 12 | H | Torquay U | D | 2-2 | 1-0 | 16 | Elito (pen) [4], Scott [85] | 1227 |
| 39 | 16 | H | Burton Alb | D | 1-1 | 0-1 | 16 | Scott [51] | 1364 |
| 40 | 23 | A | Fleetwood T | L | 1-2 | 1-1 | 17 | Elito (pen) [5] | 2019 |
| 41 | 29 | A | Barnet | D | 0-0 | 0-0 | 16 | | 3680 |
| 42 | Apr 1 | H | Bristol R | L | 2-4 | 1-3 | 17 | Strevens [29], Reed [73] | 2082 |
| 43 | 6 | A | Exeter C | W | 1-0 | 1-0 | 17 | Doe [5] | 3755 |
| 44 | 13 | H | Oxford U | L | 0-1 | 0-1 | 17 | | 1788 |
| 45 | 20 | A | Aldershot T | L | 0-1 | 0-0 | 21 | | 2861 |
| 46 | 27 | H | York C | L | 0-1 | 0-0 | 22 | | 3781 |

**Final League Position: 22**

### GOALSCORERS

*League (55):* Howell 9, Williams 8 (2 pens), Gayle 7 (1 pen), Elito 6 (3 pens), Wilkinson 6, Spillane 4 (2 pens), Doe 3, Saunders 3, Bingham 2, Scott 2, Ilesanmi 1, Ogogo 1, Reed 1, Strevens 1, Woodall 1.
*FA Cup (0).*
*Capital One Cup (0).*
*Johnstone's Paint Trophy (3):* Scott 1, Spillane 1 (1 pen), Woodall 1.

| Lewington C 41 | Hoyte G 23+3 | Spillane M 24 | Doe S 46 | Ilesanmi F 46 | Bingham B 12+6 | Howell L 46 | Ogogo A 46 | Elito M 43+3 | Gayle D 16+2 | Woodall B 9+19 | Williams S 29+4 | Green Danny J —+6 | Scott J 11+7 | Wilkinson L 42+1 | Green Dominic 1+9 | Saunders M 32 | Reed J 12+10 | Maher K 7+1 | Caprice J —+8 | Edmans R —+1 | Dennis L —+6 | Shields S —+1 | Strevens B 10+4 | Seabright J 3+1 | Miles J 2 | Silva T 4 | Shariff M 1+3 | Gracco G —+1 | Fortune J —+1 | Match No |
|---|---|---|---|---|---|---|---|---|---|---|---|---|---|---|---|---|---|---|---|---|---|---|---|---|---|---|---|---|---|---|
| 1 | 2 | 3 | 4 | 5 | 6 | $7^2$ | 8 | 9 | 10 | $11^1$ | 12 | 13 | | | | | | | | | | | | | | | | | | 1 |
| 1 | 2 | 4 | 3 | 5 | 8 | $6^2$ | 7 | 9 | 10 | $11^1$ | 12 | 13 | | | | | | | | | | | | | | | | | | 2 |
| 1 | 2 | 4 | 3 | 5 | 8 | $6^1$ | 7 | 10 | $9^2$ | | 11 | 12 | 13 | | | | | | | | | | | | | | | | | 3 |
| 1 | 2 | $3^2$ | 8 | 4 | $6^3$ | 9 | 7 | 10 | 11 | 12 | $5^1$ | | | 13 | 14 | | | | | | | | | | | | | | | 4 |
| 1 | 2 | 7 | 4 | 5 | 8 | 6 | $9^1$ | $11^3$ | 13 | $10^2$ | | | 14 | $3^8$ | 12 | | | | | | | | | | | | | | | 5 |
| 1 | 2 | 8 | 4 | 5 | 6 | 7 | $11^1$ | $10^2$ | 9 | | 12 | 13 | | 3 | | 3 | | | | | | | | | | | | | | 6 |
| 1 | 4 | 7 | 3 | 5 | 14 | 8 | 6 | $9^1$ | $10^2$ | $11^1$ | 12 | | 13 | 2 | | | | | | | | | | | | | | | | 7 |
| 1 | $2^1$ | 8 | 4 | 5 | | 7 | 6 | 11 | 12 | | 10 | 13 | $9^2$ | 3 | | | | | | | | | | | | | | | | 8 |
| 1 | 7 | 4 | 5 | 6 | 8 | 2 | 12 | $11^2$ | 13 | 9 | | | | 3 | | $10^1$ | | | | | | | | | | | | | | 9 |
| 1 | 3 | 4 | 5 | $6^2$ | 7 | 9 | 8 | 13 | | 10 | | 12 | | $11^1$ | | 2 | | | | | | | | | | | | | | 10 |
| 1 | 8 | 4 | 5 | 6 | 7 | 2 | $9^1$ | 11 | 12 | 10 | | | | 3 | | | | | | | | | | | | | | | | 11 |
| 1 | 8 | 3 | 5 | 7 | 2 | 6 | 11 | | 10 | | | | | 4 | | 9 | | | | | | | | | | | | | | 12 |
| 1 | 13 | $7^2$ | 3 | 4 | 8 | 6 | $5^1$ | 10 | 11 | | | | | 2 | 12 | $9^3$ | 14 | | | | | | | | | | | | | 13 |
| 1 | 12 | 7 | 3 | 5 | 6 | 2 | $9^2$ | 11 | 14 | $10^3$ | | | | 4 | 13 | $8^1$ | | | | | | | | | | | | | | 14 |
| 1 | 6 | 3 | 5 | 8 | 2 | $9^2$ | 10 | 14 | $11^3$ | | | | | 4 | 12 | $7^1$ | 13 | | | | | | | | | | | | | 15 |
| 1 | | 4 | 5 | 8 | 2 | 9 | 10 | 12 | $11^1$ | | | | | 3 | | 6 | $7^8$ | | | | | | | | | | | | | 16 |
| 1 | 7 | 3 | 5 | 13 | 6 | 2 | 9 | 11 | 12 | | | | | $4^2$ | | 8 | $10^1$ | | | | | | | | | | | | | 17 |
| 1 | 8 | 4 | 5 | 12 | 7 | 2 | 9 | 11 | 13 | | | | | 3 | | $6^1$ | $10^2$ | | | | | | | | | | | | | 18 |
| 1 | 7 | 3 | 5 | 8 | 2 | 11 | 12 | 10 | | | | | | 4 | | 6 | $9^1$ | | | | | | | | | | | | | 19 |
| 1 | $7^2$ | 4 | 5 | 8 | 2 | $9^3$ | 12 | 11 | | | | | 14 | 3 | | 6 | $10^1$ | 13 | | | | | | | | | | | | 20 |
| 1 | 6 | 4 | 5 | 9 | 2 | $7^2$ | 12 | 10 | | | | | | 3 | | 8 | $11^1$ | 13 | | | | | | | | | | | | 21 |
| 1 | 7 | 3 | 5 | 6 | 2 | 9 | 12 | 11 | | | | | | 4 | | 8 | $10^1$ | | | | | | | | | | | | | 22 |
| 1 | $7^1$ | 3 | 5 | 8 | 2 | $6^3$ | 12 | 11 | | | | | 14 | 4 | | 9 | $10^2$ | 13 | | | | | | | | | | | | 23 |
| 1 | 7 | 3 | 5 | 9 | 2 | 6 | 12 | 11 | | | | | | 4 | $10^1$ | | $8^2$ | 13 | | | | | | | | | | | | 24 |
| 1 | 7 | 4 | 5 | 9 | 2 | 6 | 12 | 10 | | | | | | 3 | | $8^2$ | $11^1$ | 13 | | | | | | | | | | | | 25 |
| 1 | 6 | 4 | 5 | 7 | 2 | 9 | $11^1$ | 10 | | | | 12 | 3 | | | 8 | | | | | | | | | | | | | | 26 |
| 1 | 6 | 4 | 5 | 7 | 2 | 9 | $10^2$ | | | | | $11^1$ | | 3 | | $8^3$ | 12 | 14 | 13 | | | | | | | | | | | 27 |
| 1 | 2 | 3 | 5 | 6 | 9 | | 10 | 7 | | | | | | 4 | | 11 | | | | | | | | | | | | | | 28 |
| 1 | 2 | 4 | 5 | 13 | 7 | 8 | $6^2$ | $11^1$ | 10 | | | | | 3 | | $9^3$ | | 14 | 12 | | | | | | | | | | | 29 |
| 1 | | 3 | 5 | 8 | 7 | 2 | $11^2$ | 12 | 9 | | | | | 4 | | 6 | $10^1$ | | | | | 13 | | | | | | | | 30 |
| 1 | 12 | 4 | 5 | $9^2$ | 7 | 2 | 6 | 13 | 10 | | | | | 3 | | $8^1$ | | | | | | | 11 | | | | | | | 31 |
| 1 | 2 | 3 | 5 | 8 | 7 | 9 | 12 | $11^1$ | | | | | | 4 | | 6 | | | | | | | 10 | | | | | | | 32 |
| 1 | $2^3$ | 3 | 5 | 8 | 7 | $9^1$ | 10 | | | | | | | 4 | 13 | $6^2$ | 14 | | 12 | | | | 11 | | | | | | | 33 |
| 1 | 2 | 4 | 5 | 8 | 7 | $9^2$ | 10 | | | | | | | 3 | 13 | $6^1$ | 12 | | | | | | 11 | | | | | | | 34 |
| 1 | 2 | 4 | 5 | 12 | 8 | 9 | $6^2$ | 10 | | | | | | 3 | | 7 | 13 | | | | | | $11^1$ | | | | | | | 35 |
| 1 | 2 | 3 | 5 | | 7 | 8 | 13 | 11 | | | | | | 4 | $9^2$ | $6^3$ | 12 | | 14 | | | | $10^1$ | | | | | | | 36 |
| 1 | 2 | 4 | 5 | 12 | 9 | 7 | $10^2$ | 11 | | | | | | 3 | 8 | $6^1$ | | | | | | | 13 | | | | | | | 37 |
| 1 | 2 | 4 | 5 | $9^2$ | $7^1$ | 8 | 11 | 10 | | | | | | 3 | 13 | 6 | | | | | | | 12 | | | | | | | 38 |
| 1 | 6 | 4 | 5 | 7 | 2 | $9^1$ | $11^2$ | | | | | | | 3 | | 8 | 13 | | | | | | 12 | 10 | | | | | | 39 |
| $1^1$ | $6^2$ | 4 | 5 | 8 | 2 | 9 | 11 | | | | | | | 3 | 14 | 7 | 13 | | | | | | $10^3$ | 12 | | | | | | 40 |
| | 9 | 4 | 5 | 8 | 2 | 11 | | | | | | | | 3 | | 7 | | | | | | | 10 | | 1 | $6^1$ | 12 | | | 41 |
| | $2^3$ | 3 | 5 | 8 | 7 | $11^1$ | | | | | | | | 4 | | 13 | | | | | | | 12 | 10 | 1 | $6^2$ | 9 | 14 | | 42 |
| | | 3 | 5 | 8 | 2 | 10 | | | | | | | | 4 | | $9^1$ | $11^2$ | 6 | | | | | 12 | 13 | 1 | $7^1$ | | 14 | | 43 |
| | | 4 | 5 | 9 | 2 | $11^3$ | | | | | | | | 3 | | $6^1$ | 8 | 7 | | | | | 12 | 14 | 1 | $10^2$ | 13 | | | 44 |
| 1 | | 3 | 5 | $9^2$ | 7 | 6 | 13 | | | 14 | | | 10 | 2 | | 4 | $11^3$ | $8^1$ | | | | | | | | | 12 | | | 45 |
| | | 4 | 5 | 9 | 8 | 2 | $6^1$ | 11 | | | | | 10 | 3 | | 12 | 7 | | | | | | | | | | i | | | 46 |

**FA Cup**
First Round   Bournemouth   (a)   0-4

**Capital One Cup**
First Round   Coventry C   (h)   0-1

**Johnstone's Paint Trophy**
First Round   Stevenage   (h)   3-2
Second Round   Southend U   (a)   0-2

# DERBY COUNTY

## FOUNDATION

Derby County was formed by members of the Derbyshire County Cricket Club in 1884, when football was booming in the area and the cricketers thought that a football club would help boost finances for the summer game. To begin with, they sported the cricket club's colours of amber, chocolate and pale blue, and went into the game at the top immediately entering the FA Cup.

*Pride Park Stadium, Pride Park, Derby DE24 8XL.*

*Telephone:* (0871) 472 1884.

*Fax:* (01332) 667 519.

*Ticket Office:* (0871) 472 1884.

*Website:* www.dcfc.co.uk

*Email:* derby.county@dcfc.co.uk

*Ground Capacity:* 33,502.

*Record Attendance:* 41,826 v Tottenham H, Division 1, 20 September 1969 (at Baseball Ground); 33,597, England v Mexico, 25 May 2001 (at Pride Park).

*Pitch Measurements:* 105m × 68m (114yd × 74yd)

*Chairman:* Andy Appleby.

*Chief Executive:* Sam Rush.

*Manager:* Nigel Clough.

*Coaches:* Gary Crosby, Andy Garner, Martin Taylor, Johnny Metgod.

*Physio:* Neil Sullivan.

*Colours:* White shirts with black trim, black shorts with white trim, white socks.

*Year Formed:* 1884.

*Turned Professional:* 1884.

*Club Nickname:* 'The Rams'.

*Grounds:* 1884, Racecourse Ground; 1895, Baseball Ground; 1997, Pride Park.

*First Football League Game:* 8 September 1888, Football League, v Bolton W (a) W 6–3 – Marshall; Latham, Ferguson, Williamson; Monks, Walter Roulstone; Bakewell (2), Cooper (2), Higgins, Harry Plackett, Lol Plackett (2).

*Record League Victory:* 9–0 v Wolverhampton W, Division 1, 10 January 1891 – Bunyan; Archie Goodall, Roberts; Walker, Chalmers, Walter Roulstone (1); Bakewell, McLachlan, Johnny Goodall (1), Holmes (2), McMillan (5). 9–0 v Sheffield W, Division 1, 21 January 1899 – Fryer; Methven, Staley; Cox, Archie Goodall, May; Oakden (1), Bloomer (6), Boag, McDonald (1), Allen, (1 og).

*Record Cup Victory:* 12–0 v Finn Harps, UEFA Cup 1st rd 1st leg, 15 September 1976 – Moseley; Thomas, Nish, Rioch (1), McFarland, Todd (King), Macken, Gemmill, Hector (5), George (3), James (3).

## HONOURS

**Football League – Division 1:**
*Champions* 1971–72, 1974–75;
*Runners-up* 1895–96, 1929–30, 1935–36, 1995–96;
**Division 2:** *Champions* 1911–12, 1914–15, 1968–69, 1986–87;
*Runners-up* 1925–26;
**Division 3 (N):** *Champions* 1956–57;
*Runners-up* 1955–56.
**FA Cup:** *Winners* 1946;
*Runners-up* 1898, 1899, 1903.
**Football League Cup:** Semi-final 1968, 2009.
**Texaco Cup:** *Winners* 1972.
**European Competitions**
**European Cup:** 1972–73, 1975–76.
**UEFA Cup:** 1974–75, 1976–77.
**Anglo-Italian Cup:** *Runners-up* 1993.

### sky SPORTS FACT FILE

Steve Bloomer headed the Derby County scoring charts every season from 1893–94 through to 1905–06. He holds the club record of 332 League and Cup goals, his tally including a 6 (against Sheffield Wednesday in January 1899), one 4 and 18 hat-tricks.

*Record Defeat:* 2–11 v Everton, FA Cup 1st rd, 1889–90.

*Most League Points (2 for a win):* 63, Division 2, 1968–69 and Division 3 (N), 1955–56 and 1956–57.

*Most League Points (3 for a win):* 84, Division 3, 1985–86, Division 3, 1986–87 and FL C, 2006–07.

*Most League Goals:* 111, Division 3 (N), 1956–57.

*Highest League Scorer in Season:* Jack Bowers, 37, Division 1, 1930–31; Ray Straw, 37 Division 3 (N), 1956–57.

*Most League Goals in Total Aggregate:* Steve Bloomer, 292, 1892–1906 and 1910–14.

*Most League Goals in One Match:* 6, Steve Bloomer v Sheffield W, Division 1, 2 January 1899.

*Most Capped Player:* Deon Burton, 42 (59), Jamaica.

*Most League Appearances:* Kevin Hector, 486, 1966–78 and 1980–82.

*Youngest League Player:* Mason Bennett, 15 years 99 days v Middlesbrough 22 October 2011.

*Record Transfer Fee Received:* £7,000,000 rising to £9,000,000 for Seth Johnson from Leeds U, October 2001.

*Record Transfer Fee Paid:* £4,000,000 to Crewe Alex for Seth Johnson, May 1999 (including sell-on).

*Football League Record:* 1888 Founder Member of the Football League; 1907–12 Division 2; 1912–14 Division 1; 1914–15 Division 2; 1915–21 Division 1; 1921–26 Division 2; 1926–53 Division 1; 1953–55 Division 2; 1955–57 Division 3 (N); 1957–69 Division 2; 1969–80 Division 1; 1980–84 Division 2; 1984–86 Division 3; 1986–87 Division 2; 1987–91 Division 1; 1991–92 Division 2; 1992–96 Division 1; 1996–2002 FA Premier League; 2002–04 Division 1; 2004–07 FL C; 2007–08 FA Premier League; 2008– FL C.

## MANAGERS

**W. D. Clark** 1896–1900
**Harry Newbould** 1900–06
**Jimmy Methven** 1906–22
**Cecil Potter** 1922–25
**George Jobey** 1925–41
**Ted Magner** 1944–46
**Stuart McMillan** 1946–53
**Jack Barker** 1953–55
**Harry Storer** 1955–62
**Tim Ward** 1962–67
**Brian Clough** 1967–73
**Dave Mackay** 1973–76
**Colin Murphy** 1977
**Tommy Docherty** 1977–79
**Colin Addison** 1979–82
**Johnny Newman** 1982
**Peter Taylor** 1982–84
**Roy McFarland** 1984
**Arthur Cox** 1984–93
**Roy McFarland** 1993–95
**Jim Smith** 1995–2001
**Colin Todd** 2001–02
**John Gregory** 2002–03
**George Burley** 2003–05
**Phil Brown** 2005–06
**Billy Davies** 2006–07
**Paul Jewell** 2007–08
**Nigel Clough** January 2009–

## LATEST SEQUENCES

*Longest Sequence of League Wins:* 9, 15.3.1969 – 19.4.1969.

*Longest Sequence of League Defeats:* 8, 12.12.1987 – 10.2.1988.

*Longest Sequence of League Draws:* 6, 26.3.1927 – 18.4.1927.

*Longest Sequence of Unbeaten League Matches:* 22, 8.3.1969 – 20.9.1969.

*Longest Sequence Without a League Win:* 36, 22.9.2007 – 30.8.2008.

*Successive Scoring Runs:* 29 from 3.12.1960.

*Successive Non-scoring Runs:* 8 from 30.10.1920.

## TEN YEAR LEAGUE RECORD

| | | P | W | D | L | F | A | Pts | Pos |
|---|---|---|---|---|---|---|---|---|---|
| 2003-04 | Div 1 | 46 | 13 | 13 | 20 | 53 | 67 | 52 | 20 |
| 2004-05 | FL C | 46 | 22 | 10 | 14 | 71 | 60 | 76 | 4 |
| 2005-06 | FL C | 46 | 10 | 20 | 16 | 53 | 67 | 50 | 20 |
| 2006-07 | FL C | 46 | 25 | 9 | 12 | 62 | 46 | 84 | 3 |
| 2007-08 | PR Lge | 38 | 1 | 8 | 29 | 20 | 89 | 11 | 20 |
| 2008-09 | FL C | 46 | 14 | 12 | 20 | 55 | 67 | 54 | 18 |
| 2009-10 | FL C | 46 | 15 | 11 | 20 | 53 | 63 | 56 | 14 |
| 2010-11 | FL C | 46 | 13 | 10 | 23 | 58 | 71 | 49 | 19 |
| 2011-12 | FL C | 46 | 18 | 10 | 18 | 50 | 58 | 64 | 12 |
| 2012-13 | FL C | 46 | 16 | 13 | 17 | 65 | 62 | 61 | 10 |

## DID YOU KNOW ?

Winger Ivan Sharpe enjoyed double success in 1912, firstly helping Derby County to the Division Two title and in July winning Olympic Gold as a member of the Great Britain team. In later life he became editor of the prestigious *Athletic News* and a well-known football journalist.

## DERBY COUNTY – FL CHAMPIONSHIP 2012–13 LEAGUE RECORD

| Match No. | Date | Venue | Opponents | Result | H/T Score | Lg Pos. | Goalscorers | Attendance |
|---|---|---|---|---|---|---|---|---|
| 1 | Aug 18 | H | Sheffield W | D 2-2 | 2-1 | 10 | Tyson [11], Buxton [27] | 27,437 |
| 2 | 21 | A | Bolton W | L 0-2 | 0-0 | 22 | | 17,050 |
| 3 | 25 | A | Wolverhampton W | D 1-1 | 0-1 | 21 | Robinson [90] | 21,861 |
| 4 | Sept 1 | H | Watford | W 5-1 | 3-0 | 14 | Keogh [16], Hendrick [36], Sammon [43], Hughes [52], Ward [67] | 20,608 |
| 5 | 15 | A | Huddersfield T | L 0-1 | 0-1 | 19 | | 15,265 |
| 6 | 18 | H | Charlton Ath | W 3-2 | 1-0 | 9 | Ward 2 (1 pen) [7, 64 (p)], Bryson [53] | 20,063 |
| 7 | 22 | H | Burnley | L 1-2 | 1-1 | 17 | Ward [20] | 21,347 |
| 8 | 30 | A | Nottingham F | W 1-0 | 0-0 | 12 | Bryson [55] | 28,707 |
| 9 | Oct 3 | A | Middlesbrough | D 2-2 | 1-1 | 13 | Robinson (pen) [16], Coutts [88] | 13,377 |
| 10 | 6 | H | Brighton & HA | D 0-0 | 0-0 | 13 | | 22,059 |
| 11 | 20 | H | Blackburn R | D 1-1 | 0-1 | 14 | Robinson [88] | 22,958 |
| 12 | 23 | A | Ipswich T | W 2-1 | 1-1 | 12 | Robinson [40], Tyson [90] | 15,417 |
| 13 | 27 | A | Peterborough U | L 0-3 | 0-1 | 13 | | 8427 |
| 14 | Nov 3 | H | Blackpool | W 4-1 | 2-0 | 11 | Robinson 2 [12, 54], Brayford [31], Sammon [65] | 22,272 |
| 15 | 6 | H | Barnsley | W 2-0 | 0-0 | 9 | O'Connor [69], Tyson [90] | 20,808 |
| 16 | 10 | A | Millwall | L 1-2 | 0-1 | 9 | Hughes [53] | 10,392 |
| 17 | 17 | A | Crystal Palace | L 0-3 | 0-1 | 13 | | 16,211 |
| 18 | 24 | H | Birmingham C | W 3-2 | 1-0 | 12 | Sammon 2 [32, 80], Tyson [84] | 21,505 |
| 19 | 27 | H | Cardiff C | D 1-1 | 0-1 | 12 | Robinson [69] | 20,911 |
| 20 | Dec 1 | A | Leicester C | L 1-4 | 1-2 | 16 | Robinson [38] | 20,680 |
| 21 | 8 | H | Leeds U | W 3-1 | 1-1 | 10 | Sammon [15], Buxton [66], Davies, B [90] | 25,034 |
| 22 | 15 | A | Bristol C | W 2-0 | 2-0 | 10 | Hendrick [34], Bryson [36] | 12,526 |
| 23 | 21 | H | Hull C | L 1-2 | 1-1 | 10 | Jacobs [45] | 25,442 |
| 24 | 26 | A | Burnley | L 0-2 | 0-1 | 12 | | 13,779 |
| 25 | 29 | A | Charlton Ath | D 1-1 | 0-1 | 11 | Ward (pen) [72] | 17,761 |
| 26 | Jan 1 | H | Middlesbrough | W 3-1 | 2-0 | 10 | Jacobs [19], Hendrick [42], Sammon [65] | 22,523 |
| 27 | 12 | A | Brighton & HA | L 1-2 | 0-2 | 12 | Hendrick [70] | 25,464 |
| 28 | 19 | H | Nottingham F | D 1-1 | 0-1 | 13 | Ward [52] | 33,010 |
| 29 | Feb 2 | H | Huddersfield T | W 3-0 | 2-0 | 9 | Bryson [24], Ward [33], Keogh [59] | 21,561 |
| 30 | 9 | A | Sheffield W | D 2-2 | 1-0 | 10 | Hendrick [23], Ward (pen) [48] | 25,765 |
| 31 | 12 | A | Hull C | L 1-2 | 0-0 | 10 | Ward [84] | 15,677 |
| 32 | 16 | H | Wolverhampton W | D 0-0 | 0-0 | 9 | | 23,036 |
| 33 | 19 | H | Bolton W | D 1-1 | 0-1 | 9 | Ward [81] | 22,145 |
| 34 | 23 | A | Watford | L 1-2 | 0-1 | 11 | Ward (pen) [73] | 14,425 |
| 35 | Mar 1 | H | Crystal Palace | L 0-1 | 0-1 | 12 | | 23,065 |
| 36 | 5 | A | Cardiff C | D 1-1 | 0-0 | 12 | Sammon [75] | 21,544 |
| 37 | 9 | A | Birmingham C | L 1-3 | 1-0 | 15 | Davies, B [40] | 15,850 |
| 38 | 16 | H | Leicester C | W 2-1 | 2-0 | 12 | Keogh [16], Martin [44] | 23,123 |
| 39 | 29 | H | Bristol C | W 3-0 | 1-0 | 12 | Hendrick [36], Ward [54], Davies, B [90] | 23,483 |
| 40 | Apr 1 | A | Leeds U | W 2-1 | 0-0 | 8 | Coutts [73], Buxton [88] | 21,384 |
| 41 | 6 | H | Ipswich T | L 0-1 | 0-0 | 10 | | 23,081 |
| 42 | 13 | A | Blackburn R | L 0-2 | 0-2 | 13 | | 13,391 |
| 43 | 16 | A | Barnsley | D 1-1 | 0-0 | 15 | Coutts [90] | 9007 |
| 44 | 20 | H | Peterborough U | W 3-1 | 1-0 | 11 | Bryson [41], Martin [50], Keogh [52] | 23,753 |
| 45 | 27 | A | Blackpool | L 1-2 | 0-1 | 13 | Davies, B [65] | 14,775 |
| 46 | May 4 | H | Millwall | W 1-0 | 0-0 | 10 | Sammon [85] | 25,021 |

**Final League Position: 10**

### GOALSCORERS

*League (65):* Ward 12 (4 pens), Robinson 8 (1 pen), Sammon 8, Hendrick 6, Bryson 5, Davies, B 4, Keogh 4, Tyson 4, Buxton 3, Coutts 3, Hughes 2, Jacobs 2, Martin 2, Brayford 1, O'Connor 1.
*FA Cup (5):* Bennett 1, Brayford 1, Davies B 1, Hendrick 1, Sammon 1.
*Capital One Cup (5):* Buxton 2, Keogh 1, Robinson 1, Tyson 1.

| Fielding F 16 | Brayford J 40 | Keogh R 46 | Buxton J 26 + 5 | Roberts G 29 | Coutts P 44 | Hendrick J 43 + 2 | Bryson C 37 | Hughes W 33 + 2 | Tyson N 4 + 12 | Ward J 23 + 2 | O'Connor J 15 + 7 | Robinson T 13 + 15 | Gjokaj V 2 + 4 | Sammon C 41 + 4 | Bennett M 1 + 5 | Jacobs M 13 + 25 | Doyle C 1 + 1 | Legzdins A 30 + 1 | Davies B 8 + 15 | O'Brien M 6 + 3 | Freeman K 10 + 9 | Hoganson M 3 + 1 | Martin C 12 + 1 | Forsyth C 10 | Match No. |
|---|---|---|---|---|---|---|---|---|---|---|---|---|---|---|---|---|---|---|---|---|---|---|---|---|---|
| 1 | 2 | 3 | 4 | 5 | 6 | 7 | 8 | $9^3$ | $10^1$ | $11^2$ | 12 | 13 | 14 | | | | | | | | | | | | 1 |
| 1 | 2 | 3 | | 5 | 6 | 8 | 7 | 12 | $11^2$ | 9 | 4 | | | $10^1$ | 13 | | | | | | | | | | 2 |
| 1 | 2 | 4 | | 5 | $6^2$ | 8 | 7 | $9^1$ | 12 | 10 | 3 | 14 | | $11^3$ | 13 | | | | | | | | | | 3 |
| 1 | 2 | 3 | 12 | $5^1$ | 6 | 8 | $7^3$ | $9^2$ | | 11 | 4 | | | 10 | | 13 | 14 | | | | | | | | 4 |
| 1 | 2 | 3 | 14 | $5^3$ | | 8 | 7 | 6 | | 10 | 4 | 13 | | $11^2$ | | 12 | $9^1$ | | | | | | | | 5 |
| 1 | 2 | 4 | 12 | 5 | 6 | 7 | 8 | $9^2$ | | 11 | $3^1$ | 13 | | 10 | | | | | | | | | | | 6 |
| 1 | 2 | 4 | 3 | 5 | 6 | 8 | 7 | $9^1$ | | 11 | | 13 | | $10^2$ | | 12 | | | | | | | | | 7 |
| 1 | 2 | 4 | 3 | $5^2$ | 6 | 8 | 7 | 9 | | $10^1$ | 13 | 14 | | $11^3$ | | 12 | | | | | | | | | 8 |
| 1 | 2 | 3 | 4 | $5^3$ | 6 | $7^2$ | 8 | 9 | $10^1$ | 14 | 11 | | | 12 | | 13 | | | | | | | | | 9 |
| | 2 | 3 | 4 | 5 | 6 | 7 | 9 | $8^1$ | | $11^2$ | | 13 | | 10 | | | | 1 | | | | | | | 10 |
| | 2 | 3 | 4 | $5^2$ | 6 | 7 | 8 | 9 | 13 | 11 | | | | $10^1$ | | 12 | | 1 | | | | | | | 11 |
| | 2 | 4 | | 5 | 6 | 7 | 8 | | 13 | 11 | 3 | | | $10^2$ | | 12 | $9^1$ | 1 | | | | | | | 12 |
| | 2 | 3 | $4^4$ | $5^2$ | 6 | $7^3$ | 8 | $9^1$ | 13 | 11 | | | 14 | 10 | | 12 | | 1 | | | | | | | 13 |
| | 2 | 3 | | 5 | 6 | $7^2$ | 8 | $9^3$ | | $11^1$ | 4 | | 14 | 10 | | 12 | | 1 | 13 | | | | | | 14 |
| | 2 | 3 | | 5 | $6^3$ | 7 | 8 | 9 | 13 | $11^1$ | 4 | | 14 | $10^2$ | | 12 | | 1 | | | | | | | 15 |
| | 2 | 3 | | 5 | 6 | 7 | 8 | 9 | | 11 | 4 | | | $10^1$ | | 12 | | 1 | | | | | | | 16 |
| | 2 | 3 | 4 | 5 | $6^2$ | 7 | 8 | 9 | 13 | $11^1$ | | | | 10 | | 12 | | 1 | | | | | | | 17 |
| | 2 | 3 | 4 | 5 | 6 | $7^3$ | 8 | $9^2$ | | 11 | | | 14 | $10^1$ | | 12 | | 1 | 13 | | | | | | 18 |
| | 2 | 3 | 4 | $5^1$ | 6 | 7 | 8 | $9^2$ | 13 | $11^3$ | | | 14 | 10 | | 12 | | 1 | | | | | | | 19 |
| | 2 | 3 | 4 | $5^1$ | 6 | 7 | 8 | $9^3$ | 13 | 11 | | | 14 | $10^2$ | | 12 | | 1 | | | | | | | 20 |
| | 2 | 3 | $4^1$ | 5 | 6 | 7 | $8^3$ | 9 | | $11^2$ | | | 14 | 10 | | | | 1 | 13 | 12 | | | | | 21 |
| | 2 | 4 | | 5 | 6 | 7 | $10^1$ | $8^3$ | | 11 | | | 14 | 9 | | | | 1 | 12 | 13 | | $3^2$ | | | 22 |
| | 2 | 3 | | $5^2$ | 6 | 7 | 8 | 9 | | 11 | 4 | | | $10^1$ | | 12 | | 1 | 13 | | | | | | 23 |
| | 2 | 4 | | 5 | 6 | 7 | 8 | 9 | | $11^2$ | | | 14 | $10^1$ | | 12 | | 1 | 13 | | | $3^3$ | | | 24 |
| | 2 | 3 | | 5 | 6 | 7 | 8 | $9^2$ | | 11 | 4 | $13^3$ | 14 | $10^1$ | | 12 | | 1 | | | | | | | 25 |
| | 2 | 3 | | | 6 | 7 | 8 | 9 | | $11^1$ | | | | $10^2$ | | 12 | | 1 | 13 | 5 | 4 | | | | 26 |
| | 2 | 3 | 4 | 5 | 6 | 7 | $8^3$ | $9^1$ | | $11^2$ | | | 14 | 10 | | 12 | | 1 | 13 | | | | | | 27 |
| | 2 | 3 | | 5 | 6 | 7 | 8 | $9^2$ | | 11 | | | | $10^1$ | | 12 | | 1 | 13 | | 4 | | | | 28 |
| | 2 | 3 | | $5^2$ | 6 | 7 | 8 | $9^3$ | | $11^1$ | | | 14 | 10 | | 12 | | 1 | 13 | | 4 | | | | 29 |
| | 2 | 3 | 4 | 5 | $6^1$ | 7 | 8 | $9^3$ | | 11 | | | 14 | $10^2$ | | 12 | | 1 | 13 | | | | | | 30 |
| | | 3 | 4 | $5^1$ | $6^3$ | 7 | 8 | 9 | | $11^1$ | | | 14 | 10 | | 12 | | 1 | 13 | | $2^2$ | | | | 31 |
| | | 3 | 4 | | 6 | 7 | $8^1$ | 9 | | 11 | | | | 10 | | 12 | | 1 | | | 2 | | | 5 | 32 |
| | | 3 | 4 | | $6^2$ | 7 | 8 | 9 | | 11 | | | | 10 | | 12 | | 1 | 13 | | 2 | | | $5^1$ | 33 |
| | | 3 | 4 | | 6 | 7 | 8 | $9^2$ | | $11^3$ | | | 14 | 10 | | 12 | | 1 | 13 | | 2 | | | $5^1$ | 34 |
| | 2 | 3 | 4 | 5 | $6^3$ | 7 | 8 | 9 | | $11^1$ | | | 14 | $10^2$ | | 12 | | 1 | 13 | | | | | | 35 |
| | 2 | 3 | 4 | | 6 | 7 | 8 | $9^1$ | | 11 | | | | | | 12 | | 1 | | | | | 10 | 5 | 36 |
| | 2 | 3 | 4 | | $6^1$ | 7 | 8 | 9 | | 11 | | | | | | 12 | | 1 | | | | | 10 | 5 | 37 |
| 1 | | 3 | 4 | | 6 | 7 | 8 | $9^1$ | | 11 | | 13 | | | | 12 | | | | | $2^2$ | | 10 | 5 | 38 |
| 1 | | 3 | 4 | | 6 | 7 | 8 | $9^1$ | | 11 | | | | | | 12 | | | | | 2 | | 10 | 5 | 39 |
| 1 | | 3 | 4 | | 6 | 7 | $8^1$ | | | 11 | | 13 | | $9^2$ | | 12 | | | | | 2 | | 10 | 5 | 40 |
| 1 | | 3 | 4 | | 6 | 7 | $8^2$ | $9^1$ | | 11 | | 13 | | | | 12 | | | | | 2 | | 10 | 5 | 41 |
| 1 | 2 | 3 | 4 | | $6^1$ | 7 | $8^2$ | 9 | | $11^3$ | | 13 | 14 | | | 12 | | | | | | | 10 | 5 | 42 |
| 1 | 2 | 4 | 3 | | 6 | 7 | 8 | $9^1$ | | $11^2$ | | 13 | 14 | | | 12 | | | | | | | $10^3$ | 5 | 43 |
| $1^2$ | 2 | 3 | 4 | | 6 | 7 | $8^3$ | $9^2$ | | $11^1$ | | 13 | 14 | 10 | | 12 | | | | | | | | 5 | 44 |
| | 2 | 3 | 4 | | 6 | $7^2$ | 8 | 9 | | $11^3$ | | 13 | 14 | $10^1$ | | 12 | | 1 | | | | | | 5 | 45 |
| | 2 | 3 | 4 | 5 | $6^2$ | 7 | 8 | 9 | | $11^1$ | | 13 | 14 | $10^3$ | | 12 | | 1 | | | | | | | 46 |

**FA Cup**

| | | | |
|---|---|---|---|
| Third Round | Tranmere R | (h) | 5-0 |
| Fourth Round | Blackburn R | (h) | 0-3 |

**Capital One Cup**

| | | | |
|---|---|---|---|
| First Round | Scunthorpe U | (h) | 5-5 |
| *(aet; lost 6-7 on pens)* | | | |

# DONCASTER ROVERS

## FOUNDATION

In 1879, Mr Albert Jenkins assembled a team to play a match against the Yorkshire Institution for the Deaf. The players remained together as Doncaster Rovers, joining the Midland Alliance in 1889 and the Midland Counties League in 1891.

*Keepmoat Stadium, Stadium Way, Lakeside, Doncaster, South Yorkshire DN4 5JW.*

*Telephone:* (01302) 764 664.

*Fax:* (01302) 363 525.

*Ticket Office:* (01302) 762 576.

*Website:* www.doncasterroversfc.co.uk

*Email:* info@doncasterroversfc.co.uk

*Ground Capacity:* 15,231.

*Record Attendance:* 37,149 v Hull C, Division 3 (N), 2 October 1948 (at Belle Vue); 15,001 v Leeds U, FL 1, 1 April 2008 (at Keepmoat Stadium).

*Pitch Measurements:* 99m × 69m (109yd × 76yd)

*Chairman:* John Ryan.

*Chief Executive:* Gavin Baldwin.

*Manager:* Paul Dickov.

*Assistant Manager:* Brian Horton.

*Fitness Coach*: Ben Rome.

*Colours:* Red and white hooped shirts, black shorts, red socks with white tops.

*Year Formed:* 1879.

*Turned Professional:* 1885.

*Club Nickname:* 'Rovers', 'Donny'.

*Grounds:* 1880–1916, Intake Ground; 1920, Benetthorpe Ground; 1922, Low Pasture, Belle Vue; 2007, Keepmoat Stadium.

## HONOURS

**Football League Division 3:** *Champions* 2003–04; **Division 3 (N):** *Champions* – 1934–35, 1946–47, 1949–50; *Runners-up* 1937–38, 1938–39; **FL 1:** *Champions* 2012–13; **Division 4:** *Champions* 1965–66, 1968–69; *Runners-up* 1983–84.

**FA Cup:** Best season: 5th rd, 1952, 1954, 1955, 1956.

**Football League Cup:** Best season: 5th rd, 1976, 2006.

**Johnstone's Paint Trophy:** *Winners* 2007.

**Football Conference:** *Champions* 2002–03

**Sheffield County Cup:** *Winners* 1891, 1912, 1936, 1938, 1956, 1968, 1976, 1986.

**Midland Counties League:** *Champions* 1897, 1899.

**Conference Trophy:** *Winners* 1999, 2000.

**Sheffield & Hallamshire Senior Cup:** *Winners* 2001, 2002.

*First Football League Game:* 7 September 1901, Division 2, v Burslem Port Vale (h) D 3–3 – Eggett; Simpson, Layton; Longden, Jones, Wright, Langham, Murphy, Price, Goodson (2), Bailey (1).

*Record League Victory:* 10–0 v Darlington, Division 4, 25 January 1964 – Potter; Raine, Meadows, Windross (1), White, Ripley (2), Robinson, Book (2), Hale (4), Jeffrey, Broadbent (1).

*Record Cup Victory:* 7–0 v Blyth Spartans, FA Cup 1st rd, 27 November 1937 – Imrie; Shaw, Rodgers, McFarlane, Bycroft, Cyril Smith, Burton (1), Killourhy (4), Morgan (2), Malam, Dutton.

## sky SPORTS FACT FILE

Alick Jeffrey made his debut for Doncaster Rovers at the age of 15 and was one of the most promising players of his era until suffering a broken leg playing for England U23s in October 1956. He later resumed his career with Rovers but was never the same player again.

*Record Defeat:* 0–12 v Small Heath, Division 2, 11 April 1903.

*Most League Points (2 for a win):* 72, Division 3 (N), 1946–47.

*Most League Points (3 for a win):* 92, Division 3, 2003–04.

*Most League Goals:* 123, Division 3 (N), 1946–47.

*Highest League Scorer in Season:* Clarrie Jordan, 42, Division 3 (N), 1946–47.

*Most League Goals in Total Aggregate:* Tom Keetley, 180, 1923–29.

*Most League Goals in One Match:* 6, Tom Keetley v Ashington, Division 3 (N), 16 February 1929.

*Most Capped Player:* Len Graham, 14, Northern Ireland.

*Most League Appearances:* Fred Emery, 417, 1925–36.

*Youngest League Player:* Alick Jeffrey, 15 years 229 days v Fulham, 15 September 1954.

*Record Transfer Fee Received:* £2,000,000 from Reading for Matthew Mills, July 2009.

*Record Transfer Fee Paid:* £1,150,000 to Sheffield U for Billy Sharp, August 2010.

*Football League Record:* 1901 Elected to Division 2; 1903 Failed re-election; 1904 Re-elected; 1905 Failed re-election; 1923 Re-elected to Division 3 (N); 1935–37 Division 2; 1937–47 Division 3 (N); 1947–48 Division 2; 1948–50 Division 3 (N); 1950–58 Division 2; 1958–59 Division 3; 1959–66 Division 4; 1966–67 Division 3; 1967–69 Division 4; 1969–71 Division 3; 1971–81 Division 4; 1981–83 Division 3; 1983–84 Division 4; 1984–88 Division 3; 1988–92 Division 4; 1992–98 Division 3; 1998–2003 Conference; 2003–04 Division 3; 2004–08 FL 1; 2008–12 FL C; 2012–13 FL 1; 2013– FL C.

## LATEST SEQUENCES

*Longest Sequence of League Wins:* 10, 22.1.1947 – 4.4.1947.

*Longest Sequence of League Defeats:* 9, 14.1.1905 – 1.4.1905.

*Longest Sequence of League Draws:* 4, 29.10.1932 – 19.11.1932.

*Longest Sequence of Unbeaten League Matches:* 20, 26.12.1968 – 12.4.1969.

*Longest Sequence Without a League Win:* 20, 9.8.1997 – 29.11.1997.

*Successive Scoring Runs:* 27 from 10.11.1934.

*Successive Non-scoring Runs:* 7 from 27.9.1947.

## MANAGERS

**Arthur Porter** 1920–21
**Harry Tufnell** 1921–22
**Arthur Porter** 1922–23
**Dick Ray** 1923–27
**David Menzies** 1928–36
**Fred Emery** 1936–40
**Bill Marsden** 1944–46
**Jackie Bestall** 1946–49
**Peter Doherty** 1949–58
**Jack Hodgson and Sid Bycroft**
  (*Joint Managers*) 1958
**Jack Crayston** 1958–59
  (*continued as Secretary-Manager to 1961*)
**Jackie Bestall** (*TM*) 1959–60
**Norman Curtis** 1960–61
**Danny Malloy** 1961–62
**Oscar Hold** 1962–64
**Bill Leivers** 1964–66
**Keith Kettleborough** 1966–67
**George Raynor** 1967–68
**Lawrie McMenemy** 1968–71
**Maurice Setters** 1971–74
**Stan Anderson** 1975–78
**Billy Bremner** 1978–85
**Dave Cusack** 1985–87
**Dave Mackay** 1987–89
**Billy Bremner** 1989–91
**Steve Beaglehole** 1991–93
**Ian Atkins** 1994
**Sammy Chung** 1994–96
**Kerry Dixon** (*Player-Manager*) 1996–97
**Dave Cowling** 1997
**Mark Weaver** 1997–98
**Ian Snodin** 1998–99
**Steve Wignall** 1999–2001
**Dave Penney** 2002–06
**Sean O'Driscoll** 2006–11
**Dean Saunders** 2011–13
**Brian Flynn** 2013
**Paul Dickov** May 2013–

## TEN YEAR LEAGUE RECORD

|         |       | P  | W  | D  | L  | F  | A  | Pts | Pos |
|---------|-------|----|----|----|----|----|----|-----|-----|
| 2003-04 | Div 3 | 46 | 27 | 11 | 8  | 79 | 37 | 92  | 1   |
| 2004-05 | FL 1  | 46 | 16 | 18 | 12 | 65 | 60 | 66  | 10  |
| 2005-06 | FL 1  | 46 | 20 | 9  | 17 | 55 | 51 | 69  | 8   |
| 2006-07 | FL 1  | 46 | 16 | 15 | 15 | 52 | 47 | 63  | 11  |
| 2007-08 | FL 1  | 46 | 23 | 11 | 12 | 65 | 41 | 80  | 3   |
| 2008-09 | FL C  | 46 | 17 | 7  | 22 | 42 | 53 | 58  | 14  |
| 2009-10 | FL C  | 46 | 15 | 15 | 16 | 59 | 58 | 60  | 12  |
| 2010-11 | FL C  | 46 | 11 | 15 | 20 | 55 | 81 | 48  | 21  |
| 2011-12 | FL C  | 46 | 8  | 12 | 26 | 43 | 80 | 36  | 24  |
| 2012-13 | FL 1  | 46 | 25 | 9  | 12 | 62 | 44 | 84  | 1   |

## DID YOU KNOW

Clarrie Jordan's record breaking tally of 42 goals in 41 Division Three North games in 1946–47 included a run of four games during which he scored three hat-tricks. He scored in 10 consecutive League matches between 22 January and 4 April.

## DONCASTER ROVERS – FOOTBALL LEAGUE ONE 2012–13 LEAGUE RECORD

| Match No. | Date | Venue | Opponents | Result | H/T Score | Lg Pos. | Goalscorers | Attendance |
|---|---|---|---|---|---|---|---|---|
| 1 | Aug 18 | A | Walsall | W 3-0 | 2-0 | 2 | Brown [5], Cotterill [26], Bennett [56] | 4205 |
| 2 | 21 | H | Bury | W 2-1 | 1-1 | 2 | Bennett [36], Brown [84] | 6380 |
| 3 | 25 | H | Crawley T | L 0-1 | 0-0 | 5 | | 6403 |
| 4 | Sept 1 | A | Yeovil T | L 1-2 | 0-0 | 9 | Paynter [90] | 3535 |
| 5 | 15 | A | Colchester U | W 2-1 | 1-1 | 9 | Cotterill [3], Bond (og) [48] | 3262 |
| 6 | 18 | A | Sheffield U | D 0-0 | 0-0 | 10 | | 17,925 |
| 7 | 22 | H | Stevenage | D 1-1 | 0-1 | 12 | Brown [79] | 5910 |
| 8 | 29 | A | Leyton Orient | W 2-0 | 2-0 | 10 | Hume [12], Cotterill [21] | 4401 |
| 9 | Oct 2 | H | Preston NE | L 1-3 | 1-1 | 11 | Cotterill [45] | 5681 |
| 10 | 6 | H | Shrewsbury T | W 1-0 | 1-0 | 10 | Paynter (pen) [4] | 6437 |
| 11 | 13 | A | Hartlepool U | D 1-1 | 0-0 | 9 | Jones, R [89] | 4406 |
| 12 | 20 | H | Brentford | W 2-1 | 0-1 | 7 | Cotterill [74], Paynter [84] | 6555 |
| 13 | 23 | A | Tranmere R | W 2-1 | 0-0 | 6 | Paynter [48], Hume [90] | 7386 |
| 14 | 27 | A | Notts Co | W 2-0 | 0-0 | 5 | Keegan [61], Brown [63] | 6750 |
| 15 | Nov 6 | H | Crewe Alex | L 0-2 | 0-1 | 6 | | 5411 |
| 16 | 10 | H | Bournemouth | L 0-1 | 0-1 | 9 | | 5951 |
| 17 | 17 | A | Portsmouth | W 1-0 | 1-0 | 8 | Hume [25] | 11,792 |
| 18 | 20 | A | Carlisle U | W 3-1 | 2-0 | 4 | Jones, R [14], Cotterill [18], Spurr [76] | 3229 |
| 19 | 24 | H | Scunthorpe U | W 4-0 | 1-0 | 3 | Ribeiro (og) [22], Cotterill [46], Jones, R [62], Paynter [64] | 8037 |
| 20 | 27 | H | Oldham Ath | W 1-0 | 0-0 | 2 | Cotterill [69] | 6066 |
| 21 | Dec 8 | A | Swindon T | D 1-1 | 1-1 | 2 | Hollands (og) [10] | 7700 |
| 22 | 15 | H | Coventry C | L 1-4 | 0-2 | 4 | Brown [76] | 6623 |
| 23 | 26 | A | Oldham Ath | W 2-1 | 1-1 | 4 | Jones, R [3], Syers [90] | 4252 |
| 24 | 29 | A | Preston NE | W 3-0 | 2-0 | 3 | Syers [1], Cotterill [30], Paynter (pen) [76] | 9626 |
| 25 | Jan 1 | H | Sheffield U | D 2-2 | 1-0 | 3 | Paynter (pen) [18], Syers [63] | 12,785 |
| 26 | 5 | H | Colchester U | W 1-0 | 0-0 | 2 | Cotterill [84] | 6373 |
| 27 | 12 | A | Stevenage | W 2-1 | 0-0 | 2 | Hume [79], Jones, R [90] | 3280 |
| 28 | 19 | H | Leyton Orient | W 2-0 | 1-0 | 2 | Jones, R [19], Brown [53] | 6438 |
| 29 | Feb 2 | A | Bury | L 0-2 | 0-2 | 2 | | 3618 |
| 30 | 9 | H | Walsall | L 1-2 | 1-1 | 2 | Paynter [16] | 7013 |
| 31 | 12 | H | Milton Keynes D | D 0-0 | 0-0 | 2 | | 6423 |
| 32 | 18 | A | Crawley T | D 1-1 | 1-1 | 2 | Husband [43] | 3267 |
| 33 | 23 | H | Yeovil T | D 1-1 | 1-1 | 4 | Paynter [45] | 6356 |
| 34 | 26 | A | Shrewsbury T | W 2-1 | 0-0 | 1 | Husband [73], Bennett [90] | 4886 |
| 35 | Mar 2 | H | Hartlepool U | W 3-0 | 1-0 | 1 | Hume [35], Coppinger [54], Paynter [81] | 7457 |
| 36 | 5 | A | Milton Keynes D | L 0-3 | 0-1 | 1 | | 6804 |
| 37 | 9 | H | Bournemouth | W 2-1 | 0-0 | 1 | Paynter [66], Husband [88] | 7178 |
| 38 | 16 | H | Portsmouth | D 1-1 | 1-0 | 1 | Brown [37] | 7604 |
| 39 | 23 | A | Scunthorpe U | W 3-2 | 2-1 | 1 | Mirfin (og) [5], Hume [39], Brown [48] | 5288 |
| 40 | 29 | A | Coventry C | L 0-1 | 0-1 | 1 | | 9000 |
| 41 | Apr 1 | H | Swindon T | W 1-0 | 0-0 | 1 | McCombe [80] | 8106 |
| 42 | 6 | H | Tranmere R | W 1-0 | 0-0 | 1 | Jones, R [63] | 7979 |
| 43 | 9 | H | Carlisle U | L 0-2 | 0-1 | 1 | | 7884 |
| 44 | 13 | A | Crewe Alex | W 2-1 | 0-0 | 1 | Paynter 2 [66, 70] | 5465 |
| 45 | 20 | H | Notts Co | L 1-0 | 0-1 | 2 | | 12,624 |
| 46 | 27 | A | Brentford | W 1-0 | 0-0 | 1 | Coppinger [90] | 12,300 |

**Final League Position: 1**

### GOALSCORERS

**League (62):** Paynter 13 (3 pens), Cotterill 10, Brown 8, Jones, R 7, Hume 6, Bennett 3, Husband 3, Syers 3, Coppinger 2, Keegan 1, McCombe 1, Spurr 1, own goals 4.
*FA Cup (4):* Blake 1, Brown 1, Hume 1, Woods Martom 1.
*Capital One Cup (4):* Syers 2, Brown 1 (1 pen), Jones R 1.
*Johnstone's Paint Trophy (2):* Ball 1, Brown 1.

| Woods G 42 | Quinn P 37 + 1 | Jones R 44 | McCombe J 33 | Spurr T 46 | Cotterill D 44 | Syers D 20 + 12 | Woods Martin 15 + 1 | Bennett K 26 + 9 | Brown C 28 + 8 | Paynter B 25 + 12 | Harper J 19 + 8 | Coppinger J 19 + 6 | Blake R — + 7 | Hume I 24 + 9 | Husband J 24 + 9 | Keegan P 22 + 3 | Martis S 3 + 6 | Ball J — + 1 | Griffin A 8 + 8 | Clingan S 1 + 5 | Sinclair E 1 + 3 | Fowler L 1 + 3 | Lundstram J 14 | Sullivan N 4 | Furman D 6 + 2 | Match No. |
|---|---|---|---|---|---|---|---|---|---|---|---|---|---|---|---|---|---|---|---|---|---|---|---|---|---|---|
| 1 | 2 | 3 | 4 | 5 | 6 | | 7 | 8 | $9^2$ | $10^3$ | $11^1$ | 12 | 13 | 14 | | | | | | | | | | | | 1 |
| 1 | 2 | 3 | 4 | 5 | 6 | | 7 | $8^1$ | 9 | $10^2$ | 11 | 12 | 13 | | | | | | | | | | | | | 2 |
| 1 | 2 | 4 | 3 | 5 | 6 | | 8 | 7 | 9 | $10^1$ | 11 | 12 | | | | | | | | | | | | | | 3 |
| 1 | 2 | 3 | 4 | 5 | 6 | 7 | $8^3$ | $9^2$ | $11^1$ | 10 | 12 | | | 13 | 14 | | | | | | | | | | | 4 |
| 1 | 2 | 3 | 4 | 6 | 7 | $5^2$ | 9 | $10^1$ | $11^3$ | | 13 | | | 14 | 12 | 8 | | | | | | | | | | 5 |
| 1 | 2 | 3 | 4 | 5 | $6^2$ | $9^1$ | 8 | $10^3$ | 11 | | 12 | | | 14 | 13 | 7 | | | | | | | | | | 6 |
| 1 | 2 | 3 | 4 | 5 | 11 | 6 | $7^2$ | $9^3$ | 10 | | 12 | | | 13 | 14 | $8^1$ | | | | | | | | | | 7 |
| 1 | 13 | 3 | 4 | 5 | $6^2$ | 7 | 12 | $9^1$ | 11 | 14 | 8 | | | $10^3$ | 2 | | | | | | | | | | | 8 |
| 1 | 2 | 3 | 4 | 5 | 6 | 7 | 8 | 9 | 10 | 11 | | | | | | | | | | | | | | | | 9 |
| 1 | 2 | | 4 | 6 | $8^2$ | | 9 | 13 | $10^1$ | 7 | | | | 11 | 5 | 12 | 3 | | | | | | | | | 10 |
| 1 | 2 | 4 | | 5 | 9 | 7 | | 6 | $10^3$ | $11^1$ | 8 | | | 13 | 14 | $3^2$ | 12 | | | | | | | | | 11 |
| 1 | 2 | 4 | | 5 | 6 | 12 | 8 | 9 | $11^2$ | 13 | 7 | | | 14 | $10^3$ | | $3^1$ | | | | | | | | | 12 |
| 1 | 2 | 3 | | 4 | $6^1$ | 12 | | 9 | | $11^3$ | 8 | | | 14 | 10 | $5^2$ | 7 | | | 13 | | | | | | 13 |
| 1 | $2^2$ | 3 | | 4 | | 7 | | 6 | 12 | $10^1$ | 8 | | | $11^3$ | 5 | 9 | | | | 13 | 14 | | | | | 14 |
| 1 | 2 | $3^1$ | | 4 | | $6^2$ | 9 | | 14 | 11 | $8^3$ | 13 | 10 | 5 | 7 | | | 12 | | | | | | | | 15 |
| 1 | 2 | | 4 | | $6^1$ | 12 | | | 10 | $9^2$ | 7 | | | 13 | 11 | 5 | | | 3 | 8 | | | | | | 16 |
| 1 | | 3 | | 5 | $6^2$ | 13 | 9 | | 12 | $10^1$ | 7 | | | $11^3$ | 2 | 8 | 14 | | 4 | | | | | | | 17 |
| 1 | | $3^1$ | | 4 | 6 | 14 | 9 | | 13 | $11^3$ | 7 | | | $10^2$ | 5 | 8 | 12 | | 2 | | | | | | | 18 |
| 1 | 2 | 4 | | 3 | 6 | 14 | $9^1$ | | 12 | 10 | $7^2$ | | | 11 | 5 | $8^3$ | | | | 13 | | | | | | 19 |
| 1 | 2 | 3 | | 4 | 6 | 13 | $9^1$ | | 10 | | $7^2$ | | | 11* | 5 | 8 | | | | | 12 | | | | | 20 |
| 1 | 2 | 3 | | 4 | 9 | | $6^1$ | $10^3$ | | | $7^2$ | | | 11 | 5 | 8 | 13 | | 14 | 12 | | | | | | 21 |
| 1 | $2^2$ | 3 | | 4 | $9^1$ | | 6 | 12 | 11 | | $7^3$ | | | 10 | 5 | 8 | | | 13 | 14 | | | | | | 22 |
| 1 | 2 | 3 | 4 | 5 | 6 | 12 | | $9^3$ | 13 | $11^2$ | 7 | | | 10 | 14 | $8^1$ | | | | | | | | | | 23 |
| 1 | 2 | 3 | 5 | 4 | $6^2$ | 8 | | $10^1$ | | $11^3$ | 9 | | | 14 | 7 | 12 | | | 13 | | | | | | | 24 |
| 1 | $2^1$ | 4 | 3 | 5 | 6 | 8 | | $9^2$ | | 10* | | 13 | | $11^3$ | | 7 | 14 | | 12 | | | | | | | 25 |
| 1 | 2 | 3 | 4 | 5 | $6^3$ | 8 | | $9^1$ | | 13 | | 10 | 14 | 7 | | | | | | $11^2$ | 12 | | | | | 26 |
| 1 | 2 | 3 | 4 | 5 | 7 | 6 | | $9^2$ | 10 | | 12 | 13 | 11 | | | $8^1$ | | | | | | | | | | 27 |
| 1 | 2 | 4 | 3 | 5 | $6^2$ | 8 | | 9 | 10 | $11^1$ | 13 | | | 7 | | | | | | | 12 | | | | | 28 |
| 1 | 2 | 3 | 4 | 5 | 6 | $7^1$ | | $9^2$ | $11^3$ | 13 | 10 | | | | 8 | | | | | | 14 | 12 | | | | 29 |
| 1 | 2 | 4 | 3 | 5 | 9 | | 13 | 10 | $11^2$ | 8 | 6 | | | | $7^1$ | | | | | | | 12 | | | | 30 |
| 1 | 2 | 4 | 3 | 5 | 9 | | 7 | | $10^2$ | 12 | 11 | | | 6 | | | | | $8^1$ | 13 | | | | | | 31 |
| 1 | 2 | 3 | 7 | 4 | 9 | | 12 | | 10 | 8 | 11 | | | 5 | | | | | | | $6^1$ | | | | | 32 |
| 1 | 2 | 4 | 3 | 5 | 6 | 13 | | 14 | | $11^3$ | | 10 | 12 | $9^1$ | 8 | | | | | | | $7^2$ | | | | 33 |
| 1 | 2 | 4 | 3 | 5 | $6^3$ | 12 | | 14 | | 13 | | 11 | $10^2$ | 9 | $7^1$ | | | | | | | 8 | | | | 34 |
| 1 | 2 | 3 | 4 | 5 | $6^2$ | 7 | | 13 | | 12 | | 11 | $10^1$ | 9 | | | | | | | | 8 | | | | 35 |
| 1 | 2 | $4^1$ | 5 | 3 | 6 | | 14 | | 13 | 7 | 10 | $11^2$ | $9^3$ | | | | 12 | | | | | 8 | | | | 36 |
| | 2 | 4 | 3 | 5 | 6 | | 13 | $11^1$ | $10^2$ | | 8 | 12 | 9 | | | | | | | | | 7 | | 1 | | 37 |
| 1 | 2 | 4 | 3 | 5 | 6 | | | 10 | $11^2$ | $7^1$ | | 13 | 9 | | | | 14 | | | | | $8^3$ | | | 12 | 38 |
| 1 | 2 | 3 | 4 | 5 | 6 | | | 11 | 12 | | 8 | $10^1$ | 9 | | | | | | | | | 7 | | | | 39 |
| 1 | | 3 | 4 | 5 | 6 | 13 | | 10 | | 7 | $11^2$ | $9^1$ | | 2 | | | | | | | | 8 | | | 12 | 40 |
| 1 | | 4 | 3 | 5 | 6 | | | $9^1$ | $11^2$ | 13 | 10 | 12 | | 2 | | | | | | | | 7 | | | 8 | 41 |
| 1 | | 4 | 3 | 5 | 6 | | | $9^1$ | 10 | 12 | 11 | | | 2 | | | | | | | | 8 | | | 7 | 42 |
| 1 | | 4 | 3 | 5 | 6 | | | $9^1$ | 11 | 12 | $10^2$ | 13 | 14 | $2^3$ | | | | | | | | 7 | | | 8 | 43 |
| | | 4 | 3 | 5 | 9 | | | 11 | 12 | 6 | $10^1$ | | | 2 | | | | | | | | 7 | 1 | | 8 | 44 |
| | | 4 | 3 | 5 | $6^2$ | 12 | | 13 | 11 | $10^3$ | 9 | 14 | | 2 | | | | | | | | $7^1$ | 1 | | 8 | 45 |
| | 2 | 3 | 4 | 5 | 9 | 14 | | $11^3$ | 13 | 6 | $10^2$ | | | 12 | | | | | | | | $7^1$ | 1 | | 8 | 46 |

**FA Cup**

| | | | | |
|---|---|---|---|---|
| First Round | Bradford PA | (h) | 3-1 | |
| Second Round | Oldham Ath | (a) | 1-3 | |

**Capital One Cup**

| | | | | |
|---|---|---|---|---|
| First Round | York C | (h) | 1-1 | |
| *(aet; won 4-2 on pens)* | | | | |
| Second Round | Hull C | (h) | 3-2 | |
| Third Round | Norwich C | (a) | 0-1 | |

**Johnstone's Paint Trophy**

| | | | | |
|---|---|---|---|---|
| Second Round | Chesterfield | (h) | 1-0 | |
| Northern Quarter-Finals | Crewe Alex | (a) | 1-1 | |
| *(aet; lost 3-5 on pens)* | | | | |

# EVERTON

## FOUNDATION

St Domingo Church Sunday School formed a football club in 1878 which played at Stanley Park. Enthusiasm was so great that in November 1879 they decided to expand membership and changed the name to Everton, playing in black shirts with a scarlet sash and nicknamed the 'Black Watch'. After wearing several other colours, royal blue was adopted in 1901.

*Goodison Park, Goodison Road, Liverpool L4 4EL.*
*Telephone:* (0871) 663 1878.

*Fax:* (0151) 286 9112.

*Ticket Office:* (0871) 663 1878.

*Website:* www.evertonfc.com

*Email:* everton@evertonfc.com

*Ground Capacity:* 39,571.

*Record Attendance:* 78,299 v Liverpool, Division 1, 18 September 1948.

*Pitch Measurements:* 100.48m × 68m (109yd × 74yd)

*Chairman:* Bill Kenwright CBE.

*Chief Executive:* Robert Elstone.

*Manager:* Roberto Martinez.

*Assistant Manager:* Graeme Jones.

*Physios:* Dominic Rogan, Matt Connery.

*Colours:* Blue shirts with white trim, white shorts with blue trim, blue socks.

*Year Formed:* 1878.

*Turned Professional:* 1885.

*Previous Name:* 1878, St Domingo FC; 1879, Everton.

*Club Nickname:* 'The Toffees'.

*Grounds:* 1878, Stanley Park; 1882, Priory Road; 1884, Anfield Road; 1892, Goodison Park.

*First Football League Game:* 8 September 1888, Football League, v Accrington (h) W 2–1 – Smalley; Dick, Ross; Holt, Jones, Dobson; Fleming (2), Waugh, Lewis, Edgar Chadwick, Farmer.

*Record League Victory:* 9–1 v Manchester C, Division 1, 3 September 1906 – Scott; Balmer, Crelley; Booth, Taylor (1), Abbott (1); Sharp, Bolton (1), Young (4), Settle (2), George Wilson. 9–1 v Plymouth Arg, Division 2, 27 December 1930 – Coggins; Williams, Cresswell; McPherson, Griffiths, Thomson; Critchley, Dunn, Dean (4), Johnson (1), Stein (4).

## HONOURS

**Football League – Division 1:**
*Champions* 1890–91, 1914–15, 1927–28, 1931–32, 1938–39, 1962–63, 1969–70, 1984–85, 1986–87;
*Runners-up* 1889–90, 1894–95, 1901–02, 1904–05, 1908–09, 1911–12, 1985–86;
**Division 2:** *Champions* 1930–31;
*Runners-up* 1953–54.
**FA Cup:** *Winners* 1906, 1933, 1966, 1984, 1995; *Runners-up* 1893, 1897, 1907, 1968, 1985, 1986, 1989, 2009.
**Football League Cup:**
*Runners-up* 1977, 1984.
**League Super Cup:** *Runners-up* 1986.
**Simod Cup:** *Runners-up* 1989.
**Zenith Data Systems Cup:**
*Runners-up* 1991.
**European Competitions**
**European Cup:** 1963–64, 1970–71.
**European Cup-Winners' Cup:**
1966–67, 1984–85 (*winners*), 1995–96.
**European Fairs Cup:** 1962–63, 1964–65, 1965–66.
**Champions League:** 2005–06.
**UEFA Cup:** 1975–76, 1978–79, 1979–80, 2005–06, 2007–08, 2008–09.
**Europa League:** 2009–10.

## sky SPORTS FACT FILE

Everton first experienced competitive European football in the 1962–63 season when they entered the Inter Cities Fairs Cup. The Toffees were drawn against Dunfermline Athletic, winning the first leg 1-0. However, Dunfermline went on to win the second leg 2-0 to progress into the next round.

**Record Cup Victory:** 11–2 v Derby Co, FA Cup 1st rd, 18 January 1890 – Smalley; Hannah, Doyle (1); Kirkwood, Holt (1), Parry; Latta, Brady (3), Geary (3), Edgar Chadwick, Millward (3).

**Record Defeat:** 4–10 v Tottenham H, Division 1, 11 October 1958.

**Most League Points (2 for a win):** 66, Division 1, 1969–70.

**Most League Points (3 for a win):** 90, Division 1, 1984–85.

**Most League Goals:** 121, Division 2, 1930–31.

**Highest League Scorer in Season:** William Ralph 'Dixie' Dean, 60, Division 1, 1927–28 (All-time League record).

**Most League Goals in Total Aggregate:** William Ralph 'Dixie' Dean, 349, 1925–37.

**Most League Goals in One Match:** 6, Jack Southworth v WBA, Division 1, 30 December 1893.

**Most Capped Player:** Neville Southall, 92, Wales.

**Most League Appearances:** Neville Southall, 578, 1981–98.

**Youngest League Player:** James Vaughan, 16 years 271 days v Crystal Palace, 10 April 2005.

**Record Transfer Fee Received:** £25,000,000 rising to £29,000,000 from Manchester U for Wayne Rooney, August 2004.

**Record Transfer Fee Paid:** £15,000,000 to Standard Liege for Marouane Fellaini, September 2008.

**Football League Record:** 1888 Founder Member of the Football League; 1930–31 Division 2; 1931–51 Division 1; 1951–54 Division 2; 1954–92 Division 1; 1992– FA Premier League.

## MANAGERS

W. E. Barclay 1888–89
*(Secretary-Manager)*
Dick Molyneux 1889–1901
*(Secretary-Manager)*
William C. Cuff 1901–18
*(Secretary-Manager)*
W. J. Sawyer 1918–19
*(Secretary-Manager)*
Thomas H. McIntosh 1919–35
*(Secretary-Manager)*
Theo Kelly 1936–48
Cliff Britton 1948–56
Ian Buchan 1956–58
Johnny Carey 1958–61
Harry Catterick 1961–73
Billy Bingham 1973–77
Gordon Lee 1977–81
Howard Kendall 1981–87
Colin Harvey 1987–90
Howard Kendall 1990–93
Mike Walker 1994
Joe Royle 1994–97
Howard Kendall 1997–98
Walter Smith 1998–2002
David Moyes 2002–13
Roberto Martinez July 2013–

## LATEST SEQUENCES

**Longest Sequence of League Wins:** 12, 24.3.1894 – 13.10.1894.

**Longest Sequence of League Defeats:** 6, 26.12.1996 – 29.1.1997.

**Longest Sequence of League Draws:** 5, 4.5.1977 – 16.5.1977.

**Longest Sequence of Unbeaten League Matches:** 20, 29.4.1978 – 16.12.1978.

**Longest Sequence Without a League Win:** 14, 6.3.1937 – 4.9.1937.

**Successive Scoring Runs:** 40 from 15.3.1930.

**Successive Non-scoring Runs:** 6 from 3.3.1951.

## TEN YEAR LEAGUE RECORD

| | | P | W | D | L | F | A | Pts | Pos |
|---|---|---|---|---|---|---|---|---|---|
| 2003-04 | PR Lge | 38 | 9 | 12 | 17 | 45 | 57 | 39 | 17 |
| 2004-05 | PR Lge | 38 | 18 | 7 | 13 | 45 | 46 | 61 | 4 |
| 2005-06 | PR Lge | 38 | 14 | 8 | 16 | 34 | 49 | 50 | 11 |
| 2006-07 | PR Lge | 38 | 15 | 13 | 10 | 52 | 36 | 58 | 6 |
| 2007-08 | PR Lge | 38 | 19 | 8 | 11 | 55 | 33 | 65 | 5 |
| 2008-09 | PR Lge | 38 | 17 | 12 | 9 | 55 | 37 | 63 | 5 |
| 2009-10 | PR Lge | 38 | 16 | 13 | 9 | 60 | 49 | 61 | 8 |
| 2010-11 | PR Lge | 38 | 13 | 15 | 10 | 51 | 45 | 54 | 7 |
| 2011-12 | PR Lge | 38 | 15 | 11 | 12 | 50 | 40 | 56 | 7 |
| 2012-13 | PR Lge | 38 | 16 | 15 | 7 | 55 | 40 | 63 | 6 |

## DID YOU KNOW ?

Everton had already clinched the First Division championship before the final game of the 1927–28 season, but 'Dixie' Dean needed a hat-trick to set a new Football League scoring record of 60 goals. He hit two early goals but had to wait until the 82nd minute to achieve his target.

## EVERTON – FA PREMIERSHIP 2012–13 LEAGUE RECORD

| Match No. | Date | Venue | Opponents | Result | H/T Score | Lg Pos. | Goalscorers | Attendance |
|---|---|---|---|---|---|---|---|---|
| 1 | Aug 20 | H | Manchester U | W 1-0 | 0-0 | 7 | Fellaini [57] | 38,415 |
| 2 | 25 | A | Aston Villa | W 3-1 | 3-0 | 3 | Pienaar [3], Fellaini [31], Jelavic [43] | 36,565 |
| 3 | Sept 1 | A | WBA | L 0-2 | 0-0 | 5 | | 25,383 |
| 4 | 17 | H | Newcastle U | D 2-2 | 1-0 | 7 | Baines [15], Anichebe [88] | 32,510 |
| 5 | 22 | A | Swansea C | W 3-0 | 2-0 | 2 | Anichebe [22], Mirallas [43], Fellaini [82] | 20,464 |
| 6 | 29 | H | Southampton | W 3-1 | 3-1 | 2 | Osman [25], Jelavic 2 [32, 38] | 37,922 |
| 7 | Oct 6 | A | Wigan Ath | D 2-2 | 1-2 | 3 | Jelavic [11], Baines (pen) [87] | 18,759 |
| 8 | 21 | A | QPR | D 1-1 | 1-1 | 4 | Julio Cesar (og) [33] | 17,959 |
| 9 | 28 | H | Liverpool | D 2-2 | 2-2 | 5 | Osman [22], Naismith [35] | 39,613 |
| 10 | Nov 3 | A | Fulham | D 2-2 | 0-1 | 4 | Fellaini 2 [55, 72] | 25,699 |
| 11 | 10 | H | Sunderland | W 2-1 | 0-1 | 4 | Fellaini [77], Jelavic [79] | 35,999 |
| 12 | 17 | A | Reading | L 1-2 | 1-0 | 5 | Naismith [10] | 24,184 |
| 13 | 24 | H | Norwich C | D 1-1 | 1-0 | 5 | Naismith [12] | 34,502 |
| 14 | 28 | H | Arsenal | D 1-1 | 1-1 | 6 | Fellaini [28] | 37,141 |
| 15 | Dec 1 | A | Manchester C | D 1-1 | 1-1 | 6 | Fellaini [33] | 47,386 |
| 16 | 9 | H | Tottenham H | W 2-1 | 0-0 | 4 | Pienaar [90], Jelavic [90] | 36,494 |
| 17 | 15 | A | Stoke C | D 1-1 | 1-0 | 4 | Shawcross (og) [36] | 27,008 |
| 18 | 22 | A | West Ham U | W 2-1 | 0-1 | 4 | Anichebe [64], Pienaar [73] | 35,005 |
| 19 | 26 | H | Wigan Ath | W 2-1 | 0-0 | 5 | Osman [52], Jagielka [77] | 38,749 |
| 20 | 30 | H | Chelsea | L 1-2 | 1-1 | 6 | Pienaar [2] | 39,485 |
| 21 | Jan 2 | A | Newcastle U | W 2-1 | 1-1 | 5 | Baines [43], Anichebe [60] | 49,391 |
| 22 | 12 | H | Swansea C | D 0-0 | 0-0 | 5 | | 35,782 |
| 23 | 21 | A | Southampton | D 0-0 | 0-0 | 5 | | 28,359 |
| 24 | 30 | H | WBA | W 2-1 | 2-0 | 5 | Baines 2 (1 pen) [29, 45 (p)] | 31,376 |
| 25 | Feb 2 | H | Aston Villa | D 3-3 | 1-2 | 5 | Anichebe [21], Fellaini 2 [69, 90] | 38,121 |
| 26 | 10 | A | Manchester U | L 0-2 | 0-2 | 6 | | 75,525 |
| 27 | 23 | A | Norwich C | L 1-2 | 1-0 | 6 | Osman [39] | 26,828 |
| 28 | Mar 2 | H | Reading | W 3-1 | 1-0 | 6 | Fellaini [42], Pienaar [59], Mirallas [66] | 35,244 |
| 29 | 16 | H | Manchester C | W 2-0 | 1-0 | 6 | Osman [32], Jelavic [90] | 36,519 |
| 30 | 30 | H | Stoke C | W 1-0 | 1-0 | 6 | Mirallas [28] | 33,977 |
| 31 | Apr 7 | A | Tottenham H | D 2-2 | 1-1 | 6 | Jagielka [15], Mirallas [53] | 36,192 |
| 32 | 13 | H | QPR | W 2-0 | 1-0 | 6 | Gibson [40], Anichebe [56] | 34,876 |
| 33 | 16 | A | Arsenal | D 0-0 | 0-0 | 6 | | 60,071 |
| 34 | 20 | A | Sunderland | L 0-1 | 0-1 | 6 | | 44,614 |
| 35 | 27 | H | Fulham | W 1-0 | 1-0 | 6 | Pienaar [16] | 34,563 |
| 36 | May 5 | H | Liverpool | D 0-0 | 0-0 | 6 | | 44,991 |
| 37 | 12 | H | West Ham U | W 2-0 | 1-0 | 6 | Mirallas 2 [6, 60] | 39,475 |
| 38 | 19 | A | Chelsea | L 1-2 | 1-1 | 6 | Naismith [14] | 41,794 |

**Final League Position: 6**

### GOALSCORERS

*League (55):* Fellaini 11, Jelavic 7, Anichebe 6, Mirallas 6, Pienaar 6, Baines 5 (2 pens), Osman 5, Naismith 4, Jagielka 2, Gibson 1, own goals 2.
*FA Cup (12):* Baines 2 (2 pens), Osman 2, Anichebe 1, Coleman 1, Fellaini 1, Heitinga 1, Jagielka 1, Jelavic 1, Mirallas 1, Pienaar 1.
*Capital One Cup (6):* Mirallas 2, Anichebe 1, Distin 1, Gueye 1, Osman 1.

| Howard T 36 | Hibbert T 4 + 2 | Jagielka P 36 | Distin S 31 + 3 | Baines L 38 | Osman L 36 | Gibson D 22 + 1 | Neville P 18 | Pienaar S 35 | Fellaini M 31 | Jelavic N 26 + 11 | Coleman S 24 + 2 | Naismith S 13 + 18 | Heitinga J 17 + 9 | Mirallas K 23 + 4 | Anichebe V 19 + 7 | Oviedo B 1 + 14 | Gueye M — + 2 | Vellios A — + 6 | Hitzlsperger T 4 + 3 | Barkley R 2 + 5 | Duffy S — + 1 | Mucha J 2 | Match No. |
|---|---|---|---|---|---|---|---|---|---|---|---|---|---|---|---|---|---|---|---|---|---|---|---|
| 1 | 2 | 3 | 4 | 5 | $6^1$ | 7 | 8 | 9 | $10^3$ | $11^2$ | 12 | 13 | 14 | | | | | | | | | | 1 |
| 1 | | 3 | 4 | 5 | 6 | $8^2$ | 2 | 7 | 11 | $10^3$ | 12 | | $9^1$ | 14 | 13 | | | | | | | | 2 |
| 1 | 12 | 3 | 4 | 5 | 6 | $7^1$ | $2^3$ | 9 | 10 | 11 | | | $8^2$ | 13 | 14 | | | | | | | | 3 |
| 1 | 2 | 3 | 4 | 5 | 7 | | 6 | 8 | 9 | $11^1$ | | 13 | $10^2$ | 12 | | | | | | | | | 4 |
| 1 | 4 | | | 5 | 6 | | 2 | $7^2$ | $9^3$ | 8 | 12 | 3 | $10^1$ | 11 | 13 | 14 | | | | | | | 5 |
| 1 | 4 | 14 | | 5 | $8^3$ | 7 | 2 | 9 | 10 | $11^1$ | 3 | | $6^2$ | 12 | 13 | | | | | | | | 6 |
| 1 | 3 | 12 | 5 | 8 | $7^2$ | 9 | 10 | 11 | 2 | 14 | $4^1$ | $6^3$ | 13 | | | | | | | | | | 7 |
| 1 | 4 | 3 | 5 | 8 | | 7 | $9^4$ | $10^2$ | 2 | 12 | 13 | $6$ | $11^1$ | | | | | | | | | | 8 |
| 1 | 3 | 4 | 5 | 7 | 8 | | 10 | 11 | 2 | $6^2$ | | $9^1$ | 13 | 12 | | | | | | | | | 9 |
| 1 | 3 | 13 | 5 | 7 | | 8 | 9 | 10 | $11^2$ | 2 | 12 | 4 | $6^1$ | | | | | | | | | | 10 |
| 1 | 3 | | 5 | | | $8^2$ | 9 | 10 | $11^3$ | 2 | 12 | 4 | $6^1$ | | | 13 | 14 | | | | | | 11 |
| 1 | 4 | | 5 | 7 | | 10 | 8 | 11 | 2 | $6^1$ | 3 | | 12 | 13 | $9^2$ | | | | | | | | 12 |
| 1 | 2 | 4 | 5 | 10 | | 6 | | 11 | | $7^1$ | 3 | | 9 | 12 | 8 | | | | | | | | 13 |
| 1 | 2 | 3 | 4 | 5 | 8 | $7^2$ | | 9 | 10 | 11 | | $6^1$ | | 12 | 13 | | | | | | | | 14 |
| 1 | 2 | 3 | 4 | 5 | 7 | 6 | | 10 | 9 | $11^2$ | | $8^1$ | 13 | 12 | | | | | | | | | 15 |
| 1 | 3 | 4 | 5 | | | $8^2$ | 7 | 9 | 10 | $11^3$ | 2 | 12 | 14 | $6^1$ | 13 | | | | | | | | 16 |
| 1 | 3 | 4 | 5 | 7 | 8 | | 9 | 10 | 11 | 2 | $6^1$ | | 12 | | | | | | | | | | 17 |
| 1 | 3 | 4 | 5 | 6 | $7^4$ | $8^1$ | $9^2$ | 10 | | 12 | 2 | | $11^3$ | 13 | | | 14 | | | | | | 18 |
| 1 | 3 | 4 | 5 | 6 | $8^1$ | 2 | 9 | | 10 | 12 | 13 | | $11^3$ | 14 | | $7^2$ | | | | | | | 19 |
| 1 | 2 | 4 | 5 | 7 | | $9^3$ | | 11 | | $6^1$ | 3 | | 10 | 14 | 12 | $8^2$ | 13 | | | | | | 20 |
| 1 | 2 | 4 | 5 | 8 | | 7 | 9 | 10 | $11^2$ | | $6^1$ | 3 | | 12 | 13 | | | | | | | | 21 |
| 1 | 3 | 4 | 5 | 8 | | $7^1$ | 9 | 10 | 11 | 2 | 12 | | $6^2$ | | | 13 | | | | | | | 22 |
| 1 | 3 | 4 | 5 | 8 | | 7 | 9 | 11 | $10^2$ | $2^1$ | 6 | | 13 | 12 | | | | | | | | | 23 |
| 1 | 2 | 4 | 5 | 8 | 12 | 7 | 9 | 10 | 13 | | 3 | $6^1$ | $11^2$ | | | | | | | | | | 24 |
| 1 | 2 | 4 | 5 | 8 | $7^3$ | 9 | 10 | 12 | | 14 | $3^1$ | $6^2$ | 11 | 13 | | | | | | | | | 25 |
| 1 | 3 | | 5 | 7 | 8 | 2 | 9 | 10 | 12 | | 13 | 4 | $6^2$ | $11^1$ | | | | | | | | | 26 |
| 1 | 3 | 4 | 5 | 7 | 8 | | $10^2$ | 9 | $11^1$ | 2 | 6 | | 12 | 13 | | | | | | | | | 27 |
| | $3^1$ | 4 | 5 | $8^2$ | 7 | | $9^3$ | 10 | 11 | 2 | | 12 | 6 | 13 | | | | 14 | | | 1 | | 28 |
| | | 4 | 5 | 8 | 7 | | $9^2$ | 10 | 13 | 2 | 12 | 2 | $6^1$ | $11^2$ | | | | | | | 1 | | 29 |
| 1 | 2 | 4 | 5 | 8 | 7 | | | 10 | 6 | 3 | | $9^1$ | 11 | | | | | 12 | | | | | 30 |
| 1 | 3 | 4 | 5 | 10 | 8 | | | 12 | 2 | 13 | 7 | $6^2$ | 11 | | | | | $9^1$ | | | | | 31 |
| 1 | 3 | 4 | 5 | $7^1$ | 8 | | 9 | 10 | 12 | 2 | 13 | 14 | $6^2$ | $11^3$ | | | | | | | | | 32 |
| 1 | 3 | 4 | 5 | 6 | | 10 | | 12 | 2 | 13 | | $9^1$ | $11^2$ | 14 | | | | $8^1$ | | | | | 33 |
| 1 | | 4 | 5 | $10^2$ | $7^1$ | 9 | 8 | 12 | 2 | 13 | 3 | $6$ | $11^3$ | | | | | 14 | | | | | 34 |
| 1 | 3 | 4 | 5 | 7 | | 9 | 8 | $10^1$ | 2 | | 6 | 11 | | 12 | | | | | | | | | 35 |
| 1 | 3 | 4 | 5 | 7 | 8 | | 9 | 10 | 12 | 2 | | $6^1$ | 11 | | | | | | | | | | 36 |
| 1 | 13 | 3 | 4 | 5 | $8^2$ | 7 | 9 | 10 | 12 | 2 | | $6^3$ | $11^1$ | 14 | | | | | | | | | 37 |
| 1 | | 3 | 4 | 5 | 7 | | 9 | 8 | 13 | 2 | $10^2$ | 12 | 6 | $11^1$ | | | | | | | | | 38 |

**FA Cup**

| | | | |
|---|---|---|---|
| Third Round | Cheltenham T | (a) | 5-1 |
| Fourth Round | Bolton W | (a) | 2-1 |
| Fifth Round | Oldham Ath | (a) | 2-2 |
| *Replay* | Oldham Ath | (h) | 3-1 |
| Sixth Round | Wigan Ath | (h) | 0-3 |

**Capital One Cup**

| | | | |
|---|---|---|---|
| Second Round | Leyton Orient | (h) | 5-0 |
| Third Round | Leeds U | (a) | 1-2 |

# EXETER CITY

## FOUNDATION

Exeter City was formed in 1904 by the amalgamation of St Sidwell's United and Exeter United. The club first played in the East Devon League and then the Plymouth & District League. After an exhibition match between West Bromwich Albion and Woolwich Arsenal, which was held to test interest as Exeter was then a rugby stronghold, it was decided to form Exeter City. At a meeting at the Red Lion Hotel in 1908, the club turned professional.

*St James Park, Stadium Way, Exeter, Devon EX4 6PX.*

*Telephone:* (01392) 411 243.

*Fax:* (01392) 413 959.

*Ticket Office:* (01392) 411 243.

*Website:* www.exetercityfc.co.uk

*Email:* reception@exetercityfc.co.uk

*Training Ground:* (01395) 232 784.

*Ground Capacity:* 8,830.

*Record Attendance:* 20,984 v Sunderland, FA Cup 6th rd (replay), 4 March 1931.

*Pitch Measurements:* 104m × 66m (114yd × 73yd)

*Chairman:* Edward Chorlton OBE.

*Vice-chairman and Chief Executive:* Julian Tagg.

*Manager:* Paul Tisdale.

*First Team Coach:* Rob Edwards.

*Physio:* Andrew Proctor.

*Colours:* Red and white striped shirts with red sleeves, black shorts, white socks with black trim.

*Year Formed:* 1904.

*Turned Professional:* 1908.

*Club Nickname:* 'The Grecians'.

*Ground:* 1904, St James Park.

*First Football League Game:* 28 August 1920, Division 3, v Brentford (h) W 3–0 – Pym; Coleburne, Feebury (1p); Crawshaw, Carrick, Mitton; Appleton, Makin, Wright (1), Vowles (1), Dockray.

*Record League Victory:* 8–1 v Coventry C, Division 3 (S), 4 December 1926 – Bailey; Pollard, Charlton; Pullen, Pool, Garrett; Purcell (2), McDevitt, Blackmore (2), Dent (2), Compton (2). 8–1 v Aldershot, Division 3 (S), 4 May 1935 – Chesters; Gray, Miller; Risdon, Webb, Angus; Jack Scott (1), Wrightson (1), Poulter (3), McArthur (1), Dryden (1), (1 og).

*Record Cup Victory:* 14–0 v Weymouth, FA Cup 1st qual rd, 3 October 1908 – Fletcher; Craig, Bulcock; Ambler, Chadwick, Wake; Parnell (1), Watson (1), McGuigan (4), Bell (6), Copestake (2).

## HONOURS

**Football League – Division 3:**
Best season: 8th, 1979–80;
**Division 3 (S):** *Runners-up* 1932–33;
**Division 4:** *Champions* 1989–90;
*Runners-up* 1976–77;
**FL 2:** *Runners-up* 2008–09.

**FA Cup:** Best season: 6th rd replay, 1931, 6th rd 1981.

**Football League Cup:** never beyond 4th rd.

**Division 3 (S) Cup:** *Winners* 1934.

## sky SPORTS FACT FILE

Stanley Rous, later to become Secretary of the Football Association and President of FIFA , played as a goalkeeper for Exeter City's reserve team in 1919 while studying locally at St Luke's College. He later qualified as a referee before becoming involved in the administration of the game.

*Record Defeat:* 0–9 v Notts Co, Division 3 (S), 16 October 1948. 0–9 v Northampton T, Division 3 (S), 12 April 1958.

*Most League Points (2 for a win):* 62, Division 4, 1976–77.

*Most League Points (3 for a win):* 89, Division 4, 1989–90.

*Most League Goals:* 88, Division 3 (S), 1932–33.

*Highest League Scorer in Season:* Fred Whitlow, 33, Division 3 (S), 1932–33.

*Most League Goals in Total Aggregate:* Tony Kellow, 129, 1976–78, 1980–83, 1985–88.

*Most League Goals in One Match:* 4, Harold 'Jazzo' Kirk v Portsmouth, Division 3 (S), 3 March 1923; 4, Fred Dent v Bristol R, Division 3 (S), 5 November 1927; 4, Fred Whitlow v Watford, Division 3 (S), 29 October 1932.

*Most Capped Player:* Dermot Curtis, 1 (17), Eire.

*Most League Appearances:* Arnold Mitchell, 495, 1952–66.

*Youngest League Player:* Cliff Bastin, 16 years 31 days v Coventry C, 14 April 1928.

*Record Transfer Fee Received:* £500,000 from Manchester C for Martin Phillips, November 1995.

*Record Transfer Fee Paid:* £65,000 to Blackpool for Tony Kellow, March 1980.

*Football League Record:* 1920 Elected to Division 3; 1921–58 Division 3 (S); 1958–64 Division 4; 1964–66 Division 3; 1966–77 Division 4; 1977–84 Division 3; 1984–90 Division 4; 1990–92 Division 3; 1992–94 Division 2; 1994–2003 Division 3; 2003–08 Conference; 2008–09 FL 2; 2009–12 FL 1; 2012– FL 2.

## LATEST SEQUENCES

*Longest Sequence of League Wins:* 7, 23.4.1977 – 20.8.1977.

*Longest Sequence of League Defeats:* 7, 14.1.1984 – 25.2.1984.

*Longest Sequence of League Draws:* 6, 13.9.1986 – 4.10.1986.

*Longest Sequence of Unbeaten League Matches:* 13, 23.8.1986 – 25.10.1986.

*Longest Sequence Without a League Win:* 18, 21.2.1995 – 19.8.1995.

*Successive Scoring Runs:* 22 from 15.9.1958.

*Successive Non-scoring Runs:* 6 from 24.11.1923.

## MANAGERS

Arthur Chadwick 1910–22
Fred Mavin 1923–27
Dave Wilson 1928–29
Billy McDevitt 1929–35
Jack English 1935–39
George Roughton 1945–52
Norman Kirkman 1952–53
Norman Dodgin 1953–57
Bill Thompson 1957–58
Frank Broome 1958–60
Glen Wilson 1960–62
Cyril Spiers 1962–63
Jack Edwards 1963–65
Ellis Stuttard 1965–66
Jock Basford 1966–67
Frank Broome 1967–69
Johnny Newman 1969–76
Bobby Saxton 1977–79
Brian Godfrey 1979–83
Gerry Francis 1983–84
Jim Iley 1984–85
Colin Appleton 1985–87
Terry Cooper 1988–91
Alan Ball 1991–94
Terry Cooper 1994–95
Peter Fox 1995–2000
Noel Blake 2000–01
John Cornforth 2001–02
Neil McNab 2002–03
Gary Peters 2003
Eamonn Dolan 2003–04
Alex Inglethorpe 2004–06
Paul Tisdale June 2006–

## TEN YEAR LEAGUE RECORD

|         |      | P  | W  | D  | L  | F  | A  | Pts | Pos |
|---------|------|----|----|----|----|----|----|-----|-----|
| 2003-04 | Conf | 42 | 19 | 12 | 11 | 71 | 51 | 69  | 6   |
| 2004-05 | Conf | 42 | 20 | 11 | 11 | 71 | 50 | 71  | 6   |
| 2005-06 | Conf | 42 | 18 | 9  | 15 | 65 | 48 | 63  | 7   |
| 2006-07 | Conf | 46 | 22 | 12 | 12 | 67 | 48 | 78  | 5   |
| 2007-08 | BSP  | 46 | 22 | 17 | 7  | 83 | 58 | 83  | 4   |
| 2008-09 | FL 2 | 46 | 22 | 13 | 11 | 65 | 50 | 79  | 2   |
| 2009-10 | FL 1 | 46 | 11 | 18 | 17 | 48 | 60 | 51  | 18  |
| 2010-11 | FL 1 | 46 | 20 | 10 | 16 | 66 | 73 | 70  | 8   |
| 2011-12 | FL 1 | 46 | 10 | 12 | 24 | 46 | 75 | 42  | 23  |
| 2012-13 | FL 2 | 46 | 18 | 10 | 18 | 63 | 62 | 64  | 10  |

## DID YOU KNOW

Henry Dyer who appeared as a full back for Exeter City in 1907–08 was among the casualties in the *Titanic* disaster. Henry was the senior assistant fourth engineer on the ill-fated liner and was aged just 24 when he lost his life.

## EXETER CITY – FOOTBALL LEAGUE TWO 2012–13 LEAGUE RECORD

| Match No. | Date | Venue | Opponents | Result | H/T Score | Lg Pos. | Goalscorers | Attendance |
|---|---|---|---|---|---|---|---|---|
| 1 | Aug 18 | H | Morecambe | L 0-3 | 0-3 | 24 | | 3792 |
| 2 | 21 | A | Aldershot T | W 2-1 | 1-1 | 13 | Cureton 2 [14, 73] | 2678 |
| 3 | 25 | A | Accrington S | W 3-0 | 1-0 | 6 | Gow 2 [14, 54], Bauza [90] | 1149 |
| 4 | Sept 1 | H | Burton Alb | W 3-0 | 2-0 | 2 | Cureton [19], Davies [41], O'Flynn [89] | 3707 |
| 5 | 8 | A | Oxford U | W 4-2 | 2-0 | 2 | Cureton 2 [11, 50], Bennett [27], O'Flynn [72] | 6405 |
| 6 | 15 | H | York C | D 1-1 | 0-0 | 4 | O'Flynn [83] | 4092 |
| 7 | 18 | H | Wycombe W | W 3-2 | 1-1 | 3 | Davies [29], Cureton [54], Coles [67] | 3365 |
| 8 | 22 | A | Southend U | L 1-2 | 0-0 | 3 | Bennett [51] | 4964 |
| 9 | 29 | H | Bristol R | L 1-2 | 0-1 | 5 | Cureton [66] | 5054 |
| 10 | Oct 2 | A | Barnet | W 2-1 | 1-0 | 4 | Cureton 2 [35, 67] | 1483 |
| 11 | 6 | H | Port Vale | L 0-2 | 0-1 | 4 | | 3938 |
| 12 | 13 | A | Northampton T | L 0-3 | 0-2 | 7 | | 4607 |
| 13 | 20 | H | Chesterfield | L 0-1 | 0-1 | 7 | | 3668 |
| 14 | 23 | A | Dagenham & R | D 1-1 | 0-1 | 11 | Cureton [51] | 1487 |
| 15 | 27 | A | Cheltenham T | L 0-3 | 0-0 | 11 | | 3545 |
| 16 | Nov 6 | H | AFC Wimbledon | W 2-0 | 1-0 | 11 | Cureton [32], O'Flynn [71] | 3249 |
| 17 | 10 | H | Fleetwood T | D 2-2 | 1-2 | 10 | Cureton [24], O'Flynn (pen) [57] | 3540 |
| 18 | 17 | A | Bradford C | W 1-0 | 1-0 | 9 | Cureton [44] | 10,434 |
| 19 | 20 | A | Gillingham | W 3-2 | 1-1 | 7 | Gow [27], Cureton 2 [54, 87] | 6851 |
| 20 | 24 | H | Rotherham U | L 0-1 | 0-1 | 9 | | 3954 |
| 21 | Dec 8 | A | Rochdale | W 3-2 | 3-0 | 7 | Baldwin [24], O'Flynn 2 [27, 38] | 1796 |
| 22 | 15 | H | Plymouth Arg | D 1-1 | 1-0 | 7 | Sercombe [34] | 6447 |
| 23 | 26 | H | Oxford U | L 1-3 | 0-1 | 10 | Cureton (pen) [67] | 4437 |
| 24 | 29 | H | Barnet | D 2-2 | 2-0 | 11 | Coles [34], Bennett [45] | 4085 |
| 25 | Jan 1 | A | Wycombe W | W 1-0 | 0-0 | 9 | O'Flynn [84] | 3679 |
| 26 | 5 | A | York C | W 2-1 | 1-1 | 5 | Rodman (og) [14], Keohane [53] | 3506 |
| 27 | 12 | H | Southend U | W 3-0 | 1-0 | 3 | O'Flynn 2 [43, 87], Bennett [80] | 3971 |
| 28 | 15 | A | Torquay U | D 1-1 | 0-1 | 3 | Gow (pen) [85] | 4476 |
| 29 | 28 | H | Torquay U | L 0-1 | 0-1 | 4 | | 4824 |
| 30 | Feb 2 | H | Aldershot T | D 0-0 | 0-0 | 7 | | 3755 |
| 31 | 9 | A | Morecambe | W 3-0 | 0-0 | 4 | Cureton 2 [61, 90], Davies [85] | 1840 |
| 32 | 15 | H | Accrington S | W 2-0 | 0-0 | 3 | Keohane 2 [79, 82] | 3924 |
| 33 | 23 | A | Burton Alb | L 2-4 | 0-3 | 7 | Bauza [70], Bennett [74] | 2823 |
| 34 | 26 | A | Port Vale | W 2-0 | 2-0 | 6 | Cureton [11], Coles [33] | 4480 |
| 35 | Mar 2 | H | Northampton T | W 3-0 | 1-0 | 4 | Nicholls, L (og) [22], Cureton [59], Gosling [83] | 4666 |
| 36 | 6 | A | Bristol R | L 0-2 | 0-1 | 6 | | 7107 |
| 37 | 9 | A | Fleetwood T | D 0-0 | 0-0 | 7 | | 2097 |
| 38 | 12 | H | Gillingham | D 0-0 | 0-0 | 7 | | 3608 |
| 39 | 16 | H | Bradford C | W 4-1 | 2-0 | 5 | Duke (og) [11], D'Ath [45], Bennett [84], O'Flynn [89] | 4199 |
| 40 | 30 | A | Plymouth Arg | L 0-1 | 0-1 | 7 | | 13,251 |
| 41 | Apr 1 | H | Rochdale | L 1-2 | 1-0 | 7 | Cureton [45] | 3979 |
| 42 | 6 | H | Dagenham & R | L 0-1 | 0-1 | 7 | | 3755 |
| 43 | 9 | A | Rotherham U | L 1-4 | 0-3 | 8 | Coles [77] | 6703 |
| 44 | 13 | A | AFC Wimbledon | D 2-2 | 1-0 | 8 | Reid 2 [36, 61] | 4749 |
| 45 | 20 | H | Cheltenham T | L 0-1 | 0-1 | 9 | | 5247 |
| 46 | 27 | A | Chesterfield | L 0-4 | 0-3 | 10 | | 5762 |

**Final League Position: 10**

### GOALSCORERS

*League (63):* Cureton 21 (1 pen), O'Flynn 11 (1 pen), Bennett 6, Coles 4, Gow 4 (1 pen), Davies 3, Keohane 3, Bauza 2, Reid 2, Baldwin 1, D'Ath 1, Gosling 1, Sercombe 1, own goals 3.
*FA Cup (0).*
*Capital One Cup (1):* O'Flynn 1.
*Johnstone's Paint Trophy (0).*

| Krysiak A 42 | Amankwaah K 27 + 7 | Baldwin P 41 | Coles D 46 | Woodman C 44 | Sercombe L 18 + 2 | Oakley M 33 + 3 | Bennett S 41 + 2 | Davies A 32 + 5 | Gow A 21 + 5 | Cureton J 38 + 2 | Bauza G 4 + 15 | Frear E — + 2 | O'Flynn J 21 + 14 | Doherty T 23 + 7 | Moore-Taylor J 4 + 3 | Chamberlain E — + 4 | Keohane J 13 + 20 | Nichols T — + 3 | Tully S 24 + 3 | Cane J — + 1 | Evans R 4 + 1 | Dawson A 2 + 5 | Reid J 3 + 1 | Gosling J 6 + 6 | Moseley M 11 | D'Ath L 7 + 1 | Rodgers A 1 + 1 | Anderson M — + 1 | Match No. |
|---|---|---|---|---|---|---|---|---|---|---|---|---|---|---|---|---|---|---|---|---|---|---|---|---|---|---|---|---|---|
| 1 | 2 | 3 | 4 | $5^2$ | 6 | 7 | $8^1$ | 9 | 10 | $11^3$ | 12 | 13 | 14 | | | | | | | | | | | | | | | | 1 |
| 1 | 2 | 3 | 4 | 5 | 6 | 12 | 7 | 9 | $10^2$ | 11 | 13 | | | $8^1$ | | | | | | | | | | | | | | | 2 |
| 1 | 2 | 3 | 4 | 5 | 6 | 7 | $8^3$ | 9 | $10^2$ | $11^1$ | 13 | | 12 | 14 | | | | | | | | | | | | | | | 3 |
| 1 | 2 | 3 | $4^3$ | 5 | 6 | 8 | 7 | 9 | $10^2$ | $11^1$ | 13 | | 12 | | | 14 | | | | | | | | | | | | | 4 |
| 1 | 2 | 3 | 4 | 5 | 6 | 8 | 7 | 9 | | | $11^1$ | 12 | | | | | $10^2$ | 13 | | | | | | | | | | | 5 |
| 1 | 2 | $4^3$ | 3 | 5 | $6^1$ | 7 | 8 | 9 | | $10^2$ | | | 11 | 12 | 14 | 13 | | | | | | | | | | | | | 6 |
| 1 | 2 | 4 | 3 | 5 | | 8 | 7 | 10 | | $11^1$ | | | $6^2$ | | | | $9^2$ | 12 | 13 | 14 | | | | | | | | | 7 |
| 1 | 2 | 3 | 4 | 5 | 6 | 7 | 9 | | | $11^1$ | | | 12 | $8^3$ | | | $10^2$ | 13 | 14 | | | | | | | | | | 8 |
| 1 | 2 | $3^1$ | 4 | 5 | | 6 | $8^2$ | 9 | $10^1$ | 11 | | | 12 | 7 | 14 | 13 | | | | | | | | | | | | | 9 |
| | 2 | 4 | 3 | 5 | | 7 | | 9 | | $11^2$ | 13 | | $10^1$ | 6 | | 12 | | | 8 | | 1 | | | | | | | | 10 |
| | 6 | 4 | 3 | 5 | 14 | 8 | | 9 | | 11 | 12 | | $10^1$ | $7^2$ | | 13 | | | $2^3$ | | 1 | | | | | | | | 11 |
| | $2^1$ | $3^3$ | 4 | 5 | 13 | 8 | 7 | 9 | 12 | 10 | | | $11^2$ | 14 | | | 6 | | | 1 | | | | | | | | | 12 |
| 1 | 13 | | 3 | | 6 | 7 | 4 | $9^3$ | | $11^1$ | 12 | 14 | 10 | $8^2$ | 5 | | | | 2 | | | | | | | | | | 13 |
| 1 | 2 | | 4 | 5 | 7 | 8 | 3 | 9 | 12 | 11 | | | | | | | 10 | $6^1$ | 2 | | | | | | | | | | 14 |
| 1 | 2 | | 4 | 5 | 7 | $8^3$ | 3 | $10^1$ | 13 | 11 | | | 12 | | | | 9 | $6^2$ | | 14 | | | | | | | | | 15 |
| 1 | | 3 | 4 | 5 | 6 | 7 | $8^2$ | | $9^1$ | $10^3$ | | | 11 | 13 | | | 12 | 14 | 2 | | | | | | | | | | 16 |
| 1 | | 3 | 4 | 5 | 6 | 7 | 9 | | 8 | 11 | | | 10 | | | | | | 2 | | | | | | | | | | 17 |
| 1 | 13 | 4 | 6 | 5 | 8 | 7 | $3^1$ | | $10^2$ | $9^3$ | 14 | | 11 | 12 | | | | | 2 | | | | | | | | | | 18 |
| 1 | | 4 | 6 | 5 | 8 | 7 | 3 | | 10 | $9^2$ | | | | $11^1$ | | 13 | 12 | | 2 | | | | | | | | | | 19 |
| 1 | | 4 | 3 | | 6 | 7 | 8 | | 10 | 11 | | | 13 | $9^1$ | 5 | | $12^2$ | | $2^3$ | | 14 | | | | | | | | 20 |
| 1 | 14 | 4 | 3 | 5 | 7 | 6 | | 12 | | $8^2$ | 11 | | $10^3$ | | | | $9^1$ | | 2 | | 13 | | | | | | | | 21 |
| 1 | 13 | 4 | 3 | 5 | 6 | $7^1$ | 8 | | | $9^2$ | 10 | | 11 | | | | 12 | | 2 | | | | | | | | | | 22 |
| 1 | 12 | 4 | 3 | 5 | $6^2$ | 7 | 8 | | | $11^3$ | 10 | | $9^1$ | | | | 14 | | 2 | | 13 | | | | | | | | 23 |
| 1 | | 3 | 4 | 5 | $6^1$ | 7 | 8 | 13 | $10^2$ | 14 | | | $11^3$ | | | | 9 | | 2 | | 12 | | | | | | | | 24 |
| 1 | | 4 | 5 | 3 | | 6 | 7 | | 9 | $10^4$ | | | 11 | | | | 8 | | 2 | | | | | | | | | | 25 |
| 1 | 12 | 3 | 4 | 5 | | 9 | 8 | 13 | $10^2$ | | | | 11 | $7^1$ | | | 6 | | 2 | | | | | | | | | | 26 |
| 1 | 13 | 3 | 4 | 5 | | 7 | 6 | $8^1$ | $10^2$ | | | | 11 | 12 | | | 9 | | $2^3$ | | 14 | | | | | | | | 27 |
| 1 | 6 | 4 | 5 | 3 | | 14 | 9 | $7^2$ | 13 | | $11^1$ | | $10^3$ | 8 | | | 12 | | 2 | | | | | | | | | | 28 |
| 1 | | 3 | 4 | 5 | | $8^3$ | 9 | 14 | 11 | 13 | 12 | | | $7^1$ | | | 6 | | 2 | | | | | $10^2$ | | | | | 29 |
| 1 | 2 | 3 | 4 | 5 | | $7^1$ | 8 | | 9 | 11 | $10^2$ | | | | | | 13 | | | | | | | 12 | $6^1$ | | | | 30 |
| 1 | 2 | 5 | 4 | 3 | | | 7 | 9 | | 11 | | | 8 | | | | 10 | | | | | | | | 6 | | | | 31 |
| $1^1$ | 2 | 3 | 4 | 5 | | | 8 | 13 | | 11 | $10^3$ | | | 7 | | | 14 | | | 12 | | | | 9 | $6^2$ | | | | 32 |
| | 2 | 3 | 4 | 5 | | 13 | 7 | $9^1$ | | 11 | 12 | 14 | 8 | | | | $10^3$ | | | | 1 | | | | $6^2$ | | | | 33 |
| 1 | 6 | 3 | 4 | 5 | | | 8 | 2 | 7 | $11^1$ | | | 12 | 10 | | | | | | | | | | | $9^\#$ | | | | 34 |
| 1 | 2 | 4 | 3 | 5 | | $8^2$ | 7 | 10 | | $11^1$ | | | 12 | 9 | | | 13 | | | | | | 6 | | | | | | 35 |
| 1 | $5^3$ | 4 | 2 | | | 7 | 6 | 8 | | 11 | 14 | | $10^2$ | $9^1$ | | | 13 | | | | | | 12 | | | | | | 36 |
| 1 | $2^1$ | 3 | 4 | 5 | | 8 | 7 | 9 | | 11 | | | 12 | | | | $10^2$ | 6 | | | | | 13 | | | | | | 37 |
| 1 | 2 | 4 | 3 | 5 | | $7^1$ | 8 | 9 | | $11^2$ | 13 | | 14 | | | | 12 | | | | | | 6 | $10^3$ | | | | | 38 |
| 1 | 2 | 4 | 3 | 5 | | | 8 | 10 | | 11 | | | | | | | 12 | 13 | | | | | $6^2$ | 7 | $9^1$ | | | | 39 |
| 1 | 2 | 3 | 4 | 5 | | | 8 | 9 | | 11 | 13 | $7^1$ | | 14 | | | | | | | | | 12 | $6^3$ | $10^2$ | | | | 40 |
| 1 | | 3 | 4 | 5 | | | 8 | 9 | | $10^3$ | $11^1$ | | | 14 | 13 | | 2 | | | | | | | $6^2$ | 7 | 12 | | | 41 |
| 1 | $2^1$ | 3 | 4 | 5 | | | 8 | 10 | | | 13 | | 11 | $7^3$ | | | 14 | | | | | 12 | | $6^2$ | 9 | | | | 42 |
| 1 | | 3 | 4 | 5 | | | 8 | 9 | | 11 | | | 12 | $7^3$ | | | 13 | | | | | | $2^1$ | | $6^2$ | 10 | 14 | | 43 |
| 1 | | 4 | 5 | 3 | | | 12 | 8 | 13 | 10 | | | $9^1$ | 7 | | | | | 2 | | | | 11 | | $6^2$ | | | | 44 |
| 1 | | 3 | 5 | | | | 12 | 6 | $9^3$ | 10 | 14 | | | 7 | 4 | | 13 | | $2^2$ | | | | | $11^1$ | | 8 | | | 45 |
| 1 | | 3 | $5^2$ | | | | 10 | 8 | 9 | | | | 4 | 12 | | | | | 2 | | | | | $11^1$ | 14 | 6 | $7^3$ | 13 | 46 |

**FA Cup**

| First Round | Bury | (a) | 0-1 |
|---|---|---|---|

**Capital One Cup**

| First Round | Crystal Palace | (h) | 1-2 |
|---|---|---|---|

**Johnstone's Paint Trophy**

| First Round | Aldershot T | (h) | 0-0 |
|---|---|---|---|

(aet; lost 3-4 on pens)

# FLEETWOOD TOWN

### FOUNDATION

Originally formed in 1908 as Fleetwood FC, it was liquidated in 1976. Re-formed as Fleetwood Town in 1977, it folded again in 1996. Once again, it was re-formed a year later as Fleetwood Wanderers, but a sponsorship deal saw the club's name immediately changed to Fleetwood Freeport through the local retail outlet centre. This sponsorship ended in 2002, but since then local energy businessman Andy Pilley took charge and the club has risen through the non-league pyramid until finally achieving Football League status in 2012 as Fleetwood Town.

*Highbury Stadium, Park Avenue, Fleetwood, Lancashire FY7 5TX.*

*Telephone:* (01253) 775 080.

*Ticket Office:* (01253) 775 080

*Website:* www.fleetwoodtownfc.com

*Email:* info@fleetwoodtownfc.com

*Ground Capacity:* 5,092.

*Record attendance:* (Before 1997) 6,150 v Rochdale, FA Cup 1st rd, 13 November 1965; (Since 1997) 5,092 v Blackpool, FA Cup 3rd rd, 7 January 2012.

*Pitch Measurements:* 102m × 67m (112yd × 74yd)

*Chairman:* Andy Pilley.

*Chief Executive:* Steve Curwood.

*Secretary:* Steve Edwards.

*Manager:* Graham Alexander.

*Assistant Manager:* Craig Madden.

*Physio:* Luke Bussey.

*Colours:* Red shirts with white sleeves, white shorts, red socks.

*Year Formed:* 1908 (re-formed 1997).

*Club Nicknames:* 'The Trawlermen', 'The Cod Army'.

*Grounds:* 1908, North Euston Hotel; 1934, Memorial Park (now Highbury Stadium).

*First Football League Game:* 18 August 2012, FL 2, v Torquay U (h) D 0–0 – Davies; Beeley, Mawene, McNulty, Howell, Nicolson, Johnson, McGuire, Ball, Parkin, Mangan.

*Record League Victory:* 13–0 v Oldham T, North West Counties Div 2, 5 December 1998.

*Record Defeat:* 0–7 v Billingham T, FA Cup 1st qual rd, 15 September 2001.

*Most League Points (3 for a win):* 60, FL 2, 2012–13.

### MANAGER

**Micky Mellon** 2008–12
**Graham Alexander** December 2012–

### sky SPORTS FACT FILE

Fleetwood Town entered the FA Cup for the first time in 2002–03. They played in the competition proper for the first time in 2006–07 when they went down 3-0 away to Salisbury City in a first round tie in front of a crowd of 2,684.

*Most League Goals:* 55, FL 2, 2012–13

*Most League Goals in Total Aggregate:* Junior Brown, 11, 2012–13.

*Most League Appearances:* Scott Davies, 45, 2012–13.

*Youngest League Player:* Jamie Allen, 17 years 227 days v Northampton T, 5 January 2013.

*Record Transfer Fee Received:* £1,000,000 from Leicester C for Jamie Vardy, May 2012.

*Record Transfer Fee Paid:* £300,000 to Kidderminster H for Jamille Matt, July 2012.

*Football League Record:* Promoted to Football League 2012– FL 2.

## LATEST SEQUENCES

*Longest Sequence of League Wins:* 4, 25.8.2012 – 15.9.2012.

*Longest Sequence of League Defeats:* 4, 6.4.2013 – onwards.

*Longest Sequence of League Draws:* 3, 27.10.2012 – 10.11.2012.

*Longest Sequence of Unbeaten League Matches:* 6, 20.10.2012 – 17.11.12.

*Longest Sequence Without a League Win:* 6, 23.3.2013 – onwards.

*Successive Scoring Runs:* 5 from 25.8.2012.

*Successive Non-scoring Runs:* 2 from 2.3.2012.

---

## HONOURS

### 1908 Foundation

**Lancashire Combination:** Champions 1923–24. *Runners-Up:* 1933–34, 1934–35.

**Northern Premier League Challenge Cup:** *Winners:* 1971.

**Lancashire Combination Cup:** *Winners:* 1926, 1932, 1933, 1934. *Runners-up:* 1953, 1967.

### 1976 Foundation

**Northern Premier League First Division:** *Champions:* 1987–88.

**North West Counties Football League First Division:** *Champions:* 1983–84.

**Northern Premier League Presiden's Cup:** *Winners:* 1990.

**FA Vase:** *Runners Cup:* 1984–85.

**Northern Premier League Challenge Cup:** *Runners-up:* 1989.

### 1997 Foundation

**FA Cup:** 3rd rd 2011–12.

**Conference:** *Champions:* 2011–12.

**Conference North:** *Runners-up and Play-off winners:* 2009–10.

**Northern Premier League Premier Division:** *Champions:* 2007–08.

**Northern Premier League First Division:** *Runners-up* (promoted): 2005–06.

**North West Counties Football League Premier Division:** *Champions:* 2004–05.

**North West Counties Football League First Divison:** *Champions:* 1998–99.

**Peter Swales Memorial Shield:** *Winners:* 2008.

**Northern Premier League Challenge Cup:** *Winners:* 2007.

**North West Counties Football League First Division Trophy:** *Winners:* 1999.

**Lancashire League West Division Reserve League:** *Winners:* 2008–09.

---

## TEN YEAR LEAGUE RECORD

| | | P | W | D | L | F | A | Pts | Pos |
|---|---|---|---|---|---|---|---|---|---|
| 2003-04 | NWC 1 | 42 | 26 | 8 | 8 | 84 | 51 | 86 | 3 |
| 2004-05 | NWC 1 | 42 | 31 | 6 | 5 | 107 | 42 | 99 | 1 |
| 2005-06 | Uni 1 | 42 | 22 | 10 | 10 | 72 | 48 | 76 | 2 |
| 2006-07 | Uni Pr | 42 | 19 | 10 | 13 | 71 | 60 | 67 | 8 |
| 2007-08 | Uni Pr | 40 | 28 | 7 | 5 | 81 | 39 | 91 | 1 |
| 2008-09 | Conf N | 42 | 17 | 11 | 14 | 70 | 66 | 62 | 8 |
| 2009-10 | Conf N | 42 | 26 | 7 | 7 | 86 | 44 | 85 | 2 |
| 2010-11 | BSP | 46 | 22 | 12 | 12 | 68 | 42 | 78 | 5 |
| 2011-12 | BSP | 46 | 31 | 10 | 5 | 102 | 48 | 103 | 1 |
| 2012-13 | FL 2 | 46 | 15 | 15 | 16 | 55 | 57 | 60 | 13 |

## DID YOU KNOW

Fleetwood Town achieved a double of the North West Counties Division Two League and League Cup competitions in the second season of their existence, 1998–99, under their sponsor's title of Fleetwood Freeport. They achieved their record score of 13-0 against Oldham Town in the same season.

## FLEETWOOD TOWN – FOOTBALL LEAGUE TWO 2012–13 LEAGUE RECORD

| Match No. | Date | Venue | Opponents | Result | H/T Score | Lg Pos. | Goalscorers | Attendance |
|---|---|---|---|---|---|---|---|---|
| 1 | Aug 18 | H | Torquay U | D 0-0 | 0-0 | 11 | | 3624 |
| 2 | 21 | A | Bradford C | L 0-1 | 0-0 | 18 | | 9224 |
| 3 | 25 | A | Burton Alb | W 1-0 | 0-0 | 13 | Howell [47] | 2349 |
| 4 | Sept 1 | H | Aldershot T | W 4-1 | 1-1 | 8 | Brown 2 [26, 81], McNulty [47], Mangan [90] | 2510 |
| 5 | 8 | A | Morecambe | W 4-0 | 1-0 | 4 | Parkin 3 [21, 50, 76], Nicholson [84] | 3232 |
| 6 | 15 | H | Northampton T | W 1-0 | 0-0 | 3 | Mangan [90] | 3027 |
| 7 | 18 | H | Port Vale | L 2-5 | 1-2 | 4 | Brown [39], Gillespie (pen) [84] | 3392 |
| 8 | 22 | A | Bristol R | D 0-0 | 0-0 | 5 | | 5079 |
| 9 | 29 | H | Barnet | W 2-1 | 1-1 | 3 | Ball (pen) [26], Barkhuizen [78] | 3615 |
| 10 | Oct 2 | A | York C | W 2-0 | 1-0 | 3 | Brown [36], Gillespie [87] | 3084 |
| 11 | 6 | A | Cheltenham T | D 2-2 | 1-0 | 3 | Ball [32], Brown [90] | 2702 |
| 12 | 13 | H | Wycombe W | L 0-1 | 0-1 | 4 | | 3612 |
| 13 | 20 | H | AFC Wimbledon | D 1-1 | 1-0 | 3 | Gillespie [10] | 2547 |
| 14 | 23 | A | Chesterfield | W 2-1 | 1-1 | 3 | Gillespie [7], Brown [90] | 4372 |
| 15 | 27 | A | Rochdale | D 0-0 | 0-0 | 4 | | 2372 |
| 16 | Nov 6 | H | Rotherham U | D 1-1 | 1-1 | 4 | Parkin [21] | 2498 |
| 17 | 10 | A | Exeter C | D 2-2 | 2-1 | 5 | McNulty [13], Nicholson [41] | 3540 |
| 18 | 17 | H | Plymouth Arg | W 3-0 | 1-0 | 4 | Ball [2], Nelson (og) [83], Brown [90] | 2657 |
| 19 | 20 | H | Accrington S | L 1-3 | 0-2 | 4 | McGuire [67] | 2472 |
| 20 | 24 | A | Dagenham & R | L 0-1 | 0-0 | 6 | | 1618 |
| 21 | Dec 8 | H | Southend U | D 0-0 | 0-0 | 8 | | 2399 |
| 22 | 15 | A | Gillingham | D 2-2 | 2-1 | 8 | Brown [20], Goodall [28] | 8571 |
| 23 | 26 | H | Morecambe | W 1-0 | 0-0 | 7 | Ball [69] | 3477 |
| 24 | 29 | H | York C | D 0-0 | 0-0 | 8 | | 2465 |
| 25 | Jan 1 | A | Port Vale | W 2-0 | 2-0 | 6 | Ball [26], Goodall [39] | 6082 |
| 26 | 5 | A | Northampton T | L 1-3 | 0-2 | 7 | Allen, J [90] | 4381 |
| 27 | 12 | H | Bristol R | L 0-3 | 0-2 | 8 | | 2811 |
| 28 | 26 | H | Oxford U | W 3-0 | 1-0 | 8 | Matt [9], Crowther [58], Parkin [86] | 2461 |
| 29 | Feb 2 | H | Bradford C | D 2-2 | 1-1 | 9 | Goodall [23], Parkin (pen) [75] | 3577 |
| 30 | 9 | A | Torquay U | W 1-0 | 1-0 | 8 | Parkin [26] | 2207 |
| 31 | 12 | A | Oxford U | W 2-1 | 1-0 | 4 | Crowther [28], Brown [55] | 5003 |
| 32 | 16 | A | Burton Alb | L 0-4 | 0-0 | 8 | | 2698 |
| 33 | 23 | A | Aldershot T | L 0-2 | 0-1 | 9 | | 2032 |
| 34 | 26 | H | Cheltenham T | D 1-1 | 0-1 | 8 | Brown [69] | 2031 |
| 35 | Mar 2 | A | Wycombe W | L 0-1 | 0-0 | 9 | | 3162 |
| 36 | 9 | H | Exeter C | D 0-0 | 0-0 | 9 | | 2097 |
| 37 | 12 | A | Accrington S | W 3-0 | 1-0 | 8 | Parkin 3 [25, 62, 70] | 1388 |
| 38 | 16 | A | Plymouth Arg | L 1-2 | 0-2 | 9 | Ball [75] | 6776 |
| 39 | 19 | A | Barnet | L 0-2 | 0-1 | 9 | | 1731 |
| 40 | 23 | H | Dagenham & R | W 2-1 | 1-1 | 8 | Brown [6], Evans [52] | 2019 |
| 41 | 30 | H | Gillingham | D 2-2 | 1-2 | 8 | Matt 2 [33, 69] | 3033 |
| 42 | Apr 1 | A | Southend U | D 1-1 | 1-0 | 8 | Goodall [2] | 5107 |
| 43 | 6 | H | Rochdale | L 0-3 | 0-1 | 10 | | 2954 |
| 44 | 13 | A | Rotherham U | L 1-2 | 1-1 | 10 | Ball [6] | 7360 |
| 45 | 20 | H | Chesterfield | L 1-3 | 0-2 | 12 | Mangan [68] | 3705 |
| 46 | 27 | A | AFC Wimbledon | L 1-2 | 0-0 | 13 | Mangan [64] | 4738 |

**Final League Position: 13**

### GOALSCORERS

*League (55):* Brown 11, Parkin 10 (1 pen), Ball 7 (1 pen), Gillespie 4 (1 pen), Goodall 4, Mangan 4, Matt 3, Crowther 2, McNulty 2, Nicholson 2, Allen, J 1, Barkhuizen 1, Evans 1, Howell 1, McGuire 1, own goal 1.
*FA Cup (5):* Ball 2, Parkin 2 (2 pens), Brown 1.
*Capital One Cup (0).*
*Johnstone's Paint Trophy (2):* McGuire 2.

| Davies S 45 | Beeley S 34 | Mawene Y 19 | McNulty S 16 | Howell D 30 | Nicholson B 18+12 | Johnson D 17+5 | McGuire J 34+3 | Ball D 28+6 | Parkin J 14+8 | Mangan A 7+5 | Brown J 40+3 | Gillespie S 9+13 | Marrow A 13+7 | Fowler L 10 | McLaughlin C 13+6 | Barkhuizen T 8+5 | Titchiner A 3+6 | Eastham A 1 | Milligan A 3+5 | Goodall A 28+1 | Edwards Rob 4 | Obeng C 4+1 | Ferguson B 6 | Branco R —+1 | Atkinson R 18 | Evans G 13+3 | Barry A 9+3 | Allen J 2+2 | Matt J 11+3 | Pond N 11+1 | McKenna P 15 | Crowther R 8+7 | Fontaine J 4+9 | Charnock K 1+2 | Gyorio M —+1 | Lucas D 1+1 | Edwards Ryan 9 | Match No. |
|---|---|---|---|---|---|---|---|---|---|---|---|---|---|---|---|---|---|---|---|---|---|---|---|---|---|---|---|---|---|---|---|---|---|---|---|---|---|---|
| 1 | 2 | 3 | 4 | 5 | 6 | 7 | 8 | 9² | 10 | 11¹ | 12 | 13 | | | | | | | | | | | | | | | | | | | | | | | | | | 1 |
| 1 | 2 | 4 | 3 | 5 | 6 | 8 | 7³ | 10¹ | 11 | 12 | 9² | 14 | 13 | | | | | | | | | | | | | | | | | | | | | | | | | 2 |
| 1 | 2 | 4 | 3 | 5 | 6 | 8 | | 10¹ | 11² | | 9 | 13 | 14 | 7³ | 12 | | | | | | | | | | | | | | | | | | | | | | | 3 |
| 1 | 2 | 4 | 3 | 5¹ | 12 | 6 | | 10³ | | 9 | 7 | 14 | 13 | 8² | | 11¹ | | | | | | | | | | | | | | | | | | | | | | 4 |
| 1 | 2 | 4 | 3 | 5 | 12 | 6 | 8¹ | | 11 | 10³ | 9 | | 13 | 7² | | 14 | | | | | | | | | | | | | | | | | | | | | | 5 |
| 1 | 2 | 3 | 4 | 5 | | 7 | 6² | | 11¹ | 10 | 8 | 12 | | 9 | 13 | | | | | | | | | | | | | | | | | | | | | | | 6 |
| 1 | 2 | 4 | | | 6¹ | 8 | | 10² | 11 | | 9 | 13 | 14 | 7³ | 12 | 3 | | | | | | | | | | | | | | | | | | | | | | 7 |
| 1 | 2 | 5 | 4 | 3 | 13 | 9¹ | 8 | | 11 | | 6² | 10 | 14 | 7¹ | 12 | | | | | | | | | | | | | | | | | | | | | | | 8 |
| 1 | 2 | 3 | 4 | 5 | | 6 | 9² | 8 | 13 | | 10 | 14 | 7¹ | | 11³ | | | | 12 | | | | | | | | | | | | | | | | | | | 9 |
| 1 | 2 | 4 | 3 | 5¹ | 13 | 8 | 7 | 11³ | | | 10 | 14 | 9 | | 6² | | | | 12 | | | | | | | | | | | | | | | | | | | 10 |
| 1 | 2 | 4 | 3¹ | | 6 | 8³ | 9 | 11²14 | | | 10 | 13 | 7 | | 12 | | | | 5 | | | | | | | | | | | | | | | | | | | 11 |
| 1 | 2 | 3 | | 9³ | 6² | 8¹ | 11 | 12 | | | 10 | 14 | 7 | | 12 | | | | 13 | 5 | 4 | | | | | | | | | | | | | | | | | 12 |
| 1 | | 4 | | 5 | 12 | 7¹ | 13 | 11 | | | 10³ | | | 6 | 2 | 8² | | | 14 | 3 | | | | | | | | | | | | | | | | | | 13 |
| 1 | | 4 | | 5 | 14 | | 8 | 12 | | | 10 | 11 | 7³ | 9² | 2 | 6¹ | | | 13 | 3 | | | | | | | | | | | | | | | | | | 14 |
| 1 | | 4 | | 5 | 13 | | 6 | 12 | | | | 11¹ | 7⁴ | 8 | 2 | 9² | | | | 3 | 10 | | | | | | | | | | | | | | | | | 15 |
| 1 | 2 | 3 | 4 | 5 | | | 8 | 11³ | 10¹ | | 12 | | 13 | 7² | 14 | | | | | | | | | | | 6 | 9 | | | | | | | | | | | 16 |
| 1 | 2 | 4 | 3 | 5 | 7 | | 9 | 11 | | | 10 | | | | | 12 | | | | | | | | | | 6¹ | 8 | | | | | | | | | | | 17 |
| 1 | 2 | 3 | 4 | 5 | 6² | 13 | 7 | 10 | | | 9 | | | | 11¹ | | | | | | | | | | | 12 | 8 | | | | | | | | | | | 18 |
| 1 | | 4 | 3 | 5 | 12 | 6¹ | 7 | 10 | | | 11 | | | 2 | | | | | | | | | | | | 9² | 8 | 13 | | | | | | | | | | 19 |
| 1 | 2 | 4 | 3 | | 7 | | 9 | 11¹ | | | 10 | | | | | 6 | 12 | | | 5 | | | | | | | 8 | | | | | | | | | | | 20 |
| 1 | 2 | | | 5 | 6 | | | 10² | | | 9 | 11 | 7 | | | 13 | 12 | | 3 | | | 8¹ | | | 4 | | | | | | | | | | | | | 21 |
| 1 | 2 | | | 5 | 6 | 12 | 13 | 10³ | | | 9 | 11² | 7 | | | 14 | 8¹ | | 3 | | | | | | 4 | | | | | | | | | | | | | 22 |
| 1 | 2 | | | 5 | 6¹ | 14 | 12 | 10 | | | 9 | 11² | 8 | | | 13 | 7³ | | 3 | | | | | | 4 | | | | | | | | | | | | | 23 |
| 1 | 2 | | | 5 | | 12 | 8 | 10² | | | 9 | 13 | 6 | | | 11 | 7¹ | | 4 | | | | | | 3 | | | | | | | | | | | | | 24 |
| 1 | 2 | | | 5 | | 8 | 9 | 11 | | | 6 | 12 | 7 | | | 10¹ | | | 4 | | | | | | 3 | | | | | | | | | | | | | 25 |
| 1 | | | | 5 | | 6² | 7¹ | 10³ | | | 9 | 8 | 2 | | 11 | | | | | | | | | | 3 | 12 | 13 | 14 | | | | | | | | | | 26 |
| 1 | 2 | | | 5¹ | 14 | | 10² | | | | 9 | | 7 | | | 4 | | | | | | | | | | 3 | 6 | 8³ | 13 | 11 | 12 | | | | | | | | 27 |
| 1 | 2 | | | | | | 8 | | 13 | | 9¹ | | | | | 14 | | | 5 | | | | | | 3 | 6 | 10³ | 11² | 4 | 7 | 12 | | | | | | | 28 |
| | 2² | | | | | | 7 | | 14 | | 9 | | | | 13 | | | | 5 | | | | | | 4 | 6¹ | 11³ | 10 | 3 | 8 | 12 | | | | | | | 29 |
| 1 | | | | 5 | | | 7 | 13 | 10¹ | | 6 | | | | | 2 | | | 3 | | | | | | 4 | | 11² | | 8 | 9³ | 12 | 14 | | | | | | 30 |
| 1 | | | | 5 | | | 7 | 10³ | | | 9² | | | | | 2 | | | 4 | | | | | | 3 | 13 | | | 8 | 6¹ | 11 | 12 | 14 | | | | | 31 |
| 1¹ | | | | | 9¹ | 6³ | 7²11 | | | | 2 | | | | | 5 | | | 4 | | | | | | | 13 | 14 | | 8 | 10 | 3 | | | | 12 | | | 32 |
| | | | | | | | 8⁸10¹ | 12 | | | 13 | | | | | 2 | | | 5⁸ | | | | | | 3 | 6 | | | 7 | 9 | 11² | | | | 1 | 4 | 33 |
| 1 | | | | 5 | | 8² | 14 | 12 | | | 13 | 9 | | | | 2 | | | 4 | | | | | | 6 | | | | 7 | 11³ | 10¹ | | | | 3 | 4 | 34 |
| 1 | 2 | | | 3 | | | 12³ | 11 | | | 6 | 9¹ | | | | 5 | | | | | | | | | 10² | 7 | | | 8 | 13 | 14 | | | | 4 | | 35 |
| 1 | 2 | | | 5¹ | 14 | | | 11² | | | 9 | | | | | 12 | | | 4 | | | | | | 10 | 6 | 13 | 3 | 7³ | 8 | | | | | 4 | | 36 |
| 1 | 2 | | | 13 | | | 7 | 10 | 11¹ | | 6 | | | | | 14 | | | 5 | | | | | | 4 | 9 | 8² | | 3³ | 8 | | | | | | | 37 |
| 1 | 5 | | | 13 | | | 8² | 11 | 10 | | 9 | | | | | 2³ | | | | | | | | | 3 | 12 | | 4 | 7⁸ | 6¹ | 14 | | | | | | 38 |
| 1 | 2 | | | 7 | | | 11² | 10³ | | | 6 | | | | | 12 | | | 5¹ | | | | | | 4 | 9 | 8 | 14 | 3 | | 13 | | | | | | | 39 |
| 1 | 2 | | | 6 | | | 8 | | | | 9² | | | | | 5 | | | | | | | | | 11 | 7 | 10¹ | 4 | | 13 | 12 | | | | 3 | | 40 |
| 1 | 2 | | | 6 | | | 8 | 12 | 13 | | 9 | | | | | 5 | | | | | | | | | 11² | 7¹ | 10 | 4 | | | | | | | 3 | | 41 |
| 1 | | | | 8 | | | 7 | | | | 9 | | | | | 5 | | | 2 | | | | | | 11² | | 10¹ | 4 | 6 | 13 | 12 | | | | 3 | | 42 |
| 1 | | | | 6 | | | 8 | | 12 | | 9 | | | | | 5 | | | 2 | | | | | | 11² | | 10 | 4⁸ | 7¹ | 13 | | | | | 3 | | 43 |
| 1 | 2² | | | 13 | | | 7³ | 11 | | | 12 | 4 | | | 6 | 5 | | | | | | | | | 8¹ | | 10 | 9 | | 14 | | | | | 3 | | 44 |
| 1 | 2 | | | | | | 8 | 10 | | | 12 | 5 | | | | 4 | | | | | | | | | 9² | | 11¹ | 7 | 6 | 13 | | | | | 3 | | 45 |
| 1 | 2³ | | | | | | 8 | 13 | | | 10 | 9 | | | | 5 | | | | | | | | | 6 | 14 | 11² | 3 | 7 | 4¹ | 12 | | | | 3 | | 46 |

**FA Cup**

| | | | |
|---|---|---|---|
| First Round | Bromley | (h) | 3-0 |
| Second Round | Aldershot T | (h) | 2-3 |

**Capital One Cup**

| | | | |
|---|---|---|---|
| First Round | Nottingham F | (h) | 0-1 |

**Johnstone's Paint Trophy**

| | | | |
|---|---|---|---|
| First Round | Rochdale | (a) | 2-2 |
| *(aet; lost 2-4 on pens)* | | | |

# FULHAM

## FOUNDATION

Churchgoers were responsible for the foundation of Fulham, which first saw the light of day as Fulham St Andrew's Church Sunday School FC in 1879. They won the West London Amateur Cup in 1887 and the championship of the West London League in its initial season of 1892–93. The name Fulham had been adopted in 1888.

*Craven Cottage, Stevenage Road, London SW6 6HH.*

*Telephone:* (0843) 208 1222.

*Fax:* (0870) 442 0236 (Motspur Park).

*Ticket Line:* (0843) 208 1234.

*Website:* www.fulhamfc.co.uk

*Email:* enquiries@fulhamfc.com

*Ground Capacity:* 26,700.

*Record Attendance:* 49,335 v Millwall, Division 2, 8 October 1938.

*Pitch Measurements:* 100m × 65m (109yd × 71yd)

*Chairman:* Mohamed Al Fayed.

*Chief Executive:* Alistair Mackintosh.

*Manager:* Martin Jol.

*Head Coach:* Michael Lindeman.

*Director of Sports Medicine and Exercise Science:* Mark Taylor.

## HONOURS

**Football League –**
**Division 1:** *Champions* 2000–01;
**Division 2:** *Champions* 1948–49, 1998–99; *Runners-up* 1958–59;
**Division 3 (S):** *Champions* 1931–32;
**Division 3:** *Runners-up* 1970–71, 1996–97.
**FA Cup:** *Runners-up* 1975.
**Football League Cup:** Best season: 5th rd, 1968, 1971, 2000, 2005.
**European Competitions**
**UEFA Cup:** 2002–03.
**Intertoto Cup:** 2002 (*winners*).
**Europa League:** 2009–10 (*runners-up*), 2011–12.

*Colours:* White shirts with thin black stripes, black shorts, white socks with black trim.

*Year Formed:* 1879.

*Turned Professional:* 1898.

*Reformed:* 1987.

*Previous Name:* 1879, Fulham St Andrew's; 1888, Fulham.

*Club Nickname:* 'The Cottagers'.

*Grounds:* 1879, Star Road, Fulham; c.1883, Eel Brook Common, 1884, Lillie Road; 1885, Putney Lower Common; 1886, Ranelagh House, Fulham; 1888, Barn Elms, Castelnau; 1889, Purser's Cross (Roskell's Field), Parsons Green Lane; 1891, Eel Brook Common; 1891, Half Moon, Putney; 1895, Captain James Field, West Brompton; 1896, Craven Cottage.

*First Football League Game:* 3 September 1907, Division 2, v Hull C (h) L 0–1 – Skene; Ross, Lindsay; Collins, Morrison, Goldie; Dalrymple, Freeman, Bevan, Hubbard, Threlfall.

*Record League Victory:* 10–1 v Ipswich T, Division 1, 26 December 1963 – Macedo; Cohen, Langley; Mullery (1), Keetch, Robson (1); Key, Cook (1), Leggat (4), Haynes, Howfield (3).

*Record Cup Victory:* 7–0 v Swansea C, FA Cup 1st rd, 11 November 1995 – Lange; Jupp (1), Herrera, Barkus (Brooker (1)), Moore, Angus, Thomas (1), Morgan, Brazil (Hamill), Conroy (3) (Bolt), Cusack (1).

*Record Defeat:* 0–10 v Liverpool, League Cup 2nd rd 1st leg, 23 September 1986.

## sky SPORTS FACT FILE

Tosh Chamberlain enjoyed a spectacular start to his Football League career for Fulham on 20 November 1954 when he scored with his first kick of the game in a 3-2 win over Lincoln City. He went on to make over 200 appearances for the Cottagers before moving on to Dover.

*Most League Points (2 for a win):* 60, Division 2, 1958–59 and Division 3, 1970–71.

*Most League Points (3 for a win):* 101, Division 2, 1998–99. 101, Division 1, 2000–01.

*Most League Goals:* 111, Division 3 (S), 1931–32.

*Highest League Scorer in Season:* Frank Newton, 43, Division 3 (S), 1931–32.

*Most League Goals in Total Aggregate:* Gordon Davies, 159, 1978–84, 1986–91.

*Most League Goals in One Match:* 5, Fred Harrison v Stockport Co, Division 2, 5 September 1908; 5, Bedford Jezzard v Hull C, Division 2, 8 October 1955; 5, Jimmy Hill v Doncaster R, Division 2, 15 March 1958; 5, Steve Earle v Halifax T, Division 3, 16 September 1969.

*Most Capped Player:* Johnny Haynes, 56, England.

*Most League Appearances:* Johnny Haynes, 594, 1952–70.

*Youngest League Player:* Matthew Briggs, 16 years 65 days v Middlesbrough, 13 May 2007.

*Record Transfer Fee Received:* £15,000,000 from Tottenham H for Moussa Dembele, August 2012.

*Record Transfer Fee Paid:* £11,500,000 to Lyon for Steve Marlet, August 2001.

*Football League Record:* 1907 Elected to Division 2; 1928–32 Division 3 (S); 1932–49 Division 2; 1949–52 Division 1; 1952–59 Division 2; 1959–68 Division 1; 1968–69 Division 2; 1969–71 Division 3; 1971–80 Division 2; 1980–82 Division 3; 1982–86 Division 2; 1986–92 Division 3; 1992–94 Division 2; 1994–97 Division 3; 1997–99 Division 2; 1999–2001 Division 1; 2001– FA Premier League.

## LATEST SEQUENCES

*Longest Sequence of League Wins:* 12, 7.5.2000 – 18.10.2000.

*Longest Sequence of League Defeats:* 11, 2.12.1961 – 24.2.1962.

*Longest Sequence of League Draws:* 6, 14.10.1995 – 18.11.1995.

*Longest Sequence of Unbeaten League Matches:* 15, 26.1.1999 – 13.4.1999.

*Longest Sequence Without a League Win:* 15, 25.2.1950 – 23.8.1950.

*Successive Scoring Runs:* 26 from 28.3.1931.

*Successive Non-scoring Runs:* 6 from 21.8.1971.

## MANAGERS

**Harry Bradshaw** 1904–09
**Phil Kelso** 1909–24
**Andy Ducat** 1924–26
**Joe Bradshaw** 1926–29
**Ned Liddell** 1929–31
**Jim McIntyre** 1931–34
**Jimmy Hogan** 1934–35
**Jack Peart** 1935–48
**Frank Osborne** 1948–64
  *(was Secretary-Manager or General Manager for most of this period and Team Manager 1953–56)*
**Bill Dodgin Snr** 1949–53
**Duggie Livingstone** 1956–58
**Bedford Jezzard** 1958–64
  *(General Manager for last two months)*
**Vic Buckingham** 1965–68
**Bobby Robson** 1968
**Bill Dodgin Jnr** 1968–72
**Alec Stock** 1972–76
**Bobby Campbell** 1976–80
**Malcolm Macdonald** 1980–84
**Ray Harford** 1984–96
**Ray Lewington** 1986–90
**Alan Dicks** 1990–91
**Don Mackay** 1991–94
**Ian Branfoot** 1994–96
  *(continued as General Manager)*
**Micky Adams** 1996–97
**Ray Wilkins** 1997–98
**Kevin Keegan** 1998–99
  *(Chief Operating Officer)*
**Paul Bracewell** 1999–2000
**Jean Tigana** 2000–03
**Chris Coleman** 2003–07
**Lawrie Sanchez** 2007
**Roy Hodgson** 2007–10
**Mark Hughes** 2010–11
**Martin Jol** June 2011–

## TEN YEAR LEAGUE RECORD

|  |  | P | W | D | L | F | A | Pts | Pos |
|---|---|---|---|---|---|---|---|---|---|
| 2003-04 | PR Lge | 38 | 14 | 10 | 14 | 52 | 46 | 52 | 9 |
| 2004-05 | PR Lge | 38 | 12 | 8 | 18 | 52 | 60 | 44 | 13 |
| 2005-06 | PR Lge | 38 | 14 | 6 | 18 | 48 | 58 | 48 | 12 |
| 2006-07 | PR Lge | 38 | 8 | 15 | 15 | 38 | 60 | 39 | 16 |
| 2007-08 | PR Lge | 38 | 8 | 12 | 18 | 38 | 60 | 36 | 17 |
| 2008-09 | PR Lge | 38 | 14 | 11 | 13 | 39 | 34 | 53 | 7 |
| 2009-10 | PR Lge | 38 | 12 | 10 | 16 | 39 | 46 | 46 | 12 |
| 2010-11 | PR Lge | 38 | 11 | 16 | 11 | 49 | 43 | 49 | 8 |
| 2011-12 | PR Lge | 38 | 14 | 10 | 14 | 48 | 51 | 52 | 9 |
| 2012-13 | PR Lge | 38 | 11 | 10 | 17 | 50 | 60 | 43 | 12 |

## DID YOU KNOW ?

Ronnie Rooke scored a hat-trick for Fulham on his debut against West Ham on 7 November 1936 and went on to net 290 goals in 309 appearances (including wartime games). As well as hitting all six in an FA Cup tie with Bury in January 1939, he had 10 four-goal tallies and 16 hat-tricks.

### FULHAM – FA PREMIERSHIP 2012–13 LEAGUE RECORD

| Match No. | Date | Venue | Opponents | Result | H/T Score | Lg Pos. | Goalscorers | Atten-dance |
|---|---|---|---|---|---|---|---|---|
| 1 | Aug 18 | H | Norwich C | W 5-0 | 2-0 | 1 | Duff [26], Petric 2 [41, 54], Kacaniklic [66], Sidwell (pen) [87] | 25,062 |
| 2 | 25 | A | Manchester U | L 2-3 | 1-3 | 5 | Duff [3], Vidic (og) [64] | 75,352 |
| 3 | Sept 1 | A | West Ham U | L 0-3 | 0-3 | 8 | | 33,458 |
| 4 | 15 | H | WBA | W 3-0 | 2-0 | 8 | Berbatov 2 (1 pen) [32, 45 (p)], Sidwell [89] | 25,691 |
| 5 | 22 | A | Wigan Ath | W 2-1 | 1-0 | 4 | Rodallega [31], Duff [68] | 19,284 |
| 6 | 29 | H | Manchester C | L 1-2 | 1-1 | 8 | Petric (pen) [10] | 25,698 |
| 7 | Oct 7 | A | Southampton | D 2-2 | 0-1 | 9 | Hooiveld (og) [70], Richardson [88] | 28,004 |
| 8 | 20 | H | Aston Villa | W 1-0 | 0-0 | 8 | Baird [84] | 25,693 |
| 9 | 27 | A | Reading | D 3-3 | 0-1 | 6 | Ruiz [61], Baird [77], Berbatov [88] | 24,093 |
| 10 | Nov 3 | H | Everton | D 2-2 | 1-0 | 7 | Ruiz [7], Sidwell [90] | 25,699 |
| 11 | 10 | A | Arsenal | D 3-3 | 2-2 | 8 | Berbatov 2 (1 pen) [29, 67 (p)], Kacaniklic [40] | 60,093 |
| 12 | 18 | H | Sunderland | L 1-3 | 0-0 | 9 | Petric [62] | 25,646 |
| 13 | 24 | A | Stoke C | L 0-1 | 0-1 | 9 | | 26,921 |
| 14 | 28 | A | Chelsea | D 0-0 | 0-0 | 11 | | 41,707 |
| 15 | Dec 1 | H | Tottenham H | L 0-3 | 0-0 | 12 | | 25,426 |
| 16 | 10 | H | Newcastle U | W 2-1 | 1-0 | 13 | Sidwell [19], Rodallega [63] | 25,270 |
| 17 | 15 | A | QPR | L 1-2 | 0-0 | 13 | Petric [88] | 18,233 |
| 18 | 22 | A | Liverpool | L 0-4 | 0-2 | 13 | | 44,570 |
| 19 | 26 | H | Southampton | D 1-1 | 1-0 | 14 | Berbatov [8] | 25,700 |
| 20 | 29 | H | Swansea C | L 1-2 | 0-1 | 14 | Ruiz [56] | 25,700 |
| 21 | Jan 1 | A | WBA | W 2-1 | 1-0 | 13 | Berbatov [39], Kacaniklic [58] | 25,436 |
| 22 | 12 | H | Wigan Ath | D 1-1 | 1-0 | 13 | Karagounis [22] | 25,442 |
| 23 | 19 | A | Manchester C | L 0-2 | 0-1 | 14 | | 47,286 |
| 24 | 30 | H | West Ham U | W 3-1 | 1-0 | 12 | Berbatov [10], Rodallega [49], O'Brien (og) [90] | 24,791 |
| 25 | Feb 2 | H | Manchester U | L 0-1 | 0-0 | 13 | | 25,670 |
| 26 | 9 | A | Norwich C | D 0-0 | 0-0 | 13 | | 26,816 |
| 27 | 23 | H | Stoke C | W 1-0 | 1-0 | 11 | Berbatov [45] | 25,458 |
| 28 | Mar 2 | A | Sunderland | D 2-2 | 2-1 | 10 | Berbatov (pen) [16], Riether [35] | 39,312 |
| 29 | 17 | A | Tottenham H | W 1-0 | 0-0 | 10 | Berbatov [52] | 36,004 |
| 30 | Apr 1 | H | QPR | W 3-2 | 3-1 | 10 | Berbatov 2 (1 pen) [8 (p), 22], Hill (og) [41] | 25,117 |
| 31 | 7 | A | Newcastle U | L 0-1 | 0-0 | 10 | | 51,847 |
| 32 | 13 | A | Aston Villa | D 1-1 | 0-0 | 10 | Delph (og) [66] | 37,011 |
| 33 | 17 | H | Chelsea | L 0-3 | 0-2 | 10 | | 25,002 |
| 34 | 20 | H | Arsenal | L 0-1 | 0-1 | 11 | | 25,700 |
| 35 | 27 | A | Everton | L 0-1 | 0-1 | 1 | | 34,563 |
| 36 | May 4 | H | Reading | L 2-4 | 0-1 | 12 | Ruiz 2 [70, 77] | 24,087 |
| 37 | 12 | H | Liverpool | L 1-3 | 1-1 | 15 | Berbatov [33] | 25,640 |
| 38 | 19 | A | Swansea C | W 3-0 | 1-0 | 12 | Kacaniklic [22], Berbatov [77], Emanuelson [90] | 20,365 |

**Final League Position: 12**

### GOALSCORERS

*League (50):* Berbatov 15 (4 pens), Petric 5 (1 pen), Ruiz 5, Kacaniklic 4, Sidwell 4 (1 pen), Duff 3, Rodallega 3, Baird 2, Emanuelson 1, Karagounis 1, Richardson 1, Riether 1, own goals 5.
*FA Cup (4):* Hangeland 1, Hughes 1, Karagounis 1, Richardson 1.
*Capital One Cup (0).*

| Schwarzer M 36 | Riether S 35 | Hangeland B 35 | Hughes A 23 + 1 | Riise J 29 + 2 | Duff D 27 + 4 | Diarra M 7 + 1 | Dembele M 2 | Kacaniklic A 16 + 4 | Ruiz B 26 + 3 | Petric M 9 + 14 | Rodallega H 14 + 15 | Kasami P — + 2 | Sidwell S 24 + 4 | Briggs M 3 + 2 | Baird C 14 + 5 | Richardson K 12 + 2 | Berbatov D 32 + 1 | Smith A — + 1 | Karagounis G 20 + 5 | Dejagah A 13 + 8 | Senderos P 18 + 3 | Frei K 2 + 5 | Kelly S — + 2 | Stockdale D 2 | Emanuelson U 5 + 8 | Manolev S 4 + 1 | Frimpong E 2 + 4 | Enoh E 8 + 1 | Match No. |
|---|---|---|---|---|---|---|---|---|---|---|---|---|---|---|---|---|---|---|---|---|---|---|---|---|---|---|---|---|---|
| 1 | 2 | 3 | 4 | 5 | $6^2$ | 7 | 8 | 9 | $10^3$ | $11^1$ | 12 | 13 | 14 | | | | | | | | | | | | | | | | 1 |
| 1 | 2 | 4 | 3 | | 6 | $7^3$ | 8 | $9^1$ | 10 | $11^2$ | 13 | | 12 | | 5 | 14 | | | | | | | | | | | | | 2 |
| 1 | 2 | 4 | 3 | 5 | 6 | 8 | | 13 | | $11^1$ | 10 | | 7 | | | | $9^2$ | | 12 | | | | | | | | | | 3 |
| 1 | 2 | 4 | 3 | 5 | $6^2$ | | | $9^1$ | | 11 | 12 | | 7 | | 8 | | 10 | 13 | | | | | | | | | | | 4 |
| 1 | 2 | 4 | 3 | 5 | 6 | | | $9^1$ | 12 | $11^2$ | | | 8 | 13 | 7 | | 10 | | | | | | | | | | | | 5 |
| 1 | 2 | 4 | 3 | 5 | 8 | | | 12 | 9 | $10^1$ | 11 | | 7 | | $6^2$ | | | | 13 | | | | | | | | | | 6 |
| 1 | 2 | 4 | 3 | 5 | 10 | | | $6^1$ | 7 | 11 | | | $9^2$ | | 8 | 12 | | | 13 | | | | | | | | | | 7 |
| 1 | 2 | 4 | 3 | 5 | | 12 | | | | $11^1$ | 9 | | $6^3$ | | 7 | $8^2$ | 10 | | 14 | 13 | | | | | | | | | 8 |
| 1 | 2 | 4 | 3 | 5 | $6^2$ | 8 | | | 12 | | $10^1$ | | 14 | | $7^3$ | 9 | 11 | | 13 | | | | | | | | | | 9 |
| 1 | 2 | 4 | 3 | $5^1$ | 6 | $7^3$ | | $9^2$ | 10 | 14 | | | 13 | | 8 | | 11 | | 12 | | | | | | | | | | 10 |
| 1 | 2 | 4 | 3 | 5 | 13 | | | 12 | 6 | | | | 8 | | 7 | $9^1$ | 10 | | $11^2$ | | | | | | | | | | 11 |
| 1 | 2 | $3^4$ | 4 | 5 | 6 | | | $9^1$ | $10^3$ | 14 | 12 | | 7 | | | | 11 | | $8^2$ | 13 | | | | | | | | | 12 |
| 1 | 2 | | 3 | 5 | 12 | | | | | 11 | 13 | | $7^2$ | | 6 | | 10 | | $8^1$ | 9 | 4 | | | | | | | | 13 |
| 1 | 2 | | 4 | 5 | 6 | $7^1$ | | | | 14 | $10^3$ | | 8 | | | | 11 | | $9^2$ | | 3 | 13 | | | | | | | 14 |
| 1 | $2^1$ | | 4 | 5 | 13 | 7 | | | | $11^3$ | 14 | | 8 | | | | 10 | | 9 | 3 | $6^2$ | 12 | | | | | | | 15 |
| 1 | 2 | 4 | 3 | 5 | 6 | | | $9^1$ | | 13 | $10^2$ | | 8 | | 7 | | 11 | | | 12 | | | | | | | | | 16 |
| 1 | $2^1$ | 3 | 4 | 5 | 6 | | | | | 13 | $11^3$ | | 7 | | 8 | $9^2$ | 10 | | 14 | | | 12 | | | | | | | 17 |
| 1 | 2 | 3 | 4 | 5 | | | | $6^1$ | | 12 | | | 8 | $9^2$ | 11 | | 7 | 10 | | 13 | | | | | | | | | 18 |
| 1 | 2 | 3 | | 5 | | | | $9^1$ | 12 | $11^3$ | | | 7 | 8 | 10 | | 14 | | $6^2$ | 4 | 13 | | | | | | | | 19 |
| | 2 | 3 | 4 | | | | | 10 | | 12 | | | 7 | 5 | 11 | | 8 | | $6^1$ | 13 | $9^2$ | 1 | | | | | | | 20 |
| | 2 | 4 | 3 | | | | | 9 | 10 | 12 | | | 7 | 5 | | | $11^2$ | | $8^1$ | 6 | 13 | 1 | | | | | | | 21 |
| 1 | 2 | 3 | 4 | | $6^2$ | | | $9^3$ | 8 | $11^1$ | 12 | | 13 | 5 | 10 | | 7 | 14 | | | | | | | | | | | 22 |
| 1 | 2 | 4 | 3 | | 6 | | | 10 | 13 | | | | 8 | 12 | $5^1$ | 11 | 7 | | $9^2$ | | | | | | | | | | 23 |
| 1 | 2 | 3 | | 5 | 6 | | | $10^2$ | 14 | 9 | | | 8 | 13 | $11^3$ | | $7^1$ | 12 | 4 | | | | | | | | | | 24 |
| 1 | 2 | $3^1$ | 12 | 5 | 6 | | | 10 | 14 | 11 | | | 8 | | | $7^2$ | $9^3$ | 4 | | | | 13 | | | | | | | 25 |
| 1 | | 4 | | 5 | 8 | | | $9^3$ | 13 | $11^2$ | 6 | | | | 10 | | | | 14 | 3 | | | | | 12 | 2 | $7^1$ | | 26 |
| 1 | 2 | 4 | | 5 | $6^2$ | | | 10 | 14 | | | | 7 | | 12 | | $11^3$ | | $8^1$ | 9 | 3 | | | | 13 | | | | 27 |
| 1 | 2 | 4 | | 5 | $6^2$ | | | 10 | | 14 | | | 7 | | | | 11 | | $8^1$ | $9^3$ | 3 | | | | 13 | | 12 | | 28 |
| 1 | 2 | 4 | | 5 | 9 | | | $11^2$ | | | | | 7 | | | | 10 | | $6^1$ | 9 | 3 | | | | 13 | | | 12 | 29 |
| 1 | 2 | 4 | | 5 | 6 | | | 10 | | | | | $8^4$ | | | | 11 | | 7 | $9^1$ | 3 | | | | $12^2$ | 13 | | | 30 |
| 1 | 2 | 3 | | 5 | 9 | | | 10 | | 13 | | | | | 11 | | 7 | | 4 | | | | | | $6^2$ | 12 | $8^1$ | | 31 |
| 1 | 2 | 4 | | 14 | $9^3$ | | | 10 | 13 | | | | $5^2$ | 11 | | | $8^1$ | | 6 | 12 | | | | | | | | | 32 |
| 1 | 2 | 4 | | $5^1$ | | | | 6 | $11^3$ | 12 | | | 10 | | $8^2$ | | 3 | 14 | 9 | | 13 | 7 | | | | | | | 33 |
| 1 | | 4 | | | | | | $9^1$ | 10 | 12 | $7^8$ | | 5 | 11 | | | 3 | 13 | $6^2$ | 2 | 8 | | | | | | | | 34 |
| 1 | | 4 | | 13 | | | | 9 | 10 | 12 | 14 | | $5^2$ | $11^1$ | $7^3$ | | 3 | | 6 | 2 | 8 | | | | | | | | 35 |
| 1 | 2 | 4 | | $5^2$ | $6^3$ | | | 14 | 10 | 12 | | | 13 | $7^1$ | | | 11 | | 3 | 9 | 8 | | | | | | | | 36 |
| 1 | 2 | 4 | 3 | 14 | 6 | | | $9^2$ | 10 | 13 | | | $5^1$ | $7^3$ | | | 11 | | 12 | 8 | | | | | | | | | 37 |
| 1 | 2 | 4 | | 5 | $6^2$ | | | 8 | 11 | 14 | | | $10^3$ | 12 | | | 3 | | | 13 | $7^1$ | 9 | | | | | | | 38 |

**FA Cup**

| | | | | |
|---|---|---|---|---|
| Third Round | Blackpool | (h) | 1-1 | |
| *Replay* | Blackpool | (a) | 2-1 | |
| Fourth Round | Manchester U | (a) | 1-4 | |

**Capital One Cup**

| | | | |
|---|---|---|---|
| Second Round | Sheffield W | (a) | 0-1 |

# GILLINGHAM

## FOUNDATION

The success of the pioneering Royal Engineers of Chatham excited the interest of the residents of the Medway Towns and led to the formation of many clubs including Excelsior. After winning the Kent Junior Cup and the Chatham District League in 1893, Excelsior decided to go for bigger things and it was at a meeting in the Napier Arms, Brompton, in 1893 that New Brompton FC came into being, buying and developing the ground which is now Priestfield Stadium. They changed their name to Gillingham in 1913, when they also changed their strip from black and white stripes to predominantly blue.

*MEMS Priestfield Stadium, Redfern Avenue, Gillingham, Kent ME7 4DD.*

*Telephone:* (01634) 300 000.

*Fax:* (01634) 850 986.

*Ticket Office:* (01634) 300 000 (option 1).

*Website:* www.gillinghamfootballclub.com

*Email:* info@priestfield.com

*Ground Capacity:* 11,440.

*Record Attendance:* 23,002 v QPR, FA Cup 3rd rd, 10 January 1948.

*Pitch Measurements:* 104m × 68m (114yd × 75yd)

*Chairman:* Paul D. P. Scally.

*Vice-chairman:* Michael Anderson.

*Manager:* Martin Allen.

*Assistant Manager:* John Schofield.

*Physio:* Gary Hemens.

*Colours:* Red shirts with blue sleeves, white shorts, blue socks.

*Year Formed:* 1893.

*Turned Professional:* 1894.

*Previous Name:* 1893, New Brompton; 1913, Gillingham.

*Club Nickname:* 'The Gills'.

*Ground:* 1893, Priestfield Stadium.

## HONOURS

**Football League –**
**Division 1:** 11th, 2002–03;
**Division 3:** *Runners-up* 1995–96;
**Division 4:** *Champions* 1963–64;
*Runners-up* 1973–74;
**FL 2:** *Champions* 2012–13.

**FA Cup:** Best season: 6th rd, 2000.

**Football League Cup:** Best season: 4th rd, 1964, 1997.

*First Football League Game:* 28 August 1920, Division 3, v Southampton (h) D 1–1 – Branfield; Robertson, Sissons; Battiste, Baxter, Wigmore; Holt, Hall, Gilbey (1), Roe, Gore.

*Record League Victory:* 10–0 v Chesterfield, Division 3, 5 September 1987 – Kite; Haylock, Pearce, Shipley (2) (Lillis), West, Greenall (1), Pritchard (2), Shearer (2), Lovell, Elsey (2), David Smith (1).

*Record Cup Victory:* 10–1 v Gorleston, FA Cup 1st rd, 16 November 1957 – Brodie; Parry, Hannaway; Riggs, Boswell, Laing; Payne, Fletcher (2), Saunders (5), Morgan (1), Clark (2).

## sky SPORTS FACT FILE

After being voted out the Football League in 1938, Gillingham returned for the 1950–51 season when they were one of two clubs elected into Division Three South when the competition was extended from 22 to 24 clubs. The Gills topped the poll on that occasion with 44 votes.

*Record Defeat:* 2–9 v Nottingham F, Division 3 (S), 18 November 1950.

*Most League Points (2 for a win):* 62, Division 4, 1973–74.

*Most League Points (3 for a win):* 85, Division 2, 1999–2000.

*Most League Goals:* 90, Division 4, 1973–74.

*Highest League Scorer in Season:* Ernie Morgan, 31, Division 3 (S), 1954–55; Brian Yeo, 31, Division 4, 1973–74.

*Most League Goals in Total Aggregate:* Brian Yeo, 135, 1963–75.

*Most League Goals in One Match:* 6, Fred Cheesmur v Merthyr T, Division 3 (S), 26 April 1930.

*Most Capped Player:* Andrew Crofts, 12 (24), Wales.

*Most League Appearances:* John Simpson, 571, 1957–72.

*Youngest League Player:* Luke Freeman, 15 years 247 days v Hartlepool U, 24 November 2007.

*Record Transfer Fee Received:* £1,500,000 from Manchester C for Robert Taylor, November 1999.

*Record Transfer Fee Paid:* £600,000 to Reading for Carl Asaba, August 1998.

*Football League Record:* 1920 Original Member of Division 3; 1921 Division 3 (S); 1938 Failed re-election; Southern League 1938–44; Kent League 1944–46; Southern League 1946–50; 1950 Re-elected to Division 3 (S); 1958–64 Division 4; 1964–71 Division 3; 1971–74 Division 4; 1974–89 Division 3; 1989–92 Division 4; 1992–96; Division 3; 1996–2000 Division 2; 2000–04 Division 1; 2004–05 FL C; 2005–08 FL 1; 2008–09 FL 2; 2009–10 FL 1; 2010–13 FL 2; 2013– FL 1.

## LATEST SEQUENCES

*Longest Sequence of League Wins:* 7, 18.12.1954 – 29.1.1955.

*Longest Sequence of League Defeats:* 10, 20.9.1988 – 5.11.1988.

*Longest Sequence of League Draws:* 5, 28.8.1993 – 18.9.1993.

*Longest Sequence of Unbeaten League Matches:* 20, 13.10.1973 – 10.2.1974.

*Longest Sequence Without a League Win:* 15, 1.4.1972 – 2.9.1972.

*Successive Scoring Runs:* 20 from 31.10.1959.

*Successive Non-scoring Runs:* 6 from 11.2.1961.

## MANAGERS

**W. Ironside Groombridge**
1896–1906 *(Secretary-Manager)*
*(previously Financial Secretary)*
**Steve Smith** 1906–08
**W. I. Groombridge** 1908–19
*(Secretary-Manager)*
**George Collins** 1919–20
**John McMillan** 1920–23
**Harry Curtis** 1923–26
**Albert Hoskins** 1926–29
**Dick Hendrie** 1929–31
**Fred Mavin** 1932–37
**Alan Ure** 1937–38
**Bill Harvey** 1938–39
**Archie Clark** 1939–58
**Harry Barratt** 1958–62
**Freddie Cox** 1962–65
**Basil Hayward** 1966–71
**Andy Nelson** 1971–74
**Len Ashurst** 1974–75
**Gerry Summers** 1975–81
**Keith Peacock** 1981–87
**Paul Taylor** 1988
**Keith Burkinshaw** 1988–89
**Damien Richardson** 1989–92
**Glenn Roeder** 1992–93
**Mike Flanagan** 1993–95
**Neil Smillie** 1995
**Tony Pulis** 1995–99
**Peter Taylor** 1999–2000
**Andy Hessenthaler** 2000–04
**Stan Ternent** 2004–05
**Neale Cooper** 2005
**Ronnie Jepson** 2005–07
**Mark Stimson** 2007–10
**Andy Hessenthaler** 2010–12
**Martin Allen** July 2012–

## TEN YEAR LEAGUE RECORD

|  |  | P | W | D | L | F | A | Pts | Pos |
|---|---|---|---|---|---|---|---|---|---|
| 2003-04 | Div 1 | 46 | 14 | 9 | 23 | 48 | 67 | 51 | 21 |
| 2004-05 | FL C | 46 | 12 | 14 | 20 | 45 | 66 | 50 | 22 |
| 2005-06 | FL 1 | 46 | 16 | 12 | 18 | 50 | 64 | 60 | 14 |
| 2006-07 | FL 1 | 46 | 17 | 8 | 21 | 56 | 77 | 59 | 16 |
| 2007-08 | FL 1 | 46 | 11 | 13 | 22 | 44 | 73 | 46 | 22 |
| 2008-09 | FL 2 | 46 | 21 | 12 | 13 | 58 | 55 | 75 | 5 |
| 2009-10 | FL 1 | 46 | 12 | 14 | 20 | 48 | 64 | 50 | 21 |
| 2010-11 | FL 2 | 46 | 17 | 17 | 12 | 67 | 57 | 68 | 8 |
| 2011-12 | FL 2 | 46 | 20 | 10 | 16 | 79 | 62 | 70 | 8 |
| 2012-13 | FL 2 | 46 | 23 | 14 | 9 | 66 | 39 | 83 | 1 |

## DID YOU KNOW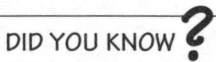

In their days as New Brompton, the Gills achieved a major FA Cup giant-killing act in January 1908. As members of the Southern League they defeated the might of First Division club Sunderland 3-1, with Charlie McGibbon netting a hat-trick.

## GILLINGHAM – FOOTBALL LEAGUE TWO 2012–13 LEAGUE RECORD

| Match No. | Date | Venue | Opponents | Result | H/T Score | Lg Pos. | Goalscorers | Attendance |
|---|---|---|---|---|---|---|---|---|
| 1 | Aug 18 | H | Bradford C | W 3-1 | 1-0 | 4 | Kedwell 2 (1 pen) [43, 54 (p)], Weston [88] | 5127 |
| 2 | 21 | A | Wycombe W | W 1-0 | 0-0 | 2 | Martin [56] | 3507 |
| 3 | 25 | A | Dagenham & R | W 2-1 | 1-1 | 2 | Burton [30], Weston [62] | 2251 |
| 4 | Sept 1 | H | Chesterfield | D 1-1 | 1-1 | 1 | Kedwell [21] | 4380 |
| 5 | 8 | A | Barnet | W 3-1 | 3-1 | 1 | Payne [10], Kedwell [11], Burton [39] | 2835 |
| 6 | 15 | H | Bristol R | W 4-0 | 3-0 | 1 | Kedwell 2 (1 pen) [5 (p), 15], Lee [45], Whelpdale [82] | 4768 |
| 7 | 18 | H | Southend U | W 1-0 | 1-0 | 1 | Kedwell (pen) [45] | 4920 |
| 8 | 22 | A | Port Vale | W 2-0 | 2-0 | 1 | Burton [11], Whelpdale [25] | 6978 |
| 9 | 29 | H | Rochdale | L 1-2 | 0-1 | 1 | Kedwell (pen) [74] | 5874 |
| 10 | Oct 2 | A | Northampton T | W 2-1 | 1-0 | 1 | Burton [44], Payne [55] | 3648 |
| 11 | 6 | A | Oxford U | D 0-0 | 0-0 | 1 | | 6690 |
| 12 | 13 | H | Aldershot T | W 4-0 | 3-0 | 1 | Allen [11], Kedwell (pen) [27], Weston [38], Whelpdale [66] | 5039 |
| 13 | 20 | H | Burton Alb | W 4-1 | 2-0 | 1 | Flanagan [22], Fish [40], Weston [59], Martin [63] | 7268 |
| 14 | 23 | A | Torquay U | L 1-2 | 0-0 | 1 | Burton [53] | 2251 |
| 15 | 27 | A | AFC Wimbledon | W 1-0 | 1-0 | 1 | Vincelot [23] | 4546 |
| 16 | Nov 6 | H | Cheltenham T | D 0-0 | 0-0 | 1 | | 6096 |
| 17 | 10 | A | Plymouth Arg | D 2-2 | 1-1 | 1 | Strevens [38], Barrett [88] | 6396 |
| 18 | 17 | H | Morecambe | W 2-1 | 1-0 | 1 | Montrose [37], Burton [90] | 5402 |
| 19 | 20 | H | Exeter C | L 2-3 | 1-1 | 1 | Whelpdale [4], Jackman [79] | 6851 |
| 20 | 24 | A | Accrington S | D 1-1 | 1-0 | 1 | Weston [42] | 1624 |
| 21 | Dec 8 | A | Rotherham U | W 2-1 | 1-0 | 1 | Burton 2 [11, 57] | 8029 |
| 22 | 15 | H | Fleetwood T | D 2-2 | 1-2 | 1 | Lee [42], Weston [65] | 8571 |
| 23 | 26 | H | Barnet | L 0-1 | 0-1 | 1 | | 7448 |
| 24 | Jan 1 | A | Southend U | W 1-0 | 1-0 | 1 | Whelpdale [3] | 7498 |
| 25 | 5 | A | Bristol R | W 2-0 | 2-0 | 1 | Whelpdale [3], Burton [44] | 6088 |
| 26 | 12 | H | Port Vale | L 1-2 | 1-2 | 2 | Kedwell [21] | 8392 |
| 27 | 26 | H | York C | D 1-1 | 0-1 | 2 | McDonald [85] | 4893 |
| 28 | 29 | H | Northampton T | W 2-0 | 1-0 | 1 | McDonald [4], Weston [84] | 5600 |
| 29 | Feb 4 | H | Wycombe W | L 0-1 | 0-0 | 2 | | 4758 |
| 30 | 9 | A | Bradford C | W 1-0 | 0-0 | 2 | McDonald [64] | 10,887 |
| 31 | 12 | H | York C | D 0-0 | 0-0 | 2 | | 2699 |
| 32 | 16 | A | Dagenham & R | W 2-1 | 1-0 | 1 | Legge [29], Burton (pen) [68] | 5611 |
| 33 | 23 | A | Chesterfield | W 1-0 | 0-0 | 1 | McDonald [50] | 5235 |
| 34 | 26 | H | Oxford U | L 0-1 | 0-0 | 1 | | 4928 |
| 35 | Mar 2 | A | Aldershot T | D 1-1 | 0-0 | 1 | Legge [75] | 3267 |
| 36 | 9 | H | Plymouth Arg | W 2-1 | 1-0 | 1 | German [31], Whelpdale [62] | 10,260 |
| 37 | 12 | A | Exeter C | D 0-0 | 0-0 | 1 | | 3608 |
| 38 | 16 | A | Morecambe | D 1-1 | 0-1 | 1 | Dack [52] | 1674 |
| 39 | 19 | A | Rochdale | D 1-1 | 0-1 | 1 | Kedwell [56] | 1551 |
| 40 | 23 | H | Accrington S | W 1-0 | 1-0 | 1 | Fish [24] | 10,097 |
| 41 | 30 | A | Fleetwood T | D 2-2 | 2-1 | 1 | Kedwell [3], Allen [43] | 3033 |
| 42 | Apr 1 | H | Rotherham U | W 1-0 | 1-0 | 1 | Burton [22] | 6796 |
| 43 | 6 | H | Torquay U | W 1-0 | 0-0 | 1 | Kedwell [48] | 7574 |
| 44 | 13 | A | Cheltenham T | L 0-1 | 0-0 | 1 | | 4939 |
| 45 | 20 | H | AFC Wimbledon | D 2-2 | 2-0 | 1 | Burton [12], Kedwell [23] | 11,172 |
| 46 | 27 | A | Burton Alb | L 2-3 | 1-2 | 1 | Weston (pen) [9], Nyafli [66] | 5426 |

**Final League Position: 1**

## GOALSCORERS

*League (66):* Kedwell 14 (5 pens), Burton 12 (1 pen), Weston 8 (1 pen), Whelpdale 7, McDonald 4, Allen 2, Fish 2, Lee 2, Legge 2, Martin 2, Payne 2, Barrett 1, Dack 1, Flanagan 1, German 1, Jackman 1, Montrose 1, Nyafli 1, Strevens 1, Vincelot 1.
*FA Cup (4):* Birchall 1, Burton 1, Fish 1, Kedwell 1 (1 pen).
*Capital One Cup (2):* Kedwell 1 (1 pen), Strevens 1.
*Johnstone's Paint Trophy (2):* Dack 1, Montrose 1.

| Nelson S 45 | Flanagan T 12+1 | Frampton A 21+9 | Fish M 43+1 | Martin J 38 | Lee C 22+9 | Montrose L 12+3 | Allen C 22+10 | Jackman D 7+3 | Burton D 31+9 | Kedwell D 27+11 | Payne J 15+4 | Weston M 19+18 | Dack B 8+8 | Barrett A 43 | Whelpdale C 37+4 | Davies C 12+2 | Strevens B 4+8 | Birchall A 7+8 | Wright D 7 | Findley R 3+4 | Vincelot R 8+1 | Forecast T 1+1 | Legge L 22 | Gregory S 13+4 | McDonald C 6+1 | Robinson A 12+2 | German A 4+3 | Richardson M 1+1 | East D 1+1 | Muggleton S 1 | Romeo M 1 | Grant H 1 | Haysman K —+1 | Nyaffi N —+1 | McKain D —+1 | Match No. |
|---|---|---|---|---|---|---|---|---|---|---|---|---|---|---|---|---|---|---|---|---|---|---|---|---|---|---|---|---|---|---|---|---|---|---|---|---|
| 1 | 2 | 3 | 4 | 5 | 6 | 7¹ | 8 | 9³ | 10² | 11 | 12 | 13 | 14 |  |  |  |  |  |  |  |  |  |  |  |  |  |  |  |  |  |  |  |  |  |  | 1 |
| 1 | 3⁴ |  | 2 | 5 | 7 |  | 12 | 14 |  | 10³ | 8 | 11 | 9¹ | 4 | 6² | 13 |  | 14 |  |  |  |  |  |  |  |  |  |  |  |  |  |  |  |  |  | 2 |
| 1 |  | 4 | 2 | 5 | 8 | 7 | 9³ |  | 10¹ | 12 | 13 | 11 |  | 6² | 3 | 14 |  |  |  |  |  |  |  |  |  |  |  |  |  |  |  |  |  |  |  | 3 |
| 1 | 3 |  | 2 | 5 | 7 | 8¹ | 13 |  | 11 | 10³ | 12 | 9 |  | 4 | 6² |  | 14 |  |  |  |  |  |  |  |  |  |  |  |  |  |  |  |  |  |  | 4 |
| 1 | 14 | 2³ | 5 | 8 |  | 9 | 10² | 11 | 6 | 12 | 3 | 7¹ | 4 | 13 |  |  |  |  |  |  |  |  |  |  |  |  |  |  |  |  |  |  |  |  |  | 5 |
| 1 |  | 2 | 5 | 6 |  | 9 | 11¹ | 10² | 7 | 12 | 3 | 14 | 4 | 13 | 8³ |  |  |  |  |  |  |  |  |  |  |  |  |  |  |  |  |  |  |  |  | 6 |
| 1 | 13 | 2 | 5 | 8¹ |  | 9³ | 11² | 10 |  | 12⁸ | 3 | 6 | 4 | 14 | 7 |  |  |  |  |  |  |  |  |  |  |  |  |  |  |  |  |  |  |  |  | 7 |
| 1 | 4 | 13 | 2 | 5 | 8² | 14 | 7³ | 11 | 12 |  | 3 | 6 |  | 9 | 10¹ |  |  |  |  |  |  |  |  |  |  |  |  |  |  |  |  |  |  |  |  | 8 |
| 1 | 3 |  | 2 | 5 | 8² | 13 | 9⁴ | 11³ | 14 |  | 12 |  |  | 4 | 6 |  |  |  |  |  | 7 | 10¹ |  |  |  |  |  |  |  |  |  |  |  |  |  | 9 |
| 1 | 4 | 13 | 2 | 5 | 9⁴ |  | 11³ | 10 | 7² | 12 |  |  |  | 3 | 6¹ |  |  |  |  |  | 8 | 14 |  |  |  |  |  |  |  |  |  |  |  |  |  | 10 |
| 1 | 4 | 14 | 2 | 5 | 12 |  | 11³ | 10 | 7 | 9² |  |  |  | 3 | 6 |  |  |  |  |  | 8¹ | 13 |  |  |  |  |  |  |  |  |  |  |  |  |  | 11 |
| 1 | 3 | 12 | 2 | 5¹ |  | 8 |  | 10 | 9² | 11³ |  |  |  | 4 | 7 |  |  | 13 |  |  | 6 | 14 |  |  |  |  |  |  |  |  |  |  |  |  |  | 12 |
| 1 | 3 |  | 2 | 5 | 8 | 9 |  | 10³ | 6¹ | 11² | 12 |  |  | 4 | 7 |  |  | 14 |  |  | 13 |  |  |  |  |  |  |  |  |  |  |  |  |  |  | 13 |
| 1 | 4 | 12 | 2 | 5¹ |  | 10 |  | 6³ | 13 | 9 |  |  |  | 3 | 8 | 7 | 14 | 11² |  |  |  |  |  |  |  |  |  |  |  |  |  |  |  |  |  | 14 |
| 1 | 4 | 5 | 2 | 12 | 8 |  |  | 10 |  | 9¹ |  |  |  | 3 | 6 |  | 11 |  | 7 |  |  |  |  |  |  |  |  |  |  |  |  |  |  |  |  | 15 |
| 1 | 5 | 2 |  | 8 |  | 13 | 12 | 10³ | 6¹ | 11² |  |  |  | 3 | 7 | 4 |  | 14 |  | 9 |  |  |  |  |  |  |  |  |  |  |  |  |  |  |  | 16 |
| 1 | 4 | 2 |  | 7¹ |  | 5 | 10³ | 13 | 6 | 12 |  |  |  | 3 | 9² |  | 11 | 14 | 8 |  |  |  |  |  |  |  |  |  |  |  |  |  |  |  |  | 17 |
| 1 | 4³ | 2 |  | 8 | 13 | 5 | 14 | 10 |  | 12 |  |  |  | 3 | 7 | 6 | 11¹ |  | 9² |  |  |  |  |  |  |  |  |  |  |  |  |  |  |  |  | 18 |
| 1 |  | 2 |  | 8¹ | 6² | 9 | 5 | 10 | 14 |  | 12 |  |  | 4 | 7 | 3 | 11³ |  | 13 |  |  |  |  |  |  |  |  |  |  |  |  |  |  |  |  | 19 |
| 1⁸ | 14 | 2 |  | 6¹ | 7 | 13 | 5 | 10³ |  | 11 |  |  |  | 4 | 9² | 3 |  |  | 8 | 12 |  |  |  |  |  |  |  |  |  |  |  |  |  |  |  | 20 |
| 1 | 4 | 2 | 5 | 8 | 12 | 7 |  | 10² | 11 | 6¹ | 13 | 14 | 3 |  |  |  |  |  | 9³ |  |  |  |  |  |  |  |  |  |  |  |  |  |  |  |  | 21 |
| 1 | 3 | 2 | 5 | 7² | 13 | 9³ |  | 11¹ | 10 | 6 | 12 |  |  | 4 |  |  | 14 |  | 8 |  |  |  |  |  |  |  |  |  |  |  |  |  |  |  |  | 22 |
| 1 |  | 2 | 5 | 9² | 6¹ | 7 |  | 11 |  | 14 | 10 |  |  | 4 | 12 | 3 |  | 13 | 8³ |  |  |  |  |  |  |  |  |  |  |  |  |  |  |  |  | 23 |
| 1 | 7 |  | 2 | 5 | 12 |  | 13 | 10³ | 14 | 8 | 9 |  |  | 4 | 6¹ |  |  | 11² |  |  | 3 |  |  |  |  |  |  |  |  |  |  |  |  |  |  | 24 |
| 1 | 6 | 2 | 3 |  |  | 14 |  | 11² | 13 | 7 | 9³ |  |  | 5 | 8 |  |  | 10¹ |  |  | 4 | 12 |  |  |  |  |  |  |  |  |  |  |  |  |  | 25 |
| 1 | 8 | 2 | 5 | 14 |  |  | 11² | 10 | 7¹ | 9 |  |  |  | 4 | 6³ |  |  | 13 |  |  | 3 | 12 |  |  |  |  |  |  |  |  |  |  |  |  |  | 26 |
| 1 | 2¹ | 13 | 5 | 9 | 8² |  |  | 10 |  | 12 |  |  |  | 4 | 7 |  |  | 11³ |  |  | 3 | 6 | 14 |  |  |  |  |  |  |  |  |  |  |  |  | 27 |
| 1 | 8 | 2 | 5 | 7³ |  | 14 |  | 11 | 13 | 9² |  |  |  | 4 | 12 |  |  |  |  |  | 3 | 6 | 10¹ |  |  |  |  |  |  |  |  |  |  |  |  | 28 |
| 1 | 8¹ | 2 | 5 | 7 |  |  | 11³ | 14 |  | 9² |  |  |  | 4 | 13 |  |  |  |  |  | 3 | 6 | 10 | 12 |  |  |  |  |  |  |  |  |  |  |  | 29 |
| 1 | 8 | 2 | 5 | 13 |  | 9¹ |  | 11 |  | 12 |  |  |  | 4 | 6 |  |  |  |  |  | 3 |  | 10² | 7 |  |  |  |  |  |  |  |  |  |  |  | 30 |
| 1 | 7 | 2 | 5 | 14 | 6¹ |  | 11² |  | 12 |  |  |  |  | 3 | 9 |  |  | 13 |  |  | 4 |  | 10 | 8³ |  |  |  |  |  |  |  |  |  |  |  | 31 |
| 1 | 7¹ | 2³ | 5 | 9 |  | 12 |  |  |  | 10 | 14 | 4 | 6 |  | 3 | 13 |  |  |  | 3 | 6 | 10² | 8 |  |  |  |  |  |  |  |  |  |  |  |  | 32 |
| 1 |  | 2¹ | 5 | 7 |  |  | 12 |  |  | 11 |  |  |  | 4 | 9 | 13 |  |  |  | 3 | 6 | 10² | 8 |  |  |  |  |  |  |  |  |  |  |  |  | 33 |
| 1 |  | 5 | 7 |  |  |  | 11 | 14 |  | 9¹ | 12 |  |  | 4 | 2 |  | 10² |  |  | 3 | 6³ |  | 8 | 13 |  |  |  |  |  |  |  |  |  |  |  | 34 |
| 1 |  | 2 | 5 | 7¹ |  |  | 11² | 10 |  | 12 |  |  |  | 8 | 6 |  |  |  |  | 4 | 3 |  | 9 | 13 |  |  |  |  |  |  |  |  |  |  |  | 35 |
| 1 |  | 2 | 5 |  |  | 12 | 10 |  |  | 6³ | 4 | 9² |  | 3 | 7 |  |  |  |  | 8 | 11¹ | 13 | 14 |  |  |  |  |  |  |  |  |  |  |  |  | 36 |
| 1 | 13 | 2 | 5 | 12 |  |  | 11 | 14 |  | 7² | 3 |  |  | 4 | 6 |  |  |  |  | 8 | 10³ |  | 9¹ |  |  |  |  |  |  |  |  |  |  |  |  | 37 |
| 1 | 6 | 2 | 5 |  |  | 12 | 14 | 11 |  | 7 | 3 | 9² |  | 4 |  |  |  |  |  | 13 | 10³ | 8¹ |  |  |  |  |  |  |  |  |  |  |  |  |  | 38 |
| 1 | 6⁴ | 2 | 5 | 12 |  | 13 | 14 | 11³ |  | 7² | 3 | 9¹ |  | 4 |  |  |  |  |  | 8 | 10 |  |  |  |  |  |  |  |  |  |  |  |  |  |  | 39 |
| 1 |  | 2 | 5 | 14 |  | 9¹ | 11² | 10 | 13 |  |  |  |  | 4 | 7 |  |  |  |  | 3 | 6³ |  | 8 | 12 |  |  |  |  |  |  |  |  |  |  |  | 40 |
| 1 |  | 2 | 5 |  |  | 9 | 13 | 10 |  | 12 |  |  |  | 4 | 6² | 7 |  | 11¹ |  | 3 | 8 |  |  |  |  |  |  |  |  |  |  |  |  |  |  | 41 |
| 1 |  | 2 | 5 |  |  | 9 | 11 | 10 |  | 12 |  |  |  | 4 | 7 |  |  |  |  | 3 | 6 | 8¹ |  |  |  |  |  |  |  |  |  |  |  |  |  | 42 |
| 1 | 12 | 2 | 5 | 14 | 7³ |  | 13 | 11 |  | 6¹ |  | 4 | 9 |  |  |  | 10² |  |  | 3 | 8 |  |  |  |  |  |  |  |  |  |  |  |  |  |  | 43 |
| 1 | 6 | 2 | 5¹ | 9² |  | 8³ | 11 | 10 |  | 13 |  | 4 | 7 |  |  |  | 14 |  |  | 3 | 12 |  |  |  |  |  |  |  |  |  |  |  |  |  |  | 44 |
| 1 | 5 | 2 |  | 9 |  | 8 | 11² | 10 |  | 12 |  | 4 | 7¹ |  |  |  | 13 |  |  | 3 | 6 |  |  |  |  |  |  |  |  |  |  |  |  |  |  | 45 |
| 1 |  | 3 |  | 7 |  |  |  | 11 | 6¹ |  |  | 4 | 10 |  |  |  |  |  | 1 |  | 8 |  |  |  |  |  |  |  |  |  | 2 | 5 | 9³ | 12² | 13 | 14 | 46 |

# HARTLEPOOL UNITED

## FOUNDATION

The inspiration for the launching of Hartlepool United was the West Hartlepool club which won the FA Amateur Cup in 1904–05. They had been in existence since 1881 and their cup success led in 1908 to the formation of the new professional concern which first joined the North-Eastern League. In those days they were Hartlepools United and won the Durham Senior Cup in their first two seasons.

*Victoria Park, Clarence Road, Hartlepool TS24 8BZ.*

*Telephone:* (01429) 272 584.

*Fax:* (01429) 863 007.

*Ticket Office:* (01429) 272 584 (option 2).

*Website:* www.hartlepoolunited.co.uk

*Email:* enquires@hartlepoolunited.co.uk

*Ground Capacity:* 7,856.

*Record Attendance:* 17,426 v Manchester U, FA Cup 3rd rd, 5 January 1957.

*Pitch Measurements:* 103m × 70m (113yd × 77yd)

*Chairman:* Ken Hodcroft.

*Chief Executive:* Russ Green.

*Manager:* Colin Cooper.

*Assistant Manager:* Craig Hignett.

*Physio:* Ian Gallagher.

*Colours:* Blue and white striped shirts with blue sleeves, blue shorts, white socks with blue trim.

*Year Formed:* 1908.

*Turned Professional:* 1908.

*Previous Names:* 1908, Hartlepools United; 1968, Hartlepool; 1977, Hartlepool United.

*Club Nickname:* 'The Pool', 'Monkey Hangers'.

*Ground:* 1908, Victoria Park.

*First Football League Game:* 27 August 1921, Division 3 (N), v Wrexham (a) W 2–0 – Gill; Thomas, Crilly; Dougherty, Hopkins, Short; Kessler, Mulholland (1), Lister (1), Robertson, Donald.

*Record League Victory:* 10–1 v Barrow, Division 4, 4 April 1959 – Oakley; Cameron, Waugh; Johnson, Moore, Anderson; Scott (1), Langland (1), Smith (3), Clark (2), Luke (2), (1 og).

*Record Cup Victory:* 6–0 v North Shields, FA Cup 1st rd, 30 November 1946 – Heywood; Brown, Gregory; Spelman, Lambert, Jones; Price, Scott (2), Sloan (4), Moses, McMahon; 6–0 v Gainsborough Trinity (a), FA Cup 1st rd, 10 November 2007 – Budtz; McCunnie, Humphreys, Liddle (1) (Antwi), Nelson, Clark, Moore (1), Sweeney, Barker (2) (Monkhouse), Mackay (Porter 1), Brown (1).

*Record Defeat:* 1–10 v Wrexham, Division 4, 3 March 1962.

## HONOURS

**Football League –**
**FL 2:** *Runners-up* 2006–07;
**Division 3:** *Runners-up* 2002–03;
**Division 3 (N):** *Runners-up* 1956–57.

**FA Cup:** Best season: 4th rd, 1955, 1978, 1989, 1993, 2005, 2009.

**Football League Cup:** Best season: 4th rd, 1975.

## sky SPORTS FACT FILE

Hartlepool United's Victoria Park ground suffered bomb damage during the First World War. A raid by Zeppelins on the evening of 27 February 1916 saw severe damage to the Clarence Road grandstand, but the club's attempts to obtain compensation from the German government were unsuccessful.

*Most League Points (2 for a win):* 60, Division 4, 1967–68.

*Most League Points (3 for a win):* 88, FL 2, 2006–07.

*Most League Goals:* 90, Division 3 (N), 1956–57.

*Highest League Scorer in Season:* William Robinson, 28, Division 3 (N), 1927–28; Joe Allon, 28, Division 4, 1990–91.

*Most League Goals in Total Aggregate:* Ken Johnson, 98, 1949–64.

*Most League Goals in One Match:* 5, Harry Simmons v Wigan Borough, Division 3 (N), 1 January 1931; 5, Bobby Folland v Oldham Ath, Division 3 (N), 15 April 1961.

*Most Capped Player:* Ambrose Fogarty, 1 (11), Republic of Ireland.

*Most League Appearances:* Richie Humphreys, 481, 2001–13.

*Youngest League Player:* David Foley, 16 years 105 days v Port Vale, 25 August 2003.

*Record Transfer Fee Received:* £750,000 from Ipswich T for Tommy Miller, July 2001.

*Record Transfer Fee Paid:* £75,000 to Northampton for Chris Freestone, March 1993; £75,000 to Notts Co for Gary Jones, March 1999; £75,000 to Mansfield T for Darrell Clarke, July 2001.

*Football League Record:* 1921 Original Member of Division 3 (N); 1958–68 Division 4; 1968–69 Division 3; 1969–91 Division 4; 1991–92 Division 3; 1992–94 Division 2; 1994–2003 Division 3; 2003–04 Division 2; 2004–06 FL 1; 2006–07 FL 2; 2007–13 FL 1; 2013– FL 2.

## LATEST SEQUENCES

*Longest Sequence of League Wins:* 9, 18.11.2006 – 1.1.2007.

*Longest Sequence of League Defeats:* 8, 27.1.1993 – 27.2.1993.

*Longest Sequence of League Draws:* 6, 30.4.2011 – 20.8.2011.

*Longest Sequence of Unbeaten League Matches:* 23, 18.11.2006 – 30.3.2007.

*Longest Sequence Without a League Win:* 20, 8.9.2012 – 26.12.2012.

*Successive Scoring Runs:* 27 from 18.11.2006.

*Successive Non-scoring Runs:* 11 from 9.1.1993.

## MANAGERS

**Alfred Priest** 1908–12
**Percy Humphreys** 1912–13
**Jack Manners** 1913–20
**Cecil Potter** 1920–22
**David Gordon** 1922–24
**Jack Manners** 1924–27
**Bill Norman** 1927–31
**Jack Carr** 1932–35
  *(had been Player-Coach from 1931)*
**Jimmy Hamilton** 1935–43
**Fred Westgarth** 1943–57
**Ray Middleton** 1957–59
**Bill Robinson** 1959–62
**Allenby Chilton** 1962–63
**Bob Gurney** 1963–64
**Alvan Williams** 1964–65
**Geoff Twentyman** 1965
**Brian Clough** 1965–67
**Angus McLean** 1967–70
**John Simpson** 1970–71
**Len Ashurst** 1971–74
**Ken Hale** 1974–76
**Billy Horner** 1976–83
**Johnny Duncan** 1983
**Mike Docherty** 1983
**Billy Horner** 1984–86
**John Bird** 1986–88
**Bobby Moncur** 1988–89
**Cyril Knowles** 1989–91
**Alan Murray** 1991–93
**Viv Busby** 1993
**John MacPhail** 1993–94
**David McCreery** 1994–95
**Keith Houchen** 1995–96
**Mick Tait** 1996–99
**Chris Turner** 1999–2002
**Mike Newell** 2002–03
**Neale Cooper** 2003–05
**Martin Scott** 2005–06
**Danny Wilson** 2006–08
**Chris Turner** 2008–10
**Mick Wadsworth** 2010–11
**Neale Cooper** 2011–12
**John Hughes** 2012–13
**Colin Cooper** May 2013–

## TEN YEAR LEAGUE RECORD

|         |       | P  | W  | D  | L  | F  | A  | Pts | Pos |
|---------|-------|----|----|----|----|----|----|-----|-----|
| 2003-04 | Div 2 | 46 | 20 | 13 | 13 | 76 | 61 | 73  | 6   |
| 2004-05 | FL 1  | 46 | 21 | 8  | 17 | 76 | 66 | 71  | 6   |
| 2005-06 | FL 1  | 46 | 11 | 17 | 18 | 44 | 59 | 50  | 21  |
| 2006-07 | FL 2  | 46 | 26 | 10 | 10 | 65 | 40 | 88  | 2   |
| 2007-08 | FL 1  | 46 | 15 | 9  | 22 | 63 | 66 | 54  | 15  |
| 2008-09 | FL 1  | 46 | 13 | 11 | 22 | 66 | 79 | 50  | 19  |
| 2009-10 | FL 1  | 46 | 14 | 11 | 21 | 59 | 67 | 50* | 20  |
| 2010-11 | FL 1  | 46 | 15 | 12 | 19 | 47 | 65 | 57  | 16  |
| 2011-12 | FL 1  | 46 | 14 | 14 | 18 | 50 | 55 | 56  | 13  |
| 2012-13 | FL 1  | 46 | 9  | 14 | 23 | 39 | 67 | 41  | 23  |

*3 pts deducted.

## DID YOU KNOW ?

H'Angus the Monkey can claim to be the only football club mascot to become mayor of the local town. Stuart Drummond, who performed the role of mascot, was elected Mayor of Hartlepool in 2002 and was twice re-elected to the post before standing down in 2013.

## HARTLEPOOL UNITED – FOOTBALL LEAGUE ONE 2012–13 LEAGUE RECORD

| Match No. | Date | Venue | Opponents | Result | | H/T Score | Lg Pos. | Goalscorers | Attendance |
|---|---|---|---|---|---|---|---|---|---|
| 1 | Aug 18 | H | Swindon T | D | 0-0 | 0-0 | 16 | | 4132 |
| 2 | 21 | A | Notts Co | L | 0-2 | 0-1 | 20 | | 4913 |
| 3 | Sept 1 | H | Scunthorpe U | W | 2-0 | 1-0 | 14 | Franks [23], James [86] | 3863 |
| 4 | 8 | H | Carlisle U | L | 1-2 | 1-0 | 17 | Poole [40] | 4474 |
| 5 | 15 | A | Bournemouth | D | 1-1 | 0-0 | 18 | Walton (pen) [73] | 5308 |
| 6 | 18 | A | Preston NE | L | 0-5 | 0-2 | 20 | | 8132 |
| 7 | 22 | H | Shrewsbury T | D | 2-2 | 1-1 | 20 | Franks [15], Monkhouse [90] | 3909 |
| 8 | 29 | A | Colchester U | L | 1-3 | 1-2 | 23 | Lynch [6] | 3471 |
| 9 | Oct 2 | H | Sheffield U | L | 1-2 | 0-1 | 23 | Howard [78] | 4027 |
| 10 | 6 | A | Crewe Alex | L | 1-2 | 1-1 | 23 | Horwood [9] | 4375 |
| 11 | 13 | H | Doncaster R | D | 1-1 | 0-0 | 23 | Austin (pen) [70] | 4406 |
| 12 | 16 | A | Leyton Orient | L | 0-1 | 0-0 | 23 | | 2664 |
| 13 | 20 | H | Crawley T | L | 0-1 | 0-1 | 23 | | 3852 |
| 14 | 23 | A | Bury | L | 1-2 | 0-1 | 24 | Noble [56] | 1877 |
| 15 | 27 | A | Brentford | D | 2-2 | 1-1 | 24 | Dean (og) [25], Craig (og) [90] | 5213 |
| 16 | Nov 7 | H | Tranmere R | L | 0-2 | 0-0 | 24 | | 3285 |
| 17 | 10 | A | Yeovil T | L | 0-1 | 0-1 | 24 | | 3095 |
| 18 | 17 | H | Coventry C | L | 0-5 | 0-0 | 24 | | 4404 |
| 19 | 20 | H | Oldham Ath | L | 1-2 | 0-1 | 24 | Sweeney [65] | 3078 |
| 20 | 24 | A | Walsall | D | 1-1 | 1-0 | 24 | Horwood (pen) [29] | 4562 |
| 21 | Dec 8 | H | Stevenage | L | 0-2 | 0-1 | 24 | | 3265 |
| 22 | 15 | A | Milton Keynes D | L | 0-1 | 0-1 | 24 | | 7164 |
| 23 | 26 | A | Carlisle U | L | 0-3 | 0-2 | 24 | | 5380 |
| 24 | 29 | A | Sheffield U | W | 3-2 | 1-1 | 24 | Howard 2 [7, 72], Humphreys [54] | 19,941 |
| 25 | Jan 1 | H | Preston NE | L | 0-1 | 0-1 | 24 | | 3829 |
| 26 | 12 | A | Shrewsbury T | D | 1-1 | 0-1 | 24 | Wyke [55] | 5101 |
| 27 | 22 | H | Bournemouth | L | 1-2 | 0-1 | 24 | Baldwin [51] | 2502 |
| 28 | 26 | A | Portsmouth | W | 3-1 | 1-0 | 24 | Baldwin [18], Poole [52], Rutherford [90] | 10,981 |
| 29 | Feb 2 | H | Notts Co | W | 2-1 | 1-0 | 24 | Poole [5], Hartley [70] | 3662 |
| 30 | 9 | A | Swindon T | D | 1-1 | 0-1 | 24 | Monkhouse [74] | 9973 |
| 31 | 12 | H | Portsmouth | D | 0-0 | 0-0 | 24 | | 3526 |
| 32 | 16 | H | Leyton Orient | W | 2-1 | 0-1 | 23 | Hartley [88], James [90] | 3773 |
| 33 | 23 | A | Scunthorpe U | W | 2-1 | 2-0 | 23 | Poole [20], Franks [37] | 3434 |
| 34 | 26 | H | Crewe Alex | W | 3-0 | 2-0 | 23 | Wyke [27], Franks [40], Monkhouse [90] | 3509 |
| 35 | Mar 2 | A | Doncaster R | L | 0-3 | 0-1 | 23 | | 7457 |
| 36 | 5 | H | Colchester U | D | 0-0 | 0-0 | 22 | | 3148 |
| 37 | 9 | H | Yeovil T | D | 0-0 | 0-0 | 22 | | 3633 |
| 38 | 16 | A | Coventry C | L | 0-1 | 0-1 | 22 | | 10,412 |
| 39 | 19 | A | Oldham Ath | L | 0-3 | 0-2 | 23 | | 3269 |
| 40 | 23 | H | Walsall | D | 0-0 | 0-0 | 24 | | 3065 |
| 41 | 29 | H | Milton Keynes D | L | 0-2 | 0-1 | 24 | | 3269 |
| 42 | Apr 1 | A | Stevenage | L | 0-1 | 0-0 | 24 | | 2903 |
| 43 | 6 | H | Bury | W | 2-0 | 1-0 | 23 | Monkhouse 2 [42, 71] | 2939 |
| 44 | 13 | A | Tranmere R | W | 1-0 | 1-0 | 23 | Austin [10] | 4721 |
| 45 | 20 | H | Brentford | D | 1-1 | 1-1 | 22 | James [25] | 3541 |
| 46 | 27 | A | Crawley T | D | 2-2 | 0-0 | 23 | Monkhouse 2 [75, 80] | 4100 |

**Final League Position: 23**

## GOALSCORERS

*League (39):* Monkhouse 7, Franks 4, Poole 4, Howard 3, James 3, Austin 2 (1 pen), Baldwin 2, Hartley 2, Horwood 2 (1 pen), Wyke 2, Humphreys 1, Lynch 1, Noble 1, Rutherford 1, Sweeney 1, Walton 1 (1 pen), own goals 2.
*FA Cup (1):* Sweeney 1.
*Capital One Cup (0).*
*Johnstone's Paint Trophy (0).*

| Flinders S 46 | Horwood E 33+4 | Collins S 41 | Hartley P 43 | Austin N 36+3 | Monkhouse A 20+15 | Sweeney A 31+3 | Walton S 32+2 | Franks J 44+1 | Howard S 28+6 | Poole J 22+14 | James L 4+22 | Luscombe N 2+11 | Baldwin J 28+4 | Murray P 16+1 | Holden D 12+5 | Lynch C 2+4 | Noble R 7+3 | Wyke C 21+4 | Humphreys R 29+2 | Richards J 9+2 | Rutherford G —+7 | Boagey Z —+1 | Hawkins L —+1 | Match No. |
|---|---|---|---|---|---|---|---|---|---|---|---|---|---|---|---|---|---|---|---|---|---|---|---|---|
| 1 | 2 | 3 | $4^3$ | 5 | 6 | 7 | 8 | $9^2$ | 10 | $11^1$ | 12 | 13 | 14 | | | | | | | | | | | 1 |
| 1 | 5 | 3 | 4 | | 9 | 8 | $7^2$ | $6^3$ | 11 | $10^1$ | 14 | 13 | 2 | 12 | | | | | | | | | | 2 |
| 1 | 5 | 3 | 4 | 2 | 9 | 8 | | $6^2$ | 11 | $10^1$ | 12 | | | 7 | 13 | | | | | | | | | 3 |
| 1 | 5 | 3 | $4^2$ | $2^4$ | 9 | 8 | | $6^1$ | 10 | $11^3$ | 14 | | 13 | 7 | 12 | | | | | | | | | 4 |
| 1 | 3 | 4 | 5 | | | 7 | $10^2$ | 9 | $8^1$ | 11 | 12 | | 2 | 6 | 13 | | | | | | | | | 5 |
| 1 | 5 | 3 | 4 | 2 | 9 | 10 | 7 | 6 | 11 | | | | | $8^1$ | 12 | | | | | | | | | 6 |
| 1 | 5 | 3 | 4 | | 13 | 7 | | $6^3$ | 11 | $10^1$ | 12 | | 2 | 8 | 14 | $9^2$ | | | | | | | | 7 |
| 1 | 5 | 3 | 4 | | 7 | 12 | 9 | 6 | 11 | 13 | | | 2 | $8^2$ | $10^1$ | | | | | | | | | 8 |
| 1 | | | 4 | 2 | 9 | 7 | | 6 | 11 | $10^1$ | 12 | | 3 | 8 | 5 | | | | | | | | | 9 |
| 1 | 12 | 3 | 4 | 2 | $9^1$ | 7 | | $6^3$ | 11 | 13 | | | 3 | 8 | 5 | 14 | $10^2$ | | | | | | | 10 |
| 1 | $9^1$ | | 4 | 2 | | 7 | | 6 | 11 | 12 | | | 3 | 8 | 5 | | $10^2$ | $13^3$ | 14 | | | | | 11 |
| 1 | | | 4 | 2 | | 7 | | $6^2$ | 11 | 12 | 14 | 3 | $8^3$ | 5 | | $10^1$ | | 9 | 13 | | | | | 12 |
| 1 | 3 | | 2 | | 7 | 8 | $6^2$ | 11 | 9 | | 12 | 4 | | 5 | | $10^1$ | | 13 | | | | | | 13 |
| 1 | 12 | 3 | 4 | 2 | | 6 | $8^3$ | 14 | 11 | | 13 | 7 | | $5^1$ | 10 | | $9^2$ | | | | | | | 14 |
| 1 | 4 | 3 | 2 | | 6 | 8 | | 11 | 12 | 13 | 7 | $9^2$ | 10 | $5^1$ | | | | | | | | | | 15 |
| 1 | 3 | 4 | 5 | | 6 | 8 | 9 | 10 | $11^1$ | 13 | | $7^2$ | 12 | | | | 2 | | | | | | | 16 |
| 1 | 4 | 3 | 5 | | 7 | 6 | $9^1$ | 11 | 10 | | 13 | $8^2$ | | 12 | | | 2 | | | | | | | 17 |
| 1 | 3 | 4 | 2 | 13 | 6 | 12 | 11 | | $9^1$ | | | $7^1$ | 5 | 10 | 14 | $8^2$ | | | | | | | | 18 |
| 1 | 5 | 3 | 4 | $2^4$ | 12 | 8 | $6^1$ | $9^2$ | 10 | | 13 | $7^3$ | 14 | 11 | | | | | | | | | | 19 |
| 1 | 5 | 3 | 4 | 10 | 9 | | $8^2$ | 11 | 13 | | | $7^1$ | 12 | 6 | 2 | | | | | | | | | 20 |
| 1 | 5 | 3 | | $9^1$ | 7 | 12 | $6^2$ | 10 | 14 | 13 | 4 | | | | | | $11^3$ | 8 | 2 | | | | | 21 |
| 1 | $3^1$ | 4 | | 9 | 7 | $6^2$ | 10 | 13 | | 5 | 12 | | | $11^3$ | 8 | 2 | 14 | | | | | | | 22 |
| 1 | 5 | 4 | 3 | $9^1$ | 7 | | 6 | $11^2$ | 12 | 13 | | | | | | $10^1$ | 8 | 2 | | | | | | 23 |
| 1 | 5 | 4 | 3 | 13 | 14 | 8 | $7^2$ | $6^3$ | 10 | 12 | | | | | | $11^1$ | 9 | 2 | | | | | | 24 |
| 1 | 5 | 3 | 4 | 12 | | 6 | $7^1$ | $10^3$ | 11 | 13 | | 14 | | | | $9^2$ | 8 | 2 | | | | | | 25 |
| 1 | 5 | 3 | 4 | 12 | | 8 | $7^2$ | 6 | 11 | 13 | | | | | | $10^1$ | 9 | 2 | | | | | | 26 |
| 1 | 5 | 3 | 4 | 2 | 14 | $6^1$ | $7^2$ | 9 | $10^3$ | 13 | | 12 | | | | 11 | 8 | | | | | | | 27 |
| 1 | 5 | 3 | 4 | 2 | | 6 | 7 | | 11 | 12 | | $8^1$ | | | | $10^2$ | 9 | | 13 | | | | | 28 |
| 1 | 5 | 3 | 4 | 2 | 14 | | 7 | $10^1$ | | $9^2$ | 13 | 6 | | 12 | | $11^3$ | 8 | | | | | | | 29 |
| 1 | 5 | 3 | 4 | 2 | 12 | | 7 | $9^2$ | | 11 | 13 | 14 | 8 | | | $10^3$ | 6 | | | | | | | 30 |
| 1 | 5 | 3 | 4 | 2 | 12 | | 6 | $9^2$ | | 10 | 13 | | 7 | | | 11 | $8^1$ | | | | | | | 31 |
| 1 | 2 | 4 | 3 | 5 | 13 | | $8^2$ | $9^1$ | 12 | $11^1$ | 14 | | 7 | | | 10 | 6 | | | | | | | 32 |
| 1 | 5 | 3 | 4 | 2 | 13 | | 7 | $11^3$ | 12 | $9^1$ | 14 | | 8 | | | $10^1$ | 6 | | | | | | | 33 |
| 1 | 2 | 3 | 4 | 5 | 12 | | $8^1$ | $9^3$ | | $11^2$ | 14 | 13 | 7 | | | 10 | 6 | | | | | | | 34 |
| 1 | 5 | 3 | 4 | 2 | | 6 | | | $11^1$ | 13 | $10^2$ | 12 | | 7 | | 9 | 8 | | | | | | | 35 |
| 1 | 5 | 3 | 4 | 2 | | | 14 | $7^3$ | $10^2$ | 13 | 9 | | | 12 | $6^1$ | 11 | 8 | | | | | | | 36 |
| 1 | 2 | 3 | 4 | 5 | | 13 | 14 | 8 | $9^3$ | 12 | $10^1$ | | | $6^2$ | | 11 | 7 | | | | | | | 37 |
| 1 | 5 | 3 | 4 | 2 | 14 | | $6^1$ | 7 | $11^3$ | 12 | 9 | 13 | | | | $10^2$ | 8 | | | | | | | 38 |
| 1 | 5 | 3 | 4 | 2 | 12 | | 8 | 7 | 6 | 11 | $10^1$ | 13 | $9^2$ | | | | | | | | | | | 39 |
| 1 | 5 | 3 | 4 | 2 | 11 | | 6 | 7 | $9^1$ | $10^2$ | | 12 | | | | 13 | 8 | | | | | | | 40 |
| 1 | $5^2$ | 3 | 4 | 2 | 11 | | $6^1$ | $7^4$ | 9 | | 12 | | 8 | | 13 | 10 | | | | | | | | 41 |
| 1 | | 3 | 4 | 2 | 11 | | 7 | $9^2$ | | 12 | | $6^1$ | | 5 | | 10 | 8 | | 13 | | | | | 42 |
| 1 | | 3 | 4 | 2 | 9 | | $8^2$ | 6 | | $10^3$ | | 7 | | 5 | | $11^1$ | 12 | | 13 | 14 | | | | 43 |
| 1 | | 3 | 4 | 2 | 9 | 12 | 7 | $6^1$ | | $11^2$ | | 8 | | 5 | | 10 | | | 13 | | | | | 44 |
| 1 | 13 | 3 | 4 | 2 | 9 | | 7 | $6^2$ | | 11 | | 8 | | 5 | | $10^1$ | 12 | | | | | | | 45 |
| 1 | 12 | 3 | 4 | 5 | 11 | | 6 | 10 | | $9^2$ | | $8^1$ | 2 | | | $7^3$ | 13 | 14 | | | | | | 46 |

**FA Cup**
First Round    Chesterfield    (a)    1-6

**Capital One Cup**
First Round    Crewe Alex    (a)    0-5

**Johnstone's Paint Trophy**
Second Round    Bradford C    (h)    0-0
(*aet; lost 2-3 on pens*)

# HUDDERSFIELD TOWN

## FOUNDATION

A meeting, attended largely by members of the Huddersfield & District FA, was held at the Imperial Hotel in 1906 to discuss the feasibility of establishing a football club in this rugby stronghold. However, it was not until a man with both the enthusiasm and the money to back the scheme came on the scene that real progress was made. This benefactor was Mr Hilton Crowther and it was at a meeting at the Albert Hotel in 1908 that the club formally came into existence with an investment of £2,000 and joined the North-Eastern League.

*John Smith's Stadium, Stadium Way, Leeds Road, Huddersfield, West Yorkshire HD1 6PX.*

*Telephone:* (0870) 4444 677.

*Fax:* (01484) 484 101.

*Ticket Office:* (01484) 484 123.

*Website:* www.htafc.com

*Email:* info@htafc.com

*Ground Capacity:* 24,554.

*Record Attendance:* 67,037 v Arsenal, FA Cup 6th rd, 27 February 1932 (at Leeds Road); 23,678 v Liverpool, FA Cup 3rd rd, 12 December 1999 (at Alfred McAlpine Stadium).

*Pitch Measurements:* 105m × 69m (115yd × 76yd)

*Chairman:* Dean Hoyle.

*Chief Executive:* Nigel Clibbens.

*Manager:* Mark Robins.

*First Team Coach:* Steve Taylor.

*Physio:* James Haycock.

*Colours:* Blue and white striped shirts, white shorts, black socks.

*Year Formed:* 1908.

*Turned Professional:* 1908.

*Club Nickname:* 'The Terriers'.

*Grounds:* 1908, Leeds Road; 1994, The Alfred McAlpine Stadium (renamed the Galpharm Stadium 2004, John Smith's Stadium in 2012).

*First Football League Game:* 3 September 1910, Division 2, v Bradford PA (a) W 1–0 – Mutch; Taylor, Morris; Beaton, Hall, Bartlett; Blackburn, Wood, Hamilton (1), McCubbin, Jee.

*Record League Victory:* 10–1 v Blackpool, Division 1, 13 December 1930 – Turner; Goodall, Spencer; Redfern, Wilson, Campbell; Bob Kelly (1), McLean (4), Robson (3), Davies (1), Smailes (1).

*Record Cup Victory:* 7–0 v Lincoln U, FA Cup 1st rd, 16 November 1991 – Clarke; Trevitt, Charlton, Donovan (2), Mitchell, Doherty, O'Regan (1), Stapleton (1) (Wright), Roberts (2), Onuora (1), Barnett (Ireland). *N.B.* 11–0 v Heckmondwike (a), FA Cup pr rd, 18 September 1909 – Doggart; Roberts, Ewing; Hooton, Stevenson, Randall; Kenworthy (2), McCreadie (1), Foster (4), Stacey (4), Jee.

### HONOURS

**Football League – Division 1:** *Champions* 1923–24, 1924–25, 1925–26; *Runners-up* 1926–27, 1927–28, 1933–34;
**Division 2:** *Champions* 1969–70; *Runners-up* 1919–20, 1952–53;
**Division 4:** *Champions* 1979–80.
**FA Cup:** *Winners* 1922; *Runners-up* 1920, 1928, 1930, 1938.
**Football League Cup:** Semi-final 1968.
**Autoglass Trophy:** *Runners-up* 1994.

## sky SPORTS FACT FILE

Club songs are not just a feature of modern football. When Huddersfield Town won the FA Cup in 1922 they had their own Cup song. 'Oh! It's Our Night Out Again Tonight' was available in sheet music and was also played by the band to entertain fans before the match.

*Record Defeat:* 1–10 v Manchester C, Division 2, 7 November 1987.

*Most League Points (2 for a win):* 66, Division 4, 1979–80.

*Most League Points (3 for a win):* 87, FL 1, 2010–11.

*Most League Goals:* 101, Division 4, 1979–80.

*Highest League Scorer in Season:* Sam Taylor, 35, Division 2, 1919–20; George Brown, 35, Division 1, 1925–26; Jordan Rhodes, 35, 2011–12.

*Most League Goals in Total Aggregate:* George Brown, 142, 1921–29; Jimmy Glazzard, 142, 1946–56.

*Most League Goals in One Match:* 5, Dave Mangnall v Derby Co, Division 1, 21 November 1931; 5, Alf Lythgoe v Blackburn R, Division 1, 13 April 1935.

*Most Capped Player:* Jimmy Nicholson, 31 (41), Northern Ireland.

*Most League Appearances:* Billy Smith, 520, 1914–34.

*Youngest League Player:* Denis Law, 16 years 303 days v Notts Co, 24 December 1956.

*Record Transfer Fee Received:* £8,000,000 from Blackburn R for Jordan Rhodes, August 2012.

*Record Transfer Fee Paid:* £1,200,000 to Bristol R for Marcus Stewart, July 1996.

*Football League Record:* 1910 Elected to Division 2; 1920–52 Division 1; 1952–53 Division 2; 1953–56 Division 1; 1956–70 Division 2; 1970–72 Division 1; 1972–73 Division 2; 1973–75 Division 3; 1975–80 Division 4; 1980–83 Division 3; 1983–88 Division 2; 1988–92 Division 3; 1992–95 Division 2; 1995–2001 Division 1; 2001–03 Division 2; 2003–04 Division 3; 2004–12 FL 1; 2012– FL C.

## LATEST SEQUENCES

*Longest Sequence of League Wins:* 11, 5.4.1920 – 4.9.1920.

*Longest Sequence of League Defeats:* 7, 8.10.1955 – 19.11.1955.

*Longest Sequence of League Draws:* 6, 3.3.1987 – 3.4.1987.

*Longest Sequence of Unbeaten League Matches:* 43, 1.1.2011 – 19.11.2011.

*Longest Sequence Without a League Win:* 22, 4.12.1971 – 29.4.1972.

*Successive Scoring Runs:* 27 from 12.3.2005.

*Successive Non-scoring Runs:* 7 from 22.1.1972.

## MANAGERS

Fred Walker 1908–10
Richard Pudan 1910–12
Arthur Fairclough 1912–19
Ambrose Langley 1919–21
Herbert Chapman 1921–25
Cecil Potter 1925–26
Jack Chaplin 1926–29
Clem Stephenson 1929–42
Ted Magner 1942–43
David Steele 1943–47
George Stephenson 1947–52
Andy Beattie 1952–56
Bill Shankly 1956–59
Eddie Boot 1960–64
Tom Johnston 1964–68
Ian Greaves 1968–74
Bobby Collins 1974
Tom Johnston 1975–78
*(had been General Manager since 1975)*
Mike Buxton 1978–86
Steve Smith 1986–87
Malcolm Macdonald 1987–88
Eoin Hand 1988–92
Ian Ross 1992–93
Neil Warnock 1993–95
Brian Horton 1995–97
Peter Jackson 1997–99
Steve Bruce 1999–2000
Lou Macari 2000–02
Mick Wadsworth 2002–03
Peter Jackson 2003–07
Andy Ritchie 2007–08
Stan Ternent 2008
Lee Clark 2008–12
Simon Grayson 2012–13
Mark Robins February 2013–

## TEN YEAR LEAGUE RECORD

|  |  | P | W | D | L | F | A | Pts | Pos |
|---|---|---|---|---|---|---|---|---|---|
| 2003-04 | Div 3 | 46 | 23 | 12 | 11 | 68 | 52 | 81 | 4 |
| 2004-05 | FL 1 | 46 | 20 | 10 | 16 | 74 | 65 | 70 | 9 |
| 2005-06 | FL 1 | 46 | 19 | 16 | 11 | 72 | 59 | 73 | 4 |
| 2006-07 | FL 1 | 46 | 14 | 17 | 15 | 60 | 69 | 59 | 15 |
| 2007-08 | FL 1 | 46 | 20 | 6 | 20 | 50 | 62 | 66 | 10 |
| 2008-09 | FL 1 | 46 | 18 | 14 | 14 | 62 | 65 | 68 | 9 |
| 2009-10 | FL 1 | 46 | 23 | 11 | 12 | 82 | 56 | 80 | 6 |
| 2010-11 | FL 1 | 46 | 25 | 12 | 9 | 77 | 48 | 87 | 3 |
| 2011-12 | FL 1 | 46 | 21 | 18 | 7 | 79 | 47 | 81 | 4 |
| 2012-13 | FL C | 46 | 15 | 13 | 18 | 53 | 73 | 58 | 19 |

## DID YOU KNOW

Huddersfield Town have only once scored more than 100 goals in a season. That was in the 1979–80 season when they won the Division Four title, scoring 101. The Terriers conceded exactly 100 goals in 1987–88 when they finished bottom of the Second Division and were relegated.

## HUDDERSFIELD TOWN – FL CHAMPIONSHIP 2012–13 LEAGUE RECORD

| Match No. | Date | Venue | Opponents | Result | H/T Score | Lg Pos. | Goalscorers | Attendance |
|---|---|---|---|---|---|---|---|---|
| 1 | Aug 17 | A | Cardiff C | L 0-1 | 0-0 | 24 | | 21,127 |
| 2 | 21 | H | Nottingham F | D 1-1 | 0-0 | 20 | Rhodes (pen) [90] | 15,434 |
| 3 | 25 | H | Burnley | W 2-0 | 1-0 | 12 | Lynch [7], Rhodes [58] | 15,483 |
| 4 | Sept 1 | A | Ipswich T | D 2-2 | 1-0 | 15 | Clayton [36], Vaughan [80] | 16,843 |
| 5 | 15 | H | Derby Co | W 1-0 | 1-0 | 8 | Ward [1] | 15,265 |
| 6 | 19 | A | Sheffield W | W 3-1 | 2-1 | 6 | Norwood [16], Novak [18], Clayton (pen) [71] | 25,230 |
| 7 | 24 | A | Blackpool | W 3-1 | 2-1 | 2 | Novak [13], Vaughan [45], Norwood [48] | 13,886 |
| 8 | 29 | H | Watford | L 2-3 | 1-0 | 6 | Norwood [25], Lee [84] | 14,564 |
| 9 | Oct 2 | H | Leicester C | L 0-2 | 0-1 | 8 | | 13,821 |
| 10 | 6 | A | Birmingham C | W 1-0 | 1-0 | 6 | Beckford [25] | 18,437 |
| 11 | 20 | H | Wolverhampton W | W 2-1 | 2-0 | 3 | Vaughan [10], Beckford [27] | 18,012 |
| 12 | 23 | A | Peterborough U | L 1-3 | 0-2 | 6 | Hammill [51] | 6348 |
| 13 | 27 | A | Millwall | L 0-4 | 0-1 | 9 | | 11,066 |
| 14 | Nov 3 | H | Bristol C | W 1-0 | 1-0 | 7 | Scannell [43] | 12,561 |
| 15 | 6 | H | Blackburn R | D 2-2 | 1-1 | 7 | Novak 2 [15, 90] | 14,597 |
| 16 | 10 | A | Barnsley | W 1-0 | 1-0 | 6 | Beckford [36] | 12,130 |
| 17 | 17 | H | Brighton & HA | L 1-2 | 0-2 | 8 | Church [90] | 13,299 |
| 18 | 24 | A | Charlton Ath | D 1-1 | 0-0 | 10 | Clayton (pen) [88] | 20,012 |
| 19 | 27 | A | Middlesbrough | L 0-3 | 0-1 | 11 | | 21,850 |
| 20 | Dec 1 | H | Leeds U | L 2-4 | 2-2 | 14 | Atkinson [12], Clayton (pen) [43] | 20,372 |
| 21 | 8 | H | Bolton W | D 2-2 | 1-0 | 15 | Knight (og) [9], Vaughan [87] | 16,372 |
| 22 | 15 | A | Hull C | L 0-2 | 0-1 | 17 | | 16,488 |
| 23 | 22 | A | Crystal Palace | D 1-1 | 0-1 | 15 | Southern [75] | 17,993 |
| 24 | 26 | H | Blackpool | D 1-1 | 0-0 | 15 | Gerrard [66] | 16,832 |
| 25 | 29 | H | Sheffield W | D 0-0 | 0-0 | 16 | | 17,494 |
| 26 | Jan 1 | A | Leicester C | L 1-6 | 0-3 | 17 | Arfield [60] | 25,913 |
| 27 | 12 | H | Birmingham C | D 1-1 | 0-1 | 17 | Hammill [90] | 14,214 |
| 28 | 19 | A | Watford | L 0-4 | 0-1 | 18 | | 12,522 |
| 29 | 30 | H | Crystal Palace | W 1-0 | 0-0 | 16 | Vaughan [65] | 13,471 |
| 30 | Feb 2 | A | Derby Co | L 0-3 | 0-2 | 17 | | 21,561 |
| 31 | 9 | H | Cardiff C | D 0-0 | 0-0 | 18 | | 15,265 |
| 32 | 19 | A | Nottingham F | L 1-6 | 1-4 | 21 | Vaughan [10] | 26,938 |
| 33 | 23 | H | Ipswich T | D 0-0 | 0-0 | 20 | | 13,083 |
| 34 | 26 | A | Burnley | W 1-0 | 0-0 | 18 | Vaughan [55] | 11,266 |
| 35 | Mar 2 | A | Brighton & HA | L 1-4 | 1-1 | 19 | Vaughan [42] | 25,831 |
| 36 | 5 | H | Middlesbrough | W 2-1 | 0-0 | 16 | Lee [86], Ward [90] | 12,705 |
| 37 | 9 | H | Charlton Ath | L 0-1 | 0-1 | 18 | | 13,591 |
| 38 | 16 | A | Leeds U | W 2-1 | 0-0 | 16 | Danns [54], Vaughan [86] | 23,814 |
| 39 | 30 | H | Hull C | L 0-1 | 0-0 | 19 | | 14,175 |
| 40 | Apr 2 | A | Bolton W | L 0-1 | 0-0 | 22 | | 17,891 |
| 41 | 6 | H | Peterborough U | D 2-2 | 1-0 | 21 | Danns [41], Wallace [69] | 14,175 |
| 42 | 13 | A | Wolverhampton W | W 3-1 | 1-1 | 19 | Scannell [27], Beckford 2 [69, 70] | 23,185 |
| 43 | 16 | A | Blackburn R | L 0-1 | 0-1 | 22 | | 15,317 |
| 44 | 20 | H | Millwall | W 3-0 | 1-0 | 19 | Beckford 2 [37, 62], Vaughan [55] | 12,415 |
| 45 | 27 | A | Bristol C | W 3-1 | 2-0 | 18 | Vaughan 3 [2, 13, 64] | 13,376 |
| 46 | May 4 | H | Barnsley | D 2-2 | 0-1 | 19 | Beckford [53], Vaughan [81] | 21,614 |

**Final League Position: 19**

### GOALSCORERS

*League (53):* Vaughan 14, Beckford 8, Clayton 4 (3 pens), Novak 4, Norwood 3, Danns 2, Hammill 2, Lee 2, Rhodes 2 (1 pen), Scannell 2, Ward 2, Arfield 1, Atkinson 1, Church 1, Gerrard 1, Lynch 1, Southern 1, Wallace 1, own goal 1.
*FA Cup (5):* Novak 2 (1 pen), Beckford 1, Clayton 1, Scannell 1.
*Capital One Cup (0).*

| Smithies A 46 | Dixon P 29+8 | Clarke P 42+1 | Hunt J 39+1 | Lynch J 20+2 | Norwood O 37+2 | Scannell S 22+12 | Clayton A 43 | Arfield S 9+12 | Southern K 24+5 | Novak L 24+11 | Gerrard A 32+6 | Spencer J —+1 | Rhodes J 2 | Ward D 17+11 | Vaughan J 31+2 | Hammill A 6+10 | Woods C 20+7 | Lee A 1+20 | Beckford J 14+7 | Robinson A 1+1 | Church S 7 | Atkinson C 3+4 | Wallace M 3+3 | Bennett I —+1 | Danns N 17 | Gobern O 13+2 | Sinnott J —+1 | Robinson T 4+2 | Match No. |
|---|---|---|---|---|---|---|---|---|---|---|---|---|---|---|---|---|---|---|---|---|---|---|---|---|---|---|---|---|---|
| 1 | 2 | 3 | 4 | 5 | 6 | $7^2$ | 8 | $9^1$ | 10 | 11 | 12 | 13 | | | | | | | | | | | | | | | | | 1 |
| 1 | $5^1$ | 3 | 2 | 4 | 6 | 9 | 7 | 12 | $8^3$ | $11^2$ | 14 | | | 10 | 13 | | | | | | | | | | | | | | 2 |
| 1 | $5^1$ | 3 | 2 | 4 | 6 | $10^1$ | 7 | | 8 | 13 | 14 | | | 11 | 12 | $9^2$ | | | | | | | | | | | | | 3 |
| 1 | $5^1$ | 3 | 2 | $4^3$ | 7 | | 9 | | 8 | $6^2$ | 12 | | | | 10 | 11 | 13 | 14 | | | | | | | | | | | 4 |
| 1 | 5 | 3 | 2 | 4 | 8 | 14 | 9 | 13 | 10 | 12 | | | | | | $7^1$ | $11^3$ | $6^2$ | | | | | | | | | | | 5 |
| 1 | 5 | 3 | 2 | $4^4$ | $7^2$ | | 8 | 9 | $11^1$ | 12 | | | | | 10 | $6^3$ | 13 | 14 | | | | | | | | | | | 6 |
| 1 | 5 | 3 | 2 | | $7^2$ | 12 | 6 | 14 | $8^3$ | 10 | 4 | | | 9 | $11^1$ | 13 | | | | | | | | | | | | | 7 |
| 1 | 5 | 3 | 2 | | $6^2$ | 12 | $7^1$ | 14 | 8 | 10 | 4 | | | 9 | | 13 | $11^3$ | | | | | | | | | | | | 8 |
| 1 | $5^2$ | 3 | 2 | | $6^3$ | 11 | $7^1$ | 14 | 8 | 10 | 4 | | | 9 | | 13 | 12 | | | | | | | | | | | | 9 |
| 1 | 14 | 3 | 2 | 7 | | 8 | 6 | 13 | 4 | | | | | $11^2$ | $9^1$ | 12 | $5^3$ | 10 | | | | | | | | | | | 10 |
| 1 | 14 | 3 | 2 | 13 | $8^1$ | 6 | 7 | 12 | 4 | | | | | 9 | $11^2$ | | $5^3$ | 10 | | | | | | | | | | | 11 |
| 1 | 13 | 4 | 2 | 7 | 14 | 6 | 8 | 3 | | | | | | $9^1$ | $11^3$ | 12 | $5^2$ | 10 | | | | | | | | | | | 12 |
| 1 | 12 | 4 | $2^4$ | 5 | 14 | 13 | 8 | 7 | $11^3$ | $3^1$ | | | | $9^2$ | 6 | | 10 | | | | | | | | | | | | 13 |
| 1 | 5 | 3 | | 4 | $8^2$ | $9^3$ | 6 | | 7 | 11 | 14 | | | 12 | $10^1$ | 2 | 13 | | | | | | | | | | | | 14 |
| 1 | 5 | 3 | | 4 | $7^2$ | 6 | 9 | | 8 | 11 | | | | 12 | $10^1$ | 2 | 13 | | | | | | | | | | | | 15 |
| 1 | 5 | 3 | 2 | 4 | | 8 | 6 | | 7 | $9^2$ | | | | 12 | | 13 | $10^1$ | 11 | | | | | | | | | | | 16 |
| 1 | 5 | 3 | 2 | 4 | $8^3$ | | 6 | 14 | $7^2$ | $10^1$ | | | | 9 | | 13 | 12 | 11 | | | | | | | | | | | 17 |
| 1 | 5 | 3 | 2 | 4 | $7^1$ | | 8 | 12 | $9^4$ | $11^2$ | | | | $10^3$ | | 14 | 13 | 6 | | | | | | | | | | | 18 |
| 1 | 5 | 4 | 2 | 3 | $7^1$ | | 8 | | $11^3$ | | 6 | | | 13 | | 14 | $9^2$ | 10 | 12 | | | | | | | | | | 19 |
| 1 | | 3 | 2 | $5^1$ | | 8 | $6^3$ | | 4 | 9 | 13 | | | 14 | 12 | $10^2$ | 11 | 7 | | | | | | | | | | | 20 |
| 1 | 5 | 3 | 2 | | 8 | 12 | 6 | | $9^3$ | 4 | | | | 14 | 11 | 13 | $10^1$ | $7^2$ | | | | | | | | | | | 21 |
| 1 | | 3 | 2 | 5 | $7^3$ | | 6 | | 8 | $10^1$ | 4 | | | $9^2$ | 11 | 14 | 13 | 12 | | | | | | | | | | | 22 |
| 1 | | 14 | 2 | 4 | $8^1$ | $6^2$ | 9 | | 7 | | $3^4$ | | | 13 | $10^3$ | 12 | 5 | 11 | | | | | | | | | | | 23 |
| 1 | | 3 | 2 | | $8^2$ | $6^3$ | 9 | | 7 | | 4 | | | 10 | 14 | $5^1$ | 11 | | | | 12 | 13 | | | | | | | 24 |
| 1 | 14 | | $2^3$ | 4 | | 13 | 6 | | 8 | | 3 | | | 12 | 9 | | 11 | | $10^2$ | $7^1$ | 5 | | | | | | | | | 25 |
| $1^1$ | 13 | | | 6 | $3^2$ | 14 | | $9^3$ | 7 | | 8 | 10 | 4 | 11 | 5 | | | | | | | 2 | 12 | | | | | | 26 |
| 1 | $5^3$ | 4 | 2 | | $8^1$ | 9 | 6 | | | 14 | 3 | | | $10^2$ | 12 | | 13 | 11 | | | | | | | 7 | | | | 27 |
| 1 | 5 | 3 | 9 | | $6^3$ | $7^1$ | 14 | 12 | 13 | 4 | | | | $10^2$ | | | 2 | 11 | | | | | | | 8 | | | | 28 |
| 1 | | 3 | 2 | | $8^1$ | 12 | 9 | 6 | | 10 | 4 | | | $11^2$ | | 5 | 14 | $13^3$ | | | | | | | 7 | | | | 29 |
| 1 | | $3^1$ | 2 | | $7^3$ | 13 | 8 | 9 | | $10^2$ | 4 | | | 11 | | 5 | 14 | | | | | | 12 | | 6 | | | | 30 |
| 1 | | 2 | 3 | | $7^1$ | 10 | 8 | 9 | | | 4 | | | $11^2$ | | 5 | 13 | | | | | | 12 | | 6 | | | | 31 |
| 1 | | 3 | 2 | 4 | $7^2$ | $9^1$ | 8 | 12 | | $10^3$ | | | | 11 | | 5 | | | | | | | | | 6 | 13 | 14 | | 32 |
| 1 | 5 | 3 | 14 | | 13 | $7^3$ | 6 | | $10^1$ | 4 | | | | 11 | | 2 | | | | | | | | | 9 | $8^2$ | | 12 | 33 |
| 1 | 2 | 3 | | | 8 | 9 | 12 | | 13 | 4 | | | | $11^2$ | | 5 | | | | | | | | | 7 | $6^1$ | | 10 | 34 |
| 1 | 5 | 3 | 2 | 14 | | 10 | 8 | 12 | 13 | $4^3$ | | | | $9^2$ | | | | | | | | | | | 7 | $6^1$ | | 11 | 35 |
| 1 | 5 | 3 | 2 | | $8^3$ | 6 | | | 10 | $4^1$ | | | | 13 | | 14 | | | 12 | | | | | | 9 | 7 | | $11^2$ | 36 |
| 1 | 5 | 3 | 2 | | $8^2$ | | 7 | 14 | 10 | 4 | | | | 13 | | 12 | | | | | | | | | 9 | $6^3$ | | $11^1$ | 37 |
| 1 | 5 | 4 | 2 | | $7^1$ | 12 | 8 | | | 3 | | | | $10^2$ | 11 | 14 | | | 13 | | | | | | 6 | $9^3$ | | | 38 |
| 1 | 2 | 4 | 5 | | $7^1$ | 13 | $9^2$ | | | 3 | | | | 12 | 10 | | $11^3$ | | | | | | | | 6 | 8 | | 14 | 39 |
| 1 | 5 | $3^3$ | $2^1$ | | 7 | 10 | | | 14 | 4 | | | | 9 | 11 | 12 | | | 13 | | | | | | $6^2$ | 8 | | | 40 |
| 1 | 5 | 3 | | | 7 | 10 | 6 | | | | | | | $11^2$ | 2 | 13 | 12 | | | 4 | | | | | 9 | $8^1$ | | | 41 |
| 1 | 5 | 3 | | | 6 | 10 | 9 | 12 | | | 4 | | | $11^3$ | 2 | 14 | 13 | | | | | | | | $8^1$ | $7^2$ | | | 42 |
| 1 | 5 | 4 | | | $7^1$ | 11 | $8^3$ | $6^2$ | | 3 | | | | 10 | 2 | 14 | 12 | | | | | | | | 9 | 13 | | | 43 |
| 1 | 13 | 3 | 2 | | 8 | 9 | 6 | 12 | 14 | 4 | | | | $10^3$ | $5^2$ | $11^1$ | | | | | | | | | 7 | | | | 44 |
| 1 | 13 | 4 | 2 | | $7^1$ | $9^2$ | 6 | 12 | 10 | 3 | | | | $11^3$ | 5 | 14 | | | | | | | | | 8 | | | | 45 |
| 1 | | 3 | 2 | | $7^1$ | $6^3$ | 9 | 12 | 14 | 4 | | | | 13 | 11 | 5 | | 10 | | | | | | | $8^4$ | | | | 46 |

**FA Cup**

| | | | |
|---|---|---|---|
| Third Round | Charlton Ath | (a) | 1-0 |
| Fourth Round | Leicester C | (h) | 1-1 |
| *Replay* | Leicester C | (a) | 2-1 |
| Fifth Round | Wigan Ath | (h) | 1-4 |

**Capital One Cup**

| | | | |
|---|---|---|---|
| First Round | Preston NE | (a) | 0-2 |

# HULL CITY

## FOUNDATION

The enthusiasts who formed Hull City in 1904 were brave men indeed. More than that, they were audacious for they immediately put the club on the map in this Rugby League fortress by obtaining a three-year agreement with the Hull Rugby League club to rent their ground! They had obtained quite a number of conversions to the dribbling code, before the Rugby League forbade the use of any of their club grounds by Association Football clubs. By that time, Hull City were well away, having entered the FA Cup in their initial season and the Football League, Second Division after only a year.

*The KC Stadium, Walton Street, Hull, East Yorkshire HU3 6HU.*

*Telephone:* (01482) 504 600.

*Fax:* (01482) 304 882.

*Ticket Office:* (01482) 505 600.

*Website:* www.hullcityafc.net

*Email:* info@hulltigers.com

*Ground Capacity:* 25,404.

*Record Attendance:* 55,019 v Manchester U, FA Cup 6th rd, 26 February 1949 (at Boothferry Park); 25,512 v Sunderland, FL C, 28 October 2007 (at KC Stadium).

*Pitch Measurements:* 104m × 71m (114yd × 78yd)

*Chairman:* Assem Allam.

*Vice-chairman:* Ehab Allam.

*Manager:* Steve Bruce.

*Assistant Manager:* Steve Agnew.

*Physio:* Stuart Leake.

*Colours:* Amber shirts with black panels, black shorts, amber socks with black tops.

*Year Formed:* 1904.

*Turned Professional:* 1905.

*Club Nickname:* 'The Tigers'.

*Grounds:* 1904, Boulevard Ground (Hull RFC); 1905, Anlaby Road (Hull CC); 1944, Boulevard Ground; 1946, Boothferry Park; 2002, Kingston Communications Stadium.

*First Football League Game:* 2 September 1905, Division 2, v Barnsley (h) W 4–1 – Spendiff; Langley, Jones; Martin, Robinson, Gordon (2); Rushton, Spence (1), Wilson (1), Howe, Raisbeck.

*Record League Victory:* 11–1 v Carlisle U, Division 3 (N), 14 January 1939 – Ellis; Woodhead, Dowen; Robinson (1), Blyth, Hardy; Hubbard (2), Richardson (2), Dickinson (2), Davies (2), Cunliffe (2).

*Record Cup Victory:* 8–2 v Stalybridge Celtic (a), FA Cup 1st rd, 26 November 1932 – Maddison; Goldsmith, Woodhead; Gardner, Hill (1), Denby; Forward (1), Duncan, McNaughton (1), Wainscoat (4), Sargeant (1).

## HONOURS

**FA Premier League:** Best season 17th, 2008–09.

**Football League – FL C:** *Runners-up* 2012–13;

**FL 1:** *Runners-up* 2004–05;

**Division 3 (N):** *Champions* 1932–33, 1948–49;

**Division 3:** *Champions* 1965–66; *Runners-up* 1958–59, 2003–04;

**Division 4:** *Runners-up* 1982–83.

**FA Cup:** Semi-final 1930.

**Football League Cup:** Best season: 4th, 1974, 1976, 1978.

**Associate Members' Cup:** *Runners-up* 1984.

## sky SPORTS FACT FILE

Hull City had two Scandinavian players on their books in the 1956–57 season. Mauno Rintanen from Finland made four appearances deputising for regular goalkeeper Billy Bly, while Viggo Jensen played in 13 games before returning to Denmark in December 1956.

*Record Defeat:* 0–8 v Wolverhampton W, Division 2, 4 November 1911.

*Most League Points (2 for a win):* 69, Division 3, 1965–66.

*Most League Points (3 for a win):* 90, Division 4, 1982–83.

*Most League Goals:* 109, Division 3, 1965–66.

*Highest League Scorer in Season:* Bill McNaughton, 39, Division 3 (N), 1932–33.

*Most League Goals in Total Aggregate:* Chris Chilton, 193, 1960–71.

*Most League Goals in One Match:* 5, Ken McDonald v Bristol C, Division 2, 17 November 1928; 5, Simon 'Slim' Raleigh v Halifax T, Division 3 (N), 26 December 1930.

*Most Capped Player:* Theo Whitmore, 28 (105), Jamaica.

*Most League Appearances:* Andy Davidson, 520, 1952–67.

*Youngest League Player:* Matthew Edeson, 16 years 63 days v Fulham, 10 October 1992.

*Record Transfer Fee Received:* £4,000,000 from Sunderland for Michael Turner, August 2009.

*Record Transfer Fee Paid:* £5,000,000 to Fulham for Jimmy Bullard, January 2009.

*Football League Record:* 1905 Elected to Division 2; 1930–33 Division 3 (N); 1933–36 Division 2; 1936–49 Division 3 (N); 1949–56 Division 2; 1956–58 Division 3 (N); 1958–59 Division 3; 1959–60 Division 2; 1960–66 Division 3; 1966–78 Division 2; 1978–81 Division 3; 1981–83 Division 4; 1983–85 Division 3; 1985–91 Division 3; 1991–92 Division 3; 1992–96 Division 2; 1996–2004 Division 3; 2004–05 FL 1; 2005–08 FL C; 2008–10 FA Premier League; 2010–13 FL C; 2013– FA Premier League.

## LATEST SEQUENCES

*Longest Sequence of League Wins:* 10, 23.2.1966 – 20.4.1966.

*Longest Sequence of League Defeats:* 8, 7.4.1934 – 8.9.1934.

*Longest Sequence of League Draws:* 5, 30.3.1929 – 15.4.1929.

*Longest Sequence of Unbeaten League Matches:* 19, 13.3.2001 – 22.9.2001.

*Longest Sequence Without a League Win:* 27, 27.3.1989 – 4.11.1989.

*Successive Scoring Runs:* 26 from 10.4.1990.

*Successive Non-scoring Runs:* 6 from 13.11.1920.

## MANAGERS

James Ramster 1904–05
  *(Secretary-Manager)*
Ambrose Langley 1905–13
Harry Chapman 1913–14
Fred Stringer 1914–16
David Menzies 1916–21
Percy Lewis 1921–23
Bill McCracken 1923–31
Haydn Green 1931–34
John Hill 1934–36
David Menzies 1936
Ernest Blackburn 1936–46
Major Frank Buckley 1946–48
Raich Carter 1948–51
Bob Jackson 1952–55
Bob Brocklebank 1955–61
Cliff Britton 1961–70
  *(continued as General Manager to 1971)*
Terry Neill 1970–74
John Kaye 1974–77
Bobby Collins 1977–78
Ken Houghton 1978–79
Mike Smith 1979–82
Bobby Brown 1982
Colin Appleton 1982–84
Brian Horton 1984–88
Eddie Gray 1988–89
Colin Appleton 1989
Stan Ternent 1989–91
Terry Dolan 1991–97
Mark Hateley 1997–98
Warren Joyce 1998–2000
Brian Little 2000–02
Jan Molby 2002
Peter Taylor 2002–06
Phil Parkinson 2006
Phil Brown *(after caretaker role December 2006)* 2007–10
Ian Dowie *(consultant)* 2010
Nigel Pearson 2010–11
Nick Barmby 2011–12
Steve Bruce June 2012–

## TEN YEAR LEAGUE RECORD

| | | P | W | D | L | F | A | Pts | Pos |
|---|---|---|---|---|---|---|---|---|---|
| 2003-04 | Div 3 | 46 | 25 | 13 | 8 | 82 | 44 | 88 | 2 |
| 2004-05 | FL 1 | 46 | 26 | 8 | 12 | 80 | 53 | 86 | 2 |
| 2005-06 | FL C | 46 | 12 | 16 | 18 | 49 | 55 | 52 | 18 |
| 2006-07 | FL C | 46 | 13 | 10 | 23 | 51 | 67 | 49 | 21 |
| 2007-08 | FL C | 46 | 21 | 12 | 13 | 65 | 47 | 75 | 3 |
| 2008-09 | PR Lge | 38 | 8 | 11 | 19 | 39 | 64 | 35 | 17 |
| 2009-10 | PR Lge | 38 | 6 | 12 | 20 | 34 | 75 | 30 | 19 |
| 2010-11 | FL C | 46 | 16 | 17 | 13 | 52 | 51 | 65 | 11 |
| 2011-12 | FL C | 46 | 19 | 11 | 16 | 47 | 44 | 68 | 8 |
| 2012-13 | FL C | 46 | 24 | 7 | 15 | 61 | 52 | 79 | 2 |

## DID YOU KNOW ?

Hull City played a series of friendly games in their inaugural season, 1904–05, but also entered the FA Cup. Their first competitive game was a preliminary round tie in that competition against Stockton and after drawing 3-3 at home they lost 4-1 in the replay.

## HULL CITY – FL CHAMPIONSHIP 2012–13 LEAGUE RECORD

| Match No. | Date | Venue | Opponents | Result | H/T Score | Lg Pos. | Goalscorers | Attendance |
|---|---|---|---|---|---|---|---|---|
| 1 | Aug 18 | H | Brighton & HA | W | 1-0 | 0-0 | 7 | Simpson $^{85}$ | 15,794 |
| 2 | 22 | A | Blackburn R | L | 0-1 | 0-0 | 16 | | 13,562 |
| 3 | 25 | A | Charlton Ath | D | 0-0 | 0-0 | 14 | | 16,202 |
| 4 | Sept 1 | H | Bolton W | W | 3-1 | 1-1 | 5 | Aluko $^{29}$, Faye $^{46}$, Quinn $^{49}$ | 15,304 |
| 5 | 15 | H | Millwall | W | 4-1 | 4-0 | 4 | Koren $^{14}$, Simpson $^{32}$, Faye $^{36}$, Aluko $^{40}$ | 14,756 |
| 6 | 18 | A | Leeds U | W | 3-2 | 2-1 | 4 | Elmohamady $^{23}$, Faye $^{29}$, Koren $^{76}$ | 19,750 |
| 7 | 23 | A | Leicester C | L | 1-3 | 1-2 | 4 | Simpson $^{26}$ | 20,815 |
| 8 | 29 | H | Peterborough U | L | 1-3 | 0-2 | 8 | Simpson $^{61}$ | 15,279 |
| 9 | Oct 2 | H | Blackpool | L | 2-3 | 1-1 | 10 | Aluko $^{39}$, Quinn $^{47}$ | 14,919 |
| 10 | 6 | A | Sheffield W | W | 1-0 | 0-0 | 10 | McLean $^{77}$ | 23,441 |
| 11 | 20 | H | Ipswich T | W | 2-1 | 0-1 | 6 | Proschwitz 2 $^{74, 90}$ | 15,983 |
| 12 | 23 | A | Middlesbrough | L | 0-2 | 0-0 | 8 | | 14,129 |
| 13 | 27 | A | Bristol C | W | 2-1 | 1-1 | 6 | Aluko $^{8}$, Skuse (og) $^{65}$ | 12,354 |
| 14 | Nov 3 | H | Barnsley | W | 1-0 | 1-0 | 5 | Aluko $^{16}$ | 15,598 |
| 15 | 6 | H | Wolverhampton W | W | 2-1 | 1-0 | 4 | Aluko $^{29}$, Simpson $^{51}$ | 14,768 |
| 16 | 10 | A | Cardiff C | L | 1-2 | 0-1 | 4 | Koren $^{90}$ | 20,058 |
| 17 | 17 | A | Birmingham C | W | 3-2 | 3-1 | 4 | Aluko 2 $^{14, 26}$, Chester $^{33}$ | 17,363 |
| 18 | 24 | H | Burnley | L | 0-1 | 0-1 | 5 | | 17,782 |
| 19 | 27 | H | Crystal Palace | D | 0-0 | 0-0 | 6 | | 16,656 |
| 20 | Dec 1 | A | Nottingham F | W | 2-1 | 1-1 | 5 | Koren (pen) $^{34}$, McShane $^{69}$ | 19,472 |
| 21 | 8 | A | Watford | W | 2-1 | 1-0 | 4 | Meyler $^{41}$, Brady $^{73}$ | 12,156 |
| 22 | 15 | H | Huddersfield T | W | 2-0 | 1-0 | 4 | Koren $^{8}$, Meyler $^{90}$ | 16,488 |
| 23 | 21 | A | Derby Co | W | 2-1 | 1-1 | 2 | Koren $^{26}$, Faye $^{50}$ | 25,442 |
| 24 | 26 | H | Leicester C | D | 0-0 | 0-0 | 2 | | 20,321 |
| 25 | 29 | H | Leeds U | W | 2-0 | 0-0 | 2 | Evans $^{52}$, Meyler $^{55}$ | 23,453 |
| 26 | Jan 1 | A | Blackpool | D | 0-0 | 0-0 | 2 | | 13,691 |
| 27 | 12 | H | Sheffield W | L | 1-3 | 0-1 | 2 | Koren $^{83}$ | 16,531 |
| 28 | 19 | A | Peterborough U | D | 1-1 | 1-0 | 3 | Newell (og) $^{33}$ | 6214 |
| 29 | Feb 2 | A | Millwall | W | 1-0 | 1-0 | 3 | Meyler $^{1}$ | 9589 |
| 30 | 9 | A | Brighton & HA | L | 0-1 | 0-0 | 4 | | 25,367 |
| 31 | 12 | H | Derby Co | W | 2-1 | 0-0 | 2 | Gedo $^{47}$, Elmohamady $^{87}$ | 15,677 |
| 32 | 16 | H | Charlton Ath | W | 1-0 | 1-0 | 2 | Gedo $^{33}$ | 16,849 |
| 33 | 19 | H | Blackburn R | W | 2-0 | 0-0 | 2 | Gedo $^{52}$, Elmohamady $^{67}$ | 15,981 |
| 34 | 23 | A | Bolton W | L | 1-4 | 0-3 | 3 | Brady $^{68}$ | 17,655 |
| 35 | Mar 2 | H | Birmingham C | W | 5-2 | 3-0 | 2 | Boyd 2 $^{1, 33}$, Gedo 2 $^{11, 76}$, Koren $^{49}$ | 17,146 |
| 36 | 5 | A | Crystal Palace | L | 2-4 | 0-1 | 3 | Simpson $^{73}$, Meyler $^{90}$ | 16,230 |
| 37 | 11 | A | Burnley | W | 1-0 | 0-0 | 2 | Quinn $^{66}$ | 10,450 |
| 38 | 16 | H | Nottingham F | L | 1-2 | 1-0 | 2 | Boyd $^{45}$ | 19,848 |
| 39 | 30 | A | Huddersfield T | W | 1-0 | 0-0 | 2 | Boyd $^{46}$ | 14,175 |
| 40 | Apr 2 | H | Watford | L | 0-1 | 0-1 | 2 | | 20,043 |
| 41 | 6 | A | Middlesbrough | W | 1-0 | 0-0 | 2 | Brady $^{62}$ | 17,901 |
| 42 | 13 | A | Ipswich T | W | 2-1 | 1-0 | 2 | Brady (pen) $^{28}$, Koren $^{83}$ | 21,988 |
| 43 | 16 | A | Wolverhampton W | L | 0-1 | 0-0 | 2 | | 19,641 |
| 44 | 19 | H | Bristol C | D | 0-0 | 0-0 | 2 | | 18,595 |
| 45 | 27 | A | Barnsley | L | 0-2 | 0-1 | 2 | | 15,744 |
| 46 | May 4 | H | Cardiff C | D | 2-2 | 0-0 | 2 | Proschwitz $^{58}$, McShane $^{63}$ | 23,812 |

**Final League Position: 2**

### GOALSCORERS

*League (61):* Koren 9 (1 pen), Aluko 8, Simpson 6, Gedo 5, Meyler 5, Boyd 4, Brady 4 (1 pen), Faye 4, Elmohamady 3, Proschwitz 3, Quinn 3, McShane 2, Chester 1, Evans 1, McLean 1, own goals 2.
*FA Cup (3):* Proschwitz 2, Cairney 1.
*Capital One Cup (3):* McLean 2, Simpson 1.

| Amos B 17 | Rosenior L 15+17 | Chester J 43+1 | Faye A 28+3 | Dudgeon J 9 | Stewart C 1+1 | McKenna P 6+3 | Koren R 37+3 | Aluko S 22+1 | McLean A 3+11 | Proschwitz N 5+22 | Evans C 23+9 | Bruce A 29+3 | Simpson J 27+16 | Cairney T —+10 | McShane P 20+5 | Elmohamady A 41 | Olofinjana S 9+3 | Quinn S 41+1 | Dawson A 3+1 | Brady R 28+4 | Meyler D 25+3 | Stockdale D 24 | Hobbs D 20+2 | Jakupovic E 5 | Oxley M —+1 | Gedo M 10+2 | Fathi A 1+6 | Boyd G 12+1 | Fryatt M 2+2 | Match No. |
|---|---|---|---|---|---|---|---|---|---|---|---|---|---|---|---|---|---|---|---|---|---|---|---|---|---|---|---|---|---|---|
| 1 | 2 | 3 | $4^2$ | 5 | 6 | 7 | 8 | 9 | $10^3$ | $11^1$ | 12 | 13 | 14 | | | | | | | | | | | | | | | | | 1 |
| 1 | $5^3$ | 2 | 4 | 9 | | $6^2$ | 7 | 10 | 14 | 11 | $8^1$ | 3 | 13 | 12 | | | | | | | | | | | | | | | | 2 |
| 1 | 5 | 2 | 4 | 9 | | 6 | 7 | 10 | | $11^2$ | 8 | $3^1$ | 13 | | 12 | | | | | | | | | | | | | | | 3 |
| 1 | | 2 | 3 | 6 | | | $9^2$ | $10^1$ | 14 | | 12 | 4 | $11^3$ | | 13 | 5 | 7 | 8 | | | | | | | | | | | | 4 |
| 1 | 14 | 2 | 3 | 9 | | | 6 | $11^3$ | 12 | | | $4^2$ | 10 | | 13 | 5 | $7^1$ | 8 | | | | | | | | | | | | 5 |
| 1 | 12 | 2 | 3 | 9 | | | $6^1$ | 10 | 13 | | 7 | 4 | $11^2$ | | | 5 | | 8 | | | | | | | | | | | | 6 |
| 1 | 12 | 2 | $3^2$ | $9^1$ | | | 6 | 10 | 14 | | $7^3$ | 4 | 11 | | | 5 | 13 | 8 | | | | | | | | | | | | 7 |
| 1 | 13 | $3^2$ | 4 | 6 | | | 7 | 11 | | 12 | | 5 | 10 | | 2 | $8^1$ | 9 | | | | | | | | | | | | | 8 |
| 1 | 12 | | 4 | $6^2$ | | | 7 | 11 | 13 | | | $5^1$ | 10 | | 3 | 2 | 8 | 9 | | | | | | | | | | | | 9 |
| 1 | 2 | | 4 | | | | 8 | $11^3$ | 12 | 13 | | | $10^1$ | | 3 | 6 | 7 | 9 | 5 | | | | | | | | | | | 10 |
| 1 | $2^1$ | 14 | $4^3$ | | | | 3 | 11 | 12 | 13 | | | 10 | | 7 | 6 | $8^2$ | 9 | 5 | | | | | | | | | | | 11 |
| 1 | $2^2$ | 3 | | | | | $8^3$ | 12 | 11 | $10^1$ | 13 | | 14 | | 4 | 6 | 7 | 9 | 5 | | | | | | | | | | | 12 |
| 1 | 6 | 3 | | | | | 12 | $7^1$ | 11 | 14 | | $8^2$ | 4 | $10^3$ | | 5 | 2 | 13 | 9 | | | | | | | | | | | 13 |
| 1 | 6 | 3 | | | | | 13 | 8 | $11^2$ | 14 | | 7 | $5^1$ | $10^3$ | | 4 | 2 | | 9 | 12 | | | | | | | | | | 14 |
| 1 | $6^1$ | 3 | 13 | | | | 14 | 8 | $11^2$ | | | 7 | $5^3$ | 10 | | 4 | 2 | 9 | | 12 | | | | | | | | | | 15 |
| 1 | 2 | 3 | 5 | | | | 8 | 11 | 14 | | | 7 | | $10^1$ | | $4^2$ | 6 | $9^3$ | | 13 | 12 | | | | | | | | | 16 |
| 1 | $9^2$ | 2 | 3 | | | | 6 | 11 | 14 | | | | 4 | $10^3$ | | 5 | $7^1$ | 8 | | 13 | 12 | | | | | | | | | 17 |
| | $6^3$ | 3 | 4 | | | | 7 | 11 | | 14 | | | $5^2$ | 10 | | 2 | $8^1$ | 9 | | 13 | 12 | 1 | | | | | | | | 18 |
| | 14 | 3 | | | | | $7^1$ | $11^2$ | 13 | 12 | 8 | 5 | | | 4 | 2 | 10 | | | $6^3$ | 9 | 1 | | | | | | | | 19 |
| | 14 | 3 | 13 | | | | $10^3$ | | $11^1$ | 12 | 7 | 2 | | | 4 | 5 | 8 | | | $9^2$ | 6 | 1 | | | | | | | | 20 |
| | 13 | 2 | | | | | $10^2$ | | 14 | 6 | 4 | 11 | | | $3^1$ | 5 | | 7 | | $9^3$ | 8 | 1 | 12 | | | | | | | 21 |
| | 13 | 3 | 14 | | | | $9^3$ | | | | | $7^1$ | 5 | 11 | 12 | | 2 | | 10 | $6^2$ | 8 | 1 | 4 | | | | | | | 22 |
| | | 2 | 4 | | | | $10^2$ | | | 12 | 7 | | $11^1$ | 13 | | 5 | | 6 | | 8 | 9 | | 3 | 1 | | | | | | 23 |
| | 13 | 2 | $3^2$ | | | | 7 | $10^1$ | 14 | | $6^1$ | 11 | | 12 | 5 | | 8 | 9 | | | 4 | 1 | | | | | | | | 24 |
| | 13 | 2 | 3 | | | | $10^1$ | $11^3$ | 12 | | 6 | 14 | | | $5^2$ | | 8 | 9 | 7 | | 4 | 1 | | | | | | | | 25 |
| | 5 | 2 | 3 | | | | $10^1$ | $11^2$ | 12 | | $7^3$ | 14 | 13 | | | 8 | 9 | 6 | | 4 | 1 | | | | | | | | | 26 |
| | 2 | 3 | | | | | 10 | 11 | 13 | $6^1$ | 12 | | | 5 | | 8 | 9 | 7 | | $4^2$ | $1^3$ | 14 | | | | | | | | 27 |
| | 5 | 2 | 14 | | | | $7^2$ | 11 | 12 | 3 | $10^1$ | 13 | | 4 | | $8^3$ | 9 | 6 | | 1 | | | | | | | | | | 28 |
| | 3 | $5^1$ | | | | | 8 | 13 | 14 | $2^3$ | 11 | 4 | 9 | | 10 | | 7 | $6^2$ | 1 | 12 | | | | | | | | | | 29 |
| | 2 | | | | | | $4^3$ | 14 | 12 | $8^1$ | $5^2$ | 6 | 7 | 9 | | 10 | 11 | 1 | 3 | | 13 | | | | | | | | | 30 |
| | 14 | 2 | | | | | $11^2$ | 13 | $7^3$ | | $10^1$ | 4 | 5 | 8 | | 9 | 6 | 1 | 3 | | 12 | | | | | | | | | 31 |
| | 2 | | | | | | 13 | | | 7 | $10^2$ | 14 | $4^1$ | 5 | | 8 | 9 | 6 | 1 | 3 | $11^3$ | 12 | | | | | | | | 32 |
| | 2 | | | | | | $10^3$ | | | $7^1$ | 4 | 13 | 5 | 12 | 8 | | 9 | 6 | 1 | 3 | $11^2$ | 14 | | | | | | | | 33 |
| | 2 | | | | | | $11^1$ | | 6 | 4 | 13 | 14 | 5 | | 8 | 9 | $10^3$ | 1 | 3 | | $7^2$ | 12 | | | | | | | | 34 |
| | 2 | | | | | | 7 | | 4 | 13 | 12 | 14 | $5^3$ | 8 | | 9 | $6^1$ | 1 | 3 | | 10 | $11^2$ | | | | | | | | 35 |
| | $2^1$ | | | | | | $6^2$ | | | 3 | 14 | 12 | 5 | $8^3$ | 9 | | 7 | 1 | 4 | | 11 | 13 | 10 | | | | | | | 36 |
| | 14 | 4 | | | | | 12 | | | $6^2$ | 13 | 2 | 5 | $8^3$ | 9 | | 7 | 1 | 3 | | $11^1$ | 10 | | | | | | | | 37 |
| | 2 | | | | | | $6^3$ | | 14 | 12 | 13 | $4^1$ | 5 | $8^2$ | 9 | | 7 | 1 | 3 | | 10 | 11 | | | | | | | | 38 |
| 12 | 2 | 6 | | | | | 8 | | 13 | $4^1$ | 10 | 14 | $5^2$ | | 9 | 7 | 1 | 3 | | | | $11^3$ | | | | | | | | 39 |
| | 2 | 4 | | | | | 6 | 14 | 13 | $7^1$ | 10 | 5 | 12 | 9 | | 1 | $3^3$ | $11^2$ | 8 | | | | | | | | | | | 40 |
| 12 | 2 | 3 | | | | | 7 | 6 | $4^1$ | 13 | 5 | 8 | 9 | 1 | | $10^2$ | 14 | $11^3$ | | | | | | | | | | | | 41 |
| | 3 | 4 | | | | | 13 | $7^1$ | $11^2$ | 5 | 8 | 9 | 6 | 1 | 2 | 12 | $10^3$ | 14 | | | | | | | | | | | | 42 |
| | 2 | $3^2$ | | | | | $11^1$ | 14 | 12 | 5 | 8 | 9 | 6 | 1 | 4 | $7^3$ | 10 | 13 | | | | | | | | | | | | 43 |
| 14 | $2^3$ | 3 | | | | | 12 | 13 | 5 | 8 | 9 | 7 | 1 | 4 | $10^1$ | 6 | $11^2$ | | | | | | | | | | | | | 44 |
| 14 | 4 | 3 | | | | | $13^{}$ | $7^3$ | 12 | 2 | 6 | 9 | 5 | 8 | 1 | $10^1$ | $11^2$ | | | | | | | | | | | | | 45 |
| 9 | 2 | 4 | | | | | 12 | | $10^1$ | 3 | 5 | 8 | $11^2$ | 7 | 1 | 13 | 6 | | | | | | | | | | | | | 46 |

**FA Cup**

| | | | |
|---|---|---|---|
| Third Round | Leyton Orient | (h) | 1-1 |
| *Replay* | Leyton Orient | (a) | 2-1 |
| Fourth Round | Barnsley | (h) | 0-1 |

**Capital One Cup**

| | | | |
|---|---|---|---|
| First Round | Rotherham U | (h) | 1-1 |
| *(aet; won 7-6 on pens)* | | | |
| Second Round | Doncaster R | (a) | 2-3 |

# IPSWICH TOWN

## FOUNDATION

Considering that Ipswich Town only reached the Football League in 1938, many people outside of East Anglia may be surprised to learn that this club was formed at a meeting held in the Town Hall as far back as 1878 when Mr T. C. Cobbold, MP, was voted president. Originally it was the Ipswich Association FC to distinguish it from the older Ipswich Football Club which played rugby. These two amalgamated in 1888 and the handling game was dropped in 1893.

*Portman Road, Ipswich, Suffolk IP1 2DA.*

*Telephone:* (01473) 400 500.

*Fax:* (01473) 400 040.

*Ticket Office:* (0844) 8011 555.

*Website:* www.itfc.co.uk

*Email:* customerservices@itfc.co.uk

*Ground Capacity:* 30,311.

*Record Attendance:* 38,010 v Leeds U, FA Cup 6th rd, 8 March 1975.

*Pitch Measurements:* 102m × 64m (112yd × 70yd)

*Managing Directors:* Ian Milne, Jonathan Symonds.

*Manager:* Mick McCarthy.

*Assistant Manager:* Terry Connor.

*Physios:* Matt Byard, Alex Chapman.

*Colours:* Blue shirts with white trim, white shorts, blue socks with white tops.

*Year Formed:* 1878.

*Turned Professional:* 1936.

*Previous Name:* Ipswich Association FC; 1888, Ipswich Town.

*Club Nicknames:* 'The Blues', 'Town', 'The Tractor Boys'.

*Grounds:* 1878, Broom Hill and Brook's Hall; 1884, Portman Road.

*First Football League Game:* 27 August 1938, Division 3 (S), v Southend U (h) W 4–2 – Burns; Dale, Parry; Perrett, Fillingham, McLuckie; Williams, Davies (1), Jones (2), Alsop (1), Little.

*Record League Victory:* 7–0 v Portsmouth, Division 2, 7 November 1964 – Thorburn; Smith, McNeil; Baxter, Bolton, Thompson; Broadfoot (1), Hegan (2), Baker (1), Leadbetter, Brogan (3). 7–0 v Southampton, Division 1, 2 February 1974 – Sivell; Burley, Mills (1), Morris, Hunter, Beattie (1), Hamilton (2), Viljoen, Johnson, Whymark (2), Lambert (1) (Woods). 7–0 v WBA, Division 1, 6 November 1976 – Sivell; Burley, Mills, Talbot, Hunter, Beattie (1), Osborne, Wark (1), Mariner (1) (Bertschin), Whymark (4), Woods.

## HONOURS

**Football League – Division 1:**
*Champions* 1961–62;
*Runners-up* 1980–81, 1981–82;
**Division 2:** *Champions* 1960–61, 1967–68, 1991–92;
**Division 3 (S):** *Champions* 1953–54, 1956–57.

**FA Cup:** *Winners* 1978.

**Football League Cup:** Semi-final 1982, 1985, 2001, 2011.

**Texaco Cup:** *Winners* 1973.

**European Competitions**
**European Cup:** 1962–63.
**European Cup-Winners' Cup:** 1978–79.
**UEFA Cup:** 1973–74, 1974–75, 1975–76, 1977–78, 1979–80, 1980–81 (*winners*), 1981–82, 1982–83, 2001–02, 2002–03.

**sky SPORTS** FACT FILE

Ipswich Town made their debut at Wembley Stadium on 13 October 1928 when they won 4-0 to Ealing in a Southern Amateur League fixture. The match attracted a crowd of around 1,200. This was one of several played by their opponents at the national stadium that season.

*Record Cup Victory:* 10–0 v Floriana, European Cup prel. rd, 25 September 1962 – Bailey; Malcolm, Compton; Baxter, Laurel, Elsworthy (1); Stephenson, Moran (2), Crawford (5), Phillips (2), Blackwood.

*Record Defeat:* 1–10 v Fulham, Division 1, 26 December 1963.

*Most League Points (2 for a win):* 64, Division 3 (S), 1953–54 and 1955–56.

*Most League Points (3 for a win):* 87, Division 1, 1999–2000.

*Most League Goals:* 106, Division 3 (S), 1955–56.

*Highest League Scorer in Season:* Ted Phillips, 41, Division 3 (S), 1956–57.

*Most League Goals in Total Aggregate:* Ray Crawford, 204, 1958–63 and 1966–69.

*Most League Goals in One Match:* 5, Alan Brazil v Southampton, Division 1, 16 February 1981.

*Most Capped Player:* Allan Hunter, 47 (53), Northern Ireland.

*Most League Appearances:* Mick Mills, 591, 1966–82.

*Youngest League Player:* Jason Dozzell, 16 years 56 days v Coventry C, 4 February 1984.

*Record Transfer Fee Received:* £8,000,000 from Sunderland for Connor Wickham, June 2011.

*Record Transfer Fee Paid:* £5,000,000 to Sampdoria for Matteo Sereni, August 2001.

*Football League Record:* 1938 Elected to Division 3 (S); 1954–55 Division 2; 1955–57 Division 3 (S); 1957–61 Division 2; 1961–64 Division 1; 1964–68 Division 2; 1968–86 Division 1; 1986–92 Division 2; 1992–95 FA Premier League; 1995–2000 Division 1; 2000–02 FA Premier League; 2002–04 Division 1; 2004– FL C.

### MANAGERS

Mick O'Brien 1936–37
Scott Duncan 1937–55
  *(continued as Secretary)*
Alf Ramsey 1955–63
Jackie Milburn 1963–64
Bill McGarry 1964–68
Bobby Robson 1969–82
Bobby Ferguson 1982–87
Johnny Duncan 1987–90
John Lyall 1990–94
George Burley 1994–2002
Joe Royle 2002–06
Jim Magilton 2006–09
Roy Keane 2009–11
Paul Jewell 2011–12
Mick McCarthy November 2012–

### LATEST SEQUENCES

*Longest Sequence of League Wins:* 8, 23.9.1953 – 31.10.1953.

*Longest Sequence of League Defeats:* 10, 4.9.1954 – 16.10.1954.

*Longest Sequence of League Draws:* 7, 10.11.1990 – 21.12.1990.

*Longest Sequence of Unbeaten League Matches:* 23, 8.12.1979 – 26.4.1980.

*Longest Sequence Without a League Win:* 21, 28.8.1963 – 14.12.1963.

*Successive Scoring Runs:* 31 from 7.3.2004.

*Successive Non-scoring Runs:* 7 from 28.2.1995.

### TEN YEAR LEAGUE RECORD

|         |       | P  | W  | D  | L  | F  | A  | Pts | Pos |
|---------|-------|----|----|----|----|----|----|-----|-----|
| 2003-04 | Div 1 | 46 | 21 | 10 | 15 | 84 | 72 | 73  | 5   |
| 2004-05 | FL C  | 46 | 24 | 13 | 9  | 85 | 56 | 85  | 3   |
| 2005-06 | FL C  | 46 | 14 | 14 | 18 | 53 | 66 | 56  | 15  |
| 2006-07 | FL C  | 46 | 18 | 8  | 20 | 64 | 59 | 62  | 14  |
| 2007-08 | FL C  | 46 | 18 | 15 | 13 | 65 | 56 | 69  | 8   |
| 2008-09 | FL C  | 46 | 17 | 15 | 14 | 62 | 53 | 66  | 9   |
| 2009-10 | FL C  | 46 | 12 | 20 | 14 | 50 | 61 | 56  | 15  |
| 2010-11 | FL C  | 46 | 18 | 8  | 20 | 62 | 68 | 62  | 13  |
| 2011-12 | FL C  | 46 | 17 | 10 | 19 | 69 | 77 | 61  | 15  |
| 2012-13 | FL C  | 46 | 16 | 12 | 18 | 48 | 61 | 60  | 14  |

### DID YOU KNOW ?

Jimmy Leadbetter made 375 first-team appearances for Ipswich Town after signing in June 1955. He was converted to a left winger by manager Alf Ramsey and operated in an unconventional deep-lying role, widely being credited as the prototype for the 'wingless wonders' approach that won the 1966 World Cup.

## IPSWICH TOWN – FL CHAMPIONSHIP 2012–13 LEAGUE RECORD

| Match No. | Date | Venue | Opponents | Result | H/T Score | Lg Pos. | Goalscorers | Attendance |
|---|---|---|---|---|---|---|---|---|
| 1 | Aug 18 | H | Blackburn R | D 1-1 | 0-1 | 15 | Lowe (og) [83] | 19,117 |
| 2 | 21 | A | Watford | W 1-0 | 0-0 | 4 | Chopra [90] | 12,422 |
| 3 | 25 | A | Blackpool | L 0-6 | 0-2 | 16 | | 14,266 |
| 4 | Sept 1 | H | Huddersfield T | D 2-2 | 0-1 | 17 | Chambers [63], Chopra [72] | 16,843 |
| 5 | 15 | A | Middlesbrough | L 0-2 | 0-1 | 22 | | 14,887 |
| 6 | 19 | H | Wolverhampton W | L 0-2 | 0-0 | 23 | | 16,540 |
| 7 | 22 | H | Charlton Ath | L 1-2 | 0-0 | 23 | Scotland [57] | 16,587 |
| 8 | 29 | A | Barnsley | D 1-1 | 1-0 | 23 | Cresswell [6] | 8571 |
| 9 | Oct 2 | A | Brighton & HA | D 1-1 | 1-0 | 23 | Murphy [27] | 24,736 |
| 10 | 6 | H | Cardiff C | L 1-2 | 1-0 | 23 | Campbell [45] | 16,434 |
| 11 | 20 | A | Hull C | L 1-2 | 1-0 | 23 | Emmanuel-Thomas [29] | 15,983 |
| 12 | 23 | H | Derby Co | L 1-2 | 1-1 | 24 | Campbell [24] | 15,417 |
| 13 | 27 | H | Sheffield W | L 0-3 | 0-1 | 24 | | 17,738 |
| 14 | Nov 3 | A | Birmingham C | W 1-0 | 1-0 | 24 | Campbell [8] | 18,063 |
| 15 | 6 | A | Crystal Palace | L 0-5 | 0-1 | 24 | | 15,517 |
| 16 | 10 | H | Burnley | W 2-1 | 0-0 | 22 | Murphy [51], Campbell [87] | 16,297 |
| 17 | 17 | A | Leicester C | L 0-6 | 0-4 | 22 | | 20,779 |
| 18 | 24 | H | Peterborough U | D 1-1 | 0-1 | 23 | Campbell (pen) [60] | 16,427 |
| 19 | 27 | H | Nottingham F | W 3-1 | 1-0 | 21 | N'Daw [30], Hyam [61], Murphy [89] | 16,200 |
| 20 | Dec 1 | A | Bolton W | W 2-1 | 0-1 | 20 | Campbell (pen) [70], Chopra [90] | 17,208 |
| 21 | 8 | H | Millwall | W 3-0 | 1-0 | 20 | Campbell 2 (1 pen) [37, 64 (p)], Murphy [50] | 17,380 |
| 22 | 15 | A | Leeds U | L 0-2 | 0-1 | 20 | | 19,185 |
| 23 | 22 | H | Bristol C | D 1-1 | 1-1 | 20 | Smith [32] | 17,290 |
| 24 | 26 | A | Charlton Ath | W 2-1 | 2-0 | 20 | Campbell [34], Murphy [45] | 18,380 |
| 25 | 29 | A | Wolverhampton W | W 2-0 | 1-0 | 19 | Cresswell [33], Campbell [64] | 28,595 |
| 26 | Jan 1 | H | Brighton & HA | L 0-3 | 0-2 | 19 | | 19,018 |
| 27 | 12 | A | Cardiff C | D 0-0 | 0-0 | 19 | | 22,724 |
| 28 | 19 | H | Barnsley | D 1-1 | 0-0 | 19 | Chambers [56] | 15,913 |
| 29 | 26 | A | Bristol C | L 1-2 | 1-0 | 21 | Murphy [30] | 12,662 |
| 30 | Feb 2 | H | Middlesbrough | W 4-0 | 1-0 | 19 | Smith 2 [38, 78], McGoldrick [47], McLean [56] | 16,389 |
| 31 | 9 | A | Blackburn R | L 0-1 | 0-0 | 20 | | 14,342 |
| 32 | 16 | H | Blackpool | W 1-0 | 0-0 | 18 | Chopra [50] | 16,673 |
| 33 | 19 | H | Watford | L 0-2 | 0-1 | 18 | | 16,821 |
| 34 | 23 | A | Huddersfield T | D 0-0 | 0-0 | 19 | | 13,083 |
| 35 | Mar 2 | H | Leicester C | W 1-0 | 0-0 | 18 | McGoldrick [85] | 17,021 |
| 36 | 5 | A | Nottingham F | L 0-1 | 0-0 | 19 | | 19,458 |
| 37 | 9 | A | Peterborough U | D 0-0 | 0-0 | 20 | | 9367 |
| 38 | 16 | H | Bolton W | W 1-0 | 0-0 | 18 | Edwards [88] | 17,034 |
| 39 | 30 | H | Leeds U | W 3-0 | 1-0 | 16 | McGoldrick 2 [45, 49], Emmanuel-Thomas [68] | 20,402 |
| 40 | Apr 1 | A | Millwall | D 0-0 | 0-0 | 17 | | 10,141 |
| 41 | 6 | A | Derby Co | W 1-0 | 0-0 | 14 | Edwards [90] | 23,081 |
| 42 | 13 | H | Hull C | L 1-2 | 0-1 | 17 | Wordsworth [55] | 21,988 |
| 43 | 16 | H | Crystal Palace | W 3-0 | 3-0 | 13 | Nouble 2 [37, 45], Cresswell [45] | 17,656 |
| 44 | 20 | A | Sheffield W | D 1-1 | 1-0 | 14 | Tabb [12] | 23,630 |
| 45 | 27 | H | Birmingham C | W 3-1 | 2-0 | 12 | Edwards [6], Chambers [17], Murphy [57] | 21,921 |
| 46 | May 4 | A | Burnley | L 0-2 | 0-0 | 14 | | 12,820 |

**Final League Position: 14**

### GOALSCORERS

*League (48):* Campbell 10 (3 pens), Murphy 7, Chopra 4, McGoldrick 4, Chambers 3, Cresswell 3, Edwards 3, Smith 3, Emmanuel-Thomas 2, Nouble 2, Hyam 1, McLean 1, N'Daw 1, Scotland 1, Tabb 1, Wordsworth 1, own goal 1.
*FA Cup (1):* Chopra 1.
*Capital One Cup (4):* Cresswell 1, Luongo 1, Scotland 1, Smith 1.

| Loach S 22 | Edwards C 42+1 | Smith T 37+1 | Chambers L 44 | Cresswell A 46 | Emmanuel-Thomas J 10+19 | Hyam L 26+4 | Luongo M 6+3 | Martin L 33+1 | Carson J 3+3 | Chopra M 14+19 | Scotland J 2+10 | Drury A 20+9 | Delaney D —+1 | Murray R —+1 | Ainsley J 1+1 | Murphy D 32+7 | Taylor P 3 | N'Daw G 32+2 | Ellington N —+2 | Higginbotham D 11+1 | Wellens R 7 | Campbell D 17 | Mohsni B —+5 | Henderson S 24 | Reo-Coker N 8+2 | Marriott J —+1 | Orr B 13 | Barnett T 2+1 | Hewitt E 2+5 | McGoldrick D 13 | McLean A 4+3 | Nouble F 6+11 | Stearman R 15 | Wordsworth A 2+5 | Brown R —+1 | Tabb J 7+2 | Kisnorbo P 1+2 | Mings T 1 | Match No. |
|---|---|---|---|---|---|---|---|---|---|---|---|---|---|---|---|---|---|---|---|---|---|---|---|---|---|---|---|---|---|---|---|---|---|---|---|---|---|---|---|
| 1 | 2 | 3 | 4 | 5 | 6¹ | 7 | 8² | 9 | 10 | 11 | 12 | 13 | | | | | | | | | | | | | | | | | | | | | | | | | | | 1 |
| 1 | 2 | 4 | 3 | 5 | 9² | 7 | 6 | 11 | 8¹ | 10³ | 12 | 13 | 14 | | | | | | | | | | | | | | | | | | | | | | | | | | 2 |
| 1 | 2 | 4 | 3 | 5 | 10¹ | 7 | 6² | 9 | 13 | 11³ | 12 | 8 | | 14 | | | | | | | | | | | | | | | | | | | | | | | | | 3 |
| 1 | | 3 | 4 | 5 | | 7 | 6 | | | 11 | 12 | 8 | | | 2 | 9 | | 10¹ | | | | | | | | | | | | | | | | | | | | | 4 |
| 1 | 2 | 4 | 3 | 5 | 14 | | 12 | 9 | | 11³ | 13 | 7¹ | | | 8² | 6 | | 10 | | | | | | | | | | | | | | | | | | | | | 5 |
| 1 | 2 | 4 | 3 | 5 | 13 | | 8 | 6 | | 11 | 12 | 14 | | | | 9² | | 10¹ | 7³ | | | | | | | | | | | | | | | | | | | | 6 |
| 1 | 2 | 4³ | 3 | 5 | 9¹ | | 7 | 6 | 13 | | 11 | 8 | | | | 10² | | | | 12 | 14 | | | | | | | | | | | | | | | | | | 7 |
| 1 | 2 | | 3 | 5 | | 7¹ | 12 | 9 | | 10³ | 8 | | | | 13 | 11 | | 6² | 14 | 4 | | | | | | | | | | | | | | | | | | | 8 |
| 1 | 2 | | 3 | 5 | 9² | | 8 | 13 | 10¹ | 12 | 6 | | | | | 11 | | 7 | | 4 | | | | | | | | | | | | | | | | | | | 9 |
| 1 | 2 | | 3 | 5 | 6 | | 13 | 9 | | | 12 | 8 | | | | 10³ | | | | 4 | 7² | 11¹ | 14 | | | | | | | | | | | | | | | | 10 |
| | 2 | | 3 | 5 | 6 | | 11¹ | | | 13 | | 14 | | | | 9³ | | | | 4 | 7 | 10³ | 12 | 1 | 8 | | | | | | | | | | | | | | 11 |
| | 2 | | 3 | 5 | 10 | | | 9 | | 12 | 13 | 6² | | | | 11 | | | | 4 | 8 | 11¹ | | 1 | 7 | | | | | | | | | | | | | | 12 |
| | 2 | | 3 | 5 | 13 | 8 | | 9 | 6² | 12 | | | | | | 11¹ | | | | 4 | 7 | 10³ | 14 | 1 | | | | | | | | | | | | | | | 13 |
| | 2 | | 4 | 5 | 14 | | 6 | | | | 13 | | | | | 11 | 7² | 3 | | 9¹ | 10³ | 12 | | 1 | 8 | | | | | | | | | | | | | | 14 |
| 2 | 12 | 4 | | 5 | 13 | | 6 | | | | 8¹ | | | | | 11² | | 14 | | 3 | 9³ | 10 | | 1 | 7 | | | | | | | | | | | | | | 15 |
| | 6 | | 4 | | 5 | 12 | | | | | | | | | | 10 | | 7 | | 8¹ | 11² | 13 | | 1 | 9 | | | | | | | | | | | | | | 16 |
| | 6 | | 3 | 5 | 12 | 13 | | 9 | | 14 | | | | | | 11¹ | | 8² | | 2 | | 10¹ | | 1 | 7 | 4 | | | | | | | | | | | | | 17 |
| | 6 | | 4 | 5 | 12 | 14 | | 9 | | 10¹ | | | | | | 13 | 7 | 3 | | 11² | | 8³ | 2 | | | | | | | | | | | | | | | | 18 |
| | 6 | 4 | 3 | 5 | 8² | | 9 | | | 14 | | 13 | | | | 12 | | 7 | | | | 11³ | | | | | | | | 2 | 10¹ | | | | | | | | 19 |
| | 6 | 4 | 3 | 5 | 12 | | 9 | | | 14 | | 8¹ | | | | 13 | | 7 | | | | 11¹ | | | | | | | | 2 | 10² | | | | | | | | 20 |
| | 6 | 4 | 3 | 5 | | | 9 | | | 13 | | 8 | | | | 10² | | 7 | | | | 11¹ | | | | | | | | 2³ | 12 | 14 | | | | | | | 21 |
| | 6 | 4 | 3 | 5 | 13 | | 9 | | | 12 | | 8 | | | | 11² | | 7 | | | | 10¹ | | | | | | | | 2³ | 14 | | | | | | | | 22 |
| | 6 | 4 | 3 | 5 | 13 | | 9 | | | 12 | | 8 | | | | 10² | | 7 | | | | 11¹ | | | | | | | | 2 | | | | | | | | | 23 |
| | 6 | 4 | 3 | 5 | 14 | 13 | 9 | | | | | 8¹ | | | | 10³ | | 7 | | | | 11² | | 1 | 12 | 2 | | | | | | | | | | | | | 24 |
| | 6 | 4 | 3 | 5 | | | 9 | | | 13 | | 7¹ | | | | 11 | | 8 | | | | 10² | | 1 | 12 | 2 | | | | | | | | | | | | | 25 |
| | 6 | 4 | 3 | 5 | 14 | | 9 | | | 12 | 13 | | | | | 11¹ | | 8³ | | | | 10² | | 1 | 7 | 2 | | | | | | | | | | | | | 26 |
| 1 | 6 | 4 | 3 | 2 | | 9 | | 8³ | | 12 | | | | | | 13 | 7 | | | | | | | 5 | | | | | | 10² | 11¹ | 14 | | | | | | | 27 |
| 1 | 6 | 4 | 3 | 5 | | 9² | | 14 | | | | | | | | 13 | 7 | | | | | | | 2 | | | | | | 11³ | 10¹ | 12 | | | | | | | 28 |
| 1 | 6 | 4 | 3 | 5 | | 8 | | 9 | | | | | | | | 11¹ | 7 | | | | | | | 2 | | | | | | 10 | 12 | | | | | | | | 29 |
| 1 | 6 | 4 | 3 | 5 | 8³ | | | | | | | 14 | | | | 9 | 7 | | | | | | | 2 | | | | | | 10² | 11¹ | 12 | 2 | 13 | | | | | 30 |
| 6³ | 4 | 3 | 5 | | 8 | | | | | 13 | | | | | | 9 | 7 | | | | | | | 1 | | | | | | 11¹ | 10² | 14 | 2 | 12 | | | | | 31 |
| 6 | 4 | 3 | 5 | | 8 | | | | | 12 | | | | | | 11 | 7 | | | | | | | 1 | | | | | | 10² | 13 | 2 | 9¹ | | | | | | 32 |
| 6 | 4 | 3 | 5 | | 8 | 9¹ | | 10 | | | | | | | | | 7 | | | | | | | 1 | | | | | | 11² | 12 | 13 | 2 | 9¹ | | | | | 33 |
| 6 | 4 | 3 | 5 | 7 | 9² | | 11³ | 13 | | | | | | | | 12 | 8 | | | | | | | 1 | | | | | | 10¹ | 14 | 2 | | | | | | | 34 |
| 6 | 4 | 3 | 5 | 12 | 7 | 9¹ | | 10² | 14 | | | | | | | 13 | 8 | | | | | | | 1 | | | | | | 11³ | | 2 | | | | | | | 35 |
| | 4 | 3 | 5 | | 8 | 9⁴ | | 10² | | 6¹ | | | | | | 11³ | 7 | | | | | | | 1 | | | | | 13 | | 14 | 2⁸ | | 12 | | | | | 36 |
| | 4 | 3 | 5 | 13 | 8 | | | 6² | | | | | | | | | 7 | | | | | | | 1 | | | 2 | 11 | 12 | 10¹ | | | | | 9 | | | | 37 |
| 6 | 4 | 3 | 5 | 12 | 8 | | 13 | 7 | | | | | | | | 10 | | | | | | | | 1 | | | | | | 11¹ | | 2 | | | | 9² | | | 38 |
| 1 | 6¹ | 4 | 3 | 5 | 12 | 7 | | 13 | 8 | | | | | | | 10³ | | | | | | | | | | | | | | 11² | | 14 | 2 | | | 9 | | | 39 |
| 1 | 12 | 4 | 3 | 5 | 6 | 7 | | 9² | 10¹ | | | | | | | | 8 | | | | | | | | | | | | | 11 | | 2 | | | | 13 | | | 40 |
| 1 | 6 | 4 | 3 | 5 | | 8 | | 14 | 7² | | | | | | | 10¹ | 13 | | | | | | | | | | | | | 11³ | | 12 | 2 | | | 9 | | | 41 |
| 1 | 6 | 4 | 3 | 5 | 14 | 7 | | 10² | | | | | | | | 11³ | 8 | | | | | | | | | | | | | 13 | 2 | 12 | | | | 9¹ | | | 42 |
| 1 | 6² | 4 | 3 | 5 | 9¹ | 7 | | 10 | | | | | | | | | 8 | | | | | | | | | | | | 14 | 11³ | 2 | 12 | | | | 13 | | | 43 |
| 1 | 6 | 4 | 3 | 5 | 13 | 8 | | 10² | | | | | | | | | 7 | | | | | | | | | | | | | 11 | 2¹ | 14 | | | | 9³ | 12 | | 44 |
| 1 | 6 | 4 | 3 | 5 | 12 | 7 | | 10² | 8 | | 14 | 13 | | | | | | | | | | | | | | | | 2 | | 11¹ | | | | | | 9³ | | | 45 |
| 1 | 6² | 9 | | 5 | | 7 | | | | | | | | | | 11 | | | | | | | | | | | 12 | 13 | | 10¹ | 4 | 8³ | | 14 | 3 | 2 | | | 46 |

**FA Cup**
Third Round    Aston Villa    (a)   1-2

**Capital One Cup**
First Round    Bristol R    (h)   3-1
Second Round    Carlisle U    (a)   1-2

# LEEDS UNITED

## FOUNDATION

Immediately the Leeds City club (founded in 1904) was wound up by the FA in October 1919, following allegations of illegal payments to players, a meeting was called by a Leeds solicitor, Mr Alf Masser, at which Leeds United was formed. They joined the Midland League, playing their first game in that competition in November 1919. It was in this same month that the new club had discussions with the directors of a virtually bankrupt Huddersfield Town who wanted to move to Leeds in an amalgamation. But Huddersfield survived even that crisis.

*Elland Road, Leeds, West Yorkshire LS11 0ES.*

*Telephone:* (0871) 334 1919.

*Fax:* (0113) 367 6050.

*Ticket Office:* (0871) 334 1992.

*Website:* www.leedsunited.com

*Email:* reception@leedsunited.com

*Ground Capacity:* 37,914.

*Record Attendance:* 57,892 v Sunderland, FA Cup 5th rd (replay), 15 March 1967.

*Pitch Measurements:* 106m × 69m (117yd × 76yd)

*Chairman:* Ken Bates.

*Chief Executive:* Shaun Harvey.

*Manager:* Brian McDermott.

*Assistant Manager:* Nigel Gibbs.

*Physio:* Harvey Sharman.

*Colours:* White shirts with blue and yellow trim, white shorts with blue and yellow trim, white socks with blue and yellow trim.

*Year Formed:* 1919, as Leeds United after disbandment (by FA order) of Leeds City (formed in 1904).

*Turned Professional:* 1920.

*Club Nickname:* 'The Whites'.

*Ground:* 1919, Elland Road.

## HONOURS

**Football League – Division 1:**
*Champions* 1968–69, 1973–74, 1991–92; *Runners-up* 1964–65, 1965–66, 1969–70, 1970–71, 1971–72; **Division 2:** *Champions* 1923–24, 1963–64, 1989–90; *Runners-up* 1927–28, 1931–32, 1955–56; **FL 1:** *Runners-up* 2009–10.

**FA Cup:** *Winners* 1972; *Runners-up* 1965, 1970, 1973.

**Football League Cup:** *Winners* 1968; *Runners-up* 1996.

**European Competitions**
**European Cup:** 1969–70, 1974–75 (*runners-up*).
**Champions League:** 1992–93, 2000–01 (*s-f*).
**European Cup-Winners' Cup:** 1972–73 (*runners-up*).
**European Fairs Cup:** 1965–66, 1966–67 (*runners-up*), 1967–68 (*winners*), 1968–69, 1970–71 (*winners*).
**UEFA Cup:** 1971–72, 1973–74, 1979–80, 1995–96, 1998–99, 1999–2000 (*s-f*), 2001–02, 2002–03.

*First Football League Game:* 28 August 1920, Division 2, v Port Vale (a) L 0–2 – Down; Duffield, Tillotson; Musgrove, Baker, Walton; Mason, Goldthorpe, Thompson, Lyon, Best.

*Record League Victory:* 8–0 v Leicester C, Division 1, 7 April 1934 – Moore; George Milburn, Jack Milburn; Edwards, Hart, Copping; Mahon (2), Firth (2), Duggan (2), Furness (2), Cochrane.

## sky SPORTS FACT FILE

The 1970 European Cup semi-final second leg between Celtic and Leeds United attracted the highest ever attendance at a UEFA club tie. A crowd of 136,505 turned out at Hampden Park to see Celtic win the game 2-1 and progress to the final with a 3-1 aggregate victory.

*Record Cup Victory:* 10–0 v Lyn (Oslo), European Cup 1st rd 1st leg, 17 September 1969 – Sprake; Reaney, Cooper, Bremner (2), Charlton, Hunter, Madeley, Clarke (2), Jones (3), Giles (2) (Bates), O'Grady (1).

*Record Defeat:* 1–8 v Stoke C, Division 1, 27 August 1934.

*Most League Points (2 for a win):* 67, Division 1, 1968–69.

*Most League Points (3 for a win):* 86, FL 1, 2009–10.

*Most League Goals:* 98, Division 2, 1927–28.

*Highest League Scorer in Season:* John Charles, 42, Division 2, 1953–54.

*Most League Goals in Total Aggregate:* Peter Lorimer, 168, 1965–79 and 1983–86.

*Most League Goals in One Match:* 5, Gordon Hodgson v Leicester C, Division 1, 1 October 1938.

*Most Capped Player:* Lucas Radebe, 58 (70), South Africa.

*Most League Appearances:* Jack Charlton, 629, 1953–73.

*Youngest League Player:* Peter Lorimer, 15 years 289 days v Southampton, 29 September 1962.

*Record Transfer Fee Received:* £30,000,000 from Manchester U for Rio Ferdinand, July 2002.

*Record Transfer Fee Paid:* £18,000,000 to West Ham United for Rio Ferdinand, November 2000.

*Football League Record:* 1920 Elected to Division 2; 1924–27 Division 1; 1927–28 Division 2; 1928–31 Division 1; 1931–32 Division 2; 1932–47 Division 1; 1947–56 Division 2; 1956–60 Division 1; 1960–64 Division 2; 1964–82 Division 1; 1982–90 Division 2; 1990–92 Division 1; 1992–2004 FA Premier League; 2004–07 FL C; 2007–10 FL 1; 2010– FL C.

## MANAGERS

**Dick Ray** 1919–20
**Arthur Fairclough** 1920–27
**Dick Ray** 1927–35
**Bill Hampson** 1935–47
**Willis Edwards** 1947–48
**Major Frank Buckley** 1948–53
**Raich Carter** 1953–58
**Bill Lambton** 1958–59
**Jack Taylor** 1959–61
**Don Revie** OBE 1961–74
**Brian Clough** 1974
**Jimmy Armfield** 1974–78
**Jock Stein** CBE 1978
**Jimmy Adamson** 1978–80
**Allan Clarke** 1980–82
**Eddie Gray** MBE 1982–85
**Billy Bremner** 1985–88
**Howard Wilkinson** 1988–96
**George Graham** 1996–98
**David O'Leary** 1998–2002
**Terry Venables** 2002–03
**Peter Reid** 2003
**Eddie Gray** *(Caretaker)* 2003–04
**Kevin Blackwell** 2004–06
**Dennis Wise** 2006–08
**Gary McAllister** 2008
**Simon Grayson** 2008–12
**Neil Warnock** 2012–13
**Brian McDermott** April 2013–

## LATEST SEQUENCES

*Longest Sequence of League Wins:* 9, 26.9.1931 – 21.11.1931.

*Longest Sequence of League Defeats:* 6, 28.12.2003 – 7.2.2004.

*Longest Sequence of League Draws:* 5, 19.4.1997 – 9.8.1997.

*Longest Sequence of Unbeaten League Matches:* 34, 26.10.1968 – 26.8.1969.

*Longest Sequence Without a League Win:* 17, 1.2.1947 – 26.5.1947.

*Successive Scoring Runs:* 30 from 27.8.1927.

*Successive Non-scoring Runs:* 6 from 30.1.1982.

## TEN YEAR LEAGUE RECORD

| | | P | W | D | L | F | A | Pts | Pos |
|---|---|---|---|---|---|---|---|---|---|
| 2003-04 | PR Lge | 38 | 8 | 9 | 21 | 40 | 79 | 33 | 19 |
| 2004-05 | FL C | 46 | 14 | 18 | 14 | 49 | 52 | 60 | 14 |
| 2005-06 | FL C | 46 | 21 | 15 | 10 | 57 | 38 | 78 | 5 |
| 2006-07 | FL C | 46 | 13 | 7 | 26 | 46 | 72 | 36* | 24 |
| 2007-08 | FL 1 | 46 | 27 | 10 | 9 | 72 | 38 | 76† | 5 |
| 2008-09 | FL 1 | 46 | 26 | 6 | 14 | 77 | 49 | 84 | 4 |
| 2009-10 | FL 1 | 46 | 25 | 11 | 10 | 77 | 44 | 86 | 2 |
| 2010-11 | FL C | 46 | 19 | 15 | 12 | 81 | 70 | 72 | 7 |
| 2011-12 | FL C | 46 | 17 | 10 | 19 | 65 | 68 | 61 | 14 |
| 2012-13 | FL C | 46 | 17 | 10 | 19 | 57 | 66 | 61 | 13 |

*\*10 pts deducted; †15 pts deducted.*

### DID YOU KNOW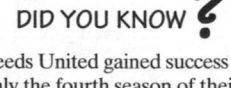

Leeds United gained success in only the fourth season of their existence when they won the Division Two title in 1923–24. Promotion was clinched with a 4-0 home win over Stockport on Easter Monday with the title secured the following Saturday when they defeated Nelson 1-0 at Elland Road.

## LEEDS UNITED – FL CHAMPIONSHIP 2012–13 LEAGUE RECORD

| Match No. | Date | Venue | Opponents | Result | H/T Score | Lg Pos. | Goalscorers | Attendance |
|---|---|---|---|---|---|---|---|---|
| 1 | Aug 18 | H | Wolverhampton W | W 1-0 | 1-0 | 8 | Becchio 17 | 23,745 |
| 2 | 21 | A | Blackpool | L 1-2 | 1-0 | 15 | Lees 16 | 14,315 |
| 3 | 25 | A | Peterborough U | W 2-1 | 1-0 | 7 | Becchio 2 7, 50 | 10,432 |
| 4 | Sept 1 | H | Blackburn R | D 3-3 | 1-2 | 7 | Diouf 41, McCormack 56, Becchio 65 | 24,411 |
| 5 | 15 | A | Cardiff C | L 1-2 | 0-0 | 9 | Austin 77 | 23,836 |
| 6 | 18 | H | Hull C | L 2-3 | 1-2 | 13 | Becchio (pen) 8, Gray 90 | 19,750 |
| 7 | 22 | H | Nottingham F | W 2-1 | 2-0 | 11 | Becchio 14, Poleon 25 | 24,292 |
| 8 | 29 | A | Bristol C | W 3-2 | 0-0 | 9 | Diouf 2 63, 80, Tonge 83 | 15,692 |
| 9 | Oct 2 | A | Bolton W | D 2-2 | 1-1 | 9 | Byram 44, Becchio (pen) 50 | 21,255 |
| 10 | 6 | H | Barnsley | W 1-0 | 1-0 | 7 | Becchio (pen) 42 | 22,569 |
| 11 | 19 | A | Sheffield W | D 1-1 | 0-1 | 6 | Tonge 77 | 28,582 |
| 12 | 23 | H | Charlton Ath | D 1-1 | 1-0 | 7 | Norris 37 | 17,484 |
| 13 | 27 | H | Birmingham C | L 0-1 | 0-0 | 11 | | 22,152 |
| 14 | Nov 2 | A | Brighton & HA | D 2-2 | 1-1 | 10 | Diouf (pen) 37, Brown 66 | 26,402 |
| 15 | 6 | A | Burnley | L 0-1 | 0-0 | 15 | | 14,470 |
| 16 | 10 | H | Watford | L 1-6 | 0-1 | 17 | Tonge (pen) 80 | 19,104 |
| 17 | 18 | A | Millwall | L 0-1 | 0-0 | 18 | | 13,117 |
| 18 | 24 | H | Crystal Palace | W 2-1 | 0-0 | 16 | Becchio 52, Green 76 | 20,964 |
| 19 | 27 | H | Leicester C | W 1-0 | 1-0 | 15 | Becchio (pen) 3 | 17,717 |
| 20 | Dec 1 | A | Huddersfield T | W 4-2 | 2-2 | 10 | Tonge 35, Becchio 2 37, 86, Norris 70 | 20,372 |
| 21 | 8 | A | Derby Co | L 1-3 | 1-1 | 14 | Green 45 | 25,034 |
| 22 | 15 | H | Ipswich T | W 2-0 | 1-0 | 12 | Thomas 19, Green 68 | 19,185 |
| 23 | 22 | H | Middlesbrough | W 2-1 | 1-1 | 8 | Becchio 2 45, 73 | 25,406 |
| 24 | 26 | A | Nottingham F | L 2-4 | 1-1 | 9 | Green 12, Somma 90 | 26,670 |
| 25 | 29 | A | Hull C | L 0-2 | 0-0 | 9 | | 23,453 |
| 26 | Jan 1 | H | Bolton W | W 1-0 | 0-0 | 8 | Becchio (pen) 66 | 22,386 |
| 27 | 12 | A | Barnsley | L 0-2 | 0-0 | 11 | | 13,999 |
| 28 | 19 | A | Bristol C | W 1-0 | 0-0 | 11 | McCormack 67 | 18,156 |
| 29 | Feb 2 | H | Cardiff C | L 0-1 | 0-0 | 12 | | 19,236 |
| 30 | 9 | A | Wolverhampton W | D 2-2 | 0-0 | 11 | Varney 64, McCormack (pen) 78 | 23,463 |
| 31 | 12 | A | Middlesbrough | L 0-1 | 0-0 | 11 | | 18,388 |
| 32 | 20 | H | Blackpool | W 2-0 | 0-0 | 9 | Norris 57, Morison 63 | 25,532 |
| 33 | 23 | A | Blackburn R | D 0-0 | 0-0 | 9 | | 18,467 |
| 34 | Mar 2 | H | Millwall | W 1-0 | 0-0 | 9 | Warnock (pen) 72 | 19,002 |
| 35 | 5 | A | Leicester C | D 1-1 | 0-0 | 10 | Byram 52 | 22,660 |
| 36 | 9 | A | Crystal Palace | D 2-2 | 0-1 | 10 | Morison 2 56, 69 | 19,976 |
| 37 | 12 | A | Peterborough U | D 1-1 | 0-1 | 10 | Byram 57 | 24,240 |
| 38 | 16 | H | Huddersfield T | L 1-2 | 0-0 | 10 | White 60 | 23,814 |
| 39 | 30 | A | Ipswich T | L 0-3 | 0-1 | 11 | | 20,402 |
| 40 | Apr 1 | H | Derby Co | L 1-2 | 0-0 | 12 | McCormack 67 | 21,384 |
| 41 | 6 | A | Charlton Ath | L 1-2 | 0-0 | 16 | Varney 81 | 18,900 |
| 42 | 13 | H | Sheffield W | W 2-1 | 0-1 | 11 | Varney 2 63, 69 | 23,936 |
| 43 | 16 | H | Burnley | W 1-0 | 0-0 | 11 | Austin 62 | 16,788 |
| 44 | 20 | A | Birmingham C | L 0-1 | 0-0 | 13 | | 17,666 |
| 45 | 27 | H | Brighton & HA | L 1-2 | 0-1 | 16 | Diouf (pen) 74 | 24,904 |
| 46 | May 4 | A | Watford | W 2-1 | 1-1 | 13 | Poleon 42, McCormack 90 | 16,968 |

**Final League Position: 13**

### GOALSCORERS

*League (57):* Becchio 15 (5 pens), Diouf 5 (2 pens), McCormack 5 (1 pen), Green 4, Tonge 4 (1 pen), Varney 4, Byram 3, Morison 3, Norris 3, Austin 2, Poleon 2, Brown 1, Gray 1, Lees 1, Somma 1, Thomas 1, Warnock 1 (1 pen), White 1.
*FA Cup (5):* McCormack 2, Becchio 1, Diouf 1 (1 pen), Varney 1.
*Capital One Cup (13):* Becchio 3 (1 pen), Austin 2, Byram 1, Diouf 1, Lees 1, McCormack 1 (1 pen), Norris 1, Tonge 1, Varney 1, White 1.

| Kenny P 46 | Byram S 42+2 | Peltier L 40+1 | Pearce J 26+7 | White A 14+10 | Green P 30+2 | Norris D 27+3 | Austin R 26+5 | Varney L 26+8 | McCormack R 25+7 | Becchio L 25+1 | Diouf E 28+8 | Lees T 38+2 | Pugh D 1+3 | Drury A 11+1 | Poleon D 1+5 | Gray A —+8 | Tonge M 32+3 | Brown M 15+9 | Hall R 2+6 | Tate A 10 | Thomas J 6 | Somma D 1+3 | Barkley R 3+1 | Habibou H 1+3 | Warnock S 16 | Morison S 13+2 | Dawson C 1 | Match No. |
|---|---|---|---|---|---|---|---|---|---|---|---|---|---|---|---|---|---|---|---|---|---|---|---|---|---|---|---|---|
| 1 | 2 | 3 | 4 | 5 | 6¹ | 7 | 8 | 9 | 10² | 11 | 12 | 13 | | | | | | | | | | | | | | | | 1 |
| 1 | 6 | 2 | 4 | 5² | | 7 | 8 | 11 | 9¹ | 10 | 12 | 3 | 13 | | | | | | | | | | | | | | | 2 |
| 1 | 12 | 2 | 3 | | | 7 | 8 | 11 | 9² | 10³ | 6¹ | 4 | | 5 | 13 | 14 | | | | | | | | | | | | 3 |
| 1 | 12 | 2 | 3 | | | 8 | 7 | 6¹ | 11 | 10 | 9 | 4 | | 5 | | | | | | | | | | | | | | 4 |
| 1 | 9 | 2 | 4 | 7 | | | 6 | 12³ | 11¹ | 10 | 13 | 5 | | 3² | 14 | | 8 | | | | | | | | | | | 5 |
| 1 | 6 | 2 | 4 | 5 | | | 8 | 9² | | 11¹ | 10 | 3 | | | 12 | 13 | 7 | | | | | | | | | | | 6 |
| 1 | 6 | 2² | 4 | 12 | | | 7 | 13 | | 10³ | 9 | 3 | | 5 | 11¹ | 14 | 8 | | | | | | | | | | | 7 |
| 1 | 2 | 5 | 4 | 6 | | | 8 | | | 11¹ | 10 | 3 | | | 12 | 9 | 7 | | | | | | | | | | | 8 |
| 1 | 6 | 4 | 3 | | | | 7 | | | 11 | 10 | 2 | | 5 | | 9 | 8 | | | | | | | | | | | 9 |
| 1 | 2 | 5 | 4 | 9 | | 12 | 7 | | | 10² | 11 | 3 | | | | 13 | 8¹ | 6 | | | | | | | | | | 10 |
| 1 | 6 | 2² | 4 | 5 | | 12 | 7¹ | 13 | | 10 | 11 | 3 | | | | 9 | 8 | | | | | | | | | | | 11 |
| 1 | 2 | | 4 | 12 | 7² | 6 | | 9¹ | | 10³ | 11 | 3. | | 5 | | 14 | 13 | 8 | | | | | | | | | | 12 |
| 1 | 2 | 5 | 3 | 12 | | 6¹ | 8 | | | 11 | 10 | 4² | 9 | | | | 7 | | 13 | | | | | | | | | 13 |
| 1 | 2 | 5 | 4 | 6 | | 14 | 8 | 11² | | 13 | 10³ | 3¹ | 12 | | | | 9 | 7 | | | | | | | | | | 14 |
| 1 | 6 | 3 | 4 | 2² | | | 8 | 13 | | 11 | 10 | | 12 | 5¹ | | | 9 | 7 | | | | | | | | | | 15 |
| 1 | 5 | 3 | 4¹ | 9² | 6¹ | 7 | 2 | 11 | | | 10³ | 12 | | | | | 8 | 14 | 13 | | | | | | | | | 16 |
| 1 | 2 | 4 | | 7 | | | 9² | 12 | 11 | 10 | 3 | | 5 | | | | 8 | | 6¹ | | | | | | | | | 17 |
| 1 | 2 | 5 | | 6 | 8 | | | 13 | 11 | 10² | 4 | | 12³ | | | | 7 | 14 | | 3 | 9¹ | | | | | | | 18 |
| 1 | 2 | 5 | | 7 | 6 | | | | | 10 | 11 | 3 | | | | | 8 | 12 | | 4 | 9¹ | | | | | | | 19 |
| 1 | 2 | 5 | | 6 | 8 | | | | 11 | 10² | | | 13 | 7³ | 14 | 12 | 4 | 9¹ | | | | | | | | | | 20 |
| 1 | 2 | 5 | 14 | 6 | 8³ | | 12 | 11² | 10 | 13 | 3 | | | | 7 | | | 9¹ | 4 | | | | | | | | | 21 |
| 1 | 2 | 5 | | 6 | 7 | | 14 | 12 | 10³ | 11¹ | 3 | | | | 8 | 13 | | 4 | 9² | | | | | | | | | 22 |
| 1 | 2 | 5³ | 14 | 12 | 6¹ | 8 | | | 11 | 10 | 4 | | | | 7 | | | 3 | 9² | 13 | | | | | | | | 23 |
| 1 | 2³ | | 13 | | 6 | | 8² | | 14 | 11 | 10³ | 3 | 5 | | | | 7 | | 4 | 9 | 12 | | | | | | | 24 |
| 1 | 9 | | 4 | 2 | 6 | 8³ | 13 | 12 | 11 | | 3 | | | | | | 7 | | 5 | 10¹ | | | | | | | | 25 |
| 1 | 2 | 5 | 3 | | 8 | 6 | 7 | | 11 | 10 | 9¹ | | | 12 | | | | 4 | | | | | | | | | | 26 |
| 1 | 2 | 5 | 3 | | 13 | 8¹ | 7 | | 12 | 10 | 11² | | | | 9 | | | 4 | | 6 | | | | | | | | 27 |
| 1 | 2 | 4 | | 5 | 12 | | 8 | | 10² | 11 | 6 | 3 | | | 13 | 7 | | | | 9¹ | | | | | | | | 28 |
| 1 | 2 | 4 | | 5 | | | 8 | 9 | 11 | | 10¹ | 3. | | | | 7 | | | 6 | 12 | | | | | | | | 29 |
| 1 | 2 | 3 | | | 8 | 7 | | 9 | 11¹ | | 4 | | | | | 6 | | 12 | | | 5 | 10 | | | | | | 30 |
| 1 | 2 | 3 | | | 8² | 7¹ | 13 | 9 | 11 | 12 | 4 | | | | | 6³ | | | | 14 | 5 | 10 | | | | | | 31 |
| 1 | 2 | 4 | 13 | | 6 | 8² | | 11 | 9 | | 3 | | | | 7¹ | 12 | | | | | 5 | 10 | | | | | | 32 |
| 1 | 2 | 4 | | 6 | 8 | | 11 | 9 | | 3 | | | | | 7 | | | | | 5 | 10 | | | | | | | 33 |
| 1 | 2 | 4 | 14 | | 7 | 6² | 11³ | 9¹ | 12 | 3 | | | | | 8 | 13 | | | | | 5 | 10 | | | | | | 34 |
| 1 | 2 | 3 | 12 | | 6 | 8 | 9 | 11¹ | | 4 | | | | | 7 | | | | | | 5 | 10 | | | | | | 35 |
| 1 | 2 | 3 | | | 7 | 6² | 13 | 10 | 9¹ | | 4 | | | | 8 | | 12 | | | 14 | 5 | 11³ | | | | | | 36 |
| 1 | 2 | 4 | 12 | | 6 | 8³ | 14 | 9 | 10 | 13 | 3¹ | | | | 7 | | | | | | 5 | 11² | | | | | | 37 |
| 1 | 2 | 4 | | 12 | 6² | | 8 | 9 | | 10 | 3 | | | | 7 | 13 | | | | 11¹ | 5 | | | | | | | 38 |
| 1 | 2 | 3 | 12 | 13 | 6¹ | 7 | | 11² | 14 | | 4■ | | | | 9³ | 8 | | | | | 5 | 10 | | | | | | 39 |
| 1 | 2 | 3 | 4 | 13 | 6 | | 8 | 9 | 12 | 11² | | | | | | | | | | | 5 | 10 | 7¹ | | | | | 40 |
| 1 | 2 | 3³ | 4 | 9¹ | 6 | 7 | 14 | 12 | 11 | | | | | | 8² | 13 | | | | | 5 | 10 | | | | | | 41 |
| 1 | 2 | | 3 | 13 | 6 | 7¹ | 8 | 9 | 10 | 12 | | 5 | | | 14 | | | | | | 4³ | 11² | | | | | | 42 |
| 1 | 2 | | 4 | | 6 | | 7 | 9 | 11¹ | 10 | 3 | | | | 8 | | | | 12 | | 5 | | | | | | | 43 |
| 1 | 2 | 12 | 3 | | 7 | | 6³ | 10 | 11 | | 8² | 4 | 14 | | 9¹ | | | | | | 5 | 13 | | | | | | 44 |
| 1 | | 2 | 4 | | 8 | | 7¹ | 11³ | 10 | | 9■ | 3 | | | 6² | 13 | | | | | 5 | 12 | | | | | | 45 |
| 1 | | 2 | 4 | 13 | 6³ | | | 9 | 11 | | | 3 | | 5 | 12 | | 7 | 8¹ | 14 | | | 10² | | | | | | 46 |

**FA Cup**

| | | | |
|---|---|---|---|
| Third Round | Birmingham C | (h) | 1-1 |
| *Replay* | Birmingham C | (a) | 2-1 |
| Fourth Round | Tottenham H | (h) | 2-1 |
| Fifth Round | Manchester C | (a) | 0-4 |

**Capital One Cup**

| | | | |
|---|---|---|---|
| First Round | Shrewsbury T | (h) | 4-0 |
| Second Round | Oxford U | (h) | 3-0 |
| Third Round | Everton | (h) | 2-1 |
| Fourth Round | Southampton | (h) | 3-0 |
| Quarter-Finals | Chelsea | (h) | 1-5 |

# LEICESTER CITY

## FOUNDATION

In 1884 a number of young footballers, who were mostly old boys of Wyggeston School, held a meeting at a house on the Roman Fosse Way and formed Leicester Fosse FC. They collected 9d (less than 4p) towards the cost of a ball, plus the same amount for membership. Their first professional, Harry Webb from Stafford Rangers, was signed in 1888 for 2s 6d (12p) per week, plus travelling expenses.

*King Power Stadium, Filbert Way, Leicester LE2 7FL.*

*Telephone:* (0844) 815 5000.

*Fax:* (0116) 247 0585.

*Ticket Office:* (0844) 815 5000.

*Website:* www.lcfc.co.uk

*Email:* sales@lcfc.co.uk

*Ground Capacity:* 32,312.

*Record Attendance:* 47,298 v Tottenham H, FA Cup 5th rd, 18 February 1928 (at Filbert Street); 32,148 v Manchester U, FA Premier League, 26 December 2003 (at Walkers Stadium).

*Pitch Measurements:* 100m × 69m (110yd × 76yd)

*Chairman:* Khun Vichai Srivaddhanaprabha.

*Chief Executive:* Susan Whelan.

*Manager:* Nigel Pearson.

*Assistant Managers:* Craig Shakespeare and Steve Walsh.

*Physio:* Dave Rennie.

*Colours:* Blue shirts with white trim, white shorts, blue socks with white trim.

*Year Formed:* 1884.

*Turned Professional:* 1888.

*Previous Name:* 1884, Leicester Fosse; 1919, Leicester City.

*Club Nickname:* 'The Foxes'.

*Grounds:* 1884, Victoria Park; 1887, Belgrave Road; 1888, Victoria Park; 1891, Filbert Street; 2002, Walkers Stadium (now known as King Power Stadium from 2011).

*First Football League Game:* 1 September 1894, Division 2, v Grimsby T (a) L 3–4 – Thraves; Smith, Bailey; Seymour, Brown, Henrys; Hill, Hughes, McArthur (1), Skea (2), Priestman.

*Record League Victory:* 10–0 v Portsmouth, Division 1, 20 October 1928 – McLaren; Black, Brown; Findlay, Carr, Watson; Adcock, Hine (3), Chandler (6), Lochhead, Barry (1).

*Record Cup Victory:* 8–1 v Coventry C (a), League Cup 5th rd, 1 December 1964 – Banks; Sjoberg, Norman (2); Roberts, King, McDerment; Hodgson (2), Cross, Goodfellow, Gibson (1), Stringfellow (2), (1 og).

## HONOURS

**Football League – Division 1:**
*Runners-up* 1928–29, 2002–03;
**Division 2:** *Champions* 1924–25, 1936–37, 1953–54, 1956–57, 1970–71, 1979–80; *Runners-up* 1907–08;
**FL 1:** *Champions* 2008–09.
**FA Cup:** *Runners-up* 1949, 1961, 1963, 1969.
**Football League Cup:** *Winners* 1964, 1997, 2000; *Runners-up* 1965, 1999.
**European Competitions**
**European Cup-Winners' Cup:** 1961–62.
**UEFA Cup:** 1997–98, 2000–01.

## sky SPORTS FACT FILE

Division Two champions Leicester City were invited to play Division One runners-up Liverpool for the FA Charity Shield in August 1971 after the previous season's double winners Arsenal declined an invitation. The Foxes won 1-0 with a goal from Steve Whitworth.

**Record Defeat:** 0–12 (as Leicester Fosse) v Nottingham F, Division 1, 21 April 1909.

**Most League Points (2 for a win):** 61, Division 2, 1956–57.

**Most League Points (3 for a win):** 96, FL 1, 2008–09.

**Most League Goals:** 109, Division 2, 1956–57.

**Highest League Scorer in Season:** Arthur Rowley, 44, Division 2, 1956–57.

**Most League Goals in Total Aggregate:** Arthur Chandler, 259, 1923–35.

**Most League Goals in One Match:** 6, John Duncan v Port Vale, Division 2, 25 December 1924; 6, Arthur Chandler v Portsmouth, Division 1, 20 October 1928.

**Most Capped Player:** John O'Neill, 39, Northern Ireland.

**Most League Appearances:** Adam Black, 528, 1920–35.

**Youngest League Player:** Dave Buchanan, 16 years 192 days v Oldham Ath, 1 January 1979.

**Record Transfer Fee Received:** £11,000,000 from Liverpool for Emile Heskey, March 2000.

**Record Transfer Fee Paid:** £5,000,000 to Wolverhampton W for Ade Akinbiyi, July 2000.

**Football League Record:** 1894 Elected to Division 2; 1908–09 Division 1; 1909–25 Division 2; 1925–35 Division 1; 1935–37 Division 2; 1937–39 Division 1; 1946–54 Division 2; 1954–55 Division 1; 1955–57 Division 2; 1957–69 Division 1; 1969–71 Division 2; 1971–78 Division 1; 1978–80 Division 2; 1980–81 Division 1; 1981–83 Division 2; 1983–87 Division 1; 1987–92 Division 2; 1992–94 Division 1; 1994–95 FA Premier League; 1995–96 Division 1; 1996–2002 FA Premier League; 2002–03 Division 1; 2003–04 FA Premier League; 2004–08 FL C; 2008–09 FL 1; 2009– FL C.

## LATEST SEQUENCES

**Longest Sequence of League Wins:** 7, 28.2.1993 – 27.3.1993.

**Longest Sequence of League Defeats:** 8, 17.3.2001 – 28.4.2001.

**Longest Sequence of League Draws:** 6, 21.8.1976 – 18.9.1976.

**Longest Sequence of Unbeaten League Matches:** 23, 1.11.2008 – 7.3.2009.

**Longest Sequence Without a League Win:** 18, 12.4.1975 – 1.11.1975.

**Successive Scoring Runs:** 31 from 12.11.1932.

**Successive Non-scoring Runs:** 7 from 21.11.1987.

### MANAGERS

Frank Gardner 1884–92
Ernest Marson 1892–94
J. Lee 1894–95
Henry Jackson 1895–97
William Clark 1897–98
George Johnson 1898–1912
Jack Bartlett 1912–14
Louis Ford 1914–15
Harry Linney 1915–19
Peter Hodge 1919–26
Willie Orr 1926–32
Peter Hodge 1932–34
Arthur Lochhead 1934–36
Frank Womack 1936–39
Tom Bromilow 1939–45
Tom Mather 1945–46
John Duncan 1946–49
Norman Bullock 1949–55
David Halliday 1955–58
Matt Gillies 1958–68
Frank O'Farrell 1968–71
Jimmy Bloomfield 1971–77
Frank McLintock 1977–78
Jock Wallace 1978–82
Gordon Milne 1982–86
Bryan Hamilton 1986–87
David Pleat 1987–91
Gordon Lee 1991
Brian Little 1991–94
Mark McGhee 1994–95
Martin O'Neill 1995–2000
Peter Taylor 2000–01
Dave Bassett 2001–02
Micky Adams 2002–04
Craig Levein 2004–06
Robert Kelly 2006–07
Martin Allen 2007
Gary Megson 2007
Ian Holloway 2007–08
Nigel Pearson 2008–10
Paulo Sousa 2010
Sven-Göran Eriksson 2010–11
Nigel Pearson November 2011–

### TEN YEAR LEAGUE RECORD

| | | P | W | D | L | F | A | Pts | Pos |
|---|---|---|---|---|---|---|---|---|---|
| 2003-04 | PR Lge | 38 | 6 | 15 | 17 | 48 | 65 | 33 | 18 |
| 2004-05 | FL C | 46 | 12 | 21 | 13 | 49 | 46 | 57 | 15 |
| 2005-06 | FL C | 46 | 13 | 15 | 18 | 51 | 59 | 54 | 16 |
| 2006-07 | FL C | 46 | 13 | 14 | 19 | 49 | 64 | 53 | 19 |
| 2007-08 | FL C | 46 | 12 | 16 | 18 | 42 | 45 | 52 | 22 |
| 2008-09 | FL 1 | 46 | 27 | 15 | 4 | 84 | 39 | 96 | 1 |
| 2009-10 | FL C | 46 | 21 | 13 | 12 | 61 | 45 | 76 | 5 |
| 2010-11 | FL C | 46 | 19 | 10 | 17 | 76 | 71 | 67 | 10 |
| 2011-12 | FL C | 46 | 18 | 12 | 16 | 66 | 55 | 66 | 9 |
| 2012-13 | FL C | 46 | 19 | 11 | 16 | 71 | 48 | 68 | 6 |

### DID YOU KNOW

Ken Keyworth hit a hat-trick in six minutes for Leicester City against Manchester United at Filbert Street on 16 April 1963. The Foxes won 4-3 to go top of the Division One table, but finished the season in fourth position.

## LEICESTER CITY – FL CHAMPIONSHIP 2012–13 LEAGUE RECORD

| Match No. | Date | | Venue | Opponents | Result | H/T Score | Lg Pos. | Goalscorers | Attendance |
|---|---|---|---|---|---|---|---|---|---|
| 1 | Aug | 18 | H | Peterborough U | W 2-0 | 0-0 | 3 | Morgan [51], King [75] | 23,863 |
| 2 | | 21 | A | Charlton Ath | L 1-2 | 0-2 | 9 | King [53] | 16,658 |
| 3 | | 25 | A | Blackburn R | L 1-2 | 0-1 | 17 | Vardy [55] | 13,935 |
| 4 | Sept | 1 | H | Blackpool | W 1-0 | 0-0 | 9 | Marshall (pen) [54] | 18,655 |
| 5 | | 16 | A | Wolverhampton W | L 1-2 | 0-2 | 16 | Konchesky [70] | 20,030 |
| 6 | | 19 | H | Burnley | W 2-1 | 0-1 | 10 | Nugent [47], Vardy [57] | 18,480 |
| 7 | | 23 | H | Hull C | W 3-1 | 2-1 | 7 | Nugent 3 [7, 42, 90] | 20,815 |
| 8 | | 29 | A | Middlesbrough | W 2-1 | 0-0 | 5 | Vardy [62], Dyer [89] | 15,679 |
| 9 | Oct | 2 | A | Huddersfield T | W 2-0 | 1-0 | 2 | Knockaert 2 [30, 60] | 13,821 |
| 10 | | 6 | H | Bristol C | W 2-0 | 1-0 | 2 | Nugent [19], Foster (og) [74] | 22,529 |
| 11 | | 20 | A | Birmingham C | D 1-1 | 0-1 | 1 | Marshall [86] | 18,271 |
| 12 | | 23 | H | Brighton & HA | W 1-0 | 1-0 | 1 | King [10] | 25,726 |
| 13 | | 27 | H | Crystal Palace | L 1-2 | 0-2 | 2 | King [90] | 23,646 |
| 14 | Nov | 3 | A | Watford | L 1-2 | 0-1 | 4 | Nugent [71] | 12,954 |
| 15 | | 6 | A | Bolton W | D 0-0 | 0-0 | 5 | | 16,754 |
| 16 | | 10 | H | Nottingham F | D 2-2 | 2-1 | 5 | Ward (og) [7], Nugent [32] | 24,793 |
| 17 | | 17 | H | Ipswich T | W 6-0 | 4-0 | 5 | Nugent 2 (1 pen) [8 ipl, 17], Dyer [27], Knockaert [44], Waghorn [53], Futacs [82] | 20,779 |
| 18 | | 24 | A | Sheffield W | W 2-0 | 1-0 | 3 | Drinkwater [41], Marshall [76] | 24,664 |
| 19 | | 27 | A | Leeds U | L 0-1 | 0-1 | 4 | | 17,717 |
| 20 | Dec | 1 | H | Derby Co | W 4-1 | 2-1 | 3 | Whitbread [6], Waghorn [23], Nugent 2 [74, 89] | 20,680 |
| 21 | | 8 | H | Barnsley | D 2-2 | 1-2 | 5 | Knockaert [9], Vardy [90] | 23,579 |
| 22 | | 15 | A | Millwall | L 0-1 | 0-0 | 5 | | 10,189 |
| 23 | | 22 | H | Cardiff C | L 0-1 | 0-1 | 5 | | 25,055 |
| 24 | | 26 | A | Hull C | D 0-0 | 0-0 | 5 | | 20,321 |
| 25 | | 29 | A | Burnley | W 1-0 | 1-0 | 5 | Nugent [31] | 13,050 |
| 26 | Jan | 1 | H | Huddersfield T | W 6-1 | 3-0 | 5 | Wood 2 [6, 24], De Laet [45], Knockaert 2 [49, 51], Waghorn [76] | 25,913 |
| 27 | | 12 | A | Bristol C | W 4-0 | 3-0 | 3 | Wood 3 [11, 18, 41], James [49] | 13,078 |
| 28 | | 18 | H | Middlesbrough | W 1-0 | 0-0 | 2 | Nugent [70] | 8585 |
| 29 | | 31 | H | Wolverhampton W | W 2-1 | 1-0 | 2 | Knockaert [24], Nugent [73] | 21,677 |
| 30 | Feb | 9 | A | Peterborough U | L 1-2 | 0-0 | 2 | Marshall [52] | 11,070 |
| 31 | | 19 | H | Charlton Ath | L 1-2 | 0-1 | 5 | Wood [69] | 19,920 |
| 32 | | 23 | A | Blackpool | D 0-0 | 0-0 | 5 | | 14,509 |
| 33 | | 26 | H | Blackburn R | W 3-0 | 2-0 | 5 | Wood [29], Kane [42], King [90] | 19,561 |
| 34 | Mar | 2 | A | Ipswich T | L 0-1 | 0-0 | 5 | | 17,021 |
| 35 | | 5 | H | Leeds U | D 1-1 | 0-0 | 5 | Keane [90] | 22,660 |
| 36 | | 9 | A | Sheffield W | L 0-1 | 0-0 | 5 | | 24,883 |
| 37 | | 12 | A | Cardiff C | D 1-1 | 0-0 | 5 | Keane [72] | 23,231 |
| 38 | | 16 | A | Derby Co | L 1-2 | 0-2 | 6 | Schlupp [62] | 23,123 |
| 39 | | 29 | H | Millwall | L 0-1 | 0-0 | 6 | | 22,365 |
| 40 | Apr | 1 | A | Barnsley | L 0-2 | 0-2 | 7 | | 10,429 |
| 41 | | 6 | A | Brighton & HA | D 1-1 | 0-0 | 7 | James [73] | 28,493 |
| 42 | | 12 | H | Birmingham C | D 2-2 | 1-0 | 7 | Davies (og) [12], Schlupp [75] | 25,554 |
| 43 | | 16 | H | Bolton W | W 3-2 | 2-1 | 6 | Wood (pen) [39], Dyer [41], Schlupp [79] | 22,442 |
| 44 | | 20 | A | Crystal Palace | D 2-2 | 1-1 | 7 | King [37], Wood [73] | 18,563 |
| 45 | | 26 | H | Watford | L 1-2 | 0-2 | 7 | Kane [61] | 25,091 |
| 46 | May | 4 | A | Nottingham F | W 3-2 | 2-1 | 6 | James [24], King [43], Knockaert [90] | 28,646 |

**Final League Position: 6**

### GOALSCORERS

*League (71):* Nugent 14 (1 pen), Wood 9 (1 pen), Knockaert 8, King 7, Marshall 4 (1 pen), Vardy 4, Dyer 3, James 3, Schlupp 3, Waghorn 3, Kane 2, Keane 2, De Laet 1, Drinkwater 1, Futacs 1, Konchesky 1, Morgan 1, Whitbread 1, own goals 3.
*FA Cup (4):* Wood 2, De Leat 1, Keane 1.
*Capital One Cup (6):* Dyer 1, Futacs 1, James 1, Knockaert 1, Marshall 1, Vardy 1.
*Championship Play-Offs (2):* Nugent 2.

| Schmeichel K 46 | De Laet R 39 + 2 | Moore L 10 + 6 | Morgan W 45 | Konchesky P 39 | Marshall B 24 + 16 | Drinkwater D 41 + 1 | James M 20 + 4 | Dyer L 27 + 15 | Beckford J 2 + 2 | Vardy J 17 + 9 | King A 35 + 7 | Knockaert A 33 + 9 | Nugent D 36 + 6 | Danns N — + 1 | St. Ledger S 8 + 1 | Schlupp J 13 + 6 | Waghorn M 9 + 15 | Futacs M — + 9 | Whitbread Z 14 + 2 | Keane M 22 | Lingard J — + 5 | Gallagher P — + 8 | Wood C 19 + 1 | Kane H 5 + 8 | Wellens R 2 | Match No. |
|---|---|---|---|---|---|---|---|---|---|---|---|---|---|---|---|---|---|---|---|---|---|---|---|---|---|---|
| 1 | 2 | 3 | 4 | 5 | 6 | 7 | 8¹ | 9² | 10³ | 11 | 12 | 13 | 14 | | | | | | | | | | | | | 1 |
| 1 | 2 | 3 | 4 | 5 | 6³ | 8 | 7² | 9 | 10¹ | 11 | 12 | 14 | 13 | | | | | | | | | | | | | 2 |
| 1 | 2 | 4 | 3 | 5 | 6³ | 8² | | 9¹ | 14 | 10 | 7 | 12 | 11 | 13 | | | | | | | | | | | | 3 |
| 1 | | 4 | 3 | 5 | 6² | 7 | | 9³ | 14 | 10 | 8 | 13 | 11 | | 2¹ | 12 | | | | | | | | | | 4 |
| 1 | 2 | 4 | 3 | 5 | 6 | 7 | 12 | 9² | | 11³ | 8¹ | 13 | 10 | | | | 14 | | | | | | | | | 5 |
| 1 | 2 | | 5 | 3 | 6¹ | 4 | 9 | 13 | | 7² | | 10 | 11³ | | 8 | 12 | 14 | | | | | | | | | 6 |
| 1 | 2 | | 4 | 5 | 6³ | 7 | 8¹ | 14 | | 10² | 12 | 9 | 11 | | 3 | 13 | | | | | | | | | | 7 |
| 1 | 2¹ | 12 | 5 | 3 | 9³ | 7 | 8² | 14 | | 10 | 13 | 6 | 11 | | 4 | | | | | | | | | | | 8 |
| 1 | 2 | 3 | 5 | 14 | 8 | | 9¹ | | | 11² | 7 | 6³ | 10 | | 4 | 12 | 13 | | | | | | | | | 9 |
| 1 | 12 | 5 | 4 | 2¹ | 13 | 8 | | 7 | | 10² | 6 | 9 | 11 | | 3³ | | | | 14 | | | | | | | 10 |
| 1 | 2 | | 5 | 3 | 13 | 8 | | 9¹ | | 12 | 7 | 6³ | 11 | | | | 10² | 14 | | 4 | | | | | | 11 |
| 1 | 2¹ | 12 | 3 | 5 | 14 | 8 | | 9 | | 13 | 7 | 6 | 11² | | | | 10³ | | | 4 | | | | | | 12 |
| 1 | 4 | | 3 | 5 | 13 | 7² | 12 | 9¹ | | 10 | 8 | 6³ | 11 | | 14 | | | | | 2 | | | | | | 13 |
| 1 | 2 | 3 | 5 | 9² | 6¹ | 8 | 12 | | | 7 | 10³ | 11 | | | | 14 | 13 | | | 4³ | | | | | | 14 |
| 1 | 2 | 13 | 3 | 5¹ | | 7 | | 9 | | | 8 | 6 | 10 | | | 12 | 11³ | | | | 4² | 14 | | | | 15 |
| 1 | 2 | | 3 | | 13 | 8 | | 9 | | | 7 | 6² | 11¹ | | | 5 | 10 | | | 4 | | 12 | | | | 16 |
| 1 | 2 | 4 | | | 13 | 5 | | 9 | | 12 | 6 | 8² | 10¹ | | | 7 | 11³ | 14 | | 3 | | | | | | 17 |
| 1 | 2 | 4 | | | 6² | 3 | | 9 | | 10¹ | 8 | 13 | | | | 5 | 11³ | 12 | 7 | | | 14 | | | | 18 |
| 1 | 2 | | 3 | | 6² | 8 | | 9 | | 10¹ | 7 | 13 | | | | 5 | 11³ | 12 | 4 | | | 14 | | | | 19 |
| 1 | 2 | | 3 | 5 | 13 | 7 | 14 | 9² | | 11¹ | 8 | 6³ | 12 | | | 10 | | | 4 | | | | | | | 20 |
| 1 | 2 | | 3 | 5 | 12 | 8 | | 9³ | | 13 | 7 | 6¹ | 10 | | | | 11² | 14 | 4 | | | | | | | 21 |
| 1 | 2 | | 3 | 5 | 12 | 8 | 14 | 9³ | | 10 | 7² | 6¹ | 11 | | | | | 13 | 4 | | | | | | | 22 |
| 1 | 5 | | 3 | 2 | 13 | 8 | | 6³ | | 11 | 7 | 9² | 10 | | | 12 | | | | 4 | 14 | | | | | 23 |
| 1 | 2¹ | 12 | 4 | 5 | 8 | 6 | 10 | | | 9³ | 7 | 11² | | | | 13 | | | 3 | | 14 | | | | | 24 |
| 1 | 2 | 4 | 3 | 5 | 8 | 7 | 6 | 10² | | 9¹ | 11³ | | | | | 12 | 14 | | | | | 13 | | | | 25 |
| 1 | 5 | | 4 | 3 | 6² | 7 | 8 | 13 | | 9³ | 12 | 10¹ | | | | | | | 2 | | 14 | 11 | | | | 26 |
| 1 | 2 | | 3 | 5 | 9³ | 7 | 8 | 12 | | | | 6¹ | | | | 13 | | | 4 | | 14 | 10² | | | | 27 |
| 1 | 2 | | 3 | 5 | 9² | 7 | 8 | 12 | 14 | 13 | | 6¹ | 10³ | | | | | | 4 | | | 11 | | | | 28 |
| 1 | 2 | | 3 | 5 | 9¹ | 8 | | 12 | | 13 | 7 | 6² | 11³ | | | | | 14 | | | | 10 | | | | 29 |
| 1 | 2 | 4 | | 5 | 9² | 8 | | 13 | | 10¹ | 6 | 7 | 11 | | | | 12 | | | 3 | | | | | | 30 |
| 1 | 2 | 4 | | 5 | 9² | 7 | 8³ | 13 | | 14 | 6¹ | 10 | | | | | | | | 3 | 12 | 11 | | | | 31 |
| 1 | 2 | 4 | | 5 | 6² | 8 | | 12 | | 14 | 7 | 13 | 10¹ | | | | | | | 3 | | 11 | 9³ | | | 32 |
| 1 | 2 | 4 | | 5 | 6 | 7 | | 12 | 13 | 8 | 9¹ | | | | | | | | | 3 | | 11³ | 10² | | | 33 |
| 1 | 2 | | 3 | 5 | 6² | 7 | | 12 | | | 8 | 9¹ | | | | | | | | 4 | 13 | 11 | 10 | | | 34 |
| 1 | 2 | 4 | | 5¹ | 13 | 6 | | 12 | | 7 | 8² | 9³ | | | | 14 | | | | 3 | | 11 | 10 | | | 35 |
| 1 | 2³ | 4 | | | 6² | 8 | | | | 7 | 12 | 10 | | 14 | 5 | | | | | 3 | 13 | 11 | 9¹ | | | 36 |
| 1 | | 3 | | | | 7 | | 6 | 13 | 8 | | 10² | | 2 | 5 | 14 | | | | 4 | 11³ | 12 | | 9¹ | | 37 |
| 1 | | 3 | 5 | 13 | 8 | | 11² | 7 | | 10 | | | | 2 | 12 | | | | | 4 | | 9³ | 14 | 6¹ | | 38 |
| 1 | 2 | | 3⁴ | 5 | | 8¹ | 7 | | | 12 | 6 | 10 | | | 9 | | | | | 4 | | 11² | 13 | | | 39 |
| 1 | 2¹ | 12 | | 5 | 13 | | 7 | 9 | | 8 | 6² | 11 | | | | 14 | | | 4 | 3 | | 10³ | | | | 40 |
| 1 | 12 | 2 | 3 | 5 | 6¹ | 7 | 8 | | | 11 | | 10³ | | | 9² | | | | | 4 | | 13 | 14 | | | 41 |
| 1 | 2 | | 3 | 5 | | 7¹ | 8 | 12 | | 6 | | 10 | | | 9 | | | | | 3 | | 11² | 13 | | | 42 |
| 1 | 2 | | 3 | 5 | | 13 | 8 | 9¹ | | 7 | 6² | 12 | | | 10³ | | | | 14 | 4 | | 11 | | | | 43 |
| 1 | 2 | | 3 | 5 | | | 8 | 9² | | 7 | 6³ | 12 | | | 10¹ | | | | | 4 | 13 | 11 | 14 | | | 44 |
| 1 | 2 | 4 | 3 | | 14 | | 8 | 6² | | 5 | 10³ | 12 | | | 9¹ | | | | | 7 | | 11 | 13 | | | 45 |
| 1 | 2¹ | 12 | 3 | | 14 | | 7 | 9² | | 8 | 6 | 10 | | | 5 | | | | | 4³ | | 11 | 13 | | | 46 |

**FA Cup**

| | | | |
|---|---|---|---|
| Third Round | Burton | (h) | 2-0 |
| Fourth Round | Huddersfield T | (a) | 1-1 |
| *Replay* | Huddersfield T | (h) | 1-2 |

**Capital One Cup**

| | | | |
|---|---|---|---|
| First Round | Torquay U | (a) | 4-0 |
| Second Round | Burton | (h) | 2-4 |

**Championship Play-Offs**

| | | | |
|---|---|---|---|
| Semi-Finals | Watford | (h) | 1-0 |
| | Watford | (a) | 1-3 |

# LEYTON ORIENT

## FOUNDATION

There is some doubt about the foundation of Leyton Orient, and, indeed, some confusion with clubs like Leyton and Clapton over their early history. As regards the foundation, the most favoured version is that Leyton Orient was formed originally by members of Homerton Theological College who established Glyn Cricket Club in 1881 and then carried on through the following winter playing football. Eventually many employees of the Orient Shipping Line became involved and so the name Orient was chosen in 1888.

*Matchroom Stadium, Brisbane Road, Leyton, London E10 5NF.*

*Telephone:* (0871) 310 1881.

*Fax:* (0871) 310 1882.

*Ticket Office:* (0871) 310 1883.

*Website:* www.leytonorient.com

*Email:* info@leytonorient.net

*Ground Capacity:* 9,311.

*Record Attendance:* 34,345 v West Ham U, FA Cup 4th rd, 25 January 1964.

*Pitch Measurements:* 105m × 73m (115yd × 80yd)

*Chairman:* Barry Hearn.

*Chief Executive:* Matthew Porter.

*Manager:* Russell Slade.

*Assistant Manager:* Kevin Nugent.

*Physio:* Nick Dawes.

*Colours:* Red shirts with white insert and striped sleeves, red shorts, red socks with white trim.

*Year Formed:* 1881.

*Turned Professional:* 1903.

*Previous Names:* 1881, Glyn Cricket and Football Club; 1886, Eagle Football Club; 1888, Orient Football Club; 1898, Clapton Orient; 1946, Leyton Orient; 1966, Orient; 1987, Leyton Orient.

*Club Nickname:* 'The O's'.

*Grounds:* 1884, Glyn Road; 1896, Whittles Athletic Ground; 1900, Millfields Road; 1930, Lea Bridge Road; 1937, Brisbane Road.

*First Football League Game:* 2 September 1905, Division 2, v Leicester Fosse (a) L 1–2 – Butler; Holmes, Codling; Lamberton, Boden, Boyle; Kingaby (1), Wootten, Leigh, Evenson, Bourne.

*Record League Victory:* 8–0 v Crystal Palace, Division 3 (S), 12 November 1955 – Welton; Lee, Earl; Blizzard, Aldous, McKnight; White (1), Facey (3), Burgess (2), Heckman, Hartburn (2). 8–0 v Rochdale, Division 4, 20 October 1987 – Wells; Howard, Dickenson (1), Smalley (1), Day, Hull, Hales (2), Castle (Sussex), Shinners (2), Godfrey (Harvey), Comfort (2). 8–0 v Colchester U, Division 4, 15 October 1988 – Wells; Howard, Dickenson, Hales (1p), Day (1), Sitton (1), Baker (1), Ward, Hull (3), Juryeff, Comfort (1). 8–0 v Doncaster R, Division 3, 28 December 1997 – Hyde; Channing, Naylor, Smith (1p), Hicks, Clark, Ling, Roger Joseph, Griffiths (3) (Harris), Richards (2) (Baker (1)), Inglethorpe (1) (Simpson).

## HONOURS

**Football League – Division 1:** 22nd, 1962–63;

**Division 2:** *Runners-up* 1961–62;

**Division 3:** *Champions* 1969–70;

**Division 3 (S):** *Champions* 1955–56; *Runners-up* 1954–55.

**FA Cup:** Semi-final 1978.

**Football League Cup:** Best season: 5th rd, 1963.

## sky SPORTS FACT FILE

Hubert Ashton played five games as a full back for Clapton Orient, as Leyton Orient were then known, in the 1926–27 season. An Essex county cricketer between 1921 and 1939, he was elected as Member of Parliament for Chelmsford in 1950 and held his seat until 1964 when he retired.

**Record Cup Victory:** 9–2 v Chester, League Cup 3rd rd, 15 October 1962 – Robertson; Charlton, Taylor; Gibbs, Bishop, Lea; Deeley (1), Waites (3), Dunmore (2), Graham (3), Wedge.

**Record Defeat:** 0–8 v Aston Villa, FA Cup 4th rd, 30 January 1929.

**Most League Points (2 for a win):** 66, Division 3 (S), 1955–56.

**Most League Points (3 for a win):** 81, FL 2, 2005–06.

**Most League Goals:** 106, Division 3 (S), 1955–56.

**Highest League Scorer in Season:** Tom Johnston, 35, Division 2, 1957–58.

**Most League Goals in Total Aggregate:** Tom Johnston, 121, 1956–58, 1959–61.

**Most League Goals in One Match:** 4, Wally Leigh v Bradford C, Division 2, 13 April 1906; 4, Albert Pape v Oldham Ath, Division 2, 1 September 1924; 4, Peter Kitchen v Millwall, Division 3, 21 April 1984.

**Most Capped Players:** Tunji Banjo, 7 (7), Nigeria; John Chiedozie, 7 (9), Nigeria; Tony Grealish, 7 (45), Republic of Ireland.

**Most League Appearances:** Peter Allen, 432, 1965–78.

**Youngest League Player:** Paul Went, 15 years 327 days v Preston NE, 4 September 1965.

**Record Transfer Fee Received:** £1,000,000 from Fulham for Gabriel Zakuani, July 2006.

**Record Transfer Fee Paid:** £175,000 to Wigan Ath for Paul Beesley, October 1989.

**Football League Record:** 1905 Elected to Division 2; 1929–56 Division 3 (S); 1956–62 Division 2; 1962–63 Division 1; 1963–66 Division 2; 1966–70 Division 3; 1970–82 Division 2; 1982–85 Division 3; 1985–89 Division 4; 1989–92 Division 3; 1992–95 Division 2; 1995–2004 Division 3; 2004–06 FL 2; 2006– FL 1.

## LATEST SEQUENCES

**Longest Sequence of League Wins:** 10, 21.1.1956 – 30.3.1956.

**Longest Sequence of League Defeats:** 9, 1.4.1995 – 6.5.1995.

**Longest Sequence of League Draws:** 6, 30.11.1974 – 28.12.1974.

**Longest Sequence of Unbeaten League Matches:** 13, 30.10.1954 – 19.2.1955.

**Longest Sequence Without a League Win:** 23, 6.10.1962 – 13.4.1963.

**Successive Scoring Runs:** 24 from 3.5.2003.

**Successive Non-scoring Runs:** 8 from 19.11.1994.

## MANAGERS

Sam Omerod 1905–06
Ike Ivenson 1906
Billy Holmes 1907–22
Peter Proudfoot 1922–29
Arthur Grimsdell 1929–30
Peter Proudfoot 1930–31
Jimmy Seed 1931–33
David Pratt 1933–34
Peter Proudfoot 1935–39
Tom Halsey 1939
Bill Wright 1939–45
Willie Hall 1945
Bill Wright 1945–46
Charlie Hewitt 1946–48
Neil McBain 1948–49
Alec Stock 1949–59
Les Gore 1959–61
Johnny Carey 1961–63
Benny Fenton 1963–64
Dave Sexton 1965
Dick Graham 1966–68
Jimmy Bloomfield 1968–71
George Petchey 1971–77
Jimmy Bloomfield 1977–81
Paul Went 1981
Ken Knighton 1981–83
Frank Clark 1983–91
  *(Managing Director)*
Peter Eustace 1991–94
Chris Turner/John Sitton 1994–95
Pat Holland 1995–96
Tommy Taylor 1996–2001
Paul Brush 2001–03
Martin Ling 2003–09
Geraint Williams 2009–10
Russell Slade April 2010–

## TEN YEAR LEAGUE RECORD

|  |  | P | W | D | L | F | A | Pts | Pos |
|---|---|---|---|---|---|---|---|---|---|
| 2003-04 | Div 3 | 46 | 13 | 14 | 19 | 48 | 65 | 53 | 19 |
| 2004-05 | FL 2 | 46 | 16 | 15 | 15 | 65 | 67 | 63 | 11 |
| 2005-06 | FL 2 | 46 | 22 | 15 | 9 | 67 | 51 | 81 | 3 |
| 2006-07 | FL 1 | 46 | 12 | 15 | 19 | 61 | 77 | 51 | 20 |
| 2007-08 | FL 1 | 46 | 16 | 12 | 18 | 49 | 63 | 60 | 14 |
| 2008-09 | FL 1 | 46 | 15 | 11 | 20 | 45 | 57 | 56 | 14 |
| 2009-10 | FL 1 | 46 | 13 | 12 | 21 | 53 | 63 | 51 | 17 |
| 2010-11 | FL 1 | 46 | 19 | 13 | 14 | 71 | 62 | 70 | 7 |
| 2011-12 | FL 1 | 46 | 13 | 11 | 22 | 48 | 75 | 50 | 20 |
| 2012-13 | FL 1 | 46 | 21 | 8 | 17 | 55 | 48 | 71 | 7 |

## DID YOU KNOW ?

Winger Fred Le May played for Thames and Watford before joining Clapton Orient for the 1932–33 season. Fred, who made 10 appearances for the O's that season, was just five foot tall and is believed to be the smallest player to have appeared in the Football League.

## LEYTON ORIENT – FOOTBALL LEAGUE ONE 2012–13 LEAGUE RECORD

| Match No. | Date | Venue | Opponents | Result | H/T Score | Lg Pos. | Goalscorers | Attendance |
|---|---|---|---|---|---|---|---|---|
| 1 | Aug 18 | A | Tranmere R | L | 1-3 | 0-1 | 21 | Symes (pen) [88] | 5063 |
| 2 | 21 | H | Stevenage | L | 0-1 | 0-1 | 23 | | 3564 |
| 3 | Sept 1 | A | Crawley T | L | 0-1 | 0-0 | 23 | | 4287 |
| 4 | 8 | A | Swindon T | W | 1-0 | 0-0 | 20 | Cook [59] | 8072 |
| 5 | 13 | H | Brentford | W | 1-0 | 0-0 | 16 | Brunt [75] | 3333 |
| 6 | 18 | H | Yeovil T | W | 4-1 | 2-0 | 13 | Chorley [3], Brunt [24], Smith, Jimmy [71], Lisbie [79] | 2876 |
| 7 | 22 | A | Crewe Alex | D | 1-1 | 1-1 | 14 | Rowlands [19] | 5183 |
| 8 | 29 | H | Doncaster R | L | 0-2 | 0-2 | 14 | | 4401 |
| 9 | Oct 2 | A | Walsall | W | 2-1 | 2-0 | 12 | Cook [11], Cox [29] | 3281 |
| 10 | 6 | H | Sheffield U | L | 0-1 | 0-0 | 14 | | 4882 |
| 11 | 13 | A | Bournemouth | L | 0-2 | 0-0 | 16 | | 5715 |
| 12 | 16 | H | Hartlepool U | W | 1-0 | 0-0 | 12 | Brunt [47] | 2664 |
| 13 | 20 | A | Oldham Ath | L | 0-2 | 0-0 | 16 | | 3919 |
| 14 | 23 | H | Colchester U | L | 0-2 | 0-1 | 18 | | 3378 |
| 15 | 27 | A | Coventry C | L | 0-1 | 0-1 | 19 | | 4741 |
| 16 | Nov 7 | A | Milton Keynes D | L | 0-1 | 0-1 | 20 | | 6985 |
| 17 | 10 | H | Shrewsbury T | W | 2-1 | 1-0 | 16 | Lisbie 2 (1 pen) [33 (p), 88] | 3822 |
| 18 | 17 | A | Carlisle U | W | 4-1 | 4-1 | 15 | Mooney 2 [18, 44], Chorley [26], Cook [38] | 3964 |
| 19 | 20 | A | Portsmouth | W | 3-2 | 1-0 | 13 | Lisbie 2 (1 pen) [32, 62 (p)], Odubajo [51] | 9955 |
| 20 | 24 | H | Preston NE | W | 2-0 | 1-0 | 13 | Baudry [43], Lisbie [61] | 4190 |
| 21 | Dec 8 | A | Bury | W | 2-0 | 1-0 | 11 | Lisbie 2 [31, 56] | 2121 |
| 22 | 15 | H | Scunthorpe U | L | 1-3 | 0-0 | 12 | Lisbie (pen) [79] | 4942 |
| 23 | 29 | H | Walsall | W | 2-1 | 1-0 | 14 | Mooney [43], Odubajo [87] | 3865 |
| 24 | Jan 1 | A | Yeovil T | L | 0-3 | 0-1 | 15 | | 3516 |
| 25 | 12 | H | Crewe Alex | D | 1-1 | 1-1 | 14 | Cook [26] | 3755 |
| 26 | 19 | A | Doncaster R | L | 0-2 | 0-1 | 15 | | 6438 |
| 27 | 22 | A | Brentford | D | 2-2 | 1-2 | 15 | Rowlands [6], Cook [86] | 4523 |
| 28 | 26 | H | Notts Co | W | 2-1 | 0-0 | 15 | Mooney [65], Baudry [68] | 3578 |
| 29 | 29 | H | Swindon T | D | 0-0 | 0-0 | 15 | | 3536 |
| 30 | Feb 2 | A | Stevenage | W | 1-0 | 1-0 | 13 | Cox [10] | 3577 |
| 31 | 9 | H | Tranmere R | W | 2-1 | 1-0 | 10 | MacDonald [9], Rowlands [67] | 4351 |
| 32 | 16 | A | Hartlepool U | L | 1-2 | 1-0 | 10 | Rowlands (pen) [8] | 3773 |
| 33 | 23 | H | Crawley T | L | 0-1 | 0-1 | 13 | | 3463 |
| 34 | 26 | A | Sheffield U | D | 0-0 | 0-0 | 12 | | 16,540 |
| 35 | Mar 2 | H | Bournemouth | W | 3-1 | 1-0 | 11 | MacDonald 2 [26, 48], Lisbie [79] | 5136 |
| 36 | 6 | A | Notts Co | D | 1-1 | 0-1 | 11 | Lisbie (pen) [66] | 4004 |
| 37 | 9 | A | Shrewsbury T | W | 2-0 | 1-0 | 11 | Baudry [33], Lisbie (pen) [52] | 5274 |
| 38 | 12 | H | Portsmouth | W | 1-0 | 0-0 | 10 | Batt [57] | 3641 |
| 39 | 16 | H | Carlisle U | W | 4-1 | 2-0 | 10 | Vincelot [32], Batt [45], Lisbie (pen) [69], Cox [89] | 4387 |
| 40 | 23 | A | Preston NE | D | 0-0 | 0-0 | 9 | | 8405 |
| 41 | 29 | A | Scunthorpe U | L | 1-2 | 1-2 | 9 | Lisbie [45] | 3052 |
| 42 | Apr 1 | H | Bury | W | 2-0 | 2-0 | 9 | Smith, Jimmy [9], Mooney [34] | 3713 |
| 43 | 6 | A | Colchester U | L | 1-2 | 1-2 | 9 | Lisbie [37] | 4704 |
| 44 | 13 | H | Milton Keynes D | W | 2-0 | 0-0 | 8 | Sawyer [81], Lisbie [90] | 4634 |
| 45 | 20 | A | Coventry C | W | 1-0 | 1-0 | 7 | Cox [45] | 11,234 |
| 46 | 27 | H | Oldham Ath | D | 1-1 | 1-0 | 7 | Smith, Jimmy [10] | 5191 |

**Final League Position: 7**

### GOALSCORERS

*League (55):* Lisbie 16 (6 pens), Cook 5, Mooney 5, Cox 4, Rowlands 4 (1 pen), Baudry 3, Brunt 3, MacDonald 3, Smith, Jimmy 3, Batt 2, Chorley 2, Odubajo 2, Sawyer 1, Symes 1 (1 pen), Vincelot 1.
*FA Cup (8):* Cox 4, Mooney 4.
*Capital One Cup (1):* Baudry 1.
*Johnstone's Paint Trophy (7):* Mooney 4, Batt 1, Odubajo 1, Symes 1 (1 pen).

| Jones J 26 | James L 26+2 | Cuthbert S 16+2 | Clarke N 32+2 | Sawyer G 34 | Baudry M 22+2 | Smith Jimmy 21+14 | Griffith A 16+5 | Cox D 39+5 | Mooney D 22+10 | Lisbie K 23+5 | Chorley B 27+1 | Symes M 5+8 | Brunt R 8+10 | Odubajo M 34+10 | Obafemi A —+8 | Allsop R 20 | McSweeney L 29+3 | Rowlands M 31+2 | Cook L 30+8 | Laird M —+1 | Wagstaff S 6+1 | Smith A —+2 | MacDonald C 17+3 | Azeez A 1 | Omozusi E 1+5 | Batt S 7+4 | Vincelot R 13+2 | Lee H —+1 | Match No. |
|---|---|---|---|---|---|---|---|---|---|---|---|---|---|---|---|---|---|---|---|---|---|---|---|---|---|---|---|---|---|
| 1 | 2 | 3¹ | 4 | 5 | 6 | 7 | 8 | 9 | 10³ | 11² | 12 | 13 | 14 |  |  |  |  |  |  |  |  |  |  |  |  |  |  |  | 1 |
| 1 | 2 |  | 4 | 5 | 6 | 9¹ | 7 | 8 | 11² |  | 3 | 10 |  | 12 | 13 |  |  |  |  |  |  |  |  |  |  |  |  |  | 2 |
|  |  |  | 4 | 5 | 14 |  | 8 | 9 | 12 | 13 | 3 | 11 |  | 6² |  | 1 | 2 | 7³ | 10¹ |  |  |  |  |  |  |  |  |  | 3 |
|  |  | 3 |  | 5 |  |  | 8 | 9 | 10 |  | 4 | 11¹ |  | 12 | 13 | 1 | 2 | 6 | 7² |  |  |  |  |  |  |  |  |  | 4 |
|  |  |  | 4 | 5 | 14 | 7 | 6 | 10 |  |  | 3 | 11¹ |  | 12 | 13 | 1 | 2 | 8³ | 9² |  |  |  |  |  |  |  |  |  | 5 |
|  |  |  | 4 | 5 |  | 8 | 7 | 6 | 13 | 10³ | 3 | 11² |  | 12 | 14 | 1 | 2 | 9¹ |  |  |  |  |  |  |  |  |  |  | 6 |
|  |  |  | 4 | 5 | 12 | 7⁴ | 6 | 10 |  |  | 3 | 13 | 11² |  | 14 | 1 | 2 | 8¹ | 9³ |  |  |  |  |  |  |  |  |  | 7 |
|  |  |  | 4 | 5 |  | 7¹ | 8 | 6 | 13 | 10 | 3 | 11² |  |  | 14 | 1 | 2 | 9³ | 12 |  |  |  |  |  |  |  |  |  | 8 |
|  |  |  | 4 | 5 | 14 |  | 6 | 8 | 7³ | 11 | 3 | 13 |  |  | 12 | 1 | 2 | 9² | 10¹ |  |  |  |  |  |  |  |  |  | 9 |
|  | 14 |  | 4 | 5 |  |  | 6¹ | 7 | 10 | 11² | 3 |  |  | 12 | 13 | 1 | 2 | 8³ | 9 |  |  |  |  |  |  |  |  |  | 10 |
|  |  |  | 4 | 5 |  | 7 | 6 | 14 |  |  | 3 | 10² | 13 | 12 |  | 1 | 2 | 8 | 9¹ |  |  |  | 11³ |  |  |  |  |  | 11 |
|  |  |  | 4 | 5 |  | 7 | 12 | 9 |  |  | 3 | 10 |  | 6¹ |  | 1 | 2 | 8 |  |  |  |  | 11 |  |  |  |  |  | 12 |
|  |  |  | 4 | 5 |  | 7 |  | 9 | 12 |  | 3 | 13 | 11² | 6¹ |  | 1 | 2 | 8 |  |  |  |  | 10 |  |  |  |  |  | 13 |
|  |  | 3 |  | 5 |  | 7 |  | 9² | 12 |  | 4 | 10¹ |  | 6 |  | 1 | 2 | 8 | 13 |  |  |  | 11 |  |  |  |  |  | 14 |
|  |  |  | 4 | 5 |  |  | 8 | 2¹ | 11 |  | 3 | 13 | 10² | 6 |  | 1 |  | 7 | 12 |  |  |  | 9 |  |  |  |  |  | 15 |
| 8 |  | 3 |  | 5 | 14 |  |  | 9² | 13 | 11 | 12 | 4 |  |  |  | 1 | 2 | 6² | 10 |  | 7¹ |  |  |  |  |  |  |  | 16 |
| 7 |  |  | 4 | 5 |  |  | 6² | 13 | 11¹ | 10 | 3 |  |  | 12 |  | 1 | 2 | 8 | 9³ |  | 14 |  |  |  |  |  |  |  | 17 |
| 9¹ |  | 3 | 2 |  | 14 |  | 12 | 6³ | 11 | 10² | 4 |  |  |  | 13 | 1 | 5 | 8 | 7 |  |  |  |  |  |  |  |  |  | 18 |
| 9 |  | 3¹ | 2 |  | 12 |  | 13 | 14 | 6² | 11 | 10 |  |  | 4 |  | 1 | 5 | 8 | 7³ |  |  |  |  |  |  |  |  |  | 19 |
| 8 |  |  | 4 | 5 |  |  | 12 | 6 | 11² | 10 | 3 |  |  |  | 13 | 1 | 2 | 7 | 9¹ |  |  |  |  |  |  |  |  |  | 20 |
| 8 |  | 3 |  | 5 |  |  | 13 | 6 | 11 | 10¹ | 4 |  |  | 12² |  | 1 | 2 | 7 | 9³ |  |  |  | 14 |  |  |  |  |  | 21 |
| 8 |  |  | 4 | 5 |  |  |  | 6 | 11 | 10³ | 3 |  |  |  | 14 | 1 | 2 | 7² | 9¹ | 12 |  |  | 13 |  |  |  |  |  | 22 |
| 1 | 8³ | 14 | 4 |  |  |  | 12 | 6 | 10 | 11² | 3 |  |  |  | 13 |  | 2 | 5 | 7 |  |  |  | 9¹ |  |  |  |  |  | 23 |
| 1 | 6 | 12 | 4 |  |  |  | 8 | 9 | 11³ |  | 3 |  |  | 10² | 14 |  | 2 | 5 | 7¹ |  |  |  | 13 |  |  |  |  |  | 24 |
| 1 | 8 | 3 | 5 | 4¹ |  |  | 7 | 6 |  | 11 |  |  |  |  | 13 |  | 2 | 9 |  |  |  |  | 10² |  |  |  | 12 |  | 25 |
| 1 | 4 | 5 |  |  |  | 7 | 8³ | 9 | 12 |  | 3 |  |  | 6 | 14 |  | 2² | 13 |  |  |  |  | 10 |  | 11¹ |  |  |  | 26 |
| 1 | 8¹ | 3 |  | 5 |  |  |  | 9 | 10 |  | 4 |  |  |  | 13 |  | 2 | 7 | 6 |  |  |  | 11² |  | 12 |  |  |  | 27 |
| 1 | 8 | 2 | 4 | 5 |  |  |  | 13 | 12 | 11 | 3 |  |  | 6 |  |  |  | 7² | 9¹ |  |  |  | 10 |  |  |  |  |  | 28 |
| 1 | 8 | 2 | 3 | 5 |  |  |  | 13 | 12 | 11 | 4 |  |  | 6 |  |  |  | 7² | 9¹ |  |  |  | 10 |  |  |  |  |  | 29 |
| 1 | 3 | 14 | 4 | 5 |  |  |  | 9 | 7 | 6 | 12 |  |  | 8² | 13 |  | 2 |  |  |  |  |  | 10³ |  | 11¹ |  |  |  | 30 |
| 1 | 8¹ | 3 | 4 | 5 |  |  |  |  | 12 | 6 | 11 |  |  | 2 |  |  |  | 7³ | 9² |  |  |  | 10 |  |  |  | 13 | 14 | 31 |
| 1 | 8 | 3 | 12 | 5¹ | 4 |  |  | 13 |  | 11² |  |  |  | 2 |  |  |  | 7 | 9 |  |  |  | 10 |  |  |  | 6³ | 14 | 32 |
| 1 | 8 | 3 | 2 |  | 4 |  |  | 14 | 6 | 11 | 12 |  |  |  |  |  | 5 | 9¹ | 7³ |  |  |  | 10² |  |  |  | 13 |  | 33 |
| 1 | 8 | 2 | 3 |  | 4 |  |  | 9 | 10 |  | 12 |  |  | 6 |  |  | 5 |  | 7 |  |  |  |  |  | 11¹ |  |  |  | 34 |
| 1 | 7² | 2 | 3 |  | 4 |  |  | 13 | 9 | 10¹ | 12 |  |  | 6 | 14 |  | 5 |  |  |  |  |  |  |  | 11³ | 8 |  |  | 35 |
| 1 | 2 | 3 | 4 |  |  |  |  | 9² | 6 | 10¹ | 13 |  |  |  | 14 |  | 5 |  |  |  |  |  |  |  | 11³ | 7 |  |  | 36 |
| 1 | 7 | 2 | 4² |  |  |  |  | 6 |  | 10¹ | 3 |  |  |  |  |  | 5 | 9 |  |  |  |  | 12 |  | 11 | 8 | 13 |  | 37 |
| 1 | 7³ | 3 |  |  | 4¹ |  |  | 6 | 13 |  |  |  |  | 2 | 14 |  | 5 | 9 |  |  |  |  | 10 |  | 11² | 8 | 12 |  | 38 |
| 1 |  | 3 | 4 |  |  |  |  | 6 | 13 | 11² |  |  |  | 2 |  |  | 5 | 9 | 7 |  |  |  | 10¹ |  |  | 8 | 12 |  | 39 |
| 1 | 7 | 3 | 4¹ |  |  |  |  | 6 | 13 | 11² |  |  |  | 2 | 14 |  | 5 | 9 |  |  |  |  | 10³ |  |  | 8 | 12 |  | 40 |
| 1 |  | 3 |  |  | 13 |  |  | 6 | 9³ | 10 |  |  |  | 2 | 14 |  | 5 | 8² | 7 |  |  |  | 4 |  | 11¹ |  | 12 |  | 41 |
| 1 | 8 | 3 | 5 | 4¹ |  | 7 | 6 |  |  | 11 |  |  |  | 2 | 14 |  |  | 9² |  |  |  |  | 10 |  | 13 |  | 12³ |  | 42 |
| 1 | 7¹ |  | 4 |  |  |  | 6 |  | 9 |  | 11 |  |  | 2 | 13 |  | 5 | 8 |  |  |  |  | 10² |  | 12 |  | 3 |  | 43 |
| 1 |  | 3 |  | 5 |  |  | 8 | 9 |  | 10 |  |  |  | 6 |  |  | 2 | 7 |  |  |  |  | 12 |  | 11¹ |  | 4 |  | 44 |
| 1 | 12 |  | 4 | 5 |  |  | 8 |  |  | 10 | 11 |  |  | 6 |  |  | 2 | 7 | 9¹ |  |  |  |  |  |  |  | 3 |  | 45 |
| 1 | 7² | 3 |  | 5 |  |  | 8 | 9 |  | 10 |  |  |  | 6 |  |  | 2¹ |  |  |  |  |  | 12 |  | 11 |  | 4 | 13 | 46 |

**FA Cup**

| First Round | Gloucester | (a) | 2-0 |
|---|---|---|---|
| Second Round | Alfreton T | (a) | 4-2 |
| Third Round | Hull C | (a) | 1-1 |
| *Replay* | Hull C | (h) | 1-2 |

**Capital One Cup**

| First Round | Charlton Ath | (a) | 1-1 |
|---|---|---|---|

*(aet; won 4-3 on pens)*

| Second Round | Everton | (a) | 0-5 |
|---|---|---|---|

**Johnstone's Paint Trophy**

| Second Round | Barnet | (h) | 1-0 |
|---|---|---|---|
| Southern Quarter-Finals | Northampton T | (a) | 3-0 |
| Southern Semi-Finals | Yeovil T | (h) | 1-0 |
| Southern Final | Southend U | (h) | 0-1 |
|  | Southend U | (a) | 2-2 |

# LIVERPOOL

## FOUNDATION

But for a dispute between Everton FC and their landlord at Anfield in 1892, there may never have been a Liverpool club. This dispute persuaded the majority of Evertonians to quit Anfield for Goodison Park, leaving the landlord, Mr John Houlding, to form a new club. He originally tried to retain the name 'Everton' but when this failed, he founded Liverpool Association FC on 15 March 1892.

*Anfield Stadium, Anfield Road, Liverpool L4 0TH.*

*Telephone:* (0843) 170 5555.

*Fax:* (0151) 260 8813.

*Ticket Office:* (0843) 170 5555.

*Website:* www.liverpoolfc.com

*Email:* (via website)

*Ground Capacity:* 45,276.

*Record Attendance:* 61,905 v Wolverhampton W, FA Cup 4th rd, 2 February 1952.

*Pitch Measurements:* 101m × 68m (110yd × 74yd)

*Chairman:* Tom Werner.

*Vice-chairman:* David Ginsberg.

*Manager:* Brendan Rodgers.

*Assistant Manager:* Colin Pascoe.

*Physio:* Chris Morgan.

*Colours:* Red shirts, red shorts, red socks.

*Year Formed:* 1892.

*Turned Professional:* 1892.

*Club Nicknames:* 'The Reds', 'Pool'.

*Ground:* 1892, Anfield.

*First Football League Game:* 2 September 1893, Division 2, v Middlesbrough Ironopolis (a) W 2–0 – McOwen; Hannah, McLean; Henderson, McQue (1), McBride; Gordon, McVean (1), Matt McQueen, Stott, Hugh McQueen.

## HONOURS

**FA Premier League:** *Runners-up* 2001–02, 2008–09.
**Football League – Division 1:**
*Champions* 1900–01, 1905–06, 1921–22, 1922–23, 1946–47, 1963–64, 1965–66, 1972–73, 1975–76, 1976–77, 1978–79, 1979–80, 1981–82, 1982–83, 1983–84, 1985–86, 1987–88, 1989–90; *Runners-up* 1898–99, 1909–10, 1968–69, 1973–74, 1974–75, 1977–78, 1984–85, 1986–87, 1988–89, 1990–91;
**Division 2:** *Champions* 1893–94, 1895–96, 1904–05, 1961–62.
**FA Cup:** *Winners* 1965, 1974, 1986, 1989, 1992, 2001, 2006; *Runners-up* 1914, 1950, 1971, 1977, 1988, 1996, 2012.
**Football League Cup:** *Winners* 1981, 1982, 1983, 1984, 1995, 2001, 2003, 2012; *Runners-up* 1978, 1987, 2005.
**League Super Cup:** *Winners* 1986.
**European Competitions**: European Cup: 1964–65, 1966–67, 1973–74, 1976–77 (*winners*), 1977–78 (*winners*), 1978–79, 1979–80, 1980–81 (*winners*), 1981–82, 1982–83, 1983–84 (*winners*), 1984–85 (*runners-up*). **Champions League:** 2001–02, 2002–03, 2004–05 (*winners*), 2005–06, 2006–07 (*runners-up*), 2007–08 (*s-f*), 2008–09 (*q-f*), 2009–10. **European Cup-Winners' Cup:** 1965–66 (*runners-up*), 1971–72, 1974–75, 1992–93, 1996–97 (*s-f*). **European Fairs Cup:** 1967–68, 1968–69, 1969–70, 1970–71. **UEFA Cup:** 1972–73 (*winners*), 1975–76 (*winners*), 1991–92, 1995–96, 1997–98, 1998–99, 2000–01 (*winners*), 2002–03, 2003–04. **Europa League:** 2009–10, 2010–11, 2012–13. **Super Cup:** 1977 (*winners*), 1978, 1984, 2001 (*winners*), 2005 (*winners*). **World Club Championship:** 1981, 1984. **FIFA Club World Cup:** 2005.

*Record League Victory:* 10–1 v Rotherham T, Division 2, 18 February 1896 – Storer; Goldie, Wilkie; McCartney, McQue, Holmes; McVean (3), Ross (2), Allan (4), Becton (1), Bradshaw.

### sky SPORTS FACT FILE

When Liverpool lost the 1914 FA Cup final to Burnley their half-back Harry Lowe missed the game but still received his runners-up medal after the club made a request to the Football Association. Harry had captained the Reds throughout the season only to be injured the week before the final.

*Record Cup Victory:* 11–0 v Stromsgodset Drammen, ECWC 1st rd 1st leg, 17 September 1974 – Clemence; Smith (1), Lindsay (1p), Thompson (2), Cormack (1), Hughes (1), Boersma (2), Hall, Heighway (1), Kennedy (1), Callaghan (1).

*Record Defeat:* 1–9 v Birmingham C, Division 2, 11 December 1954.

*Most League Points (2 for a win):* 68, Division 1, 1978–79.

*Most League Points (3 for a win):* 90, Division 1, 1987–88.

*Most League Goals:* 106, Division 2, 1895–96.

*Highest League Scorer in Season:* Roger Hunt, 41, Division 2, 1961–62.

*Most League Goals in Total Aggregate:* Roger Hunt, 245, 1959–69.

*Most League Goals in One Match:* 5, Andy McGuigan v Stoke C, Division 1, 4 January 1902; 5, John Evans v Bristol R, Division 2, 15 September 1954; 5, Ian Rush v Luton T, Division 1, 29 October 1983.

*Most Capped Player:* Steven Gerrard, 102, England.

*Most League Appearances:* Ian Callaghan, 640, 1960–78.

*Youngest League Player:* Jack Robinson, 16 years 250 days v Hull C, 9 May 2010.

| MANAGERS |
|---|
| W. E. Barclay 1892–96 |
| Tom Watson 1896–1915 |
| David Ashworth 1920–23 |
| Matt McQueen 1923–28 |
| George Patterson 1928–36 |
| *(continued as Secretary)* |
| George Kay 1936–51 |
| Don Welsh 1951–56 |
| Phil Taylor 1956–59 |
| Bill Shankly 1959–74 |
| Bob Paisley 1974–83 |
| Joe Fagan 1983–85 |
| Kenny Dalglish 1985–91 |
| Graeme Souness 1991–94 |
| Roy Evans 1994–98 |
| *(then Joint Manager)* |
| Gerard Houllier 1998–2004 |
| Rafael Benitez 2004–10 |
| Roy Hodgson 2010–11 |
| Kenny Dalglish 2011–12 |
| Brendan Rodgers June 2012– |

*Record Transfer Fee Received:* £50,000,000 from Chelsea for Fernando Torres, January 2011.

*Record Transfer Fee Paid:* £35,000,000 to Newcastle U for Andy Carroll, January 2011.

*Football League Record:* 1893 Elected to Division 2; 1894–95 Division 1; 1895–96 Division 2; 1896–1904 Division 1; 1904–05 Division 2; 1905–54 Division 1; 1954–62 Division 2; 1962–92 Division 1; 1992– FA Premier League.

## LATEST SEQUENCES

*Longest Sequence of League Wins:* 12, 21.4.1990 – 6.10.1990.

*Longest Sequence of League Defeats:* 9, 29.4.1899 – 14.10.1899.

*Longest Sequence of League Draws:* 6, 19.2.1975 – 19.3.1975.

*Longest Sequence of Unbeaten League Matches:* 31, 4.5.1987 – 16.3.1988.

*Longest Sequence Without a League Win:* 14, 12.12.1953 – 20.3.1954.

*Successive Scoring Runs:* 29 from 27.4.1957.

*Successive Non-scoring Runs:* 5 from 22.12.1906.

## TEN YEAR LEAGUE RECORD

| | | P | W | D | L | F | A | Pts | Pos |
|---|---|---|---|---|---|---|---|---|---|
| 2003-04 | PR Lge | 38 | 16 | 12 | 10 | 55 | 37 | 60 | 4 |
| 2004-05 | PR Lge | 38 | 17 | 7 | 14 | 52 | 41 | 58 | 5 |
| 2005-06 | PR Lge | 38 | 25 | 7 | 6 | 57 | 25 | 82 | 3 |
| 2006-07 | PR Lge | 38 | 20 | 8 | 10 | 57 | 27 | 68 | 3 |
| 2007-08 | PR Lge | 38 | 21 | 13 | 4 | 67 | 28 | 76 | 4 |
| 2008-09 | PR Lge | 38 | 25 | 11 | 2 | 77 | 27 | 86 | 2 |
| 2009-10 | PR Lge | 38 | 18 | 9 | 11 | 61 | 35 | 63 | 7 |
| 2010-11 | PR Lge | 38 | 17 | 7 | 14 | 59 | 44 | 58 | 6 |
| 2011-12 | PR Lge | 38 | 14 | 10 | 14 | 47 | 40 | 52 | 8 |
| 2012-13 | PR Lge | 38 | 16 | 13 | 9 | 71 | 43 | 61 | 7 |

## DID YOU KNOW ?

Inside left Gordon Wallace scored Liverpool's first European Cup goal when he netted the opener against Icelandic club KR Reykjavik in a preliminary round tie in August 1964. He added a second goal in the Reds' 5-0 victory in his only appearance for the club in the competition.

## LIVERPOOL – FA PREMIERSHIP 2012–13 LEAGUE RECORD

| Match No. | Date | Venue | Opponents | Result | H/T Score | Lg Pos. | Goalscorers | Attendance |
|---|---|---|---|---|---|---|---|---|
| 1 | Aug 18 | A | WBA | L 0-3 | 0-1 | 18 | | 26,039 |
| 2 | 26 | H | Manchester C | D 2-2 | 1-0 | 16 | Skrtel [34], Suarez [66] | 44,942 |
| 3 | Sept 2 | A | Arsenal | L 0-2 | 0-1 | 18 | | 44,932 |
| 4 | 15 | A | Sunderland | D 1-1 | 0-1 | 17 | Suarez [71] | 41,997 |
| 5 | 23 | H | Manchester U | L 1-2 | 0-0 | 18 | Gerrard [46] | 44,263 |
| 6 | 29 | A | Norwich C | W 5-2 | 2-0 | 14 | Suarez 3 [2, 38, 57], Sahin [47], Barnett (og) [68] | 26,831 |
| 7 | Oct 7 | H | Stoke C | D 0-0 | 0-0 | 14 | | 44,531 |
| 8 | 20 | H | Reading | W 1-0 | 1-0 | 11 | Sterling [29] | 44,874 |
| 9 | 28 | A | Everton | D 2-2 | 2-2 | 12 | Baines (og) [14], Suarez [20] | 39,613 |
| 10 | Nov 4 | H | Newcastle U | D 1-1 | 0-1 | 12 | Suarez [67] | 44,803 |
| 11 | 11 | A | Chelsea | D 1-1 | 0-1 | 13 | Suarez [73] | 41,627 |
| 12 | 17 | H | Wigan Ath | W 3-0 | 0-0 | 11 | Suarez 2 [47, 58], Jose Enrique [65] | 44,913 |
| 13 | 25 | A | Swansea C | D 0-0 | 0-0 | 11 | | 20,621 |
| 14 | 28 | A | Tottenham H | L 1-2 | 0-2 | 12 | Bale (og) [72] | 36,162 |
| 15 | Dec 1 | H | Southampton | W 1-0 | 1-0 | 11 | Agger [43] | 44,525 |
| 16 | 9 | A | West Ham U | W 3-2 | 1-2 | 10 | Johnson [11], Cole [76], Shelvey [79] | 35,005 |
| 17 | 15 | H | Aston Villa | L 1-3 | 0-2 | 12 | Gerrard [87] | 44,607 |
| 18 | 22 | H | Fulham | W 4-0 | 2-0 | 8 | Skrtel [8], Gerrard [36], Downing [51], Suarez [90] | 44,570 |
| 19 | 26 | A | Stoke C | L 1-3 | 1-2 | 10 | Gerrard (pen) [2] | 27,490 |
| 20 | 30 | A | QPR | W 3-0 | 3-0 | 9 | Suarez 2 [10, 16], Agger [28] | 18,304 |
| 21 | Jan 2 | H | Sunderland | W 3-0 | 2-0 | 8 | Sterling [19], Suarez 2 [26, 52] | 44,228 |
| 22 | 13 | A | Manchester U | L 1-2 | 0-1 | 8 | Sturridge [57] | 75,501 |
| 23 | 19 | H | Norwich C | W 5-0 | 2-0 | 7 | Henderson [26], Suarez [36], Sturridge [59], Gerrard [66], Bennett, R (og) [74] | 44,901 |
| 24 | 30 | A | Arsenal | D 2-2 | 1-0 | 7 | Suarez [5], Henderson [60] | 60,089 |
| 25 | Feb 3 | A | Manchester C | D 2-2 | 1-1 | 7 | Sturridge [29], Gerrard [73] | 47,301 |
| 26 | 11 | H | WBA | L 0-2 | 0-0 | 9 | | 44,752 |
| 27 | 17 | H | Swansea C | W 5-0 | 1-0 | 7 | Gerrard (pen) [34], Coutinho [46], Jose Enrique [50], Suarez [56], Sturridge (pen) [71] | 44,832 |
| 28 | Mar 2 | A | Wigan Ath | W 4-0 | 3-0 | 7 | Downing [2], Suarez 3 [18, 34, 49] | 20,804 |
| 29 | 10 | H | Tottenham H | W 3-2 | 1-1 | 6 | Suarez [21], Downing [66], Gerrard (pen) [82] | 44,752 |
| 30 | 16 | A | Southampton | L 1-3 | 1-2 | 7 | Coutinho [45] | 32,070 |
| 31 | 31 | A | Aston Villa | W 2-1 | 0-1 | 7 | Henderson [47], Gerrard (pen) [60] | 42,037 |
| 32 | Apr 7 | H | West Ham U | D 0-0 | 0-0 | 7 | | 45,007 |
| 33 | 13 | A | Reading | D 0-0 | 0-0 | 7 | | 24,139 |
| 34 | 21 | H | Chelsea | D 2-2 | 0-1 | 7 | Sturridge [52], Suarez [90] | 45,009 |
| 35 | 27 | A | Newcastle U | W 6-0 | 2-0 | 7 | Agger [3], Henderson 2 [17, 76], Sturridge 2 [54, 60], Borini [74] | 52,351 |
| 36 | May 5 | H | Everton | D 0-0 | 0-0 | 7 | | 44,991 |
| 37 | 12 | A | Fulham | W 3-1 | 1-1 | 7 | Sturridge 3 [36, 62, 85] | 25,640 |
| 38 | 19 | H | QPR | W 1-0 | 1-0 | 7 | Coutinho [23] | 44,792 |

**Final League Position: 7**

### GOALSCORERS

*League (71):* Suarez 23, Sturridge 10 (1 pen), Gerrard 9 (4 pens), Henderson 5, Agger 3, Coutinho 3, Downing 3, Jose Enrique 2, Skrtel 2, Sterling 2, Borini 1, Cole 1, Johnson 1, Sahin 1, Shelvey 1, own goals 4.
*FA Cup (4):* Suarez 2, Allen 1, Sturridge 1.
*Capital One Cup (3):* Sahin 2, Suarez 1.
*Europa League (20):* Shelvey 4, Suarez 4, Downing 2, Allen 1, Borini 1, Coates 1, Cole 1, Gerrard 1, Henderson 1, Johnson 1, Wisdom 1, own goals 2.

| Reina J 31 | Kelly M 4 | Skrtel M 23+2 | Agger D 35 | Johnson G 36 | Lucas 24+2 | Allen J 21+6 | Gerrard S 36 | Downing S 25+4 | Suarez L 33 | Borini F 5+8 | Carragher J 16+8 | Cole J —+6 | Carroll A —+2 | Coates S 2+3 | Sterling R 19+5 | Shelvey J 9+10 | Jose Enrique 25+4 | Sahin N 7 | Suso 8+6 | Henderson J 16+14 | Wisdom A 12 | Assaidi O —+4 | Jones B 7 | Sturridge D 11+3 | Coutinho P 12+1 | Coady C —+1 | Ibe J 1 | Match No. |
|---|---|---|---|---|---|---|---|---|---|---|---|---|---|---|---|---|---|---|---|---|---|---|---|---|---|---|---|---|
| 1 | 2 | 3 | $4^8$ | 5 | $6^2$ | 7 | 8 | $9^1$ | 10 | 11 | 12 | $13^3$ | 14 | | | | | | | | | | | | | | | 1 |
| 1 | $2^2$ | 3 | | 5 | $6^1$ | 7 | 9 | | 11 | $8^3$ | | 14 | | 4 | 10 | 12 | 13 | | | | | | | | | | | 2 |
| | | 3 | 4 | 2 | | 7 | 6 | 12 | 10 | $9^1$ | | | | | 11 | 13 | 5 | $8^2$ | | | | | | | | | | 3 |
| 1 | 2 | 3 | 4 | 5 | | 7 | 6 | 12 | 10 | $9^1$ | | | | | 11 | 8 | | | | | | | | | | | | 4 |
| 1 | 2 | 3 | $4^3$ | 5 | | 7 | 6 | | 10 | $9^1$ | 14 | | | | $11^2$ | $8^8$ | | | 12 | 13 | | | | | | | | 5 |
| 1 | | 4 | 3 | $5^2$ | | | 8 | 10 | | 11 | | | 14 | | 6 | | | $7^2$ | $9^1$ | 13 | 2 | 12 | | | | | | 6 |
| 1 | | 3 | 4 | 5 | | 7 | 6 | | 10 | | | 12 | | | 11 | | | $8^2$ | $9^1$ | | 2 | 13 | | | | | | 7 |
| | | 3 | 4 | 5 | | 7 | 6 | | 10 | | | | | | $11^3$ | 12 | 13 | $8^1$ | $9^2$ | 14 | 2 | | 1 | | | | | 8 |
| | | 3 | 4 | | | 9 | 8 | | 11 | | | | | | 12 | 10 | 13 | 5 | $7^1$ | $6^2$ | 14 | $2^3$ | 1 | | | | | 9 |
| | | 3 | 4 | | | 7 | 6 | 13 | 10 | | | | | | 11 | 12 | 5 | $8^2$ | $9^1$ | | 2 | | 1 | | | | | 10 |
| | | | 4 | 5 | | 6 | 7 | | | 3 | | | | 8 | | 10 | | | $9^1$ | 12 | 2 | | 1 | | | | | 11 |
| 1 | | 4 | $3^2$ | 6 | | 8 | 7 | | $10^3$ | | | 13 | | | 9 | 14 | 5 | | | $11^1$ | 12 | 2 | | | | | | 12 |
| 1 | | 3 | 4 | 2 | | 8 | 7 | $6^2$ | 11 | | | 13 | | | 10 | 12 | 5 | | $9^1$ | | | | | | | | | 13 |
| 1 | | 4 | 3 | 2 | | 8 | 7 | $5^2$ | 10 | | | | | | 9 | 12 | 11 | | | $6^1$ | | 13 | | | | | | 14 |
| 1 | | 3 | 4 | 2 | | $6^2$ | $7^1$ | 9 | | 11 | | 13 | | | 10 | 8 | 5 | | 12 | | | | | | | | | 15 |
| 1 | | 3 | 4 | 2 | | $7^2$ | $6^3$ | 8 | 11 | | | 12 | | 14 | 9 | 10 | $5^1$ | | 13 | | | | | | | | | 16 |
| 1 | | 3 | 4 | 2 | | $7^2$ | 8 | 6 | 5 | 10 | | 12 | | | 11 | $9^1$ | | | 13 | | | | | | | | | 17 |
| 1 | | 3 | 4 | 2 | | $7^3$ | 13 | 6 | 11 | 10 | | 14 | | | 12 | $8^2$ | 5 | | $9^1$ | | | | | | | | | 18 |
| 1 | | 3 | 4 | 2 | | $7^2$ | | 6 | $8^3$ | 11 | | 14 | | | 12 | 9 | 5 | | $10^1$ | 13 | | | | | | | | 19 |
| 1 | | 3 | 4 | 2 | 12 | 6 | 9 | 8 | 11 | | | 14 | | | 10 | | $5^2$ | | 13 | $7^1$ | | | | | | | | 20 |
| 1 | | $3^3$ | 4 | 5 | 7 | 12 | 6 | 9 | 10 | | | 14 | | | $11^1$ | | | | 13 | $8^2$ | 2 | | | | | | | 21 |
| 1 | | 3 | 4 | 5 | $6^1$ | $9^3$ | 8 | 7 | 11 | 13 | | | | | $10^2$ | | | | | 14 | 2 | | 12 | | | | | 22 |
| | | 4 | 5 | $7^1$ | 14 | 6 | 11 | 9 | 13 | 3 | | | | | 12 | | | | | $8^3$ | 2 | | 1 | $10^1$ | | | | 23 |
| 1 | | 3 | 2 | 6 | | 7 | 9 | 10 | | 4 | | | | | 12 | | | | | 8 | | 5 | | $11^1$ | | | | 24 |
| 1 | 12 | 3 | 2 | 6 | 13 | 7 | 8 | 10 | | 4 | | | | | $5^1$ | | | | 9 | | | | | $11^2$ | | | | 25 |
| 1 | | 4 | 2 | 6 | | 7 | $9^1$ | 11 | 13 | 3 | | | | | 12 | $10^1$ | 5 | | | $8^2$ | | | | 14 | | | | 26 |
| 1 | | 4 | 2 | $8^2$ | 13 | 7 | 6 | $10^3$ | 14 | 3 | | | | | | | 5 | | | 12 | | | | 11 | $9^1$ | | | 27 |
| 1 | | 4 | 2 | 7 | 8 | 6 | 9 | 10 | | 3 | | | | | | | 5 | | | 12 | | | | | $11^1$ | | | 28 |
| | | 4 | 2 | 6 | 12 | 7 | 8 | 9 | | 3 | | | | | | | 5 | | | 13 | | | 1 | $11^2$ | $10^1$ | | | 29 |
| | | 4 | 3 | 2 | 12 | $6^1$ | 8 | 7 | 10 | | | | | | | | 5 | | | 13 | | | 1 | $11^2$ | 9 | | | 30 |
| 1 | | 3 | 2 | 6 | | 7 | 10 | 11 | | 4 | | | | | 12 | | 5 | | | 8 | | | | | $9^1$ | | | 31 |
| 1 | | 4 | 2 | 7 | | 6 | $8^1$ | 11 | | 4 | | | | | | | 5 | | | $9^2$ | | 13 | | 12 | 10 | | | 32 |
| 1 | | 3 | 2 | 6 | | 7 | 12 | 10 | | 4 | | | | | | | 5 | | | $6^1$ | | | | 11 | 9 | | | 33 |
| 1 | | 4 | 2 | 7 | | 6 | $8^2$ | 11 | | 3 | | | | | | 13 | 5 | | | 9 | | | | 12 | $10^1$ | | | 34 |
| 1 | | 4 | 2 | 8 | | $7^1$ | 11 | | 12 | 3 | | | | | | 14 | 5 | 13 | | 6 | | | | $10^2$ | $9^3$ | | | 35 |
| 1 | 13 | 4 | 2 | 6 | | 7 | $8^2$ | | 12 | 3 | | | | | | | 5 | | | $9^1$ | | | | 11 | 10 | | | 36 |
| 1 | | 5 | 7 | | | | 9 | | 13 | 4 | | 3 | | $8^2$ | 12 | | | 6 | $2^1$ | | | | | 10 | $11^3$ | 14 | | 37 |
| 1 | | 4 | | 2 | 7 | | 6 | | 12 | $3^3$ | | | 14 | | | | 5 | 8 | | | | | | 11 | $10^2$ | | $9^1$ | 38 |

**FA Cup**
| | | | |
|---|---|---|---|
| Third Round | Mansfield T | (a) | 2-1 |
| Fourth Round | Oldham Ath | (a) | 2-3 |

**Capital One Cup**
| | | | |
|---|---|---|---|
| Third Round | WBA | (a) | 2-1 |
| Fourth Round | Swansea C | (h) | 1-3 |

**Europa League**
| | | | |
|---|---|---|---|
| Third Qualifying Round | FC Gomel | (a) | 1-0 |
| | FC Gomel | (h) | 3-0 |
| Play-off Round | Hearts | (a) | 1-0 |
| | Hearts | (h) | 1-1 |
| Group A | Young Boys | (a) | 5-3 |
| | Udinese | (h) | 2-3 |
| | Anzhi Makhachkala | (h) | 1-0 |
| | Anzhi Makhachkala | (a) | 0-1 |
| | Young Boys | (h) | 2-2 |
| | Udinese | (a) | 1-0 |
| Second Round | Zenit St Petersburg | (a) | 0-2 |
| | Zenit St Petersburg | (h) | 3-1 |

# MANCHESTER CITY

## FOUNDATION

Manchester City was formed as a limited company in 1894 after their predecessors Ardwick had been forced into bankruptcy. However, many historians like to trace the club's lineage as far back as 1880 when St Mark's Church, West Gorton added a football section to their cricket club. They amalgamated with Belle Vue for one season before splitting again under the name Gorton Association FC in 1884–85. In 1887 Gorton AFC turned professional and moved ground to Hyde Road under the new name Ardwick AFC.

*Etihad Stadium, Etihad Campus, Manchester M11 3FF.*
*Telephone:* (0161) 444 1894.
*Fax:* (0161) 438 7999.
*Ticket Office:* (0161) 444 1894.
*Website:* www.mcfc.co.uk
*Email:* mcfc@mcfc.co.uk
*Ground Capacity:* 47,405.
*Record Attendance:* 84,569 v Stoke C, FA Cup 6th rd, 3 March 1934 (at Maine Road; British record for any game outside London or Glasgow); 47,370 v Tottenham H, FA Premier League, 5 May 2010 (at City of Manchester Stadium).
*Pitch Measurements:* 105m × 68m (114yd × 74yd)
*Chairman:* Khaldoon Al Mubarak.
*Chief Executive:* Ferran Soriano.
*Manager:* Manuel Pellegrini
*Assistant Managers:* Ruben Cousillas Fuse, Brian Kidd.
*Fitness Coach:* Jose Cabello.
*Colours:* Sky blue shirts, white shorts, sky blue socks with black tops.
*Year Formed:* 1887 as Ardwick FC; 1894 as Manchester City.
*Turned Professional:* 1887 as Ardwick FC.
*Previous Names:* 1880, St Mark's Church, West Gorton; 1884, Gorton; 1887, Ardwick; 1894, Manchester City.
*Club Nicknames:* 'The Blues', 'The Citizens'.

## HONOURS

**FA Premier League**: *Champions* 2011–12; *Runners-up* 2012–13.
**Football League – Division 1:** *Champions* 1936–37, 1967–68, 2001–02; *Runners-up* 1903–04, 1920–21, 1976–77, 1999–2000; **Division 2:** *Champions* 1898–99, 1902–03, 1909–10, 1927–28, 1946–47, 1965–66; *Runners-up* 1895–96, 1950–51, 1988–89.
**FA Cup:** *Winners* 1904, 1934, 1956, 1969, 2011; *Runners-up* 1926, 1933, 1955, 1981, 2013.
**Football League Cup:** *Winners* 1970, 1976; *Runners-up* 1974.
**Full Members Cup:** *Runners-up* 1986.
**European Competitions**
**Champions League:** 2011–12, 2012–13. **European Cup:** 1968–69.
**European Cup-Winners' Cup:** 1969–70 (*winners*), 1970–71.
**UEFA Cup:** 1972–73, 1976–77, 1977–78, 1978–79, 2003–04, 2008–09.
**Europa League:** 2010–11, 2011–12.

*Grounds:* 1880, Clowes Street; 1881, Kirkmanshulme Cricket Ground; 1882, Queens Road; 1884, Pink Bank Lane; 1887, Hyde Road (1894–1923 as City); 1923, Maine Road; 2003, City of Manchester Stadium (now know as Etihad Stadium from 2011).
*First Football League Game:* 3 September 1892, Division 2, v Bootle (h) W 7–0 – Douglas; McVickers, Robson; Middleton, Russell, Hopkins; Davies (3), Morris (2), Angus (1), Weir (1), Milarvie.
*Record League Victory:* 10–1 v Huddersfield T, Division 2, 7 November 1987 – Nixon; Gidman, Hinchcliffe, Clements, Lake, Redmond, White (3), Stewart (3), Adcock (3), McNab (1), Simpson.
*Record Cup Victory:* 10–1 v Swindon T, FA Cup 4th rd, 29 January 1930 – Barber; Felton, McCloy; Barrass, Cowan, Heinemann; Toseland, Marshall (5), Tait (3), Johnson (1), Brook (1).

## sky SPORTS FACT FILE

With Old Trafford unavailable due to wartime damage, Manchester City shared their Maine Road ground with their rivals United in the first three post-war seasons. The two met in Division One action in both 1947–48 and 1948–49, with all four games being drawn, three goalless.

*Record Defeat:* 1–9 v Everton, Division 1, 3 September 1906.

*Most League Points (2 for a win):* 62, Division 2, 1946–47.

*Most League Points (3 for a win):* 99, Division 1, 2001–02.

*Most League Goals:* 108, Division 2, 1926–27, 108, Division 1, 2001–02.

*Highest League Scorer in Season:* Tommy Johnson, 38, Division 1, 1928–29.

*Most League Goals in Total Aggregate:* Tommy Johnson, 158, 1919–30.

*Most League Goals in One Match:* 5, Fred Williams v Darwen, Division 2, 18 February 1899; 5, Tom Browell v Burnley, Division 2, 24 October 1925; 5, Tom Johnson v Everton, Division 1, 15 September 1928; 5, George Smith v Newport Co, Division 2, 1 June 1947.

*Most Capped Player:* Colin Bell, 48, England.

*Most League Appearances:* Alan Oakes, 565, 1959–76.

*Youngest League Player:* Glyn Pardoe, 15 years 314 days v Birmingham C, 11 April 1962.

*Record Transfer Fee Received:* £21,000,000 from Chelsea for Shaun Wright-Phillips, July 2005.

*Record Transfer Fee Paid:* £38,000,000 to Atletico Madrid for Sergio Aguero, July 2011.

*Football League Record:* 1892 Ardwick elected founder member of Division 2; 1894 Newly-formed Manchester C elected to Division 2; Division 1 1899–1902, 1903–09, 1910–26, 1928–38, 1947–50, 1951–63, 1966–83, 1985–87, 1989–92; Division 2 1902–03, 1909–10, 1926–28, 1938–47, 1950–51, 1963–66, 1983–85, 1987–89; 1992–96 FA Premier League; 1996–98 Division 1; 1998–99 Division 2; 1999–2000 Division 1; 2000–01 FA Premier League; 2001–02 Division 1; 2002– FA Premier League.

## LATEST SEQUENCES

*Longest Sequence of League Wins:* 9, 8.4.1912 – 28.9.1912.

*Longest Sequence of League Defeats:* 8, 23.8.1995 – 14.10.1995.

*Longest Sequence of League Draws:* 7, 5.10.2009 – 28.11.2009.

*Longest Sequence of Unbeaten League Matches:* 22, 16.11.1946 – 19.4.1947.

*Longest Sequence Without a League Win:* 17, 26.12.1979 – 7.4.1980.

*Successive Scoring Runs:* 44 from 3.10.1936.

*Successive Non-scoring Runs:* 6 from 30.1.1971.

## MANAGERS

**Joshua Parlby** 1893–95
*(Secretary-Manager)*
**Sam Omerod** 1895–1902
**Tom Maley** 1902–06
**Harry Newbould** 1906–12
**Ernest Magnall** 1912–24
**David Ashworth** 1924–25
**Peter Hodge** 1926–32
**Wilf Wild** 1932–46
*(continued as Secretary to 1950)*
**Sam Cowan** 1946–47
**John 'Jock' Thomson** 1947–50
**Leslie McDowall** 1950–63
**George Poyser** 1963–65
**Joe Mercer** 1965–71
*(continued as General Manager to 1972)*
**Malcolm Allison** 1972–73
**Johnny Hart** 1973
**Ron Saunders** 1973–74
**Tony Book** 1974–79
**Malcolm Allison** 1979–80
**John Bond** 1980–83
**John Benson** 1983
**Billy McNeill** 1983–86
**Jimmy Frizzell** 1986–87
*(continued as General Manager)*
**Mel Machin** 1987–89
**Howard Kendall** 1989–90
**Peter Reid** 1990–93
**Brian Horton** 1993–95
**Alan Ball** 1995–96
**Steve Coppell** 1996
**Frank Clark** 1996–98
**Joe Royle** 1998–2001
**Kevin Keegan** 2001–05
**Stuart Pearce** 2005–07
**Sven-Göran Eriksson** 2007–08
**Mark Hughes** 2008–09
**Roberto Mancini** 2009–13
**Manuel Pellegrini** June 2013–

## TEN YEAR LEAGUE RECORD

|  |  | P | W | D | L | F | A | Pts | Pos |
|---|---|---|---|---|---|---|---|---|---|
| 2003-04 | PR Lge | 38 | 9 | 14 | 15 | 55 | 54 | 41 | 16 |
| 2004-05 | PR Lge | 38 | 13 | 13 | 12 | 47 | 39 | 52 | 8 |
| 2005-06 | PR Lge | 38 | 13 | 4 | 21 | 43 | 48 | 43 | 15 |
| 2006-07 | PR Lge | 38 | 11 | 9 | 18 | 29 | 44 | 42 | 14 |
| 2007-08 | PR Lge | 38 | 15 | 10 | 13 | 45 | 53 | 55 | 9 |
| 2008-09 | PR Lge | 38 | 15 | 5 | 18 | 58 | 50 | 50 | 10 |
| 2009-10 | PR Lge | 38 | 18 | 13 | 7 | 73 | 45 | 67 | 5 |
| 2010-11 | PR Lge | 38 | 21 | 8 | 9 | 60 | 33 | 71 | 3 |
| 2011-12 | PR Lge | 38 | 28 | 5 | 5 | 93 | 29 | 89 | 1 |
| 2012-13 | PR Lge | 38 | 23 | 9 | 6 | 66 | 34 | 78 | 2 |

## DID YOU KNOW

Manchester City achieved a unique feat in the 1957–58 season when they scored 104 goals and conceded 100. This was the first time a team had both scored and conceded a century of Football League goals in the same season.

## MANCHESTER CITY – FA PREMIERSHIP 2012–13 LEAGUE RECORD

| Match No. | Date | Venue | Opponents | Result | H/T Score | Lg Pos. | Goalscorers | Attendance |
|---|---|---|---|---|---|---|---|---|
| 1 | Aug 19 | H | Southampton | W 3-2 | 1-0 | 5 | Tevez [40], Dzeko [72], Nasri [80] | 46,190 |
| 2 | 26 | A | Liverpool | D 2-2 | 0-1 | 5 | Toure, Y [63], Tevez [80] | 44,942 |
| 3 | Sept 1 | H | QPR | W 3-1 | 1-0 | 4 | Toure, Y [16], Dzeko [61], Tevez [90] | 45,579 |
| 4 | 15 | A | Stoke C | D 1-1 | 1-1 | 4 | Javi Garcia [35] | 27,101 |
| 5 | 23 | H | Arsenal | D 1-1 | 1-0 | 7 | Lescott [40] | 47,318 |
| 6 | 29 | A | Fulham | W 2-1 | 1-1 | 4 | Aguero [43], Dzeko [87] | 25,698 |
| 7 | Oct 6 | H | Sunderland | W 3-0 | 1-0 | 2 | Kolarov [5], Aguero [60], Milner [89] | 47,036 |
| 8 | 20 | A | WBA | W 2-1 | 0-0 | 3 | Dzeko 2 [80, 90] | 24,891 |
| 9 | 27 | H | Swansea C | W 1-0 | 0-0 | 2 | Tevez [61] | 46,801 |
| 10 | Nov 3 | A | West Ham U | D 0-0 | 0-0 | 3 | | 35,005 |
| 11 | 11 | H | Tottenham H | W 2-1 | 0-1 | 2 | Aguero [65], Dzeko [88] | 47,208 |
| 12 | 17 | H | Aston Villa | W 5-0 | 1-0 | 1 | Silva [43], Aguero 2 (1 pen) [54 (pl), 67], Tevez 2 (1 pen) [65 (pl), 74] | 47,072 |
| 13 | 25 | A | Chelsea | D 0-0 | 0-0 | 2 | | 41,792 |
| 14 | 28 | A | Wigan Ath | W 2-0 | 0-0 | 2 | Balotelli [69], Milner [72] | 19,623 |
| 15 | Dec 1 | A | Everton | D 1-1 | 1-1 | 2 | Tevez (pen) [43] | 47,386 |
| 16 | 9 | H | Manchester U | L 2-3 | 0-2 | 2 | Toure, Y [60], Zabaleta [86] | 47,166 |
| 17 | 15 | A | Newcastle U | W 3-1 | 2-0 | 2 | Aguero [10], Javi Garcia [39], Toure, Y [78] | 49,579 |
| 18 | 22 | H | Reading | W 1-0 | 0-0 | 2 | Barry [90] | 47,007 |
| 19 | 26 | A | Sunderland | L 0-1 | 0-0 | 2 | | 42,190 |
| 20 | 29 | A | Norwich C | W 4-3 | 2-1 | 2 | Dzeko 2 [2, 5], Aguero [50], Bunn (og) [67] | 26,827 |
| 21 | Jan 1 | H | Stoke C | W 3-0 | 1-0 | 2 | Zabaleta [43], Dzeko [56], Aguero (pen) [74] | 47,192 |
| 22 | 13 | A | Arsenal | W 2-0 | 2-0 | 2 | Milner [21], Dzeko [32] | 60,107 |
| 23 | 19 | A | Fulham | W 2-0 | 1-0 | 2 | Silva 2 [2, 69] | 47,286 |
| 24 | 29 | A | QPR | D 0-0 | 0-0 | 2 | | 17,894 |
| 25 | Feb 3 | H | Liverpool | D 2-2 | 1-1 | 2 | Dzeko [23], Aguero [78] | 47,301 |
| 26 | 9 | A | Southampton | L 1-3 | 1-2 | 2 | Dzeko [39] | 31,738 |
| 27 | 24 | H | Chelsea | W 2-0 | 0-0 | 2 | Toure, Y [63], Tevez [85] | 47,256 |
| 28 | Mar 4 | H | Aston Villa | W 1-0 | 1-0 | 2 | Tevez [45] | 33,217 |
| 29 | 16 | A | Everton | L 0-2 | 0-1 | 2 | | 36,519 |
| 30 | 30 | H | Newcastle U | W 4-0 | 2-0 | 2 | Tevez [41], Silva [45], Kompany [56], Toure, Y [69] | 47,201 |
| 31 | Apr 8 | A | Manchester U | W 2-1 | 0-0 | 2 | Milner [51], Aguero [78] | 75,498 |
| 32 | 17 | H | Wigan Ath | W 1-0 | 0-0 | 2 | Tevez [83] | 47,106 |
| 33 | 21 | A | Tottenham H | L 1-3 | 1-0 | 2 | Nasri [5] | 36,121 |
| 34 | 27 | H | West Ham U | W 2-1 | 1-0 | 2 | Aguero [28], Toure, Y [83] | 47,189 |
| 35 | May 4 | A | Swansea C | D 0-0 | 0-0 | 2 | | 20,242 |
| 36 | 7 | H | WBA | W 1-0 | 1-0 | 2 | Dzeko [35] | 46,158 |
| 37 | 14 | A | Reading | W 2-0 | 1-0 | 2 | Aguero [40], Dzeko [88] | 22,859 |
| 38 | 19 | H | Norwich C | L 2-3 | 1-1 | 2 | Rodwell 2 [29, 59] | 47,054 |

**Final League Position: 2**

### GOALSCORERS

*League (66):* Dzeko 14, Aguero 12 (2 pens), Tevez 11 (2 pens), Toure, Y 7, Milner 4, Silva 4, Javi Garcia 2, Nasri 2, Rodwell 2, Zabaleta 2, Balotelli 1, Barry 1, Kolarov 1, Kompany 1, Lescott 1, own goal 1.
*FA Cup (15):* Tevez 5, Aguero 3 (1 pen), Barry 1, Kolarov 1, Lopes 1, Nasri 1, Silva 1, Toure 1, Zabaleta 1.
*Capital One Cup (2):* Balotelli 1, Kolarov 1.
*Community Shield (3):* Nasri 1, Tevez 1, Toure 1.
*UEFA Champions League (7):* Aguero 2 (1 pen), Balotelli 1 (1 pen), Dzeko 1, Kolarov 1, Nasri 1, Toure L 1.

| Hart J 38 | Zabaleta P 29 + 1 | Kompany V 26 | Lescott J 17 + 9 | Clichy G 26 + 2 | Silva D 29 + 3 | Rodwell J 6 + 5 | Toure Y 32 | Nasri S 22 + 6 | Aguero S 22 + 8 | Tevez C 28 + 6 | Dzeko E 16 + 16 | Balotelli M 7 + 7 | Kolarov A 11 + 9 | Toure K 10 + 5 | De Jong N 1 | Milner J 19 + 7 | Razak A — + 3 | Maicon S 4 + 5 | Javi Garcia F 17 + 7 | Sinclair S 2 + 9 | Barry G 27 + 4 | Nastasic M 21 | Richards M 7 | Rekik K 1 | Match No. |
|---|---|---|---|---|---|---|---|---|---|---|---|---|---|---|---|---|---|---|---|---|---|---|---|---|---|
| 1 | 2 | 3 | 4 | 5 | $6^2$ | 7 | 8 | 9 | $10^1$ | $11^3$ | 12 | 13 | 14 | | | | | | | | | | | | 1 |
| 1 | 2 | 3 | | | 14 | 12 | 6 | $10^1$ | 9 | 13 | $11^2$ | 5 | 4 | 7 | $8^3$ | | | | | | | | | | 2 |
| 1 | $2^1$ | 3 | 4 | | $6^2$ | 8 | 7 | $9^3$ | 10 | 11 | 5 | 12 | 13 | 14 | | | | | | | | | | | 3 |
| 1 | | 3 | 4 | 5 | 13 | | 7 | 6 | $11^1$ | 14 | $10^3$ | | | | | 2 | 8 | $9^2$ | 12 | | | | | | 4 |
| 1 | 2 | 3 | 4 | 5 | 8 | 12 | 7 | | $10^3$ | 13 | $11^2$ | 14 | | | | 6 | $9^1$ | | | | | | | | 5 |
| 1 | 2 | 3 | | 5 | 8 | | 9 | 13 | 10 | $11^1$ | 14 | 12 | | | | $6^3$ | $7^2$ | 4 | | | | | | | 6 |
| 1 | 2 | | 4 | 13 | $9^3$ | 14 | 7 | | 12 | $10^2$ | | $11^1$ | 5 | | | 6 | | | 8 | | 3 | | | | 7 |
| 1 | | 4 | 3 | 5 | | | 9 | 8 | 12 | $11^3$ | 13 | $10^1$ | 14 | $6^4$ | | $7^2$ | | 2 | | | | | | | 8 |
| 1 | | 4 | 14 | 5 | | | 7 | 6 | $11^3$ | 10 | | 12 | $9^1$ | 13 | | 8 | 3 | $2^2$ | | | | | | | 9 |
| 1 | | 3 | | 5 | | 7 | $8^3$ | 12 | $9^2$ | 10 | $11^1$ | | 4 | | | 13 | 14 | 6 | 2 | | | | | | 10 |
| 1 | 2 | 3 | | 5 | 8 | | 6 | | $11^3$ | $9^2$ | 13 | 10 | | | | 12 | 14 | 7 | $4^1$ | | | | | | 11 |
| 1 | | 3 | | $5^2$ | $8^3$ | | 6 | 10 | $11^1$ | 9 | 12 | 13 | | | | 2 | 14 | 7 | 4 | | | | | | 12 |
| 1 | 2 | 4 | | | 6 | | 7 | | $10^2$ | 12 | $9^1$ | 13 | 5 | | | 11 | | | 8 | 3 | | | | | 13 |
| 1 | 5 | 3 | | | 8 | | 7 | | $10^2$ | | 11 | 13 | 14 | $12^2$ | | 2 | $6^1$ | | 9 | 4 | | | | | 14 |
| 1 | 12 | 3 | 4 | | 8 | | 6 | 10 | 13 | $9^2$ | $11^3$ | 14 | $5^1$ | | | 2 | | | 7 | | | | | | 15 |
| 1 | 2 | $3^1$ | | 5 | 6 | | $7^3$ | 9 | 10 | 13 | 14 | $11^2$ | | 12 | | | | | 8 | 4 | | | | | 16 |
| 1 | 2 | 14 | 5 | 6 | | 8 | $9^1$ | 10 | $11^3$ | 13 | | $12^2$ | 4 | | | 7 | | | | 3 | | | | | 17 |
| 1 | 2 | | | | 9 | | 8 | | 10 | $11^2$ | 12 | | 3 | | 14 | $7^1$ | 13 | 6 | 4 | | $5^3$ | | | | 18 |
| 1 | 2 | 3 | 14 | | 9 | | 8 | | 10 | $11^1$ | 12 | | $4^2$ | | 6 | $7^3$ | 13 | 5 | | | | | | | 19 |
| 1 | 2 | 3 | 13 | 5 | $9^1$ | | 6 | $10^5$ | $8^3$ | | $11^2$ | | | | 12 | 14 | | 7 | 4 | | | | | | 20 |
| 1 | 2 | 3 | 4 | 5 | $9^2$ | | 7 | | $11^1$ | 12 | $10^3$ | | | 6 | 14 | | | 13 | 8 | | | | | | 21 |
| 1 | 2 | $3^4$ | 12 | 5 | $9^3$ | | | | $10^1$ | $11^2$ | 13 | 14 | | 8 | | 6 | | 7 | 4 | | | | | | 22 |
| 1 | $2^1$ | 3 | 14 | 5 | $10^3$ | | | 12 | 13 | $9^2$ | 11 | | | 8 | | 7 | | 6 | 4 | | | | | | 23 |
| 1 | 2 | | 3 | 5 | 10 | 13 | | $8^1$ | 11 | $9^2$ | 12 | | | $6^3$ | | | 4 | 14 | 7 | | | | | | 24 |
| 1 | 2 | | 3 | 5 | $9^2$ | | 14 | 10 | | 11 | | 12 | | 6 | | 13 | 7 | | $8^3$ | $4^1$ | | | | | 25 |
| 1 | 2 | | $3^2$ | 5 | $9^3$ | | 7 | $6^1$ | 10 | | 11 | | 13 | 12 | | 14 | 4 | | 8 | | | | | | 26 |
| 1 | 2 | | 14 | 5 | $11^3$ | $8^1$ | 7 | 13 | $10^2$ | 12 | | | 3 | 9 | | 6 | | | | 4 | | | | | 27 |
| 1 | 2 | | 5 | $10^3$ | $7^1$ | 9 | 13 | | $11^2$ | 12 | | | 3 | 8 | | 6 | | 14 | 4 | | | | | | 28 |
| 1 | 2 | | 13 | 10 | | | 12 | | 9 | 11 | 5 | $3^3$ | $8^2$ | | | 6 | 14 | $7^1$ | 4 | | | | | | 29 |
| 1 | 2 | $4^2$ | 3 | 5 | $8^3$ | | 6 | $10^1$ | 12 | $9^1$ | 11 | | | | | 13 | 14 | 7 | | | | | | | 30 |
| 1 | 2 | 4 | 13 | 5 | $10^2$ | | 7 | $9^1$ | 12 | $11^3$ | | | | | | 8 | 14 | | 6 | 3 | | | | | 31 |
| 1 | | 4 | 3 | | 9 | 8 | $11^1$ | 10 | 12 | 5 | | | 13 | | | $7^2$ | 14 | 6 | | $2^3$ | | | | | 32 |
| 1 | 2 | 3 | 14 | $5^3$ | | 6 | 10 | | 9 | $11^2$ | 12 | | | $8^1$ | | | 13 | 7 | 4 | | | | | | 33 |
| 1 | 2 | 3 | 4 | 5 | $8^1$ | | 6 | $9^3$ | 11 | $10^2$ | | 14 | | 12 | | 13 | | 7 | | | | | | | 34 |
| 1 | 2 | 3 | | 5 | $10^3$ | 14 | $6^1$ | 8 | $11^2$ | 13 | 12 | | | 7 | | | | 9 | 4 | | | | | | 35 |
| 1 | | 4 | | $7^2$ | | $10^1$ | | $9^1$ | 11 | 5 | 3 | | 8 | 14 | 13 | 6 | | | 12 | | 2 | | | | 36 |
| 1 | | 4 | 5 | 9 | | 6 | $11^3$ | 10 | 14 | | $3^1$ | | 8 | 12 | 13 | $7^2$ | | | 2 | | | | | | 37 |
| 1 | 2 | | 4 | 13 | $7^2$ | 6 | 9 | 12 | $10^1$ | 11 | | 5 | | 8 | | | | | 3 | | | | | | 38 |

**FA Cup**

| | | | |
|---|---|---|---|
| Third Round | Watford | (h) | 3-0 |
| Fourth Round | Stoke C | (a) | 1-0 |
| Fifth Round | Leeds U | (h) | 4-0 |
| Sixth Round | Barnsley | (h) | 5-0 |
| Semi-Finals | Chelsea | | 2-1 |
| (*at Wembley*) | | | |
| Final (*at Wembley*) | Wigan Ath | | 0-1 |

**Capital One Cup**

| | | | |
|---|---|---|---|
| Third Round | Aston Villa | (h) | 2-4 |

**Community Shield**

| | | |
|---|---|---|
| (*at Villa Park*) | Chelsea | 3-2 |

**UEFA Champions League**

| | | | |
|---|---|---|---|
| Group D | Real Madrid | (a) | 2-3 |
| | Borussia Dortmund | (h) | 1-1 |
| | Ajax | (a) | 1-3 |
| | Ajax | (h) | 2-2 |
| | Real Madrid | (h) | 1-1 |
| | Borussia Dortmund | (a) | 0-1 |

# MANCHESTER UNITED

## FOUNDATION

Manchester United was formed as comparatively recently as 1902 after their predecessors, Newton Heath, went bankrupt. However, it is usual to give the date of the club's foundation as 1878 when the dining room committee of the carriage and waggon works of the Lancashire and Yorkshire Railway Company formed Newton Heath L and YR Cricket and Football Club. They won the Manchester Cup in 1886 and as Newton Heath FC were admitted to the Second Division in 1892.

*Old Trafford, Sir Matt Busby Way, Manchester M16 0RA.*

*Telephone:* (0161) 868 8000.

*Fax:* (0161) 868 8804.

*Ticket Office:* (0161) 868 8000.

*Website:* www.manutd.com

*Email:* enquiries@manutd.co.uk

*Ground Capacity:* 75,765.

*Record Attendance:* 76,098 v Blackburn R, FA Premier League, 31 March 2007.

*Ground Record Attendance:* 76,962 Wolverhampton W v Grimsby T, FA Cup semi-final, 25 March 1939.

*Pitch Measurements:* 105m × 68m (114yd × 74yd)

*Co-Chairmen:* Joel and Avram Glazer.

*Chief Executive:* Ed Woodward.

*Manager:* David Moyes.

*Assistant Manager:* Steve Round.

*Physio:* Rob Swire.

*Colours:* Red shirts with black trim, white shorts with red side panels, black socks.

*Year Formed:* 1878 as Newton Heath LYR; 1902, Manchester United.

*Turned Professional:* 1885.

*Previous Name:* 1880, Newton Heath; 1902, Manchester United.

*Club Nickname:* 'Red Devils'.

*Grounds:* 1880, North Road, Monsall Road; 1893, Bank Street; 1910, Old Trafford (played at Maine Road 1941–49).

## HONOURS

**FA Premier League:** *Champions* 1992–93, 1993–94, 1995–96, 1996–97, 1998–99, 1999–2000, 2000–01, 2002–03, 2006–07, 2007–08, 2008–09, 2010–11, 2012–13; *Runners-up* 1994–95, 1997–98, 2005–06, 2009–10, 2011–12.
**Football League – Division 1:** *Champions* 1907–08, 1910–11, 1951–52, 1955–56, 1956–57, 1964–65, 1966–67; *Runners-up* 1946–47, 1947–48, 1948–49, 1950–51, 1958–59, 1963–64, 1967–68, 1979–80, 1987–88, 1991–92.
**Division 2:** *Champions* 1935–36, 1974–75; *Runners-up* 1896–97, 1905–06, 1924–25, 1937–38.
**FA Cup:** *Winners* 1909, 1948, 1963, 1977, 1983, 1985, 1990, 1994, 1996, 1999, 2004; *Runners-up* 1957, 1958, 1976, 1979, 1995, 2005, 2007.
**Football League Cup:** *Winners* 1992, 2006, 2009, 2010; *Runners-up* 1983, 1991, 1994, 2003.
**European Competitions**
**European Cup:** 1956–57 (*s-f*), 1957–58 (*s-f*), 1965–66 (*s-f*), 1967–68 (*winners*), 1968–69 (*s-f*). **Champions League:** 1993–94, 1994–95, 1996–97 (*s-f*), 1997–98, 1998–99 (*winners*), 1999–2000, 2000–01, 2001–02 (*s-f*), 2002–03, 2003–04, 2004–05, 2005–06, 2006–07 (*s-f*), 2007–08 (*winners*), 2008–09 (*runners-up*), 2009–10, 2010–11 (*runners-up*), 2011–12, 2012–13. **European Cup-Winners' Cup:** 1963–64, 1977–78, 1983–84, 1990–91 (*winners*). 1991–92. **Inter Cities Fairs Cup:** 1964–65. **UEFA Cup:** 1976–77, 1980–81, 1982–83, 1984–85, 1992–93, 1995–96. **Europa League:** 2011–12. **Super Cup:** 1991 (*winners*), 1999, 2008. **World Club Championship:** 1968, 1999 (*winners*). **FIFA Club World Cup:** 2008 (*winners*).
*NB: In 1958–59 FA refused permission to compete in European Cup.*

## sky SPORTS FACT FILE

Manchester United only escaped relegation to Division Three North on the final day of the 1933–34 season when they won 2-0 at Millwall. United began the game in the bottom two but victory at The Den saw them leapfrog Millwall who went down alongside already relegated Lincoln City.

*First Football League Game:* 3 September 1892, Division 1, v Blackburn R (a) L 3–4 – Warner; Clements, Brown; Perrins, Stewart, Erentz; Farman (1), Coupar (1), Donaldson (1), Carson, Mathieson.

*Record League Victory (as Newton Heath):* 10–1 v Wolverhampton W, Division 1, 15 October 1892 – Warner; Mitchell, Clements; Perrins, Stewart (3), Erentz; Farman (1), Hood (1), Donaldson (3), Carson (1), Hendry (1).

*Record League Victory (as Manchester U):* 9–0 v Ipswich T, FA Premier League, 4 March 1995 – Schmeichel; Keane (1) (Sharpe), Irwin, Bruce (Butt), Kanchelskis, Pallister, Cole (5), Ince (1), McClair, Hughes (2), Giggs.

*Record Cup Victory:* 10–0 v RSC Anderlecht, European Cup prel. rd 2nd leg, 26 September 1956 – Wood; Foulkes, Byrne; Colman, Jones, Edwards; Berry (1), Whelan (2), Taylor (3), Viollet (4), Pegg.

*Record Defeat:* 0–7 v Blackburn R, Division 1, 10 April 1926; 0–7 v Aston Villa, Division 1, 27 December 1930; 0–7 v Wolverhampton W, Division 2, 26 December 1931.

*Most League Points (2 for a win):* 64, Division 1, 1956–57.

*Most League Points (3 for a win):* 92, FA Premier League, 1993–94.

*Most League Goals:* 103, Division 1, 1956–57 and 1958–59.

*Highest League Scorer in Season:* Dennis Viollet, 32, 1959–60.

*Most League Goals in Total Aggregate:* Bobby Charlton, 199, 1956–73.

*Most Capped Player:* Bobby Charlton, 106, England.

*Most League Appearances:* Ryan Giggs, 660, 1991–.

*Youngest League Player:* Jeff Whitefoot, 16 years 105 days v Portsmouth, 15 April 1950.

*Record Transfer Fee Received:* £80,000,000 from Real Madrid for Cristiano Ronaldo, June 2009.

*Record Transfer Fee Paid:* £30,750,000 to Tottenham H for Dimitar Berbatov, September 2008.

*Football League Record:* 1892 Newton Heath elected to Division 1; 1894–1906 Division 2; 1906–22 Division 1; 1922–25 Division 2; 1925–31 Division 1; 1931–36 Division 2; 1936–37 Division 1; 1937–38 Division 2; 1938–74 Division 1; 1974–75 Division 2; 1975–92 Division 1; 1992– FA Premier League.

## MANAGERS

**J. Ernest Mangnall** 1903–12
**John Bentley** 1912–14
**John Robson** 1914–21
  *(Secretary-Manager from 1916)*
**John Chapman** 1921–26
**Clarence Hilditch** 1926–27
**Herbert Bamlett** 1927–31
**Walter Crickmer** 1931–32
**Scott Duncan** 1932–37
**Walter Crickmer** 1937–45
  *(Secretary-Manager)*
**Matt Busby** 1945–69
  *(continued as General Manager*
  *then Director)*
**Wilf McGuinness** 1969–70
**Sir Matt Busby** 1970–71
**Frank O'Farrell** 1971–72
**Tommy Docherty** 1972–77
**Dave Sexton** 1977–81
**Ron Atkinson** 1981–86
**Sir Alex Ferguson** 1986–2013
**David Moyes** July 2013–

## LATEST SEQUENCES

*Longest Sequence of League Wins:* 14, 15.10.1904 – 3.1.1905.

*Longest Sequence of League Defeats:* 14, 26.4.1930 – 25.10.1930.

*Longest Sequence of League Draws:* 6, 30.10.1988 – 27.11.1988.

*Longest Sequence of Unbeaten League Matches:* 29, 26.12.1998 – 25.9.1999.

*Longest Sequence Without a League Win:* 16, 19.4.1930 – 25.10.1930.

*Successive Scoring Runs:* 36 from 3.12.2007.

*Successive Non-scoring Runs:* 5 from 22.2.1902.

## TEN YEAR LEAGUE RECORD

|         |        | P  | W  | D  | L | F  | A  | Pts | Pos |
|---------|--------|----|----|----|---|----|----|-----|-----|
| 2003-04 | PR Lge | 38 | 23 | 6  | 9 | 64 | 35 | 75  | 3   |
| 2004-05 | PR Lge | 38 | 22 | 11 | 5 | 58 | 26 | 77  | 3   |
| 2005-06 | PR Lge | 38 | 25 | 8  | 5 | 72 | 34 | 83  | 2   |
| 2006-07 | PR Lge | 38 | 28 | 5  | 5 | 83 | 27 | 89  | 1   |
| 2007-08 | PR Lge | 38 | 27 | 6  | 5 | 80 | 22 | 87  | 1   |
| 2008-09 | PR Lge | 38 | 28 | 6  | 4 | 68 | 24 | 90  | 1   |
| 2009-10 | PR Lge | 38 | 27 | 4  | 7 | 86 | 28 | 85  | 2   |
| 2010-11 | PR Lge | 38 | 23 | 11 | 4 | 78 | 37 | 80  | 1   |
| 2011-12 | PR Lge | 38 | 28 | 5  | 5 | 89 | 33 | 89  | 2   |
| 2012-13 | PR Lge | 38 | 28 | 5  | 5 | 86 | 43 | 89  | 1   |

**DID YOU KNOW ?**

When Manchester United entered the European Cup for the first time in 1956–57 they played their early home games at Manchester City's Maine Road ground because Old Trafford did not have floodlights. Lights were installed in March 1957, enabling the semi-final against Real Madrid to be played at Old Trafford.

## MANCHESTER UNITED – FA PREMIERSHIP 2012–13 LEAGUE RECORD

| Match No. | Date | Venue | Opponents | Result | H/T Score | Lg Pos. | Goalscorers | Attendance |
|---|---|---|---|---|---|---|---|---|
| 1 | Aug 20 | A | Everton | L | 0-1 | 0-0 | 16 | | 38,415 |
| 2 | 25 | H | Fulham | W | 3-2 | 3-1 | 7 | Van Persie [10], Kagawa [35], Da Silva [41] | 75,352 |
| 3 | Sept 2 | A | Southampton | W | 3-2 | 1-1 | 5 | Van Persie 3 [23,87,90] | 31,609 |
| 4 | 15 | H | Wigan Ath | W | 4-0 | 0-0 | 2 | Scholes [51], Hernandez [63], Buttner [66], Powell [82] | 75,142 |
| 5 | 23 | A | Liverpool | W | 2-1 | 0-0 | 2 | Da Silva [51], Van Persie (pen) [81] | 44,263 |
| 6 | 29 | H | Tottenham H | L | 2-3 | 0-2 | 3 | Nani [51], Kagawa [54] | 75,566 |
| 7 | Oct 7 | A | Newcastle U | W | 3-0 | 2-0 | 2 | Evans [8], Evra [15], Cleverley [71] | 52,203 |
| 8 | 20 | H | Stoke C | W | 4-2 | 2-1 | 2 | Rooney 2 [27,65], Van Persie [44], Welbeck [46] | 75,585 |
| 9 | 28 | A | Chelsea | W | 3-2 | 2-1 | 2 | Luiz (og) [4], Van Persie [12], Hernandez [75] | 41,644 |
| 10 | Nov 3 | H | Arsenal | W | 2-1 | 1-0 | 1 | Van Persie [3], Evra [67] | 75,492 |
| 11 | 10 | A | Aston Villa | W | 3-2 | 0-1 | 1 | Hernandez 2 [58,87], Vlaar (og) [63] | 40,538 |
| 12 | 17 | A | Norwich C | L | 0-1 | 0-0 | 2 | | 26,840 |
| 13 | 24 | H | QPR | W | 3-1 | 0-0 | 1 | Evans [64], Fletcher [68], Hernandez [72] | 75,603 |
| 14 | 28 | H | West Ham U | W | 1-0 | 1-0 | 1 | Van Persie [1] | 75,572 |
| 15 | Dec 1 | A | Reading | W | 4-3 | 4-3 | 1 | Anderson [13], Rooney 2 (1 pen) [16(pl),30], Van Persie [34] | 24,095 |
| 16 | 9 | H | Manchester C | W | 3-2 | 2-0 | 1 | Rooney 2 [16,29], Van Persie [90] | 47,166 |
| 17 | 15 | H | Sunderland | W | 3-1 | 2-0 | 1 | Van Persie [16], Cleverley [19], Rooney [59] | 75,582 |
| 18 | 23 | A | Swansea C | D | 1-1 | 1-1 | 1 | Evra [16] | 20,650 |
| 19 | 26 | H | Newcastle U | W | 4-3 | 1-2 | 1 | Evans [25], Evra [58], Van Persie [71], Hernandez [90] | 75,596 |
| 20 | 29 | H | WBA | W | 2-0 | 1-0 | 1 | McAuley (og) [9], Van Persie [90] | 75,595 |
| 21 | Jan 1 | A | Wigan Ath | W | 4-0 | 2-0 | 1 | Hernandez 2 [35,63], Van Persie 2 [43,88] | 20,342 |
| 22 | 13 | H | Liverpool | W | 2-1 | 1-0 | 1 | Van Persie [19], Vidic [54] | 75,501 |
| 23 | 20 | A | Tottenham H | D | 1-1 | 1-0 | 1 | Van Persie [25] | 35,956 |
| 24 | 30 | H | Southampton | W | 2-1 | 2-1 | 1 | Rooney 2 [8,27] | 75,600 |
| 25 | Feb 2 | A | Fulham | W | 1-0 | 0-0 | 1 | Rooney [79] | 25,670 |
| 26 | 10 | H | Everton | W | 2-0 | 2-0 | 1 | Giggs [13], Van Persie [45] | 75,525 |
| 27 | 23 | A | QPR | W | 2-0 | 1-0 | 1 | Da Silva [23], Giggs [80] | 18,337 |
| 28 | Mar 2 | H | Norwich C | W | 4-0 | 1-0 | 1 | Kagawa 3 [45,76,87], Rooney [90] | 75,586 |
| 29 | 16 | H | Reading | W | 1-0 | 1-0 | 1 | Rooney [21] | 75,605 |
| 30 | 30 | A | Sunderland | W | 1-0 | 1-0 | 1 | Bramble (og) [27] | 43,760 |
| 31 | Apr 8 | H | Manchester C | L | 1-2 | 0-0 | 1 | Kompany (og) [59] | 75,498 |
| 32 | 14 | A | Stoke C | W | 2-0 | 1-0 | 1 | Carrick [4], Van Persie (pen) [66] | 27,191 |
| 33 | 17 | A | West Ham U | D | 2-2 | 1-1 | 1 | Valencia [31], Van Persie [77] | 34,692 |
| 34 | 22 | H | Aston Villa | W | 3-0 | 3-0 | 1 | Van Persie 3 [2,13,33] | 75,591 |
| 35 | 28 | A | Arsenal | D | 1-1 | 1-1 | 1 | Van Persie (pen) [44] | 60,112 |
| 36 | May 5 | H | Chelsea | L | 0-1 | 0-0 | 1 | | 75,500 |
| 37 | 12 | H | Swansea C | W | 2-1 | 1-0 | 1 | Hernandez [39], Ferdinand [87] | 75,572 |
| 38 | 19 | A | WBA | D | 5-5 | 3-1 | 1 | Kagawa [6], Olsson (og) [9], Buttner [30], Van Persie [53], Hernandez [63] | 26,438 |

**Final League Position: 1**

### GOALSCORERS

*League (86):* Van Persie 26 (3 pens), Rooney 12 (1 pen), Hernandez 10, Kagawa 6, Evra 4, Da Silva 3, Evans 3, Buttner 2, Cleverley 2, Giggs 2, Anderson 1, Carrick 1, Ferdinand 1, Fletcher 1, Nani 1, Powell 1, Scholes 1, Valencia 1, Vidic 1, Welbeck 1, own goals 6.

*FA Cup (11):* Hernandez 4, Rooney 3, Cleverley 1, Giggs 1 (1 pen), Nani 1, Van Persie 1.

*Capital One Cup (6):* Giggs 2 (1 pen), Anderson 1, Cleverley 1, Hernandez 1, Nani 1.

*UEFA Champions League (11):* Hernandez 3, Van Persie 3, Carrick 1, Evans 1, Rooney 1 (1 pen), Welbeck 1, own goal 1.

| De Gea D 28 | Valencia A 24+6 | Carrick M 34+2 | Vidic N 18+1 | Evra P 34 | Nani 7+4 | Cleverley T 18+4 | Scholes P 8+8 | Kagawa S 17+3 | Rooney W 22+5 | Welbeck D 13+14 | Van Persie R 35+3 | Young A 17+2 | Anderson 9+8 | Da Silva R 27+1 | Giggs R 12+10 | Lindegaard A 10 | Ferdinand R 26+2 | Hernandez J 9+13 | Buttner A 4+1 | Powell N —+2 | Evans J 21+2 | Smalling C 10+5 | Fletcher D 2+1 | Jones P 13+4 | Match No. |
|---|---|---|---|---|---|---|---|---|---|---|---|---|---|---|---|---|---|---|---|---|---|---|---|---|---|
| 1 | 2 | 3 | 4 | 5 | $6^2$ | $7^3$ | 8 | 9 | 10 | $11^1$ | 12 | 13 | 14 | | | | | | | | | | | | 1 |
| 1 | 8 | 3 | 4 | 5 | 6 | | | $9^2$ | 13 | 12 | 11 | $10^1$ | $7^3$ | 2 | 14 | | | | | | | | | | 2 |
| | 6 | 8 | 4 | 5 | 13 | $7^1$ | 12 | $11^2$ | | $9^3$ | 10 | | | 2 | | 1 | 3 | 14 | | | | | | | 3 |
| | 8 | $4^3$ | | | 6 | $7^1$ | | 11 | 12 | | $9^2$ | | 2 | | | 1 | 3 | 10 | 5 | | 13 | 14 | | | 4 |
| | 8 | 6 | | 5 | $10^1$ | 12 | | $9^2$ | | 14 | 11 | | $2^3$ | 7 | | 1 | 3 | 13 | | | 4 | | | | 5 |
| | 7 | 5 | | 6 | 8 | $9^2$ | 12 | 13 | 11 | | 2 | $10^1$ | | 1 | | | $3^3$ | 14 | | | 4 | | | | 6 |
| 1 | 12 | 7 | | 5 | 6 | 13 | $10^1$ | $9^2$ | 8 | $11^3$ | | | 2 | 14 | | | 3 | | | | 4 | | | | 7 |
| 1 | $6^2$ | 8 | | 5 | 13 | $7^1$ | | 11 | $9^3$ | 10 | 12 | | 2 | | | | 3 | 14 | | | 4 | | | | 8 |
| 1 | 6 | 7 | | 5 | $8^1$ | | | $10^2$ | 11 | 9 | | 2 | 13 | | | | 3 | 12 | | | 4 | | | | 9 |
| 1 | $6^2$ | 7 | | 5 | 13 | $8^1$ | | 10 | 11 | 9 | 12 | | 2 | | | | 3 | | | | 4 | | | | 10 |
| 1 | 6 | 7 | | 5 | 13 | $8^2$ | | $10^3$ | 11 | $9^1$ | 14 | | 2 | | | | 3 | 12 | | | | 4 | | | 11 |
| | $6^1$ | 7 | | 5 | 12 | | | 13 | 10 | 9 | 14 | 2 | 8 | 1 | | | $3^3$ | $11^2$ | | | | 4 | | | 12 |
| | | 5 | | | $8^2$ | | 9 | $10^3$ | 11 | $6^1$ | 13 | 2 | | 1 | 4 | 12 | | | 14 | 3 | | 7 | | | 13 |
| | 6 | 5 | | | $8^1$ | | $9^2$ | 13 | 10 | 12 | $7^3$ | 2 | | 1 | | 11 | | | 4 | 3 | | 14 | | | 14 |
| | 8 | 5 | | | | | 10 | 14 | $11^3$ | 9 | $7^2$ | $2^1$ | | 1 | 3 | | | 4 | 12 | 6 | 13 | | | | 15 |
| 1 | $6^2$ | 7 | | 5 | $8^3$ | | | 10 | 14 | 11 | 9 | | 2 | | | | 3 | | | $4^1$ | 12 | 13 | | | 16 |
| 1 | 6 | $7^1$ | 13 | 5 | $8^2$ | 12 | | 10 | | 11 | 9 | | 14 | $4^2$ | | | | | | 3 | | 2 | | | 17 |
| 1 | $6^1$ | 7 | 4 | 5 | $8^3$ | 14 | | $10^2$ | | 11 | 9 | | 13 | | | | 12 | | | 3 | | 2 | | | 18 |
| 1 | 6 | 7 | | 5 | 12 | $8^1$ | | 10 | | 9 | | | | 3 | $11^2$ | | 4 | 2 | 13 | | | | | | 19 |
| 1 | 8 | 6 | 3 | 5 | $7^2$ | 13 | $9^1$ | | 11 | 12 | 10 | | | 4 | 2 | | | | | | | | | | 20 |
| 1 | $7^2$ | 5 | | | 8 | | 12 | | 14 | 10 | $6^2$ | | 2 | 9 | $3^1$ | 11 | | 4 | 13 | | | | | | 21 |
| 1 | 12 | 6 | $4^3$ | 5 | 7 | | | $9^2$ | | 10 | 11 | $8^1$ | | 2 | | | 3 | | | | 14 | 13 | | | 22 |
| 1 | 13 | 7 | 4 | 5 | $8^2$ | | | $9^1$ | 12 | 10 | 11 | | 2 | | | | 3 | | | | | 6 | | | 23 |
| 1 | | 7 | 4 | 5 | 14 | | | $9^3$ | 10 | 6 | 11 | $8^2$ | 13 | | 12 | | | $3^1$ | 2 | | | | | | 24 |
| | $6^1$ | 8 | | 5 | $9^9$ | $7^2$ | | 10 | 14 | 11 | | | 2 | 13 | 3 | 12 | | | | 4 | | | | | 25 |
| 1 | 6 | 12 | 3 | 5 | 7 | | | 10 | | 11 | | | 2 | 9 | | | | | $4^2$ | 13 | $8^1$ | | | | 26 |
| 1 | 14 | 7 | 4 | 5 | 6 | | | 13 | 12 | $10^1$ | $9^3$ | | 2 | 8 | 3 | $11^2$ | | | | | | | | | 27 |
| 1 | 6 | 8 | 3 | 5 | 13 | | | 9 | 10 | 12 | $11^1$ | $7^2$ | | 4 | 2 | | | | | | | | | | 28 |
| 1 | | 12 | 4 | | 13 | 10 | 6 | 11 | $9^1$ | $8^2$ | 7 | 3 | 5 | | 2 | | | | | | | | | | 29 |
| 1 | 6 | 7 | 3 | | 14 | $10^1$ | 13 | 11 | 9 | $8^3$ | $2^1$ | | 5 | 12 | 4 | | | | | | | | | | 30 |
| 1 | 12 | 7 | | 5 | 14 | $10^2$ | $9^1$ | 11 | $6^3$ | | 2 | 8 | 3 | 13 | | | | | | 4 | | | | | 31 |
| 1 | 6 | 7 | 4 | 5 | 9 | 8 | 12 | 11 | | $3^1$ | $10^1$ | | 2 | | | | | | | | | | | | 32 |
| 1 | 6 | 7 | 4 | 5 | $9^2$ | $10^1$ | | 11 | | 2 | 12 | 3 | 13 | | | | | | | | 8 | | | | 33 |
| 1 | 8 | 6 | | 5 | 10 | $9^1$ | 12 | 11 | | 2 | 7 | | 4 | | | | | | | 3 | | | | | 34 |
| 1 | 6 | 7 | | 5 | $9^2$ | | | $10^3$ | 11 | 12 | $2^1$ | 13 | 3 | 14 | | 4 | | | | 8 | | | | | 35 |
| $9^3$ | | 4 | 5 | $8^1$ | 13 | | 10 | $7^2$ | $2^4$ | 11 | 1 | 14 | 12 | 3 | | 6 | | | | | | | | | 36 |
| 1 | 12 | 6 | 4 | 5 | $7^1$ | 9 | $8^2$ | 11 | 13 | 14 | 3 | $10^3$ | | 2 | | | | | | | | | | | 37 |
| | 2 | 7 | | | $8^1$ | 13 | $9^2$ | | 10 | 6 | 12 | 1 | 14 | 11 | 5 | $3^3$ | | 4 | | | | | | | 38 |

**FA Cup**

| | | | |
|---|---|---|---|
| Third Round | West Ham U | (a) | 2-2 |
| *Replay* | West Ham U | (h) | 1-0 |
| Fourth Round | Fulham | (h) | 4-1 |
| Fifth Round | Reading | (h) | 2-1 |
| Sixth Round | Chelsea | (h) | 2-2 |
| *Replay* | Chelsea | (a) | 0-1 |

**Capital One Cup**

| | | | |
|---|---|---|---|
| Third Round | Newcastle U | (h) | 2-1 |
| Fourth Round | Chelsea | (a) | 4-5 |

**UEFA Champions League**

| | | | |
|---|---|---|---|
| Group H | Galatasaray | (h) | 1-0 |
| | CFR Cluj | (a) | 2-1 |
| | Braga | (h) | 3-2 |
| | Braga | (a) | 3-1 |
| | Galatasaray | (a) | 0-1 |
| | CFR Cluj | (h) | 0-1 |
| Knock-out Round | Real Madrid | (a) | 1-1 |
| | Real Madrid | (h) | 1-2 |

# MANSFIELD TOWN

## FOUNDATION

The club was formed as Mansfield Wesleyans in 1897, and changed their name to Mansfield Wesley in 1906 and Mansfield Town in 1910. This was after the Mansfield Wesleyan Chapel trustees had requested that the club change its name as 'it has no longer had any connection with either the chapel or school'. The new club participated in the Notts and Derby District League, but in the following season 1911–12 joined the Central Alliance.

*One Call Stadium, Quarry Lane, Mansfield, Nottinghamshire NG18 5DA.*

*Telephone:* (01623) 482 482.

*Fax:* (01623) 482 495.

*Ticket Office:* (01623) 482 482.

*Website:* www.mansfieldtown.net

*Email:* info@mansfieldtown.net

*Ground Capacity:* 8,186.

*Record Attendance:* 24,467 v Nottingham F, FA Cup 3rd rd, 10 January 1953.

*Pitch Measurements:* 103m × 64m (113yd × 70yd)

*Chairman:* John Radford.

*Chief Executive:* Carolyn Radford.

*Manager:* Paul Cox.

*Assistant Manager:* Adam Murray.

*Physio:* Simon Murphy.

*Colours:* Yellow and blue striped shirts, yellow shorts, yellow socks with blue trim.

*Year Formed:* 1897.

*Turned Professional:* 1906.

*Ltd Co.:* 1922.

*Previous Name:* 1897, Mansfield Wesleyans; 1906, Mansfield Wesley; 1910, Mansfield Town.

*Grounds:* 1897–99, Westfield Lane; 1899–1901, Ratcliffe Gate; 1901–12, Newgate Lane; 1912–16, Ratcliffe Gate; 1916, Field Mill (renamed One Call Stadium, 2012).

*Club Nickname:* 'The Stags'.

*First Football League Game:* 29 August 1931, Division 3 (S), v Swindon T (h) W 3–2 – Wilson; Clifford, England; Wake, Davis, Blackburn; Gilhespy, Readman (1), Johnson, Broom (2), Baxter.

*Record League Victory:* 9–2 v Rotherham U, Division 3 (N), 27 December 1932 – Wilson; Anthony, England; Davies, S. Robinson, Slack; Prior, Broom, Readman (3), Hoyland (3), Bowater (3).

*Record Cup Victory:* 8–0 v Scarborough (a), FA Cup 1st rd, 22 November 1952 – Bramley; Chessell, Bradley; Field, Plummer, Lewis; Scott, Fox (3), Marron (2), Sid Watson (1), Adam (2).

*Record Defeat:* 1–8 v Walsall, Division 3 (N), 19 January 1933.

## HONOURS

**Football League: Division 2:** Best season: 21st, 1977–78; **Division 3:** *Champions* 1976–77; Promoted to **Division 2** (3rd) 2001–02; **Division 4:** *Champions* 1974–75; **Division 3 (N):** *Runners-up* 1950–51.

**FA Cup:** Best season: 6th rd, 1969.

**Football League Cup:** Best season: 5th rd, 1976.

**Freight Rover Trophy:** *Winners* 1987.

**Conference:** *Winners* 2012–13.

## sky SPORTS FACT FILE

Mansfield Town reached the FA Cup quarter-finals in 1968–69, defeating Tow Law Town, Rotherham United, Sheffield United, Southend and West Ham before going down to Leicester City in the sixth round. They were rewarded for their exploits with the *Daily Mirror*'s Giant Killing Cup.

*Most League Points (2 for a win):* 68, Division 4, 1974–75.

*Most League Points (3 for a win):* 81, Division 4, 1985–86.

*Most League Goals:* 108, Division 4, 1962–63.

*Highest League Scorer in Season:* Ted Harston, 55, Division 3 (N), 1936–37.

*Most League Goals in Total Aggregate:* Harry Johnson, 104, 1931–36.

*Most League Goals in One Match:* 7, Ted Harston v Hartlepools U, Division 3N, 23 January 1937.

*Most Capped Player:* John McClelland, 6 (53), Northern Ireland.

*Most League Appearances:* Rod Arnold, 440, 1970–83.

*Youngest League Player:* Cyril Poole, 15 years 351 days v New Brighton, 27 February 1937.

*Record Transfer Fee Received:* £655,000 from Tottenham H for Colin Calderwood, July 1993.

*Record Transfer Fee Paid:* £150,000 to Carlisle U for Lee Peacock, October 1997.

*Football League Record:* 1931 Elected to Division 3 (S); 1932–37 Division 3 (N); 1937–47 Division 3 (S); 1947–58 Division 3 (N); 1958–60 Division 3; 1960–63 Division 4; 1963–72 Division 3; 1972–75 Division 4; 1975–77 Division 3; 1977–78 Division 2; 1978–80 Division 3; 1980–86 Division 4; 1986–91 Division 3; 1991–92 Division 4; 1992–93 Division 2; 1993–2002 Division 3; 2002–03 Division 2; 2003–04 Division 3; 2004–08 FL 2; 2008–13 Blue Square Premier; 2013– FL 2.

## LATEST SEQUENCES

*Longest Sequence of League Wins:* 7, 13.9.1991 – 26.10.1991.

*Longest Sequence of League Defeats:* 7, 18.1.1947 – 15.3.1947.

*Longest Sequence of League Draws:* 5, 18.10.1986 – 22.11.1986.

*Longest Sequence of Unbeaten League Matches:* 20, 14.2.1976 – 21.8.1976.

*Longest Sequence Without a League Win:* 14, 25.3.2000 – 2.9.2000.

*Successive Scoring Runs:* 27 from 1.10.1962.

*Successive Non-scoring Runs:* 8 from 25.3.2000.

## MANAGERS

John Baynes 1922–25
Ted Davison 1926–28
Jack Hickling 1928–33
Henry Martin 1933–35
Charlie Bell 1935
Harold Wightman 1936
Harold Parkes 1936–38
Jack Poole 1938–44
Lloyd Barke 1944–45
Roy Goodall 1945–49
Freddie Steele 1949–51
George Jobey 1952–53
Stan Mercer 1953–55
Charlie Mitten 1956–58
Sam Weaver 1958–60
Raich Carter 1960–63
Tommy Cummings 1963–67
Tommy Eggleston 1967–70
Jock Basford 1970–71
Danny Williams 1971–74
Dave Smith 1974–76
Peter Morris 1976–78
Billy Bingham 1978–79
Mick Jones 1979–81
Stuart Boam 1981–83
Ian Greaves 1983–89
George Foster 1989–93
Andy King 1993–96
Steve Parkin 1996–99
Billy Dearden 1999–2002
Stuart Watkiss 2002
Keith Curle 2002–05
Carlton Palmer 2005
Peter Shirtliff 2005–06
Billy Dearden 2006–08
Paul Holland 2008
Billy McEwan 2008
David Holdsworth 2008–10
Duncan Russell 2010–11
Paul Cox May 2011–

## TEN YEAR LEAGUE RECORD

|  |  | P | W | D | L | F | A | Pts | Pos |
|---|---|---|---|---|---|---|---|---|---|
| 2003-04 | Div 3 | 46 | 22 | 9 | 15 | 76 | 62 | 75 | 5 |
| 2004-05 | FL 2 | 46 | 15 | 15 | 16 | 56 | 56 | 60 | 13 |
| 2005-06 | FL 2 | 46 | 13 | 15 | 18 | 59 | 66 | 54 | 16 |
| 2006-07 | FL 2 | 46 | 14 | 12 | 20 | 58 | 63 | 54 | 17 |
| 2007-08 | FL 2 | 46 | 11 | 9 | 26 | 48 | 68 | 42 | 23 |
| 2008-09 | BSP | 46 | 19 | 9 | 18 | 57 | 55 | 62 | 12 |
| 2009-10 | BSP | 44 | 17 | 11 | 16 | 69 | 60 | 62 | 9 |
| 2010-11 | BSP | 46 | 17 | 10 | 19 | 73 | 75 | 61 | 13 |
| 2011-12 | BSP | 46 | 25 | 14 | 7 | 87 | 48 | 89 | 3 |
| 2012-13 | BSP | 46 | 30 | 5 | 11 | 92 | 52 | 95 | 1 |

## DID YOU KNOW

Winger John Mitten understudied his father Charlie on the wing at Mansfield Town during the 1957–58 season. Charlie, who was the Stags' player-manager at the time, made 38 appearances and John just three, although the two never played in the same team.

# MIDDLESBROUGH

## FOUNDATION

A previous belief that Middlesbrough Football Club was founded at a tripe supper at the Corporation Hotel has proved to be erroneous. In fact, members of Middlesbrough Cricket Club were responsible for forming it at a meeting in the gymnasium of the Albert Park Hotel in 1875.

*Riverside Stadium, Middlesbrough TS3 6RS.*

*Telephone:* (0844) 499 6789.

*Fax:* (01642) 757 697.

*Ticket Office:* (0844) 499 1234.

*Website:* www.mfc.co.uk

*Email:* enquiries@mfc.co.uk

*Ground Capacity:* 34,998.

*Record Attendance:* 53,536 v Newcastle U, Division 1, 27 December 1949 (at Ayresome Park); 34,814 v Newcastle U, FA Premier League, 5 March 2003 (at Riverside Stadium).

*Pitch Measurements:* 105m × 68m (115yd × 75yd)

*Chairman:* Steve Gibson.

*Chief Executive:* Neil Bausor.

*Manager:* Tony Mowbray.

*Assistant Manager:* Mark Venus.

*Head of Medical:* Chris Moseley.

*Colours:* Red shirts with white trim, red shorts with white trim, red socks with white trim.

*Year Formed:* 1876; re-formed 1986.

*Turned Professional:* 1889; became amateur 1892, and professional again, 1899.

*Club Nickname:* 'Boro'.

*Grounds:* 1877, Old Archery Ground, Albert Park; 1879, Breckon Hill; 1882, Linthorpe Road Ground; 1903, Ayresome Park; 1995, Riverside Stadium.

*First Football League Game:* 2 September 1899, Division 2, v Lincoln C (a) L 0–3 – Smith; Shaw, Ramsey; Allport, McNally, McCracken; Wanless, Longstaffe, Gettins, Page, Pugh.

*Record League Victory:* 9–0 v Brighton & HA, Division 2, 23 August 1958 – Taylor; Bilcliff, Robinson; Harris (2p), Phillips, Walley; Day, McLean, Clough (5), Peacock (2), Holliday.

*Record Cup Victory:* 7–0 v Hereford U, Coca-Cola Cup 2nd rd, 1st leg, 18 September 1996 – Miller; Fleming (1), Branco (1), Whyte, Vickers, Whelan, Emerson (1), Mustoe, Stamp, Juninho, Ravanelli (4).

## HONOURS

**Football League – Division 1:**
*Champions* 1994–95;
*Runners-up* 1997–98;
**Division 2:** *Champions* 1926–27, 1928–29, 1973–74;
*Runners-up* 1901–02, 1991–92;
**Division 3:** *Runners-up* 1966–67, 1986–87.

**FA Cup:** *Runners-up* 1997.

**Football League Cup:** *Winners* 2004; *Runners-up* 1997, 1998.

**Amateur Cup:** *Winners* 1895, 1898.

**Anglo-Scottish Cup:** *Winners* 1976.

**Zenith Data Systems Cup:** *Runners-up* 1990.

**European Competitions**
**UEFA Cup:** 2004–05, 2005–06 (*runners-up*).

## sky SPORTS FACT FILE

Middlesbrough were involved in the highest scoring drawn match in Football League history. On 22 October 1960 they drew 6-6 away to Charlton Athletic. Boro were 6-4 up at one point before being pegged back. Brian Clough scored a hat-trick in the game.

**Record Defeat:** 0–9 v Blackburn R, Division 2, 6 November 1954.

**Most League Points (2 for a win):** 65, Division 2, 1973–74.

**Most League Points (3 for a win):** 94, Division 3, 1986–87.

**Most League Goals:** 122, Division 2, 1926–27.

**Highest League Scorer in Season:** George Camsell, 59, Division 2, 1926–27 (Second Division record).

**Most League Goals in Total Aggregate:** George Camsell, 325, 1925–39.

**Most League Goals in One Match:** 5, John Wilkie v Gainsborough T, Division 2, 2 March 1901; 5, Andy Wilson v Nottingham F, Division 1, 6 October 1923; 5, George Camsell v Manchester C, Division 2, 25 December 1926; 5, George Camsell v Aston Villa, Division 1, 9 September 1935; 5, Brian Clough v Brighton & HA, Division 2, 22 August 1958.

**Most Capped Player:** Wilf Mannion, 26, England.

**Most League Appearances:** Tim Williamson, 563, 1902–23.

**Youngest League Player:** Luke Williams, 16 years 200 days v Barnsley, 18 December 2009.

**Record Transfer Fee Received:** £12,000,000 from Atletico Madrid for Juninho, July 1997; £12,000,000 from Aston Villa for Stewart Downing, July 2009.

**Record Transfer Fee Paid:** £12,000,000 to Heerenveen for Afonso Alves, January 2008.

**Football League Record:** 1899 Elected to Division 2; 1902–24 Division 1; 1924–27 Division 2; 1927–28 Division 1; 1928–29 Division 2; 1929–54 Division 1; 1954–66 Division 2; 1966–67 Division 3; 1967–74 Division 2; 1974–82 Division 1; 1982–86 Division 2; 1986–87 Division 3; 1987–88 Division 2; 1988–89 Division 1; 1989–92 Division 2; 1992–93 FA Premier League; 1993–95 Division 1; 1995–97 FA Premier League; 1997–98 Division 1; 1998–2009 FA Premier League; 2009– FL C.

### MANAGERS

John Robson 1899–1905
Alex Mackie 1905–06
Andy Aitken 1906–09
J. Gunter 1908–10
  (Secretary-Manager)
Andy Walker 1910–11
Tom McIntosh 1911–19
Jimmy Howie 1920–23
Herbert Bamlett 1923–26
Peter McWilliam 1927–34
Wilf Gillow 1934–44
David Jack 1944–52
Walter Rowley 1952–54
Bob Dennison 1954–63
Raich Carter 1963–66
Stan Anderson 1966–73
Jack Charlton 1973–77
John Neal 1977–81
Bobby Murdoch 1981–82
Malcolm Allison 1982–84
Willie Maddren 1984–86
Bruce Rioch 1986–90
Colin Todd 1990–91
Lennie Lawrence 1991–94
Bryan Robson 1994–2001
Steve McClaren 2001–06
Gareth Southgate 2006–09
Gordon Strachan 2009–10
Tony Mowbray October 2010–

## LATEST SEQUENCES

**Longest Sequence of League Wins:** 9, 16.2.1974 – 6.4.1974.

**Longest Sequence of League Defeats:** 8, 26.12.1995 – 17.2.1996.

**Longest Sequence of League Draws:** 8, 3.4.1971 – 1.5.1971.

**Longest Sequence of Unbeaten League Matches:** 24, 8.9.1973 – 19.1.1974.

**Longest Sequence Without a League Win:** 19, 3.10.1981 – 6.3.1982.

**Successive Scoring Runs:** 26 from 21.9.1946.

**Successive Non-scoring Runs:** 5 from 17.1.2009.

### TEN YEAR LEAGUE RECORD

| | | | P | W | D | L | F | A | Pts | Pos |
|---|---|---|---|---|---|---|---|---|---|---|
| 2003-04 | PR Lge | | 38 | 13 | 9 | 16 | 44 | 52 | 48 | 11 |
| 2004-05 | PR Lge | | 38 | 14 | 13 | 11 | 53 | 46 | 55 | 7 |
| 2005-06 | PR Lge | | 38 | 12 | 9 | 17 | 48 | 58 | 45 | 14 |
| 2006-07 | PR Lge | | 38 | 12 | 10 | 16 | 44 | 49 | 46 | 12 |
| 2007-08 | PR Lge | | 38 | 10 | 12 | 16 | 43 | 53 | 42 | 13 |
| 2008-09 | PR Lge | | 38 | 7 | 11 | 20 | 28 | 57 | 32 | 19 |
| 2009-10 | FL C | | 46 | 16 | 14 | 16 | 58 | 50 | 62 | 11 |
| 2010-11 | FL C | | 46 | 17 | 11 | 18 | 68 | 68 | 62 | 12 |
| 2011-12 | FL C | | 46 | 18 | 16 | 12 | 52 | 51 | 70 | 7 |
| 2012-13 | FL C | | 46 | 18 | 5 | 23 | 61 | 70 | 59 | 16 |

### DID YOU KNOW

Viv Anderson became Middlesbrough's oldest debutant when he lined up against West Bromwich Albion at The Hawthorns on 1 April 1995. Viv, who had joined the club's management team the previous summer, was 38 years and 215 days old at the time.

## MIDDLESBROUGH – FL CHAMPIONSHIP 2012–13 LEAGUE RECORD

| Match No. | Date | Venue | Opponents | Result | H/T Score | Lg Pos. | Goalscorers | Attendance |
|---|---|---|---|---|---|---|---|---|
| 1 | Aug 18 | A | Barnsley | L 0-1 | 0-1 | 20 | | 12,203 |
| 2 | 21 | H | Burnley | W 3-2 | 1-1 | 12 | Bailey [42], Reach [79], Williams, L [88] | 15,559 |
| 3 | 25 | H | Crystal Palace | W 2-1 | 1-0 | 6 | Hines [41], Zemmama [52] | 15,494 |
| 4 | Sept 1 | A | Millwall | L 1-3 | 1-2 | 11 | Emnes (pen) [43] | 9576 |
| 5 | 15 | H | Ipswich T | W 2-0 | 1-0 | 7 | Williams, L [34], Carayol [90] | 14,887 |
| 6 | 18 | A | Blackpool | L 1-4 | 1-2 | 8 | Bikey [45] | 12,746 |
| 7 | 21 | A | Blackburn R | W 2-1 | 1-0 | 6 | Jutkiewicz 2 [7, 61] | 13,405 |
| 8 | 29 | H | Leicester C | L 1-2 | 0-0 | 11 | Bailey [50] | 15,679 |
| 9 | Oct 3 | H | Derby Co | D 2-2 | 1-1 | 11 | Jutkiewicz 2 [19, 82] | 13,377 |
| 10 | 6 | A | Watford | W 2-1 | 1-1 | 11 | Emnes [30], McDonald [77] | 12,006 |
| 11 | 20 | A | Brighton & HA | W 1-0 | 1-0 | 7 | Emnes [21] | 26,293 |
| 12 | 23 | H | Hull C | W 2-0 | 0-0 | 3 | Haroun [59], Miller [66] | 14,129 |
| 13 | 27 | H | Bolton W | W 2-1 | 0-1 | 3 | McDonald 2 [67, 85] | 16,200 |
| 14 | Nov 3 | A | Charlton Ath | W 4-1 | 1-1 | 2 | Woodgate [27], McDonald [53], Ledesma [63], Smallwood [90] | 17,744 |
| 15 | 6 | A | Nottingham F | D 0-0 | 0-0 | 2 | | 20,150 |
| 16 | 9 | H | Sheffield W | W 3-1 | 1-0 | 1 | Hoyte [13], Miller [60], Jutkiewicz [76] | 28,229 |
| 17 | 17 | A | Cardiff C | L 0-1 | 0-1 | 3 | | 21,578 |
| 18 | 24 | H | Bristol C | L 1-3 | 1-1 | 4 | Miller [35] | 20,585 |
| 19 | 27 | H | Huddersfield T | W 3-0 | 1-0 | 3 | McDonald 2 [28, 85], Ledesma [66] | 21,850 |
| 20 | 30 | A | Birmingham C | L 2-3 | 1-1 | 3 | Leadbitter [14], McDonald [62] | 15,322 |
| 21 | Dec 8 | A | Peterborough U | W 3-2 | 2-1 | 3 | Haroun 2 [9, 20], Miller [76] | 6612 |
| 22 | 15 | H | Wolverhampton W | W 2-0 | 0-0 | 3 | Emnes (pen) [89], McDonald [90] | 15,662 |
| 23 | 22 | A | Leeds U | L 1-2 | 1-1 | 4 | Jutkiewicz [30] | 25,406 |
| 24 | 26 | H | Blackburn R | W 1-0 | 0-0 | 3 | Jutkiewicz [67] | 22,882 |
| 25 | 29 | H | Blackpool | W 4-2 | 2-0 | 3 | Miller [14], Smallwood [36], McDonald [62], Reach [88] | 18,164 |
| 26 | Jan 1 | A | Derby Co | L 1-3 | 0-2 | 4 | Jutkiewicz [90] | 22,523 |
| 27 | 12 | H | Watford | L 1-2 | 0-1 | 5 | McDonald [90] | 17,499 |
| 28 | 18 | A | Leicester C | L 0-1 | 0-0 | 5 | | 8585 |
| 29 | Feb 2 | A | Ipswich T | L 0-4 | 0-1 | 6 | | 16,389 |
| 30 | 9 | H | Barnsley | L 2-3 | 0-1 | 6 | Carayol [50], Main [62] | 15,034 |
| 31 | 12 | H | Leeds U | W 1-0 | 0-0 | 6 | Main [81] | 18,388 |
| 32 | 16 | A | Crystal Palace | L 1-4 | 0-1 | 6 | Haroun [80] | 17,213 |
| 33 | 19 | A | Burnley | D 0-0 | 0-0 | 6 | | 12,394 |
| 34 | 23 | H | Millwall | L 1-2 | 0-2 | 7 | Main [75] | 15,377 |
| 35 | Mar 2 | H | Cardiff C | W 2-1 | 2-0 | 7 | Dyer [13], Ameobi [17] | 15,440 |
| 36 | 5 | A | Huddersfield T | L 1-2 | 0-0 | 8 | McDonald [78] | 12,705 |
| 37 | 9 | A | Bristol C | L 0-2 | 0-1 | 9 | | 13,524 |
| 38 | 16 | H | Birmingham C | L 0-1 | 0-0 | 9 | | 14,348 |
| 39 | 30 | A | Wolverhampton W | L 2-3 | 1-1 | 9 | Leadbitter 2 [25, 52] | 21,277 |
| 40 | Apr 2 | H | Peterborough U | D 0-0 | 0-0 | 9 | | 13,683 |
| 41 | 6 | A | Hull C | L 0-1 | 0-0 | 9 | | 17,901 |
| 42 | 13 | H | Brighton & HA | L 0-2 | 0-0 | 10 | | 14,925 |
| 43 | 16 | H | Nottingham F | W 1-0 | 1-0 | 10 | Carayol [42] | 13,861 |
| 44 | 20 | A | Bolton W | L 1-2 | 0-0 | 12 | Dyer [56] | 18,420 |
| 45 | 27 | A | Charlton Ath | D 2-2 | 0-2 | 12 | Emnes [76], McDonald [87] | 15,011 |
| 46 | May 4 | A | Sheffield W | L 0-2 | 0-2 | 16 | | 31,375 |

**Final League Position: 16**

## GOALSCORERS

*League (61):* McDonald 12, Jutkiewicz 8, Emnes 5 (2 pens), Miller 5, Haroun 4, Carayol 3, Leadbitter 3, Main 3, Bailey 2, Dyer 2, Ledesma 2, Reach 2, Smallwood 2, Williams, L 2, Ameobi 1, Bikey 1, Hines 1, Hoyte 1, Woodgate 1, Zemmama 1.

*FA Cup (6):* Jutkiewicz 2, Zemmama 2, Halliday 1, Miller 1.

*Capital One Cup (8):* Ledesma 2, Carayol 1, Emnes 1, McDonald 1, Park 1, Smallwood 1, Zemmama 1.

| Steele J 46 | Hoyte J 29+2 | Woodgate J 24 | Williams R 21+2 | Friend G 34 | Haroun F 20+3 | Leadbitter G 42 | Arca J 1 | Ledesma E 14+14 | Emnes M 19+5 | Bailey N 19+9 | Reach A 9+7 | Halliday A 13+6 | Zemmama M 4+13 | McEachran J 35+3 | Main C 6+7 | Smallwood R 13+9 | Williams L 3+8 | Hines S 17+4 | Miller I 14+11 | Bikey A 31+2 | Thomson K 5+4 | Jutkiewicz L 18+6 | Carayol M 12+6 | McManus S 7 | McDonald S 25+7 | Parnaby S 10+4 | Dyer K 7+2 | Ameobi S 7+2 | Burgess C 1 | Gibson B —+1 | Morris B —+1 | Match No. |
|---|---|---|---|---|---|---|---|---|---|---|---|---|---|---|---|---|---|---|---|---|---|---|---|---|---|---|---|---|---|---|---|---|
| 1 | 2 | 3 | 4 | 5¹ | 6³ | 7 | 8² | 9 | 10 | 11 | 12 | 13 | 14 | | | | | | | | | | | | | | | | | | | 1 |
| 1 | 2 | 3 | 4 | 5 | | 7 | | 10¹ | | 6² | 9 | | 12 | 8 | 11³ | 13 | 14 | | | | | | | | | | | | | | | 2 |
| 1 | 5 | | 4 | 2 | 10³ | 8 | | | | 6 | | | 9 | 7² | 13 | 14 | 12 | | 3 | 11¹ | | | | | | | | | | | | 3 |
| 1 | 2 | 3 | | 5 | 9² | 8 | | 12 | 11 | | | 6¹ | 7 | | 13 | 14 | 4 | 10³ | | | | | | | | | | | | | | 4 |
| 1 | 2 | 4 | | 5 | | 7 | | | | 8 | | | 14 | 9 | | 11² | | 10¹ | 3 | 6³ | 12 | 13 | | | | | | | | | | 5 |
| 1 | 2 | 4 | | 3 | 6 | | | 14 | 10¹ | | | 13 | | 8 | | 11³ | 5 | 7 | 12 | 9² | | | | | | | | | | | | 6 |
| 1 | 2 | 3¹ | | 5 | | 8² | | 10 | 13 | | | | 14 | 9 | | 12 | | 4 | 6 | 11 | 7³ | | | | | | | | | | | 7 |
| 1 | 5 | 3¹ | | 2 | | 9 | | | 14 | | | 7 | | 11² | 6 | 13 | 12 | | 4 | 8³ | 10 | | | | | | | | | | | 8 |
| 1 | 2 | | | 5 | 14 | 6 | | 12 | | 9 | | 13³ | 7¹ | | 10 | 3 | | 4 | 8² | 11 | | | | | | | | | | | | 9 |
| 1 | 2¹ | | | 5 | 9² | 6 | | 13 | 10 | 7 | | 8 | | | 14 | | | 3 | | 11³ | | 4 | 12 | | | | | | | | | 10 |
| 1 | | 4 | | 5 | 9 | 8 | | 10² | 7 | 14 | | | 6¹ | | 13 | | 12 | | 3 | | 2 | 11³ | | | | | | | | | | 11 |
| 1 | | | | 5 | 6 | 7 | | 14 | 11 | 13 | 9¹ | | | 8² | | 3 | 10³ | 4 | | | 12 | 2 | | | | | | | | | | 12 |
| 1 | | | | 5 | 6 | 7 | | 13 | 11¹ | | 9² | 14 | | 8³ | | 3 | 10 | 4 | | | 12 | 2 | | | | | | | | | | 13 |
| 1 | 13 | 4 | | 5 | 11² | 6 | | 8¹ | | 9 | | | | 7³ | 14 | | 3 | | | 12 | | 10 | 2 | | | | | | | | | 14 |
| 1 | 12 | | | 5 | 7 | 8 | | 13 | | 6 | | | 14 | 9 | | 4 | | | 11² | | | 10³ | 2¹ | | | | | | | | | 15 |
| 1 | 5 | 4¹ | | 2 | 14 | 8 | | 9 | 6³ | | | | 7 | | | | 12 | 10² | 3 | | | 13 | 11 | | | | | | | | | 16 |
| 1 | 2 | | 4³ | 9¹ | 6 | | | 7 | 13 | 14 | | | 8 | 12 | | 5 | | 3 | | 10² | | 11 | | | | | | | | | | 17 |
| 1 | 5 | | | | 7 | | | 9 | 6 | | | | 8¹ | | | 14 | 4 | 10³ | 3 | 13 | 11² | 12 | 2 | | | | | | | | | 18 |
| 1 | 2 | | | | 6² | 7 | | 5 | 14 | 7³ | | | 13³ | 8 | | 3 | 12 | 13 | 4 | 11¹ | | 10 | | | | | | | | | | 19 |
| 1 | 2 | | | | 9 | | | 6¹ | 8 | | | 5 | 14 | 7³ | | 12 | 3 | 13 | 4 | | | 11 | | | | | | | | | | 20 |
| 1 | 4 | | | 7¹ | 6 | | | 9 | 10² | | | 2 | | 8³ | 12 | | 13 | 5 | 14 | | | 11 | 3 | | | | | | | | | 21 |
| 1 | 5 | 3 | 2³ | | 8 | | | 12 | 13 | | | 7 | | 9 | 6¹ | 4 | 10² | | | | | 11 | 14 | | | | | | | | | 22 |
| 1 | 2² | 3 | | | 8 | | | 13 | 11 | | 14 | 7 | | 9¹ | 4 | | | | | | | 6³ | 12 | | | | | | | | | 23 |
| 1 | 5 | 3 | 12 | 2 | | | | 6 | 9³ | 14 | | | 7² | 13 | | | 4¹ | 10 | | | | 11 | | | | | | | | | | 24 |
| 1 | 2¹ | 3 | 4 | | | 7 | | | 6³ | 8 | 13 | 5 | | 9 | | | 10² | | | 14 | | 11 | 12 | | | | | | | | | 25 |
| 1 | | 4¹ | 3 | | | 7³ | | | 6 | 9 | 5 | | | 8 | 13 | | 14 | | 12 | 10 | | 11² | 2 | | | | | | | | | 26 |
| 1 | | 5 | 2 | 6 | 7 | | | 9³ | | 3 | 12 | | 14 | 8¹ | | | 4 | 13 | | | | 11² | 10 | | | | | | | | | 27 |
| 1 | 2¹ | | | 9 | 5 | 10 | 8 | | 6 | 13 | | | | 7² | | | | 3 | | 4 | 12 | 11³ | | | | | | | | | | 28 |
| 1 | 3¹ | 4 | 5 | 6 | 8 | | | 9¹ | 10² | | | 13 | | 12 | | | 14 | 2 | | 11 | | | 7 | | | | | | | | | 29 |
| 1 | | 7 | 2 | | 6 | | | 8¹ | | 3 | | 13 | 14 | | 12 | | 5 | | 4 | 11¹ | 10 | | 9² | | | | | | | | | 30 |
| 1 | | 4¹ | 7 | 2 | 10 | 8 | | | 14 | | 12 | | 9² | 11■ | | | 13 | 3 | | | 6³ | | | 5 | | | | | | | | 31 |
| 1 | | 8 | 4 | 9 | 7 | | | 13 | | 5 | | 6³ | | | | 14 | 3 | | 10² | 11 | | 2¹ | 12 | | | | | | | | | 32 |
| 1 | | 6 | 5 | | 8 | | | 11² | 2 | | 10³ | | 9 | 13 | 7¹ | | 14 | 3 | | 12 | 4 | | | | | | | | | | | 33 |
| 1 | | 7¹ | 5 | | 8 | | | 10³ | 2 | | | | 9 | 11 | | | 13 | 4 | | 12 | 3 | 14 | 6² | | | | | | | | | 34 |
| 1 | | | 2 | | 7 | | | 12 | 13 | 5 | | | 8 | 14 | | 3 | 11³ | | | | 4 | 10 | 6² | 9¹ | | | | | | | | 35 |
| 1 | | 13 | 5 | 5¹ | 6 | | | 12 | | 7 | | | 8¹ | 14 | 2² | 4 | 11³ | | 3 | 9 | | | | 10 | | | | | | | | 36 |
| 1 | | 3 | 8 | 5¹ | | | | 14 | 10² | 2³ | | 12 | | 13 | 7 | | | | 6 | 4 | 11 | | 9 | | | | | | | | | 37 |
| 1 | 2³ | 5 | | 4 | 9 | 6 | | | | 8 | | 14 | | 12 | 3 | 11¹ | 13 | | 10 | | | | | 7² | | | | | | | | 38 |
| 1 | 5 | 4³ | | 9 | | 7 | | | | 8² | 14 | | | 3 | | 10 | 6¹ | 2 | 11 | 12 | 13 | | | | | | | | | | | 39 |
| 1 | 5 | | 4 | 2¹ | 6 | 7 | | 12 | | | | | 8 | 13 | | 11³ | 3 | | 14 | 10² | | 9 | | | | | | | | | | 40 |
| 1 | 2 | 4¹ | 3 | 9 | 7 | | | 5 | 14 | | | | 8 | | | 11 | 12 | | 10² | 6³ | | | | | | | | | | | | 41 |
| 1 | 2 | 4 | 3 | 9² | 7 | | | 5 | 6¹ | 14 | 11 | 8³ | | | | 13 | 10 | | 12 | | | | | | | | | | | | | 42 |
| 1 | 2 | 4 | 13 | | | | | 12 | 14 | 5 | | 8¹ | 7 | | 3 | | | 9 | | 11 | | 6³ | 10² | | | | | | | | | 43 |
| 1 | 2 | 4■ | 3 | | | | | 12 | 14 | 5 | | 6¹ | 7 | | | 13 | | 10 | 9 | | 8³ | 11² | | | | | | | | | | 44 |
| 1 | 5 | | 4 | | 7 | | | 13 | 11³ | 6² | 2 | | | 10¹ | 8 | | 14 | 3 | | 9 | 12 | | | | | | | | | | | 45 |
| 1 | 2 | | 4 | | 7 | | | | | 13 | 5³ | | | 10 | 8¹ | | | 3 | | 6² | | 11 | | | 9 | 12 | 14 | | | | | 46 |

## FA Cup

| | | | |
|---|---|---|---|
| Third Round | Hastings U | (h) | 4-1 |
| Fourth Round | Aldershot T | (h) | 2-1 |
| Fifth Round | Chelsea | (h) | 0-2 |

## Capital One Cup

| | | | |
|---|---|---|---|
| First Round | Bury | (a) | 2-1 |
| Second Round | Gillingham | (a) | 2-0 |
| Third Round | Preston NE | (a) | 3-1 |
| Fourth Round | Sunderland | (a) | 1-0 |
| Quarter-Finals | Swansea C | (a) | 0-1 |

# MILLWALL

## FOUNDATION

Formed in 1885 as Millwall Rovers by employees of Morton & Co, a jam and marmalade factory in West Ferry Road. The founders were predominantly Scotsmen. Their first headquarters was The Islanders pub in Tooke Street, Millwall. Their first trophy was the East End Cup in 1887.

*The Den, Zampa Road, London SE16 3LN.*

*Telephone:* (020) 7232 1222. *Fax:* (020) 7231 3663.

*Ticket Office:* (0844) 826 2004.

*Website:* www.millwallfc.co.uk

*Email:* questions@millwallplc.com

*Ground Capacity:* 19,734.

*Record Attendance:* 48,672 v Derby Co, FA Cup 5th rd, 20 February 1937 (at The Den, Cold Blow Lane); 20,093 v Arsenal, FA Cup 3rd rd, 10 January 1994 (at The Den, Bermondsey).

*Pitch Measurements:* 105m × 68m (114yd × 74yd)

*Chairman:* John G. Berylson.

*Chief Executive:* Andy Ambler.

*Manager:* Steve Lomas.

*Assistant Manager:* Joe Gallen.

*Physio:* Bobby Bacic.

*Colours:* Blue shirts, white shorts, blue socks.

*Year Formed:* 1885.

*Turned Professional:* 1893.

*Previous Names:* 1885, Millwall Rovers; 1889, Millwall Athletic; 1899, Millwall; 1985, Millwall Football & Athletic Company.

*Club Nickname:* 'The Lions'.

*Grounds:* 1885, Glengall Road, Millwall; 1886, Back of 'Lord Nelson'; 1890, East Ferry Road; 1901, North Greenwich; 1910, The Den, Cold Blow Lane; 1993, The Den, Bermondsey.

*First Football League Game:* 28 August 1920, Division 3, v Bristol R (h) W 2–0 – Lansdale; Fort, Hodge; Voisey (1), Riddell, McAlpine; Waterall, Travers, Broad (1), Sutherland, Dempsey.

*Record League Victory:* 9–1 v Torquay U, Division 3 (S), 29 August 1927 – Lansdale, Tilling, Hill, Amos, Bryant (3), Graham, Chance, Hawkins (3), Landells (1), Phillips (2), Black. 9–1 v Coventry C, Division 3 (S), 19 November 1927 – Lansdale, Fort, Hill, Amos, Collins (1), Graham, Chance, Landells (1), Cock (2), Phillips (2), Black.

*Record Cup Victory:* 7–0 v Gateshead, FA Cup 2nd rd, 12 December 1936 – Yuill; Ted Smith, Inns; Brolly, Hancock, Forsyth; Thomas (1), Mangnall (1), Ken Burditt (2), McCartney (2), Thorogood (1).

*Record Defeat:* 1–9 v Aston Villa, FA Cup 4th rd, 28 January 1946.

## HONOURS

**Football League – Division 1:**
Best season: 3rd, 1993–94;
**Division 2:** *Champions* 1987–88, 2000–01; **Division 3 (S):**
*Champions* 1927–28, 1937–38;
*Runners-up* 1952–53;
**Division 3:** *Runners–up* 1965–66, 1984–85;
**Division 4:** *Champions* 1961–62;
*Runners-up* 1964–65.

**FA Cup:** *Runners-up* 2004; *Semi-final* 1900, 1903, 1937 (first Division 3 side to reach semi-final), 2013.

**Football League Cup:** Best season: 5th rd, 1974, 1977, 1995.

**Football League Trophy:** *Winners* 1983.

**Auto Windscreens Shield:**
*Runners-up* 1999.

**European Competitions**
**UEFA Cup:** 2004–05.

## sky SPORTS FACT FILE

The Third Division game between Workington and Millwall played at Borough Park on 28 January 1966 was broadcast on closed circuit television at The Den. While a crowd of 4,323 attended the match, a further 9,000 watched on the screens back in London. The game finished in a 0-0 draw.

*Most League Points (2 for a win):* 65, Division 3 (S), 1927–28 and Division 3, 1965–66.

*Most League Points (3 for a win):* 93, Division 2, 2000–01.

*Most League Goals:* 127, Division 3 (S), 1927–28.

*Highest League Scorer in Season:* Richard Parker, 37, Division 3 (S), 1926–27.

*Most League Goals in Total Aggregate:* Neil Harris, 124, 1995–2004; 2006–11.

*Most League Goals in One Match:* 5, Richard Parker v Norwich C, Division 3 (S), 28 August 1926.

*Most Capped Player:* Eamonn Dunphy, 22 (23), Republic of Ireland.

*Most League Appearances:* Barry Kitchener, 523, 1967–82.

*Youngest League Player:* Moses Ashikodi, 15 years 240 days v Brighton & HA, 22 February 2003.

*Record Transfer Fee Received:* £2,800,000 from Norwich C for Steve Morison, June 2011.

*Record Transfer Fee Paid:* £800,000 to Derby Co for Paul Goddard, December 1989.

*Football League Record:* 1920 Original Members of Division 3; 1921 Division 3 (S); 1928–34 Division 2; 1934–38 Division 3 (S); 1938–48 Division 2; 1948–58 Division 3 (S); 1958–62 Division 4; 1962–64 Division 3; 1964–65 Division 4; 1965–66 Division 3; 1966–75 Division 2; 1975–76 Division 3; 1976–79 Division 2; 1979–85 Division 2; 1985–88 Division 2; 1988–90 Division 1; 1990–92 Division 2; 1992–96 Division 1; 1996–2001 Division 2; 2001–04 Division 1; 2004–06 FL C; 2006–10 FL 1; 2010– FL C.

## LATEST SEQUENCES

*Longest Sequence of League Wins:* 10, 10.3.1928 – 25.4.1928.

*Longest Sequence of League Defeats:* 11, 10.4.1929 – 16.9.1929.

*Longest Sequence of League Draws:* 5, 22.12.1973 – 12.1.1974.

*Longest Sequence of Unbeaten League Matches:* 19, 22.8.1959 – 31.10.1959.

*Longest Sequence Without a League Win:* 20, 26.12.1989 – 5.5.1990.

*Successive Scoring Runs:* 22 from 8.12.1923.

*Successive Non-scoring Runs:* 6 from 20.12.1947.

## MANAGERS

**F. B. Kidd** 1894–99
*(Hon. Treasurer/Manager)*
**E. R. Stopher** 1899–1900
*(Hon. Treasurer/Manager)*
**George Saunders** 1900–11
*(Hon. Treasurer/Manager)*
**Herbert Lipsham** 1911–19
**Robert Hunter** 1919–33
**Bill McCracken** 1933–36
**Charlie Hewitt** 1936–40
**Bill Voisey** 1940–44
**Jack Cock** 1944–48
**Charlie Hewitt** 1948–56
**Ron Gray** 1956–57
**Jimmy Seed** 1958–59
**Reg Smith** 1959–61
**Ron Gray** 1961–63
**Billy Gray** 1963–66
**Benny Fenton** 1966–74
**Gordon Jago** 1974–77
**George Petchey** 1978–80
**Peter Anderson** 1980–82
**George Graham** 1982–86
**John Docherty** 1986–90
**Bob Pearson** 1990
**Bruce Rioch** 1990–92
**Mick McCarthy** 1992–96
**Jimmy Nicholl** 1996–97
**John Docherty** 1997
**Billy Bonds** 1997–98
**Keith Stevens** 1998–2000
*(then Joint Manager)*
*(plus* **Alan McLeary** 1999–2000)
**Mark McGhee** 2000–03
**Dennis Wise** 2003–05
**Steve Claridge** 2005
**Colin Lee** 2005
**David Tuttle** 2005–06
**Nigel Spackman** 2006
**Willie Donachie** 2006–07
**Kenny Jackett** 2007–13
**Steve Lomas** May 2013–

## TEN YEAR LEAGUE RECORD

|         |       | P  | W  | D  | L  | F  | A  | Pts | Pos |
|---------|-------|----|----|----|----|----|----|-----|-----|
| 2003-04 | Div 1 | 46 | 18 | 15 | 13 | 55 | 48 | 69  | 10  |
| 2004-05 | FL C  | 46 | 18 | 12 | 16 | 51 | 45 | 66  | 10  |
| 2005-06 | FL C  | 46 | 8  | 17 | 21 | 35 | 61 | 40  | 23  |
| 2006-07 | FL 1  | 46 | 19 | 9  | 18 | 59 | 62 | 66  | 10  |
| 2007-08 | FL 1  | 46 | 14 | 10 | 22 | 45 | 60 | 52  | 17  |
| 2008-09 | FL 1  | 46 | 25 | 7  | 14 | 63 | 53 | 82  | 5   |
| 2009-10 | FL 1  | 46 | 24 | 13 | 9  | 76 | 44 | 85  | 3   |
| 2010-11 | FL C  | 46 | 18 | 13 | 15 | 62 | 48 | 67  | 9   |
| 2011-12 | FL C  | 46 | 15 | 12 | 19 | 55 | 57 | 57  | 16  |
| 2012-13 | FL C  | 46 | 15 | 11 | 20 | 51 | 62 | 56  | 20  |

## DID YOU KNOW ?

Roger Wynter was the star of Millwall's success in the London *Evening Standard* five-a-side tournament in April 1983 scoring eight goals and keeping Teddy Sheringham on the bench. He failed to make the first team at The Den, but later played in indoor soccer in the USA for Pittsburgh Spirit.

## MILLWALL – FL CHAMPIONSHIP 2012–13 LEAGUE RECORD

| Match No. | Date | Venue | Opponents | | Result | H/T Score | Lg Pos. | Goalscorers | Attendance |
|---|---|---|---|---|---|---|---|---|---|
| 1 | Aug 18 | H | Blackpool | L | 0-2 | 0-1 | 23 | | 11,010 |
| 2 | 21 | A | Peterborough U | W | 2-1 | 1-1 | 17 | Malone [43], Henderson [64] | 6188 |
| 3 | 25 | A | Sheffield W | L | 2-3 | 2-1 | 19 | Henry [35], Trotter [43] | 24,752 |
| 4 | Sept 1 | H | Middlesbrough | W | 3-1 | 2-1 | 10 | Trotter [25], Keogh 2 [35, 86] | 9576 |
| 5 | 15 | A | Hull C | L | 1-4 | 0-4 | 16 | Henderson [63] | 14,756 |
| 6 | 18 | H | Cardiff C | L | 0-2 | 0-0 | 21 | | 9295 |
| 7 | 22 | H | Brighton & HA | L | 1-2 | 0-1 | 22 | Wood [79] | 12,191 |
| 8 | 29 | A | Burnley | D | 2-2 | 1-2 | 21 | Trotter [3], Henderson [90] | 11,192 |
| 9 | Oct 2 | A | Bristol C | D | 1-1 | 1-1 | 22 | Henderson [38] | 12,010 |
| 10 | 6 | H | Bolton W | W | 2-1 | 1-0 | 20 | Henderson 2 [17, 90] | 10,116 |
| 11 | 20 | A | Crystal Palace | D | 2-2 | 1-2 | 19 | Trotter (pen) [42], Beevers [77] | 16,124 |
| 12 | 23 | H | Birmingham C | D | 3-3 | 3-1 | 19 | Wood 2 [11, 18], Taylor, C [13] | 9258 |
| 13 | 27 | H | Huddersfield T | W | 4-0 | 1-0 | 15 | Wood 2 [28, 61], Henry [79], Trotter [88] | 11,066 |
| 14 | Nov 3 | A | Nottingham F | W | 4-1 | 1-1 | 14 | Trotter [3], Henderson [60], Wood [76], Keogh [84] | 24,160 |
| 15 | 6 | A | Watford | D | 0-0 | 0-0 | 14 | | 11,293 |
| 16 | 10 | H | Derby Co | W | 2-1 | 1-0 | 10 | Feeney [33], Keogh [76] | 10,392 |
| 17 | 18 | H | Leeds U | W | 1-0 | 0-0 | 9 | Wood [85] | 13,117 |
| 18 | 24 | A | Blackburn R | W | 2-0 | 0-0 | 6 | Wood [71], Henry [90] | 13,898 |
| 19 | 27 | A | Wolverhampton W | W | 1-0 | 0-0 | 5 | Keogh [79] | 18,174 |
| 20 | Dec 1 | H | Charlton Ath | D | 0-0 | 0-0 | 7 | | 18,013 |
| 21 | 8 | A | Ipswich T | L | 0-3 | 0-1 | 7 | | 17,380 |
| 22 | 15 | H | Leicester C | W | 1-0 | 0-0 | 6 | Taylor, C [67] | 10,189 |
| 23 | 18 | A | Brighton & HA | D | 2-2 | 1-0 | 6 | Wood 2 [25, 57] | 24,773 |
| 24 | 22 | H | Barnsley | L | 1-2 | 0-1 | 7 | Wood [80] | 10,118 |
| 25 | 29 | A | Cardiff C | L | 0-1 | 0-1 | 8 | | 24,263 |
| 26 | Jan 1 | H | Bristol C | W | 2-1 | 1-0 | 7 | N'Guessan [19], Smith, A [75] | 9784 |
| 27 | 12 | A | Bolton W | D | 1-1 | 1-1 | 7 | Keogh (pen) [9] | 16,985 |
| 28 | 19 | H | Burnley | L | 0-2 | 0-1 | 9 | | 9384 |
| 29 | 29 | A | Barnsley | L | 0-2 | 0-0 | 9 | | 7844 |
| 30 | Feb 2 | H | Hull C | L | 0-1 | 0-1 | 10 | | 9589 |
| 31 | 9 | A | Blackpool | L | 1-2 | 1-0 | 12 | Henry [32] | 12,653 |
| 32 | 19 | H | Peterborough U | L | 1-5 | 1-2 | 14 | Henry [13] | 8769 |
| 33 | 23 | A | Middlesbrough | W | 2-1 | 2-0 | 13 | Friend (og) [25], Woolford [40] | 15,377 |
| 34 | Mar 2 | A | Leeds U | L | 0-1 | 0-0 | 14 | | 19,002 |
| 35 | 5 | A | Wolverhampton W | L | 0-2 | 0-1 | 15 | | 8727 |
| 36 | 16 | H | Charlton Ath | W | 2-0 | 0-0 | 15 | Easter [58], Lowry [64] | 18,514 |
| 37 | 29 | A | Leicester C | W | 1-0 | 0-0 | 14 | Dunne [87] | 22,365 |
| 38 | Apr 1 | H | Ipswich T | D | 0-0 | 0-0 | 14 | | 10,141 |
| 39 | 6 | A | Birmingham C | D | 1-1 | 0-0 | 15 | Taylor, C [70] | 15,302 |
| 40 | 9 | H | Sheffield W | L | 1-2 | 1-1 | 16 | Abdou [2] | 9084 |
| 41 | 16 | H | Watford | L | 1-0 | 0-0 | 16 | Batt [83] | 9366 |
| 42 | 20 | A | Huddersfield T | L | 0-3 | 0-1 | 17 | | 12,415 |
| 43 | 23 | H | Blackburn R | L | 1-2 | 1-0 | 18 | Osborne [14] | 8607 |
| 44 | 27 | H | Nottingham F | L | 0-1 | 0-1 | 19 | | 12,330 |
| 45 | 30 | H | Crystal Palace | D | 0-0 | 0-0 | 19 | | 12,745 |
| 46 | May 4 | A | Derby Co | L | 0-1 | 0-0 | 20 | | 25,021 |

**Final League Position: 20**

### GOALSCORERS

*League (51):* Wood 11, Henderson 7, Keogh 6 (1 pen), Trotter 6 (1 pen), Henry 5, Taylor, C 3, Abdou 1, Batt 1, Beevers 1, Dunne 1, Easter 1, Feeney 1, Lowry 1, Malone 1, N'Guessan 1, Osborne 1, Smith, A 1, Woolford 1, own goal 1.
*FA Cup (7):* Shittu 2, Feeney 1, Henry 1, Hulse 1, Marquis 1, N'Guessan 1.
*Capital One Cup (2):* Batt 1, Ward 1.

| Taylor M 6 | Smith J 13+4 | Shittu D 38+1 | Ward D 1 | Lowry S 37+2 | Henry J 33+2 | Trotter L 34+2 | Wright J 19+5 | Malone S 13+2 | Henderson D 16+4 | Keogh A 24+13 | Dunne A 22+3 | Feeney L 12+10 | Osborne K 13 | Abdou N 36+3 | Batt S 4+12 | Racon T —+1 | Robinson P 2+1 | Taylor C 17+5 | Wood C 18+1 | Forde D 40 | Beevers M 35 | Smith A 24+1 | N'Guessan D 6+7 | Woolford M 8+7 | Tyson N 1+3 | Marquis J 6+4 | Hulse R 7+4 | Afobe B 5 | Saville G 2+1 | Chaplow R 4 | Easter J 5+4 | St. Ledger S 5+1 | Match No. |
|---|---|---|---|---|---|---|---|---|---|---|---|---|---|---|---|---|---|---|---|---|---|---|---|---|---|---|---|---|---|---|---|---|---|
| 1 | 2[2] | 3[1] | 4 | 5 | 6 | 7 | 8 | 9 | 10 | 11 | 12 | 13 | | | | | | | | | | | | | | | | | | | | | 1 |
| 1 | | | | 4 | 9[1] | 8 | 6 | 5 | 10 | 11 | 2 | | | 3 | 7 | 12 | | | | | | | | | | | | | | | | | 2 |
| 1 | | | | 3 | 6 | 7 | 9[1] | 5 | 10 | 11 | 2 | | | 4 | 8 | | 12 | | | | | | | | | | | | | | | | 3 |
| 1 | | | | 4 | 6[2] | 7 | 8 | 5 | 11[1] | 10 | 2 | 13 | | 3 | 9 | | 12 | | | | | | | | | | | | | | | | 4 |
| 1 | 13 | | | 3 | 5 | 6 | 7 | 9 | 10 | 11 | 12 | | | 4[1] | 8 | | | 2[2] | | | | | | | | | | | | | | | 5 |
| 1 | | | | 5 | 6[3] | 8 | 7[1] | 4 | 11[2] | 10 | 2 | | | 3 | 9 | 14 | | | 12 | 13 | | | | | | | | | | | | | 6 |
| 1 | | | | 3 | 6 | 9 | 7[1] | 5[2] | 14 | 10[3] | 2 | | | 4 | 8 | | 13 | 12[4] | 11 | 1 | | | | | | | | | | | | | 7 |
| | 12 | 3 | | 2 | 9 | 8 | 6[2] | 14 | 11[3] | 5 | | 7 | 13 | 4[1] | | | | 10 | | 1 | | | | | | | | | | | | | 8 |
| | 5 | 3 | | 4 | 6 | 7 | 9[2] | 10 | 12 | 2 | | | | 8 | | | | 13 | 11[1] | 1 | | | | | | | | | | | | | 9 |
| | 5 | 2 | | | 6[2] | | 9[3] | 10 | 12 | 3 | | | | 8 | 14 | | | 13 | 11[1] | 1 | 4 | | | | | | | | | | | | 10 |
| | 7 | 3 | | 8 | 13 | 5[1] | 6 | | | 2 | 12 | | | 10[2] | 14 | | | 9 | 11[3] | 1 | 4 | | | | | | | | | | | | 11 |
| | 5[1] | 3 | | 12 | | 7 | 6[2] | | 10 | 2 | | 13 | | 8 | | | | 9 | 11 | 1 | 4 | | | | | | | | | | | | 12 |
| | | 3 | | 5 | 6[1] | 8 | 12 | | 11 | | 2 | 7 | | | | | | 9 | 10 | 1 | 4 | | | | | | | | | | | | 13 |
| | | 3 | | 5 | 6 | 7 | | | 10[1] | 12 | | | | 8 | | | | 9 | 11 | 1 | 4 | 2 | | | | | | | | | | | 14 |
| | | 3 | | 5 | 7[1] | 6 | 12 | | 10[2] | 13 | | | 14 | 9 | | | | 8[3] | 11 | 1 | 4 | 2 | | | | | | | | | | | 15 |
| | | 4 | | 5 | | 6 | 12 | | 10 | 8 | | 7 | | | | | | 9[1] | 11 | 1 | 3 | 2 | | | | | | | | | | | 16 |
| | | 3 | | 5 | 12 | 8 | 7 | | 10 | | | 6[1] | | 8 | | | | 9[2] | 11 | 1 | 4 | 2 | 13 | | | | | | | | | | 17 |
| | | 3 | | 5 | 6 | | 7 | 12 | 11 | | | | | 8 | | | | 9[1] | 10 | 1 | 4 | 2 | | | | | | | | | | | 18 |
| | 13 | 3 | | 5 | | 8 | | | 10[2] | | | 6[1] | | 7 | | | | 9 | 11 | 1 | 4 | 2 | 12 | | | | | | | | | | 19 |
| | | 3 | | 5 | | 8 | | | 10 | | | 6[1] | | 7 | | | | 9 | 11 | 1 | 4 | 2 | 12 | | | | | | | | | | 20 |
| | | 3 | | 5 | 6 | 8 | 13 | | 10 | | | 7[2] | | | | | | 9[1] | 11 | 1 | 4 | 2 | 12 | | | | | | | | | | 21 |
| | | 3 | | 5 | 6 | 7 | | | 9[1] | | | 13 | | 8 | 14 | | | 12 | 11[3] | 1 | 4 | 2 | 10[2] | | | | | | | | | | 22 |
| | 10 | 3 | | 5 | 6 | 8 | 7 | | | | | 13 | | 12 | | | | 9[1] | 11[2] | 1 | 4 | 2 | | | | | | | | | | | 23 |
| | 12 | 3 | | 5 | 6 | 8 | 7 | | | | | 11[2] | | 9[1] | | | | 10 | | 1 | 4 | 2[3] | 13 | | | | | | | | | | 24 |
| | | 3 | | 2 | 6 | 7 | | | 9[1] | 10 | | 12 | | 8 | 13 | | | | | 1 | 4 | 5 | 11[2] | | | | | | | | | | 25 |
| | 12 | 3 | | 5 | 6 | 7 | | | 10[1] | | | 9 | | 8 | 13 | | | | | 1 | 4 | 2 | 11[2] | | | | | | | | | | 26 |
| | | 3 | | | 6 | 8 | 5 | | 12 | 10[1] | | 7 | | | | | | | | 1 | 4 | 2 | 11 | 9 | | | | | | | | | 27 |
| | 5 | 4 | | | 6 | 7 | | | 11 | | | 9 | | | | | | | | 1 | 3 | 2 | 10[2] | 8[1] | 12 | 13 | | | | | | | 28 |
| | | 3 | | 12 | 7 | 8 | | | 10[1] | | | 9[3] | | 4[2] | 6 | | | | | 1 | 5 | 2 | | 14 | | 11 | 13 | | | | | | 29 |
| | | 3 | | 10 | 6 | 9 | 8[2] | | 12 | | | 7 | | | | | | | | 1 | 5 | 2 | 14 | 4[3] | | 11 | 13 | | | | | | 30 |
| | | 3 | | 5 | 6 | 7 | | | 12 | | | 13 | | 8 | | | | | | 1 | 4 | 2 | | 9[2] | | 11 | 10[1] | | | | | | 31 |
| | | | | 5[1] | 6 | 7 | | 11 | 13 | | | | | 3 | 8 | | | | | 1 | 4 | 2[2] | 12 | | | 14 | 10[3] | 9[1] | | | | | 32 |
| | | 3 | | | 6 | 8 | | | | | 2 | | | 4 | 7 | | | | | 1 | 5 | | 9 | | | 10 | | | | | 11 | | 33 |
| | | 3 | | 5 | 6 | | 7[3] | | 12 | 2 | | | | 8 | | | | | | 1 | 4 | | 9 | 13 | 10[1] | 11[2] | 14 | | | | | | 34 |
| | | 3 | | 5 | 14 | | 7[3] | | 12 | | | | | 8 | | | 6 | | | 1 | 4 | 2 | 9 | 13 | 10[2] | 11[1] | | | | | | | 35 |
| | 7 | 3 | | 5 | | 8 | | | | | 2 | | | 4[1] | 14 | | 9 | | | 1 | | | 12 | 10[2] | | 11 | | | | | 6[3] | 13 | 36 |
| | 8[2] | 3 | | 4 | 7 | | | | 10[3] | 2 | | 13 | | | | | | | | 1 | | 5 | | 14 | | 12 | 11[1] | | | 6 | 9 | | 37 |
| | 8[3] | 3 | | 5 | 7 | | 6[2] | | | 2 | | 13 | | | | | | | | 1 | 4 | | 10[1] | 12 | | | 9 | | 11 | 14 | | | 38 |
| | | 3 | | 5 | | 8 | | | | 2 | 9[2] | 11 | | | | | | | | 1 | 4 | | 12 | | 10 | | | | 6[1] | 13 | 7 | | 39 |
| | | 3 | | 5 | 13 | | | | 14 | 2 | | 7 | 12 | | | | 6 | | | 1 | 4 | | | 11[2] | | | 9[1] | | | 10[3] | 8 | | 40 |
| | 8 | 3 | | 5 | 6 | | | | 11 | | | 7 | 13 | 9[1] | | | | | | 1 | 4 | 2 | | 12 | | | | | | | 10[2] | | 41 |
| | 6 | 3 | | | 9 | | | | 10[3] | | | 14 | | 4 | 8 | | 11[1] | | | 1 | 5 | 2 | | 7[2] | | | 13 | | | | 12 | | 42 |
| | 8 | 3 | | | 6 | | | | 12 | | 2 | 14 | | 9[3] | 4 | | 7 | 13 | | 1 | 5 | | | 11[1] | | | | | | | 10[2] | | 43 |
| | | 6 | | | | | | | 13 | | 2 | 14 | | 4 | 7 | | 11[1] | | | 1 | 3 | 5 | 10[2] | 12 | | | 9[3] | | | | | 8 | 44 |
| | | 4 | | 3 | 6[1] | 14 | 7 | | 10 | | 2 | 9 | | 11[2] | | | | | | 1 | 5 | | 13[3] | 12 | | | | | | | | 8 | 45 |
| | | 3 | | 5 | | 8 | 7[2] | | 11 | | 2 | 10 | | 13 | 6[1] | | | | | 1 | 4 | | | 14 | | | | | | 12 | | 9[3] | 46 |

**FA Cup**

| | | | |
|---|---|---|---|
| Third Round | Preston NE | (h) | 1-0 |
| Fourth Round | Aston Villa | (h) | 2-1 |
| Fifth Round | Luton T | (a) | 3-0 |
| Sixth Round | Blackburn R | (h) | 0-0 |
| *Replay* | Blackburn R | (a) | 1-0 |
| Semi-Finals | Wigan Ath | (h) | 0-2 |
| *(at Wembley)* | | | |

**Capital One Cup**

| | | | |
|---|---|---|---|
| First Round | Crawley T | (h) | 2-2 |
| *(aet; lost 1-4 on pens)* | | | |

# MILTON KEYNES DONS

## FOUNDATION

In July 2004 Wimbledon became MK Dons and relocated to Milton Keynes. In 2007 it recognised itself as a new club with no connection to the old Wimbledon FC. In August of that year the replica trophies and other Wimbledon FC memorabilia were returned to the London Borough of Merton.

*Stadiummk, Stadium Way West, Milton Keynes, Buckinghamshire MK1 1ST.*

*Telephone:* (01908) 622 922.

*Fax:* (01908) 622 933.

*Ticket Office:* (01908) 622 900.

*Website:* www.mkdons.com

*Email:* info@mkdons.com

*Ground Capacity:* 22,233.

## HONOURS

**Football League – FL 2:**
*Champions* 2007–08.

**Johnstone's Paint Trophy:**
*Winners* 2008.

**FA Cup:** Best season: 5th rd, 2013.

**Football League Cup:** Best season: 3rd rd, 2007, 2011, 2012.

*Record Attendance:* 8,306 v Tottenham H, League Cup 3rd rd, 25 October 2006 (at National Hockey Stadium); 17,717 v Leicester C, FL 1, 28 February 2009 (at Stadiummk).

*Ground Record Attendance:* 20,222, England U21 v Bulgaria U21, 16 November 2007.

*Pitch Measurements:* 105m × 67m (115yd × 74yd)

*Chairman:* Pete Winkelman.

*Manager:* Karl Robinson.

*Assistant Manager:* Mick Harford.

*Head of Sports Medicine:* Simon Crampton.

*Colours:* White shirts with red trim, white shorts, white socks.

*Year Formed:* 2004.

*Turned Professional:* 2004.

*Club Nickname:* 'The Dons'.

*Grounds:* 2003, The National Hockey Stadium; 2007, Stadiummk.

*First Football League Game:* 7 August 2004, FL 1, v Barnsley (h) D 1–1 – Rachubka; Palmer, Lewington, Harding, Williams, Oyedele, Kamara, Smith, Smart (Herve), McLeod (1) (Hornuss), Small.

*Record League Victory:* 6–2 v Oldham Ath, FL 1, 14 March 2009 – Gueret; Cummings, O'Hanlon, Llera, Lewington, Leven, Chadwick (Johnson), Navarro (1) (Belson), Baldock (2) (Gerba (1)), Wilbraham (1), Puncheon (1); 6–2 v Chesterfield, FL 1, 28 August 2011 – Martin; Smith A, Lewington, Chicksen, MacKenzie, Williams (Chadwick) (1), Ibhehre, Gleeson, Baldock (3) (O'Shea (1 pen)), Bowditch (1), Balanta (Powell).

## sky SPORTS FACT FILE

Striker Izale McLeod scored Milton Keynes Dons first-ever Football League goal under their new name when he netted a second-half equaliser to earn a draw against Barnsley in August 2004. He went on to finish the season as the club's leading scorer with a total of 18 goals.

**Record Cup Victory:** 6–0 v Nantwich T, FA Cup 1st rd, 12 November 2011 – Martin; Chicksen, Baldock G, Doumbe (1), Flanagan, Williams S, Powell (1) (O'Shea (1), Chadwick (Galloway), Bowditch (2), MacDonald (Williams G (1)), Balanta.

**Record Defeat:** 0–5 v Hartlepool U, FL 1, 31 January 2005; 0–5 v Huddersfield T, FL 1, 18 February 2006; 0–5 v Tottenham H, Carling Cup 3rd rd, 24 October 2006; 0–5 v Rochdale, FL 2, 27 January 2007; 0–5 v Carlisle U, FL 1, 13 February 2010.

| MANAGERS |
|---|
| **Stuart Murdock** 2002–04 |
| **Danny Wilson** 2004–06 |
| **Martin Allen** 2006–07 |
| **Paul Ince** 2007–08 |
| **Roberto Di Matteo** 2008–09 |
| **Paul Ince** 2009–10 |
| **Karl Robinson** May 2010– |

**Most League Goals in One Match:** 3, Clive Platt v Barnet, FL 2, 20 January 2007; 3, Mark Wright v Bury, FL 2, 2 February 2008; 3, Aaron Wilbraham v Cheltenham T, FL 1, 31 January 2009; 3, Sam Baldock v Colchester U, FL 1, 12 March 2011; 3, Sam Baldock v Chesterfield, FL 1, 20 August 2012; 3, Dean Bowditch v Bury, FL 1, 22 September 2012.

**Record Transfer Fee Received:** £1,000,000 from West Ham U for Sam Baldock, August 2011.

**Most League Points (3 for a win):** 97, FL 2, 2007–08.

**Most League Goals:** 84, FL 1, 2011–12.

**Highest League Scorer in Season:** Izale McLeod, 21, 2006–07.

**Most League Goals in Total Aggregate:** Izale McLeod, 55, 2004–07; 2012–13.

**Most Capped Player:** Ali Gerba (29), Canada.

**Most League Appearances:** Dean Lewington, 385, 2004–13.

**Youngest League Player:** Brendon Galloway, 16 years 42 days v Rochdale, 28 April 2012.

**Football League Record:** 2004–06 FL 1; 2006–08 FL 2; 2008– FL 1.

## LATEST SEQUENCES

**Longest Sequence of League Wins:** 8, 7.9.2007 – 20.10.2007.
**Longest Sequence of League Defeats:** 4, 10.8.2004 – 28.8.2004.
**Longest Sequence of League Draws:** 4, 21.2.2009 – 10.3.2009; 12.2.2013 – 2.3.2013.
**Longest Sequence of Unbeaten League Matches:** 18, 29.1.2008 – 3.5.2008.
**Longest Sequence Without a League Win:** 11, 13.3.2010 – 2.5.2010.
**Successive Scoring Runs:** 18 from 7.4.2007.
**Successive Non-scoring Runs:** 4, 17.12.2005 – 2.1.2006.

## TEN YEAR LEAGUE RECORD

| | | P | W | D | L | F | A | Pts | Pos |
|---|---|---|---|---|---|---|---|---|---|
| 2003-04* | Div 1 | 46 | 8 | 5 | 33 | 41 | 89 | 29 | 24 |
| 2004-05 | FL 1 | 46 | 12 | 15 | 19 | 54 | 68 | 51 | 20 |
| 2005-06 | FL 1 | 46 | 12 | 14 | 20 | 45 | 66 | 50 | 22 |
| 2006-07 | FL 2 | 46 | 25 | 9 | 12 | 76 | 58 | 84 | 4 |
| 2007-08 | FL 2 | 46 | 29 | 10 | 7 | 82 | 37 | 97 | 1 |
| 2008-09 | FL 1 | 46 | 26 | 9 | 11 | 83 | 47 | 87 | 3 |
| 2009-10 | FL 1 | 46 | 17 | 9 | 20 | 60 | 68 | 60 | 12 |
| 2010-11 | FL 1 | 46 | 23 | 8 | 15 | 67 | 60 | 77 | 5 |
| 2011-12 | FL 1 | 46 | 22 | 14 | 10 | 84 | 47 | 80 | 5 |
| 2012-13 | FL 1 | 46 | 19 | 13 | 14 | 62 | 45 | 70 | 8 |

*As Wimbledon.*

## DID YOU KNOW ?

Clive Platt was the first Milton Keynes Dons player to notch a hat-trick in a Football League game. He scored all three goals in a home win over Barnet in January 2007 and ended the season with a tally of 18 League goals for the club.

## MILTON KEYNES DONS – FOOTBALL LEAGUE ONE 2012–13 LEAGUE RECORD

| Match No. | Date | Venue | Opponents | Result | H/T Score | Lg Pos. | Goalscorers | Attendance |
|---|---|---|---|---|---|---|---|---|
| 1 | Aug 18 | H | Oldham Ath | W 2-0 | 1-0 | 4 | Potter [34], Powell [59] | 7409 |
| 2 | 21 | A | Bournemouth | D 1-1 | 0-1 | 6 | Powell [62] | 5407 |
| 3 | 25 | A | Swindon T | L 0-1 | 0-1 | 10 | | 8299 |
| 4 | Sept 1 | H | Carlisle U | W 2-0 | 1-0 | 8 | Chadwick [12], Lowe [65] | 7227 |
| 5 | 8 | A | Walsall | L 0-1 | 0-1 | 10 | | 3657 |
| 6 | 15 | H | Yeovil T | W 1-0 | 0-0 | 8 | MacDonald [75] | 7235 |
| 7 | 18 | H | Notts Co | D 1-1 | 0-1 | 7 | O'Shea [68] | 7121 |
| 8 | 22 | A | Bury | W 4-1 | 1-0 | 4 | Bowditch 3 [33, 55, 66], Chadwick [90] | 2321 |
| 9 | 29 | H | Crewe Alex | W 1-0 | 1-0 | 3 | MacDonald [8] | 11,037 |
| 10 | Oct 2 | A | Coventry C | D 1-1 | 1-1 | 5 | Gleeson [42] | 9848 |
| 11 | 6 | H | Portsmouth | D 2-2 | 1-2 | 5 | Webster (og) [40], Potter [72] | 10,409 |
| 12 | 14 | A | Preston NE | D 0-0 | 0-0 | 7 | | 8327 |
| 13 | 20 | H | Stevenage | L 0-1 | 0-1 | 8 | | 9190 |
| 14 | 23 | A | Crawley T | L 0-2 | 0-1 | 10 | | 2853 |
| 15 | 27 | A | Scunthorpe U | W 3-0 | 2-0 | 8 | Chadwick 2 [17, 30], Smith [60] | 2737 |
| 16 | Nov 7 | H | Leyton Orient | W 1-0 | 1-0 | 8 | Lowe [41] | 6985 |
| 17 | 10 | H | Sheffield U | W 1-0 | 0-0 | 7 | Williams (pen) [90] | 9835 |
| 18 | 16 | A | Tranmere R | W 1-0 | 0-0 | 2 | Gleeson [87] | 10,587 |
| 19 | 20 | A | Shrewsbury T | D 2-2 | 1-0 | 3 | Balanta [45], Bowditch [90] | 4747 |
| 20 | 24 | H | Colchester U | W 5-1 | 2-0 | 2 | Chadwick 2 [28, 64], Williams (pen) [37], Otsemobor [61], Lowe [82] | 7443 |
| 21 | Dec 8 | A | Brentford | L 2-3 | 1-1 | 6 | Lowe [14], Gleeson [53] | 5833 |
| 22 | 15 | H | Hartlepool U | W 1-0 | 1-0 | 5 | Lowe [16] | 7164 |
| 23 | 26 | H | Walsall | L 2-4 | 2-3 | 6 | Lowe [6], Bowditch [31] | 8700 |
| 24 | 29 | H | Coventry C | L 2-3 | 2-1 | 7 | Powell [15], Lowe [38] | 13,620 |
| 25 | Jan 1 | A | Notts Co | W 2-1 | 2-0 | 6 | Potter [6], Powell [13] | 5325 |
| 26 | 12 | H | Bury | D 1-1 | 1-0 | 6 | Bowditch [15] | 7384 |
| 27 | 29 | A | Yeovil T | L 1-2 | 1-1 | 10 | Kay [35] | 3152 |
| 28 | Feb 2 | H | Bournemouth | L 0-3 | 0-2 | 11 | | 9233 |
| 29 | 9 | A | Oldham Ath | L 1-3 | 1-2 | 13 | Powell [39] | 4094 |
| 30 | 12 | A | Doncaster R | D 0-0 | 0-0 | 12 | | 6423 |
| 31 | 23 | A | Carlisle U | D 1-1 | 1-0 | 14 | Chicksen [36] | 4283 |
| 32 | 26 | A | Portsmouth | D 1-1 | 1-1 | 13 | Williams [27] | 9815 |
| 33 | Mar 2 | H | Preston NE | D 1-1 | 1-1 | 13 | Chicksen [2] | 8412 |
| 34 | 5 | H | Doncaster R | W 3-0 | 1-0 | 11 | McLeod [40], Powell [56], Gleeson [83] | 6804 |
| 35 | 9 | A | Sheffield U | D 0-0 | 0-0 | 12 | | 17,936 |
| 36 | 12 | H | Shrewsbury T | L 2-3 | 1-2 | 13 | Lowe 2 [27, 47] | 6622 |
| 37 | 16 | H | Tranmere R | W 3-0 | 2-0 | 12 | Lewington [9], Gleeson [43], Potter [51] | 9682 |
| 38 | 19 | A | Crewe Alex | L 1-2 | 1-1 | 13 | Bamford [31] | 3770 |
| 39 | 29 | A | Hartlepool U | W 2-0 | 1-0 | 11 | Bamford [7], Bowditch [62] | 3269 |
| 40 | Apr 1 | H | Brentford | W 2-0 | 1-0 | 10 | Bowditch [14], Gleeson [85] | 10,455 |
| 41 | 6 | H | Crawley T | D 0-0 | 0-0 | 10 | | 7746 |
| 42 | 9 | H | Swindon T | W 2-0 | 1-0 | 9 | Doumbe [58], Lowe [89] | 8608 |
| 43 | 13 | A | Leyton Orient | L 0-2 | 0-0 | 10 | | 4634 |
| 44 | 16 | A | Colchester U | W 2-0 | 1-0 | 7 | Powell [11], Bamford [78] | 3175 |
| 45 | 20 | A | Scunthorpe U | L 0-1 | 0-1 | 9 | | 9752 |
| 46 | 27 | A | Stevenage | W 2-0 | 1-0 | 8 | Bamford [33], Lowe [77] | 3801 |

**Final League Position: 8**

### GOALSCORERS

*League (62):* Lowe 11, Bowditch 8, Powell 7, Chadwick 6, Gleeson 6, Bamford 4, Potter 4, Williams 3 (2 pens), Chicksen 2, MacDonald 2, Balanta 1, Doumbe 1, Kay 1, Lewington 1, McLeod 1, O'Shea 1, Otsemobor 1, Smith 1, own goal 1.
*FA Cup (14):* Williams 3 (2 pens), Bowditch 2, Alli 1, Chicksen 1, Gleeson 1, Harley 1, Lowe 1, O'Shea 1, Otsemobor 1, Potter 1, own goal 1.
*Capital One Cup (3):* Chadwick 2, Bowditch 1.
*Johnstone's Paint Trophy (0).*

| Martin D 31 | Chicksen A 25+7 | Lewington D 38 | MacKenzie G 10+1 | Kay A 31+2 | Powell D 25+9 | Potter D 46 | Chadwick L 30+6 | O'Shea J 5+6 | Bowditch D 38+1 | Lowe R 28+14 | MacDonald C 7+12 | Ibehre J —+3 | Smith A 9+18 | Otsemobor J 33+2 | Williams S 43+1 | Gleeson S 27+3 | Bullard J —+2 | Doumbe S 15+9 | Allan S 2+2 | Balanta A 11+1 | Bamford P 11+3 | Ismail Z 1+6 | Sekajja I —+1 | Alli D 1+1 | Harley R 8 | McLeod 15+8 | Lines C 11+5 | McLoughlin I 15+1 | Baldock G —+2 | Galloway B —+1 | Rasulo G —+1 | Match No. |
|---|---|---|---|---|---|---|---|---|---|---|---|---|---|---|---|---|---|---|---|---|---|---|---|---|---|---|---|---|---|---|---|---|
| 1 | 2 | 3 | 4 | 5¹ | 6 | 7 | 8³ | 9 | 10¹ | 11² | 12 | 13 | 14 | | | | | | | | | | | | | | | | | | | 1 |
| 1 | 3 | 4 | 5 | | 6 | 7 | 12 | 14 | 9³ | 11² | 10¹ | 13 | 8⁴ | 2 | | | | | | | | | | | | | | | | | | 2 |
| 1 | 5³ | 3⁴ | 4 | | 10 | 7 | 8 | 9 | 6 | 11² | 13 | 14 | | 2 | 12 | | | | | | | | | | | | | | | | | 3 |
| 1 | 3 | | 4 | | 6³ | 8 | 9¹ | 14 | 10 | 11² | 12 | | | 2 | 5 | 7 | 13 | | | | | | | | | | | | | | | 4 |
| 1 | 5 | | 4 | | 8 | 7 | 9² | 13 | 10³ | 11¹ | 12 | | 14 | 2 | 3 | 6 | | | | | | | | | | | | | | | | 5 |
| 1 | 5 | 3¹ | 12 | | 6 | 8 | 10 | | 9³ | 11² | 13 | | | 2 | 4 | 7 | 14 | | | | | | | | | | | | | | | 6 |
| 1 | | 3 | 4 | 5¹ | 6 | 8 | 10² | 12 | | 13 | 11³ | | 14 | 2 | 9 | 7 | | | | | | | | | | | | | | | | 7 |
| 1 | 5 | 3 | 14 | | 7 | 9 | 10 | 8³ | 12 | 11¹ | | | | 2² | 4 | 6 | | 13 | | | | | | | | | | | | | | 8 |
| 1 | 2 | 3 | | 4 | 12 | 8 | 9² | 6¹ | 10 | 14 | 11³ | | | | 5 | 7 | | 13 | | | | | | | | | | | | | | 9 |
| 1 | 5 | | 4 | | 8³ | 6 | 10¹ | 9 | 14 | 11² | | | | 2 | 5 | 7 | | | | | | | | | | | | | | | | 10 |
| 1 | 3 | | 4 | 6 | 8 | 9 | | 10 | | 11² | | | 12 | 2¹ | 5 | 7 | | 13 | | | | | | | | | | | | | | 11 |
| 1 | 5 | | | | 7 | 10 | | 8 | 12 | 13 | | | 11¹ | 2 | 3 | 6 | | 4 | 9² | | | | | | | | | | | | | 12 |
| 1 | 13 | 3 | | | 8 | 9 | 10³ | | 14 | 12 | | | 11² | 2¹ | 5 | 7 | | 4 | 6 | | | | | | | | | | | | | 13 |
| 1 | 13 | 2 | | 4 | 8 | 6 | 10³ | | | 12 | 11¹ | | 14 | 5 | 7 | | | 3 | | 9² | | | | | | | | | | | | 14 |
| 1 | 12 | 5 | | 4 | 9¹ | 8 | 7³ | 14 | | 13 | | | 11² | 2 | 3 | 6 | | | 10 | | | | | | | | | | | | | | 15 |
| 1 | 12 | 3 | | 4³ | | 8 | 9 | | 6¹ | 11² | 13 | | | 2 | 5 | 7 | | 14 | 10 | | | | | | | | | | | | | 16 |
| 1 | 10 | | 2 | | 6 | 7 | | 11 | 9¹ | | | | 12 | 4 | 3 | 5 | | 13 | 8² | | | | | | | | | | | | | 17 |
| 1 | 4 | | 3 | 13 | 8 | 7³ | | 10 | 11¹ | | | | 12 | 2 | 5 | 6 | | 14 | 9² | | | | | | | | | | | | | 18 |
| 1 | 12 | 5¹ | | 4 | 13 | 7 | 9³ | 8 | | 14 | | | 11 | 2 | 3 | 6 | | | 10² | | | | | | | | | | | | | 19 |
| 1 | 5 | | | | 4 | 7 | 9² | | 8³ | 12 | | | | 2 | 3 | 6 | | | 10 | 11¹ | 13 | 14 | | | | | | | | | | 20 |
| 1 | 5 | | 3 | 12 | 9 | 8² | | | 11³ | 13 | | | 14 | 2 | 4 | 7 | | | 10 | 6¹ | | | | | | | | | | | | 21 |
| 1 | 3 | | 4 | | 8 | 9 | | 6 | 11² | 13 | | | | 5 | 7 | | 2 | 10¹ | 12 | | | | | | | | | | | | | 22 |
| 1 | 2 | 3 | | 4 | 6² | 8 | | 10 | 11 | | | | 14 | 9 | | 5³ | | 7¹ | 12 | 13 | | | | | | | | | | | | 23 |
| 1 | 2 | 5 | | 3 | 6 | 8 | | 10 | 11³ | 14 | | | 7¹ | 4 | | | | 12 | 13 | 9² | | | | | | | | | | | | 24 |
| 1 | 2 | 5 | 14 | 3 | 6 | 8 | | 10¹ | 11³ | | | | 12 | 4 | | 13 | | 7² | | | 9 | | | | | | | | | | | 25 |
| 1 | 2 | 3 | | 4 | 6² | 7 | | 9 | 10 | | | | 12 | 5 | | | | 13 | | 8 | 11¹ | | | | | | | | | | | 26 |
| 1 | 9 | 5 | | 4⁴ | | 6 | 10¹ | | 14 | 2³ | 3 | | | 13 | | | | | | 7² | 11 | 12 | | | | | | | | | | 27 |
| 1 | 10¹ | 3 | | | 8 | | 6 | 11⁴ | | 13 | 2 | 5 | | 4² | | | 14 | | | 7 | 12 | 9³ | | | | | | | | | | 28 |
| 1 | 14 | 5 | 4 | | 6 | 7 | 12 | 9 | | 11³ | 2 | 3 | | | | | | | | 10¹ | 13 | 8² | | | | | | | | | | 29 |
| 1 | 12 | 5 | 3 | | 6 | 7 | 10¹ | 9 | | | 2 | 4 | | | | | | | | 8 | 11 | | | | | | | | | | | 30 |
| 1¹ | 10 | 5 | 3³ | 2 | 13 | 9 | 6 | | 11 | | | | 4 | | 14 | | | | | 7² | | 8 | 12 | | | | | | | | | 31 |
| | 2 | 5 | 3 | 4 | 6 | 8 | 10 | | 13 | | | | 14 | 7³ | | | | | | 9² | 11¹ | 12 | 1 | | | | | | | | | 32 |
| | 10 | 5 | | 3 | 8 | 6 | 9 | | 12 | 11² | | | | 2¹ | 4 | | | | | 13 | 7 | 1 | | | | | | | | | | 33 |
| | 2 | 3 | | 4 | 6 | 8 | 9¹ | | 10² | 11³ | | | | 5 | 14 | 13 | | | | 12 | 7 | 1 | | | | | | | | | | 34 |
| | 2 | 5 | | 3 | 6¹ | 9 | | | 10 | 11³ | | | 8² | | 4 | 14 | 12 | | 13 | | 7 | 1 | | | | | | | | | | 35 |
| | 10 | 3 | | 4 | | 8 | | 6 | 9 | | | | 14 | 5 | 12 | | 2¹ | | 13 | | 11² | 7³ | 1 | | | | | | | | | 36 |
| | 2 | 5¹ | | 3 | | 8 | | 10 | 9 | | | | | 12 | 4 | 6³ | | | | 11² | | 14 | 7 | 1 | 13 | | | | | | | 37 |
| | 5 | | 4⁴ | | 7 | | | 9¹ | 10² | | | | 14 | 2³ | 3 | 8 | | | | 11 | | 13 | 6 | 1 | 12 | | | | | | | 38 |
| | 5³ | | | 12 | 8 | 13 | 9 | 11 | | | | | 10¹ | 2 | 4 | 7 | | 3 | | 6² | | | | 1 | | 14 | | | | | | 39 |
| | 3 | | | 12 | 8 | 13 | 10² | 11¹ | | | | | 14 | 2 | 5 | 7 | | 4 | | 6³ | | | 9 | 1 | | | | | | | | 40 |
| | 3 | | | 6¹ | 8 | 12 | 10 | 11 | | | | | 2 | 5 | 7 | 4 | | 9 | | | | | | 1 | | | | | | | | 41 |
| | 10 | 5 | | | 7 | 9² | | 8 | 13 | | | | 14 | 2 | 4 | 6¹ | | 3 | | 11³ | | | | 12 | 1 | | | | | | | 42 |
| | 10² | 5 | | | 13 | 6 | 12 | | 8 | 11¹ | | | | 2³ | 4 | | | 3 | | 9 | | | | 14 | 7 | 1 | | | | | | 43 |
| | | 5¹ | | 12 | 8² | 6 | 9³ | | 10 | 13 | | | | 2 | 4 | 7 | | 3 | | 11 | | | | 14 | 1 | | | | | | | 44 |
| | | | | 4 | 8 | 7 | 9¹ | | 10 | 12 | | | | 2¹ | 5 | 6 | 3² | | | 11 | | | | 14 | 13 | 1 | | | | | | 45 |
| | | | | 8 | 5 | 7 | 9¹ | | 11 | 12 | | | | 2 | 4 | 6³ | 3 | | | 10² | | | 13 | | | 1 | | | | 14 | 46 |

**FA Cup**

| | | | | |
|---|---|---|---|---|
| First Round | Cambridge C | (a) | 0-0 | |
| *Replay* | Cambridge C | (h) | 6-1 | |
| Second Round | AFC Wimbledon | (h) | 2-1 | |
| Third Round | Sheffield W | (a) | 0-0 | |
| *Replay* | Sheffield W | (h) | 2-0 | |
| Fourth Round | QPR | (a) | 4-2 | |
| Fifth Round | Barnsley | (h) | 0-3 | |

**Capital One Cup**

| | | | |
|---|---|---|---|
| First Round | Cheltenham T | (a) | 1-1 |
| *(aet; won 5-3 on pens)* | | | |
| Second Round | Blackburn R | (h) | 2-1 |
| Third Round | Sunderland | (h) | 0-2 |

**Johnstone's Paint Trophy**

| | | | |
|---|---|---|---|
| First Round | Northampton T | (a) | 0-1 |

# MORECAMBE

## FOUNDATION

Several attempts to start a senior football club in a rugby stronghold finally succeeded on 7 May 1920 at the West View Hotel, Morecambe and a team competed in the Lancashire Combination for 1920–21. The club shared with a local cricket club at Woodhill Lane for the first season and a crowd of 3,000 watched the first game. The club moved to Roseberry Park, the name of which was changed to Christie Park after J.B. Christie who as President had purchased the ground.

*Globe Arena, Christie Way, Westgate, Morecambe, Lancashire LA4 4TB.*

*Telephone:* (01524) 411 797.

*Fax:* (01524) 832 230.

*Ticket Office:* (01524) 411 797.

*Website:* www.morecambefc.com

*Email:* office@morecambefc.com

*Ground Capacity:* 6,400.

*Record Attendance:* 9,383 v Weymouth, FA Cup 3rd rd, 6 January 1962 (at Christie Park). 5,003 v Burnley, Lge Cup 2nd rd, 24 August 2010 (at Globe Arena).

*Pitch Measurements:* 100m × 69m (110yd × 76yd)

*Chairman:* Peter McGuigan.

*Manager:* Jim Bentley.

*Assistant Manager:* Ken McKenna.

*Physio:* Simon Farnworth.

*Colours:* Red panelled shirts with white trim, white shorts, red socks.

*Year Formed:* 1920.

*Turned Professional:* 1920.

*Club Nickname:* 'The Shrimps'.

*Grounds:* 1920, Woodhill Lane; 1921, Christie Park; 2010, Globe Arena.

*First Football League game:* 11 August 2007, FL 2, v Barnet (h) D 0–0 – Lewis; Yates, Adams, Artell, Bentley, Stanley, Baker (Burns), Sorvel, Twiss (Newby), Curtis, Hunter (Thompson).

## HONOURS

**Football League FL 2:** Best season: 4th, 2009–10.
**FA Cup:** Best season: 3rd rd, 1962, 2001, 2003.
**Football League Cup:** Best season: 3rd rd, 2008.
**Northern Premier League:** *Runners-up* – 1994–95.
**Presidents Cup:** *Winners* 1991–92.
**FA Trophy:** *Winners* 1973–74.
**Lancs Senior Cup:** *Winners* 1967–68.
**Lancs Combination** – *Champions* 1924–25, 1961–62, 1962–63, 1967–68. *Runners-up* 1925–26.
**Lancs Combination Cup:** *Winners* 1926–27, 1945–46, 1964–65, 1966–67, 1967–68. *Runners-up* 1923–24, 1924–25, 1962–63.
**Lancs Junior Cup:** *Winners* 1927, 1928, 1962, 1963, 1969, 1986, 1987, 1994, 1996, 1999, 2004.

## sky SPORTS FACT FILE

Morecambe were members of the Lancashire Combination from their foundation in 1920 through until 1968. The Shrimps won both the Combination and the Combination League Cup in each of their final two seasons in the competition after which they became founder members of the Northern Premier League.

**Record League Victory:** 6–0 v Crawley T, FL 2, 10 September 2011 – Roche; Reid, Wilson (pen), McCready, Haining (Parrish), Fenton (1), Drummond, McDonald, Price (Jevons), Carlton (3) (Alessandra), Ellison (1).

**Record Cup Victory:** 6–2 v Nelson (a), Lancashire Trophy, 27 January 2004.

**Record Defeat:** 2–7 v Port Vale, FL 2, 30 April 2011.

**Most League Points (3 for a win):** 73, FL 2, 2009–10.

**Most League Goals:** 73, FL 2, 2009–10.

**Highest League Scorer in Season:** Phil Jevons, 18, 2009–10.

**Most League Goals in Total Aggregate:** Stuart Drummond, 34, 2007–13.

**Most League Goals in One Match:** 3, Jon Newby v Rotherham U, FL 2, 29 March 2008.

**Most League Appearances:** Stuart Drummond, 228, 2007–13.

**Youngest League Player:** Aaron McGowan, 16 years 263 days, 20 April 2013.

**Record Transfer Fee Received:** £225,000 from Stockport C for Carl Baker, July 2008.

**Record Transfer Fee Paid:** Undisclosed to Southport for Carl Baker, July 2007.

**Football League Record:** 2006–07 Promoted from Conference; 2007– FL 2.

## MANAGERS

Jimmy Milne 1947–48
Albert Dainty 1955–56
Ken Horton 1956–61
Joe Dunn 1961–64
Geoff Twentyman 1964–65
Ken Waterhouse 1965–69
Ronnie Clayton 1969–70
Gerry Irving/Ronnie Mitchell 1970
Ken Waterhouse 1970–72
Dave Roberts 1972–75
Alan Spavin 1975–76
Johnny Johnson 1976–77
Tommy Ferber 1977–78
Mick Hogarth 1978–79
Don Curbage 1979–81
Jim Thompson 1981
Les Rigby 1981–84
Sean Gallagher 1984–85
Joe Wojciechowicz 1985–88
Eric Whalley 1988
Billy Wright 1988–89
Lawrie Milligan 1989
Bryan Griffiths 1989–93
Leighton James 1994
Jim Harvey 1994–2006
Sammy McIlroy 2006–11
Jim Bentley May 2011–

## LATEST SEQUENCES

**Longest Sequence of League Wins:** 7, 31.10.2009 – 12.12.2009.

**Longest Sequence of League Defeats:** 4, 23.2.2008 – 12.3.2008.

**Longest Sequence of League Draws:** 4, 13.9.2008 – 4.10.2008.

**Longest Sequence of Unbeaten League Matches:** 12, 31.1.2009 – 21.3.2009.

**Longest Sequence Without a League Win:** 10, 5.4.2008 – 30.8.2008.

**Successive Scoring Runs:** 17 from 13.8.2011 – 19.11.2011.

**Successive Non-scoring Runs:** 3 from 26.11.2001 – 17.12.2011.

## TEN YEAR LEAGUE RECORD

|  |  | P | W | D | L | F | A | Pts | Pos |
|---|---|---|---|---|---|---|---|---|---|
| 2003-04 | Conf | 42 | 20 | 7 | 15 | 66 | 66 | 67 | 7 |
| 2004-05 | Conf | 42 | 19 | 14 | 9 | 69 | 50 | 71 | 7 |
| 2005-06 | Conf | 42 | 22 | 8 | 12 | 68 | 41 | 74 | 5 |
| 2006-07 | Conf | 46 | 23 | 12 | 11 | 64 | 46 | 81 | 3 |
| 2007-08 | FL 2 | 46 | 16 | 12 | 18 | 59 | 63 | 60 | 11 |
| 2008-09 | FL 2 | 46 | 15 | 18 | 13 | 53 | 56 | 63 | 11 |
| 2009-10 | FL 2 | 46 | 20 | 13 | 13 | 73 | 64 | 73 | 4 |
| 2010-11 | FL 2 | 46 | 13 | 12 | 21 | 54 | 73 | 51 | 20 |
| 2011-12 | FL 2 | 46 | 14 | 14 | 18 | 63 | 57 | 56 | 15 |
| 2012-13 | FL 2 | 46 | 15 | 13 | 18 | 55 | 61 | 58 | 16 |

## DID YOU KNOW ?

Morecambe won promotion to the Football League in May 2007 when they beat Exeter City 2-1 in the Conference play-off final at Wembley with goals from Gary Thompson and Danny Carlton in front of a crowd of 40,043.

## MORECAMBE – FOOTBALL LEAGUE TWO 2012–13 LEAGUE RECORD

| Match No. | Date | Venue | Opponents | Result | H/T Score | Lg Pos. | Goalscorers | Attendance |
|---|---|---|---|---|---|---|---|---|
| 1 | Aug 18 | A | Exeter C | W 3-0 | 3-0 | 1 | Fleming 2 [14, 24], Reid [32] | 3792 |
| 2 | 21 | H | York C | D 2-2 | 0-0 | 4 | Brodie (pen) [53], Drummond [74] | 2063 |
| 3 | 25 | H | Port Vale | L 1-3 | 1-1 | 11 | Ellison [32] | 2164 |
| 4 | Sept 1 | A | Bristol R | W 3-0 | 0-0 | 6 | McDonald [52], Fenton [57], Ellison [62] | 5207 |
| 5 | 8 | H | Fleetwood T | L 0-4 | 0-1 | 12 | | 3232 |
| 6 | 15 | A | Aldershot T | D 0-0 | 0-0 | 13 | | 1960 |
| 7 | 18 | A | Bradford C | L 1-3 | 0-1 | 17 | Redshaw [82] | 9054 |
| 8 | 22 | H | Plymouth Arg | L 2-3 | 1-0 | 18 | Redshaw [4], Brodie (pen) [51] | 1865 |
| 9 | 28 | A | Cheltenham T | L 0-2 | 0-1 | 19 | | 2563 |
| 10 | Oct 2 | H | Chesterfield | W 2-0 | 1-0 | 17 | McDonald [45], Alessandra [52] | 1285 |
| 11 | 6 | H | Burton Alb | D 0-0 | 0-0 | 17 | | 1585 |
| 12 | 13 | A | Rochdale | W 2-1 | 1-0 | 16 | Redshaw 2 [10, 66] | 2493 |
| 13 | 20 | H | Southend U | W 1-0 | 0-0 | 14 | Redshaw [88] | 1643 |
| 14 | 23 | A | Rotherham U | L 1-2 | 1-0 | 14 | Ellison [30] | 5632 |
| 15 | 27 | A | Torquay U | L 0-1 | 0-1 | 17 | | 2457 |
| 16 | Nov 6 | H | Accrington S | D 0-0 | 0-0 | 17 | | 1410 |
| 17 | 10 | H | Barnet | W 4-1 | 2-0 | 15 | Ellison [6], Fleming [10], Brodie 2 (2 pens) [81, 86] | 1653 |
| 18 | 17 | A | Gillingham | L 1-2 | 0-1 | 15 | Redshaw [69] | 5402 |
| 19 | 20 | A | Northampton T | L 0-3 | 0-0 | 17 | | 4013 |
| 20 | 24 | H | AFC Wimbledon | W 3-1 | 2-0 | 16 | Ellison 3 [7, 34, 79] | 1616 |
| 21 | Dec 8 | A | Wycombe W | D 2-2 | 0-1 | 16 | Brodie [59], Redshaw [90] | 3238 |
| 22 | 15 | H | Oxford U | D 1-1 | 0-0 | 16 | Ellison [78] | 1385 |
| 23 | 26 | A | Fleetwood T | L 0-1 | 0-0 | 17 | | 3477 |
| 24 | 29 | A | Chesterfield | D 1-1 | 1-1 | 18 | McCready [29] | 6358 |
| 25 | Jan 1 | H | Bradford C | D 0-0 | 0-0 | 18 | | 3635 |
| 26 | 8 | H | Dagenham & R | W 2-1 | 0-1 | 17 | Burrow [53], Parrish [76] | 4029 |
| 27 | 12 | A | Plymouth Arg | L 1-2 | 0-2 | 18 | Williams [80] | 6401 |
| 28 | 18 | A | Cheltenham T | D 0-0 | 0-0 | 17 | | 1586 |
| 29 | 26 | H | Dagenham & R | W 2-1 | 0-0 | 16 | Drummond [81], Williams [83] | 1370 |
| 30 | Feb 2 | A | York C | W 4-1 | 1-1 | 12 | Alessandra [23], Ellison [74], Redshaw 2 [87, 90] | 3138 |
| 31 | 9 | H | Exeter C | L 0-3 | 0-0 | 14 | | 1840 |
| 32 | 12 | H | Aldershot T | W 2-1 | 0-0 | 12 | Risser (og) [72], McDonald [85] | 1226 |
| 33 | 16 | A | Port Vale | W 1-0 | 0-0 | 10 | Alessandra [63] | 5513 |
| 34 | 23 | A | Bristol R | D 1-1 | 1-0 | 10 | Redshaw [2] | 1736 |
| 35 | 26 | H | Burton Alb | L 2-3 | 0-2 | 10 | Redshaw (pen) [81], Holroyd [90] | 2170 |
| 36 | Mar 2 | H | Rochdale | W 3-0 | 1-0 | 10 | McCready [9], Ellison [60], Fleming [63] | 2028 |
| 37 | 9 | A | Barnet | L 1-4 | 1-0 | 13 | Redshaw [33] | 2012 |
| 38 | 12 | H | Northampton T | D 1-1 | 0-0 | 13 | Redshaw [57] | 1366 |
| 39 | 16 | H | Gillingham | D 1-1 | 1-0 | 13 | Redshaw [42] | 1674 |
| 40 | 23 | A | AFC Wimbledon | L 0-2 | 0-2 | 13 | | 3902 |
| 41 | 29 | A | Oxford U | D 1-1 | 1-0 | 13 | Redshaw [90] | 5523 |
| 42 | Apr 1 | H | Wycombe W | L 0-1 | 0-0 | 14 | | 1702 |
| 43 | 6 | H | Rotherham U | W 2-1 | 0-0 | 14 | Threlfall [56], Ellison [90] | 2197 |
| 44 | 12 | A | Accrington S | L 0-2 | 0-1 | 15 | | 2473 |
| 45 | 20 | A | Torquay U | L 0-2 | 0-1 | 16 | | 2033 |
| 46 | 27 | A | Southend U | W 1-0 | 1-0 | 16 | Fleming [34] | 5081 |

**Final League Position: 16**

## GOALSCORERS

*League (55):* Redshaw 15 (1 pen), Ellison 11, Brodie 5 (4 pens), Fleming 5, Alessandra 3, McDonald 3, Drummond 2, McCready 2, Williams 2, Burrow 1, Fenton 1, Holroyd 1, Parrish 1, Reid 1, Threlfall 1, own goal 1.
*FA Cup (3):* Ellison 1, Fleming 1, McDonald 1.
*Capital One Cup (2):* Alessandra 1, Fleming 1.
*Johnstone's Paint Trophy (4):* Brodie 1 (1 pen), Ellison 1, Mustoe 1, Redshaw 1.

| Roche B 42 | Reid I 9+9 | McCready C 37+3 | Parrish A 23+2 | Haining W 33+3 | Threlfall R 20+5 | Drummond S 41+3 | Fleming A 29+3 | McDonald G 40+3 | Brodie R 15+8 | Ellison K 38+2 | Carlton D —+2 | Burrow J 12+20 | Redshaw J 25+15 | Wright A 39+1 | Alessandra L 31+9 | Fenton N 37+1 | Arestidou A 4+2 | Mustoe J 10+1 | Parkinson D —+3 | McGee J 1+2 | Williams R 10+6 | Holroyd C 8+8 | Mwasile J 1+4 | Doyle C 1+3 | McGowan A —+1 | Match No. |
|---|---|---|---|---|---|---|---|---|---|---|---|---|---|---|---|---|---|---|---|---|---|---|---|---|---|---|
| 1 | $2^2$ | 3 | 4 | 5 | 6 | 7 | 8 | 9 | $10^1$ | $11^3$ | 12 | 13 | 14 | | | | | | | | | | | | | 1 |
| 1 | $7^1$ | 3 | 2 | $4^3$ | 5 | 6 | 9 | $8^2$ | 11 | 10 | | 12 | 13 | 14 | | | | | | | | | | | | 2 |
| 1 | 3 | 2 | | 5 | $7^3$ | 8 | 14 | $10^1$ | 11 | | | 12 | 13 | 6 | $9^2$ | 4 | | | | | | | | | | 3 |
| 1 | | 8 | 5 | 4 | 3 | 14 | | 9 | 12 | $11^2$ | $13^3$ | $7^1$ | | 6 | | 10 | 2 | | | | | | | | | 4 |
| 1 | 14 | 2 | 5 | 4 | 8 | | $7^3$ | $10^2$ | 11 | | | 13 | 12 | 6 | $9^1$ | 3 | | | | | | | | | | 5 |
| 1 | 14 | 3 | $6^3$ | 4 | 5 | 9 | 7 | | 12 | 13 | | $11^1$ | $10^2$ | 8 | | 2 | | | | | | | | | | 6 |
| 1 | 2 | | $6^3$ | 7 | $8^2$ | 14 | $11^1$ | 10 | | | | 13 | 12 | 9 | | 3 | | | | | | | | | | 7 |
| 1 | $6^3$ | | 2 | 4 | 5 | 14 | | 8 | 12 | 9 | | $10^2$ | $11^1$ | 7 | 13 | 3 | | | | | | | | | | 8 |
| 1 | | 4 | 2 | | 5 | | 9 | 7 | 11 | $10^4$ | | | 12 | 6 | $8^1$ | 3 | | | | | | | | | | 9 |
| 1 | | 4 | | 12 | $5^1$ | 7 | 6 | 8 | 10 | | | 13 | $11^2$ | 2 | 9 | 3 | | | | | | | | | | 10 |
| 1 | | 12 | 3 | | $2^1$ | | 7 | 8 | 6 | $11^2$ | | 13 | 10 | 5 | 9 | 4 | 1 | | | | | | | | | 11 |
| 1 | | 13 | 3 | | 7 | 8 | 6 | 12 | $11^2$ | | | 5 | $10^3$ | 2 | $9^1$ | 4 | 14 | | | | | | | | | 12 |
| 1 | | 14 | 13 | 3 | | 8 | 7 | 6 | $12^4$ | 11 | | | $10^3$ | 2 | $9^1$ | 4 | $5^2$ | | | | | | | | | 13 |
| 1 | 13 | $3^2$ | | 4 | | 6 | 7 | 8 | | 11 | | 12 | $10^1$ | 5 | | 2 | 9 | | | | | | | | | 14 |
| 1 | 12 | 3 | | 2 | | 7 | 8 | 9 | | $11^2$ | | 5 | 10 | $4^1$ | | 6 | 13 | | | | | | | | | 15 |
| 1 | | 13 | | $3^2$ | | 7 | 8 | 6 | 12 | 11 | | $10^1$ | 2 | 9 | 4 | 5 | | | | | | | | | | 16 |
| | 13 | 4 | | | 6 | 7 | $8^1$ | 11 | | $9^1$ | 12 | | 2 | $10^2$ | 3 | 1 | 5 | 14 | | | | | | | | 17 |
| 1 | $6^2$ | 3 | 2 | | 13 | 7 | 8 | $9$ | $10^1$ | 11 | | 12 | 5 | | 4 | | | | | | | | | | | 18 |
| 1 | $9^1$ | 3 | | | 6 | 8 | 7 | $10^2$ | 11 | | | 13 | 2 | 12 | | 4 | 5 | | | | | | | | | 19 |
| 1 | 12 | 3 | 2 | 14 | | 7 | | 8 | 13 | 11 | | $10^2$ | 6 | $9^1$ | 4 | | $5^3$ | | | | | | | | | 20 |
| $11$ | $5^3$ | 4 | | $3^2$ | | 6 | | 8 | 11 | 10 | | 14 | 7 | 13 | 2 | $12$ | 9 | | | | | | | | | 21 |
| 1 | | 3 | 14 | 12 | | 7 | 8 | 6 | 9 | 11 | | $10^2$ | 2 | 13 | $4^1$ | | $5^3$ | | | | | | | | | 22 |
| 1 | $6^1$ | 3 | | | 9 | 7 | $8^2$ | 11 | 10 | | | 12 | 2 | 13 | 4 | | 5 | | | | | | | | | 23 |
| 1 | 12 | 4 | 2 | 3 | | | 8 | $10^3$ | $11^2$ | 13 | | 5 | 9 | | | | | 14 | | $6^1$ | | | | | | 24 |
| 1 | 14 | 3 | 2 | | 12 | $6^1$ | | 7 | 13 | 10 | | $11^2$ | $9^3$ | 5 | 8 | 4 | | | | | | | | | | 25 |
| 1 | | 3 | 2 | | | 6 | 13 | 7 | | 10 | | $11^2$ | $9^1$ | 5 | 8 | 4 | | 12 | | | | | | | | 26 |
| 1 | $6^1$ | | $2^4$ | 3 | $5^3$ | 12 | 7 | $8^2$ | | 9 | | 11 | 14 | 10 | | 4 | | | | | 13 | | | | | 27 |
| 1 | | 3 | | 2 | 5 | 7 | $8^6$ | 6 | | 11 | | $10^1$ | | 9 | | 4 | | | | | 13 | 12 | | | | 28 |
| 1 | | 4 | 5 | $3^3$ | | 6 | | 7 | | 11 | | 14 | 12 | 8 | $9^1$ | 2 | | | | | 13 | $10^3$ | | | | 29 |
| 1 | | 4 | 2 | 5 | | 8 | | 6 | | 9 | | 13 | 12 | $11^1$ | 3 | | | | | | 7 | $10^2$ | | | | 30 |
| 1 | | 2 | 3 | | | 7 | $6^2$ | 9 | | 13 | | 12 | 5 | $10^1$ | 4 | | | | | | 8 | $11^3$ | 14 | | | 31 |
| 1 | | 3 | | 2 | | 7 | | 6 | | 11 | | 12 | $10^1$ | 5 | $9^2$ | 4 | | | | | 8 | 13 | | | | 32 |
| 1 | 5 | 3 | 4 | | | 9 | | 8 | $6^3$ | | | $12$ | $10^1$ | $7^4$ | $11^2$ | 2 | | | | | 14 | 13 | | | | 33 |
| 1 | | 3 | $5^1$ | 2 | 12 | 7 | 14 | 6 | | 11 | | 10 | | $9^2$ | 4 | | | | | | $8^3$ | 13 | | | | 34 |
| 1 | | 3 | 2 | 5 | $6^1$ | 7 | 8 | | | $11^2$ | | $10^3$ | 14 | 13 | 4 | | | | | | 12 | 9 | | | | 35 |
| 1 | $3^3$ | 2 | | 6 | $7^2$ | | 12 | | | 13 | 10 | 5 | 11 | 4 | | 8 | $9^1$ | | | | | 14 | | | | 36 |
| $1^1$ | | 4 | 2 | 7 | | 6 | | $11^3$ | | 10 | 5 | $9^1$ | 3 | 12 | | | | 14 | | | $8^2$ | 13 | | | | 37 |
| | | 3 | $5^1$ | 2 | 12 | 6 | | 7 | | 11 | | 10 | 8 | $9^2$ | 4 | 1 | | | | | | 13 | | | | 38 |
| 1 | | 3 | $2^1$ | 12 | 7 | 14 | $6^3$ | | | 13 | 10 | 5 | 11 | 4 | | | | | | | $8^2$ | 9 | | | | 39 |
| 1 | | 3 | | 5 | 4 | 7 | 8 | | | 13 | 11 | 6 | $9^2$ | $2^1$ | | | | | | | | $10^3$ | 14 | 12 | | 40 |
| 1 | | 3 | 4 | 5 | 6 | 7 | $8^3$ | | 11 | | 13 | $12$ | $10^2$ | | | | | | | | | $9^1$ | 14 | | | 41 |
| | 4 | | 3 | 5 | 7 | 8 | | 9 | | $11^1$ | 10 | 2 | 12 | | 1 | | | | | | 6 | | | | | 42 |
| 1 | 4 | $2^1$ | 3 | 5 | 7 | 6 | 8 | | 11 | | 10 | 9 | 12 | | | | | | | | | | | | | 43 |
| 1 | 3 | | $4^1$ | 5 | 7 | 6 | $8^3$ | 9 | | $10^3$ | 11 | 2 | | | | | | | | | 14 | 13 | 12 | | | 44 |
| 1 | | | 5 | 3 | 7 | $6^3$ | 11 | | 12 | $10^2$ | 2 | $9^1$ | | | | | | | | | 8 | | 13 | $4^4$ | 14 | 45 |
| 1 | | 2 | 3 | 5 | 4 | 6 | 14 | | | $13$ | $10^3$ | 7 | $9^1$ | | | | | | | | 8 | 12 | $11^2$ | | | 46 |

# NEWCASTLE UNITED

## FOUNDATION

In October 1882 a club called Stanley, which had been formed in 1881, changed its name to Newcastle East End to avoid confusion with two other local clubs, Stanley Nops and Stanley Albion. Shortly afterwards another club, Rosewood, merged with them. Newcastle West End had been formed in August 1882 and they played on a pitch which was part of the Town Moor. They moved to Brandling Park in 1885 and St James' Park 1886 (home of Newcastle Rangers). West End went out of existence after a bad run and the remaining committee men invited East End to move to St James' Park. They accepted and, at a meeting in Bath Lane Hall in 1892, changed their name to Newcastle United.

*St James' Park, Newcastle-upon-Tyne NE1 4ST.*

*Telephone:* (0191) 201 8400.

*Fax:* (0191) 201 8600.

*Ticket Office:* (0844) 372 1892.

*Website:* www.nufc.co.uk

*Email:* admin@nufc.co.uk

*Ground Capacity:* 52,405.

*Record Attendance:* 68,386 v Chelsea, Division 1, 3 September 1930.

*Pitch Measurements:* 105m × 68m (114yd × 74yd)

*Manager:* Alan Pardew.

*Assistant Manager:* John Carver.

*Physio:* Derek Wright.

*Colours:* Black and white striped shirts, black shorts with white trim, black socks.

*Year Formed:* 1881.

*Turned Professional:* 1889.

*Previous Names:* 1881, Stanley; 1882, Newcastle East End; 1892, Newcastle United.

*Club Nickname:* 'The Magpies', 'The Toon'.

*Grounds:* 1881, South Byker; 1886, Chillingham Road, Heaton; 1892, St James' Park.

*First Football League Game:* 2 September 1893, Division 2, v Royal Arsenal (a) D 2–2 – Ramsay; Jeffery, Miller; Crielly, Graham, McKane; Bowman, Crate (1), Thompson, Sorley (1), Wallace. Graham not Crate scored according to some reports.

*Record League Victory:* 13–0 v Newport Co, Division 2, 5 October 1946 – Garbutt; Cowell, Graham; Harvey, Brennan, Wright; Milburn (2), Bentley (1), Wayman (4), Shackleton (6), Pearson.

## HONOURS

**FA Premier League:**
*Runners-up* 1995–96, 1996–97.

**Football League – Division 1:**
*Champions* 1904–05, 1906–07, 1908–09, 1926–27, 1992–93;
**Division 2:** *Champions* 1964–65;
*Runners-up* 1897–98, 1947–48;
**FL C:** *Champions* 2009–10.

**FA Cup:** *Winners* 1910, 1924, 1932, 1951, 1952, 1955; *Runners-up* 1905, 1906, 1908, 1911, 1974, 1998, 1999.

**Football League Cup:**
*Runners-up* 1976.

**Texaco Cup:** *Winners* 1974, 1975.

**European Competitions**
**Champions League:** 1997–98, 2002–03, 2003–04. **European Fairs Cup:** 1968–69 (*winners*), 1969–70, 1970–71.
**UEFA Cup:** 1977–78, 1994–95, 1996–97, 1999–2000, 2003–04 (*s-f*), 2004–05, 2006–07.
**European Cup Winners' Cup:** 1998–99.
**Europa League:** 2012–13.
**Anglo-Italian Cup:** 1972–73 (*winners*).
**Intertoto Cup:** 2001 (*runners-up*), 2005, 2006 (*winners*).

## sky SPORTS FACT FILE

Colin Veitch was a key figure in the successful Newcastle United team of the early 1900s. He was also active in the theatre with the Clarion Dramatic Society and Newcastle People's Theatre and an acquaintance of the playwright George Bernard Shaw.

*Record Cup Victory:* 9–0 v Southport (at Hillsborough), FA Cup 4th rd, 1 February 1932 – McInroy; Nelson, Fairhurst; McKenzie, Davidson, Weaver (1); Boyd (1), Jimmy Richardson (3), Cape (2), McMenemy (1), Lang (1).

*Record Defeat:* 0–9 v Burton Wanderers, Division 2, 15 April 1895.

*Most League Points (2 for a win):* 57, Division 2, 1964–65.

*Most League Points (3 for a win):* 102, FL C, 2009–10.

*Most League Goals:* 98, Division 1, 1951–52.

*Highest League Scorer in Season:* Hughie Gallacher, 36, Division 1, 1926–27.

*Most League Goals in Total Aggregate:* Jackie Milburn, 177, 1946–57.

*Most League Goals in One Match:* 6, Len Shackleton v Newport Co, Division 2, 5 October 1946.

*Most Capped Player:* Shay Given, 82 (125), Republic of Ireland.

*Most League Appearances:* Jim Lawrence, 432, 1904–22.

*Youngest League Player:* Steve Watson, 16 years 223 days v Wolverhampton W, 10 November 1990.

*Record Transfer Fee Received:* £35,000,000 from Liverpool for Andy Carroll, January 2011.

*Record Transfer Fee Paid:* £16,000,000 to Real Madrid for Michael Owen, September 2005.

*Football League Record:* 1893 Elected to Division 2; 1898–1934 Division 1; 1934–48 Division 2; 1948–61 Division 1; 1961–65 Division 2; 1965–78 Division 1; 1978–84 Division 2; 1984–89 Division 1; 1989–92 Division 2; 1992–93 Division 1; 1993–2009 FA Premier League; 2009–10 FL C; 2010– FA Premier League.

## LATEST SEQUENCES

*Longest Sequence of League Wins:* 13, 25.4.1992 – 18.10.1992.

*Longest Sequence of League Defeats:* 10, 23.8.1977 – 15.10.1977.

*Longest Sequence of League Draws:* 4, 20.1.1990 – 24.2.1990.

*Longest Sequence of Unbeaten League Matches:* 17, 13.2.2010 – 2.5.2010.

*Longest Sequence Without a League Win:* 21, 14.1.1978 – 23.8.1978.

*Successive Scoring Runs:* 25 from 15.4.1939.

*Successive Non-scoring Runs:* 6 from 31.12.1938.

## MANAGERS

**Frank Watt** 1895–32
 *(Secretary-Manager)*
**Andy Cunningham** 1930–35
**Tom Mather** 1935–39
**Stan Seymour** 1939–47
 *(Hon. Manager)*
**George Martin** 1947–50
**Stan Seymour** 1950–54
 *(Hon. Manager)*
**Duggie Livingstone** 1954–56
**Stan Seymour** 1956–58
 *(Hon. Manager)*
**Charlie Mitten** 1958–61
**Norman Smith** 1961–62
**Joe Harvey** 1962–75
**Gordon Lee** 1975–77
**Richard Dinnis** 1977
**Bill McGarry** 1977–80
**Arthur Cox** 1980–84
**Jack Charlton** 1984
**Willie McFaul** 1985–88
**Jim Smith** 1988–91
**Ossie Ardiles** 1991–92
**Kevin Keegan** 1992–97
**Kenny Dalglish** 1997–98
**Ruud Gullit** 1998–99
**Sir Bobby Robson** 1999–2004
**Graeme Souness** 2004–06
**Glenn Roeder** 2006–07
**Sam Allardyce** 2007–08
**Kevin Keegan** 2008
**Joe Kinnear** 2008–09
**Alan Shearer** 2009
**Chris Hughton** 2009–10
**Alan Pardew** December 2010–

## TEN YEAR LEAGUE RECORD

| | | P | W | D | L | F | A | Pts | Pos |
|---|---|---|---|---|---|---|---|---|---|
| 2003-04 | PR Lge | 38 | 13 | 17 | 8 | 52 | 40 | 56 | 5 |
| 2004-05 | PR Lge | 38 | 10 | 14 | 14 | 47 | 57 | 44 | 14 |
| 2005-06 | PR Lge | 38 | 17 | 7 | 14 | 47 | 42 | 58 | 7 |
| 2006-07 | PR Lge | 38 | 11 | 10 | 17 | 38 | 47 | 43 | 13 |
| 2007-08 | PR Lge | 38 | 11 | 10 | 17 | 45 | 65 | 43 | 12 |
| 2008-09 | PR Lge | 38 | 7 | 13 | 18 | 40 | 59 | 34 | 18 |
| 2009-10 | FL C | 46 | 30 | 12 | 4 | 90 | 35 | 102 | 1 |
| 2010-11 | PR Lge | 38 | 11 | 13 | 14 | 56 | 57 | 46 | 12 |
| 2011-12 | PR Lge | 38 | 19 | 8 | 11 | 56 | 51 | 65 | 5 |
| 2012-13 | PR Lge | 38 | 11 | 8 | 19 | 45 | 68 | 41 | 16 |

## DID YOU KNOW

Newcastle United first gained experience of European football in the 1960–61 season when they took part in the Friendship Cup. On 10 August 1960 they won 3-2 away to Racing Club de Paris, then on 28 September they ran out 2-1 winners in the home leg.

## NEWCASTLE UNITED – FA PREMIERSHIP 2012–13 LEAGUE RECORD

| Match No. | Date | Venue | Opponents | Result | H/T Score | Lg Pos. | Goalscorers | Attendance |
|---|---|---|---|---|---|---|---|---|
| 1 | Aug 18 | H | Tottenham H | W 2-1 | 0-0 | 4 | Ba [55], Ben Arfa (pen) [80] | 52,385 |
| 2 | 25 | A | Chelsea | L 0-2 | 0-2 | 9 | | 41,718 |
| 3 | Sept 2 | H | Aston Villa | D 1-1 | 0-1 | 10 | Ben Arfa [59] | 48,245 |
| 4 | 17 | A | Everton | D 2-2 | 0-1 | 11 | Ba 2 [49, 90] | 32,510 |
| 5 | 23 | H | Norwich C | W 1-0 | 1-0 | 10 | Ba [19] | 49,402 |
| 6 | 29 | A | Reading | D 2-2 | 0-0 | 9 | Ba 2 [58, 83] | 24,097 |
| 7 | Oct 7 | H | Manchester U | L 0-3 | 0-2 | 10 | | 52,203 |
| 8 | 21 | A | Sunderland | D 1-1 | 1-0 | 11 | Cabaye [3] | 47,456 |
| 9 | 28 | H | WBA | W 2-1 | 1-0 | 10 | Ba [35], Cisse [90] | 49,731 |
| 10 | Nov 4 | A | Liverpool | D 1-1 | 1-0 | 10 | Cabaye [43] | 44,803 |
| 11 | 11 | H | West Ham U | L 0-1 | 0-1 | 10 | | 51,855 |
| 12 | 17 | H | Swansea C | L 1-2 | 0-0 | 12 | Ba [90] | 49,403 |
| 13 | 25 | A | Southampton | L 0-2 | 0-1 | 14 | | 31,410 |
| 14 | 28 | A | Stoke C | L 1-2 | 0-0 | 14 | Cisse [47] | 26,793 |
| 15 | Dec 3 | H | Wigan Ath | W 3-0 | 2-0 | 14 | Ba 2 (1 pen) [13 (p), 21], Bigirimana [71] | 43,858 |
| 16 | 10 | A | Fulham | L 1-2 | 0-1 | 14 | Ben Arfa [54] | 25,270 |
| 17 | 15 | H | Manchester C | L 1-3 | 0-2 | 15 | Ba [51] | 49,579 |
| 18 | 22 | H | QPR | W 1-0 | 0-0 | 14 | Ameobi, Shola [81] | 50,180 |
| 19 | 26 | A | Manchester U | L 3-4 | 2-1 | 15 | Perch [4], Evans (og) [28], Cisse [68] | 75,596 |
| 20 | 29 | A | Arsenal | L 3-7 | 1-1 | 15 | Ba 2 [43, 69], Marveaux [59] | 60,087 |
| 21 | Jan 2 | H | Everton | L 1-2 | 1-1 | 15 | Cisse [2] | 49,391 |
| 22 | 12 | A | Norwich C | D 0-0 | 0-0 | 16 | | 26,752 |
| 23 | 19 | H | Reading | L 1-2 | 1-0 | 16 | Cabaye [35] | 49,411 |
| 24 | 29 | A | Aston Villa | W 2-1 | 2-0 | 15 | Cisse [19], Cabaye [31] | 30,334 |
| 25 | Feb 2 | H | Chelsea | W 3-2 | 1-0 | 15 | Gutierrez [41], Sissoko 2 [68, 90] | 52,314 |
| 26 | 9 | A | Tottenham H | L 1-2 | 1-1 | 16 | Gouffran [24] | 36,244 |
| 27 | 24 | H | Southampton | W 4-2 | 2-1 | 14 | Sissoko [33], Cisse [42], Cabaye (pen) [67], Hooiveld (og) [79] | 52,259 |
| 28 | Mar 2 | A | Swansea C | L 0-1 | 0-0 | 15 | | 20,405 |
| 29 | 10 | H | Stoke C | W 2-1 | 0-0 | 13 | Cabaye [73], Cisse [90] | 50,703 |
| 30 | 17 | A | Wigan Ath | L 1-2 | 0-1 | 13 | Santon [72] | 22,297 |
| 31 | 30 | A | Manchester C | L 0-4 | 0-2 | 15 | | 47,201 |
| 32 | Apr 7 | H | Fulham | W 1-0 | 0-0 | 13 | Cisse [90] | 51,847 |
| 33 | 14 | H | Sunderland | L 0-3 | 0-1 | 13 | | 52,355 |
| 34 | 20 | A | WBA | D 1-1 | 1-0 | 16 | Gouffran [8] | 25,671 |
| 35 | 27 | H | Liverpool | L 0-6 | 0-2 | 16 | | 52,351 |
| 36 | May 4 | A | West Ham U | D 0-0 | 0-0 | 16 | | 34,962 |
| 37 | 12 | A | QPR | W 2-1 | 2-1 | 13 | Ben Arfa (pen) [18], Gouffran [35] | 17,278 |
| 38 | 19 | H | Arsenal | L 0-1 | 0-0 | 16 | | 52,354 |

**Final League Position: 16**

### GOALSCORERS

*League (45):* Ba 13 (1 pen), Cisse 8, Cabaye 6 (1 pen), Ben Arfa 4 (2 pens), Gouffran 3, Sissoko 3, Ameobi, Shola 1, Bigirimana 1, Gutierrez 1, Marveaux 1, Perch 1, Santon 1, own goals 2.
*FA Cup (0).*
*Capital One Cup (1):* Cisse 1.
*Europa League (13):* Cisse 4, Ameobi 3 (1 pen), Anita 1, Marveaux 1, Obertan 1, Taylor R 1, Vuckic 1, own goal 1.

| Krul T 24 | Simpson D 18+1 | Taylor S 24+1 | Perch J 19+8 | Santon D 31 | Ben Arfa H 16+3 | Tiote C 22+2 | Cabaye Y 25+1 | Gutierrez J 34 | Cisse P 35+1 | Ba D 19+1 | Anita V 17+8 | Obertan G 4+10 | Coloccini F 22 | Taylor R —+1 | Marveaux S 10+12 | Bigirimana G 3+10 | Harper S 5+1 | Williamson M 19 | Ameobi Shola 4+19 | Tavernier J —+2 | Ferguson S 4+5 | Ameobi Sam 1+7 | Ranger N —+2 | Debuchy M 14 | Gouffran Y 14+1 | Sissoko M 12 | Yanga-Mbiwa M 11+3 | Elliot R 9+1 | Haidara M 2+2 | Campbell A —+3 | Gosling D —+3 | Match No. |
|---|---|---|---|---|---|---|---|---|---|---|---|---|---|---|---|---|---|---|---|---|---|---|---|---|---|---|---|---|---|---|---|---|
| 1 | 2 | 3 | 4 | 5 | 6 | 7 | $8^1$ | 9 | 10 | $11^2$ | 12 | 13 | | | | | | | | | | | | | | | | | | | | 1 |
| 1 | $2^1$ | 4 | 14 | $5^2$ | 6 | $7^3$ | 9 | 11 | 10 | 8 | | | 3 | | 12 | 13 | | | | | | | | | | | | | | | | 2 |
| 1 | $2^1$ | 4 | | 5 | 6 | 7 | $9^2$ | 11 | $10^3$ | 8 | 14 | | 3 | | 13 | 12 | | | | | | | | | | | | | | | | 3 |
| | | 3 | 2 | 5 | 11 | | $6^3$ | 8 | $10^2$ | 12 | 7 | | | | $9^1$ | 14 | 1 | 4 | 13 | | | | | | | | | | | | | 4 |
| | | 4 | 2 | 5 | $6^3$ | 13 | 8 | 9 | $10^1$ | 11 | $7^2$ | 12 | | | | | 1 | 3 | 14 | | | | | | | | | | | | | 5 |
| | | $4^1$ | 2 | 5 | 6 | 7 | | 9 | $10^2$ | 11 | | | | $8^3$ | | | 1 | 3 | 13 | 12 | 14 | | | | | | | | | | | 6 |
| | | 3 | 2 | | 6 | $7^3$ | 8 | 9 | $10^2$ | 11 | 13 | | 14 | | | | 1 | 4 | 12 | $5^1$ | | | | | | | | | | | | 7 |
| 1 | 2 | 13 | 12 | 5 | $9^3$ | $8$ | 7 | 6 | 10 | | 14 | | | $4^2$ | | | | 3 | $11^1$ | | | | | | | | | | | | | 8 |
| 1 | $2^1$ | | 8 | 5 | 6 | | 7 | 9 | 12 | $10^3$ | | 13 | 3 | | | | | 4 | $11^2$ | | 14 | | | | | | | | | | | 9 |
| 1 | 12 | 3 | $6^1$ | 5 | 9 | | $7^3$ | 8 | 10 | $11^2$ | 2 | | $4^4$ | | | | | | 14 | 13 | | | | | | | | | | | | 10 |
| 1 | $2^3$ | 3 | | 5 | 6 | | $7^3$ | 8 | $10^2$ | 11 | 12 | 14 | | | | | | 4 | 13 | | 9 | | | | | | | | | | | 11 |
| 1 | $2^2$ | 3 | | 5 | 6 | 8 | | | 11 | | 7 | | 14 | 13 | | | | 4 | 12 | $9^1$ | $10^3$ | | | | | | | | | | | 12 |
| 1 | 2 | $3^3$ | 14 | 5 | | 7 | | 8 | 11 | 10 | $6^2$ | | | 13 | | | | 4 | | $9^1$ | 12 | | | | | | | | | | | 13 |
| 1 | 2 | | 7 | 5 | | 8 | | 9 | $11^2$ | 10 | $6^1$ | | 3 | | | | | 4 | | 13 | 12 | | | | | | | | | | | 14 |
| 1 | 2 | | | $5^2$ | | $7^1$ | | $9^3$ | 11 | 10 | 8 | | 4 | | $6$ | 12 | | 3 | | 13 | 14 | | | | | | | | | | | 15 |
| 1 | 2 | | | $9^1$ | $7^3$ | | 6 | 10 | 11 | $8^2$ | | | 3 | | 13 | 14 | | 4 | 12 | | | | | | | | | | | | | 16 |
| 1 | $2^3$ | | 6 | 5 | | $7^1$ | | 9 | $10^2$ | 11 | 8 | | 4 | | 12 | | | 3 | 13 | | 14 | | | | | | | | | | | 17 |
| 1 | 2 | | 8 | 5 | | $7^3$ | | $9^1$ | $11^2$ | 10 | 6 | 12 | 3 | | 14 | | | 4 | 13 | | | | | | | | | | | | | 18 |
| 1 | 2 | | 7 | 5 | | | | $9^3$ | $10^2$ | 6 | 12 | 4 | | | 11 | $8^1$ | | 3 | 13 | | 14 | | | | | | | | | | | 19 |
| 1 | $2^2$ | | 4 | 5 | | 8 | | 11 | 10 | | 6 | 3 | | | $9^3$ | $7^1$ | | | | 12 | 14 | 13 | | | | | | | | | | 20 |
| 1 | | $2^3$ | 5 | | $8^2$ | | 11 | | 7 | $6^1$ | 4 | | | | 9 | 12 | | 3 | 10 | | | | 13 | 14 | | | | | | | | 21 |
| 1 | | 6 | 5 | | | 12 | 10 | 11 | $7^2$ | $8^1$ | 4 | | | | 9 | 13 | | 3 | | | | 2 | | | | | | | | | | 22 |
| 1 | | 12 | 3 | | | $6^2$ | 10 | 8 | $7^3$ | 14 | 2 | | | | $9^1$ | 13 | | 5 | 11 | | | 4 | | | | | | | | | | 23 |
| 1 | 3 | $6^1$ | 5 | | | | 7 | 10 | 11 | 13 | 4 | | | | | | | | 12 | | | | | 2 | $8^2$ | $9^3$ | 14 | | | | | 24 |
| 1 | 3 | 6 | 5 | | | | 7 | 10 | 11 | | 4 | | 12 | | | | | | | | | | | 2 | $8^1$ | $9^2$ | 13 | | | | | 25 |
| 1 | 4 | $6^2$ | 5 | | 13 | 8 | | $9^3$ | 11 | | 3 | | 12 | | | | | 14 | | | | | | 2 | $10^1$ | 7 | | | | | | 26 |
| | 4 | 13 | 5 | | 6 | $7^2$ | 9 | 11 | | 14 | | $3^1$ | | | 12 | | | | | | | | | 2 | $10^3$ | 8 | 12 | 1 | | | | 27 |
| | 3 | | 5 | | $9^2$ | 7 | 10 | 11 | | | | | 13 | | | | | 12 | | | | | | 2 | 6 | 8 | 4 | 1 | | | | 28 |
| | 3 | | $5^2$ | | $7^1$ | 6 | 8 | 11 | | | | | 13 | | | | | | 12 | | | | | 2 | $10^3$ | 9 | 4 | 1 | 12 | 14 | | 29 |
| | 3 | 13 | 5 | | 7 | | 8 | 11 | | | | | 6 | | | | | 14 | | | | | | $2^1$ | $9^3$ | 10 | 4 | 1 | $12^2$ | | | 30 |
| | 2 | 3 | 12 | | | $7^3$ | 5 | 11 | | 6 | $8^1$ | | 14 | | | | | | | | | | | | $10^2$ | 9 | 4 | 1 | | | 13 | 31 |
| 1 | $2^3$ | 4 | | $5^1$ | | 7 | 9 | 10 | | 12 | | | 6 | | | | | 13 | | | | | | $11^2$ | 8 | 3 | | 14 | | | | 32 |
| $1^2$ | | | | | 14 | 7 | $8^3$ | 5 | 11 | | | | 6 | | | | | 12 | | | | | | 2 | $9^1$ | 10 | 4 | 13 | | | | 33 |
| | 3 | 6 | | 13 | | | $7^3$ | 10 | 11 | | | | | | | | | 12 | | | | | | 2 | $8^1$ | 9 | 4 | 1 | $5^2$ | 14 | | 34 |
| | 3 | $9^2$ | | 12 | $7^3$ | 8 | 10 | 11 | | 14 | | | | | | | | | | | | | | $2^1$ | 13 | 6 | 4 | 1 | 5 | | | 35 |
| | 2 | 3 | | | $6^1$ | 8 | 7 | 10 | 11 | | | 4 | | | | | | 12 | | | | | | | $9^2$ | | 5 | 1 | | | 13 | 36 |
| | | 12 | | | $9^3$ | $7^1$ | 6 | 8 | 10 | | | 13 | 3 | | | | | $14$ | 4 | | | | | | $11^2$ | | 5 | $1$ | | | | 37 |
| | | 3 | | | 6 | 8 | $7^1$ | 9 | 11 | | 12 | | 4 | | 13 | | | 1 | | | | | | | $10^2$ | | $5^3$ | | | 14 | | 38 |

**FA Cup**

Third Round    Brighton & HA    (a)    0-2

**Capital One Cup**

Third Round    Manchester U    (a)    1-2

**Europa League**

| | | | |
|---|---|---|---|
| Play-off Round | Atromitos | (a) | 1-1 |
| | Atromitos | (h) | 1-0 |
| Group D | Maritimo | (a) | 0-0 |
| | Bordeaux | (h) | 3-0 |
| | Club Brugge | (h) | 1-0 |
| | Club Brugge | (a) | 2-2 |
| | Maritimo | (h) | 1-1 |
| | Bordeaux | (a) | 0-2 |
| Second Round | FC Metalist Kharkiv | (h) | 0-0 |
| | FC Metalist Kharkiv | (a) | 1-0 |
| Third Round | Anzhi Makhachkala | (a) | 0-0 |
| | Anzhi Makhachkala | (h) | 1-0 |
| Quarter-Finals | Benfica | (a) | 1-3 |
| | Benfica | (h) | 1-1 |

# NEWPORT COUNTY

## FOUNDATION

In 1912 Newport County were formed following a meeting at The Tredegar Arms Hotel. A professional football club had existed in the town called Newport FC, but they ceased to exist in 1907. The first season as Newport County was in the second division of the Southern League. They started life playing at Somerton Park where they remained through their League years. They were elected to the Football League for the beginning of the 1920–21 season as founder members of Division 3. At the end of the 1987–88 season, they were relegated from the Football League and replaced by Lincoln City. On February 27 1989, Newport County went out of business and from the ashes Newport AFC was born. Starting down the pyramid in the Hellenic League, they eventually gained promotion to the Conference in 2011 and were promoted to the Football League after a play-off with Wrexham in 2013.

*Rodney Parade, Newport, South Wales NP19 0UU.*

*Telephone:* (01633) 670 690.

*Ticket Office:* (01633) 674 990.

*Website:* www.newport-county.co.uk

*Email:* office@newport-county.co.uk

*Ground Capacity:* 5,511.

*Record Attendance:* 24,268 v Cardiff C, Division 3 (S), 16 October 1937 (Somerton Park); 4,660 v Swansea C, FA Cup 1st rd, 11 November 2006 (Newport Stadium); 6,615 v Grimsby T, Conference National Play-off Semi-final, 28 April 2013 (Rodney Parade).

*Pitch Measurements:* 102m × 65m (112yd × 72yd)

*Chairman:* Les Scadding.

*Chief Executive:* Dave Boddy.

*Manager:* Justin Edinburgh.

*Assistant Manager:* Jimmy Dack.

*Physio:* Wayne Jones.

*Colours:* Amber shirts with black trim, black shorts, black socks with amber hoops.

*Year Formed:* 1912.

*Turned Professional:* 1912.

*Club Nicknames:* 'The Exiles', 'The Ironsides', 'The Port', 'The County'.

## HONOURS

**Football League – Division 3 (S): Champions** 1938–39.

**FA Cup:** Best season: 5th rd, 1949.

**Football League Cup:** Never past 3rd rd.

**Welsh Cup:** *Winners* 1980; *Runners-up* 1963, 1987.

**FA Trophy:** *Runners-up* 2012.

**European Competitions European Cup Winners' Cup:** 1980–81 (*quarter-finals*).

## sky SPORTS FACT FILE

Newport County, under their former title Newport AFC, played their first FA Cup tie on 29 August 1992. They won 3-0 away to Dawlish Town in a preliminary round tie and progressed to the fourth qualifying round before going down to Sutton United.

*Grounds:* 1912–89, 1990–92, Somerton Park, 1992–94, Meadow Park Stadium; 1994, Newport Stadium, 2012, Rodney Parade.

*First Football League Game:* 28 August 1920, Division 3, v Reading (h) L 0–1.

*Record League Victory:* 10-0 v Merthyr T, Division 3(S), 10 April 1930 – Martin (5), Gittins (2), Thomas (1), Bagley (1), Lawson (1).

*Record Cup Victory:* 7-0 v Working, FA Cup 1st rd, 24 November 1928 – Young (3), Pugh (2) Gittins (1), Reid (1).

*Record Defeat:* 0–13 v Newcastle U, Division 2, 5 October 1946.

*Most League Points (2 for a win):* 61, Division 4, 1979–80.

*Most League Points (3 for a win):* 78, Division 3, 1982–83.

*Most League Goals:* 85, Division 4, 1964–65.

*Highest League Scorer in Season:* Tudor Martin, 34, Division 3 (S), 1929–30.

*Most League Goals in Total Aggregate:* Reg Parker, 99, 1948–54.

*Most League Goals in One Match:* 5, Tudor Martin v Merthyr T, Dvision 3 (S), 10 April 1930.

*Most Capped Player:* Nigel Vaughan, 3 (10), Wales.

*Most League Appearances:* Len Weare, 526, 1955–70.

*Record Transfer Fee Received:* £160,000 from Chelsea for Roger Freestone, March 1987.

*Record Transfer Fee Paid:* £80,000 to Swansea C for Alan Waddle, January 1981.

*Football League Record:* 1920 Original member of Division 3; 1921–31 Divsion 3 (S) – dropped out of Football League; 1932 Re-elected to Division 3 (S); 1932–39 Division 3 (S); 1946–47 Division 2; 1947–58 Division 3 (S); 1958–62 Division 3; 1962–80 Division 4; 1980–87 Division 3; 1987–88 Division 4 (relegated from Football League); 2011 promoted to Conference; 2011–13 Conference; 2013– FL 2.

## MANAGERS

Davy McDougle 1912–13
  *(Player-Manager)*
Sam Hollis 1913–17
Harry Parkes 1919–22
Jimmy Hindmarsh 1922–35
Louis Page 1935–36
Tom Bromilow 1936–37
Billy McCandless 1937–45
Tom Bromilow 1945–50
Fred Stansfield 1950–53
Billy Lucas 1953–61
Bobby Evans 1961–62
Billy Lucas 1962–67
Leslie Graham 1967–69
Bobby Ferguson 1969–70
  *(Player-Manager)*
Billy Lucas 1970–74
Brian Harris 1974–75
Dave Elliott 1975–76
  *(Player-Manager)*
Jimmy Scoular 1976–77
Colin Addison 1977–78
Len Ashurst 1978–82
Colin Addison 1982–85
Bobby Smith 1985–86
John Relish 1986
Jimmy Mullen 1986–87
John Lewis 1987
Brian Eastick 1987–88
David Williams 1988
Eddie May 1988
John Mahoney 1988–89
John Relish 1989–93
Graham Rogers 1993–96
Chris Price 1997
Tim Harris 1997–2002
Peter Nicholas 2002–04
John Cornforth 2004–05
Peter Beadle 2005–08
Dean Holdsworth 2008–11
Anthony Hudson 2011
Justin Edinburgh October 2011–

## TEN YEAR LEAGUE RECORD

|  |  | P | W | D | L | F | A | Pts | Pos |
|---|---|---|---|---|---|---|---|---|---|
| 2003-04 | SLP | 42 | 15 | 14 | 13 | 52 | 50 | 59 | 7 |
| 2004-05 | Conf S | 42 | 13 | 11 | 18 | 56 | 61 | 50 | 18 |
| 2005-06 | Conf S | 42 | 12 | 8 | 22 | 50 | 67 | 44 | 18 |
| 2006-07 | Conf S | 42 | 21 | 7 | 14 | 83 | 57 | 70 | 6 |
| 2007-08 | Conf S | 42 | 18 | 12 | 12 | 64 | 49 | 66 | 9 |
| 2008-09 | Conf S | 42 | 16 | 11 | 15 | 50 | 51 | 59 | 10 |
| 2009-10 | Conf S | 42 | 32 | 7 | 3 | 93 | 26 | 103 | 1 |
| 2010-11 | BSP | 46 | 18 | 15 | 13 | 78 | 60 | 69 | 9 |
| 2011-12 | BSP | 46 | 11 | 14 | 21 | 53 | 65 | 47 | 19 |
| 2012–13 | BSP | 46 | 25 | 10 | 11 | 85 | 60 | 85 | 3 |

## DID YOU KNOW ?

Chris Lilygreen made 31 appearances for the old Newport County club between 1983 and 1985. After spells with a number of non-league clubs including Yeovil Town and Bath City he signed for the newly formed Newport AFC and finished the Exiles' inaugural season as top scorer with 28 goals.

# NORTHAMPTON TOWN

## FOUNDATION

Formed in 1897 by schoolteachers connected with the Northampton & District Elementary Schools' Association, they survived a financial crisis at the end of their first year when they were £675 in the red and became members of the Midland League – a fast move indeed for a new club. They achieved Southern League membership in 1901.

*Sixfields Stadium, Upton Way, Northampton NN5 5QA.*

*Telephone:* (01604) 683 700.

*Fax:* (01604) 751 613.

*Ticket Office:* (01604) 683 777.

*Website:* www.ntfc.co.uk

*Email:* gareth.willsher@ntfc.tv

*Ground Capacity:* 7,300.

*Record Attendance:* 24,523 v Fulham, Division 1, 23 April 1966 (at County Ground); 7,557 v Manchester C, Division 2, 26 September 1998 (at Sixfields Stadium).

*Pitch Measurements:* 106m × 65m (116yd × 72yd)

*Chairman:* David Cardoza.

*Manager:* Aidy Boothroyd.

*Assistant Manager:* Andy King.

*Physio:* Stuart Barker.

*Colours:* Claret shirts, white shorts with claret trim, white socks with claret trim.

*Year Formed:* 1897.

*Turned Professional:* 1901.

*Grounds:* 1897, County Ground; 1994, Sixfields Stadium.

*Club Nickname:* 'The Cobblers'.

*First Football League Game:* 28 August 1920, Division 3, v Grimsby T (a) L 0–2 – Thorpe; Sproston, Hewison; Jobey, Tomkins, Pease; Whitworth, Lockett, Thomas, Freeman, MacKechnie.

*Record League Victory:* 10–0 v Walsall, Division 3 (S), 5 November 1927 – Hammond; Watson, Jeffs; Allen, Brett, Odell; Daley, Smith (3), Loasby (3), Hoten (1), Wells (3).

*Record Cup Victory:* 10–0 v Sutton T, FA Cup prel rd, 7 December 1907 – Cooch; Drennan, Lloyd Davies, Tirrell (1), McCartney, Hickleton, Badenock (3), Platt (3), Lowe (1), Chapman (2), McDiarmid.

*Record Defeat:* 0–11 v Southampton, Southern League, 28 December 1901.

## HONOURS

**Football League – Division 1:** 21st, 1965–66;
**Division 2:** *Runners-up* 1964–65;
**Division 3:** *Champions* 1962–63;
**Division 3 (S):** *Runners-up* 1927–28, 1949–50;
**Division 4:** *Champions* 1986–87; *Runners-up* 1975–76;
**FL 2:** *Runners-up* 2005–06.
**FA Cup:** Best season: 5th rd, 1934, 1950, 1970.
**Football League Cup:** Best season: 5th rd, 1965, 1967.

## sky SPORTS FACT FILE

Bernard Vann, who played at centre forward for Northampton Town in the 1906–07 season, was one of only a few footballers to win the Victoria Cross. He received the award for conspicuous bravery during the First World War, but sadly he was killed in action just four days later.

*Most League Points (2 for a win):* 68, Division 4, 1975–76.

*Most League Points (3 for a win):* 99, Division 4, 1986–87.

*Most League Goals:* 109, Division 3, 1962–63 and Division 3 (S), 1952–53.

*Highest League Scorer in Season:* Cliff Holton, 36, Division 3, 1961–62.

*Most League Goals in Total Aggregate:* Jack English, 135, 1947–60.

*Most League Goals in One Match:* 5, Ralph Hoten v Crystal Palace, Division 3 (S), 27 October 1928.

*Most Capped Player:* Edwin Lloyd Davies, 12 (16), Wales.

*Most League Appearances:* Tommy Fowler, 521, 1946–61.

*Youngest League Player:* Adrian Mann, 16 years 297 days v Bury, 5 May 1984.

*Record Transfer Fee Received:* £470,000 from Blackburn R for Mark Bunn, September 2008.

*Record Transfer Fee Paid:* £165,000 to Oldham Ath for Josh Low, July 2003.

*Football League Record:* 1920 Original Member of Division 3; 1921 Division 3 (S); 1958–61 Division 4; 1961–63 Division 3; 1963–65 Division 2; 1965–66 Division 1; 1966–67 Division 3; 1967–69 Division 3; 1969–76 Division 4; 1976–77 Division 3; 1977–87 Division 4; 1987–90 Division 3; 1990–92 Division 4; 1992–97 Division 3; 1997–99 Division 2; 1999–2000 Division 3; 2000–03 Division 2; 2003–04 Division 3; 2004–06 FL 2; 2006–09 FL 1; 2009– FL 2.

## LATEST SEQUENCES

*Longest Sequence of League Wins:* 8, 27.8.1960 – 19.9.1960.

*Longest Sequence of League Defeats:* 8, 26.10.1935 – 21.12.1935.

*Longest Sequence of League Draws:* 6, 18.9.1983 – 15.10.1983.

*Longest Sequence of Unbeaten League Matches:* 21, 27.9.1986 – 6.2.1987.

*Longest Sequence Without a League Win:* 18, 26.3.1969 – 20.9.1969.

*Successive Scoring Runs:* 27 from 23.8.1986.

*Successive Non-scoring Runs:* 7 from 7.4.1939.

## MANAGERS

Arthur Jones 1897–1907
  *(Secretary-Manager)*
Herbert Chapman 1907–12
Walter Bull 1912–13
Fred Lessons 1913–19
Bob Hewison 1920–25
Jack Tresadern 1925–30
Jack English 1931–35
Syd Puddefoot 1935–37
Warney Cresswell 1937–39
Tom Smith 1939–49
Bob Dennison 1949–54
Dave Smith 1954–59
David Bowen 1959–67
Tony Marchi 1967–68
Ron Flowers 1968–69
Dave Bowen 1969–72
  *(continued as General Manager and Secretary 1972–85 when joined the board)*
Billy Baxter 1972–73
Bill Dodgin Jnr 1973–76
Pat Crerand 1976–77
By committee 1977
Bill Dodgin Jnr 1977
John Petts 1977–78
Mike Keen 1978–79
Clive Walker 1979–80
Bill Dodgin Jnr 1980–82
Clive Walker 1982–84
Tony Barton 1984–85
Graham Carr 1985–90
Theo Foley 1990–92
Phil Chard 1992–93
John Barnwell 1993–94
Ian Atkins 1995–99
Kevin Wilson 1999–2001
Kevan Broadhurst 2001–03
Terry Fenwick 2003
Martin Wilkinson 2003
Colin Calderwood 2003–06
John Gorman 2006
Stuart Gray 2007–09
Ian Sampson 2009–11
Gary Johnson 2011
Aidy Boothroyd November 2011–

## TEN YEAR LEAGUE RECORD

|         |       | P  | W  | D  | L  | F  | A  | Pts | Pos |
|---------|-------|----|----|----|----|----|----|-----|-----|
| 2003-04 | Div 3 | 46 | 22 | 9  | 15 | 58 | 51 | 75  | 6   |
| 2004-05 | FL 2  | 46 | 20 | 12 | 14 | 62 | 51 | 72  | 7   |
| 2005-06 | FL 2  | 46 | 22 | 17 | 7  | 63 | 37 | 83  | 2   |
| 2006-07 | FL 1  | 46 | 15 | 14 | 17 | 48 | 51 | 59  | 14  |
| 2007-08 | FL 1  | 46 | 17 | 15 | 14 | 60 | 55 | 66  | 9   |
| 2008-09 | FL 1  | 46 | 12 | 13 | 21 | 61 | 65 | 49  | 21  |
| 2009-10 | FL 2  | 46 | 18 | 13 | 15 | 62 | 53 | 67  | 11  |
| 2010-11 | FL 2  | 46 | 11 | 19 | 16 | 63 | 71 | 52  | 16  |
| 2011-12 | FL 2  | 46 | 12 | 12 | 22 | 56 | 79 | 48  | 20  |
| 2012-13 | FL 2  | 46 | 21 | 10 | 15 | 64 | 55 | 73  | 6   |

## DID YOU KNOW

Half back Graham Carr made 96 first-team appearances for Northampton Town between 1962 and 1968, later returning to the County Ground as manager between 1985 and 1990. He is the father of the comedian and chat show host Alan Carr.

## NORTHAMPTON TOWN – FOOTBALL LEAGUE TWO 2012–13 LEAGUE RECORD

| Match No. | Date | Venue | Opponents | Result | H/T Score | Lg Pos. | Goalscorers | Atten- dance |
|---|---|---|---|---|---|---|---|---|
| 1 | Aug 18 | A | Rochdale | D 0-0 | 0-0 | 12 | | 2558 |
| 2 | 21 | H | Rotherham U | W 2-1 | 1-1 | 6 | Hackett [26], Nicholls, A [86] | 4171 |
| 3 | 25 | H | Southend U | D 3-3 | 0-0 | 9 | Akinfenwa [65], Artell [82], Nicholls, A [86] | 4562 |
| 4 | Sept 1 | A | Plymouth Arg | L 2-3 | 1-0 | 13 | Nicholls, A [26], Artell [90] | 6037 |
| 5 | 8 | H | AFC Wimbledon | W 2-0 | 0-0 | 8 | Nicholls, A [60], Hackett [72] | 4235 |
| 6 | 15 | A | Fleetwood T | L 0-1 | 0-0 | 12 | | 3027 |
| 7 | 18 | A | Dagenham & R | W 1-0 | 0-0 | 7 | Akinfenwa [50] | 1429 |
| 8 | 22 | H | Chesterfield | D 0-0 | 0-0 | 9 | | 4709 |
| 9 | 29 | A | Burton Alb | D 3-3 | 0-1 | 13 | Langmead [63], Artell [75], Nicholls, A [83] | 2857 |
| 10 | Oct 2 | H | Gillingham | L 1-2 | 0-1 | 13 | Akinfenwa [82] | 3648 |
| 11 | 6 | A | Bristol R | L 1-3 | 0-0 | 15 | Akinfenwa [75] | 5166 |
| 12 | 13 | H | Exeter C | W 3-0 | 2-0 | 12 | Akinfenwa [25], Langmead [39], Nicholls, A [84] | 4607 |
| 13 | 19 | A | Barnet | L 0-4 | 0-0 | 12 | | 2721 |
| 14 | 23 | H | Bradford C | L 0-1 | 0-0 | 17 | | 3541 |
| 15 | 27 | H | Port Vale | W 2-0 | 0-0 | 14 | Nicholls, A [20], Moult [43] | 5061 |
| 16 | Nov 6 | A | York C | D 1-1 | 0-1 | 14 | Akinfenwa [58] | 3039 |
| 17 | 10 | A | Accrington S | W 4-2 | 1-1 | 12 | Akinfenwa 3 [17, 69, 76], Robinson [67] | 1441 |
| 18 | 17 | H | Wycombe W | W 3-1 | 1-0 | 11 | Akinfenwa 2 (1 pen) [24, 61 (p)], Hackett [65] | 4764 |
| 19 | 20 | H | Morecambe | W 3-0 | 0-0 | 9 | Akinfenwa [56], Ellison (og) [61], Demontagnac [90] | 4013 |
| 20 | 24 | A | Oxford U | L 1-2 | 0-1 | 10 | Platt [76] | 6635 |
| 21 | Dec 8 | H | Cheltenham T | L 2-3 | 2-2 | 12 | Akinfenwa [2], Jones (og) [14] | 4625 |
| 22 | 15 | A | Torquay U | D 1-1 | 0-0 | 13 | Langmead [90] | 2302 |
| 23 | 22 | H | Aldershot T | W 2-0 | 0-0 | 9 | Robinson [49], Platt [90] | 4574 |
| 24 | Jan 1 | H | Dagenham & R | W 3-1 | 2-0 | 10 | Ogogo (og) [36], Hackett [39], Langmead [52] | 4368 |
| 25 | 5 | H | Fleetwood T | W 3-1 | 2-0 | 9 | Robinson 2 [7, 41], Platt [53] | 4381 |
| 26 | 12 | A | Chesterfield | L 0-3 | 0-3 | 10 | | 5467 |
| 27 | 19 | H | Burton Alb | W 1-0 | 0-0 | 6 | Akinfenwa [69] | 4090 |
| 28 | 22 | A | Aldershot T | W 2-1 | 2-1 | 3 | Hackett (pen) [22], Carlisle [35] | 1191 |
| 29 | 29 | A | Gillingham | L 0-2 | 0-1 | 4 | | 5600 |
| 30 | Feb 2 | A | Rotherham U | L 1-3 | 0-1 | 8 | Carlisle [90] | 7739 |
| 31 | 9 | H | Rochdale | W 3-1 | 1-0 | 6 | Platt [32], Langmead [69], Akinfenwa (pen) [76] | 5110 |
| 32 | 16 | A | Southend U | W 2-1 | 1-0 | 7 | O'Donovan [11], Langmead [90] | 5406 |
| 33 | 19 | A | AFC Wimbledon | D 1-1 | 0-1 | 6 | Akinfenwa (pen) [76] | 4129 |
| 34 | 23 | H | Plymouth Arg | W 1-0 | 0-0 | 4 | Platt [72] | 5382 |
| 35 | 26 | H | Bristol R | W 1-0 | 0-0 | 4 | Harding [88] | 4077 |
| 36 | Mar 2 | A | Exeter C | L 0-3 | 0-1 | 5 | | 4666 |
| 37 | 9 | H | Accrington S | W 2-0 | 2-0 | 4 | Hackett [9], O'Donovan [30] | 4746 |
| 38 | 12 | A | Morecambe | D 1-1 | 0-0 | 4 | Langmead [89] | 1366 |
| 39 | 23 | H | Oxford U | W 1-0 | 1-0 | 4 | Harding [45] | 6151 |
| 40 | 29 | H | Torquay U | W 1-0 | 0-0 | 3 | O'Donovan [85] | 5166 |
| 41 | Apr 1 | A | Cheltenham T | L 0-1 | 0-1 | 3 | | 4042 |
| 42 | 6 | A | Bradford C | L 0-1 | 0-1 | 3 | | 10,389 |
| 43 | 13 | H | York C | L 0-2 | 0-1 | 6 | | 6608 |
| 44 | 16 | A | Wycombe W | D 0-0 | 0-0 | 6 | | 3615 |
| 45 | 20 | A | Port Vale | D 2-2 | 1-1 | 6 | Carlisle [2], O'Donovan [69] | 12,496 |
| 46 | 27 | H | Barnet | W 2-0 | 0-0 | 6 | O'Donovan [67], Guttridge [73] | 7471 |

**Final League Position: 6**

### GOALSCORERS
*League (64):* Akinfenwa 16 (3 pens), Langmead 7, Nicholls, A 7, Hackett 6 (1 pen), O'Donovan 5, Platt 5, Robinson 4, Artell 3, Carlisle 3, Harding 2, Demontagnac 1, Guttridge 1, Moult 1, own goals 3.
*FA Cup (4):* Demontagnac 1 (1 pen), Langmead 1, Moult 1, Platt 1.
*Capital One Cup (3):* Artell 1, Nicholls A 1, Platt 1.
*Johnstone's Paint Trophy (3):* Akinfenwa 1 (1 pen), Mukendi 1, Robinson 1.
*League Two Play-Offs (2):* Guttridge 1, O'Donovan 1.

| Nicholls L 46 | Johnson J 16 + 4 | Langmead K 39 | Artell D 10 + 1 | Widdowson J 39 | Hackett C 39 + 2 | Tozer B 45 + 1 | Guttridge L 20 + 5 | Harding B 35 | Platt C 25 + 11 | Nicholls A 15 | Mukendi H — + 7 | Akinfenwa A 30 + 11 | East D 12 + 2 | Demontagnac I 17 + 10 | Moult L 4 + 9 | Wilson L 2 + 3 | Roofe K 4 + 2 | Charles A 8 + 1 | Huws E 9 + 1 | Hornby L 19 + 6 | Robinson J 13 + 12 | Moyo D 2 + 3 | Carlisle C 26 | Oyeleke E 1 + 1 | O'Donovan R 15 + 1 | Collins L 13 + 2 | Cameron N 2 + 1 | Dias C — + 1 | Match No. |
|---|---|---|---|---|---|---|---|---|---|---|---|---|---|---|---|---|---|---|---|---|---|---|---|---|---|---|---|---|---|
| 1 | 2 | 3 | 4 | 5 | 6 | 7 | 8¹ | 9 | 10 | 11 | 12 | | | | | | | | | | | | | | | | | | 1 |
| 1 | 2 | 3 | 4 | 5 | 8 | 9 | 7¹ | 6 | 11 | 10 | | | 12 | | | | | | | | | | | | | | | | 2 |
| 1 | 2 | 3 | 4 | 5 | 6 | 8 | 7¹ | 9 | 11 | 10 | | | 12 | | | | | | | | | | | | | | | | 3 |
| 1 | | 3 | 4 | 5 | 6³ | 7 | 8 | 9² | 12 | 10 | 14 | 11¹ | 2 | 13 | | | | | | | | | | | | | | | 4 |
| 1 | | 3 | 4 | 5 | 6³ | 8 | | 9 | 11² | 10 | 14 | 12 | 2 | 13 | 7¹ | | | | | | | | | | | | | | 5 |
| 1 | | 4 | 3 | 5 | 6 | 8 | | 7 | 10 | 9 | | 2⁸ | 11¹ | 12 | | | | | | | | | | | | | | | 6 |
| 1 | 2 | 3 | 4 | 5 | 6 | 12 | 8 | 7¹ | 13 | 11 | 14 | 10² | | 9³ | | | | | | | | | | | | | | | 7 |
| 1 | | 3 | 4 | 5 | 6 | 7 | 8 | | 11 | 10 | | 2 | 9¹ | 12 | | | | | | | | | | | | | | | 8 |
| 1 | 12 | 3 | 4 | 5 | 6² | 7 | 8 | | 11 | 10 | | 2¹ | 9³ | 14 | | 13 | | | | | | | | | | | | | 9 |
| 1 | 2¹ | 3 | 4 | 5 | 12 | 8 | 6³ | | 11 | 10 | | 13 | 9² | 14 | 7 | | | | | | | | | | | | | | 10 |
| 1 | | 4 | 13 | 3 | 7 | 6 | | | 11 | 14 | 10 | 2¹ | 8² | 12 | 9³ | 5⁸ | | | | | | | | | | | | | 11 |
| 1 | | 3 | | 5 | 2 | 8 | | 10³ | 9 | | | 11² | 6¹ | 14 | 13 | | | | | 7 | 12 | | 4 | | | | | | 12 |
| 1 | | 3 | | 5 | 2¹ | 7 | | 10² | 9 | 13 | | 11 | | 14 | 12 | | | | | 6³ | 4 | | 8 | | | | | | 13 |
| 1 | | 3 | | 5 | | 8 | | 10¹ | 9 | | | 11 | 2 | | 12 | | | | | 6 | 4 | | 7 | | | | | | 14 |
| 1 | | 3 | | 5 | | 8 | | | 10¹ | | | 11 | 2 | 13 | 12 | 9⁸ | | | | 4 | 7 | | 6 | | | | | | 15 |
| 1 | 3¹ | 4 | | 5 | 6 | 7 | | 10 | | | | 11 | 2 | | 9⁸ | | | | | 8 | 12 | | | | | | | | 16 |
| 1 | | 3 | | 5 | 9 | 4 | | 11¹ | | 14 | 10³ | 2 | 13 | | 6² | | | | | 7 | 8 | 12 | | | | | | | 17 |
| 1 | | 3 | | 5 | 6 | 4 | | 7 | 12 | | 10² | 2 | 9¹ | | | 14 | | | | 8 | 11³ | 13 | | | | | | | 18 |
| 1 | | 3 | | 5 | 6 | 2 | | 7 | 12 | | 10¹ | | 9 | 13 | | | 14 | | | 8³ | 11² | | 4 | | | | | | 19 |
| 1 | | | 4 | | 11 | 5 | | 8 | 12 | | 10 | 2 | 9¹ | | | | | | | 7 | 6 | 3⁸ | | | | | | | 20 |
| 1 | | 3 | | 5¹ | 6 | 2 | | 9 | 13 | | 10 | 14 | 11¹ | | | 8 | | | | 7² | 12 | | 4 | | | | | | 21 |
| 1 | | 4 | | | 7 | 2 | | 6 | 10 | | 11 | | | 3 | 9 | 8¹ | 12 | | | | | 5 | | | | | | | 22 |
| 1 | | 3 | | | 6 | 2 | | 9 | 10 | | 11¹ | | | 5 | 8 | 7 | 12 | | | | | 4 | | | | | | | 23 |
| 1 | | 3 | | 5 | 6 | 2 | 12 | 8 | 10² | | 11 | | 13 | | 4 | 7¹ | 9 | | | | | | | | | | | | 24 |
| 1 | | 3 | | 5 | 6 | 2 | 7¹ | 8 | 11² | | 10 | 14 | 13 | | | 12 | 9³ | 4 | | | | | | | | | | | 25 |
| 1 | | 3 | | 5 | 6 | 2 | 8 | 7² | 11 | | 10¹ | 13 | | | | 12 | 9 | 4 | | | | | | | | | | | 26 |
| 1 | | 3 | | 5 | 6 | 2 | 7 | 8 | 11¹ | | 10 | 12 | | | | 13 | 9² | 4 | | | | | | | | | | | 27 |
| 1 | | 3 | | 5 | 10 | 6 | 2 | 7 | 11 | | | | | | | 9 | 8 | 4 | | | | | | | | | | | 28 |
| 1 | | 3 | | 5 | 6 | 2 | 8¹ | 9 | 10 | | 12 | 13 | | | | 7 | 11² | 4 | | | | | | | | | | | 29 |
| 1 | | 4 | | 5 | 6 | 2 | 8 | 7 | 13 | | 11 | | | 10² | | 3 | 9¹ | 12 | | | | | | | | | | | 30 |
| 1 | | 3 | | 5² | 6 | 2 | 7³ | 8 | 10 | | 11¹ | | | 14 | 13 | 4 | 9 | 12 | | | | | | | | | | | 31 |
| 1 | 2 | 3 | | 9 | 6 | 5 | 8 | 7 | 10² | | 12 | | | | | | | | | | | | | | 13 | 11 | 4¹ | | 32 |
| 1 | 2 | 5 | | 6 | 12 | 8 | | 13 | | 10 | 7² | | | | | 9 | 14 | | | | | | 3 | | 11³ | 4¹ | | | 33 |
| 1 | 2¹ | 3 | | 6 | 8 | | | 9 | 10² | | 12 | | | | | 7 | 13 | | | | | | 4 | | 11 | 5 | | | 34 |
| 1 | 14 | 3 | | 2 | 13 | 8 | | 10³ | | | 11¹ | 12 | | | | 7 | 6² | | | | | | 4 | | 9 | 5 | | | 35 |
| 1 | | 3 | | 9² | 2 | 10 | 7 | 13 | | 11 | | | | | | 8¹ | 12 | | | | | | 4 | | 6 | 5 | | | 36 |
| 1 | 12 | 3 | | 5 | 6³ | 2 | 8 | 10² | | 13 | | 9 | | | | 7¹ | 14 | | | | | | 4 | | 11 | | | | 37 |
| 1 | 2² | 4 | | 9 | 6 | 8 | | 7 | 13 | | 12 | 10 | | | | 3 | | | | | | | 11 | | 5¹ | | | | 38 |
| 1 | 2² | 3¹ | | 5 | 6³ | 7 | 13 | 8 | 10 | | 11 | 9 | | | | 14 | 4 | | | | | | 12 | | | | | | 39 |
| 1 | 2 | | | 5 | 6³ | 7 | 8 | 10¹ | 12 | | 9² | 13 | | | | 3 | 11 | | | | | | 4 | | 14 | | | | 40 |
| 1 | 2 | | | 5¹ | 6 | 7 | 12 | 8 | 10 | | 9 | | | | | 3 | 11 | | | | | | 4 | | | | | | 41 |
| 1 | 2 | | | 6 | 7 | 8 | 9 | 13 | 10¹ | | 12 | | | | | 3 | 11 | | | | | | 4 | | 5² | | | | 42 |
| 1 | 2 | | | 5² | 6¹ | 7 | 12 | 8 | 13 | | 10 | 9³ | 14 | | | 4 | 11 | | | | | | 3 | | | | | | 43 |
| 1 | 12 | | | 5¹ | 6 | 2 | 8 | 9 | 10 | | 7² | 13 | | | | 4 | 11 | | | | | | 3 | | | | | | 44 |
| 1 | 5 | | | 10 | 2 | 7 | 6 | 8 | | | 11 | | | | | 4 | 9 | | | | | | 3 | | | | | | 45 |
| 1 | 2 | | | 7² | 8 | 12 | | 6 | 9 | | 11¹ | | | | | 4 | 10 | | | | | | 5 | | 3 | | | 13 | 46 |

**FA Cup**

| | | | | |
|---|---|---|---|---|
| First Round | Bradford C | (h) | 1-1 | |
| *Replay* | Bradford C | (a) | 3-3 | |
| *(aet; lost 2-4 on pens)* | | | | |

**Capital One Cup**

| | | | |
|---|---|---|---|
| First Round | Cardiff C | (h) | 2-1 |
| Second Round | Wolverhampton W | (h) | 1-3 |

**Johnstone's Paint Trophy**

| | | | |
|---|---|---|---|
| First Round | Milton Keynes D | (h) | 1-0 |
| Second Round | Colchester U | (h) | 2-1 |
| Southern Quarter-Finals | Leyton Orient | (h) | 0-3 |

**League Two Play-Offs**

| | | | |
|---|---|---|---|
| Semi-Finals | Cheltenham T | (a) | 1-0 |
| | Cheltenham T | (h) | 1-0 |
| Final *(at Wembley)* | Bradford C | | 0-3 |

# NORWICH CITY

## FOUNDATION

Formed in 1902, largely through the initiative of two local schoolmasters who called a meeting at the Criterion Cafe, they were shocked by an FA Commission which in 1904 declared the club professional and ejected them from the FA Amateur Cup. However, this only served to strengthen their determination. New officials were appointed and a professional club established at a meeting in the Agricultural Hall in March 1905.

*Carrow Road, Norwich, Norfolk NR1 1JE.*

*Telephone:* (01603) 760 760.

*Fax:* (01603) 613 886.

*Ticket Office:* (0844) 826 1902.

*Website:* www.canaries.co.uk

*Email:* reception@ncfc-canaries.co.uk

*Ground Capacity:* 27,224.

*Record Attendance:* 25,037 v Sheffield W, FA Cup 5th rd, 16 February 1935 (at The Nest); 43,984 v Leicester C, FA Cup 6th rd, 30 March 1963 (at Carrow Road).

*Pitch Measurements:* 105m × 68m (114yd × 74yd)

*Chairman:* Alan Bowkett.

*Joint Majority Shareholders:* Delia Smith and Michael Wynn-Jones.

*Manager:* Chris Hughton.

*Assistant Manager:* Colin Calderwood.

*Physio:* Neal Reynolds.

## HONOURS

**FA Premier League:** Best season: 3rd 1992–93.

**Football League – Division 1:**
*Champions* 2003–04;
**FL C:** *Runners-up* 2010–11;
**Division 2:** *Champions* 1971–72, 1985–86;
**FL 1:** *Champions* 2009–10;
**Division 3 (S):** *Champions* 1933–34;
*Runners-up* 1950–51;
**Division 3:** *Runners-up* 1959–60.

**FA Cup:** Semi-finals 1959, 1989, 1992.

**Football League Cup:** *Winners* 1962, 1985; *Runners-up* 1973, 1975.

**European Competitions**
**UEFA Cup:** 1993–94.

*Colours:* Yellow shirts with green trim, green shorts with yellow trim, yellow socks with green trim.

*Year Formed:* 1902.

*Turned Professional:* 1905.

*Club Nickname:* 'The Canaries'.

*Grounds:* 1902, Newmarket Road; 1908, The Nest, Rosary Road; 1935, Carrow Road.

*First Football League Game:* 28 August 1920, Division 3, v Plymouth Arg (a) D 1–1 – Skermer; Gray, Gadsden; Wilkinson, Addy, Martin; Laxton, Kidger, Parker, Whitham (1), Dobson.

*Record League Victory:* 10–2 v Coventry C, Division 3 (S), 15 March 1930 – Jarvie; Hannah, Graham; Brown, O'Brien, Lochhead (1); Porter (1), Anderson, Hunt (5), Scott (2), Slicer (1).

*Record Cup Victory:* 8–0 v Sutton U, FA Cup 4th rd, 28 January 1989 – Gunn; Culverhouse, Bowen, Butterworth, Linighan, Townsend (Crook), Gordon, Fleck (3), Allen (4), Phelan, Putney (1).

## sky SPORTS FACT FILE

On 29 October 1938, King George VI watched Norwich City's home game against Millwall at Carrow Road which was the first time a reigning monarch had attended a Division Two game. The Canaries went down to a 2-0 defeat in front of 21,500 spectators.

*Record Defeat:* 2–10 v Swindon T, Southern League, 5 September 1908.

*Most League Points (2 for a win):* 64, Division 3 (S), 1950–51.

*Most League Points (3 for a win):* 95, FL 1, 2009–10.

*Most League Goals:* 99, Division 3 (S), 1952–53.

*Highest League Scorer in Season:* Ralph Hunt, 31, Division 3 (S), 1955–56.

*Most League Goals in Total Aggregate:* Johnny Gavin, 122, 1945–54, 1955–58.

*Most League Goals in One Match:* 5, Tommy Hunt v Coventry C, Division 3 (S), 15 March 1930; 5, Roy Hollis v Walsall, Division 3 (S), 29 December 1951.

*Most Capped Player:* Mark Bowen, 35 (41), Wales.

*Most League Appearances:* Ron Ashman, 592, 1947–64.

*Youngest League Player:* Ryan Jarvis, 16 years 282 days v Walsall, 19 April 2003.

*Record Transfer Fee Received:* £7,250,000 from West Ham U for Dean Ashton, January 2006.

*Record Transfer Fee Paid:* £8,500,000 to Sporting Lisbon for Ricky van Wolfswinkel, July 2013.

*Football League Record:* 1920 Original Member of Division 3; 1921 Division 3 (S): 1934–39 Division 2; 1946–58 Division 3 (S); 1958–60 Division 3; 1960–72 Division 2; 1972–74 Division 1; 1974–75 Division 2; 1975–81 Division 1; 1981–82 Division 2; 1982–85 Division 1; 1985–86 Division 2; 1986–92 Division 1; 1992–95 FA Premier League; 1995–2004 Division 1; 2004–05 FA Premier League; 2005–09 FL C; 2009–10 FL 1; 2010–11 FL C; 2011– FA Premier League.

## LATEST SEQUENCES

*Longest Sequence of League Wins:* 10, 23.11.1985 – 25.1.1986.

*Longest Sequence of League Defeats:* 7, 1.4.1995 – 6.5.1995.

*Longest Sequence of League Draws:* 7, 15.1.1994 – 26.2.1994.

*Longest Sequence of Unbeaten League Matches:* 20, 31.8.1950 – 30.12.1950.

*Longest Sequence Without a League Win:* 25, 22.9.1956 – 23.2.1957.

*Successive Scoring Runs:* 25 from 31.8.1963.

*Successive Non-scoring Runs:* 5 from 21.2.1925.

## MANAGERS

John Bowman 1905–07
James McEwen 1907–08
Arthur Turner 1909–10
Bert Stansfield 1910–15
Major Frank Buckley 1919–20
Charles O'Hagan 1920–21
Albert Gosnell 1921–26
Bert Stansfield 1926
Cecil Potter 1926–29
James Kerr 1929–33
Tom Parker 1933–37
Bob Young 1937–39
Jimmy Jewell 1939
Bob Young 1939–45
Duggie Lochhead 1945–46
Cyril Spiers 1946–47
Duggie Lochhead 1947–50
Norman Low 1950–55
Tom Parker 1955–57
Archie Macaulay 1957–61
Willie Reid 1961–62
George Swindin 1962
Ron Ashman 1962–66
Lol Morgan 1966–69
Ron Saunders 1969–73
John Bond 1973–80
Ken Brown 1980–87
Dave Stringer 1987–92
Mike Walker 1992–94
John Deehan 1994–95
Martin O'Neill 1995
Gary Megson 1995–96
Mike Walker 1996–98
Bruce Rioch 1998–2000
Bryan Hamilton 2000
Nigel Worthington 2000–06
Peter Grant 2006–07
Glenn Roeder 2007–09
Bryan Gunn 2009
Paul Lambert 2009–12
Chris Hughton June 2012–

## TEN YEAR LEAGUE RECORD

|         |        | P  | W  | D  | L  | F  | A  | Pts | Pos |
|---------|--------|----|----|----|----|----|----|-----|-----|
| 2003-04 | Div 1  | 46 | 28 | 10 | 8  | 79 | 39 | 94  | 1   |
| 2004-05 | PR Lge | 38 | 7  | 12 | 19 | 42 | 77 | 33  | 19  |
| 2005-06 | FL C   | 46 | 18 | 8  | 20 | 56 | 65 | 62  | 9   |
| 2006-07 | FL C   | 46 | 16 | 9  | 21 | 56 | 71 | 57  | 16  |
| 2007-08 | FL C   | 46 | 15 | 10 | 21 | 49 | 59 | 55  | 17  |
| 2008-09 | FL C   | 46 | 12 | 10 | 24 | 57 | 70 | 46  | 22  |
| 2009-10 | FL 1   | 46 | 29 | 8  | 9  | 89 | 47 | 95  | 1   |
| 2010-11 | FL C   | 46 | 23 | 15 | 8  | 83 | 58 | 84  | 2   |
| 2011-12 | PR Lge | 38 | 12 | 11 | 15 | 52 | 66 | 47  | 12  |
| 2012-13 | PR Lge | 38 | 10 | 14 | 14 | 41 | 58 | 44  | 11  |

## DID YOU KNOW ?

Norwich City won the Football League Cup in 1961–62 beating Rochdale 4–0 on aggregate over the two legs. The Canaries reached the fifth round of the FA Cup in the same season, with their run including a 2–1 replay victory at local rivals Ipswich Town.

## NORWICH CITY – FA PREMIERSHIP 2012–13 LEAGUE RECORD

| Match No. | Date | | Venue | Opponents | Result | H/T Score | Lg Pos. | Goalscorers | Attendance |
|---|---|---|---|---|---|---|---|---|---|
| 1 | Aug | 18 | A | Fulham | L 0-5 | 0-2 | 19 | | 25,062 |
| 2 | | 25 | H | QPR | D 1-1 | 1-1 | 16 | Jackson [11] | 26,317 |
| 3 | Sept | 1 | A | Tottenham H | D 1-1 | 0-0 | 15 | Snodgrass [85] | 36,142 |
| 4 | | 15 | H | West Ham U | D 0-0 | 0-0 | 15 | | 26,806 |
| 5 | | 23 | A | Newcastle U | L 0-1 | 0-1 | 17 | | 49,402 |
| 6 | | 29 | H | Liverpool | L 2-5 | 0-2 | 18 | Morison [61], Holt [87] | 26,831 |
| 7 | Oct | 6 | A | Chelsea | L 1-4 | 1-3 | 19 | Holt [11] | 41,784 |
| 8 | | 20 | H | Arsenal | W 1-0 | 1-0 | 15 | Holt [19] | 26,825 |
| 9 | | 27 | A | Aston Villa | D 1-1 | 0-1 | 16 | Turner [79] | 33,184 |
| 10 | Nov | 3 | H | Stoke C | W 1-0 | 1-0 | 14 | Johnson [44] | 26,072 |
| 11 | | 10 | A | Reading | D 0-0 | 0-0 | 15 | | 24,080 |
| 12 | | 17 | H | Manchester U | W 1-0 | 0-0 | 13 | Pilkington [60] | 26,840 |
| 13 | | 24 | A | Everton | D 1-1 | 0-1 | 13 | Bassong [90] | 34,502 |
| 14 | | 28 | A | Southampton | D 1-1 | 1-1 | 13 | Snodgrass [45] | 29,325 |
| 15 | Dec | 2 | H | Sunderland | W 2-1 | 2-1 | 12 | Bassong [8], Pilkington [37] | 26,228 |
| 16 | | 8 | A | Swansea C | W 4-3 | 3-0 | 11 | Whittaker [16], Bassong [40], Holt [44], Snodgrass [77] | 20,294 |
| 17 | | 15 | H | Wigan Ath | W 2-1 | 1-0 | 7 | Pilkington [15], Hoolahan [64] | 26,677 |
| 18 | | 22 | A | WBA | L 1-2 | 1-1 | 10 | Snodgrass [23] | 25,799 |
| 19 | | 26 | H | Chelsea | L 0-1 | 0-1 | 11 | | 26,831 |
| 20 | | 29 | H | Manchester C | L 3-4 | 1-2 | 11 | Pilkington [15], Martin, R 2 [63, 75] | 26,827 |
| 21 | Jan | 1 | A | West Ham U | L 1-2 | 0-2 | 12 | Martin, R [90] | 35,005 |
| 22 | | 12 | H | Newcastle U | D 0-0 | 0-0 | 12 | | 26,752 |
| 23 | | 19 | A | Liverpool | L 0-5 | 0-2 | 13 | | 44,901 |
| 24 | | 30 | H | Tottenham H | D 1-1 | 1-0 | 14 | Hoolahan [32] | 26,818 |
| 25 | Feb | 2 | A | QPR | D 0-0 | 0-0 | 14 | | 17,543 |
| 26 | | 9 | H | Fulham | D 0-0 | 0-0 | 14 | | 26,816 |
| 27 | | 23 | H | Everton | W 2-1 | 0-1 | 12 | Kamara [84], Holt [90] | 26,828 |
| 28 | Mar | 2 | A | Manchester U | L 0-4 | 0-1 | 13 | | 75,586 |
| 29 | | 9 | H | Southampton | D 0-0 | 0-0 | 13 | | 26,783 |
| 30 | | 17 | A | Sunderland | D 1-1 | 1-1 | 12 | Hoolahan [26] | 38,625 |
| 31 | | 30 | A | Wigan Ath | L 0-1 | 0-0 | 14 | | 17,784 |
| 32 | Apr | 6 | H | Swansea C | D 2-2 | 1-1 | 13 | Snodgrass [40], Turner [60] | 26,372 |
| 33 | | 13 | A | Arsenal | L 1-3 | 0-0 | 14 | Turner [56] | 60,095 |
| 34 | | 20 | H | Reading | W 2-1 | 0-0 | 13 | Bennett, R [50], Bennett, E [52] | 26,460 |
| 35 | | 27 | A | Stoke C | L 0-1 | 0-0 | 14 | | 27,488 |
| 36 | May | 4 | H | Aston Villa | L 1-2 | 0-0 | 15 | Holt (pen) [74] | 26,842 |
| 37 | | 12 | H | WBA | W 4-0 | 1-0 | 12 | Snodgrass [25], Holt [62], McAuley (og) [65], Howson [90] | 26,837 |
| 38 | | 19 | A | Manchester C | W 3-2 | 1-1 | 11 | Pilkington [26], Holt [54], Howson [65] | 47,054 |

**Final League Position: 11**

### GOALSCORERS

*League (41):* Holt 8 (1 pen), Snodgrass 6, Pilkington 5, Bassong 3, Hoolahan 3, Martin, R 3, Turner 3, Howson 2, Bennett, E 1, Bennett, R 1, Jackson 1, Johnson 1, Kamara 1, Morison 1, Whittaker 1, own goal 1.
*FA Cup (3):* Bennett E 1, Jackson 1, Snodgrass 1.
*Capital One Cup (6):* Hoolahan 1 (1 pen), Jackson 1, Lappin 1, Morison 1, Tettey 1, own goal 1.

| Ruddy J 15 | Martin R 30 + 1 | Bennett R 10 + 5 | Turner M 25 + 1 | Tierney M 1 | Pilkington A 25 + 5 | Howson J 22 + 8 | Johnson B 37 | Surman A 4 | Snodgrass S 35 + 2 | Holt G 28 + 6 | Morison S 4 + 15 | Bennett E 9 + 15 | Hoolahan W 28 + 5 | Bassong S 34 | Barnet L 6 + 2 | Garrido J 34 | Jackson S 5 + 8 | Martin C — + 1 | Kane H 1 + 2 | Tettey A 21 + 6 | Whittaker S 12 + 1 | Bunn M 22 + 1 | Fox D — + 2 | Becchio L 2 + 6 | Kamara K 7 + 4 | Camp L 1 + 2 | Match No. |
|---|---|---|---|---|---|---|---|---|---|---|---|---|---|---|---|---|---|---|---|---|---|---|---|---|---|---|---|
| 1 | 2 | 3 | 4 | 5 | 6 | 7 | 8 | 9$^1$ | 10$^2$ | 11$^3$ | 12 | 13 | 14 | | | | | | | | | | | | | | 1 |
| 1 | 2 | | | | 9 | 7 | 8 | | 10$^2$ | 6 | 11$^1$ | 12 | | | | 3 | 4 | 5 | | 13 | | | | | | | 2 |
| 1 | 2 | | | | 9 | 7 | 6 | | 8 | 10 | 12 | | | | 3 | 4 | 5 | | | 11$^1$ | | | | | | | 3 |
| 1 | 2 | | | | | 7 | 8 | 9 | 6 | 10$^2$ | 12 | | | | 4 | 3 | 5 | 11$^1$ | | 13 | | | | | | | 4 |
| 1 | 2 | | 12 | | | 7 | 8 | 9$^3$ | 6 | 13 | 11$^1$ | | 10 | | 4$^2$ | 3 | 5 | 14 | | | | | | | | | 5 |
| 1 | 2 | | 3 | | | 7 | 8 | 9$^2$ | 6 | 12 | 10$^3$ | | 13 | | | 4 | 5 | 11$^1$ | | | | | | | | | 6 |
| 1 | 2 | 14 | | | 12 | 7 | 9$^1$ | | | 11$^2$ | 13 | 6 | 8 | 4$^3$ | 3 | 5 | | | 10 | | | | | | | | 7 |
| 1 | 2 | 13 | 3 | | 10 | | 7 | | 12 | 11$^2$ | 14 | 6$^1$ | 8$^3$ | 4 | | 5 | | | 9 | | | | | | | | 8 |
| 1 | 2$^1$ | 12 | 4 | | 9 | | 8$^2$ | | 13 | 11 | 14 | 6$^2$ | 10 | 3 | | 5 | | | 7 | | | | | | | | 9 |
| 1 | | 12 | 4$^1$ | | 9 | 8 | | 6 | 11 | 14 | | 10$^3$ | 3 | 13 | 5$^2$ | | | 7 | 2 | | | | | | | | 10 |
| 1 | | 3 | | | 9 | | 8 | | 6$^2$ | 11$^1$ | 12 | 13 | 10 | 4 | | 5 | | | 7 | 2 | | | | | | | 11 |
| 1 | | 4 | | | 9 | 13 | 7 | | 6$^3$ | 11$^1$ | 12 | 14 | 10$^2$ | 3 | | 5 | | | 8 | 2 | | | | | | | 12 |
| 1$^2$ | | 4 | | | 10 | | 6 | | 8$^3$ | 11 | 12 | | 9$^1$ | 3 | | 5 | 14 | | 7 | 2 | 13 | | | | | | 13 |
| | 3 | | | | 9 | 14 | 7 | | 6$^2$ | 11$^1$ | 12 | 13 | 10$^3$ | 4 | | 5 | | | 8 | 2 | 1 | | | | | 14 |
| | 4 | | | | 9 | 13 | 8 | | 6$^1$ | 11 | | 12 | 10$^2$ | 3 | | 5 | | | 7 | 2 | 1 | | | | | 15 |
| 2 | | | | | 9 | 8 | 6 | | 7 | 11$^1$ | 12 | | 10 | 3 | 13 | 5 | | | 4$^2$ | 1 | | | | | | 16 |
| | 3 | | | | 9$^3$ | 12 | 8 | | 6 | 11$^2$ | 14 | 13 | 10$^1$ | 4 | | 5 | | | 7 | 2 | 1 | | | | | 17 |
| 12 | | 4 | | | 10 | 13 | 9 | | 6 | | 11 | | 8$^2$ | 3 | | 5 | 14 | | 7$^3$ | 2$^1$ | 1 | | | | | 18 |
| 2 | | 3 | | | 9$^1$ | 13 | 8$^2$ | | 6 | 11 | 12 | 14 | 10$^3$ | 4 | | 5 | | | 7 | | 1 | | | | | 19 |
| 2 | | 3 | | | 9 | 13 | 8 | | 6 | 11$^1$ | | | 10$^3$ | 4 | | 5 | 14 | 12 | 7$^2$ | | 1 | | | | | 20 |
| 2 | 5 | 4 | | | 9 | 7$^3$ | | | 6 | | 12 | 10$^2$ | 3 | | 13 | 11$^1$ | 8 | | 1 | 14 | | | | | | 21 |
| 2 | | 4 | | | 6 | | 7 | | 9$^2$ | 12 | | 13 | 10 | 3 | | 5 | 11$^1$ | | 8 | | 1 | | | | | 22 |
| 2 | 3 | 4 | | | 13 | 8 | 7 | | 6$^1$ | 12 | | | | 3 | | 5 | | | 10 | | 1 | | | | | 23 |
| 2 | | 4 | | | 9 | 12 | 7 | | 6 | 11 | | | 10$^1$ | 3 | | 5 | | | 8 | | 1 | | | | | 24 |
| 2 | | 4 | | | 9$^1$ | | 8 | | 6 | 11 | | | 12 | 10$^2$ | 3 | | 5 | | | 7 | 1 | 13 | | | | 25 |
| 2 | | 4 | | | | 8 | 6 | | 9$^1$ | 10 | 3 | | | 5 | 12 | | | | 7 | | 1 | 11$^2$ | 13 | | | 26 |
| 2 | | 4 | | | 13 | 6 | 7 | | 9 | 10 | | | 8$^2$ | 3 | | 5 | | | | | 1 | 11$^1$ | 12 | | | 27 |
| 2 | | 4 | | | 9 | 8 | 7 | | 6$^2$ | 11$^3$ | | | 13 | 10$^1$ | 3 | | 5 | | | | 1 | 14 | 12 | | | 28 |
| 2 | | 4 | | | 9$^1$ | 8 | 7 | | 6 | 11 | | | 12 | 3 | | 5 | | | | | 1 | 13 | 10$^2$ | | | 29 |
| | 2 | | | | | 8 | 7 | | 9$^3$ | 13 | | 6 | 10$^1$ | 3 | | 5 | | | 14 | 1$^■$ | | 11$^2$ | 12 | | | 30 |
| 2 | | 3 | | | | 6$^2$ | 7 | | 8 | 12 | | 9 | 10$^3$ | 4 | | 5 | | | 13 | | | 14 | 11$^1$ | 1 | | 31 |
| 2 | | 4 | | | | 7$^3$ | 8 | | 9 | 13 | | 6 | 10$^2$ | 3 | | 5 | | | 14 | | | 11 | 12 | | | 32 |
| 2 | | 4 | | | | 6 | 7$^1$ | | 9 | 11 | | | | 3 | | 13 | | | 8$^2$ | 5 | 1 | 12 | 10 | | | 33 |
| 2 | 12 | 4$^1$ | | 14 | 7 | 8 | | 9$^3$ | 11 | | 6$^2$ | | 3 | | 5 | | | 13 | | 1 | | 10 | | | 34 |
| 2 | 3 | | | 14 | 9 | 8 | | 9$^2$ | 11 | | 13 | 12 | 4$^3$ | | | 5 | | | 6$^1$ | 5 | 1 | | 10 | | | 35 |
| 2 | 4 | | | | 9 | 8 | 7 | | 6$^2$ | 11 | | 13 | 10$^1$ | 3 | | 5$^3$ | 14 | | | | 1 | | 12 | | | 36 |
| 1 | 2 | 3 | | | | 9 | 7 | 8 | 6$^1$ | 11$^3$ | | 13 | 10$^2$ | 4 | | 5 | | | 12 | | | 14 | | | | 37 |
| 1 | | 3 | 4 | | | 9$^2$ | 8 | 7$^1$ | | 6 | 11$^3$ | | 13 | 10 | | 5 | | | 12 | 2 | | 14 | | | | 38 |

**FA Cup**

| | | | |
|---|---|---|---|
| Third Round | Peterborough U | (a) | 3-0 |
| Fourth Round | Luton T | (h) | 0-1 |

**Capital One Cup**

| | | | |
|---|---|---|---|
| Second Round | Scunthorpe U | (h) | 2-1 |
| Third Round | Doncaster R | (h) | 1-0 |
| Fourth Round | Tottenham H | (h) | 2-1 |
| Quarter-Finals | Aston Villa | (h) | 1-4 |

# NOTTINGHAM FOREST

## FOUNDATION

One of the oldest football clubs in the world, Nottingham Forest was formed at a meeting in the Clinton Arms in 1865. Known originally as the Forest Football Club, the game which first drew the founders together was 'shinney', a form of hockey. When they determined to change to football in 1865, one of their first moves was to buy a set of red caps to wear on the field.

*The City Ground, Nottingham NG2 5FJ.*
*Telephone:* (0115) 982 4444.
*Fax:* (0115) 982 4455.
*Ticket Office:* (0871) 226 1980.
*Website:* www.nottinghamforest.co.uk
*Email:* info@nottinghamforest.co.uk
*Ground Capacity:* 30,540.
*Record Attendance:* 49,946 v Manchester U, Division 1, 28 October 1967.
*Pitch Measurements:* 105m × 71m (115yd × 78yd)
*Chairman:* Fawaz Mubarak Al-Hasawi.
*Manager:* Billy Davies.
*Assistant Manager:* David Kelly.
*Physio:* Andrew Balderston.
*Colours:* Red shirt with white trim, white shorts, red socks.
*Year Formed:* 1865.
*Turned Professional:* 1889.
*Previous Name:* Forest Football Club.
*Club Nickname:* 'The Reds'.
*Grounds:* 1865, Forest Racecourse; 1879, The Meadows; 1880, Trent Bridge Cricket Ground; 1882, Parkside, Lenton; 1885, Gregory, Lenton; 1890, Town Ground; 1898, City Ground.

## HONOURS

**Football League – Division 1:**
*Champions* 1977–78, 1997–98;
*Runners-up* 1966–67, 1978–79, 1993–94; **FL 1:** *Runners-up* 2007–08;
**Division 2:** *Champions* 1906–07, 1921–22; *Runners-up* 1956–57;
**Division 3 (S):** *Champions* 1950–51.
**FA Cup:** *Winners* 1898, 1959; *Runners-up* 1991.
**Football League Cup:** *Winners* 1978, 1979, 1989, 1990; *Runners-up* 1980, 1992.
**Anglo-Scottish Cup:** *Winners* 1977.
**Simod Cup:** *Winners* 1989.
**Zenith Data Systems Cup:** *Winners:* 1992.
**European Competitions**
**European Cup:** 1978–79 (*winners*), 1979–80 (*winners*), 1980–81.
**European Fairs Cup:** 1961–62, 1967–68. **UEFA Cup:** 1983–84, 1984–85, 1995–96. **Super Cup:** 1979 (*winners*), 1980.
**World Club Championship:** 1980.

*First Football League Game:* 3 September 1892, Division 1, v Everton (a) D 2–2 – Brown; Earp, Scott; Hamilton, Albert Smith, McCracken; McCallum, 'Tich' Smith, Higgins (2), Pike, McInnes.

*Record League Victory:* 12–0 v Leicester Fosse, Division 1, 12 April 1909 – Iremonger; Dudley, Maltby; Hughes (1), Needham, Armstrong; Hooper (3), Marrison, West (3), Morris (2), Spouncer (3 incl. 1p).

*Record Cup Victory:* 14–0 v Clapton (away), FA Cup 1st rd, 17 January 1891 – Brown; Earp, Scott; Albert Smith, Russell, Jeacock; McCallum (2), 'Tich' Smith (1), Higgins (5), Lindley (4), Shaw (2).

*Record Defeat:* 1–9 v Blackburn R, Division 2, 10 April 1937.

*Most League Points (2 for a win):* 70, Division 3 (S), 1950–51.

*Most League Points (3 for a win):* 94, Division 1, 1997–98.

## sky SPORTS FACT FILE

The First Division game between Nottingham Forest and Leeds United on 24 August 1968 was abandoned at half time after fire broke out in the centre stand. The teams were drawing 1-1 at the time. Forest were forced to play home games at Meadow Lane on a temporary basis.

*Most League Goals:* 110, Division 3 (S), 1950–51.

*Highest League Scorer in Season:* Wally Ardron, 36, Division 3 (S), 1950–51.

*Most League Goals in Total Aggregate:* Grenville Morris, 199, 1898–1913.

*Most League Goals in One Match:* 4, Enoch West v Sunderland, Division 1, 9 November 1907; 4, Tommy Gibson v Burnley, Division 2, 25 January 1913; 4, Tom Peacock v Port Vale, Division 2, 23 December 1933; 4, Tom Peacock v Barnsley, Division 2, 9 November 1935; 4, Tom Peacock v Port Vale, Division 2, 23 November 1935; 4, Tom Peacock v Doncaster R, Division 2, 26 December 1935; 4, Tommy Capel v Gillingham, Division 3 (S), 18 November 1950; 4, Wally Ardron v Hull C, Division 2, 26 December 1952; 4, Tommy Wilson v Barnsley, Division 2, 9 February 1957; 4, Peter Withe v Ipswich T, Division 1, 4 October 1977; 4, Marlon Harewood v Stoke C, Division 1, 22 February 2003.

*Most Capped Player:* Stuart Pearce, 76 (78), England.

*Most League Appearances:* Bob McKinlay, 614, 1951–70.

*Youngest League Player:* Craig Westcarr, 16 years 257 days v Burnley, 13 October 2001.

*Record Transfer Fee Received:* £8,500,000 from Liverpool for Stan Collymore, June 1995.

*Record Transfer Fee Paid:* £4,500,000 to Celtic for Pierre van Hooijdonk, March 1997.

*Football League Record:* 1892 Elected to Division 1; 1906–07 Division 2; 1907–11 Division 1; 1911–22 Division 2; 1922–25 Division 1; 1925–49 Division 2; 1949–51 Division 3 (S); 1951–57 Division 2; 1957–72 Division 1; 1972–77 Division 2; 1977–92 Division 1; 1992–93 FA Premier League; 1993–94 Division 1; 1994–97 FA Premier League; 1997–98 Division 1; 1998–99 FA Premier League; 1999–2004 Division 1; 2004–05 FL C; 2005–08 FL 1; 2008– FL C.

## MANAGERS

Harry Radford 1889–97
*(Secretary-Manager)*
Harry Haslam 1897–1909
*(Secretary-Manager)*
Fred Earp 1909–12
Bob Masters 1912–25
John Baynes 1925–29
Stan Hardy 1930–31
Noel Watson 1931–36
Harold Wightman 1936–39
Billy Walker 1939–60
Andy Beattie 1960–63
Johnny Carey 1963–68
Matt Gillies 1969–72
Dave Mackay 1972
Allan Brown 1973–75
Brian Clough 1975–93
Frank Clark 1993–96
Stuart Pearce 1996–97
Dave Bassett 1997–99
*(previously General Manager)*
Ron Atkinson 1999
David Platt 1999–2001
Paul Hart 2001–04
Joe Kinnear 2004
Gary Megson 2005–06
Colin Calderwood 2006–08
Billy Davies 2009–11
Steve McClaren 2011
Steve Cotterill 2011–12
Sean O'Driscoll 2012
Alex McLeish 2012–13
Billy Davies February 2013–

## LATEST SEQUENCES

*Longest Sequence of League Wins:* 7, 9.5.1979 – 1.9.1979.

*Longest Sequence of League Defeats:* 14, 21.3.1913 – 27.9.1913.

*Longest Sequence of League Draws:* 7, 29.4.1978 – 2.9.1978.

*Longest Sequence of Unbeaten League Matches:* 42, 26.11.1977 – 25.11.1978.

*Longest Sequence Without a League Win:* 19, 8.9.1998 – 16.1.1999.

*Successive Scoring Runs:* 22 from 28.3.1931.

*Successive Non-scoring Runs:* 7 from 13.12.2003.

## TEN YEAR LEAGUE RECORD

| | | P | W | D | L | F | A | Pts | Pos |
|---|---|---|---|---|---|---|---|---|---|
| 2003-04 | Div 1 | 46 | 15 | 15 | 16 | 61 | 58 | 60 | 14 |
| 2004-05 | FL C | 46 | 9 | 17 | 20 | 42 | 66 | 44 | 23 |
| 2005-06 | FL 1 | 46 | 19 | 12 | 15 | 67 | 52 | 69 | 7 |
| 2006-07 | FL 1 | 46 | 23 | 13 | 10 | 65 | 41 | 82 | 4 |
| 2007-08 | FL 1 | 46 | 22 | 16 | 8 | 64 | 32 | 82 | 2 |
| 2008-09 | FL C | 46 | 13 | 14 | 19 | 50 | 65 | 53 | 19 |
| 2009-10 | FL C | 46 | 22 | 13 | 11 | 65 | 40 | 79 | 3 |
| 2010-11 | FL C | 46 | 20 | 15 | 11 | 69 | 50 | 75 | 6 |
| 2011-12 | FL C | 46 | 14 | 8 | 24 | 48 | 63 | 50 | 19 |
| 2012-13 | FL C | 46 | 17 | 16 | 13 | 63 | 59 | 67 | 8 |

## DID YOU KNOW ?

Sam Widdowson, who played for Nottingham Forest between 1878 and 1885, is credited as the man who introduced shin guards into the game in the 1870s. Sam, who also played cricket for Nottinghamshire, used a pair of cut-down cricket pads to protect his legs against hacking.

## NOTTINGHAM FOREST – FL CHAMPIONSHIP 2012–13 LEAGUE RECORD

| Match No. | Date | Venue | Opponents | Result | | H/T Score | Lg Pos. | Goalscorers | Attendance |
|---|---|---|---|---|---|---|---|---|---|
| 1 | Aug 18 | H | Bristol C | W | 1-0 | 0-0 | 9 | Guedioura [71] | 21,575 |
| 2 | 21 | A | Huddersfield T | D | 1-1 | 0-0 | 5 | Cox [68] | 15,434 |
| 3 | 24 | A | Bolton W | D | 2-2 | 1-1 | 2 | McGugan [15], Reid [57] | 17,361 |
| 4 | Sept 1 | H | Charlton Ath | W | 2-1 | 1-0 | 3 | McGugan [17], Hutchinson [75] | 19,745 |
| 5 | 15 | H | Birmingham C | D | 2-2 | 0-0 | 6 | Cox [73], Ibanez (og) [86] | 22,738 |
| 6 | 18 | H | Crystal Palace | D | 1-1 | 0-0 | 6 | Blackstock [81] | 13,153 |
| 7 | 22 | A | Leeds U | L | 1-2 | 0-2 | 10 | Blackstock [60] | 24,292 |
| 8 | 30 | H | Derby Co | L | 0-1 | 0-0 | 17 | | 28,707 |
| 9 | Oct 3 | H | Blackburn R | D | 0-0 | 0-0 | 16 | | 18,748 |
| 10 | 6 | A | Peterborough U | W | 1-0 | 0-0 | 12 | Reid [51] | 10,469 |
| 11 | 20 | H | Cardiff C | W | 3-1 | 2-0 | 11 | Reid [25], Ayala [27], Sharp [47] | 21,491 |
| 12 | 23 | A | Blackpool | D | 2-2 | 1-0 | 10 | Sharp [25], Blackstock [90] | 13,228 |
| 13 | 27 | A | Barnsley | W | 4-1 | 3-1 | 7 | Halford [35], Cox [42], Cohen [45], Jenas [77] | 10,186 |
| 14 | Nov 3 | H | Millwall | L | 1-4 | 1-1 | 8 | Sharp [22] | 24,160 |
| 15 | 6 | H | Middlesbrough | D | 0-0 | 0-0 | 11 | | 20,150 |
| 16 | 10 | A | Leicester C | D | 2-2 | 1-2 | 11 | Guedioura [22], Cox (pen) [67] | 24,793 |
| 17 | 17 | H | Sheffield W | W | 1-0 | 0-0 | 9 | Llera (og) [75] | 24,584 |
| 18 | 24 | A | Wolverhampton W | W | 2-1 | 1-1 | 7 | Sharp [16], Guedioura [57] | 22,527 |
| 19 | 27 | A | Ipswich T | L | 1-3 | 0-1 | 9 | Blackstock [58] | 16,200 |
| 20 | Dec 1 | H | Hull C | L | 1-2 | 1-1 | 9 | Sharp (pen) [43] | 19,472 |
| 21 | 8 | H | Burnley | W | 2-0 | 0-0 | 9 | Blackstock [59], Sharp [76] | 19,672 |
| 22 | 15 | A | Brighton & HA | D | 0-0 | 0-0 | 9 | | 26,684 |
| 23 | 22 | A | Watford | L | 0-2 | 0-2 | 11 | | 15,143 |
| 24 | 26 | H | Leeds U | W | 4-2 | 1-1 | 8 | Sharp 2 (1 pen) [44 (p), 54], Austin (og) [57], Blackstock [61] | 26,670 |
| 25 | 29 | H | Crystal Palace | D | 2-2 | 1-1 | 7 | Reid [45], Sharp [90] | 23,703 |
| 26 | Jan 1 | A | Blackburn R | L | 0-3 | 0-0 | 11 | | 15,490 |
| 27 | 12 | H | Peterborough U | W | 2-1 | 1-0 | 9 | Halford [28], Ward [83] | 22,777 |
| 28 | 19 | A | Derby Co | D | 1-1 | 1-0 | 10 | Cohen [31] | 33,010 |
| 29 | 26 | H | Watford | L | 0-3 | 0-2 | 10 | | 20,732 |
| 30 | Feb 2 | A | Birmingham C | L | 1-2 | 0-1 | 11 | Sharp (pen) [90] | 17,738 |
| 31 | 9 | A | Bristol C | L | 0-2 | 0-0 | 13 | | 13,768 |
| 32 | 16 | H | Bolton W | D | 1-1 | 0-0 | 11 | Reid [59] | 24,409 |
| 33 | 19 | H | Huddersfield T | W | 6-1 | 4-1 | 8 | Majewski 3 [21, 37, 43], Ward [24], Lansbury [55], Henderson [90] | 26,938 |
| 34 | 23 | A | Charlton Ath | W | 2-0 | 0-0 | 8 | Majewski [53], Lansbury [61] | 18,697 |
| 35 | Mar 2 | A | Sheffield W | W | 1-0 | 1-0 | 8 | Majewski [27] | 23,220 |
| 36 | 5 | H | Ipswich T | W | 1-0 | 0-0 | 7 | McGugan [84] | 19,458 |
| 37 | 9 | H | Wolverhampton W | W | 3-1 | 1-0 | 6 | Lansbury 2 [31, 67], McGugan [90] | 23,350 |
| 38 | 16 | A | Hull C | W | 2-1 | 0-1 | 5 | Henderson [55], McGugan [84] | 19,848 |
| 39 | 30 | H | Brighton & HA | D | 2-2 | 0-0 | 5 | McGugan [82], Lansbury [90] | 28,124 |
| 40 | Apr 1 | A | Burnley | D | 1-1 | 0-0 | 5 | McGugan (pen) [90] | 13,618 |
| 41 | 6 | A | Blackpool | D | 1-1 | 0-1 | 5 | McGugan (pen) [81] | 22,814 |
| 42 | 13 | A | Cardiff C | L | 0-3 | 0-1 | 7 | | 26,588 |
| 43 | 16 | A | Middlesbrough | L | 0-1 | 0-1 | 8 | | 13,861 |
| 44 | 20 | H | Barnsley | D | 0-0 | 0-0 | 8 | | 22,230 |
| 45 | 27 | A | Millwall | W | 1-0 | 0-0 | 7 | Halford [8] | 12,330 |
| 46 | May 4 | H | Leicester C | L | 2-3 | 1-2 | 8 | Cox [3], Ward [50] | 28,646 |

**Final League Position: 8**

### GOALSCORERS

*League (63):* Sharp 10 (3 pens), McGugan 8 (2 pens), Blackstock 6, Cox 5 (1 pen), Lansbury 5, Majewski 5, Reid 5, Guedioura 3, Halford 3, Ward 3, Cohen 2, Henderson 2, Ayala 1, Hutchinson 1, Jenas 1, own goals 3.
*FA Cup (2):* Sharp 1, own goal 1.
*Capital One Cup (2):* Blackstock 1, Cox 1.

| Camp L 26 | Moloney B 7+6 | Halford G 34+3 | Collins D 37+3 | Harding D 26+1 | McGugan L 13+17 | Guedioura A 30+5 | Gillett S 24+1 | Reid A 40+2 | Majewski R 21+10 | Blackstock D 21+16 | Cox S 32+7 | Lascelles J —+2 | Greening J —+5 | Tudgay M —+3 | Moussi G 6+12 | Hutchinson S 6+3 | Ayala D 12 | Sharp B 30+9 | Coppinger J 2+4 | Lansbury H 24+8 | Cohen C 36+2 | Jenas J 1+5 | Ward E 29+2 | Hutton A 7 | Darlow K 20 | Jara Reyes G 15+2 | Henderson D 7+4 | Match No. |
|---|---|---|---|---|---|---|---|---|---|---|---|---|---|---|---|---|---|---|---|---|---|---|---|---|---|---|---|---|
| 1 | 2 | 3 | 4 | 5 | 6[1] | 7 | 8 | 9[2] | 10[3] | 11 | 12 | 13 | 14 |  |  |  |  |  |  |  |  |  |  |  |  |  |  | 1 |
| 1 | 2 | 4 | 3 | 5 | 8[2] | 9 | 7 | 6 | 10[1] | 11[3] |  |  |  | 12 | 13 | 14 |  |  |  |  |  |  |  |  |  |  |  | 2 |
| 1 | 2 | 4 | 3 | 5 | 7[2] | 8[1] | 6 | 9 | 11 | 10 |  |  | 13 |  | 12 |  |  |  |  |  |  |  |  |  |  |  |  | 3 |
| 1 |  | 5 | 4 |  | 6[2] | 7 | 8 | 9[3] | 10 | 11[1] |  |  |  |  | 13 |  | 2 | 3 | 12 | 14 |  |  |  |  |  |  |  | 4 |
| 1 | 3 | 5 | 13 | 6 | 8[2] | 7[3] | 9 | 14 | 10[1] | 12 |  |  |  |  | 2 |  | 4 | 11 |  |  |  |  |  |  |  |  |  | 5 |
| 1 | 6 | 3 | 5 | 8[3] | 12[1] | 7 | 9 | 14 | 13 | 10 |  |  |  |  | 2[1] |  | 4 | 11[2] |  |  |  |  |  |  |  |  |  | 6 |
| 1 | 2 | 3 | 5 | 12 |  | 7 |  | 9[1] |  | 11 | 10 |  |  |  |  |  | 8[2] |  |  | 6[3] | 13 |  |  |  |  |  |  | 7 |
| 1 | 14 | 2[3] | 4 | 5 | 7[2] |  | 6 | 9[1] |  | 11* | 10 |  |  |  |  |  | 3 | 12 |  | 13 | 8 |  |  |  |  |  |  | 8 |
| 1 | 2 | 3 | 5 | 7[2] |  | 8 | 10[3] | 12 |  | 4 | 11 | 14 | 6[1] |  | 9 | 13 |  |  |  |  |  |  |  |  |  |  |  | 9 |
| 1 | 12 | 2 | 4 | 5 | 6[2] |  | 7 | 8 | 14 |  | 11[3] |  |  |  | 3[1] | 10 |  |  |  | 9 | 13 |  |  |  |  |  |  | 10 |
| 1 | 14 | 2 | 4 | 5 |  | 8* | 7 | 9[1] | 12[3] | 10[1] | 13 | 3 | 11 |  | 6 |  |  |  |  |  |  |  |  |  |  |  |  | 11 |
| 1 | 12 | 2 | 4 | 5 |  | 6[3] | 9 | 8[2] | 14 | 10 |  |  |  |  | 3[1] | 11 |  |  |  | 7 | 13 |  |  |  |  |  |  | 12 |
| 1 | 2 | 4[2] | 3 | 5 |  |  | 7 | 8[3] | 9[1] |  | 11 |  |  |  | 10 | 14 |  |  |  | 6 | 12 | 13 |  |  |  |  |  | 13 |
| 1 | 2 |  | 4 | 5 | 14 | 12 | 7[3] | 9[2] | 8[1] | 13 | 10 |  |  |  | 11 |  |  |  |  | 6 |  | 3 |  |  |  |  |  | 14 |
| 1 | 13 | 2 | 4 | 5[2] |  |  | 7 | 8 | 9[1] | 12 | 11[3] |  |  |  | 10 |  |  | 14 | 6 |  |  |  | 3 |  |  |  |  | 15 |
| 1 | 4 | 2 | 3 |  |  | 9[1] | 6[3] | 7[2] | 14 | 11 |  |  |  |  | 10 |  |  | 13 | 8 | 12 | 5 |  |  |  |  |  |  | 16 |
| 1 | 6 | 2 | 3 | 13 | 5 | 8[1] | 10 | 11 | 12 | 9 |  |  |  |  | 7[2] |  |  |  | 11 | 12 | 9 | 7[2] | 4 |  |  |  |  | 17 |
| 1 | 14 | 3 | 5 |  | 8 | 6 |  | 12 | 11[1] | 13 |  |  |  |  | 10[3] |  |  | 9[2] | 7 |  | 4 | 2 |  |  |  |  |  | 18 |
| 1 | 4 | 5[3] | 14 | 7 | 6[2] | 13 |  | 11 |  |  |  |  |  |  | 10 | 12 | 9[1] | 8 |  | 3 | 2 |  |  |  |  |  |  | 19 |
| 1 | 4 | 5 | 12 | 7 | 8[1] | 10 |  | 13 |  |  |  |  |  |  | 11 | 6 | 9[2] |  |  | 3 | 2 |  |  |  |  |  |  | 20 |
| 1 | 4 | 5 | 7[3] | 14 | 8[2] | 9 |  | 10 |  |  |  |  |  |  | 13 |  | 11 | 6[1] | 12 | 3 | 2 |  |  |  |  |  |  | 21 |
| 1 | 12 | 3 | 2[1] |  | 6[2] | 14 | 8[3] | 10 |  |  |  |  |  |  | 4 |  | 9 | 11 | 13 | 7 |  | 5 |  |  |  |  |  | 22 |
| 1 | 13 | 2 | 5[1] | 12 |  | 9[2] |  | 14 | 10[3] |  |  |  |  |  | 7 |  | 3* | 11 |  | 8 |  | 4 | 6 |  |  |  |  | 23 |
| 1 | 5 | 4 |  | 7 | 9[3] | 8[1] |  | 11 | 13 |  |  |  |  |  | 12 |  | 10[2] |  | 14 | 6 |  | 3 | 2 |  |  |  |  | 24 |
| 1 | 2 | 4 | 5 | 12 | 7[3] |  | 9 | 8[1] | 11 | 14 |  |  |  |  | 10 |  | 13 | 6[2] |  | 3 |  |  |  |  |  |  |  | 25 |
| 1 | 2 | 3 | 5 |  | 8[2] |  | 9 |  | 13 | 11 |  |  |  |  | 7 |  | 4 | 10 |  | 6[1] | 12 |  |  |  |  |  |  | 26 |
|  | 3 | 5 |  | 7 |  |  | 8[2] |  | 11 |  |  |  |  | 12 | 13 |  |  | 10 |  | 9[1] | 6 |  | 4 |  | 1 | 2 |  | 27 |
|  | 5 | 4 |  |  | 7[2] |  |  | 9[1] | 12 | 11 |  |  | 13 |  |  |  |  | 10 |  | 6 | 8 |  | 3 |  | 1 | 2 |  | 28 |
|  | 5 | 4 |  | 6[1] | 12 | 13 | 10[3] | 9[2] |  |  |  |  |  |  |  |  |  | 11 |  | 7 | 8 |  | 3 |  | 1 | 2 | 14 | 29 |
|  | 4 | 3 | 5 |  |  | 9 | 12 | 14 | 13 |  |  | 7[1] |  |  |  |  |  | 11 |  | 8 | 6[3] |  | 3 |  | 1 | 2 | 10[2] | 30 |
|  | 3 | 4 | 5[1] | 14 | 7 |  | 9 | 8[3] | 10 | 13 |  |  |  |  |  |  |  | 11 |  | 6 |  | 12 |  |  | 1 | 2[2] |  | 31 |
|  | 4 |  | 13 | 7 |  | 9 | 8 | 12 | 10[3] |  |  |  |  |  |  |  |  | 11[1] |  | 6[2] | 5 |  | 3 |  | 1 | 2 | 14 | 32 |
|  | 4 | 12 | 13 | 7 |  | 9 | 8 | 11[3] | 10 |  |  |  |  |  |  |  |  | 6[5] |  | 5 |  |  | 3[1] |  | 1 | 2 | 14 | 33 |
|  | 4 |  | 12 | 7 |  | 9[1] | 8 | 10[2] | 14 |  |  |  |  |  |  |  |  | 13 |  | 6[1] | 5 |  | 3 |  | 1 | 2 | 11 | 34 |
|  | 3[3] |  |  | 7 |  | 9 | 8[1] | 11 | 10[2] | 14 |  |  |  | 12 |  |  | 13 |  |  | 6[1] | 5 |  | 4 |  | 1 | 2 |  | 35 |
|  | 4 |  | 12 | 7[2] |  | 9 | 8 | 11 | 10 | 13 |  |  |  | 14 |  |  |  |  |  | 6[1] | 5 |  | 3 |  | 1 | 2[3] |  | 36 |
|  | 14 | 4 |  | 12 | 7 |  | 9[3] | 8[2] | 11 | 10 |  |  | 13 |  |  |  |  |  |  | 6 | 5 |  | 3 |  | 1 | 2 |  | 37 |
|  | 4 |  | 13 | 7 |  | 9[1] | 6[2] | 14 | 11 |  |  |  |  |  |  |  |  | 12 |  | 8 | 5 |  | 3 |  | 1 | 2 | 10[3] | 38 |
|  | 4 |  | 13 | 7[3] |  | 9 | 8[2] | 11 |  |  |  |  |  |  | 2[1] |  |  | 14 |  | 6 | 5 |  | 3 |  | 1 | 12 | 10 | 39 |
|  | 4 |  | 10 |  |  | 7[3] | 14 | 9[1] | 13 |  |  |  |  | 5 |  |  |  | 11[2] |  | 8 | 6 |  | 3 |  | 1 | 2 | 12 | 40 |
|  | 3 |  | 12 | 7[3] |  | 9[1] | 8[2] | 13 | 11 |  |  |  |  |  |  |  |  | 14 |  | 6 | 5 |  | 4 |  | 1 | 2 | 10* | 41 |
|  | 3[2] | 13 |  | 7 | 6[3] |  | 9[1] | 11 |  |  |  |  |  | 12 | 14 |  |  | 8 |  | 2 | 4 |  | 1 | 5 | 10* |  |  | 42 |
|  | 4 |  | 8 | 6[1] |  | 9[3] | 12 | 14 | 10 |  |  |  |  |  |  |  | 5[2] | 11 |  | 7 | 2 |  | 3 |  | 1 | 13 |  | 43 |
|  | 4 | 12 | 13 | 7 |  | 9 | 8[3] | 14 | 10 |  |  |  |  |  |  |  | 2[1] | 11 |  | 6[2] | 5 |  | 3 |  | 1 |  |  | 44 |
|  | 2 | 4 | 5 | 12 | 7 |  | 6[3] | 8[1] | 10 | 13 |  | 14 |  |  |  |  |  | 11[2] |  | 9 |  |  | 3 |  | 1 |  |  | 45 |
|  | 2[1] | 4 | 5 | 13 | 7[3] |  | 9[2] | 12 | 11 |  |  |  |  |  |  |  |  | 14 |  | 8 | 6 |  | 3 |  | 1 |  | 10 | 46 |

**FA Cup**
Third Round    Oldham Ath      (h)   2-3

**Capital One Cup**
First Round    Fleetwood T    (a)   1-0
Second Round    Wigan Ath    (h)   1-4

# NOTTS COUNTY

## FOUNDATION

According to the official history of Notts County 'the true date of Notts' foundation has to be the meeting at the George Hotel on 7 December 1864'. However, there is documented evidence of continuous play from 1862, when club members played organised matches amongst themselves in The Park in Nottingham. They are the world's oldest professional football club.

*Meadow Lane Stadium, Meadow Lane, Nottingham NG2 3HJ.*

*Telephone:* (0115) 952 9000.

*Fax:* (0115) 955 3994.

*Ticket Office:* (0115) 955 7204.

*Website:* www.nottscountyfc.co.uk

*Email:* office@nottscountyfc.co.uk

*Ground Capacity:* 20,280.

*Record Attendance:* 47,310 v York C, FA Cup 6th rd, 12 March 1955.

*Pitch Measurements:* 104m × 69m (114yd × 76yd)

*Executive Chairman:* Ray Trew.

*Chief Executive:* James Rodwell.

*Manager:* Chris Kiwomya.

*First Team Coach:* Andy Watson.

*Physio:* Rebecca Knight.

*Colours:* Black and white striped shirts, black shorts, black socks.

## HONOURS

**Football League – Division 1:**
Best season: 3rd, 1890–91, 1900–01;
**Division 2:** *Champions* 1896–97, 1913–14, 1922–23;
*Runners-up* 1894–95, 1980–81;
**Division 3 (S):** *Champions* 1930–31, 1949–50; *Runners-up* 1936–37;
**Division 3:** *Champions* 1997–98;
*Runners-up* 1972–73;
**Division 4:** *Champions* 1970–71;
*Runners-up* 1959–60;
**FL 2:** *Champions* 2009–10.
**FA Cup:** *Winners* 1894;
*Runners-up* 1891.
**Football League Cup:** Best season: 5th rd, 1964, 1973, 1976.
**Anglo-Italian Cup:** *Winners* 1995;
*Runners-up* 1994.

*Year Formed:* 1862* (*see Foundation*). *Turned Professional:* 1885.

*Club Nickname:* 'The Magpies'.

*Grounds:* 1862, The Park; 1864, The Meadows; 1877, Beeston Cricket Ground; 1880, Castle Ground; 1883, Trent Bridge; 1910, Meadow Lane.

*First Football League Game:* 15 September 1888, Football League, v Everton (a) L 1–2 – Holland; Guttridge, McLean; Brown, Warburton, Shelton; Hodder, Harker, Jardine, Albert Moore (1), Wardle.

*Record League Victory:* 11–1 v Newport Co, Division 3 (S), 15 January 1949 – Smith; Southwell, Purvis; Gannon, Baxter, Adamson; Houghton (1), Sewell (4), Lawton (4), Pimbley, Johnston (2).

*Record Cup Victory:* 15–0 v Rotherham T (at Trent Bridge), FA Cup 1st rd, 24 October 1885 – Sherwin; Snook, Henry Thomas Moore; Dobson (1), Emmett (1), Chapman; Gunn (1), Albert Moore (2), Jackson (3), Daft (2), Cursham (4), (1 og).

*Record Defeat:* 1–9 v Blackburn R, Division 1, 16 November 1889. 1–9 v Aston Villa, Division 1, 29 September 1888. 1–9 v Portsmouth, Division 2, 9 April 1927.

*Most League Points (2 for a win):* 69, Division 4, 1970–71.

## sky SPORTS FACT FILE

On 25 May 1922 Notts County played St Mirren in Barcelona for the Landome Trophy and lost 2-1. Almost exactly 55 years later the two clubs met again, playing for the Queen's Silver Jubilee Festival Cup in Gibraltar. On this occasion the Magpies were successful, winning 4-3 over two legs.

**Most League Points (3 for a win):** 99, Division 3, 1997–98.

**Most League Goals:** 107, Division 4, 1959–60.

**Highest League Scorer in Season:** Tom Keetley, 39, Division 3 (S), 1930–31.

**Most League Goals in Total Aggregate:** Les Bradd, 125, 1967–78.

**Most League Goals in One Match:** 5, Robert Jardine v Burnley, Division 1, 27 October 1888; 5, Daniel Bruce v Port Vale, Division 2, 26 February 1895; 5, Bertie Mills v Barnsley, Division 2, 19 November 1927.

**Most Capped Player:** Kevin Wilson, 15 (42), Northern Ireland.

**Most League Appearances:** Albert Iremonger, 564, 1904–26.

**Youngest League Player:** Tony Bircumshaw, 16 years 54 days v Brentford, 3 April 1961.

**Record Transfer Fee Received:** £2,500,000 from Derby Co for Craig Short, September 1992.

**Record Transfer Fee Paid:** £800,000 to Manchester C for Kasper Schmeichel, July 2009.

**Football League Record:** 1888 Founder Member of the Football League; 1893–97 Division 2; 1897–1913 Division 1; 1913–14 Division 2; 1914–20 Division 1; 1920–23 Division 2; 1923–26 Division 1; 1926–30 Division 2; 1930–31 Division 3 (S); 1931–35 Division 2; 1935–50 Division 3 (S); 1950–58 Division 2; 1958–59 Division 3; 1959–60 Division 4; 1960–64 Division 3; 1964–71 Division 4; 1971–73 Division 3; 1973–81 Division 2; 1981–84 Division 1; 1984–85 Division 2; 1985–90 Division 3; 1990–91 Division 2; 1991–95 Division 1; 1995–97 Division 2; 1997–98 Division 3; 1998–2004 Division 2; 2004–10 FL 2; 2010– FL 1.

## LATEST SEQUENCES

**Longest Sequence of League Wins:** 10, 3.12.1997 – 31.1.1998.

**Longest Sequence of League Defeats:** 7, 3.9.1983 – 16.10.1983.

**Longest Sequence of League Draws:** 6, 16.8.2008 – 20.9.2008.

**Longest Sequence of Unbeaten League Matches:** 19, 26.4.1930 – 6.12.1930.

**Longest Sequence Without a League Win:** 20, 3.12.1996 – 31.3.1997.

**Successive Scoring Runs:** 35 from 26.4.1930.

**Successive Non-scoring Runs:** 9 from 15.3.2011 – 16.4.2011.

## MANAGERS

Edwin Browne 1883–93
Tom Featherstone 1893
Tom Harris 1893–1913
Albert Fisher 1913–27
Horace Henshall 1927–34
Charlie Jones 1934
David Pratt 1935
Percy Smith 1935–36
Jimmy McMullan 1936–37
Harry Parkes 1938–39
Tony Towers 1939–42
Frank Womack 1942–43
Major Frank Buckley 1944–46
Arthur Stollery 1946–49
Eric Houghton 1949–53
George Poyser 1953–57
Tommy Lawton 1957–58
Frank Hill 1958–61
Tim Coleman 1961–63
Eddie Lowe 1963–65
Tim Coleman 1965–66
Jack Burkitt 1966–67
Andy Beattie *(General Manager)* 1967
Billy Gray 1967–68
Jack Wheeler (*Caretaker Manager*) 1968–69
Jimmy Sirrel 1969–75
Ron Fenton 1975–77
Jimmy Sirrel 1978–82 *(continued as General Manager to 1984)*
Howard Wilkinson 1982–83
Larry Lloyd 1983–84
Richie Barker 1984–85
Jimmy Sirrel 1985–87
John Barnwell 1987–88
Neil Warnock 1989–93
Mick Walker 1993–94
Russell Slade 1994–95
Howard Kendall 1995
Colin Murphy 1995–96 *(General Manager)*
Steve Thompson 1995–96
Sam Allardyce 1997–99
Gary Brazil 1999–2000
Jocky Scott 2000–01
Gary Brazil 2001–02
Billy Dearden 2002–04
Gary Mills 2004
Ian Richardson 2004–05
Gudjon Thordarson 2005–06
Steve Thompson 2006–07
Ian McParland 2007–09
Hans Backe 2009
Sven-Göran Eriksson 2009–10 *(Director of Football)*
Steve Cotterill 2010
Craig Short 2010
Paul Ince 2010–11
Martin Allen 2011–12
Keith Curle 2012–13
Chris Kiwomya February 2013–

## TEN YEAR LEAGUE RECORD

|         |       | P  | W  | D  | L  | F  | A  | Pts | Pos |
|---------|-------|----|----|----|----|----|----|-----|-----|
| 2003-04 | Div 2 | 46 | 10 | 12 | 24 | 50 | 78 | 42  | 23  |
| 2004-05 | FL 2  | 46 | 13 | 13 | 20 | 46 | 62 | 52  | 19  |
| 2005-06 | FL 2  | 46 | 12 | 16 | 18 | 48 | 63 | 52  | 21  |
| 2006-07 | FL 2  | 46 | 16 | 14 | 16 | 55 | 53 | 62  | 13  |
| 2007-08 | FL 2  | 46 | 10 | 18 | 18 | 37 | 53 | 48  | 21  |
| 2008-09 | FL 2  | 46 | 11 | 14 | 21 | 49 | 69 | 47  | 19  |
| 2009-10 | FL 2  | 46 | 27 | 12 | 7  | 96 | 31 | 93  | 1   |
| 2010-11 | FL 1  | 46 | 14 | 8  | 24 | 46 | 60 | 50  | 19  |
| 2011-12 | FL 1  | 46 | 21 | 10 | 15 | 75 | 63 | 73  | 7   |
| 2012-13 | FL 1  | 46 | 16 | 17 | 13 | 61 | 49 | 65  | 12  |

## DID YOU KNOW

Goalkeeper George Smith was the first-ever winner of the Notts County Supporters' Club Player of the Year in 1964–65. George was an ever-present for the Magpies that season and in total made 352 first-team appearances between 1955 and 1966.

## NOTTS COUNTY – FOOTBALL LEAGUE ONE 2012–13 LEAGUE RECORD

| Match No. | Date | Venue | Opponents | Result | H/T Score | Lg Pos. | Goalscorers | Attendance |
|---|---|---|---|---|---|---|---|---|
| 1 | Aug 18 | A | Crewe Alex | W 2-1 | 1-0 | 5 | Zoko [40], Arquin [58] | 5718 |
| 2 | 21 | H | Hartlepool U | W 2-0 | 1-0 | 3 | Zoko [17], Bishop [86] | 4913 |
| 3 | 25 | H | Walsall | L 0-1 | 0-0 | 6 | | 5851 |
| 4 | Sept 1 | A | Bury | W 2-0 | 1-0 | 3 | Hughes, L [2], Judge [90] | 2725 |
| 5 | 8 | H | Shrewsbury T | W 3-2 | 0-0 | 1 | Zoko [57], Hughes, J [64], Hughes, L [87] | 6774 |
| 6 | 15 | A | Oldham Ath | D 2-2 | 0-0 | 2 | Labadie [46], Campbell-Ryce [82] | 4039 |
| 7 | 18 | A | Milton Keynes D | D 1-1 | 1-0 | 3 | Bishop [27] | 7121 |
| 8 | 22 | H | Portsmouth | W 3-0 | 1-0 | 2 | Arquin 2 [5, 57], Judge [47] | 6834 |
| 9 | 29 | A | Sheffield U | D 1-1 | 0-0 | 2 | Hughes, L [76] | 18,814 |
| 10 | Oct 2 | H | Stevenage | L 1-2 | 0-0 | 4 | Campbell-Ryce (pen) [71] | 4927 |
| 11 | 6 | H | Tranmere R | L 0-1 | 0-1 | 7 | | 7260 |
| 12 | 13 | A | Carlisle U | W 4-0 | 0-0 | 5 | Hughes, J [11], Bishop [27], Zoko [54], Campbell-Ryce (pen) [57] | 4731 |
| 13 | 20 | A | Coventry C | W 2-1 | 1-0 | 5 | Boucaud [39], Arquin [84] | 11,882 |
| 14 | 23 | H | Bournemouth | D 3-3 | 2-0 | 5 | Hughes, J [21], Arquin [32], Campbell-Ryce (pen) [84] | 4584 |
| 15 | 27 | H | Doncaster R | L 0-2 | 0-0 | 6 | | 6750 |
| 16 | Nov 6 | A | Colchester U | W 2-0 | 2-0 | 5 | Bishop [17], Judge [44] | 3051 |
| 17 | 10 | H | Crawley T | D 1-1 | 1-1 | 5 | Bishop [12] | 5685 |
| 18 | 17 | A | Scunthorpe U | D 2-2 | 1-2 | 7 | Hughes, L 2 [34, 82] | 4553 |
| 19 | 20 | A | Preston NE | D 0-0 | 0-0 | 8 | | 8013 |
| 20 | 24 | H | Swindon T | W 1-0 | 1-0 | 6 | Judge [28] | 6383 |
| 21 | Dec 8 | A | Yeovil T | D 0-0 | 0-0 | 7 | | 3355 |
| 22 | 15 | H | Brentford | L 1-2 | 1-1 | 8 | Craig (og) [20] | 5307 |
| 23 | 26 | A | Shrewsbury T | D 2-2 | 2-1 | 10 | Hughes, L [24], Campbell-Ryce [45] | 6474 |
| 24 | Jan 1 | H | Milton Keynes D | L 1-2 | 0-2 | 13 | Campbell-Ryce (pen) [56] | 5325 |
| 25 | 19 | A | Sheffield U | D 1-1 | 0-1 | 14 | Judge [80] | 7061 |
| 26 | 22 | H | Oldham Ath | W 1-0 | 1-0 | 12 | Showunmi [35] | 3409 |
| 27 | 26 | A | Leyton Orient | L 1-2 | 0-0 | 12 | Hughes, J [78] | 3578 |
| 28 | 29 | A | Portsmouth | W 2-0 | 0-0 | 9 | Hughes, J [81], Zoko [88] | 10,276 |
| 29 | Feb 2 | A | Hartlepool U | L 1-2 | 0-1 | 10 | Campbell-Ryce [52] | 3662 |
| 30 | 5 | A | Stevenage | L 0-2 | 0-0 | 10 | | 2550 |
| 31 | 9 | H | Crewe Alex | D 1-1 | 0-1 | 11 | Cofie [57] | 5450 |
| 32 | 16 | A | Walsall | D 1-1 | 0-1 | 11 | Arquin [66] | 4416 |
| 33 | 22 | H | Bury | W 4-1 | 0-1 | 9 | Kelly [58], Zoko 2 [61, 65], Campbell-Ryce (pen) [74] | 5795 |
| 34 | 26 | A | Tranmere R | D 1-1 | 0-1 | 10 | Bishop [74] | 4703 |
| 35 | Mar 2 | H | Carlisle U | W 1-0 | 1-0 | 10 | Judge [35] | 5553 |
| 36 | 6 | H | Leyton Orient | D 1-1 | 1-0 | 10 | Bishop [31] | 4004 |
| 37 | 9 | A | Crawley T | D 0-0 | 0-0 | 10 | | 3689 |
| 38 | 12 | H | Preston NE | L 0-1 | 0-1 | 11 | | 3587 |
| 39 | 16 | A | Scunthorpe U | W 1-0 | 0-0 | 11 | Leacock [81] | 4634 |
| 40 | 23 | A | Swindon T | D 0-0 | 0-0 | 11 | | 8415 |
| 41 | 29 | A | Brentford | L 1-2 | 0-1 | 10 | Judge [74] | 7412 |
| 42 | Apr 1 | H | Yeovil T | L 1-2 | 0-1 | 11 | Judge (pen) [49] | 5004 |
| 43 | 6 | A | Bournemouth | L 1-3 | 1-2 | 11 | Hughes, J [2] | 7551 |
| 44 | 13 | H | Colchester U | W 3-1 | 1-1 | 12 | Hughes, J [18], Arquin [77], Nangle [90] | 4306 |
| 45 | 20 | A | Doncaster R | W 1-0 | 1-0 | 11 | Labadie [14] | 12,624 |
| 46 | 27 | H | Coventry C | D 2-2 | 1-0 | 12 | Waite [34], Pearce [54] | 7608 |

**Final League Position: 12**

### GOALSCORERS

*League (61):* Campbell-Ryce 8 (5 pens), Judge 8 (1 pen), Arquin 7, Bishop 7, Hughes, J 7, Zoko 7, Hughes, L 6, Labadie 2, Boucaud 1, Cofie 1, Kelly 1, Leacock 1, Nangle 1, Pearce 1, Showunmi 1, Waite 1, own goal 1.
*FA Cup (3):* Arquin 2, Zoko 1.
*Capital One Cup (0).*
*Johnstone's Paint Trophy (3):* Regan 1, Showunmi 1, Stewart 1.

| Bialkowski B 40 | Kelly J 20 + 2 | Leacock D 42 | Williams T 1 | Sheehan A 32 + 1 | Hughes J 39 + 5 | Bishop N 40 + 1 | Liddle G 46 | Zoko F 25 + 13 | Judge A 38 + 1 | Arquin Y 27 + 14 | Labadie J 8 + 16 | Hughes L 7 + 11 | Mahon G 3 + 9 | Boucaud A 38 + 1 | Waite T 3 + 5 | Showunmi E 9 + 13 | Nangle R — + 7 | Regan C 9 + 2 | Campbell-Ryce J 34 + 3 | Wholey J — + 1 | Bencherif H 1 + 10 | Stewart J 7 | Eastham A 3 + 1 | Stewart D 2 + 1 | Iwelumo C 5 | Smith M 4 + 1 | Spiess F 6 + 1 | Cofie J 6 + 1 | Blyth J 2 + 2 | Hollis H 5 + 1 | Thompson C 1 + 1 | Tempest G 1 + 2 | Pilkington K — + 1 | Pearce K 2 | Match No. |
|---|---|---|---|---|---|---|---|---|---|---|---|---|---|---|---|---|---|---|---|---|---|---|---|---|---|---|---|---|---|---|---|---|---|---|---|
| 1 | 2 | 3 | $4^1$ | 5 | 6 | 7 | 8 | $9^2$ | 10 | $11^8$ | $12^3$ | 13 | 14 | | | | | | | | | | | | | | | | | | | | | | 1 |
| 1 | 2 | 3 | | 5 | 9 | 8 | 4 | $10^1$ | 6 | | 12 | $11^3$ | 13 | $7^2$ | 14 | | | | | | | | | | | | | | | | | | | | 2 |
| 1 | 2 | 3 | | $5^3$ | 9 | 7 | 4 | | 6 | | $10^1$ | 11 | 13 | $8^3$ | 14 | 12 | | | | | | | | | | | | | | | | | | | 3 |
| 1 | 2 | 3 | | 5 | 6 | $7^2$ | 4 | $9^1$ | 10 | | 12 | $11^3$ | 13 | 8 | | | 14 | | | | | | | | | | | | | | | | | | 4 |
| 1 | 2 | 3 | | $5^1$ | 8 | 6 | 4 | $9^2$ | 11 | 10 | 14 | 13 | | $7^3$ | | | 12 | | | | | | | | | | | | | | | | | | 5 |
| 1 | 2 | 3 | | | 7 | 4 | $9^1$ | 10 | $6^2$ | 12 | $11^3$ | | $8^8$ | | 13 | | 5 | 14 | | | | | | | | | | | | | | | | | 6 |
| 1 | 2 | 5 | | | 12 | 8 | 4 | $10^2$ | 7 | $11^3$ | 9 | 13 | | | 14 | | 3 | $6^1$ | | | | | | | | | | | | | | | | | 7 |
| 1 | 2 | 3 | | | 8 | $7^1$ | 4 | 11 | $9^3$ | 10 | 6 | | | $5^2$ | 12 | 13 | 14 | | | | | | | | | | | | | | | | | | 8 |
| 1 | $2^2$ | 3 | | | 7 | 9 | 4 | $10^1$ | 8 | 11 | 13 | 12 | 14 | 5 | $6^3$ | | | | | | | | | | | | | | | | | | | | 9 |
| 1 | | 3 | $13^8$ | 5 | 7 | 4 | $11^2$ | 9 | 12 | 14 | | 8 | $10^1$ | 2 | $6^3$ | | | | | | | | | | | | | | | | | | | | 10 |
| 1 | | 3 | | $8^1$ | 7 | 4 | 13 | 9 | $10^2$ | 12 | | 6 | 14 | 2 | $11^3$ | | 5 | | | | | | | | | | | | | | | | | | 11 |
| 1 | | 3 | | 8 | $7^2$ | 5 | 12 | $9^1$ | 11 | | 6 | 14 | 2 | $10^3$ | | 4 | 13 | | | | | | | | | | | | | | | | | | 12 |
| 1 | | 2 | | 7 | 5 | 8 | $10^1$ | 11 | 12 | 13 | 9 | | $6^2$ | 4 | 3 | | | | | | | | | | | | | | | | | | | | 13 |
| 1 | | 3 | | 8 | 6 | 4 | $11^1$ | 10 | 12 | 7 | 9 | 5 | 2 | | | | | | | | | | | | | | | | | | | | | | 14 |
| 1 | | $3^1$ | | 8 | 6 | 2 | $11^2$ | 13 | 10 | 12 | $7^3$ | 14 | 9 | 5 | 4 | | | | | | | | | | | | | | | | | | | | 15 |
| 1 | | 4 | | 5 | 6 | 2 | $9^1$ | $8^3$ | 10 | 12 | 14 | 7 | $11^2$ | 13 | 3 | | | | | | | | | | | | | | | | | | | | 16 |
| 1 | | 3 | | 5 | 6 | 2 | $11^1$ | 8 | 10 | 12 | 7 | 13 | $9^2$ | 4 | | | | | | | | | | | | | | | | | | | | | 17 |
| 1 | | 3 | 5 | $7^3$ | 6 | 2 | 14 | 11 | 12 | 13 | 10 | 8 | $9^1$ | $4^2$ | | | | | | | | | | | | | | | | | | | | | 18 |
| 1 | | 4 | 5 | 11 | 6 | 3 | $9^1$ | $7^3$ | $10^4$ | 14 | 12 | 8 | 2 | $13^8$ | | | | | | | | | | | | | | | | | | | | | 19 |
| 1 | $2^2$ | 3 | | 5 | 8 | 6 | 4 | $11^1$ | 9 | 14 | 12 | $7^3$ | 13 | 10 | | | | | | | | | | | | | | | | | | | | | 20 |
| 1 | | 4 | | 5 | 6 | 9 | 3 | 12 | $8^3$ | $10^2$ | 14 | $7^1$ | 13 | 2 | 11 | | | | | | | | | | | | | | | | | | | | 21 |
| 1 | 2 | $3^1$ | | 5 | 8 | 6 | 4 | 11 | | 13 | | $7^2$ | 14 | 9 | $12$ | $10^3$ | | | | | | | | | | | | | | | | | | | 22 |
| 1 | 2 | | | 5 | 7 | 4 | | 9 | 13 | 14 | $10^1$ | 8 | 12 | $6^3$ | | $11^2$ | 3 | | | | | | | | | | | | | | | | | | 23 |
| 1 | $2^3$ | | | 7 | 4 | 13 | 9 | 12 | | 10 | 8 | 14 | $6^2$ | 5 | $11^1$ | 3 | | | | | | | | | | | | | | | | | | | 24 |
| 1 | | 3 | | 4 | 8 | 6 | 2 | $11^8$ | 9 | $10^1$ | 7 | | | 5 | 12 | | | | | | | | | | | | | | | | | | | | 25 |
| 1 | | 3 | | 4 | 8 | 6 | 2 | | 9 | $11^3$ | 13 | 7 | $10^1$ | 14 | $5^2$ | 12 | | | | | | | | | | | | | | | | | | | 26 |
| $1^1$ | | 3 | | 4 | 9 | 5 | 2 | $8^3$ | $11^2$ | 6 | $10^1$ | 13 | 7 | 14 | | | 12 | | | | | | | | | | | | | | | | | | 27 |
| | 12 | 3 | | 2 | 8 | $6^8$ | 4 | $10^3$ | $9^1$ | 11 | 13 | 14 | $7^2$ | 5 | | | 1 | | | | | | | | | | | | | | | | | | 28 |
| | 12 | 3 | | 4 | 9 | | 2 | $11^3$ | 7 | $10^2$ | $8^1$ | 6 | 14 | 5 | 13 | | 1 | | | | | | | | | | | | | | | | | | 29 |
| | | 4 | | 2 | 6 | | 3 | $11^1$ | 5 | 10 | $7^2$ | 8 | 12 | 9 | 13 | | 1 | | | | | | | | | | | | | | | | | | 30 |
| | 2 | 3 | | 5 | 8 | | 4 | 13 | 11 | 12 | $7^1$ | 6 | 14 | $9^2$ | | | 1 | $10^3$ | | | | | | | | | | | | | | | | | 31 |
| 1 | | 3 | | 4 | $8^3$ | 6 | 2 | 13 | 9 | 12 | 14 | 7 | | 5 | | | | $11^2$ | $10^1$ | | | | | | | | | | | | | | | | 32 |
| 1 | 2 | $3^3$ | | 5 | 13 | 7 | 4 | 12 | 9 | $10^1$ | | $8^2$ | | 6 | | | | 11 | 14 | | | | | | | | | | | | | | | | 33 |
| 1 | $2^1$ | 3 | | 5 | 12 | 7 | 4 | $10^3$ | 9 | 13 | | 8 | | 6 | 14 | | | $11^2$ | | | | | | | | | | | | | | | | | 34 |
| 1 | | 3 | | 4 | 8 | 6 | 2 | $10^3$ | 9 | 12 | 13 | 7 | | $5^2$ | | | | $11^1$ | 14 | | | | | | | | | | | | | | | | 35 |
| 1 | | 3 | | 5 | 13 | 7 | 2 | $10^2$ | 9 | 12 | | 8 | | 6 | | | | $11^1$ | 4 | | | | | | | | | | | | | | | | 36 |
| 1 | | | | 2 | 9 | 7 | 5 | 12 | | | | 8 | 13 | $6^3$ | $10^1$ | | | 3 | 14 | $11^2$ | 4 | | | | | | | | | | | | | | 37 |
| 1 | | | | 5 | 8 | 6 | 2 | $11^2$ | | 13 | | 7 | $10^3$ | $9^1$ | | | 3 | | 14 | 4 | 12 | | | | | | | | | | | | | | 38 |
| 1 | | 3 | | 5 | 9 | 7 | 2 | 12 | 6 | $11^1$ | | $8^7$ | 14 | $10^3$ | | | | 4 | 13 | | | | | | | | | | | | | | | | 39 |
| 1 | $2^3$ | 3 | | 5 | 6 | 7 | 4 | | 8 | 12 | | 9 | | $11^2$ | | | 13 | | 14 | | | | $10^1$ | | | | | | | | | | | | 40 |
| $1^1$ | 2 | 3 | | 5 | $10^2$ | 7 | 4 | 14 | 8 | 11 | | 9 | | 13 | | | $6^3$ | | | | | | 12 | | | | | | | | | | | | 41 |
| | 2 | 4 | | 5 | 12 | 8 | 3 | 14 | 9 | $11^2$ | | $7^3$ | 13 | 10 | | | $6^1$ | | | | | 1 | | | | | | | | | | | | | 42 |
| 1 | $2^3$ | 4 | | 5 | 10 | 9 | 3 | | 14 | $8^1$ | | $7^8$ | 13 | $11^2$ | | | 6 | | | | | | 12 | | | | | | | | | | | | 43 |
| 1 | | 3 | | 5 | 8 | | 2 | | 12 | 7 | | $11^1$ | $10^1$ | 13 | 9 | | | | | | | | | 4 | $6^2$ | | | | | | | | | | 44 |
| | | 3 | | 5 | 7 | | 2 | 12 | 6 | 10 | 8 | | $11^1$ | | | $9^2$ | 13 | | | | 1 | | | | | | | | | | | 4 | | | 45 |
| 1 | | 3 | | 5 | 8 | 13 | 2 | | 9 | 10 | $7^2$ | | 12 | $11^1$ | | | 6 | | | | | | | | | | | | | | | | 4 | | 46 |

**FA Cup**

| | | | |
|---|---|---|---|
| First Round | Portsmouth | (a) | 2-0 |
| Second Round | Rotherham U | (a) | 1-1 |
| *Replay* | Rotherham U | (h) | 0-3 |

**Capital One Cup**

| | | | |
|---|---|---|---|
| First Round | Bradford C | (h) | 0-1 |

**Johnstone's Paint Trophy**

| | | | |
|---|---|---|---|
| First Round | Scunthorpe U | (a) | 2-1 |
| Second Round | Sheffield U | (h) | 1-4 |

# OLDHAM ATHLETIC

## FOUNDATION

It was in 1895 that John Garland, the landlord of the Featherstall and Junction Hotel, decided to form a football club. As Pine Villa they played in the Oldham Junior League. In 1899 the local professional club, Oldham County, went out of existence and one of the liquidators persuaded Pine Villa to take over their ground at Sheepfoot Lane and change their name to Oldham Athletic.

*Boundary Park, Furtherwood Road, Oldham OL1 2PA.*

*Telephone:* (0161) 624 4972.

*Fax:* (0161) 627 5915.

*Ticket Office:* (0161) 785 5150.

*Website:* www.oldhamathletic.co.uk

*Email:* enquiries@oldhamathletic.co.uk

*Ground Capacity:* 10,840.

*Record Attendance:* 46,471 v Sheffield W, FA Cup 4th rd, 25 January 1930.

*Pitch Measurements:* 96m × 65m (106yd × 72yd)

*Chairman:* Simon Corney.

*Chief Executive:* Neil Joy.

*Manager:* Lee Johnson.

*Head of Sports Medicine:* Jon Guy.

*Colours:* Blue shirts, blue shorts, blue socks.

*Year Formed:* 1895.

*Turned Professional:* 1899.

*Previous Name:* 1895, Pine Villa; 1899, Oldham Athletic.

*Club Nickname:* 'The Latics'.

*Grounds:* 1895, Sheepfoot Lane; 1900, Hudson Field; 1906, Sheepfoot Lane; 1907, Boundary Park.

*First Football League Game:* 9 September 1907, Division 2, v Stoke (a) W 3–1 – Hewitson; Hodson, Hamilton; Fay, Walders, Wilson; Ward, Billy Dodds (1), Newton (1), Hancock, Swarbrick (1).

*Record League Victory:* 11–0 v Southport, Division 4, 26 December 1962 – Bollands; Branagan, Marshall; McCall, Williams, Scott; Ledger (1), Johnstone, Lister (6), Colquhoun (1), Whitaker (3).

*Record Cup Victory:* 10–1 v Lytham, FA Cup 1st rd, 28 November 1925 – Gray; Wynne, Grundy; Adlam, Heaton, Naylor (1), Douglas, Pynegar (2), Ormston (2), Barnes (3), Watson (2).

*Record Defeat:* 4–13 v Tranmere R, Division 3 (N), 26 December 1935.

*Most League Points (2 for a win):* 62, Division 3, 1973–74.

## HONOURS

**Football League – Division 1:**
*Runners-up* 1914–15;
**Division 2:** *Champions* 1990–91;
*Runners-up* 1909–10;
**Division 3 (N):** *Champions* 1952–53;
**Division 2:** *Champions* 1973–74;
**Division 4:** *Runners-up* 1962–63.
**FA Cup:** Semi-final 1913, 1990, 1994.
**Football League Cup:**
*Runners-up* 1990.

## sky SPORTS FACT FILE

Oldham Athletic toured Central Europe in 1911. In addition to games with local teams they met Lancashire rivals Blackburn Rovers in two exhibition games. The Latics won 1-0 in Budapest but three days later they lost 5-2 in Vienna.

*Most League Points (3 for a win):* 88, Division 2, 1990–91.

*Most League Goals:* 95, Division 4, 1962–63.

*Highest League Scorer in Season:* Tom Davis, 33, Division 3 (N), 1936–37.

*Most League Goals in Total Aggregate:* Roger Palmer, 141, 1980–94.

*Most League Goals in One Match:* 7, Eric Gemmell v Chester, Division 3 (N), 19 January 1952.

*Most Capped Player:* Gunnar Halle, 24 (64), Norway.

*Most League Appearances:* Ian Wood, 525, 1966–80.

*Youngest League Player:* Wayne Harrison, 15 years 11 months v Notts Co, 27 October 1984.

*Record Transfer Fee Received:* £1,700,000 from Aston Villa for Earl Barrett, February 1992.

*Record Transfer Fee Paid:* £750,000 to Aston Villa for Ian Olney, June 1992.

*Football League Record:* 1907 Elected to Division 2; 1910–23 Division 1; 1923–35 Division 2; 1935–53 Division 3 (N); 1953–54 Division 2; 1954–58 Division 3 (N); 1958–63 Division 4; 1963–69 Division 3; 1969–71 Division 4; 1971–74 Division 3; 1974–91 Division 2; 1991–92 Division 1; 1992–94 FA Premier League; 1994–97 Division 1; 1997–2004 Division 2; 2004– FL 1.

## LATEST SEQUENCES

*Longest Sequence of League Wins:* 10, 12.1.1974 – 12.3.1974.

*Longest Sequence of League Defeats:* 8, 15.12.1934 – 2.2.1935.

*Longest Sequence of League Draws:* 5, 26.12.1982 – 15.1.1983.

*Longest Sequence of Unbeaten League Matches:* 20, 1.5.1990 – 10.11.1990.

*Longest Sequence Without a League Win:* 17, 4.9.1920 – 18.12.1920.

*Successive Scoring Runs:* 25 from 15.1.1927.

*Successive Non-scoring Runs:* 6 from 4.2.1922.

## MANAGERS

David Ashworth 1906–14
Herbert Bamlett 1914–21
Charlie Roberts 1921–22
David Ashworth 1923–24
Bob Mellor 1924–27
Andy Wilson 1927–32
Bob Mellor 1932–33
Jimmy McMullan 1933–34
Bob Mellor 1934–45
  *(continued as Secretary to 1953)*
Frank Womack 1945–47
Billy Wootton 1947–50
George Hardwick 1950–56
Ted Goodier 1956–58
Norman Dodgin 1958–60
Danny McLennan 1960
Jack Rowley 1960–63
Les McDowall 1963–65
Gordon Hurst 1965–66
Jimmy McIlroy 1966–68
Jack Rowley 1968–69
Jimmy Frizzell 1970–82
Joe Royle 1982–94
Graeme Sharp 1994–97
Neil Warnock 1997–98
Andy Ritchie 1998–2001
Mick Wadsworth 2001–02
Iain Dowie 2002–03
Brian Talbot 2004–05
Ronnie Moore 2005–06
John Sheridan 2006–09
Joe Royle 2009
Dave Penney 2009–10
Paul Dickov 2010–13
Lee Johnson March 2013–

## TEN YEAR LEAGUE RECORD

|  |  | P | W | D | L | F | A | Pts | Pos |
|---|---|---|---|---|---|---|---|---|---|
| 2003-04 | Div 2 | 46 | 12 | 21 | 13 | 66 | 60 | 57 | 15 |
| 2004-05 | FL 1 | 46 | 14 | 10 | 22 | 60 | 73 | 52 | 19 |
| 2005-06 | FL 1 | 46 | 18 | 11 | 17 | 58 | 60 | 65 | 10 |
| 2006-07 | FL 1 | 46 | 21 | 12 | 13 | 69 | 47 | 75 | 6 |
| 2007-08 | FL 1 | 46 | 18 | 13 | 15 | 58 | 46 | 67 | 8 |
| 2008-09 | FL 1 | 46 | 16 | 17 | 13 | 66 | 65 | 65 | 10 |
| 2009-10 | FL 1 | 46 | 13 | 13 | 20 | 39 | 57 | 52 | 16 |
| 2010-11 | FL 1 | 46 | 13 | 17 | 16 | 53 | 60 | 56 | 17 |
| 2011-12 | FL 1 | 46 | 14 | 12 | 20 | 50 | 66 | 54 | 16 |
| 2012-13 | FL 1 | 46 | 14 | 9 | 23 | 46 | 59 | 51 | 19 |

## DID YOU KNOW ?

When Oldham Athletic defeated Yeovil Town 1-0 on 16 April 2013 the win provided an early success for manager Lee Johnson against a team managed by his father, Gary. This is only the second father and son pairing that have faced each other as managers in Football League action.

## OLDHAM ATHLETIC – FOOTBALL LEAGUE ONE 2012–13 LEAGUE RECORD

| Match No. | Date | Venue | Opponents | Result | | H/T Score | Lg Pos. | Goalscorers | Attendance |
|---|---|---|---|---|---|---|---|---|---|
| 1 | Aug 18 | A | Milton Keynes D | L | 0-2 | 0-1 | 22 | | 7409 |
| 2 | 21 | H | Walsall | D | 1-1 | 1-0 | 19 | M'Changama [36] | 3496 |
| 3 | 25 | H | Stevenage | L | 0-1 | 0-1 | 22 | | 3142 |
| 4 | Sept 1 | A | Portsmouth | W | 1-0 | 0-0 | 15 | Ertl (og) [59] | 12,635 |
| 5 | 15 | H | Notts Co | D | 2-2 | 0-0 | 20 | Derbyshire [49], Baxter [85] | 4039 |
| 6 | 18 | H | Scunthorpe U | D | 1-1 | 1-1 | 18 | Derbyshire [40] | 2969 |
| 7 | 22 | A | Brentford | L | 0-1 | 0-1 | 19 | | 5251 |
| 8 | 29 | H | Coventry C | L | 0-1 | 0-0 | 21 | | 4022 |
| 9 | Oct 2 | A | Crewe Alex | W | 2-0 | 0-0 | 19 | Tarkowski [61], Derbyshire [79] | 3935 |
| 10 | 6 | H | Preston NE | W | 3-1 | 1-0 | 16 | Baxter [27], Montano [58], Furman [69] | 5496 |
| 11 | 13 | A | Sheffield U | D | 1-1 | 0-0 | 15 | Smith, M [90] | 18,188 |
| 12 | 20 | H | Leyton Orient | W | 2-0 | 0-0 | 13 | Derbyshire [77], Baxter [83] | 3919 |
| 13 | 23 | A | Carlisle U | L | 1-3 | 0-0 | 17 | Baxter (pen) [85] | 3310 |
| 14 | 27 | A | Crawley T | D | 1-1 | 0-0 | 17 | Baxter [67] | 3375 |
| 15 | Nov 6 | H | Bury | L | 1-2 | 0-1 | 18 | Simpson, R [90] | 4120 |
| 16 | 10 | H | Tranmere R | L | 0-1 | 0-0 | 19 | | 5159 |
| 17 | 17 | A | Bournemouth | L | 1-4 | 0-0 | 21 | Smith, M [86] | 6118 |
| 18 | 20 | A | Hartlepool U | W | 2-1 | 1-0 | 18 | Baxter 2 [17, 90] | 3078 |
| 19 | 24 | H | Shrewsbury T | W | 1-0 | 1-0 | 16 | Grounds [13] | 3886 |
| 20 | 27 | A | Doncaster R | L | 0-1 | 0-0 | 16 | | 6066 |
| 21 | Dec 8 | A | Colchester U | W | 2-0 | 1-0 | 16 | Mvoto [33], Wilson (og) [61] | 2987 |
| 22 | 15 | H | Swindon T | L | 0-2 | 0-2 | 16 | | 3345 |
| 23 | 22 | A | Yeovil T | L | 1-4 | 1-2 | 16 | Baxter [3] | 3492 |
| 24 | 26 | H | Doncaster R | L | 1-2 | 1-1 | 17 | M'Changama [27] | 4252 |
| 25 | 29 | H | Crewe Alex | L | 1-2 | 0-0 | 18 | Taylor [82] | 3451 |
| 26 | Jan 1 | A | Scunthorpe U | D | 2-2 | 1-2 | 19 | Byrne [35], Baxter (pen) [65] | 3116 |
| 27 | 12 | H | Brentford | L | 0-2 | 0-1 | 19 | | 4615 |
| 28 | 19 | A | Coventry C | L | 1-2 | 0-0 | 19 | Smith, M [89] | 10,108 |
| 29 | 22 | A | Notts Co | L | 0-1 | 0-1 | 19 | | 3409 |
| 30 | Feb 2 | A | Walsall | L | 1-3 | 1-1 | 20 | Barnard [19] | 4672 |
| 31 | 9 | H | Milton Keynes D | W | 3-1 | 2-1 | 21 | Barnard [22], Mvoto [44], Iwelumo [53] | 4094 |
| 32 | 19 | A | Stevenage | W | 2-1 | 0-1 | 20 | Furman [46], Tarkowski [60] | 2748 |
| 33 | 23 | H | Portsmouth | W | 1-0 | 1-0 | 19 | Baxter [11] | 4527 |
| 34 | Mar 2 | H | Sheffield U | L | 0-2 | 0-0 | 21 | | 6426 |
| 35 | 9 | A | Tranmere R | L | 0-1 | 0-0 | 21 | | 5560 |
| 36 | 16 | H | Bournemouth | L | 0-1 | 0-1 | 21 | | 3540 |
| 37 | 19 | H | Hartlepool U | W | 3-0 | 2-0 | 20 | Simpson, R [17], Mvoto [27], Baxter [69] | 3269 |
| 38 | 29 | A | Swindon T | D | 1-1 | 0-0 | 21 | Barnard [68] | 10,040 |
| 39 | Apr 1 | H | Colchester U | D | 1-1 | 0-1 | 20 | Baxter [68] | 4244 |
| 40 | 6 | A | Carlisle U | L | 1-2 | 0-2 | 20 | Baxter (pen) [73] | 4271 |
| 41 | 9 | A | Preston NE | L | 0-2 | 0-0 | 20 | | 9080 |
| 42 | 13 | A | Bury | W | 1-0 | 0-0 | 20 | Smith, M [79] | 4558 |
| 43 | 16 | H | Yeovil T | W | 1-0 | 1-0 | 19 | Smith, M [45] | 3888 |
| 44 | 20 | A | Crawley T | W | 2-1 | 0-0 | 18 | Smith, M [56], Mvoto [90] | 4794 |
| 45 | 23 | A | Shrewsbury T | L | 0-1 | 0-0 | 19 | | 5332 |
| 46 | 27 | A | Leyton Orient | D | 1-1 | 0-1 | 19 | Millar [46] | 5191 |

**Final League Position: 19**

### GOALSCORERS

*League (46):* Baxter 13 (3 pens), Smith, M 6, Derbyshire 4, Mvoto 4, Barnard 3, Furman 2, M'Changama 2, Simpson, R 2, Tarkowski 2, Byrne 1, Grounds 1, Iwelumo 1, Millar 1, Montano 1, Taylor 1, own goals 2.
*FA Cup (14):* Smith M 4, Baxter 2, Derbyshire 2, Simpson R 2, Wabara 2, Montano 1, Obita 1.
*Capital One Cup (2):* Mvoto 1, Slew 1.
*Johnstone's Paint Trophy (1):* Smith M 1.

| Cisak A 10 | Byrne C 32 + 3 | Mvoto J 42 | Tarkowski J 17 + 4 | Grounds J 44 | Croft L 44 + 1 | Furman D 24 + 4 | M'Changama Y 10 + 6 | Montano C 25 + 5 | Slew J 3 | Simpson R 23 + 14 | Taylor D 1 + 7 | Hughes C — + 3 | Winchester C 6 + 3 | Smith M 14 + 20 | Brown C 20 + 5 | Wabara R 25 | Wesolowski J 32 + 1 | Derbyshire M 18 | Baxter J 34 + 5 | Sutherland C 1 + 9 | Bouzanis D 36 | Jacob L — + 1 | Millar K 2 + 10 | Mellor D 4 + 1 | Iwelumo C 4 + 3 | Barnard L 14 | Obita J 4 + 4 | Smith K 9 + 1 | Reid B 3 + 4 | Belezika G 3 | Cooper J 1 | Gosset D 1 + 1 | Truelove J — + 1 | Match No. |
|---|---|---|---|---|---|---|---|---|---|---|---|---|---|---|---|---|---|---|---|---|---|---|---|---|---|---|---|---|---|---|---|---|---|---|
| 1 | 2 | 3 | 4 | 5 | 6 | 7 | 8 | 9¹ | 10² | 11 | 12 |  |  |  |  |  |  |  |  |  |  |  |  |  |  |  |  |  |  |  |  |  |  | 1 |
| 1 | 2 | 3 | 4 | 5 | 6 | 7 | 8 | 9² | 10¹ | 11 | 12 | 13 |  |  |  |  |  |  |  |  |  |  |  |  |  |  |  |  |  |  |  |  |  | 2 |
| 1 | 2 | 4 | 3² | 5 | 6 | 7 | 8 | 9³ | 10 |  |  |  | 14 | 11¹ | 12 | 13 |  |  |  |  |  |  |  |  |  |  |  |  |  |  |  |  |  | 3 |
| 1 | 3⁴ | 4 | 13 | 5 | 6 | 7 | 8 | 9 | 10¹ | 11² |  |  |  |  | 12 | 2 |  |  |  |  |  |  |  |  |  |  |  |  |  |  |  |  |  | 4 |
| 1 | 4 | 3 |  | 5 | 6 |  | 8 | 9³ |  | 10¹ |  |  |  |  | 12 | 2 | 7 | 11² | 13 | 14 |  |  |  |  |  |  |  |  |  |  |  |  |  | 5 |
|  | 4 | 3 |  | 5 | 6 |  | 8 | 9 |  | 12 |  |  |  | 11¹ |  | 2 | 7² | 10 | 13 |  | 1 |  |  |  |  |  |  |  |  |  |  |  |  | 6 |
|  | 4² | 3 |  | 2 | 9 |  | 8 | 6 |  | 11 |  |  |  | 13 |  | 5 | 7¹ | 10 | 12 |  | 1 |  |  |  |  |  |  |  |  |  |  |  |  | 7 |
|  | 4² | 3 |  | 5 | 6 |  | 8 | 9 |  | 12 |  |  |  | 13 |  | 2 | 7¹ | 10 | 11 |  | 1 |  |  |  |  |  |  |  |  |  |  |  |  | 8 |
|  | 3 | 4¹ | 12 | 5 | 6 |  | 8 | 9 |  |  |  |  |  | 13 |  | 2 | 7 | 10 | 11² |  | 1 |  |  |  |  |  |  |  |  |  |  |  |  | 9 |
|  | 4 | 3¹ |  | 5 | 6 |  | 8 | 9³ |  |  |  |  | 14 | 13 | 12 | 2 | 7 | 10 | 11² |  | 1 |  |  |  |  |  |  |  |  |  |  |  |  | 10 |
|  | 4 | 3 |  | 5 | 6 |  |  | 9 |  | 12 |  |  |  | 7¹ |  | 2 | 8 | 11 | 10 |  | 1 |  |  |  |  |  |  |  |  |  |  |  |  | 11 |
|  | 4 | 3 |  | 5 | 6 |  |  | 9² |  |  |  |  |  | 8¹ | 12 | 2 | 7 | 10 | 11 | 13 | 1 |  |  |  |  |  |  |  |  |  |  |  |  | 12 |
|  | 4³ | 3 |  | 5 | 6 |  | 8 | 9² |  |  |  |  |  | 14 | 12 | 2 | 7 | 10¹ | 11 | 13 | 1 |  |  |  |  |  |  |  |  |  |  |  |  | 13 |
|  | 4 | 3⁴ | 12 | 2 | 6 | 13 | 8¹ |  |  | 11 |  |  |  | 14 |  | 5 | 7 | 10³ | 9² |  | 1 |  |  |  |  |  |  |  |  |  |  |  |  | 14 |
|  | 4 | 3 |  | 5 | 6 |  | 12 | 9¹ | 8 |  |  |  |  | 13 |  | 2 | 7³ | 11 | 10² | 14 | 1 |  |  |  |  |  |  |  |  |  |  |  |  | 15 |
|  | 4² | 3 |  | 5 | 6³ |  | 8 | 13 | 9 |  |  |  |  |  | 12 | 2 | 7 | 10 | 11 | 14 | 1 |  |  |  |  |  |  |  |  |  |  |  |  | 16 |
|  | 4 | 3 |  | 5 | 6² | 7³ | 8¹ | 9 |  |  |  |  | 14 |  | 12 | 2 |  | 10 | 11 | 13 | 1 |  |  |  |  |  |  |  |  |  |  |  |  | 17 |
|  | 4 | 3 |  |  | 6² | 7 | 12 | 9¹ |  |  |  |  | 14 | 13 |  | 2 | 5 | 8³ | 10 | 11 | 1 |  |  |  |  |  |  |  |  |  |  |  |  | 18 |
|  | 3 | 4 |  | 9 | 6 |  | 8 |  |  |  |  |  |  | 11 | 5 | 2 | 7 | 10 |  |  | 1 |  |  |  |  |  |  |  |  |  |  |  |  | 19 |
|  | 4 | 3 |  |  | 6² | 7 |  | 9³ |  |  |  |  |  | 13 | 12 | 2 | 5 | 8¹ | 10 | 11 | 1 | 14 |  |  |  |  |  |  |  |  |  |  |  | 20 |
| 1 | 12 | 3 |  | 5 | 6³ |  | 8 | 9² |  |  |  |  | 14 | 13 |  | 2¹ | 4 | 7 | 10 | 11 |  |  |  |  |  |  |  |  |  |  |  |  |  | 21 |
| 1 | 3¹ | 4 |  | 5 | 6 |  | 8 | 9³ |  |  |  |  | 14 | 13 | 12 | 2 | 7² | 11 | 10 |  |  |  |  |  |  |  |  |  |  |  |  |  |  | 22 |
|  | 2 | 4 |  | 5 | 9 | 7 | 12 | 6¹ |  |  |  |  |  | 13 | 10 | 3 | 8² | 11 |  |  | 1 |  |  |  |  |  |  |  |  |  |  |  |  | 23 |
|  | 4 | 3 |  | 5 | 6 |  | 8 | 9¹ | 12 |  |  |  |  |  | 10 | 2 | 4 | 7 | 11 |  | 1 |  |  |  |  |  |  |  |  |  |  |  |  | 24 |
|  |  | 3 |  | 5 | 6³ |  | 8 | 9¹ | 12 |  |  | 13 |  |  | 10 | 2² | 4 | 7 | 11 |  | 1 |  |  |  | 14 |  |  |  |  |  |  |  |  | 25 |
|  | 4 | 3 |  | 5 | 6² |  | 8 | 9¹ | 12 |  |  |  |  | 13 | 10 | 2 | 7* |  | 11 |  | 1 |  |  |  |  |  |  |  |  |  |  |  |  | 26 |
|  | 5² | 4 | 3 |  | 6 |  | 8¹ | 9 |  | 12 |  |  | 14 |  |  | 2 | 7³ | 11 | 10 | 13 | 1 |  |  |  |  |  |  |  |  |  |  |  |  | 27 |
|  | 3 | 4 |  | 5 | 6³ | 7 |  | 9¹ |  | 12 |  |  | 14 |  | 10 | 2 |  | 11 |  | 13 | 1 |  |  |  |  |  | 8² |  |  |  |  |  |  | 28 |
|  | 4 | 3 |  | 5 | 12 | 7¹ |  | 9 |  |  |  |  | 14 | 13 | 10² | 2 | 8 | 11 | 6³ |  | 1 |  |  |  |  |  |  |  |  |  |  |  |  | 29 |
|  | 3 | 4 |  | 5 | 6² |  |  |  |  |  |  |  |  | 14 | 8¹ | 2³ | 7 | 9 | 13 |  | 1 |  |  |  |  | 10 | 11 | 12 |  |  |  |  |  | 30 |
|  | 14 | 3 | 4 | 5 | 6¹ |  |  |  |  |  |  |  |  |  | 12 | 2³ | 8 | 9 | 13 |  | 1 |  |  |  |  |  | 11 | 10 | 7² |  |  |  |  | 31 |
| 1 | 4² | 3 |  | 5 | 6 | 7 | 8 | 9¹ |  | 11 |  |  |  | 13 | 12³ | 2 |  |  |  | 14 |  |  |  |  | 10 |  |  |  |  |  |  |  |  | 32 |
|  | 14 | 4 | 3⁵ | 5 | 6 | 7 |  |  |  |  |  |  |  | 13 | 12 | 2 | 8 |  |  |  | 1 |  |  |  |  |  | 10¹ | 11² | 9 |  |  |  |  | 33 |
| 1 | 4 | 3 |  | 5 | 6 |  | 8 | 9 |  |  |  |  |  | 11 | 2² |  | 7¹ | 10 |  |  |  |  |  |  |  |  | 13 | 12 |  |  |  |  |  | 34 |
|  | 3 | 4 |  | 5 | 6 |  |  |  |  | 12 |  |  |  | 14 | 10¹ | 2 | 7³ | 8 |  |  | 1 |  | 13 |  |  |  | 11 | 9² |  |  |  |  |  | 35 |
|  | 3 | 4 |  | 5 | 6¹ |  |  |  |  |  |  | 13 | 14 |  |  | 2 | 7 | 8 |  |  | 1 |  |  |  |  | 12 | 10³ | 11 | 9² |  |  |  |  | 36 |
|  | 3 | 4 |  | 5 | 8¹ |  |  |  | 10² |  |  |  |  |  |  | 2 | 6 | 9 |  |  | 1 |  |  |  |  | 12 | 14 | 11³ | 13 | 7 |  |  |  | 37 |
|  | 3 | 4 |  | 5 | 8¹ |  |  |  | 12 |  |  |  | 14 |  | 10² | 2 | 6 | 9 |  |  | 1 |  |  |  |  |  | 13 | 11³ |  | 7 |  |  |  | 38 |
|  | 4 | 3 |  | 5 | 8 |  |  |  |  |  |  |  |  |  | 10 | 2² | 6 | 9 |  |  | 1 |  |  |  |  |  | 11 | 12 | 7 | 13 |  |  |  | 39 |
|  | 3 | 4 |  | 5 |  |  |  |  |  |  |  |  |  | 13 | 10² | 2³ | 6 | 9 |  |  | 1 |  |  |  |  | 12 | 14 | 11¹ | 7 | 8 |  |  |  | 40 |
|  | 4¹ | 3 | 12 | 5 | 6 |  |  |  |  |  |  |  |  | 14 | 9 |  | 7 | 8 |  |  | 1 |  |  |  |  |  | 13 | 11² | 10 | 2³ |  |  |  | 41 |
|  | 3 | 4 |  | 5 | 6 |  |  | 9³ |  |  |  |  |  | 11¹ | 13 | 2 |  |  |  |  | 1 |  |  |  |  | 12 | 8 | 10² | 7 | 14 |  |  |  | 42 |
|  | 4 |  |  | 5 | 6² |  |  | 9 |  |  |  |  |  |  | 10¹ | 2 |  |  |  |  | 1 |  |  |  |  | 12 | 8 | 11 | 7 | 13 | 3 |  |  | 43 |
|  |  | 3 |  | 5 | 6 |  |  | 9 |  |  |  |  |  |  | 10² | 2 |  |  |  | 13 | 1 |  |  |  |  | 12 | 8 | 11¹ | 7 |  |  | 4 |  | 44 |
| 1 | 2 | 3 |  | 5¹ | 6 |  |  | 9 |  | 12 |  |  | 8² |  |  |  |  | 10 |  |  |  |  |  |  |  |  | 11 |  | 13 | 7³ |  | 4 | 14 | 45 |
|  |  | 3 |  | 5 | 6 |  |  |  |  | 12 |  |  | 9¹ |  | 10 | 2³ |  | 8 |  |  | 1 |  |  |  |  |  |  | 11² | 7 | 13 |  | 4 | 14 | 46 |

**FA Cup**

|  |  | |  |
|---|---|---|---|
| First Round | Kidderminster H | (a) | 2-0 |
| Second Round | Doncaster R | (h) | 3-1 |
| Third Round | Nottingham F | (a) | 3-2 |
| Fourth Round | Liverpool | (h) | 3-2 |
| Fifth Round | Everton | (h) | 2-2 |
| *Replay* | Everton | (a) | 1-3 |

**Capital One Cup**

|  |  | |  |
|---|---|---|---|
| First Round | Sheffield W | (h) | 2-4 |

**Johnstone's Paint Trophy**

|  |  | |  |
|---|---|---|---|
| First Round | Chesterfield | (a) | 1-2 |

# OXFORD UNITED

## FOUNDATION

There had been an Oxford United club around the time of World War I but only in the Oxfordshire Thursday League and there is no connection with the modern club which began as Headington in 1893, adding 'United' a year later. Playing first on Quarry Fields and subsequently Wootten's Fields, they owe much to a Dr Hitchings for their early development.

*The Kassam Stadium, Grenoble Road, Oxford OX4 4XP.*

*Telephone:* (01865) 337 500.

*Fax:* (01865) 337 501.

*Ticket Office:* (01865) 337 533.

*Website:* www.oufc.co.uk

*Email:* admin@oufc.co.uk

*Ground Capacity:* 12,500.

*Record Attendance:* 22,730 v Preston NE, FA Cup 6th rd, 29 February 1964 (at Manor Ground); 12,243 v Leyton Orient, FL 2, 6 May 2006 (at The Kassam Stadium).

*Pitch Measurements:* 102m × 71m (112yd × 78yd)

*Executive Chairman:* Ian Lenagan.

*Manager:* Chris Wilder.

*Assistant Manager:* Mickey Lewis.

*Physio:* Andy Lord.

*Colours:* Yellow shirts, yellow shorts, yellow socks.

*Year Formed:* 1893.

*Turned Professional:* 1949.

*Previous Names:* 1893, Headington; 1894, Headington United; 1960, Oxford United.

*Club Nickname:* 'The U's'.

*Grounds:* 1893, Headington Quarry; 1894, Wootten's Fields; 1898, Sandy Lane Ground; 1902, Britannia Field; 1909, Sandy Lane; 1910, Quarry Recreation Ground; 1914, Sandy Lane; 1922, The Paddock Manor Road; 1925, Manor Ground; 2001, The Kassam Stadium.

*First Football League Game:* 18 August 1962, Division 4, v Barrow (a) L 2–3 – Medlock; Beavon, Quartermain; Ron Atkinson, Kyle, Jones; Knight, Graham Atkinson (1), Houghton (1), Cornwell, Colfar.

*Record League Victory:* 7–0 v Barrow, Division 4, 19 December 1964 – Fearnley; Beavon, Quartermain; Ron Atkinson (1), Kyle, Jones; Morris, Booth (3), Willey (1), Graham Atkinson (1), Harrington (1).

*Record Cup Victory:* 9–1 v Dorchester T, FA Cup 1st rd, 11 November 1995 – Whitehead; Wood (2), Mike Ford (1), Smith, Elliott, Gilchrist, Rush (1), Massey (Murphy), Moody (3), Bobby Ford (1), Angel (Beauchamp (1)).

## HONOURS

**Football League – Division 1:** Best season: 12th, 1997–98; **Division 2:** *Champions* 1984–85; *Runners-up* 1995–96; **Division 3:** *Champions* 1967–68, 1983–84.

**FA Cup:** Best season: 6th rd, 1964 (shared record for 4th Division club).

**Football League Cup:** *Winners* 1986.

## sky SPORTS FACT FILE

Scots-born Eddie McIlvenney who captained the USA team that defeated England in the 1950 World Cup finished his playing career with Oxford United in their Southern League days. Eddie made regular appearances in the second half of the 1957–58 season and in the opening months of the following campaign.

*Record Defeat:* 0–7 v Sunderland, Division 1, 19 September 1998.

*Most League Points (2 for a win):* 61, Division 4, 1964–65.

*Most League Points (3 for a win):* 95, Division 3, 1983–84.

*Most League Goals:* 91, Division 3, 1983–84.

*Highest League Scorer in Season:* John Aldridge, 30, Division 2, 1984–85.

*Most League Goals in Total Aggregate:* Graham Atkinson, 77, 1962–73.

*Most League Goals in One Match:* 4, Tony Jones v Newport Co, Division 4, 22 September 1962; 4, Arthur Longbottom v Darlington, Division 4, 26 October 1963; 4, Richard Hill v Walsall, Division 2, 26 December 1988; 4, John Durnin v Luton T, 14 November 1992; 4, Tom Craddock v Accrington S, FL 2, 20 October 2011.

*Most Capped Player:* Jim Magilton, 18 (52), Northern Ireland.

*Most League Appearances:* John Shuker, 478, 1962–77.

*Youngest League Player:* Jason Seacole, 16 years 149 days v Mansfield T, 7 September 1976.

*Record Transfer Fee Received:* £1,600,000 from Leicester C for Matt Elliott, January 1997.

*Record Transfer Fee Paid:* £475,000 to Aberdeen for Dean Windass, August 1998.

*Football League Record:* 1962 Elected to Division 4; 1965–68 Division 3; 1968–76 Division 2; 1976–84 Division 3; 1984–85 Division 2; 1985–88 Division 1; 1988–92 Division 2; 1992–94 Division 1; 1994–96 Division 2; 1996–99 Division 1; 1999–2001 Division 2; 2001–04 Division 3; 2004–06 FL 2; 2006–10 Conference; 2010– FL 2.

## MANAGERS

**Harry Thompson** 1949–58
*(Player-Manager)* 1949-51
**Arthur Turner** 1959–69
*(continued as General Manager to 1972)*
**Ron Saunders** 1969
**Gerry Summers** 1969–75
**Mick Brown** 1975–79
**Bill Asprey** 1979–80
**Ian Greaves** 1980–82
**Jim Smith** 1982–85
**Maurice Evans** 1985–88
**Mark Lawrenson** 1988
**Brian Horton** 1988–93
**Denis Smith** 1993–97
**Malcolm Crosby** 1997–98
**Malcolm Shotton** 1998–99
**Micky Lewis** 1999–2000
**Denis Smith** 2000
**David Kemp** 2000–01
**Mark Wright** 2001
**Ian Atkins** 2001–04
**Graham Rix** 2004
**Ramon Diaz** 2004–05
**Brian Talbot** 2005–06
**Darren Patterson** 2006
**Jim Smith** 2006–07
**Darren Patterson** 2007–08
**Chris Wilder** December 2008–

## LATEST SEQUENCES

*Longest Sequence of League Wins:* 6, 6.4.1985 – 24.4.1985.

*Longest Sequence of League Defeats:* 7, 4.5.1991 – 7.9.1991.

*Longest Sequence of League Draws:* 5, 7.10.1978 – 28.10.1978.

*Longest Sequence of Unbeaten League Matches:* 20, 17.3.1984 – 29.9.1984.

*Longest Sequence Without a League Win:* 27, 14.11.1987 – 27.8.1988.

*Successive Scoring Runs:* 17 from 10.9.1983.

*Successive Non-scoring Runs:* 6 from 26.3.1988.

## TEN YEAR LEAGUE RECORD

| | | P | W | D | L | F | A | Pts | Pos |
|---|---|---|---|---|---|---|---|---|---|
| 2003-04 | Div 3 | 46 | 18 | 17 | 11 | 55 | 44 | 71 | 9 |
| 2004-05 | FL 2 | 46 | 16 | 11 | 19 | 50 | 63 | 59 | 15 |
| 2005-06 | FL 2 | 46 | 11 | 16 | 19 | 43 | 57 | 49 | 23 |
| 2006-07 | Conf | 46 | 22 | 15 | 9 | 66 | 33 | 81 | 2 |
| 2007-08 | BSP | 46 | 20 | 11 | 15 | 56 | 48 | 71 | 9 |
| 2008-09 | BSP | 46 | 24 | 10 | 12 | 72 | 51 | 77* | 7 |
| 2009-10 | BSP | 44 | 25 | 11 | 8 | 64 | 31 | 86 | 3 |
| 2010-11 | FL 2 | 46 | 17 | 12 | 17 | 58 | 60 | 63 | 12 |
| 2011-12 | FL 2 | 46 | 17 | 17 | 12 | 59 | 48 | 68 | 9 |
| 2012-13 | FL 2 | 46 | 19 | 8 | 19 | 60 | 61 | 65 | 9 |

*5 pts deducted.

## DID YOU KNOW **?**

On 15 October 1969, Oxford United won for the first time on the ground of a First Division team. Nottingham Forest provided the venue in a League Cup tie which was decided in the 71st minute when Ken Skeen first headed, then followed up by successfully hitting in the rebound.

## OXFORD UNITED – FOOTBALL LEAGUE TWO 2012–13 LEAGUE RECORD

| Match No. | Date | Venue | Opponents | Result | | H/T Score | Lg Pos. | Goalscorers | Attendance |
|---|---|---|---|---|---|---|---|---|---|
| 1 | Aug 18 | A | Bristol R | W | 2-0 | 2-0 | 8 | Forster-Caskey [22], Potter [32] | 7451 |
| 2 | 21 | H | Southend U | W | 2-0 | 0-0 | 1 | Craddock 2 [54, 87] | 6001 |
| 3 | 25 | A | Plymouth Arg | W | 2-1 | 2-0 | 1 | Smalley 2 [20, 23] | 6906 |
| 4 | Sept 1 | A | York C | L | 1-3 | 1-2 | 3 | McLaughlin (og) [23] | 4015 |
| 5 | 8 | H | Exeter C | L | 2-4 | 0-2 | 6 | Forster-Caskey (pen) [55], Potter [63] | 6405 |
| 6 | 15 | A | Burton Alb | L | 0-4 | 0-2 | 11 | | 2389 |
| 7 | 18 | A | Cheltenham T | L | 1-2 | 0-1 | 16 | Leven (pen) [80] | 3037 |
| 8 | 22 | H | Bradford C | L | 0-2 | 0-0 | 17 | | 6032 |
| 9 | 29 | A | Rotherham U | L | 1-3 | 1-1 | 17 | Rigg [8] | 7258 |
| 10 | Oct 2 | H | AFC Wimbledon | W | 3-2 | 1-2 | 16 | Forster-Caskey [9], Smalley [55], Potter [81] | 5206 |
| 11 | 6 | H | Gillingham | D | 0-0 | 0-0 | 16 | | 6690 |
| 12 | 15 | A | Port Vale | L | 0-3 | 0-1 | 19 | | 4596 |
| 13 | 20 | H | Accrington S | W | 5-0 | 3-0 | 18 | Craddock 4 [12, 23, 36, 71], Potter [78] | 5403 |
| 14 | 23 | A | Rochdale | L | 0-2 | 0-0 | 18 | | 1619 |
| 15 | 27 | A | Wycombe W | W | 3-1 | 1-0 | 15 | Constable [4], Craddock [46], Mullins [62] | 5498 |
| 16 | Nov 6 | H | Dagenham & R | L | 2-3 | 0-1 | 18 | Craddock 2 [60, 65] | 5074 |
| 17 | 10 | H | Torquay U | D | 0-0 | 0-0 | 17 | | 5773 |
| 18 | 17 | A | Chesterfield | L | 1-2 | 1-1 | 18 | Mullins [2] | 5433 |
| 19 | 20 | A | Barnet | D | 2-2 | 1-1 | 18 | Rigg [6], Whing [46] | 1626 |
| 20 | 24 | H | Northampton T | W | 2-1 | 1-0 | 18 | Constable [15], Pittman [79] | 6635 |
| 21 | Dec 8 | A | Aldershot T | D | 1-1 | 1-0 | 18 | Chapman [33] | 5721 |
| 22 | 15 | A | Morecambe | D | 1-1 | 0-0 | 18 | Worley [88] | 1385 |
| 23 | 26 | A | Exeter C | W | 3-1 | 1-0 | 16 | Constable 2 [18, 50], Leven [52] | 4437 |
| 24 | 29 | A | AFC Wimbledon | W | 3-0 | 2-0 | 14 | Rigg [32], Potter [37], Craddock [64] | 4401 |
| 25 | Jan 1 | H | Cheltenham T | W | 1-0 | 1-0 | 13 | Leven (pen) [10] | 6951 |
| 26 | 12 | A | Bradford C | W | 2-1 | 1-1 | 12 | Rigg [18], Leven (pen) [90] | 10,087 |
| 27 | 26 | A | Fleetwood T | L | 0-3 | 0-1 | 12 | | 2461 |
| 28 | 29 | H | Burton Alb | D | 1-1 | 0-0 | 12 | Constable [50] | 4906 |
| 29 | Feb 2 | A | Southend U | L | 0-1 | 0-0 | 13 | | 5596 |
| 30 | 9 | H | Bristol R | L | 0-2 | 0-0 | 15 | | 7608 |
| 31 | 12 | H | Fleetwood T | L | 1-2 | 0-1 | 15 | Davis [89] | 5003 |
| 32 | 16 | A | Plymouth Arg | W | 1-0 | 1-0 | 13 | Constable [16] | 7189 |
| 33 | 23 | H | York C | D | 0-0 | 0-0 | 13 | | 5808 |
| 34 | 26 | A | Gillingham | W | 1-0 | 0-0 | 11 | Potter [84] | 4928 |
| 35 | Mar 2 | H | Port Vale | W | 2-1 | 1-1 | 11 | Potter [10], Smalley [76] | 6322 |
| 36 | 5 | H | Rotherham U | L | 0-4 | 0-4 | 12 | | 5169 |
| 37 | 9 | A | Torquay U | W | 3-1 | 0-0 | 10 | Constable [50], Batt (pen) [54], Heslop [90] | 2504 |
| 38 | 12 | H | Barnet | W | 1-0 | 0-0 | 9 | Raynes [90] | 5027 |
| 39 | 16 | H | Chesterfield | L | 0-1 | 0-1 | 10 | | 6003 |
| 40 | 23 | A | Northampton T | L | 0-1 | 0-1 | 10 | | 6151 |
| 41 | 29 | H | Morecambe | D | 1-1 | 0-0 | 10 | Potter [60] | 5523 |
| 42 | Apr 1 | A | Aldershot T | L | 2-3 | 0-1 | 12 | Davies [66], Pittman [85] | 2927 |
| 43 | 6 | A | Wycombe W | L | 0-1 | 0-1 | 13 | | 6777 |
| 44 | 13 | A | Dagenham & R | W | 1-0 | 1-0 | 11 | Potter [40] | 1788 |
| 45 | 20 | H | Rochdale | W | 3-0 | 0-0 | 10 | Whing [53], Constable [76], Potter [90] | 6014 |
| 46 | 27 | A | Accrington S | W | 3-0 | 0-0 | 9 | Constable [64], Smalley (pen) [67], Rigg [90] | 2028 |

**Final League Position: 9**

### GOALSCORERS

*League (60):* Craddock 10, Potter 10, Constable 9, Rigg 5, Smalley 5 (1 pen), Leven 4 (3 pens), Forster-Caskey 3 (1 pen), Mullins 2, Pittman 2, Whing 2, Batt 1 (1 pen), Chapman 1, Davies 1, Davis 1, Heslop 1, Raynes 1, Worley 1, own goal 1.
*FA Cup (7):* Constable 3, Leven 1, Pittman 1, Raynes 1, Rigg 1.
*Capital One Cup (0).*
*Johnstone's Paint Trophy (9):* Constable 2, Craddock 2, Leven 1 (1 pen), Marsh 1, Potter 1, Rigg 1, Worley 1.

| Clarke R 23+1 | Batt D 37 | Raynes M 36+2 | Wright J 42 | Capaldi T 24+5 | Chapman A 22+4 | Forster-Caskey J 13+3 | Cox L 14 | Rigg S 41+3 | Potter A 39+4 | Constable J 29+10 | Heslop S 14+10 | Smalley D 16+11 | Craddock T 22+10 | Evans A —+1 | Pitman J 2+13 | Boateng D 1+1 | Marsh T —+2 | Leven P 16+4 | O'Brien L 11+4 | Brown W 4 | Worley H 2+7 | Mullins J 8 | Whing A 19+3 | Davis L 19+4 | Parker J 5+10 | Duberry M 9+2 | Montrose L 5 | Richards J 4 | Crocombe M 4 | McCormick L 15 | Davies S 10+2 | Long S —+1 | Match No. |
|---|---|---|---|---|---|---|---|---|---|---|---|---|---|---|---|---|---|---|---|---|---|---|---|---|---|---|---|---|---|---|---|---|---|
| 1 | 2 | 3 | 4 | 5 | 6¹ | 7 | 8 | 9 | 10³ | 11² | 12 | 13 | 14 | | | | | | | | | | | | | | | | | | | | 1 |
| 1 | 2 | 4 | 3 | 5 | 7 | 8 | 6¹ | 11 | 9² | 10 | 12 | 13 | | | | | | | | | | | | | | | | | | | | | 2 |
| 1 | 2 | 3 | 4 | 5 | 7 | 8² | | 9 | 6 | 13 | 12 | 10¹ | 11³ | | | | | | | | | | | | | | | | | | | | 3 |
| 1 | 2 | 3 | 4 | 5 | 7 | 8 | | 11³ | 10 | 13 | 6¹ | 9² | 12 | 14 | | | | | | | | | | | | | | | | | | | 4 |
| 1 | 2 | 3 | 4 | 5 | 7 | 8 | | 11² | 9 | 14³ | 6¹ | 10³ | 12 | 13 | | | | | | | | | | | | | | | | | | | 5 |
| 1 | 2 | 3 | 4 | 5 | 9 | 10¹ | 7 | 8 | 11³ | 12 | | 13 | 6² | 14 | | | | | | | | | | | | | | | | | | | 6 |
| 1 | 2 | 3 | 4 | 5 | 8 | 7 | | 12 | 14 | 6² | 10 | 9³ | 11¹ | 13 | | | | | | | | | | | | | | | | | | | 7 |
| 1 | 2 | 3 | 4 | 8 | | 7 | | 12 | 9 | 10 | 6² | 11 | | | 13 | | | | 5¹ | | | | | | | | | | | | | | 8 |
| | 5 | 2 | 3 | 8 | 6³ | 7 | | 11 | 10 | 14 | | 12 | 9¹ | | | | | 13 | | 1 | 4² | | | | | | | | | | | | 9 |
| 14 | 2 | 3¹ | 4 | | 8 | 7² | 9 | 6 | | 13 | 10 | 11 | | | | | | 5 | 13 | 12 | | | | | | | | | | | | | 10 |
| 1 | 2¹ | | 4 | | 6 | 8 | | 11 | 9³ | 14 | 7 | 10² | 13 | | 12 | | | 5 | | | 3 | | | | | | | | | | | | 11 |
| 1 | | | 3 | 12 | 6 | 8 | | 9 | 13 | 11 | 7² | 10³ | | | | | | 5¹ | | | 2 | 4 | 14 | | | | | | | | | | 12 |
| | 4 | | | 5¹ | 14 | 8² | 7 | 9 | 6 | 11 | | 10 | | | | | | 13 | 12 | | | 3 | 2³ | | | | | | | | | | 13 |
| 1 | | 3 | | 5 | | 7² | | 9 | 6¹ | 10 | 12 | | 11 | | 13 | | | 8 | | | | 4 | 2 | | | | | | | | | | 14 |
| 1 | | 3 | 5 | 8 | 12 | | | 9¹ | 6 | 10 | | | 11² | 13 | | | | 7³ | | | 14 | 4 | 2 | | | | | | | | | | 15 |
| 1 | | 3 | 4 | 5² | 7 | | | 8¹ | 6 | 8 | 9 | 10 | 11 | | 12 | | | 9 | | | | 2³ | 13 | | | | | | | | | | 16 |
| 1 | | 3 | | 13 | | | | 8 | 9 | 10 | 6² | | 11¹ | | 12 | | | 7 | | | | 4 | 2 | 5 | | | | | | | | | 17 |
| 1 | | | 4 | 5 | 14 | | 9¹ | 7 | 12 | 10³ | 11 | 6² | | | 13 | | | 8 | | | | 3 | 2 | | | | | | | | | | 18 |
| 1 | | | 4 | 5 | 7 | | | 9 | 10 | 11 | 6¹ | | | | 12 | | | 8 | | | | 3 | 2 | | | | | | | | | | 19 |
| 1 | | 3 | 4 | 5 | | 6¹ | 7 | 9² | 11 | 10 | | | | | 12 | | | 8 | | | | 13 | 2 | | | | | | | | | | 20 |
| 1 | 2 | 3 | 4 | 5 | 7 | | | 10 | 6² | 11 | 13⁸ | | 12 | | | | | 8 | | | | | 9¹ | | | | | | | | | | 21 |
| 1 | 2 | 3 | 4 | 5² | 7 | 14 | | 9¹ | 6 | 11 | | 10³ | | | | | | 8 | | | | 13 | | 12 | | | | | | | | | 22 |
| 1 | 2 | 3 | 4 | 12 | | 14 | 7 | 9 | 6 | 10 | | 11² | | | | | | 8³ | | | | | 5¹ | 13 | | | | | | | | | 23 |
| 1 | 2 | 3 | 4 | | | 7 | | 9² | 6³ | 10² | 12 | | 11¹ | | | | | 8 | 5 | | | | | 13 | 14 | | | | | | | | 24 |
| 1 | 2 | | 4 | 13 | | 7 | | 9² | 6³ | 10 | | | 11¹ | | | | | 8 | 5 | | 14 | | | 12 | 3 | | | | | | | | 25 |
| | 6 | 2 | 4 | | | | | 9 | 5 | | | | | | 11 | 1 | | | 7 | | | | | | 3 | 8 | 10 | | | | | | 26 |
| | 5 | 3¹ | 4 | 8 | 12 | | | 11 | 9 | | 6² | 14 | 13 | | 7 | 1 | | | | | | | | 2 | | 10³ | | | | | | | 27 |
| | 2 | 12 | 4 | 13 | 7 | | | 9 | 6 | 10 | | 14 | 11³ | | 8² | 5 | | | | | | | | | 3¹ | | | 1 | | | | | 28 |
| | 2 | 3 | 4 | | 7 | | | 9¹ | 6 | 10 | | | 13 | | 8 | 5² | | | | | | | | | | | | 1 | | | | | 29 |
| | 2 | 4³ | 3 | 8² | 6 | | | 9 | 12 | 10 | | | | | | | | 14 | | | | | 5 | 13 | | 7 | 11¹ | 1 | | | | | 30 |
| | 2 | 3 | 4 | | 7 | | | 9 | 6 | 11 | | | 10¹ | | | | | | | | | | 5 | 12 | | 8 | | 1 | | | | | 31 |
| | 2 | 3 | 4 | | 7³ | | | 9¹ | | 11 | | 12 | 10² | | 13 | | | | | | | | 14 | 5 | 6 | 8 | | 1 | | | | | 32 |
| | 2 | 4 | 3 | | 7 | | | 9² | 12 | 10 | | 13 | 11¹ | | | | | | | | | | | 5 | 6 | 8 | | 1 | | | | | 33 |
| | 2 | 3 | 4 | 6 | 8 | | | 10 | 7 | 12 | | 9² | 11¹ | | | | | | | | | | 5 | 13 | | | | 1 | | | | | 34 |
| | 2 | 3 | 4 | 8 | 7¹ | | | 9 | 6³ | 13 | | | 10 | | | | | | | | | | 12 | 5 | 11² | | | 1 | | | 14 | | 35 |
| | 5 | 2 | 4 | 14 | | | | 11 | 9 | | | 6¹ | 10 | | | | | | | | | | 7³ | 8 | 13 | 3² | | 1 | | | 12 | | 36 |
| | 2 | 3 | 4 | 9² | | | | 8¹ | 11 | 10 | 14 | 13 | | | | | | 5 | | | | | 6 | | 12³ | | | 1 | | | 7 | | 37 |
| | 2 | 3 | 4 | | | | | 9³ | 11 | 10 | | 12 | 14 | | | | | 5² | | | | | 7 | 13 | 6¹ | | | 1 | | | 8 | | 38 |
| | 2 | 3¹ | 4 | | | | | 9¹ | 6 | 10 | | 11² | 12 | | | | | | | | | | 14 | 8 | 5 | 13 | | 1 | | | 7 | | 39 |
| | 2 | 3 | 4 | | | | | 9¹ | 6 | 10 | | 12 | 11 | | | | | | | | | | | 7 | 5 | | | 1 | | | 8 | | 40 |
| | 2 | 3 | 4 | | | | | 9 | 6 | 10 | | | 11¹ | | | | | | | | | | | 8 | 5 | 12 | | 1 | | | 7 | | 41 |
| | 2 | 3⁴ | 4 | | | | | 8³ | 10 | 13 | 7¹ | 11 | 11 | 14 | 12² | | | | | | | | 9 | 5 | | | 1 | | | 6 | | 42 |
| | 2 | | 4 | | | | | 6 | 10² | 12 | 11 | 11 | 9 | | | | | 7 | 5 | 13 | 3 | | | | 1 | | | 8 | | | | | 43 |
| | 2 | 14 | 4 | | | | | 13 | 10 | 12 | 11³ | | | | | | | 5² | | | 8 | 9 | 6¹ | 3 | | 1 | | | 7 | | | | 44 |
| | 2 | 4 | | 9¹ | | | | 10 | 6 | 12 | | 11³ | | 14 | | | | 13 | | | 7 | 5² | 3 | | 1 | | | 8 | | | | | 45 |
| | 2¹ | 4 | | | | | | 9 | 6 | 10³ | 12 | 11² | | | 13 | | | | | | | 7 | 5 | | | | 1 | | | 8 | 14 | | 46 |

**FA Cup**

| First Round | Barnet | (a) | 2-0 |
|---|---|---|---|
| Second Round | Accrington S | (a) | 3-3 |
| *Replay* | Accrington S | (h) | 2-0 |
| Third Round | Sheffield U | (h) | 0-3 |

**Capital One Cup**

| First Round | Bournemouth | (h) | 0-0 |
|---|---|---|---|
| Second Round | Leeds U | (a) | 0-3 |

*(aet; won 5-3 on pens)*

**Johnstone's Paint Trophy**

| First Round | Swindon T | (h) | 1-0 |
|---|---|---|---|
| Second Round | Cheltenham T | (a) | 4-2 |
| Southern Quarter-Finals | Plymouth Arg | (a) | 1-1 |

*(aet; won 3-1 on pens)*

| Southern Semi-Finals | Southend U | (h) | 3-3 |
|---|---|---|---|

*(aet; lost 3-5 on pens)*

# PETERBOROUGH UNITED

## FOUNDATION

The old Peterborough & Fletton club, founded in 1923, was suspended by the FA during season 1932–33 and disbanded. Local enthusiasts determined to carry on and in 1934 a new professional club, Peterborough United, was formed and entered the Midland League the following year. Peterborough's first success came in 1939–40, but from 1955–56 to 1959–60 they won five successive titles. During the 1958–59 season they were undefeated in the Midland League. They reached the third round of the FA Cup, won the Northamptonshire Senior Cup, the Maunsell Cup and were runners-up in the East Anglian Cup.

*London Road Stadium, London Road, Peterborough PE2 8AL.*

*Telephone:* (01733) 563 947. *Fax:* (01733) 344 140.

*Ticket Office:* (0844) 847 1934.

*Website:* www.theposh.com

*Email:* info@theposh.com

*Ground Capacity:* 11,494.

*Record Attendance:* 30,096 v Swansea T, FA Cup 5th rd, 20 February 1965.

*Pitch Measurements:* 102m × 69m (112yd × 76yd)

*Chairman:* Darragh MacAnthony.

*Chief Executive:* Bob Symns.

*Manager:* Darren Ferguson.

*Assistant Manager:* Kevin Russell.

*Physio:* Chris Burton.

*Colours:* Blue shirts, white shorts, white socks with blue trim.

*Year Formed:* 1934.

*Turned Professional:* 1934.

*Club Nickname:* 'The Posh'.

*Ground:* 1934, London Road Stadium.

*First Football League Game:* 20 August 1960, Division 4, v Wrexham (h) W 3–0 – Walls; Stafford, Walker; Rayner, Rigby, Norris; Hails, Emery (1), Bly (1), Smith, McNamee (1).

*Record League Victory:* 9–1 v Barnet (a) Division 3, 5 September 1998 – Griemink; Hooper (1), Drury (Farell), Gill, Bodley, Edwards, Davies, Payne, Grazioli (5), Quinn (2) (Rowe), Houghton (Etherington) (1).

*Record Cup Victory:* 9–1 v Rushden T, FA Cup 1st qual rd, 6 October 1945 – Hilliard; Bryan, Parrott, Warner, Hobbs, Woods, Polhill (1), Fairchild, Laxton (6), Tasker (1), Rodgers (1); 9–1 v Kingstonian, FA Cup 1st rd, 25 November 1992. Match ordered to be replayed by FA. Peterborough won replay 1–0.

## HONOURS

**Football League – Division 1:** Best season: 10th, 1992–93;

**Division 2:** 1991–92 (play-offs);

**FL 1:** *Runners-up* 2008–09;

**FL 2:** *Runners-up* 2007–08;

**Division 4:** *Champions* 1960–61, 1973–74.

**FA Cup:** Best season: 6th rd, 1965.

**Football League Cup:** Semi-final 1966.

## sky SPORTS FACT FILE

Dennis Emery holds the all-time record for goals scored for Peterborough United. He netted a total of 231 goals from 308 competitive appearances between 1954 and 1963. His tally includes 53 goals in 1957–58 and 51 in 1956–57, with Posh winning the Midland League title on both occasions.

*Record Defeat:* 1–8 v Northampton T, FA Cup 2nd rd (2nd replay), 18 December 1946.

*Most League Points (2 for a win):* 66, Division 4, 1960–61.

*Most League Points (3 for a win):* 92, FL 2, 2007–08.

*Most League Goals:* 134, Division 4, 1960–61.

*Highest League Scorer in Season:* Terry Bly, 52, Division 4, 1960–61.

*Most League Goals in Total Aggregate:* Jim Hall, 122, 1967–75.

*Most League Goals in One Match:* 5, Guiliano Grazioli v Barnet, Division 3, 5 September 1998.

*Most Capped Player:* Craig Morgan, 19 (23), Wales.

*Most League Appearances:* Tommy Robson, 482, 1968–81.

*Youngest League Player:* Matthew Etherington, 15 years 262 days v Brentford, 3 May 1997.

*Record Transfer Fee Received:* £3,200,000 from Norwich C for Ryan Bennett, July 2012.

*Record Transfer Fee Paid:* £1,100,000 to Crawley T for Tyrone Barnett, July 2012.

*Football League Record:* 1960 Elected to Division 4; 1961–68 Division 3, when they were demoted for financial irregularities; 1968–74 Division 4; 1974–79 Division 3; 1979–91 Division 4; 1991–92 Division 3; 1992–94 Division 1; 1994–97 Division 2; 1997–2000 Division 3; 2000–04 Division 2; 2004–05 FL 1; 2005–08 FL 2; 2008–09 FL 1; 2009–10 FL C; 2010–11 FL 1; 2011–13 FL C; 2013– FL 1.

## LATEST SEQUENCES

*Longest Sequence of League Wins:* 9, 1.2.1992 – 14.3.1992.

*Longest Sequence of League Defeats:* 8, 12.1.2008 – 12.4.2008.

*Longest Sequence of League Draws:* 8, 18.12.1971 – 12.2.1972.

*Longest Sequence of Unbeaten League Matches:* 17, 17.12.1960 – 8.4.1961.

*Longest Sequence Without a League Win:* 17, 23.9.1978 – 30.12.1978.

*Successive Scoring Runs:* 33 from 20.9.1960.

*Successive Non-scoring Runs:* 6 from 13.8.2002.

## MANAGERS

Jock Porter 1934–36
Fred Taylor 1936–37
Vic Poulter 1937–38
Sam Haden 1938–48
Jack Blood 1948–50
Bob Gurney 1950–52
Jack Fairbrother 1952–54
George Swindin 1954–58
Jimmy Hagan 1958–62
Jack Fairbrother 1962–64
Gordon Clark 1964–67
Norman Rigby 1967–69
Jim Iley 1969–72
Noel Cantwell 1972–77
John Barnwell 1977–78
Billy Hails 1978–79
Peter Morris 1979–82
Martin Wilkinson 1982–83
John Wile 1983–86
Noel Cantwell 1986–88 *(continued as General Manager)*
Mick Jones 1988–89
Mark Lawrenson 1989–90
Dave Booth 1990–91
Chris Turner 1991–92
Lil Fuccillo 1992–93
Chris Turner 1993–94
John Still 1994–95
Mick Halsall 1995–96
Barry Fry 1996–2005
Mark Wright 2005–06
Steve Bleasdale 2006
Keith Alexander 2006–07
Darren Ferguson 2007–09
Mark Cooper 2009–10
Jim Gannon 2010
Gary Johnson 2010–11
Darren Ferguson January 2011–

## TEN YEAR LEAGUE RECORD

|         |       | P  | W  | D  | L  | F   | A  | Pts | Pos |
|---------|-------|----|----|----|----|-----|----|-----|-----|
| 2003-04 | Div 2 | 46 | 12 | 16 | 18 | 58  | 58 | 52  | 18  |
| 2004-05 | FL 1  | 46 | 9  | 12 | 25 | 49  | 73 | 39  | 23  |
| 2005-06 | FL 2  | 46 | 17 | 11 | 18 | 57  | 49 | 62  | 9   |
| 2006-07 | FL 2  | 46 | 18 | 11 | 17 | 70  | 61 | 65  | 10  |
| 2007-08 | FL 2  | 46 | 28 | 8  | 10 | 84  | 43 | 92  | 2   |
| 2008-09 | FL 1  | 46 | 26 | 11 | 9  | 78  | 54 | 89  | 2   |
| 2009-10 | FL C  | 46 | 8  | 10 | 28 | 46  | 80 | 34  | 24  |
| 2010-11 | FL 1  | 46 | 23 | 10 | 13 | 106 | 75 | 79  | 4   |
| 2011-12 | FL C  | 46 | 13 | 11 | 22 | 67  | 77 | 50  | 18  |
| 2012-13 | FL C  | 46 | 15 | 9  | 22 | 66  | 75 | 54  | 22  |

## DID YOU KNOW

When Peterborough United played Lincoln City at London Road on Boxing Day 1978 the teams had a combined record of 33 games without a win. Posh lost 1-0 that day and it was not until 13 January that they finally achieved a victory, beating Chester 2-1 at home.

## PETERBOROUGH UNITED – FL CHAMPIONSHIP 2012–13 LEAGUE RECORD

| Match No. | Date | Venue | Opponents | Result | H/T Score | Lg Pos. | Goalscorers | Attendance |
|---|---|---|---|---|---|---|---|---|
| 1 | Aug 18 | A | Leicester C | L 0-2 | 0-0 | 24 | | 23,863 |
| 2 | 21 | H | Millwall | L 1-2 | 1-1 | 23 | Boyd [11] | 6188 |
| 3 | 25 | H | Leeds U | L 1-2 | 0-1 | 23 | Bostwick [73] | 10,432 |
| 4 | Sept 1 | A | Birmingham C | L 0-1 | 0-1 | 24 | | 14,929 |
| 5 | 15 | A | Burnley | L 2-5 | 2-2 | 24 | Tomlin (pen) [20], Mendez-Laing [23] | 10,979 |
| 6 | 18 | H | Bristol C | L 1-2 | 0-0 | 24 | Tomlin (pen) [90] | 5435 |
| 7 | 22 | H | Wolverhampton W | L 0-2 | 0-1 | 24 | | 9280 |
| 8 | 29 | H | Hull C | W 3-1 | 2-0 | 24 | Sinclair 3 [24, 29, 73] | 15,279 |
| 9 | Oct 2 | A | Barnsley | W 2-0 | 2-0 | 24 | Boyd [2], Barnett [10] | 8319 |
| 10 | 6 | H | Nottingham F | L 0-1 | 0-0 | 24 | | 10,469 |
| 11 | 20 | A | Watford | L 0-1 | 0-0 | 24 | | 15,950 |
| 12 | 23 | H | Huddersfield T | W 3-1 | 2-0 | 23 | Boyd 2 [16, 24], Ntlhe [48] | 6348 |
| 13 | 27 | H | Derby Co | W 3-0 | 1-0 | 21 | Bostwick [30], Berahino 2 [86, 90] | 8427 |
| 14 | Nov 3 | A | Sheffield W | L 1-2 | 0-0 | 22 | Boyd [79] | 22,406 |
| 15 | 6 | A | Brighton & HA | L 0-1 | 0-0 | 22 | | 23,703 |
| 16 | 10 | H | Crystal Palace | L 1-2 | 1-0 | 23 | McCann [6] | 9691 |
| 17 | 17 | H | Blackburn R | L 1-4 | 0-3 | 24 | Tomlin [88] | 5997 |
| 18 | 24 | A | Ipswich T | D 1-1 | 1-0 | 24 | Tomlin [8] | 16,427 |
| 19 | 27 | A | Charlton Ath | L 0-2 | 0-0 | 24 | | 17,377 |
| 20 | Dec 1 | H | Blackpool | L 1-4 | 0-0 | 24 | Gayle [71] | 5633 |
| 21 | 8 | H | Middlesbrough | L 2-3 | 1-2 | 24 | Gayle 2 [38, 52] | 6612 |
| 22 | 15 | A | Cardiff C | W 2-1 | 1-0 | 24 | Bostwick [22], Gayle [47] | 22,073 |
| 23 | 22 | H | Bolton W | W 5-4 | 2-1 | 24 | Tomlin [2], Gayle [6], Thorne [47], Little [69], Zakuani [83] | 6600 |
| 24 | 26 | A | Wolverhampton W | W 3-0 | 2-0 | 22 | Tomlin [17], Rowe [43], Gayle [69] | 23,033 |
| 25 | 29 | A | Bristol C | L 2-4 | 1-2 | 23 | McCann (pen) [19], Gayle [89] | 12,991 |
| 26 | Jan 1 | H | Barnsley | W 2-1 | 1-0 | 21 | Bostwick [28], Rowe [87] | 7339 |
| 27 | 12 | A | Nottingham F | L 1-2 | 0-1 | 22 | Wootton [60] | 22,777 |
| 28 | 19 | H | Hull C | D 1-1 | 0-1 | 22 | McCann (pen) [79] | 6214 |
| 29 | Feb 2 | H | Burnley | D 2-2 | 0-1 | 24 | Rowe 2 [65, 69] | 6648 |
| 30 | 9 | H | Leicester C | W 2-1 | 0-0 | 24 | Petrucci [74], McCann [88] | 11,070 |
| 31 | 19 | A | Millwall | W 5-1 | 2-1 | 23 | Tomlin 2 [7, 55], Rowe [32], Mendez-Laing [59], Boyd [88] | 8769 |
| 32 | 23 | H | Birmingham C | L 0-2 | 0-1 | 24 | | 8350 |
| 33 | 26 | A | Bolton W | L 0-1 | 0-1 | 24 | | 15,675 |
| 34 | Mar 2 | A | Blackburn R | W 3-2 | 3-0 | 22 | Gayle 3 [11, 14, 27] | 13,192 |
| 35 | 5 | H | Charlton Ath | D 2-2 | 1-0 | 23 | Swanson [24], Bostwick [71] | 6050 |
| 36 | 9 | H | Ipswich T | D 0-0 | 0-0 | 23 | | 9367 |
| 37 | 12 | A | Leeds U | D 1-1 | 1-0 | 22 | Gayle [15] | 24,240 |
| 38 | 16 | A | Blackpool | W 1-0 | 1-0 | 22 | Ferdinand [45] | 13,037 |
| 39 | 30 | H | Cardiff C | W 2-1 | 0-1 | 21 | McCann 2 (2 pens) [72, 79] | 9236 |
| 40 | Apr 2 | A | Middlesbrough | D 0-0 | 0-0 | 22 | | 13,683 |
| 41 | 6 | A | Huddersfield T | D 2-2 | 0-1 | 22 | Tomlin [50], Gayle [86] | 14,175 |
| 42 | 13 | H | Watford | W 3-2 | 1-0 | 21 | Swanson [29], Gayle [61], Tomlin [67] | 10,848 |
| 43 | 16 | H | Brighton & HA | D 0-0 | 0-0 | 20 | | 8780 |
| 44 | 20 | A | Derby Co | L 1-3 | 0-1 | 21 | McCann (pen) [64] | 23,753 |
| 45 | 27 | H | Sheffield W | W 1-0 | 0-0 | 21 | McCann [64] | 13,938 |
| 46 | May 4 | A | Crystal Palace | L 2-3 | 1-1 | 22 | Tomlin [28], Mendez-Laing [63] | 22,154 |

**Final League Position: 22**

### GOALSCORERS
*League (66):* Gayle 13, Tomlin 11 (2 pens), McCann 8 (5 pens), Boyd 6, Bostwick 5, Rowe 5, Mendez-Laing 3, Sinclair 3, Berahino 2, Swanson 2, Barnett 1, Ferdinand 1, Little 1, Ntlhe 1, Petrucci 1, Thorne 1, Wootton 1, Zakuani 1.
*FA Cup (0).*
*Capital One Cup (6):* Taylor 2, Tomlin 2, Boyd 1, Newell 1.

| Olejnik R 46 | Ntlhe K 9+3 | Brisley S 23+5 | Zakuani G 30+3 | Alcock C 23+4 | Tomlin L 39+3 | Bostwick M 39 | Newell J 21+9 | Frecklington L 4+1 | Taylor P 2+1 | Boyd G 30+1 | Sinclair E 5+7 | McCann G 28+12 | Little M 38+2 | Swanson D 10+17 | Barnett T 10+8 | Mendez-Laing N 13+8 | Ferdinand K 15+17 | Knight-Percival N 29+2 | Gordon J 1+2 | Rowe T 30+1 | Berahino S 7+3 | Anderson J —+1 | Thorne G 7 | Gayle D 28+1 | Kearns D —+1 | Wootton S 2 | Petrucci D 4 | Pritchard A 2+4 | Payne J 11+3 | Cuvelier F —+1 | Match No. |
|---|---|---|---|---|---|---|---|---|---|---|---|---|---|---|---|---|---|---|---|---|---|---|---|---|---|---|---|---|---|---|---|
| 1 | 2 | 3 | 4 | 5² | 6 | 7 | 8¹ | 9² | 10 | 11 | 12 | 13 | 14 | | | | | | | | | | | | | | | | | | 1 |
| 1 | 5 | 3 | 4 | 2 | 10 | 6 | 8¹ | 7³ | 11² | 9 | 13 | 12 | | 14 | | | | | | | | | | | | | | | | | 2 |
| 1 | 5 | 3 | 4 | 2² | 10 | 6 | 7¹ | | 14 | 9 | 11³ | 8 | 13 | 12 | | | | | | | | | | | | | | | | | 3 |
| 1 | 5² | 3 | 4¹ | 13 | 10 | 8 | | 12 | | 9 | | 14 | 7 | | 2 | 6³ | 11 | | | | | | | | | | | | | | 4 |
| 1 | 3¹ | 12 | 5 | 9 | 4 | 6 | | 10² | 13 | 7 | | 2³ | | 11 | 8 | 14 | | | | | | | | | | | | | | | 5 |
| 1 | 5 | 3 | | 11 | 7 | 13 | 9¹ | 12 | 8² | 2 | | 10 | 6 | | | 4 | | | | | | | | | | | | | | | 6 |
| 1 | 5 | 3 | | 11² | 7 | 9³ | 13 | 8¹ | 2 | | 10 | 6 | 12 | 4 | 14 | | | | | | | | | | | | | | | | 7 |
| 1 | 12 | 6 | | 5 | 14 | 7 | | 10 | 11 | 13 | 2 | | 9³ | | 8¹ | 4 | | 3² | | | | | | | | | | | | | 8 |
| 1 | | 4 | 14 | 5 | | 7 | | 6² | 11¹ | 13 | 2 | | 10 | | 8³ | 3 | | 9 | 12 | | | | | | | | | | | | 9 |
| 1 | | 3 | | 5 | 14 | 8 | | 9 | 11² | | 2¹ | 12 | 10 | | 7 | 4 | | 6³ | 13 | | | | | | | | | | | | 10 |
| 1 | 12 | 3 | | 2² | | 5 | | 6 | 11³ | 13 | 9 | | 10 | | 8 | 4 | | 7¹ | 14 | | | | | | | | | | | | 11 |
| 1 | 8 | 3 | | 2 | 9² | 6 | 14 | 11 | 12 | 7³ | 5 | | | | 13 | 4 | | 10¹ | | | | | | | | | | | | | 12 |
| 1 | 6 | 4 | | 3 | 9² | 7 | | 11¹ | 13 | 8 | 2 | 12 | | | | 5 | | 10 | | | | | | | | | | | | | 13 |
| 1 | 8¹ | 3 | | 5 | 10 | 4 | 12 | | 7 | | 9² | 2 | 13 | 14 | 6 | | | 11³ | | | | | | | | | | | | | 14 |
| 1 | | 3 | 14 | 2 | 13 | 5 | 7³ | | 11 | | 6¹ | 4 | | 9 | 12 | 8 | | 10² | | | | | | | | | | | | | 15 |
| 1 | | 3 | | 2 | 9¹ | 6 | 8 | | 11 | | 7 | 5³ | 12 | 13 | 14 | 4 | | 10² | | | | | | | | | | | | | 16 |
| 1 | | 3 | | 2² | 9 | 6 | 8 | | 11 | | 7 | 5¹ | | | 12 | 4 | | 10 | 13 | | | | | | | | | | | | 17 |
| 1 | | 3 | | 7 | 5 | 6 | | | 10 | | 8 | 2 | | | | 4 | | 11¹ | | 9 | | | 12 | | | | | | | | 18 |
| 1 | 4¹ | | | 11 | 5 | 6 | | | 8 | | 7 | 2 | 12 | | | 3 | | | | 9 | | | 10 | | | | | | | | 19 |
| 1 | | 3 | | 2² | 9 | | 8 | | 10¹ | | 7 | 5³ | 13 | | | 14 | 4 | | 12 | 6 | | | 11 | | | | | | | | 20 |
| 1 | | 3 | | 10 | 4 | 5 | | 9 | | | 2 | 13 | | | 12 | 7² | | 6¹ | | 8 | 11 | | | | | | | | | | 21 |
| 1 | 14 | 2 | 12 | 5 | 3 | 7² | | 10 | | | 8 | | | | 13 | 4¹ | | 6³ | | 9 | 11 | | | | | | | | | | 22 |
| 1 | | 3 | 13 | 11 | 2 | 9¹ | | 8 | | | 5² | | | | 12 | 4 | | 7 | | 6 | 10 | | | | | | | | | | 23 |
| 1 | | 3 | | 10² | 4 | 6¹ | | 7 | | 14 | 5 | 14 | | | 13 | 2 | | 9 | | 8³ | 11 | | | | | | | | | | 24 |
| 1 | 12 | 3 | | 10¹ | 2 | 8³ | | 6 | | 7² | 5 | 14 | | | 13 | 4¹ | | 9 | | | 11 | | | | | | | | | | 25 |
| 1 | 4³ | 3 | | 10² | 2 | 8¹ | | 6 | | | 5 | 12 | | | 7 | 14 | | 9 | | | 11 | 13 | | | | | | | | | 26 |
| 1 | 4³ | | | | 3 | 7² | | 6 | | 13 | 5 | | | 14 | 8¹ | | 12 | 9 | | | 11 | | | | | 2 | 10 | | | | 27 |
| 1 | 4² | | | 2 | 8 | | | 6 | | 12 | 5 | 14 | | | 13 | | 10³ | 9 | | | 11 | | | | | 3 | 7¹ | | | | 28 |
| 1 | | 3 | | 11³ | 2 | 8² | | 6 | | 7 | 5 | | | | 13 | | 4¹ | 9 | | | 10 | | | | | | | 12 | 14 | | 29 |
| 1 | | 3 | | 10 | 4 | | | 9 | | 8 | 2 | | | | 6¹ | 13 | | 5 | | | 11 | | | | | 7 | 12² | | | | 30 |
| 1 | | 3 | | 11³ | 4 | 14 | | 7 | | 8 | 5 | 12 | | | 9¹ | 2² | | 6 | | | 10 | | | | | | 13 | | | | 31 |
| 1 | | 3 | | 10 | 4 | 9¹ | | 8 | | 2 | 12 | | | | 6 | 7 | | 5 | | | 11 | | | | | | | | | | 32 |
| 1 | | 4 | 14 | 11 | 3 | 13 | | 7 | | 2³ | 9² | | | | 6¹ | | | 5 | | | 10 | | | 8¹ | | | 12 | | | | 33 |
| 1 | | 4 | | 10 | 3 | 13 | | 7 | | 2 | 9² | | | | 6¹ | 12 | | 5 | | | 11 | | | | | | | | 8 | | 34 |
| 1 | 13 | 4² | | 6 | 3 | | | 8¹ | | 2 | 9³ | 14 | 10 | 12 | | | | 5 | | | 11 | | | | | | | | 7 | | 35 |
| 1 | 13 | 4 | | 10 | 3 | 12 | | 8² | | 2 | 9³ | 14 | 6¹ | | | | | 5 | | | 11 | | | | | | | | 7 | | 36 |
| 1 | | 4 | | 10 | 3 | | | 12 | | 2 | 9¹ | 13 | 7² | | 5 | | | 6 | | | 11 | | | | | | | | 8 | | 37 |
| 1 | 14 | 3 | | 8 | 2³ | 12 | | | | 5 | | 11¹² | 13 | 6 | 4¹ | | | 9 | | | 10 | | | | | | | | 7 | | 38 |
| 1 | | 4 | 3 | 10³ | | 7¹ | | | | 13 | 2 | | 14 | 12 | 9² | 5 | | 6 | | | 11 | | | | | | | | 8 | | 39 |
| 1 | | 3 | 2 | 10 | | 6¹ | | 12 | | 7 | 13 | | | | 8 | 4 | | 5 | | | 11 | | | | | | | | 9² | | 40 |
| 1 | | 3 | 2 | 9 | | 6³ | | 5 | | 13 | 14 | 10² | | 12 | 4 | | | 8 | | | 11 | | | | | | | | 7¹ | | 41 |
| 1 | 12 | 3 | 2 | 10³ | | 7 | | 5¹ | | 8² | | 9 | | 6 | 4 | | | 9 | | | 11 | | | | | | | 13 | | 14 | 42 |
| 1 | 2 | 3 | | 5 | 10 | | | 7 | | 8¹ | | 12 | 6 | | 4 | | | 9 | | | 11 | | | | | | | | | | 43 |
| 1 | 3 | 4¹ | 2 | 11 | | 12 | | 7³ | | 13 | 8² | 5 | | 6 | | | | 10 | | | | | | | | | | 14 | 9 | | 44 |
| 1 | | 4 | 2 | 10 | 3 | 12 | | 8³ | | 13 | | 6¹ | 14 | | 5 | | | 11 | | | | | | | | | | 9² | 7 | | 45 |
| 1 | | 3 | 5 | 9 | 4 | | | 6 | | | 13 | 10 | | 12 | 7 | | | 8 | | | | | | | | | | 2¹ | 11² | | 46 |

**FA Cup**  
Third Round     Norwich C     (h)     0-3

**Capital One Cup**  
First Round     Southend U     (h)     4-0  
Second Round     Reading     (a)     2-3

# PLYMOUTH ARGYLE

## FOUNDATION

The club was formed in September 1886 as the Argyle Athletic Club by former public and private school pupils who wanted to continue playing the game. The meeting was held in a room above the Borough Arms (a coffee house), Bedford Street, Plymouth. It was common then to choose a local street/terrace as a club name and Argyle or Argyll was a fashionable name throughout the land due to Queen Victoria's great interest in Scotland.

**Home Park, Plymouth, Devon PL2 3DQ.**

*Telephone:* (01752) 562 561.

*Fax:* (01752) 606 167.

*Ticket Office:* (0845) 872 3335.

*Website:* www.pafc.co.uk

*Email:* argyle@pafc.co.uk

*Ground Capacity:* 16,388.

*Record Attendance:* 43,596 v Aston Villa, Division 2, 10 October 1936.

*Pitch Measurements:* 102m × 66m (112yd × 73yd)

*Chairman:* James Brent.

*Manager:* John Sheridan.

*First Team Coach:* Gary Owers.

*Physio:* Paul Atkinson.

*Colours:* Dark green shirts with white trim, white shorts with green trim, white socks with green trim.

*Year Formed:* 1886.

*Turned Professional:* 1903.

*Previous Name:* 1886, Argyle Athletic Club; 1903, Plymouth Argyle.

*Club Nickname:* 'The Pilgrims'.

*Ground:* 1886, Home Park.

*First Football League Game:* 28 August 1920, Division 3, v Norwich C (h) D 1–1 – Craig; Russell, Atterbury; Logan, Dickinson, Forbes; Kirkpatrick, Jack, Bowler, Heeps (1), Dixon.

*Record League Victory:* 8–1 v Millwall, Division 2, 16 January 1932 – Harper; Roberts, Titmuss, Mackay, Pullan, Reed; Grozier, Bowden (2), Vidler (3), Leslie (1), Black (1), (1 og). 8–1 v Hartlepool U (a), Division 2, 7 May 1994 – Nicholls; Patterson (Naylor), Hill, Burrows, Comyn, McCall (1), Barlow, Castle (1), Landon (3), Marshall (1), Dalton (2).

*Record Cup Victory:* 6–0 v Corby T, FA Cup 3rd rd, 22 January 1966 – Leiper; Book, Baird; Williams, Nelson, Newman; Jones (1), Jackson (1), Bickle (3), Piper (1), Jennings.

## HONOURS

**Football League – Division 2:** *Champions* 2003–04;

**Division 3 (S):** *Champions* 1929–30, 1951–52; *Runners-up* 1921–22, 1922–23, 1923–24, 1924–25, 1925–26, 1926–27 (record of six consecutive years);

**Division 3:** *Champions* 1958–59, 2001–02; *Runners-up* 1974–75, 1985–86.

**FA Cup:** Semi-final 1984.

**Football League Cup:** Semi-final 1965, 1974.

## sky SPORTS FACT FILE

The two Christmas holiday games between Plymouth Argyle and Charlton Athletic in 1960 saw the teams share an astonishing 20 goals. Argyle went down 6-4 at the Valley on Boxing Day but 24 hours later they defeated Charlton by an identical score with Wilf Carter netting five times.

*Record Defeat:* 0–9 v Stoke C, Division 2, 17 December 1960.

*Most League Points (2 for a win):* 68, Division 3 (S), 1929–30.

*Most League Points (3 for a win):* 102, Division 3, 2001–02.

*Most League Goals:* 107, Division 3 (S), 1925–26 and 1951–52.

*Highest League Scorer in Season:* Jack Cock, 32, Division 3 (S), 1926–27.

*Most League Goals in Total Aggregate:* Sammy Black, 180, 1924–38.

*Most League Goals in One Match:* 5, Wilf Carter v Charlton Ath, Division 2, 27 December 1960.

*Most Capped Player:* Moses Russell, 20 (23), Wales.

*Most League Appearances:* Kevin Hodges, 530, 1978–92.

*Youngest League Player:* Lee Phillips, 16 years 43 days v Gillingham, 29 October 1996.

*Record Transfer Fee Received:* £3,000,000 from Hull C for Peter Halmosi, July 2008.

*Record Transfer Fee Paid:* £500,000 to Cardiff C for Steve MacLean, January 2008; £500,000 to QPR for Simon Walton, August 2008.

*Football League Record:* 1920 Original Member of Division 3; 1921–30 Division 3 (S); 1930–50 Division 2; 1950–52 Division 3 (S); 1952–56 Division 2; 1956–58 Division 3 (S); 1958–59 Division 3; 1959–68 Division 2; 1968–75 Division 3; 1975–77 Division 2; 1977–86 Division 3; 1986–95 Division 2; 1995–96 Division 3; 1996–98 Division 2; 1998–2002 Division 3; 2002–04 Division 2; 2004–10 FL C; 2010–11 FL 1; 2011– FL 2.

## LATEST SEQUENCES

*Longest Sequence of League Wins:* 9, 8.3.1986 – 12.4.1986.

*Longest Sequence of League Defeats:* 9, 12.10.1963 – 7.12.1963.

*Longest Sequence of League Draws:* 5, 26.2.2000 – 14.3.2000.

*Longest Sequence of Unbeaten League Matches:* 22, 20.4.1929 – 21.12.1929.

*Longest Sequence Without a League Win:* 13, 27.4.1963 – 2.10.1963.

*Successive Scoring Runs:* 39 from 15.4.1939.

*Successive Non-scoring Runs:* 5 from 20.9.1947.

## MANAGERS

Frank Brettell 1903–05
Bob Jack 1905–06
Bill Fullerton 1906–07
Bob Jack 1910–38
Jack Tresadern 1938–47
Jimmy Rae 1948–55
Jack Rowley 1955–60
Neil Dougall 1961
Ellis Stuttard 1961–63
Andy Beattie 1963–64
Malcolm Allison 1964–65
Derek Ufton 1965–68
Billy Bingham 1968–70
Ellis Stuttard 1970–72
Tony Waiters 1972–77
Mike Kelly 1977–78
Malcolm Allison 1978–79
Bobby Saxton 1979–81
Bobby Moncur 1981–83
Johnny Hore 1983–84
Dave Smith 1984–88
Ken Brown 1988–90
David Kemp 1990–92
Peter Shilton 1992–95
Steve McCall 1995
Neil Warnock 1995–97
Mick Jones 1997–98
Kevin Hodges 1998–2000
Paul Sturrock 2000–04
Bobby Williamson 2004–05
Tony Pulis 2005–06
Ian Holloway 2006–07
Paul Sturrock 2007–09
Paul Mariner 2009–10
Peter Reid 2010–11
Carl Fletcher 2011–13
John Sheridan January 2013–

## TEN YEAR LEAGUE RECORD

|  |  | P | W | D | L | F | A | Pts | Pos |
|---|---|---|---|---|---|---|---|---|---|
| 2003-04 | Div 2 | 46 | 26 | 12 | 8 | 85 | 41 | 90 | 1 |
| 2004-05 | FL C | 46 | 14 | 11 | 21 | 52 | 64 | 53 | 17 |
| 2005-06 | FL C | 46 | 13 | 17 | 16 | 39 | 46 | 56 | 14 |
| 2006-07 | FL C | 46 | 17 | 16 | 13 | 63 | 62 | 67 | 11 |
| 2007-08 | FL C | 46 | 17 | 13 | 16 | 60 | 50 | 64 | 10 |
| 2008-09 | FL C | 46 | 13 | 12 | 21 | 44 | 57 | 51 | 21 |
| 2009-10 | FL C | 46 | 11 | 8 | 27 | 43 | 68 | 41 | 23 |
| 2010-11 | FL 1 | 46 | 15 | 7 | 24 | 51 | 74 | 42* | 23 |
| 2011-12 | FL 2 | 46 | 10 | 16 | 20 | 47 | 64 | 46 | 21 |
| 2012-13 | FL 2 | 46 | 13 | 13 | 20 | 46 | 55 | 52 | 21 |

*10 pts deducted.

## DID YOU KNOW ?

Plymouth Argyle reached the last four of the FA Cup in the 1983–84 season while playing in the old Third Division. Their cup campaign began in the first round at Southend United in November and only ended when they went down 1-0 to Watford in the semi-final at Villa Park.

## PLYMOUTH ARGYLE – FOOTBALL LEAGUE TWO 2012–13 LEAGUE RECORD

| Match No. | Date | Venue | Opponents | Result | H/T Score | Lg Pos. | Goalscorers | Atten-dance |
|---|---|---|---|---|---|---|---|---|
| 1 | Aug 18 | H | Aldershot T | L | 0-2 | 0-1 | 21 | | 7020 |
| 2 | 21 | A | Dagenham & R | D | 0-0 | 0-0 | 22 | | 1878 |
| 3 | 25 | A | Oxford U | L | 1-2 | 0-2 | 23 | Williams [74] | 6906 |
| 4 | Sept 1 | H | Northampton T | W | 3-2 | 0-1 | 15 | Feeney [47], Griffiths, R [59], Nelson [74] | 6037 |
| 5 | 8 | A | Torquay U | D | 0-0 | 0-0 | 17 | | 4932 |
| 6 | 15 | H | Port Vale | L | 1-3 | 1-0 | 19 | Williams [18] | 6080 |
| 7 | 18 | H | Bristol R | D | 1-1 | 1-0 | 19 | Hourihane [35] | 6303 |
| 8 | 22 | A | Morecambe | W | 3-2 | 0-1 | 16 | Jenkins [72], Feeney 2 (2 pens) [80, 87] | 1865 |
| 9 | 29 | H | Southend U | D | 1-1 | 0-0 | 16 | MacDonald [50] | 6269 |
| 10 | Oct 2 | A | Wycombe W | D | 1-1 | 0-1 | 18 | Madjo [50] | 3161 |
| 11 | 6 | H | AFC Wimbledon | L | 1-2 | 0-1 | 19 | Griffiths, R [89] | 6271 |
| 12 | 13 | A | Barnet | W | 4-1 | 2-1 | 18 | Griffiths, R (pen) [2], Blanchard [11], Cowan-Hall [62], Young [90] | 3229 |
| 13 | 20 | H | Rochdale | W | 3-1 | 2-0 | 15 | Madjo 2 (2 pens) [4, 90], Gurrieri [7] | 6261 |
| 14 | 23 | A | Cheltenham T | L | 1-2 | 1-1 | 15 | Hourihane [30] | 3058 |
| 15 | 27 | A | Rotherham U | L | 0-1 | 0-0 | 18 | | 7233 |
| 16 | Nov 7 | H | Burton Alb | L | 1-2 | 0-0 | 19 | Cowan-Hall [49] | 5219 |
| 17 | 10 | A | Gillingham | D | 2-2 | 1-1 | 19 | Nelson [33], Young [79] | 6396 |
| 18 | 17 | A | Fleetwood T | L | 0-3 | 0-1 | 19 | | 2657 |
| 19 | 20 | A | Bradford C | L | 0-1 | 0-1 | 19 | | 8843 |
| 20 | 24 | H | Chesterfield | L | 0-1 | 0-0 | 20 | | 5711 |
| 21 | Dec 8 | H | York C | W | 2-0 | 1-0 | 20 | Fyfield (og) [45], Chadwick [90] | 5881 |
| 22 | 15 | A | Exeter C | D | 1-1 | 0-1 | 20 | Lennox [73] | 6447 |
| 23 | 22 | A | Accrington S | D | 1-1 | 1-0 | 20 | Bhasera [27] | 2012 |
| 24 | 26 | H | Torquay U | D | 1-1 | 0-0 | 20 | Harvey [90] | 10,003 |
| 25 | 29 | H | Wycombe W | L | 0-1 | 0-1 | 20 | | 6983 |
| 26 | Jan 1 | A | Bristol R | L | 1-2 | 0-2 | 21 | Hourihane [62] | 7332 |
| 27 | 5 | A | Port Vale | L | 0-4 | 0-1 | 23 | | 5139 |
| 28 | 12 | H | Morecambe | W | 2-1 | 2-0 | 22 | Hourihane [10], Cowan-Hall [16] | 6401 |
| 29 | 26 | H | Accrington S | D | 0-0 | 0-0 | 22 | | 6509 |
| 30 | Feb 2 | H | Dagenham & R | D | 0-0 | 0-0 | 22 | | 6234 |
| 31 | 9 | A | Aldershot T | W | 2-1 | 2-1 | 20 | Banton 2 [5, 40] | 3241 |
| 32 | 16 | H | Oxford U | L | 0-1 | 0-1 | 21 | | 7189 |
| 33 | 23 | A | Northampton T | L | 0-1 | 0-0 | 24 | | 5382 |
| 34 | 26 | A | AFC Wimbledon | D | 1-1 | 1-1 | 24 | Banton [26] | 4480 |
| 35 | Mar 2 | H | Barnet | W | 2-1 | 1-1 | 23 | Hourihane [36], Murray [49] | 8210 |
| 36 | 9 | A | Gillingham | L | 1-2 | 0-1 | 24 | Banton [77] | 10,260 |
| 37 | 12 | H | Bradford C | D | 0-0 | 0-0 | 23 | | 5609 |
| 38 | 16 | H | Fleetwood T | W | 2-1 | 2-0 | 21 | Wotton (pen) [25], Banton [39] | 6776 |
| 39 | 19 | A | Southend U | W | 2-0 | 0-0 | 20 | Wotton (pen) [57], Reid [75] | 4674 |
| 40 | 30 | H | Exeter C | W | 1-0 | 1-0 | 20 | Banton [45] | 13,251 |
| 41 | Apr 1 | A | York C | L | 0-2 | 0-2 | 22 | | 4682 |
| 42 | 6 | H | Cheltenham T | W | 2-0 | 1-0 | 18 | Reid [40], Hector (og) [54] | 7941 |
| 43 | 13 | A | Burton Alb | L | 0-1 | 0-0 | 19 | | 4392 |
| 44 | 16 | A | Chesterfield | W | 2-1 | 2-0 | 17 | Bryan [21], Nelson [26] | 4988 |
| 45 | 20 | H | Rotherham U | L | 0-1 | 0-0 | 19 | | 10,648 |
| 46 | 27 | A | Rochdale | L | 0-1 | 0-0 | 21 | | 4272 |

**Final League Position: 21**

## GOALSCORERS

*League (46):* Banton 6, Hourihane 5, Cowan-Hall 3, Feeney 3 (2 pens), Griffiths, R 3 (1 pen), Madjo 3 (2 pens), Nelson 3, Reid 2, Williams 2, Wotton 2 (2 pens), Young 2, Bhasera 1, Blanchard 1, Bryan 1, Chadwick 1, Gurrieri 1, Harvey 1, Jenkins 1, Lennox 1, MacDonald 1, Murray 1, own goals 2.
*FA Cup (0).*
*Capital One Cup (4):* Chadwick 1, Cowan-Hall 1, Gorman 1, Williams 1 (1 pen).
*Johnstone's Paint Trophy (3):* Cowan-Hall 1, Gurrieri 1, MacDonald 1.

| Cole J 33+1 | Nelson C 25+2 | Purse D 21 | Blanchard M 38+2 | Bhasera O 40+2 | Gurrieri A 22+6 | Wotton P 17+2 | Hourihane C 42 | Gorman J 1+1 | Chadwick N 10+18 | Lecointe M 3+3 | Young L 26+6 | Cowan-Hall P 25+15 | Feeney W 12+9 | Berry D 27+1 | Williams R 13+2 | MacDonald A 14+2 | Griffiths R 6+8 | Lennox J 4+7 | Madjo G 9+5 | Jenkins R 2 | Griffiths S 4 | Lowry J 6+3 | Gilmartin R 13 | Harvey T 2+8 | Molesley M 3+2 | Branston G 19 | Murray R 6+7 | Charles A 9+2 | Reid R 18 | Banton J 14 | Cox L 10 | Ugwu C 2+4 | Richards J —+1 | Bryan J 10 | Match No. |
|---|---|---|---|---|---|---|---|---|---|---|---|---|---|---|---|---|---|---|---|---|---|---|---|---|---|---|---|---|---|---|---|---|---|---|---|
| 1 | 2 | 3 | 4 | 5 | $6^2$ | 7 | 8 | $9^1$ | 10 | $11^3$ | 12 | 13 | 14 | | | | | | | | | | | | | | | | | | | | | | 1 |
| 1 | 2 | 3 | 4 | 5 | $9^3$ | 7 | 8 | 14 | $10^2$ | $11^1$ | 6 | 12 | 13 | | | | | | | | | | | | | | | | | | | | | | 2 |
| 1 | $2^1$ | $4^3$ | 3 | 5 | $11^2$ | 7 | 8 | | 14 | | 6 | 9 | 10 | 12 | 13 | | | | | | | | | | | | | | | | | | | | 3 |
| 1 | 14 | 3 | 4 | 9 | | $7^2$ | 8 | | | | 6 | $10^1$ | 11 | 2 | 5 | 12 | $13^3$ | | | | | | | | | | | | | | | | | | 4 |
| 1 | 4 | 3 | | 14 | | 7 | 8 | | 12 | | $6^1$ | | $10^2$ | 2 | 5 | 11 | $9^3$ | 13 | | | | | | | | | | | | | | | | | 5 |
| 1 | 3 | 4 | | 9 | | $7^1$ | 8 | | 12 | | $6^2$ | | 10 | 2 | 5 | 11 | 13 | | | | | | | | | | | | | | | | | | 6 |
| 1 | 3 | 4 | | 9 | | | 8 | | | | $10^1$ | 7 | 12 | 13 | 2 | 5 | $6^2$ | 11 | | | | | | | | | | | | | | | | | 7 |
| 1 | 4 | 3 | | $9^1$ | | 7 | | | | | 12 | 10 | | 2 | 5 | 6 | | 11 | 8 | | | | | | | | | | | | | | | | 8 |
| 1 | 3 | 4 | 9 | | | | 8 | | 14 | | 7 | 12 | $11^1$ | 2 | 5 | $6^3$ | 13 | $10^2$ | | | | | | | | | | | | | | | | | 9 |
| 1 | 2 | 5 | 3 | $4^3$ | | | 8 | | 14 | | 12 | $10^1$ | 6 | 7 | 13 | $11^2$ | 9 | | | | | | | | | | | | | | | | | | 10 |
| 1 | 4 | 3 | | $9^1$ | | | $8^3$ | | 14 | | 7 | 11 | | $2^2$ | 5 | 6 | 10 | 13 | 12 | | | | | | | | | | | | | | | | 11 |
| 1 | 3 | 4 | 12 | | | | 8 | | 14 | | 7 | 9 | | 2 | | $6^2$ | $10^3$ | 13 | $11^1$ | | 5 | | | | | | | | | | | | | | 12 |
| 1 | 13 | 3 | 4 | $10^2$ | | | 8 | | | | 7 | $9^1$ | | 2 | | 6 | | 12 | 11 | | 5 | | | | | | | | | | | | | | 13 |
| 1 | 3 | 4 | 12 | 8 | | 7 | | | 13 | | $9^3$ | | | 2 | | 6 | $10^1$ | $11^2$ | | 5 | 14 | | | | | | | | | | | | | | 14 |
| 1 | 4 | | 3 | 14 | $9^2$ | | | | 13 | | 7 | 10 | 12 | 2 | | $6^1$ | 13 | 14 | $11^2$ | 5 | $8^3$ | | | | | | | | | | | | | | 15 |
| 1 | 3 | | 4 | 5 | 9 | | | | | | 7 | 12 | 10 | 2 | | $6^1$ | 13 | 14 | $11^2$ | | $8^3$ | | | | | | | | | | | | | | 16 |
| | 4 | 3 | | 5 | 12 | | 8 | | 13 | | 6 | 9 | $11^1$ | 2 | | $10^2$ | | | | 7 | 1 | | | | | | | | | | | | | | 17 |
| | 4 | $3^1$ | 14 | 5 | | | 8 | | 10 | | 6 | $9^3$ | $11^1$ | 2 | 12 | | 13 | | | $7^2$ | 1 | | | | | | | | | | | | | | 18 |
| | 4 | | 3 | 5 | 10 | | 7 | | 11 | | | $6^1$ | 13 | 2 | $9^2$ | | | | | 8 | 1 | 12 | | | | | | | | | | | | | 19 |
| | 3 | | 4 | 5 | $9^1$ | | 8 | | $11^3$ | | | $6^2$ | | 2 | | 10 | 13 | 12 | 14 | | 1 | | 7 | | | | | | | | | | | | 20 |
| | 2 | 3 | 4 | 5 | $9^2$ | | 8 | | 12 | | 6 | $10^3$ | | 2 | | $11^1$ | 14 | | | 13 | 1 | | 7 | | | | | | | | | | | | 21 |
| | 2 | 3 | $4^⁕$ | 5 | $8^1$ | $7^3$ | 13 | | 6 | | | 14 | | 12 | $11^2$ | 10 | | | | | 1 | | 9 | | | | | | | | | | | | 22 |
| | 3 | 4 | | 9 | | | 8 | | | | 7 | 13 | 12 | 2 | 5 | $11^1$ | $6^2$ | | | | 1 | | | | | | | | | | | | | | 23 |
| | 2 | 3 | 5 | 4 | | | 9 | | $10^1$ | | 8 | 11 | | 6 | 12 | | | | | | 1 | 7 | | | | | | | | | | | | | 24 |
| | 2 | 3 | 4 | $9^3$ | | | 8 | | $10^2$ | | 7 | 6 | 12 | 5 | 13 | | | | | | 1 | $11^1$ | 14 | | | | | | | | | | | | 25 |
| | 5 | 2 | 4 | | | | 7 | | 10 | | $8^3$ | 9 | $11^2$ | 3 | $6^1$ | 13 | 12 | | | | 1 | | 14 | | | | | | | | | | | | 26 |
| | 4 | 3 | 6 | | $9^2$ | 7 | $11^⁕$ | | | | $8^1$ | 10 | 12 | 2 | 5 | | | | | 13 | 1 | | | | | | | | | | | | | | 27 |
| | 3 | $8^3$ | 5 | 13 | 7 | | | | 14 | | 6 | $10^1$ | 2 | | | | | | | $9^2$ | 1 | 12 | | 4 | 11 | | | | | | | | | | 28 |
| 12 | 3 | $7^2$ | 9 | | | 8 | | | 13 | | 6 | | 2 | | | | | | | $1^1$ | 14 | | | 4 | $10^3$ | 5 | 11 | | | | | | | | 29 |
| 1 | | | 5 | 12 | | | 8 | | | 13 | 7 | 6 | | 2 | | | | | | | | 14 | | 3 | $10^2$ | 4 | $11^3$ | $9^1$ | | | | | | | 30 |
| 1 | | 13 | 5 | | $7^2$ | 8 | | | | | 6 | | | 2 | | | | | | | | | 3 | | | 4 | $10^1$ | 9 | 11 | 12 | | | | | 31 |
| 1 | | | 5 | | | 8 | | | | | 6 | | | 2 | | | | | | | | | 4 | 12 | 3 | 10 | 9 | 7 | $11^1$ | | | | | | 32 |
| 1 | | 2 | 5 | 13 | $8^2$ | 9 | | | | | $6^1$ | | | | | | | | | | | | 3 | 14 | 4 | $11^3$ | 10 | 7 | 12 | | | | | | 33 |
| 1 | | 2 | 5 | | | 8 | | | 13 | | | | | | | | | | | | | | 3 | 6 | 4 | 10 | $9^1$ | 7 | $11^2$ | 12 | | | | | 34 |
| 1 | | 2 | 5 | $9^3$ | | 8 | | | | | 12 | 13 | | | | | | | | | | | 3 | 11 | 4 | $10^2$ | 6 | $7^1$ | 14 | | | | | | 35 |
| 1 | | 2 | 5 | $8^2$ | | $6^3$ | | | | | 14 | 13 | | | | | | | | | | | 4 | $9^1$ | 3 | 10 | 11 | 7 | 12 | | | | | | 36 |
| 1 | | 2 | 5 | $9^3$ | 3 | 8 | | | 12 | | | 13 | | | | | | | | | | | 14 | | 4 | | $11^1$ | 10 | 7 | | | $6^2$ | | | 37 |
| 1 | | 2 | 5 | $6^1$ | 4 | 8 | | | 13 | | | 12 | | | | | | | | | | | 3 | | | | $11^2$ | 10 | 7 | | | 9 | | | 38 |
| 1 | | 2 | 5 | 14 | 12 | 8 | | | | | $6^2$ | | | | | | | | | | | | 4 | 13 | $3^1$ | 11 | $10^3$ | 7 | | | | 9 | | | 39 |
| 1 | | 2 | 5 | $6^3$ | 4 | 8 | | | 12 | | 14 | | | | | | | | | | | | 3 | 13 | | 11 | $10^2$ | $7^1$ | | | | 9 | | | 40 |
| 1 | | 2 | 5 | | 4 | 7 | | | 12 | | 8 | $6^3$ | | | | | | | | | | | 13 | 3 | 14 | 12 | $11^1$ | $9^2$ | | | | 10 | | | 41 |
| 1 | 4 | 2 | 5 | 9 | $7^1$ | | | | 8 | | 13 | | | | | | | | | | | | 3 | 14 | 12 | $11^3$ | $10^2$ | 6 | | | | | | | 42 |
| 1 | 8 | 3 | 5 | $6^2$ | | | | | 13 | | 7 | 12 | | 2 | | | | | | | | | 4 | | | | $11^1$ | 10 | | | | 9 | | | 43 |
| 1 | 7 | | 5 | 11 | 3 | 8 | | | 12 | | | 6 | | 2 | | | | | | | | | 4 | | | | $10^1$ | | | | | 9 | | | 44 |
| 1 | $7^2$ | 2 | 5 | 10 | 3 | 8 | | | 13 | | | $6^1$ | | | | | | | | | | | 14 | | | | $11^3$ | | | | 4 | 12 | 9 | | 45 |
| 1 | 8 | | $3^⁕$ | $6^3$ | $11^2$ | 7 | 5 | | 12 | | | | | 2 | | | | | | | | | 13 | | | | 4 | | 14 | $10^1$ | | 9 | | | 46 |

**FA Cup**

| | | | |
|---|---|---|---|
| First Round | Dorchester T | (a) | 0-1 |

**Capital One Cup**

| | | | |
|---|---|---|---|
| First Round | Portsmouth | (h) | 3-0 |
| Second Round | Burnley | (a) | 1-1 |

*(aet; lost 2-3 on pens)*

**Johnstone's Paint Trophy**

| | | | |
|---|---|---|---|
| Second Round | Aldershot T | (h) | 2-1 |
| Southern Quarter-Finals | Oxford U | (h) | 1-1 |

*(aet; lost 1-3 on pens)*

# PORT VALE

## FOUNDATION

Port Vale Football Club was formed in 1876 and took its name from the venue of the inaugural meeting at 'Port Vale House' situated in a suburb of Stoke-on-Trent. Upon moving to Burslem in 1884 the club changed its name to 'Burslem Port Vale' and after several seasons in the Midland League became founder members of the Football League Division Two in 1892. The prefix 'Burslem' was dropped from the name as a new ground several miles away was acquired.

*Vale Park, Hamil Road, Burslem, Stoke-on-Trent, Staffordshire ST6 1AW.*

*Telephone:* (01782) 655 800.

*Fax:* (01782) 834 981.

*Ticket Office:* (0171) 222 1950.

*Website:* www.port-vale.co.uk

*Email:* enquiries@port-vale.co.uk

*Ground Capacity:* 19,148.

*Record Attendance:* 22,993 v Stoke C, Division 2, 6 March 1920 (at Recreation Ground); 49,768 v Aston Villa, FA Cup 5th rd, 20 February 1960 (at Vale Park).

*Pitch Measurements:* 104m × 70m (114yd × 77yd)

*Chairman:* Norman Smurthwaite.

*Manager:* Micky Adams.

*Assistant Manager:* Mark Grew.

*Physio:* Andrew Foster.

*Colours:* White shirts with black trim, black shorts with white trim, black socks with white trim.

*Year Formed:* 1876.

*Turned Professional:* 1885.

*Previous Names:* 1876, Port Vale; 1884, Burslem Port Vale; 1909, Port Vale.

*Club Nickname:* 'Valiants'.

*Grounds:* 1876, Limekin Lane, Longport; 1881, Westport; 1884, Moorland Road, Burslem; 1886, Athletic Ground, Cobridge; 1913, Recreation Ground, Hanley; 1950, Vale Park.

*First Football League Game:* 3 September 1892, Division 2, v Small Heath (a) L 1–5 – Frail; Clutton, Elson; Farrington, McCrindle, Delves; Walker, Scarratt, Bliss (1), Jones. (Only 10 men).

*Record League Victory:* 9–1 v Chesterfield, Division 2, 24 September 1932 – Leckie; Shenton, Poyser; Sherlock, Round, Jones; McGrath, Mills, Littlewood (6), Kirkham (2), Morton (1).

*Record Cup Victory:* 7–1 v Irthlingborough, FA Cup 1st rd, 12 January 1907 – Matthews; Dunn, Hamilton; Eardley, Baddeley, Holyhead; Carter, Dodds (2), Beats, Mountford (2), Coxon (3).

*Record Defeat:* 0–10 v Sheffield U, Division 2, 10 December 1892. 0–10 v Notts Co, Division 2, 26 February 1895.

## HONOURS

**Football League – Division 2:** *Runners-up* 1993–94;

**Division 3 (N):** *Champions* 1929–30, 1953–54; *Runners-up* 1952–53;

**Division 4:** *Champions* 1958–59.

**FA Cup:** Semi-final 1954, when in Division 3.

**Football League Cup:** Best season: 4th rd, 2007.

**Autoglass Trophy:** *Winners* 1993.

**Anglo-Italian Cup:** *Runners-up* 1996.

**LDV Vans Trophy:** *Winners* 2001.

## sky SPORTS FACT FILE

Goalkeeper Arthur Jepson made 92 appearances, including wartime matches, for Port Vale between 1938 and 1946. He was also a talented cricketer, taking over 1,000 wickets for Nottinghamshire between 1938 and 1959, later going on to umpire in Test matches.

*Most League Points (2 for a win):* 69, Division 3 (N), 1953–54.

*Most League Points (3 for a win):* 89, Division 2, 1992–93.

*Most League Goals:* 110, Division 4, 1958–59.

*Highest League Scorer in Season:* Wilf Kirkham 38, Division 2, 1926–27.

*Most League Goals in Total Aggregate:* Wilf Kirkham, 154, 1923–29, 1931–33.

*Most League Goals in One Match:* 6, Stewart Littlewood v Chesterfield, Division 2, 24 September 1922.

*Most Capped Player:* Chris Birchall, 22 (39), Trinidad & Tobago.

*Most League Appearances:* Roy Sproson, 761, 1950–72.

*Youngest League Player:* Malcolm McKenzie, 15 years 347 days v Newport Co, 12 April 1966.

*Record Transfer Fee Received:* £2,000,000 from Wimbledon for Gareth Ainsworth, October 1998.

*Record Transfer Fee Paid:* £500,000 to Lincoln C for Gareth Ainsworth, September 1997.

*Football League Record:* 1892 Original Member of Division 2. Failed re-election in 1896; Re-elected 1898; Resigned 1907; Returned in Oct, 1919, when they took over the fixtures of Leeds City; 1929–30 Division 3 (N); 1930–36 Division 2; 1936–38 Division 3 (N); 1938–52 Division 3 (S); 1952–54 Division 3 (N); 1954–57 Division 2; 1957–58 Division 3 (S); 1958–59 Division 4; 1959–65 Division 3; 1965–70 Division 4; 1970–78 Division 3; 1978–83 Division 4; 1983–84 Division 3; 1984–86 Division 4; 1986–89 Division 3; 1989–94 Division 2; 1994–2000 Division 1; 2000–04 Division 2; 2004–08 FL 1; 2008–13 FL 2; 2013– FL 1.

## LATEST SEQUENCES

*Longest Sequence of League Wins:* 8, 8.4.1893 – 30.9.1893.

*Longest Sequence of League Defeats:* 9, 9.3.1957 – 20.4.1957.

*Longest Sequence of League Draws:* 6, 26.4.1981 – 12.9.1981.

*Longest Sequence of Unbeaten League Matches:* 19, 5.5.1969 – 8.11.1969.

*Longest Sequence Without a League Win:* 17, 7.12.1991 – 21.3.1992.

*Successive Scoring Runs:* 22 from 12.9.1992.

*Successive Non-scoring Runs:* 4 from 10.2.1896.

## MANAGERS

**Sam Gleaves** 1896–1905
*(Secretary-Manager)*
**Tom Clare** 1905–11
**A. S. Walker** 1911–12
**H. Myatt** 1912–14
**Tom Holford** 1919–24
*(continued as Trainer)*
**Joe Schofield** 1924–30
**Tom Morgan** 1930–32
**Tom Holford** 1932–35
**Warney Cresswell** 1936–37
**Tom Morgan** 1937–38
**Billy Frith** 1945–46
**Gordon Hodgson** 1946–51
**Ivor Powell** 1951
**Freddie Steele** 1951–57
**Norman Low** 1957–62
**Freddie Steele** 1962–65
**Jackie Mudie** 1965–67
**Sir Stanley Matthews**
*(General Manager)* 1965–68
**Gordon Lee** 1968–74
**Roy Sproson** 1974–77
**Colin Harper** 1977
**Bobby Smith** 1977–78
**Dennis Butler** 1978–79
**Alan Bloor** 1979
**John McGrath** 1980–83
**John Rudge** 1983–99
**Brian Horton** 1999–2004
**Martin Foyle** 2004–07
**Lee Sinnott** 2007–08
**Dean Glover** 2008–09
**Micky Adams** 2009–10
**Jim Gannon** 2011
**Micky Adams** May 2011–

## TEN YEAR LEAGUE RECORD

|  |  | P | W | D | L | F | A | Pts | Pos |
|---|---|---|---|---|---|---|---|---|---|
| 2003-04 | Div 2 | 46 | 21 | 10 | 15 | 73 | 63 | 73 | 7 |
| 2004-05 | FL 1 | 46 | 17 | 5 | 24 | 49 | 59 | 56 | 18 |
| 2005-06 | FL 1 | 46 | 16 | 12 | 18 | 49 | 54 | 60 | 13 |
| 2006-07 | FL 1 | 46 | 18 | 6 | 22 | 64 | 65 | 60 | 12 |
| 2007-08 | FL 1 | 46 | 9 | 11 | 26 | 47 | 81 | 38 | 23 |
| 2008-09 | FL 2 | 46 | 13 | 9 | 24 | 44 | 66 | 48 | 18 |
| 2009-10 | FL 2 | 46 | 17 | 17 | 12 | 61 | 50 | 68 | 10 |
| 2010-11 | FL 2 | 46 | 17 | 14 | 15 | 54 | 49 | 65 | 11 |
| 2011-12 | FL 2 | 46 | 20 | 9 | 17 | 68 | 60 | 59* | 12 |
| 2012-13 | FL 2 | 46 | 21 | 15 | 10 | 87 | 52 | 78 | 3 |

*10 pts deducted.

## DID YOU KNOW ?

Port Vale returned to the Football League in October 1919 after a 12-year absence, taking the place of Leeds City who were expelled. Vale inherited 10 points from the Yorkshire club and finished the season in a mid-table position, adding a further 30 points themselves.

## PORT VALE – FOOTBALL LEAGUE TWO 2012–13 LEAGUE RECORD

| Match No. | Date | Venue | Opponents | Result | H/T Score | Lg Pos. | Goalscorers | Attendance |
|---|---|---|---|---|---|---|---|---|
| 1 | Aug 18 | H | Barnet | W 3-0 | 2-0 | 2 | Dodds [8], Myrie-Williams (pen) [20], Pope [75] | 4608 |
| 2 | 21 | A | Accrington S | L 0-2 | 0-1 | 10 | | 1946 |
| 3 | 25 | A | Morecambe | W 3-1 | 1-1 | 5 | Morsy [1], McCombe [89], Pope [90] | 2164 |
| 4 | Sept 1 | H | Torquay U | D 1-1 | 0-1 | 7 | Saah (og) [69] | 4721 |
| 5 | 8 | H | Rotherham U | W 6-2 | 4-1 | 3 | Dodds [5], Pope 4 [16,21,68,78], Vincent [28] | 5544 |
| 6 | 15 | A | Plymouth Arg | W 3-1 | 0-1 | 2 | Myrie-Williams (pen) [66], Vincent [74], Williamson [78] | 6080 |
| 7 | 18 | A | Fleetwood T | W 5-2 | 2-1 | 2 | Pope 2 [29,60], Vincent [34], Dodds 2 [67,78] | 3392 |
| 8 | 22 | H | Gillingham | L 0-2 | 0-2 | 2 | | 6978 |
| 9 | 29 | A | Bradford C | W 1-0 | 1-0 | 2 | Pope [37] | 11,030 |
| 10 | Oct 2 | H | Dagenham & R | D 1-1 | 0-0 | 2 | Myrie-Williams [75] | 4355 |
| 11 | 6 | A | Exeter C | W 2-0 | 1-0 | 2 | Pope 2 [40,62] | 3938 |
| 12 | 15 | H | Oxford U | W 3-0 | 1-0 | 2 | Pope [30], Vincent [51], Morsy [62] | 4596 |
| 13 | 20 | H | Wycombe W | W 4-1 | 0-1 | 2 | Williamson [59], Pope 2 [66,87], Vincent [90] | 5303 |
| 14 | 23 | A | Burton Alb | D 1-1 | 0-0 | 2 | Williamson [75] | 3975 |
| 15 | 27 | A | Northampton T | L 0-2 | 0-2 | 2 | | 5061 |
| 16 | Nov 6 | H | Rochdale | D 2-2 | 1-0 | 2 | Pope 2 [27,62] | 4139 |
| 17 | 10 | A | Southend U | D 0-0 | 0-0 | 2 | | 4876 |
| 18 | 17 | H | York C | D 2-2 | 2-0 | 2 | Burge [30], Myrie-Williams (pen) [44] | 5380 |
| 19 | 20 | H | Bristol R | W 4-0 | 3-0 | 2 | Pope 3 [20,22,67], Williamson [35] | 4177 |
| 20 | 24 | A | Aldershot T | W 3-1 | 1-1 | 2 | Williamson [17], Burge [47], Myrie-Williams (pen) [76] | 1992 |
| 21 | Dec 8 | H | Chesterfield | L 0-2 | 0-1 | 2 | | 5298 |
| 22 | 15 | A | Cheltenham T | D 1-1 | 0-0 | 2 | Dodds [67] | 3670 |
| 23 | 26 | A | Rotherham U | W 2-1 | 0-0 | 2 | Dodds [56], Pope [63] | 10,502 |
| 24 | 29 | A | Dagenham & R | W 3-2 | 3-1 | 1 | Pope [4], Myrie-Williams [9], Dodds [39] | 1697 |
| 25 | Jan 1 | H | Fleetwood T | L 0-2 | 0-2 | 2 | | 6082 |
| 26 | 5 | H | Plymouth Arg | W 4-0 | 1-0 | 2 | Myrie-Williams [32], Pope 2 [55,83], Williamson [77] | 5139 |
| 27 | 12 | A | Gillingham | W 2-1 | 2-1 | 1 | Pope [4], Hughes [20] | 8392 |
| 28 | 24 | A | AFC Wimbledon | D 2-2 | 1-2 | 1 | Jones [44], Pope [58] | 3395 |
| 29 | Feb 2 | H | Accrington S | W 3-0 | 0-0 | 1 | Hughes 2 [50,66], Purse [54] | 5172 |
| 30 | 5 | H | AFC Wimbledon | W 3-0 | 2-0 | 1 | Hughes [13], Vincent 2 [35,75] | 5567 |
| 31 | 9 | A | Barnet | D 0-0 | 0-0 | 1 | | 2398 |
| 32 | 16 | H | Morecambe | L 0-1 | 0-0 | 2 | | 5513 |
| 33 | 23 | A | Torquay U | W 1-0 | 1-0 | 2 | Andrew [28] | 2679 |
| 34 | 26 | H | Exeter C | L 0-2 | 0-2 | 2 | | 4480 |
| 35 | Mar 2 | A | Oxford U | L 1-2 | 1-1 | 2 | Loft [16] | 6322 |
| 36 | 5 | H | Bradford C | D 0-0 | 0-0 | 2 | | 4281 |
| 37 | 9 | H | Southend U | L 1-2 | 0-2 | 2 | Hughes [64] | 4858 |
| 38 | 12 | A | Bristol R | L 0-2 | 0-2 | 3 | | 5111 |
| 39 | 16 | A | York C | W 2-0 | 1-0 | 2 | Myrie-Williams [7], Hughes [48] | 3945 |
| 40 | 29 | H | Cheltenham T | W 3-2 | 1-0 | 2 | Pope 3 [19,58,74] | 5867 |
| 41 | Apr 1 | A | Chesterfield | D 2-2 | 1-2 | 2 | Purse [5], Pope [85] | 6669 |
| 42 | 5 | H | Burton Alb | W 7-1 | 3-0 | 2 | Hughes 3 (2 pens) [12,22 (pl),51 (pl)], Birchall [25], Pope [56], Williamson 2 [73,90] | 10,978 |
| 43 | 9 | H | Aldershot T | D 1-1 | 1-0 | 2 | Myrie-Williams [45] | 6197 |
| 44 | 13 | A | Rochdale | D 2-2 | 1-1 | 2 | Chilvers [89], Pope [34] | 5042 |
| 45 | 20 | H | Northampton T | D 2-2 | 1-1 | 2 | Chilvers [39], Collins (og) [86] | 12,496 |
| 46 | 27 | A | Wycombe W | D 1-1 | 0-1 | 3 | Hughes [79] | 7120 |

**Final League Position: 3**

### GOALSCORERS

*League (87):* Pope 31, Hughes 10 (2 pens), Myrie-Williams 9 (4 pens), Williamson 8, Dodds 7, Vincent 7, Burge 2, Chilvers 2, Morsy 2, Purse 2, Andrew 1, Birchall 1, Jones 1, Loft 1, McCombe 1, own goals 2.
*FA Cup (4):* McDonald 1, Pope 1, Vincent 1, Williamson 1.
*Capital One Cup (1):* Shuker 1.
*Johnstone's Paint Trophy (4):* Myrie-Williams 2 (1 pen), Burge 1, Pope 1.

| Neal C 46 | Duffy R 35+1 | McCombe J 31+1 | McDonald C 20+2 | Loft D 32 | Myrie-Williams J 43+1 | Morsy S 21+7 | Shuker C 14+15 | Vincent A 32+2 | Pope T 46 | Dodds L 25+5 | Yates A 20+6 | Williamson B 8+25 | Burge R 23+7 | Taylor R 15+13 | Murphy D 1+2 | Owen G 1+1 | Lloyd R —+6 | James K 3+3 | Davis J 3+4 | McAllister S —+2 | Chilvers L 19+1 | Andrew C 7+15 | Birchall C 5+6 | Purse D 17 | Hughes L 13+5 | Jones D 16 | Griffith A 10 | Match No. |
|---|---|---|---|---|---|---|---|---|---|---|---|---|---|---|---|---|---|---|---|---|---|---|---|---|---|---|---|---|
| 1 | 2¹ | 3 | 4 | 5 | 6 | 7 | 8³ | 9² | 10 | 11 | 12 | 13 | 14 | | | | | | | | | | | | | | | 1 |
| 1 | 2¹ | 3 | 4 | 5 | 6 | 7 | 8² | 9³ | 11 | 10 | 12 | 14 | 13 | | | | | | | | | | | | | | | 2 |
| 1 | 2 | 3 | 4 | 5 | 6¹ | 8 | 7³ | 9 | 11 | 10² | | 13 | 12 | 14 | | | | | | | | | | | | | | 3 |
| 1 | 2 | 3 | 4 | 5 | 6 | 7 | 8² | 9 | 11 | 10³ | | 14 | 13 | 12 | | | | | | | | | | | | | | 4 |
| 1 | 2 | 3 | 4¹ | 5 | 6² | 7 | 8 | 9³ | 11 | 10 | | | 14 | 13 | 12 | | | | | | | | | | | | | 5 |
| 1 | 2 | 4 | 3 | 5 | 6 | 8 | 7² | 9³ | 11 | 10¹ | 12 | 13 | 14 | | | | | | | | | | | | | | | 6 |
| 1 | 2 | 4 | 3 | 5 | 6³ | 7¹ | 8 | 9² | 11 | 10 | | 14 | 12 | 13 | | | | | | | | | | | | | | 7 |
| 1 | 2 | 3 | 4 | 5 | 6 | 7² | 8¹ | 9 | 11 | 10² | | 14 | 12 | 13 | | | | | | | | | | | | | | 8 |
| 1 | 2¹ | 4 | 3 | 7 | 6 | 13 | | 9² | 11 | 10 | 12 | | 8 | 5 | | | | | | | | | | | | | | 9 |
| 1 | 2³ | 3 | 4 | 5 | 6 | 7 | 12 | 9 | 11 | 10² | 14 | 13 | 8¹ | | | | | | | | | | | | | | | 10 |
| 1 | 2 | 4 | 3 | 8¹ | 6 | 7 | 13 | 9² | 11 | 10 | | 12 | 5 | | | 14 | | | | | | | | | | | | 11 |
| 1 | 2² | 3 | 4 | | 6 | 7 | 12 | 9 | 11 | 10³ | 13 | 14 | 8 | 5 | | | | | | | | | | | | | | 12 |
| 1 | 2 | 3 | 4 | | 6² | | 7³ | 9 | 11 | 10 | | 12 | | 5 | 8¹ | 13 | 14 | | | | | | | | | | | 13 |
| 1 | 2¹ | 4 | 3³ | | 6 | 8 | 7² | 9 | 11 | 10 | 12 | 13 | | 5 | | | | | 14 | | | | | | | | | 14 |
| 1 | | 3 | | | 6 | | 7³ | | 9 | 10 | | 2 | 11¹ | 8 | 5 | 4² | 14 | 13 | 12 | | | | | | | | | 15 |
| 1 | | | 4 | 5¹ | 6 | | 7⁴ | | 9 | 11 | | 2 | 10² | 8 | 12 | 13³ | 14 | 3 | | | | | | | | | | 16 |
| 1 | 13 | | | | 6² | | 12 | 9 | 10 | 7 | | 2 | 11¹ | 8 | 5² | | 3 | | | | | 12 | | | | | | 17 |
| 1 | 6 | 3 | 4 | | | 9 | 7¹ | | 10 | 11 | 13 | 2 | 8 | 5² | | | | | | | | 12 | | | | | | 18 |
| 1 | 5 | 3 | 4³ | | 6 | | | | 9 | 10¹ | | 2 | 11 | 7² | | | | 12 | 8 | 14 | 13 | | | | | | | 19 |
| 1 | 5 | 3 | 4¹ | | | | 7³ | | 14 | 10 | 9 | 13 | 2 | 11² | 6 | | | | 8 | | 12 | | | | | | | 20 |
| 1 | 2 | 3 | 4 | 5² | 6 | | | | 13 | 9 | 10 | 14 | | 7 | 12 | | | | 8² | | | 11¹ | | | | | | 21 |
| 1 | 2 | 3 | | 5 | | 7 | 13 | 6¹ | 11 | 10³ | | 12 | 8 | 9² | | | | | | | 4 | 14 | | | | | | 22 |
| 1 | 2 | 3 | | 5 | 9² | 7 | | | 11 | 10¹ | 6 | | 8 | 13 | | | | | | | 4 | 12 | | | | | | 23 |
| 1 | 2 | 3 | 13 | | 6¹ | 7 | | | 10 | 9² | | 5 | 8 | 12 | | | | | | | 4 | 11 | | | | | | 24 |
| 1 | 2³ | 3¹ | 12 | | 6 | 7 | | | 14 | 10 | 11 | 5 | 8 | 13 | | | | | | | 4 | 9² | | | | | | 25 |
| 1 | | | 8 | | 6¹ | 7 | 9² | 10 | | 2 | 11³ | | 5 | | | | 13 | | 4 | | 3 | 14 | 12 | | | | | 26 |
| 1 | 5 | | 8 | | 6² | | 9³ | 10 | | 2 | 12 | | 7 | 14 | | | | | | | 3 | 13 | | 4 | 11¹ | | | 27 |
| 1 | 2 | | 8³ | | 6 | 14 | | 9¹ | 11 | | 13 | | 7 | | | | | | | | 3 | 12 | | 4 | 10² | 5 | | 28 |
| 1 | 2 | | 8 | | 6³ | | 13 | | 9 | 11 | 12 | | 7² | | | | | | | | 4 | 14 | | 3 | 10¹ | 5 | | 29 |
| 1 | 2 | | 8 | | 6² | | 9³ | | 11 | | 12 | | 7 | | | | | | | | 4 | 14 | 13 | 3 | 10¹ | 5 | | 30 |
| 1 | 3 | | 8 | | 6 | | 12 | 14 | 9² | 11 | | | 7³ | | | | | | | | 4 | 13 | | 3 | 10¹ | 5 | | 31 |
| 1 | 3 | | 8 | | 6 | | 13 | | 9³ | 11 | 2² | 12 | 7 | | | | | | | | | 14 | | 4 | 10¹ | 5 | | 32 |
| 1 | 2 | 3 | 8 | | 6 | | 12 | 9 | 10 | | | | 7¹ | | | | | | | | | 11 | | 4 | | | 8 | 33 |
| 1 | 2 | 3³ | 8 | | 6 | | | 9¹ | 10 | 13 | | | 7 | 12 | | | | | | | | 11² | | 4 | 14 | 5 | | 34 |
| 1 | 2 | 4 | 7 | | 6 | 14 | | | 10 | 13 | | | 11¹ | 8³ | | | | | | | | 9² | | 3 | 12 | 5 | | 35 |
| 1 | 2 | | 8⁴ | | 6² | | 12 | 9¹ | 10 | | 11³ | | | | | | | | | | 3 | 14 | | 4 | 13 | 5 | 7 | 36 |
| 1 | 2 | | | 13 | 6² | | | 9³ | 10 | | | | 5 | | | | | | | | 4 | 14 | 12 | 3¹ | 11 | | 8 | 37 |
| 1 | 4³ | 3 | | | 9 | 14 | | | 10² | 5 | 2 | | 8¹ | | | | | | | | 7 | 13 | 11 | | 12 | | 6 | 38 |
| 1 | 4 | | | | 6² | 14 | 9³ | | 11 | 2 | 12 | | 5 | | | | | | | | 3 | 13 | 8 | | 10¹ | | 7 | 39 |
| 1 | 3 | | | | 6 | | 9¹ | | 10 | 2 | 12 | | 8 | | | | | | | | 4 | 13 | | | 11¹ | 5 | 7 | 40 |
| 1 | | | 8 | | 6 | 14 | 13 | 9¹ | 10 | 2 | | | | | | | | | | | 4 | 11³ | 12 | 3 | | 5 | 7² | 41 |
| 1 | | | 7 | | 6² | 14 | | | 11 | 2 | 13 | | | | | | | | | | 4 | 9 | | 3 | 10¹ | 5 | 8³ | 42 |
| 1 | 4³ | | 8 | | 6 | | | | 10 | 2 | 13 | | | | | | | | | 14 | 12 | 9² | 3 | | 11 | 5 | 7 | 43 |
| 1 | | | 8 | 13 | 6² | | 9³ | | 11 | 2 | 12 | | | | | | | | | | 4 | 14 | | 3 | 10¹ | 5 | 7 | 44 |
| 1 | | | 8 | 13 | 6 | 14 | | 9¹ | 10 | 2 | | | | | | | | | | | 4 | 12 | | 3¹ | 11 | 5 | 7² | 45 |
| 1 | 2³ | 3 | | 7 | | | | 9 | 11 | 10² | 12 | | 14 | 8¹ | | | | | | | 4 | 13 | 6 | | | 5 | | 46 |

**FA Cup**

| | | | |
|---|---|---|---|
| First Round | Forest Green R | (a) | 3-2 |
| Second Round | Sheffield U | (a) | 1-2 |

**Capital One Cup**

| | | | |
|---|---|---|---|
| First Round | Burnley | (h) | 1-3 |

**Johnstone's Paint Trophy**

| | | | |
|---|---|---|---|
| First Round | Tranmere R | (h) | 2-0 |
| Second Round | Walsall | (a) | 2-2 |
| *(aet; won 6-5 on pens)* | | | |
| Northern Quarter-Finals | Bradford C | (h) | 0-2 |

# PORTSMOUTH

## FOUNDATION

At a meeting held in his High Street, Portsmouth offices in 1898, solicitor Alderman J. E. Pink and five other business and professional men agreed to buy some ground close to Goldsmith Avenue for £4,950 which they developed into Fratton Park in record breaking time. A team of professionals was signed up by manager Frank Brettell and entry to the Southern League obtained for the new club's September 1899 kick-off.

*Fratton Park, Frogmore Road, Portsmouth, Hampshire PO4 8RA.*

*Telephone:* (02392) 731 204.

*Fax:* (02392) 734 129.

*Ticket Office:* (0844) 847 1898.

*Website:* www.portsmouthfc.co.uk

*Email:* info@portsmouthfc.co.uk

*Ground Capacity:* 21,178.

*Record Attendance:* 51,385 v Derby Co, FA Cup 6th rd, 26 February 1949.

*Pitch Measurements:* 105m × 66m (115yd × 73yd)

*Chairman:* Iain McInnes.

*Chief Executive:* Mark Catlin.

*Manager:* Guy Whittingham.

*Assistant Manager/Head of Sports Performance:* Steve Allen.

*Colours:* Blue shirts with white trim, white shorts, red socks.

*Year Formed:* 1898.

*Turned Professional:* 1898.

*Club Nickname:* 'Pompey'.

*Ground:* 1898, Fratton Park.

*First Football League Game:* 28 August 1920, Division 3, v Swansea T (h) W 3–0 – Robson; Probert, Potts; Abbott, Harwood, Turner; Thompson, Stringfellow (1), Reid (1), James (1), Beedie.

*Record League Victory:* 9–1 v Notts Co, Division 2, 9 April 1927 – McPhail; Clifford, Ted Smith; Reg Davies (1), Foxall, Moffat; Forward (1), Mackie (2), Haines (3), Watson, Cook (2).

*Record Cup Victory:* 7–0 v Stockport Co, FA Cup 3rd rd, 8 January 1949 – Butler; Rookes, Ferrier; Scoular, Flewin, Dickinson; Harris (3), Barlow, Clarke (2), Phillips (2), Froggatt.

*Record Defeat:* 0–10 v Leicester C, Division 1, 20 October 1928.

*Most League Points (2 for a win):* 65, Division 3, 1961–62.

## HONOURS

**Football League – Division 1:**
*Champions* 1948–49, 1949–50, 2002–03;
**Division 2:** *Runners-up* 1926–27, 1986–87;
**Division 3 (S):** *Champions* 1923–24;
**Division 3:** *Champions* 1961–62, 1982–83.
**FA Cup:** *Winners* 1939, 2008; *Runners-up* 1929, 1934, 2010.
**Football League Cup:** Best season: 5th rd, 1961, 1986, 1994, 2010.
**European Competitions**
**UEFA Cup:** 2008–09.

## sky SPORTS FACT FILE

Portsmouth had their only experience of competitive European football in 2008-09 when they qualified for the UEFA Cup. Pompey won through to the Group stage where they defeated Heerenveen and drew 2-2 with AC Milan at Fratton Park but it was not enough to progress into the knock-out stages.

*Most League Points (3 for a win):* 98, Division 1, 2002–03.

*Most League Goals:* 97, Division 1, 2002–03.

*Highest League Scorer in Season:* Guy Whittingham, 42, Division 1, 1992–93.

*Most League Goals in Total Aggregate:* Peter Harris, 194, 1946–60.

*Most League Goals in One Match:* 5, Alf Strange v Gillingham, Division 3, 27 January 1923; 5, Peter Harris v Aston Villa, Division 1, 3 September 1958.

*Most Capped Player:* Jimmy Dickinson, 48, England.

*Most League Appearances:* Jimmy Dickinson, 764, 1946–65.

*Youngest League Player:* Clive Green, 16 years 259 days v Wrexham, 21 August 1976.

*Record Transfer Fee Received:* £20,000,000 from Real Madrid for Lassana Diarra, January 2009.

*Record Transfer Fee Paid:* Reported fee of £11,000,000 to Liverpool for Peter Crouch, July 2008.

*Football League Record:* 1920 Original Member of Division 3; 1921 Division 3 (S); 1924–27 Division 2; 1927–59 Division 1; 1959–61 Division 2; 1961–62 Division 3; 1962–76 Division 2; 1976–78 Division 3; 1978–80 Division 4; 1980–83 Division 3; 1983–87 Division 2; 1987–88 Division 1; 1988–92 Division 2; 1992–2003 Division 1; 2003–10 FA Premier League; 2010–12 FL C; 2012–13 FL 1; 2013– FL 2.

## LATEST SEQUENCES

*Longest Sequence of League Wins:* 7, 17.8.2002 – 17.9.2002.

*Longest Sequence of League Defeats:* 9, 21.10.1975 – 6.12.1975; 26.12.2012 – 9.2.2013.

*Longest Sequence of League Draws:* 5, 16.12.2000 – 13.1.2001.

*Longest Sequence of Unbeaten League Matches:* 15, 18.4.1924 – 18.10.1924.

*Longest Sequence Without a League Win:* 25, 29.11.1958 – 22.8.1959.

*Successive Scoring Runs:* 23 from 30.8.1930.

*Successive Non-scoring Runs:* 6 from 14.1.1939.

## MANAGERS

Frank Brettell 1898–1901
Bob Blyth 1901–04
Richard Bonney 1905–08
Bob Brown 1911–20
John McCartney 1920–27
Jack Tinn 1927–47
Bob Jackson 1947–52
Eddie Lever 1952–58
Freddie Cox 1958–61
George Smith 1961–70
Ron Tindall 1970–73
    *(General Manager to 1974)*
John Mortimore 1973–74
Ian St John 1974–77
Jimmy Dickinson 1977–79
Frank Burrows 1979–82
Bobby Campbell 1982–84
Alan Ball 1984–89
John Gregory 1989–90
Frank Burrows 1990–91
Jim Smith 1991–95
Terry Fenwick 1995–98
Alan Ball 1998–99
Tony Pulis 2000
Steve Claridge 2000–01
Graham Rix 2001–02
Harry Redknapp 2002–04
Velimir Zajec 2004–05
Alain Perrin 2005
Harry Redknapp 2005–08
Tony Adams 2008–09
Paul Hart 2009
Avram Grant 2009–10
Steve Cotterill 2010–11
Michael Appleton 2011–12
Guy Whittingham
    November 2012–

## TEN YEAR LEAGUE RECORD

| | | P | W | D | L | F | A | Pts | Pos |
|---|---|---|---|---|---|---|---|---|---|
| 2003-04 | PR Lge | 38 | 12 | 9 | 17 | 47 | 54 | 45 | 13 |
| 2004-05 | PR Lge | 38 | 10 | 9 | 19 | 43 | 59 | 39 | 16 |
| 2005-06 | PR Lge | 38 | 10 | 8 | 20 | 37 | 62 | 38 | 17 |
| 2006-07 | PR Lge | 38 | 14 | 12 | 12 | 45 | 42 | 54 | 9 |
| 2007-08 | PR Lge | 38 | 16 | 9 | 13 | 48 | 40 | 57 | 8 |
| 2008-09 | PR Lge | 38 | 10 | 11 | 17 | 38 | 57 | 41 | 14 |
| 2009-10 | PR Lge | 38 | 7 | 7 | 24 | 34 | 66 | 19* | 20 |
| 2010-11 | FL C | 46 | 15 | 13 | 18 | 53 | 60 | 58 | 16 |
| 2011-12 | FL C | 46 | 13 | 11 | 22 | 50 | 59 | 40† | 22 |
| 2012-13 | FL 1 | 46 | 10 | 12 | 24 | 51 | 69 | 32‡ | 24 |

*\*9 pts deducted; † 10 pts deducted; ‡10 pts deducted.*

## DID YOU KNOW ?

Portsmouth only joined the Football League in 1920 but after entering the Third Division rapidly won promotion through to top-flight football in less than a decade. During this period Pompey also reached an FA Cup final for the first time in 1929 losing 2-0 to Bolton Wanderers.

## PORTSMOUTH – FOOTBALL LEAGUE ONE 2012–13 LEAGUE RECORD

| Match No. | Date | Venue | Opponents | Result | H/T Score | Lg Pos. | Goalscorers | Attendance |
|---|---|---|---|---|---|---|---|---|
| 1 | Aug 18 | H | Bournemouth | D | 1-1 | 1-0 | 10 | McLeod [19] | 17,703 |
| 2 | 21 | A | Colchester U | D | 2-2 | 1-1 | 12 | Rodgers [30], Obita [86] | 4335 |
| 3 | 25 | A | Carlisle U | L | 2-4 | 0-1 | 20 | Harris [90], Clifford [90] | 5120 |
| 4 | Sept 1 | H | Oldham Ath | L | 0-1 | 0-0 | 21 | | 12,635 |
| 5 | 9 | A | Crawley T | W | 3-0 | 0-0 | 16 | Harris [74], Rodgers [83], McLeod [85] | 5058 |
| 6 | 15 | H | Walsall | L | 1-2 | 0-0 | 17 | McLeod [69] | 11,767 |
| 7 | 18 | H | Swindon T | L | 1-2 | 0-1 | 19 | Michalik [90] | 12,121 |
| 8 | 22 | A | Notts Co | L | 0-3 | 0-1 | 21 | | 6834 |
| 9 | 29 | H | Scunthorpe U | W | 2-1 | 1-1 | 17 | Gyepes [12], Thomas [89] | 10,995 |
| 10 | Oct 2 | A | Yeovil T | W | 2-1 | 1-0 | 14 | McLeod [13], Gyepes [79] | 4769 |
| 11 | 6 | A | Milton Keynes D | D | 2-2 | 2-1 | 17 | McLeod [4], Gyepes [20] | 10,409 |
| 12 | 13 | H | Crewe Alex | W | 2-0 | 2-0 | 12 | Thomas [2], McLeod (pen) [18] | 11,829 |
| 13 | 20 | H | Shrewsbury T | W | 3-1 | 0-0 | 11 | Thomas [55], McLeod 2 [58, 90] | 13,051 |
| 14 | 23 | A | Stevenage | L | 1-2 | 0-1 | 14 | Harley [51] | 4012 |
| 15 | 29 | A | Sheffield U | L | 0-1 | 0-0 | 15 | | 18,946 |
| 16 | Nov 6 | H | Brentford | L | 0-1 | 0-1 | 17 | | 11,328 |
| 17 | 10 | A | Bury | L | 0-2 | 0-1 | 18 | | 3280 |
| 18 | 17 | H | Doncaster R | L | 0-1 | 0-1 | 19 | | 11,792 |
| 19 | 20 | H | Leyton Orient | L | 2-3 | 0-1 | 21 | McLeod (pen) [57], Allan [65] | 9955 |
| 20 | 24 | A | Coventry C | D | 1-1 | 0-1 | 20 | McLeod [90] | 11,295 |
| 21 | Dec 8 | A | Tranmere R | D | 2-2 | 0-1 | 20 | Gyepes [50], Jervis [75] | 5591 |
| 22 | 15 | H | Preston NE | D | 0-0 | 0-0 | 21 | | 12,376 |
| 23 | 26 | H | Crawley T | L | 1-2 | 1-1 | 21 | Benson [11] | 13,169 |
| 24 | 29 | H | Yeovil T | L | 1-2 | 0-2 | 21 | Benson [54] | 12,370 |
| 25 | Jan 1 | A | Swindon T | L | 0-5 | 0-0 | 21 | | 11,381 |
| 26 | 4 | A | Walsall | L | 0-2 | 0-2 | 21 | | 4038 |
| 27 | 26 | H | Hartlepool U | L | 1-3 | 0-1 | 23 | Wallace [67] | 10,981 |
| 28 | 29 | H | Notts Co | L | 0-2 | 0-0 | 23 | | 10,276 |
| 29 | Feb 2 | H | Colchester U | L | 2-3 | 1-3 | 23 | Wallace [5], Keene [73] | 11,132 |
| 30 | 5 | A | Scunthorpe U | L | 1-2 | 1-1 | 23 | Walker [45] | 2596 |
| 31 | 9 | A | Bournemouth | L | 0-2 | 0-0 | 23 | | 9135 |
| 32 | 12 | A | Hartlepool U | D | 0-0 | 0-0 | 23 | | 3526 |
| 33 | 16 | H | Carlisle U | D | 1-1 | 0-0 | 24 | Walker (pen) [78] | 11,466 |
| 34 | 23 | A | Oldham Ath | L | 0-1 | 0-1 | 24 | | 4527 |
| 35 | 26 | H | Milton Keynes D | D | 1-1 | 1-1 | 24 | Connolly, D [22] | 9815 |
| 36 | Mar 2 | A | Crewe Alex | W | 2-1 | 2-0 | 24 | Agyemang [6], Connolly, D [29] | 5120 |
| 37 | 9 | H | Bury | W | 2-0 | 0-0 | 23 | Connolly, D 2 [50, 65] | 11,493 |
| 38 | 12 | A | Leyton Orient | L | 0-1 | 0-0 | 23 | | 3641 |
| 39 | 16 | A | Doncaster R | D | 1-1 | 0-1 | 23 | Wallace [75] | 7604 |
| 40 | 23 | H | Coventry C | W | 2-0 | 1-0 | 22 | Wallace [15], Agyemang [76] | 12,601 |
| 41 | 29 | A | Preston NE | D | 1-1 | 1-0 | 22 | Wallace [3] | 9464 |
| 42 | Apr 1 | H | Tranmere R | W | 1-0 | 0-0 | 22 | Connolly, D [53] | 12,014 |
| 43 | 6 | A | Stevenage | D | 0-0 | 0-0 | 22 | | 12,036 |
| 44 | 13 | A | Brentford | L | 2-3 | 1-1 | 22 | Connolly, D [26], Cooper [58] | 9149 |
| 45 | 20 | H | Sheffield U | W | 3-0 | 3-0 | 24 | Cooper [21], Connolly, D [24], Wallace [32] | 18,433 |
| 46 | 27 | A | Shrewsbury T | L | 2-3 | 0-2 | 24 | Harris [61], Agyemang [78] | 8021 |

**Final League Position: 24**

### GOALSCORERS

*League (51):* McLeod 10 (2 pens), Connolly, D 7, Wallace 6, Gyepes 4, Agyemang 3, Harris 3, Thomas 3, Benson 2, Cooper 2, Rodgers 2, Walker 2 (1 pen), Allan 1, Clifford 1, Harley 1, Jervis 1, Keene 1, Michalik 1, Obita 1.
*FA Cup (0).*
*Capital One Cup (0).*
*Johnstone's Paint Trophy (3):* Howard 1, McLeod 1, Rodgers 1.

| Andersen M 18 | Dumbuya M 22+1 | Sutherland F —+1 | Long K 5 | Connolly P 4 | Sodje S 9 | Harley J 23 | Djilali K 1 | Racon T 16 | Howard B 23 | Williamson L 19+3 | Compton J 7+5 | Agyemang P 15 | Rodgers L 6+4 | Akinde J 3+8 | McLeod I 23+1 | Clifford C —+2 | Harris A 7+19 | Webster A 10+8 | Walker L 16+10 | Obita J 2+6 | Russell D 17 | Ertl J 33+4 | Gyepes G 34+1 | Thompson J 2 | Michalik L 17+1 | Maloney J 1+8 | Thomas W 6 | Buzsaky A 5+1 | Awford N —+1 | Dickinson C 6 | Allan S 6+3 | Eastwood S 27 | Mendez-Laing N 5+3 | Benson P 7 | Rocha R 19+2 | Cisak A 1 | Jervis J 1+2 | Connolly D 15+2 | Wallace J 19+3 | Cooper S 13+1 | Butler D 15+2 | Reed A 5+5 | Keene J 6+3 | Moutaouakil Y 17+2 | Match No. |
|---|---|---|---|---|---|---|---|---|---|---|---|---|---|---|---|---|---|---|---|---|---|---|---|---|---|---|---|---|---|---|---|---|---|---|---|---|---|---|---|---|---|---|---|---|---|
| 1 | 2 | 3 | 4 | 5 | 6[3] | 7 | 8[1] | 9[2] | 10 | 11 | 12 | 13 | 14 | | | | | | | | | | | | | | | | | | | | | | | | | | | | | | | | 1 |
| 1 | 2 | 3 | 4 | 5 | | 8 | 6[1] | 9[2] | 11 | 10 | | 12 | 7 | 13 | | | | | | | | | | | | | | | | | | | | | | | | | | | | | | | 2 |
| 1 | 6 | 3[8] | 4 | 5 | | 8 | | 9 | 11[3] | 10[2] | 14 | 13 | 2[1] | 7 | 12 | | | | | | | | | | | | | | | | | | | | | | | | | | | | | | 3 |
| 1 | 6 | | 3 | 5 | | 7 | | 9 | 13 | 11 | | 12 | | 8[1] | 2[8] | 4 | 10[2] | | | | | | | | | | | | | | | | | | | | | | | | | | | | 4 |
| 1 | | 3 | | 5 | 8[3] | 6 | | 9[2] | 11 | 10 | | 13 | 12 | 14 | | 7 | | 2[1] | 4 | | | | | | | | | | | | | | | | | | | | | | | | | | 5 |
| 1 | 2 | 3[1] | | 5 | 8 | 6 | 13 | 10 | 11 | | 9[2] | | 12 | | 7 | | 4 | | | | | | | | | | | | | | | | | | | | | | | | | | | 6 |
| 1 | 2 | | | 5 | 7 | 6 | 9[2] | 13 | 10 | | 12 | | 11[1] | 8 | 3 | | 4 | | | | | | | | | | | | | | | | | | | | | | | | | | | 7 |
| 1 | 2 | | | 5 | 7 | 6 | 9[3] | 11[2] | 10[1] | | 12 | | 14 | 13 | 8 | 3 | 4 | | | | | | | | | | | | | | | | | | | | | | | | | | | 8 |
| 1 | 6 | | | 5[1] | 8 | 9 | | 10 | | | 12 | 2 | | 14 | 7[2] | 13 | 3 | 4 | 11[3] | | | | | | | | | | | | | | | | | | | | | | | | | | 9 |
| 1 | 9 | | | 5 | 6 | 8 | | 11[2] | | | 12 | 2 | | 13 | | 7 | 4 | 3 | 10[1] | | | | | | | | | | | | | | | | | | | | | | | | | | 10 |
| 1 | 2 | | | 9 | 8[2] | 6 | | 10 | | | 3 | | 13 | | 7 | 4 | 5 | 11[1] | 12 | | | | | | | | | | | | | | | | | | | | | | | | | | 11 |
| 1 | | | | 5 | 7 | 9 | 12 | 13 | 10[2] | | 2 | | | | 6 | 4 | 3 | 11 | 8[1] | | | | | | | | | | | | | | | | | | | | | | | | | | 12 |
| 1 | 5 | | | 6[1] | 8 | 2 | 13 | | 11 | | 12 | | | | 7 | 4 | 3 | 10 | 9[2] | | | | | | | | | | | | | | | | | | | | | | | | | | 13 |
| 1 | 12 | | | 2 | 7 | 6 | | 10 | | | 5 | | | | 4 | 3 | 11 | 8[1] | 9 | | | | | | | | | | | | | | | | | | | | | | | | | | 14 |
| 1 | 2 | | | 9[1] | 7 | | 13 | 10 | | | 12 | | | | 8[2] | 3 | 4 | | 6 | 5 | 11 | | | | | | | | | | | | | | | | | | | | | | | | 15 |
| | 2 | | | 9[2] | 7 | 8 | | 11 | | | 12 | 6[1] | 13 | | 4 | | 3 | 10 | 5 | | 1 | | | | | | | | | | | | | | | | | | | | | | | | 16 |
| 1 | 2 | | | 9[2] | 7 | 6 | 13 | | 11 | | 10 | | 14 | | 8[1] | 12 | 4[1] | 3 | | 5 | | | | | | | | | | | | | | | | | | | | | | | | 17 |
| 1 | 2 | | | | 7 | 8[1] | 13 | | 10 | | 12 | | | | 9 | 5 | 3 | | 4[2] | | 6 | 11 | | | | | | | | | | | | | | | | | | | | | | | 18 |
| 1 | | | | 5 | 7 | | | | 11 | | | | | | 8[2] | 13 | 4[1] | | 3 | 2 | 6 | 9 | 10 | 12 | | | | | | | | | | | | | | | | | | | | | 19 |
| | 2[3] | | | 5 | 7 | | | 10 | | | 14 | | | | 8 | 9 | 3 | | 6[1] | 12 | 11[2] | 4 | 1 | 13 | | | | | | | | | | | | | | | | | | | | | 20 |
| | 2 | | | 5 | 8 | 13 | | 11[3] | | | 7[2] | 6 | 3 | | 14 | 1 | 9[1] | 10 | 4 | 12 | | | | | | | | | | | | | | | | | | | | | | | | 21 |
| | 2 | | | 5 | 8 | 13 | | 10 | | | 9[2] | 7 | 3 | | 6 | 1 | 12 | 4 | | 11[1] | | | | | | | | | | | | | | | | | | | | | | | | 22 |
| | 5 | | | 2 | 8 | 14 | | 13 | | | 7 | 6[2] | 4[1] | | 12 | 9 | 1 | 10[3] | 11 | 3 | | | | | | | | | | | | | | | | | | | | | | | | 23 |
| | 2 | | | | 8[2] | 6 | | 11[1] | | | 12 | 5 | 9 | | 7 | 14 | 3 | 13 | 1 | 10 | 4[3] | | | | | | | | | | | | | | | | | | | | | | | | 24 |
| | 2 | | | 5 | | 6 | | 11[3] | 4 | | 9[1] | 8 | 7 | | 3 | 10[2] | 1 | 14 | | 12 | 13 | | | | | | | | | | | | | | | | | | | | | | | | 25 |
| | 2 | | | | 7 | | | 13 | 5[3] | | 9[1] | 8 | 4 | | 3 | 12 | 1 | 6[2] | 10 | 11 | 14 | | | | | | | | | | | | | | | | | | | | | | | | 26 |
| | | 14 | | | | | | 12 | | | 8 | 7[3] | 3 | | 1 | | 4 | | | 10 | 6 | 2[2] | 5 | 9[1] | 11 | 13 | | | | | | | | | | | | | | | | | | | 27 |
| | | | | | | | 6[1] | | 12 | | 7 | 3 | | | 1 | | 4 | | | 10 | 9 | 5[2] | 2 | 13 | 11 | 8 | | | | | | | | | | | | | | | | | | 28 |
| | | | 3 | | | | | 9 | | | 13 | 7 | 12 | | 1 | | 4[1] | | | 11[2] | 6 | 8[3] | 5 | 14 | 10 | 2 | | | | | | | | | | | | | | | | | | 29 |
| | | | 3 | | | | 10[1] | 5[2] | 9 | | 7 | 4 | | | 1 | | 8 | 12 | 13 | 6 | 11 | 2 | | | | | | | | | | | | | | | | | | | | | | 30 |
| | | | | | | 9[2] | 10[1] | 11 | | 14 | 8 | 3 | | | 1 | | 4 | | | 13 | 7[3] | 5 | 6 | 12 | 2 | | | | | | | | | | | | | | | | | | | 31 |
| | | | 3 | | | 11 | 6[1] | 12 | | | 5 | | | | 1 | | 9 | | | 7 | 2 | 8 | 10 | 4 | | | | | | | | | | | | | | | | | | | | 32 |
| | | | 3 | | | 9 | 11 | 14 | | | 13 | 7 | | | 1 | | 4 | | | 8[3] | 2[1] | 5 | 6 | 10[2] | 12 | | | | | | | | | | | | | | | | | | | 33 |
| | | | 4[8] | | | 8 | 11[2] | 10 | | | 9[1] | 7 | 3 | | 1 | | 13 | 6 | 5 | 12 | 14 | 2[3] | | | | | | | | | | | | | | | | | | | | | | 34 |
| | | | 7[1] | | | 11 | | 14 | 13 | 9[3] | 8 | 4 | | | 1 | | 3 | 10 | 6 | 5 | 12 | 2[2] | | | | | | | | | | | | | | | | | | | | | | 35 |
| | | | 8 | | | 10[3] | 14 | | | | 6[2] | 7 | 3 | | 1 | | 4 | 11[1] | 9 | 5 | 13 | 12 | 2 | | | | | | | | | | | | | | | | | | | | | 36 |
| | | | 8 | | | 11 | | | | | 9 | 7 | 3 | 12 | 1 | | 4 | 10[1] | 6 | 5 | 2 | | | | | | | | | | | | | | | | | | | | | | | 37 |
| | | | 8 | | | 11 | 13 | 9[1] | | | 7 | 3 | 12 | | 1 | | 4 | 10 | 6 | 5[2] | 2 | | | | | | | | | | | | | | | | | | | | | | | 38 |
| | | | 7 | | | 10 | 12 | | | 13 | 9[1] | 8 | 4 | | 1 | | 3 | 11 | 6 | 5[2] | 2 | | | | | | | | | | | | | | | | | | | | | | | 39 |
| | | | 8 | | | 10[2] | 13 | | | | 9[1] | 7 | 4 | 12 | 1 | | 3 | 11 | 6 | 5 | 2 | | | | | | | | | | | | | | | | | | | | | | | 40 |
| | | | 8 | | | 10[3] | 14 | | | | 6[1] | 7 | 3 | | 1 | | 4 | 11[2] | 9 | 5 | 12 | 2 | | | | | | | | | | | | | | | | | | | | | | 41 |
| | | | 4[3] | | | 8 | 10[2] | 13 | | | 12 | 7 | 3 | 6[1] | 1 | | 14 | 11 | 9 | 5 | 2 | | | | | | | | | | | | | | | | | | | | | | | 42 |
| | | | 8 | | | | 11[2] | 12 | 14 | 9[1] | 7 | 3 | 13 | | 1 | | 4 | 10 | 6 | 5 | 2[3] | | | | | | | | | | | | | | | | | | | | | | | 43 |
| | | | 9 | | | 8 | 10[1] | 12 | | | 3 | 4 | 13 | | 1 | | 11 | 7 | 6[2] | 5 | 2 | | | | | | | | | | | | | | | | | | | | | | | 44 |
| | | | 3 | | | 8 | 11[1] | 12 | | | 7[3] | 4 | 13 | 14 | 1 | | 10 | 6[2] | 9 | 5 | 2 | | | | | | | | | | | | | | | | | | | | | | | 45 |
| | | | 4 | | | 7 | 10 | 11 | 12 | | 8 | 3[1] | 13 | | 1 | | 6 | 9 | 5 | 2[2] | | | | | | | | | | | | | | | | | | | | | | | | 46 |

**FA Cup**

First Round  Notts Co  (h)  0-2

**Capital One Cup**

First Round  Plymouth Arg  (a)  0-3

**Johnstone's Paint Trophy**

First Round  Bournemouth  (h)  2-2
*(aet; won 4-3 on pens)*

Second Round  Wycombe W  (h)  1-3

# PRESTON NORTH END

## FOUNDATION

North End Cricket and Rugby Club, which was formed in 1863, indulged in most sports before taking up soccer in about 1879. In 1881 they decided to stick to football to the exclusion of other sports and even a 16–0 drubbing by Blackburn Rovers in an invitation game at Deepdale, a few weeks after taking this decision, did not deter them for they immediately became affiliated to the Lancashire FA.

*Deepdale Stadium, Sir Tom Finney Way, Deepdale, Preston, Lancashire PR1 6RU.*
*Telephone:* (0844) 856 1964.
*Fax:* (01772) 693 366.
*Ticket Office:* (0844) 856 1966.
*Website:* www.pne.co.uk
*Email:* enquiries@pne.co.uk
*Ground Capacity:* 23,404.
*Record Attendance:* 42,684 v Arsenal, Division 1, 23 April 1938.
*Pitch Measurements:* 100m × 70m (110yd × 77yd)
*Directors:* Kevin Abbott, Anthony Hughes, Paul Newsham, David Robinson, David Taylor.
*Manager:* Simon Grayson.
*Assistant Manager:* Glynn Snodin.
*Head Physio:* Matthew Jackson.
*Colours:* White shirts, blue shorts, white socks.
*Year Formed:* 1880.
*Turned Professional:* 1885.
*Club Nicknames:* 'The Lilywhites', 'North End'.
*Ground:* 1881, Deepdale.

## HONOURS

**Football League – Division 1:**
*Champions* 1888–89 (first champions) 1889–90; *Runners-up* 1890–91, 1891–92, 1892–93, 1905–06, 1952–53, 1957–58;
**Division 2:** *Champions* 1903–04, 1912–13, 1950–51, 1999–2000; *Runners-up* 1914–15, 1933–34;
**Division 3:** *Champions* 1970–71, 1995–96;
**Division 4:** *Runners-up* 1986–87.
**FA Cup:** *Winners* 1889, 1938; *Runners-up* 1888, 1922, 1937, 1954, 1964.
**Football League Cup:** Best season: 4th rd, 2003.
**Double Performed:** 1888–89.
**Football League Cup:** Best season: 4th rd, 1963, 1966, 1972, 1981.

*First Football League Game:* 8 September 1888, Football League, v Burnley (h) W 5–2 – Trainer; Howarth, Holmes; Robertson, William Graham, Johnny Graham; Gordon (1), Jimmy Ross (2), Goodall, Dewhurst (2), Drummond.
*Record League Victory:* 10–0 v Stoke, Division 1, 14 September 1889 – Trainer; Howarth, Holmes; Kelso, Russell (1), Johnny Graham; Gordon, Jimmy Ross (2), Nick Ross (3), Thomson (2), Drummond (2).
*Record Cup Victory:* 26–0 v Hyde, FA Cup 1st rd, 15 October 1887 – Addision; Howarth, Nick Ross; Russell (1), Thomson (5), Johnny Graham (1); Gordon (5), Jimmy Ross (8), John Goodall (1), Dewhurst (3), Drummond (2).
*Record Defeat:* 0–7 v Blackpool, Division 1, 1 May 1948.
*Most League Points (2 for a win):* 61, Division 3, 1970–71.
*Most League Points (3 for a win):* 95, Division 2, 1999–2000.
*Most League Goals:* 100, Division 2, 1927–28 and Division 1, 1957–58.

## sky SPORTS FACT FILE

Club captain Fred Dewhurst set up Preston's first FA Cup final victory when he netted the opening goal in their 3-0 win over Wolverhampton back in 1889. Jimmy Ross and Sam Thomson completed the scoring for North End who had already clinched the Football League title.

*Highest League Scorer in Season:* Ted Harper, 37, Division 2, 1932–33.

*Most League Goals in Total Aggregate:* Tom Finney, 187, 1946–60.

*Most League Goals in One Match:* 4, Jimmy Ross v Stoke, Division 1, 6 October 1888; 4, Nick Ross v Derby Co, Division 1, 11 January 1890; 4, George Drummond v Notts Co, Division 1, 12 December 1891; 4, Frank Becton v Notts Co, Division 1, 31 March 1893; 4, George Harrison v Grimsby T, Division 2, 3 November 1928; 4, Alex Reid v Port Vale, Division 2, 23 February 1929; 4, James McClelland v Reading, Division 2, 6 September 1930; 4, Dick Rowley v Notts Co, Division 2, 16 April 1932; 4, Ted Harper v Burnley, Division 2, 29 August 1932; 4, Ted Harper v Lincoln C, Division 2, 11 March 1933; 4, Charlie Wayman v QPR, Division 2, 25 December 1950; 4, Alex Bruce v Colchester U, Division 3, 28 February 1978.

*Most Capped Player:* Tom Finney, 76, England.

*Most League Appearances:* Alan Kelly, 447, 1961–75.

*Youngest League Player:* Steve Doyle, 16 years 166 days v Tranmere R, 15 November 1974.

*Record Transfer Fee Received:* £6,000,000 from Portsmouth for David Nugent, August 2007.

*Record Transfer Fee Paid:* £1,500,000 to Manchester U for David Healy, December 2000.

*Football League Record:* 1888 Founder Member of League; 1901–04 Division 2; 1904–12 Division 1; 1912–13 Division 2; 1913–14 Division 1; 1914–15 Division 2; 1919–25 Division 1; 1925–34 Division 2; 1934–49 Division 1; 1949–51 Division 2; 1951–61 Division 1; 1961–70 Division 2; 1970–71 Division 3; 1971–74 Division 2; 1974–78 Division 3; 1978–81 Division 2; 1981–85 Division 3; 1985–87 Division 4; 1987–92 Division 3; 1992–93 Division 2; 1993–96 Division 3; 1996–2000 Division 2; 2000–04 Division 1; 2004–11 FL C; 2011– FL 1.

## LATEST SEQUENCES

*Longest Sequence of League Wins:* 14, 25.12.1950 – 27.3.1951.

*Longest Sequence of League Defeats:* 8, 22.9.1984 – 27.10.1984.

*Longest Sequence of League Draws:* 6, 24.2.1979 – 20.3.1979.

*Longest Sequence of Unbeaten League Matches:* 23, 8.9.1888 – 14.9.1889.

*Longest Sequence Without a League Win:* 15, 14.4.1923 – 20.10.1923.

*Successive Scoring Runs:* 30 from 15.11.1952.

*Successive Non-scoring Runs:* 6 from 8.4.1897.

## MANAGERS

Charlie Parker 1906–15
Vincent Hayes 1919–23
Jim Lawrence 1923–25
Frank Richards 1925–27
Alex Gibson 1927–31
Lincoln Hayes 1931–32
*Run by committee* 1932–36
Tommy Muirhead 1936–37
*Run by committee* 1937–49
Will Scott 1949–53
Scot Symon 1953–54
Frank Hill 1954–56
Cliff Britton 1956–61
Jimmy Milne 1961–68
Bobby Seith 1968–70
Alan Ball Snr 1970–73
Bobby Charlton 1973–75
Harry Catterick 1975–77
Nobby Stiles 1977–81
Tommy Docherty 1981
Gordon Lee 1981–83
Alan Kelly 1983–85
Tommy Booth 1985–86
Brian Kidd 1986
John McGrath 1986–90
Les Chapman 1990–92
Sam Allardyce 1992 (*Caretaker*)
John Beck 1992–94
Gary Peters 1994–98
David Moyes 1998–2002
Kelham O'Hanlon 2002
  (*Caretaker*)
Craig Brown 2002–04
Billy Davies 2004–06
Paul Simpson 2006–07
Alan Irvine 2007–09
Darren Ferguson 2010
Phil Brown 2011
Graham Westley 2012–13
Simon Grayson February 2013–

## TEN YEAR LEAGUE RECORD

| | | P | W | D | L | F | A | Pts | Pos |
|---|---|---|---|---|---|---|---|---|---|
| 2003-04 | Div 1 | 46 | 15 | 14 | 17 | 69 | 71 | 59 | 15 |
| 2004-05 | FL C | 46 | 21 | 12 | 13 | 67 | 58 | 75 | 5 |
| 2005-06 | FL C | 46 | 20 | 20 | 6 | 59 | 30 | 80 | 4 |
| 2006-07 | FL C | 46 | 22 | 8 | 16 | 64 | 53 | 74 | 7 |
| 2007-08 | FL C | 46 | 15 | 11 | 20 | 50 | 56 | 56 | 15 |
| 2008-09 | FL C | 46 | 21 | 11 | 14 | 66 | 54 | 74 | 6 |
| 2009-10 | FL C | 46 | 13 | 15 | 18 | 58 | 73 | 54 | 17 |
| 2010-11 | FL C | 46 | 10 | 12 | 24 | 54 | 79 | 42 | 22 |
| 2011-12 | FL 1 | 46 | 13 | 15 | 18 | 54 | 68 | 54 | 15 |
| 2012-13 | FL 1 | 46 | 14 | 17 | 15 | 54 | 49 | 59 | 14 |

## DID YOU KNOW

David Beckham scored on each of his first two appearances for Preston North End when he spent time on loan at the club in the 1994–95 season. Just eight days after his final game for North End he made his Premier League debut for Manchester United.

## PRESTON NORTH END – FOOTBALL LEAGUE ONE 2012-13 LEAGUE RECORD

| Match No. | Date | Venue | Opponents | Result | H/T Score | Lg Pos. | Goalscorers | Attendance |
|---|---|---|---|---|---|---|---|---|
| 1 | Aug 18 | H | Colchester U | D 0-0 | 0-0 | 17 | | 10,034 |
| 2 | 21 | A | Shrewsbury T | L 0-1 | 0-1 | 17 | | 6444 |
| 3 | 25 | A | Bournemouth | D 1-1 | 0-0 | 19 | Sodje [76] | 5329 |
| 4 | Sept 2 | H | Swindon T | W 4-1 | 3-0 | 12 | Sodje [5], Wroe [10], Beavon [43], Welsh [68] | 10,372 |
| 5 | 8 | A | Bury | W 2-1 | 1-0 | 7 | Sodje [30], Cansdell-Sherriff [66] | 5213 |
| 6 | 15 | H | Crawley T | L 1-2 | 0-0 | 11 | Huntington [90] | 9812 |
| 7 | 18 | H | Hartlepool U | W 5-0 | 2-0 | 5 | Byrom [28], Beavon [29], King [65], Laird 2 [84, 87] | 8132 |
| 8 | 22 | A | Walsall | L 1-3 | 1-1 | 11 | Byrom [10] | 4189 |
| 9 | 29 | H | Yeovil T | W 3-2 | 0-1 | 9 | Monakana [57], Ayling (og) [64], Burn (og) [86] | 8520 |
| 10 | Oct 2 | A | Doncaster R | W 3-1 | 1-1 | 7 | King [33], Laird [60], Beavon [71] | 5681 |
| 11 | 6 | A | Oldham Ath | L 1-3 | 0-1 | 8 | Sodje [90] | 5496 |
| 12 | 14 | H | Milton Keynes D | D 0-0 | 0-0 | 8 | | 8327 |
| 13 | 20 | H | Sheffield U | L 0-1 | 0-1 | 9 | | 11,536 |
| 14 | 23 | A | Scunthorpe U | W 3-2 | 3-1 | 8 | Wroe 3 [1, 28, 36] | 2671 |
| 15 | 27 | A | Tranmere R | D 1-1 | 0-0 | 9 | Huntington [50] | 7732 |
| 16 | Nov 6 | H | Carlisle U | D 1-1 | 0-1 | 10 | Cummins [90] | 9249 |
| 17 | 10 | A | Stevenage | W 4-1 | 2-1 | 10 | Beavon [6], King [32], Monakana [58], Wroe [72] | 3740 |
| 18 | 17 | H | Brentford | D 1-1 | 0-0 | 10 | Laird [62] | 8804 |
| 19 | 20 | H | Notts Co | D 0-0 | 0-0 | 10 | | 8013 |
| 20 | 24 | A | Leyton Orient | L 0-2 | 0-1 | 11 | | 4190 |
| 21 | Dec 8 | H | Crewe Alex | L 1-3 | 0-1 | 14 | Huntington [89] | 8542 |
| 22 | 15 | A | Portsmouth | D 0-0 | 0-0 | 15 | | 12,376 |
| 23 | 22 | A | Coventry C | D 1-1 | 0-1 | 15 | Holmes [77] | 12,230 |
| 24 | 26 | H | Bury | D 0-0 | 0-0 | 14 | | 12,014 |
| 25 | 29 | H | Doncaster R | L 0-3 | 0-2 | 15 | | 9626 |
| 26 | Jan 1 | A | Hartlepool U | W 1-0 | 1-0 | 14 | Mousinho [45] | 3829 |
| 27 | 13 | H | Walsall | L 1-3 | 0-2 | 16 | Wright [90] | 9823 |
| 28 | 26 | H | Coventry C | D 2-2 | 1-1 | 16 | Cummins [30], Wroe [60] | 8474 |
| 29 | Feb 2 | H | Shrewsbury T | L 1-2 | 1-0 | 17 | Beavon [43] | 8331 |
| 30 | 9 | A | Colchester U | L 0-1 | 0-0 | 17 | | 3215 |
| 31 | 12 | A | Yeovil T | L 1-3 | 1-0 | 17 | Beardsley [30] | 3661 |
| 32 | 16 | H | Bournemouth | W 2-0 | 2-0 | 17 | Beavon [19], Wright [31] | 8899 |
| 33 | 23 | A | Swindon T | D 1-1 | 0-0 | 18 | Hayhurst [51] | 9145 |
| 34 | Mar 2 | A | Milton Keynes D | D 1-1 | 1-1 | 17 | Hayhurst [7] | 8412 |
| 35 | 9 | H | Stevenage | W 2-0 | 2-0 | 17 | Holmes [6], Hayhurst [16] | 9000 |
| 36 | 12 | A | Notts Co | W 1-0 | 1-0 | 15 | Hollis (og) [34] | 3587 |
| 37 | 16 | A | Brentford | L 0-1 | 0-0 | 16 | | 6512 |
| 38 | 23 | H | Leyton Orient | D 0-0 | 0-0 | 16 | | 8405 |
| 39 | 29 | H | Portsmouth | D 1-1 | 0-1 | 16 | Keane [77] | 9464 |
| 40 | Apr 1 | A | Crewe Alex | L 0-1 | 0-1 | 16 | | 6366 |
| 41 | 6 | H | Scunthorpe U | W 3-0 | 1-0 | 16 | Holmes [38], Wroe [77], King [90] | 8118 |
| 42 | 9 | H | Oldham Ath | W 2-0 | 0-0 | 15 | Wroe (pen) [73], Hayhurst [90] | 9080 |
| 43 | 13 | A | Carlisle U | D 1-1 | 1-1 | 14 | Monakana [12] | 5965 |
| 44 | 20 | H | Tranmere R | W 1-0 | 1-0 | 13 | Monakana [45] | 10,467 |
| 45 | 23 | A | Crawley T | L 0-1 | 0-1 | 14 | | 3026 |
| 46 | 27 | A | Sheffield U | D 0-0 | 0-0 | 14 | | 19,888 |

**Final League Position: 14**

### GOALSCORERS

*League (54):* Wroe 8 (1 pen), Beavon 6, Hayhurst 4, King 4, Laird 4, Monakana 4, Sodje 4, Holmes 3, Huntington 3, Byrom 2, Cummins 2, Wright 2, Beardsley 1, Cansdell-Sherriff 1, Keane 1, Mousinho 1, Welsh 1, own goals 3.
*FA Cup (5):* Amoo 1, Beavon 1, Byrom 1, Monakana 1, Robertson 1.
*Capital One Cup (7):* Wroe 3, King 2, Monakana 1, Sodje 1.
*Johnstone's Paint Trophy (10):* Beavon 2, Sodje 2, Beardsley 1, Cummins 1, Foster 1, Huntington 1, King 1, Procter 1.

| Stuckmann T 22 | Keane K 22 + 4 | Laird S 19 | Huntington P 34 + 3 | Cansdell-Sherriff S 14 + 1 | Monakana A 23 + 15 | Wroe N 36 + 2 | Mousinho J 16 + 8 | King J 33 + 3 | Buchanan D 27 + 6 | Beardsley C 12 + 7 | Amoo D 6 + 11 | Welsh J 32 + 4 | Procter A 6 + 9 | Holmes L 23 + 5 | Sodje A 5 + 9 | Cummins G 5 + 14 | Wright B 37 + 1 | Beavon S 30 + 1 | Byrom J 12 + 10 | Hayhurst W 18 + 3 | Simonsen S 10 | Robertson C 16 + 5 | Elding A 2 + 3 | Kane T 3 | Foster L 3 + 3 | Trundle L — + 1 | Garner J 9 + 5 | Connolly P 14 + 1 | Davies B 3 | Rudd D 14 | Match No. |
|---|---|---|---|---|---|---|---|---|---|---|---|---|---|---|---|---|---|---|---|---|---|---|---|---|---|---|---|---|---|---|---|
| 1 | 2 | 3 | 4 | 5 | 6 | 7 | 8² | 9³ | 10¹ | 11 | 12 | 13 | 14 | | | | | | | | | | | | | | | | | | 1 |
| 1 | 2 | 5 | 3 | 4 | 6 | 7 | | 10¹ | | 11 | 13 | 8 | | 9² | 12³ | 14 | | | | | | | | | | | | | | | 2 |
| 1 | | 5 | 3 | 4 | 6 | 12 | 7 | 9³ | 14 | 10 | 11² | | 8¹ | 13 | 2 | | | | | | | | | | | | | | | | 3 |
| 1 | 2 | 3 | 4 | 5 | 8³ | 6 | | | | | 12 | 14 | 7 | 13 | | 11² | 9 | 10¹ | | | | | | | | | | | | | 4 |
| 1 | 6¹ | 5 | 3 | 4 | 9² | 8 | | | | 14 | 13 | 7 | | 10³ | | 2 | 11 | 12 | | | | | | | | | | | | | 5 |
| 1 | | 9 | 3 | 4 | 6³ | 8 | | 5¹ | | 13 | 7 | | 11 | | 2² | 10 | 12 | 14 | | | | | | | | | | | | | 6 |
| | 5 | | 4 | 7 | 14 | 12 | | 10¹ | 6² | 2 | | 13 | | 3 | 11 | 8³ | 9 | 1 | | | | | | | | | | | | | 7 |
| | 5 | 3² | 4 | 13 | 9 | 8³ | | 14 | 7 | | 12 | | 2 | 11 | 6 | 10¹ | 1 | | | | | | | | | | | | | | 8 |
| 1 | 2 | 5 | 3 | | 6³ | | 7 | 13 | 12 | 10² | 14 | | | 4 | 11 | 8 | 9¹ | | | | | | | | | | | | | | 9 |
| 1 | | 9 | 3¹ | 12 | 13 | | 7 | 2 | 5³ | 11 | 6² | 14 | | 4 | 10 | 8 | | | | | | | | | | | | | | | 10 |
| 1 | | 5 | 3⁴ | 12 | 13 | 8 | 2 | 9² | 10³ | 6¹ | | 14 | | 4 | 11 | 7 | | | | | | | | | | | | | | | 11 |
| 1 | 2 | 5 | 3¹ | | 6 | 8 | 13 | | | 7 | | | 10³ | 14 | 4 | 11 | | 9² | | 12 | | | | | | | | | | | 12 |
| 1 | 2 | 5 | 12 | | 9 | 6³ | 7 | | 10² | 13 | 8 | | | 14 | 4¹ | 11 | | 3 | | | | | | | | | | | | | 13 |
| | 2 | 5 | 4 | 7 | 9¹ | 6 | | 10 | | | 12³ | 8 | 13 | | | 11² | 14 | | 1 | 3 | | | | | | | | | | | 14 |
| | 2 | 9 | 3 | 5 | 6¹ | 8 | | 10 | | | | 7 | | | | 11 | 12 | | 1 | 4 | | | | | | | | | | | 15 |
| | 2 | 9 | 3 | | | 7 | | 11³ | | | 6² | | | 12 | 13 | 14 | 5¹ | 10 | 8 | | 1 | 4 | | | | | | | | | 16 |
| | 2 | 3 | | 6² | 7 | 12 | 9³ | 13 | | | 5 | | | 8¹ | | 14 | 10 | 11 | | 1 | 4 | | | | | | | | | | 17 |
| | 2 | 3 | 4 | | 9 | 6 | 11³ | 12 | | | 7 | | | 8¹ | | | 10² | 14 | | 1 | 5 | 13 | | | | | | | | | 18 |
| | 2¹ | 5 | 4 | | 9 | 6 | 8² | | | | 7 | | | 13 | 10³ | 14 | 12 | 11 | | 1 | 3 | | | | | | | | | | 19 |
| | | 3 | | | 8 | | 10² | 5 | | | 7 | | | 9 | 13 | 12 | 2¹ | 11³ | | 1 | 4 | 14 | 6 | | | | | | | | 20 |
| 1 | | 3 | 5 | 9¹ | 7³ | 10 | | | 12 | 8 | | 6 | 13 | | | | 14 | | | 4 | 11 | 2² | | | | | | | | | 21 |
| 1 | | | 5 | 6³ | | 12 | 2 | 9 | 10 | | | 7² | 14 | | 3 | 13 | 8 | | | 4 | 11¹ | | | | | | | | | | 22 |
| 1 | | | 14 | | 6 | 2 | 5 | 12 | 11³ | 13 | | 7¹ | 9 | | 10² | 3 | | 8 | | | 4 | | | | | | | | | | 23 |
| 1 | | | 12 | | 2 | 9 | 5 | 10³ | 14 | 7 | | 6¹ | | | 4 | | 8 | 11² | | | | 3 | 13 | | | | | | | | 24 |
| 1 | | 3¹ | | 6 | 2 | 5 | 10² | 7 | 8³ | | | 4 | | 11 | 14 | 9 | | | 13 | 12 | | | | | | | | | | | 25 |
| | | 5 | | | 8³ | 7 | 11 | 9² | | 2 | 14 | | | 4¹ | 10 | 13 | | 1 | 12 | | 6 | 3 | | | | | | | | | 26 |
| 1 | | | 6¹ | 8 | | 2² | 5 | | 7 | | | 9³ | | 13 | 4 | 10 | 12 | 14 | | 3 | | 11 | | | | | | | | | 27 |
| 1 | | | 6 | 7 | | 10 | 14 | | 12 | 9 | | 11² | 5 | 8¹ | | 3 | | | 13 | 2 | 4³ | | | | | | | | | 1 | 28 |
| 1 | | 14 | 13 | 7 | 4 | | 12 | 9 | | 11² | 5 | 10 | 8¹ | | 9² | 3 | | | 2 | 6³ | | | | | | | | | | 1 | 29 |
| 1 | | 14 | 13 | 7 | | 5 | 12 | 8 | 6¹ | 9² | 10³ | 4⁴ | | | 3 | | | 11 | 2 | | | | | | | | | | | 1 | 30 |
| | 14 | 3 | 6 | | 12 | 11³ | 8 | 7² | 9 | 13 | | | 4 | | | 10 | 2 | 5¹ | 1 | | | | | | | | | | | | 31 |
| 6 | | 3 | 14 | 8 | 4 | 5 | 12 | 7 | | 9² | | 2 | 10¹ | 11³ | | 13 | | | | | | | | | | | | | | 1 | 32 |
| 2 | | 3 | | | 7 | 10 | 5 | 13 | 8 | 12 | 6¹ | | 4 | 11² | | 9³ | 14 | | | | | | | | | | | | | 1 | 33 |
| | | 3 | 12 | 8 | | 10 | 2² | | 7 | | 9³ | | 4 | 11¹ | 6 | | 13 | | | | | 14 | 5 | | | | | | | 1 | 34 |
| | | 3 | | | 8 | 13 | 11¹ | 5 | 12 | | 7² | 6 | | | 4 | 10 | 9 | | | | | | 12 | | | | 10² | 2 | | 1 | 35 |
| | | 3 | | 8 | 14 | | 5 | | | | 7³ | 6 | | 13 | 4¹ | 11 | 9 | | 12 | | | | | | | | | 2 | | 1 | 36 |
| 13 | | 3 | | 8 | 12 | 9¹ | 5 | | | 7¹ | | 6² | 14 | | 10 | 4 | | | | | | | | | | | 11 | 2 | | 1 | 37 |
| 2 | | 3 | 13 | 7 | 8 | 10³ | 5 | | | 6 | 14 | 4 | 11¹ | | 9² | | | | | | | | | | | | 12 | | | 1 | 38 |
| 2 | | 3 | 14 | 8 | 7¹ | 11 | 5 | | | 6³ | 12 | 4 | | | 9 | | | | | | | | | | | | 10² | 13 | | 1 | 39 |
| 7 | | 4 | 6² | 8 | | 13 | 5 | | 9 | | 11³ | 3 | | | 12 | | | | | | | | 14 | | | | 10³ | 2 | 5¹ | 1 | 40 |
| 7² | | 4 | 13 | 8 | | 6 | 5 | 12 | | 9¹ | | 10 | | | 3 | 11³ | | | | | | | | | | | 14 | 2 | 6¹ | 1 | 41 |
| 2 | | 3 | 12 | 7³ | 14 | 10 | 5 | | | 8 | | 13 | 4 | 11² | | 9 | | | | | | | | | | | 6¹ | | | 1 | 42 |
| 1 | | 3 | 9¹ | 8⁴ | 6 | 11 | 5 | | | 7 | 12 | | 13 | 4 | | | | | | | | | | | | | 10² | 2 | | | 43 |
| | 13 | 3 | 6² | | 8 | 10 | 5 | | | 7 | | 12 | | 4 | | 14 | 9³ | | | | | | | | | | 11¹ | 2 | | 1 | 44 |
| 1 | 12 | 3 | 9² | 14 | 8 | 10 | 5 | | | 7 | | 13 | | 2 | | 6³ | 11 | | | | | | | | | | 4¹ | | | 1 | 45 |
| | 2³ | 3 | 13 | 9 | 7 | 11 | 5 | | | 8 | 14 | 10 | | | | 4¹ | | | 6² | | | | | | | | 12 | | | 1 | 46 |

**FA Cup**

| First Round | Yeovil T | (h) | 3-0 |
|---|---|---|---|
| Second Round | Gillingham | (h) | 2-0 |
| Third Round | Millwall | (a) | 0-1 |

**Capital One Cup**

| First Round | Huddersfield T | (h) | 2-0 |
|---|---|---|---|
| Second Round | Crystal Palace | (h) | 4-1 |
| Third Round | Middlesbrough | (h) | 1-3 |

**Johnstone's Paint Trophy**

| First Round | Carlisle U | (a) | 1-1 |
|---|---|---|---|
| *(aet; won 3-1 on pens)* | | | |
| Second Round | Morecambe | (a) | 4-2 |
| Third Round | Bury | (a) | 3-3 |
| *(aet; won 5-4 on pens)* | | | |
| Quarter-Finals | Coventry C | (a) | 2-3 |

# QUEENS PARK RANGERS

## FOUNDATION

There is an element of doubt about the date of the foundation of this club, but it is believed that in either 1885 or 1886 it was formed through the amalgamation of Christchurch Rangers and St Jude's Institute FC. The leading light was George Wodehouse, whose family maintained a connection with the club until comparatively recent times. Most of the players came from the Queen's Park district so this name was adopted after a year as St Jude's Institute.

*Loftus Road Stadium, South Africa Road, Shepherds Bush, London W12 7PJ.*

*Telephone:* (020) 8743 0262.

*Fax:* (020) 8749 0994.

*Ticket Office:* (0844) 447 7007.

*Website:* www.qpr.co.uk

*Email:* feedback@qpr.co.uk

*Ground Capacity:* 18,439.

*Record Attendance:* 41,097 v Leeds U, FA Cup 3rd rd, 9 January 1932 (at White City); 35,353 v Leeds U, Division 1, 27 April 1974 (at Loftus Road).

*Pitch Measurements:* 100m × 65.85m (109yd × 72yd)

*Chairman:* Tony Fernandes.

*Chief Executive:* Phil Beard.

*Manager:* Harry Redknapp.

*Assistant Manager:* Kevin Bond.

*Physio:* Nigel Cox.

*Colours:* Blue and white hooped shirts, white shorts with blue trim, white socks.

*Year Formed:* 1885* (*see Foundation*).

*Turned Professional:* 1898.

*Previous Name:* 1885, St Jude's; 1887, Queens Park Rangers. *Club Nicknames:* 'Rangers', 'The Hoops', 'Rs'.

*Grounds:* 1885* (*see Foundation*), Welford's Fields; 1888–99, London Scottish Ground, Brondesbury, Home Farm, Kensal Rise Green, Gun Club Wormwood Scrubs, Kilburn Cricket Ground; 1899, Kensal Rise Athletic Ground; 1901, Latimer Road, Notting Hill; 1904, Agricultural Society, Park Royal; 1907, Park Royal Ground; 1917, Loftus Road; 1931, White City; 1933, Loftus Road; 1962, White City; 1963, Loftus Road.

*First Football League Game:* 28 August 1920, Division 3, v Watford (h) L 1–2 – Price; Blackman, Wingrove; McGovern, Grant, O'Brien; Faulkner, Birch (1), Smith, Gregory, Middlemiss.

*Record League Victory:* 9–2 v Tranmere R, Division 3, 3 December 1960 – Drinkwater; Woods, Ingham; Keen, Rutter, Angell; Lazarus (2), Bedford (2), Evans (2), Andrews (1), Clark (2).

*Record Cup Victory:* 8–1 v Bristol R (a), FA Cup 1st rd, 27 November 1937 – Gilfillan; Smith, Jefferson; Lowe, James, March; Cape, Mallett, Cheetham (3), Fitzgerald (3) Bott (2). 8–1 v Crewe Alex, Milk Cup 1st rd, 3 October 1983 – Hucker; Neill, Dawes, Waddock (1), McDonald (1), Fenwick, Micklewhite (1), Stewart (1), Allen (1), Stainrod (3), Gregory.

## HONOURS

**Football League – Division 1:**
*Runners-up* 1975–76;

**FL C:** *Champions* 2010–11;

**Division 2:** *Champions* 1982–83;
*Runners-up* 1967–68, 1972–73, 2003–04;

**Division 3 (S):** *Champions* 1947–48;
*Runners-up* 1946–47;

**Division 3:** *Champions* 1966–67.

**FA Cup:** *Runners-up* 1982.

**Football League Cup:** *Winners* 1967;
*Runners-up* 1986.

**European Competitions**
**UEFA Cup:** 1976–77, 1984–85.

## sky SPORTS FACT FILE

George Goddard scored five Football League hat-tricks for Queens Park Rangers in 1929–30 when the club finished in third place in Division Three South. He finished the campaign with 37 goals from 41 League appearances and added a further hat-trick in the London Challenge Cup tie against Millwall.

*Record Defeat:* 1–8 v Mansfield T, Division 3, 15 March 1965. 1–8 v Manchester U, Division 1, 19 March 1969.

*Most League Points (2 for a win):* 67, Division 3, 1966–67.

*Most League Points (3 for a win):* 88, FL C, 2010–11.

*Most League Goals:* 111, Division 3, 1961–62.

*Highest League Scorer in Season:* George Goddard, 37, Division 3 (S), 1929–30.

*Most League Goals in Total Aggregate:* George Goddard, 172, 1926–34.

*Most League Goals in One Match:* 4, George Goddard v Merthyr T, Division 3 (S), 9 March 1929; 4, George Goddard v Swindon T, Division 3 (S), 12 April 1930; 4, George Goddard v Exeter C, Division 3 (S), 20 December 1930; 4, George Goddard v Watford, Division 3 (S), 19 September 1931; 4, Tom Cheetham v Aldershot, Division 3 (S), 14 September 1935; 4, Tom Cheetham v Aldershot, Division 3 (S), 12 November 1938.

*Most Capped Player:* Alan McDonald, 52, Northern Ireland.

*Most League Appearances:* Tony Ingham, 519, 1950–63.

*Youngest League Player:* Frank Sibley, 16 years 97 days v Bristol C, 10 March 1964.

*Record Transfer Fee Received:* £12,000,000 from Anzhi Makhachkala for Chris Samba, July 2013.

*Record Transfer Fee Paid:* £12,500,000 to Anzhi Makhachkala for Chris Samba, January 2013.

*Football League Record:* 1920 Original Members of Division 3; 1921–48 Division 3 (S); 1948–52 Division 2; 1952–58 Division 3 (S); 1958–67 Division 3; 1967–68 Division 2; 1968–69 Division 1; 1969–73 Division 2; 1973–79 Division 1; 1979–83 Division 2; 1983–92 Division 1; 1992–96 FA Premier League; 1996–2001 Division 1; 2001–04 Division 2; 2004–11 FL C; 2011–13 FA Premier League; 2013– FL C.

## LATEST SEQUENCES

*Longest Sequence of League Wins:* 8, 7.11.1931 – 28.12.1931.

*Longest Sequence of League Defeats:* 9, 25.2.1969 – 5.4.1969.

*Longest Sequence of League Draws:* 6, 29.1.2000 – 5.3.2000.

*Longest Sequence of Unbeaten League Matches:* 20, 11.3.1972 – 23.9.1972.

*Longest Sequence Without a League Win:* 20, 7.12.1968 – 7.4.1969.

*Successive Scoring Runs:* 33 from 9.12.1961.

*Successive Non-scoring Runs:* 6 from 18.3.1939.

## MANAGERS

James Cowan 1906–13
Jimmy Howie 1913–20
Ned Liddell 1920–24
Will Wood 1924–25
    *(had been Secretary since 1903)*
Bob Hewison 1925–31
John Bowman 1931
Archie Mitchell 1931–33
Mick O'Brien 1933–35
Billy Birrell 1935–39
Ted Vizard 1939–44
Dave Mangnall 1944–52
Jack Taylor 1952–59
Alec Stock 1959–65
    *(General Manager to 1968)*
Bill Dodgin Jnr 1968
Tommy Docherty 1968
Les Allen 1968–71
Gordon Jago 1971–74
Dave Sexton 1974–77
Frank Sibley 1977–78
Steve Burtenshaw 1978–79
Tommy Docherty 1979–80
Terry Venables 1980–84
Gordon Jago 1984
Alan Mullery 1984
Frank Sibley 1984–85
Jim Smith 1985–88
Trevor Francis 1988–89
Don Howe 1989–91
Gerry Francis 1991–94
Ray Wilkins 1994–96
Stewart Houston 1996–97
Ray Harford 1997–98
Gerry Francis 1998–2001
Ian Holloway 2001–06
Gary Waddock 2006
John Gregory 2006–07
Luigi Di Canio 2007–08
Iain Dowie 2008
Paulo Sousa 2008–09
Jim Magilton 2009
Paul Hart 2009–10
Neil Warnock 2010–12
Mark Hughes 2012
Harry Redknapp November 2012–

## TEN YEAR LEAGUE RECORD

| | | P | W | D | L | F | A | Pts | Pos |
|---|---|---|---|---|---|---|---|---|---|
| 2003-04 | Div 2 | 46 | 22 | 17 | 7 | 80 | 45 | 83 | 2 |
| 2004-05 | FL C | 46 | 17 | 11 | 18 | 54 | 58 | 62 | 11 |
| 2005-06 | FL C | 46 | 12 | 14 | 20 | 50 | 65 | 50 | 21 |
| 2006-07 | FL C | 46 | 14 | 11 | 21 | 54 | 68 | 53 | 18 |
| 2007-08 | FL C | 46 | 14 | 16 | 16 | 60 | 66 | 58 | 14 |
| 2008-09 | FL C | 46 | 15 | 16 | 15 | 42 | 44 | 61 | 11 |
| 2009-10 | FL C | 46 | 14 | 15 | 17 | 58 | 65 | 57 | 13 |
| 2010-11 | FL C | 46 | 24 | 16 | 6 | 71 | 32 | 88 | 1 |
| 2011-12 | PR Lge | 38 | 10 | 7 | 21 | 43 | 66 | 37 | 17 |
| 2012-13 | PR Lge | 38 | 4 | 13 | 21 | 30 | 60 | 25 | 20 |

## DID YOU KNOW ?

Mike Keen was the only player to appear in all 58 competitive games for Queens Park Rangers in 1966–67 when they won the Division Three title and the League Cup. QPR finished 12 points in the League and defeated West Bromwich Albion to lift the League Cup.

## QUEENS PARK RANGERS – FA PREMIERSHIP 2012–13 LEAGUE RECORD

| Match No. | Date | Venue | Opponents | Result | H/T Score | Lg Pos. | Goalscorers | Attendance |
|---|---|---|---|---|---|---|---|---|
| 1 | Aug 18 | H | Swansea C | L | 0-5 | 0-1 | 20 | | 18,072 |
| 2 | 25 | A | Norwich C | D | 1-1 | 1-1 | 17 | Zamora [19] | 26,317 |
| 3 | Sept 1 | A | Manchester C | L | 1-3 | 0-1 | 18 | Zamora [59] | 45,579 |
| 4 | 15 | H | Chelsea | D | 0-0 | 0-0 | 18 | | 18,271 |
| 5 | 23 | A | Tottenham H | L | 1-2 | 1-0 | 19 | Zamora [33] | 36,052 |
| 6 | Oct 1 | H | West Ham U | L | 1-2 | 0-2 | 20 | Taarabt [57] | 17,363 |
| 7 | 6 | A | WBA | L | 2-3 | 1-2 | 20 | Taarabt [35], Granero [90] | 23,987 |
| 8 | 21 | H | Everton | D | 1-1 | 1-1 | 20 | Baines (og) [2] | 17,959 |
| 9 | 27 | A | Arsenal | L | 0-1 | 0-0 | 20 | | 60,103 |
| 10 | Nov 4 | H | Reading | D | 1-1 | 0-1 | 19 | Cisse [66] | 16,797 |
| 11 | 10 | A | Stoke C | L | 0-1 | 0-0 | 20 | | 27,529 |
| 12 | 17 | H | Southampton | L | 1-3 | 0-2 | 20 | Hoilett [49] | 18,174 |
| 13 | 24 | A | Manchester U | L | 1-3 | 0-0 | 20 | Mackie [52] | 75,603 |
| 14 | 27 | A | Sunderland | D | 0-0 | 0-0 | 20 | | 36,513 |
| 15 | Dec 1 | H | Aston Villa | D | 1-1 | 1-1 | 20 | Mackie [18] | 17,387 |
| 16 | 8 | A | Wigan Ath | D | 2-2 | 1-1 | 20 | Nelsen [26], Cisse [71] | 17,163 |
| 17 | 15 | H | Fulham | W | 2-1 | 0-0 | 19 | Taarabt 2 [52, 68] | 18,233 |
| 18 | 22 | A | Newcastle U | L | 0-1 | 0-0 | 19 | | 50,180 |
| 19 | 26 | H | WBA | L | 1-2 | 0-1 | 20 | Cisse [68] | 17,782 |
| 20 | 30 | H | Liverpool | L | 0-3 | 0-3 | 20 | | 18,304 |
| 21 | Jan 2 | A | Chelsea | W | 1-0 | 0-0 | 20 | Wright-Phillips [78] | 41,634 |
| 22 | 12 | H | Tottenham H | D | 0-0 | 0-0 | 20 | | 18,018 |
| 23 | 19 | A | West Ham U | D | 1-1 | 1-0 | 20 | Remy [14] | 34,962 |
| 24 | 29 | A | Manchester C | D | 0-0 | 0-0 | 20 | | 17,894 |
| 25 | Feb 2 | H | Norwich C | D | 0-0 | 0-0 | 20 | | 17,543 |
| 26 | 9 | A | Swansea C | L | 1-4 | 0-2 | 20 | Zamora [48] | 20,529 |
| 27 | 23 | H | Manchester U | L | 0-2 | 0-1 | 20 | | 18,337 |
| 28 | Mar 2 | A | Southampton | W | 2-1 | 1-1 | 20 | Remy [14], Bothroyd [77] | 31,728 |
| 29 | 9 | H | Sunderland | W | 3-1 | 1-1 | 20 | Remy [30], Townsend [70], Jenas [90] | 18,169 |
| 30 | 16 | A | Aston Villa | L | 2-3 | 1-1 | 20 | Jenas [23], Townsend [73] | 38,594 |
| 31 | Apr 1 | A | Fulham | L | 2-3 | 1-3 | 19 | Taarabt [45], Remy [51] | 25,117 |
| 32 | 7 | H | Wigan Ath | D | 1-1 | 0-0 | 19 | Remy [85] | 16,658 |
| 33 | 13 | A | Everton | L | 0-2 | 0-1 | 19 | | 34,876 |
| 34 | 20 | H | Stoke C | L | 0-2 | 0-1 | 19 | | 17,391 |
| 35 | 28 | A | Reading | D | 0-0 | 0-0 | 19 | | 23,388 |
| 36 | May 4 | H | Arsenal | L | 0-1 | 0-1 | 20 | | 18,178 |
| 37 | 12 | H | Newcastle U | L | 1-2 | 1-2 | 20 | Remy (pen) [11] | 17,278 |
| 38 | 19 | A | Liverpool | L | 0-1 | 0-1 | 20 | | 44,792 |

**Final League Position: 20**

### GOALSCORERS

*League (30):* Remy 6 (1 pen), Taarabt 5, Zamora 4, Cisse 3, Jenas 2, Mackie 2, Townsend 2, Bothroyd 1, Granero 1, Hoilett 1, Nelsen 1, Wright-Phillips 1, own goal 1.
*FA Cup (4):* Bothroyd 2, Da Silva 1, Dyer 1.
*Capital One Cup (5):* Bosingwa 1, Cisse 1, Hoilett 1, Wright-Phillips 1, Zamora 1.

| Green R 14+2 | Onuoha N 15+8 | Ferdinand A 10+3 | Hill C 31 | Da Silva F 13+8 | Taarabt A 25+6 | Park J 15+5 | Diakite S 11+3 | Hoilett J 15+11 | Mackie J 17+12 | Cisse D 12+6 | Wright-Phillips S 14+6 | Johnson A 2+1 | Derry S 10+8 | Traore A 24+2 | Zamora B 16+5 | Bosingwa J 22+1 | Nelsen R 21 | Granero E 19+5 | Faurlin A 10+1 | Dyer K 1+3 | Julio Cesar S 24 | Mbia S 29 | Remy L 13+1 | Bothroyd J 2+2 | Samba C 10 | Townsend A 12 | Jenas J 8+4 | Ben Haim T 2+1 | Harriman M 1 | Match No. |
|---|---|---|---|---|---|---|---|---|---|---|---|---|---|---|---|---|---|---|---|---|---|---|---|---|---|---|---|---|---|---|
| 1 | 2 | 3 | $4^1$ | 5 | 6 | 7 |  | $8^3$ | 9 | 10 | $11^2$ | 12 | 13 | 14 |  |  |  |  |  |  |  |  |  |  |  |  |  |  |  | 1 |
| 1 | 12 | 4 | $3^1$ | 5 |  | 8 | $7^3$ | 9 | 6 | 10 |  |  | 14 | $2^2$ | 11 | 13 |  |  |  |  |  |  |  |  |  |  |  |  |  | 2 |
| 1 | 12 | $3^1$ |  | 5 |  | 8 |  |  | 14 | 6 | 11 |  | 10 | 2 | 4 | $7^3$ | $9^2$ | 13 |  |  |  |  |  |  |  |  |  |  |  | 3 |
| 12 | 3 |  | $5^1$ |  | 9 |  |  | 13 | 14 | $6^3$ | $10^2$ |  | 11 | 2 | 4 | 7 | 8 |  | 1 |  |  |  |  |  |  |  |  |  |  | 4 |
| 2 |  | 4 |  | 9 |  |  | 10 | 14 | 13 | $6^3$ |  |  | $11^2$ | $5^1$ | 3 | 8 | 7 | 12 | 1 |  |  |  |  |  |  |  |  |  |  | 5 |
| $5^3$ |  | 2 |  | 13 | $9^1$ | $12^*$ | 14 |  | 11 | $6^2$ |  |  | 10 |  | 3 | 7 | 8 |  | 1 | 4 |  |  |  |  |  |  |  |  |  | 6 |
|  | 3 | $5^1$ |  | 9 | 10 |  | 14 | 13 |  | $8^2$ |  | 12 | 11 | 2 | 4 | 6 |  | 1 | $7^3$ | - |  |  |  |  |  |  |  |  |  | 7 |
| 13 | 14 |  |  | 9 | 8 | 3 | 10 |  | 12 |  | $5^2$ | $11^3$ | 2 | $4^3$ | 7 |  | 1 | 6 |  |  |  |  |  |  |  |  |  |  |  | 8 |
| 13 |  |  | 10 |  | 7 | 9 | 14 | 12 | $6^3$ |  | $5^2$ | $11^3$ | 2 | 4 | 8 |  | 1 | $3^4$ |  |  |  |  |  |  |  |  |  |  |  | 9 |
| 13 | 3 |  | 9 |  | 8 | 10 | $6^1$ | 11 |  | $5^2$ | 12 | 2 | 4 | 7 |  | 1 |  |  |  |  |  |  |  |  |  |  |  |  |  | 10 |
|  | 3 |  | 10 |  | 6 | 9 | 11 |  | 5 | 12 | 2 | 4 | 8 | $7^1$ |  | 1 |  |  |  |  |  |  |  |  |  |  |  |  |  | 11 |
|  | 3 | 14 | 9 | $6^2$ | 10 | 12 | 11 | 13 | 5 | $2^3$ | 4 | 8 | $7^1$ |  | 1 |  |  |  |  |  |  |  |  |  |  |  |  |  |  | 12 |
| 12 | 2 | $9^2$ |  | 13 | 8 | 11 | 6 | $5^1$ |  | 3 | 14 | $7^3$ | 10 | 1 | 4 |  |  |  |  |  |  |  |  |  |  |  |  |  |  | 13 |
| 12 |  | 3 | $9^3$ | 13 | $8^2$ |  | 10 | 11 | 14 | 5 | 2 | 4 | 6 | $1^1$ | 7 |  |  |  |  |  |  |  |  |  |  |  |  |  |  | 14 |
| 1 |  | 4 | 10 | 13 | $7^3$ | 14 | 11 |  | 9 | 12 | 5 | 2 | 3 | $8^2$ | $6^1$ |  |  |  |  |  |  |  |  |  |  |  |  |  |  | 15 |
| 1 |  | 4 | 14 | $11^1$ | $6^2$ | 10 | 12 | 9 | 7 | 5 | $2^3$ | 3 | 13 | $8$ |  |  |  |  |  |  |  |  |  |  |  |  |  |  |  | 16 |
| 1 | 5 | 13 | 3 | 12 | 9 | 11 | $10^2$ | $8^1$ | 2 | 4 | 6 | 7 |  |  |  |  |  |  |  |  |  |  |  |  |  |  |  |  |  | 17 |
| 1 | 3 | 5 | 2 | 10 | 13 | 6 | $11^2$ | 12 | 14 | 4 | $8^1$ | $9^3$ | 7 |  |  |  |  |  |  |  |  |  |  |  |  |  |  |  |  | 18 |
| 1 | 3 | 4 | $2^1$ | 9 | 12 | 13 | 8 | 11 | 10 | 5 | $7^2$ | 6 |  |  |  |  |  |  |  |  |  |  |  |  |  |  |  |  |  | 19 |
| 2 |  | 4 | 14 | 10 | $7^2$ | 6 | $11^1$ | $9^3$ | 12 | 5 | 3 | 13 | 1 | 8 |  |  |  |  |  |  |  |  |  |  |  |  |  |  |  | 20 |
| 2 |  | 4 | 5 | $10^3$ | 14 | $8^1$ | 11 | 12 | 7 | 3 | $9^2$ | 13 | 1 | 6 |  |  |  |  |  |  |  |  |  |  |  |  |  |  |  | 21 |
| 2 |  | 3 | 5 | 10 | 7 | 11 | 9 | 8 | 4 | 1 | 6 |  |  |  |  |  |  |  |  |  |  |  |  |  |  |  |  |  |  | 22 |
| 2 |  | 4 | 5 | $9^3$ | 14 | $8^2$ | $10^1$ | 6 | 12 | 3 | 1 | 7 | 11 | 13 |  |  |  |  |  |  |  |  |  |  |  |  |  |  |  | 23 |
| 2 |  | 4 | 8 | 9 | 12 | 7 | 5 | 14 | 3 | $10^1$ | 13 | 1 | $6^3$ | $11^2$ |  |  |  |  |  |  |  |  |  |  |  |  |  |  |  | 24 |
|  | 4 | $2^3$ | 10 | 11 | $6^1$ | 8 | 5 | 12 | 1 | $7^2$ | 3 | 9 | 13 | 14 |  |  |  |  |  |  |  |  |  |  |  |  |  |  |  | 25 |
| 2 |  | 4 | 10 | $11^2$ | 14 | $7^1$ | 5 | 13 | 12 | 1 | 8 | 3 | 6 | $9^3$ |  |  |  |  |  |  |  |  |  |  |  |  |  |  |  | 26 |
|  | 4 | 9 | 14 | 8 | 5 | $11^2$ | 2 | $7^1$ | 1 | 6 | 13 | 3 | $10^3$ | 12 |  |  |  |  |  |  |  |  |  |  |  |  |  |  |  | 27 |
| 13 |  | 4 | 14 | 6 | 9 | 5 | 2 | $7^1$ | $1^2$ | 8 | 11 | $10^3$ | 3 | 12 |  |  |  |  |  |  |  |  |  |  |  |  |  |  |  | 28 |
| 1 |  | 4 | 5 | 7 | $9^2$ | 12 | 13 | $10^1$ | 2 | 8 | $11^3$ | 3 | 6 | 14 |  |  |  |  |  |  |  |  |  |  |  |  |  |  |  | 29 |
|  | 4 | $5^2$ | 13 | $6^3$ | 12 | 14 | $10^1$ | 2 | 1 | 7 | 9 | 3 | 11 | 8 |  |  |  |  |  |  |  |  |  |  |  |  |  |  |  | 30 |
| 12 | $4^1$ | $9^2$ | 13 | 14 | $5^3$ | 10 | 2 | 1 | 7 | 11 | 3 | 6 | 8 |  |  |  |  |  |  |  |  |  |  |  |  |  |  |  |  | 31 |
| 12 | 4 | 13 | $9^2$ | 14 | $5^1$ | $11^*$ | 2 | 1 | 8 | $10^3$ | 3 | 6 | 7 |  |  |  |  |  |  |  |  |  |  |  |  |  |  |  |  | 32 |
| 5 | 4 | 12 | $8^1$ | 13 | 10 | 2 | $9^2$ | 1 | 11 | 3 | 6 | 7 |  |  |  |  |  |  |  |  |  |  |  |  |  |  |  |  |  | 33 |
| 1 | 3 | $9^2$ | 11 | 12 | 7 | 2 | 6 | 10 | 13 | 4 | $8^1$ | 5 |  |  |  |  |  |  |  |  |  |  |  |  |  |  |  |  |  | 34 |
| 1 | 4 | 3 | 13 | $9^1$ | 12 | 14 | 5 | $2^2$ | 7 | $8^3$ | 10 | 11 | 6 |  |  |  |  |  |  |  |  |  |  |  |  |  |  |  |  | 35 |
| 1 | 3 | 4 | 14 | 13 | $10^2$ | 12 | $5^3$ | 11 | $8^1$ | 9 | 6 | 7 | 2 |  |  |  |  |  |  |  |  |  |  |  |  |  |  |  |  | 36 |
| 1 | 4 | 3 | 13 | 14 | $9^3$ | 12 | 5 | 11 | $2^2$ | $8^1$ | 10 | 6 | 7 |  |  |  |  |  |  |  |  |  |  |  |  |  |  |  |  | 37 |
| 1 | 3 | 4 | $6^3$ | 14 | 13 | 7 | 5 | $10^2$ | 12 | 8 | $9^1$ | 11 | 2 |  |  |  |  |  |  |  |  |  |  |  |  |  |  |  |  | 38 |

**FA Cup**

|  |  | |  |
|---|---|---|---|
| Third Round | WBA | (h) | 1-1 |
| *Replay* | WBA | (a) | 1-0 |
| Fourth Round | Milton Keynes D | (h) | 2-4 |

**Capital One Cup**

|  |  | |  |
|---|---|---|---|
| Second Round | Walsall | (h) | 3-0 |
| Third Round | Reading | (h) | 2-3 |

# READING

## FOUNDATION

Reading was formed as far back as 1871 at a public meeting held at the Bridge Street Rooms. They first entered the FA Cup as early as 1877 when they amalgamated with the Reading Hornets. The club was further strengthened in 1889 when Earley FC joined them. They were the first winners of the Berks & Bucks Cup in 1878–79.

*Madejski Stadium, Junction 11, M4, Reading, Berkshire RG2 0FL.*

*Telephone:* (0118) 968 1100.

*Fax:* (0118) 968 1101.

*Ticket Office:* (0844) 249 1871.

*Website:* www.readingfc.co.uk

*Email:* customerservice@readingfc.co.uk

*Ground Capacity:* 24,197.

*Record Attendance:* 33,042 v Brentford, FA Cup 5th rd, 19 February 1927 (at Elm Park); 24,122 v Aston Villa, FA Premier League, 10 February 2007 (at Madejski Stadium).

*Pitch Measurements:* 105m × 68m (114yd × 74yd)

*Chairman:* Sir John Madejski

*Chief Executive:* Nigel Howe.

*Manager:* Nigel Adkins.

*Assistant Manager:* Andy Crosby.

*Physio:* Luke Anthony.

*Colours:* Blue and white hooped shirts with blue sleeves, blue shorts, white socks with blue trim.

*Year Formed:* 1871.

*Turned Professional:* 1895.

*Club Nickname:* 'The Royals'.

*Grounds:* 1871, Reading Recreation; Reading Cricket Ground; 1882, Coley Park; 1889, Caversham Cricket Ground; 1896, Elm Park; 1998, Madejski Stadium.

*First Football League Game:* 28 August 1920, Division 3, v Newport Co (a) W 1–0 – Crawford; Smith, Horler; Christie, Mavin, Getgood; Spence, Weston, Yarnell, Bailey (1), Andrews.

*Record League Victory:* 10–2 v Crystal Palace, Division 3 (S), 4 September 1946 – Groves; Glidden, Gulliver; McKenna, Ratcliffe, Young; Chitty, Maurice Edelston (3), McPhee (4), Barney (1), Deverell (2).

*Record Cup Victory:* 6–0 v Leyton, FA Cup 2nd rd, 12 December 1925 – Duckworth; Eggo, McConnell; Wilson, Messer, Evans; Smith (2), Braithwaite (1), Davey (1), Tinsley, Robson (2).

*Record Defeat:* 0–18 v Preston NE, FA Cup 1st rd, 1893–94.

## HONOURS

**FA Premier League:** Best season: 8th 2006–07.

**Football League – FL C:**
*Champions* 2005–06, 2011–12;
Division 1: *Runners-up* 1994–95;
Division 2: *Champions* 1993–94;
*Runners-up* 2001–02;
Division 3: *Champions* 1985–86;
Division 3 (S): *Champions* 1925–26;
*Runners-up* 1931–32, 1934–35, 1948–49, 1951–52;
Division 4: *Champions* 1978–79.

**FA Cup:** Semi-final 1927.

**Football League Cup:** Best season: 5th rd, 1996, 1998.

**Simod Cup:** *Winners* 1988.

## sky SPORTS FACT FILE

Reading won their first 13 League games of the 1985-86 season to create a new Football League record. The first team to break the sequence was Wolverhampton Wanderers who drew 2-2 at Elm Park on 23 October. The Royals finished the campaign as Division Three champions.

*Most League Points (2 for a win):* 65, Division 4, 1978–79.

*Most League Points (3 for a win):* 106, Championship, 2005–06 (Football League Record).

*Most League Goals:* 112, Division 3 (S), 1951–52.

*Highest League Scorer in Season:* Ronnie Blackman, 39, Division 3 (S), 1951–52.

*Most League Goals in Total Aggregate:* Ronnie Blackman, 158, 1947–54.

*Most League Goals in One Match:* 6, Arthur Bacon v Stoke C, Division 2, 3 April 1931.

*Most Capped Player:* Kevin Doyle, 26 (50), Republic of Ireland.

*Most League Appearances:* Martin Hicks, 500, 1978–91.

*Youngest League Player:* Peter Castle, 16 years 49 days v Watford, 30 April 2003.

*Record Transfer Fee Received:* £7,000,000 from TSG 1899 Hoffenheim for Gylfi Sigurdsson, August 2010.

*Record Transfer Fee Paid:* £2,500,000 to Nantes for Emerse Fae, August 2007.

*Football League Record:* 1920 Original Member of Division 3; 1921–26 Division 3 (S); 1926–31 Division 2; 1931–58 Division 3 (S); 1958–71 Division 3; 1971–76 Division 4; 1976–77 Division 3; 1977–79 Division 4; 1979–83 Division 3; 1983–84 Division 4; 1984–86 Division 3; 1986–88 Division 2; 1988–92 Division 3; 1992–94 Division 2; 1994–98 Division 1; 1998–2002 Division 2; 2002–04 Division 1; 2004–06 FL C; 2006–08 FA Premier League; 2008–12 FL C; 2012–13 FA Premier League; 2013– FL C.

## LATEST SEQUENCES

*Longest Sequence of League Wins:* 13, 17.8.1985 – 19.10.1985.

*Longest Sequence of League Defeats:* 8, 29.12.2007 – 24.2.2008.

*Longest Sequence of League Draws:* 6, 23.3.2002 – 20.4.2002.

*Longest Sequence of Unbeaten League Matches:* 33, 9.8.2005 – 14.2.2006.

*Longest Sequence Without a League Win:* 14, 30.4.1927 – 29.10.1927.

*Successive Scoring Runs:* 32 from 1.10.1932.

*Successive Non-scoring Runs:* 6 from 13.4.1925.

## MANAGERS

**Thomas Sefton** 1897–1901
*(Secretary-Manager)*
**James Sharp** 1901–02
**Harry Matthews** 1902–20
**Harry Marshall** 1920–22
**Arthur Chadwick** 1923–25
**H. S. Bray** 1925–26
*(Secretary only since 1922 and 1926–35)*
**Andrew Wylie** 1926–31
**Joe Smith** 1931–35
**Billy Butler** 1935–39
**John Cochrane** 1939
**Joe Edelston** 1939–47
**Ted Drake** 1947–52
**Jack Smith** 1952–55
**Harry Johnston** 1955–63
**Roy Bentley** 1963–69
**Jack Mansell** 1969–71
**Charlie Hurley** 1972–77
**Maurice Evans** 1977–84
**Ian Branfoot** 1984–89
**Ian Porterfield** 1989–91
**Mark McGhee** 1991–94
**Jimmy Quinn/Mick Gooding** 1994–97
**Terry Bullivant** 1997–98
**Tommy Burns** 1998–99
**Alan Pardew** 1999–2003
**Steve Coppell** 2003–09
**Brendan Rodgers** 2009
**Brian McDermott** 2009–13
**Nigel Adkins** March 2013–

## TEN YEAR LEAGUE RECORD

| | | P | W | D | L | F | A | Pts | Pos |
|---|---|---|---|---|---|---|---|---|---|
| 2003-04 | Div 1 | 46 | 20 | 10 | 16 | 55 | 57 | 70 | 9 |
| 2004-05 | FL C | 46 | 19 | 13 | 14 | 51 | 44 | 70 | 7 |
| 2005-06 | FL C | 46 | 31 | 13 | 2 | 99 | 32 | 106 | 1 |
| 2006-07 | PR Lge | 38 | 16 | 7 | 15 | 52 | 47 | 55 | 8 |
| 2007-08 | PR Lge | 38 | 10 | 6 | 22 | 41 | 66 | 36 | 18 |
| 2008-09 | FL C | 46 | 21 | 14 | 11 | 72 | 40 | 77 | 4 |
| 2009-10 | FL C | 46 | 17 | 12 | 17 | 68 | 63 | 63 | 9 |
| 2010-11 | FL C | 46 | 20 | 17 | 9 | 77 | 51 | 77 | 5 |
| 2011-12 | FL C | 46 | 27 | 8 | 11 | 69 | 41 | 89 | 1 |
| 2012-13 | PR Lge | 38 | 6 | 10 | 22 | 43 | 73 | 28 | 19 |

## DID YOU KNOW

Maurice Edelston made over 200 peacetime appearances for Reading in the immediate post-war period. Capped nine times by England Amateurs and five times in wartime internationals, he became one of the leading commentators on the game for BBC Radio from the 1960s onwards.

## READING – FA PREMIERSHIP 2012–13 LEAGUE RECORD

| Match No. | Date | Venue | Opponents | Result | H/T Score | Lg Pos. | Goalscorers | Attendance |
|---|---|---|---|---|---|---|---|---|
| 1 | Aug 18 | H | Stoke C | D | 1-1 | 0-1 | 6 | Le Fondre (pen) [90] | 23,973 |
| 2 | 22 | A | Chelsea | L | 2-4 | 2-1 | 12 | Pogrebnyak [25], Guthrie [29] | 41,733 |
| 3 | Sept 16 | H | Tottenham H | L | 1-3 | 0-1 | 19 | Robson-Kanu [90] | 24,160 |
| 4 | 22 | A | WBA | L | 0-1 | 0-0 | 20 | | 23,854 |
| 5 | 29 | H | Newcastle U | D | 2-2 | 0-0 | 19 | Kebe [58], Hunt [62] | 24,097 |
| 6 | Oct 6 | A | Swansea C | D | 2-2 | 2-0 | 17 | Pogrebnyak [31], Hunt [44] | 20,336 |
| 7 | 20 | A | Liverpool | L | 0-1 | 0-1 | 19 | | 44,874 |
| 8 | 27 | H | Fulham | D | 3-3 | 1-0 | 18 | Leigertwood [26], McCleary [85], Robson-Kanu [90] | 24,093 |
| 9 | Nov 4 | A | QPR | D | 1-1 | 1-0 | 18 | Gorkss [16] | 16,797 |
| 10 | 10 | H | Norwich C | D | 0-0 | 0-0 | 18 | | 24,080 |
| 11 | 17 | H | Everton | W | 2-1 | 0-1 | 17 | Le Fondre 2 (1 pen) [51, 79 (p)] | 24,184 |
| 12 | 24 | A | Wigan Ath | L | 2-3 | 1-0 | 18 | Morrison [35], Al Habsi (og) [80] | 15,436 |
| 13 | 27 | A | Aston Villa | L | 0-1 | 0-0 | 19 | | 28,692 |
| 14 | Dec 1 | H | Manchester U | L | 3-4 | 3-4 | 19 | Robson-Kanu [8], Le Fondre [19], Morrison [23] | 24,095 |
| 15 | 8 | A | Southampton | L | 0-1 | 0-0 | 19 | | 29,331 |
| 16 | 11 | A | Sunderland | L | 0-3 | 0-2 | 19 | | 37,723 |
| 17 | 17 | H | Arsenal | L | 2-5 | 0-3 | 20 | Le Fondre [66], Kebe [71] | 24,125 |
| 18 | 22 | A | Manchester C | L | 0-1 | 0-0 | 20 | | 47,007 |
| 19 | 26 | H | Swansea C | D | 0-0 | 0-0 | 19 | | 24,050 |
| 20 | 29 | H | West Ham U | W | 1-0 | 1-0 | 19 | Pogrebnyak [5] | 24,183 |
| 21 | Jan 1 | A | Tottenham H | L | 1-3 | 1-1 | 19 | Pogrebnyak [4] | 36,180 |
| 22 | 12 | H | WBA | W | 3-2 | 0-1 | 19 | Kebe [82], Le Fondre (pen) [88], Pogrebnyak [90] | 23,495 |
| 23 | 19 | A | Newcastle U | W | 2-1 | 0-1 | 18 | Le Fondre 2 [71, 77] | 49,411 |
| 24 | 30 | H | Chelsea | D | 2-2 | 0-1 | 17 | Le Fondre 2 [87, 90] | 24,097 |
| 25 | Feb 2 | H | Sunderland | W | 2-1 | 1-1 | 17 | Kebe 2 [7, 85] | 23,829 |
| 26 | 9 | A | Stoke C | L | 1-2 | 0-0 | 17 | Mariappa [83] | 26,737 |
| 27 | 23 | H | Wigan Ath | L | 0-3 | 0-2 | 19 | | 22,321 |
| 28 | Mar 2 | A | Everton | L | 1-3 | 0-1 | 19 | Robson-Kanu [84] | 35,244 |
| 29 | 9 | A | Aston Villa | L | 1-2 | 1-2 | 19 | Baker (og) [32] | 24,102 |
| 30 | 16 | A | Manchester U | L | 0-1 | 0-1 | 19 | | 75,605 |
| 31 | 30 | A | Arsenal | L | 1-4 | 0-1 | 20 | Robson-Kanu [68] | 60,082 |
| 32 | Apr 6 | H | Southampton | L | 0-2 | 0-1 | 20 | | 24,108 |
| 33 | 13 | H | Liverpool | D | 0-0 | 0-0 | 20 | | 24,139 |
| 34 | 20 | A | Norwich C | L | 1-2 | 0-0 | 20 | McCleary [72] | 26,460 |
| 35 | 28 | H | QPR | D | 0-0 | 0-0 | 20 | | 23,388 |
| 36 | May 4 | H | Fulham | W | 4-2 | 1-0 | 19 | Robson-Kanu 2 (1 pen) [12 (p), 62], Le Fondre [75], Karacan [83] | 24,087 |
| 37 | 14 | H | Manchester C | L | 0-2 | 0-1 | 19 | | 22,859 |
| 38 | 19 | A | West Ham U | L | 2-4 | 0-2 | 19 | McCleary [53], Le Fondre [55] | 34,973 |

**Final League Position: 19**

### GOALSCORERS

*League (43):* Le Fondre 12 (3 pens), Robson-Kanu 7 (1 pen), Kebe 5, Pogrebnyak 5, McCleary 3, Hunt 2, Morrison 2, Gorkss 1, Guthrie 1, Karacan 1, Leigertwood 1, Mariappa 1, own goals 2.
*FA Cup (8):* Hunt 3, Leigertwood 1, McAnuff 1, McCleary 1, Le Fondre 2 (1 pen).
*Capital One Cup (11):* Pogrebnyak 3, Gorkss 1, Gunter 1, Hunt 1, Leigertwood 1, Roberts 1, Shorey 1, own goals 2.

| Federici A 21 | Gunter C 20 | Pearce A 18 + 1 | Gorkss K 14 | Harte I 15 + 1 | Leigertwood M 29 + 1 | Robson-Kanu H 13 + 12 | Guthrie D 19 + 2 | McAnuff J 38 | Le Fondre A 11 + 23 | Pogrebnyak P 26 + 3 | McCleary G 15 + 16 | Hunt N 10 + 14 | Karacan J 21 | McCarthy A 13 | Shorey N 16 + 1 | Cummings S 9 | Mariappa A 29 | Kebe J 16 + 2 | Roberts J 8 + 3 | Tabb J 12 | Morrison S 15 + 1 | Samuel D — + 1 | Carrico D 1 + 2 | Kelly S 16 | Akpan H 6 + 3 | Blackman N 3 + 8 | Taylor S 4 | Match No. |
|---|---|---|---|---|---|---|---|---|---|---|---|---|---|---|---|---|---|---|---|---|---|---|---|---|---|---|---|---|
| 1 | 2 | 3 | 4 | 5 | 6 | 7$^1$ | 8 | 9 | 10 | 11$^2$ | 12 | 13 | | | | | | | | | | | | | | | | 1 |
| 1 | 2 | 3 | 4 | 5 | 8 | 14 | 9 | 7 | 12 | 11$^2$ | 10$^3$ | 13 | 6$^1$ | | | | | | | | | | | | | | | 2 |
| | 2 | 3 | 4 | 5 | 7 | 14 | 9$^3$ | 10 | 12 | 11$^2$ | 6 | 13 | 8$^1$ | 1 | | | | | | | | | | | | | | 3 |
| | 2$^2$ | 4 | 3 | | 8 | 13 | 7 | 9 | 11 | 10$^1$ | 6 | 12 | | 1 | 5 | | | | | | | | | | | | | 4 |
| | | 3 | | | 8 | | | 9 | 14 | 10$^2$ | 12 | 11$^3$ | 7 | 1 | 5 | 2 | 4 | 6$^1$ | 13 | | | | | | | | | 5 |
| | | 4 | 4 | | | 14 | | 6 | 13 | 10$^2$ | | 11$^1$ | 7 | 1 | 2 | 5 | 3 | 9 | 12 | 8$^3$ | | | | | | | | 6 |
| | | 3 | | | 8 | | 7$^3$ | 10 | 13 | 11$^2$ | 12 | | 9$^1$ | 1 | 5 | 2 | 4 | 6 | 14 | | | | | | | | | 7 |
| | | 3 | | | 8 | 13 | | 10 | 14 | 6$^3$ | 12 | | | 1 | 5 | 2 | 4 | 9$^2$ | 11 | 7$^1$ | | | | | | | | 8 |
| | 2 | | 4 | | 7 | 13 | | 9$^2$ | 14 | 6$^1$ | | 11 | | 1 | 5 | | 12 | 10$^3$ | | | 8 | 3 | | | | | | 9 |
| 1 | 2 | | 4 | | 7 | | | 9 | 14 | 13 | 6$^2$ | 11$^1$ | | | 5 | | 12 | 10$^3$ | | | 8 | 3 | | | | | | 10 |
| 1 | 2 | | 4 | | 7 | 6 | | 9 | 11$^1$ | | | 12 | | | 5 | | 10 | | | | 8 | 3 | | | | | | 11 |
| 1 | 2 | | 4 | | 7 | 6 | | 9 | 10 | 13 | 12 | | | | 5 | | 11$^2$ | 8$^1$ | | | 8 | 3 | | | | | | 12 |
| 1 | | | | | 7 | 6$^2$ | | 9 | 11 | 13 | 12 | | | | 5 | 2 | 4 | 10$^1$ | | | 8 | 3 | | | | | | 13 |
| 1 | | | | | 7 | 6$^3$ | | 9$^2$ | 10 | 12 | 13 | 14 | | | 5 | 2 | 3 | 11$^1$ | | | 8 | 4 | | | | | | 14 |
| 1 | 12 | | | | 7 | 6$^2$ | | 9 | 11 | | 14 | 13 | | | 5 | 2 | 3 | 10 | | | 8$^2$ | 4$^1$ | | | | | | 15 |
| 1 | 3 | | | | 8 | | | 9 | 11 | 6$^1$ | 10 | | | | 5 | 2 | 4 | | | | 7 | 12 | | | | | | 16 |
| 1 | 3 | | | | 7 | 12 | | 6 | 13 | 11$^2$ | 14 | 10$^1$ | | | 5 | 2 | 4 | 9$^3$ | | | 8 | | | | | | | 17 |
| 1 | 2 | 3 | | 5$^2$ | 7 | | 12 | 6 | | 11 | | | | 8$^1$ | | 13 | 4 | 10 | 9 | | | | | | | | | 18 |
| 1 | 2 | 3 | | 5 | 7 | 13 | 10 | 9$^1$ | 12 | 11$^2$ | | | | 8 | | | 4 | 6 | | | | | | | | | | 19 |
| 1 | 2 | | 4 | 5 | 6 | 13 | | 9$^1$ | 10 | 11 | | 12 | 7 | | | | 3 | 8$^2$ | | | | | | | | | | 20 |
| 1 | 2 | 3 | | 5 | 8 | | 12 | 9 | 10$^2$ | 13 | 11$^3$ | 14 | 7$^1$ | | | | 4 | 6 | | | | | | | | | | 21 |
| 1 | 2 | | 4 | 5 | | | | 9 | 10 | 13 | 11 | 12 | 7$^2$ | | | | 3 | 6 | | | | | | 8$^1$ | | | | 22 |
| 1 | 2 | | 4 | 6 | | | | 10$^2$ | 9 | 13 | 11 | | 7$^1$ | | | | 3 | | | | 8 | | | | 5 | 12 | | 23 |
| 1 | 3 | | | 5 | 8 | | | 9$^1$ | 10$^2$ | 13 | 11 | 12 | 7$^3$ | | | | 4 | 6 | | | | | | 2 | 14 | | | 24 |
| 1 | 3 | | | 5 | 7 | | | 8 | 12 | 10$^2$ | 9$^1$ | | | | | | 4 | 6 | | | | | | 2 | 11 | 13 | | 25 |
| 1 | 3 | | | 5 | 8 | | | 9$^2$ | 12 | 11$^3$ | 13 | 14 | | | | | 4 | 6 | | | | | | 2 | 7 | 10$^1$ | | 26 |
| 1 | | | | 5 | 8 | | | 10 | 12 | 11$^8$ | 14 | 13 | 9$^3$ | | | | 3 | 6$^2$ | | | | | 4 | 2 | 7$^1$ | | | 27 |
| | 4 | | | 5 | 7 | 12 | | 9 | 10 | 11$^2$ | | | | | | | 3 | 6 | | | | | | 2 | 8 | 13 | 1 | 28 |
| | 3 | | | 5 | 8$^3$ | 6 | 14 | 9 | 11 | 12 | 10$^2$ | | | | | | 4 | | | | | | | 2 | 7$^1$ | 13 | 1 | 29 |
| | 3 | | | | 7 | 9$^2$ | 8 | 12 | 10 | 11$^1$ | 6 | | | 5 | | | 4 | | | | 14 | | | 2$^3$ | | 13 | 1 | 30 |
| | 3 | | | 6 | 10$^2$ | 8 | 9 | 11$^1$ | 14 | 12 | 7$^2$ | | | 7$^2$ | 5 | | 4 | | | | | | | 2 | | 13 | 1 | 31 |
| 1 | 5 | | | 12 | 6$^1$ | 8$^2$ | 10 | 11 | 13 | 14 | 7 | | | | | | 3 | | | | | | 4 | 2 | 9$^1$ | | | 32 |
| | 2 | | | | 8 | 9 | 14 | 10$^2$ | 6 | 11$^3$ | 7$^1$ | 1 | | | | | 3 | | | | | | 4 | 12 | 5 | 13 | | 33 |
| | 2 | | | | 7 | 9 | | 11 | 6 | | 8 | 1 | | | | | 3 | | | | | | 4 | 5 | 10 | | | 34 |
| | 2 | | 14 | | 12 | 8 | 9 | 13 | 10 | 6$^2$ | 7 | 1 | | | | | 3 | | | | | | 4 | 5$^3$ | 11$^1$ | | | 35 |
| | 5 | | | | 9$^3$ | 6 | 10$^2$ | 12 | 11 | 8 | 7 | 1 | | | | | 4 | | 7 | | | | 3 | 14 | 2 | 13 | | 36 |
| | 2 | | | | 10 | 7 | 9$^2$ | 12 | 11$^1$ | 8 | 6 | 1 | | | | | 4 | | | | | | 3 | 5 | | 13 | | 37 |
| | 2 | | 4 | | 11$^2$ | 8 | 9 | 12 | 10$^1$ | 6 | 7 | 1 | | | | | | | | | | | | 5 | | 13 | | 38 |

**FA Cup**

| Third Round | Crawley T | (a) | 3-1 |
|---|---|---|---|
| Fourth Round | Sheffield U | (h) | 4-0 |
| Fifth Round | Manchester U | (a) | 1-2 |

**Capital One Cup**

| Second Round | Peterborough U | (h) | 3-2 |
|---|---|---|---|
| Third Round | QPR | (a) | 3-2 |
| Fourth Round | Arsenal | (h) | 5-7 |

# ROCHDALE

## FOUNDATION

Considering the love of rugby in their area, it is not surprising that Rochdale had difficulty in establishing an Association Football club. The earlier Rochdale Town club formed in 1900 went out of existence in 1907 when the present club was immediately established and joined the Manchester League, before graduating to the Lancashire Combination in 1908.

*Spotland Stadium, Willbutts Lane, Rochdale*
*OL11 5DS.*

*Telephone:* (0844) 826 1907.

*Fax:* (01706) 648 466.

*Ticket Office:* (0844) 826 1907 (option 8).

*Website:* www.rochdaleafc.co.uk

*Email:* admin@rochdaleafc.co.uk

*Ground Capacity:* 10,037.

*Record Attendance:* 24,231 v Notts Co, FA Cup 2nd rd, 10 December 1949.

*Pitch Measurements:* 104m × 69m (114yd × 76yd)

*Chairman:* Chris Dunphy.

*Chief Executive:* Colin Garlick.

*Manager:* Keith Hill.

*Assistant Manager:* Chris Beech.

*Fitness Coach:* Ross Preston.

*Colours:* Black and blue striped shirts, white shorts, blue socks with black trim.

*Year Formed:* 1907.

*Turned Professional:* 1907.

*Club Nickname:* 'The Dale'.

*Ground:* 1907, St Clements Playing Fields (original name Spotland).

*First Football League Game:* 27 August 1921, Division 3 (N), v Accrington Stanley (h) W 6–3 – Crabtree; Nuttall, Sheehan; Hill, Farrer, Yarwood; Hoad, Sandiford, Dennison (2), Owens (3), Carney (1).

*Record League Victory:* 8–1 v Chesterfield, Division 3 (N), 18 December 1926 – Hill; Brown, Ward; Hillhouse, Parkes, Braidwood; Hughes, Bertram, Whitehurst (5), Schofield (2), Martin (1).

*Record Cup Victory:* 8–2 v Crook T, FA Cup 1st rd, 26 November 1927 – Moody; Hopkins, Ward; Braidwood, Parkes, Barker; Tompkinson, Clennell (3) Whitehurst (4), Hall, Martin (1).

*Record Defeat:* 1–9 v Tranmere R, Division 3 (N), 25 December 1931.

*Most League Points (2 for a win):* 62, Division 3 (N), 1923–24.

## HONOURS

**Football League – FL 1:** Best season: 9th 2010–11; **FL 2:** Best season: 3rd 2009–10 (promoted to FL 1); **Division 3 (N):** *Runners-up* 1923–24, 1926–27.

**FA Cup:** Best season: 5th rd, 1990, 2003.

**Football League Cup:** *Runners-up* 1962.

## sky SPORTS FACT FILE

In the 1931–32 season Rochdale finished bottom of Division Three North. In a run of 26 games from 14 November to the end of the campaign they lost 25, with the only exception being a 1-1 draw at New Brighton on 19 March.

*Most League Points (3 for a win):* 82, FL 2, 2009–10.

*Most League Goals:* 105, Division 3 (N), 1926–27.

*Highest League Scorer in Season:* Albert Whitehurst, 44, Division 3 (N), 1926–27.

*Most League Goals in Total Aggregate:* Reg Jenkins, 119, 1964–73.

*Most League Goals in One Match:* 6, Tommy Tippett v Hartlepools U, Division 3 (N), 21 April 1930.

*Most Capped Player:* Leo Bertos, 6 (39), New Zealand.

*Most League Appearances:* Gary Jones, 470, 1998–2001; 2003–12.

*Youngest League Player:* Zac Hughes, 16 years 105 days v Exeter C, 19 September 1987.

*Record Transfer Fee Received:* £600,000 from WBA for Craig Dawson, August 2010.

*Record Transfer Fee Paid:* £150,000 to Stoke C for Paul Connor, March 2001.

*Football League Record:* 1921 Elected to Division 3 (N); 1958–59 Division 3; 1959–69 Division 4; 1969–74 Division 3; 1974–92 Division 4; 1992–2004 Division 3; 2004–10 FL 2; 2010–12 FL 1; 2012– FL 2.

## LATEST SEQUENCES

*Longest Sequence of League Wins:* 8, 29.9.1969 – 3.11.1969.

*Longest Sequence of League Defeats:* 17, 14.11.1931 – 12.3.1932.

*Longest Sequence of League Draws:* 6, 17.8.1968 – 14.9.1968.

*Longest Sequence of Unbeaten League Matches:* 20, 15.9.1923 – 19.1.1924.

*Longest Sequence Without a League Win:* 28, 14.11.1931 – 29.8.1932.

*Successive Scoring Runs:* 29 from 8.1.1927.

*Successive Non-scoring Runs:* 9 from 14.3.1980.

## MANAGERS

Billy Bradshaw 1920
*Run by committee 1920–22*
Tom Wilson 1922–23
Jack Peart 1923–30
Will Cameron 1930–31
Herbert Hopkinson 1932–34
Billy Smith 1934–35
Ernest Nixon 1935–37
Sam Jennings 1937–38
Ted Goodier 1938–52
Jack Warner 1952–53
Harry Catterick 1953–58
Jack Marshall 1958–60
Tony Collins 1960–68
Bob Stokoe 1967–68
Len Richley 1968–70
Dick Conner 1970–73
Walter Joyce 1973–76
Brian Green 1976–77
Mike Ferguson 1977–78
Doug Collins 1979
Bob Stokoe 1979–80
Peter Madden 1980–83
Jimmy Greenhoff 1983–84
Vic Halom 1984–86
Eddie Gray 1986–88
Danny Bergara 1988–89
Terry Dolan 1989–91
Dave Sutton 1991–94
Mick Docherty 1994–96
Graham Barrow 1996–99
Steve Parkin 1999–2001
John Hollins 2001–02
Paul Simpson 2002–03
Alan Buckley 2003
Steve Parkin 2003–06
Keith Hill 2007–11
    *(caretaker from December 2006)*
Steve Eyre 2011
John Coleman 2012–13
Keith Hill January 2013–

## TEN YEAR LEAGUE RECORD

| | | P | W | D | L | F | A | Pts | Pos |
|---|---|---|---|---|---|---|---|---|---|
| 2003-04 | Div 3 | 46 | 12 | 14 | 20 | 49 | 58 | 50 | 21 |
| 2004-05 | FL 2 | 46 | 16 | 18 | 12 | 54 | 48 | 66 | 9 |
| 2005-06 | FL 2 | 46 | 14 | 14 | 18 | 66 | 69 | 56 | 14 |
| 2006-07 | FL 2 | 46 | 18 | 12 | 16 | 70 | 50 | 66 | 9 |
| 2007-08 | FL 2 | 46 | 23 | 11 | 12 | 77 | 54 | 80 | 5 |
| 2008-09 | FL 2 | 46 | 19 | 13 | 14 | 70 | 59 | 70 | 6 |
| 2009-10 | FL 2 | 46 | 25 | 7 | 14 | 82 | 48 | 82 | 3 |
| 2010-11 | FL 1 | 46 | 18 | 14 | 14 | 63 | 55 | 68 | 9 |
| 2011-12 | FL 1 | 46 | 8 | 14 | 24 | 47 | 81 | 38 | 24 |
| 2012-13 | FL 2 | 46 | 16 | 13 | 17 | 68 | 70 | 61 | 12 |

## DID YOU KNOW

Rochdale were undefeated at home during the 1923–24 campaign when they finished runners-up in Division Three North. The first visiting team to score at Spotland that season were Barrow who went down 3-1 on 15 December.

## ROCHDALE – FOOTBALL LEAGUE TWO 2012–13 LEAGUE RECORD

| Match No. | Date | Venue | Opponents | Result | H/T Score | Lg Pos. | Goalscorers | Attendance |
|---|---|---|---|---|---|---|---|---|
| 1 | Aug 18 | H | Northampton T | D 0-0 | 0-0 | 13 | | 2558 |
| 2 | 21 | A | Chesterfield | D 1-1 | 0-0 | 16 | Tutte [49] | 4595 |
| 3 | 25 | A | Torquay U | L 2-4 | 1-2 | 19 | Tutte [8], Putterill [85] | 2731 |
| 4 | Sept 1 | H | Barnet | W 2-0 | 2-0 | 14 | Grimes [17], Adebola [34] | 2021 |
| 5 | 8 | H | Burton Alb | L 0-1 | 0-0 | 16 | | 2199 |
| 6 | 15 | A | AFC Wimbledon | W 2-1 | 2-0 | 14 | Adebola [10], Grant [39] | 3529 |
| 7 | 18 | A | Rotherham U | W 3-2 | 1-0 | 8 | Adebola [45], Grant (pen) [75], McIntyre [79] | 6683 |
| 8 | 22 | H | Dagenham & R | D 2-2 | 2-0 | 10 | Adebola [33], Grant [37] | 2120 |
| 9 | 29 | A | Gillingham | W 2-1 | 1-0 | 7 | Tutte [15], Grant [59] | 5874 |
| 10 | Oct 2 | H | Bradford C | D 0-0 | 0-0 | 8 | | 3461 |
| 11 | 6 | A | Accrington S | W 3-2 | 2-1 | 5 | Donnelly [1], Grimes (pen) [32], Kennedy [83] | 2678 |
| 12 | 13 | H | Morecambe | L 1-2 | 0-1 | 6 | Donnelly [73] | 2493 |
| 13 | 20 | A | Plymouth Arg | L 1-3 | 0-2 | 8 | Adebola [76] | 6261 |
| 14 | 23 | H | Oxford U | W 2-0 | 0-0 | 6 | Donnelly [78], Grant [87] | 1619 |
| 15 | 27 | H | Fleetwood T | D 0-0 | 0-0 | 9 | | 2372 |
| 16 | Nov 6 | A | Port Vale | D 2-2 | 0-1 | 8 | Grant [73], Tutte [87] | 4139 |
| 17 | 10 | A | Wycombe W | W 2-1 | 1-1 | 6 | Grimes [5], Grant [90] | 3020 |
| 18 | 17 | H | Bristol R | W 2-1 | 1-1 | 5 | Tutte [27], Grant [59] | 2204 |
| 19 | 24 | A | Southend U | L 1-3 | 0-0 | 8 | Gornell [50] | 5216 |
| 20 | Dec 1 | H | York C | L 2-3 | 0-3 | 9 | Bennett [61], Grant (pen) [83] | 2411 |
| 21 | 8 | A | Exeter C | L 2-3 | 0-3 | 11 | Gornell 2 [66, 90] | 1796 |
| 22 | 15 | A | Aldershot T | L 2-4 | 1-3 | 15 | Grimes 2 [12, 60] | 1910 |
| 23 | 21 | H | Cheltenham T | W 4-1 | 2-0 | 9 | Grant [38], Grimes 2 [45, 67], Adebola [69] | 1605 |
| 24 | 26 | A | Burton Alb | L 2-3 | 1-2 | 13 | Cavanagh [42], Grant [54] | 2994 |
| 25 | 29 | A | Bradford C | W 4-2 | 4-2 | 10 | Gornell 2 [6, 40], Tutte [27], Grimes [33] | 11,198 |
| 26 | Jan 1 | H | Rotherham U | L 1-2 | 1-0 | 12 | Grimes [29] | 3408 |
| 27 | 5 | H | AFC Wimbledon | L 0-1 | 0-0 | 12 | | 2071 |
| 28 | 12 | A | Dagenham & R | L 1-2 | 0-0 | 14 | Tutte [72] | 2289 |
| 29 | 25 | A | Cheltenham T | D 0-0 | 0-0 | 14 | | 2348 |
| 30 | Feb 2 | H | Chesterfield | D 1-1 | 0-0 | 14 | Grant [66] | 2746 |
| 31 | 9 | A | Northampton T | L 1-3 | 0-1 | 16 | Kennedy [65] | 5110 |
| 32 | 16 | H | Torquay U | W 1-0 | 1-0 | 16 | Bennett [18] | 2351 |
| 33 | 23 | A | Barnet | D 0-0 | 0-0 | 14 | | 1870 |
| 34 | 26 | A | Accrington S | L 0-3 | 0-0 | 15 | | 1780 |
| 35 | Mar 2 | A | Morecambe | L 0-3 | 0-1 | 16 | | 2028 |
| 36 | 9 | H | Wycombe W | W 4-1 | 1-1 | 16 | Henderson [19], Harriman (og) [48], Donnelly 2 [78, 85] | 1979 |
| 37 | 12 | A | York C | D 0-0 | 0-0 | 17 | | 2929 |
| 38 | 16 | A | Bristol R | L 1-2 | 0-0 | 17 | Rose [75] | 6691 |
| 39 | 19 | H | Gillingham | D 1-1 | 1-0 | 17 | Donnelly [12] | 1551 |
| 40 | 29 | H | Aldershot T | D 1-1 | 0-0 | 17 | Donnelly [52] | 2280 |
| 41 | Apr 1 | A | Exeter C | W 2-1 | 0-1 | 16 | Henderson [87], Grant [90] | 3979 |
| 42 | 6 | A | Fleetwood T | W 3-0 | 1-0 | 16 | Henderson [9], Donnelly [61], Kennedy [89] | 2954 |
| 43 | 10 | H | Southend U | W 4-2 | 1-0 | 13 | Rose [34], Grant 2 [51, 74], Grimes [77] | 1758 |
| 44 | 13 | A | Port Vale | D 2-2 | 1-1 | 14 | Chilvers (og) [31], Kennedy [90] | 5042 |
| 45 | 20 | A | Oxford U | L 0-3 | 0-0 | 15 | | 6014 |
| 46 | 27 | H | Plymouth Arg | W 1-0 | 0-0 | 12 | Bunney [78] | 4272 |

**Final League Position: 12**

### GOALSCORERS

*League (68):* Grant 15 (2 pens), Grimes 10 (1 pen), Donnelly 8, Tutte 7, Adebola 6, Gornell 5, Kennedy 4, Henderson 3, Bennett 2, Rose 2, Bunney 1, Cavanagh 1, McIntyre 1, Putterill 1, own goals 2.
*FA Cup (1):* Kennedy 1.
*Capital One Cup (3):* Kennedy 2 (2 pens), Tutte 1.
*Johnstone's Paint Trophy (3):* Grant 1 (1 pen), Grimes 1, Putterill 1.

| Lillis J 46 | Pearson M 8+1 | Edwards Ryan 25+1 | Edwards P 43+1 | McIntyre K 37+1 | Cavanagh P 30+1 | Kennedy J 44+2 | Tutte A 37 | Donnelly G 26+17 | Grimes A 27+11 | Adebola D 22+4 | Putterill R 1+17 | Craney I —+6 | Curran C —+4 | Barry-Murphy B 6+2 | Grant R 35+1 | Rafferty J 20+1 | Bennett R 31+2 | Logan J —+5 | Gornell T 16+3 | Haworth A 3+4 | Cansdell-Sheriff S 16+1 | Rose M 10+4 | Jones R 2+1 | Henderson I 12 | Thompson J 5+2 | Camps C —+2 | Thomas W 2 | Gray R 1+1 | O'Connor D 1 | Tanser S —+1 | Bunney J —+1 | Match No. |
|---|---|---|---|---|---|---|---|---|---|---|---|---|---|---|---|---|---|---|---|---|---|---|---|---|---|---|---|---|---|---|---|---|
| 1 | 2 | 3 | 4 | 5 | 6 | 7 | 8 | $9^1$ | 10 | 11 | 12 | | | | | | | | | | | | | | | | | | | | | 1 |
| 1 | 6 | 4 | 3 | 5 | 2 | 7 | 8 | 10 | 9 | $11^1$ | 12 | | | | | | | | | | | | | | | | | | | | | 2 |
| 1 | 2 | 3 | $4^2$ | 5 | 7 | 8 | 6 | 10 | 9 | $11^3$ | 12 | 13 | 14 | | | | | | | | | | | | | | | | | | | 3 |
| 1 | 2 | 3 | 4 | 5 | | 7 | 8 | 10 | $6^2$ | 11 | 13 | | | $9^1$ | 12 | | | | | | | | | | | | | | | | | 4 |
| 1 | 2 | 3 | 4 | 5 | $7^3$ | $8^1$ | 6 | 13 | 12 | 11 | $9^2$ | | 14 | | 10 | | | | | | | | | | | | | | | | | 5 |
| 1 | | 3 | 4 | 8 | | 6 | $7^2$ | 14 | $9^1$ | $11^3$ | 12 | 13 | | | 10 | 2 | 5 | | | | | | | | | | | | | | | 6 |
| 1 | | 3 | 4 | 5 | | 6 | 8 | 9 | | $10^1$ | 12 | | | | 11 | 2 | 7 | | | | | | | | | | | | | | | 7 |
| 1 | 13 | 3 | 7 | $5^1$ | | 8 | 6 | 12 | $9^2$ | $10^1$ | | | 14 | | $11^3$ | 2 | 4 | | | | | | | | | | | | | | | 8 |
| 1 | 5 | 3 | 7 | | | 8 | 6 | 9 | | $10^1$ | 12 | | | | 11 | 2 | 4 | | | | | | | | | | | | | | | 9 |
| 1 | | 4 | 7 | 5 | | $8^1$ | 6 | 9 | | 10 | 12 | | | | $11^{\blacksquare}$ | 2 | 3 | | | | | | | | | | | | | | | 10 |
| 1 | | 4 | 7 | 5 | | 6 | 8 | $9^2$ | $11^1$ | $10^3$ | 13 | 14 | 12 | | | 2 | 3 | | | | | | | | | | | | | | | 11 |
| 1 | | $8^1$ | 5 | 7 | 12 | 6 | 11 | 9 | 10 | | | | | | | 2 | 4 | | | | | | | | | | | | | | | 12 |
| 1 | | 4 | 7 | 5 | $2^1$ | 8 | 6 | 13 | $11^2$ | 10 | | | | | 9 | | 3 | 12 | | | | | | | | | | | | | | 13 |
| 1 | | 4 | 13 | 5 | 6 | 8 | 7 | 12 | $9^2$ | $10^1$ | | | | | 11 | 2 | 3 | | | | | | | | | | | | | | | 14 |
| 1 | | 4 | 2 | 5 | 6 | 7 | 8 | 11 | $10^1$ | 12 | | | | | 9 | | 3 | | | | | | | | | | | | | | | 15 |
| 1 | | 4 | 5 | $8^2$ | 3 | 7 | 6 | 9 | 12 | $10^1$ | 13 | | | | 11 | | 2 | | | | | | | | | | | | | | | 16 |
| 1 | | 4 | | 5 | 8 | 6 | $7^3$ | 12 | $10^2$ | 13 | 14 | | | | 9 | 2 | 3 | | $11^1$ | | | | | | | | | | | | | 17 |
| 1 | | 4 | 2 | 5 | 7 | 8 | 6 | 12 | 13 | $10^1$ | | | | | 9 | | 3 | | $11^2$ | | | | | | | | | | | | | 18 |
| 1 | | 4 | 2 | 5 | 7 | 6 | 8 | 12 | | $10^1$ | | | | | 9 | | 3 | | 11 | | | | | | | | | | | | | 19 |
| 1 | | 2 | 3 | 5 | 7 | $8^2$ | 6 | 12 | 13 | $10^1$ | | | | | 11 | 4 | 9 | | | | | | | | | | | | | | | 20 |
| 1 | | 3 | 5 | | 8 | 7 | 6 | 11 | | 12 | | | | | 10 | $2^1$ | 4 | | $9^{\blacksquare}$ | | | | | | | | | | | | | 21 |
| 1 | 3 | 12 | 2 | 8 | $4^2$ | 6 | 7 | $10^3$ | 9 | 11 | 13 | 14 | | | $5^1$ | | | | | | | | | | | | | | | | | 22 |
| 1 | | 3 | 5 | 2 | 6 | $7^3$ | 9 | 12 | 8 | $11^3$ | 13 | 14 | | | $10^2$ | 4 | | | | | | | | | | | | | | | | 23 |
| 1 | | 3 | 4 | 5 | $7^2$ | 6 | 8 | 12 | 9 | $10^1$ | 13 | | | | 11 | 2 | | | | | | | | | | | | | | | | 24 |
| 1 | | 4 | 3 | 5 | 7 | 6 | 8 | 12 | $11^3$ | | 14 | | | | 9 | $2^2$ | 13 | | $10^1$ | | | | | | | | | | | | | 25 |
| 1 | | 3 | 4 | 5 | 7 | 8 | 6 | 13 | $9^2$ | | | | | | 11 | $2^1$ | 12 | | 10 | | | | | | | | | | | | | 26 |
| 1 | | 4 | $5^3$ | 7 | 8 | 6 | 12 | $11^1$ | 14 | 13 | | | | | 9 | $2^{\blacksquare}$ | 3 | | $10^2$ | | | | | | | | | | | | | 27 |
| 1 | $2^1$ | | 4 | 5 | 7 | 12 | 6 | | | 13 | | | | $8^2$ | 10 | | 3 | | 11 | | | | | | | | | | | | | 28 |
| 1 | | 4 | 5 | 7 | 8 | 6 | | $11^2$ | 12 | | | | | | 9 | 2 | 3 | | $10^1$ | 13 | | | | | | | | | | | | 29 |
| 1 | | 7 | 5 | | 8 | 6 | 12 | $9^2$ | $10^1$ | | | | | 14 | $11^{\blacksquare}$ | 2 | 4 | | | | 13 | $3^3$ | | | | | | | | | | 30 |
| 1 | | 4 | 5 | 13 | 7 | $10^1$ | 9 | 12 | | | | | | | | $2^2$ | 3 | 14 | $11^3$ | 6 | 8 | | | | | | | | | | | 31 |
| 1 | | 4 | 5 | | 8 | 9 | $11^1$ | 12 | | | | | | 7 | | | 2 | 10 | $6^2$ | 3 | 13 | | | | | | | | | | | 32 |
| 1 | | 3 | 5 | | 7 | 6 | $11^1$ | 13 | | | | | | $8^2$ | | | 2 | 10 | $9^3$ | 4 | 12 | 14 | | | | | | | | | | 33 |
| 1 | | 4 | | 7 | 9 | 13 | 11 | | | | | | | $8^3$ | | | 2 | 14 | $10^2$ | 12 | 3 | 5 | $6^1$ | | | | | | | | | 34 |
| 1 | | 4 | 13 | 7 | | | 14 | | | | | | | $6^2$ | 10 | | 2 | | $11^3$ | | 3 | $5^1$ | 8 | 9 | 12 | | | | | | | 35 |
| 1 | | 3 | 5 | | 8 | 7 | 12 | | | | | | | 9 | | | 2 | | $10^1$ | | 4 | 13 | | 11 | $6^2$ | | | | | | | 36 |
| 1 | | 4 | 5 | | 7 | 8 | 10 | 12 | | | | | | 11 | | | 2 | | | | 13 | 3 | | $9^1$ | $6^2$ | | | | | | | 37 |
| 1 | | 4 | 5 | | 6 | 7 | $9^1$ | 13 | | | | | | 10 | | | $2^2$ | | | | 3 | 12 | 11 | 8 | | | | | | | | 38 |
| 1 | | 3 | 5 | 7 | 6 | | 10 | 12 | | | | | | 2 | | | | | | | 4 | 11 | | $8^1$ | 9 | | | | | | | 39 |
| 1 | | 3 | 5 | 7 | 8 | | 10 | | | | | | | 11 | | | | | | | 4 | 2 | | 9 | 6 | | | | | | | 40 |
| 1 | | 3 | $5^1$ | 7 | $8^2$ | | 11 | 6 | | | | | | 10 | 12 | | | | | | 4 | 2 | | 9 | 13 | | | | | | | 41 |
| 1 | | 3 | | $8^2$ | 7 | | $10^1$ | 11 | | | | | 13 | 6 | 2 | | | 12 | | 4 | 5 | 9 | | | | | | | | | | 42 |
| 1 | | 3 | | 8 | 7 | | $10^1$ | 11 | | | | | | 6 | 2 | | | 12 | | 4 | 5 | 9 | | | | | | | | | | 43 |
| 1 | | 3 | | 8 | 7 | | $11^2$ | $10^1$ | | | | | | 6 | 2 | | 14 | 13 | | 4 | 5 | $9^3$ | | 12 | | | | | | | | 44 |
| 1 | | 4 | | 8 | $7^3$ | | 10 | $11^2$ | | | | | | 6 | $2^1$ | | 14 | | | 13 | 5 | 9 | | | | 3 | 12 | | | | | 45 |
| 1 | | | 7 | 8 | | | $11^2$ | | | | | | | $6^3$ | | | | | | 4 | 5 | 9 | | 14 | 2 | 10 | $3^1$ | 12 | 13 | | | 46 |

**FA Cup**  
First Round · Morecambe · (a) · 1-1  
*Replay* · Morecambe · (h) · 0-1

**Capital One Cup**  
First Round · Barnsley · (h) · 3-4

**Johnstone's Paint Trophy**  
First Round · Fleetwood T · (h) · 2-2  
*(aet; won 4-2 on pens)*  
Second Round · Bury · (h) · 1-1  
*(aet; lost 4-5 on pens)*

# ROTHERHAM UNITED

## FOUNDATION

Rotherham were formed in 1870 before becoming Town in the late 1880s. Thornhill United were founded in 1877 and changed their name to Rotherham County in 1905. The Town amalgamated with Rotherham County to form Rotherham United in 1925.

*New York Stadium, New York Way, Rotherham, South Yorkshire S60 1AH*

*Telephone:* (0844) 4140 733.

*Fax:* (0844) 4140 744.

*Ticket Office:* (0844) 4140 733.

*Website:* www.themillers.co.uk

*Email:* office@rotherhamunited.net

*Ground Capacity:* 12,009.

*Record Attendance:* 25,170 v Sheffield U, Division 2, 13 December 1952 (at Millmoor); 7,082 v Aldershot T, FL 2 Play-offs semi-final 2nd leg, 19 May 2010 (at Don Valley); 11,441 v Burton Alb, FL 2, 18 August 2012 (at New York Stadium).

*Pitch Measurements:* 100m × 65m (110yd × 72yd)

*Chairman:* Tony Stewart.

*Manager:* Steve Evans.

*Assistant Manager:* Paul Raynor.

*Head of Medical:* Denis Circuit.

*Colours:* Red shirts with white trim, white shorts, red socks with white trim.

*Year Formed:* 1870. *Turned Professional:* 1905. *Club Nickname:* 'The Millers'.

*Previous Names:* 1877, Thornhill United; 1905, Rotherham County; 1925, amalgamated with Rotherham Town under Rotherham United.

*Grounds:* 1870, Red House Ground; 1907, Millmoor; 2008, Don Valley Stadium; 2012, New York Stadium.

*First Football League Game:* 2 September 1893, Division 2, Rotherham T v Lincoln C (a) D 1–1 – McKay; Thickett, Watson; Barr, Brown, Broadhead; Longden, Cutts, Leatherbarrow, McCormick, Pickering, (1 og). 30 August 1919, Division 2, Rotherham Co v Nottingham F (h) W 2–0 – Branston; Alton, Baines; Bailey, Coe, Stanton; Lee (1), Cawley (1), Glennon, Lees, Lamb.

*Record League Victory:* 8–0 v Oldham Ath, Division 3 (N), 26 May 1947 – Warnes; Selkirk, Ibbotson; Edwards, Horace Williams, Danny Williams; Wilson (2), Shaw (1), Ardron (3), Guest (1), Hainsworth (1).

*Record Cup Victory:* 6–0 v Spennymoor U, FA Cup 2nd rd, 17 December 1977 – McAlister; Forrest, Breckin, Womble, Stancliffe, Green, Finney, Phillips (3), Gwyther (2) (Smith), Goodfellow, Crawford (1). 6–0 v Wolverhampton W, FA Cup 1st rd, 16 November 1985 – O'Hanlon; Forrest, Dungworth, Gooding (1), Smith (1), Pickering, Birch (2), Emerson, Tynan (1), Simmons (1), Pugh. 6–0 v Kings Lynn, FA Cup 2nd rd, 6 December 1997 – Mimms; Clark, Hurst (Goodwin), Garner (1) (Hudson) (1), Warner (Bass), Richardson (1), Berry (1), Thompson, Druce (1), Glover (1), Roscoe.

*Record Defeat:* 1–11 v Bradford C, Division 3 (N), 25 August 1928.

## HONOURS

**Football League – Division 2:**
*Runners-up* 2000–01;
**Division 3:** *Champions* 1980–81;
*Runners-up* 1999–2000;
**Division 3 (N):** *Champions* 1950–51;
*Runners-up* 1946–47, 1947–48, 1948–49;
**Division 4:** *Champions* 1988–89;
*Runners-up* 1991–92.

**FL 2:** *Runners-up* 2012–13

**FA Cup:** Best season: 5th rd, 1953, 1968.

**Football League Cup:**
*Runners-up* 1961.

**Auto Windscreens Shield:**
*Winners* 1996.

## sky SPORTS FACT FILE

Rotherham United defeated Arsenal 2-0 in an FA Cup third round second replay at Hillsborough in January 1960. The three ties attracted an aggregate attendance of more than 138,000 with the 57,598 gate for the Highbury game being the largest the Millers have played in front of.

*Most League Points (2 for a win):* 71, Division 3 (N), 1950–51.

*Most League Points (3 for a win):* 91, Division 2, 2000–01.

*Most League Goals:* 114, Division 3 (N), 1946–47.

*Highest League Scorer in Season:* Wally Ardron, 38, Division 3 (N), 1946–47.

*Most League Goals in Total Aggregate:* Gladstone Guest, 130, 1946–56.

*Most League Goals in One Match:* 4, Roland Bastow v York C, Division 3 (N), 9 November 1935; 4, Roland Bastow v Rochdale, Division 3 (N), 7 March 1936; 4, Wally Ardron v Crewe Alex, Division 3 (N), 5 October 1946; 4, Wally Ardron v Carlisle U, Division 3 (N), 13 September 1947; 4, Wally Ardron v Hartlepools U, Division 3 (N), 13 October 1948; 4, Ian Wilson v Liverpool, Division 2, 2 May 1955; 4, Carl Gilbert v Swansea C, Division 3, 28 September 1971; 4, Carl Airey v Chester, Division 3, 31 August 1987; 4, Shaun Goater v Hartlepool U, Division 3, 9 April 1994; 4, Lee Glover v Hull C, Division 3, 28 December 1997; 4, Darren Byfield v Millwall, Division 1, 10 August 2002; 4, Adam Le Fondre v Cheltenham T, FL 2, 21 August 2010.

*Most Capped Player:* Shaun Goater, 14 (36), Bermuda.

*Most League Appearances:* Danny Williams, 459, 1946–62.

*Youngest League Player:* Kevin Eley, 16 years 72 days v Scunthorpe U, 15 May 1984.

*Record Transfer Fee Received:* £850,000 from Cardiff C for Alan Lee, August 2003.

*Record Transfer Fee Paid:* £160,000 to Peterborough U for Lee Frecklington, January 2013.

*Football League Record:* 1893 Rotherham Town elected to Division 2; 1896 Failed re-election; 1919 Rotherham County elected to Division 2; 1923–51 Division 3 (N); 1951–68 Division 2; 1968–73 Division 3; 1973–75 Division 4; 1975–81 Division 3; 1981–83 Division 2; 1983–88 Division 3; 1988–89 Division 4; 1989–91 Division 3; 1991–92 Division 4; 1992–97 Division 2; 1997–2000 Division 3; 2000–01 Division 2; 2001–04 Division 1; 2004–05 FL C; 2005–07 FL 1; 2007–13 FL 2; 2013– FL 1.

## MANAGERS

Billy Heald 1925–29 *(Secretary only for several years)*
Stanley Davies 1929–30
Billy Heald 1930–33
Reg Freeman 1934–52
Andy Smailes 1952–58
Tom Johnston 1958–62
Danny Williams 1962–65
Jack Mansell 1965–67
Tommy Docherty 1967–68
Jimmy McAnearney 1968–73
Jimmy McGuigan 1973–79
Ian Porterfield 1979–81
Emlyn Hughes 1981–83
George Kerr 1983–85
Norman Hunter 1985–87
Dave Cusack 1987–88
Billy McEwan 1988–91
Phil Henson 1991–94
Archie Gemmill/John McGovern 1994–96
Danny Bergara 1996–97
Ronnie Moore 1997–2005
Mick Harford 2005
Alan Knill 2005–07
Mark Robins 2007–09
Ronnie Moore 2009–11
Andy Scott 2011–12
Steve Evans April 2012–

## LATEST SEQUENCES

*Longest Sequence of League Wins:* 9, 2.2.1982 – 6.3.1982.

*Longest Sequence of League Defeats:* 8, 7.4.1956 – 18.8.1956.

*Longest Sequence of League Draws:* 6, 13.10.1969 – 22.11.1969.

*Longest Sequence of Unbeaten League Matches:* 18, 13.10.1969 – 7.2.1970.

*Longest Sequence Without a League Win:* 21, 9.5.2004 – 20.11.2004.

*Successive Scoring Runs:* 30 from 3.4.1954.

*Successive Non-scoring Runs:* 6 from 21.8.2004.

## TEN YEAR LEAGUE RECORD

|         |       | P  | W  | D  | L  | F  | A  | Pts | Pos |
|---------|-------|----|----|----|----|----|----|-----|-----|
| 2003-04 | Div 1 | 46 | 13 | 15 | 18 | 53 | 61 | 54  | 17  |
| 2004-05 | FL C  | 46 | 5  | 14 | 27 | 35 | 69 | 29  | 24  |
| 2005-06 | FL 1  | 46 | 12 | 16 | 18 | 52 | 62 | 52  | 20  |
| 2006-07 | FL 1  | 46 | 13 | 9  | 24 | 58 | 75 | 38  | 23  |
| 2007-08 | FL 2  | 46 | 21 | 11 | 14 | 62 | 58 | 64* | 9   |
| 2008-09 | FL 2  | 46 | 21 | 12 | 13 | 60 | 46 | 58† | 14  |
| 2009-10 | FL 2  | 46 | 21 | 10 | 15 | 55 | 52 | 73  | 5   |
| 2010-11 | FL 2  | 46 | 17 | 15 | 14 | 75 | 60 | 66  | 9   |
| 2011-12 | FL 2  | 46 | 18 | 13 | 15 | 67 | 63 | 67  | 10  |
| 2012-13 | FL 2  | 46 | 24 | 7  | 15 | 74 | 59 | 79  | 2   |

*\*10 pts deducted; †17 pts deducted.*

## DID YOU KNOW ?

Rotherham United enjoyed success in 1945–46, the final season of the emergency wartime competitions. They won the Division Three North East title on goal average from Darlington and then defeated Chester 5-4 over two legs to win the Division Three North Cup.

## ROTHERHAM UNITED – FOOTBALL LEAGUE TWO 2012–13 LEAGUE RECORD

| Match No. | Date | Venue | Opponents | Result | H/T Score | Lg Pos. | Goalscorers | Attendance |
|---|---|---|---|---|---|---|---|---|
| 1 | Aug 18 | H | Burton Alb | W 3-0 | 2-0 | 3 | Nardiello (pen) [5], Odejayi [11], Pringle [75] | 11,441 |
| 2 | 21 | A | Northampton T | L 1-2 | 1-1 | 7 | Pringle [42] | 4171 |
| 3 | 25 | A | Chesterfield | D 1-1 | 0-1 | 10 | Odejayi [51] | 7232 |
| 4 | Sept 1 | H | Bradford C | W 4-0 | 3-0 | 5 | O'Connor [1], Evans 2 [24, 86], Pringle [34] | 11,199 |
| 5 | 8 | A | Port Vale | L 2-6 | 1-4 | 10 | O'Connor [31], Nardiello (pen) [54] | 5544 |
| 6 | 15 | H | Torquay U | W 1-0 | 1-0 | 6 | Revell [34] | 7405 |
| 7 | 18 | H | Rochdale | L 2-3 | 0-1 | 10 | Revell [59], Nardiello [65] | 6683 |
| 8 | 22 | A | Barnet | D 0-0 | 0-0 | 12 | | 1821 |
| 9 | 29 | H | Oxford U | W 3-1 | 1-1 | 10 | O'Connor 2 (1 pen) [30 (p), 74], Taylor [88] | 7258 |
| 10 | Oct 6 | A | York C | D 0-0 | 0-0 | 10 | | 5417 |
| 11 | 13 | H | Southend U | L 0-3 | 0-0 | 13 | | 7328 |
| 12 | 20 | A | Aldershot T | W 3-0 | 1-0 | 9 | Frecklington [34], Harris [56], Revell [82] | 1953 |
| 13 | 23 | H | Morecambe | W 2-1 | 0-1 | 7 | Nardiello 2 [64, 66] | 5632 |
| 14 | 27 | H | Plymouth Arg | W 1-0 | 0-0 | 6 | Agard [73] | 7233 |
| 15 | Nov 6 | A | Fleetwood T | D 1-1 | 1-1 | 6 | Arnason [19] | 2498 |
| 16 | 10 | A | Dagenham & R | L 0-5 | 0-2 | 9 | | 1720 |
| 17 | 17 | H | Cheltenham T | W 4-2 | 3-2 | 8 | Nardiello 2 [4, 29], Pringle [20], Frecklington [90] | 6705 |
| 18 | 20 | H | Wycombe W | L 2-3 | 2-1 | 11 | Nardiello [1], Bradley [35] | 5688 |
| 19 | 24 | A | Exeter C | W 1-0 | 1-0 | 7 | Sharps [42] | 3954 |
| 20 | 27 | A | Accrington S | W 2-1 | 1-1 | 4 | Nardiello 2 [5, 48] | 1424 |
| 21 | Dec 8 | H | Gillingham | L 1-2 | 0-1 | 5 | Taylor [69] | 8029 |
| 22 | 15 | A | AFC Wimbledon | W 1-0 | 0-0 | 4 | Agard [79] | 3718 |
| 23 | 26 | H | Port Vale | L 1-2 | 0-0 | 6 | Agard [83] | 10,502 |
| 24 | 29 | H | Accrington S | W 4-1 | 1-1 | 5 | Eckersley (og) [15], Nardiello 2 [63, 74], O'Connor [77] | 7304 |
| 25 | Jan 1 | A | Rochdale | W 2-1 | 0-1 | 3 | Odejayi [78], Cameron [90] | 3408 |
| 26 | 12 | H | Barnet | L 0-2 | 0-1 | 4 | | 7434 |
| 27 | 26 | H | Bristol R | L 1-3 | 0-1 | 9 | Noble [73] | 6582 |
| 28 | Feb 2 | H | Northampton T | W 3-1 | 1-0 | 6 | Nardiello (pen) [42], Pringle [75], Noble [79] | 7739 |
| 29 | 9 | A | Burton Alb | L 0-2 | 0-1 | 9 | | 3967 |
| 30 | 12 | A | Torquay U | W 3-1 | 0-0 | 7 | Frecklington [46], Revell [59], Odejayi [90] | 1178 |
| 31 | 16 | A | Chesterfield | W 1-0 | 0-0 | 6 | Mullins [57] | 11,143 |
| 32 | 19 | A | Bristol R | W 2-1 | 0-0 | 3 | Odejayi [60], Frecklington [62] | 8646 |
| 33 | 26 | H | York C | D 1-1 | 0-0 | 5 | Nardiello [90] | 7666 |
| 34 | Mar 2 | A | Southend U | D 1-1 | 0-0 | 7 | Mullins [88] | 4983 |
| 35 | 5 | A | Oxford U | W 4-0 | 4-0 | 4 | Noble [30], Arnason [33], Mullins [41], Pringle [44] | 5169 |
| 36 | 9 | H | Dagenham & R | L 1-2 | 0-0 | 6 | Nardiello [66] | 7309 |
| 37 | 12 | A | Wycombe W | D 2-2 | 0-1 | 5 | Nardiello 2 [51, 64] | 2581 |
| 38 | 16 | A | Cheltenham T | L 0-3 | 0-2 | 7 | | 3241 |
| 39 | 29 | H | AFC Wimbledon | W 1-0 | 0-0 | 6 | Revell [77] | 7594 |
| 40 | Apr 1 | A | Gillingham | L 0-1 | 0-1 | 6 | | 6796 |
| 41 | 6 | A | Morecambe | L 1-2 | 0-0 | 6 | Revell [64] | 2197 |
| 42 | 9 | H | Exeter C | W 4-1 | 3-0 | 6 | Pringle [2], Nardiello [28], O'Connor [30], Morgan, C [51] | 6703 |
| 43 | 13 | H | Fleetwood T | W 2-1 | 1-1 | 5 | Nardiello [3], Agard [62] | 7360 |
| 44 | 16 | A | Bradford C | W 2-0 | 0-0 | 3 | Frecklington (pen) [80], Agard [90] | 13,461 |
| 45 | 20 | A | Plymouth Arg | W 1-0 | 0-0 | 3 | Agard [76] | 10,648 |
| 46 | 27 | H | Aldershot T | W 2-0 | 0-0 | 2 | Mullins [64], Frecklington [90] | 11,300 |

**Final League Position: 2**

### GOALSCORERS

*League (74):* Nardiello 19 (3 pens), Pringle 7, Agard 6, Frecklington 6 (1 pen), O'Connor 6 (1 pen), Revell 6, Odejayi 5, Mullins 4, Noble 3, Arnason 2, Evans 2, Taylor 2, Bradley 1, Cameron 1, Harris 1, Morgan, C 1, Sharps 1, own goal 1.
*FA Cup (8):* Frecklington 3 (1 pen), Bradley 2, Pringle 2, Nardiello 1.
*Capital One Cup (1):* Ainsworth 1.
*Johnstone's Paint Trophy (0).*

| Shearer S 19 | Noble D 20 + 2 | Mullins J 29 | Sharps I 23 | Wilson L 5 | Taylor J 17 + 3 | Amason K 33 | O'Connor M 32 + 3 | Nardiello D 29 + 7 | Pringle B 39 + 2 | Odejayi K 17 + 25 | Bradley M 21 + 6 | Ainsworth L 8 + 8 | Revell A 34 + 7 | Agard K 12 + 18 | Evans G 9 + 4 | Rose M 1 + 4 | Hunt N 6 + 3 | Tonge D 9 + 2 | Morgan C 20 + 1 | Harris R 5 | Denton A — + 1 | Warrington A 27 | Frecklington L 27 + 4 | Morris J 5 | Devitt J 1 | Rooney L 2 + 1 | Cameron C 5 + 10 | Walker N — + 2 | Ridehalgh L 19 + 1 | O'Connell J 1 + 2 | Morgan A 1 | Kearns D 5 + 5 | Davis C 15 | Slew J 2 + 5 | Skarz J 8 | Match No. |
|---|---|---|---|---|---|---|---|---|---|---|---|---|---|---|---|---|---|---|---|---|---|---|---|---|---|---|---|---|---|---|---|---|---|---|---|---|
| 1 | 2 | 3¹ | 4 | 5 | 6 | 7 | 8² | 9³ | 10 | 11 | 12 | 13 | 14 | | | | | | | | | | | | | | | | | | | | | | | 1 |
| 1 | 8 | | 4 | 5 | 7 | 3 | 6² | 10¹ | | 9 | 11³ | 2 | | 14 | 12 | 13 | | | | | | | | | | | | | | | | | | | | 2 |
| 1 | 7 | | 4 | 5 | 6 | 3 | | 10³ | 11 | | 2 | | 9¹ | 13 | 12 | 8² | 14 | | | | | | | | | | | | | | | | | | | 3 |
| 1 | 6 | | 4 | 5 | 13 | 3 | 7² | 11¹ | 8³ | 10 | | 2 | 14 | 12 | | 9 | | | | | | | | | | | | | | | | | | | | 4 |
| 1 | 6 | 4 | 3 | 5¹ | | | 8 | 11 | | 7 | 10 | | 14 | | 9³ | | | 2² | 12 | 13 | | | | | | | | | | | | | | | | 5 |
| 1 | | 4 | | 7 | | | 8 | 12 | 9 | 10 | | | 11¹ | 13 | 6² | | | 2 | 5 | 3 | | | | | | | | | | | | | | | | 6 |
| 1 | | 3 | | 8 | | | 7 | 13 | 9 | 11² | | | 12 | 10 | 14 | 6¹ | | 2³ | 5 | 4 | | | | | | | | | | | | | | | | 7 |
| 1 | | 3 | | 7 | | | 8 | | 6 | 11² | 5³ | 12 | 10⁴ | 13 | | 9¹ | 14 | 2 | 4 | | | | | | | | | | | | | | | | | 8 |
| 1 | | 3 | 13 | 7 | | 8³ | | 9² | 10 | 14 | 6 | | 12 | 11¹ | | 2 | | 4 | 5 | | | | | | | | | | | | | | | | | 9 |
| 1 | | 3 | | 8 | 7 | | | 10¹ | 11 | | 6 | | 12 | 9 | | 2 | | 4 | 5 | | | | | | | | | | | | | | | | | 10 |
| 1 | 14 | 4 | | 7 | | 8 | 12 | 10 | 11² | | 6¹ | | 9³ | | 2 | | 3 | 5 | 13 | | | | | | | | | | | | | | | | | 11 |
| | | 3 | 13 | 7¹ | 11¹ | 8 | | 14 | 6 | 10 | 12 | | | | 2 | 4 | 5 | 1 | 9³ | | | | | | | | | | | | | | | | | 12 |
| | | 3 | | 7 | 11¹ | 9² | 12 | | 6 | 10 | 13 | | | | 2 | 4 | 5 | 1 | 8 | | | | | | | | | | | | | | | | | 13 |
| | | 3 | | 8 | 11³ | 9 | 14 | 12 | | 10 | 13 | 6² | | | 2¹ | 4 | | 1 | 7 | 5 | | | | | | | | | | | | | | | | 14 |
| | | 3 | | 8² | 13 | | 9 | 10 | 2 | 11 | | | | 4 | | 1 | 7 | 5 | 6¹ | | | | | | | | | | | | | | | | | 15 |
| | | 3 | | 6 | 14 | 9 | 11³ | 2 | 10 | | 13 | 12 | 4¹ | | 1 | 8 | 5 | 7² | | | | | | | | | | | | | | | | | | 16 |
| | | 3 | 7 | 12 | 11² | 9 | 13 | 2 | 10 | | | | 4¹ | | 1 | 8 | 5 | | 6³ | 14 | | | | | | | | | | | | | | | | 17 |
| | | 3 | 4 | | 11 | 9 | 13 | 2 | 10² | | 12 | 14 | | | 1 | 8¹ | 5 | | 7³ | 6 | | | | | | | | | | | | | | | | 18 |
| | 4 | 3 | 7 | | 9 | 10¹ | 6 | 2 | 11 | | 12⁴ | | | | 1 | | | | 8² | | 5 | 13 | | | | | | | | | | | | | | 19 |
| | 4 | 3 | 7 | | 8 | 9¹ | 10 | 2 | 11 | | | | | | 1 | 12 | | 13 | 6² | 5 | | | | | | | | | | | | | | | | 20 |
| | 2 | 4¹ | 7 | 3 | 8² | 6³ | 10 | 14 | 11 | | | | | | 1 | 9 | | 13 | 5 | 12 | | | | | | | | | | | | | | | | 21 |
| | 2 | 4 | 7 | 3 | 8² | 10³ | 6¹ | 14 | 11 | 13 | | | | | 1 | 9 | | 12 | 5 | | | | | | | | | | | | | | | | | 22 |
| | 4 | | 7 | 3 | 8¹ | 9³ | 6² | 14 | 2 | 11 | 12 | | | | 1 | 10 | | 13 | | 5 | | | | | | | | | | | | | | | | 23 |
| | 3 | | 7 | 4 | 8 | 12 | | 13 | 2 | 11² | 6 | | | | 1 | 10³ | | 9¹ | 14 | 5 | | | | | | | | | | | | | | | | 24 |
| | 3 | | 6 | 11 | 7 | | 5² | 10 | 2 | 13 | 8¹ | | | | 1 | 9 | | 12 | 4 | | | | | | | | | | | | | | | | | 25 |
| | 4 | 3 | | 7 | | 13 | 9¹ | 10³ | 2 | 14 | 6 | | | | 1 | 8 | | | | 5 | | 11² | 12 | | | | | | | | | | | | | 26 |
| 14 | 4 | | | 6 | 8 | 11¹ | 9 | 13 | | 10² | | | | | 2 | | | 1 | 7³ | | 12 | 5 | | | 3⁴ | | | | | | | | | | | 27 |
| 8² | 3 | | | 4 | 7¹ | 9³ | 6 | 11 | 2 | | | | | 12 | | | | 1 | | | 14 | 5 | | | 13 | 10 | | | | | | | | | | 28 |
| 8¹ | 3 | | | 4 | 7⁸ | 9³ | 6² | 10 | 2 | 14 | | | | | | | | 1 | 12 | | | 5 | | | 13 | 11¹ | | | | | | | | | | 29 |
| | 9 | | | 4 | | 10¹ | | 12 | 2 | | 11² | 6³ | | | | | | 1 | 7 | | 14 | 5 | | | 8 | 3 | 13 | | | | | | | | | 30 |
| 6 | 3 | | | 7 | | 11² | | 12 | 2 | | 10¹ | | | | | | | 1 | 8 | | 14 | 5 | | | 9³ | 4 | 13 | | | | | | | | | 31 |
| 6² | 3 | | | 7 | | | 12 | 2 | | 10³ | 11 | | | | | | | 1 | 8 | | 13 | 5 | | | 9¹ | 4 | 14 | | | | | | | | | 32 |
| 8³ | 3 | | | 7 | | 9 | 14 | 12 | 2 | 11² | 10¹ | | | | | | | 1 | 6 | | | 5 | | | | 4 | 13 | | | | | | | | | 33 |
| 8 | 2 | | | 4 | 6 | 11 | 9¹ | 13 | | 10² | | | | | | | | 1 | 7 | | 12 | 5³ | | | | 3 | 14 | | | | | | | | | 34 |
| 7 | 2 | | | 4 | 6 | 10³ | 8 | 14 | 12 | 11³ | 13 | | | | | | | 1 | 9 | | | 5 | | | | 3¹ | | | | | | | | | | 35 |
| 8 | 2 | | | 4⁸ | 6 | 11 | 9³ | 13 | 12 | 10² | 14 | | | | | | | 1 | 7 | | | 5¹ | | | | 3 | | | | | | | | | | 36 |
| 9 | 5 | | | 8 | 10¹ | 6³ | 13 | 11² | 14 | | 2 | | | | | | | 1 | 7 | | | 3 | | | 12 | 4 | | | | | | | | | | 37 |
| 7¹ | 2 | | | 8 | 10 | 6³ | 13 | 11² | 14 | | | | | 4 | | | | 1 | 9 | | | 5 | | | 12 | 3 | | | | | | | | | | 38 |
| 1 | 8¹ | 2 | | | 7 | | 11² | | 13 | 12 | 10 | 14 | | | | | | | 4 | | | 6 | | | | | | | 9³ | 3 | | | | 5 | | 39 |
| 1 | 8² | 2 | | | 7 | 12 | 11³ | 13 | 14 | | 6¹ | 10 | | | | | | | 4 | | | | | | | | | | 9 | 3 | | | | 5 | | 40 |
| 1 | | 3⁸ | | | 8 | 7 | | 10 | 13 | 2¹ | 6 | 11² | 9 | | | | | | 12 | 4 | | | | | | | | | | | | | | 5 | | 41 |
| 1 | 8 | | | | 4 | 7³ | 10 | 9 | 13 | 12 | 11² | 6¹ | | | | | | | 2 | 3 | | | 14 | | | | | | | | | | | 5 | | 42 |
| 1 | 8 | 2 | | | 3 | 7 | 11¹ | 9 | 14 | 13 | 10³ | 6² | | | | | | | 4 | | | | 12 | | | | | | | | | | | 5 | | 43 |
| 1 | | 2 | | | 7 | 8¹ | 10 | | 11 | 6 | 12 | | | | | | | | 4 | | | | 9 | | | | | | | | | 3 | | 5 | | 44 |
| 1 | | 2 | | | 7 | 8 | | 9 | 13 | 11² | 10 | | | | | | | | 4 | | | | 6¹ | | | | 12 | | | | | 3 | | 5 | | 45 |
| 1 | 6³ | 2 | | | 3 | 7 | 12 | 9 | 13 | 11² | 8¹ | 14 | | | | | | | 10 | | | | | | | | | | | | | 4 | | 5 | | 46 |

**FA Cup**

| | | | | |
|---|---|---|---|---|
| First Round | Stevenage | (h) | 3-2 |
| Second Round | Notts Co | (h) | 1-1 |
| *Replay* | Notts Co | (a) | 3-0 |
| Third Round | Aldershot T | (a) | 1-3 |

**Capital One Cup**

First Round    Hull C    (a)    1-1
(*aet; lost 6-7 on pens*)

**Johnstone's Paint Trophy**

First Round    York C    (h)    0-1

# SCUNTHORPE UNITED

## FOUNDATION

The year of foundation for Scunthorpe United has often been quoted as 1910, but the club can trace its history back to 1899 when Brumby Hall FC, who played on the Old Showground, consolidated their position by amalgamating with some other clubs and changing their name to Scunthorpe United. The year 1910 was when that club amalgamated with North Lindsey United as Scunthorpe and Lindsey United. The link is Mr W. T. Lockwood whose chairmanship covers both years.

*Glanford Park, Jack Brownsword Way, Scunthorpe, North Lincolnshire DN15 8TD.*

*Telephone:* (0871) 221 1899.

*Fax:* (01724) 857 986.

*Ticket Office:* (0871) 221 1899 (option 1).

*Website:* www.scunthorpe-united.co.uk

*Email:* admin@scunthorpe-united.co.uk

*Ground Capacity:* 9,144.

*Record Attendance:* 23,935 v Portsmouth, FA Cup 4th rd, 30 January 1954 (at Old Showground); 9,077 v Manchester U, League Cup 3rd rd, 22 September 2010 (at Glanford Park).

*Pitch Measurements:* 101m × 66m (111yd × 73yd)

*Chairman:* Peter Swann.

*Vice-chairman:* Rex Garton.

*Manager:* Brian Laws.

*Assistant Manager:* Russ Wilcox.

*Physio:* Darren Mouatt.

*Colours:* Claret and light blue shirts, claret shorts, light blue socks.

*Year Formed:* 1899.

*Turned Professional:* 1912.

*Previous Names:* Amalgamated first with Brumby Hall then North Lindsey United to become Scunthorpe and Lindsey United, 1910; 1958, Scunthorpe United.

*Club Nickname:* 'The Iron'.

*Grounds:* 1899, Old Showground; 1988, Glanford Park.

*First Football League Game:* 19 August 1950, Division 3 (N), v Shrewsbury T (h) D 0–0 – Thompson; Barker, Brownsword; Allen, Taylor, McCormick; Mosby, Payne, Gorin, Rees, Boyes.

*Record League Victory:* 8–1 v Luton T, Division 3, 24 April 1965 – Sidebottom; Horstead, Hemstead; Smith, Neale, Lindsey; Bramley (1), Scott, Thomas (5), Mahy (1), Wilson (1). 8–1 v Torquay U (a), Division 3, 28 October 1995 – Samways; Housham, Wilson, Ford (1), Knill (1), Hope (Nicholson), Thornber, Bullimore (Walsh), McFarlane (4) (Young), Eyre (2), Paterson.

## HONOURS

**Football League – FL 1:**
*Champions* 2006–07;
**FL 2:** *Runners-up* 2004–05;
**Division 3 (N):** *Champions* 1957–58.

**FA Cup:** Best season: 5th rd, 1958, 1970.

**Football League Cup:** Best season: 4th rd, 2010.

**Johnstone's Paint Trophy:** *Runners-up* 2008–09.

## sky SPORTS FACT FILE

Jack Haigh made 360 first-team appearances for Scunthorpe United between 1952 and 1960. One of his best performances came in an FA Cup tie at Newcastle in January 1958 when he was knocked unconscious twice but still managed to get up to score, earning himself the nickname 'The Iron Man'.

**Record Cup Victory:** 9–0 v Boston U, FA Cup 1st rd, 21 November 1953 – Malan; Hubbard, Brownsword; Sharpe, White, Bushby; Mosby (1), Haigh (3), Whitfield (2), Gregory (1), Mervyn Jones (2).

**Record Defeat:** 0–8 v Carlisle U, Division 3 (N), 25 December 1952.

**Most League Points (2 for a win):** 66, Division 3 (N), 1956–57, 1957–58.

**Most League Points (3 for a win):** 91, FL 1, 2006–07.

**Most League Goals:** 88, Division 3 (N), 1957–58.

**Highest League Scorer in Season:** Barrie Thomas, 31, Division 2, 1961–62.

**Most League Goals in Total Aggregate:** Steve Cammack, 110, 1979–81, 1981–86.

**Most League Goals in One Match:** 5, Barrie Thomas v Luton T, Division 3, 24 April 1965.

**Most Capped Player:** Grant McCann, 10 (39), Northern Ireland.

**Most League Appearances:** Jack Brownsword, 595, 1950–65.

**Youngest League Player:** Mike Farrell, 16 years 240 days v Workington, 8 November 1975.

**Record Transfer Fee Received:** £2,500,000 from Celtic for Gary Hooper, August 2010.

**Record Transfer Fee Paid:** £700,000 to Hibernian for Rob Jones, July 2009.

**Football League Record:** 1950 Elected to Division 3 (N); 1958–64 Division 2; 1964–68 Division 3; 1968–72 Division 4; 1972–73 Division 3; 1973–83 Division 4; 1983–84 Division 3; 1984–92 Division 4; 1992–99 Division 3; 1999–2000 Division 2; 2000–04 Division 3; 2004–05 FL 2; 2005–07 FL 1; 2007–08 FL C; 2008–09 FL 1; 2009–11 FL C; 2011–13 FL 1; 2013– FL 2.

## MANAGERS

Harry Allcock 1915–53
*(Secretary-Manager)*
Tom Crilly 1936–37
Bernard Harper 1946–48
Leslie Jones 1950–51
Bill Corkhill 1952–56
Ron Suart 1956–58
Tony McShane 1959
Bill Lambton 1959
Frank Soo 1959–60
Dick Duckworth 1960–64
Fred Goodwin 1964–66
Ron Ashman 1967–73
Ron Bradley 1973–74
Dick Rooks 1974–76
Ron Ashman 1976–81
John Duncan 1981–83
Allan Clarke 1983–84
Frank Barlow 1984–87
Mick Buxton 1987–91
Bill Green 1991–93
Richard Money 1993–94
David Moore 1994–96
Mick Buxton 1996–97
Brian Laws 1997–2004; 2004–06
Nigel Adkins 2006–10
Ian Baraclough 2010–11
Alan Knill 2011–12
Brian Laws November 2012–

## LATEST SEQUENCES

**Longest Sequence of League Wins:** 7, 27.1.2007 – 3.3.2007.

**Longest Sequence of League Defeats:** 8, 29.11.1997 – 20.1.1998.

**Longest Sequence of League Draws:** 6, 2.1.1984 – 25.2.1984.

**Longest Sequence of Unbeaten League Matches:** 19, 22.12.2006 – 6.4.2007.

**Longest Sequence Without a League Win:** 14, 22.3.1975 – 6.9.1975.

**Successive Scoring Runs:** 24 from 13.1.2007.

**Successive Non-scoring Runs:** 7 from 19.4.1975.

## TEN YEAR LEAGUE RECORD

|         |       | P  | W  | D  | L  | F  | A  | Pts | Pos |
|---------|-------|----|----|----|----|----|----|-----|-----|
| 2003-04 | Div 3 | 46 | 11 | 16 | 19 | 69 | 72 | 49  | 22  |
| 2004-05 | FL 2  | 46 | 22 | 14 | 10 | 69 | 42 | 80  | 2   |
| 2005-06 | FL 1  | 46 | 15 | 15 | 16 | 68 | 73 | 60  | 12  |
| 2006-07 | FL 1  | 46 | 26 | 13 | 7  | 73 | 35 | 91  | 1   |
| 2007-08 | FL C  | 46 | 11 | 13 | 22 | 46 | 69 | 46  | 23  |
| 2008-09 | FL 1  | 46 | 22 | 10 | 14 | 82 | 63 | 76  | 6   |
| 2009-10 | FL C  | 46 | 14 | 10 | 22 | 62 | 84 | 52  | 20  |
| 2010-11 | FL C  | 46 | 12 | 6  | 28 | 43 | 87 | 42  | 24  |
| 2011-12 | FL 1  | 46 | 10 | 22 | 14 | 55 | 59 | 52  | 18  |
| 2012-13 | FL 1  | 46 | 13 | 9  | 24 | 49 | 73 | 48  | 21  |

## DID YOU KNOW

Scunthorpe United were one of four clubs to join the Football League for the 1950–51 season when the competition expanded to 92 clubs. The Iron still had to play in the fourth qualifying round of the FA Cup and went down 1-0 to Southern League club Hereford United.

## SCUNTHORPE UNITED – FOOTBALL LEAGUE ONE 2012–13 LEAGUE RECORD

| Match No. | Date | Venue | Opponents | Result | | H/T Score | Lg Pos. | Goalscorers | Attendance |
|---|---|---|---|---|---|---|---|---|---|
| 1 | Aug 18 | A | Crawley T | L | 0-3 | 0-1 | 23 | | 3172 |
| 2 | 21 | H | Crewe Alex | L | 1-2 | 1-1 | 24 | Grella [15] | 3215 |
| 3 | 25 | H | Yeovil T | L | 0-4 | 0-1 | 24 | | 3279 |
| 4 | Sept 1 | A | Hartlepool U | L | 0-2 | 0-1 | 24 | | 3863 |
| 5 | 8 | H | Sheffield U | D | 1-1 | 0-0 | 24 | Clarke [60] | 5533 |
| 6 | 15 | A | Shrewsbury T | W | 1-0 | 1-0 | 21 | Clarke [5] | 5623 |
| 7 | 18 | A | Oldham Ath | D | 1-1 | 1-1 | 21 | Clarke [3] | 2969 |
| 8 | 22 | H | Colchester U | W | 1-0 | 0-0 | 18 | Clarke (pen) [76] | 3133 |
| 9 | 29 | A | Portsmouth | L | 1-2 | 1-1 | 19 | Clarke [6] | 10,995 |
| 10 | Oct 2 | H | Tranmere R | L | 1-3 | 1-0 | 21 | Hawley [15] | 2768 |
| 11 | 6 | A | Stevenage | L | 0-1 | 0-0 | 22 | | 2953 |
| 12 | 13 | H | Brentford | D | 1-1 | 0-1 | 22 | Clarke [77] | 3008 |
| 13 | 20 | A | Swindon T | D | 1-1 | 0-1 | 22 | Hawley [56] | 7388 |
| 14 | 23 | H | Preston NE | L | 2-3 | 1-3 | 22 | Clarke [42], Hawley [72] | 2671 |
| 15 | 27 | H | Milton Keynes D | L | 0-3 | 0-2 | 22 | | 2737 |
| 16 | Nov 6 | A | Walsall | W | 4-1 | 2-0 | 22 | Canavan 2 [13, 50], Duffy [31], Clarke [75] | 2787 |
| 17 | 10 | A | Coventry C | W | 2-1 | 1-1 | 21 | Clarke 2 (1 pen) [43 (p), 76] | 9892 |
| 18 | 17 | H | Notts Co | D | 2-2 | 2-1 | 22 | Ribeiro [13], Mozika [45] | 4553 |
| 19 | 20 | H | Bury | L | 1-2 | 0-1 | 23 | Clarke [52] | 3027 |
| 20 | 24 | A | Doncaster R | L | 0-4 | 0-1 | 23 | | 8037 |
| 21 | Dec 8 | H | Bournemouth | L | 1-2 | 0-2 | 23 | Hawley (pen) [64] | 2875 |
| 22 | 15 | A | Leyton Orient | W | 3-1 | 0-0 | 22 | Ribeiro [61], Hawley [69], Mozika [80] | 4942 |
| 23 | 26 | A | Sheffield U | L | 0-3 | 0-1 | 23 | | 21,819 |
| 24 | 29 | A | Tranmere R | L | 0-1 | 0-0 | 23 | | 6044 |
| 25 | Jan 1 | H | Oldham Ath | D | 2-2 | 2-1 | 23 | Canavan [16], Duffy [19] | 3116 |
| 26 | 5 | H | Shrewsbury T | D | 0-0 | 0-0 | 21 | | 3044 |
| 27 | 12 | A | Colchester U | W | 2-1 | 1-0 | 20 | Ryan [41], Hawley [46] | 3258 |
| 28 | 26 | A | Carlisle U | D | 1-1 | 0-0 | 21 | Hawley [52] | 3829 |
| 29 | Feb 2 | A | Crewe Alex | L | 0-1 | 0-0 | 22 | | 4302 |
| 30 | 5 | H | Portsmouth | W | 2-1 | 1-1 | 20 | Sodje 2 [40, 85] | 2596 |
| 31 | 9 | H | Crawley T | W | 2-1 | 0-0 | 20 | Ryan [67], Canavan [79] | 3124 |
| 32 | 12 | H | Carlisle U | W | 3-1 | 2-1 | 18 | Sodje 2 [17, 90], Reid [22] | 3112 |
| 33 | 16 | A | Yeovil T | L | 0-3 | 0-1 | 19 | | 4163 |
| 34 | 23 | H | Hartlepool U | L | 1-2 | 0-2 | 20 | Alabi [77] | 3434 |
| 35 | 26 | H | Stevenage | W | 1-0 | 0-0 | 19 | Duffy [66] | 2382 |
| 36 | Mar 2 | A | Brentford | L | 0-1 | 0-0 | 20 | | 5400 |
| 37 | 9 | H | Coventry C | L | 1-2 | 1-1 | 20 | Sodje [8] | 3676 |
| 38 | 16 | A | Notts Co | L | 0-1 | 0-0 | 20 | | 4634 |
| 39 | 23 | H | Doncaster R | L | 2-3 | 1-2 | 21 | Duffy [41], Hawley [85] | 5288 |
| 40 | 29 | H | Leyton Orient | W | 2-1 | 2-1 | 20 | Sodje [3], Canavan [42] | 3052 |
| 41 | Apr 1 | A | Bournemouth | L | 0-1 | 0-1 | 21 | | 7465 |
| 42 | 6 | A | Preston NE | L | 0-3 | 0-1 | 21 | | 8118 |
| 43 | 13 | H | Walsall | D | 1-1 | 0-0 | 21 | Canavan [88] | 4049 |
| 44 | 16 | A | Bury | L | 1-2 | 1-0 | 21 | Hawley [45] | 1567 |
| 45 | 20 | A | Milton Keynes D | W | 1-0 | 1-0 | 21 | Hawley [41] | 9752 |
| 46 | 27 | H | Swindon T | W | 3-1 | 0-0 | 21 | Collins [87], Duffy (pen) [90], Hawley [90] | 6020 |

**Final League Position: 21**

### GOALSCORERS

*League (49):* Clarke 11 (2 pens), Hawley 11 (1 pen), Canavan 6, Sodje 6, Duffy 5 (1 pen), Mozika 2, Ribeiro 2, Ryan 2, Alabi 1, Collins 1, Grella 1, Reid 1.
*FA Cup (0).*
*Capital One Cup (6):* Grant 2 (1 pen), Barcham 1, Duffy 1, Grella 1, Jennings 1.
*Johnstone's Paint Trophy (1):* Duffy 1.

| | Slocombe S 29 | Ribeiro C 27+1 | Mirfin D 23+7 | Newey T 45 | Kennedy C 11+6 | Ryan J 41+4 | Walker J 21+2 | Duffy M 43 | Barcham A 23+11 | Grella M 10+15 | Jennings C 2+10 | Gibbons R 7 | Keegan J —+3 | Canavan N 38+2 | Prutton D 13 | Clarke L 14+1 | Hawley K 37+2 | Sedgwick C —+4 | Severn J —+1 | Reid P 26 | Collins M 26+3 | Mildenhall S 9 | Mozika D 8+3 | Ellington N 2+4 | McChrystal M 3 | Wootton J —+1 | Djeziri A 1+3 | Adelakun H —+2 | Godden M 5+3 | Sodje A 13+3 | Nolan E 11+1 | Alabi J —+9 | Holmen Johansen E 8 | Forde A 7+1 | Match No. |
|---|---|---|---|---|---|---|---|---|---|---|---|---|---|---|---|---|---|---|---|---|---|---|---|---|---|---|---|---|---|---|---|---|---|---|---|
| | 1 | 2 | 3 | 4 | 5 | 6 | 7 | 8[1] | 9[1] | 10 | 11 | 12 | | | | | | | | | | | | | | | | | | | | | | | 1 |
| | 1 | 2 | 3 | 4 | 5 | 8 | 6[2] | | | 7[1] | 10 | 11 | 12 | 9 | 13 | | | | | | | | | | | | | | | | | | | | 2 |
| | 1 | 2 | 3 | | 5[3] | 7[2] | 6 | | 9 | 13 | 10[1] | 11 | 12 | 8 | 14 | 4 | | | | | | | | | | | | | | | | | | | 3 |
| | 1 | 2 | 3 | 5 | | 7[1] | 8[1] | 9 | 11[2] | | 10 | 12 | | | 13 | 4 | 6 | | | | | | | | | | | | | | | | | | 4 |
| | 1 | 2 | 3 | 5 | 14 | 7 | 6 | 9[3] | | 10[2] | 11[1] | | | 4 | | 8 | 12 | 13 | | | | | | | | | | | | | | | | | 5 |
| | 1 | 2 | 3 | 5 | | 6[2] | 7 | 9 | | | 12 | | | 4 | | 8 | 10 | 11[1] | 13 | | | | | | | | | | | | | | | | 6 |
| | 1 | 2 | 3 | 5 | 9[3] | | 7 | 6[1] | 12 | 13 | | | | 4 | | 8 | 10 | 11[2] | 14 | | | | | | | | | | | | | | | | 7 |
| | 1 | 2 | 3 | 5 | 9[1] | | 7 | 6 | 12 | 13 | | | | 4 | | 8 | 10 | 11[2] | | | | | | | | | | | | | | | | | 8 |
| | 1[1] | 2[3] | 3 | 5 | 9 | | 7 | 6[2] | 14 | | | | | 4 | | 8 | 10 | 11 | 13 | 12 | | | | | | | | | | | | | | | 9 |
| | 1 | 2 | 3 | 5 | 9 | | 7 | 6[1] | 12 | 13 | | | | 4 | | 8[2] | 10 | 11 | | | | | | | | | | | | | | | | | 10 |
| | 1 | 2 | 3 | 5 | | 6[1] | 7 | 9 | | 11 | 8 | | | 4 | | 10 | 12 | | | | | | | | | | | | | | | | | | 11 |
| | 1 | 2 | 3[8] | 5 | 13 | | 6[2] | 9 | | 11[1] | 12 | 7 | | 4 | | 8 | 10 | | | | | | | | | | | | | | | | | | 12 |
| | 1 | 2 | | 5 | | | 9[1] | | 6 | 12 | | | 8[2] | 4 | | 7 | 11 | 10 | | | 3 | 13 | | | | | | | | | | | | | 13 |
| | 1 | 2 | 12 | 5 | | | 9[3] | | 6 | | 14 | 7[2] | | 4 | | 8 | 10 | 11 | | | 3[1] | 13 | | | | | | | | | | | | | 14 |
| | 1 | 2 | 3 | 5 | 13 | | 7 | 6 | | 12 | 11[2] | | | | | 8[1] | 10 | | | 4 | 9 | | | | | | | | | | | | | | 15 |
| | | 2 | | 5 | 12 | 14 | 7[2] | 6[3] | 9[1] | | | | | 3 | 8[1] | | 10 | 11 | | 4 | | 1 | 13 | | | | | | | | | | | | 16 |
| | | 2[1] | | 5 | 12 | 8 | 7[2] | 6 | 9 | | | | | 4 | | | 10 | 11 | | 3 | | 1 | 13 | | | | | | | | | | | | 17 |
| | | 2 | | 5 | 12 | 8[1] | | 6 | 9 | | | | | 4 | | | 10[2] | 11 | | 3[4] | | 1 | 7 | 13 | | | | | | | | | | | 18 |
| | | 2 | | 5 | 12 | 14 | 8 | 6 | 9[1] | | | | | 4 | | | 10 | 11[2] | | | | 1 | 7[3] | 13 | 3 | | | | | | | | | | 19 |
| | | 2 | | 5 | | 9[1] | 7[3] | 6 | 13 | | | | | 4 | | 8 | 10 | 12 | | | | 1 | 14 | 11[2] | 3 | | | | | | | | | | 20 |
| | | 2 | | 5 | | 7[3] | | 6 | 9[1] | 10[2] | | | | 4 | | | 11 | | | | 12 | | | | | 3 | 13 | 14 | | | | | | | 21 |
| | | 2 | | 5 | | 7[1] | | 6 | 10 | | | | | 4 | | | 11 | | | | 3 | 9 | 1 | 8 | | | 12 | | | | | | | | 22 |
| | | 2 | | 5 | 14 | 9[1] | | 6[3] | 10 | | | | | 4 | | | 11[2] | | | | 3 | 7 | 1 | 8 | 12 | | 13 | | | | | | | | 23 |
| | | 2 | | 5 | | | | | 10 | | | | 8[1] | 3 | | | 11 | | | | 4 | 9 | 1 | | | | 6[2] | 12 | 13 | | | | | | 24 |
| | 1 | 2 | | 5 | | 7[1] | | 6 | 10 | | | | | 4 | | | 11 | | | | 3 | 9 | 1 | 8 | 12 | | | | | | | | | | 25 |
| | 1 | 2 | | 5 | | 9 | | 6 | 12 | 13 | | | | 4 | | | 10 | | | | 3 | 8 | 7[1] | 11[2] | | | | | | | | | | | 26 |
| | 1 | 13 | 2 | 5 | 7[2] | | | 9 | 11 | | | | | 4 | | | 6 | | | | 3 | 8 | | | | | 12 | 10[1] | | | | | | | 27 |
| | 1 | 13 | 5 | 2 | 8 | | | 12 | | | | | | 3 | | | 11 | | | | 4 | 6 | | | | | | 10 | | | | | | | 28 |
| | 1 | | 2 | 5 | 6 | | | 7 | 9[2] | 12 | | | | 4 | | | 10 | | | | 3 | 8 | | | | | 13 | 11[1] | | | | | | | 29 |
| | 1 | | 2 | 5 | 7[2] | 13 | | 6 | 9[1] | 12 | | | | 4 | | | 10 | | | | 3 | 8 | | | | | | 11 | | | | | | | 30 |
| | 1 | 13 | 5 | 2 | 9 | 12 | | 6[2] | | 7[1] | | | | 4 | | | 10 | | | | 3 | 8 | | | | | | 11 | | | | | | | 31 |
| | 1 | 12 | 2 | 5 | 9 | 7 | | 6[1] | | | | | | 4 | | | 11 | | | | 3 | 8 | | | | | | 10 | | | | | | | 32 |
| | 1 | | 2 | 5[1] | 6 | 7 | | 8[2] | 13 | | 12 | | | 3 | | | 11 | | | | 4 | 9 | | | | | | 10[1] | 14 | | | | | | 33 |
| | 1 | | 3 | 5 | | 9 | | 8[1] | 6 | 12 | | | | 4 | | | 10 | | | | | 7 | | | | | | | 11[2] | 2 | 13 | | | | 34 |
| | 1 | | 3 | 5 | | 9 | | 8[1] | 6 | 10 | | | | 4 | | | 11 | | | | | 7 | | | | | | | | 2 | 12 | | | | 35 |
| | 1 | | 3 | 5 | | 9 | | 7[1] | 6 | 11[2] | | 13 | 14 | 4 | | | 10[3] | | | | | 8 | | | | | | | 10[1] | 2 | 12 | 1 | | | 36 |
| | | | 3 | 5 | | 8 | | 6 | 9[2] | | | 13 | | 4 | | | 11 | | | | 4 | 7 | | | | | | | 10[1] | 2 | 12 | 1 | | | 37 |
| | | | 3 | 5 | | 8 | | 6 | 13 | | | | | 12 | | | 11 | | | | 4[1] | 7 | | | | | | | 10 | 2 | | 1 | | 9[2] | 38 |
| | | 3[1] | | 5 | | 8 | | 6 | 13 | 14 | | | | 12 | | | 11 | | | | 4 | 7 | | | | | | | 10[1] | 3 | | 1 | | 9[2] | 39 |
| | | 12 | | 5 | | 8 | | 6 | 9[3] | | | | | 4 | | | 11[2] | | | | 3[1] | 7 | | | | | | | 10 | 2 | 13 | 1 | | 14 | 40 |
| | | 3 | | 5 | | 8 | | 6 | 10[3] | | 14 | | | 4 | | | 7 | | | | | | | | | | | | 13 | 2 | 12 | 1 | | 9[1] | 41 |
| | 2 | 3 | | 5 | | 8 | | 6 | 9[1] | 12 | | | | 4 | | | 7 | | | | | | | | | | | 11[2] | 10 | | 13 | 1 | | | 42 |
| | | | | 5 | | 7 | | 6 | | 13 | | | | 4 | | | 11[1] | | | | 3 | 8 | | | | | | | 10 | 12 | 2 | 1 | | 9[2] | 43 |
| | | 12 | | 5 | | 7 | | 6 | | 13 | | | | 4[1] | | | 11[3] | | | | 3 | 8 | | | | | | | 10 | 14 | 2 | 1 | | 9[2] | 44 |
| | 1 | 2 | 3 | 5 | | 8 | | 6 | | | | | | | | | 11 | | | | 4 | 7 | | | | | | | 10[1] | | 12 | | 9 | | 45 |
| | 1 | 13 | 3 | 5 | | 7[1] | | 6 | | | | | | | | | 10 | | | | 4 | 8 | | | | | | | 14 | 11[2] | 2 | 12 | 9[3] | | 46 |

**FA Cup**

| | | | | |
|---|---|---|---|---|
| First Round | Gillingham | (a) | 0-4 | |

**Capital One Cup**

| | | | | |
|---|---|---|---|---|
| First Round | Derby Co | (a) | 5-5 | |
| *(aet; won 7-6 on pens)* | | | | |
| Second Round | Norwich C | (a) | 1-2 | |

**Johnstone's Paint Trophy**

| | | | |
|---|---|---|---|
| First Round | Notts Co | (h) | 1-2 |

# SHEFFIELD UNITED

## FOUNDATION

In March 1889, Yorkshire County Cricket Club formed Sheffield United six days after an FA Cup semi-final between Preston North End and West Bromwich Albion had finally convinced Charles Stokes, a member of the cricket club, that the formation of a professional football club would prove successful at Bramall Lane. The United's first secretary, Mr J. B. Wostinholm, was also secretary of the cricket club.

*Bramall Lane Ground, Cherry Street, Bramall Lane, Sheffield, South Yorkshire S2 4SU.*

*Telephone:* (0871) 995 1899.

*Fax:* (0871) 663 2430.

*Ticket Office:* (0871) 995 1889.

*Website:* www.sufc.co.uk

*Email:* info@sufc.co.uk

*Ground Capacity:* 32,609.

*Record Attendance:* 68,287 v Leeds U, FA Cup 5th rd, 15 February 1936.

*Pitch Measurements:* 102m × 65m (112yd × 72yd)

*Chairman (Football Club):* David Green.

*Manager:* David Weir.

*Assistant Manager (Performance):* Adam Owen.

*Physio:* Paul Teather.

*Colours:* Red and white striped shirts, black shorts with red and white trim, white socks with red trim.

*Year Formed:* 1889.

*Turned Professional:* 1889.

*Club Nickname:* 'The Blades'.

*Ground:* 1889, Bramall Lane.

## HONOURS

**Football League**
**Division 1:** *Champions* 1897–98;
*Runners-up* 1896–97, 1899–1900;
**Division 2:** *Champions* 1952–53;
*Runners-up* 1892–93, 1938–39,
1960–61, 1970–71, 1989–90;
**FL C:** *Runners-up* 2005–06;
**Division 3:** *Runners-up* 1988–89;
**Division 4:** *Champions* 1981–82.
**FA Cup:** *Winners* 1899, 1902, 1915,
1925; *Runners-up* 1901, 1936.
**Football League Cup:** semi-final 2003.

*First Football League Game:* 3 September 1892, Division 2, v Lincoln C (h) W 4–2 – Lilley; Witham, Cain; Howell, Hendry, Needham (1); Wallace, Dobson, Hammond (3), Davies, Drummond.

*Record League Victory:* 10–0 v Burslem Port Vale (a), Division 2, 10 December 1892 – Howlett; Witham, Lilley; Howell, Hendry, Needham; Drummond (1), Wallace (1), Hammond (4), Davies (2), Watson (2).

*Record Cup Victory:* 6–1 v Scarborough (a), FA Cup 1st qualifying rd, 5 October 1889 – Howlett; Stringer, Gilmartin, Mack, Hobson, Hudson, Galbraith (2), Robertson (1), Fraser (2), Duncan, Mosforth (1). 6–1 v Loughborough, FA Cup 4th qualifying rd, 6 December 1890. 6–1 v Lincoln C, League Cup, 22 August 2000 – Tracey; Uhlenbeek, Weber, Woodhouse (Ford), Murphy, Sandford, Devlin (pen), Ribeiro (Santos), Bent (3), Kelly (1) (Thompson), Jagielka, og (1).

## sky SPORTS FACT FILE

Arthur Brown was just 18 years old when he made his full international debut for England against Wales back in 1904. Arthur, who joined United from Gainsborough Trinity, went on to complete a century of Football League goals for the Blades before moving on to play for Sunderland.

**Record Defeat:** 0–13 v Bolton W, FA Cup 2nd rd, 1 February 1890.

**Most League Points (2 for a win):** 60, Division 2, 1952–53.

**Most League Points (3 for a win):** 96, Division 4, 1981–82.

**Most League Goals:** 102, Division 1, 1925–26.

**Highest League Scorer in Season:** Jimmy Dunne, 41, Division 1, 1930–31.

**Most League Goals in Total Aggregate:** Harry Johnson, 205, 1919–30.

**Most League Goals in One Match:** 5, Harry Hammond v Bootle, Division 2, 26 November 1892; 5, Harry Johnson v West Ham U, Division 1, 26 December 1927.

**Most Capped Player:** Billy Gillespie, 25, Northern Ireland.

**Most League Appearances:** Joe Shaw, 629, 1948–66.

**Youngest League Player:** Steve Hawes, 17 years 47 days v WBA, 2 September 1995.

**Record Transfer Fee Received:** £4,000,000 from Everton for Phil Jagielka, July 2007; £4,000,000 from Tottenham H for Kyle Naughton, July 2009; £4,000,000 from Tottenham H for Kyle Walker, July 2009.

**Record Transfer Fee Paid:** £4,000,000 to Everton for James Beattie, August 2007.

**Football League Record:** 1892 Elected to Division 2; 1893–1934 Division 1; 1934–39 Division 2; 1946–49 Division 1; 1949–53 Division 2; 1953–56 Division 1; 1956–61 Division 2; 1961–68 Division 1; 1968–71 Division 2; 1971–76 Division 1; 1976–79 Division 2; 1979–81 Division 3; 1981–82 Division 4; 1982–84 Division 3; 1984–88 Division 2; 1988–89 Division 3; 1989–90 Division 2; 1990–92 Division 1; 1992–94 FA Premier League; 1994–2004 Division 1; 2004–06 FL C; 2006–07 FA Premier League; 2007–11 FL C; 2011– FL 1.

## MANAGERS

**J. B. Wostinholm** 1889–99
  *(Secretary-Manager)*
**John Nicholson** 1899–1932
**Ted Davison** 1932–52
**Reg Freeman** 1952–55
**Joe Mercer** 1955–58
**Johnny Harris** 1959–68
  *(continued as General Manager to 1970)*
**Arthur Rowley** 1968–69
**Johnny Harris** *(General Manager resumed Team Manager duties)* 1969–73
**Ken Furphy** 1973–75
**Jimmy Sirrel** 1975–77
**Harry Haslam** 1978–81
**Martin Peters** 1981
**Ian Porterfield** 1981–86
**Billy McEwan** 1986–88
**Dave Bassett** 1988–95
**Howard Kendall** 1995–97
**Nigel Spackman** 1997–98
**Steve Bruce** 1998–99
**Adrian Heath** 1999
**Neil Warnock** 1999–2007
**Bryan Robson** 2007–08
**Kevin Blackwell** 2008–10
**Gary Speed** 2010
**Micky Adams** 2010–11
**Danny Wilson** 2011–13
**David Weir** June 2013–

## LATEST SEQUENCES

*Longest Sequence of League Wins:* 8, 14.9.1960 – 22.10.1960.

*Longest Sequence of League Defeats:* 7, 19.8.1975 – 20.9.1975.

*Longest Sequence of League Draws:* 6, 6.5.2001 – 8.9.2001.

*Longest Sequence of Unbeaten League Matches:* 22, 2.9.1899 – 13.1.1900.

*Longest Sequence Without a League Win:* 19, 27.9.1975 – 7.2.1976.

*Successive Scoring Runs:* 34 from 30.3.1956.

*Successive Non-scoring Runs:* 6 from 4.12.1993.

## TEN YEAR LEAGUE RECORD

| | | P | W | D | L | F | A | Pts | Pos |
|---|---|---|---|---|---|---|---|---|---|
| 2003-04 | Div 1 | 46 | 20 | 11 | 15 | 65 | 56 | 71 | 8 |
| 2004-05 | FL C | 46 | 18 | 13 | 15 | 57 | 56 | 67 | 8 |
| 2005-06 | FL C | 46 | 26 | 12 | 8 | 76 | 46 | 90 | 2 |
| 2006-07 | PR Lge | 38 | 10 | 8 | 20 | 32 | 55 | 38 | 18 |
| 2007-08 | FL C | 46 | 17 | 15 | 14 | 56 | 51 | 66 | 9 |
| 2008-09 | FL C | 46 | 22 | 14 | 10 | 64 | 39 | 80 | 3 |
| 2009-10 | FL C | 46 | 17 | 14 | 15 | 62 | 55 | 65 | 8 |
| 2010-11 | FL C | 46 | 11 | 9 | 26 | 44 | 79 | 42 | 23 |
| 2011-12 | FL 1 | 46 | 27 | 9 | 10 | 92 | 51 | 90 | 3 |
| 2012-13 | FL 1 | 46 | 19 | 18 | 9 | 56 | 42 | 75 | 5 |

## DID YOU KNOW ?

Graham Shaw, who made over 400 Football League appearances for Sheffield United, was a former ABA junior boxing champion. Graham made his debut for the Blades in 1952 when he played in the Sheffield derby match at Hillsborough and went on to win five England caps.

## SHEFFIELD UNITED – FOOTBALL LEAGUE ONE 2012–13 LEAGUE RECORD

| Match No. | Date | Venue | Opponents | Result | H/T Score | Lg Pos. | Goalscorers | Attendance |
|---|---|---|---|---|---|---|---|---|
| 1 | Aug 18 | H | Shrewsbury T | W 1-0 | 1-0 | 6 | McAllister [4] | 18,286 |
| 2 | 21 | A | Coventry C | D 1-1 | 0-0 | 7 | Blackman [84] | 12,621 |
| 3 | 25 | A | Colchester U | D 1-1 | 1-0 | 8 | Cofie [17] | 4017 |
| 4 | Sept 1 | H | Bournemouth | W 5-3 | 3-1 | 5 | Flynn 2 [24, 31], Cofie [43], Cresswell [60], Blackman (pen) [90] | 18,790 |
| 5 | 8 | A | Scunthorpe U | D 1-1 | 0-0 | 4 | Collins [83] | 5533 |
| 6 | 15 | H | Bury | D 1-1 | 1-1 | 7 | Blackman [10] | 16,866 |
| 7 | 18 | H | Doncaster R | D 0-0 | 0-0 | 6 | | 17,925 |
| 8 | 22 | A | Yeovil T | W 1-0 | 0-0 | 6 | Collins [55] | 4117 |
| 9 | 29 | H | Notts Co | D 1-1 | 0-0 | 7 | Kitson [51] | 18,814 |
| 10 | Oct 2 | A | Hartlepool U | W 2-1 | 1-0 | 6 | Kitson [27], Gallagher [89] | 4027 |
| 11 | 6 | A | Leyton Orient | W 1-0 | 0-0 | 3 | Blackman [59] | 4882 |
| 12 | 13 | H | Oldham Ath | D 1-1 | 0-0 | 3 | Blackman (pen) [52] | 18,188 |
| 13 | 20 | A | Preston NE | W 1-0 | 1-0 | 3 | Kitson [43] | 11,536 |
| 14 | 23 | H | Walsall | W 1-0 | 1-0 | 3 | Blackman (pen) [14] | 15,744 |
| 15 | 29 | H | Portsmouth | W 1-0 | 0-0 | 2 | Blackman (pen) [66] | 18,946 |
| 16 | Nov 6 | A | Swindon T | D 0-0 | 0-0 | 1 | | 8354 |
| 17 | 10 | A | Milton Keynes D | L 0-1 | 0-0 | 2 | | 9835 |
| 18 | 17 | H | Stevenage | W 4-1 | 1-1 | 2 | Porter 2 [19, 87], Miller 2 [55, 70] | 17,984 |
| 19 | 20 | H | Crewe Alex | D 3-3 | 2-2 | 2 | Miller [4], Maguire [30], Blackman [51] | 16,000 |
| 20 | 24 | A | Brentford | L 0-2 | 0-2 | 4 | | 7763 |
| 21 | Dec 8 | A | Carlisle U | W 3-1 | 2-0 | 3 | Flynn [16], Blackman [34], Collins [84] | 4892 |
| 22 | 15 | H | Tranmere R | D 0-0 | 0-0 | 3 | | 19,163 |
| 23 | 22 | A | Crawley T | W 2-0 | 1-0 | 1 | McMahon 2 [29, 72] | 4604 |
| 24 | 26 | H | Scunthorpe U | W 3-0 | 1-0 | 1 | Miller [4], Kitson [56], Blackman (pen) [84] | 21,819 |
| 25 | 29 | H | Hartlepool U | L 2-3 | 1-1 | 2 | Doyle [30], Maguire [90] | 19,941 |
| 26 | Jan 1 | A | Doncaster R | D 2-2 | 0-1 | 2 | Blackman (pen) [80], Kitson [89] | 12,785 |
| 27 | 12 | H | Yeovil T | L 0-2 | 0-0 | 4 | | 20,454 |
| 28 | 19 | A | Notts Co | D 1-1 | 1-0 | 5 | Maguire [2] | 7061 |
| 29 | Feb 1 | H | Coventry C | L 1-2 | 0-1 | 6 | Kitson [72] | 17,511 |
| 30 | 9 | A | Shrewsbury T | W 2-1 | 0-0 | 5 | Doyle [63], Kitson [72] | 7232 |
| 31 | 12 | A | Bury | W 2-0 | 1-0 | 5 | Forte [38], Murphy [60] | 3064 |
| 32 | 16 | H | Colchester U | W 3-0 | 1-0 | 2 | Robson (pen) [4], McDonald [73], Kitson [90] | 16,860 |
| 33 | 23 | A | Bournemouth | W 1-0 | 1-0 | 1 | Murphy [20] | 8497 |
| 34 | 26 | H | Leyton Orient | D 0-0 | 0-0 | 2 | | 16,540 |
| 35 | Mar 2 | A | Oldham Ath | W 2-0 | 0-0 | 2 | Doyle [57], Kitson [86] | 6426 |
| 36 | 9 | H | Milton Keynes D | D 0-0 | 0-0 | 2 | | 17,936 |
| 37 | 16 | A | Stevenage | L 0-4 | 0-1 | 6 | | 3483 |
| 38 | 29 | A | Tranmere R | W 1-0 | 1-0 | 5 | Taylor (og) [42] | 9145 |
| 39 | Apr 1 | H | Carlisle U | D 0-0 | 0-0 | 4 | | 19,005 |
| 40 | 6 | A | Walsall | D 1-1 | 0-1 | 5 | Porter [65] | 7042 |
| 41 | 9 | H | Crawley T | L 0-2 | 0-0 | 5 | | 18,680 |
| 42 | 13 | A | Swindon T | W 2-0 | 1-0 | 5 | Porter [37], Kitson [82] | 19,298 |
| 43 | 16 | H | Brentford | D 2-2 | 0-1 | 3 | Robson (pen) [62], Kitson [68] | 23,431 |
| 44 | 20 | A | Portsmouth | L 0-3 | 0-3 | 6 | | 18,433 |
| 45 | 23 | A | Crewe Alex | L 0-1 | 0-0 | 6 | | 5379 |
| 46 | 27 | H | Preston NE | D 0-0 | 0-0 | 5 | | 19,888 |

**Final League Position: 5**

### GOALSCORERS

*League (56):* Blackman 11 (6 pens), Kitson 11, Miller 4, Porter 4, Collins 3, Doyle 3, Flynn 3, Maguire 3, Cofie 2, McMahon 2, Murphy 2, Robson 2 (2 pens), Cresswell 1, Forte 1, Gallagher 1, McAllister 1, McDonald 1, own goal 1.
*FA Cup (7):* Blackman 2, Miller 2, Kitson 1, McMahon 1, Porter 1.
*Capital One Cup (2):* Blackman 1, Collins 1.
*Johnstone's Paint Trophy (5):* Maguire 2, Miller 2, McAllister 1.
*League One Play-Offs (1):* McFadzean 1.

| Howard M 11 | McMahon T 38 | Collins N 38+1 | Maguire H 44 | Williams M 14+4 | McAllister D 10+4 | Doyle M 43 | McDonald K 45 | Quinn S 3 | Cofie J 8+8 | Blackman N 28 | Miller S 7+8 | Hill M 34 | Flynn R 36 | Cresswell R 2+14 | Westlake D 8+3 | Gallagher P 6 | Kitson D 30+3 | Porter C 13+8 | Long G 35+1 | Ironside J 1+11 | Chapell J —+2 | Higginbotham D 13+2 | Kennedy T 1 | Whitehouse E 1+2 | Murphy J 15+2 | Philliskirk D —+1 | Forte J 7+5 | Robson B 10+7 | Poleon D 3+4 | De Girolamo D —+2 | McFadzean C 2+6 | Match No. |
|---|---|---|---|---|---|---|---|---|---|---|---|---|---|---|---|---|---|---|---|---|---|---|---|---|---|---|---|---|---|---|---|---|
| 1 | 2 | 3 | 4 | 5 | 6 | 7 | 8 | 9 | 10¹ | 11 | 12 | | | | | | | | | | | | | | | | | | | | | 1 |
| 1 | 5 | 3 | 4 | | 6 | 8 | 7 | 9 | 11¹ | 10 | 12 | 2 | | | | | | | | | | | | | | | | | | | | 2 |
| 1 | 2 | 4 | 3 | | 6 | 7 | 9 | 8 | 10¹ | 11 | 12 | 5 | | | | | | | | | | | | | | | | | | | | 3 |
| 1 | 2 | 4 | 3 | | 6 | 7 | 8 | | 10¹ | 11 | | 5 | | | | | 9 | 12 | | | | | | | | | | | | | | 4 |
| 1 | 2 | 4 | 3 | 12 | 6² | 7⁸ | 8 | | 10³ | 11 | 14 | 5¹ | 9⁴ | 13 | | | | | | | | | | | | | | | | | | 5 |
| 1 | 7 | 4 | 3 | | 9 | | 8 | | 11¹ | 10 | | 5 | | | | | 12 | 2² | 6 | 13 | | | | | | | | | | | | 6 |
| 1 | 2 | 4 | 3 | 8 | 9 | | 7 | | 13 | 10 | | 5 | | | | | 11¹ | 6² | 12 | | | | | | | | | | | | | 7 |
| 1 | 2 | 4 | 3 | 13 | 7 | | 8 | | 10 | | | 5 | | 9 | | | 6² | 11¹ | 12 | | | | | | | | | | | | | 8 |
| 1 | 2 | 4 | 3 | | 8 | | 7 | | 13 | 10 | | 5 | 9 | | | | 6² | 11¹ | 12 | | | | | | | | | | | | | 9 |
| 1 | 2 | 4 | 3 | | 7 | | 8 | | 12 | 10¹ | | 5 | 9 | 13 | | | 6 | 11² | | | | | | | | | | | | | | 10 |
| 1¹ | 2 | | 3 | 5 | 7 | | 8 | | 10² | | | 4 | 6 | 14 | | | 9 | 11³ | 13 | 12 | | | | | | | | | | | | 11 |
| | 2 | | 3 | 5 | 7 | | 8 | | 9¹ | 11 | | 4 | 6 | 12 | | | 10 | | 1 | | | | | | | | | | | | | 12 |
| | 2 | 13 | 3 | 5 | 9² | 6 | 8 | | 11³ | 14 | | 4 | 7 | | | | 10¹ | 12 | 1 | | | | | | | | | | | | | 13 |
| | 2 | | 3 | 5 | 6¹ | 7 | 8 | | 12 | 11² | 13 | 4 | 9 | | | | 10³ | 14 | 1 | | | | | | | | | | | | | 14 |
| | 2 | 4 | 3 | 9² | 8 | 7 | | | 10¹ | 13 | | 5 | 6 | 12 | | | 11 | | 1 | | | | | | | | | | | | | 15 |
| | 2 | 4 | 3 | 9 | | 7 | 8 | | 11¹ | | | 5 | 6 | 12 | | | 10 | | 1 | | | | | | | | | | | | | 16 |
| | 2¹ | 5 | 4 | 9 | 13 | 8 | 7 | | 10³ | 14 | 3² | 6 | | 12 | | | 11 | | 1 | | | | | | | | | | | | | 17 |
| | 4 | 3 | 5 | | 8 | 7 | | 12 | 11 | 9² | | 6 | 13 | 2 | | | 10¹ | | 1 | | | | | | | | | | | | | 18 |
| | 4 | 3 | 5 | 12 | 8 | 7 | | | 9 | 11 | | 6¹ | | | | | 10 | | 1 | | | | | | | | | | | | | 19 |
| | 5¹ | 6 | 3 | | 7 | 9 | | | 11 | 2 | | 4 | 8 | 13 | 12 | | 10² | | 1 | | | | | | | | | | | | | 20 |
| | 4 | 3 | | 12 | 8 | 7¹ | | | 6 | 11 | | 5 | 9 | | 2 | | 10² | 1 | 13 | | | | | | | | | | | | | 21 |
| | 2 | 4 | 3 | 9² | 13 | 8 | | | 6 | 10 | | 5 | 7 | | | | 12 | 11¹ | 1 | | | | | | | | | | | | | 22 |
| | 11 | 10 | 2 | 14 | | 5 | 7 | | 13 | 6³ | 8² | 3 | 4 | | | | 9¹ | | 1 | 12 | | | | | | | | | | | | 23 |
| | 2 | 4² | 3 | 13 | | 8 | 7 | | 12 | 6 | 10¹ | 5 | 9 | 14 | | | 11³ | | 1 | | | | | | | | | | | | | 24 |
| | | 3 | 5 | | | 7² | 8 | | 10¹ | 6 | | 4 | 9 | 14 | 2 | | 11³ | | 1 | 13 | 12 | | | | | | | | | | | 25 |
| | 2 | | | | | 7 | 8 | | 12 | 10 | | 5 | 6² | | | | 11 | | 1 | 13 | | 3 | 4 | 9¹ | | | | | | | | 26 |
| | 2 | | 3 | 5³ | | 7 | 8 | | | 6 | | 9¹ | 13 | | | | 10² | | 1 | 12 | | 4 | | 11 | 14 | | | | | | | 27 |
| | 2 | | 3 | | | 8 | 7 | | | 6 | | 9 | 5 | | | | 11¹ | | 1 | 12 | | 4 | | 10 | | | | | | | | 28 |
| | 2 | 4 | 3 | | | 8 | 7 | | | 6 | | | | | | | 10 | 11¹ | 1 | | | 5 | | 9² | | 12 | 13 | | | | | 29 |
| | 2 | 4 | 3 | | | 8 | 7 | | | 6 | | | | | | | 10² | | 1 | 13 | | 5 | | 9¹ | | 11 | 12 | | | | | 30 |
| | 2 | 4 | 3 | | | 8 | 7 | | | 6 | | | | | | | 10² | | 1 | 13 | | 5 | | 9 | | 11¹ | 12 | | | | | 31 |
| | 2 | 4 | 3 | | | 8 | 7 | | | 6² | | | | | | | 10 | | 1 | | | 5 | | 11 | | 9¹ | 12 | 13 | | | | 32 |
| | 2 | 4 | 3 | | | 8 | 7 | | | 6 | | | | | | | 10 | | 1 | | | 5 | | 11 | | 9¹ | 12 | | | | | 33 |
| | 2 | 4 | 3 | | | 8 | 7 | | | 6 | 13 | | | | | | 11² | | 1 | | | 5 | | 9³ | | 10¹ | 14 | 12 | | | | 34 |
| | 2 | 3 | 4 | | | 8 | 7 | | | 5 | 9 | | | | | | 11 | | 1 | | | | | 9¹ | 6 | 10¹ | 12 | | | | | 35 |
| | 2 | 4 | 3 | | | 8 | 7 | | | 5 | 6 | | | | | | 11 | | 1 | | | | | 9¹ | 12 | 10² | 13 | | | | | 36 |
| | 4 | 11 | 2 | | | 7 | 8 | | | 3 | 6¹ | | | | | | 10 | | 1 | | | 5² | | 13 | 9 | | 12 | | | | | 37 |
| | 2 | 4 | 3 | | | 7 | 8 | | | 5 | 9 | | | | | | 11 | | 1 | | | 6¹ | | 10 | 12 | | | | | | | 38 |
| | 2 | 4 | 3 | | | 8 | 7 | | | 5¹ | | | | | | | 10³ | 1 | 14 | | 12 | | 13 | 9 | 6 | 11² | | | | | | 39 |
| | | 4 | 3 | | | 8 | 7 | | | 5 | | | | | | | 10¹ | 12 | 1 | 2 | | 9 | | 11 | 6² | | 13 | | | | | 40 |
| | | 4 | 3 | | | 8³ | 7 | | | 2 | 6 | | | | | 11 | 12 | | 1 | 5 | | 9¹ | | 10² | 14 | | 13 | | | | | 41 |
| | 2 | 4 | 3 | | | | | | | 5 | 6 | | | | | | 10 | 11³ | 1 | 14 | | 13 | | 9¹ | | 12 | | | | | | 42 |
| | 2 | 4 | 3⁸ | | | 7² | 8 | | | 5 | 6¹ | | | | | | 10³ | 11 | 1 | 14 | | 9 | | 12 | 13 | | | | | | | 43 |
| | 2³ | 4 | | | | 7 | 8 | | | 5 | 6² | 14 | | | | | 11¹ | 10 | 1 | | 3 | | 9 | | 13 | 12 | | | | | | 44 |
| | | 3 | 4 | | | 7 | 9 | | | | 2 | | | | | | 10 | | 1 | 13 | 14 | 5¹ | | 12 | | 11² | 8⁴ | | 6 | | | 45 |
| | | 4 | 3 | | | 8 | 7³ | | | 5 | | | | | | | 10¹ | 12 | 1 | 11 | | 14 | | 6 | | 13 | | 9² | | | | 46 |

**FA Cup**

| | | | | |
|---|---|---|---|---|
| First Round | Bristol R | (a) | 2-1 | |
| Second Round | Port Vale | (h) | 2-1 | |
| Third Round | Oxford U | (a) | 3-0 | |
| Fourth Round | Reading | (a) | 0-4 | |

**Capital One Cup**

| | | | |
|---|---|---|---|
| First Round | Burton | (h) | 2-2 |

*(aet; lost 4-5 on pens)*

**Johnstone's Paint Trophy**

| | | | |
|---|---|---|---|
| Second Round | Notts Co | (a) | 4-1 |
| Northern Quarter-Finals | Coventry C | (a) | 1-1 |

*(aet; lost 1-4 on pens)*

**League One Play-Offs**

| | | | |
|---|---|---|---|
| Semi-Finals | Yeovil T | (h) | 1-0 |
| | Yeovil T | (a) | 0-2 |

# SHEFFIELD WEDNESDAY

## FOUNDATION

Sheffield being one of the principal centres of early Association Football, this club was formed as long ago as 1867 by the Sheffield Wednesday Cricket Club (formed 1825) and their colours from the start were blue and white. The inaugural meeting was held at the Adelphi Hotel and the original committee included Charles Stokes who was subsequently a founder member of Sheffield United.

*Hillsborough Stadium, Sheffield, South Yorkshire S6 1SW.*

*Telephone:* (0871) 995 1867.

*Fax:* (0114) 221 2122.

*Ticket Office:* (0871) 900 1867.

*Website:* www.swfc.co.uk

*Email:* enquiries@swfc.co.uk

*Ground Capacity:* 39,732.

*Record Attendance:* 72,841 v Manchester C, FA Cup 5th rd, 17 February 1934.

*Pitch Measurements:* 105m × 68m (115yd × 75yd)

*Chairman:* Milan Mandaric.

*Vice-chairman:* Paul Aldridge.

*Manager:* Dave Jones.

*Assistant Manager:* Paul Wilkinson.

*Head Physio:* Paul Smith.

*Colours:* Blue and white striped shirts, black shorts, black socks.

*Year Formed:* 1867 (fifth oldest League club).

*Turned Professional:* 1887.

*Previous Name:* The Wednesday until 1929.

*Club Nickname:* 'The Owls'.

*Grounds:* 1867, Highfield; 1869, Myrtle Road; 1877, Sheaf House; 1887, Olive Grove; 1899, Owlerton (since 1912 known as Hillsborough). Some games were played at Endcliffe in the 1880s. Until 1895 Bramall Lane was used for some games.

*First Football League Game:* 3 September 1892, Division 1, v Notts Co (a) W 1–0 – Allan; Tom Brandon (1), Mumford; Hall, Betts, Harry Brandon; Spiksley, Brady, Davis, Bob Brown, Dunlop.

*Record League Victory:* 9–1 v Birmingham, Division 1, 13 December 1930 – Brown; Walker, Blenkinsop; Strange, Leach, Wilson; Hooper (3), Seed (2), Ball (2), Burgess (1), Rimmer (1).

*Record Cup Victory:* 12–0 v Halliwell, FA Cup 1st rd, 17 January 1891 – Smith; Thompson, Brayshaw; Harry Brandon (1), Betts, Cawley (2); Winterbottom, Mumford (2), Bob Brandon (1), Woolhouse (5), Ingram (1).

## HONOURS

**Football League – Division 1:**
*Champions* 1902–03, 1903–04, 1928–29, 1929–30;
*Runners-up* 1960–61;
**Division 2:** *Champions* 1899–1900, 1925–26, 1951–52, 1955–56, 1958–59;
*Runners-up* 1949–50, 1983–84.
**FL 1:** *Runners-up* 2011–12.
**FA Cup:** *Winners* 1896, 1907, 1935;
*Runners-up* 1890, 1966, 1993.

**Football League Cup:** *Winners* 1991;
*Runners-up* 1993.

**European Competitions**
**European Fairs Cup:** 1961–62, 1963–64. **UEFA Cup:** 1992–93.
**Intertoto Cup:** 1995.

## sky SPORTS FACT FILE

The legendary Sheffield Wednesday winger Fred Spiksley always laundered his own kit and was an immaculate off-field dresser. En route to Accrington in 1891 he was delayed and met a couple of Wednesday players. He stayed and went on to make 324 appearances and score 116 goals.

**Record Defeat:** 0–10 v Aston Villa, Division 1, 5 October 1912.

**Most League Points (2 for a win):** 62, Division 2, 1958–59.

**Most League Points (3 for a win):** 93, FL 1, 2011–12.

**Most League Goals:** 106, Division 2, 1958–59.

**Highest League Scorer in Season:** Derek Dooley, 46, Division 2, 1951–52.

**Most League Goals in Total Aggregate:** Andrew Wilson, 199, 1900–20.

**Most League Goals in One Match:** 6, Doug Hunt v Norwich C, Division 2, 19 November 1938.

**Most Capped Player:** Nigel Worthington, 50 (66), Northern Ireland.

**Most League Appearances:** Andrew Wilson, 501, 1900–20.

**Youngest League Player:** Peter Fox, 15 years 269 days v Orient, 31 March 1973.

**Record Transfer Fee Received:** £3,000,000 from WBA for Chris Brunt, August 2007.

**Record Transfer Fee Paid:** £4,500,000 to Celtic for Paolo Di Canio, August 1997.

**Football League Record:** 1892 Elected to Division 1; 1899–1900 Division 2; 1900–20 Division 1; 1920–26 Division 2; 1926–37 Division 1; 1937–50 Division 2; 1950–51 Division 1; 1951–52 Division 2; 1952–55 Division 1; 1955–56 Division 2; 1956–58 Division 1; 1958–59 Division 2; 1959–70 Division 1; 1970–75 Division 2; 1975–80 Division 3; 1980–84 Division 2; 1984–90 Division 1; 1990–91 Division 2; 1991–92 Division 1; 1992–2000 FA Premier League; 2000–03 Division 1; 2003–04 Division 2; 2004–05 FL 1; 2005–10 FL C; 2010–12 FL 1; 2012– FL C.

## MANAGERS

Arthur Dickinson 1891–1920
*(Secretary-Manager)*
Robert Brown 1920–33
Billy Walker 1933–37
Jimmy McMullan 1937–42
Eric Taylor 1942–58
  *(continued as General Manager to 1974)*
Harry Catterick 1958–61
Vic Buckingham 1961–64
Alan Brown 1964–68
Jack Marshall 1968–69
Danny Williams 1969–71
Derek Dooley 1971–73
Steve Burtenshaw 1974–75
Len Ashurst 1975–77
Jackie Charlton 1977–83
Howard Wilkinson 1983–88
Peter Eustace 1988–89
Ron Atkinson 1989–91
Trevor Francis 1991–95
David Pleat 1995–97
Ron Atkinson 1997–98
Danny Wilson 1998–2000
Peter Shreeves *(Acting)* 2000
Paul Jewell 2000–01
Peter Shreeves 2001
Terry Yorath 2001–02
Chris Turner 2002–04
Paul Sturrock 2004–06
Brian Laws 2006–09
Alan Irvine 2010–11
Gary Megson 2011–12
Dave Jones March 2012–

## LATEST SEQUENCES

**Longest Sequence of League Wins:** 9, 23.4.1904 – 15.10.1904.

**Longest Sequence of League Defeats:** 8, 9.9.2000 – 17.10.2000.

**Longest Sequence of League Draws:** 7, 15.3.2008 – 14.4.2008.

**Longest Sequence of Unbeaten League Matches:** 19, 10.12.1960 – 8.4.1961.

**Longest Sequence Without a League Win:** 20, 11.1.1975 – 30.8.1975.

**Successive Scoring Runs:** 40 from 14.11.1959.

**Successive Non-scoring Runs:** 8 from 8.3.1975.

## TEN YEAR LEAGUE RECORD

|         |       | P  | W  | D  | L  | F  | A  | Pts | Pos |
|---------|-------|----|----|----|----|----|----|-----|-----|
| 2003-04 | Div 2 | 46 | 13 | 14 | 19 | 48 | 64 | 53  | 16  |
| 2004-05 | FL 1  | 46 | 19 | 15 | 12 | 77 | 59 | 72  | 5   |
| 2005-06 | FL C  | 46 | 13 | 13 | 20 | 39 | 52 | 52  | 19  |
| 2006-07 | FL C  | 46 | 20 | 11 | 15 | 70 | 66 | 71  | 9   |
| 2007-08 | FL C  | 46 | 14 | 13 | 19 | 54 | 55 | 55  | 16  |
| 2008-09 | FL C  | 46 | 16 | 13 | 17 | 51 | 58 | 61  | 12  |
| 2009-10 | FL C  | 46 | 11 | 14 | 21 | 49 | 69 | 47  | 22  |
| 2010-11 | FL 1  | 46 | 16 | 10 | 20 | 67 | 67 | 58  | 15  |
| 2011-12 | FL 1  | 46 | 28 | 9  | 9  | 81 | 48 | 93  | 2   |
| 2012-13 | FL C  | 46 | 16 | 10 | 20 | 53 | 61 | 58  | 18  |

## DID YOU KNOW

Fixtures between Sheffield Wednesday and Everton have produced 10 or more goals on three occasions, each with a different result. The teams drew 5-5 at Owlerton in November 1904, Wednesday lost 9-3 at Goodison in October 1931 and won 6-4 at home in September 1936.

## SHEFFIELD WEDNESDAY – FL CHAMPIONSHIP 2012–13 LEAGUE RECORD

| Match No. | Date | Venue | Opponents | Result | H/T Score | Lg Pos. | Goalscorers | Attendance |
|---|---|---|---|---|---|---|---|---|
| 1 | Aug 18 | A | Derby Co | D 2-2 | 1-2 | 11 | O'Grady [39], Johnson, R [90] | 27,437 |
| 2 | 21 | H | Birmingham C | W 3-2 | 2-0 | 2 | Johnson, R [14], Rodri [39], Johnson, J [89] | 25,379 |
| 3 | 25 | H | Millwall | W 3-2 | 1-2 | 2 | Johnson, J [19], Llera 2 [68, 90] | 24,752 |
| 4 | Sept 1 | A | Crystal Palace | L 1-2 | 0-1 | 6 | Antonio [50] | 14,043 |
| 5 | 14 | A | Brighton & HA | L 0-3 | 0-1 | 8 | | 26,594 |
| 6 | 19 | H | Huddersfield T | L 1-3 | 1-2 | 17 | Johnson, R [37] | 25,230 |
| 7 | 22 | H | Bolton W | L 1-2 | 0-1 | 21 | Barkley (pen) [62] | 26,598 |
| 8 | 29 | A | Wolverhampton W | L 0-1 | 0-1 | 22 | | 23,591 |
| 9 | Oct 2 | A | Burnley | D 3-3 | 1-2 | 21 | O'Grady 2 [23, 64], Antonio [85] | 12,122 |
| 10 | 6 | H | Hull C | L 0-1 | 0-0 | 22 | | 23,441 |
| 11 | 19 | H | Leeds U | D 1-1 | 1-0 | 22 | Bothroyd [44] | 28,582 |
| 12 | 24 | A | Blackburn R | L 0-1 | 0-1 | 23 | | 13,782 |
| 13 | 27 | A | Ipswich T | W 3-0 | 1-0 | 22 | Barkley 2 [2, 59], Antonio [81] | 17,738 |
| 14 | Nov 3 | H | Peterborough U | W 2-1 | 0-0 | 19 | Barkley [46], Llera [76] | 22,406 |
| 15 | 6 | H | Blackpool | L 0-2 | 0-1 | 20 | | 19,978 |
| 16 | 9 | A | Middlesbrough | L 1-3 | 0-1 | 20 | Madine [49] | 28,229 |
| 17 | 17 | A | Nottingham F | L 0-1 | 0-1 | 21 | | 24,584 |
| 18 | 24 | H | Leicester C | L 0-2 | 0-1 | 22 | | 24,664 |
| 19 | 27 | H | Watford | L 1-4 | 1-1 | 23 | Antonio [4] | 18,922 |
| 20 | Dec 2 | A | Cardiff C | L 0-1 | 0-0 | 23 | | 22,034 |
| 21 | 8 | H | Bristol C | L 2-3 | 1-1 | 23 | Llera [3], Madine [79] | 20,449 |
| 22 | 15 | A | Barnsley | W 1-0 | 1-0 | 23 | O'Grady [35] | 12,484 |
| 23 | 22 | H | Charlton Ath | W 2-0 | 1-0 | 21 | McCabe [20], Helan [90] | 20,517 |
| 24 | 26 | A | Bolton W | W 1-0 | 1-0 | 21 | Sidibe [25] | 22,292 |
| 25 | 29 | A | Huddersfield T | D 0-0 | 0-0 | 21 | | 17,494 |
| 26 | Jan 1 | H | Burnley | L 0-2 | 0-0 | 22 | | 23,677 |
| 27 | 12 | A | Hull C | W 3-1 | 1-0 | 21 | Johnson, R [24], Jakupovic (og) [86], Antonio [90] | 16,531 |
| 28 | 19 | H | Wolverhampton W | D 0-0 | 0-0 | 21 | | 21,142 |
| 29 | 26 | A | Charlton Ath | W 2-1 | 0-0 | 20 | Johnson, R [84], Lita [89] | 20,292 |
| 30 | Feb 2 | H | Brighton & HA | W 3-1 | 2-0 | 18 | Lita [5], Pugh [34], Antonio [56] | 22,044 |
| 31 | 9 | H | Derby Co | D 2-2 | 0-1 | 19 | Antonio [51], Llera [57] | 25,765 |
| 32 | 19 | A | Birmingham C | D 0-0 | 0-0 | 19 | | 15,738 |
| 33 | 23 | H | Crystal Palace | W 1-0 | 0-0 | 18 | Lita [81] | 23,475 |
| 34 | Mar 2 | H | Nottingham F | L 0-1 | 0-1 | 19 | | 23,220 |
| 35 | 5 | A | Watford | L 1-2 | 1-0 | 19 | Antonio [19] | 12,727 |
| 36 | 9 | A | Leicester C | W 1-0 | 0-0 | 18 | Wickham [70] | 24,883 |
| 37 | 16 | H | Cardiff C | L 0-2 | 0-1 | 21 | | 24,191 |
| 38 | 30 | H | Barnsley | W 2-1 | 0-0 | 20 | Madine [65], Johnson, R [77] | 29,697 |
| 39 | Apr 1 | A | Bristol C | D 1-1 | 1-0 | 21 | Johnson, J [36] | 19,148 |
| 40 | 6 | H | Blackburn R | W 3-2 | 2-1 | 18 | Johnson, J 2 [20, 78], Lita (pen) [35] | 24,660 |
| 41 | 9 | A | Millwall | W 2-1 | 1-1 | 14 | Llera [40], Maguire [90] | 9084 |
| 42 | 13 | A | Leeds U | L 1-2 | 1-0 | 16 | Johnson, J [27] | 23,936 |
| 43 | 16 | A | Blackpool | D 0-0 | 0-0 | 18 | | 13,845 |
| 44 | 20 | H | Ipswich T | D 1-1 | 0-1 | 18 | Lita [58] | 23,630 |
| 45 | 27 | A | Peterborough U | L 0-1 | 0-0 | 20 | | 13,938 |
| 46 | May 4 | H | Middlesbrough | W 2-0 | 2-0 | 18 | Howard [9], Lita [31] | 31,375 |

**Final League Position: 18**

## GOALSCORERS

*League (53):* Antonio 8, Johnson, J 6, Johnson, R 6, Lita 6 (1 pen), Llera 6, Barkley 4 (1 pen), O'Grady 4, Madine 3, Bothroyd 1, Helan 1, Howard 1, Maguire 1, McCabe 1, Pugh 1, Rodri 1, Sidibe 1, Wickham 1, own goal 1.
*FA Cup (0).*
*Capital One Cup (5):* O'Grady 2, Antonio 1, Johnson J 1, Madine 1 (1 pen).

| Kirkland C 46 | Buxton L 40 | Llera M 41 | Gardner A 37 | Johnson R 16 | Antonio M 37 | McCabe R 16+6 | Semedo J 17+9 | Johnson J 21+20 | Pecnik N 5+5 | O'Grady C 14+7 | Madine G 10+20 | Beevers M 5+1 | Rodri L 5+6 | Maguire C 1+9 | Jones D 9 | Mayor D 1+7 | Mattock J 6+1 | Taylor M 10+1 | Bothroyd J 14 | Barkley R 12+1 | Lee K 16+7 | Corry P 6 | Helan J 27+1 | Sidibe M 5+4 | Lines C 4+2 | Prutton D 22 | Coke G 15+1 | Pugh D 16 | Lita L 13+4 | Wickham C 4+2 | Holden S 4 | Olofinjana S 6 | Howard S 5+3 | Match No. |
|---|---|---|---|---|---|---|---|---|---|---|---|---|---|---|---|---|---|---|---|---|---|---|---|---|---|---|---|---|---|---|---|---|---|---|
| 1 | 2 | 3 | 4² | 5 | 6 | 7 | 8 | 9 | 10¹ | 11 | 12 | 13 | | | | | | | | | | | | | | | | | | | | | | 1 |
| 1 | 2 | 3 | | 5 | 9³ | 8 | 7 | 6 | 13 | 10² | 12 | 4 | 11¹ | 14 | | | | | | | | | | | | | | | | | | | | 2 |
| 1 | 2 | 4 | | 5 | 9 | 8² | 7 | 6 | 13 | 12 | 10¹ | 3 | 11 | | | | | | | | | | | | | | | | | | | | | 3 |
| 1 | 2 | 3 | | 11 | 7 | 6 | 10² | 13 | 8 | 12 | 4 | 9³ | 5 | 14 | | | | | | | | | | | | | | | | | | | | 4 |
| 1 | | 4 | | 6 | 8 | 7 | 9² | 13 | | 14 | 5 | 11¹ | | 2 | 3 | 10³ | 12 | | | | | | | | | | | | | | | | | | 5 |
| 1 | | | 5 | 6 | 13 | 7² | 9 | 12 | 14 | 10¹ | 4 | 2⁸ | 3 | 11³ | 8 | | | | | | | | | | | | | | | | | | | 6 |
| 1 | | 3 | | 6 | 7¹ | 12 | 13 | 8 | 14 | | 10² | 5 | | 4 | 11³ | 9 | 2 | | | | | | | | | | | | | | | | | 7 |
| 1 | | 4 | | 6 | | 7 | 2 | 9¹ | 11 | | 13 | | 12 | 5 | 3 | 10² | 8 | | | | | | | | | | | | | | | | | 8 |
| 1 | | 4 | | 6 | 12 | 7 | 2 | 9¹ | 10² | 13 | | | 5 | 3 | 11 | 8 | | | | | | | | | | | | | | | | | | 9 |
| 1 | 2 | 4 | 3 | 6 | 8³ | 7 | 13 | | 10¹ | 12 | | | 14 | 5 | | 11² | 9 | | | | | | | | | | | | | | | | | 10 |
| 1 | 2 | 4 | 3 | 6 | | 7 | | 10¹ | 13 | | | | 5 | 12 | | 11 | 8 | 9² | | | | | | | | | | | | | | | | 11 |
| 1 | 2 | 4 | | 6 | | 7 | 10 | | 13 | 11 | | 12 | 5² | | 3 | | 8 | 9¹ | | | | | | | | | | | | | | | | 12 |
| 1 | 2 | 4 | 3 | 10 | | 6 | 12 | | 11² | 13 | | | 5 | | | 7 | 8 | 9¹ | | | | | | | | | | | | | | | | 13 |
| 1 | 2 | 4 | 3 | | 6 | 12 | 7 | 14 | 11² | 13 | | | 5 | | | 10³ | 9 | 8¹ | | | | | | | | | | | | | | | | 14 |
| 1 | 2 | 4 | 3 | | 6 | 7² | 9 | 12 | | 11¹ | | | 13 | 5 | | 10 | 8 | | | | | | | | | | | | | | | | | 15 |
| 1 | 2 | 3 | 4 | | 10 | 14 | 8 | 12 | | 13 | 11 | | 5 | | | | 6¹ | 7³ | 9² | | | | | | | | | | | | | | | 16 |
| 1 | 2 | | 4 | 5 | 9 | | 7 | 12 | 8¹ | | 10 | | | 3² | 13 | | 11 | 6 | | | | | | | | | | | | | | | | 17 |
| 1 | 2 | | 3 | | 6 | 8¹ | 7 | 9 | | 13 | | 14 | | | | 4 | 11² | | | 5 | 10³ | 12 | | | | | | | | | | | | 18 |
| 1 | 2³ | 4 | 3¹ | | 6 | 8² | 13 | 14 | | | | | | | | 12 | 11 | | | 9 | 5 | 10 | 7 | | | | | | | | | | | 19 |
| 1 | 2 | 5 | | 6 | | | 13 | | | 10³ | 12 | | 14 | | 8² | | 3 | | | 4 | 11¹ | 7 | 9 | | | | | | | | | | | 20 |
| 1 | 2 | 4 | | 6 | | | 9² | | | 11¹ | 10 | | 13 | | | 12 | 3 | | | 5 | | 7 | 8 | | | | | | | | | | | 21 |
| 1 | 2 | 4 | 3 | 6 | 13 | | 9¹ | | | 11 | 10² | | | | 12 | | | | | 5 | 14 | 8³ | 7 | | | | | | | | | | | 22 |
| 1 | 2 | 4 | 3 | 5 | 6 | 7 | | | | 11² | 10³ | | | | | 13 | | | | 11 | 9 | 10² | | 8¹ | | | | | | | | | | 23 |
| 1 | 2 | 4 | 3 | 5¹ | 6³ | 7 | | 14 | | 12 | | | | | | 13 | | | | 11 | 9 | 10² | 8 | | | | | | | | | | | 24 |
| 1 | 2 | 3 | 4 | 5 | 11² | 8 | | 13 | | | 10¹ | | | | | | | | | 6 | 9 | 12 | 7 | | | | | | | | | | | 25 |
| 1 | 2 | 4 | 3 | | 6 | 8 | | 13 | | 12 | | | | | 7 | | | | | 9 | 5 | 10¹ | 11² | | | | | | | | | | | 26 |
| 1 | 2 | 4 | 3 | 5 | 10 | 7¹ | 12 | 11² | | | | | | | | | | | | 6 | 9 | 13 | | 8 | | | | | | | | | | 27 |
| 1 | 2 | 4 | 3 | 5 | 10 | | | 11¹ | | 12 | | | | | | | | | | 6 | 9 | | 7 | 8 | | | | | | | | | | 28 |
| 1 | 2 | 4 | 3 | 5 | 10 | | 14 | 11³ | | 13 | | | | | | | | | | 6¹ | | | 7 | 8 | 9² | 12 | | | | | | | | 29 |
| 1 | 2 | 4 | 3 | | 10 | | 13 | | | 12 | | | | | | | | | | 6 | 9¹ | | 7 | 8 | 5 | 11² | | | | | | | | 30 |
| 1 | 2 | 4 | 3 | | 10 | | | 13 | | | | | | | | | | | | 6¹ | 9² | | 7 | 8 | 5 | 11 | 12 | | | | | | | 31 |
| 1 | 2 | 4 | | 6 | 14 | | 12 | | | 13 | | | | | | | 3 | | | | 5 | | 7 | 8³ | 9 | 10² | 11¹ | | | | | | | 32 |
| 1 | 2 | 4 | 3 | | 9³ | | | 14 | | 12 | | | | | | | | | | 6² | 13 | | 7 | 8 | 5 | 11 | 10¹ | | | | | | | 33 |
| 1 | 2 | 4 | 3 | 6 | | | 12 | | | 14 | | | | | | | | | | 13 | 9 | | 7³ | 8 | 5² | 10 | 11¹ | | | | | | | 34 |
| 1 | 2 | 4 | 3 | | 10 | | 12 | 13 | | | | | | | | | | | | 7 | 6 | | 8³ | 9¹ | 5² | 14 | 11 | | | | | | | 35 |
| 1 | 2 | 3 | 4 | 5¹ | 11 | | 13 | | | | | | | | | | | | | 9 | 6 | | 8 | | 7 | 10² | 12 | | | | | | | 36 |
| 1 | 2 | 4 | 3 | 5 | 6³ | | | 13 | | | 12 | | 14 | | | | | | | 10 | 9² | | 7 | | 8¹ | 11 | | | | | | | | 37 |
| 1 | 2⁸ | 4 | 3 | 5 | | | 12 | | | 10 | | 14 | | | | | | | | | 9 | | 13 | | 8¹ | 11³ | | 6² | 7 | | | | | 38 |
| 1 | | 4 | 3 | 5 | | 14 | 9¹ | | | 13 | | | | | | | | | | 2 | 11 | | 6 | 8³ | 7 | 12 | | | 10² | | | | | 39 |
| 1 | 2 | 4 | 3 | 5 | | | 10¹ | | | | | | | | 14 | | | | | 12 | 9 | | 6 | | 11² | 7¹ | 8 | 13 | | | | | 40 |
| 1 | 2 | 4 | 3 | | 12 | | | | | 13 | | | | | | | | | | 6 | 9² | | 8 | 5 | 10¹ | | 7 | 11 | | | | | 41 |
| 1 | 2 | 4 | 3 | 5 | | | 10² | | | | | | | | 14 | | | | | 12 | 9 | | 7 | 8¹ | 11 | 6³ | | 13 | | | | | 42 |
| 1 | 2 | 3 | 4 | | 9² | | | | | | | | | | 13 | | | | | 12 | 11 | | 8 | 7 | 5 | 6¹ | | 10 | | | | | 43 |
| 1 | 2 | 4 | 3 | | 9² | | | | | | | | | | 13 | | | | | 6¹ | 10 | | 8 | 5 | 11 | | 7 | 12 | | | | | 44 |
| 1 | 2 | 4 | 3 | | 7³ | | | | | 14 | | | | | 6 | | | | | 12 | 10² | | 8 | 5 | 13 | | 9 | 11³ | | | | | 45 |
| 1 | 2 | 4 | 3 | | 13 | | 6¹ | | | 14 | | | | | | | | | | 12 | 9 | | 8 | | 5 | 10³ | | 7² | 11 | | | | | 46 |

# SHREWSBURY TOWN

## FOUNDATION

Shrewsbury School having provided a number of the early England and Wales international players it is not surprising that there was a Town club as early as 1876 which won the Birmingham Senior Cup in 1879. However, the present Shrewsbury Town club was formed in 1886 and won the Welsh FA Cup as early as 1891.

*Greenhous Meadow, Oteley Road, Shrewsbury, Shropshire SY2 6ST.*

*Telephone:* (01743) 289 177.

*Fax:* (01743) 246 942.

*Ticket Office:* (01743) 273 943.

*Website:* www.shrewsburytown.com

*Email:* info@shrewsburytown.co.uk

*Ground Capacity:* 9,875.

*Record Attendance:* 18,917 v Walsall, Division 3, 26 April 1961 (at Gay Meadow); 8,429 v Bury, FL 2 Play-off semi-final, 7 May 2009 (at ProStar Stadium).

*Pitch Measurements:* 105m × 70m (115yd × 77yd)

*Chairman:* Roland Wycherley.

*Manager:* Graham Turner.

*First Team Coach:* John Trewick.

*Physio:* Chris Skitt.

## HONOURS

**Football League – Division 2:** Best season: 8th, 1983–84, 1984–85; **Division 3:** *Champions* 1978–79, 1993–94; **Division 4:** *Runners-up* 1974–75. **FL 2:** *Runners-up* 2011–12.

**FA Cup:** Best season: 6th rd, 1979, 1982.

**Football League Cup:** Semi-final 1961.

**Welsh Cup:** *Winners* 1891, 1938, 1977, 1979, 1984, 1985; *Runners-up* 1931, 1948, 1980.

**Auto Windscreens Shield:** *Runners-up* 1996.

*Colours:* Blue and yellow striped shirts with blue sleeves, blue shorts, blue socks.

*Year Formed:* 1886.

*Turned Professional:* 1896.

*Club Nicknames:* 'Town', 'Blues', 'Salop'. The name 'Salop' is a colloquialism for the county of Shropshire. Since Shrewsbury is the only club in Shropshire, cries of 'Come on Salop' are frequently used!

*Grounds:* 1886, Old Racecourse Ground; 1889, Ambler's Field; 1893, Sutton Lane; 1895, Barracks Ground; 1910, Gay Meadow; 2007, New Meadow (re-named Greenhous Meadow 2010).

*First Football League Game:* 19 August 1950, Division 3 (N), v Scunthorpe U (a) D 0–0 – Egglestone; Fisher, Lewis; Wheatley, Depear, Robinson; Griffin, Hope, Jackson, Brown, Barker.

*Record League Victory:* 7–0 v Swindon T, Division 3 (S), 6 May 1955 – McBride; Bannister, Skeech; Wallace, Maloney, Candlin; Price, O'Donnell (1), Weigh (4), Russell, McCue (2); 7–0 v Gillingham, FL 2, 13 September 2008 – Daniels; Herd, Tierney, Davies (2), Jackson (1) (Langmead), Coughlan (1), Cansdell-Sherriff (1), Thornton, Hibbert (1) (Hindmarch), Holt (pen), McIntyre (Ashton).

*Record Cup Victory:* 11–2 v Marine, FA Cup 1st rd, 11 November 1995 – Edwards; Seabury (Dempsey (1)), Withe (1), Evans (1), Whiston (2), Scott (1), Woods, Stevens (1), Spink (3) (Anthrobus), Walton, Berkley, (1 og).

## sky SPORTS FACT FILE

Shrewsbury Town entered the FA Amateur Cup in 1895–96. They reached the semi-final stage only to lose 2-0 to Royal Artillery, Portsmouth in a match played on neutral ground at Reading. The Shrews had three second-half goals disallowed.

*Record Defeat:* 1–8 v Norwich C, Division 3 (S), 13 September 1952; 1–8 v Coventry C, Division 3, 22 October 1963.

*Most League Points (2 for a win):* 62, Division 4, 1974–75.

*Most League Points (3 for a win):* 88, FL 2, 2011–12.

*Most League Goals:* 101, Division 4, 1958–59.

*Highest League Scorer in Season:* Arthur Rowley, 38, Division 4, 1958–59.

*Most League Goals in Total Aggregate:* Arthur Rowley, 152, 1958–65 (thus completing his League record of 434 goals).

*Most League Goals in One Match:* 5, Alf Wood v Blackburn R, Division 3, 2 October 1971.

*Most Capped Player:* Jimmy McLaughlin, 5 (12), Northern Ireland; Bernard McNally, 5, Northern Ireland.

*Most League Appearances:* Mickey Brown, 418, 1986–91; 1992–94; 1996–2001.

*Youngest League Player:* Graham French, 16 years 177 days v Reading, 30 September 1961.

*Record Transfer Fee Received:* £600,000 from Manchester C for Joe Hart, May 2006.

*Record Transfer Fee Paid:* £170,000 to Nottingham F for Grant Holt, June 2008.

*Football League Record:* 1950 Elected to Division 3 (N); 1951–58 Division 3 (S); 1958–59 Division 4; 1959–74 Division 3; 1974–75 Division 4; 1975–79 Division 3; 1979–89 Division 2; 1989–94 Division 3; 1994–97 Division 2; 1997–2003 Division 3; 2003–04 Conference; 2004–12 FL 2; 2012– FL 1.

## LATEST SEQUENCES

*Longest Sequence of League Wins:* 7, 28.10.1995 – 16.12.1995.

*Longest Sequence of League Defeats:* 11, 9.4.2003 – 14.8.2004.

*Longest Sequence of League Draws:* 6, 30.10.1963 – 14.12.1963.

*Longest Sequence of Unbeaten League Matches:* 16, 30.10.1993 – 26.2.1994.

*Longest Sequence Without a League Win:* 18, 8.3.2003 – 14.8.2004.

*Successive Scoring Runs:* 28 from 7.9.1960.

*Successive Non-scoring Runs:* 6 from 1.1.1991.

### MANAGERS

**W. Adams** 1905–12
*(Secretary-Manager)*
**A. Weston** 1912–34
*(Secretary-Manager)*
**Jack Roscamp** 1934–35
**Sam Ramsey** 1935–36
**Ted Bousted** 1936–40
**Leslie Knighton** 1945–49
**Harry Chapman** 1949–50
**Sammy Crooks** 1950–54
**Walter Rowley** 1955–57
**Harry Potts** 1957–58
**Johnny Spuhler** 1958
**Arthur Rowley** 1958–68
**Harry Gregg** 1968–72
**Maurice Evans** 1972–73
**Alan Durban** 1974–78
**Richie Barker** 1978
**Graham Turner** 1978–84
**Chic Bates** 1984–87
**Ian McNeill** 1987–90
**Asa Hartford** 1990–91
**John Bond** 1991–93
**Fred Davies** 1994–97
*(previously Caretaker-Manager 1993–94)*
**Jake King** 1997–99
**Kevin Ratcliffe** 1999–2003
**Jimmy Quinn** 2003–04
**Gary Peters** 2004–08
**Paul Simpson** 2008–10
**Graham Turner** June 2010–

### TEN YEAR LEAGUE RECORD

| | | P | W | D | L | F | A | Pts | Pos |
|---|---|---|---|---|---|---|---|---|---|
| 2003-04 | Conf. | 42 | 20 | 14 | 8 | 67 | 42 | 74 | 3 |
| 2004-05 | FL 2 | 46 | 11 | 16 | 19 | 48 | 53 | 49 | 21 |
| 2005-06 | FL 2 | 46 | 16 | 13 | 17 | 55 | 55 | 61 | 10 |
| 2006-07 | FL 2 | 46 | 18 | 17 | 11 | 68 | 46 | 71 | 7 |
| 2007-08 | FL 2 | 46 | 12 | 14 | 20 | 56 | 65 | 50 | 18 |
| 2008-09 | FL 2 | 46 | 17 | 18 | 11 | 61 | 44 | 69 | 7 |
| 2009-10 | FL 2 | 46 | 17 | 12 | 17 | 55 | 54 | 63 | 12 |
| 2010-11 | FL 2 | 46 | 22 | 13 | 11 | 72 | 49 | 79 | 4 |
| 2011-12 | FL 2 | 46 | 26 | 10 | 10 | 66 | 41 | 88 | 2 |
| 2012-13 | FL 1 | 46 | 13 | 16 | 17 | 54 | 60 | 55 | 16 |

### DID YOU KNOW ?

Shrewsbury Town have regularly entered the Welsh Cup throughout their history and have won the trophy on six occasions. The last time was in May 1985 when they defeated Bangor City 5-1 over two legs in the final.

## SHREWSBURY TOWN – FOOTBALL LEAGUE ONE 2012-13 LEAGUE RECORD

| Match No. | Date | Venue | Opponents | Result | H/T Score | Lg Pos. | Goalscorers | Attendance |
|---|---|---|---|---|---|---|---|---|
| 1 | Aug 18 | A | Sheffield U | L | 0-1 | 0-1 | 20 | | 18,286 |
| 2 | 21 | H | Preston NE | W | 1-0 | 1-0 | 11 | Parry [4] | 6444 |
| 3 | 25 | H | Tranmere R | D | 1-1 | 1-0 | 11 | Morgan [45] | 6253 |
| 4 | Sept 1 | A | Stevenage | D | 1-1 | 1-1 | 12 | Parry [5] | 2374 |
| 5 | 8 | A | Notts Co | L | 2-3 | 0-0 | 16 | Richards (pen) [61], Grandison [62] | 6774 |
| 6 | 15 | H | Scunthorpe U | L | 0-1 | 0-1 | 19 | | 5623 |
| 7 | 18 | H | Coventry C | W | 4-1 | 2-0 | 16 | Jones [3], Parry [21], Richards (pen) [62], Morgan [64] | 5960 |
| 8 | 22 | A | Hartlepool U | D | 2-2 | 1-1 | 16 | Morgan 2 [27, 82] | 3909 |
| 9 | 29 | H | Swindon T | L | 0-1 | 0-0 | 16 | | 6303 |
| 10 | Oct 2 | H | Brentford | D | 0-0 | 0-0 | 15 | | 4384 |
| 11 | 6 | A | Doncaster R | L | 0-1 | 0-1 | 18 | | 6437 |
| 12 | 14 | H | Walsall | W | 1-0 | 1-0 | 15 | Parry [25] | 6495 |
| 13 | 20 | A | Portsmouth | L | 1-3 | 0-0 | 20 | Morgan [61] | 13,051 |
| 14 | 23 | H | Yeovil T | L | 1-3 | 0-1 | 20 | Richards (pen) [81] | 4711 |
| 15 | 27 | H | Colchester U | D | 2-2 | 0-1 | 20 | Hall 2 [79, 82] | 5066 |
| 16 | Nov 6 | A | Bournemouth | L | 1-2 | 1-2 | 21 | Richards (pen) [14] | 5022 |
| 17 | 10 | A | Leyton Orient | L | 1-2 | 0-1 | 23 | Taylor [70] | 3822 |
| 18 | 17 | H | Crewe Alex | W | 1-0 | 1-0 | 20 | Summerfield [43] | 6169 |
| 19 | 20 | H | Milton Keynes D | D | 2-2 | 0-1 | 20 | Rodgers [65], Wright [72] | 4747 |
| 20 | 24 | A | Oldham Ath | L | 0-1 | 0-1 | 22 | | 3886 |
| 21 | Dec 8 | A | Crawley T | D | 2-2 | 2-1 | 21 | Richards [14], Taylor [34] | 2770 |
| 22 | 15 | H | Carlisle U | W | 2-1 | 1-1 | 20 | Taylor [22], Parry [64] | 5260 |
| 23 | 21 | D | Bury | D | 2-2 | 1-1 | 17 | Wildig [1], Taylor [68] | 2536 |
| 24 | 26 | H | Notts Co | D | 2-2 | 1-2 | 19 | Rodgers [19], Taylor [81] | 6474 |
| 25 | 29 | H | Brentford | D | 0-0 | 0-0 | 19 | | 5715 |
| 26 | Jan 1 | A | Coventry C | W | 1-0 | 0-0 | 18 | Morgan [63] | 15,185 |
| 27 | 5 | A | Scunthorpe U | D | 0-0 | 0-0 | 17 | | 3044 |
| 28 | 12 | H | Hartlepool U | D | 1-1 | 1-0 | 17 | Taylor [23] | 5101 |
| 29 | 19 | A | Swindon T | L | 0-2 | 0-0 | 18 | | 7754 |
| 30 | 26 | H | Bury | D | 0-0 | 0-0 | 18 | | 4795 |
| 31 | Feb 2 | A | Preston NE | W | 2-1 | 0-1 | 18 | Taylor [64], Richards (pen) [90] | 8331 |
| 32 | 9 | H | Sheffield U | L | 1-2 | 0-0 | 18 | McGinn [88] | 7232 |
| 33 | 15 | A | Tranmere R | W | 2-0 | 1-0 | 17 | Porter [10], Gayle [67] | 9127 |
| 34 | 23 | H | Stevenage | W | 2-1 | 1-1 | 17 | Parry [31], Morgan [86] | 4818 |
| 35 | 26 | H | Doncaster R | L | 1-2 | 0-0 | 17 | Eaves [90] | 4886 |
| 36 | Mar 2 | A | Walsall | L | 1-3 | 0-1 | 18 | McAllister [77] | 5496 |
| 37 | 9 | H | Leyton Orient | L | 0-2 | 0-1 | 18 | | 5274 |
| 38 | 12 | A | Milton Keynes D | W | 3-2 | 2-1 | 18 | Eaves 2 [16, 19], Kay (og) [69] | 6622 |
| 39 | 16 | A | Crewe Alex | D | 1-1 | 1-1 | 18 | Summerfield [28] | 5106 |
| 40 | 29 | A | Carlisle U | D | 2-2 | 0-0 | 18 | Richards [63], Mambo [76] | 4472 |
| 41 | Apr 1 | H | Crawley T | W | 3-0 | 0-0 | 18 | Eaves 3 [48, 67, 85] | 5196 |
| 42 | 6 | A | Yeovil T | L | 1-2 | 1-2 | 18 | McGinn [21] | 4473 |
| 43 | 13 | H | Bournemouth | L | 0-3 | 0-1 | 18 | | 6047 |
| 44 | 20 | A | Colchester U | D | 0-0 | 0-0 | 19 | | 5862 |
| 45 | 23 | H | Oldham Ath | W | 1-0 | 0-0 | 18 | Jacobson [49] | 5332 |
| 46 | 27 | H | Portsmouth | W | 3-2 | 2-0 | 16 | Goldson [6], Jacobson [37], Asante [56] | 8021 |

**Final League Position: 16**

### GOALSCORERS

*League (54):* Morgan 7, Richards 7 (5 pens), Taylor 7, Eaves 7, Parry 6, Hall 2, Jacobson 2, McGinn 2, Rodgers 2, Summerfield 2, Asante 1, Gayle 1, Goldson 1, Grandison 1, Jones 1, Mambo 1, McAllister 1, Porter 1, Wildig 1, Wright 1, own goal 1.
*FA Cup (1):* Summerfield 1.
*Capital One Cup (0).*
*Johnstone's Paint Trophy (1):* Hall 1.

| Weale C 46 | Grandison J 30 | Hector M 8 | Jones D 38 | Purdie R 12+11 | Parry P 23+8 | Summerfield L 30+6 | Richards M 43 | Wright M 12+5 | Gornell T 9+3 | Morgan M 37+3 | Hall A 4+11 | Bradshaw T 6+15 | Wildig A 16+5 | Taylor J 30+7 | Hazell R 3 | Doble R 1+4 | Jacobson J 29+1 | Collins L 8 | Winnall S 3+1 | Helan J 3 | Proctor J 2 | Bennett J 4 | Rodgers L 13+2 | Gayle C 18 | Goldson C 14+3 | Mambo Y 13+2 | McGinn S 12+6 | McAllister D 14+1 | Edwards R 4 | Porter C 4+1 | Eaves T 10 | Hurst J 4 | Asante A 3+4 | Woods R —+2 | Match No. |
|---|---|---|---|---|---|---|---|---|---|---|---|---|---|---|---|---|---|---|---|---|---|---|---|---|---|---|---|---|---|---|---|---|---|---|---|
| 1 | 2 | 3 | 4 | 5 | 6 | $7^1$ | $8^3$ | 9 | $10^2$ | 11 | 12 | 13 | 14 | | | | | | | | | | | | | | | | | | | | | | 1 |
| 1 | 2 | 4 | 3 | 5 | $6^3$ | $8^1$ | 7 | 9 | $10^2$ | 11 | 12 | | 14 | | | | 13 | | | | | | | | | | | | | | | | | | 2 |
| 1 | 2 | 4 | 3 | 5 | 6 | $7^1$ | 8 | 9 | $10^2$ | 11 | 12 | 13 | | | | | | | | | | | | | | | | | | | | | | | 3 |
| 1 | 2 | | 4 | 5 | 9 | 3 | 8 | 7 | $10^1$ | 11 | 12 | | | | | | 6 | | | | | | | | | | | | | | | | | | 4 |
| 1 | 2 | | 3 | 5 | 6 | $7^2$ | 8 | 9 | $11^1$ | 10 | 12 | 13 | | | | | 4 | | | | | | | | | | | | | | | | | | 5 |
| 1 | 2 | | 3 | $5^1$ | 6 | 7 | 8 | $9^2$ | $10^2$ | 11 | 12 | 13 | 14 | | | | 4 | | | | | | | | | | | | | | | | | | 6 |
| 1 | 2 | 4 | 3 | | 9 | 7 | $8^1$ | 12 | $11^2$ | 10 | | 6 | 13 | | | | 5 | | | | | | | | | | | | | | | | | | 7 |
| 1 | 2 | 4 | 3 | | 9 | 7 | 8 | 12 | $10^1$ | 11 | | 6 | | | | | 5 | | | | | | | | | | | | | | | | | | 8 |
| 1 | 2 | 4 | 3 | | $6^2$ | 7 | 9 | 12 | 14 | 10 | $8^1$ | 13 | | | | | 5 | | $11^3$ | | | | | | | | | | | | | | | | 9 |
| 1 | 2 | | 3 | | 6 | 7 | 5 | $9^2$ | 12 | 11 | 8 | 13 | | | | | 4 | | $10^1$ | | | | | | | | | | | | | | | | 10 |
| 1 | 2 | | 3 | | 6 | 8 | 5 | $9^2$ | $11^1$ | 10 | 13 | $7^3$ | 12 | | 14 | | 4 | | | | | | | | | | | | | | | | | | 11 |
| 1 | 2 | | 3 | $11^1$ | 7 | | 5 | 12 | 10 | | 8 | 13 | 6 | $9^2$ | | | 4 | | | | | | | | | | | | | | | | | | 12 |
| 1 | 2 | | 3 | 11 | 7 | | 5 | 12 | $10^4$ | | 8 | 13 | $6^2$ | $9^1$ | | | 4 | | | | | | | | | | | | | | | | | | 13 |
| 1 | 2 | | 3 | 14 | 6 | 7 | 8 | | $11^2$ | $9^3$ | | 13 | 12 | | | | 5 | 4 | $10^1$ | | | | | | | | | | | | | | | | 14 |
| 1 | 2 | | 3 | 12 | 10 | 7 | $8^2$ | | | | | 13 | | | | | $5^1$ | 4 | 9 | 11 | | | | | | | | | | | | | | | 15 |
| 1 | 2 | | 3 | | 12 | | $7^2$ | | 10 | 13 | | 8 | 6 | | | | 4 | | 9 | $11^1$ | 5 | | | | | | | | | | | | | | 16 |
| 1 | 2 | | 3 | 5 | 12 | 8 | 7 | | 10 | | | | 6 | | | | | $9^1$ | | 4 | 11 | | | | | | | | | | | | | | 17 |
| 1 | 2 | 3 | | | 7 | 8 | 9 | | 10 | | 12 | 6 | | | | | 5 | | 4 | $11^1$ | | | | | | | | | | | | | | | 18 |
| 1 | 2 | 3 | | | 7 | 8 | 9 | | 10 | | | 6 | | | | | 5 | | 4 | 11 | | | | | | | | | | | | | | | 19 |
| 1 | 3 | 4 | | | 7 | 8 | $9^1$ | | 10 | | 12 | 6 | | | 13 | | 5 | | | | | | $11^2$ | 2 | | | | | | | | | | | 20 |
| 1 | 3 | 4 | | 12 | 7 | 8 | $6^1$ | | 10 | | | 13 | | 9 | | | | | | | | | $11^2$ | 2 | 5 | | | | | | | | | | 21 |
| 1 | 2 | 3 | 12 | $9^1$ | 8 | | 11 | | 13 | 7 | 6 | | | $10^2$ | 5 | 4 | | | | | | | | | | | | | | | | | | | 22 |
| 1 | 3 | 4 | 12 | $6^1$ | 8 | | 10 | | 7 | $9^2$ | 13 | 14 | | | | | | | | | | | $11^3$ | 2 | 5 | | | | | | | | | | 23 |
| 1 | 3 | 4 | 13 | $9^2$ | 8 | | 10 | 12 | 14 | $7^1$ | 6 | | | | | | | | | | | | $11^3$ | 5 | 2 | | | | | | | | | | 24 |
| 1 | 3 | 4 | 9 | 8 | | | 10 | 12 | 13 | $7^1$ | 6 | | | | | | | | | | | | $11^2$ | 5 | 2 | | | | | | | | | | 25 |
| 1 | 3 | 4 | 9 | 7 | | | 10 | 12 | 13 | $8^1$ | $6^3$ | | | 5 | | | | | | | | | $11^2$ | 2 | 14 | | | | | | | | | | 26 |
| 1 | 3 | 4 | 9 | 7 | | | 10 | $8^2$ | 12 | 6 | | | | 5 | | | | | | | | | $11^1$ | 2 | 13 | | | | | | | | | | 27 |
| 1 | 4 | 3 | $9^2$ | 14 | 8 | | $11^3$ | 12 | 6 | | | | | 5 | | | | | | | | | $10^1$ | 2 | 13 | 7 | | | | | | | | | 28 |
| 1 | $4^1$ | 3 | $6^3$ | 7 | | | 11 | $10^2$ | 9 | | | | | 5 | | | | | | | | | 14 | 2 | 12 | 13 | 8 | | | | | | | | 29 |
| 1 | 3 | | $9^4$ | 13 | 8 | | 11 | $10^1$ | 6 | | | | | 5 | | | | | | | | | | 2 | 4 | 12 | 7 | | | | | | | | 30 |
| 1 | 4 | 13 | 12 | 8 | | | 11 | $9^2$ | $5^1$ | | | | | | | | | | | | | | 10 | 2 | 3 | 6 | 7 | | | | | | | | 31 |
| 1 | 3 | 11 | 12 | 9 | | | 13 | $6^1$ | $10^2$ | 5 | | | | | | | | | | | | | | 2 | 4 | 7 | 8 | | | | | | | | 32 |
| 1 | 3 | 13 | $6^2$ | 9 | 10¹ | | 5 | | | | | | | | | | | | | | | | 12 | 2 | 8 | 7 | 4 | 11 | | | | | | | 33 |
| 1 | 3 | $6^1$ | 9 | 13 | 12 | | 5 | | | | | | | | | | | | | | | | 2 | 7 | 8 | 4 | 11 | $10^2$ | | | | | | | 34 |
| 1 | 3 | $6^2$ | 12 | 9 | 13 | 14 | 5 | | | | | | | | | | | | | | | | 2 | $7^3$ | $8^4$ | 4 | $10^1$ | 11 | | | | | | | 35 |
| 1 | 3 | 13 | $6^1$ | 12 | 9 | 10 | 5 | | | | | | | | | | | | | | | | 2 | $7^2$ | 8 | 4 | 11 | | | | | | | | 36 |
| 1 | 3 | 13 | 7 | 9 | 12 | 6 | 5 | | | | | | | | | | | | | | | | 2 | 4 | 8 | $11^1$ | 10 | | | | | | | | 37 |
| 1 | 4 | 12 | 13 | 7 | 6 | $10^1$ | $9^2$ | 3 | | | | | | | | | | | | | | | 2 | 5 | 8 | 14 | $11^3$ | | | | | | | | 38 |
| 1 | 4 | 14 | 7 | 9 | $10^3$ | 6 | 5 | | | | | | | | | | | | | | | | $2^1$ | 12 | 3 | 13 | $8^2$ | 11 | | | | | | | 39 |
| 1 | $3^1$ | | 7 | 9 | $10^2$ | 6 | 5 | | | | | | | | | | | | | | | | 12 | 4 | 8 | 11 | 2 | 13 | | | | | | | 40 |
| 1 | | 12 | 7 | 6 | 14 | $10^2$ | $9^3$ | 5 | | | | | | | | | | | | | | | 4 | 3 | $8^1$ | 11 | $2^1$ | 13 | | | | | | | 41 |
| 1 | | 12 | 8 | 9 | $10^2$ | 6 | 5 | | | | | | | | | | | | | | | | 4 | 3 | 7 | 11 | $2^1$ | 13 | | | | | | | 42 |
| 1 | $2^3$ | | $9^2$ | 6 | $11^1$ | 7 | 3 | | | | | | | | | | | | | | | | 14 | 4 | 8 | 13 | 10 | 5 | 12 | | | | | | 43 |
| 1 | | | | | | 10 | 9 | 6 | | 5 | | | | | | | | | | | | | 2 | 3 | 4 | 8 | 7 | | | | | | 11 | | 44 |
| 1 | | 12 | 8 | | | 10 | $9^2$ | 6 | | 5 | | | | | | | | | | | | | 2 | 4 | 3 | 7 | | | | | | | $11^1$ | 13 | 45 |
| 1 | | 14 | 7 | | | $10^3$ | $9^2$ | 6 | | 5 | | | | | | | | | | | | | 2 | 3 | 4 | 12 | 8 | | | | | | $11^1$ | 13 | 46 |

**FA Cup**
First Round — Hereford U — (a) — 1-3

**Capital One Cup**
First Round — Leeds U — (a) — 0-4

**Johnstone's Paint Trophy**
Second Round — Crewe Alex — (h) — 1-2

# SOUTHAMPTON

## FOUNDATION

The club was formed by members of the St Mary's Church of England Young Men's Association at a meeting of the Y.M.A. in November 1885 and it was named as such. For the sake of brevity this was usually shortened to St Mary's Y.M.A. The rector Canon Albert Basil Orme Wilberforce was elected president. The name was changed to plain St Mary's during 1887–88 and did not become Southampton St Mary's until 1894, the inaugural season in the Southern League.

*St Mary's Stadium, Britannia Road, Southampton, Hampshire SO14 5FP.*

*Telephone:* (0845) 688 9448.

*Fax:* (0845) 688 9445.

*Ticket Office:* (0845) 688 9288.

*Website:* www.saintsfc.co.uk

*Email:* sfc@saintsfc.co.uk

*Ground Capacity:* 32,689.

*Record Attendance:* 31,044 v Manchester U, Division 1, 8 October 1969 (at The Dell); 32,151 v Arsenal, FA Premier League, 29 December 2003 (at St Mary's).

*Pitch Measurements:* 105m × 68m (114yd × 74yd)

*Executive Chairman:* Nicola Cortese.

*Manager:* Mauricio Pochettino.

*Assistant Manager:* Jesús Pérez.

*Physio:* Matt Radcliffe.

*Colours:* Red shirt with thin white stripes, red shorts, red socks with white hoops.

*Year Formed:* 1885.

*Turned Professional:* 1894.

*Previous Names:* 1885, St Mary's Young Men's Association; 1887–88, St Mary's; 1894–95 Southampton St Mary's; 1897, Southampton.

*Club Nickname:* 'Saints'.

*Grounds:* 1885, 'The Common' (from 1887 also used the County Cricket Ground and Antelope Cricket Ground); 1889, Antelope Cricket Ground; 1896 The County Cricket Ground; 1898, The Dell; 2001, St Mary's.

*First Football League Game:* 28 August 1920, Division 3, v Gillingham (a) D 1–1 – Allen; Parker, Titmuss; Shelley, Campbell, Turner; Barratt, Dominy (1), Rawlings, Moore, Foxall.

*Record League Victory:* 9–3 v Wolverhampton W, Division 2, 18 September 1965 – Godfrey; Jones, Williams; Walker, Knapp, Huxford; Paine (2), O'Brien (1), Melia, Chivers (4), Sydenham (2).

*Record Cup Victory:* 7–1 v Ipswich T, FA Cup 3rd rd, 7 January 1961 – Reynolds; Davies, Traynor, Conner, Page, Huxford, Paine (1), O'Brien (3 incl. 1p), Reeves, Mulgrew (2), Penk (1).

## HONOURS

**Football League – FL C:** *Runners-up* 2011–12; **Division 1:** *Runners-up* 1983–84; **Division 2:** *Runners-up* 1965–66, 1977–78;
**Division 3:** *Champions* 1959–60: *Runners-up* 1920–21;
**Division 3 (S):** *Champions* 1921–22.

**FA Cup:** *Winners* 1976; *Runners-up* 1900, 1902, 2003.

**Football League Cup:** *Runners-up* 1979.

**Zenith Data Systems Cup:** *Runners-up* 1992.

**Johnstone's Paint Trophy:** *Winners* 2009–10.

**European Competitions European Fairs Cup:** 1969–70.
**UEFA Cup:** 1971–72, 1981–82, 1982–83, 1984–85, 2003–04.
**European Cup-Winners' Cup:** 1976–77.

## sky SPORTS FACT FILE

Southampton defeated Rotherham United 6-1 at The Dell on 27 April 1964. The teams met again on 21 November 1964 and the score was exactly the same. George O'Brien registered a hat-trick for Saints on both occasions.

**Record Defeat:** 0–8 v Tottenham H, Division 2, 28 March 1936; 0–8 v Everton, Division 1, 20 November 1971.

**Most League Points (2 for a win):** 61, Division 3 (S), 1921–22 and Division 3, 1959–60.

**Most League Points (3 for a win):** 92, FL 1, 2010–11.

**Most League Goals:** 112, Division 3 (S), 1957–58.

**Highest League Scorer in Season:** Derek Reeves, 39, Division 3, 1959–60.

**Most League Goals in Total Aggregate:** Mike Channon, 185, 1966–77, 1979–82.

**Most League Goals in One Match:** 5, Charlie Wayman v Leicester C, Division 2, 23 October 1948.

**Most Capped Player:** Peter Shilton, 49 (125), England.

**Most League Appearances:** Terry Paine, 713, 1956–74.

**Youngest League Player:** Theo Walcott, 16 years 143 days v Wolverhampton W, 6 August 2005.

**Record Transfer Fee Received:** £10,000,000 (plus add-ons) from Arsenal for Alex Oxlade-Chamberlain, August 2011.

**Record Transfer Fee Paid:** £12,000,000 to Bologna for Gaston Ramirez, August 2012.

**Football League Record:** 1920 Original Member of Division 3; 1921–22 Division 3 (S); 1922–53 Division 2; 1953–58 Division 3 (S); 1958–60 Division 3; 1960–66 Division 2; 1966–74 Division 1; 1974–78 Division 2; 1978–92 Division 1; 1992–2005 FA Premier League; 2005–09 FL C; 2009–11 FL 1; 2011–12 FL C; 2012– FA Premier League.

## LATEST SEQUENCES

**Longest Sequence of League Wins:** 10, 16.4.2011 – 20.8.2011.

**Longest Sequence of League Defeats:** 5, 16.8.1998 – 12.9.1998.

**Longest Sequence of League Draws:** 8, 29.8.2005 – 15.10.2005.

**Longest Sequence of Unbeaten League Matches:** 19, 5.9.1921 – 31.12.1921.

**Longest Sequence Without a League Win:** 20, 30.8.1969 – 27.12.1969.

**Successive Scoring Runs:** 28 from 10.2.2008.

**Successive Non-scoring Runs:** 5 from 1.9.1937.

## MANAGERS

Cecil Knight 1894–95
*(Secretary-Manager)*
Charles Robson 1895–97
Er Arnfield 1897–1911
*(Secretary-Manager)*
*(continued as Secretary)*
George Swift 1911–12
Er Arnfield 1912–19
Jimmy McIntyre 1919–24
Arthur Chadwick 1925–31
George Kay 1931–36
George Gross 1936–37
Tom Parker 1937–43
*J. R. Sarjantson stepped down*
*from the board to act as*
*Secretary-Manager 1943–47 with*
*the next two listed being Team*
*Managers during this period*
Arthur Dominy 1943–46
Bill Dodgin Snr 1946–49
Sid Cann 1949–51
George Roughton 1952–55
Ted Bates 1955–73
Lawrie McMenemy 1973–85
Chris Nicholl 1985–91
Ian Branfoot 1991–94
Alan Ball 1994–95
Dave Merrington 1995–96
Graeme Souness 1996–97
Dave Jones 1997–2000
Glenn Hoddle 2000–01
Stuart Gray 2001
Gordon Strachan 2001–04
Paul Sturrock 2004
Steve Wigley 2004
Harry Redknapp 2004–05
George Burley 2005–08
Nigel Pearson 2008
Jan Poortvliet 2008–09
Mark Wotte 2009
Alan Pardew 2009–10
Nigel Adkins 2010–13
Mauricio Pochettino January 2013–

## TEN YEAR LEAGUE RECORD

| | | P | W | D | L | F | A | Pts | Pos |
|---|---|---|---|---|---|---|---|---|---|
| 2003-04 | PR Lge | 38 | 12 | 11 | 15 | 44 | 45 | 47 | 12 |
| 2004-05 | PR Lge | 38 | 6 | 14 | 18 | 45 | 66 | 32 | 20 |
| 2005-06 | FL C | 46 | 13 | 19 | 14 | 49 | 50 | 58 | 12 |
| 2006-07 | FL C | 46 | 21 | 12 | 13 | 77 | 53 | 75 | 6 |
| 2007-08 | FL C | 46 | 13 | 15 | 18 | 56 | 72 | 54 | 20 |
| 2008-09 | FL C | 46 | 10 | 15 | 21 | 46 | 69 | 45 | 23 |
| 2009-10 | FL 1 | 46 | 23 | 14 | 9 | 85 | 47 | 73* | 7 |
| 2010-11 | FL 1 | 46 | 28 | 8 | 10 | 86 | 38 | 92 | 2 |
| 2011-12 | FL C | 46 | 26 | 10 | 10 | 85 | 46 | 88 | 2 |
| 2012-13 | PR Lge | 38 | 9 | 14 | 15 | 49 | 60 | 41 | 14 |

*\*10 pts deducted.*

### DID YOU KNOW

Alf Charles made a single appearance for Southampton against Bradford City in January 1937. He originally came to England with the 1933 West Indies cricket team, acting as valet for Learie Constantine. His first senior club had been Everton, one of the top clubs in Trinidad, not the Goodison-based outfit.

## SOUTHAMPTON – FA PREMIERSHIP 2012–13 LEAGUE RECORD

| Match No. | Date | Venue | Opponents | Result | H/T Score | Lg Pos. | Goalscorers | Attendance |
|---|---|---|---|---|---|---|---|---|
| 1 | Aug 19 | A | Manchester C | L | 2-3 | 0-1 | 14 | Lambert [59], Davis, S [68] | 46,190 |
| 2 | 25 | H | Wigan Ath | L | 0-2 | 0-0 | 18 | | 29,604 |
| 3 | Sept 2 | H | Manchester U | L | 2-3 | 1-1 | 20 | Lambert [16], Schneiderlin [55] | 31,609 |
| 4 | 15 | A | Arsenal | L | 1-6 | 1-4 | 20 | Fox [46] | 60,097 |
| 5 | 22 | H | Aston Villa | W | 4-1 | 0-1 | 17 | Lambert 2 (1 pen) [58, 90 (p)], Clyne [63], Puncheon [72] | 30,713 |
| 6 | 29 | A | Everton | L | 1-3 | 1-3 | 17 | Ramirez [6] | 37,922 |
| 7 | Oct 7 | H | Fulham | D | 2-2 | 1-0 | 17 | Fonte 2 [4, 90] | 28,004 |
| 8 | 20 | A | West Ham U | L | 1-4 | 0-0 | 18 | Lallana [63] | 34,925 |
| 9 | 28 | H | Tottenham H | L | 1-2 | 0-2 | 19 | Rodriguez [66] | 31,944 |
| 10 | Nov 5 | A | WBA | L | 0-2 | 0-1 | 20 | | 25,635 |
| 11 | 10 | H | Swansea C | D | 1-1 | 0-0 | 19 | Schneiderlin [64] | 30,501 |
| 12 | 17 | A | QPR | W | 3-1 | 2-0 | 19 | Lambert [23], Puncheon [45], Ferdinand (og) [83] | 18,174 |
| 13 | 25 | H | Newcastle U | W | 2-0 | 1-0 | 17 | Lallana [34], Ramirez [60] | 31,410 |
| 14 | 28 | H | Norwich C | D | 1-1 | 1-1 | 18 | Lambert [32] | 29,325 |
| 15 | Dec 1 | A | Liverpool | L | 0-1 | 0-1 | 18 | | 44,525 |
| 16 | 8 | H | Reading | W | 1-0 | 0-0 | 15 | Puncheon [61] | 29,331 |
| 17 | 22 | H | Sunderland | L | 0-1 | 0-1 | 17 | | 31,275 |
| 18 | 26 | A | Fulham | D | 1-1 | 0-1 | 17 | Lambert (pen) [85] | 25,700 |
| 19 | 29 | A | Stoke C | D | 3-3 | 3-1 | 18 | Lambert [10], Rodriguez [24], Wilkinson (og) [36] | 26,391 |
| 20 | Jan 1 | H | Arsenal | D | 1-1 | 1-1 | 17 | Ramirez [34] | 31,743 |
| 21 | 12 | A | Aston Villa | W | 1-0 | 1-0 | 15 | Lambert (pen) [34] | 32,500 |
| 22 | 16 | A | Chelsea | D | 2-2 | 0-2 | 15 | Lambert [58], Puncheon [75] | 38,484 |
| 23 | 21 | H | Everton | D | 0-0 | 0-0 | 15 | | 28,359 |
| 24 | 30 | A | Manchester U | L | 1-2 | 1-2 | 16 | Rodriguez [3] | 75,600 |
| 25 | Feb 2 | A | Wigan Ath | D | 2-2 | 0-1 | 16 | Lambert [64], Schneiderlin [85] | 18,598 |
| 26 | 9 | H | Manchester C | W | 3-1 | 2-1 | 15 | Puncheon [7], Davis, S [22], Barry (og) [48] | 31,738 |
| 27 | 24 | A | Newcastle U | L | 2-4 | 1-2 | 16 | Schneiderlin [3], Lambert [50] | 52,259 |
| 28 | Mar 2 | H | QPR | L | 1-2 | 1-1 | 16 | Ramirez [45] | 31,728 |
| 29 | 9 | A | Norwich C | D | 0-0 | 0-0 | 16 | | 26,783 |
| 30 | 16 | H | Liverpool | W | 3-1 | 2-1 | 15 | Schneiderlin [6], Lambert [33], Rodriguez [80] | 32,070 |
| 31 | 30 | H | Chelsea | W | 2-1 | 2-1 | 12 | Rodriguez [23], Lambert [35] | 31,779 |
| 32 | Apr 6 | A | Reading | W | 2-0 | 1-0 | 11 | Rodriguez [35], Lallana [72] | 24,108 |
| 33 | 13 | H | West Ham U | D | 1-1 | 0-0 | 11 | Ramirez [59] | 31,984 |
| 34 | 20 | A | Swansea C | D | 0-0 | 0-0 | 12 | | 20,561 |
| 35 | 27 | H | WBA | L | 0-3 | 0-1 | 13 | | 31,946 |
| 36 | May 4 | A | Tottenham H | L | 0-1 | 0-0 | 14 | | 36,190 |
| 37 | 12 | A | Sunderland | D | 1-1 | 0-0 | 14 | Puncheon [76] | 41,988 |
| 38 | 19 | H | Stoke C | D | 1-1 | 0-0 | 14 | Lambert [57] | 31,539 |

**Final League Position: 14**

### GOALSCORERS

*League (49):* Lambert 15 (3 pens), Puncheon 6, Rodriguez 6, Ramirez 5, Schneiderlin 5, Lallana 3, Davis, S 2, Fonte 2, Clyne 1, Fox 1, own goals 3.
*FA Cup (1):* Rodriguez 1.
*Capital One Cup (6):* Rodriguez 2 (1 pen), Lee 1, Puncheon 1, Reeves 1, Sharp 1.

| Davis K 9+1 | Clyne N 34 | Fonte J 25+2 | Hooiveld J 23+2 | Fox D 14+6 | Ward-Prowse J 4+11 | Lallana A 26+4 | Schneiderlin M 36 | Puncheon J 25+7 | Rodriguez J 24+11 | Do Prado G 8+10 | Lambert R 35+3 | Davis S 22+10 | Sharp B —+2 | Mayuka E 1+10 | Yoshida M 31+1 | Ramirez G 20+6 | Gazzaniga P 9 | Richardson F 2+3 | Reeves B —+3 | Chaplow R —+3 | Boruc A 20 | Shaw L 22+3 | Cork J 28 | De Ridder S —+4 | Match No. |
|---|---|---|---|---|---|---|---|---|---|---|---|---|---|---|---|---|---|---|---|---|---|---|---|---|---|
| 1 | 2 | 3 | 4 | 5 | 6² | 7 | 8 | 9³ | 10¹ | 11 | 12 | 13 | 14 |  |  |  |  |  |  |  |  |  |  |  | 1 |
| 1 | 2 | 3 | 4 | 5 | 12 | 8 | 7 |  | 10² | 9 | 11 | 6¹ | 13 |  |  |  |  |  |  |  |  |  |  |  | 2 |
| 1 | 2 | 3 | 4 | 5 | 9 | 10³ | 8 | 6¹ | 14 | 13 | 11² | 7 |  |  |  | 12 |  |  |  |  |  |  |  |  | 3 |
| 1 | 2 | 4 | 3¹ | 5 | 7 | 10 | 8 | 6 | 14 | 11³ | 9² |  |  |  |  | 12 | 13 |  |  |  |  |  |  |  | 4 |
|  | 2 |  | 4 | 5¹ | 14 | 9 | 7 | 6² | 10 | 8³ | 13 |  |  |  | 3 | 11 | 1 | 12 |  |  |  |  |  |  | 5 |
|  |  | 5² | 3 | 8 | 9³ | 11¹ | 10 | 7 | 12 | 4 | 6 |  |  |  | 1 | 2 | 13 | 14 |  |  |  |  |  |  | 6 |
|  | 4 | 12 | 5 | 9 | 7 | 6¹ | 10 | 14 | 11² | 8 | 3 |  |  |  | 1 | 2³ | 13 |  |  |  |  |  |  |  | 7 |
|  | 2 | 4 | 3 | 14 | 9 | 7 | 6² | 10¹ | 11 | 13 | 8³ | 12 |  |  | 5 |  | 1 |  |  |  |  |  |  |  | 8 |
|  | 2 | 4 | 5³ | 9 | 7 | 6¹ | 11 | 13 | 10 | 8² | 12 |  |  |  | 3 | 14 | 1 |  |  |  |  |  |  |  | 9 |
|  | 2 | 3 | 5³ | 9 | 6 | 10¹ | 13 | 11 | 7 | 12 | 4 | 8² | 1 |  |  | 14 |  |  |  |  |  |  |  |  | 10 |
|  | 2 | 4 | 12 | 9 | 8 | 6 | 10 | 3 | 11 | 1 |  |  |  |  |  |  |  |  |  |  |  | 5¹ | 7 |  | 11 |
|  | 2 | 3 | 13 | 10 | 6 | 8 | 14 | 11³ | 12 | 4 | 9¹ | 1 |  |  |  |  |  |  |  |  |  | 5² | 7 |  | 12 |
|  | 2 | 3 | 14 | 9 | 8 | 6 | 12 | 11¹ | 13 | 4 | 10² | 1 |  |  |  |  |  |  |  |  |  | 5³ | 7 |  | 13 |
|  | 2 | 4 |  | 9 | 7 | 6² | 13 | 10 | 3 | 11 | 1 | 12 |  |  |  |  |  |  |  |  |  | 5¹ | 8 |  | 14 |
|  | 2 | 4 |  | 9 | 8 | 6² | 13 | 11 | 12 | 3 | 10 | 1 |  |  |  |  |  |  |  |  |  | 5 | 7¹ |  | 15 |
| 1 | 2 | 3 |  | 9¹ | 8 | 6 | 10² | 13 | 11 | 4 | 12 |  |  |  |  |  |  |  |  |  |  | 5 | 7 |  | 16 |
| 1 | 2 | 4 |  | 8² | 6³ | 14 | 10 | 13 | 9¹ | 3 | 11 |  |  |  |  |  |  |  |  |  |  | 5 | 7 | 12 | 17 |
| 1 | 2 | 3 |  | 6 | 9 | 12 | 13 | 11 | 8¹ | 4 | 10² |  |  |  |  |  |  |  |  |  |  | 5 | 7 |  | 18 |
| 1 |  | 4 | 2 | 12 | 7 | 6² | 9 | 10 | 11 | 3 |  |  |  |  | 13 |  |  |  |  |  |  | 5¹ | 8 |  | 19 |
|  | 4 |  | 13 | 8 | 6 | 12 | 11³ | 10¹ | 7 | 3 | 9² |  |  |  |  |  |  |  |  |  | 1 | 5 | 2 | 14 | 20 |
|  | 2 | 4 | 12 | 8 | 9² | 6 | 11 | 13 | 3 | 10¹ |  |  |  |  |  |  |  |  |  |  | 1 | 5³ | 7 | 14 | 21 |
|  | 2 | 4 |  | 8 | 9 | 11¹ | 10³ | 12 | 7² | 3 | 14 | 13 |  |  |  |  |  |  |  |  | 1 | 5 | 6 | 14 | 22 |
|  | 2 | 4 |  | 8 | 6³ | 12 | 11¹ | 10 | 13 | 3 | 9² |  |  |  |  |  |  |  |  |  | 1 | 5 | 7 | 14 | 23 |
|  | 2 | 4 | 5³ | 12 | 6 | 8¹ | 9 | 11 | 13 | 3 | 10² |  |  |  |  |  |  |  |  |  | 1 | 14 | 7 |  | 24 |
|  | 2² | 4 | 14 | 13 | 6 | 8³ | 10 | 11 | 12 | 3 | 9¹ |  |  |  |  |  |  |  |  |  | 1 | 5 | 7 |  | 25 |
|  | 2 | 4 | 5² | 14 | 12 | 7 | 9 | 10 | 11 | 8³ | 3 | 13 |  |  |  |  |  |  |  |  | 1 |  | 6 |  | 26 |
|  | 2 | 3 | 12 | 9 | 7 | 14 | 10³ | 11 | 6² | 4 | 13 |  |  |  |  |  |  |  |  |  | 1 | 5¹ | 8 |  | 27 |
|  | 2 | 3 | 5² | 14 | 10¹ | 9 | 6 | 12 | 11 | 4 | 7³ |  |  |  |  |  |  |  |  |  | 1 | 13 | 8 |  | 28 |
|  | 3 | 4 |  | 13 | 10² | 6 | 14 | 7³ | 12 | 11 | 2 | 9¹ |  |  |  |  |  |  |  |  | 1 | 5 | 8 |  | 29 |
|  | 2 | 12 | 4¹ | 10³ | 6 | 8 | 14 | 11 | 13 | 3 | 9² |  |  |  |  |  |  |  |  |  | 1 | 5 | 7 |  | 30 |
| 12 | 2 | 4 | 14 | 13 | 7 | 6² | 10 | 11 | 9³ | 3 |  |  |  |  |  |  |  |  |  |  | 1¹ | 5 | 8 |  | 31 |
|  | 2 | 4 | 12 | 7 | 10 | 13 | 11 | 9² | 3 | 6¹ |  |  |  |  |  |  |  |  |  |  | 1 | 5 | 8 |  | 32 |
|  | 2 | 4 | 5 | 10¹ | 8 | 13 | 12 | 11 | 9 | 3 | 6² |  |  |  |  |  |  |  |  |  | 1 |  | 7 |  | 33 |
|  | 2 | 4 | 5 | 9² | 6 | 13 | 10³ | 11¹ | 8 | 14 | 3 | 12 |  |  |  |  |  |  |  |  | 1 |  | 7 |  | 34 |
|  | 2 | 14 | 4 | 5⁴ | 11² | 6 | 10 | 9³ | 7 | 13 | 3 | 12 |  |  |  |  |  |  |  |  | 1 |  | 8¹ |  | 35 |
|  | 2 | 4 | 3 |  | 10² | 13 | 8 | 9¹ | 11 | 7 | 12 |  |  |  |  |  |  |  |  |  | 1 | 5 | 6 |  | 36 |
|  | 2 | 4 | 3 |  | 13 | 9¹ | 7 | 12 | 10 | 11 | 6 |  |  |  |  |  |  |  |  |  | 1 | 5 | 8² |  | 37 |
| 1 | 2 | 3 | 4 |  | 13 | 9¹ | 7 | 12 | 10 | 11 | 6² | 14 |  |  |  |  |  |  |  |  |  | 5 | 8³ |  | 38 |

**FA Cup**

| | | | | |
|---|---|---|---|---|
| Third Round | Chelsea | (h) | 1-5 | |

**Capital One Cup**

| | | | |
|---|---|---|---|
| Second Round | Stevenage | (a) | 4-1 |
| Third Round | Sheffield W | (h) | 2-0 |
| Fourth Round | Leeds U | (a) | 0-3 |

# SOUTHEND UNITED

## FOUNDATION

The leading club in Southend around the turn of the 20th century was Southend Athletic, but they were an amateur concern. Southend United was a more ambitious professional club when they were founded in 1906, employing Bob Jack as secretary-manager and immediately joining the Second Division of the Southern League.

*Roots Hall Stadium, Victoria Avenue, Southend-on-Sea, Essex SS2 6NQ.*

*Telephone:* (01702) 304 050.

*Fax:* (01702) 304 124.

*Ticket Office:* (08444) 770 077.

*Website:* www.southendunited.co.uk

*Email:* info@southend-united.co.uk

*Ground Capacity:* 11,927.

*Record Attendance:* 22,862 v Tottenham H, FA Cup 3rd rd replay, 11 January 1936 (at Southend Stadium); 31,090 v Liverpool, FA Cup 3rd rd, 10 January 1979 (at Roots Hall).

*Pitch Measurements:* 100m × 67m (110yd × 74yd)

*Chairman:* Ronald Martin.

*Chief Executive:* Steve Kavanagh.

*Manager:* Phil Brown.

*Assistant Manager:* Graham Coughlan.

*Physio:* Ben Clarkson.

*Colours:* Navy blue shirts with white trim, navy blue shorts, white socks.

*Year Formed:* 1906.

*Turned Professional:* 1906.

*Club Nicknames:* 'The Blues', 'The Shrimpers'.

## HONOURS

**Football League – Division 1:** Best season: 13th, 1994–95;

**FL 1:** *Champions* 2005–06;

**Division 3:** *Runners-up* 1990–91;

**Division 4:** *Champions* 1980–81; *Runners-up* 1971–72, 1977–78.

**FA Cup:** Best season: old 3rd rd, 1921; 5th rd, 1926, 1952, 1976, 1993.

**Football League Cup:** Quarter-final 2007.

**LDV Vans Trophy:** *Runners-up* 2004, 2005.

**Johnstone's Paint Trophy:** *Runners-up* 2013.

*Grounds:* 1906, Roots Hall, Prittlewell; 1920, Kursaal; 1934, Southend Stadium; 1955, Roots Hall Football Ground.

*First Football League Game:* 28 August 1920, Division 3, v Brighton & HA (a) W 2–0 – Capper; Reid, Newton; Wileman, Henderson, Martin; Nicholls, Nuttall, Fairclough (2), Myers, Dorsett.

*Record League Victory:* 9–2 v Newport Co, Division 3 (S), 5 September 1936 – McKenzie; Nelson, Everest (1); Deacon, Turner, Carr; Bolan, Lane (1), Goddard (4), Dickinson (2), Oswald (1).

*Record Cup Victory:* 10–1 v Golders Green, FA Cup 1st rd, 24 November 1934 – Moore; Morfitt, Kelly; Mackay, Joe Wilson, Carr (1); Lane (1), Johnson (5), Cheesmuir (2), Deacon (1), Oswald. 10–1 v Brentwood, FA Cup 2nd rd, 7 December 1968 – Roberts; Bentley, Birks; McMillan (1) Beesley, Kurila; Clayton, Chisnall, Moore (4), Best (5), Hamilton. 10–1 v Aldershot, Leyland DAF Cup Prel rd, 6 November 1990 – Sansome; Austin, Powell, Cornwell, Prior (1), Tilson (3), Cawley, Butler, Ansah (1), Benjamin (1), Angell (4).

## sky SPORTS FACT FILE

In March 1936 Southend United travelled to Haarlem for a midweek friendly fixture against a Netherlands B international team under floodlights. The Shrimpers conceded two goals in each half, going down by a 4-0 margin.

*Record Defeat:* 1–9 v Brighton & HA, Division 3, 27 November 1965.

*Most League Points (2 for a win):* 67, Division 4, 1980–81.

*Most League Points (3 for a win):* 85, Division 3, 1990–91.

*Most League Goals:* 92, Division 3 (S), 1950–51.

*Highest League Scorer in Season:* Jim Shankly, 31, 1928–29; Sammy McCrory, 1957–58, both in Division 3 (S).

*Most League Goals in Total Aggregate:* Roy Hollis, 122, 1953–60.

*Most League Goals in One Match:* 5, Jim Shankly v Merthyr T, Division 3 (S), 1 March 1930.

*Most Capped Player:* George Mackenzie, 9, Eire.

*Most League Appearances:* Sandy Anderson, 452, 1950–63.

*Youngest League Player:* Phil O'Connor, 16 years 76 days v Lincoln C, 26 December 1969.

*Record Transfer Fee Received:* £4,200,000 from Nottingham F for Stan Collymore, June 1993.

*Record Transfer Fee Paid:* £750,000 to Crystal Palace for Stan Collymore, November 1992.

*Football League Record:* 1920 Original Member of Division 3; 1921–58 Division 3 (S); 1958–66 Division 3; 1966–72 Division 4; 1972–76 Division 3; 1976–78 Division 4; 1978–80 Division 3; 1980–81 Division 4; 1981–84 Division 3; 1984–87 Division 4; 1987–89 Division 3; 1989–90 Division 4; 1990–91 Division 3; 1991–92 Division 2; 1992–97 Division 1; 1997–98 Division 2; 1998–2004 Division 3; 2004–05 FL 2; 2005–06 FL 1; 2006–07 FL C; 2007–10 FL 1; 2010– FL 2.

## LATEST SEQUENCES

*Longest Sequence of League Wins:* 8, 29.8.2005 – 9.10.2005.

*Longest Sequence of League Defeats:* 6, 29.8.1987 – 19.9.1987.

*Longest Sequence of League Draws:* 6, 30.1.1982 – 19.2.1982.

*Longest Sequence of Unbeaten League Matches:* 16, 20.2.1932 – 29.8.1932.

*Longest Sequence Without a League Win:* 17, 31.12.1983 – 14.4.1984.

*Successive Scoring Runs:* 24 from 23.3.1929.

*Successive Non-scoring Runs:* 6 from 28.10.1933.

## MANAGERS

**Bob Jack** 1906–10
**George Molyneux** 1910–11
**O. M. Howard** 1911–12
**Joe Bradshaw** 1912–19
**Ned Liddell** 1919–20
**Tom Mather** 1920–21
**Ted Birnie** 1921–34
**David Jack** 1934–40
**Harry Warren** 1946–56
**Eddie Perry** 1956–60
**Frank Broome** 1960
**Ted Fenton** 1961–65
**Alvan Williams** 1965–67
**Ernie Shepherd** 1967–69
**Geoff Hudson** 1969–70
**Arthur Rowley** 1970–76
**Dave Smith** 1976–83
**Peter Morris** 1983–84
**Bobby Moore** 1984–86
**Dave Webb** 1986–87
**Dick Bate** 1987
**Paul Clark** 1987–88
**Dave Webb** (*General Manager*) 1988–92
**Colin Murphy** 1992–93
**Barry Fry** 1993
**Peter Taylor** 1993–95
**Steve Thompson** 1995
**Ronnie Whelan** 1995–97
**Alvin Martin** 1997–99
**Alan Little** 1999–2000
**David Webb** 2000–01
**Rob Newman** 2001–03
**Steve Wignall** 2003
**Steve Tilson** 2003–10
**Paul Sturrock** 2010–13
**Phil Brown** March 2013–

## TEN YEAR LEAGUE RECORD

|  |  | P | W | D | L | F | A | Pts | Pos |
|---|---|---|---|---|---|---|---|---|---|
| 2003-04 | Div 3 | 46 | 14 | 12 | 20 | 51 | 63 | 54 | 17 |
| 2004-05 | FL 2 | 46 | 22 | 12 | 12 | 65 | 46 | 78 | 4 |
| 2005-06 | FL 1 | 46 | 23 | 13 | 10 | 72 | 43 | 82 | 1 |
| 2006-07 | FL C | 46 | 10 | 12 | 24 | 47 | 80 | 42 | 22 |
| 2007-08 | FL 1 | 46 | 22 | 10 | 14 | 70 | 55 | 76 | 6 |
| 2008-09 | FL 1 | 46 | 21 | 8 | 17 | 58 | 61 | 71 | 8 |
| 2009-10 | FL 1 | 46 | 10 | 13 | 23 | 51 | 72 | 43 | 23 |
| 2010-11 | FL 2 | 46 | 16 | 13 | 17 | 62 | 56 | 61 | 13 |
| 2011-12 | FL 2 | 46 | 25 | 8 | 13 | 77 | 48 | 83 | 4 |
| 2012-13 | FL 2 | 46 | 16 | 13 | 17 | 61 | 55 | 61 | 11 |

## DID YOU KNOW ?

Southend United's first-ever manager was Bob Jack, a Scot who began his career with Alloa Athletic, appointed in the summer of 1906. Some 28 years later his son David Jack, who won nine caps for England, was appointed to the same position, remaining in post until August 1940.

## SOUTHEND UNITED – FOOTBALL LEAGUE TWO 2012–13 LEAGUE RECORD

| Match No. | Date | | Venue | Opponents | | Result | H/T Score | Lg Pos. | Goalscorers | Atten- dance |
|---|---|---|---|---|---|---|---|---|---|---|
| 1 | Aug | 18 | H | Accrington S | L | 0-1 | 0-0 | 16 | | 4673 |
| 2 | | 21 | A | Oxford U | L | 0-2 | 0-0 | 24 | | 6001 |
| 3 | | 25 | A | Northampton T | D | 3-3 | 0-0 | 21 | Assombalonga [57], Ferdinand [78], Cresswell [90] | 4562 |
| 4 | Sept | 1 | H | Wycombe W | W | 1-0 | 1-0 | 16 | Assombalonga [7] | 4787 |
| 5 | | 8 | H | Dagenham & R | W | 3-1 | 2-1 | 13 | Assombalonga 2 [18, 37], Cresswell [70] | 5348 |
| 6 | | 15 | A | Cheltenham T | W | 3-1 | 1-1 | 8 | Clohessy [44], Assombalonga [49], Phillips [52] | 2751 |
| 7 | | 18 | A | Gillingham | L | 0-1 | 0-1 | 13 | | 4920 |
| 8 | | 22 | H | Exeter C | W | 2-1 | 0-0 | 8 | Corr [78], Eastwood [88] | 4964 |
| 9 | | 29 | A | Plymouth Arg | D | 1-1 | 0-0 | 11 | Assombalonga [54] | 6269 |
| 10 | Oct | 2 | H | Burton Alb | L | 0-1 | 0-0 | 12 | | 4150 |
| 11 | | 6 | H | Barnet | D | 2-2 | 0-0 | 12 | Eastwood (pen) [67], Hurst [84] | 5025 |
| 12 | | 13 | A | Rotherham U | W | 3-0 | 0-0 | 9 | Assombalonga 2 [51, 65], Martin [72] | 7328 |
| 13 | | 20 | A | Morecambe | L | 0-1 | 0-0 | 11 | | 1643 |
| 14 | | 23 | H | Aldershot T | L | 1-2 | 0-1 | 12 | Phillips [68] | 4225 |
| 15 | | 27 | H | York C | D | 0-0 | 0-0 | 13 | | 5397 |
| 16 | Nov | 6 | A | Bristol R | W | 3-2 | 2-1 | 12 | Tomlin [40], Hurst [44], Cresswell [64] | 4721 |
| 17 | | 10 | H | Port Vale | D | 0-0 | 0-0 | 11 | | 4876 |
| 18 | | 17 | A | Torquay U | W | 4-1 | 3-0 | 10 | Tomlin 2 [10, 47], Assombalonga 2 [39, 45] | 2449 |
| 19 | | 20 | A | AFC Wimbledon | W | 4-0 | 1-0 | 8 | Tomlin 2 [43, 67], Cresswell [61], Corr [88] | 3753 |
| 20 | | 24 | H | Rochdale | W | 3-1 | 0-0 | 4 | Assombalonga [57], Tomlin [59], Laird [77] | 5216 |
| 21 | Dec | 8 | A | Fleetwood T | D | 0-0 | 0-0 | 6 | | 2399 |
| 22 | | 15 | H | Bradford C | D | 2-2 | 0-1 | 6 | Cresswell [80], Tomlin [90] | 5142 |
| 23 | | 21 | H | Chesterfield | W | 3-0 | 0-0 | 4 | Cresswell [51], Tomlin 2 [61, 69] | 5273 |
| 24 | | 26 | A | Dagenham & R | W | 3-0 | 2-0 | 4 | Tomlin 2 [1, 14], Hurst [55] | 3555 |
| 25 | | 29 | A | Burton Alb | L | 0-2 | 0-2 | 4 | | 2636 |
| 26 | Jan | 1 | H | Gillingham | L | 0-1 | 0-1 | 5 | | 7498 |
| 27 | | 12 | A | Exeter C | L | 0-3 | 0-1 | 7 | | 3971 |
| 28 | | 26 | A | Chesterfield | W | 1-0 | 0-0 | 7 | Tomlin [83] | 4817 |
| 29 | Feb | 2 | H | Oxford U | W | 1-0 | 0-0 | 5 | Leonard [85] | 5596 |
| 30 | | 9 | A | Accrington S | D | 1-1 | 0-0 | 7 | Hurst [82] | 1589 |
| 31 | | 12 | H | Cheltenham T | L | 1-2 | 0-2 | 9 | Reeves [90] | 3908 |
| 32 | | 16 | H | Northampton T | L | 1-2 | 0-1 | 9 | Lund [65] | 5406 |
| 33 | | 23 | A | Wycombe W | W | 2-1 | 0-1 | 8 | Corr [53], Assombalonga [85] | 3518 |
| 34 | | 26 | A | Barnet | L | 0-2 | 0-1 | 9 | | 2211 |
| 35 | Mar | 2 | H | Rotherham U | D | 1-1 | 0-0 | 8 | Hurst [73] | 4983 |
| 36 | | 9 | A | Port Vale | W | 2-1 | 2-0 | 8 | Clohessy (pen) [19], Assombalonga [31] | 4858 |
| 37 | | 12 | H | AFC Wimbledon | L | 1-3 | 1-1 | 10 | Clohessy (pen) [29] | 4236 |
| 38 | | 16 | H | Torquay U | D | 1-1 | 1-1 | 8 | Eastwood [9] | 4891 |
| 39 | | 19 | H | Plymouth Arg | L | 0-2 | 0-0 | 8 | | 4674 |
| 40 | | 29 | A | Bradford C | D | 2-2 | 2-0 | 8 | Tomlin [10], Assombalonga [11] | 10,598 |
| 41 | Apr | 1 | H | Fleetwood T | D | 1-1 | 0-1 | 10 | Corr [86] | 5107 |
| 42 | | 10 | A | Rochdale | L | 2-4 | 0-1 | 12 | Phillips [46], Corr [90] | 1758 |
| 43 | | 13 | H | Bristol R | D | 0-0 | 0-0 | 13 | | 4612 |
| 44 | | 16 | A | Aldershot T | W | 2-0 | 0-0 | 10 | Corr [70], Assombalonga (pen) [78] | 2568 |
| 45 | | 20 | A | York C | L | 1-2 | 1-2 | 11 | Leonard [22] | 5975 |
| 46 | | 27 | H | Morecambe | L | 0-1 | 0-1 | 11 | | 5081 |

**Final League Position: 11**

### GOALSCORERS

*League (61):* Assombalonga 15 (1 pen), Tomlin 13, Corr 6, Cresswell 6, Hurst 5, Clohessy 3 (2 pens), Eastwood 3 (1 pen), Phillips 3, Leonard 2, Ferdinand 1, Laird 1, Lund 1, Martin 1, Reeves 1.
*FA Cup (8):* Corr 4, Tomlin 2, Eastwood 1, Laird 1.
*Capital One Cup (0).*
*Johnstone's Paint Trophy (12):* Corr 3, Cresswell 2, Assombalonga 1, Clohessy 1, Hurst 1, Leonard 1, Mkandawire 1, Reeves 1, Tomlin 1 (1 pen).

| Belford C 4 | Clohessy S 46 | Phillips M 19 + 2 | Barker C 28 + 3 | Prosser L 23 + 2 | Leonard R 16 + 6 | Ferdinand K 3 | Timlin M 25 | Hall R 1 + 1 | Tomlin G 28 + 5 | Assombalonga B 40 + 3 | Cresswell R 42 + 1 | Spicer J 10 + 3 | Harris N — + 7 | Straker A 21 + 7 | Hurst K 41 + 3 | Martin D 10 + 4 | Smith P 34 | Benyon E 2 + 3 | Bentley D 8 + 1 | Eastwood F 10 + 16 | Corr B 13 + 19 | Coughlan G — + 1 | Clarke-Harris J — + 3 | Woodyard A 4 + 1 | Laird M 22 + 1 | Mkandawire T 18 | Donnelly S — + 2 | Spillane M 9 | Lavery C — + 3 | Reeves B 7 + 3 | Mayor D 4 + 1 | Mohsni B 8 | Lund M 10 + 2 | Pinnock M — + 2 | Njie S — + 1 | Match No. |
|---|---|---|---|---|---|---|---|---|---|---|---|---|---|---|---|---|---|---|---|---|---|---|---|---|---|---|---|---|---|---|---|---|---|---|---|---|
| 1 | 2 | 3 | 4 | 5 | $6^3$ | $7^2$ | 8 | 9 | 10 | $11^1$ | 12 | 13 | 14 | | | | | | | | | | | | | | | | | | | | | | | 1 |
| 1 | 2 | 3 | 14 | | $6^2$ | 10 | $8^4$ | 12 | 11 | 13 | 4 | 7 | | $5^3$ | $9^1$ | | | | | | | | | | | | | | | | | | | | | 2 |
| 1 | 2 | 3 | 13 | 5 | $6^2$ | 8 | | | 11 | 10 | 4 | 7 | | 12 | $9^1$ | | | | | | | | | | | | | | | | | | | | 3 |
| 1 | 2 | 3 | | 5 | $6^2$ | | 8 | | 11 | 10 | 4 | 7 | 13 | 12 | $9^1$ | | | | | | | | | | | | | | | | | | | | 4 |
| | 2 | 3 | 5 | | | | 8 | | $11^3$ | $10^2$ | 4 | 7 | 13 | 12 | 6 | $9^1$ | 1 | 14 | | | | | | | | | | | | | | | | | 5 |
| | 2 | 3 | 5 | | | | 8 | | 11 | 10 | 4 | 6 | | 12 | 7 | $9^1$ | 1 | | | | | | | | | | | | | | | | | | 6 |
| | 2 | $5^2$ | 3 | | | | 8 | | 11 | 10 | 4 | 7 | | 13 | 6 | $9^3$ | 1 | $11^1$ | 14 | 12 | | | | | | | | | | | | | | | 7 |
| | 2 | | 5 | 4 | 13 | | 8 | | | 10 | 3 | $7^3$ | | | 6 | $9^2$ | | $11^1$ | 1 | 12 | 14 | | | | | | | | | | | | | | 8 |
| | 2 | | 5 | 4 | 12 | | 7 | | | 10 | 3 | $8^3$ | | | 6 | $9^1$ | | $11^2$ | 1 | 13 | $14^4$ | | | | | | | | | | | | | | 9 |
| | 2 | | 5 | 4 | | | | | | 8 | 3 | $7^4$ | | | 6 | 9 | | | 1 | 10 | | | | | | | | | | | | | | | 10 |
| | 2 | | 5 | 4 | | | 7 | | | 11 | 10 | 3 | | | $8^1$ | 6 | 12 | 1 | | 9 | | | | | | | | | | | | | | | 11 |
| | 2 | | 5 | | 11 | | 7 | | | 9 | $10^2$ | $3^1$ | | | 8 | 6 | 4 | 1 | | | | | 12 | 13 | | | | | | | | | | | 12 |
| | 2 | 14 | 4 | | | $7^3$ | | $8^1$ | | 6 | 11 | 3 | 12 | | 5 | 9 | $10^2$ | 1 | | | | | 13 | | | | | | | | | | | | 13 |
| | 2 | $3^2$ | 5 | | | | | | | 11 | 10 | 4 | $8^1$ | | 13 | 6 | $9^3$ | 1 | | 12 | | | 14 | 7 | | | | | | | | | | | 14 |
| | 2 | | 4 | | | | | | | 9 | 11 | 3 | | | 5 | $6^2$ | 13 | 1 | | $10^1$ | 12 | | | 8 | 7 | | | | | | | | | | 15 |
| | 2 | 3 | 5 | | 12 | | 6 | | | $11^1$ | $10^2$ | 4 | | | 9 | | 1 | | | 13 | | | | | 7 | 8 | | | | | | | | | 16 |
| | 2 | 3 | 5 | | | | 9 | | | 11 | $10^2$ | 4 | | | $6^1$ | | 1 | | | 13 | 12 | | | | 7 | 8 | | | | | | | | | 17 |
| | 2 | 4 | $5^2$ | 13 | | | | | | $10^1$ | $11^3$ | 3 | | | 7 | | 1 | | | 14 | 12 | | | | 9 | 6 | | | | | | | | | 18 |
| | 2 | 3 | $5^2$ | 13 | | | | | | 11 | $10^1$ | 4 | | | 7 | | 1 | | | 12 | | | | | 8 | 6 | | | | | | | | | 19 |
| | 2 | 3 | 5 | | | | | | | 9 | 11 | 10 | 4 | | 7 | | 1 | | | | | | | | 8 | 6 | | | | | | | | | 20 |
| | 2 | | 5 | 4 | | | | | | $10^2$ | $11^3$ | 3 | | | $9^1$ | 6 | | | | 14 | 12 | | | | 7 | 8 | 13 | | | | | | | | 21 |
| | 2 | | $5^2$ | 4 | | | | | | 9 | 10 | 11 | 3 | | | 6 | | 1 | | 13 | 12 | | | | 8 | $7^1$ | | | | | | | | | 22 |
| | 2 | | $5^3$ | 4 | | | | | | $11^1$ | $10^2$ | 3 | | 14 | 6 | | 1 | | | 12 | 13 | | | | 7 | 8 | | | | | | | | | 23 |
| | 2 | | 5 | 4 | | | | | | $11^2$ | $10^1$ | 3 | | | 6 | | 1 | | | 13 | 12 | | | | 7 | 8 | | | | | | | | | 24 |
| | 2 | 13 | 5 | 4 | | | | | | 9 | 11 | 3 | | | 6 | 12 | 1 | | | 14 | $10^2$ | | | | $8^3$ | $7^1$ | | | | | | | | | 25 |
| | 2 | | 5 | 4 | | | | | | 9 | 11 | $10^2$ | 3 | | | 6 | | 1 | | 13 | 12 | | | | $7^1$ | $8^3$ | 14 | | | | | | | | 26 |
| | 2 | 4 | 5 | | | | | | | 9 | 11 | | 3 | 14 | 6 | 12 | 1 | 13 | | $10^3$ | | | | | $7^2$ | $8^1$ | | | | | | | | | 27 |
| | 2 | 4 | 5 | | | 6 | | | | 8 | 11 | | 3 | | 9 | 1 | | | | 10 | | | | | | 7 | | | | | | | | | 28 |
| | 2 | 3 | 5 | | 13 | | | | | $11^1$ | | 4 | | | $9^3$ | | 1 | | | 10 | | | $6^2$ | | 7 | 12 | 14 | | | | | | | | 29 |
| | 2 | 4 | | | $9^1$ | | | | | $11^3$ | $3^4$ | | | 5 | 6 | | 1 | | | 12 | | | 14 | 8 | 7 | 13 | $10^2$ | | | | | | | | 30 |
| | 2 | | 4 | 13 | | | | | | 12 | | | | 5 | 6 | | 1 | | | 10 | | | $8^2$ | $7^1$ | 3 | 14 | 11 | $9^3$ | | | | | | | 31 |
| | 2 | | 4 | | | | | | | $10^3$ | | | 13 | 5 | 6 | | 1 | | | 12 | 11 | | | | $7^2$ | | 14 | $9^1$ | $3^4$ | 8 | | | | | 32 |
| | 2 | $3^1$ | 4 | $9^2$ | | | | | | 11 | 5 | | | 12 | 8 | | 1 | | | 10 | | | | | 7 | | 14 | $6^3$ | | 13 | | | | | 33 |
| | 2 | | 3 | 12 | | | | | | $11^2$ | 4 | | | 5 | 6 | | 1 | | | 13 | 10 | | | | $7^1$ | | $9^3$ | 14 | | 8 | | | | | 34 |
| | 2 | | 4 | 6 | | | | | | $11^2$ | 3 | | | 5 | 7 | | 1 | | | 13 | 12 | | | | | | $9^1$ | 10 | 8 | | | | | | 35 |
| | 2 | | 4 | 6 | | | | | | $11^2$ | 3 | | 12 | 5 | 10 | | 1 | | | 13 | | | | | 9 | | | | $8^1$ | 7 | | | | | 36 |
| | 2 | | 4 | $9^1$ | | | | | | 11 | 3 | | 14 | 12 | $5^3$ | 6 | | 1 | | 13 | | | | | $7^2$ | | | | 10 | 8 | | | | | 37 |
| | 2 | | | | | | | | | 12 | 11 | | | 5 | 6 | | 1 | | $10^1$ | | | | | | 7 | 4 | | 9 | | 3 | 8 | | | | 38 |
| | 2 | | | | | | | | | 13 | $11^2$ | 4 | | 5 | 6 | | 1 | | $10^1$ | 12 | | | | | 8 | 7 | | 9 | | 3 | | | | | 39 |
| | 2 | | 4 | | | | | | | 11 | $10^3$ | 3 | | 5 | 6 | | 1 | | | 13 | 14 | | | | | 8 | | $9^1$ | | $7^2$ | 12 | | | | 40 |
| | 2 | 3 | | | | | | | | 11 | 10 | 4 | | 5 | 6 | | 1 | | | $9^1$ | 13 | | | | 12 | 7 | | | | $8^2$ | | | | | 41 |
| | 2 | 4 | 5 | | | | | | | 12 | 11 | 3 | | | $6^2$ | | 1 | | | 13 | 10 | | | | 8 | 7 | | $9^1$ | | | | | | | 42 |
| | 2 | | | $6^2$ | | | | | | 12 | 11 | 3 | | 5 | 13 | | 1 | | $9^1$ | 10 | | | | | 7 | 4 | | | | 8 | | | | | 43 |
| | 2 | 12 | | 6 | | | | | | 9 | 4 | | 3 | | | | 1 | | $11^1$ | $8^2$ | | | | | 10 | 5 | | | | 7 | 13 | | | | 44 |
| | 2 | | 4 | 6 | | | | | | 12 | $9^2$ | 3 | | 5 | 13 | | 1 | | | $10^1$ | 11 | | | | $8^1$ | | | | | 7 | | | | | 45 |
| | 2 | | 4 | 8 | | | | | | $9^2$ | 12 | 3 | | 5 | 6 | | 1 | | | $11^1$ | $10^3$ | | | | | | | | | 7 | 13 | 14 | | | 46 |

**FA Cup**

| | | | | |
|---|---|---|---|---|
| First Round | Stockport Co | | (h) | 3-0 |
| Second Round | Bury | | (a) | 1-1 |
| *Replay* | Bury | | (h) | 1-1 |
| *(aet; won 3-2 on pens)* | | | | |
| Third Round | Brentford | | (h) | 2-2 |
| *Replay* | Brentford | | (a) | 1-2 |

**Capital One Cup**

| | | | | |
|---|---|---|---|---|
| First Round | Peterborough U | | (a) | 0-4 |

**Johnstone's Paint Trophy**

| | | | | |
|---|---|---|---|---|
| First Round | AFC Wimbledon | | (h) | 2-1 |
| Second Round | Dagenham & R | | (h) | 2-0 |
| Southern Quarter-Finals | Brentford | | (h) | 2-1 |
| Southern Semi-Finals | Oxford U | | (a) | 3-3 |
| *(aet; won 5-3 on pens)* | | | | |
| Southern Final | Leyton Orient | | (a) | 1-0 |
| | Leyton Orient | | (h) | 2-2 |
| Final *(at Wembley)* | Crewe Alex | | | 0-2 |

# STEVENAGE

## FOUNDATION

There have been several clubs associated with the town of Stevenage. Stevenage Town was formed in 1884. They absorbed Stevenage Rangers in 1955 and later played at Broadhall Way. The club went into liquidation in 1968 and Stevenage Athletic was formed, but they, too, followed a similar path in 1976. Then Stevenage Borough was founded. The Broadhall Way pitch was dug up and remained unused for three years. Thus the new club started its life in the modest surrounds of the King George V playing fields with a roped-off ground in the Chiltern League. A change of competition followed to the Wallspan Southern Combination and by 1980 the club returned to the council-owned Broadhall Way when "Borough" was added to the name. Entry into the United Counties League was so successful the league and cup were won in the first season. On to the Isthmian League Division Two and the climb up the pyramid continued. In 1995–96 Stevenage Borough won the Conference but was denied a place in the Football League as the ground did not measure up to the competition's standards. Subsequent improvements changed this and the 7,100 capacity venue became one of the best appointed grounds in non-league football. After winning elevation to the Football League the club dropped Borough from its title.

*Lamex Stadium, Broadhall Way, Stevenage, Hertfordshire SG2 8RH.*

*Telephone:* (01438) 223223.

*Fax:* (01438) 743666.

*Ticket Office:* (0871) 855 1696.

*Website:* stevenagefc.com

*Email:* adamc@stevenagefc.com

*Ground Capacity:* 6,722.

*Record Attendance:* 6,489 v Kidderminster H, Conference, 25 January 1997.

*Pitch Measurements:* 100m × 64m (110yd × 70yd)

*Chairman:* Phil Wallace.

*Manager:* Graham Westley.

*Assistant Manager:* Dino Maamria.

*Physio:* Paul Dando.

*Colours:* White shirts with red trim, red shorts, red socks with white tops.

*Nickname:* 'The Boro'.

## HONOURS

**Football League – FL 2:** Best season: 6th 2010–11 promoted to FL 1.
**FA Cup:** Best season: 5th rd, 2012.
**Football League Cup:** Best season: 2nd rd, 2012.
**Blue Square Premier League:** *Champions* 2009–10.
**Conference:** *Champions* 1995–96.
**FA Trophy:** *Winners* 2007, 2009; *Runners-up* 2002, 2010.
**Herts Senior Cup:** *Winners* 2009.
**Isthmian League Premier Division:** *Champions* 1993–94.
**Isthmian League Division 1:** *Champions*: 1991–92.
**Isthmian League Division 2 (N):** *Champions*: 1985–86, 1990–91.
**United Counties League Division 1:** *Champions* 1980–81.
**United Counties League Cup:** *Winners* 1981.

## sky SPORTS FACT FILE

Stevenage did the double in their first season in the United Counties League in 1980–81. Borough scored 106 goals and lost just two games in winning the Division One title by six clear points. They then went on to defeat Thrapston Venturas 3-0 in the Division One cup final.

*Previous Name:* Stevenage Borough.

*Grounds:* 1976, King George V playing fields; 1980, Broadhall Way.

*First Football League Game:* 7 August 2010, FL 2, v Macclesfield T (h) D 2–2 – Day; Henry, Laird, Bostwick, Roberts, Foster, Wilson (Sinclair), Byrom, Griffin (1), Winn (Odubade), Vincenti (1) (Beardsley).

*Year Formed:* 1976.

*Turned Professional:* 1976.

*Record League Victory:* 6–0 v Yeovil T, FL 2, 14 April 2012 – Day; Lascelles (1), Laird, Roberts (1), Ashton (1), Shroot (Mousinho), Wilson (Myrie-Williams), Long, Agyemang (1), Reid (Slew), Freeman (2).

*Record Victory:* 11–1 v British Timken Ath 1980–81.

*Record Defeat:* 0–7 v Southwick 1987–88.

*Most League Points (3 for a win):* 73, FL 1, 2011–12.

*Most League Goals:* 69, FL 1, 2011–12.

*Highest League Scorer in Season:* Lucas Akins, 10, 2012–13.

*Most Goals in Total Aggregate:* Mark Roberts, 14, 2010–13.

*Most League Goals in One Match:* 3, Chris Holroyd v Hereford U, FL 2, 28 September 2010; 3, Dani Lopez v Sheffield U, FL 1, 16 March 2013.

*Most Capped Player:* Marcus Haber, 2 (7), Canada.

*Most League Appearances:* Mark Roberts, 132, 2010–13.

*Record Transfer Fee Received:* £260,000 from Peterborough U for George Boyd, January 2007.

*Record Transfer Fee Paid:* £20,000 to Hereford United for Richard Leadbetter, February 1999.

*Football League Record:* 2010–11 FL 2; 2011– FL 1.

### MANAGERS

Derek Montgomery 1976–83
Frank Cornwell 1983–87
John Bailey 1987–88
Brian Wilcox 1988–90
Paul Fairclough 1990–98
Richard Hill 1998–2000
Steve Wignall 2000
Paul Fairclough 2000–02
Wayne Turner 2002–03
Graham Westley 2003–06
Mark Stimson 2006–07
Peter Taylor 2007–08
Graham Westley 2008–12
Gary Smith 2012–13
Graham Westley March 2013–

## LATEST SEQUENCES

*Longest Sequence of League Wins:* 6, 12.3.2011 – 2.4.2011.

*Longest Sequence of League Defeats:* 6, 9.2.2013 – 2.3.2013.

*Longest Sequence of League Draws:* 5, 17.3.2012 – 31.3.2012.

*Longest Sequence of Unbeaten League Matches:* 17, 9.4.2012 – 6.10.2012.

*Longest Sequence Without a League Win:* 6, 9.2.2013 – 2.3.2013.

*Successive Scoring Runs:* 17 from 9.4.2012.

*Successive Non-scoring Runs:* 4 from 6.4.2013.

## TEN YEAR LEAGUE RECORD

|  |  | P | W | D | L | F | A | Pts | Pos |
|---|---|---|---|---|---|---|---|---|---|
| 2003-04 | Conf | 42 | 18 | 9 | 15 | 58 | 52 | 63 | 8 |
| 2004-05 | Conf | 42 | 22 | 6 | 14 | 65 | 52 | 72 | 5 |
| 2005-06 | Conf | 42 | 19 | 12 | 11 | 62 | 47 | 69 | 6 |
| 2006-07 | Conf | 46 | 20 | 10 | 16 | 76 | 66 | 70 | 8 |
| 2007-08 | BSP | 46 | 24 | 7 | 15 | 82 | 55 | 79 | 6 |
| 2008-09 | BSP | 46 | 23 | 12 | 11 | 73 | 54 | 81 | 5 |
| 2009-10 | BSP | 44 | 30 | 9 | 5 | 79 | 24 | 99 | 1 |
| 2010-11 | FL 2 | 46 | 18 | 15 | 13 | 62 | 45 | 69 | 6 |
| 2011-12 | FL 1 | 46 | 18 | 19 | 9 | 69 | 44 | 73 | 6 |
| 2012-13 | FL 1 | 46 | 15 | 9 | 22 | 47 | 64 | 54 | 18 |

### DID YOU KNOW ?

Stevenage progressed through six rounds of the FA Cup in 1996–97 before finally going out 2-0 to Birmingham City in the third round. Borough began their campaign by defeating Arlesey Town 3-0, and then achieved wins against Baldock Town, Braintree Town, Gravesend & Northfleet, Hayes and Leyton Orient.

## STEVENAGE – FOOTBALL LEAGUE ONE 2012–13 LEAGUE RECORD

| Match No. | Date | Venue | Opponents | Result | H/T Score | Lg Pos. | Goalscorers | Atten-dance |
|---|---|---|---|---|---|---|---|---|
| 1 | Aug 18 | H | Carlisle U | D 1-1 | 0-0 | 11 | Shroot [88] | 2736 |
| 2 | 21 | A | Leyton Orient | W 1-0 | 1-0 | 8 | Akins [23] | 3564 |
| 3 | 25 | A | Oldham Ath | W 1-0 | 1-0 | 4 | Akins (pen) [33] | 3142 |
| 4 | Sept 1 | H | Shrewsbury T | D 1-1 | 1-1 | 6 | Charles [24] | 2374 |
| 5 | 9 | A | Coventry C | W 2-1 | 1-1 | 3 | Shroot [21], Haber [71] | 9458 |
| 6 | 15 | H | Crewe Alex | D 2-2 | 1-2 | 3 | Freeman [27], Shroot [81] | 2826 |
| 7 | 18 | H | Walsall | W 3-1 | 1-0 | 2 | Shroot [24], Tansey [72], Akins [86] | 2634 |
| 8 | 22 | A | Doncaster R | D 1-1 | 1-0 | 3 | Risser [16] | 5910 |
| 9 | 29 | H | Bury | D 2-2 | 0-1 | 5 | Haber [54], Tansey [56] | 2660 |
| 10 | Oct 2 | A | Notts Co | W 2-1 | 0-0 | 2 | Akins (pen) [83], Shroot [90] | 4927 |
| 11 | 6 | H | Scunthorpe U | W 1-0 | 0-0 | 2 | Tansey [75] | 2953 |
| 12 | 13 | A | Colchester U | L 0-1 | 0-0 | 2 | | 4045 |
| 13 | 20 | A | Milton Keynes D | W 1-0 | 1-0 | 2 | Akins [27] | 9190 |
| 14 | 23 | H | Portsmouth | W 2-1 | 1-0 | 2 | Morais 2 [14, 61] | 4012 |
| 15 | 27 | H | Swindon T | L 0-4 | 0-3 | 3 | | 4518 |
| 16 | Nov 6 | A | Yeovil T | W 3-1 | 1-1 | 2 | Morais [2], Akins [48], Dunne [63] | 2900 |
| 17 | 10 | H | Preston NE | L 1-4 | 1-2 | 3 | Tansey [15] | 3740 |
| 18 | 17 | A | Sheffield U | L 1-4 | 1-1 | 5 | Roberts [45] | 17,984 |
| 19 | 20 | A | Bournemouth | D 1-1 | 1-0 | 5 | Tansey [27] | 5504 |
| 20 | 24 | H | Tranmere R | D 1-1 | 0-0 | 7 | Tansey [90] | 3069 |
| 21 | Dec 8 | A | Hartlepool U | W 2-0 | 1-0 | 5 | Haber [19], Akins (pen) [60] | 3265 |
| 22 | 15 | H | Crawley T | L 1-2 | 0-0 | 6 | Shroot [55] | 3066 |
| 23 | 26 | H | Coventry C | L 1-3 | 1-0 | 9 | Akins (pen) [32] | 4102 |
| 24 | Jan 1 | A | Walsall | L 0-1 | 0-0 | 12 | | 3301 |
| 25 | 5 | H | Crewe Alex | W 2-1 | 0-1 | 9 | Akins [55], Haber [60] | 4262 |
| 26 | 12 | H | Doncaster R | L 1-2 | 0-0 | 11 | Dunne [66] | 3280 |
| 27 | Feb 2 | H | Leyton Orient | L 0-1 | 0-1 | 15 | | 3577 |
| 28 | 5 | H | Notts Co | W 2-0 | 1-0 | 13 | Hoskins [1], Haber [89] | 2550 |
| 29 | 9 | A | Carlisle U | L 1-2 | 1-2 | 14 | Haber [22] | 3944 |
| 30 | 12 | A | Brentford | L 0-2 | 0-1 | 14 | | 7022 |
| 31 | 19 | H | Oldham Ath | L 1-2 | 1-0 | 15 | Dunne [9] | 2748 |
| 32 | 23 | H | Shrewsbury T | L 1-2 | 1-1 | 15 | Dunne [20] | 4818 |
| 33 | 26 | A | Scunthorpe U | L 0-1 | 0-0 | 15 | | 2382 |
| 34 | Mar 2 | H | Colchester U | L 0-2 | 0-0 | 15 | | 3144 |
| 35 | 5 | H | Brentford | W 1-0 | 0-0 | 15 | Haber [75] | 2794 |
| 36 | 9 | A | Preston NE | L 0-2 | 0-2 | 15 | | 9000 |
| 37 | 12 | H | Bournemouth | L 0-1 | 0-1 | 16 | | 2418 |
| 38 | 16 | H | Sheffield U | W 4-0 | 1-0 | 15 | Lopez 3 [41, 50, 64], Akins [69] | 3483 |
| 39 | 19 | A | Bury | L 0-2 | 0-0 | 15 | | 1396 |
| 40 | 24 | A | Tranmere R | L 1-3 | 1-3 | 15 | Freeman [12] | 4342 |
| 41 | 29 | A | Crawley T | D 1-1 | 1-0 | 15 | Roberts [40] | 3395 |
| 42 | Apr 1 | H | Hartlepool U | W 1-0 | 0-0 | 15 | Ehmer [76] | 2903 |
| 43 | 6 | A | Portsmouth | D 0-0 | 0-0 | 15 | | 12,036 |
| 44 | 13 | H | Yeovil T | L 0-2 | 0-0 | 17 | | 3516 |
| 45 | 20 | A | Swindon T | L 0-3 | 0-1 | 17 | | 9515 |
| 46 | 27 | H | Milton Keynes D | L 0-2 | 0-1 | 18 | | 3801 |

**Final League Position: 18**

### GOALSCORERS

*League (47):* Akins 10 (4 pens), Haber 7, Shroot 6, Tansey 6, Dunne 4, Lopez 3, Morais 3, Freeman 2, Roberts 2, Charles 1, Ehmer 1, Hoskins 1, Risser 1.
*FA Cup (2):* Dunne 1, Morais 1.
*Capital One Cup (4):* Dunne 1, Roberts 1, Thalassitis 1, own goal 1.
*Johnstone's Paint Trophy (2):* Roberts 1, Shroot 1.

| Day C 16+1 | Gray D 42 | Roberts M 44 | N'Gala B 21+4 | Charles D 33+4 | Morais F 21+7 | Dunne J 40+2 | Tansey G 26+11 | Grant A 34+7 | Freeman L 26+13 | Haber M 33+9 | Akins L 41+5 | Shroot R 11+15 | Thalassitis M —+2 | Ashton J 8 | Rogers R 1+5 | Agyemang P 5+9 | Risser O 5+7 | Lopez D 7+3 | Comminges M 19+2 | Arnold S 30 | Hills L 9+2 | Beleck S 6+7 | Hoskins S 6+8 | Chorley B 8 | Mahon G 8+1 | Jeffrey A —+1 | Ehmer M 5+1 | Deacon R —+1 | Ball M 1+1 | N'Guissan J —+1 | Match No. |
|---|---|---|---|---|---|---|---|---|---|---|---|---|---|---|---|---|---|---|---|---|---|---|---|---|---|---|---|---|---|---|---|
| 1 | 2 | 3 | 4 | 5 | $6^2$ | 7 | $8^1$ | 9 | 10 | $11^3$ | 12 | 13 | 14 | | | | | | | | | | | | | | | | | | 1 |
| 1 | 2 | | 4 | 5 | 13 | 8 | 12 | 7 | $6^2$ | $11^3$ | 9 | $10^1$ | 14 | 3 | | | | | | | | | | | | | | | | | 2 |
| 1 | 2 | 3 | | 5 | $10^2$ | 8 | 12 | 7 | $6^1$ | 11 | 9 | | | 4 | 13 | | | | | | | | | | | | | | | | 3 |
| 1 | 2 | | 4 | 5 | 12 | 8 | $7^1$ | 9 | $6^3$ | 10 | 14 | | | 3 | | $11^2$ | 13 | | | | | | | | | | | | | | 4 |
| 1 | 2 | 5 | 12 | 3 | | 8 | | 7 | 10 | 14 | 9 | $6^2$ | | $4^1$ | | $11^3$ | 13 | | | | | | | | | | | | | | 5 |
| 1 | 2 | | 4 | 5 | | 8 | 13 | $7^3$ | 9 | 11 | $6^2$ | 12 | | 3 | | $10^1$ | 14 | | | | | | | | | | | | | | 6 |
| 1 | 2 | | 4 | | | 8 | 13 | 7 | $6^2$ | $11^3$ | 9 | | | 3 | | $10^1$ | 14 | | 5 | | | | | | | | | | | | 7 |
| 1 | 5 | 3 | 13 | $10^1$ | | 8 | 12 | 9 | | $11^2$ | 7 | | | 4 | | 6 | | | 2 | | | | | | | | | | | | 8 |
| 1 | 2 | | 4 | 5 | 13 | 8 | 6 | $7^2$ | $10^3$ | 11 | 9 | | 14 | $3^1$ | | 12 | | | | | | | | | | | | | | | 9 |
| | $2^3$ | 3 | | 6 | $9^2$ | 12 | 7 | $8^1$ | 13 | 11 | 10 | | 14 | | | 5 | | | 4 | 1 | | | | | | | | | | | 10 |
| | 3 | | 14 | 4 | $9^2$ | 7 | 8 | 12 | 13 | 11 | 6 | | $10^3$ | | | $5^1$ | | | 2 | 1 | | | | | | | | | | | 11 |
| 2 | 3 | | 4 | 5 | $10^2$ | 7 | 9 | $6^3$ | 13 | 11 | $8^3$ | | 14 | | | | | | | 1 | | | | | | | | | | | 12 |
| | 2 | 3 | 4 | 5 | $10^2$ | 7 | 9 | $8^1$ | | 11 | | | | | | 13 | 6 | | 12 | 1 | | | | | | | | | | | 13 |
| | 2 | 3 | 4 | 5 | 9 | $7^1$ | 8 | 12 | $6^2$ | 11 | $10^3$ | | | | | 14 | 13 | | | 1 | | | | | | | | | | | 14 |
| | 2 | 3 | 4 | 5 | $10^3$ | 7 | 8 | 12 | 6 | $11^2$ | $9^1$ | | | | | 13 | 14 | | | 1 | | | | | | | | | | | 15 |
| | 2 | 3 | 4 | 5 | $9^3$ | 8 | 13 | $7^2$ | 6 | 12 | 10 | | | | | $11^1$ | 14 | | | 1 | | | | | | | | | | | 16 |
| | 2 | 3 | 4 | 5 | 13 | 7 | 8 | $9^1$ | $6^2$ | $11^3$ | 10 | | 14 | | | | | | 12 | 1 | | | | | | | | | | | 17 |
| | 2 | 3 | 4 | 10 | | $8^1$ | 13 | $7^2$ | 6 | $11^3$ | 12 | | 14 | | | 9 | | | | 1 | 5 | | | | | | | | | | 18 |
| | 2 | 3 | 4 | 5 | 9 | $8^3$ | | 7 | 6 | $11^2$ | | | 14 | | | | | 12 | 13 | 1 | $10^1$ | | | | | | | | | | 19 |
| | 2 | 3 | 4 | 5 | $10^1$ | $7^3$ | 8 | 9 | 6 | $11^2$ | 12 | | 14 | | | | | | 13 | 1 | | | | | | | | | | | 20 |
| | $2^3$ | 3 | 4 | 10 | | 8 | 7 | $9^1$ | 6 | $11^2$ | | | 14 | | | | 13 | | 5 | 1 | 12 | | | | | | | | | | 21 |
| | 2 | 3 | 4 | 13 | | 8 | 7 | 12 | 6 | $11^3$ | 10 | | | | | $9^1$ | | | | 1 | $5^2$ | | | | | | | | | | 22 |
| | 2 | 3 | 4 | 5 | $10^1$ | 7 | 13 | 12 | $6^3$ | 11 | 8 | | 14 | | | $9^2$ | | | | 1 | | | | | | | | | | | 23 |
| | 2 | 3 | 4 | | 9 | 7 | 13 | 12 | 6 | $11^1$ | 8 | | | | | | | | 5 | 1 | $10^2$ | | | | | | | | | | 24 |
| | $2^2$ | 3 | 4 | $10^1$ | 13 | 8 | 7 | 9 | 6 | $11^3$ | | | 14 | | | | | | 5 | 1 | 12 | | | | | | | | | | 25 |
| | 2 | 5 | 14 | 3 | 13 | $7^2$ | 8 | 9 | 6 | | 10 | | | | | | | | $4^3$ | 1 | $11^1$ | 12 | | | | | | | | | 26 |
| | 2 | 3 | 5 | 10 | | 7 | | 9 | $6^2$ | | $8^1$ | | | | | | | | 13 | 1 | 12 | 11 | 4 | | | | | | | | 27 |
| | 2 | 3 | | 9 | 13 | 8 | 7 | 12 | $6^1$ | | | | 14 | | | | | | 5 | 1 | $11^3$ | $10^2$ | 4 | | | | | | | | 28 |
| 12 | 2 | 3 | | | 13 | 7 | 8 | 9 | $6^3$ | $11^2$ | | | 14 | | | | | | 5 | 1 | $10^1$ | | 4 | | | | | | | | 29 |
| 1 | 2 | 3 | | 13 | | 7 | 8 | $9^1$ | 6 | $11^3$ | | | 14 | | | | | | 5 | | 12 | $10^2$ | 4 | | | | | | | | 30 |
| 1 | 2 | | 4 | | | 8 | 13 | 7 | $6^2$ | 11 | 9 | | | | | | | | 5 | | 12 | $10^1$ | 3 | | | | | | | | 31 |
| 1 | 5 | 3 | 2 | $10^1$ | | 8 | 12 | $7^3$ | | 11 | | | | | | | | | | | | $9^1$ | 13 | 14 | 4 | 6 | | | | | 32 |
| 1 | 2 | 3 | 5 | $10^3$ | | 7 | 8 | $9^2$ | | 12 | | | 14 | | | | | | | | | 11 | 13 | | 4 | 6 | | | | | 33 |
| 1 | 2 | 3 | 5 | 10 | | 8 | 13 | $7^2$ | $6^1$ | 11 | | | 14 | | | | | | | | 12 | | $9^3$ | 4 | | | | | | 34 |
| | 2 | 3 | 4 | | 13 | | 12 | $7^2$ | $6^1$ | 11 | 9 | | 14 | | | | | | 5 | 1 | | $10^3$ | 8 | | | | | | | | 35 |
| | 2 | 5 | 4 | | | 7 | 13 | | 6 | $11^2$ | 9 | | 14 | | | | | | 3 | 1 | 12 | $10^1$ | $8^3$ | | | | | | | | 36 |
| | | $3^3$ | 4 | 10 | | 8 | 12 | 7 | 6 | | $9^2$ | | | | | | | | 2 | 1 | 5 | | 12 | 11 | | 13 | | | | | 37 |
| | | 3 | 4 | | | 8 | 13 | 7 | $6^3$ | $11^1$ | | | | | | | | 2 | $10^3$ | 1 | 5 | 12 | 14 | | | 9 | | | | | 38 |
| | 2 | 3 | 4 | 12 | | 8 | 14 | | 6 | | 9 | | | | | | | 13 | $10^3$ | 1 | $5^2$ | $11^1$ | 7 | | | | | | | | 39 |
| | 2 | 3 | 4 | 5 | | 8 | 13 | $7^2$ | 6 | 11 | 9 | | | | | | | | $10^1$ | 1 | 12 | | | | | | | | | | 40 |
| | 2 | 3 | 4 | $10^2$ | 13 | | 12 | $7^1$ | 6 | 11 | 9 | | | | | | | | $5^3$ | 1 | | | 8 | | | | | | | | 41 |
| | 5 | 3 | 4 | 10 | 13 | 2 | 12 | $7^1$ | 6 | $11^3$ | | | | | | | | | $9^2$ | | | | 8 | 14 | | | | | | | 42 |
| | 2 | 3 | 4 | 10 | $9^3$ | 8 | 12 | $7^2$ | 6 | | | | | | | $11^1$ | 14 | | | 1 | | 13 | 5 | | | | | | | | 43 |
| | 2 | 3 | 4 | 10 | | $8^3$ | 12 | 7 | $6^2$ | | 9 | | | | | $11^1$ | 14 | | | 1 | | 13 | 5 | | | | | | | | 44 |
| 1 | | 3 | 4 | 12 | | 8 | | $7^1$ | 6 | | 10 | | 14 | | | | | | 11 | 2 | $5^3$ | | | | | $9^2$ | 13 | | | | 45 |
| 1 | 2 | 3 | $4^1$ | 5 | | 7 | 14 | | $6^2$ | 9 | 10 | | | | | | | | | | 12 | | | | 8 | $11^3$ | 13 | | | | 46 |

**FA Cup**

| | | | | |
|---|---|---|---|---|
| First Round | Rotherham U | (a) | 2-3 | |

**Capital One Cup**

| | | | | |
|---|---|---|---|---|
| First Round | AFC Wimbledon | (h) | 3-1 | |
| Second Round | Southampton | (h) | 1-4 | |

**Johnstone's Paint Trophy**

| | | | | |
|---|---|---|---|---|
| First Round | Dagenham & R | (a) | 2-3 | |

# STOKE CITY

## FOUNDATION

The date of the formation of this club has long been in doubt. The year 1863 was claimed, but more recent research by local club historian Wade Martin has uncovered nothing earlier than 1868, when a couple of Old Carthusians, who were apprentices at the local works of the old North Staffordshire Railway Company, met with some others from that works, to form Stoke Ramblers. It should also be noted that the old Stoke club went bankrupt in 1908 when a new club was formed.

*Britannia Stadium, Stanley Matthews Way, Stoke-on-Trent, Staffordshire ST4 4EG.*

*Telephone:* (01782) 367 598.

*Fax:* (01782) 592 221.

*Ticket Office:* (01782) 367 599.

*Website:* www.stokecityfc.com

*Email:* info@stokecityfc.com

*Ground Capacity:* 27,740.

*Record Attendance:* 51,380 v Arsenal, Division 1, 29 March 1937 (at Victoria Ground); 28,218 v Everton, Division 2, 5 January 2002 (at Britannia Stadium).

*Pitch Measurements:* 100m × 64m (109yd × 69yd)

*Chairman:* Peter Coates.

*Chief Executive:* Tony Scholes.

*Manager:* Mark Hughes.

*Assistant Manager:* Mark Bowen.

*Physio:* Dave Watson.

*Colours:* Red and white striped shirts with red sleeves with red trim, white shorts with red trim, white socks.

*Year Formed:* 1863* (*see Foundation*).

*Turned Professional:* 1885.

*Previous Names:* 1868, Stoke Ramblers; 1870, Stoke; 1925, Stoke City.

*Club Nickname:* 'The Potters'.

*Grounds:* 1875, Sweeting's Field; 1878, Victoria Ground (previously known as the Athletic Club Ground); 1997, Britannia Stadium.

*First Football League Game:* 8 September 1888, Football League, v WBA (h) L 0–2 – Rowley; Clare, Underwood; Ramsey, Shutt, Smith; Sayer, McSkimming, Staton, Edge, Tunnicliffe.

*Record League Victory:* 10–3 v WBA, Division 1, 4 February 1937 – Doug Westland; Brigham, Harbot; Tutin, Turner (1p), Kirton; Matthews, Antonio (2), Freddie Steele (5), Jimmy Westland, Johnson (2).

*Record Cup Victory:* 7–1 v Burnley, FA Cup 2nd rd (replay), 20 February 1896 – Clawley; Clare, Eccles; Turner, Grewe, Robertson; Willie Maxwell, Dickson, Alan Maxwell (3), Hyslop (4), Schofield.

## HONOURS

**Football League – Division 1:**
Best season: 4th, 1935–36, 1946–47;

**FL C:** *Runners-up* 2007–08;

**Division 2:** *Champions* 1932–33, 1962–63, 1992–93;
*Runners-up* 1921–22;

**Division 3 (N):** *Champions* 1926–27.

**FA Cup:** *Runners-up* 2011.

**Football League Cup:** *Winners* 1972;
*Runners-up* 1964.

**Autoglass Trophy:** *Winners*: 1992.

**Auto Windscreens Shield:**
*Winners*: 2000.

**European Competitions**
**UEFA Cup:** 1972–73, 1974–75.
**Europa League:** 2011–12.

## sky SPORTS FACT FILE

On the day after the 1949–50 season ended two Stoke City players, Neil Franklin and George Mountford, flew out of the country en route for Colombia where they signed for the Santa Fe club. Both were punished by the FA on their return for joining a club outside FIFA's jurisdiction.

*Record Defeat:* 0–10 v Preston NE, Division 1, 14 September 1889.

*Most League Points (2 for a win):* 63, Division 3 (N), 1926–27.

*Most League Points (3 for a win):* 93, Division 2, 1992–93.

*Most League Goals:* 92, Division 3 (N), 1926–27.

*Highest League Scorer in Season:* Freddie Steele, 33, Division 1, 1936–37.

*Most League Goals in Total Aggregate:* Freddie Steele, 142, 1934–49.

*Most League Goals in One Match:* 7, Neville Coleman v Lincoln C, Division 2, 23 February 1957.

*Most Capped Player:* Glen Whelan, 49, Republic of Ireland.

*Most League Appearances:* Eric Skeels, 506, 1958–76.

*Youngest League Player:* Peter Bullock, 16 years 163 days v Swansea C, 19 April 1958.

*Record Transfer Fee Received:* £4,500,000 from VfL Wolfsburg for Tuncay Sanli, January 2011.

*Record Transfer Fee Paid:* £10,000,000 to Tottenham H for Peter Crouch, August 2011.

*Football League Record:* 1888 Founder Member of Football League; 1890 Not re-elected; 1891 Re-elected; relegated in 1907, and after one year in Division 2, resigned for financial reasons; 1919 re-elected to Division 2; 1922–23 Division 1; 1923–26 Division 2; 1926–27 Division 3 (N); 1927–33 Division 2; 1933–53 Division 1; 1953–63 Division 2; 1963–77 Division 1; 1977–79 Division 2; 1979–85 Division 1; 1985–90 Division 2; 1990–92 Division 3; 1992–93 Division 2; 1993–98 Division 1; 1998–2002 Division 2; 2002–04 Division 1; 2004–08 FL C; 2008– FA Premier League.

## LATEST SEQUENCES

*Longest Sequence of League Wins:* 8, 30.3.1895 – 21.9.1895.

*Longest Sequence of League Defeats:* 11, 6.4.1985 – 17.8.1985.

*Longest Sequence of League Draws:* 5, 21.3.1987 – 11.4.1987; 13.5.2012 – 15.9.2012.

*Longest Sequence of Unbeaten League Matches:* 25, 5.9.1992 – 20.2.1993.

*Longest Sequence Without a League Win:* 17, 22.4.1989 – 14.10.1989.

*Successive Scoring Runs:* 21 from 24.12.1921.

*Successive Non-scoring Runs:* 8 from 29.12.1984.

## MANAGERS

Tom Slaney 1874–83
*(Secretary-Manager)*
Walter Cox 1883–84
*(Secretary-Manager)*
Harry Lockett 1884–90
Joseph Bradshaw 1890–92
Arthur Reeves 1892–95
William Rowley 1895–97
H. D. Austerberry 1897–1908
A. J. Barker 1908–14
Peter Hodge 1914–15
Joe Schofield 1915–19
Arthur Shallcross 1919–23
John 'Jock' Rutherford 1923
Tom Mather 1923–35
Bob McGrory 1935–52
Frank Taylor 1952–60
Tony Waddington 1960–77
George Eastham 1977–78
Alan A'Court 1978
Alan Durban 1978–81
Richie Barker 1981–83
Bill Asprey 1984–85
Mick Mills 1985–89
Alan Ball 1989–91
Lou Macari 1991–93
Joe Jordan 1993–94
Lou Macari 1994–97
Chic Bates 1997–98
Chris Kamara 1998
Brian Little 1998–99
Gary Megson 1999
Gudjon Thordarson 1999–2002
Steve Cotterill 2002
Tony Pulis 2002–05
Johan Boskamp 2005–06
Tony Pulis 2006–13
Mark Hughes May 2013–

## TEN YEAR LEAGUE RECORD

|         |        | P  | W  | D  | L  | F  | A  | Pts | Pos |
|---------|--------|----|----|----|----|----|----|-----|-----|
| 2003-04 | Div 1  | 46 | 18 | 12 | 16 | 58 | 55 | 66  | 11  |
| 2004-05 | FL C   | 46 | 17 | 10 | 19 | 36 | 38 | 61  | 12  |
| 2005-06 | FL C   | 46 | 17 | 7  | 22 | 54 | 63 | 58  | 13  |
| 2006-07 | FL C   | 46 | 19 | 16 | 11 | 62 | 41 | 73  | 8   |
| 2007-08 | FL C   | 46 | 21 | 16 | 9  | 69 | 55 | 79  | 2   |
| 2008-09 | PR Lge | 38 | 12 | 9  | 17 | 38 | 55 | 45  | 12  |
| 2009-10 | PR Lge | 38 | 11 | 14 | 13 | 34 | 48 | 47  | 11  |
| 2010-11 | PR Lge | 38 | 13 | 7  | 18 | 46 | 48 | 46  | 13  |
| 2011-12 | PR Lge | 38 | 11 | 12 | 15 | 36 | 53 | 45  | 14  |
| 2012-13 | PR Lge | 38 | 9  | 15 | 14 | 34 | 45 | 42  | 13  |

## DID YOU KNOW ?

George Eastham scored just five goals in a seven-year spell with Stoke City. One of these proved to be the winner in the 1972 Football League Cup final against Chelsea. Aged 35 years and 161 days, he was the oldest player and oldest scorer in a Wembley final.

## STOKE CITY – FA PREMIERSHIP 2012–13 LEAGUE RECORD

| Match No. | Date | Venue | Opponents | Result | H/T Score | Lg Pos. | Goalscorers | Attendance |
|---|---|---|---|---|---|---|---|---|
| 1 | Aug 18 | A | Reading | D | 1-1 | 1-0 | 7 | Kightly [34] | 23,973 |
| 2 | 26 | H | Arsenal | D | 0-0 | 0-0 | 11 | | 27,072 |
| 3 | Sept 1 | A | Wigan Ath | D | 2-2 | 1-1 | 10 | Walters (pen) [40], Crouch [76] | 16,247 |
| 4 | 15 | H | Manchester C | D | 1-1 | 1-1 | 10 | Crouch [15] | 27,101 |
| 5 | 22 | A | Chelsea | L | 0-1 | 0-0 | 13 | | 41,112 |
| 6 | 29 | H | Swansea C | W | 2-0 | 2-0 | 12 | Crouch 2 [12, 36] | 27,330 |
| 7 | Oct 7 | A | Liverpool | D | 0-0 | 0-0 | 12 | | 44,531 |
| 8 | 20 | A | Manchester U | L | 2-4 | 1-2 | 13 | Rooney (og) [11], Kightly [58] | 75,585 |
| 9 | 27 | H | Sunderland | D | 0-0 | 0-0 | 12 | | 27,055 |
| 10 | Nov 3 | A | Norwich C | L | 0-1 | 0-1 | 15 | | 26,072 |
| 11 | 10 | H | QPR | W | 1-0 | 0-0 | 12 | Adam [52] | 27,529 |
| 12 | 19 | A | West Ham U | D | 1-1 | 1-0 | 14 | Walters [13] | 35,005 |
| 13 | 24 | H | Fulham | W | 1-0 | 1-0 | 11 | Adam [26] | 26,921 |
| 14 | 28 | H | Newcastle U | W | 2-1 | 0-0 | 9 | Walters [81], Jerome [85] | 26,793 |
| 15 | Dec 1 | A | WBA | W | 1-0 | 0-0 | 9 | Whitehead [75] | 24,739 |
| 16 | 8 | A | Aston Villa | D | 0-0 | 0-0 | 9 | | 30,110 |
| 17 | 15 | H | Everton | D | 1-1 | 0-1 | 9 | Jones [52] | 27,008 |
| 18 | 22 | A | Tottenham H | D | 0-0 | 0-0 | 9 | | 35,702 |
| 19 | 26 | H | Liverpool | W | 3-1 | 2-1 | 8 | Walters 2 [5, 49], Jones [12] | 27,490 |
| 20 | 29 | H | Southampton | D | 3-3 | 1-3 | 8 | Jones [16], Upson [67], Jerome [90] | 26,391 |
| 21 | Jan 1 | A | Manchester C | L | 0-3 | 0-1 | 9 | | 47,192 |
| 22 | 12 | H | Chelsea | L | 0-4 | 0-1 | 10 | | 27,348 |
| 23 | 19 | A | Swansea C | L | 1-3 | 0-0 | 10 | Owen [90] | 19,603 |
| 24 | 29 | H | Wigan Ath | D | 2-2 | 1-0 | 10 | Shawcross [23], Crouch [48] | 24,421 |
| 25 | Feb 2 | A | Arsenal | L | 0-1 | 0-0 | 10 | | 59,872 |
| 26 | 9 | H | Reading | W | 2-1 | 0-0 | 10 | Huth [67], Jerome [81] | 26,737 |
| 27 | 23 | A | Fulham | L | 0-1 | 0-1 | 10 | | 25,458 |
| 28 | Mar 2 | H | West Ham U | L | 0-1 | 0-1 | 11 | | 26,250 |
| 29 | 10 | A | Newcastle U | L | 1-2 | 0-0 | 11 | Walters (pen) [67] | 50,703 |
| 30 | 16 | H | WBA | D | 0-0 | 0-0 | 10 | | 26,317 |
| 31 | 30 | A | Everton | L | 0-1 | 0-1 | 13 | | 33,977 |
| 32 | Apr 6 | H | Aston Villa | L | 1-3 | 0-1 | 14 | Kightly [80] | 27,544 |
| 33 | 14 | H | Manchester U | L | 0-2 | 0-1 | 16 | | 27,191 |
| 34 | 20 | A | QPR | W | 2-0 | 1-0 | 15 | Crouch [42], Walters (pen) [77] | 17,391 |
| 35 | 27 | H | Norwich C | W | 1-0 | 0-0 | 12 | Adam [46] | 27,488 |
| 36 | May 6 | A | Sunderland | D | 1-1 | 1-0 | 11 | Walters [9] | 38,130 |
| 37 | 12 | H | Tottenham H | L | 1-2 | 1-1 | 11 | Nzonzi [3] | 27,531 |
| 38 | 19 | A | Southampton | D | 1-1 | 0-0 | 13 | Crouch [47] | 31,539 |

**Final League Position: 13**

### GOALSCORERS

*League (34):* Walters 8 (3 pens), Crouch 7, Adam 3, Jerome 3, Jones 3, Kightly 3, Huth 1, Nzonzi 1, Owen 1, Shawcross 1, Upson 1, Whitehead 1, own goal 1.
*FA Cup (4):* Walters 2, Jerome 1, Jones 1.
*Capital One Cup (3):* Crouch 1, Jones 1, Walters 1.

| Begovic A 38 | Huth R 35 | Wilkinson A 19+5 | Whelan G 31+1 | Wilson M 19 | Shawcross R 37 | Kightly M 14+8 | Whitehead D 12+14 | Etherington M 21+10 | Walters J 38 | Crouch P 23+6 | Jerome C 8+18 | Delap R —+1 | Palacios W —+4 | Pennant J 1 | Cameron G 29+6 | Shotton R 20+3 | Adam C 22+5 | Nzonzi S 35 | Owen M —+8 | Jones K 10+16 | Edu M —+1 | Upson M 1 | Shea B —+2 | Match No. |
|---|---|---|---|---|---|---|---|---|---|---|---|---|---|---|---|---|---|---|---|---|---|---|---|---|
| 1 | 2 | 3 | 4³ | 5 | 6 | 7¹ | 8* | 9² | 10 | 11 | 12 | 13 | 14 | | | | | | | | | | | 1 |
| 1 | 3 | 2 | 8³ | 5 | 4 | 9 | | | 10 | 11² | 12 | | 14 | | 6¹ | 7 | 13 | | | | | | | 2 |
| 1 | 3 | 2¹ | 6 | 5 | 4 | 9² | 8 | | 11 | 10 | 13 | | | | 7 | 12 | | | | | | | | 3 |
| 1 | 4 | 2 | 7 | 5 | 3 | 10¹ | | | 12 | 6 | 11³ | | | | 13 | | | 9² | 8 | 14 | | | | 4 |
| 1 | 2 | | 8 | 5 | 3 | 6² | | | 13 | 10 | 11³ | | | | 4 | | | 7¹ | 9 | 12 | 14 | | | 5 |
| 1 | 3 | | 7² | 5 | 4 | 10 | 13 | 12 | 6 | 11³ | | | | | 2 | | | 9¹ | 8 | | 14 | | | 6 |
| 1 | 3 | | 8¹ | 5 | 4 | 10² | 12 | 13 | 6 | 11 | | | | | 2 | | | 9³ | 7 | | 14 | | | 7 |
| 1 | 3 | | 5 | 4 | 10² | 7³ | 12 | 8¹ | 11 | | | | 14 | | 2 | | | 9 | 6 | 13 | | | | 8 |
| 1 | 4 | 12 | 5¹ | 3 | 6 | 7 | 13 | 10² | 11 | | | | | | 2 | | | 8³ | 9 | 14 | | | | 9 |
| 1 | 3 | 5³ | 14 | | 4 | 9¹ | 6 | 12 | 11² | 10 | | | | | 2 | | | 7 | 8 | | 13 | | | 10 |
| 1 | 3 | 2 | 8 | | 4 | 12 | 14 | 10¹ | 7 | 11² | | | | | 5 | | | 9³ | 6 | | 13 | | | 11 |
| 1 | 3 | 5¹ | 6² | | 4 | 14 | | 11³ | 9 | 10 | | 13 | | | 2 | 12 | | 7 | 8 | | | | | 12 |
| 1 | 4 | | 8 | 3 | 12 | 14 | 9¹ | 6 | 11² | | | | | | 2 | 5 | 10³ | 7 | | 13 | | | | 13 |
| 1 | 3 | | 8 | 4 | 13 | | 9³ | 6 | 11¹ | 14 | | | | | 5 | 2 | 10² | 7 | | 12 | | | | 14 |
| 1 | 4 | | 9 | 3 | 12 | 13 | 10¹ | 6 | | | | | | | 5 | 2 | 8² | 7 | | 11 | | | | 15 |
| 1 | 3 | | 9 | 4 | | 7 | 10¹ | 6 | 13 | 12 | | | | | 5 | 2ᵃ | | 8 | | 11² | | | | 16 |
| 1 | 4 | 2 | 7 | 3 | 14 | | 9³ | 6 | 13 | 12 | | | | | 5 | | 10¹ | 8 | | 11² | | | | 17 |
| 1 | 4 | 2 | 8 | 3 | | 12 | 9³ | 11 | 14 | 13 | | | | | 5 | 6¹ | | 7 | | 10² | | | | 18 |
| 1 | 4 | 5 | 8 | 3 | 6¹ | 12 | 9³ | 10 | 13 | | | | | | 2 | 14 | | 7 | | 11² | | | | 19 |
| 1 | 3 | 5² | 7 | | 6³ | 13 | 9¹ | 10 | 14 | 12 | | | | | | 2 | 8ᵃ | | | 11 | | | 4 | 20 |
| 1 | 3 | 5 | 9 | 4 | | 13 | 12 | 6 | | 10 | | | | | 2 | | | 7² | 8 | 11¹ | | | | 21 |
| 1 | 4 | 5 | 7 | 3 | 14 | 13 | 9³ | 6 | | 12 | | | | | 2 | | | 10² | 8 | 11¹ | | | | 22 |
| 1 | 3 | | 7 | 4 | | 2 | 6³ | 10 | 11¹ | 12 | | | | | 5 | | | 9² | 8 | 14 | 13 | | | 23 |
| 1 | 4 | 13 | 6 | 3 | | 5 | 9 | 10 | 11³ | 12 | | | | | 2 | | | 8¹ | 7² | 14 | | | | 24 |
| 1 | 4 | 5 | 9 | 3 | | | 10 | 6² | 11¹ | 13 | | | | 7³ | 2 | | | 8 | 14 | 12 | | | | 25 |
| 1 | 4 | 5³ | 8 | 3 | 6¹ | | 9 | 10 | 11² | 12 | | | | 14 | 2 | | | 7 | | 13 | | | | 26 |
| 1 | 3 | | 8 | 5 | 4 | | 10¹ | 6 | 11³ | 13 | | | | 9² | 2 | | | 7 | | 14 | | | 12 | 27 |
| 1 | | 5 | 7³ | 4 | 3 | 9¹ | | 6² | 11 | 10 | | | | | 2 | 14 | | 8 | | 13 | | | 12 | 28 |
| 1 | | 5 | 7 | 4 | 3 | 13 | | 9 | 11¹ | 10² | | | | | 2 | 6 | | 8 | | 12 | | | | 29 |
| 1 | | 7¹ | 4 | 3 | | 12 | 9 | 10 | 11² | 6³ | | | | | 5 | 2 | 14 | 8 | | 13 | | | | 30 |
| 1 | 4 | | 7 | 5 | 3 | | | 9 | 10² | 11 | | | | | 2¹ | 6 | 12 | 8 | | 13 | | | | 31 |
| 1 | 4 | | 5² | 3 | 12 | 8 | 9¹ | 10 | | 13 | | | | | 2 | 6 | 14 | 7 | | 11 | | | | 32 |
| 1 | 4 | 5 | 7 | 3 | | | 10² | 14 | 12 | | | | | | 2¹ | 6 | 9 | 8 | 13 | 11³ | | | | 33 |
| 1 | 3 | 12 | 6 | 5¹ | 4 | 13 | | 9 | 10³ | 11 | | | | | 14 | 2 | 7² | 8 | | | | | | 34 |
| 1 | 4 | 5¹ | 8² | | 3 | 13 | 14 | 6 | 11 | 10³ | | | | | 12 | 2 | 9 | 7 | | | | | | 35 |
| 1 | 4 | | 5¹ | | 3 | 8 | 13 | 9 | 10³ | 11 | | | | | 12 | 2 | 7² | 6 | | 14 | | | | 36 |
| 1 | 4 | 12 | | 5 | 3 | | 7 | 9¹ | 10 | 11² | 13 | | | | 14 | 2³ | 6ᵃ | 8 | | | | | | 37 |
| 1 | 4 | 12 | | 5¹ | 3 | | 7 | 9² | 11³ | 10 | 13 | | | | 6 | 2 | | 8 | 14 | | | | | 38 |

**FA Cup**

| | | | | |
|---|---|---|---|---|
| Third Round | Crystal Palace | (a) | 0-0 | |
| *Replay* | Crystal Palace | (h) | 4-1 | |
| Fourth Round | Manchester C | (h) | 0-1 | |

**Capital One Cup**

| | | | |
|---|---|---|---|
| Second Round | Swindon T | (h) | 3-4 |

# SUNDERLAND

## FOUNDATION

A Scottish schoolmaster named James Allan, working at Hendon Board School, took the initiative in the foundation of Sunderland in 1879 when they were formed as The Sunderland and District Teachers' Association FC at a meeting in the Adults School, Norfolk Street. Due to financial difficulties, they quickly allowed members from outside the teaching profession and so became Sunderland AFC in October 1880.

*Stadium of Light, Sunderland, Tyne and Wear SR5 1SU.*

*Telephone:* (0871) 911 1200.

*Fax:* (0191) 551 5123.

*Ticket Office:* (0871) 911 1973.

*Website:* www.safc.com

*Email:* enquiries@safc.com

*Ground Capacity:* 48,707.

*Record Attendance:* 75,118 v Derby Co, FA Cup 6th rd replay, 8 March 1933 (at Roker Park); 48,353 v Liverpool, FA Premier League, 13 April 2002 (at Stadium of Light). (FA Premier League figure 46,062.)

*Pitch Measurements:* 105m × 68m (114yd × 74yd)

*Chairman:* Ellis Short.

*Chief Executive:* Margaret Byrne.

*Head Coach:* Paolo Di Canio.

*First Team Coach:* Fabrizio Piccareta.

*Physio:* Dave Galley.

*Colours:* Red and white striped shirts, black shorts, black socks with red tops.

*Year Formed:* 1879.

*Turned Professional:* 1886.

*Previous Names:* 1879, Sunderland and District Teachers AFC; 1880, Sunderland.

*Club Nickname:* 'The Black Cats'.

*Grounds:* 1879, Blue House Field, Hendon; 1882, Groves Field, Ashbrooke; 1883, Horatio Street; 1884, Abbs Field, Fulwell; 1886, Newcastle Road; 1898, Roker Park; 1997, Stadium of Light.

*First Football League Game:* 13 September 1890, Football League, v Burnley (h) L 2–3 – Kirtley; Porteous, Oliver; Wilson, Auld, Gibson; Spence (1), Miller, Campbell (1), Scott, Davy Hannah.

*Record League Victory:* 9–1 v Newcastle U (a), Division 1, 5 December 1908 – Roose; Forster, Melton; Daykin, Thomson, Low; Mordue (1), Hogg (3), Brown, Holley (3), Bridgett (2).

*Record Cup Victory:* 11–1 v Fairfield, FA Cup 1st rd, 2 February 1895 – Doig; McNeill, Johnston; Dunlop, McCreadie (1), Wilson; Gillespie (1), Millar (5), Campbell, Jimmy Hannah (3), Scott (1).

## HONOURS

**Football League: Division 1:** *Champions* 1891–92, 1892–93, 1894–95, 1901–02, 1912–13, 1935–36, 1995–96, 1998–99; *Runners-up* 1893–94, 1897–98, 1900–01, 1922–23, 1934–35; **Division 2:** *Champions* 1975–76; *Runners-up* 1963–64, 1979–80. **FL C:** *Champions* 2004–05, 2006–07; **Division 3:** *Champions* 1987–88.

**FA Cup:** *Winners* 1937, 1973; *Runners-up* 1913, 1992.

**Football League Cup:** *Runners-up* 1985.

**European Competitions European Cup-Winners' Cup:** 1973–74.

## sky SPORTS FACT FILE

Colin Grainger, who played 120 games for Sunderland between 1957 and 1960, was known as 'The Singing Winger'. He made two records for HMV, as well as appearing on the Winifred Atwell show on television and deputising for Ronnie Hilton on a couple of occasions.

**Record Defeat:** 0–8 v Sheff Wed, Division 1, 26 December 1911; 0–8 v West Ham U, Division 1, 19 October 1968; 0–8 v Watford, Division 1, 25 September 1982.

**Most League Points (2 for a win):** 61, Division 2, 1963–64.

**Most League Points (3 for a win):** 105, Division 1, 1998–99.

**Most League Goals:** 109, Division 1, 1935–36.

**Highest League Scorer in Season:** Dave Halliday, 43, Division 1, 1928–29.

**Most League Goals in Total Aggregate:** Charlie Buchan, 209, 1911–25.

**Most League Goals in One Match:** 5, Charlie Buchan v Liverpool, Division 1, 7 December 1919; 5, Bobby Gurney v Bolton W, Division 1, 7 December 1935; 5, Dominic Sharkey v Norwich C, Division 2, 20 February 1962.

**Most Capped Player:** Charlie Hurley, 38 (40), Republic of Ireland.

**Most League Appearances:** Jim Montgomery, 537, 1962–77.

**Youngest League Player:** Derek Forster, 15 years 184 days v Leicester C, 22 August 1964.

**Record Transfer Fee Received:** £19,000,000 (rising to £24,000,000) from Aston Villa for Darren Bent, January 2011.

**Record Transfer Fee Paid:** £14,000,000 to Wolverhampton W for Steven Fletcher, August 2012.

**Football League Record:** 1890 Elected to Division 1; 1958–64 Division 2; 1964–70 Division 1; 1970–76 Division 2; 1976–77 Division 1; 1977–80 Division 2; 1980–85 Division 1; 1985–87 Division 2; 1987–88 Division 3; 1988–90 Division 2; 1990–91 Division 1; 1991–92 Division 2; 1992–96 Division 1; 1996–97 FA Premier League; 1997–99 Division 1; 1999–2003 FA Premier League; 2003–04 Division 1; 2004–05 FL C; 2005–06 FA Premier League; 2006–07 FL C; 2007– FA Premier League.

| MANAGERS |
|---|
| Tom Watson 1888–96 |
| Bob Campbell 1896–99 |
| Alex Mackie 1899–1905 |
| Bob Kyle 1905–28 |
| Johnny Cochrane 1928–39 |
| Bill Murray 1939–57 |
| Alan Brown 1957–64 |
| George Hardwick 1964–65 |
| Ian McColl 1965–68 |
| Alan Brown 1968–72 |
| Bob Stokoe 1972–76 |
| Jimmy Adamson 1976–78 |
| Ken Knighton 1979–81 |
| Alan Durban 1981–84 |
| Len Ashurst 1984–85 |
| Lawrie McMenemy 1985–87 |
| Denis Smith 1987–91 |
| Malcolm Crosby 1991–93 |
| Terry Butcher 1993 |
| Mick Buxton 1993–95 |
| Peter Reid 1995–2002 |
| Howard Wilkinson 2002–03 |
| Mick McCarthy 2003–06 |
| Niall Quinn 2006 |
| Roy Keane 2006–08 |
| Ricky Sbragia 2008–09 |
| Steve Bruce 2009–11 |
| Martin O'Neill 2011–13 |
| Paolo Di Canio March 2013– |

## LATEST SEQUENCES

**Longest Sequence of League Wins:** 13, 14.11.1891 – 2.4.1892.

**Longest Sequence of League Defeats:** 17, 18.1.2003 – 16.8.2003.

**Longest Sequence of League Draws:** 6, 26.3.1949 – 19.4.1949.

**Longest Sequence of Unbeaten League Matches:** 19, 3.5.1998 – 14.11.1998.

**Longest Sequence Without a League Win:** 22, 21.12.2002 – 16.8.2003.

**Successive Scoring Runs:** 29 from 8.11.1997.

**Successive Non-scoring Runs:** 10 from 27.11.1976.

## TEN YEAR LEAGUE RECORD

| | | P | W | D | L | F | A | Pts | Pos |
|---|---|---|---|---|---|---|---|---|---|
| 2003-04 | Div 1 | 46 | 22 | 13 | 11 | 62 | 45 | 79 | 3 |
| 2004-05 | FL C | 46 | 29 | 7 | 10 | 76 | 41 | 94 | 1 |
| 2005-06 | PR Lge | 38 | 3 | 6 | 29 | 26 | 69 | 15 | 20 |
| 2006-07 | FL C | 46 | 27 | 7 | 12 | 76 | 47 | 88 | 1 |
| 2007-08 | PR Lge | 38 | 11 | 6 | 21 | 36 | 59 | 39 | 15 |
| 2008-09 | PR Lge | 38 | 9 | 9 | 20 | 34 | 54 | 36 | 16 |
| 2009-10 | PR Lge | 38 | 11 | 11 | 16 | 48 | 56 | 44 | 13 |
| 2010-11 | PR Lge | 38 | 12 | 11 | 15 | 45 | 56 | 47 | 10 |
| 2011-12 | PR Lge | 38 | 11 | 12 | 15 | 45 | 46 | 45 | 13 |
| 2012-13 | PR Lge | 38 | 9 | 12 | 17 | 41 | 54 | 39 | 17 |

## DID YOU KNOW ?

Vic Halom, a member of the Sunderland team that won the FA Cup in 1973, later turned to politics. He stood as a candidate for the Liberal Democrats for the Sunderland North seat in the 1992 General Election, finishing in third place with 5,389 votes.

## SUNDERLAND – FA PREMIERSHIP 2012–13 LEAGUE RECORD

| Match No. | Date | Venue | Opponents | Result | H/T Score | Lg Pos. | Goalscorers | Attendance |
|---|---|---|---|---|---|---|---|---|
| 1 | Aug 18 | A | Arsenal | D 0-0 | 0-0 | 9 | | 60,078 |
| 2 | Sept 1 | A | Swansea C | D 2-2 | 2-1 | 12 | Fletcher 2 [40, 45] | 20,350 |
| 3 | 15 | H | Liverpool | D 1-1 | 1-0 | 14 | Fletcher [29] | 41,997 |
| 4 | 22 | A | West Ham U | D 1-1 | 1-0 | 12 | Fletcher [9] | 33,052 |
| 5 | 29 | H | Wigan Ath | W 1-0 | 0-0 | 13 | Fletcher [51] | 37,742 |
| 6 | Oct 6 | A | Manchester C | L 0-3 | 0-1 | 13 | | 47,036 |
| 7 | 21 | H | Newcastle U | D 1-1 | 0-1 | 14 | Ba (og) [86] | 47,456 |
| 8 | 27 | A | Stoke C | D 0-0 | 0-0 | 14 | | 27,055 |
| 9 | Nov 3 | H | Aston Villa | L 0-1 | 0-0 | 16 | | 41,515 |
| 10 | 10 | A | Everton | L 1-2 | 1-0 | 16 | Johnson [45] | 35,999 |
| 11 | 18 | A | Fulham | W 3-1 | 0-0 | 15 | Fletcher [50], Cuellar [65], Sessegnon [70] | 25,646 |
| 12 | 24 | H | WBA | L 2-4 | 0-2 | 16 | Gardner [73], Sessegnon [87] | 36,390 |
| 13 | 27 | H | QPR | D 0-0 | 0-0 | 16 | | 36,513 |
| 14 | Dec 2 | A | Norwich C | L 1-2 | 1-2 | 17 | Gardner [44] | 26,228 |
| 15 | 8 | H | Chelsea | L 1-3 | 0-2 | 18 | Johnson [66] | 39,273 |
| 16 | 11 | H | Reading | W 3-0 | 2-0 | 15 | McClean [3], Fletcher [28], Sessegnon [90] | 37,723 |
| 17 | 15 | A | Manchester U | L 1-3 | 0-2 | 16 | Campbell [72] | 75,582 |
| 18 | 22 | A | Southampton | W 1-0 | 1-0 | 15 | Fletcher [42] | 31,275 |
| 19 | 26 | H | Manchester C | W 1-0 | 0-0 | 13 | Johnson [53] | 42,190 |
| 20 | 29 | H | Tottenham H | L 1-2 | 1-0 | 13 | O'Shea [40] | 41,168 |
| 21 | Jan 2 | A | Liverpool | L 0-3 | 0-2 | 14 | | 44,228 |
| 22 | 12 | H | West Ham U | W 3-0 | 1-0 | 14 | Larsson [12], Johnson [47], McClean [74] | 39,918 |
| 23 | 19 | A | Wigan Ath | W 3-2 | 3-1 | 11 | Gardner (pen) [17], Fletcher 2 [20, 42] | 19,219 |
| 24 | 29 | H | Swansea C | D 0-0 | 0-0 | 11 | | 35,628 |
| 25 | Feb 2 | A | Reading | L 1-2 | 1-1 | 12 | Gardner (pen) [29] | 23,829 |
| 26 | 9 | H | Arsenal | L 0-1 | 0-1 | 13 | | 46,402 |
| 27 | 23 | A | WBA | L 1-2 | 0-1 | 14 | Sessegnon [79] | 25,924 |
| 28 | Mar 2 | H | Fulham | D 2-2 | 1-2 | 14 | Gardner (pen) [37], Sessegnon [70] | 39,312 |
| 29 | 9 | A | QPR | L 1-3 | 1-1 | 14 | Fletcher [20] | 18,169 |
| 30 | 17 | H | Norwich C | D 1-1 | 1-1 | 15 | Gardner (pen) [40] | 38,625 |
| 31 | 30 | H | Manchester U | L 0-1 | 0-1 | 16 | | 43,760 |
| 32 | Apr 7 | A | Chelsea | L 1-2 | 1-0 | 17 | Azpilicueta (og) [45] | 41,500 |
| 33 | 14 | A | Newcastle U | W 3-0 | 1-0 | 15 | Sessegnon [27], Johnson [74], Vaughan [82] | 52,355 |
| 34 | 20 | H | Everton | W 1-0 | 1-0 | 14 | Sessegnon [45] | 44,614 |
| 35 | 29 | A | Aston Villa | L 1-6 | 1-2 | 15 | Rose [32] | 37,428 |
| 36 | May 6 | H | Stoke C | D 1-1 | 0-1 | 15 | O'Shea [63] | 38,130 |
| 37 | 12 | H | Southampton | D 1-1 | 0-0 | 17 | Bardsley [68] | 41,988 |
| 38 | 19 | A | Tottenham H | L 0-1 | 0-0 | 17 | | 36,063 |

**Final League Position: 17**

## GOALSCORERS

*League (41):* Fletcher 11, Sessegnon 7, Gardner 6 (4 pens), Johnson 5, McClean 2, O'Shea 2, Bardsley 1, Campbell 1, Cuellar 1, Larsson 1, Rose 1, Vaughan 1, own goals 2.
*FA Cup (2):* Gardner 1, Wickham 1.
*Capital One Cup (4):* McClean 3, Gardner 1.

| Mignolet S 38 | Gardner C 32 + 1 | Cuellar C 26 | O'Shea J 34 | Richardson K 1 | Larsson S 36 + 2 | Colback J 30 + 5 | Cattermole L 10 | McClean J 24 + 12 | Sessegnon S 34 + 1 | Campbell F 1 + 11 | Saha L — + 11 | Elmohamady A — + 2 | Meyler D — + 3 | Johnson A 35 | Fletcher S 28 | Rose D 25 + 2 | Bramble T 12 + 4 | Vaughan D 6 + 18 | Bardsley P 11 + 7 | Wickham C 3 + 9 | Kilgallon M 6 | McFadden J — + 3 | N'Diaye A 15 + 1 | Graham D 11 + 2 | Mangane K — + 2 | Mandron M — + 2 | Knott B — + 1 | Mitchell A — + 1 | Match No. |
|---|---|---|---|---|---|---|---|---|---|---|---|---|---|---|---|---|---|---|---|---|---|---|---|---|---|---|---|---|---|
| 1 | 2 | 3 | 4 | 5 | 6³ | 7 | 8 | 9 | 10¹ | 11² | 12 | 13 | 14 | | | | | | | | | | | | | | | | 1 |
| 1 | 2 | 3 | 4 | | 7 | 5 | 8¹ | 9 | 10³ | 14 | 13 | | 12 | 6 | 11² | | | | | | | | | | | | | | 2 |
| 1 | 2 | 3¹ | 4 | | 6 | 7 | 8 | 9 | 10 | 13 | 14 | | | | 11³ | 5² | 12 | | | | | | | | | | | | 3 |
| 1 | 2 | | 3 | | 6¹ | 7 | 8 | 9 | 10² | 13³ | | | 14 | | 11 | 5 | 4 | 12 | | | | | | | | | | | 4 |
| 1 | 2 | | 3 | | 7 | 8 | | 9 | 10 | | | | | 6¹ | 11 | 5 | 4 | 12 | | | | | | | | | | | 5 |
| 1 | 2 | 4 | 3 | | 7 | 8 | | 9 | 10³ | 14 | 13 | | | 6² | 11 | 5¹ | | 12 | | | | | | | | | | | 6 |
| 1 | 2 | 4 | 3 | | 7 | 8 | | 9 | 10¹ | 12 | | | | 6² | 11 | 5 | 13 | | | | | | | | | | | | 7 |
| 1 | 2 | 4 | 3 | | 6¹ | 8 | 7 | 10 | 12 | 14 | | | | 9³ | 11 | 5² | | | 13 | | | | | | | | | | 8 |
| 1 | 8¹ | 4 | 3 | | 6 | 5 | 7 | 13 | 11² | 14 | 12 | | | 9 | 10 | | | | 2³ | | | | | | | | | | 9 |
| 1 | 2 | 4 | 3 | | 7 | 8³ | | 9 | 11 | 12 | | | | 6² | 10¹ | 5 | 13 | 14 | | | | | | | | | | | 10 |
| 1 | | 3 | 4 | | 9¹ | 8² | 7 | 12 | 10 | | | | | 6 | 11 | 5 | 13 | | 2 | | | | | | | | | | 11 |
| 1 | 12 | 4 | 3² | | 6 | 8³ | 7¹ | 13 | 10 | | 14 | | | 9 | 11 | 5 | | | 2 | | | | | | | | | | 12 |
| 1 | 8³ | 4 | | | 6 | 12 | | 7¹ | 13 | 10 | | 14 | | 9² | 11 | 5 | | | 2 | 3 | | | | | | | | | 13 |
| 1 | 7 | 4 | | | 8³ | | | 9 | 10 | 13 | | | | 6 | 11¹ | 5 | | | 2 | 12 | 3 | | | | | | | | 14 |
| 1 | 7 | 3 | 4 | | 8² | 12 | | 9 | 10 | | 13 | | | 6 | | 5 | | | 2¹ | 11 | | | | | | | | | 15 |
| 1 | 2 | 4 | 3 | | 8 | 5 | | 9 | 10 | | | | | 6¹ | 11 | 7² | 14 | 13 | 12³ | | | | | | | | | | 16 |
| 1 | 7 | 2 | 4 | | 6 | 3³ | | 9 | 10 | 13 | | | | 8² | 11¹ | 5 | | | 12 | 14 | | | | | | | | | 17 |
| 1 | 2 | 3 | 4 | | 8¹ | 7 | | 9 | 10³ | 13 | | | | 6² | 11 | 5 | | 14 | 12 | | | | | | | | | | 18 |
| 1 | 6 | 3 | | | 2¹ | 8 | | 7 | 10 | 12 | | | | 9 | 11 | 5² | | 13 | 4 | | | | | | | | | | 19 |
| 1 | 2 | 4 | 3² | | 7³ | 8 | | 9 | 10 | 12 | | | | 6 | 11 | | 13 | | | | | | 14 | 5¹ | | | | | 20 |
| 1 | 2 | 3 | | | 7² | 8 | | 9 | 10¹ | 12 | | | | 6 | 11 | 5³ | 14 | | | | | | 4 | 13 | | | | | 21 |
| 1 | 2 | | 3 | | 8 | 5 | | 9 | 11³ | | | | | 6² | 10¹ | | 4 | 7 | | 12 | | | 14 | 13 | | | | | 22 |
| 1 | 2 | | 3 | | 6 | 5 | | 12 | 11² | 14 | | | | 9¹ | 10 | 4 | 8³ | 13 | | 7 | | | | | | | | | 23 |
| 1 | 2 | | 4 | | 9 | 5 | | 12 | 10 | | | | | 6² | 11 | 3 | 8 | 13 | | 7¹ | | | | | | | | | 24 |
| 1 | 7 | | 4 | | 6¹ | 5 | | 13 | 11³ | | | | | 9 | 10 | 12 | 3 | 8² | | | | | 2 | 14 | | | | | 25 |
| 1 | 2 | | 4 | | 12 | 9 | 7¹ | | 6 | | | | | 10 | 11 | 5³ | 3 | 14 | | | | | 8² | 13 | | | | | 26 |
| 1 | 2 | | 5 | | 8¹ | 7 | | 13 | 6 | | | | | 9² | 11 | 3 | 12 | | | | | | 4 | 10 | | | | | 27 |
| 1 | 2 | | 5 | | 8 | 5 | | 12 | 6 | | | | | 9 | 10 | 4 | | | | | | | 7 | 11¹ | | | | | 28 |
| 1 | 2 | | 4 | | 7 | 5³ | | | 6 | | | | | 9 | 10 | 12 | 3 | 13 | 14 | | | | 8² | 11¹ | | | | | 29 |
| 1 | 2 | 4¹ | 3 | | 8 | | | 13 | 9 | | | | | 6² | 10 | 5 | 12 | 7 | | 14 | | | | 11² | | | | | 30 |
| 1 | 7 | | 4 | | 13 | 14 | | 9 | 10 | | | | | 6¹ | | 5³ | 3 | | 2² | 12 | | | 8 | 11 | | | | | 31 |
| 1 | 7² | | 4 | | 8¹ | 13 | | 12 | 9 | | | | | 10 | | 5 | | 2 | 11 | 3 | | | | 6 | | | | | 32 |
| 1 | | 4³ | 3 | | 8 | 12 | | 9² | 10 | | | | | 6 | | 5 | 13 | 2¹ | | 7 | | | 11 | | 14 | | | | 33 |
| 1 | | 4 | 3 | | 2¹ | 8 | | 9 | 11² | | | | | 6 | | 5 | 12 | | | 7 | | | 10 | | 13 | | | | 34 |
| 1 | 8³ | 4 | 3 | | 6¹ | | | 12 | 10⁴ | | | | | 9 | | 5 | 14 | 2 | | 7 | | | 11² | | 13 | | | | 35 |
| 1 | 7² | 3 | 4 | | 6¹ | 2 | | 9 | | | | | | 10² | | 5 | 12 | 13 | | 8 | | | 11 | | | | | | 36 |
| 1 | | 4 | 3 | | 6² | 8 | | 9¹ | | | | | | 10 | | 5 | 13 | 2 | 12 | 7 | | | 11 | | | | | | 37 |
| 1 | | 4 | 3 | | 6 | 2 | | 5¹ | | | | | | 9 | | | 7⁸ | | 10² | 8 | 11³ | | | | | 13 | 12 | 14 | 38 |

**FA Cup**

| | | | | |
|---|---|---|---|---|
| Third Round | Bolton W | (a) | 2-2 | |
| *Replay* | Bolton W | (h) | 0-2 | |

**Capital One Cup**

| | | | |
|---|---|---|---|
| Second Round | Morecambe | (h) | 2-0 |
| Third Round | Milton Keynes D | (a) | 2-0 |
| Fourth Round | Middlesbrough | (h) | 0-1 |

# SWANSEA CITY

## FOUNDATION

The earliest Association Football in Wales was played in the northern part of the country and no international took place in the south until 1894, when a local paper still thought it necessary to publish an outline of the rules and an illustration of the pitch markings. There had been an earlier Swansea club, but this has no connection with Swansea Town (now City) formed at a public meeting in June 1912.

*Liberty Stadium, Morfa, Landore, Swansea SA1 2FA.*
*Telephone:* (01792) 616 600.
*Fax:* (01792) 616 606.
*Ticket Office:* (0844) 815 6665.
*Website:* www.swanseacity.net
*Email:* info@swanseacityfc.co.uk
*Ground Capacity:* 20,745.
*Record Attendance:* 32,796 v Arsenal, FA Cup 4th rd, 17 February 1968 (at Vetch Field); 19,288 v Yeovil T, FL 1, 11 November 2005 (at Liberty Stadium).
*Pitch Measurements:* 105m × 68m (114yd × 74yd)
*Chairman:* Huw Jenkins.
*Vice-chairman:* Leigh Dineen.
*Manager:* Michael Laudrup.
*Assistant Manager:* Morten Wieghorst.
*Head Physio:* Kate Rees.
*Colours:* White shirts with gold trim, white shorts with gold trim, white socks with gold trim.
*Year Formed:* 1912.
*Turned Professional:* 1912.
*Previous Name:* 1912, Swansea Town; 1970, Swansea City.
*Club Nicknames:* 'The Swans', 'The Jacks'.
*Grounds:* 1912, Vetch Field; 2005, Liberty Stadium.
*First Football League Game:* 28 August 1920, Division 3, v Portsmouth (a) L 0–3 – Crumley; Robson, Evans; Smith, Holdsworth, Williams; Hole, Ivor Jones, Edmundson, Rigsby, Spottiswood.
*Record League Victory:* 8–0 v Hartlepool U, Division 4, 1 April 1978 – Barber; Evans, Bartley, Lally (1) (Morris), May, Bruton, Kevin Moore, Robbie James (3 incl. 1p), Curtis (3), Toshack (1), Chappell.
*Record Cup Victory:* 12–0 v Sliema W (Malta), ECWC 1st rd 1st leg, 15 September 1982 – Davies; Marustik, Hadziabdic (1), Irwin (1), Kennedy, Rajkovic (1), Loveridge (2) (Leighton James), Robbie James, Charles (2), Stevenson (1), Latchford (1) (Walsh (3)).
*Record Defeat:* 0–8 v Liverpool, FA Cup 3rd rd, 9 January 1990; 0–8 v Monaco, ECWC, 1st rd 2nd leg, 1 October 1991.

## HONOURS

**Football League – Division 1:**
Best season: 6th, 1981–82;
**FL 1:** *Champions* 2007–08;
**Division 35(S):** *Champions* 1924–25, 1948–49; **Division 3:**
*Champions* 1999–2000.

**FA Cup:** Semi-finals 1926, 1964.

**Football League Cup:** *Winners* 2013.

**Welsh Cup:** *Winners* 11 times;
*Runners-up* 8 times.

**Autoglass Trophy:** *Winners* 1994, 2006.

**Football League Trophy:**
*Winners* 2006.

**European Competitions**
**European Cup-Winners' Cup:**
1961–62, 1966–67, 1981–82, 1982–83, 1983–84, 1989–90, 1991–92.

## sky SPORTS FACT FILE

Defender Wyndham Evans appeared for Swansea City in all four divisions between 1977 and 1981 when the club rose from the Fourth Division to the old First Division. In total he spent 15 seasons with the Swans making 389 League appearances.

*Most League Points (2 for a win):* 62, Division 3 (S), 1948–49.

*Most League Points (3 for a win):* 92, FL 1, 2007–08.

*Most League Goals:* 90, Division 2, 1956–57.

*Highest League Scorer in Season:* Cyril Pearce, 35, Division 2, 1931–32.

*Most League Goals in Total Aggregate:* Ivor Allchurch, 166, 1949–58, 1965–68.

*Most League Goals in One Match:* 5, Jack Fowler v Charlton Ath, Division 3S, 27 December 1924.

*Most Capped Player:* Ivor Allchurch, 42 (68), Wales.

*Most League Appearances:* Wilfred Milne, 585, 1919–37.

*Youngest League Player:* Nigel Dalling, 15 years 289 days v Southport, 6 December 1974.

*Record Transfer Fee Received:* £15,000,000 from Liverpool for Joe Allen, August 2012.

*Record Transfer Fee Paid:* £5,550,000 to Valencia for Pablo Hernandez, August 2012.

*Football League Record:* 1920 Original Member of Division 3; 1921–25 Division 3 (S); 1925–47 Division 2; 1947–49 Division 3 (S); 1949–65 Division 2; 1965–67 Division 3; 1967–70 Division 4; 1970–73 Division 3; 1973–78 Division 4; 1978–79 Division 3; 1979–81 Division 2; 1981–83 Division 1; 1983–84 Division 2; 1984–86 Division 3; 1986–88 Division 4; 1988–92 Division 3; 1992–96 Division 2; 1996–2000 Division 3; 2000–01 Division 2; 2001–04 Division 3; 2004–05 FL 2; 2005–08 FL 1; 2008–11 FL C; 2011– FA Premier League.

## LATEST SEQUENCES

*Longest Sequence of League Wins:* 9, 27.11.1999 – 22.01.2000.

*Longest Sequence of League Defeats:* 9, 26.1.1991 – 19.3.1991.

*Longest Sequence of League Draws:* 8, 25.11.2008 – 28.12.2008.

*Longest Sequence of Unbeaten League Matches:* 19, 19.10.1970 – 9.3.1971.

*Longest Sequence Without a League Win:* 15, 25.3.1989 – 2.9.1989.

*Successive Scoring Runs:* 27 from 28.8.1947.

*Successive Non-scoring Runs:* 6 from 6.2.1996.

## MANAGERS

Walter Whittaker 1912–14
William Bartlett 1914–15
Joe Bradshaw 1919–26
Jimmy Thomson 1927–31
Neil Harris 1934–39
Haydn Green 1939–47
Bill McCandless 1947–55
Ron Burgess 1955–58
Trevor Morris 1958–65
Glyn Davies 1965–66
Billy Lucas 1967–69
Roy Bentley 1969–72
Harry Gregg 1972–75
Harry Griffiths 1975–77
John Toshack 1978–83
    (resigned October re-appointed
    in December) 1983–84
Colin Appleton 1984
John Bond 1984–85
Tommy Hutchison 1985–86
Terry Yorath 1986–89
Ian Evans 1989–90
Terry Yorath 1990–91
Frank Burrows 1991–95
Bobby Smith 1995
Kevin Cullis 1996
Jan Molby 1996–97
Micky Adams 1997
Alan Cork 1997–98
John Hollins 1998–2001
Colin Addison 2001–02
Nick Cusack 2002
Brian Flynn 2002–04
Kenny Jackett 2004–07
Roberto Martinez 2007–09
Paulo Sousa 2009–10
Brendan Rodgers 2010–12
Michael Laudrup June 2012–

## TEN YEAR LEAGUE RECORD

|  |  | P | W | D | L | F | A | Pts | Pos |
|---|---|---|---|---|---|---|---|---|---|
| 2003-04 | Div 3 | 46 | 15 | 14 | 17 | 58 | 61 | 59 | 10 |
| 2004-05 | FL 2 | 46 | 24 | 8 | 14 | 62 | 43 | 80 | 3 |
| 2005-06 | FL 1 | 46 | 18 | 17 | 11 | 78 | 55 | 71 | 6 |
| 2006-07 | FL 1 | 46 | 20 | 12 | 14 | 69 | 53 | 72 | 7 |
| 2007-08 | FL 1 | 46 | 27 | 11 | 8 | 82 | 42 | 92 | 1 |
| 2008-09 | FL C | 46 | 16 | 20 | 10 | 63 | 50 | 68 | 8 |
| 2009-10 | FL C | 46 | 17 | 18 | 11 | 40 | 37 | 69 | 7 |
| 2010-11 | FL C | 46 | 24 | 8 | 14 | 69 | 42 | 80 | 3 |
| 2011-12 | PR Lge | 38 | 12 | 11 | 15 | 44 | 51 | 47 | 11 |
| 2012-13 | PR Lge | 38 | 11 | 13 | 14 | 47 | 51 | 46 | 9 |

## DID YOU KNOW ?

Ben Benyon appeared for Swansea in their first season in the Football League in 1920–21 just a few months after earning two Welsh Rugby Union international caps while playing for Swansea RFC. After two seasons at the Vetch Field he joined Oldham Rugby League club.

## SWANSEA CITY – FA PREMIERSHIP 2012–13 LEAGUE RECORD

| Match No. | Date | Venue | Opponents | Result | | H/T Score | Lg Pos. | Goalscorers | Attendance |
|---|---|---|---|---|---|---|---|---|---|
| 1 | Aug 18 | A | QPR | W | 5-0 | 1-0 | 2 | Michu 2 [8, 53], Dyer 2 [63, 71], Sinclair [81] | 18,072 |
| 2 | 25 | H | West Ham U | W | 3-0 | 2-0 | 2 | Rangel [20], Michu [29], Graham [64] | 20,424 |
| 3 | Sept 1 | H | Sunderland | D | 2-2 | 1-2 | 2 | Routledge [45], Michu [66] | 20,350 |
| 4 | 15 | A | Aston Villa | L | 0-2 | 0-1 | 5 | | 34,005 |
| 5 | 22 | H | Everton | L | 0-3 | 0-2 | 9 | | 20,464 |
| 6 | 29 | A | Stoke C | L | 0-2 | 0-2 | 11 | | 27,330 |
| 7 | Oct 6 | H | Reading | D | 2-2 | 0-2 | 11 | Michu [71], Routledge [78] | 20,336 |
| 8 | 20 | H | Wigan Ath | W | 2-1 | 0-0 | 10 | Hernandez [65], Michu [67] | 19,696 |
| 9 | 27 | A | Manchester C | L | 0-1 | 0-0 | 10 | | 46,801 |
| 10 | Nov 3 | H | Chelsea | D | 1-1 | 0-0 | 11 | Hernandez [88] | 20,527 |
| 11 | 10 | A | Southampton | D | 1-1 | 0-0 | 11 | Dyer [73] | 30,501 |
| 12 | 17 | A | Newcastle U | W | 2-1 | 0-0 | 10 | Michu [58], de Guzman [87] | 49,403 |
| 13 | 25 | H | Liverpool | D | 0-0 | 0-0 | 9 | | 20,621 |
| 14 | 28 | H | WBA | W | 3-1 | 3-1 | 8 | Michu [9], Routledge 2 [11, 39] | 20,377 |
| 15 | Dec 1 | A | Arsenal | W | 2-0 | 0-0 | 7 | Michu 2 [88, 90] | 60,098 |
| 16 | 8 | H | Norwich C | L | 3-4 | 0-3 | 8 | Michu 2 [51, 90], de Guzman [59] | 20,294 |
| 17 | 16 | A | Tottenham H | L | 0-1 | 0-0 | 10 | | 35,783 |
| 18 | 23 | H | Manchester U | D | 1-1 | 1-1 | 11 | Michu [29] | 20,650 |
| 19 | 26 | A | Reading | D | 0-0 | 0-0 | 9 | | 24,050 |
| 20 | 29 | A | Fulham | W | 2-1 | 1-0 | 9 | Graham [19], de Guzman [52] | 25,700 |
| 21 | Jan 1 | H | Aston Villa | D | 2-2 | 1-1 | 8 | Routledge [9], Graham [90] | 20,406 |
| 22 | 12 | A | Everton | D | 0-0 | 0-0 | 9 | | 35,782 |
| 23 | 19 | H | Stoke C | W | 3-1 | 0-0 | 9 | Davies [49], de Guzman 2 [57, 80] | 19,603 |
| 24 | 29 | A | Sunderland | D | 0-0 | 0-0 | 8 | | 35,628 |
| 25 | Feb 2 | A | West Ham U | L | 0-1 | 0-0 | 8 | | 34,962 |
| 26 | 9 | H | QPR | W | 4-1 | 2-0 | 7 | Michu 2 [6, 67], Rangel [18], Hernandez [50] | 20,529 |
| 27 | 17 | A | Liverpool | L | 0-5 | 0-1 | 8 | | 44,832 |
| 28 | Mar 2 | H | Newcastle U | W | 1-0 | 0-0 | 8 | Moore [85] | 20,405 |
| 29 | 9 | A | WBA | L | 1-2 | 1-1 | 9 | Moore [33] | 24,832 |
| 30 | 16 | H | Arsenal | L | 0-2 | 0-0 | 9 | | 20,583 |
| 31 | 30 | H | Tottenham H | L | 1-2 | 0-2 | 9 | Michu [71] | 20,604 |
| 32 | Apr 6 | A | Norwich C | D | 2-2 | 1-1 | 9 | Michu [35], Moore [75] | 26,372 |
| 33 | 20 | H | Southampton | D | 0-0 | 0-0 | 9 | | 20,561 |
| 34 | 28 | A | Chelsea | L | 0-2 | 0-2 | 9 | | 41,780 |
| 35 | May 4 | H | Manchester C | D | 0-0 | 0-0 | 9 | | 20,242 |
| 36 | 7 | A | Wigan Ath | W | 3-2 | 0-1 | 9 | Rangel [50], Shechter [59], Tiendalli [76] | 18,850 |
| 37 | 12 | A | Manchester U | L | 1-2 | 0-1 | 9 | Michu [49] | 75,572 |
| 38 | 19 | H | Fulham | L | 0-3 | 0-1 | 9 | | 20,365 |

**Final League Position: 9**

### GOALSCORERS

*League (47):* Michu 18, de Guzman 5, Routledge 5, Dyer 3, Graham 3, Hernandez 3, Moore 3, Rangel 3, Davies 1, Shechter 1, Sinclair 1, Tiendalli 1.
*FA Cup (2):* Graham 1, Michu 1.
*Capital One Cup (17):* De Guzman 3 (1 pen), Dyer 3, Graham 3, Michu 3, Moore 2, Chico 1, Monk 1, own goal 1.

| Vorm M 26 | Rangel A 30+3 | Williams A 37 | Chico 26 | Taylor N 4+2 | de Guzman J 33+4 | Michu M 35 | Britton L 30+3 | Dyer N 25+12 | Graham D 10+8 | Routledge W 30+6 | Agustien K 4+14 | Sinclair S —+1 | Gower M —+1 | Moore L 4+13 | Davies B 33+4 | Tate A 2+1 | Ki S 20+9 | Hernandez P 27+3 | Shechter I 7+11 | Tremmel G 12+2 | Monk G 10+1 | Tiendalli D 11+3 | Lamah R 1+4 | Bartley K 1+1 | Match No. |
|---|---|---|---|---|---|---|---|---|---|---|---|---|---|---|---|---|---|---|---|---|---|---|---|---|---|
| 1 | 2 | 3 | 4 | 5 | $6^1$ | $7^3$ | 8 | $9^2$ | 10 | 11 | 12 | 13 | 14 | | | | | | | | | | | | 1 |
| 1 | 2 | 4 | 3 | | $5^3$ | $7^1$ | 8 | 6 | 9 | 11 | $10^2$ | | | | | | 13 | 14 | | | | | | | 2 |
| 1 | 2 | 3 | $4^4$ | $5^1$ | | 8 | $10^3$ | 7 | 6 | 11 | $9^2$ | | | | | | 12 | 13 | 14 | | | | | | 3 |
| 1 | 2 | 4 | | | | 7 | 8 | $6^3$ | 9 | $11^2$ | $10^1$ | | | 13 | 5 | 3 | 12 | 14 | | | | | | | 4 |
| 1 | 2 | 4 | | | | 7 | 8 | 13 | $12^4$ | $11^3$ | 10 | | | | 5 | $3^2$ | 6 | $9^1$ | 14 | | | | | | 5 |
| 1 | 2 | 4 | 3 | | | $9^2$ | 7 | 6 | 11 | 12 | | | | 13 | 5 | | 8 | $10^1$ | | | | | | | 6 |
| 1 | 2 | 4 | 3 | | 14 | $8^3$ | 7 | $6^2$ | $11^1$ | 10 | | | | 12 | 5 | | 9 | 13 | | | | | | | 7 |
| 1 | 2 | 4 | 3 | | | $7^2$ | 11 | 9 | 12 | 13 | 6 | | | | 5 | | 8 | $10^1$ | | | | | | | 8 |
| $1^1$ | 2 | 4 | 3 | | | 9 | 11 | $8^2$ | 14 | 13 | 7 | | | | 5 | | 6 | $10^2$ | | 12 | | | | | 9 |
| | 2 | 4 | | | | 8 | $11^3$ | $7^2$ | 13 | 12 | $6^1$ | | | | 5 | | 9 | 10 | 14 | 1 | 3 | | | | 10 |
| | 2 | | 3 | | | $8^3$ | 10 | $7^2$ | 12 | $11^1$ | 14 | | | | 5 | | 6 | 9 | 13 | 1 | 4 | | | | 11 |
| | 2 | | 3 | | | 7 | $9^3$ | 6 | 8 | 14 | 12 | 13 | | | 5 | | 10 | $11^2$ | | 1 | 4 | | | | 12 |
| | 2 | 3 | 4 | | $9^3$ | 8 | 7 | 13 | $10^2$ | 14 | | | | | 5 | | 12 | 6 | $11^1$ | 1 | | | | | 13 |
| | 2 | 3 | 4 | | 13 | $11^3$ | 6 | $9^1$ | 10 | 14 | | | | 12 | 5 | | 8 | $7^2$ | | 1 | | | | | 14 |
| | 2 | 4 | 3 | | | $9^2$ | 11 | 7 | 6 | | | | | 12 | 5 | | 8 | $10^1$ | | 1 | | | 13 | | 15 |
| | 2 | 4 | 3 | | | 8 | 10 | | 6 | $11^1$ | 7 | | | | 5 | | 9 | | 12 | | 1 | | | | 16 |
| | | 4 | 3 | | 9 | 11 | 6 | $8^3$ | 14 | 10 | 12 | | | 13 | 5 | | $7^2$ | | | | 1 | 2 | | | 17 |
| 1 | | 4 | 3 | | $9^2$ | 11 | $7^1$ | 6 | 10 | $8^3$ | | | | 13 | 5 | | 12 | | 14 | | | 2 | | | 18 |
| 1 | | 4 | 3 | | 13 | $11^3$ | $7^1$ | 6 | 10 | 12 | | | $9^2$ | | 5 | | 8 | | 14 | | | 2 | | | 19 |
| | 2 | | 3 | | 6 | 14 | 8 | 11 | $10^1$ | $7^3$ | | | | | | | 13 | | 12 | $9^2$ | 1 | 4 | 5 | | 20 |
| 1 | 2 | 3 | 4 | | $9^1$ | 8 | $7^3$ | 13 | 11 | $6^2$ | 14 | | | | 5 | | 12 | 10 | | | | 2 | | | 21 |
| 1 | 8 | 4 | 3 | | 12 | $10^3$ | $9^1$ | 14 | 13 | 6 | | | | | 5 | | 7 | $11^2$ | | | | 2 | | | 22 |
| 1 | 2 | 4 | | | | 7 | $9^3$ | 14 | 13 | 10 | | | | | 5 | | 8 | $6^1$ | $11^2$ | | 3 | 12 | | | 23 |
| | | 3 | 4 | | | 7 | 11 | $8^3$ | 6 | 14 | | | | | 5 | | 12 | $9^1$ | $10^1$ | 1 | | 2 | 13 | | 24 |
| | 2 | 4 | 3 | | | 6 | 10 | $7^1$ | 13 | $11^2$ | | | | 12 | 5 | | 8 | 9 | | | 1 | | | | 25 |
| 1 | 2 | 4 | $3^1$ | | | 7 | $11^3$ | 10 | | $9^2$ | | 13 | | 14 | 5 | | 8 | 6 | | | | | | 12 | 26 |
| 1 | 14 | 8 | | | | | 6 | 13 | | 12 | 7 | | | | 5 | | | $11^2$ | $10^3$ | | 3 | 2 | $9^1$ | 4 | 27 |
| 1 | 2 | | 3 | | | 9 | 11 | $7^2$ | $10^1$ | 8 | | | | 13 | 5 | | 12 | $6^3$ | | | 4 | 14 | | | 28 |
| 1 | 2 | 4 | | | | 7 | 10 | | 12 | | | | $9^3$ | $11^1$ | 5 | | 8 | $6^4$ | 14 | | 3 | 13 | | | 29 |
| 1 | 2 | | 3 | | | 8 | 11 | 7 | $6^2$ | 12 | | | | 13 | 5 | | $9^1$ | 10 | | | 4 | | | | 30 |
| 1 | | 4 | $3^2$ | | | $7^1$ | 11 | 6 | 9 | 8 | | | | | 5 | | 12 | $10^3$ | 14 | | 13 | 2 | | | 31 |
| 1 | 13 | 4 | 3 | | | 7 | 8 | | | $11^3$ | | | $9^1$ | 10 | $5^2$ | | 6 | 12 | | | | 2 | 14 | | 32 |
| 1 | 2 | 4 | 3 | | | 7 | 9 | 6 | 10 | 12 | | | | $11^1$ | 5 | | 13 | $8^2$ | | | | | | | 33 |
| 1 | 2 | 4 | 3 | 14 | | 9 | 11 | $7^2$ | 12 | $8^1$ | | | | | $5^3$ | | 6 | 10 | | | 13 | | | | 34 |
| 1 | 2 | 4 | 3 | | | 7 | $11^2$ | 6 | $9^1$ | $8^1$ | 12 | | | 13 | 5 | | 10 | | | | 14 | | | | 35 |
| $1^3$ | 6 | 4 | | | | 8 | 7 | 12 | 9 | 13 | | | | | 5 | | | $11^2$ | $10^1$ | 14 | 3 | 2 | | | 36 |
| | 13 | 4 | 3 | $2^1$ | | 9 | $11^2$ | 8 | 6 | 7 | 14 | | | | 12 | | $10^3$ | | | 1 | | 5 | | | 37 |
| 1 | 2 | 4 | 3 | 14 | | $9^2$ | 11 | 7 | 10 | 8 | | | | 13 | $5^3$ | | | $6^1$ | 12 | | | | | | 38 |

**FA Cup**

| | | | |
|---|---|---|---|
| Third Round | Arsenal | (h) | 2-2 |
| *Replay* | Arsenal | (a) | 0-1 |

**Capital One Cup**

| | | | |
|---|---|---|---|
| Second Round | Barnsley | (h) | 3-1 |
| Third Round | Crawley T | (a) | 3-2 |
| Fourth Round | Liverpool | (a) | 3-1 |
| Quarter-Finals | Middlesbrough | (h) | 1-0 |
| Semi-Finals | Chelsea | (a) | 2-0 |
| | Chelsea | (h) | 0-0 |
| Final (*at Wembley*) | Bradford C | | 5-0 |

# SWINDON TOWN

## FOUNDATION

It is generally accepted that Swindon Town came into being in 1881, although there is no firm evidence that the club's founder, Rev. William Pitt, captain of the Spartans (an offshoot of a cricket club), changed his club's name to Swindon Town before 1883, when the Spartans amalgamated with St Mark's Young Men's Friendly Society.

*The County Ground, County Road, Swindon, Wiltshire SN1 2ED.*

*Telephone:* (0871) 876 1879.

*Fax:* (0844) 880 1112.

*Ticket Office:* (0871) 876 1969.

*Website:* www.swindontownfc.co.uk

*Email:* boxoffice@swindontownfc.co.uk

*Ground Capacity:* 14,983.

*Record Attendance:* 32,000 v Arsenal, FA Cup 3rd rd, 15 January 1972.

*Pitch Measurements:* 100m × 64m (110yd × 70yd)

*Chairman:* Jed McCrory.

*General Manager:* Steve Murrall.

*Manager:* Kevin MacDonald.

*Assistant Manager:* Mark Cooper.

*Physio:* Paul Godfrey.

*Colours:* Red shirts with white trim, white shorts with red trim, red socks with white trim.

*Year Formed:* 1881* (*see Foundation*).

*Turned Professional:* 1894.

*Club Nickname:* 'The Robins'.

*Grounds:* 1881, The Croft; 1896, County Ground.

*First Football League Game:* 28 August 1920, Division 3, v Luton T (h) W 9–1 – Nash; Kay, Macconachie; Langford, Hawley, Wareing; Jefferson (1), Fleming (4), Rogers, Batty (2), Davies (1), (1 og).

*Record League Victory:* 9–1 v Luton T, Division 3 (S), 28 August 1920 – Nash; Kay, Macconachie; Langford, Hawley, Wareing; Jefferson (1), Fleming (4), Rogers, Batty (2), Davies (1), (1 og).

*Record Cup Victory:* 10–1 v Farnham U Breweries (away), FA Cup 1st rd (replay), 28 November 1925 – Nash; Dickenson, Weston, Archer, Bew, Adey; Denyer (2), Wall (1), Richardson (4), Johnson (3), Davies.

## HONOURS

**Football League: FL 2:** *Champions* 2011–12;
**Division 2:** *Champions* 1995–96;
**Division 3:** *Runners-up* 1962–63, 1968–69;
**Division 4:** *Champions* 1985–86.
**FA Cup:** Semi-finals 1910, 1912.
**Football League Cup:** *Winners* 1969.
**Johnstone's Paint Trophy:** *Runners-up* 2012.
**Anglo-Italian Cup:** *Winners* 1970.

## sky SPORTS FACT FILE

In May 1910 Swindon Town travelled to Paris where they played against Barnsley for the Dubonnet Cup, an invitation trophy. The match was played at the Parc des Princes and the Robins won 2-1 with both goals coming from Harold Fleming.

*Record Defeat:* 1–10 v Manchester C, FA Cup 4th rd (replay), 25 January 1930.

*Most League Points (2 for a win):* 64, Division 3, 1968–69.

*Most League Points (3 for a win):* 102, Division 4, 1985–86.

*Most League Goals:* 100, Division 3 (S), 1926–27.

*Highest League Scorer in Season:* Harry Morris, 47, Division 3 (S), 1926–27.

*Most League Goals in Total Aggregate:* Harry Morris, 216, 1926–33.

*Most League Goals in One Match:* 5, Harry Morris v QPR, Division 3 (S), 18 December 1926; 5, Harry Morris v Norwich C, Division 3, 26 April 1930; 5, Keith East v Mansfield T, Division 3, 20 November 1965.

*Most Capped Player:* Rod Thomas, 30 (50), Wales.

*Most League Appearances:* John Trollope, 770, 1960–80.

*Youngest League Player:* Paul Rideout, 16 years 107 days v Hull C, 29 November 1980.

*Record Transfer Fee Received:* £1,500,000 from Manchester C for Kevin Horlock, January 1997; £1,500,000 from WBA for Simon Cox, July 2009.

*Record Transfer Fee Paid:* £800,000 to West Ham U for Joey Beauchamp, August 1994.

*Football League Record:* 1920 Original Member of Division 3; 1921–58 Division 3 (S); 1958–63 Division 3; 1963–65 Division 2; 1965–69 Division 3; 1969–74 Division 2; 1974–82 Division 3; 1982–86 Division 4; 1986–87 Division 3; 1987–92 Division 2; 1992–93 Division 1; 1993–94 FA Premier League; 1994–95 Division 1; 1995–96 Division 2; 1996–2000 Division 1; 2000–04 Division 2; 2004–06 FL 1; 2006–07 FL 2; 2007–11 FL 1; 2011–12 FL 2; 2012– FL 1.

## MANAGERS

Sam Allen 1902–33
Ted Vizard 1933–39
Neil Harris 1939–41
Louis Page 1945–53
Maurice Lindley 1953–55
Bert Head 1956–65
Danny Williams 1965–69
Fred Ford 1969–71
Dave Mackay 1971–72
Les Allen 1972–74
Danny Williams 1974–78
Bobby Smith 1978–80
John Trollope 1980–83
Ken Beamish 1983–84
Lou Macari 1984–89
Ossie Ardiles 1989–91
Glenn Hoddle 1991–93
John Gorman 1993–94
Steve McMahon 1994–98
Jimmy Quinn 1998–2000
Colin Todd 2000
Andy King 2000–01
Roy Evans 2001
Andy King 2001–05
Iffy Onuora 2005–06
Dennis Wise 2006
Paul Sturrock 2006–07
Maurice Malpas 2008
Danny Wilson 2008–11
Paul Hart 2011
Paolo Di Canio 2011–13
Kevin MacDonald March 2013–

## LATEST SEQUENCES

*Longest Sequence of League Wins:* 10, 31.12.2011 – 28.2.2012

*Longest Sequence of League Defeats:* 8, 29.8.2005 – 8.10.2005.

*Longest Sequence of League Draws:* 6, 22.11.1991 – 28.12.1991.

*Longest Sequence of Unbeaten League Matches:* 22, 12.1.1986 – 23.8.86.

*Longest Sequence Without a League Win:* 19, 30.10.1999 – 4.3.2000.

*Successive Scoring Runs:* 31 from 17.4.1926.

*Successive Non-scoring Runs:* 5 from 16.11.1963.

## TEN YEAR LEAGUE RECORD

|         |       | P  | W  | D  | L  | F  | A  | Pts | Pos |
|---------|-------|----|----|----|----|----|----|-----|-----|
| 2003-04 | Div 2 | 46 | 20 | 13 | 13 | 76 | 58 | 73  | 5   |
| 2004-05 | FL 1  | 46 | 17 | 12 | 17 | 66 | 68 | 63  | 12  |
| 2005-06 | FL 1  | 46 | 11 | 15 | 20 | 46 | 65 | 48  | 23  |
| 2006-07 | FL 2  | 46 | 25 | 10 | 11 | 58 | 38 | 85  | 3   |
| 2007-08 | FL 1  | 46 | 16 | 13 | 17 | 63 | 56 | 61  | 13  |
| 2008-09 | FL 1  | 46 | 12 | 17 | 17 | 68 | 71 | 53  | 15  |
| 2009-10 | FL 1  | 46 | 22 | 16 | 8  | 73 | 57 | 82  | 5   |
| 2010-11 | FL 1  | 46 | 9  | 14 | 23 | 50 | 72 | 41  | 24  |
| 2011-12 | FL 2  | 46 | 29 | 6  | 11 | 75 | 32 | 93  | 1   |
| 2012-13 | FL 1  | 46 | 20 | 14 | 12 | 72 | 39 | 74  | 6   |

## DID YOU KNOW ?

Titus Okere, a member of the Nigeria squad that toured Britain in 1949, signed a professional contract with Swindon Town in January 1953. A speedy winger, he played for the reserve and 'A' teams but did not play first-team football and left the club at the end of the season.

## SWINDON TOWN – FOOTBALL LEAGUE ONE 2012–13 LEAGUE RECORD

| Match No. | Date | Venue | Opponents | Result | H/T Score | Lg Pos. | Goalscorers | Attendance |
|---|---|---|---|---|---|---|---|---|
| 1 | Aug 18 | A | Hartlepool U | D 0-0 | 0-0 | 18 | | 4132 |
| 2 | 21 | H | Crawley T | W 3-0 | 2-0 | 4 | Ritchie 25, Miller 45, De Vita 63 | 7658 |
| 3 | 25 | H | Milton Keynes D | W 1-0 | 1-0 | 3 | Ritchie 45 | 8299 |
| 4 | Sept 2 | A | Preston NE | L 1-4 | 0-3 | 8 | De Vita 58 | 10,372 |
| 5 | 8 | H | Leyton Orient | L 0-1 | 0-0 | 11 | | 8072 |
| 6 | 15 | A | Carlisle U | D 2-2 | 2-2 | 12 | Rooney, A 29, Benson 32 | 4987 |
| 7 | 18 | A | Portsmouth | W 2-1 | 1-0 | 8 | Ritchie 45, Williams 55 | 12,121 |
| 8 | 22 | H | Bournemouth | W 4-0 | 2-0 | 5 | Ritchie 2 12, 67, Williams 25, Rooney, A 85 | 8533 |
| 9 | 29 | A | Shrewsbury T | W 1-0 | 0-0 | 4 | Ferry 79 | 6303 |
| 10 | Oct 2 | H | Colchester U | L 0-1 | 0-0 | 8 | | 7443 |
| 11 | 6 | A | Bury | W 1-0 | 1-0 | 4 | Collins 1 | 2683 |
| 12 | 13 | H | Coventry C | D 2-2 | 0-2 | 6 | Roberts 77, Collins 80 | 9808 |
| 13 | 20 | H | Scunthorpe U | D 1-1 | 1-0 | 6 | Collins 18 | 7388 |
| 14 | 23 | A | Crewe Alex | L 1-2 | 1-2 | 7 | De Vita 25 | 4010 |
| 15 | 27 | A | Stevenage | W 4-0 | 3-0 | 7 | De Vita 17, Ritchie 31, Storey 38, Rooney, A 62 | 4518 |
| 16 | Nov 6 | H | Sheffield U | D 0-0 | 0-0 | 7 | | 8354 |
| 17 | 10 | A | Walsall | W 2-0 | 1-0 | 6 | Ferry 1, Ritchie 62 | 4139 |
| 18 | 17 | H | Yeovil T | W 4-1 | 3-1 | 3 | Williams 24, Collins 2 28, 90, Ward 43 | 8112 |
| 19 | 20 | H | Brentford | L 0-1 | 0-0 | 6 | | 7431 |
| 20 | 24 | A | Notts Co | L 0-1 | 0-1 | 8 | | 6383 |
| 21 | Dec 8 | H | Doncaster R | D 1-1 | 1-1 | 8 | Ritchie 8 | 7700 |
| 22 | 15 | A | Oldham Ath | W 2-0 | 2-0 | 7 | De Vita 2 28, 31 | 3345 |
| 23 | 21 | H | Tranmere R | W 5-0 | 4-0 | 5 | Hollands 4, De Vita 7, Williams 2 21, 51, Ritchie 33 | 8885 |
| 24 | Jan 1 | A | Portsmouth | W 5-0 | 0-0 | 5 | Collins 4 61, 66, 73, 83, Hollands 69 | 11,381 |
| 25 | 5 | H | Carlisle U | W 4-0 | 2-0 | 5 | Williams 2 16, 55, Collins 36, De Vita 80 | 9162 |
| 26 | 12 | A | Bournemouth | D 1-1 | 0-1 | 5 | Williams 85 | 8777 |
| 27 | 19 | H | Shrewsbury T | W 2-0 | 0-0 | 3 | Martin (pen) 49, Williams 53 | 7754 |
| 28 | 29 | A | Leyton Orient | D 0-0 | 0-0 | 3 | | 3536 |
| 29 | Feb 2 | H | Crawley T | D 1-1 | 0-1 | 4 | Rooney, A (pen) 59 | 3558 |
| 30 | 5 | A | Colchester U | W 1-0 | 0-0 | 3 | Collins 53 | 3214 |
| 31 | 9 | H | Hartlepool U | D 1-1 | 1-0 | 3 | Ferry 15 | 9973 |
| 32 | 19 | A | Tranmere R | W 3-1 | 0-0 | 1 | Collins 48, Roberts 2 71, 90 | 5223 |
| 33 | 23 | H | Preston NE | D 1-1 | 0-0 | 2 | Rooney, A 75 | 9145 |
| 34 | 26 | H | Bury | L 0-1 | 0-1 | 4 | | 7508 |
| 35 | Mar 2 | A | Coventry C | W 2-1 | 0-1 | 3 | Williams 86, Ward 90 | 14,280 |
| 36 | 9 | H | Walsall | D 2-2 | 1-1 | 3 | Williams 11, Ferry 79 | 8407 |
| 37 | 12 | A | Brentford | L 1-2 | 1-0 | 4 | Ferry 32 | 5867 |
| 38 | 19 | A | Yeovil T | W 2-0 | 0-0 | 3 | Rooney, A (pen) 77, Collins 90 | 5207 |
| 39 | 23 | H | Notts Co | D 0-0 | 0-0 | 2 | | 8415 |
| 40 | 29 | H | Oldham Ath | D 1-1 | 0-0 | 4 | Rooney, A 71 | 10,040 |
| 41 | Apr 1 | A | Doncaster R | L 0-1 | 0-0 | 5 | | 8106 |
| 42 | 9 | A | Milton Keynes D | L 0-2 | 0-0 | 6 | | 8608 |
| 43 | 13 | A | Sheffield U | L 0-2 | 0-1 | 6 | | 19,298 |
| 44 | 16 | H | Crewe Alex | W 4-1 | 3-0 | 6 | Rooney, A 2 5, 25, Luongo 18, Collins 71 | 7169 |
| 45 | 20 | H | Stevenage | W 3-0 | 1-0 | 5 | Flint 2 22, 73, Roberts 53 | 9515 |
| 46 | 27 | A | Scunthorpe U | L 1-3 | 0-0 | 6 | Collins 83 | 6020 |

**Final League Position: 6**

### GOALSCORERS

*League (72):* Collins 15, Williams 11, Ritchie 9, Rooney, A 9 (2 pens), De Vita 8, Ferry 5, Roberts 4, Flint 2, Hollands 2, Ward 2, Benson 1, Luongo 1, Martin 1 (1 pen), Miller 1, Storey 1.
*FA Cup (0).*
*Capital One Cup (12):* Collins 3, Benson 2, Navarro 2, Storey 2, Archibald-Henville 1, Flint 1, Williams 1.
*Johnstone's Paint Trophy (0).*
*League One Play-Offs (4):* Devera 1, Flint 1, Luongo 1, Rooney A 1.

| Foderingham W 46 | Devera J 23 + 2 | McCormack A 38 + 2 | Archibald-Henville T 3 + 2 | McEveley J 27 + 1 | Ritchie M 26 + 1 | Miller T 28 + 6 | Navarro A 12 + 5 | De Vita R 24 + 12 | Benson P 6 + 3 | Williams A 38 + 2 | Rooney L 1 + 10 | Ferry S 32 + 10 | Collins J 27 + 18 | Flint A 28 + 1 | Storey M 2 + 6 | Bedwell L — + 1 | Bostock J 6 + 2 | Bessone F 4 + 1 | Rooney A 11 + 18 | Ward D 39 | Roberts G 29 + 10 | Coke G 1 + 3 | Thompson N 23 + 3 | Thompson L 2 + 2 | Martin C 6 + 6 | Hollands D 8 + 2 | Luongo M 7 | Parrett D 3 | Byrne N 6 + 1 | Francis M — + 2 | Waldon C — + 1 | *Match No.* |
|---|---|---|---|---|---|---|---|---|---|---|---|---|---|---|---|---|---|---|---|---|---|---|---|---|---|---|---|---|---|---|---|---|
| 1 | 2 | 3 | 4 | 5 | 6 | 7 | $8^{2}$ | $9^{1}$ | $10^{3}$ | 11 | 12 | 13 | 14 | | | | | | | | | | | | | | | | | | | 1 |
| 1 | 2 | 4 | | 5 | 6 | $8^{3}$ | 12 | $9^{1}$ | 13 | $11^{2}$ | 14 | 7 | 10 | 3 | | | | | | | | | | | | | | | | | | 2 |
| 1 | 2 | 4 | | 5 | 6 | 8 | 12 | $9^{1}$ | | 11 | | 7 | $10^{2}$ | 3 | 13 | | | | | | | | | | | | | | | | | 3 |
| $1^{1}$ | 2 | 4 | | 5 | | 7 | $8^{3}$ | 6 | | 10 | $9^{2}$ | 14 | 11 | 3 | | 12 | 13 | | | | | | | | | | | | | | | 4 |
| 1 | 2 | 4 | | | 6 | 8 | $7^{1}$ | 9 | 14 | $11^{3}$ | | 12 | $10^{2}$ | 3 | | | | 5 | 13 | | | | | | | | | | | | | 5 |
| 1 | 2 | 3 | | 5 | 6 | 8 | | | $9^{2}$ | 11 | | $7^{3}$ | 13 | | | | | | $10^{1}$ | 4 | 12 | 14 | | | | | | | | | | 6 |
| 1 | | 3 | | $5^{3}$ | 6 | 7 | $8^{2}$ | | | 11 | | | $10^{1}$ | | | | | 14 | 12 | 4 | 9 | 13 | 2 | | | | | | | | | 7 |
| 1 | | 3 | | 5 | 6 | 8 | $7^{2}$ | | | $10^{3}$ | | 13 | $11^{1}$ | | | | | | 12 | 4 | 9 | 14 | 2 | | | | | | | | | 8 |
| 1 | | 4 | | 5 | 6 | 13 | | $9^{1}$ | | 10 | | 8 | $11^{3}$ | | | | | 2 | 14 | 3 | 12 | $7^{2}$ | | | | | | | | | | 9 |
| 1 | | 4 | 3 | 5 | 6 | 8 | $7^{2}$ | $9^{3}$ | $10^{1}$ | 11 | | 13 | 12 | | | | | 2 | 14 | | | | | | | | | | | | | 10 |
| 1 | 14 | | | 5 | 6 | 7 | | | 13 | $11^{1}$ | | 8 | $10^{2}$ | 3 | | | | 9 | 12 | 4 | | | $2^{3}$ | | | | | | | | | 11 |
| 1 | | | | 5 | $6^{3}$ | 8 | 14 | | $11^{2}$ | | | 7 | 13 | 3 | | | $10^{1}$ | | 12 | 4 | 9 | | 2 | | | | | | | | | 12 |
| 1 | | 12 | 13 | 5 | 6 | 8 | | | $11^{1}$ | | | 7 | $10^{3}$ | 3■ | | | | | 14 | 4 | 9 | | $2^{2}$ | | | | | | | | | 13 |
| 1 | 2 | 3 | 4 | 5 | 13 | 7 | | $6^{2}$ | | | | 8 | 11 | | 12 | | | | $10^{1}$ | | 9 | | | | | | | | | | | 14 |
| 1 | 4 | 7 | | | $11^{1}$ | 2 | | 8 | $10^{3}$ | | | 14 | | 5 | $6^{2}$ | | 9 | | 13 | 3 | 12 | | | | | | | | | | | 15 |
| 1 | 4 | | 14 | 5 | 6 | | | 12 | | 11 | | 7 | $10^{2}$ | | 13 | | | | | 3 | $9^{1}$ | | 2 | $8^{3}$ | | | | | | | | 16 |
| 1 | 4 | | | 5 | 6 | | | 13 | | 11 | | 7 | $10^{1}$ | | 12 | | $8^{3}$ | | | 3 | $9^{2}$ | | 2 | 14 | | | | | | | | 17 |
| 1 | 4 | 2 | | 5 | 6 | | | 14 | | $11^{1}$ | | 7 | 10 | | | | $8^{2}$ | | | 3 | $9^{3}$ | | | | 12 | 13 | | | | | | 18 |
| 1 | 3 | | | 5 | 6 | | | | | | | $7^{2}$ | $10^{1}$ | | 12 | | 13 | | 14 | 4 | $9^{3}$ | | 2 | | 11 | 8 | | | | | | 19 |
| 1 | 3 | 2 | | 5 | 6 | | | $9^{3}$ | | 11 | | 7 | $10^{2}$ | | | | $8^{1}$ | | | 4 | 14 | | | | 13 | 12 | | | | | | 20 |
| 1 | 5 | | | | 6 | | | $9^{3}$ | | 10 | | 13 | 12 | 3 | | | 7 | | | 4 | 14 | | | 2 | $11^{1}$ | $8^{2}$ | | | | | | 21 |
| 1 | 3 | 5 | | | 6 | 14 | | $9^{1}$ | | 10 | | $7^{3}$ | 13 | | | | | | | 4 | 12 | | 2 | | $11^{2}$ | 8 | | | | | | 22 |
| 1 | 3 | 5 | | | 6 | 12 | | $9^{2}$ | | $10^{3}$ | | $7^{1}$ | 14 | | | | | | | 4 | 13 | | 2 | | 11 | 8 | | | | | | 23 |
| 1 | 3 | 5 | | | 6 | $7^{2}$ | | $9^{1}$ | | 10 | | 13 | 14 | | | | | | | 4 | 12 | | 2 | | $11^{3}$ | 8 | | | | | | 24 |
| 1 | 3 | 5 | | | $6^{2}$ | 14 | | 13 | | $11^{1}$ | | $7^{3}$ | 10 | | | | | | | 4 | 9 | | 2 | | 12 | 8 | | | | | | 25 |
| 1 | 3 | 5 | | | 9 | $7^{3}$ | | 13 | | 11 | | 14 | $10^{1}$ | | | | | | | 4 | $6^{2}$ | | 2 | | 12 | 8 | | | | | | 26 |
| 1 | | $5^{3}$ | | 14 | 6 | 12 | | | | 10 | | 7 | 13 | 3 | | | | | | 4 | 9 | | 2 | | $11^{2}$ | $8^{1}$ | | | | | | 27 |
| 1 | $3^{1}$ | 5 | | | 6 | 7 | | $9^{3}$ | | 11 | | 8 | $10^{2}$ | 12 | | | | | | 4 | 14 | | 2 | | 13 | | | | | | | 28 |
| 1 | | 7 | | $5^{1}$ | | 8 | | 11 | | 9 | | 2 | $10^{2}$ | 3 | | | | | 12 | 4 | $6^{3}$ | | 13 | | 14 | | | | | | | 29 |
| 1 | | 14 | | 5 | | 8 | $7^{2}$ | $9^{1}$ | | 11 | | 13 | 12 | 3 | | | | | $10^{3}$ | 4 | 6 | | 2 | | | | | | | | | 30 |
| 1 | | 5 | | | | 8 | | 9 | | $10^{2}$ | | 7 | 12 | 3 | 13 | | | | $11^{1}$ | 4 | 6 | | 2 | | | | | | | | | 31 |
| 1 | | 2 | | 5 | | 8 | 13 | $6^{3}$ | | 12 | | $7^{2}$ | 10 | 3 | $11^{1}$ | | | | | 4 | 9 | | 14 | | | | | | | | | 32 |
| 1 | | 2 | | 5 | | 8 | 12 | $9^{2}$ | | 11 | | $7^{1}$ | 10 | 3 | | | | | 13 | 4 | 6 | | | | | | | | | | | 33 |
| 1 | | 2 | | 5 | | 8 | $7^{1}$ | $9^{2}$ | | 11 | 14 | | 10 | 3 | | | | | 13 | 4 | $6^{3}$ | | 12 | | | | | | | | | 34 |
| 1 | | 2 | | 5 | | 7 | | 14 | | 11 | 12 | $8^{1}$ | $10^{2}$ | 4 | | | | | 13 | 3 | $6^{3}$ | | 9 | | | | | | | | | 35 |
| 1 | 14 | 7 | | 5 | | 8 | | 13 | | 11 | | 6 | $10^{1}$ | 3 | | | | | 12 | 4 | $9^{2}$ | | $2^{3}$ | | | | | | | | | 36 |
| 1 | | 6 | | 5 | | $8^{2}$ | | 14 | | $10^{3}$ | 12 | 7 | 13 | 3 | | | | | 11 | 4 | $9^{1}$ | | 2 | | | | | | | | | 37 |
| 1 | | 9 | | 5 | | 7 | | 13 | | $11^{3}$ | 14 | $8^{1}$ | 12 | 4 | | | | | 6 | 3 | $10^{2}$ | | 2 | | | | | | | | | 38 |
| 1 | | 5 | | | | $9^{1}$ | 7 | 14 | | 6 | | 8 | 13 | 3 | | | | | $11^{3}$ | 4 | $10^{2}$ | | 2 | 12 | | | | | | | | 39 |
| 1 | | 5 | | | | | 7 | | | $10^{3}$ | | 6 | 14 | 3 | | | | | 13 | 4 | $11^{2}$ | | $2^{1}$ | | | | 8 | 9 | 12 | | | 40 |
| 1 | | 5 | | | | | $8^{1}$ | 13 | | | | 9 | 11 | 3 | | | | | 6 | 4 | 12 | | | | | | 7 | $10^{2}$ | 2 | | | 41 |
| 1 | | 5 | | | | | $7^{1}$ | 13 | | 10 | | 6 | 12 | 4 | | | | | 14 | 3 | $11^{2}$ | | | | | | 8 | $9^{3}$ | 2 | | | 42 |
| 1 | | 5 | | | | | | $9^{1}$ | | 11 | 13 | 8 | $10^{3}$ | 4 | | | | | 12 | 3 | $6^{2}$ | | | | | | 7 | | 2 | 14 | | 43 |
| 1 | 5 | 7 | | | | | | | | $10^{2}$ | 14 | $6^{1}$ | 12 | 3 | | | | | $11^{3}$ | 4 | 9 | | | | | | 8 | | 2 | 13 | | 44 |
| 1 | 2 | 7 | | | | | | 6 | | $10^{3}$ | 13 | | 12 | 3 | | | | | $11^{1}$ | 4 | $9^{2}$ | | | | | | 8 | | 5 | | 14 | 45 |
| 1 | 2 | 7 | | | | 13 | | $6^{2}$ | | 12 | 14 | | 11 | 3 | | | | | $10^{1}$ | 4 | $9^{3}$ | | | | | | 8 | | 5 | | | 46 |

**FA Cup**

| | | | |
|---|---|---|---|
| First Round | Macclesfield T | (h) | 0-2 |

**Capital One Cup**

| | | | |
|---|---|---|---|
| First Round | Brighton & HA | (h) | 3-0 |
| Second Round | Stoke C | (a) | 4-3 |
| Third Round | Burnley | (h) | 3-1 |
| Fourth Round | Aston Villa | (h) | 2-3 |

**Johnstone's Paint Trophy**

| | | | |
|---|---|---|---|
| First Round | Oxford U | (a) | 0-1 |

**League One Play-Offs**

| | | | |
|---|---|---|---|
| Semi-Finals | Brentford | (h) | 1-1 |
| | Brentford | (a) | 3-3 |

*(aet; lost 4-5 on pens)*

# TORQUAY UNITED

## FOUNDATION

The idea of establishing a Torquay club was agreed by old boys of Torquay College and Torbay College, while sitting in Princess Gardens listening to the band. A proper meeting was subsequently held at Tor Abbey Hotel at which officers were elected. This was on 1 May 1899 and the club's first competition was the Eastern League (later known as the East Devon League). As an amateur club it played at Teignmouth Road, Torquay Recreation Ground and Cricket Field Road before settling down for four years at Torquay Cricket Ground where the rugby club now plays. They became Torquay United in 1921 after merging with Babbacombe FC.

*Plainmoor, Torquay, Devon TQ1 3PS.*

*Telephone:* (01803) 328 666 (option 0).

*Fax:* (01803) 323 976.

*Ticket Office:* (01803) 328 666 (option 0).

*Website:* www.torquayunited.com

*Email:* reception@torquayunited.com

*Ground Capacity:* 6,145.

*Record Attendance:* 21,908 v Huddersfield T, FA Cup 4th rd, 29 January 1955.

*Pitch Measurements:* 100m × 67m (110yd × 74yd)

*Chairman:* Simon Baker.

*Manager Director:* Bill Phillips.

*Manager:* Alan Knill.

*Assistant Manager:* Shaun Taylor.

*Physio:* Damian Davey.

*Colours:* Yellow shirts with blue trim, yellow shorts, yellow socks.

*Year Formed:* 1899.

*Turned Professional:* 1921.

*Previous Name:* 1910, Torquay Town; 1921, Torquay United.

*Club Nickname:* 'The Gulls'.

*Grounds:* 1899, Teignmouth Road; 1900, Torquay Recreation Ground; 1904, Cricket Field Road; 1906, Torquay Cricket Ground; 1910, Plainmoor Ground.

*First Football League Game:* 27 August 1927, Division 3 (S), v Exeter C (h) D 1–1 – Millsom; Cook, Smith; Wellock, Wragg, Connor, Mackey, Turner (1), Jones, McGovern, Thomson.

*Record League Victory:* 9–0 v Swindon T, Division 3 (S), 8 March 1952 – George Webber; Topping, Ralph Calland; Brown, Eric Webber, Towers; Shaw (1), Marchant (1), Tommy Northcott (2), Collins (3), Edds (2).

## HONOURS

**Football League – Division 3 (S):** *Runners-up* 1956–57.

**FA Cup:** Best season: 4th rd, 1949, 1955, 1971, 1983, 1990, 2009, 2011.

**Football League Cup:** never past 3rd rd.

**Sherpa Van Trophy:** *Runners-up* 1989.

## sky SPORTS FACT FILE

Torquay United struggled badly in their inaugural Football League season. They played their first-ever away game at Millwall on 29 August 1927 going down by a 9-1 margin, and finished the campaign bottom of the Division Three South table.

*Record Cup Victory:* 7–1 v Northampton T, FA Cup 1st rd, 14 November 1959 – Gill; Penford, Downs; Bettany, George Northcott, Rawson; Baxter, Cox, Tommy Northcott (1), Bond (3), Pym (3).

*Record Defeat:* 2–10 v Fulham, Division 3 (S), 7 September 1931; 2–10 v Luton T, Division 3 (S), 2 September 1933.

*Most League Points (2 for a win):* 60, Division 4, 1959–60.

*Most League Points (3 for a win):* 81, Division 3, 2003–04.

*Most League Goals:* 89, Division 3 (S), 1956–57.

*Highest League Scorer in Season:* Sammy Collins, 40, Division 3 (S), 1955–56.

*Most League Goals in Total Aggregate:* Sammy Collins, 204, 1948–58.

*Most League Goals in One Match:* 5, Robin Stubbs v Newport Co, Division 4, 19 October 1963.

*Most Capped Player:* Tony Bedeau, 4, Grenada.

*Most League Appearances:* Dennis Lewis, 443, 1947–59.

*Youngest League Player:* David Byng, 16 years 36 days v Walsall, 14 August 1993.

*Record Transfer Fee Received:* £650,000 from Crewe Alex for Rodney Jack, June 1998.

*Record Transfer Fee Paid:* £75,000 to Peterborough U for Leon Constantine, December 2004.

*Football League Record:* 1927 Elected to Division 3 (S); 1958–60 Division 4; 1960–62 Division 3; 1962–66 Division 4; 1966–72 Division 3; 1972–91 Division 4; 1991–2004 Division 3; 2004–05 FL 1; 2005–07 FL 2; 2007–09 Blue Square Pr; 2009– FL 2.

## LATEST SEQUENCES

*Longest Sequence of League Wins:* 8, 24.1.1998 – 3.3.1998.

*Longest Sequence of League Defeats:* 8, 30.9.1995 – 18.11.1995.

*Longest Sequence of League Draws:* 8, 25.10.1969 – 13.12.1969.

*Longest Sequence of Unbeaten League Matches:* 15, 5.5.1990 – 3.11.1990.

*Longest Sequence Without a League Win:* 19, 23.9.2006 – 20.1.2007.

*Successive Scoring Runs:* 19 from 3.10.1953.

*Successive Non-scoring Runs:* 7 from 8.1.1972.

## MANAGERS

Percy Mackrill 1927–29
A. H. Hoskins 1929
*(Secretary-Manager)*
Frank Womack 1929–32
Frank Brown 1932–38
Alf Steward 1938–40
Billy Butler 1945–46
Jack Butler 1946–47
John McNeil 1947–50
Bob John 1950
Alex Massie 1950–51
Eric Webber 1951–65
Frank O'Farrell 1965–68
Alan Brown 1969–71
Jack Edwards 1971–73
Malcolm Musgrove 1973–76
Frank O'Farrell 1976–77
Mike Green 1977–81
Frank O'Farrell 1981–82
*(continued as General Manager to 1983)*
Bruce Rioch 1982–84
Dave Webb 1984–85
John Sims 1985
Stuart Morgan 1985–87
Cyril Knowles 1987–89
Dave Smith 1989–91
John Impey 1991
Ivan Golac 1992
Paul Compton 1992–93
Don O'Riordan 1993–95
Eddie May 1995–96
Kevin Hodges *(Head Coach)* 1996–98
Wes Saunders 1998–2001
Roy McFarland 2001–02
Leroy Rosenior 2002–06
Ian Atkins 2006
John Cornforth 2006
Lubos Kubik 2006–07
Keith Curle 2007
Leroy Rosenior 2007
Paul Buckle 2007–11
Martin Ling 2011–13
Alan Knill May 2013–

## TEN YEAR LEAGUE RECORD

| | | P | W | D | L | F | A | Pts | Pos |
|---|---|---|---|---|---|---|---|---|---|
| 2003-04 | Div 3 | 46 | 23 | 12 | 11 | 68 | 44 | 81 | 3 |
| 2004-05 | FL 1 | 46 | 12 | 15 | 19 | 55 | 79 | 51 | 21 |
| 2005-06 | FL 2 | 46 | 13 | 13 | 20 | 53 | 66 | 52 | 20 |
| 2006-07 | FL 2 | 46 | 7 | 14 | 25 | 36 | 63 | 35 | 24 |
| 2007-08 | BSP | 46 | 26 | 8 | 12 | 83 | 57 | 86 | 3 |
| 2008-09 | BSP | 46 | 23 | 14 | 9 | 72 | 47 | 83 | 4 |
| 2009-10 | FL 2 | 46 | 14 | 15 | 17 | 64 | 55 | 57 | 17 |
| 2010-11 | FL 2 | 46 | 17 | 18 | 11 | 74 | 53 | 68* | 7 |
| 2011-12 | FL 2 | 46 | 23 | 12 | 11 | 63 | 50 | 81 | 5 |
| 2012-13 | FL 2 | 46 | 13 | 14 | 19 | 55 | 62 | 53 | 19 |

*1 pt deducted.

## DID YOU KNOW ?

Torquay United were undefeated at home during the 1956-57 season, winning 19 of the 23 games and scoring 71 goals. They finished the campaign as runners-up in Division Three South on goal average to Ipswich Town and with only the champions moving up missed out on promotion.

## TORQUAY UNITED – FOOTBALL LEAGUE TWO 2012–13 LEAGUE RECORD

| Match No. | Date | Venue | Opponents | Result | H/T Score | Lg Pos. | Goalscorers | Attendance |
|---|---|---|---|---|---|---|---|---|
| 1 | Aug 18 | A | Fleetwood T | D | 0-0 | 0-0 | | 3624 |
| 2 | 21 | H | Cheltenham T | D | 2-2 | 2-1 | 15 | Downes [22], Howe [23] | 2517 |
| 3 | 25 | H | Rochdale | W | 4-2 | 2-1 | 8 | Bodin [12], Downes [34], Howe 2 [60,68] | 2731 |
| 4 | Sept 1 | A | Port Vale | D | 1-1 | 1-0 | 11 | Morris [39] | 4721 |
| 5 | 8 | H | Plymouth Arg | D | 0-0 | 0-0 | 11 | | 4932 |
| 6 | 15 | A | Rotherham U | L | 0-1 | 0-1 | 17 | | 7405 |
| 7 | 18 | A | AFC Wimbledon | W | 1-0 | 1-0 | 12 | Howe [34] | 3350 |
| 8 | 22 | H | Burton Alb | D | 1-1 | 1-0 | 14 | Howe [18] | 2438 |
| 9 | 29 | A | Chesterfield | D | 1-1 | 0-0 | 15 | Howe [52] | 5117 |
| 10 | Oct 2 | H | Aldershot T | W | 4-3 | 0-2 | 9 | Bodin [48], Jarvis [69], Yeoman [84], Howe [89] | 2358 |
| 11 | 6 | A | Wycombe W | L | 1-2 | 1-1 | 11 | Howe [42] | 4205 |
| 12 | 13 | H | Accrington S | W | 3-1 | 1-0 | 10 | Howe (pen) [5], Bodin [67], Mansell [80] | 2474 |
| 13 | 20 | A | Bristol R | L | 2-3 | 0-2 | 10 | Howe [53], Downes [59] | 6331 |
| 14 | 23 | H | Gillingham | W | 2-1 | 0-0 | 8 | Craig [56], Nicholson [85] | 2251 |
| 15 | 27 | H | Morecambe | W | 1-0 | 1-0 | 7 | Stevens [30] | 2457 |
| 16 | Nov 6 | A | Barnet | L | 0-1 | 0-0 | 7 | | 1544 |
| 17 | 10 | A | Oxford U | D | 0-0 | 0-0 | 8 | | 5773 |
| 18 | 17 | H | Southend U | L | 1-4 | 0-3 | 12 | Jarvis [52] | 2449 |
| 19 | 24 | A | York C | W | 2-0 | 1-0 | 13 | Stevens [10], Oastler [61] | 3174 |
| 20 | Dec 1 | H | Dagenham & R | W | 2-1 | 1-0 | 8 | Stevens [36], Ogogo (og) [80] | 2069 |
| 21 | 8 | A | Bradford C | L | 0-1 | 0-0 | 10 | | 9347 |
| 22 | 15 | H | Northampton T | D | 1-1 | 0-0 | 11 | Jarvis [62] | 2302 |
| 23 | 26 | A | Plymouth Arg | D | 1-1 | 0-0 | 12 | Downes [78] | 10,003 |
| 24 | Jan 1 | H | AFC Wimbledon | L | 2-3 | 1-2 | 15 | Mansell [9], Howe [90] | 2618 |
| 25 | 12 | A | Burton Alb | L | 1-2 | 1-0 | 16 | Jarvis [43] | 2356 |
| 26 | 15 | H | Exeter C | D | 1-1 | 1-0 | 16 | Howe (pen) [15] | 4476 |
| 27 | 28 | A | Exeter C | W | 1-0 | 1-0 | 13 | Howe (pen) [17] | 4824 |
| 28 | Feb 2 | A | Cheltenham T | L | 1-2 | 0-1 | 16 | Howe [88] | 2961 |
| 29 | 9 | H | Fleetwood T | L | 0-1 | 0-1 | 17 | | 2207 |
| 30 | 12 | H | Rotherham U | L | 1-3 | 0-0 | 18 | Bodin (pen) [90] | 1178 |
| 31 | 16 | H | Rochdale | L | 0-1 | 0-1 | 19 | | 2351 |
| 32 | 19 | A | Aldershot T | L | 0-1 | 0-0 | 19 | | 2095 |
| 33 | 23 | H | Port Vale | L | 0-1 | 0-1 | 19 | | 2679 |
| 34 | 26 | H | Wycombe W | L | 1-2 | 1-0 | 20 | Jarvis [37] | 1793 |
| 35 | Mar 2 | A | Accrington S | D | 0-0 | 0-0 | 20 | | 1197 |
| 36 | 9 | H | Oxford U | L | 1-3 | 0-0 | 22 | Downes [58] | 2504 |
| 37 | 12 | A | Dagenham & R | D | 2-2 | 0-1 | 22 | Labadie [71], Howe (pen) [89] | 1227 |
| 38 | 16 | A | Southend U | D | 1-1 | 1-1 | 20 | Labadie [45] | 4891 |
| 39 | 19 | H | Chesterfield | W | 2-1 | 2-0 | 19 | Labadie [2], Howe [8] | 2047 |
| 40 | 23 | H | York C | W | 2-1 | 2-0 | 19 | Benyon [6], Jarvis [23] | 2871 |
| 41 | 29 | A | Northampton T | L | 0-1 | 0-0 | 19 | | 5166 |
| 42 | Apr 1 | H | Bradford C | L | 1-3 | 1-2 | 21 | Labadie [3] | 2569 |
| 43 | 6 | A | Gillingham | L | 0-1 | 0-0 | 22 | | 7574 |
| 44 | 16 | H | Barnet | W | 3-2 | 1-0 | 20 | Benyon [25], Bodin [60], Saah [71] | 2722 |
| 45 | 20 | A | Morecambe | W | 2-0 | 1-0 | 18 | Drummond (og) [28], Yeoman [69] | 2033 |
| 46 | 27 | H | Bristol R | D | 3-3 | 0-1 | 19 | Benyon 2 [52,68], Jarvis [62] | 5666 |

**Final League Position: 19**

### GOALSCORERS

*League (55):* Howe 16 (4 pens), Jarvis 7, Bodin 5 (1 pen), Downes 5, Benyon 4, Labadie 4, Stevens 3, Mansell 2, Yeoman 2, Craig 1, Morris 1, Nicholson 1, Oastler 1, Saah 1, own goals 2.
*FA Cup (0).*
*Capital One Cup (0).*
*Johnstone's Paint Trophy (2):* Jarvis 2.

| Poke M 43 | Oastler J 37 + 1 | Downes A 38 | Saah B 43 | Nicholson K 41 + 1 | Mansell L 42 | Lathrope D 21 + 7 | Morris I 9 + 2 | Bodin B 40 + 3 | Howe R 42 | Cruise T 6 + 10 | Macklin L 3 + 13 | Easton C 18 + 3 | Jarvis R 26 + 12 | Thompson N 3 + 15 | Craig N 28 + 2 | Mackenzie K 1 | Leadbitter D 9 + 4 | Stevens D 15 + 8 | Yeoman A 4 + 9 | Rice M 3 + 2 | Halpin S — + 2 | MacDonald A 10 + 4 | Benyon E 12 + 3 | Labadie J 7 | Chapell J 5 + 1 | Match No. |
|---|---|---|---|---|---|---|---|---|---|---|---|---|---|---|---|---|---|---|---|---|---|---|---|---|---|---|
| 1 | 2 | 3 | 4 | 5 | 6 | 7 | 8 | 9 | 10 | $11^1$ | 12 | | | | | | | | | | | | | | | 1 |
| 1 | 2 | 4 | 3 | 5 | 8 | $6^1$ | 9 | 10 | $11^3$ | 13 | $7^2$ | 12 | 14 | | | | | | | | | | | | | 2 |
| 1 | 2 | 4* | 3 | 5 | 7 | | | 9 | $10^3$ | $11^2$ | 12 | 6 | 13 | $8^1$ | 14 | | | | | | | | | | | 3 |
| 1 | 2 | | 4 | 5 | 7 | 6 | | $10^3$ | $9^2$ | 14 | 13 | $11^1$ | | | 8 | | 3 | 12 | | | | | | | | 4 |
| 1 | 2 | 4 | 3 | 5 | 8 | $7^2$ | 9 | | 11 | 13 | | 12 | | | 6 | | $10^1$ | | | | | | | | | 5 |
| 1 | 2 | 3 | 4 | 5 | 8 | | | 9 | 10 | 13 | | 12 | | | $6^1$ | | $11^2$ | | | | | | | | | 6 |
| 1 | 2 | 3 | 4 | 5 | 6 | | 8 | 9 | 10 | | | 7 | 12 | | 11 | | | | | | | | | | | 7 |
| 1 | 2 | 3 | 4 | 5 | 7 | | 8 | $9^2$ | 11 | | | 6 | 13 | | | | $10^1$ | 12 | | | | | | | | 8 |
| 1 | 2 | 3 | 4 | 5 | 7 | | | 9 | 11 | 12 | | $6^2$ | 13 | $8^1$ | 14 | | $10^3$ | | | | | | | | | 9 |
| 1 | 2 | 3 | 4 | 5 | 8 | | | 10 | 11 | 12 | | | $7^2$ | | 6 | | $9^1$ | 13 | | | | | | | | 10 |
| 1 | 2 | 3 | 4 | 5 | 7 | | | $10^3$ | 11 | | | $8^2$ | 13 | $9^1$ | 6 | | 12 | | 14 | | | | | | | 11 |
| 1 | 2 | 4 | 3 | 5 | 6 | 7 | | 9 | 11 | 14 | $12^3$ | | 13 | $8^2$ | | | $10^1$ | | | | | | | | | 12 |
| 1 | 2* | 4 | 5 | 3 | 7 | $6^1$ | | $9^2$ | 11 | 14 | | 8 | 13 | | | | $10^3$ | 12 | | | | | | | | 13 |
| 1 | | 4 | 3 | 5 | 7 | 6 | | 10 | 11 | 12 | | 8 | | | $2^1$ | | 9 | | | | | | | | | 14 |
| 1 | | 3 | 4 | 5 | 7 | 6 | | $9^1$ | $11^3$ | 13 | 14 | 12 | | 8 | 2 | | $10^2$ | | | | | | | | | 15 |
| $1^1$ | 2 | 3 | 4 | 5 | 9 | $8^3$ | | 10 | 11 | | | $6^2$ | 14 | | 7 | | 13 | 12 | | | | | | | | 16 |
| | 2 | 4 | 3 | 5 | 6 | $8^2$ | | 11 | 7 | | | $10^1$ | 9 | | 12 | 1 | | 13 | | | | | | | | 17 |
| | 2 | 3 | 4 | 5 | 7 | $6^2$ | | $10^3$ | 11 | 14 | | $8^1$ | 12 | | 13 | | 9 | | | 1 | | | | | | 18 |
| 1 | 2 | 3 | 4 | 5 | 12 | 6 | | $11^3$ | | 13 | | 7 | | $10^1$ | 8 | | $9^2$ | | 14 | | | | | | | 19 |
| 1 | 2 | 4 | 3 | 5 | | | 14 | $8^3$ | 11 | | | 6 | $9^2$ | | 12 | | 7 | $10^1$ | 13 | | | | | | | 20 |
| 1 | | 4 | 3* | 5 | | | 14 | $6^1$ | 11 | | | 7 | | $8^3$ | 12 | | 9 | $10^2$ | 2 | 13 | | | | | | 21 |
| 1 | 2 | 4 | 3 | | 6 | | | 13 | 11 | | | 9 | $10^2$ | | 12 | | 8 | $7^1$ | 5 | | | | | | | 22 |
| 1 | 2 | 4 | 5 | | $7^2$ | | 13 | $9^1$ | 11 | | | 6 | | 8 | 10 | | 12 | 3 | | | | | | | | 23 |
| 1 | 2 | 4 | 3 | | 6 | | 14 | 10 | $7^3$ | 13 | | $8^1$ | $9^2$ | | 11 | | 12 | | 5 | | | | | | | 24 |
| 1 | 2 | 4 | 3 | 5 | 7 | $6^3$ | | 12 | 11 | | | $9^2$ | 14 | 8 | | | $10^1$ | 13 | | | | | | | | 25 |
| 1 | 2 | 4 | 5 | 3 | 6 | 7 | | $9^2$ | 11 | | | $8^1$ | 12 | | | | 10 | 13 | | | | | | | | 26 |
| 1 | 2 | 4 | 3 | 5 | 7 | | 8 | $9^2$ | 11 | 13 | | 10 | | | $6^1$ | | 12 | | | | | | | | | 27 |
| 1 | $2^2$ | 4 | 3 | 5 | 7 | 6 | 8 | | 11 | 13 | | 12 | | | 9 | | $10^1$ | | | | | | | | | 28 |
| 1 | | 3 | 4 | 5 | 7 | 6 | | 9 | 11 | 13 | | $8^2$ | | | 2 | | 12 | $10^1$ | | | | | | | | 29 |
| 1 | | 3 | 4 | 5 | 7 | 6 | | 9 | 13 | | | 8 | | | $10^1$ | | 2 | | 12 | | | $11^2$ | | | | 30 |
| 1 | | $4^2$ | 3 | 5 | 7 | | | $9^3$ | 11 | 12 | | 8 | | | 10 | | $6^1$ | | 2 | | | 13 | 14 | | | 31 |
| 1 | 2 | 3 | | 5 | 6 | | 12 | 9 | 11 | | | 4 | | | 8 | | 10 | | | | | $7^1$ | | | | 32 |
| 1 | $3^1$ | 4 | 5 | | 7 | | | $9^2$ | 10 | 13 | | 8 | | | 6 | | 2 | | | | | 12 | 11 | | | 33 |
| 1 | 12 | 3 | | 5 | 7 | | | 9 | 10 | | | $8^1$ | | | 6 | | 2 | | | | | 4 | 11 | | | 34 |
| 1 | 2 | 3 | | 5 | 7 | | 8 | 9 | 10 | | | $6^1$ | | | 12 | | | | | | | 4 | 11 | | | 35 |
| 1 | 2 | 4 | 3 | 5 | 6 | | | 9 | 10 | 12 | | $7^1$ | 13 | | | | | | | | | 11 | $8^2$ | | | 36 |
| 1 | 2 | 3* | 4 | | 8 | | | 9 | 10 | | | 5 | 13 | | $6^2$ | | | | | | | 12 | $11^1$ | 7 | | 37 |
| 1 | 2 | 3 | | | 7 | | 13 | 9 | 11 | | | 5 | 12 | | $10^2$ | | | | | | | 4 | | 8 | $6^1$ | 38 |
| 1 | 2 | 3 | | | 7 | | | 10 | | | | 5 | 14 | | $6^2$ | | 12 | | 13 | | | 4 | $11^1$ | 8 | $9^3$ | 39 |
| 1 | 2 | 3 | | 12 | 7 | | 13 | 10 | | | | 5* | | | 6 | | | | | | | 4 | $11^1$ | 8 | $9^2$ | 40 |
| 1 | 2 | 3 | | 5 | 8 | | 12 | 10 | | | | 6 | | | | | | | | | | 4 | 11 | 7 | $9^1$ | 41 |
| $1^1$ | 2 | 3 | | | 8 | | | $9^3$ | 10 | | | 5 | 14 | | $6^2$ | | | | 12 | | | 4 | 11 | 7 | 13 | 42 |
| | 2 | 3 | 4 | 5 | 8 | $7^1$ | $6^3$ | 9 | 10 | | | | | | | | | 13 | 14 | 1 | | 12 | $11^2$ | | | 43 |
| 1 | 2 | 4 | 3 | 5 | 8 | 7 | 13 | 9 | 11 | | | $6^2$ | | | | | | | | | | 12 | $10^1$ | | | 44 |
| 1 | 2 | 4 | 3 | 5 | 7 | 8 | | $9^2$ | 11 | | | 6 | 13 | | | | | | | | | 12 | $10^1$ | | | 45 |
| 1 | 2 | 4 | 3 | 5 | 7 | 8 | | 9 | | | | 6 | | | | | | | | | | 10 | 11 | | | 46 |

**FA Cup**
First Round — Harrogate T — (h) — 0-1

**Capital One Cup**
First Round — Leicester C — (h) — 0-4

**Johnstone's Paint Trophy**
Second Round — Yeovil T — (h) — 2-2
*(aet; lost 4-5 on pens)*

# TOTTENHAM HOTSPUR

## FOUNDATION

The Hotspur Football Club was formed from an older cricket club in 1882. Most of the founders were old boys of St John's Presbyterian School and Tottenham Grammar School. The Casey brothers were well to the fore as the family provided the club's first goalposts (painted blue and white) and their first ball. They soon adopted the local YMCA as their meeting place, but after a couple of moves settled at the Red House, which is still their headquarters, although now known simply as 748 High Road.

*White Hart Lane, Bill Nicholson Way, 748 High Road, Tottenham, London N17 0AP.*

*Telephone:* (0844) 499 5000.

*Fax:* (020) 3544 8563.

*Ticket Office:* (0844) 844 0102.

*Website:* www.tottenhamhotspur.com

*Email:* website@tottenhamhotspur.com

*Ground Capacity:* 36,284.

*Record Attendance:* 75,038 v Sunderland, FA Cup 6th rd, 5 March 1938.

*Pitch Measurements:* 100m × 67m (109yd × 73yd)

*Chairman:* Daniel Levy.

*Head Coach:* Andre Villas-Boas.

*Assistant Head Coach:* Steffen Freund.

*Head Physio:* Geoff Scott.

*Colours:* White shirts, white shorts, white socks with black trim.

*Year Formed:* 1882. *Turned Professional:* 1895.

*Previous Name:* 1882, Hotspur Football Club; 1884, Tottenham Hotspur.

*Club Nickname:* 'Spurs'.

*Grounds:* 1882, Tottenham Marshes; 1888, Northumberland Park; 1899, White Hart Lane.

## HONOURS

**Football League – Division 1:** *Champions* 1950–51, 1960–61; *Runners-up* 1921–22, 1951–52, 1956–57, 1962–63; **Division 2:** *Champions* 1919–20, 1949–50; *Runners-up* 1908–09, 1932–33.

**FA Cup:** *Winners* 1901 (as non-League club), 1921, 1961, 1962, 1967, 1981, 1982, 1991; *Runners-up* 1987.

**Football League Cup:** *Winners* 1971, 1973, 1999, 2008; *Runners-up* 1982, 2002, 2009.

**European Competitions**
**European Cup:** 1961–62.
**Champions League:** 2010–11.
**European Cup-Winners' Cup:** 1962–63 (*winners*), 1963–64, 1967–68, 1981–82, 1982–83, 1991–92.
**UEFA Cup:** 1971–72 (*winners*), 1972–73, 1973–74 (*runners-up*), 1983–84 (*winners*), 1984–85, 1999–2000, 2006–07, 2007–08, 2008–09. **Europa League:** 2011–12, 2012–13. **Intertoto Cup:** 1995.

*First Football League Game:* 1 September 1908, Division 2, v Wolverhampton W (h) W 3–0 – Hewitson; Coquet, Burton; Morris (1), Danny Steel, Darnell; Walton, Woodward (2), Macfarlane, Bobby Steel, Middlemiss.

*Record League Victory:* 9–0 v Bristol R, Division 2, 22 October 1977 – Daines; Naylor, Holmes, Hoddle (1), McAllister, Perryman, Pratt, McNab, Moores (3), Lee (4), Taylor (1).

*Record Cup Victory:* 13–2 v Crewe Alex, FA Cup 4th rd (replay), 3 February 1960 – Brown; Hills, Henry; Blanchflower, Norman, Mackay; White, Harmer (1), Smith (4), Allen (5), Jones (3 incl. 1p).

## sky SPORTS FACT FILE

Vivian Woodward, who scored Tottenham Hotspur's first-ever Football League goal, was a full England international who captained the Great Britain team to victory in the 1908 and 1912 Olympic Games. He also worked as an architect and joined the board of directors while still a player at White Hart Lane.

**Record Defeat:** 0–8 v Cologne, UEFA Intertoto Cup, 22 July 1995.

**Most League Points (2 for a win):** 70, Division 2, 1919–20.

**Most League Points (3 for a win):** 77, Division 1, 1984–85.

**Most League Goals:** 115, Division 1, 1960–61.

**Highest League Scorer in Season:** Jimmy Greaves, 37, Division 1, 1962–63.

**Most League Goals in Total Aggregate:** Jimmy Greaves, 220, 1961–70.

**Most League Goals in One Match:** 5, Ted Harper v Reading, Division 2, 30 August 1930; 5, Alf Stokes v Birmingham C, Division 1, 18 September 1957; 5, Bobby Smith v Aston Villa, Division 1, 29 March 1958; 5, Jermain Defoe v Wigan Ath, FA Premier League, 22 November 2009.

**Most Capped Player:** Pat Jennings, 74 (119), Northern Ireland.

**Most League Appearances:** Steve Perryman, 655, 1969–86.

**Youngest League Player:** Ally Dick, 16 years 301 days v Manchester C, 20 February 1982.

**Record Transfer Fee Received:** £33,000,000 from Real Madrid for Luka Modric, August 2012.

**Record Transfer Fee Paid:** £17,000,000 to Blackburn R for David Bentley, July 2008 and £17,000,000 to Corinthians for Paulinho, July 2013.

**Football League Record:** 1908 Elected to Division 2; 1909–15 Division 1; 1919–20 Division 2; 1920–28 Division 1; 1928–33 Division 2; 1933–35 Division 1; 1935–50 Division 2; 1950–77 Division 1; 1977–78 Division 2; 1978–92 Division 1; 1992– FA Premier League.

## MANAGERS

Frank Brettell 1898–99
John Cameron 1899–1906
Fred Kirkham 1907–08
Peter McWilliam 1912–27
Billy Minter 1927–29
Percy Smith 1930–35
Jack Tresadern 1935–38
Peter McWilliam 1938–42
Arthur Turner 1942–46
Joe Hulme 1946–49
Arthur Rowe 1949–55
Jimmy Anderson 1955–58
Bill Nicholson 1958–74
Terry Neill 1974–76
Keith Burkinshaw 1976–84
Peter Shreeves 1984–86
David Pleat 1986–87
Terry Venables 1987–91
Peter Shreeves 1991–92
Doug Livermore 1992–93
Ossie Ardiles 1993–94
Gerry Francis 1994–97
Christian Gross *(Head Coach)* 1997–98
George Graham 1998–2001
Glenn Hoddle 2001–03
David Pleat *(Caretaker)* 2003–04
Jacques Santini 2004
Martin Jol 2004–07
Juande Ramos 2007–08
Harry Redknapp 2008–12
Andre Villas-Boas July 2012–

## LATEST SEQUENCES

**Longest Sequence of League Wins:** 13, 23.4.1960 – 1.10.1960.

**Longest Sequence of League Defeats:** 7, 1.1.1994 – 27.2.1994.

**Longest Sequence of League Draws:** 6, 9.1.1999 – 27.2.1999.

**Longest Sequence of Unbeaten League Matches:** 22, 31.8.1949 – 31.12.1949.

**Longest Sequence Without a League Win:** 16, 29.12.1934 – 13.4.1935.

**Successive Scoring Runs:** 32 from 24.2.1962.

**Successive Non-scoring Runs:** 6 from 28.12.1985.

## TEN YEAR LEAGUE RECORD

| | | P | W | D | L | F | A | Pts | Pos |
|---|---|---|---|---|---|---|---|---|---|
| 2003-04 | PR Lge | 38 | 13 | 6 | 19 | 47 | 57 | 45 | 14 |
| 2004-05 | PR Lge | 38 | 14 | 10 | 14 | 47 | 41 | 52 | 9 |
| 2005-06 | PR Lge | 38 | 18 | 11 | 9 | 53 | 38 | 65 | 5 |
| 2006-07 | PR Lge | 38 | 17 | 9 | 12 | 57 | 54 | 60 | 5 |
| 2007-08 | PR Lge | 38 | 11 | 13 | 14 | 66 | 61 | 46 | 11 |
| 2008-09 | PR Lge | 38 | 14 | 9 | 15 | 45 | 45 | 51 | 8 |
| 2009-10 | PR Lge | 38 | 21 | 7 | 10 | 67 | 41 | 70 | 4 |
| 2010-11 | PR Lge | 38 | 16 | 14 | 8 | 55 | 46 | 62 | 5 |
| 2011-12 | PR Lge | 38 | 20 | 9 | 9 | 66 | 41 | 69 | 4 |
| 2012-13 | PR Lge | 38 | 21 | 9 | 8 | 66 | 46 | 72 | 5 |

## DID YOU KNOW

Tottenham Hotspur's legendary manager Bill Nicholson's first game in charge of the club saw them 6-1 up at half-time against Everton in October 1958. Spurs eventually won the game 10-4 with Bobby Smith netting four goals and the other four forwards also finding the net.

## TOTTENHAM HOTSPUR – FA PREMIERSHIP 2012–13 LEAGUE RECORD

| Match No. | Date | Venue | Opponents | Result | H/T Score | Lg Pos. | Goalscorers | Atten-dance |
|---|---|---|---|---|---|---|---|---|
| 1 | Aug 18 | A | Newcastle U | L | 1-2 | 0-0 | 16 | Defoe [76] | 52,385 |
| 2 | 25 | H | WBA | D | 1-1 | 0-0 | 14 | Assou-Ekotto [74] | 36,166 |
| 3 | Sept 1 | H | Norwich C | D | 1-1 | 0-0 | 14 | Dembele [68] | 36,142 |
| 4 | 16 | A | Reading | W | 3-1 | 1-0 | 10 | Defoe 2 [18, 74], Bale [71] | 24,160 |
| 5 | 23 | H | QPR | W | 2-1 | 0-1 | 8 | Faurlin (og) [60], Defoe [61] | 36,052 |
| 6 | 29 | A | Manchester U | W | 3-2 | 2-0 | 5 | Evans (og) [2], Bale [32], Dempsey [52] | 75,566 |
| 7 | Oct 7 | H | Aston Villa | W | 2-0 | 0-0 | 5 | Caulker [58], Lennon [67] | 35,802 |
| 8 | 20 | H | Chelsea | L | 2-4 | 0-1 | 5 | Gallas [47], Defoe [54] | 36,060 |
| 9 | 28 | A | Southampton | W | 2-1 | 2-0 | 4 | Bale [15], Dempsey [39] | 31,944 |
| 10 | Nov 3 | H | Wigan Ath | L | 0-1 | 0-0 | 5 | | 35,534 |
| 11 | 11 | A | Manchester C | L | 1-2 | 1-0 | 7 | Caulker [21] | 47,208 |
| 12 | 17 | A | Arsenal | L | 2-5 | 1-3 | 8 | Adebayor [10], Bale [71] | 60,111 |
| 13 | 25 | H | West Ham U | W | 3-1 | 1-0 | 7 | Defoe 2 [44, 64], Bale [58] | 36,043 |
| 14 | 28 | H | Liverpool | W | 2-1 | 2-0 | 5 | Lennon [7], Bale [16] | 36,162 |
| 15 | Dec 1 | A | Fulham | W | 3-0 | 0-0 | 4 | Sandro [55], Defoe 2 [72, 77] | 25,426 |
| 16 | 9 | A | Everton | L | 1-2 | 0-0 | 5 | Dempsey [76] | 36,494 |
| 17 | 16 | H | Swansea C | W | 1-0 | 0-0 | 4 | Vertonghen [75] | 35,783 |
| 18 | 22 | H | Stoke C | D | 0-0 | 0-0 | 5 | | 35,702 |
| 19 | 26 | A | Aston Villa | W | 4-0 | 0-0 | 4 | Defoe [57], Bale 3 [61, 73, 84] | 36,863 |
| 20 | 29 | A | Sunderland | W | 2-1 | 0-1 | 3 | Cuellar (og) [48], Lennon [51] | 41,168 |
| 21 | Jan 1 | H | Reading | W | 3-1 | 1-1 | 3 | Dawson [9], Adebayor [51], Dempsey [79] | 36,180 |
| 22 | 12 | A | QPR | D | 0-0 | 0-0 | 4 | | 18,018 |
| 23 | 20 | H | Manchester U | D | 1-1 | 0-1 | 4 | Dempsey [90] | 35,956 |
| 24 | 30 | A | Norwich C | D | 1-1 | 0-1 | 4 | Bale [80] | 26,818 |
| 25 | Feb 3 | A | WBA | W | 1-0 | 0-0 | 4 | Bale [67] | 24,978 |
| 26 | 9 | H | Newcastle U | W | 2-1 | 1-1 | 4 | Bale 2 [5, 78] | 36,244 |
| 27 | 25 | A | West Ham U | W | 3-2 | 1-1 | 3 | Bale 2 [13, 90], Sigurdsson [76] | 35,005 |
| 28 | Mar 3 | A | Arsenal | W | 2-1 | 2-0 | 3 | Bale [37], Lennon [39] | 36,170 |
| 29 | 10 | A | Liverpool | L | 2-3 | 1-1 | 3 | Vertonghen 2 [45, 53] | 44,752 |
| 30 | 17 | H | Fulham | L | 0-1 | 0-0 | 4 | | 36,004 |
| 31 | 30 | A | Swansea C | W | 2-1 | 2-0 | 3 | Vertonghen [7], Bale [21] | 20,604 |
| 32 | Apr 7 | H | Everton | D | 2-2 | 1-1 | 4 | Adebayor [1], Sigurdsson [87] | 36,192 |
| 33 | 21 | H | Manchester C | W | 3-1 | 0-1 | 5 | Dempsey [75], Defoe [79], Bale [82] | 36,121 |
| 34 | 27 | A | Wigan Ath | D | 2-2 | 1-1 | 5 | Bale [9], Boyce (og) [90] | 22,326 |
| 35 | May 4 | H | Southampton | W | 1-0 | 0-0 | 5 | Bale [86] | 36,190 |
| 36 | 8 | A | Chelsea | D | 2-2 | 1-2 | 5 | Adebayor [26], Sigurdsson [80] | 41,581 |
| 37 | 12 | A | Stoke C | W | 2-1 | 1-1 | 5 | Dempsey [20], Adebayor [83] | 27,531 |
| 38 | 19 | H | Sunderland | W | 1-0 | 0-0 | 5 | Bale [90] | 36,063 |

**Final League Position: 5**

### GOALSCORERS

*League (66):* Bale 21, Defoe 11, Dempsey 7, Adebayor 5, Lennon 4, Vertonghen 4, Sigurdsson 3, Caulker 2, Assou-Ekotto 1, Dawson 1, Dembele 1, Gallas 1, Sandro 1, own goals 4.
*FA Cup (4):* Dempsey 3, Bale 1.
*Capital One Cup (4):* Bale 1, Sigurdsson 1, Townsend 1, Vertonghen 1.
*Europa League (19):* Defoe 4, Adebayor 3, Bale 3, Sigurdsson 3, Dempsey 2, Dawson 1, Dembele 1, Vertonghen 1, own goal 1.

| Friedel B 11 | Walker K 36 | Kaboul Y 1 | Gallas W 16 + 3 | Assou-Ekotto B 12 + 3 | Livermore J 4 + 7 | Sandro 22 | Lennon A 33 + 1 | Sigurdsson G 12 + 21 | Bale G 33 | Defoe J 27 + 7 | Van der Vaart R 1 + 1 | Kane H — + 1 | Vertonghen J 34 | Adebayor E 18 + 7 | Jenas J — + 1 | Dembele M 26 + 4 | Huddlestone T 11 + 9 | Naughton K 13 + 1 | Dempsey C 22 + 7 | Townsend A — + 5 | Caulker S 17 + 1 | Dawson M 23 + 4 | Lloris H 27 | Carroll T — + 7 | Falque I — + 1 | Parker S 15 + 6 | Holtby L 4 + 7 | Match No. |
|---|---|---|---|---|---|---|---|---|---|---|---|---|---|---|---|---|---|---|---|---|---|---|---|---|---|---|---|---|
| 1 | 2 | 3 | 4 | 5 | 6 | 7² | 8 | 9¹ | 10 | 11 | 12 | 13 | | | | | | | | | | | | | | | | 1 |
| 1 | 2 | | 3 | 5 | 6 | 7² | 8 | 13 | 10 | 11³ | 9¹ | | 4 | 12 | 14 | | | | | | | | | | | | | 2 |
| 1 | 2 | | 3 | 5 | 6 | 7¹ | 8 | 9² | 10 | 11³ | | | 4 | 13 | | 12 | 14█ | | | | | | | | | | | 3 |
| 1 | 2 | | 4 | | | 8 | 6³ | 7¹ | 10² | 11 | | | 3 | | | 9 | 12 | 5 | 13 | 14 | | | | | | | | 4 |
| 1 | 2 | | 3 | | | 7 | 6³ | 9¹ | 5 | 11 | | | 4 | 8 | | 13 | | 10² | 14 | 12 | | | | | | | | 5 |
| 1 | 2 | | 4 | | | 7 | 6 | 12 | 10 | 11 | | | 5 | 8² | | 13 | | 9¹ | | 3 | 14 | | | | | | | 6 |
| | 2 | | 3 | | | 8 | 6³ | 13 | 9 | 10¹ | | | 5 | 12 | | 7 | 11² | 14 | 4 | | | 1 | | | | | | 7 |
| 1 | 2 | | 3 | | 12 | 7 | 8 | 9 | | 11 | | | 5 | 13 | | 6¹ | | 10² | | | 4 | | | | | | | 8 |
| 1 | 2 | | 4 | | 12 | 6 | 8 | 13 | 10 | 11² | | | 5 | | | | 7¹ | 9³ | 3 | | 14 | | | | | | | 9 |
| 1 | 2³ | 3 | | | | 6¹ | 9 | 12 | 11 | 10² | | | 5 | 13 | | 7 | | 8 | | | 4 | | | 14 | | | | 10 |
| 1 | 2¹ | 3 | | | | 6 | 8³ | 9 | 13 | | | | 5 | 11² | | 7 | 14 | 10 | | | 4 | 12 | | | | | | 11 |
| | 2¹ | 3 | | | | 7 | 6 | 9 | 11 | | | | 4 | 10█ | | | 8³ | 5² | 12 | | | 13 | 1 | 14 | | | | 12 |
| | 2 | | | | 13 | 7² | 8¹ | 14 | 10 | 11³ | | | 5 | 12 | | 6 | | | 9 | | 4 | 3 | 1 | | | | | 13 |
| | 2 | | 3 | | | 7 | 6 | 12 | 9 | 11 | | | 5 | 8² | | 13 | | | 10¹ | | | 4 | 1 | | | | | 14 |
| | | 12 | | | | 8 | 6 | 13 | 9² | 10 | | | 5 | 7³ | | 2 | 11 | | | | 4 | 3¹ | 1 | 14 | | | | 15 |
| | 2 | | 3 | | | 9 | 6¹ | 13 | | 11³ | | | 5 | 10 | | 8² | 12 | | 7 | | | 4 | 1 | | | 14 | | 16 |
| | 2 | | 3 | | | 7 | 6 | 12 | | 11 | | | 4 | 10² | | 8³ | | 5 | 9¹ | 13 | | | 1 | | | 14 | | 17 |
| | 2 | | | | | 7 | 6¹ | 12 | 9 | 10 | | | 5 | 11 | | 8² | | | | | 4 | 3 | 1 | | | 13 | | 18 |
| | 2 | | 3 | | | 8 | 6 | 13 | 9³ | 10 | | | 4 | 11² | | 7¹ | | 5 | | 14 | | | 1 | | | 12 | | 19 |
| | 2 | | | | | 7 | 6² | 14 | 9³ | 11¹ | | | 10 | 8 | | 5 | 12 | | | | 4 | 3 | 1 | | | 13 | | 20 |
| | 2 | 14 | | | | 7 | 6 | 9² | | 11 | | | 4 | 10³ | | 8¹ | | 5 | 13 | | | 3 | 1 | | | 12 | | 21 |
| | 2 | | | | | 8¹ | 6³ | 14 | 9 | 11 | | | 4 | 10² | | 7 | | 5 | 13 | | | 3 | 1 | | | 12 | | 22 |
| | 2 | | 12 | | | 6 | | 9 | 11 | | | | | 8 | 13 | 5¹ | 10 | | | | 4 | 3 | 1 | | | 7² | | 23 |
| | 2 | | 5 | | | 6² | 13 | 9 | 11 | | | | 3 | 8 | | | 10¹ | | | | | 4 | 1 | | | 7 | 12 | 24 |
| | 2² | 13 | 5 | | | 6³ | 14 | 9 | 11¹ | | | | 4 | 7 | | | 10 | | | | | 3 | 1 | | | 8 | 12 | 25 |
| | 2 | | 13 | | 14 | 6 | | 11 | | | | | | | 12 | 8³ | | 5² | 10 | | 4 | 3 | 1 | | | 7 | 9¹ | 26 |
| | 2 | | | | 14 | 8 | | 12 | 9 | | | | 5 | 11 | | 7² | | | | | 4 | 3 | 1 | 13 | | 6³ | 10¹ | 27 |
| | 2 | | | 14 | 5 | 13 | 8³ | 10 | 9 | 12 | | | 4 | 11¹ | | | | 6² | | | | 3 | 1 | | | 7 | | 28 |
| | 2 | | 5² | | 7¹ | | | 10 | 8 | 11 | | | 3 | | | 9 | | | | | 4 | | 1 | 13 | | 6 | 12 | 29 |
| | 2 | | 5 | | | | 8² | | 9 | 13 | | | 6 | 10 | | 11³ | 2 | | 12 | | 4 | 3¹ | 1 | 14 | | 7 | | 30 |
| 1 | 2 | | | | | | 10 | 9² | 8 | 12 | | | 4 | 11¹ | | 7 | | 5 | | | | 3 | | | | 6 | 13 | 31 |
| | 2 | | | | | 6 | | | | | | | 5 | 11 | | 8¹ | 12 | | 10 | | 4 | 3 | 1 | 13 | | 7² | 9 | 32 |
| | 2 | | 5 | | | 6¹ | | 9 | 14 | | | | 4 | 11³ | | 7 | 13 | | 10 | | | 3 | 1 | | | 8² | 12 | 33 |
| | 2 | | 13 | | | 14 | | 8 | 11 | | | | 4 | 9¹ | | 7 | | 5² | 10 | | | 3 | 1 | | | 6³ | 12 | 34 |
| | 2 | | 5 | | | 6² | 14 | 10 | 11 | | | | 4 | 13 | | 8¹ | 7 | | 9³ | | | 3 | 1 | | | | 12 | 35 |
| | 2 | | 5 | | | 8¹ | 12 | 9 | | | | | 4 | 11 | | 7 | | | 13 | | | 3 | 1 | | | 6 | 10² | 36 |
| | 2 | | | | | 6² | 14 | 10 | 13 | | | | 5 | 11 | | 12 | 7 | | 9³ | | 4 | 3 | 1 | | | | 8¹ | 37 |
| | 2 | | 5³ | | | 6 | 14 | 10 | 13 | | | | 3 | 11 | | 12 | 8 | | 9² | | 4 | | 1 | | | | 7¹ | 38 |

**FA Cup**

| | | | |
|---|---|---|---|
| Third Round | Coventry C | (h) | 3-0 |
| Fourth Round | Leeds U | (a) | 1-2 |

**Capital One Cup**

| | | | |
|---|---|---|---|
| Third Round | Carlisle U | (a) | 3-0 |
| Fourth Round | Norwich C | (a) | 1-2 |

**Europa League**

| | | | |
|---|---|---|---|
| Group J | Lazio | (h) | 0-0 |
| | Panathinaikos | (a) | 1-1 |
| | Maribor | (a) | 1-1 |
| | Maribor | (h) | 3-1 |
| | Lazio | (a) | 0-0 |
| | Panathinaikos | (h) | 3-1 |
| Second Round | Lyon | (h) | 2-1 |
| | Lyon | (a) | 1-1 |
| Third Round | Inter Milan | (h) | 3-0 |
| | Inter Milan | (a) | 1-4 |
| Quarter-Finals | FC Basel | (h) | 2-2 |
| | FC Basel | (a) | 2-2 |

*(aet; lost 1-4 on pens)*

# TRANMERE ROVERS

## FOUNDATION

Formed in 1884 as Belmont they adopted their present title the following year and eventually joined their first league, the West Lancashire League, in 1889–90, the same year as their first success in the Wirral Challenge Cup. The club almost folded in 1899–1900 when all the players left en bloc to join a rival club, but they survived the crisis and went from strength to strength, winning the 'Combination' title in 1907–08 and the Lancashire Combination in 1913–14. They joined the Football League in 1921 from the Central League.

*Prenton Park, Prenton Road West, Birkenhead, Merseyside CH42 9PY.*

*Telephone:* (0871) 221 2001.

*Fax:* (0151) 609 0606.

*Ticket Office:* (0871) 221 2001.

*Website:* www.tranmererovers.co.uk

*Email:* info@tranmererovers.co.uk

*Ground Capacity:* 16,151.

*Record Attendance:* 24,424 v Stoke C, FA Cup 4th rd, 5 February 1972.

*Pitch Measurements:* 102m × 65m (112yd × 72yd)

*Chairman:* Peter Johnson.

*Chief Executive:* Mick Horton.

*Manager:* Ronnie Moore.

*First Team Coach:* John McMahon.

*Physio:* Gregg Blundell.

*Colours:* White shirts, white shorts, white socks with blue trim.

*Year Formed:* 1884.

*Turned Professional:* 1912.

*Previous Name:* 1884, Belmont AFC; 1885, Tranmere Rovers.

*Club Nickname:* 'Rovers'.

*Grounds:* 1884, Steeles Field; 1887, Ravenshaws Field/Old Prenton Park; 1912, Prenton Park.

*First Football League Game:* 27 August 1921, Division 3 (N), v Crewe Alex (h) W 4–1 – Bradshaw; Grainger, Stuart (1); Campbell, Milnes (1), Heslop; Moreton, Groves (1), Hyam, Ford (1), Hughes.

*Record League Victory:* 13–4 v Oldham Ath, Division 3 (N), 26 December 1935 – Gray; Platt, Fairhurst; McLaren, Newton, Spencer; Eden, MacDonald (1), Bell (9), Woodward (2), Urmson (1).

*Record Cup Victory:* 13–0 v Oswestry U, FA Cup 2nd prel rd, 10 October 1914 – Ashcroft; Stevenson, Bullough, Hancock, Taylor, Holden (1), Moreton (1), Cunningham (2), Smith (5), Leck (3), Gould (1).

## HONOURS

**Football League Division 1:**
Best season: 4th, 1992–93;

**Division 3 (N):** *Champions* 1937–38;

**Division 4:** *Runners-up* 1988–89.

**FA Cup:** Best season: 6th rd, 2000, 2001, 2004.

**Football League Cup:**
*Runners-up* 2000.

**Welsh Cup:** *Winners* 1935;
*Runners-up* 1934.

**Leyland DAF Cup:** *Winners* 1990;
*Runners-up* 1991.

## sky SPORTS FACT FILE

In 1938–39 Tranmere Rovers had their first season in the old Division Two after winning Division Three North. The campaign ended in relegation with Rovers winning just six games all at home. They managed just a single point from their 21 away fixtures and finished bottom of the table.

**Record Defeat:** 1–9 v Tottenham H, FA Cup 3rd rd (replay), 14 January 1953.

**Most League Points (2 for a win):** 60, Division 4, 1964–65.

**Most League Points (3 for a win):** 80, Division 4, 1988–89; Division 3, 1989–90; Division 2, 2002–03.

**Most League Goals:** 111, Division 3 (N), 1930–31.

**Highest League Scorer in Season:** Bunny Bell, 35, Division 3 (N), 1933–34.

**Most League Goals in Total Aggregate:** Ian Muir, 142, 1985–95.

**Most League Goals in One Match:** 9, Bunny Bell v Oldham Ath, Division 3 (N), 26 December 1935.

**Most Capped Player:** John Aldridge, 30 (69), Republic of Ireland.

**Most League Appearances:** Harold Bell, 595, 1946–64 (incl. League record 401 consecutive appearances).

**Youngest League Player:** Iain Hume, 16 years 167 days v Swindon T, 15 April 2000.

**Record Transfer Fee Received:** £3,300,000 from Everton for Steve Simonsen, September 1998.

**Record Transfer Fee Paid:** £500,000 to Aston Villa for Shaun Teale, July 1995.

**Football League Record:** 1921 Original Member of Division 3 (N): 1938–39 Division 2; 1946–58 Division 3 (N); 1958–61 Division 3; 1961–67 Division 4; 1967–75 Division 3; 1975–76 Division 4; 1976–79 Division 3; 1979–89 Division 4; 1989–91 Division 3; 1991–92 Division 2; 1992–2001 Division 1; 2001–04 Division 2; 2004– FL 1.

## MANAGERS

Bert Cooke 1912–35
Jackie Carr 1935–36
Jim Knowles 1936–39
Bill Ridding 1939–45
Ernie Blackburn 1946–55
Noel Kelly 1955–57
Peter Farrell 1957–60
Walter Galbraith 1961
Dave Russell 1961–69
Jackie Wright 1969–72
Ron Yeats 1972–75
John King 1975–80
Bryan Hamilton 1980–85
Frank Worthington 1985–87
Ronnie Moore 1987
John King 1987–96
John Aldridge 1996–2001
Dave Watson 2001–02
Ray Mathias 2002–03
Brian Little 2003–06
Ronnie Moore 2006–09
John Barnes 2009
Les Parry 2009–12
Ronnie Moore March 2012–

## LATEST SEQUENCES

**Longest Sequence of League Wins:** 9, 9.2.1990 – 19.3.1990.

**Longest Sequence of League Defeats:** 8, 29.10.1938 – 17.12.1938.

**Longest Sequence of League Draws:** 5, 26.12.1997 – 31.1.1998.

**Longest Sequence of Unbeaten League Matches:** 18, 16.3.1970 – 4.9.1970.

**Longest Sequence Without a League Win:** 16, 8.11.1969 – 14.3.1970.

**Successive Scoring Runs:** 32 from 24.2.1934.

**Successive Non-scoring Runs:** 7 from 20.12.1997.

## TEN YEAR LEAGUE RECORD

|  |  | P | W | D | L | F | A | Pts | Pos |
|---|---|---|---|---|---|---|---|---|---|
| 2003-04 | Div 2 | 46 | 17 | 16 | 13 | 59 | 56 | 67 | 8 |
| 2004-05 | FL 1 | 46 | 22 | 13 | 11 | 73 | 55 | 79 | 3 |
| 2005-06 | FL 1 | 46 | 13 | 15 | 18 | 50 | 52 | 54 | 18 |
| 2006-07 | FL 1 | 46 | 18 | 13 | 15 | 58 | 53 | 67 | 9 |
| 2007-08 | FL 1 | 46 | 18 | 11 | 17 | 52 | 47 | 65 | 11 |
| 2008-09 | FL 1 | 46 | 21 | 11 | 14 | 62 | 49 | 74 | 7 |
| 2009-10 | FL 1 | 46 | 14 | 9 | 23 | 45 | 72 | 51 | 19 |
| 2010-11 | FL 1 | 46 | 15 | 11 | 20 | 53 | 60 | 56 | 17 |
| 2011-12 | FL 1 | 46 | 14 | 14 | 18 | 49 | 53 | 56 | 12 |
| 2012-13 | FL 1 | 46 | 19 | 10 | 17 | 58 | 48 | 67 | 11 |

## DID YOU KNOW ?

Stan Rowlands became Tranmere Rovers' first full international when he represented Wales against England in March 1914. Rovers were playing in the Lancashire Combination at the time and finished the season as champions. The game was to prove Stan's only appearance for his country.

# TRANMERE ROVERS – FOOTBALL LEAGUE ONE 2012–13 LEAGUE RECORD

| Match No. | Date | Venue | Opponents | Result | H/T Score | Lg Pos. | Goalscorers | Attendance |
|---|---|---|---|---|---|---|---|---|
| 1 | Aug 18 | H | Leyton Orient | W 3-1 | 1-0 | 3 | Bakayogo [34], Akpa Akpro 2 [57, 65] | 5063 |
| 2 | 21 | A | Carlisle U | W 3-0 | 2-0 | 1 | Robinson 3 [12, 19, 66] | 4192 |
| 3 | 25 | A | Shrewsbury T | D 1-1 | 0-1 | 2 | Akpa Akpro [88] | 6253 |
| 4 | Sept 1 | H | Colchester U | W 4-0 | 1-0 | 1 | Cassidy 3 [40, 49, 77], Bakayogo [58] | 4711 |
| 5 | 8 | A | Crewe Alex | D 0-0 | 0-0 | 2 | | 5740 |
| 6 | 15 | H | Coventry C | W 2-0 | 0-0 | 1 | Cassidy [79], Robinson [83] | 6087 |
| 7 | 18 | H | Bury | W 3-0 | 1-0 | 1 | Robinson 2 (2 pens) [36, 68], Cassidy [71] | 4976 |
| 8 | 22 | A | Crawley T | W 5-2 | 2-2 | 1 | Holmes [2], Cassidy 2 [39, 53], Akpa Akpro [46], Robinson [90] | 3099 |
| 9 | 29 | H | Brentford | D 1-1 | 0-0 | 1 | Akpa Akpro [60] | 5720 |
| 10 | Oct 2 | A | Scunthorpe U | W 3-1 | 0-1 | 1 | Wallace [64], Akpa Akpro 2 [66, 88] | 2768 |
| 11 | 6 | A | Notts Co | W 1-0 | 1-0 | 1 | Thompson [22] | 7260 |
| 12 | 13 | H | Yeovil T | W 3-2 | 1-2 | 1 | Wallace [45], Cassidy [51], Holmes [78] | 6344 |
| 13 | 20 | A | Bournemouth | L 1-3 | 1-0 | 1 | Jervis [39] | 6233 |
| 14 | 23 | H | Doncaster R | L 1-2 | 0-0 | 1 | Cassidy [87] | 7386 |
| 15 | 27 | H | Preston NE | D 1-1 | 0-0 | 1 | Cassidy [85] | 7732 |
| 16 | Nov 7 | A | Hartlepool U | W 2-0 | 0-0 | 1 | Robinson (pen) [79], Stockton [90] | 3285 |
| 17 | 10 | A | Oldham Ath | W 1-0 | 0-0 | 1 | McGurk [54] | 5159 |
| 18 | 16 | H | Milton Keynes D | L 0-1 | 0-0 | 1 | | 10,587 |
| 19 | 20 | H | Walsall | D 0-0 | 0-0 | 1 | | 4717 |
| 20 | 24 | A | Stevenage | D 1-1 | 0-0 | 1 | Cassidy [78] | 3069 |
| 21 | Dec 8 | H | Portsmouth | D 2-2 | 1-0 | 1 | Taylor [31], O'Halloran [74] | 5591 |
| 22 | 15 | A | Sheffield U | D 0-0 | 0-0 | 1 | | 19,163 |
| 23 | 21 | A | Swindon T | L 0-5 | 0-4 | 1 | | 8885 |
| 24 | 26 | H | Crewe Alex | W 2-1 | 0-1 | 2 | McGurk [58], Power [63] | 7252 |
| 25 | 29 | H | Scunthorpe U | W 1-0 | 0-0 | 1 | Stockton [59] | 6044 |
| 26 | Jan 1 | A | Bury | W 1-0 | 0-0 | 1 | Robinson [56] | 3208 |
| 27 | 12 | H | Crawley T | W 2-0 | 2-0 | 1 | Amoo [30], Jones, P (og) [39] | 5011 |
| 28 | 16 | H | Coventry C | L 0-1 | 0-1 | 1 | | 9668 |
| 29 | 19 | A | Brentford | W 2-1 | 1-0 | 1 | Robinson (pen) [42], McGurk [66] | 6948 |
| 30 | Feb 2 | H | Carlisle U | L 0-1 | 0-1 | 1 | | 5713 |
| 31 | 9 | A | Leyton Orient | L 1-2 | 0-1 | 1 | O'Halloran [75] | 4351 |
| 32 | 15 | H | Shrewsbury T | L 0-2 | 0-1 | 3 | | 9127 |
| 33 | 19 | H | Swindon T | L 1-3 | 0-0 | 6 | Daniels [78] | 5223 |
| 34 | 23 | A | Colchester U | W 5-1 | 2-1 | 3 | Power [11], Akpa Akpro [41], Taylor [65], Stockton [85], O'Halloran (pen) [90] | 3077 |
| 35 | 26 | H | Notts Co | D 1-1 | 1-0 | 3 | Bell-Baggie [29] | 4703 |
| 36 | Mar 2 | A | Yeovil T | L 0-1 | 0-0 | 6 | | 4862 |
| 37 | 9 | H | Oldham Ath | W 1-0 | 0-0 | 4 | Power [61] | 5560 |
| 38 | 12 | A | Walsall | L 0-2 | 0-0 | 5 | | 3775 |
| 39 | 16 | A | Milton Keynes D | L 0-3 | 0-2 | 7 | | 9682 |
| 40 | 24 | H | Stevenage | W 3-1 | 3-1 | 5 | Bakayogo 2 [10, 38], Gibson [16] | 4342 |
| 41 | 29 | H | Sheffield U | L 0-1 | 0-1 | 6 | | 9145 |
| 42 | Apr 1 | A | Portsmouth | L 0-1 | 0-0 | 7 | | 12,014 |
| 43 | 6 | A | Doncaster R | L 0-1 | 0-0 | 7 | | 7979 |
| 44 | 13 | H | Hartlepool U | L 0-1 | 0-1 | 9 | | 4721 |
| 45 | 20 | A | Preston NE | L 0-1 | 0-0 | 10 | | 10,467 |
| 46 | 27 | H | Bournemouth | D 0-0 | 0-0 | 11 | | 6745 |

**Final League Position: 11**

## GOALSCORERS

**League (58):** Cassidy 11, Robinson 10 (4 pens), Akpa Akpro 8, Bakayogo 4, McGurk 3, O'Halloran 3 (1 pen), Power 3, Stockton 3, Holmes 2, Taylor 2, Wallace 2, Amoo 1, Bell-Baggie 1, Daniels 1, Gibson 1, Jervis 1, Thompson 1, own goal 1.
**FA Cup (5):** Stockton 2, McGurk 1, Power 1, Thompson 1.
**Capital One Cup (2):** Bell-Baggie 1, Stockton 1.
**Johnstone's Paint Trophy (0).**

| Fon Williams O 45 | Holmes D 43 | Taylor A 44 | Gibson B 28 | Bakayogo Z 46 | Thompson J 7 + 12 | Palmer L 42 + 1 | Wallace J 19 | Robinson A 33 | Cassidy J 26 | Akpa Akpro J 27 + 1 | Bell-Baggie A 20 + 11 | Stockton C 5 + 26 | Power M 25 + 2 | Golobart R 1 | Kirby J — + 4 | McGurk A 20 + 7 | Harrison D 4 + 9 | Kay M 3 + 3 | Black P 2 + 8 | Jervis J 4 | Eccleston N 1 | Goodison J 9 + 1 | O'Halloran M 17 + 6 | Daniels D 10 + 3 | Amoo D 6 + 5 | Corry P 5 + 1 | Sidibe M 10 | McGinty S 3 | Mooney J 1 | Match No. |
|---|---|---|---|---|---|---|---|---|---|---|---|---|---|---|---|---|---|---|---|---|---|---|---|---|---|---|---|---|---|---|
| 1 | 2 | 3 | 4 | 5 | 6 | 7 | 8 | 9$^1$ | 10 | 11$^2$ | 12 | 13 | | | | | | | | | | | | | | | | | | 1 |
| 1 | 2 | 3 | 4 | 5 | 6$^3$ | 7 | 8 | 9$^2$ | 10 | 11$^1$ | 13 | 12 | 14 | | | | | | | | | | | | | | | | | 2 |
| 1 | 2 | 3 | 4 | 5 | 6$^1$ | 7 | 8 | 9 | 10$^2$ | 11 | 12 | 13 | | | | | | | | | | | | | | | | | | 3 |
| 1 | 2 | | 4 | 5 | | 7 | 8 | 9$^1$ | 10$^2$ | 11 | 6 | 13 | | 3 | 12 | | | | | | | | | | | | | | | 4 |
| 1 | 2 | 3 | 4 | 5 | | 8 | 7 | 9 | 10 | 11 | 6$^1$ | | | | | 12 | | | | | | | | | | | | | | 5 |
| 1 | 2 | 3 | 4 | 5 | 12 | 8 | 7$^3$ | 9 | 10 | 11 | 6$^1$ | | | | 14 | | 13 | | | | | | | | | | | | | 6 |
| 1 | 2 | 3 | 4 | 5 | 12 | 8 | 7 | 9$^3$ | 11 | 10$^2$ | 6$^1$ | 13 | | | 14 | | | | | | | | | | | | | | | 7 |
| 1 | 5 | 2 | 4 | 3 | 9$^1$ | 7 | 6 | 8$^2$ | 10 | 11 | | | | | | 12 | 13 | | | | | | | | | | | | | 8 |
| 1 | 2 | 3 | 4 | 5 | 6$^1$ | 8 | 7$^2$ | 9 | 10 | 11 | | | | | | 12 | 13 | | | | | | | | | | | | | 9 |
| 1 | 2 | 3 | 4 | 5 | | 7 | 8 | 9 | 10 | 11 | 6 | | | | | 12 | | | | | | | | | | | | | | 10 |
| 1 | 2 | 3 | 4 | 5 | 12 | 7 | 8 | | 10 | 11$^1$ | 6 | | | | | 9 | | | | | | | | | | | | | | 11 |
| 1 | 2 | 3 | 4 | 5 | 9$^1$ | 7 | 8 | | 11 | | 6 | 12 | | | | 10$^2$ | | 13 | | | | | | | | | | | | 12 |
| 1 | 2 | 3 | 4 | 5 | 13 | 8 | 7 | | 10 | | 6$^2$ | | | | | 9 | | 12 | 11$^1$ | | | | | | | | | | | 13 |
| 1 | 2 | 3 | 4 | 5 | 12 | 8 | 7 | 9$^1$ | 10 | | 6 | 13 | | | | 11$^2$ | | | | | | | | | | | | | | 14 |
| 1 | 2 | 3 | 4 | 5 | 13 | 8 | 7 | | 10 | | 6 | 12 | | | | 9$^1$ | | | 11$^2$ | | | | | | | | | | | 15 |
| 1 | 2 | 3 | 4 | 5 | | 7 | 8 | 9 | 10 | | 6$^1$ | 13 | | | | 12 | | | 11$^2$ | | | | | | | | | | | 16 |
| 1 | 2$^1$ | 3 | 4 | 5 | 6$^2$ | 7 | 8 | | 10 | | 14 | | | | | 9 | 13 | 12 | 11$^3$ | | | | | | | | | | | 17 |
| 1 | 2 | 3 | 4 | 5 | 6 | 7 | 8 | | 10 | | 13 | | | | | 9$^2$ | 12 | | 11$^1$ | | | | | | | | | | | 18 |
| 1 | 2 | 3 | 4 | 5 | | 8$^3$ | | 9 | 10 | | 11$^1$ | 14 | | | | 13 | 6$^2$ | 7 | 12 | | | | | | | | | | | 19 |
| 1 | 2 | | 5 | 4 | | 6 | 7 | 8$^1$ | 9 | | 10 | | | | | 12 | | | | | | 3 | 11 | | | | | | | 20 |
| 1 | 2 | 3 | | 5 | | 6 | | 8 | 11 | | 12 | | | | | 9$^1$ | 7 | | | | | 4 | 10 | | | | | | | 21 |
| 1 | 5 | 3 | | 6 | 12 | 2 | | 11$^1$ | 10 | | | 7 | | | | 9 | | | | | | 4 | 8 | | | | | | | 22 |
| 1 | 2$^1$ | 3 | | 5$^3$ | | 7 | | 10 | 11 | | 8 | | | | | 9 | 12 | 14 | | | | 4$^2$ | 6 | 13 | | | | | | 23 |
| 1 | 2 | 3 | | 5 | 12 | 7 | | 9$^1$ | 10 | | 8 | | | | | 6 | | | | | | 11 | 4 | | | | | | | 24 |
| 1 | 2 | 3 | | 5 | 13 | 7 | | 9 | 10 | 12 | 8 | | | | | 6$^2$ | | | | | | 11$^1$ | 4 | | | | | | | 25 |
| 1 | 2 | 3 | | 5 | 13 | 8 | | 9$^2$ | 10 | | | | | | | 6$^1$ | | | | | | 11 | 4 | | | | | | | 26 |
| 1 | 2 | 3 | | 5 | | 7 | | 9$^1$ | | 12 | | | | | | 6$^2$ | 13 | | | | | 11 | 4 | 10 | | | | | | 27 |
| 1 | 2 | 3 | | 5 | | 7 | | | | 11 | 14 | 12 | 8 | | | 13 | 6$^1$ | | | | | 10$^2$ | 4 | 9$^3$ | | | | | | 28 |
| 1 | 2 | 3 | | 5 | | 7 | | 8$^2$ | 9 | 13 | 12 | 6 | | | | 11$^3$ | | | | | | 14 | 4 | 10 | | | | | | 29 |
| 1 | 2 | 3 | | 5 | | 7 | | 9 | | 11$^4$ | 14 | 12 | 8$^2$ | | | 6$^4$ | | | | | | 13 | 4 | 10$^1$ | | | | | | 30 |
| 1 | 2 | 3 | | 5 | | 8 | | 9 | | 12 | 10 | 7 | | | | 6$^2$ | | | | | | 13 | 4 | 11$^1$ | | | | | | 31 |
| 1 | 2$^2$ | 3 | | 5 | | 7$^4$ | | 9 | | 10$^1$ | 8 | 6 | | | | 13 | | | | | | 11$^3$ | 4 | 14 | 12 | | | | | 32 |
| 1 | | 3 | | 5 | | | | 9 | | 12 | 10$^2$ | 8 | | | | | | 2 | 13 | | | 6 | 4 | 11$^1$ | 7 | | | | | 33 |
| 1 | | 3 | | 5 | | | | 9$^2$ | 11 | | 12 | 8 | | | | | | 2 | 13 | | | 4 | 6 | | 7 | 10$^1$ | | | | 34 |
| 1 | | 3 | | 5 | | | | 9$^1$ | 11 | | 6$^3$ | 12 | 7 | | | | | 2 | 14 | | | 4$^2$ | 10 | 13 | 8 | | | | | 35 |
| 1 | 2 | 3 | | 5 | | 7 | | | 11 | | 9$^3$ | 12 | 7 | | | | | | | | | 4 | 6$^2$ | | 14 | 8 | 10$^1$ | | | 36 |
| 1 | 2 | 3 | | 5 | | 7 | | | 11 | | 9$^3$ | 13 | 6 | | | | 14 | | | | | 4 | 10$^1$ | | 12 | 8$^2$ | | | | 37 |
| 1 | 2 | 3 | | 5 | | 7 | | | 11 | | 9$^3$ | 13 | 6 | | | | | | | | | 4$^1$ | 10$^2$ | 12 | 14 | 8 | | | | 38 |
| 1 | 2 | 5 | 4 | 9$^2$ | | 7 | | | 11 | 12 | 13 | 6 | | | | 8$^1$ | 3 | | | | | | | | 10 | | | | | 39 |
| 1 | 2 | 3 | 4 | 9$^2$ | | 7 | | | 11 | | 6$^1$ | 8 | | | | | 5 | | | | | 12 | 13 | | 10 | | | | | 40 |
| 1 | 2 | 3 | 4 | 9 | | 7 | | | 11 | | 6$^1$ | 8 | | | | 12 | | | | | | | | | | | 10 | 5 | | 41 |
| 1 | 2 | 3 | 4 | 9$^1$ | | 7 | | | 11 | | 6 | 12 | 8 | | | | | | | | | | | | | | 10 | 5 | | 42 |
| 1 | 2 | 4 | 3 | 9 | 12 | 8 | | | 11 | | 10 | 6$^1$ | 7$^3$ | | | | | | | | | 14 | 13 | | | | 5$^2$ | | | 43 |
| 1 | 2 | 3 | 4 | 5 | 12 | 7 | | 9$^3$ | 11 | | 6$^2$ | 13 | 8 | | | | | | | | | | 14 | | | | 10$^1$ | | | 44 |
| 1 | 2 | 3 | 4 | 5 | | 7 | | 9 | 11 | 12 | 13 | 8 | | | | | | | | | | | 6$^1$ | | | | 10$^2$ | | | 45 |
| | 2 | 4 | 3 | 5 | | 7$^3$ | | 6$^2$ | 9 | 12 | 10 | 8 | | | | | 13 | 14 | | | | | 11$^1$ | | | | | | 1 | 46 |

**FA Cup**

| | | | |
|---|---|---|---|
| First Round | Braintree T | (a) | 3-0 |
| Second Round | Chesterfield | (h) | 2-1 |
| Third Round | Derby Co | (a) | 0-5 |

**Capital One Cup**

| | | | |
|---|---|---|---|
| First Round | Chesterfield | (a) | 2-1 |
| Second Round | Aston Villa | (a) | 0-3 |

**Johnstone's Paint Trophy**

| | | | |
|---|---|---|---|
| First Round | Port Vale | (a) | 0-2 |

# WALSALL

## FOUNDATION

Two of the leading clubs around Walsall in the 1880s were Walsall Swifts (formed 1877) and Walsall Town (formed 1879). The Swifts were winners of the Birmingham Senior Cup in 1881, while the Town reached the 4th round (5th round modern equivalent) of the FA Cup in 1883. These clubs amalgamated as Walsall Town Swifts in 1888, becoming simply Walsall in 1895.

*Banks's Stadium, Bescot Crescent, Walsall WS1 4SA.*
*Telephone:* (01922) 622 791. *Fax:* (01922) 613 202.
*Ticket Office:* (01922) 651 414/416.
*Website:* www.saddlers.co.uk
*Email:* info@walsallfc.co.uk
*Ground Capacity:* 10,989.
*Record Attendance:* 25,453 v Newcastle U, Division 2, 29 August 1961 (at Fellows Park); 11,049 v Rotherham U, Division 1, 9 May 2004 (at Bescot Stadium).
*Pitch Measurements:* 100m × 66m (110yd × 73yd)
*Chairman:* Jeff Bonser.
*Chief Executive:* Stefan Gamble.
*Manager:* Dean Smith.
*First Team Coach:* Richard O'Kelly.
*Physio:* Jon Whitney.
*Colours:* Red shirts with black trim, red shorts, red and white socks.
*Year Formed:* 1888.
*Turned Professional:* 1888.
*Previous Names:* Walsall Swifts (founded 1877) and Walsall Town (founded 1879) amalgamated in 1888 as Walsall Town Swifts; 1895, Walsall.
*Club Nickname:* 'The Saddlers'.
*Grounds:* 1888, Fellows Park; 1990, Bescot Stadium.
*First Football League Game:* 3 September 1892, Division 2, v Darwen (h) L 1–2 – Hawkins; Withington, Pinches; Robinson, Whitrick, Forsyth; Marshall, Holmes, Turner, Gray (1), Pangbourn.
*Record League Victory:* 10–0 v Darwen, Division 2, 4 March 1899 – Tennent; Ted Peers (1), Davies; Hickinbotham, Jenkyns, Taggart; Dean (3), Vail (2), Aston (4), Martin, Griffin.
*Record Cup Victory:* 7–0 v Macclesfield T (a), FA Cup 2nd rd, 6 December 1997 – Walker; Evans, Marsh, Viveash (1), Ryder, Peron, Boli (2 incl. 1p) (Ricketts), Porter (2), Keates, Watson (Platt), Hodge (2 incl. 1p).
*Record Defeat:* 0–12 v Small Heath, 17 December 1892; 0–12 v Darwen, 26 December 1896, both Division 2.
*Most League Points (2 for a win):* 65, Division 4, 1959–60.
*Most League Points (3 for a win):* 89, FL 2, 2006–07.
*Most League Goals:* 102, Division 4, 1959–60.
*Highest League Scorer in Season:* Gilbert Alsop, 40, Division 3 (N), 1933–34 and 1934–35.

## HONOURS

**Football League –**
**Division 2:** *Runners-up*, 1998–99;
**FL 2:** *Champions* 2006–07;
**Division 3:** *Runners-up* 1960–61, 1994–95;
**Division 4:** *Champions* 1959–60;
*Runners-up* 1979–80.
**FA Cup:** Best season: 5th rd, 1939, 1975, 1978, 1987, 2002, 2003 and last 16 1889.
**Football League Cup:** Semi-final 1984.

## sky SPORTS FACT FILE

When Walsall won the Fourth Division title in 1959–60 they won 18 of their first 24 League fixtures. They finished in rather dismal fashion, just 5 wins from 15 games, but that great start was sufficient to win them the championship.

*Most League Goals in Total Aggregate:* Tony Richards, 184, 1954–63; Colin Taylor, 184, 1958–63, 1964–68, 1969–73.

*Most League Goals in One Match:* 5, Gilbert Alsop v Carlisle U, Division 3 (N), 2 February 1935; 5, Bill Evans v Mansfield T, Division 3 (N), 5 October 1935; 5, Johnny Devlin v Torquay U, Division 3 (S), 1 September 1949.

*Most Capped Player:* Mick Kearns, 15 (18), Republic of Ireland.

*Most League Appearances:* Colin Harrison, 467, 1964–82.

*Youngest League Player:* Geoff Morris, 16 years 218 days v Scunthorpe U, 14 September 1965.

*Record Transfer Fee Received:* £1,000,000 from Coventry C for Scott Dann, January 2008.

*Record Transfer Fee Paid:* £175,000 to Birmingham C for Alan Buckley, June 1979.

*Football League Record:* 1892 Elected to Division 2; 1895 Failed re-election; 1896–1901 Division 2; 1901 Failed re-election; 1921 Original Member of Division 3 (N); 1927–31 Division 3 (S); 1931–36 Division 3 (N); 1936–58 Division 3 (S); 1958–60 Division 4; 1960–61 Division 3; 1961–63 Division 2; 1963–79 Division 3; 1979–80 Division 4; 1980–88 Division 3; 1988–89 Division 2; 1989–90 Division 3; 1990–92 Division 4; 1992–95 Division 3; 1995–99 Division 2; 1999–2000 Division 1; 2000–01 Division 2; 2001–04 Division 1; 2004–06 FL 1; 2006–07 FL 2; 2007– FL 1.

## LATEST SEQUENCES

*Longest Sequence of League Wins:* 7, 10.10.1959 – 21.11.1959.

*Longest Sequence of League Defeats:* 15, 29.10.1988 – 4.2.1989.

*Longest Sequence of League Draws:* 5, 7.5.1988 – 17.9.1988.

*Longest Sequence of Unbeaten League Matches:* 21, 6.11.1979 – 22.3.1980.

*Longest Sequence Without a League Win:* 18, 15.10.1988 – 4.2.1989.

*Successive Scoring Runs:* 27 from 9.2.1928.

*Successive Non-scoring Runs:* 5 from 8.10.1927.

## MANAGERS

H. Smallwood 1888–91 *(Secretary-Manager)*
A. G. Burton 1891–93
J. H. Robinson 1893–95
C. H. Ailso 1895–96 *(Secretary-Manager)*
A. E. Parsloe 1896–97 *(Secretary-Manager)*
L. Ford 1897–98 *(Secretary-Manager)*
G. Hughes 1898–99 *(Secretary-Manager)*
L. Ford 1899–1901 *(Secretary-Manager)*
J. E. Shutt 1908–13 *(Secretary-Manager)*
Haydn Price 1914–20
Joe Burchell 1920–26
David Ashworth 1926–27
Jack Torrance 1927–28
James Kerr 1928–29
Sid Scholey 1929–30
Peter O'Rourke 1930–32
Bill Slade 1932–34
Andy Wilson 1934–37
Tommy Lowes 1937–44
Harry Hibbs 1944–51
Tony McPhee 1951
Brough Fletcher 1952–53
Major Frank Buckley 1953–55
John Love 1955–57
Billy Moore 1957–64
Alf Wood 1964
Reg Shaw 1964–68
Dick Graham 1968
Ron Lewin 1968–69
Billy Moore 1969–72
John Smith 1972–73
Ronnie Allen 1973
Doug Fraser 1973–77
Dave Mackay 1977–78
Alan Ashman 1978
Frank Sibley 1979
Alan Buckley 1979–86
Neil Martin *(Joint Manager with Buckley)* 1981–82
Tommy Coakley 1986–88
John Barnwell 1989–90
Kenny Hibbitt 1990–94
Chris Nicholl 1994–97
Jan Sorensen 1997–98
Ray Graydon 1998–2002
Colin Lee 2002–04
Paul Merson 2004–06
Kevin Broadhurst 2006
Richard Money 2006–08
Jimmy Mullen 2008–09
Chris Hutchings 2009–10
Dean Smith January 2011–

## TEN YEAR LEAGUE RECORD

|  |  | P | W | D | L | F | A | Pts | Pos |
|---|---|---|---|---|---|---|---|---|---|
| 2003-04 | Div 1 | 46 | 13 | 12 | 21 | 45 | 65 | 51 | 22 |
| 2004-05 | FL 1 | 46 | 16 | 12 | 18 | 65 | 69 | 60 | 14 |
| 2005-06 | FL 1 | 46 | 11 | 14 | 21 | 47 | 70 | 47 | 24 |
| 2006-07 | FL 2 | 46 | 25 | 14 | 7 | 66 | 34 | 89 | 1 |
| 2007-08 | FL 1 | 46 | 16 | 16 | 14 | 52 | 46 | 64 | 12 |
| 2008-09 | FL 1 | 46 | 17 | 10 | 19 | 61 | 66 | 61 | 13 |
| 2009-10 | FL 1 | 46 | 16 | 14 | 16 | 60 | 63 | 62 | 10 |
| 2010-11 | FL 1 | 46 | 12 | 12 | 22 | 56 | 75 | 48 | 20 |
| 2011-12 | FL 1 | 46 | 10 | 20 | 16 | 51 | 57 | 50 | 19 |
| 2012-13 | FL 1 | 46 | 17 | 17 | 12 | 65 | 58 | 68 | 9 |

## DID YOU KNOW

Allan Clarke, who was leading scorer for Walsall in 1964–65 and 1965–66, was from a famous footballing family. Three of his brothers, Derek, Wayne and Kelvin, also played for the Saddlers while a fifth brother, Frank, began his career with Shrewsbury Town.

## WALSALL – FOOTBALL LEAGUE ONE 2012–13 LEAGUE RECORD

| Match No. | Date | Venue | Opponents | Result | H/T Score | Lg Pos. | Goalscorers | Attendance |
|---|---|---|---|---|---|---|---|---|
| 1 | Aug 18 | H | Doncaster R | L | 0-3 | 0-2 | 24 | | 4205 |
| 2 | 21 | A | Oldham Ath | D | 1-1 | 0-1 | 22 | Bowerman [79] | 3496 |
| 3 | 25 | A | Notts Co | W | 1-0 | 0-0 | 13 | Butler [80] | 5851 |
| 4 | Sept 1 | H | Brentford | D | 2-2 | 2-0 | 13 | Paterson [28], Bowerman [29] | 3434 |
| 5 | 8 | H | Milton Keynes D | W | 1-0 | 1-0 | 9 | Holden [17] | 3657 |
| 6 | 15 | A | Portsmouth | W | 2-1 | 0-0 | 5 | Baxendale [56], Cuvelier [63] | 11,767 |
| 7 | 18 | A | Stevenage | L | 1-3 | 0-1 | 9 | Bowerman [59] | 2634 |
| 8 | 22 | H | Preston NE | W | 3-1 | 1-1 | 7 | Baxendale [38], Bowerman 2 (1 pen) [55 (p), 58] | 4189 |
| 9 | 29 | A | Bournemouth | W | 2-1 | 1-0 | 6 | Butler [41], Bowerman [90] | 4951 |
| 10 | Oct 2 | H | Leyton Orient | L | 1-2 | 0-2 | 9 | Grigg (pen) [58] | 3281 |
| 11 | 6 | H | Carlisle U | L | 1-2 | 1-1 | 11 | Paterson [17] | 3964 |
| 12 | 14 | A | Shrewsbury T | L | 0-1 | 0-1 | 11 | | 6495 |
| 13 | 20 | H | Crewe Alex | D | 2-2 | 2-1 | 12 | Paterson [12], Cuvelier [26] | 3836 |
| 14 | 23 | A | Sheffield U | L | 0-1 | 0-1 | 15 | | 15,744 |
| 15 | 27 | A | Bury | D | 1-1 | 1-1 | 13 | Grigg [7] | 2514 |
| 16 | Nov 6 | H | Scunthorpe U | L | 1-4 | 0-2 | 16 | Grigg [90] | 2787 |
| 17 | 10 | H | Swindon T | L | 0-2 | 0-1 | 17 | | 4139 |
| 18 | 17 | A | Crawley T | D | 2-2 | 1-1 | 17 | Brandy [14], Hemmings [74] | 3039 |
| 19 | 20 | A | Tranmere R | D | 0-0 | 0-0 | 17 | | 4717 |
| 20 | 24 | H | Hartlepool U | D | 1-1 | 0-1 | 19 | Holden [49] | 4562 |
| 21 | Dec 8 | A | Coventry C | L | 1-5 | 1-3 | 19 | Adams (og) [16] | 10,986 |
| 22 | 15 | H | Yeovil T | D | 2-2 | 1-0 | 18 | Paterson [13], Grigg [72] | 3160 |
| 23 | 22 | H | Colchester U | W | 1-0 | 0-0 | 17 | Brandy [61] | 3006 |
| 24 | 26 | A | Milton Keynes D | W | 4-2 | 3-2 | 16 | Brandy [15], Grigg 2 [25, 43], Paterson [90] | 8700 |
| 25 | 29 | A | Leyton Orient | L | 1-2 | 0-1 | 16 | Mantom [79] | 3865 |
| 26 | Jan 1 | H | Stevenage | W | 1-0 | 0-0 | 16 | Paterson [87] | 3301 |
| 27 | 4 | H | Portsmouth | W | 2-0 | 0-0 | 14 | Brandy [29], Grigg [40] | 4038 |
| 28 | 13 | A | Preston NE | W | 3-1 | 2-0 | 12 | Brandy [18], Downing [38], Baxendale [56] | 9823 |
| 29 | 19 | H | Bournemouth | W | 3-1 | 2-0 | 10 | Mantom [27], Grigg 2 (2 pens) [45, 79] | 3173 |
| 30 | 26 | A | Colchester U | L | 0-2 | 0-0 | 11 | | 2865 |
| 31 | Feb 2 | H | Oldham Ath | W | 3-1 | 1-1 | 9 | Baxendale [40], Paterson 2 [74, 90] | 4672 |
| 32 | 9 | A | Doncaster R | W | 2-1 | 1-1 | 9 | Butler [2], Brandy [81] | 7013 |
| 33 | 16 | H | Notts Co | D | 1-1 | 1-0 | 9 | Grigg (pen) [29] | 4416 |
| 34 | 23 | A | Brentford | D | 0-0 | 0-0 | 9 | | 4781 |
| 35 | 26 | H | Carlisle U | W | 3-0 | 1-0 | 9 | Grigg 3 (1 pen) [3 (p), 66, 86] | 3266 |
| 36 | Mar 2 | H | Shrewsbury T | W | 3-1 | 1-0 | 8 | Grigg 2 (1 pen) [30 (p), 54], Westcarr [47] | 5496 |
| 37 | 9 | A | Swindon T | D | 2-2 | 1-1 | 9 | Grigg (pen) [32], Paterson [90] | 8407 |
| 38 | 12 | H | Tranmere R | W | 2-0 | 0-0 | 8 | Grigg (pen) [50], Westcarr [57] | 3775 |
| 39 | 16 | H | Crawley T | D | 2-2 | 0-0 | 9 | Paterson [90], Grigg [90] | 5003 |
| 40 | 23 | A | Hartlepool U | D | 0-0 | 0-0 | 8 | | 3065 |
| 41 | 29 | A | Yeovil T | D | 0-0 | 0-0 | 8 | | 5594 |
| 42 | Apr 1 | H | Coventry C | W | 4-0 | 1-0 | 8 | Paterson 2 [33, 87], Westcarr 2 (1 pen) [54 (p), 74] | 7504 |
| 43 | 6 | H | Sheffield U | D | 1-1 | 1-0 | 8 | Westcarr [44] | 7042 |
| 44 | 13 | A | Scunthorpe U | D | 1-1 | 0-0 | 7 | Grigg [54] | 4049 |
| 45 | 20 | H | Bury | D | 1-1 | 1-0 | 8 | Brandy [22] | 4745 |
| 46 | 27 | A | Crewe Alex | L | 0-2 | 0-0 | 9 | | 6547 |

**Final League Position: 9**

### GOALSCORERS

*League (65):* Grigg 19 (8 pens), Paterson 12, Brandy 7, Bowerman 6 (1 pen), Westcarr 5 (1 pen), Baxendale 4, Butler 3, Cuvelier 2, Holden 2, Mantom 2, Downing 1, Hemmings 1, own goal 1.
*FA Cup (3):* Bowerman 1, Paterson 1, Taundry 1.
*Capital One Cup (1):* Hemmings 1.
*Johnstone's Paint Trophy (2):* Cuvelier 1 (1 pen), Grigg 1.

| Grof D 10 | Chambers J 16+6 | Holden D 24+1 | Butler A 41 | Purkiss B 25+2 | Featherstone N 24+7 | Chambers A 34+3 | Paterson J 46 | Hemmings A 10+18 | Cuvelier F 16+3 | Grigg W 38+3 | Brandy F 27+7 | Baxendale J 23+9 | Bowerman G 10+18 | Williams A —+6 | Taylor A 34 | Downing P 27+4 | Jones J 1+2 | Taundry R 10+7 | Darlow K 9 | Benning M 6+4 | Mantom S 29 | McCarey A 14 | Westcarr C 18+6 | McLoughlin I 6 | George B 1 | Johnstone S 7 | Sawyers R —+4 | Match No. |
|---|---|---|---|---|---|---|---|---|---|---|---|---|---|---|---|---|---|---|---|---|---|---|---|---|---|---|---|---|
| 1 | 2 | 3 | 4 | 5 | 6 | 7 | 8[1] | 9[2] | 10 | 11 | 12[3] | 13 | 14 |  |  |  |  |  |  |  |  |  |  |  |  |  |  | 1 |
| 1 | 5 | 3 | 4 | 2 | 7[1] | 8 | 6 | 9 | 10 | 11[2] |  | 13 | 12 |  |  |  |  |  |  |  |  |  |  |  |  |  |  | 2 |
| 1 | 2 | 3 | 4 | 5 | 9[1] | 8 | 7 | 10 | 6 | 11 |  |  | 12 |  |  |  |  |  |  |  |  |  |  |  |  |  |  | 3 |
| 1 |  | 4 | 3 | 2 | 7 | 6[3] | 8[1] | 9 | 10 |  | 12 | 11[2] | 13 |  | 5 | 14 |  |  |  |  |  |  |  |  |  |  |  | 4 |
| 1 |  | 4 | 3 | 2 | 7 | 6 | 9[2] | 8 |  |  | 10[1] | 11[3] | 14 |  | 5 |  | 12 | 13 |  |  |  |  |  |  |  |  |  | 5 |
| 1 |  | 4 | 3 | 2 | 7 | 9 | 11[2] | 6 | 12 | 8[1] | 10 |  |  |  | 5 |  |  | 13 |  |  |  |  |  |  |  |  |  | 6 |
| 1 |  | 5 | 3 | 2 | 7 | 11 | 6[1] | 8 | 12 | 9[2] | 10 | 13 | 4[3] |  | 14 |  |  |  |  |  |  |  |  |  |  |  |  | 7 |
|  |  | 4 | 3 | 2 | 9 |  | 6[2] |  | 7 | 10[3] |  | 8[1] | 11 |  | 5 | 14 | 13 | 12 | 1 |  |  |  |  |  |  |  |  | 8 |
|  | 5 | 4 |  | 2 | 8 |  | 10 |  | 6 | 9[2] | 13 | 7[1] | 11 |  | 3 |  |  | 12 | 1 |  |  |  |  |  |  |  |  | 9 |
|  | 3 | 4 |  | 2[2] | 8 |  | 9[2] | 13 | 7 | 10 | 12 | 6[1] | 11 |  | 5 |  |  | 14 | 1 |  |  |  |  |  |  |  |  | 10 |
|  | 4 | 3 |  | 2[1] | 8 |  | 9 | 13 | 7 | 10 | 14 | 6[2] | 11[3] |  | 5 |  |  | 12 | 1 |  |  |  |  |  |  |  |  | 11 |
|  | 4 | 3 |  |  | 7 | 8 | 9 | 12 | 10[1] |  | 14 | 6[2] | 11[3] | 13 | 5 |  |  | 2 | 1 |  |  |  |  |  |  |  |  | 12 |
|  | 3 | 4 | 13 |  | 9[1] | 8 | 10 |  | 7 | 11[3] | 14 | 6 | 12 |  | 5[2] |  |  | 2 | 1 |  |  |  |  |  |  |  |  | 13 |
|  | 4[4] | 3 |  |  | 8 | 9 | 10[2] | 13 | 7 | 11[3] |  | 6[1] | 14 |  | 5 | 12 |  | 2 | 1 |  |  |  |  |  |  |  |  | 14 |
| 1 | 12 | 3 |  |  | 9 | 7 | 6[3] | 14 | 8 | 11 | 10[3] | 13 |  |  | 5[1] | 4 |  | 2 |  |  |  |  |  |  |  |  |  | 15 |
| 1 | 2[2] | 3 | 4 |  | 8 | 7 | 10 | 12 |  | 6[3] | 11 | 14 |  |  |  | 9[1] |  | 5 |  |  | 13 |  |  |  |  |  |  | 16 |
| 1 | 4 | 3 |  |  | 8[3] | 7 | 11[2] | 13 |  | 10 | 12 | 9[1] | 14 |  |  | 2 |  |  |  |  | 5 | 6 |  |  |  |  |  | 17 |
|  | 4 | 3 |  |  | 6[1] | 12 | 9 | 8[2] |  | 11[3] | 10 | 13 | 14 |  | 5 | 2 |  |  |  |  |  | 1 | 7 |  |  |  |  | 18 |
|  | 3 |  |  |  | 7 | 14 | 6 | 9[1] |  | 10[3] | 11[2] | 12 | 13 |  | 5 | 4 |  |  |  |  | 2 | 1 | 8 |  |  |  |  | 19 |
|  | 3 | 4 |  |  | 6 | 8 | 10[1] |  |  | 11[2] | 9 |  | 13 |  | 5 | 2 |  |  |  |  | 7 | 1 | 12 |  |  |  |  | 20 |
|  | 3 | 4[4] |  |  | 7[3] | 12 | 6[1] | 14 |  | 11 | 9[2] |  |  |  | 5 | 13 |  | 2 |  |  | 8 | 1 | 10 |  |  |  |  | 21 |
|  |  | 4 |  | 2 | 8 |  | 6[2] | 10 | 9[1] |  | 12 |  |  |  | 5 | 3 |  |  |  | 13 | 7 | 1 | 11 |  |  |  |  | 22 |
|  |  | 4 |  | 2 | 8 |  | 9[2] | 13 |  | 11[1] | 10 | 12 |  |  | 5 | 3 |  |  |  |  | 7 | 1 | 6 |  |  |  |  | 23 |
|  |  | 4 |  | 2 | 7 |  | 9 | 12 |  | 11 | 6 |  |  |  | 3 | 5 |  |  |  |  | 8 | 1 | 10[1] |  |  |  |  | 24 |
|  |  | 3 |  | 2 | 7 |  | 9[3] | 14 | 12 | 11[2] | 10[1] |  | 13 |  | 5 | 4 |  |  |  |  | 8 | 1 | 6 |  |  |  |  | 25 |
|  |  | 3 |  | 2 | 8 |  | 11 |  | 6[2] | 10[3] | 12 | 14 |  |  | 5[1] | 4 |  |  | 1 |  | 13 | 7 | 9 |  |  |  |  | 26 |
|  | 13 |  | 4 | 2 |  |  | 8 | 9 |  | 10 | 11[1] | 12 |  |  | 3 |  |  |  |  |  | 5[2] | 1 | 7 | 6 |  |  |  | 27 |
|  | 13 |  | 4 | 2 |  |  | 8 | 9 | 12 | 11[3] | 10[2] | 6[3] | 14 |  |  | 3 |  |  |  |  | 5 | 1 | 7 |  |  |  |  | 28 |
|  | 12 |  | 4 | 2 |  | 7 | 9 |  |  | 10 | 11[4] | 6[1] |  |  | 5 | 3 |  |  |  |  | 8 | 1 |  |  |  |  |  | 29 |
|  | 3 |  |  | 2 | 8[2] | 7 | 10 | 12 |  | 11 | 6[1] | 13 |  |  | 5 | 4 |  |  |  |  | 9 | 1 |  |  |  |  |  | 30 |
|  | 13 |  | 4 | 2 |  | 7 | 9 |  |  | 10 | 11[2] | 6[1] |  |  | 5 | 3 |  |  |  |  | 8 | 1 | 12 |  |  |  |  | 31 |
|  | 12 | 3 |  | 2[1] | 14 | 8 | 9 |  |  | 11 | 10[3] | 6[2] |  |  | 5 | 4 |  |  |  |  | 7 | 1 | 13 |  |  |  |  | 32 |
|  | 2 | 3 |  |  |  | 7 | 9 |  | 10 | 11 | 12 |  |  |  | 5 | 4 |  |  |  |  | 8 | 1 | 6[1] |  |  |  |  | 33 |
|  |  | 3 | 13 |  |  | 7 | 9 |  |  | 11 | 10[2] | 6[1] |  |  | 5 | 4 |  |  |  |  | 8 | 1 | 12 |  | 2 |  |  | 34 |
|  | 12 | 3 | 14 | 2 | 7[1] | 6 | 9[3] |  |  | 11 |  | 13 |  |  | 5 | 4 |  |  |  |  | 8 | 1 | 10[2] |  |  |  |  | 35 |
|  | 12 | 3 |  | 2 | 6[2] | 8 | 9 |  |  | 11 |  | 13 |  |  | 5 | 4 |  |  |  |  | 7 | 1 | 10[1] |  |  |  |  | 36 |
|  | 5 | 3 | 12 |  | 6[2] | 7 | 9 | 13 |  | 10 |  |  |  |  | 4 | 2 |  |  |  |  | 8 | 1 | 11[1] |  |  |  |  | 37 |
|  | 5 |  | 12 |  | 6[1] | 7 | 9 |  |  | 11 |  |  |  |  | 3 | 2 |  |  |  |  | 8 | 1 | 10[1] |  |  |  |  | 38 |
|  | 2 | 4 | 12 |  | 6[2] | 7 | 9 | 13 |  | 11 |  |  |  |  | 5 | 3 |  |  |  |  | 8 | 1 | 10[1] |  |  |  |  | 39 |
|  | 5[2] | 3 | 13 |  | 10[1] | 7 | 9 | 12 | 6 |  | 14 |  |  |  | 4 | 2 |  |  |  |  | 8 |  | 11[3] |  |  | 1 |  | 40 |
|  | 2 | 4 |  |  | 6 | 8 | 9 | 12 |  | 11 |  |  |  |  | 5 | 3 |  |  |  |  | 7 |  | 10[2] |  |  | 1 | 13 | 41 |
|  | 2 | 4 |  |  | 7 |  | 10 | 12 |  | 11[2] | 8[1] |  |  |  | 5 | 3 |  |  |  |  | 6 |  | 9 |  |  | 1 | 13 | 42 |
|  |  | 4 |  | 2 | 7 |  | 9 | 13 |  | 11[3] | 8[2] |  |  |  | 5[1] | 3 |  |  |  |  | 12 |  | 6 | 10 |  | 1 | 14 | 43 |
|  | 5 | 3 |  | 2 | 6 |  | 10 |  |  | 11 | 12 |  |  |  | 4 |  |  |  |  |  | 8 |  | 7 | 9[1] |  | 1 |  | 44 |
|  | 5 | 3 |  | 2 | 8 |  | 9[1] | 12 | 10[2] | 11 | 6[3] |  |  |  |  | 4 |  |  |  | 13 | 7 |  |  |  |  | 1 | 14 | 45 |
|  | 2 | 3 |  |  | 8 | 7 | 10 | 13 | 6[1] | 11 | 9[2] |  |  |  | 5 | 4 |  |  |  |  | 12 |  |  |  |  | 1 |  | 46 |

**FA Cup**

| First Round | Lincoln C | (a) | 1-1 |
|---|---|---|---|
| *Replay* | Lincoln C | (h) | 2-3 |

**Capital One Cup**

| First Round | Brentford | (h) | 1-0 |
|---|---|---|---|
| Second Round | QPR | (a) | 0-3 |

**Johnstone's Paint Trophy**

| Second Round | Port Vale | (h) | 2-2 |
|---|---|---|---|
| *(aet; lost 5-6 on pens)* | | | |

# WATFORD

## FOUNDATION

The club was formed as Watford Rovers in 1881. The name was changed to West Herts in 1893 and then the name Watford was adopted after rival club Watford St Mary's was absorbed in 1898.

*Vicarage Road Stadium, Vicarage Road, Watford, Hertfordshire WD18 0ER.*

*Telephone:* (0844) 856 1881.

*Fax:* (01923) 496 001.

*Ticket Office:* (0844) 856 1881.

*Website:* www.watfordfc.com

*Email:* yourvoice@watfordfc.com

*Ground Capacity:* 17,477.

*Record Attendance:* 34,099 v Manchester U, FA Cup 4th rd (replay), 3 February 1969.

*Pitch Measurements:* 105m × 68m (115yd × 75yd)

*Chairman:* Raffaele Riva.

*Chief Executive:* Scott Duxbury.

*Head Coach:* Gianfranco Zola OBE.

*Assistant Coaches:* Adolfo Sormani, Giancarlo Corradini.

*Head of Medicine:* Marco Cesarini.

*Colours:* Yellow shirts with red and black trim, black shorts with red trim, black socks with red trim.

*Year Formed:* 1881.

*Turned Professional:* 1897.

*Previous Names:* 1881, Watford Rovers; 1893, West Herts; 1898, Watford.

*Club Nickname:* 'The Hornets'.

*Grounds:* 1883, Vicarage Meadow, Rose and Crown Meadow; 1889, Colney Butts; 1890, Cassio Road; 1922, Vicarage Road.

*First Football League Game:* 28 August 1920, Division 3, v QPR (a) W 2–1 – Williams; Horseman, Fred Gregory; Bacon, Toone, Wilkinson; Bassett, Ronald (1), Hoddinott, White (1), Waterall.

*Record League Victory:* 8–0 v Sunderland, Division 1, 25 September 1982 – Sherwood; Rice, Rostron, Taylor, Terry, Bolton, Callaghan (2), Blissett (4), Jenkins (2), Jackett, Barnes.

*Record Cup Victory:* 10–1 v Lowestoft T, FA Cup 1st rd, 27 November 1926 – Yates; Prior, Fletcher (1); Frank Smith, Bert Smith, Strain; Stephenson, Warner (3), Edmonds (3), Swan (1), Daniels (1), (1 og).

*Record Defeat:* 0–10 v Wolverhampton W, FA Cup 1st rd (replay), 24 January 1912.

## HONOURS

**Football League – Division 1:**
*Runners-up* 1982–83;
**Division 2:** *Champions* 1997–98;
*Runners-up* 1981–82;
**Division 3:** *Champions* 1968–69;
*Runners-up* 1978–79;
**Division 4:** *Champions* 1977–78.

**FA Cup:** *Runners-up* 1984, semi-finals 1970, 1984, 1987, 2003, 2007.

**Football League Cup:** Semi-final 1979, 2005.

**European Competitions**
**UEFA Cup:** 1983–84.

## sky SPORTS FACT FILE

Two of the earliest black professional footballers were brothers Eddie and Jack Cother who played for Watford from the late 1890s. Their father was of Indian origin and Jack, the more proficient player, made over 100 Southern League appearances for the Hornets between 1898 and 1905.

*Most League Points (2 for a win):* 71, Division 4, 1977–78.

*Most League Points (3 for a win):* 88, Division 2, 1997–98.

*Most League Goals:* 92, Division 4, 1959–60.

*Highest League Scorer in Season:* Cliff Holton, 42, Division 4, 1959–60.

*Most League Goals in Total Aggregate:* Luther Blissett, 148, 1976–83, 1984–88, 1991–92.

*Most League Goals in One Match:* 5, Eddie Mummery v Newport Co, Division 3 (S), 5 January 1924.

*Most Capped Players:* John Barnes, 31 (79), England; Kenny Jackett, 31, Wales.

*Most League Appearances:* Luther Blissett, 415, 1976–83, 1984–88, 1991–92.

*Youngest League Player:* Keith Mercer, 16 years 125 days v Tranmere R, 16 February 1973.

*Record Transfer Fee Received:* £9,600,000 from Aston Villa for Ashley Young, January 2007.

*Record Transfer Fee Paid:* £3,250,000 to WBA for Nathan Ellington, August 2007.

*Football League Record:* 1920 Original Member of Division 3; 1921–58 Division 3 (S); 1958–60 Division 4; 1960–69 Division 3; 1969–72 Division 2; 1972–75 Division 3; 1975–78 Division 4; 1978–79 Division 3; 1979–82 Division 2; 1982–88 Division 1; 1988–92 Division 2; 1992–96 Division 1; 1996–98 Division 2; 1998–99 Division 1; 1999–2000 FA Premier League; 2000–04 Division 1; 2004–06 FL C; 2006–07 FA Premier League; 2007– FL C.

## LATEST SEQUENCES

*Longest Sequence of League Wins:* 7, 28.8.2000 – 14.10.2000.

*Longest Sequence of League Defeats:* 9, 26.12.1972 – 27.2.1973.

*Longest Sequence of League Draws:* 7, 30.11.1996 – 27.1.1997.

*Longest Sequence of Unbeaten League Matches:* 22, 1.10.1996 – 1.3.1997.

*Longest Sequence Without a League Win:* 19, 27.11.1971 – 8.4.1972.

*Successive Scoring Runs:* 22 from 20.8.1985.

*Successive Non-scoring Runs:* 7 from 18.12.1971.

## MANAGERS

John Goodall 1903–10
Harry Kent 1910–26
Fred Pagnam 1926–29
Neil McBain 1929–37
Bill Findlay 1938–47
Jack Bray 1947–48
Eddie Hapgood 1948–50
Ron Gray 1950–51
Haydn Green 1951–52
Len Goulden 1952–55
    (*General Manager to 1956*)
Johnny Paton 1955–56
Neil McBain 1956–59
Ron Burgess 1959–63
Bill McGarry 1963–64
Ken Furphy 1964–71
George Kirby 1971–73
Mike Keen 1973–77
Graham Taylor 1977–87
Dave Bassett 1987–88
Steve Harrison 1988–90
Colin Lee 1990
Steve Perryman 1990–93
Glenn Roeder 1993–96
Kenny Jackett 1996–97
Graham Taylor 1997–2001
Gianluca Vialli 2001–02
Ray Lewington 2002–05
Adrian Boothroyd 2005–08
Brendan Rodgers 2008–09
Malky Mackay 2009–11
Sean Dyche 2011–12
Gianfranco Zola July 2012–

## TEN YEAR LEAGUE RECORD

| | | P | W | D | L | F | A | Pts | Pos |
|---|---|---|---|---|---|---|---|---|---|
| 2003-04 | Div 1 | 46 | 15 | 12 | 19 | 54 | 68 | 57 | 16 |
| 2004-05 | FL C | 46 | 12 | 16 | 18 | 52 | 59 | 52 | 18 |
| 2005-06 | FL C | 46 | 22 | 15 | 9 | 77 | 53 | 81 | 3 |
| 2006-07 | PR Lge | 38 | 5 | 13 | 20 | 29 | 59 | 28 | 20 |
| 2007-08 | FL C | 46 | 18 | 16 | 12 | 62 | 56 | 70 | 6 |
| 2008-09 | FL C | 46 | 16 | 10 | 20 | 68 | 72 | 58 | 13 |
| 2009-10 | FL C | 46 | 14 | 12 | 20 | 61 | 68 | 54 | 16 |
| 2010-11 | FL C | 46 | 16 | 13 | 17 | 77 | 71 | 61 | 14 |
| 2011-12 | FL C | 46 | 16 | 16 | 14 | 56 | 64 | 64 | 11 |
| 2012-13 | FL C | 46 | 23 | 8 | 15 | 85 | 58 | 77 | 3 |

## DID YOU KNOW ?

Centre forward Frank Hoddinott led the scoring charts for Watford in their first Football League season, 1920–21, with 22 goals. On 12 February 1921 he became the first Hornets player to win a full international cap when he lined up for Wales against Scotland at Aberdeen.

## WATFORD – FL CHAMPIONSHIP 2012–13 LEAGUE RECORD

| Match No. | Date | Venue | Opponents | Result | H/T Score | Lg Pos. | Goalscorers | Attendance |
|---|---|---|---|---|---|---|---|---|
| 1 | Aug 18 | A | Crystal Palace | W 3-2 | 1-2 | 4 | Taylor [22], Abdi [88], Vydra [90] | 17,109 |
| 2 | 21 | H | Ipswich T | L 0-1 | 0-0 | 13 | | 12,422 |
| 3 | 25 | H | Birmingham C | W 2-0 | 2-0 | 5 | Abdi (pen) [4], Vydra [17] | 11,022 |
| 4 | Sept 1 | A | Derby Co | L 1-5 | 0-3 | 12 | Vydra [74] | 20,608 |
| 5 | 15 | A | Bolton W | L 1-2 | 0-2 | 18 | Doyley [58] | 16,608 |
| 6 | 18 | H | Brighton & HA | L 0-1 | 0-0 | 20 | | 11,894 |
| 7 | 22 | H | Bristol C | D 2-2 | 0-0 | 20 | Wilson, J (og) [59], Vydra [72] | 11,886 |
| 8 | 29 | A | Huddersfield T | W 3-2 | 0-1 | 18 | Forestieri [68], Hall [83], Deeney (pen) [87] | 14,564 |
| 9 | Oct 2 | A | Charlton Ath | W 2-1 | 1-1 | 11 | Hoban [29], Abdi [70] | 15,585 |
| 10 | 6 | H | Middlesbrough | L 1-2 | 1-1 | 14 | Deeney [1] | 12,006 |
| 11 | 20 | H | Peterborough U | W 1-0 | 0-0 | 13 | Vydra (pen) [90] | 15,950 |
| 12 | 23 | A | Cardiff C | L 1-2 | 1-0 | 15 | Hoban [28] | 20,077 |
| 13 | 27 | A | Blackburn R | L 0-1 | 0-0 | 16 | | 13,233 |
| 14 | Nov 3 | H | Leicester C | W 2-1 | 1-0 | 15 | Abdi [14], Forestieri [68] | 12,954 |
| 15 | 6 | H | Millwall | D 0-0 | 0-0 | 16 | | 11,293 |
| 16 | 10 | A | Leeds U | W 6-1 | 1-0 | 12 | Vydra 2 [28, 83], Abdi [61], Yeates [75], Deeney [90], Murray [90] | 19,104 |
| 17 | 17 | H | Wolverhampton W | W 2-1 | 1-0 | 10 | Chalobah [35], Deeney [68] | 13,588 |
| 18 | 24 | A | Blackpool | D 2-2 | 2-0 | 11 | Anya [4], Deeney [21] | 13,076 |
| 19 | 27 | A | Sheffield W | W 4-1 | 1-1 | 8 | Forestieri [18], Geijo [67], Deeney [75], Yeates [83] | 18,922 |
| 20 | Dec 1 | H | Barnsley | W 4-1 | 1-0 | 6 | Deeney 2 [10, 66], Yeates [59], Vydra (pen) [83] | 11,335 |
| 21 | 8 | H | Hull C | L 1-2 | 0-1 | 6 | Deeney [90] | 12,156 |
| 22 | 15 | A | Burnley | D 1-1 | 1-1 | 7 | Chalobah [11] | 14,896 |
| 23 | 22 | H | Nottingham F | W 2-0 | 2-0 | 6 | Vydra 2 [15, 40] | 15,143 |
| 24 | 29 | A | Brighton & HA | W 3-1 | 0-0 | 6 | Deeney [54], Vydra 2 [68, 69] | 26,727 |
| 25 | Jan 1 | A | Charlton Ath | L 3-4 | 1-2 | 6 | Pudil [11], Abdi (pen) [53], Geijo [68] | 14,221 |
| 26 | 12 | A | Middlesbrough | W 2-1 | 1-0 | 6 | Vydra 2 [45, 83] | 17,499 |
| 27 | 19 | H | Huddersfield T | W 4-0 | 1-0 | 6 | Deeney (pen) [45], Vydra 2 [57, 74], Battocchio [86] | 12,522 |
| 28 | 26 | A | Nottingham F | W 3-0 | 2-0 | 4 | Vydra 2 [20, 72], Deeney [34] | 20,732 |
| 29 | 29 | A | Bristol C | L 0-2 | 0-1 | 4 | | 13,586 |
| 30 | Feb 2 | H | Bolton W | W 2-1 | 1-1 | 4 | Vydra [36], Abdi [70] | 13,223 |
| 31 | 8 | H | Crystal Palace | D 2-2 | 2-0 | 3 | Abdi [6], Chalobah [14] | 15,079 |
| 32 | 16 | A | Birmingham C | W 4-0 | 2-0 | 3 | Deeney 2 [38, 62], Anya [43], Abdi [89] | 18,933 |
| 33 | 19 | A | Ipswich T | W 2-0 | 1-0 | 3 | Anya [18], Chalobah [72] | 16,821 |
| 34 | 23 | H | Derby Co | W 2-1 | 1-0 | 2 | Vydra [35], Ekstrand [68] | 14,425 |
| 35 | Mar 1 | A | Wolverhampton W | D 1-1 | 1-0 | 2 | Abdi [41] | 18,571 |
| 36 | 5 | H | Sheffield W | W 2-1 | 0-1 | 2 | Forestieri 2 [53, 63] | 12,727 |
| 37 | 9 | H | Blackpool | L 1-2 | 1-0 | 2 | Battocchio [27] | 13,857 |
| 38 | 16 | A | Barnsley | L 0-1 | 0-1 | 3 | | 9076 |
| 39 | 29 | H | Burnley | D 3-3 | 2-2 | 3 | Deeney [6], Forestieri 2 [29, 72] | 15,435 |
| 40 | Apr 2 | A | Hull C | W 1-0 | 1-0 | 3 | Deeney [41] | 20,043 |
| 41 | 6 | H | Cardiff C | D 0-0 | 0-0 | 3 | | 15,550 |
| 42 | 13 | A | Peterborough U | L 2-3 | 0-1 | 3 | Yeates [85], Forestieri [90] | 10,848 |
| 43 | 16 | A | Millwall | L 0-1 | 0-0 | 3 | | 9366 |
| 44 | 20 | H | Blackburn R | W 4-0 | 0-0 | 3 | Deeney 2 [52, 61], Abdi [67], Briggs [75] | 13,775 |
| 45 | 26 | A | Leicester C | W 2-1 | 2-0 | 3 | Deeney [41], Chalobah [43] | 25,091 |
| 46 | May 4 | H | Leeds U | L 1-2 | 1-1 | 3 | Abdi [45] | 16,968 |

**Final League Position: 3**

### GOALSCORERS

*League (85):* Vydra 20 (2 pens), Deeney 19 (2 pens), Abdi 12 (2 pens), Forestieri 8, Chalobah 5, Yeates 4, Anya 3, Battocchio 2, Geijo 2, Hoban 2, Briggs 1, Doyley 1, Ekstrand 1, Hall 1, Murray 1, Pudil 1, Taylor 1, own goal 1.
*FA Cup (0).*
*Capital One Cup (2):* Anya 1, Iwelumo 1.
*Championship Play-Offs (3):* Vydra 2, Deeney 1.

| Almunia M 39 | Dickinson C 2 + 2 | Taylor M 3 | Nosworthy N 18 + 1 | Doyley L 28 + 6 | Yeates M 18 + 11 | Hogg J 31 + 7 | Eustace J 2 + 3 | Murray S 8 + 7 | Abdi A 36 + 2 | Garner J 2 | Vydra M 27 + 14 | Iwelumo C 4 + 3 | Smith C 2 + 5 | Hodson L 1 + 1 | Pudil D 35 + 2 | Anya I 18 + 7 | Beleck S —— + 5 | Cassetti M 36 + 2 | Battocchio C 15 + 7 | Neuton P 7 + 1 | Forestieri F 19 + 9 | Chalobah N 34 + 4 | Deeney T 33 + 7 | Hall F 19 + 2 | Hoban T 19 | Ekstrand J 29 + 3 | Geijo A 7 + 11 | Thompson A —— + 4 | Fanchone J 1 | Mujangi Bia G —— + 3 | Forsyth C 1 + 1 | Bond J 7 + 1 | Briggs M 5 + 2 | Buaben P —— + 1 | Bonham J —— + 1 | Match No. |
|---|---|---|---|---|---|---|---|---|---|---|---|---|---|---|---|---|---|---|---|---|---|---|---|---|---|---|---|---|---|---|---|---|---|---|---|---|
| 1 | 2 | 3 | 4 | 5 | 6 | 7 | 8¹ | 9³ | 10 | 11² | 12 | 13 | 14 | | | | | | | | | | | | | | | | | | | | | | | 1 |
| 1 | | 3 | 4 | | 6³ | 7 | | 9² | 8 | 11¹ | 10 | 12 | | | 5 | | | 2 | | | | 13 | 14 | | | | | | | | | | | | | 2 |
| 1 | 12 | 3 | 4 | 2 | 6 | 7 | | 9³ | 8 | 11¹ | 10² | | 14 | | 5 | | | 13 | | | | | | | | | | | | | | | | | | 3 |
| 1 | 3 | | 4 | 2 | 7³ | 6 | | 9² | 8 | 11 | 10 | | | | 5¹ | 12 | | | | | | 13 | 14 | | | | | | | | | | | | | 4 |
| 1 | | 4 | 2 | | 6³ | 7 | | 9¹ | 8² | 11 | 10 | 13 | | | 5 | 14 | | | | | 3 | 12 | | | | | | | | | | | | | | 5 |
| 1 | | 4 | 12 | 6 | 7 | | | 8 | 10 | 9³ | | | | | 5 | 14 | 2¹ | | 3 | 11² | 13 | | | | | | | | | | | | | | | 6 |
| 1 | | 4 | 14 | 6 | | 7 | 8 | 10 | | | | | | | 5 | | | 2³ | 3² | 11¹ | 9 | 12 | 13 | | | | | | | | | | | | | 7 |
| 1 | | | 12 | 7 | | | 14 | 8¹ | | | | | 13 | | 5 | | | 2 | 3 | 11³ | 9 | 10 | 4 | 6 | | | | | | | | | | | | 8 |
| 1 | 13 | | | 7 | | | 8 | | 14 | | | | | | 9 | | | 5 | 4¹ | 11¹ | 6² | 10³ | 3 | 2 | 12 | | | | | | | | | | | 9 |
| 1 | | | 13 | 6 | | 14 | 7² | 11⁴ | | | | | | | 2 | | | 5 | 3³ | 9 | 10¹ | 4 | 8 | 12 | | | | | | | | | | | | 10 |
| 1 | | 3 | 14 | 5 | | 7¹ | 12 | | | | | | | | 6 | | | 11³ | 9 | 10² | 2 | 4 | 13 | | | | | | | | | | | | | 11 |
| 1 | | 4 | 9 | 8 | | 10¹ | | | | | | | | | 2⁴ | 12 | | 6² | | | 7¹ | 14 | 3 | 5 | | 11³ | 13 | | | | | | | | | 12 |
| 1 | | 2 | 7² | 6 | | 8 | | | | | | | | | 5 | 13 | | 11³ | | | 10 | 3 | 4 | 12 | 14 | | 9¹ | | | | | | | | | 13 |
| 1 | | 4 | | 7 | | 8² | | | | | | 12 | 13 | | 6 | 14 | | 2 | | | 11¹ | 9 | 10 | 3³ | 5 | | | | | | | | | | | 14 |
| 1 | | 2 | | 7 | | 8 | | | | | | 13 | | | 6 | 12 | | 5¹ | | | 11² | 9 | 10 | 3 | 4 | 14 | | | | | | | | | | 15 |
| 1 | | 2 | 9 | 13 | | 14 | 6² | | 11 | | 8³ | | | | 5 | | | 7 | | | 12 | 3 | 4 | 10¹ | | | | | | | | | | | | 16 |
| 1 | | 2³ | 6² | 7 | | | | | | | | 12 | 13 | | 9 | | | 5¹ | | | 11 | 8 | 10 | 4 | 3 | 14 | | | | | | | | | | 17 |
| 1 | | | 8² | | | 13 | | | 11³ | | | | | | 5 | 9¹ | | 12 | 6 | | 14 | 7 | 10 | 3 | 2 | 4 | | | | | | | | | | 18 |
| 1 | 13 | | 9³ | 8 | | 14 | | | | | | | | | 6² | | | 2 | | | 11¹ | 7 | 12 | 3 | 4 | 5 | 10 | | | | | | | | | 19 |
| 1 | | | 6 | 7 | | | | | | | | | | | 12 | | | 9² | | | 5 | 13 | | | 8 | 10³ | 2³ | 3 | 4 | | | | | | | 20 |
| 1 | | | 6 | 7 | | | | 13 | | | | | | | 11 | | | 9² | 14 | | 5 | | 8 | 10 | 2³ | 4 | 3¹ | | 10² | | | | | | | 21 |
| 1 | | | 12 | 8 | | | | | 6 | | | | 13 | | 9³ | 14 | | 5 | | | 7¹ | 11 | | 3 | 4 | 2 | 10² | | | | | | | | | 22 |
| 1 | | | 7 | | | | | | | | | 8² | 11¹ | | 6 | | 12 | 5 | 13 | | 9³ | 10 | | 2 | 3 | 4 | | | | 14 | | | | | | 23 |
| 1 | | | 7 | | | | | | 9³ | | | | 10 | | 3 | 8² | | 14 | 12 | | 6 | 11 | | 2¹ | 4 | 5 | | | 13 | | | | | | | 24 |
| 1 | | | 12 | | | | | 5¹ | 7¹ | | | 13 | | | 6² | | | 9 | | 2 | 11 | 8 | 14 | 3 | 4 | 10 | | | | | | | | | | 25 |
| 1 | 4 | 2 | 13 | | | 12 | | | 6 | | | 11² | | | 9 | | | 5 | 7 | | | 8¹ | 10 | | | 3 | | | | | | | | | | 26 |
| 1 | 3 | 2 | | | | 12 | | | 6 | | | 11² | | | 5 | 7 | | 13 | 8¹ | 10³ | | | | | | 4 | 14 | | | | | 9 | | | | 27 |
| 1 | 4 | 2 | 14 | 13 | | | | | 6 | | | 11 | | | 9 | 5¹ | 7² | 8³ | | | 10 | 12 | | | | 3 | | | | | | | | | | 28 |
| 1 | | 3 | | | | 7 | 8³ | 5¹ | 9 | | | | | | 6 | | | 11 | 14 | 13 | 2 | | | | | 4 | 10² | | | | | | | | | 29 |
| 1 | 12 | 3 | | 13 | 14 | | | | 6 | | | 11 | | | 5 | | | 7 | 8³ | | 9² | 10 | 2 | 4¹ | | | | | | | | | | | | 30 |
| 1 | | 3 | | 8 | | 7 | | | | | | 10¹ | | | 9 | | | 5 | 13 | 12 | 6² | 11 | 2 | 4 | | | | | | | | | | | | 31 |
| 1 | 3 | | 4 | | | 14 | 13 | | 6 | | | 11³ | | | 9¹ | 5² | | 2 | 8 | | | 7 | 10 | | | | 12 | | | | | | | | | 32 |
| 1 | 3 | 2 | 14 | | | 8 | | | 6 | | | 5 | | | 9² | 5 | | 11¹ | 7 | | 10³ | 4 | | | | | | 13 | | | | | | | | 33 |
| 1¹ | | 3 | 2 | | | 13 | | | 6 | | | 10³ | | | 9 | 5 | 7 | | | | 8 | 14 | | | | 4 | 11² | | | 12 | | | | | | 34 |
| 1 | | 3 | 2 | | | 13 | | | 6 | | | 11¹ | | | 14 | 9³ | | 5 | 8 | | 12 | 7² | 10 | 4 | | | | | | | | 1 | | | | 35 |
| 1 | | 3 | 14 | | | 9¹ | | | 7 | | | 11 | | | 8² | 5³ | | 2 | 6 | | 12 | 13 | 10 | 4 | | | | | | | | 1 | | | | 36 |
| 1 | | 4 | 2 | 5 | | 8 | | | 12 | | | 6² | | | 7³ | | | 9 | 11¹ | | 10 | 13 | 14 | | | | | | | | | 1 | 3 | | | 37 |
| 1 | | 3 | 2 | 6¹ | | 8³ | | | 11 | | | 9² | | | 5 | 7 | | 14 | 12 | | 10 | 4 | | | | | | 13 | | | | 1 | | | | 38 |
| 1 | | | 12 | | | 8 | | | 13 | | | 9² | | | 5¹ | 7 | | 11 | 6 | | 10³ | 2 | | 4 | 14 | | | | | | | 1 | 3 | | | 39 |
| 1 | | | 12 | | | 6 | | | 11³ | | | 13 | | | 9 | 5 | | 7 | 8 | | 10 | 2¹ | | 4 | | | | | | | | 1 | 3² | 14 | | 40 |
| 1 | | | 2 | | | 12 | | | | | | 5 | | | 11² | 9 | | 5 | 6¹ | 13 | 7 | 10 | | 4 | | | | | | | | | | 8 | | 41 |
| 1 | | | 2 | 13 | | 6³ | | | 8 | | | 12 | | | 9 | 5 | 4 | | 11 | | 7² | 10 | | 3¹ | 14 | | | | | | | | | | | 42 |
| 1 | | | 2 | 6² | | 13 | | | 11 | | | 7³ | | | 9 | 3 | | 14 | 8 | | 10¹ | 4 | | 12 | | | | | | 5 | | | | | | 43 |
| 1 | | | 2 | 9 | | 14 | | | 7 | | | 13 | | | 5 | 6³ | | 3 | 11² | | 8 | 10 | | 4¹ | | | | | | 12 | | | | | | 44 |
| 1 | | 4 | 13 | 2 | | 8³ | | | 6 | | | 5 | | | 7¹ | 9 | | 14 | 10² | | 3 | 11 | | 12 | | | | | | | | | | | | 45 |
| 1 | | 2 | 14 | 5³ | | 9 | | | 13 | | | 6 | | | 7² | 3 | | 11 | 9 | | 10 | 4 | | 12 | | | | | 11¹ | 12 | | | | | | 46 |

# WEST BROMWICH ALBION

## FOUNDATION

There is a well known story that when employees of Salter's Spring Works in West Bromwich decided to form a football club, they had to send someone to the nearby Association Football stronghold of Wednesbury to purchase a football. A weekly subscription of 2d (less than 1p) was imposed and the name of the new club was West Bromwich Strollers.

*The Hawthorns, West Bromwich, West Midlands B71 4LF.*

*Telephone:* (0871) 271 1100.

*Fax:* (0871) 271 9851.

*Ticket Office:* (0121) 227 2227.

*Website:* www.wbafc.co.uk

*Email:* enquiries@wbafc.co.uk

*Ground Capacity:* 26,445.

*Record Attendance:* 64,815 v Arsenal, FA Cup 6th rd, 6 March 1937.

*Pitch Measurements:* 105m × 68m (114yd × 74yd)

*Chairman:* Jeremy Peace.

*Chief Executive:* Mark Jenkins.

*Head Coach:* Steve Clarke.

*Assistant Head Coaches:* Keith Downing, Kevin Keen.

*Physio:* Richie Rawlins.

*Colours:* Navy blue and white striped shirts, white shorts with navy blue trim, white socks with navy blue hoops.

*Year Formed:* 1878.

*Turned Professional:* 1885.

*Previous Name:* 1878, West Bromwich Strollers; 1881, West Bromwich Albion.

*Club Nicknames:* 'The Throstles', 'The Baggies', 'Albion'.

*Grounds:* 1878, Coopers Hill; 1879, Dartmouth Park; 1881, Bunns Field, Walsall Street; 1882, Four Acres (Dartmouth Cricket Club); 1885, Stoney Lane; 1900, The Hawthorns.

*First Football League Game:* 8 September 1888, Football League, v Stoke (a) W 2–0 – Roberts; Jack Horton, Green; Ezra Horton, Perry, Bayliss; Bassett, Woodhall (1), Hendry, Pearson, Wilson (1).

*Record League Victory:* 12–0 v Darwen, Division 1, 4 April 1892 – Reader; Jack Horton, McCulloch; Reynolds (2), Perry, Groves; Bassett (3), McLeod, Nicholls (1), Pearson (4), Geddes (1), (1 og).

*Record Cup Victory:* 10–1 v Chatham (away), FA Cup 3rd rd, 2 March 1889 – Roberts; Jack Horton, Green; Timmins (1), Charles Perry, Ezra Horton; Bassett (2), Walter Perry (1), Bayliss (2), Pearson, Wilson (3), (1 og).

## HONOURS

**Football League – Division 1:**
*Champions* 1919–20;
*Runners-up* 1924–25, 1953–54, 2001–02, 2003–04.
**FL C:** *Champions* 2007–08;
*Runners-up* 2009–10.
**Division 2:** *Champions* 1901–02, 1910–11; *Runners-up* 1930–31, 1948–49.
**FA Cup:** *Winners* 1888, 1892, 1931, 1954, 1968; *Runners-up* 1886, 1887, 1895, 1912, 1935.
**Football League Cup:** *Winners* 1966; *Runners-up* 1967, 1970.
**European Competitions**
**European Cup-Winners' Cup:** 1968–69.
**European Fairs Cup:** 1966–67.
**UEFA Cup:** 1978–79, 1979–80, 1981–82.

## sky SPORTS FACT FILE

On 19 May 1888 West Bromwich Albion took on Scottish Cup holders Renton at 'Second' Hampden Park in a match billed as the World's Championship. The match was played in torrential rain and the referee twice took the players off the field. The Baggies lost the match 4-1.

*Record Defeat:* 3–10 v Stoke C, Division 1, 4 February 1937.

*Most League Points (2 for a win):* 60, Division 1, 1919–20.

*Most League Points (3 for a win):* 91, FL C, 2009–10.

*Most League Goals:* 105, Division 2, 1929–30.

*Highest League Scorer in Season:* William 'Ginger' Richardson, 39, Division 1, 1935–36.

*Most League Goals in Total Aggregate:* Tony Brown, 218, 1963–79.

*Most League Goals in One Match:* 6, Jimmy Cookson v Blackpool, Division 2, 17 September 1927.

*Most Capped Player:* Stuart Williams, 33 (43), Wales.

*Most League Appearances:* Tony Brown, 574, 1963–80.

*Youngest League Player:* Charlie Wilson, 16 years 73 days v Oldham Ath, 1 October 1921.

*Record Transfer Fee Received:* £8,000,000 from Aston Villa for Curtis Davies, July 2008.

*Record Transfer Fee Paid:* £4,700,000 to Mallorca for Borja Valero, August 2008.

*Football League Record:* 1888 Founder Member of Football League; 1901–02 Division 2; 1902–04 Division 1; 1904–11 Division 2; 1911–27 Division 1; 1927–31 Division 2; 1931–38 Division 1; 1938–49 Division 2; 1949–73 Division 1; 1973–76 Division 2; 1976–86 Division 1; 1986–91 Division 2; 1991–92 Division 3; 1992–93 Division 2; 1993–2002 Division 1; 2002–03 FA Premier League; 2003–04 Division 1; 2004–06 FA Premier League; 2006–08 FL C; 2008–09 FA Premier League; 2009–10 FL C; 2010– FA Premier League.

## LATEST SEQUENCES

*Longest Sequence of League Wins:* 11, 5.4.1930 – 8.9.1930.

*Longest Sequence of League Defeats:* 11, 28.10.1995 – 26.12.1995.

*Longest Sequence of League Draws:* 5, 30.8.1999 – 3.10.1999.

*Longest Sequence of Unbeaten League Matches:* 17, 7.9.1957 – 7.12.1957.

*Longest Sequence Without a League Win:* 15, 16.10.2004 – 25.9.2004.

*Successive Scoring Runs:* 36 from 26.4.1958.

*Successive Non-scoring Runs:* 4 from 15.2.1913.

## MANAGERS

Louis Ford 1890–92
*(Secretary-Manager)*
Henry Jackson 1892–94
*(Secretary-Manager)*
Edward Stephenson 1894–95
*(Secretary-Manager)*
Clement Keys 1895–96
*(Secretary-Manager)*
Frank Heaven 1896–1902
*(Secretary-Manager)*
Fred Everiss 1902–48
Jack Smith 1948–52
Jesse Carver 1952
Vic Buckingham 1953–59
Gordon Clark 1959–61
Archie Macaulay 1961–63
Jimmy Hagan 1963–67
Alan Ashman 1967–71
Don Howe 1971–75
Johnny Giles 1975–77
Ronnie Allen 1977
Ron Atkinson 1978–81
Ronnie Allen 1981–82
Ron Wylie 1982–84
Johnny Giles 1984–85
Nobby Stiles 1985–86
Ron Saunders 1986–87
Ron Atkinson 1987–88
Brian Talbot 1988–91
Bobby Gould 1991–92
Ossie Ardiles 1992–93
Keith Burkinshaw 1993–94
Alan Buckley 1994–97
Ray Harford 1997
Denis Smith 1997–1999
Brian Little 1999–2000
Gary Megson 2000–04
Bryan Robson 2004–06
Tony Mowbray 2006–09
Roberto Di Matteo 2009–11
Roy Hodgson 2011–12
Steve Clarke June 2012–

## TEN YEAR LEAGUE RECORD

|  |  | P | W | D | L | F | A | Pts | Pos |
|---|---|---|---|---|---|---|---|---|---|
| 2003-04 | Div 1 | 46 | 25 | 11 | 10 | 64 | 42 | 86 | 2 |
| 2004-05 | PR Lge | 38 | 6 | 16 | 16 | 36 | 61 | 34 | 17 |
| 2005-06 | PR Lge | 38 | 7 | 9 | 22 | 31 | 58 | 30 | 19 |
| 2006-07 | FL C | 46 | 22 | 10 | 14 | 81 | 55 | 76 | 4 |
| 2007-08 | FL C | 46 | 23 | 12 | 11 | 88 | 55 | 81 | 1 |
| 2008-09 | PR Lge | 38 | 8 | 8 | 22 | 36 | 67 | 32 | 20 |
| 2009-10 | FL C | 46 | 26 | 13 | 7 | 89 | 48 | 91 | 2 |
| 2010-11 | PR Lge | 38 | 12 | 11 | 15 | 56 | 71 | 47 | 11 |
| 2011-12 | PR Lge | 38 | 13 | 8 | 17 | 45 | 52 | 47 | 10 |
| 2012-13 | PR Lge | 38 | 14 | 7 | 17 | 53 | 57 | 49 | 8 |

## DID YOU KNOW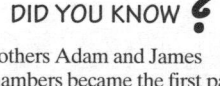

Brothers Adam and James Chambers became the first pair of twins to represent England at international level when they were selected for the squad for the FIFA World Youth Championships in Nigeria in 1999. They both came off the bench against Cameroon on 8 April. England lost the game 1-0.

## WEST BROMWICH ALBION – FA PREMIERSHIP 2012–13 LEAGUE RECORD

| Match No. | Date | Venue | Opponents | Result | H/T Score | Lg Pos. | Goalscorers | Attendance |
|---|---|---|---|---|---|---|---|---|
| 1 | Aug 18 | H | Liverpool | W 3-0 | 1-0 | 3 | Gera [43], Odemwingie (pen) [64], Lukaku [77] | 26,039 |
| 2 | 25 | A | Tottenham H | D 1-1 | 0-0 | 4 | Morrison [90] | 36,166 |
| 3 | Sept 1 | H | Everton | W 2-0 | 0-0 | 3 | Long [65], McAuley [82] | 25,383 |
| 4 | 15 | A | Fulham | L 0-3 | 0-2 | 6 | | 25,691 |
| 5 | 22 | H | Reading | W 1-0 | 0-0 | 3 | Lukaku [71] | 23,854 |
| 6 | 30 | A | Aston Villa | D 1-1 | 0-0 | 6 | Long [51] | 34,489 |
| 7 | Oct 6 | H | QPR | W 3-2 | 2-1 | 4 | Morrison [5], Gera [22], Mulumbu [85] | 23,987 |
| 8 | 20 | H | Manchester C | L 1-2 | 0-0 | 6 | Long [67] | 24,891 |
| 9 | 28 | A | Newcastle U | L 1-2 | 0-1 | 8 | Lukaku [55] | 49,731 |
| 10 | Nov 5 | H | Southampton | W 2-0 | 1-0 | 5 | Odemwingie 2 [36, 60] | 25,635 |
| 11 | 10 | A | Wigan Ath | W 2-1 | 2-1 | 5 | Morrison [31], Caldwell (og) [43] | 17,812 |
| 12 | 17 | H | Chelsea | W 2-1 | 1-1 | 4 | Long [10], Odemwingie [50] | 25,933 |
| 13 | 24 | A | Sunderland | W 4-2 | 2-0 | 3 | Gera [30], Long [44], Lukaku (pen) [81], Fortune [90] | 36,390 |
| 14 | 28 | A | Swansea C | L 1-3 | 1-3 | 4 | Lukaku [45] | 20,377 |
| 15 | Dec 1 | H | Stoke C | L 0-1 | 0-0 | 5 | | 24,739 |
| 16 | 8 | A | Arsenal | L 0-2 | 0-1 | 5 | | 60,083 |
| 17 | 16 | H | West Ham U | D 0-0 | 0-0 | 6 | | 24,816 |
| 18 | 22 | H | Norwich C | W 2-1 | 1-1 | 6 | Gera [43], Lukaku [82] | 25,799 |
| 19 | 26 | A | QPR | W 2-1 | 1-0 | 6 | Brunt [29], Green (og) [49] | 17,782 |
| 20 | 29 | A | Manchester U | L 0-2 | 0-1 | 7 | | 75,595 |
| 21 | Jan 1 | H | Fulham | L 1-2 | 0-1 | 7 | Lukaku [49] | 25,436 |
| 22 | 12 | A | Reading | L 2-3 | 1-0 | 7 | Lukaku 2 [19, 69] | 23,495 |
| 23 | 19 | H | Aston Villa | D 2-2 | 0-2 | 8 | Brunt [49], Odemwingie [83] | 25,583 |
| 24 | 30 | A | Everton | L 1-2 | 0-2 | 9 | Long [65] | 31,376 |
| 25 | Feb 3 | H | Tottenham H | L 0-1 | 0-0 | 9 | | 24,978 |
| 26 | 11 | A | Liverpool | W 2-0 | 0-0 | 8 | McAuley [81], Lukaku [91] | 44,752 |
| 27 | 23 | H | Sunderland | W 2-1 | 1-0 | 7 | Lukaku 2 (1 pen) [35 (p), 75] | 25,924 |
| 28 | Mar 2 | A | Chelsea | L 0-1 | 0-1 | 9 | | 41,548 |
| 29 | 9 | H | Swansea C | W 2-1 | 1-1 | 7 | Lukaku [40], de Guzman (og) [61] | 24,832 |
| 30 | 16 | A | Stoke C | D 0-0 | 0-0 | 8 | | 26,317 |
| 31 | 30 | A | West Ham U | L 1-3 | 0-2 | 8 | Dorrans (pen) [88] | 34,966 |
| 32 | Apr 6 | H | Arsenal | L 1-2 | 0-1 | 8 | Morrison (pen) [71] | 26,144 |
| 33 | 20 | H | Newcastle U | D 1-1 | 0-1 | 8 | Jones [64] | 25,671 |
| 34 | 27 | A | Southampton | W 3-0 | 1-0 | 8 | Fortune [6], Lukaku [67], Long [77] | 31,946 |
| 35 | May 4 | H | Wigan Ath | L 2-3 | 1-1 | 8 | Long [29], McAuley [50] | 25,756 |
| 36 | 7 | A | Manchester C | L 0-1 | 0-1 | 8 | | 46,158 |
| 37 | 12 | A | Norwich C | L 0-4 | 0-1 | 8 | | 26,837 |
| 38 | 19 | H | Manchester U | D 5-5 | 1-3 | 8 | Morrison [40], Lukaku 3 [50, 81, 86], Mulumbu [81] | 26,438 |

**Final League Position: 8**

### GOALSCORERS

*League (53):* Lukaku 17 (2 pens), Long 8, Morrison 5 (1 pen), Odemwingie 5 (1 pen), Gera 4, McAuley 3, Brunt 2, Fortune 2, Mulumbu 2, Dorrans 1 (1 pen), Jones 1, own goals 3.
*FA Cup (1):* Long 1.
*Capital One Cup (5):* Long 2, Brunt 1, Ghanassy 1, Tamas 1.

| Foster B 30 | Reid S 11 | McAuley G 36 | Olsson J 36 | Ridgewell L 28+2 | Morrison J 33+2 | Yacob C 29+1 | Mulumbu Y 28 | Odemwingie P 13+12 | Long S 25+9 | Gera Z 14+2 | Fortune M 9+12 | Lukaku R 20+15 | Brunt C 23+8 | Dorrans G 21+5 | Rosenberg M 5+19 | Jones B 24+3 | Popov G 10+2 | Tamas G 7+4 | Jara Reyes G —+1 | Myhill B 8 | Thorne G 3+2 | Thomas J 4+6 | Brown I —+1 | Dawson C 1 | Match No. |
|---|---|---|---|---|---|---|---|---|---|---|---|---|---|---|---|---|---|---|---|---|---|---|---|---|---|
| 1 | 2 | 3 | 4 | 5 | 6[3] | 7 | 8 | 9 | 10 | 11[2] | 12 | 13 | 14 | | | | | | | | | | | | 1 |
| 1 | 2 | 3 | 4 | 5 | 9 | 7 | 6 | | 11[1] | | 10[3] | 12 | 13 | 8[2] | 14 | | | | | | | | | | 2 |
| 1 | 2[1] | 4 | 3 | 5 | 7 | 6 | 8 | 13 | 10[3] | 11 | 14 | 9[2] | 12 | | | | | | | | | | | | 3 |
| 1 | | 3 | 4 | 5 | 9 | 7[3] | 6 | 8[1] | 11[2] | | | 10[1] | 12 | 13 | | 14 | 2 | | | | | | | | 4 |
| 1 | | 3 | 4 | 5 | 6[1] | 8 | 7 | | 12 | 10[2] | | 11[3] | 9 | 13 | 14 | 2 | | | | | | | | | 5 |
| 1 | | 3 | 4 | | 6 | 8 | 7 | 11[3] | 10 | | | 14 | 9[1] | 12 | | | 2[2] | 5 | 13 | | | | | | 6 |
| 1 | | 3 | 4 | | 9 | 6 | 7 | 10[3] | 11[2] | 8 | | 14 | | 13 | | | 5 | 2[1] | 12 | | | | | | 7 |
| 1 | | 4 | 3 | 5 | 6[2] | 9 | 7 | 12 | 11[3] | 13 | 10 | 14 | | 8[1] | | | | | 2 | | | | | | 8 |
| 1 | | 3 | 4 | 5 | 6 | | 8 | 10 | 12 | 7[3] | | 11[1] | | 9[2] | 13 | 14 | 2 | | | | | | | | 9 |
| 1 | | 3 | 4 | 5 | 7 | 6 | | 8[1] | 11[2] | 9 | 14 | 13 | 12 | 10[1] | | 2 | | | | | | | | | 10 |
| | | 3 | 4 | 5 | 9[1] | 7 | 6 | 12 | 11[2] | 13 | | 8[3] | 10 | | | 14 | 2 | | | 1 | | | | | 11 |
| | | 3 | 5 | 6[2] | 7 | 8 | 11 | 10[3] | 9[1] | | 13 | 12 | 14 | 2 | | | 4 | | | 1 | | | | | 12 |
| | | 4 | 3 | 5 | 8[3] | 7 | | 6[2] | 11[1] | 10 | 12 | 13 | 9 | | 2 | | 14 | | | 1 | | | | | 13 |
| | | 2 | 3 | 4 | 7 | 6 | 8 | 10 | | | | 11 | 9 | | | 5 | | | | 1 | | | | | 14 |
| | 2 | 3 | 4 | | 6[3] | 7 | 13 | 11 | 10[2] | | 12 | 14 | 8 | 9[1] | | 5 | | | | 1 | | | | | 15 |
| | 2 | 4 | 3 | 5[1] | 7 | | 8 | 10[2] | 11 | 9[3] | | 13 | 6 | | 14 | | 12 | | | 1 | | | | | 16 |
| | | 3 | 4 | | 7 | | 8 | 10 | 11[2] | 9[1] | | 12 | 6 | | 13 | 2 | 5 | | | 1 | | | | | 17 |
| 1 | | 3 | 4 | | 6 | | | 8 | 13 | 9[2] | 12 | 11[3] | 7 | 10[1] | | 2 | 5 | 14 | | | | | | | 18 |
| 1 | | 3 | 4 | 12 | 7[3] | | 6 | | 13 | 9 | 8 | 11[2] | 10 | | 2 | 5[1] | 14 | | | | | | | | 19 |
| 1 | | 3 | | 5 | 13 | | | 10 | 11 | | 14 | 12 | 7[2] | 9[3] | 8[1] | 2 | | 4 | | | 6 | | | | 20 |
| 1 | | 4 | | 5 | 9 | | 7 | 13 | 12 | 8[2] | 10[1] | 11 | 6[3] | | | 2 | | 3 | | | 14 | | | | 21 |
| 1 | | 3 | 4 | 5 | 9 | | | | | 11 | 7 | 8[1] | 12 | 2 | | | | | | | 6 | 10 | | | 22 |
| 1 | | 3 | 4 | 5 | 6 | 8[1] | | 11 | | 10 | 9[3] | 7[2] | 13 | 2 | | | | | | | 14 | 12 | | | 23 |
| 1 | | 3 | 4 | | 6[2] | 12 | | 13 | | 11 | 9 | 7 | 14 | 2 | 5 | | | | | | 8[1] | 10[2] | | | 24 |
| 1 | 2 | 4 | 3 | 12 | 8 | 7[3] | | | 10 | | 14 | 11[1] | 9 | 6[2] | 13 | | 5[8] | | | | | | | | 25 |
| 1 | 2 | 3 | 4 | 5 | 9 | 6 | 7 | | 11[7] | | 13 | 12 | 10 | 8[1] | | | | | | | | | | | 26 |
| 1 | 2 | 3 | 4 | 5 | 6[2] | 7 | 8 | 14 | 10[1] | | 13 | 11[3] | 9 | 12 | | | | | | | | | | | 27 |
| 1 | 2 | 4 | 3 | 5 | 8 | 6[3] | 7 | 12 | 11 | | 10[1] | | 9[2] | 14 | | | | | | | 13 | | | | 28 |
| 1 | | 3 | 4 | 5 | 9[2] | 6 | 7 | 12 | | | 13 | 11[1] | 10 | 8[3] | | 2 | | | | | 14 | | | | 29 |
| 1 | | 3 | 4 | 5 | 8[3] | 7 | 9 | 12 | 13 | | 14 | 11[2] | 10 | | | 2 | | | | | 6[1] | | | | 30 |
| 1 | | 2 | 5 | 3 | | 6[2] | 8[4] | 13 | 10[1] | | 14 | 11 | 9 | 7[3] | 12 | 4 | | | | | | | | | 31 |
| 1 | | 3 | 4 | 5 | 9 | 6 | | | 11 | | 13 | 7 | 8[1] | 12 | 2 | | | | | | | 10[3] | | | 32 |
| 1 | | 3 | 4 | | 8 | 7[1] | | 12 | | 10[2] | 11[3] | 9 | 6 | 13 | 2 | 5 | | | | | | 14 | | | 33 |
| 1 | 2 | 4 | 3 | 5 | 9[1] | 6 | | 11[3] | | 8[4] | 10[2] | | 7 | 14 | 12 | | | | | | 13 | | | | 34 |
| 1 | | 3 | 4 | 5 | 12 | 6 | 7[3] | 9 | | 11[1] | | 8 | 10[2] | 2 | | | | | | | 13 | 14 | | | 35 |
| | | 4 | 9 | 7 | 8[1] | 6 | 13 | 14 | 11 | | 12 | 10[2] | 5 | | 2[3] | | 1 | | | | | | 3 | | 36 |
| 1 | 2[2] | 3 | 4 | | 6 | 7 | 8 | 14 | 10 | | 11[3] | 13 | | 9[1] | 12 | 5 | | | | | | | | | 37 |
| 1 | | 3 | 4 | 5[1] | 9[2] | 6 | 7 | | 11[3] | | 14 | 12 | 10 | 8 | 13 | 2 | | | | | | | | | 38 |

**FA Cup**

| | | | | |
|---|---|---|---|---|
| Third Round | QPR | (a) | 1-1 |
| *Replay* | QPR | (h) | 0-1 |

**Capital One Cup**

| | | | | |
|---|---|---|---|---|
| Second Round | Yeovil T | (a) | 4-2 |
| Third Round | Liverpool | (h) | 1-2 |

# WEST HAM UNITED

## FOUNDATION

Thames Iron Works FC was formed by employees of this famous shipbuilding company in 1895 and entered the FA Cup in their initial season at Chatham and the London League in their second. The committee wanted to introduce professional players, so Thames Iron Works was wound up in June 1900 and relaunched a month later as West Ham United.

*The Boleyn Ground, Upton Park, Green Street, London E13 9AZ.*

*Telephone:* (0871) 222 2700.

*Fax:* (020) 8548 2758.

*Ticket Office:* (0871) 529 1966.

*Website:* www.whufc.com

*Email:* customerservices@westhamunited.co.uk

*Ground Capacity:* 35,016.

*Record Attendance:* 42,322 v Tottenham H, Division 1, 17 October 1970.

*Pitch Measurements:* 100.58m × 66.84m (109yd × 73yd)

*Joint Chairmen:* David Sullivan and David Gold.

*Vice-chairman:* Karren Brady.

*Manager:* Sam Allardyce.

*Assistant Manager:* Neil McDonald.

*Head of Sports Medicine:* Andy Rolls.

*Colours:* Claret shirts with sky blue trim, white shorts, claret socks.

*Year Formed:* 1895.

*Turned Professional:* 1900.

*Previous Name:* 1895, Thames Iron Works FC; 1900, West Ham United.

*Club Nicknames:* 'The Hammers', 'The Irons'.

*Grounds:* 1895, Memorial Recreation Ground, Canning Town; 1904, Boleyn Ground.

*First Football League Game:* 30 August 1919, Division 2, v Lincoln C (h) D 1–1 – Hufton; Cope, Lee; Lane, Fenwick, McCrae; David Smith, Moyes (1), Puddefoot, Morris, Bradshaw.

*Record League Victory:* 8–0 v Rotherham U, Division 2, 8 March 1958 – Gregory; Bond, Wright; Malcolm, Brown, Lansdowne; Grice, Smith (2), Keeble (2), Dick (4), Musgrove. 8–0 v Sunderland, Division 1, 19 October 1968 – Ferguson; Bonds, Charles; Peters, Stephenson, Moore (1); Redknapp, Boyce, Brooking (1), Hurst (6), Sissons.

## HONOURS

**Football League – Division 1:**
*Runners-up* 1992–93
**Division 2:** *Champions* 1957–58, 1980–81; *Runners-up* 1922–23, 1990–91.
**FA Cup:** *Winners* 1964, 1975, 1980; *Runners-up* 1923, 2006.
**Football League Cup:**
*Runners-up* 1966, 1981.
**European Competitions**
**European Cup-Winners' Cup:**
1964–65 (*winners*), 1965–66, 1975–76 (*runners-up*), 1980–81.
**UEFA Cup:** 1999–2000; 2006–07.
**Intertoto Cup:** 1999 (*winners*).

## sky SPORTS FACT FILE

Goalkeeper Jim Standen enjoyed a unique double success in the summer of 1964. Firstly he gained an FA Cup winners' medal as a member of the West Ham United team that defeated Preston. He then helped Worcestershire win cricket's County Championship, taking 64 wickets at an average of 13.00.

*Record Cup Victory:* 10–0 v Bury, League Cup 2nd rd (2nd leg), 25 October 1983 – Parkes; Stewart (1), Walford, Bonds (Orr), Martin (1), Devonshire (2), Allen, Cottee (4), Swindlehurst, Brooking (2), Pike.

*Record Defeat:* 2–8 v Blackburn R, Division 1, 26 December 1963.

*Most League Points (2 for a win):* 66, Division 2, 1980–81.

*Most League Points (3 for a win):* 88, Division 1, 1992–93.

*Most League Goals:* 101, Division 2, 1957–58.

*Highest League Scorer in Season:* Vic Watson, 42, Division 1, 1929–30.

*Most League Goals in Total Aggregate:* Vic Watson, 298, 1920–35.

*Most League Goals in One Match:* 6, Vic Watson v Leeds U, Division 1, 9 February 1929; 6, Geoff Hurst v Sunderland, Division 1, 19 October 1968.

*Most Capped Player:* Bobby Moore, 108, England.

*Most League Appearances:* Billy Bonds, 663, 1967–88.

*Youngest League Player:* Billy Williams, 16 years 221 days v Blackpool, 6 May 1922.

*Record Transfer Fee Received:* £18,000,000 from Leeds U for Rio Ferdinand, November 2000.

*Record Transfer Fee Paid:* £15,000,000 to Liverpool for Andy Carroll, July 2013.

*Football League Record:* 1919 Elected to Division 2; 1923–32 Division 1; 1932–58 Division 2; 1958–78 Division 1; 1978–81 Division 2; 1981–89 Division 1; 1989–91 Division 2; 1991–93 Division 1; 1993–2003 FA Premier League; 2003–04 Division 1; 2004–05 FL C; 2005–11 FA Premier League; 2011–12 FL C; 2012– FA Premier League.

| MANAGERS |
|---|
| **Syd King** 1902–32 |
| **Charlie Paynter** 1932–50 |
| **Ted Fenton** 1950–61 |
| **Ron Greenwood** 1961–74 |
| *(continued as General Manager to 1977)* |
| **John Lyall** 1974–89 |
| **Lou Macari** 1989–90 |
| **Billy Bonds** 1990–94 |
| **Harry Redknapp** 1994–2001 |
| **Glenn Roeder** 2001–03 |
| **Alan Pardew** 2003–06 |
| **Alan Curbishley** 2006–08 |
| **Gianfranco Zola** 2008–10 |
| **Avram Grant** 2010–11 |
| **Sam Allardyce** June 2011– |

## LATEST SEQUENCES

*Longest Sequence of League Wins:* 9, 19.10.1985 – 14.12.1985.

*Longest Sequence of League Defeats:* 9, 28.3.1932 – 29.8.1932.

*Longest Sequence of League Draws:* 5, 15.10.2003 – 1.11.2003.

*Longest Sequence of Unbeaten League Matches:* 27, 27.12.80 – 10.10.81.

*Longest Sequence Without a League Win:* 17, 31.1.1976 – 21.8.1976.

*Successive Scoring Runs:* 27 from 5.10.1957.

*Successive Non-scoring Runs:* 5 from 1.5.1971.

### TEN YEAR LEAGUE RECORD

|  |  | P | W | D | L | F | A | Pts | Pos |
|---|---|---|---|---|---|---|---|---|---|
| 2003-04 | Div 1 | 46 | 19 | 17 | 10 | 67 | 45 | 74 | 4 |
| 2004-05 | FL C | 46 | 21 | 10 | 15 | 66 | 56 | 73 | 6 |
| 2005-06 | PR Lge | 38 | 16 | 7 | 15 | 52 | 55 | 55 | 9 |
| 2006-07 | PR Lge | 38 | 12 | 5 | 21 | 35 | 59 | 41 | 15 |
| 2007-08 | PR Lge | 38 | 13 | 10 | 15 | 42 | 50 | 49 | 10 |
| 2008-09 | PR Lge | 38 | 14 | 9 | 15 | 42 | 45 | 51 | 9 |
| 2009-10 | PR Lge | 38 | 8 | 11 | 19 | 47 | 66 | 35 | 17 |
| 2010-11 | PR Lge | 38 | 7 | 12 | 19 | 43 | 70 | 33 | 20 |
| 2011-12 | FL C | 46 | 24 | 14 | 8 | 81 | 48 | 86 | 3 |
| 2012-13 | PR Lge | 38 | 12 | 10 | 16 | 45 | 53 | 46 | 10 |

## DID YOU KNOW ?

West Ham United defender Jim Barrett had one of the shortest ever international careers. He spent just four minutes on the pitch for England against Ireland in 1928 before being forced off through injury and never appeared for his country again.

## WEST HAM UNITED – FA PREMIERSHIP 2012–13 LEAGUE RECORD

| Match No. | Date | | Venue | Opponents | Result | | H/T Score | Lg Pos. | Goalscorers | Atten-dance |
|---|---|---|---|---|---|---|---|---|---|---|
| 1 | Aug | 18 | H | Aston Villa | W | 1-0 | 1-0 | 5 | Nolan [40] | 34,172 |
| 2 | | 25 | A | Swansea C | L | 0-3 | 0-2 | 10 | | 20,424 |
| 3 | Sept | 1 | H | Fulham | W | 3-0 | 3-0 | 6 | Nolan [1], Reid [29], Taylor [41] | 33,458 |
| 4 | | 15 | A | Norwich C | D | 0-0 | 0-0 | 7 | | 26,806 |
| 5 | | 22 | H | Sunderland | D | 1-1 | 0-1 | 8 | Nolan [90] | 33,052 |
| 6 | Oct | 1 | A | QPR | W | 2-1 | 2-0 | 7 | Jarvis [3], Vaz Te [35] | 17,363 |
| 7 | | 6 | H | Arsenal | L | 1-3 | 1-1 | 8 | Diame [21] | 34,974 |
| 8 | | 20 | H | Southampton | W | 4-1 | 0-0 | 7 | Noble 2 (1 pen) [46, 72 (p)], Nolan [48], Maiga [87] | 34,925 |
| 9 | | 27 | A | Wigan Ath | L | 1-2 | 0-1 | 9 | Tomkins [90] | 19,090 |
| 10 | Nov | 3 | H | Manchester C | D | 0-0 | 0-0 | 8 | | 35,005 |
| 11 | | 11 | A | Newcastle U | W | 1-0 | 1-0 | 6 | Nolan [37] | 51,855 |
| 12 | | 19 | H | Stoke C | D | 1-1 | 0-1 | 7 | O'Brien [48] | 35,005 |
| 13 | | 25 | A | Tottenham H | L | 1-3 | 0-1 | 8 | Carroll [82] | 36,043 |
| 14 | | 28 | A | Manchester U | L | 0-1 | 0-1 | 10 | | 75,572 |
| 15 | Dec | 1 | H | Chelsea | W | 3-1 | 0-1 | 8 | Cole, C [63], Diame [86], Maiga [90] | 35,005 |
| 16 | | 9 | H | Liverpool | L | 2-3 | 2-1 | 11 | Noble (pen) [36], Gerrard (og) [43] | 35,005 |
| 17 | | 16 | A | WBA | D | 0-0 | 0-0 | 11 | | 24,816 |
| 18 | | 22 | H | Everton | L | 1-2 | 1-0 | 12 | Cole, C [14] | 35,005 |
| 19 | | 29 | A | Reading | L | 0-1 | 0-1 | 12 | | 24,183 |
| 20 | Jan | 1 | H | Norwich C | W | 2-1 | 2-0 | 11 | Noble (pen) [3], O'Brien [26] | 35,005 |
| 21 | | 12 | A | Sunderland | L | 0-3 | 0-1 | 11 | | 39,918 |
| 22 | | 19 | H | QPR | D | 1-1 | 0-1 | 12 | Cole, J [68] | 34,962 |
| 23 | | 23 | A | Arsenal | L | 1-5 | 1-1 | 12 | Collison [18] | 60,081 |
| 24 | | 30 | A | Fulham | L | 1-3 | 0-1 | 13 | Nolan [48] | 24,791 |
| 25 | Feb | 2 | H | Swansea C | W | 1-0 | 0-0 | 11 | Carroll [77] | 34,962 |
| 26 | | 10 | A | Aston Villa | L | 1-2 | 0-0 | 11 | Westwood (og) [87] | 30,503 |
| 27 | | 25 | H | Tottenham H | L | 2-3 | 1-1 | 14 | Carroll (pen) [25], Cole, J [58] | 35,005 |
| 28 | Mar | 2 | A | Stoke C | W | 1-0 | 1-0 | 12 | Collison [45] | 26,250 |
| 29 | | 17 | A | Chelsea | L | 0-2 | 0-1 | 14 | | 41,639 |
| 30 | | 30 | H | WBA | W | 3-1 | 2-0 | 11 | Carroll 2 [16, 80], O'Neil [28] | 34,966 |
| 31 | Apr | 7 | A | Liverpool | D | 0-0 | 0-0 | 12 | | 45,007 |
| 32 | | 13 | A | Southampton | D | 1-1 | 0-0 | 12 | Carroll [66] | 31,984 |
| 33 | | 17 | H | Manchester U | D | 2-2 | 1-1 | 11 | Vaz Te [17], Diame [55] | 34,692 |
| 34 | | 20 | H | Wigan Ath | W | 2-0 | 1-0 | 10 | Jarvis [21], Nolan [80] | 34,544 |
| 35 | | 27 | A | Manchester C | L | 1-2 | 0-1 | 10 | Carroll [90] | 47,189 |
| 36 | May | 4 | H | Newcastle U | D | 0-0 | 0-0 | 10 | | 34,962 |
| 37 | | 12 | A | Everton | L | 0-2 | 0-1 | 10 | | 39,475 |
| 38 | | 19 | H | Reading | W | 4-2 | 2-0 | 10 | Nolan 3 [23, 79, 87], Vaz Te [34] | 34,973 |

**Final League Position: 10**

### GOALSCORERS

*League (45):* Nolan 10, Carroll 7 (1 pen), Noble 4 (3 pens), Diame 3, Vaz Te 3, Cole, C 2, Cole, J 2, Collison 2, Jarvis 2, Maiga 2, O'Brien 2, O'Neil 1, Reid 1, Taylor 1, Tomkins 1, own goals 2.
*FA Cup (2):* Collins 2.
*Capital One Cup (3):* Maiga 2, Maynard 1.

| Jaaskelainen J 38 | Demel G 28+3 | Reid W 36 | Collins J 29 | McCartney G 9+3 | Noble M 25+3 | Diame M 31+2 | Nolan K 35 | Vaz Te R 18+6 | Cole C 14+13 | Taylor M 14+14 | O'Brien J 32+1 | Tomkins J 18+8 | Maiga M 2+15 | Jarvis M 29+3 | Diarra A 1+2 | Carroll A 22+2 | Hall R —+1 | Benayoun Y 4+2 | O'Neil G 17+7 | Spence J —+4 | Collison J 5+12 | Potts D 1+1 | Cole J 7+4 | Chamakh M 2+1 | Pogatetz E 1+5 | Match No. |
|---|---|---|---|---|---|---|---|---|---|---|---|---|---|---|---|---|---|---|---|---|---|---|---|---|---|---|
| 1 | 2 | 3 | 4 | $5^1$ | 6 | 7 | $8^2$ | 9 | $10^3$ | 11 | 12 | 13 | 14 | | | | | | | | | | | | | 1 |
| 1 | 10 | 2 | 4 | 5 | 8 | $9^3$ | 7 | 12 | $11^2$ | | | $3^1$ | 13 | 6 | 14 | | | | | | | | | | | 2 |
| 1 | $2^3$ | 3 | $4^1$ | | 7 | 6 | 8 | 10 | 13 | 9 | 5 | 12 | | | | $11^2$ | 14 | | | | | | | | | 3 |
| 1 | 2 | 3 | 4 | | 7 | 6 | 9 | $8^1$ | $11^1$ | $10^2$ | 5 | 13 | 12 | | | | | 14 | | | | | | | | 4 |
| 1 | 2 | 4 | 3 | | 7 | 6 | 8 | $9^1$ | $10^3$ | $11^2$ | 5 | 14 | 12 | | | | | 13 | | | | | | | | 5 |
| 1 | 2 | $3^1$ | 4 | 13 | 6 | 7 | 9 | 8 | $11^3$ | $5^2$ | 12 | | 10 | | | 14 | | | | | | | | | | 6 |
| 1 | $2^2$ | 4 | 3 | 5 | 6 | $7^3$ | 9 | $8^1$ | 14 | 12 | | 13 | 10 | | | 11 | | | | | | | | | | 7 |
| 1 | | 4 | 3 | 5 | 6 | $7^1$ | 9 | | | $2^3$ | 13 | 10 | | | | $11^2$ | | 8 | 12 | 14 | | | | | | 8 |
| 1 | | 4 | 3 | 5 | $7^2$ | $9^3$ | 8 | 13 | | 2 | 12 | 6 | | | | 11 | | $10^1$ | 14 | | | | | | | 9 |
| 1 | 3 | $4^3$ | 5 | | | 7 | $8^1$ | 10 | 13 | 2 | | 6 | | | | $11^2$ | | 9 | 12 | 14 | | | | | | 10 |
| 1 | 14 | 3 | $5^3$ | | 8 | 7 | 10 | | | 11 | 2 | 4 | | | | 12 | | $9^1$ | $6^2$ | 13 | | | | | | 11 |
| 1 | 12 | 3 | 5 | | 6 | 8 | 7 | | 14 | 13 | $2^1$ | 4 | | | | $11^3$ | | $10^2$ | 9 | | | | | | | 12 |
| 1 | | 4 | 5 | | 9 | 7 | $10^3$ | 14 | 13 | 2 | 3 | $6^1$ | 12 | | | 11 | | $8^2$ | | | | | | | | 13 |
| 1 | 2 | 3 | 4 | | $7^3$ | 10 | | 12 | 6 | 5 | 8 | 13 | | $9^2$ | | $11^1$ | | 14 | | | | | | | | 14 |
| 1 | 2 | 4 | 3 | | 7 | 13 | 9 | | $11^3$ | 12 | | 5 | | $6^2$ | 14 | 10 | | $8^1$ | | | | | | | | 15 |
| 1 | $2^1$ | 4 | 3 | 12 | 9 | $7^2$ | 8 | | 11 | $6^3$ | 5 | 13 | | 14 | | 10 | | | | | | | | | | 16 |
| 1 | $2^2$ | 3 | 4 | | 6 | | 9 | | 11 | 10 | 5 | 13 | 12 | | | $8^1$ | | 7 | | | | | | | | 17 |
| 1 | | 4 | 3 | | 6 | | 9 | | $11^8$ | 8 | $5^2$ | 2 | 12 | $10^3$ | | | | $7^1$ | 13 | 14 | | | | | | 18 |
| 1 | | 4 | 3 | | $6^3$ | | 9 | | 13 | 11 | $8^1$ | 5 | 2 | | | 14 | | 10 | $7^2$ | 12 | | | | | | 19 |
| 1 | 2 | 3 | | | 6 | | | $10^2$ | 11 | 8 | $5^1$ | 4 | 13 | $9^3$ | | | | 12 | 14 | 7 | | | | | | 20 |
| 1 | 2 | 4 | $3^1$ | | | | 9 | | 13 | $11^3$ | 12 | 10 | | 7 | | | | | $6^2$ | | 5 | 8 | 14 | | | 21 |
| 1 | 2 | 4 | | | 6 | 7 | $9^2$ | 13 | 12 | | 5 | 3 | | | | 10 | | | 8 | | | | $11^1$ | | | 22 |
| 1 | 2 | $4^1$ | | | 6 | 14 | 7 | $11^3$ | 10 | 9 | 5 | 3 | | | | | | | 12 | | | $8^2$ | 13 | | | 23 |
| 1 | $2^2$ | 3 | | | 7 | 6 | 8 | | 12 | 13 | 5 | 4 | | | | 9 | | | | | | | $10^3$ | $11^1$ | | 24 |
| 1 | | 4 | | | 6 | $7^2$ | $9^3$ | 8 | | 5 | 2 | 3 | $10^1$ | 11 | | | | | 13 | | | | 12 | 14 | | 25 |
| 1 | 12 | 3 | | | $6^3$ | 7 | 8 | 13 | 14 | $9^2$ | $2^1$ | 4 | | | | | | | 11 | | | | 10 | 5 | | 26 |
| 1 | $2^2$ | 3 | 4 | | | $7^3$ | $8^1$ | | 12 | 5 | | 9 | 10 | | | 6 | | | 14 | | | | 11 | | 13 | 27 |
| 1 | 2 | 4 | 3 | | | | 9 | | 13 | | $10^3$ | 5 | | $6^2$ | | 11 | | | 8 | | | | 12 | $7^1$ | 14 | 28 |
| 1 | 5 | 3 | $4^2$ | | $8^1$ | | 9 | 14 | 12 | 2 | 13 | | | 11 | | 10 | | | 7 | | | | 6 | | | 29 |
| 1 | $2^2$ | 3 | 4 | 13 | | $7^3$ | $8^1$ | 11 | | 12 | 5 | | | 9 | | 10 | | | 6 | | | | 14 | | | 30 |
| 1 | 2 | 4 | | | 6 | | $9^1$ | $8^2$ | 11 | 12 | 5 | $3^3$ | | | | 10 | | | 7 | | | | 13 | | 14 | 31 |
| 1 | 2 | 4 | | | 6 | | 9 | $8^3$ | 14 | 5 | $3^2$ | $10^1$ | | | | 11 | | | 7 | | | | 12 | 13 | | 32 |
| 1 | 2 | 4 | 3 | | 12 | $6^3$ | $7^2$ | 11 | 13 | 5 | | | | 9 | | 10 | | | | | $8^1$ | | 14 | | | 33 |
| 1 | 2 | 4 | 3 | | 12 | $6^3$ | 9 | $8^2$ | 5 | | | | | 10 | | 11 | | | | | $7^1$ | | 14 | | 13 | 34 |
| 1 | 5 | 3 | 4 | | | 7 | $9^2$ | $8^1$ | 14 | 13 | $2^3$ | | | | | 10 | | 11 | | | 6 | | 12 | | | 35 |
| 1 | $2^2$ | 4 | 3 | | 6 | | 9 | $8^1$ | 13 | 5 | | $10^3$ | | | | 11 | | | | | 7 | | 12 | | 14 | 36 |
| 1 | 2 | 4 | 3 | | 14 | $6^1$ | 9 | 12 | | 5 | | 10 | | | | 11 | | | | | $7^3$ | | $8^2$ | | 13 | 37 |
| 1 | 2 | 4 | 3 | | 7 | 6 | 8 | $9^2$ | 14 | $5^3$ | | 13 | | | | 10 | | | | | | | 12 | | $11^1$ | 38 |

**FA Cup**

| | | | |
|---|---|---|---|
| Third Round | Manchester U | (h) | 2-2 |
| *Replay* | Manchester U | (a) | 0-1 |

**Capital One Cup**

| | | | |
|---|---|---|---|
| Second Round | Crewe Alex | (h) | 2-0 |
| Third Round | Wigan Ath | (h) | 1-4 |

# WIGAN ATHLETIC

## FOUNDATION

Following the demise of Wigan Borough and their resignation from the Football League in 1931, a public meeting was called in Wigan at the Queen's Hall in May 1932 at which a new club, Wigan Athletic, was founded in the hope of carrying on in the Football League. With this in mind, they bought Springfield Park for £2,250, but failed to gain admission to the Football League until 46 years later.

*The DW Stadium, Loire Drive, Wigan, Lancashire WN5 0UZ.*

*Telephone:* (01942) 774 000.

*Fax:* (01942) 770 477.

*Ticket Office:* (0871) 663 3552.

*Website:* www.wiganlatics.co.uk

*Email:* feedback@wiganathletic.com

*Ground Capacity:* 25,133.

*Record Attendance:* 27,526 v Hereford U, 12 December 1953 (at Springfield Park); 25,133 v Manchester U, FA Premier League, 11 May 2008 (at DW Stadium).

*Pitch Measurements:* 105m × 68m (114yd × 74yd)

*Chairman:* David Whelan.

*Chief Executive:* Jonathan Jackson.

*Manager:* Owen Coyle.

*Assistant Manager:* Sandy Stewart.

*Physio:* Andy Mitchell.

*Colours:* Blue and white striped shirts with blue sleeves, blue shorts, blue socks with black trim.

*Year Formed:* 1932.

*Turned Professional:* 1932.

*Club Nickname:* 'The Latics'.

*Grounds:* 1932, Springfield Park; 1999, JJB Stadium (renamed the DW Stadium in 2009).

*First Football League Game:* 19 August 1978, Division 4, v Hereford U (a) D 0–0 – Brown; Hinnigan, Gore, Gillibrand, Ward, Davids, Corrigan, Purdie, Houghton, Wilkie, Wright.

*Record League Victory:* 7–1 v Scarborough, Division 3, 11 March 1997 – Lee Butler; John Butler, Sharp (Morgan), Greenall, McGibbon (Biggins (1)), Martinez (1), Diaz (2), Jones (Lancashire (1)), Lowe (2), Rogers, Kilford.

*Record Cup Victory:* 6–0 v Carlisle U (a), FA Cup 1st rd, 24 November 1934 – Caunce; Robinson, Talbot; Paterson, Watson, Tufnell; Armes (2), Robson (1), Roberts (2), Felton, Scott (1).

*Record Defeat:* 1–9 v Tottenham H, FA Premier League, 22 November 2009.

## HONOURS

**Football League – FL C:**
*Runners-up* 2004–05;
**Division 2:** *Champions* 2002–03;
**Division 3:** *Champions* 1996–97.

**FA Cup:** *Winners* 2013.

**Football League Cup:**
*Runners-up* 2006.

**Freight Rover Trophy:** *Winners* 1985.

**Auto Windscreens Shield:**
*Winners* 1999.

## sky SPORTS FACT FILE

Wigan Athletic came close to election to the Football League in 1950. With two places available the Latics tied with Workington for second place on 19 votes, with Scunthorpe United two votes behind. The ballot went to a third round with the Lincolnshire club defeating Wigan by 30 to 18.

**Most League Points (2 for a win):** 55, Division 4, 1978–79 and 1979–80.

**Most League Points (3 for a win):** 100, Division 2, 2002–03.

**Most League Goals:** 84, Division 3, 1996–97.

**Highest League Scorer in Season:** Graeme Jones, 31, Division 3, 1996–97.

**Most League Goals in Total Aggregate:** Andy Liddell, 70, 1998–2004.

**Most League Goals in One Match:** Not more than three goals by one player.

**Most Capped Players:** Kevin Kilbane, 22 (110), Republic of Ireland; Henri Camara, 22 (99), Senegal.

**Most League Appearances:** Kevin Langley, 317, 1981–86, 1990–94.

**Youngest League Player:** Steve Nugent, 16 years 132 days v Leyton Orient, 16 September 1989.

**Record Transfer Fee Received:** £15,250,000 from Manchester U for Antonio Valencia, June 2009.

**Record Transfer Fee Paid:** £6,000,000 to Newcastle U for Charles N'Zogbia, February 2009; £6,000,000 to Estudiantes for Mauro Boselli, August 2010.

**Football League Record:** 1978 Elected to Division 4; 1982–92 Division 3; 1992–93 Division 2; 1993–97 Division 3; 1997–2003 Division 2; 2003–04 Division 1; 2004–05 FL C; 2005–13 FA Premier League; 2013– FL C.

## LATEST SEQUENCES

**Longest Sequence of League Wins:** 11, 2.11.2002 – 18.1.2003.

**Longest Sequence of League Defeats:** 8, 13.12.2006 – 30.1.2007.

**Longest Sequence of League Draws:** 6, 11.12.2001 – 5.1.2002.

**Longest Sequence of Unbeaten League Matches:** 25, 8.5.1999 – 3.1.2000.

**Longest Sequence Without a League Win:** 14, 9.5.1989 – 17.10.1989.

**Successive Scoring Runs:** 24 from 27.4.1996.

**Successive Non-scoring Runs:** 4 from 15.4.1995.

### MANAGERS

Charlie Spencer 1932–37
Jimmy Milne 1946–47
Bob Pryde 1949–52
Ted Goodier 1952–54
Walter Crook 1954–55
Ron Suart 1955–56
Billy Cooke 1956
Sam Barkas 1957
Trevor Hitchen 1957–58
Malcolm Barrass 1958–59
Jimmy Shirley 1959
Pat Murphy 1959–60
Allenby Chilton 1960
Johnny Ball 1961–63
Allan Brown 1963–66
Alf Craig 1966–67
Harry Leyland 1967–68
Alan Saunders 1968
Ian McNeill 1968–70
Gordon Milne 1970–72
Les Rigby 1972–74
Brian Tiler 1974–76
Ian McNeill 1976–81
Larry Lloyd 1981–83
Harry McNally 1983–85
Bryan Hamilton 1985–86
Ray Mathias 1986–89
Bryan Hamilton 1989–93
Dave Philpotts 1993
Kenny Swain 1993–94
Graham Barrow 1994–95
John Deehan 1995–98
Ray Mathias 1998–99
John Benson 1999–2000
Bruce Rioch 2000–01
Steve Bruce 2001
Paul Jewell 2001–07
Chris Hutchings 2007
Steve Bruce 2007–09
Roberto Martinez 2009–13
Owen Coyle June 2013–

### TEN YEAR LEAGUE RECORD

| | | P | W | D | L | F | A | Pts | Pos |
|---|---|---|---|---|---|---|---|---|---|
| 2003-04 | Div 1 | 46 | 18 | 17 | 11 | 60 | 45 | 71 | 7 |
| 2004-05 | FL C | 46 | 25 | 12 | 9 | 79 | 35 | 87 | 2 |
| 2005-06 | PR Lge | 38 | 15 | 6 | 17 | 45 | 52 | 51 | 10 |
| 2006-07 | PR Lge | 38 | 10 | 8 | 20 | 37 | 59 | 38 | 17 |
| 2007-08 | PR Lge | 38 | 10 | 10 | 18 | 34 | 51 | 40 | 14 |
| 2008-09 | PR Lge | 38 | 12 | 9 | 17 | 34 | 45 | 45 | 11 |
| 2009-10 | PR Lge | 38 | 9 | 9 | 20 | 37 | 79 | 36 | 16 |
| 2010-11 | PR Lge | 38 | 9 | 15 | 14 | 40 | 61 | 42 | 16 |
| 2011-12 | PR Lge | 38 | 11 | 10 | 17 | 42 | 62 | 43 | 15 |
| 2012-13 | PR Lge | 38 | 9 | 9 | 20 | 47 | 73 | 36 | 18 |

### DID YOU KNOW

Wigan Athletic reached the FA Cup rounds proper for the first occasion in 1933–34. Drawn to play Carlisle United away the Latics won 6-1, a record win by a non-league side over Football League opposition. They then beat Torquay United before losing at home to Millwall in round 3.

## WIGAN ATHLETIC – FA PREMIERSHIP 2012–13 LEAGUE RECORD

| Match No. | Date | Venue | Opponents | Result | | H/T Score | Lg Pos. | Goalscorers | Attendance |
|---|---|---|---|---|---|---|---|---|---|
| 1 | Aug 19 | H | Chelsea | L | 0-2 | 0-2 | 17 | | 19,738 |
| 2 | 25 | A | Southampton | W | 2-0 | 0-0 | 8 | Di Santo [51], Kone [89] | 29,604 |
| 3 | Sept 1 | H | Stoke C | D | 2-2 | 1-1 | 7 | Maloney (pen) [5], Di Santo [49] | 16,247 |
| 4 | 15 | A | Manchester U | L | 0-4 | 0-0 | 13 | | 75,142 |
| 5 | 22 | H | Fulham | L | 1-2 | 0-1 | 15 | Kone [90] | 19,284 |
| 6 | 29 | A | Sunderland | L | 0-1 | 0-0 | 16 | | 37,742 |
| 7 | Oct 6 | H | Everton | D | 2-2 | 2-1 | 16 | Kone [10], Di Santo [23] | 18,759 |
| 8 | 20 | A | Swansea C | L | 1-2 | 0-0 | 16 | Boyce [69] | 19,696 |
| 9 | 27 | H | West Ham U | W | 2-1 | 1-0 | 15 | Ramis [8], McArthur [47] | 19,090 |
| 10 | Nov 3 | A | Tottenham H | W | 1-0 | 0-0 | 12 | Watson, B [56] | 35,534 |
| 11 | 10 | H | WBA | L | 1-2 | 1-2 | 14 | Kone [44] | 17,812 |
| 12 | 17 | A | Liverpool | L | 0-3 | 0-0 | 15 | | 44,913 |
| 13 | 24 | H | Reading | W | 3-2 | 0-1 | 15 | Gomez 3 [58, 68, 90] | 15,436 |
| 14 | 28 | H | Manchester C | L | 0-2 | 0-0 | 15 | | 19,623 |
| 15 | Dec 3 | A | Newcastle U | L | 0-3 | 0-2 | 16 | | 43,858 |
| 16 | 8 | H | QPR | D | 2-2 | 1-1 | 17 | McCarthy 2 [19, 74] | 17,163 |
| 17 | 15 | A | Norwich C | L | 1-2 | 0-1 | 18 | Maloney [51] | 26,677 |
| 18 | 22 | H | Arsenal | L | 0-1 | 0-0 | 18 | | 21,754 |
| 19 | 26 | A | Everton | L | 1-2 | 0-0 | 18 | Kone [82] | 38,749 |
| 20 | 29 | A | Aston Villa | W | 3-0 | 1-0 | 16 | Ramis [3], Boyce [52], Kone [56] | 33,374 |
| 21 | Jan 1 | H | Manchester U | L | 0-4 | 0-2 | 18 | | 20,342 |
| 22 | 12 | A | Fulham | D | 1-1 | 0-1 | 17 | Di Santo [71] | 25,442 |
| 23 | 19 | H | Sunderland | L | 2-3 | 1-3 | 19 | Vaughan (og) [5], Henriquez [79] | 19,219 |
| 24 | 29 | A | Stoke C | D | 2-2 | 0-1 | 17 | McArthur [50], Di Santo [61] | 24,421 |
| 25 | Feb 2 | H | Southampton | D | 2-2 | 1-0 | 18 | Caldwell [25], Maloney [90] | 18,598 |
| 26 | 9 | A | Chelsea | L | 1-4 | 0-1 | 18 | Maloney [58] | 41,562 |
| 27 | 23 | A | Reading | W | 3-0 | 2-0 | 17 | Kone 2 [44, 45], Figueroa [48] | 22,321 |
| 28 | Mar 2 | H | Liverpool | L | 0-4 | 0-3 | 17 | | 20,804 |
| 29 | 17 | H | Newcastle U | W | 2-1 | 1-0 | 18 | Beausejour [18], Kone [90] | 22,297 |
| 30 | 30 | H | Norwich C | W | 1-0 | 0-0 | 17 | Kone [81] | 17,784 |
| 31 | Apr 7 | A | QPR | D | 1-1 | 0-0 | 18 | Maloney [90] | 16,658 |
| 32 | 17 | A | Manchester C | L | 0-1 | 0-0 | 18 | | 47,106 |
| 33 | 20 | A | West Ham U | L | 0-2 | 0-1 | 18 | | 34,544 |
| 34 | 27 | H | Tottenham H | D | 2-2 | 1-1 | 18 | Boyce [11], McManaman [49] | 22,326 |
| 35 | May 4 | A | WBA | W | 3-2 | 1-1 | 18 | Kone [39], McArthur [58], McManaman [90] | 25,756 |
| 36 | 7 | H | Swansea C | L | 2-3 | 1-0 | 18 | Espinoza [45], McCarthy [53] | 18,850 |
| 37 | 14 | A | Arsenal | L | 1-4 | 1-1 | 18 | Maloney [45] | 60,068 |
| 38 | 19 | H | Aston Villa | D | 2-2 | 2-1 | 18 | Boyce [21], Baker (og) [45] | 23,001 |

**Final League Position: 18**

### GOALSCORERS

*League (47):* Kone 11, Maloney 6 (1 pen), Di Santo 5, Boyce 4, Gomez 3, McArthur 3, McCarthy 3, McManaman 2, Ramis 2, Beausejour 1, Caldwell 1, Espinoza 1, Figueroa 1, Henriquez 1, Watson, B 1, own goals 2.
*FA Cup (13):* Gomez 3 (1 pen), McManaman 3, Kone 2, Boselli 1, Figueroa 1, Maloney 1, McArthur 1, Watson B 1.
*Capital One Cup (8):* Boselli 3, Gomez 2 (1 pen), Figueroa 1, McManaman 1, Ramis 1.

| Al Habsi A 29 | Alcaraz A 8 + 2 | Caldwell G 25 | Ramis I 16 | Boyce E 36 | McCarthy J 38 | McArthur J 24 + 10 | Figueroa M 33 | Maloney S 34 + 2 | Di Santo F 24 + 11 | Moses V 1 | Gomez J 17 + 15 | Kone A 32 + 2 | Watson B 7 + 5 | Beausejour J 32 + 2 | Boselli M 1 + 6 | Jones D 8 + 5 | Miyaichi R — + 4 | McManaman C 8 + 12 | Stam R 11 + 6 | Lopez A 3 + 2 | Espinoza R 6 + 6 | Henriquez A — + 4 | Golobart R 2 + 1 | Scharner P 14 | Robles B 9 | Fyvie F — + 1 | Campabadal E — + 1 | Match No. |
|---|---|---|---|---|---|---|---|---|---|---|---|---|---|---|---|---|---|---|---|---|---|---|---|---|---|---|---|---|
| 1 | 2 | 3 | 4 | 5 | 6 | $7^3$ | 8 | 9 | $10^2$ | 11 | 12 | 13 | 14 | | | | | | | | | | | | | | | 1 |
| 1 | 2 | 3 | 4 | 5 | 6 | 7 | 8 | $11^2$ | $10^1$ | | 12 | $9^3$ | 13 | 14 | | | | | | | | | | | | | | 2 |
| 1 | | 3 | 2 | 5 | 7 | $6^2$ | 4 | 11 | $10^3$ | | . | 9 | 13 | $8^1$ | 12 | 14 | | | | | | | | | | | | 3 |
| 1 | | 3 | 4 | 2 | 7 | 8 | 5 | $6^1$ | 11 | | 12 | 10 | | $9^2$ | 13 | | | | | | | | | | | | | 4 |
| 1 | $3^2$ | 4 | $2^3$ | 7 | | 5 | 10 | | | | $9^1$ | 11 | 8 | 6 | 12 | | | 13 | 14 | | | | | | | | | 5 |
| 1 | | 3 | 2 | $5^3$ | 6 | 7 | 4 | $11^1$ | 12 | | 10 | 9 | 8 | | 14 | 13 | | | | | | | | | | | | 6 |
| 1 | | 3 | 2 | 5 | 6 | 7 | 4 | 11 | $10^1$ | | | 9 | | 8 | | | | 12 | | | | | | | | | | 7 |
| 1 | 2 | | 4 | 7 | 5 | $6^2$ | $3^1$ | 10 | $11^2$ | | 14 | 9 | 12 | 8 | 13 | | | | | | | | | | | | | 8 |
| 1 | | 3 | 2 | 5 | 6 | 7 | 4 | 11 | $10^1$ | | | 9 | 12 | 8 | | | | | | | | | | | | | | 9 |
| 1 | | 3 | 2 | 5 | 6 | | 4 | 11 | $10^1$ | | | 9 | 12 | 7 | 8 | | | | | | | | | | | | | 10 |
| 1 | | 3 | 2 | 5 | 6 | | 4 | 11 | $10^3$ | | 14 | 9 | $7^2$ | 8 | 13 | | | | 12 | | | | | | | | | 11 |
| 1 | $3^2$ | 2 | 5 | 7 | | | 4 | 9 | $10^3$ | | 13 | 11 | $6^1$ | 8 | 12 | 14 | | | | | | | | | | | | 12 |
| 1 | $3^2$ | 2 | 6 | 14 | | | 4 | $11^1$ | 12 | | 9 | 10 | | 8 | | | $7^3$ | | | 5 | 13 | | | | | | | 13 |
| | | 3 | 6 | 12 | 5 | | 11 | | | | 8 | 9 | 10 | $7^1$ | | | 13 | | $2^2$ | 4 | | | | | | | | 14 |
| | $4^2$ | 3 | 8 | 12 | 5 | | $10^3$ | | | | $6^1$ | 11 | 9 | 7 | | | 14 | | 2 | 13 | | | | | | | | 15 |
| | | 2 | 6 | 7 | | | 12 | $10^2$ | | | 9 | 11 | | 8 | 13 | $4^1$ | | | 5 | 3 | | | | | | | | 16 |
| | | 2 | $7^2$ | 6 | 4 | 13 | 14 | | | | $10^1$ | 9 | | 8 | $11^3$ | 12 | | | 5 | 3 | | | | | | | | 17 |
| | | 4 | 8 | 7 | 3 | $6^2$ | $10^1$ | | | | 13 | 11 | | 5 | | 9 | | 12 | 2 | | | | | | | | | 18 |
| 1 | 3 | | 2 | 6 | 8 | 4 | 10 | 12 | | | 13 | 11 | | 9 | | | | $5^2$ | | | | | | | | | | 19 |
| 1 | | 3 | 2 | 5 | 6 | | 12 | 4 | 11 | | 13 | $9^3$ | | $8^2$ | | $7^1$ | | 14 | | | | | | | | | | 20 |
| 1 | | 3 | 2 | 5 | 6 | 7 | 4 | $10^3$ | $9^2$ | | 13 | 11 | | 8 | | | | 14 | 12 | | | | | | | | | 21 |
| 1 | | 3 | $4^2$ | 8 | 9 | 6 | 2 | 10 | 11 | | 12 | | | 5 | | $7^1$ | | 13 | | | | | | | | | | 22 |
| 1 | | 3 | | $2^2$ | 6 | 7 | 4 | 11 | $10^3$ | | 9 | | | 8 | 14 | | | $5^1$ | | 12 | 13 | | | | | | | 23 |
| 1 | | 3 | | $5^1$ | 7 | 6 | 4 | 10 | 11 | | | $9^2$ | | | | | 13 | 12 | 8 | | 2 | | | | | | | 24 |
| 1 | | 3 | | $6^3$ | 7 | 4 | 11 | 10 | | | 12 | 9 | | 8 | | | 13 | $5^1$ | | | $9^2$ | 14 | | 2 | | | | 25 |
| | 4 | | | 6 | 7 | 5 | 10 | 11 | | | 12 | | | 8 | | 13 | | $2^2$ | $9^1$ | | 3 | | | | | | | 26 |
| 1 | 13 | 3 | | 6 | 8 | 4 | 7 | $11^1$ | | | 12 | 10 | | 9 | | | | | | | 2 | | | | | | | 27 |
| 1 | 13 | $3^1$ | | 5 | 6 | 7 | 4 | 11 | $10^2$ | | 9 | $8^3$ | | | | | | 14 | 12 | | 2 | | | | | | | 28 |
| | | 3 | | 5 | 6 | 12 | 4 | 9 | 13 | | 7 | 10 | $8^2$ | $11^1$ | | | | | | | | | | 2 | 1 | | | 29 |
| | | 3 | | 5 | 6 | 12 | 4 | 9 | 13 | | 7 | $11^2$ | 8 | $10^1$ | | | | | | | | | | 2 | 1 | | | 30 |
| | | 2 | | 5 | 6 | 12 | $4^3$ | 11 | 13 | | 7 | 10 | $8^1$ | $9^2$ | | | | | | | | | 14 | 3 | 1 | | | 31 |
| | | 2 | | 5 | 7 | 13 | 4 | $11^3$ | $10^1$ | | $6^2$ | 9 | 8 | 12 | | | | | | | | | 14 | 3 | 1 | | | 32 |
| | $4^1$ | 3 | | 5 | 6 | 13 | 8 | 11 | 14 | | $7^3$ | 10 | 12 | $9^2$ | | | | | | | | | | 2 | 1 | | | 33 |
| | | 2 | | 6 | 7 | $4^1$ | | 11 | 13 | | $5^3$ | 10 | | 8 | | | | $9^2$ | 12 | | 14 | | | 3 | 1 | | | 34 |
| | | 3 | | 6 | 13 | | | 11 | | | $8^1$ | 10 | | 7 | | $5^3$ | | 9 | $2^2$ | | 14 | | 12 | 4 | 1 | | | 35 |
| | | 3 | | 2 | 6 | | 8 | 9 | | | 12 | 13 | | 11 | | $7^2$ | | $10^1$ | 14 | | 5 | | | 4 | 1 | | | 36 |
| | | 4 | | 2 | | | 8 | 9 | | | $7^3$ | 12 | | $11^2$ | 10 | 13 | | $6^1$ | 5 | | 14 | | | 3 | 1 | | | 37 |
| 1 | | 2 | | 6 | 8 | | | 11 | | | $9^1$ | 10 | | $7^2$ | | 5 | | 13 | | | 3 | | | 4 | | 12 | 14 | 38 |

**FA Cup**

| | | | | |
|---|---|---|---|---|
| Third Round | Bournemouth | (h) | 1-1 | |
| *Replay* | Bournemouth | (a) | 1-0 | |
| Fourth Round | Macclesfield T | (a) | 1-0 | |
| Fifth Round | Huddersfield T | (a) | 4-1 | |
| Sixth Round | Everton | (a) | 3-0 | |
| Semi-Finals | Millwall | | 2-0 | |
| *(at Wembley)* | | | | |
| Final *(at Wembley)* | Manchester C | | 1-0 | |

**Capital One Cup**

| | | | |
|---|---|---|---|
| Second Round | Nottingham F | (a) | 4-1 |
| Third Round | West Ham U | (a) | 4-1 |
| Fourth Round | Bradford C | (h) | 0-0 |
| *(aet; lost 2-4 on pens)* | | | |

# WOLVERHAMPTON WANDERERS

## FOUNDATION

Enthusiasts of the game at St Luke's School, Blakenhall formed a club in 1877. In the same neighbourhood a cricket club called Blakenhall Wanderers had a football section. Several St Luke's footballers played cricket for them and shortly before the start of the 1879–80 season the two amalgamated and Wolverhampton Wanderers FC was brought into being.

*Molineux Stadium, Waterloo Road, Wolverhampton WV1 4QR.*

*Telephone:* (0871) 222 2220.

*Fax:* (01902) 687 006.

*Ticket Office:* (0871) 222 1877.

*Website:* wolves.co.uk

*Email:* info@wolves.co.uk

*Ground Capacity:* 30,852.

*Record Attendance:* 61,315 v Liverpool, FA Cup 5th rd, 11 February 1939.

*Pitch Measurements:* 106m × 67m (116yd × 74yd)

*Chairman:* Steve Morgan OBE.

*Chief Executive:* Jez Moxey.

*Head Coach:* Kenny Jackett.

*Head of Medical:* Phil Hayward.

*Colours:* Gold shirts with black trim, black shorts with gold trim, gold socks with black trim.

*Year Formed:* 1877* (*see Foundation*).

*Turned Professional:* 1888.

*Previous Names:* 1879, St Luke's combined with Wanderers Cricket Club to become Wolverhampton Wanderers (1923) Ltd. New limited companies followed in 1982 and 1986 (current).

*Club Nickname:* 'Wolves'.

## HONOURS

**Football League – Division 1:**
*Champions* 1953–54, 1957–58, 1958–59; *Runners-up* 1937–38, 1938–39, 1949–50, 1954–55, 1959–60;
**Division 2:** *Champions* 1931–32, 1976–77; *Runners-up* 1966–67, 1982–83; **FL C:** *Champions* 2008–09;
**Division 3 (N):** *Champions* 1923–24;
**Division 3:** *Champions* 1988–89;
**Division 4:** *Champions* 1987–88.

**FA Cup:** *Winners* 1893, 1908, 1949, 1960; *Runners-up* 1889, 1896, 1921, 1939.

**Football League Cup:** *Winners* 1974, 1980.

**Texaco Cup:** *Winners* 1971.

**Sherpa Van Trophy:** *Winners* 1988.

**European Competitions**
**European Cup:** 1958–59, 1959–60.
**European Cup-Winners' Cup:** 1960–61. **UEFA Cup:** 1971–72 (*runners-up*), 1973–74, 1974–75, 1980–81.

*Grounds:* 1877, Windmill Field; 1879, John Harper's Field; 1881, Dudley Road; 1889, Molineux.

*First Football League Game:* 8 September 1888, Football League, v Aston Villa (h) D 1–1 – Baynton; Baugh, Mason; Fletcher, Allen, Lowder; Hunter, Cooper, Anderson, White, Cannon, (1 og).

*Record League Victory:* 10–1 v Leicester C, Division 1, 15 April 1938 – Sidlow; Morris, Dowen; Galley, Cullis, Gardiner; Maguire (1), Horace Wright, Westcott (4), Jones (1), Dorsett (4).

*Record Cup Victory:* 14–0 v Crosswell's Brewery, FA Cup 2nd rd, 13 November 1886 – Ike Griffiths; Baugh, Mason; Pearson, Allen (1), Lowder; Hunter (4), Knight (2), Brodie (4), Bernie Griffiths (2), Wood. Plus one goal 'scrambled through'.

## sky SPORTS FACT FILE

Cameron Buchanan created history when he lined up for Wolverhampton Wanderers against West Bromwich Albion in a wartime match on 26 September 1942. Aged just 14 years and 57 days he is believed to be the youngest player ever to appear in a senior match in England.

*Record Defeat:* 1–10 v Newton Heath, Division 1, 15 October 1892.

*Most League Points (2 for a win):* 64, Division 1, 1957–58.

*Most League Points (3 for a win):* 92, Division 3, 1988–89.

*Most League Goals:* 115, Division 2, 1931–32.

*Highest League Scorer in Season:* Dennis Westcott, 38, Division 1, 1946–47.

*Most League Goals in Total Aggregate:* Steve Bull, 250, 1986–99.

*Most League Goals in One Match:* 5, Joe Butcher v Accrington, Division 1, 19 November 1892; 5, Tom Phillipson v Barnsley, Division 2, 26 April 1926; 5, Tom Phillipson v Bradford C, Division 2, 25 December 1926; 5, Billy Hartill v Notts Co, Division 2, 12 October 1929; 5, Billy Hartill v Aston Villa, Division 1, 3 September 1934.

*Most Capped Player:* Billy Wright, 105, England (70 consecutive).

*Most League Appearances:* Derek Parkin, 501, 1967–82.

*Youngest League Player:* Jimmy Mullen, 16 years 43 days v Leeds U, 18 February 1939.

*Record Transfer Fee Received:* £14,000,000 from Sunderland for Steven Fletcher, August 2012.

*Record Transfer Fee Paid:* £6,500,000 to Reading for Kevin Doyle, June 2009; £6,500,000 to Burnley for Steven Fletcher, June 2010.

*Football League Record:* 1888 Founder Member of Football League: 1906–23 Division 2; 1923–24 Division 3 (N); 1924–32 Division 2; 1932–65 Division 1; 1965–67 Division 2; 1967–76 Division 1; 1976–77 Division 2; 1977–82 Division 1; 1982–83 Division 2; 1983–84 Division 1; 1984–85 Division 2; 1985–86 Division 3; 1986–88 Division 4; 1988–89 Division 3; 1989–92 Division 2; 1992–2003 Division 1; 2003–04 FA Premier League; 2004–09 FL C; 2009–12 FA Premier League; 2012–13 FL C; 2013– FL 1.

## MANAGERS

George Worrall 1877–85
*(Secretary-Manager)*
John Addenbrooke 1885–1922
George Jobey 1922–24
Albert Hoskins 1924–26
*(had been Secretary since 1922)*
Fred Scotchbrook 1926–27
Major Frank Buckley 1927–44
Ted Vizard 1944–48
Stan Cullis 1948–64
Andy Beattie 1964–65
Ronnie Allen 1966–68
Bill McGarry 1968–76
Sammy Chung 1976–78
John Barnwell 1978–81
Ian Greaves 1982
Graham Hawkins 1982–84
Tommy Docherty 1984–85
Bill McGarry 1985
Sammy Chapman 1985–86
Brian Little 1986
Graham Turner 1986–94
Graham Taylor 1994–95
Mark McGhee 1995–98
Colin Lee 1998–2000
Dave Jones 2001–04
Glenn Hoddle 2004–06
Mick McCarthy 2006–12
Stale Solbakken 2012–13
Dean Saunders 2013
Kenny Jackett May 2013–

## LATEST SEQUENCES

*Longest Sequence of League Wins:* 8, 15.10.1988 – 26.11.1988.

*Longest Sequence of League Defeats:* 8, 5.12.1981 – 13.2.1982.

*Longest Sequence of League Draws:* 6, 22.4.1995 – 20.8.1995.

*Longest Sequence of Unbeaten League Matches:* 21, 15.1.2005 – 13.8.2005.

*Longest Sequence Without a League Win:* 19, 1.12.1984 – 6.4.1985.

*Successive Scoring Runs:* 41 from 20.12.1958.

*Successive Non-scoring Runs:* 7 from 2.2.1985.

## TEN YEAR LEAGUE RECORD

| | | P | W | D | L | F | A | Pts | Pos |
|---|---|---|---|---|---|---|---|---|---|
| 2003-04 | PR Lge | 38 | 7 | 12 | 19 | 38 | 77 | 33 | 20 |
| 2004-05 | FL C | 46 | 15 | 21 | 10 | 72 | 59 | 66 | 9 |
| 2005-06 | FL C | 46 | 16 | 19 | 11 | 50 | 42 | 67 | 7 |
| 2006-07 | FL C | 46 | 22 | 10 | 14 | 59 | 56 | 76 | 5 |
| 2007-08 | FL C | 46 | 18 | 16 | 12 | 53 | 48 | 70 | 7 |
| 2008-09 | FL C | 46 | 27 | 9 | 10 | 80 | 52 | 90 | 1 |
| 2009-10 | PR Lge | 38 | 9 | 11 | 18 | 32 | 56 | 38 | 15 |
| 2010-11 | PR Lge | 38 | 11 | 7 | 20 | 46 | 66 | 40 | 17 |
| 2011-12 | PR Lge | 38 | 5 | 10 | 23 | 40 | 82 | 25 | 20 |
| 2012-13 | FL C | 46 | 14 | 9 | 23 | 55 | 69 | 51 | 23 |

The highest average attendance achieved by Wolverhampton Wanderers in the pre-1939 era was 30,316 in the 1937–38 season. This was exceeded in each of the first 15 post-war seasons, with an all-time high figure of 45,346 being achieved in 1949–50.

## WOLVERHAMPTON WANDERERS – FL CHAMPIONSHIP 2012–13 LEAGUE RECORD

| Match No. | Date | Venue | Opponents | Result | H/T Score | Lg Pos. | Goalscorers | Attendance |
|---|---|---|---|---|---|---|---|---|
| 1 | Aug 18 | A | Leeds U | L | 0-1 | 0-1 | 21 | | 23,745 |
| 2 | 21 | H | Barnsley | W | 3-1 | 1-0 | 10 | Ward [8], Ebanks-Blake [61], Edwards [70] | 24,400 |
| 3 | 25 | H | Derby Co | D | 1-1 | 1-0 | 11 | Doyle [35] | 21,861 |
| 4 | Sept 2 | A | Cardiff C | L | 1-3 | 1-2 | 19 | Sako [10] | 22,020 |
| 5 | 16 | H | Leicester C | W | 2-1 | 2-0 | 10 | Ebanks-Blake [13], Stearman [21] | 20,030 |
| 6 | 19 | A | Ipswich T | W | 2-0 | 0-0 | 8 | Smith (og) [69], Doumbia [77] | 16,540 |
| 7 | 22 | A | Peterborough U | W | 2-0 | 1-0 | 5 | Ebanks-Blake (pen) [33], Sigurdarson [82] | 9280 |
| 8 | 29 | H | Sheffield W | W | 1-0 | 1-0 | 3 | Sako [43] | 23,591 |
| 9 | Oct 2 | H | Crystal Palace | L | 1-2 | 0-0 | 5 | Ebanks-Blake [53] | 19,561 |
| 10 | 6 | A | Blackburn R | W | 1-0 | 0-0 | 3 | Sako [78] | 17,034 |
| 11 | 20 | A | Huddersfield T | L | 1-2 | 0-2 | 5 | Ebanks-Blake [63] | 18,012 |
| 12 | 23 | H | Bolton W | D | 2-2 | 2-1 | 5 | Doyle 2 [27, 30] | 20,915 |
| 13 | 27 | H | Charlton Ath | D | 1-1 | 1-0 | 8 | Sako [12] | 22,198 |
| 14 | Nov 3 | A | Burnley | L | 0-2 | 0-1 | 9 | | 12,295 |
| 15 | 6 | A | Hull C | L | 1-2 | 0-1 | 13 | Chester (og) [67] | 14,768 |
| 16 | 10 | H | Brighton & HA | D | 3-3 | 1-1 | 15 | Sako [22], Doumbia [61], Johnson [90] | 21,583 |
| 17 | 17 | A | Watford | L | 1-2 | 0-1 | 16 | Sako [54] | 13,588 |
| 18 | 24 | H | Nottingham F | L | 1-2 | 1-1 | 17 | Sigurdarson [5] | 22,527 |
| 19 | 27 | H | Millwall | L | 0-1 | 0-0 | 18 | | 18,174 |
| 20 | Dec 1 | A | Bristol C | W | 4-1 | 4-0 | 17 | Ebanks-Blake [21], Doyle 2 [25, 41], Sigurdarson [44] | 13,892 |
| 21 | 8 | H | Birmingham C | W | 1-0 | 1-0 | 16 | King (og) [34] | 21,339 |
| 22 | 15 | A | Middlesbrough | L | 0-2 | 0-0 | 18 | | 15,662 |
| 23 | 21 | A | Blackpool | W | 2-1 | 1-0 | 13 | Ebanks-Blake 2 (1 pen) [3, 72 (p)] | 14,556 |
| 24 | 26 | H | Peterborough U | L | 0-3 | 0-2 | 14 | | 23,033 |
| 25 | 29 | H | Ipswich T | L | 0-2 | 0-1 | 17 | | 28,595 |
| 26 | Jan 1 | A | Crystal Palace | L | 1-3 | 0-2 | 18 | Ebanks-Blake [75] | 17,453 |
| 27 | 11 | H | Blackburn R | D | 1-1 | 0-1 | 17 | Johnson [74] | 20,264 |
| 28 | 19 | A | Sheffield W | D | 0-0 | 0-0 | 17 | | 21,142 |
| 29 | 26 | H | Blackpool | L | 1-2 | 1-1 | 18 | Ebanks-Blake [15] | 20,100 |
| 30 | 31 | A | Leicester C | L | 1-2 | 0-1 | 19 | Sako [51] | 21,677 |
| 31 | Feb 9 | H | Leeds U | D | 2-2 | 0-0 | 21 | Peltier (og) [57], Batth [90] | 23,463 |
| 32 | 16 | A | Derby Co | D | 0-0 | 0-0 | 21 | | 23,036 |
| 33 | 19 | A | Barnsley | L | 1-2 | 1-0 | 22 | Sigurdarson [7] | 10,972 |
| 34 | 24 | H | Cardiff C | L | 1-2 | 0-1 | 22 | Sako [70] | 20,930 |
| 35 | Mar 1 | H | Watford | D | 1-1 | 0-1 | 22 | Sako [90] | 18,571 |
| 36 | 5 | A | Millwall | W | 2-0 | 1-0 | 21 | Edwards [9], Ebanks-Blake [61] | 8727 |
| 37 | 9 | A | Nottingham F | L | 1-3 | 0-1 | 21 | Doherty [65] | 23,350 |
| 38 | 16 | H | Bristol C | W | 2-1 | 0-1 | 23 | Ebanks-Blake [76], Doyle [78] | 21,711 |
| 39 | 30 | H | Middlesbrough | W | 3-2 | 1-1 | 22 | McManus (og) [17], Sigurdarson [48], Doyle [70] | 21,277 |
| 40 | Apr 1 | A | Birmingham C | W | 3-2 | 3-0 | 18 | Hunt [20], Ebanks-Blake 2 (1 pen) [27, 37 (p)] | 19,630 |
| 41 | 6 | A | Bolton W | L | 0-2 | 0-2 | 19 | | 18,432 |
| 42 | 13 | A | Huddersfield T | L | 1-3 | 1-1 | 23 | Ward [4] | 23,185 |
| 43 | 16 | H | Hull C | W | 1-0 | 0-0 | 21 | Doyle [55] | 19,641 |
| 44 | 20 | A | Charlton Ath | L | 1-2 | 0-0 | 22 | Doyle [66] | 19,023 |
| 45 | 27 | H | Burnley | L | 1-2 | 0-1 | 23 | Dicko [88] | 24,199 |
| 46 | May 4 | A | Brighton & HA | L | 0-2 | 0-2 | 23 | | 30,003 |

**Final League Position: 23**

### GOALSCORERS

*League (55):* Ebanks-Blake 14 (3 pens), Doyle 9, Sako 9, Sigurdarson 5, Doumbia 2, Edwards 2, Johnson 2, Ward 2, Batth 1, Dicko 1, Doherty 1, Hunt 1, Stearman 1, own goals 5.
*FA Cup (0).*
*Capital One Cup (4):* Batth 1, Ebanks-Blake 1, Nouble 1, Sako 1.

| Ikeme C 38 | Zubar R 7+1 | Stearman R 8+4 | Johnson S 42 | Ward S 37+2 | Forde A 1+11 | Henry K 36+3 | Doumbia T 27+6 | Jarvis M 2 | Doyle K 40+2 | Ebanks-Blake S 31+9 | Peszko S 7+6 | Sigurdarson B 22+15 | Edwards D 14+10 | Berra C 30 | Davis D 12+16 | Elokobi G 1+1 | Jonsson E —+1 | Sako B 36+1 | Nouble F —+2 | Boukari R 2+2 | Margreiter G —+1 | Foley K 24+2 | Batth D 5+7 | Pennant J 10+5 | De Vries D 8+2 | O'Hara J 15+5 | Cassidy J 3+3 | Hunt S 8+4 | Gorkss K 15 | Robinson J 11 | Hammill A —+4 | Doherty M 13 | Dicko N 1+3 | McAlinden L —+1 | Match No. |
|---|---|---|---|---|---|---|---|---|---|---|---|---|---|---|---|---|---|---|---|---|---|---|---|---|---|---|---|---|---|---|---|---|---|---|---|
| 1 | 2 | 3³ | 4 | 5 | 6¹ | 7 | 8 | 9 | 10 | 11² | 12 | 13 | 14 |  |  |  |  |  |  |  |  |  |  |  |  |  |  |  |  |  |  |  |  |  | 1 |
| 1 | 2 |  | 3 | 5 |  | 7¹ | 8³ | 9 | 10 | 11² | 6 | 13 | 12 | 4 | 14 |  |  |  |  |  |  |  |  |  |  |  |  |  |  |  |  |  |  |  | 2 |
| 1 | 2 |  | 3 | 5 | 12 |  | 9³ |  | 10 | 11 | 6 |  | 7² | 4 | 8¹ | 13 | 14 |  |  |  |  |  |  |  |  |  |  |  |  |  |  |  |  |  | 3 |
| 1 | 2¹ | 13 | 3 | 5 | 14 |  | 9 |  | 10 | 11 |  | 7³ | 6² | 4 |  |  |  | 8 | 12 |  |  |  |  |  |  |  |  |  |  |  |  |  |  |  | 4 |
| 1 | 2 |  | 3 | 5 |  | 8 | 7¹ |  | 10 | 11³ | 6² | 14 | 12 | 4 |  |  |  | 9 |  |  |  | 13 |  |  |  |  |  |  |  |  |  |  |  |  | 5 |
| 1 | 2 |  | 3 | 5 |  | 7² | 13 |  | 10³ | 12 |  | 11¹ | 8 | 4 |  |  |  | 9 |  | 6 | 14 |  |  |  |  |  |  |  |  |  |  |  |  |  | 6 |
| 1 | 14 | 4 | 5 |  |  | 8 | 7 |  | 11 | 10² | 6¹ | 13 |  | 3 |  |  |  | 9 |  | 12 |  | 2³ |  |  |  |  |  |  |  |  |  |  |  |  | 7 |
| 1 |  |  | 3 | 5 |  | 8 | 7 |  | 10³ | 11² | 12 | 13 |  | 4 |  |  |  | 9 | 6¹ | 2 | 14 |  |  |  |  |  |  |  |  |  |  |  |  |  | 8 |
| 1 |  |  | 4 | 5 |  | 8¹ | 7 |  | 11 | 10 | 6² | 13 | 14 | 3 | 12 |  |  | 9 |  | 2³ |  |  |  |  |  |  |  |  |  |  |  |  |  |  | 9 |
| 1 | 13 | 2¹ | 3 | 9 | 12 | 8 | 7 |  | 11³ |  |  |  |  | 4 | 6² |  |  | 10 |  | 5 | 14 |  |  |  |  |  |  |  |  |  |  |  |  |  | 10 |
| 1 |  |  | 3 | 5 |  | 8 |  |  | 10 | 11 |  |  | 12 | 4 | 7¹ |  |  | 9 |  | 2 | 6 |  |  |  |  |  |  |  |  |  |  |  |  |  | 11 |
| 1 | 14 |  | 3 | 5 |  | 8 | 7 |  | 10³ | 11¹ |  | 12 | 13 | 4 |  |  |  | 9 |  | 2 | 6² |  |  |  |  |  |  |  |  |  |  |  |  |  | 12 |
| 1 |  |  | 3 | 5 | 14 | 7² | 8 |  | 10 | 11¹ |  | 12 | 13 | 4 |  |  |  | 9 |  | 2 | 6³ |  |  |  |  |  |  |  |  |  |  |  |  |  | 13 |
| 1 |  | 4² | 5 | 12 | 8 | 9 |  |  | 10 | 11 |  | 13 | 3 |  |  |  |  | 7 |  | 2 | 6¹ |  |  |  |  |  |  |  |  |  |  |  |  |  | 14 |
| 1 | 2³ | 4 | 5 | 12 | 8 | 7¹ |  | 11 | 13 |  | 10² | 6 | 3 |  |  |  |  | 9 |  |  | 14 |  |  |  |  |  |  |  |  |  |  |  |  |  | 15 |
| 1 |  |  | 3 | 5 |  | 8⁴ | 12 |  | 10 | 11¹ |  | 13 | 7³ | 4 | 14 |  |  | 9 |  | 2 | 6² |  |  |  |  |  |  |  |  |  |  |  |  |  | 16 |
| 1 |  | 2 | 3 | 5 |  | 7² |  |  | 10³ | 14 |  | 11 | 8 | 4⁴ | 13 |  |  | 9 |  |  |  | 12 | 6¹ |  |  |  |  |  |  |  |  |  |  |  | 17 |
| 1 |  |  | 3 | 5 | 14 | 7² |  |  | 10 | 12 |  | 9 | 8 | 4 | 13 |  |  | 11 |  | 2³ | 6¹ |  |  |  |  |  |  |  |  |  |  |  |  |  | 18 |
| 1¹ | 2³ | 3 | 5 | 13 |  | 11 | 14 |  | 8 | 7 |  | 4 | 9 |  | 10 |  |  |  |  | 6² | 12 |  |  |  |  |  |  |  |  |  |  |  |  |  | 19 |
| 1 |  |  | 3 | 5 | 13 | 8 |  | 11² | 10 |  | 6³ | 7¹ | 4 | 12 |  |  |  | 9 | 14 |  |  | 2 |  |  |  |  |  |  |  |  |  |  |  |  | 20 |
| 1 |  |  | 3 | 5 |  | 7 | 6¹ |  | 11 | 10² |  | 8 | 4 | 12 |  |  |  | 9 |  | 2 | 13 |  |  |  |  |  |  |  |  |  |  |  |  |  | 21 |
| 1 |  |  | 3 | 5 |  | 7 | 6² |  | 11 | 10¹ |  | 8 | 4 | 12 |  |  |  | 9 |  | 2 | 13 |  |  |  |  |  |  |  |  |  |  |  |  |  | 22 |
| 1 | 14 | 3 | 5 | 13 | 7 | 8¹ |  | 10 | 11 |  |  | 4 | 12 |  |  |  | 9³ |  | 2 | 6² |  |  |  |  |  |  |  |  |  |  |  |  |  |  | 23 |
| 1 |  |  | 3 | 5¹ |  | 7 | 8 |  | 11 | 10³ |  | 12 | 4 | 14 |  |  |  | 9 |  | 2 | 6² | 13 |  |  |  |  |  |  |  |  |  |  |  |  | 24 |
| 1 |  |  | 3 | 5 |  | 7¹ | 13 |  | 10³ | 11 |  | 6 | 4 | 8² |  |  |  | 9 |  | 2 | 14 | 12 |  |  |  |  |  |  |  |  |  |  |  |  | 25 |
| 1 | 2 | 3 | 5 | 13 | 7 |  |  | 11 | 10 |  | 4 | 8¹ |  | 9² |  |  | 6³ |  | 14 | 12 |  |  |  |  |  |  |  |  |  |  |  |  |  |  | 26 |
| 1 | 2¹ |  | 3 | 5 |  | 7 |  |  | 10 | 14 | 12 |  | 4 | 8² |  |  |  | 9 |  | 6 |  | 13 | 11³ |  |  |  |  |  |  |  |  |  |  |  | 27 |
| 1 | 2 |  | 3 | 5 |  | 7 |  |  | 11 | 10² | 14 |  | 4 | 8¹ |  |  |  | 9³ |  | 6 |  | 12 | 13 |  |  |  |  |  |  |  |  |  |  |  | 28 |
| 1 | 2¹ | 3⁸ |  | 7 |  |  |  |  | 10³ | 11 | 6² | 13 |  | 4 | 14 |  |  | 9 |  | 5 |  |  | 8 | 12 |  |  |  |  |  |  |  |  |  |  | 29 |
| 1 |  |  | 5 |  | 7² | 6³ |  |  | 11 | 12 | 10¹ | 13 |  | 4 | 14 |  |  | 9 |  | 2 | 3 |  | 8 |  |  |  |  |  |  |  |  |  |  |  | 30 |
| 1 |  |  | 5 |  | 7² | 6¹ |  |  | 11 | 10 |  | 12 | 13 | 4 |  |  |  | 9 |  | 2 | 3 |  | 8 |  |  |  |  |  |  |  |  |  |  |  | 31 |
| 1 |  |  | 5 |  | 7 |  |  |  | 11¹ | 12 | 14 | 10 | 6³ |  | 13 |  |  | 9 |  | 2 | 4 |  | 8² |  | 3 |  |  |  |  |  |  |  |  |  | 32 |
| 1 |  |  |  | 7 |  |  |  |  | 11 | 10³ | 6² |  | 12 |  |  |  |  | 9 |  | 2 | 4 |  | 8¹ | 14 |  | 3 | 5 | 13 |  |  |  |  |  |  | 33 |
| 1 |  | 3 |  | 7 | 6¹ |  |  |  | 13 | 12 |  | 11 |  |  |  |  |  | 10 |  | 14 | 2² |  | 8 |  |  | 4 | 9 |  | 5³ |  |  |  |  |  | 34 |
| 1 |  | 3 |  | 7³ |  |  |  |  | 11¹ | 12 |  | 10 |  |  | 14 |  |  | 9 |  |  |  |  | 8 | 13 | 6² | 4 | 5 |  | 2 |  |  |  |  |  | 35 |
| 1 |  | 4 | 5 | 8 |  |  |  |  | 11 |  |  | 13 | 6 |  |  |  |  | 9¹ |  |  |  |  | 7 | 10² | 12 | 3 |  |  | 2 |  |  |  |  |  | 36 |
| 1 |  | 3 | 5⁹ | 8² | 13 |  |  |  | 14 | 11 |  | 10⁶ | 6 | 12 |  |  |  | 9 |  |  |  |  | 7¹ |  |  | 4 |  |  | 2 |  |  |  |  |  | 37 |
| 1³ |  | 3 |  |  |  |  |  |  | 11 | 10 |  | 13 | 6² | 8 |  | 9¹ |  |  |  |  |  |  | 14 | 7 |  | 12 | 4 | 5 |  | 2 |  |  |  |  | 38 |
|  |  | 3 | 14 |  |  |  |  |  | 12 |  |  | 10² | 11 | 6 |  | 7 |  |  |  |  |  |  |  | 13 |  | 1 | 8¹ |  | 9³ | 4 | 5 |  | 2 |  | 39 |
|  |  | 3 |  |  |  |  |  |  | 12 |  |  | 11 | 10² | 6 |  | 7 |  |  |  |  |  |  |  | 14 |  | 1 | 8¹ |  | 9³ | 4 | 5 |  | 2 | 13 | 40 |
|  |  | 3 |  |  |  |  |  |  | 12 | 13 | 10 |  | 6 |  | 8¹ |  |  |  |  |  |  |  |  |  |  | 1 | 7³ | 11² | 9 | 4 | 5 | 14 | 2 |  | 41 |
|  |  | 3 | 9¹ |  |  |  |  |  | 7 | 12 |  | 10 |  |  | 11² |  |  |  |  |  |  |  |  |  |  | 1 | 8⁴ |  | 6 | 4 | 5 | 14 | 2 | 13 | 42 |
|  |  | 3 | 9¹ |  |  |  |  |  | 7 | 8 |  | 10 |  |  | 11² |  |  |  |  |  |  | 12 | 13 |  |  | 1 |  |  | 6 | 4 | 5 |  | 2 |  | 43 |
|  |  | 4 | 5² |  |  |  |  |  | 6 | 8 |  | 10 |  |  | 11 |  |  |  |  |  |  |  | 13 |  |  | 1 |  |  | 9¹ | 3 | 7 | 12 | 2 |  | 44 |
|  |  | 3 | 9¹ |  |  |  |  |  | 8 | 7 |  | 11 |  |  | 10² |  |  | 12 |  |  |  |  |  |  |  | 1 |  |  | 6³ | 4 | 5 |  | 2 | 13 | 45 |
|  |  | 4 | 14 |  |  |  |  |  | 7 | 9 |  | 11 |  |  | 13 |  | 5³ |  | 6¹ |  |  |  |  |  |  | 1 | 8 |  | 12 | 3 |  |  | 2² | 10 | 46 |

**FA Cup**
Third Round     Luton T     (a)   0-1

**Capital One Cup**
First Round     Aldershot T     (h)   1-1
*(aet; won 7-6 on pens)*
Second Round     Northampton T     (a)   3-1
Third Round     Chelsea     (a)   0-6

# WYCOMBE WANDERERS

## FOUNDATION

In 1887 a group of young furniture trade workers called a meeting at the Steam Engine public house with the aim of forming a football club and entering junior football. It is thought that they were named after the famous FA Cup winners, The Wanderers, who had visited the town in 1877 for a tie with the original High Wycombe club. It is also possible that they played informally before their formation, although there is no proof of this.

*Adams Park, Hillbottom Road, High Wycombe, Buckinghamshire HP12 4HJ.*

*Telephone:* (01494) 472 100. *Fax:* (01494) 527 633.

*Ticket Office:* (01494) 441 118.

*Website:* www.wwfc.com

*Email:* wwfc@wwfc.com

*Ground Capacity:* 10,000.

*Record Attendance:* 15,850 v St Albans C, FA Amateur Cup 4th rd, 25 February 1950 (at Loakes Park); 9,921 v Fulham, FA Cup 3rd rd, 9 January 2002 (at Adams Park).

*Pitch Measurements:* 105m × 68m (115yd × 75yd)

*Joint Chairmen:* Ivor L. Beeks, Don Woodward.

*Manager:* Gareth Ainsworth.

*Assistant Manager:* Richard Dobson.

*Physio:* Theo Farley.

*Colours:* Light blue and dark blue quartered shirts, dark blue shorts, dark blue socks.

*Year Formed:* 1887.

*Turned Professional:* 1974.

*Club Nicknames:* 'The Chairboys' (after High Wycombe's tradition of furniture making), 'The Blues'.

*Grounds:* 1887, The Rye; 1893, Spring Meadow; 1895, Loakes Park; 1899, Daws Hill Park; 1901, Loakes Park; 1990, Adams Park.

*First Football League Game:* 14 August 1993, Division 3 v Carlisle U (a) D 2–2: Hyde; Cousins, Horton (Langford), Kerr, Crossley, Ryan, Carroll, Stapleton, Thompson, Scott, Guppy (1) (Hutchinson), (1 og).

*Record League Victory:* 5–0 v Burnley, Division 2, 15 April 1997 – Parkin; Cousins, Bell, Kavanagh, McCarthy, Forsyth, Carroll (2p) (Simpson), Scott (Farrell), Stallard (1), McGavin (1) (Read (1)), Brown. 5–0 v Northampton T, Division 2, 4 January 2003 – Talia; Senda, Ryan, Thomson, McCarthy, Johnson, Bulman, Simpson (1), Faulconbridge (Harris), Dixon (1) (Roberts 3), Brown (Currie).

*Record Cup Victory:* 5–0 v Hitchin T (a), FA Cup 2nd rd, 3 December 1994 – Hyde; Cousins, Brown, Crossley, Evans, Ryan (1), Carroll, Bell (1), Thompson, Garner (3) (Hemmings), Stapleton (Langford).

## HONOURS

**Football League – Division 2:** Best season: 6th, 1994–95; **FL 2:** Best season: 3rd, 2008–09 (promoted to FL 1), 2010–11 (promoted to FL 1).

**FA Amateur Cup:** *Winners* 1931.

**FA Trophy:** *Winners* 1991, 1993.

**GM Vauxhall Conference:** *Winners* 1992–93.

**FA Cup:** semi-final 2001.

**Football League Cup:** semi-final 2007.

## sky SPORTS FACT FILE

Manager Martin O'Neill led Wycombe Wanderers to the Football Conference title in 1992–93, thus earning the club promotion to the Football League. The Chairboys also won the FA Trophy that season, defeating Runcorn 4-1 in the Wembley final.

**Record Defeat:** 0–7 v Shrewsbury T, Johnstone's Paint Trophy, 7 October 2008.

**Most League Points (3 for a win):** 80, FL 2, 2010-11.

**Most League Goals:** 72, FL 2, 2005–06.

**Highest League Goalscorer in Season:** Scott McGleish, 25, 2007–08.

**Most League Goals in Total Aggregate:** Nathan Tyson, 42, 2004–06.

**Most League Goals in One Match:** 3, Miquel Desouza v Bradford C, Division 2, 2 September 1995; 3, John Williams v Stockport Co, Division 2, 24 February 1996; 3, Mark Stallard v Walsall, Division 2, 21 October 1997; 3, Sean Devine v Reading, Division 2, 2 October 1999; 3, Sean Divine v Bury, Division 2, 26 February 2000; 3, Stuart Roberts v Northampton T, Division 2, 4 January 2003; 3, Nathan Tyson v Lincoln C, FL 2, 5 March 2005; 3, Nathan Tyson v Kidderminster H, FL 2, 2 April 2005; 3, Nathan Tyson v Stockport Co, FL 2, 10 September 2005; 3, Kevin Betsy v Mansfield T, FL 2, 24 September 2005; 3, Scott McGleish v Mansfield T, FL 2, 8 January 2008; 3, Stuart Roberts v Northampton T, Division 2, 4 January 2003.

**Most Capped Player:** Mark Rogers, 7, Canada.

**Most League Appearances:** Steve Brown, 371, 1994–2004.

**Youngest League Player:** Jordon Ibe, 15 years 311 days v Hartlepool U, 15 October 2011.

**Record Transfer Fee Received:** £600,000 from Nottingham F for Nathan Tyson, January 2006.

**Record Transfer Fee Paid:** £200,000 to Barnet for Sean Devine, 15 April 1999.

**Football League Record:** 1993 Promoted to Division 3 from GM Vauxhall Conference; 1993–94 Division 3; 1994–2004 Division 2; 2004–09 FL 2; 2009–10 FL 1; 2010–11 FL 2; 2011–12 FL 1; 2012– FL 2.

## MANAGERS

First coach appointed 1951.
*Prior to Brian Lee's appointment in 1969 the team was selected by a Match Committee which met every Monday evening.*

James McCormack 1951–52
Sid Cann 1952–61
Graham Adams 1961–62
Don Welsh 1962–64
Barry Darvill 1964–68
Brian Lee 1969–76
Ted Powell 1976–77
John Reardon 1977–78
Andy Williams 1978–80
Mike Keen 1980–84
Paul Bence 1984–86
Alan Gane 1986–87
Peter Suddaby 1987–88
Jim Kelman 1988–90
Martin O'Neill 1990–95
Alan Smith 1995–96
John Gregory 1996–98
Neil Smillie 1998–99
Lawrie Sanchez 1999–2003
Tony Adams 2003–04
John Gorman 2004–06
Paul Lambert 2006–08
Peter Taylor 2008–09
Gary Waddock 2009–12
Gareth Ainsworth November 2012–

## LATEST SEQUENCES

**Longest Sequence of League Wins:** 6, 19.8.2006 – 16.9.2006.

**Longest Sequence of League Defeats:** 6, 18.3.2006 – 17.4.2006.

**Longest Sequence of League Draws:** 5, 24.1.2004 – 21.2.2004.

**Longest Sequence of Unbeaten League Matches:** 21, 6.8.2005 – 10.12.2005.

**Longest Sequence Without a League Win:** 13, 16.8.2003 – 18.10.2003 and 10.1.2004 – 20.3.2004.

**Successive Scoring Runs:** 15 from 28.12.2004.

**Successive Non-scoring Runs:** 5 from 15.10.1996.

## TEN YEAR LEAGUE RECORD

|  |  | P | W | D | L | F | A | Pts | Pos |
|---|---|---|---|---|---|---|---|---|---|
| 2003-04 | Div 2 | 46 | 6 | 19 | 21 | 50 | 75 | 37 | 24 |
| 2004-05 | FL 2 | 46 | 17 | 14 | 15 | 58 | 52 | 65 | 10 |
| 2005-06 | FL 2 | 46 | 18 | 17 | 11 | 72 | 56 | 71 | 6 |
| 2006-07 | FL 2 | 46 | 16 | 14 | 16 | 52 | 47 | 62 | 12 |
| 2007-08 | FL 2 | 46 | 22 | 12 | 12 | 56 | 42 | 78 | 7 |
| 2008-09 | FL 2 | 46 | 20 | 18 | 8 | 54 | 33 | 78 | 3 |
| 2009-10 | FL 1 | 46 | 10 | 15 | 21 | 56 | 76 | 45 | 22 |
| 2010-11 | FL 2 | 46 | 22 | 14 | 10 | 69 | 50 | 80 | 3 |
| 2011-12 | FL 1 | 46 | 11 | 10 | 25 | 65 | 88 | 43 | 21 |
| 2012-13 | FL 2 | 46 | 17 | 9 | 20 | 50 | 60 | 60 | 15 |

## DID YOU KNOW ?

Frank Adams, after whom Adams Park is named, was a centre half and captain for Wycombe Wanderers and a successful businessman. He purchased the Chairboys' former ground Loakes Park and presented it to the club in April 1947.

## WYCOMBE WANDERERS – FOOTBALL LEAGUE TWO 2012–13 LEAGUE RECORD

| Match No. | Date | Venue | Opponents | Result | H/T Score | Lg Pos. | Goalscorers | Attendance |
|---|---|---|---|---|---|---|---|---|
| 1 | Aug 18 | A | York C | W | 3-1 | 2-0 | 5 | Bloomfield [28], Wood [44], Beavon [53] | 4591 |
| 2 | 21 | H | Gillingham | L | 0-1 | 0-0 | 11 | | 3507 |
| 3 | Sept 1 | A | Southend U | L | 0-1 | 0-1 | 18 | | 4787 |
| 4 | 8 | H | Cheltenham T | D | 1-1 | 1-1 | 18 | Lowe (og) [3] | 3667 |
| 5 | 15 | A | Chesterfield | L | 1-3 | 0-2 | 20 | Trotman (og) [72] | 5113 |
| 6 | 18 | A | Exeter C | L | 2-3 | 1-1 | 20 | Ainsworth [4], Morgan [52] | 3365 |
| 7 | 22 | H | AFC Wimbledon | L | 0-1 | 0-1 | 21 | | 4260 |
| 8 | 29 | A | Dagenham & R | L | 0-3 | 0-1 | 23 | | 1680 |
| 9 | Oct 2 | H | Plymouth Arg | D | 1-1 | 1-0 | 23 | McClure [12] | 3161 |
| 10 | 6 | H | Torquay U | W | 2-1 | 1-1 | 22 | Doherty [33], Scowen [63] | 4205 |
| 11 | 13 | A | Fleetwood T | W | 1-0 | 1-0 | 20 | Andrade [9] | 3612 |
| 12 | 20 | A | Port Vale | L | 1-4 | 1-0 | 21 | Grant (pen) [20] | 5303 |
| 13 | 23 | H | Barnet | D | 0-0 | 0-0 | 22 | | 3244 |
| 14 | 27 | H | Oxford U | L | 1-3 | 0-1 | 22 | Grant (pen) [49] | 5498 |
| 15 | Nov 6 | A | Aldershot T | D | 0-0 | 0-0 | 22 | | 2042 |
| 16 | 10 | H | Rochdale | L | 1-2 | 1-1 | 22 | Grant [25] | 3020 |
| 17 | 17 | A | Northampton T | L | 1-3 | 0-1 | 24 | Grant (pen) [72] | 4764 |
| 18 | 20 | A | Rotherham U | W | 3-2 | 1-2 | 23 | Winfield [29], McClure 2 [50, 55] | 5688 |
| 19 | 24 | H | Burton Alb | W | 3-0 | 1-0 | 19 | McClure 2 [13, 63], Grant (pen) [58] | 3191 |
| 20 | Dec 1 | H | Bristol R | W | 2-0 | 1-0 | 19 | Grant [11], Ainsworth [55] | 3740 |
| 21 | 8 | A | Morecambe | D | 2-2 | 1-0 | 19 | Morgan 2 [22, 50] | 3238 |
| 22 | 15 | A | Accrington S | W | 2-0 | 2-0 | 17 | Andrade [11], McClure [34] | 1050 |
| 23 | 26 | A | Cheltenham T | L | 0-4 | 0-2 | 19 | | 3501 |
| 24 | 29 | A | Plymouth Arg | W | 1-0 | 1-0 | 17 | McClure [11] | 6983 |
| 25 | Jan 1 | H | Exeter C | L | 0-1 | 0-0 | 19 | | 3679 |
| 26 | 5 | H | Chesterfield | W | 2-1 | 1-1 | 17 | Hause [45], Kuffour [55] | 3492 |
| 27 | 12 | A | AFC Wimbledon | D | 2-2 | 1-2 | 17 | Kuffour [8], McClure [72] | 4507 |
| 28 | 19 | H | Dagenham & R | W | 1-0 | 1-0 | 16 | Wood [32] | 2365 |
| 29 | Feb 4 | A | Gillingham | W | 1-0 | 0-0 | 14 | McClure [86] | 4758 |
| 30 | 9 | H | York C | W | 4-0 | 2-0 | 11 | Morgan 2 (2 pens) [3, 45], Grant [58], Winfield [78] | 3383 |
| 31 | 12 | H | Bradford C | L | 0-3 | 0-1 | 13 | | 3068 |
| 32 | 16 | A | Bristol R | L | 0-1 | 0-1 | 14 | | 7324 |
| 33 | 23 | H | Southend U | L | 1-2 | 1-0 | 15 | Morgan [7] | 3518 |
| 34 | 26 | A | Torquay U | W | 2-1 | 0-1 | 12 | Wood [76], McClure [81] | 1793 |
| 35 | Mar 2 | H | Fleetwood T | W | 1-0 | 0-0 | 13 | Stewart [90] | 3162 |
| 36 | 9 | A | Rochdale | L | 1-4 | 1-1 | 14 | Lewis [16] | 1979 |
| 37 | 12 | H | Rotherham U | D | 2-2 | 1-0 | 14 | Grant [7], Doherty [81] | 2581 |
| 38 | 19 | A | Bradford C | L | 0-1 | 0-1 | 15 | | 8047 |
| 39 | 29 | H | Accrington S | L | 0-1 | 0-0 | 15 | | 4577 |
| 40 | Apr 1 | A | Morecambe | W | 1-0 | 0-0 | 15 | Lewis [55] | 1702 |
| 41 | 6 | A | Oxford U | W | 1-0 | 1-0 | 15 | Grant [19] | 6777 |
| 42 | 9 | A | Burton Alb | L | 0-2 | 0-0 | 15 | | 2202 |
| 43 | 13 | H | Aldershot T | W | 2-1 | 0-0 | 15 | McClure [50], Grant [75] | 4290 |
| 44 | 16 | A | Northampton T | D | 0-0 | 0-0 | 14 | | 3615 |
| 45 | 20 | A | Barnet | L | 0-1 | 0-0 | 14 | | 6001 |
| 46 | 27 | H | Port Vale | D | 1-1 | 1-0 | 15 | Morgan (pen) [31] | 7120 |

**Final League Position: 15**

## GOALSCORERS

*League (50):* McClure 11, Grant 10 (4 pens), Morgan 7 (3 pens), Wood 3, Ainsworth 2, Andrade 2, Doherty 2, Kuffour 2, Lewis 2, Winfield 2, Beavon 1, Bloomfield 1, Hause 1, Scowen 1, Stewart 1, own goals 2.
*FA Cup (1):* Spring 1.
*Capital One Cup (0).*
*Johnstone's Paint Trophy (3):* Morgan 2, Grant 1.

| Bull N 9 | Stewart A 15+4 | Doherty G 22+1 | Johnson L 18+2 | Bassey G 3 | Bloomfield M 2 | Lewis S 44 | Spring M 19+6 | Wood S 33+2 | Grant J 40+1 | Beavon S 2 | Oli D 6+4 | Winfield D 28+1 | Logan R 3+5 | Angol L —+3 | Thompson A 2 | Parsons M 4 | Kuffour J 22+10 | Ainsworth G 12+13 | Dunne C 38 | Kewley-Graham J 2+5 | Morgan D 29+4 | Taylor O 1+5 | Parish E 2 | Foster D 9 | Archer J 27 | Scowen J 34 | McClure M 22+5 | Morias J —+19 | Andrade B 15+8 | Azeez A —+4 | Ehui G —+2 | Hause K 8+1 | McCoy M 8+1 | Harriman M 19+1 | Ingram M 8 | Match No. |
|---|---|---|---|---|---|---|---|---|---|---|---|---|---|---|---|---|---|---|---|---|---|---|---|---|---|---|---|---|---|---|---|---|---|---|---|---|
| 1 | 2 | 3 | 4 | 5 | $6^2$ | 7 | 8 | 9 | $10^1$ | $11^3$ | 12 | 13 | 14 | | | | | | | | | | | | | | | | | | | | | | | 1 |
| 1 | 2 | 4 | 3 | $5^3$ | $8^2$ | 6 | 10 | $7^1$ | 9 | 11 | 12 | 13 | 14 | | | | | | | | | | | | | | | | | | | | | | | 2 |
| 1 | $4^2$ | 3 | 13 | 5 | | 8 | 7 | | 6 | | | $11^3$ | | $10^1$ | | 12 | 2 | 9 | 12 | 14 | | | | | | | | | | | | | | | | 3 |
| 1 | | 4 | 3 | | | 6 | $7^2$ | | 9 | | | $10^1$ | | 12 | | | 5 | 11 | 13 | | 2 | 8 | | | | | | | | | | | | | | 4 |
| 1 | 12 | 3 | $4^■$ | | | 6 | 7 | | 8 | | | | | | | | $2^2$ | $10^1$ | $11^3$ | 14 | 5 | | | 9 | 13 | | | | | | | | | | | 5 |
| | 4 | | | | | 7 | 8 | $9^3$ | | | | 3 | 10 | 13 | | 5 | 12 | $6^1$ | | | $11^2$ | 14 | 1 | 2 | | | | | | | | | | | | 6 |
| | 4 | 3 | | | | $7^■$ | 8 | | | | | | $10^2$ | 13 | | 11 | $6^3$ | 5 | 12 | 9 | 14 | 1 | 2 | | | | | | | | | | | | | 7 |
| | 3 | 4 | | | | 8 | 7 | | 13 | | | | | | | $9^3$ | | 5 | | $11^2$ | $10^1$ | | 2 | 1 | 6 | 12 | 14 | | | | | | | | | 8 |
| | 5 | 4 | | | | 7 | 13 | | 9 | | | | | | | $11^3$ | $6^2$ | 3 | | 12 | | | 2 | 1 | 8 | $10^1$ | 14 | | | | | | | | | 9 |
| | 4 | 3 | | | | $7^2$ | 13 | | 9 | | | | | | | 11 | $6^3$ | 5 | | 12 | | | 2 | 1 | 8 | $10^1$ | 14 | | | | | | | | | 10 |
| 1 | | 3 | 4 | | | 8 | 12 | | $9^1$ | | | | | | | 10 | | 5 | | 11 | | | 2 | | 7 | | 6 | | | | | | | | | 11 |
| 1 | | 4 | 3 | | | 8 | 12 | | $6^2$ | | | | | | | $11^1$ | | 5 | | 10 | | | 2 | | $9^3$ | 13 | 14 | $7^1$ | | | | | | | | 12 |
| 1 | 2 | 4 | | | | 7 | | 12 | 9 | | | | 3 | 14 | | | $6^2$ | 5 | | $10^1$ | | | | | 8 | $11^3$ | 13 | | | | | | | | | 13 |
| 1 | 2 | 4 | | | | 7 | 14 | $9^3$ | 10 | | | | 3 | 12 | | | $11^1$ | $6^2$ | 5 | | | | | | 8 | | 13 | | | | | | | | | 14 |
| | | | | | | 7 | 10 | 5 | 9 | | | $11^2$ | 3 | | | | $6^1$ | 2 | | | 13 | | | 1 | 4 | | 12 | 8 | | | | | | | | 15 |
| | | | 4 | | | 7 | | 5 | 9 | | | 10 | 3 | | | | 2 | | | $11^1$ | | | | 1 | 8 | | 12 | 6 | | | | | | | | 16 |
| | | | 4 | | | 7 | | $9^1$ | 6 | | | $11^2$ | 3 | | | | 5 | | | 10 | | 2 | 1 | 8 | 13 | | 12 | | | | | | | | | 17 |
| | | | 3 | | | 8 | | 12 | $6^1$ | | | | 4 | | | | 14 | 5 | 13 | 10 | | | $2^2$ | 1 | 7 | 11 | | $9^3$ | | | | | | | | 18 |
| | | | 4 | | | 2 | | 5 | $9^1$ | | | | 3 | | | | | 7 | 10 | | | | | 1 | $8^3$ | $11^2$ | 13 | 6 | 12 | 14 | | | | | | 19 |
| | | | 4 | | | 7 | | 5 | $6^1$ | | | | 3 | | | | 12 | 2 | | 10 | | | | 1 | $8^1$ | $11^2$ | | 9 | 13 | | | | | | | 20 |
| | | | | | | 7 | | 5 | $9^■$ | | | | 4 | | | | | 2 | 13 | $10^2$ | | | | 1 | 8 | $11^1$ | | 6 | | 3 | 12 | | | | | 21 |
| | | | | | | 7 | | 5 | | | | 13 | | | | 12 | $6^2$ | 4 | 14 | $10^1$ | | | | 1 | 8 | $11^■$ | | $9^3$ | | 3 | 2 | | | | | 22 |
| | 13 | | | | | 7 | | 5 | | | | $10^3$ | | | | 11 | 6 | $3^1$ | | | | | | 1 | $8^2$ | | 14 | 9 | | 12 | 4 | 2 | | | | 23 |
| | 3 | | | | | 7 | 8 | 5 | | | | | | | | 10 | $6^2$ | | | | 12 | | | 1 | | $11^1$ | 13 | 9 | 12 | | 4 | 2 | | | | 24 |
| | 5 | | | | | 7 | 8 | 3 | 6 | | | | | | | $10^1$ | | | | 12 | | | | 1 | | $11^2$ | | 9 | 13 | | 4 | $2^3$ | 14 | | | 25 |
| | 12 | | | | | $7^2$ | | 9 | 6 | | | | 5 | | | | 11 | 13 | 3 | $10^1$ | | | | 1 | 8 | | | | | 4 | | 2 | | | | 26 |
| | | | | | | 8 | | 9 | $6^1$ | | | | 4 | | | | $11^2$ | | 3 | 10 | | | | 1 | 7 | 12 | | 13 | | 5 | | 2 | | | | 27 |
| | 4 | | | | | 7 | | 9 | 6 | | | | 3 | | | | $11^2$ | 13 | 5 | $10^1$ | | | | 1 | 8 | | 12 | | | | | 2 | | | | 28 |
| | 4 | | | | | 8 | | 9 | 6 | | | | 3 | | | | $10^1$ | | 5 | 11 | | | | 1 | 7 | 12 | | | | | | 2 | | | | 29 |
| | 4 | | | | | 7 | | 9 | $6^1$ | | | | 3 | | | | 13 | 14 | 5 | $10^2$ | | | | 1 | 8 | $11^3$ | | 12 | | | | 2 | | | | 30 |
| | 4 | | | | | 7 | | 9 | 6 | | | | 3 | | | | 13 | | 5 | 10 | | | | 1 | 8 | $11^1$ | | $12^2$ | | | | 2 | | | | 31 |
| | 5 | | | | | 6 | 13 | 7 | $8^1$ | | | 14 | 2 | | | | 10 | | 3 | 12 | | | | 1 | | $11^3$ | | | | | | $9^2$ | 4 | | | 32 |
| | 4 | | | | | 7 | 8 | 9 | $6^2$ | | | | 5 | | | | 12 | | 3 | $10^1$ | | | | 1 | | 11 | 13 | | | | | | 2 | | | 33 |
| | 13 | | | | | 7 | | 5 | $9^1$ | | | | 3 | | | | | 12 | 4 | 10 | | | | 1 | 8 | 11 | | $6^2$ | | | | 2 | | | 34 |
| | 3 | | | | | 7 | | 9 | | | | | 4 | | | | | $6^1$ | 5 | $10^3$ | | | | 1 | 8 | $11^2$ | 13 | 12 | | 14 | | 2 | | | | 35 |
| | 3 | | | | | 8 | | 9 | 6 | | | | 4 | | | | 13 | | 5 | $10^2$ | | | | 1 | 7 | $11^1$ | 12 | | | | | 2 | | | 36 |
| | 14 | | | | | 7 | | 4 | 6 | | | | $2^3$ | | | | 12 | 13 | 5 | 10 | | | | 1 | $8^1$ | $11^1$ | | $9^2$ | | | | 3 | | | 37 |
| | 4 | | | | | 7 | | 9 | $6^1$ | | | | 3 | | | | 12 | 5 | | $11^2$ | | | | 1 | 8 | 10 | 13 | | | | | 2 | | | 38 |
| | 4 | 3 | | | | 7 | | 9 | $6^2$ | | | | | | | | $10^1$ | 13 | | | | | | | 8 | 11 | 12 | | | | 2 | 5 | 1 | | 39 |
| | 4 | | | | | 6 | 7 | 10 | 8 | | | | 3 | | | | 11 | | 5 | | | | | 9 | | | | | | | 2 | | 1 | | 40 |
| | 4 | | | | | 8 | 7 | 9 | 6 | | | | 3 | | | | 10 | | 5 | | | | | 11 | | | | | | | 2 | | 1 | | 41 |
| | 3 | | | | | 7 | | $9^2$ | 10 | | | | 4 | | | | $11^3$ | $6^1$ | 5 | 13 | | | 14 | | 8 | 12 | | | | | 2 | | 1 | | 42 |
| | 4 | 12 | | | | 7 | | $9^2$ | 6 | | | | $3^1$ | | | | 14 | 5 | | $10^3$ | | | | | 8 | 11 | 13 | | | | 2 | | 1 | | 43 |
| | 4 | 3 | | | | 6 | 7 | | 9 | | | | | | | | 13 | 5 | | $10^2$ | | | | | 8 | $11^1$ | 12 | | | | 2 | | 1 | | 44 |
| | 4 | 3 | | | | 6 | 7 | $10^2$ | 8 | | | | | | | | $11^1$ | 5 | | | | | | | 9 | 13 | 12 | | | | 2 | 1 | | 45 |
| | | | | | | 7 | 8 | 9 | 10 | | | | 3 | | | | 12 | 5 | 11 | | | | | | $6^1$ | | | | 4 | 2 | | 1 | | 46 |

# YEOVIL TOWN

## FOUNDATION

One of the prime movers of Yeovil football was Ernest J. Sercombe. His association with the club began in 1895 as a playing member of Yeovil Casuals, of which team he became vice-captain and in his last season 1899–1900, he was chosen to play for Somerset against Devon. Upon the reorganisation of the club, he became secretary of the old Yeovil Town FC and with the amalgamation with Petters United in 1914, he continued to serve until his resignation in 1930.

*Huish Park, Lufton Way, Yeovil, Somerset BA22 8YF.*

*Telephone:* (01935) 423 662.

*Fax:* (01935) 847 886.

*Ticket Office:* (01935) 847 888.

*Website:* www.ytfc.net

*Email:* jcotton@ytfc.net

*Ground Capacity:* 9,565.

*Record Attendance:* 16,318 v Sunderland, FA Cup 4th rd, 29 January 1949 (at Huish); 9,527 v Leeds U, FL 1, 25 April 2008 (at Huish Park).

*Pitch Measurements:* 105m × 65m (115yd × 72yd)

*Chairman:* John R. Fry.

*Chief Executive:* Martyn Starnes.

*Manager:* Gary Johnson.

*Assistant Manager:* Terry Skiverton.

*Physio:* Mike Miccichi.

*Colours:* Green and white hooped shirts, white shorts, green and white hooped socks.

*Year Formed:* 1895.

*Turned Professional:* 1921.

*Previous Names:* 1895, Yeovil Casuals; 1907, Yeovil Town; 1915, Yeovil & Petters United; 1946, Yeovil Town.

*Club Nickname:* 'The Glovers'.

*Grounds:* 1895, Pen Mill Ground; 1921, Huish; 1990, Huish Park.

*First Football League Game:* 9 August 2003, Division 3 v Rochdale (a) W 3-1: Weale; Williams (Lindegaard), Crittenden, Lockwood, O'Brien, Pluck (Rodrigues), Gosling (El Kholti), Way, Jackson, Gall (2), Johnson (1).

*Record League Victory:* 6–1 v Oxford U, FL 2, 18 September 2004 – Weale; Rose, O'Brien, Way, Skiverton, Fontaine, Caceres (Tarachulski), Johnson, Jevons (3), Stoicers (2) (Mirza), Terry (Gall 1).

## HONOURS

**Football League – FL 2:**
*Winners* 2004–05.

**Conference:** *Champions* 2002–03.

**FA Cup:** 5th rd 1949.

**League Cup:** never past 2nd rd.

**Southern League:**
*Champions* 1954–55, 1963–64, 1970–71; *Runners-up*: 1923–24, 1931–32, 1934–35, 1969–70, 1972–73.

**Southern League Cup:**
*Winners* 1948–49, 1954–55, 1960–61, 1965–66; *Runners-up*: 1946–47, 1955–56.

**Isthmian League:** *Winners* 1987–88; *Runners-up*: 1985–86, 1986–87, 1996–97.

**AC Delco Cup:** *Winners* 1987–88.

**Bob Lord Trophy:** *Winners* 1989–90.

**FA Trophy:** *Winners* 2002.

**London Combination:**
*Runners-up* 1930–31, 1932–33.

## sky SPORTS FACT FILE

In April 1933 Yeovil & Petters United faced the Czechoslovakian national team in a friendly at the old Huish ground. The Glovers, who competed in the Western Section of the Southern League at the time, came out on top with an impressive 8-3 victory.

*Record Cup Victory:* 12–1 v Westbury United, FA Cup 1st qual rd, 1923–24.

*Record Defeat:* 0–8 v Manchester United, FA Cup 5th rd, 12 February 1949.

*Most League Points (3 for a win):* 83, FL 2, 2004–05.

*Most League Goals:* 90, FL 2, 2004–05.

*Highest League Goalscorer in Season:* Phil Jevons, 27, 2004–05.

*Most League Goals in Total Aggregate:* Phil Jevons, 42, 2004–06.

*Most League Goals in One Match:* 3, Phil Jevons v Oxford U, FL 2, 18 September 2004; 3, Phil Jevons v Chester C, FL 2, 30 October 2004; 3, Phil Jevons v Bristol R, FL 2, 12 February 2005; 3, Arron Davies v Chesterfield, FL 1, 4 March 2006.

*Most Capped Players:* Andrejs Stolcers, 1 (81), Latvia; Arron Davies, 1, Wales.

*Most League Appearances:* Terry Skiverton, 195, 2003–09.

*Record Transfer Fee Received:* £1,200,000 from Nottingham F for Arron Davies and Chris Cohen, July 2007.

*Record Transfer Fee Paid:* £250,000 to Quilmes AC for Pablo Bastianini, August 2005.

*Football League Record:* 2003 Promoted to Division 3 from Conference; 2003–04 Division 3; 2004–05 FL 2; 2005–13 FL 1; 2013– FL C.

## LATEST SEQUENCES

*Longest Sequence of League Wins:* 8, 29.12.2012 – 16.2.2013.

*Longest Sequence of League Defeats:* 6, 8.9.2012 – 2.10.2012.

*Longest Sequence of League Draws:* 3, 16.4.2011 – 25.4.2011.

*Longest Sequence of Unbeaten League Matches:* 9, 29.12.2012 – 23.2.2013.

*Longest Sequence Without a League Win:* 10, 17.9.2011 – 19.11.2011.

*Successive Scoring Runs:* 22 from 30.10.2004.

*Successive Non-scoring Runs:* 3 from 21.1.2006.

### MANAGERS

Jack Gregory 1922–28
Tommy Lawes 1928–29
Dave Pratt 1929–33
Louis Page 1933–35
Dave Halliday 1935–38
Billy Kingdon 1938–46
Alec Stock 1946–49
George Patterson 1949–51
Harry Lowe 1951–53
Ike Clarke 1953–57
Norman Dodgin 1957
Jimmy Baldwin 1957–60
Basil Hayward 1960–64
Glyn Davies 1964–65
Joe McDonald 1965–67
Ron Saunders 1967–69
Mike Hughes 1969–72
Cecil Irwin 1972–75
Stan Harland 1975–81
Barry Lloyd 1978–81
Malcolm Allison 1981
Jimmy Giles 1981–83
Trevor Finnigan/Mike Hughes 1983
Steve Coles 1983–84
Ian McFarlane 1984
Gerry Gow 1984–87
Brian Hall 1987–90
Clive Whitehead 1990–91
Steve Rutter 1991–93
Brian Hall 1994–95
Graham Roberts 1995–98
Colin Lippiatt 1998–99
Steve Thompson 1999–2000
Dave Webb 2000
Gary Johnson 2001–05
Steve Thompson 2005–06
Russell Slade 2006–09
Terry Skiverton 2009–12
Gary Johnson January 2012–

### TEN YEAR LEAGUE RECORD

|         |       | P  | W  | D  | L  | F  | A  | Pts | Pos |
|---------|-------|----|----|----|----|----|----|-----|-----|
| 2003-04 | Div 3 | 46 | 23 | 5  | 18 | 70 | 57 | 74  | 8   |
| 2004-05 | FL 2  | 46 | 25 | 8  | 13 | 90 | 65 | 83  | 1   |
| 2005-06 | FL 1  | 46 | 15 | 11 | 20 | 54 | 62 | 56  | 15  |
| 2006-07 | FL 1  | 46 | 23 | 10 | 13 | 55 | 39 | 79  | 5   |
| 2007-08 | FL 1  | 46 | 14 | 10 | 22 | 38 | 59 | 52  | 18  |
| 2008-09 | FL 1  | 46 | 12 | 15 | 19 | 41 | 66 | 51  | 17  |
| 2009-10 | FL 1  | 46 | 13 | 14 | 19 | 55 | 59 | 53  | 15  |
| 2010-11 | FL 1  | 46 | 16 | 11 | 19 | 56 | 66 | 59  | 14  |
| 2011-12 | FL 1  | 46 | 14 | 12 | 20 | 59 | 80 | 54  | 17  |
| 2012-13 | FL 1  | 46 | 23 | 8  | 15 | 71 | 56 | 77  | 4   |

### DID YOU KNOW ?

Yeovil & Petters United first applied for election to the Football League in 1927 when they bid for a place in Division Three South. Their efforts proved unsuccessful with Watford unanimously elected and Torquay narrowly ousting Aberdare in a second round of voting. Yeovil received just a single vote.

## YEOVIL TOWN – FOOTBALL LEAGUE ONE 2012–13 LEAGUE RECORD

| Match No. | Date | Venue | Opponents | Result | H/T Score | Lg Pos. | Goalscorers | Attendance |
|---|---|---|---|---|---|---|---|---|
| 1 | Aug 18 | H | Coventry C | D | 1-1 | 1-1 | 12 | Hinds [21] | 6006 |
| 2 | 21 | A | Brentford | W | 3-1 | 1-0 | 5 | Hayter 2 [23, 80], Craig (og) [84] | 5269 |
| 3 | 25 | A | Scunthorpe U | W | 4-0 | 1-0 | 1 | Marsh-Brown [37], Reid [50], Ugwu 2 [88, 90] | 3279 |
| 4 | Sept 1 | H | Doncaster R | W | 2-1 | 0-0 | 2 | Hayter [56], Ugwu [84] | 3535 |
| 5 | 8 | H | Bournemouth | L | 0-1 | 0-1 | 3 | | 5238 |
| 6 | 15 | A | Milton Keynes D | L | 0-1 | 0-0 | 6 | | 7235 |
| 7 | 18 | A | Leyton Orient | L | 1-4 | 0-2 | 11 | Foley [55] | 2876 |
| 8 | 22 | H | Sheffield U | L | 0-1 | 0-0 | 13 | | 4117 |
| 9 | 29 | A | Preston NE | L | 2-3 | 1-0 | 13 | Williams (pen) [6], Burn [87] | 8520 |
| 10 | Oct 2 | H | Portsmouth | L | 1-2 | 0-1 | 16 | Reid (pen) [69] | 4769 |
| 11 | 6 | H | Colchester U | W | 3-1 | 2-1 | 13 | Madden 2 [20, 34], Hayter [78] | 3002 |
| 12 | 13 | A | Tranmere R | L | 2-3 | 2-1 | 14 | Madden [9], Foley [29] | 6344 |
| 13 | 20 | H | Bury | W | 2-1 | 1-0 | 14 | Webster [34], Foley [76] | 3386 |
| 14 | 23 | A | Shrewsbury T | W | 3-1 | 1-0 | 11 | Madden 2 [9, 70], Hayter [60] | 4711 |
| 15 | 27 | A | Crewe Alex | W | 1-0 | 1-0 | 10 | Webster [40] | 4176 |
| 16 | Nov 6 | H | Stevenage | L | 1-3 | 1-1 | 11 | Madden [6] | 2900 |
| 17 | 10 | H | Hartlepool U | W | 1-0 | 1-0 | 11 | Edwards [7] | 3095 |
| 18 | 17 | A | Swindon T | L | 1-4 | 1-3 | 12 | Hayter [41] | 8112 |
| 19 | 20 | A | Crawley T | W | 1-0 | 0-0 | 12 | Hunt (og) [90] | 2912 |
| 20 | 24 | H | Carlisle U | L | 1-3 | 0-1 | 12 | Reid [65] | 3394 |
| 21 | Dec 8 | H | Notts Co | D | 0-0 | 0-0 | 13 | | 3355 |
| 22 | 15 | A | Walsall | D | 2-2 | 0-1 | 14 | Reid [78], Foley [90] | 3160 |
| 23 | 22 | H | Oldham Ath | W | 4-1 | 2-1 | 11 | Williams 2 (1 pen) [39 (pl), 44], Hayter [77], Madden [88] | 3492 |
| 24 | 26 | A | Bournemouth | L | 0-3 | 0-1 | 12 | | 8016 |
| 25 | 29 | A | Portsmouth | W | 2-1 | 2-0 | 12 | Blizzard [15], Webster [38] | 12,370 |
| 26 | Jan 1 | H | Leyton Orient | W | 3-0 | 1-0 | 9 | Madden 2 [41, 74], Hayter [59] | 3516 |
| 27 | 12 | A | Sheffield U | W | 2-0 | 0-0 | 8 | Madden 2 [49, 66] | 20,454 |
| 28 | 29 | H | Milton Keynes D | W | 2-1 | 1-1 | 7 | Madden 2 [26, 78] | 3152 |
| 29 | Feb 2 | H | Brentford | W | 3-0 | 2-0 | 7 | Madden [34], Upson [41], Burn [84] | 4106 |
| 30 | 9 | A | Coventry C | W | 1-0 | 1-0 | 7 | Madden [45] | 11,277 |
| 31 | 12 | H | Preston NE | W | 3-1 | 0-1 | 7 | Hayter [73], Ralph [80], Madden [90] | 3661 |
| 32 | 16 | H | Scunthorpe U | W | 3-0 | 1-0 | 3 | Webster [28], Hayter (pen) [72], Madden [75] | 4163 |
| 33 | 23 | A | Doncaster R | D | 1-1 | 1-1 | 5 | Madden [6] | 6356 |
| 34 | 26 | A | Colchester U | L | 0-2 | 0-1 | 6 | | 2367 |
| 35 | Mar 2 | H | Tranmere R | W | 1-0 | 0-0 | 5 | Upson [58] | 4862 |
| 36 | 9 | A | Hartlepool U | D | 0-0 | 0-0 | 5 | | 3633 |
| 37 | 12 | H | Crawley T | D | 2-2 | 2-0 | 6 | Webster [5], Madden [18] | 3338 |
| 38 | 19 | H | Swindon T | L | 0-2 | 0-0 | 7 | | 5207 |
| 39 | 23 | A | Carlisle U | D | 3-3 | 1-1 | 7 | Dawson [25], Madden [51], Hayter [78] | 3809 |
| 40 | 29 | H | Walsall | D | 0-0 | 0-0 | 7 | | 5594 |
| 41 | Apr 1 | A | Notts Co | W | 2-1 | 1-0 | 6 | Madden [45], Dolan [52] | 5004 |
| 42 | 6 | H | Shrewsbury T | W | 2-1 | 2-1 | 3 | Hayter (pen) [11], Madden [32] | 4473 |
| 43 | 13 | A | Stevenage | W | 2-0 | 0-0 | 4 | Foley [53], Hayter [81] | 3516 |
| 44 | 16 | A | Oldham Ath | L | 0-1 | 0-1 | 5 | | 3888 |
| 45 | 20 | H | Crewe Alex | W | 1-0 | 1-0 | 4 | Edwards [1] | 5293 |
| 46 | 27 | A | Bury | L | 2-3 | 0-3 | 4 | Hayter [58], Dawson [90] | 2440 |

**Final League Position: 4**

### GOALSCORERS

*League (71):* Madden 22, Hayter 14 (2 pens), Foley 5, Webster 5, Reid 4 (1 pen), Ugwu 3, Williams 3 (2 pens), Burn 2, Dawson 2, Edwards 2, Upson 2, Blizzard 1, Dolan 1, Hinds 1, Marsh-Brown 1, Ralph 1, own goals 2.
*FA Cup (0).*
*Capital One Cup (5):* Hinds 2, Reid 2, Marsh-Brown 1.
*Johnstone's Paint Trophy (7):* Upson 3, Foley 2, Hayter 2.
*League One Play-Offs (4):* Burn 1, Dawson 1, Madden 1, Upson 1.

| Stech M 46 | Ayling L 38+1 | McAllister J 33+1 | Hinds R 15+4 | Webster B 43+1 | Blizzard D 15+9 | Upson E 41 | Hayter J 42+2 | Reid R 7+12 | Ugwu C 4+11 | Foley S 37+4 | Marsh-Brown K 14+7 | Ralph N 5+9 | Young L 2+13 | Ince R 1+1 | Smith K 16+1 | Nkumu A —+1 | Williams G 9+15 | Edwards J 32+3 | Burn D 34 | Madden P 35 | Johnson D 3+2 | Bennett D —+1 | Dolan M 6+2 | Dawson K 20 | Appiah K 1+4 | Fletcher W —+1 | Gordon B 1+2 | Cook J —+1 | Balanta A 4+2 | Maksimenko V 2+1 | Match No. |
|---|---|---|---|---|---|---|---|---|---|---|---|---|---|---|---|---|---|---|---|---|---|---|---|---|---|---|---|---|---|---|---|
| 1 | 2 | 3 | 4 | 5 | 6 | 7 | $8^3$ | 9 | $10^1$ | $11^2$ | 12 | 13 | 14 | | | | | | | | | | | | | | | | | | 1 |
| 1 | 2 | 5 | 3 | 4 | 7 | 8 | 11 | $10^3$ | 14 | $9^1$ | $6^2$ | 13 | 12 | | | | | | | | | | | | | | | | | | 2 |
| 1 | 2 | 5 | 3 | 4 | 7 | 8 | 10 | $11^2$ | 13 | $9^3$ | $6^1$ | 14 | 12 | | | | | | | | | | | | | | | | | | 3 |
| 1 | 2 | 5 | 3 | 4 | 7 | 8 | $10^2$ | 11 | 13 | 9 | $6^1$ | | 12 | | | | | | | | | | | | | | | | | | 4 |
| 1 | 2 | | 3 | 4 | $7^1$ | 8 | 10 | $11^2$ | 13 | 9 | $6^3$ | 5 | 14 | 12 | | | | | | | | | | | | | | | | | 5 |
| 1 | $2^3$ | | 3 | 4 | 7 | 8 | $10^2$ | 12 | $11^1$ | 9 | 14 | 5 | 6 | | | | 13 | | | | | | | | | | | | | | 6 |
| 1 | 13 | | 3 | | $7^2$ | 8 | 10 | 11 | 12 | 9 | $6^1$ | 5 | | | $4^3$ | 2 | 14 | | | | | | | | | | | | | | 7 |
| 1 | 2 | 5 | 3 | 4 | $6^3$ | 7 | 9 | 12 | $11^2$ | 14 | | | | | 8 | | 10 | 13 | | | | | | | | | | | | | 8 |
| 1 | $2^3$ | 5 | | 4 | 8 | 7 | $10^1$ | $11^1$ | 12 | 9 | 6 | 13 | 14 | | | | | | 3 | | | | | | | | | | | | 9 |
| 1 | 9 | $2^2$ | 3 | | 6 | 7 | $10^1$ | 11 | 13 | | $12^3$ | 5 | 14 | | 8 | | 4 | | | | | | | | | | | | | | 10 |
| 1 | | 5 | 3 | | 7 | 10 | | | | 9 | 6 | | | | 8 | | 2 | 4 | 11 | | | | | | | | | | | | 11 |
| 1 | | 5 | 3 | | 7 | | $11^1$ | $9^2$ | 13 | | 6 | | | | 8 | | 2 | 4 | 10 | | | | | | | | | | | | 12 |
| 1 | | $5^2$ | | 4 | 7 | $10^3$ | 14 | 9 | 13 | | $6^1$ | 12 | | | 8 | | 2 | 3 | 11 | | | | | | | | | | | | 13 |
| 1 | | $5^1$ | | 4 | 7 | 10 | $11^3$ | 9 | 12 | | 6 | 13 | 14 | | $8^2$ | | 2 | 3 | | | | | | | | | | | | | 14 |
| 1 | | 5 | 3 | | 7 | $10^1$ | | 9 | 13 | | $6^2$ | 12 | | | 8 | | 2 | 4 | 11 | | | | | | | | | | | | 15 |
| 1 | | 5 | 3 | | | $10^2$ | 13 | 9 | | | $6^1$ | 12 | | | 8 | | 2 | 4 | 11 | 7 | | | | | | | | | | | 16 |
| 1 | 2 | 5 | 3 | | | $10^1$ | 13 | $9^2$ | 12 | | 6 | | | | 8 | | | 4 | 11 | 7 | | | | | | | | | | | 17 |
| 1 | 2 | 5 | 3 | | | $10^2$ | 13 | $9^3$ | 12 | | 14 | | | | 8 | | 6 | 4 | 11 | $7^1$ | | | | | | | | | | | 18 |
| 1 | 2 | 5 | 3 | | | $11^2$ | 12 | $9^1$ | 7 | | 13 | | | | 8 | | 6 | 4 | 10 | | | | | | | | | | | | 19 |
| 1 | $2^3$ | | 3 | | 7 | 10 | 12 | $11^1$ | 9 | | $6^2$ | 5 | 14 | | 8 | | 13 | 4 | | | | | | | | | | | | | 20 |
| 1 | 2 | 5 | 3 | | 7 | 12 | | 9 | | | $10^1$ | | | | 8 | | 6 | 4 | 11 | | | | | | | | | | | | 21 |
| 1 | 2 | 5 | 3 | | $7^2$ | 13 | 12 | 14 | 9 | | $8^3$ | | | | 11 | | 6 | 4 | $10^1$ | | | | | | | | | | | | 22 |
| 1 | 2 | 5 | 3 | 4 | 12 | 8 | 10 | 13 | $9^1$ | | | | | | $6^2$ | | 7 | | | 11 | | | | | | | | | | | 23 |
| 1 | 2 | 9 | $3^2$ | $4^3$ | 7 | 8 | 10 | 12 | 14 | | 13 | | | | $6^1$ | | 5 | | 11 | | | | | | | | | | | | 24 |
| 1 | 2 | 9 | 3 | 4 | 7 | 8 | 10 | 12 | | | | | | | 6 | | 5 | | $11^1$ | | | | | | | | | | | | 25 |
| 1 | 2 | $9^2$ | 3 | 4 | 7 | 8 | $10^3$ | 13 | 14 | | 12 | | | | $6^1$ | | 5 | | 11 | | | | | | | | | | | | 26 |
| 1 | 2 | 5 | | 3 | 12 | 7 | 10 | | 9 | | | | | | | | 4 | 11 | | | $6^1$ | | 8 | | | | | | | | 27 |
| 1 | 2 | 5 | | 3 | | 8 | $10^2$ | | 9 | | 13 | | | | | | 4 | 11 | | | $7^1$ | | 6 | 12 | | | | | | | 28 |
| 1 | 2 | 5 | | 3 | 14 | $8^3$ | $10^2$ | | 9 | | 12 | | | | | | 4 | 11 | | | $7^1$ | | 6 | 13 | | | | | | | 29 |
| 1 | 2 | 5 | | 3 | 12 | 7 | 10 | | $9^1$ | | | | | | | | 8 | 4 | 11 | | | | | 6 | | | | | | | 30 |
| 1 | 2 | 5 | | 3 | | 8 | $10^3$ | | $9^1$ | | 13 | 12 | | | | | 7 | 4 | 11 | | | | | $6^2$ | 14 | | | | | | 31 |
| 1 | 2 | $5^2$ | | 3 | | 8 | $10^2$ | | $7^1$ | 14 | 12 | | | | | | 6 | 4 | 11 | | | | | 9 | 13 | | | | | | 32 |
| 1 | 2 | $5^3$ | | 3 | | 8 | $11^1$ | 12 | | | $9^2$ | 13 | 14 | | | | 7 | 4 | 10 | | | | | 6 | | | | | | | 33 |
| 1 | 2 | | | 3 | | 7 | | | | | $9^1$ | | 5 | 12 | | | 13 | 8 | 4 | 10 | 14 | | | $6^3$ | $11^2$ | | | | | | 34 |
| 1 | 2 | 5 | | 3 | | 7 | 10 | | 9 | | | | | | | | 8 | 4 | 11 | | | | | 6 | | | | | | | 35 |
| 1 | 2 | 5 | | 3 | | 7 | $11^2$ | | $9^1$ | | 14 | | | | | | 12 | 8 | 4 | 10 | | | | $6^3$ | 13 | | | | | | 36 |
| 1 | 2 | $5^1$ | | 3 | 13 | 7 | $10^3$ | | 12 | | 14 | | | | | | 8 | 4 | 11 | | | | | 6 | | | $9^2$ | | | | 37 |
| 1 | 2 | $5^1$ | 4 | | | 8 | 10 | | 14 | | | | | | | | $9^2$ | 7 | 3 | 11 | | | | $6^3$ | | | 12 | 13 | | | 38 |
| 1 | 2 | | 3 | | $7^1$ | 8 | 11 | | 9 | | | | | | | | 5 | 4 | 10 | | | | | 6 | | | 12 | | | | 39 |
| 1 | 2 | | 3 | | 7 | 10 | | | $6^1$ | | | | | | | | 5 | 4 | 11 | | | | 12 | 8 | | | | | 9 | | 40 |
| 1 | 2 | 14 | 3 | | 7 | $10^3$ | 12 | 13 | | | | | | | | | 5 | 4 | 11 | | | | | $8^1$ | 6 | | | | $9^2$ | | 41 |
| 1 | 2 | 14 | 3 | | 8 | $10^3$ | 12 | 13 | | | | | | | | | 5 | 4 | 11 | | | | | $7^2$ | $6^1$ | | | | 9 | | 42 |
| 1 | 2 | 13 | 3 | 12 | 4 | $11^2$ | | 5 | | | | | | | | | 8 | $7^3$ | 6 | | | | | $10^1$ | 9 | | | | | | 43 |
| 1 | 2 | 13 | $3^3$ | 4 | | 7 | 10 | | $9^2$ | | | | | | 12 | | 5 | | 11 | | | | | 8 | | | | | $6^1$ | 14 | 44 |
| 1 | 2 | | $4^1$ | | 6 | 11 | 7 | | $5^2$ | 12 | | 14 | | | | | 8 | | 10 | | | | | 9 | | | | | $13^3$ | 3 | 45 |
| 1 | | 3 | 13 | | 5 | 7 | $10^2$ | | 8 | | 2 | | | | 12 | | $8^1$ | $11^3$ | 6 | | | | | | | | | | 14 | 4 | 46 |

**FA Cup**

| | | | | |
|---|---|---|---|---|
| First Round | Preston NE | (a) | 0-3 | |

**Capital One Cup**

| First Round | Colchester U | (h) | 3-0 |
|---|---|---|---|
| Second Round | WBA | (h) | 2-4 |

**Johnstone's Paint Trophy**

| First Round | Bristol R | (a) | 3-0 |
|---|---|---|---|
| Second Round | Torquay U | (a) | 2-2 |

*(aet; won 5-4 on pens)*

| Southern Quarter-Finals | Wycombe W | (h) | 2-0 |
|---|---|---|---|
| Southern Semi-Finals | Leyton Orient | (a) | 0-1 |

**League One Play-Offs**

| Semi-Finals | Sheffield U | (a) | 0-1 |
|---|---|---|---|
| | Sheffield U | (h) | 2-0 |
| Final (*at Wembley*) | Brentford | | 2-1 |

# YORK CITY

## FOUNDATION

Although there was a York City club formed in 1903 by a soccer enthusiast from Darlington, this has no connection with the modern club because it went out of existence during World War I. Unlike many others of that period who restarted in 1919, York City did not re-form until 1922 and the tendency now is to ignore the modern club's pre-1922 existence.

*Bootham Crescent, York YO30 7AQ.*

*Telephone:* (01904) 624 447.

*Fax:* (01904) 631 457.

*Ticket Office:* (01904) 624 447 (ext 2).

*Website:* www.yorkcityfootballclub.co.uk

*Email:* enquiries@yorkcityfootballclub.co.uk

*Ground Capacity:* 8,105.

*Record Attendance:* 28,123 v Huddersfield T, FA Cup 6th rd, 5 March 1938.

*Pitch Measurements:* 105m × 68m (115yd × 75yd)

*Chairman:* Jason McGill.

*Manager:* Nigel Worthington.

*Assistant Manager:* Steve Torpey.

*Physio:* Jeff Miller.

*Colours:* Red shirts with white sleeves, blue shorts, white socks with blue trim.

*Year Formed:* 1922.

*Turned Professional:* 1922.

*Ltd Co.:* 1922.

*Club Nickname:* 'Minstermen'.

*Previous Grounds:* 1922, Fulfordgate; 1932, Bootham Crescent.

*First Football League Game:* 31 August 1929, Division 3 (N), v Wigan Borough (a) W 2–0 – Farmery; Archibald, Johnson; Beck, Davis, Thompson; Evans, Gardner, Cowie (1), Smailes, Stockill (1).

*Record League Victory:* 9–1 v Southport, Division 3 (N), 2 February 1957 – Forgan; Phillips, Howe; Brown (1), Cairney, Mollatt; Hill, Bottom (4 incl. 1p), Wilkinson (2), Wragg (1), Fenton (1).

*Record Cup Victory:* 6–0 v South Shields (a), FA Cup 1st rd, 16 November 1968 – Widdowson; Baker (1p), Richardson; Carr, Jackson, Burrows; Taylor, Ross (3), MacDougall (2), Hodgson, Boyer.

*Record Defeat:* 0–12 v Chester, Division 3 (N), 1 February 1936.

*Most League Points (2 for a win):* 62, Division 4, 1964–65.

## HONOURS

**Football League – Division 3:** *Promoted* 1973–74 (3rd); **Division 4:** *Champions* 1983–84. 1992–93 *(play-offs).*
**FA Cup:** *Semi-finals* 1955, *when in Division 3.*
**Football League Cup:** Best season: 5th rd, 1962.
**FA Trophy:** *Winners* 2012; *Runners-up* 2009.

## sky SPORTS FACT FILE

In September 1990 York City forward David Longhurst collapsed and died during the Fourth Division game with Lincoln City at Bootham Crescent. He was the first player to die during a Football League match since 1927. An inquest later revealed he had suffered from a rare heart condition.

*Most League Points (3 for a win):* 101, Division 4, 1983–84.

*Most League Goals:* 96, Division 4, 1983–84.

*Highest League Scorer in Season:* Bill Fenton, 31, Division 3 (N), 1951–52; Arthur Bottom, 31, Division 3 (N), 1954–55 and 1955–56.

*Most League Goals in Total Aggregate:* Norman Wilkinson, 125, 1954–66.

*Most League Goals in One Match:* 5, Alf Patrick v Rotherham U, Division 3N, 20 November 1948.

*Most Capped Player:* Peter Scott, 7 (10), Northern Ireland.

*Most League Appearances:* Barry Jackson, 481, 1958–70.

*Youngest League Player:* Reg Stockill, 15 years 281 days v Wigan Borough, 31 August 1929.

*Record Transfer Fee Received:* £1,000,000 from Manchester U for Jonathan Greening, March 1998.

*Record Transfer Fee Paid:* £140,000 to Burnley for Adrian Randall, December 1995.

*Football League Record:* 1929 Elected to Division 3 (N); 1958–59 Division 4; 1959–60 Division 3; 1960–65 Division 4; 1965–66 Division 3; 1966–71 Division 4; 1971–74 Division 3; 1974–76 Division 2; 1976–77 Division 3; 1977–84 Division 4; 1984–88 Division 3; 1988–92 Division 4; 1992–93 Division 3; 1993–99 Division 2; 1999–04 Division 3; 2004–07 Conference; 2007–12 Blue Square Premier; 2012– FL 2.

## LATEST SEQUENCES

*Longest Sequence of League Wins:* 7, 31.10.1964 – 26.12.1964.

*Longest Sequence of League Defeats:* 8, 14.11.1966 – 31.12.1966.

*Longest Sequence of League Draws:* 6, 26.12.1992 – 22.1.1993.

*Longest Sequence of Unbeaten League Matches:* 21, 10.9.1973 – 12.1.1974.

*Longest Sequence Without a League Win:* 21, 17.1.2004 – 18.8.2012.

*Successive Scoring Runs:* 24 from 3.3.1984.

*Successive Non-scoring Runs:* 7 from 28.8.1972.

## MANAGERS

Bill Sherrington 1924–60
*(was Secretary for most of this time but virtually Secretary-Manager for a long pre-war spell)*
John Collier 1929–36
Tom Mitchell 1936–50
Dick Duckworth 1950–52
Charlie Spencer 1952–53
Jimmy McCormick 1953–54
Sam Bartram 1956–60
Tom Lockie 1960–67
Joe Shaw 1967–68
Tom Johnston 1968–75
Wilf McGuinness 1975–77
Charlie Wright 1977–80
Barry Lyons 1980–81
Denis Smith 1982–87
Bobby Saxton 1987–88
John Bird 1988–91
John Ward 1991–93
Alan Little 1993–99
Neil Thompson 1999–2000
Terry Dolan 2000–03
Chris Brass 2003–04
Billy McEwan 2005–07
Colin Walker 2007–08
Martin Foyle 2008–10
Gary Mills 2010–13
Nigel Worthington March 2013–

## TEN YEAR LEAGUE RECORD

|         |       | P  | W  | D  | L  | F  | A  | Pts | Pos |
|---------|-------|----|----|----|----|----|----|-----|-----|
| 2003-04 | Div 3 | 46 | 10 | 14 | 22 | 35 | 66 | 44  | 24  |
| 2004-05 | Conf  | 42 | 11 | 10 | 21 | 39 | 66 | 43  | 17  |
| 2005-06 | Conf  | 42 | 17 | 12 | 13 | 63 | 48 | 63  | 8   |
| 2006-07 | Conf  | 46 | 23 | 11 | 12 | 65 | 45 | 80  | 4   |
| 2007-08 | BSP   | 46 | 17 | 11 | 18 | 71 | 74 | 62  | 14  |
| 2008-09 | BSP   | 46 | 11 | 19 | 16 | 47 | 51 | 52  | 17  |
| 2009-10 | BSP   | 44 | 22 | 12 | 10 | 62 | 35 | 78  | 5   |
| 2010-11 | BSP   | 46 | 19 | 14 | 13 | 55 | 50 | 71  | 8   |
| 2011-12 | BSP   | 46 | 23 | 14 | 9  | 81 | 45 | 83  | 4   |
| 2012-13 | FL 2  | 46 | 12 | 19 | 15 | 50 | 60 | 55  | 17  |

## DID YOU KNOW

In the 1946–47 season the York City squad included two players recruited from the Polish Army who had been stationed locally. Goalkeeper Edouard Wojtczak made eight appearances whilst winger Eryk Kubicki played five times.

## YORK CITY – FOOTBALL LEAGUE TWO 2012–13 LEAGUE RECORD

| Match No. | Date | Venue | Opponents | Result | H/T Score | Lg Pos. | Goalscorers | Attendance |
|---|---|---|---|---|---|---|---|---|
| 1 | Aug 18 | H | Wycombe W | L | 1-3 | 0-2 | 18 | Walker [54] | 4591 |
| 2 | 21 | A | Morecambe | D | 2-2 | 0-0 | 19 | Smith, C [58], Chambers [87] | 2063 |
| 3 | 25 | A | Barnet | W | 3-1 | 3-1 | 12 | Parslow [7], Chambers [16], Coulson [45] | 1889 |
| 4 | Sept 1 | H | Oxford U | W | 3-1 | 2-1 | 9 | Coulson [1], Chambers [15], McLaughlin [54] | 4015 |
| 5 | 8 | H | Chesterfield | D | 2-2 | 1-2 | 7 | Coulson [40], Walker [90] | 5119 |
| 6 | 15 | A | Exeter C | D | 1-1 | 0-0 | 9 | Coulson [52] | 4092 |
| 7 | 19 | A | Burton Alb | L | 1-3 | 1-1 | 15 | McLaughlin [9] | 2368 |
| 8 | 22 | H | Cheltenham T | D | 0-0 | 0-0 | 15 | | 3477 |
| 9 | 29 | A | Aldershot T | W | 2-0 | 0-0 | 12 | Blair [49], Walker (pen) [52] | 2176 |
| 10 | Oct 2 | H | Fleetwood T | L | 0-2 | 0-1 | 14 | | 3084 |
| 11 | 6 | H | Rotherham U | D | 0-0 | 0-0 | 14 | | 5417 |
| 12 | 13 | A | Bradford C | D | 1-1 | 1-0 | 14 | Chambers [44] | 11,883 |
| 13 | 20 | H | Dagenham & R | W | 3-2 | 2-1 | 12 | Chambers 2 [19, 37], Blair [65] | 3391 |
| 14 | 23 | A | Accrington S | W | 1-0 | 0-0 | 9 | Walker [83] | 1506 |
| 15 | 27 | A | Southend U | D | 0-0 | 0-0 | 10 | | 5397 |
| 16 | Nov 6 | H | Northampton T | D | 1-1 | 1-0 | 10 | Blair [23] | 3039 |
| 17 | 10 | H | AFC Wimbledon | L | 0-3 | 0-0 | 13 | | 3585 |
| 18 | 17 | A | Port Vale | D | 2-2 | 0-2 | 13 | Rodman [67], Reed, J [89] | 5380 |
| 19 | 24 | H | Torquay U | L | 0-2 | 0-1 | 17 | | 3174 |
| 20 | Dec 1 | A | Rochdale | W | 3-2 | 3-0 | 14 | Potts 2 [7, 35], Walker [19] | 2411 |
| 21 | 8 | H | Plymouth Arg | L | 0-2 | 0-1 | 15 | | 5881 |
| 22 | 15 | H | Bristol R | W | 4-1 | 4-1 | 14 | Kenneth (og) [14], Chambers 2 [16, 33], Walker [19] | 3109 |
| 23 | 26 | A | Chesterfield | L | 0-3 | 0-0 | 15 | | 7322 |
| 24 | 29 | A | Fleetwood T | D | 0-0 | 0-0 | 16 | | 2465 |
| 25 | Jan 1 | H | Burton Alb | W | 3-0 | 2-0 | 14 | Walker (pen) [13], McLaughlin [36], Blair [81] | 3863 |
| 26 | 5 | H | Exeter C | L | 1-2 | 1-1 | 15 | Potts [19] | 3506 |
| 27 | 12 | A | Cheltenham T | D | 1-1 | 0-0 | 15 | Walker [84] | 2881 |
| 28 | 19 | H | Aldershot T | D | 0-0 | 0-0 | 15 | | 2757 |
| 29 | 26 | A | Gillingham | D | 1-1 | 1-0 | 15 | Lee (og) [17] | 4893 |
| 30 | Feb 2 | H | Morecambe | L | 1-4 | 1-1 | 17 | Walker (pen) [28] | 3138 |
| 31 | 9 | A | Wycombe W | L | 0-4 | 0-2 | 18 | | 3383 |
| 32 | 12 | H | Gillingham | D | 0-0 | 0-0 | 17 | | 2699 |
| 33 | 16 | A | Barnet | L | 1-2 | 1-1 | 17 | Stephens (og) [7] | 3594 |
| 34 | 23 | A | Oxford U | D | 0-0 | 0-0 | 17 | | 5808 |
| 35 | 26 | A | Rotherham U | D | 1-1 | 0-0 | 17 | Blair [63] | 7666 |
| 36 | Mar 2 | H | Bradford C | L | 0-2 | 0-0 | 18 | | 5678 |
| 37 | 9 | A | AFC Wimbledon | L | 2-3 | 1-1 | 19 | Smith, C 2 [29, 72] | 4349 |
| 38 | 12 | H | Rochdale | D | 0-0 | 0-0 | 19 | | 2929 |
| 39 | 16 | H | Port Vale | L | 0-2 | 0-1 | 19 | | 3945 |
| 40 | 23 | A | Torquay U | L | 1-2 | 0-2 | 23 | Cresswell (pen) [73] | 2871 |
| 41 | 30 | A | Bristol R | D | 0-0 | 0-0 | 23 | | 7378 |
| 42 | Apr 1 | H | Plymouth Arg | W | 2-0 | 2-0 | 23 | Chambers [20], Cresswell [29] | 4682 |
| 43 | 6 | H | Accrington S | D | 1-1 | 1-0 | 23 | Reed, A [45] | 4446 |
| 44 | 13 | A | Northampton T | W | 2-0 | 1-0 | 20 | Chambers [7], Johnson (og) [85] | 6608 |
| 45 | 20 | H | Southend U | W | 2-1 | 2-1 | 20 | Reed, A [1], Blair [41] | 5975 |
| 46 | 27 | A | Dagenham & R | W | 1-0 | 0-0 | 17 | Smith, C [68] | 3781 |

**Final League Position: 17**

### GOALSCORERS

*League (50):* Chambers 10, Walker 9 (3 pens), Blair 6, Coulson 4, Smith, C 4, McLaughlin 3, Potts 3, Cresswell 2 (1 pen), Reed, A 2, Parslow 1, Reed, J 1, Rodman 1, own goals 4.
*FA Cup (4):* Reed J 3, own goal 1.
*Capital One Cup (1):* Coulson 1.
*Johnstone's Paint Trophy (1):* Blair 1.

| Ingham M 46 | Parslow D 44+1 | Smith C 45 | Doig C 13+1 | Fyfield J 23+4 | Smith J 8+4 | Bullock L 1+11 | McLaughlin P 26+4 | Chambers A 36+2 | Walker J 36+7 | Coulson M 13+6 | Blair M 35+9 | Potts M 12+2 | McReady J —+4 | Blanchett D 2+2 | Oyebanjo L 22+8 | Carlisle C 10 | Taylor C 3+1 | Challinor J 5+13 | Reed J 4+13 | Johnson O —+4 | Kearns D 8+1 | Kerr S 26+2 | Rodman A 12+6 | Allan T 1+4 | McGurk D 11 | Everson B —+2 | O'Connell J 18 | Obeng C 4 | McDaid D —+4 | McGrath J 9 | Rankine M 5+3 | Carson J 5 | Cresswell R 5 | Platt T 6+1 | Reed A 6 | Match No. |
|---|---|---|---|---|---|---|---|---|---|---|---|---|---|---|---|---|---|---|---|---|---|---|---|---|---|---|---|---|---|---|---|---|---|---|---|---|
| 1 | 2 | 3 | 4 | 5 | 6 | $7^1$ | $8^2$ | 9 | 10 | $11^3$ | 12 | 13 | 14 | | | | | | | | | | | | | | | | | | | | | | | 1 |
| 1 | 2 | 4 | 3 | | 7 | 14 | $8^1$ | 11 | $10^3$ | $9^2$ | 12 | | 13 | | | 5 | 6 | | | | | | | | | | | | | | | | | | | 2 |
| 1 | 6 | 3 | 4 | 12 | | $7^2$ | 14 | 8 | 10 | $9^3$ | 11 | 13 | | | | $5^1$ | 6 | | | | | | | | | | | | | | | | | | | 3 |
| 1 | 7 | 3 | | 13 | 6 | | 8 | $10^3$ | $9^1$ | $11^2$ | 12 | | | | | | | 2 | 4 | 5 | 14 | | | | | | | | | | | | | | | 4 |
| 1 | 7 | 3 | | 12 | $6^2$ | | 11 | 10 | $8^3$ | 9 | | | | | | | | 2 | 4 | $5^1$ | 13 | 14 | | | | | | | | | | | | | | 5 |
| 1 | 7 | 3 | | $6^1$ | 14 | | $8^3$ | $11^2$ | 10 | 9 | 13 | | | | | | | 2 | 4 | 5 | 12 | | | | | | | | | | | | | | | 6 |
| 1 | 7 | 3 | 12 | 5 | $6^2$ | | $8^3$ | 9 | 10 | 11 | 13 | 14 | | | | | | 2 | $4^1$ | | | | | | | | | | | | | | | | | 7 |
| 1 | 7 | $3^1$ | 4 | 5 | $6^2$ | 12 | 8 | 11 | 10 | 9 | 14 | | $13^3$ | | | | | 2 | | | | | | | | | | | | | | | | | | 8 |
| 1 | 4 | 3 | 6 | 5 | | $7^2$ | 11 | $10^3$ | $9^1$ | 8 | | | | | | | | 2 | | | 12 | 13 | 14 | | | | | | | | | | | | | 9 |
| 1 | $7^2$ | 3 | 4 | 5 | 13 | | $8^3$ | 11 | 10 | $9^1$ | 6 | | | | | 14 | 2 | | | | 12 | | | | | | | | | | | | | | | 10 |
| 1 | 7 | 3 | 4 | 5 | | | $8^1$ | 11 | 10 | $9^2$ | 6 | | | | | | 2 | | | | 12 | 13 | | | | | | | | | | | | | | 11 |
| 1 | 13 | 3 | | 5 | | | 9 | 10 | 12 | 6 | | | | | | 4 | | | 2 | $11^1$ | | $8^2$ | 7 | | | | | | | | | | | | | 12 |
| 1 | 2 | 3 | | 5 | 12 | | 8 | $10^3$ | $9^1$ | 6 | | | | | 14 | 4 | | | 13 | | | 11 | $7^2$ | | | | | | | | | | | | | 13 |
| 1 | 2 | 3 | | 5 | 14 | | 12 | 11 | 10 | $9^1$ | $8^2$ | | | | | 4 | | | 13 | | | 7 | $6^1$ | | | | | | | | | | | | | 14 |
| 1 | 2 | 3 | | 5 | 12 | | $9^1$ | 10 | 11 | | 7 | | | | | 13 | 4 | | | | | | $8^2$ | 6 | | | | | | | | | | | | | 15 |
| 1 | 2 | 3 | | 5 | | | $6^1$ | 11 | $10^3$ | | 9 | | | | | 13 | 4 | | | 12 | 14 | 8 | $7^2$ | | | | | | | | | | | | | 16 |
| 1 | | 3 | | 5 | | | | $9^2$ | $10^3$ | | 11 | | | | | 2 | 4 | | 12 | 14 | 13 | 6 | 7 | $8^1$ | | | | | | | | | | | | | 17 |
| 1 | 7 | 3 | 4 | 5 | | | | $9^1$ | 13 | | 6 | | | | | 2 | | | | | 12 | 11 | 8 | $10^2$ | | | | | | | | | | | | 18 |
| 1 | $7^1$ | 3 | 4 | 5 | | | | 13 | 14 | | 11 | | | | | 2 | | | | | 6 | $10^2$ | 8 | 12 | $9^3$ | | | | | | | | | | | 19 |
| 1 | 2 | 3 | 4 | 5 | | | $8^2$ | 11 | $10^3$ | | 9 | $6^1$ | | | | 13 | | | 12 | 14 | | 7 | | | | | | | | | | | | | | 20 |
| 1 | 2 | 3 | $4^3$ | 5 | | | $8^1$ | 11 | 10 | | 9 | $7^2$ | | 14 | | 12 | 13 | | | | | 6 | | | | | | | | | | | | | | 21 |
| 1 | 2 | 3 | $4^2$ | 5 | 12 | | $8^1$ | $9^3$ | 10 | | 11 | 6 | | | | | | | | | | 7 | 14 | 13 | | | | | | | | | | | | 22 |
| 1 | 2 | 3 | $4^2$ | 5 | | | 8 | | 10 | | 9 | $6^3$ | | 14 | | | | 12 | | | | 7 | $11^1$ | 13 | | | | | | | | | | | | 23 |
| 1 | 2 | 3 | | 5 | | 13 | 9 | | 11 | | 7 | $8^2$ | | 12 | | | | | | | | 6 | $10^1$ | | 4 | | | | | | | | | | | 24 |
| 1 | 2 | 3 | | 5 | 13 | 8 | | 10¹ | | | 11 | $6^3$ | | 14 | | | | | | | | $7^2$ | 9 | | 4 | | | | | | | | | | | 25 |
| 1 | 2 | 3 | $5^1$ | | | 8 | | $10^2$ | | | 9 | $7^3$ | | 12 | | | | | | | | 6 | 11 | 13 | 4 | | | | | | | | | | | 26 |
| 1 | 2 | 4 | | 5 | | | $7^3$ | 10 | | | 11 | $6^2$ | | 9 | | | | 13 | 14 | | | 8 | | | 12 | | $3^1$ | | | | | | | | | 27 |
| 1 | 2 | 3 | | 5 | | | $8^1$ | 10 | | | 11 | 6 | | 12 | | | | | $9^2$ | | | 7 | | | | 4 | 13 | | | | | | | | | 28 |
| 1 | 2 | 3 | | | | 13 | 7 | 10 | | | 11 | 8 | | $5^1$ | | | | 12 | | | | 6 | $9^2$ | | | 4 | | | | | | | | | | 29 |
| 1 | 5 | | 13 | | | | $8^2$ | 10 | | | 9 | $6^1$ | 14 | | | | | | | | | 7 | $11^3$ | | | 4 | | | 2 | 12 | | | | | | 30 |
| 1 | 5 | 9 | | 3 | | | $10^2$ | 12 | 11 | | 6 | $8^1$ | | | | | | | | | | $7^3$ | 13 | | | 4 | | | 2 | 14 | | | | | | 31 |
| 1 | 3 | | | 5 | | | 13 | $11^2$ | | | 9 | | | | | | | $6^1$ | | | | 7 | 12 | | | 4 | 2 | | | 8 | 10 | | | | | 32 |
| 1 | 2 | 3 | | 5 | | | | $9^1$ | 13 | | 11 | | | | | | | 2 | | | | $7^3$ | 12 | | 14 | 4 | 6 | | | 8 | $10^2$ | | | | | 33 |
| 1 | 5 | 3 | | | 12 | | | $11^1$ | $10^2$ | | 6 | | | | | | | 2 | | | | 7 | 9 | | | 4 | | | | 8 | 13 | | | | | 34 |
| 1 | 5 | 3 | | | | | 12 | 13 | $11^2$ | $10^3$ | 6 | | | | | | | 2 | | | | 7 | $9^1$ | | | 4 | | | | 8 | 14 | | | | | 35 |
| 1 | 5 | 3 | | | | | | 14 | $11^1$ | 10 | 6 | | | | | | | 2 | | | | 7 | $9^3$ | | | 4 | | 12 | | $8^2$ | 13 | | | | | 36 |
| 1 | 5 | 3 | 2 | | | | | $6^2$ | 10 | 13 | $9^1$ | | | | | | | | | | | 7 | 12 | | | 4 | | | | 8 | 11 | | | | | 37 |
| 1 | 2 | 4 | | 5 | | | | $9^1$ | $11^2$ | | 6 | | | | | | | 13 | | | | 8 | 12 | | | 3 | | | | 7 | 10 | | | | | 38 |
| 1 | 2 | 3 | | $5^3$ | | | | 14 | $6^1$ | $10^1$ | 13 | | | | | | | 12 | | | | 7 | | | | 4 | | | | 8 | 11 | 9 | | | | 39 |
| 1 | 2 | 3 | | | | | | $8^1$ | 11 | | 7 | | | | | | | 2 | | | | 4 | 5 | | | 9 | | | | 6 | 10 | 12 | | | | 40 |
| 1 | 4 | 2 | | | | | | $9^1$ | 12 | | | | | | | | | 5 | | | | 3 | 7 | | | 6 | 11 | | 8 | 10 | | | | | | 41 |
| 1 | 8 | 3 | | | | | | $10^1$ | 12 | 13 | | | | | | | | 2 | | | | 4 | 5 | | | 6 | $11^2$ | 7 | 9 | | | | | | | 42 |
| 1 | 6 | 3 | | | | | | $10^2$ | 14 | 12 | 13 | | | | | | | 2 | | | | $4^1$ | 5 | | | 7 | $11^3$ | 8 | 9 | | | | | | | 43 |
| 1 | 9 | 4 | | | | | | 10 | 12 | | 6 | | | | | | | 2 | | | | | 5 | | 3 | | | | | | | | $11^1$ | 7 | 8 | 44 |
| 1 | 7 | 3 | | | | | | 9 | $10^2$ | 14 | $11^3$ | | | | | | | 2 | | | | 12 | | | | 4 | 5 | 13 | | | | | | 8 | $6^1$ | 45 |
| 1 | 7 | 3 | | | | | | 9 | $10^2$ | 12 | $11^1$ | | | | | | | 2 | | | | | 13 | | | 4 | 5 | | | | | | | 6 | 8 | 46 |

**FA Cup**
First Round — AFC Wimbledon — (h) — 1-1
*Replay* — AFC Wimbledon — (a) — 3-4

**Capital One Cup**
First Round — Doncaster R — (a) — 1-1
*(aet; lost 2-4 on pens)*

**Johnstone's Paint Trophy**
First Round — Rotherham U — (a) — 1-0
Second Round — Coventry C — (h) — 0-4

# ENGLISH LEAGUE PLAYERS DIRECTORY

*Players listed represent those with their clubs during the 2012–13 season.*

*Players are listed alphabetically on pages 550–556.*

The number alongside each player corresponds to the team number heading. (Abadaki, Godwin 68 = team 68 (Rochdale)). Club names in italic indicate loans.

## ACCRINGTON S (1)

**ALDRED, Tom (D)**     25   0
H: 6 2   W: 13 02   b.Bolton 11-9-90
*Source:* Scholar.

| | | | | |
|---|---|---|---|---|
| 2008-09 | Carlisle U | 0 | 0 | |
| 2009-10 | Carlisle U | 5 | 0 | 5 0 |
| 2010-11 | Watford | 0 | 0 | |
| 2010-11 | *Stockport Co* | 7 | 0 | 7 0 |
| 2011-12 | Watford | 0 | 0 | |
| 2011-12 | Colchester U | 0 | 0 | |
| 2011-12 | *Torquay U* | 0 | 0 | |
| 2012-13 | Colchester U | 0 | 0 | |
| 2012-13 | Accrington S | 13 | 0 | 13 0 |

**AMOND, Padraig (F)**     197   53
H: 5 11   W: 12 05   b.Carlow 15-4-88
*Honours:* Eire Under-21.

| | | | | |
|---|---|---|---|---|
| 2006 | Shamrock R | 10 | 1 | |
| 2007 | Shamrock R | 6 | 1 | |
| 2007 | *Kildare Co* | 13 | 5 | 13 5 |
| 2008 | Shamrock R | 26 | 9 | |
| 2009 | Shamrock R | 20 | 4 | 62 15 |
| 2010 | Sligo R | 27 | 17 | 27 17 |
| 2010-11 | Pacos | 0 | 0 | |
| 2011-12 | Accrington S | 42 | 7 | 17 0 |
| 2012-13 | Accrington S | 36 | 9 | 78 16 |

**BARNETT, Charlie (M)**     132   7
H: 5 7   W: 11 07   b.Liverpool 19-9-88
*Source:* Scholar.

| | | | | |
|---|---|---|---|---|
| 2006-07 | Liverpool | 0 | 0 | |
| 2007-08 | Liverpool | 0 | 0 | |
| 2008-09 | Tranmere R | 29 | 3 | |
| 2009-10 | Tranmere R | 7 | 1 | 36 4 |
| 2010-11 | Accrington S | 40 | 2 | |
| 2011-12 | Accrington S | 42 | 1 | |
| 2012-13 | Accrington S | 14 | 0 | 96 3 |

**BEATTIE, James (F)**     443 131
H: 6 1   W: 13 06   b.Lancaster 27-2-78
*Source:* Trainee. *Honours:* England Under-21, 5 full caps.

| | | | | |
|---|---|---|---|---|
| 1994-95 | Blackburn R | 0 | 0 | |
| 1995-96 | Blackburn R | 0 | 0 | |
| 1996-97 | Blackburn R | 1 | 0 | |
| 1997-98 | Blackburn R | 3 | 0 | 4 0 |
| 1998-99 | Southampton | 35 | 5 | |
| 1999-2000 | Southampton | 18 | 0 | |
| 2000-01 | Southampton | 37 | 11 | |
| 2001-02 | Southampton | 28 | 12 | |
| 2002-03 | Southampton | 38 | 23 | |
| 2003-04 | Southampton | 37 | 14 | |
| 2004-05 | Southampton | 11 | 3 | 204 68 |
| 2004-05 | Everton | 11 | 1 | |
| 2005-06 | Everton | 32 | 10 | |
| 2006-07 | Everton | 33 | 2 | 76 13 |
| 2007-08 | Sheffield U | 39 | 22 | |
| 2008-09 | Sheffield U | 23 | 12 | |
| 2008-09 | Stoke C | 16 | 7 | |
| 2009-10 | Stoke C | 22 | 3 | 38 10 |
| 2010-11 | Rangers | 7 | 0 | 7 0 |
| 2010-11 | *Blackpool* | 9 | 0 | 9 0 |
| 2011-12 | Sheffield U | 18 | 0 | |
| 2012-13 | Sheffield U | 0 | 0 | 80 34 |
| 2012-13 | Accrington S | 25 | 6 | 25 6 |

**BOCO, Romuald (F)**     93   13
H: 5 10   W: 10 13   b.Bernay 8-7-85
*Source:* Niort. *Honours:* Benin 39 full caps, 9 goals.

| | | | | |
|---|---|---|---|---|
| 2006-07 | Accrington S | 32 | 3 | |
| 2007-08 | Accrington S | 11 | 0 | |
| 2008-09 | Accrington S | 0 | 0 | |
| 2009-10 | Burton Alb | 8 | 0 | 8 0 |
| From Sligo | | | | |
| 2012-13 | Accrington S | 42 | 10 | 85 13 |

**CARVER, Marcus (F)**     13   0
H: 5 11   W: 11 11   b.Blackburn 22-10-93
*Source:* Scholar.

| | | | | |
|---|---|---|---|---|
| 2011-12 | Accrington S | 2 | 0 | |
| 2012-13 | Accrington S | 11 | 0 | 13 0 |

**CHIPPENDALE, Aiden (M)**     12   0
H: 5 8   W: 10 10   b.Bradford 24-5-92
*Source:* Scholar.

| | | | | |
|---|---|---|---|---|
| 2010-11 | Huddersfield T | 1 | 0 | |
| 2011-12 | Huddersfield T | 0 | 0 | 1 0 |
| 2011-12 | *Inverness CT* | 5 | 0 | 5 0 |
| 2012-13 | Accrington S | 6 | 0 | 6 0 |

**CLARK, Luke (D)**     8   0
H: 5 10   W: 11 05   b.Preston 24-5-94
*Source:* Scholar.

| | | | | |
|---|---|---|---|---|
| 2011-12 | Preston NE | 2 | 0 | 2 0 |
| 2012-13 | Accrington S | 6 | 0 | 6 0 |

**DAWBER, Andrew (G)**     2   0
b. 20-11-94

| | | | | |
|---|---|---|---|---|
| 2012-13 | Accrington S | 2 | 0 | 2 0 |

**DIXON, Bohan (M)**     6   0
H: 6 4   W: 11 07   b.Liverpool 17-10-93

| | | | | |
|---|---|---|---|---|
| 2012-13 | Accrington S | 6 | 0 | 6 0 |

**DUNBAVIN, Ian (G)**     243   0
H: 6 1   W: 12 10   b.Knowsley 27-5-80
*Source:* Trainee.

| | | | | |
|---|---|---|---|---|
| 1998-99 | Liverpool | 0 | 0 | |
| 1999-2000 | Liverpool | 0 | 0 | |
| 1999-2000 | Shrewsbury T | 7 | 0 | |
| 2000-01 | Shrewsbury T | 22 | 0 | |
| 2001-02 | Shrewsbury T | 34 | 0 | |
| 2002-03 | Shrewsbury T | 33 | 0 | |
| 2003-04 | Shrewsbury T | 0 | 0 | 96 0 |
| From Halifax T. | | | | |
| 2006-07 | Accrington S | 23 | 0 | |
| 2007-08 | Accrington S | 23 | 0 | |
| 2008-09 | Accrington S | 4 | 0 | |
| 2009-10 | Accrington S | 27 | 0 | |
| 2010-11 | Accrington S | 25 | 0 | |
| 2011-12 | Accrington S | 25 | 0 | |
| 2012-13 | Accrington S | 20 | 0 | 147 0 |

**ECKERSLEY, Tom (D)**     2   0
b.Sale 6-12-91
*Source:* Scholar.

| | | | | |
|---|---|---|---|---|
| 2011-12 | Bolton W | 0 | 0 | |
| 2012-13 | Accrington S | 2 | 0 | 2 0 |

**GRAY, James (F)**     16   2
H: 5 11   b.Stockton on Tees 17-10-92
*Honours:* Northern Ireland Under-21.

| | | | | |
|---|---|---|---|---|
| 2012-13 | Accrington S | 16 | 2 | 16 2 |

**HATFIELD, Will (M)**     49   5
H: 5 8   W: 10 00   b.Liversedge 10-10-91
*Source:* Scholar.

| | | | | |
|---|---|---|---|---|
| 2009-10 | Leeds U | 0 | 0 | |
| 2010-11 | Leeds U | 0 | 0 | |
| 2011-12 | Leeds U | 0 | 0 | |
| 2011-12 | Accrington S | 17 | 3 | |
| 2012-13 | Accrington S | 32 | 2 | 49 5 |

**HUGHES, Bryan (M)**     487 55
H: 5 10   W: 11 08   b.Liverpool 19-6-76
*Source:* Trainee. *Honours:* England Under-21.

| | | | | |
|---|---|---|---|---|
| 1993-94 | Wrexham | 11 | 0 | |
| 1994-95 | Wrexham | 38 | 9 | |
| 1995-96 | Wrexham | 22 | 0 | |
| 1996-97 | Wrexham | 23 | 3 | 94 12 |
| 1996-97 | Birmingham C | 11 | 0 | |
| 1997-98 | Birmingham C | 40 | 5 | |
| 1998-99 | Birmingham C | 28 | 3 | |
| 1999-2000 | Birmingham C | 45 | 10 | |
| 2000-01 | Birmingham C | 45 | 4 | |
| 2001-02 | Birmingham C | 31 | 7 | |
| 2002-03 | Birmingham C | 22 | 2 | |
| 2003-04 | Birmingham C | 26 | 3 | 248 34 |
| 2004-05 | Charlton Ath | 17 | 1 | |
| 2005-06 | Charlton Ath | 33 | 3 | |
| 2006-07 | Charlton Ath | 24 | 1 | 74 5 |
| 2007-08 | Hull C | 35 | 1 | |
| 2008-09 | Hull C | 6 | 0 | |
| 2009-10 | Hull C | 0 | 0 | 41 1 |
| 2009-10 | *Derby Co* | 3 | 0 | 3 0 |
| 2010-11 | Burton Alb | 1 | 0 | 1 0 |
| From Grimsby T. | | | | |
| 2011 | IBV | 5 | 0 | 5 0 |
| 2011-12 | Accrington S | 21 | 3 | |
| 2012-13 | Accrington S | 0 | 0 | 21 3 |

**HUNT, Nicky (D)**     204   2
H: 6 1   W: 13 07   b.Westhoughton 3-9-83
*Source:* Scholar. *Honours:* England Under-21.

| | | | | |
|---|---|---|---|---|
| 2000-01 | Bolton W | 1 | 0 | |
| 2001-02 | Bolton W | 0 | 0 | |
| 2002-03 | Bolton W | 0 | 0 | |
| 2003-04 | Bolton W | 31 | 1 | |
| 2004-05 | Bolton W | 29 | 0 | |
| 2005-06 | Bolton W | 20 | 0 | |
| 2006-07 | Bolton W | 33 | 0 | |
| 2007-08 | Bolton W | 14 | 0 | |
| 2008-09 | Bolton W | 0 | 0 | |
| 2008-09 | *Birmingham C* | 11 | 0 | 11 0 |
| 2009-10 | Bolton W | 0 | 0 | 128 1 |
| 2009-10 | *Derby Co* | 21 | 0 | 21 0 |
| 2010-11 | Bristol C | 7 | 0 | |
| 2011-12 | Bristol C | 0 | 0 | 7 0 |
| 2011-12 | Preston NE | 17 | 1 | 17 1 |
| 2012-13 | Rotherham U | 9 | 0 | 9 0 |
| 2012-13 | Accrington S | 11 | 0 | 11 0 |

**JEFFERS, Francis (F)**     233 39
H: 5 9   W: 11 09   b.Liverpool 25-1-81
*Source:* Trainee. *Honours:* England Schools, Youth, Under-21, 1 full cap, 1 goal.

| | | | | |
|---|---|---|---|---|
| 1997-98 | Everton | 1 | 0 | |
| 1998-99 | Everton | 15 | 6 | |
| 1999-2000 | Everton | 21 | 6 | |
| 2000-01 | Everton | 12 | 6 | |
| 2001-02 | Arsenal | 6 | 2 | |
| 2002-03 | Arsenal | 16 | 2 | |
| 2003-04 | Arsenal | 0 | 0 | 22 4 |
| 2003-04 | *Everton* | 18 | 0 | 67 18 |
| 2004-05 | Charlton Ath | 20 | 3 | |
| 2005-06 | Charlton Ath | 0 | 0 | 20 3 |
| 2005-06 | *Rangers* | 8 | 0 | 8 0 |
| 2006-07 | Blackburn R | 10 | 0 | 10 0 |
| 2006-07 | *Ipswich T* | 9 | 4 | 9 4 |
| 2007-08 | Sheffield W | 10 | 2 | |
| 2008-09 | Sheffield W | 31 | 3 | |
| 2009-10 | Sheffield W | 13 | 0 | 54 5 |
| 2010-11 | Newcastle Jets | 1 | 0 | |
| 2010-11 | Motherwell | 10 | 1 | 10 1 |
| 2011-12 | Newcastle Jets | 17 | 1 | 26 2 |
| 2012-13 | Floriana | 0 | 0 | |
| 2012-13 | Accrington S | 7 | 2 | 7 2 |

**JOYCE, Luke (M)**     181   6
H: 5 11   W: 12 03   b.Bolton 9-7-87
*Source:* Scholar.

| | | | | |
|---|---|---|---|---|
| 2005-06 | Wigan Ath | 0 | 0 | |
| 2005-06 | Carlisle U | 0 | 0 | |
| 2006-07 | Carlisle U | 16 | 1 | |
| 2007-08 | Carlisle U | 3 | 1 | |
| 2008-09 | Carlisle U | 7 | 0 | 26 2 |
| 2009-10 | Accrington S | 41 | 1 | |
| 2010-11 | Accrington S | 27 | 1 | |
| 2011-12 | Accrington S | 43 | 2 | |
| 2012-13 | Accrington S | 44 | 0 | 155 4 |

**LIDDLE, Michael (D)**    67   0
H: 5 6   W: 11 00   b.Hounslow 25-12-89
*Source:* Scholar. *Honours:* Eire Under-21.

| | | | | | |
|---|---|---|---|---|---|
| 2007-08 | Sunderland | 0 | 0 | | |
| 2008-09 | Sunderland | 0 | 0 | | |
| 2008-09 | *Carlisle U* | 22 | 0 | 22 | 0 |
| 2009-10 | Sunderland | 0 | 0 | | |
| 2010-11 | Sunderland | 0 | 0 | | |
| 2010-11 | *Leyton Orient* | 1 | 0 | 1 | 0 |
| 2011-12 | Sunderland | 0 | 0 | | |
| 2011-12 | *Accrington S* | 12 | 0 | | |
| 2012-13 | Accrington S | 32 | 0 | 44 | 0 |

**LINDFIELD, Craig (F)**    135   11
H: 6 0   W: 10 05   b.Greasby 7-9-88
*Source:* Scholar. *Honours:* England Youth.

| | | | | | |
|---|---|---|---|---|---|
| 2006-07 | Liverpool | 0 | 0 | | |
| 2007-08 | Liverpool | 0 | 0 | | |
| 2007-08 | *Notts Co* | 3 | 1 | 3 | 1 |
| 2007-08 | *Chester C* | 7 | 0 | 7 | 0 |
| 2008-09 | Liverpool | 0 | 0 | | |
| 2008-09 | *Bournemouth* | 3 | 1 | 3 | 1 |
| 2008-09 | *Accrington S* | 20 | 2 | | |
| 2009-10 | Liverpool | 0 | 0 | | |
| 2009-10 | *Macclesfield T* | 18 | 2 | 18 | 2 |
| 2010-11 | Accrington S | 16 | 0 | | |
| 2011-12 | Accrington S | 39 | 4 | | |
| 2012-13 | Accrington S | 29 | 1 | 104 | 7 |

**LINGANZI, Amine (M)**    19   0
H: 6 1   W: 10 00   b.Algiers 16-11-89

| | | | | | |
|---|---|---|---|---|---|
| 2008-09 | St Etienne | 3 | 0 | | |
| 2009-10 | St Etienne | 0 | 0 | 3 | 0 |
| 2009-10 | Blackburn R | 1 | 0 | | |
| 2010-11 | Blackburn R | 1 | 0 | | |
| 2010-11 | *Preston NE* | 1 | 0 | 1 | 0 |
| 2011-12 | Blackburn R | 0 | 0 | | |
| 2012-13 | Blackburn R | 0 | 0 | 2 | 0 |
| 2012-13 | Accrington S | 13 | 0 | 13 | 0 |

**MILLER, George (M)**    32   3
H: 5 9   W: 12 02   b.Eccleston 25-11-91
*Source:* Scholar.

| | | | | | |
|---|---|---|---|---|---|
| 2009-10 | Preston NE | 0 | 0 | | |
| 2010-11 | Preston NE | 1 | 0 | | |
| 2011-12 | Preston NE | 6 | 0 | 7 | 0 |
| 2012-13 | Accrington S | 25 | 3 | 25 | 3 |

**MOLYNEUX, Lee (D)**    52   8
H: 6 1   W: 12 09   b.Liverpool 24-2-89
*Source:* Scholar. *Honours:* England Schools, Youth.

| | | | | | |
|---|---|---|---|---|---|
| 2005-06 | Everton | 0 | 0 | | |
| 2006-07 | Everton | 0 | 0 | | |
| 2007-08 | Everton | 0 | 0 | | |
| 2008-09 | Southampton | 4 | 0 | | |
| 2009-10 | Southampton | 0 | 0 | 4 | 0 |
| 2010-11 | Plymouth Arg | 9 | 0 | 9 | 0 |
| 2012-13 | Accrington S | 39 | 8 | 39 | 8 |

**MURPHY, Peter (D)**    111   9
H: 6 0   W: 11 10   b.Liverpool 13-2-90
*Source:* Scholar.

| | | | | | |
|---|---|---|---|---|---|
| 2007-08 | Accrington S | 2 | 0 | | |
| 2008-09 | Accrington S | 3 | 0 | | |
| 2009-10 | Accrington S | 10 | 0 | | |
| 2010-11 | Accrington S | 13 | 0 | | |
| 2011-12 | Accrington S | 38 | 4 | | |
| 2012-13 | Accrington S | 45 | 5 | 111 | 9 |

**NSIALA, Aristote (D)**    46   0
H: 6 4   W: 14 09   b.DR Congo 25-3-92
*Source:* Scholar.

| | | | | | |
|---|---|---|---|---|---|
| 2009-10 | Everton | 0 | 0 | | |
| 2010-11 | Everton | 0 | 0 | | |
| 2010-11 | *Macclesfield T* | 10 | 0 | 10 | 0 |
| 2011-12 | Everton | 0 | 0 | | |
| 2011-12 | *Accrington S* | 19 | 0 | | |
| 2012-13 | Accrington S | 17 | 0 | 36 | 0 |

**RICHARDSON, Leam (D)**    205   2
H: 5 7   W: 11 04   b.Leeds 19-11-79
*Source:* Trainee.

| | | | | | |
|---|---|---|---|---|---|
| 1997-98 | Blackburn R | 0 | 0 | | |
| 1998-99 | Blackburn R | 0 | 0 | | |
| 1999-2000 | Blackburn R | 0 | 0 | | |
| 2000-01 | Bolton W | 12 | 0 | | |
| 2001-02 | Bolton W | 1 | 0 | | |
| 2001-02 | *Notts Co* | 21 | 0 | 21 | 0 |
| 2002-03 | Bolton W | 0 | 0 | 13 | 0 |

| | | | | | |
|---|---|---|---|---|---|
| 2002-03 | *Blackpool* | 20 | 0 | | |
| 2003-04 | Blackpool | 28 | 0 | | |
| 2004-05 | Blackpool | 23 | 0 | 71 | 0 |
| 2006-07 | Accrington S | 38 | 0 | | |
| 2007-08 | Accrington S | 37 | 1 | | |
| 2008-09 | Accrington S | 11 | 0 | | |
| 2009-10 | Accrington S | 2 | 0 | | |
| 2010-11 | Accrington S | 11 | 1 | | |
| 2011-12 | Accrington S | 1 | 0 | | |
| 2012-13 | Accrington S | 0 | 0 | 100 | 2 |

**SAMPSON, Jack (F)**    14   0
H: 6 2   W: 12 04   b.Wigan 14-4-93
*Source:* Scholar. *Honours:* England Youth.

| | | | | | |
|---|---|---|---|---|---|
| 2010-11 | Bolton W | 0 | 0 | | |
| 2011-12 | Bolton W | 0 | 0 | | |
| 2011-12 | *Southend U* | 9 | 0 | 9 | 0 |
| 2012-13 | Bolton W | 0 | 0 | | |
| 2012-13 | Accrington S | 5 | 0 | 5 | 0 |

**STOCKDALE, Adam (M)**    0   0
b. 14-10-93

| | | | | |
|---|---|---|---|---|
| 2012-13 | Accrington S | 0 | 0 | |

**WILSON, Laurence (D)**    263   16
H: 5 10   W: 10 09   b.Huyton 10-10-86
*Source:* Scholar. *Honours:* England Youth.

| | | | | | |
|---|---|---|---|---|---|
| 2004-05 | Everton | 0 | 0 | | |
| 2005-06 | Everton | 0 | 0 | | |
| 2005-06 | *Mansfield T* | 15 | 1 | 15 | 1 |
| 2006-07 | Chester C | 41 | 1 | | |
| 2007-08 | Chester C | 40 | 2 | | |
| 2008-09 | Chester C | 34 | 1 | 115 | 4 |
| 2009-10 | Morecambe | 41 | 3 | | |
| 2010-11 | Morecambe | 38 | 3 | | |
| 2011-12 | Morecambe | 30 | 5 | 109 | 11 |
| 2012-13 | *Rotherham U* | 5 | 0 | 5 | 0 |
| 2012-13 | Accrington S | 19 | 0 | 19 | 0 |

**WINNARD, Dean (D)**    159   3
H: 5 9   W: 10 04   b.Wigan 20-8-89

| | | | | | |
|---|---|---|---|---|---|
| 2006-07 | Blackburn R | 0 | 0 | | |
| 2007-08 | Blackburn R | 0 | 0 | | |
| 2008-09 | Blackburn R | 0 | 0 | | |
| 2009-10 | Accrington S | 44 | 0 | | |
| 2010-11 | Accrington S | 45 | 1 | | |
| 2011-12 | Accrington S | 30 | 1 | | |
| 2012-13 | Accrington S | 40 | 1 | 159 | 3 |

**Scholars**
Atkinson, Connor Michael; Barker, Dalian Aaron; Clarke, Joseph Paul; Dawson, Joseph Michael; Doig, James Kevin; Goulding, Liam John; Greaves, Luke Andrew James; Hennigan, Daniel Stephen; Hudson, Nathan Paul; Jeffries, Jason Joseph; Jenkins, James Edward; Martini-Horrocks, Louis; Peake, Joshua Gary; Proctor, Benjamin Stephen; Willison, Jack David; Wolland, Kieran Fred.

# AFC WIMBLEDON (2)

**ANTWI, Will (D)**    69   1
H: 6 1   W: 13 07   b.London 19-10-82
*Source:* Scholar. *Honours:* Ghana 1 full cap.

| | | | | | |
|---|---|---|---|---|---|
| 2002-03 | Crystal Palace | 4 | 0 | | |
| 2003-04 | Crystal Palace | 0 | 0 | 4 | 0 |
| *From Aldershot T* | | | | | |
| 2005-06 | Wycombe W | 5 | 0 | | |
| 2006-07 | Wycombe W | 25 | 1 | | |
| 2007-08 | Wycombe W | 6 | 0 | | |
| 2008-09 | Wycombe W | 6 | 0 | 42 | 1 |
| *From Dagenham & R, Luton T, Grimsby T* | | | | | |
| 2012-13 | AFC Wimbledon | 23 | 0 | 23 | 0 |

**BALKESTEIN, Pim (D)**    111   4
H: 6 3   W: 12 00   b.Gouda 29-4-87
*Source:* Heerenveen.

| | | | | | |
|---|---|---|---|---|---|
| 2008-09 | Ipswich T | 20 | 0 | | |
| 2009-10 | Ipswich T | 9 | 0 | 29 | 0 |
| 2009-10 | *Brentford* | 14 | 1 | | |
| 2010-11 | Brentford | 20 | 1 | | |
| 2011-12 | Brentford | 5 | 0 | 39 | 2 |
| 2011-12 | *Rochdale* | 13 | 0 | 13 | 0 |
| 2011-12 | *AFC Wimbledon* | 6 | 0 | | |
| 2012-13 | AFC Wimbledon | 24 | 2 | 30 | 2 |

**BENNETT, Alan (D)**    180   6
H: 6 2   W: 12 08   b.Cork 4-10-81
*Honours:* Eire Under-21, B, 2 full caps.

| | | | | | |
|---|---|---|---|---|---|
| 2006-07 | Reading | 0 | 0 | | |
| 2007-08 | Reading | 0 | 0 | | |
| 2007-08 | *Southampton* | 10 | 0 | 10 | 0 |
| 2007-08 | *Brentford* | 11 | 1 | | |
| 2008-09 | Reading | 0 | 0 | | |
| 2008-09 | *Brentford* | 44 | 1 | | |
| 2009-10 | Brentford | 13 | 0 | 68 | 2 |
| 2009-10 | *Wycombe W* | 6 | 1 | | |
| 2010-11 | Wycombe W | 17 | 0 | 23 | 1 |
| 2011-12 | Cheltenham T | 44 | 2 | | |
| 2012-13 | Cheltenham T | 17 | 0 | 61 | 2 |
| 2012-13 | AFC Wimbledon | 18 | 1 | 18 | 1 |

**BROWN, Sebastian (G)**    60   0
H: 6 2   W: 13 07   b.Carshalton 24-11-89
*Source:* Scholar.

| | | | | | |
|---|---|---|---|---|---|
| 2008-09 | Brentford | 0 | 0 | | |
| 2009-10 | Brentford | 0 | 0 | | |
| 2011-12 | AFC Wimbledon | 44 | 0 | | |
| 2012-13 | AFC Wimbledon | 16 | 0 | 60 | 0 |

**CUMMINGS, Warren (D)**    294   7
H: 5 9   W: 11 05   b.Aberdeen 15-10-80
*Source:* Trainee. *Honours:* Scotland Under-21, 1 full cap.

| | | | | | |
|---|---|---|---|---|---|
| 1999-2000 | Chelsea | 0 | 0 | | |
| 2000-01 | Chelsea | 0 | 0 | | |
| 2000-01 | *Bournemouth* | 10 | 1 | | |
| 2000-01 | *WBA* | 3 | 0 | | |
| 2001-02 | Chelsea | 0 | 0 | | |
| 2001-02 | *WBA* | 14 | 0 | 17 | 0 |
| 2002-03 | Chelsea | 0 | 0 | | |
| 2002-03 | *Bournemouth* | 20 | 0 | | |
| 2003-04 | Bournemouth | 42 | 2 | | |
| 2004-05 | Bournemouth | 30 | 2 | | |
| 2005-06 | Bournemouth | 0 | 0 | | |
| 2006-07 | Bournemouth | 31 | 0 | | |
| 2007-08 | Bournemouth | 32 | 2 | | |
| 2008-09 | Bournemouth | 32 | 0 | | |
| 2009-10 | Bournemouth | 34 | 0 | | |
| 2010-11 | Bournemouth | 14 | 0 | | |
| 2011-12 | Bournemouth | 14 | 0 | 259 | 7 |
| 2011-12 | *Crawley T* | 9 | 0 | 9 | 0 |
| 2012-13 | AFC Wimbledon | 9 | 0 | 9 | 0 |

**DARKO, Jessie (F)**    12   0
H: 6 2   W: 12 09   b.13-3-93

| | | | | | |
|---|---|---|---|---|---|
| 2012-13 | Cardiff C | 0 | 0 | | |
| 2012-13 | AFC Wimbledon | 12 | 0 | 12 | 0 |

**DJILALI, Kieran (M)**    64   4
H: 6 3   W: 13 02   b.Lambeth 22-1-91
*Source:* Scholar.

| | | | | | |
|---|---|---|---|---|---|
| 2008-09 | Crystal Palace | 6 | 0 | | |
| 2009-10 | Crystal Palace | 8 | 1 | | |
| 2009-10 | *Chesterfield* | 8 | 1 | | |
| 2010-11 | Crystal Palace | 14 | 0 | 28 | 1 |
| 2010-11 | *Chesterfield* | 10 | 1 | 18 | 2 |
| 2011-12 | AFC Wimbledon | 12 | 1 | | |
| 2012-13 | AFC Wimbledon | 5 | 0 | 17 | 1 |
| 2012-13 | *Portsmouth* | 1 | 0 | 1 | 0 |

**FENLON, Jim (M)**    17   1
b. 3-3-94

| | | | | | |
|---|---|---|---|---|---|
| 2012-13 | AFC Wimbledon | 17 | 1 | 17 | 1 |

**HARRIS, Louis (M)**    9   0
H: 6 0   W: 12 05   b.Sutton Coldfield 7-12-92
*Source:* Scholar.

| | | | | | |
|---|---|---|---|---|---|
| 2011-12 | Wolverhampton W | 0 | 0 | | |
| 2011-12 | *Notts Co* | 2 | 0 | 2 | 0 |
| 2012-13 | AFC Wimbledon | 7 | 0 | 7 | 0 |

**HUSSEY, Chris (D)**    77   0
H: 5 10   W: 10 03   b.Hammersmith 2-1-89
*Source:* Scholar. *Honours:* AFC Wimbledon.

| | | | | | |
|---|---|---|---|---|---|
| 2009-10 | Coventry C | 8 | 0 | | |
| 2010-11 | Coventry C | 11 | 0 | | |
| 2010-11 | *Crewe Alex* | 0 | 0 | | |
| 2011-12 | Coventry C | 29 | 0 | | |
| 2012-13 | Coventry C | 10 | 0 | 58 | 0 |
| 2012-13 | AFC Wimbledon | 19 | 0 | 19 | 0 |

**JAIMEZ-RUIZ, Mikhael (G)** 45 0
H: 6 0  W: 12 00  b.Merida 12-7-84
*Source:* Northwood. *Honours:* Venezuela 1
full cap.

| | | | | |
|---|---|---|---|---|
| 2008-09 | Aldershot T | 14 | 0 | |
| 2009-10 | Aldershot T | 30 | 0 | 44 0 |
| From Dover Ath | | | | |
| 2012-13 | AFC Wimbledon | 1 | 0 | 1 0 |

**JOHNSON, Huw (F)** 9 0
b.Hammersmith 22-6-93
*Source:* Youth.

| | | | | |
|---|---|---|---|---|
| 2011-12 | AFC Wimbledon | 1 | 0 | |
| 2012-13 | AFC Wimbledon | 8 | 0 | 9 0 |

**JOLLEY, Christian (F)** 52 7
H: 6 0  W: 10 00  b.Fleet 12-5-88
*Source:* Kingstonian.

| | | | | |
|---|---|---|---|---|
| 2011-12 | AFC Wimbledon | 37 | 7 | |
| 2012-13 | AFC Wimbledon | 15 | 0 | 52 7 |

**KIERNAN, Brendan (M)** 15 0
H: 5 9  W: 11 11  b.Lambeth 10-11-92
*Source:* Youth.

| | | | | |
|---|---|---|---|---|
| 2011-12 | AFC Wimbledon | 9 | 0 | |
| 2012-13 | AFC Wimbledon | 6 | 0 | 15 0 |

**LONG, Stacy (M)** 99 7
H: 5 8  W: 10 00  b.Farnborough 11-1-85
*Source:* Scholar. *Honours:* England Under-20,
Youth.

| | | | | |
|---|---|---|---|---|
| 2001-02 | Charlton Ath | 0 | 0 | |
| 2002-03 | Charlton Ath | 0 | 0 | |
| 2003-04 | Charlton Ath | 0 | 0 | |
| 2004-05 | Charlton Ath | 0 | 0 | |
| 2005-06 | Notts Co | 19 | 1 | 19 0 |
| From Ebbsfleet U. | | | | |
| 2010-11 | Stevenage | 22 | 2 | |
| 2011-12 | Stevenage | 30 | 1 | 52 3 |
| 2012-13 | AFC Wimbledon | 28 | 3 | 28 3 |

**McNAUGHTON, Callum (D)** 19 0
H: 6 2  W: 13 05  b.Harlow 25-10-91
*Source:* Scholar.

| | | | | |
|---|---|---|---|---|
| 2010-11 | West Ham U | 0 | 0 | |
| 2011-12 | West Ham U | 0 | 0 | |
| 2011-12 | AFC Wimbledon | 18 | 0 | |
| 2012-13 | AFC Wimbledon | 1 | 0 | 19 0 |

**MERRIFIELD, Frankie (M)** 5 0
b. 8-1-94

| | | | | |
|---|---|---|---|---|
| 2011-12 | AFC Wimbledon | 0 | 0 | |
| 2012-13 | AFC Wimbledon | 5 | 0 | 5 0 |

**MIDSON, Jack (F)** 119 39
H: 5 8  W: 11 07  b.Stevenage 21-7-83
*Source:* Stevenage B, Chelmsford C (loan),
Dagenham & R, Hemel Hempstead (loan),
Bishop's Stortford, Histon.

| | | | | |
|---|---|---|---|---|
| 2010-11 | Oxford U | 21 | 6 | 21 6 |
| 2010-11 | Southend U | 4 | 2 | 4 2 |
| 2010-11 | Barnet | 5 | 0 | 5 0 |
| 2011-12 | AFC Wimbledon | 46 | 18 | |
| 2012-13 | AFC Wimbledon | 43 | 13 | 89 31 |

**MITCHEL-KING, Mat (D)** 93 2
H: 6 4  W: 13 00  b.Reading 12-9-83
*Source:* Cambridge C, Mildenhall T, Histon.

| | | | | |
|---|---|---|---|---|
| 2009-10 | Crewe Alex | 32 | 0 | |
| 2010-11 | Crewe Alex | 14 | 0 | 46 0 |
| 2011-12 | AFC Wimbledon | 24 | 0 | |
| 2012-13 | AFC Wimbledon | 23 | 2 | 47 2 |

**MOORE, Luke (F)** 72 13
H: 5 11  W: 11 07  b.Gravesend 27-4-88
*Source:* Ebbsfleet U.

| | | | | |
|---|---|---|---|---|
| 2011-12 | AFC Wimbledon | 37 | 9 | |
| 2012-13 | AFC Wimbledon | 35 | 4 | 72 13 |

**MOORE, Sammy (M)** 90 10
H: 5 8  W: 9 00  b.Dover 7-9-87
*Source:* Scholar.

| | | | | |
|---|---|---|---|---|
| 2006-07 | Ipswich T | 1 | 0 | |
| 2007-08 | Ipswich T | 0 | 0 | |
| 2007-08 | Brentford | 20 | 2 | 20 2 |
| 2008-09 | Ipswich T | 0 | 0 | 1 0 |
| 2011-12 | AFC Wimbledon | 41 | 6 | |
| 2012-13 | AFC Wimbledon | 28 | 2 | 69 8 |

**OSANO, Curtis (D)** 17 0
H: 5 11  W: 11 03  b.Nakuru 8-3-87
*Honours:* From Aldershot T, Woking,
Rushden & D, Luton T

| | | | | |
|---|---|---|---|---|
| 2012-13 | AFC Wimbledon | 17 | 0 | 17 0 |

**PELL, Harry (M)** 64 5
H: 6 4  W: 13 05  b.Tilbury 21-10-91
*Source:* Charlton Ath Scholar.

| | | | | |
|---|---|---|---|---|
| 2010-11 | Bristol R | 10 | 0 | 10 0 |
| 2010-11 | Hereford U | 7 | 0 | |
| 2011-12 | Hereford U | 30 | 3 | 37 3 |
| 2012-13 | AFC Wimbledon | 17 | 2 | 17 2 |

**PRIOR, Jason (F)** 9 0
H: 6 1  W: 11 11  b.Portsmouth 20-12-88
*Source:* Bognor Regis T.

| | | | | |
|---|---|---|---|---|
| 2011-12 | AFC Wimbledon | 3 | 0 | |
| 2012-13 | AFC Wimbledon | 6 | 0 | 9 0 |

**SAINTE-LUCE, Kevin (M)** 14 2
H: 5 10  W: 11 11  b.Paris 28-4-93

| | | | | |
|---|---|---|---|---|
| 2012-13 | Cardiff C | 0 | 0 | |
| 2012-13 | AFC Wimbledon | 14 | 2 | 14 2 |

**STRUTTON, Charlie (F)** 14 0
b.Brent 17-4-89
*Source:* Chalfont St Peter.

| | | | | |
|---|---|---|---|---|
| 2011-12 | AFC Wimbledon | 0 | 0 | |
| 2012-13 | AFC Wimbledon | 14 | 0 | 14 0 |

**SULLIVAN, John (G)** 48 0
H: 5 10  W: 11 04  b.Brighton 8-3-88
*Source:* Scholar.

| | | | | |
|---|---|---|---|---|
| 2005-06 | Brighton & HA | 0 | 0 | |
| 2006-07 | Brighton & HA | 0 | 0 | |
| 2007-08 | Brighton & HA | 0 | 0 | |
| 2008-09 | Brighton & HA | 13 | 0 | 13 0 |
| 2009-10 | Millwall | 0 | 0 | |
| 2010-11 | Millwall | 0 | 0 | |
| 2010-11 | Yeovil T | 13 | 0 | 13 0 |
| 2010-11 | Charlton Ath | 4 | 0 | |
| 2011-12 | Charlton Ath | 3 | 0 | |
| 2012-13 | Charlton Ath | 0 | 0 | 7 0 |
| 2012-13 | Colchester U | 4 | 0 | 4 0 |
| 2012-13 | AFC Wimbledon | 11 | 0 | 11 0 |

**SWEENEY, Daniel (M)** 1 0
b. 25-4-94

| | | | | |
|---|---|---|---|---|
| 2012-13 | AFC Wimbledon | 1 | 0 | 1 0 |

**SWEENEY, Peter (M)** 254 16
H: 6 0  W: 12 11  b.Glasgow 25-9-84
*Source:* Scholar. *Honours:* Scotland Youth,
Under-21, B.

| | | | | |
|---|---|---|---|---|
| 2001-02 | Millwall | 1 | 0 | |
| 2002-03 | Millwall | 5 | 1 | |
| 2003-04 | Millwall | 29 | 2 | |
| 2004-05 | Millwall | 24 | 2 | 59 5 |
| 2005-06 | Stoke C | 17 | 1 | |
| 2006-07 | Stoke C | 13 | 1 | |
| 2006-07 | Yeovil T | 8 | 0 | 8 0 |
| 2007-08 | Stoke C | 5 | 0 | 35 2 |
| 2007-08 | Walsall | 7 | 0 | 7 0 |
| 2007-08 | Leeds U | 9 | 0 | |
| 2008-09 | Leeds U | 0 | 0 | 9 0 |
| 2008-09 | Grimsby T | 8 | 0 | |
| 2009-10 | Grimsby T | 40 | 4 | 48 4 |
| 2010-11 | Bury | 25 | 0 | |
| 2011-12 | Bury | 41 | 4 | |
| 2012-13 | Bury | 16 | 1 | 82 5 |
| 2012-13 | AFC Wimbledon | 6 | 0 | 6 0 |

**YOUGA, Kelly (M)** 100 2
H: 6 1  W: 12 00  b.Bangui 22-9-85
*Source:* Lyon. *Honours:* Central African
Republic 3 full caps.

| | | | | |
|---|---|---|---|---|
| 2005-06 | Charlton Ath | 0 | 0 | |
| 2005-06 | Bristol C | 4 | 0 | 4 0 |
| 2006-07 | Charlton Ath | 0 | 0 | |
| 2006-07 | Bradford C | 11 | 0 | 11 0 |
| 2007-08 | Charlton Ath | 11 | 0 | |
| 2007-08 | Scunthorpe U | 19 | 1 | 19 1 |
| 2008-09 | Charlton Ath | 33 | 1 | |
| 2009-10 | Charlton Ath | 18 | 0 | |
| 2010-11 | Charlton Ath | 0 | 0 | |
| 2011-12 | Charlton Ath | 0 | 0 | 62 1 |
| 2011-12 | Yeovil T | 1 | 0 | 1 0 |
| 2012-13 | AFC Wimbledon | 3 | 0 | 3 0 |

**YUSSUFF, Rashid (M)** 71 7
H: 6 1  W: 10 07  b.Poplar 23-9-89

| | | | | |
|---|---|---|---|---|
| 2007-08 | Charlton Ath | 0 | 0 | |
| 2008-09 | Charlton Ath | 0 | 0 | |
| 2009-10 | Gillingham | 8 | 0 | |
| 2010-11 | Gillingham | 0 | 0 | 8 0 |
| 2011-12 | AFC Wimbledon | 40 | 4 | |
| 2012-13 | AFC Wimbledon | 23 | 3 | 63 7 |

**Players retained or with offer of contract**
Bamba, Youssouf Naghi.

**Scholars**
Basker, Harlan Jay; Beere, Thomas Keith
Robert; Craig, Charlie Ryan; Cunnington,
Matthew Adam; Fayers, Charlie Edward
Lowell George; Jacquart, Chace Daniel;
Lindo, Duvaine Ricardo; Nightingale,
William John Robert; Oakley, George;
Obaye-Daley, Oluseyi; Pearse, Daniel;
Roberts, Owen Bryan; Tarbie, Kieron;
Vlietinck, Christopher David; Williams-
Mitchell, Khan Ishmael Noir.

# ALDERSHOT T (3)

**BERGQVIST, Doug (D)** 7 0
H: 6 0  W: 13 07  b.Stockholm 29-3-93
*Source:* Scholar.

| | | | | |
|---|---|---|---|---|
| 2010-11 | Aldershot T | 1 | 0 | |
| 2011-12 | Aldershot T | 2 | 0 | |
| 2012-13 | Aldershot T | 4 | 0 | 7 0 |

**BROWN, Troy (D)** 70 6
H: 6 1  W: 12 01  b.Croydon 17-9-90
*Source:* Fulham Scholar. *Honours:* Wales
Under-21.

| | | | | |
|---|---|---|---|---|
| 2009-10 | Ipswich T | 1 | 0 | |
| 2010-11 | Ipswich T | 12 | 0 | 13 0 |
| 2011-12 | Rotherham U | 6 | 1 | 6 1 |
| 2011-12 | Aldershot T | 17 | 2 | |
| 2012-13 | Aldershot T | 34 | 3 | 51 5 |

**CADOGAN, Kieron (M)** 59 4
H: 6 4  W: 12 07  b.Tooting 3-8-90
*Source:* Scholar.

| | | | | |
|---|---|---|---|---|
| 2007-08 | Crystal Palace | 0 | 0 | |
| 2008-09 | Crystal Palace | 4 | 1 | |
| 2009-10 | Crystal Palace | 0 | 0 | |
| 2009-10 | Burton Alb | 2 | 0 | 2 0 |
| 2010-11 | Crystal Palace | 16 | 1 | |
| 2011-12 | Crystal Palace | 1 | 0 | |
| 2011-12 | Rotherham U | 13 | 1 | 13 1 |
| 2012-13 | Crystal Palace | 0 | 0 | 21 2 |
| 2012-13 | Aldershot T | 23 | 1 | 23 1 |

**CONNOLLY, Reece (F)** 16 0
H: 6 0  W: 11 09  b.Frimley 22-1-92
*Source:* Scholar.

| | | | | |
|---|---|---|---|---|
| 2009-10 | Aldershot T | 3 | 0 | |
| 2010-11 | Aldershot T | 5 | 0 | |
| 2011-12 | Aldershot T | 7 | 0 | |
| 2012-13 | Aldershot T | 1 | 0 | 16 0 |

**COOKSLEY, Harry (M)** 1 0
H: 6 1  W: 11 07  b.Guildford 15-11-94

| | | | | |
|---|---|---|---|---|
| 2012-13 | Aldershot T | 1 | 0 | 1 0 |

**DONNELLY, Scott (M)** 119 21
H: 5 8  W: 11 10  b.Hammersmith 25-12-87
*Source:* Scholar.

| | | | | |
|---|---|---|---|---|
| 2004-05 | QPR | 2 | 0 | |
| 2005-06 | QPR | 8 | 0 | |
| 2006-07 | QPR | 3 | 0 | 13 0 |
| From Wealdstone. | | | | |
| 2008-09 | Aldershot T | 20 | 1 | |
| 2009-10 | Aldershot T | 43 | 13 | |
| 2010-11 | Swansea C | 1 | 0 | |
| 2010-11 | Wycombe W | 18 | 3 | |
| 2011-12 | Swansea C | 0 | 0 | 1 0 |
| 2011-12 | Wycombe W | 18 | 4 | 36 7 |
| 2012-13 | Aldershot T | 4 | 0 | 67 14 |
| 2012-13 | Southend U | 2 | 0 | 2 0 |

**FORBES, Terrell (D)** 452 4
H: 5 11  W: 12 07  b.Southwark 17-8-81
*Source:* Trainee.

| | | | | |
|---|---|---|---|---|
| 1999-2000 | West Ham U | 0 | 0 | |
| 1999-2000 | Bournemouth | 3 | 0 | 3 0 |

|  |  | | | | |
|---|---|--:|--:|--:|--:|
| 2000-01 | West Ham U | 0 | 0 | | |
| 2001-02 | QPR | 43 | 0 | | |
| 2002-03 | QPR | 38 | 0 | | |
| 2003-04 | QPR | 30 | 0 | | |
| 2004-05 | QPR | 3 | 0 | 114 | 0 |
| 2004-05 | Grimsby T | 33 | 0 | 33 | 0 |
| 2005-06 | Oldham Ath | 39 | 0 | 39 | 0 |
| 2006-07 | Yeovil T | 46 | 0 | | |
| 2007-08 | Yeovil T | 41 | 0 | | |
| 2008-09 | Yeovil T | 38 | 0 | | |
| 2009-10 | Yeovil T | 38 | 1 | 163 | 1 |
| 2010-11 | Leyton Orient | 34 | 2 | | |
| 2011-12 | Leyton Orient | 39 | 0 | 73 | 2 |
| 2012-13 | Chesterfield | 17 | 1 | 17 | 1 |
| 2012-13 | Aldershot T | 10 | 0 | 10 | 0 |

**GOULDING, Jeff (F)**   147 23
H: 6 2   W: 11 11   b.Sutton 13-5-84
*Source:* Croydon, Egham T, Aldershot T, Hayes, Yeading, Fisher Ath.

|  |  | | | | |
|---|---|--:|--:|--:|--:|
| 2008-09 | Bournemouth | 27 | 3 | | |
| 2009-10 | Bournemouth | 17 | 1 | 44 | 4 |
| 2010-11 | Cheltenham T | 39 | 10 | | |
| 2011-12 | Cheltenham T | 35 | 5 | | |
| 2012-13 | Cheltenham T | 19 | 3 | 93 | 18 |
| 2012-13 | Aldershot T | 10 | 1 | 10 | 1 |

**HERD, Ben (D)**   308 4
H: 5 9   W: 10 12   b.Welwyn 21-6-85
*Source:* Scholar.

|  |  | | | | |
|---|---|--:|--:|--:|--:|
| 2002-03 | Watford | 0 | 0 | | |
| 2003-04 | Watford | 0 | 0 | | |
| 2004-05 | Watford | 0 | 0 | | |
| 2005-06 | Shrewsbury T | 46 | 2 | | |
| 2006-07 | Shrewsbury T | 31 | 1 | | |
| 2007-08 | Shrewsbury T | 45 | 0 | | |
| 2008-09 | Shrewsbury T | 21 | 0 | 143 | 0 |
| 2009-10 | Aldershot T | 34 | 0 | | |
| 2010-11 | Aldershot T | 43 | 1 | | |
| 2011-12 | Aldershot T | 45 | 0 | | |
| 2012-13 | Aldershot T | 43 | 0 | 165 | 1 |

**HOLDSWORTH, Jordan (M)**   0 0
|  |  | | | | |
|---|---|--:|--:|--:|--:|
| 2012-13 | Aldershot T | 0 | 0 | | |

**HYLTON, Danny (F)**   154 30
H: 6 0   W: 11 13   b.Camden 25-2-89
*Source:* Youth.

|  |  | | | | |
|---|---|--:|--:|--:|--:|
| 2008-09 | Aldershot T | 29 | 5 | | |
| 2009-10 | Aldershot T | 21 | 3 | | |
| 2010-11 | Aldershot T | 33 | 5 | | |
| 2011-12 | Aldershot T | 44 | 13 | | |
| 2012-13 | Aldershot T | 27 | 4 | 154 | 30 |

**LANCASHIRE, Oliver (D)**   99 2
H: 6 1   W: 11 10   b.Basingstoke 13-12-88
*Source:* Scholar.

|  |  | | | | |
|---|---|--:|--:|--:|--:|
| 2006-07 | Southampton | 0 | 0 | | |
| 2007-08 | Southampton | 0 | 0 | | |
| 2008-09 | Southampton | 11 | 0 | | |
| 2009-10 | Southampton | 2 | 0 | 13 | 0 |
| 2009-10 | *Grimsby T* | 25 | 1 | 25 | 1 |
| 2010-11 | Walsall | 29 | 0 | | |
| 2011-12 | Walsall | 20 | 1 | 49 | 1 |
| 2012-13 | Aldershot T | 12 | 0 | 12 | 0 |

**MADJO, Guy (F)**   102 30
H: 6 0   W: 13 05   b.Cameroon 1-6-84
*Honours:* Cameroon Under-23.

|  |  | | | | |
|---|---|--:|--:|--:|--:|
| 2005-06 | Bristol C | 5 | 0 | 5 | 0 |

From Forest Green R, Stafford R, Crawley (loan)

|  |  | | | | |
|---|---|--:|--:|--:|--:|
| 2007-08 | *Cheltenham T* | 5 | 0 | 5 | 0 |
| 2007-08 | Shrewsbury T | 15 | 3 | | |
| 2008-09 | Shrewsbury T | 0 | 0 | 15 | 3 |
| 2008-09 | Guangdong S C | 18 | 10 | 18 | 10 |
| 2009-10 | Bylis Ballsh | 15 | 2 | 15 | 2 |
| 2011-12 | Stevenage | 1 | 0 | 1 | 0 |
| 2011-12 | *Port Vale* | 6 | 4 | 6 | 4 |
| 2011-12 | Aldershot T | 20 | 8 | | |
| 2012-13 | Aldershot T | 3 | 0 | 23 | 8 |
| 2012-13 | *Plymouth Arg* | 14 | 3 | 14 | 3 |

**McNAMEE, Anthony (M)**   232 8
H: 5 6   W: 10 03   b.Kensington 13-7-84
*Source:* Scholar. *Honours:* England Youth, Under-20.

|  |  | | | | |
|---|---|--:|--:|--:|--:|
| 2001-02 | Watford | 7 | 1 | | |
| 2002-03 | Watford | 23 | 0 | | |
| 2003-04 | Watford | 2 | 0 | | |
| 2004-05 | Watford | 14 | 0 | | |
| 2005-06 | Watford | 38 | 1 | | |
| 2006-07 | Watford | 7 | 0 | | |
| 2006-07 | *Crewe Alex* | 5 | 0 | 5 | 0 |
| 2007-08 | Watford | 0 | 0 | 91 | 2 |
| 2007-08 | Swindon T | 19 | 2 | | |
| 2008-09 | Swindon T | 43 | 0 | | |
| 2009-10 | Swindon T | 17 | 1 | 79 | 3 |
| 2009-10 | Norwich C | 17 | 1 | | |
| 2010-11 | Norwich C | 17 | 0 | 34 | 1 |
| 2011-12 | Milton Keynes D | 7 | 0 | 7 | 0 |
| 2011-12 | Wycombe W | 15 | 2 | 15 | 2 |
| 2012-13 | Macclesfield T | 0 | 0 | | |
| 2012-13 | Aldershot T | 1 | 0 | 1 | 0 |

**MEKKI, Adam (M)**   62 3
H: 5 9   W: 11 00   b.Chester 24-12-91
*Source:* Scholar.

|  |  | | | | |
|---|---|--:|--:|--:|--:|
| 2009-10 | Aldershot T | 0 | 0 | | |
| 2010-11 | Aldershot T | 8 | 0 | | |
| 2011-12 | Aldershot T | 25 | 1 | | |
| 2012-13 | Aldershot T | 29 | 2 | 62 | 3 |

**MORRIS, Aaron (D)**   99 2
H: 6 1   W: 12 05   b.Cardiff 30-12-89
*Source:* Scholar. *Honours:* Wales Youth, Under-21.

|  |  | | | | |
|---|---|--:|--:|--:|--:|
| 2008-09 | Cardiff C | 0 | 0 | | |
| 2009-10 | Cardiff C | 1 | 0 | 1 | 0 |
| 2010-11 | Aldershot T | 22 | 0 | | |
| 2011-12 | Aldershot T | 39 | 2 | | |
| 2012-13 | Aldershot T | 37 | 0 | 98 | 2 |

**MORRIS, Glenn (G)**   183 0
H: 6 0   W: 12 03   b.Woolwich 20-12-83
*Source:* Scholar.

|  |  | | | | |
|---|---|--:|--:|--:|--:|
| 2001-02 | Leyton Orient | 2 | 0 | | |
| 2002-03 | Leyton Orient | 23 | 0 | | |
| 2003-04 | Leyton Orient | 27 | 0 | | |
| 2004-05 | Leyton Orient | 12 | 0 | | |
| 2005-06 | Leyton Orient | 9 | 0 | | |
| 2006-07 | Leyton Orient | 3 | 0 | | |
| 2007-08 | Leyton Orient | 16 | 0 | | |
| 2008-09 | Leyton Orient | 26 | 0 | | |
| 2009-10 | Leyton Orient | 11 | 0 | 124 | 0 |
| 2010-11 | Southend U | 33 | 0 | | |
| 2011-12 | Southend U | 24 | 0 | | |
| 2012-13 | Southend U | 0 | 0 | 57 | 0 |
| 2012-13 | Aldershot T | 2 | 0 | 2 | 0 |

**PAYNE, Josh (M)**   85 6
H: 6 0   W: 11 09   b.Basingstoke 25-11-90
*Source:* Scholar.

|  |  | | | | |
|---|---|--:|--:|--:|--:|
| 2008-09 | West Ham U | 2 | 0 | | |
| 2008-09 | *Cheltenham T* | 11 | 1 | 11 | 1 |
| 2009-10 | West Ham U | 0 | 0 | | |
| 2009-10 | Colchester U | 3 | 0 | 3 | 0 |
| 2009-10 | Wycombe W | 3 | 1 | 3 | 1 |
| 2010-11 | West Ham U | 0 | 0 | 2 | 0 |
| 2010-11 | Doncaster R | 0 | 0 | | |
| 2010-11 | Oxford U | 28 | 1 | | |
| 2011-12 | Oxford U | 6 | 0 | 34 | 1 |
| 2011-12 | Aldershot T | 17 | 2 | | |
| 2012-13 | Aldershot T | 15 | 1 | 32 | 3 |

**RANKINE, Michael (F)**   78 4
H: 6 1   W: 14 12   b.Doncaster 15-1-85
*Source:* Doncaster R, Barrow.

|  |  | | | | |
|---|---|--:|--:|--:|--:|
| 2004-05 | Scunthorpe U | 21 | 1 | | |
| 2005-06 | Scunthorpe U | 0 | 0 | 21 | 1 |

From Armthorpe W, Alfreton T, Rushden & D.

|  |  | | | | |
|---|---|--:|--:|--:|--:|
| 2008-09 | *Bournemouth* | 3 | 0 | 3 | 0 |

From York C.

|  |  | | | | |
|---|---|--:|--:|--:|--:|
| 2011-12 | Aldershot T | 22 | 2 | | |
| 2012-13 | Aldershot T | 24 | 1 | 46 | 3 |
| 2012-13 | *York C* | 8 | 0 | 8 | 0 |

**REID, Craig (F)**   102 19
H: 5 10   W: 11 10   b.Coventry 17-12-85
*Source:* Ipswich T Scholar.

|  |  | | | | |
|---|---|--:|--:|--:|--:|
| 2004-05 | Coventry C | 0 | 0 | | |
| 2005-06 | Coventry C | 0 | 0 | | |
| 2006-07 | Cheltenham T | 6 | 0 | | |
| 2007-08 | Cheltenham T | 8 | 0 | 14 | 0 |

From Grays Ath, Newport Co.

|  |  | | | | |
|---|---|--:|--:|--:|--:|
| 2010-11 | Stevenage | 20 | 2 | | |
| 2011-12 | Stevenage | 29 | 6 | | |
| 2012-13 | Stevenage | 0 | 0 | 49 | 8 |
| 2012-13 | Aldershot T | 39 | 11 | 39 | 11 |

**RISSER, Oliver (M)**   197 9
H: 6 3   W: 13 10   b.Windhoek 17-9-80
*Honours:* Namibia 27 full caps.

|  |  | | | | |
|---|---|--:|--:|--:|--:|
| 2003-04 | Bor Dortmund II | 20 | 1 | | |
| 2004-05 | Bor Dortmund II | 13 | 0 | 33 | 1 |
| 2005-06 | Sandhausen | 28 | 0 | 28 | 0 |
| 2006 | Breidablik | 6 | 0 | 6 | 0 |
| 2006-07 | Bonner | 32 | 2 | 32 | 2 |
| 2007-08 | Hannover II | 7 | 0 | 7 | 0 |
| 2008 | Manglerud Star | 7 | 1 | 7 | 1 |
| 2009 | Lyn | 7 | 0 | | |
| 2010 | Lyn | 11 | 1 | 18 | 1 |
| 2010 | Kuopio | 8 | 0 | 8 | 0 |
| 2011-12 | Swindon T | 32 | 3 | | |
| 2012-13 | Swindon T | 0 | 0 | 32 | 3 |
| 2012-13 | *Stevenage* | 12 | 1 | 12 | 1 |
| 2012-13 | Aldershot T | 14 | 0 | 14 | 0 |

**ROBERTS, Jordan (M)**   9 0
H: 5 11   W: 12 13   b.Watford 5-1-94
*Source:* Scholar.

|  |  | | | | |
|---|---|--:|--:|--:|--:|
| 2011-12 | Aldershot T | 4 | 0 | | |
| 2012-13 | Aldershot T | 5 | 0 | 9 | 0 |

**RODMAN, Alex (F)**   61 8
H: 6 2   W: 12 08   b.Sutton Coldfield 15-2-87
*Source:* Leamington, Grantham T, Lincoln U, Gainsborough T, Tamworth.

|  |  | | | | |
|---|---|--:|--:|--:|--:|
| 2010-11 | Aldershot T | 14 | 5 | | |
| 2011-12 | Aldershot T | 18 | 1 | | |
| 2012-13 | Aldershot T | 11 | 1 | 43 | 7 |
| 2012-13 | *York C* | 18 | 1 | 18 | 1 |

**STANLEY, Craig (M)**   205 17
H: 5 8   W: 10 08   b.Bedworth 3-3-83
*Source:* Scholar.

|  |  | | | | |
|---|---|--:|--:|--:|--:|
| 2002-03 | Walsall | 0 | 0 | | |
| 2003-04 | Walsall | 0 | 0 | | |
| 2003-04 | *Raith R* | 20 | 1 | 20 | 1 |

From Hereford U.

|  |  | | | | |
|---|---|--:|--:|--:|--:|
| 2007-08 | Morecambe | 41 | 2 | | |
| 2008-09 | Morecambe | 24 | 5 | | |
| 2009-10 | Morecambe | 40 | 4 | | |
| 2010-11 | Morecambe | 22 | 2 | 127 | 13 |
| 2010-11 | *Torquay U* | 19 | 1 | 19 | 1 |
| 2011-12 | Bristol R | 1 | 1 | 34 | 1 |
| 2012-13 | Aldershot T | 5 | 1 | 5 | 1 |

**TONKIN, Anthony (D)**   207 0
H: 5 11   W: 12 02   b.Newlyn 17-1-80
*Source:* Yeovil T.

|  |  | | | | |
|---|---|--:|--:|--:|--:|
| 2002-03 | Stockport Co | 24 | 0 | | |
| 2003-04 | Stockport Co | 0 | 0 | 24 | 0 |
| 2003-04 | Crewe Alex | 26 | 0 | | |
| 2004-05 | Crewe Alex | 35 | 0 | | |
| 2005-06 | Crewe Alex | 27 | 0 | 88 | 0 |
| 2006-07 | Yeovil T | 5 | 0 | 5 | 0 |

From Forest Green R, Cambridge U.

|  |  | | | | |
|---|---|--:|--:|--:|--:|
| 2010-11 | Oxford U | 39 | 0 | | |
| 2011-12 | Oxford U | 14 | 0 | 53 | 0 |
| 2012-13 | Aldershot T | 37 | 0 | 37 | 0 |

**VINCENTI, Peter (F)**   109 15
H: 6 2   W: 11 13   b.St Peter 7-7-86
*Source:* St Peter.

|  |  | | | | |
|---|---|--:|--:|--:|--:|
| 2007-08 | Millwall | 0 | 0 | | |
| 2010-11 | Stevenage | 5 | 1 | 5 | 1 |
| 2010-11 | Aldershot T | 23 | 6 | | |
| 2011-12 | Aldershot T | 42 | 6 | | |
| 2012-13 | Aldershot T | 39 | 2 | 104 | 14 |

**WEBBE, Bobby (M)**   0 0
H: 5 9   W: 11 11   b.Sutton 31-12-94
|  |  | | | | |
|---|---|--:|--:|--:|--:|
| 2012-13 | Aldershot T | 0 | 0 | | |

**WORNER, Ross (G)**   31 0
H: 6 1   W: 12 05   b.Hindhead 3-10-89
*Source:* Woking.

|  |  | | | | |
|---|---|--:|--:|--:|--:|
| 2010-11 | Charlton Ath | 8 | 0 | 8 | 0 |
| 2011-12 | Aldershot T | 22 | 0 | | |
| 2012-13 | Aldershot T | 1 | 0 | 23 | 0 |

**YOUNG, Jamie (G)**   184 0
H: 5 11   W: 13 00   b.Brisbane 25-8-85
*Source:* Scholar. *Honours:* England Youth, Under-20.

|  |  | | | | |
|---|---|--:|--:|--:|--:|
| 2003-04 | Reading | 1 | 0 | | |
| 2004-05 | Reading | 0 | 0 | | |
| 2005-06 | Reading | 0 | 0 | 1 | 0 |
| 2005-06 | *Rushden & D* | 20 | 0 | 20 | 0 |

| | | | | | |
|---|---|---|---|---|---|
| 2006-07 | Wycombe W | 19 | 0 | | |
| 2007-08 | Wycombe W | 4 | 0 | | |
| 2008-09 | Wycombe W | 15 | 0 | | |
| 2009-10 | Wycombe W | 1 | 0 | 39 | 0 |
| 2009-10 | Aldershot T | 9 | 0 | | |
| 2010-11 | Aldershot T | 46 | 0 | | |
| 2011-12 | Aldershot T | 25 | 0 | | |
| 2012-13 | Aldershot T | 44 | 0 | 124 | 0 |

**Scholars**
Beckles-Richards, Reece Devante Dennis; Blair, Elliott; Brice, Adam Luke; Douglas, Meshack; Gerrard, Robert Daniel; Grosvenor, Nicholas D'angeld Ricardo; Halliday, Kofi; Howard, Jack; McDonald, Mitchell David; Metcalfe, Jack Jordan; Murphy, Rory David; Rudolph, Matthew; Stojsavljevic, Milan; Williams, Luke.

# ARSENAL (4)

**AFOBE, Benik (F)**      **56**   **7**
H: 5 10   W: 11 00   b.Leyton 12-2-93
*Source:* Scholar. *Honours:* England Youth, Under-21.

| | | | | | |
|---|---|---|---|---|---|
| 2009-10 | Arsenal | 0 | 0 | | |
| 2010-11 | Arsenal | 0 | 0 | | |
| 2010-11 | *Huddersfield T* | 28 | 5 | 28 | 5 |
| 2011-12 | Arsenal | 0 | 0 | | |
| 2011-12 | *Reading* | 3 | 0 | 3 | 0 |
| 2012-13 | Arsenal | 0 | 0 | | |
| 2012-13 | *Bolton W* | 20 | 2 | 20 | 2 |
| 2012-13 | *Millwall* | 5 | 0 | 5 | 0 |

**AKPOM, Chuba (F)**      **0**   **0**
b.London 9-10-95

| | | | |
|---|---|---|---|
| 2012-13 | Arsenal | 0 | 0 |

**ANDRE SANTOS, Clarindo (D)**    **220**   **29**
H: 5 10   W: 11 13   b.Sao Paulo 8-3-83
*Honours:* Brazil 24 full caps.

| | | | | | |
|---|---|---|---|---|---|
| 2004 | Figueirense | 30 | 2 | | |
| 2005 | Flamengo | 24 | 0 | | |
| 2006 | Flamengo | 0 | 0 | 24 | 0 |
| 2006 | Atletico Mineiro | 15 | 0 | 15 | 0 |
| 2007 | Figueirense | 31 | 6 | 61 | 8 |
| 2008 | Corinthians | 34 | 9 | | |
| 2009 | Corinthians | 5 | 0 | 39 | 9 |
| 2009-10 | Fenerbahce | 27 | 5 | | |
| 2010-11 | Fenerbahce | 25 | 5 | 52 | 10 |
| 2011-12 | Arsenal | 15 | 2 | | |
| 2012-13 | Arsenal | 8 | 0 | 23 | 2 |
| 2013 | *Gremio* | 6 | 0 | 6 | 0 |

**ANEKE, Chuks (M)**      **43**   **7**
H: 6 3   W: 13 01   b.Newham 3-7-93
*Source:* Scholar. *Honours:* England Youth.

| | | | | | |
|---|---|---|---|---|---|
| 2010-11 | Arsenal | 0 | 0 | | |
| 2011-12 | Arsenal | 0 | 0 | | |
| 2011-12 | *Stevenage* | 6 | 0 | 6 | 0 |
| 2011-12 | *Preston NE* | 7 | 1 | 7 | 1 |
| 2012-13 | Arsenal | 0 | 0 | | |
| 2012-13 | *Crewe Alex* | 30 | 6 | 30 | 6 |

**ANGHA, Martin (D)**      **0**   **0**
H: 6 2   W: 12 10   b.Switzerland 22-1-94
*Source:* Zurich.

| | | | |
|---|---|---|---|
| 2010-11 | Arsenal | 0 | 0 |
| 2011-12 | Arsenal | 0 | 0 |
| 2012-13 | Arsenal | 0 | 0 |

**ANSAH, Zak (F)**      **0**   **0**
H: 5 10   W: 11 00   b.Sidcup 4-5-94
*Source:* Scholar.

| | | | |
|---|---|---|---|
| 2010-11 | Arsenal | 0 | 0 |
| 2011-12 | Arsenal | 0 | 0 |
| 2012-13 | Arsenal | 0 | 0 |

**ARSHAVIN, Andrei (F)**      **353**   **77**
H: 5 8   W: 9 11   b.St Petersburg 29-5-81
*Honours:* Russia 75 full caps, 17 goals.

| | | | |
|---|---|---|---|
| 1999 | Zenit | 0 | 0 |
| 2000 | Zenit | 10 | 0 |
| 2001 | Zenit | 29 | 4 |
| 2002 | Zenit | 30 | 4 |
| 2003 | Zenit | 27 | 5 |
| 2004 | Zenit | 28 | 6 |
| 2005 | Zenit | 29 | 9 |
| 2006 | Zenit | 28 | 7 |

| | | | | | |
|---|---|---|---|---|---|
| 2007 | Zenit | 30 | 10 | | |
| 2008 | Zenit | 27 | 6 | | |
| 2008-09 | Arsenal | 12 | 6 | | |
| 2009-10 | Arsenal | 30 | 10 | | |
| 2010-11 | Arsenal | 37 | 6 | | |
| 2011-12 | Arsenal | 19 | 1 | | |
| 2011-12 | *Zenit* | 10 | 3 | 248 | 54 |
| 2012-13 | Arsenal | 7 | 0 | 105 | 23 |

**ARTETA, Mikel (M)**      **374**   **57**
H: 5 9   W: 10 08   b.San Sebastian 26-3-82
*Honours:* Spain Youth, Under-21.

| | | | | | |
|---|---|---|---|---|---|
| 1999-2000 | Barcelona B | 26 | 1 | | |
| 2000-01 | Barcelona B | 16 | 2 | 42 | 3 |
| 2000-01 | Paris St Germain | 6 | 1 | | |
| 2001-02 | Paris St Germain | 25 | 1 | 31 | 2 |
| 2002-03 | Rangers | 27 | 4 | | |
| 2003-04 | Rangers | 23 | 8 | 50 | 12 |
| 2004-05 | Real Sociedad | 14 | 1 | 14 | 1 |
| 2004-05 | Everton | 12 | 1 | | |
| 2005-06 | Everton | 29 | 1 | | |
| 2006-07 | Everton | 35 | 9 | | |
| 2007-08 | Everton | 28 | 1 | | |
| 2008-09 | Everton | 26 | 5 | | |
| 2009-10 | Everton | 13 | 6 | | |
| 2010-11 | Everton | 29 | 3 | | |
| 2011-12 | Everton | 2 | 1 | 174 | 27 |
| 2011-12 | Arsenal | 29 | 6 | | |
| 2012-13 | Arsenal | 34 | 6 | 63 | 12 |

**BELLERIN, Hector (D)**      **0**   **0**
H: 5 10   W: 11 09   b.Barcelona 19-3-95

| | | | |
|---|---|---|---|
| 2012-13 | Arsenal | 0 | 0 |

**BENDTNER, Nicklas (F)**      **178**   **41**
H: 6 2   W: 13 00   b.Copenhagen 16-1-88
*Source:* Scholar. *Honours:* Denmark Youth, Under-21, 55 full caps, 22 goals.

| | | | | | |
|---|---|---|---|---|---|
| 2005-06 | Arsenal | 0 | 0 | | |
| 2006-07 | Arsenal | 0 | 0 | | |
| 2006-07 | *Birmingham C* | 42 | 11 | 42 | 11 |
| 2007-08 | Arsenal | 27 | 5 | | |
| 2008-09 | Arsenal | 31 | 9 | | |
| 2009-10 | Arsenal | 23 | 6 | | |
| 2010-11 | Arsenal | 17 | 2 | | |
| 2011-12 | Arsenal | 1 | 0 | | |
| 2011-12 | *Sunderland* | 28 | 8 | 28 | 8 |
| 2012-13 | Arsenal | 0 | 0 | 99 | 22 |
| 2012-13 | *Juventus* | 9 | 0 | 9 | 0 |

**BOATENG, Daniel (D)**      **4**   **0**
H: 6 0   W: 12 04   b.Enfield 2-9-92
*Source:* Scholar.

| | | | | | |
|---|---|---|---|---|---|
| 2010-11 | Arsenal | 0 | 0 | | |
| 2011-12 | Arsenal | 0 | 0 | | |
| 2011-12 | *Swindon T* | 2 | 0 | 2 | 0 |
| 2012-13 | Arsenal | -0 | 0 | | |
| 2012-13 | *Oxford U* | 2 | 0 | 2 | 0 |

**CAMPBELL, Joel (F)**      **8**   **0**
H: 5 10   W: 12 00   b.Costa Rica 26-6-92
*Honours:* Costa Rica Youth, 14 full caps, 6 goals.

| | | | | | |
|---|---|---|---|---|---|
| 2009-10 | Saprissa | 1 | 0 | | |
| 2010-11 | Saprissa | 2 | 0 | 3 | 0 |
| 2010-11 | *Puntarenas* | 5 | 0 | 5 | 0 |
| 2011-12 | *Lorient* | 0 | 0 | | |
| 2012-13 | Arsenal | 0 | 0 | | |

**CAZORLA, Santi (M)**      **290**   **51**
H: 5 5   W: 10 07   b.Lugo De Llanera 13-12-84
*Honours:* Spain Under-21, 55 full caps, 8 goals.

| | | | | | |
|---|---|---|---|---|---|
| 2003-04 | Villarreal | 2 | 0 | | |
| 2004-05 | Villarreal | 28 | 2 | | |
| 2005-06 | Villarreal | 23 | 0 | | |
| 2006-07 | *Recreativo Huelva* | 34 | 5 | 34 | 5 |
| 2007-08 | Villarreal | 36 | 5 | | |
| 2008-09 | Villarreal | 30 | 8 | | |
| 2009-10 | Villarreal | 24 | 5 | | |
| 2010-11 | Villarreal | 37 | 5 | 180 | 25 |
| 2011-12 | Malaga | 38 | 9 | | |
| 2012-13 | Malaga | 0 | 0 | 38 | 9 |
| 2012-13 | Arsenal | 38 | 12 | 38 | 12 |

**CHAMAKH, Marouane (F)**      **273**   **64**
H: 6 1   W: 11 00   b.Tonnens 10-1-84
*Honours:* Morocco 62 full caps, 17 goals.

| | | | | | |
|---|---|---|---|---|---|
| 2002-03 | Bordeaux | 10 | 1 | | |
| 2003-04 | Bordeaux | 25 | 6 | | |
| 2004-05 | Bordeaux | 33 | 10 | | |
| 2005-06 | Bordeaux | 29 | 7 | | |
| 2006-07 | Bordeaux | 29 | 5 | | |
| 2007-08 | Bordeaux | 32 | 4 | | |
| 2008-09 | Bordeaux | 34 | 13 | | |
| 2009-10 | Bordeaux | 38 | 10 | 230 | 56 |
| 2010-11 | Arsenal | 29 | 7 | | |
| 2011-12 | Arsenal | 11 | 1 | | |
| 2012-13 | Arsenal | 0 | 0 | 40 | 8 |
| 2012-13 | *West Ham U* | 3 | 0 | 3 | 0 |

**COQUELIN, Francis (M)**      **45**   **1**
H: 5 10   W: 11 08   b.Laval 13-5-91
*Source:* Laval. *Honours:* France Under-21.

| | | | | | |
|---|---|---|---|---|---|
| 2008-09 | Arsenal | 0 | 0 | | |
| 2009-10 | Arsenal | 0 | 0 | | |
| 2010-11 | Arsenal | 0 | 0 | | |
| 2010-11 | *Lorient* | 24 | 1 | 24 | 1 |
| 2011-12 | Arsenal | 10 | 0 | | |
| 2012-13 | Arsenal | 11 | 0 | 21 | 0 |

**DALLISON, Tom (M)**      **0**   **0**
H: 5 10   W: 14 01   b. 2-2-96

| | | | |
|---|---|---|---|
| 2012-13 | Arsenal | 0 | 0 |

**DIABY, Abou (M)**      **133**   **15**
H: 6 2   W: 12 04   b.Paris 11-5-86
*Honours:* France Youth, Under-21, 16 full caps, 1 goal.

| | | | | | |
|---|---|---|---|---|---|
| 2004-05 | Auxerre | 5 | 0 | | |
| 2005-06 | Auxerre | 5 | 1 | 10 | 1 |
| 2005-06 | Arsenal | 12 | 1 | | |
| 2006-07 | Arsenal | 12 | 1 | | |
| 2007-08 | Arsenal | 15 | 1 | | |
| 2008-09 | Arsenal | 24 | 3 | | |
| 2009-10 | Arsenal | 29 | 6 | | |
| 2010-11 | Arsenal | 16 | 2 | | |
| 2011-12 | Arsenal | 4 | 0 | | |
| 2012-13 | Arsenal | 11 | 0 | 123 | 14 |

**DJOUROU, Johan (D)**      **113**   **1**
H: 6 2   W: 12 05   b.Ivory Coast 18-1-87
*Source:* Scholar. *Honours:* Switzerland Youth, Under-20, Under-21, 38 full caps, 1 goal.

| | | | | | |
|---|---|---|---|---|---|
| 2004-05 | Arsenal | 7 | 0 | | |
| 2005-06 | Arsenal | 7 | 0 | | |
| 2006-07 | Arsenal | 21 | 0 | | |
| 2007-08 | Arsenal | 2 | 0 | | |
| 2007-08 | *Birmingham C* | 13 | 0 | 13 | 0 |
| 2008-09 | Arsenal | 15 | 0 | | |
| 2009-10 | Arsenal | 1 | 0 | | |
| 2010-11 | Arsenal | 22 | 1 | | |
| 2011-12 | Arsenal | 18 | 0 | | |
| 2012-13 | Arsenal | 0 | 0 | 86 | 1 |
| 2012-13 | *Hannover 96* | 14 | 0 | 14 | 0 |

**EASTMOND, Craig (D)**      **36**   **2**
H: 6 0   W: 11 11   b.Wandsworth 9-12-90
*Source:* Scholar.

| | | | | | |
|---|---|---|---|---|---|
| 2009-10 | Arsenal | 4 | 0 | | |
| 2010-11 | Arsenal | 0 | 0 | | |
| 2010-11 | *Millwall* | 6 | 0 | 6 | 0 |
| 2011-12 | Arsenal | 0 | 0 | | |
| 2011-12 | *Wycombe W* | 14 | 0 | 14 | 0 |
| 2012-13 | Arsenal | 0 | 0 | 4 | 0 |
| 2012-13 | *Colchester U* | 12 | 2 | 12 | 2 |

**EBECILIO, Kyle (M)**      **0**   **0**
H: 5 11   W: 12 02   b.Rotterdam 17-2-94
*Source:* Feyenoord. *Honours:* Holland Youth.

| | | | |
|---|---|---|---|
| 2010-11 | Arsenal | 0 | 0 |
| 2011-12 | Arsenal | 0 | 0 |
| 2012-13 | Arsenal | 0 | 0 |

Transferred to FC Twente May 2013

**EISFELD, Thomas (M)**      **0**   **0**
H: 5 10   W: 10 03   b.Finsterwalde 18-1-93
*Source:* Borussia Dortmund.

| | | | |
|---|---|---|---|
| 2011-12 | Arsenal | 0 | 0 |
| 2012-13 | Arsenal | 0 | 0 |

**FABIANSKI, Lukasz (G)**    84   0
H: 6 3   W: 13 01   b.Costrzyn nad Odra 18-4-85
*Honours:* Poland Under-21, 21 full caps.

| | | | | |
|---|---|---|---|---|
| 2005-06 | Legia | 30 | 0 | |
| 2006-07 | Legia | 23 | 0 | 53   0 |
| 2007-08 | Arsenal | 3 | 0 | |
| 2008-09 | Arsenal | 6 | 0 | |
| 2009-10 | Arsenal | 4 | 0 | |
| 2010-11 | Arsenal | 14 | 0 | |
| 2011-12 | Arsenal | 0 | 0 | |
| 2012-13 | Arsenal | 4 | 0 | 31   0 |

**FRIMPONG, Emmanuel (M)**    23   0
H: 5 11   W: 10 07   b.Ghana 10-1-92
*Source:* Scholar. *Honours:* England Youth, Ghana 1 full cap.

| | | | | |
|---|---|---|---|---|
| 2008-09 | Arsenal | 0 | 0 | |
| 2009-10 | Arsenal | 0 | 0 | |
| 2010-11 | Arsenal | 0 | 0 | |
| 2011-12 | Arsenal | 6 | 0 | |
| 2011-12 | *Wolverhampton W* | 5 | 0 | 5   0 |
| 2012-13 | Arsenal | 0 | 0 | 6   0 |
| 2012-13 | *Charlton Ath* | 6 | 0 | 6   0 |
| 2012-13 | *Fulham* | 6 | 0 | 6   0 |

**GALINDO, Samuel (M)**    19   0
H: 6 3   W: 12 00   b.Bolivia 18-4-92
*Source:* Real America. *Honours:* Bolivia Youth, 2 full caps.

| | | | | |
|---|---|---|---|---|
| 2010-11 | Arsenal | 0 | 0 | |
| 2010-11 | *Salamanca* | 7 | 0 | 7   0 |
| 2011-12 | Arsenal | 0 | 0 | |
| 2011-12 | *Gimnastic* | 12 | 0 | 12   0 |
| 2012-13 | Arsenal | 0 | 0 | |

**GERVINHO (F)**    233   60
H: 5 10   W: 10 10   b.Anyama 27-5-87
*Honours:* Ivory Coast 45 full caps, 13 goals.

| | | | | |
|---|---|---|---|---|
| 2005-06 | Beveren | 32 | 6 | |
| 2006-07 | Beveren | 29 | 8 | 61   14 |
| 2007-08 | Le Mans | 26 | 2 | |
| 2008-09 | Le Mans | 33 | 7 | 59   9 |
| 2009-10 | Lille | 32 | 13 | |
| 2010-11 | Lille | 35 | 15 | 67   28 |
| 2011-12 | Arsenal | 28 | 4 | |
| 2012-13 | Arsenal | 18 | 5 | 46   9 |

**GIBBS, Kieran (M)**    68   1
H: 5 10   W: 10 02   b.Lambeth 26-9-89
*Source:* Scholar. *Honours:* England Youth, Under-21, 2 full caps.

| | | | | |
|---|---|---|---|---|
| 2007-08 | Arsenal | 0 | 0 | |
| 2007-08 | *Norwich C* | 7 | 0 | 7   0 |
| 2008-09 | Arsenal | 8 | 0 | |
| 2009-10 | Arsenal | 3 | 0 | |
| 2010-11 | Arsenal | 7 | 0 | |
| 2011-12 | Arsenal | 16 | 1 | |
| 2012-13 | Arsenal | 27 | 0 | 61   1 |

**GIROUD, Olivier (F)**    186   75
H: 6 3   W: 13 11   b.Chambery 30-9-86
*Honours:* France 19 full caps, 3 goals.

| | | | | |
|---|---|---|---|---|
| 2005-06 | Grenoble | 3 | 0 | |
| 2006-07 | Grenoble | 15 | 2 | 18   2 |
| 2008-09 | Tours | 23 | 8 | |
| 2009-10 | Tours | 38 | 21 | 61   29 |
| 2010-11 | Montpellier | 37 | 12 | |
| 2011-12 | Montpellier | 36 | 21 | 73   33 |
| 2012-13 | Arsenal | 34 | 11 | 34   11 |

**GNABRY, Serge (M)**    1   0
H: 5 9   W: 11 06   b.Stuttgart 14-7-95

| | | | | |
|---|---|---|---|---|
| 2012-13 | Arsenal | 1 | 0 | 1   0 |

**HAJROVIC, Sead (D)**    10   0
H: 6 0   W: 12 08   b.Brugg 4-6-93
*Source:* Scholar.

| | | | | |
|---|---|---|---|---|
| 2010-11 | Arsenal | 0 | 0 | |
| 2011-12 | Arsenal | 0 | 0 | |
| 2011-12 | *Barnet* | 10 | 0 | 10   0 |
| 2012-13 | Arsenal | 0 | 0 | |

**HAYDEN, Isaac (D)**    0   0
b.Chelmsford 22-3-95
*Source:* Scholar.

| | | | | |
|---|---|---|---|---|
| 2011-12 | Arsenal | 0 | 0 | |
| 2012-13 | Arsenal | 0 | 0 | |

**HENDERSON, Conor (M)**    2   0
H: 6 1   W: 11 13   b.Sidcup 8-9-91
*Source:* Scholar. *Honours:* Eire Youth, Under-21.

| | | | | |
|---|---|---|---|---|
| 2008-09 | Arsenal | 0 | 0 | |
| 2009-10 | Arsenal | 0 | 0 | |
| 2010-11 | Arsenal | 0 | 0 | |
| 2011-12 | Arsenal | 0 | 0 | |
| 2012-13 | Arsenal | 0 | 0 | |
| 2012-13 | *Coventry C* | 2 | 0 | 2   0 |

**ILIEV, Dejan (G)**    0   0
H: 6 5   b.Strumica 25-2-95
*Source:* Belascia. *Honours:* Macedonia Youth, Under-21.

| | | | | |
|---|---|---|---|---|
| 2012-13 | Arsenal | 0 | 0 | |

**IWOBI, Alex (M)**    0   0
H: 5 11   W: 11 11   b. 3-5-96

| | | | | |
|---|---|---|---|---|
| 2012-13 | Arsenal | 0 | 0 | |

**JEBB, Jack (M)**    0   0
b. 11-9-95

| | | | | |
|---|---|---|---|---|
| 2012-13 | Arsenal | 0 | 0 | |

**JENKINSON, Carl (D)**    31   0
H: 6 1   W: 12 02   b.Harlow 8-2-92
*Source:* Scholar. *Honours:* Finland Youth, Under-21, England Youth, 1 full cap.

| | | | | |
|---|---|---|---|---|
| 2010-11 | *Charlton Ath* | 8 | 0 | 8   0 |
| 2010-11 | Arsenal | 0 | 0 | |
| 2011-12 | Arsenal | 9 | 0 | |
| 2012-13 | Arsenal | 14 | 0 | 23   0 |

**KAMARA, Glen (F)**    0   0
H: 5 10   W: 13 00   b. 28-10-95

| | | | | |
|---|---|---|---|---|
| 2012-13 | Arsenal | 0 | 0 | |

**KOSCIELNY, Laurent (D)**    231   15
H: 6 1   W: 11 11   b.Tulle 10-9-85
*Honours:* France 10 full caps.

| | | | | |
|---|---|---|---|---|
| 2004-05 | Guingamp | 11 | 0 | |
| 2005-06 | Guingamp | 9 | 0 | |
| 2006-07 | Guingamp | 21 | 0 | 41   0 |
| 2007-08 | Tours | 33 | 1 | |
| 2008-09 | Tours | 34 | 5 | 67   6 |
| 2009-10 | Lorient | 35 | 3 | 35   3 |
| 2010-11 | Arsenal | 30 | 2 | |
| 2011-12 | Arsenal | 33 | 2 | |
| 2012-13 | Arsenal | 25 | 2 | 88   6 |

**LIPMAN, Austin (M)**    0   0

| | | | | |
|---|---|---|---|---|
| 2012-13 | Arsenal | 0 | 0 | |

**MANNONE, Vito (G)**    48   0
H: 6 0   W: 11 08   b.Milan 2-3-88
*Source:* Atalanta.

| | | | | |
|---|---|---|---|---|
| 2005-06 | Arsenal | 0 | 0 | |
| 2006-07 | Arsenal | 0 | 0 | |
| 2006-07 | *Barnsley* | 2 | 0 | 2   0 |
| 2007-08 | Arsenal | 0 | 0 | |
| 2008-09 | Arsenal | 1 | 0 | |
| 2009-10 | Arsenal | 5 | 0 | |
| 2010-11 | Arsenal | 0 | 0 | |
| 2010-11 | *Hull C* | 10 | 0 | |
| 2011-12 | Arsenal | 0 | 0 | |
| 2011-12 | *Hull C* | 21 | 0 | 31   0 |
| 2012-13 | Arsenal | 9 | 0 | 15   0 |

**MARTINEZ, Damian (G)**    1   0
H: 6 3   W: 13 05   b.Mar del Plata 2-9-92
*Source:* Independiente.

| | | | | |
|---|---|---|---|---|
| 2010-11 | Arsenal | 0 | 0 | |
| 2011-12 | Arsenal | 0 | 0 | |
| 2011-12 | *Oxford U* | 1 | 0 | 1   0 |
| 2012-13 | Arsenal | 0 | 0 | |

**MEADE, Jernade (M)**    0   0
H: 5 8   W: 11 09   b.Luton 25-10-92
*Source:* Scholar.

| | | | | |
|---|---|---|---|---|
| 2011-12 | Arsenal | 0 | 0 | |
| 2012-13 | Arsenal | 0 | 0 | |

**MERTESACKER, Per (D)**    275   22
H: 6 6   W: 14 -02   b.Hannover 29-9-84
*Honours:* Germany Under-21, 90 full caps, 2 goals.

| | | | | |
|---|---|---|---|---|
| 2003-04 | Hannover | 13 | 0 | |
| 2004-05 | Hannover | 31 | 2 | |
| 2005-06 | Hannover | 30 | 5 | 74   7 |
| 2006-07 | Werder Bremen | 25 | 2 | |
| 2007-08 | Werder Bremen | 32 | 1 | |
| 2008-09 | Werder Bremen | 23 | 2 | |
| 2009-10 | Werder Bremen | 33 | 5 | |
| 2010-11 | Werder Bremen | 29 | 2 | |
| 2011-12 | Werder Bremen | 4 | 0 | 146   12 |
| 2011-12 | Arsenal | 21 | 0 | |
| 2012-13 | Arsenal | 34 | 3 | 55   3 |

**MIQUEL, Ignasi (D)**    5   0
H: 6 4   W: 13 05   b.Barcelona 28-9-92
*Source:* Scholar.

| | | | | |
|---|---|---|---|---|
| 2009-10 | Arsenal | 0 | 0 | |
| 2010-11 | Arsenal | 0 | 0 | |
| 2011-12 | Arsenal | 4 | 0 | |
| 2012-13 | Arsenal | 1 | 0 | 5   0 |

**MIYAICHI, Ryo (F)**    16   0
H: 6 0   W: 11 02   b.Okazaki 14-12-92
*Source:* Chukyodai Chuyko High School.
*Honours:* Japan Youth, 2 full caps.

| | | | | |
|---|---|---|---|---|
| 2010-11 | Arsenal | 0 | 0 | |
| 2011-12 | Arsenal | 0 | 0 | |
| 2011-12 | *Bolton W* | 12 | 0 | 12   0 |
| 2012-13 | Arsenal | 0 | 0 | |
| 2012-13 | *Wigan Ath* | 4 | 0 | 4   0 |

**MONREAL, Nacho (D)**    183   4
H: 5 10   W: 11 04   b.Pamplona 26-2-86
*Honours:* Spain Under-21, 13 full caps.

| | | | | |
|---|---|---|---|---|
| 2006-07 | Osasuna | 11 | 0 | |
| 2007-08 | Osasuna | 27 | 0 | |
| 2008-09 | Osasuna | 28 | 0 | |
| 2009-10 | Osasuna | 31 | 1 | |
| 2010-11 | Osasuna | 31 | 1 | 128   2 |
| 2011-12 | Malaga | 31 | 0 | |
| 2012-13 | Malaga | 14 | 1 | 45   1 |
| 2012-13 | Arsenal | 10 | 1 | 10   1 |

**MONTEIRO, Elton (D)**    0   0
H: 6 3   W: 13 05   b.Sion 22-2-94
*Source:* Scholar.

| | | | | |
|---|---|---|---|---|
| 2010-11 | Arsenal | 0 | 0 | |
| 2011-12 | Arsenal | 0 | 0 | |
| 2012-13 | Arsenal | 0 | 0 | |

**OLSSON, Kristoffer (M)**    0   0
b.Vrinnevi 30-6-95
*Source:* IFK Norrkopings. *Honours:* Sweden Youth.

| | | | | |
|---|---|---|---|---|
| 2012-13 | Arsenal | 0 | 0 | |

**ORMONDE-OTTEWILL, Brandon (D)** 0   0
b. 21-12-95
*Source:* Scholar. *Honours:* England Youth.

| | | | | |
|---|---|---|---|---|
| 2012-13 | Arsenal | 0 | 0 | |

**OXLADE-CHAMBERLAIN, Alex (M)** 77   12
H: 5 11   W: 11 00   b.Portsmouth 15-8-93
*Source:* Scholar. *Honours:* England Under-21, 12 full caps, 3 goals.

| | | | | |
|---|---|---|---|---|
| 2009-10 | Southampton | 7 | 0 | |
| 2010-11 | Southampton | 34 | 9 | 36   9 |
| 2011-12 | Arsenal | 16 | 2 | |
| 2012-13 | Arsenal | 25 | 1 | 41   3 |

**PARK, Chu-Young (F)**    183   51
H: 6 0   W: 11 11   b.Daegu 10-7-85
*Honours:* South Korea Youth, Under-23, 58 full caps, 24 goals.

| | | | | |
|---|---|---|---|---|
| 2005 | Seoul | 19 | 12 | |
| 2006 | Seoul | 26 | 7 | |
| 2007 | Seoul | 11 | 2 | |
| 2008 | Seoul | 13 | 2 | 69   23 |
| 2008-09 | Monaco | 31 | 5 | |
| 2009-10 | Monaco | 27 | 8 | |
| 2010-11 | Monaco | 33 | 12 | 91   25 |
| 2011-12 | Arsenal | 1 | 0 | |
| 2012-13 | Arsenal | 0 | 0 | 1   0 |
| 2012-13 | *Celta Vigo* | 22 | 3 | 22   3 |

**PODOLSKI, Lukas (F)**    255   102
H: 6 0   W: 13 00   b.Gleiwitz, Poland 4-6-85
*Honours:* Germany Youth, Under-21, 110 full caps, 43 goals.

| | | | | |
|---|---|---|---|---|
| 2003-04 | Cologne | 19 | 10 | |
| 2004-05 | Cologne | 12 | 21 | |
| 2005-06 | Cologne | 32 | 12 | |
| 2006-07 | Bayern Munich | 22 | 4 | |
| 2007-08 | Bayern Munich | 25 | 5 | |
| 2008-09 | Bayern Munich | 24 | 6 | 71   15 |
| 2009-10 | Cologne | 27 | 2 | |

| Season | Club | Apps | Gls | Tot A | Tot G |
|---|---|---|---|---|---|
| 2010-11 | Cologne | 32 | 13 | | |
| 2011-12 | Cologne | 29 | 18 | 151 | 76 |
| 2012-13 | Arsenal | 33 | 11 | 33 | 11 |

**RAMSEY, Aaron (M)**    131   9
H: 5 9   W: 10 07   b.Caerphilly 26-12-90
*Source:* School. *Honours:* Wales Youth, Under-21, 26 full caps, 6 goals.

| Season | Club | Apps | Gls | Tot A | Tot G |
|---|---|---|---|---|---|
| 2006-07 | Cardiff C | 1 | 0 | | |
| 2007-08 | Cardiff C | 15 | 1 | | |
| 2008-09 | Arsenal | 9 | 0 | | |
| 2009-10 | Arsenal | 18 | 3 | | |
| 2010-11 | Arsenal | 7 | 1 | | |
| 2010-11 | *Nottingham F* | 5 | 0 | 5 | 0 |
| 2010-11 | *Cardiff C* | 6 | 1 | 22 | 2 |
| 2011-12 | Arsenal | 34 | 2 | | |
| 2012-13 | Arsenal | 36 | 1 | 104 | 7 |

**ROSICKY, Tomas (M)**    318   42
H: 5 10   W: 10 10   b.Prague 4-10-80
*Honours:* Czech Republic Under-21, 91 full caps, 20 goals.

| Season | Club | Apps | Gls | Tot A | Tot G |
|---|---|---|---|---|---|
| 1998-99 | Sparta Prague | 3 | 0 | | |
| 1999-2000 | Sparta Prague | 24 | 5 | | |
| 2000-01 | Sparta Prague | 14 | 3 | 41 | 8 |
| 2000-01 | Borussia Dortmund | 15 | 0 | | |
| 2001-02 | Borussia Dortmund | 30 | 5 | | |
| 2002-03 | Borussia Dortmund | 30 | 3 | | |
| 2003-04 | Borussia Dortmund | 19 | 2 | | |
| 2004-05 | Borussia Dortmund | 27 | 4 | | |
| 2005-06 | Borussia Dortmund | 28 | 5 | 149 | 19 |
| 2006-07 | Arsenal | 26 | 3 | | |
| 2007-08 | Arsenal | 18 | 6 | | |
| 2008-09 | Arsenal | 0 | 0 | | |
| 2009-10 | Arsenal | 25 | 3 | | |
| 2010-11 | Arsenal | 21 | 0 | | |
| 2011-12 | Arsenal | 28 | 1 | | |
| 2012-13 | Arsenal | 10 | 2 | 128 | 15 |

**SAGNA, Bakari (D)**    265   3
H: 5 10   W: 11 05   b.Sens 14-2-83
*Source:* Auxerre B. *Honours:* France Under-21, 34 full caps.

| Season | Club | Apps | Gls | Tot A | Tot G |
|---|---|---|---|---|---|
| 2003-04 | Auxerre | 0 | 0 | | |
| 2004-05 | Auxerre | 26 | 0 | | |
| 2005-06 | Auxerre | 23 | 0 | | |
| 2006-07 | Auxerre | 38 | 0 | 87 | 0 |
| 2007-08 | Arsenal | 29 | 1 | | |
| 2008-09 | Arsenal | 35 | 0 | | |
| 2009-10 | Arsenal | 35 | 0 | | |
| 2010-11 | Arsenal | 33 | 1 | | |
| 2011-12 | Arsenal | 21 | 1 | | |
| 2012-13 | Arsenal | 25 | 0 | 178 | 3 |

**SHEA, James (G)**    1   0
H: 5 11   W: 12 00   b.Islington 16-6-91
*Source:* Scholar.

| Season | Club | Apps | Gls | Tot A | Tot G |
|---|---|---|---|---|---|
| 2009-10 | Arsenal | 0 | 0 | | |
| 2010-11 | Arsenal | 0 | 0 | | |
| 2011-12 | Arsenal | 0 | 0 | | |
| 2011-12 | *Dagenham & R* | 1 | 0 | 1 | 0 |
| 2012-13 | Arsenal | 0 | 0 | | |

**SIEMANN, Leander (M)**    0   0
b.Berlin 25-10-95
*Source:* Hertha Berlin.

| Season | Club | Apps | Gls | Tot A | Tot G |
|---|---|---|---|---|---|
| 2012-13 | Arsenal | 0 | 0 | | |

**SILVA, Wellington (M)**    18   3
H: 5 6   W: 10 00   b.Rio de Janeiro 6-1-93
*Source:* Fluminense. *Honours:* Brazil Youth.

| Season | Club | Apps | Gls | Tot A | Tot G |
|---|---|---|---|---|---|
| 2010-11 | Arsenal | 0 | 0 | | |
| 2010-11 | *Levante* | 2 | 0 | 2 | 0 |
| 2011-12 | Arsenal | 0 | 0 | | |
| 2011-12 | *Alcoyano* | 16 | 3 | 16 | 3 |
| 2012-13 | Arsenal | 0 | 0 | | |

**SQUILLACI, Sebastien (D)**    323   22
H: 6 0   W: 11 13   b.Toulon 11-8-80
*Honours:* France 21 full caps.

| Season | Club | Apps | Gls | Tot A | Tot G |
|---|---|---|---|---|---|
| 1997-98 | Toulon | 6 | 0 | 6 | 0 |
| 1998-99 | Monaco | 0 | 0 | | |
| 1999-2000 | Monaco | 0 | 0 | | |
| 2000-01 | Ajaccio | 36 | 2 | | |
| 2001-02 | Ajaccio | 33 | 5 | 69 | 7 |
| 2002-03 | Monaco | 34 | 2 | | |
| 2003-04 | Monaco | 27 | 5 | | |
| 2004-05 | Monaco | 28 | 2 | | |
| 2005-06 | Monaco | 26 | 1 | 115 | 10 |
| 2006-07 | Lyon | 28 | 3 | | |
| 2007-08 | Lyon | 34 | 0 | 62 | 3 |
| 2008-09 | Sevilla | 32 | 0 | | |
| 2009-10 | Sevilla | 16 | 1 | 48 | 1 |
| 2010-11 | Arsenal | 22 | 1 | | |
| 2011-12 | Arsenal | 1 | 0 | | |
| 2012-13 | Arsenal | 0 | 0 | 23 | 1 |

**SZCZESNY, Wojciech (G)**    106   0
H: 5 10   W: 11 11   b.Warsaw 18-4-90
*Source:* Scholar. *Honours:* Poland 12 full caps.

| Season | Club | Apps | Gls | Tot A | Tot G |
|---|---|---|---|---|---|
| 2007-08 | Arsenal | 0 | 0 | | |
| 2008-09 | Arsenal | 0 | 0 | | |
| 2009-10 | Arsenal | 0 | 0 | | |
| 2009-10 | *Brentford* | 28 | 0 | 28 | 0 |
| 2010-11 | Arsenal | 15 | 0 | | |
| 2011-12 | Arsenal | 38 | 0 | | |
| 2012-13 | Arsenal | 25 | 0 | 78 | 0 |

**UADE, Arinse (D)**    0   0
H: 6 0   W: 12 03   b. 26-12-95

| Season | Club | Apps | Gls | Tot A | Tot G |
|---|---|---|---|---|---|
| 2012-13 | Arsenal | 0 | 0 | | |

**VERMAELEN, Thomas (D)**    208   22
H: 6 0   W: 11 11   b.Antwerp 14-11-85
*Source:* Ekeren, Antwerp. *Honours:* Belgium Under-21, 42 full caps, 1 goal.

| Season | Club | Apps | Gls | Tot A | Tot G |
|---|---|---|---|---|---|
| 2003-04 | Ajax | 1 | 0 | | |
| 2004-05 | *RKC Waalwijk* | 13 | 2 | 13 | 2 |
| 2005-06 | Ajax | 24 | 3 | | |
| 2006-07 | Ajax | 23 | 0 | | |
| 2007-08 | Ajax | 20 | 0 | | |
| 2008-09 | Ajax | 31 | 4 | 99 | 7 |
| 2009-10 | Arsenal | 33 | 7 | | |
| 2010-11 | Arsenal | 5 | 0 | | |
| 2011-12 | Arsenal | 29 | 6 | | |
| 2012-13 | Arsenal | 29 | 0 | 96 | 13 |

**WALCOTT, Theo (F)**    202   44
H: 5 9   W: 11 01   b.Stanmore 16-3-89
*Source:* Scholar. *Honours:* England Youth, Under-21, B, 33 full caps, 4 goals.

| Season | Club | Apps | Gls | Tot A | Tot G |
|---|---|---|---|---|---|
| 2005-06 | Southampton | 21 | 4 | 21 | 4 |
| 2005-06 | Arsenal | 0 | 0 | | |
| 2006-07 | Arsenal | 16 | 0 | | |
| 2007-08 | Arsenal | 25 | 4 | | |
| 2008-09 | Arsenal | 22 | 2 | | |
| 2009-10 | Arsenal | 23 | 3 | | |
| 2010-11 | Arsenal | 28 | 9 | | |
| 2011-12 | Arsenal | 35 | 8 | | |
| 2012-13 | Arsenal | 32 | 14 | 181 | 40 |

**WATT, Sanchez (M)**    56   5
H: 5 11   W: 12 00   b.Hackney 14-2-91
*Source:* Scholar. *Honours:* England Youth.

| Season | Club | Apps | Gls | Tot A | Tot G |
|---|---|---|---|---|---|
| 2008-09 | Arsenal | 0 | 0 | | |
| 2009-10 | Arsenal | 0 | 0 | | |
| 2009-10 | *Southend U* | 4 | 0 | 4 | 0 |
| 2009-10 | *Leeds U* | 6 | 0 | | |
| 2010-11 | Arsenal | 0 | 0 | | |
| 2010-11 | *Leeds U* | 22 | 1 | 28 | 1 |
| 2011-12 | Arsenal | 0 | 0 | | |
| 2011-12 | *Sheffield W* | 4 | 0 | 4 | 0 |
| 2011-12 | *Crawley T* | 14 | 2 | 14 | 2 |
| 2012-13 | Arsenal | 0 | 0 | | |
| 2012-13 | *Colchester U* | 6 | 2 | 6 | 2 |

**WILSHERE, Jack (M)**    76   2
H: 5 7   W: 11 03   b.Stevenage 1-1-92
*Source:* Scholar. *Honours:* England Youth, Under-21, 7 full caps.

| Season | Club | Apps | Gls | Tot A | Tot G |
|---|---|---|---|---|---|
| 2008-09 | Arsenal | 1 | 0 | | |
| 2009-10 | Arsenal | 0 | 0 | | |
| 2009-10 | *Bolton W* | 14 | 1 | 14 | 1 |
| 2010-11 | Arsenal | 35 | 1 | | |
| 2011-12 | Arsenal | 0 | 0 | | |
| 2012-13 | Arsenal | 25 | 0 | 62 | 1 |

**WYNTER, Jordan (M)**    0   0

| Season | Club | Apps | Gls | Tot A | Tot G |
|---|---|---|---|---|---|
| 2012-13 | Arsenal | 0 | 0 | | |

**YENNARIS, Nico (D)**    3   0
H: 5 7   W: 10 03   b.Leytonstone 23-5-93
*Source:* Scholar. *Honours:* England Youth.

| Season | Club | Apps | Gls | Tot A | Tot G |
|---|---|---|---|---|---|
| 2010-11 | Arsenal | 0 | 0 | | |
| 2011-12 | Arsenal | 1 | 0 | | |
| 2011-12 | *Notts Co* | 2 | 0 | 2 | 0 |
| 2012-13 | Arsenal | 0 | 0 | 1 | 0 |

**Scholars**
Dallison-Lisbon, Thomas Albert; Dawkins, Tarum; Iwobi, Alex; Jeffrey, Anthony Lamar Malcolm; Kamara, Glen; Mugabo, Alfred Martin; Uade, Obasiarinse Idehaloise; Vickers, Josh.

# ASTON VILLA (5)

**AGBONLAHOR, Gabriel (F)**    253   62
H: 5 11   W: 12 05   b.Birmingham 13-10-86
*Source:* Scholar. *Honours:* England Under-20, Under-21, 3 full caps.

| Season | Club | Apps | Gls | Tot A | Tot G |
|---|---|---|---|---|---|
| 2005-06 | Aston Villa | 9 | 1 | | |
| 2005-06 | *Watford* | 2 | 0 | 2 | 0 |
| 2005-06 | *Sheffield W* | 8 | 0 | 8 | 0 |
| 2006-07 | Aston Villa | 38 | 9 | | |
| 2007-08 | Aston Villa | 37 | 11 | | |
| 2008-09 | Aston Villa | 36 | 11 | | |
| 2009-10 | Aston Villa | 36 | 13 | | |
| 2010-11 | Aston Villa | 26 | 3 | | |
| 2011-12 | Aston Villa | 33 | 5 | | |
| 2012-13 | Aston Villa | 28 | 9 | 243 | 62 |

**ALBRIGHTON, Marc (M)**    67   7
H: 6 2   W: 12 06   b.Tamworth 18-11-89
*Source:* Scholar. *Honours:* England Youth, Under-20, Under-21.

| Season | Club | Apps | Gls | Tot A | Tot G |
|---|---|---|---|---|---|
| 2008-09 | Aston Villa | 0 | 0 | | |
| 2009-10 | Aston Villa | 3 | 0 | | |
| 2010-11 | Aston Villa | 29 | 5 | | |
| 2011-12 | Aston Villa | 26 | 2 | | |
| 2012-13 | Aston Villa | 9 | 0 | 67 | 7 |

**BAKER, Nathan (D)**    62   0
H: 6 2   W: 11 11   b.Worcester 23-4-91
*Source:* Scholar. *Honours:* England Youth, Under-20, Under-21.

| Season | Club | Apps | Gls | Tot A | Tot G |
|---|---|---|---|---|---|
| 2008-09 | Aston Villa | 0 | 0 | | |
| 2009-10 | Aston Villa | 0 | 0 | | |
| 2009-10 | *Lincoln C* | 18 | 0 | 18 | 0 |
| 2010-11 | Aston Villa | 4 | 0 | | |
| 2011-12 | Aston Villa | 8 | 0 | | |
| 2011-12 | *Millwall* | 6 | 0 | 6 | 0 |
| 2012-13 | Aston Villa | 26 | 0 | 38 | 0 |

**BANNAN, Barry (D)**    101   3
H: 5 10   W: 10 08   b.Glasgow 1-12-89
*Source:* Scholar. *Honours:* Scotland Under-21, 12 full caps.

| Season | Club | Apps | Gls | Tot A | Tot G |
|---|---|---|---|---|---|
| 2008-09 | Aston Villa | 0 | 0 | | |
| 2008-09 | *Derby Co* | 10 | 1 | 10 | 1 |
| 2009-10 | Aston Villa | 0 | 0 | | |
| 2009-10 | *Blackpool* | 20 | 1 | 20 | 1 |
| 2010-11 | Aston Villa | 12 | 0 | | |
| 2010-11 | *Leeds U* | 7 | 0 | 7 | 0 |
| 2011-12 | Aston Villa | 28 | 1 | | |
| 2012-13 | Aston Villa | 24 | 0 | 64 | 1 |

**BENNETT, Joe (D)**    110   1
H: 5 10   W: 10 04   b.Rochdale 28-3-90
*Source:* Scholar. *Honours:* England Under-20, Under-21.

| Season | Club | Apps | Gls | Tot A | Tot G |
|---|---|---|---|---|---|
| 2008-09 | Middlesbrough | 1 | 0 | | |
| 2009-10 | Middlesbrough | 12 | 0 | | |
| 2010-11 | Middlesbrough | 31 | 0 | | |
| 2011-12 | Middlesbrough | 41 | 1 | | |
| 2012-13 | Middlesbrough | 0 | 0 | 85 | 1 |
| 2012-13 | Aston Villa | 25 | 0 | 25 | 0 |

**BENT, Darren (F)**    362   151
H: 5 11   W: 12 07   b.Wandsworth 6-2-84
*Source:* Scholar. *Honours:* England Youth, Under-21, 13 full caps, 4 goals.

| Season | Club | Apps | Gls | Tot A | Tot G |
|---|---|---|---|---|---|
| 2001-02 | Ipswich T | 5 | 1 | | |
| 2002-03 | Ipswich T | 35 | 12 | | |
| 2003-04 | Ipswich T | 37 | 16 | | |
| 2004-05 | Ipswich T | 45 | 20 | 122 | 49 |
| 2005-06 | Charlton Ath | 36 | 18 | | |
| 2006-07 | Charlton Ath | 32 | 13 | 68 | 31 |
| 2007-08 | Tottenham H | 27 | 6 | | |
| 2008-09 | Tottenham H | 33 | 12 | | |
| 2009-10 | Tottenham H | 0 | 0 | 60 | 18 |
| 2009-10 | Sunderland | 38 | 24 | | |
| 2010-11 | Sunderland | 20 | 8 | 58 | 32 |
| 2010-11 | Aston Villa | 16 | 9 | | |
| 2011-12 | Aston Villa | 22 | 9 | | |
| 2012-13 | Aston Villa | 16 | 3 | 54 | 21 |

**BENTEKE, Christian (F)** 138 55
H: 6 3 W: 13 00 b.Kinshasa 3-12-90
*Honours:* Belgium Youth, Under-21, 14 full caps, 6 goals.

| | | | | | |
|---|---|--:|--:|--:|--:|
| 2007-08 | Genk | 7 | 0 | | |
| 2008-09 | Genk | 3 | 0 | | |
| 2008-09 | Standard Liege | 9 | 3 | | |
| 2009-10 | *KV Kortrijk* | 24 | 9 | 24 | 9 |
| 2010-11 | Standard Liege | 5 | 0 | | |
| 2010-11 | *KV Mechelen* | 15 | 5 | 15 | 5 |
| 2011-12 | Standard Liege | 4 | 0 | 18 | 3 |
| 2011-12 | Genk | 32 | 16 | | |
| 2012-13 | Genk | 5 | 3 | 47 | 19 |
| 2012-13 | Aston Villa | 34 | 19 | 34 | 19 |

**BOWERY, Jordan (F)** 93 10
H: 6 1 W: 12 00 b.Nottingham 2-7-91
*Source:* Scholar.

| | | | | | |
|---|---|--:|--:|--:|--:|
| 2008-09 | Chesterfield | 3 | 0 | | |
| 2009-10 | Chesterfield | 10 | 0 | | |
| 2010-11 | Chesterfield | 27 | 1 | | |
| 2011-12 | Chesterfield | 40 | 8 | | |
| 2012-13 | Chesterfield | 3 | 1 | 83 | 10 |
| 2012-13 | Aston Villa | 10 | 0 | 10 | 0 |

**BURKE, Graham (F)** 0 0
H: 5 11 W: 11 11 b.Dublin 21-9-93
*Source:* Scholar. *Honours:* Eire Youth, Under-21.

| | | | |
|---|---|--:|--:|
| 2010-11 | Aston Villa | 0 | 0 |
| 2011-12 | Aston Villa | 0 | 0 |
| 2012-13 | Aston Villa | 0 | 0 |

**CARRUTHERS, Samir (F)** 3 0
H: 5 8 W: 11 00 b.Islington 4-4-93
*Source:* Scholar. *Honours:* Eire Youth, Under-21.

| | | | | | |
|---|---|--:|--:|--:|--:|
| 2011-12 | Aston Villa | 3 | 0 | | |
| 2012-13 | Aston Villa | 0 | 0 | 3 | 0 |

**CLARK, Ciaran (D)** 64 5
H: 6 2 W: 12 00 b.Harrow 26-9-89
*Source:* Scholar. *Honours:* England Youth, Under-20. Eire 6 full caps, 1 goal.

| | | | | | |
|---|---|--:|--:|--:|--:|
| 2008-09 | Aston Villa | 0 | 0 | | |
| 2009-10 | Aston Villa | 1 | 0 | | |
| 2010-11 | Aston Villa | 19 | 3 | | |
| 2011-12 | Aston Villa | 15 | 1 | | |
| 2012-13 | Aston Villa | 29 | 1 | 64 | 5 |

**CROOKS, Alfie (F)** 0 0
*Source:* Scholar.

| | | | |
|---|---|--:|--:|
| 2012-13 | Aston Villa | 0 | 0 |

**DELFOUNESO, Nathan (F)** 86 9
H: 6 1 W: 12 04 b.Birmingham 2-2-91
*Source:* Scholar. *Honours:* England Youth, Under-21.

| | | | | | |
|---|---|--:|--:|--:|--:|
| 2007-08 | Aston Villa | 0 | 0 | | |
| 2008-09 | Aston Villa | 4 | 0 | | |
| 2009-10 | Aston Villa | 9 | 1 | | |
| 2010-11 | Aston Villa | 11 | 1 | | |
| 2010-11 | *Burnley* | 11 | 1 | 11 | 1 |
| 2011-12 | Aston Villa | 6 | 0 | | |
| 2011-12 | *Leicester C* | 4 | 0 | 4 | 0 |
| 2012-13 | Aston Villa | 1 | 0 | 31 | 2 |
| 2012-13 | *Blackpool* | 40 | 6 | 40 | 6 |

**DELPH, Fabian (D)** 99 6
H: 5 8 W: 11 00 b.Bradford 21-11-89
*Source:* Scholar. *Honours:* England Youth, Under-21.

| | | | | | |
|---|---|--:|--:|--:|--:|
| 2006-07 | Leeds U | 1 | 0 | | |
| 2007-08 | Leeds U | 1 | 0 | | |
| 2008-09 | Leeds U | 42 | 6 | | |
| 2009-10 | Aston Villa | 8 | 0 | | |
| 2010-11 | Aston Villa | 7 | 0 | | |
| 2011-12 | Aston Villa | 11 | 0 | | |
| 2011-12 | *Leeds U* | 5 | 0 | 49 | 6 |
| 2012-13 | Aston Villa | 24 | 0 | 50 | 0 |

**DEMPSEY, Robin (D)** 0 0
b. 1-2-96
*Source:* Scholar. *Honours:* Republic of Ireland Youth.

| | | | |
|---|---|--:|--:|
| 2012-13 | Aston Villa | 0 | 0 |

**DONACIEN, Janoi (D)** 0 0
b.St Lucia

| | | | |
|---|---|--:|--:|
| 2011-12 | Aston Villa | 0 | 0 |
| 2012-13 | Aston Villa | 0 | 0 |

**DRENNAN, Michael (F)** 0 0
b.Kilkenny 2-2-94
*Source:* Scholar. *Honours:* Eire Youth.

| | | | |
|---|---|--:|--:|
| 2010-11 | Aston Villa | 0 | 0 |
| 2011-12 | Aston Villa | 0 | 0 |
| 2012-13 | Aston Villa | 0 | 0 |

**DUNNE, Richard (D)** 451 12
H: 6 2 W: 15 10 b.Dublin 21-9-79
*Source:* Trainee. *Honours:* Eire Schools, Youth, Under-21, B, 77 full caps, 8 goals.

| | | | | | |
|---|---|--:|--:|--:|--:|
| 1996-97 | Everton | 7 | 0 | | |
| 1997-98 | Everton | 3 | 0 | | |
| 1998-99 | Everton | 16 | 0 | | |
| 1999-2000 | Everton | 31 | 0 | | |
| 2000-01 | Everton | 3 | 0 | 60 | 0 |
| 2000-01 | Manchester C | 25 | 0 | | |
| 2001-02 | Manchester C | 43 | 1 | | |
| 2002-03 | Manchester C | 25 | 0 | | |
| 2003-04 | Manchester C | 29 | 0 | | |
| 2004-05 | Manchester C | 35 | 2 | | |
| 2005-06 | Manchester C | 32 | 3 | | |
| 2006-07 | Manchester C | 38 | 1 | | |
| 2007-08 | Manchester C | 36 | 0 | | |
| 2008-09 | Manchester C | 31 | 1 | | |
| 2009-10 | Manchester C | 2 | 0 | 296 | 8 |
| 2009-10 | Aston Villa | 35 | 3 | | |
| 2010-11 | Aston Villa | 32 | 0 | | |
| 2011-12 | Aston Villa | 28 | 1 | | |
| 2012-13 | Aston Villa | 0 | 0 | 95 | 4 |

**EL AHMADI, Karim (M)** 203 8
H: 6 1 W: 12 03 b.Enschede 27-1-85
*Honours:* Morroco Youth, 19 full caps, 1 goal.

| | | | | | |
|---|---|--:|--:|--:|--:|
| 2003-04 | FC Twente | 7 | 0 | | |
| 2004-05 | FC Twente | 19 | 1 | | |
| 2005-06 | FC Twente | 8 | 0 | | |
| 2006-07 | FC Twente | 22 | 2 | | |
| 2007-08 | FC Twente | 33 | 0 | 89 | 3 |
| 2008-09 | Feyenoord | 22 | 2 | | |
| 2009-10 | Feyenoord | 26 | 0 | | |
| 2010-11 | Feyenoord | 15 | 0 | | |
| 2011-12 | Feyenoord | 31 | 2 | 94 | 4 |
| 2012-13 | Aston Villa | 20 | 1 | 20 | 1 |

**GARDNER, Gary (M)** 20 1
H: 6 2 W: 12 13 b.Solihull 29-6-92
*Source:* Scholar. *Honours:* England Youth, Under-20, Under-21.

| | | | | | |
|---|---|--:|--:|--:|--:|
| 2009-10 | Aston Villa | 0 | 0 | | |
| 2010-11 | Aston Villa | 0 | 0 | | |
| 2011-12 | Aston Villa | 14 | 0 | | |
| 2011-12 | *Coventry C* | 4 | 1 | 4 | 1 |
| 2012-13 | Aston Villa | 2 | 0 | 16 | 0 |

**GIVEN, Shay (G)** 462 0
H: 6 0 W: 13 03 b.Lifford 20-4-76
*Source:* Celtic. *Honours:* Eire Youth, Under-21, 125 full caps.

| | | | | | |
|---|---|--:|--:|--:|--:|
| 1994-95 | Blackburn R | 0 | 0 | | |
| 1994-95 | *Swindon T* | 0 | 0 | | |
| 1995-96 | Blackburn R | 0 | 0 | | |
| 1995-96 | *Swindon T* | 5 | 0 | 5 | 0 |
| 1995-96 | *Sunderland* | 17 | 0 | 17 | 0 |
| 1996-97 | Blackburn R | 2 | 0 | 2 | 0 |
| 1997-98 | Newcastle U | 24 | 0 | | |
| 1998-99 | Newcastle U | 31 | 0 | | |
| 1999-2000 | Newcastle U | 14 | 0 | | |
| 2000-01 | Newcastle U | 34 | 0 | | |
| 2001-02 | Newcastle U | 38 | 0 | | |
| 2002-03 | Newcastle U | 38 | 0 | | |
| 2003-04 | Newcastle U | 38 | 0 | | |
| 2004-05 | Newcastle U | 36 | 0 | | |
| 2005-06 | Newcastle U | 38 | 0 | | |
| 2006-07 | Newcastle U | 22 | 0 | | |
| 2007-08 | Newcastle U | 19 | 0 | | |
| 2008-09 | Newcastle U | 22 | 0 | 354 | 0 |
| 2008-09 | Manchester C | 15 | 0 | | |
| 2009-10 | Manchester C | 35 | 0 | | |
| 2010-11 | Manchester C | 0 | 0 | 50 | 0 |
| 2011-12 | Aston Villa | 32 | 0 | | |
| 2012-13 | Aston Villa | 2 | 0 | 34 | 0 |

**GRAHAM, Jordan (M)** 0 0
b.Coventry 5-3-95
*Source:* Scholar.

| | | | |
|---|---|--:|--:|
| 2011-12 | Aston Villa | 0 | 0 |
| 2012-13 | Aston Villa | 0 | 0 |

**GRANT, Aidan (G)** 0 0
H: 6 0 b.South Shields 27-3-95
*Source:* Newcastle U.

| | | | |
|---|---|--:|--:|
| 2012-13 | Aston Villa | 0 | 0 |

**GREALISH, Jack (M)** 0 0
b.Birmingham 10-9-95
*Source:* Scholar. *Honours:* Republic of Ireland Youth.

| | | | |
|---|---|--:|--:|
| 2012-13 | Aston Villa | 0 | 0 |

**GUZAN, Brad (G)** 139 0
H: 6 4 W: 14 11 b.Chicago 9-9-84
*Honours:* USA 22 full caps.

| | | | | | |
|---|---|--:|--:|--:|--:|
| 2005 | Chivas USA | 24 | 0 | | |
| 2006 | Chivas USA | 13 | 0 | | |
| 2007 | Chivas USA | 27 | 0 | | |
| 2008 | Chivas USA | 15 | 0 | 79 | 0 |
| 2008-09 | Aston Villa | 1 | 0 | | |
| 2009-10 | Aston Villa | 0 | 0 | | |
| 2010-11 | Aston Villa | 0 | 0 | | |
| 2010-11 | *Hull C* | 16 | 0 | 16 | 0 |
| 2011-12 | Aston Villa | 7 | 0 | | |
| 2012-13 | Aston Villa | 36 | 0 | 44 | 0 |

**HERD, Chris (M)** 69 7
H: 5 9 W: 11 04 b.Perth 4-4-89
*Source:* Scholar. *Honours:* Australia Youth.

| | | | | | |
|---|---|--:|--:|--:|--:|
| 2007-08 | Aston Villa | 0 | 0 | | |
| 2007-08 | *Port Vale* | 11 | 2 | 11 | 2 |
| 2007-08 | *Wycombe W* | 4 | 0 | 4 | 0 |
| 2008-09 | Aston Villa | 0 | 0 | | |
| 2009-10 | Aston Villa | 0 | 0 | | |
| 2009-10 | *Lincoln C* | 20 | 4 | 20 | 4 |
| 2010-11 | Aston Villa | 0 | 0 | | |
| 2011-12 | Aston Villa | 19 | 1 | | |
| 2012-13 | Aston Villa | 9 | 0 | 34 | 1 |

**HOLMAN, Brett (M)** 230 61
H: 5 10 W: 11 10 b.Bankstown 27-3-84
*Honours:* Australia Youth, Under-23, 53 full caps, 8 goals.

| | | | | | |
|---|---|--:|--:|--:|--:|
| 2002-03 | Excelsior | 29 | 6 | | |
| 2004-05 | Excelsior | 10 | 12 | | |
| 2005-06 | Excelsior | 11 | 14 | 50 | 32 |
| 2006-07 | NEC | 32 | 7 | | |
| 2007-08 | NEC | 27 | 6 | 59 | 13 |
| 2008-09 | AZ | 15 | 1 | | |
| 2009-10 | AZ | 23 | 5 | | |
| 2010-11 | AZ | 26 | 4 | | |
| 2011-12 | AZ | 30 | 5 | 94 | 15 |
| 2012-13 | Aston Villa | 27 | 1 | 27 | 1 |

**HUTTON, Alan (D)** 199 3
H: 6 1 W: 11 05 b.Glasgow 30-11-84
*Honours:* Scotland Under-21, 32 full caps.

| | | | | | |
|---|---|--:|--:|--:|--:|
| 2004-05 | Rangers | 10 | 0 | | |
| 2005-06 | Rangers | 19 | 0 | | |
| 2006-07 | Rangers | 33 | 1 | | |
| 2007-08 | Rangers | 20 | 0 | 82 | 1 |
| 2007-08 | Tottenham H | 14 | 0 | | |
| 2008-09 | Tottenham H | 8 | 0 | | |
| 2009-10 | Tottenham H | 8 | 0 | | |
| 2009-10 | *Sunderland* | 11 | 0 | 11 | 0 |
| 2010-11 | Tottenham H | 21 | 2 | | |
| 2011-12 | Tottenham H | 0 | 0 | 51 | 2 |
| 2011-12 | Aston Villa | 31 | 0 | | |
| 2012-13 | Aston Villa | 0 | 0 | 31 | 0 |
| 2012-13 | *Nottingham F* | 7 | 0 | 7 | 0 |
| 2012-13 | *Mallorca* | 17 | 0 | 17 | 0 |

**IRELAND, Stephen (F)** 187 17
H: 5 8 W: 10 07 b.Cork 22-8-86
*Source:* Scholar. *Honours:* Eire Youth, Under-21, 6 full caps, 4 goals.

| | | | | | |
|---|---|--:|--:|--:|--:|
| 2005-06 | Manchester C | 24 | 0 | | |
| 2006-07 | Manchester C | 24 | 1 | | |
| 2007-08 | Manchester C | 33 | 4 | | |
| 2008-09 | Manchester C | 35 | 9 | | |
| 2009-10 | Manchester C | 22 | 2 | | |
| 2010-11 | Manchester C | 0 | 0 | 138 | 16 |
| 2010-11 | Aston Villa | 10 | 0 | | |
| 2010-11 | *Newcastle U* | 2 | 0 | 2 | 0 |
| 2011-12 | Aston Villa | 24 | 1 | | |
| 2012-13 | Aston Villa | 13 | 0 | 47 | 1 |

**JOHNSON, Daniel (M)** 5 0
H: 5 8 W: 10 07 b.Kingston, Jam 8-10-92
*Source:* Scholar.

| | | | | | |
|---|---|--:|--:|--:|--:|
| 2010-11 | Aston Villa | 0 | 0 | | |
| 2011-12 | Aston Villa | 0 | 0 | | |
| 2012-13 | Aston Villa | 0 | 0 | | |
| 2012-13 | *Yeovil T* | 5 | 0 | 5 | 0 |

**LICHAJ, Eric (D)**    63   2
H: 5 11   W: 12 07   b.Chicago 17-11-88
*Source:* Univ of North Carolina, Chicago Magic. *Honours:* USA 8 full caps.

| | | | | | |
|---|---|---|---|---|---|
| 2007-08 | Aston Villa | 0 | 0 | | |
| 2008-09 | Aston Villa | 0 | 0 | | |
| 2009-10 | Aston Villa | 0 | 0 | | |
| 2009-10 | Lincoln C | 6 | 0 | 6 | 0 |
| 2009-10 | Leyton Orient | 9 | 1 | 9 | 1 |
| 2010-11 | Aston Villa | 5 | 0 | | |
| 2010-11 | Leeds U | 16 | 0 | 16 | 0 |
| 2011-12 | Aston Villa | 10 | 1 | | |
| 2012-13 | Aston Villa | 17 | 0 | 32 | 1 |

**LOWTON, Matt (M)**    120   12
H: 5 11   W: 12 04   b.Chesterfield 9-6-89
*Source:* Scholar.

| | | | | | |
|---|---|---|---|---|---|
| 2008-09 | Sheffield U | 0 | 0 | | |
| 2009-10 | Sheffield U | 2 | 0 | | |
| 2009-10 | Ferencvaros | 5 | 0 | 5 | 0 |
| 2010-11 | Sheffield U | 32 | 4 | | |
| 2011-12 | Sheffield U | 44 | 6 | 78 | 10 |
| 2012-13 | Aston Villa | 37 | 2 | 37 | 2 |

**MAKOUN, Jean II (M)**    328   30
H: 5 8   W: 10 12   b.Yaounde 29-5-83
*Honours:* Cameroon 62 full caps, 3 goals.

| | | | | | |
|---|---|---|---|---|---|
| 2001-02 | Lille B | 20 | 9 | | |
| 2002-03 | Lille B | 13 | 0 | 33 | 9 |
| 2002-03 | Lille | 10 | 0 | | |
| 2003-04 | Lille | 32 | 1 | | |
| 2004-05 | Lille | 33 | 0 | | |
| 2005-06 | Lille | 31 | 5 | | |
| 2006-07 | Lille | 33 | 1 | | |
| 2007-08 | Lille | 26 | 2 | 165 | 9 |
| 2008-09 | Lyon | 35 | 6 | | |
| 2009-10 | Lyon | 28 | 1 | | |
| 2010-11 | Lyon | 13 | 1 | 76 | 8 |
| 2010-11 | Aston Villa | 7 | 0 | | |
| 2011-12 | Aston Villa | 0 | 0 | | |
| 2011-12 | Olympiacos | 19 | 2 | 19 | 2 |
| 2012-13 | Aston Villa | 0 | 0 | 7 | 0 |
| 2012-13 | Rennes | 28 | 2 | 28 | 2 |

**MARSHALL, Andy (G)**    390   0
H: 6 3   W: 14 08   b.Bury St Edmunds 14-4-75
*Source:* Trainee. *Honours:* England Youth, Under-21.

| | | | | | |
|---|---|---|---|---|---|
| 1993-94 | Norwich C | 0 | 0 | | |
| 1994-95 | Norwich C | 21 | 0 | | |
| 1995-96 | Norwich C | 3 | 0 | | |
| 1996-97 | Norwich C | 7 | 0 | | |
| 1996-97 | Bournemouth | 11 | 0 | 11 | 0 |
| 1996-97 | Gillingham | 5 | 0 | 5 | 0 |
| 1997-98 | Norwich C | 42 | 0 | | |
| 1998-99 | Norwich C | 37 | 0 | | |
| 1999-2000 | Norwich C | 44 | 0 | | |
| 2000-01 | Norwich C | 41 | 0 | 195 | 0 |
| 2001-02 | Ipswich T | 13 | 0 | | |
| 2002-03 | Ipswich T | 40 | 0 | | |
| 2003-04 | Ipswich T | 0 | 0 | 53 | 0 |
| 2003-04 | Millwall | 16 | 0 | | |
| 2004-05 | Millwall | 22 | 0 | | |
| 2005-06 | Millwall | 29 | 0 | 67 | 0 |
| 2006-07 | Coventry C | 41 | 0 | | |
| 2007-08 | Coventry C | 16 | 0 | | |
| 2008-09 | Coventry C | 2 | 0 | 59 | 0 |
| 2009-10 | Aston Villa | 0 | 0 | | |
| 2010-11 | Aston Villa | 0 | 0 | | |
| 2011-12 | Aston Villa | 0 | 0 | | |
| 2012-13 | Aston Villa | 0 | 0 | | |

**N'ZOGBIA, Charles (M)**    251   28
H: 5 9   W: 11 00   b.Le Havre 28-5-86
*Honours:* France Youth, Under-21, 2 full caps, 1 goal.

| | | | | | |
|---|---|---|---|---|---|
| 2004-05 | Newcastle U | 14 | 0 | | |
| 2005-06 | Newcastle U | 32 | 5 | | |
| 2006-07 | Newcastle U | 22 | 0 | | |
| 2007-08 | Newcastle U | 31 | 3 | | |
| 2008-09 | Newcastle U | 18 | 1 | 117 | 9 |
| 2008-09 | Wigan Ath | 13 | 1 | | |
| 2009-10 | Wigan Ath | 34 | 8 | | |
| 2010-11 | Wigan Ath | 34 | 9 | 83 | 15 |
| 2011-12 | Aston Villa | 30 | 2 | | |
| 2012-13 | Aston Villa | 21 | 2 | 51 | 4 |

**PETROV, Stilian (M)**    451   65
H: 5 11   W: 11 09   b.Sofia 5-7-79
*Source:* FC Montana. *Honours:* Bulgaria 106 full caps, 8 goals.

| | | | | | |
|---|---|---|---|---|---|
| 1997-98 | CSKA Sofia | 10 | 0 | | |
| 1998-99 | CSKA Sofia | 29 | 3 | 39 | 3 |
| 1999-2000 | Celtic | 29 | 1 | | |
| 2000-01 | Celtic | 28 | 7 | | |
| 2001-02 | Celtic | 27 | 6 | | |
| 2002-03 | Celtic | 34 | 12 | | |
| 2003-04 | Celtic | 35 | 6 | | |
| 2004-05 | Celtic | 37 | 11 | | |
| 2005-06 | Celtic | 37 | 10 | 227 | 53 |
| 2006-07 | Aston Villa | 30 | 2 | | |
| 2007-08 | Aston Villa | 28 | 1 | | |
| 2008-09 | Aston Villa | 36 | 1 | | |
| 2009-10 | Aston Villa | 37 | 0 | | |
| 2010-11 | Aston Villa | 27 | 1 | | |
| 2011-12 | Aston Villa | 27 | 4 | | |
| 2012-13 | Aston Villa | 0 | 0 | 185 | 9 |

**SIEGRIST, Benjamin (G)**    0   0
H: 6 4   W: 13 05   b.Basle 31-1-92
*Source:* Scholar. *Honours:* Switzerland Youth.

| | | | |
|---|---|---|---|
| 2008-09 | Aston Villa | 0 | 0 |
| 2009-10 | Aston Villa | 0 | 0 |
| 2010-11 | Aston Villa | 0 | 0 |
| 2011-12 | Aston Villa | 0 | 0 |
| 2012-13 | Aston Villa | 0 | 0 |

**STEVENS, Enda (D)**    84   0
H: 6 0   W: 12 04   b.Dublin 9-7-90
*Honours:* Republic of Ireland Under-21.

| | | | | | |
|---|---|---|---|---|---|
| 2008 | UCD | 2 | 0 | 2 | 0 |
| 2009 | St Patrick's Ath | 30 | 0 | 30 | 0 |
| 2010 | Shamrock R | 18 | 0 | | |
| 2011 | Shamrock R | 27 | 0 | 45 | 0 |
| 2011-12 | Aston Villa | 0 | 0 | | |
| 2012-13 | Aston Villa | 7 | 0 | 7 | 0 |

**STIEBER, Andras (M)**    0   0
b.Zarvar 8-10-91

| | | | |
|---|---|---|---|
| 2010-11 | Aston Villa | 0 | 0 |
| 2011-12 | Aston Villa | 0 | 0 |
| 2012-13 | Aston Villa | 0 | 0 |

**SYLLA, Yacouba (M)**    75   0
H: 6 0   W: 12 07   b.Etampes 29-11-90

| | | | | | |
|---|---|---|---|---|---|
| 2010-11 | Clermont Foot | 20 | 0 | | |
| 2011-12 | Clermont Foot | 23 | 0 | | |
| 2012-13 | Clermont Foot | 21 | 0 | 64 | 0 |
| 2012-13 | Aston Villa | 11 | 0 | 11 | 0 |

**VLAAR, Ron (D)**    169   10
H: 5 11   W: 12 05   b.Hensbroek 16-2-85
*Honours:* Holland Under-21, 16 full caps, 1 goal.

| | | | | | |
|---|---|---|---|---|---|
| 2004-05 | AZ | 3 | 0 | | |
| 2005-06 | AZ | 7 | 0 | 10 | 0 |
| 2005-06 | Feyenoord | 16 | 0 | | |
| 2006-07 | Feyenoord | 20 | 1 | | |
| 2007-08 | Feyenoord | 4 | 1 | | |
| 2009-10 | Feyenoord | 32 | 4 | | |
| 2010-11 | Feyenoord | 26 | 2 | | |
| 2011-12 | Feyenoord | 34 | 0 | | |
| 2012-13 | Feyenoord | 0 | 0 | 132 | 8 |
| 2012-13 | Aston Villa | 27 | 2 | 27 | 2 |

**WEIMANN, Andreas (F)**    66   13
H: 5 9   W: 11 09   b.Vienna 5-8-91
*Source:* Scholar. *Honours:* Austria Under-21, 6 full caps.

| | | | | | |
|---|---|---|---|---|---|
| 2008-09 | Aston Villa | 0 | 0 | | |
| 2009-10 | Aston Villa | 0 | 0 | | |
| 2010-11 | Aston Villa | 1 | 0 | | |
| 2010-11 | Watford | 18 | 4 | | |
| 2011-12 | Aston Villa | 14 | 2 | | |
| 2011-12 | Watford | 3 | 0 | 21 | 4 |
| 2012-13 | Aston Villa | 30 | 7 | 45 | 9 |

**WESTWOOD, Ashley (M)**    158   14
H: 5 10   W: 11 00   b.Nantwich 1-4-90
*Source:* Scholar.

| | | | | | |
|---|---|---|---|---|---|
| 2008-09 | Crewe Alex | 2 | 0 | | |
| 2009-10 | Crewe Alex | 36 | 6 | | |
| 2010-11 | Crewe Alex | 46 | 5 | | |
| 2011-12 | Crewe Alex | 41 | 3 | | |
| 2012-13 | Crewe Alex | 0 | 0 | 128 | 14 |
| 2012-13 | Aston Villa | 30 | 0 | 30 | 0 |

**WILLIAMS, Derrick (D)**    1   0
H: 5 11   W: 11 11   b.Waterford 17-1-93
*Source:* Scholar. *Honours:* Eire Youth, Under-21.

| | | | | | |
|---|---|---|---|---|---|
| 2009-10 | Aston Villa | 0 | 0 | | |
| 2010-11 | Aston Villa | 0 | 0 | | |
| 2011-12 | Aston Villa | 0 | 0 | | |
| 2012-13 | Aston Villa | 1 | 0 | 1 | 0 |

**Scholars**
Bateman, Liam Vere; Calder, Riccardo; Cowans, Henry Gordon Mander; Hill, Craig Dennis; Kinsella, Lewis; Lewis, Bradley; Lyden, Jordan; O'Brien, Daniel William; Robinson, Callum Jack; Sellars, Jerell; Strain, Thomas James; Toner, Kevin Stephen; Watkins, Bradley; Webb, Joshua John; Wildin, Courtney James; Zazrivec, Tomas.

# BARNET (6)

**ABDULLA, Ahmed (M)**    6   0
H: 5 8   W: 10 11   b.Saudi Arabia 12-11-91

| | | | | | |
|---|---|---|---|---|---|
| 2011-12 | Swindon T | 0 | 0 | | |
| 2011-12 | Dagenham & R | 0 | 0 | | |
| 2012-13 | Barnet | 6 | 0 | 6 | 0 |

**ALLEN, Iffy (M)**    2   0
H: 5 9   b.Lambeth 15-3-94

| | | | | | |
|---|---|---|---|---|---|
| 2012-13 | Barnet | 2 | 0 | 2 | 0 |

**ATIENO, Taiwo (F)**    135   24
H: 6 2   W: 12 13   b.Brixton 6-8-85
*Source:* Scholar.

| | | | | | |
|---|---|---|---|---|---|
| 2003-04 | Walsall | 3 | 0 | | |
| 2004-05 | Walsall | 0 | 0 | | |
| 2004-05 | Rochdale | 13 | 2 | 13 | 2 |
| 2004-05 | Chester C | 4 | 1 | 4 | 1 |
| 2005-06 | Walsall | 2 | 0 | 5 | 0 |
| 2005-06 | Darlington | 3 | 0 | 3 | 0 |
| 2007 | Puerto Rico Is | 10 | 5 | | |
| 2008 | Puerto Rico Is | 22 | 4 | 32 | 9 |

From Charleston Battery.

| | | | | | |
|---|---|---|---|---|---|
| 2009 | Rochester Rhinos | 17 | 2 | 17 | 2 |
| 2010-11 | Luton T | 13 | 3 | 13 | 3 |
| 2010-11 | Stevenage | 1 | 0 | 1 | 0 |
| 2011-12 | Torquay U | 43 | 6 | | |
| 2012-13 | Torquay U | 0 | 0 | 43 | 6 |
| 2012-13 | Barnet | 4 | 1 | 4 | 1 |

**BEATTIE, Craig (F)**    173   32
H: 6 0   W: 11 07   b.Glasgow 16-1-84
*Honours:* Scotland Under-21, 7 full caps, 1 goal.

| | | | | | |
|---|---|---|---|---|---|
| 2003-04 | Celtic | 10 | 1 | | |
| 2004-05 | Celtic | 11 | 4 | | |
| 2005-06 | Celtic | 14 | 6 | | |
| 2006-07 | Celtic | 16 | 2 | 51 | 13 |
| 2007-08 | WBA | 21 | 3 | | |
| 2007-08 | Preston NE | 2 | 0 | 2 | 0 |
| 2008-09 | WBA | 7 | 1 | | |
| 2008-09 | Crystal Palace | 15 | 5 | 15 | 5 |
| 2008-09 | Sheffield U | 13 | 1 | 13 | 1 |
| 2009-10 | WBA | 3 | 0 | 31 | 4 |
| 2009-10 | Swansea C | 23 | 3 | | |
| 2010-11 | Swansea C | 22 | 4 | | |
| 2011-12 | Swansea C | 0 | 0 | 45 | 7 |
| 2011-12 | Watford | 4 | 1 | 4 | 1 |
| 2011-12 | Hearts | 5 | 1 | 5 | 1 |
| 2012-13 | St Johnstone | 2 | 0 | 2 | 0 |
| 2012-13 | Barnet | 5 | 0 | 5 | 0 |

**BROWN, Jordan (D)**    31   0
H: 5 10   W: 12 00   b.Benfleet 11-10-91
*Source:* Scholar.

| | | | | | |
|---|---|---|---|---|---|
| 2010-11 | West Ham U | 0 | 0 | | |
| 2011-12 | West Ham U | 0 | 0 | | |
| 2011-12 | Aldershot T | 3 | 0 | 3 | 0 |
| 2011-12 | Crewe Alex | 7 | 0 | 7 | 0 |
| 2012-13 | Barnet | 21 | 0 | 21 | 0 |

**BYRNE, Mark (M)**    113   14
H: 5 9   W: 11 00   b.Dublin 9-11-88
*Source:* Crumlin U.

| | | | |
|---|---|---|---|
| 2006-07 | Nottingham F | 0 | 0 |
| 2007-08 | Nottingham F | 1 | 0 |
| 2008-09 | Nottingham F | 1 | 0 |
| 2009-10 | Nottingham F | 0 | 0 |

| 2010-11 | Nottingham F | 0 | 0 | 2 | 0 |
|---|---|---|---|---|---|
| 2010-11 | Barnet | 28 | 6 | | |
| 2011-12 | Barnet | 43 | 5 | | |
| 2012-13 | Barnet | 40 | 3 | 111 | 14 |

**COWLER, Sam (G)** 2 0
H: 6 3  W: 11 00  b.Colchester 26-10-92

| 2012-13 | Barnet | 2 | 0 | 2 | 0 |
|---|---|---|---|---|---|

**CRAWFORD, Harry (F)** 43 4
H: 6 1  W: 12 04  b.Watford 10-12-91
*Source:* Scholar.

| 2009-10 | Southend U | 7 | 1 | | |
|---|---|---|---|---|---|
| 2010-11 | Southend U | 23 | 2 | | |
| 2011-12 | Southend U | 3 | 0 | | |
| 2012-13 | Southend U | 0 | 0 | 33 | 3 |
| 2012-13 | Barnet | 10 | 1 | 10 | 1 |

**DAVIDS, Edgar (M)** 414 36
H: 5 6  W: 10 09  b.Paramaribo (Suriname) 13-3-73
*Honours:* Holland Under-21, 74 full caps, 6 goals.

| 1991-92 | Ajax | 13 | 9 | | |
|---|---|---|---|---|---|
| 1992-93 | Ajax | 28 | 1 | | |
| 1993-94 | Ajax | 15 | 2 | | |
| 1994-95 | Ajax | 22 | 5 | | |
| 1995-96 | Ajax | 28 | 7 | | |
| 1996-97 | AC Milan | 15 | 0 | | |
| 1997-98 | AC Milan | 3 | 0 | 18 | 0 |
| 1997-98 | Juventus | 20 | 1 | | |
| 1998-99 | Juventus | 27 | 1 | | |
| 1999-2000 | Juventus | 27 | 1 | | |
| 2000-01 | Juventus | 26 | 1 | | |
| 2001-02 | Juventus | 28 | 2 | | |
| 2002-03 | Juventus | 26 | 1 | | |
| 2003-04 | Juventus | 5 | 0 | 159 | 8 |
| 2003-04 | Barcelona | 18 | 1 | 18 | 1 |
| 2004-05 | Inter Milan | 14 | 0 | 14 | 0 |
| 2005-06 | Tottenham H | 31 | 1 | | |
| 2006-07 | Tottenham H | 9 | 0 | 40 | 1 |
| 2006-07 | Ajax | 11 | 1 | | |
| 2007-08 | Ajax | 14 | 0 | 131 | 25 |
| 2010-11 | Crystal Palace | 6 | 0 | 6 | 0 |
| 2012-13 | Barnet | 28 | 1 | 28 | 1 |

**EDGAR, Anthony (M)** 24 2
H: 5 8  W: 11 00  b.Newham 30-9-90
*Source:* Scholar.

| 2009-10 | West Ham U | 0 | 0 | | |
|---|---|---|---|---|---|
| 2009-10 | Bournemouth | 3 | 0 | 3 | 0 |
| 2010-11 | West Ham U | 0 | 0 | | |
| 2011-12 | Yeovil T | 10 | 1 | 10 | 1 |
| 2012-13 | Barnet | 11 | 1 | 11 | 1 |

**FULLER, Barry (D)** 188 1
H: 5 10  W: 11 10  b.Ashford 25-9-84
*Source:* Scholar.

| 2004-05 | Charlton Ath | 0 | 0 | | |
|---|---|---|---|---|---|
| 2005-06 | Charlton Ath | 0 | 0 | | |
| 2005-06 | Barnet | 15 | 1 | | |

From Stevenage B.

| 2007-08 | Gillingham | 10 | 0 | | |
|---|---|---|---|---|---|
| 2008-09 | Gillingham | 37 | 0 | | |
| 2009-10 | Gillingham | 36 | 0 | | |
| 2010-11 | Gillingham | 42 | 0 | | |
| 2011-12 | Gillingham | 9 | 0 | | |
| 2012-13 | Gillingham | 0 | 0 | 134 | 0 |
| 2012-13 | Barnet | 39 | 0 | 54 | 1 |

**GAMBIN, Luke (M)** 11 2
b.Surrey 16-3-93
*Source:* Scholar.

| 2011-12 | Barnet | 1 | 0 | | |
|---|---|---|---|---|---|
| 2012-13 | Barnet | 10 | 2 | 11 | 2 |

**HOLMES, Ricky (M)** 91 15
H: 6 2  W: 11 11  b.Southend 19-6-87
*Source:* Southend U, Chelmsford C.

| 2010-11 | Barnet | 25 | 2 | | |
|---|---|---|---|---|---|
| 2011-12 | Barnet | 41 | 8 | | |
| 2012-13 | Barnet | 25 | 5 | 91 | 15 |

**HOLWIJN, Melvin (F)** 124 40
H: 5 11  W: 11 10  b.Amsterdam 2-1-80

| 1998-99 | Stormvogels Telstar | 19 | 2 | | |
|---|---|---|---|---|---|
| 1999-2000 | Stormvogels Telstar | 21 | 3 | | |
| 2000-01 | Stormvogels Telstar | 27 | 9 | | |
| 2002-03 | FC Volendam | 1 | 1 | 1 | 1 |
| 2003-04 | Iraklis | 13 | 0 | | |
| 2004-05 | Iraklis | 4 | 0 | 17 | 0 |
| 2006-07 | Stormvogels Telstar | 10 | 14 | | |
| 2007-08 | Stormvogels Telstar | 5 | 7 | | |
| 2008-09 | Stormvogels Telstar | 2 | 2 | | |
| 2010-11 | Stormvogels Telstar | 2 | 2 | | |
| 2011-12 | Stormvogels Telstar | 19 | 0 | 105 | 39 |
| 2012-13 | Barnet | 1 | 0 | 1 | 0 |

**HYDE, Jake (F)** 104 29
H: 6 1  W: 13 02  b.Slough 1-7-90
*Source:* Swindon T.

| 2009-10 | Barnet | 34 | 6 | | |
|---|---|---|---|---|---|
| 2010-11 | Dundee | 2 | 3 | | |
| 2010-11 | Dunfermline Ath | 2 | 0 | 2 | 0 |
| 2011-12 | Dundee | 26 | 6 | 28 | 9 |
| 2012-13 | Barnet | 40 | 14 | 74 | 20 |

**JOHN, Collins (F)** 179 36
H: 5 11  W: 12 03  b.Zwandru (Lib) 7-10-85
*Honours:* Holland Under-21, 2 full caps.

| 2002-03 | FC Twente | 17 | 2 | | |
|---|---|---|---|---|---|
| 2003-04 | FC Twente | 18 | 9 | 35 | 11 |
| 2003-04 | Fulham | 8 | 4 | | |
| 2004-05 | Fulham | 27 | 4 | | |
| 2005-06 | Fulham | 35 | 11 | | |
| 2006-07 | Fulham | 23 | 1 | | |
| 2007-08 | Fulham | 2 | 0 | | |
| 2007-08 | Leicester C | 11 | 2 | 11 | 2 |
| 2007-08 | Watford | 5 | 0 | 5 | 0 |
| 2008-09 | Fulham | 0 | 0 | 95 | 20 |
| 2008-09 | NEC | 5 | 0 | 5 | 0 |
| 2009-10 | Roeselare | 11 | 0 | 11 | 0 |
| 2009-10 | Chicago Fire | 7 | 1 | | |
| 2010-11 | Chicago Fire | 9 | 2 | 16 | 3 |
| 2012-13 | Barnet | 1 | 0 | 1 | 0 |

**JOHNSON, Elliot (D)** 26 1
b.Edgware 17-8-94

| 2012-13 | Barnet | 26 | 1 | 26 | 1 |
|---|---|---|---|---|---|

**KABBA, Steven (F)** 219 46
H: 5 10  W: 11 03  b.Lambeth 7-3-81
*Source:* Trainee.

| 1999-2000 | Crystal Palace | 1 | 0 | | |
|---|---|---|---|---|---|
| 2000-01 | Crystal Palace | 1 | 0 | | |
| 2001-02 | Crystal Palace | 4 | 0 | | |
| 2001-02 | Luton T | 3 | 0 | 3 | 0 |
| 2002-03 | Crystal Palace | 4 | 1 | 10 | 1 |
| 2002-03 | Grimsby T | 13 | 6 | 13 | 6 |
| 2002-03 | Sheffield U | 25 | 7 | | |
| 2003-04 | Sheffield U | 1 | 0 | | |
| 2004-05 | Sheffield U | 11 | 2 | | |
| 2005-06 | Sheffield U | 34 | 9 | | |
| 2006-07 | Sheffield U | 7 | 0 | 78 | 18 |
| 2006-07 | Watford | 11 | 0 | | |
| 2007-08 | Watford | 14 | 1 | | |
| 2008-09 | Watford | 0 | 0 | 25 | 1 |
| 2008-09 | Blackpool | 17 | 2 | 17 | 2 |
| 2008-09 | Oldham Ath | 8 | 0 | 8 | 0 |
| 2009-10 | Brentford | 10 | 0 | 10 | 0 |
| 2009-10 | Burton Alb | 23 | 6 | 23 | 6 |
| 2010-11 | Barnet | 23 | 11 | | |
| 2011-12 | Barnet | 9 | 1 | | |
| 2012-13 | Barnet | 0 | 0 | 32 | 12 |

**KAMARA, Ishmail (F)** 1 0
H: 6 1

| 2012-13 | Barnet | 1 | 0 | 1 | 0 |
|---|---|---|---|---|---|

**KAMDJO, Clovis (D)** 114 5
H: 5 11  W: 12 02  b.Cameroon 15-12-90
*Source:* Reading Youth. *Honours:* Cameroon Youth.

| 2009-10 | Barnet | 15 | 0 | | |
|---|---|---|---|---|---|
| 2010-11 | Barnet | 32 | 1 | | |
| 2011-12 | Barnet | 41 | 3 | | |
| 2012-13 | Barnet | 26 | 1 | 114 | 5 |

**KUIPERS, Michels (G)** 281 0
H: 6 2  W: 14 03  b.Amsterdam 26-6-74
*Source:* SDW Amsterdam.

| 1998-99 | Bristol R | 1 | 0 | | |
|---|---|---|---|---|---|
| 1999-2000 | Bristol R | 0 | 0 | 1 | 0 |
| 2000-01 | Brighton & HA | 34 | 0 | | |
| 2001-02 | Brighton & HA | 39 | 0 | | |
| 2002-03 | Brighton & HA | 21 | 0 | | |
| 2003-04 | Brighton & HA | 10 | 0 | | |
| 2003-04 | Hull C | 3 | 0 | 3 | 0 |
| 2004-05 | Brighton & HA | 30 | 0 | | |
| 2005-06 | Brighton & HA | 5 | 0 | | |
| 2005-06 | Boston U | 15 | 0 | 15 | 0 |
| 2006-07 | Brighton & HA | 14 | 0 | | |
| 2007-08 | Brighton & HA | 46 | 0 | | |
| 2008-09 | Brighton & HA | 28 | 0 | | |
| 2009-10 | Brighton & HA | 20 | 0 | | |
| 2010-11 | Brighton & HA | 0 | 0 | 247 | 0 |
| 2011-12 | Crawley T | 15 | 0 | | |
| 2012-13 | Crawley T | 0 | 0 | 15 | 0 |
| 2012-13 | Barnet | 0 | 0 | | |

**LOWE, Jamal (F)** 8 0
H: 6 0  b.27-1-94

| 2012-13 | Barnet | 8 | 0 | 8 | 0 |
|---|---|---|---|---|---|

**MARSH-BROWN, Keanu (F)** 66 5
H: 5 11  W: 12 04  b.Hammersmith 10-8-92
*Source:* Scholar.

| 2009-10 | Fulham | 0 | 0 | | |
|---|---|---|---|---|---|
| 2010-11 | Fulham | 0 | 0 | | |
| 2010-11 | Milton Keynes D | 17 | 2 | 17 | 2 |
| 2010-11 | Dundee U | 1 | 0 | | |
| 2011-12 | Fulham | 0 | 0 | | |
| 2011-12 | Oldham Ath | 11 | 1 | 11 | 1 |
| 2011-12 | Dundee U | 11 | 0 | 12 | 0 |
| 2012-13 | Yeovil T | 21 | 1 | 21 | 1 |
| 2012-13 | Barnet | 5 | 1 | 5 | 1 |

**N'TOKO, Chiro (D)** 21 3
H: 6 3  W: 12 11  b.Kinshasa 31-1-88

| 2007-08 | AGOVV | 3 | 2 | | |
|---|---|---|---|---|---|
| 2008-09 | AGOVV | 1 | 0 | | |
| 2009-10 | AGOVV | 1 | 1 | 5 | 3 |
| 2010-11 | ADO Den Haag | 4 | 0 | | |
| 2011-12 | ADO Den Haag | 10 | 0 | 14 | 0 |
| 2012-13 | Barnet | 2 | 0 | 2 | 0 |

**NURSE, Jon (M)** 205 30
H: 5 9  W: 12 04  b.Barbados 1-3-81
*Source:* Stevenage B. *Honours:* Barbados 4 full caps.

| 2007-08 | Dagenham & R | 30 | 1 | | |
|---|---|---|---|---|---|
| 2008-09 | Dagenham & R | 34 | 4 | | |
| 2009-10 | Dagenham & R | 38 | 7 | | |
| 2010-11 | Dagenham & R | 38 | 10 | | |
| 2011-12 | Dagenham & R | 39 | 5 | 179 | 27 |
| 2012-13 | Barnet | 26 | 3 | 26 | 3 |

**O'BRIEN, Liam (G)** 21 0
H: 6 1  W: 12 06  b.Ruislip 30-11-91
*Source:* Scholar. *Honours:* England Youth.

| 2008-09 | Portsmouth | 0 | 0 | | |
|---|---|---|---|---|---|
| 2009-10 | Portsmouth | 0 | 0 | | |
| 2010-11 | Barnet | 8 | 0 | | |
| 2011-12 | Barnet | 10 | 0 | | |
| 2012-13 | Barnet | 3 | 0 | 21 | 0 |

**OSTER, John (M)** 420 26
H: 5 9  W: 10 08  b.Boston 8-12-78
*Source:* Trainee. *Honours:* Wales Youth, Under-21, B, 13 full caps.

| 1996-97 | Grimsby T | 24 | 3 | | |
|---|---|---|---|---|---|
| 1997-98 | Everton | 31 | 1 | | |
| 1998-99 | Everton | 9 | 0 | 40 | 1 |
| 1999-2000 | Sunderland | 10 | 0 | | |
| 2000-01 | Sunderland | 8 | 0 | | |
| 2001-02 | Sunderland | 0 | 0 | | |
| 2001-02 | Barnsley | 2 | 0 | 2 | 0 |
| 2002-03 | Sunderland | 3 | 0 | | |
| 2002-03 | Grimsby T | 17 | 6 | 41 | 9 |
| 2003-04 | Sunderland | 38 | 5 | | |
| 2004-05 | Sunderland | 9 | 0 | 68 | 5 |
| 2004-05 | Leeds U | 8 | 1 | 8 | 1 |
| 2004-05 | Burnley | 15 | 1 | 15 | 1 |
| 2005-06 | Reading | 33 | 1 | | |
| 2006-07 | Reading | 25 | 1 | | |
| 2007-08 | Reading | 18 | 0 | 76 | 2 |
| 2008-09 | Crystal Palace | 31 | 3 | 31 | 3 |
| 2009-10 | Doncaster R | 40 | 1 | | |
| 2010-11 | Doncaster R | 41 | 0 | | |
| 2011-12 | Doncaster R | 30 | 1 | | |
| 2012-13 | Doncaster R | 0 | 0 | 111 | 2 |
| 2012-13 | Barnet | 28 | 2 | 28 | 2 |

**SAVILLE, Jack (D)** 23 1
H: 6 3  W: 12 00  b.Camberley 2-4-91
*Source:* Chelsea Scholar.

| 2009-10 | Southampton | 0 | 0 | | |
|---|---|---|---|---|---|
| 2010-11 | Southampton | 0 | 0 | | |
| 2011-12 | Southampton | 0 | 0 | | |
| 2011-12 | Barnet | 17 | 0 | | |
| 2012-13 | Barnet | 6 | 1 | 23 | 1 |

**SENDA, Danny (D)**    388   10
H: 5 10   W: 10 02   b.Harrow 17-4-81
*Source:* Southampton Trainee. *Honours:*
England Youth.

| | | | | | |
|---|---|---|---|---|---|
| 1998-99 | Wycombe W | 6 | 0 | | |
| 1999-2000 | Wycombe W | 27 | 1 | | |
| 2000-01 | Wycombe W | 31 | 2 | | |
| 2001-02 | Wycombe W | 43 | 0 | | |
| 2002-03 | Wycombe W | 41 | 2 | | |
| 2003-04 | Wycombe W | 40 | 0 | | |
| 2004-05 | Wycombe W | 44 | 4 | | |
| 2005-06 | Wycombe W | 44 | 0 | 276 | 9 |
| 2006-07 | Millwall | 36 | 0 | | |
| 2007-08 | Millwall | 40 | 1 | | |
| 2008-09 | Millwall | 0 | 0 | 76 | 1 |
| 2010-11 | Torquay U | 2 | 0 | 2 | 0 |
| 2010-11 | Bristol R | 15 | 0 | 15 | 0 |
| 2011-12 | Barnet | 19 | 0 | | |
| 2012-13 | Barnet | 0 | 0 | 19 | 0 |

**STACK, Graham (G)**    144   0
H: 6 2   W: 12 06   b.Hampstead 26-9-81
*Honours:* Eire Youth, Under-21.

| | | | | | |
|---|---|---|---|---|---|
| 2004-05 | Arsenal | 0 | 0 | | |
| 2004-05 | *Millwall* | 26 | 0 | 26 | 0 |
| 2005-06 | Reading | 1 | 0 | | |
| 2006-07 | Reading | 0 | 0 | | |
| 2006-07 | *Leeds U* | 12 | 0 | 12 | 0 |
| 2007-08 | Reading | 0 | 0 | 1 | 0 |
| 2007-08 | *Wolverhampton W* | 2 | 0 | 2 | 0 |
| 2008-09 | Plymouth Arg | 5 | 0 | 5 | 0 |
| 2009-10 | Hibernian | 20 | 0 | | |
| 2010-11 | Hibernian | 6 | 0 | | |
| 2011-12 | Hibernian | 30 | 0 | 56 | 0 |
| 2012-13 | Barnet | 42 | 0 | 42 | 0 |

**STEPHENS, David (D)**    72   1
H: 5 10   W: 11 04   b.Welwyn Garden City
8-7-91
*Source:* Scholar. *Honours:* Wales Under-21.

| | | | | | |
|---|---|---|---|---|---|
| 2009-10 | Norwich C | 0 | 0 | | |
| 2009-10 | Lincoln C | 3 | 0 | 3 | 0 |
| 2010-11 | Hibernian | 10 | 0 | | |
| 2011-12 | Hibernian | 16 | 0 | | |
| 2012-13 | Hibernian | 1 | 0 | 27 | 0 |
| 2012-13 | Barnet | 42 | 1 | 42 | 1 |

**SYKES, George (F)**    3   0
H: 6 4   b.Buckhurst Hill 14-9-94

| | | | | | |
|---|---|---|---|---|---|
| 2012-13 | Barnet | 3 | 0 | 3 | 0 |

**VILHETE, Mauro (M)**    30   0
H: 5 8   W: 11 09   b.Sintra 10-5-93
*Source:* Scholar.

| | | | | | |
|---|---|---|---|---|---|
| 2009-10 | Barnet | 2 | 0 | | |
| 2010-11 | Barnet | 20 | 0 | | |
| 2011-12 | Barnet | 3 | 0 | | |
| 2012-13 | Barnet | 5 | 0 | 30 | 0 |

**VOSE, Dominic (M)**    2   0
b.Lambeth 23-11-93
*Source:* Academy.

| | | | | | |
|---|---|---|---|---|---|
| 2010-11 | West Ham U | 0 | 0 | | |
| 2011-12 | West Ham U | 0 | 0 | | |
| 2012-13 | Barnet | 2 | 0 | 2 | 0 |

**WARREN, Freddie (M)**    2   0
b.Barking 2-11-92
*Source:* Scholar.

| | | | | | |
|---|---|---|---|---|---|
| 2011-12 | Charlton Ath | 0 | 0 | | |
| 2012-13 | Barnet | 2 | 0 | 2 | 0 |

**WESTON, Curtis (M)**    221   17
H: 5 11   W: 11 09   b.Greenwich 24-1-87
*Source:* Scholar.

| | | | | | |
|---|---|---|---|---|---|
| 2003-04 | Millwall | 1 | 0 | | |
| 2004-05 | Millwall | 3 | 0 | | |
| 2005-06 | Millwall | 0 | 0 | 4 | 0 |
| 2006-07 | Swindon T | 27 | 1 | 27 | 1 |
| 2007-08 | Leeds U | 7 | 1 | | |
| 2007-08 | *Scunthorpe U* | 7 | 0 | 7 | 0 |
| 2008-09 | Leeds U | 0 | 0 | 7 | 1 |
| 2008-09 | Gillingham | 45 | 5 | | |
| 2009-10 | Gillingham | 39 | 6 | | |
| 2010-11 | Gillingham | 33 | 4 | | |
| 2011-12 | Gillingham | 30 | 0 | 147 | 15 |
| 2012-13 | Barnet | 29 | 0 | 29 | 0 |

**YIADOM, Andy (M)**    46   4
H: 5 11   W: 11 11   b.Holloway 2-12-91
*Source:* Watford Scholar, Hayes & Yeading
U, Braintree T.

| | | | | | |
|---|---|---|---|---|---|
| 2011-12 | Barnet | 7 | 1 | | |
| 2012-13 | Barnet | 39 | 3 | 46 | 4 |

**Scholars**
Abrahams, Tanasheh James Benjamin Vic;
Adewale-Duckrell, Ikponmwonsa
Nosagleagbon M; Allen, Ifeanyi Decosta;
Barnes, Dillon; Charles, James Robert;
Guthmy, Kamal Swalehdin; Hackett, Jamal
Dwayne; Khlaf, Zacharia James; Lowe, Jamal
Akua; McCluskey, George Timothy; Redley,
Ramario Nathaniel; Sykes, George Robert
James; Thomas, Ishmael Nathaniel.

# BARNSLEY (7)

**ALNWICK, Ben (G)**    57   0
H: 6 2   W: 13 12   b.Prudhoe 1-1-87
*Source:* Scholar. *Honours:* England Youth,
Under-21.

| | | | | | |
|---|---|---|---|---|---|
| 2003-04 | Sunderland | 0 | 0 | | |
| 2004-05 | Sunderland | 3 | 0 | | |
| 2005-06 | Sunderland | 5 | 0 | | |
| 2006-07 | Sunderland | 11 | 0 | 19 | 0 |
| 2006-07 | Tottenham H | 0 | 0 | | |
| 2007-08 | Tottenham H | 0 | 0 | | |
| 2007-08 | *Luton T* | 4 | 0 | 4 | 0 |
| 2007-08 | *Leicester C* | 8 | 0 | 8 | 0 |
| 2008-09 | Tottenham H | 0 | 0 | | |
| 2008-09 | *Carlisle U* | 6 | 0 | 6 | 0 |
| 2009-10 | Tottenham H | 1 | 0 | | |
| 2009-10 | *Norwich C* | 3 | 0 | 3 | 0 |
| 2010-11 | Tottenham H | 0 | 0 | | |
| 2010-11 | *Leeds U* | 0 | 0 | | |
| 2010-11 | *Doncaster R* | 0 | 0 | | |
| 2011-12 | Tottenham H | 0 | 0 | | |
| 2011-12 | *Leyton Orient* | 6 | 0 | 6 | 0 |
| 2012-13 | Tottenham H | 0 | 0 | 1 | 0 |
| 2012-13 | Barnsley | 10 | 0 | 10 | 0 |

**BOLAND, Antoine (M)**    0   0
b. 30-12-94
*Source:* Scholar.

| | | | |
|---|---|---|---|
| 2012-13 | Barnsley | 0 | 0 |

**CLARK, Jordan (F)**    8   0
H: 6 0   W: 11 07   b.Barnsley 22-9-93

| | | | | | |
|---|---|---|---|---|---|
| 2010-11 | Barnsley | 4 | 0 | | |
| 2011-12 | Barnsley | 2 | 0 | | |
| 2012-13 | Barnsley | 0 | 0 | 6 | 0 |
| 2012-13 | *Chesterfield* | 2 | 0 | 2 | 0 |

**CRANIE, Martin (D)**    208   1
H: 6 1   W: 12 09   b.Yeovil 23-9-86
*Source:* Scholar. *Honours:* England Youth,
Under-20, Under-21.

| | | | | | |
|---|---|---|---|---|---|
| 2003-04 | Southampton | 1 | 0 | | |
| 2004-05 | Southampton | 3 | 0 | | |
| 2004-05 | *Bournemouth* | 3 | 0 | 3 | 0 |
| 2005-06 | Southampton | 11 | 0 | | |
| 2006-07 | Southampton | 1 | 0 | 16 | 0 |
| 2006-07 | *Yeovil T* | 12 | 0 | 12 | 0 |
| 2007-08 | Portsmouth | 2 | 0 | | |
| 2007-08 | *QPR* | 6 | 0 | 6 | 0 |
| 2008-09 | Portsmouth | 0 | 0 | | |
| 2008-09 | *Charlton Ath* | 19 | 0 | 19 | 0 |
| 2009-10 | Portsmouth | 0 | 0 | 2 | 0 |
| 2009-10 | Coventry C | 40 | 1 | | |
| 2010-11 | Coventry C | 36 | 0 | | |
| 2011-12 | Coventry C | 38 | 0 | 114 | 1 |
| 2012-13 | Barnsley | 36 | 0 | 36 | 0 |

**CYWKA, Thomasz (M)**    81   10
H: 5 10   W: 11 09   b.Gliwice 27-6-88
*Source:* Gwarek Zabrze. *Honours:* Poland
Youth, Under-21.

| | | | | | |
|---|---|---|---|---|---|
| 2006-07 | Wigan Ath | 0 | 0 | | |
| 2006-07 | *Oldham Ath* | 4 | 0 | 4 | 0 |
| 2007-08 | Wigan Ath | 0 | 0 | | |
| 2008-09 | Wigan Ath | 0 | 0 | | |
| 2009-10 | Wigan Ath | 0 | 0 | | |
| 2009-10 | *Derby Co* | 5 | 0 | | |
| 2010-11 | *Derby Co* | 31 | 4 | | |

**2011-12   Derby Co   8   1   44   5**

| | | | | | |
|---|---|---|---|---|---|
| 2011-12 | Derby Co | 8 | 1 | 44 | 5 |
| 2011-12 | Reading | 4 | 0 | 4 | 0 |
| 2012-13 | Barnsley | 29 | 5 | 29 | 5 |

**DAGNALL, Chris (F)**    308   76
H: 5 8   W: 12 03   b.Liverpool 15-4-86
*Source:* Scholar.

| | | | | | |
|---|---|---|---|---|---|
| 2003-04 | Tranmere R | 10 | 1 | | |
| 2004-05 | Tranmere R | 23 | 6 | | |
| 2005-06 | Tranmere R | 6 | 0 | 39 | 7 |
| 2005-06 | Rochdale | 21 | 3 | | |
| 2006-07 | Rochdale | 37 | 17 | | |
| 2007-08 | Rochdale | 14 | 7 | | |
| 2008-09 | Rochdale | 40 | 7 | | |
| 2009-10 | Rochdale | 45 | 20 | 157 | 54 |
| 2010-11 | Scunthorpe U | 37 | 5 | | |
| 2011-12 | Scunthorpe U | 23 | 4 | 60 | 9 |
| 2011-12 | Barnsley | 9 | 0 | | |
| 2011-12 | *Bradford C* | 7 | 1 | 7 | 1 |
| 2012-13 | Barnsley | 36 | 5 | 45 | 5 |

**DAWSON, Stephen (M)**    309   17
H: 5 9   W: 11 09   b.Dublin 4-12-85
*Source:* Scholar. *Honours:* Eire Under-21.

| | | | | | |
|---|---|---|---|---|---|
| 2003-04 | Leicester C | 0 | 0 | | |
| 2004-05 | Leicester C | 0 | 0 | | |
| 2005-06 | Mansfield T | 40 | 1 | | |
| 2006-07 | Mansfield T | 34 | 1 | | |
| 2007-08 | Mansfield T | 43 | 2 | 117 | 4 |
| 2008-09 | Bury | 43 | 2 | | |
| 2009-10 | Bury | 45 | 4 | 88 | 6 |
| 2010-11 | Leyton Orient | 40 | 2 | | |
| 2011-12 | Leyton Orient | 20 | 1 | 60 | 3 |
| 2011-12 | Barnsley | 12 | 0 | | |
| 2012-13 | Barnsley | 32 | 4 | 44 | 4 |

**DONE, Matt (M)**    206   10
H: 5 10   W: 10 04   b.Oswestry 22-6-88
*Source:* Scholar.

| | | | | | |
|---|---|---|---|---|---|
| 2005-06 | Wrexham | 6 | 0 | | |
| 2006-07 | Wrexham | 34 | 1 | | |
| 2007-08 | Wrexham | 26 | 0 | 66 | 1 |
| 2008-09 | Hereford U | 36 | 0 | | |
| 2009-10 | Hereford U | 20 | 0 | 56 | 0 |
| 2010-11 | Rochdale | 33 | 5 | 33 | 5 |
| 2011-12 | Barnsley | 31 | 4 | | |
| 2012-13 | Barnsley | 13 | 0 | 44 | 4 |
| 2012-13 | *Hibernian* | 7 | 0 | 7 | 0 |

**EDWARDS, Rob (D)**    213   5
H: 6 1   W: 11 10   b.Telford 25-12-82
*Source:* Trainee. *Honours:* Wales Youth, 15
full caps.

| | | | | | |
|---|---|---|---|---|---|
| 1999-2000 | Aston Villa | 0 | 0 | | |
| 2000-01 | Aston Villa | 0 | 0 | | |
| 2001-02 | Aston Villa | 0 | 0 | | |
| 2002-03 | Aston Villa | 8 | 0 | | |
| 2003-04 | Aston Villa | 0 | 0 | 8 | 0 |
| 2003-04 | *Crystal Palace* | 7 | 1 | 7 | 1 |
| 2003-04 | *Derby Co* | 11 | 1 | 11 | 1 |
| 2004-05 | Wolverhampton W | 17 | 0 | | |
| 2005-06 | Wolverhampton W | 42 | 0 | | |
| 2006-07 | Wolverhampton W | 33 | 0 | | |
| 2007-08 | Wolverhampton W | 8 | 1 | 100 | 1 |
| 2008-09 | Blackpool | 36 | 2 | | |
| 2009-10 | Blackpool | 21 | 0 | | |
| 2010-11 | Blackpool | 2 | 0 | 59 | 2 |
| 2010-11 | *Norwich C* | 3 | 0 | 3 | 0 |
| 2011-12 | Barnsley | 17 | 0 | | |
| 2012-13 | Barnsley | 0 | 0 | 17 | 0 |
| 2012-13 | *Fleetwood T* | 4 | 0 | 4 | 0 |
| 2012-13 | *Shrewsbury T* | 4 | 0 | 4 | 0 |

**ETUHU, Kelvin (F)**    73   4
H: 5 11   W: 11 02   b.Kano 30-5-88
*Source:* Scholar.

| | | | | | |
|---|---|---|---|---|---|
| 2005-06 | Manchester C | 0 | 0 | | |
| 2006-07 | Manchester C | 0 | 0 | | |
| 2006-07 | *Rochdale* | 4 | 2 | 4 | 2 |
| 2007-08 | Manchester C | 6 | 1 | | |
| 2007-08 | *Leicester C* | 4 | 0 | 4 | 0 |
| 2008-09 | Manchester C | 4 | 0 | | |
| 2009-10 | Manchester C | 0 | 0 | | |
| 2009-10 | *Cardiff C* | 16 | 0 | 16 | 0 |
| 2010-11 | Manchester C | 0 | 0 | 10 | 1 |
| 2011-12 | Kavala | 0 | 0 | | |
| 2011-12 | Portsmouth | 13 | 1 | | |
| 2012-13 | Portsmouth | 0 | 0 | 13 | 1 |
| 2012-13 | Barnsley | 26 | 0 | 26 | 0 |

**FOSTER, Stephen (D)** 461 25
H: 6 0  W: 11 05  b.Warrington 10-9-80
Source: Trainee. Honours: England Schools.

|  |  | | | | |
|---|---|---|---|---|---|
| 1998-99 | Crewe Alex | 1 | 0 | | |
| 1999-2000 | Crewe Alex | 0 | 0 | | |
| 2000-01 | Crewe Alex | 30 | 0 | | |
| 2001-02 | Crewe Alex | 34 | 5 | | |
| 2002-03 | Crewe Alex | 35 | 4 | | |
| 2003-04 | Crewe Alex | 45 | 2 | | |
| 2004-05 | Crewe Alex | 34 | 1 | | |
| 2005-06 | Crewe Alex | 39 | 3 | 218 | 15 |
| 2006-07 | Burnley | 17 | 0 | | |
| 2007-08 | Burnley | 0 | 0 | 17 | 0 |
| 2007-08 | Barnsley | 41 | 1 | | |
| 2008-09 | Barnsley | 38 | 3 | | |
| 2009-10 | Barnsley | 42 | 2 | | |
| 2010-11 | Barnsley | 33 | 1 | | |
| 2011-12 | Barnsley | 41 | 1 | | |
| 2012-13 | Barnsley | 31 | 2 | 226 | 10 |

**GOLBOURNE, Scott (M)** 210 5
H: 5 8  W: 11 08  b.Bristol 29-2-88
Source: Scholar. Honours: England Youth.

|  |  | | | | |
|---|---|---|---|---|---|
| 2004-05 | Bristol C | 9 | 0 | | |
| 2005-06 | Bristol C | 5 | 0 | 14 | 0 |
| 2005-06 | Reading | 1 | 0 | | |
| 2006-07 | Reading | 0 | 0 | | |
| 2006-07 | Wycombe W | 34 | 1 | 34 | 1 |
| 2007-08 | Reading | 1 | 0 | | |
| 2007-08 | *Bournemouth* | 5 | 0 | 5 | 0 |
| 2008-09 | Reading | 0 | 0 | 2 | 0 |
| 2008-09 | *Oldham Ath* | 8 | 0 | 8 | 0 |
| 2009-10 | Exeter C | 34 | 0 | | |
| 2010-11 | Exeter C | 44 | 2 | | |
| 2011-12 | Exeter C | 26 | 0 | 104 | 2 |
| 2011-12 | Barnsley | 12 | 1 | | |
| 2012-13 | Barnsley | 31 | 1 | 43 | 2 |

**GONZALEZ, David (G)** 257 0
H: 6 4  W: 13 01  b.Medellin 20-7-82
Honours: Colombia 2 full caps.

|  |  | | | | |
|---|---|---|---|---|---|
| 2001 | At Nacional | 0 | 0 | | |
| 2002 | Independiente | 21 | 0 | | |
| 2003 | Independiente | 38 | 0 | | |
| 2004 | Independiente | 46 | 0 | | |
| 2005 | Independiente | 22 | 0 | 127 | 0 |
| 2006 | Dep Cali | 35 | 0 | | |
| 2007 | Dep Cali | 22 | 0 | 57 | 0 |
| 2007-08 | Rize | 24 | 0 | 24 | 0 |
| 2009 | Huracan | 30 | 0 | 30 | 0 |
| 2009-10 | Manchester C | 0 | 0 | | |
| 2010-11 | Manchester C | 0 | 0 | | |
| 2010-11 | *Leeds U* | 0 | 0 | | |
| 2010-11 | *Aberdeen* | 0 | 0 | | |
| 2011-12 | Manchester C | 0 | 0 | | |
| 2011-12 | Brighton & HA | 2 | 0 | 2 | 0 |
| 2011-12 | *Aberdeen* | 14 | 0 | 14 | 0 |
| 2012-13 | Barnsley | 3 | 0 | 3 | 0 |

**HAREWOOD, Marlon (F)** 451 124
H: 6 1  W: 13 07  b.Hampstead 25-8-79
Source: Trainee.

|  |  | | | | |
|---|---|---|---|---|---|
| 1996-97 | Nottingham F | 0 | 0 | | |
| 1997-98 | Nottingham F | 1 | 0 | | |
| 1998-99 | Nottingham F | 23 | 1 | | |
| 1998-99 | *Ipswich T* | 6 | 1 | 6 | 1 |
| 1999-2000 | Nottingham F | 34 | 4 | | |
| 2000-01 | Nottingham F | 33 | 3 | | |
| 2001-02 | Nottingham F | 28 | 11 | | |
| 2002-03 | Nottingham F | 44 | 20 | | |
| 2003-04 | Nottingham F | 19 | 12 | | |
| 2003-04 | West Ham U | 28 | 13 | | |
| 2004-05 | West Ham U | 45 | 17 | | |
| 2005-06 | West Ham U | 37 | 14 | | |
| 2006-07 | West Ham U | 32 | 3 | 142 | 47 |
| 2007-08 | Aston Villa | 23 | 5 | | |
| 2008-09 | Aston Villa | 6 | 0 | | |
| 2008-09 | *Wolverhampton W* | 5 | 0 | 5 | 0 |
| 2009-10 | Aston Villa | 0 | 0 | 29 | 5 |
| 2009-10 | *Newcastle U* | 15 | 5 | 15 | 5 |
| 2010-11 | Blackpool | 16 | 5 | 16 | 5 |
| 2010-11 | *Barnsley* | 10 | 4 | | |
| 2011 | Guangzhou | 10 | 4 | 10 | 4 |
| 2011-12 | Nottingham F | 4 | 0 | 186 | 51 |
| 2012-13 | Barnsley | 32 | 2 | 42 | 6 |

**HASSELL, Bobby (D)** 423 10
H: 5 10  W: 12 00  b.Derby 4-6-80
Source: Trainee.

|  |  | | | | |
|---|---|---|---|---|---|
| 1997-98 | Mansfield T | 9 | 0 | | |
| 1998-99 | Mansfield T | 3 | 0 | | |
| 1999-2000 | Mansfield T | 11 | 1 | | |
| 2000-01 | Mansfield T | 40 | 1 | | |
| 2001-02 | Mansfield T | 43 | 1 | | |
| 2002-03 | Mansfield T | 20 | 0 | | |
| 2003-04 | Mansfield T | 34 | 0 | 160 | 3 |
| 2004-05 | Barnsley | 39 | 0 | | |
| 2005-06 | Barnsley | 28 | 2 | | |
| 2006-07 | Barnsley | 39 | 2 | | |
| 2007-08 | Barnsley | 20 | 0 | | |
| 2008-09 | Barnsley | 40 | 0 | | |
| 2009-10 | Barnsley | 24 | 1 | | |
| 2010-11 | Barnsley | 37 | 1 | | |
| 2011-12 | Barnsley | 19 | 0 | | |
| 2012-13 | Barnsley | 17 | 1 | 263 | 7 |

**JONES, Andrai (D)** 24 0
H: 5 11  W: 10 10  b.Liverpool 1-1-92
Source: Scholar.

|  |  | | | | |
|---|---|---|---|---|---|
| 2010-11 | Bury | 1 | 0 | | |
| 2011-12 | Bury | 11 | 0 | | |
| 2012-13 | Bury | 10 | 0 | 22 | 0 |
| 2012-13 | Barnsley | 2 | 0 | 2 | 0 |

**KENNEDY, Tom (D)** 335 14
H: 5 10  W: 11 01  b.Bury 24-6-85
Source: Scholar.

|  |  | | | | |
|---|---|---|---|---|---|
| 2002-03 | Bury | 0 | 0 | | |
| 2003-04 | Bury | 27 | 0 | | |
| 2004-05 | Bury | 46 | 1 | | |
| 2005-06 | Bury | 33 | 4 | | |
| 2006-07 | Bury | 37 | 0 | 143 | 5 |
| 2007-08 | Rochdale | 43 | 2 | | |
| 2008-09 | Rochdale | 45 | 4 | | |
| 2009-10 | Rochdale | 44 | 3 | | |
| 2010-11 | Leicester C | 1 | 0 | | |
| 2010-11 | *Rochdale* | 6 | 0 | 138 | 9 |
| 2010-11 | *Peterborough U* | 14 | 0 | | |
| 2011-12 | Leicester C | 5 | 0 | | |
| 2011-12 | *Peterborough U* | 10 | 0 | 24 | 0 |
| 2012-13 | Leicester C | 0 | 0 | 6 | 0 |
| 2012-13 | Barnsley | 24 | 0 | 24 | 0 |

**McNULTY, Jim (D)** 149 5
H: 6 1  W: 12 00  b.Runcorn 13-2-85
Source: Wrexham Scholar, Caernarfon T.
Honours: Scotland Youth.

|  |  | | | | |
|---|---|---|---|---|---|
| 2006-07 | Macclesfield T | 15 | 0 | | |
| 2007-08 | Macclesfield T | 19 | 1 | 34 | 1 |
| 2007-08 | Stockport Co | 11 | 0 | | |
| 2008-09 | Stockport Co | 26 | 1 | 37 | 1 |
| 2008-09 | Brighton & HA | 5 | 1 | | |
| 2009-10 | Brighton & HA | 8 | 0 | | |
| 2009-10 | *Scunthorpe U* | 3 | 0 | | |
| 2010-11 | Brighton & HA | 0 | 0 | 13 | 1 |
| 2010-11 | *Scunthorpe U* | 6 | 0 | 9 | 0 |
| 2011-12 | Barnsley | 44 | 2 | | |
| 2012-13 | Barnsley | 12 | 0 | 56 | 2 |

**MELLIS, Jacob (M)** 63 8
H: 5 11  W: 10 11  b.Nottingham 8-1-91
Source: Scholar. Honours: England Youth.

|  |  | | | | |
|---|---|---|---|---|---|
| 2009-10 | Chelsea | 0 | 0 | | |
| 2009-10 | *Southampton* | 12 | 0 | 12 | 0 |
| 2010-11 | Chelsea | 0 | 0 | | |
| 2010-11 | *Barnsley* | 15 | 2 | | |
| 2012-13 | Barnsley | 36 | 6 | 51 | 8 |

**MIDO (F)** 217 71
H: 6 2  W: 13 00  b.Cairo 23-2-83
Honours: Egypt 51 full caps, 19 goals.

|  |  | | | | |
|---|---|---|---|---|---|
| 1999-2000 | Zamalek | 4 | 3 | | |
| 2000-01 | Gent | 21 | 11 | 21 | 11 |
| 2001-02 | Ajax | 24 | 12 | | |
| 2002-03 | Ajax | 16 | 9 | | |
| 2002-03 | Celta Vigo | 8 | 4 | 8 | 4 |
| 2003-04 | Marseille | 22 | 7 | 22 | 7 |
| 2003-04 | Roma | 8 | 0 | 8 | 0 |
| 2004-05 | Tottenham H | 9 | 2 | | |
| 2005-06 | Tottenham H | 27 | 11 | | |
| 2006-07 | Tottenham H | 12 | 1 | 48 | 14 |
| 2007-08 | Middlesbrough | 22 | 9 | | |
| 2008-09 | Middlesbrough | 13 | 4 | | |
| 2008-09 | *Wigan Ath* | 12 | 2 | 12 | 2 |
| 2009-10 | Zamalek | 15 | 1 | 19 | 4 |

|  |  | | | | |
|---|---|---|---|---|---|
| 2009-10 | Middlesbrough | 0 | 0 | 25 | 6 |
| 2009-10 | *West Ham U* | 9 | 0 | 9 | 0 |
| 2010-11 | Ajax | 4 | 2 | 44 | 23 |
| 2012-13 | Barnsley | 1 | 0 | 1 | 0 |

**NOBLE-LAZARUS, Reuben (F)** 33 2
H: 5 11  W: 13 07  b.Huddersfield 16-8-93
Source: Youth.

|  |  | | | | |
|---|---|---|---|---|---|
| 2008-09 | Barnsley | 2 | 0 | | |
| 2009-10 | Barnsley | 2 | 0 | | |
| 2010-11 | Barnsley | 7 | 1 | | |
| 2011-12 | Barnsley | 8 | 0 | | |
| 2012-13 | Barnsley | 14 | 1 | 33 | 2 |

**O'BRIEN, Jim (F)** 182 10
H: 6 0  W: 11 11  b.Alexandria 28-9-87

|  |  | | | | |
|---|---|---|---|---|---|
| 2006-07 | Celtic | 0 | 0 | | |
| 2006-07 | *Dunfermline Ath* | 13 | 1 | 13 | 1 |
| 2007-08 | Celtic | 1 | 0 | 1 | 0 |
| 2007-08 | *Dundee U* | 10 | 0 | 10 | 0 |
| 2008-09 | Motherwell | 29 | 1 | | |
| 2009-10 | Motherwell | 35 | 3 | 64 | 4 |
| 2010-11 | Barnsley | 33 | 1 | | |
| 2011-12 | Barnsley | 31 | 2 | | |
| 2012-13 | Barnsley | 30 | 2 | 94 | 5 |

**PERKINS, David (D)** 240 14
H: 5 6  W: 11 06  b.Heysham 21-6-82

|  |  | | | | |
|---|---|---|---|---|---|
| 2006-07 | Rochdale | 18 | 0 | | |
| 2007-08 | Rochdale | 40 | 4 | 58 | 4 |
| 2008-09 | Colchester U | 38 | 5 | | |
| 2009-10 | Colchester U | 5 | 1 | | |
| 2009-10 | *Chesterfield* | 13 | 1 | 13 | 1 |
| 2009-10 | *Stockport Co* | 22 | 0 | 22 | 0 |
| 2010-11 | Colchester U | 36 | 1 | 79 | 7 |
| 2011-12 | Barnsley | 33 | 1 | | |
| 2012-13 | Barnsley | 35 | 1 | 68 | 2 |

**ROSE, Danny (F)** 13 1
H: 5 8  W: 9 00  b.Barnsley 10-12-93
Source: Scholar.

|  |  | | | | |
|---|---|---|---|---|---|
| 2010-11 | Barnsley | 1 | 0 | | |
| 2011-12 | Barnsley | 4 | 0 | | |
| 2012-13 | Barnsley | 8 | 1 | 13 | 1 |

**SCOTLAND, Jason (F)** 343 111
H: 5 8  W: 11 10  b.Morvant 18-2-79
Source: San Juan Jabloteh, Defence Force.
Honours: Trinidad & Tobago 41 full caps, 8 goals.

|  |  | | | | |
|---|---|---|---|---|---|
| 2003-04 | Dundee U | 21 | 4 | | |
| 2004-05 | Dundee U | 29 | 3 | 50 | 7 |
| 2005-06 | St Johnstone | 31 | 15 | | |
| 2006-07 | St Johnstone | 35 | 18 | 66 | 33 |
| 2007-08 | Swansea C | 45 | 24 | | |
| 2008-09 | Swansea C | 45 | 21 | | |
| 2009-10 | Swansea C | 0 | 0 | 90 | 45 |
| 2009-10 | *Wigan Ath* | 32 | 1 | | |
| 2010-11 | Wigan Ath | 0 | 0 | 32 | 1 |
| 2010-11 | *Ipswich T* | 39 | 10 | | |
| 2011-12 | Ipswich T | 36 | 8 | | |
| 2012-13 | Ipswich T | 12 | 1 | 87 | 19 |
| 2012-13 | Barnsley | 18 | 6 | 18 | 6 |

**SILVA, Toni (M)** 20 1
H: 6 0  W: 11 09  b.Guinea-Bissau 15-9-93
Honours: Portugal Youth.

|  |  | | | | |
|---|---|---|---|---|---|
| 2010-11 | Liverpool | 0 | 0 | | |
| 2011-12 | Liverpool | 0 | 0 | | |
| 2011-12 | *Northampton T* | 15 | 1 | 15 | 1 |
| 2012-13 | Liverpool | 0 | 0 | | |
| 2012-13 | Barnsley | 1 | 0 | 1 | 0 |
| 2012-13 | *Dagenham & R* | 4 | 0 | 4 | 0 |

**STEELE, Luke (G)** 219 0
H: 6 2  W: 12 00  b.Peterborough 24-9-84
Source: Scholar. Honours: England Youth, Under-20.

|  |  | | | | |
|---|---|---|---|---|---|
| 2001-02 | Peterborough U | 2 | 0 | 2 | 0 |
| 2001-02 | Manchester U | 0 | 0 | | |
| 2002-03 | Manchester U | 0 | 0 | | |
| 2003-04 | Manchester U | 0 | 0 | | |
| 2004-05 | Manchester U | 0 | 0 | | |
| 2004-05 | *Coventry C* | 32 | 0 | | |
| 2005-06 | Manchester U | 0 | 0 | | |
| 2006-07 | WBA | 0 | 0 | | |
| 2006-07 | *Coventry C* | 5 | 0 | 37 | 0 |
| 2007-08 | WBA | 2 | 0 | 2 | 0 |
| 2007-08 | *Barnsley* | 14 | 0 | | |
| 2008-09 | Barnsley | 10 | 0 | | |

| 2009-10 | Barnsley | 39 | 0 | | |
| 2010-11 | Barnsley | 46 | 0 | | |
| 2011-12 | Barnsley | 36 | 0 | | |
| 2012-13 | Barnsley | 33 | 0 | 178 | 0 |

**WISEMAN, Scott (D)** 237 3
H: 6 0　W: 11 06　b.Hull 9-10-85
*Source:* Scholar. *Honours:* England Youth, Under-20.

| 2003-04 | Hull C | 2 | 0 | | |
| 2004-05 | Hull C | 3 | 0 | | |
| 2004-05 | *Boston U* | 2 | 0 | 2 | 0 |
| 2005-06 | Hull C | 11 | 0 | | |
| 2006-07 | Hull C | 0 | 0 | 16 | 0 |
| 2006-07 | *Rotherham U* | 18 | 1 | 18 | 1 |
| 2006-07 | *Darlington* | 10 | 0 | | |
| 2007-08 | Darlington | 7 | 0 | 17 | 0 |
| 2008-09 | Rochdale | 32 | 0 | | |
| 2009-10 | Rochdale | 36 | 1 | | |
| 2010-11 | Rochdale | 37 | 0 | 105 | 1 |
| 2011-12 | Barnsley | 43 | 1 | | |
| 2012-13 | Barnsley | 36 | 0 | 79 | 1 |

**Players retained or with offer of contract**
Brito, E Silva Toni.

**Scholars**
Abbott, Bradley Ian; Alderson, Joshua Jack; Alexander-Salmon, Omari Keith Jayden; Biggins, Harrison; Chadderton, Elliot; Cooke, Joshua James Alan; Freeman, Dean Thomas; MacKey, Conor Laurence; Maris, George Thomas; McKnight, Darren James; Moore, Jamie Stephen; Ngoma, Kenna; Oates, Rhys Derek; Pilkington, Callum Jon; Shillito, McCauley Jake; Smith, George Thomas; Sousa, Erico Henrique; Williams, Thomas James.

# BIRMINGHAM C (8)

**AMBROSE, Darren (M)** 304 55
H: 6 0　W: 11 00　b.Harlow 29-2-84
*Source:* Scholar. *Honours:* England Youth, Under-20, Under-21.

| 2001-02 | Ipswich T | 1 | 0 | | |
| 2002-03 | Ipswich T | 29 | 8 | | |
| 2002-03 | Newcastle U | 1 | 0 | | |
| 2003-04 | Newcastle U | 24 | 2 | | |
| 2004-05 | Newcastle U | 12 | 3 | 37 | 5 |
| 2005-06 | Charlton Ath | 28 | 3 | | |
| 2006-07 | Charlton Ath | 26 | 3 | | |
| 2007-08 | Charlton Ath | 37 | 7 | | |
| 2008-09 | Charlton Ath | 21 | 0 | 112 | 13 |
| 2008-09 | *Ipswich T* | 9 | 0 | 39 | 8 |
| 2009-10 | Crystal Palace | 46 | 15 | | |
| 2010-11 | Crystal Palace | 28 | 7 | | |
| 2011-12 | Crystal Palace | 36 | 7 | 110 | 29 |
| 2012-13 | Birmingham C | 6 | 0 | 6 | 0 |

**ARTHUR, Koby (M)** 2 0
H: 5 6　W: 10 09　b.Kumasi 3-1-96

| 2012-13 | Birmingham C | 2 | 0 | 2 | 0 |

**ASANTE, Akwasi (F)** 11 2
H: 5 7　W: 10 00　b.Amsterdam 22-9-92
*Source:* Scholar.

| 2010-11 | Birmingham C | 0 | 0 | | |
| 2011-12 | Birmingham C | 0 | 0 | | |
| 2011-12 | *Northampton T* | 4 | 1 | 4 | 1 |
| 2012-13 | Birmingham C | 0 | 0 | | |
| 2012-13 | *Shrewsbury T* | 7 | 1 | 7 | 1 |

**BELL, Amari (D)** 0 0
H: 5 11　W: 12 00　b. 5-5-94
*Source:* Scholar.

| 2012-13 | Birmingham C | 0 | 0 | | |

**BURKE, Chris (M)** 284 46
H: 5 9　W: 10 10　b.Glasgow 2-12-83
*Honours:* Scotland Under-21, B, 5 full caps, 2 goals.

| 2001-02 | Rangers | 2 | 1 | | |
| 2002-03 | Rangers | 0 | 0 | | |
| 2003-04 | Rangers | 20 | 3 | | |
| 2004-05 | Rangers | 12 | 0 | | |
| 2005-06 | Rangers | 27 | 4 | | |
| 2006-07 | Rangers | 22 | 2 | | |
| 2007-08 | Rangers | 11 | 2 | | |
| 2008-09 | Rangers | 1 | 0 | 95 | 11 |
| 2008-09 | Cardiff C | 14 | 1 | | |
| 2009-10 | Cardiff C | 44 | 9 | | |
| 2010-11 | Cardiff C | 44 | 5 | 102 | 15 |
| 2011-12 | Birmingham C | 46 | 12 | | |
| 2012-13 | Birmingham C | 41 | 8 | 87 | 20 |

**CALDWELL, Steven (D)** 323 12
H: 6 2　W: 13 12　b.Stirling 12-9-80
*Source:* Trainee. *Honours:* Scotland Youth, Under-21, B, 12 full caps.

| 1997-98 | Newcastle U | 0 | 0 | | |
| 1998-99 | Newcastle U | 0 | 0 | | |
| 1999-2000 | Newcastle U | 0 | 0 | | |
| 2000-01 | Newcastle U | 9 | 0 | | |
| 2001-02 | Newcastle U | 0 | 0 | | |
| 2001-02 | *Blackpool* | 6 | 0 | 6 | 0 |
| 2001-02 | *Bradford C* | 9 | 0 | 9 | 0 |
| 2002-03 | Newcastle U | 14 | 1 | | |
| 2003-04 | Newcastle U | 5 | 0 | 28 | 1 |
| 2003-04 | *Leeds U* | 13 | 1 | 13 | 1 |
| 2004-05 | Sunderland | 41 | 4 | | |
| 2005-06 | Sunderland | 24 | 0 | | |
| 2006-07 | Sunderland | 11 | 0 | 76 | 4 |
| 2006-07 | Burnley | 17 | 0 | | |
| 2007-08 | Burnley | 29 | 2 | | |
| 2008-09 | Burnley | 45 | 2 | | |
| 2009-10 | Burnley | 13 | 1 | | |
| 2010-11 | Burnley | 0 | 0 | 104 | 5 |
| 2010-11 | *Wigan Ath* | 10 | 0 | 10 | 0 |
| 2011-12 | Birmingham C | 43 | 0 | | |
| 2012-13 | Birmingham C | 34 | 1 | 77 | 1 |

Transferred to Toronto FC May 2013

**CARR, Stephen (D)** 410 8
H: 5 9　W: 11 13　b.Dublin 29-8-76
*Source:* Trainee. *Honours:* Eire Schools, Youth, Under-21, 44 full caps.

| 1993-94 | Tottenham H | 1 | 0 | | |
| 1994-95 | Tottenham H | 0 | 0 | | |
| 1995-96 | Tottenham H | 0 | 0 | | |
| 1996-97 | Tottenham H | 26 | 0 | | |
| 1997-98 | Tottenham H | 38 | 0 | | |
| 1998-99 | Tottenham H | 37 | 0 | | |
| 1999-2000 | Tottenham H | 34 | 3 | | |
| 2000-01 | Tottenham H | 28 | 3 | | |
| 2001-02 | Tottenham H | 0 | 0 | | |
| 2002-03 | Tottenham H | 30 | 0 | | |
| 2003-04 | Tottenham H | 32 | 1 | 226 | 7 |
| 2004-05 | Newcastle U | 26 | 1 | | |
| 2005-06 | Newcastle U | 19 | 0 | | |
| 2006-07 | Newcastle U | 23 | 0 | | |
| 2007-08 | Newcastle U | 0 | 0 | | |
| 2008-09 | Newcastle U | 0 | 0 | 78 | 1 |
| 2008-09 | Birmingham C | 13 | 0 | | |
| 2009-10 | Birmingham C | 35 | 0 | | |
| 2010-11 | Birmingham C | 38 | 0 | | |
| 2011-12 | Birmingham C | 20 | 0 | | |
| 2012-13 | Birmingham C | 0 | 0 | 106 | 0 |

**DAVIES, Curtis (D)** 271 18
H: 6 2　W: 11 13　b.Waltham Forest 15-3-85
*Source:* Scholar. *Honours:* England Under-21.

| 2003-04 | Luton T | 6 | 0 | | |
| 2004-05 | Luton T | 44 | 1 | | |
| 2005-06 | Luton T | 6 | 1 | 56 | 2 |
| 2005-06 | WBA | 33 | 2 | | |
| 2006-07 | WBA | 32 | 0 | | |
| 2007-08 | WBA | 0 | 0 | 65 | 2 |
| 2007-08 | *Aston Villa* | 12 | 1 | | |
| 2008-09 | Aston Villa | 35 | 1 | | |
| 2009-10 | Aston Villa | 2 | 1 | | |
| 2010-11 | Aston Villa | 0 | 0 | 49 | 3 |
| 2010-11 | *Leicester C* | 12 | 0 | 12 | 0 |
| 2011-12 | Birmingham C | 6 | 0 | | |
| 2012-13 | Birmingham C | 41 | 6 | 89 | 11 |

**DEAMAN, Jack (D)** 0 0
H: 6 3　W: 11 11　b.Camden 18-5-93
*Source:* Wrexham Scholar.

| 2011-12 | Birmingham C | 0 | 0 | | |
| 2012-13 | Birmingham C | 0 | 0 | | |
| 2012-13 | *Cheltenham T* | 0 | 0 | | |

**DELFOUNESO, Emmitt (D)** 0 0
H: 6 2　W: 12 11　b.Birmingham 28-1-94

| 2012-13 | Birmingham C | 0 | 0 | | |

**DIOP, Papa Bouba (M)** 260 26
H: 6 4　W: 14 12　b.Dakar 28-1-78
*Source:* Espoir, Jaraaf, Vevey Sports.
*Honours:* Senegal 63 full caps, 11 goals.

| 1999-2000 | Neuchatel Xamax | 0 | 0 | | |
| 2000-01 | Neuchatel Xamax | 18 | 4 | 18 | 4 |
| 2000-01 | Grasshoppers | 11 | 1 | | |
| 2001-02 | Grasshoppers | 18 | 4 | 29 | 5 |
| 2001-02 | Lens | 5 | 0 | | |
| 2002-03 | Lens | 16 | 3 | | |
| 2003-04 | Lens | 26 | 3 | 47 | 6 |
| 2004-05 | Fulham | 29 | 6 | | |
| 2005-06 | Fulham | 22 | 2 | | |
| 2006-07 | Fulham | 23 | 0 | | |
| 2007-08 | Fulham | 2 | 0 | 76 | 8 |
| 2007-08 | Portsmouth | 25 | 0 | | |
| 2008-09 | Portsmouth | 16 | 0 | | |
| 2009-10 | Portsmouth | 12 | 0 | 53 | 0 |
| 2010-11 | AEK Athens | 19 | 1 | 19 | 1 |
| 2011-12 | West Ham U | 16 | 1 | 16 | 1 |
| 2012-13 | Birmingham C | 2 | 1 | 2 | 1 |

**DOYLE, Colin (G)** 47 0
H: 6 5　W: 14 05　b.Cork 12-8-85
*Honours:* Eire Youth, Under-21, 1 full cap.

| 2004-05 | Birmingham C | 0 | 0 | | |
| 2004-05 | *Chester C* | 0 | 0 | | |
| 2005-06 | *Nottingham F* | 3 | 0 | 3 | 0 |
| 2005-06 | *Millwall* | 14 | 0 | 14 | 0 |
| 2006-07 | Birmingham C | 19 | 0 | | |
| 2007-08 | Birmingham C | 3 | 0 | | |
| 2008-09 | Birmingham C | 2 | 0 | | |
| 2009-10 | Birmingham C | 0 | 0 | | |
| 2010-11 | Birmingham C | 1 | 0 | | |
| 2011-12 | Birmingham C | 2 | 0 | | |
| 2012-13 | Birmingham C | 0 | 0 | 30 | 0 |

**ELLIOTT, Wade (M)** 545 58
H: 5 10　W: 10 03　b.Eastleigh 14-12-78
*Source:* Bashley.

| 1999-2000 | Bournemouth | 12 | 3 | | |
| 2000-01 | Bournemouth | 36 | 9 | | |
| 2001-02 | Bournemouth | 46 | 8 | | |
| 2002-03 | Bournemouth | 44 | 4 | | |
| 2003-04 | Bournemouth | 39 | 3 | | |
| 2004-05 | Bournemouth | 43 | 4 | 220 | 31 |
| 2005-06 | Burnley | 36 | 3 | | |
| 2006-07 | Burnley | 42 | 4 | | |
| 2007-08 | Burnley | 46 | 2 | | |
| 2008-09 | Burnley | 42 | 4 | | |
| 2009-10 | Burnley | 38 | 4 | | |
| 2010-11 | Burnley | 44 | 2 | | |
| 2011-12 | Burnley | 4 | 0 | 252 | 19 |
| 2011-12 | Birmingham C | 29 | 2 | | |
| 2012-13 | Birmingham C | 44 | 6 | 73 | 8 |

**FAHEY, Keith (M)** 265 31
H: 5 10　W: 12 07　b.Dublin 15-1-83
*Source:* Arsenal Trainee. *Honours:* Eire 16 full caps, 3 goals.

| 1999-2000 | Aston Villa | 0 | 0 | | |
| 2000-01 | Aston Villa | 0 | 0 | | |
| 2001-02 | Aston Villa | 0 | 0 | | |
| 2002-03 | Aston Villa | 0 | 0 | | |
| 2003 | St Patrick's Ath | 0 | 0 | | |
| 2004 | St Patrick's Ath | 33 | 5 | | |
| 2005 | St Patrick's Ath | 14 | 3 | | |
| 2005 | Drogheda U | 14 | 2 | | |
| 2006 | Drogheda U | 8 | 0 | 22 | 2 |
| 2006 | St Patrick's Ath | 13 | 3 | | |
| 2007 | St Patrick's Ath | 32 | 1 | | |
| 2008 | St Patrick's Ath | 30 | 8 | 122 | 20 |
| 2008-09 | Birmingham C | 19 | 4 | | |
| 2009-10 | Birmingham C | 34 | 0 | | |
| 2010-11 | Birmingham C | 24 | 1 | | |
| 2011-12 | Birmingham C | 35 | 4 | | |
| 2012-13 | Birmingham C | 9 | 0 | 121 | 9 |

**FRY, James (D)** 0 0
H: 5 11　W: 12 03　b.Solihull 3-2-95

| 2012-13 | Birmingham C | 0 | 0 | | |

**GNAHORE, Eddy (M)** 0 0
H: 6 2　W: 13 05　b.Paris 14-11-93
*Source:* Scholar. *Honours:* France Youth.

| 2011-12 | Birmingham C | 0 | 0 | | |
| 2012-13 | Birmingham C | 0 | 0 | | |

**GOMIS, Morgaro (M)**  196  8
H: 5 9  W: 11 00  b.Le Blanc-Mesnil 14-7-85
*Source:* Windsor & E, Dagenham & R, Barnet, Lewes. *Honours:* Senegal 1 full cap.

|  |  | | | | |
|---|---|---|---|---|---|
| 2006-07 | Cowdenbeath | 15 | 2 | 15 | 2 |
| 2006-07 | Dundee U | 12 | 0 | | |
| 2007-08 | Dundee U | 36 | 1 | | |
| 2008-09 | Dundee U | 37 | 0 | | |
| 2009-10 | Dundee U | 31 | 4 | | |
| 2010-11 | Dundee U | 34 | 1 | 150 | 6 |
| 2011-12 | Birmingham C | 16 | 0 | | |
| 2012-13 | Birmingham C | 15 | 0 | 31 | 0 |

**HALES, Reece (F)**  0  0
H: 6 1  W: 12 07  b.Birmingham 12-2-95

|  |  | | | | |
|---|---|---|---|---|---|
| 2012-13 | Birmingham C | 0 | 0 | | |

**HANCOX, Mitch (D)**  19  0
H: 5 10  W: 11 03  b.Solihull 9-11-93
*Source:* Scholar.

|  |  | | | | |
|---|---|---|---|---|---|
| 2011-12 | Birmingham C | 0 | 0 | | |
| 2012-13 | Birmingham C | 19 | 0 | 19 | 0 |

**HENRY-FRANCIS, Marcel (F)**  0  0
H: 6 1  W: 13 02  b.London 25-5-94

|  |  | | | | |
|---|---|---|---|---|---|
| 2012-13 | Birmingham C | 0 | 0 | | |

**HIGGINS, Ryan (M)**  0  0
H: 5 9  W: 11 12  b.Liverpool 1-5-94

|  |  | | | | |
|---|---|---|---|---|---|
| 2012-13 | Birmingham C | 0 | 0 | | |

**IBANEZ, Pablo (D)**  259  12
H: 6 3  W: 13 07  b.Madrigueras 3-8-81
*Honours:* Spain Under-21, 23 full caps.

|  |  | | | | |
|---|---|---|---|---|---|
| 2002-03 | Albacete | 38 | 1 | | |
| 2003-04 | Albacete | 31 | 1 | 74 | 2 |
| 2004-05 | Atletico Madrid | 35 | 3 | | |
| 2005-06 | Atletico Madrid | 35 | 2 | | |
| 2006-07 | Atletico Madrid | 24 | 2 | | |
| 2007-08 | Atletico Madrid | 34 | 1 | | |
| 2008-09 | Atletico Madrid | 21 | 1 | | |
| 2009-10 | Atletico Madrid | 7 | 0 | 156 | 9 |
| 2010-11 | WBA | 10 | 1 | 10 | 1 |
| 2011-12 | Birmingham C | 13 | 0 | | |
| 2012-13 | Birmingham C | 6 | 0 | 19 | 0 |

**JERVIS, Jake (F)**  52  12
H: 6 3  W: 12 13  b.Birmingham 17-9-91
*Source:* Scholar.

|  |  | | | | |
|---|---|---|---|---|---|
| 2009-10 | Birmingham C | 0 | 0 | | |
| 2009-10 | *Hereford U* | 7 | 2 | | |
| 2010-11 | Birmingham C | 0 | 0 | | |
| 2010-11 | *Notts Co* | 10 | 0 | 10 | 0 |
| 2010-11 | *Hereford U* | 4 | 0 | 11 | 2 |
| 2011-12 | Birmingham C | 0 | 0 | | |
| 2011-12 | *Swindon T* | 12 | 3 | 12 | 3 |
| 2011-12 | *Preston NE* | 5 | 2 | 5 | 2 |
| 2012-13 | Birmingham C | 2 | 0 | 2 | 0 |
| 2012-13 | *Carlisle U* | 5 | 3 | 5 | 3 |
| 2012-13 | *Tranmere R* | 4 | 1 | 4 | 1 |
| 2012-13 | *Portsmouth* | 3 | 1 | 3 | 1 |

Transferred to Elazigspor January 2013

**KING, Marlon (F)**  440  149
H: 5 10  W: 12 10  b.Dulwich 26-4-80
*Source:* Trainee. *Honours:* Jamaica 20 full caps, 12 goals.

|  |  | | | | |
|---|---|---|---|---|---|
| 1998-99 | Barnet | 22 | 6 | | |
| 1999-2000 | Barnet | 31 | 8 | 53 | 14 |
| 2000-01 | Gillingham | 38 | 15 | | |
| 2001-02 | Gillingham | 42 | 17 | | |
| 2002-03 | Gillingham | 10 | 4 | | |
| 2003-04 | Gillingham | 11 | 4 | 101 | 40 |
| 2003-04 | Nottingham F | 24 | 5 | | |
| 2004-05 | Nottingham F | 26 | 5 | | |
| 2004-05 | *Leeds U* | 9 | 0 | 9 | 0 |
| 2005-06 | Nottingham F | 0 | 0 | 50 | 10 |
| 2005-06 | Watford | 41 | 21 | | |
| 2006-07 | Watford | 13 | 4 | | |
| 2007-08 | Watford | 27 | 11 | 81 | 36 |
| 2007-08 | Wigan Ath | 15 | 1 | | |
| 2008-09 | Wigan Ath | 0 | 0 | | |
| 2008-09 | Hull C | 20 | 5 | 20 | 5 |
| 2008-09 | *Middlesbrough* | 13 | 2 | 13 | 2 |
| 2009-10 | Wigan Ath | 3 | 0 | 18 | 1 |
| 2010-11 | Coventry C | 28 | 12 | 28 | 12 |
| 2011-12 | Birmingham C | 40 | 16 | | |
| 2012-13 | Birmingham C | 27 | 13 | 67 | 29 |

**LEE, Oliver (M)**  40  3
H: 5 11  W: 12 07  b.Hornchurch 11-7-91
*Source:* Scholar.

|  |  | | | | |
|---|---|---|---|---|---|
| 2009-10 | West Ham U | 0 | 0 | | |
| 2010-11 | West Ham U | 0 | 0 | | |
| 2010-11 | *Dagenham & R* | 5 | 0 | | |
| 2011-12 | West Ham U | 0 | 0 | | |
| 2011-12 | *Dagenham & R* | 16 | 3 | 21 | 3 |
| 2011-12 | *Gillingham* | 8 | 0 | 8 | 0 |
| 2012-13 | Barnet | 11 | 0 | 11 | 0 |
| 2012-13 | Birmingham C | 0 | 0 | | |

**LOVENKRANDS, Peter (F)**  305  76
H: 5 11  W: 11 02  b.Copenhagen 29-1-80
*Honours:* Denmark Youth, 22 full caps, 1 goal.

|  |  | | | | |
|---|---|---|---|---|---|
| 1998-99 | AB Copenhagen | 18 | 2 | | |
| 1999-2000 | AB Copenhagen | 14 | 5 | 32 | 7 |
| 2000-01 | Rangers | 8 | 0 | | |
| 2001-02 | Rangers | 18 | 2 | | |
| 2002-03 | Rangers | 28 | 9 | | |
| 2003-04 | Rangers | 25 | 8 | | |
| 2004-05 | Rangers | 17 | 3 | | |
| 2005-06 | Rangers | 33 | 14 | 129 | 36 |
| 2006-07 | Schalke | 24 | 6 | | |
| 2007-08 | Schalke | 20 | 0 | 44 | 6 |
| 2008-09 | Schalke B | 3 | 2 | 3 | 2 |
| 2008-09 | Newcastle U | 12 | 3 | | |
| 2009-10 | Newcastle U | 29 | 13 | | |
| 2010-11 | Newcastle U | 25 | 6 | | |
| 2011-12 | Newcastle U | 9 | 0 | 75 | 22 |
| 2012-13 | Birmingham C | 22 | 3 | 22 | 3 |

**MULLINS, Hayden (D)**  551  27
H: 5 11  W: 11 12  b.Reading 27-3-79
*Source:* Trainee. *Honours:* England Under-21.

|  |  | | | | |
|---|---|---|---|---|---|
| 1996-97 | Crystal Palace | 0 | 0 | | |
| 1997-98 | Crystal Palace | 0 | 0 | | |
| 1998-99 | Crystal Palace | 40 | 5 | | |
| 1999-2000 | Crystal Palace | 45 | 10 | | |
| 2000-01 | Crystal Palace | 41 | 1 | | |
| 2001-02 | Crystal Palace | 43 | 0 | | |
| 2002-03 | Crystal Palace | 43 | 2 | | |
| 2003-04 | Crystal Palace | 10 | 0 | 222 | 18 |
| 2003-04 | West Ham U | 27 | 0 | | |
| 2004-05 | West Ham U | 37 | 1 | | |
| 2005-06 | West Ham U | 35 | 0 | | |
| 2006-07 | West Ham U | 30 | 2 | | |
| 2007-08 | West Ham U | 34 | 0 | | |
| 2008-09 | West Ham U | 17 | 1 | 180 | 4 |
| 2008-09 | Portsmouth | 17 | 0 | | |
| 2009-10 | Portsmouth | 18 | 0 | | |
| 2010-11 | Portsmouth | 45 | 2 | | |
| 2011-12 | Portsmouth | 34 | 1 | 114 | 3 |
| 2011-12 | *Reading* | 8 | 0 | | |
| 2012-13 | Birmingham C | 28 | 2 | 28 | 2 |

**MURPHY, David (D)**  230  11
H: 6 1  W: 12 03  b.Hartlepool 1-3-84
*Source:* Scholar. *Honours:* England Youth.

|  |  | | | | |
|---|---|---|---|---|---|
| 2001-02 | Middlesbrough | 5 | 0 | | |
| 2002-03 | Middlesbrough | 8 | 0 | | |
| 2003-04 | Middlesbrough | 0 | 0 | 13 | 0 |
| 2003-04 | *Barnsley* | 10 | 2 | 10 | 2 |
| 2004-05 | Hibernian | 27 | 1 | | |
| 2005-06 | Hibernian | 30 | 1 | | |
| 2006-07 | Hibernian | 33 | 0 | | |
| 2007-08 | Hibernian | 17 | 2 | 107 | 4 |
| 2007-08 | Birmingham C | 14 | 1 | | |
| 2008-09 | Birmingham C | 30 | 0 | | |
| 2009-10 | Birmingham C | 10 | 0 | | |
| 2010-11 | Birmingham C | 10 | 0 | | |
| 2011-12 | Birmingham C | 33 | 4 | | |
| 2012-13 | Birmingham C | 13 | 0 | 100 | 5 |

**PACKWOOD, Will (M)**  5  0
H: 6 3  W: 12 08  b.Concord 21-5-93
*Source:* Scholar. *Honours:* USA Youth.

|  |  | | | | |
|---|---|---|---|---|---|
| 2011-12 | Birmingham C | 0 | 0 | | |
| 2012-13 | Birmingham C | 5 | 0 | 5 | 0 |

**REDMOND, Nathan (M)**  62  7
H: 5 8  W: 11 11  b.Birmingham 6-3-94
*Source:* Scholar. *Honours:* England Youth, Under-21.

|  |  | | | | |
|---|---|---|---|---|---|
| 2011-12 | Birmingham C | 24 | 5 | | |
| 2012-13 | Birmingham C | 38 | 2 | 62 | 7 |

**REILLY, Callum (M)**  18  1
H: 6 1  W: 12 03  b.Warrington 3-10-93
*Honours:* Eire Under-21.

|  |  | | | | |
|---|---|---|---|---|---|
| 2012-13 | Birmingham C | 18 | 1 | 18 | 1 |

**ROBINSON, Paul (D)**  555  12
H: 5 9  W: 11 12  b.Watford 14-12-78
*Source:* Trainee. *Honours:* England Under-21.

|  |  | | | | |
|---|---|---|---|---|---|
| 1996-97 | Watford | 12 | 0 | | |
| 1997-98 | Watford | 22 | 2 | | |
| 1998-99 | Watford | 29 | 0 | | |
| 1999-2000 | Watford | 32 | 0 | | |
| 2000-01 | Watford | 39 | 0 | | |
| 2001-02 | Watford | 38 | 3 | | |
| 2002-03 | Watford | 37 | 3 | | |
| 2003-04 | Watford | 10 | 0 | 219 | 8 |
| 2003-04 | WBA | 31 | 0 | | |
| 2004-05 | WBA | 30 | 1 | | |
| 2005-06 | WBA | 33 | 0 | | |
| 2006-07 | WBA | 42 | 2 | | |
| 2007-08 | WBA | 43 | 1 | | |
| 2008-09 | WBA | 35 | 0 | | |
| 2009-10 | WBA | 0 | 0 | 214 | 4 |
| 2009-10 | *Bolton W* | 25 | 0 | | |
| 2010-11 | Bolton W | 35 | 0 | | |
| 2011-12 | Bolton W | 17 | 0 | 77 | 0 |
| 2011-12 | *Leeds U* | 10 | 0 | 10 | 0 |
| 2012-13 | Birmingham C | 35 | 0 | 35 | 0 |

**ROONEY, Adam (F)**  205  71
H: 5 9  W: 12 03  b.Dublin 21-4-87
*Source:* Scholar. *Honours:* Eire Youth, Under-21.

|  |  | | | | |
|---|---|---|---|---|---|
| 2005-06 | Stoke C | 5 | 4 | | |
| 2006-07 | Stoke C | 10 | 0 | | |
| 2006-07 | *Yeovil T* | 3 | 0 | 3 | 0 |
| 2007-08 | Stoke C | 0 | 0 | 15 | 4 |
| 2007-08 | *Chesterfield* | 22 | 7 | 22 | 7 |
| 2007-08 | *Bury* | 16 | 3 | 16 | 3 |
| 2008-09 | Inverness CT | 30 | 5 | | |
| 2009-10 | Inverness CT | 35 | 24 | | |
| 2010-11 | Inverness CT | 37 | 15 | 102 | 44 |
| 2011-12 | Birmingham C | 18 | 4 | | |
| 2012-13 | Birmingham C | 0 | 0 | 18 | 4 |
| 2012-13 | *Swindon T* | 29 | 9 | 29 | 9 |

**SPECTOR, Jonathan (D)**  184  1
H: 6 0  W: 12 08  b.Chicago 1-3-86
*Source:* Chicago Sockers. *Honours:* USA Youth, 34 full caps.

|  |  | | | | |
|---|---|---|---|---|---|
| 2003-04 | Manchester U | 0 | 0 | | |
| 2004-05 | Manchester U | 3 | 0 | | |
| 2005-06 | Manchester U | 0 | 0 | 3 | 0 |
| 2005-06 | *Charlton Ath* | 20 | 0 | 20 | 0 |
| 2006-07 | West Ham U | 25 | 0 | | |
| 2007-08 | West Ham U | 26 | 0 | | |
| 2008-09 | West Ham U | 9 | 0 | | |
| 2009-10 | West Ham U | 27 | 0 | | |
| 2010-11 | West Ham U | 14 | 1 | 101 | 1 |
| 2011-12 | Birmingham C | 31 | 0 | | |
| 2012-13 | Birmingham C | 29 | 0 | 60 | 0 |

**TOWNSEND, Nick (G)**  0  0
H: 5 11  W: 13 11  b.Solihull 1-11-94

|  |  | | | | |
|---|---|---|---|---|---|
| 2012-13 | Birmingham C | 0 | 0 | | |

**ZIGIC, Nikola (F)**  371  201
H: 6 8  W: 14 02  b.Backa Topola 25-9-80
*Honours:* Serbia 57 full caps, 20 goals.

|  |  | | | | |
|---|---|---|---|---|---|
| 1998-99 | Backa Topola | 14 | 8 | | |
| 1999-2000 | Backa Topola | 28 | 28 | | |
| 2000-01 | Backa Topola | 30 | 30 | | |
| 2001-02 | Backa Topola | 4 | 2 | 76 | 68 |
| 2001-02 | Mornar Bar | 23 | 15 | 23 | 15 |
| 2002-03 | Kolubara | 8 | 3 | 8 | 3 |
| 2002-03 | Spartak Subotica | 11 | 14 | 11 | 14 |
| 2003-04 | Red Star Belgrade | 28 | 19 | | |
| 2004-05 | Red Star Belgrade | 25 | 15 | | |
| 2005-06 | Red Star Belgrade | 23 | 11 | | |
| 2006-07 | Red Star Belgrade | 3 | 2 | 79 | 47 |
| 2006-07 | Santander | 32 | 11 | | |
| 2007-08 | Valencia | 15 | 1 | | |
| 2008-09 | Santander | 19 | 13 | 51 | 24 |
| 2009-10 | Valencia | 13 | 4 | 28 | 5 |
| 2010-11 | Birmingham C | 25 | 5 | | |
| 2011-12 | Birmingham C | 35 | 11 | | |
| 2012-13 | Birmingham C | 35 | 9 | 95 | 25 |

**Scholars**
Adams, Charlee Shaun; Brown, Reece;
Dacres-Cogley, Joshua Jacob; Delfouneso,
Emmitt Daniel; Ebanks, Deqwon Lee; Fry,
James Michael Engelbretsen; Gray, Demarai;
Hales, Reece Brett; Hawker, Joshua Michael;
Kalenda, Jean; Kelly, Nathaniel; McGee,
George David; Moseley, Bobby James;
Preston, Callum; Solomon-Otabor, Viv Efosa;
Thomson, Callum James; Townsend, Nicholas
Peter; Trueman, Connal Joe; Truslove, Liam;
Webb, Reece.

## BLACKBURN R (9)

**BEST, Leon (F)**　　　　　　**203  48**
H: 6 1　W: 13 03　b.Nottingham 19-9-86
Source: Scholar. Honours: Eire Youth,
Under-21, 7 full caps.

| 2004-05 | Southampton | 3 | 0 | | |
| 2004-05 | QPR | 5 | 0 | 5 | 0 |
| 2005-06 | Southampton | 3 | 0 | | |
| 2005-06 | Sheffield W | 13 | 2 | 13 | 2 |
| 2006-07 | Southampton | 9 | 4 | 15 | 4 |
| 2006-07 | Bournemouth | 15 | 3 | 15 | 3 |
| 2006-07 | Yeovil T | 15 | 10 | 15 | 10 |
| 2007-08 | Coventry C | 34 | 8 | | |
| 2008-09 | Coventry C | 31 | 2 | | |
| 2009-10 | Coventry C | 27 | 9 | 92 | 19 |
| 2009-10 | Newcastle U | 13 | 0 | | |
| 2010-11 | Newcastle U | 11 | 6 | | |
| 2011-12 | Newcastle U | 18 | 4 | 42 | 10 |
| 2012-13 | Blackburn R | 6 | 0 | 6 | 0 |

**DANN, Scott (D)**　　　　　　**229  17**
H: 6 2　W: 12 00　b.Liverpool 14-2-87
Source: Scholar. Honours: England Under-21.

| 2004-05 | Walsall | 1 | 0 | | |
| 2005-06 | Walsall | 0 | 0 | | |
| 2006-07 | Walsall | 30 | 4 | | |
| 2007-08 | Walsall | 28 | 3 | 59 | 7 |
| 2007-08 | Coventry C | 16 | 0 | | |
| 2008-09 | Coventry C | 31 | 3 | 47 | 3 |
| 2009-10 | Birmingham C | 30 | 0 | | |
| 2010-11 | Birmingham C | 20 | 2 | | |
| 2011-12 | Birmingham C | 0 | 0 | 50 | 2 |
| 2011-12 | Blackburn R | 27 | 1 | | |
| 2012-13 | Blackburn R | 46 | 4 | 73 | 5 |

**DUNN, David (M)**　　　　　　**342  53**
H: 5 9　W: 12 03　b.Gt Harwood 27-12-79
Source: Trainee. Honours: England Youth,
Under-21, 1 full cap.

| 1997-98 | Blackburn R | 0 | 0 | | |
| 1998-99 | Blackburn R | 15 | 1 | | |
| 1999-2000 | Blackburn R | 22 | 2 | | |
| 2000-01 | Blackburn R | 42 | 12 | | |
| 2001-02 | Blackburn R | 29 | 7 | | |
| 2002-03 | Blackburn R | 28 | 8 | | |
| 2003-04 | Birmingham C | 21 | 2 | | |
| 2004-05 | Birmingham C | 11 | 2 | | |
| 2005-06 | Birmingham C | 15 | 2 | | |
| 2006-07 | Birmingham C | 11 | 1 | 58 | 7 |
| 2006-07 | Blackburn R | 11 | 0 | | |
| 2007-08 | Blackburn R | 31 | 1 | | |
| 2008-09 | Blackburn R | 15 | 1 | | |
| 2009-10 | Blackburn R | 23 | 9 | | |
| 2010-11 | Blackburn R | 27 | 2 | | |
| 2011-12 | Blackburn R | 26 | 2 | | |
| 2012-13 | Blackburn R | 15 | 1 | 284 | 46 |

**EDWARDS, Ryan (D)**　　　　　**35  0**
b.Liverpool 7-10-93
Source: Scholar.

| 2011-12 | Blackburn R | 0 | 0 | | |
| 2012-13 | Rochdale | 26 | 0 | 26 | 0 |
| 2012-13 | Blackburn R | 0 | 0 | | |
| 2012-13 | Fleetwood T | 9 | 0 | 9 | 0 |

**ETUHU, Dickson (M)**　　　　　**339  28**
H: 6 2　W: 13 04　b.Kano 8-6-82
Source: Scholar. Honours: Nigeria 20 full
caps.

| 1999-2000 | Manchester C | 0 | 0 | | |
| 2000-01 | Manchester C | 0 | 0 | | |
| 2001-02 | Manchester C | 12 | 0 | 12 | 0 |
| 2001-02 | Preston NE | 16 | 3 | | |
| 2002-03 | Preston NE | 39 | 6 | | |

| 2003-04 | Preston NE | 31 | 3 | | |
| 2004-05 | Preston NE | 35 | 3 | | |
| 2005-06 | Preston NE | 13 | 2 | 134 | 17 |
| 2005-06 | Norwich C | 19 | 0 | | |
| 2006-07 | Norwich C | 43 | 6 | 62 | 6 |
| 2007-08 | Sunderland | 20 | 1 | | |
| 2008-09 | Sunderland | 0 | 0 | 20 | 1 |
| 2008-09 | Fulham | 21 | 1 | | |
| 2009-10 | Fulham | 20 | 0 | | |
| 2010-11 | Fulham | 28 | 2 | | |
| 2011-12 | Fulham | 22 | 0 | | |
| 2012-13 | Fulham | 0 | 0 | 91 | 3 |
| 2012-13 | Blackburn R | 20 | 1 | 20 | 1 |

**EVANS, Micah (F)**　　　　　　**27  3**
b.Manchester 3-3-93
Source: Blackburn R Scholar.

| 2011-12 | Blackburn R | 0 | 0 | | |
| 2011-12 | Accrington S | 23 | 3 | 23 | 3 |
| 2012-13 | Blackburn R | 0 | 0 | | |
| 2012-13 | Chesterfield | 4 | 0 | 4 | 0 |

**FORMICA, Mauro (M)**　　　　**132  23**
H: 5 9　W: 10 01　b.Rosario 4-4-88
Honours: Argentina Youth.

| 2007-08 | Newell's Old Boys | 4 | 0 | | |
| 2008-09 | Newell's Old Boys | 19 | 7 | | |
| 2009-10 | Newell's Old Boys | 36 | 8 | | |
| 2010-11 | Newell's Old Boys | 16 | 2 | 75 | 17 |
| 2010-11 | Blackburn R | 0 | 0 | | |
| 2011-12 | Blackburn R | 34 | 4 | | |
| 2012-13 | Blackburn R | 15 | 1 | 49 | 5 |
| 2012-13 | Palermo | 8 | 1 | 8 | 1 |

**FORRESTER, Anton (F)**　　　　**0  0**
H: 6 0　W: 12 00　b.Liverpool 11-2-94
Source: Scholar.

| 2010-11 | Everton | 0 | 0 | | |
| 2011-12 | Everton | 0 | 0 | | |
| 2012-13 | Blackburn R | 0 | 0 | | |

**GIVET, Gael (D)**　　　　　　**322  11**
H: 5 11　W: 11 11　b.Arles 9-10-81
Honours: France 13 full caps.

| 2000-01 | Monaco | 1 | 0 | | |
| 2001-02 | Monaco | 23 | 2 | | |
| 2002-03 | Monaco | 23 | 1 | | |
| 2003-04 | Monaco | 33 | 2 | | |
| 2004-05 | Monaco | 34 | 0 | | |
| 2005-06 | Monaco | 32 | 2 | | |
| 2006-07 | Monaco | 32 | 1 | 178 | 8 |
| 2007-08 | Marseille | 29 | 0 | | |
| 2008-09 | Marseille | 0 | 0 | 29 | 0 |
| 2008-09 | Blackburn R | 14 | 0 | | |
| 2009-10 | Blackburn R | 34 | 2 | | |
| 2010-11 | Blackburn R | 29 | 1 | | |
| 2011-12 | Blackburn R | 22 | 0 | | |
| 2012-13 | Blackburn R | 16 | 0 | 115 | 3 |

**GOODWILLIE, David (F)**　　　**168  39**
H: 5 9　W: 11 02　b.Stirling 28-3-89
Honours: Scotland Youth, Under-21, 3 full
caps, 1 goal.

| 2005-06 | Dundee U | 10 | 1 | | |
| 2006-07 | Dundee U | 17 | 0 | | |
| 2007-08 | Dundee U | 2 | 0 | | |
| 2007-08 | Raith R | 23 | 9 | 23 | 9 |
| 2008-09 | Dundee U | 16 | 3 | | |
| 2009-10 | Dundee U | 33 | 8 | | |
| 2010-11 | Dundee U | 37 | 16 | | |
| 2011-12 | Dundee U | 1 | 0 | 116 | 28 |
| 2011-12 | Blackburn R | 20 | 2 | | |
| 2012-13 | Blackburn R | 8 | 0 | 28 | 2 |
| 2012-13 | Crystal Palace | 1 | 0 | 1 | 0 |

**HANLEY, Grant (D)**　　　　　**70  3**
H: 6 2　W: 12 00　b.Dumfries 20-11-91
Source: Scholar. Honours: Scotland Youth,
Under-21, 7 full caps, 1 goal.

| 2008-09 | Blackburn R | 0 | 0 | | |
| 2009-10 | Blackburn R | 1 | 0 | | |
| 2010-11 | Blackburn R | 7 | 0 | | |
| 2011-12 | Blackburn R | 23 | 1 | | |
| 2012-13 | Blackburn R | 39 | 2 | 70 | 3 |

**HANLEY, Raheem (D)**　　　　**0  0**
H: 5 8　W: 11 00　b.Blackburn 24-3-94
Source: Manchester U Scholar.

| 2011-12 | Blackburn R | 0 | 0 | | |
| 2012-13 | Blackburn R | 0 | 0 | | |

**HENLEY, Adam (D)**　　　　　**22  0**
H: 5 10　W: 12 02　b.Knoxville 14-6-94
Source: Scholar. Honours: Wales Youth,
Under-21.

| 2011-12 | Blackburn R | 7 | 0 | | |
| 2012-13 | Blackburn R | 15 | 0 | 22 | 0 |

**HENRIQUE, Nuno (D)**　　　　**9  0**
H: 6 1　W: 12 07　b.Fafe 19-10-86

| 2011-12 | Feirense | 7 | 0 | 7 | 0 |
| 2012-13 | Academica | 2 | 0 | 2 | 0 |
| 2012-13 | Blackburn R | 0 | 0 | | |

**JORGE, Paulo (M)**　　　　　　**1  0**
H: 5 10　W: 11 01　b.Braga 18-1-93

| 2012-13 | Blackburn R | 1 | 0 | 1 | 0 |

**JUNIOR, Edinho (F)**　　　　　**7  2**
H: 5 11　W: 11 10　b.Faro 7-3-94

| 2012-13 | Blackburn R | 1 | 0 | 1 | 0 |
| 2012-13 | Shillong Lajong | 6 | 2 | 6 | 2 |

**KAZIM-RICHARDS, Colin (F)**　**247  26**
H: 6 1　W: 10 09　b.Leyton 26-8-86
Source: Scholar. Honours: Turkey Under-21,
35 full caps, 2 goals.

| 2004-05 | Bury | 30 | 3 | 30 | 3 |
| 2005-06 | Brighton & HA | 42 | 6 | | |
| 2006-07 | Brighton & HA | 1 | 0 | 43 | 6 |
| 2006-07 | Sheffield U | 27 | 1 | 27 | 1 |
| 2007-08 | Fenerbahce | 28 | 0 | | |
| 2008-09 | Fenerbahce | 21 | 2 | | |
| 2009-10 | Fenerbahce | 11 | 3 | | |
| 2009-10 | Toulouse | 15 | 2 | 15 | 2 |
| 2010-11 | Fenerbahce | 5 | 0 | 65 | 5 |
| 2010-11 | Galatasaray | 13 | 3 | | |
| 2011-12 | Galatasaray | 18 | 2 | 31 | 5 |
| 2011-12 | Olympiacos | 8 | 1 | 8 | 1 |
On loan from Galatasaray
| 2012-13 | Blackburn R | 28 | 3 | 28 | 3 |

**KEAN, Jake (G)**　　　　　　**52  0**
H: 6 4　W: 11 13　b.Derby 4-2-91
Source: Derby Co Scholar.

| 2010-11 | Blackburn R | 0 | 0 | | |
| 2010-11 | Hartlepool U | 19 | 0 | 19 | 0 |
| 2011-12 | Blackburn R | 1 | 0 | | |
| 2011-12 | Rochdale | 14 | 0 | 14 | 0 |
| 2012-13 | Blackburn R | 18 | 0 | 19 | 0 |

**KING, Josh (F)**　　　　　　**44  3**
H: 5 11　W: 11 09　b.Oslo 15-1-92
Source: Scholar. Honours: Norway Youth,
Under-21, 6 full caps, 1 goal.

| 2008-09 | Manchester U | 0 | 0 | | |
| 2009-10 | Manchester U | 0 | 0 | | |
| 2010-11 | Manchester U | 0 | 0 | | |
| 2010-11 | Preston NE | 8 | 0 | 8 | 0 |
| 2011-12 | Manchester U | 0 | 0 | | |
| 2011-12 | Moenchengladbach | 2 | 0 | 2 | 0 |
| 2011-12 | Hull C | 18 | 1 | 18 | 1 |
| 2012-13 | Manchester U | 0 | 0 | | |
| 2012-13 | Blackburn R | 16 | 2 | 16 | 2 |

**LENIHAN, Darragh (M)**　　　**0  0**
b.Dublin 16-3-94
Source: Belvedere. Honours: Eire Youth.

| 2011-12 | Blackburn R | 0 | 0 | | |
| 2012-13 | Blackburn R | 0 | 0 | | |

**LOWE, Jason (M)**　　　　　　**76  2**
H: 6 0　W: 12 08　b.Wigan 2-9-91
Source: Scholar. Honours: England Under-20,
Under-21.

| 2009-10 | Blackburn R | 0 | 0 | | |
| 2010-11 | Blackburn R | 1 | 0 | | |
| 2010-11 | Oldham Ath | 7 | 2 | 7 | 2 |
| 2011-12 | Blackburn R | 32 | 0 | | |
| 2012-13 | Blackburn R | 36 | 0 | 69 | 0 |

**MOLINA, Hugo (D)**　　　　　**0  0**
b.Spain 30-11-93
Source: Scholar.

| 2011-12 | Blackburn R | 0 | 0 | | |
| 2012-13 | Blackburn R | 0 | 0 | | |

**MORRIS, Josh (M)**　　　　　**26  0**
H: 5 9　W: 10 00　b.Preston 30-9-91
Source: Scholar. Honours: England Under-20.

| 2010-11 | Blackburn R | 4 | 0 | | |
| 2011-12 | Blackburn R | 2 | 0 | | |
| 2011-12 | Yeovil T | 5 | 0 | 5 | 0 |

| 2012-13 | Blackburn R | 10 | 0 | 16 | 0 |
| 2012-13 | *Rotherham U* | 5 | 0 | 5 | 0 |

**MURPHY, Danny (M)**    600 79
H: 5 10   W: 11 09   b.Chester 18-3-77
*Source:* Trainee. *Honours:* England Schools, Youth, Under-21, 9 full caps, 1 goal.

| 1993-94 | Crewe Alex | 12 | 2 | | |
| 1994-95 | Crewe Alex | 35 | 5 | | |
| 1995-96 | Crewe Alex | 42 | 10 | | |
| 1996-97 | Crewe Alex | 45 | 10 | | |
| 1997-98 | Liverpool | 16 | 0 | | |
| 1998-99 | Liverpool | 1 | 0 | | |
| 1998-99 | *Crewe Alex* | 16 | 1 | 150 | 28 |
| 1999-2000 | Liverpool | 23 | 3 | | |
| 2000-01 | Liverpool | 27 | 4 | | |
| 2001-02 | Liverpool | 36 | 6 | | |
| 2002-03 | Liverpool | 36 | 7 | | |
| 2003-04 | Liverpool | 31 | 5 | 170 | 25 |
| 2004-05 | Charlton Ath | 38 | 3 | | |
| 2005-06 | Charlton Ath | 18 | 4 | 56 | 7 |
| 2005-06 | Tottenham H | 10 | 0 | | |
| 2006-07 | Tottenham H | 12 | 1 | | |
| 2007-08 | Tottenham H | 0 | 0 | 22 | 1 |
| 2007-08 | Fulham | 33 | 5 | | |
| 2008-09 | Fulham | 38 | 5 | | |
| 2009-10 | Fulham | 25 | 5 | | |
| 2010-11 | Fulham | 37 | 0 | | |
| 2011-12 | Fulham | 36 | 2 | 169 | 17 |
| 2012-13 | Blackburn R | 33 | 1 | 33 | 1 |

**NUNES, Fabio (M)**    6 0
H: 5 9   W: 11 10   b.portimao 24-7-92

| 2012-13 | Blackburn R | 6 | 0 | 6 | 0 |

**NUNO GOMES, Miguel (F)**    451 172
H: 5 11   W: 11 04   b.Amarante 5-7-76

| 1994-95 | Boavista | 17 | 1 | | |
| 1995-96 | Boavista | 28 | 7 | | |
| 1996-97 | Boavista | 34 | 15 | 79 | 23 |
| 1997-98 | Benfica | 33 | 18 | | |
| 1998-99 | Benfica | 34 | 24 | | |
| 1999-2000 | Benfica | 34 | 18 | | |
| 2000-01 | Fiorentina | 30 | 10 | | |
| 2001-02 | Fiorentina | 23 | 5 | 53 | 15 |
| 2002-03 | Benfica | 19 | 9 | | |
| 2003-04 | Benfica | 21 | 7 | | |
| 2004-05 | Benfica | 22 | 7 | | |
| 2005-06 | Benfica | 28 | 14 | | |
| 2006-07 | Benfica | 23 | 6 | | |
| 2007-08 | Benfica | 25 | 7 | | |
| 2008-09 | Benfica | 24 | 7 | | |
| 2009-10 | Benfica | 13 | 3 | | |
| 2010-11 | Benfica | 6 | 4 | 282 | 124 |
| 2011-12 | *Braga* | 19 | 6 | 19 | 6 |
| 2012-13 | Blackburn R | 18 | 4 | 18 | 4 |

**O'CONNELL, Jack (D)**    21 0
b.Liverpool 29-3-94

| 2012-13 | Blackburn R | 0 | 0 | | |
| 2012-13 | *Rotherham U* | 3 | 0 | 3 | 0 |
| 2012-13 | *York C* | 18 | 0 | 18 | 0 |

**O'CONNOR, Anthony (D)**    46 0
H: 6 2   W: 12 06   b.Cork 25-10-92
*Source:* Scholar. *Honours:* Eire Youth, Under-21.

| 2010-11 | Blackburn R | 0 | 0 | | |
| 2011-12 | Blackburn R | 0 | 0 | | |
| 2012-13 | Blackburn R | 0 | 0 | | |
| 2012-13 | *Burton Alb* | 46 | 0 | 46 | 0 |

**O'SULLIVAN, John (M)**    1 0
b.Birmingham 18-9-93
*Source:* Scholar. *Honours:* Eire Youth, Under-21.

| 2011-12 | Blackburn R | 0 | 0 | | |
| 2012-13 | Blackburn R | 1 | 0 | 1 | 0 |

**OLSSON, Marcus (M)**    135 13
H: 5 11   W: 10 10   b.Gavle 17-5-88
*Honours:* Sweden Under-21, 2 full caps.

| 2008 | Halmstad | 21 | 2 | | |
| 2009 | Halmstad | 20 | 4 | | |
| 2010 | Halmstad | 30 | 4 | | |
| 2011 | Halmstad | 29 | 2 | 100 | 12 |
| 2011-12 | Blackburn R | 12 | 0 | | |
| 2012-13 | Blackburn R | 23 | 1 | 35 | 1 |

**OLSSON, Martin (D)**    117 3
H: 5 7   W: 12 12   b.Gavle 17-5-88
*Source:* Hogaborg. *Honours:* Sweden Under-21, 15 full caps, 4 goals.

| 2005-06 | Blackburn R | 0 | 0 | | |
| 2006-07 | Blackburn R | 0 | 0 | | |
| 2007-08 | Blackburn R | 2 | 0 | | |
| 2008-09 | Blackburn R | 9 | 0 | | |
| 2009-10 | Blackburn R | 21 | 1 | | |
| 2010-11 | Blackburn R | 29 | 2 | | |
| 2011-12 | Blackburn R | 27 | 0 | | |
| 2012-13 | Blackburn R | 29 | 0 | 117 | 3 |

**ORR, Bradley (D)**    316 13
H: 6 0   W: 11 11   b.Liverpool 1-11-82
*Source:* Scholar.

| 2001-02 | Newcastle U | 0 | 0 | | |
| 2002-03 | Newcastle U | 0 | 0 | | |
| 2003-04 | Newcastle U | 0 | 0 | | |
| 2003-04 | *Burnley* | 4 | 0 | 4 | 0 |
| 2004-05 | Bristol C | 37 | 0 | | |
| 2005-06 | Bristol C | 38 | 1 | | |
| 2006-07 | Bristol C | 35 | 4 | | |
| 2007-08 | Bristol C | 42 | 4 | | |
| 2008-09 | Bristol C | 38 | 1 | | |
| 2009-10 | Bristol C | 39 | 2 | 229 | 12 |
| 2010-11 | QPR | 33 | 1 | | |
| 2011-12 | QPR | 6 | 0 | 39 | 1 |
| 2011-12 | Blackburn R | 12 | 0 | | |
| 2012-13 | Blackburn R | 19 | 0 | 31 | 0 |
| 2012-13 | *Ipswich T* | 13 | 0 | 13 | 0 |

**OSAWE, Osayamen (F)**    2 0
b.Blackburn 13-9-93

| 2012-13 | Blackburn R | 0 | 0 | | |
| 2012-13 | *Accrington S* | 2 | 0 | 2 | 0 |

**PAYNE, Tim (F)**    0 0
H: 5 10   W: 11 05   b.New Zealand 10-1-94
*Source:* Waitakere U. *Honours:* New Zealand Youth, 9 full caps, 2 goals.

| 2011-12 | Blackburn R | 0 | 0 | | |
| 2012-13 | Blackburn R | 0 | 0 | | |

**PEDERSEN, Morten (F)**    451 80
H: 5 11   W: 11 00   b.Vadso 8-9-81
*Honours:* Norway Youth, Under-21, 74 full caps, 16 goals.

| 1997 | Norlid | 21 | 0 | | |
| 1998 | Pola | 20 | 4 | 20 | 4 |
| 1999 | Norlid | 19 | 0 | 40 | 0 |
| 2000 | Tromso | 10 | 3 | | |
| 2001 | Tromso | 26 | 5 | | |
| 2002 | Tromso | 23 | 18 | | |
| 2003 | Tromso | 26 | 8 | | |
| 2004 | Tromso | 18 | 7 | 103 | 41 |
| 2004-05 | Blackburn R | 19 | 4 | | |
| 2005-06 | Blackburn R | 34 | 9 | | |
| 2006-07 | Blackburn R | 36 | 6 | | |
| 2007-08 | Blackburn R | 37 | 4 | | |
| 2008-09 | Blackburn R | 33 | 1 | | |
| 2009-10 | Blackburn R | 33 | 3 | | |
| 2010-11 | Blackburn R | 35 | 4 | | |
| 2011-12 | Blackburn R | 33 | 3 | | |
| 2012-13 | Blackburn R | 28 | 1 | 288 | 35 |

**RHODES, Jordan (F)**    196 109
H: 6 1   W: 11 03   b.Oldham 5-2-90
*Source:* Academy. *Honours:* Scotland Under-21, 9 full caps, 3 goals.

| 2007-08 | Ipswich T | 8 | 1 | | |
| 2008-09 | Ipswich T | 2 | 0 | 10 | 1 |
| 2008-09 | *Rochdale* | 5 | 2 | 5 | 2 |
| 2008-09 | *Brentford* | 7 | 4 | 14 | 7 |
| 2009-10 | Huddersfield T | 45 | 19 | | |
| 2010-11 | Huddersfield T | 40 | 35 | | |
| 2011-12 | Huddersfield T | 40 | 35 | | |
| 2012-13 | Huddersfield T | 2 | 2 | 124 | 72 |
| 2012-13 | Blackburn R | 43 | 27 | 43 | 27 |

**RIBEIRO, Bruno (D)**    16 0
H: 5 6   W: 10 07   b.Sao Paulo 1-4-83

| 2009-10 | Gremio | 7 | 0 | | |
| 2010-11 | Gremio | 4 | 0 | 11 | 0 |
| 2012-13 | Blackburn R | 5 | 0 | 5 | 0 |
| 2012-13 | *Linense* | 0 | 0 | | |

**ROBINSON, Paul (G)**    393 1
H: 6 1   W: 14 07   b.Beverley 15-10-79
*Source:* Trainee. *Honours:* England Under-21, 41 full caps.

| 1996-97 | Leeds U | 0 | 0 | | |
| 1997-98 | Leeds U | 0 | 0 | | |
| 1998-99 | Leeds U | 5 | 0 | | |
| 1999-2000 | Leeds U | 0 | 0 | | |
| 2000-01 | Leeds U | 16 | 0 | | |
| 2001-02 | Leeds U | 0 | 0 | | |
| 2002-03 | Leeds U | 38 | 0 | | |
| 2003-04 | Leeds U | 36 | 0 | 95 | 0 |
| 2003-04 | Tottenham H | 0 | 0 | | |
| 2004-05 | Tottenham H | 36 | 0 | | |
| 2005-06 | Tottenham H | 38 | 0 | | |
| 2006-07 | Tottenham H | 38 | 1 | | |
| 2007-08 | Tottenham H | 25 | 0 | 137 | 1 |
| 2008-09 | Blackburn R | 35 | 0 | | |
| 2009-10 | Blackburn R | 35 | 0 | | |
| 2010-11 | Blackburn R | 36 | 0 | | |
| 2011-12 | Blackburn R | 34 | 0 | | |
| 2012-13 | Blackburn R | 21 | 0 | 161 | 0 |

**ROCHINA, Ruben (F)**    69 10
H: 5 11   W: 11 00   b.Sagunto 23-3-91
*Honours:* Spain Youth.

| 2008-09 | Barcelona B | 10 | 2 | | |
| 2009-10 | Barcelona B | 3 | 0 | 13 | 2 |
| 2010-11 | Blackburn R | 4 | 0 | | |
| 2011-12 | Blackburn R | 18 | 2 | | |
| 2012-13 | Blackburn R | 19 | 5 | 41 | 7 |
| 2012-13 | *Real Zaragoza* | 15 | 1 | 15 | 1 |

**ROSADO, Diogo (M)**    19 2
H: 6 1   W: 12 11   b.Peniche 21-2-90

| 2011-12 | Sporting Lisbon | 0 | 0 | | |
| 2011-12 | *Feirense* | 17 | 2 | 17 | 2 |
| 2012-13 | Sporting Lisbon | 0 | 0 | | |
| 2012-13 | Blackburn R | 2 | 0 | 2 | 0 |

**SANDOMIERSKI, Grzegorz (G)**    8 0
H: 6 5   W: 13 08   b.Bialystok 5-9-89
*Honours:* Poland Youth Under-21, 3 full caps.

| 2012-13 | Genk | 0 | 0 | | |

On loan from Genk

| 2012-13 | Blackburn R | 8 | 0 | 8 | 0 |

**SLEW, Jordan (F)**    31 3
H: 6 3   W: 12 11   b.Sheffield 7-9-92
*Source:* Scholar.

| 2010-11 | Sheffield U | 7 | 2 | | |
| 2011-12 | Sheffield U | 4 | 1 | 11 | 3 |
| 2011-12 | Blackburn R | 1 | 0 | | |
| 2011-12 | *Stevenage* | 9 | 0 | 9 | 0 |
| 2012-13 | Blackburn R | 0 | 0 | 1 | 0 |
| 2012-13 | *Oldham Ath* | 3 | 0 | 3 | 0 |
| 2012-13 | *Rotherham U* | 7 | 0 | 7 | 0 |

**USAI, Sebastian (G)**    4 0
H: 6 3   W: 10 01   b.Brisbane 28-2-90
*Source:* Brisbane Strikers.

| 2010-11 | N Queensland F | 4 | 0 | 4 | 0 |
| 2011-12 | Blackburn R | 0 | 0 | | |
| 2012-13 | Blackburn R | 0 | 0 | | |

**VUKCEVIC, Simon (M)**    173 29
H: 5 10   W: 12 02   b.Podgorica 29-1-86
*Honours:* Serbia Under-21, 42 full caps, 2 goals. Montenegro Under-21, 42 full caps, 2 goals.

| 2002-03 | Partizan Belgrade | 1 | 0 | | |
| 2003-04 | Partizan Belgrade | 12 | 0 | | |
| 2004-05 | Partizan Belgrade | 26 | 10 | | |
| 2005-06 | Partizan Belgrade | 13 | 3 | 52 | 13 |
| 2006 | Saturn Moscow O | 24 | 0 | | |
| 2007 | Saturn Moscow O | 4 | 1 | 28 | 1 |
| 2007-08 | Sporting Lisbon | 26 | 7 | | |
| 2008-09 | Sporting Lisbon | 13 | 4 | | |
| 2009-10 | Sporting Lisbon | 14 | 1 | | |
| 2010-11 | Sporting Lisbon | 24 | 2 | 77 | 14 |
| 2011-12 | Blackburn R | 7 | 1 | | |
| 2012-13 | Blackburn R | 9 | 0 | 16 | 1 |

**WILLIAMSON, Lee (M)**    420 36
H: 5 10   W: 10 04   b.Derby 7-6-82
*Source:* Trainee.

| 1999-2000 | Mansfield T | 4 | 0 | | |
| 2000-01 | Mansfield T | 15 | 0 | | |
| 2001-02 | Mansfield T | 46 | 3 | | |
| 2002-03 | Mansfield T | 40 | 0 | | |
| 2003-04 | Mansfield T | 35 | 0 | | |
| 2004-05 | Mansfield T | 4 | 0 | 144 | 3 |

| | | | | | |
|---|---|---|---|---|---|
| 2004-05 | Northampton T | 37 | 0 | **37** | **0** |
| 2005-06 | Rotherham U | 37 | 4 | | |
| 2006-07 | Rotherham U | 19 | 5 | **56** | **9** |
| 2006-07 | Watford | 5 | 0 | | |
| 2007-08 | Watford | 32 | 2 | | |
| 2008-09 | Watford | 34 | 2 | **71** | **4** |
| 2008-09 | *Preston NE* | 5 | 1 | **5** | **1** |
| 2009-10 | Sheffield U | 20 | 3 | | |
| 2010-11 | Sheffield U | 16 | 3 | | |
| 2011-12 | Sheffield U | 40 | 13 | | |
| 2012-13 | Sheffield U | 0 | 0 | **76** | **19** |
| 2012-13 | Portsmouth | 22 | 0 | **22** | **0** |
| 2012-13 | Blackburn R | 9 | 0 | **9** | **0** |

**Scholars**
Anderson, Jordan Jacob; Bauress, Bradley Stephen; Beesley, William; Brown, Thomas Hayden; Butterwick, William Peter; Daly, Kellen Joseph; Haley, Curtis Oliver; Harris, Callum Lee; Humphreys, Ryan Christopher; Laverty, Daniel Joseph; MacLaren, Jamie; Osawe, Osayamen; Paul, Thomas; Pero, Deniz; Preston, Jordan Robert; Raya, Martin David; Rittenberg, Dean James; Torres, Martinez Yeray; Urwin, Matthew William; Vicars, Ian Paul; Wassi, Brice; Wylie, Peter James John.

# BLACKPOOL (10)

**ALMOND, Louis (F)**    **4**   **0**
H: 5 11   W: 12 00   b.Blackburn 5-1-92
Source: Scholar.

| | | | | | |
|---|---|---|---|---|---|
| 2009-10 | Blackpool | 0 | 0 | | |
| 2009-10 | *Cheltenham T* | 4 | 0 | **4** | **0** |
| 2010-11 | Blackpool | 0 | 0 | | |
| 2011-12 | Blackpool | 0 | 0 | | |
| 2012-13 | Blackpool | 0 | 0 | | |

**BANVO, Anderson (F)**    **0**   **0**
H: 6 1   b.Paris 4-2-94
Source: Paris St Germain. Honours: Ivory Coast Youth.

| | | | |
|---|---|---|---|
| 2012-13 | Blackpool | 0 | 0 |

**BAPTISTE, Alex (D)**    **344**   **13**
H: 6 0   W: 11 11   b.Sutton-in-Ashfield 31-1-86
Source: Scholar.

| | | | | | |
|---|---|---|---|---|---|
| 2002-03 | Mansfield T | 4 | 0 | | |
| 2003-04 | Mansfield T | 17 | 0 | | |
| 2004-05 | Mansfield T | 41 | 1 | | |
| 2005-06 | Mansfield T | 41 | 1 | | |
| 2006-07 | Mansfield T | 46 | 3 | | |
| 2007-08 | Mansfield T | 25 | 0 | **174** | **5** |
| 2008-09 | Blackpool | 21 | 1 | | |
| 2009-10 | Blackpool | 42 | 3 | | |
| 2010-11 | Blackpool | 21 | 2 | | |
| 2011-12 | Blackpool | 43 | 1 | | |
| 2012-13 | Blackpool | 43 | 1 | **170** | **8** |

**BARKHUIZEN, Tom (F)**    **51**   **12**
H: 5 9   W: 11 00   b.Blackpool 4-7-93
Source: Scholar.

| | | | | | |
|---|---|---|---|---|---|
| 2011-12 | Blackpool | 0 | 0 | | |
| 2011-12 | *Hereford U* | 38 | 11 | **38** | **11** |
| 2012-13 | Blackpool | 0 | 0 | | |
| 2012-13 | *Fleetwood T* | 13 | 1 | **13** | **1** |

**BASHAM, Chris (M)**    **77**   **4**
H: 5 11   W: 12 08   b.Hebburn 20-7-88
Source: Scholar.

| | | | | | |
|---|---|---|---|---|---|
| 2007-08 | Bolton W | 0 | 0 | | |
| 2007-08 | *Rochdale* | 13 | 0 | **13** | **0** |
| 2008-09 | Bolton W | 11 | 1 | | |
| 2009-10 | Bolton W | 8 | 0 | **19** | **1** |
| 2010-11 | Blackpool | 2 | 0 | | |
| 2011-12 | Blackpool | 17 | 2 | | |
| 2012-13 | Blackpool | 26 | 1 | **45** | **3** |

**BROADFOOT, Kirk (D)**    **264**   **16**
H: 6 3   W: 13 13   b.Irvine 8-8-84

| | | | | | |
|---|---|---|---|---|---|
| 2002-03 | St Mirren | 23 | 1 | | |
| 2003-04 | St Mirren | 31 | 3 | | |
| 2004-05 | St Mirren | 36 | 4 | | |
| 2005-06 | St Mirren | 27 | 2 | | |
| 2006-07 | St Mirren | 37 | 3 | **154** | **13** |
| 2007-08 | Rangers | 15 | 1 | | |
| 2008-09 | Rangers | 27 | 0 | | |
| 2009-10 | Rangers | 12 | 0 | | |
| 2010-11 | Rangers | 8 | 0 | | |
| 2011-12 | Rangers | 16 | 0 | **78** | **1** |
| 2012-13 | Blackpool | 32 | 2 | **32** | **2** |

**BRUNA, Gerardo (M)**    **2**   **0**
H: 5 8   W: 10 02   b.Mendoza 29-1-91
Source: Real Madrid.

| | | | | | |
|---|---|---|---|---|---|
| 2007-08 | Liverpool | 0 | 0 | | |
| 2008-09 | Liverpool | 0 | 0 | | |
| 2009-10 | Liverpool | 0 | 0 | | |
| 2010-11 | Liverpool | 0 | 0 | | |
| 2011-12 | Liverpool | 1 | 0 | | |
| 2012-13 | Blackpool | 1 | 0 | **2** | **0** |

**CAPRICE, Jake (M)**    **8**   **0**
H: 5 10   W: 11 07   b.Lambeth 11-11-92
Source: Scholar.

| | | | | | |
|---|---|---|---|---|---|
| 2011-12 | Crystal Palace | 0 | 0 | | |
| 2012-13 | Blackpool | 0 | 0 | | |
| 2012-13 | *Dagenham & R* | 8 | 0 | **8** | **0** |

**CATHCART, Craig (D)**    **138**   **5**
H: 6 2   W: 11 06   b.Belfast 6-2-89
Source: Scholar. Honours: Northern Ireland Youth, Under-21, 14 full caps.

| | | | | | |
|---|---|---|---|---|---|
| 2005-06 | Manchester U | 0 | 0 | | |
| 2006-07 | Manchester U | 0 | 0 | | |
| 2007-08 | Manchester U | 0 | 0 | | |
| 2007-08 | *Antwerp* | 13 | 2 | **13** | **2** |
| 2008-09 | Manchester U | 0 | 0 | | |
| 2008-09 | *Plymouth Arg* | 31 | 1 | **31** | **1** |
| 2009-10 | Manchester U | 0 | 0 | | |
| 2009-10 | *Watford* | 12 | 0 | **12** | **0** |
| 2010-11 | Blackpool | 30 | 1 | | |
| 2011-12 | Blackpool | 27 | 0 | | |
| 2012-13 | Blackpool | 25 | 1 | **82** | **2** |

**CRAINEY, Stephen (D)**    **312**   **4**
H: 5 9   W: 9 11   b.Glasgow 22-6-81
Honours: Scotland B, Under-21, 12 full caps.

| | | | | | |
|---|---|---|---|---|---|
| 1999-2000 | Celtic | 9 | 0 | | |
| 2000-01 | Celtic | 2 | 0 | | |
| 2001-02 | Celtic | 15 | 0 | | |
| 2002-03 | Celtic | 13 | 0 | | |
| 2003-04 | Celtic | 2 | 0 | **41** | **0** |
| 2003-04 | *Southampton* | 5 | 0 | **5** | **0** |
| 2004-05 | Leeds U | 9 | 0 | | |
| 2005-06 | Leeds U | 24 | 0 | | |
| 2006-07 | Leeds U | 19 | 0 | **52** | **0** |
| 2007-08 | Blackpool | 40 | 1 | | |
| 2008-09 | Blackpool | 17 | 0 | | |
| 2009-10 | Blackpool | 41 | 0 | | |
| 2010-11 | Blackpool | 31 | 0 | | |
| 2011-12 | Blackpool | 42 | 3 | | |
| 2012-13 | Blackpool | 43 | 0 | **214** | **4** |

**DJEZIRI, Adda (F)**    **14**   **2**
H: 6 3   W: 13 04   b.Denmark 3-8-88

| | | | | | |
|---|---|---|---|---|---|
| 2008-09 | Vejle | 6 | 2 | **6** | **2** |
| 2011-12 | Koge | 4 | 0 | **4** | **0** |
| 2012-13 | Blackpool | 0 | 0 | | |
| 2012-13 | *Scunthorpe U* | 4 | 0 | **4** | **0** |

**EARDLEY, Neal (M)**    **217**   **12**
H: 5 11   W: 11 10   b.Llandudno 6-11-88
Source: Scholar. Honours: Wales Under-21, 16 full caps.

| | | | | | |
|---|---|---|---|---|---|
| 2005-06 | Oldham Ath | 1 | 0 | | |
| 2006-07 | Oldham Ath | 36 | 2 | | |
| 2007-08 | Oldham Ath | 42 | 6 | | |
| 2008-09 | Oldham Ath | 34 | 2 | | |
| 2009-10 | Oldham Ath | 0 | 0 | **113** | **10** |
| 2009-10 | Blackpool | 24 | 0 | | |
| 2010-11 | Blackpool | 31 | 1 | | |
| 2011-12 | Blackpool | 26 | 1 | | |
| 2012-13 | Blackpool | 23 | 0 | **104** | **2** |

**EASTHAM, Ashley (D)**    **79**   **2**
H: 6 3   W: 12 06   b.Preston 22-3-91
Source: Scholar.

| | | | | | |
|---|---|---|---|---|---|
| 2009-10 | Blackpool | 1 | 0 | | |
| 2009-10 | *Cheltenham T* | 20 | 0 | | |
| 2010-11 | Blackpool | 0 | 0 | | |
| 2010-11 | *Cheltenham T* | 9 | 0 | **29** | **0** |
| 2010-11 | *Carlisle U* | 0 | 0 | | |
| 2011-12 | Blackpool | 0 | 0 | | |
| 2011-12 | *Bury* | 25 | 2 | | |
| 2012-13 | Blackpool | 0 | 0 | **1** | **0** |
| 2012-13 | *Fleetwood T* | 1 | 0 | **1** | **0** |

| | | | | | |
|---|---|---|---|---|---|
| 2012-13 | *Notts Co* | 4 | 0 | **4** | **0** |
| 2012-13 | *Bury* | 19 | 0 | **44** | **2** |

**ECCLESTON, Nathan (F)**    **46**   **6**
H: 5 10   W: 12 00   b.Manchester 30-12-90
Source: Scholar.

| | | | | | |
|---|---|---|---|---|---|
| 2007-08 | Liverpool | 0 | 0 | | |
| 2008-09 | Liverpool | 0 | 0 | | |
| 2009-10 | Liverpool | 0 | 0 | | |
| 2009-10 | *Huddersfield T* | 11 | 1 | **11** | **1** |
| 2010-11 | Liverpool | 1 | 0 | | |
| 2010-11 | *Charlton Ath* | 21 | 3 | **21** | **3** |
| 2011-12 | Liverpool | 0 | 0 | | |
| 2011-12 | *Rochdale* | 5 | 1 | **5** | **1** |
| 2012-13 | Liverpool | 0 | 0 | **2** | **0** |
| 2012-13 | Blackpool | 6 | 1 | **6** | **1** |
| 2012-13 | *Tranmere R* | 1 | 0 | **1** | **0** |

**EVATT, Ian (D)**    **386**   **18**
H: 6 3   W: 13 12   b.Coventry 19-11-81
Source: Trainee.

| | | | | | |
|---|---|---|---|---|---|
| 1998-99 | Derby Co | 0 | 0 | | |
| 1999-2000 | Derby Co | 0 | 0 | | |
| 2000-01 | Derby Co | 1 | 0 | | |
| 2001-02 | *Northampton T* | 11 | 0 | **11** | **0** |
| 2001-02 | Derby Co | 3 | 0 | | |
| 2002-03 | Derby Co | 30 | 0 | **34** | **0** |
| 2003-04 | Chesterfield | 43 | 5 | | |
| 2004-05 | Chesterfield | 41 | 4 | **84** | **9** |
| 2005-06 | QPR | 27 | 0 | | |
| 2006-07 | QPR | 0 | 0 | **27** | **0** |
| 2006-07 | Blackpool | 44 | 0 | | |
| 2007-08 | Blackpool | 29 | 0 | | |
| 2008-09 | Blackpool | 33 | 1 | | |
| 2009-10 | Blackpool | 36 | 4 | | |
| 2010-11 | Blackpool | 38 | 1 | | |
| 2011-12 | Blackpool | 39 | 3 | | |
| 2012-13 | Blackpool | 11 | 0 | **230** | **9** |

**FERGUSON, Barry (M)**    **465**   **48**
H: 5 7   W: 9 10   b.Hamilton 2-2-78
Source: Rangers SABC. Honours: Scotland Under-21, 45 full caps, 3 goals.

| | | | | | |
|---|---|---|---|---|---|
| 1994-95 | Rangers | 0 | 0 | | |
| 1995-96 | Rangers | 0 | 0 | | |
| 1996-97 | Rangers | 1 | 0 | | |
| 1997-98 | Rangers | 7 | 0 | | |
| 1998-99 | Rangers | 23 | 1 | | |
| 1999-2000 | Rangers | 31 | 4 | | |
| 2000-01 | Rangers | 30 | 2 | | |
| 2001-02 | Rangers | 22 | 1 | | |
| 2002-03 | Rangers | 36 | 16 | | |
| 2003-04 | Rangers | 3 | 0 | | |
| 2003-04 | Blackburn R | 15 | 1 | | |
| 2004-05 | Blackburn R | 21 | 2 | **36** | **3** |
| 2004-05 | Rangers | 13 | 2 | | |
| 2005-06 | Rangers | 32 | 5 | | |
| 2006-07 | Rangers | 32 | 4 | | |
| 2007-08 | Rangers | 38 | 7 | | |
| 2008-09 | Rangers | 22 | 2 | **290** | **44** |
| 2009-10 | Birmingham C | 37 | 0 | | |
| 2010-11 | Birmingham C | 35 | 0 | **72** | **0** |
| 2011-12 | Blackpool | 42 | 1 | | |
| 2012-13 | Blackpool | 19 | 0 | **61** | **1** |
| 2012-13 | *Fleetwood T* | 6 | 0 | **6** | **0** |

**GILKS, Matthew (G)**    **316**   **0**
H: 6 3   W: 13 12   b.Rochdale 4-6-82
Source: Scholar. Honours: Scotland 2 full caps.

| | | | | | |
|---|---|---|---|---|---|
| 2000-01 | Rochdale | 3 | 0 | | |
| 2001-02 | Rochdale | 19 | 0 | | |
| 2002-03 | Rochdale | 20 | 0 | | |
| 2003-04 | Rochdale | 12 | 0 | | |
| 2004-05 | Rochdale | 30 | 0 | | |
| 2005-06 | Rochdale | 46 | 0 | | |
| 2006-07 | Rochdale | 46 | 0 | **176** | **0** |
| 2007-08 | Norwich C | 0 | 0 | | |
| 2008-09 | Bradford | 5 | 0 | | |
| 2008-09 | *Shrewsbury T* | 4 | 0 | **4** | **0** |
| 2009-10 | Blackpool | 26 | 0 | | |
| 2010-11 | Blackpool | 18 | 0 | | |
| 2011-12 | Blackpool | 42 | 0 | | |
| 2012-13 | Blackpool | 45 | 0 | **136** | **0** |

**GOMES, Tiago (M)**    **157**   **12**
H: 5 11   W: 11 12   b.Vila Franca de Xira 18-8-85

| | | | |
|---|---|---|---|
| 2006-07 | Amadora | 26 | 2 |

## GRANDIN, Elliot (F) — 141 18

(continued)

|  |  | | | | |
|---|---|---|---|---|---|
| 2007-08 | Amadora | 21 | 1 | 47 | 3 |
| 2008-09 | *Steaua Bucuresti* | 6 | 0 | 6 | 0 |
| 2009-10 | Hercules | 33 | 7 | | |
| 2010-11 | Hercules | 29 | 2 | | |
| 2011-12 | Hercules | 17 | 0 | 79 | 9 |
| 2012-13 | Blackpool | 25 | 0 | 25 | 0 |

**GRANDIN, Elliot (F)**    141 18
H: 5 10  W: 10 07  b.Caen 17-10-87

|  |  | | | | |
|---|---|---|---|---|---|
| 2004-05 | Caen | 1 | 0 | | |
| 2005-06 | Caen | 19 | 3 | | |
| 2006-07 | Caen | 23 | 2 | | |
| 2007-08 | Caen | 12 | 1 | 55 | 6 |
| 2007-08 | Marseille | 8 | 0 | | |
| 2008-09 | Marseille | 8 | 2 | 16 | 2 |
| 2008-09 | *Grenoble* | 8 | 0 | 8 | 0 |
| 2009-10 | CSKA Sofia | 10 | 4 | | |
| 2010-11 | CSKA Sofia | 1 | 0 | 11 | 4 |
| 2010-11 | Blackpool | 23 | 1 | | |
| 2011-12 | Blackpool | 7 | 2 | | |
| 2011-12 | *Nice* | 9 | 0 | 9 | 0 |
| 2012-13 | Blackpool | 12 | 3 | 42 | 6 |

**HALSTEAD, Mark (G)**    3 0
H: 6 3  W: 14 00  b.Blackpool 1-9-90
*Source:* Scholar.

|  |  | | | | |
|---|---|---|---|---|---|
| 2009-10 | Blackpool | 0 | 0 | | |
| 2010-11 | Blackpool | 1 | 0 | | |
| 2011-12 | Blackpool | 0 | 0 | | |
| 2012-13 | Blackpool | 2 | 0 | 3 | 0 |

**HARRIS, Robert (D)**    169 11
H: 5 8  W: 10 00  b.Glasgow 28-8-87

|  |  | | | | |
|---|---|---|---|---|---|
| 2004-05 | Clyde | 1 | 0 | | |
| 2005-06 | Clyde | 20 | 0 | | |
| 2006-07 | Clyde | 24 | 0 | 45 | 0 |
| 2007-08 | Queen of the S | 26 | 2 | | |
| 2008-09 | Queen of the S | 21 | 2 | | |
| 2009-10 | Queen of the S | 32 | 4 | | |
| 2010-11 | Queen of the S | 31 | 2 | 110 | 10 |
| 2011-12 | Blackpool | 5 | 0 | | |
| 2012-13 | Blackpool | 4 | 0 | 9 | 0 |
| 2012-13 | *Rotherham U* | 5 | 1 | 5 | 1 |

**INCE, Tom (M)**    44 18
H: 5 10  W: 10 06  b.Stockport 30-1-92
*Source:* Liverpool. *Honours:* England Youth, Under-21.

|  |  | | | | |
|---|---|---|---|---|---|
| 2011-12 | Blackpool | 0 | 0 | | |
| 2012-13 | Blackpool | 44 | 18 | 44 | 18 |

**KETTINGS, Chris (G)**    2 0
H: 6 2  W: 12 04  b.Bolton 25-10-92
*Source:* Scholar. *Honours:* Scotland Youth, Under-21.

|  |  | | | | |
|---|---|---|---|---|---|
| 2011-12 | Blackpool | 0 | 0 | | |
| 2011-12 | *Birmingham C* | 0 | 0 | | |
| 2011-12 | *Morecambe* | 2 | 0 | 2 | 0 |
| 2012-13 | Blackpool | 0 | 0 | | |

**MARTINEZ, Angel (M)**    176 10
H: 5 9  W: 11 13  b.Girona 31-1-86
*Honours:* Spain Youth, Under-21.

|  |  | | | | |
|---|---|---|---|---|---|
| 2006-07 | Espanyol B | 27 | 5 | 27 | 5 |
| 2006-07 | Espanyol | 7 | 0 | | |
| 2007-08 | Espanyol | 28 | 2 | | |
| 2008-09 | Espanyol | 15 | 0 | 50 | 2 |
| 2009-10 | Rayo Vallecano | 27 | 2 | 27 | 2 |
| 2010-11 | Girona | 36 | 0 | 36 | 0 |
| 2011-12 | Blackpool | 15 | 1 | | |
| 2012-13 | Blackpool | 21 | 0 | 36 | 1 |

**NOGUERA, Alberto (F)**    3 0
H: 5 10  W: 11 04  b.Madrid 24-9-89

|  |  | | | | |
|---|---|---|---|---|---|
| 2010-11 | Atletico Madrid | 2 | 0 | 2 | 0 |
| 2012-13 | Blackpool | 1 | 0 | 1 | 0 |

**OSBOURNE, Isaiah (M)**    104 2
H: 6 2  W: 12 06  b.Birmingham 5-11-87
*Source:* Scholar.

|  |  | | | | |
|---|---|---|---|---|---|
| 2005-06 | Aston Villa | 0 | 0 | | |
| 2006-07 | Aston Villa | 11 | 0 | | |
| 2007-08 | Aston Villa | 8 | 0 | | |
| 2008-09 | Aston Villa | 0 | 0 | | |
| 2008-09 | *Nottingham F* | 8 | 0 | 8 | 0 |
| 2009-10 | Aston Villa | 0 | 0 | | |
| 2009-10 | *Middlesbrough* | 9 | 0 | 9 | 0 |
| 2010-11 | Aston Villa | 0 | 0 | 19 | 0 |
| 2010-11 | *Sheffield W* | 10 | 0 | 10 | 0 |
| 2011-12 | Hibernian | 30 | 1 | 30 | 1 |
| 2012-13 | Blackpool | 28 | 1 | 28 | 1 |

**PHILLIPS, Kevin (F)**    564 244
H: 5 7  W: 11 00  b.Hitchin 25-7-73
*Source:* Baldock T. *Honours:* England B, 8 full caps.

|  |  | | | | |
|---|---|---|---|---|---|
| 1994-95 | Watford | 16 | 9 | | |
| 1995-96 | Watford | 27 | 11 | | |
| 1996-97 | Watford | 16 | 4 | 59 | 24 |
| 1997-98 | Sunderland | 43 | 29 | | |
| 1998-99 | Sunderland | 26 | 23 | | |
| 1999-2000 | Sunderland | 36 | 30 | | |
| 2000-01 | Sunderland | 34 | 14 | | |
| 2001-02 | Sunderland | 37 | 11 | | |
| 2002-03 | Sunderland | 32 | 6 | 208 | 113 |
| 2003-04 | Southampton | 34 | 12 | | |
| 2004-05 | Southampton | 30 | 10 | 64 | 22 |
| 2005-06 | Aston Villa | 23 | 4 | | |
| 2006-07 | Aston Villa | 0 | 0 | 23 | 4 |
| 2006-07 | WBA | 36 | 16 | | |
| 2007-08 | WBA | 35 | 22 | 71 | 38 |
| 2008-09 | Birmingham C | 36 | 14 | | |
| 2009-10 | Birmingham C | 19 | 4 | | |
| 2010-11 | Birmingham C | 14 | 1 | 69 | 19 |
| 2011-12 | Blackpool | 38 | 16 | | |
| 2012-13 | Blackpool | 18 | 2 | 56 | 18 |
| 2012-13 | *Crystal Palace* | 14 | 6 | 14 | 6 |

**PHILLIPS, Matthew (M)**    178 25
H: 6 0  W: 12 10  b.Aylesbury 13-3-91
*Source:* Scholar. *Honours:* England Youth, Under-20. Scotland 2 full caps.

|  |  | | | | |
|---|---|---|---|---|---|
| 2007-08 | Wycombe W | 2 | 0 | | |
| 2008-09 | Wycombe W | 37 | 3 | | |
| 2009-10 | Wycombe W | 36 | 5 | | |
| 2010-11 | Wycombe W | 3 | 0 | 78 | 8 |
| 2010-11 | Blackpool | 27 | 1 | | |
| 2011-12 | Blackpool | 33 | 7 | | |
| 2011-12 | *Sheffield U* | 6 | 5 | 6 | 5 |
| 2012-13 | Blackpool | 34 | 4 | 94 | 12 |

**ROBERTSON, Scott (M)**    252 22
H: 5 8  W: 11 04  b.Dundee 7-4-85

|  |  | | | | |
|---|---|---|---|---|---|
| 2003-04 | Dundee | 0 | 0 | | |
| 2003-04 | *Peterhead* | 16 | 3 | | |
| 2004-05 | Dundee | 9 | 0 | | |
| 2004-05 | *Peterhead* | 13 | 1 | 29 | 4 |
| 2005-06 | Dundee | 35 | 1 | | |
| 2006-07 | Dundee | 29 | 2 | | |
| 2007-08 | Dundee | 30 | 5 | 103 | 8 |
| 2008-09 | Dundee U | 23 | 3 | | |
| 2009-10 | Dundee U | 13 | 0 | | |
| 2010-11 | Dundee U | 34 | 0 | | |
| 2011-12 | Dundee U | 37 | 6 | 107 | 9 |
| 2012-13 | Blackpool | 1 | 0 | 1 | 0 |
| 2012-13 | Hibernian | 12 | 1 | 12 | 1 |

**SYLVESTRE, Ludovic (M)**    186 21
H: 6 0  W: 11 09  b.Le Blanc-Mesnil 5-2-84

|  |  | | | | |
|---|---|---|---|---|---|
| 2005-06 | Barcelona B | 20 | 0 | 20 | 0 |
| 2005-06 | Barcelona | 2 | 0 | 2 | 0 |
| 2006-07 | Sparta Prague | 19 | 0 | | |
| 2007-08 | Sparta Prague | 6 | 0 | 25 | 0 |
| 2007-08 | *Viktoria Plzen* | 14 | 3 | 14 | 3 |
| 2008-09 | Mlada Boleslav | 29 | 4 | | |
| 2009-10 | Mlada Boleslav | 27 | 7 | | |
| 2010-11 | Mlada Boleslav | 4 | 1 | 60 | 12 |
| 2010-11 | Blackpool | 8 | 0 | | |
| 2011-12 | Blackpool | 28 | 1 | | |
| 2012-13 | Blackpool | 29 | 5 | 65 | 6 |

**TAYLOR-FLETCHER, Gary (F)**    403 85
H: 6 0  W: 11 00  b.Widnes 4-6-81
*Source:* Northwich Vic. *Honours:* England Schools.

|  |  | | | | |
|---|---|---|---|---|---|
| 2000-01 | Hull C | 5 | 0 | 5 | 0 |
| 2001-02 | Leyton Orient | 9 | 0 | | |
| 2002-03 | Leyton Orient | 12 | 1 | 21 | 1 |
| 2003-04 | Lincoln C | 42 | 16 | | |
| 2004-05 | Lincoln C | 38 | 11 | 80 | 27 |
| 2005-06 | Huddersfield T | 43 | 10 | | |
| 2006-07 | Huddersfield T | 39 | 11 | 82 | 21 |
| 2007-08 | Blackpool | 42 | 6 | | |
| 2008-09 | Blackpool | 38 | 5 | | |
| 2009-10 | Blackpool | 32 | 6 | | |
| 2010-11 | Blackpool | 31 | 6 | | |
| 2011-12 | Blackpool | 37 | 8 | | |
| 2012-13 | Blackpool | 35 | 5 | 215 | 36 |

**TOMSETT, Liam (M)**    15 1
H: 6 3  W: 11 07  b.Ulverston 1-11-92
*Source:* Scholar.

|  |  | | | | |
|---|---|---|---|---|---|
| 2011-12 | Blackpool | 0 | 0 | | |
| 2011-12 | *Ayr U* | 15 | 1 | 15 | 1 |
| 2012-13 | Blackpool | 0 | 0 | | |

**Scholars**

Blackett, Romone Carlisle Joseph; Charles, Dion; Clayton, Mitchell James; Cole, Adeyinka Aduragbemi; Cross, Louis Maurice Corrin; Fraser, Jon James; Gardikiotis, Alexander; Gardikiotis, Odisseas Dean; Hunt, Connor Charles; Johnson-Schuster, Marcus Kayne; Ling, Joshua Ashley; Lomax, George John Paul; McGahey, Harrison; N'Daw, Emmanuel; Pachipis, Andreas; Ready, Conor David; Rowley, Ashley James; Shaw, Kieran John; Spruin, Gavin; Staunton-Turner, Sam Christopher.

# BOLTON W (11)

**ALONSO, Marcus (D)**    75 8
H: 6 2  W: 13 05  b.Madrid 28-12-90

|  |  | | | | |
|---|---|---|---|---|---|
| 2008-09 | RM Castilla | 11 | 0 | | |
| 2009-10 | RM Castilla | 28 | 3 | 39 | 3 |
| 2009-10 | Real Madrid | 1 | 0 | 1 | 0 |
| 2010-11 | Bolton W | 4 | 0 | | |
| 2011-12 | Bolton W | 5 | 1 | | |
| 2012-13 | Bolton W | 26 | 4 | 35 | 5 |

**ANDREWS, Keith (M)**    329 41
H: 6 0  W: 12 04  b.Dublin 13-9-80
*Source:* Trainee. *Honours:* Eire Youth, 35 full caps, 3 goals.

|  |  | | | | |
|---|---|---|---|---|---|
| 1997-98 | Wolverhampton W | 0 | 0 | | |
| 1998-99 | Wolverhampton W | 0 | 0 | | |
| 1999-2000 | Wolverhampton W | 2 | 0 | | |
| 2000-01 | Wolverhampton W | 22 | 0 | | |
| 2000-01 | *Oxford U* | 4 | 1 | 4 | 1 |
| 2001-02 | Wolverhampton W | 11 | 0 | | |
| 2002-03 | Wolverhampton W | 9 | 0 | | |
| 2003-04 | Wolverhampton W | 1 | 0 | | |
| 2003-04 | *Stoke C* | 16 | 0 | 16 | 0 |
| 2003-04 | *Walsall* | 10 | 2 | 10 | 2 |
| 2004-05 | Wolverhampton W | 20 | 0 | 65 | 0 |
| 2005-06 | Hull C | 26 | 0 | | |
| 2006-07 | Hull C | 3 | 0 | 29 | 0 |
| 2006-07 | Milton Keynes D | 34 | 6 | | |
| 2007-08 | Milton Keynes D | 41 | 12 | | |
| 2008-09 | Milton Keynes D | 1 | 0 | 76 | 18 |
| 2008-09 | Blackburn R | 33 | 4 | | |
| 2009-10 | Blackburn R | 32 | 1 | | |
| 2010-11 | Blackburn R | 5 | 0 | | |
| 2011-12 | Blackburn R | 0 | 0 | 70 | 5 |
| 2011-12 | *Ipswich T* | 20 | 9 | 20 | 9 |
| 2011-12 | WBA | 14 | 2 | 14 | 2 |
| 2012-13 | Bolton W | 25 | 4 | 25 | 4 |

**BOGDAN, Adam (G)**    66 0
H: 6 4  W: 14 02  b.Budapest 27-9-87
*Source:* Vasas. *Honours:* Hungary Youth, Under-21, 14 full caps.

|  |  | | | | |
|---|---|---|---|---|---|
| 2007-08 | Bolton W | 0 | 0 | | |
| 2008-09 | Bolton W | 0 | 0 | | |
| 2009-10 | Bolton W | 0 | 0 | | |
| 2009-10 | *Crewe Alex* | 1 | 0 | 1 | 0 |
| 2010-11 | Bolton W | 4 | 0 | | |
| 2011-12 | Bolton W | 20 | 0 | | |
| 2012-13 | Bolton W | 41 | 0 | 65 | 0 |

**BOLGER, Cian (D)**    48 2
H: 6 4  W: 12 05  b.Co. Kildare 12-3-92
*Source:* Scholar.

|  |  | | | | |
|---|---|---|---|---|---|
| 2009-10 | Leicester C | 0 | 0 | | |
| 2010-11 | Leicester C | 0 | 0 | | |
| 2010-11 | *Bristol R* | 6 | 0 | | |
| 2011-12 | Leicester C | 0 | 0 | | |
| 2011-12 | *Bristol R* | 39 | 2 | | |
| 2012-13 | Leicester C | 0 | 0 | | |
| 2012-13 | *Bristol R* | 3 | 0 | 48 | 2 |
| 2012-13 | Bolton W | 0 | 0 | | |

## DAVIES, Craig (F) — 292 77
H: 6 2  W: 13 05  b.Burton-on-Trent 9-1-86
Source: Manchester C. Honours: Wales Youth, Under-21, 6 full caps.

|  |  | | | | |
|---|---|---|---|---|---|
| 2004-05 | Oxford U | 28 | 6 | | |
| 2005-06 | Oxford U | 20 | 2 | 48 | 8 |
| 2005-06 | Verona | 0 | 0 | | |
| 2006-07 | Wolverhampton W | 23 | 0 | 23 | 0 |
| 2007-08 | Oldham Ath | 32 | 10 | | |
| 2008-09 | Oldham Ath | 12 | 0 | 44 | 10 |
| 2008-09 | *Stockport Co* | 9 | 5 | 9 | 5 |
| 2008-09 | Brighton & HA | 16 | 1 | | |
| 2009-10 | Brighton & HA | 5 | 0 | 21 | 1 |
| 2009-10 | *Yeovil T* | 4 | 0 | 4 | 0 |
| 2009-10 | Port Vale | 24 | 7 | 24 | 7 |
| 2010-11 | Chesterfield | 41 | 23 | 41 | 23 |
| 2011-12 | Barnsley | 40 | 11 | | |
| 2012-13 | Barnsley | 20 | 8 | 60 | 19 |
| 2012-13 | Bolton W | 18 | 4 | 18 | 4 |

## DAVIES, Kevin (F) — 619 118
H: 6 0  W: 12 10  b.Sheffield 26-3-77
Source: Trainee. Honours: England Youth, Under-21, 1 full cap.

|  |  | | | | |
|---|---|---|---|---|---|
| 1993-94 | Chesterfield | 24 | 4 | | |
| 1994-95 | Chesterfield | 41 | 11 | | |
| 1995-96 | Chesterfield | 30 | 4 | | |
| 1996-97 | Chesterfield | 34 | 3 | 129 | 22 |
| 1996-97 | Southampton | 0 | 0 | | |
| 1997-98 | Southampton | 25 | 9 | | |
| 1998-99 | Blackburn R | 21 | 1 | | |
| 1999-2000 | Blackburn R | 2 | 0 | 23 | 1 |
| 1999-2000 | Southampton | 23 | 6 | | |
| 2000-01 | Southampton | 27 | 1 | | |
| 2001-02 | Southampton | 23 | 2 | | |
| 2002-03 | Southampton | 9 | 1 | 107 | 19 |
| 2002-03 | *Millwall* | 9 | 3 | 9 | 3 |
| 2003-04 | Bolton W | 38 | 9 | | |
| 2004-05 | Bolton W | 35 | 8 | | |
| 2005-06 | Bolton W | 37 | 7 | | |
| 2006-07 | Bolton W | 30 | 8 | | |
| 2007-08 | Bolton W | 32 | 3 | | |
| 2008-09 | Bolton W | 38 | 11 | | |
| 2009-10 | Bolton W | 37 | 7 | | |
| 2010-11 | Bolton W | 38 | 8 | | |
| 2011-12 | Bolton W | 31 | 6 | | |
| 2012-13 | Bolton W | 35 | 6 | 351 | 73 |

## DAVIES, Mark (M) — 144 13
H: 5 11  W: 11 08  b.Willenhall 18-2-88
Source: Scholar. Honours: England Youth.

|  |  | | | | |
|---|---|---|---|---|---|
| 2004-05 | Wolverhampton W | 0 | 0 | | |
| 2005-06 | Wolverhampton W | 20 | 1 | | |
| 2006-07 | Wolverhampton W | 0 | 0 | | |
| 2007-08 | Wolverhampton W | 0 | 0 | | |
| 2008-09 | Wolverhampton W | 0 | 0 | 27 | 1 |
| 2008-09 | *Leicester C* | 7 | 1 | 7 | 1 |
| 2008-09 | Bolton W | 10 | 0 | | |
| 2009-10 | Bolton W | 17 | 0 | | |
| 2010-11 | Bolton W | 24 | 1 | | |
| 2011-12 | Bolton W | 35 | 4 | | |
| 2012-13 | Bolton W | 24 | 6 | 110 | 11 |

## EAGLES, Chris (M) — 273 46
H: 5 10  W: 11 07  b.Hemel Hempstead 19-11-85
Source: Trainee. Honours: England Youth.

|  |  | | | | |
|---|---|---|---|---|---|
| 2003-04 | Manchester U | 0 | 0 | | |
| 2004-05 | Manchester U | 0 | 0 | | |
| 2004-05 | Watford | 13 | 1 | | |
| 2005-06 | Manchester U | 0 | 0 | | |
| 2005-06 | Sheffield W | 25 | 3 | 25 | 3 |
| 2005-06 | *Watford* | 17 | 3 | 30 | 4 |
| 2006-07 | Manchester U | 2 | 1 | | |
| 2006-07 | *NEC Nijmegen* | 15 | 1 | 15 | 1 |
| 2007-08 | Manchester U | 0 | 0 | 6 | 1 |
| 2008-09 | Burnley | 43 | 8 | | |
| 2009-10 | Burnley | 34 | 2 | | |
| 2010-11 | Burnley | 43 | 11 | 120 | 21 |
| 2011-12 | Bolton W | 34 | 4 | | |
| 2012-13 | Bolton W | 43 | 12 | 77 | 16 |

## EAVES, Tom (M) — 44 13
H: 6 3  W: 13 07  b.Liverpool 14-1-92
Source: Scholar.

|  |  | | | | |
|---|---|---|---|---|---|
| 2009-10 | Oldham Ath | 15 | 0 | | |
| 2010-11 | Bolton W | 0 | 0 | | |
| 2010-11 | *Oldham Ath* | 0 | 0 | 15 | 0 |
| 2011-12 | Bolton W | 0 | 0 | | |
| 2012-13 | Bolton W | 3 | 0 | 3 | 0 |
| 2012-13 | *Bristol R* | 16 | 7 | 16 | 7 |
| 2012-13 | *Shrewsbury T* | 10 | 6 | 10 | 6 |

## GREGUS, Jan (M) — 65 1
H: 6 2  W: 10 13  b.Nitra 29-1-91
Honours: Slovakia Youth, Under-21.

|  |  | | | | |
|---|---|---|---|---|---|
| 2009-10 | Banik Ostrava | 11 | 0 | | |
| 2010-11 | Banik Ostrava | 21 | 0 | | |
| 2011-12 | Banik Ostrava | 26 | 1 | | |
| 2012-13 | Banik Ostrava | 7 | 0 | 65 | 1 |

On loan from Banik Ostrava

|  |  | | | | |
|---|---|---|---|---|---|
| 2012-13 | Bolton W | 0 | 0 | | |

## HOLDEN, Stuart (M) — 121 17
H: 5 10  W: 11 07  b.Aberdeen 1-8-85
Source: Clemson Tigers. Honours: USA 17 full caps, 2 goals.

|  |  | | | | |
|---|---|---|---|---|---|
| 2005-06 | Sunderland | 0 | 0 | | |
| 2006 | Houston D | 13 | 1 | | |
| 2007 | Houston D | 21 | 5 | | |
| 2008 | Houston D | 27 | 3 | | |
| 2009 | Houston D | 26 | 6 | 87 | 15 |
| 2009-10 | Bolton W | 2 | 0 | | |
| 2010-11 | Bolton W | 26 | 2 | | |
| 2011-12 | Bolton W | 0 | 0 | | |
| 2012-13 | Bolton W | 2 | 0 | 30 | 2 |
| 2012-13 | *Sheffield W* | 4 | 0 | 4 | 0 |

## KNIGHT, Aaron (M) — 0 0

|  |  | | | | |
|---|---|---|---|---|---|
| 2012-13 | Bolton W | 0 | 0 | | |

## KNIGHT, Zat (D) — 335 7
H: 6 6  W: 15 02  b.Solihull 2-5-80
Source: Rushall Olympic. Honours: England Under-21, 2 full caps.

|  |  | | | | |
|---|---|---|---|---|---|
| 1998-99 | Fulham | 0 | 0 | | |
| 1999-2000 | Fulham | 0 | 0 | | |
| 1999-2000 | *Peterborough U* | 8 | 0 | 8 | 0 |
| 2000-01 | Fulham | 0 | 0 | | |
| 2001-02 | Fulham | 10 | 0 | | |
| 2002-03 | Fulham | 17 | 0 | | |
| 2003-04 | Fulham | 31 | 0 | | |
| 2004-05 | Fulham | 35 | 1 | | |
| 2005-06 | Fulham | 30 | 0 | | |
| 2006-07 | Fulham | 23 | 2 | | |
| 2007-08 | Fulham | 4 | 0 | 150 | 3 |
| 2007-08 | Aston Villa | 27 | 1 | | |
| 2008-09 | Aston Villa | 13 | 1 | | |
| 2009-10 | Aston Villa | 0 | 0 | 40 | 2 |
| 2009-10 | Bolton W | 35 | 1 | | |
| 2010-11 | Bolton W | 34 | 1 | | |
| 2011-12 | Bolton W | 25 | 0 | | |
| 2012-13 | Bolton W | 43 | 0 | 137 | 2 |

## LAINTON, Robert (G) — 0 0
H: 6 2  W: 12 06  b.Ashton-under-Lyne 12-10-89
Source: Scholar.

|  |  | | | | |
|---|---|---|---|---|---|
| 2009-10 | Bolton W | 0 | 0 | | |
| 2010-11 | Bolton W | 0 | 0 | | |
| 2011-12 | Bolton W | 0 | 0 | | |
| 2012-13 | Bolton W | 0 | 0 | | |

## LEE, Chung Yong (M) — 159 21
H: 5 11  W: 10 09  b.Seoul 2-7-88
Honours: South Korea 42 full caps, 5 goals.

|  |  | | | | |
|---|---|---|---|---|---|
| 2006 | FC Seoul | 2 | 0 | | |
| 2007 | FC Seoul | 15 | 3 | | |
| 2008 | FC Seoul | 20 | 5 | | |
| 2009 | FC Seoul | 14 | 2 | 51 | 10 |
| 2009-10 | Bolton W | 34 | 4 | | |
| 2010-11 | Bolton W | 31 | 3 | | |
| 2011-12 | Bolton W | 2 | 0 | | |
| 2012-13 | Bolton W | 41 | 4 | 108 | 11 |

## LESTER, Chris (M) — 0 0
b.Salford 27-10-94
Honours: Northern Ireland Under-21.

|  |  | | | | |
|---|---|---|---|---|---|
| 2012-13 | Bolton W | 0 | 0 | | |

## LONERGAN, Andrew (G) — 253 1
H: 6 4  W: 13 02  b.Preston 19-10-83
Source: Scholar. Honours: Eire Youth, England Youth, Under-20.

|  |  | | | | |
|---|---|---|---|---|---|
| 2000-01 | Preston NE | 1 | 0 | | |
| 2001-02 | Preston NE | 0 | 0 | | |
| 2002-03 | Preston NE | 0 | 0 | | |
| 2002-03 | *Darlington* | 2 | 0 | 2 | 0 |
| 2003-04 | Preston NE | 8 | 0 | | |
| 2004-05 | Preston NE | 23 | 1 | | |
| 2005-06 | Preston NE | 0 | 0 | | |
| 2005-06 | *Wycombe W* | 2 | 0 | 2 | 0 |
| 2006-07 | Preston NE | 13 | 0 | | |
| 2006-07 | *Swindon T* | 1 | 0 | 1 | 0 |
| 2007-08 | Preston NE | 43 | 0 | | |
| 2008-09 | Preston NE | 46 | 0 | | |
| 2009-10 | Preston NE | 45 | 0 | | |
| 2010-11 | Preston NE | 29 | 0 | 208 | 1 |
| 2011-12 | Leeds U | 35 | 0 | 35 | 0 |
| 2012-13 | Bolton W | 5 | 0 | 5 | 0 |

## LYNCH, Jay (G) — 0 0
H: 6 2  W: 13 04  b.Salford 31-3-93

|  |  | | | | |
|---|---|---|---|---|---|
| 2012-13 | Bolton W | 0 | 0 | | |

## McKEE, Joe (M) — 3 0
H: 5 11  W: 10 05  b.Linlithgow 30-10-92
Source: Scholar. Honours: Scotland Youth.

|  |  | | | | |
|---|---|---|---|---|---|
| 2009-10 | Livingston | 1 | 0 | 1 | 0 |
| 2009-10 | Burnley | 0 | 0 | | |
| 2010-11 | Burnley | 0 | 0 | | |
| 2011-12 | Burnley | 0 | 0 | | |
| 2011-12 | *St Mirren* | 2 | 0 | 2 | 0 |
| 2012-13 | Bolton W | 0 | 0 | | |

## MEARS, Tyrone (D) — 230 7
H: 5 11  W: 11 10  b.Stockport 18-2-83
Source: Manchester C Juniors. Honours: Jamaica 1 full cap.

|  |  | | | | |
|---|---|---|---|---|---|
| 2000-01 | Manchester C | 0 | 0 | | |
| 2001-02 | Manchester C | 1 | 0 | 1 | 0 |
| 2002-03 | Preston NE | 22 | 1 | | |
| 2003-04 | Preston NE | 12 | 1 | | |
| 2004-05 | Preston NE | 4 | 0 | | |
| 2005-06 | Preston NE | 32 | 2 | 70 | 4 |
| 2006-07 | West Ham U | 5 | 0 | 5 | 0 |
| 2006-07 | *Derby Co* | 13 | 1 | | |
| 2007-08 | Derby Co | 25 | 1 | | |
| 2008-09 | Derby Co | 3 | 0 | 41 | 2 |
| 2008-09 | *Marseille* | 4 | 0 | 4 | 0 |
| 2009-10 | Burnley | 38 | 0 | | |
| 2010-11 | Burnley | 44 | 1 | | |
| 2011-12 | Burnley | 0 | 0 | 82 | 1 |
| 2011-12 | Bolton W | 1 | 0 | | |
| 2012-13 | Bolton W | 26 | 0 | 27 | 0 |

## MEDO, Mohamed (M) — 25 14
H: 5 9  W: 10 12  b.Serabu 27-12-81
Honours: Sierra Leone Youth, 5 full caps, 1 goal.

|  |  | | | | |
|---|---|---|---|---|---|
| 2007-08 | HJK Helsinki | 4 | 4 | | |
| 2008-09 | HJK Helsinki | 4 | 4 | | |
| 2009-10 | HJK Helsinki | 3 | 3 | | |
| 2010-11 | HJK Helsinki | 2 | 2 | 13 | 13 |
| 2012-13 | Partizan Belgrade | 0 | 0 | | |
| 2012-13 | Bolton W | 12 | 1 | 12 | 1 |

## MILLS, Matthew (D) — 210 12
H: 6 3  W: 12 12  b.Swindon 14-7-86
Source: Scholar. Honours: England Youth.

|  |  | | | | |
|---|---|---|---|---|---|
| 2004-05 | Southampton | 0 | 0 | | |
| 2004-05 | *Coventry C* | 4 | 0 | 4 | 0 |
| 2004-05 | *Bournemouth* | 12 | 3 | 12 | 3 |
| 2005-06 | Southampton | 4 | 0 | 4 | 0 |
| 2005-06 | Manchester C | 1 | 0 | | |
| 2006-07 | Manchester C | 1 | 0 | | |
| 2006-07 | Colchester U | 9 | 0 | 9 | 0 |
| 2007-08 | Manchester C | 0 | 0 | 2 | 0 |
| 2007-08 | Doncaster R | 34 | 3 | | |
| 2008-09 | Doncaster R | 41 | 0 | | |
| 2009-10 | Doncaster R | 0 | 0 | 75 | 3 |
| 2009-10 | Reading | 23 | 2 | | |
| 2010-11 | Reading | 38 | 2 | 61 | 4 |
| 2011-12 | Leicester C | 25 | 1 | 25 | 1 |
| 2012-13 | Bolton W | 18 | 1 | 18 | 1 |

## MUAMBA, Fabrice (M) — 201 5
H: 6 1  W: 11 10  b.DR Congo 6-4-88
Source: Scholar. Honours: England Youth, Under-21.

|  |  | | | | |
|---|---|---|---|---|---|
| 2005-06 | Arsenal | 0 | 0 | | |
| 2006-07 | Arsenal | 0 | 0 | | |
| 2006-07 | Birmingham C | 34 | 0 | | |
| 2007-08 | Birmingham C | 37 | 2 | 71 | 2 |
| 2008-09 | Bolton W | 38 | 0 | | |
| 2009-10 | Bolton W | 36 | 1 | | |
| 2010-11 | Bolton W | 36 | 1 | | |
| 2011-12 | Bolton W | 20 | 1 | | |
| 2012-13 | Bolton W | 0 | 0 | 130 | 3 |

**NGOG, David (F)**   145 21
H: 6 3  W: 12 04  b.Paris 1-4-89
*Honours:* France Youth, Under-21.

| Season | Club | Apps | Gls | Tot A | Tot G |
|---|---|---|---|---|---|
| 2006-07 | Paris St Germain | 4 | 0 | | |
| 2007-08 | Paris St Germain | 14 | 1 | 18 | 1 |
| 2008-09 | Liverpool | 14 | 2 | | |
| 2009-10 | Liverpool | 24 | 5 | | |
| 2010-11 | Liverpool | 25 | 2 | | |
| 2011-12 | Liverpool | 0 | 0 | 63 | 9 |
| 2011-12 | Bolton W | 33 | 3 | | |
| 2012-13 | Bolton W | 31 | 8 | 64 | 11 |

**O'HALLORAN, Michael (F)**   31 3
H: 6 2  W: 12 06  b.Glasgow 6-1-91
*Source:* Scholar. *Honours:* Scotland Under-21.

| Season | Club | Apps | Gls | Tot A | Tot G |
|---|---|---|---|---|---|
| 2009-10 | Bolton W | 0 | 0 | | |
| 2010-11 | Bolton W | 0 | 0 | | |
| 2011-12 | Bolton W | 0 | 0 | | |
| 2011-12 | *Sheffield U* | 7 | 0 | 7 | 0 |
| 2012-13 | Bolton W | 0 | 0 | | |
| 2012-13 | *Carlisle U* | 1 | 0 | 1 | 0 |
| 2012-13 | *Tranmere R* | 23 | 3 | 23 | 3 |

**ODELUSI, Sanmi (F)**   1 0
b.London 11-6-93

| Season | Club | Apps | Gls | Tot A | Tot G |
|---|---|---|---|---|---|
| 2012-13 | Bolton W | 1 | 0 | 1 | 0 |

**PETROV, Martin (F)**   379 72
H: 6 0  W: 12 02  b.Vzatza 15-1-79
*Honours:* Bulgaria 88 full caps, 19 goals.

| Season | Club | Apps | Gls | Tot A | Tot G |
|---|---|---|---|---|---|
| 1996-97 | CSKA Sofia | 3 | 0 | | |
| 1997-98 | CSKA Sofia | 4 | 0 | 7 | 0 |
| 1998-99 | Servette | 12 | 2 | | |
| 1999-2000 | Servette | 31 | 9 | | |
| 2000-01 | Servette | 32 | 11 | 75 | 22 |
| 2001-02 | Wolfsburg | 32 | 6 | | |
| 2002-03 | Wolfsburg | 26 | 2 | | |
| 2003-04 | Wolfsburg | 28 | 8 | | |
| 2004-05 | Wolfsburg | 30 | 12 | 116 | 28 |
| 2005-06 | Atletico Madrid | 36 | 1 | | |
| 2006-07 | Atletico Madrid | 13 | 2 | 49 | 3 |
| 2007-08 | Manchester C | 34 | 5 | | |
| 2008-09 | Manchester C | 9 | 0 | | |
| 2009-10 | Manchester C | 16 | 4 | 59 | 9 |
| 2010-11 | Bolton W | 28 | 3 | | |
| 2011-12 | Bolton W | 31 | 4 | | |
| 2012-13 | Bolton W | 14 | 3 | 73 | 10 |

Transferred to Espanyol January 2013

**PRATLEY, Darren (M)**   280 34
H: 6 1  W: 10 12  b.Barking 22-4-85
*Source:* Scholar.

| Season | Club | Apps | Gls | Tot A | Tot G |
|---|---|---|---|---|---|
| 2001-02 | Fulham | 0 | 0 | | |
| 2002-03 | Fulham | 0 | 0 | | |
| 2003-04 | Fulham | 1 | 0 | | |
| 2004-05 | Fulham | 0 | 0 | | |
| 2004-05 | *Brentford* | 14 | 1 | | |
| 2005-06 | Fulham | 0 | 0 | 1 | 0 |
| 2005-06 | *Brentford* | 32 | 4 | 46 | 5 |
| 2006-07 | Swansea C | 28 | 1 | | |
| 2007-08 | Swansea C | 42 | 5 | | |
| 2008-09 | Swansea C | 37 | 4 | | |
| 2009-10 | Swansea C | 36 | 7 | | |
| 2010-11 | Swansea C | 34 | 9 | 177 | 26 |
| 2011-12 | Bolton W | 25 | 1 | | |
| 2012-13 | Bolton W | 31 | 2 | 56 | 3 |

**REAM, Tim (D)**   187 7
H: 6 1  W: 11 05  b.St Louis 5-10-87
*Honours:* USA 7 full caps.

| Season | Club | Apps | Gls | Tot A | Tot G |
|---|---|---|---|---|---|
| 2006 | St Louis Billikens | 19 | 0 | | |
| 2007 | St Louis Billikens | 19 | 0 | | |
| 2008 | St Louis Billikens | 22 | 0 | | |
| 2008 | Chicago Fire | 12 | 0 | | |
| 2009 | Chicago Fire | 7 | 0 | 19 | 0 |
| 2009 | St Louis Billikens | 22 | 6 | 82 | 6 |
| 2010 | New York RB | 30 | 1 | | |
| 2011 | New York RB | 28 | 0 | 58 | 1 |
| 2011-12 | Bolton W | 13 | 0 | | |
| 2012-13 | Bolton W | 15 | 0 | 28 | 0 |

**RICKETTS, Sam (D)**   340 4
H: 6 1  W: 12 01  b.Aylesbury 11-10-81
*Source:* Trainee. *Honours:* Wales 48 full caps.

| Season | Club | Apps | Gls | Tot A | Tot G |
|---|---|---|---|---|---|
| 1999-2000 | Oxford U | 0 | 0 | | |
| 2000-01 | Oxford U | 14 | 0 | | |
| 2001-02 | Oxford U | 29 | 1 | | |
| 2002-03 | Oxford U | 2 | 0 | 45 | 1 |

From Telford U

| Season | Club | Apps | Gls | Tot A | Tot G |
|---|---|---|---|---|---|
| 2004-05 | Swansea C | 42 | 0 | | |
| 2005-06 | Swansea C | 44 | 1 | 86 | 1 |
| 2006-07 | Hull C | 40 | 1 | | |
| 2007-08 | Hull C | 44 | 0 | | |
| 2008-09 | Hull C | 29 | 0 | | |
| 2009-10 | Hull C | 0 | 0 | 113 | 1 |
| 2009-10 | Bolton W | 27 | 0 | | |
| 2010-11 | Bolton W | 17 | 0 | | |
| 2011-12 | Bolton W | 20 | 1 | | |
| 2012-13 | Bolton W | 32 | 0 | 96 | 1 |

**RILEY, Joe (D)**   3 0
H: 6 0  W: 11 02  b.Salford 13-10-91
*Source:* Scholar.

| Season | Club | Apps | Gls | Tot A | Tot G |
|---|---|---|---|---|---|
| 2011-12 | Bolton W | 3 | 0 | | |
| 2012-13 | Bolton W | 0 | 0 | 3 | 0 |

**SORDELL, Marvin (F)**   108 26
H: 5 9  W: 12 06  b.Pinner 17-2-91
*Source:* Scholar. *Honours:* England Under-21.

| Season | Club | Apps | Gls | Tot A | Tot G |
|---|---|---|---|---|---|
| 2009-10 | Watford | 6 | 1 | | |
| 2009-10 | *Tranmere R* | 8 | 1 | 8 | 1 |
| 2010-11 | Watford | 43 | 12 | | |
| 2011-12 | Watford | 26 | 8 | 75 | 21 |
| 2011-12 | Bolton W | 3 | 0 | | |
| 2012-13 | Bolton W | 22 | 4 | 25 | 4 |

**VELA, Joshua (M)**   7 0
H: 5 11  W: 11 07  b.Salford 14-12-93
*Source:* Scholar.

| Season | Club | Apps | Gls | Tot A | Tot G |
|---|---|---|---|---|---|
| 2010-11 | Bolton W | 0 | 0 | | |
| 2011-12 | Bolton W | 3 | 0 | | |
| 2012-13 | Bolton W | 4 | 0 | 7 | 0 |

**WHEATER, David (D)**   198 14
H: 6 5  W: 12 12  b.Redcar 14-2-87
*Source:* Scholar. *Honours:* England Youth, Under-21.

| Season | Club | Apps | Gls | Tot A | Tot G |
|---|---|---|---|---|---|
| 2004-05 | Middlesbrough | 0 | 0 | | |
| 2005-06 | Middlesbrough | 6 | 0 | | |
| 2005-06 | *Doncaster R* | 7 | 1 | 7 | 1 |
| 2006-07 | Middlesbrough | 2 | 1 | | |
| 2006-07 | *Wolverhampton W* | 1 | 0 | 1 | 0 |
| 2006-07 | *Darlington* | 15 | 2 | 15 | 2 |
| 2007-08 | Middlesbrough | 34 | 3 | | |
| 2008-09 | Middlesbrough | 32 | 1 | | |
| 2009-10 | Middlesbrough | 42 | 0 | | |
| 2010-11 | Middlesbrough | 24 | 3 | 140 | 9 |
| 2010-11 | Bolton W | 7 | 0 | | |
| 2011-12 | Bolton W | 24 | 2 | | |
| 2012-13 | Bolton W | 4 | 0 | 35 | 2 |

**WYLDE, Gregg (M)**   80 4
H: 5 9  W: 11 04  b.Kirkintilloch 23-3-91

| Season | Club | Apps | Gls | Tot A | Tot G |
|---|---|---|---|---|---|
| 2009-10 | Rangers | 4 | 0 | | |
| 2010-11 | Rangers | 30 | 0 | | |
| 2011-12 | Rangers | 42 | 4 | 76 | 4 |
| 2012-13 | Bolton W | 0 | 0 | | |
| 2012-13 | *Bury* | 4 | 0 | 4 | 0 |

**Players retained or with offer of contract**
Kamara, Mohammed.

**Scholars**
Bailey, Sam Lewis; Ball, James Cameron; Campbell, Harry Joseph Gordon; Clough, Zach Paul John; Dennis, Elliott Ben; Fielding, Lewis; Gibson, James Robert; Hamer, Saul Michael; Hampson, Benjamin Christopher; Hendrie, Jordan Lee; Holding, Robert Samuel; Kelly, James Alexander; Lester, Christopher James; Maher, Niall Callum James Peter; Matthews, Glenn William; Newby, Elliot Christian; Sievers, Jan-Ole; Threlkeld, Oscar George; Torres, Guillermo Garcia; Walker, Thomas James; Wolstenholme, Dyllon Alan; Woodland, Luke; Youngs, Thomas Ronald.

# BOURNEMOUTH (12)

**ADDISON, Miles (D)**   110 4
H: 6 2  W: 13 03  b.Newham 7-1-89
*Source:* Scholar. *Honours:* England Under-21.

| Season | Club | Apps | Gls | Tot A | Tot G |
|---|---|---|---|---|---|
| 2005-06 | Derby Co | 2 | 0 | | |
| 2006-07 | Derby Co | 0 | 0 | | |
| 2007-08 | Derby Co | 1 | 0 | | |
| 2008-09 | Derby Co | 28 | 1 | | |
| 2009-10 | Derby Co | 13 | 2 | | |
| 2010-11 | Derby Co | 21 | 0 | | |
| 2011-12 | Derby Co | 0 | 0 | | |
| 2011-12 | *Barnsley* | 11 | 0 | 11 | 0 |
| 2011-12 | Bournemouth | 14 | 1 | | |
| 2012-13 | Derby Co | 0 | 0 | 65 | 3 |
| 2012-13 | Bournemouth | 20 | 0 | 34 | 1 |

**ALLSOP, Ryan (G)**   30 0
H: 6 2  W: 12 06  b.Birmingham 17-6-92

| Season | Club | Apps | Gls | Tot A | Tot G |
|---|---|---|---|---|---|
| 2012-13 | *Leyton Orient* | 20 | 0 | 20 | 0 |
| 2012-13 | Bournemouth | 10 | 0 | 10 | 0 |

**ARTER, Harry (M)**   94 14
H: 5 9  W: 11 07  b.Sidcup 28-12-89
*Source:* Scholar.

| Season | Club | Apps | Gls | Tot A | Tot G |
|---|---|---|---|---|---|
| 2007-08 | Charlton Ath | 0 | 0 | | |
| 2008-09 | Charlton Ath | 0 | 0 | | |

From Woking.

| Season | Club | Apps | Gls | Tot A | Tot G |
|---|---|---|---|---|---|
| 2010-11 | Bournemouth | 18 | 0 | | |
| 2010-11 | *Carlisle U* | 5 | 1 | 5 | 1 |
| 2011-12 | Bournemouth | 34 | 5 | | |
| 2012-13 | Bournemouth | 37 | 8 | 89 | 13 |

**BASSELE, Aristide (M)**   0 0
b.London 15-6-94

| Season | Club | Apps | Gls | Tot A | Tot G |
|---|---|---|---|---|---|
| 2012-13 | Bournemouth | 0 | 0 | | |

**BUCHEL, Benjamin (G)**   0 0
H: 6 2  W: 11 08  b.Ruggel 4-7-89
*Honours:* Liechtenstein Youth, Under-21, 5 full caps.

| Season | Club | Apps | Gls | Tot A | Tot G |
|---|---|---|---|---|---|
| 2012-13 | Bournemouth | 0 | 0 | | |

**CARMICHAEL, Josh (M)**   4 0
H: 6 0  W: 12 06  b.Poole 27-9-94
*Source:* Youth.

| Season | Club | Apps | Gls | Tot A | Tot G |
|---|---|---|---|---|---|
| 2011-12 | Bournemouth | 1 | 0 | | |
| 2012-13 | Bournemouth | 3 | 0 | 4 | 0 |

**CHIEDOZIE, Jordan (M)**   0 0
H: 5 11  W: 11 06  b.Owerri 5-5-90

| Season | Club | Apps | Gls | Tot A | Tot G |
|---|---|---|---|---|---|
| 2012-13 | Bournemouth | 0 | 0 | | |

**COOK, Steve (D)**   62 1
H: 6 1  W: 12 13  b.Hastings 19-4-91
*Source:* Scholar.

| Season | Club | Apps | Gls | Tot A | Tot G |
|---|---|---|---|---|---|
| 2008-09 | Brighton & HA | 2 | 0 | | |
| 2009-10 | Brighton & HA | 0 | 0 | | |
| 2010-11 | Brighton & HA | 0 | 0 | | |
| 2011-12 | Brighton & HA | 1 | 0 | 3 | 0 |
| 2011-12 | Bournemouth | 26 | 0 | | |
| 2012-13 | Bournemouth | 33 | 1 | 59 | 1 |

**DANIELS, Charlie (M)**   210 11
H: 6 1  W: 12 12  b.Harlow 7-9-86
*Source:* Scholar.

| Season | Club | Apps | Gls | Tot A | Tot G |
|---|---|---|---|---|---|
| 2005-06 | Tottenham H | 0 | 0 | | |
| 2006-07 | Tottenham H | 0 | 0 | | |
| 2006-07 | *Chesterfield* | 2 | 0 | 2 | 0 |
| 2007-08 | Tottenham H | 0 | 0 | | |
| 2007-08 | *Leyton Orient* | 31 | 2 | | |
| 2008-09 | Tottenham H | 0 | 0 | | |
| 2008-09 | *Gillingham* | 5 | 1 | 5 | 1 |
| 2008-09 | *Leyton Orient* | 21 | 2 | | |
| 2009-10 | Leyton Orient | 41 | 0 | | |
| 2010-11 | Leyton Orient | 42 | 0 | | |
| 2011-12 | Leyton Orient | 13 | 0 | 148 | 4 |
| 2011-12 | Bournemouth | 21 | 2 | | |
| 2012-13 | Bournemouth | 34 | 4 | 55 | 6 |

**DAVIDS, Lorenzo (M)**   154 5
H: 5 8  W: 11 08  b.Paramaribo 4-9-86

| Season | Club | Apps | Gls | Tot A | Tot G |
|---|---|---|---|---|---|
| 2006-07 | NEC | 8 | 0 | | |
| 2007-08 | NEC | 29 | 2 | | |
| 2008-09 | NEC | 34 | 0 | | |
| 2009-10 | NEC | 31 | 1 | | |
| 2010-11 | NEC | 29 | 2 | 131 | 5 |
| 2011-12 | Augsburg | 20 | 0 | 20 | 0 |
| 2012-13 | Bournemouth | 3 | 0 | 3 | 0 |

Transferred to Randers FC February 2013

**DEMOUGE, Frank (F)**   244 84
H: 6 3  W: 12 03  b.Nijmegen 25-6-82

| Season | Club | Apps | Gls | Tot A | Tot G |
|---|---|---|---|---|---|
| 2001-02 | NEC | 25 | 7 | | |
| 2002-03 | NEC | 29 | 3 | | |
| 2003-04 | NEC | 23 | 4 | | |
| 2004-05 | NEC | 5 | 0 | | |
| 2005-06 | NEC | 1 | 0 | 83 | 14 |
| 2005-06 | Eindhoven | 8 | 9 | 8 | 9 |
| 2006-07 | FC Den Bosch | 9 | 12 | 9 | 12 |
| 2007-08 | Willem II | 23 | 8 | | |
| 2008-09 | Willem II | 32 | 14 | | |
| 2009-10 | Willem II | 30 | 7 | | |

| 2010-11 | Willem II | 3 | 1 | 88 | 30 |
|---|---|---|---|---|---|
| 2010-11 | FC Utrecht | 20 | 6 | | |
| 2011-12 | FC Utrecht | 23 | 7 | 43 | 13 |
| 2012-13 | Bournemouth | 2 | 0 | 2 | 0 |
| 2012-13 | Roda JC | 11 | 6 | 11 | 6 |

**ELPHICK, Tommy (M)**    187   9
H: 5 11   W: 11 07   b.Brighton 7-9-87
*Source:* Scholar.

| 2005-06 | Brighton & HA | 1 | 0 | | |
|---|---|---|---|---|---|
| 2006-07 | Brighton & HA | 3 | 0 | | |
| 2007-08 | Brighton & HA | 39 | 2 | | |
| 2008-09 | Brighton & HA | 39 | 1 | | |
| 2009-10 | Brighton & HA | 44 | 3 | | |
| 2010-11 | Brighton & HA | 27 | 1 | | |
| 2011-12 | Brighton & HA | 0 | 0 | | |
| 2012-13 | Brighton & HA | 0 | 0 | 153 | 7 |
| 2012-13 | Bournemouth | 34 | 2 | 34 | 2 |

**FLAHAVAN, Darryl (G)**    355   0
H: 5 11   W: 12 05   b.Southampton 9-9-77
*Source:* Trainee.
From Woking.

| 2000-01 | Southend U | 29 | 0 | | |
|---|---|---|---|---|---|
| 2001-02 | Southend U | 41 | 0 | | |
| 2002-03 | Southend U | 41 | 0 | | |
| 2003-04 | Southend U | 37 | 0 | | |
| 2004-05 | Southend U | 28 | 0 | | |
| 2005-06 | Southend U | 43 | 0 | | |
| 2006-07 | Southend U | 46 | 0 | | |
| 2007-08 | Southend U | 26 | 0 | 291 | 0 |
| 2008-09 | Crystal Palace | 1 | 0 | | |
| 2008-09 | Leeds U | 0 | 0 | | |
| 2009-10 | Crystal Palace | 1 | 0 | | |
| 2009-10 | Oldham Ath | 18 | 0 | 18 | 0 |
| 2010-11 | Crystal Palace | 0 | 0 | 2 | 0 |
| 2011-12 | Bournemouth | 44 | 0 | | |
| 2012-13 | Bournemouth | 0 | 0 | 44 | 0 |

**FLETCHER, Steve (F)**    704   112
H: 6 2   W: 14 09   b.Hartlepool 26-7-72
*Source:* Trainee.

| 1990-91 | Hartlepool U | 14 | 2 | | |
|---|---|---|---|---|---|
| 1991-92 | Hartlepool U | 18 | 2 | 32 | 4 |
| 1992-93 | Bournemouth | 31 | 4 | | |
| 1993-94 | Bournemouth | 36 | 6 | | |
| 1994-95 | Bournemouth | 40 | 6 | | |
| 1995-96 | Bournemouth | 7 | 1 | | |
| 1996-97 | Bournemouth | 35 | 7 | | |
| 1997-98 | Bournemouth | 42 | 12 | | |
| 1998-99 | Bournemouth | 39 | 8 | | |
| 1999-2000 | Bournemouth | 36 | 7 | | |
| 2000-01 | Bournemouth | 45 | 9 | | |
| 2001-02 | Bournemouth | 2 | 0 | | |
| 2002-03 | Bournemouth | 35 | 5 | | |
| 2003-04 | Bournemouth | 41 | 9 | | |
| 2004-05 | Bournemouth | 36 | 9 | | |
| 2005-06 | Bournemouth | 27 | 4 | | |
| 2006-07 | Bournemouth | 41 | 1 | | |
| 2007-08 | Chesterfield | 38 | 5 | 38 | 5 |

From Crawley T.

| 2008-09 | Bournemouth | 21 | 4 | | |
|---|---|---|---|---|---|
| 2009-10 | Bournemouth | 45 | 4 | | |
| 2010-11 | Bournemouth | 38 | 6 | | |
| 2011-12 | Bournemouth | 20 | 1 | | |
| 2011-12 | Plymouth Arg | 6 | 0 | 6 | 0 |
| 2012-13 | Bournemouth | 11 | 0 | 628 | 103 |

**FOGDEN, Wes (F)**    56   4
H: 5 8   W: 10 04   b.Brighton 12-4-88
*Source:* Scholar.

| 2006-07 | Brighton & HA | 0 | 0 | | |
|---|---|---|---|---|---|
| 2007-08 | Brighton & HA | 3 | 0 | 3 | 0 |

From Dorchester T, Havant & Waterlooville.

| 2011-12 | Bournemouth | 27 | 3 | | |
|---|---|---|---|---|---|
| 2012-13 | Bournemouth | 26 | 1 | 53 | 4 |

**FRANCIS, Simon (D)**    351   7
H: 6 0   W: 12 06   b.Nottingham 16-2-85
*Source:* Scholar. *Honours:* England Youth, Under-20.

| 2002-03 | Bradford C | 25 | 1 | | |
|---|---|---|---|---|---|
| 2003-04 | Bradford C | 30 | 0 | 55 | 1 |
| 2003-04 | Sheffield U | 5 | 0 | | |
| 2004-05 | Sheffield U | 6 | 0 | | |
| 2005-06 | Sheffield U | 1 | 0 | 12 | 0 |
| 2005-06 | Grimsby T | 5 | 0 | 5 | 0 |
| 2005-06 | Tranmere R | 17 | 1 | 17 | 1 |
| 2006-07 | Southend U | 40 | 1 | | |

| 2007-08 | Southend U | 27 | 2 | | |
|---|---|---|---|---|---|
| 2008-09 | Southend U | 45 | 0 | | |
| 2009-10 | Southend U | 45 | 1 | 157 | 4 |
| 2010-11 | Charlton Ath | 34 | 0 | | |
| 2011-12 | Charlton Ath | 0 | 0 | 34 | 0 |
| 2011-12 | Bournemouth | 29 | 0 | | |
| 2012-13 | Bournemouth | 42 | 1 | 71 | 1 |

**FRASER, Ryan (M)**    26   0
H: 5 4   W: 10 13   b.Aberdeen 24-2-94
*Honours:* Scotland Youth, Under-21.

| 2010-11 | Aberdeen | 2 | 0 | | |
|---|---|---|---|---|---|
| 2011-12 | Aberdeen | 3 | 0 | | |
| 2012-13 | Aberdeen | 16 | 0 | 21 | 0 |
| 2012-13 | Bournemouth | 5 | 0 | 5 | 0 |

**GILKES, Harrison (M)**    0   0

| 2012-13 | Bournemouth | 0 | 0 | | |
|---|---|---|---|---|---|

**GRABBAN, Lewis (F)**    195   48
H: 6 0   W: 11 03   b.Croydon 12-1-88
*Source:* Scholar.

| 2005-06 | Crystal Palace | 0 | 0 | | |
|---|---|---|---|---|---|
| 2006-07 | Crystal Palace | 8 | 1 | | |
| 2006-07 | Oldham Ath | 9 | 0 | 9 | 0 |
| 2007-08 | Crystal Palace | 2 | 0 | 10 | 1 |
| 2007-08 | Motherwell | 6 | 0 | 6 | 0 |
| 2007-08 | Millwall | 13 | 3 | | |
| 2008-09 | Millwall | 31 | 6 | | |
| 2009-10 | Millwall | 11 | 0 | | |
| 2009-10 | Brentford | 7 | 2 | | |
| 2010-11 | Millwall | 1 | 0 | 56 | 9 |
| 2010-11 | Brentford | 22 | 5 | 29 | 7 |
| 2011-12 | Rotherham U | 43 | 18 | 43 | 18 |
| 2012-13 | Bournemouth | 42 | 13 | 42 | 13 |

**HUGHES, Richard (M)**    295   16
H: 6 0   W: 12 13   b.Glasgow 25-6-79
*Source:* Atalanta. *Honours:* Scotland Youth, Under-21, 5 full caps.

| 1998-99 | Bournemouth | 44 | 2 | | |
|---|---|---|---|---|---|
| 1999-2000 | Bournemouth | 21 | 2 | | |
| 2000-01 | Bournemouth | 44 | 8 | | |
| 2001-02 | Bournemouth | 22 | 2 | | |
| 2002-03 | Portsmouth | 6 | 0 | | |
| 2002-03 | Grimsby T | 12 | 1 | 12 | 1 |
| 2003-04 | Portsmouth | 11 | 0 | | |
| 2004-05 | Portsmouth | 16 | 0 | | |
| 2005-06 | Portsmouth | 26 | 0 | | |
| 2006-07 | Portsmouth | 18 | 0 | | |
| 2007-08 | Portsmouth | 13 | 0 | | |
| 2008-09 | Portsmouth | 20 | 0 | | |
| 2009-10 | Portsmouth | 10 | 0 | | |
| 2010-11 | Portsmouth | 11 | 0 | 131 | 0 |
| 2012-13 | Bournemouth | 21 | 1 | 152 | 15 |

**JALAL, Shwan (G)**    168   0
H: 6 2   W: 14 02   b.Baghdad 14-8-83
*Source:* Hastings T.

| 2001-02 | Tottenham H | 0 | 0 | | |
|---|---|---|---|---|---|
| 2002-03 | Tottenham H | 0 | 0 | | |
| 2003-04 | Tottenham H | 0 | 0 | | |

From Woking.

| 2006-07 | Sheffield W | 0 | 0 | | |
|---|---|---|---|---|---|
| 2006-07 | Peterborough U | 1 | 0 | | |
| 2007-08 | Peterborough U | 7 | 0 | | |
| 2007-08 | Morecambe | 12 | 0 | 12 | 0 |
| 2008-09 | Peterborough U | 0 | 0 | 8 | 0 |
| 2008-09 | Bournemouth | 41 | 0 | | |
| 2009-10 | Bournemouth | 44 | 0 | | |
| 2010-11 | Bournemouth | 43 | 0 | | |
| 2011-12 | Bournemouth | 3 | 0 | | |
| 2012-13 | Bournemouth | 17 | 0 | 148 | 0 |

**JAMES, David (G)**    788   0
H: 6 5   W: 15 07   b.Welwyn 1-8-70
*Source:* Trainee. *Honours:* England Youth, Under-21, B, 53 full caps.

| 1988-89 | Watford | 0 | 0 | | |
|---|---|---|---|---|---|
| 1989-90 | Watford | 0 | 0 | | |
| 1990-91 | Watford | 46 | 0 | | |
| 1991-92 | Watford | 43 | 0 | 89 | 0 |
| 1992-93 | Liverpool | 29 | 0 | | |
| 1993-94 | Liverpool | 14 | 0 | | |
| 1994-95 | Liverpool | 42 | 0 | | |
| 1995-96 | Liverpool | 38 | 0 | | |
| 1996-97 | Liverpool | 38 | 0 | | |
| 1997-98 | Liverpool | 27 | 0 | | |
| 1998-99 | Liverpool | 26 | 0 | 214 | 0 |
| 1999-2000 | Aston Villa | 29 | 0 | | |

| 2000-01 | Aston Villa | 38 | 0 | 67 | 0 |
|---|---|---|---|---|---|
| 2001-02 | West Ham U | 26 | 0 | | |
| 2002-03 | West Ham U | 38 | 0 | | |
| 2003-04 | West Ham U | 27 | 0 | 91 | 0 |
| 2003-04 | Manchester C | 17 | 0 | | |
| 2004-05 | Manchester C | 38 | 0 | | |
| 2005-06 | Manchester C | 38 | 0 | 93 | 0 |
| 2006-07 | Portsmouth | 38 | 0 | | |
| 2007-08 | Portsmouth | 35 | 0 | | |
| 2008-09 | Portsmouth | 36 | 0 | | |
| 2009-10 | Portsmouth | 25 | 0 | 134 | 0 |
| 2010-11 | Bristol C | 45 | 0 | | |
| 2011-12 | Bristol C | 36 | 0 | 81 | 0 |
| 2012-13 | Bournemouth | 19 | 0 | 19 | 0 |

**MACDONALD, Shaun (M)**    138   10
H: 6 1   W: 11 04   b.Swansea 17-6-88
*Source:* Scholar. *Honours:* Wales Youth, Under-21, 1 full cap.

| 2005-06 | Swansea C | 7 | 0 | | |
|---|---|---|---|---|---|
| 2006-07 | Swansea C | 8 | 0 | | |
| 2007-08 | Swansea C | 1 | 0 | | |
| 2008-09 | Swansea C | 5 | 0 | | |
| 2008-09 | Yeovil T | 4 | 2 | | |
| 2009-10 | Swansea C | 3 | 0 | | |
| 2009-10 | Yeovil T | 31 | 3 | | |
| 2010-11 | Swansea C | 0 | 0 | | |
| 2010-11 | Yeovil T | 26 | 4 | 61 | 9 |
| 2011-12 | Swansea C | 0 | 0 | 24 | 0 |
| 2011-12 | Bournemouth | 25 | 1 | | |
| 2012-13 | Bournemouth | 28 | 0 | 53 | 1 |

**McDERMOTT, Donal (F)**    63   7
H: 6 6   W: 12 00   b.Co. Meath 19-10-89
*Source:* Scholar. *Honours:* Eire Youth.

| 2007-08 | Manchester C | 0 | 0 | | |
|---|---|---|---|---|---|
| 2008-09 | Manchester C | 0 | 0 | | |
| 2008-09 | Milton Keynes D | 1 | 0 | 1 | 0 |
| 2009-10 | Manchester C | 0 | 0 | | |
| 2009-10 | Chesterfield | 15 | 5 | 15 | 5 |
| 2009-10 | Scunthorpe U | 9 | 0 | 9 | 0 |
| 2010-11 | Manchester C | 0 | 0 | | |
| 2010-11 | Bournemouth | 9 | 1 | | |
| 2011-12 | Huddersfield T | 9 | 0 | 9 | 0 |
| 2011-12 | Bournemouth | 14 | 1 | | |
| 2012-13 | Bournemouth | 6 | 0 | 29 | 2 |

**McQUOID, Josh (F)**    136   15
H: 5 9   W: 10 10   b.Southampton 15-12-89
*Source:* Scholar. *Honours:* Northern Ireland Under-21, B, 5 full caps.

| 2006-07 | Bournemouth | 2 | 0 | | |
|---|---|---|---|---|---|
| 2007-08 | Bournemouth | 5 | 0 | | |
| 2008-09 | Bournemouth | 16 | 0 | | |
| 2009-10 | Bournemouth | 29 | 1 | | |
| 2010-11 | Bournemouth | 17 | 9 | | |
| 2010-11 | Millwall | 11 | 1 | | |
| 2011-12 | Millwall | 5 | 0 | 16 | 1 |
| 2011-12 | Burnley | 17 | 1 | 17 | 1 |
| 2012-13 | Bournemouth | 34 | 3 | 103 | 13 |

**MEADES, Jonathan (M)**    26   1
H: 6 1   W: 13 00   b.Cardiff 2-3-92
*Source:* Scholar. *Honours:* Wales Youth, Under-21.

| 2010-11 | Cardiff C | 0 | 0 | | |
|---|---|---|---|---|---|
| 2011-12 | Cardiff C | 0 | 0 | | |
| 2012-13 | Bournemouth | 0 | 0 | | |
| 2012-13 | AFC Wimbledon | 26 | 1 | 26 | 1 |

**O'KANE, Eunan (M)**    156   17
H: 5 8   W: 13 04   b.Derry 10-7-90
*Honours:* Northern Ireland Schools, Youth, Under-21. Eire Under-21.

| 2007-08 | Everton | 0 | 0 | | |
|---|---|---|---|---|---|
| 2008-09 | Everton | 0 | 0 | | |
| 2009-10 | Coleraine | 13 | 4 | 13 | 4 |
| 2009-10 | Torquay U | 16 | 1 | | |
| 2010-11 | Torquay U | 45 | 6 | | |
| 2011-12 | Torquay U | 45 | 5 | | |
| 2012-13 | Torquay U | 0 | 0 | 106 | 12 |
| 2012-13 | Bournemouth | 37 | 1 | 37 | 1 |

**PARTINGTON, Joe (M)**    52   2
H: 5 11   W: 11 13   b.Portsmouth 1-4-90
*Source:* Scholar. *Honours:* Wales Youth, Under-21.

| 2007-08 | Bournemouth | 6 | 1 | | |
|---|---|---|---|---|---|
| 2008-09 | Bournemouth | 11 | 1 | | |
| 2009-10 | Bournemouth | 11 | 0 | | |

| | | | | | |
|---|---|---|---|---|---|
| 2010-11 | Bournemouth | 5 | 0 | | |
| 2011-12 | Bournemouth | 5 | 0 | | |
| 2012-13 | Bournemouth | 14 | 0 | 52 | 2 |

**PITMAN, Brett (F)**         277 97
H: 6 0   W: 11 00   b.Jersey 31-1-88
*Source:* St Pauls (Jersey).

| | | | | | |
|---|---|---|---|---|---|
| 2005-06 | Bournemouth | 19 | 1 | | |
| 2006-07 | Bournemouth | 29 | 5 | | |
| 2007-08 | Bournemouth | 39 | 6 | | |
| 2008-09 | Bournemouth | 39 | 17 | | |
| 2009-10 | Bournemouth | 46 | 26 | | |
| 2010-11 | Bournemouth | 2 | 3 | | |
| 2010-11 | Bristol C | 39 | 13 | | |
| 2011-12 | Bristol C | 35 | 7 | | |
| 2012-13 | Bristol C | 3 | 0 | 77 | 20 |
| 2012-13 | Bournemouth | 26 | 19 | 200 | 77 |

**PUGH, Marc (M)**         261 48
H: 5 11   W: 11 04   b.Bacup 2-4-87
*Source:* Scholar.

| | | | | | |
|---|---|---|---|---|---|
| 2005-06 | Burnley | 0 | 0 | | |
| 2005-06 | Bury | 6 | 1 | | |
| 2006-07 | Bury | 35 | 3 | 41 | 4 |
| 2007-08 | Shrewsbury T | 37 | 4 | | |
| 2008-09 | Shrewsbury T | 7 | 0 | 44 | 4 |
| 2008-09 | Luton T | 4 | 0 | 4 | 0 |
| 2008-09 | *Hereford U* | 9 | 1 | | |
| 2009-10 | Hereford U | 40 | 13 | 49 | 14 |
| 2010-11 | Bournemouth | 41 | 12 | | |
| 2011-12 | Bournemouth | 42 | 8 | | |
| 2012-13 | Bournemouth | 40 | 6 | 123 | 26 |

**PURCHES, Stephen (D)**        387 15
H: 5 11   W: 11 13   b.Ilford 14-1-80

| | | | | | |
|---|---|---|---|---|---|
| 1998-99 | West Ham U | 0 | 0 | | |
| 1999-2000 | West Ham U | 0 | 0 | | |
| 2000-01 | Bournemouth | 34 | 0 | | |
| 2001-02 | Bournemouth | 41 | 2 | | |
| 2002-03 | Bournemouth | 44 | 3 | | |
| 2003-04 | Bournemouth | 42 | 3 | | |
| 2004-05 | Bournemouth | 14 | 1 | | |
| 2005-06 | Bournemouth | 26 | 0 | | |
| 2006-07 | Bournemouth | 43 | 1 | | |
| 2007-08 | Leyton Orient | 37 | 1 | | |
| 2008-09 | Leyton Orient | 42 | 3 | | |
| 2009-10 | Leyton Orient | 31 | 1 | 110 | 5 |
| 2010-11 | Bournemouth | 9 | 0 | | |
| 2011-12 | Bournemouth | 24 | 0 | | |
| 2012-13 | Bournemouth | 0 | 0 | 277 | 10 |

**RITCHIE, Matt (M)**         184 43
H: 5 8   W: 11 00   b.Gosport 10-9-89
*Source:* Scholar.

| | | | | | |
|---|---|---|---|---|---|
| 2008-09 | Portsmouth | 0 | 0 | | |
| 2008-09 | *Dagenham & R* | 37 | 11 | 37 | 11 |
| 2009-10 | Portsmouth | 2 | 0 | | |
| 2009-10 | *Notts Co* | 16 | 3 | 16 | 3 |
| 2009-10 | *Swindon T* | 4 | 0 | | |
| 2010-11 | Portsmouth | 5 | 0 | 7 | 0 |
| 2010-11 | Swindon T | 36 | 7 | | |
| 2011-12 | Swindon T | 40 | 10 | | |
| 2012-13 | Swindon T | 27 | 9 | 107 | 26 |
| 2012-13 | Bournemouth | 17 | 3 | 17 | 3 |

**SHERINGHAM, Charlie (F)**     6 1
H: 6 1   W: 11 06   b.Chingford 17-4-88
From Ipswich T Scholar, LA Galaxy, C
Palace Baltimore (loan), Cambridge C,
Welling U, Bishop's Stortford, Histon (loan),
Dartford.

| | | | | | |
|---|---|---|---|---|---|
| 2011-12 | Bournemouth | 6 | 1 | | |
| 2012-13 | Bournemouth | 0 | 0 | 6 | 1 |

**STOCKLEY, Jayden (F)**       25 3
H: 6 2   W: 12 07   b.Poole 10-10-93
*Source:* School.

| | | | | | |
|---|---|---|---|---|---|
| 2009-10 | Bournemouth | 2 | 0 | | |
| 2010-11 | Bournemouth | 4 | 0 | | |
| 2011-12 | Bournemouth | 10 | 0 | | |
| 2011-12 | *Accrington S* | 9 | 3 | 9 | 3 |
| 2012-13 | Bournemouth | 0 | 0 | 16 | 0 |

**STRUGNELL, Dan (D)**        1 0
H: 6 1   W: 12 00   b.Christchurch 30-6-92
*Source:* Youth.

| | | | | | |
|---|---|---|---|---|---|
| 2011-12 | Bournemouth | 1 | 0 | | |
| 2012-13 | Bournemouth | 0 | 0 | 1 | 0 |

**THOMAS, Wesley (F)**      143 42
H: 5 10   W: 11 00   b.Barking 23-1-87
*Source:* QPR Youth, Waltham Forest,
Thurrock, Fisher Ath.

| | | | | | |
|---|---|---|---|---|---|
| 2008-09 | Dagenham & R | 5 | 0 | | |
| 2009-10 | Dagenham & R | 23 | 3 | 28 | 3 |
| 2010-11 | Cheltenham T | 41 | 18 | 41 | 18 |
| 2011-12 | Crawley T | 6 | 1 | 6 | 1 |
| 2011-12 | Bournemouth | 36 | 11 | | |
| 2012-13 | Bournemouth | 6 | 0 | 42 | 11 |
| 2012-13 | *Portsmouth* | 6 | 3 | 6 | 3 |
| 2012-13 | *Blackpool* | 9 | 3 | 9 | 3 |
| 2012-13 | *Birmingham C* | 11 | 3 | 11 | 3 |

**TUBBS, Matt (F)**         70 20
H: 5 9   W: 11 00   b.Salisbury 15-7-84
*Source:* Bolton W Scholar.
On loan from Salisbury C.

| | | | | | |
|---|---|---|---|---|---|
| 2008-09 | Bournemouth | 8 | 1 | | |
| 2009-10 | Bournemouth | 0 | 0 | | |
| 2011-12 | *Crawley T* | 24 | 12 | 24 | 12 |
| 2011-12 | Bournemouth | 7 | 1 | | |
| 2012-13 | Bournemouth | 31 | 6 | 46 | 8 |

**WAKEFIELD, Josh (M)**      3 0
H: 5 11   W: 11 05   b.Frimley 6-11-93
*Source:* Youth.

| | | | | | |
|---|---|---|---|---|---|
| 2011-12 | Bournemouth | 2 | 0 | | |
| 2012-13 | Bournemouth | 1 | 0 | 3 | 0 |
| 2012-13 | *Dagenham & R* | 0 | 0 | | |

**ZUBAR, Stephane (D)**      120 3
H: 6 1   W: 12 11   b.Guadeloupe 9-10-86
*Honours:* Guadeloupe 2 full caps.

| | | | | | |
|---|---|---|---|---|---|
| 2006-07 | Caen | 0 | 0 | | |
| 2006-07 | Pau | 10 | 0 | 10 | 0 |
| 2007-08 | Caen | 0 | 0 | | |
| 2007-08 | FC Brussels | 11 | 0 | 11 | 0 |
| 2008-09 | Vaslui | 10 | 0 | | |
| 2009-10 | Vaslui | 26 | 1 | 36 | 1 |
| 2010-11 | Plymouth Arg | 29 | 2 | | |
| 2011-12 | Plymouth Arg | 4 | 0 | 33 | 2 |
| 2011-12 | Bournemouth | 22 | 0 | | |
| 2012-13 | Bournemouth | 2 | 0 | 24 | 0 |
| 2012-13 | *Bury* | 6 | 0 | 6 | 0 |

**Scholars**
Banaghan, Macually James; Blackman, Daryl
Henry Antony; Blackmore, Lewis Leon
Marcus; Buckley, Callum Ralph; Cargill,
Baily James; Collins, Chad Richard; Davis,
Charlie Eric Wayne; Goodship, Brandon;
Harris, Anthony; Kaye, Joshua Joseph;
Kirkwood, Samuel Jack; Lindsay, Lewis;
McCarthy, Jake; Roberts, Kieran Matthew;
Tierney, Edward George; Turner, Thomas
John; Walsh, Mason Anthony; West, Jamie
David.

# BRADFORD C (13)

**ATKINSON, Will (M)**      137 13
H: 5 10   W: 10 07   b.Beverley 14-10-88
*Source:* Scholar.

| | | | | | |
|---|---|---|---|---|---|
| 2006-07 | Hull C | 0 | 0 | | |
| 2007-08 | Hull C | 0 | 0 | | |
| 2007-08 | *Port Vale* | 4 | 0 | 4 | 0 |
| 2007-08 | *Mansfield T* | 12 | 0 | 12 | 0 |
| 2008-09 | Hull C | 0 | 0 | | |
| 2009-10 | Hull C | 2 | 1 | | |
| 2009-10 | *Rochdale* | 15 | 3 | | |
| 2010-11 | Hull C | 4 | 0 | | |
| 2010-11 | *Rotherham U* | 3 | 1 | 3 | 1 |
| 2010-11 | *Rochdale* | 21 | 2 | 36 | 5 |
| 2011-12 | Hull C | 0 | 0 | 6 | 1 |
| 2011-12 | *Plymouth Arg* | 22 | 4 | 22 | 4 |
| 2011-12 | *Bradford C* | 12 | 1 | | |
| 2012-13 | Bradford C | 42 | 1 | 54 | 2 |

**BASS, Forrayah (M)**       0 0
b. 12-3-95

| | | | | | |
|---|---|---|---|---|---|
| 2012-13 | Bradford C | 0 | 0 | | |

**CONNELL, Alan (F)**      276 60
H: 6 0   W: 12 00   b.Enfield 5-2-83
*Source:* Ipswich T Trainee.

| | | | | | |
|---|---|---|---|---|---|
| 2002-03 | Bournemouth | 13 | 6 | | |
| 2003-04 | Bournemouth | 7 | 0 | | |
| 2004-05 | Bournemouth | 34 | 2 | | |

| | | | | | |
|---|---|---|---|---|---|
| 2005-06 | Torquay U | 22 | 7 | 22 | 7 |
| 2006-07 | Hereford U | 44 | 9 | 44 | 9 |
| 2007-08 | Brentford | 42 | 12 | | |
| 2008-09 | Brentford | 2 | 0 | 44 | 12 |
| 2008-09 | Bournemouth | 12 | 0 | | |
| 2009-10 | Bournemouth | 38 | 5 | 104 | 13 |

From Grimsby T.

| | | | | | |
|---|---|---|---|---|---|
| 2011-12 | Swindon T | 32 | 11 | 32 | 11 |
| 2012-13 | Bradford C | 30 | 8 | 30 | 8 |

**DARBY, Stephen (D)**       106 0
H: 5 9   W: 10 00   b.Liverpool 6-10-88
*Source:* Scholar. *Honours:* England Youth.

| | | | | | |
|---|---|---|---|---|---|
| 2006-07 | Liverpool | 0 | 0 | | |
| 2007-08 | Liverpool | 0 | 0 | | |
| 2008-09 | Liverpool | 0 | 0 | | |
| 2009-10 | Liverpool | 1 | 0 | | |
| 2009-10 | *Swindon T* | 12 | 0 | 12 | 0 |
| 2010-11 | Liverpool | 0 | 0 | | |
| 2010-11 | *Notts Co* | 23 | 0 | 23 | 0 |
| 2011-12 | Liverpool | 0 | 0 | 1 | 0 |
| 2011-12 | *Rochdale* | 35 | 0 | 35 | 0 |
| 2012-13 | Bradford C | 35 | 0 | 35 | 0 |

**DAVIES, Andrew (D)**      187 9
H: 6 3   W: 14 08   b.Stockton 17-12-84
*Source:* Scholar. *Honours:* England Youth,
Under-20, Under-21.

| | | | | | |
|---|---|---|---|---|---|
| 2002-03 | Middlesbrough | 1 | 0 | | |
| 2003-04 | Middlesbrough | 10 | 0 | | |
| 2004-05 | Middlesbrough | 3 | 0 | | |
| 2004-05 | *QPR* | 9 | 0 | 9 | 0 |
| 2005-06 | Middlesbrough | 12 | 0 | | |
| 2005-06 | *Derby Co* | 23 | 3 | 23 | 3 |
| 2006-07 | Middlesbrough | 23 | 0 | | |
| 2007-08 | Middlesbrough | 4 | 0 | | |
| 2007-08 | Southampton | 23 | 0 | | |
| 2008-09 | Southampton | 0 | 0 | 23 | 0 |
| 2008-09 | Stoke C | 2 | 0 | | |
| 2008-09 | *Preston NE* | 5 | 0 | 5 | 0 |
| 2009-10 | Stoke C | 0 | 0 | | |
| 2009-10 | *Sheffield U* | 8 | 0 | 8 | 0 |
| 2010-11 | Stoke C | 0 | 0 | | |
| 2010-11 | *Walsall* | 3 | 0 | 3 | 0 |
| 2010-11 | *Middlesbrough* | 6 | 0 | 59 | 0 |
| 2011-12 | Stoke C | 0 | 0 | 2 | 0 |
| 2011-12 | *Crystal Palace* | 1 | 0 | 1 | 0 |
| 2011-12 | *Bradford C* | 26 | 2 | | |
| 2012-13 | Bradford C | 28 | 4 | 54 | 6 |

**DOYLE, Nathan (M)**      194 4
H: 5 11   W: 12 06   b.Derby 12-1-87
*Source:* Scholar. *Honours:* England Youth,
Under-20.

| | | | | | |
|---|---|---|---|---|---|
| 2003-04 | Derby Co | 2 | 0 | | |
| 2004-05 | Derby Co | 3 | 0 | | |
| 2005-06 | Derby Co | 4 | 0 | | |
| 2005-06 | *Notts Co* | 12 | 0 | 12 | 0 |
| 2006-07 | Derby Co | 0 | 0 | 9 | 0 |
| 2006-07 | *Bradford C* | 28 | 0 | | |
| 2006-07 | Hull C | 1 | 0 | | |
| 2007-08 | Hull C | 1 | 0 | | |
| 2008-09 | Hull C | 3 | 0 | | |
| 2009-10 | Hull C | 0 | 0 | 5 | 0 |
| 2009-10 | Barnsley | 34 | 0 | | |
| 2010-11 | Barnsley | 43 | 2 | | |
| 2011-12 | Barnsley | 21 | 0 | 98 | 2 |
| 2011-12 | *Preston NE* | 5 | 0 | 5 | 0 |
| 2012-13 | Bradford C | 37 | 2 | 65 | 2 |

**DUKE, Matt (G)**        109 0
H: 6 5   W: 13 04   b.Sheffield 16-7-77
*Source:* Alfreton T.

| | | | | | |
|---|---|---|---|---|---|
| 1999-2000 | Sheffield U | 0 | 0 | | |
| 2000-01 | Sheffield U | 0 | 0 | | |
| 2001-02 | Sheffield U | 0 | 0 | | |
| 2004-05 | Hull C | 2 | 0 | | |
| 2005-06 | Hull C | 2 | 0 | | |
| 2005-06 | *Stockport Co* | 3 | 0 | 3 | 0 |
| 2005-06 | *Wycombe W* | 5 | 0 | 5 | 0 |
| 2006-07 | Hull C | 1 | 0 | | |
| 2007-08 | Hull C | 3 | 0 | | |
| 2008-09 | Hull C | 10 | 0 | | |
| 2009-10 | Hull C | 11 | 0 | | |
| 2010-11 | Hull C | 21 | 0 | 50 | 0 |
| 2011-12 | Bradford C | 18 | 0 | | |
| 2011-12 | *Northampton T* | 9 | 0 | 9 | 0 |
| 2012-13 | Bradford C | 24 | 0 | 42 | 0 |

**ERANGEY, Connor (M)**     0   0
| | | | | | |
|---|---|---|---|---|---|
| 2012-13 | Bradford C | 0 | 0 | | |

**GRAY, Andy (F)**    482 107
H: 6 1   W: 13 00   b.Harrogate 15-11-77
*Source:* Trainee. *Honours:* Scotland Youth, B, 2 full caps.
| | | | | | |
|---|---|---|---|---|---|
| 1995-96 | Leeds U | 15 | 0 | | |
| 1996-97 | Leeds U | 7 | 0 | | |
| 1997-98 | Leeds U | 0 | 0 | | |
| 1997-98 | *Bury* | 6 | 1 | **6** | **1** |
| 1998-99 | Leeds U | 0 | 0 | | |
| 1998-99 | Nottingham F | 8 | 0 | | |
| 1998-99 | *Preston NE* | 5 | 0 | **5** | **0** |
| 1998-99 | *Oldham Ath* | 4 | 0 | **4** | **0** |
| 1999-2000 | Nottingham F | 22 | 0 | | |
| 2000-01 | Nottingham F | 18 | 0 | | |
| 2001-02 | Nottingham F | 16 | 1 | **64** | **1** |
| 2002-03 | Bradford U | 44 | 15 | | |
| 2003-04 | Bradford C | 33 | 5 | | |
| 2003-04 | Sheffield U | 14 | 9 | | |
| 2004-05 | Sheffield U | 43 | 15 | | |
| 2005-06 | Sheffield U | 1 | 1 | **58** | **25** |
| 2005-06 | Sunderland | 21 | 1 | **21** | **1** |
| 2005-06 | Burnley | 9 | 3 | | |
| 2006-07 | Burnley | 35 | 14 | | |
| 2007-08 | Burnley | 25 | 11 | **69** | **28** |
| 2007-08 | Charlton Ath | 16 | 2 | | |
| 2008-09 | Charlton Ath | 27 | 7 | | |
| 2009-10 | Charlton Ath | 2 | 0 | **45** | **9** |
| 2009-10 | Barnsley | 30 | 6 | | |
| 2010-11 | Barnsley | 34 | 7 | | |
| 2011-12 | Barnsley | 32 | 8 | **96** | **21** |
| 2012-13 | Leeds U | 8 | 1 | **30** | **1** |
| 2012-13 | Bradford C | 7 | 0 | **84** | **20** |

**HANNAH, Ross (F)**    19   2
H: 5 9   W: 11 11   b.Sheffield 14-5-86
*Source:* Gainsborough T, Stocksbridge PS, Belper T, Matlock T.
| | | | | | |
|---|---|---|---|---|---|
| 2011-12 | Bradford C | 18 | 2 | | |
| 2012-13 | Bradford C | 1 | 0 | **19** | **2** |

**HANSON, James (F)**    152 41
H: 6 4   W: 12 04   b.Bradford 9-11-87
*Source:* Eccleshill U, Guiseley.
| | | | | | |
|---|---|---|---|---|---|
| 2009-10 | Bradford C | 34 | 12 | | |
| 2010-11 | Bradford C | 36 | 6 | | |
| 2011-12 | Bradford C | 39 | 13 | | |
| 2012-13 | Bradford C | 43 | 10 | **152** | **41** |

**HEPWORTH, Calum (M)**    0   0
b. 25-1-96
| | | | | | |
|---|---|---|---|---|---|
| 2012-13 | Bradford C | 0 | 0 | | |

**HINES, Zavon (F)**    82   5
H: 5 10   W: 10 07   b.Jamaica 27-12-88
*Source:* Scholar. *Honours:* England Under-21.
| | | | | | |
|---|---|---|---|---|---|
| 2007-08 | West Ham U | 0 | 0 | | |
| 2007-08 | Coventry C | 7 | 1 | **7** | **1** |
| 2008-09 | West Ham U | 4 | 0 | | |
| 2009-10 | West Ham U | 13 | 1 | | |
| 2010-11 | West Ham U | 9 | 0 | **22** | **1** |
| 2011-12 | Burnley | 13 | 0 | **13** | **0** |
| 2011-12 | *Bournemouth* | 8 | 1 | **8** | **1** |
| 2012-13 | Bradford C | 32 | 2 | **32** | **2** |

**JONES, Gary (M)**    573 78
H: 5 11   W: 12 05   b.Birkenhead 3-6-77
*Source:* Caernarfon T.
| | | | | | |
|---|---|---|---|---|---|
| 1997-98 | Swansea C | 8 | 0 | **8** | **0** |
| 1997-98 | Rochdale | 17 | 2 | | |
| 1998-99 | Rochdale | 20 | 0 | | |
| 1999-2000 | Rochdale | 39 | 7 | | |
| 2000-01 | Rochdale | 44 | 8 | | |
| 2001-02 | Rochdale | 20 | 5 | | |
| 2001-02 | Barnsley | 25 | 1 | | |
| 2002-03 | Barnsley | 31 | 1 | | |
| 2003-04 | Barnsley | 0 | 0 | **56** | **2** |
| 2003-04 | Rochdale | 26 | 4 | | |
| 2004-05 | Rochdale | 39 | 8 | | |
| 2005-06 | Rochdale | 42 | 4 | | |
| 2006-07 | Rochdale | 27 | 3 | | |
| 2007-08 | Rochdale | 43 | 7 | | |
| 2008-09 | Rochdale | 28 | 0 | | |
| 2009-10 | Rochdale | 34 | 4 | | |
| 2010-11 | Rochdale | 46 | 17 | | |
| 2011-12 | Rochdale | 45 | 5 | **470** | **74** |
| 2012-13 | Bradford C | 39 | 2 | **39** | **2** |

**McARDLE, Rory (D)**    242 10
H: 6 1   W: 11 04   b.Doncaster 1-5-87
*Source:* Scholar. *Honours:* Northern Ireland Youth, Under-21, 2 full caps.
| | | | | | |
|---|---|---|---|---|---|
| 2005-06 | Sheffield W | 0 | 0 | | |
| 2005-06 | *Rochdale* | 19 | 1 | | |
| 2006-07 | Sheffield W | 1 | 0 | **1** | **0** |
| 2006-07 | Rochdale | 25 | 0 | | |
| 2007-08 | Rochdale | 43 | 3 | | |
| 2008-09 | Rochdale | 41 | 2 | | |
| 2009-10 | Rochdale | 20 | 0 | **148** | **6** |
| 2010-11 | Aberdeen | 28 | 2 | | |
| 2011-12 | Aberdeen | 25 | 0 | **53** | **2** |
| 2012-13 | Bradford C | 40 | 2 | **40** | **2** |

**McHUGH, Carl (D)**    16   1
b.Co. Donegal 5-2-93
*Source:* Scholar. *Honours:* Eire Youth.
| | | | | | |
|---|---|---|---|---|---|
| 2011-12 | Reading | 0 | 0 | | |
| 2012-13 | Bradford C | 16 | 1 | **16** | **1** |

**McLAUGHLIN, Jon (G)**    79   0
H: 6 2   W: 13 00   b.Edinburgh 9-9-87
*Source:* Harrogate T.
| | | | | | |
|---|---|---|---|---|---|
| 2008-09 | Bradford C | 1 | 0 | | |
| 2009-10 | Bradford C | 7 | 0 | | |
| 2010-11 | Bradford C | 25 | 0 | | |
| 2011-12 | Bradford C | 23 | 0 | | |
| 2012-13 | Bradford C | 23 | 0 | **79** | **0** |

**MEREDITH, James (D)**    36   1
H: 6 1   W: 11 06   b.Albury, Australia 4-4-88
*Source:* Scholar.
| | | | | | |
|---|---|---|---|---|---|
| 2006-07 | Derby Co | 0 | 0 | | |
| 2006-07 | *Chesterfield* | 1 | 0 | **1** | **0** |
| 2007-08 | *Shrewsbury T* | 3 | 0 | **3** | **0** |
| From York C | | | | | |
| 2012-13 | Bradford C | 32 | 1 | **32** | **1** |

**NELSON, Michael (D)**    449 30
H: 6 2   W: 13 03   b.Gateshead 15-3-82
*Source:* Bishop Auckland.
| | | | | | |
|---|---|---|---|---|---|
| 2000-01 | Bury | 2 | 1 | | |
| 2001-02 | Bury | 31 | 2 | | |
| 2002-03 | Bury | 39 | 5 | **72** | **8** |
| 2003-04 | Hartlepool U | 40 | 3 | | |
| 2004-05 | Hartlepool U | 43 | 1 | | |
| 2005-06 | Hartlepool U | 43 | 2 | | |
| 2006-07 | Hartlepool U | 42 | 1 | | |
| 2007-08 | Hartlepool U | 45 | 2 | | |
| 2008-09 | Hartlepool U | 46 | 5 | **259** | **14** |
| 2009-10 | Norwich C | 31 | 3 | | |
| 2010-11 | Norwich C | 8 | 2 | **39** | **5** |
| 2010-11 | Scunthorpe U | 20 | 0 | | |
| 2011-12 | Scunthorpe U | 10 | 1 | **30** | **1** |
| 2011-12 | Kilmarnock | 15 | 1 | | |
| 2012-13 | Kilmarnock | 21 | 1 | **36** | **2** |
| 2012-13 | Bradford C | 13 | 0 | **13** | **0** |

**OLIVER, Luke (D)**    141   4
H: 6 6   W: 14 05   b.Acton 1-5-84
*Source:* Brook House.
| | | | | | |
|---|---|---|---|---|---|
| 2002-03 | Wycombe W | 2 | 0 | | |
| 2003-04 | Wycombe W | 2 | 0 | | |
| From Woking | | | | | |
| 2005-06 | Yeovil T | 3 | 0 | **3** | **0** |
| From Stevenage B. | | | | | |
| 2008-09 | Wycombe W | 8 | 0 | | |
| 2009-10 | Wycombe W | 23 | 0 | **35** | **0** |
| 2009-10 | *Bradford C* | 7 | 2 | | |
| 2010-11 | Bradford C | 42 | 1 | | |
| 2011-12 | Bradford C | 39 | 1 | | |
| 2012-13 | Bradford C | 15 | 0 | **103** | **4** |

**RAVENHILL, Ricky (M)**    333 22
H: 5 10   W: 11 02   b.Doncaster 16-1-81
*Source:* Barnsley Trainee.
| | | | | | |
|---|---|---|---|---|---|
| 2003-04 | Doncaster R | 36 | 3 | | |
| 2004-05 | Doncaster R | 35 | 3 | | |
| 2005-06 | Doncaster R | 27 | 3 | **98** | **9** |
| 2006-07 | Chester C | 3 | 0 | **3** | **0** |
| 2006-07 | Grimsby T | 17 | 2 | **17** | **2** |
| 2006-07 | Darlington | 15 | 1 | | |
| 2007-08 | Darlington | 35 | 3 | | |
| 2008-09 | Darlington | 38 | 2 | **88** | **6** |
| 2008-09 | Notts Co | 9 | 0 | | |
| 2009-10 | Notts Co | 40 | 3 | | |
| 2010-11 | Notts Co | 34 | 0 | | |
| 2011-12 | Notts Co | 5 | 0 | **79** | **3** |

**REID, Kyel (M)**    172 14
H: 5 10   W: 12 05   b.Deptford 26-11-87
*Source:* Scholar. *Honours:* England Youth.
| | | | | | |
|---|---|---|---|---|---|
| 2004-05 | West Ham U | 0 | 0 | | |
| 2005-06 | West Ham U | 2 | 0 | | |
| 2006-07 | West Ham U | 0 | 0 | | |
| 2006-07 | *Barnsley* | 26 | 2 | **26** | **2** |
| 2007-08 | West Ham U | 1 | 0 | | |
| 2007-08 | *Crystal Palace* | 2 | 0 | **2** | **0** |
| 2008-09 | West Ham U | 0 | 0 | **3** | **0** |
| 2008-09 | *Blackpool* | 7 | 0 | **7** | **0** |
| 2008-09 | *Wolverhampton W* | 8 | 1 | **8** | **1** |
| 2009-10 | Sheffield U | 7 | 0 | **7** | **0** |
| 2009-10 | *Charlton Ath* | 17 | 4 | | |
| 2010-11 | Charlton Ath | 32 | 1 | **49** | **5** |
| 2011-12 | Bradford C | 37 | 4 | | |
| 2012-13 | Bradford C | 33 | 2 | **70** | **6** |

**THOMPSON, Gary (M)**    192 33
H: 6 0   W: 14 02   b.Kendal 24-11-80
*Source:* Scholar.
| | | | | | |
|---|---|---|---|---|---|
| 2007-08 | Morecambe | 40 | 7 | **40** | **7** |
| 2008-09 | Scunthorpe U | 24 | 3 | | |
| 2009-10 | Scunthorpe U | 36 | 9 | | |
| 2010-11 | Scunthorpe U | 12 | 1 | | |
| 2011-12 | Scunthorpe U | 39 | 7 | **111** | **20** |
| 2012-13 | Bradford C | 41 | 6 | **41** | **6** |

**WELLS, Nahki (F)**    75 28
H: 5 7   W: 11 00   b.Bermuda 1-6-90
*Source:* Bermuda T Hornets, Bermuda Hogges.
*Honours:* Bermuda 6 full caps.
| | | | | | |
|---|---|---|---|---|---|
| 2010-11 | Carlisle U | 3 | 0 | **3** | **0** |
| 2011-12 | Bradford C | 33 | 10 | | |
| 2012-13 | Bradford C | 39 | 18 | **72** | **28** |

**Scholars**
Bass, Forrayah George Warrington N; Bentley, Jack; Boote, Andrew Stephen; Bott, Thomas David; Bower, Connor Patrick James; Brown, Scott David; Curtis, Nathan Robert; Erangey, Connor James Ryan; Harrison, Kyle Michael; Hepworth, Calum; Hiza, Robert Jonathan; McBurnie, Oliver; Morrison, Stuart; Stockdill, Jack Peter; Swain, Louie Robert.

# BRENTFORD (14)

**ADAMS, Charlie (M)**    1   0
H: 5 6   W: 9 10   b.London 16-5-94
| | | | | | |
|---|---|---|---|---|---|
| 2012-13 | Brentford | 1 | 0 | **1** | **0** |

**BARRON, Scott (D)**    137   2
H: 5 9   W: 9 08   b.Preston 2-9-85
*Source:* Scholar.
| | | | | | |
|---|---|---|---|---|---|
| 2003-04 | Ipswich T | 0 | 0 | | |
| 2004-05 | Ipswich T | 0 | 0 | | |
| 2005-06 | Ipswich T | 15 | 0 | | |
| 2006-07 | Ipswich T | 0 | 0 | **15** | **0** |
| 2006-07 | *Wrexham* | 3 | 0 | **3** | **0** |
| 2007-08 | Millwall | 12 | 0 | | |
| 2008-09 | Millwall | 14 | 0 | | |
| 2009-10 | Millwall | 23 | 0 | | |
| 2010-11 | Millwall | 38 | 2 | | |
| 2011-12 | Millwall | 20 | 0 | | |
| 2012-13 | Millwall | 0 | 0 | **107** | **2** |
| 2012-13 | Brentford | 12 | 0 | **12** | **0** |

**CRAIG, Tony (D)**    280   7
H: 6 0   W: 10 03   b.Greenwich 20-4-85
*Source:* Scholar.
| | | | | | |
|---|---|---|---|---|---|
| 2002-03 | Millwall | 2 | 1 | | |
| 2003-04 | Millwall | 9 | 0 | | |
| 2004-05 | Millwall | 10 | 0 | | |
| 2004-05 | *Wycombe W* | 14 | 0 | **14** | **0** |
| 2005-06 | Millwall | 28 | 0 | | |
| 2006-07 | Millwall | 30 | 1 | | |
| 2007-08 | *Crystal Palace* | 13 | 0 | **13** | **0** |
| 2007-08 | *Millwall* | 5 | 1 | | |
| 2008-09 | Millwall | 44 | 2 | | |
| 2009-10 | Millwall | 30 | 2 | | |
| 2010-11 | Millwall | 24 | 0 | | |
| 2011-12 | Millwall | 23 | 0 | **205** | **7** |
| 2011-12 | *Leyton Orient* | 4 | 0 | **4** | **0** |
| 2012-13 | Brentford | 44 | 0 | **44** | **0** |

**DALLAS, Stuart (M)**    28 24
H: 6 0   W: 12 09   b.Cookstown 19-4-91

| 2010-11 | Crusaders | 13 | 16 | | |
| 2011-12 | Crusaders | 8 | 8 | 21 | 24 |
| 2012-13 | Brentford | 7 | 0 | 7 | 0 |

**DEAN, Harlee (M)**    71 4
H: 6 0   W: 11 10   b.Basingstoke 26-7-91
*Source:* Scholar.

| 2008-09 | Dagenham & R | 0 | 0 | | |
| 2009-10 | Dagenham & R | 1 | 0 | 1 | 0 |
| 2010-11 | Southampton | 0 | 0 | | |
| 2011-12 | Southampton | 0 | 0 | | |
| 2011-12 | *Brentford* | 26 | 1 | | |
| 2012-13 | Brentford | 44 | 3 | 70 | 4 |

**DIAGOURAGA, Toumani (M)**    247 10
H: 6 2   W: 11 05   b.Paris 10-6-87
*Source:* Scholar.

| 2004-05 | Watford | 0 | 0 | | |
| 2005-06 | Watford | 1 | 0 | | |
| 2005-06 | *Swindon T* | 8 | 0 | 8 | 0 |
| 2006-07 | Watford | 0 | 0 | | |
| 2006-07 | *Rotherham U* | 7 | 0 | 7 | 0 |
| 2007-08 | Watford | 0 | 0 | 1 | 0 |
| 2007-08 | *Hereford U* | 1 | 0 | | |
| 2008-09 | Hereford U | 45 | 2 | 86 | 4 |
| 2009-10 | Peterborough U | 19 | 0 | 19 | 0 |
| 2009-10 | *Brentford* | 20 | 0 | | |
| 2010-11 | Brentford | 32 | 1 | | |
| 2011-12 | Brentford | 35 | 4 | | |
| 2012-13 | Brentford | 39 | 1 | 126 | 6 |

**DONALDSON, Clayton (F)**    226 81
H: 6 1   W: 11 07   b.Bradford 7-2-84
*Source:* Scholar.

| 2002-03 | Hull C | 2 | 0 | | |
| 2003-04 | Hull C | 0 | 0 | | |
| 2004-05 | Hull C | 0 | 0 | 2 | 0 |
From York C
| 2007-08 | Hibernian | 17 | 5 | 17 | 5 |
| 2008-09 | Crewe Alex | 37 | 6 | | |
| 2009-10 | Crewe Alex | 37 | 13 | | |
| 2010-11 | Crewe Alex | 43 | 28 | 117 | 47 |
| 2011-12 | Brentford | 46 | 11 | | |
| 2012-13 | Brentford | 44 | 18 | 90 | 29 |

**DOUGLAS, Jonathan (M)**    363 22
H: 5 11   W: 11 11   b.Monaghan 22-11-81
*Source:* Trainee. *Honours:* Eire Under-21, 8
full caps.

| 1999-2000 | Blackburn R | 0 | 0 | | |
| 2000-01 | Blackburn R | 0 | 0 | | |
| 2001-02 | Blackburn R | 0 | 0 | | |
| 2002-03 | Blackburn R | 1 | 0 | | |
| 2002-03 | *Chesterfield* | 7 | 1 | 7 | 1 |
| 2003-04 | Blackpool | 16 | 3 | 16 | 3 |
| 2003-04 | Blackburn R | 14 | 1 | | |
| 2004-05 | Blackburn R | 1 | 0 | | |
| 2004-05 | *Gillingham* | 10 | 0 | 10 | 0 |
| 2005-06 | Blackburn R | 0 | 0 | | |
| 2005-06 | *Leeds U* | 40 | 5 | | |
| 2006-07 | Blackburn R | 0 | 0 | 16 | 1 |
| 2006-07 | Leeds U | 35 | 1 | | |
| 2007-08 | Leeds U | 24 | 3 | | |
| 2008-09 | Leeds U | 43 | 1 | 142 | 10 |
| 2009-10 | Swindon T | 43 | 0 | | |
| 2010-11 | Swindon T | 39 | 1 | 82 | 1 |
| 2011-12 | Brentford | 46 | 2 | | |
| 2012-13 | Brentford | 44 | 4 | 90 | 6 |

**EL ALAGUI, Farid (F)**    44 21
H: 6 1   W: 13 00   b.Marmande 28-8-85

| 2011-12 | Falkirk | 33 | 18 | 33 | 18 |
| 2012-13 | Brentford | 11 | 3 | 11 | 3 |

**FORRESTER, Harry (F)**    62 8
H: 5 9   W: 11 03   b.Milton Keynes 2-1-91
*Source:* Watford Scholar.

| 2007-08 | Aston Villa | 0 | 0 | | |
| 2008-09 | Aston Villa | 0 | 0 | | |
| 2009-10 | Aston Villa | 0 | 0 | | |
| 2010-11 | Aston Villa | 0 | 0 | | |
| 2010-11 | *Kilmarnock* | 7 | 0 | 7 | 0 |
| 2011-12 | Brentford | 19 | 0 | | |
| 2012-13 | Brentford | 36 | 8 | 55 | 8 |

**FORSHAW, Adam (M)**    51 3
H: 6 1   W: 11 02   b.Liverpool 8-10-91
*Source:* Scholar.

| 2009-10 | Everton | 0 | 0 | | |
| 2010-11 | Everton | 1 | 0 | | |
| 2011-12 | Everton | 0 | 0 | 1 | 0 |
| 2011-12 | *Brentford* | 7 | 0 | | |
| 2012-13 | Brentford | 43 | 3 | 50 | 3 |

**GERMAN, Antonio (F)**    40 4
H: 5 10   W: 12 03   b.Wembley 26-12-91
*Source:* Scholar.

| 2008-09 | QPR | 3 | 0 | | |
| 2009-10 | QPR | 13 | 2 | | |
| 2009-10 | *Aldershot T* | 3 | 0 | 3 | 0 |
| 2010-11 | QPR | 2 | 0 | | |
| 2010-11 | *Southend U* | 4 | 0 | 4 | 0 |
| 2010-11 | *Yeovil T* | 4 | 0 | 4 | 0 |
| 2011-12 | QPR | 0 | 0 | 18 | 2 |
From Stockport Co, Bromley.
| 2011-12 | Brentford | 2 | 0 | | |
| 2012-13 | Brentford | 2 | 1 | 4 | 1 |
| 2012-13 | *Gillingham* | 7 | 1 | 7 | 1 |

**GOUNET, Antoine (G)**    0 0
H: 6 2   W: 13 03   b.France 16-10-88
*Source:* Tours.

| 2011-12 | Brentford | 0 | 0 | | |
| 2012-13 | Brentford | 0 | 0 | | |

**HAYES, Paul (F)**    396 91
H: 6 0   W: 12 12   b.Dagenham 20-9-83
*Source:* Norwich C Scholar.

| 2002-03 | Scunthorpe U | 18 | 8 | | |
| 2003-04 | Scunthorpe U | 35 | 2 | | |
| 2004-05 | Scunthorpe U | 46 | 18 | | |
| 2005-06 | Barnsley | 45 | 6 | | |
| 2006-07 | Barnsley | 30 | 5 | | |
| 2006-07 | *Huddersfield T* | 4 | 1 | 4 | 1 |
| 2007-08 | Scunthorpe U | 40 | 8 | | |
| 2008-09 | Scunthorpe U | 44 | 17 | | |
| 2009-10 | Scunthorpe U | 45 | 9 | 228 | 62 |
| 2010-11 | Preston NE | 23 | 2 | 23 | 2 |
| 2010-11 | *Barnsley* | 7 | 0 | 82 | 11 |
| 2011-12 | Charlton Ath | 19 | 3 | 19 | 3 |
| 2011-12 | *Wycombe W* | 6 | 6 | 6 | 6 |
| 2012-13 | Brentford | 23 | 4 | 23 | 4 |
| 2012-13 | *Crawley T* | 11 | 2 | 11 | 2 |

**LEE, Richard (G)**    154 0
H: 6 0   W: 12 06   b.Oxford 5-10-82
*Source:* Scholar. *Honours:* England Under-20.

| 2000-01 | Watford | 0 | 0 | | |
| 2001-02 | Watford | 0 | 0 | | |
| 2002-03 | Watford | 4 | 0 | | |
| 2003-04 | Watford | 0 | 0 | | |
| 2004-05 | Watford | 33 | 0 | | |
| 2005-06 | Watford | 0 | 0 | | |
| 2005-06 | *Blackburn R* | 0 | 0 | | |
| 2006-07 | Watford | 10 | 0 | | |
| 2007-08 | Watford | 35 | 0 | | |
| 2008-09 | Watford | 10 | 0 | | |
| 2009-10 | Watford | 0 | 0 | 92 | 0 |
| 2010-11 | Brentford | 22 | 0 | | |
| 2011-12 | Brentford | 37 | 0 | | |
| 2012-13 | Brentford | 3 | 0 | 62 | 0 |

**LOGAN, Shaleum (D)**    122 5
H: 6 1   W: 12 07   b.Wythenshawe 29-1-88
*Source:* Scholar.

| 2006-07 | Manchester C | 0 | 0 | | |
| 2007-08 | Manchester C | 0 | 0 | | |
| 2007-08 | *Grimsby T* | 5 | 2 | 5 | 2 |
| 2007-08 | *Scunthorpe U* | 4 | 0 | 4 | 0 |
| 2007-08 | *Stockport Co* | 7 | 0 | 7 | 0 |
| 2008-09 | Manchester C | 1 | 0 | | |
| 2009-10 | Manchester C | 0 | 0 | | |
| 2009-10 | *Tranmere R* | 33 | 0 | 33 | 0 |
| 2010-11 | Manchester C | 0 | 0 | | |
| 2011-12 | Brentford | 27 | 3 | | |
| 2012-13 | Brentford | 45 | 0 | 72 | 3 |

**MAWSON, Alfie (D)**    0 0
b. 19-1-94

| 2012-13 | Brentford | 0 | 0 | | |

**MOORE, Simon (G)**    64 0
H: 6 3   W: 12 02   b.Sandown 19-5-90
*Source:* Farnborough T.

| 2009-10 | Brentford | 1 | 0 | | |

| 2010-11 | Brentford | 10 | 0 | | |
| 2011-12 | Brentford | 10 | 0 | | |
| 2012-13 | Brentford | 43 | 0 | 64 | 0 |

**NORRIS, Luke (F)**    1 0
H: 6 1   W: 13 05   b.Stevenage 3-6-93
*Source:* Hitchin T.

| 2011-12 | Brentford | 1 | 0 | | |
| 2012-13 | Brentford | 0 | 0 | 1 | 0 |

**O'CONNOR, Kevin (F)**    411 32
H: 5 11   W: 12 00   b.Blackburn 24-2-82
*Source:* Trainee. *Honours:* Eire Youth,
Under-21.

| 1999-2000 | Brentford | 6 | 0 | | |
| 2000-01 | Brentford | 11 | 1 | | |
| 2001-02 | Brentford | 25 | 0 | | |
| 2002-03 | Brentford | 45 | 5 | | |
| 2003-04 | Brentford | 43 | 1 | | |
| 2004-05 | Brentford | 37 | 2 | | |
| 2005-06 | Brentford | 30 | 7 | | |
| 2006-07 | Brentford | 39 | 6 | | |
| 2007-08 | Brentford | 37 | 3 | | |
| 2008-09 | Brentford | 28 | 0 | | |
| 2009-10 | Brentford | 43 | 4 | | |
| 2010-11 | Brentford | 41 | 2 | | |
| 2011-12 | Brentford | 14 | 1 | | |
| 2012-13 | Brentford | 12 | 0 | 411 | 32 |

**OYELEKE, Emmanuel (M)**    3 0
H: 5 9   W: 11 11   b.Wandsworth 24-12-92
*Source:* Scholar.

| 2011-12 | Brentford | 1 | 0 | | |
| 2012-13 | Brentford | 0 | 0 | 1 | 0 |
| 2012-13 | *Northampton T* | 2 | 0 | 2 | 0 |

**PIERRE, Aaron (D)**    0 0
H: 6 1   W: 13 12   b.Southall 17-2-93
*Source:* Fulham Scholar.

| 2011-12 | Brentford | 0 | 0 | | |
| 2012-13 | Brentford | 0 | 0 | | |

**REEVES, Jake (M)**    20 0
H: 5 8   W: 11 11   b.Lewisham 30-6-93
*Source:* Scholar.

| 2010-11 | Brentford | 1 | 0 | | |
| 2011-12 | Brentford | 8 | 0 | | |
| 2012-13 | Brentford | 6 | 0 | 15 | 0 |
| 2012-13 | *AFC Wimbledon* | 5 | 0 | 5 | 0 |

**SAUNDERS, Sam (M)**    177 30
H: 5 6   W: 11 04   b.Erith 29-8-83
*Source:* Welling U, Hastings T, Ashford T,
Carshalton Ath.

| 2007-08 | Dagenham & R | 22 | 0 | | |
| 2008-09 | Dagenham & R | 40 | 14 | 62 | 14 |
| 2009-10 | Brentford | 26 | 1 | | |
| 2010-11 | Brentford | 21 | 2 | | |
| 2011-12 | Brentford | 37 | 10 | | |
| 2012-13 | Brentford | 31 | 3 | 115 | 16 |

**Scholars**
Beale, Sam; Bryan, Richard Edward; Clarke,
Joshua Joseph Jason Ishmel; Herbert, Max;
Hippolyte, Myles Elliot Zach; Lavender,
Lewis Henry; Maloney, Joseph Francis;
Miller-Rodney, Tyrell; Moore, Montell;
Onovwigun, Michael; Pilbeam, George;
Rowe, Fabian Troy; Stockwell, Joshua James;
Stone, Lionel Junior Richard; Taylor, Joseph
Stuart; Tomasevic, Stefan.

# BRIGHTON & HA (15)

**AGDESTEIN, Torbjorn (F)**    6 0
H: 6 0   W: 12 10   b.Norway 18-9-91
*Source:* Stord.

| 2010-11 | Brighton & HA | 0 | 0 | | |
| 2011-12 | Brighton & HA | 4 | 0 | | |
| 2012-13 | Brighton & HA | 2 | 0 | 6 | 0 |

**ANKERGREN, Casper (G)**    272 0
H: 6 3   W: 14 07   b.Koge 9-11-79
*Source:* Koge. *Honours:* Denmark Youth,
Under-21.

| 2001-02 | Brondby | 1 | 0 | | |
| 2002-03 | Brondby | 16 | 0 | | |
| 2003-04 | Brondby | 1 | 0 | | |
| 2004-05 | Brondby | 32 | 0 | | |
| 2005-06 | Brondby | 18 | 0 | | |

| 2006-07 | Brondby | 18 | 0 | **86** | **0** |
| 2006-07 | Leeds U | 14 | 0 | | |
| 2007-08 | Leeds U | 43 | 0 | | |
| 2008-09 | Leeds U | 33 | 0 | | |
| 2009-10 | Leeds U | 29 | 0 | **119** | **0** |
| 2010-11 | Brighton & HA | 45 | 0 | | |
| 2011-12 | Brighton & HA | 19 | 0 | | |
| 2012-13 | Brighton & HA | 3 | 0 | **67** | **0** |

**ASMUNDSSON, Emil (M)**        **0 0**
b. 8-1-95
Source: Fylkir Reykjavik. *Honours:* Iceland Youth.

| 2012-13 | Brighton & HA | 0 | 0 | | |

**BARKER, George (F)**        **4 0**
H: 5 8   W: 11 02   b.Portsmouth 26-9-91
Source: Scholar.

| 2010-11 | Brighton & HA | 0 | 0 | | |
| 2011-12 | Brighton & HA | 0 | 0 | | |
| 2012-13 | Brighton & HA | 3 | 0 | **3** | **0** |
| 2012-13 | Barnet | 1 | 0 | **1** | **0** |

**BARNES, Ashley (F)**        **155 43**
H: 6 0   W: 12 00   b.Bath 30-10-89
Source: Paulton R.

| 2006-07 | Plymouth Arg | 0 | 0 | | |
| 2007-08 | Plymouth Arg | 0 | 0 | | |
| 2008-09 | Plymouth Arg | 15 | 1 | | |
| 2009-10 | Plymouth Arg | 7 | 1 | **22** | **2** |
| 2009-10 | Torquay U | 6 | 0 | **6** | **0** |
| 2009-10 | *Brighton & HA* | 8 | 4 | | |
| 2010-11 | Brighton & HA | 42 | 18 | | |
| 2011-12 | Brighton & HA | 43 | 11 | | |
| 2012-13 | Brighton & HA | 34 | 8 | **127** | **41** |

**BREZOVAN, Peter (G)**        **136 0**
H: 6 6   W: 14 13   b.Bratislava 9-12-79
Source: PS Bratislava, Vinohrady, Devin, Slovan Breclav, Zigma Olomouc. *Honours:* Slovakia U-21.

| 2002-03 | Brno | 10 | 0 | | |
| 2003-04 | Brno | 2 | 0 | | |
| 2004-05 | Inter Bratislava | 8 | 0 | **8** | **0** |
| 2005-06 | Brno | 7 | 0 | **19** | **0** |
| 2006-07 | Swindon T | 14 | 0 | | |
| 2007-08 | Swindon T | 31 | 0 | | |
| 2008-09 | Swindon T | 21 | 0 | **66** | **0** |
| 2009-10 | Brighton & HA | 20 | 0 | | |
| 2010-11 | Brighton & HA | 2 | 0 | | |
| 2011-12 | Brighton & HA | 20 | 0 | | |
| 2012-13 | Brighton & HA | 1 | 0 | **43** | **0** |

**BRIDCUTT, Liam (M)**        **151 2**
H: 5 9   W: 11 07   b.Reading 8-5-89
Source: Scholar. *Honours:* Scotland 1 full cap.

| 2007-08 | Chelsea | 0 | 0 | | |
| 2007-08 | Yeovil T | 9 | 0 | **9** | **0** |
| 2008-09 | Chelsea | 0 | 0 | | |
| 2008-09 | Watford | 6 | 0 | **6** | **0** |
| 2009-10 | Chelsea | 0 | 0 | | |
| 2009-10 | Stockport Co | 15 | 0 | **15** | **0** |
| 2010-11 | Chelsea | 0 | 0 | | |
| 2010-11 | Brighton & HA | 37 | 2 | | |
| 2011-12 | Brighton & HA | 43 | 0 | | |
| 2012-13 | Brighton & HA | 41 | 0 | **121** | **2** |

**BUCKLEY, Will (F)**        **163 34**
H: 6 0   W: 13 00   b.Oldham 12-8-88
Source: Curzon Ashton.

| 2007-08 | Rochdale | 7 | 0 | | |
| 2008-09 | Rochdale | 37 | 10 | | |
| 2009-10 | Rochdale | 15 | 3 | **59** | **13** |
| 2009-10 | Watford | 6 | 1 | | |
| 2010-11 | Watford | 34 | 4 | **39** | **5** |
| 2011-12 | Brighton & HA | 29 | 8 | | |
| 2012-13 | Brighton & HA | 36 | 8 | **65** | **16** |

**CALDERON, Inigo (D)**        **328 20**
H: 5 10   W: 12 02   b.Vitoria 4-1-82

| 2002-03 | Alaves B | 35 | 1 | | |
| 2003-04 | Alaves B | 33 | 0 | **68** | **1** |
| 2004-05 | Alicante | 25 | 0 | | |
| 2005-06 | Alicante | 31 | 4 | | |
| 2006-07 | Alicante | 28 | 1 | **84** | **5** |
| 2007-08 | Alaves | 20 | 0 | | |
| 2008-09 | Alaves | 33 | 2 | **53** | **2** |
| 2009-10 | Brighton & HA | 19 | 1 | | |
| 2010-11 | Brighton & HA | 44 | 7 | | |
| 2011-12 | Brighton & HA | 32 | 4 | | |
| 2012-13 | Brighton & HA | 28 | 0 | **123** | **12** |

**CROFTS, Andrew (D)**        **319 30**
H: 5 10   W: 12 09   b.Chatham 29-5-84
Source: Trainee. *Honours:* Wales Youth, Under-21, 24 full caps.

| 2000-01 | Gillingham | 1 | 0 | | |
| 2001-02 | Gillingham | 0 | 0 | | |
| 2002-03 | Gillingham | 0 | 0 | | |
| 2003-04 | Gillingham | 8 | 0 | | |
| 2004-05 | Gillingham | 27 | 2 | | |
| 2005-06 | Gillingham | 45 | 2 | | |
| 2006-07 | Gillingham | 43 | 8 | | |
| 2007-08 | Gillingham | 41 | 5 | | |
| 2008-09 | Gillingham | 9 | 0 | **174** | **17** |
| 2008-09 | Peterborough U | 9 | 0 | **9** | **0** |
| 2009-10 | Brighton & HA | 44 | 5 | | |
| 2010-11 | Norwich C | 44 | 8 | | |
| 2011-12 | Norwich C | 24 | 0 | | |
| 2012-13 | Norwich C | 0 | 0 | **68** | **8** |
| 2012-13 | Brighton & HA | 24 | 0 | **68** | **5** |

**DICKENSON, Brennan (F)**        **18 3**
H: 6 0   W: 12 07   b.Ferndown 26-2-93

| 2012-13 | Brighton & HA | 0 | 0 | | |
| 2012-13 | Chesterfield | 11 | 1 | **11** | **1** |
| 2012-13 | AFC Wimbledon | 7 | 2 | **7** | **2** |

**DICKER, Gary (M)**        **261 11**
H: 6 0   W: 12 00   b.Dublin 31-7-86
*Honours:* Eire Under-21.

| 2004 | UCD | 9 | 1 | | |
| 2005 | UCD | 31 | 2 | | |
| 2006 | UCD | 28 | 2 | **68** | **5** |
| 2006-07 | Birmingham C | 0 | 0 | | |
| 2007-08 | Stockport Co | 30 | 0 | | |
| 2008-09 | Stockport Co | 25 | 0 | **55** | **0** |
| 2008-09 | *Brighton & HA* | 9 | 1 | | |
| 2009-10 | Brighton & HA | 42 | 2 | | |
| 2010-11 | Brighton & HA | 46 | 3 | | |
| 2011-12 | Brighton & HA | 18 | 0 | | |
| 2012-13 | Brighton & HA | 23 | 0 | **138** | **6** |

**DOBBIE, Stephen (F)**        **274 90**
H: 5 10   W: 11 00   b.Glasgow 5-12-82

| 2002-03 | Rangers | 0 | 0 | | |
| 2002-03 | Northern Spirit | 3 | 3 | **3** | **3** |
| 2003-04 | Hibernian | 28 | 2 | | |
| 2004-05 | Hibernian | 7 | 0 | **35** | **2** |
| 2004-05 | St Johnstone | 8 | 2 | | |
| 2005-06 | St Johnstone | 20 | 1 | **28** | **3** |
| 2006-07 | Dumbarton | 17 | 10 | **17** | **10** |
| 2006-07 | Queen of the S | 15 | 10 | | |
| 2007-08 | Queen of the S | 36 | 16 | | |
| 2008-09 | Queen of the S | 32 | 23 | **83** | **49** |
| 2009-10 | Swansea C | 6 | 0 | | |
| 2009-10 | Blackpool | 16 | 4 | | |
| 2010-11 | Swansea C | 41 | 9 | | |
| 2011-12 | Swansea C | 8 | 0 | | |
| 2011-12 | Blackpool | 7 | 5 | **23** | **9** |
| 2012-13 | Swansea C | 0 | 0 | **55** | **9** |
| 2012-13 | Brighton & HA | 15 | 2 | **15** | **2** |
| 2012-13 | Crystal Palace | 15 | 3 | **15** | **3** |

**DUNK, Lewis (D)**        **45 0**
H: 6 3   W: 12 02   b.Brighton 1-12-91
Source: Scholar.

| 2009-10 | Brighton & HA | 1 | 0 | | |
| 2010-11 | Brighton & HA | 5 | 0 | | |
| 2011-12 | Brighton & HA | 31 | 0 | | |
| 2012-13 | Brighton & HA | 8 | 0 | **45** | **0** |

**EL-ABD, Adam (D)**        **291 5**
H: 5 10   W: 13 05   b.Brighton 11-9-84
Source: Scholar. *Honours:* Egypt 1 full cap.

| 2003-04 | Brighton & HA | 11 | 0 | | |
| 2004-05 | Brighton & HA | 16 | 0 | | |
| 2005-06 | Brighton & HA | 29 | 0 | | |
| 2006-07 | Brighton & HA | 42 | 1 | | |
| 2007-08 | Brighton & HA | 35 | 1 | | |
| 2008-09 | Brighton & HA | 31 | 0 | | |
| 2009-10 | Brighton & HA | 35 | 1 | | |
| 2010-11 | Brighton & HA | 37 | 1 | | |
| 2011-12 | Brighton & HA | 23 | 0 | | |
| 2012-13 | Brighton & HA | 32 | 1 | **291** | **5** |

**FORSTER-CASKEY, Jake (M)**        **24 4**
H: 5 10   W: 10 00   b.Southend 25-4-94
Source: Scholar. *Honours:* England Youth.

| 2009-10 | Brighton & HA | 1 | 0 | | |
| 2010-11 | Brighton & HA | 0 | 0 | | |

| 2011-12 | Brighton & HA | 4 | 1 | | |
| 2012-13 | Brighton & HA | 3 | 0 | **8** | **1** |
| 2012-13 | Oxford U | 16 | 3 | **16** | **3** |

**GREER, Gordon (D)**        **329 9**
H: 6 2   W: 12 05   b.Glasgow 14-12-80
Source: Port Glasgow. *Honours:* Scotland B.

| 2000-01 | Clyde | 30 | 0 | **30** | **0** |
| 2000-01 | Blackburn R | 0 | 0 | | |
| 2001-02 | Blackburn R | 0 | 0 | | |
| 2002-03 | Blackburn R | 0 | 0 | | |
| 2002-03 | Stockport Co | 5 | 1 | **5** | **1** |
| 2003-04 | Kilmarnock | 25 | 0 | | |
| 2004-05 | Kilmarnock | 22 | 1 | | |
| 2005-06 | Kilmarnock | 27 | 2 | | |
| 2006-07 | Kilmarnock | 33 | 0 | **107** | **3** |
| 2007-08 | Doncaster R | 11 | 1 | | |
| 2008-09 | Doncaster R | 1 | 0 | **12** | **1** |
| 2008-09 | Swindon T | 19 | 1 | | |
| 2009-10 | Swindon T | 44 | 1 | **63** | **2** |
| 2010-11 | Brighton & HA | 32 | 0 | | |
| 2011-12 | Brighton & HA | 42 | 1 | | |
| 2012-13 | Brighton & HA | 38 | 1 | **112** | **2** |

**HARLEY, Ryan (M)**        **145 26**
H: 5 11   W: 11 00   b.Bristol 22-1-85
Source: Scholar.

| 2004-05 | Bristol C | 2 | 0 | | |
| 2005-06 | Bristol C | 0 | 0 | **2** | **0** |
| 2008-09 | Exeter C | 31 | 4 | | |
| 2009-10 | Exeter C | 44 | 10 | | |
| 2010-11 | Exeter C | 21 | 6 | | |
| 2010-11 | Swansea C | 0 | 0 | | |
| 2010-11 | Exeter C | 21 | 4 | **117** | **24** |
| 2011-12 | Swansea C | 0 | 0 | | |
| 2011-12 | Brighton & HA | 16 | 2 | | |
| 2012-13 | Brighton & HA | 2 | 0 | **18** | **2** |
| 2012-13 | Milton Keynes D | 8 | 0 | **8** | **0** |

**HOSKINS, Will (F)**        **218 52**
H: 5 11   W: 11 02   b.Nottingham 6-5-86
Source: Scholar. *Honours:* England Youth, Under-20.

| 2003-04 | Rotherham U | 4 | 2 | | |
| 2004-05 | Rotherham U | 22 | 2 | | |
| 2005-06 | Rotherham U | 23 | 4 | | |
| 2006-07 | Rotherham U | 24 | 15 | | |
| 2006-07 | Watford | 9 | 0 | | |
| 2007-08 | Watford | 1 | 0 | | |
| 2007-08 | Millwall | 10 | 2 | **10** | **2** |
| 2007-08 | Nottingham F | 2 | 0 | **2** | **0** |
| 2008-09 | Watford | 32 | 4 | | |
| 2009-10 | Watford | 18 | 3 | **60** | **7** |
| 2010-11 | Bristol R | 43 | 17 | **43** | **17** |
| 2011-12 | Brighton & HA | 7 | 1 | | |
| 2011-12 | Sheffield U | 12 | 2 | **12** | **2** |
| 2011-12 | Rotherham U | 0 | 0 | **73** | **23** |
| 2012-13 | Brighton & HA | 11 | 0 | **18** | **1** |

**KASIM, Yaser (M)**        **1 0**
H: 5 11   W: 11 07   b.Bagdad 10-5-91
Source: Tottenham H Scholar.

| 2010-11 | Brighton & HA | 1 | 0 | | |
| 2011-12 | Brighton & HA | 0 | 0 | | |
| 2012-13 | Brighton & HA | 0 | 0 | **1** | **0** |

**KUSZCZAK, Tomasz (G)**        **119 0**
H: 6 3   W: 13 03   b.Krosno Odrzansia 20-3-82
Source: Uerdingen. *Honours:* Poland Youth, Under-21, 11 full caps.

| 2001-02 | Hertha Berlin | 0 | 0 | | |
| 2002-03 | Hertha Berlin | 0 | 0 | | |
| 2003-04 | Hertha Berlin | 0 | 0 | | |
| 2004-05 | WBA | 3 | 0 | | |
| 2005-06 | WBA | 28 | 0 | | |
| 2006-07 | WBA | 0 | 0 | **31** | **0** |
| 2006-07 | Manchester U | 6 | 0 | | |
| 2007-08 | Manchester U | 9 | 0 | | |
| 2008-09 | Manchester U | 4 | 0 | | |
| 2009-10 | Manchester U | 8 | 0 | | |
| 2010-11 | Manchester U | 5 | 0 | | |
| 2011-12 | Manchester U | 0 | 0 | **32** | **0** |
| 2011-12 | Watford | 13 | 0 | **13** | **0** |
| 2012-13 | Brighton & HA | 43 | 0 | **43** | **0** |

**LOPEZ, David (M)**        **224 31**
H: 5 11   W: 11 06   b.Logrono 10-9-82

| 2004-05 | Osasuna | 12 | 1 | | |
| 2005-06 | Osasuna | 34 | 6 | | |

| | | | | | |
|---|---|---|---|---|---|
| 2006-07 | Osasuna | 31 | 4 | **77** | **11** |
| 2007-08 | Athletic Bilbao | 30 | 1 | | |
| 2008-09 | Athletic Bilbao | 29 | 3 | | |
| 2009-10 | Athletic Bilbao | 17 | 0 | | |
| 2010-11 | Athletic Bilbao | 28 | 6 | | |
| 2011-12 | Athletic Bilbao | 12 | 1 | **116** | **11** |
| 2012-13 | Brighton & HA | 31 | 9 | **31** | **9** |

**LUALUA, Kazenga (F)** 83 10
H: 5 11 W: 12 00 b.Kinshasa 10-12-90
*Source:* Scholar.

| | | | | | |
|---|---|---|---|---|---|
| 2007-08 | Newcastle U | 2 | 0 | | |
| 2008-09 | Newcastle U | 3 | 0 | | |
| 2008-09 | *Doncaster R* | 4 | 0 | **4** | **0** |
| 2009-10 | Newcastle U | 1 | 0 | | |
| 2009-10 | *Brighton & HA* | 11 | 0 | | |
| 2010-11 | Newcastle U | 2 | 0 | | |
| 2010-11 | *Brighton & HA* | 11 | 4 | | |
| 2011-12 | Newcastle U | 0 | 0 | **8** | **0** |
| 2011-12 | Brighton & HA | 27 | 1 | | |
| 2012-13 | Brighton & HA | 22 | 5 | **71** | **10** |

**MACKAIL-SMITH, Craig (F)** 259 100
H: 6 3 W: 12 04 b.Watford 25-2-84
*Source:* Dagenham & R. *Honours:* Scotland 7 full caps, 1 goal.

| | | | | | |
|---|---|---|---|---|---|
| 2006-07 | Peterborough U | 15 | 8 | | |
| 2007-08 | Peterborough U | 36 | 12 | | |
| 2008-09 | Peterborough U | 46 | 23 | | |
| 2009-10 | Peterborough U | 43 | 10 | | |
| 2010-11 | Peterborough U | 45 | 27 | **185** | **80** |
| 2011-12 | Brighton & HA | 45 | 9 | | |
| 2012-13 | Brighton & HA | 29 | 11 | **74** | **20** |

**MAKSIMENKO, Vitalijs (D)** 3 0
H: 6 1 W: 11 11 b.Riga 8-12-90
*Honours:* Latvia Youth, Under-21, 2 full caps.

| | | | | | |
|---|---|---|---|---|---|
| 2012-13 | Skonto FC | 0 | 0 | | |
| 2012-13 | Brighton & HA | 0 | 0 | | |
| 2012-13 | *Yeovil T* | 3 | 0 | **3** | **0** |

**MARCH, Solly (M)** 0 0
b.Lewes 26-7-94

| | | | |
|---|---|---|---|
| 2012-13 | Brighton & HA | 0 | 0 |

**OATWAY, Charlie (M)** 0 0
H: 5 11 W: 10 08 b.London 11-8-91

| | | | |
|---|---|---|---|
| 2012-13 | Brighton & HA | 0 | 0 |

**ORLANDI, Andrea (M)** 175 14
H: 6 0 W: 12 01 b.Barcelona 3-8-84

| | | | | | |
|---|---|---|---|---|---|
| 2005-06 | Alaves | 0 | 0 | | |
| 2005-06 | *Barcelona* | 1 | 0 | **1** | **0** |
| 2005-06 | Barcelona B | 32 | 4 | | |
| 2006-07 | Barcelona B | 35 | 1 | **67** | **5** |
| 2007-08 | Swansea C | 8 | 0 | | |
| 2008-09 | Swansea C | 11 | 1 | | |
| 2009-10 | Swansea C | 30 | 1 | | |
| 2010-11 | Swansea C | 20 | 0 | | |
| 2011-12 | Swansea C | 3 | 1 | | |
| 2012-13 | Swansea C | 0 | 0 | **72** | **3** |
| 2012-13 | Brighton & HA | 35 | 6 | **35** | **6** |

**PAINTER, Marcos (D)** 165 1
H: 5 11 W: 12 04 b.Solihull 17-8-86
*Source:* Scholar. *Honours:* Eire Youth, Under-21.

| | | | | | |
|---|---|---|---|---|---|
| 2005-06 | Birmingham C | 4 | 0 | | |
| 2006-07 | Birmingham C | 1 | 0 | **5** | **0** |
| 2006-07 | Swansea C | 23 | 0 | | |
| 2007-08 | Swansea C | 30 | 0 | | |
| 2008-09 | Swansea C | 11 | 0 | | |
| 2009-10 | Swansea C | 4 | 0 | **68** | **0** |
| 2009-10 | *Brighton & HA* | 19 | 0 | | |
| 2010-11 | Brighton & HA | 46 | 1 | | |
| 2011-12 | Brighton & HA | 20 | 0 | | |
| 2012-13 | Brighton & HA | 5 | 0 | **90** | **1** |
| 2012-13 | *Bournemouth* | 2 | 0 | **2** | **0** |

**RICHARDS, Courtney (M)** 0 0
*Source:* Coventry C.

| | | | |
|---|---|---|---|
| 2012-13 | Brighton & HA | 0 | 0 |

**SALTOR, Bruno (D)** 232 2
H: 5 10 W: 11 10 b.Masnou (Barca) 1-10-80

| | | | | | |
|---|---|---|---|---|---|
| 2001-02 | Espanyol | 1 | 0 | **1** | **0** |
| 2001-02 | *Gimnastic* | 12 | 0 | **12** | **0** |
| 2004-05 | Lleida | 1 | 1 | | |
| 2005-06 | Lleida | 38 | 0 | **39** | **1** |
| 2006-07 | Almeria | 23 | 0 | | |
| 2007-08 | Almeria | 34 | 0 | | |
| 2008-09 | Almeria | 34 | 0 | **91** | **0** |
| 2009-10 | Valencia | 26 | 0 | | |
| 2010-11 | Valencia | 19 | 0 | | |
| 2011-12 | Valencia | 14 | 0 | **59** | **0** |
| 2012-13 | Brighton & HA | 30 | 1 | **30** | **1** |

**SMITH, Grant (M)** 0 0

| | | | |
|---|---|---|---|
| 2012-13 | Brighton & HA | 0 | 0 |

**ULLOA, Jose (F)** 194 84
H: 6 1 W: 11 10 b.General Roca 26-7-86

| | | | | | |
|---|---|---|---|---|---|
| 2004-05 | San Lorenzo | 0 | 0 | | |
| 2005-06 | San Lorenzo | 22 | 3 | | |
| 2006-07 | San Lorenzo | 6 | 0 | **25** | **3** |
| 2007-08 | Arsenal Sarandi | 6 | 1 | **6** | **1** |
| 2007-08 | Olimpo | 8 | 1 | **8** | **1** |
| 2008-09 | Castellon | 33 | 17 | | |
| 2009-10 | Castellon | 32 | 14 | | |
| 2010-11 | Castellon | 1 | 0 | **66** | **31** |
| 2010-11 | Almeria | 34 | 7 | | |
| 2011-12 | Almeria | 28 | 29 | | |
| 2012-13 | Almeria | 10 | 3 | **72** | **39** |
| 2012-13 | Brighton & HA | 17 | 9 | **17** | **9** |

**VICENTE, Rodriguez (M)** 325 50
H: 5 9 W: 11 05 b.Valencia 16-7-81
*Honours:* Spain Youth, Under-21, 38 full caps, 3 goals.

| | | | | | |
|---|---|---|---|---|---|
| 1997-98 | Levante | 3 | 1 | | |
| 1998-99 | Levante | 16 | 1 | | |
| 1999-2000 | Levante | 35 | 7 | **54** | **9** |
| 2000-01 | Valencia | 33 | 5 | | |
| 2001-02 | Valencia | 31 | 1 | | |
| 2002-03 | Valencia | 28 | 1 | | |
| 2003-04 | Valencia | 33 | 12 | | |
| 2004-05 | Valencia | 12 | 3 | | |
| 2005-06 | Valencia | 21 | 3 | | |
| 2006-07 | Valencia | 16 | 4 | | |
| 2007-08 | Valencia | 17 | 0 | | |
| 2008-09 | Valencia | 27 | 6 | | |
| 2009-10 | Valencia | 11 | 0 | | |
| 2010-11 | Valencia | 13 | 1 | **242** | **36** |
| 2011-12 | Brighton & HA | 17 | 3 | | |
| 2012-13 | Brighton & HA | 12 | 2 | **29** | **5** |

**Scholars**
Barry, Bradley Oliver; Benham, Matthew Richard; Colquhoun, Luke Ray; Cooper, Ryan Alan; Cousins, George William; Davis, Jason Mytton; Deen, Robin; Gray, Benjamin Nigel David; Harris, Charles Haddon; Hunt, Robert Donald; Lall, Dylan; Levy, Elliot Samuel; MacFarlane, Jack; Muitt, James Andrew; Peake, Jacob John; Rea, Glen Charles; Shonk, Jack Stephen; Walton, Christian Timothy; Wiltshire, Cameron Anthony; Wray, Oliver.

# BRISTOL C (16)

**ADOMAH, Albert (F)** 243 36
H: 6 1 W: 11 08 b.Lambeth 13-12-87
*Source:* Harrow Borough. *Honours:* Ghana 8 full caps, 1 goal.

| | | | | | |
|---|---|---|---|---|---|
| 2007-08 | Barnet | 22 | 5 | | |
| 2008-09 | Barnet | 45 | 9 | | |
| 2009-10 | Barnet | 45 | 5 | **112** | **19** |
| 2010-11 | Bristol C | 46 | 5 | | |
| 2011-12 | Bristol C | 45 | 5 | | |
| 2012-13 | Bristol C | 40 | 7 | **131** | **17** |

**AJALA, Toby (M)** 14 0
H: 5 9 W: 11 11 b. 27-7-91

| | | | | | |
|---|---|---|---|---|---|
| 2012-13 | AFC Wimbledon | 12 | 0 | **12** | **0** |
| 2012-13 | Bristol C | 2 | 0 | **2** | **0** |

**AMADI-HOLLOWAY, Aaron (D)** 0 0
H: 6 2 W: 13 00 b.Newark 21-2-93
*Source:* Bath C.

| | | | |
|---|---|---|---|
| 2012-13 | Bristol C | 0 | 0 |

**ANDERSON, Paul (M)** 176 19
H: 5 9 W: 10 04 b.Leicester 23-7-88
*Source:* Scholar. *Honours:* England Youth.

| | | | |
|---|---|---|---|
| 2005-06 | Hull C | 0 | 0 |
| 2005-06 | Liverpool | 0 | 0 |
| 2006-07 | Liverpool | 0 | 0 |
| 2007-08 | Liverpool | 0 | 0 |

| | | | | | |
|---|---|---|---|---|---|
| 2007-08 | *Swansea C* | 31 | 7 | **31** | **7** |
| 2008-09 | Liverpool | 0 | 0 | | |
| 2008-09 | *Nottingham F* | 26 | 2 | | |
| 2009-10 | Nottingham F | 37 | 4 | | |
| 2010-11 | Nottingham F | 36 | 3 | | |
| 2011-12 | Nottingham F | 17 | 0 | | |
| 2012-13 | Nottingham F | 0 | 0 | **116** | **9** |
| 2012-13 | Bristol C | 29 | 3 | **29** | **3** |

**BALDOCK, Sam (F)** 157 48
H: 5 7 W: 10 07 b.Buckingham 15-3-89
*Source:* Scholar. *Honours:* England Under-20.

| | | | | | |
|---|---|---|---|---|---|
| 2005-06 | Milton Keynes D | 0 | 0 | | |
| 2006-07 | Milton Keynes D | 1 | 0 | | |
| 2007-08 | Milton Keynes D | 5 | 0 | | |
| 2008-09 | Milton Keynes D | 40 | 12 | | |
| 2009-10 | Milton Keynes D | 20 | 5 | | |
| 2010-11 | Milton Keynes D | 30 | 12 | | |
| 2011-12 | Milton Keynes D | 4 | 4 | **100** | **33** |
| 2011-12 | West Ham U | 23 | 5 | | |
| 2012-13 | West Ham U | 0 | 0 | **23** | **5** |
| 2012-13 | Bristol C | 34 | 10 | **34** | **10** |

**BATES, Matthew (D)** 126 6
H: 5 10 W: 12 03 b.Stockton 10-12-86
*Source:* Scholar. *Honours:* England Youth, Under-20.

| | | | | | |
|---|---|---|---|---|---|
| 2003-04 | Middlesbrough | 0 | 0 | | |
| 2004-05 | Middlesbrough | 2 | 0 | | |
| 2004-05 | *Darlington* | 4 | 0 | **4** | **0** |
| 2005-06 | Middlesbrough | 16 | 0 | | |
| 2006-07 | Middlesbrough | 1 | 0 | | |
| 2006-07 | *Ipswich T* | 2 | 0 | **2** | **0** |
| 2007-08 | Middlesbrough | 0 | 0 | | |
| 2007-08 | *Norwich C* | 3 | 0 | **3** | **0** |
| 2008-09 | Middlesbrough | 17 | 1 | | |
| 2009-10 | Middlesbrough | 0 | 0 | | |
| 2010-11 | Middlesbrough | 31 | 3 | | |
| 2011-12 | Middlesbrough | 37 | 2 | **104** | **6** |
| 2012-13 | Bristol C | 13 | 0 | **13** | **0** |

**BATTEN, Jack (M)** 0 0

| | | | |
|---|---|---|---|
| 2012-13 | Bristol C | 0 | 0 |

**BRYAN, Joe (D)** 24 1
H: 5 7 W: 11 05 b.Bristol 17-9-93
*Source:* Scholar.

| | | | | | |
|---|---|---|---|---|---|
| 2011-12 | Bristol C | 1 | 0 | | |
| 2012-13 | Bristol C | 13 | 0 | **14** | **0** |
| 2012-13 | *Plymouth Arg* | 10 | 1 | **10** | **1** |

**BURNS, Wes (F)** 6 0
b.Cardiff 28-12-95

| | | | | | |
|---|---|---|---|---|---|
| 2012-13 | Bristol C | 6 | 0 | **6** | **0** |

**CAREY, Lewis (G)** 0 0
H: 6 0 W: 11 00 b.Tunbridge Wells 2-6-93
*Source:* Scholar.

| | | | |
|---|---|---|---|
| 2011-12 | Bristol C | 0 | 0 |
| 2012-13 | Bristol C | 0 | 0 |

**CAREY, Louis (D)** 580 12
H: 5 10 W: 11 00 b.Bristol 20-1-77
*Source:* Trainee. *Honours:* Scotland Under-21.

| | | | | | |
|---|---|---|---|---|---|
| 1995-96 | Bristol C | 23 | 0 | | |
| 1996-97 | Bristol C | 42 | 0 | | |
| 1997-98 | Bristol C | 38 | 0 | | |
| 1998-99 | Bristol C | 41 | 0 | | |
| 1999-2000 | Bristol C | 22 | 0 | | |
| 2000-01 | Bristol C | 46 | 3 | | |
| 2001-02 | Bristol C | 35 | 0 | | |
| 2002-03 | Bristol C | 24 | 1 | | |
| 2003-04 | Bristol C | 41 | 1 | | |
| 2004-05 | *Coventry C* | 23 | 0 | **23** | **0** |
| 2004-05 | Bristol C | 14 | 0 | | |
| 2005-06 | Bristol C | 38 | 3 | | |
| 2006-07 | Bristol C | 38 | 2 | | |
| 2007-08 | Bristol C | 33 | 0 | | |
| 2008-09 | Bristol C | 28 | 0 | | |
| 2009-10 | Bristol C | 37 | 2 | | |
| 2010-11 | Bristol C | 21 | 0 | | |
| 2011-12 | Bristol C | 20 | 0 | | |
| 2012-13 | Bristol C | 16 | 0 | **557** | **12** |

**CUNNINGHAM, Greg (D)** 72 1
H: 6 0 W: 11 00 b.Galway 31-1-91
*Source:* Scholar. *Honours:* Eire Youth, Under-21, 4 full caps.

| | | | |
|---|---|---|---|
| 2008-09 | Manchester C | 0 | 0 |

| 2009-10 | Manchester C | 2 | 0 | | |
| 2010-11 | Manchester C | 0 | 0 | | |
| 2010-11 | *Leicester C* | 13 | 0 | 13 | 0 |
| 2011-12 | Manchester C | 0 | 0 | | |
| 2011-12 | *Nottingham F* | 27 | 0 | 27 | 0 |
| 2012-13 | Manchester C | 0 | 0 | 2 | 0 |
| 2012-13 | Bristol C | 30 | 1 | 30 | 1 |

**DAVIES, Steve (F)** 180 38
H: 6 0 W: 12 00 b.Liverpool 29-12-87
Source: Scholar.

| 2005-06 | Tranmere R | 22 | 2 | | |
| 2006-07 | Tranmere R | 28 | 1 | | |
| 2007-08 | Tranmere R | 10 | 2 | 60 | 5 |
| 2008-09 | Derby Co | 19 | 3 | | |
| 2009-10 | Derby Co | 18 | 1 | | |
| 2010-11 | Derby Co | 20 | 5 | | |
| 2011-12 | Derby Co | 26 | 11 | | |
| 2012-13 | Derby Co | 0 | 0 | 83 | 20 |
| 2012-13 | Bristol C | 37 | 13 | 37 | 13 |

**DOBIE, Luke (M)** 4 0
b.Ormskirk 7-10-92
Source: Everton Scholar.

| 2011-12 | Middlesbrough | 0 | 0 | | |
| 2011-12 | *Accrington S* | 4 | 0 | 4 | 0 |
| 2012-13 | Bristol C | 0 | 0 | | |

**ELLIOTT, Marvin (M)** 362 24
H: 6 0 W: 12 02 b.Wandsworth 15-9-84
Source: Scholar. Honours: Jamaica 1 full cap.

| 2001-02 | Millwall | 0 | 0 | | |
| 2002-03 | Millwall | 1 | 0 | | |
| 2003-04 | Millwall | 21 | 0 | | |
| 2004-05 | Millwall | 41 | 1 | | |
| 2005-06 | Millwall | 39 | 2 | | |
| 2006-07 | Millwall | 42 | 0 | 144 | 3 |
| 2007-08 | Bristol C | 45 | 5 | | |
| 2008-09 | Bristol C | 28 | 3 | | |
| 2009-10 | Bristol C | 39 | 1 | | |
| 2010-11 | Bristol C | 46 | 8 | | |
| 2011-12 | Bristol C | 28 | 2 | | |
| 2012-13 | Bristol C | 32 | 2 | 218 | 21 |

**FONTAINE, Liam (D)** 285 6
H: 5 11 W: 12 00 b.Beckenham 7-1-86
Source: Trainee. Honours: England Youth, Under-20.

| 2003-04 | Fulham | 0 | 0 | | |
| 2004-05 | Fulham | 1 | 0 | | |
| 2004-05 | *Yeovil T* | 15 | 0 | | |
| 2005-06 | Fulham | 0 | 0 | 1 | 0 |
| 2005-06 | *Yeovil T* | 10 | 0 | 25 | 0 |
| 2005-06 | *Bristol C* | 15 | 0 | | |
| 2006-07 | Bristol C | 30 | 0 | | |
| 2007-08 | Bristol C | 38 | 1 | | |
| 2008-09 | Bristol C | 42 | 2 | | |
| 2009-10 | Bristol C | 36 | 2 | | |
| 2010-11 | Bristol C | 31 | 0 | | |
| 2011-12 | Bristol C | 26 | 0 | | |
| 2012-13 | Bristol C | 41 | 1 | 259 | 6 |

**FOSTER, Ricky (D)** 299 8
H: 5 9 W: 12 00 b.Aberdeen 31-7-85
Honours: Scotland Under-21.

| 2002-03 | Aberdeen | 2 | 0 | | |
| 2003-04 | Aberdeen | 18 | 1 | | |
| 2004-05 | Aberdeen | 25 | 1 | | |
| 2005-06 | Aberdeen | 25 | 1 | | |
| 2006-07 | Aberdeen | 37 | 3 | | |
| 2007-08 | Aberdeen | 33 | 1 | | |
| 2008-09 | Aberdeen | 34 | 0 | | |
| 2009-10 | Aberdeen | 37 | 0 | | |
| 2010-11 | Aberdeen | 1 | 0 | | |
| 2010-11 | *Rangers* | 15 | 0 | 15 | 0 |
| 2011-12 | Aberdeen | 22 | 1 | 234 | 8 |
| 2011-12 | Bristol C | 20 | 0 | | |
| 2012-13 | Bristol C | 30 | 0 | 50 | 0 |

**GERKEN, Dean (G)** 169 0
H: 6 3 W: 12 08 b.Southend 22-5-85
Source: Scholar.

| 2003-04 | Colchester U | 1 | 0 | | |
| 2004-05 | Colchester U | 13 | 0 | | |
| 2005-06 | Colchester U | 7 | 0 | | |
| 2006-07 | Colchester U | 27 | 0 | | |
| 2007-08 | Colchester U | 40 | 0 | | |
| 2008-09 | Colchester U | 21 | 0 | 109 | 0 |
| 2008-09 | *Darlington* | 7 | 0 | 7 | 0 |
| 2009-10 | Bristol C | 39 | 0 | | |
| 2010-11 | Bristol C | 1 | 0 | | |
| 2011-12 | Bristol C | 10 | 0 | | |
| 2012-13 | Bristol C | 3 | 0 | 53 | 0 |

**HALL, Lewis (M)** 0 0

| 2012-13 | Bristol C | 0 | 0 | | |

**HEATON, Tom (G)** 135 0
H: 6 1 W: 13 12 b.Chester 15-4-86
Source: Trainee. Honours: England Youth, Under-21.

| 2003-04 | Manchester U | 0 | 0 | | |
| 2004-05 | Manchester U | 0 | 0 | | |
| 2005-06 | Manchester U | 0 | 0 | | |
| 2005-06 | *Swindon T* | 14 | 0 | 14 | 0 |
| 2006-07 | Manchester U | 0 | 0 | | |
| 2007-08 | Manchester U | 0 | 0 | | |
| 2008-09 | Manchester U | 0 | 0 | | |
| 2008-09 | *Cardiff C* | 21 | 0 | | |
| 2009-10 | Manchester U | 0 | 0 | | |
| 2009-10 | *Rochdale* | 12 | 0 | 12 | 0 |
| 2009-10 | *Wycombe W* | 16 | 0 | 16 | 0 |
| 2010-11 | Cardiff C | 27 | 0 | | |
| 2011-12 | Cardiff C | 2 | 0 | 50 | 0 |
| 2012-13 | Bristol C | 43 | 0 | 43 | 0 |

**HOWARD, Brian (M)** 321 40
H: 5 8 W: 11 00 b.Winchester 23-1-83
Source: Trainee. Honours: England Schools, Youth, Under-20.

| 1999-2000 | Southampton | 0 | 0 | | |
| 2000-01 | Southampton | 0 | 0 | | |
| 2001-02 | Southampton | 0 | 0 | | |
| 2002-03 | Southampton | 0 | 0 | | |
| 2003-04 | Swindon T | 35 | 4 | | |
| 2004-05 | Swindon T | 35 | 5 | 70 | 9 |
| 2005-06 | Barnsley | 31 | 5 | | |
| 2006-07 | Barnsley | 42 | 8 | | |
| 2007-08 | Barnsley | 41 | 13 | | |
| 2008-09 | Barnsley | 7 | 1 | 121 | 27 |
| 2008-09 | Sheffield U | 26 | 2 | | |
| 2009-10 | Sheffield U | 4 | 0 | 30 | 2 |
| 2009-10 | Reading | 34 | 2 | | |
| 2010-11 | Reading | 24 | 0 | | |
| 2011-12 | Reading | 1 | 0 | 59 | 2 |
| 2011-12 | *Millwall* | 12 | 0 | 12 | 0 |
| 2012-13 | Portsmouth | 23 | 0 | 23 | 0 |
| 2012-13 | Bristol C | 6 | 0 | 6 | 0 |

**JORDAN, Rhys (M)** 0 0

| 2012-13 | Bristol C | 0 | 0 | | |

**KELLY, Liam (M)** 119 15
H: 6 2 W: 13 11 b.Milton Keynes 10-2-90
Honours: Scotland Under-21, 1 full cap.

| 2009-10 | Kilmarnock | 15 | 1 | | |
| 2010-11 | Kilmarnock | 32 | 7 | | |
| 2011-12 | Kilmarnock | 34 | 1 | | |
| 2012-13 | Kilmarnock | 19 | 6 | 100 | 15 |
| 2012-13 | Bristol C | 19 | 0 | 19 | 0 |

**KILKENNY, Neil (M)** 256 14
H: 5 8 W: 10 08 b.Enfield 19-12-85
Source: Arsenal Trainee. Honours: England Youth, Under-20, Australia Under-23, 14 full caps.

| 2003-04 | Birmingham C | 0 | 0 | | |
| 2004-05 | Birmingham C | 0 | 0 | | |
| 2004-05 | *Oldham Ath* | 27 | 4 | | |
| 2005-06 | Birmingham C | 18 | 0 | | |
| 2006-07 | Birmingham C | 8 | 0 | | |
| 2007-08 | Birmingham C | 0 | 0 | 26 | 0 |
| 2007-08 | *Oldham Ath* | 20 | 1 | 47 | 5 |
| 2007-08 | Leeds U | 16 | 1 | | |
| 2008-09 | Leeds U | 30 | 4 | | |
| 2009-10 | Leeds U | 35 | 2 | | |
| 2010-11 | Leeds U | 37 | 1 | 118 | 8 |
| 2011-12 | Bristol C | 41 | 1 | | |
| 2012-13 | Bristol C | 24 | 0 | 65 | 1 |

**KING, Tom (M)** 0 0

| 2012-13 | Bristol C | 0 | 0 | | |

**KRANS, Kevin (M)** 0 0

| 2012-13 | Bristol C | 0 | 0 | | |

**MOLONEY, Brendan (M)** 89 2
H: 6 1 W: 11 12 b.Killarney 18-1-89
Source: Scholar. Honours: Eire Under-21.

| 2005-06 | Nottingham F | 0 | 0 | | |
| 2006-07 | Nottingham F | 1 | 0 | | |
| 2007-08 | Nottingham F | 2 | 0 | | |
| 2007-08 | *Chesterfield* | 9 | 1 | 9 | 1 |
| 2008-09 | Nottingham F | 12 | 0 | | |
| 2009-10 | Nottingham F | 0 | 0 | | |
| 2009-10 | *Notts Co* | 18 | 1 | 18 | 1 |
| 2009-10 | *Scunthorpe U* | 3 | 0 | 3 | 0 |
| 2010-11 | Nottingham F | 6 | 0 | | |
| 2011-12 | Nottingham F | 8 | 0 | | |
| 2012-13 | Nottingham F | 13 | 0 | 42 | 0 |
| 2012-13 | Bristol C | 17 | 0 | 17 | 0 |

**MORRIS, Jody (M)** 319 15
H: 5 5 W: 10 06 b.London 22-12-78
Source: Trainee. Honours: England Schools, Youth, Under-21.

| 1995-96 | Chelsea | 1 | 0 | | |
| 1996-97 | Chelsea | 12 | 0 | | |
| 1997-98 | Chelsea | 12 | 1 | | |
| 1998-99 | Chelsea | 18 | 1 | | |
| 1999-2000 | Chelsea | 30 | 3 | | |
| 2000-01 | Chelsea | 21 | 0 | | |
| 2001-02 | Chelsea | 5 | 0 | | |
| 2002-03 | Chelsea | 25 | 4 | 124 | 5 |
| 2003-04 | Leeds U | 12 | 0 | 12 | 0 |
| 2003-04 | Rotherham U | 10 | 1 | 10 | 1 |
| 2004-05 | Millwall | 37 | 5 | | |
| 2005-06 | Millwall | 24 | 0 | | |
| 2006-07 | Millwall | 4 | 0 | 65 | 5 |
| 2007-08 | St Johnstone | 5 | 1 | | |
| 2008-09 | St Johnstone | 14 | 0 | | |
| 2009-10 | St Johnstone | 34 | 2 | | |
| 2010-11 | St Johnstone | 23 | 0 | | |
| 2011-12 | St Johnstone | 28 | 1 | 104 | 4 |
| 2012-13 | Bristol C | 4 | 0 | 4 | 0 |

**NYATANGA, Lewin (D)** 233 10
H: 6 2 W: 12 08 b.Burton 18-8-88
Source: Scholar. Honours: Wales Under-21, 34 full caps.

| 2005-06 | Derby Co | 24 | 1 | | |
| 2006-07 | Derby Co | 7 | 1 | | |
| 2006-07 | *Sunderland* | 11 | 0 | 11 | 0 |
| 2006-07 | *Barnsley* | 10 | 1 | | |
| 2007-08 | Derby Co | 2 | 1 | | |
| 2007-08 | *Barnsley* | 41 | 1 | 51 | 2 |
| 2008-09 | Derby Co | 30 | 1 | 63 | 4 |
| 2009-10 | Bristol C | 37 | 1 | | |
| 2010-11 | Bristol C | 20 | 1 | | |
| 2010-11 | *Peterborough U* | 3 | 0 | 3 | 0 |
| 2011-12 | Bristol C | 29 | 0 | | |
| 2012-13 | Bristol C | 19 | 2 | 105 | 4 |

**PEARSON, Stephen (M)** 316 27
H: 6 0 W: 11 01 b.Lanark 2-10-82
Honours: Scotland Under-21, B, 10 full caps.

| 2000-01 | Motherwell | 6 | 0 | | |
| 2001-02 | Motherwell | 27 | 2 | | |
| 2002-03 | Motherwell | 29 | 6 | | |
| 2003-04 | Motherwell | 18 | 4 | 80 | 12 |
| 2003-04 | Celtic | 17 | 3 | | |
| 2004-05 | Celtic | 8 | 0 | | |
| 2005-06 | Celtic | 18 | 2 | | |
| 2006-07 | Celtic | 13 | 1 | 56 | 6 |
| 2006-07 | Derby Co | 9 | 0 | | |
| 2007-08 | Derby Co | 24 | 0 | | |
| 2007-08 | *Stoke C* | 4 | 0 | 4 | 0 |
| 2008-09 | Derby Co | 12 | 1 | | |
| 2009-10 | Derby Co | 37 | 1 | | |
| 2010-11 | Derby Co | 30 | 1 | | |
| 2011-12 | Derby Co | 0 | 0 | 112 | 3 |
| 2011-12 | Bristol C | 28 | 3 | | |
| 2012-13 | Bristol C | 36 | 3 | 64 | 6 |

**PERNTREOU, Kleiton (M)** 0 0

| 2012-13 | Bristol C | 0 | 0 | | |

**REID, Bobby (M)** 13 1
H: 5 7 W: 10 10 b.Bristol 1-3-93
Source: Scholar.

| 2010-11 | Bristol C | 1 | 0 | | |
| 2011-12 | Bristol C | 0 | 0 | | |
| 2011-12 | *Cheltenham T* | 1 | 0 | 1 | 0 |
| 2012-13 | Bristol C | 4 | 1 | 5 | 1 |
| 2012-13 | *Oldham Ath* | 7 | 0 | 7 | 0 |

**SKUSE, Cole (M)** 279 9
H: 6 1 W: 11 05 b.Bristol 29-3-86
Source: Scholar.

| 2004-05 | Bristol C | 7 | 0 | | |
| 2005-06 | Bristol C | 38 | 2 | | |

| 2006-07 | Bristol C | 42 | 0 | | |
|---|---|---|---|---|---|
| 2007-08 | Bristol C | 25 | 0 | | |
| 2008-09 | Bristol C | 33 | 2 | | |
| 2009-10 | Bristol C | 43 | 2 | | |
| 2010-11 | Bristol C | 30 | 1 | | |
| 2011-12 | Bristol C | 36 | 2 | | |
| 2012-13 | Bristol C | 25 | 0 | 279 | 9 |

**STEAD, Jon (F)** 354 84
H: 6 3  W: 13 03  b.Huddersfield 7-4-83
Source: Scholar. Honours: England Under-21.

| 2001-02 | Huddersfield T | 0 | 0 | | |
|---|---|---|---|---|---|
| 2002-03 | Huddersfield T | 42 | 6 | | |
| 2003-04 | Huddersfield T | 26 | 16 | 68 | 22 |
| 2003-04 | Blackburn R | 13 | 6 | | |
| 2004-05 | Blackburn R | 29 | 2 | 42 | 8 |
| 2005-06 | Sunderland | 30 | 1 | | |
| 2006-07 | Sunderland | 5 | 1 | 35 | 2 |
| 2006-07 | *Derby Co* | 17 | 3 | 17 | 3 |
| 2006-07 | Sheffield U | 14 | 5 | | |
| 2007-08 | Sheffield U | 24 | 3 | | |
| 2008-09 | Sheffield U | 1 | 0 | 39 | 8 |
| 2008-09 | Ipswich T | 39 | 12 | | |
| 2009-10 | Ipswich T | 22 | 6 | | |
| 2009-10 | *Coventry C* | 10 | 2 | 10 | 2 |
| 2010-11 | Ipswich T | 3 | 1 | 64 | 19 |
| 2010-11 | Bristol C | 27 | 9 | | |
| 2011-12 | Bristol C | 24 | 6 | | |
| 2012-13 | Bristol C | 28 | 5 | 79 | 20 |

**TAYLOR, Ryan (F)** 171 23
H: 6 2  W: 10 10  b.Rotherham 4-5-88
Source: Scholar.

| 2005-06 | Rotherham U | 1 | 0 | | |
|---|---|---|---|---|---|
| 2006-07 | Rotherham U | 10 | 0 | | |
| 2007-08 | Rotherham U | 35 | 6 | | |
| 2008-09 | Rotherham U | 33 | 4 | | |
| 2009-10 | Rotherham U | 19 | 0 | | |
| 2009-10 | *Exeter C* | 7 | 0 | 7 | 0 |
| 2010-11 | Rotherham U | 34 | 11 | 132 | 21 |
| 2011-12 | Bristol C | 7 | 1 | | |
| 2012-13 | Bristol C | 25 | 1 | 32 | 2 |

**WILSON, James (D)** 58 0
H: 6 2  W: 11 05  b.Chepstow 26-2-89
Source: Scholar. Honours: Wales Youth, Under-21.

| 2005-06 | Bristol C | 0 | 0 | | |
|---|---|---|---|---|---|
| 2006-07 | Bristol C | 0 | 0 | | |
| 2007-08 | Bristol C | 0 | 0 | | |
| 2008-09 | Bristol C | 2 | 0 | | |
| 2008-09 | *Brentford* | 14 | 0 | | |
| 2009-10 | Bristol C | 0 | 0 | | |
| 2009-10 | *Brentford* | 13 | 0 | 27 | 0 |
| 2010-11 | Bristol C | 2 | 0 | | |
| 2011-12 | Bristol C | 21 | 0 | | |
| 2012-13 | Bristol C | 6 | 0 | 31 | 0 |

**WILSON, Mark (D)** 367 14
H: 5 11  W: 10 07  b.Glasgow 5-6-84

| 1995-96 | Berwick R | 24 | 1 | | |
|---|---|---|---|---|---|
| 1996-97 | Berwick R | 4 | 0 | 28 | 1 |
| 1996-97 | Alloa Ath | 16 | 0 | | |
| 1997-98 | Alloa Ath | 17 | 0 | | |
| 1998-99 | Alloa Ath | 24 | 1 | | |
| 1999-2000 | Alloa Ath | 21 | 0 | | |
| 2000-01 | Alloa Ath | 4 | 0 | 82 | 1 |
| 2001-02 | Stenhousemuir | 13 | 0 | | |
| 2002-03 | Stenhousemuir | 27 | 1 | | |
| 2002-03 | Stenhousemuir | 21 | 2 | 34 | 2 |
| 2003-04 | Dundee U | 32 | 3 | | |
| 2004-05 | Dundee U | 37 | 4 | | |
| 2005-06 | Dundee U | 21 | 0 | 117 | 0 |
| 2005-06 | Celtic | 15 | 0 | | |
| 2006-07 | Celtic | 12 | 0 | | |
| 2007-08 | Celtic | 11 | 0 | | |
| 2008-09 | Celtic | 18 | 0 | | |
| 2009-10 | Celtic | 10 | 0 | | |
| 2010-11 | Celtic | 25 | 2 | | |
| 2011-12 | Celtic | 7 | 0 | 98 | 2 |
| 2012-13 | Bristol C | 8 | 0 | 8 | 0 |

**Scholars**
Abbott, Christopher David; Cable, Conor James; Cline, William Christopher; Costa, Castanheira Dylan Costa; Gooden, Shelton Luke Ricardo; Gordon, Elan Jermaine Anthony; Horgan, Jamie Alexander; John, Miles Bradley; Mitchell, Pierce Jonty; Paice, Harry; Pollard, Tyson John; Simms, Jamal Kwesi.

# BRISTOL R (17)

**ANYINSAH, Joe (M)** 175 27
H: 5 8  W: 11 00  b.Bristol 8-10-84
Source: Scholar.

| 2001-02 | Bristol C | 0 | 0 | | |
|---|---|---|---|---|---|
| 2002-03 | Bristol C | 0 | 0 | | |
| 2003-04 | Bristol C | 0 | 0 | | |
| 2004-05 | Bristol C | 7 | 0 | 7 | 0 |
| 2005-06 | Preston NE | 3 | 0 | | |
| 2005-06 | *Bury* | 3 | 0 | 3 | 0 |
| 2006-07 | Preston NE | 3 | 0 | | |
| 2007-08 | Preston NE | 0 | 0 | | |
| 2007-08 | *Carlisle U* | 12 | 3 | | |
| 2007-08 | *Crewe Alex* | 8 | 0 | 8 | 0 |
| 2008-09 | Preston NE | 0 | 0 | 6 | 0 |
| 2008-09 | *Brighton & HA* | 11 | 0 | 11 | 0 |
| 2008-09 | Carlisle U | 19 | 4 | | |
| 2009-10 | Carlisle U | 28 | 9 | | |
| 2010-11 | Carlisle U | 0 | 0 | 59 | 16 |
| 2010-11 | Charlton Ath | 19 | 3 | 19 | 3 |
| 2011-12 | Bristol R | 31 | 4 | | |
| 2012-13 | Bristol R | 31 | 4 | 62 | 8 |

**BROGHAMMER, Fabian (D)** 36 3
H: 5 10  W: 11 00

| 2012-13 | Bristol R | 36 | 3 | 36 | 3 |
|---|---|---|---|---|---|

**BROWN, Lee (M)** 82 10
H: 6 0  W: 12 06  b.Bromley 10-8-90
Source: Scholar.

| 2008-09 | QPR | 0 | 0 | | |
|---|---|---|---|---|---|
| 2009-10 | QPR | 1 | 0 | | |
| 2010-11 | QPR | 0 | 0 | 1 | 0 |
| 2011-12 | Bristol R | 42 | 7 | | |
| 2012-13 | Bristol R | 39 | 3 | 81 | 10 |

**BROWN, Wayne (M)** 96 13
H: 5 9  W: 12 05  b.Kingston 6-8-88
Source: Scholar.

| 2006-07 | Fulham | 0 | 0 | | |
|---|---|---|---|---|---|
| 2007-08 | Fulham | 0 | 0 | | |
| 2007-08 | *Brentford* | 11 | 1 | 11 | 1 |
| 2008-09 | Fulham | 1 | 0 | | |
| 2009 | *TPS Turku* | 25 | 9 | 25 | 9 |
| 2009-10 | Fulham | 0 | 0 | 1 | 0 |
| 2009-10 | *Bristol R* | 4 | 0 | | |
| 2010-11 | Bristol R | 25 | 3 | | |
| 2011-12 | Bristol R | 12 | 0 | | |
| 2012-13 | Bristol R | 18 | 0 | 59 | 3 |

Transferred to TPS March 2013

**BRUNT, Ryan (F)** 51 9
H: 6 1  W: 11 11  b.Birmingham 26-5-93
Source: Scholar.

| 2011-12 | Stoke C | 0 | 0 | | |
|---|---|---|---|---|---|
| 2011-12 | *Tranmere R* | 15 | 1 | 15 | 1 |
| 2012-13 | Stoke C | 0 | 0 | | |
| 2012-13 | *Leyton Orient* | 18 | 3 | 18 | 3 |
| 2012-13 | Bristol R | 18 | 5 | 18 | 5 |

**CLARKE, Ollie (M)** 6 0
H: 5 11  W: 11 11  b.Bristol 29-6-92

| 2009-10 | Bristol R | 0 | 0 | | |
|---|---|---|---|---|---|
| 2010-11 | Bristol R | 1 | 0 | | |
| 2011-12 | Bristol R | 0 | 0 | | |
| 2012-13 | Bristol R | 5 | 0 | 6 | 0 |

**CLARKSON, David (F)** 315 67
H: 5 10  W: 10 03  b.Airdrie 10-9-85
Honours: Scotland Under-21, B, 2 full caps, 1 goal.

| 2002-03 | Motherwell | 19 | 3 | | |
|---|---|---|---|---|---|
| 2003-04 | Motherwell | 38 | 12 | | |
| 2004-05 | Motherwell | 35 | 3 | | |
| 2005-06 | Motherwell | 32 | 4 | | |
| 2006-07 | Motherwell | 29 | 2 | | |
| 2007-08 | Motherwell | 35 | 12 | | |
| 2008-09 | Motherwell | 33 | 13 | 221 | 49 |
| 2009-10 | Bristol C | 26 | 4 | | |
| 2010-11 | Bristol C | 34 | 0 | | |
| 2011-12 | Bristol C | 4 | 0 | 64 | 11 |
| 2011-12 | *Brentford* | 4 | 1 | 4 | 1 |
| 2012-13 | Bristol R | 26 | 6 | 26 | 6 |

**CLUCAS, Seanan (M)** 22 0
H: 5 10  W: 12 00  b.Dungannon 8-11-92
Source: Scholar. Honours: Northern Ireland Youth, Under-21.

| 2011-12 | Preston NE | 1 | 0 | 1 | 0 |
|---|---|---|---|---|---|
| 2011-12 | *Burton Alb* | 2 | 0 | 2 | 0 |
| 2012-13 | Bristol R | 19 | 0 | 19 | 0 |

**GILL, Matthew (M)** 319 16
H: 5 11  W: 11 10  b.Cambridge 8-11-80
Source: Trainee.

| 1997-98 | Peterborough U | 2 | 0 | | |
|---|---|---|---|---|---|
| 1998-99 | Peterborough U | 26 | 0 | | |
| 1999-2000 | Peterborough U | 20 | 1 | | |
| 2000-01 | Peterborough U | 17 | 1 | | |
| 2001-02 | Peterborough U | 12 | 2 | | |
| 2002-03 | Peterborough U | 41 | 1 | | |
| 2003-04 | Peterborough U | 33 | 0 | | |
| 2004-05 | Notts Co | 43 | 0 | | |
| 2005-06 | Notts Co | 14 | 0 | 57 | 0 |
| 2008-09 | Exeter C | 43 | 9 | 43 | 9 |
| 2009-10 | Norwich C | 8 | 0 | | |
| 2010-11 | Norwich C | 4 | 0 | 12 | 0 |
| 2010-11 | *Peterborough U* | 4 | 0 | 155 | 5 |
| 2010-11 | Walsall | 8 | 2 | 8 | 2 |
| 2011-12 | Bristol R | 33 | 0 | | |
| 2012-13 | Bristol R | 11 | 0 | 44 | 0 |

**GODDARD, Jordan (M)** 0 0
b.Wolverhampton 9-9-93
Source: Scholar.

| 2011-12 | Bristol R | 0 | 0 | | |
|---|---|---|---|---|---|
| 2012-13 | Bristol R | 0 | 0 | | |

**GOUGH, Conor (G)** 2 0
H: 6 5  W: 14 00  b.Ilford 9-8-93
Source: Scholar.

| 2011-12 | Charlton Ath | 0 | 0 | | |
|---|---|---|---|---|---|
| 2011-12 | *Bristol R* | 1 | 0 | | |
| 2012-13 | Bristol R | 1 | 0 | 2 | 0 |

**HARDING, Mitch (F)** 6 0
b.Weston-Super-Mare 27-1-94
Source: Scholar.

| 2011-12 | Bristol R | 1 | 0 | | |
|---|---|---|---|---|---|
| 2012-13 | Bristol R | 5 | 0 | 6 | 0 |

**HARRISON, Ellis (F)** 14 3
H: 5 11  W: 12 06  b.Newport 1-2-94
Source: Scholar.

| 2010-11 | Bristol R | 1 | 0 | | |
|---|---|---|---|---|---|
| 2011-12 | Bristol R | 0 | 0 | | |
| 2012-13 | Bristol R | 13 | 3 | 14 | 3 |

**HARROLD, Matt (F)** 297 59
H: 6 1  W: 11 10  b.Leyton 25-7-84
Source: Harlow T.

| 2003-04 | Brentford | 13 | 2 | | |
|---|---|---|---|---|---|
| 2004-05 | Brentford | 19 | 0 | 32 | 2 |
| 2004-05 | Grimsby T | 6 | 2 | 6 | 2 |
| 2005-06 | Yeovil T | 42 | 9 | | |
| 2006-07 | Yeovil T | 5 | 0 | 47 | 9 |
| 2006-07 | Southend U | 36 | 3 | | |
| 2007-08 | Southend U | 16 | 0 | | |
| 2008-09 | Southend U | 0 | 0 | 52 | 3 |
| 2008-09 | Wycombe W | 37 | 9 | | |
| 2009-10 | Wycombe W | 36 | 8 | 73 | 17 |
| 2010-11 | Shrewsbury T | 41 | 8 | 41 | 8 |
| 2011-12 | Bristol R | 40 | 16 | | |
| 2012-13 | Bristol R | 6 | 2 | 46 | 18 |

**HUNTER, Shaquille (M)** 0 0
H: 5 10  W: 11 03  b.Bristol 29-8-95

| 2012-13 | Bristol R | 0 | 0 | | |
|---|---|---|---|---|---|

**KENNETH, Garry (D)** 188 7
H: 6 4  W: 13 00  b.Dundee 21-6-87

| 2004-05 | Dundee U | 11 | 0 | | |
|---|---|---|---|---|---|
| 2005-06 | Dundee U | 16 | 1 | | |
| 2006-07 | Dundee U | 11 | 1 | | |
| 2006-07 | *Cowdenbeath* | 7 | 0 | 7 | 0 |
| 2007-08 | Dundee U | 19 | 1 | | |
| 2008-09 | Dundee U | 25 | 1 | | |
| 2009-10 | Dundee U | 28 | 1 | | |
| 2010-11 | Dundee U | 28 | 1 | | |
| 2011-12 | Dundee U | 25 | 0 | 163 | 6 |
| 2012-13 | Bristol R | 18 | 1 | 18 | 1 |

**LOCKYER, Tom (D)** 4 0
b.Bristol 30-12-94

| 2012-13 | Bristol R | 4 | 0 | 4 | 0 |
|---|---|---|---|---|---|

**McCHRYSTAL, Mark (D)**  139  3
H: 6 1   W: 13 07   b.Derry 26-6-84
*Source:* Scholar. *Honours:* Northern Ireland Under-21.

| | | | | |
|---|---|---|---|---|
| 2001-02 | Wolverhampton W | 0 | 0 | |
| 2003 | Derry C | 5 | 0 | |
| 2003 | *Institute* | 6 | 0 | 6  0 |
| 2004 | Derry C | 9 | 1 | |
| 2005 | Derry C | 9 | 0 | |
| 2006-07 | Partick Th | 15 | 1 | 15  1 |
| 2007 | Derry C | 3 | 0 | |
| 2008 | Derry C | 11 | 0 | |
| 2009 | Derry C | 13 | 0 | 50  1 |
| 2009-10 | Lisburn Distillery | 3 | 0 | 3  0 |
| 2010-11 | Tranmere R | 23 | 0 | |
| 2011-12 | Tranmere R | 18 | 1 | |
| 2012-13 | Tranmere R | 0 | 0 | 41  1 |
| 2012-13 | *Scunthorpe U* | 3 | 0 | 3  0 |
| 2012-13 | Bristol R | 21 | 0 | 21  0 |

**MILDENHALL, Steve (G)**  355  1
H: 6 4   W: 14 01   b.Swindon 13-5-78
*Source:* Trainee.

| | | | | |
|---|---|---|---|---|
| 1996-97 | Swindon T | 1 | 0 | |
| 1997-98 | Swindon T | 4 | 0 | |
| 1998-99 | Swindon T | 0 | 0 | |
| 1999-2000 | Swindon T | 5 | 0 | |
| 2000-01 | Swindon T | 23 | 0 | 33  0 |
| 2001-02 | Notts Co | 26 | 0 | |
| 2002-03 | Notts Co | 21 | 0 | |
| 2003-04 | Notts Co | 28 | 0 | |
| 2004-05 | Notts Co | 1 | 0 | 76  0 |
| 2004-05 | Oldham Ath | 6 | 0 | 6  0 |
| 2005-06 | Grimsby T | 46 | 1 | 46  1 |
| 2006-07 | Yeovil T | 46 | 0 | |
| 2007-08 | Yeovil T | 29 | 0 | 75  0 |
| 2008-09 | Southend U | 34 | 0 | |
| 2009-10 | Southend U | 44 | 0 | |
| 2010-11 | Southend U | 0 | 0 | 78  0 |
| 2010-11 | Millwall | 0 | 0 | |
| 2011-12 | Millwall | 10 | 0 | |
| 2012-13 | Millwall | 0 | 0 | 10  0 |
| 2012-13 | *Scunthorpe U* | 9 | 0 | 9  0 |
| 2012-13 | Bristol R | 22 | 0 | 22  0 |

**NORBURN, Oliver (M)**  40  3
b.Leicester 26-10-92
*Source:* Scholar.

| | | | | |
|---|---|---|---|---|
| 2011-12 | Leicester C | 0 | 0 | |
| 2011-12 | *Bristol R* | 5 | 0 | |
| 2012-13 | Bristol R | 35 | 3 | 40  3 |

**PARKES, Tom (D)**  86  2
H: 6 3   W: 12 05   b.Sutton-in-Ashfield 15-1-92
*Source:* Scholar.

| | | | | |
|---|---|---|---|---|
| 2008-09 | Leicester C | 0 | 0 | |
| 2009-10 | Leicester C | 0 | 0 | |
| 2009-10 | *Burton Alb* | 22 | 1 | |
| 2010-11 | Leicester C | 0 | 0 | |
| 2010-11 | *Yeovil T* | 1 | 0 | 1  0 |
| 2010-11 | *Burton Alb* | 5 | 0 | |
| 2011-12 | Leicester C | 0 | 0 | |
| 2011-12 | *Burton Alb* | 4 | 0 | 31  1 |
| 2011-12 | *Bristol R* | 14 | 0 | |
| 2012-13 | Leicester C | 0 | 0 | |
| 2012-13 | Bristol R | 40 | 1 | 54  1 |

**PATERSON, Jim (M)**  336  12
H: 5 11   W: 12 13   b.Airdrie 25-9-79
*Source:* Dundee U BC. *Honours:* Scotland Under-21.

| | | | | |
|---|---|---|---|---|
| 1998-99 | Dundee U | 15 | 0 | |
| 1999-2000 | Dundee U | 8 | 1 | |
| 2000-01 | Dundee U | 6 | 1 | |
| 2001-02 | Dundee U | 27 | 2 | |
| 2002-03 | Dundee U | 33 | 1 | |
| 2003-04 | Dundee U | 16 | 0 | 105  5 |
| 2004-05 | Motherwell | 35 | 3 | |
| 2005-06 | Motherwell | 19 | 1 | |
| 2006-07 | Motherwell | 34 | 1 | |
| 2007-08 | Motherwell | 20 | 0 | 108  5 |
| 2007-08 | Plymouth Arg | 8 | 1 | |
| 2008-09 | Plymouth Arg | 17 | 0 | |
| 2009-10 | Plymouth Arg | 12 | 0 | |
| 2009-10 | *Aberdeen* | 7 | 0 | 7  0 |
| 2010-11 | Plymouth Arg | 28 | 0 | 65  1 |
| 2011 | Shamrock R | 8 | 0 | 8  0 |
| 2011-12 | Bristol R | 17 | 1 | |
| 2012-13 | Bristol R | 26 | 0 | 43  1 |

**RICHARDS, Eliot (M)**  90  14
H: 5 9   W: 11 09   b.New Tredegar 1-9-91
*Source:* Scholar. *Honours:* Wales Youth.

| | | | | |
|---|---|---|---|---|
| 2009-10 | Bristol R | 5 | 0 | |
| 2010-11 | Bristol R | 13 | 1 | |
| 2011-12 | Bristol R | 32 | 7 | |
| 2012-13 | Bristol R | 40 | 6 | 90  14 |

**RIORDAN, Derek (F)**  267  99
H: 6 2   W: 10 03   b.Edinburgh 16-1-83

| | | | | |
|---|---|---|---|---|
| 2001-02 | Hibernian | 6 | 0 | |
| 2002-03 | Hibernian | 10 | 3 | |
| 2002-03 | *Cowdenbeath* | 2 | 3 | 2  3 |
| 2003-04 | Hibernian | 34 | 15 | |
| 2004-05 | Hibernian | 37 | 20 | |
| 2005-06 | Hibernian | 36 | 16 | |
| 2006-07 | Celtic | 16 | 4 | |
| 2007-08 | Celtic | 8 | 1 | 24  5 |
| 2008-09 | Hibernian | 32 | 12 | |
| 2009-10 | Hibernian | 37 | 13 | |
| 2010-11 | Hibernian | 33 | 11 | 225  90 |
| 2011-12 | Shanghai S | 1 | 1 | 1  1 |
| 2011-12 | St Johnstone | 4 | 0 | 4  0 |
| 2012-13 | Bristol R | 11 | 0 | 11  0 |

**SANTOS, Alefe (M)**  1  0
b. 28-1-95

| | | | | |
|---|---|---|---|---|
| 2012-13 | Bristol R | 1 | 0 | 1  0 |

**SMITH, Michael (D)**  233  17
H: 5 11   W: 11 02   b.Ballyclare 4-9-88
*Honours:* Northern Ireland Under-23.

| | | | | |
|---|---|---|---|---|
| 2005-06 | Ballyclare Com | 1 | 0 | |
| 2006-07 | Ballyclare Com | 25 | 2 | |
| 2007-08 | Ballyclare Com | 39 | 1 | |
| 2008-09 | Ballyclare Com | 27 | 7 | 92  10 |
| 2008-09 | Ballymena U | 12 | 1 | |
| 2009-10 | Ballymena U | 37 | 2 | |
| 2010-11 | Ballymena U | 34 | 3 | 83  6 |
| 2011-12 | Bristol R | 20 | 0 | |
| 2012-13 | Bristol R | 38 | 1 | 58  1 |

**TOUNKARA, Oumare (F)**  61  10
H: 6 1   W: 12 08   b.Paris 25-5-90
*Source:* Sedan.

| | | | | |
|---|---|---|---|---|
| 2009-10 | Sunderland | 0 | 0 | |
| 2010-11 | Sunderland | 0 | 0 | |
| 2010-11 | *Oldham Ath* | 44 | 7 | |
| 2011-12 | Sunderland | 0 | 0 | |
| 2011-12 | *Oldham Ath* | 8 | 1 | |
| 2012-13 | Oldham Ath | 0 | 0 | 52  8 |
| 2012-13 | Bristol R | 9 | 2 | 9  2 |

**VIRGO, Adam (D)**  256  21
H: 6 2   W: 13 12   b.Brighton 25-1-83
*Source:* Juniors. *Honours:* Scotland B.

| | | | | |
|---|---|---|---|---|
| 2000-01 | Brighton & HA | 6 | 0 | |
| 2001-02 | Brighton & HA | 6 | 0 | |
| 2002-03 | Brighton & HA | 3 | 0 | |
| 2002-03 | *Exeter C* | 9 | 0 | 9  0 |
| 2003-04 | Brighton & HA | 22 | 1 | |
| 2004-05 | Brighton & HA | 36 | 8 | |
| 2005-06 | Celtic | 10 | 0 | |
| 2006-07 | Celtic | 0 | 0 | 10  0 |
| 2006-07 | Coventry C | 15 | 1 | |
| 2007-08 | Coventry C | 0 | 0 | 15  1 |
| 2007-08 | Colchester U | 36 | 1 | 36  1 |
| 2008-09 | Brighton & HA | 36 | 3 | |
| 2009-10 | Brighton & HA | 25 | 1 | 134  13 |
| 2010-11 | Yeovil T | 33 | 5 | 33  5 |
| 2011-12 | Bristol R | 9 | 1 | |
| 2012-13 | Bristol R | 10 | 0 | 19  1 |

**WOODARDS, Danny (D)**  211  2
H: 5 11   W: 11 01   b.Forest Gate 7-10-83
*Source:* Trainee.

| | | | | |
|---|---|---|---|---|
| 2003-04 | Chelsea | 0 | 0 | |
| 2004-05 | Chelsea | 0 | 0 | |
| 2005-06 | Chelsea | 0 | 0 | |
| From Exeter C. | | | | |
| 2006-07 | Crewe Alex | 11 | 0 | |
| 2007-08 | Crewe Alex | 36 | 0 | |
| 2008-09 | Crewe Alex | 37 | 0 | 84  0 |
| 2009-10 | Milton Keynes D | 37 | 1 | |
| 2010-11 | Milton Keynes D | 37 | 1 | 66  1 |
| 2011-12 | Bristol R | 39 | 1 | |
| 2012-13 | Bristol R | 22 | 2 | 61  3 |

**Scholars**
Anderson, Treyvond Theophilus; Bryan, Aaron Victor; Douglas, Chad Castrus; Finn, Connor Anthony Alan; Gonzalez-Barra, Carlos; Greenslade, Daniel; Kamara, Samuel Ishmael; Keary, Patrick; Lockyer, Thomas Alun; Lucas, James Alexander; Macey, Matthew Ryan; Santos, D'Abadia Alefe; Southway, Joshua Edward; Thomas, Dominic William; Ward-Baptiste, Aaron James.

---

# BURNLEY (18)

**ANDERSON, Tom (D)**  0  0
b.Burnley 2-9-93
*Source:* Scholar.

| | | | |
|---|---|---|---|
| 2011-12 | Burnley | 0 | 0 |
| 2012-13 | Burnley | 0 | 0 |

**AUSTIN, Charlie (F)**  136  72
H: 6 2   W: 13 03   b.Hungerford 5-7-89
*Source:* Poole T.

| | | | | |
|---|---|---|---|---|
| 2009-10 | Swindon T | 33 | 19 | |
| 2010-11 | Swindon T | 21 | 12 | 54  31 |
| 2010-11 | Burnley | 4 | 0 | |
| 2011-12 | Burnley | 41 | 16 | |
| 2012-13 | Burnley | 37 | 25 | 82  41 |

**BARTLEY, Marvyn (M)**  178  6
H: 6 1   W: 12 04   b.Reading 4-7-86
*Source:* Hampton & Richmond B.

| | | | | |
|---|---|---|---|---|
| 2007-08 | Bournemouth | 20 | 1 | |
| 2008-09 | Bournemouth | 33 | 1 | |
| 2009-10 | Bournemouth | 34 | 0 | |
| 2010-11 | Bournemouth | 26 | 1 | 113  3 |
| 2010-11 | Burnley | 5 | 0 | |
| 2011-12 | Burnley | 39 | 3 | |
| 2012-13 | Burnley | 21 | 0 | 65  3 |

**COLEMAN, Alex (D)**  0  0
b.Bury 17-12-93
*Source:* Scholar.

| | | | |
|---|---|---|---|
| 2011-12 | Burnley | 0 | 0 |
| 2012-13 | Burnley | 0 | 0 |

**CONLAN, Luke (D)**  0  0
b.Portaferry 31-10-94
*Source:* Scholar.

| | | | |
|---|---|---|---|
| 2011-12 | Burnley | 0 | 0 |
| 2012-13 | Burnley | 0 | 0 |

**DUFF, Michael (D)**  457  18
H: 6 1   W: 11 08   b.Belfast 11-1-78
*Source:* Trainee. *Honours:* Northern Ireland 24 full caps.

| | | | | |
|---|---|---|---|---|
| 1999-2000 | Cheltenham T | 31 | 2 | |
| 2000-01 | Cheltenham T | 39 | 5 | |
| 2001-02 | Cheltenham T | 45 | 3 | |
| 2002-03 | Cheltenham T | 44 | 2 | |
| 2003-04 | Cheltenham T | 42 | 0 | 201  12 |
| 2004-05 | Burnley | 42 | 0 | |
| 2005-06 | Burnley | 41 | 0 | |
| 2006-07 | Burnley | 44 | 2 | |
| 2007-08 | Burnley | 8 | 1 | |
| 2008-09 | Burnley | 27 | 1 | |
| 2009-10 | Burnley | 11 | 0 | |
| 2010-11 | Burnley | 28 | 1 | |
| 2011-12 | Burnley | 31 | 0 | |
| 2012-13 | Burnley | 24 | 1 | 256  6 |

**EDGAR, David (D)**  106  7
H: 6 2   W: 12 13   b.Ontario 19-5-87
*Source:* Scholar. *Honours:* Canada Youth, Under-20, 17 full caps, 1 goal.

| | | | | |
|---|---|---|---|---|
| 2005-06 | Newcastle U | 0 | 0 | |
| 2006-07 | Newcastle U | 3 | 1 | |
| 2007-08 | Newcastle U | 5 | 0 | |
| 2008-09 | Newcastle U | 11 | 1 | |
| 2009-10 | Newcastle U | 0 | 0 | 19  2 |
| 2009-10 | Burnley | 4 | 0 | |
| 2009-10 | *Swansea C* | 5 | 1 | 5  1 |
| 2010-11 | Burnley | 7 | 0 | |
| 2011-12 | Burnley | 44 | 2 | |
| 2012-13 | Burnley | 27 | 2 | 82  4 |

**ERRINGTON, Jack (D)**  0  0
b.Wallsend 9-12-94
*Source:* Scholar.

| | | | |
|---|---|---|---|
| 2011-12 | Burnley | 0 | 0 |
| 2012-13 | Burnley | 0 | 0 |

**GRANT, Lee (G)**    341   0
H: 6 3   W: 13 01   b.Hemel Hempstead 27-1-83
*Source:* Scholar. *Honours:* England Youth, Under-21.

| | | | | | |
|---|---|---|---|---|---|
| 2000-01 | Derby Co | 0 | 0 | | |
| 2001-02 | Derby Co | 0 | 0 | | |
| 2002-03 | Derby Co | 29 | 0 | | |
| 2003-04 | Derby Co | 36 | 0 | | |
| 2004-05 | Derby Co | 2 | 0 | | |
| 2005-06 | Derby Co | 0 | 0 | | |
| 2005-06 | *Burnley* | 1 | 0 | | |
| 2005-06 | *Oldham Ath* | 16 | 0 | 16 | 0 |
| 2006-07 | Derby Co | 7 | 0 | 74 | 0 |
| 2007-08 | Sheffield W | 44 | 0 | | |
| 2008-09 | Sheffield W | 46 | 0 | | |
| 2009-10 | Sheffield W | 46 | 0 | 136 | 0 |
| 2010-11 | Burnley | 25 | 0 | | |
| 2011-12 | Burnley | 43 | 0 | | |
| 2012-13 | Burnley | 46 | 0 | 115 | 0 |

**HEWITT, Steven (M)**    1   0
H: 5 7   W: 11 00   b.Manchester 5-12-93
*Source:* Scholar.

| | | | | | |
|---|---|---|---|---|---|
| 2011-12 | Burnley | 1 | 0 | | |
| 2012-13 | Burnley | 0 | 0 | 1 | 0 |

**HOWIESON, Cameron (M)**    2   0
H: 5 9   W: 11 00   b.Dunedin 22-12-94
*Source:* Scholar. *Honours:* New Zealand Youth, 4 full caps.

| | | | | | |
|---|---|---|---|---|---|
| 2011-12 | Burnley | 2 | 0 | | |
| 2012-13 | Doncaster R | 0 | 0 | | |
| 2012-13 | Burnley | 0 | 0 | 2 | 0 |

**INGS, Danny (F)**    74   13
H: 5 10   W: 11 07   b.Winchester 16-3-92
*Source:* Youth.

| | | | | | |
|---|---|---|---|---|---|
| 2009-10 | Bournemouth | 0 | 0 | | |
| 2010-11 | Bournemouth | 26 | 7 | | |
| 2011-12 | Bournemouth | 1 | 0 | 27 | 7 |
| 2011-12 | Burnley | 15 | 3 | | |
| 2012-13 | Burnley | 32 | 3 | 47 | 6 |

**JACKSON, Joe (F)**    1   0
H: 5 11   W: 10 07   b.Barrow 3-2-93
*Source:* Scholar.

| | | | | | |
|---|---|---|---|---|---|
| 2011-12 | Burnley | 1 | 0 | | |
| 2012-13 | Burnley | 0 | 0 | 1 | 0 |

**JENSEN, Brian (G)**    318   0
H: 6 1   W: 12 04   b.Copenhagen 8-6-75
*Source:* Hvidovre, B93.

| | | | | | |
|---|---|---|---|---|---|
| 1997-98 | AZ | 0 | 0 | | |
| 1998-99 | AZ | 1 | 0 | 1 | 0 |
| 1999-2000 | WBA | 12 | 0 | | |
| 2000-01 | WBA | 33 | 0 | | |
| 2001-02 | WBA | 1 | 0 | | |
| 2002-03 | WBA | 0 | 0 | 46 | 0 |
| 2003-04 | Burnley | 46 | 0 | | |
| 2004-05 | Burnley | 27 | 0 | | |
| 2005-06 | Burnley | 39 | 0 | | |
| 2006-07 | Burnley | 31 | 0 | | |
| 2007-08 | Burnley | 19 | 0 | | |
| 2008-09 | Burnley | 45 | 0 | | |
| 2009-10 | Burnley | 38 | 0 | | |
| 2010-11 | Burnley | 21 | 0 | | |
| 2011-12 | Burnley | 4 | 0 | | |
| 2012-13 | Burnley | 1 | 0 | 271 | 0 |

**LAFFERTY, Danny (D)**    89   8
H: 6 0   W: 12 08   b.Derry 1-4-90
*Honours:* Northern Ireland Youth, Under-21, B, 4 full caps.

| | | | | | |
|---|---|---|---|---|---|
| 2009-10 | Celtic | 0 | 0 | | |
| 2009-10 | Ayr U | 14 | 1 | 14 | 1 |
| 2010 | Derry C | 12 | 0 | | |
| 2011 | Derry C | 34 | 7 | 46 | 7 |
| 2011-12 | Burnley | 5 | 0 | | |
| 2012-13 | Burnley | 24 | 0 | 29 | 0 |

**LONG, Kevin (D)**    90   4
H: 6 3   W: 13 01   b.Cork 18-8-90

| | | | | | |
|---|---|---|---|---|---|
| 2009 | Cork C | 16 | 0 | 16 | 0 |
| 2009-10 | Burnley | 0 | 0 | | |
| 2010-11 | Burnley | 0 | 0 | | |
| 2010-11 | *Accrington S* | 15 | 0 | | |
| 2011-12 | Burnley | 0 | 0 | | |
| 2011-12 | *Accrington S* | 24 | 4 | 39 | 4 |
| 2011-12 | *Rochdale* | 16 | 0 | | |
| 2012-13 | Burnley | 14 | 0 | 14 | 0 |
| 2012-13 | *Portsmouth* | 5 | 0 | 5 | 0 |

**LOVE, Archie (M)**    0   0
b.Manchester 12-1-93
*Source:* Scholar.

| | | | |
|---|---|---|---|
| 2011-12 | Burnley | 0 | 0 |
| 2012-13 | Burnley | 0 | 0 |

**MACDONALD, Alex (F)**    81   8
H: 5 7   W: 11 04   b.Warrington 14-4-90
*Source:* Scholar. *Honours:* Scotland Youth, Under-21.

| | | | | | |
|---|---|---|---|---|---|
| 2007-08 | Burnley | 2 | 0 | | |
| 2008-09 | Burnley | 3 | 0 | | |
| 2009-10 | Burnley | 0 | 0 | | |
| 2009-10 | *Falkirk* | 11 | 1 | 11 | 1 |
| 2010-11 | Burnley | 0 | 0 | | |
| 2010-11 | *Inverness CT* | 10 | 1 | 10 | 1 |
| 2011-12 | Burnley | 5 | 0 | | |
| 2011-12 | *Plymouth Arg* | 18 | 4 | | |
| 2012-13 | Burnley | 1 | 0 | 11 | 0 |
| 2012-13 | *Plymouth Arg* | 16 | 1 | 34 | 5 |
| 2012-13 | *Burton Alb* | 15 | 1 | 15 | 1 |

**MARNEY, Dean (M)**    271   16
H: 5 10   W: 11 09   b.Barking 31-1-84
*Source:* Scholar. *Honours:* England Under-21.

| | | | | | |
|---|---|---|---|---|---|
| 2002-03 | Tottenham H | 0 | 0 | | |
| 2002-03 | *Swindon T* | 9 | 0 | 9 | 0 |
| 2003-04 | Tottenham H | 3 | 0 | | |
| 2003-04 | *QPR* | 2 | 0 | 2 | 0 |
| 2004-05 | Tottenham H | 5 | 2 | | |
| 2004-05 | *Gillingham* | 3 | 0 | 3 | 0 |
| 2005-06 | Tottenham H | 0 | 0 | 8 | 2 |
| 2005-06 | *Norwich C* | 13 | 0 | 13 | 0 |
| 2006-07 | Hull C | 37 | 2 | | |
| 2007-08 | Hull C | 41 | 6 | | |
| 2008-09 | Hull C | 31 | 0 | | |
| 2009-10 | Hull C | 16 | 1 | 125 | 9 |
| 2009-10 | Burnley | 0 | 0 | | |
| 2010-11 | Burnley | 36 | 3 | | |
| 2011-12 | Burnley | 37 | 0 | | |
| 2012-13 | Burnley | 38 | 2 | 111 | 5 |

**McCANN, Chris (M)**    238   27
H: 6 1   W: 11 11   b.Dublin 21-7-87
*Source:* Scholar. *Honours:* Eire Youth.

| | | | | | |
|---|---|---|---|---|---|
| 2005-06 | Burnley | 23 | 2 | | |
| 2006-07 | Burnley | 38 | 5 | | |
| 2007-08 | Burnley | 35 | 5 | | |
| 2008-09 | Burnley | 44 | 6 | | |
| 2009-10 | Burnley | 7 | 0 | | |
| 2010-11 | Burnley | 4 | 1 | | |
| 2011-12 | Burnley | 46 | 4 | | |
| 2012-13 | Burnley | 41 | 4 | 238 | 27 |

**MEE, Ben (D)**    65   1
H: 5 11   W: 11 09   b.Sale 21-9-89
*Source:* Scholar. *Honours:* England Youth, Under-20, Under-21.

| | | | | | |
|---|---|---|---|---|---|
| 2007-08 | Manchester C | 0 | 0 | | |
| 2008-09 | Manchester C | 0 | 0 | | |
| 2009-10 | Manchester C | 0 | 0 | | |
| 2010-11 | Manchester C | 0 | 0 | | |
| 2010-11 | *Leicester C* | 15 | 0 | 15 | 0 |
| 2011-12 | Manchester C | 0 | 0 | | |
| 2011-12 | Burnley | 31 | 0 | | |
| 2012-13 | Burnley | 19 | 1 | 50 | 1 |

**O'NEILL, Luke (D)**    6   0
H: 6 0   W: 11 04   b.Slough 20-8-91

| | | | | | |
|---|---|---|---|---|---|
| 2009-10 | Leicester C | 1 | 0 | 1 | 0 |
| 2009-10 | *Tranmere R* | 4 | 0 | 4 | 0 |

From Kettering (loan), Mansfield

| | | | | | |
|---|---|---|---|---|---|
| 2012-13 | Burnley | 1 | 0 | 1 | 0 |

**PATERSON, Martin (F)**    200   49
H: 5 9   W: 10 11   b.Tunstall 13-5-87
*Source:* Scholar. *Honours:* Northern Ireland Youth, Under-21, 15 full caps.

| | | | | | |
|---|---|---|---|---|---|
| 2004-05 | Stoke C | 3 | 0 | | |
| 2005-06 | Stoke C | 3 | 0 | | |
| 2006-07 | Stoke C | 9 | 1 | 15 | 1 |
| 2006-07 | *Grimsby T* | 15 | 6 | 15 | 6 |
| 2007-08 | Scunthorpe U | 40 | 13 | 40 | 13 |
| 2008-09 | Burnley | 43 | 12 | | |
| 2009-10 | Burnley | 23 | 4 | | |
| 2010-11 | Burnley | 11 | 2 | | |
| 2011-12 | Burnley | 14 | 3 | | |
| 2012-13 | Burnley | 39 | 8 | 130 | 29 |

**PORTER, George (F)**    54   2
H: 5 10   W: 12 06   b.Sidcup 27-6-92
*Source:* Cray W.

| | | | | | |
|---|---|---|---|---|---|
| 2010-11 | Leyton Orient | 1 | 0 | | |
| 2011-12 | Leyton Orient | 34 | 1 | 35 | 1 |
| 2012-13 | Burnley | 0 | 0 | | |
| 2012-13 | *Colchester U* | 19 | 1 | 19 | 1 |

**RICHARDS, Dane (M)**    185   26
H: 5 7   W: 10 11   b.Montego Bay 14-12-83
*Honours:* Jamaica 51 full caps, 10 goals.

| | | | | | |
|---|---|---|---|---|---|
| 2007 | New York RB | 30 | 2 | | |
| 2008 | New York RB | 27 | 4 | | |
| 2009 | New York RB | 27 | 3 | | |
| 2010 | New York RB | 27 | 5 | | |
| 2011 | New York RB | 30 | 7 | | |
| 2012 | New York RB | 17 | 1 | 158 | 22 |
| 2012 | Vancouver W | 13 | 3 | 13 | 3 |
| 2012-13 | Burnley | 1 | 0 | 1 | 0 |
| 2013 | *Bodo/Glimt* | 13 | 1 | 13 | 1 |

**SHACKELL, Jason (D)**    300   10
H: 6 4   W: 13 06   b.Stevenage 27-9-83
*Source:* Scholar.

| | | | | | |
|---|---|---|---|---|---|
| 2002-03 | Norwich C | 2 | 0 | | |
| 2003-04 | Norwich C | 6 | 0 | | |
| 2004-05 | Norwich C | 11 | 0 | | |
| 2005-06 | Norwich C | 17 | 0 | | |
| 2006-07 | Norwich C | 43 | 3 | | |
| 2007-08 | Norwich C | 39 | 0 | | |
| 2008-09 | Norwich C | 15 | 0 | 133 | 3 |
| 2008-09 | Wolverhampton W | 12 | 0 | | |
| 2009-10 | Wolverhampton W | 0 | 0 | 12 | 0 |
| 2009-10 | *Doncaster R* | 21 | 1 | 21 | 1 |
| 2010-11 | Barnsley | 44 | 3 | | |
| 2011-12 | Barnsley | 0 | 0 | 44 | 3 |
| 2011-12 | Derby Co | 46 | 1 | 46 | 1 |
| 2012-13 | Burnley | 44 | 2 | 44 | 2 |

**STANISLAS, Junior (M)**    114   12
H: 6 0   W: 12 00   b.Kidbrooke 26-11-89
*Source:* Scholar. *Honours:* England Youth, Under-21.

| | | | | | |
|---|---|---|---|---|---|
| 2007-08 | West Ham U | 0 | 0 | | |
| 2008-09 | West Ham U | 9 | 2 | | |
| 2008-09 | *Southend U* | 6 | 1 | 6 | 1 |
| 2009-10 | West Ham U | 26 | 3 | | |
| 2010-11 | West Ham U | 6 | 1 | | |
| 2011-12 | West Ham U | 1 | 0 | 42 | 6 |
| 2011-12 | Burnley | 31 | 0 | | |
| 2012-13 | Burnley | 35 | 5 | 66 | 5 |

**STEWART, Jon (G)**    4   0
H: 6 2   W: 13 01   b.Hayes 13-3-89
*Source:* Swindon T Scholar, Weymouth.

| | | | | | |
|---|---|---|---|---|---|
| 2008-09 | Portsmouth | 0 | 0 | | |
| 2009-10 | Portsmouth | 0 | 0 | | |
| 2010-11 | Bournemouth | 4 | 0 | | |
| 2011-12 | Bournemouth | 0 | 0 | 4 | 0 |
| 2011-12 | Burnley | 0 | 0 | | |
| 2012-13 | Burnley | 0 | 0 | | |

**STOCK, Brian (M)**    368   34
H: 5 11   W: 11 02   b.Winchester 24-12-81
*Source:* Trainee. *Honours:* Wales Under-21, 3 full caps.

| | | | | | |
|---|---|---|---|---|---|
| 1999-2000 | Bournemouth | 5 | 0 | | |
| 2000-01 | Bournemouth | 1 | 0 | | |
| 2001-02 | Bournemouth | 26 | 2 | | |
| 2002-03 | Bournemouth | 27 | 2 | | |
| 2003-04 | Bournemouth | 19 | 3 | | |
| 2004-05 | Bournemouth | 41 | 6 | | |
| 2005-06 | Bournemouth | 26 | 3 | 145 | 16 |
| 2005-06 | Preston NE | 6 | 1 | | |
| 2006-07 | Preston NE | 0 | 0 | 8 | 1 |
| 2006-07 | Doncaster R | 36 | 3 | | |
| 2007-08 | Doncaster R | 40 | 5 | | |
| 2008-09 | Doncaster R | 36 | 6 | | |
| 2009-10 | Doncaster R | 15 | 0 | | |
| 2010-11 | Doncaster R | 37 | 2 | | |
| 2011-12 | Doncaster R | 26 | 1 | | |
| 2012-13 | *Doncaster R* | 0 | 0 | 190 | 17 |
| 2012-13 | Burnley | 25 | 0 | 25 | 0 |

**TREACY, Keith (M)**    133   14
H: 6 0   W: 13 02   b.Dublin 13-9-88
*Source:* Scholar. *Honours:* Eire Youth, Under-21, 6 full caps.

| | | | | | |
|---|---|---|---|---|---|
| 2005-06 | Blackburn R | 0 | 0 | | |
| 2006-07 | Blackburn R | 0 | 0 | | |
| 2006-07 | *Stockport Co* | 4 | 0 | 4 | 0 |

| 2007-08 | Blackburn R | 0 | 0 | | |
|---|---|---|---|---|---|
| 2008-09 | Blackburn R | 12 | 0 | | |
| 2009-10 | Blackburn R | 0 | 0 | 12 | 0 |
| 2009-10 | *Sheffield U* | 16 | 1 | 16 | 1 |
| 2009-10 | Preston NE | 17 | 2 | | |
| 2010-11 | Preston NE | 38 | 7 | 55 | 9 |
| 2011-12 | Burnley | 24 | 2 | | |
| 2011-12 | *Sheffield W* | 7 | 1 | 7 | 1 |
| 2012-13 | Burnley | 15 | 1 | 39 | 3 |

**TRIPPIER, Keiran (D)** 133 5
H: 5 10 W: 11 00 b.Bury 19-9-90
*Source:* Scholar. *Honours:* England Youth, Under-20, Under-21.

| 2007-08 | Manchester C | 0 | 0 | | |
|---|---|---|---|---|---|
| 2008-09 | Manchester C | 0 | 0 | | |
| 2009-10 | Manchester C | 0 | 0 | | |
| 2009-10 | *Barnsley* | 3 | 0 | | |
| 2010-11 | Manchester C | 0 | 0 | | |
| 2010-11 | *Barnsley* | 39 | 2 | 42 | 2 |
| 2011-12 | Manchester C | 0 | 0 | | |
| 2011-12 | Burnley | 46 | 3 | | |
| 2012-13 | Burnley | 45 | 0 | 91 | 3 |

**VOKES, Sam (F)** 189 34
H: 6 1 W: 13 10 b.Lymington 21-10-89
*Source:* Scholar. *Honours:* Wales Under-21, 25 full caps, 5 goals.

| 2006-07 | Bournemouth | 13 | 4 | | |
|---|---|---|---|---|---|
| 2007-08 | Bournemouth | 41 | 12 | 54 | 16 |
| 2008-09 | Wolverhampton W | 36 | 6 | | |
| 2009-10 | Wolverhampton W | 5 | 0 | | |
| 2009-10 | *Leeds U* | 8 | 1 | 8 | 1 |
| 2010-11 | Wolverhampton W | 2 | 0 | | |
| 2010-11 | *Bristol C* | 1 | 0 | 1 | 0 |
| 2010-11 | *Sheffield U* | 6 | 1 | 6 | 1 |
| 2010-11 | *Norwich C* | 4 | 1 | 4 | 1 |
| 2011-12 | Wolverhampton W | 4 | 0 | | |
| 2011-12 | *Burnley* | 9 | 2 | | |
| 2011-12 | *Brighton & HA* | 14 | 3 | 14 | 3 |
| 2012-13 | Wolverhampton W | 0 | 0 | 47 | 6 |
| 2012-13 | Burnley | 46 | 4 | 55 | 6 |

**WALLACE, Ross (M)** 290 32
H: 5 6 W: 9 12 b.Dundee 23-5-85
*Source:* Celtic S Form. *Honours:* Scotland Youth, Under-21, B, 1 full cap.

| 2001-02 | Celtic | 0 | 0 | | |
|---|---|---|---|---|---|
| 2002-03 | Celtic | 0 | 0 | | |
| 2003-04 | Celtic | 8 | 1 | | |
| 2004-05 | Celtic | 16 | 0 | | |
| 2005-06 | Celtic | 11 | 0 | | |
| 2006-07 | Celtic | 2 | 0 | 37 | 1 |
| 2006-07 | Sunderland | 32 | 6 | | |
| 2007-08 | Sunderland | 21 | 2 | | |
| 2008-09 | Sunderland | 0 | 0 | 53 | 8 |
| 2008-09 | Preston NE | 39 | 5 | | |
| 2009-10 | Preston NE | 41 | 7 | 80 | 12 |
| 2010-11 | Burnley | 40 | 3 | | |
| 2011-12 | Burnley | 44 | 5 | | |
| 2012-13 | Burnley | 36 | 3 | 120 | 11 |

**Scholars**
Daly, Luke Thomas; Dummigan, Cameron; Gallagher, Luke; Galvin, Evan; Gilchrist, Jason Lee; Holt, Charlie George; Jakovleks, Callum David; Lowe, Nathan Patrick; Ly, Kevin Lap Chi; Mitchell, Conor; Nuttall, Lewis Lee; Richardson, Callum John; Whitmore, Alexander James.

# BURTON ALB (19)

**BELL, Lee (M)** 278 12
H: 5 11 W: 12 04 b.Alsager 26-1-83
*Source:* Scholar.

| 2000-01 | Crewe Alex | 0 | 0 | | |
|---|---|---|---|---|---|
| 2001-02 | Crewe Alex | 0 | 0 | | |
| 2002-03 | Crewe Alex | 17 | 1 | | |
| 2003-04 | Crewe Alex | 3 | 0 | | |
| 2004-05 | Crewe Alex | 17 | 0 | | |
| 2005-06 | Crewe Alex | 17 | 2 | | |
| 2006-07 | Crewe Alex | 0 | 0 | | |
| 2007-08 | Mansfield T | 23 | 1 | 23 | 1 |
| 2008-09 | Macclesfield T | 41 | 1 | | |
| 2009-10 | Macclesfield T | 42 | 2 | 83 | 3 |
| 2010-11 | Crewe Alex | 45 | 1 | | |
| 2011-12 | Crewe Alex | 30 | 0 | | |
| 2012-13 | Crewe Alex | 0 | 0 | 129 | 4 |
| 2012-13 | Burton Alb | 43 | 4 | 43 | 4 |

**CORBETT, Andy (F)** 120 2
H: 6 0 W: 11 07 b.Worcester 20-2-82

| 1999-2000 | Kidderminster H | 6 | 0 | | |
|---|---|---|---|---|---|
| 2001-02 | Kidderminster H | 2 | 0 | 8 | 0 |

From Solihull B, Nuneaton B.

| 2009-10 | Burton Alb | 34 | 1 | | |
|---|---|---|---|---|---|
| 2010-11 | Burton Alb | 40 | 1 | | |
| 2011-12 | Burton Alb | 33 | 0 | | |
| 2012-13 | Burton Alb | 5 | 0 | 112 | 2 |
| 2012-13 | *Hereford U* | 0 | 0 | | |

**DIAMOND, Zander (D)** 264 22
H: 6 2 W: 11 07 b.Alexandria 3-12-85
*Honours:* Scotland Under-21.

| 2003-04 | Aberdeen | 19 | 2 | | |
|---|---|---|---|---|---|
| 2004-05 | Aberdeen | 29 | 3 | | |
| 2005-06 | Aberdeen | 33 | 0 | | |
| 2006-07 | Aberdeen | 21 | 0 | | |
| 2007-08 | Aberdeen | 26 | 3 | | |
| 2008-09 | Aberdeen | 28 | 4 | | |
| 2009-10 | Aberdeen | 16 | 3 | | |
| 2010-11 | Aberdeen | 32 | 1 | 204 | 16 |
| 2011-12 | Oldham Ath | 23 | 2 | 23 | 2 |
| 2012-13 | Burton Alb | 37 | 4 | 37 | 4 |

**DYER, Jack (M)** 50 1
H: 5 9 W: 11 00 b.Sutton Coldfield 11-12-91
*Source:* Aston Villa Scholar.

| 2010-11 | Burton Alb | 5 | 0 | | |
|---|---|---|---|---|---|
| 2011-12 | Burton Alb | 17 | 1 | | |
| 2012-13 | Burton Alb | 28 | 0 | 50 | 1 |

**HOLNESS, Marcus (D)** 130 5
H: 6 0 W: 12 02 b.Swinton 8-12-88
*Source:* Scholar.

| 2007-08 | Oldham Ath | 0 | 0 | | |
|---|---|---|---|---|---|
| 2007-08 | *Rochdale* | 19 | 0 | | |
| 2008-09 | Rochdale | 8 | 0 | | |
| 2009-10 | Rochdale | 11 | 0 | | |
| 2010-11 | Rochdale | 46 | 1 | | |
| 2011-12 | Rochdale | 24 | 3 | 108 | 4 |
| 2012-13 | Burton Alb | 22 | 1 | 22 | 1 |

**KEE, Billy (F)** 141 43
H: 5 9 W: 11 04 b.Loughborough 1-12-90
*Honours:* Northern Ireland Youth, Under-21.

| 2009-10 | Leicester C | 0 | 0 | | |
|---|---|---|---|---|---|
| 2009-10 | *Accrington S* | 37 | 9 | 37 | 9 |
| 2010-11 | Torquay U | 40 | 9 | | |
| 2011-12 | Torquay U | 4 | 0 | 44 | 9 |
| 2011-12 | Burton Alb | 20 | 12 | | |
| 2012-13 | Burton Alb | 40 | 13 | 60 | 25 |

**LYNESS, Dean (G)** 15 0
H: 6 3 W: 11 12 b.Birmingham 20-7-91

| 2012-13 | Burton Alb | 15 | 0 | 15 | 0 |
|---|---|---|---|---|---|

**MAGHOMA, Jacques (M)** 155 26
H: 5 9 W: 11 06 b.Lubumbashi 23-10-87
*Source:* Scholar. *Honours:* DR Congo 3 full caps, 2 goals.

| 2005-06 | Tottenham H | 0 | 0 | | |
|---|---|---|---|---|---|
| 2006-07 | Tottenham H | 0 | 0 | | |
| 2007-08 | Tottenham H | 0 | 0 | | |
| 2008-09 | Tottenham H | 0 | 0 | | |
| 2009-10 | Burton Alb | 35 | 3 | | |
| 2010-11 | Burton Alb | 41 | 4 | | |
| 2011-12 | Burton Alb | 36 | 4 | | |
| 2012-13 | Burton Alb | 43 | 15 | 155 | 26 |

**McCRORY, Damien (M)** 145 2
H: 6 2 W: 12 10 b.Limerick 22-2-90
*Honours:* Eire Youth.

| 2008-09 | Plymouth Arg | 0 | 0 | | |
|---|---|---|---|---|---|
| 2008-09 | *Port Vale* | 12 | 0 | | |
| 2009-10 | Plymouth Arg | 0 | 0 | | |
| 2009-10 | *Port Vale* | 5 | 0 | 17 | 0 |
| 2009-10 | *Grimsby T* | 10 | 0 | 10 | 0 |
| 2009-10 | Dagenham & R | 20 | 0 | | |
| 2010-11 | Dagenham & R | 34 | 0 | | |
| 2011-12 | Dagenham & R | 33 | 1 | 76 | 1 |
| 2012-13 | Burton Alb | 41 | 1 | 42 | 1 |

**McGRATH, John (M)** 173 4
H: 5 10 W: 10 04 b.Limerick 27-3-80
*Source:* Belvedere. *Honours:* Eire Under-21.

| 1999-2000 | Aston Villa | 0 | 0 | | |
|---|---|---|---|---|---|
| 2000-01 | Aston Villa | 3 | 0 | | |
| 2001-02 | Aston Villa | 0 | 0 | | |
| 2002-03 | Aston Villa | 0 | 0 | 3 | 0 |
| 2003-04 | Doncaster R | 11 | 0 | | |
| 2004-05 | Doncaster R | 0 | 0 | 11 | 0 |
| 2004-05 | *Shrewsbury T* | 8 | 0 | 8 | 0 |
| 2004-05 | *Kidderminster H* | 19 | 0 | 19 | 0 |
| 2005-06 | Limerick | 0 | 0 | | |

From Weymouth, Tamworth.

| 2009-10 | Burton Alb | 45 | 1 | | |
|---|---|---|---|---|---|
| 2010-11 | Burton Alb | 41 | 3 | | |
| 2011-12 | Burton Alb | 31 | 0 | | |
| 2012-13 | Burton Alb | 6 | 0 | 123 | 4 |
| 2012-13 | *York C* | 9 | 0 | 9 | 0 |

**PALMER, Chris (D)** 216 14
H: 5 7 W: 11 00 b.Derby 16-10-83
*Source:* Scholar.

| 2003-04 | Derby Co | 0 | 0 | | |
|---|---|---|---|---|---|
| 2004-05 | Notts Co | 25 | 4 | | |
| 2005-06 | Notts Co | 29 | 1 | 54 | 5 |
| 2006-07 | Wycombe W | 32 | 0 | | |
| 2007-08 | Wycombe W | 1 | 0 | 33 | 0 |
| 2007-08 | *Darlington* | 4 | 0 | 4 | 0 |
| 2008-09 | Walsall | 44 | 1 | 44 | 1 |
| 2009-10 | Gillingham | 20 | 1 | | |
| 2010-11 | Gillingham | 18 | 4 | 38 | 5 |
| 2011-12 | Burton Alb | 34 | 3 | | |
| 2012-13 | Burton Alb | 9 | 0 | 43 | 3 |

**PALMER, Matthew (M)** 2 0
H: 5 10 W: 12 06 b.Derby 1-8-93

| 2012-13 | Burton Alb | 2 | 0 | 2 | 0 |
|---|---|---|---|---|---|

**PATERSON, Matthew (F)** 86 14
H: 5 10 W: 10 10 b.Dunfermline 18-10-89
*Source:* Scholar. *Honours:* Scotland Youth.

| 2008-09 | Southampton | 11 | 1 | | |
|---|---|---|---|---|---|
| 2009-10 | Southampton | 7 | 1 | 18 | 2 |
| 2009-10 | *Southend U* | 16 | 2 | | |
| 2010-11 | Southend U | 11 | 0 | | |
| 2010-11 | *Stockport Co* | 10 | 3 | 10 | 3 |
| 2011-12 | Southend U | 0 | 0 | 27 | 2 |
| 2012-13 | Burton Alb | 31 | 7 | 31 | 7 |

**PHILLIPS, Jimmy (M)** 87 1
H: 5 7 W: 10 00 b.Stoke 20-9-89
*Source:* Scholar.

| 2008-09 | Stoke C | 0 | 0 | | |
|---|---|---|---|---|---|
| 2009-10 | Burton Alb | 24 | 1 | | |
| 2010-11 | Burton Alb | 23 | 0 | | |
| 2011-12 | Burton Alb | 33 | 0 | | |
| 2012-13 | Burton Alb | 7 | 0 | 87 | 1 |

**SHARPS, Ian (D)** 455 17
H: 6 3 W: 14 07 b.Warrington 23-10-80
*Source:* Trainee.

| 1998-99 | Tranmere R | 1 | 0 | | |
|---|---|---|---|---|---|
| 1999-2000 | Tranmere R | 0 | 0 | | |
| 2000-01 | Tranmere R | 0 | 0 | | |
| 2001-02 | Tranmere R | 29 | 0 | | |
| 2002-03 | Tranmere R | 30 | 3 | | |
| 2003-04 | Tranmere R | 27 | 1 | | |
| 2004-05 | Tranmere R | 44 | 1 | | |
| 2005-06 | Tranmere R | 39 | 1 | 170 | 6 |
| 2006-07 | Rotherham U | 38 | 2 | | |
| 2007-08 | Rotherham U | 33 | 2 | | |
| 2008-09 | Rotherham U | 45 | 4 | | |
| 2009-10 | Rotherham U | 44 | 0 | | |
| 2010-11 | Shrewsbury T | 43 | 1 | | |
| 2011-12 | Shrewsbury T | 43 | 1 | 86 | 2 |
| 2012-13 | Rotherham U | 23 | 1 | 183 | 9 |
| 2012-13 | Burton Alb | 16 | 0 | 16 | 0 |

**STANTON, Nathan (D)** 439 1
H: 5 9 W: 12 06 b.Nottingham 6-5-81
*Source:* Trainee. *Honours:* England Youth.

| 1997-98 | Scunthorpe U | 1 | 0 | | |
|---|---|---|---|---|---|
| 1998-99 | Scunthorpe U | 4 | 0 | | |
| 1999-2000 | Scunthorpe U | 34 | 0 | | |
| 2000-01 | Scunthorpe U | 38 | 0 | | |
| 2001-02 | Scunthorpe U | 42 | 0 | | |
| 2002-03 | Scunthorpe U | 42 | 0 | | |
| 2003-04 | Scunthorpe U | 33 | 0 | | |
| 2004-05 | Scunthorpe U | 21 | 0 | | |
| 2005-06 | Scunthorpe U | 22 | 0 | 237 | 0 |
| 2006-07 | Rochdale | 35 | 0 | | |
| 2007-08 | Rochdale | 27 | 0 | | |
| 2008-09 | Rochdale | 39 | 0 | | |
| 2009-10 | Rochdale | 38 | 0 | 139 | 0 |

| | | | | | |
|---|---|---|---|---|---|
| 2010-11 | Burton Alb | 23 | 0 | | |
| 2011-12 | Burton Alb | 22 | 0 | | |
| 2012-13 | Burton Alb | 18 | 1 | 63 | 1 |

**TAYLOR, Cleveland (M)**    344   27
H: 5 8  W: 10 07  b.Leicester 9-9-83
*Source:* Scholar. *Honours:* Jamaica Youth.

| | | | | | |
|---|---|---|---|---|---|
| 2001-02 | Bolton W | 0 | 0 | | |
| 2002-03 | Bolton W | 0 | 0 | | |
| 2002-03 | *Exeter C* | 3 | 0 | 3 | 0 |
| 2003-04 | Bolton W | 0 | 0 | | |
| 2003-04 | Scunthorpe U | 20 | 3 | | |
| 2004-05 | Scunthorpe U | 44 | 6 | | |
| 2005-06 | Scunthorpe U | 45 | 3 | | |
| 2006-07 | Scunthorpe U | 45 | 3 | | |
| 2007-08 | Scunthorpe U | 20 | 0 | 174 | 15 |
| 2007-08 | Carlisle U | 18 | 0 | | |
| 2008-09 | Carlisle U | 42 | 3 | | |
| 2009-10 | Carlisle U | 1 | 0 | 61 | 3 |
| 2009-10 | Brentford | 12 | 1 | 12 | 1 |
| 2009-10 | *Burton Alb* | 24 | 4 | | |
| 2010-11 | St Johnstone | 21 | 1 | 21 | 1 |
| 2011-12 | Burton Alb | 31 | 2 | | |
| 2012-13 | Burton Alb | 18 | 1 | 73 | 7 |

**TOMLINSON, Stuart (G)**    119   0
H: 6 1  W: 11 02  b.Ellesmere Port 10-5-85
*Source:* Scholar.

| | | | | | |
|---|---|---|---|---|---|
| 2002-03 | Crewe Alex | 1 | 0 | | |
| 2003-04 | Crewe Alex | 1 | 0 | | |
| 2004-05 | Crewe Alex | 0 | 0 | | |
| 2005-06 | Crewe Alex | 2 | 0 | | |
| 2006-07 | Crewe Alex | 7 | 0 | | |
| 2007-08 | Crewe Alex | 0 | 0 | | |
| 2008-09 | Crewe Alex | 9 | 0 | | |
| 2009-10 | Crewe Alex | 0 | 0 | 20 | 0 |
| From Barrow. | | | | | |
| 2010-11 | Port Vale | 36 | 0 | | |
| From Barrow. | | | | | |
| 2011-12 | Port Vale | 38 | 0 | | |
| 2012-13 | Port Vale | 0 | 0 | 74 | 0 |
| 2012-13 | Burton Alb | 25 | 0 | 25 | 0 |

**WEBSTER, Aaron (D)**    110   18
H: 6 1  W: 12 00  b.Burton-on-Trent
19-12-80
*Source:* Youth.

| | | | | | |
|---|---|---|---|---|---|
| 2009-10 | Burton Alb | 24 | 4 | | |
| 2010-11 | Burton Alb | 42 | 11 | | |
| 2011-12 | Burton Alb | 35 | 3 | | |
| 2012-13 | Burton Alb | 9 | 0 | 110 | 18 |

**WEIR, Robbie (M)**    99   8
H: 5 9  W: 11 07  b.Belfast 9-12-88
*Source:* Scholar. *Honours:* Northern Ireland
Under-21, B.

| | | | | | |
|---|---|---|---|---|---|
| 2007-08 | Sunderland | 0 | 0 | | |
| 2008-09 | Sunderland | 0 | 0 | | |
| 2009-10 | Sunderland | 0 | 0 | | |
| 2010-11 | Sunderland | 0 | 0 | | |
| 2010-11 | *Tranmere R* | 18 | 0 | | |
| 2011-12 | Tranmere R | 39 | 3 | 57 | 3 |
| 2012-13 | Burton Alb | 42 | 5 | 42 | 5 |

**YUSSUF, Abdi (F)**    25   1
H: 6 1  W: 11 13  b.Zanzibar 3-10-92
*Source:* Scholar.

| | | | | | |
|---|---|---|---|---|---|
| 2010-11 | Leicester C | 0 | 0 | | |
| 2011-12 | Burton Alb | 17 | 1 | | |
| 2012-13 | Burton Alb | 8 | 0 | 25 | 1 |

**ZOLA, Calvin (F)**    273   68
H: 6 3  W: 14 06  b.Kinshasa 31-12-84
*Source:* Scholar.

| | | | | | |
|---|---|---|---|---|---|
| 2001-02 | Newcastle U | 0 | 0 | | |
| 2002-03 | Newcastle U | 0 | 0 | | |
| 2003-04 | Newcastle U | 0 | 0 | | |
| 2003-04 | *Oldham Ath* | 25 | 5 | 25 | 5 |
| 2004-05 | Tranmere R | 15 | 2 | | |
| 2005-06 | Tranmere R | 22 | 4 | | |
| 2006-07 | Tranmere R | 29 | 5 | | |
| 2007-08 | Tranmere R | 30 | 5 | 96 | 16 |
| 2008-09 | Crewe Alex | 27 | 5 | | |
| 2009-10 | Crewe Alex | 34 | 15 | | |
| 2010-11 | Crewe Alex | 6 | 1 | 67 | 21 |
| 2010-11 | *Burton Alb* | 18 | 3 | | |
| 2011-12 | Burton Alb | 36 | 12 | | |
| 2012-13 | Burton Alb | 31 | 11 | 85 | 26 |

**Scholars**
Austin, Harry Lewis; Cowdrill, Benjamin
Alan; Croucher, Samuel Michael Eric; Currie,
Isaac Konata; Didlick, Talon Noden; Doyle-
Charles, Joseph; Horton, Alex Thomas;
Markall, Ben; O'Mahoney, Kyle Haydn;
Palmer, Matthew Thomas; Patterson, Devarn;
Slade, Liam John; Stanley-Browne, Leandro
Jamaal; Yates, Shae Steven.

# BURY (20)

**BELFORD, Cameron (G)**    100   0
H: 6 1  W: 11 10  b.Nuneaton 16-10-88
*Source:* Coventry C Scholar.

| | | | | | |
|---|---|---|---|---|---|
| 2007-08 | Bury | 1 | 0 | | |
| 2008-09 | Bury | 1 | 0 | | |
| 2009-10 | Bury | 7 | 0 | | |
| 2010-11 | Bury | 39 | 0 | | |
| 2011-12 | Bury | 23 | 0 | | |
| 2011-12 | *Southend U* | 13 | 0 | | |
| 2012-13 | Bury | 7 | 0 | 78 | 0 |
| 2012-13 | *Southend U* | 4 | 0 | 17 | 0 |
| 2012-13 | *Accrington S* | 5 | 0 | 5 | 0 |

**BISHOP, Andy (F)**    292   79
H: 6 0  W: 10 10  b.Cannock 19-10-82
*Source:* Scholar.

| | | | | | |
|---|---|---|---|---|---|
| 2002-03 | Walsall | 3 | 0 | | |
| 2002-03 | *Kidderminster H* | 29 | 5 | | |
| 2003-04 | *Kidderminster H* | 11 | 2 | 40 | 7 |
| 2003-04 | *Rochdale* | 10 | 1 | 10 | 1 |
| 2003-04 | *Yeovil T* | 5 | 2 | 5 | 2 |
| From York C. | | | | | |
| 2006-07 | Bury | 43 | 15 | | |
| 2007-08 | Bury | 44 | 19 | | |
| 2008-09 | Bury | 42 | 16 | | |
| 2009-10 | Bury | 25 | 3 | | |
| 2010-11 | Bury | 19 | 4 | | |
| 2011-12 | Bury | 40 | 8 | | |
| 2012-13 | Bury | 24 | 4 | 237 | 69 |

**BYRNE, Shane (M)**    17   0
H: 5 10  W: 12 02  b.Dublin 25-4-93
*Source:* Scholar. *Honours:* Eire Youth.

| | | | | | |
|---|---|---|---|---|---|
| 2010-11 | Leicester C | 0 | 0 | | |
| 2011-12 | Leicester C | 0 | 0 | | |
| 2011-12 | *Bury* | 14 | 0 | | |
| 2012-13 | Bury | 3 | 0 | 17 | 0 |

**CAROLE, Sebastien (M)**    132   6
H: 5 7  W: 11 04  b.Pontoise 8-9-82
*Source:* Monaco.

| | | | | | |
|---|---|---|---|---|---|
| 2003-04 | West Ham U | 1 | 0 | 1 | 0 |
| 2004-05 | Chateauroux | 11 | 1 | 11 | 1 |
| 2005-06 | Brighton & HA | 40 | 2 | | |
| 2006-07 | Leeds U | 17 | 0 | | |
| 2007-08 | Leeds U | 28 | 3 | 45 | 3 |
| 2008-09 | Darlington | 6 | 0 | 6 | 0 |
| 2008-09 | Brighton & HA | 12 | 0 | | |
| 2009-10 | Tranmere R | 4 | 0 | 4 | 0 |
| 2009-10 | Brighton & HA | 9 | 0 | 61 | 2 |
| 2012-13 | Bury | 4 | 0 | 4 | 0 |

**CARRINGTON, Mark (M)**    121   9
H: 6 0  W: 11 00  b.Warrington 4-5-87
*Source:* Scholar.

| | | | | | |
|---|---|---|---|---|---|
| 2006-07 | Crewe Alex | 3 | 0 | | |
| 2007-08 | Crewe Alex | 9 | 0 | | |
| 2008-09 | Crewe Alex | 17 | 2 | 29 | 2 |
| 2009-10 | Milton Keynes D | 20 | 4 | | |
| 2010-11 | Milton Keynes D | 2 | 0 | 32 | 6 |
| 2010-11 | Hamilton A | 12 | 0 | 12 | 0 |
| 2011-12 | Bury | 21 | 1 | | |
| 2012-13 | Bury | 27 | 0 | 48 | 1 |

**CARSON, Trevor (G)**    91   0
H: 6 0  W: 14 11  b.Downpatrick 5-3-88
*Source:* Scholar. *Honours:* Northern Ireland
Youth, Under-21, B.

| | | | | | |
|---|---|---|---|---|---|
| 2004-05 | Sunderland | 0 | 0 | | |
| 2005-06 | Sunderland | 0 | 0 | | |
| 2006-07 | Sunderland | 0 | 0 | | |
| 2007-08 | Sunderland | 0 | 0 | | |
| 2008-09 | Sunderland | 0 | 0 | | |
| 2008-09 | *Chesterfield* | 18 | 0 | 18 | 0 |
| 2009-10 | Sunderland | 0 | 0 | | |
| 2010-11 | Sunderland | 0 | 0 | | |

| | | | | | |
|---|---|---|---|---|---|
| 2010-11 | *Lincoln C* | 16 | 0 | 16 | 0 |
| 2011-12 | *Brentford* | 1 | 0 | 1 | 0 |
| 2011-12 | Sunderland | 0 | 0 | | |
| 2011-12 | *Hull C* | 0 | 0 | | |
| 2011-12 | Bury | 17 | 0 | | |
| 2012-13 | Bury | 39 | 0 | 56 | 0 |

**FAGAN, Craig (F)**    291   47
H: 5 11  W: 11 11  b.Birmingham 11-12-82
*Source:* Scholar.

| | | | | | |
|---|---|---|---|---|---|
| 2001-02 | Birmingham C | 0 | 0 | | |
| 2002-03 | Birmingham C | 1 | 0 | | |
| 2002-03 | *Bristol C* | 6 | 1 | 6 | 1 |
| 2003-04 | Birmingham C | 0 | 0 | 1 | 0 |
| 2003-04 | Colchester U | 37 | 9 | | |
| 2004-05 | Colchester U | 26 | 8 | 63 | 17 |
| 2004-05 | Hull C | 12 | 4 | | |
| 2005-06 | Hull C | 41 | 5 | | |
| 2006-07 | Hull C | 27 | 6 | | |
| 2006-07 | Derby Co | 17 | 1 | | |
| 2007-08 | Derby Co | 22 | 0 | 39 | 1 |
| 2007-08 | *Hull C* | 8 | 0 | | |
| 2008-09 | Hull C | 22 | 3 | | |
| 2009-10 | Hull C | 25 | 2 | | |
| 2010-11 | Hull C | 5 | 0 | 140 | 20 |
| 2011-12 | Bradford C | 31 | 7 | 31 | 7 |
| 2012-13 | Bury | 11 | 1 | 11 | 1 |

**FUTCHER, Ben (D)**    322   21
H: 6 7  W: 12 05  b.Manchester 20-2-81
*Source:* Trainee.

| | | | | | |
|---|---|---|---|---|---|
| 1999-2000 | Oldham Ath | 5 | 0 | | |
| 2000-01 | Oldham Ath | 5 | 0 | | |
| 2001-02 | Oldham Ath | 0 | 0 | 10 | 0 |
| From Stalybridge C, Doncaster R | | | | | |
| 2002-03 | Lincoln C | 43 | 8 | | |
| 2003-04 | Lincoln C | 43 | 2 | | |
| 2004-05 | Lincoln C | 35 | 3 | 121 | 13 |
| 2005-06 | Boston U | 14 | 0 | 14 | 0 |
| 2005-06 | Grimsby T | 15 | 2 | | |
| 2006-07 | Grimsby T | 4 | 0 | 19 | 2 |
| 2006-07 | Peterborough U | 25 | 3 | 25 | 3 |
| 2007-08 | Bury | 40 | 0 | | |
| 2008-09 | Bury | 34 | 2 | | |
| 2009-10 | Bury | 32 | 0 | | |
| 2010-11 | Bury | 11 | 1 | | |
| 2010-11 | *Oxford U* | 6 | 0 | 6 | 0 |
| 2011-12 | Bury | 0 | 0 | | |
| 2011-12 | *Macclesfield T* | 10 | 0 | 10 | 0 |
| 2012-13 | Bury | 0 | 0 | 117 | 3 |

**HARRAD, Shaun (F)**    174   51
H: 5 10  W: 12 04  b.Nottingham 11-12-84
*Source:* Scholar.

| | | | | | |
|---|---|---|---|---|---|
| 2002-03 | Notts Co | 5 | 0 | | |
| 2003-04 | Notts Co | 8 | 0 | | |
| 2004-05 | Notts Co | 16 | 1 | 29 | 1 |
| 2009-10 | Burton Alb | 42 | 21 | | |
| 2010-11 | Burton Alb | 20 | 10 | 62 | 31 |
| 2010-11 | Northampton T | 18 | 6 | | |
| 2011-12 | Northampton T | 0 | 0 | 18 | 6 |
| 2011-12 | Bury | 26 | 2 | | |
| 2011-12 | *Rotherham U* | 8 | 3 | 8 | 3 |
| 2012-13 | Bury | 0 | 0 | 26 | 2 |
| 2012-13 | *Cheltenham T* | 31 | 8 | 31 | 8 |

**HEALY, David (F)**    378   91
H: 5 8  W: 10 08  b.Downpatrick 5-8-79
*Honours:* Northern Ireland Youth, Under-21,
95 full caps, 36 goals.

| | | | | | |
|---|---|---|---|---|---|
| 1999-2000 | Manchester U | 0 | 0 | | |
| 1999-2000 | *Port Vale* | 16 | 3 | 16 | 3 |
| 2000-01 | Manchester U | 1 | 0 | 1 | 0 |
| 2000-01 | Preston NE | 22 | 9 | | |
| 2001-02 | Preston NE | 44 | 10 | | |
| 2002-03 | Preston NE | 24 | 5 | | |
| 2002-03 | *Norwich C* | 13 | 2 | 13 | 2 |
| 2003-04 | Preston NE | 38 | 15 | | |
| 2004-05 | Preston NE | 11 | 5 | 139 | 44 |
| 2004-05 | Leeds U | 28 | 7 | | |
| 2005-06 | Leeds U | 42 | 12 | | |
| 2006-07 | Leeds U | 41 | 10 | 111 | 29 |
| 2007-08 | Fulham | 30 | 4 | 30 | 4 |
| 2008-09 | Sunderland | 10 | 1 | | |
| 2009-10 | Sunderland | 3 | 0 | | |
| 2009-10 | *Ipswich T* | 12 | 1 | 12 | 1 |
| 2010-11 | Sunderland | 0 | 0 | 13 | 1 |
| 2010-11 | *Doncaster R* | 8 | 2 | 8 | 2 |
| 2010-11 | Rangers | 8 | 1 | | |

| | | | | |
|---|---|---|---|---|
| 2011-12 | Rangers | 11 | 3 | 19 4 |
| 2012-13 | Bury | 16 | 1 | 16 1 |

**HOLDEN, Euan (D)** 1 0
H: 6 1  W: 12 11  b.Aberdeen 2-2-88
*Source:* Stockport Co.

| | | | | |
|---|---|---|---|---|
| 2012-13 | Bury | 1 | 0 | 1 0 |

**HUGHES, Mark (D)** 210 10
H: 6 1  W: 13 03  b.Liverpool 9-12-86
*Source:* Scholar.

| | | | | |
|---|---|---|---|---|
| 2004-05 | Everton | 0 | 0 | |
| 2005-06 | Everton | 0 | 0 | |
| 2005-06 | *Stockport Co* | 3 | 1 | 3 1 |
| 2006-07 | Everton | 1 | 0 | 1 0 |
| 2006-07 | Northampton T | 17 | 2 | |
| 2007-08 | Northampton T | 35 | 1 | |
| 2008-09 | Northampton T | 41 | 1 | 93 4 |
| 2009-10 | Walsall | 26 | 1 | 26 1 |
| 2010-11 | N Queensland F | 30 | 4 | 30 4 |
| 2011-12 | Bury | 25 | 0 | |
| 2012-13 | Bury | 27 | 0 | 52 0 |
| 2012-13 | *Accrington S* | 5 | 0 | 5 0 |

**JOHN-LEWIS, Lemell (M)** 155 17
H: 5 10  W: 11 10  b.Hammersmith 17-5-89
*Source:* Scholar.

| | | | | |
|---|---|---|---|---|
| 2006-07 | Lincoln C | 0 | 0 | |
| 2007-08 | Lincoln C | 21 | 3 | |
| 2008-09 | Lincoln C | 27 | 4 | |
| 2009-10 | Lincoln C | 24 | 1 | 72 8 |
| 2010-11 | Bury | 39 | 2 | |
| 2011-12 | Bury | 28 | 5 | |
| 2012-13 | Bury | 16 | 2 | 83 9 |

**JONES, Craig (M)** 134 27
H: 5 7  W: 10 13  b.Chester 20-3-87

| | | | | |
|---|---|---|---|---|
| 2004-05 | Airbus UK | 1 | 0 | |
| 2005-06 | Airbus UK | 7 | 6 | 9 8 |
| 2007-08 | Rhyl | 27 | 8 | |
| 2008-09 | Rhyl | 14 | 2 | 41 10 |
| 2008-09 | Connah's Quay | 12 | 0 | 12 0 |
| 2009-10 | New Saints FC | 26 | 7 | 26 7 |
| 2010-11 | Port Talbot | 4 | 0 | |
| 2011-12 | Port Talbot | 7 | 0 | 21 1 |
| 2012-13 | Bury | 25 | 1 | 25 1 |

**LOCKWOOD, Adam (D)** 250 16
H: 6 0  W: 12 07  b.Wakefield 26-10-81
*Source:* Reading Trainee.

| | | | | |
|---|---|---|---|---|
| 2003-04 | Yeovil T | 43 | 4 | |
| 2004-05 | Yeovil T | 10 | 0 | |
| 2005-06 | Yeovil T | 20 | 0 | 73 4 |
| 2005-06 | *Torquay U* | 9 | 3 | 9 3 |
| 2006-07 | Doncaster R | 44 | 2 | |
| 2007-08 | Doncaster R | 39 | 3 | |
| 2008-09 | Doncaster R | 22 | 0 | |
| 2009-10 | Doncaster R | 16 | 2 | |
| 2010-11 | Doncaster R | 16 | 1 | |
| 2011-12 | Doncaster R | 14 | 0 | 151 8 |
| 2012-13 | Bury | 17 | 1 | 17 1 |

**MARSHALL, Marcus (F)** 96 5
H: 5 10  W: 11 06  b.Hammersmith 7-10-89
*Source:* Scholar.

| | | | | |
|---|---|---|---|---|
| 2007-08 | Blackburn R | 0 | 0 | |
| 2008-09 | Blackburn R | 0 | 0 | |
| 2009-10 | Blackburn R | 0 | 0 | |
| 2009-10 | *Rotherham U* | 22 | 0 | |
| 2010-11 | Rotherham U | 36 | 3 | |
| 2011-12 | Rotherham U | 14 | 1 | 73 4 |
| 2011-12 | *Macclesfield T* | 14 | 1 | 14 1 |
| 2012-13 | Bury | 9 | 0 | 9 0 |

**MEZAGUE, Valery (M)** 197 22
H: 6 0  W: 11 12  b.Marseille 8-12-83

| | | | | |
|---|---|---|---|---|
| 2001-02 | Montpellier | 5 | 0 | |
| 2002-03 | Montpellier | 26 | 6 | |
| 2003-04 | Montpellier | 13 | 1 | |
| 2004-05 | Portsmouth | 11 | 0 | 11 0 |
| 2005-06 | Montpellier | 8 | 3 | 52 10 |
| 2005-06 | Sochaux | 16 | 0 | |
| 2006-07 | Sochaux | 9 | 0 | |
| 2007-08 | Le Havre | 28 | 4 | 28 4 |
| 2008-09 | Sochaux | 9 | 0 | 34 0 |
| 2008-09 | Chateauroux | 16 | 3 | 16 3 |
| 2009-10 | Vannes OC | 32 | 4 | |
| 2010-11 | Vannes OC | 14 | 1 | 46 5 |
| 2011-12 | Panetolikos | 3 | 0 | 3 0 |
| 2012-13 | Bury | 7 | 0 | 7 0 |

**PICKEN, Phil (D)** 239 2
H: 5 9  W: 10 07  b.Droylsden 12-11-85
*Source:* Scholar.

| | | | | |
|---|---|---|---|---|
| 2004-05 | Manchester U | 0 | 0 | |
| 2005-06 | Manchester U | 0 | 0 | |
| 2005-06 | *Chesterfield* | 32 | 1 | |
| 2006-07 | Chesterfield | 39 | 1 | |
| 2007-08 | Chesterfield | 37 | 0 | |
| 2008-09 | Chesterfield | 11 | 0 | |
| 2008-09 | *Notts Co* | 22 | 0 | 22 0 |
| 2009-10 | Chesterfield | 21 | 0 | 140 2 |
| 2010-11 | Bury | 38 | 0 | |
| 2011-12 | Bury | 37 | 0 | |
| 2012-13 | Bury | 2 | 0 | 77 0 |

**PRATT, Tom (F)** 2 0
H: 5 10  W: 11 08  b.Manchester 3-6-95

| | | | | |
|---|---|---|---|---|
| 2012-13 | Bury | 2 | 0 | 2 0 |

**REGAN, Carl (D)** 310 3
H: 5 11  W: 11 12  b.Liverpool 14-1-80
*Source:* Trainee. *Honours:* England Youth.

| | | | | |
|---|---|---|---|---|
| 1997-98 | Everton | 0 | 0 | |
| 1998-99 | Everton | 0 | 0 | |
| 1999-2000 | Everton | 0 | 0 | |
| 2000-01 | Barnsley | 27 | 0 | |
| 2001-02 | Barnsley | 10 | 0 | |
| 2002-03 | Barnsley | 0 | 0 | 37 0 |
| 2002-03 | Hull C | 38 | 0 | |
| 2003-04 | Hull C | 0 | 0 | 38 0 |

From Droylsden.

| | | | | |
|---|---|---|---|---|
| 2004-05 | Chester C | 6 | 0 | |
| 2005-06 | Chester C | 41 | 0 | 47 0 |
| 2006-07 | Macclesfield T | 38 | 2 | |
| 2007-08 | Macclesfield T | 20 | 0 | 58 2 |
| 2007-08 | Milton Keynes D | 9 | 1 | |
| 2008-09 | Milton Keynes D | 27 | 0 | 36 1 |
| 2009-10 | Bristol R | 35 | 0 | |
| 2010-11 | Bristol R | 21 | 0 | 56 0 |
| 2010-11 | Notts Co | 4 | 0 | |
| 2011-12 | Shrewsbury T | 13 | 0 | 13 0 |
| 2012-13 | Notts Co | 11 | 0 | 15 0 |
| 2012-13 | Bury | 10 | 0 | 10 0 |

**SCHUMACHER, Steven (M)** 308 43
H: 5 10  W: 11 00  b.Liverpool 30-4-84
*Source:* Scholar. *Honours:* England Youth.

| | | | | |
|---|---|---|---|---|
| 2000-01 | Everton | 0 | 0 | |
| 2001-02 | Everton | 0 | 0 | |
| 2002-03 | Everton | 0 | 0 | |
| 2003-04 | Everton | 0 | 0 | |
| 2003-04 | *Carlisle U* | 4 | 0 | 4 0 |
| 2004-05 | Bradford C | 43 | 6 | |
| 2005-06 | Bradford C | 30 | 1 | |
| 2006-07 | Bradford C | 44 | 6 | 117 13 |
| 2007-08 | Crewe Alex | 26 | 1 | |
| 2008-09 | Crewe Alex | 15 | 2 | |
| 2009-10 | Crewe Alex | 32 | 4 | 73 7 |
| 2010-11 | Bury | 43 | 9 | |
| 2011-12 | Bury | 32 | 6 | |
| 2012-13 | Bury | 39 | 8 | 114 23 |

**SOARES, Tom (M)** 225 18
H: 6 0  W: 11 04  b.Reading 10-7-86
*Source:* Scholar. *Honours:* England Youth, Under-20, Under-21.

| | | | | |
|---|---|---|---|---|
| 2003-04 | Crystal Palace | 3 | 0 | |
| 2004-05 | Crystal Palace | 44 | 0 | |
| 2005-06 | Crystal Palace | 44 | 1 | |
| 2006-07 | Crystal Palace | 37 | 3 | |
| 2007-08 | Crystal Palace | 39 | 6 | |
| 2008-09 | Crystal Palace | 4 | 1 | 149 11 |
| 2008-09 | Stoke C | 7 | 0 | |
| 2008-09 | *Charlton Ath* | 11 | 1 | 11 1 |
| 2009-10 | Stoke C | 0 | 0 | |
| 2009-10 | *Sheffield W* | 25 | 2 | 25 2 |
| 2010-11 | Stoke C | 0 | 0 | |
| 2011-12 | Stoke C | 0 | 0 | 7 0 |
| 2011-12 | *Hibernian* | 10 | 2 | 10 2 |
| 2012-13 | Bury | 23 | 2 | 23 2 |

**SODJE, Efe (D)** 531 35
H: 6 1  W: 12 00  b.Greenwich 5-10-72
*Source:* Delta Steel Pioneer, Stevenage Bor.
*Honours:* Nigeria 9 full caps, 1 goal.

| | | | | |
|---|---|---|---|---|
| 1997-98 | Macclesfield T | 41 | 3 | |
| 1998-99 | Macclesfield T | 42 | 3 | 83 6 |
| 1999-2000 | Luton T | 9 | 0 | 9 0 |
| 1999-2000 | Colchester U | 3 | 0 | 3 0 |
| 2000-01 | Crewe Alex | 32 | 0 | |
| 2001-02 | Crewe Alex | 36 | 2 | |
| 2002-03 | Crewe Alex | 30 | 1 | 98 3 |
| 2003-04 | Huddersfield T | 39 | 4 | |
| 2004-05 | Huddersfield T | 28 | 1 | 67 5 |
| 2004-05 | Yeovil T | 6 | 2 | |
| 2005-06 | Yeovil T | 19 | 1 | 25 3 |
| 2005-06 | Southend U | 13 | 1 | |
| 2006-07 | Southend U | 24 | 1 | 37 2 |
| 2007-08 | Gillingham | 13 | 0 | 13 0 |
| 2007-08 | *Bury* | 16 | 1 | |
| 2008-09 | Bury | 41 | 7 | |
| 2009-10 | Bury | 39 | 2 | |
| 2010-11 | Bury | 40 | 3 | |
| 2011-12 | Bury | 41 | 2 | |
| 2012-13 | Bury | 19 | 1 | 196 16 |

**WORRALL, David (M)** 176 11
H: 6 0  W: 11 03  b.Manchester 12-6-90
*Source:* Scholar.

| | | | | |
|---|---|---|---|---|
| 2006-07 | Bury | 1 | 0 | |
| 2007-08 | Bury | 0 | 0 | |
| 2007-08 | WBA | 0 | 0 | |
| 2008-09 | *Accrington S* | 4 | 0 | 4 0 |
| 2008-09 | *Shrewsbury T* | 9 | 0 | 9 0 |
| 2009-10 | WBA | 0 | 0 | |
| 2009-10 | Bury | 40 | 4 | |
| 2010-11 | Bury | 40 | 2 | |
| 2011-12 | Bury | 41 | 3 | |
| 2012-13 | Bury | 41 | 2 | 163 11 |

**Scholars**
Beastall, Luke Graham; Bickett, Liam Matthew; Clarke, Levi Thomas; Cliffe, Jake Oliver; Cook, Matthew John Barton; Dickinson, Samuel Jack; Keane, Connor Owen; Kennedy, Luis Jordan; Nasseri, Navid; Pratt, Thomas Ryan; Prickett, Matthew John; Rouine, Thomas Elliot; Thornton, Joseph Luke; Toth, Tommy Lee; Walker, Regan Craig; Willis, Connor Nathan.

# CARDIFF C (21)

**BELLAMY, Craig (F)** 436 133
H: 5 9  W: 10 12  b.Cardiff 13-7-79
*Source:* Trainee. *Honours:* Wales Schools, Youth, Under-21, 73 full caps, 19 goals.

| | | | | |
|---|---|---|---|---|
| 1996-97 | Norwich C | 3 | 0 | |
| 1997-98 | Norwich C | 36 | 13 | |
| 1998-99 | Norwich C | 40 | 17 | |
| 1999-2000 | Norwich C | 4 | 2 | |
| 2000-01 | Norwich C | 1 | 0 | 84 32 |
| 2000-01 | Coventry C | 34 | 6 | 34 6 |
| 2001-02 | Newcastle U | 27 | 9 | |
| 2002-03 | Newcastle U | 29 | 7 | |
| 2003-04 | Newcastle U | 16 | 4 | |
| 2004-05 | Newcastle U | 21 | 7 | 93 27 |
| 2004-05 | *Celtic* | 12 | 7 | 12 7 |
| 2005-06 | Blackburn R | 27 | 13 | 27 13 |
| 2006-07 | Liverpool | 27 | 7 | |
| 2007-08 | West Ham U | 8 | 2 | |
| 2008-09 | West Ham U | 16 | 5 | 24 7 |
| 2008-09 | Manchester C | 8 | 3 | |
| 2009-10 | Manchester C | 32 | 10 | |
| 2010-11 | Manchester C | 0 | 0 | |
| 2010-11 | *Cardiff C* | 35 | 11 | |
| 2011-12 | Manchester C | 0 | 0 | 40 13 |
| 2011-12 | Liverpool | 27 | 6 | |
| 2012-13 | Liverpool | 0 | 0 | 54 13 |
| 2012-13 | Cardiff C | 33 | 4 | 68 15 |

**CAMPBELL, Frazier (F)** 116 29
H: 5 11  W: 12 04  b.Huddersfield 13-9-87
*Source:* Scholar. *Honours:* England Youth, Under-21, 1 full cap.

| | | | | |
|---|---|---|---|---|
| 2005-06 | Manchester U | 0 | 0 | |
| 2006-07 | Manchester U | 0 | 0 | |
| 2007-08 | Manchester U | 1 | 0 | |
| 2007-08 | *Hull C* | 34 | 15 | 34 15 |
| 2008-09 | Manchester U | 1 | 0 | |
| 2008-09 | *Tottenham H* | 10 | 1 | 10 1 |
| 2009-10 | Manchester U | 0 | 0 | 2 0 |
| 2009-10 | Sunderland | 31 | 4 | |
| 2010-11 | Sunderland | 3 | 0 | |
| 2011-12 | Sunderland | 12 | 1 | |
| 2012-13 | Sunderland | 12 | 1 | 58 6 |
| 2012-13 | Cardiff C | 12 | 7 | 12 7 |

**CONNOLLY, Matthew (D)** 179 10
H: 6 1  W: 11 03  b.Barnet 24-9-87
*Source:* Scholar. *Honours:* England Youth.

|  |  | | | | |
|---|---|---|---|---|---|
| 2005-06 | Arsenal | 0 | 0 | | |
| 2006-07 | Arsenal | 0 | 0 | | |
| 2006-07 | *Bournemouth* | 5 | 1 | 5 | 1 |
| 2007-08 | Arsenal | 0 | 0 | | |
| 2007-08 | *Colchester U* | 16 | 2 | 16 | 2 |
| 2007-08 | QPR | 20 | 0 | | |
| 2008-09 | QPR | 35 | 0 | | |
| 2009-10 | QPR | 19 | 2 | | |
| 2010-11 | QPR | 36 | 0 | | |
| 2011-12 | QPR | 6 | 0 | | |
| 2011-12 | *Reading* | 6 | 0 | 6 | 0 |
| 2012-13 | QPR | 0 | 0 | 116 | 2 |
| 2012-13 | Cardiff C | 36 | 5 | 36 | 5 |

**CONWAY, Craig (M)** 255 25
H: 5 7  W: 10 07  b.Irvine 2-5-85
*Honours:* Scotland 4 full caps.

|  |  | | | | |
|---|---|---|---|---|---|
| 2002-03 | Ayr U | 1 | 0 | | |
| 2003-04 | Ayr U | 6 | 0 | | |
| 2004-05 | Ayr U | 23 | 3 | | |
| 2005-06 | Ayr U | 31 | 4 | 61 | 7 |
| 2006-07 | Dundee U | 30 | 0 | | |
| 2007-08 | Dundee U | 15 | 1 | | |
| 2008-09 | Dundee U | 36 | 5 | | |
| 2009-10 | Dundee U | 33 | 4 | | |
| 2010-11 | Dundee U | 22 | 3 | 136 | 13 |
| 2011-12 | Cardiff C | 31 | 3 | | |
| 2012-13 | Cardiff C | 27 | 2 | 58 | 5 |

**COULSON, Luke (D)** 0 0
H: 5 10  W: 11 01  b.St Helens 6-3-94

|  |  | | |
|---|---|---|---|
| 2012-13 | Cardiff C | 0 | 0 |

**COWIE, Don (M)** 381 44
H: 5 5  W: 8 05  b.Inverness 15-2-83
*Honours:* Scotland 10 full caps.

|  |  | | | | |
|---|---|---|---|---|---|
| 2000-01 | Ross Co | 1 | 0 | | |
| 2001-02 | Ross Co | 18 | 0 | | |
| 2002-03 | Ross Co | 30 | 1 | | |
| 2003-04 | Ross Co | 23 | 0 | | |
| 2004-05 | Ross Co | 34 | 5 | | |
| 2005-06 | Ross Co | 32 | 4 | | |
| 2006-07 | Ross Co | 28 | 7 | 166 | 17 |
| 2007-08 | Inverness CT | 37 | 9 | | |
| 2008-09 | Inverness CT | 22 | 3 | 59 | 12 |
| 2008-09 | Watford | 10 | 3 | | |
| 2009-10 | Watford | 41 | 2 | | |
| 2010-11 | Watford | 37 | 4 | 88 | 9 |
| 2011-12 | Cardiff C | 43 | 4 | | |
| 2012-13 | Cardiff C | 25 | 2 | 68 | 6 |

**GESTEDE, Rudy (F)** 93 15
H: 6 4  W: 13 07  b.Nancy 10-10-88
*Honours:* France Youth.

|  |  | | | | |
|---|---|---|---|---|---|
| 2008-09 | Metz | 5 | 0 | | |
| 2009-10 | Cannes | 22 | 4 | 22 | 4 |
| 2010-11 | Metz | 11 | 3 | 16 | 3 |
| 2010-11 | Metz B | 3 | 1 | 3 | 1 |
| 2011-12 | Cardiff C | 25 | 2 | | |
| 2012-13 | Cardiff C | 27 | 5 | 52 | 7 |

**GUNNARSSON, Aron (M)** 210 19
H: 5 9  W: 11 00  b.Akureyri 22-9-89
*Honours:* Iceland Youth, Under-21, 32 full caps.

|  |  | | | | |
|---|---|---|---|---|---|
| 2007-08 | AZ | 1 | 0 | 1 | 0 |
| 2008-09 | Coventry C | 40 | 1 | | |
| 2009-10 | Coventry C | 40 | 1 | | |
| 2010-11 | Coventry C | 42 | 4 | 122 | 6 |
| 2011-12 | Cardiff C | 42 | 5 | | |
| 2012-13 | Cardiff C | 45 | 8 | 87 | 13 |

**HARRIS, Kedeem (M)** 19 0
H: 5 9  W: 10 08  b.Westminster 8-6-93
*Source:* Scholar.

|  |  | | | | |
|---|---|---|---|---|---|
| 2009-10 | Wycombe W | 2 | 0 | | |
| 2010-11 | Wycombe W | 0 | 0 | | |
| 2011-12 | Wycombe W | 17 | 0 | 19 | 0 |
| 2011-12 | Cardiff C | 0 | 0 | | |
| 2012-13 | Cardiff C | 0 | 0 | | |

**HAWKINS, Ronnie (M)** 0 0

|  |  | | |
|---|---|---|---|
| 2012-13 | Cardiff C | 0 | 0 |

**HEALEY, Rhys (M)** 0 0

|  |  | | |
|---|---|---|---|
| 2012-13 | Cardiff C | 0 | 0 |

**HELGUSON, Heidar (F)** 424 133
H: 5 10  W: 12 09  b.Akureyri 22-8-77
*Source:* Throttur. *Honours:* Iceland Youth, Under-21, 55 full caps, 12 goals.

|  |  | | | | |
|---|---|---|---|---|---|
| 1998 | Lillestrom | 19 | 2 | | |
| 1999 | Lillestrom | 25 | 16 | 44 | 18 |
| 1999-2000 | Watford | 16 | 6 | | |
| 2000-01 | Watford | 33 | 8 | | |
| 2001-02 | Watford | 34 | 6 | | |
| 2002-03 | Watford | 30 | 11 | | |
| 2003-04 | Watford | 22 | 8 | | |
| 2004-05 | Watford | 39 | 16 | | |
| 2005-06 | Fulham | 27 | 8 | | |
| 2006-07 | Fulham | 30 | 4 | 57 | 12 |
| 2007-08 | Bolton W | 6 | 2 | | |
| 2008-09 | Bolton W | 1 | 0 | 7 | 2 |
| 2008-09 | QPR | 20 | 5 | | |
| 2009-10 | QPR | 5 | 1 | | |
| 2009-10 | *Watford* | 29 | 11 | 203 | 66 |
| 2010-11 | QPR | 34 | 13 | | |
| 2011-12 | QPR | 16 | 8 | | |
| 2012-13 | QPR | 0 | 0 | 75 | 27 |
| 2012-13 | Cardiff C | 38 | 8 | 38 | 8 |

**HUDSON, Mark (D)** 317 21
H: 6 1  W: 12 01  b.Guildford 30-3-82
*Source:* Trainee.

|  |  | | | | |
|---|---|---|---|---|---|
| 1998-99 | Fulham | 0 | 0 | | |
| 1999-2000 | Fulham | 0 | 0 | | |
| 2000-01 | Fulham | 0 | 0 | | |
| 2001-02 | Fulham | 0 | 0 | | |
| 2002-03 | Fulham | 0 | 0 | | |
| 2003-04 | Fulham | 0 | 0 | | |
| 2003-04 | *Oldham Ath* | 15 | 0 | 15 | 0 |
| 2003-04 | *Crystal Palace* | 14 | 0 | | |
| 2004-05 | Crystal Palace | 7 | 1 | | |
| 2005-06 | Crystal Palace | 15 | 0 | | |
| 2006-07 | Crystal Palace | 39 | 4 | | |
| 2007-08 | Crystal Palace | 45 | 2 | 120 | 7 |
| 2008-09 | Charlton Ath | 43 | 3 | 43 | 3 |
| 2009-10 | Cardiff C | 27 | 2 | | |
| 2010-11 | Cardiff C | 40 | 0 | | |
| 2011-12 | Cardiff C | 39 | 5 | | |
| 2012-13 | Cardiff C | 33 | 4 | 139 | 11 |

**JOHN, Declan (M)** 6 0
H: 5 10  W: 11 10  b.Merthyr Tydfil 30-6-95

|  |  | | | | |
|---|---|---|---|---|---|
| 2010-11 | Llanelli | 1 | 0 | 1 | 0 |
| 2011-12 | Afan Lido | 5 | 0 | 5 | 0 |
| 2012-13 | Cardiff C | 0 | 0 | | |

**KIM, Bo-Kyung (M)** 96 25
H: 5 10  W: 11 06  b.Oita 6-10-89
*Honours:* South Korea Youth, 17 full caps, 2 goals.

|  |  | | | | |
|---|---|---|---|---|---|
| 2010 | Oita Trinita | 27 | 8 | 27 | 8 |
| 2011 | Cerezo Osaka | 26 | 8 | | |
| 2012 | Cerezo Osaka | 15 | 7 | 41 | 15 |
| 2012-13 | Cardiff C | 28 | 2 | 28 | 2 |

**KISS, Filip (M)** 83 11
H: 6 1  W: 11 11  b.Dunajska 13-10-90
*Honours:* Slovakia Youth, Under-21.

|  |  | | | | |
|---|---|---|---|---|---|
| 2009-10 | Petrzalka | 25 | 4 | 25 | 4 |
| 2010-11 | Slovan Bratislava | 29 | 6 | | |
| 2011-12 | Slovan Bratislava | 1 | 0 | 30 | 6 |
| 2011-12 | *Cardiff C* | 26 | 1 | | |
| 2012-13 | Cardiff C | 2 | 0 | 28 | 1 |

**LAPPIN, Simon (M)** 277 13
H: 5 11  W: 9 06  b.Glasgow 25-1-83
*Honours:* Scotland Under-21.

|  |  | | | | |
|---|---|---|---|---|---|
| 2001-02 | St Mirren | 1 | 0 | | |
| 2002-03 | St Mirren | 34 | 0 | | |
| 2003-04 | St Mirren | 24 | 4 | | |
| 2004-05 | St Mirren | 34 | 1 | | |
| 2005-06 | St Mirren | 35 | 3 | | |
| 2006-07 | St Mirren | 24 | 1 | 152 | 9 |
| 2007-08 | Norwich C | 14 | 1 | | |
| 2007-08 | *Motherwell* | 14 | 2 | 14 | 2 |
| 2007-08 | Norwich C | 15 | 1 | | |
| 2008-09 | Norwich C | 5 | 0 | | |
| 2009-10 | Norwich C | 44 | 0 | | |
| 2010-11 | Norwich C | 27 | 0 | | |
| 2011-12 | Norwich C | 4 | 0 | | |
| 2012-13 | Norwich C | 0 | 0 | 109 | 2 |
| 2012-13 | Cardiff C | 2 | 0 | 2 | 0 |

**LEWIS, Joe (G)** 191 0
H: 6 5  W: 12 10  b.Bungay 6-10-87
*Source:* Scholar. *Honours:* England Youth, Under-21.

|  |  | | | | |
|---|---|---|---|---|---|
| 2004-05 | Norwich C | 0 | 0 | | |
| 2005-06 | Norwich C | 0 | 0 | | |
| 2006-07 | Norwich C | 0 | 0 | | |
| 2006-07 | *Stockport Co* | 5 | 0 | 5 | 0 |
| 2007-08 | Norwich C | 0 | 0 | | |
| 2007-08 | *Morecambe* | 19 | 0 | 19 | 0 |
| 2007-08 | Peterborough U | 22 | 0 | | |
| 2008-09 | Peterborough U | 46 | 0 | | |
| 2009-10 | Peterborough U | 43 | 0 | | |
| 2010-11 | Peterborough U | 45 | 0 | | |
| 2011-12 | Peterborough U | 11 | 0 | 167 | 0 |
| 2012-13 | Cardiff C | 0 | 0 | | |

**MARSHALL, David (G)** 274 0
H: 6 3  W: 13 04  b.Glasgow 5-3-85
*Source:* Celtic Youth. *Honours:* Scotland Youth, Under-21, B, 6 full caps.

|  |  | | | | |
|---|---|---|---|---|---|
| 2003-04 | Celtic | 11 | 0 | | |
| 2004-05 | Celtic | 18 | 0 | | |
| 2005-06 | Celtic | 4 | 0 | | |
| 2006-07 | Celtic | 2 | 0 | 35 | 0 |
| 2006-07 | Norwich C | 2 | 0 | | |
| 2007-08 | Norwich C | 46 | 0 | | |
| 2008-09 | Norwich C | 46 | 0 | 94 | 0 |
| 2008-09 | Cardiff C | 0 | 0 | | |
| 2009-10 | Cardiff C | 43 | 0 | | |
| 2010-11 | Cardiff C | 11 | 0 | | |
| 2011-12 | Cardiff C | 45 | 0 | | |
| 2012-13 | Cardiff C | 46 | 0 | 145 | 0 |

**MASON, Joe (F)** 120 25
H: 5 9  W: 11 11  b.Plymouth 13-5-91
*Honours:* Eire Youth, Under-21.

|  |  | | | | |
|---|---|---|---|---|---|
| 2009-10 | Plymouth Arg | 19 | 3 | | |
| 2010-11 | Plymouth Arg | 34 | 7 | 53 | 10 |
| 2011-12 | Cardiff C | 39 | 9 | | |
| 2012-13 | Cardiff C | 28 | 6 | 67 | 15 |

**MATHURIN-HARRIS, Kadeem (M)** 0 0

|  |  | | |
|---|---|---|---|
| 2012-13 | Cardiff C | 0 | 0 |

**MAYNARD, Nicky (F)** 202 79
H: 5 11  W: 11 00  b.Winsford 11-12-86
*Source:* Scholar.

|  |  | | | | |
|---|---|---|---|---|---|
| 2005-06 | Crewe Alex | 1 | 1 | | |
| 2006-07 | Crewe Alex | 31 | 16 | | |
| 2007-08 | Crewe Alex | 27 | 14 | 59 | 31 |
| 2008-09 | Bristol C | 43 | 11 | | |
| 2009-10 | Bristol C | 42 | 20 | | |
| 2010-11 | Bristol C | 13 | 6 | | |
| 2011-12 | Bristol C | 27 | 8 | 125 | 45 |
| 2011-12 | West Ham U | 14 | 2 | | |
| 2012-13 | West Ham U | 0 | 0 | 14 | 2 |
| 2012-13 | Cardiff C | 4 | 1 | 4 | 1 |

**McNAUGHTON, Kevin (D)** 425 4
H: 5 10  W: 10 06  b.Dundee 28-8-82
*Honours:* Scotland Under-21, 4 full caps.

|  |  | | | | |
|---|---|---|---|---|---|
| 1999-2000 | Aberdeen | 0 | 0 | | |
| 2000-01 | Aberdeen | 33 | 0 | | |
| 2001-02 | Aberdeen | 34 | 0 | | |
| 2002-03 | Aberdeen | 22 | 1 | | |
| 2003-04 | Aberdeen | 17 | 0 | | |
| 2004-05 | Aberdeen | 35 | 2 | | |
| 2005-06 | Aberdeen | 34 | 0 | 175 | 3 |
| 2006-07 | Cardiff C | 42 | 0 | | |
| 2007-08 | Cardiff C | 35 | 1 | | |
| 2008-09 | Cardiff C | 39 | 0 | | |
| 2009-10 | Cardiff C | 21 | 0 | | |
| 2010-11 | Cardiff C | 44 | 0 | | |
| 2011-12 | Cardiff C | 42 | 0 | | |
| 2012-13 | Cardiff C | 27 | 0 | 250 | 1 |

**McPHAIL, Stephen (M)** 351 10
H: 5 8  W: 11 04  b.Westminster 9-12-79
*Source:* Trainee. *Honours:* Eire Youth, B, Under-21, 10 full caps, 1 goal.

|  |  | | | | |
|---|---|---|---|---|---|
| 1996-97 | Leeds U | 0 | 0 | | |
| 1997-98 | Leeds U | 4 | 0 | | |
| 1998-99 | Leeds U | 17 | 0 | | |
| 1999-2000 | Leeds U | 24 | 2 | | |
| 2000-01 | Leeds U | 7 | 0 | | |
| 2001-02 | Leeds U | 1 | 0 | | |
| 2001-02 | *Millwall* | 3 | 0 | 3 | 0 |
| 2002-03 | Leeds U | 13 | 0 | | |

| | | | | | |
|---|---|---|---|---|---|
| 2003-04 | Leeds U | 12 | 1 | 78 | 3 |
| 2003-04 | *Nottingham F* | 14 | 0 | 14 | 0 |
| 2004-05 | Barnsley | 36 | 2 | | |
| 2005-06 | Barnsley | 34 | 2 | 70 | 4 |
| 2006-07 | Cardiff C | 43 | 0 | | |
| 2007-08 | Cardiff C | 43 | 3 | | |
| 2008-09 | Cardiff C | 32 | 0 | | |
| 2009-10 | Cardiff C | 21 | 0 | | |
| 2010-11 | Cardiff C | 28 | 0 | | |
| 2011-12 | Cardiff C | 19 | 0 | | |
| 2012-13 | Cardiff C | 0 | 0 | 186 | 3 |

**MUTCH, Jordon (M)** 89 9
H: 5 9  W: 10 03  b.Derby 2-12-91
*Source:* Scholar. *Honours:* England Youth, Under-21.

| | | | | | |
|---|---|---|---|---|---|
| 2007-08 | Birmingham C | 0 | 0 | | |
| 2008-09 | Birmingham C | 0 | 0 | | |
| 2009-10 | Birmingham C | 0 | 0 | | |
| 2009-10 | *Hereford U* | 3 | 0 | 3 | 0 |
| 2009-10 | *Doncaster R* | 17 | 2 | 17 | 2 |
| 2010-11 | Birmingham C | 3 | 0 | | |
| 2010-11 | *Watford* | 23 | 5 | 23 | 5 |
| 2011-12 | Birmingham C | 21 | 2 | 24 | 2 |
| 2012-13 | Cardiff C | 22 | 0 | 22 | 0 |

**NOONE, Craig (M)** 153 18
H: 6 3  W: 12 07  b.Kirkby 17-11-87
*Source:* Skelmersdale U, Burscough, Southport.

| | | | | | |
|---|---|---|---|---|---|
| 2008-09 | Plymouth Arg | 21 | 1 | | |
| 2009-10 | Plymouth Arg | 17 | 1 | | |
| 2009-10 | *Exeter C* | 7 | 2 | 7 | 2 |
| 2010-11 | Plymouth Arg | 17 | 3 | 55 | 5 |
| 2010-11 | Brighton & HA | 23 | 2 | | |
| 2011-12 | Brighton & HA | 33 | 2 | | |
| 2012-13 | Brighton & HA | 3 | 0 | 59 | 4 |
| 2012-13 | Cardiff C | 32 | 7 | 32 | 7 |

**NUGENT, Ben (D)** 12 1
H: 6 1  W: 13 00  b.Street 28-11-93

| | | | | | |
|---|---|---|---|---|---|
| 2012-13 | Cardiff C | 12 | 1 | 12 | 1 |

**OSHILAJA, Adedeji (D)** 0 0
H: 5 11  W: 11 10  b.Bermondsey 16-7-93

| | | | |
|---|---|---|---|
| 2012-13 | Cardiff C | 0 | 0 |

**PARISH, Elliot (G)** 11 0
H: 6 2  W: 13 00  b.Towcester 20-5-90
*Source:* Scholar. *Honours:* England Youth, Under-20.

| | | | | | |
|---|---|---|---|---|---|
| 2008-09 | Aston Villa | 0 | 0 | | |
| 2009-10 | Aston Villa | 0 | 0 | | |
| 2010-11 | Aston Villa | 0 | 0 | | |
| 2010-11 | *Lincoln C* | 9 | 0 | 9 | 0 |
| 2011-12 | Aston Villa | 0 | 0 | | |
| 2011-12 | Cardiff C | 0 | 0 | | |
| 2012-13 | *Wycombe W* | 2 | 0 | 2 | 0 |
| 2012-13 | Cardiff C | 0 | 0 | | |

**RALLS, Joe (M)** 14 1
H: 5 10  W: 11 00  b.Farnborough 13-10-93
*Source:* Scholar. *Honours:* England Youth.

| | | | | | |
|---|---|---|---|---|---|
| 2011-12 | Cardiff C | 10 | 1 | | |
| 2012-13 | Cardiff C | 4 | 0 | 14 | 1 |

**SMITH, Tommy (F)** 491 94
H: 5 8  W: 11 04  b.Hemel Hempstead 22-5-80
*Source:* Trainee. *Honours:* England Youth, Under-21.

| | | | | | |
|---|---|---|---|---|---|
| 1997-98 | Watford | 1 | 0 | | |
| 1998-99 | Watford | 8 | 2 | | |
| 1999-2000 | Watford | 22 | 2 | | |
| 2000-01 | Watford | 43 | 11 | | |
| 2001-02 | Watford | 40 | 11 | | |
| 2002-03 | Watford | 35 | 7 | | |
| 2003-04 | Watford | 0 | 0 | | |
| 2003-04 | Sunderland | 35 | 4 | 35 | 4 |
| 2004-05 | Derby Co | 42 | 11 | | |
| 2005-06 | Derby Co | 43 | 8 | | |
| 2006-07 | Derby Co | 5 | 1 | 90 | 20 |
| 2006-07 | Watford | 32 | 1 | | |
| 2007-08 | Watford | 44 | 7 | | |
| 2008-09 | Watford | 44 | 17 | | |
| 2009-10 | Watford | 4 | 2 | 273 | 60 |
| 2009-10 | Portsmouth | 16 | 1 | | |
| 2010-11 | Portsmouth | 3 | 0 | 19 | 1 |
| 2010-11 | QPR | 33 | 6 | | |
| 2011-12 | QPR | 17 | 2 | | |

| | | | | | |
|---|---|---|---|---|---|
| 2012-13 | QPR | 0 | 0 | 50 | 8 |
| 2012-13 | Cardiff C | 24 | 1 | 24 | 1 |

**TAYLOR, Andrew (D)** 253 5
H: 5 10  W: 11 04  b.Hartlepool 1-8-86
*Source:* Trainee. *Honours:* England Youth, Under-20, Under-21.

| | | | | | |
|---|---|---|---|---|---|
| 2003-04 | Middlesbrough | 0 | 0 | | |
| 2004-05 | Middlesbrough | 0 | 0 | | |
| 2005-06 | Middlesbrough | 13 | 0 | | |
| 2005-06 | *Bradford C* | 24 | 0 | 24 | 0 |
| 2006-07 | Middlesbrough | 34 | 0 | | |
| 2007-08 | Middlesbrough | 19 | 0 | | |
| 2008-09 | Middlesbrough | 26 | 0 | | |
| 2009-10 | Middlesbrough | 12 | 0 | | |
| 2010-11 | Middlesbrough | 21 | 3 | 125 | 3 |
| 2010-11 | *Watford* | 19 | 1 | 19 | 1 |
| 2011-12 | Cardiff C | 42 | 1 | | |
| 2012-13 | Cardiff C | 43 | 0 | 85 | 1 |

**TURNER, Ben (D)** 149 7
H: 6 4  W: 14 04  b.Birmingham 21-1-88
*Source:* Scholar. *Honours:* England Youth.

| | | | | | |
|---|---|---|---|---|---|
| 2005-06 | Coventry C | 1 | 0 | | |
| 2006-07 | Coventry C | 1 | 0 | | |
| 2006-07 | *Peterborough U* | 8 | 0 | 8 | 0 |
| 2006-07 | *Oldham Ath* | 1 | 0 | 1 | 0 |
| 2007-08 | Coventry C | 19 | 0 | | |
| 2008-09 | Coventry C | 24 | 0 | | |
| 2009-10 | Coventry C | 13 | 0 | | |
| 2010-11 | Coventry C | 14 | 4 | 72 | 4 |
| 2011-12 | Cardiff C | 37 | 2 | | |
| 2012-13 | Cardiff C | 31 | 1 | 68 | 3 |

**VELIKONJA, Etien (F)** 22 24
H: 5  W: 11 04  b.Sempeter Pri Gorici 26-12-88
*Honours:* Slovenia Youth, Under-21, 3 full caps.

| | | | | | |
|---|---|---|---|---|---|
| 2010-11 | HiT Gorica | 2 | 3 | 2 | 3 |
| 2010-11 | Maribor | 6 | 6 | | |
| 2011-12 | Maribor | 11 | 15 | 17 | 21 |
| 2012-13 | Cardiff C | 3 | 0 | 3 | 0 |

**WHITTINGHAM, Peter (M)** 339 64
H: 5 10  W: 9 13  b.Nuneaton 8-9-84
*Source:* Trainee. *Honours:* England Youth, Under-20, Under-21.

| | | | | | |
|---|---|---|---|---|---|
| 2002-03 | Aston Villa | 4 | 0 | | |
| 2003-04 | Aston Villa | 32 | 0 | | |
| 2004-05 | Aston Villa | 13 | 1 | | |
| 2004-05 | *Burnley* | 7 | 0 | 7 | 0 |
| 2005-06 | Aston Villa | 4 | 0 | | |
| 2005-06 | *Derby Co* | 11 | 0 | 11 | 0 |
| 2006-07 | Aston Villa | 3 | 0 | 56 | 1 |
| 2006-07 | Cardiff C | 19 | 4 | | |
| 2007-08 | Cardiff C | 41 | 5 | | |
| 2008-09 | Cardiff C | 33 | 3 | | |
| 2009-10 | Cardiff C | 41 | 20 | | |
| 2010-11 | Cardiff C | 45 | 11 | | |
| 2011-12 | Cardiff C | 46 | 12 | | |
| 2012-13 | Cardiff C | 40 | 8 | 265 | 63 |

**Scholars**
Bowen, Jaye Ricky; Enzam, Yora; Griffiths, Dane Ryan; Hill, Gethyn; James, Thomas Lynn; Matthews, Liam Robert; O'Sullivan, Thomas Paul; Owen, Kane Andrei Timothy; Richards, David Matthew; Roche, Tyler Paul; Southam, Macauley Anthony; Watkins, Benjamin Lewis; Watkins, Curtis James; Wharton, Theo; Wickham, Bradley; Williams, Bradley Jason; Yorwerth, Joshua.

## CARLISLE U (22)

**BECK, Mark (F)** 29 4
H: 6 5  W: 12 08  b.Sunderland 2-2-94
*Source:* Scholar.

| | | | | | |
|---|---|---|---|---|---|
| 2011-12 | Carlisle U | 2 | 0 | | |
| 2012-13 | Carlisle U | 27 | 4 | 29 | 4 |

**BERRETT, James (M)** 165 23
H: 5 10  W: 10 13  b.Halifax 13-1-89
*Source:* Scholar. *Honours:* Eire Youth, Under-21.

| | | | | | |
|---|---|---|---|---|---|
| 2006-07 | Huddersfield T | 2 | 0 | | |
| 2007-08 | Huddersfield T | 15 | 1 | | |
| 2008-09 | Huddersfield T | 9 | 1 | | |
| 2009-10 | Huddersfield T | 9 | 0 | 35 | 2 |
| 2010-11 | Carlisle U | 46 | 10 | | |
| 2011-12 | Carlisle U | 42 | 9 | | |
| 2012-13 | Carlisle U | 42 | 2 | 130 | 21 |

**BUGNO, Alessio (D)** 42 1
H: 5 11  W: 12 04  b.Magenta 23-3-90

| | | | | | |
|---|---|---|---|---|---|
| 2010-11 | Monza | 17 | 1 | | |
| 2011-12 | Monza | 23 | 0 | 40 | 1 |
| 2012-13 | Carlisle U | 2 | 0 | 2 | 0 |

Transferred to Monza January 2013

**CADAMARTERI, Danny (F)** 349 37
H: 5 7  W: 13 05  b.Cleckheaton 12-10-79
*Source:* Trainee. *Honours:* England Youth, Under-21.

| | | | | | |
|---|---|---|---|---|---|
| 1996-97 | Everton | 1 | 0 | | |
| 1997-98 | Everton | 26 | 4 | | |
| 1998-99 | Everton | 30 | 4 | | |
| 1999-2000 | Everton | 17 | 1 | | |
| 1999-2000 | *Fulham* | 5 | 1 | 5 | 1 |
| 2000-01 | Everton | 16 | 4 | | |
| 2001-02 | Everton | 3 | 0 | 93 | 13 |
| 2001-02 | Bradford C | 14 | 2 | | |
| 2002-03 | Bradford C | 20 | 0 | | |
| 2003-04 | Bradford C | 18 | 3 | | |
| 2004-05 | Leeds U | 0 | 0 | | |
| 2004-05 | Sheffield U | 21 | 1 | 21 | 1 |
| 2005-06 | Bradford C | 39 | 2 | | |
| 2006-07 | Bradford C | 0 | 0 | 91 | 7 |
| 2006-07 | *Doncaster R* | 6 | 1 | 6 | 1 |
| 2006-07 | Leicester C | 9 | 0 | 9 | 0 |
| 2007-08 | Huddersfield T | 12 | 3 | | |
| 2008-09 | Huddersfield T | 32 | 2 | | |
| 2009-10 | Huddersfield T | 0 | 0 | | |
| 2009-10 | Dundee U | 21 | 4 | | |
| 2010-11 | Dundee U | 8 | 0 | 29 | 4 |
| 2010-11 | Huddersfield T | 11 | 3 | | |
| 2011-12 | Huddersfield T | 15 | 0 | 70 | 8 |
| 2012-13 | Carlisle U | 25 | 2 | 25 | 2 |

**CHANTLER, Chris (M)** 37 0
H: 5 8  W: 11 00  b.Cheadle Hulme 16-12-90
*Source:* Scholar.

| | | | | | |
|---|---|---|---|---|---|
| 2009-10 | Manchester C | 0 | 0 | | |
| 2010-11 | Manchester C | 0 | 0 | | |
| 2011-12 | Manchester C | 0 | 0 | | |
| 2011-12 | Carlisle U | 12 | 0 | | |
| 2012-13 | Carlisle U | 25 | 0 | 37 | 0 |

**COLLIN, Adam (G)** 133 0
H: 6 2  W: 12 00  b.Penrith 9-12-84
*Source:* Trainee.

| | | | |
|---|---|---|---|
| 2003-04 | Newcastle U | 0 | 0 |
| 2003-04 | *Oldham Ath* | 0 | 0 |

From Workington.

| | | | | | |
|---|---|---|---|---|---|
| 2009-10 | Carlisle U | 29 | 0 | | |
| 2010-11 | Carlisle U | 46 | 0 | | |
| 2011-12 | Carlisle U | 46 | 0 | | |
| 2012-13 | Carlisle U | 12 | 0 | 133 | 0 |

**EDWARDS, Mike (D)** 508 27
H: 6 0  W: 12 10  b.Hessle 25-4-80
*Source:* Trainee.

| | | | | | |
|---|---|---|---|---|---|
| 1997-98 | Hull C | 21 | 0 | | |
| 1998-99 | Hull C | 30 | 0 | | |
| 1999-2000 | Hull C | 40 | 1 | | |
| 2000-01 | Hull C | 42 | 4 | | |
| 2001-02 | Hull C | 39 | 1 | | |
| 2002-03 | Hull C | 6 | 0 | 178 | 6 |
| 2002-03 | Colchester U | 5 | 0 | 5 | 0 |
| 2003-04 | Grimsby T | 33 | 1 | 33 | 1 |
| 2004-05 | Notts Co | 9 | 0 | | |
| 2005-06 | Notts Co | 46 | 7 | | |
| 2006-07 | Notts Co | 45 | 3 | | |
| 2007-08 | Notts Co | 19 | 1 | | |
| 2008-09 | Notts Co | 43 | 2 | | |
| 2009-10 | Notts Co | 40 | 5 | | |
| 2010-11 | Notts Co | 37 | 1 | | |
| 2011-12 | Notts Co | 30 | 1 | 269 | 20 |
| 2012-13 | Carlisle U | 23 | 0 | 23 | 0 |

**GILLESPIE, Mark (G)** 36 0
H: 6 3  W: 13 07  b.Newcastle 27-3-92
*Source:* Scholar.

| | | | | | |
|---|---|---|---|---|---|
| 2009-10 | Carlisle U | 1 | 0 | | |
| 2010-11 | Carlisle U | 0 | 0 | | |
| 2011-12 | Carlisle U | 0 | 0 | | |
| 2012-13 | Carlisle U | 35 | 0 | 36 | 0 |

**KAVANAGH, Graham (M)**    537   76
H: 5 10   W: 13 03   b.Dublin 2-12-73
*Source:* Home Farm. *Honours:* Eire Schools, Youth, Under-21, B, 16 full caps, 1 goal.

| | | | | |
|---|---|---|---|---|
| 1991-92 | Middlesbrough | 0 | 0 | |
| 1992-93 | Middlesbrough | 10 | 0 | |
| 1993-94 | Middlesbrough | 11 | 2 | |
| 1993-94 | *Darlington* | 5 | 0 | 5   0 |
| 1994-95 | Middlesbrough | 7 | 0 | |
| 1995-96 | Middlesbrough | 7 | 1 | |
| 1996-97 | Middlesbrough | 0 | 0 | 35   3 |
| 1996-97 | Stoke C | 38 | 4 | |
| 1997-98 | Stoke C | 44 | 5 | |
| 1998-99 | Stoke C | 36 | 11 | |
| 1999-2000 | Stoke C | 45 | 7 | |
| 2000-01 | Stoke C | 43 | 8 | 206   35 |
| 2001-02 | Cardiff C | 43 | 13 | |
| 2002-03 | Cardiff C | 44 | 5 | |
| 2003-04 | Cardiff C | 27 | 7 | |
| 2004-05 | Cardiff C | 28 | 3 | 142   28 |
| 2004-05 | Wigan Ath | 11 | 0 | |
| 2005-06 | Wigan Ath | 35 | 0 | |
| 2006-07 | Wigan Ath | 2 | 0 | 48   0 |
| 2006-07 | Sunderland | 14 | 1 | |
| 2007-08 | Sunderland | 0 | 0 | |
| 2007-08 | *Sheffield W* | 23 | 2 | 23   2 |
| 2008-09 | Sunderland | 0 | 0 | 14   1 |
| 2008-09 | Carlisle U | 34 | 5 | |
| 2009-10 | Carlisle U | 29 | 2 | |
| 2010-11 | Carlisle U | 1 | 0 | |
| 2011-12 | Carlisle U | 0 | 0 | |
| 2012-13 | Carlisle U | 0 | 0 | 64   7 |

**LIVESEY, Danny (D)**    281   17
H: 6 3   W: 13 01   b.Salford 31-12-84
*Source:* Trainee.

| | | | | |
|---|---|---|---|---|
| 2002-03 | Bolton W | 2 | 0 | |
| 2003-04 | Bolton W | 0 | 0 | |
| 2003-04 | *Notts Co* | 11 | 0 | 11   0 |
| 2003-04 | *Rochdale* | 13 | 0 | 13   0 |
| 2004-05 | Bolton W | 0 | 0 | 2   0 |
| 2004-05 | *Blackpool* | 1 | 0 | 1   0 |
| 2005-06 | Carlisle U | 36 | 4 | |
| 2006-07 | Carlisle U | 31 | 1 | |
| 2007-08 | Carlisle U | 45 | 6 | |
| 2008-09 | Carlisle U | 27 | 0 | |
| 2009-10 | Carlisle U | 38 | 2 | |
| 2010-11 | Carlisle U | 10 | 0 | |
| 2011-12 | Carlisle U | 28 | 1 | |
| 2012-13 | Carlisle U | 39 | 3 | 254   17 |

**LOY, Rory (F)**    78   10
H: 5 10   W: 10 07   b.Dumfries 19-3-88
*Honours:* Scotland Under-21.

| | | | | |
|---|---|---|---|---|
| 2008-09 | Rangers | 1 | 0 | |
| 2008-09 | *Dunfermline Ath* | 18 | 3 | 18   3 |
| 2009-10 | Rangers | 0 | 0 | |
| 2009-10 | *St Mirren* | 8 | 0 | 8   0 |
| 2010-11 | Rangers | 0 | 0 | 2   0 |
| 2010-11 | Carlisle U | 17 | 1 | |
| 2011-12 | Carlisle U | 20 | 3 | |
| 2012-13 | Carlisle U | 13 | 3 | 50   7 |

**MADDEN, Patrick (F)**    134   44
H: 6 0   W: 11 13   b.Dublin 4-3-90
*Honours:* Eire Youth, Under-21.

| | | | | |
|---|---|---|---|---|
| 2008 | Bohemians | 18 | 4 | |
| 2009 | Bohemians | 2 | 0 | |
| 2009 | Shelbourne | 13 | 6 | 13   6 |
| 2010 | Bohemians | 34 | 10 | 54   14 |
| 2010-11 | Carlisle U | 18 | 1 | |
| 2011-12 | Carlisle U | 18 | 1 | |
| 2012-13 | Carlisle U | 1 | 1 | 32   2 |
| 2012-13 | *Yeovil T* | 35 | 22 | 35   22 |

**MANSET, Mathieu (F)**    99   17
H: 6 1   W: 13 08   b.Metz 5-8-89
*Source:* Le Havre.

| | | | | |
|---|---|---|---|---|
| 2009-10 | Hereford U | 29 | 3 | |
| 2010-11 | Hereford U | 21 | 7 | 50   10 |
| 2010-11 | Reading | 13 | 2 | |
| 2011-12 | Reading | 15 | 3 | 28   5 |
| 2011-12 | *Shanghai S* | 9 | 1 | 9   1 |
| 2012-13 | FC Sion | 5 | 1 | 5   1 |
| 2012-13 | Carlisle U | 7 | 0 | 7   0 |

**McGOVERN, John-Paul (M)**    348   22
H: 5 10   W: 12 02   b.Glasgow 3-10-80
*Source:* Celtic BC.

| | | | | |
|---|---|---|---|---|
| 2001-02 | Celtic | 0 | 0 | |
| 2002-03 | Celtic | 0 | 0 | |
| 2002-03 | *Sheffield U* | 15 | 1 | 15   1 |
| 2003-04 | Celtic | 0 | 0 | |
| 2004-05 | Sheffield W | 46 | 6 | |
| 2005-06 | Sheffield W | 7 | 0 | 53   6 |
| 2006-07 | Milton Keynes D | 44 | 3 | |
| 2007-08 | Milton Keynes D | 3 | 0 | 47   3 |
| 2007-08 | Swindon T | 41 | 2 | |
| 2008-09 | Swindon T | 26 | 2 | |
| 2009-10 | Swindon T | 45 | 1 | |
| 2010-11 | Swindon T | 38 | 3 | 150   8 |
| 2011-12 | Carlisle U | 45 | 3 | |
| 2012-13 | Carlisle U | 38 | 1 | 83   4 |

**MILLER, Lee (F)**    376   107
H: 6 0   W: 11 07   b.Lanark 18-5-83
*Source:* Form S. *Honours:* Scotland 3 full caps.

| | | | | |
|---|---|---|---|---|
| 2000-01 | Falkirk | 0 | 0 | |
| 2001-02 | Falkirk | 27 | 11 | |
| 2002-03 | Falkirk | 34 | 17 | 61   28 |
| 2003-04 | Bristol C | 42 | 8 | |
| 2004-05 | Bristol C | 7 | 0 | 49   8 |
| 2004-05 | Hearts | 18 | 8 | 18   8 |
| 2005-06 | Dundee U | 34 | 8 | |
| 2006-07 | Dundee U | 3 | 0 | 37   8 |
| 2006-07 | Aberdeen | 32 | 4 | |
| 2007-08 | Aberdeen | 36 | 12 | |
| 2008-09 | Aberdeen | 34 | 10 | |
| 2009-10 | Aberdeen | 18 | 3 | 120   29 |
| 2009-10 | Middlesbrough | 10 | 0 | |
| 2010-11 | Middlesbrough | 1 | 0 | |
| 2010-11 | *Notts Co* | 6 | 2 | 6   2 |
| 2010-11 | *Scunthorpe U* | 18 | 1 | 18   1 |
| 2011-12 | Middlesbrough | 0 | 0 | 11   0 |
| 2011-12 | Carlisle U | 33 | 14 | |
| 2012-13 | Carlisle U | 23 | 9 | 56   23 |

**MURPHY, Peter (M)**    395   16
H: 5 10   W: 12 10   b.Dublin 27-10-80
*Source:* Trainee. *Honours:* Eire Youth, Under-21, 1 full cap.

| | | | | |
|---|---|---|---|---|
| 1998-99 | Blackburn R | 0 | 0 | |
| 1999-2000 | Blackburn R | 0 | 0 | |
| 2000-01 | Blackburn R | 0 | 0 | |
| 2000-01 | *Halifax T* | 21 | 1 | 21   1 |
| 2001-02 | Blackburn R | 0 | 0 | |
| 2001-02 | Carlisle U | 40 | 0 | |
| 2002-03 | Carlisle U | 40 | 2 | |
| 2003-04 | Carlisle U | 35 | 1 | |
| 2004-05 | Carlisle U | 0 | 0 | |
| 2005-06 | Carlisle U | 44 | 2 | |
| 2006-07 | Carlisle U | 40 | 2 | |
| 2007-08 | Carlisle U | 36 | 3 | |
| 2008-09 | Carlisle U | 28 | 0 | |
| 2009-10 | Carlisle U | 16 | 0 | |
| 2010-11 | Carlisle U | 34 | 3 | |
| 2011-12 | Carlisle U | 40 | 1 | |
| 2012-13 | Carlisle U | 21 | 1 | 374   15 |

**NOBLE, Liam (M)**    96   15
H: 5 9   W: 10 05   b.Newcastle 8-5-91
*Source:* Scholar.

| | | | | |
|---|---|---|---|---|
| 2009-10 | Sunderland | 0 | 0 | |
| 2010-11 | Sunderland | 0 | 0 | |
| 2010-11 | *Carlisle U* | 21 | 3 | |
| 2011-12 | Sunderland | 0 | 0 | |
| 2011-12 | Carlisle U | 40 | 6 | |
| 2012-13 | Carlisle U | 35 | 6 | 96   15 |

**O'HANLON, Sean (D)**    304   26
H: 6 1   W: 12 04   b.Liverpool 2-1-83

| | | | | |
|---|---|---|---|---|
| 2003-04 | Swindon T | 21 | 1 | |
| 2004-05 | Swindon T | 40 | 3 | |
| 2005-06 | Swindon T | 40 | 4 | 101   8 |
| 2006-07 | Milton Keynes D | 38 | 4 | |
| 2007-08 | Milton Keynes D | 43 | 4 | |
| 2008-09 | Milton Keynes D | 40 | 3 | |
| 2009-10 | Milton Keynes D | 6 | 0 | |
| 2010-11 | Milton Keynes D | 34 | 4 | 161   15 |
| 2011-12 | Hibernian | 22 | 2 | |
| 2012-13 | Hibernian | 1 | 0 | 23   2 |
| 2012-13 | Carlisle U | 19 | 1 | 19   1 |

**POTTS, Brad (M)**    27   0
H: 6 2   W: 12 09   b.Carlisle 3-7-94

| | | | | |
|---|---|---|---|---|
| 2012-13 | Carlisle U | 27 | 0 | 27   0 |

**ROBSON, Matty (D)**    279   24
H: 5 10   W: 11 02   b.Spennymoor 23-1-85
*Source:* Scholar.

| | | | | |
|---|---|---|---|---|
| 2002-03 | Hartlepool U | 0 | 0 | |
| 2003-04 | Hartlepool U | 23 | 1 | |
| 2004-05 | Hartlepool U | 27 | 2 | |
| 2005-06 | Hartlepool U | 19 | 1 | |
| 2006-07 | Hartlepool U | 20 | 2 | |
| 2007-08 | Hartlepool U | 17 | 1 | |
| 2008-09 | Hartlepool U | 29 | 2 | 135   9 |
| 2009-10 | Carlisle U | 39 | 4 | |
| 2010-11 | Carlisle U | 42 | 2 | |
| 2011-12 | Carlisle U | 27 | 2 | |
| 2012-13 | Carlisle U | 36 | 7 | 144   15 |

**SALMON, Alex (F)**    2   0
H: 5 11   W: 11 07   b.Liverpool 9-7-94

| | | | | |
|---|---|---|---|---|
| 2012-13 | Carlisle U | 2 | 0 | 2   0 |

**SIMEK, Frankie (D)**    241   2
H: 6 0   W: 11 06   b.St Louis 13-10-84
*Source:* Trainee. *Honours:* USA 5 full caps.

| | | | | |
|---|---|---|---|---|
| 2002-03 | Arsenal | 0 | 0 | |
| 2003-04 | Arsenal | 0 | 0 | |
| 2004-05 | Arsenal | 0 | 0 | |
| 2004-05 | *QPR* | 5 | 0 | 5   0 |
| 2004-05 | *Bournemouth* | 8 | 0 | 8   0 |
| 2005-06 | Sheffield W | 43 | 1 | |
| 2006-07 | Sheffield W | 41 | 1 | |
| 2007-08 | Sheffield W | 17 | 0 | |
| 2008-09 | Sheffield W | 6 | 0 | |
| 2009-10 | Sheffield W | 12 | 0 | 119   2 |
| 2010-11 | Carlisle U | 46 | 0 | |
| 2011-12 | Carlisle U | 25 | 0 | |
| 2012-13 | Carlisle U | 38 | 0 | 109   0 |

**SYMINGTON, David (M)**    31   3
H: 5 8   W: 12 03   b.Carlisle 28-1-94

| | | | | |
|---|---|---|---|---|
| 2012-13 | Carlisle U | 31 | 3 | 31   3 |

**THIRLWELL, Paul (M)**    326   8
H: 5 11   W: 12 08   b.Washington 13-2-79
*Source:* Trainee. *Honours:* England Under-21.

| | | | | |
|---|---|---|---|---|
| 1996-97 | Sunderland | 0 | 0 | |
| 1997-98 | Sunderland | 0 | 0 | |
| 1998-99 | Sunderland | 2 | 0 | |
| 1999-2000 | Sunderland | 8 | 0 | |
| 1999-2000 | *Swindon T* | 12 | 0 | 12   0 |
| 2000-01 | Sunderland | 5 | 0 | |
| 2001-02 | Sunderland | 14 | 0 | |
| 2002-03 | Sunderland | 19 | 0 | |
| 2003-04 | Sunderland | 29 | 0 | 77   0 |
| 2004-05 | Sheffield U | 30 | 1 | 30   1 |
| 2005-06 | Derby Co | 21 | 0 | |
| 2006-07 | Derby Co | 0 | 0 | 21   0 |
| 2006-07 | Carlisle U | 30 | 0 | |
| 2007-08 | Carlisle U | 13 | 0 | |
| 2008-09 | Carlisle U | 34 | 4 | |
| 2009-10 | Carlisle U | 28 | 1 | |
| 2010-11 | Carlisle U | 23 | 1 | |
| 2011-12 | Carlisle U | 26 | 1 | |
| 2012-13 | Carlisle U | 32 | 0 | 186   7 |

**TODD, Josh (M)**    1   0
H: 5 10   W: 12 03   b.Carlisle 11-6-94

| | | | | |
|---|---|---|---|---|
| 2012-13 | Carlisle U | 1 | 0 | 1   0 |

**WELSH, Andy (M)**    306   14
H: 5 8   W: 10 03   b.Manchester 24-11-83
*Source:* Scholar. *Honours:* Scotland Youth.

| | | | | |
|---|---|---|---|---|
| 2001-02 | Stockport Co | 15 | 0 | |
| 2002-03 | Stockport Co | 13 | 2 | |
| 2002-03 | *Macclesfield T* | 6 | 2 | 6   2 |
| 2003-04 | Stockport Co | 34 | 1 | |
| 2004-05 | Stockport Co | 13 | 0 | 75   3 |
| 2004-05 | Sunderland | 7 | 1 | |
| 2005-06 | Sunderland | 14 | 0 | |
| 2005-06 | *Leicester C* | 10 | 1 | |
| 2006-07 | Sunderland | 0 | 0 | 21   1 |
| 2006-07 | *Leicester C* | 7 | 0 | 17   1 |
| 2007 | Toronto Lynx | 20 | 1 | 20   1 |
| 2007-08 | Blackpool | 21 | 0 | |
| 2008-09 | Blackpool | 0 | 0 | 21   0 |
| 2008-09 | Yeovil T | 37 | 0 | |
| 2009-10 | Yeovil T | 42 | 2 | |

|  |  | | | | |
|---|---|--:|--:|--:|--:|
| 2010-11 | Yeovil T | 34 | 4 | 113 | 6 |
| 2011-12 | Carlisle U | 21 | 0 | | |
| 2012-13 | Carlisle U | 12 | 0 | 33 | 0 |

**Scholars**
Berwick, Thomas Joseph; Brass, Lewis Alan Shaun; Brough, Patrick John; Chisholm, Jake; Clarey, Jamie Luke; Dempsey, Kyle Michael; Dixon, Daniel Louis; Gwinnutt, Brandon Lee; Lynch, Jack William; McEvoy, Evan Christopher; Minor, Dale Jon; Morse, Dillon; Parker, Jordan; Salmon, Alex Mark; Staunch, Bradley; Non, Contract; Caig, Antony.

## CHARLTON ATH (23)

**AJAYI, Semi (D)** 0 0
H: 6 4 W: 13 00 b.Croydon 9-11-93

|  |  | | | | |
|---|---|--:|--:|--:|--:|
| 2012-13 | Charlton Ath | 0 | 0 | | |

**AZEEZ, Adebayo (F)** 5 0
H: 6 0 W: 12 07 b.Orpington 8-1-94

|  |  | | | | |
|---|---|--:|--:|--:|--:|
| 2012-13 | Charlton Ath | 0 | 0 | | |
| 2012-13 | Wycombe W | 4 | 0 | 4 | 0 |
| 2012-13 | Leyton Orient | 1 | 0 | 1 | 0 |

**BUTTON, David (G)** 95 0
H: 6 3 W: 13 00 b.Stevenage 27-2-89
*Source:* Scholar. *Honours:* England Youth.

|  |  | | | | |
|---|---|--:|--:|--:|--:|
| 2005-06 | Tottenham H | 0 | 0 | | |
| 2006-07 | Tottenham H | 0 | 0 | | |
| 2007-08 | Rochdale | 0 | 0 | | |
| 2007-08 | Tottenham H | 0 | 0 | | |
| 2008-09 | Tottenham H | 0 | 0 | | |
| 2008-09 | Bournemouth | 4 | 0 | 4 | 0 |
| 2008-09 | Luton T | 0 | 0 | | |
| 2008-09 | Dagenham & R | 3 | 0 | 3 | 0 |
| 2009-10 | Tottenham H | 0 | 0 | | |
| 2009-10 | Crewe Alex | 10 | 0 | 10 | 0 |
| 2009-10 | Shrewsbury T | 26 | 0 | 26 | 0 |
| 2010-11 | Tottenham H | 0 | 0 | | |
| 2010-11 | Plymouth Arg | 30 | 0 | 30 | 0 |
| 2011-12 | Tottenham H | 0 | 0 | | |
| 2011-12 | Leyton Orient | 1 | 0 | 1 | 0 |
| 2011-12 | Doncaster R | 7 | 0 | 7 | 0 |
| 2011-12 | Barnsley | 9 | 0 | 9 | 0 |
| 2012-13 | Tottenham H | 0 | 0 | | |
| 2012-13 | Charlton Ath | 5 | 0 | 5 | 0 |

**COOK, Jordan (F)** 38 5
H: 5 10 W: 10 10 b.Hetton-le-Hole 20-3-90
*Source:* Scholar.

|  |  | | | | |
|---|---|--:|--:|--:|--:|
| 2007-08 | Sunderland | 0 | 0 | | |
| 2008-09 | Sunderland | 0 | 0 | | |
| 2009-10 | Sunderland | 0 | 0 | | |
| 2009-10 | Darlington | 5 | 0 | 5 | 0 |
| 2010-11 | Sunderland | 3 | 0 | | |
| 2010-11 | Walsall | 8 | 1 | 8 | 1 |
| 2011-12 | Sunderland | 0 | 0 | 3 | 0 |
| 2011-12 | Carlisle U | 14 | 4 | 14 | 4 |
| 2012-13 | Charlton Ath | 7 | 0 | 7 | 0 |
| 2012-13 | Yeovil T | 1 | 0 | 1 | 0 |

**CORT, Leon (D)** 393 38
H: 6 3 W: 13 01 b.Bermondsey 11-9-79
*Source:* Dulwich H. *Honours:* Guyana 6 full caps, 1 goal.

|  |  | | | | |
|---|---|--:|--:|--:|--:|
| 1997-98 | Millwall | 0 | 0 | | |
| 1998-99 | Millwall | 0 | 0 | | |
| 1999-2000 | Millwall | 0 | 0 | | |
| 2000-01 | Millwall | 0 | 0 | | |
| 2001-02 | Southend U | 45 | 4 | | |
| 2002-03 | Southend U | 46 | 6 | | |
| 2003-04 | Southend U | 46 | 1 | 137 | 11 |
| 2004-05 | Hull C | 44 | 4 | | |
| 2005-06 | Hull C | 42 | 4 | 86 | 10 |
| 2006-07 | Crystal Palace | 37 | 7 | | |
| 2007-08 | Crystal Palace | 12 | 0 | 49 | 7 |
| 2007-08 | Stoke C | 33 | 8 | | |
| 2008-09 | Stoke C | 11 | 0 | | |
| 2009-10 | Stoke C | 0 | 0 | 44 | 8 |
| 2009-10 | Burnley | 15 | 0 | | |
| 2010-11 | Burnley | 4 | 0 | | |
| 2010-11 | Preston NE | 13 | 0 | 13 | 0 |
| 2011-12 | Burnley | 0 | 0 | 19 | 0 |
| 2011-12 | Charlton Ath | 15 | 0 | | |
| 2012-13 | Charlton Ath | 30 | 2 | 45 | 2 |

**COUSINS, Jordan (D)** 0 0
H: 5 10 W: 11 05 b.Greenwich 6-3-94
*Source:* Scholar. *Honours:* England Youth.

|  |  | | | | |
|---|---|--:|--:|--:|--:|
| 2011-12 | Charlton Ath | 0 | 0 | | |
| 2012-13 | Charlton Ath | 0 | 0 | | |

**DERVITE, Dorian (D)** 59 3
H: 6 3 W: 13 06 b.Lille 25-7-88
*Honours:* France Youth.

|  |  | | | | |
|---|---|--:|--:|--:|--:|
| 2008-09 | Southend U | 18 | 0 | 18 | 0 |
| 2010-11 | Villarreal B | 9 | 0 | | |
| 2011-12 | Villarreal B | 2 | 0 | 11 | 0 |
| 2012-13 | Villarreal | 0 | 0 | | |
| 2012-13 | Charlton Ath | 30 | 3 | 30 | 3 |

**EVINA, Cedric (D)** 42 2
H: 5 11 W: 12 08 b.Cameroon 16-11-91
*Source:* Scholar.

|  |  | | | | |
|---|---|--:|--:|--:|--:|
| 2009-10 | Arsenal | 0 | 0 | | |
| 2010-11 | Arsenal | 0 | 0 | | |
| 2010-11 | Oldham Ath | 27 | 2 | 27 | 2 |
| 2011-12 | Charlton Ath | 3 | 0 | | |
| 2012-13 | Charlton Ath | 12 | 0 | 15 | 0 |

**FEELY, Kevin (D)** 28 1
H: 5 10 W: 11 07 b.Dublin 30-8-92

|  |  | | | | |
|---|---|--:|--:|--:|--:|
| 2011 | Bohemians | 5 | 0 | | |
| 2012 | Bohemians | 23 | 1 | 28 | 1 |
| 2012-13 | Charlton Ath | 0 | 0 | | |

**FOX, Morgan (D)** 0 0
H: 6 1 W: 12 03 b.Chelmsford 21-9-93

|  |  | | | | |
|---|---|--:|--:|--:|--:|
| 2012-13 | Charlton Ath | 0 | 0 | | |

**FULLER, Ricardo (F)** 371 95
H: 6 3 W: 12 10 b.Kingston, Jamaica 31-10-79
*Source:* Tivoli Gardens. *Honours:* Jamaica 73 full caps, 9 goals.

|  |  | | | | |
|---|---|--:|--:|--:|--:|
| 2000-01 | Crystal Palace | 8 | 0 | 8 | 0 |
| 2001-02 | Hearts | 27 | 8 | 27 | 8 |

From Tivoli Gardens.

|  |  | | | | |
|---|---|--:|--:|--:|--:|
| 2002-03 | Preston NE | 8 | 0 | | |
| 2003-04 | Preston NE | 38 | 17 | | |
| 2004-05 | Preston NE | 2 | 1 | 58 | 27 |
| 2004-05 | Portsmouth | 31 | 1 | 31 | 1 |
| 2005-06 | Southampton | 30 | 9 | | |
| 2005-06 | Ipswich T | 3 | 2 | 3 | 2 |
| 2006-07 | Southampton | 1 | 0 | 31 | 9 |
| 2006-07 | Stoke C | 30 | 10 | | |
| 2007-08 | Stoke C | 42 | 15 | | |
| 2008-09 | Stoke C | 34 | 11 | | |
| 2009-10 | Stoke C | 35 | 3 | | |
| 2010-11 | Stoke C | 28 | 4 | | |
| 2011-12 | Stoke C | 0 | 0 | 182 | 43 |
| 2012-13 | Charlton Ath | 31 | 5 | 31 | 5 |

**GREEN, Danny (M)** 136 28
H: 5 11 W: 12 00 b.Harlow 9-7-88
*Source:* Bishop's Stortford.

|  |  | | | | |
|---|---|--:|--:|--:|--:|
| 2006-07 | Northampton T | 0 | 0 | | |
| 2007-08 | Nottingham F | 0 | 0 | | |

From Bishop's Stortford.

|  |  | | | | |
|---|---|--:|--:|--:|--:|
| 2009-10 | Dagenham & R | 46 | 13 | | |
| 2010-11 | Dagenham & R | 41 | 11 | 87 | 24 |
| 2011-12 | Charlton Ath | 32 | 3 | | |
| 2012-13 | Charlton Ath | 17 | 1 | 49 | 4 |

**HAMER, Ben (G)** 175 0
H: 5 11 W: 12 04 b.Chard 20-11-87
*Source:* Crawley T.

|  |  | | | | |
|---|---|--:|--:|--:|--:|
| 2006-07 | Reading | 0 | 0 | | |
| 2007-08 | Reading | 0 | 0 | | |
| 2007-08 | Brentford | 20 | 0 | | |
| 2008-09 | Reading | 0 | 0 | | |
| 2008-09 | Brentford | 45 | 0 | | |
| 2009-10 | Reading | 0 | 0 | | |
| 2010-11 | Reading | 0 | 0 | | |
| 2010-11 | Brentford | 10 | 0 | 75 | 0 |
| 2010-11 | Exeter C | 18 | 0 | 18 | 0 |
| 2011-12 | Charlton Ath | 41 | 0 | | |
| 2012-13 | Charlton Ath | 41 | 0 | 82 | 0 |

**HARRIOTT, Callum (M)** 17 2
H: 5 5 W: 10 05 b.Norbury 4-3-94
*Source:* Scholar.

|  |  | | | | |
|---|---|--:|--:|--:|--:|
| 2010-11 | Charlton Ath | 3 | 0 | | |
| 2011-12 | Charlton Ath | 0 | 0 | | |
| 2012-13 | Charlton Ath | 14 | 2 | 17 | 2 |

**HAYNES, Danny (F)** 236 42
H: 5 11 W: 12 04 b.Peckham 19-1-88
*Source:* Scholar. *Honours:* England Youth.

|  |  | | | | |
|---|---|--:|--:|--:|--:|
| 2005-06 | Ipswich T | 19 | 3 | | |
| 2006-07 | Ipswich T | 31 | 7 | | |
| 2006-07 | Millwall | 5 | 2 | 5 | 2 |
| 2007-08 | Ipswich T | 40 | 7 | | |
| 2008-09 | Ipswich T | 24 | 0 | 114 | 17 |
| 2009-10 | Bristol C | 38 | 7 | | |
| 2010-11 | Bristol C | 13 | 1 | 51 | 8 |
| 2010-11 | Barnsley | 20 | 6 | | |
| 2011-12 | Barnsley | 12 | 0 | 32 | 6 |
| 2011-12 | Charlton Ath | 14 | 2 | | |
| 2012-13 | Charlton Ath | 20 | 7 | 34 | 9 |

**HOLLANDS, Danny (M)** 270 34
H: 6 0 W: 11 11 b.Ashford (Middlesex) 6-11-85
*Source:* Trainee.

|  |  | | | | |
|---|---|--:|--:|--:|--:|
| 2003-04 | Chelsea | 0 | 0 | | |
| 2004-05 | Chelsea | 0 | 0 | | |
| 2005-06 | Chelsea | 0 | 0 | | |
| 2005-06 | Torquay U | 10 | 1 | 10 | 1 |
| 2006-07 | Bournemouth | 33 | 1 | | |
| 2007-08 | Bournemouth | 37 | 4 | | |
| 2008-09 | Bournemouth | 42 | 6 | | |
| 2009-10 | Bournemouth | 39 | 6 | | |
| 2010-11 | Bournemouth | 42 | 7 | 193 | 24 |
| 2011-12 | Charlton Ath | 43 | 7 | | |
| 2012-13 | Charlton Ath | 14 | 0 | 57 | 7 |
| 2012-13 | Swindon T | 10 | 2 | 10 | 2 |

**HOLMES-DENNIS, Tareiq (M)** 0 0

|  |  | | | | |
|---|---|--:|--:|--:|--:|
| 2012-13 | Charlton Ath | 0 | 0 | | |

**HUGHES, Andy (M)** 537 39
H: 5 11 W: 12 01 b.Stockport 2-1-78
*Source:* Trainee.

|  |  | | | | |
|---|---|--:|--:|--:|--:|
| 1995-96 | Oldham Ath | 15 | 1 | | |
| 1996-97 | Oldham Ath | 8 | 0 | | |
| 1997-98 | Oldham Ath | 10 | 0 | 33 | 1 |
| 1997-98 | Notts Co | 15 | 2 | | |
| 1998-99 | Notts Co | 30 | 3 | | |
| 1999-2000 | Notts Co | 35 | 7 | | |
| 2000-01 | Notts Co | 30 | 5 | 110 | 17 |
| 2001-02 | Reading | 39 | 6 | | |
| 2002-03 | Reading | 43 | 9 | | |
| 2003-04 | Reading | 43 | 3 | | |
| 2004-05 | Reading | 41 | 0 | 166 | 18 |
| 2005-06 | Norwich C | 36 | 2 | | |
| 2006-07 | Norwich C | 36 | 0 | 72 | 2 |
| 2007-08 | Leeds U | 40 | 1 | | |
| 2008-09 | Leeds U | 27 | 0 | | |
| 2009-10 | Leeds U | 39 | 0 | | |
| 2010-11 | Leeds U | 10 | 0 | 116 | 1 |
| 2010-11 | Scunthorpe U | 19 | 0 | 19 | 0 |
| 2011-12 | Charlton Ath | 15 | 0 | | |
| 2012-13 | Charlton Ath | 6 | 0 | 21 | 0 |

**JACKSON, Johnnie (M)** 311 56
H: 6 1 W: 12 00 b.Camden 15-8-82
*Source:* Trainee. *Honours:* England Youth, Under-20.

|  |  | | | | |
|---|---|--:|--:|--:|--:|
| 1999-2000 | Tottenham H | 0 | 0 | | |
| 2000-01 | Tottenham H | 0 | 0 | | |
| 2001-02 | Tottenham H | 0 | 0 | | |
| 2002-03 | Tottenham H | 0 | 0 | | |
| 2002-03 | Swindon T | 13 | 1 | 13 | 1 |
| 2002-03 | Colchester U | 8 | 0 | | |
| 2003-04 | Tottenham H | 11 | 1 | | |
| 2003-04 | Coventry C | 5 | 2 | 5 | 2 |
| 2004-05 | Tottenham H | 8 | 0 | | |
| 2004-05 | Watford | 15 | 0 | 15 | 0 |
| 2005-06 | Tottenham H | 1 | 0 | 20 | 1 |
| 2005-06 | Derby Co | 6 | 0 | 6 | 0 |
| 2006-07 | Colchester U | 32 | 2 | | |
| 2007-08 | Colchester U | 46 | 7 | | |
| 2008-09 | Colchester U | 29 | 4 | | |
| 2009-10 | Colchester U | 0 | 0 | 115 | 13 |
| 2009-10 | Notts Co | 24 | 2 | 24 | 2 |
| 2009-10 | Charlton Ath | 4 | 0 | | |
| 2010-11 | Charlton Ath | 30 | 13 | | |
| 2011-12 | Charlton Ath | 36 | 12 | | |
| 2012-13 | Charlton Ath | 43 | 12 | 113 | 37 |

**JORDAN, Bradley (M)** 0 0
H: 5 8 W: 10 09 b.Ashford 21-1-94

|  |  | | | | |
|---|---|--:|--:|--:|--:|
| 2012-13 | Charlton Ath | 0 | 0 | | |

**KERKAR, Salim (F)** 40 3
H: 5 11  W: 9 10  b.Givors 4-8-87
| 2006-07 | Gueugnon | 1 | 0 | 1 | 0 |
| 2010-11 | Rangers | 1 | 0 | | |
| 2011-12 | Rangers | 15 | 1 | 16 | 1 |
| 2011-12 | Ajman | 1 | 1 | 1 | 1 |
| 2012-13 | Charlton Ath | 22 | 1 | 22 | 1 |

**KERMORGANT, Yann (F)** 268 71
H: 6 0  W: 13 03  b.Vannes 8-11-81
*Source:* Vannes.
| 2004-05 | Chatellerault | 29 | 14 | 29 | 14 |
| 2005-06 | Grenoble | 26 | 6 | | |
| 2006-07 | Grenoble | 32 | 10 | 58 | 16 |
| 2007-08 | Reims | 33 | 4 | | |
| 2008-09 | Reims | 34 | 9 | 67 | 13 |
| 2009-10 | Leicester C | 20 | 1 | | |
| 2010-11 | Leicester C | 0 | 0 | 20 | 1 |
| 2010-11 | Arles-Avignon | 26 | 3 | 26 | 3 |
| 2011-12 | Charlton Ath | 36 | 12 | | |
| 2012-13 | Charlton Ath | 32 | 12 | 68 | 24 |

**LENNON, Harry (M)** 0 0
| 2012-13 | Charlton Ath | 0 | 0 | | |

**MORRISON, Michael (D)** 178 10
H: 6 0  W: 12 00  b.Bury St Edmunds 3-3-88
*Source:* Cambridge U.
| 2008-09 | Leicester C | 35 | 3 | | |
| 2009-10 | Leicester C | 31 | 2 | | |
| 2010-11 | Leicester C | 11 | 0 | 77 | 5 |
| 2010-11 | Sheffield W | 12 | 0 | 12 | 0 |
| 2011-12 | Charlton Ath | 45 | 4 | | |
| 2012-13 | Charlton Ath | 44 | 1 | 89 | 5 |

**OSBORNE, Harry (D)** 0 0
H: 6 0  W: 12 03  b.Greenwich 3-3-94
*Source:* Scholar.
| 2011-12 | Charlton Ath | 0 | 0 | | |
| 2012-13 | Charlton Ath | 0 | 0 | | |

**PHILLIPS, Dillon (M)** 0 0
| 2012-13 | Charlton Ath | 0 | 0 | | |

**POPE, Nick (G)** 1 0
H: 6 3  W: 11 13  b.Cambridge 19-4-92
*Source:* Bury T.
| 2011-12 | Charlton Ath | 0 | 0 | | |
| 2012-13 | Charlton Ath | 1 | 0 | 1 | 0 |

**POYET, Diego (M)** 0 0
b. 8-4-95
*Source:* Scholar.
| 2011-12 | Charlton Ath | 0 | 0 | | |
| 2012-13 | Charlton Ath | 0 | 0 | | |

**PRITCHARD, Bradley (M)** 62 3
H: 6 1  W: 14 02  b.Zimbabwe 19-12-85
*Source:* Nuneaton Bor, Tamworth, Hayes & Yeading U.
| 2011-12 | Charlton Ath | 20 | 0 | | |
| 2012-13 | Charlton Ath | 42 | 3 | 62 | 3 |

**SHO-SILVA, Oluwatobi (M)** 0 0
| 2012-13 | Charlton Ath | 0 | 0 | | |

**SMITH, Michael (F)** 14 4
H: 6 4  W: 11 02  b.Wallsend 17-10-91
*Source:* Darlington.
| 2011-12 | Charlton Ath | 0 | 0 | | |
| 2011-12 | *Accrington S* | 6 | 3 | 6 | 3 |
| 2012-13 | Charlton Ath | 0 | 0 | | |
| 2012-13 | *Colchester U* | 8 | 1 | 8 | 1 |

**SOLLY, Chris (D)** 113 2
H: 5 8  W: 10 07  b.Rochester 20-1-91
*Source:* Scholar.
| 2008-09 | Charlton Ath | 1 | 0 | | |
| 2009-10 | Charlton Ath | 9 | 0 | | |
| 2010-11 | Charlton Ath | 14 | 1 | | |
| 2011-12 | Charlton Ath | 44 | 0 | | |
| 2012-13 | Charlton Ath | 45 | 1 | 113 | 2 |

**STEPHENS, Dale (M)** 139 20
H: 5 7  W: 11 04  b.Bolton 12-6-89
*Source:* Scholar.
| 2006-07 | Bury | 3 | 0 | | |
| 2007-08 | Bury | 6 | 1 | 9 | 1 |
| 2008-09 | Oldham Ath | 14 | 0 | | |
| 2009-10 | Oldham Ath | 26 | 2 | | |
| 2009-10 | *Rochdale* | 6 | 1 | 6 | 1 |
| 2010-11 | Oldham Ath | 34 | 9 | 60 | 11 |

---

| 2010-11 | *Southampton* | 6 | 0 | 6 | 0 |
| 2011-12 | Charlton Ath | 30 | 5 | | |
| 2012-13 | Charlton Ath | 28 | 2 | 58 | 7 |

**TAYLOR, Matthew (D)** 158 9
H: 6 0  W: 12 04  b.Chorley 30-1-82
*Source:* Burscough, Rossendale U, Matlock T, Hucknall T, Guiseley, Team Bath.
| 2008-09 | Exeter C | 31 | 2 | | |
| 2009-10 | Exeter C | 46 | 5 | | |
| 2010-11 | Exeter C | 28 | 2 | 105 | 9 |
| 2011-12 | Charlton Ath | 41 | 0 | | |
| 2012-13 | Charlton Ath | 12 | 0 | 53 | 0 |

**WAGSTAFF, Scott (M)** 129 17
H: 5 10  W: 10 03  b.Maidstone 31-3-90
*Source:* Scholar.
| 2007-08 | Charlton Ath | 2 | 0 | | |
| 2008-09 | Charlton Ath | 2 | 0 | | |
| 2008-09 | *Bournemouth* | 5 | 0 | 5 | 0 |
| 2009-10 | Charlton Ath | 30 | 4 | | |
| 2010-11 | Charlton Ath | 40 | 8 | | |
| 2011-12 | Charlton Ath | 34 | 4 | | |
| 2012-13 | Charlton Ath | 9 | 1 | 117 | 17 |
| 2012-13 | *Leyton Orient* | 7 | 0 | 7 | 0 |

**WIGGINS, Rhoys (D)** 133 3
H: 5 8  W: 11 05  b.Uxbridge 4-11-87
*Source:* Scholar. *Honours:* Wales Youth, Under-21.
| 2006-07 | Crystal Palace | 0 | 0 | | |
| 2007-08 | Crystal Palace | 0 | 0 | | |
| 2008-09 | Crystal Palace | 1 | 0 | 1 | 0 |
| 2008-09 | *Bournemouth* | 13 | 0 | | |
| 2009-10 | Norwich C | 0 | 0 | | |
| 2009-10 | *Bournemouth* | 19 | 0 | | |
| 2010-11 | Bournemouth | 35 | 2 | 67 | 2 |
| 2011-12 | Charlton Ath | 45 | 1 | | |
| 2012-13 | Charlton Ath | 20 | 0 | 65 | 1 |

**WILSON, Lawrie (D)** 118 12
H: 5 11  W: 11 00  b.London 11-9-87
*Source:* Charlton Ath.
| 2006-07 | Colchester U | 0 | 0 | | |
| 2010-11 | Stevenage | 42 | 5 | | |
| 2011-12 | Stevenage | 46 | 5 | 88 | 10 |
| 2012-13 | Charlton Ath | 30 | 2 | 30 | 2 |

**WRIGHT-PHILLIPS, Bradley (F)** 272 78
H: 5 10  W: 10 07  b.Lewisham 12-3-85
*Source:* Scholar. *Honours:* England Youth, Under-20.
| 2002-03 | Manchester C | 0 | 0 | | |
| 2003-04 | Manchester C | 0 | 0 | | |
| 2004-05 | Manchester C | 14 | 1 | | |
| 2005-06 | Manchester C | 18 | 1 | 32 | 2 |
| 2006-07 | Southampton | 39 | 8 | | |
| 2007-08 | Southampton | 39 | 8 | | |
| 2008-09 | Southampton | 33 | 6 | 111 | 22 |
| 2009-10 | Plymouth Arg | 15 | 4 | | |
| 2010-11 | Plymouth Arg | 17 | 13 | 32 | 17 |
| 2010-11 | Charlton Ath | 21 | 9 | | |
| 2011-12 | Charlton Ath | 42 | 22 | | |
| 2012-13 | Charlton Ath | 19 | 1 | 82 | 32 |
| 2012-13 | *Brentford* | 15 | 5 | 15 | 5 |

**Scholars**
Adeloye, Oluwatomisin; Brown, Ellis Ryan; Derry, Thomas Robinson; Doherty, Harry Daniel; Gerard, Harry Nicholas Stephen; Kennedy, Mikhail Caolan Patrick; Martin, Brian Micheal; Muldoon, Oliver James; Neavin, Darien Aaron; O'Hanlon, Cathal; Pyke, Levander; Shehaj, Lamce; Stewart, Greig; Thomas, Terell Mondasia.

## CHELSEA (24)

**AKE, Nathan (M)** 3 0
H: 5 11  W: 11 01  b.Den Haag 18-2-95
| 2012-13 | Chelsea | 3 | 0 | 3 | 0 |

**AZPILICUETA, Cesar (D)** 173 1
H: 5 10  W: 10 13  b.Pamplona 28-8-89
*Honours:* Spain Youth, Under-21, 3 full caps.
| 2006-07 | Osasuna | 1 | 0 | | |
| 2007-08 | Osasuna | 37 | 0 | | |
| 2008-09 | Osasuna | 36 | 0 | | |
| 2009-10 | Osasuna | 33 | 0 | 99 | 0 |
| 2010-11 | Marseille | 15 | 0 | | |

---

| 2011-12 | Marseille | 30 | 1 | | |
| 2012-13 | Marseille | 2 | 0 | 47 | 1 |
| 2012-13 | Chelsea | 27 | 0 | 27 | 0 |

**BA, Demba (F)** 215 105
H: 6 2  W: 12 13  b.Sevres 25-5-85
*Honours:* Senegal 18 full caps, 4 goals.
| 2005-06 | Rouen | 26 | 22 | 26 | 22 |
| 2006-07 | Mouscron | 10 | 8 | | |
| 2007-08 | Mouscron | 2 | 0 | 12 | 8 |
| 2007-08 | Hoffenheim | 30 | 12 | | |
| 2008-09 | Hoffenheim | 33 | 14 | | |
| 2009-10 | Hoffenheim | 17 | 5 | | |
| 2010-11 | Hoffenheim | 17 | 6 | 97 | 37 |
| 2010-11 | West Ham U | 12 | 7 | 12 | 7 |
| 2011-12 | Newcastle U | 34 | 16 | | |
| 2012-13 | Newcastle U | 20 | 13 | 54 | 29 |
| 2012-13 | Chelsea | 14 | 2 | 14 | 2 |

**BAKER, Lewis (M)** 0 0
| 2012-13 | Chelsea | 0 | 0 | | |

**BAMFORD, Patrick (F)** 16 4
H: 6 1  W: 11 02  b.Newark 5-9-93
*Source:* Scholar. *Honours:* England Youth.
| 2010-11 | Nottingham F | 0 | 0 | | |
| 2011-12 | Nottingham F | 2 | 0 | 2 | 0 |
| 2011-12 | Chelsea | 0 | 0 | | |
| 2012-13 | Chelsea | 0 | 0 | | |
| 2012-13 | *Milton Keynes D* | 14 | 4 | 14 | 4 |

**BENAYOUN, Yossi (M)** 415 112
H: 5 10  W: 11 00  b.Beer Sheva 6-6-80
*Honours:* Israel 92 full caps, 24 goals.
| 1997-98 | Hapoel Beer Sheva | 25 | 15 | 25 | 15 |
| 1998-99 | Maccabi Haifa | 29 | 16 | | |
| 1999-2000 | Maccabi Haifa | 38 | 19 | | |
| 2000-01 | Maccabi Haifa | 37 | 13 | | |
| 2001-02 | Maccabi Haifa | 26 | 7 | 130 | 55 |
| 2002-03 | Santander | 31 | 4 | | |
| 2003-04 | Santander | 35 | 7 | | |
| 2004-05 | Santander | 0 | 0 | 66 | 11 |
| 2005-06 | West Ham U | 34 | 5 | | |
| 2006-07 | West Ham U | 29 | 3 | | |
| 2007-08 | Liverpool | 30 | 4 | | |
| 2008-09 | Liverpool | 32 | 8 | | |
| 2009-10 | Liverpool | 30 | 6 | 92 | 18 |
| 2010-11 | Chelsea | 7 | 1 | | |
| 2011-12 | Chelsea | 1 | 0 | | |
| 2011-12 | *Arsenal* | 19 | 4 | 19 | 4 |
| 2012-13 | Chelsea | 6 | 0 | 14 | 1 |
| 2012-13 | *West Ham U* | 6 | 0 | 69 | 8 |

**BERTRAND, Ryan (D)** 172 1
H: 5 10  W: 11 00  b.Southwark 5-8-89
*Source:* Scholar. *Honours:* England Youth, Under-21, 2 full caps.
| 2006-07 | Chelsea | 0 | 0 | | |
| 2006-07 | *Bournemouth* | 5 | 0 | 5 | 0 |
| 2007-08 | Chelsea | 0 | 0 | | |
| 2007-08 | *Oldham Ath* | 21 | 0 | 21 | 0 |
| 2007-08 | *Norwich C* | 18 | 0 | | |
| 2008-09 | Chelsea | 0 | 0 | | |
| 2008-09 | *Norwich C* | 38 | 0 | 56 | 0 |
| 2009-10 | Chelsea | 0 | 0 | | |
| 2009-10 | *Reading* | 44 | 1 | 44 | 1 |
| 2010-11 | Chelsea | 1 | 0 | | |
| 2010-11 | *Nottingham F* | 19 | 0 | 19 | 0 |
| 2011-12 | Chelsea | 7 | 0 | | |
| 2012-13 | Chelsea | 19 | 0 | 27 | 0 |

**BLACKMAN, Jamal (G)** 0 0
b.Croydon 27-10-93
*Source:* Scholar. *Honours:* England Youth.
| 2011-12 | Chelsea | 0 | 0 | | |
| 2012-13 | Chelsea | 0 | 0 | | |

**CAHILL, Gary (D)** 237 20
H: 6 2  W: 12 06  b.Dronfield 19-12-85
*Source:* Trainee. *Honours:* England Youth, Under-20, Under-21, 15 full caps, 2 goals.
| 2003-04 | Aston Villa | 0 | 0 | | |
| 2004-05 | Aston Villa | 0 | 0 | | |
| 2004-05 | *Burnley* | 27 | 1 | 27 | 1 |
| 2005-06 | Aston Villa | 7 | 1 | | |
| 2006-07 | Aston Villa | 20 | 0 | | |
| 2007-08 | Aston Villa | 10 | 0 | 28 | 1 |
| 2007-08 | *Sheffield U* | 16 | 2 | 16 | 2 |
| 2007-08 | Bolton W | 13 | 0 | | |
| 2008-09 | Bolton W | 33 | 3 | | |
| 2009-10 | Bolton W | 29 | 5 | | |
| 2010-11 | Bolton W | 36 | 3 | | |

| | | | | |
|---|---|---|---|---|
| 2011-12 | Bolton W | 19 | 2 | 130 13 |
| 2011-12 | Chelsea | 10 | 1 | |
| 2012-13 | Chelsea | 26 | 2 | 36 3 |

**CECH, Petr (G)** 420 0
H: 6 5　W: 14 07　b.Plzen 20-5-82
*Honours:* Czech Republic Youth, Under-20, Under-21, 101 full caps.

| | | | | |
|---|---|---|---|---|
| 1998-99 | Viktoria Plzen | 0 | 0 | |
| 1999-2000 | Chmel | 1 | 0 | |
| 2000-01 | Chmel | 26 | 0 | 27 0 |
| 2001-02 | Sparta Prague | 26 | 0 | 26 0 |
| 2002-03 | Rennes | 37 | 0 | |
| 2003-04 | Rennes | 38 | 0 | 75 0 |
| 2004-05 | Chelsea | 35 | 0 | |
| 2005-06 | Chelsea | 34 | 0 | |
| 2006-07 | Chelsea | 20 | 0 | |
| 2007-08 | Chelsea | 26 | 0 | |
| 2008-09 | Chelsea | 35 | 0 | |
| 2009-10 | Chelsea | 34 | 0 | |
| 2010-11 | Chelsea | 38 | 0 | |
| 2011-12 | Chelsea | 34 | 0 | |
| 2012-13 | Chelsea | 36 | 0 | 292 0 |

**CHALOBAH, Nathaniel (D)** 38 5
H: 6 1　W: 11 11　b.Sierra Leone 12-12-94
*Source:* Scholar. *Honours:* England Youth, Under-21.

| | | | | |
|---|---|---|---|---|
| 2010-11 | Chelsea | 0 | 0 | |
| 2011-12 | Chelsea | 0 | 0 | |
| 2012-13 | Chelsea | 0 | 0 | |
| 2012-13 | *Watford* | 38 | 5 | 38 5 |

**CLIFFORD, Billy (M)** 18 1
H: 5 7　W: 10 03　b.Slough 18-10-92
*Source:* Scholar.

| | | | | |
|---|---|---|---|---|
| 2010-11 | Chelsea | 0 | 0 | |
| 2011-12 | Chelsea | 0 | 0 | |
| 2012-13 | Chelsea | 0 | 0 | |
| 2012-13 | *Colchester U* | 18 | 1 | 18 1 |

**COLE, Ashley (D)** 382 16
H: 5 8　W: 10 05　b.Stepney 20-12-80
*Source:* Trainee. *Honours:* England Schools, Youth, Under-21, B, 103 full caps, 1 goal.

| | | | | |
|---|---|---|---|---|
| 1998-99 | Arsenal | 0 | 0 | |
| 1999-2000 | Arsenal | 1 | 0 | |
| 1999-2000 | *Crystal Palace* | 14 | 1 | 14 1 |
| 2000-01 | Arsenal | 17 | 3 | |
| 2001-02 | Arsenal | 29 | 2 | |
| 2002-03 | Arsenal | 31 | 1 | |
| 2003-04 | Arsenal | 32 | 0 | |
| 2004-05 | Arsenal | 35 | 2 | |
| 2005-06 | Arsenal | 11 | 0 | |
| 2006-07 | Arsenal | 0 | 0 | 156 8 |
| 2006-07 | Chelsea | 23 | 0 | |
| 2007-08 | Chelsea | 27 | 1 | |
| 2008-09 | Chelsea | 34 | 1 | |
| 2009-10 | Chelsea | 27 | 4 | |
| 2010-11 | Chelsea | 38 | 0 | |
| 2011-12 | Chelsea | 32 | 0 | |
| 2012-13 | Chelsea | 31 | 1 | 212 16 |

**COURTOIS, Thibaut (G)** 115 0
H: 6 6　W: 14 02　b.Bree 11-5-92
*Honours:* Belgium Youth, 10 full caps.

| | | | | |
|---|---|---|---|---|
| 2008-09 | Genk | 1 | 0 | |
| 2009-10 | Genk | 0 | 0 | |
| 2010-11 | Genk | 40 | 0 | 41 0 |
| 2011-12 | Chelsea | 0 | 0 | |
| 2011-12 | *Atletico Madrid* | 37 | 0 | |
| 2012-13 | Chelsea | 0 | 0 | |
| 2012-13 | *Atletico Madrid* | 37 | 0 | 74 0 |

**DAVEY, Alex (M)** 0 0

| | | | | |
|---|---|---|---|---|
| 2012-13 | Chelsea | 0 | 0 | |

**DAVILA, Ulises (M)** 70 7
b.Guadalajara 13-4-91
*Honours:* Mexico Youth.

| | | | | |
|---|---|---|---|---|
| 2008-09 | Tapatio | 18 | 3 | 18 3 |
| 2009-10 | Guadalajara | 7 | 0 | |
| 2010-11 | Guadalajara | 8 | 0 | 15 0 |
| 2011-12 | Chelsea | 0 | 0 | |
| 2011-12 | *Vitesse* | 2 | 0 | 2 0 |
| 2012-13 | Chelsea | 0 | 0 | |
| 2012-13 | *Sabadell* | 35 | 4 | 35 4 |

**DE BRUYNE, Kevin (M)** 112 24
H: 5 11　W: 12 00　b.Ghent 28-6-91
*Honours:* Belgium Youth, Under-21, 13 full caps, 3 goals.

| | | | | |
|---|---|---|---|---|
| 2008-09 | Genk | 2 | 0 | |
| 2009-10 | Genk | 30 | 3 | |
| 2010-11 | Genk | 32 | 5 | |
| 2011-12 | Genk | 15 | 6 | 79 14 |
| 2011-12 | Chelsea | 0 | 0 | |
| 2012-13 | Chelsea | 0 | 0 | |
| 2012-13 | *Werder Bremen* | 33 | 10 | 33 10 |

**DELAC, Matej (G)** 53 0
b.Bosnia 20-8-92
*Source:* Vitesse.

| | | | | |
|---|---|---|---|---|
| 2009-10 | Inter Zapresic | 38 | 0 | |
| 2010-11 | Chelsea | 0 | 0 | |
| 2011-12 | Chelsea | 0 | 0 | |
| 2011-12 | *Dynamo Ceske* | 1 | 0 | 1 0 |
| 2012-13 | Chelsea | 0 | 0 | |
| 2012-13 | *Inter Zapresic* | 14 | 0 | 52 0 |

**ESSIEN, Michael (M)** 321 37
H: 5 10　W: 13 06　b.Accra 3-12-82
*Source:* Liberty Accra. *Honours:* Ghana 52 full caps, 9 goals.

| | | | | |
|---|---|---|---|---|
| 2000-01 | Bastia | 13 | 1 | |
| 2001-02 | Bastia | 24 | 4 | |
| 2002-03 | Bastia | 29 | 6 | 66 11 |
| 2003-04 | Lyon | 34 | 3 | |
| 2004-05 | Lyon | 37 | 4 | 71 7 |
| 2005-06 | Chelsea | 31 | 2 | |
| 2006-07 | Chelsea | 33 | 2 | |
| 2007-08 | Chelsea | 27 | 6 | |
| 2008-09 | Chelsea | 11 | 1 | |
| 2009-10 | Chelsea | 14 | 3 | |
| 2010-11 | Chelsea | 33 | 3 | |
| 2011-12 | Chelsea | 14 | 0 | |
| 2012-13 | Chelsea | 0 | 0 | 163 17 |
| 2012-13 | *Real Madrid* | 21 | 2 | 21 2 |

**FERREIRA, Paulo (D)** 306 4
H: 6 0　W: 11 13　b.Cascais 18-1-79
*Honours:* Portugal Under-21, 62 full caps.

| | | | | |
|---|---|---|---|---|
| 1997-98 | Estoril | 1 | 0 | |
| 1998-99 | Estoril | 16 | 0 | |
| 1999-2000 | Estoril | 18 | 2 | 35 2 |
| 2000-01 | Vitoria Setubal | 34 | 2 | |
| 2001-02 | Vitoria Setubal | 34 | 0 | 68 2 |
| 2002-03 | Porto | 30 | 0 | |
| 2003-04 | Porto | 32 | 0 | 62 0 |
| 2004-05 | Chelsea | 29 | 0 | |
| 2005-06 | Chelsea | 21 | 0 | |
| 2006-07 | Chelsea | 24 | 0 | |
| 2007-08 | Chelsea | 18 | 0 | |
| 2008-09 | Chelsea | 7 | 0 | |
| 2009-10 | Chelsea | 13 | 0 | |
| 2010-11 | Chelsea | 21 | 0 | |
| 2011-12 | Chelsea | 6 | 0 | |
| 2012-13 | Chelsea | 2 | 0 | 141 0 |

**HAZARD, Eden (M)** 180 45
H: 5 7　W: 8 11　b.La Louviere 7-1-91
*Honours:* Belgium Youth, 37 full caps, 5 goals.

| | | | | |
|---|---|---|---|---|
| 2007-08 | Lille | 3 | 0 | |
| 2008-09 | Lille | 30 | 4 | |
| 2009-10 | Lille | 37 | 5 | |
| 2010-11 | Lille | 38 | 7 | |
| 2011-12 | Lille | 38 | 20 | 146 36 |
| 2012-13 | Chelsea | 34 | 9 | 34 9 |

**HAZARD, Thorgan (M)** 48 5
H: 5 8　W: 10 11　b.La Louviere 29-3-93

| | | | | |
|---|---|---|---|---|
| 2011-12 | Lens | 14 | 0 | 14 0 |
| 2012-13 | Chelsea | 0 | 0 | |
| 2012-13 | *Zulte-Waregem* | 34 | 5 | 34 5 |

**HILARIO (G)** 253 2
H: 6 2　W: 13 05　b.San Pedro da Cova 21-10-75
*Honours:* Portugal Under-21, B, 1 full cap.

| | | | | |
|---|---|---|---|---|
| 1994-95 | Naval | 27 | 0 | 27 0 |
| 1995-96 | Academica | 33 | 2 | |
| 1996-97 | Porto | 18 | 0 | |
| 1997-98 | Porto | 3 | 0 | |
| 1998-99 | Amadora | 27 | 0 | 27 0 |
| 1999-2000 | Porto | 19 | 0 | |
| 2000-01 | Porto | 0 | 0 | |
| 2001-02 | Varzim | 24 | 0 | 24 0 |

| | | | | |
|---|---|---|---|---|
| 2002-03 | Porto | 0 | 0 | 40 0 |
| 2002-03 | Academica | 10 | 0 | 43 2 |
| 2003-04 | Nacional | 29 | 0 | |
| 2004-05 | Nacional | 32 | 0 | |
| 2005-06 | Nacional | 11 | 0 | 72 0 |
| 2006-07 | Chelsea | 11 | 0 | |
| 2007-08 | Chelsea | 3 | 0 | |
| 2008-09 | Chelsea | 1 | 0 | |
| 2009-10 | Chelsea | 3 | 0 | |
| 2010-11 | Chelsea | 0 | 0 | |
| 2011-12 | Chelsea | 2 | 0 | |
| 2012-13 | Chelsea | 0 | 0 | 20 0 |

**HUTCHINSON, Sam (M)** 14 1
H: 6 0　W: 11 07　b.Windsor 3-8-89
*Source:* Scholar. *Honours:* England Youth.

| | | | | |
|---|---|---|---|---|
| 2006-07 | Chelsea | 1 | 0 | |
| 2007-08 | Chelsea | 0 | 0 | |
| 2008-09 | Chelsea | 0 | 0 | |
| 2009-10 | Chelsea | 2 | 0 | |
| 2010-11 | Chelsea | 0 | 0 | |
| 2011-12 | Chelsea | 2 | 0 | |
| 2012-13 | Chelsea | 0 | 0 | 5 0 |
| 2012-13 | *Nottingham F* | 9 | 1 | 9 1 |

**INCE, Rohan (D)** 2 0
H: 6 3　W: 12 08　b.Whitechapel 8-11-92
*Source:* Scholar.

| | | | | |
|---|---|---|---|---|
| 2010-11 | Chelsea | 0 | 0 | |
| 2011-12 | Chelsea | 0 | 0 | |
| 2012-13 | Chelsea | 0 | 0 | |
| 2012-13 | *Yeovil T* | 2 | 0 | 2 0 |

**IVANOVIC, Branislav (M)** 269 25
H: 6 0　W: 12 04　b.Sremska Mitreovica 22-2-84
*Honours:* Serbia Under-21, 61 full caps, 7 goals.

| | | | | |
|---|---|---|---|---|
| 2002-03 | Sremska | 19 | 2 | 19 2 |
| 2003-04 | OFK Belgrade | 13 | 0 | |
| 2004-05 | OFK Belgrade | 27 | 2 | |
| 2005-06 | OFK Belgrade | 15 | 3 | 55 5 |
| 2006 | Lokomotiv Moscow | 28 | 2 | |
| 2007 | Lokomotiv Moscow | 26 | 3 | 54 5 |
| 2007-08 | Chelsea | 0 | 0 | |
| 2008-09 | Chelsea | 16 | 0 | |
| 2009-10 | Chelsea | 28 | 1 | |
| 2010-11 | Chelsea | 34 | 4 | |
| 2011-12 | Chelsea | 29 | 3 | |
| 2012-13 | Chelsea | 34 | 5 | 141 13 |

**KAKUTA, Gael (F)** 53 6
H: 5 8　W: 10 03　b.Lille 21-6-91
*Source:* Lens. *Honours:* Chelsea Scholar. France Youth, Under-21.

| | | | | |
|---|---|---|---|---|
| 2008-09 | Chelsea | 0 | 0 | |
| 2009-10 | Chelsea | 1 | 0 | |
| 2010-11 | Chelsea | 5 | 0 | |
| 2010-11 | *Fulham* | 7 | 1 | 7 1 |
| 2011-12 | Chelsea | 0 | 0 | |
| 2011-12 | *Bolton W* | 4 | 0 | 4 0 |
| 2011-12 | *Dijon* | 14 | 4 | 14 4 |
| 2012-13 | Chelsea | 0 | 0 | 6 0 |
| 2012-13 | *Vitesse* | 22 | 1 | 22 1 |

**KALAS, Tomas (D)** 39 1
H: 6 0　W: 12 00　b.Olomouc 15-5-93
*Source:* Sigma Olomouc. *Honours:* Czech Republic Under-21.

| | | | | |
|---|---|---|---|---|
| 2009-10 | Sigma Olomouc | 1 | 0 | |
| 2010-11 | Chelsea | 0 | 0 | |
| 2010-11 | *Sigma Olomouc* | 4 | 0 | 5 0 |
| 2011-12 | Chelsea | 0 | 0 | |
| 2012-13 | Chelsea | 0 | 0 | |
| 2012-13 | *Vitesse* | 34 | 1 | 34 1 |

**KANE, Todd (D)** 17 0
H: 5 11　W: 11 00　b.Huntingdon 17-9-93
*Source:* Scholar. *Honours:* England Youth.

| | | | | |
|---|---|---|---|---|
| 2011-12 | Chelsea | 0 | 0 | |
| 2012-13 | Chelsea | 0 | 0 | |
| 2012-13 | *Preston NE* | 3 | 0 | 3 0 |
| 2012-13 | *Blackburn R* | 14 | 0 | 14 0 |

**LALKOVIC, Milan (F)** 16 0
b.Kosice 9-12-92
*Source:* Scholar. *Honours:* Slovakia Youth, Under-21.

| | | | | |
|---|---|---|---|---|
| 2010-11 | Chelsea | 0 | 0 | |
| 2011-12 | Chelsea | 0 | 0 | |

| Season | Club | Apps | Gls | Tot A | Tot G |
|---|---|---|---|---|---|
| 2011-12 | *Doncaster R* | 6 | 0 | 6 | 0 |
| 2011-12 | *Den Haag* | 2 | 0 | 2 | 0 |
| 2012-13 | Chelsea | 0 | 0 | | |
| 2012-13 | *Vitoria Guimaraes* | 8 | 0 | 8 | 0 |

**LAMPARD, Frank (M)** 560 166
H: 6 0  W: 14 02  b.Romford 20-6-78
*Source:* Trainee. *Honours:* England Youth, Under-21, B, 97 full caps, 29 goals.

| Season | Club | Apps | Gls | Tot A | Tot G |
|---|---|---|---|---|---|
| 1994-95 | West Ham U | 0 | 0 | | |
| 1995-96 | West Ham U | 0 | 0 | | |
| 1995-96 | Swansea C | 9 | 1 | 9 | 1 |
| 1996-97 | West Ham U | 13 | 0 | | |
| 1997-98 | West Ham U | 31 | 5 | | |
| 1998-99 | West Ham U | 38 | 5 | | |
| 1999-2000 | West Ham U | 34 | 7 | | |
| 2000-01 | West Ham U | 30 | 7 | 148 | 24 |
| 2001-02 | Chelsea | 37 | 5 | | |
| 2002-03 | Chelsea | 38 | 6 | | |
| 2003-04 | Chelsea | 38 | 10 | | |
| 2004-05 | Chelsea | 38 | 13 | | |
| 2005-06 | Chelsea | 35 | 16 | | |
| 2006-07 | Chelsea | 37 | 11 | | |
| 2007-08 | Chelsea | 24 | 10 | | |
| 2008-09 | Chelsea | 37 | 12 | | |
| 2009-10 | Chelsea | 36 | 22 | | |
| 2010-11 | Chelsea | 24 | 10 | | |
| 2011-12 | Chelsea | 30 | 11 | | |
| 2012-13 | Chelsea | 29 | 15 | 403 | 141 |

**LOFTUS-CHEEK, Ruben (M)** 0 0
b. 23-1-96

| Season | Club | Apps | Gls |
|---|---|---|---|
| 2012-13 | Chelsea | 0 | 0 |

**LUIZ, David (D)** 170 11
H: 6 2  W: 13 03  b.Sao Paulo 22-4-87
*Honours:* Brazil Youth, 28 full caps.

| Season | Club | Apps | Gls | Tot A | Tot G |
|---|---|---|---|---|---|
| 2005 | Vitoria | 0 | 0 | | |
| 2006 | Vitoria | 26 | 1 | 26 | 1 |
| 2006-07 | Benfica | 10 | 0 | | |
| 2007-08 | Benfica | 8 | 0 | | |
| 2008-09 | Benfica | 19 | 2 | | |
| 2009-10 | Benfica | 29 | 2 | | |
| 2010-11 | Benfica | 16 | 0 | 82 | 4 |
| 2010-11 | Chelsea | 12 | 2 | | |
| 2011-12 | Chelsea | 20 | 2 | | |
| 2012-13 | Chelsea | 30 | 2 | 62 | 6 |

**LUKAKU, Romelu (F)** 116 50
H: 6 3  W: 13 00  b.Antwerp 13-5-93
*Honours:* Belgium Under-21, 21 full caps, 3 goals.

| Season | Club | Apps | Gls | Tot A | Tot G |
|---|---|---|---|---|---|
| 2008-09 | Anderlecht | 1 | 0 | | |
| 2009-10 | Anderlecht | 33 | 15 | | |
| 2010-11 | Anderlecht | 37 | 16 | | |
| 2011-12 | Anderlecht | 2 | 2 | 73 | 33 |
| 2011-12 | Chelsea | 8 | 0 | | |
| 2012-13 | Chelsea | 0 | 0 | 8 | 0 |
| 2012-13 | WBA | 35 | 17 | 35 | 17 |

**MALOUDA, Florent (M)** 438 80
H: 6 0  W: 11 06  b.Guyane 13-6-80
*Honours:* France 80 full caps, 9 goals.

| Season | Club | Apps | Gls | Tot A | Tot G |
|---|---|---|---|---|---|
| 1996-97 | Chateauroux | 2 | 0 | | |
| 1997-98 | Chateauroux | 1 | 0 | | |
| 1998-99 | Chateauroux | 28 | 3 | | |
| 1999-2000 | Chateauroux | 28 | 2 | 59 | 5 |
| 2000-01 | Guingamp | 23 | 1 | | |
| 2001-02 | Guingamp | 32 | 4 | | |
| 2002-03 | Guingamp | 37 | 10 | 92 | 15 |
| 2003-04 | Lyon | 35 | 4 | | |
| 2004-05 | Lyon | 37 | 5 | | |
| 2005-06 | Lyon | 31 | 6 | | |
| 2006-07 | Lyon | 35 | 10 | 138 | 25 |
| 2007-08 | Chelsea | 21 | 2 | | |
| 2008-09 | Chelsea | 31 | 6 | | |
| 2009-10 | Chelsea | 33 | 12 | | |
| 2010-11 | Chelsea | 38 | 13 | | |
| 2011-12 | Chelsea | 26 | 2 | | |
| 2012-13 | Chelsea | 0 | 0 | 149 | 35 |

**MARIN, Marko (M)** 154 17
H: 5 7  W: 9 12  b.Gradiska 13-3-89
*Honours:* Germany Youth, Under-21, 16 full caps, 1 goal.

| Season | Club | Apps | Gls | Tot A | Tot G |
|---|---|---|---|---|---|
| 2006-07 | Moenchengladbach | 3 | 0 | | |
| 2007-08 | Moenchengladbach | 25 | 4 | | |
| 2008-09 | Moenchengladbach | 33 | 4 | 61 | 8 |
| 2009-10 | Werder Bremen | 32 | 4 | | |
| 2010-11 | Werder Bremen | 34 | 3 | | |
| 2011-12 | Werder Bremen | 21 | 1 | 87 | 8 |
| 2012-13 | Chelsea | 6 | 1 | 6 | 1 |

**MATA, Juan (M)** 237 61
H: 5 7  W: 11 00  b.Ocon de Villafranca 28-4-88
*Honours:* Spain Youth, Under-21, 27 full caps, 8 goals.

| Season | Club | Apps | Gls | Tot A | Tot G |
|---|---|---|---|---|---|
| 2006-07 | Real Madrid B | 39 | 10 | 39 | 10 |
| 2007-08 | Valencia | 24 | 5 | | |
| 2008-09 | Valencia | 37 | 11 | | |
| 2009-10 | Valencia | 35 | 9 | | |
| 2010-11 | Valencia | 33 | 8 | 129 | 33 |
| 2011-12 | Chelsea | 34 | 6 | | |
| 2012-13 | Chelsea | 35 | 12 | 69 | 18 |

**McEACHRAN, Josh (M)** 53 0
H: 5 10  W: 10 03  b.Oxford 1-3-93
*Source:* Scholar. *Honours:* England Under-21.

| Season | Club | Apps | Gls | Tot A | Tot G |
|---|---|---|---|---|---|
| 2010-11 | Chelsea | 9 | 0 | | |
| 2011-12 | Chelsea | 2 | 0 | | |
| 2011-12 | Swansea C | 4 | 0 | 4 | 0 |
| 2012-13 | Chelsea | 0 | 0 | 11 | 0 |
| 2012-13 | Middlesbrough | 38 | 0 | 38 | 0 |

**MEIRELES, Raul (M)** 274 23
H: 5 10  W: 10 12  b.Oporto 17-3-83
*Honours:* Portugal Under-21, 68 full caps, 8 goals.

| Season | Club | Apps | Gls | Tot A | Tot G |
|---|---|---|---|---|---|
| 2001-02 | Aves | 16 | 0 | | |
| 2002-03 | Aves | 26 | 1 | 42 | 1 |
| 2003-04 | Boavista | 29 | 0 | 29 | 0 |
| 2004-05 | Porto | 13 | 0 | | |
| 2005-06 | Porto | 18 | 2 | | |
| 2006-07 | Porto | 25 | 3 | | |
| 2007-08 | Porto | 28 | 4 | | |
| 2008-09 | Porto | 28 | 4 | | |
| 2009-10 | Porto | 25 | 2 | 137 | 15 |
| 2010-11 | Liverpool | 33 | 5 | | |
| 2011-12 | Liverpool | 2 | 0 | 35 | 5 |
| 2011-12 | Chelsea | 28 | 2 | | |
| 2012-13 | Chelsea | 3 | 0 | 31 | 2 |

Transferred to Fenerbahce September 2012

**MIKEL, John Obi (M)** 188 1
H: 6 0  W: 13 05  b.Plateau State 22-4-87
*Source:* Plateau U. *Honours:* Nigeria Youth, 46 full caps, 3 goals.

| Season | Club | Apps | Gls | Tot A | Tot G |
|---|---|---|---|---|---|
| 2005 | Lyn | 6 | 1 | 6 | 1 |
| 2006-07 | Chelsea | 22 | 0 | | |
| 2007-08 | Chelsea | 29 | 0 | | |
| 2008-09 | Chelsea | 34 | 0 | | |
| 2009-10 | Chelsea | 25 | 0 | | |
| 2010-11 | Chelsea | 28 | 0 | | |
| 2011-12 | Chelsea | 22 | 0 | | |
| 2012-13 | Chelsea | 22 | 0 | 182 | 0 |

**MOSES, Victor (M)** 155 20
H: 5 10  W: 11 07  b.Lagos 12-12-90
*Source:* Scholar. *Honours:* England Youth, Under-21, Nigeria 12 full caps 4 goals.

| Season | Club | Apps | Gls | Tot A | Tot G |
|---|---|---|---|---|---|
| 2007-08 | Crystal Palace | 13 | 3 | | |
| 2008-09 | Crystal Palace | 27 | 2 | | |
| 2009-10 | Crystal Palace | 18 | 6 | 58 | 11 |
| 2009-10 | Wigan Ath | 14 | 1 | | |
| 2010-11 | Wigan Ath | 21 | 1 | | |
| 2011-12 | Wigan Ath | 38 | 6 | | |
| 2012-13 | Wigan Ath | 1 | 0 | 74 | 8 |
| 2012-13 | Chelsea | 23 | 1 | 23 | 1 |

**MUSONDA, Lamisha (M)** 0 0
H: 5 6  b.Brussels 27-3-92

| Season | Club | Apps | Gls |
|---|---|---|---|
| 2012-13 | Chelsea | 0 | 0 |

**MUSONDA, Tika (M)** 0 0
b.Brussels 18-1-94

| Season | Club | Apps | Gls |
|---|---|---|---|
| 2012-13 | Chelsea | 0 | 0 |

**NKUMU, Archange (M)** 1 0
H: 6 2  W: 11 00  b.Tottenham 5-11-93
*Source:* Scholar.

| Season | Club | Apps | Gls | Tot A | Tot G |
|---|---|---|---|---|---|
| 2011-12 | Chelsea | 0 | 0 | | |
| 2012-13 | Chelsea | 0 | 0 | | |
| 2012-13 | Yeovil T | 1 | 0 | 1 | 0 |
| 2012-13 | Colchester U | 0 | 0 | | |

**OMERUO, Kenneth (D)** 0 0
H: 6 1  W: 12 00  b.Nigeria 17-10-93
*Source:* Standard Liege Youth. *Honours:* Nigeria Youth.

| Season | Club | Apps | Gls |
|---|---|---|---|
| 2011-12 | Chelsea | 0 | 0 |
| 2012-13 | Chelsea | 0 | 0 |

**OSCAR, Emboaba (M)** 72 14
H: 5 11  W: 10 04  b.Americana 9-9-91
*Honours:* Brazil Youth, 22 full caps 6 goals.

| Season | Club | Apps | Gls | Tot A | Tot G |
|---|---|---|---|---|---|
| 2008-09 | Sao Paulo | 1 | 0 | | |
| 2009-10 | Sao Paulo | 3 | 0 | 4 | 0 |
| 2010-11 | Internacional | 7 | 2 | | |
| 2011-12 | Internacional | 27 | 8 | 34 | 10 |
| 2012-13 | Chelsea | 34 | 4 | 34 | 4 |

**PAPPOE, Daniel (D)** 0 0
b.Accra 30-12-93
*Source:* Scholar.

| Season | Club | Apps | Gls |
|---|---|---|---|
| 2011-12 | Chelsea | 0 | 0 |
| 2012-13 | Chelsea | 0 | 0 |

**PIAZON, Lucas (M)** 1 0
H: 6 0  W: 11 11  b.Curitiba 20-1-94
*Source:* Scholar.

| Season | Club | Apps | Gls | Tot A | Tot G |
|---|---|---|---|---|---|
| 2011-12 | Chelsea | 0 | 0 | | |
| 2012-13 | Chelsea | 1 | 0 | 1 | 0 |
| 2012-13 | *Malaga* | 0 | 0 | | |

**PIREZ, Jhon (F)** 0 0
b.Montevideo 20-2-93
*Source:* Scholar. *Honours:* Uruguay Youth.

| Season | Club | Apps | Gls |
|---|---|---|---|
| 2011-12 | Chelsea | 0 | 0 |
| 2012-13 | Chelsea | 0 | 0 |

**RAMIRES (M)** 195 29
H: 5 11  W: 10 03  b.Rio de Janeiro 24-3-87
*Honours:* Brazil 34 full caps, 3 goals.

| Season | Club | Apps | Gls | Tot A | Tot G |
|---|---|---|---|---|---|
| 2006 | Joinville | 14 | 3 | 14 | 3 |
| 2007 | Cruzeiro | 32 | 3 | | |
| 2008 | Cruzeiro | 25 | 6 | | |
| 2009 | Cruzeiro | 4 | 1 | 61 | 10 |
| 2009-10 | Benfica | 26 | 4 | 26 | 4 |
| 2010-11 | Chelsea | 29 | 2 | | |
| 2011-12 | Chelsea | 30 | 5 | | |
| 2012-13 | Chelsea | 35 | 5 | 94 | 12 |

**ROMEU, Oriol (M)** 72 1
H: 6 0  W: 12 06  b.Ulldecona 24-9-91
*Honours:* Spain Youth, Under-21.

| Season | Club | Apps | Gls | Tot A | Tot G |
|---|---|---|---|---|---|
| 2008-09 | Barcelona B | 5 | 0 | | |
| 2009-10 | Barcelona B | 26 | 0 | | |
| 2010-11 | Barcelona B | 18 | 1 | 49 | 1 |
| 2010-11 | Barcelona | 1 | 0 | 1 | 0 |
| 2011-12 | Chelsea | 16 | 0 | | |
| 2012-13 | Chelsea | 6 | 0 | 22 | 0 |

**SAVILLE, George (M)** 3 0
H: 5 9  W: 11 07  b.Camberley 1-6-93
*Source:* Scholar.

| Season | Club | Apps | Gls | Tot A | Tot G |
|---|---|---|---|---|---|
| 2010-11 | Chelsea | 0 | 0 | | |
| 2011-12 | Chelsea | 0 | 0 | | |
| 2012-13 | Chelsea | 0 | 0 | | |
| 2012-13 | Millwall | 3 | 0 | 3 | 0 |

**TERRY, John (D)** 393 32
H: 6 1  W: 14 02  b.Barking 7-12-80
*Source:* Trainee. *Honours:* England Under-21, 78 full caps, 6 goals.

| Season | Club | Apps | Gls | Tot A | Tot G |
|---|---|---|---|---|---|
| 1997-98 | Chelsea | 0 | 0 | | |
| 1998-99 | Chelsea | 2 | 0 | | |
| 1999-2000 | Chelsea | 4 | 0 | | |
| 1999-2000 | *Nottingham F* | 6 | 0 | 6 | 0 |
| 2000-01 | Chelsea | 22 | 1 | | |
| 2001-02 | Chelsea | 33 | 1 | | |
| 2002-03 | Chelsea | 20 | 3 | | |
| 2003-04 | Chelsea | 33 | 2 | | |
| 2004-05 | Chelsea | 36 | 3 | | |
| 2005-06 | Chelsea | 36 | 4 | | |
| 2006-07 | Chelsea | 28 | 1 | | |
| 2007-08 | Chelsea | 23 | 1 | | |
| 2008-09 | Chelsea | 35 | 1 | | |
| 2009-10 | Chelsea | 37 | 2 | | |
| 2010-11 | Chelsea | 33 | 3 | | |
| 2011-12 | Chelsea | 31 | 6 | | |
| 2012-13 | Chelsea | 14 | 4 | 387 | 32 |

**TORRES, Fernando (F)** 358 155
H: 5 9  W: 12 03  b.Madrid 20-3-84
*Honours:* Spain Youth, Under-21, 104 full caps, 36 goals.

| Season | Club | Apps | Gls | Tot A | Tot G |
|---|---|---|---|---|---|
| 2002-03 | Atletico Madrid | 29 | 13 | | |
| 2003-04 | Atletico Madrid | 35 | 19 | | |
| 2004-05 | Atletico Madrid | 38 | 16 | | |
| 2005-06 | Atletico Madrid | 36 | 13 | | |
| 2006-07 | Atletico Madrid | 36 | 14 | 174 | 75 |
| 2007-08 | Liverpool | 33 | 24 | | |

|  |  | | | | |
|---|---|--:|--:|--:|--:|
| 2008-09 | Liverpool | 24 | 14 | | |
| 2009-10 | Liverpool | 22 | 18 | | |
| 2010-11 | Liverpool | 23 | 9 | 102 | 65 |
| 2010-11 | Chelsea | 14 | 1 | | |
| 2011-12 | Chelsea | 32 | 6 | | |
| 2012-13 | Chelsea | 36 | 8 | 82 | 15 |

**TURNBULL, Ross (G)** 98 0
H: 6 4  W: 15 00  b.Bishop Auckland 4-1-85
Source: Trainee. Honours: England Youth, Under-20.

|  |  | | | | |
|---|---|--:|--:|--:|--:|
| 2002-03 | Middlesbrough | 0 | 0 | | |
| 2003-04 | Middlesbrough | 0 | 0 | | |
| 2003-04 | *Darlington* | 1 | 0 | 1 | 0 |
| 2003-04 | *Barnsley* | 3 | 0 | | |
| 2004-05 | Middlesbrough | 0 | 0 | | |
| 2004-05 | *Bradford C* | 2 | 0 | 2 | 0 |
| 2004-05 | *Barnsley* | 23 | 0 | 26 | 0 |
| 2005-06 | Middlesbrough | 2 | 0 | | |
| 2005-06 | *Crewe Alex* | 29 | 0 | 29 | 0 |
| 2006-07 | Middlesbrough | 0 | 0 | | |
| 2007-08 | Middlesbrough | 3 | 0 | | |
| 2007-08 | *Cardiff C* | 6 | 0 | 6 | 0 |
| 2008-09 | Middlesbrough | 22 | 0 | | |
| 2009-10 | Middlesbrough | 0 | 0 | 27 | 0 |
| 2009-10 | Chelsea | 2 | 0 | | |
| 2010-11 | Chelsea | 0 | 0 | | |
| 2011-12 | Chelsea | 2 | 0 | | |
| 2012-13 | Chelsea | 3 | 0 | 7 | 0 |

**VAN AANHOLT, Patrick (D)** 84 2
H: 5 9  W: 10 08  b.Den Bosch 3-7-88
Honours: Holland Youth, Under-21.

|  |  | | | | |
|---|---|--:|--:|--:|--:|
| 2007-08 | Chelsea | 0 | 0 | | |
| 2008-09 | Chelsea | 0 | 0 | | |
| 2009-10 | Chelsea | 2 | 0 | | |
| 2009-10 | *Coventry C* | 20 | 0 | 20 | 0 |
| 2009-10 | *Newcastle U* | 7 | 0 | 7 | 0 |
| 2010-11 | Chelsea | 0 | 0 | | |
| 2010-11 | *Leicester C* | 12 | 1 | 12 | 1 |
| 2011-12 | Chelsea | 0 | 0 | | |
| 2011-12 | *Wigan Ath* | 3 | 0 | 3 | 0 |
| 2011-12 | *Vitesse* | 9 | 0 | | |
| 2012-13 | Chelsea | 0 | 0 | 2 | 0 |
| 2012-13 | *Vitesse* | 31 | 1 | 40 | 1 |

**WALKER, Sam (G)** 78 0
H: 6 5  W: 14 00  b.Gravesend 2-10-91
Source: Scholar.

|  |  | | | | |
|---|---|--:|--:|--:|--:|
| 2009-10 | Chelsea | 0 | 0 | | |
| 2010-11 | Chelsea | 0 | 0 | | |
| 2010-11 | *Barnet* | 7 | 0 | 7 | 0 |
| 2011-12 | Chelsea | 0 | 0 | | |
| 2011-12 | *Northampton T* | 21 | 0 | 21 | 0 |
| 2011-12 | *Yeovil T* | 20 | 0 | 20 | 0 |
| 2012-13 | Chelsea | 0 | 0 | | |
| 2012-13 | *Bristol R* | 11 | 0 | 11 | 0 |
| 2012-13 | *Colchester U* | 19 | 0 | 19 | 0 |

**Players retained or with offer of contract**
Feruz, Islam; Nditi, Adam Eric Richard; Oliveira Dos Santos, Wallace; Osmanovic, Anjur; Swift, John David; Van Homoet Bruma, Jeffrey Kevin.

**Scholars**
Beeney, Mitchell Ryan; Christensen, Andreas Bodtker; Cole George; Conroy, Dion John; Dabo, Fankaty Sheikam; Gnahore, Ambrose Gnahoua; Houghton, Jordan; Kandi, Chike; Killip, Ben; Kiwomya, Andrew Alexander; Mitchell, Reece Steven; Muleba, Jonathan; Ssewankambo, Isak Ssali; Starkey, Jesse Aaron; Wright, Kevin.

# CHELTENHAM T (25)

**ANDREW, Danny (D)** 66 4
H: 5 11  W: 11 06  b.Holbeach 23-12-90

|  |  | | | | |
|---|---|--:|--:|--:|--:|
| 2009-10 | Peterborough U | 2 | 0 | 2 | 0 |
| 2009-10 | *Cheltenham T* | 10 | 0 | | |
| 2010-11 | Cheltenham T | 43 | 4 | | |
| 2011-12 | Cheltenham T | 10 | 0 | | |
| 2012-13 | Cheltenham T | 1 | 0 | 64 | 4 |

**BROWN, Scott P (G)** 207 0
H: 6 2  W: 13 01  b.Wolverhampton 26-4-85
Source: Wolverhampton W Trainee.
From Welshpool T

|  |  | | | | |
|---|---|--:|--:|--:|--:|
| 2003-04 | Bristol C | 0 | 0 | | |
| 2004-05 | Cheltenham T | 0 | 0 | | |
| 2005-06 | Cheltenham T | 1 | 0 | | |
| 2006-07 | Cheltenham T | 11 | 0 | | |
| 2007-08 | Cheltenham T | 0 | 0 | | |
| 2008-09 | Cheltenham T | 35 | 0 | | |
| 2009-10 | Cheltenham T | 46 | 0 | | |
| 2010-11 | Cheltenham T | 46 | 0 | | |
| 2011-12 | Cheltenham T | 22 | 0 | | |
| 2012-13 | Cheltenham T | 46 | 0 | 207 | 0 |

**CARTER, Darren (M)** 246 18
H: 6 2  W: 12 03  b.Solihull 18-12-83
Source: Scholar. Honours: England Youth, Under-20.

|  |  | | | | |
|---|---|--:|--:|--:|--:|
| 2001-02 | Birmingham C | 13 | 1 | | |
| 2002-03 | Birmingham C | 12 | 0 | | |
| 2003-04 | Birmingham C | 5 | 0 | | |
| 2004-05 | Birmingham C | 15 | 2 | 45 | 3 |
| 2004-05 | *Sunderland* | 10 | 1 | 10 | 1 |
| 2005-06 | WBA | 20 | 1 | | |
| 2006-07 | WBA | 33 | 3 | 53 | 4 |
| 2007-08 | Preston NE | 39 | 4 | | |
| 2008-09 | Preston NE | 18 | 0 | | |
| 2009-10 | Preston NE | 23 | 0 | | |
| 2010-11 | Preston NE | 14 | 0 | 94 | 4 |
| 2010-11 | *Millwall* | 10 | 0 | 10 | 0 |
| 2012-13 | Cheltenham T | 34 | 6 | 34 | 6 |

**DEERING, Sam (M)** 98 5
H: 5 5  W: 10 00  b.Stepney 26-2-91
Source: Oxford U Scholar.

|  |  | | | | |
|---|---|--:|--:|--:|--:|
| 2010-11 | Oxford U | 6 | 0 | 6 | 0 |
| 2010-11 | *Barnet* | 16 | 2 | | |
| 2011-12 | Barnet | 44 | 3 | 60 | 5 |
| 2012-13 | Cheltenham T | 32 | 0 | 32 | 0 |

**DUFFY, Darryl (F)** 283 74
H: 5 11  W: 12 01  b.Glasgow 16-4-84
Honours: Scotland Under-21, B.

|  |  | | | | |
|---|---|--:|--:|--:|--:|
| 2003-04 | Rangers | 1 | 0 | 1 | 0 |
| 2003-04 | *Brechin C* | 8 | 3 | 8 | 3 |
| 2004-05 | Falkirk | 35 | 17 | | |
| 2005-06 | Falkirk | 21 | 9 | 56 | 26 |
| 2005-06 | Hull C | 15 | 3 | | |
| 2006-07 | Hull C | 5 | 0 | | |
| 2006-07 | *Hartlepool U* | 10 | 5 | 10 | 5 |
| 2006-07 | *Swansea C* | 8 | 5 | | |
| 2007-08 | Swansea C | 20 | 1 | 28 | 6 |
| 2008-09 | Bristol R | 43 | 13 | | |
| 2009-10 | Bristol R | 30 | 4 | | |
| 2009-10 | *Carlisle U* | 8 | 1 | 8 | 1 |
| 2010-11 | Bristol R | 3 | 0 | 76 | 17 |
| 2010-11 | *Hibernian* | 7 | 0 | 7 | 0 |
| 2011-12 | Cheltenham T | 41 | 11 | | |
| 2012-13 | Cheltenham T | 24 | 2 | 65 | 13 |

**ELLIOTT, Steve (D)** 444 24
H: 6 1  W: 14 00  b.Derby 29-10-78
Source: Trainee. Honours: England Under-21.

|  |  | | | | |
|---|---|--:|--:|--:|--:|
| 1996-97 | Derby Co | 0 | 0 | | |
| 1997-98 | Derby Co | 0 | 0 | | |
| 1998-99 | Derby Co | 11 | 0 | | |
| 1999-2000 | Derby Co | 20 | 0 | | |
| 2000-01 | Derby Co | 6 | 0 | | |
| 2001-02 | Derby Co | 6 | 0 | | |
| 2002-03 | Derby Co | 23 | 1 | | |
| 2003-04 | Derby Co | 4 | 0 | 73 | 1 |
| 2003-04 | *Blackpool* | 28 | 0 | 28 | 0 |
| 2004-05 | Bristol R | 41 | 2 | | |
| 2005-06 | Bristol R | 45 | 2 | | |
| 2006-07 | Bristol R | 39 | 5 | | |
| 2007-08 | Bristol R | 33 | 3 | | |
| 2008-09 | Bristol R | 39 | 3 | | |
| 2009-10 | Bristol R | 21 | 1 | 218 | 16 |
| 2010-11 | Cheltenham T | 41 | 1 | | |
| 2011-12 | Cheltenham T | 38 | 2 | | |
| 2012-13 | Cheltenham T | 46 | 4 | 125 | 7 |

**GRAHAM, Bagasan (M)** 8 0
H: 5 11  W: 11 05  b.Plaistow 6-10-92
Source: QPR Scholar.

|  |  | | | | |
|---|---|--:|--:|--:|--:|
| 2011-12 | Cheltenham T | 7 | 0 | | |
| 2012-13 | Cheltenham T | 1 | 0 | 8 | 0 |

**HANKS, Joe (M)** 1 0
b.Gloucester 2-3-95

|  |  | | | | |
|---|---|--:|--:|--:|--:|
| 2012-13 | Cheltenham T | 1 | 0 | 1 | 0 |

**HARRISON, Byron (F)** 95 21
H: 6 3  W: 13 02  b.Wandsworth 15-6-87
Source: Havant & Waterlooville, Worthing, Boreham Wood, Harrow B, Ashford T, Carshalton Ath.

|  |  | | | | |
|---|---|--:|--:|--:|--:|
| 2010-11 | Stevenage | 20 | 8 | | |
| 2011-12 | Stevenage | 18 | 2 | 38 | 10 |
| 2011-12 | AFC Wimbledon | 19 | 2 | | |
| 2012-13 | AFC Wimbledon | 21 | 8 | 40 | 10 |
| 2012-13 | Cheltenham T | 17 | 1 | 17 | 1 |

**HECTOR, Michael (D)** 72 6
H: 6 4  W: 12 13  b.Newham 19-7-92
Source: Scholar.

|  |  | | | | |
|---|---|--:|--:|--:|--:|
| 2009-10 | Reading | 0 | 0 | | |
| 2010-11 | Reading | 0 | 0 | | |
| 2011 | *Dundalk* | 11 | 2 | 11 | 2 |
| 2011-12 | Reading | 0 | 0 | | |
| 2011-12 | *Barnet* | 27 | 2 | 27 | 2 |
| 2012-13 | Reading | 0 | 0 | | |
| 2012-13 | *Shrewsbury T* | 8 | 0 | 8 | 0 |
| 2012-13 | *Aldershot T* | 8 | 1 | 8 | 1 |
| 2012-13 | Cheltenham T | 18 | 1 | 18 | 1 |

**HOOMAN, Harry (D)** 8 0
H: 5 11  W: 12 06  b.Worcester 27-4-91
Source: Scholar.

|  |  | | | | |
|---|---|--:|--:|--:|--:|
| 2009-10 | Shrewsbury T | 2 | 0 | | |
| 2010-11 | Shrewsbury T | 0 | 0 | 2 | 0 |
| 2011-12 | Cheltenham T | 2 | 0 | | |
| 2012-13 | Cheltenham T | 4 | 0 | 6 | 0 |

**JOMBATI, Sido (D)** 73 3
H: 6 0  W: 11 11  b.Lisbon 20-8-87
Source: Exeter C, Weymouth, Basingstoke T, Bath C.

|  |  | | | | |
|---|---|--:|--:|--:|--:|
| 2011-12 | Cheltenham T | 36 | 2 | | |
| 2012-13 | Cheltenham T | 37 | 1 | 73 | 3 |

**JONES, Billy (D)** 242 9
H: 6 1  W: 11 05  b.Chatham 26-3-83
Source: Trainee.

|  |  | | | | |
|---|---|--:|--:|--:|--:|
| 2000-01 | Leyton Orient | 1 | 0 | | |
| 2001-02 | Leyton Orient | 16 | 0 | | |
| 2002-03 | Leyton Orient | 24 | 0 | | |
| 2003-04 | Leyton Orient | 31 | 0 | | |
| 2004-05 | Leyton Orient | 0 | 0 | 72 | 0 |
| 2004-05 | Kidderminster H | 12 | 0 | | |
| 2005-06 | Kidderminster H | 0 | 0 | | |
| 2006-07 | Kidderminster H | 0 | 0 | 12 | 0 |
| 2007-08 | Crewe Alex | 22 | 0 | | |
| 2008-09 | Crewe Alex | 38 | 6 | | |
| 2009-10 | Crewe Alex | 11 | 2 | 71 | 8 |
| 2010-11 | Exeter C | 29 | 0 | | |
| 2011-12 | Exeter C | 19 | 1 | 48 | 1 |
| 2012-13 | Cheltenham T | 39 | 0 | 39 | 0 |

**LOWE, Keith (D)** 195 11
H: 6 2  W: 13 03  b.Wolverhampton 13-9-85
Source: Scholar.

|  |  | | | | |
|---|---|--:|--:|--:|--:|
| 2004-05 | Wolverhampton W | 11 | 0 | | |
| 2005-06 | Wolverhampton W | 3 | 0 | | |
| 2005-06 | *Burnley* | 16 | 0 | 16 | 0 |
| 2005-06 | *QPR* | 1 | 0 | 1 | 0 |
| 2005-06 | *Swansea C* | 4 | 0 | 4 | 0 |
| 2006-07 | Wolverhampton W | 0 | 0 | | |
| 2006-07 | *Brighton & HA* | 0 | 0 | | |
| 2006-07 | *Cheltenham T* | 16 | 1 | | |
| 2007-08 | Wolverhampton W | 0 | 0 | | |
| 2007-08 | *Port Vale* | 28 | 3 | 28 | 3 |
| 2008-09 | Wolverhampton W | 0 | 0 | 14 | 0 |
| 2009-10 | Hereford U | 19 | 1 | 19 | 1 |
| 2010-11 | Cheltenham T | 36 | 1 | | |
| 2011-12 | Cheltenham T | 30 | 1 | | |
| 2012-13 | Cheltenham T | 31 | 4 | 113 | 7 |

**McGLASHAN, Jermaine (M)** 122 11
H: 5 7  W: 10 00  b.Croydon 14-4-88
Source: Ashford T (Middlesex).

|  |  | | | | |
|---|---|--:|--:|--:|--:|
| 2010-11 | Aldershot T | 38 | 1 | | |
| 2011-12 | Aldershot T | 23 | 4 | 61 | 5 |
| 2011-12 | Cheltenham T | 16 | 2 | | |
| 2012-13 | Cheltenham T | 45 | 4 | 61 | 6 |

**MOHAMED, Kaid (F)** 202 47
H: 5 11  W: 12 06  b.Cardiff 23-7-84
Source: Carmarthen T.

|  |  | | | | |
|---|---|--:|--:|--:|--:|
| 2003-04 | Cwmbran T | 29 | 3 | | |
| 2004-05 | Cwmbran T | 15 | 2 | | |
| 2004-05 | Llanelli | 3 | 1 | | |

|  |  | | | | |
|---|---|---|---|---|---|
| 2005-06 | Carmarthen T | 14 | 4 | | |
| 2005-06 | Cwmbran T | 11 | 7 | 55 | 12 |
| 2006-07 | Llanelli | 5 | 0 | 8 | 1 |
| 2006-07 | Carmarthen T | 30 | 15 | 44 | 19 |
| 2007-08 | Swindon T | 11 | 0 | 11 | 0 |

From Forest Green R, Bath C, AFC Wimbledon.

| | | | | | |
|---|---|---|---|---|---|
| 2011-12 | Cheltenham T | 45 | 11 | | |
| 2012-13 | Cheltenham T | 39 | 4 | 84 | 15 |

**PACK, Marlon (M)**    150 15
H: 6 2   W: 11 09   b.Portsmouth 25-3-91
*Source:* Scholar.

| | | | | | |
|---|---|---|---|---|---|
| 2008-09 | Portsmouth | 0 | 0 | | |
| 2009-10 | Portsmouth | 0 | 0 | | |
| 2009-10 | Wycombe W | 8 | 0 | 8 | 0 |
| 2009-10 | Dagenham & R | 17 | 1 | 17 | 1 |
| 2010-11 | Portsmouth | 1 | 0 | 1 | 0 |
| 2010-11 | *Cheltenham T* | 38 | 2 | | |
| 2011-12 | Cheltenham T | 43 | 5 | | |
| 2012-13 | Cheltenham T | 43 | 7 | 124 | 14 |

**PENN, Russ (M)**    167 9
H: 5 11   W: 12 13   b.Dudley 8-11-85
*Source:* Scunthorpe U, Kidderminster H.
*Honours:* England C.

| | | | | | |
|---|---|---|---|---|---|
| 2009-10 | Burton Alb | 40 | 4 | | |
| 2010-11 | Burton Alb | 41 | 3 | 81 | 7 |
| 2011-12 | Cheltenham T | 43 | 1 | | |
| 2012-13 | Cheltenham T | 43 | 1 | 86 | 2 |

**ROBERTS, Connor (G)**    0 0
b.Wrexham 8-12-92
*Source:* Scholar. *Honours:* Wales Youth.

| | | | | | |
|---|---|---|---|---|---|
| 2009-10 | Everton | 0 | 0 | | |
| 2010-11 | Everton | 0 | 0 | | |
| 2011-12 | Everton | 0 | 0 | | |
| 2012-13 | Colwyn Bay | 0 | 0 | | |
| 2012-13 | Cheltenham T | 0 | 0 | | |

**TAYLOR, Jason (M)**    261 17
H: 6 1   W: 11 03   b.Ashton-under-Lyne 28-1-87
*Source:* Scholar.

| | | | | | |
|---|---|---|---|---|---|
| 2005-06 | Oldham Ath | 0 | 0 | | |
| 2005-06 | *Stockport Co* | 9 | 0 | | |
| 2006-07 | Stockport Co | 45 | 1 | | |
| 2007-08 | Stockport Co | 42 | 4 | | |
| 2008-09 | Stockport Co | 8 | 1 | 104 | 6 |
| 2008-09 | Rotherham U | 15 | 1 | | |
| 2009-10 | Rotherham U | 2 | 0 | | |
| 2009-10 | *Rochdale* | 23 | 1 | 23 | 1 |
| 2010-11 | Rotherham U | 42 | 5 | | |
| 2011-12 | Rotherham U | 39 | 2 | | |
| 2012-13 | Rotherham U | 20 | 2 | 118 | 10 |
| 2012-13 | Cheltenham T | 16 | 0 | 16 | 0 |

**WILLIAMS, Ed (M)**    0 0

| | | | | | |
|---|---|---|---|---|---|
| 2012-13 | Cheltenham T | 0 | 0 | | |

**ZEBROSKI, Chris (F)**    211 40
H: 6 1   W: 11 08   b.Swindon 29-10-86
*Source:* Cirencester T, Scholar.

| | | | | | |
|---|---|---|---|---|---|
| 2005-06 | Plymouth Arg | 4 | 0 | | |
| 2006-07 | Plymouth Arg | 0 | 0 | 4 | 0 |
| 2006-07 | Millwall | 25 | 3 | | |
| 2007-08 | Millwall | 0 | 0 | 25 | 3 |
| 2008-09 | Wycombe W | 33 | 7 | | |
| 2009-10 | Wycombe W | 15 | 2 | 48 | 9 |
| 2009-10 | Torquay U | 30 | 6 | | |
| 2010-11 | Torquay U | 44 | 14 | 74 | 20 |
| 2011-12 | Bristol R | 39 | 3 | | |
| 2012-13 | Bristol R | 0 | 0 | 39 | 3 |
| 2012-13 | Cheltenham T | 21 | 5 | 21 | 5 |

**Scholars**
Bowen, James Malcolm Robert; Dale, Robson Louis; Donaghue, Owen Patrick; Gonzalo, Michael Joseph; Hamilton, Spencer Jon; Hanks, Joseph Peter; Keightley, Elliott Nigel; Kirkpatrick-Jones, Zachary Daniel; Kotwica, Zackariah Daniel; Marshall, Callum; Morana, Lewis Daniel; Powell, Adam Thomas; Reaney, Dale Edward; Rivers, Harvey Charles; Thomas, Keiron; Whitehead, Kieran John; Williams, Harry John Robert; Williams, Edward Christopher.

# CHESTERFIELD (26)

**ALLOTT, Mark (M)**    587 52
H: 5 11   W: 11 07   b.Middleton 3-10-77
*Source:* Trainee.

| | | | | | |
|---|---|---|---|---|---|
| 1995-96 | Oldham Ath | 0 | 0 | | |
| 1996-97 | Oldham Ath | 5 | 1 | | |
| 1997-98 | Oldham Ath | 22 | 2 | | |
| 1998-99 | Oldham Ath | 41 | 7 | | |
| 1999-2000 | Oldham Ath | 32 | 10 | | |
| 2000-01 | Oldham Ath | 39 | 7 | | |
| 2001-02 | Oldham Ath | 15 | 4 | | |
| 2001-02 | Chesterfield | 21 | 4 | | |
| 2002-03 | Chesterfield | 33 | 0 | | |
| 2003-04 | Chesterfield | 40 | 2 | | |
| 2004-05 | Chesterfield | 45 | 2 | | |
| 2005-06 | Chesterfield | 43 | 3 | | |
| 2006-07 | Chesterfield | 39 | 0 | | |
| 2007-08 | Oldham Ath | 42 | 4 | | |
| 2008-09 | Oldham Ath | 45 | 3 | 241 | 38 |
| 2009-10 | Chesterfield | 45 | 2 | | |
| 2010-11 | Chesterfield | 36 | 0 | | |
| 2011-12 | Chesterfield | 36 | 1 | | |
| 2012-13 | Chesterfield | 8 | 0 | 346 | 14 |

**BARRINGTON, Josh (G)**    0 0
b. 20-12-94

| | | | | | |
|---|---|---|---|---|---|
| 2012-13 | Chesterfield | 0 | 0 | | |

**BOA MORTE, Luis (F)**    347 47
H: 5 9   W: 12 06   b.Lisbon 4-8-77
*Source:* Sporting Lisbon, Lourihanense (loan). *Honours:* Portugal Youth, Under-21, 28 full caps, 1 goal.

| | | | | | |
|---|---|---|---|---|---|
| 1997-98 | Arsenal | 15 | 0 | | |
| 1998-99 | Arsenal | 8 | 0 | | |
| 1999-2000 | Arsenal | 2 | 0 | 25 | 0 |
| 1999-2000 | Southampton | 14 | 1 | | |
| 2000-01 | Southampton | 0 | 0 | 14 | 1 |
| 2000-01 | *Fulham* | 39 | 18 | | |
| 2001-02 | Fulham | 23 | 1 | | |
| 2002-03 | Fulham | 29 | 2 | | |
| 2003-04 | Fulham | 33 | 9 | | |
| 2004-05 | Fulham | 31 | 8 | | |
| 2005-06 | Fulham | 35 | 6 | | |
| 2006-07 | Fulham | 15 | 0 | 205 | 44 |
| 2006-07 | West Ham U | 14 | 1 | | |
| 2007-08 | West Ham U | 27 | 0 | | |
| 2008-09 | West Ham U | 27 | 0 | | |
| 2009-10 | West Ham U | 1 | 1 | | |
| 2010-11 | West Ham U | 22 | 0 | | |
| 2011-12 | West Ham U | 0 | 0 | 91 | 2 |
| 2012-13 | Chesterfield | 12 | 0 | 12 | 0 |

**BODEN, Scott (F)**    111 15
H: 5 11   W: 11 00   b.Sheffield 19-12-89
*Source:* IFK Marlehamn.

| | | | | | |
|---|---|---|---|---|---|
| 2008-09 | Chesterfield | 11 | 2 | | |
| 2009-10 | Chesterfield | 35 | 6 | | |
| 2010-11 | Chesterfield | 23 | 3 | | |
| 2011-12 | Chesterfield | 35 | 4 | | |
| 2011-12 | *Macclesfield T* | 7 | 0 | 7 | 0 |
| 2012-13 | Chesterfield | 9 | 0 | 104 | 15 |
| 2012-13 | *Alfreton T* | 0 | 0 | | |

**BRINDLEY, Richard (D)**    12 0
H: 5 10   W: 11 09   b.Coventry 30-11-87

| | | | | | |
|---|---|---|---|---|---|
| 2012-13 | Chesterfield | 12 | 0 | 12 | 0 |

**BROADHEAD, Jack (D)**    0 0
b. 2-10-94

| | | | | | |
|---|---|---|---|---|---|
| 2012-13 | Chesterfield | 0 | 0 | | |

**CLAY, Craig (M)**    27 1
H: 5 11   W: 11 07   b.Nottingham 5-5-92
*Source:* Scholar.

| | | | | | |
|---|---|---|---|---|---|
| 2010-11 | Chesterfield | 3 | 1 | | |
| 2011-12 | Chesterfield | 5 | 0 | | |
| 2012-13 | Chesterfield | 19 | 0 | 27 | 1 |

**COOPER, Liam (D)**    50 3
H: 6 2   W: 13 07   b.Hull 30-8-91
*Source:* Scholar. *Honours:* Scotland Youth.

| | | | | | |
|---|---|---|---|---|---|
| 2008-09 | Hull C | 0 | 0 | | |
| 2009-10 | Hull C | 2 | 0 | | |
| 2010-11 | Hull C | 2 | 0 | | |
| 2010-11 | Carlisle U | 6 | 1 | 6 | 1 |
| 2011-12 | Hull C | 7 | 0 | | |
| 2011-12 | *Huddersfield T* | 4 | 0 | 4 | 0 |
| 2012-13 | Hull C | 0 | 0 | 11 | 0 |
| 2012-13 | Chesterfield | 29 | 2 | 29 | 2 |

**DARIKWA, Tendayi (M)**    38 5
H: 6 2   W: 12 02   b.Nottingham 13-12-91
*Source:* Scholar.

| | | | | | |
|---|---|---|---|---|---|
| 2010-11 | Chesterfield | 0 | 0 | | |
| 2011-12 | Chesterfield | 2 | 0 | | |
| 2012-13 | Chesterfield | 36 | 5 | 38 | 5 |

**GNANDUILLET, Armand (F)**    13 3
H: 6 4   W: 13 12   b.Angers 13-2-92

| | | | | | |
|---|---|---|---|---|---|
| 2012-13 | Chesterfield | 13 | 3 | 13 | 3 |

**HAZEL, Jacob (F)**    2 0
H: 5 9   W: 11 04   b.Halifax 15-4-94

| | | | | | |
|---|---|---|---|---|---|
| 2012-13 | Chesterfield | 2 | 0 | 2 | 0 |

**HIRD, Samuel (D)**    203 3
H: 5 7   W: 10 12   b.Askern 7-9-87
*Source:* Scholar.

| | | | | | |
|---|---|---|---|---|---|
| 2005-06 | Leeds U | 0 | 0 | | |
| 2006-07 | Leeds U | 0 | 0 | | |
| 2006-07 | *Doncaster R* | 5 | 0 | | |
| 2007-08 | Doncaster R | 4 | 0 | | |
| 2007-08 | *Grimsby T* | 17 | 0 | 17 | 0 |
| 2008-09 | Doncaster R | 37 | 1 | | |
| 2009-10 | Doncaster R | 36 | 0 | | |
| 2010-11 | Doncaster R | 32 | 0 | | |
| 2011-12 | Doncaster R | 31 | 0 | 145 | 1 |
| 2012-13 | Chesterfield | 41 | 2 | 41 | 2 |

**LEE, Tommy (G)**    257 0
H: 6 2   W: 12 00   b.Keighley 3-1-86
*Source:* Scholar.

| | | | | | |
|---|---|---|---|---|---|
| 2005-06 | Manchester U | 0 | 0 | | |
| 2005-06 | *Macclesfield T* | 11 | 0 | | |
| 2006-07 | Macclesfield T | 34 | 0 | | |
| 2007-08 | Macclesfield T | 18 | 0 | 63 | 0 |
| 2007-08 | *Rochdale* | 11 | 0 | 11 | 0 |
| 2008-09 | Chesterfield | 28 | 0 | | |
| 2009-10 | Chesterfield | 42 | 0 | | |
| 2010-11 | Chesterfield | 46 | 0 | | |
| 2011-12 | Chesterfield | 35 | 0 | | |
| 2012-13 | Chesterfield | 32 | 0 | 183 | 0 |

**LESTER, Jack (F)**    560 146
H: 5 9   W: 12 08   b.Sheffield 8-10-75
*Source:* Trainee. *Honours:* England Schools.

| | | | | | |
|---|---|---|---|---|---|
| 1994-95 | Grimsby T | 7 | 0 | | |
| 1995-96 | Grimsby T | 5 | 0 | | |
| 1996-97 | Grimsby T | 22 | 5 | | |
| 1996-97 | *Doncaster R* | 11 | 1 | 11 | 1 |
| 1997-98 | Grimsby T | 40 | 4 | | |
| 1998-99 | Grimsby T | 33 | 4 | | |
| 1999-2000 | Grimsby T | 26 | 4 | 133 | 17 |
| 1999-2000 | Nottingham F | 15 | 2 | | |
| 2000-01 | Nottingham F | 19 | 7 | | |
| 2001-02 | Nottingham F | 32 | 5 | | |
| 2002-03 | Nottingham F | 33 | 7 | | |
| 2003-04 | Sheffield U | 32 | 12 | | |
| 2004-05 | Sheffield U | 12 | 0 | 44 | 12 |
| 2004-05 | Nottingham F | 3 | 1 | | |
| 2005-06 | Nottingham F | 38 | 5 | | |
| 2006-07 | Nottingham F | 35 | 6 | 175 | 33 |
| 2007-08 | Chesterfield | 36 | 23 | | |
| 2008-09 | Chesterfield | 37 | 20 | | |
| 2009-10 | Chesterfield | 29 | 11 | | |
| 2010-11 | Chesterfield | 40 | 17 | | |
| 2011-12 | Chesterfield | 21 | 3 | | |
| 2012-13 | Chesterfield | 34 | 9 | 197 | 83 |

**O'DONNELL, Richard (G)**    44 0
H: 6 2   W: 13 05   b.Sheffield 12-9-88
*Source:* Scholar.

| | | | | | |
|---|---|---|---|---|---|
| 2007-08 | Sheffield W | 0 | 0 | | |
| 2007-08 | *Rotherham U* | 0 | 0 | | |
| 2007-08 | *Oldham Ath* | 4 | 0 | 4 | 0 |
| 2008-09 | Sheffield W | 0 | 0 | | |
| 2009-10 | Sheffield W | 0 | 0 | | |
| 2010-11 | Sheffield W | 9 | 0 | | |
| 2011-12 | Sheffield W | 6 | 0 | 15 | 0 |
| 2011-12 | *Macclesfield T* | 11 | 0 | 11 | 0 |
| 2012-13 | Chesterfield | 14 | 0 | 14 | 0 |

**RANDALL, Mark (M)**    83 3
H: 6 0   W: 12 12   b.Milton Keynes 28-9-89
*Source:* Scholar. *Honours:* England Youth.

| | | | | | |
|---|---|---|---|---|---|
| 2006-07 | Arsenal | 0 | 0 | | |
| 2007-08 | Arsenal | 1 | 0 | | |

|  |  | | | | |
|---|---|---|---|---|---|
| 2007-08 | Burnley | 10 | 0 | 10 | 0 |
| 2008-09 | Arsenal | 1 | 0 | | |
| 2009-10 | Arsenal | 0 | 0 | | |
| 2009-10 | Milton Keynes D | 16 | 0 | 16 | 0 |
| 2010-11 | Arsenal | 0 | 0 | 2 | 0 |
| 2010-11 | Rotherham U | 10 | 1 | 10 | 1 |
| 2011-12 | Chesterfield | 16 | 1 | | |
| 2012-13 | Chesterfield | 29 | 1 | 45 | 2 |

**RICHARDS, Marc (F)**    373 117
H: 6 2   W: 12 06   b.Wolverhampton 8-7-82
*Source:* Trainee. *Honours:* England Youth, Under-20.

|  |  | | | | |
|---|---|---|---|---|---|
| 1999-2000 | Blackburn R | 0 | 0 | | |
| 2000-01 | Blackburn R | 0 | 0 | | |
| 2001-02 | Blackburn R | 0 | 0 | | |
| 2001-02 | Crewe Alex | 4 | 0 | 4 | 0 |
| 2001-02 | Oldham Ath | 5 | 0 | 5 | 0 |
| 2001-02 | Halifax T | 5 | 0 | 5 | 0 |
| 2002-03 | Blackburn R | 0 | 0 | | |
| 2002-03 | Swansea C | 17 | 7 | 17 | 7 |
| 2003-04 | Northampton T | 41 | 8 | | |
| 2004-05 | Northampton T | 12 | 2 | | |
| 2004-05 | Rochdale | 5 | 2 | 5 | 2 |
| 2005-06 | Northampton T | 0 | 0 | 53 | 10 |
| 2005-06 | Barnsley | 38 | 12 | | |
| 2006-07 | Barnsley | 31 | 6 | 69 | 18 |
| 2007-08 | Port Vale | 29 | 5 | | |
| 2008-09 | Port Vale | 30 | 10 | | |
| 2009-10 | Port Vale | 46 | 20 | | |
| 2010-11 | Port Vale | 40 | 16 | | |
| 2011-12 | Port Vale | 36 | 17 | 181 | 68 |
| 2012-13 | Chesterfield | 34 | 12 | 34 | 12 |

**SMITH, Nathan (D)**    168 1
H: 5 11   W: 12 00   b.Enfield 11-1-87
*Source:* Potters Bar T. *Honours:* Jamaica 1 full cap.

|  |  | | | | |
|---|---|---|---|---|---|
| 2007-08 | Yeovil T | 7 | 0 | | |
| 2008-09 | Yeovil T | 33 | 1 | | |
| 2009-10 | Yeovil T | 34 | 0 | | |
| 2010-11 | Yeovil T | 40 | 0 | 114 | 1 |
| 2011-12 | Chesterfield | 25 | 0 | | |
| 2012-13 | Chesterfield | 29 | 0 | 54 | 0 |

**TALBOT, Drew (F)**    257 23
H: 5 10   W: 11 00   b.Barnsley 19-7-86
*Source:* Dodworth Colliery.

|  |  | | | | |
|---|---|---|---|---|---|
| 2003-04 | Sheffield W | 0 | 0 | | |
| 2004-05 | Sheffield W | 21 | 4 | | |
| 2005-06 | Sheffield W | 0 | 0 | | |
| 2006-07 | Sheffield W | 8 | 0 | 29 | 4 |
| 2006-07 | Scunthorpe U | 3 | 1 | 3 | 1 |
| 2006-07 | Luton T | 15 | 3 | | |
| 2006-07 | Luton T | 27 | 0 | | |
| 2007-08 | Luton T | 7 | 0 | 49 | 3 |
| 2008-09 | Chesterfield | 17 | 2 | | |
| 2009-10 | Chesterfield | 30 | 6 | | |
| 2010-11 | Chesterfield | 44 | 3 | | |
| 2011-12 | Chesterfield | 43 | 2 | | |
| 2012-13 | Chesterfield | 42 | 2 | 176 | 15 |

**TOGWELL, Sam (M)**    307 12
H: 5 11   W: 12 04   b.Beaconsfield 14-10-84
*Source:* Scholar.

|  |  | | | | |
|---|---|---|---|---|---|
| 2002-03 | Crystal Palace | 1 | 0 | | |
| 2003-04 | Crystal Palace | 0 | 0 | | |
| 2004-05 | Crystal Palace | 0 | 0 | | |
| 2004-05 | Oxford U | 4 | 0 | 4 | 0 |
| 2004-05 | Northampton T | 8 | 0 | 8 | 0 |
| 2005-06 | Crystal Palace | 0 | 0 | 1 | 0 |
| 2005-06 | Port Vale | 27 | 2 | 27 | 2 |
| 2006-07 | Barnsley | 44 | 1 | | |
| 2007-08 | Barnsley | 22 | 1 | 66 | 2 |
| 2008-09 | Scunthorpe U | 40 | 2 | | |
| 2009-10 | Scunthorpe U | 41 | 2 | | |
| 2010-11 | Scunthorpe U | 36 | 0 | | |
| 2011-12 | Scunthorpe U | 39 | 1 | 156 | 5 |
| 2012-13 | Chesterfield | 45 | 3 | 45 | 3 |

**TROTMAN, Neal (D)**    150 6
H: 6 3   W: 13 08   b.Manchester 11-3-87
*Source:* Burnley Scholar.

|  |  | | | | |
|---|---|---|---|---|---|
| 2006-07 | Oldham Ath | 1 | 0 | | |
| 2006-07 | Oldham Ath | 17 | 1 | | |
| 2007-08 | Preston NE | 3 | 0 | | |
| 2008-09 | Preston NE | 0 | 0 | | |
| 2008-09 | Colchester U | 6 | 0 | 6 | 0 |
| 2009-10 | Preston NE | 0 | 0 | | |
| 2009-10 | Southampton | 18 | 2 | 18 | 2 |
| 2009-10 | Huddersfield T | 21 | 2 | 21 | 2 |
| 2010-11 | Preston NE | 0 | 0 | 3 | 0 |
| 2010-11 | Oldham Ath | 18 | 0 | 36 | 1 |
| 2011-12 | Rochdale | 12 | 0 | 12 | 0 |
| 2011-12 | Chesterfield | 23 | 1 | | |
| 2012-13 | Chesterfield | 31 | 0 | 54 | 1 |

**WAFULA, Jonathan (F)**    1 0
b.Alfreton 17-6-94

|  |  | | | | |
|---|---|---|---|---|---|
| 2012-13 | Chesterfield | 1 | 0 | 1 | 0 |

**WESTCARR, Craig (F)**    197 38
H: 5 11   W: 11 04   b.Nottingham 29-1-85
*Source:* Scholar. *Honours:* England Youth.

|  |  | | | | |
|---|---|---|---|---|---|
| 2001-02 | Nottingham F | 8 | 0 | | |
| 2002-03 | Nottingham F | 11 | 1 | | |
| 2003-04 | Nottingham F | 3 | 0 | | |
| 2004-05 | Nottingham F | 1 | 0 | 23 | 1 |
| 2004-05 | Lincoln C | 6 | 1 | 6 | 1 |
| 2004-05 | Milton Keynes D | 4 | 0 | 4 | 0 |

From Cambridge U, Kettering T.

|  |  | | | | |
|---|---|---|---|---|---|
| 2009-10 | Notts Co | 42 | 9 | | |
| 2010-11 | Notts Co | 41 | 12 | | |
| 2011-12 | Notts Co | 4 | 0 | 87 | 21 |
| 2011-12 | Chesterfield | 38 | 8 | | |
| 2012-13 | Chesterfield | 15 | 2 | 53 | 10 |
| 2012-13 | Walsall | 24 | 5 | 24 | 5 |

**WHITAKER, Danny (M)**    443 66
H: 5 10   W: 11 00   b.Wilmslow 14-11-80
*Source:* Wilmslow Sports.

|  |  | | | | |
|---|---|---|---|---|---|
| 2000-01 | Macclesfield T | 0 | 0 | | |
| 2001-02 | Macclesfield T | 16 | 2 | | |
| 2002-03 | Macclesfield T | 41 | 10 | | |
| 2003-04 | Macclesfield T | 36 | 5 | | |
| 2004-05 | Macclesfield T | 36 | 2 | | |
| 2005-06 | Macclesfield T | 42 | 4 | 171 | 23 |
| 2006-07 | Port Vale | 45 | 7 | | |
| 2007-08 | Port Vale | 41 | 7 | 86 | 14 |
| 2008-09 | Oldham Ath | 39 | 6 | | |
| 2009-10 | Oldham Ath | 41 | 2 | 80 | 8 |
| 2010-11 | Chesterfield | 46 | 15 | | |
| 2011-12 | Chesterfield | 30 | 5 | | |
| 2012-13 | Chesterfield | 30 | 1 | 106 | 21 |

**Scholars**
Barrington, Joshua John; Bowland, Bradley John; Brock, Oliver; Clarke, Matthew Ryan; Colton, Thomas Edward; Edridge, Regan William John; Fereday, Mark Howard; Hewitt, Alex James Joel; Johnson, Fabian Jacob; Mason, Cameron Francis; Mathers, Joseph Jordan; McNicholas, Jamie; Noel, Cormac Etienne Hayden; Partridge, Benjamin Jon; Scully, Joshua Daniel; Slack, Jordan Andrew; Whittaker, Timothy Mark.

# COLCHESTER U (27)

**BEAN, Marcus (M)**    294 19
H: 5 11   W: 11 06   b.Hammersmith 2-11-84
*Source:* Scholar.

|  |  | | | | |
|---|---|---|---|---|---|
| 2002-03 | QPR | 7 | 0 | | |
| 2003-04 | QPR | 31 | 1 | | |
| 2004-05 | QPR | 20 | 1 | | |
| 2004-05 | Swansea C | 8 | 0 | | |
| 2005-06 | QPR | 9 | 0 | 67 | 2 |
| 2005-06 | Swansea C | 9 | 1 | 17 | 1 |
| 2005-06 | Blackpool | 17 | 1 | | |
| 2006-07 | Blackpool | 6 | 0 | | |
| 2007-08 | Blackpool | 0 | 0 | 23 | 1 |
| 2007-08 | Rotherham U | 12 | 1 | 12 | 1 |
| 2008-09 | Brentford | 44 | 9 | | |
| 2009-10 | Brentford | 31 | 0 | | |
| 2010-11 | Brentford | 37 | 3 | | |
| 2011-12 | Brentford | 32 | 2 | 144 | 14 |
| 2012-13 | Colchester U | 31 | 0 | 31 | 0 |

**BOND, Andy (M)**    114 10
H: 5 10   W: 11 07   b.Wigan 16-3-86
*Source:* Crewe Alex Scholar, Barrow.

|  |  | | | | |
|---|---|---|---|---|---|
| 2010-11 | Colchester U | 43 | 7 | | |
| 2011-12 | Colchester U | 40 | 3 | | |
| 2012-13 | Colchester U | 27 | 0 | 110 | 10 |
| 2012-13 | Crewe Alex | 4 | 0 | 4 | 0 |

**COKER, Ben (D)**    41 0
H: 5 11   W: 11 09   b.Hatfield 17-6-89
*Source:* Bury T.

|  |  | | | | |
|---|---|---|---|---|---|
| 2010-11 | Colchester U | 20 | 0 | | |
| 2011-12 | Colchester U | 20 | 0 | | |
| 2012-13 | Colchester U | 1 | 0 | 41 | 0 |

**COUSINS, Mark (G)**    58 0
H: 6 2   W: 12 02   b.Chelmsford 9-1-87
*Source:* Scholar.

|  |  | | | | |
|---|---|---|---|---|---|
| 2005-06 | Colchester U | 0 | 0 | | |
| 2006-07 | Colchester U | 0 | 0 | | |
| 2007-08 | Colchester U | 2 | 0 | | |
| 2008-09 | Colchester U | 9 | 0 | | |
| 2009-10 | Colchester U | 0 | 0 | | |
| 2010-11 | Colchester U | 14 | 0 | | |
| 2011-12 | Colchester U | 10 | 0 | | |
| 2012-13 | Colchester U | 23 | 0 | 58 | 0 |

**DUGUID, Karl (M)**    522 47
H: 5 11   W: 11 06   b.Letchworth 21-3-78
*Source:* Trainee.

|  |  | | | | |
|---|---|---|---|---|---|
| 1995-96 | Colchester U | 16 | 1 | | |
| 1996-97 | Colchester U | 20 | 3 | | |
| 1997-98 | Colchester U | 21 | 3 | | |
| 1998-99 | Colchester U | 33 | 4 | | |
| 1999-2000 | Colchester U | 41 | 12 | | |
| 2000-01 | Colchester U | 41 | 5 | | |
| 2001-02 | Colchester U | 41 | 4 | | |
| 2002-03 | Colchester U | 27 | 3 | | |
| 2003-04 | Colchester U | 30 | 2 | | |
| 2004-05 | Colchester U | 0 | 0 | | |
| 2005-06 | Colchester U | 35 | 0 | | |
| 2006-07 | Colchester U | 43 | 5 | | |
| 2007-08 | Colchester U | 39 | 1 | | |
| 2008-09 | Plymouth Arg | 39 | 1 | | |
| 2009-10 | Plymouth Arg | 42 | 1 | | |
| 2010-11 | Plymouth Arg | 26 | 0 | 107 | 2 |
| 2011-12 | Colchester U | 25 | 3 | | |
| 2012-13 | Colchester U | 5 | 0 | 415 | 45 |

**EASTMAN, Tom (D)**    70 5
H: 6 3   W: 13 12   b.Clacton 21-10-91
*Source:* Scholar.

|  |  | | | | |
|---|---|---|---|---|---|
| 2009-10 | Ipswich T | 1 | 0 | | |
| 2010-11 | Ipswich T | 9 | 0 | 10 | 0 |
| 2011-12 | Colchester U | 25 | 3 | | |
| 2011-12 | Crawley T | 6 | 0 | 6 | 0 |
| 2012-13 | Colchester U | 29 | 2 | 54 | 5 |

**GILBEY, Alex (M)**    3 0
H: 6 0   W: 11 07   b.Dagenham 9-12-94
*Source:* Scholar.

|  |  | | | | |
|---|---|---|---|---|---|
| 2011-12 | Colchester U | 0 | 0 | | |
| 2012-13 | Colchester U | 3 | 0 | 3 | 0 |

**HEATH, Matt (D)**    249 16
H: 6 4   W: 13 13   b.Leicester 1-11-81
*Source:* Scholar.

|  |  | | | | |
|---|---|---|---|---|---|
| 2000-01 | Leicester C | 0 | 0 | | |
| 2001-02 | Leicester C | 5 | 0 | | |
| 2002-03 | Leicester C | 11 | 3 | | |
| 2003-04 | Leicester C | 13 | 0 | | |
| 2003-04 | Stockport Co | 8 | 0 | 8 | 0 |
| 2004-05 | Leicester C | 22 | 3 | 51 | 6 |
| 2005-06 | Coventry C | 25 | 1 | | |
| 2006-07 | Coventry C | 7 | 0 | 32 | 1 |
| 2006-07 | Leeds U | 26 | 3 | | |
| 2007-08 | Leeds U | 26 | 1 | 52 | 4 |
| 2007-08 | Colchester U | 5 | 0 | | |
| 2008-09 | Colchester U | 14 | 0 | | |
| 2008-09 | Brighton & HA | 6 | 1 | 6 | 1 |
| 2009-10 | Colchester U | 18 | 0 | | |
| 2009-10 | Southend U | 4 | 0 | 4 | 0 |
| 2010-11 | Colchester U | 27 | 2 | | |
| 2011-12 | Colchester U | 26 | 2 | | |
| 2012-13 | Colchester U | 6 | 0 | 96 | 4 |

**IBEHRE, Jabo (F)**    396 71
H: 6 2   W: 13 13   b.Islington 28-1-83
*Source:* Trainee.

|  |  | | | | |
|---|---|---|---|---|---|
| 1999-2000 | Leyton Orient | 3 | 0 | | |
| 2000-01 | Leyton Orient | 5 | 2 | | |
| 2001-02 | Leyton Orient | 28 | 4 | | |
| 2002-03 | Leyton Orient | 25 | 5 | | |
| 2003-04 | Leyton Orient | 35 | 4 | | |
| 2004-05 | Leyton Orient | 19 | 2 | | |
| 2005-06 | Leyton Orient | 33 | 8 | | |
| 2006-07 | Leyton Orient | 30 | 4 | | |

| | | | | | |
|---|---|--:|--:|--:|--:|
| 2007-08 | Leyton Orient | 31 | 7 | 209 | 36 |
| 2008-09 | Walsall | 39 | 10 | 39 | 10 |
| 2009-10 | Milton Keynes D | 10 | 1 | | |
| 2009-10 | *Southend U* | 4 | 0 | 4 | 0 |
| 2009-10 | *Stockport Co* | 20 | 5 | 20 | 5 |
| 2010-11 | Milton Keynes D | 42 | 3 | | |
| 2011-12 | Milton Keynes D | 39 | 8 | | |
| 2012-13 | Milton Keynes D | 3 | 0 | 94 | 12 |
| 2012-13 | Colchester U | 30 | 8 | 30 | 8 |

**IZZET, Kem (M)**    422 18
H: 5 7   W: 10 05   b.Mile End 29-9-80
*Source:* Trainee.

| | | | | | |
|---|---|--:|--:|--:|--:|
| 1998-99 | Charlton Ath | 0 | 0 | | |
| 1999-2000 | Charlton Ath | 0 | 0 | | |
| 2000-01 | Charlton Ath | 0 | 0 | | |
| 2000-01 | Colchester U | 6 | 1 | | |
| 2001-02 | Colchester U | 40 | 3 | | |
| 2002-03 | Colchester U | 45 | 8 | | |
| 2003-04 | Colchester U | 44 | 3 | | |
| 2004-05 | Colchester U | 4 | 0 | | |
| 2005-06 | Colchester U | 33 | 0 | | |
| 2006-07 | Colchester U | 45 | 1 | | |
| 2007-08 | Colchester U | 39 | 1 | | |
| 2008-09 | Colchester U | 43 | 1 | | |
| 2009-10 | Colchester U | 37 | 0 | | |
| 2010-11 | Colchester U | 41 | 0 | | |
| 2011-12 | Colchester U | 34 | 0 | | |
| 2012-13 | Colchester U | 11 | 0 | 422 | 18 |

**LADAPO, Freddie (F)**    4 0
H: 6 0   W: 12 06   b.Romford 1-2-93
*Source:* Scholar.

| | | | | | |
|---|---|--:|--:|--:|--:|
| 2011-12 | Colchester U | 0 | 0 | | |
| 2012-13 | Colchester U | 4 | 0 | 4 | 0 |

**MASSEY, Gavin (F)**    71 9
H: 5 11   W: 11 06   b.Watford 14-10-92
*Source:* Scholar.

| | | | | | |
|---|---|--:|--:|--:|--:|
| 2009-10 | Watford | 1 | 0 | | |
| 2010-11 | Watford | 3 | 0 | | |
| 2011-12 | Watford | 3 | 0 | | |
| 2011-12 | *Yeovil T* | 16 | 3 | 16 | 3 |
| 2011-12 | *Colchester U* | 8 | 0 | | |
| 2012-13 | Watford | 0 | 0 | 7 | 0 |
| 2012-13 | Colchester U | 40 | 6 | 48 | 6 |

**MELAUGH, Ryan (M)**    0 0
H: 5 11   W: 11 01   b.Harlow 28-8-94

| | | | | | |
|---|---|--:|--:|--:|--:|
| 2012-13 | Colchester U | 0 | 0 | | |

**MORRISON, Clinton (F)**    559 150
H: 6 0   W: 12 00   b.Tooting 14-5-79
*Source:* Trainee. *Honours:* Eire Under-21, 36 full caps, 9 goals.

| | | | | | |
|---|---|--:|--:|--:|--:|
| 1996-97 | Crystal Palace | 0 | 0 | | |
| 1997-98 | Crystal Palace | 1 | 1 | | |
| 1998-99 | Crystal Palace | 37 | 12 | | |
| 1999-2000 | Crystal Palace | 29 | 13 | | |
| 2000-01 | Crystal Palace | 45 | 14 | | |
| 2001-02 | Crystal Palace | 45 | 22 | | |
| 2002-03 | Birmingham C | 28 | 6 | | |
| 2003-04 | Birmingham C | 32 | 4 | | |
| 2004-05 | Birmingham C | 26 | 4 | | |
| 2005-06 | Birmingham C | 1 | 0 | 87 | 14 |
| 2005-06 | Crystal Palace | 40 | 13 | | |
| 2006-07 | Crystal Palace | 41 | 12 | | |
| 2007-08 | Crystal Palace | 43 | 16 | 281 | 103 |
| 2008-09 | Coventry C | 45 | 10 | | |
| 2009-10 | Coventry C | 46 | 11 | 91 | 21 |
| 2010-11 | Sheffield W | 35 | 6 | | |
| 2011-12 | Sheffield W | 19 | 1 | 54 | 7 |
| 2011-12 | *Milton Keynes D* | 6 | 3 | 6 | 3 |
| 2011-12 | *Brentford* | 8 | 0 | 8 | 0 |
| 2012-13 | Colchester U | 32 | 2 | 32 | 2 |

**O'TOOLE, John (M)**    156 16
H: 6 2   W: 13 07   b.Harrow 30-9-88
*Honours:* Eire Under-21.

| | | | | | |
|---|---|--:|--:|--:|--:|
| 2007-08 | Watford | 35 | 3 | | |
| 2008-09 | Watford | 22 | 7 | | |
| 2008-09 | *Sheffield U* | 9 | 1 | 9 | 1 |
| 2009-10 | Watford | 0 | 0 | 57 | 10 |
| 2009-10 | Colchester U | 31 | 2 | | |
| 2010-11 | Colchester U | 11 | 0 | | |
| 2011-12 | Colchester U | 15 | 0 | | |
| 2012-13 | Colchester U | 15 | 0 | 72 | 2 |
| 2012-13 | *Bristol R* | 18 | 3 | 18 | 3 |

**OKUONGHAE, Magnus (D)**    220 8
H: 6 3   W: 13 04   b.Nigeria 16-2-86
*Source:* Scholar.

| | | | | | |
|---|---|--:|--:|--:|--:|
| 2003-04 | Rushden & D | 1 | 0 | | |
| 2004-05 | Rushden & D | 0 | 0 | | |
| 2005-06 | Rushden & D | 21 | 1 | | |
| 2006-07 | Rushden & D | 0 | 0 | 22 | 1 |
| 2007-08 | Dagenham & R | 10 | 0 | | |
| 2008-09 | Dagenham & R | 45 | 2 | 55 | 2 |
| 2009-10 | Colchester U | 44 | 0 | | |
| 2010-11 | Colchester U | 14 | 2 | | |
| 2011-12 | Colchester U | 42 | 0 | | |
| 2012-13 | Colchester U | 43 | 3 | 143 | 5 |

**OLUFEMI, Tosin (M)**    1 0
H: 5 8   W: 10 13   b.Hackney 13-5-94

| | | | | | |
|---|---|--:|--:|--:|--:|
| 2012-13 | Colchester U | 1 | 0 | 1 | 0 |

**PHILLIPS, Shaun (G)**    0 0
H: 6 3   W: 13 00   b.Colchester 7-3-94

| | | | | | |
|---|---|--:|--:|--:|--:|
| 2012-13 | Colchester U | 0 | 0 | | |

**ROSE, Michael (D)**    260 17
H: 5 11   W: 12 04   b.Salford 28-7-82
*Source:* Trainee.

| | | | | | |
|---|---|--:|--:|--:|--:|
| 1999-2000 | Manchester U | 0 | 0 | | |
| 2000-01 | Manchester U | 0 | 0 | | |
| 2001-02 | Manchester U | 0 | 0 | | |

From Hereford U

| | | | | | |
|---|---|--:|--:|--:|--:|
| 2004-05 | Yeovil T | 40 | 1 | | |
| 2005-06 | Yeovil T | 1 | 0 | 41 | 1 |
| 2005-06 | *Cheltenham T* | 3 | 0 | 3 | 0 |
| 2005-06 | *Scunthorpe U* | 15 | 0 | 15 | 0 |
| 2006-07 | Stockport Co | 25 | 3 | | |
| 2007-08 | Stockport Co | 28 | 3 | | |
| 2008-09 | Stockport Co | 27 | 0 | | |
| 2009-10 | Stockport Co | 24 | 2 | 104 | 8 |
| 2009-10 | *Norwich C* | 12 | 1 | 12 | 1 |
| 2010-11 | Swindon T | 35 | 3 | 35 | 3 |
| 2011-12 | Colchester U | 0 | 0 | | |
| 2011-12 | Colchester U | 14 | 0 | | |
| 2012-13 | Colchester U | 22 | 2 | 36 | 2 |
| 2012-13 | *Rochdale* | 14 | 2 | 14 | 2 |

**SANDERSON, Jordan (M)**    1 0
H: 6 0   W: 11 02   b.Chingford 7-8-93
*Source:* Scholar.

| | | | | | |
|---|---|--:|--:|--:|--:|
| 2010-11 | Colchester U | 1 | 0 | | |
| 2011-12 | Colchester U | 0 | 0 | | |
| 2012-13 | Colchester U | 0 | 0 | 1 | 0 |

**SEARS, Freddie (F)**    129 11
H: 5 8   W: 10 01   b.Hornchurch 27-11-89
*Source:* Scholar. *Honours:* England Youth, Under-21.

| | | | | | |
|---|---|--:|--:|--:|--:|
| 2007-08 | West Ham U | 7 | 1 | | |
| 2008-09 | West Ham U | 17 | 0 | | |
| 2009-10 | West Ham U | 1 | 0 | | |
| 2009-10 | *Crystal Palace* | 18 | 0 | 18 | 0 |
| 2009-10 | *Coventry C* | 10 | 0 | 10 | 0 |
| 2010-11 | West Ham U | 11 | 1 | | |
| 2010-11 | *Scunthorpe U* | 9 | 0 | 9 | 0 |
| 2011-12 | West Ham U | 10 | 0 | 46 | 2 |
| 2011-12 | *Colchester U* | 11 | 2 | | |
| 2012-13 | Colchester U | 35 | 7 | 46 | 9 |

**WHITE, John (D)**    232 0
H: 6 0   W: 12 01   b.Maldon 26-7-86
*Source:* Scholar.

| | | | | | |
|---|---|--:|--:|--:|--:|
| 2004-05 | Colchester U | 20 | 0 | | |
| 2005-06 | Colchester U | 35 | 0 | | |
| 2006-07 | Colchester U | 16 | 0 | | |
| 2007-08 | Colchester U | 21 | 0 | | |
| 2008-09 | Colchester U | 26 | 0 | | |
| 2009-10 | Colchester U | 39 | 0 | | |
| 2009-10 | *Southend U* | 5 | 0 | 5 | 0 |
| 2010-11 | Colchester U | 22 | 0 | | |
| 2011-12 | Colchester U | 26 | 0 | | |
| 2012-13 | Colchester U | 22 | 0 | 227 | 0 |

**WILSON, Brian (D)**    304 16
H: 5 10   W: 11 00   b.Manchester 9-5-83
*Source:* Scholar.

| | | | | | |
|---|---|--:|--:|--:|--:|
| 2001-02 | Stoke C | 1 | 0 | | |
| 2002-03 | Stoke C | 3 | 0 | | |
| 2003-04 | Stoke C | 2 | 0 | 6 | 0 |
| 2003-04 | Cheltenham T | 43 | 3 | | |
| 2004-05 | Cheltenham T | 43 | 3 | | |
| 2005-06 | Cheltenham T | 43 | 9 | | |
| 2006-07 | Cheltenham T | 25 | 2 | 125 | 14 |

| | | | | | |
|---|---|--:|--:|--:|--:|
| 2006-07 | Bristol C | 19 | 0 | | |
| 2007-08 | Bristol C | 18 | 1 | | |
| 2008-09 | Bristol C | 20 | 0 | | |
| 2009-10 | Bristol C | 3 | 0 | 60 | 1 |
| 2010-11 | Colchester U | 26 | 1 | | |
| 2011-12 | Colchester U | 46 | 0 | | |
| 2012-13 | Colchester U | 41 | 0 | 113 | 1 |

**WRIGHT, David (D)**    451 8
H: 5 11   W: 11 01   b.Warrington 1-5-80
*Source:* Trainee. *Honours:* England Youth.

| | | | | | |
|---|---|--:|--:|--:|--:|
| 1997-98 | Crewe Alex | 3 | 0 | | |
| 1998-99 | Crewe Alex | 20 | 1 | | |
| 1999-2000 | Crewe Alex | 45 | 0 | | |
| 2000-01 | Crewe Alex | 42 | 0 | | |
| 2001-02 | Crewe Alex | 30 | 0 | | |
| 2002-03 | Crewe Alex | 31 | 1 | | |
| 2003-04 | Crewe Alex | 40 | 1 | 211 | 3 |
| 2004-05 | Wigan Ath | 31 | 0 | | |
| 2005-06 | Wigan Ath | 2 | 0 | | |
| 2005-06 | *Norwich C* | 5 | 0 | 5 | 0 |
| 2006-07 | Wigan Ath | 12 | 0 | 45 | 0 |
| 2006-07 | Ipswich T | 19 | 1 | | |
| 2007-08 | Ipswich T | 41 | 2 | | |
| 2008-09 | Ipswich T | 34 | 1 | | |
| 2009-10 | Ipswich T | 26 | 1 | 120 | 5 |
| 2010-11 | Crystal Palace | 28 | 0 | | |
| 2011-12 | Crystal Palace | 22 | 0 | | |
| 2012-13 | Crystal Palace | 1 | 0 | 51 | 0 |
| 2012-13 | *Gillingham* | 7 | 0 | 7 | 0 |
| 2012-13 | Colchester U | 12 | 0 | 12 | 0 |

**WRIGHT, Drey (M)**    21 3
H: 5 9   W: 10 11   b.Greenwich 30-4-94

| | | | | | |
|---|---|--:|--:|--:|--:|
| 2012-13 | Colchester U | 21 | 3 | 21 | 3 |

**Scholars**
Blanche, Toby Jack; Bonne, Macauley Miles; Brown, Matthew; Clarke, Conor Patrick; Curtis, Jack John Charles Richard; Kent, Frankie; Lapslie, Thomas William Cavendish; Mafuta, Augustin Panga; Nwachuku, Nnamdi Prince; O'Donoghue, Michael Derry; Roast, Billy Frederick; Rogers, Callum Ron; Simmons, Jack Charles; Szmodics, Samuel Joseph.

# COVENTRY C (28)

**ADAMS, Blair (D)**    45 0
H: 5 11   W: 11 05   b.South Shields 8-9-91
*Source:* Scholar. *Honours:* England Under-20.

| | | | | | |
|---|---|--:|--:|--:|--:|
| 2010-11 | Sunderland | 0 | 0 | | |
| 2011-12 | Sunderland | 0 | 0 | | |
| 2011-12 | *Brentford* | 7 | 0 | 7 | 0 |
| 2011-12 | *Northampton T* | 22 | 0 | 22 | 0 |
| 2012-13 | Sunderland | 0 | 0 | | |
| 2012-13 | Coventry C | 16 | 0 | 16 | 0 |

**BAKER, Carl (M)**    207 36
H: 6 2   W: 12 06   b.Prescot 26-12-82
*Source:* Southport.

| | | | | | |
|---|---|--:|--:|--:|--:|
| 2007-08 | Morecambe | 42 | 10 | 42 | 10 |
| 2008-09 | Stockport Co | 22 | 3 | | |
| 2009-10 | Stockport Co | 20 | 9 | 42 | 12 |
| 2009-10 | Coventry C | 22 | 0 | | |
| 2010-11 | Coventry C | 32 | 1 | | |
| 2011-12 | Coventry C | 26 | 1 | | |
| 2012-13 | Coventry C | 43 | 12 | 123 | 14 |

**BARTON, Adam (M)**    72 4
H: 5 11   W: 12 01   b.Clitheroe 7-1-91
*Source:* Scholar. *Honours:* Eire Under-21. Northern Ireland 1 full cap.

| | | | | | |
|---|---|--:|--:|--:|--:|
| 2008-09 | Preston NE | 0 | 0 | | |
| 2009-10 | Preston NE | 1 | 0 | | |
| 2010-11 | Preston NE | 33 | 1 | | |
| 2011-12 | Preston NE | 16 | 0 | | |
| 2012-13 | Preston NE | 0 | 0 | 50 | 1 |
| 2012-13 | Coventry C | 22 | 3 | 22 | 3 |

**BELL, David (M)**    315 22
H: 5 10   W: 11 05   b.Wellingborough 21-4-84
*Source:* Trainee. *Honours:* Eire Youth, Under-21.

| | | | | | |
|---|---|--:|--:|--:|--:|
| 2001-02 | Rushden & D | 0 | 0 | | |
| 2002-03 | Rushden & D | 30 | 3 | | |
| 2003-04 | Rushden & D | 37 | 1 | | |

| 2004-05 | Rushden & D | 40 | 3 | | |
| 2005-06 | Rushden & D | 14 | 3 | **121** | **10** |
| 2005-06 | Luton T | 9 | 0 | | |
| 2006-07 | Luton T | 34 | 3 | | |
| 2007-08 | Luton T | 32 | 4 | **75** | **7** |
| 2007-08 | *Leicester C* | 6 | 0 | **6** | **0** |
| 2008-09 | Norwich C | 19 | 0 | **19** | **0** |
| 2008-09 | Coventry C | 9 | 1 | | |
| 2009-10 | Coventry C | 28 | 2 | | |
| 2010-11 | Coventry C | 22 | 2 | | |
| 2011-12 | Coventry C | 28 | 0 | | |
| 2012-13 | Coventry C | 7 | 0 | **94** | **5** |

**BURGE, Lee (G)**     **0**   **0**
H: 5 11 W: 11 00 b.Hereford 9-1-93
*Source:* Scholar.

| 2011-12 | Coventry C | 0 | 0 | | |
| 2012-13 | Coventry C | 0 | 0 | | |

**CAMERON, Nathan (D)**     **51**   **0**
H: 6 2 W: 12 04 b.Birmingham 21-11-91
*Source:* Scholar.

| 2009-10 | Coventry C | 0 | 0 | | |
| 2010-11 | Coventry C | 25 | 0 | | |
| 2011-12 | Coventry C | 14 | 0 | | |
| 2012-13 | Coventry C | 9 | 0 | **48** | **0** |
| 2012-13 | *Northampton T* | 3 | 0 | **3** | **0** |

**CHRISTIE, Cyrus (D)**     **68**   **2**
H: 6 2 W: 12 03 b.Coventry 30-9-92
*Source:* Scholar.

| 2011-12 | Coventry C | 37 | 0 | | |
| 2012-13 | Coventry C | 31 | 2 | **68** | **2** |

**CLARKE, Jordan (D)**     **72**   **2**
H: 6 0 W: 11 02 b.Coventry 19-11-91
*Source:* Scholar. *Honours:* England Youth.

| 2009-10 | Coventry C | 12 | 0 | | |
| 2010-11 | Coventry C | 21 | 1 | | |
| 2011-12 | Coventry C | 19 | 1 | | |
| 2012-13 | Coventry C | 20 | 0 | **72** | **2** |

**CLARKE, Leon (F)**     **261**   **72**
H: 6 2 W: 14 02 b.Birmingham 10-2-85
*Source:* Scholar.

| 2003-04 | Wolverhampton W | 0 | 0 | | |
| 2003-04 | *Kidderminster H* | 4 | 0 | **4** | **0** |
| 2004-05 | Wolverhampton W | 28 | 7 | | |
| 2005-06 | Wolverhampton W | 24 | 1 | | |
| 2005-06 | *QPR* | 1 | 0 | | |
| 2005-06 | *Plymouth Arg* | 5 | 0 | **5** | **0** |
| 2006-07 | Wolverhampton W | 22 | 5 | **74** | **13** |
| 2006-07 | Sheffield W | 10 | 1 | | |
| 2006-07 | *Oldham Ath* | 5 | 3 | **5** | **3** |
| 2007-08 | Sheffield W | 8 | 3 | | |
| 2007-08 | *Southend U* | 16 | 8 | **16** | **8** |
| 2008-09 | Sheffield W | 29 | 8 | | |
| 2009-10 | Sheffield W | 36 | 6 | **83** | **18** |
| 2010-11 | QPR | 13 | 0 | **14** | **0** |
| 2010-11 | *Preston NE* | 6 | 1 | **6** | **1** |
| 2011-12 | Swindon T | 2 | 0 | **2** | **0** |
| 2011-12 | Chesterfield | 14 | 9 | **14** | **9** |
| 2011-12 | Charlton Ath | 7 | 0 | | |
| 2011-12 | *Crawley T* | 4 | 1 | **4** | **1** |
| 2012-13 | Charlton Ath | 0 | 0 | **7** | **0** |
| 2012-13 | *Scunthorpe U* | 15 | 11 | **15** | **11** |
| 2012-13 | Coventry C | 12 | 8 | **12** | **8** |

**DANIELS, Billy (F)**     **4**   **0**
H: 6 0 W: 11 07 b.Bristol 3-7-94

| 2012-13 | Coventry C | 4 | 0 | **4** | **0** |

**DUNN, Chris (G)**     **101**   **0**
H: 6 5 W: 13 11 b.Brentwood 23-10-87
*Source:* Scholar.

| 2006-07 | Northampton T | 0 | 0 | | |
| 2007-08 | Northampton T | 1 | 0 | | |
| 2008-09 | Northampton T | 29 | 0 | | |
| 2009-10 | Northampton T | 29 | 0 | | |
| 2010-11 | Northampton T | 39 | 0 | **98** | **0** |
| 2011-12 | Coventry C | 2 | 0 | | |
| 2012-13 | Coventry C | 1 | 0 | **3** | **0** |

**EDJENGUELE, William (D)**     **89**   **4**
H: 6 2 W: 13 00 b.Paris 7-5-87

| 2008-09 | Neuchatel Xamax | 23 | 0 | | |
| 2009-10 | Neuchatel Xamax | 15 | 1 | **38** | **1** |
| 2011-12 | Panetolikos | 18 | 2 | **18** | **2** |
| 2012-13 | Coventry C | 33 | 1 | **33** | **1** |

**ELLIOTT, Stephen (F)**     **242**   **50**
H: 5 9 W: 11 08 b.Dublin 6-1-84
*Source:* School. *Honours:* Eire Youth, Under-21, 9 full caps, 1 goal.

| 2003-04 | Manchester C | 2 | 0 | **2** | **0** |
| 2004-05 | Sunderland | 42 | 15 | | |
| 2005-06 | Sunderland | 15 | 2 | | |
| 2006-07 | Sunderland | 24 | 5 | **81** | **22** |
| 2007-08 | Wolverhampton W | 29 | 4 | **29** | **4** |
| 2008-09 | Preston NE | 37 | 6 | | |
| 2009-10 | Preston NE | 9 | 1 | **46** | **7** |
| 2009-10 | *Norwich C* | 10 | 2 | **10** | **2** |
| 2010-11 | Hearts | 30 | 8 | | |
| 2011-12 | Hearts | 26 | 3 | **56** | **11** |
| 2012-13 | Coventry C | 18 | 4 | **18** | **4** |

**FLECK, John (M)**     **83**   **5**
H: 5 9 W: 11 05 b.Glasgow 24-8-91
*Honours:* Scotland Youth, Under-21.

| 2007-08 | Rangers | 1 | 0 | | |
| 2008-09 | Rangers | 8 | 1 | | |
| 2009-10 | Rangers | 15 | 1 | | |
| 2010-11 | Rangers | 13 | 0 | | |
| 2011-12 | Rangers | 4 | 0 | **41** | **2** |
| 2011-12 | Blackpool | 7 | 0 | **7** | **0** |
| 2012-13 | Coventry C | 35 | 3 | **35** | **3** |
On loan from Rangers.

**GARNER, Louis (M)**     **0**   **0**
H: 5 10 W: 11 07 b.Manchester 31-10-94

| 2012-13 | Coventry C | 0 | 0 | | |

**HAYNES, Ryan (D)**     **1**   **0**
H: 5 7 W: 10 10 b.Northampton 27-9-95

| 2012-13 | Coventry C | 1 | 0 | **1** | **0** |

**JENNINGS, Steven (M)**     **283**   **8**
H: 5 5 W: 12 00 b.Liverpool 28-10-84
*Source:* Scholar.

| 2003-04 | Tranmere R | 4 | 0 | | |
| 2004-05 | Tranmere R | 11 | 0 | | |
| 2005-06 | Tranmere R | 38 | 1 | | |
| 2006-07 | Tranmere R | 2 | 0 | | |
| 2006-07 | *Hereford U* | 11 | 0 | **11** | **0** |
| 2007-08 | Tranmere R | 41 | 2 | | |
| 2008-09 | Tranmere R | 44 | 3 | **140** | **6** |
| 2009-10 | Motherwell | 29 | 2 | | |
| 2010-11 | Motherwell | 30 | 0 | | |
| 2011-12 | Motherwell | 34 | 0 | **93** | **2** |
| 2012-13 | Coventry C | 39 | 0 | **39** | **0** |

**KILBANE, Kevin (M)**     **539**   **37**
H: 6 1 W: 13 05 b.Preston 1-2-77
*Source:* Trainee. *Honours:* Eire Under-21, 110 full caps, 8 goals.

| 1993-94 | Preston NE | 0 | 0 | | |
| 1994-95 | Preston NE | 0 | 0 | | |
| 1995-96 | Preston NE | 11 | 1 | | |
| 1996-97 | Preston NE | 36 | 2 | **47** | **3** |
| 1997-98 | WBA | 43 | 4 | | |
| 1998-99 | WBA | 44 | 6 | | |
| 1999-2000 | WBA | 19 | 5 | **106** | **15** |
| 1999-2000 | Sunderland | 20 | 1 | | |
| 2000-01 | Sunderland | 30 | 4 | | |
| 2001-02 | Sunderland | 28 | 2 | | |
| 2002-03 | Sunderland | 30 | 1 | | |
| 2003-04 | Sunderland | 5 | 0 | **113** | **8** |
| 2003-04 | Everton | 30 | 3 | | |
| 2004-05 | Everton | 38 | 1 | | |
| 2005-06 | Everton | 34 | 0 | | |
| 2006-07 | Everton | 2 | 0 | **104** | **4** |
| 2006-07 | Wigan Ath | 31 | 1 | | |
| 2007-08 | Wigan Ath | 35 | 1 | | |
| 2008-09 | Wigan Ath | 10 | 0 | **76** | **2** |
| 2008-09 | Hull C | 16 | 0 | | |
| 2009-10 | Hull C | 21 | 1 | | |
| 2010-11 | Hull C | 14 | 0 | | |
| 2010-11 | *Huddersfield T* | 24 | 2 | **24** | **2** |
| 2011-12 | Hull C | 0 | 0 | **51** | **2** |
| 2011-12 | *Derby Co* | 9 | 1 | **9** | **1** |
| 2012-13 | Coventry C | 9 | 0 | **9** | **0** |

**LOBJOIT, Leon (M)**     **0**   **0**
b.London 4-1-95

| 2012-13 | Coventry C | 0 | 0 | | |

**MALAGA, Kevin (D)**     **5**   **0**
H: 6 2 W: 12 09 b.Toulon 24-6-87

| 2009-10 | Auxerre | 1 | 0 | **1** | **0** |
| 2010-11 | Nice | 1 | 0 | | |
| 2011-12 | Nice | 1 | 0 | **2** | **0** |
| 2012-13 | Coventry C | 2 | 0 | **2** | **0** |

**McDONALD, Cody (F)**     **115**   **40**
H: 5 10 W: 11 03 b.Witham 30-5-86
*Source:* Dartford.

| 2008-09 | Norwich C | 7 | 1 | | |
| 2009-10 | Norwich C | 17 | 3 | | |
| 2010-11 | Norwich C | 0 | 0 | | |
| 2010-11 | *Gillingham* | 41 | 25 | | |
| 2011-12 | Norwich C | 0 | 0 | **24** | **4** |
| 2011-12 | Coventry C | 23 | 4 | | |
| 2012-13 | Coventry C | 20 | 3 | **43** | **7** |
| 2012-13 | *Gillingham* | 7 | 4 | **48** | **29** |

**McSHEFFREY, Gary (F)**     **372**   **89**
H: 5 8 W: 10 06 b.Coventry 13-8-82
*Source:* Trainee. *Honours:* England Youth, Under-20.

| 1998-99 | Coventry C | 1 | 0 | | |
| 1999-2000 | Coventry C | 3 | 0 | | |
| 2000-01 | Coventry C | 0 | 0 | | |
| 2001-02 | *Stockport Co* | 5 | 1 | **5** | **1** |
| 2001-02 | Coventry C | 8 | 1 | | |
| 2002-03 | Coventry C | 29 | 4 | | |
| 2003-04 | Coventry C | 19 | 11 | | |
| 2003-04 | *Luton T* | 18 | 9 | | |
| 2004-05 | Coventry C | 37 | 12 | | |
| 2004-05 | *Luton T* | 5 | 1 | **23** | **10** |
| 2005-06 | Coventry C | 43 | 15 | | |
| 2006-07 | Coventry C | 3 | 1 | | |
| 2006-07 | Birmingham C | 40 | 13 | | |
| 2007-08 | Birmingham C | 32 | 3 | | |
| 2008-09 | Birmingham C | 6 | 0 | | |
| 2008-09 | *Nottingham F* | 4 | 0 | **4** | **0** |
| 2009-10 | Birmingham C | 9 | 0 | **83** | **16** |
| 2009-10 | *Leeds U* | 10 | 1 | **10** | **1** |
| 2010-11 | Coventry C | 33 | 8 | | |
| 2011-12 | Coventry C | 39 | 8 | | |
| 2012-13 | Coventry C | 32 | 1 | **247** | **61** |

**MOUSSA, Franck (M)**     **169**   **20**
H: 5 8 W: 10 08 b.Brussels 24-7-89
*Source:* Scholar.

| 2005-06 | Southend U | 1 | 0 | | |
| 2006-07 | Southend U | 4 | 0 | | |
| 2007-08 | Southend U | 16 | 0 | | |
| 2008-09 | Southend U | 26 | 2 | | |
| 2008-09 | *Wycombe W* | 9 | 0 | **9** | **0** |
| 2009-10 | Southend U | 43 | 5 | **90** | **7** |
| 2010-11 | Leicester C | 8 | 1 | | |
| 2010-11 | *Doncaster R* | 14 | 2 | **14** | **2** |
| 2011-12 | Leicester C | 0 | 0 | **8** | **1** |
| 2011-12 | Chesterfield | 10 | 4 | **10** | **4** |
| 2012-13 | Nottingham F | 0 | 0 | | |
| 2012-13 | Coventry C | 38 | 6 | **38** | **6** |

**MURPHY, Joe (G)**     **399**   **0**
H: 6 2 W: 13 06 b.Dublin 21-8-81
*Source:* Trainee. *Honours:* Eire Youth, Under-21, 2 full caps.

| 1999-2000 | Tranmere R | 21 | 0 | | |
| 2000-01 | Tranmere R | 20 | 0 | | |
| 2001-02 | Tranmere R | 22 | 0 | **63** | **0** |
| 2002-03 | WBA | 2 | 0 | | |
| 2003-04 | WBA | 3 | 0 | | |
| 2004-05 | WBA | 0 | 0 | **5** | **0** |
| 2004-05 | Walsall | 25 | 0 | | |
| 2005-06 | Sunderland | 0 | 0 | | |
| 2005-06 | Walsall | 14 | 0 | **39** | **0** |
| 2006-07 | Scunthorpe U | 45 | 0 | | |
| 2007-08 | Scunthorpe U | 45 | 0 | | |
| 2008-09 | Scunthorpe U | 42 | 0 | | |
| 2009-10 | Scunthorpe U | 40 | 0 | | |
| 2010-11 | Scunthorpe U | 29 | 0 | **201** | **0** |
| 2011-12 | Coventry C | 46 | 0 | | |
| 2012-13 | Coventry C | 45 | 0 | **91** | **0** |

**PHILLIPS, Aaron (D)**     **0**   **0**
b. 20-11-93

| 2012-13 | Coventry C | 0 | 0 | | |

**PHILLISKIRK, Daniel (M)**     **10**   **0**
H: 5 10 W: 11 05 b.Oldham 10-4-91
*Source:* Scholar.

| 2008-09 | Chelsea | 0 | 0 | | |
| 2009-10 | Chelsea | 0 | 0 | | |
| 2010-11 | Chelsea | 0 | 0 | | |
| 2010-11 | *Oxford U* | 1 | 0 | | |
| 2010-11 | *Sheffield U* | 3 | 0 | | |

**STEWART** (continued)

|  |  | | | | |
|---|---|--:|--:|--:|--:|
| 2011-12 | Sheffield U | 0 | 0 | | |
| 2011-12 | *Oxford U* | 4 | 0 | **5** | **0** |
| 2012-13 | Sheffield U | 1 | 0 | **4** | **0** |
| 2012-13 | Coventry C | 1 | 0 | **1** | **0** |

**STEWART, Jordan (D)** 299 11
H: 6 0  W: 12 09  b.Birmingham 3-3-82
*Source:* Trainee. *Honours:* England Youth, Under-21.

|  |  | | | | |
|---|---|--:|--:|--:|--:|
| 1999-2000 | Leicester C | 1 | 0 | | |
| 1999-2000 | *Bristol R* | 4 | 0 | **4** | **0** |
| 2000-01 | Leicester C | 0 | 0 | | |
| 2001-02 | Leicester C | 12 | 0 | | |
| 2002-03 | Leicester C | 37 | 4 | | |
| 2003-04 | Leicester C | 25 | 1 | | |
| 2004-05 | Leicester C | 35 | 1 | **110** | **6** |
| 2005-06 | Watford | 35 | 0 | | |
| 2006-07 | Watford | 31 | 0 | | |
| 2007-08 | Watford | 39 | 2 | **105** | **2** |
| 2008-09 | Derby Co | 26 | 2 | **26** | **2** |
| 2009-10 | Sheffield U | 23 | 0 | **23** | **0** |
| 2010-11 | Xanthi | 14 | 1 | **14** | **1** |
| 2011-12 | Millwall | 4 | 0 | **4** | **0** |
| 2012-13 | Notts Co | 7 | 0 | **7** | **0** |
| 2012-13 | Coventry C | 6 | 0 | **6** | **0** |

**THOMAS, Conor (M)** 38 1
H: 6 1  W: 11 05  b.Coventry 29-10-93
*Source:* Scholar. *Honours:* England Youth.

|  |  | | | | |
|---|---|--:|--:|--:|--:|
| 2010-11 | *Liverpool* | 0 | 0 | | |
| 2010-11 | Coventry C | 0 | 0 | | |
| 2011-12 | Coventry C | 27 | 1 | | |
| 2012-13 | Coventry C | 11 | 0 | **38** | **1** |

**WILLIS, Jordan (D)** 4 0
H: 5 11  W: 11 00  b.Coventry 24-8-94
*Source:* Scholar. *Honours:* England Youth.

|  |  | | | | |
|---|---|--:|--:|--:|--:|
| 2011-12 | Coventry C | 3 | 0 | | |
| 2012-13 | Coventry C | 1 | 0 | **4** | **0** |

**WILSON, Callum (M)** 12 1
H: 5 11  W: 10 06  b.Coventry 27-2-92
*Source:* Scholar.

|  |  | | | | |
|---|---|--:|--:|--:|--:|
| 2009-10 | Coventry C | 0 | 0 | | |
| 2010-11 | Coventry C | 1 | 0 | | |
| 2011-12 | Coventry C | 0 | 0 | | |
| 2012-13 | Coventry C | 11 | 1 | **12** | **1** |

**WOOD, Richard (D)** 288 15
H: 6 3  W: 12 13  b.Ossett 5-7-85
*Source:* Scholar.

|  |  | | | | |
|---|---|--:|--:|--:|--:|
| 2002-03 | Sheffield W | 3 | 1 | | |
| 2003-04 | Sheffield W | 12 | 0 | | |
| 2004-05 | Sheffield W | 34 | 1 | | |
| 2005-06 | Sheffield W | 30 | 1 | | |
| 2006-07 | Sheffield W | 12 | 0 | | |
| 2007-08 | Sheffield W | 27 | 2 | | |
| 2008-09 | Sheffield W | 42 | 0 | | |
| 2009-10 | Sheffield W | 11 | 2 | **171** | **7** |
| 2009-10 | Coventry C | 24 | 3 | | |
| 2010-11 | Coventry C | 40 | 1 | | |
| 2011-12 | Coventry C | 17 | 1 | | |
| 2012-13 | Coventry C | 36 | 3 | **117** | **8** |

# CRAWLEY T (29)

**ADAMS, Nicky (F)** 251 27
H: 5 10  W: 11 00  b.Bolton 16-10-86
*Source:* Scholar. *Honours:* Wales Under-21.

|  |  | | | | |
|---|---|--:|--:|--:|--:|
| 2005-06 | Bury | 15 | 1 | | |
| 2006-07 | Bury | 19 | 1 | | |
| 2007-08 | Bury | 43 | 12 | **77** | **14** |
| 2008-09 | Leicester C | 12 | 0 | | |
| 2008-09 | Rochdale | 14 | 1 | | |
| 2009-10 | Leicester C | 18 | 0 | **30** | **0** |
| 2009-10 | *Leyton Orient* | 6 | 0 | **6** | **0** |
| 2010-11 | Brentford | 7 | 0 | **7** | **0** |
| 2010-11 | Rochdale | 30 | 0 | | |
| 2011-12 | Rochdale | 41 | 4 | **85** | **5** |
| 2012-13 | Crawley T | 46 | 8 | **46** | **8** |

**ALEXANDER, Gary (F)** 528 152
H: 6 0  W: 13 04  b.Lambeth 15-8-79
*Source:* Trainee.

|  |  | | | | |
|---|---|--:|--:|--:|--:|
| 1998-99 | West Ham U | 0 | 0 | | |
| 1999-2000 | West Ham U | 0 | 0 | | |
| 1999-2000 | *Exeter C* | 37 | 16 | **37** | **16** |
| 2000-01 | Swindon T | 37 | 7 | **37** | **7** |
| 2001-02 | Hull C | 43 | 17 | | |
| 2002-03 | Hull C | 25 | 6 | **68** | **23** |
| 2002-03 | Leyton Orient | 17 | 2 | | |
| 2003-04 | Leyton Orient | 44 | 15 | | |
| 2004-05 | Leyton Orient | 28 | 9 | | |
| 2005-06 | Leyton Orient | 46 | 14 | | |
| 2006-07 | Leyton Orient | 44 | 12 | **179** | **52** |
| 2007-08 | Millwall | 36 | 7 | | |
| 2008-09 | Millwall | 35 | 11 | | |
| 2009-10 | Millwall | 15 | 1 | **86** | **19** |
| 2010-11 | Brentford | 38 | 9 | | |
| 2011-12 | Brentford | 24 | 12 | **62** | **21** |
| 2011-12 | *Crawley T* | 14 | 7 | | |
| 2012-13 | Crawley T | 27 | 4 | **41** | **11** |
| 2012-13 | *AFC Wimbledon* | 18 | 3 | **18** | **3** |

**BRODIE, Richard (F)** 23 5
H: 6 2  W: 13 00  b.Gateshead 8-7-87
*Source:* Whickham, Newcastle Benfield, York C.

|  |  | | | | |
|---|---|--:|--:|--:|--:|
| 2011-12 | Crawley T | 0 | 0 | | |
| 2012-13 | Crawley T | 0 | 0 | | |
| 2012-13 | Morecambe | 23 | 5 | **23** | **5** |

**BULMAN, Dannie (M)** 284 18
H: 5 9  W: 11 12  b.Ashford 24-1-79
*Source:* Ashford T.

|  |  | | | | |
|---|---|--:|--:|--:|--:|
| 1998-99 | Wycombe W | 11 | 1 | | |
| 1999-2000 | Wycombe W | 29 | 1 | | |
| 2000-01 | Wycombe W | 36 | 4 | | |
| 2001-02 | Wycombe W | 46 | 5 | | |
| 2002-03 | Wycombe W | 42 | 3 | | |
| 2003-04 | Wycombe W | 38 | 0 | **202** | **14** |

From Stevenage, Crawley T.

|  |  | | | | |
|---|---|--:|--:|--:|--:|
| 2010-11 | *Oxford U* | 5 | 0 | **5** | **0** |
| 2011-12 | Crawley T | 41 | 3 | | |
| 2012-13 | Crawley T | 36 | 1 | **77** | **4** |

**CLARKE, Billy (F)** 181 36
H: 5 7  W: 10 01  b.Cork 13-12-87
*Source:* Scholar. *Honours:* Eire Youth, Under-21.

|  |  | | | | |
|---|---|--:|--:|--:|--:|
| 2004-05 | Ipswich T | 0 | 0 | | |
| 2005-06 | Ipswich T | 2 | 0 | | |
| 2005-06 | *Colchester U* | 6 | 0 | **6** | **0** |
| 2006-07 | Ipswich T | 27 | 3 | | |
| 2007-08 | Ipswich T | 20 | 0 | | |
| 2007-08 | *Falkirk* | 8 | 1 | **8** | **1** |
| 2008-09 | Ipswich T | 0 | 0 | **49** | **3** |
| 2008-09 | *Darlington* | 20 | 8 | **20** | **8** |
| 2008-09 | *Northampton T* | 5 | 3 | **5** | **3** |
| 2008-09 | *Brentford* | 8 | 6 | **8** | **6** |
| 2009-10 | Blackpool | 18 | 1 | | |
| 2010-11 | Blackpool | 0 | 0 | | |
| 2011-12 | Blackpool | 9 | 0 | **27** | **1** |
| 2011-12 | *Sheffield U* | 5 | 1 | **5** | **1** |
| 2011-12 | Crawley T | 17 | 3 | | |
| 2012-13 | Crawley T | 36 | 10 | **53** | **13** |

**CONNOLLY, Mark (D)** 41 2
H: 6 1  W: 12 01  b.Monaghan 16-12-91
*Source:* Wolverhampton W Scholar. *Honours:* Eire Youth, Under-21.

|  |  | | | | |
|---|---|--:|--:|--:|--:|
| 2009-10 | Bolton W | 0 | 0 | | |
| 2009-10 | *St Johnstone* | 1 | 0 | **1** | **0** |
| 2010-11 | Bolton W | 0 | 0 | | |
| 2011-12 | Bolton W | 0 | 0 | | |
| 2011-12 | *Macclesfield T* | 7 | 0 | **7** | **0** |
| 2012-13 | Crawley T | 33 | 2 | **33** | **2** |

**COOPER, Shaun (D)** 259 3
H: 5 10  W: 10 05  b.Newport (IW) 5-10-83
*Source:* School.

|  |  | | | | |
|---|---|--:|--:|--:|--:|
| 2000-01 | Portsmouth | 0 | 0 | | |
| 2001-02 | Portsmouth | 7 | 0 | | |
| 2002-03 | Portsmouth | 0 | 0 | | |
| 2003-04 | Portsmouth | 0 | 0 | | |
| 2003-04 | *Leyton Orient* | 9 | 0 | **9** | **0** |
| 2004-05 | Portsmouth | 0 | 0 | | |
| 2004-05 | *Kidderminster H* | 10 | 0 | **10** | **0** |
| 2005-06 | Portsmouth | 0 | 0 | | |
| 2005-06 | Bournemouth | 35 | 0 | | |
| 2006-07 | Bournemouth | 33 | 0 | | |
| 2007-08 | Bournemouth | 38 | 1 | | |
| 2008-09 | Bournemouth | 37 | 0 | | |
| 2009-10 | Bournemouth | 6 | 0 | | |
| 2010-11 | Bournemouth | 36 | 0 | | |
| 2011-12 | Bournemouth | 26 | 0 | **211** | **1** |
| 2012-13 | Crawley T | 8 | 0 | **8** | **0** |
| 2012-13 | *Portsmouth* | 14 | 2 | **21** | **2** |

**DOLLERY, Jon (D)** 0 0
H: 5 10  W: 11 10  b.Haywards 7-9-93

|  |  | | | | |
|---|---|--:|--:|--:|--:|
| 2012-13 | Crawley T | 0 | 0 | | |

**DUMBUYA, Mustapha (D)** 76 0
H: 5 7  W: 11 00  b.Sierra Leone 7-8-87
*Source:* Potters Bar T. *Honours:* Sierra Leone 3 full caps.

|  |  | | | | |
|---|---|--:|--:|--:|--:|
| 2009-10 | Doncaster R | 3 | 0 | | |
| 2010-11 | Doncaster R | 23 | 0 | | |
| 2011-12 | Doncaster R | 10 | 0 | | |
| 2011-12 | *Crystal Palace* | 2 | 0 | **2** | **0** |
| 2012-13 | Doncaster R | 0 | 0 | **36** | **0** |
| 2012-13 | Portsmouth | 23 | 0 | **23** | **0** |
| 2012-13 | Crawley T | 15 | 0 | **15** | **0** |

**ELFORD-ALLIYU, Lateef (F)** 45 7
H: 5 8  W: 10 12  b.Ibadan 1-6-92
*Source:* Scholar.

|  |  | | | | |
|---|---|--:|--:|--:|--:|
| 2009-10 | WBA | 0 | 0 | | |
| 2009-10 | *Hereford U* | 1 | 0 | **1** | **0** |
| 2010-11 | WBA | 0 | 0 | | |
| 2010-11 | *Tranmere R* | 16 | 5 | | |
| 2011-12 | WBA | 0 | 0 | | |
| 2011-12 | *Tranmere R* | 4 | 0 | **20** | **5** |
| 2011-12 | *Bury* | 13 | 2 | | |
| 2012-13 | Bury | 5 | 0 | **18** | **2** |
| 2012-13 | Crawley T | 6 | 0 | **6** | **0** |

**ESSAM, Connor (D)** 27 1
H: 6 0  W: 12 00  b.Sheerness 9-7-92
*Source:* Scholar.

|  |  | | | | |
|---|---|--:|--:|--:|--:|
| 2010-11 | Gillingham | 0 | 0 | | |
| 2011-12 | Gillingham | 18 | 0 | | |
| 2012-13 | Gillingham | 0 | 0 | **18** | **0** |
| 2012-13 | Crawley T | 9 | 1 | **9** | **1** |

**EVANS, Daniel (F)** 0 0
H: 5 10  W: 11 11  b.Peterborough 24-11-93
*Source:* Peterborough U Scholar.

|  |  | | | | |
|---|---|--:|--:|--:|--:|
| 2011-12 | Crawley T | 0 | 0 | | |
| 2012-13 | Crawley T | 0 | 0 | | |

**HUNT, David (M)** 266 11
H: 5 11  W: 11 09  b.Dulwich 10-9-82
*Source:* Scholar.

|  |  | | | | |
|---|---|--:|--:|--:|--:|
| 2002-03 | Crystal Palace | 2 | 0 | **2** | **0** |
| 2003-04 | Leyton Orient | 38 | 1 | | |
| 2004-05 | Leyton Orient | 27 | 0 | **65** | **1** |
| 2005-06 | Northampton T | 4 | 0 | | |
| 2005-06 | Northampton T | 40 | 3 | | |
| 2006-07 | Northampton T | 29 | 0 | **73** | **3** |
| 2007-08 | Shrewsbury T | 27 | 2 | | |
| 2008-09 | Shrewsbury T | 2 | 0 | **29** | **2** |
| 2008-09 | Brentford | 20 | 2 | | |
| 2009-10 | Brentford | 24 | 3 | | |
| 2010-11 | Brentford | 3 | 0 | **47** | **5** |
| 2011-12 | Crawley T | 27 | 0 | | |
| 2012-13 | Crawley T | 23 | 0 | **50** | **0** |

**JONES, Mike (M)** 226 23
H: 5 11  W: 12 04  b.Birkenhead 15-8-87
*Source:* Scholar.

|  |  | | | | |
|---|---|--:|--:|--:|--:|
| 2005-06 | Tranmere R | 1 | 0 | | |
| 2006-07 | Tranmere R | 0 | 0 | | |
| 2006-07 | *Shrewsbury T* | 13 | 1 | **13** | **1** |
| 2007-08 | Tranmere R | 9 | 1 | **10** | **1** |
| 2008-09 | Bury | 46 | 4 | | |
| 2009-10 | Bury | 41 | 5 | | |
| 2010-11 | Bury | 42 | 8 | | |
| 2011-12 | Bury | 24 | 3 | **153** | **20** |
| 2011-12 | Sheffield W | 10 | 0 | | |
| 2012-13 | Sheffield W | 0 | 0 | **10** | **0** |
| 2012-13 | Crawley T | 40 | 1 | **40** | **1** |

**JONES, Paul (G)** 172 0
H: 6 3  W: 13 00  b.Maidstone 28-6-86
*Source:* Leyton Orient Scholar.

|  |  | | | | |
|---|---|--:|--:|--:|--:|
| 2008-09 | Exeter C | 46 | 0 | | |
| 2009-10 | Exeter C | 26 | 0 | | |
| 2010-11 | Exeter C | 18 | 0 | **90** | **0** |
| 2010-11 | *Peterborough U* | 1 | 0 | | |
| 2011-12 | Peterborough U | 35 | 0 | **36** | **0** |
| 2012-13 | Crawley T | 46 | 0 | **46** | **0** |

**MALINS, Alex (D)** 0 0
H: 5 7  W: 10 10  b.Horsham 10-11-94

|  |  | | | | |
|---|---|--:|--:|--:|--:|
| 2012-13 | Crawley T | 0 | 0 | | |

**McFADZEAN, Kyle (D)** 54 5
H: 6 1　W: 13 04　b.Sheffield 20-2-87
*Source:* Scholar.
| | | | | |
|---|---|---|---|---|
| 2004-05 | Sheffield U | 0 | 0 | |
| 2005-06 | Sheffield U | 0 | 0 | |
| 2006-07 | Sheffield U | 0 | 0 | |
| From Alfreton T | | | | |
| 2011-12 | Crawley T | 37 | 2 | |
| 2012-13 | Crawley T | 17 | 3 | 54　5 |

**PROCTOR, Jamie (F)** 64 11
H: 6 2　W: 12 03　b.Preston 25-3-92
*Source:* Scholar.
| | | | | |
|---|---|---|---|---|
| 2009-10 | Preston NE | 1 | 0 | |
| 2010-11 | Preston NE | 5 | 1 | |
| 2010-11 | *Stockport Co* | 7 | 0 | 7　0 |
| 2011-12 | Preston NE | 31 | 3 | |
| 2012-13 | Preston NE | 0 | 0 | 37　4 |
| 2012-13 | Swansea C | 0 | 0 | |
| 2012-13 | *Shrewsbury T* | 2 | 0 | 2　0 |
| 2012-13 | Crawley T | 18 | 7 | 18　7 |

**SADLER, Matthew (D)** 246 2
H: 5 11　W: 11 08　b.Birmingham 26-2-85
*Source:* Scholar. *Honours:* England Youth.
| | | | | |
|---|---|---|---|---|
| 2001-02 | Birmingham C | 0 | 0 | |
| 2002-03 | Birmingham C | 2 | 0 | |
| 2003-04 | Birmingham C | 0 | 0 | |
| 2003-04 | *Northampton T* | 7 | 0 | 7　0 |
| 2004-05 | Birmingham C | 0 | 0 | |
| 2005-06 | Birmingham C | 8 | 0 | |
| 2006-07 | Birmingham C | 36 | 0 | |
| 2007-08 | Birmingham C | 5 | 0 | 51　0 |
| 2007-08 | Watford | 15 | 0 | |
| 2008-09 | Watford | 15 | 0 | |
| 2009-10 | Watford | 0 | 0 | |
| 2009-10 | *Stockport Co* | 20 | 0 | 20　0 |
| 2010-11 | Watford | 0 | 0 | 30　0 |
| 2010-11 | *Shrewsbury T* | 46 | 0 | 46　0 |
| 2011-12 | Walsall | 46 | 1 | 46　1 |
| 2012-13 | Crawley T | 46 | 1 | 46　1 |

**SIMPSON, Josh (M)** 114 9
H: 5 10　W: 12 02　b.Cambridge 6-3-87
*Source:* Cambridge C, Cambridge U, Histon.
| | | | | |
|---|---|---|---|---|
| 2009-10 | Peterborough U | 21 | 2 | |
| 2010-11 | Peterborough U | 0 | 0 | 21　2 |
| 2010-11 | *Southend U* | 17 | 1 | 17　1 |
| 2011-12 | Crawley T | 40 | 2 | |
| 2012-13 | Crawley T | 36 | 4 | 76　6 |

**SMITH, Jonte (F)** 4 0
H: 6 1　W: 10 12　b.Bermuda 10-7-94
| | | | | |
|---|---|---|---|---|
| 2012-13 | Crawley T | 4 | 0 | 4　0 |

**SPARROW, Matt (M)** 400 46
H: 5 11　W: 10 06　b.Wembley 3-10-81
*Source:* Scholar.
| | | | | |
|---|---|---|---|---|
| 1999-2000 | Scunthorpe U | 11 | 0 | |
| 2000-01 | Scunthorpe U | 11 | 4 | |
| 2001-02 | Scunthorpe U | 24 | 1 | |
| 2002-03 | Scunthorpe U | 42 | 9 | |
| 2003-04 | Scunthorpe U | 38 | 3 | |
| 2004-05 | Scunthorpe U | 44 | 5 | |
| 2005-06 | Scunthorpe U | 39 | 5 | |
| 2006-07 | Scunthorpe U | 29 | 4 | |
| 2007-08 | Scunthorpe U | 32 | 1 | |
| 2008-09 | Scunthorpe U | 36 | 4 | |
| 2009-10 | Scunthorpe U | 30 | 1 | 336　37 |
| 2010-11 | Brighton & HA | 29 | 4 | |
| 2011-12 | Brighton & HA | 18 | 2 | 47　6 |
| 2012-13 | Crawley T | 17 | 3 | 17　3 |

**TORRES, Sergio (M)** 179 11
H: 6 2　W: 12 04　b.Mar del Plata 8-11-83
*Source:* Basingstoke T.
| | | | | |
|---|---|---|---|---|
| 2005-06 | Wycombe W | 24 | 1 | |
| 2006-07 | Wycombe W | 20 | 0 | |
| 2007-08 | Wycombe W | 42 | 5 | 86　6 |
| 2008-09 | Peterborough U | 15 | 1 | |
| 2009-10 | Peterborough U | 9 | 0 | |
| 2009-10 | *Lincoln C* | 8 | 1 | 8　1 |
| 2010-11 | Peterborough U | 0 | 0 | 24　1 |
| 2011-12 | Crawley T | 38 | 3 | |
| 2012-13 | Crawley T | 23 | 0 | 61　3 |

**WALSH, Joe (D)** 30 2
H: 5 11　W: 11 00　b.Cardiff 15-5-92
*Source:* Scholar. *Honours:* Wales Youth, Under-21.
| | | | | |
|---|---|---|---|---|
| 2010-11 | Swansea C | 0 | 0 | |
| 2011-12 | Swansea C | 0 | 0 | |
| 2012-13 | Crawley T | 30 | 2 | 30　2 |

**WICKHAM, Aaron (M)** 0 0
H: 5 10　W: 12 02　b.Camden 11-12-93
*Source:* Peterborough U Scholar.
| | | | |
|---|---|---|---|
| 2011-12 | Crawley T | 0 | 0 |
| 2012-13 | Crawley T | 0 | 0 |

**Scholars**
Baker-Richardson, Courtney Romello; Bako, Elisha Thomas; Donald, Alex Ramsey; Fagan, Shane Joseph; Finch, Jack Jonathon; Fletcher, Ricky Lee; Forrester, Jordan Kyle John; Frederick, Jemal; Garner, Louis; Gott, Alex George; Haynes, Ryan Matthew; Lawton, Ivor James John; Lobjoit, Leon Alan; Maund, Benjamin James William; Moore-Azille, Tarik Armani Carlos; Pegg, Joseph William Samuel; Quinn, Ryan John; Rankin, Lewis John Clark Brown; Smith, Jordan Nathaniel; Smith, Ryan Anthony.

# CREWE ALEX (30)

**BATEMAN, Paris (D)** 0 0
H: 5 11　W: 11 11　b.Crewe 26-12-93
| | | | |
|---|---|---|---|
| 2012-13 | Crewe Alex | 0 | 0 |

**CLAYTON, Harry (F)** 0 0
H: 5 11　W: 11 11　b.Crewe 15-2-93
*Source:* Scholar.
| | | | |
|---|---|---|---|
| 2011-12 | Crewe Alex | 0 | 0 |
| 2012-13 | Crewe Alex | 0 | 0 |

**CLAYTON, Max (F)** 61 7
H: 5 9　W: 11 00　b.Crewe 9-8-94
*Source:* Scholar. *Honours:* England Youth.
| | | | | |
|---|---|---|---|---|
| 2010-11 | Crewe Alex | 2 | 0 | |
| 2011-12 | Crewe Alex | 24 | 3 | |
| 2012-13 | Crewe Alex | 35 | 4 | 61　7 |

**COLCLOUGH, Ryan (F)** 18 1
H: 6 3　W: 13 01　b.Budapest 27-12-94
| | | | | |
|---|---|---|---|---|
| 2012-13 | Crewe Alex | 18 | 1 | 18　1 |

**DANIELS, Brendon (M)** 7 0
H: 5 11　W: 11 09　b.Stoke 24-9-93
*Source:* Scholar.
| | | | | |
|---|---|---|---|---|
| 2011-12 | Crewe Alex | 0 | 0 | |
| 2012-13 | Crewe Alex | 7 | 0 | 7　0 |

**DAVIS, Harry (D)** 85 6
H: 6 2　W: 12 04　b.Burnley 24-9-91
*Source:* Scholar.
| | | | | |
|---|---|---|---|---|
| 2009-10 | Crewe Alex | 1 | 0 | |
| 2010-11 | Crewe Alex | 1 | 0 | |
| 2011-12 | Crewe Alex | 41 | 5 | |
| 2012-13 | Crewe Alex | 42 | 1 | 85　6 |

**DUGDALE, Adam (D)** 83 4
H: 6 3　W: 12 07　b.Liverpool 12-9-87
*Source:* Scholar.
| | | | | |
|---|---|---|---|---|
| 2006-07 | Crewe Alex | 0 | 0 | |
| 2006-07 | *Accrington S* | 2 | 0 | 2　0 |
| From Southport, Droylsden, Montagnee, Barrow, AFC Telford U. | | | | |
| 2010-11 | Crewe Alex | 20 | 1 | |
| 2011-12 | Crewe Alex | 43 | 3 | |
| 2012-13 | Crewe Alex | 18 | 0 | 81　4 |

**ELLINGTON, Nathan (F)** 455 122
H: 5 10　W: 13 01　b.Bradford 2-7-81
*Source:* Walton & Hersham.
| | | | | |
|---|---|---|---|---|
| 1998-99 | Bristol R | 10 | 1 | |
| 1999-2000 | Bristol R | 37 | 4 | |
| 2000-01 | Bristol R | 42 | 15 | |
| 2001-02 | Bristol R | 27 | 15 | 116　35 |
| 2001-02 | Wigan Ath | 3 | 2 | |
| 2002-03 | Wigan Ath | 44 | 15 | |
| 2003-04 | Wigan Ath | 44 | 18 | |
| 2004-05 | Wigan Ath | 45 | 24 | 134　59 |
| 2005-06 | WBA | 31 | 5 | |
| 2006-07 | WBA | 34 | 9 | |
| 2007-08 | WBA | 3 | 0 | 68　14 |

| | | | | | |
|---|---|---|---|---|---|
| 2007-08 | Watford | 34 | 4 | | |
| 2008-09 | Watford | 0 | 0 | | |
| 2008-09 | *Derby Co* | 27 | 3 | 27　3 | |
| 2009-10 | Watford | 17 | 1 | | |
| 2009-10 | *Xanthi* | 10 | 4 | 10　4 | |
| 2010-11 | Watford | 0 | 0 | 51　5 | |
| 2010-11 | *Preston NE* | 18 | 2 | 18　2 | |
| 2011-12 | Ipswich T | 15 | 0 | | |
| 2012-13 | Ipswich T | 2 | 0 | 17　0 | |
| 2012-13 | *Scunthorpe U* | 6 | 0 | 6　0 | |
| 2012-13 | Crewe Alex | 8 | 0 | 8　0 | |

**ELLIS, Mark (D)** 133 13
H: 6 2　W: 12 04　b.Kingsbridge 30-9-88
*Source:* Exeter C.
| | | | | |
|---|---|---|---|---|
| 2007-08 | Bolton W | 0 | 0 | |
| 2009-10 | Torquay U | 27 | 3 | |
| 2010-11 | Torquay U | 27 | 2 | |
| 2011-12 | Torquay U | 35 | 3 | 89　8 |
| 2012-13 | Crewe Alex | 44 | 5 | 44　5 |

**GARRATT, Ben (G)** 1 0
H: 6 1　W: 10 06　b.Market Drayton 25-4-94
*Source:* Scholar. *Honours:* England Youth.
| | | | | |
|---|---|---|---|---|
| 2011-12 | Crewe Alex | 0 | 0 | |
| 2012-13 | Crewe Alex | 1 | 0 | 1　0 |

**GUTHRIE, Jon (D)** 2 0
H: 5 10　W: 11 00　b.Devizes 1-2-93
*Source:* Pewsey Vale.
| | | | | |
|---|---|---|---|---|
| 2011-12 | Crewe Alex | 0 | 0 | |
| 2012-13 | Crewe Alex | 2 | 0 | 2　0 |

**LEITCH-SMITH, AJ (F)** 101 22
H: 5 11　W: 12 04　b.Crewe 6-3-90
*Source:* Scholar.
| | | | | |
|---|---|---|---|---|
| 2008-09 | Crewe Alex | 0 | 0 | |
| 2009 | *IBV* | 18 | 5 | 18　5 |
| 2009-10 | Crewe Alex | 1 | 0 | |
| 2010-11 | Crewe Alex | 16 | 5 | |
| 2011-12 | Crewe Alex | 38 | 8 | |
| 2012-13 | Crewe Alex | 28 | 4 | 83　17 |

**MARTIN, Alan (G)** 48 0
H: 6 0　W: 11 11　b.Glasgow 1-1-89
*Source:* Motherwell. *Honours:* Scotland Youth, Under-21.
| | | | | |
|---|---|---|---|---|
| 2007-08 | Leeds U | 0 | 0 | |
| 2008-09 | Leeds U | 0 | 0 | |
| 2009-10 | Leeds U | 0 | 0 | |
| 2009-10 | *Accrington S* | 7 | 0 | 7　0 |
| 2010-11 | Leeds U | 0 | 0 | |
| 2010-11 | *Ayr U* | 15 | 0 | 15　0 |
| 2011-12 | Crewe Alex | 0 | 0 | |
| 2012-13 | Crewe Alex | 26 | 0 | 26　0 |

**MELLOR, Kelvin (D)** 48 1
H: 5 10　W: 11 09　b.Copenhagen 25-1-91
*Source:* Nantwich T.
| | | | | |
|---|---|---|---|---|
| 2007-08 | Crewe Alex | 0 | 0 | |
| 2008-09 | Crewe Alex | 0 | 0 | |
| 2009-10 | Crewe Alex | 0 | 0 | |
| 2010-11 | Crewe Alex | 1 | 0 | |
| 2011-12 | Crewe Alex | 12 | 1 | |
| 2012-13 | Crewe Alex | 35 | 0 | 48　1 |

**MOORE, Byron (M)** 222 27
H: 6 0　W: 10 06　b.Stoke 24-8-88
*Source:* Scholar.
| | | | | |
|---|---|---|---|---|
| 2006-07 | Crewe Alex | 0 | 0 | |
| 2007-08 | Crewe Alex | 33 | 3 | |
| 2008-09 | Crewe Alex | 36 | 3 | |
| 2009-10 | Crewe Alex | 32 | 3 | |
| 2010-11 | Crewe Alex | 38 | 6 | |
| 2011-12 | Crewe Alex | 42 | 8 | |
| 2012-13 | Crewe Alex | 41 | 4 | 222　27 |

**MURPHY, Luke (M)** 161 21
H: 6 1　W: 11 05　b.Alsager 21-10-89
*Source:* Scholar.
| | | | | |
|---|---|---|---|---|
| 2008-09 | Crewe Alex | 9 | 1 | |
| 2009-10 | Crewe Alex | 32 | 3 | |
| 2010-11 | Crewe Alex | 39 | 3 | |
| 2011-12 | Crewe Alex | 42 | 8 | |
| 2012-13 | Crewe Alex | 39 | 6 | 161　21 |

**NOLAN, Liam (D)** 0 0
H: 5 9　W: 10 12　b.Liverpool 20-9-94
| | | | |
|---|---|---|---|
| 2012-13 | Crewe Alex | 0 | 0 |

**OSMAN, Abdul (M)** 160 8
H: 6 0  W: 11 00  b.Accra 27-2-87
*Source:* Hampton & Richmond B, Maidenhead U.

| | | | | |
|---|---|---|---|---|
| 2007-08 | Gretna | 18 | 1 | 18 1 |
| 2008-09 | Northampton T | 36 | 2 | |
| 2009-10 | Northampton T | 30 | 2 | |
| 2010-11 | Northampton T | 38 | 3 | |
| 2011-12 | Northampton T | 0 | 0 | 104 7 |
| 2012-13 | Crewe Alex | 38 | 0 | 38 0 |

**PHILLIPS, Steve (G)** 501 0
H: 6 1  W: 11 10  b.Bath 6-5-78
*Source:* Paulton R.

| | | | | |
|---|---|---|---|---|
| 1996-97 | Bristol C | 0 | 0 | |
| 1997-98 | Bristol C | 0 | 0 | |
| 1998-99 | Bristol C | 15 | 0 | |
| 1999-2000 | Bristol C | 21 | 0 | |
| 2000-01 | Bristol C | 42 | 0 | |
| 2001-02 | Bristol C | 22 | 0 | |
| 2002-03 | Bristol C | 46 | 0 | |
| 2003-04 | Bristol C | 46 | 0 | |
| 2004-05 | Bristol C | 46 | 0 | |
| 2005-06 | Bristol C | 19 | 0 | 257 0 |
| 2006-07 | Bristol R | 44 | 0 | |
| 2007-08 | Bristol R | 46 | 0 | |
| 2008-09 | Bristol R | 46 | 0 | |
| 2009-10 | Bristol R | 0 | 0 | 136 0 |
| 2009-10 | *Shrewsbury T* | 11 | 0 | 11 0 |
| 2009-10 | *Crewe Alex* | 28 | 0 | |
| 2010-11 | Crewe Alex | 3 | 0 | |
| 2011-12 | Crewe Alex | 46 | 0 | |
| 2012-13 | Crewe Alex | 20 | 0 | 97 0 |

**POGBA, Mathias (F)** 34 12
H: 6 3  W: 12 13  b.Conakry 19-8-90

| | | | | |
|---|---|---|---|---|
| 2010-11 | Wrexham | 0 | 0 | |
| 2012-13 | Crewe Alex | 34 | 12 | 34 12 |

**RAY, George (D)** 4 0
H: 5 10  W: 11 03  b.Warrington 13-10-93
*Source:* Scholar.

| | | | | |
|---|---|---|---|---|
| 2011-12 | Crewe Alex | 0 | 0 | |
| 2012-13 | Crewe Alex | 4 | 0 | 4 0 |

**ROBERTSON, Gregor (D)** 234 4
H: 6 0  W: 12 04  b.Edinburgh 19-1-84
*Honours:* Scotland Under-21.

| | | | | |
|---|---|---|---|---|
| 2000-01 | Nottingham F | 0 | 0 | |
| 2001-02 | Nottingham F | 0 | 0 | |
| 2002-03 | Nottingham F | 0 | 0 | |
| 2003-04 | Nottingham F | 16 | 0 | |
| 2004-05 | Nottingham F | 20 | 0 | 36 0 |
| 2005-06 | Rotherham U | 35 | 1 | |
| 2006-07 | Rotherham U | 18 | 0 | 53 1 |
| 2007-08 | Chesterfield | 35 | 1 | |
| 2008-09 | Chesterfield | 38 | 2 | |
| 2009-10 | Chesterfield | 10 | 0 | |
| 2010-11 | Chesterfield | 21 | 0 | |
| 2011-12 | Chesterfield | 12 | 0 | 116 3 |
| 2012-13 | Crewe Alex | 29 | 0 | 29 0 |

**SHELLEY, Danny (D)** 73 8
H: 5 9  W: 10 08  b.Stoke 29-12-90
*Source:* Scholar.

| | | | | |
|---|---|---|---|---|
| 2008-09 | Crewe Alex | 3 | 0 | |
| 2009-10 | Crewe Alex | 19 | 1 | |
| 2010-11 | Crewe Alex | 25 | 6 | |
| 2011-12 | Crewe Alex | 26 | 1 | |
| 2012-13 | Crewe Alex | 0 | 0 | 73 8 |

**TOOTLE, Matt (D)** 141 2
H: 5 9  W: 11 00  b.Widnes 11-10-90
*Source:* Scholar.

| | | | | |
|---|---|---|---|---|
| 2009-10 | Crewe Alex | 28 | 1 | |
| 2010-11 | Crewe Alex | 39 | 0 | |
| 2011-12 | Crewe Alex | 37 | 0 | |
| 2012-13 | Crewe Alex | 37 | 1 | 141 2 |

**TURTON, Oliver (D)** 23 0
H: 5 11  W: 11 11  b.Manchester 6-12-92
*Source:* Scholar.

| | | | | |
|---|---|---|---|---|
| 2010-11 | Crewe Alex | 1 | 0 | |
| 2011-12 | Crewe Alex | 2 | 0 | |
| 2012-13 | Crewe Alex | 20 | 0 | 23 0 |

**WATERS, Billy (M)** 0 0
H: 5 9  W: 11 07  b.Epsom 15-10-94

| | | | |
|---|---|---|---|
| 2012-13 | Crewe Alex | 0 | 0 |

**WEST, Michael (M)** 8 0
H: 5 9  W: 12 06  b.Maidstone 9-2-91
*Source:* Ebbsfleet U.

| | | | | |
|---|---|---|---|---|
| 2012-13 | Crewe Alex | 8 | 0 | 8 0 |

**WHITE, Andrew (D)** 0 0
H: 5 7  W: 11 00  b.Chester 8-10-92
*Source:* Scholar.

| | | | |
|---|---|---|---|
| 2011-12 | Crewe Alex | 0 | 0 |
| 2012-13 | Crewe Alex | 0 | 0 |

**Players retained or with offer of contract**
Williams, Anthony Simon.

**Scholars**
Cunningham, Jake Aiden; Eden, Jack William; Isaacs, Bradley James; John, Louis Tyler; Kouadio, William; Laing, Alex Neil; Malins, Alexander Jordan; Melford-Rowe, Emmanuel Joshua; Melville, Scott Andrew; Richefond, Ryan James; Robinson, Malachi Tramaine Jahvan; Rowson, Sean James; Thomas, Cecil Jee; Woon, William Ernest Henry.

## CRYSTAL PALACE (31)

**APPIAH, Kwesi (F)** 13 0
H: 5 11  W: 12 08  b.Thamesmead 12-8-90
*Source:* Margate, Ebbsfleet U.

| | | | | |
|---|---|---|---|---|
| 2008-09 | Peterborough U | 0 | 0 | |

From Brackley T, Thurrock, Margate.

| | | | | |
|---|---|---|---|---|
| 2011-12 | Crystal Palace | 4 | 0 | |
| 2012-13 | Crystal Palace | 2 | 0 | 6 0 |
| 2012-13 | *Aldershot T* | 2 | 0 | 2 0 |
| 2012-13 | *Yeovil T* | 5 | 0 | 5 0 |

**BANTON, Jason (F)** 15 6
H: 5 10  W: 11 05  b.Tottenham 15-12-92
*Source:* Scholar.

| | | | | |
|---|---|---|---|---|
| 2009-10 | Blackburn R | 0 | 0 | |
| 2010-11 | Blackburn R | 0 | 0 | |
| 2010-11 | Liverpool | 0 | 0 | |
| 2011-12 | Liverpool | 0 | 0 | |
| 2011-12 | *Burton Alb* | 1 | 0 | 1 0 |
| 2012-13 | Crystal Palace | 0 | 0 | |
| 2012-13 | *Plymouth Arg* | 14 | 6 | 14 6 |

**BLAKE, Darcy (M)** 107 0
H: 5 10  W: 12 05  b.New Tredegar 13-12-88
*Source:* Scholar. *Honours:* Wales Youth, Under-21, 14 full caps, 1 goal.

| | | | | |
|---|---|---|---|---|
| 2005-06 | Cardiff C | 1 | 0 | |
| 2006-07 | Cardiff C | 10 | 0 | |
| 2007-08 | Cardiff C | 8 | 0 | |
| 2008-09 | Cardiff C | 7 | 0 | |
| 2009-10 | Cardiff C | 18 | 0 | |
| 2009-10 | *Plymouth Arg* | 7 | 0 | 7 0 |
| 2010-11 | Cardiff C | 26 | 0 | |
| 2011-12 | Cardiff C | 30 | 0 | |
| 2012-13 | Cardiff C | 0 | 0 | 90 0 |
| 2012-13 | Crystal Palace | 10 | 0 | 10 0 |

**BOATENG, Hiram (M)** 0 0
b. 8-1-96

| | | | |
|---|---|---|---|
| 2012-13 | Crystal Palace | 0 | 0 |

**BOLASIE, Yannick (M)** 159 17
H: 6 2  W: 13 02  b.DR Congo 24-5-89

| | | | | |
|---|---|---|---|---|
| 2008-09 | Plymouth Arg | 0 | 0 | |
| 2008-09 | Barnet | 20 | 3 | |
| 2009-10 | Plymouth Arg | 16 | 1 | |
| 2009-10 | Barnet | 22 | 2 | 42 5 |
| 2010-11 | Plymouth Arg | 35 | 7 | 51 8 |
| 2011-12 | Bristol C | 23 | 1 | |
| 2012-13 | Bristol C | 0 | 0 | 23 1 |
| 2012-13 | Crystal Palace | 43 | 3 | 43 3 |

**CHAMBERS, Michael (D)** 0 0
H: 6 2  b.Cardiff 15-2-94
*Source:* Dulwich Hamlet.

| | | | |
|---|---|---|---|
| 2011-12 | Crystal Palace | 0 | 0 |
| 2012-13 | Crystal Palace | 0 | 0 |

**DE SILVA, Kyle (F)** 10 0
H: 5 10  W: 11 05  b.Croydon 29-11-93
*Source:* Scholar.

| | | | | |
|---|---|---|---|---|
| 2010-11 | Crystal Palace | 0 | 0 | |
| 2011-12 | Crystal Palace | 6 | 0 | |
| 2012-13 | Crystal Palace | 1 | 0 | 7 0 |
| 2012-13 | *Barnet* | 3 | 0 | 3 0 |

**DELANEY, Damien (D)** 445 13
H: 6 3  W: 14 00  b.Cork 20-7-81
*Source:* Cork C. *Honours:* Eire 7 full caps.

| | | | | |
|---|---|---|---|---|
| 2000-01 | Leicester C | 5 | 0 | |
| 2001-02 | Leicester C | 3 | 0 | |
| 2001-02 | *Stockport Co* | 12 | 1 | 12 1 |
| 2001-02 | *Huddersfield T* | 2 | 0 | 2 0 |
| 2002-03 | Leicester C | 0 | 0 | 8 0 |
| 2002-03 | *Mansfield T* | 7 | 0 | 7 0 |
| 2002-03 | Hull C | 30 | 1 | |
| 2003-04 | Hull C | 46 | 2 | |
| 2004-05 | Hull C | 43 | 1 | |
| 2005-06 | Hull C | 46 | 0 | |
| 2006-07 | Hull C | 37 | 1 | |
| 2007-08 | Hull C | 22 | 0 | 224 5 |
| 2007-08 | QPR | 17 | 1 | |
| 2008-09 | QPR | 37 | 1 | |
| 2009-10 | QPR | 0 | 0 | 54 2 |
| 2009-10 | Ipswich T | 36 | 0 | |
| 2010-11 | Ipswich T | 32 | 2 | |
| 2011-12 | Ipswich T | 29 | 0 | |
| 2012-13 | Ipswich T | 1 | 0 | 98 2 |
| 2012-13 | Crystal Palace | 40 | 3 | 40 3 |

**DIKGACOI, Kagisho (M)** 182 15
H: 5 11  W: 12 10  b.Brandfort 24-11-84
*Honours:* South Africa 46 full caps, 2 goals.

| | | | | |
|---|---|---|---|---|
| 2004-05 | Bloemfontein YT | 10 | 0 | 10 0 |
| 2005-06 | Lamontville GA | 9 | 0 | |
| 2006-07 | Lamontville GA | 25 | 0 | |
| 2007-08 | Lamontville GA | 23 | 4 | |
| 2008-09 | Lamontville GA | 23 | 4 | 80 8 |
| 2009-10 | Fulham | 12 | 0 | |
| 2010-11 | Fulham | 1 | 0 | 13 0 |
| 2010-11 | *Crystal Palace* | 13 | 1 | |
| 2011-12 | Crystal Palace | 27 | 2 | |
| 2012-13 | Crystal Palace | 39 | 4 | 79 7 |

**EASTER, Jermaine (F)** 319 74
H: 5 9  W: 12 02  b.Cardiff 15-1-82
*Source:* Trainee. *Honours:* Wales Youth, 10 full caps.

| | | | | |
|---|---|---|---|---|
| 2000-01 | Wolverhampton W | 0 | 0 | |
| 2000-01 | Hartlepool U | 4 | 0 | |
| 2001-02 | Hartlepool U | 12 | 2 | |
| 2002-03 | Hartlepool U | 8 | 0 | |
| 2003-04 | Hartlepool U | 3 | 0 | 27 2 |
| 2003-04 | Cambridge U | 15 | 2 | |
| 2004-05 | Cambridge U | 24 | 6 | 39 8 |
| 2004-05 | Boston U | 9 | 3 | 9 3 |
| 2005-06 | Stockport Co | 19 | 8 | 19 8 |
| 2005-06 | Wycombe W | 15 | 2 | |
| 2006-07 | Wycombe W | 38 | 17 | |
| 2007-08 | Wycombe W | 6 | 2 | 59 21 |
| 2007-08 | Plymouth Arg | 32 | 6 | |
| 2008-09 | Plymouth Arg | 4 | 0 | 36 6 |
| 2008-09 | *Millwall* | 5 | 1 | |
| 2008-09 | *Colchester U* | 5 | 2 | 5 2 |
| 2009-10 | Milton Keynes D | 36 | 14 | |
| 2010-11 | Milton Keynes D | 14 | 0 | 50 14 |
| 2010-11 | *Swansea C* | 6 | 1 | 6 1 |
| 2010-11 | Crystal Palace | 14 | 1 | |
| 2011-12 | Crystal Palace | 33 | 5 | |
| 2012-13 | Crystal Palace | 8 | 1 | 55 7 |
| 2012-13 | *Millwall* | 9 | 1 | 14 2 |

**FITZSIMONS, Ross (G)** 0 0
H: 6 1  W: 11 10  b.Hammersmith 28-5-94

| | | | |
|---|---|---|---|
| 2012-13 | Crystal Palace | 0 | 0 |

**GABBIDON, Daniel (D)** 340 11
H: 6 0  W: 13 05  b.Cwmbran 8-8-79
*Source:* Trainee. *Honours:* Wales Youth, Under-21, 46 full caps.

| | | | | |
|---|---|---|---|---|
| 1998-99 | WBA | 2 | 0 | |
| 1999-2000 | WBA | 18 | 0 | |
| 2000-01 | WBA | 0 | 0 | 20 0 |
| 2000-01 | Cardiff C | 43 | 3 | |
| 2001-02 | Cardiff C | 44 | 3 | |
| 2002-03 | Cardiff C | 24 | 0 | |
| 2003-04 | Cardiff C | 41 | 3 | |
| 2004-05 | Cardiff C | 45 | 1 | 197 10 |
| 2005-06 | West Ham U | 32 | 0 | |
| 2006-07 | West Ham U | 18 | 0 | |
| 2007-08 | West Ham U | 10 | 0 | |
| 2008-09 | West Ham U | 5 | 0 | |
| 2009-10 | West Ham U | 10 | 0 | |
| 2010-11 | West Ham U | 26 | 0 | 96 0 |

| 2011-12 | QPR | 17 | 0 | 17 | 0 |
|---|---|---|---|---|---|
| 2012-13 | Crystal Palace | 10 | 1 | 10 | 1 |

**GARVAN, Owen (M)**    239 23
H: 6 0   W: 10 07   b.Dublin 29-1-88
*Source:* Scholar. *Honours:* Eire Youth, Under-21.

| 2005-06 | Ipswich T | 32 | 3 | | |
|---|---|---|---|---|---|
| 2006-07 | Ipswich T | 27 | 1 | | |
| 2007-08 | Ipswich T | 43 | 2 | | |
| 2008-09 | Ipswich T | 37 | 7 | | |
| 2009-10 | Ipswich T | 25 | 0 | 164 | 13 |
| 2010-11 | Crystal Palace | 26 | 3 | | |
| 2011-12 | Crystal Palace | 22 | 3 | | |
| 2012-13 | Crystal Palace | 27 | 4 | 75 | 10 |

**INNISS, Ryan (D)**    0 0
H: 6 5   W: 13 02   b.Kent 5-6-95

| 2012-13 | Crystal Palace | 0 | 0 | | |
|---|---|---|---|---|---|

**JEDINAK, Mile (M)**    265 33
H: 6 2   W: 13 12   b.Sydney 3-8-84
*Honours:* Australia Youth, 34 full caps, 3 goals.

| 2000-01 | Sydney U | 3 | 0 | | |
|---|---|---|---|---|---|
| 2001-02 | Sydney U | 7 | 1 | | |
| 2002-03 | Sydney U | 18 | 2 | | |
| 2003-04 | Varteks | 0 | 0 | | |
| 2004-05 | Sydney U | 24 | 3 | | |
| 2005-06 | Sydney U | 30 | 6 | 82 | 12 |
| 2006-07 | Central Coast M | 8 | 0 | | |
| 2007-08 | Central Coast M | 22 | 2 | | |
| 2008-09 | Central Coast M | 15 | 6 | 45 | 8 |
| 2008-09 | Genclerbirligi | 15 | 1 | | |
| 2009-10 | Genclerbirligi | 2 | 0 | | |
| 2009-10 | Antalya | 28 | 5 | 28 | 5 |
| 2010-11 | Genclerbirligi | 21 | 3 | 38 | 4 |
| 2011-12 | Crystal Palace | 31 | 1 | | |
| 2012-13 | Crystal Palace | 41 | 3 | 72 | 4 |

**KING, Tom (G)**    0 0
b.Plymouth 9-3-95
*Source:* Scholar.

| 2011-12 | Crystal Palace | 0 | 0 | | |
|---|---|---|---|---|---|
| 2012-13 | Crystal Palace | 0 | 0 | | |

**MARROW, Alex (M)**    82 1
H: 6 1   W: 13 00   b.Tyldesley 21-1-90
*Source:* Ashton Ath.

| 2007-08 | Blackburn R | 0 | 0 | | |
|---|---|---|---|---|---|
| 2008-09 | Blackburn R | 0 | 0 | | |
| 2009-10 | Blackburn R | 0 | 0 | | |
| 2009-10 | Oldham Ath | 32 | 1 | 32 | 1 |
| 2010-11 | Blackburn R | 0 | 0 | | |
| 2010-11 | Crystal Palace | 21 | 0 | | |
| 2011-12 | Crystal Palace | 1 | 0 | | |
| 2011-12 | Preston NE | 4 | 0 | 4 | 0 |
| 2012-13 | Crystal Palace | 4 | 0 | 26 | 0 |
| 2012-13 | Fleetwood T | 20 | 0 | 20 | 0 |

**McCARTHY, Patrick (D)**    252 11
H: 6 2   W: 13 07   b.Dublin 31-5-83
*Source:* Scholar. *Honours:* Eire Youth, B, Under-21.

| 2000-01 | Manchester C | 0 | 0 | | |
|---|---|---|---|---|---|
| 2001-02 | Manchester C | 0 | 0 | | |
| 2002-03 | Manchester C | 0 | 0 | | |
| 2002-03 | Boston U | 12 | 0 | 12 | 0 |
| 2002-03 | Notts Co | 6 | 0 | 6 | 0 |
| 2003-04 | Manchester C | 0 | 0 | | |
| 2004-05 | Manchester C | 0 | 0 | | |
| 2004-05 | Leicester C | 12 | 0 | | |
| 2005-06 | Leicester C | 38 | 2 | | |
| 2006-07 | Leicester C | 22 | 1 | 72 | 3 |
| 2007-08 | Charlton Ath | 29 | 2 | 29 | 2 |
| 2008-09 | Crystal Palace | 27 | 3 | | |
| 2009-10 | Crystal Palace | 20 | 0 | | |
| 2010-11 | Crystal Palace | 43 | 1 | | |
| 2011-12 | Crystal Palace | 43 | 2 | | |
| 2012-13 | Crystal Palace | 0 | 0 | 133 | 6 |

**MORITZ, Andre (M)**    121 24
H: 6 2   W: 13 00   b.Florianopolis 6-8-86

| 2007-08 | Kasimpasa | 20 | 4 | | |
|---|---|---|---|---|---|
| 2009-10 | Kasimpasa | 21 | 9 | 41 | 13 |
| 2010-11 | Kayserispor | 21 | 2 | 21 | 2 |
| 2011-12 | Mersin Idmanyurdu | 32 | 4 | 32 | 4 |
| 2012-13 | Crystal Palace | 27 | 5 | 27 | 5 |

**MOXEY, Dean (D)**    166 7
H: 6 2   W: 11 00   b.Exeter 14-1-86
*Source:* Scholar.

| 2008-09 | Exeter C | 43 | 4 | 43 | 4 |
|---|---|---|---|---|---|
| 2009-10 | Derby Co | 30 | 0 | | |
| 2010-11 | Derby Co | 22 | 2 | 52 | 2 |
| 2010-11 | Crystal Palace | 17 | 1 | | |
| 2011-12 | Crystal Palace | 24 | 0 | | |
| 2012-13 | Crystal Palace | 30 | 0 | 71 | 1 |

**MURRAY, Glenn (F)**    290 121
H: 6 1   W: 12 12   b.Maryport 25-9-83
*Source:* Wilmington Hammerheads, Workington.

| 2005-06 | Carlisle U | 26 | 3 | | |
|---|---|---|---|---|---|
| 2006-07 | Carlisle U | 1 | 0 | 27 | 3 |
| 2006-07 | Stockport Co | 11 | 3 | 11 | 3 |
| 2006-07 | Rochdale | 31 | 16 | | |
| 2007-08 | Rochdale | 23 | 9 | 54 | 25 |
| 2007-08 | Brighton & HA | 21 | 9 | | |
| 2008-09 | Brighton & HA | 23 | 11 | | |
| 2009-10 | Brighton & HA | 32 | 12 | | |
| 2010-11 | Brighton & HA | 42 | 22 | 118 | 54 |
| 2011-12 | Crystal Palace | 38 | 6 | | |
| 2012-13 | Crystal Palace | 42 | 30 | 80 | 36 |

**O'KEEFE, Stuart (M)**    32 0
H: 5 8   W: 10 00   b.Eye 4-3-91
*Source:* Ipswich T Scholar.

| 2008-09 | Southend U | 3 | 0 | | |
|---|---|---|---|---|---|
| 2009-10 | Southend U | 7 | 0 | | |
| 2010-11 | Southend U | 0 | 0 | 10 | 0 |
| 2010-11 | Crystal Palace | 4 | 0 | | |
| 2011-12 | Crystal Palace | 13 | 0 | | |
| 2012-13 | Crystal Palace | 5 | 0 | 22 | 0 |

**PARR, Jonathan (M)**    198 10
H: 6 0   W: 11 11   b.Oslo 21-10-88
*Honours:* Norway Youth, Under-21, 9 full caps.

| 2006 | Lyn | 11 | 0 | 11 | 0 |
|---|---|---|---|---|---|
| 2007 | Aalesund | 19 | 1 | | |
| 2008 | Aalesund | 24 | 4 | | |
| 2009 | Aalesund | 27 | 2 | | |
| 2010 | Aalesund | 25 | 0 | | |
| 2011 | Aalesund | 15 | 1 | 110 | 8 |
| 2011-12 | Crystal Palace | 39 | 2 | | |
| 2012-13 | Crystal Palace | 38 | 0 | 77 | 2 |

**PARSONS, Matthew (D)**    18 0
H: 5 10   W: 11 09   b.Catford 23-12-91
*Source:* Scholar.

| 2010-11 | Crystal Palace | 2 | 0 | | |
|---|---|---|---|---|---|
| 2010-11 | Barnet | 8 | 0 | 8 | 0 |
| 2011-12 | Crystal Palace | 4 | 0 | | |
| 2012-13 | Crystal Palace | 0 | 0 | 6 | 0 |
| 2012-13 | Wycombe W | 4 | 0 | 4 | 0 |

**PRICE, Lewis (G)**    102 0
H: 6 3   W: 13 05   b.Bournemouth 19-7-84
*Source:* Southampton Academy. *Honours:* Wales Youth, Under-21, 11 full caps.

| 2002-03 | Ipswich T | 0 | 0 | | |
|---|---|---|---|---|---|
| 2003-04 | Ipswich T | 1 | 0 | | |
| 2004-05 | Ipswich T | 8 | 0 | | |
| 2004-05 | Cambridge U | 6 | 0 | 6 | 0 |
| 2005-06 | Ipswich T | 25 | 0 | | |
| 2006-07 | Ipswich T | 34 | 0 | 68 | 0 |
| 2007-08 | Derby Co | 6 | 0 | | |
| 2008-09 | Derby Co | 0 | 0 | | |
| 2008-09 | Milton Keynes D | 2 | 0 | 2 | 0 |
| 2008-09 | Luton T | 1 | 0 | 1 | 0 |
| 2009-10 | Derby Co | 0 | 0 | 6 | 0 |
| 2009-10 | Brentford | 13 | 0 | 13 | 0 |
| 2010-11 | Crystal Palace | 1 | 0 | | |
| 2011-12 | Crystal Palace | 5 | 0 | | |
| 2012-13 | Crystal Palace | 0 | 0 | 6 | 0 |

**RAMAGE, Peter (D)**    190 6
H: 6 3   W: 11 02   b.Whitley Bay 22-11-83
*Source:* Trainee.

| 2003-04 | Newcastle U | 0 | 0 | | |
|---|---|---|---|---|---|
| 2004-05 | Newcastle U | 4 | 0 | | |
| 2005-06 | Newcastle U | 23 | 0 | | |
| 2006-07 | Newcastle U | 21 | 0 | | |
| 2007-08 | Newcastle U | 3 | 0 | 51 | 0 |
| 2008-09 | QPR | 31 | 0 | | |
| 2009-10 | QPR | 33 | 2 | | |
| 2010-11 | QPR | 4 | 0 | | |
| 2011-12 | QPR | 0 | 0 | 68 | 2 |
| 2011-12 | Crystal Palace | 17 | 0 | | |
| 2011-12 | Birmingham C | 14 | 0 | 14 | 0 |
| 2012-13 | Crystal Palace | 40 | 4 | 57 | 4 |

**SEKAJJA, Ibra (F)**    7 1
H: 5 11   W: 11 00   b.Uganda 31-10-92
*Source:* Scholar.

| 2010-11 | Crystal Palace | 1 | 1 | | |
|---|---|---|---|---|---|
| 2011-12 | Crystal Palace | 1 | 0 | | |
| 2012-13 | Crystal Palace | 0 | 0 | 2 | 1 |
| 2012-13 | Milton Keynes D | 1 | 0 | 1 | 0 |
| 2012-13 | Barnet | 4 | 0 | 4 | 0 |

**SPERONI, Julian (G)**    378 0
H: 6 0   W: 11 00   b.Buenos Aires 18-5-79
*Honours:* Argentina Under-20, Under-21.

| 1999-2000 | Platense | 2 | 0 | | |
|---|---|---|---|---|---|
| 2000-01 | Platense | 0 | 0 | 2 | 0 |
| 2001-02 | Dundee | 17 | 0 | | |
| 2002-03 | Dundee | 38 | 0 | | |
| 2003-04 | Dundee | 37 | 0 | 92 | 0 |
| 2004-05 | Crystal Palace | 6 | 0 | | |
| 2005-06 | Crystal Palace | 4 | 0 | | |
| 2006-07 | Crystal Palace | 5 | 0 | | |
| 2007-08 | Crystal Palace | 46 | 0 | | |
| 2008-09 | Crystal Palace | 45 | 0 | | |
| 2009-10 | Crystal Palace | 45 | 0 | | |
| 2010-11 | Crystal Palace | 45 | 0 | | |
| 2011-12 | Crystal Palace | 42 | 0 | | |
| 2012-13 | Crystal Palace | 46 | 0 | 284 | 0 |

**TAYLOR, Quade (M)**    0 0
H: 6 3   W: 11 00   b.Tooting 11-12-93
*Source:* Dulwich H.

| 2010-11 | Crystal Palace | 0 | 0 | | |
|---|---|---|---|---|---|
| 2011-12 | Crystal Palace | 0 | 0 | | |
| 2012-13 | Crystal Palace | 0 | 0 | | |

**WARD, Joel (D)**    135 7
H: 6 2   W: 11 13   b.Emsworth 29-10-89
*Source:* Scholar.

| 2008-09 | Portsmouth | 0 | 0 | | |
|---|---|---|---|---|---|
| 2008-09 | Bournemouth | 21 | 1 | 21 | 1 |
| 2009-10 | Portsmouth | 3 | 0 | | |
| 2010-11 | Portsmouth | 42 | 3 | | |
| 2011-12 | Portsmouth | 44 | 3 | 89 | 6 |
| 2012-13 | Crystal Palace | 25 | 0 | 25 | 0 |

**WILBRAHAM, Aaron (F)**    420 91
H: 6 3   W: 12 04   b.Knutsford 21-10-79
*Source:* Trainee.

| 1997-98 | Stockport Co | 7 | 1 | | |
|---|---|---|---|---|---|
| 1998-99 | Stockport Co | 26 | 0 | | |
| 1999-2000 | Stockport Co | 26 | 4 | | |
| 2000-01 | Stockport Co | 36 | 12 | | |
| 2001-02 | Stockport Co | 21 | 3 | | |
| 2002-03 | Stockport Co | 15 | 7 | | |
| 2003-04 | Stockport Co | 41 | 8 | 172 | 35 |
| 2004-05 | Hull C | 19 | 2 | 19 | 2 |
| 2004-05 | Oldham Ath | 4 | 2 | 4 | 2 |
| 2005-06 | Milton Keynes D | 31 | 4 | | |
| 2005-06 | Bradford C | 5 | 1 | 5 | 1 |
| 2006-07 | Milton Keynes D | 32 | 7 | | |
| 2007-08 | Milton Keynes D | 35 | 10 | | |
| 2008-09 | Milton Keynes D | 35 | 10 | | |
| 2009-10 | Milton Keynes D | 35 | 10 | | |
| 2010-11 | Milton Keynes D | 10 | 2 | 176 | 49 |
| 2010-11 | Norwich C | 12 | 1 | | |
| 2011-12 | Norwich C | 11 | 1 | 23 | 2 |
| 2012-13 | Crystal Palace | 21 | 0 | 21 | 0 |

**WILLIAMS, Jon (M)**    43 0
H: 5 6   W: 10 00   b.Tunbridge Wells 9-10-93
*Source:* Scholar. *Honours:* Wales Youth, Under-21, 2 full caps.

| 2010-11 | Crystal Palace | 0 | 0 | | |
|---|---|---|---|---|---|
| 2011-12 | Crystal Palace | 14 | 0 | | |
| 2012-13 | Crystal Palace | 29 | 0 | 43 | 0 |

**WYNTER, Alex (M)**    0 0
H: 6 0   W: 13 04   b.Camberwell 15-9-93
*Source:* Scholar.

| 2009-10 | Crystal Palace | 0 | 0 | | |
|---|---|---|---|---|---|
| 2010-11 | Crystal Palace | 0 | 0 | | |
| 2011-12 | Crystal Palace | 0 | 0 | | |
| 2012-13 | Crystal Palace | 0 | 0 | | |

**Players retained or with offer of contract**
Allassani, Reise Malcolm; Gray, Jake Stephen; Kaikai, Sulaiman Borbor; Sow, Ghassimu.

**Scholars**
Black, Sonny Jamaal; Croll, Luke Alan; Dymond, Connor William; Gabsi, Elijah Yousef Septe; Gregory, David Michael; Johnson-Cole, William Moses Bernard; Khinda-John, Kiran; Palmer, Javen; Williams, Jerome Craig; Woodley, Kieran Luke; Wright, Douglas William.

## DAGENHAM & R (32)

**BINGHAM, Billy (D)**    53   4
H: 5 11   W: 11 02   b.Welling 15-7-90
*Source:* Crystal Palace.

| 2008-09 | Dagenham & R | 0 | 0 | | |
| 2009-10 | Dagenham & R | 2 | 0 | | |
| 2010-11 | Dagenham & R | 6 | 0 | | |
| 2011-12 | Dagenham & R | 27 | 2 | | |
| 2012-13 | Dagenham & R | 18 | 2 | 53 | 4 |

**DENNIS, Louis (F)**    6   0
H: 6 1   W: 10 12   b.Hendon 9-10-92
*Source:* Youth.

| 2011-12 | Dagenham & R | 0 | 0 | | |
| 2012-13 | Dagenham & R | 6 | 0 | 6 | 0 |

**DOE, Scott (D)**    167   9
H: 6 0   W: 11 06   b.Reading 6-11-88
*Source:* Swindon T Scholar, Weymouth.

| 2009-10 | Dagenham & R | 42 | 0 | | |
| 2010-11 | Dagenham & R | 38 | 0 | | |
| 2011-12 | Dagenham & R | 41 | 6 | | |
| 2012-13 | Dagenham & R | 46 | 3 | 167 | 9 |

**EDMANS, Rob (F)**    4   0
H: 6 5   W: 12 08   b.Greenwich 25-1-87
*Source:* Witham T, Chelmsford C.

| 2011-12 | Dagenham & R | 3 | 0 | | |
| 2012-13 | Dagenham & R | 1 | 0 | 4 | 0 |
| 2012-13 | *Macclesfield T* | 0 | 0 | | |
| 2012-13 | *Chelmsford* | 0 | 0 | | |

**ELITO, Medy (M)**    113   16
H: 6 2   W: 13 00   b.Kinshasa 20-3-90
*Source:* Scholar. *Honours:* England Youth.

| 2007-08 | Colchester U | 11 | 1 | | |
| 2008-09 | Colchester U | 5 | 0 | | |
| 2009-10 | Colchester U | 3 | 0 | | |
| 2009-10 | *Cheltenham T* | 12 | 3 | | |
| 2010-11 | Colchester U | 0 | 0 | 19 | 1 |
| 2010-11 | *Dagenham & R* | 10 | 2 | | |
| 2010-11 | *Cheltenham T* | 2 | 0 | 14 | 3 |
| 2011-12 | Dagenham & R | 24 | 4 | | |
| 2012-13 | Dagenham & R | 46 | 6 | 80 | 12 |

**FORTUNE, Jon (D)**    231   9
H: 6 2   W: 12 12   b.Islington 23-8-80
*Source:* Trainee.

| 1998-99 | Charlton Ath | 0 | 0 | | |
| 1999-2000 | Charlton Ath | 0 | 0 | | |
| 1999-2000 | *Mansfield T* | 4 | 0 | | |
| 2000-01 | Charlton Ath | 0 | 0 | | |
| 2000-01 | *Mansfield T* | 14 | 0 | 18 | 0 |
| 2001-02 | Charlton Ath | 19 | 0 | | |
| 2002-03 | Charlton Ath | 26 | 1 | | |
| 2003-04 | Charlton Ath | 28 | 2 | | |
| 2004-05 | Charlton Ath | 31 | 2 | | |
| 2005-06 | Charlton Ath | 11 | 0 | | |
| 2006-07 | Charlton Ath | 14 | 1 | | |
| 2006-07 | *Stoke C* | 14 | 1 | 14 | 1 |
| 2007-08 | Charlton Ath | 26 | 2 | | |
| 2008-09 | Charlton Ath | 17 | 0 | | |
| 2009-10 | Charlton Ath | 0 | 0 | | |
| 2009-10 | Sheffield U | 5 | 1 | | |
| 2010-11 | Sheffield U | 0 | 0 | 5 | 1 |
| 2010-11 | Charlton Ath | 16 | 0 | | |
| 2011-12 | Charlton Ath | 0 | 0 | 182 | 7 |
| 2011-12 | Exeter C | 5 | 0 | 5 | 0 |
| 2012-13 | Barnet | 6 | 0 | 6 | 0 |
| 2012-13 | Dagenham & R | 1 | 0 | 1 | 0 |

**GAYLE, Ian (D)**    0   0
b.Welling 23-10-92
*Source:* Youth.

| 2011-12 | Dagenham & R | 0 | 0 | | |
| 2012-13 | Dagenham & R | 0 | 0 | | |

**GRACCO, Gianluca (F)**    1   0
b.Naples 19-6-90

| 2012-13 | Dagenham & R | 1 | 0 | 1 | 0 |

**GREEN, Danny J (M)**    17   1
H: 6 0   W: 12 06   b.Harlow 4-8-90
*Source:* Billericay T.

| 2010-11 | Dagenham & R | 3 | 0 | | |
| 2011-12 | Dagenham & R | 8 | 1 | | |
| 2012-13 | Dagenham & R | 6 | 0 | 17 | 1 |

**GREEN, Dominic (F)**    77   6
H: 5 6   W: 11 02   b.Newham 5-7-89
*Source:* Scholar.

| 2007-08 | Dagenham & R | 12 | 0 | | |
| 2008-09 | Dagenham & R | 2 | 1 | | |
| 2008-09 | Peterborough U | 16 | 1 | | |
| 2009-10 | Peterborough U | 11 | 1 | | |
| 2009-10 | *Chesterfield* | 10 | 2 | 10 | 2 |
| 2010-11 | Peterborough U | 0 | 0 | 27 | 2 |
| 2011-12 | Dagenham & R | 16 | 1 | | |
| 2012-13 | Dagenham & R | 10 | 0 | 40 | 2 |

**HOWELL, Luke (D)**    135   11
H: 5 10   W: 10 05   b.Heathfield 5-1-87
*Source:* Scholar.

| 2006-07 | Gillingham | 1 | 0 | 1 | 0 |
| 2007-08 | Milton Keynes D | 8 | 0 | | |
| 2008-09 | Milton Keynes D | 15 | 1 | | |
| 2009-10 | Milton Keynes D | 29 | 0 | | |
| 2010-11 | Milton Keynes D | 1 | 0 | 53 | 1 |
| 2010-11 | Lincoln C | 25 | 1 | 25 | 1 |
| 2011-12 | Dagenham & R | 10 | 0 | | |
| 2012-13 | Dagenham & R | 46 | 9 | 56 | 9 |

**HOYTE, Gavin (D)**    67   0
H: 5 11   W: 11 00   b.Waltham Forest 6-6-90
*Source:* Scholar. *Honours:* England Youth, Under-20.

| 2007-08 | Arsenal | 0 | 0 | | |
| 2008-09 | Arsenal | 1 | 0 | | |
| 2008-09 | Watford | 7 | 0 | 7 | 0 |
| 2009-10 | Arsenal | 0 | 0 | | |
| 2009-10 | *Brighton & HA* | 18 | 0 | 18 | 0 |
| 2010-11 | Arsenal | 0 | 0 | | |
| 2010-11 | *Lincoln C* | 12 | 0 | 12 | 0 |
| 2011-12 | Arsenal | 0 | 0 | 1 | 0 |
| 2011-12 | *AFC Wimbledon* | 3 | 0 | 3 | 0 |
| 2012-13 | Dagenham & R | 26 | 0 | 26 | 0 |

**ILESANMI, Femi (D)**    88   1
H: 6 1   W: 11 13   b.Southwark 18-4-91
*Source:* QPR Scholar, Ashford T (M'sex).

| 2010-11 | Dagenham & R | 25 | 0 | | |
| 2011-12 | Dagenham & R | 17 | 0 | | |
| 2012-13 | Dagenham & R | 46 | 1 | 88 | 1 |

**LEWINGTON, Chris (G)**    85   0
H: 6 1   W: 12 00   b.Sidcup 23-8-88
*Source:* Erith & B, Dulwich H, Fisher Ath, Sittingbourne, Leatherhead.

| 2009-10 | Dagenham & R | 0 | 0 | | |
| 2010-11 | Dagenham & R | 3 | 0 | | |
| 2011-12 | Dagenham & R | 41 | 0 | | |
| 2012-13 | Dagenham & R | 41 | 0 | 85 | 0 |

**MAHER, Kevin (M)**    496   23
H: 6 0   W: 12 13   b.Ilford 17-10-76
*Source:* Trainee. *Honours:* Eire Under-21.

| 1995-96 | Tottenham H | 0 | 0 | | |
| 1996-97 | Tottenham H | 0 | 0 | | |
| 1997-98 | Tottenham H | 0 | 0 | | |
| 1997-98 | Southend U | 18 | 1 | | |
| 1998-99 | Southend U | 34 | 4 | | |
| 1999-2000 | Southend U | 24 | 0 | | |
| 2000-01 | Southend U | 41 | 2 | | |
| 2001-02 | Southend U | 36 | 5 | | |
| 2002-03 | Southend U | 42 | 2 | | |
| 2003-04 | Southend U | 42 | 1 | | |
| 2004-05 | Southend U | 42 | 1 | | |
| 2005-06 | Southend U | 44 | 1 | | |
| 2006-07 | Southend U | 41 | 5 | | |
| 2007-08 | Southend U | 19 | 0 | 383 | 22 |
| 2007-08 | *Gillingham* | 7 | 0 | | |
| 2008-09 | Oldham Ath | 28 | 1 | 28 | 1 |
| 2009-10 | Gillingham | 26 | 0 | | |
| 2010-11 | Gillingham | 36 | 0 | 69 | 0 |
| 2011-12 | Dagenham & R | 8 | 0 | | |
| 2012-13 | Dagenham & R | 8 | 0 | 16 | 0 |

**OGOGO, Abu (D)**    158   6
H: 5 8   W: 10 02   b.Epsom 3-11-89
*Source:* Scholar.

| 2007-08 | Arsenal | 0 | 0 | | |
| 2008-09 | Arsenal | 0 | 0 | | |
| 2008-09 | *Barnet* | 9 | 1 | 9 | 1 |
| 2009-10 | Dagenham & R | 30 | 2 | | |
| 2010-11 | Dagenham & R | 33 | 1 | | |
| 2011-12 | Dagenham & R | 40 | 1 | | |
| 2012-13 | Dagenham & R | 46 | 1 | 149 | 5 |

**OSBORN, Alex (F)**    0   0
H: 5 9   W: 11 00   b.Walthamstow 29-7-93
*Source:* Grays Ath.

| 2010-11 | Dagenham & R | 0 | 0 | | |
| 2011-12 | Dagenham & R | 0 | 0 | | |
| 2012-13 | Dagenham & R | 0 | 0 | | |

**REED, Jake (F)**    29   1
H: 5 9   W: 11 07   b.Great Yarmouth 13-5-91
*Source:* Great Yarmouth T.

| 2011-12 | Dagenham & R | 7 | 0 | | |
| 2012-13 | Dagenham & R | 22 | 1 | 29 | 1 |

**SANTOS, Ricardo (D)**    0   0
b.Almada 18-6-95

| 2012-13 | Dagenham & R | 0 | 0 | | |

**SAUNDERS, Matthew (M)**    55   7
H: 5 11   W: 11 05   b.Chertsey 12-9-89
*Source:* Scholar.

| 2008-09 | Fulham | 0 | 0 | | |
| 2009-10 | Fulham | 0 | 0 | | |
| 2009-10 | *Lincoln C* | 18 | 3 | 18 | 3 |
| 2010-11 | Fulham | 0 | 0 | | |
| 2011-12 | Fulham | 0 | 0 | | |
| 2011-12 | Dagenham & R | 5 | 1 | | |
| 2012-13 | Dagenham & R | 32 | 3 | 37 | 4 |

**SCOTT, Josh (F)**    94   14
H: 6 1   W: 12 00   b.Camden 10-5-85
*Source:* Hayes, Hayes & Yeading U.

| 2009-10 | Dagenham & R | 40 | 10 | | |
| 2010-11 | Dagenham & R | 16 | 1 | | |
| 2011-12 | Dagenham & R | 20 | 1 | | |
| 2012-13 | Dagenham & R | 18 | 2 | 94 | 14 |

**SEABRIGHT, Jordan (G)**    4   0
H: 6 2   W: 12 06   b.Poole 1-5-94
*Source:* Youth.

| 2011-12 | Bournemouth | 0 | 0 | | |
| 2012-13 | Bournemouth | 0 | 0 | | |
| 2012-13 | Dagenham & R | 4 | 0 | 4 | 0 |

**SHIELDS, Sean (F)**    1   0
b.Enfield 20-1-92
*Source:* St Albans. *Honours:* Northern Ireland Under-21.

| 2012-13 | Dagenham & R | 1 | 0 | 1 | 0 |

**STREVENS, Ben (M)**    288   57
H: 6 1   W: 12 00   b.Edgware 24-5-80
*Source:* Wingate & Finchley.

| 1998-99 | Barnet | 0 | 0 | | |
| 1999-2000 | Barnet | 6 | 0 | | |
| 2000-01 | Barnet | 28 | 4 | | |
| 2005-06 | Barnet | 35 | 5 | 69 | 9 |

From Crawley T.

| 2007-08 | Dagenham & R | 46 | 15 | | |
| 2008-09 | Dagenham & R | 46 | 14 | | |
| 2009-10 | Brentford | 25 | 6 | 25 | 6 |
| 2010-11 | Wycombe W | 40 | 7 | | |
| 2011-12 | Wycombe W | 36 | 4 | 76 | 11 |
| 2012-13 | Gillingham | 12 | 1 | 12 | 1 |
| 2012-13 | Dagenham & R | 14 | 1 | 106 | 30 |

**WILKINSON, Luke (D)**    43   6
H: 6 2   W: 11 09   b.Wells 2-12-92
*Source:* Bristol C Scholar.

| 2009-10 | Portsmouth | 0 | 0 | | |
| 2010-11 | Dagenham & R | 0 | 0 | | |
| 2011-12 | Dagenham & R | 0 | 0 | | |
| 2012-13 | Dagenham & R | 43 | 6 | 43 | 6 |

**WILLIAMS, Sam (F)**    148   22
H: 5 11   W: 10 08   b.Greenwich 9-6-87
*Source:* Scholar.

| 2004-05 | Aston Villa | 0 | 0 | | |
| 2005-06 | Aston Villa | 0 | 0 | | |
| 2005-06 | *Wrexham* | 15 | 2 | 15 | 2 |
| 2006-07 | Aston Villa | 0 | 0 | | |

| | | | | |
|---|---|---|---|---|
| 2006-07 | Brighton & HA | 3 | 1 | 3 1 |
| 2007-08 | Aston Villa | 0 | 0 | |
| 2008-09 | Aston Villa | 0 | 0 | |
| 2008-09 | Colchester U | 1 | 0 | 1 0 |
| 2008-09 | Walsall | 5 | 1 | 5 1 |
| 2008-09 | Brentford | 11 | 2 | 11 2 |
| 2009-10 | Yeovil T | 34 | 4 | |
| 2010-11 | Yeovil T | 36 | 2 | 70 6 |
| 2011-12 | Dagenham & R | 10 | 2 | |
| 2012-13 | Dagenham & R | 33 | 8 | 43 10 |

**WOODALL, Brian (F)** 67 12
H: 5 10  W: 11 09  b.Bielefeld 28-12-87
Source: SC Herford, Hinckley U, Gresley R, Atherstone T, Coventry Sphinx, Gresley.

| | | | |
|---|---|---|---|
| 2011-12 | Dagenham & R | 39 | 11 |
| 2012-13 | Dagenham & R | 28 | 1  67 12 |

**Scholars**
Almeida, Santos Ricardo Alexandre; Connors, Jack Stuart; Davies, Cain Adrian; Efambe, Rouchy Ayenge; Ferguson, Nathan James Decalvia; Jordan-Daniel, Shaquille Aaron; Kashket, Reiss Max; Martinsen-Hickman, Tristan Nicholas; Monsheju, Timothy; Nouble, Joel Jonathan; Pykes, Kurtis; Rumens, Daniel; Sidhu, Jordan; Stewart, Montana; Tweddell, Harrison; Walker, Omari; Webber, Christopher Daniel.

# DERBY CO (33)

**ATKINS, Ross (G)** 50 0
H: 6 0  W: 13 00  b.Derby 3-11-89
Source: Scholar.

| | | | | |
|---|---|---|---|---|
| 2008-09 | Derby Co | 0 | 0 | |
| 2009-10 | Derby Co | 0 | 0 | |
| 2010-11 | Derby Co | 1 | 0 | |
| 2011-12 | Derby Co | 0 | 0 | |
| 2011-12 | Burton Alb | 45 | 0 | |
| 2012-13 | Derby Co | 0 | 0 | 1 0 |
| 2012-13 | Burton Alb | 4 | 0 | 49 0 |

**BAILEY, James (M)** 134 3
H: 6 0  W: 12 05  b.Bollington 18-9-88
Source: Scholar.

| | | | | |
|---|---|---|---|---|
| 2006-07 | Crewe Alex | 0 | 0 | |
| 2007-08 | Crewe Alex | 1 | 0 | |
| 2008-09 | Crewe Alex | 24 | 0 | |
| 2009-10 | Crewe Alex | 21 | 0 | 46 0 |
| 2010-11 | Derby Co | 36 | 1 | |
| 2011-12 | Derby Co | 22 | 0 | |
| 2012-13 | Derby Co | 0 | 0 | 58 1 |
| 2012-13 | Coventry C | 30 | 2 | 30 2 |

**BARKER, Shaun (D)** 355 18
H: 6 2  W: 12 08  b.Nottingham 19-9-82
Source: Scholar.

| | | | | |
|---|---|---|---|---|
| 2002-03 | Rotherham U | 11 | 0 | |
| 2003-04 | Rotherham U | 36 | 2 | |
| 2004-05 | Rotherham U | 33 | 2 | |
| 2005-06 | Rotherham U | 43 | 3 | 123 7 |
| 2006-07 | Blackpool | 45 | 3 | |
| 2007-08 | Blackpool | 46 | 2 | |
| 2008-09 | Blackpool | 43 | 0 | 134 5 |
| 2009-10 | Derby Co | 35 | 5 | |
| 2010-11 | Derby Co | 43 | 1 | |
| 2011-12 | Derby Co | 20 | 0 | |
| 2012-13 | Derby Co | 0 | 0 | 98 6 |

**BENNETT, Mason (F)** 15 0
H: 5 10  W: 10 02  b.Shirebrook 15-7-96
Source: Scholar.

| | | | | |
|---|---|---|---|---|
| 2011-12 | Derby Co | 9 | 0 | |
| 2012-13 | Derby Co | 6 | 0 | 15 0 |

**BRAYFORD, John (D)** 190 4
H: 5 8  W: 11 02  b.Stoke 29-12-87
Source: Burton Alb.

| | | | | |
|---|---|---|---|---|
| 2008-09 | Crewe Alex | 36 | 2 | |
| 2009-10 | Crewe Alex | 45 | 0 | 81 2 |
| 2010-11 | Derby Co | 46 | 1 | |
| 2011-12 | Derby Co | 23 | 0 | |
| 2012-13 | Derby Co | 40 | 1 | 109 2 |

**BRYSON, Craig (M)** 294 31
H: 5 7  W: 10 00  b.Rutherglen 6-11-86
Honours: Scotland Under-21, 1 full cap.

| | | | |
|---|---|---|---|
| 2003-04 | Clyde | 0 | 0 |

| | | | | |
|---|---|---|---|---|
| 2004-05 | Clyde | 28 | 3 | |
| 2005-06 | Clyde | 33 | 2 | |
| 2006-07 | Clyde | 34 | 3 | 95 8 |
| 2007-08 | Kilmarnock | 19 | 4 | |
| 2008-09 | Kilmarnock | 33 | 2 | |
| 2009-10 | Kilmarnock | 33 | 4 | |
| 2010-11 | Kilmarnock | 33 | 2 | 118 12 |
| 2011-12 | Derby Co | 44 | 6 | |
| 2012-13 | Derby Co | 37 | 5 | 81 11 |

**BUXTON, Jake (D)** 223 11
H: 6 1  W: 13 05  b.Sutton-in-Ashfield 4-3-85
Source: Scholar.

| | | | | |
|---|---|---|---|---|
| 2002-03 | Mansfield T | 3 | 0 | |
| 2003-04 | Mansfield T | 9 | 1 | |
| 2004-05 | Mansfield T | 30 | 1 | |
| 2005-06 | Mansfield T | 39 | 0 | |
| 2006-07 | Mansfield T | 30 | 1 | |
| 2007-08 | Mansfield T | 40 | 2 | |
| 2008-09 | Mansfield T | 0 | 0 | 151 5 |

From Burton Alb.

| | | | | |
|---|---|---|---|---|
| 2008-09 | Derby Co | 0 | 0 | |
| 2009-10 | Derby Co | 19 | 1 | |
| 2010-11 | Derby Co | 1 | 0 | |
| 2011-12 | Derby Co | 21 | 2 | |
| 2012-13 | Derby Co | 31 | 3 | 72 6 |

**COUTTS, Paul (M)** 174 7
H: 5 9  W: 11 11  b.Aberdeen 22-7-88
Source: Cove R. Honours: Scotland Under-21.

| | | | | |
|---|---|---|---|---|
| 2008-09 | Peterborough U | 37 | 0 | |
| 2009-10 | Peterborough U | 16 | 0 | 53 0 |
| 2009-10 | Preston NE | 13 | 1 | |
| 2010-11 | Preston NE | 23 | 1 | |
| 2011-12 | Preston NE | 41 | 2 | 77 4 |
| 2012-13 | Derby Co | 44 | 3 | 44 3 |

**DAVIES, Ben (M)** 351 66
H: 5 7  W: 12 03  b.Birmingham 27-5-81
Source: Walsall trainee.

| | | | | |
|---|---|---|---|---|
| 2000-01 | Kidderminster H | 3 | 0 | |
| 2001-02 | Kidderminster H | 9 | 0 | 12 0 |
| 2004-05 | Chester C | 44 | 2 | |
| 2005-06 | Chester C | 45 | 7 | 89 9 |
| 2006-07 | Shrewsbury T | 43 | 12 | |
| 2007-08 | Shrewsbury T | 27 | 6 | |
| 2008-09 | Shrewsbury T | 42 | 12 | 112 30 |
| 2009-10 | Notts Co | 45 | 15 | |
| 2010-11 | Notts Co | 22 | 5 | 67 20 |
| 2010-11 | Derby Co | 13 | 1 | |
| 2011-12 | Derby Co | 35 | 2 | |
| 2012-13 | Derby Co | 23 | 4 | 71 7 |

**DEENEY, Saul (G)** 52 0
H: 6 0  W: 12 13  b.Londonderry 12-3-83
Source: Scholar. Honours: Eire Youth, Under-21.

| | | | | |
|---|---|---|---|---|
| 2000-01 | Notts Co | 0 | 0 | |
| 2001-02 | Notts Co | 0 | 0 | |
| 2002-03 | Notts Co | 7 | 0 | |
| 2003-04 | Notts Co | 3 | 0 | |
| 2004-05 | Notts Co | 32 | 0 | |
| 2005-06 | Notts Co | 0 | 0 | |
| 2006-07 | Notts Co | 7 | 0 | |
| 2007-08 | Notts Co | 0 | 0 | |
| 2008-09 | Notts Co | 0 | 0 | 49 0 |
| 2009-10 | Derby Co | 3 | 0 | |
| 2010-11 | Derby Co | 0 | 0 | |
| 2011-12 | Derby Co | 0 | 0 | |
| 2012-13 | Derby Co | 0 | 0 | 3 0 |

**DOYLE, Conor (F)** 22 0
H: 6 2  W: 12 04  b.Mckinney 13-10-91
Source: Creighton Univ. Honours: Eire Under-21.

| | | | | |
|---|---|---|---|---|
| 2010-11 | Derby Co | 14 | 0 | |
| 2011-12 | Derby Co | 6 | 0 | |
| 2012-13 | Derby Co | 2 | 0 | 22 0 |

**FIELDING, Frank (G)** 165 0
H: 5 11  W: 12 00  b.Blackburn 4-4-88
Source: Scholar. Honours: England Youth, Under-21.

| | | | | |
|---|---|---|---|---|
| 2006-07 | Blackburn R | 0 | 0 | |
| 2007-08 | Blackburn R | 0 | 0 | |
| 2007-08 | Wycombe W | 36 | 0 | 36 0 |
| 2008-09 | Blackburn R | 0 | 0 | |
| 2008-09 | Northampton T | 12 | 0 | 12 0 |

| | | | | |
|---|---|---|---|---|
| 2008-09 | Rochdale | 23 | 0 | |
| 2009-10 | Blackburn R | 0 | 0 | |
| 2009-10 | Rochdale | 18 | 0 | 41 0 |
| 2010-11 | Blackburn R | 0 | 0 | |
| 2010-11 | Derby Co | 16 | 0 | |
| 2011-12 | Derby Co | 44 | 0 | |
| 2012-13 | Derby Co | 16 | 0 | 76 0 |

**FREEMAN, Kieron (D)** 38 1
H: 5 10  W: 12 05  b.Nottingham 21-3-92
Source: Scholar. Honours: Wales Youth, Under-21.

| | | | | |
|---|---|---|---|---|
| 2010-11 | Nottingham F | 0 | 0 | |
| 2011-12 | Nottingham F | 0 | 0 | |
| 2011-12 | Notts Co | 19 | 1 | 19 1 |
| 2012-13 | Derby Co | 19 | 0 | 19 0 |

**GJOKAJ, Valentin (D)** 6 0
H: 6 3  W: 11 12  b.Switzerland 23-8-93

| | | | | |
|---|---|---|---|---|
| 2012-13 | Derby Co | 6 | 0 | 6 0 |
| 2012-13 | Carlisle U | 0 | 0 | |

**HENDRICK, Jeff (M)** 91 9
H: 6 1  W: 11 11  b.Dublin 31-1-92
Source: Scholar. Honours: Eire Youth, Under-21, 4 full caps.

| | | | | |
|---|---|---|---|---|
| 2010-11 | Derby Co | 4 | 0 | |
| 2011-12 | Derby Co | 42 | 3 | |
| 2012-13 | Derby Co | 45 | 6 | 91 9 |

**HOGANSON, Michael (D)** 4 0
H: 5 11  W: 10 10  b.Newcastle 3-10-93

| | | | | |
|---|---|---|---|---|
| 2012-13 | Derby Co | 4 | 0 | 4 0 |

**HUGHES, Will (M)** 38 2
H: 6 1  W: 11 08  b.Weybridge 7-4-95
Source: Scholar. Honours: England Youth, Under-21.

| | | | | |
|---|---|---|---|---|
| 2011-12 | Derby Co | 3 | 0 | |
| 2012-13 | Derby Co | 35 | 2 | 38 2 |

**JACOBS, Michael (M)** 125 13
H: 5 9  W: 11 08  b.Rothwell 23-3-92
Source: Scholar.

| | | | | |
|---|---|---|---|---|
| 2009-10 | Northampton T | 0 | 0 | |
| 2010-11 | Northampton T | 41 | 5 | |
| 2011-12 | Northampton T | 46 | 6 | 87 11 |
| 2012-13 | Derby Co | 38 | 2 | 38 2 |

**KEOGH, Richard (D)** 279 13
H: 6 0  W: 11 02  b.Harlow 11-8-86
Source: Scholar. Honours: Eire Under-21, 2 full caps, 1 goal.

| | | | | |
|---|---|---|---|---|
| 2004-05 | Stoke C | 0 | 0 | |
| 2005-06 | Bristol C | 9 | 1 | |
| 2005-06 | Wycombe W | 3 | 0 | 3 0 |
| 2006-07 | Bristol C | 31 | 2 | |
| 2007-08 | Bristol C | 0 | 0 | 40 3 |
| 2007-08 | Huddersfield T | 9 | 1 | 9 1 |
| 2007-08 | Carlisle U | 7 | 0 | |
| 2007-08 | Cheltenham T | 10 | 0 | 10 0 |
| 2008-09 | Carlisle U | 32 | 1 | |
| 2009-10 | Carlisle U | 41 | 3 | 80 4 |
| 2010-11 | Coventry C | 46 | 1 | |
| 2011-12 | Coventry C | 45 | 0 | 91 1 |
| 2012-13 | Derby Co | 46 | 4 | 46 4 |

**LEGZDINS, Adam (G)** 88 0
H: 6 1  W: 14 02  b.Penkridge 28-11-86
Source: Scholar.

| | | | | |
|---|---|---|---|---|
| 2006-07 | Birmingham C | 0 | 0 | |
| 2007-08 | Birmingham C | 0 | 0 | |
| 2008-09 | Crewe Alex | 0 | 0 | |
| 2009-10 | Crewe Alex | 6 | 0 | 6 0 |
| 2010-11 | Burton Alb | 46 | 0 | |
| 2011-12 | Derby Co | 4 | 0 | |
| 2011-12 | Burton Alb | 1 | 0 | 47 0 |
| 2012-13 | Derby Co | 31 | 0 | 35 0 |

**LELAN, Josh (D)** 0 0
b.Derby 21-12-94

| | | | |
|---|---|---|---|
| 2012-13 | Derby Co | 0 | 0 |

**MORCH, Mats (G)** 0 0
b.Mandal

| | | | |
|---|---|---|---|
| 2010-11 | Derby Co | 0 | 0 |
| 2011-12 | Derby Co | 0 | 0 |
| 2012-13 | Derby Co | 0 | 0 |

## NAYLOR, Tom (D) 13 0
H: 5 11   W: 11 05   b.Sutton-in-Ashfield 28-6-91
*Source:* Mansfield T.

| | | | | |
|---|---|---|---|---|
| 2011-12 | Derby Co | 8 | 0 | |
| 2012-13 | Derby Co | 0 | 0 | 8 0 |
| 2012-13 | *Bradford C* | 5 | 0 | 5 0 |

## O'BRIEN, Mark (D) 32 0
H: 5 11   W: 12 02   b.Dublin 20-11-92
*Source:* Cherry Orchard. *Honours:* Eire Youth.

| | | | | |
|---|---|---|---|---|
| 2008-09 | Derby Co | 1 | 0 | |
| 2009-10 | Derby Co | 0 | 0 | |
| 2010-11 | Derby Co | 2 | 0 | |
| 2011-12 | Derby Co | 20 | 0 | |
| 2012-13 | Derby Co | 9 | 0 | 32 0 |

## O'CONNOR, James (D) 292 6
H: 5 10   W: 12 05   b.Birmingham 20-11-84
*Source:* Scholar.

| | | | | |
|---|---|---|---|---|
| 2003-04 | Aston Villa | 0 | 0 | |
| 2004-05 | Aston Villa | 0 | 0 | |
| 2004-05 | *Port Vale* | 13 | 0 | 13 0 |
| 2004-05 | Bournemouth | 6 | 0 | |
| 2005-06 | Bournemouth | 39 | 1 | 45 1 |
| 2006-07 | Doncaster R | 40 | 1 | |
| 2007-08 | Doncaster R | 40 | 0 | |
| 2008-09 | Doncaster R | 32 | 1 | |
| 2009-10 | Doncaster R | 38 | 0 | |
| 2010-11 | Doncaster R | 34 | 2 | |
| 2011-12 | Doncaster R | 28 | 0 | 212 4 |
| 2012-13 | Derby Co | 22 | 1 | 22 1 |

## ROBERTS, Gareth (D) 533 22
H: 5 8   W: 11 12   b.Wrexham 6-2-78
*Source:* Trainee. *Honours:* Wales Under-21, B, 9 full caps.

| | | | | |
|---|---|---|---|---|
| 1995-96 | Liverpool | 0 | 0 | |
| 1996-97 | Liverpool | 0 | 0 | |
| 1997-98 | Liverpool | 0 | 0 | |
| 1998-99 | Liverpool | 0 | 0 | |
| 1998-99 | Panionios | 15 | 0 | 15 0 |
| 1999-2000 | Tranmere R | 37 | 1 | |
| 2000-01 | Tranmere R | 34 | 0 | |
| 2001-02 | Tranmere R | 45 | 2 | |
| 2002-03 | Tranmere R | 37 | 4 | |
| 2003-04 | Tranmere R | 44 | 1 | |
| 2004-05 | Tranmere R | 40 | 3 | |
| 2005-06 | Tranmere R | 44 | 2 | 281 13 |
| 2006-07 | Doncaster R | 30 | 1 | |
| 2007-08 | Doncaster R | 37 | 3 | |
| 2008-09 | Doncaster R | 32 | 1 | |
| 2009-10 | Doncaster R | 42 | 3 | 141 8 |
| 2010-11 | Derby Co | 26 | 0 | |
| 2011-12 | Derby Co | 41 | 1 | |
| 2012-13 | Derby Co | 29 | 0 | 96 1 |

## ROBINSON, Theo (F) 204 56
H: 5 9   W: 10 03   b.Birmingham 22-1-89
*Source:* Scholar. *Honours:* Jamaica, 5 full caps.

| | | | | |
|---|---|---|---|---|
| 2005-06 | Watford | 1 | 0 | |
| 2006-07 | Watford | 1 | 0 | |
| 2007-08 | Watford | 0 | 0 | |
| 2007-08 | *Hereford U* | 43 | 13 | 43 13 |
| 2008-09 | Watford | 0 | 0 | 5 0 |
| 2008-09 | *Southend U* | 21 | 7 | 21 7 |
| 2009-10 | Huddersfield T | 37 | 13 | |
| 2010-11 | Huddersfield T | 1 | 0 | |
| 2010-11 | Millwall | 11 | 3 | 11 3 |
| 2010-11 | *Derby Co* | 13 | 2 | |
| 2011-12 | Derby Co | 39 | 10 | |
| 2012-13 | Derby Co | 28 | 8 | 80 20 |
| 2012-13 | *Huddersfield T* | 6 | 0 | 44 13 |

## SAMMON, Conor (F) 227 42
H: 5 10   W: 11 11   b.Dublin 13-4-87
*Honours:* Eire Under-21, 7 full caps.

| | | | | |
|---|---|---|---|---|
| 2005 | UCD | 7 | 0 | |
| 2006 | UCD | 31 | 7 | |
| 2007 | UCD | 31 | 6 | 69 13 |
| 2008 | Derry C | 16 | 3 | 16 3 |
| 2008-09 | Kilmarnock | 17 | 1 | |
| 2009-10 | Kilmarnock | 25 | 6 | |
| 2010-11 | Kilmarnock | 23 | 15 | 65 17 |
| 2010-11 | Wigan Ath | 7 | 1 | |
| 2011-12 | Wigan Ath | 25 | 0 | |
| 2012-13 | Wigan Ath | 0 | 0 | 32 1 |
| 2012-13 | Derby Co | 45 | 8 | 45 8 |

## TYSON, Nathan (F) 357 84
H: 5 10   W: 10 02   b.Reading 4-5-82
*Source:* Trainee. *Honours:* England Under-20.

| | | | | |
|---|---|---|---|---|
| 1999-2000 | Reading | 1 | 0 | |
| 2000-01 | Reading | 0 | 0 | |
| 2001-02 | Reading | 1 | 0 | |
| 2001-02 | *Swansea C* | 11 | 1 | 11 1 |
| 2001-02 | *Cheltenham T* | 8 | 1 | 8 1 |
| 2002-03 | Reading | 23 | 1 | |
| 2003-04 | Reading | 8 | 0 | 33 1 |
| 2003-04 | Wycombe W | 21 | 9 | |
| 2004-05 | Wycombe W | 42 | 22 | |
| 2005-06 | Wycombe W | 15 | 11 | 78 42 |
| 2005-06 | Nottingham F | 28 | 10 | |
| 2006-07 | Nottingham F | 24 | 7 | |
| 2007-08 | Nottingham F | 34 | 9 | |
| 2008-09 | Nottingham F | 35 | 5 | |
| 2009-10 | Nottingham F | 33 | 2 | |
| 2010-11 | Nottingham F | 30 | 2 | 184 35 |
| 2011-12 | Derby Co | 23 | 0 | |
| 2012-13 | Derby Co | 16 | 4 | 39 4 |
| 2012-13 | *Millwall* | 4 | 0 | 4 0 |

## WARD, Jamie (M) 239 69
H: 5 5   W: 9 04   b.Birmingham 12-5-86
*Source:* Scholar. *Honours:* Northern Ireland Youth, Under-21, 4 full caps.

| | | | | |
|---|---|---|---|---|
| 2003-04 | Aston Villa | 0 | 0 | |
| 2004-05 | Aston Villa | 0 | 0 | |
| 2005-06 | Aston Villa | 0 | 0 | |
| 2005-06 | *Stockport Co* | 9 | 1 | 9 1 |
| 2006-07 | Torquay U | 25 | 9 | 25 9 |
| 2006-07 | Chesterfield | 9 | 3 | |
| 2007-08 | Chesterfield | 35 | 12 | |
| 2008-09 | Chesterfield | 23 | 14 | 67 29 |
| 2008-09 | Sheffield U | 16 | 2 | |
| 2009-10 | Sheffield U | 28 | 7 | |
| 2010-11 | Sheffield U | 19 | 0 | 63 9 |
| 2010-11 | Derby Co | 13 | 5 | |
| 2011-12 | Derby Co | 37 | 4 | |
| 2012-13 | Derby Co | 25 | 12 | 75 21 |

**Players retained or with offer of contract**
Hayes, Dylan Brendan; Wixted, Adam Joseph.

**Scholars**
Bennett, Mason Kane; Berry, Samuel Dean; Bola, Kayode; Carrigy, Daryl Matthew; Dales, Andrew; Dawkins, Niall George; Etheridge, Ross; Hanson, James William; Johnson, Andre; Nash, Joshua Samuel James; Rawson, Farrend James; Revan, Kurtis; Sharpe, Rhys; Spiriak, Jakub; Thomas, Kwame Blair; Wassall, Ayrton Elijah.

# DONCASTER R (34)

## BAGAYOKO, Mamadou (F) 335 92
H: 6 3   W: 12 06   b.Paris 21-5-79
*Honours:* Mali 31 full caps, 4 goals.

| | | | | |
|---|---|---|---|---|
| 1997-98 | Dunkerque | 3 | 0 | |
| 1998-99 | Dunkerque | 4 | 0 | 7 0 |
| 1998-99 | Sens | 34 | 29 | 34 29 |
| 1999-2000 | Strasbourg B | 10 | 3 | |
| 1999-2000 | Strasbourg | 11 | 0 | |
| 2000-01 | Strasbourg B | 13 | 3 | 23 6 |
| 2000-01 | Strasbourg | 16 | 0 | |
| 2001-02 | Strasbourg | 21 | 2 | |
| 2002-03 | Strasbourg | 17 | 2 | 65 4 |
| 2003-04 | Ajaccio | 34 | 8 | 34 8 |
| 2004-05 | Nantes | 30 | 7 | |
| 2005-06 | Nice | 32 | 5 | |
| 2006-07 | *Al-Wahda* | 29 | 13 | 29 13 |
| 2007-08 | Nantes | 21 | 10 | |
| 2008-09 | Nantes | 26 | 7 | 77 24 |
| 2009-10 | Nice | 23 | 1 | |
| 2010-11 | Nice | 5 | 0 | 60 6 |
| 2011-12 | PAS Giannina | 1 | 0 | 1 0 |
| 2011-12 | Doncaster R | 5 | 2 | |
| 2012-13 | Doncaster R | 0 | 0 | 5 2 |

## BALL, Jordan (F) 1 0
b.Mansfield 12-9-93

| | | | | |
|---|---|---|---|---|
| 2012-13 | Doncaster R | 1 | 0 | 1 0 |

## BENNETT, Kyle (F) 103 9
H: 5 5   W: 9 08   b.Telford 9-9-90
*Source:* Scholar. *Honours:* England Youth.

| | | | | |
|---|---|---|---|---|
| 2007-08 | Wolverhampton W | 0 | 0 | |
| 2008-09 | Wolverhampton W | 0 | 0 | |
| 2009-10 | Wolverhampton W | 0 | 0 | |
| 2010-11 | Bury | 32 | 2 | 32 2 |
| 2011-12 | Doncaster R | 36 | 4 | |
| 2012-13 | Doncaster R | 35 | 3 | 71 7 |

## BLAKE, Robbie (F) 578 145
H: 5 9   W: 12 00   b.Middlesbrough 4-3-76
*Source:* Trainee.

| | | | | |
|---|---|---|---|---|
| 1994-95 | Darlington | 9 | 0 | |
| 1995-96 | Darlington | 29 | 11 | |
| 1996-97 | Darlington | 30 | 10 | 68 21 |
| 1996-97 | Bradford C | 5 | 0 | |
| 1997-98 | Bradford C | 34 | 8 | |
| 1998-99 | Bradford C | 39 | 16 | |
| 1999-2000 | Bradford C | 28 | 2 | |
| 2000-01 | Bradford C | 21 | 4 | |
| 2000-01 | *Nottingham F* | 11 | 1 | 11 1 |
| 2001-02 | Bradford C | 26 | 10 | 153 40 |
| 2001-02 | Burnley | 10 | 0 | |
| 2002-03 | Burnley | 41 | 13 | |
| 2003-04 | Burnley | 45 | 19 | |
| 2004-05 | Burnley | 24 | 10 | |
| 2004-05 | Birmingham C | 11 | 2 | 11 2 |
| 2005-06 | Leeds U | 41 | 11 | |
| 2006-07 | Leeds U | 36 | 8 | 77 19 |
| 2007-08 | Burnley | 45 | 9 | |
| 2008-09 | Burnley | 46 | 8 | |
| 2009-10 | Burnley | 31 | 2 | 242 61 |
| 2010-11 | Bolton W | 8 | 1 | |
| 2011-12 | Bolton W | 1 | 0 | 9 1 |
| 2012-13 | Doncaster R | 7 | 0 | 7 0 |

## BROWN, Chris (F) 272 49
H: 6 3   W: 13 01   b.Doncaster 11-12-84
*Source:* Trainee. *Honours:* England Youth.

| | | | | |
|---|---|---|---|---|
| 2002-03 | Sunderland | 0 | 0 | |
| 2003-04 | Sunderland | 0 | 0 | |
| 2003-04 | *Doncaster R* | 22 | 10 | |
| 2004-05 | Sunderland | 37 | 5 | |
| 2005-06 | Sunderland | 13 | 1 | |
| 2005-06 | *Hull C* | 13 | 1 | 13 1 |
| 2006-07 | Sunderland | 16 | 3 | 66 9 |
| 2006-07 | Norwich C | 4 | 0 | |
| 2007-08 | Norwich C | 14 | 1 | 18 1 |
| 2007-08 | Preston NE | 17 | 5 | |
| 2008-09 | Preston NE | 30 | 6 | |
| 2009-10 | Preston NE | 43 | 6 | |
| 2010-11 | Preston NE | 16 | 1 | 106 18 |
| 2011-12 | Doncaster R | 11 | 2 | |
| 2012-13 | Doncaster R | 36 | 8 | 69 20 |

## CLINGAN, Sammy (M) 279 19
H: 5 11   W: 11 06   b.Belfast 13-1-84
*Source:* Scholar. *Honours:* Northern Ireland Schools, Youth, Under-21, Under-23, 34 full caps.

| | | | | |
|---|---|---|---|---|
| 2001-02 | Wolverhampton W | 0 | 0 | |
| 2002-03 | Wolverhampton W | 0 | 0 | |
| 2003-04 | Wolverhampton W | 0 | 0 | |
| 2004-05 | Wolverhampton W | 0 | 0 | |
| 2004-05 | *Chesterfield* | 15 | 2 | |
| 2005-06 | Wolverhampton W | 0 | 0 | |
| 2005-06 | *Chesterfield* | 21 | 1 | 36 3 |
| 2005-06 | Nottingham F | 15 | 0 | |
| 2006-07 | Nottingham F | 28 | 0 | |
| 2007-08 | Nottingham F | 42 | 1 | 85 1 |
| 2008-09 | Norwich C | 40 | 6 | |
| 2009-10 | Norwich C | 0 | 0 | 40 6 |
| 2009-10 | Coventry C | 34 | 5 | |
| 2010-11 | Coventry C | 28 | 0 | |
| 2011-12 | Coventry C | 36 | 2 | 98 7 |
| 2012-13 | Doncaster R | 6 | 0 | 6 0 |
| 2012-13 | Kilmarnock | 14 | 2 | 14 2 |

## COPPINGER, James (F) 393 42
H: 5 7   W: 10 03   b.Middlesbrough 10-1-81
*Source:* Darlington Trainee. *Honours:* England Youth.

| | | | | |
|---|---|---|---|---|
| 1997-98 | Newcastle U | 0 | 0 | |
| 1998-99 | Newcastle U | 0 | 0 | |
| 1999-2000 | Newcastle U | 0 | 0 | |
| 1999-2000 | *Hartlepool U* | 10 | 3 | |
| 2000-01 | Newcastle U | 1 | 0 | |

|  |  | | | | |
|---|---|--:|--:|--:|--:|
| 2001-02 | Newcastle U | 0 | 0 | **1** | **0** |
| 2001-02 | *Hartlepool U* | 14 | 2 | **24** | **5** |
| 2002-03 | Exeter C | 43 | 5 | | |
| 2003-04 | Exeter C | 0 | 0 | **43** | **5** |
| 2004-05 | Doncaster R | 31 | 0 | | |
| 2005-06 | Doncaster R | 36 | 5 | | |
| 2006-07 | Doncaster R | 39 | 4 | | |
| 2007-08 | Doncaster R | 39 | 3 | | |
| 2008-09 | Doncaster R | 32 | 5 | | |
| 2009-10 | Doncaster R | 39 | 4 | | |
| 2010-11 | Doncaster R | 40 | 7 | | |
| 2011-12 | Doncaster R | 38 | 2 | | |
| 2012-13 | Doncaster R | 25 | 2 | **319** | **32** |
| 2012-13 | *Nottingham F* | 6 | 0 | **6** | **0** |

**COTTERILL, David (F)**    **239 31**
H: 5 9   W: 11 02   b.Cardiff 4-12-87
*Source:* Scholar. *Honours:* Wales Youth, Under-21, 19 full caps, 1 goal.

|  |  | | | | |
|---|---|--:|--:|--:|--:|
| 2004-05 | Bristol C | 12 | 0 | | |
| 2005-06 | Bristol C | 45 | 7 | | |
| 2006-07 | Bristol C | 5 | 1 | **62** | **8** |
| 2006-07 | Wigan Ath | 16 | 1 | | |
| 2007-08 | Wigan Ath | 2 | 0 | **18** | **1** |
| 2007-08 | *Sheffield U* | 16 | 0 | | |
| 2008-09 | Sheffield U | 24 | 4 | | |
| 2009-10 | Sheffield U | 14 | 2 | **54** | **6** |
| 2009-10 | Swansea C | 21 | 3 | | |
| 2010-11 | Swansea C | 14 | 1 | | |
| 2010-11 | *Portsmouth* | 15 | 1 | **15** | **1** |
| 2011-12 | Swansea C | 0 | 0 | **35** | **4** |
| 2011-12 | Barnsley | 11 | 1 | **11** | **1** |
| 2012-13 | Doncaster R | 44 | 10 | **44** | **10** |

**FOWLER, Lee (M)**    **80 0**
H: 5 7   W: 9 13   b.Cardiff 10-6-83
*Source:* Scholar. *Honours:* Wales Youth, Under-21.

|  |  | | | | |
|---|---|--:|--:|--:|--:|
| 2001-02 | Coventry C | 13 | 0 | | |
| 2002-03 | Coventry C | 1 | 0 | **14** | **0** |
| 2003-04 | Huddersfield T | 29 | 0 | | |
| 2004-05 | Huddersfield T | 20 | 0 | **49** | **0** |

From Scarborough, Burton Alb, Forest Green R, Wrexham

|  |  | | | | |
|---|---|--:|--:|--:|--:|
| 2012-13 | Fleetwood T | 10 | 0 | **10** | **0** |
| 2012-13 | *Doncaster R* | 4 | 0 | **4** | **0** |
| 2012-13 | *Burton Alb* | 3 | 0 | **3** | **0** |

**GRIFFIN, Andy (D)**    **339 6**
H: 5 9   W: 11 9   b.Billinge 7-3-79
*Source:* Trainee. *Honours:* England Youth, Under-21.

|  |  | | | | |
|---|---|--:|--:|--:|--:|
| 1996-97 | Stoke C | 34 | 1 | | |
| 1997-98 | Stoke C | 23 | 1 | | |
| 1997-98 | Newcastle U | 4 | 0 | | |
| 1998-99 | Newcastle U | 14 | 0 | | |
| 1999-2000 | Newcastle U | 3 | 1 | | |
| 2000-01 | Newcastle U | 19 | 0 | | |
| 2001-02 | Newcastle U | 4 | 0 | | |
| 2002-03 | Newcastle U | 27 | 1 | | |
| 2003-04 | Newcastle U | 5 | 0 | **76** | **2** |
| 2004-05 | Portsmouth | 22 | 0 | | |
| 2005-06 | Portsmouth | 22 | 0 | | |
| 2006-07 | Portsmouth | 0 | 0 | **44** | **0** |
| 2006-07 | *Stoke C* | 33 | 2 | | |
| 2007-08 | *Derby Co* | 15 | 0 | **15** | **0** |
| 2007-08 | Stoke C | 15 | 0 | | |
| 2008-09 | Stoke C | 20 | 0 | | |
| 2009-10 | Stoke C | 0 | 0 | **125** | **4** |
| 2009-10 | *Reading* | 21 | 0 | | |
| 2010-11 | Reading | 33 | 0 | | |
| 2011-12 | Reading | 9 | 0 | **63** | **0** |
| 2012-13 | Doncaster R | 16 | 0 | **16** | **0** |

**HARPER, James (M)**    **410 30**
H: 5 10   W: 11 02   b.Chelmsford 9-11-80
*Source:* Trainee.

|  |  | | | | |
|---|---|--:|--:|--:|--:|
| 1999-2000 | Arsenal | 0 | 0 | | |
| 2000-01 | Arsenal | 0 | 0 | | |
| 2000-01 | *Cardiff C* | 3 | 0 | **3** | **0** |
| 2000-01 | Reading | 12 | 1 | | |
| 2001-02 | Reading | 26 | 1 | | |
| 2002-03 | Reading | 36 | 2 | | |
| 2003-04 | Reading | 39 | 1 | | |
| 2004-05 | Reading | 41 | 3 | | |
| 2005-06 | Reading | 45 | 7 | | |
| 2006-07 | Reading | 38 | 3 | | |
| 2007-08 | Reading | 38 | 6 | | |
| 2008-09 | Reading | 34 | 1 | | |
| 2009-10 | Reading | 3 | 0 | **312** | **25** |
| 2009-10 | Sheffield U | 34 | 4 | **34** | **4** |
| 2010-11 | Hull C | 28 | 1 | | |
| 2011-12 | Hull C | 1 | 0 | **29** | **1** |
| 2011-12 | *Wycombe W* | 5 | 0 | **5** | **0** |
| 2012-13 | Doncaster R | 27 | 0 | **27** | **0** |

**HUSBAND, James (D)**    **36 3**
H: 5 10   W: 10 00   b.Leeds 3-1-94
*Source:* Scholar.

|  |  | | | | |
|---|---|--:|--:|--:|--:|
| 2011-12 | Doncaster R | 3 | 0 | | |
| 2012-13 | Doncaster R | 33 | 3 | **36** | **3** |

**JONES, Rob (D)**    **300 29**
H: 6 7   W: 12 02   b.Stockton 30-11-79
*Source:* Gateshead.

|  |  | | | | |
|---|---|--:|--:|--:|--:|
| 2002-03 | Stockport Co | 0 | 0 | | |
| 2003-04 | Stockport Co | 16 | 2 | **16** | **2** |
| 2003-04 | *Macclesfield T* | 1 | 0 | **1** | **0** |
| 2004-05 | Grimsby T | 20 | 1 | | |
| 2005-06 | Grimsby T | 40 | 4 | **60** | **5** |
| 2006-07 | Hibernian | 34 | 4 | | |
| 2007-08 | Hibernian | 30 | 0 | | |
| 2008-09 | Hibernian | 32 | 4 | **96** | **8** |
| 2009-10 | Scunthorpe U | 28 | 1 | | |
| 2010-11 | Scunthorpe U | 14 | 1 | **42** | **2** |
| 2010-11 | *Sheffield W* | 8 | 1 | | |
| 2011-12 | Sheffield W | 33 | 4 | **41** | **5** |
| 2012-13 | Doncaster R | 44 | 7 | **44** | **7** |

**KEEGAN, Paul (M)**    **198 13**
H: 5 11   W: 11 05   b.Dublin 5-7-84
*Source:* Home Farm. *Honours:* Eire Youth, Under-21.

|  |  | | | | |
|---|---|--:|--:|--:|--:|
| 2000-01 | Leeds U | 0 | 0 | | |
| 2001-02 | Leeds U | 0 | 0 | | |
| 2002-03 | Leeds U | 0 | 0 | | |
| 2003-04 | Leeds U | 0 | 0 | | |
| 2003-04 | *Scunthorpe U* | 2 | 0 | **2** | **0** |
| 2004-05 | Leeds U | 0 | 0 | | |
| 2005 | Drogheda | 11 | 0 | | |
| 2006 | Drogheda | 25 | 4 | | |
| 2007 | Drogheda | 30 | 1 | | |
| 2008 | Drogheda | 27 | 1 | **93** | **6** |
| 2009 | Bohemians | 34 | 2 | | |
| 2010 | Bohemians | 32 | 4 | **66** | **6** |
| 2010-11 | Doncaster R | 10 | 0 | | |
| 2011-12 | Doncaster R | 2 | 0 | | |
| 2012-13 | Doncaster R | 25 | 1 | **37** | **1** |

**MARTIS, Shelton (D)**    **216 7**
H: 6 0   W: 11 11   b.Willemstad 29-11-82
*Honours:* Netherlands Antilles 1 full cap.

|  |  | | | | |
|---|---|--:|--:|--:|--:|
| 2002-03 | Excelsior | 12 | 0 | | |
| 2003-04 | Excelsior | 10 | 0 | **22** | **0** |
| 2004-05 | Eindhoven | 32 | 0 | **32** | **0** |
| 2005-06 | Darlington | 40 | 2 | | |
| 2006-07 | Darlington | 20 | 0 | **42** | **2** |
| 2006-07 | Hibernian | 26 | 0 | **26** | **0** |
| 2007-08 | WBA | 2 | 0 | | |
| 2007-08 | *Scunthorpe U* | 3 | 0 | **3** | **0** |
| 2008-09 | WBA | 7 | 0 | | |
| 2008-09 | *Doncaster R* | 5 | 1 | | |
| 2009-10 | WBA | 13 | 2 | **22** | **2** |
| 2009-10 | Doncaster R | 14 | 1 | | |
| 2010-11 | Doncaster R | 26 | 1 | | |
| 2011-12 | Doncaster R | 15 | 0 | | |
| 2012-13 | Doncaster R | 9 | 0 | **69** | **3** |

**MAXTED, Jonathan (G)**    **0 0**
H: 6 0   W: 11 03   b. 26-10-93

|  |  | | | | |
|---|---|--:|--:|--:|--:|
| 2012-13 | Doncaster R | 0 | 0 | | |

**McCOMBE, Jamie (D)**    **362 26**
H: 6 5   W: 12 05   b.Scunthorpe 1-1-83
*Source:* Scholar.

|  |  | | | | |
|---|---|--:|--:|--:|--:|
| 2001-02 | Scunthorpe U | 17 | 0 | | |
| 2002-03 | Scunthorpe U | 31 | 1 | | |
| 2003-04 | Scunthorpe U | 15 | 0 | **63** | **1** |
| 2003-04 | Lincoln C | 8 | 0 | | |
| 2004-05 | Lincoln C | 41 | 3 | | |
| 2005-06 | Lincoln C | 38 | 4 | **87** | **7** |
| 2006-07 | Bristol C | 41 | 4 | | |
| 2007-08 | Bristol C | 34 | 3 | | |
| 2008-09 | Bristol C | 28 | 1 | | |
| 2009-10 | Bristol C | 16 | 1 | **119** | **9** |
| 2010-11 | Huddersfield T | 34 | 5 | | |
| 2011-12 | Huddersfield T | 20 | 3 | | |
| 2011-12 | *Preston NE* | 6 | 0 | **6** | **0** |
| 2012-13 | Huddersfield T | 0 | 0 | **54** | **8** |
| 2012-13 | Doncaster R | 33 | 1 | **33** | **1** |

**PAYNTER, Billy (F)**    **384 98**
H: 6 1   W: 14 01   b.Liverpool 13-7-84
*Source:* Schoolboy.

|  |  | | | | |
|---|---|--:|--:|--:|--:|
| 2000-01 | Port Vale | 1 | 0 | | |
| 2001-02 | Port Vale | 7 | 0 | | |
| 2002-03 | Port Vale | 31 | 5 | | |
| 2003-04 | Port Vale | 44 | 13 | | |
| 2004-05 | Port Vale | 45 | 10 | | |
| 2005-06 | Port Vale | 16 | 2 | **144** | **30** |
| 2005-06 | Hull C | 22 | 3 | **22** | **3** |
| 2006-07 | Southend U | 9 | 0 | | |
| 2006-07 | *Bradford C* | 15 | 4 | **15** | **4** |
| 2007-08 | Southend U | 0 | 0 | **9** | **0** |
| 2007-08 | Swindon T | 36 | 8 | | |
| 2008-09 | Swindon T | 42 | 11 | | |
| 2009-10 | Swindon T | 42 | 26 | **120** | **45** |
| 2010-11 | Leeds U | 22 | 1 | | |
| 2011-12 | Leeds U | 5 | 2 | | |
| 2011-12 | *Brighton & HA* | 10 | 0 | **10** | **0** |
| 2012-13 | Leeds U | 0 | 0 | **27** | **3** |
| 2012-13 | Doncaster R | 37 | 13 | **37** | **13** |

**QUINN, Paul (D)**    **245 4**
H: 6 0   W: 11 04   b.Wishaw 21-7-85
*Honours:* Scotland Under-21.

|  |  | | | | |
|---|---|--:|--:|--:|--:|
| 2002-03 | Motherwell | 4 | 0 | | |
| 2003-04 | Motherwell | 26 | 0 | | |
| 2004-05 | Motherwell | 23 | 0 | | |
| 2005-06 | Motherwell | 18 | 0 | | |
| 2006-07 | Motherwell | 26 | 0 | | |
| 2007-08 | Motherwell | 31 | 2 | | |
| 2008-09 | Motherwell | 33 | 1 | **161** | **3** |
| 2009-10 | Cardiff C | 22 | 0 | | |
| 2010-11 | Cardiff C | 23 | 1 | | |
| 2011-12 | Cardiff C | 1 | 0 | **46** | **1** |
| 2012-13 | Doncaster R | 38 | 0 | **38** | **0** |

**SPURR, Tommy (D)**    **257 6**
H: 6 1   W: 11 05   b.Leeds 13-9-87
*Source:* Scholar.

|  |  | | | | |
|---|---|--:|--:|--:|--:|
| 2005-06 | Sheffield W | 2 | 0 | | |
| 2006-07 | Sheffield W | 36 | 0 | | |
| 2007-08 | Sheffield W | 41 | 2 | | |
| 2008-09 | Sheffield W | 41 | 2 | | |
| 2009-10 | Sheffield W | 46 | 1 | | |
| 2010-11 | Sheffield W | 26 | 0 | **192** | **5** |
| 2011-12 | Doncaster R | 19 | 0 | | |
| 2012-13 | Doncaster R | 46 | 1 | **65** | **1** |

**SULLIVAN, Neil (G)**    **560 0**
H: 6 2   W: 12 00   b.Sutton 24-2-70
*Source:* Trainee. *Honours:* Scotland 28 full caps.

|  |  | | | | |
|---|---|--:|--:|--:|--:|
| 1988-89 | Wimbledon | 0 | 0 | | |
| 1989-90 | Wimbledon | 0 | 0 | | |
| 1990-91 | Wimbledon | 1 | 0 | | |
| 1991-92 | Wimbledon | 1 | 0 | | |
| 1991-92 | *Crystal Palace* | 1 | 0 | **1** | **0** |
| 1992-93 | Wimbledon | 1 | 0 | | |
| 1993-94 | Wimbledon | 2 | 0 | | |
| 1994-95 | Wimbledon | 11 | 0 | | |
| 1995-96 | Wimbledon | 16 | 0 | | |
| 1996-97 | Wimbledon | 36 | 0 | | |
| 1997-98 | Wimbledon | 38 | 0 | | |
| 1998-99 | Wimbledon | 38 | 0 | | |
| 1999-2000 | Wimbledon | 37 | 0 | **181** | **0** |
| 2000-01 | Tottenham H | 35 | 0 | | |
| 2001-02 | Tottenham H | 29 | 0 | | |
| 2002-03 | Tottenham H | 0 | 0 | **64** | **0** |
| 2003-04 | Chelsea | 4 | 0 | **4** | **0** |
| 2004-05 | Leeds U | 46 | 0 | | |
| 2005-06 | Leeds U | 42 | 0 | | |
| 2006-07 | Leeds U | 7 | 0 | **95** | **0** |
| 2006-07 | *Doncaster R* | 16 | 0 | | |
| 2007-08 | Doncaster R | 46 | 0 | | |
| 2008-09 | Doncaster R | 46 | 0 | | |
| 2009-10 | Doncaster R | 45 | 0 | | |
| 2010-11 | Doncaster R | 31 | 0 | | |
| 2011-12 | Doncaster R | 9 | 0 | | |
| 2012-13 | Doncaster R | 4 | 0 | **197** | **0** |
| 2012-13 | *AFC Wimbledon* | 18 | 0 | **18** | **0** |

**SYERS, Dave (M)**    **87 13**
H: 6 0   W: 11 07   b.Leeds 30-11-87
*Source:* Ossett Alb, Farsley C, Harrogate T.

|  |  | | | | |
|---|---|--:|--:|--:|--:|
| 2010-11 | Bradford C | 37 | 8 | | |
| 2011-12 | Bradford C | 18 | 2 | **55** | **10** |
| 2012-13 | Doncaster R | 32 | 3 | **32** | **3** |

**WAKEFIELD, Liam (D)**    0   0
H: 6 0   W: 11 00   b.Doncaster 9-4-94

| | | | | |
|---|---|---|---|---|
| 2012-13 | Doncaster R | 0 | 0 | |

**WILSON, Mark (M)**    235   10
H: 5 10   W: 12 07   b.Scunthorpe 9-2-79
*Source:* Trainee. *Honours:* England Schools, Youth, Under-21.

| | | | | | |
|---|---|---|---|---|---|
| 1995-96 | Manchester U | 0 | 0 | | |
| 1996-97 | Manchester U | 0 | 0 | | |
| 1997-98 | Manchester U | 0 | 0 | | |
| 1997-98 | *Wrexham* | 13 | 4 | 13 | 4 |
| 1998-99 | Manchester U | 0 | 0 | | |
| 1999-2000 | Manchester U | 3 | 0 | | |
| 2000-01 | Manchester U | 0 | 0 | 3 | 0 |
| 2001-02 | Middlesbrough | 10 | 0 | | |
| 2002-03 | Middlesbrough | 6 | 0 | | |
| 2002-03 | *Stoke C* | 4 | 0 | 4 | 0 |
| 2003-04 | Middlesbrough | 0 | 0 | | |
| 2003-04 | *Swansea C* | 12 | 2 | 12 | 2 |
| 2003-04 | *Sheffield W* | 3 | 0 | 3 | 0 |
| 2004-05 | Middlesbrough | 0 | 0 | 16 | 0 |
| 2004-05 | *Doncaster R* | 3 | 0 | | |
| 2004-05 | *Livingston* | 5 | 0 | 5 | 0 |
| 2005 | Dallas | 8 | 0 | | |
| 2006 | Dallas | 12 | 1 | 20 | 1 |
| 2006-07 | Doncaster R | 22 | 1 | | |
| 2007-08 | Doncaster R | 31 | 1 | | |
| 2008-09 | Doncaster R | 22 | 1 | | |
| 2008-09 | *Tranmere R* | 5 | 0 | 5 | 0 |
| 2009-10 | Doncaster R | 35 | 0 | | |
| 2010-11 | Doncaster R | 28 | 0 | | |
| 2011-12 | Doncaster R | 3 | 0 | | |
| 2011-12 | *Walsall* | 4 | 0 | 4 | 0 |
| 2011-12 | *Oxford U* | 6 | 0 | 6 | 0 |
| 2012-13 | Doncaster R | 0 | 0 | 144 | 3 |

**WOODS, Gary (G)**    73   0
H: 6 1   W: 11 00   b.Kettering 1-10-90
*Source:* Manchester U Scholar.

| | | | | | |
|---|---|---|---|---|---|
| 2008-09 | Doncaster R | 1 | 0 | | |
| 2009-10 | Doncaster R | 0 | 0 | | |
| 2010-11 | Doncaster R | 16 | 0 | | |
| 2011-12 | Doncaster R | 14 | 0 | | |
| 2012-13 | Doncaster R | 42 | 0 | 73 | 0 |

**WOODS, Martin (M)**    168   11
H: 5 11   W: 11 13   b.Airdrie 1-1-86
*Source:* Trainee. *Honours:* Scotland Youth, Under-21.

| | | | | | |
|---|---|---|---|---|---|
| 2002-03 | Leeds U | 0 | 0 | | |
| 2003-04 | Leeds U | 0 | 0 | | |
| 2004-05 | Leeds U | 1 | 0 | 1 | 0 |
| 2004-05 | *Hartlepool U* | 6 | 0 | 6 | 0 |
| 2005-06 | Sunderland | 7 | 0 | 7 | 0 |
| 2006-07 | Rotherham U | 36 | 4 | 36 | 4 |
| 2007-08 | Doncaster R | 15 | 0 | | |
| 2007-08 | *Yeovil T* | 3 | 0 | 3 | 0 |
| 2008-09 | Doncaster R | 41 | 0 | | |
| 2009-10 | Doncaster R | 24 | 4 | | |
| 2010-11 | Doncaster R | 15 | 1 | | |
| 2011-12 | Doncaster R | 16 | 0 | 115 | 7 |

**WOODS, Michael (M)**    5   1
H: 6 0   W: 12 07   b.Pocklington 6-4-90
*Source:* Scholar. *Honours:* England Youth.

| | | | | | |
|---|---|---|---|---|---|
| 2006-07 | Chelsea | 0 | 0 | | |
| 2007-08 | Chelsea | 0 | 0 | | |
| 2008-09 | Chelsea | 0 | 0 | | |
| 2009-10 | Chelsea | 0 | 0 | | |
| 2010-11 | Chelsea | 0 | 0 | | |
| 2010-11 | *Notts Co* | 0 | 0 | | |
| 2011-12 | Chelsea | 0 | 0 | | |
| 2011-12 | *Yeovil T* | 5 | 1 | 5 | 1 |
| 2012-13 | Doncaster R | 0 | 0 | | |

**Scholars**
Askins Benjamin Jack; Binns, Jordan Thomas; Brown, Scott Peter; Burnyeat, Ryan Mark; Busby, Aaron Michael; Dawson, Jacob Thomas; Ferguson, Lewis Edward; Finnegan, Evan Christopher; Lund, Spencer Declan; Meade, Joshua Ryan; Middleton, Harry Oliver; Myers, Callum James; Peterson, Alex; Steadman, Jack Alan; Terrell, Callum Burton; Whincop, Christopher; Whitehouse, Billy Haywood.

# EVERTON (35)

**ANICHEBE, Victor (F)**    130   17
H: 6 1   W: 13 00   b.Nigeria 23-4-88
*Source:* Scholar. *Honours:* Nigeria Under-23, 10 full caps, 1 goal.

| | | | | | |
|---|---|---|---|---|---|
| 2005-06 | Everton | 2 | 1 | | |
| 2006-07 | Everton | 19 | 3 | | |
| 2007-08 | Everton | 27 | 1 | | |
| 2008-09 | Everton | 17 | 1 | | |
| 2009-10 | Everton | 11 | 1 | | |
| 2010-11 | Everton | 16 | 0 | | |
| 2011-12 | Everton | 12 | 4 | | |
| 2012-13 | Everton | 26 | 6 | 130 | 17 |

**BAINES, Leighton (D)**    344   20
H: 5 8   W: 11 00   b.Liverpool 11-12-84
*Source:* Trainee. *Honours:* England Under-21, 17 full caps, 1 goal.

| | | | | | |
|---|---|---|---|---|---|
| 2002-03 | Wigan Ath | 6 | 0 | | |
| 2003-04 | Wigan Ath | 26 | 0 | | |
| 2004-05 | Wigan Ath | 41 | 1 | | |
| 2005-06 | Wigan Ath | 37 | 0 | | |
| 2006-07 | Wigan Ath | 35 | 3 | | |
| 2007-08 | Wigan Ath | 0 | 0 | 145 | 4 |
| 2007-08 | Everton | 22 | 0 | | |
| 2008-09 | Everton | 31 | 1 | | |
| 2009-10 | Everton | 37 | 1 | | |
| 2010-11 | Everton | 38 | 5 | | |
| 2011-12 | Everton | 33 | 4 | | |
| 2012-13 | Everton | 38 | 5 | 199 | 16 |

**BARKLEY, Ross (M)**    30   4
H: 6 2   W: 12 00   b.Liverpool 5-12-93
*Source:* Scholar. *Honours:* England Youth, Under-21.

| | | | | | |
|---|---|---|---|---|---|
| 2010-11 | Everton | 0 | 0 | | |
| 2011-12 | Everton | 6 | 0 | | |
| 2012-13 | Everton | 7 | 0 | 13 | 0 |
| 2012-13 | *Sheffield W* | 13 | 4 | 13 | 4 |
| 2012-13 | *Leeds U* | 4 | 0 | 4 | 0 |

**BIDWELL, Jake (D)**    64   0
H: 6 0   W: 11 00   b.Southport 21-3-93
*Source:* Scholar. *Honours:* England Youth.

| | | | | | |
|---|---|---|---|---|---|
| 2009-10 | Everton | 0 | 0 | | |
| 2010-11 | Everton | 0 | 0 | | |
| 2011-12 | Everton | 0 | 0 | | |
| 2011-12 | *Brentford* | 24 | 0 | | |
| 2012-13 | Everton | 0 | 0 | | |
| 2012-13 | *Brentford* | 40 | 0 | 64 | 0 |

**BROWNING, Tyias (D)**    0   0
H: 5 11   W: 12 00   b.Liverpool 27-5-94
*Source:* Scholar.

| | | | | |
|---|---|---|---|---|
| 2011-12 | Everton | 0 | 0 | |
| 2012-13 | Everton | 0 | 0 | |

**COLEMAN, Seamus (D)**    90   5
H: 6 4   W: 10 07   b.Donegal 11-10-88
*Source:* Sligo R. *Honours:* Eire Under-21, Under-23, 14 full caps.

| | | | | | |
|---|---|---|---|---|---|
| 2008-09 | Everton | 0 | 0 | | |
| 2009-10 | Everton | 3 | 0 | | |
| 2009-10 | *Blackpool* | 9 | 1 | 9 | 1 |
| 2010-11 | Everton | 34 | 4 | | |
| 2011-12 | Everton | 18 | 0 | | |
| 2012-13 | Everton | 26 | 0 | 81 | 4 |

**DISTIN, Sylvain (D)**    498   11
H: 6 3   W: 14 06   b.Bagnolet 16-12-77

| | | | | | |
|---|---|---|---|---|---|
| 1998-99 | Tours | 26 | 3 | 26 | 3 |
| 1999-2000 | Gueugnon | 33 | 1 | 33 | 1 |
| 2000-01 | Paris St Germain | 28 | 0 | 28 | 0 |
| 2001-02 | Newcastle U | 28 | 0 | 28 | 0 |
| 2002-03 | Manchester C | 34 | 0 | | |
| 2003-04 | Manchester C | 38 | 2 | | |
| 2004-05 | Manchester C | 38 | 1 | | |
| 2005-06 | Manchester C | 31 | 0 | | |
| 2006-07 | Manchester C | 37 | 2 | 178 | 5 |
| 2007-08 | Portsmouth | 36 | 0 | | |
| 2008-09 | Portsmouth | 38 | 0 | | |
| 2009-10 | Portsmouth | 3 | 0 | 77 | 0 |
| 2009-10 | Everton | 29 | 0 | | |
| 2010-11 | Everton | 38 | 2 | | |
| 2011-12 | Everton | 27 | 0 | | |
| 2012-13 | Everton | 34 | 0 | 128 | 2 |

**DUFFY, Shane (D)**    24   2
H: 6 4   W: 12 00   b.Derry 1-1-92
*Source:* Scholar. *Honours:* Northern Ireland Under-21, Eire Under-21.

| | | | | | |
|---|---|---|---|---|---|
| 2008-09 | Everton | 0 | 0 | | |
| 2009-10 | Everton | 0 | 0 | | |
| 2010-11 | Everton | 0 | 0 | | |
| 2010-11 | *Burnley* | 1 | 0 | 1 | 0 |
| 2011-12 | Everton | 4 | 0 | | |
| 2011-12 | *Scunthorpe U* | 18 | 2 | 18 | 2 |
| 2012-13 | Everton | 1 | 0 | 5 | 0 |

**FELLAINI, Marouane (M)**    200   31
H: 6 4   W: 13 05   b.Brussels 22-11-87
*Honours:* Belgium Youth, 42 full caps, 7 goals.

| | | | | | |
|---|---|---|---|---|---|
| 2006-07 | Standard Liege | 29 | 0 | | |
| 2007-08 | Standard Liege | 30 | 6 | | |
| 2008-09 | Standard Liege | 3 | 0 | 62 | 6 |
| 2008-09 | Everton | 30 | 8 | | |
| 2009-10 | Everton | 23 | 2 | | |
| 2010-11 | Everton | 20 | 1 | | |
| 2011-12 | Everton | 34 | 3 | | |
| 2012-13 | Everton | 31 | 11 | 138 | 25 |

**GARBUTT, Luke (D)**    34   2
H: 5 10   W: 11 07   b.Harrogate 21-5-93
*Source:* Scholar. *Honours:* England Youth.

| | | | | | |
|---|---|---|---|---|---|
| 2010-11 | Everton | 0 | 0 | | |
| 2011-12 | Everton | 0 | 0 | | |
| 2011-12 | *Cheltenham T* | 34 | 2 | 34 | 2 |
| 2012-13 | Everton | 0 | 0 | | |

**GIBSON, Darron (M)**    86   6
H: 6 0   W: 12 04   b.Derry 25-10-87
*Source:* Scholar. *Honours:* Eire Youth, Under-21, 19 full caps, 1 goal.

| | | | | | |
|---|---|---|---|---|---|
| 2005-06 | Manchester U | 0 | 0 | | |
| 2006-07 | Manchester U | 0 | 0 | | |
| 2007-08 | Manchester U | 0 | 0 | | |
| 2007-08 | *Wolverhampton W* | 21 | 1 | 21 | 1 |
| 2008-09 | Manchester U | 3 | 1 | | |
| 2009-10 | Manchester U | 15 | 2 | | |
| 2010-11 | Manchester U | 12 | 0 | | |
| 2011-12 | Manchester U | 1 | 0 | 31 | 3 |
| 2011-12 | Everton | 11 | 1 | | |
| 2012-13 | Everton | 23 | 1 | 34 | 2 |

**GUEYE, Magaye (F)**    58   10
H: 5 10   W: 11 07   b.Paris 6-7-90
*Honours:* France Youth, Under-21.

| | | | | | |
|---|---|---|---|---|---|
| 2008-09 | Strasbourg | 3 | 0 | | |
| 2009-10 | Strasbourg | 24 | 9 | 27 | 9 |
| 2010-11 | Everton | 5 | 0 | | |
| 2011-12 | Everton | 17 | 1 | | |
| 2012-13 | Everton | 2 | 0 | 24 | 1 |
| 2012-13 | *Brest* | 7 | 0 | 7 | 0 |

**HEITINGA, Johnny (D)**    293   10
H: 5 11   W: 11 05   b.Alphen aan den Rijn 15-11-83
*Honours:* Holland 87 full caps, 7 goals.

| | | | | | |
|---|---|---|---|---|---|
| 2000-01 | Ajax | 0 | 0 | | |
| 2001-02 | Ajax | 15 | 0 | | |
| 2002-03 | Ajax | 1 | 0 | | |
| 2003-04 | Ajax | 26 | 3 | | |
| 2004-05 | Ajax | 26 | 1 | | |
| 2005-06 | Ajax | 19 | 1 | | |
| 2006-07 | Ajax | 32 | 0 | | |
| 2007-08 | Ajax | 33 | 0 | 152 | 5 |
| 2008-09 | Atletico Madrid | 27 | 3 | 27 | 3 |
| 2009-10 | Everton | 31 | 0 | | |
| 2010-11 | Everton | 27 | 1 | | |
| 2011-12 | Everton | 30 | 1 | | |
| 2012-13 | Everton | 26 | 0 | 114 | 2 |

**HIBBERT, Tony (D)**    259   0
H: 5 9   W: 11 05   b.Liverpool 20-2-81
*Source:* Trainee.

| | | | | |
|---|---|---|---|---|
| 1998-99 | Everton | 0 | 0 | |
| 1999-2000 | Everton | 0 | 0 | |
| 2000-01 | Everton | 3 | 0 | |
| 2001-02 | Everton | 10 | 0 | |
| 2002-03 | Everton | 24 | 0 | |
| 2003-04 | Everton | 25 | 0 | |
| 2004-05 | Everton | 36 | 0 | |
| 2005-06 | Everton | 29 | 0 | |
| 2006-07 | Everton | 13 | 0 | |
| 2007-08 | Everton | 24 | 0 | |

|  |  | | | | |
|---|---|---|---|---|---|
| 2008-09 | Everton | 17 | 0 | | |
| 2009-10 | Everton | 20 | 0 | | |
| 2010-11 | Everton | 20 | 0 | | |
| 2011-12 | Everton | 32 | 0 | | |
| 2012-13 | Everton | 6 | 0 | 259 | 0 |

**HITZLSPERGER, Thomas (M)** 259 31
H: 6 0  W: 12 07  b.Munich 5-4-82
*Source:* Bayern Munich. *Honours:* Germany Youth, Under-21, 52 full caps, 6 goals.

|  |  | | | | |
|---|---|---|---|---|---|
| 2000-01 | Aston Villa | 1 | 0 | | |
| 2001-02 | Aston Villa | 12 | 1 | | |
| 2001-02 | *Chesterfield* | 5 | 0 | 5 | 0 |
| 2002-03 | Aston Villa | 26 | 2 | | |
| 2003-04 | Aston Villa | 32 | 3 | | |
| 2004-05 | Aston Villa | 28 | 2 | 99 | 8 |
| 2005-06 | Stuttgart | 26 | 2 | | |
| 2006-07 | Stuttgart | 30 | 7 | | |
| 2007-08 | Stuttgart | 25 | 5 | | |
| 2008-09 | Stuttgart | 32 | 5 | | |
| 2009-10 | Stuttgart | 12 | 1 | 125 | 20 |
| 2009-10 | Lazio | 6 | 1 | 6 | 1 |
| 2010-11 | West Ham U | 11 | 2 | 11 | 2 |
| 2011-12 | Wolfsburg | 6 | 0 | 6 | 0 |
| 2012-13 | Everton | 7 | 0 | 7 | 0 |

**HOWARD, Tim (G)** 390 1
H: 6 3  W: 14 12  b.North Brunswick 6-3-79
*Honours:* USA Under-21, Under-23, 88 full caps.

|  |  | | | | |
|---|---|---|---|---|---|
| 1998 | NY/NJ MetroStars | 1 | 0 | | |
| 1999 | NY/NJ MetroStars | 9 | 0 | | |
| 2000 | NY/NJ MetroStars | 9 | 0 | | |
| 2001 | NY/NJ MetroStars | 26 | 0 | | |
| 2002 | NY/NJ MetroStars | 27 | 0 | | |
| 2003 | NY/NJ MetroStars | 13 | 0 | 85 | 0 |
| 2003-04 | Manchester U | 32 | 0 | | |
| 2004-05 | Manchester U | 12 | 0 | | |
| 2005-06 | Manchester U | 1 | 0 | | |
| 2006-07 | Manchester U | 0 | 0 | 45 | 0 |
| 2006-07 | Everton | 36 | 0 | | |
| 2007-08 | Everton | 36 | 0 | | |
| 2008-09 | Everton | 38 | 0 | | |
| 2009-10 | Everton | 38 | 0 | | |
| 2010-11 | Everton | 38 | 0 | | |
| 2011-12 | Everton | 38 | 1 | | |
| 2012-13 | Everton | 36 | 0 | 260 | 1 |

**JAGIELKA, Phil (D)** 433 24
H: 6 0  W: 13 01  b.Manchester 17-8-82
*Source:* Scholar. *Honours:* England Youth, Under-20, Under-21, B, 18 full caps, 1 goal.

|  |  | | | | |
|---|---|---|---|---|---|
| 1999-2000 | Sheffield U | 1 | 0 | | |
| 2000-01 | Sheffield U | 15 | 0 | | |
| 2001-02 | Sheffield U | 23 | 3 | | |
| 2002-03 | Sheffield U | 42 | 0 | | |
| 2003-04 | Sheffield U | 43 | 3 | | |
| 2004-05 | Sheffield U | 46 | 0 | | |
| 2005-06 | Sheffield U | 46 | 8 | | |
| 2006-07 | Sheffield U | 38 | 4 | 254 | 18 |
| 2007-08 | Everton | 34 | 1 | | |
| 2008-09 | Everton | 34 | 0 | | |
| 2009-10 | Everton | 12 | 0 | | |
| 2010-11 | Everton | 33 | 1 | | |
| 2011-12 | Everton | 30 | 2 | | |
| 2012-13 | Everton | 36 | 2 | 179 | 6 |

**JELAVIC, Nikica (F)** 223 79
H: 6 2  W: 13 12  b.Capljina 27-8-85
*Honours:* Croatia Youth, 26 full caps, 5 goals.

|  |  | | | | |
|---|---|---|---|---|---|
| 2002-03 | Hajduk Split | 2 | 0 | | |
| 2003-04 | Hajduk Split | 2 | 0 | | |
| 2004-05 | Hajduk Split | 0 | 0 | | |
| 2005-06 | Hajduk Split | 9 | 0 | | |
| 2006-07 | Hajduk Split | 22 | 5 | 35 | 5 |
| 2007-08 | Waregem | 23 | 3 | 23 | 3 |
| 2008-09 | Rapid Vienna | 34 | 7 | | |
| 2009-10 | Rapid Vienna | 33 | 17 | | |
| 2010-11 | Rapid Vienna | 13 | 2 | 70 | 25 |
| 2010-11 | Rangers | 23 | 16 | | |
| 2011-12 | Rangers | 22 | 14 | 45 | 30 |
| 2011-12 | Everton | 13 | 9 | | |
| 2012-13 | Everton | 37 | 7 | 50 | 16 |

**JUNIOR, Francisco (M)** 0 0
H: 5 4  W: 10 02  b.Bissau 18-1-92
*Honours:* Portugal Youth, Under-21.

|  |  | | |
|---|---|---|---|
| 2012-13 | Everton | 0 | 0 |

**KENNEDY, Matthew (M)** 14 0
H: 5 9  W: 10 02  b.Irvine 1-11-94
*Honours:* Scotland Youth, Under-21.

|  |  | | | | |
|---|---|---|---|---|---|
| 2011-12 | Kilmarnock | 11 | 0 | | |
| 2012-13 | Kilmarnock | 3 | 0 | 14 | 0 |
| 2012-13 | Everton | 0 | 0 | | |

**LUNDSTRAM, John (M)** 14 0
H: 5 11  W: 11 09  b.Liverpool 18-2-94
*Source:* Scholar. *Honours:* England Youth.

|  |  | | | | |
|---|---|---|---|---|---|
| 2011-12 | Everton | 0 | 0 | | |
| 2012-13 | Everton | 0 | 0 | | |
| 2012-13 | *Doncaster R* | 14 | 0 | 14 | 0 |

**McALENY, Conor (F)** 5 0
H: 5 10  W: 12 05  b.Liverpool 12-8-92
*Source:* Scholar.

|  |  | | | | |
|---|---|---|---|---|---|
| 2009-10 | Everton | 0 | 0 | | |
| 2010-11 | Everton | 0 | 0 | | |
| 2011-12 | Everton | 2 | 0 | | |
| 2011-12 | *Scunthorpe U* | 3 | 0 | 3 | 0 |
| 2012-13 | Everton | 0 | 0 | 2 | 0 |

**MIRALLAS, Kevin (F)** 204 53
H: 6 0  W: 11 10  b.Leige 5-10-87
*Honours:* Belgium Youth, Under-21, 34 full caps, 6 goals.

|  |  | | | | |
|---|---|---|---|---|---|
| 2004-05 | Lille | 1 | 1 | | |
| 2005-06 | Lille | 15 | 1 | | |
| 2006-07 | Lille | 23 | 2 | | |
| 2007-08 | Lille | 35 | 6 | 74 | 10 |
| 2008-09 | St Etienne | 30 | 3 | | |
| 2009-10 | St Etienne | 23 | 0 | 53 | 3 |
| 2010-11 | *Olympiacos* | 26 | 14 | | |
| 2011-12 | *Olympiacos* | 24 | 20 | | |
| 2012-13 | *Olympiacos* | 0 | 0 | 50 | 34 |
| 2012-13 | Everton | 27 | 6 | 27 | 6 |

**MUCHA, Jan (G)** 129 0
H: 6 2  W: 12 00  b.Bela nad Cirochou 5-12-82
*Honours:* Slovakia 33 full caps.

|  |  | | | | |
|---|---|---|---|---|---|
| 2002-03 | Zilina | 8 | 0 | | |
| 2003-04 | Zilina | 12 | 0 | | |
| 2004-05 | Zilina | 12 | 0 | 32 | 0 |
| 2005-06 | Legia | 0 | 0 | | |
| 2006-07 | Legia | 7 | 0 | | |
| 2007-08 | Legia | 29 | 0 | | |
| 2008-09 | Legia | 29 | 0 | | |
| 2009-10 | Legia | 30 | 0 | 95 | 0 |
| 2010-11 | Everton | 0 | 0 | | |
| 2011-12 | Everton | 0 | 0 | | |
| 2012-13 | Everton | 2 | 0 | 2 | 0 |

**NAISMITH, Steven (F)** 231 61
H: 5 10  W: 11 04  b.Irvine 14-9-86
*Honours:* Scotland Under-21, B, 22 full caps, 2 goals.

|  |  | | | | |
|---|---|---|---|---|---|
| 2003-04 | Kilmarnock | 1 | 0 | | |
| 2004-05 | Kilmarnock | 24 | 1 | | |
| 2005-06 | Kilmarnock | 36 | 13 | | |
| 2006-07 | Kilmarnock | 37 | 15 | | |
| 2007-08 | Kilmarnock | 4 | 0 | 102 | 29 |
| 2007-08 | Rangers | 21 | 5 | | |
| 2008-09 | Rangers | 7 | 0 | | |
| 2009-10 | Rangers | 28 | 3 | | |
| 2010-11 | Rangers | 31 | 11 | | |
| 2011-12 | Rangers | 11 | 9 | 98 | 28 |
| 2012-13 | Everton | 31 | 4 | 31 | 4 |

**NEVILLE, Phil (M)** 505 9
H: 5 11  W: 12 00  b.Bury 21-1-77
*Source:* Trainee. *Honours:* England Schools, Youth, B, Under-21, 59 full caps.

|  |  | | | | |
|---|---|---|---|---|---|
| 1994-95 | Manchester U | 2 | 0 | | |
| 1995-96 | Manchester U | 24 | 0 | | |
| 1996-97 | Manchester U | 18 | 0 | | |
| 1997-98 | Manchester U | 30 | 1 | | |
| 1998-99 | Manchester U | 28 | 0 | | |
| 1999-2000 | Manchester U | 29 | 0 | | |
| 2000-01 | Manchester U | 29 | 1 | | |
| 2001-02 | Manchester U | 28 | 2 | | |
| 2002-03 | Manchester U | 25 | 1 | | |
| 2003-04 | Manchester U | 31 | 0 | | |
| 2004-05 | Manchester U | 19 | 0 | 263 | 4 |
| 2005-06 | Everton | 34 | 0 | | |
| 2006-07 | Everton | 35 | 1 | | |
| 2007-08 | Everton | 37 | 2 | | |
| 2008-09 | Everton | 37 | 0 | | |

|  |  | | | | |
|---|---|---|---|---|---|
| 2009-10 | Everton | 23 | 0 | | |
| 2010-11 | Everton | 31 | 1 | | |
| 2011-12 | Everton | 27 | 0 | | |
| 2012-13 | Everton | 18 | 0 | 242 | 4 |

**OSMAN, Leon (F)** 313 43
H: 5 8  W: 10 09  b.Billinge 17-5-81
*Source:* Trainee. *Honours:* England Schools, Youth, 2 full caps.

|  |  | | | | |
|---|---|---|---|---|---|
| 1998-99 | Everton | 0 | 0 | | |
| 1999-2000 | Everton | 0 | 0 | | |
| 2000-01 | Everton | 0 | 0 | | |
| 2001-02 | Everton | 0 | 0 | | |
| 2002-03 | Everton | 2 | 0 | | |
| 2002-03 | *Carlisle U* | 12 | 1 | 12 | 1 |
| 2003-04 | Everton | 4 | 1 | | |
| 2003-04 | *Derby Co* | 17 | 3 | 17 | 3 |
| 2004-05 | Everton | 29 | 6 | | |
| 2005-06 | Everton | 35 | 3 | | |
| 2006-07 | Everton | 34 | 3 | | |
| 2007-08 | Everton | 28 | 4 | | |
| 2008-09 | Everton | 34 | 6 | | |
| 2009-10 | Everton | 26 | 2 | | |
| 2010-11 | Everton | 26 | 4 | | |
| 2011-12 | Everton | 30 | 5 | | |
| 2012-13 | Everton | 36 | 5 | 284 | 39 |

**OVIEDO, Bryan (M)** 59 2
H: 5 8  W: 10 13  b.Alajuela 18-2-90
*Honours:* Costa Rica Under-20, 23 full caps, 1 goal.

|  |  | | | | |
|---|---|---|---|---|---|
| 2009-10 | FC Copenhagen | 3 | 0 | | |
| 2010-11 | FC Copenhagen | 1 | 0 | | |
| 2010-11 | *Nordsjaelland* | 14 | 0 | 14 | 0 |
| 2011-12 | FC Copenhagen | 22 | 2 | | |
| 2012-13 | FC Copenhagen | 4 | 0 | 30 | 2 |
| 2012-13 | Everton | 15 | 0 | 15 | 0 |

**PIENAAR, Steven (M)** 282 34
H: 5 10  W: 10 06  b.Westbury 17-3-82
*Honours:* South Africa 60 full caps, 3 goals.

|  |  | | | | |
|---|---|---|---|---|---|
| 2001-02 | Ajax | 8 | 1 | | |
| 2002-03 | Ajax | 31 | 5 | | |
| 2003-04 | Ajax | 16 | 3 | | |
| 2004-05 | Ajax | 24 | 4 | | |
| 2005-06 | Ajax | 15 | 2 | 94 | 15 |
| 2006-07 | Bor Dortmund | 25 | 0 | 25 | 0 |
| 2007-08 | Everton | 28 | 2 | | |
| 2008-09 | Everton | 28 | 2 | | |
| 2009-10 | Everton | 30 | 4 | | |
| 2010-11 | Everton | 18 | 1 | | |
| 2010-11 | Tottenham H | 8 | 0 | | |
| 2011-12 | Tottenham H | 2 | 0 | | |
| 2011-12 | *Everton* | 14 | 4 | | |
| 2012-13 | Tottenham H | 0 | 0 | 10 | 0 |
| 2012-13 | Everton | 35 | 6 | 153 | 19 |

**SPRINGTHORPE, Mason (D)** 0 0
H: 6 2  W: 11 05  b.Shrewsbury 1-11-94
*Source:* Scholar.

|  |  | | |
|---|---|---|---|
| 2011-12 | Everton | 0 | 0 |
| 2012-13 | Everton | 0 | 0 |

**STONES, John (D)** 24 0
H: 6 2  W: 11 00  b.Barnsley 28-5-94
*Source:* Scholar.

|  |  | | | | |
|---|---|---|---|---|---|
| 2011-12 | Barnsley | 2 | 0 | | |
| 2011-12 | Barnsley | 22 | 0 | 24 | 0 |
| 2012-13 | Everton | 0 | 0 | | |

**VELLIOS, Apostolos (F)** 44 7
H: 6 3  W: 12 06  b.Salonika 8-1-92
*Honours:* Greece Youth, Under-21.

|  |  | | | | |
|---|---|---|---|---|---|
| 2008-09 | Iraklis | 1 | 0 | | |
| 2009-10 | Iraklis | 9 | 2 | | |
| 2010-11 | Iraklis | 12 | 2 | 22 | 4 |
| 2010-11 | Everton | 3 | 0 | | |
| 2011-12 | Everton | 13 | 3 | | |
| 2012-13 | Everton | 6 | 0 | 22 | 3 |

**YOBO, Joseph (D)** 380 12
H: 6 1  W: 13 00  b.Kano 6-9-80
*Source:* Mechelen. *Honours:* Nigeria B, 95 full caps, 7 goals.

|  |  | | | | |
|---|---|---|---|---|---|
| 1998-99 | Standard Liege | 0 | 0 | | |
| 1999-2000 | Standard Liege | 18 | 0 | | |
| 2000-01 | Standard Liege | 30 | 2 | 48 | 2 |
| 2001-02 | Marseille | 23 | 0 | 23 | 0 |
| 2002-03 | Everton | 24 | 0 | | |
| 2003-04 | Everton | 28 | 2 | | |
| 2004-05 | Everton | 27 | 0 | | |
| 2005-06 | Everton | 29 | 1 | | |

| | | | | | |
|---|---|---|---|---|---|
| 2006-07 | Everton | 38 | 2 | | |
| 2007-08 | Everton | 30 | 1 | | |
| 2008-09 | Everton | 27 | 1 | | |
| 2009-10 | Everton | 17 | 1 | | |
| 2010-11 | Everton | 0 | 0 | | |
| 2010-11 | *Fenerbahce* | 30 | 1 | | |
| 2011-12 | Everton | 0 | 0 | | |
| 2011-12 | *Fenerbahce* | 39 | 1 | | |
| 2012-13 | Everton | 0 | 0 | 220 | 8 |
| 2012-13 | *Fenerbahce* | 20 | 0 | 89 | 2 |

**Players retained or with offer of contract**
Duffus, Courtney; Green, George William; Hope, Hallam Robert; McLaughlin, Ben Padraic.

**Scholars**
Adelson, Jake Joseph Clifford; Grant, Conor James; Griffiths, Russell John; Jones, Gethin Wynne; Langton, Curtis John; Long, Christopher; Pennington, Matthew; Shannon, Oliver John William; Touray, Ibou Omar.

# EXETER C (36)

**AMANKWAAH, Kevin (D)**   298 7
H: 6 1 W: 12 12 b.Harrow 19-5-82
*Source:* Scholar. *Honours:* England Youth.

| | | | | | |
|---|---|---|---|---|---|
| 1999-2000 | Bristol C | 5 | 0 | | |
| 2000-01 | Bristol C | 14 | 0 | | |
| 2001-02 | Bristol C | 24 | 1 | | |
| 2002-03 | Bristol C | 1 | 0 | | |
| 2002-03 | *Torquay U* | 6 | 0 | 6 | 0 |
| 2003-04 | Bristol C | 5 | 0 | | |
| 2003-04 | *Cheltenham T* | 12 | 0 | 12 | 0 |
| 2004-05 | Bristol C | 5 | 0 | 54 | 1 |
| 2004-05 | Yeovil T | 15 | 0 | | |
| 2005-06 | Yeovil T | 38 | 1 | 53 | 1 |
| 2006-07 | Swansea C | 29 | 0 | | |
| 2007-08 | Swansea C | 0 | 0 | 29 | 0 |
| 2008-09 | Swindon T | 31 | 2 | | |
| 2009-10 | Swindon T | 36 | 3 | | |
| 2010-11 | Swindon T | 19 | 0 | | |
| 2011-12 | Swindon T | 0 | 0 | 86 | 5 |
| 2011-12 | Burton Alb | 8 | 0 | 8 | 0 |
| 2011-12 | Rochdale | 16 | 0 | 16 | 0 |
| 2012-13 | Exeter C | 34 | 0 | 34 | 0 |

**ANDERSON, Myles (D)**   7 0
H: 6 0 W: 12 08 b.Westminster 9-1-90
*Source:* Leyton Orient.

| | | | | | |
|---|---|---|---|---|---|
| 2010-11 | Aberdeen | 1 | 0 | 1 | 0 |
| 2011-12 | Blackburn R | 0 | 0 | | |
| 2012-13 | Blackburn R | 0 | 0 | | |
| 2012-13 | *Aldershot T* | 5 | 0 | 5 | 0 |
| 2012-13 | Exeter C | 1 | 0 | 1 | 0 |

**BALDWIN, Pat (D)**   284 3
H: 6 3 W: 12 07 b.City of London 12-11-82
*Source:* Chelsea Academy.

| | | | | | |
|---|---|---|---|---|---|
| 2002-03 | Colchester U | 19 | 0 | | |
| 2003-04 | Colchester U | 4 | 0 | | |
| 2004-05 | Colchester U | 38 | 0 | | |
| 2005-06 | Colchester U | 25 | 0 | | |
| 2006-07 | Colchester U | 38 | 1 | | |
| 2007-08 | Colchester U | 26 | 0 | | |
| 2008-09 | Colchester U | 35 | 0 | | |
| 2009-10 | Colchester U | 7 | 0 | | |
| 2009-10 | *Bristol R* | 6 | 0 | 6 | 0 |
| 2009-10 | *Southend U* | 18 | 1 | | |
| 2010-11 | Colchester U | 11 | 0 | | |
| 2011-12 | Colchester U | 5 | 0 | 208 | 1 |
| 2011-12 | Southend U | 2 | 0 | 20 | 1 |
| 2011-12 | *Exeter C* | 9 | 0 | | |
| 2012-13 | Exeter C | 41 | 1 | 50 | 1 |

**BAUZA, Guillem (F)**   117 19
H: 5 11 W: 12 01 b.Palma de Mallorca 25-10-84
*Source:* Mallorca, Espanyol.

| | | | | | |
|---|---|---|---|---|---|
| 2007-08 | Swansea C | 28 | 7 | | |
| 2008-09 | Swansea C | 15 | 2 | | |
| 2009-10 | Swansea C | 6 | 0 | 49 | 9 |
| 2010-11 | Hereford U | 12 | 2 | 12 | 2 |
| 2010-11 | Northampton T | 10 | 4 | 10 | 4 |
| 2011-12 | Exeter C | 27 | 2 | | |
| 2012-13 | Exeter C | 19 | 2 | 46 | 4 |

**BENNETT, Scott (D)**   59 9
H: 5 10 W: 12 10 b.Newquay 30-11-90
*Source:* Scholar.

| | | | | | |
|---|---|---|---|---|---|
| 2008-09 | Exeter C | 0 | 0 | | |
| 2009-10 | Exeter C | 0 | 0 | | |
| 2010-11 | Exeter C | 1 | 0 | | |
| 2011-12 | Exeter C | 15 | 3 | | |
| 2012-13 | Exeter C | 43 | 6 | 59 | 9 |

**CANE, Jacob (M)**   1 0
b.Exeter 20-5-94

| | | | | | |
|---|---|---|---|---|---|
| 2012-13 | Exeter C | 1 | 0 | 1 | 0 |

**CHAMBERLAIN, Elliott (F)**   4 0
b.Bermuda 29-4-92
*Source:* Scholar. *Honours:* Wales Youth, Under-21.

| | | | | | |
|---|---|---|---|---|---|
| 2009-10 | Leicester C | 0 | 0 | | |
| 2010-11 | Leicester C | 0 | 0 | | |
| 2011-12 | Leicester C | 0 | 0 | | |
| 2012-13 | Exeter C | 4 | 0 | 4 | 0 |

**COLES, Danny (D)**   361 14
H: 6 1 W: 11 05 b.Bristol 31-10-81
*Source:* Scholarship.

| | | | | | |
|---|---|---|---|---|---|
| 1999-2000 | Bristol C | 1 | 0 | | |
| 2000-01 | Bristol C | 2 | 0 | | |
| 2001-02 | Bristol C | 23 | 0 | | |
| 2002-03 | Bristol C | 39 | 2 | | |
| 2003-04 | Bristol C | 45 | 2 | | |
| 2004-05 | Bristol C | 38 | 1 | 148 | 5 |
| 2005-06 | Hull C | 9 | 0 | | |
| 2006-07 | Hull C | 21 | 0 | | |
| 2007-08 | Hull C | 1 | 0 | 31 | 0 |
| 2007-08 | *Hartlepool U* | 3 | 0 | 3 | 0 |
| 2007-08 | Bristol R | 24 | 1 | | |
| 2008-09 | Bristol R | 5 | 1 | | |
| 2009-10 | Bristol R | 36 | 1 | | |
| 2010-11 | Bristol R | 37 | 0 | 102 | 3 |
| 2011-12 | Exeter C | 31 | 2 | | |
| 2012-13 | Exeter C | 46 | 4 | 77 | 6 |

**CURETON, Jamie (F)**   637 226
H: 5 8 W: 10 07 b.Bristol 28-8-75
*Source:* Trainee. *Honours:* England Youth.

| | | | | | |
|---|---|---|---|---|---|
| 1992-93 | Norwich C | 0 | 0 | | |
| 1993-94 | Norwich C | 0 | 0 | | |
| 1994-95 | Norwich C | 17 | 4 | | |
| 1995-96 | Norwich C | 12 | 2 | | |
| 1995-96 | *Bournemouth* | 5 | 0 | 5 | 0 |
| 1996-97 | Norwich C | 0 | 0 | | |
| 1996-97 | Bristol R | 38 | 11 | | |
| 1997-98 | Bristol R | 43 | 13 | | |
| 1998-99 | Bristol R | 46 | 25 | | |
| 1999-2000 | Bristol R | 46 | 22 | | |
| 2000-01 | Bristol R | 1 | 1 | 174 | 72 |
| 2000-01 | Reading | 43 | 26 | | |
| 2001-02 | Reading | 38 | 15 | | |
| 2002-03 | Reading | 27 | 9 | 108 | 50 |
| From Busan Icons. | | | | | |
| 2003-04 | QPR | 13 | 2 | | |
| 2004-05 | QPR | 30 | 4 | 43 | 6 |
| 2005-06 | Swindon T | 30 | 7 | 30 | 7 |
| 2005-06 | *Colchester U* | 8 | 4 | | |
| 2006-07 | Colchester U | 44 | 23 | 52 | 27 |
| 2007-08 | Norwich C | 41 | 12 | | |
| 2008-09 | Norwich C | 22 | 2 | | |
| 2008-09 | *Barnsley* | 8 | 2 | 8 | 2 |
| 2009-10 | Norwich C | 6 | 2 | 98 | 22 |
| 2009-10 | *Shrewsbury T* | 12 | 0 | 12 | 0 |
| 2010-11 | Exeter C | 41 | 17 | | |
| 2011-12 | Leyton Orient | 19 | 1 | 19 | 1 |
| 2011-12 | *Exeter C* | 7 | 1 | | |
| 2012-13 | Exeter C | 40 | 21 | 88 | 39 |

**DAVIES, Arron (M)**   228 31
H: 5 9 W: 11 00 b.Cardiff 22-6-84
*Source:* Trainee. *Honours:* Wales Under-21, 1 full cap.

| | | | | | |
|---|---|---|---|---|---|
| 2002-03 | Southampton | 0 | 0 | | |
| 2003-04 | Southampton | 0 | 0 | | |
| 2003-04 | *Barnsley* | 4 | 0 | 4 | 0 |
| 2004-05 | Southampton | 0 | 0 | | |
| 2004-05 | Yeovil T | 23 | 8 | | |
| 2005-06 | Yeovil T | 39 | 8 | | |
| 2006-07 | Yeovil T | 39 | 6 | | |
| 2007-08 | Nottingham F | 19 | 1 | | |
| 2008-09 | Nottingham F | 13 | 0 | | |
| 2009-10 | Nottingham F | 0 | 0 | 32 | 1 |
| 2009-10 | *Brighton & HA* | 7 | 0 | 7 | 0 |
| 2009-10 | Yeovil T | 10 | 0 | 111 | 22 |
| 2010-11 | Peterborough U | 22 | 1 | 22 | 1 |
| 2011-12 | Northampton T | 15 | 4 | 15 | 4 |
| 2012-13 | Exeter C | 37 | 3 | 37 | 3 |

**DAWSON, Aaron (M)**   9 0
H: 5 10 W: 10 10 b.Exmouth 24-3-92
*Source:* Scholar.

| | | | | | |
|---|---|---|---|---|---|
| 2010-11 | Exeter C | 0 | 0 | | |
| 2011-12 | Exeter C | 2 | 0 | | |
| 2012-13 | Exeter C | 7 | 0 | 9 | 0 |

**DOHERTY, Tommy (M)**   348 9
H: 5 8 W: 9 12 b.Bristol 17-3-79
*Source:* Trainee. *Honours:* Northern Ireland 9 full caps.

| | | | | | |
|---|---|---|---|---|---|
| 1997-98 | Bristol C | 30 | 2 | | |
| 1998-99 | Bristol C | 23 | 1 | | |
| 1999-2000 | Bristol C | 1 | 0 | | |
| 2000-01 | Bristol C | 0 | 0 | | |
| 2001-02 | Bristol C | 34 | 1 | | |
| 2002-03 | Bristol C | 38 | 0 | | |
| 2003-04 | Bristol C | 33 | 2 | | |
| 2004-05 | Bristol C | 29 | 1 | 188 | 7 |
| 2005-06 | QPR | 15 | 0 | | |
| 2005-06 | *Yeovil T* | 1 | 0 | 1 | 0 |
| 2006-07 | QPR | 0 | 0 | 15 | 0 |
| 2006-07 | *Wycombe W* | 26 | 2 | | |
| 2007-08 | Wycombe W | 24 | 0 | | |
| 2008-09 | Wycombe W | 34 | 0 | | |
| 2009-10 | Wycombe W | 12 | 0 | 96 | 2 |
| 2010-11 | Bradford C | 18 | 0 | 18 | 0 |
| From Newport Co, Bath C | | | | | |
| 2012-13 | Exeter C | 30 | 0 | 30 | 0 |

**EVANS, Rhys (G)**   263 0
H: 6 1 W: 13 10 b.Swindon 27-1-82
*Source:* Trainee. *Honours:* England Schools, Youth, Under-20, Under-21.

| | | | | | |
|---|---|---|---|---|---|
| 1999-2000 | Chelsea | 0 | 0 | | |
| 1999-2000 | *Bristol R* | 4 | 0 | | |
| 2000-01 | Chelsea | 0 | 0 | | |
| 2001-02 | Chelsea | 0 | 0 | | |
| 2001-02 | *QPR* | 11 | 0 | 11 | 0 |
| 2002-03 | Chelsea | 0 | 0 | | |
| 2002-03 | *Leyton Orient* | 7 | 0 | 7 | 0 |
| 2003-04 | Swindon T | 41 | 0 | | |
| 2004-05 | Swindon T | 45 | 0 | | |
| 2005-06 | Swindon T | 32 | 0 | 118 | 0 |
| 2006-07 | Blackpool | 32 | 0 | | |
| 2007-08 | Blackpool | 0 | 0 | 32 | 0 |
| 2007-08 | *Bradford C* | 4 | 0 | | |
| 2007-08 | *Millwall* | 21 | 0 | 21 | 0 |
| 2008-09 | Bradford C | 45 | 0 | 49 | 0 |
| 2009-10 | Bristol R | 3 | 0 | 7 | 0 |
| 2010-11 | Southend U | 13 | 0 | 13 | 0 |
| 2012-13 | Exeter C | 5 | 0 | 5 | 0 |

**FREAR, Elliott (F)**   12 0
H: 5 8 W: 10 01 b.Exeter 11-9-90
*Source:* Scholar.

| | | | | | |
|---|---|---|---|---|---|
| 2009-10 | Exeter C | 0 | 0 | | |
| 2010-11 | Exeter C | 0 | 0 | | |
| 2011-12 | Exeter C | 10 | 0 | | |
| 2012-13 | Exeter C | 2 | 0 | 12 | 0 |

**GOSLING, Jake (M)**   12 1
b.Newquay 11-8-93
*Source:* Scholar.

| | | | | | |
|---|---|---|---|---|---|
| 2011-12 | Exeter C | 0 | 0 | | |
| 2012-13 | Exeter C | 12 | 1 | 12 | 1 |

**GOW, Alan (M)**   283 57
H: 6 0 W: 11 00 b.Clydebank 9-10-82
*Honours:* Scotland B.

| | | | | | |
|---|---|---|---|---|---|
| 2000-01 | Clydebank | 3 | 0 | | |
| 2001-02 | Clydebank | 5 | 0 | 8 | 0 |
| 2002-03 | Airdrie U | 27 | 5 | | |
| 2003-04 | Airdrie U | 32 | 12 | | |
| 2004-05 | Airdrie U | 26 | 9 | 85 | 26 |
| 2005-06 | Falkirk | 34 | 6 | | |
| 2006-07 | Falkirk | 36 | 7 | 70 | 13 |
| 2007-08 | Rangers | 0 | 0 | | |
| 2008-09 | Blackpool | 17 | 5 | 17 | 5 |
| 2008-09 | Norwich C | 13 | 0 | 13 | 0 |
| 2009-10 | Plymouth Arg | 14 | 2 | 14 | 2 |
| 2009-10 | *Hibernian* | 7 | 0 | 7 | 0 |
| 2010-11 | Motherwell | 15 | 1 | 15 | 1 |
| 2010-11 | Notts Co | 16 | 1 | 16 | 1 |

| 2010-11 | East Bengal | 5 | 2 | 5 | 2 |
| 2011-12 | Exeter C | 7 | 3 | | |
| 2012-13 | Exeter C | 26 | 4 | 33 | 7 |

**KEOHANE, Jimmy (M)** 37 3
H: 5 11 W: 11 05 b.Wexford 22-1-91
*Source:* Wexford.

| 2010-11 | Bristol C | 0 | 0 | | |
| 2011-12 | Bristol C | 0 | 0 | | |
| 2011-12 | Exeter C | 4 | 0 | | |
| 2012-13 | Exeter C | 33 | 3 | 37 | 3 |

**KRYSIAK, Artur (G)** 135 0
H: 6 1 W: 12 00 b.Lodz 11-8-89
*Source:* LKS Lodz. *Honours:* Poland Youth.

| 2006-07 | Birmingham C | 0 | 0 | | |
| 2007-08 | *Gretna* | 4 | 0 | 4 | 0 |
| 2007-08 | Birmingham C | 0 | 0 | | |
| 2008-09 | Birmingham C | 0 | 0 | | |
| 2008-09 | *Motherwell* | 1 | 0 | 1 | 0 |
| 2008-09 | *Swansea C* | 2 | 0 | 2 | 0 |
| 2009-10 | Birmingham C | 0 | 0 | | |
| 2009-10 | *Burton Alb* | 38 | 0 | 38 | 0 |
| 2010-11 | Exeter C | 10 | 0 | | |
| 2011-12 | Exeter C | 38 | 0 | | |
| 2012-13 | Exeter C | 42 | 0 | 90 | 0 |

**MICKLEWRIGHT, Jamie (M)** 0 0

| 2012-13 | Exeter C | 0 | 0 | | |

**MOLESLEY, Mark (M)** 76 6
H: 6 1 W: 12 07 b.Hillingdon 11-3-81
*Source:* Hayes & Y, Cambridge C, Aldershot T, Stevenage Bor, Grays Ath.

| 2008-09 | Bournemouth | 29 | 4 | | |
| 2009-10 | Bournemouth | 10 | 1 | | |
| 2010-11 | Bournemouth | 2 | 0 | | |
| 2011-12 | Bournemouth | 11 | 0 | | |
| 2011-12 | *Aldershot T* | 8 | 1 | 8 | 1 |
| 2012-13 | Bournemouth | 0 | 0 | 52 | 5 |
| 2012-13 | *Plymouth Arg* | 5 | 0 | 5 | 0 |
| 2012-13 | Exeter C | 11 | 0 | 11 | 0 |

**MOORE-TAYLOR, Jordan (D)** 7 0
b. 21-1-94

| 2012-13 | Exeter C | 7 | 0 | 7 | 0 |

**NICHOLS, Tom (F)** 11 1
H: 5 10 W: 10 10 b.Wellington 1-9-93
*Source:* Scholar.

| 2010-11 | Exeter C | 0 | 0 | | |
| 2011-12 | Exeter C | 7 | 1 | | |
| 2012-13 | Exeter C | 3 | 0 | 11 | 1 |

**O'FLYNN, John (F)** 318 116
H: 5 11 W: 11 11 b.Cobh 11-7-82
*Source:* Scholar, Cork C. *Honours:* Eire Under-21.

| 2001-02 | Peterborough U | 0 | 0 | | |
| 2002-03 | Cork C | 27 | 15 | | |
| 2003 | Cork C | 23 | 15 | | |
| 2004 | Cork C | 28 | 12 | | |
| 2005 | Cork C | 21 | 11 | | |
| 2006 | Cork C | 15 | 6 | | |
| 2007 | Cork C | 25 | 5 | | |
| 2008 | Cork C | 19 | 4 | 158 | 68 |
| 2008-09 | Barnet | 34 | 17 | | |
| 2009-10 | Barnet | 36 | 12 | 70 | 29 |
| 2010-11 | Exeter C | 31 | 6 | | |
| 2011-12 | Exeter C | 24 | 2 | | |
| 2012-13 | Exeter C | 35 | 11 | 90 | 19 |

**OAKLEY, Matthew (M)** 497 33
H: 5 10 W: 12 06 b.Peterborough 17-8-77
*Source:* Trainee. *Honours:* England Under-21.

| 1994-95 | Southampton | 1 | 0 | | |
| 1995-96 | Southampton | 10 | 0 | | |
| 1996-97 | Southampton | 28 | 3 | | |
| 1997-98 | Southampton | 33 | 1 | | |
| 1998-99 | Southampton | 22 | 2 | | |
| 1999-2000 | Southampton | 31 | 3 | | |
| 2000-01 | Southampton | 35 | 1 | | |
| 2001-02 | Southampton | 27 | 1 | | |
| 2002-03 | Southampton | 31 | 0 | | |
| 2003-04 | Southampton | 7 | 0 | | |
| 2004-05 | Southampton | 7 | 0 | | |
| 2005-06 | Southampton | 29 | 2 | 261 | 14 |
| 2006-07 | Derby Co | 37 | 6 | | |
| 2007-08 | Derby Co | 19 | 3 | 56 | 9 |

| 2007-08 | Leicester C | 20 | 0 | | |
| 2008-09 | Leicester C | 45 | 8 | | |
| 2009-10 | Leicester C | 38 | 0 | | |
| 2010-11 | Leicester C | 34 | 2 | | |
| 2011-12 | Leicester C | 0 | 0 | 137 | 10 |
| 2011-12 | *Exeter C* | 7 | 0 | | |
| 2012-13 | Exeter C | 36 | 0 | 43 | 0 |

**REID, Jamie (F)** 4 2
b.Torquay 15-7-94
*Honours:* Northern Ireland Under-21.

| 2012-13 | Exeter C | 4 | 2 | 4 | 2 |

**RODGERS, Anton (M)** 2 0
H: 5 7 b.Reading 26-1-93
*Source:* Chelsea Scholar.

| 2011-12 | Brighton & HA | 0 | 0 | | |
| 2012-13 | Exeter C | 2 | 0 | 2 | 0 |

**SERCOMBE, Liam (M)** 152 14
H: 5 10 W: 10 10 b.Exeter 25-4-90
*Source:* Scholar.

| 2008-09 | Exeter C | 29 | 2 | | |
| 2009-10 | Exeter C | 28 | 1 | | |
| 2010-11 | Exeter C | 42 | 3 | | |
| 2011-12 | Exeter C | 33 | 7 | | |
| 2012-13 | Exeter C | 20 | 1 | 152 | 14 |

**TILLSON, Jordan (D)** 0 0

| 2012-13 | Exeter C | 0 | 0 | | |

**TULLY, Steve (D)** 294 5
H: 5 8 W: 11 02 b.Paignton 10-2-80
*Source:* Trainee.

| 1997-98 | Torquay U | 9 | 0 | | |
| 1998-99 | Torquay U | 37 | 2 | | |
| 1999-2000 | Torquay U | 13 | 0 | | |
| 2000-01 | Torquay U | 29 | 1 | | |
| 2001-02 | Torquay U | 18 | 0 | 106 | 3 |

From Weymouth.

| 2008-09 | Exeter C | 36 | 0 | | |
| 2009-10 | Exeter C | 38 | 1 | | |
| 2010-11 | Exeter C | 43 | 1 | | |
| 2011-12 | Exeter C | 44 | 0 | | |
| 2012-13 | Exeter C | 27 | 0 | 188 | 2 |

**WANNELL, Jacob (D)** 0 0

| 2012-13 | Exeter C | 0 | 0 | | |

**WOODMAN, Craig (D)** 344 6
H: 5 9 W: 10 11 b.Tiverton 22-12-82
*Source:* Trainee.

| 1999-2000 | Bristol C | 0 | 0 | | |
| 2000-01 | Bristol C | 2 | 0 | | |
| 2001-02 | Bristol C | 6 | 0 | | |
| 2002-03 | Bristol C | 10 | 0 | | |
| 2003-04 | Bristol C | 21 | 0 | | |
| 2004-05 | Bristol C | 3 | 0 | | |
| 2004-05 | *Mansfield T* | 8 | 1 | 8 | 1 |
| 2004-05 | *Torquay U* | 22 | 1 | | |
| 2005-06 | Bristol C | 37 | 1 | | |
| 2005-06 | *Torquay U* | 2 | 0 | 24 | 1 |
| 2006-07 | Bristol C | 11 | 0 | 90 | 1 |
| 2007-08 | Wycombe W | 29 | 0 | | |
| 2008-09 | Wycombe W | 46 | 1 | | |
| 2009-10 | Wycombe W | 44 | 1 | 119 | 2 |
| 2010-11 | Brentford | 41 | 1 | | |
| 2011-12 | Brentford | 18 | 0 | 59 | 1 |
| 2012-13 | Exeter C | 44 | 0 | 44 | 0 |

**Players retained or with offer of contract**
Jagger, Cane Jacob.

**Scholars**
Brown, Sam; Byrne, James Joseph; Densu, Irvin Fred Nana Kwame Addo G; Duncan, Kamarl Christopher; Grimes, Matthew Jacob; Heidari, Hussein; Jay, Matthew William; Pope, Jason Warren; Pym, Christy James; Riley-Lowe, Connor; Watkins, Oliver George Arthur; Young, Roderick Orlando; Non, Contract; Edwards, Robert William; Tisdale, Paul Robert.

# FLEETWOOD T (37)

**ALLEN, Jamie (M)** 4 1

| 2012-13 | Fleetwood T | 4 | 1 | 4 | 1 |

**ATKINSON, Rob (D)** 132 5
H: 6 1 W: 12 03 b.Beverley 29-4-87
*Source:* Scholar.

| 2003-04 | Barnsley | 1 | 0 | | |
| 2004-05 | Barnsley | 1 | 0 | | |
| 2005-06 | Barnsley | 0 | 0 | | |
| 2006-07 | Barnsley | 6 | 0 | | |
| 2007-08 | Barnsley | 0 | 0 | 8 | 0 |
| 2007-08 | *Rochdale* | 2 | 0 | 2 | 0 |
| 2007-08 | Grimsby T | 24 | 1 | | |
| 2008-09 | Grimsby T | 31 | 2 | | |
| 2009-10 | Grimsby T | 37 | 2 | 92 | 5 |
| 2012-13 | Fleetwood T | 18 | 0 | 18 | 0 |
| 2012-13 | *Accrington S* | 12 | 0 | 12 | 0 |

**BALL, David (F)** 107 21
H: 6 0 W: 11 08 b.Whitefield 14-12-89
*Source:* Scholar.

| 2007-08 | Manchester C | 0 | 0 | | |
| 2008-09 | Manchester C | 0 | 0 | | |
| 2009-10 | Manchester C | 0 | 1 | | |
| 2010-11 | Manchester C | 0 | 0 | | |
| 2010-11 | *Swindon T* | 18 | 2 | 18 | 2 |
| 2010-11 | Peterborough U | 19 | 5 | | |
| 2011-12 | Peterborough U | 22 | 4 | | |
| 2011-12 | *Rochdale* | 14 | 3 | 14 | 3 |
| 2012-13 | Peterborough U | 0 | 0 | 41 | 9 |
| 2012-13 | Fleetwood T | 34 | 7 | 34 | 7 |

**BARRY, Anthony (M)** 119 1
H: 5 7 W: 10 00 b.Liverpool 29-5-86
*Source:* Everton.

| 2004-05 | Coventry C | 0 | 0 | | |

From Accrington S

| 2005-06 | Yeovil T | 4 | 0 | | |
| 2006-07 | Yeovil T | 24 | 0 | | |
| 2007-08 | Yeovil T | 36 | 0 | 64 | 0 |
| 2008-09 | Chester C | 43 | 1 | 43 | 1 |
| 2012-13 | Fleetwood T | 12 | 0 | 12 | 0 |

**BEELEY, Shaun (D)** 34 0
H: 5 10 W: 11 05

| 2012-13 | Fleetwood T | 34 | 0 | 34 | 0 |

**BRANCO, Rodrigo (F)** 1 0
H: 6 2 W: 10 12 b. 14-7-91

| 2012-13 | Fleetwood T | 1 | 0 | 1 | 0 |

**BROWN, Junior (D)** 44 11
H: 5 9 W: 10 09 b.Crewe 7-5-89

| 2006-07 | Crewe Alex | 0 | 0 | | |
| 2007-08 | Crewe Alex | 1 | 0 | 1 | 0 |
| 2012-13 | Fleetwood T | 43 | 11 | 43 | 11 |

**CHARNOCK, Kieran (D)** 102 1
H: 6 1 W: 13 07 b.Preston 3-8-84
*Source:* Scholar.

| 2002-03 | Wigan Ath | 0 | 0 | | |

From Southport, Northwich Vic.

| 2007-08 | Peterborough U | 10 | 0 | | |
| 2008-09 | Peterborough U | 2 | 0 | 12 | 0 |
| 2008-09 | *Accrington S* | 34 | 0 | 34 | 0 |
| 2009-10 | Torquay U | 24 | 0 | | |
| 2010-11 | Torquay U | 4 | 0 | 28 | 0 |
| 2010-11 | Morecambe | 21 | 1 | | |
| 2011-12 | Morecambe | 4 | 0 | 25 | 1 |
| 2012-13 | Fleetwood T | 3 | 0 | 3 | 0 |

**CROWTHER, Ryan (M)** 15 2
H: 5 11 b.Stockport 17-9-88

| 2012-13 | Fleetwood T | 15 | 2 | 15 | 2 |

**DAVIES, Scott (G)** 56 0
H: 6 0 W: 10 13 b.Blackpool 27-2-87

| 2007-08 | Morecambe | 10 | 0 | | |
| 2008-09 | Morecambe | 0 | 0 | | |
| 2009-10 | Morecambe | 1 | 0 | 11 | 0 |
| 2012-13 | Fleetwood T | 45 | 0 | 45 | 0 |

**EVANS, Gary (F)** 222 43
H: 6 0 W: 12 08 b.Stockport 26-4-88
*Source:* Crewe Alex.

| 2007-08 | Macclesfield T | 42 | 7 | | |
| 2008-09 | Macclesfield T | 40 | 12 | 82 | 19 |
| 2009-10 | Bradford C | 43 | 11 | | |
| 2010-11 | Bradford C | 36 | 3 | 79 | 14 |
| 2011-12 | Rotherham U | 32 | 7 | | |
| 2012-13 | Rotherham U | 13 | 2 | 45 | 9 |
| 2012-13 | Fleetwood T | 16 | 1 | 16 | 1 |

**FONTAINE, Jean-Michel (F)**    13   0
H: 6 3   W: 12 06   b.Saint-Pierre 28-8-88

|  |  | | | | |
|---|---|---|---|---|---|
| 2012-13 | Fleetwood T | 13 | 0 | 13 | 0 |

**GILLESPIE, Steven (F)**    218   59
H: 5 9   W: 11 02   b.Liverpool 4-6-84
*Source:* Liverpool Scholar.

|  |  | | | | |
|---|---|---|---|---|---|
| 2004-05 | Bristol C | 8 | 0 | | |
| 2004-05 | Cheltenham T | 12 | 5 | | |
| 2005-06 | Bristol C | 4 | 1 | 12 | 1 |
| 2005-06 | Cheltenham T | 14 | 5 | | |
| 2006-07 | Cheltenham T | 23 | 5 | | |
| 2007-08 | Cheltenham T | 37 | 14 | 86 | 29 |
| 2008-09 | Colchester U | 17 | 4 | | |
| 2009-10 | Colchester U | 30 | 1 | | |
| 2010-11 | Colchester U | 18 | 9 | | |
| 2011-12 | Colchester U | 33 | 11 | 98 | 25 |
| 2012-13 | Fleetwood T | 22 | 4 | 22 | 4 |

**GOODALL, Alan (D)**    241   16
H: 5 9   W: 11 06   b.Birkenhead 2-12-81
*Source:* Bangor C.

|  |  | | | | |
|---|---|---|---|---|---|
| 2004-05 | Rochdale | 34 | 2 | | |
| 2005-06 | Rochdale | 40 | 3 | | |
| 2006-07 | Rochdale | 46 | 3 | | |
| 2007-08 | Luton T | 29 | 1 | 29 | 1 |
| 2008-09 | Chesterfield | 28 | 3 | | |
| 2009-10 | Chesterfield | 17 | 0 | 45 | 3 |
| 2010-11 | Rochdale | 5 | 0 | 125 | 8 |
| 2010-11 | Stockport Co | 13 | 0 | 13 | 0 |
| 2012-13 | Fleetwood T | 29 | 4 | 29 | 4 |

**GYORIO, Mozesh (M)**    1   0
H: 5 11   W: 12 02   b.Backa Topola 1-8-89

|  |  | | | | |
|---|---|---|---|---|---|
| 2012-13 | Fleetwood T | 1 | 0 | 1 | 0 |

**HOGAN, Liam (D)**    0   0
H: 6 0   W: 12 02   b. 8-2-89
*Source:* FC Halifax.

|  |  | | |
|---|---|---|---|
| 2012-13 | Fleetwood T | 0 | 0 |

**HOWELL, Dean (D)**    96   6
H: 6 1   W: 12 05   b.Burton-on-Trent 29-11-80
*Source:* Trainee.

|  |  | | | | |
|---|---|---|---|---|---|
| 1999-2000 | Notts Co | 1 | 0 | 1 | 0 |
| 2000-01 | Crewe Alex | 1 | 0 | 1 | 0 |
| 2000-01 | *Rochdale* | 3 | 0 | 3 | 0 |
| From Southport, Morecambe, Halifax X | | | | | |
| 2005-06 | Colchester U | 4 | 0 | 4 | 0 |
| From Halifax, Weymouth, Grays, Rushden | | | | | |
| 2008-09 | Aldershot T | 14 | 0 | | |
| 2008-09 | *Bury* | 3 | 0 | 3 | 0 |
| 2009-10 | Aldershot T | 3 | 1 | | |
| 2010-11 | Aldershot T | 0 | 0 | 17 | 1 |
| 2011-12 | Crawley T | 37 | 3 | 37 | 3 |
| 2012-13 | Fleetwood T | 30 | 1 | 30 | 1 |

**JOHNSON, Damien (M)**    335   9
H: 5 9   W: 11 09   b.Lisburn 18-11-78
*Source:* Trainee. *Honours:* Northern Ireland Youth, Under-21, 56 full caps.

|  |  | | | | |
|---|---|---|---|---|---|
| 1995-96 | Blackburn R | 0 | 0 | | |
| 1996-97 | Blackburn R | 0 | 0 | | |
| 1997-98 | Blackburn R | 0 | 0 | | |
| 1997-98 | *Nottingham F* | 6 | 0 | 6 | 0 |
| 1998-99 | Blackburn R | 21 | 1 | | |
| 1999-2000 | Blackburn R | 16 | 1 | | |
| 2000-01 | Blackburn R | 16 | 0 | | |
| 2001-02 | Blackburn R | 7 | 1 | 60 | 3 |
| 2001-02 | Birmingham C | 8 | 1 | | |
| 2002-03 | Birmingham C | 30 | 1 | | |
| 2003-04 | Birmingham C | 35 | 1 | | |
| 2004-05 | Birmingham C | 36 | 0 | | |
| 2005-06 | Birmingham C | 31 | 0 | | |
| 2006-07 | Birmingham C | 26 | 1 | | |
| 2007-08 | Birmingham C | 17 | 0 | | |
| 2008-09 | Birmingham C | 9 | 0 | | |
| 2009-10 | Birmingham C | 1 | 0 | 193 | 4 |
| 2009-10 | Plymouth Arg | 20 | 2 | | |
| 2010-11 | Plymouth Arg | 0 | 0 | | |
| 2010-11 | *Huddersfield T* | 16 | 0 | | |
| 2011-12 | Plymouth Arg | 0 | 0 | | |
| 2011-12 | *Huddersfield T* | 18 | 0 | 34 | 0 |
| 2012-13 | Plymouth Arg | 0 | 0 | 20 | 2 |
| 2012-13 | Fleetwood T | 22 | 0 | 22 | 0 |

**KINSELLA, Gerard (M)**    0   0
b.Liverpool 13-11-91

|  |  | | |
|---|---|---|---|
| 2012-13 | Fleetwood T | 0 | 0 |

**LUCAS, David (G)**    308   0
H: 6 1   W: 13 07   b.Preston 23-11-77
*Source:* Trainee. *Honours:* England Youth.

|  |  | | | | |
|---|---|---|---|---|---|
| 1995-96 | Preston NE | 1 | 0 | | |
| 1995-96 | *Darlington* | 6 | 0 | | |
| 1996-97 | Preston NE | 2 | 0 | | |
| 1996-97 | *Darlington* | 7 | 0 | 13 | 0 |
| 1996-97 | *Scunthorpe U* | 6 | 0 | 6 | 0 |
| 1997-98 | Preston NE | 6 | 0 | | |
| 1998-99 | Preston NE | 30 | 0 | | |
| 1999-2000 | Preston NE | 6 | 0 | | |
| 2000-01 | Preston NE | 29 | 0 | | |
| 2001-02 | Preston NE | 24 | 0 | | |
| 2002-03 | Preston NE | 21 | 0 | | |
| 2003-04 | Preston NE | 2 | 0 | 121 | 0 |
| 2003-04 | Sheffield W | 17 | 0 | | |
| 2004-05 | Sheffield W | 34 | 0 | | |
| 2005-06 | Sheffield W | 18 | 0 | | |
| 2006-07 | Sheffield W | 0 | 0 | 69 | 0 |
| 2007-08 | Barnsley | 3 | 0 | | |
| 2007-08 | Barnsley | 0 | 0 | 3 | 0 |
| 2007-08 | Leeds U | 3 | 0 | | |
| 2008-09 | Leeds U | 13 | 0 | 16 | 0 |
| 2009-10 | Swindon T | 41 | 0 | | |
| 2010-11 | Swindon T | 21 | 0 | 62 | 0 |
| 2011-12 | Rochdale | 16 | 0 | 16 | 0 |
| 2012-13 | Birmingham C | 0 | 0 | | |
| 2012-13 | Fleetwood T | 2 | 0 | 2 | 0 |

**MANGAN, Andy (F)**    75   13
H: 6 0   W: 11 09   b.Liverpool 30-8-86
*Source:* Scholar.

|  |  | | | | |
|---|---|---|---|---|---|
| 2003-04 | Blackpool | 2 | 0 | | |
| 2004-05 | Blackpool | 0 | 0 | 2 | 0 |
| From Hyde | | | | | |
| 2006-07 | Accrington S | 34 | 4 | | |
| 2007-08 | *Bury* | 20 | 4 | 20 | 4 |
| 2007-08 | *Accrington S* | 7 | 1 | 41 | 5 |
| From Forest Green R, Wrexham | | | | | |
| 2012-13 | Fleetwood T | 12 | 4 | 12 | 4 |

**MATT, Jamille (F)**    14   3
b.Walsall 20-10-89
*Source:* Kidderminster H.

|  |  | | | | |
|---|---|---|---|---|---|
| 2012-13 | Fleetwood T | 14 | 3 | 14 | 3 |

**MAWENE, Youl (D)**    295   11
H: 6 1   W: 13 00   b.Caen 16-7-79

|  |  | | | | |
|---|---|---|---|---|---|
| 1999-2000 | Lens | 6 | 0 | 6 | 0 |
| 2000-01 | Derby Co | 8 | 0 | | |
| 2001-02 | Derby Co | 17 | 1 | | |
| 2002-03 | Derby Co | 0 | 0 | | |
| 2003-04 | Derby Co | 30 | 0 | 55 | 1 |
| 2004-05 | Preston NE | 46 | 2 | | |
| 2005-06 | Preston NE | 30 | 1 | | |
| 2006-07 | Preston NE | 0 | 0 | | |
| 2007-08 | Preston NE | 38 | 3 | | |
| 2008-09 | Preston NE | 41 | 2 | | |
| 2009-10 | Preston NE | 19 | 0 | 174 | 8 |
| 2010-11 | Panserraikos | 19 | 0 | 19 | 0 |
| 2011-12 | Aberdeen | 22 | 2 | 22 | 2 |
| 2012-13 | Fleetwood T | 19 | 0 | 19 | 0 |

**MAXWELL, Chris (G)**    0   0
b.Wrexham 30-7-90
*Source:* Wrexham.

|  |  | | |
|---|---|---|---|
| 2012-13 | Fleetwood T | 0 | 0 |

**McGUIRE, Jamie (M)**    37   1
H: 5 7   W: 10 13   b.Birkenhead 13-11-83
*Source:* Scholar.

|  |  | | | | |
|---|---|---|---|---|---|
| 2001-02 | Tranmere R | 0 | 0 | | |
| 2002-03 | Tranmere R | 0 | 0 | | |
| 2003-04 | Tranmere R | 0 | 0 | | |
| From Northwich Vic (loan), Droylsden | | | | | |
| 2012-13 | Fleetwood T | 37 | 1 | 37 | 1 |

**McLAUGHLIN, Conor (D)**    47   0
H: 6 0   W: 11 02   b.Belfast 26-7-91
*Source:* Scholar. *Honours:* Northern Ireland Under-21, 1 full cap.

|  |  | | | | |
|---|---|---|---|---|---|
| 2009-10 | Preston NE | 0 | 0 | | |
| 2010-11 | Preston NE | 0 | 0 | | |
| 2011-12 | Preston NE | 17 | 0 | 24 | 0 |
| 2011-12 | *Shrewsbury T* | 4 | 0 | 4 | 0 |
| 2012-13 | Fleetwood T | 19 | 0 | 19 | 0 |

**McNULTY, Steve (D)**    16   2
H: 6 1   W: 13 11   b.Liverpool 26-9-83
*Source:* Barrow.

|  |  | | | | |
|---|---|---|---|---|---|
| 2012-13 | Fleetwood T | 16 | 2 | 16 | 2 |

**MILLIGAN, Jamie (M)**    42   1
H: 5 6   W: 9 11   b.Blackpool 3-1-80
*Source:* Trainee. *Honours:* England Youth.

|  |  | | | | |
|---|---|---|---|---|---|
| 1998-99 | Everton | 3 | 0 | | |
| 1999-2000 | Everton | 1 | 0 | 4 | 0 |
| 2000-01 | Blackpool | 6 | 0 | | |
| 2001-02 | Blackpool | 17 | 0 | | |
| 2002-03 | Blackpool | 7 | 1 | 30 | 1 |
| From Leigh, Hyde | | | | | |
| 2012-13 | Fleetwood T | 8 | 0 | 8 | 0 |

**NICHOLSON, Barry (M)**    407   47
H: 5 7   W: 9 01   b.Dumfries 24-8-78
*Honours:* Scotland Under-21, 3 full caps.

|  |  | | | | |
|---|---|---|---|---|---|
| 1995-96 | Rangers | 0 | 0 | | |
| 1996-97 | Rangers | 0 | 0 | | |
| 1997-98 | Rangers | 0 | 0 | | |
| 1998-99 | Rangers | 6 | 0 | | |
| 1999-2000 | Rangers | 2 | 0 | 8 | 0 |
| 2000-01 | Dunfermline Ath | 36 | 3 | | |
| 2001-02 | Dunfermline Ath | 37 | 7 | | |
| 2002-03 | Dunfermline Ath | 38 | 5 | | |
| 2003-04 | Dunfermline Ath | 36 | 5 | | |
| 2004-05 | Dunfermline Ath | 27 | 3 | 174 | 23 |
| 2005-06 | Aberdeen | 33 | 2 | | |
| 2006-07 | Aberdeen | 31 | 6 | | |
| 2007-08 | Aberdeen | 38 | 5 | 102 | 13 |
| 2008-09 | Preston NE | 37 | 3 | | |
| 2009-10 | Preston NE | 4 | 0 | | |
| 2010-11 | Preston NE | 22 | 4 | | |
| 2011-12 | Preston NE | 30 | 2 | 93 | 9 |
| 2012-13 | Fleetwood T | 30 | 2 | 30 | 2 |

**PARKIN, Jon (F)**    388   105
H: 6 4   W: 13 07   b.Barnsley 30-12-81
*Source:* Scholarship.

|  |  | | | | |
|---|---|---|---|---|---|
| 1998-99 | Barnsley | 2 | 0 | | |
| 1999-2000 | Barnsley | 0 | 0 | | |
| 2000-01 | Barnsley | 4 | 0 | | |
| 2001-02 | Barnsley | 4 | 0 | 10 | 0 |
| 2001-02 | *Hartlepool U* | 1 | 0 | 1 | 0 |
| 2002-03 | York C | 18 | 2 | | |
| 2002-03 | York C | 41 | 10 | | |
| 2003-04 | York C | 15 | 2 | 74 | 14 |
| 2004-05 | Macclesfield T | 12 | 1 | | |
| 2005-06 | Macclesfield T | 11 | 7 | 65 | 30 |
| 2005-06 | Hull C | 18 | 5 | | |
| 2006-07 | Hull C | 29 | 6 | 47 | 11 |
| 2006-07 | Stoke C | 6 | 3 | | |
| 2007-08 | Stoke C | 29 | 2 | | |
| 2008-09 | Stoke C | 0 | 0 | 35 | 5 |
| 2008-09 | Preston NE | 39 | 11 | | |
| 2009-10 | Preston NE | 43 | 10 | | |
| 2010-11 | Preston NE | 19 | 7 | 101 | 28 |
| 2010-11 | Cardiff C | 11 | 1 | | |
| 2011-12 | Cardiff C | 0 | 0 | 11 | 1 |
| 2011-12 | *Doncaster R* | 5 | 0 | 5 | 0 |
| 2011-12 | *Huddersfield T* | 3 | 0 | 3 | 0 |
| 2011-12 | Scunthorpe U | 14 | 6 | 14 | 6 |
| 2012-13 | Fleetwood T | 22 | 10 | 22 | 10 |

**POND, Nathan (M)**    12   0
H: 6 3   W: 11 00   b.Preston 5-1-85

|  |  | | | | |
|---|---|---|---|---|---|
| 2012-13 | Fleetwood T | 12 | 0 | 12 | 0 |

**ROSE, Danny (M)**    34   2
H: 5 7   W: 10 04   b.Bristol 21-2-88

|  |  | | | | |
|---|---|---|---|---|---|
| 2006-07 | Manchester U | 0 | 0 | | |
| 2007-08 | Manchester U | 0 | 0 | | |
| From Oxford U, Newport Co | | | | | |
| 2012-13 | Fleetwood T | 0 | 0 | | |
| 2012-13 | *Aldershot T* | 34 | 2 | 34 | 2 |

**TITCHINER, Alex (F)**    9   0
H: 6 6   W: 13 12   b.Wales 13-6-91
*Source:* Witton Alb, Colwyn B (loan).

|  |  | | | | |
|---|---|---|---|---|---|
| 2012-13 | Fleetwood T | 9 | 0 | 9 | 0 |

**Scholars**
Barrett, Dominic; Bromley, Robbie; Cartwright, Max Jonathan; Deacon, Keano; Lazenbury, Jordan; Martin, Oliver; Olapade, Lanre; Rajab, Abdul Rahman; Wainwright, Aden; Willoughby, Kurt Henry.

## FULHAM (38)

**ALTMAN, Omri (M)**    0   0
H: 5 10   W: 11 11   b.Tel Aviv 23-3-94
Source: Scholar. Honours: Israel Youth.

| | | | |
|---|---|---|---|
| 2011-12 | Fulham | 0 | 0 |
| 2012-13 | Fulham | 0 | 0 |

**ARTHURWORREY, Stephen (D)**   0   0
H: 6 4   W: 13 12   b.Hackney 15-10-94
Source: Scholar.

| | | | |
|---|---|---|---|
| 2011-12 | Fulham | 0 | 0 |
| 2012-13 | Fulham | 0 | 0 |

**BAIRD, Chris (D)**     213   7
H: 5 10   W: 11 11   b.Ballymoney 25-2-82
Source: Scholar. Honours: Northern Ireland
Youth, Under-21, 61 full caps.

| | | | | | |
|---|---|---|---|---|---|
| 2000-01 | Southampton | 0 | 0 | | |
| 2001-02 | Southampton | 0 | 0 | | |
| 2002-03 | Southampton | 3 | 0 | | |
| 2003-04 | Southampton | 4 | 0 | | |
| 2003-04 | Walsall | 10 | 0 | 10 | 0 |
| 2003-04 | Watford | 8 | 0 | 8 | 0 |
| 2004-05 | Southampton | 0 | 0 | | |
| 2005-06 | Southampton | 17 | 0 | | |
| 2006-07 | Southampton | 44 | 3 | 68 | 3 |
| 2007-08 | Fulham | 18 | 0 | | |
| 2008-09 | Fulham | 10 | 0 | | |
| 2009-10 | Fulham | 32 | 0 | | |
| 2010-11 | Fulham | 29 | 2 | | |
| 2011-12 | Fulham | 19 | 0 | | |
| 2012-13 | Fulham | 19 | 2 | 127 | 4 |

**BANYA, Charlie (M)**     0   0
H: 5 7   W: 9 08   b.Tulse Hill 18-9-93
Source: Scholar.

| | | | |
|---|---|---|---|
| 2011-12 | Fulham | 0 | 0 |
| 2012-13 | Fulham | 0 | 0 |

**BERBATOV, Dimitar (F)**    415   184
H: 6 2   W: 12 06   b.Blagoevgrad 30-1-81
Honours: Bulgaria Under-21, 78 full caps, 8
goals.

| | | | | | |
|---|---|---|---|---|---|
| 1998-99 | CSKA Sofia | 11 | 3 | | |
| 1999-2000 | CSKA Sofia | 27 | 14 | | |
| 2000-01 | CSKA Sofia | 12 | 8 | 50 | 25 |
| 2000-01 | Leverkusen | 6 | 0 | | |
| 2001-02 | Leverkusen | 24 | 8 | | |
| 2002-03 | Leverkusen | 24 | 4 | | |
| 2003-04 | Leverkusen | 33 | 16 | | |
| 2004-05 | Leverkusen | 33 | 20 | | |
| 2005-06 | Leverkusen | 34 | 21 | 154 | 69 |
| 2006-07 | Tottenham H | 33 | 12 | | |
| 2007-08 | Tottenham H | 36 | 15 | | |
| 2008-09 | Tottenham H | 1 | 0 | 70 | 27 |
| 2008-09 | Manchester U | 31 | 9 | | |
| 2009-10 | Manchester U | 33 | 12 | | |
| 2010-11 | Manchester U | 32 | 20 | | |
| 2011-12 | Manchester U | 12 | 7 | | |
| 2012-13 | Manchester U | 0 | 0 | 108 | 48 |
| 2012-13 | Fulham | 33 | 15 | 33 | 15 |

**BETTINELLI, Marcus (G)**    0   0
b.Camberwell 24-5-92
Source: Scholar.

| | | | |
|---|---|---|---|
| 2010-11 | Fulham | 0 | 0 |
| 2011-12 | Fulham | 0 | 0 |
| 2012-13 | Fulham | 0 | 0 |

**BRIGGS, Matthew (D)**     28   1
H: 6 1   W: 11 12   b.Wandsworth 6-3-91
Source: School. Honours: England Youth,
Under-20, Under-21.

| | | | | | |
|---|---|---|---|---|---|
| 2006-07 | Fulham | 1 | 0 | | |
| 2007-08 | Fulham | 0 | 0 | | |
| 2008-09 | Fulham | 0 | 0 | | |
| 2009-10 | Fulham | 0 | 0 | | |
| 2009-10 | Leyton Orient | 1 | 0 | 1 | 0 |
| 2010-11 | Fulham | 3 | 0 | | |
| 2011-12 | Fulham | 2 | 0 | | |
| 2011-12 | Peterborough U | 5 | 0 | 5 | 0 |
| 2012-13 | Fulham | 5 | 0 | 11 | 0 |
| 2012-13 | Bristol C | 4 | 0 | 4 | 0 |
| 2012-13 | Watford | 7 | 1 | 7 | 1 |

**BRISTER, Alex (M)**     0   0
b.Epsom 19-12-93
Source: Scholar.

| | | | |
|---|---|---|---|
| 2011-12 | Fulham | 0 | 0 |
| 2012-13 | Fulham | 0 | 0 |

**BURN, Dan (D)**     38   2
H: 6 6   W: 13 00   b.Blyth 1-5-92
Source: Scholar.

| | | | | | |
|---|---|---|---|---|---|
| 2009-10 | Darlington | 4 | 0 | 4 | 0 |
| 2010-11 | Fulham | 0 | 0 | | |
| 2011-12 | Fulham | 0 | 0 | | |
| 2012-13 | Fulham | 0 | 0 | | |
| 2012-13 | Yeovil T | 34 | 2 | 34 | 2 |

**CHRISTENSEN, Lasse Vigen (M)**   0   0
H: 5 10   W: 10 04   b.Esbjerg 15-8-94

| | | | |
|---|---|---|---|
| 2012-13 | Fulham | 0 | 0 |

**DALLA VALLE, Lauri (F)**    43   10
H: 5 9   W: 11 03   b.Joensuu 14-9-91
Honours: Finland Youth, Under-21.

| | | | | | |
|---|---|---|---|---|---|
| 2007 | JIPPO | 8 | 0 | 8 | 0 |
| 2008-09 | Liverpool | 0 | 0 | | |
| 2009-10 | Liverpool | 0 | 0 | | |
| 2010-11 | Fulham | 0 | 0 | | |
| 2010-11 | Bournemouth | 8 | 2 | 8 | 2 |
| 2011-12 | Fulham | 0 | 0 | | |
| 2011-12 | Dundee U | 12 | 3 | 12 | 3 |
| 2011-12 | Exeter C | 5 | 0 | 5 | 0 |
| 2012-13 | Fulham | 0 | 0 | | |
| 2012-13 | Crewe Alex | 10 | 5 | 10 | 5 |

**DAVIES, Simon (M)**     368   33
H: 5 10   W: 11 07   b.Haverfordwest
23-10-79
Source: Trainee. Honours: Wales Youth,
Under-21, B, 58 full caps, 6 goals.

| | | | | | |
|---|---|---|---|---|---|
| 1997-98 | Peterborough U | 6 | 0 | | |
| 1998-99 | Peterborough U | 43 | 4 | | |
| 1999-2000 | Peterborough U | 16 | 2 | 65 | 6 |
| 1999-2000 | Tottenham H | 3 | 0 | | |
| 2000-01 | Tottenham H | 13 | 2 | | |
| 2001-02 | Tottenham H | 31 | 4 | | |
| 2002-03 | Tottenham H | 36 | 5 | | |
| 2003-04 | Tottenham H | 17 | 2 | | |
| 2004-05 | Tottenham H | 21 | 0 | 121 | 13 |
| 2005-06 | Everton | 30 | 1 | | |
| 2006-07 | Everton | 15 | 0 | 45 | 1 |
| 2006-07 | Fulham | 14 | 2 | | |
| 2007-08 | Fulham | 37 | 5 | | |
| 2008-09 | Fulham | 33 | 2 | | |
| 2009-10 | Fulham | 17 | 0 | | |
| 2010-11 | Fulham | 30 | 4 | | |
| 2011-12 | Fulham | 6 | 0 | | |
| 2012-13 | Fulham | 0 | 0 | 137 | 13 |

**DEJAGAH, Ashkan (M)**    175   19
H: 5 11   W: 11 08   b.Tehran 5-7-86
Honours: Germany Youth, Under-21, Iran 7
full caps, 2 goals.

| | | | | | |
|---|---|---|---|---|---|
| 2004-05 | Hertha Berlin | 1 | 0 | | |
| 2005-06 | Hertha Berlin | 3 | 0 | | |
| 2006-07 | Hertha Berlin | 22 | 1 | 26 | 1 |
| 2007-08 | Wolfsburg | 31 | 8 | | |
| 2008-09 | Wolfsburg | 27 | 3 | | |
| 2009-10 | Wolfsburg | 22 | 1 | | |
| 2010-11 | Wolfsburg | 21 | 3 | | |
| 2011-12 | Wolfsburg | 26 | 3 | | |
| 2012-13 | Wolfsburg | 1 | 0 | 128 | 18 |
| 2012-13 | Fulham | 21 | 0 | 21 | 0 |

**DELLA-VERDE, Lyle (M)**    0   0
b.Leeds 9-1-95
Source: Scholar.

| | | | |
|---|---|---|---|
| 2011-12 | Fulham | 0 | 0 |
| 2012-13 | Fulham | 0 | 0 |

**DIARRA, Mahamadou (M)**    355   27
H: 6 0   W: 11 13   b.Bamako 18-5-81
Honours: Mali 65 full caps, 6 goals.

| | | | | | |
|---|---|---|---|---|---|
| 1996 | CSK Bamako | 0 | 0 | | |
| 1997 | CSK Bamako | 24 | 6 | | |
| 1998 | CSK Bamako | 0 | 0 | 24 | 6 |
| 1998-99 | OFI Crete | 21 | 2 | 21 | 2 |
| 1999-2000 | Vitesse | 16 | 2 | | |
| 2000-01 | Vitesse | 29 | 4 | | |
| 2001-02 | Vitesse | 24 | 3 | 69 | 9 |
| 2002-03 | Lyon | 25 | 0 | | |
| 2003-04 | Lyon | 28 | 1 | | |
| 2004-05 | Lyon | 36 | 2 | | |
| 2005-06 | Lyon | 32 | 3 | | |
| 2006-07 | Lyon | 2 | 0 | 123 | 6 |
| 2006-07 | Real Madrid | 33 | 3 | | |
| 2007-08 | Real Madrid | 30 | 0 | | |
| 2008-09 | Real Madrid | 9 | 0 | | |
| 2009-10 | Real Madrid | 15 | 0 | | |
| 2010-11 | Real Madrid | 3 | 0 | 90 | 3 |
| 2010-11 | Monaco | 9 | 0 | 9 | 0 |
| 2011-12 | Fulham | 11 | 1 | | |
| 2012-13 | Fulham | 8 | 0 | 19 | 1 |

**DUFF, Damien (F)**     449   61
H: 5 9   W: 12 06   b.Ballyboden 2-3-79
Source: Lourdes Celtic. Honours: Eire
Schools, Youth, Under-20, B, 100 full caps, 8
goals.

| | | | | | |
|---|---|---|---|---|---|
| 1995-96 | Blackburn R | 0 | 0 | | |
| 1996-97 | Blackburn R | 1 | 0 | | |
| 1997-98 | Blackburn R | 26 | 4 | | |
| 1998-99 | Blackburn R | 28 | 1 | | |
| 1999-2000 | Blackburn R | 39 | 5 | | |
| 2000-01 | Blackburn R | 32 | 1 | | |
| 2001-02 | Blackburn R | 32 | 7 | | |
| 2002-03 | Blackburn R | 26 | 9 | 184 | 27 |
| 2003-04 | Chelsea | 23 | 5 | | |
| 2004-05 | Chelsea | 30 | 6 | | |
| 2005-06 | Chelsea | 28 | 3 | 81 | 14 |
| 2006-07 | Newcastle U | 22 | 1 | | |
| 2007-08 | Newcastle U | 16 | 0 | | |
| 2008-09 | Newcastle U | 30 | 3 | | |
| 2009-10 | Newcastle U | 1 | 1 | 69 | 5 |
| 2009-10 | Fulham | 32 | 6 | | |
| 2010-11 | Fulham | 24 | 4 | | |
| 2011-12 | Fulham | 28 | 2 | | |
| 2012-13 | Fulham | 31 | 3 | 115 | 15 |

**EMANUELSON, Urby (M)**    233   21
H: 5 8   W: 10 11   b.Amsterdam 16-6-86
Honours: Holland Youth, Under-21, B, 17
full caps.

| | | | | | |
|---|---|---|---|---|---|
| 2004-05 | Ajax | 2 | 0 | | |
| 2005-06 | Ajax | 25 | 1 | | |
| 2006-07 | Ajax | 30 | 3 | | |
| 2007-08 | Ajax | 31 | 3 | | |
| 2008-09 | Ajax | 32 | 4 | | |
| 2009-10 | Ajax | 31 | 5 | | |
| 2010-11 | Ajax | 18 | 1 | 169 | 17 |
| 2010-11 | AC Milan | 9 | 0 | | |
| 2011-12 | AC Milan | 30 | 2 | | |
| 2012-13 | AC Milan | 12 | 1 | 51 | 3 |
| | On loan from AC Milan | | | | |
| 2012-13 | Fulham | 13 | 1 | 13 | 1 |

**ENOH, Eyong (M)**     138   4
H: 5 11   W: 11 12   b.Kumba 23-3-86
Honours: Cameroon 31 full caps, 2 goals.

| | | | | | |
|---|---|---|---|---|---|
| 2006-07 | Ajax Cape Town | 4 | 0 | | |
| 2007-08 | Ajax Cape Town | 27 | 1 | 31 | 1 |
| 2008-09 | Ajax | 19 | 1 | | |
| 2009-10 | Ajax | 27 | 1 | | |
| 2010-11 | Ajax | 27 | 1 | | |
| 2011-12 | Ajax | 22 | 0 | | |
| 2012-13 | Ajax | 3 | 0 | 98 | 3 |
| | On loan from Ajax | | | | |
| 2012-13 | Fulham | 9 | 0 | 9 | 0 |

**ETHERIDGE, Neil (G)**    12   0
H: 6 3   W: 14 00   b.Enfield 7-2-90
Source: Scholar. Honours: England Youth,
Philippines 26 full caps.

| | | | | | |
|---|---|---|---|---|---|
| 2008-09 | Fulham | 0 | 0 | | |
| 2009-10 | Fulham | 0 | 0 | | |
| 2010-11 | Fulham | 0 | 0 | | |
| 2011-12 | Fulham | 0 | 0 | | |
| 2012-13 | Fulham | 0 | 0 | | |
| 2012-13 | Bristol R | 12 | 0 | 12 | 0 |

**FREI, Kerim (M)**     26   0
H: 5 7   W: 10 05   b.Feldkirch 19-11-93
Source: Scholar. Honours: Switzerland Youth,
Under-21, Turkey Youth, 4 full caps.

| | | | | | |
|---|---|---|---|---|---|
| 2010-11 | Fulham | 0 | 0 | | |
| 2011-12 | Fulham | 16 | 0 | | |
| 2012-13 | Fulham | 7 | 0 | 23 | 0 |
| 2012-13 | Cardiff C | 3 | 0 | 3 | 0 |

**GRIMMER, Jack (M)**     4   0
H: 6 0   W: 12 06   b.Aberdeen 25-1-94
Honours: Scotland Youth.

| | | | | | |
|---|---|---|---|---|---|
| 2009-10 | Aberdeen | 2 | 0 | | |
| 2010-11 | Aberdeen | 2 | 0 | | |
| 2011-12 | Aberdeen | 0 | 0 | 4 | 0 |

|  |  | | | | |
|---|---|---|---|---|---|
| 2011-12 | Fulham | 0 | 0 | | |
| 2012-13 | Fulham | 0 | 0 | | |

**GRYGERA, Zdenek (D)** 309 17
H: 6 1 W: 12 04 b.Prilepy u Holesova 14-5-80
*Honours:* Czech Republic 65 full caps, 2 goals.

|  |  | | | | |
|---|---|---|---|---|---|
| 1997-98 | Zlin | 20 | 1 | 20 | 1 |
| 1998-99 | Drnovice | 25 | 0 | | |
| 1999-2000 | Drnovice | 29 | 3 | 54 | 3 |
| 2000-01 | Sparta Prague | 15 | 0 | | |
| 2001-02 | Sparta Prague | 21 | 1 | | |
| 2002-03 | Sparta Prague | 29 | 1 | 65 | 2 |
| 2003-04 | Ajax | 20 | 0 | | |
| 2004-05 | Ajax | 18 | 4 | | |
| 2005-06 | Ajax | 18 | 1 | | |
| 2006-07 | Ajax | 22 | 3 | 78 | 8 |
| 2007-08 | Juventus | 24 | 1 | | |
| 2008-09 | Juventus | 31 | 2 | | |
| 2009-10 | Juventus | 19 | 0 | | |
| 2010-11 | Juventus | 13 | 0 | 87 | 3 |
| 2011-12 | Fulham | 5 | 0 | | |
| 2012-13 | Fulham | 0 | 0 | 5 | 0 |

**HANGELAND, Brede (D)** 371 17
H: 6 4 W: 13 05 b.Houston 20-6-81
*Honours:* Norway Under-21, 84 full caps, 4 goals.

|  |  | | | | |
|---|---|---|---|---|---|
| 2000 | Vidar | 0 | 0 | | |
| 2001 | Viking | 22 | 0 | | |
| 2002 | Viking | 26 | 2 | | |
| 2003 | Viking | 26 | 1 | | |
| 2004 | Viking | 14 | 3 | | |
| 2005 | Viking | 26 | 0 | 114 | 6 |
| 2005-06 | FC Copenhagen | 13 | 1 | | |
| 2006-07 | FC Copenhagen | 32 | 0 | | |
| 2007-08 | FC Copenhagen | 18 | 2 | 63 | 3 |
| 2007-08 | Fulham | 15 | 0 | | |
| 2008-09 | Fulham | 37 | 1 | | |
| 2009-10 | Fulham | 32 | 1 | | |
| 2010-11 | Fulham | 37 | 6 | | |
| 2011-12 | Fulham | 38 | 0 | | |
| 2012-13 | Fulham | 35 | 0 | 194 | 8 |

**HUGHES, Aaron (D)** 442 5
H: 6 0 W: 11 02 b.Cookstown 8-11-79
*Source:* Trainee. *Honours:* Northern Ireland Youth, B, 86 full caps, 1 goal.

|  |  | | | | |
|---|---|---|---|---|---|
| 1996-97 | Newcastle U | 0 | 0 | | |
| 1997-98 | Newcastle U | 4 | 0 | | |
| 1998-99 | Newcastle U | 14 | 0 | | |
| 1999-2000 | Newcastle U | 27 | 2 | | |
| 2000-01 | Newcastle U | 35 | 0 | | |
| 2001-02 | Newcastle U | 34 | 0 | | |
| 2002-03 | Newcastle U | 35 | 1 | | |
| 2003-04 | Newcastle U | 34 | 0 | | |
| 2004-05 | Newcastle U | 22 | 1 | 205 | 4 |
| 2005-06 | Aston Villa | 35 | 0 | | |
| 2006-07 | Aston Villa | 19 | 0 | 54 | 0 |
| 2007-08 | Fulham | 30 | 0 | | |
| 2008-09 | Fulham | 38 | 0 | | |
| 2009-10 | Fulham | 34 | 0 | | |
| 2010-11 | Fulham | 38 | 1 | | |
| 2011-12 | Fulham | 19 | 0 | | |
| 2012-13 | Fulham | 24 | 0 | 183 | 1 |

**KACANIKLIC, Alex (M)** 42 5
H: 5 11 W: 10 05 b.Helsingborg 13-8-91
*Source:* Scholar. *Honours:* Sweden Youth, 10 full caps, 2 goals.

|  |  | | | | |
|---|---|---|---|---|---|
| 2008-09 | Liverpool | 0 | 0 | | |
| 2009-10 | Liverpool | 0 | 0 | | |
| 2010-11 | Fulham | 0 | 0 | | |
| 2011-12 | Fulham | 4 | 0 | | |
| 2011-12 | *Watford* | 12 | 1 | 12 | 1 |
| 2012-13 | Fulham | 20 | 4 | 24 | 4 |
| 2012-13 | *Burnley* | 6 | 0 | 6 | 0 |

**KARAGOUNIS, Giorgos (M)** 212 20
H: 5 9 W: 11 08 b.Pyrgos 6-3-77
*Honours:* Greece 125 full caps, 9 goals.

|  |  | | | | |
|---|---|---|---|---|---|
| 2000-01 | Panathinaikos | 1 | 1 | | |
| 2001-02 | Panathinaikos | 3 | 3 | | |
| 2002-03 | Panathinaikos | 13 | 3 | | |
| 2003-04 | Inter Milan | 9 | 0 | | |
| 2004-05 | Inter Milan | 11 | 0 | 20 | 0 |
| 2005-06 | Benfica | 19 | 1 | | |
| 2006-07 | Benfica | 26 | 2 | 45 | 3 |
| 2007-08 | Panathinaikos | 27 | 2 | | |
| 2008-09 | Panathinaikos | 15 | 3 | | |
| 2009-10 | Panathinaikos | 23 | 2 | | |
| 2010-11 | Panathinaikos | 22 | 1 | | |
| 2011-12 | Panathinaikos | 18 | 1 | 122 | 16 |
| 2012-13 | Fulham | 25 | 1 | 25 | 1 |

**KASAMI, Pajtim (M)** 49 3
H: 6 2 W: 11 00 b.Macedonia 2-6-92
*Honours:* Switzerland Youth, Under-21.

|  |  | | | | |
|---|---|---|---|---|---|
| 2009-10 | Bellinzona | 10 | 2 | 10 | 2 |
| 2010-11 | Palermo | 14 | 0 | 14 | 0 |
| 2011-12 | Fulham | 7 | 0 | | |
| 2012-13 | Fulham | 2 | 0 | 9 | 0 |
| 2012-13 | *Lucerne* | 16 | 1 | 16 | 1 |

**KAVANAGH, Sean (D)** 0 0
b.Dublin 20-1-94
*Source:* Scholar. *Honours:* Eire Youth.

|  |  | | |
|---|---|---|---|
| 2011-12 | Fulham | 0 | 0 |
| 2012-13 | Fulham | 0 | 0 |

**MANOLEV, Stanislav (D)** 81 3
H: 6 0 W: 11 04 b.Blagoevgrad 16-12-85
*Honours:* Bulgaria Under-21, 31 full caps, 4 goals.

|  |  | | | | |
|---|---|---|---|---|---|
| 2009-10 | PSV | 30 | 2 | | |
| 2010-11 | PSV | 21 | 0 | | |
| 2011-12 | PSV | 23 | 1 | | |
| 2012-13 | PSV | 2 | 0 | 76 | 3 |
| On loan from PSV | | | | | |
| 2012-13 | Fulham | 5 | 0 | 5 | 0 |

**MINKWITZ, Ronny (M)** 0 0
b.Duisburg 9-12-93
*Source:* Scholar.

|  |  | | |
|---|---|---|---|
| 2010-11 | Fulham | 0 | 0 |
| 2011-12 | Fulham | 0 | 0 |
| 2012-13 | Fulham | 0 | 0 |

**NA BANGNA, Buomesca (M)** 0 0
H: 5 9 W: 10 03 b.Guinea-Bissau 6-5-93
*Source:* Chelsea Scholar.

|  |  | | |
|---|---|---|---|
| 2011-12 | Fulham | 0 | 0 |
| 2012-13 | Fulham | 0 | 0 |

**OBERSCHMIDT, Max (G)** 0 0
b.Germany 25-1-95
*Source:* Scholar.

|  |  | | |
|---|---|---|---|
| 2011-12 | Fulham | 0 | 0 |
| 2012-13 | Fulham | 0 | 0 |

**PETRIC, Mladen (F)** 256 105
H: 6 1 W: 12 09 b.Dubrave 1-1-81
*Honours:* Croatia 45 full caps, 13 goals.

|  |  | | | | |
|---|---|---|---|---|---|
| 2002-03 | Grasshoppers | 5 | 5 | | |
| 2003-04 | Grasshoppers | 28 | 6 | 33 | 11 |
| 2004-05 | Basle | 17 | 5 | | |
| 2005-06 | Basle | 31 | 15 | | |
| 2006-07 | Basle | 24 | 18 | 72 | 38 |
| 2007-08 | Borussia Dortmund | 29 | 13 | 29 | 13 |
| 2008-09 | Hamburg | 25 | 12 | | |
| 2009-10 | Hamburg | 26 | 8 | | |
| 2010-11 | Hamburg | 22 | 11 | | |
| 2011-12 | Hamburg | 26 | 7 | 99 | 38 |
| 2012-13 | Fulham | 23 | 5 | 23 | 5 |

**PRITCHARD, Josh (M)** 0 0
H: 5 9 W: 11 02 b.Stockport 23-9-92
*Source:* Scholar.

|  |  | | |
|---|---|---|---|
| 2011-12 | Fulham | 0 | 0 |
| 2012-13 | Fulham | 0 | 0 |

**RICHARDSON, Kieran (M)** 201 20
H: 5 9 W: 11 13 b.Greenwich 21-10-84
*Source:* Scholar. *Honours:* England Under-21, 8 full caps, 2 goals.

|  |  | | | | |
|---|---|---|---|---|---|
| 2002-03 | Manchester U | 2 | 0 | | |
| 2003-04 | Manchester U | 2 | 0 | | |
| 2004-05 | Manchester U | 2 | 0 | | |
| 2004-05 | *WBA* | 12 | 3 | 12 | 3 |
| 2005-06 | Manchester U | 22 | 1 | | |
| 2006-07 | Manchester U | 15 | 1 | 41 | 2 |
| 2007-08 | Sunderland | 17 | 3 | | |
| 2008-09 | Sunderland | 32 | 4 | | |
| 2009-10 | Sunderland | 29 | 1 | | |
| 2010-11 | Sunderland | 26 | 4 | | |
| 2011-12 | Sunderland | 29 | 2 | | |
| 2012-13 | Sunderland | 1 | 0 | 134 | 14 |
| 2012-13 | Fulham | 14 | 1 | 14 | 1 |

**RIETHER, Sascha (D)** 293 11
H: 5 8 W: 10 13 b.Lahr 23-3-83

|  |  | | | | |
|---|---|---|---|---|---|
| 2002-03 | SC Freiburg | 6 | 0 | | |
| 2003-04 | SC Freiburg | 33 | 3 | | |
| 2004-05 | SC Freiburg | 23 | 1 | | |
| 2005-06 | SC Freiburg | 30 | 0 | | |
| 2006-07 | SC Freiburg | 17 | 0 | 109 | 4 |
| 2007-08 | Wolfsburg | 27 | 1 | | |
| 2008-09 | Wolfsburg | 28 | 2 | | |
| 2009-10 | Wolfsburg | 33 | 1 | | |
| 2010-11 | Wolfsburg | 28 | 2 | 116 | 6 |
| 2011-12 | Cologne | 33 | 0 | 33 | 0 |
| On loan from Cologne | | | | | |
| 2012-13 | Fulham | 35 | 1 | 35 | 1 |

**RIISE, John Arne (M)** 469 37
H: 6 1 W: 14 00 b.Molde 24-9-80
*Honours:* Norway Youth, Under-21, 110 full caps, 15 goals.

|  |  | | | | |
|---|---|---|---|---|---|
| 1997 | Aalesund | 8 | 1 | | |
| 1998 | Aalesund | 17 | 4 | 25 | 5 |
| 1998-99 | Monaco | 7 | 0 | | |
| 1999-2000 | Monaco | 21 | 1 | | |
| 2000-01 | Monaco | 16 | 3 | 44 | 4 |
| 2001-02 | Liverpool | 38 | 7 | | |
| 2002-03 | Liverpool | 37 | 6 | | |
| 2003-04 | Liverpool | 28 | 0 | | |
| 2004-05 | Liverpool | 37 | 6 | | |
| 2005-06 | Liverpool | 32 | 1 | | |
| 2006-07 | Liverpool | 33 | 1 | | |
| 2007-08 | Liverpool | 29 | 0 | 234 | 21 |
| 2008-09 | Roma | 31 | 2 | | |
| 2009-10 | Roma | 36 | 5 | | |
| 2010-11 | Roma | 32 | 0 | 99 | 7 |
| 2011-12 | Fulham | 36 | 0 | | |
| 2012-13 | Fulham | 31 | 0 | 67 | 0 |

**RODALLEGA, Hugo (F)** 298 104
H: 5 11 W: 11 05 b.Valle del Cauca 25-7-85
*Honours:* Colombia 43 full caps, 8 goals.

|  |  | | | | |
|---|---|---|---|---|---|
| 2004 | Quindio | 32 | 31 | 32 | 31 |
| 2005 | Dep Cali | 26 | 12 | 26 | 12 |
| 2005-06 | Monterrey | 14 | 3 | | |
| 2006-07 | Atlas | 17 | 5 | 17 | 5 |
| 2006-07 | Monterrey | 15 | 1 | 29 | 4 |
| 2007-08 | Necaxa | 36 | 16 | | |
| 2008-09 | Necaxa | 19 | 9 | 53 | 25 |
| 2008-09 | Wigan Ath | 15 | 3 | | |
| 2009-10 | Wigan Ath | 38 | 10 | | |
| 2010-11 | Wigan Ath | 36 | 9 | | |
| 2011-12 | Wigan Ath | 23 | 2 | 112 | 24 |
| 2012-13 | Fulham | 29 | 3 | 29 | 3 |

**RUIZ, Bryan (M)** 265 89
H: 6 2 W: 12 04 b.Alajuela 18-8-85
*Honours:* Costa Rica 55 full caps, 11 goals.

|  |  | | | | |
|---|---|---|---|---|---|
| 2004-05 | Alajuelense | 31 | 13 | | |
| 2005-06 | Alajuelense | 35 | 8 | 66 | 21 |
| 2006-07 | Gent | 15 | 3 | | |
| 2007-08 | Gent | 31 | 11 | | |
| 2008-09 | Gent | 32 | 12 | 78 | 26 |
| 2009-10 | Twente | 34 | 24 | | |
| 2010-11 | Twente | 27 | 9 | | |
| 2011-12 | Twente | 4 | 2 | 65 | 35 |
| 2011-12 | Twente | 27 | 2 | | |
| 2012-13 | Fulham | 29 | 5 | 56 | 7 |

**SCHWARZER, Mark (G)** 616 0
H: 6 4 W: 14 07 b.Sydney 6-10-72
*Honours:* Australia Youth, Under-20, Under-23, 108 full caps.

|  |  | | | | |
|---|---|---|---|---|---|
| 1990-91 | Marconi Stallions | 1 | 0 | | |
| 1991-92 | Marconi Stallions | 9 | 0 | | |
| 1992-93 | Marconi Stallions | 23 | 0 | | |
| 1993-94 | Marconi Stallions | 25 | 0 | 58 | 0 |
| 1994-95 | Dynamo Dresden | 2 | 0 | 2 | 0 |
| 1995-96 | Kaiserslautern | 4 | 0 | | |
| 1996-97 | Kaiserslautern | 0 | 0 | 4 | 0 |
| 1996-97 | Bradford C | 13 | 0 | 13 | 0 |
| 1997-98 | Middlesbrough | 7 | 0 | | |
| 1998-99 | Middlesbrough | 35 | 0 | | |
| 1999-2000 | Middlesbrough | 34 | 0 | | |
| 2000-01 | Middlesbrough | 31 | 0 | | |
| 2001-02 | Middlesbrough | 38 | 0 | | |
| 2002-03 | Middlesbrough | 38 | 0 | | |
| 2003-04 | Middlesbrough | 36 | 0 | | |
| 2004-05 | Middlesbrough | 31 | 0 | | |

| | | | | |
|---|---|---|---|---|
| 2005-06 | Middlesbrough | 27 | 0 | |
| 2006-07 | Middlesbrough | 36 | 0 | |
| 2007-08 | Middlesbrough | 34 | 0 | 367 0 |
| 2008-09 | Fulham | 38 | 0 | |
| 2009-10 | Fulham | 37 | 0 | |
| 2010-11 | Fulham | 31 | 0 | |
| 2011-12 | Fulham | 30 | 0 | |
| 2012-13 | Fulham | 36 | 0 | 172 0 |

**SENDEROS, Philippe (D)** 151 8
H: 6 1 W: 13 10 b.Geneva 14-2-85
*Honours:* Switzerland Youth, Under-20, Under-21, 47 full caps, 5 goals.

| | | | | |
|---|---|---|---|---|
| 2001-02 | Servette | 3 | 0 | |
| 2002-03 | Servette | 23 | 3 | 26 3 |
| 2003-04 | Arsenal | 0 | 0 | |
| 2004-05 | Arsenal | 13 | 0 | |
| 2005-06 | Arsenal | 20 | 2 | |
| 2006-07 | Arsenal | 14 | 0 | |
| 2007-08 | Arsenal | 17 | 2 | |
| 2008-09 | Arsenal | 0 | 0 | |
| 2008-09 | *AC Milan* | 14 | 0 | 14 0 |
| 2009-10 | Arsenal | 0 | 0 | 64 4 |
| 2009-10 | *Everton* | 2 | 0 | 2 0 |
| 2010-11 | Fulham | 3 | 0 | |
| 2011-12 | Fulham | 21 | 1 | |
| 2012-13 | Fulham | 21 | 0 | 45 1 |

**SIDWELL, Steve (M)** 324 48
H: 5 10 W: 11 00 b.Wandsworth 14-12-82
*Source:* Scholar. *Honours:* England Under-20, Under-21.

| | | | | |
|---|---|---|---|---|
| 2001-02 | Arsenal | 0 | 0 | |
| 2001-02 | *Brentford* | 30 | 4 | 30 4 |
| 2002-03 | Arsenal | 0 | 0 | |
| 2002-03 | *Brighton & HA* | 12 | 5 | 12 5 |
| 2002-03 | Reading | 13 | 2 | |
| 2003-04 | Reading | 43 | 8 | |
| 2004-05 | Reading | 44 | 5 | |
| 2005-06 | Reading | 33 | 10 | |
| 2006-07 | Reading | 35 | 4 | 168 29 |
| 2007-08 | Chelsea | 15 | 0 | 15 0 |
| 2008-09 | Aston Villa | 16 | 3 | |
| 2009-10 | Aston Villa | 25 | 0 | |
| 2010-11 | Aston Villa | 4 | 0 | 45 3 |
| 2010-11 | Fulham | 12 | 2 | |
| 2011-12 | Fulham | 14 | 1 | |
| 2012-13 | Fulham | 28 | 4 | 54 7 |

**SMITH, Alex (D)** 3 0
H: 5 9 W: 8 09 b.Clapham 31-10-91
*Source:* Scholar.

| | | | | |
|---|---|---|---|---|
| 2009-10 | Fulham | 0 | 0 | |
| 2010-11 | Fulham | 0 | 0 | |
| 2011-12 | Fulham | 0 | 0 | |
| 2012-13 | Fulham | 1 | 0 | 1 0 |
| 2012-13 | *Leyton Orient* | 2 | 0 | 2 0 |

**STOCKDALE, David (G)** 145 0
H: 6 3 W: 13 04 b.Leeds 20-9-85
*Source:* Scholar.

| | | | | |
|---|---|---|---|---|
| 2002-03 | York C | 1 | 0 | |
| 2003-04 | York C | 0 | 0 | 1 0 |
| 2006-07 | Darlington | 6 | 0 | |
| 2007-08 | Darlington | 41 | 0 | 47 0 |
| 2008-09 | Fulham | 0 | 0 | |
| 2008-09 | *Rotherham U* | 8 | 0 | 8 0 |
| 2008-09 | *Leicester C* | 8 | 0 | 8 0 |
| 2009-10 | Fulham | 1 | 0 | |
| 2009-10 | *Plymouth Arg* | 21 | 0 | 21 0 |
| 2010-11 | Fulham | 7 | 0 | |
| 2011-12 | Fulham | 8 | 0 | |
| 2011-12 | *Ipswich T* | 18 | 0 | 18 0 |
| 2012-13 | Fulham | 2 | 0 | 18 0 |
| 2012-13 | *Hull C* | 24 | 0 | 24 0 |

**TANKOVIC, Muamer (F)** 0 0
H: 5 11 W: 11 06 b.Norrkoping 22-2-95
*Source:* Scholar.

| | | | |
|---|---|---|---|
| 2011-12 | Fulham | 0 | 0 |
| 2012-13 | Fulham | 0 | 0 |

**TROTTA, Marcello (F)** 32 14
H: 6 1 W: 12 12 b.Caserta 29-9-92
*Source:* Napoli. *Honours:* Italy Youth.

| | | | | |
|---|---|---|---|---|
| 2009-10 | Fulham | 0 | 0 | |
| 2010-11 | Fulham | 0 | 0 | |
| 2011-12 | Fulham | 1 | 0 | |
| 2011-12 | *Wycombe W* | 8 | 8 | 8 8 |
| 2011-12 | *Watford* | 1 | 0 | 1 0 |

| | | | | |
|---|---|---|---|---|
| 2012-13 | Fulham | 0 0 | 1 | 0 |
| 2012-13 | *Brentford* | 22 6 | 22 | 6 |

**WILLIAMS, George (F)** 2 0
H: 5 10 W: 12 04 b.Milton Keynes 7-9-95
*Source:* Scholar. *Honours:* Wales Youth.

| | | | |
|---|---|---|---|
| 2011-12 | Milton Keynes D | 2 0 | 2 0 |
| 2012-13 | Fulham | 0 | 0 |

**WILLIAMS, Ryan (F)** 4 0
H: 5 11 W: 12 00 b.Perth 28-10-93
*Source:* Scholar.

| | | | |
|---|---|---|---|
| 2011-12 | Portsmouth | 4 0 | 4 0 |
| 2011-12 | Fulham | 0 | 0 |
| 2012-13 | Fulham | 0 | 0 |

**WOODROW, Cauley (F)** 0 0
b.Hemel Hempstead 2-12-94
*Source:* Scholar.

| | | | |
|---|---|---|---|
| 2011-12 | Fulham | 0 | 0 |
| 2012-13 | Fulham | 0 | 0 |

**Players retained or with offer of contract**
David, Christofer; Donnelly, Liam Francis Peadar; Evans, Jordan Anthony John; Hyndman, Emerson; Islamovic, Dino; Joronen, Jesse Pekka; O'Halloran, Dean; o'Reilly, Daniel; Passley, Josh.

**Scholars**
Baba, Noe; Burgess, Cameron; Dembele, Moussa; Richards, Tom Oliver; Sambou, Solomon.

# GILLINGHAM (39)

**ALLEN, Charlie (M)** 41 2
H: 6 0 W: 11 10 b.Slough 24-3-92
*Source:* Brentford Scholar, Billericay T, Dagenham & R.

| | | | | |
|---|---|---|---|---|
| 2011-12 | Notts Co | 9 | 0 | 9 0 |
| 2012-13 | Gillingham | 32 | 2 | 32 2 |

**BARRETT, Adam (D)** 511 38
H: 5 10 W: 12 00 b.Dagenham 29-11-79
*Source:* Leyton Orient Trainee.

| | | | | |
|---|---|---|---|---|
| 1998-99 | Plymouth Arg | 1 | 0 | |
| 1999-2000 | Plymouth Arg | 42 | 3 | |
| 2000-01 | Plymouth Arg | 9 | 0 | 52 3 |
| 2000-01 | Mansfield T | 8 | 1 | |
| 2001-02 | Mansfield T | 29 | 0 | 37 1 |
| 2002-03 | Bristol R | 45 | 1 | |
| 2003-04 | Bristol R | 45 | 4 | 90 5 |
| 2004-05 | Southend U | 43 | 11 | |
| 2005-06 | Southend U | 45 | 3 | |
| 2006-07 | Southend U | 28 | 3 | |
| 2007-08 | Southend U | 45 | 6 | |
| 2008-09 | Southend U | 45 | 2 | |
| 2009-10 | Southend U | 41 | 2 | 247 27 |
| 2010-11 | Crystal Palace | 7 | 0 | 7 0 |
| 2010-11 | *Leyton Orient* | 14 | 0 | 14 0 |
| 2011-12 | Bournemouth | 21 | 1 | |
| 2012-13 | Bournemouth | 0 | 0 | 21 1 |
| 2012-13 | Gillingham | 43 | 1 | 43 1 |

**BIRCHALL, Adam (F)** 167 25
H: 5 7 W: 10 09 b.Maidstone 2-12-84
*Source:* Trainee. *Honours:* Wales Under-21.

| | | | | |
|---|---|---|---|---|
| 2002-03 | Arsenal | 0 | 0 | |
| 2003-04 | Arsenal | 0 | 0 | |
| 2004-05 | Arsenal | 0 | 0 | |
| 2004-05 | *Wycombe W* | 12 | 4 | 12 4 |
| 2005-06 | Mansfield T | 31 | 2 | |
| 2006-07 | Mansfield T | 5 | 0 | 36 2 |
| 2006-07 | Barnet | 23 | 6 | |
| 2007-08 | Barnet | 42 | 11 | |
| 2008-09 | Barnet | 39 | 2 | 104 19 |
| From Dover Ath. | | | | |
| 2011-12 | Gillingham | 0 | 0 | |
| 2012-13 | Gillingham | 15 | 0 | 15 0 |

**BURTON, Deon (F)** 558 134
H: 5 10 W: 11 08 b.Ashford 25-10-76
*Source:* Trainee. *Honours:* Jamaica 51 full caps, 9 goals.

| | | | |
|---|---|---|---|
| 1993-94 | Portsmouth | 2 | 0 |
| 1994-95 | Portsmouth | 7 | 2 |
| 1995-96 | Portsmouth | 32 | 7 |
| 1996-97 | Portsmouth | 21 | 1 |

| | | | | |
|---|---|---|---|---|
| 1996-97 | *Cardiff C* | 5 | 2 | 5 2 |
| 1997-98 | Derby Co | 29 | 3 | |
| 1998-99 | Derby Co | 21 | 9 | |
| 1998-99 | *Barnsley* | 3 | 0 | 3 0 |
| 1999-2000 | Derby Co | 19 | 4 | |
| 2000-01 | Derby Co | 32 | 5 | |
| 2001-02 | Derby Co | 17 | 1 | |
| 2001-02 | *Stoke C* | 12 | 2 | 12 2 |
| 2002-03 | Derby Co | 7 | 3 | 125 25 |
| 2002-03 | Portsmouth | 15 | 4 | |
| 2003-04 | Portsmouth | 1 | 0 | 78 14 |
| 2003-04 | *Walsall* | 3 | 0 | 3 0 |
| 2003-04 | *Swindon T* | 4 | 1 | 4 1 |
| 2004-05 | Brentford | 40 | 10 | 40 10 |
| 2005-06 | Rotherham U | 24 | 12 | 24 12 |
| 2005-06 | Sheffield W | 17 | 3 | |
| 2006-07 | Sheffield W | 42 | 12 | |
| 2007-08 | Sheffield W | 40 | 7 | |
| 2008-09 | Sheffield W | 17 | 1 | 116 23 |
| 2008-09 | Charlton Ath | 20 | 5 | |
| 2009-10 | Charlton Ath | 39 | 13 | 59 18 |
| 2010-11 | Gabala | 28 | 9 | |
| 2011-12 | Gabala | 21 | 6 | 49 15 |
| 2012-13 | Gillingham | 40 | 12 | 40 12 |

**CARTER, Joe (D)** 0 0
b.Buckhurst Hill 20-11-92
*Source:* Charlton Ath Scholar.

| | | | |
|---|---|---|---|
| 2011-12 | Gillingham | 0 | 0 |
| 2012-13 | Gillingham | 0 | 0 |

**DACK, Bradley (M)** 16 1
b.Greenwich 31-12-93

| | | | |
|---|---|---|---|
| 2012-13 | Gillingham | 16 1 | 16 1 |

**DAVIES, Callum (D)** 17 0
H: 6 1 W: 11 11 b.Sittingbourne 8-2-93
*Source:* Scholar.

| | | | | |
|---|---|---|---|---|
| 2010-11 | Gillingham | 1 | 0 | |
| 2011-12 | Gillingham | 2 | 0 | |
| 2012-13 | Gillingham | 14 | 0 | 17 0 |

**EAST, Danny (D)** 16 0
H: 5 10 W: 11 03 b.Hessle 26-12-91
*Source:* Scholar.

| | | | | |
|---|---|---|---|---|
| 2011-12 | Hull C | 0 | 0 | |
| 2012-13 | Hull C | 0 | 0 | |
| 2012-13 | *Northampton T* | 14 | 0 | 14 0 |
| 2012-13 | Gillingham | 2 | 0 | 2 0 |

**FISH, Matt (D)** 67 3
b.Croydon 5-1-89
*Source:* Crystal Palace Scholar, Dover Ath.

| | | | | |
|---|---|---|---|---|
| 2011-12 | Gillingham | 23 | 1 | |
| 2012-13 | Gillingham | 44 | 2 | 67 3 |

**FLITNEY, Ross (G)** 80 0
H: 6 3 W: 12 07 b.Hitchin 1-6-84
*Source:* Scholar.

| | | | | |
|---|---|---|---|---|
| 2003-04 | Fulham | 0 | 0 | |
| 2003-04 | *Brighton & HA* | 3 | 0 | 3 0 |
| 2004-05 | Fulham | 0 | 0 | |
| 2004-05 | *Doncaster R* | 0 | 0 | |
| 2005-06 | Barnet | 35 | 0 | |
| 2006-07 | Barnet | 15 | 0 | 50 0 |
| From Grays Ath, Croydon Ath, Dover Ath. | | | | |
| 2011-12 | Gillingham | 27 | 0 | |
| 2012-13 | Gillingham | 0 | 0 | 27 0 |

**FRAMPTON, Andrew (D)** 332 8
H: 5 11 W: 10 10 b.Wimbledon 3-9-79
*Source:* Trainee.

| | | | | |
|---|---|---|---|---|
| 1998-99 | Crystal Palace | 6 | 0 | |
| 1999-2000 | Crystal Palace | 9 | 0 | |
| 2000-01 | Crystal Palace | 10 | 0 | |
| 2001-02 | Crystal Palace | 2 | 0 | |
| 2002-03 | Crystal Palace | 1 | 0 | 28 0 |
| 2002-03 | Brentford | 15 | 0 | |
| 2003-04 | Brentford | 16 | 0 | |
| 2004-05 | Brentford | 35 | 0 | |
| 2005-06 | Brentford | 36 | 3 | |
| 2006-07 | Brentford | 32 | 1 | 134 4 |
| 2007-08 | Millwall | 30 | 1 | |
| 2008-09 | Millwall | 37 | 1 | |
| 2009-10 | Millwall | 21 | 2 | |
| 2010-11 | Millwall | 0 | 0 | 88 4 |
| 2010-11 | *Leyton Orient* | 1 | 0 | 1 0 |
| 2010-11 | *Swindon T* | 23 | 0 | 23 0 |
| 2011-12 | Gillingham | 28 | 0 | |
| 2012-13 | Gillingham | 30 | 0 | 58 0 |

**GRANT, Harry (M)** 1 0
2012-13 Gillingham 1 0 1 0

**GREGORY, Steven (D)** 64 2
H: 6 1 W: 12 04 b.Haddenham 19-3-87
*Source:* Scholar.
2005-06 Wycombe W 1 0
2006-07 Wycombe W 3 0 4 0
From AFC Wimbledon, Hayes & Yeading U.
2011-12 Bournemouth 28 2
2012-13 Bournemouth 0 0 28 2
2012-13 *AFC Wimbledon* 15 0 15 0
2012-13 Gillingham 17 0 17 0

**HAYSMAN, Kane (M)** 1 0
2012-13 Gillingham 1 0 1 0

**JACKMAN, Danny (D)** 311 21
H: 5 4 W: 10 00 b.Worcester 3-1-83
*Source:* Scholar.
2000-01 Aston Villa 0 0
2001-02 Aston Villa 0 0
2001-02 *Cambridge U* 7 1 7 1
2002-03 Aston Villa 0 0
2003-04 Aston Villa 0 0
2003-04 Stockport Co 27 2
2004-05 Stockport Co 33 2 60 4
2005-06 Gillingham 42 0
2006-07 Gillingham 31 1
2007-08 Northampton T 39 1
2008-09 Northampton T 43 8
2009-10 Northampton T 0 0 82 9
2009-10 Gillingham 22 0
2010-11 Gillingham 17 1
2011-12 Gillingham 40 4
2012-13 Gillingham 10 1 162 7

**KEDWELL, Danny (F)** 78 26
H: 5 11 W: 12 13 b.Gillingham 3-8-83
*Source:* Chatham T, Tonbridge Angels, Fisher Ath, Lordswood, Maidstone U, Herne Bay, Welling U, Grays Ath, AFC Wimbledon.
2011-12 Gillingham 40 12
2012-13 Gillingham 38 14 78 26

**LEE, Charlie (M)** 226 23
H: 5 11 W: 11 07 b.Whitechapel 5-1-87
*Source:* Scholar.
2005-06 Tottenham H 0 0
2006-07 Tottenham H 0 0
2006-07 *Millwall* 5 0 5 0
2007-08 Peterborough U 42 6
2008-09 Peterborough U 44 5
2009-10 Peterborough U 33 2
2010-11 Peterborough U 34 1 153 14
2010-11 *Gillingham* 4 1
2011-12 Gillingham 33 6
2012-13 Gillingham 31 2 68 9

**LEGGE, Leon (D)** 116 11
H: 6 1 W: 11 02 b.Bexhill 1-7-85
*Source:* Eastbourne UA, Hailsham T, Lewes, Tonbridge Angels.
2009-10 Brentford 29 2
2010-11 Brentford 30 3
2011-12 Brentford 28 4
2012-13 Brentford 7 0 94 9
2012-13 Gillingham 22 2 22 2

**MARTIN, Joe (M)** 112 4
H: 6 0 W: 12 13 b.Dagenham 29-11-88
*Source:* Scholar. *Honours:* England Youth.
2005-06 Tottenham H 0 0
2006-07 Tottenham H 0 0
2007-08 Tottenham H 0 0
2007-08 *Blackpool* 1 0
2008-09 Blackpool 15 0
2009-10 Blackpool 6 0 22 0
2010-11 Gillingham 17 1
2011-12 Gillingham 35 1
2012-13 Gillingham 38 2 90 4

**McKAIN, Devante (F)** 1 0
b. 26-6-94
2012-13 Gillingham 1 0 1 0

**MILLER, Ashley (F)** 6 1
H: 5 7 W: 10 03 b.Dover 8-6-94
*Source:* Scholar.
2010-11 Gillingham 1 0
2011-12 Gillingham 5 1
2012-13 Gillingham 0 0 6 1

**MONTROSE, Lewis (M)** 124 9
H: 6 0 W: 12 00 b.Manchester 17-11-88
*Source:* Scholar.
2006-07 Wigan Ath 0 0
2007-08 Wigan Ath 0 0
2008-09 Wigan Ath 0 0
2008-09 *Cheltenham T* 5 0 5 0
2008-09 *Chesterfield* 12 0 12 0
2009-10 Wycombe W 14 0
2010-11 Wycombe W 36 4 50 4
2011-12 Gillingham 37 4
2012-13 Gillingham 15 1 52 5
2012-13 *Oxford U* 5 0 5 0

**MUGGLETON, Sam (D)** 1 0
b.Melton Mowbray 17-11-95
2012-13 Gillingham 1 0 1 0

**NELSON, Stuart (G)** 270 0
H: 6 1 W: 12 12 b.Stroud 17-9-81
*Source:* Doncaster R, Hucknall T.
2003-04 Brentford 9 0
2004-05 Brentford 43 0
2005-06 Brentford 45 0
2006-07 Brentford 19 0 116 0
2007-08 Leyton Orient 30 0 30 0
2008-09 Norwich C 0 0
2010-11 Notts Co 33 0
2011-12 Notts Co 46 0 79 0
2012-13 Gillingham 45 0 45 0

**NYAFLI, Nathan (F)** 1 1
b. 24-12-93
2012-13 Gillingham 1 1 1 1

**PAYNE, Jack (M)** 115 5
H: 5 9 W: 9 02 b.Gravesend 5-12-91
*Source:* Scholar.
2008-09 Gillingham 2 0
2009-10 Gillingham 19 0
2010-11 Gillingham 31 1
2011-12 Gillingham 30 2
2012-13 Gillingham 19 2 101 5
2012-13 *Peterborough U* 14 0 14 0

**ROMEO, Mahlon (M)** 1 0
b. 19-9-95
2012-13 Gillingham 1 0 1 0

**WEBSTER, Charlie (M)** 0 0
2012-13 Gillingham 0 0

**WESTON, Myles (M)** 218 23
H: 5 11 W: 12 05 b.Lewisham 12-3-88
*Source:* Scholar.
2006-07 Charlton Ath 0 0
2006-07 *Notts Co* 4 0
2007-08 Notts Co 25 0
2008-09 Notts Co 44 3 73 3
2009-10 Brentford 40 8
2010-11 Brentford 42 3
2011-12 Brentford 26 1
2012-13 Brentford 0 0 108 12
2012-13 Gillingham 37 8 37 8

**WHELPDALE, Chris (M)** 209 34
H: 6 0 W: 12 08 b.Harold Wood 27-1-87
*Source:* Billericay T.
2007-08 Peterborough U 35 3
2008-09 Peterborough U 39 7
2009-10 Peterborough U 39 1
2010-11 Peterborough U 22 1 125 12
2010-11 *Gillingham* 4 3
2011-12 Gillingham 39 12
2012-13 Gillingham 41 7 84 22

**Scholars**
Beale, Frankie James; Blanchard, Aidan James; Butcher, Stephen James; Coates, Alfie Michael George; Freiter, Michael Thomas John; Hare, Joshua Darren; Haysman, Kane Cruz; Hessenthaler, Jakob Andrew; Lee, Oliver James; Maughan, Joshua Max; Millbank, Aaron Craig; Muggleton, Samuel Alexander; Nalder, Luke Justin; Nyafli, Setor Kofi; O'Neill, Daniel Karl Mark; Parter, Jack Terence; Romeo, Mahlon Beresford Baker; Sellens, Jack Aaron; Staunton, Joshua Michael; Webster, Charlie Ronald.

# HARTLEPOOL U (40)

**AUSTIN, Neil (D)** 358 13
H: 5 10 W: 11 09 b.Barnsley 26-4-83
*Source:* Trainee. *Honours:* England Youth, Under-20.
1999-2000 Barnsley 0 0
2000-01 Barnsley 0 0
2001-02 Barnsley 0 0
2002-03 Barnsley 34 0
2003-04 Barnsley 37 0
2004-05 Barnsley 15 0
2005-06 Barnsley 38 0
2006-07 Barnsley 24 0 148 0
2007-08 Darlington 29 2
2008-09 Darlington 33 3 62 5
2009-10 Hartlepool U 39 3
2010-11 Hartlepool U 24 2
2011-12 Hartlepool U 46 1
2012-13 Hartlepool U 39 2 148 8

**BALDWIN, Jack (D)** 49 2
H: 6 1 W: 11 00 b.Barking 30-6-93
*Source:* Faversham T.
2011-12 Hartlepool U 17 0
2012-13 Hartlepool U 32 2 49 2

**BOAGEY, Zak (F)** 1 0
H: 5 7 W: 12 08 b.Hartlepool 11-10-94
2012-13 Hartlepool U 1 0 1 0

**COLLINS, Sam (D)** 494 19
H: 6 2 W: 14 03 b.Pontefract 5-6-77
*Source:* Trainee.
1994-95 Huddersfield T 0 0
1995-96 Huddersfield T 0 0
1996-97 Huddersfield T 4 0
1997-98 Huddersfield T 10 0
1998-99 Huddersfield T 23 0 37 0
1999-2000 Bury 19 0
2000-01 Bury 34 2
2001-02 Bury 29 0 82 2
2002-03 Port Vale 44 5
2003-04 Port Vale 43 4
2004-05 Port Vale 33 2
2005-06 Port Vale 15 0 135 11
2005-06 Hull C 17 0
2006-07 Hull C 6 0
2007-08 Hull C 0 0 23 0
2007-08 *Swindon T* 4 0 4 0
2007-08 Hartlepool U 10 2
2008-09 Hartlepool U 40 1
2009-10 Hartlepool U 44 0
2010-11 Hartlepool U 42 2
2011-12 Hartlepool U 36 1
2012-13 Hartlepool U 41 0 213 6

**FLINDERS, Scott (G)** 215 1
H: 6 4 W: 13 00 b.Rotherham 12-6-86
*Source:* Scholar. *Honours:* England Youth, Under-20.
2004-05 Barnsley 11 0
2005-06 Barnsley 3 0 14 0
2006-07 Crystal Palace 8 0
2006-07 *Gillingham* 9 0 9 0
2006-07 *Brighton & HA* 12 0 12 0
2007-08 Crystal Palace 0 0
2007-08 *Yeovil T* 9 0 9 0
2008-09 Crystal Palace 0 0 8 0
2009-10 Hartlepool U 46 0
2010-11 Hartlepool U 26 1
2011-12 Hartlepool U 45 0
2012-13 Hartlepool U 46 0 163 1

**FODEN, Mark (G)** 0 0
H: 5 11 W: 12 08 b.Newcastle 1-11-95
2012-13 Hartlepool U 0 0

**FRANKS, Jonathan (F)** 88 10
H: 5 9 W: 11 03 b.Stockton 8-4-90
*Source:* Scholar. *Honours:* England Youth.
2007-08 Middlesbrough 1 0
2008-09 Middlesbrough 1 0
2009-10 Middlesbrough 23 3
2010-11 Middlesbrough 0 0
2011-12 Middlesbrough 0 0 28 3
2011-12 *Oxford U* 1 0 1 0
2011-12 *Yeovil T* 14 3 14 3
2012-13 Hartlepool U 45 4 45 4

## HARTLEY, Peter (D) — 178 10
H: 6 0 W: 12 06 b.Hartlepool 3-4-88
*Source:* Scholar.

|  |  | | | | |
|---|---|---|---|---|---|
| 2006-07 | Sunderland | 1 | 0 | | |
| 2007-08 | Sunderland | 0 | 0 | | |
| 2007-08 | Chesterfield | 12 | 0 | 12 | 0 |
| 2008-09 | Sunderland | 0 | 0 | 1 | 0 |
| 2009-10 | Hartlepool U | 38 | 2 | | |
| 2010-11 | Hartlepool U | 40 | 2 | | |
| 2011-12 | Hartlepool U | 44 | 4 | | |
| 2012-13 | Hartlepool U | 43 | 2 | 165 | 10 |

## HAWKINS, Lewis (M) — 2 0
H: 5 10 W: 12 04 b.Middlesbrough 15-6-93
*Source:* Scholar.

| 2011-12 | Hartlepool U | 1 | 0 | | |
|---|---|---|---|---|---|
| 2012-13 | Hartlepool U | 1 | 0 | 2 | 0 |

## HOLDEN, Darren (D) — 21 0
H: 5 11 W: 11 00 b.Krugersdorp 27-8-93
*Source:* Scholar.

| 2010-11 | Hartlepool U | 1 | 0 | | |
|---|---|---|---|---|---|
| 2011-12 | Hartlepool U | 3 | 0 | | |
| 2012-13 | Hartlepool U | 17 | 0 | 21 | 0 |

## HORWOOD, Evan (D) — 244 6
H: 6 0 W: 10 06 b.Billingham 10-3-86
*Source:* Scholar.

| 2004-05 | Sheffield U | 0 | 0 | | |
|---|---|---|---|---|---|
| 2004-05 | *Stockport Co* | 10 | 0 | 10 | 0 |
| 2005-06 | Sheffield U | 0 | 0 | | |
| 2005-06 | *Scunthorpe U* | 0 | 0 | | |
| 2005-06 | *Chester C* | 1 | 0 | 1 | 0 |
| 2006-07 | Sheffield U | 0 | 0 | | |
| 2006-07 | *Darlington* | 20 | 0 | 20 | 0 |
| 2007-08 | Sheffield U | 0 | 0 | | |
| 2007-08 | Gretna | 15 | 1 | 15 | 1 |
| 2008-09 | Carlisle U | 19 | 0 | | |
| 2008-09 | Carlisle U | 24 | 0 | | |
| 2009-10 | Carlisle U | 32 | 0 | 75 | 0 |
| 2010-11 | Hartlepool U | 45 | 2 | | |
| 2011-12 | Hartlepool U | 41 | 1 | | |
| 2012-13 | Hartlepool U | 37 | 2 | 123 | 5 |

## HOWARD, Steve (F) — 692 189
H: 6 3 W: 15 00 b.Durham 10-5-76
*Source:* Tow Law T. *Honours:* Scotland B.

| 1995-96 | Hartlepool U | 39 | 7 | | |
|---|---|---|---|---|---|
| 1996-97 | Hartlepool U | 32 | 8 | | |
| 1997-98 | Hartlepool U | 43 | 7 | | |
| 1998-99 | Hartlepool U | 28 | 5 | | |
| 1998-99 | Northampton T | 12 | 0 | | |
| 1999-2000 | Northampton T | 41 | 10 | | |
| 2000-01 | Northampton T | 33 | 8 | 86 | 18 |
| 2000-01 | Luton T | 12 | 3 | | |
| 2001-02 | Luton T | 42 | 24 | | |
| 2002-03 | Luton T | 41 | 22 | | |
| 2003-04 | Luton T | 34 | 14 | | |
| 2004-05 | Luton T | 40 | 18 | | |
| 2005-06 | Luton T | 43 | 14 | 212 | 95 |
| 2006-07 | Derby Co | 43 | 16 | | |
| 2007-08 | Derby Co | 20 | 1 | 63 | 17 |
| 2007-08 | Leicester C | 21 | 6 | | |
| 2008-09 | Leicester C | 41 | 13 | | |
| 2009-10 | Leicester C | 36 | 5 | | |
| 2010-11 | Leicester C | 29 | 4 | | |
| 2011-12 | Leicester C | 20 | 0 | 147 | 28 |
| 2012-13 | Sheffield W | 34 | 3 | 176 | 30 |
| 2012-13 | *Sheffield W* | 8 | 1 | 8 | 1 |

## HUMPHREYS, Richie (M) — 577 45
H: 5 11 W: 12 07 b.Sheffield 30-11-77
*Source:* Trainee. *Honours:* England Youth, Under-21.

| 1995-96 | Sheffield W | 5 | 0 | | |
|---|---|---|---|---|---|
| 1996-97 | Sheffield W | 29 | 3 | | |
| 1997-98 | Sheffield W | 7 | 0 | | |
| 1998-99 | Sheffield W | 19 | 1 | | |
| 1999-2000 | Sheffield W | 0 | 0 | | |
| 1999-2000 | *Scunthorpe U* | 6 | 2 | 6 | 2 |
| 1999-2000 | *Cardiff C* | 9 | 2 | 9 | 2 |
| 2000-01 | Sheffield W | 7 | 0 | 67 | 4 |
| 2000-01 | Cambridge U | 7 | 3 | 7 | 3 |
| 2001-02 | Hartlepool U | 46 | 5 | | |
| 2002-03 | Hartlepool U | 46 | 11 | | |
| 2003-04 | Hartlepool U | 46 | 3 | | |
| 2004-05 | Hartlepool U | 46 | 3 | | |
| 2005-06 | Hartlepool U | 46 | 2 | | |
| 2006-07 | Hartlepool U | 38 | 3 | | |
| 2006-07 | *Port Vale* | 7 | 0 | 7 | 0 |
| 2007-08 | Hartlepool U | 45 | 3 | | |
| 2008-09 | Hartlepool U | 45 | 0 | | |
| 2009-10 | Hartlepool U | 38 | 0 | | |
| 2010-11 | Hartlepool U | 25 | 2 | | |
| 2011-12 | Hartlepool U | 29 | 1 | | |
| 2012-13 | Hartlepool U | 31 | 1 | 481 | 34 |

## JAMES, Luke (M) — 45 6
H: 6 0 W: 12 08 b.Amble 4-11-94
*Source:* Scholar.

| 2011-12 | Hartlepool U | 19 | 3 | | |
|---|---|---|---|---|---|
| 2012-13 | Hartlepool U | 26 | 3 | 45 | 6 |

## LUSCOMBE, Nathan (M) — 26 1
H: 5 8 W: 11 07 b.Gateshead 6-11-89
*Source:* Scholar.

| 2008-09 | Sunderland | 0 | 0 | | |
|---|---|---|---|---|---|
| 2009-10 | Sunderland | 0 | 0 | | |
| 2010-11 | Sunderland | 0 | 0 | | |
| 2011-12 | Hartlepool U | 13 | 1 | | |
| 2012-13 | Hartlepool U | 13 | 0 | 26 | 1 |

## McHUGH, Adam (G) — 6 0
H: 6 1 W: 12 11 b.Bishop Auckland 29-5-92

| 2011-12 | St Mirren | 0 | 0 | | |
|---|---|---|---|---|---|
| 2011-12 | *Forfar Ath* | 6 | 0 | 6 | 0 |
| 2012-13 | Hartlepool U | 0 | 0 | | |

## MONKHOUSE, Andy (M) — 400 54
H: 6 1 W: 11 06 b.Leeds 23-10-80
*Source:* Trainee.

| 1998-99 | Rotherham U | 5 | 1 | | |
|---|---|---|---|---|---|
| 1999-2000 | Rotherham U | 0 | 0 | | |
| 2000-01 | Rotherham U | 12 | 0 | | |
| 2001-02 | Rotherham U | 38 | 2 | | |
| 2002-03 | Rotherham U | 20 | 0 | | |
| 2003-04 | Rotherham U | 27 | 3 | | |
| 2004-05 | Rotherham U | 14 | 2 | | |
| 2005-06 | Rotherham U | 12 | 1 | 128 | 9 |
| 2006-07 | Swindon T | 10 | 2 | 10 | 2 |
| 2006-07 | Hartlepool U | 26 | 7 | | |
| 2007-08 | Hartlepool U | 25 | 2 | | |
| 2008-09 | Hartlepool U | 44 | 6 | | |
| 2009-10 | Hartlepool U | 43 | 11 | | |
| 2010-11 | Hartlepool U | 44 | 7 | | |
| 2011-12 | Hartlepool U | 45 | 3 | | |
| 2012-13 | Hartlepool U | 35 | 7 | 262 | 43 |

## NISH, Colin (F) — 346 80
H: 6 3 W: 11 07 b.Edinburgh 7-3-81

| 1998-99 | Dunfermline Ath | 2 | 0 | | |
|---|---|---|---|---|---|
| 1999-2000 | Dunfermline Ath | 2 | 0 | | |
| 1999-2000 | *Alloa Ath* | 13 | 5 | | |
| 2000-01 | Dunfermline Ath | 4 | 0 | | |
| 2000-01 | *Alloa Ath* | 10 | 3 | 23 | 8 |
| 2001-02 | Dunfermline Ath | 14 | 0 | | |
| 2002-03 | Dunfermline Ath | 0 | 0 | 22 | 0 |
| 2002-03 | Clyde | 15 | 5 | 15 | 5 |
| 2003-04 | Kilmarnock | 30 | 9 | | |
| 2004-05 | Kilmarnock | 26 | 4 | | |
| 2005-06 | Kilmarnock | 34 | 7 | | |
| 2006-07 | Kilmarnock | 33 | 13 | | |
| 2007-08 | Kilmarnock | 22 | 7 | 145 | 40 |
| 2007-08 | Hibernian | 15 | 4 | | |
| 2008-09 | Hibernian | 31 | 7 | | |
| 2009-10 | Hibernian | 32 | 9 | | |
| 2010-11 | Hibernian | 20 | 1 | 98 | 21 |
| 2011-12 | Hartlepool U | 19 | 4 | | |
| 2012-13 | Hartlepool U | 0 | 0 | 19 | 4 |
| 2012-13 | *Dundee* | 24 | 2 | 24 | 2 |

## POOLE, James (F) — 75 12
H: 5 11 W: 12 05 b.Stockport 20-3-90
*Source:* Scholar.

| 2008-09 | Manchester C | 0 | 0 | | |
|---|---|---|---|---|---|
| 2009-10 | Manchester C | 0 | 0 | | |
| 2009-10 | *Bury* | 9 | 0 | 9 | 0 |
| 2010-11 | Manchester C | 0 | 0 | | |
| 2010-11 | *Hartlepool U* | 0 | 0 | | |
| 2011-12 | Hartlepool U | 27 | 7 | | |
| 2012-13 | Hartlepool U | 36 | 4 | 66 | 12 |

## RAFFERTY, Andy (G) — 2 0
H: 6 6 W: 13 07 b.Sidcup 27-5-88
*Source:* Guisborough T.

| 2010-11 | Hartlepool U | 1 | 0 | | |
|---|---|---|---|---|---|
| 2011-12 | Hartlepool U | 1 | 0 | | |
| 2012-13 | Hartlepool U | 0 | 0 | 2 | 0 |

## RICHARDS, Jordan (M) — 13 0
H: 5 9 W: 11 05 b.Sunderland 25-4-93
*Source:* Scholar.

| 2011-12 | Hartlepool U | 2 | 0 | | |
|---|---|---|---|---|---|
| 2012-13 | Hartlepool U | 11 | 0 | 13 | 0 |

## ROWBOTHAM, Josh (M) — 2 0
H: 5 11 W: 11 00 b.Stockton 7-1-94
*Source:* Scholar.

| 2010-11 | Hartlepool U | 1 | 0 | | |
|---|---|---|---|---|---|
| 2011-12 | Hartlepool U | 1 | 0 | | |
| 2012-13 | Hartlepool U | 0 | 0 | 2 | 0 |

## RUTHERFORD, Greg (M) — 8 1
H: 5 10 W: 12 06 b.North Shields 17-5-94
*Source:* Scholar.

| 2011-12 | Hartlepool U | 1 | 0 | | |
|---|---|---|---|---|---|
| 2012-13 | Hartlepool U | 7 | 1 | 8 | 1 |

## SWEENEY, Anthony (M) — 366 52
H: 6 0 W: 11 07 b.Stockton 5-9-83
*Source:* Scholar.

| 2001-02 | Hartlepool U | 2 | 0 | | |
|---|---|---|---|---|---|
| 2002-03 | Hartlepool U | 4 | 0 | | |
| 2003-04 | Hartlepool U | 11 | 1 | | |
| 2004-05 | Hartlepool U | 44 | 13 | | |
| 2005-06 | Hartlepool U | 35 | 5 | | |
| 2006-07 | Hartlepool U | 35 | 4 | | |
| 2007-08 | Hartlepool U | 36 | 4 | | |
| 2008-09 | Hartlepool U | 44 | 5 | | |
| 2009-10 | Hartlepool U | 42 | 2 | | |
| 2010-11 | Hartlepool U | 40 | 9 | | |
| 2011-12 | Hartlepool U | 39 | 8 | | |
| 2012-13 | Hartlepool U | 34 | 1 | 366 | 52 |

## WALTON, Simon (M) — 201 17
H: 6 1 W: 13 05 b.Sherburn-in-Elmet 13-9-87
*Source:* Scholar. *Honours:* England Youth.

| 2004-05 | Leeds U | 30 | 3 | | |
|---|---|---|---|---|---|
| 2005-06 | Leeds U | 4 | 0 | 34 | 3 |
| 2006-07 | Charlton Ath | 0 | 0 | | |
| 2006-07 | *Ipswich T* | 19 | 3 | 19 | 3 |
| 2006-07 | *Cardiff C* | 6 | 0 | 6 | 0 |
| 2007-08 | QPR | 5 | 0 | 5 | 0 |
| 2007-08 | *Hull C* | 10 | 0 | 10 | 0 |
| 2008-09 | Plymouth Arg | 13 | 0 | | |
| 2008-09 | *Blackpool* | 1 | 0 | 1 | 0 |
| 2009-10 | Plymouth Arg | 0 | 0 | | |
| 2009-10 | *Crewe Alex* | 31 | 1 | 31 | 1 |
| 2010-11 | Plymouth Arg | 7 | 1 | | |
| 2010-11 | *Sheffield U* | 0 | 0 | | |
| 2011-12 | Plymouth Arg | 41 | 8 | 61 | 9 |
| 2012-13 | Hartlepool U | 34 | 1 | 34 | 1 |

### Scholars
Bridges, Andrew; Brown, Aaron; Foden, Mark Andrew; Green, Lewis Anthony; Halpin, Connor James; Harbottle, Rhys Lee; Hedley, Kerry Michael; Jones, Daniel John; Mitchinson, Thomas Peter; Nearney, Joshua William; Nellis, Keelan Paul; Scott, Dominic James; Tuck, Ryan James; Turner, Daniel; Walker, Bradley; Wignall, Benjamin Christopher George; Wright, Jonathan.

# HUDDERSFIELD T (41)

## ALLINSON, Lloyd (G) — 0 0
H: 6 2 W: 13 00 b.Rothwell 7-9-93
*Source:* Scholar.

| 2010-11 | Huddersfield T | 0 | 0 | | |
|---|---|---|---|---|---|
| 2011-12 | Huddersfield T | 0 | 0 | | |
| 2012-13 | Huddersfield T | 0 | 0 | | |

## ARFIELD, Scott (M) — 204 20
H: 5 10 W: 10 01 b.Livingston 1-11-88
*Honours:* Scotland Under-21, B.

| 2007-08 | Falkirk | 35 | 3 | | |
|---|---|---|---|---|---|
| 2008-09 | Falkirk | 37 | 7 | | |
| 2009-10 | Falkirk | 36 | 3 | 108 | 13 |
| 2010-11 | Huddersfield T | 40 | 4 | | |
| 2011-12 | Huddersfield T | 35 | 2 | | |
| 2012-13 | Huddersfield T | 21 | 1 | 96 | 7 |

## ATKINSON, Chris (M) — 25 6
H: 6 1 W: 11 13 b.13-2-92
*Source:* Scholar.

| 2010-11 | Huddersfield T | 2 | 0 | | |
|---|---|---|---|---|---|

|  |  | | | | |
|---|---|---|---|---|---|
| 2011-12 | Huddersfield T | 1 | 0 | | |
| 2012-13 | Huddersfield T | 7 | 1 | 10 | 1 |
| 2012-13 | *Chesterfield* | 15 | 5 | 15 | 5 |

### BENNETT, Ian (G) — 448 0
H: 6 0  W: 12 10  b.Worksop 10-10-71
*Source:* Newcastle U Trainee.

|  |  | | | | |
|---|---|---|---|---|---|
| 1991-92 | Peterborough U | 7 | 0 | | |
| 1992-93 | Peterborough U | 46 | 0 | | |
| 1993-94 | Peterborough U | 19 | 0 | 72 | 0 |
| 1993-94 | Birmingham C | 22 | 0 | | |
| 1994-95 | Birmingham C | 46 | 0 | | |
| 1995-96 | Birmingham C | 24 | 0 | | |
| 1996-97 | Birmingham C | 40 | 0 | | |
| 1997-98 | Birmingham C | 45 | 0 | | |
| 1998-99 | Birmingham C | 10 | 0 | | |
| 1999-2000 | Birmingham C | 21 | 0 | | |
| 2000-01 | Birmingham C | 45 | 0 | | |
| 2001-02 | Birmingham C | 18 | 0 | | |
| 2002-03 | Birmingham C | 10 | 0 | | |
| 2003-04 | Birmingham C | 6 | 0 | | |
| 2004-05 | Birmingham C | 0 | 0 | 287 | 0 |
| 2004-05 | *Sheffield U* | 5 | 0 | | |
| 2004-05 | *Coventry C* | 6 | 0 | 6 | 0 |
| 2005-06 | Leeds U | 4 | 0 | | |
| 2006-07 | Leeds U | 0 | 0 | 4 | 0 |
| 2006-07 | Sheffield U | 2 | 0 | | |
| 2007-08 | Sheffield U | 7 | 0 | | |
| 2008-09 | Sheffield U | 2 | 0 | | |
| 2009-10 | Sheffield U | 5 | 0 | 21 | 0 |
| 2010-11 | Huddersfield T | 24 | 0 | | |
| 2011-12 | Huddersfield T | 33 | 0 | | |
| 2012-13 | Huddersfield T | 1 | 0 | 58 | 0 |

### BURKE, James (D) — 0 0
H: 5 11  W: 13 03  b.Shepley 16-4-94

|  |  | | |
|---|---|---|---|
| 2012-13 | Huddersfield T | 0 | 0 |

### CLARKE, Peter (D) — 419 34
H: 6 0  W: 12 00  b.Southport 3-1-82
*Source:* Trainee. *Honours:* England Schools, Youth, Under-20, Under-21.

|  |  | | | | |
|---|---|---|---|---|---|
| 1998-99 | Everton | 0 | 0 | | |
| 1999-2000 | Everton | 0 | 0 | | |
| 2000-01 | Everton | 1 | 0 | | |
| 2001-02 | Everton | 7 | 0 | | |
| 2002-03 | Everton | 0 | 0 | | |
| 2002-03 | *Blackpool* | 16 | 3 | | |
| 2002-03 | *Port Vale* | 13 | 1 | 13 | 1 |
| 2003-04 | Everton | 1 | 0 | | |
| 2003-04 | *Coventry C* | 5 | 0 | 5 | 0 |
| 2004-05 | Everton | 0 | 0 | 9 | 0 |
| 2004-05 | Blackpool | 38 | 5 | | |
| 2005-06 | Blackpool | 46 | 6 | 100 | 14 |
| 2006-07 | Southend U | 38 | 2 | | |
| 2007-08 | Southend U | 45 | 4 | | |
| 2008-09 | Southend U | 43 | 4 | 126 | 10 |
| 2009-10 | Huddersfield T | 46 | 5 | | |
| 2010-11 | Huddersfield T | 46 | 4 | | |
| 2011-12 | Huddersfield T | 31 | 0 | | |
| 2012-13 | Huddersfield T | 43 | 0 | 166 | 9 |

### CLARKE, Tom (D) — 112 3
H: 6 0  W: 11 02  b.Sowerby Bridge 21-12-87
*Source:* Scholar. *Honours:* England Youth.

|  |  | | | | |
|---|---|---|---|---|---|
| 2004-05 | Huddersfield T | 12 | 0 | | |
| 2005-06 | Huddersfield T | 17 | 1 | | |
| 2006-07 | Huddersfield T | 9 | 0 | | |
| 2007-08 | Huddersfield T | 3 | 0 | | |
| 2008-09 | Huddersfield T | 15 | 1 | | |
| 2008-09 | *Bradford C* | 6 | 0 | 6 | 0 |
| 2009-10 | Huddersfield T | 21 | 0 | | |
| 2010-11 | Huddersfield T | 5 | 1 | | |
| 2011-12 | Huddersfield T | 14 | 0 | | |
| 2011-12 | *Leyton Orient* | 10 | 0 | 10 | 0 |
| 2012-13 | Huddersfield T | 0 | 0 | 96 | 3 |

### CLAYTON, Adam (M) — 131 12
H: 5 9  W: 11 11  b.Manchester 14-1-89
*Source:* Scholar. *Honours:* England Under-20.

|  |  | | | | |
|---|---|---|---|---|---|
| 2007-08 | Manchester C | 0 | 0 | | |
| 2008-09 | Manchester C | 0 | 0 | | |
| 2009-10 | Manchester C | 0 | 0 | | |
| 2009-10 | *Carlisle U* | 28 | 1 | 28 | 1 |
| 2010-11 | Leeds U | 4 | 0 | | |
| 2010-11 | *Peterborough U* | 7 | 0 | 7 | 0 |
| 2010-11 | *Milton Keynes D* | 6 | 1 | 6 | 1 |
| 2011-12 | Leeds U | 43 | 6 | 47 | 6 |
| 2012-13 | Huddersfield T | 43 | 4 | 43 | 4 |

### COLGAN, Nick (G) — 283 0
H: 6 1  W: 12 00  b.Drogheda 19-9-73
*Source:* Drogheda. *Honours:* Eire Schools, Youth, Under-21, B, 9 full caps.

|  |  | | | | |
|---|---|---|---|---|---|
| 1992-93 | Chelsea | 0 | 0 | | |
| 1993-94 | Chelsea | 0 | 0 | | |
| 1993-94 | *Crewe Alex* | 0 | 0 | | |
| 1994-95 | Chelsea | 0 | 0 | | |
| 1994-95 | *Grimsby T* | 0 | 0 | | |
| 1995-96 | Chelsea | 0 | 0 | | |
| 1995-96 | *Millwall* | 0 | 0 | | |
| 1996-97 | Chelsea | 1 | 0 | | |
| 1997-98 | Chelsea | 0 | 0 | 1 | 0 |
| 1997-98 | *Brentford* | 5 | 0 | 5 | 0 |
| 1997-98 | *Reading* | 5 | 0 | 5 | 0 |
| 1998-99 | Bournemouth | 0 | 0 | | |
| 1999-2000 | Hibernian | 24 | 0 | | |
| 2000-01 | Hibernian | 37 | 0 | | |
| 2001-02 | Hibernian | 30 | 0 | | |
| 2002-03 | Hibernian | 30 | 0 | | |
| 2003-04 | Hibernian | 0 | 0 | 121 | 0 |
| 2003-04 | *Stockport Co* | 15 | 0 | 15 | 0 |
| 2004-05 | Barnsley | 13 | 0 | | |
| 2005-06 | Barnsley | 43 | 0 | | |
| 2006-07 | Barnsley | 44 | 0 | | |
| 2007-08 | Barnsley | 1 | 0 | 101 | 0 |
| 2007-08 | Ipswich T | 0 | 0 | | |
| 2008-09 | Sunderland | 0 | 0 | | |
| 2009-10 | Grimsby T | 35 | 0 | 35 | 0 |
| 2011-12 | Huddersfield T | 0 | 0 | | |
| 2012-13 | Huddersfield T | 0 | 0 | | |

### CROOKS, Matt (M) — 0 0
H: 6 0  W: 11 05  b.Leeds 20-1-94
*Source:* Scholar.

|  |  | | |
|---|---|---|---|
| 2011-12 | Huddersfield T | 0 | 0 |
| 2012-13 | Huddersfield T | 0 | 0 |

### DIXON, Paul (D) — 250 6
H: 5 9  W: 11 01  b.Aberdeen 11-10-86
*Honours:* Scotland Under-21, 3 full caps.

|  |  | | | | |
|---|---|---|---|---|---|
| 2005-06 | Dundee | 29 | 2 | | |
| 2006-07 | Dundee | 33 | 0 | | |
| 2007-08 | Dundee | 30 | 0 | 92 | 2 |
| 2008-09 | Dundee U | 29 | 1 | | |
| 2009-10 | Dundee U | 25 | 0 | | |
| 2010-11 | Dundee U | 30 | 0 | | |
| 2011-12 | Dundee U | 37 | 3 | 121 | 4 |
| 2012-13 | Huddersfield T | 37 | 0 | 37 | 0 |

### GERRARD, Anthony (D) — 301 16
H: 6 2  W: 13 07  b.Huyton 6-2-86
*Source:* Scholar. *Honours:* Eire Youth.

|  |  | | | | |
|---|---|---|---|---|---|
| 2004-05 | Everton | 0 | 0 | | |
| 2004-05 | *Walsall* | 8 | 0 | | |
| 2005-06 | Walsall | 34 | 0 | | |
| 2006-07 | Walsall | 35 | 1 | | |
| 2007-08 | Walsall | 44 | 3 | | |
| 2008-09 | Walsall | 42 | 3 | 163 | 7 |
| 2009-10 | Cardiff C | 39 | 2 | | |
| 2010-11 | Cardiff C | 0 | 0 | | |
| 2010-11 | *Hull C* | 41 | 5 | 41 | 5 |
| 2011-12 | Cardiff C | 20 | 1 | | |
| 2012-13 | Cardiff C | 0 | 0 | 59 | 3 |
| 2012-13 | Huddersfield T | 38 | 1 | 38 | 1 |

### GOBERN, Oscar (M) — 59 3
H: 5 11  W: 10 10  b.Birmingham 26-1-91
*Source:* Scholar. *Honours:* England Youth.

|  |  | | | | |
|---|---|---|---|---|---|
| 2008-09 | Southampton | 6 | 0 | | |
| 2009-10 | Southampton | 0 | 0 | | |
| 2009-10 | *Milton Keynes D* | 2 | 0 | 2 | 0 |
| 2010-11 | Southampton | 11 | 1 | 21 | 1 |
| 2011-12 | Huddersfield T | 21 | 2 | | |
| 2012-13 | Huddersfield T | 15 | 0 | 36 | 2 |

### HIGGINBOTHAM, Kallum (M) — 160 15
H: 5 11  W: 10 10  b.Manchester 15-6-89

|  |  | | | | |
|---|---|---|---|---|---|
| 2007-08 | Rochdale | 33 | 3 | | |
| 2008-09 | Rochdale | 7 | 1 | | |
| 2008-09 | *Accrington S* | 12 | 0 | 12 | 0 |
| 2009-10 | Rochdale | 29 | 3 | 69 | 7 |
| 2010-11 | Falkirk | 30 | 2 | | |
| 2011-12 | Falkirk | 20 | 5 | 50 | 7 |
| 2011-12 | Huddersfield T | 4 | 0 | | |
| 2011-12 | *Barnsley* | 5 | 0 | 5 | 0 |
| 2012-13 | Huddersfield T | 0 | 0 | 4 | 0 |

|  |  | | | | |
|---|---|---|---|---|---|
| 2012-13 | *Carlisle U* | 10 | 0 | 10 | 0 |
| 2012-13 | *Motherwell* | 10 | 1 | 10 | 1 |

### HUNT, Jack (D) — 122 2
H: 5 9  W: 11 02  b.Rothwell 6-12-90
*Source:* Scholar.

|  |  | | | | |
|---|---|---|---|---|---|
| 2009-10 | Huddersfield T | 0 | 0 | | |
| 2010-11 | Huddersfield T | 19 | 1 | | |
| 2010-11 | *Chesterfield* | 20 | 0 | 20 | 0 |
| 2011-12 | Huddersfield T | 43 | 1 | | |
| 2012-13 | Huddersfield T | 40 | 0 | 102 | 2 |

### LEE, Alan (F) — 481 103
H: 6 2  W: 13 09  b.Galway 21-8-78
*Source:* Trainee. *Honours:* Eire Under-21, 10 full caps.

|  |  | | | | |
|---|---|---|---|---|---|
| 1995-96 | Aston Villa | 0 | 0 | | |
| 1996-97 | Aston Villa | 0 | 0 | | |
| 1997-98 | Aston Villa | 0 | 0 | | |
| 1998-99 | Aston Villa | 0 | 0 | | |
| 1998-99 | *Torquay U* | 7 | 2 | 7 | 2 |
| 1998-99 | *Port Vale* | 11 | 2 | 11 | 2 |
| 1999-2000 | Burnley | 15 | 0 | | |
| 2000-01 | Burnley | 0 | 0 | 15 | 0 |
| 2000-01 | Rotherham U | 31 | 13 | | |
| 2001-02 | Rotherham U | 38 | 9 | | |
| 2002-03 | Rotherham U | 41 | 15 | | |
| 2003-04 | Rotherham U | 1 | 0 | 111 | 37 |
| 2003-04 | Cardiff C | 23 | 3 | | |
| 2004-05 | Cardiff C | 38 | 5 | | |
| 2005-06 | Cardiff C | 25 | 2 | 86 | 10 |
| 2005-06 | Ipswich T | 14 | 4 | | |
| 2006-07 | Ipswich T | 41 | 16 | | |
| 2007-08 | Ipswich T | 45 | 11 | | |
| 2008-09 | Ipswich T | 3 | 0 | 103 | 31 |
| 2008-09 | Crystal Palace | 16 | 3 | | |
| 2008-09 | *Norwich C* | 7 | 2 | 7 | 2 |
| 2009-10 | Crystal Palace | 42 | 6 | | |
| 2010-11 | Crystal Palace | 3 | 1 | 61 | 10 |
| 2010-11 | Huddersfield T | 28 | 0 | | |
| 2011-12 | Huddersfield T | 31 | 7 | | |
| 2012-13 | Huddersfield T | 21 | 2 | 80 | 9 |

### LEONARD, Max (F) — 0 0
H: 5 10  W: 11 01  b.Longwood 4-7-94

|  |  | | |
|---|---|---|---|
| 2012-13 | Huddersfield T | 0 | 0 |

### LYNCH, Joel (D) — 181 6
H: 6 1  W: 12 10  b.Eastbourne 3-10-87
*Source:* Scholar. *Honours:* England Youth, Wales 1 full cap.

|  |  | | | | |
|---|---|---|---|---|---|
| 2005-06 | Brighton & HA | 16 | 1 | | |
| 2006-07 | Brighton & HA | 39 | 0 | | |
| 2007-08 | Brighton & HA | 22 | 1 | | |
| 2008-09 | Brighton & HA | 2 | 0 | 79 | 2 |
| 2008-09 | *Nottingham F* | 23 | 0 | | |
| 2009-10 | Nottingham F | 10 | 0 | | |
| 2010-11 | Nottingham F | 12 | 0 | | |
| 2011-12 | Nottingham F | 35 | 3 | 80 | 3 |
| 2012-13 | Huddersfield T | 22 | 1 | 22 | 1 |

### NORWOOD, Oliver (M) — 78 6
H: 5 11  W: 11 13  b.Burnley 12-4-91
*Source:* Scholar. *Honours:* Northern Ireland Youth, Under-21, 9 full caps.

|  |  | | | | |
|---|---|---|---|---|---|
| 2009-10 | Manchester U | 0 | 0 | | |
| 2010-11 | Manchester U | 0 | 0 | | |
| 2010-11 | *Carlisle U* | 6 | 0 | 6 | 0 |
| 2011-12 | Manchester U | 0 | 0 | | |
| 2011-12 | *Scunthorpe U* | 15 | 1 | 15 | 1 |
| 2011-12 | *Coventry C* | 18 | 2 | 18 | 2 |
| 2012-13 | Huddersfield T | 39 | 3 | 39 | 3 |

### NOVAK, Lee (F) — 144 34
H: 6 0  W: 12 04  b.Newcastle 28-9-88
*Source:* Gateshead.

|  |  | | | | |
|---|---|---|---|---|---|
| 2008-09 | Huddersfield T | 0 | 0 | | |
| 2009-10 | Huddersfield T | 37 | 12 | | |
| 2010-11 | Huddersfield T | 31 | 5 | | |
| 2011-12 | Huddersfield T | 41 | 13 | | |
| 2012-13 | Huddersfield T | 35 | 4 | 144 | 34 |

### RIDEHALGH, Liam (D) — 85 1
H: 5 10  W: 11 05  b.Halifax 20-4-91
*Source:* Scholar.

|  |  | | | | |
|---|---|---|---|---|---|
| 2009-10 | Huddersfield T | 0 | 0 | | |
| 2010-11 | Huddersfield T | 20 | 0 | | |
| 2011-12 | Huddersfield T | 0 | 0 | | |
| 2011-12 | *Swindon T* | 11 | 0 | 11 | 0 |
| 2011-12 | *Chesterfield* | 20 | 1 | | |

| | | | |
|---|---|---|---|
| 2012-13 | Huddersfield T | 0 | 0 | 20 | 0 |
| 2012-13 | *Chesterfield* | 14 | 0 | 34 | 1 |
| 2012-13 | *Rotherham U* | 20 | 0 | 20 | 0 |

**ROBINSON, Anton (M)**                    147  11
H: 5 9   W: 10 03   b.Harrow 17-2-86
Source: Millwall Scholar.

| 2004-05 | Millwall | 0 | 0 | | |
| 2005-06 | Millwall | 0 | 0 | | |

From Ex C, Eastb B, Fish A, Weymouth.

| 2008-09 | Bournemouth | 17 | 1 | | |
| 2009-10 | Bournemouth | 44 | 4 | | |
| 2010-11 | Bournemouth | 45 | 5 | 106 | 10 |
| 2011-12 | Huddersfield T | 25 | 1 | | |
| 2012-13 | Huddersfield T | 2 | 0 | 27 | 1 |
| 2012-13 | *Gillingham* | 14 | 0 | 14 | 0 |

**SCANNELL, Sean (F)**                    164  14
H: 5 9   W: 11 07   b.Croydon 19-9-90
Source: Scholar. Honours: Eire Youth, Under-21.

| 2007-08 | Crystal Palace | 23 | 2 | | |
| 2008-09 | Crystal Palace | 25 | 2 | | |
| 2009-10 | Crystal Palace | 26 | 2 | | |
| 2010-11 | Crystal Palace | 19 | 2 | | |
| 2011-12 | Crystal Palace | 37 | 4 | 130 | 12 |
| 2012-13 | Huddersfield T | 34 | 2 | 34 | 2 |

**SINNOTT, Jordan (M)**                    1  0
H: 5 11   W: 11 12   b. 14-2-94

| 2012-13 | Huddersfield T | 1 | 0 | 1 | 0 |

**SMITH, Tommy (D)**                    0  0
b. 14-4-92

| 2012-13 | Huddersfield T | 0 | 0 | | |

**SMITHIES, Alex (G)**                    156  0
H: 6 1   W: 10 01   b.Huddersfield 25-3-90
Source: Scholar. Honours: England Youth.

| 2006-07 | Huddersfield T | 0 | 0 | | |
| 2007-08 | Huddersfield T | 2 | 0 | | |
| 2008-09 | Huddersfield T | 27 | 0 | | |
| 2009-10 | Huddersfield T | 46 | 0 | | |
| 2010-11 | Huddersfield T | 22 | 0 | | |
| 2011-12 | Huddersfield T | 13 | 0 | | |
| 2012-13 | Huddersfield T | 46 | 0 | 156 | 0 |

**SOUTHERN, Keith (M)**                    359  26
H: 5 10   W: 12 06   b.Gateshead 24-4-81
Source: Trainee.

| 1998-99 | Everton | 0 | 0 | | |
| 1999-2000 | Everton | 0 | 0 | | |
| 2000-01 | Everton | 0 | 0 | | |
| 2001-02 | Everton | 0 | 0 | | |
| 2002-03 | Everton | 0 | 0 | | |
| 2002-03 | Blackpool | 38 | 1 | | |
| 2003-04 | Blackpool | 28 | 2 | | |
| 2004-05 | Blackpool | 27 | 6 | | |
| 2005-06 | Blackpool | 42 | 2 | | |
| 2006-07 | Blackpool | 39 | 5 | | |
| 2007-08 | Blackpool | 30 | 3 | | |
| 2008-09 | Blackpool | 35 | 3 | | |
| 2009-10 | Blackpool | 45 | 2 | | |
| 2010-11 | Blackpool | 21 | 0 | | |
| 2011-12 | Blackpool | 25 | 1 | 330 | 25 |
| 2012-13 | Huddersfield T | 29 | 1 | 29 | 1 |

**SPENCER, James (F)**                    76  18
H: 6 1   W: 13 00   b.Leeds 13-12-91
Source: Scholar.

| 2008-09 | Huddersfield T | 0 | 0 | | |
| 2009-10 | Huddersfield T | 0 | 0 | | |
| 2010-11 | Huddersfield T | 0 | 0 | | |
| 2010-11 | *Morecambe* | 32 | 8 | 32 | 8 |
| 2011-12 | Huddersfield T | 0 | 0 | | |
| 2011-12 | *Cheltenham T* | 41 | 10 | 41 | 10 |
| 2012-13 | Huddersfield T | 1 | 0 | 1 | 0 |
| 2012-13 | *Brentford* | 2 | 0 | 2 | 0 |

**WALLACE, Murray (D)**                    25  3
H: 6 2   W: 11 07   b.Glasgow 10-1-93
Honours: Scotland Under-20, Under-21.

| 2011-12 | Falkirk | 19 | 2 | 19 | 2 |
| 2011-12 | Huddersfield T | 0 | 0 | | |
| 2012-13 | Huddersfield T | 6 | 1 | 6 | 1 |

**WARD, Danny (M)**                    109  16
H: 5 11   W: 12 05   b.Bradford 11-12-91
Source: Leeds U.

| 2008-09 | Bolton W | 0 | 0 | | |
| 2009-10 | Bolton W | 2 | 0 | | |

| | | | |
|---|---|---|---|
| 2009-10 | *Swindon T* | 28 | 7 | 28 | 7 |
| 2010-11 | Bolton W | 0 | 0 | 2 | 0 |
| 2010-11 | *Coventry C* | 5 | 0 | 5 | 0 |
| 2010-11 | Huddersfield T | 7 | 3 | | |
| 2011-12 | Huddersfield T | 39 | 4 | | |
| 2012-13 | Huddersfield T | 28 | 2 | 74 | 9 |

**WOODS, Calum (D)**                    181  10
H: 5 11   W: 11 07   b.Liverpool 5-2-87
Source: Liverpool Scholar. Honours: England Youth.

| 2006-07 | Dunfermline Ath | 12 | 0 | | |
| 2007-08 | Dunfermline Ath | 25 | 0 | | |
| 2008-09 | Dunfermline Ath | 30 | 5 | | |
| 2009-10 | Dunfermline Ath | 29 | 2 | | |
| 2010-11 | Dunfermline Ath | 32 | 3 | 128 | 10 |
| 2011-12 | Huddersfield T | 26 | 0 | | |
| 2012-13 | Huddersfield T | 27 | 0 | 53 | 0 |

**Players retained or with offer of contract**
Charles, Jake David; Hopson, Dale Anthony; McIntyre, Robbie; Mullin, Paul Philip.

**Scholars**
Boyle, William Sam Douglas Harry; Briggs, Thomas; Cham, Hatib; Conway, George Thomas; Cox, Ryan John Timothy; Goddard, Kedesh Malachi; Guthrie, Sam Alan; Holmes, Benjamin; Holmes, Duane Octavious; Morton, Daniel; Muhamed, Nawfal; Starkey, Michael Jay; Turner, Jacob Liam; Wilczynski, Edward William; Wilkinson, Joseph; Wright, Joseph Harris.

## HULL C (42)

**ALUKO, Sone (M)**                    147  30
H: 5 8   W: 9 10   b.Birmingham 19-2-89
Source: Scholar. Honours: England Schools, Youth, Nigeria 3 full caps.

| 2005-06 | Birmingham C | 0 | 0 | | |
| 2006-07 | Birmingham C | 0 | 0 | | |
| 2007-08 | Birmingham C | 0 | 0 | | |
| 2007-08 | *Aberdeen* | 20 | 3 | | |
| 2008-09 | Birmingham C | 0 | 0 | | |
| 2008-09 | *Blackpool* | 1 | 0 | 1 | 0 |
| 2008-09 | Aberdeen | 32 | 2 | | |
| 2009-10 | Aberdeen | 22 | 3 | | |
| 2010-11 | Aberdeen | 28 | 2 | 102 | 10 |
| 2011-12 | Rangers | 21 | 12 | 21 | 12 |
| 2012-13 | Hull C | 23 | 8 | 23 | 8 |

**ARMSTRONG, James (M)**                    0  0
b.Sunderland 10-5-93
Source: Scholar.

| 2011-12 | Sunderland | 0 | 0 | | |
| 2012-13 | Sunderland | 0 | 0 | | |
| 2012-13 | Hull C | 0 | 0 | | |

**BRADLEY, Sonny (D)**                    58  1
H: 6 0   W: 11 05   b.Hedon 14-6-92
Source: Scholar.

| 2011-12 | Hull C | 2 | 0 | | |
| 2011-12 | *Aldershot T* | 14 | 0 | | |
| 2012-13 | Hull C | 0 | 0 | 2 | 0 |
| 2012-13 | *Aldershot T* | 42 | 1 | 56 | 1 |

**BRADY, Robert (M)**                    71  7
H: 5 9   W: 10 12   b.Belfast 14-1-92
Source: Scholar. Honours: Eire Youth, Under-21, 5 full caps, 1 goal.

| 2008-09 | Manchester U | 0 | 0 | | |
| 2009-10 | Manchester U | 0 | 0 | | |
| 2010-11 | Manchester U | 0 | 0 | | |
| 2011-12 | Manchester U | 0 | 0 | | |
| 2011-12 | *Hull C* | 39 | 3 | | |
| 2012-13 | Manchester U | 0 | 0 | | |
| 2012-13 | Hull C | 32 | 4 | 71 | 7 |

**BRUCE, Alex (D)**                    217  3
H: 6 0   W: 11 06   b.Norwich 28-9-84
Source: Trainee. Honours: Eire B, Under-21, 2 full caps, Northern Ireland 1 full cap.

| 2002-03 | Blackburn R | 0 | 0 | | |
| 2003-04 | Blackburn R | 0 | 0 | | |
| 2004-05 | Blackburn R | 0 | 0 | | |
| 2004-05 | *Oldham Ath* | 12 | 0 | 12 | 0 |
| 2004-05 | Birmingham C | 0 | 0 | | |
| 2004-05 | *Sheffield W* | 6 | 0 | 6 | 0 |

| | | | |
|---|---|---|---|
| 2005-06 | Birmingham C | 6 | 0 | 6 | 0 |
| 2005-06 | *Tranmere R* | 11 | 0 | 11 | 0 |
| 2006-07 | Ipswich T | 41 | 0 | | |
| 2007-08 | Ipswich T | 36 | 0 | | |
| 2008-09 | Ipswich T | 25 | 1 | | |
| 2009-10 | Ipswich T | 13 | 1 | | |
| 2009-10 | *Leicester C* | 3 | 0 | 3 | 0 |
| 2010-11 | Ipswich T | 0 | 0 | 115 | 2 |
| 2010-11 | Leeds U | 21 | 1 | | |
| 2011-12 | Leeds U | 8 | 0 | 29 | 1 |
| 2011-12 | *Huddersfield T* | 3 | 0 | 3 | 0 |
| 2012-13 | Hull C | 32 | 0 | 32 | 0 |

**CAIRNEY, Tom (M)**                    70  2
H: 6 0   W: 11 05   b.Nottingham 20-1-91
Source: Scholar. Honours: Scotland Youth, Under-21.

| 2009-10 | Hull C | 11 | 1 | | |
| 2010-11 | Hull C | 22 | 1 | | |
| 2011-12 | Hull C | 27 | 0 | | |
| 2012-13 | Hull C | 10 | 0 | 70 | 2 |

**CHESTER, James (D)**                    135  6
H: 5 11   W: 11 04   b.Warrington 23-1-89
Source: Scholar.

| 2007-08 | Manchester U | 0 | 0 | | |
| 2008-09 | Manchester U | 0 | 0 | | |
| 2008-09 | *Peterborough U* | 5 | 0 | 5 | 0 |
| 2009-10 | Manchester U | 0 | 0 | | |
| 2009-10 | *Plymouth Arg* | 3 | 0 | 3 | 0 |
| 2010-11 | Manchester U | 0 | 0 | | |
| 2010-11 | *Carlisle U* | 18 | 2 | 18 | 2 |
| 2010-11 | Hull C | 21 | 1 | | |
| 2011-12 | Hull C | 44 | 2 | | |
| 2012-13 | Hull C | 44 | 1 | 109 | 4 |

**CULLEN, Mark (F)**                    42  2
H: 5 9   W: 11 11   b.Ashington 24-4-92
Source: Scholar.

| 2009-10 | Hull C | 3 | 1 | | |
| 2010-11 | Hull C | 17 | 0 | | |
| 2010-11 | *Bradford C* | 4 | 0 | 4 | 0 |
| 2011-12 | Hull C | 4 | 0 | | |
| 2011-12 | *Bury* | 4 | 0 | | |
| 2012-13 | Hull C | 0 | 0 | 24 | 1 |
| 2012-13 | *Bury* | 10 | 1 | 14 | 1 |

**DAWSON, Andy (D)**                    488  16
H: 5 9   W: 11 02   b.Leyburn 20-10-78
Source: Trainee.

| 1995-96 | Nottingham F | 0 | 0 | | |
| 1996-97 | Nottingham F | 0 | 0 | | |
| 1997-98 | Nottingham F | 0 | 0 | | |
| 1998-99 | Nottingham F | 0 | 0 | | |
| 1998-99 | Scunthorpe U | 24 | 0 | | |
| 1999-2000 | Scunthorpe U | 43 | 2 | | |
| 2000-01 | Scunthorpe U | 41 | 4 | | |
| 2001-02 | Scunthorpe U | 44 | 0 | | |
| 2002-03 | Scunthorpe U | 43 | 2 | 195 | 8 |
| 2003-04 | Hull C | 33 | 3 | | |
| 2004-05 | Hull C | 34 | 0 | | |
| 2005-06 | Hull C | 18 | 0 | | |
| 2006-07 | Hull C | 38 | 2 | | |
| 2007-08 | Hull C | 29 | 1 | | |
| 2008-09 | Hull C | 25 | 1 | | |
| 2009-10 | Hull C | 35 | 1 | | |
| 2010-11 | Hull C | 45 | 0 | | |
| 2011-12 | Hull C | 32 | 0 | | |
| 2012-13 | Hull C | 4 | 0 | 293 | 8 |

**DEVITT, Jamie (F)**                    70  11
H: 5 10   W: 10 05   b.Dublin 6-7-90
Source: Cherry Orchard BC, Hull C Scholar. Honours: Eire Youth, Under-21.

| 2007-08 | Hull C | 0 | 0 | | |
| 2008-09 | Hull C | 0 | 0 | | |
| 2009-10 | Hull C | 0 | 0 | | |
| 2009-10 | *Darlington* | 6 | 1 | 6 | 1 |
| 2009-10 | *Shrewsbury T* | 9 | 2 | 9 | 2 |
| 2009-10 | *Grimsby T* | 15 | 5 | 15 | 5 |
| 2010-11 | Hull C | 16 | 0 | | |
| 2011-12 | Hull C | 0 | 0 | | |
| 2011-12 | *Bradford C* | 7 | 1 | 7 | 1 |
| 2011-12 | *Accrington S* | 16 | 2 | 16 | 2 |
| 2012-13 | Hull C | 0 | 0 | 16 | 0 |
| 2012-13 | *Rotherham U* | 1 | 0 | 1 | 0 |

**DUDGEON, Joe (D)** 35 0
H: 5 9  W: 11 02  b.Leeds 26-11-90
*Source:* Scholar. *Honours:* Northern Ireland Under-21.

| | | | | | |
|---|---|---|---|---|---|
| 2009-10 | Manchester U | 0 | 0 | | |
| 2010-11 | Manchester U | 0 | 0 | | |
| 2010-11 | *Carlisle U* | 2 | 0 | 2 | 0 |
| 2011-12 | Hull C | 24 | 0 | | |
| 2012-13 | Hull C | 9 | 0 | 33 | 0 |

**EVANS, Corry (M)** 94 6
H: 5 8  W: 10 12  b.Belfast 30-7-90
*Source:* Scholar. *Honours:* Northern Ireland Under-21, B, 18 full caps, 1 goal.

| | | | | | |
|---|---|---|---|---|---|
| 2007-08 | Manchester U | 0 | 0 | | |
| 2008-09 | Manchester U | 0 | 0 | | |
| 2009-10 | Manchester U | 0 | 0 | | |
| 2010-11 | Manchester U | 0 | 0 | | |
| 2010-11 | *Carlisle U* | 1 | 0 | 1 | 0 |
| 2010-11 | *Hull C* | 18 | 3 | | |
| 2011-12 | Hull C | 43 | 2 | | |
| 2012-13 | Hull C | 32 | 1 | 93 | 6 |

**FATHI, Ahmed (D)** 50 6
H: 5 9  W: 11 06  b.Cairo 10-11-84
*Source:* Ismaily SC. *Honours:* Egypt Youth, 97 full caps, 3 goals.

| | | | | | |
|---|---|---|---|---|---|
| 2006-07 | Sheffield U | 3 | 0 | 3 | 0 |
| 2010-11 | Al Ahly Cairo | 26 | 4 | | |
| 2011-12 | Al Ahly Cairo | 14 | 2 | 40 | 6 |

On loan from Al Ahly Cairo

| | | | | | |
|---|---|---|---|---|---|
| 2012-13 | Hull C | 7 | 0 | 7 | 0 |

**FAYE, Aboulaye (M)** 317 18
H: 6 2  W: 13 10  b.Dakar 26-2-78
*Source:* Ndiambour Louga. *Honours:* Senegal 35 full caps, 3 goals.

| | | | | | |
|---|---|---|---|---|---|
| 2001-02 | Jeanne D'Arc | 32 | 4 | 32 | 4 |
| 2002-03 | Lens | 15 | 0 | | |
| 2003-04 | Lens | 19 | 0 | 34 | 0 |
| 2004-05 | Istres | 28 | 0 | 28 | 0 |
| 2005-06 | Bolton W | 27 | 1 | | |
| 2006-07 | Bolton W | 32 | 2 | | |
| 2007-08 | Bolton W | 1 | 0 | 60 | 3 |
| 2007-08 | Newcastle U | 22 | 1 | 22 | 1 |
| 2008-09 | Stoke C | 36 | 3 | | |
| 2009-10 | Stoke C | 31 | 2 | | |
| 2010-11 | Stoke C | 14 | 1 | 81 | 6 |
| 2011-12 | West Ham U | 29 | 0 | 29 | 0 |
| 2012-13 | Hull C | 31 | 4 | 31 | 4 |

**FRYATT, Matty (F)** 320 104
H: 5 10  W: 11 00  b.Nuneaton 5-3-86
*Source:* Scholar. *Honours:* England Youth.

| | | | | | |
|---|---|---|---|---|---|
| 2002-03 | Walsall | 0 | 0 | | |
| 2003-04 | Walsall | 11 | 1 | | |
| 2003-04 | *Carlisle U* | 10 | 1 | 10 | 1 |
| 2004-05 | Walsall | 36 | 15 | | |
| 2005-06 | Walsall | 23 | 11 | 70 | 27 |
| 2005-06 | Leicester C | 19 | 6 | | |
| 2006-07 | Leicester C | 32 | 3 | | |
| 2007-08 | Leicester C | 30 | 2 | | |
| 2008-09 | Leicester C | 46 | 27 | | |
| 2009-10 | Leicester C | 29 | 11 | | |
| 2010-11 | Leicester C | 12 | 2 | 168 | 51 |
| 2010-11 | Hull C | 22 | 9 | | |
| 2011-12 | Hull C | 46 | 16 | | |
| 2012-13 | Hull C | 4 | 0 | 72 | 25 |

**GEDO, Mohamed (F)** 50 17
b.Damanhur 30-10-84
*Honours:* Egypt 31 full caps, 17 goals.

| | | | | | |
|---|---|---|---|---|---|
| 2010-11 | Al Ahly Cairo | 24 | 8 | | |
| 2011-12 | Al Ahly Cairo | 14 | 4 | 38 | 12 |
| 2012-13 | Hull C | 12 | 5 | 12 | 5 |

**HOBBS, Jack (D)** 201 3
H: 6 3  W: 13 05  b.Portsmouth 18-8-88
*Source:* Scholar. *Honours:* England Youth.

| | | | | | |
|---|---|---|---|---|---|
| 2004-05 | Lincoln C | 1 | 0 | 1 | 0 |
| 2005-06 | Liverpool | 0 | 0 | | |
| 2006-07 | Liverpool | 0 | 0 | | |
| 2007-08 | Liverpool | 2 | 0 | | |
| 2007-08 | *Scunthorpe U* | 9 | 1 | 9 | 1 |
| 2008-09 | Liverpool | 0 | 0 | 2 | 0 |
| 2008-09 | Leicester C | 44 | 1 | | |
| 2009-10 | Leicester C | 44 | 0 | | |
| 2010-11 | Leicester C | 26 | 0 | 114 | 1 |
| 2010-11 | *Hull C* | 13 | 0 | | |

| | | | | | |
|---|---|---|---|---|---|
| 2011-12 | Hull C | 40 | 1 | | |
| 2012-13 | Hull C | 22 | 0 | 75 | 1 |

**JAKUPOVIC, Eldin (G)** 118 1
H: 6 3  W: 13 00  b.Kozarac 2-10-84

| | | | | | |
|---|---|---|---|---|---|
| 2004-05 | Grasshoppers | 8 | 0 | | |
| 2005-06 | FC Thun | 23 | 0 | 23 | 0 |
| 2007-08 | Grasshoppers | 23 | 1 | | |
| 2008-09 | Grasshoppers | 32 | 0 | 63 | 1 |
| 2010-11 | Olympiacos Volou | 26 | 0 | 26 | 0 |
| 2011-12 | Aris Salonika | 1 | 0 | 1 | 0 |
| 2012-13 | Hull C | 5 | 0 | 5 | 0 |

**KOREN, Robert (M)** 463 94
H: 5 10  W: 11 03  b.Ljubljana 20-9-80
*Honours:* Slovenia Under-21, 61 full caps, 5 goals.

| | | | | | |
|---|---|---|---|---|---|
| 1999-2000 | Dravograd | 31 | 2 | | |
| 2000-01 | Dravograd | 31 | 9 | 62 | 11 |
| 2001-02 | Publikum | 31 | 5 | | |
| 2002-03 | Publikum | 32 | 12 | | |
| 2003-04 | Publikum | 15 | 5 | 78 | 22 |
| 2004 | Lillestrom | 23 | 1 | | |
| 2005 | Lillestrom | 26 | 8 | | |
| 2006 | Lillestrom | 26 | 10 | 75 | 19 |
| 2006-07 | WBA | 18 | 1 | | |
| 2007-08 | WBA | 40 | 9 | | |
| 2008-09 | WBA | 35 | 1 | | |
| 2009-10 | WBA | 34 | 5 | 127 | 16 |
| 2010-11 | Hull C | 40 | 7 | | |
| 2011-12 | Hull C | 41 | 10 | | |
| 2012-13 | Hull C | 40 | 9 | 121 | 26 |

**McKENNA, Paul (M)** 554 33
H: 5 7  W: 11 12  b.Eccleston 20-10-77
*Source:* Trainee.

| | | | | | |
|---|---|---|---|---|---|
| 1995-96 | Preston NE | 0 | 0 | | |
| 1996-97 | Preston NE | 5 | 1 | | |
| 1997-98 | Preston NE | 5 | 0 | | |
| 1998-99 | Preston NE | 36 | 0 | | |
| 1999-2000 | Preston NE | 24 | 2 | | |
| 2000-01 | Preston NE | 44 | 5 | | |
| 2001-02 | Preston NE | 38 | 4 | | |
| 2002-03 | Preston NE | 41 | 3 | | |
| 2003-04 | Preston NE | 39 | 6 | | |
| 2004-05 | Preston NE | 39 | 3 | | |
| 2005-06 | Preston NE | 41 | 2 | | |
| 2006-07 | Preston NE | 33 | 2 | | |
| 2007-08 | Preston NE | 33 | 0 | | |
| 2008-09 | Preston NE | 34 | 2 | 422 | 30 |
| 2009-10 | Nottingham F | 35 | 1 | | |
| 2010-11 | Nottingham F | 32 | 2 | 67 | 3 |
| 2011-12 | Hull C | 41 | 0 | | |
| 2012-13 | Hull C | 9 | 0 | 50 | 0 |
| 2012-13 | *Fleetwood T* | 15 | 0 | 15 | 0 |

**McLEAN, Aaron (F)** 280 83
H: 5 9  W: 10 10  b.Hammersmith 25-5-83
*Source:* Trainee.

| | | | | | |
|---|---|---|---|---|---|
| 1999-2000 | Leyton Orient | 3 | 0 | | |
| 2000-01 | Leyton Orient | 2 | 1 | | |
| 2001-02 | Leyton Orient | 27 | 1 | | |
| 2002-03 | Leyton Orient | 8 | 0 | 40 | 2 |

From Aldershot T, Grays Ath.

| | | | | | |
|---|---|---|---|---|---|
| 2006-07 | Peterborough U | 16 | 7 | | |
| 2007-08 | Peterborough U | 45 | 29 | | |
| 2008-09 | Peterborough U | 42 | 18 | | |
| 2009-10 | Peterborough U | 35 | 7 | | |
| 2010-11 | Peterborough U | 19 | 10 | 157 | 71 |
| 2010-11 | Hull C | 23 | 3 | | |
| 2011-12 | Hull C | 39 | 5 | | |
| 2012-13 | Hull C | 14 | 1 | 76 | 9 |
| 2012-13 | *Ipswich T* | 7 | 1 | 7 | 1 |

**McSHANE, Paul (D)** 208 10
H: 6 0  W: 11 05  b.Wicklow 6-1-86
*Source:* Trainee. *Honours:* Eire Youth, Under-21, 31 full caps.

| | | | | | |
|---|---|---|---|---|---|
| 2002-03 | Manchester U | 0 | 0 | | |
| 2003-04 | Manchester U | 0 | 0 | | |
| 2004-05 | Manchester U | 0 | 0 | | |
| 2004-05 | *Walsall* | 4 | 1 | 4 | 1 |
| 2005-06 | Manchester U | 0 | 0 | | |
| 2005-06 | Brighton & HA | 38 | 3 | 38 | 3 |
| 2006-07 | WBA | 32 | 2 | 32 | 2 |
| 2007-08 | Sunderland | 21 | 0 | | |
| 2008-09 | Sunderland | 3 | 0 | | |
| 2008-09 | *Hull C* | 17 | 1 | | |
| 2009-10 | Sunderland | 0 | 0 | 24 | 0 |

| | | | | | |
|---|---|---|---|---|---|
| 2009-10 | Hull C | 27 | 0 | | |
| 2010-11 | Hull C | 19 | 0 | | |
| 2010-11 | *Barnsley* | 10 | 1 | 10 | 1 |
| 2011-12 | Hull C | 1 | 0 | | |
| 2011-12 | *Crystal Palace* | 11 | 0 | 11 | 0 |
| 2012-13 | Hull C | 25 | 2 | 89 | 3 |

**MEYLER, David (M)** 55 5
H: 6 3  W: 11 09  b.Cork 29-5-89
*Honours:* Eire Under-21, 4 full caps.

| | | | | | |
|---|---|---|---|---|---|
| 2008 | Cork C | 2 | 0 | 2 | 0 |
| 2008-09 | Sunderland | 0 | 0 | | |
| 2009-10 | Sunderland | 10 | 0 | | |
| 2010-11 | Sunderland | 7 | 0 | | |
| 2011-12 | Sunderland | 7 | 0 | | |
| 2012-13 | Sunderland | 3 | 0 | 25 | 0 |
| 2012-13 | Hull C | 28 | 5 | 28 | 5 |

**OLOFINJANA, Seyi (M)** 266 36
H: 6 4  W: 11 10  b.Lagos 30-6-80
*Source:* Kwara United Ilorin. *Honours:* Nigeria 44 full caps.

| | | | | | |
|---|---|---|---|---|---|
| 2003 | Brann | 25 | 9 | | |
| 2004 | Brann | 9 | 2 | 34 | 11 |
| 2004-05 | Wolverhampton W | 42 | 5 | | |
| 2005-06 | Wolverhampton W | 13 | 0 | | |
| 2006-07 | Wolverhampton W | 44 | 8 | | |
| 2007-08 | Wolverhampton W | 36 | 3 | 135 | 16 |
| 2008-09 | Stoke C | 18 | 2 | | |
| 2009-10 | Stoke C | 0 | 0 | 18 | 2 |
| 2009-10 | Hull C | 19 | 1 | | |
| 2010-11 | Hull C | 0 | 0 | | |
| 2010-11 | *Cardiff C* | 39 | 6 | 39 | 6 |
| 2011-12 | Hull C | 3 | 0 | | |
| 2012-13 | Hull C | 12 | 0 | 34 | 1 |
| 2012-13 | *Sheffield W* | 6 | 0 | 6 | 0 |

**OXLEY, Mark (G)** 7 0
H: 5 11  W: 11 05  b.Aston 2-6-90
*Source:* Rotherham U Scholar. *Honours:* England Youth.

| | | | | | |
|---|---|---|---|---|---|
| 2008-09 | Hull C | 0 | 0 | | |
| 2009-10 | Hull C | 0 | 0 | | |
| 2009-10 | *Grimsby T* | 3 | 0 | 3 | 0 |
| 2010-11 | Hull C | 0 | 0 | | |
| 2011-12 | Hull C | 0 | 0 | | |
| 2012-13 | Hull C | 1 | 0 | 1 | 0 |
| 2012-13 | *Burton Alb* | 3 | 0 | 3 | 0 |

**PROSCHWITZ, Nick (F)** 90 28
H: 6 3  W: 12 11  b.Weibenfels 28-11-86

| | | | | | |
|---|---|---|---|---|---|
| 2010-11 | FC Thun | 31 | 8 | 31 | 8 |
| 2011-12 | Paderborn | 32 | 17 | 32 | 17 |
| 2012-13 | Hull C | 27 | 3 | 27 | 3 |

**QUINN, Stephen (M)** 279 23
H: 5 6  W: 9 08  b.Dublin 4-4-86
*Source:* Trainee. *Honours:* Eire Under-21, 2 full caps.

| | | | | | |
|---|---|---|---|---|---|
| 2005-06 | Sheffield U | 0 | 0 | | |
| 2005-06 | *Milton Keynes D* | 15 | 0 | 15 | 0 |
| 2005-06 | *Rotherham U* | 16 | 0 | 16 | 0 |
| 2006-07 | Sheffield U | 15 | 2 | | |
| 2007-08 | Sheffield U | 19 | 2 | | |
| 2008-09 | Sheffield U | 43 | 7 | | |
| 2009-10 | Sheffield U | 44 | 4 | | |
| 2010-11 | Sheffield U | 37 | 1 | | |
| 2011-12 | Sheffield U | 45 | 4 | | |
| 2012-13 | Sheffield U | 3 | 0 | 206 | 20 |
| 2012-13 | Hull C | 42 | 3 | 42 | 3 |

**ROSENIOR, Liam (D)** 306 3
H: 5 10  W: 11 05  b.Wandsworth 9-7-84
*Source:* Scholar. *Honours:* England Youth, Under-20, Under-21.

| | | | | | |
|---|---|---|---|---|---|
| 2001-02 | Bristol C | 1 | 0 | | |
| 2002-03 | Bristol C | 21 | 2 | | |
| 2003-04 | Bristol C | 0 | 0 | 22 | 2 |
| 2003-04 | Fulham | 0 | 0 | | |
| 2003-04 | *Torquay U* | 10 | 0 | 10 | 0 |
| 2004-05 | Fulham | 17 | 0 | | |
| 2005-06 | Fulham | 24 | 0 | | |
| 2006-07 | Fulham | 38 | 0 | | |
| 2007-08 | Fulham | 0 | 0 | 79 | 0 |
| 2007-08 | Reading | 17 | 0 | | |
| 2008-09 | Reading | 42 | 0 | | |
| 2009-10 | Reading | 5 | 0 | | |
| 2009-10 | *Ipswich T* | 29 | 1 | 29 | 1 |
| 2010-11 | Reading | 0 | 0 | 64 | 0 |
| 2010-11 | Hull C | 26 | 0 | | |

2011-12 Hull C 44 0
2012-13 Hull C 32 0 **102 0**

**SIMPSON, Jay (F)** **187 35**
H: 5 11  W: 13 04  b.Enfield 1-12-88
*Source:* Scholar. *Honours:* England Youth.
2007-08 Arsenal 0 0
2007-08 *Millwall* 41 6
2008-09 Arsenal 0 0
2008-09 *WBA* 13 1 **13 1**
2009-10 Arsenal 0 0
2009-10 *QPR* 39 12 **39 12**
2010-11 Hull C 32 6
2011-12 Hull C 3 0
2011-12 *Millwall* 16 4 **57 10**
2012-13 Hull C 43 6 **78 12**

**STEWART, Cameron (M)** **68 1**
H: 5 8  W: 11 05  b.Manchester 8-4-91
*Source:* Scholar. *Honours:* England Youth.
2009-10 Manchester U 0 0
2010-11 Manchester U 0 0
2010-11 *Yeovil T* 5 0 **5 0**
2010-11 Hull C 14 0
2011-12 Hull C 31 1
2012-13 Hull C 2 0 **47 1**
2012-13 *Burnley* 9 0 **9 0**
2012-13 *Blackburn R* 7 0 **7 0**

**TOWNSEND, Conor (D)** **20 1**
H: 5 4  W: 9 11  b.Hessle 4-3-93
*Source:* Scholar.
2011-12 Hull C 0 0
2012-13 Hull C 0 0
2012-13 *Chesterfield* 20 1 **20 1**

**WILSON, Dougie (M)** **0 0**
b. 3-3-94
2012-13 Hull C 0 0

**Players retained or with offer of contract**
Aimson, William Stewart; Jahraldo-Martin, Callum; Margetts, Jonathon Gary.

**Scholars**
Barlow, Jack Thomas; Chambers, Daniel Lewis; Clappison, Benjamin Lewis; Clark, Max Oliver; Cracknell, Joseph; Davie, Thomas Antony; Dawson, Leon Stanley; Dixon, Matthew; Doran, Niall Alexander; Fallowfield, Ryan Jack Glenn; McCawl, Eoghan Martin; McElroy, Paul James; O'Connor, Sam James; Ricketts, Bradley Robert; Sutton, Joel Andrew; Topliss, Sam David; Watson, Rory.

# IPSWICH T (43)

**AINSLEY, Jack (D)** **4 0**
H: 5 11  W: 11 00  b.Ipswich 17-9-90
*Source:* Scholar.
2009-10 Ipswich T 0 0
2010-11 Ipswich T 1 0
2011-12 Ipswich T 1 0
2012-13 Ipswich T 2 0 **4 0**

**BROWN, Jason (G)** **164 0**
H: 5 11  W: 15 04  b.Southwark 18-5-82
*Source:* Charlton Ath Scholar. *Honours:* Wales Youth, Under-21, 2 full caps.
2001-02 Gillingham 10 0
2002-03 Gillingham 39 0
2003-04 Gillingham 22 0
2004-05 Gillingham 16 0
2005-06 Gillingham 39 0 **126 0**
2006-07 Blackburn R 1 0
2007-08 Blackburn R 4 0
2008-09 Blackburn R 4 0
2009-10 Blackburn R 4 0
2010-11 Blackburn R 0 0 **9 0**
2010-11 *Leeds U* 4 0 **4 0**
2010-11 *Leyton Orient* 3 0 **3 0**
2011-12 Aberdeen 20 0
2012-13 Aberdeen 2 0 **22 0**
2012-13 Ipswich T 0 0

**CARSON, Josh (M)** **36 5**
H: 5 9  W: 11 00  b.Ballymena 3-6-93
*Source:* Scholar. *Honours:* Northern Ireland Youth, Under-21, 4 full caps.
2010-11 Ipswich T 9 3
2011-12 Ipswich T 16 2
2012-13 Ipswich T 6 0 **31 5**
2012-13 *York C* 5 0 **5 0**

**CHAMBERS, Luke (D)** **373 21**
H: 6 1  W: 11 13  b.Kettering 29-8-85
*Source:* Scholar.
2002-03 Northampton T 1 0
2003-04 Northampton T 24 0
2004-05 Northampton T 27 0
2005-06 Northampton T 43 0
2006-07 Northampton T 29 1 **124 1**
2006-07 Nottingham F 14 0
2007-08 Nottingham F 42 6
2008-09 Nottingham F 39 2
2009-10 Nottingham F 23 3
2010-11 Nottingham F 44 6
2011-12 Nottingham F 43 0 **205 17**
2012-13 Ipswich T 44 3 **44 3**

**CHOPRA, Michael (F)** **329 105**
H: 5 9  W: 10 10  b.Newcastle 23-12-83
*Source:* Scholar. *Honours:* England Youth, Under-20, Under-21.
2000-01 Newcastle U 0 0
2001-02 Newcastle U 0 0
2002-03 Newcastle U 1 0
2002-03 *Watford* 5 5 **5 5**
2003-04 Newcastle U 6 0
2003-04 *Nottingham F* 5 0 **5 0**
2004-05 Newcastle U 1 0
2004-05 *Barnsley* 39 17 **39 17**
2005-06 Newcastle U 13 1 **21 1**
2006-07 Cardiff C 42 22
2007-08 Sunderland 33 6
2008-09 Sunderland 6 2 **39 8**
2008-09 *Cardiff C* 27 9
2009-10 Cardiff C 41 16
2010-11 Cardiff C 32 9 **142 56**
2011-12 Ipswich T 45 14
2012-13 Ipswich T 33 4 **78 18**

**CRESSWELL, Aaron (D)** **160 9**
H: 5 7  W: 10 05  b.Liverpool 15-12-89
*Source:* Scholar.
2008-09 Tranmere R 13 1
2009-10 Tranmere R 14 0
2010-11 Tranmere R 43 4 **70 5**
2011-12 Ipswich T 44 1
2012-13 Ipswich T 46 3 **90 4**

**DRURY, Andy (M)** **98 11**
H: 5 11  W: 12 06  b.Sittingbourne 28-11-83
*Source:* Sittingbourne, Ebbsfleet U, Lewes, Stevenage Bor, Luton T.
2010-11 Luton T 23 6 **23 6**
2010-11 *Ipswich T* 12 0
2011-12 Ipswich T 21 2
2011-12 *Crawley T* 13 3 **13 3**
2012-13 Ipswich T 29 0 **62 2**

**EDWARDS, Carlos (M)** **451 44**
H: 5 8  W: 11 02  b.Port of Spain 24-10-78
*Source:* Defence Force. *Honours:* Trinidad & Tobago 83 full caps, 4 goals.
2000-01 Wrexham 36 4
2001-02 Wrexham 26 5
2002-03 Wrexham 44 8
2003-04 Wrexham 42 5
2004-05 Wrexham 18 1 **166 23**
2005-06 Luton T 42 2
2006-07 Luton T 26 6 **68 8**
2006-07 *Sunderland* 15 5
2007-08 Sunderland 13 0
2008-09 Sunderland 22 0
2008-09 *Wolverhampton W* 6 0 **6 0**
2009-10 Sunderland 0 0 **50 5**
2009-10 *Ipswich T* 28 2
2010-11 Ipswich T 45 3
2011-12 Ipswich T 45 0
2012-13 Ipswich T 43 3 **161 8**

**EMMANUEL-THOMAS, Jay (M)** **111 16**
H: 5 9  W: 11 05  b.Forest Gate 27-12-90
*Source:* Scholar. *Honours:* England Youth.
2008-09 Arsenal 0 0
2009-10 Arsenal 0 0
2009-10 *Blackpool* 11 1 **11 1**
2009-10 *Doncaster R* 14 5 **14 5**
2010-11 Arsenal 1 0 **1 0**
2010-11 *Cardiff C* 14 2 **14 2**
2011-12 Ipswich T 42 6
2012-13 Ipswich T 29 2 **71 8**

**HEWITT, Elliott (D)** **29 0**
H: 5 11  W: 11 10  b.Rhyl 30-5-94
*Source:* Scholar.
2010-11 Macclesfield T 1 0
2011-12 Macclesfield T 21 0 **22 0**
2012-13 Ipswich T 7 0 **7 0**

**HYAM, Luke (M)** **48 1**
H: 5 10  W: 11 05  b.Ipswich 24-10-91
*Source:* Scholar.
2010-11 Ipswich T 10 0
2011-12 Ipswich T 8 0
2012-13 Ipswich T 30 1 **48 1**

**LOACH, Scott (G)** **198 0**
H: 6 1  W: 13 01  b.Nottingham 27-5-88
*Source:* Lincoln C Scholar. *Honours:* England Under-21.
2006-07 Watford 0 0
2007-08 Watford 0 0
2007-08 *Morecambe* 2 0 **2 0**
2007-08 *Bradford C* 20 0 **20 0**
2008-09 Watford 31 0
2009-10 Watford 46 0
2010-11 Watford 46 0
2011-12 Watford 31 0 **154 0**
2012-13 Ipswich T 22 0 **22 0**

**MARRIOTT, Jack (F)** **1 0**
H: 5 8  W: 11 03  b.Beverley 9-9-94
2012-13 Ipswich T 1 0 **1 0**

**MARTIN, Lee (M)** **172 12**
H: 5 10  W: 10 03  b.Taunton 9-2-87
*Source:* Scholar. *Honours:* England Youth.
2004-05 Manchester U 0 0
2005-06 Manchester U 0 0
2006-07 Manchester U 0 0
2006-07 *Rangers* 7 0 **7 0**
2006-07 *Stoke C* 13 1 **13 1**
2007-08 Manchester U 0 0
2007-08 *Plymouth Arg* 12 2 **12 2**
2007-08 *Sheffield U* 6 0 **6 0**
2008-09 Manchester U 1 0
2008-09 *Nottingham F* 13 1 **13 1**
2009-10 Manchester U 0 0 **1 0**
2009-10 *Ipswich T* 16 1
2010-11 Ipswich T 16 0
2010-11 *Charlton Ath* 20 2 **20 2**
2011-12 Ipswich T 34 5
2012-13 Ipswich T 34 0 **100 6**

**MINGS, Tyrone (D)** **1 0**
H: 6 3  W: 12 00  b.Bath 19-3-93
2012-13 Ipswich T 1 0 **1 0**

**MURPHY, Daryl (F)** **223 34**
H: 6 2  W: 13 12  b.Waterford 15-3-83
*Honours:* Eire Youth, Under-21, 9 full caps.
2000-01 Luton T 0 0
2001-02 Luton T 0 0
2005-06 Sunderland 18 1
2005-06 *Sheffield W* 4 0 **4 0**
2006-07 Sunderland 38 10
2007-08 Sunderland 28 3
2008-09 Sunderland 23 0
2009-10 Sunderland 3 0 **110 14**
2009-10 *Ipswich T* 18 6
2010-11 Celtic 18 3
2011-12 *Ipswich T* 33 4
2012-13 Celtic 1 0 **19 3**
On loan from Celtic
2012-13 Ipswich T 39 7 **90 17**

**MURRAY, Ronan (F)** **49 5**
H: 5 7  W: 11 00  b.Mayo 12-9-91
*Source:* Scholar. *Honours:* Eire Under-21.
2010-11 Ipswich T 8 0

| | | | | | |
|---|---|---|---|---|---|
| 2010-11 | *Torquay U* | 7 | 1 | **7** | **1** |
| 2011-12 | Ipswich T | 0 | 0 | | |
| 2011-12 | *Swindon T* | 20 | 3 | **20** | **3** |
| 2012-13 | Ipswich T | 1 | 0 | **9** | **0** |
| 2012-13 | *Plymouth Arg* | 13 | 1 | **13** | **1** |

**N'DAW, Guirane (M)**     255   9
H: 6 2   W: 12 06   b.Rufisque 24-4-84
*Honours:* Senegal 43 full caps, 4 goals.

| | | | | | |
|---|---|---|---|---|---|
| 2001-02 | Sochaux B | 0 | 0 | | |
| 2002-03 | Sochaux | 1 | 0 | | |
| 2003-04 | Sochaux | 8 | 0 | | |
| 2004-05 | Sochaux | 16 | 0 | | |
| 2005-06 | Sochaux | 30 | 1 | | |
| 2006-07 | Sochaux | 37 | 1 | | |
| 2007-08 | Sochaux | 30 | 3 | **122** | **5** |
| 2008-09 | Nantes | 32 | 3 | **32** | **3** |
| 2009-10 | *St Etienne* | 34 | 0 | | |
| 2010-11 | St Etienne | 5 | 0 | | |
| 2010-11 | *Zaragoza* | 9 | 0 | **9** | **0** |
| 2011-12 | *Birmingham C* | 19 | 0 | **19** | **0** |
| 2012-13 | St Etienne | 0 | 0 | **39** | **0** |

On loan from St Etienne

| | | | | | |
|---|---|---|---|---|---|
| 2012-13 | Ipswich T | 34 | 1 | **34** | **1** |

**NOUBLE, Frank (F)**     81   10
H: 6 3   W: 12 08   b.Lewisham 24-9-91
*Source:* Chelsea Scholar. *Honours:* England Youth.

| | | | | | |
|---|---|---|---|---|---|
| 2009-10 | West Ham U | 8 | 0 | | |
| 2009-10 | *WBA* | 3 | 0 | **3** | **0** |
| 2009-10 | *Swindon T* | 8 | 0 | **8** | **0** |
| 2010-11 | West Ham U | 2 | 0 | | |
| 2010-11 | *Swansea C* | 6 | 1 | **6** | **1** |
| 2010-11 | *Barnsley* | 4 | 0 | | |
| 2010-11 | *Charlton Ath* | 9 | 1 | **9** | **1** |
| 2011-12 | West Ham U | 3 | 1 | **13** | **1** |
| 2011-12 | *Gillingham* | 13 | 5 | **13** | **5** |
| 2011-12 | *Barnsley* | 6 | 0 | **10** | **0** |
| 2012-13 | Wolverhampton W | 2 | 0 | **2** | **0** |
| 2012-13 | Ipswich T | 17 | 2 | **17** | **2** |

**PETERS, Jaime (M)**     124   5
H: 5 7   W: 10 12   b.Ontario 4-5-87
*Source:* Kaiserslautern. *Honours:* Canada Youth, Under-20, Under-23, 26 full caps, 1 goal.

| | | | | | |
|---|---|---|---|---|---|
| 2005-06 | Ipswich T | 13 | 0 | | |
| 2006-07 | Ipswich T | 23 | 2 | | |
| 2007-08 | Ipswich T | 5 | 0 | | |
| 2007-08 | *Yeovil T* | 14 | 1 | **14** | **1** |
| 2008-09 | Ipswich T | 3 | 0 | | |
| 2008-09 | *Gillingham* | 3 | 0 | **3** | **0** |
| 2009-10 | Ipswich T | 32 | 1 | | |
| 2010-11 | Ipswich T | 23 | 1 | | |
| 2011-12 | Ipswich T | 0 | 0 | | |
| 2011-12 | *Bournemouth* | 8 | 0 | **8** | **0** |
| 2012-13 | Ipswich T | 0 | 0 | **99** | **4** |

**REO-COKER, Nigel (M)**     327   21
H: 5 8   W: 12 03   b.Southwark 14-5-84
*Source:* Scholar. *Honours:* England Youth, Under-20, Under-21.

| | | | | | |
|---|---|---|---|---|---|
| 2001-02 | Wimbledon | 1 | 0 | | |
| 2002-03 | Wimbledon | 32 | 2 | | |
| 2003-04 | Wimbledon | 25 | 4 | **58** | **6** |
| 2003-04 | West Ham U | 15 | 2 | | |
| 2004-05 | West Ham U | 39 | 3 | | |
| 2005-06 | West Ham U | 31 | 5 | | |
| 2006-07 | West Ham U | 35 | 1 | **120** | **11** |
| 2007-08 | Aston Villa | 36 | 0 | | |
| 2008-09 | Aston Villa | 26 | 1 | | |
| 2009-10 | Aston Villa | 10 | 0 | | |
| 2010-11 | Aston Villa | 30 | 0 | **102** | **1** |
| 2011-12 | Bolton W | 37 | 3 | **37** | **3** |
| 2012-13 | Ipswich T | 10 | 0 | **10** | **0** |

Transferred to Vancouver Whitecaps February 2013

**SMITH, Tommy (D)**     116   6
H: 6 2   W: 12 02   b.Macclesfield 31-3-90
*Source:* Scholar. *Honours:* England Youth. New Zealand 15 full caps, 1 goal.

| | | | | | |
|---|---|---|---|---|---|
| 2007-08 | Ipswich T | 0 | 0 | | |
| 2008-09 | Ipswich T | 2 | 0 | | |
| 2009-10 | Ipswich T | 14 | 0 | | |
| 2009-10 | *Brentford* | 8 | 0 | **8** | **0** |
| 2010-11 | Ipswich T | 22 | 3 | | |
| 2010-11 | *Colchester U* | 6 | 0 | **6** | **0** |

| | | | | | |
|---|---|---|---|---|---|
| 2011-12 | Ipswich T | 26 | 3 | | |
| 2012-13 | Ipswich T | 38 | 3 | **102** | **9** |

**TAYLOR, Paul (F)**     64   12
H: 5 11   W: 11 02   b.Liverpool 4-11-87
*Source:* Vauxhall M.

| | | | | | |
|---|---|---|---|---|---|
| 2008-09 | Chester C | 9 | 0 | **9** | **0** |
| 2009-10 | Montegnee | 1 | 0 | **1** | **0** |
| 2009-10 | Charleoi | 3 | 0 | **3** | **0** |
| 2010-11 | Anderlecht | 0 | 0 | | |
| 2010-11 | Peterborough U | 1 | 0 | | |
| 2011-12 | Peterborough U | 44 | 12 | | |
| 2012-13 | Peterborough U | 3 | 0 | **48** | **12** |
| 2012-13 | Ipswich T | 3 | 0 | **3** | **0** |

**WORDSWORTH, Anthony (M)**     184   36
H: 6 1   W: 12 00   b.Camden 3-1-89
*Source:* Scholar.

| | | | | | |
|---|---|---|---|---|---|
| 2007-08 | Colchester U | 3 | 0 | | |
| 2008-09 | Colchester U | 30 | 3 | | |
| 2009-10 | Colchester U | 41 | 11 | | |
| 2010-11 | Colchester U | 35 | 5 | | |
| 2011-12 | Colchester U | 44 | 13 | | |
| 2012-13 | Colchester U | 24 | 3 | **177** | **35** |
| 2012-13 | Ipswich T | 7 | 1 | **7** | **1** |

**Scholars**
Acott, Lewis Ian; Berkane, Amir; Bishop, Edward James; Crowe, Michael Thomas Tallaksen; Galvin, Cory; Hammond, Kyle James; Lawrence, Byron Alfredo; Leddy, Jonathan Patrick Cahill; Marriott, Jack David; October, David Francis; Robinson, Joe Alan; Sowunmi, Omar Kolawole Olufemi; Thompson, Rory Peter Francis; Timlin, Mark Anthony; Willbye, Jack Thomas; Winter, Thomas James.

# LEEDS U (44)

**ASHDOWN, Jamie (G)**     145   0
H: 6 1   W: 13 05   b.Reading 30-11-80
*Source:* Scholar.

| | | | | | |
|---|---|---|---|---|---|
| 1999-2000 | Reading | 0 | 0 | | |
| 2000-01 | Reading | 1 | 0 | | |
| 2001-02 | Reading | 1 | 0 | | |
| 2001-02 | *Arsenal* | 1 | 0 | | |
| 2002-03 | *Bournemouth* | 2 | 0 | **2** | **0** |
| 2003-04 | Reading | 10 | 0 | **13** | **0** |
| 2003-04 | *Rushden & D* | 19 | 0 | **19** | **0** |
| 2004-05 | Portsmouth | 16 | 0 | | |
| 2005-06 | Portsmouth | 17 | 0 | | |
| 2006-07 | Portsmouth | 0 | 0 | | |
| 2006-07 | *Norwich C* | 2 | 0 | **2** | **0** |
| 2007-08 | Portsmouth | 3 | 0 | | |
| 2008-09 | Portsmouth | 0 | 0 | | |
| 2009-10 | Portsmouth | 6 | 0 | | |
| 2010-11 | Portsmouth | 46 | 0 | | |
| 2011-12 | Portsmouth | 21 | 0 | **109** | **0** |
| 2012-13 | Leeds U | 0 | 0 | | |

**AUSTIN, Rodolph (M)**     121   17
H: 6 0   W: 12 03   b.Clarendon 1-6-85
*Honours:* Jamaica 53 full caps, 4 goals.

| | | | | | |
|---|---|---|---|---|---|
| 2008-09 | SK Brann | 19 | 2 | | |
| 2009-10 | SK Brann | 20 | 2 | | |
| 2010-11 | SK Brann | 22 | 1 | | |
| 2011-12 | SK Brann | 29 | 10 | **90** | **15** |
| 2012-13 | Leeds U | 31 | 2 | **31** | **2** |

**BROWN, Michael (M)**     492   38
H: 5 9   W: 12 04   b.Hartlepool 25-1-77
*Source:* Trainee. *Honours:* England Under-21.

| | | | | | |
|---|---|---|---|---|---|
| 1994-95 | Manchester C | 0 | 0 | | |
| 1995-96 | Manchester C | 21 | 0 | | |
| 1996-97 | Manchester C | 11 | 0 | | |
| 1996-97 | *Hartlepool U* | 6 | 1 | **6** | **1** |
| 1997-98 | Manchester C | 26 | 0 | | |
| 1998-99 | Manchester C | 31 | 2 | | |
| 1999-2000 | Manchester C | 0 | 0 | **89** | **2** |
| 1999-2000 | *Portsmouth* | 4 | 0 | | |
| 1999-2000 | Sheffield U | 24 | 3 | | |
| 2000-01 | Sheffield U | 36 | 1 | | |
| 2001-02 | Sheffield U | 36 | 5 | | |
| 2002-03 | Sheffield U | 40 | 16 | | |
| 2003-04 | Sheffield U | 15 | 2 | **151** | **27** |

| | | | | | |
|---|---|---|---|---|---|
| 2003-04 | Tottenham H | 17 | 1 | | |
| 2004-05 | Tottenham H | 24 | 1 | | |
| 2005-06 | Tottenham H | 9 | 0 | **50** | **2** |
| 2005-06 | Fulham | 7 | 0 | | |
| 2006-07 | Fulham | 34 | 0 | **41** | **0** |
| 2007-08 | Wigan Ath | 31 | 0 | | |
| 2008-09 | Wigan Ath | 25 | 0 | | |
| 2009-10 | Wigan Ath | 2 | 0 | **58** | **0** |
| 2009-10 | Portsmouth | 32 | 0 | | |
| 2010-11 | Portsmouth | 21 | 2 | **49** | **4** |
| 2011-12 | Leeds U | 24 | 1 | | |
| 2012-13 | Leeds U | 24 | 1 | **48** | **2** |

**BYRAM, Samuel (M)**     44   3
H: 5 11   W: 11 04   b.Thurrock 16-9-93

| | | | | | |
|---|---|---|---|---|---|
| 2012-13 | Leeds U | 44 | 3 | **44** | **3** |

**CAIRNS, Alex (G)**     1   0
H: 6 0   W: 11 05   b.Doncaster 4-1-93
*Source:* Scholar.

| | | | | | |
|---|---|---|---|---|---|
| 2011-12 | Leeds U | 1 | 0 | | |
| 2012-13 | Leeds U | 0 | 0 | **1** | **0** |

**CONNOLLY, Paul (D)**     307   2
H: 6 0   W: 11 09   b.Liverpool 29-9-83
*Source:* Scholar.

| | | | | | |
|---|---|---|---|---|---|
| 2000-01 | Plymouth Arg | 1 | 0 | | |
| 2001-02 | Plymouth Arg | 0 | 0 | | |
| 2002-03 | Plymouth Arg | 2 | 0 | | |
| 2003-04 | Plymouth Arg | 29 | 0 | | |
| 2004-05 | Plymouth Arg | 19 | 0 | | |
| 2005-06 | Plymouth Arg | 31 | 0 | | |
| 2006-07 | Plymouth Arg | 38 | 0 | | |
| 2007-08 | Plymouth Arg | 42 | 1 | **162** | **1** |
| 2008-09 | Derby Co | 40 | 1 | | |
| 2009-10 | Derby Co | 21 | 0 | **61** | **1** |
| 2009-10 | *Sheffield U* | 7 | 0 | **7** | **0** |
| 2010-11 | Leeds U | 30 | 0 | | |
| 2011-12 | Leeds U | 28 | 0 | | |
| 2012-13 | Leeds U | 0 | 0 | **58** | **0** |
| 2012-13 | *Portsmouth* | 4 | 0 | **4** | **0** |
| 2012-13 | *Preston NE* | 15 | 0 | **15** | **0** |

**DAWSON, Chris (M)**     1   0
b.Dewsbury 2-9-94

| | | | | | |
|---|---|---|---|---|---|
| 2012-13 | Leeds U | 1 | 0 | **1** | **0** |

**DIOUF, El Hadji (F)**     413   59
H: 5 11   W: 11 11   b.Dakar 15-1-81
*Honours:* Senegal 57 full caps, 16 goals.

| | | | | | |
|---|---|---|---|---|---|
| 1998-99 | Sochaux | 15 | 0 | **15** | **0** |
| 1999-2000 | Rennes | 28 | 1 | **28** | **1** |
| 2000-01 | Lens | 28 | 8 | | |
| 2001-02 | Lens | 26 | 10 | **54** | **18** |
| 2002-03 | Liverpool | 29 | 3 | | |
| 2003-04 | Liverpool | 26 | 0 | | |
| 2004-05 | Liverpool | 0 | 0 | **55** | **3** |
| 2004-05 | *Bolton W* | 27 | 9 | | |
| 2005-06 | Bolton W | 20 | 3 | | |
| 2006-07 | Bolton W | 33 | 5 | | |
| 2007-08 | Bolton W | 34 | 4 | **114** | **21** |
| 2008-09 | Sunderland | 14 | 0 | **14** | **0** |
| 2008-09 | Blackburn R | 14 | 1 | | |
| 2009-10 | Blackburn R | 26 | 3 | | |
| 2010-11 | Blackburn R | 20 | 0 | | |
| 2010-11 | *Rangers* | 15 | 1 | **15** | **1** |
| 2011-12 | Blackburn R | 0 | 0 | **60** | **4** |
| 2011-12 | Doncaster R | 22 | 6 | | |
| 2012-13 | Doncaster R | 0 | 0 | **22** | **6** |
| 2012-13 | Leeds U | 36 | 5 | **36** | **5** |

**DRURY, Adam (D)**     486   6
H: 5 10   W: 11 09   b.Cambridge 29-8-78
*Source:* Trainee.

| | | | | | |
|---|---|---|---|---|---|
| 1995-96 | Peterborough U | 1 | 0 | | |
| 1996-97 | Peterborough U | 5 | 1 | | |
| 1997-98 | Peterborough U | 31 | 0 | | |
| 1998-99 | Peterborough U | 40 | 0 | | |
| 1999-2000 | Peterborough U | 42 | 1 | | |
| 2000-01 | Peterborough U | 29 | 0 | **148** | **2** |
| 2000-01 | Norwich C | 6 | 0 | | |
| 2001-02 | Norwich C | 35 | 0 | | |
| 2002-03 | Norwich C | 45 | 2 | | |
| 2003-04 | Norwich C | 42 | 0 | | |
| 2004-05 | Norwich C | 33 | 1 | | |
| 2005-06 | Norwich C | 39 | 0 | | |
| 2006-07 | Norwich C | 39 | 0 | | |
| 2007-08 | Norwich C | 9 | 0 | | |
| 2008-09 | Norwich C | 11 | 0 | | |
| 2009-10 | Norwich C | 35 | 0 | | |

| 2010-11 | Norwich C | 20 | 1 | | |
| 2011-12 | Norwich C | 12 | 0 | 326 | 4 |
| 2012-13 | Leeds U | 12 | 0 | 12 | 0 |

**GREEN, Paul (M)**     355   37
H: 5 9   W: 10 02   b.Pontefract 10-4-83
*Source:* Scholar. *Honours:* Eire 16 full caps, 1 goal.

| 2003-04 | Doncaster R | 43 | 8 | | |
| 2004-05 | Doncaster R | 42 | 7 | | |
| 2005-06 | Doncaster R | 34 | 3 | | |
| 2006-07 | Doncaster R | 41 | 2 | | |
| 2007-08 | Doncaster R | 38 | 5 | 198 | 25 |
| 2008-09 | Derby Co | 29 | 3 | | |
| 2009-10 | Derby Co | 33 | 2 | | |
| 2010-11 | Derby Co | 36 | 2 | | |
| 2011-12 | Derby Co | 27 | 1 | 125 | 8 |
| 2012-13 | Leeds U | 32 | 4 | 32 | 4 |

**HABIBOU, Habib (F)**     75   24
H: 6 4   W: 12 08   b.Bria 16-4-87

| 2009-10 | Charleroi | 18 | 5 | 18 | 5 |
| 2010-11 | Zulte-Waregem | 26 | 11 | | |
| 2011-12 | Zulte-Waregem | 13 | 2 | | |
| 2012-13 | Zulte-Waregem | 14 | 6 | 53 | 19 |
| 2012-13 | Leeds U | 4 | 0 | 4 | 0 |

**HALL, Ryan (M)**     103   21
H: 5 10   W: 10 04   b.Dulwich 4-1-88
*Source:* Scholar.

| 2005-06 | Crystal Palace | 0 | 0 | | |
| 2006-07 | Crystal Palace | 0 | 0 | | |
| 2007-08 | Crystal Palace | 1 | 0 | 1 | 0 |
| 2007-08 | *Dagenham & R* | 8 | 2 | 8 | 2 |
| From Bromley. | | | | | |
| 2010-11 | Southend U | 41 | 9 | | |
| 2011-12 | Southend U | 43 | 10 | | |
| 2012-13 | Southend U | 2 | 0 | 86 | 19 |
| 2012-13 | Leeds U | 8 | 0 | 8 | 0 |

**KENNY, Paddy (G)**     534   0
H: 6 1   W: 14 01   b.Halifax 17-5-78
*Source:* Bradford PA. *Honours:* Eire 7 full caps.

| 1998-99 | Bury | 0 | 0 | | |
| 1999-2000 | Bury | 46 | 0 | | |
| 2000-01 | Bury | 46 | 0 | | |
| 2001-02 | Bury | 41 | 0 | | |
| 2002-03 | Bury | 0 | 0 | 133 | 0 |
| 2002-03 | Sheffield U | 45 | 0 | | |
| 2003-04 | Sheffield U | 27 | 0 | | |
| 2004-05 | Sheffield U | 40 | 0 | | |
| 2005-06 | Sheffield U | 46 | 0 | | |
| 2006-07 | Sheffield U | 34 | 0 | | |
| 2007-08 | Sheffield U | 40 | 0 | | |
| 2008-09 | Sheffield U | 44 | 0 | | |
| 2009-10 | Sheffield U | 2 | 0 | 278 | 0 |
| 2010-11 | QPR | 44 | 0 | | |
| 2011-12 | QPR | 33 | 0 | 77 | 0 |
| 2012-13 | Leeds U | 46 | 0 | 46 | 0 |

**KILLOCK, Ross (D)**     0   0
b. 12-7-94
*Source:* Alfreton T.

| 2012-13 | Leeds U | 0 | 0 | | |

**KISNORBO, Patrick (D)**     293   14
H: 6 1   W: 11 11   b.Melbourne 24-3-81
*Honours:* Australia Schools, Under-20, Under-23, 18 full caps, 1 goal.

| 2000-01 | South Melbourne | 25 | 0 | | |
| 2001-02 | South Melbourne | 23 | 2 | | |
| 2002-03 | South Melbourne | 19 | 1 | 67 | 3 |
| 2003-04 | Hearts | 31 | 0 | | |
| 2004-05 | Hearts | 17 | 1 | 48 | 1 |
| 2005-06 | Leicester C | 37 | 1 | | |
| 2006-07 | Leicester C | 40 | 5 | | |
| 2007-08 | Leicester C | 41 | 3 | | |
| 2008-09 | Leicester C | 8 | 0 | 126 | 9 |
| 2009-10 | Leeds U | 29 | 1 | | |
| 2010-11 | Leeds U | 1 | 0 | | |
| 2011-12 | Leeds U | 19 | 0 | | |
| 2012-13 | Leeds U | 0 | 0 | 49 | 1 |
| 2012-13 | *Ipswich T* | 3 | 0 | 3 | 0 |

**LEES, Tom (D)**     166   7
H: 6 1   W: 12 04   b.Warwick 28-11-90
*Honours:* England Under-21.

| 2008-09 | Leeds U | 0 | 0 | | |
| 2009-10 | Leeds U | 0 | 0 | | |

| 2009-10 | *Accrington S* | 39 | 0 | 39 | 0 |
| 2010-11 | Leeds U | 0 | 0 | | |
| 2010-11 | *Bury* | 45 | 4 | 45 | 4 |
| 2011-12 | Leeds U | 42 | 2 | | |
| 2012-13 | Leeds U | 40 | 1 | 82 | 3 |

**McCORMACK, Ross (F)**     250   67
H: 5 9   W: 11 00   b.Glasgow 18-8-86
*Honours:* Scotland Youth, Under-21, B, 8 full caps, 2 goals.

| 2003-04 | Rangers | 2 | 1 | | |
| 2004-05 | Rangers | 1 | 0 | | |
| 2005-06 | Rangers | 8 | 1 | 11 | 2 |
| 2005-06 | Doncaster R | 19 | 4 | 19 | 4 |
| 2006-07 | Motherwell | 12 | 2 | | |
| 2007-08 | Motherwell | 36 | 9 | 48 | 11 |
| 2008-09 | Cardiff C | 38 | 21 | | |
| 2009-10 | Cardiff C | 34 | 4 | | |
| 2010-11 | Cardiff C | 2 | 0 | 74 | 25 |
| 2010-11 | Leeds U | 21 | 2 | | |
| 2011-12 | Leeds U | 45 | 18 | | |
| 2012-13 | Leeds U | 32 | 5 | 98 | 25 |

**MORISON, Steven (F)**     174   51
H: 6 2   W: 13 07   b.Enfield 29-8-83
*Source:* Scholar. *Honours:* Wales 20 full caps, 1 goal.

| 2001-02 | Northampton T | 1 | 0 | | |
| 2002-03 | Northampton T | 13 | 1 | | |
| 2003-04 | Northampton T | 5 | 1 | | |
| 2004-05 | Northampton T | 4 | 1 | 23 | 3 |
| From Stevenage B. | | | | | |
| 2008-09 | Millwall | 0 | 0 | | |
| 2009-10 | Millwall | 43 | 20 | | |
| 2010-11 | Millwall | 40 | 15 | 83 | 35 |
| 2011-12 | Norwich C | 34 | 9 | | |
| 2012-13 | Norwich C | 19 | 1 | 53 | 10 |
| 2012-13 | Leeds U | 15 | 3 | 15 | 3 |

**NORRIS, David (M)**     408   52
H: 5 7   W: 11 06   b.Stamford 22-2-81
*Source:* Boston U.

| 1999-2000 | Bolton W | 0 | 0 | | |
| 2000-01 | Bolton W | 0 | 0 | | |
| 2001-02 | Bolton W | 0 | 0 | | |
| 2001-02 | *Hull C* | 6 | 1 | 6 | 1 |
| 2002-03 | Bolton W | 0 | 0 | | |
| 2002-03 | Plymouth Arg | 33 | 6 | | |
| 2003-04 | Plymouth Arg | 45 | 5 | | |
| 2004-05 | Plymouth Arg | 35 | 3 | | |
| 2005-06 | Plymouth Arg | 45 | 2 | | |
| 2006-07 | Plymouth Arg | 41 | 6 | | |
| 2007-08 | Plymouth Arg | 27 | 5 | 226 | 27 |
| 2007-08 | Ipswich T | 9 | 1 | | |
| 2008-09 | Ipswich T | 37 | 3 | | |
| 2009-10 | Ipswich T | 24 | 1 | | |
| 2010-11 | Ipswich T | 36 | 8 | 106 | 13 |
| 2011-12 | Portsmouth | 40 | 8 | 40 | 8 |
| 2012-13 | Leeds U | 30 | 3 | 30 | 3 |

**PEARCE, Jason (D)**     238   9
H: 5 11   W: 12 00   b.Hillingdon 6-12-87
*Source:* Scholar.

| 2006-07 | Portsmouth | 0 | 0 | | |
| 2007-08 | Bournemouth | 33 | 1 | | |
| 2008-09 | Bournemouth | 44 | 2 | | |
| 2009-10 | Bournemouth | 39 | 1 | | |
| 2010-11 | Bournemouth | 46 | 3 | 162 | 7 |
| 2011-12 | Portsmouth | 43 | 2 | 43 | 2 |
| 2011-12 | Leeds U | 0 | 0 | | |
| 2012-13 | Leeds U | 33 | 0 | 33 | 0 |

**PELTIER, Lee (D)**     237   4
H: 5 10   W: 12 00   b.Liverpool 11-12-86
*Source:* Scholar.

| 2004-05 | Liverpool | 0 | 0 | | |
| 2005-06 | Liverpool | 0 | 0 | | |
| 2006-07 | Liverpool | 0 | 0 | | |
| 2006-07 | *Hull C* | 7 | 0 | 7 | 0 |
| 2007-08 | Liverpool | 0 | 0 | | |
| 2007-08 | Yeovil T | 34 | 0 | | |
| 2008-09 | Yeovil T | 35 | 1 | 69 | 1 |
| 2009-10 | Huddersfield T | 42 | 0 | | |
| 2010-11 | Huddersfield T | 38 | 1 | 80 | 1 |
| 2011-12 | Leicester C | 40 | 2 | | |
| 2012-13 | Leicester C | 0 | 0 | 40 | 2 |
| 2012-13 | Leeds U | 41 | 0 | 41 | 0 |

**POLEON, Dominic (F)**     20   4
H: 6 3   W: 12 13   b.Newham 7-9-93

| 2012-13 | Leeds U | 6 | 2 | 6 | 2 |
| 2012-13 | *Bury* | 7 | 2 | 7 | 2 |
| 2012-13 | *Sheffield U* | 7 | 0 | 7 | 0 |

**PUGH, Danny (M)**     229   13
H: 6 0   W: 12 10   b.Cheadle Hulme 19-10-82
*Source:* Scholar.

| 2000-01 | Manchester U | 0 | 0 | | |
| 2001-02 | Manchester U | 0 | 0 | | |
| 2002-03 | Manchester U | 1 | 0 | | |
| 2003-04 | Manchester U | 0 | 0 | 1 | 0 |
| 2004-05 | Leeds U | 38 | 5 | | |
| 2005-06 | Leeds U | 12 | 0 | | |
| 2006-07 | Preston NE | 45 | 4 | | |
| 2007-08 | Preston NE | 7 | 0 | | |
| 2007-08 | Stoke C | 30 | 0 | | |
| 2008-09 | Stoke C | 17 | 0 | | |
| 2009-10 | Stoke C | 7 | 1 | | |
| 2010-11 | Stoke C | 10 | 0 | | |
| 2010-11 | *Preston NE* | 5 | 0 | 57 | 4 |
| 2011-12 | Stoke C | 3 | 0 | 67 | 1 |
| 2011-12 | Leeds U | 34 | 2 | | |
| 2012-13 | Leeds U | 4 | 0 | 88 | 7 |
| 2012-13 | *Sheffield W* | 16 | 1 | 16 | 1 |

**RACHUBKA, Paul (G)**     274   0
H: 6 1   W: 13 05   b.San Luis Opispo 21-5-81
*Source:* Trainee. *Honours:* England Youth, Under-20.

| 1999-2000 | Manchester U | 0 | 0 | | |
| 2000-01 | Manchester U | 1 | 0 | | |
| 2001-02 | Manchester U | 0 | 0 | 1 | 0 |
| 2001-02 | *Oldham Ath* | 16 | 0 | 16 | 0 |
| 2001-02 | Charlton Ath | 0 | 0 | | |
| 2002-03 | Charlton Ath | 0 | 0 | | |
| 2003-04 | Charlton Ath | 0 | 0 | | |
| 2003-04 | *Huddersfield T* | 13 | 0 | | |
| 2004-05 | Charlton Ath | 0 | 0 | | |
| 2004-05 | *Milton Keynes D* | 4 | 0 | 4 | 0 |
| 2004-05 | *Northampton T* | 10 | 0 | 10 | 0 |
| 2005-06 | Huddersfield T | 29 | 0 | | |
| 2006-07 | Huddersfield T | 34 | 0 | | |
| 2006-07 | Huddersfield T | 0 | 0 | 76 | 0 |
| 2006-07 | *Peterborough U* | 4 | 0 | 4 | 0 |
| 2006-07 | *Blackpool* | 8 | 0 | | |
| 2007-08 | Blackpool | 46 | 0 | | |
| 2008-09 | Blackpool | 42 | 0 | | |
| 2009-10 | Blackpool | 20 | 0 | | |
| 2010-11 | Blackpool | 2 | 0 | 118 | 0 |
| 2011-12 | Leeds U | 6 | 0 | | |
| 2011-12 | *Tranmere R* | 10 | 0 | 10 | 0 |
| 2011-12 | *Leyton Orient* | 8 | 0 | 8 | 0 |
| 2012-13 | Leeds U | 0 | 0 | 6 | 0 |
| 2012-13 | *Accrington S* | 21 | 0 | 21 | 0 |

**ROGERS, Robbie (F)**     141   20
H: 5 10   W: 12 13   b.Los Angeles 12-5-87
*Honours:* USA Youth, Under-23, 18 full caps, 2 goals.

| 2005 | Orange County BS | 3 | 0 | 3 | 0 |
| 2006 | Maryland Terrapins | 22 | 7 | 22 | 7 |
| 2006-07 | Heerenveen | 0 | 0 | | |
| 2007 | Columbus Crew | 10 | 3 | | |
| 2008 | Columbus Crew | 27 | 6 | | |
| 2009 | Columbus Crew | 22 | 1 | | |
| 2010 | Columbus Crew | 20 | 1 | | |
| 2011 | Columbus Crew | 27 | 2 | 106 | 13 |
| 2011-12 | Leeds U | 4 | 0 | | |
| 2012-13 | Leeds U | 0 | 0 | 4 | 0 |
| 2012-13 | *Stevenage* | 6 | 0 | 6 | 0 |
| Transferred to LA Galaxy May 2013 | | | | | |

**SOMMA, Davide (F)**     107   24
H: 6 1   W: 12 13   b.Johannesburg 26-3-85
*Honours:* South Africa 3 full caps, 1 goal.

| 2005-06 | Pro Vasto | 20 | 2 | | |
| 2006-07 | Pro Vasto | 19 | 0 | 39 | 2 |
| 2007-08 | Olbia | 15 | 1 | 15 | 1 |
| 2008 | San Jose Eq | 3 | 0 | 3 | 0 |
| 2009-10 | Leeds U | 0 | 0 | | |
| 2009-10 | *Chesterfield* | 3 | 0 | 3 | 0 |
| 2009-10 | *Lincoln C* | 14 | 9 | 14 | 9 |
| 2010-11 | Leeds U | 29 | 11 | | |
| 2011-12 | Leeds U | 0 | 0 | | |
| 2012-13 | Leeds U | 4 | 1 | 33 | 12 |

**TAYLOR, Charlie (D)**   16   0
H: 5 9   W: 11 00   b.York 18-9-93
Source: Scholar. Honours: England Youth.

| Season | Club | Apps | Gls | Tot A | Tot G |
|---|---|---|---|---|---|
| 2011-12 | Leeds U | 2 | 0 | | |
| 2011-12 | *Bradford C* | 3 | 0 | 3 | 0 |
| 2012-13 | Leeds U | 0 | 0 | 2 | 0 |
| 2012-13 | *York C* | 4 | 0 | 4 | 0 |
| 2012-13 | *Inverness CT* | 7 | 0 | 7 | 0 |

**THOMPSON, Zac (M)**   38   1
H: 5 10   W: 11 00   b.Billinge 5-1-93
Source: Everton Scholar.

| Season | Club | Apps | Gls | Tot A | Tot G |
|---|---|---|---|---|---|
| 2010-11 | Leeds U | 0 | 0 | | |
| 2011-12 | Leeds U | 9 | 0 | | |
| 2012-13 | Leeds U | 0 | 0 | 9 | 0 |
| 2012-13 | *Bury* | 29 | 1 | 29 | 1 |

**TONGE, Michael (M)**   349   28
H: 6 0   W: 11 10   b.Manchester 7-4-83
Source: Scholar. Honours: England Youth, Under-20, Under-21.

| Season | Club | Apps | Gls | Tot A | Tot G |
|---|---|---|---|---|---|
| 2000-01 | Sheffield U | 2 | 0 | | |
| 2001-02 | Sheffield U | 30 | 3 | | |
| 2002-03 | Sheffield U | 44 | 6 | | |
| 2003-04 | Sheffield U | 46 | 4 | | |
| 2004-05 | Sheffield U | 34 | 2 | | |
| 2005-06 | Sheffield U | 30 | 3 | | |
| 2006-07 | Sheffield U | 27 | 2 | | |
| 2007-08 | Sheffield U | 45 | 1 | | |
| 2008-09 | Sheffield U | 4 | 0 | 262 | 21 |
| 2008-09 | Stoke C | 10 | 0 | | |
| 2009-10 | Stoke C | 0 | 0 | | |
| 2009-10 | *Preston NE* | 7 | 0 | | |
| 2009-10 | *Derby Co* | 18 | 2 | 18 | 2 |
| 2010-11 | Stoke C | 2 | 0 | | |
| 2010-11 | *Preston NE* | 5 | 1 | 12 | 1 |
| 2011-12 | Stoke C | 0 | 0 | | |
| 2011-12 | *Barnsley* | 10 | 0 | 10 | 0 |
| 2012-13 | Stoke C | 0 | 0 | 12 | 0 |
| 2012-13 | Leeds U | 35 | 4 | 35 | 4 |

**TURNER, Lewis (M)**   0   0
H: 5 10   W: 11 00   b.Garforth 3-9-92
Source: Scholar.

| Season | Club | Apps | Gls |
|---|---|---|---|
| 2011-12 | Leeds U | 0 | 0 |
| 2012-13 | Leeds U | 0 | 0 |

**TURNER, Nathan (D)**   0   0
b.Garforth 3-9-92
Source: Scholar.

| Season | Club | Apps | Gls |
|---|---|---|---|
| 2011-12 | Leeds U | 0 | 0 |
| 2012-13 | Leeds U | 0 | 0 |

**VARNEY, Luke (F)**   301   64
H: 5 11   W: 11 00   b.Leicester 28-9-82
Source: Quorn.

| Season | Club | Apps | Gls | Tot A | Tot G |
|---|---|---|---|---|---|
| 2002-03 | Crewe Alex | 0 | 0 | | |
| 2003-04 | Crewe Alex | 8 | 1 | | |
| 2004-05 | Crewe Alex | 26 | 4 | | |
| 2005-06 | Crewe Alex | 27 | 5 | | |
| 2006-07 | Crewe Alex | 34 | 17 | 95 | 27 |
| 2007-08 | Charlton Ath | 39 | 8 | | |
| 2008-09 | Charlton Ath | 18 | 2 | 57 | 10 |
| 2008-09 | *Sheffield W* | 4 | 2 | | |
| 2008-09 | Derby Co | 10 | 1 | | |
| 2009-10 | Derby Co | 1 | 0 | | |
| 2009-10 | *Sheffield W* | 39 | 9 | 43 | 11 |
| 2010-11 | Derby Co | 1 | 0 | 12 | 1 |
| 2010-11 | *Blackpool* | 30 | 5 | 30 | 5 |
| 2011-12 | Portsmouth | 30 | 6 | 30 | 6 |
| 2012-13 | Leeds U | 34 | 4 | 34 | 4 |

**WARNOCK, Stephen (D)**   299   13
H: 5 7   W: 11 09   b.Ormskirk 12-12-81
Source: Trainee. Honours: England Schools, Youth, 2 full caps.

| Season | Club | Apps | Gls | Tot A | Tot G |
|---|---|---|---|---|---|
| 1998-99 | Liverpool | 0 | 0 | | |
| 1999-2000 | Liverpool | 0 | 0 | | |
| 2000-01 | Liverpool | 0 | 0 | | |
| 2001-02 | Liverpool | 0 | 0 | | |
| 2002-03 | Liverpool | 0 | 0 | | |
| 2002-03 | *Bradford C* | 12 | 1 | 12 | 1 |
| 2003-04 | Liverpool | 0 | 0 | | |
| 2003-04 | *Coventry C* | 44 | 3 | 44 | 3 |
| 2004-05 | Liverpool | 19 | 0 | | |
| 2005-06 | Liverpool | 20 | 1 | | |
| 2006-07 | Liverpool | 1 | 0 | 40 | 1 |
| 2006-07 | Blackburn R | 13 | 1 | | |
| 2007-08 | Blackburn R | 37 | 1 | | |
| 2008-09 | Blackburn R | 37 | 3 | | |
| 2009-10 | Blackburn R | 1 | 0 | 88 | 5 |
| 2009-10 | Aston Villa | 30 | 0 | | |
| 2010-11 | Aston Villa | 19 | 0 | | |
| 2011-12 | Aston Villa | 35 | 2 | | |
| 2012-13 | Aston Villa | 0 | 0 | 84 | 2 |
| 2012-13 | *Bolton W* | 15 | 0 | 15 | 0 |
| 2012-13 | *Leeds U* | 16 | 1 | 16 | 1 |

**WHITE, Aidan (D)**   99   5
H: 5 7   W: 10 00   b.Otley 10-10-91
Source: Scholar. Honours: England Youth. Eire Under-21.

| Season | Club | Apps | Gls | Tot A | Tot G |
|---|---|---|---|---|---|
| 2008-09 | Leeds U | 5 | 0 | | |
| 2009-10 | Leeds U | 8 | 0 | | |
| 2010-11 | Leeds U | 2 | 0 | | |
| 2010-11 | *Oldham Ath* | 24 | 4 | 24 | 4 |
| 2011-12 | Leeds U | 36 | 0 | | |
| 2012-13 | Leeds U | 24 | 1 | 75 | 1 |

**Players retained or with offer of contract**
Snodin, Jordan Lee.

**Scholars**
Amiri, Ali; Atkinson, Daniel Joseph; Booker, Luke Thomas; Coker, Afolabi; Coyle, Lewie Jacob; Denton, Tyler Jake; Dixon, Bradley John; Grimes, Eric Julian; Mowatt, Alex James; Parkin, Luke; Phillips, Kalvin Mark; Purver, Alex William; Roper, Corey Lee Russell; Skelton, Jake Daniel; Stokes, Eoghan; Tiesse, Bi-Le Smith; Walters, Lewis Henrique Paul.

## LEICESTER C (45)

**BECKFORD, Jermaine (F)**   246   105
H: 6 2   W: 13 02   b.Ealing 9-12-83
Source: Wealdstone. Honours: Jamaica 5 full caps, 1 goal.

| Season | Club | Apps | Gls | Tot A | Tot G |
|---|---|---|---|---|---|
| 2005-06 | Leeds U | 5 | 0 | | |
| 2006-07 | Leeds U | 5 | 0 | | |
| 2006-07 | *Carlisle U* | 4 | 1 | 4 | 1 |
| 2006-07 | *Scunthorpe U* | 18 | 8 | 18 | 8 |
| 2007-08 | Leeds U | 40 | 20 | | |
| 2008-09 | Leeds U | 34 | 26 | | |
| 2009-10 | Leeds U | 42 | 25 | 126 | 71 |
| 2010-11 | Everton | 32 | 8 | | |
| 2011-12 | Everton | 2 | 0 | 34 | 8 |
| 2011-12 | Leicester C | 39 | 9 | | |
| 2011-12 | Leicester C | 4 | 0 | 43 | 9 |
| 2012-13 | *Huddersfield T* | 21 | 8 | 21 | 8 |

**BLYTH, Jacob (F)**   6   0
b.Nuneaton 14-8-92

| Season | Club | Apps | Gls | Tot A | Tot G |
|---|---|---|---|---|---|
| 2012-13 | Leicester C | 0 | 0 | | |
| 2012-13 | *Burton Alb* | 2 | 0 | 2 | 0 |
| 2012-13 | *Notts Co* | 4 | 0 | 4 | 0 |

**CAIN, Michael (M)**   0   0
b. 4-12-94
Source: Luton T Youth.

| Season | Club | Apps | Gls |
|---|---|---|---|
| 2011-12 | Leicester C | 0 | 0 |
| 2012-13 | Leicester C | 0 | 0 |

**CLIFFORD, Conor (M)**   26   1
H: 5 8   W: 10 08   b.Dublin 1-10-91
Source: Scholar. Honours: Eire Youth, Under-21.

| Season | Club | Apps | Gls | Tot A | Tot G |
|---|---|---|---|---|---|
| 2008-09 | Chelsea | 0 | 0 | | |
| 2009-10 | Chelsea | 0 | 0 | | |
| 2010-11 | Chelsea | 0 | 0 | | |
| 2010-11 | *Plymouth Arg* | 7 | 0 | 7 | 0 |
| 2010-11 | *Notts Co* | 9 | 0 | 9 | 0 |
| 2011-12 | Chelsea | 0 | 0 | | |
| 2011-12 | *Yeovil T* | 7 | 0 | 7 | 0 |
| 2012-13 | Chelsea | 0 | 0 | | |
| 2012-13 | *Portsmouth* | 2 | 1 | 2 | 1 |
| 2012-13 | *Crawley T* | 1 | 0 | 1 | 0 |
| 2012-13 | Leicester C | 0 | 0 | | |

**DANNS, Neil (M)**   287   52
H: 5 10   W: 10 12   b.Liverpool 23-11-82
Source: Scholar.

| Season | Club | Apps | Gls | Tot A | Tot G |
|---|---|---|---|---|---|
| 2000-01 | Blackburn R | 0 | 0 | | |
| 2001-02 | Blackburn R | 0 | 0 | | |
| 2002-03 | Blackburn R | 2 | 0 | | |
| 2003-04 | Blackpool | 12 | 2 | 12 | 2 |
| 2003-04 | Blackburn R | 1 | 0 | | |
| 2003-04 | *Hartlepool U* | 9 | 1 | 9 | 1 |
| 2004-05 | Blackburn R | 0 | 0 | 3 | 0 |
| 2004-05 | Colchester U | 32 | 11 | | |
| 2005-06 | Colchester U | 41 | 8 | 73 | 19 |
| 2006-07 | Birmingham C | 29 | 3 | | |
| 2007-08 | Birmingham C | 2 | 0 | 31 | 3 |
| 2007-08 | *Crystal Palace* | 4 | 0 | | |
| 2008-09 | Crystal Palace | 20 | 2 | | |
| 2009-10 | Crystal Palace | 42 | 8 | | |
| 2010-11 | Crystal Palace | 37 | 8 | 103 | 18 |
| 2011-12 | Leicester C | 29 | 5 | | |
| 2012-13 | Leicester C | 1 | 0 | 30 | 5 |
| 2012-13 | *Bristol C* | 9 | 2 | 9 | 2 |
| 2012-13 | *Huddersfield T* | 17 | 2 | 17 | 2 |

**DE LAET, Ritchie (D)**   83   2
H: 6 1   W: 12 02   b.Antwerp 28-11-88
Source: Antwerp. Honours: Belgium Under-21, 2 full caps.

| Season | Club | Apps | Gls | Tot A | Tot G |
|---|---|---|---|---|---|
| 2007-08 | Stoke C | 0 | 0 | | |
| 2008-09 | Stoke C | 0 | 0 | | |
| 2008-09 | Manchester U | 1 | 0 | | |
| 2009-10 | Manchester U | 2 | 0 | | |
| 2010-11 | Manchester U | 0 | 0 | | |
| 2010-11 | *Sheffield U* | 6 | 0 | 6 | 0 |
| 2010-11 | *Preston NE* | 5 | 0 | 5 | 0 |
| 2010-11 | *Portsmouth* | 22 | 0 | 22 | 0 |
| 2011-12 | Manchester U | 0 | 0 | 3 | 0 |
| 2011-12 | *Norwich C* | 6 | 1 | 6 | 1 |
| 2012-13 | Leicester C | 41 | 1 | 41 | 1 |

**DRINKWATER, Daniel (M)**   132   6
H: 5 10   W: 11 00   b.Manchester 5-3-90
Source: Scholar. Honours: England Youth.

| Season | Club | Apps | Gls | Tot A | Tot G |
|---|---|---|---|---|---|
| 2008-09 | Manchester U | 0 | 0 | | |
| 2009-10 | Manchester U | 0 | 0 | | |
| 2009-10 | *Huddersfield T* | 33 | 2 | 33 | 2 |
| 2010-11 | Manchester U | 0 | 0 | | |
| 2010-11 | *Cardiff C* | 9 | 0 | 9 | 0 |
| 2010-11 | *Watford* | 12 | 0 | 12 | 0 |
| 2011-12 | Manchester U | 0 | 0 | | |
| 2011-12 | *Barnsley* | 17 | 1 | 17 | 1 |
| 2011-12 | Leicester C | 19 | 2 | | |
| 2012-13 | Leicester C | 42 | 1 | 61 | 3 |

**DYER, Lloyd (M)**   331   42
H: 5 8   W: 10 03   b.Birmingham 13-9-82
Source: Aston Villa Juniors.

| Season | Club | Apps | Gls | Tot A | Tot G |
|---|---|---|---|---|---|
| 2001-02 | WBA | 0 | 0 | | |
| 2002-03 | WBA | 0 | 0 | | |
| 2003-04 | WBA | 17 | 2 | | |
| 2003-04 | *Kidderminster H* | 7 | 1 | 7 | 1 |
| 2004-05 | WBA | 6 | 0 | | |
| 2004-05 | *Coventry C* | 6 | 0 | 6 | 0 |
| 2005-06 | WBA | 0 | 0 | 21 | 2 |
| 2005-06 | *QPR* | 15 | 0 | 15 | 0 |
| 2005-06 | *Millwall* | 6 | 0 | 6 | 0 |
| 2006-07 | Milton Keynes D | 41 | 5 | | |
| 2007-08 | Milton Keynes D | 45 | 11 | 86 | 16 |
| 2008-09 | Leicester C | 44 | 10 | | |
| 2009-10 | Leicester C | 33 | 3 | | |
| 2010-11 | Leicester C | 35 | 3 | | |
| 2011-12 | Leicester C | 36 | 4 | | |
| 2012-13 | Leicester C | 42 | 3 | 190 | 23 |

**FUTACS, Marko (F)**   90   14
H: 6 5   W: 14 00   b.Budapest 22-2-90
Honours: Hungary Youth, Under-21.

| Season | Club | Apps | Gls | Tot A | Tot G |
|---|---|---|---|---|---|
| 2008-09 | Nancy B | 12 | 3 | 12 | 3 |
| 2009-10 | Werder Bremen II | 13 | 3 | 13 | 3 |
| 2010-11 | Ingolstadt | 23 | 2 | 23 | 2 |
| 2011-12 | Portsmouth | 29 | 5 | 29 | 5 |
| 2012-13 | Leicester C | 9 | 1 | 9 | 1 |
| 2012-13 | *Blackpool* | 4 | 0 | 4 | 0 |

**GALLAGHER, Paul (F)**   288   57
H: 6 1   W: 11 00   b.Glasgow 9-8-84
Source: Trainee. Honours: Scotland Under-21, B, 1 full cap.

| Season | Club | Apps | Gls | Tot A | Tot G |
|---|---|---|---|---|---|
| 2002-03 | Blackburn R | 1 | 0 | | |
| 2003-04 | Blackburn R | 26 | 3 | | |
| 2004-05 | Blackburn R | 16 | 2 | | |
| 2005-06 | Blackburn R | 1 | 0 | | |
| 2005-06 | *Stoke C* | 37 | 11 | | |
| 2006-07 | Blackburn R | 16 | 1 | | |
| 2007-08 | Blackburn R | 0 | 0 | | |
| 2007-08 | *Preston NE* | 19 | 1 | 19 | 1 |
| 2007-08 | *Stoke C* | 7 | 0 | 44 | 11 |
| 2008-09 | Blackburn R | 0 | 0 | | |

| 2008-09 | Plymouth Arg | 40 | 13 | **40** | **13** |
| 2009-10 | Blackburn R | 1 | 0 | **61** | **6** |
| 2009-10 | Leicester C | 41 | 7 | | |
| 2010-11 | Leicester C | 41 | 10 | | |
| 2011-12 | Leicester C | 28 | 8 | | |
| 2012-13 | Leicester C | 8 | 0 | **118** | **25** |
| 2012-13 | Sheffield U | 6 | 1 | **6** | **1** |

**HOPPER, Tom (F)**     **22** **3**
H: 6 1   W: 12 00   b.Boston 14-12-93
Source: Scholar. Honours: England Youth.

| 2011-12 | Leicester C | 0 | 0 | | |
| 2012-13 | Leicester C | 0 | 0 | | |
| 2012-13 | Bury | 22 | 3 | **22** | **3** |

**JAMES, Matthew (M)**     **52** **5**
H: 6 0   W: 11 12   b.Bacup 22-7-91
Source: Scholar. Honours: England Youth, Under-20.

| 2007-08 | Manchester U | 0 | 0 | | |
| 2008-09 | Manchester U | 0 | 0 | | |
| 2009-10 | Manchester U | 0 | 0 | | |
| 2009-10 | Preston NE | 18 | 2 | | |
| 2010-11 | Manchester U | 0 | 0 | | |
| 2010-11 | Preston NE | 10 | 0 | **28** | **2** |
| 2011-12 | Manchester U | 0 | 0 | | |
| 2012-13 | Leicester C | 24 | 3 | **24** | **3** |

**KING, Andy (M)**     **216** **45**
H: 6 0   W: 11 10   b.Barnstaple 29-10-88
Source: Scholar. Honours: Wales Youth, Under-21, 18 full caps, 1 goal.

| 2007-08 | Leicester C | 11 | 1 | | |
| 2008-09 | Leicester C | 45 | 9 | | |
| 2009-10 | Leicester C | 43 | 9 | | |
| 2010-11 | Leicester C | 45 | 15 | | |
| 2011-12 | Leicester C | 30 | 4 | | |
| 2012-13 | Leicester C | 42 | 7 | **216** | **45** |

**KNOCKAERT, Anthony (M)**     **76** **18**
H: 5 8   W: 10 11   b.Lille 20-11-91
Honours: France Youth, Under-21.

| 2011-12 | Guingamp | 34 | 10 | **34** | **10** |
| 2012-13 | Leicester C | 42 | 8 | **42** | **8** |

**KONCHESKY, Paul (D)**     **428** **12**
H: 5 10   W: 11 07   b.Barking 15-5-81
Source: Trainee. Honours: England Youth, Under-20, Under-21, 2 full caps.

| 1997-98 | Charlton Ath | 3 | 0 | | |
| 1998-99 | Charlton Ath | 2 | 0 | | |
| 1999-2000 | Charlton Ath | 8 | 0 | | |
| 2000-01 | Charlton Ath | 23 | 0 | | |
| 2001-02 | Charlton Ath | 34 | 1 | | |
| 2002-03 | Charlton Ath | 30 | 3 | | |
| 2003-04 | Charlton Ath | 21 | 0 | | |
| 2003-04 | Tottenham H | 12 | 0 | **12** | **0** |
| 2004-05 | Charlton Ath | 28 | 1 | **149** | **5** |
| 2005-06 | West Ham U | 37 | 1 | | |
| 2006-07 | West Ham U | 22 | 0 | **59** | **1** |
| 2007-08 | Fulham | 33 | 0 | | |
| 2008-09 | Fulham | 36 | 1 | | |
| 2009-10 | Fulham | 27 | 1 | | |
| 2010-11 | Fulham | 1 | 0 | **97** | **2** |
| 2010-11 | Liverpool | 15 | 0 | **15** | **0** |
| 2010-11 | Nottingham F | 15 | 1 | **15** | **1** |
| 2011-12 | Leicester C | 42 | 2 | | |
| 2012-13 | Leicester C | 39 | 1 | **81** | **3** |

**LARRAURI, Pier (F)**     **0** **0**
H: 5 9   W: 11 12   b.Siena 26-3-94
Honours: Italy Youth.

| 2011-12 | Leicester C | 0 | 0 | | |
| 2012-13 | Leicester C | 0 | 0 | | |

**LOGAN, Conrad (G)**     **134** **0**
H: 6 2   W: 14 00   b.Letterkenny 18-4-86
Source: Scholar. Honours: Eire Youth.

| 2003-04 | Leicester C | 0 | 0 | | |
| 2004-05 | Leicester C | 0 | 0 | | |
| 2005-06 | Leicester C | 0 | 0 | | |
| 2005-06 | Boston U | 13 | 0 | **13** | **0** |
| 2006-07 | Leicester C | 18 | 0 | | |
| 2007-08 | Leicester C | 0 | 0 | | |
| 2007-08 | Stockport Co | 34 | 0 | | |
| 2008-09 | Leicester C | 0 | 0 | | |
| 2008-09 | Luton T | 22 | 0 | **22** | **0** |
| 2008-09 | Stockport Co | 7 | 0 | **41** | **0** |
| 2009-10 | Leicester C | 2 | 0 | | |
| 2010-11 | Leicester C | 3 | 0 | | |

| 2010-11 | Bristol R | 16 | 0 | **16** | **0** |
| 2011-12 | Leicester C | 0 | 0 | | |
| 2011-12 | Rotherham U | 19 | 0 | **19** | **0** |
| 2012-13 | Leicester C | 0 | 0 | **23** | **0** |

**MARSHALL, Ben (F)**     **152** **22**
H: 5 11   W: 11 13   b.Salford 29-3-91
Source: Crewe Alex Scholar. Honours: England Under-21.

| 2009-10 | Stoke C | 0 | 0 | | |
| 2009-10 | Northampton T | 15 | 2 | **15** | **2** |
| 2009-10 | Cheltenham T | 6 | 2 | **6** | **2** |
| 2009-10 | Carlisle U | 20 | 3 | | |
| 2010-11 | Stoke C | 0 | 0 | | |
| 2010-11 | Carlisle U | 33 | 3 | **53** | **6** |
| 2011-12 | Stoke C | 0 | 0 | | |
| 2011-12 | Sheffield W | 22 | 5 | **22** | **5** |
| 2011-12 | Leicester C | 16 | 3 | | |
| 2012-13 | Leicester C | 40 | 4 | **56** | **7** |

**MOORE, Liam (D)**     **42** **0**
H: 6 1   W: 13 08   b.Loughborough 31-1-93
Source: Scholar. Honours: England Youth, Under-21.

| 2011-12 | Leicester C | 2 | 0 | | |
| 2011-12 | Bradford C | 17 | 0 | **17** | **0** |
| 2012-13 | Leicester C | 16 | 0 | **18** | **0** |
| 2012-13 | Brentford | 7 | 0 | **7** | **0** |

**MORGAN, Wes (D)**     **419** **14**
H: 6 2   W: 14 00   b.Nottingham 21-1-84
Source: Dunkirk.

| 2002-03 | Nottingham F | 0 | 0 | | |
| 2002-03 | Kidderminster H | 5 | 1 | **5** | **1** |
| 2003-04 | Nottingham F | 32 | 2 | | |
| 2004-05 | Nottingham F | 43 | 1 | | |
| 2005-06 | Nottingham F | 43 | 2 | | |
| 2006-07 | Nottingham F | 38 | 0 | | |
| 2007-08 | Nottingham F | 42 | 1 | | |
| 2008-09 | Nottingham F | 42 | 1 | | |
| 2009-10 | Nottingham F | 44 | 3 | | |
| 2010-11 | Nottingham F | 46 | 1 | | |
| 2011-12 | Nottingham F | 22 | 1 | **352** | **12** |
| 2011-12 | Leicester C | 17 | 0 | | |
| 2012-13 | Leicester C | 45 | 1 | **62** | **1** |

**NUGENT, Dave (F)**     **374** **102**
H: 5 11   W: 12 13   b.Liverpool 2-5-85
Source: Scholar. Honours: England Youth, Under-20, Under-21, 1 full cap, 1 goal.

| 2001-02 | Bury | 5 | 0 | | |
| 2002-03 | Bury | 31 | 4 | | |
| 2003-04 | Bury | 26 | 3 | | |
| 2004-05 | Bury | 26 | 11 | **88** | **18** |
| 2004-05 | Preston NE | 18 | 8 | | |
| 2005-06 | Preston NE | 32 | 10 | | |
| 2006-07 | Preston NE | 44 | 15 | **94** | **33** |
| 2007-08 | Portsmouth | 15 | 0 | | |
| 2008-09 | Portsmouth | 16 | 3 | | |
| 2009-10 | Portsmouth | 3 | 0 | | |
| 2009-10 | Burnley | 30 | 6 | **30** | **6** |
| 2010-11 | Portsmouth | 44 | 13 | **78** | **16** |
| 2011-12 | Leicester C | 42 | 15 | | |
| 2012-13 | Leicester C | 42 | 14 | **84** | **29** |

**PANAYIOTOU, Harry (F)**     **1** **1**
b.Leicester 28-10-94
Source: Scholar.

| 2011-12 | Leicester C | 1 | 1 | | |
| 2012-13 | Leicester C | 0 | 0 | **1** | **1** |

**SCHLUPP, Jeffrey (M)**     **49** **11**
H: 5 8   W: 11 00   b.Hamburg 23-12-92
Source: Scholar. Honours: Ghana 1 full cap.

| 2010-11 | Leicester C | 0 | 0 | | |
| 2011-12 | Brentford | 9 | 6 | **9** | **6** |
| 2011-12 | Leicester C | 21 | 2 | | |
| 2012-13 | Leicester C | 19 | 3 | **40** | **5** |

**SCHMEICHEL, Kasper (G)**     **251** **0**
H: 6 1   W: 13 00   b.Copenhagen 5-11-86
Source: Scholar. Honours: Denmark Youth, Under-20, Under-21.

| 2003-04 | Manchester C | 0 | 0 | | |
| 2004-05 | Manchester C | 0 | 0 | | |
| 2005-06 | Manchester C | 0 | 0 | | |
| 2005-06 | Darlington | 4 | 0 | **4** | **0** |
| 2005-06 | Bury | 15 | 0 | | |
| 2006-07 | Manchester C | 0 | 0 | | |
| 2006-07 | Falkirk | 15 | 0 | **15** | **0** |

| 2006-07 | Bury | 14 | 0 | **29** | **0** |
| 2007-08 | Manchester C | 7 | 0 | | |
| 2007-08 | Cardiff C | 14 | 0 | **14** | **0** |
| 2007-08 | Coventry C | 9 | 0 | **9** | **0** |
| 2008-09 | Manchester C | 1 | 0 | | |
| 2009-10 | Manchester C | 0 | 0 | **8** | **0** |
| 2009-10 | Notts Co | 43 | 0 | **43** | **0** |
| 2010-11 | Leeds U | 37 | 0 | **37** | **0** |
| 2011-12 | Leicester C | 46 | 0 | | |
| 2012-13 | Leicester C | 46 | 0 | **92** | **0** |

**SMITH, Adam (G)**     **0** **0**
H: 5 11   W: 11 00   b.Sunderland 23-11-92
Source: Scholar.

| 2010-11 | Leicester C | 0 | 0 | | |
| 2011-12 | Leicester C | 0 | 0 | | |
| 2011-12 | Chesterfield | 0 | 0 | | |
| 2011-12 | Bristol R | 0 | 0 | | |
| 2012-13 | Leicester C | 0 | 0 | | |

**ST LEDGER, Sean (D)**     **320** **13**
H: 6 0   W: 11 09   b.Solihull 28-12-84
Source: Scholar. Honours: Eire 36 full caps, 3 goals.

| 2002-03 | Peterborough U | 1 | 0 | | |
| 2003-04 | Peterborough U | 2 | 0 | | |
| 2004-05 | Peterborough U | 33 | 0 | | |
| 2005-06 | Peterborough U | 43 | 1 | **79** | **1** |
| 2006-07 | Preston NE | 41 | 1 | | |
| 2007-08 | Preston NE | 37 | 1 | | |
| 2008-09 | Preston NE | 46 | 5 | | |
| 2009-10 | Preston NE | 30 | 2 | | |
| 2009-10 | Middlesbrough | 15 | 2 | **15** | **2** |
| 2010-11 | Preston NE | 31 | 1 | **185** | **10** |
| 2011-12 | Leicester C | 26 | 0 | | |
| 2012-13 | Leicester C | 9 | 0 | **35** | **0** |
| 2012-13 | Millwall | 6 | 0 | **6** | **0** |

**TAFT, George (D)**     **0** **0**
H: 5 9   W: 11 09   b.Leicester 29-7-93
Source: Scholar. Honours: England Youth.

| 2010-11 | Leicester C | 0 | 0 | | |
| 2011-12 | Leicester C | 0 | 0 | | |
| 2012-13 | Leicester C | 0 | 0 | | |

**VARDY, Jamie (F)**     **26** **4**
H: 5 10   W: 11 12   b.Sheffield 11-1-87
Source: Stocksbridge, FC Halifax, Fleetwood T.

| 2012-13 | Leicester C | 26 | 4 | **26** | **4** |

**WAGHORN, Martyn (F)**     **119** **22**
H: 5 9   W: 13 01   b.South Shields 23-1-90
Source: Scholar. Honours: England Youth, Under-21.

| 2007-08 | Sunderland | 3 | 0 | | |
| 2008-09 | Sunderland | 0 | 0 | | |
| 2008-09 | Charlton Ath | 7 | 1 | **7** | **1** |
| 2009-10 | Sunderland | 0 | 0 | | |
| 2009-10 | Leicester C | 43 | 12 | | |
| 2010-11 | Sunderland | 2 | 0 | **6** | **0** |
| 2010-11 | Leicester C | 30 | 4 | | |
| 2011-12 | Leicester C | 4 | 1 | | |
| 2011-12 | Hull C | 5 | 1 | **5** | **1** |
| 2012-13 | Leicester C | 24 | 3 | **101** | **20** |

**WELLENS, Richard (M)**     **495** **37**
H: 5 9   W: 11 06   b.Manchester 26-3-80
Source: Trainee. Honours: England Youth.

| 1996-97 | Manchester U | 0 | 0 | | |
| 1997-98 | Manchester U | 0 | 0 | | |
| 1998-99 | Manchester U | 0 | 0 | | |
| 1999-2000 | Manchester U | 0 | 0 | | |
| 1999-2000 | Blackpool | 8 | 0 | | |
| 2000-01 | Blackpool | 36 | 8 | | |
| 2001-02 | Blackpool | 36 | 1 | | |
| 2002-03 | Blackpool | 39 | 1 | | |
| 2003-04 | Blackpool | 41 | 3 | | |
| 2004-05 | Blackpool | 28 | 3 | **188** | **16** |
| 2005-06 | Oldham Ath | 45 | 4 | | |
| 2006-07 | Oldham Ath | 44 | 4 | **87** | **8** |
| 2007-08 | Doncaster R | 45 | 6 | | |
| 2008-09 | Doncaster R | 39 | 3 | **84** | **9** |
| 2009-10 | Leicester C | 41 | 1 | | |
| 2010-11 | Leicester C | 45 | 2 | | |
| 2011-12 | Leicester C | 41 | 1 | | |
| 2012-13 | Leicester C | 2 | 0 | **129** | **4** |
| 2012-13 | Ipswich T | 7 | 0 | **7** | **0** |

## WHITBREAD, Zak (D)    160   5
H: 6 2   W: 12 07   b.Houston 4-3-84
*Honours:* USA Under-23.

|  |  | | | | |
|---|---|---|---|---|---|
| 2002-03 | Liverpool | 0 | 0 | | |
| 2003-04 | Liverpool | 0 | 0 | | |
| 2004-05 | Liverpool | 0 | 0 | | |
| 2005-06 | Liverpool | 0 | 0 | | |
| 2005-06 | Millwall | 25 | 0 | | |
| 2006-07 | Millwall | 14 | 0 | | |
| 2007-08 | Millwall | 23 | 3 | | |
| 2008-09 | Millwall | 38 | 0 | | |
| 2009-10 | Millwall | 0 | 0 | 100 | 3 |
| 2009-10 | Norwich C | 4 | 0 | | |
| 2010-11 | Norwich C | 22 | 1 | | |
| 2011-12 | Norwich C | 18 | 0 | 44 | 1 |
| 2012-13 | Leicester C | 16 | 1 | 16 | 1 |

## WOOD, Chris (F)    138   41
H: 6 3   W: 12 10   b.Auckland 7-12-91
*Honours:* New Zealand Youth, Under-23, 30 full caps, 10 goals.

|  |  | | | | |
|---|---|---|---|---|---|
| 2008-09 | WBA | 2 | 0 | | |
| 2009-10 | WBA | 18 | 1 | | |
| 2010-11 | WBA | 1 | 0 | | |
| 2010-11 | *Barnsley* | 7 | 0 | 7 | 0 |
| 2010-11 | *Brighton & HA* | 29 | 8 | 29 | 8 |
| 2011-12 | WBA | 0 | 0 | | |
| 2011-12 | *Birmingham C* | 23 | 9 | 23 | 9 |
| 2011-12 | *Bristol C* | 19 | 3 | 19 | 3 |
| 2012-13 | WBA | 0 | 0 | 21 | 1 |
| 2012-13 | *Millwall* | 19 | 11 | 19 | 11 |
| 2012-13 | Leicester C | 20 | 9 | 20 | 9 |

**Players retained or with offer of contract**
Dodoo, Joseph; Paul, Alexander; Pearson, James.

**Scholars**
Anton, Jamie Richard; Awuah, Reiss; Casey, Dylan; Downes, Luke; Elder, Callum Roddie; Greenway-Tambini, Louis; King, Macaulay; McCourt, Jak; Paratore, Robert; Pepe-Ngoma, Herve; Samba, Eddy; Smith, Joshua Luke; Stankevicius, Simonas.

# LEYTON ORIENT (46)

## BAUDRY, Mathieu (D)    71   5
H: 6 2   W: 12 08   b.Le Havre 24-2-88

|  |  | | | | |
|---|---|---|---|---|---|
| 2007-08 | Troyes | 2 | 1 | | |
| 2008-09 | Troyes | 17 | 0 | | |
| 2009-10 | Troyes | 7 | 0 | 26 | 1 |
| 2010-11 | Bournemouth | 3 | 1 | | |
| 2011-12 | Bournemouth | 7 | 0 | 10 | 1 |
| 2011-12 | *Dagenham & R* | 11 | 0 | 11 | 0 |
| 2012-13 | Leyton Orient | 24 | 3 | 24 | 3 |

## BUTCHER, Lee (G)    32   0
H: 6 1   W: 12 02   b.Waltham Forest 11-10-88
*Source:* Tottenham H.

|  |  | | | | |
|---|---|---|---|---|---|
| 2010-11 | Leyton Orient | 9 | 0 | | |
| 2011-12 | Leyton Orient | 23 | 0 | | |
| 2012-13 | Leyton Orient | 0 | 0 | 32 | 0 |

## CLARKE, Nathan (D)    343   9
H: 6 2   W: 12 00   b.Halifax 30-11-83
*Source:* Scholar.

|  |  | | | | |
|---|---|---|---|---|---|
| 2001-02 | Huddersfield T | 36 | 1 | | |
| 2002-03 | Huddersfield T | 3 | 0 | | |
| 2003-04 | Huddersfield T | 26 | 1 | | |
| 2004-05 | Huddersfield T | 37 | 0 | | |
| 2005-06 | Huddersfield T | 46 | 0 | | |
| 2006-07 | Huddersfield T | 16 | 0 | | |
| 2007-08 | Huddersfield T | 44 | 2 | | |
| 2008-09 | Huddersfield T | 38 | 3 | | |
| 2009-10 | Huddersfield T | 17 | 1 | | |
| 2010-11 | Huddersfield T | 1 | 0 | | |
| 2010-11 | *Colchester U* | 18 | 0 | 18 | 0 |
| 2011-12 | Huddersfield T | 0 | 0 | 264 | 8 |
| 2011-12 | *Oldham Ath* | 16 | 1 | 16 | 1 |
| 2011-12 | *Bury* | 11 | 0 | 11 | 0 |
| 2012-13 | Leyton Orient | 34 | 0 | 34 | 0 |

## COOK, Lee (M)    308   26
H: 5 8   W: 11 10   b.Hammersmith 3-8-82
*Source:* Aylesbury U.

|  |  | | | | |
|---|---|---|---|---|---|
| 1999-2000 | Watford | 0 | 0 | | |
| 2000-01 | Watford | 4 | 0 | | |
| 2001-02 | Watford | 10 | 0 | | |
| 2002-03 | Watford | 4 | 0 | | |
| 2002-03 | *York C* | 7 | 1 | 7 | 1 |
| 2002-03 | QPR | 13 | 1 | | |
| 2003-04 | Watford | 41 | 7 | 59 | 7 |
| 2004-05 | QPR | 42 | 2 | | |
| 2005-06 | QPR | 40 | 4 | | |
| 2006-07 | QPR | 37 | 3 | | |
| 2007-08 | Fulham | 0 | 0 | | |
| 2007-08 | Charlton Ath | 9 | 0 | | |
| 2008-09 | Fulham | 0 | 0 | | |
| 2008-09 | QPR | 34 | 1 | | |
| 2009-10 | QPR | 16 | 1 | | |
| 2010-11 | QPR | 0 | 0 | | |
| 2011-12 | QPR | 0 | 0 | 182 | 12 |
| 2011-12 | *Leyton Orient* | 9 | 1 | | |
| 2011-12 | *Charlton Ath* | 4 | 0 | 13 | 0 |
| 2012-13 | Leyton Orient | 38 | 5 | 47 | 6 |

## COX, Dean (M)    273   38
H: 5 4   W: 9 08   b.Cuckfield 12-8-87
*Source:* Scholar.

|  |  | | | | |
|---|---|---|---|---|---|
| 2005-06 | Brighton & HA | 1 | 0 | | |
| 2006-07 | Brighton & HA | 42 | 6 | | |
| 2007-08 | Brighton & HA | 42 | 6 | | |
| 2008-09 | Brighton & HA | 40 | 4 | | |
| 2009-10 | Brighton & HA | 21 | 0 | 146 | 16 |
| 2010-11 | Leyton Orient | 45 | 11 | | |
| 2011-12 | Leyton Orient | 38 | 7 | | |
| 2012-13 | Leyton Orient | 44 | 4 | 127 | 22 |

## CUTHBERT, Scott (D)    164   7
H: 6 2   W: 12 05   b.Alexandria 15-6-87
*Honours:* Scotland Youth, Under-21, B.

|  |  | | | | |
|---|---|---|---|---|---|
| 2004-05 | Celtic | 0 | 0 | | |
| 2005-06 | Celtic | 0 | 0 | | |
| 2006-07 | Celtic | 0 | 0 | | |
| 2006-07 | *Livingston* | 4 | 1 | 4 | 1 |
| 2007-08 | Celtic | 0 | 0 | | |
| 2008-09 | Celtic | 0 | 0 | | |
| 2008-09 | *St Mirren* | 29 | 0 | 29 | 0 |
| 2009-10 | Swindon T | 39 | 3 | | |
| 2010-11 | Swindon T | 41 | 2 | 80 | 5 |
| 2011-12 | Leyton Orient | 33 | 1 | | |
| 2012-13 | Leyton Orient | 18 | 0 | 51 | 1 |

## JAMES, Lloyd (M)    156   3
H: 5 11   W: 11 01   b.Bristol 16-2-88
*Source:* Scholar. *Honours:* Wales Youth, Under-21.

|  |  | | | | |
|---|---|---|---|---|---|
| 2005-06 | Southampton | 0 | 0 | | |
| 2006-07 | Southampton | 0 | 0 | | |
| 2007-08 | Southampton | 0 | 0 | | |
| 2008-09 | Southampton | 41 | 0 | | |
| 2009-10 | Southampton | 30 | 2 | 71 | 2 |
| 2010-11 | Colchester U | 28 | 0 | | |
| 2011-12 | Colchester U | 23 | 1 | 51 | 1 |
| 2011-12 | *Crawley T* | 6 | 0 | 6 | 0 |
| 2012-13 | Leyton Orient | 28 | 0 | 28 | 0 |

## JONES, Jamie (G)    123   0
H: 6 2   W: 14 05   b.Kirkby 18-2-89
*Source:* Scholar.

|  |  | | | | |
|---|---|---|---|---|---|
| 2007-08 | Everton | 0 | 0 | | |
| 2008-09 | Leyton Orient | 20 | 0 | | |
| 2009-10 | Leyton Orient | 36 | 0 | | |
| 2010-11 | Leyton Orient | 35 | 0 | | |
| 2011-12 | Leyton Orient | 6 | 0 | | |
| 2012-13 | Leyton Orient | 26 | 0 | 123 | 0 |

## LAIRD, Marc (M)    147   11
H: 6 1   W: 10 07   b.Edinburgh 23-1-86
*Source:* Trainee.

|  |  | | | | |
|---|---|---|---|---|---|
| 2003-04 | Manchester C | 0 | 0 | | |
| 2004-05 | Manchester C | 0 | 0 | | |
| 2005-06 | Manchester C | 0 | 0 | | |
| 2006-07 | Manchester C | 0 | 0 | | |
| 2006-07 | *Northampton T* | 6 | 0 | 6 | 0 |
| 2007-08 | Manchester C | 0 | 0 | | |
| 2007-08 | *Port Vale* | 7 | 1 | 7 | 1 |
| 2007-08 | Millwall | 17 | 1 | | |
| 2008-09 | Millwall | 38 | 5 | | |
| 2009-10 | Millwall | 20 | 0 | | |
| 2010-11 | Millwall | 1 | 0 | 76 | 6 |
| 2010-11 | *Brentford* | 4 | 1 | 4 | 1 |
| 2011-12 | *Walsall* | 8 | 0 | 8 | 0 |
| 2011-12 | Leyton Orient | 22 | 2 | | |
| 2012-13 | Leyton Orient | 1 | 0 | 23 | 2 |
| 2012-13 | *Southend U* | 23 | 1 | 23 | 1 |

## LEE, Harry (M)    1   0
H: 6 0   W: 11 09   b.Hackney 20-3-95

|  |  | | | | |
|---|---|---|---|---|---|
| 2012-13 | Leyton Orient | 1 | 0 | 1 | 0 |

## LISBIE, Kevin (F)    388   90
H: 5 10   W: 11 06   b.Hackney 17-10-78
*Source:* Trainee. *Honours:* England Youth. Jamaica 10 full caps, 2 goals.

|  |  | | | | |
|---|---|---|---|---|---|
| 1996-97 | Charlton Ath | 25 | 1 | | |
| 1997-98 | Charlton Ath | 17 | 1 | | |
| 1998-99 | Charlton Ath | 1 | 0 | | |
| 1998-99 | *Gillingham* | 7 | 4 | 7 | 4 |
| 1999-2000 | Charlton Ath | 0 | 0 | | |
| 1999-2000 | *Reading* | 2 | 0 | 2 | 0 |
| 2000-01 | Charlton Ath | 18 | 0 | | |
| 2000-01 | *QPR* | 2 | 0 | 2 | 0 |
| 2001-02 | Charlton Ath | 22 | 5 | | |
| 2002-03 | Charlton Ath | 32 | 4 | | |
| 2003-04 | Charlton Ath | 9 | 4 | | |
| 2004-05 | Charlton Ath | 17 | 1 | | |
| 2005-06 | Charlton Ath | 6 | 0 | | |
| 2005-06 | *Norwich C* | 6 | 1 | 6 | 1 |
| 2005-06 | *Derby Co* | 7 | 1 | 7 | 1 |
| 2006-07 | Charlton Ath | 8 | 0 | 155 | 16 |
| 2007-08 | Colchester U | 42 | 17 | | |
| 2008-09 | Ipswich T | 41 | 6 | | |
| 2009-10 | Ipswich T | 0 | 0 | | |
| 2009-10 | *Colchester U* | 41 | 13 | 83 | 30 |
| 2010-11 | Ipswich T | 0 | 0 | | |
| 2010-11 | *Millwall* | 20 | 4 | 20 | 4 |
| 2011-12 | Ipswich T | 0 | 0 | 41 | 6 |
| 2011-12 | Leyton Orient | 37 | 12 | | |
| 2012-13 | Leyton Orient | 28 | 16 | 65 | 28 |

## MACDONALD, Charlie (F)    235   59
H: 5 8   W: 12 10   b.Southwark 13-2-81
*Source:* Trainee.

|  |  | | | | |
|---|---|---|---|---|---|
| 1998-99 | Charlton Ath | 0 | 0 | | |
| 1999-2000 | Charlton Ath | 3 | 0 | | |
| 2000-01 | Charlton Ath | 3 | 0 | | |
| 2000-01 | *Cheltenham T* | 8 | 2 | 8 | 2 |
| 2001-02 | Charlton Ath | 2 | 1 | 8 | 1 |
| 2001-02 | *Torquay U* | 5 | 0 | 5 | 0 |
| 2001-02 | *Colchester U* | 4 | 1 | 4 | 1 |

From Margate, Stevenage, Crawley T, Gravesend & N.

|  |  | | | | |
|---|---|---|---|---|---|
| 2007-08 | Southend U | 25 | 1 | 25 | 1 |
| 2008-09 | Brentford | 38 | 16 | | |
| 2009-10 | Brentford | 40 | 15 | | |
| 2010-11 | Brentford | 30 | 9 | | |
| 2011-12 | Brentford | 0 | 0 | 111 | 40 |
| 2011-12 | Milton Keynes D | 35 | 9 | | |
| 2012-13 | Milton Keynes D | 3 | 0 | 54 | 11 |
| 2012-13 | Leyton Orient | 20 | 3 | 20 | 3 |

## McSWEENEY, Leon (F)    203   13
H: 5 10   W: 10 11   b.Cork 19-2-83
*Source:* Cork C.

|  |  | | | | |
|---|---|---|---|---|---|
| 2001-02 | Leicester C | 0 | 0 | | |
| 2002-03 | Leicester C | 0 | 0 | | |

From Scarborough, Hucknall T, Hednesford T, Ilkeston T.

|  |  | | | | |
|---|---|---|---|---|---|
| 2007 | Cork C | 18 | 5 | 18 | 5 |
| 2007-08 | Stockport Co | 11 | 1 | | |
| 2008-09 | Stockport Co | 36 | 4 | 47 | 5 |
| 2009-10 | Hartlepool U | 31 | 1 | | |
| 2010-11 | Hartlepool U | 46 | 2 | 77 | 3 |
| 2011-12 | Leyton Orient | 29 | 0 | | |
| 2012-13 | Leyton Orient | 32 | 0 | 61 | 0 |

## MOONEY, David (F)    249   70
H: 6 2   W: 12 06   b.Dublin 30-10-84
*Source:* Shamrock R, Longford T. *Honours:* Eire Under-23.

|  |  | | | | |
|---|---|---|---|---|---|
| 2005 | Longford T | 13 | 4 | | |
| 2005 | Shamrock R | 14 | 2 | 14 | 2 |
| 2006 | Longford T | 21 | 3 | | |
| 2007 | Longford T | 32 | 19 | 66 | 26 |
| 2008 | Cork C | 22 | 15 | 22 | 15 |
| 2008-09 | Reading | 0 | 0 | | |
| 2008-09 | *Stockport Co* | 2 | 0 | 2 | 0 |
| 2008-09 | *Norwich C* | 9 | 3 | 9 | 3 |
| 2009-10 | Reading | 0 | 0 | | |
| 2009-10 | *Charlton Ath* | 28 | 5 | 28 | 5 |
| 2010-11 | Reading | 0 | 0 | | |
| 2010-11 | *Colchester U* | 39 | 9 | 39 | 9 |
| 2011-12 | Leyton Orient | 37 | 5 | | |
| 2012-13 | Leyton Orient | 32 | 5 | 69 | 10 |

**OBAFEMI, Affy (F)**    9   0
H: 6 2  W: 13 02  b.London 25-11-94
Source: Scholar.

| | | | | | |
|---|---|--:|--:|--:|--:|
| 2011-12 | Leyton Orient | 1 | 0 | | |
| 2012-13 | Leyton Orient | 8 | 0 | 9 | 0 |

**ODUBAJO, Moses (M)**    47   3
H: 5 9  W: 11 05  b.Greenwich 28-7-93
Source: Scholar.

| | | | | | |
|---|---|--:|--:|--:|--:|
| 2011-12 | Leyton Orient | 3 | 1 | | |
| 2012-13 | Leyton Orient | 44 | 2 | 47 | 3 |

**OMOZUSI, Elliot (D)**    94   0
H: 5 11  W: 12 09  b.Hackney 15-12-88
Source: Scholar. Honours: England Youth.

| | | | | | |
|---|---|--:|--:|--:|--:|
| 2005-06 | Fulham | 0 | 0 | | |
| 2006-07 | Fulham | 0 | 0 | | |
| 2007-08 | Fulham | 8 | 0 | | |
| 2008-09 | Fulham | 0 | 0 | | |
| 2008-09 | Norwich C | 21 | 0 | 21 | 0 |
| 2009-10 | Fulham | 0 | 0 | 8 | 0 |
| 2009-10 | *Charlton Ath* | 9 | 0 | 9 | 0 |
| 2010-11 | Leyton Orient | 40 | 0 | | |
| 2011-12 | Leyton Orient | 10 | 0 | | |
| 2012-13 | Leyton Orient | 6 | 0 | 56 | 0 |

**ROWLANDS, Martin (M)**    400   59
H: 5 9  W: 10 10  b.Hammersmith 8-2-79
Source: Farnborough T. Honours: Eire Under-21, 5 full caps.

| | | | | | |
|---|---|--:|--:|--:|--:|
| 1998-99 | Brentford | 36 | 4 | | |
| 1999-2000 | Brentford | 40 | 6 | | |
| 2000-01 | Brentford | 32 | 2 | | |
| 2001-02 | Brentford | 23 | 7 | | |
| 2002-03 | Brentford | 18 | 1 | 149 | 20 |
| 2003-04 | QPR | 42 | 10 | | |
| 2004-05 | QPR | 35 | 3 | | |
| 2005-06 | QPR | 14 | 2 | | |
| 2006-07 | QPR | 29 | 10 | | |
| 2007-08 | QPR | 44 | 6 | | |
| 2008-09 | QPR | 24 | 2 | | |
| 2009-10 | QPR | 6 | 0 | | |
| 2010-11 | QPR | 4 | 0 | | |
| 2010-11 | *Millwall* | 1 | 0 | 1 | 0 |
| 2011-12 | QPR | 0 | 0 | 198 | 33 |
| 2011-12 | *Wycombe W* | 10 | 0 | 10 | 0 |
| 2011-12 | *Colchester U* | 9 | 2 | 9 | 2 |
| 2012-13 | Leyton Orient | 33 | 4 | 33 | 4 |

**SAWYER, Gary (D)**    192   6
H: 6 0  W: 11 08  b.Bideford 5-7-85
Source: Scholar.

| | | | | | |
|---|---|--:|--:|--:|--:|
| 2004-05 | Plymouth Arg | 0 | 0 | | |
| 2005-06 | Plymouth Arg | 0 | 0 | | |
| 2006-07 | Plymouth Arg | 22 | 0 | | |
| 2007-08 | Plymouth Arg | 31 | 1 | | |
| 2008-09 | Plymouth Arg | 13 | 3 | | |
| 2009-10 | Plymouth Arg | 29 | 1 | 95 | 5 |
| 2009-10 | *Bristol C* | 2 | 0 | 2 | 0 |
| 2010-11 | Bristol R | 37 | 0 | | |
| 2011-12 | Bristol R | 24 | 0 | 61 | 0 |
| 2012-13 | Leyton Orient | 34 | 1 | 34 | 1 |

**SMITH, Jimmy (M)**    211   24
H: 6 0  W: 10 03  b.Newham 7-1-87
Source: Scholar. Honours: England Youth.

| | | | | | |
|---|---|--:|--:|--:|--:|
| 2004-05 | Chelsea | 0 | 0 | | |
| 2005-06 | Chelsea | 1 | 0 | | |
| 2006-07 | Chelsea | 0 | 0 | | |
| 2006-07 | *QPR* | 29 | 6 | 29 | 6 |
| 2007-08 | Chelsea | 0 | 0 | | |
| 2007-08 | *Norwich C* | 9 | 0 | 9 | 0 |
| 2008-09 | Chelsea | 0 | 0 | 1 | 0 |
| 2008-09 | *Sheffield W* | 12 | 0 | 12 | 0 |
| 2008-09 | *Leyton Orient* | 16 | 0 | | |
| 2009-10 | Leyton Orient | 40 | 2 | | |
| 2010-11 | Leyton Orient | 31 | 7 | | |
| 2011-12 | Leyton Orient | 38 | 6 | | |
| 2012-13 | Leyton Orient | 35 | 3 | 160 | 18 |

**SYMES, Michael (F)**    229   53
H: 6 3  W: 12 04  b.Gt Yarmouth 31-10-83
Source: Scholar.

| | | | | | |
|---|---|--:|--:|--:|--:|
| 2001-02 | Everton | 0 | 0 | | |
| 2002-03 | Everton | 0 | 0 | | |
| 2003-04 | Everton | 0 | 0 | | |
| 2003-04 | *Crewe Alex* | 4 | 1 | 4 | 1 |
| 2004-05 | Bradford C | 12 | 2 | | |
| 2004-05 | *Darlington* | 0 | 0 | | |
| 2005-06 | Bradford C | 3 | 1 | | |
| 2005-06 | *Stockport Co* | 1 | 0 | 1 | 0 |
| 2006-07 | Bradford C | 0 | 0 | 15 | 3 |
| 2006-07 | Shrewsbury T | 33 | 9 | | |
| 2007-08 | Shrewsbury T | 21 | 3 | | |
| 2007-08 | *Macclesfield T* | 14 | 1 | 14 | 1 |
| 2008-09 | Shrewsbury T | 8 | 2 | 62 | 14 |
| 2008-09 | *Bournemouth* | 5 | 0 | | |
| 2008-09 | *Accrington S* | 7 | 1 | | |
| 2009-10 | Accrington S | 41 | 13 | 48 | 14 |
| 2010-11 | Bournemouth | 22 | 8 | | |
| 2011-12 | Bournemouth | 15 | 3 | 42 | 11 |
| 2011-12 | *Rochdale* | 15 | 4 | 15 | 4 |
| 2012-13 | Leyton Orient | 13 | 1 | 13 | 1 |
| 2012-13 | *Burton Alb* | 15 | 4 | 15 | 4 |

**VANDERHYDE, De-Reece (D)**    0   0
H: 5 11  W: 12 08  b.London 5-4-95

| | | | |
|---|---|--:|--:|
| 2012-13 | Leyton Orient | 0 | 0 |

**VINCELOT, Romain (M)**    160   17
H: 5 9  W: 11 02  b.Poitiers 29-10-85

| | | | | | |
|---|---|--:|--:|--:|--:|
| 2004-05 | Chamois Niortais | 3 | 0 | 3 | 0 |
| 2005-06 | Chamois Niortais | 28 | 1 | | |
| 2006-07 | Chamois Niortais | 9 | 0 | | |
| 2007-08 | Chamois Niortais | 6 | 0 | 43 | 1 |
| 2008-09 | Gueugnon | 20 | 0 | 20 | 0 |
| 2009-10 | Dagenham & R | 9 | 1 | | |
| 2010-11 | Dagenham & R | 46 | 12 | 55 | 13 |
| 2011-12 | Brighton & HA | 15 | 1 | | |
| 2012-13 | Brighton & HA | 0 | 0 | 15 | 1 |
| 2012-13 | *Gillingham* | 9 | 1 | 9 | 1 |
| 2012-13 | Leyton Orient | 15 | 1 | 15 | 1 |

**Scholars**
Egbeku, Elyon Enitan; Finney, Alex; Foley, Joseph Augustine; Georgiou, Harrison Samuel Grover; Grace, Sean Christopher; Grainger, Charlie Martin; Lee, Harry Bertie; Nikolaou, Andys Antreas; Obafemi, Afolabi Adedoyin Olamilekan O; Okimeji, Lawson; Sandy, Sinclaire; Uzun, Josh; Vanderhyde, De'reece Aaron Floyd; Wickings, George James.

# LIVERPOOL (47)

**ADORJAN, Krisztian (F)**    0   0
b.Budapest 19-1-93
Source: Scholar.

| | | | |
|---|---|--:|--:|
| 2010-11 | Liverpool | 0 | 0 |
| 2011-12 | Liverpool | 0 | 0 |
| 2012-13 | Liverpool | 0 | 0 |

**AGGER, Daniel (D)**    189   12
H: 6 2  W: 12 06  b.Hvidovre 12-12-84
Honours: Denmark Youth, Under-20, Under-21, 55 full caps, 7 goals.

| | | | | | |
|---|---|--:|--:|--:|--:|
| 2004-05 | Brondby | 26 | 5 | | |
| 2005-06 | Brondby | 8 | 0 | 34 | 5 |
| 2005-06 | Liverpool | 4 | 0 | | |
| 2006-07 | Liverpool | 27 | 2 | | |
| 2007-08 | Liverpool | 5 | 0 | | |
| 2008-09 | Liverpool | 18 | 1 | | |
| 2009-10 | Liverpool | 23 | 0 | | |
| 2010-11 | Liverpool | 16 | 0 | | |
| 2011-12 | Liverpool | 27 | 1 | | |
| 2012-13 | Liverpool | 35 | 3 | 155 | 7 |

**ALLEN, Joe (M)**    154   7
H: 5 6  W: 9 10  b.Carmarthen 14-3-90
Source: Scholar. Honours: Wales Under-21, 13 full caps.

| | | | | | |
|---|---|--:|--:|--:|--:|
| 2006-07 | Swansea C | 1 | 0 | | |
| 2007-08 | Swansea C | 6 | 0 | | |
| 2008-09 | Swansea C | 23 | 1 | | |
| 2009-10 | Swansea C | 21 | 0 | | |
| 2010-11 | Swansea C | 40 | 2 | | |
| 2011-12 | Swansea C | 36 | 4 | | |
| 2012-13 | Swansea C | 0 | 0 | 127 | 7 |
| 2012-13 | Liverpool | 27 | 0 | 27 | 0 |

**ASSAIDI, Oussama (F)**    103   29
H: 5 10  W: 10 13  b.Beni Boughari 15-8-88
Honours: Holland Under-20, Morroco 13 full caps, 1 goal.

| | | | | | |
|---|---|--:|--:|--:|--:|
| 2007-08 | Almere City FC | 3 | 3 | 3 | 3 |
| 2008-09 | De Graafschap | 13 | 1 | | |
| 2009-10 | De Graafschap | 3 | 5 | 16 | 6 |
| 2009-10 | Heerenveen | 21 | 1 | | |
| 2010-11 | Heerenveen | 31 | 9 | | |
| 2011-12 | Heerenveen | 27 | 10 | | |
| 2012-13 | Heerenveen | 1 | 0 | 80 | 20 |
| 2012-13 | Liverpool | 4 | 0 | 4 | 0 |

**BAIO, Yalany (D)**    0   0
b.Guinea-Bissau 10-10-94
Source: Scholar.

| | | | |
|---|---|--:|--:|
| 2011-12 | Liverpool | 0 | 0 |
| 2012-13 | Liverpool | 0 | 0 |

**BIJEV, Villyan (F)**    18   4
H: 6 0  W: 11 11  b.Fresno 3-1-93
Source: California Odyssey.

| | | | | | |
|---|---|--:|--:|--:|--:|
| 2011-12 | Liverpool | 0 | 0 | | |
| 2011-12 | *Dusseldorf* | 17 | 4 | 17 | 4 |
| 2012 | *IK Start* | 1 | 0 | 1 | 0 |
| 2012-13 | Liverpool | 0 | 0 | | |

**BORINI, Fabio (F)**    50   16
H: 5 10  W: 11 08  b.Bentivoglio 23-3-91
Source: Scholar. Honours: Italy Youth, Under-21, 1 full cap.

| | | | | | |
|---|---|--:|--:|--:|--:|
| 2008-09 | Chelsea | 0 | 0 | | |
| 2009-10 | Chelsea | 4 | 0 | | |
| 2010-11 | Chelsea | 0 | 0 | 4 | 0 |
| 2010-11 | Swansea C | 9 | 6 | 9 | 6 |
| 2011-12 | Roma | 24 | 9 | 24 | 9 |
| 2012-13 | Liverpool | 13 | 1 | 13 | 1 |

**CARRAGHER, Jamie (D)**    508   3
H: 5 9  W: 12 01  b.Liverpool 28-1-78
Source: Trainee. Honours: England Youth, Under-21, B, 38 full caps.

| | | | | | |
|---|---|--:|--:|--:|--:|
| 1995-96 | Liverpool | 0 | 0 | | |
| 1996-97 | Liverpool | 2 | 1 | | |
| 1997-98 | Liverpool | 20 | 0 | | |
| 1998-99 | Liverpool | 34 | 1 | | |
| 1999-2000 | Liverpool | 36 | 0 | | |
| 2000-01 | Liverpool | 34 | 0 | | |
| 2001-02 | Liverpool | 33 | 0 | | |
| 2002-03 | Liverpool | 35 | 0 | | |
| 2003-04 | Liverpool | 22 | 0 | | |
| 2004-05 | Liverpool | 38 | 0 | | |
| 2005-06 | Liverpool | 36 | 0 | | |
| 2006-07 | Liverpool | 35 | 1 | | |
| 2007-08 | Liverpool | 35 | 0 | | |
| 2008-09 | Liverpool | 38 | 0 | | |
| 2009-10 | Liverpool | 37 | 0 | | |
| 2010-11 | Liverpool | 28 | 0 | | |
| 2011-12 | Liverpool | 21 | 0 | | |
| 2012-13 | Liverpool | 24 | 0 | 508 | 3 |

**CARROLL, Andy (F)**    159   45
H: 6 4  W: 11 00  b.Gateshead 6-1-89
Source: Scholar. Honours: England Youth, Under-21, 9 full caps, 2 goals.

| | | | | | |
|---|---|--:|--:|--:|--:|
| 2006-07 | Newcastle U | 4 | 0 | | |
| 2007-08 | Newcastle U | 4 | 0 | | |
| 2007-08 | *Preston NE* | 11 | 1 | 11 | 1 |
| 2008-09 | Newcastle U | 14 | 3 | | |
| 2009-10 | Newcastle U | 39 | 17 | | |
| 2010-11 | Newcastle U | 19 | 11 | 80 | 31 |
| 2010-11 | Liverpool | 7 | 2 | | |
| 2011-12 | Liverpool | 35 | 4 | | |
| 2012-13 | Liverpool | 2 | 0 | 44 | 6 |
| 2012-13 | *West Ham U* | 24 | 7 | 24 | 7 |

**COADY, Conor (D)**    1   0
H: 6 1  W: 11 05  b.Liverpool 25-2-93
Source: Scholar. Honours: England Youth.

| | | | | | |
|---|---|--:|--:|--:|--:|
| 2010-11 | Liverpool | 0 | 0 | | |
| 2011-12 | Liverpool | 0 | 0 | | |
| 2012-13 | Liverpool | 1 | 0 | 1 | 0 |

**COATES, Sebastian (D)**    67   5
H: 6 5  W: 13 12  b.Montevideo 7-10-90
Honours: Uruguay Youth, Under-20, Under-23, 12 full caps, 1 goal.

| | | | | | |
|---|---|--:|--:|--:|--:|
| 2008-09 | Nacional | 6 | 1 | | |
| 2009-10 | Nacional | 21 | 2 | | |
| 2010-11 | Nacional | 27 | 1 | | |
| 2011-12 | Nacional | 1 | 0 | 55 | 4 |
| 2011-12 | Liverpool | 7 | 1 | | |
| 2012-13 | Liverpool | 5 | 0 | 12 | 1 |

**COUTINHO, Phillippe (M)**    63   12
H: 5 7  W: 10 09  b.Rio de Janeiro 12-6-92

| | | | | | |
|---|---|--:|--:|--:|--:|
| 2009-10 | Vasco da Gama | 7 | 1 | 7 | 1 |

| Season | Club | Apps | Gls | Tot A | Tot G |
|---|---|---|---|---|---|
| 2010-11 | Inter Milan | 12 | 1 | | |
| 2011-12 | Inter Milan | 5 | 1 | | |
| 2011-12 | *Espanyol* | 16 | 5 | **16** | **5** |
| 2012-13 | Inter Milan | 10 | 1 | **27** | **3** |
| 2012-13 | Liverpool | 13 | 3 | **13** | **3** |

**DOWNING, Stewart (M)** 316 32
H: 5 11 W: 10 04 b.Middlesbrough 22-7-84
Source: Scholar. Honours: England Youth, Under-21, B, 34 full caps.

| Season | Club | Apps | Gls | Tot A | Tot G |
|---|---|---|---|---|---|
| 2001-02 | Middlesbrough | 3 | 0 | | |
| 2002-03 | Middlesbrough | 2 | 0 | | |
| 2003-04 | Middlesbrough | 20 | 0 | | |
| 2003-04 | *Sunderland* | 7 | 3 | **7** | **3** |
| 2004-05 | Middlesbrough | 35 | 5 | | |
| 2005-06 | Middlesbrough | 12 | 1 | | |
| 2006-07 | Middlesbrough | 34 | 2 | | |
| 2007-08 | Middlesbrough | 38 | 9 | | |
| 2008-09 | Middlesbrough | 37 | 0 | **181** | **17** |
| 2009-10 | Aston Villa | 25 | 2 | | |
| 2010-11 | Aston Villa | 38 | 7 | **63** | **9** |
| 2011-12 | Liverpool | 36 | 0 | | |
| 2012-13 | Liverpool | 29 | 3 | **65** | **3** |

**DUNN, Jack (M)** 0 0
b.Liverpool 19-11-94
Source: Scholar. Honours: England Youth.

| Season | Club | Apps | Gls |
|---|---|---|---|
| 2011-12 | Liverpool | 0 | 0 |
| 2012-13 | Liverpool | 0 | 0 |

**FERNANDEZ, Jesus (F)** 0 0
H: 5 9 W: 11 00 b.Cadiz 19-11-93
Source: Scholar.

| Season | Club | Apps | Gls |
|---|---|---|---|
| 2011-12 | Liverpool | 0 | 0 |
| 2012-13 | Liverpool | 0 | 0 |

**FLANAGAN, John (D)** 12 0
H: 5 11 W: 12 06 b.Liverpool 1-1-93
Source: Scholar. Honours: England Youth, Under-21.

| Season | Club | Apps | Gls | Tot A | Tot G |
|---|---|---|---|---|---|
| 2010-11 | Liverpool | 7 | 0 | | |
| 2011-12 | Liverpool | 5 | 0 | | |
| 2012-13 | Liverpool | 0 | 0 | **12** | **0** |

**GERRARD, Steven (M)** 441 98
H: 6 0 W: 12 05 b.Huyton 30-5-80
Source: Trainee. Honours: England Youth, Under-21, 102 full caps, 19 goals.

| Season | Club | Apps | Gls | Tot A | Tot G |
|---|---|---|---|---|---|
| 1997-98 | Liverpool | 0 | 0 | | |
| 1998-99 | Liverpool | 12 | 0 | | |
| 1999-2000 | Liverpool | 29 | 1 | | |
| 2000-01 | Liverpool | 33 | 7 | | |
| 2001-02 | Liverpool | 28 | 3 | | |
| 2002-03 | Liverpool | 34 | 5 | | |
| 2003-04 | Liverpool | 34 | 4 | | |
| 2004-05 | Liverpool | 30 | 7 | | |
| 2005-06 | Liverpool | 32 | 10 | | |
| 2006-07 | Liverpool | 36 | 7 | | |
| 2007-08 | Liverpool | 34 | 11 | | |
| 2008-09 | Liverpool | 31 | 16 | | |
| 2009-10 | Liverpool | 33 | 9 | | |
| 2010-11 | Liverpool | 21 | 4 | | |
| 2011-12 | Liverpool | 18 | 5 | | |
| 2012-13 | Liverpool | 36 | 9 | **441** | **98** |

**GULACSI, Peter (G)** 50 0
H: 6 3 W: 13 01 b.Budapest 6-5-90
Source: MTK. Honours: Hungary Youth, Under-21.

| Season | Club | Apps | Gls | Tot A | Tot G |
|---|---|---|---|---|---|
| 2007-08 | Liverpool | 0 | 0 | | |
| 2008-09 | Liverpool | 0 | 0 | | |
| 2008-09 | *Hereford U* | 18 | 0 | **18** | **0** |
| 2009-10 | Liverpool | 0 | 0 | | |
| 2009-10 | *Tranmere R* | 5 | 0 | | |
| 2010-11 | Liverpool | 0 | 0 | | |
| 2010-11 | *Tranmere R* | 12 | 0 | **17** | **0** |
| 2011-12 | Liverpool | 0 | 0 | | |
| 2011-12 | *Hull C* | 15 | 0 | **15** | **0** |
| 2012-13 | Liverpool | 0 | 0 | | |

**HENDERSON, Jordan (M)** 148 12
H: 6 0 W: 10 07 b.Sunderland 17-6-90
Source: Scholar. Honours: England Youth, Under-20, Under-21, 5 full caps.

| Season | Club | Apps | Gls | Tot A | Tot G |
|---|---|---|---|---|---|
| 2008-09 | Sunderland | 1 | 0 | | |
| 2008-09 | *Coventry C* | 10 | 1 | **10** | **1** |
| 2009-10 | Sunderland | 33 | 1 | | |
| 2010-11 | Sunderland | 37 | 3 | **71** | **4** |
| 2011-12 | Liverpool | 37 | 2 | | |
| 2012-13 | Liverpool | 30 | 5 | **67** | **7** |

**IBE, Jordan (F)** 8 1
H: 5 9 W: 11 00 b.Southwark 8-12-95
Source: Schoolboy.

| Season | Club | Apps | Gls | Tot A | Tot G |
|---|---|---|---|---|---|
| 2011-12 | *Wycombe W* | 7 | 1 | **7** | **1** |
| 2011-12 | Liverpool | 0 | 0 | | |
| 2012-13 | Liverpool | 1 | 0 | **1** | **0** |

**JOHNSON, Glen (D)** 261 14
H: 6 0 W: 13 04 b.Greenwich 23-8-84
Source: Scholar. Honours: England Youth, Under-20, Under-21, 48 full caps, 1 goal.

| Season | Club | Apps | Gls | Tot A | Tot G |
|---|---|---|---|---|---|
| 2001-02 | West Ham U | 0 | 0 | | |
| 2002-03 | West Ham U | 15 | 0 | **15** | **0** |
| 2002-03 | *Millwall* | 8 | 0 | **8** | **0** |
| 2003-04 | Chelsea | 19 | 3 | | |
| 2004-05 | Chelsea | 17 | 0 | | |
| 2005-06 | Chelsea | 4 | 0 | | |
| 2006-07 | Chelsea | 0 | 0 | | |
| 2006-07 | Portsmouth | 26 | 0 | | |
| 2007-08 | Chelsea | 2 | 0 | **42** | **3** |
| 2007-08 | Portsmouth | 29 | 1 | | |
| 2008-09 | Portsmouth | 29 | 3 | | |
| 2009-10 | Portsmouth | 0 | 0 | **84** | **4** |
| 2009-10 | Liverpool | 25 | 3 | | |
| 2010-11 | Liverpool | 28 | 2 | | |
| 2011-12 | Liverpool | 23 | 1 | | |
| 2012-13 | Liverpool | 36 | 1 | **112** | **7** |

**JONES, Brad (G)** 108 0
H: 6 3 W: 12 01 b.Armidale 19-3-82
Source: Trainee. Honours: Australia Under-20, Under-23, 3 full caps.

| Season | Club | Apps | Gls | Tot A | Tot G |
|---|---|---|---|---|---|
| 1998-99 | Middlesbrough | 0 | 0 | | |
| 1999-2000 | Middlesbrough | 0 | 0 | | |
| 2000-01 | Middlesbrough | 0 | 0 | | |
| 2001-02 | Middlesbrough | 0 | 0 | | |
| 2002 | *Shelbourne* | 2 | 0 | **2** | **0** |
| 2002-03 | Middlesbrough | 0 | 0 | | |
| 2002-03 | *Stockport Co* | 1 | 0 | **1** | **0** |
| 2003-04 | Middlesbrough | 1 | 0 | | |
| 2003-04 | *Blackpool* | 5 | 0 | | |
| 2003-04 | *Rotherham U* | 1 | 0 | | |
| 2004-05 | Middlesbrough | 5 | 0 | | |
| 2004-05 | *Blackpool* | 12 | 0 | **17** | **0** |
| 2005-06 | Middlesbrough | 9 | 0 | | |
| 2006-07 | Middlesbrough | 2 | 0 | | |
| 2006-07 | *Sheffield W* | 15 | 0 | **15** | **0** |
| 2007-08 | Middlesbrough | 1 | 0 | | |
| 2008-09 | Middlesbrough | 16 | 0 | | |
| 2009-10 | Middlesbrough | 24 | 0 | **58** | **0** |
| 2010-11 | Liverpool | 0 | 0 | | |
| 2010-11 | *Derby Co* | 7 | 0 | **7** | **0** |
| 2011-12 | Liverpool | 1 | 0 | | |
| 2012-13 | Liverpool | 7 | 0 | **8** | **0** |

**JOSE ENRIQUE (D)** 239 4
H: 6 0 W: 12 00 b.Valencia 23-1-86
Honours: Spain Under-21.

| Season | Club | Apps | Gls | Tot A | Tot G |
|---|---|---|---|---|---|
| 2004-05 | *Levante* | 19 | 1 | **19** | **1** |
| 2005-06 | Valencia | 0 | 0 | | |
| 2005-06 | *Celta Vigo* | 14 | 0 | **14** | **0** |
| 2006-07 | *Villarreal* | 23 | 0 | **23** | **0** |
| 2007-08 | Newcastle U | 23 | 0 | | |
| 2008-09 | Newcastle U | 26 | 0 | | |
| 2009-10 | Newcastle U | 34 | 1 | | |
| 2010-11 | Newcastle U | 36 | 0 | **119** | **1** |
| 2011-12 | Liverpool | 35 | 0 | | |
| 2012-13 | Liverpool | 29 | 2 | **64** | **2** |

**KELLY, Martin (D)** 35 1
H: 6 3 W: 12 02 b.Bolton 27-4-90
Source: Scholar. Honours: England Youth, Under-20, Under-21, 1 full cap.

| Season | Club | Apps | Gls | Tot A | Tot G |
|---|---|---|---|---|---|
| 2007-08 | Liverpool | 0 | 0 | | |
| 2008-09 | Liverpool | 0 | 0 | | |
| 2008-09 | *Huddersfield T* | 7 | 1 | **7** | **1** |
| 2009-10 | Liverpool | 1 | 0 | | |
| 2010-11 | Liverpool | 11 | 0 | | |
| 2011-12 | Liverpool | 12 | 0 | | |
| 2012-13 | Liverpool | 4 | 0 | **28** | **0** |

**LUCAS (M)** 182 5
H: 5 10 W: 11 09 b.Dourados 9-1-87
Honours: Brazil Under-20, Under-21.

| Season | Club | Apps | Gls | Tot A | Tot G |
|---|---|---|---|---|---|
| 2005 | Gremio | 3 | 0 | | |
| 2006 | Gremio | 30 | 4 | **33** | **4** |
| 2007-08 | Liverpool | 18 | 0 | | |
| 2008-09 | Liverpool | 25 | 1 | | |
| 2009-10 | Liverpool | 35 | 0 | | |
| 2010-11 | Liverpool | 33 | 0 | | |
| 2011-12 | Liverpool | 12 | 0 | | |
| 2012-13 | Liverpool | 26 | 0 | **149** | **1** |

**MERSIN, Yusuf (G)** 0 0
b.Greenwich 23-9-94
Source: Scholar.

| Season | Club | Apps | Gls |
|---|---|---|---|
| 2011-12 | Liverpool | 0 | 0 |
| 2012-13 | Liverpool | 0 | 0 |

**MORGAN, Adam (F)** 1 0
H: 5 10 W: 11 03 b.Liverpool 21-4-94
Source: Scholar. Honours: England Youth.

| Season | Club | Apps | Gls | Tot A | Tot G |
|---|---|---|---|---|---|
| 2011-12 | Liverpool | 0 | 0 | | |
| 2012-13 | Liverpool | 0 | 0 | | |
| 2012-13 | *Rotherham U* | 1 | 0 | **1** | **0** |

**MUKENDI, Henoc (F)** 7 0
H: 6 3 W: 12 11 b.Congo DR 20-1-93

| Season | Club | Apps | Gls | Tot A | Tot G |
|---|---|---|---|---|---|
| 2012-13 | Liverpool | 0 | 0 | | |
| 2012-13 | *Northampton T* | 7 | 0 | **7** | **0** |

**NGOO, Michael (F)** 15 4
b.Walthamstow 23-10-92
Source: Southend U Scholar. Honours: England Youth, Under-20.

| Season | Club | Apps | Gls | Tot A | Tot G |
|---|---|---|---|---|---|
| 2009-10 | Liverpool | 0 | 0 | | |
| 2010-11 | Liverpool | 0 | 0 | | |
| 2011-12 | Liverpool | 0 | 0 | | |
| 2012-13 | Liverpool | 0 | 0 | | |
| 2012-13 | *Hearts* | 15 | 4 | **15** | **4** |

**PACHECO, Daniel (F)** 41 7
H: 5 6 W: 10 07 b.Malaga 5-1-91
Honours: Spain Youth, Under-21.

| Season | Club | Apps | Gls | Tot A | Tot G |
|---|---|---|---|---|---|
| 2007-08 | Liverpool | 0 | 0 | | |
| 2008-09 | Liverpool | 0 | 0 | | |
| 2009-10 | Liverpool | 4 | 0 | | |
| 2010-11 | Liverpool | 0 | 0 | | |
| 2010-11 | *Norwich C* | 6 | 2 | **6** | **2** |
| 2011-12 | Liverpool | 0 | 0 | | |
| 2011-12 | *Rayo Vallecano* | 11 | 0 | | |
| 2012-13 | *Rayo Vallecano* | 0 | 0 | **11** | **0** |
| 2012-13 | Liverpool | 0 | 0 | **5** | **0** |
| 2012-13 | *Huesca* | 19 | 5 | **19** | **5** |

**PELOSI, Marc (D)** 0 0
b.Bad Sackingen 17-6-94
Source: DeAnza Force.

| Season | Club | Apps | Gls |
|---|---|---|---|
| 2011-12 | Liverpool | 0 | 0 |
| 2012-13 | Liverpool | 0 | 0 |

**PETERSSON, Kristoffer (M)** 0 0
b.Gothenburg 28-11-94
Source: Scholar.

| Season | Club | Apps | Gls |
|---|---|---|---|
| 2011-12 | Liverpool | 0 | 0 |
| 2012-13 | Liverpool | 0 | 0 |

**REINA, Jose (G)** 454 0
H: 6 2 W: 14 06 b.Madrid 31-8-82
Honours: Spain Youth, Under-21, 27 full caps.

| Season | Club | Apps | Gls | Tot A | Tot G |
|---|---|---|---|---|---|
| 1999-2000 | Barcelona B | 30 | 0 | **30** | **0** |
| 2000-01 | Barcelona | 19 | 0 | | |
| 2001-02 | Barcelona | 11 | 0 | **30** | **0** |
| 2002-03 | Villarreal | 33 | 0 | | |
| 2003-04 | Villarreal | 38 | 0 | | |
| 2004-05 | Villarreal | 38 | 0 | **109** | **0** |
| 2005-06 | Liverpool | 33 | 0 | | |
| 2006-07 | Liverpool | 35 | 0 | | |
| 2007-08 | Liverpool | 38 | 0 | | |
| 2008-09 | Liverpool | 38 | 0 | | |
| 2009-10 | Liverpool | 38 | 0 | | |
| 2010-11 | Liverpool | 38 | 0 | | |
| 2011-12 | Liverpool | 34 | 0 | | |
| 2012-13 | Liverpool | 31 | 0 | **285** | **0** |

**ROBINSON, Jack (D)** 14 0
H: 5 11 W: 10 08 b.Warrington 1-9-93
Source: Scholar. Honours: England Youth, Under-21.

| Season | Club | Apps | Gls | Tot A | Tot G |
|---|---|---|---|---|---|
| 2009-10 | Liverpool | 1 | 0 | | |
| 2010-11 | Liverpool | 2 | 0 | | |
| 2011-12 | Liverpool | 0 | 0 | | |
| 2012-13 | Liverpool | 0 | 0 | **3** | **0** |
| 2012-13 | *Wolverhampton W* | 11 | 0 | **11** | **0** |

**RODDAN, Craig (M)** 0 0
b.Kirkby 22-4-93
Source: Scholar.

| Season | Club | Apps | Gls |
|---|---|---|---|
| 2011-12 | Liverpool | 0 | 0 |
| 2012-13 | Liverpool | 0 | 0 |

**SAHIN, Nuri (M)** 188 23
H: 5 10  W: 10 02  b.Ludenscheid 5-9-88
*Honours:* Turkey Youth, Under-21, 41 full caps, 2 goals.
2005-06 Borussia Dortmund 23 1
2006-07 Borussia Dortmund 24 0
2007-08 Feyenoord 28 6 28 6
2008-09 Borussia Dortmund 24 2
2009-10 Borussia Dortmund 33 4
2010-11 Borussia Dortmund 30 6
2011-12 Real Madrid 4 0
2012-13 Real Madrid 0 0 4 0
On loan from Real Madrid
2012-13 Liverpool 7 1 7 1
2012-13 Borussia Dortmund 15 3 149 16

**SAMA, Stephen (D)** 0 0
H: 6 2  b.Cameroon 5-3-93
*Source:* Scholar.
2009-10 Liverpool 0 0
2010-11 Liverpool 0 0
2011-12 Liverpool 0 0
2012-13 Liverpool 0 0

**SHELVEY, Jonjo (M)** 99 15
H: 6 1  W: 11 02  b.Romford 27-2-92
*Source:* Scholar. *Honours:* England Youth, Under-21, 1 full cap.
2007-08 Charlton Ath 2 0
2008-09 Charlton Ath 16 3
2009-10 Charlton Ath 24 4 42 7
2010-11 Liverpool 15 0
2011-12 Liverpool 13 1
2011-12 Blackpool 10 6 10 6
2012-13 Liverpool 19 1 47 2

**SKRTEL, Martin (D)** 260 10
H: 6 3  W: 12 10  b.Handlova 15-12-84
*Honours:* Slovakia 61 full caps, 5 goals.
2002-03 Trencin 1 0
2003-04 Trencin 34 0 35 0
2004 Zenit 7 0
2005 Zenit 18 1
2006 Zenit 26 1
2007 Zenit 23 1 74 3
2007-08 Liverpool 14 0
2008-09 Liverpool 21 0
2009-10 Liverpool 19 1
2010-11 Liverpool 38 2
2011-12 Liverpool 34 2
2012-13 Liverpool 25 2 151 7

**SMITH, Bradley (D)** 0 0
b.New South Wales 9-4-94
*Source:* Scholar.
2011-12 Liverpool 0 0
2012-13 Liverpool 0 0

**SOKOLIK, Jakub (D)** 0 0
H: 5 6  b.Ostrava 28-8-93
*Source:* Scholar.
2010-11 Liverpool 0 0
2011-12 Liverpool 0 0
2012-13 Liverpool 0 0

**SPEARING, Jay (M)** 74 3
H: 5 6  W: 11 01  b.Wallasey 25-11-88
*Source:* Scholar.
2006-07 Liverpool 0 0
2007-08 Liverpool 0 0
2008-09 Liverpool 0 0
2009-10 Liverpool 3 0
2009-10 Leicester C 7 1 7 1
2010-11 Liverpool 11 0
2011-12 Liverpool 16 0
2012-13 Liverpool 0 0 30 0
2012-13 Bolton W 37 2 37 2

**STERLING, Raheem (F)** 27 2
H: 5 7  W: 10 00  b.Kingston 8-12-94
*Source:* Scholar. *Honours:* England Youth, Under-21, 1 full cap.
2011-12 Liverpool 3 0
2012-13 Liverpool 24 2 27 2

**STURRIDGE, Daniel (F)** 110 36
H: 6 2  W: 12 00  b.Birmingham 1-9-89
*Source:* Scholar. *Honours:* England Youth, Under-21, 6 full caps, 1 goal.
2006-07 Manchester C 2 0
2007-08 Manchester C 3 1
2008-09 Manchester C 16 4
2009-10 Manchester C 0 0 21 5
2009-10 Chelsea 13 1
2010-11 Chelsea 13 0
2010-11 Bolton W 12 8 12 8
2011-12 Chelsea 30 11
2012-13 Chelsea 7 1 63 13
2012-13 Liverpool 14 10 14 10

**SUAREZ, Luis (F)** 243 139
H: 5 11  W: 12 10  b.Salto 24-1-87
*Honours:* Uruguay Under-23, 69 full caps, 34 goals.
2005-06 Nacional 27 10 27 10
2006-07 Groningen 29 10 29 10
2007-08 Ajax 33 17
2008-09 Ajax 31 22
2009-10 Ajax 33 35
2010-11 Ajax 13 7 110 81
2010-11 Liverpool 13 4
2011-12 Liverpool 31 11
2012-13 Liverpool 33 23 77 38

**SUSO (M)** 34 7
H: 5 8  W: 10 12  b.Cadiz 19-11-93
2010-11 Cadiz B 20 7 20 7
2010-11 Liverpool 0 0
2011-12 Liverpool 0 0
2012-13 Liverpool 14 0 14 0

**TEIXEIRA, Joao Carlos (M)** 0 0
b.Braga 18-1-93
*Source:* Sporting Lisbon Youth. *Honours:* Portugal Youth.
2011-12 Liverpool 0 0
2012-13 Liverpool 0 0

**WARD, Danny (G)** 0 0
H: 5 11  W: 13 12  b.Wrexham 22-6-93
*Source:* Wrexham. *Honours:* Wales Youth, Under-21.
2011-12 Liverpool 0 0
2012-13 Liverpool 0 0

**WILSON, Danny (D)** 36 1
H: 6 2  W: 12 06  b.Livingston 27-12-91
*Honours:* Scotland Youth, Under-21, 5 full caps, 1 goal.
2009-10 Rangers 14 1 14 1
2010-11 Liverpool 2 0
2011-12 Liverpool 0 0
2011-12 Blackpool 6 0 6 0
2012-13 Liverpool 0 0 2 0
2012-13 Bristol C 1 0 1 0
2012-13 Hearts 13 0 13 0

**WISDOM, Andre (D)** 12 0
H: 6 1  W: 12 04  b.Leeds 9-5-93
*Source:* Scholar. *Honours:* England Youth, Under-21.
2009-10 Liverpool 0 0
2010-11 Liverpool 0 0
2011-12 Liverpool 0 0
2012-13 Liverpool 12 0 12 0

**YESIL, Samed (F)** 1 0
H: 5 10  W: 10 13  b.Dusseldorf 25-5-94
2011-12 Bayer Leverkusen 1 0 1 0
2012-13 Liverpool 0 0

**Players retained or with offer of contract**
Huertas, Ortiz Jose Ignacio; Lussey, Jordan; McLaughlin, Ryan; Randall, Connor Steven.

**Scholars**
Brannagan, Cameron; Burke, Nathan; Cleary, Daniel; Crump, Ryan; Fulton, Ryan; Heaton, Niall Michael; Jones, Lloyd Richard; Maguire, Joseph; O'Hanlon, Alex Joseph; Trickett-Smith, Daniel Thomas; Williams, Michael Jordan.

# MANCHESTER C (48)

**ABU, Mohammed (M)** 0 0
b.Ghana 14-11-91
*Source:* SC Accra. *Honours:* Ghana 4 full caps.
2010-11 Manchester C 0 0
2011-12 Manchester C 0 0
2012-13 Manchester C 0 0

**AGUERO, Sergio (F)** 293 132
H: 5 8  W: 11 09  b.Buenos Aires 2-6-88
*Honours:* Argentina Youth, Under-23, 43 full caps, 18 goals.
2002-03 Independiente 1 0
2003-04 Independiente 5 0
2004-05 Independiente 12 5
2005-06 Independiente 36 18 54 23
2006-07 Atletico Madrid 38 6
2007-08 Atletico Madrid 37 19
2008-09 Atletico Madrid 37 17
2009-10 Atletico Madrid 31 12
2010-11 Atletico Madrid 32 20 175 74
2011-12 Manchester C 34 23
2012-13 Manchester C 30 12 64 35

**BALOTELLI, Mario (F)** 115 40
H: 6 2  W: 13 08  b.Palermo 12-8-90
*Honours:* Italy Under-21, 25 full caps, 10 goals.
2005-06 Lumezzane 2 0 2 0
2006-07 Internazionale 0 0
2007-08 Internazionale 11 3
2008-09 Internazionale 22 8
2009-10 Internazionale 26 9 59 20
2010-11 Manchester C 17 6
2011-12 Manchester C 23 13
2012-13 Manchester C 14 1 54 20
Transferred to AC Milan January 2013

**BARRY, Gareth (M)** 497 47
H: 5 11  W: 12 06  b.Hastings 23-2-81
*Source:* Trainee. *Honours:* England Youth, B, Under-21, 53 full caps, 3 goals.
1997-98 Aston Villa 2 0
1998-99 Aston Villa 32 2
1999-2000 Aston Villa 30 1
2000-01 Aston Villa 30 0
2001-02 Aston Villa 20 0
2002-03 Aston Villa 35 3
2003-04 Aston Villa 36 3
2004-05 Aston Villa 34 7
2005-06 Aston Villa 36 3
2006-07 Aston Villa 35 8
2007-08 Aston Villa 37 9
2008-09 Aston Villa 38 5 365 41
2009-10 Manchester C 34 2
2010-11 Manchester C 33 2
2011-12 Manchester C 34 1
2012-13 Manchester C 31 1 132 6

**BOYATA, Dedryck (D)** 29 1
H: 6 2  W: 12 00  b.Brussels 8-9-90
*Source:* Scholar. *Honours:* Belgium Under-21, 1 full cap.
2008-09 Manchester C 0 0
2009-10 Manchester C 3 0
2010-11 Manchester C 7 0
2011-12 Manchester C 0 0
2011-12 Bolton W 14 1 14 1
2012-13 Manchester C 0 0 10 0
2012-13 FC Twente 5 0 5 0

**BRIDGE, Wayne (D)** 353 6
H: 5 10  W: 12 13  b.Southampton 5-8-80
*Source:* Trainee. *Honours:* England Youth, Under-21, 36 full caps, 1 goal.
1997-98 Southampton 0 0
1998-99 Southampton 23 0
1999-2000 Southampton 19 1
2000-01 Southampton 38 0
2001-02 Southampton 38 0
2002-03 Southampton 34 1 152 2
2003-04 Chelsea 33 1
2004-05 Chelsea 15 0
2005-06 Chelsea 0 0
2005-06 Fulham 12 0 12 0
2006-07 Chelsea 22 0
2007-08 Chelsea 11 0
2008-09 Chelsea 6 0 87 1
2009-10 Manchester C 16 0
2010-11 Manchester C 3 0
2010-11 West Ham U 15 0 15 0
2011-12 Manchester C 0 0
2011-12 Sunderland 8 0 8 0
2012-13 Manchester C 0 0 42 0
2012-13 Brighton & HA 37 3 37 3

**BUNN, Harry (F)** 22 1
H: 5 9  W: 11 10  b.Oldham 25-11-92
*Source:* Scholar.

| Season | Club | App | Gls | App | Gls |
|---|---|---|---|---|---|
| 2010-11 | Manchester C | 0 | 0 | | |
| 2011-12 | Manchester C | 0 | 0 | | |
| 2011-12 | Rochdale | 6 | 0 | 6 | 0 |
| 2011-12 | Preston NE | 1 | 1 | 1 | 1 |
| 2011-12 | Oldham Ath | 11 | 0 | | |
| 2012-13 | Manchester C | 0 | 0 | | |
| 2012-13 | Oldham Ath | 0 | 0 | 11 | 0 |
| 2012-13 | Crewe Alex | 4 | 0 | 4 | 0 |

**CLICHY, Gael (D)** 243 1
H: 5 9  W: 10 04  b.Toulouse 26-7-85
*Source:* Cannes. *Honours:* France Under-21, B, 17 full caps.

| Season | Club | App | Gls | App | Gls |
|---|---|---|---|---|---|
| 2003-04 | Arsenal | 12 | 0 | | |
| 2004-05 | Arsenal | 15 | 0 | | |
| 2005-06 | Arsenal | 7 | 0 | | |
| 2006-07 | Arsenal | 27 | 0 | | |
| 2007-08 | Arsenal | 38 | 0 | | |
| 2008-09 | Arsenal | 31 | 1 | | |
| 2009-10 | Arsenal | 24 | 0 | | |
| 2010-11 | Arsenal | 33 | 0 | 187 | 1 |
| 2011-12 | Manchester C | 28 | 0 | | |
| 2012-13 | Manchester C | 28 | 0 | 56 | 0 |

**DE JONG, Nigel (D)** 266 12
H: 5 8  W: 11 05  b.Amsterdam 30-11-84
*Honours:* Holland 67 full caps, 1 goal.

| Season | Club | App | Gls | App | Gls |
|---|---|---|---|---|---|
| 2002-03 | Ajax | 17 | 0 | | |
| 2003-04 | Ajax | 32 | 1 | | |
| 2004-05 | Ajax | 31 | 5 | | |
| 2005-06 | Hamburg | 12 | 0 | | |
| 2005-06 | Ajax | 16 | 2 | 96 | 8 |
| 2006-07 | Hamburg | 18 | 1 | | |
| 2007-08 | Hamburg | 29 | 1 | | |
| 2008-09 | Hamburg | 7 | 0 | 66 | 3 |
| 2008-09 | Manchester C | 16 | 0 | | |
| 2009-10 | Manchester C | 34 | 0 | | |
| 2010-11 | Manchester C | 32 | 1 | | |
| 2011-12 | Manchester C | 21 | 0 | | |
| 2012-13 | Manchester C | 1 | 0 | 104 | 1 |

Transferred to AC Milan August 2012

**DONYOH, Godsway (F)** 7 0
H: 5 11  W: 11 01  b. 14-10-94

| Season | Club | App | Gls | App | Gls |
|---|---|---|---|---|---|
| 2012-13 | Manchester C | 0 | 0 | | |
| 2012-13 | Djurgarden | 7 | 0 | 7 | 0 |

**DRURY, Adam (M)** 12 0
b.Grimsby 21-9-93
*Source:* Scholar.

| Season | Club | App | Gls | App | Gls |
|---|---|---|---|---|---|
| 2010-11 | Manchester C | 0 | 0 | | |
| 2011-12 | Manchester C | 0 | 0 | | |
| 2012-13 | Manchester C | 0 | 0 | | |
| 2012-13 | Burton Alb | 12 | 0 | 12 | 0 |

**DZEKO, Edin (F)** 259 119
H: 6 3  W: 13 00  b.Doboj 17-3-86
*Honours:* Bosnia Youth, Under-21, 52 full caps, 29 goals.

| Season | Club | App | Gls | App | Gls |
|---|---|---|---|---|---|
| 2004-05 | Zeljeznicar | 13 | 1 | 13 | 1 |
| 2005-06 | Usti nad Labem | 15 | 6 | 15 | 6 |
| 2005-06 | Teplice | 13 | 3 | | |
| 2006-07 | Teplice | 30 | 13 | 43 | 16 |
| 2007-08 | Wolfsburg | 28 | 8 | | |
| 2008-09 | Wolfsburg | 32 | 26 | | |
| 2009-10 | Wolfsburg | 34 | 22 | | |
| 2010-11 | Wolfsburg | 17 | 10 | 111 | 66 |
| 2010-11 | Manchester C | 15 | 2 | | |
| 2011-12 | Manchester C | 30 | 14 | | |
| 2012-13 | Manchester C | 32 | 14 | 77 | 30 |

**ELABDELLAOUI, Omar (M)** 0 0
b.Norway 5-12-91
*Source:* Scholar.

| Season | Club | App | Gls | App | Gls |
|---|---|---|---|---|---|
| 2009-10 | Manchester C | 0 | 0 | | |
| 2010-11 | Manchester C | 0 | 0 | | |
| 2011-12 | Manchester C | 0 | 0 | | |
| 2012-13 | Manchester C | 0 | 0 | | |

**EVANS, George (M)** 0 0
H: 6 0  W: 11 12  b.Cheadle 13-1-96

| Season | Club | App | Gls | App | Gls |
|---|---|---|---|---|---|
| 2012-13 | Manchester C | 0 | 0 | | |

**GUIDETTI, John (F)** 13 4
H: 5 11  W: 12 06  b.Stockholm 15-4-92
*Source:* Scholar. *Honours:* Sweden Youth, Under-21, 1 full cap.

| Season | Club | App | Gls | App | Gls |
|---|---|---|---|---|---|
| 2009-10 | Manchester C | 0 | 0 | | |
| 2009-10 | Brommapojkana | 8 | 3 | 8 | 3 |
| 2010-11 | Manchester C | 0 | 0 | | |
| 2010-11 | Burnley | 5 | 1 | 5 | 1 |
| 2011-12 | Manchester C | 0 | 0 | | |
| 2012-13 | Manchester C | 0 | 0 | | |

**HART, Joe (G)** 263 0
H: 6 3  W: 13 03  b.Shrewsbury 19-4-87
*Source:* Scholar. *Honours:* England Youth, Under-21, 32 full caps.

| Season | Club | App | Gls | App | Gls |
|---|---|---|---|---|---|
| 2004-05 | Shrewsbury T | 6 | 0 | | |
| 2005-06 | Shrewsbury T | 46 | 0 | 52 | 0 |
| 2006-07 | Manchester C | 1 | 0 | | |
| 2006-07 | Tranmere R | 6 | 0 | 6 | 0 |
| 2006-07 | Blackpool | 5 | 0 | 5 | 0 |
| 2007-08 | Manchester C | 26 | 0 | | |
| 2008-09 | Manchester C | 23 | 0 | | |
| 2009-10 | Manchester C | 0 | 0 | | |
| 2009-10 | Birmingham C | 36 | 0 | 36 | 0 |
| 2010-11 | Manchester C | 38 | 0 | | |
| 2011-12 | Manchester C | 38 | 0 | | |
| 2012-13 | Manchester C | 38 | 0 | 164 | 0 |

**HELAN, Jeremy (M)** 33 1
H: 5 11  W: 12 00  b.Paris 9-5-92
*Source:* Rennes. *Honours:* France Youth.

| Season | Club | App | Gls | App | Gls |
|---|---|---|---|---|---|
| 2009-10 | Manchester C | 0 | 0 | | |
| 2010-11 | Manchester C | 0 | 0 | | |
| 2011-12 | Manchester C | 0 | 0 | | |
| 2011-12 | Carlisle U | 2 | 0 | 2 | 0 |
| 2012-13 | Manchester C | 0 | 0 | | |
| 2012-13 | Shrewsbury T | 3 | 0 | 3 | 0 |
| 2012-13 | Sheffield W | 28 | 1 | 28 | 1 |

**HENSHALL, Alex (M)** 7 0
b.Swindon 15-2-94
*Source:* Scholar.

| Season | Club | App | Gls | App | Gls |
|---|---|---|---|---|---|
| 2010-11 | Manchester C | 0 | 0 | | |
| 2011-12 | Manchester C | 0 | 0 | | |
| 2012-13 | Manchester C | 0 | 0 | | |
| 2012-13 | Chesterfield | 7 | 0 | 7 | 0 |

**HUWS, Emyr (M)** 10 0
b.Llanelli 30-9-93
*Source:* Scholar. *Honours:* Wales Youth.

| Season | Club | App | Gls | App | Gls |
|---|---|---|---|---|---|
| 2010-11 | Manchester C | 0 | 0 | | |
| 2011-12 | Manchester C | 0 | 0 | | |
| 2012-13 | Manchester C | 0 | 0 | | |
| 2012-13 | Northampton T | 10 | 0 | 10 | 0 |

**IBRAHIM, Abdisalam (M)** 41 4
H: 6 0  W: 11 02  b.Somalia 4-5-91
*Source:* Scholar. *Honours:* Norway Youth, Under-21.

| Season | Club | App | Gls | App | Gls |
|---|---|---|---|---|---|
| 2008-09 | Manchester C | 0 | 0 | | |
| 2009-10 | Manchester C | 1 | 0 | | |
| 2010-11 | Manchester C | 0 | 0 | | |
| 2010-11 | Scunthorpe U | 11 | 0 | 11 | 0 |
| 2011-12 | Manchester C | 0 | 0 | | |
| 2011-12 | NEC Nijmegen | 8 | 1 | 8 | 1 |
| 2012 | Stromsgodset | 11 | 3 | | |
| 2012-13 | Manchester C | 0 | 0 | 1 | 0 |
| 2013 | Stromsgodset | 10 | 0 | 21 | 3 |

**JAVI GARCIA, Francisco (M)** 186 16
H: 6 2  W: 13 02  b.Madrid 8-2-87
*Honours:* Spain Youth, Under-21, 1 full cap.

| Season | Club | App | Gls | App | Gls |
|---|---|---|---|---|---|
| 2004-05 | Real Madrid | 3 | 0 | | |
| 2005-06 | RM Castilla | 28 | 4 | | |
| 2006-07 | RM Castilla | 17 | 2 | 45 | 6 |
| 2007-08 | Osasuna | 25 | 2 | 25 | 2 |
| 2008-09 | Real Madrid | 15 | 0 | 18 | 0 |
| 2009-10 | Benfica | 26 | 3 | | |
| 2010-11 | Benfica | 24 | 2 | | |
| 2011-12 | Benfica | 24 | 2 | | |
| 2012-13 | Benfica | 2 | 0 | 74 | 6 |
| 2012-13 | Manchester C | 24 | 2 | 24 | 2 |

**JOHANSEN, Eirik (G)** 0 0
H: 6 4  W: 14 00  b.Tonsberg 12-7-92
*Honours:* Norway Youth.

| Season | Club | App | Gls | App | Gls |
|---|---|---|---|---|---|
| 2010-11 | Manchester C | 0 | 0 | | |
| 2011-12 | Manchester C | 0 | 0 | | |
| 2012-13 | Manchester C | 0 | 0 | | |

**KENNEDY, Kieran (D)** 0 0
b.Urmston 23-9-93
*Source:* Scholar. *Honours:* England Youth.

| Season | Club | App | Gls | App | Gls |
|---|---|---|---|---|---|
| 2011-12 | Manchester C | 0 | 0 | | |
| 2012-13 | Manchester C | 0 | 0 | | |

**KOLAROV, Aleksandar (D)** 220 17
H: 6 2  W: 13 05  b.Belgrade 10-11-85
*Honours:* Serbia Under-21, 41 full caps, 2 goals.

| Season | Club | App | Gls | App | Gls |
|---|---|---|---|---|---|
| 2004-05 | Cukaricki | 27 | 2 | | |
| 2005-06 | Cukaricki | 17 | 0 | 44 | 2 |
| 2005-06 | OFK Belgrade | 11 | 1 | | |
| 2006-07 | OFK Belgrade | 27 | 4 | 38 | 5 |
| 2007-08 | Lazio | 24 | 1 | | |
| 2008-09 | Lazio | 25 | 2 | | |
| 2009-10 | Lazio | 33 | 3 | 82 | 6 |
| 2010-11 | Manchester C | 24 | 1 | | |
| 2011-12 | Manchester C | 12 | 2 | | |
| 2012-13 | Manchester C | 20 | 1 | 56 | 4 |

**KOMPANY, Vincent (D)** 243 12
H: 6 3  W: 13 05  b.Brussels 10-4-86
*Honours:* Belgium 55 full caps, 4 goals.

| Season | Club | App | Gls | App | Gls |
|---|---|---|---|---|---|
| 2004-05 | Anderlecht | 29 | 2 | | |
| 2005-06 | Anderlecht | 32 | 2 | 61 | 4 |
| 2006-07 | Hamburg | 6 | 0 | | |
| 2007-08 | Hamburg | 22 | 1 | | |
| 2008-09 | Hamburg | 1 | 0 | 29 | 1 |
| 2008-09 | Manchester C | 34 | 1 | | |
| 2009-10 | Manchester C | 25 | 2 | | |
| 2010-11 | Manchester C | 37 | 0 | | |
| 2011-12 | Manchester C | 31 | 3 | | |
| 2012-13 | Manchester C | 26 | 1 | 153 | 7 |

**LAWLOR, Ian (G)** 0 0
b.Dublin 27-10-94
*Source:* Scholar. *Honours:* Eire Youth.

| Season | Club | App | Gls | App | Gls |
|---|---|---|---|---|---|
| 2011-12 | Manchester C | 0 | 0 | | |
| 2012-13 | Manchester C | 0 | 0 | | |

**LESCOTT, Jolean (D)** 422 34
H: 6 2  W: 13 00  b.Birmingham 16-8-82
*Source:* Trainee. *Honours:* England Youth, Under-20, Under-21, B, 26 full caps, 1 goal.

| Season | Club | App | Gls | App | Gls |
|---|---|---|---|---|---|
| 1999-2000 | Wolverhampton W | 0 | 0 | | |
| 2000-01 | Wolverhampton W | 37 | 2 | | |
| 2001-02 | Wolverhampton W | 44 | 5 | | |
| 2002-03 | Wolverhampton W | 44 | 1 | | |
| 2003-04 | Wolverhampton W | 0 | 0 | | |
| 2004-05 | Wolverhampton W | 41 | 4 | | |
| 2005-06 | Wolverhampton W | 46 | 1 | 212 | 13 |
| 2006-07 | Everton | 38 | 2 | | |
| 2007-08 | Everton | 38 | 8 | | |
| 2008-09 | Everton | 36 | 4 | | |
| 2009-10 | Everton | 1 | 0 | 113 | 14 |
| 2009-10 | Manchester C | 18 | 1 | | |
| 2010-11 | Manchester C | 22 | 3 | | |
| 2011-12 | Manchester C | 31 | 2 | | |
| 2012-13 | Manchester C | 26 | 1 | 97 | 7 |

**MAICON, Sisenando (D)** 241 21
H: 6 0  W: 12 00  b.Criciuma 26-7-81
*Honours:* Brazil Under-20, 66 full caps, 6 goals.

| Season | Club | App | Gls | App | Gls |
|---|---|---|---|---|---|
| 2004-05 | Monaco | 30 | 4 | | |
| 2005-06 | Monaco | 27 | 1 | 57 | 5 |
| 2006-07 | Inter Milan | 32 | 2 | | |
| 2007-08 | Inter Milan | 31 | 1 | | |
| 2008-09 | Inter Milan | 27 | 4 | | |
| 2009-10 | Inter Milan | 33 | 6 | | |
| 2010-11 | Inter Milan | 28 | 1 | | |
| 2011-12 | Inter Milan | 24 | 2 | 175 | 16 |
| 2012-13 | Manchester C | 9 | 0 | 9 | 0 |

**McGIVERN, Ryan (D)** 96 2
H: 5 10  W: 11 07  b.Newry 8-1-90
*Source:* Scholar. *Honours:* Northern Ireland Youth, Under-21, B, 19 full caps.

| Season | Club | App | Gls | App | Gls |
|---|---|---|---|---|---|
| 2007-08 | Manchester C | 0 | 0 | | |
| 2008-09 | Manchester C | 0 | 0 | | |
| 2008-09 | Morecambe | 5 | 1 | 5 | 1 |
| 2009-10 | Manchester C | 0 | 0 | | |
| 2009-10 | Leicester C | 12 | 0 | 12 | 0 |
| 2010-11 | Manchester C | 1 | 0 | | |
| 2011-12 | Walsall | 15 | 0 | 15 | 0 |
| 2011-12 | Manchester C | 0 | 0 | | |
| 2011-12 | Crystal Palace | 5 | 0 | 5 | 0 |
| 2011-12 | Bristol C | 31 | 0 | 31 | 0 |
| 2012-13 | Manchester C | 0 | 0 | 1 | 0 |
| 2012-13 | Hibernian | 27 | 1 | 27 | 1 |

**MILNER, James (M)** 332 32
H: 5 9 W: 11 00 b.Leeds 4-1-86
Source: Trainee. Honours: FA Schools, Youth, England Under-20, Under-21, 38 full caps, 1 goal.

| 2002-03 | Leeds U | 18 | 2 | | |
| 2003-04 | Leeds U | 30 | 3 | 48 | 5 |
| 2003-04 | Swindon T | 6 | 2 | 6 | 2 |
| 2004-05 | Newcastle U | 25 | 1 | | |
| 2005-06 | Newcastle U | 3 | 0 | | |
| 2005-06 | Aston Villa | 27 | 1 | | |
| 2006-07 | Newcastle U | 35 | 3 | | |
| 2007-08 | Newcastle U | 29 | 2 | | |
| 2008-09 | Newcastle U | 2 | 0 | 94 | 6 |
| 2008-09 | Aston Villa | 36 | 3 | | |
| 2009-10 | Aston Villa | 36 | 7 | | |
| 2010-11 | Aston Villa | 1 | 1 | 100 | 16 |
| 2010-11 | Manchester C | 32 | 0 | | |
| 2011-12 | Manchester C | 26 | 3 | | |
| 2012-13 | Manchester C | 26 | 4 | 84 | 7 |

**NASRI, Samir (M)** 265 36
H: 5 9 W: 11 11 b.Marseille 26-6-87
Honours: France Youth, Under-21, 35 full caps, 4 goals.

| 2004-05 | Marseille | 24 | 1 | | |
| 2005-06 | Marseille | 30 | 1 | | |
| 2006-07 | Marseille | 37 | 3 | | |
| 2007-08 | Marseille | 30 | 6 | 121 | 11 |
| 2008-09 | Arsenal | 29 | 6 | | |
| 2009-10 | Arsenal | 26 | 2 | | |
| 2010-11 | Arsenal | 30 | 10 | | |
| 2011-12 | Arsenal | 1 | 0 | 86 | 18 |
| 2011-12 | Manchester C | 30 | 5 | | |
| 2012-13 | Manchester C | 28 | 2 | 58 | 7 |

**NASTASIC, Matija (D)** 47 2
H: 6 2 W: 12 05 b.Valjevo 28-3-93
Honours: Serbia Youth, Under-21, 9 full caps.

| 2011-12 | Fiorentina | 25 | 2 | | |
| 2012-13 | Fiorentina | 1 | 0 | 26 | 2 |
| 2012-13 | Manchester C | 21 | 0 | 21 | 0 |

**NIMELY, Alex (F)** 29 1
H: 5 11 W: 11 03 b.Monrovia 11-5-91
Source: Mighty Barolle, Cotonsport Garoua, Manchester C Scholar. Honours: Liberia Youth. England Under-20.

| 2008-09 | Manchester C | 0 | 0 | | |
| 2009-10 | Manchester C | 1 | 0 | | |
| 2010-11 | Manchester C | 0 | 0 | | |
| 2011-12 | Manchester C | 0 | 0 | | |
| 2011-12 | Middlesbrough | 9 | 0 | 9 | 0 |
| 2011-12 | Coventry C | 17 | 1 | 17 | 1 |
| 2012-13 | Manchester C | 0 | 0 | 1 | 0 |
| 2012-13 | Crystal Palace | 2 | 0 | 2 | 0 |

**NUHU, Razak (D)** 40 1
b.Ghana 14-4-91

| 2010-11 | Manchester C | 0 | 0 | | |
| 2011 | Stromsgodset | 11 | 0 | | |
| 2011-12 | Manchester C | 0 | 0 | | |
| 2012 | Stromsgodset | 25 | 1 | | |
| 2012-13 | Manchester C | 0 | 0 | | |
| 2013 | Stromsgodset | 4 | 0 | 40 | 1 |

**PANTILIMON, Costel (G)** 102 0
H: 6 5 W: 15 02 b.Bacau 1-2-87
Honours: Romania Youth, Under-21, 16 full caps.

| 2005-06 | Aerostar Bacau | 9 | 0 | 9 | 0 |
| 2006-07 | Poli Timisoara | 8 | 0 | | |
| 2007-08 | Poli Timisoara | 5 | 0 | 13 | 0 |
| 2008-09 | Timisoara | 31 | 0 | | |
| 2009-10 | Timisoara | 21 | 0 | | |
| 2010-11 | Timisoara | 28 | 0 | 80 | 0 |
| 2011-12 | Manchester C | 0 | 0 | | |
| 2012-13 | Manchester C | 0 | 0 | | |

**PLUMMER, Ellis (D)** 0 0
b.Denton 2-9-94
Source: Scholar.

| 2011-12 | Manchester C | 0 | 0 | | |
| 2012-13 | Manchester C | 0 | 0 | | |

**RAZAK, Abdul (M)** 16 0
H: 5 10 W: 11 02 b.Abidjan 11-11-92
Source: Scholar. Honours: Ivory Coast 4 full caps.

| 2010-11 | Manchester C | 1 | 0 | | |
| 2011-12 | Manchester C | 1 | 0 | | |
| 2011-12 | Portsmouth | 3 | 0 | 3 | 0 |
| 2011-12 | Brighton & HA | 6 | 0 | 6 | 0 |
| 2012-13 | Manchester C | 3 | 0 | 5 | 0 |
| 2012-13 | Charlton Ath | 2 | 0 | 2 | 0 |

**REKIK, Karim (D)** 14 0
H: 6 0 W: 12 00 b.Den Haag 2-12-94
Source: Scholar. Honours: Holland Youth.

| 2011-12 | Manchester C | 0 | 0 | | |
| 2011-12 | Portsmouth | 8 | 0 | 8 | 0 |
| 2012-13 | Manchester C | 1 | 0 | 1 | 0 |
| 2012-13 | Blackburn R | 5 | 0 | 5 | 0 |

**RICHARDS, Micah (D)** 177 7
H: 5 11 W: 13 00 b.Birmingham 24-6-88
Source: Scholar. Honours: England Youth, Under-21, 13 full caps, 1 goal.

| 2005-06 | Manchester C | 13 | 0 | | |
| 2006-07 | Manchester C | 28 | 1 | | |
| 2007-08 | Manchester C | 25 | 0 | | |
| 2008-09 | Manchester C | 34 | 1 | | |
| 2009-10 | Manchester C | 23 | 3 | | |
| 2010-11 | Manchester C | 18 | 1 | | |
| 2011-12 | Manchester C | 29 | 1 | | |
| 2012-13 | Manchester C | 7 | 0 | 177 | 7 |

**RODWELL, Jack (D)** 96 6
H: 6 2 W: 12 08 b.Southport 11-3-91
Source: Scholar. Honours: England Youth, Under-21, 3 full caps.

| 2007-08 | Everton | 2 | 0 | | |
| 2008-09 | Everton | 19 | 0 | | |
| 2009-10 | Everton | 26 | 2 | | |
| 2010-11 | Everton | 24 | 0 | | |
| 2011-12 | Everton | 14 | 2 | | |
| 2012-13 | Everton | 0 | 0 | 85 | 4 |
| 2012-13 | Manchester C | 11 | 2 | 11 | 2 |

**RUSNAK, Albert (M)** 0 0
b.Kosice 7-7-94
Source: Scholar.

| 2011-12 | Manchester C | 0 | 0 | | |
| 2012-13 | Manchester C | 0 | 0 | | |

**SCAPUZZI, Luca (F)** 51 1
H: 6 0 W: 11 11 b.Milan 15-4-91

| 2009-10 | Portogruaro | 22 | 0 | | |
| 2010-11 | Portogruaro | 7 | 0 | 29 | 0 |
| 2011-12 | Manchester C | 0 | 0 | | |
| 2011-12 | Oldham Ath | 10 | 1 | 10 | 1 |
| 2011-12 | Portsmouth | 2 | 0 | 2 | 0 |
| 2012-13 | Manchester C | 0 | 0 | | |
| 2012-13 | Varese | 10 | 0 | 10 | 0 |

**SILVA, David (F)** 305 44
H: 5 7 W: 10 07 b.Arguineguin 8-1-86
Honours: Spain 74 full caps, 20 goals.

| 2003-04 | Mestalla | 14 | 1 | 14 | 1 |
| 2004-05 | Eibar | 35 | 5 | 35 | 5 |
| 2005-06 | Celta Vigo | 34 | 3 | 34 | 3 |
| 2006-07 | Valencia | 36 | 5 | | |
| 2007-08 | Valencia | 34 | 4 | | |
| 2008-09 | Valencia | 19 | 4 | | |
| 2009-10 | Valencia | 30 | 8 | 119 | 21 |
| 2010-11 | Manchester C | 35 | 4 | | |
| 2011-12 | Manchester C | 36 | 6 | | |
| 2012-13 | Manchester C | 32 | 4 | 103 | 14 |

**SINCLAIR, Scott (F)** 165 34
H: 5 10 W: 10 00 b.Bath 26-3-89
Source: Bristol R Schoolboy. Honours: England Youth, Under-21.

| 2004-05 | Bristol R | 2 | 0 | 2 | 0 |
| 2005-06 | Chelsea | 0 | 0 | | |
| 2006-07 | Chelsea | 2 | 0 | | |
| 2006-07 | Plymouth Arg | 15 | 2 | 15 | 2 |
| 2007-08 | Chelsea | 1 | 0 | | |
| 2007-08 | QPR | 9 | 1 | 9 | 1 |
| 2007-08 | Charlton Ath | 3 | 0 | 3 | 0 |
| 2007-08 | Crystal Palace | 6 | 2 | 6 | 2 |
| 2008-09 | Chelsea | 2 | 0 | | |
| 2009-10 | Chelsea | 0 | 0 | | |
| 2009-10 | Wigan Ath | 18 | 1 | 18 | 1 |
| 2010-11 | Swansea C | 43 | 19 | | |
| 2011-12 | Swansea C | 38 | 8 | | |
| 2012-13 | Swansea C | 1 | 1 | 82 | 28 |
| 2012-13 | Manchester C | 11 | 0 | 11 | 0 |

**SUAREZ, Denis (M)** 0 0
H: 5 11 W: 10 12 b.Tui 6-1-94
Source: Celta Vigo Youth.

| 2011-12 | Manchester C | 0 | 0 | | |
| 2012-13 | Manchester C | 0 | 0 | | |

**SWAN, George (D)** 0 0
b.Normanton 12-9-94
Source: Scholar.

| 2011-12 | Manchester C | 0 | 0 | | |
| 2012-13 | Manchester C | 0 | 0 | | |

**TEVEZ, Carlos (F)** 306 130
H: 5 8 W: 11 11 b.Buenos Aires 5-2-84
Source: All Boys. Honours: Argentina Youth, Under-20, Under-23, 59 full caps, 13 goals.

| 2001-02 | Boca Juniors | 11 | 1 | | |
| 2002-03 | Boca Juniors | 32 | 11 | | |
| 2003-04 | Boca Juniors | 23 | 12 | | |
| 2004-05 | Boca Juniors | 9 | 2 | 75 | 26 |
| 2005 | Corinthians | 29 | 20 | 29 | 20 |
| 2006-07 | West Ham U | 26 | 7 | 26 | 7 |
| 2007-08 | Manchester U | 34 | 14 | | |
| 2008-09 | Manchester U | 29 | 5 | | |
| 2009-10 | Manchester U | 0 | 0 | 63 | 19 |
| 2009-10 | Manchester C | 35 | 23 | | |
| 2010-11 | Manchester C | 31 | 20 | | |
| 2011-12 | Manchester C | 13 | 4 | | |
| 2012-13 | Manchester C | 34 | 11 | 113 | 58 |

**TOURE, Kolo (D)** 307 11
H: 5 10 W: 13 08 b.Sokoura Bouake 19-3-81
Source: ASEC Mimosas. Honours: Ivory Coast 103 full caps, 6 goals.

| 2001-02 | Arsenal | 0 | 0 | | |
| 2002-03 | Arsenal | 26 | 2 | | |
| 2003-04 | Arsenal | 37 | 1 | | |
| 2004-05 | Arsenal | 35 | 0 | | |
| 2005-06 | Arsenal | 33 | 0 | | |
| 2006-07 | Arsenal | 35 | 3 | | |
| 2007-08 | Arsenal | 30 | 2 | | |
| 2008-09 | Arsenal | 29 | 1 | | |
| 2009-10 | Arsenal | 0 | 0 | 225 | 9 |
| 2009-10 | Manchester C | 31 | 1 | | |
| 2010-11 | Manchester C | 22 | 1 | | |
| 2011-12 | Manchester C | 14 | 0 | | |
| 2012-13 | Manchester C | 15 | 0 | 82 | 2 |

**TOURE, Yaya (M)** 323 39
H: 6 3 W: 14 02 b.Sokoura Bouake 13-5-83
Honours: Ivory Coast 78 full caps, 16 goals.

| 2001-02 | Beveren | 28 | 0 | | |
| 2002-03 | Beveren | 30 | 3 | | |
| 2003-04 | Beveren | 12 | 0 | 70 | 3 |
| 2003-04 | Metalurgs Donetsk | 11 | 1 | | |
| 2004-05 | Metalurgs Donetsk | 22 | 2 | 33 | 3 |
| 2005-06 | Olympiacos | 20 | 3 | 20 | 3 |
| 2006-07 | Monaco | 27 | 5 | 27 | 5 |
| 2007-08 | Barcelona | 26 | 1 | | |
| 2008-09 | Barcelona | 25 | 2 | | |
| 2009-10 | Barcelona | 23 | 1 | 74 | 4 |
| 2010-11 | Manchester C | 35 | 8 | | |
| 2011-12 | Manchester C | 32 | 6 | | |
| 2012-13 | Manchester C | 32 | 7 | 99 | 21 |

**WABARA, Reece (D)** 33 0
H: 6 0 W: 12 06 b.Birmingham 28-12-91
Honours: England Under-20.

| 2008-09 | Manchester C | 0 | 0 | | |
| 2009-10 | Manchester C | 0 | 0 | | |
| 2010-11 | Manchester C | 1 | 0 | | |
| 2011-12 | Manchester C | 0 | 0 | | |
| 2011-12 | Ipswich T | 6 | 0 | 6 | 0 |
| 2012-13 | Manchester C | 0 | 0 | 1 | 0 |
| 2012-13 | Oldham Ath | 25 | 0 | 25 | 0 |
| 2012-13 | Blackpool | 1 | 0 | 1 | 0 |

**WRIGHT, Richard (G)** 380 0
H: 6 2 W: 14 04 b.Ipswich 5-11-77
Source: Trainee. Honours: England Schools, Youth, Under-21, 2 full caps.

| 1994-95 | Ipswich T | 3 | 0 | | |
| 1995-96 | Ipswich T | 23 | 0 | | |
| 1996-97 | Ipswich T | 40 | 0 | | |
| 1997-98 | Ipswich T | 46 | 0 | | |
| 1998-99 | Ipswich T | 46 | 0 | | |
| 1999-2000 | Ipswich T | 46 | 0 | | |
| 2000-01 | Ipswich T | 36 | 0 | | |

| 2001-02 | Arsenal | 12 | 0 | 12 | 0 |
|---|---|---|---|---|---|
| 2002-03 | Everton | 33 | 0 | | |
| 2003-04 | Everton | 4 | 0 | | |
| 2004-05 | Everton | 7 | 0 | | |
| 2005-06 | Everton | 15 | 0 | | |
| 2006-07 | Everton | 1 | 0 | 60 | 0 |
| 2007-08 | West Ham U | 0 | 0 | | |
| 2007-08 | *Southampton* | 7 | 0 | 7 | 0 |
| 2008-09 | Ipswich T | 46 | 0 | | |
| 2009-10 | Ipswich T | 12 | 0 | | |
| 2010-11 | Ipswich T | 0 | 0 | | |
| 2010-11 | *Sheffield U* | 2 | 0 | 2 | 0 |
| 2011-12 | Ipswich T | 1 | 0 | 299 | 0 |
| 2012-13 | Manchester C | 0 | 0 | | |

**ZABALETA, Pablo (D)**    279 17
H: 5 8 W: 10 12 b.Buenos Aires 16-1-85
*Honours:* Argentina Youth, Under-23, 31 full caps.

| 2002-03 | San Lorenzo | 11 | 0 | | |
|---|---|---|---|---|---|
| 2003-04 | San Lorenzo | 27 | 3 | | |
| 2004-05 | San Lorenzo | 28 | 5 | 66 | 8 |
| 2005-06 | Espanyol | 27 | 2 | | |
| 2006-07 | Espanyol | 21 | 0 | | |
| 2007-08 | Espanyol | 32 | 1 | 80 | 3 |
| 2008-09 | Manchester C | 29 | 1 | | |
| 2009-10 | Manchester C | 27 | 0 | | |
| 2010-11 | Manchester C | 26 | 2 | | |
| 2011-12 | Manchester C | 21 | 1 | | |
| 2012-13 | Manchester C | 30 | 2 | 133 | 6 |

**Players retained or with offer of contract**
Adjei-Boateng, Bismark; Agyiri, Thomas; Bytyqi, Sinan; Cole, Devante; Facey, Shay; Fofana Seko, Mohamed; Hutton, Louis Jack; Kwakwa, Enoch; Mayifuila, Jordy Hiwula; Oduro, Dominic.

**Scholars**
Barbosa Intima Jorge Fernando; Bossaerts, Mathias; Byrne, Jack; Glendon, George; Gunn, Angus Fraser James; Hardy, James; Horsfield, James; Jones, Samuel James Cooper; Kuate, Wato; Leigh, Greg; McHale, Dominic Michael; Mesquita Lopes, Marcos Paulo; Ntcham, Jules Olivier; O'Brien, Billy Thomas; Pozo La Rosa, Jose Angel; Sharpe, Liam James; Smith-Brown, Ashley.

# MANCHESTER U (49)

**AMOS, Ben (G)**    35 0
H: 6 1 W: 13 00 b.Macclesfield 10-4-90
*Source:* Scholar. *Honours:* England Youth, Under-21.

| 2007-08 | Manchester U | 0 | 0 | | |
|---|---|---|---|---|---|
| 2008-09 | Manchester U | 0 | 0 | | |
| 2009-10 | Manchester U | 0 | 0 | | |
| 2009-10 | *Peterborough U* | 1 | 0 | 1 | 0 |
| 2010-11 | Manchester U | 0 | 0 | | |
| 2010-11 | *Oldham Ath* | 16 | 0 | 16 | 0 |
| 2011-12 | Manchester U | 1 | 0 | | |
| 2012-13 | Manchester U | 0 | 0 | | |
| 2012-13 | *Hull C* | 17 | 0 | 17 | 0 |

**ANDERSON (M)**    123 8
H: 5 8 W: 10 07 b.Porto Alegre 13-4-88
*Honours:* Brazil Youth, Under-23, 8 full caps.

| 2004-05 | Gremio | 5 | 1 | 5 | 1 |
|---|---|---|---|---|---|
| 2005-06 | Porto | 3 | 0 | | |
| 2006-07 | Porto | 15 | 2 | 18 | 2 |
| 2007-08 | Manchester U | 24 | 0 | | |
| 2008-09 | Manchester U | 17 | 0 | | |
| 2009-10 | Manchester U | 14 | 1 | | |
| 2010-11 | Manchester U | 18 | 1 | | |
| 2011-12 | Manchester U | 10 | 2 | | |
| 2012-13 | Manchester U | 17 | 1 | 100 | 5 |

**BEBE (F)**    49 5
H: 6 3 W: 11 11 b.Agualva-cacem 12-7-90
*Honours:* Portugal Under-21.

| 2009-10 | Amadora | 26 | 4 | 26 | 4 |
|---|---|---|---|---|---|
| 2010-11 | Guimaraes | 0 | 0 | | |
| 2010-11 | Manchester U | 2 | 0 | | |
| 2011-12 | Manchester U | 0 | 0 | | |
| 2011-12 | *Besiktas* | 4 | 0 | 4 | 0 |
| 2012-13 | Manchester U | 0 | 0 | 2 | 0 |
| 2012-13 | *Rio Ave* | 17 | 1 | 17 | 1 |

**BLACKETT, Tyler (D)**    0 0
H: 6 1 W: 11 12 b. 2-4-94

| 2012-13 | Manchester U | 0 | 0 | | |
|---|---|---|---|---|---|

**BROWN, Reece (D)**    28 0
H: 6 2 W: 13 02 b.Manchester 1-11-91
*Honours:* England Under-20.

| 2010-11 | *Bradford C* | 3 | 0 | 3 | 0 |
|---|---|---|---|---|---|
| 2010-11 | Manchester U | 0 | 0 | | |
| 2011-12 | Manchester U | 0 | 0 | | |
| 2011-12 | *Doncaster R* | 3 | 0 | 3 | 0 |
| 2011-12 | *Oldham Ath* | 15 | 0 | 15 | 0 |
| 2012-13 | Manchester U | 0 | 0 | | |
| 2012-13 | *Coventry C* | 6 | 0 | 6 | 0 |
| 2012-13 | *Ipswich T* | 1 | 0 | 1 | 0 |

**BUTTNER, Alexander (D)**    111 12
H: 5 8 W: 11 10 b.Doetinchem 11-2-89

| 2007-08 | Vitesse | 1 | 0 | | |
|---|---|---|---|---|---|
| 2008-09 | Vitesse | 23 | 3 | | |
| 2009-10 | Vitesse | 26 | 2 | | |
| 2010-11 | Vitesse | 24 | 0 | | |
| 2011-12 | Vitesse | 32 | 5 | 106 | 10 |
| 2012-13 | Manchester U | 5 | 2 | 5 | 2 |

**CARRICK, Michael (M)**    424 25
H: 6 1 W: 11 10 b.Wallsend 28-7-81
*Source:* Trainee. *Honours:* England Youth, Under-21, B, 29 full caps.

| 1998-99 | West Ham U | 0 | 0 | | |
|---|---|---|---|---|---|
| 1999-2000 | West Ham U | 8 | 1 | | |
| 1999-2000 | *Swindon T* | 6 | 2 | 6 | 2 |
| 1999-2000 | *Birmingham C* | 2 | 0 | 2 | 0 |
| 2000-01 | West Ham U | 33 | 1 | | |
| 2001-02 | West Ham U | 30 | 2 | | |
| 2002-03 | West Ham U | 30 | 1 | | |
| 2003-04 | West Ham U | 35 | 1 | | |
| 2004-05 | West Ham U | 0 | 0 | 136 | 6 |
| 2004-05 | Tottenham H | 29 | 0 | | |
| 2005-06 | Tottenham H | 35 | 2 | 64 | 2 |
| 2006-07 | Manchester U | 33 | 3 | | |
| 2007-08 | Manchester U | 31 | 2 | | |
| 2008-09 | Manchester U | 28 | 4 | | |
| 2009-10 | Manchester U | 30 | 3 | | |
| 2010-11 | Manchester U | 28 | 0 | | |
| 2011-12 | Manchester U | 30 | 2 | | |
| 2012-13 | Manchester U | 36 | 1 | 216 | 15 |

**CLEVERLEY, Tom (M)**    105 18
H: 5 9 W: 10 07 b.Basingstoke 12-8-89
*Source:* Scholar. *Honours:* England Youth, Under-20, Under-21, 9 full caps.

| 2007-08 | Manchester U | 0 | 0 | | |
|---|---|---|---|---|---|
| 2008-09 | Manchester U | 0 | 0 | | |
| 2008-09 | *Leicester C* | 15 | 2 | 15 | 2 |
| 2009-10 | Manchester U | 0 | 0 | | |
| 2009-10 | *Watford* | 33 | 11 | 33 | 11 |
| 2010-11 | Manchester U | 0 | 0 | | |
| 2010-11 | *Wigan Ath* | 25 | 3 | 25 | 3 |
| 2011-12 | Manchester U | 10 | 0 | | |
| 2012-13 | Manchester U | 22 | 2 | 32 | 2 |

**COFIE, John (F)**    23 3
H: 6 0 W: 12 11 b.Aboso 21-1-93
*Source:* Scholar.

| 2010-11 | Manchester U | 0 | 0 | | |
|---|---|---|---|---|---|
| 2011-12 | Manchester U | 0 | 0 | | |
| 2012-13 | Manchester U | 0 | 0 | | |
| 2012-13 | *Sheffield U* | 16 | 2 | 16 | 2 |
| 2012-13 | *Notts Co* | 7 | 1 | 7 | 1 |

**COLE, Larnell (M)**    0 0
H: 5 4 W: 12 04 b.Manchester 9-3-93
*Source:* Scholar. *Honours:* England Youth.

| 2011-12 | Manchester U | 0 | 0 | | |
|---|---|---|---|---|---|
| 2012-13 | Manchester U | 0 | 0 | | |

**DA SILVA, Fabio (M)**    42 1
H: 5 8 W: 10 03 b.Rio de Janeiro 9-7-90
*Source:* Fluminense. *Honours:* Brazil 2 full caps.

| 2008-09 | Manchester U | 3 | 0 | | |
|---|---|---|---|---|---|
| 2009-10 | Manchester U | 5 | 0 | | |
| 2010-11 | Manchester U | 11 | 1 | | |
| 2011-12 | Manchester U | 5 | 0 | | |
| 2012-13 | Manchester U | 0 | 0 | 21 | 1 |
| 2012-13 | *QPR* | 21 | 0 | 21 | 0 |

**DA SILVA, Rafael (D)**    80 5
H: 5 8 W: 10 03 b.Rio de Janeiro 9-7-90
*Source:* Fluminense. *Honours:* Brazil Youth, 2 full caps.

| 2008-09 | Manchester U | 16 | 1 | | |
|---|---|---|---|---|---|
| 2009-10 | Manchester U | 8 | 1 | | |
| 2010-11 | Manchester U | 16 | 0 | | |
| 2011-12 | Manchester U | 12 | 0 | | |
| 2012-13 | Manchester U | 28 | 3 | 80 | 5 |

**DAEHLI, Mats (M)**    0 0
b.Oslo 2-3-95
*Source:* Scholar.

| 2011-12 | Manchester U | 0 | 0 | | |
|---|---|---|---|---|---|
| 2012-13 | Manchester U | 0 | 0 | | |

**DE GEA, David (G)**    114 0
H: 6 3 W: 12 13 b.Madrid 7-11-90
*Honours:* Spain Youth, Under-21.

| 2009-10 | Atletico Madrid | 19 | 0 | | |
|---|---|---|---|---|---|
| 2010-11 | Atletico Madrid | 38 | 0 | 57 | 0 |
| 2011-12 | Manchester U | 29 | 0 | | |
| 2012-13 | Manchester U | 28 | 0 | 57 | 0 |

**EKANGAMENE, Charni (M)**    0 0
b.Antwerp 16-2-94
*Source:* Scholar. *Honours:* Belgium Youth.

| 2011-12 | Manchester U | 0 | 0 | | |
|---|---|---|---|---|---|
| 2012-13 | Manchester U | 0 | 0 | | |

**EVANS, Jonny (D)**    147 7
H: 6 2 W: 12 02 b.Belfast 3-1-88
*Source:* Scholar. *Honours:* Northern Ireland Schools, Youth, Under-21, 34 full caps, 1 goal.

| 2004-05 | Manchester U | 0 | 0 | | |
|---|---|---|---|---|---|
| 2005-06 | Manchester U | 0 | 0 | | |
| 2006-07 | Manchester U | 0 | 0 | | |
| 2006-07 | *Antwerp* | 14 | 2 | 14 | 2 |
| 2006-07 | *Sunderland* | 18 | 1 | | |
| 2007-08 | *Sunderland* | 15 | 0 | 33 | 1 |
| 2008-09 | Manchester U | 17 | 0 | | |
| 2009-10 | Manchester U | 18 | 0 | | |
| 2010-11 | Manchester U | 13 | 0 | | |
| 2011-12 | Manchester U | 29 | 1 | | |
| 2012-13 | Manchester U | 23 | 3 | 100 | 4 |

**EVRA, Patrice (D)**    426 11
H: 5 8 W: 11 10 b.Dakar 15-5-81
*Honours:* France 49 full caps.

| 1998-99 | Marsala | 24 | 3 | 24 | 3 |
|---|---|---|---|---|---|
| 1999-2000 | Monza | 3 | 0 | 3 | 0 |
| 2000-01 | Nice | 5 | 0 | | |
| 2001-02 | Nice | 34 | 1 | 39 | 1 |
| 2002-03 | Monaco | 36 | 1 | | |
| 2003-04 | Monaco | 33 | 0 | | |
| 2004-05 | Monaco | 36 | 0 | | |
| 2005-06 | Monaco | 15 | 0 | 120 | 1 |
| 2005-06 | Manchester U | 11 | 0 | | |
| 2006-07 | Manchester U | 24 | 1 | | |
| 2007-08 | Manchester U | 33 | 0 | | |
| 2008-09 | Manchester U | 28 | 0 | | |
| 2009-10 | Manchester U | 38 | 0 | | |
| 2010-11 | Manchester U | 35 | 1 | | |
| 2011-12 | Manchester U | 37 | 0 | | |
| 2012-13 | Manchester U | 34 | 4 | 240 | 6 |

**FERDINAND, Rio (D)**    489 11
H: 6 2 W: 13 12 b.Peckham 7-11-78
*Source:* Scholar. *Honours:* England Youth, Under-21, B, 81 full caps, 3 goals.

| 1995-96 | West Ham U | 1 | 0 | | |
|---|---|---|---|---|---|
| 1996-97 | West Ham U | 15 | 2 | | |
| 1996-97 | *Bournemouth* | 10 | 0 | 10 | 0 |
| 1997-98 | West Ham U | 35 | 0 | | |
| 1998-99 | West Ham U | 31 | 0 | | |
| 1999-2000 | West Ham U | 33 | 0 | | |
| 2000-01 | West Ham U | 12 | 0 | 127 | 2 |
| 2000-01 | Leeds U | 23 | 2 | | |
| 2001-02 | Leeds U | 31 | 0 | 54 | 2 |
| 2002-03 | Manchester U | 28 | 0 | | |
| 2003-04 | Manchester U | 20 | 0 | | |
| 2004-05 | Manchester U | 31 | 0 | | |
| 2005-06 | Manchester U | 37 | 3 | | |
| 2006-07 | Manchester U | 33 | 1 | | |
| 2007-08 | Manchester U | 35 | 2 | | |
| 2008-09 | Manchester U | 24 | 0 | | |
| 2009-10 | Manchester U | 19 | 0 | | |
| 2010-11 | Manchester U | 19 | 0 | | |
| 2011-12 | Manchester U | 30 | 0 | | |
| 2012-13 | Manchester U | 28 | 1 | 298 | 7 |

**FLETCHER, Darren (M)**  200  18
H: 6 0  W: 11 09  b.Edinburgh 1-2-84
Source: Scholar. Honours: Scotland
Under-21, B, 61 full caps, 5 goals.

| | | | | |
|---|---|---|---|---|
| 2000-01 | Manchester U | 0 | 0 | |
| 2001-02 | Manchester U | 0 | 0 | |
| 2002-03 | Manchester U | 0 | 0 | |
| 2003-04 | Manchester U | 22 | 0 | |
| 2004-05 | Manchester U | 18 | 3 | |
| 2005-06 | Manchester U | 27 | 1 | |
| 2006-07 | Manchester U | 24 | 3 | |
| 2007-08 | Manchester U | 16 | 0 | |
| 2008-09 | Manchester U | 26 | 3 | |
| 2009-10 | Manchester U | 30 | 4 | |
| 2010-11 | Manchester U | 26 | 2 | |
| 2011-12 | Manchester U | 8 | 1 | |
| 2012-13 | Manchester U | 3 | 1 | 200 18 |

**GIGGS, Ryan (F)**  660  114
H: 5 11  W: 11 02  b.Cardiff 29-11-73
Source: School. Honours: England Schools,
Wales Youth, Under-21, 64 full caps, 12 goals.

| | | | | |
|---|---|---|---|---|
| 1990-91 | Manchester U | 2 | 1 | |
| 1991-92 | Manchester U | 38 | 4 | |
| 1992-93 | Manchester U | 41 | 9 | |
| 1993-94 | Manchester U | 38 | 13 | |
| 1994-95 | Manchester U | 29 | 1 | |
| 1995-96 | Manchester U | 33 | 11 | |
| 1996-97 | Manchester U | 26 | 3 | |
| 1997-98 | Manchester U | 29 | 8 | |
| 1998-99 | Manchester U | 24 | 3 | |
| 1999-2000 | Manchester U | 30 | 6 | |
| 2000-01 | Manchester U | 31 | 5 | |
| 2001-02 | Manchester U | 25 | 7 | |
| 2002-03 | Manchester U | 36 | 8 | |
| 2003-04 | Manchester U | 33 | 7 | |
| 2004-05 | Manchester U | 32 | 5 | |
| 2005-06 | Manchester U | 27 | 3 | |
| 2006-07 | Manchester U | 30 | 4 | |
| 2007-08 | Manchester U | 31 | 3 | |
| 2008-09 | Manchester U | 28 | 2 | |
| 2009-10 | Manchester U | 25 | 5 | |
| 2010-11 | Manchester U | 25 | 2 | |
| 2011-12 | Manchester U | 25 | 2 | |
| 2012-13 | Manchester U | 2 | 2 | 660 114 |

**HENRIQUEZ, Angelo (F)**  21  12
H: 5 10  W: 10 11  b.Santiago 13-4-94
Honours: Chile Youth, Under-20, 2 full caps,
4 goal.

| | | | | |
|---|---|---|---|---|
| 2012 | Universidad de Chile | 17 | 11 | 17 11 |
| 2012-13 | Manchester U | 0 | 0 | |
| 2012-13 | Wigan Ath | 4 | 1 | 4 1 |

**HERNANDEZ, Javier (F)**  184  70
H: 5 8  W: 9 11  b.Guadalajara 1-6-88
Honours: Mexico Youth, 53 full caps, 35
goals.

| | | | | |
|---|---|---|---|---|
| 2005-06 | Tapatio | 11 | 0 | |
| 2006-07 | Tapatio | 12 | 3 | |
| 2006-07 | Guadalajara | 7 | 1 | |
| 2007-08 | Guadalajara | 5 | 0 | |
| 2007-08 | Tapatio | 15 | 6 | |
| 2008-09 | Tapatio | 7 | 2 | 45 11 |
| 2008-09 | Guadalajara | 22 | 4 | |
| 2009-10 | Guadalajara | 28 | 21 | 62 26 |
| 2010-11 | Manchester U | 27 | 13 | |
| 2011-12 | Manchester U | 28 | 10 | |
| 2012-13 | Manchester U | 22 | 10 | 77 33 |

**JANUZAJ, Adrian (M)**  0  0
H: 5 11  W: 11 11  b.Brussels 5-2-95
Source: Scholar.

| | | | |
|---|---|---|---|
| 2011-12 | Manchester U | 0 | 0 |
| 2012-13 | Manchester U | 0 | 0 |

**JOHNSTONE, Samuel (G)**  19  0
H: 6 0  W: 12 10  b.Preston 25-3-93
Source: Scholar. Honours: England Youth.

| | | | | |
|---|---|---|---|---|
| 2009-10 | Manchester U | 0 | 0 | |
| 2010-11 | Manchester U | 0 | 0 | |
| 2011-12 | Manchester U | 0 | 0 | |
| 2011-12 | Scunthorpe U | 12 | 0 | 12 0 |
| 2012-13 | Manchester U | 0 | 0 | |
| 2012-13 | Walsall | 7 | 0 | 7 0 |

**JONES, Phil (D)**  81  1
H: 5 11  W: 11 02  b.Preston 21-2-92
Source: Scholar. Honours: England Youth,
Under-21, 7 full caps.

| | | | | |
|---|---|---|---|---|
| 2009-10 | Blackburn R | 9 | 0 | |
| 2010-11 | Blackburn R | 26 | 0 | 35 0 |
| 2011-12 | Manchester U | 29 | 1 | |
| 2012-13 | Manchester U | 17 | 0 | 46 1 |

**KAGAWA, Shinji (M)**  80  34
H: 5 8  W: 10 00  b.Tarumi-ku 17-3-89
Honours: Japan Youth, Under-23, 45 full
caps, 14 goals.

| | | | | |
|---|---|---|---|---|
| 2009-10 | Cerezo Osaka | 11 | 7 | 11 7 |
| 2010-11 | Borussia Dortmund | 18 | 8 | |
| 2011-12 | Borussia Dortmund | 31 | 13 | 49 21 |
| 2012-13 | Manchester U | 20 | 6 | 20 6 |

**KEANE, Michael (D)**  22  2
H: 5 7  W: 12 13  b.Stockport 11-1-93
Source: Scholar. Honours: Eire Youth,
England Youth, Under-21

| | | | | |
|---|---|---|---|---|
| 2011-12 | Manchester U | 0 | 0 | |
| 2012-13 | Manchester U | 0 | 0 | |
| 2012-13 | Leicester C | 22 | 2 | 22 2 |

**KEANE, Will (F)**  1  0
H: 6 2  W: 11 05  b.Stockport 11-1-93
Source: Scholar. Honours: England Youth,
Under-21.

| | | | | |
|---|---|---|---|---|
| 2009-10 | Manchester U | 0 | 0 | |
| 2010-11 | Manchester U | 0 | 0 | |
| 2011-12 | Manchester U | 1 | 0 | |
| 2012-13 | Manchester U | 0 | 0 | 1 0 |

**LINDEGAARD, Anders (G)**  90  0
H: 6 4  W: 12 08  b.Odense 13-4-84
Honours: Denmark Youth, 5 full caps.

| | | | | |
|---|---|---|---|---|
| 2003-04 | Odense | 0 | 0 | |
| 2004-05 | Odense | 0 | 0 | |
| 2005-06 | Odense | 0 | 0 | |
| 2006-07 | Odense | 1 | 0 | |
| 2007-08 | Odense | 1 | 0 | |
| 2008-09 | Kolding | 10 | 0 | 10 0 |
| 2009 | Aalesund | 26 | 0 | |
| 2009 | Odense | 4 | 0 | 6 0 |
| 2010 | Aalesund | 30 | 0 | 56 0 |
| 2010-11 | Manchester U | 0 | 0 | |
| 2011-12 | Manchester U | 8 | 0 | |
| 2012-13 | Manchester U | 10 | 0 | 18 0 |

**LINGARD, Jesse (M)**  5  0
H: 5 3  W: 11 11  b.Warrington 15-12-92
Source: Scholar.

| | | | | |
|---|---|---|---|---|
| 2011-12 | Manchester U | 0 | 0 | |
| 2012-13 | Manchester U | 0 | 0 | |
| 2012-13 | Leicester C | 5 | 0 | 5 0 |

**MACHEDA, Federico (F)**  50  4
H: 6 0  W: 11 13  b.Rome 22-8-91
Source: Scholar. Honours: Italy Under-21.

| | | | | |
|---|---|---|---|---|
| 2008-09 | Manchester U | 4 | 2 | |
| 2009-10 | Manchester U | 5 | 1 | |
| 2010-11 | Manchester U | 7 | 1 | |
| 2010-11 | Sampdoria | 14 | 0 | 14 0 |
| 2011-12 | Manchester U | 3 | 0 | |
| 2011-12 | QPR | 3 | 0 | 3 0 |
| 2012-13 | Manchester U | 0 | 0 | 19 4 |
| 2012-13 | Stuttgart | 14 | 0 | 14 0 |

**McCULLOUGH, Luke (D)**  1  0
b.Portadown 15-2-94

| | | | | |
|---|---|---|---|---|
| 2012-13 | Manchester U | 0 | 0 | |
| 2012-13 | Cheltenham T | 1 | 0 | 1 0 |

**NANI (M)**  193  35
H: 5 9  W: 10 04  b.Cape Verde 17-11-86
Honours: Portugal Under-21, 66 full caps, 13
goals.

| | | | | |
|---|---|---|---|---|
| 2005-06 | Sporting Lisbon | 29 | 4 | |
| 2006-07 | Sporting Lisbon | 29 | 5 | 58 9 |
| 2007-08 | Manchester U | 26 | 3 | |
| 2008-09 | Manchester U | 13 | 1 | |
| 2009-10 | Manchester U | 23 | 4 | |
| 2010-11 | Manchester U | 33 | 9 | |
| 2011-12 | Manchester U | 29 | 8 | |
| 2012-13 | Manchester U | 11 | 1 | 135 26 |

**PETRUCCI, Davide (M)**  4  1
H: 6 2  W: 13 10  b.Rome 5-10-91
Source: Scholar.

| | | | | |
|---|---|---|---|---|
| 2008-09 | Manchester U | 0 | 0 | |
| 2009-10 | Manchester U | 0 | 0 | |
| 2010-11 | Manchester U | 0 | 0 | |
| 2011-12 | Manchester U | 0 | 0 | |
| 2012-13 | Manchester U | 0 | 0 | |
| 2012-13 | Peterborough U | 4 | 1 | 4 1 |

**POWELL, Nick (F)**  57  15
H: 6 0  W: 10 05  b.Crewe 23-3-94
Source: Scholar. Honours: England Youth,
England Under-21.

| | | | | |
|---|---|---|---|---|
| 2010-11 | Crewe Alex | 17 | 0 | |
| 2011-12 | Crewe Alex | 38 | 14 | 55 14 |
| 2012-13 | Manchester U | 2 | 1 | 2 1 |

**ROONEY, Wayne (F)**  345  156
H: 5 10  W: 12 13  b.Liverpool 24-10-85
Source: Scholar. Honours: FA Schools,
England Youth, 83 full caps, 36 goals.

| | | | | |
|---|---|---|---|---|
| 2002-03 | Everton | 33 | 6 | |
| 2003-04 | Everton | 34 | 9 | 67 15 |
| 2004-05 | Manchester U | 29 | 11 | |
| 2005-06 | Manchester U | 36 | 16 | |
| 2006-07 | Manchester U | 35 | 14 | |
| 2007-08 | Manchester U | 27 | 12 | |
| 2008-09 | Manchester U | 30 | 12 | |
| 2009-10 | Manchester U | 32 | 26 | |
| 2010-11 | Manchester U | 28 | 11 | |
| 2011-12 | Manchester U | 34 | 27 | |
| 2012-13 | Manchester U | 27 | 12 | 278 141 |

**SCHOLES, Paul (M)**  499  107
H: 5 7  W: 11 00  b.Salford 16-11-74
Source: Trainee. Honours: England Youth, 66
full caps, 14 goals.

| | | | | |
|---|---|---|---|---|
| 1992-93 | Manchester U | 0 | 0 | |
| 1993-94 | Manchester U | 0 | 0 | |
| 1994-95 | Manchester U | 17 | 5 | |
| 1995-96 | Manchester U | 26 | 10 | |
| 1996-97 | Manchester U | 24 | 3 | |
| 1997-98 | Manchester U | 31 | 8 | |
| 1998-99 | Manchester U | 31 | 6 | |
| 1999-2000 | Manchester U | 31 | 9 | |
| 2000-01 | Manchester U | 32 | 6 | |
| 2001-02 | Manchester U | 35 | 8 | |
| 2002-03 | Manchester U | 33 | 14 | |
| 2003-04 | Manchester U | 28 | 9 | |
| 2004-05 | Manchester U | 33 | 9 | |
| 2005-06 | Manchester U | 20 | 2 | |
| 2006-07 | Manchester U | 30 | 6 | |
| 2007-08 | Manchester U | 24 | 1 | |
| 2008-09 | Manchester U | 21 | 2 | |
| 2009-10 | Manchester U | 28 | 3 | |
| 2010-11 | Manchester U | 22 | 1 | |
| 2011-12 | Manchester U | 17 | 4 | |
| 2012-13 | Manchester U | 16 | 1 | 499 107 |

**SMALLING, Chris (D)**  63  1
H: 6 4  W: 14 02  b.Greenwich 22-11-89
Source: Maidstone U. Honours: England
Youth, Under-21, 6 full caps.

| | | | | |
|---|---|---|---|---|
| 2008-09 | Fulham | 1 | 0 | |
| 2009-10 | Fulham | 12 | 0 | 13 0 |
| 2010-11 | Manchester U | 16 | 0 | |
| 2011-12 | Manchester U | 19 | 1 | |
| 2012-13 | Manchester U | 15 | 0 | 50 1 |

**THORPE, Tom (D)**  0  0
H: 6 0  W: 14 00  b.Manchester 13-1-93
Source: Scholar. Honours: England Youth.

| | | | |
|---|---|---|---|
| 2010-11 | Manchester U | 0 | 0 |
| 2011-12 | Manchester U | 0 | 0 |
| 2012-13 | Manchester U | 0 | 0 |

**TUNNICLIFFE, Ryan (M)**  29  0
H: 6 0  W: 14 02  b.Bury 30-12-92
Source: Scholar.

| | | | | |
|---|---|---|---|---|
| 2009-10 | Manchester U | 0 | 0 | |
| 2010-11 | Manchester U | 0 | 0 | |
| 2011-12 | Manchester U | 0 | 0 | |
| 2011-12 | Peterborough U | 27 | 0 | 27 0 |
| 2012-13 | Manchester U | 0 | 0 | |
| 2012-13 | Barnsley | 2 | 0 | 2 0 |

**VALENCIA, Antonio (M)**  274  29
H: 5 10  W: 12 04  b.Lago Agrio 5-8-85
Honours: Ecuador Under-21, Under-23, 62
full caps, 8 goals.

| | | | | |
|---|---|---|---|---|
| 2002 | El Nacional | 1 | 0 | |
| 2003 | El Nacional | 26 | 2 | |
| 2004 | El Nacional | 41 | 9 | |
| 2005 | El Nacional | 14 | 4 | 83 15 |
| 2005-06 | Villarreal | 2 | 0 | 2 0 |
| 2005-06 | Recreativo | 4 | 0 | 4 0 |
| 2006-07 | Wigan Ath | 22 | 1 | |
| 2007-08 | Wigan Ath | 31 | 3 | |

| 2008-09 | Wigan Ath | 31 | 3 | **84** | **7** |
|---|---|---|---|---|---|
| 2009-10 | Manchester U | 34 | 5 | | |
| 2010-11 | Manchester U | 10 | 1 | | |
| 2011-12 | Manchester U | 27 | 4 | | |
| 2012-13 | Manchester U | 30 | 1 | **101** | **11** |

**VAN PERSIE, Robin (F)**     **293 136**
H: 6 0   W: 11 00   b.Rotterdam 6-8-83
*Source:* Excelsior. *Honours:* Holland
Under-21, 76 full caps, 35 goals.

| 2001-02 | Feyenoord | 10 | 0 | | |
|---|---|---|---|---|---|
| 2002-03 | Feyenoord | 23 | 8 | | |
| 2003-04 | Feyenoord | 28 | 6 | **61** | **14** |
| 2004-05 | Arsenal | 26 | 5 | | |
| 2005-06 | Arsenal | 24 | 5 | | |
| 2006-07 | Arsenal | 22 | 11 | | |
| 2007-08 | Arsenal | 15 | 7 | | |
| 2008-09 | Arsenal | 28 | 11 | | |
| 2009-10 | Arsenal | 16 | 9 | | |
| 2010-11 | Arsenal | 25 | 18 | | |
| 2011-12 | Arsenal | 38 | 30 | | |
| 2012-13 | Arsenal | 0 | 0 | **194** | **96** |
| 2012-13 | Manchester U | 38 | 26 | **38** | **26** |

**VERMIJL, Marnick (D)**     **0 0**
H: 5 11   W: 11 12   b.Overpelt 13-1-92
*Honours:* Belgium Youth.

| 2010-11 | Manchester U | 0 | 0 | | |
|---|---|---|---|---|---|
| 2011-12 | Manchester U | 0 | 0 | | |
| 2012-13 | Manchester U | 0 | 0 | | |

**VIDIC, Nemanja (D)**     **320 37**
H: 6 1   W: 13 02   b.Uzice 21-10-81
*Honours:* Serbia 56 full caps, 2 goals.

| 2000-01 | Subotica | 27 | 6 | **27** | **6** |
|---|---|---|---|---|---|
| 2001-02 | Red Star Belgrade | 22 | 2 | | |
| 2002-03 | Red Star Belgrade | 26 | 5 | | |
| 2003-04 | Red Star Belgrade | 20 | 5 | **68** | **12** |
| 2004 | Spartak Moscow | 12 | 2 | | |
| 2005 | Spartak Moscow | 27 | 2 | **39** | **4** |
| 2005-06 | Manchester U | 11 | 0 | | |
| 2006-07 | Manchester U | 25 | 3 | | |
| 2007-08 | Manchester U | 32 | 1 | | |
| 2008-09 | Manchester U | 34 | 4 | | |
| 2009-10 | Manchester U | 24 | 1 | | |
| 2010-11 | Manchester U | 35 | 5 | | |
| 2011-12 | Manchester U | 6 | 0 | | |
| 2012-13 | Manchester U | 19 | 1 | **186** | **15** |

**WELBECK, Danny (F)**     **99 19**
H: 6 1   W: 11 07   b.Manchester 26-11-90
*Source:* Scholar. *Honours:* England Youth,
Under-21, 16 full caps, 5 goals.

| 2007-08 | Manchester U | 0 | 0 | | |
|---|---|---|---|---|---|
| 2008-09 | Manchester U | 3 | 1 | | |
| 2009-10 | Manchester U | 5 | 0 | | |
| 2009-10 | *Preston NE* | 8 | 2 | **8** | **2** |
| 2010-11 | Manchester U | 0 | 0 | | |
| 2010-11 | *Sunderland* | 26 | 6 | **26** | **6** |
| 2011-12 | Manchester U | 30 | 9 | | |
| 2012-13 | Manchester U | 27 | 1 | **65** | **11** |

**WOOTTON, Scott (D)**     **33 2**
H: 6 2   W: 13 00   b.Birkenhead 12-9-91
*Source:* Scholar.

| 2009-10 | Manchester U | 0 | 0 | | |
|---|---|---|---|---|---|
| 2010-11 | Manchester U | 0 | 0 | | |
| 2010-11 | *Tranmere R* | 7 | 1 | **7** | **1** |
| 2011-12 | Manchester U | 0 | 0 | | |
| 2011-12 | *Peterborough U* | 11 | 0 | | |
| 2011-12 | *Nottingham F* | 13 | 0 | **13** | **0** |
| 2012-13 | Manchester U | 0 | 0 | | |
| 2012-13 | *Peterborough U* | 2 | 1 | **13** | **1** |

**YOUNG, Ashley (M)**     **299 55**
H: 5 10   W: 10 03   b.Stevenage 9-7-85
*Source:* Juniors. *Honours:* England Under-21,
29 full caps, 7 goals.

| 2002-03 | Watford | 0 | 0 | | |
|---|---|---|---|---|---|
| 2003-04 | Watford | 5 | 3 | | |
| 2004-05 | Watford | 34 | 0 | | |
| 2005-06 | Watford | 39 | 13 | | |
| 2006-07 | Watford | 20 | 3 | **98** | **19** |
| 2006-07 | Aston Villa | 13 | 2 | | |
| 2007-08 | Aston Villa | 37 | 9 | | |
| 2008-09 | Aston Villa | 36 | 7 | | |
| 2009-10 | Aston Villa | 37 | 5 | | |
| 2010-11 | Aston Villa | 34 | 7 | **157** | **30** |
| 2011-12 | Manchester U | 25 | 6 | | |
| 2012-13 | Manchester U | 19 | 0 | **44** | **6** |

**ZAHA, Wilfried (F)**     **126 13**
H: 5 11   W: 10 05   b.Ivory Coast 10-11-92
*Source:* Scholar. *Honours:* England Under-21,
1 full cap.

| 2009-10 | Crystal Palace | 1 | 0 | | |
|---|---|---|---|---|---|
| 2010-11 | Crystal Palace | 41 | 4 | | |
| 2011-12 | Crystal Palace | 41 | 6 | | |
| 2012-13 | Crystal Palace | 43 | 6 | **126** | **13** |
| 2012-13 | Manchester U | 0 | 0 | | |

**Players retained or with offer of contract**
Almeida Da Cunha, Luis Carlos; Byrne, Sam
John; Dias Correia, Tiago Manuel; Gollin,
Pierluigi; Hoelgebaum Pereira Andreas
Hugo; James, Reece; Lawrence, Thomas
Morris; Wilson, James Antony.

**Scholars**
Barber, Benjamin Thomas; Barmby, Jack;
Castro Pereira Joel Dinis; Dalley, Declan
Michael; Evans, Callum Leeroy; Fletcher,
Ashley Michael; Goss, Sean Richard;
Grimshaw, Liam David; Harrop, Josh;
Ioannou, Nicholas Dimitris; Love, Donald
Alistair; McConnell, Ryan Peter; McNair,
Patrick James Coleman; Pearson, Benjamin
David; Rothwell, Joseph Matthew; Rowley,
Louis James; Rudge, Jack James; Sutherland,
Jonathan David; Weir, James Michael;
Willock, Matthew.

# MIDDLESBROUGH (50)

**ARCA, Julio (M)**     **353 25**
H: 5 9   W: 11 13   b.Quilmes 31-1-81
*Honours:* Argentina Youth, Under-21.

| 1999-2000 | Argentinos Jun | 19 | 0 | | |
|---|---|---|---|---|---|
| 2000-01 | Argentinos Jun | 17 | 1 | **36** | **1** |
| 2000-01 | Sunderland | 27 | 2 | | |
| 2001-02 | Sunderland | 22 | 1 | | |
| 2002-03 | Sunderland | 13 | 0 | | |
| 2003-04 | Sunderland | 31 | 4 | | |
| 2004-05 | Sunderland | 40 | 9 | | |
| 2005-06 | Sunderland | 24 | 1 | **157** | **17** |
| 2006-07 | Middlesbrough | 21 | 2 | | |
| 2007-08 | Middlesbrough | 24 | 2 | | |
| 2008-09 | Middlesbrough | 18 | 0 | | |
| 2009-10 | Middlesbrough | 34 | 0 | | |
| 2010-11 | Middlesbrough | 32 | 3 | | |
| 2011-12 | Middlesbrough | 30 | 0 | | |
| 2012-13 | Middlesbrough | 1 | 0 | **160** | **7** |

**ATKINSON, David (D)**     **0 0**
b.Shildon 27-4-93
*Source:* Scholar. *Honours:* England Youth.

| 2010-11 | Middlesbrough | 0 | 0 | | |
|---|---|---|---|---|---|
| 2011-12 | Middlesbrough | 0 | 0 | | |
| 2012-13 | Middlesbrough | 0 | 0 | | |

**BAILEY, Nicky (M)**     **320 50**
H: 5 10   W: 12 06   b.Hammersmith 10-6-84
*Source:* Sutton U.

| 2005-06 | Barnet | 45 | 7 | | |
|---|---|---|---|---|---|
| 2006-07 | Barnet | 44 | 5 | **89** | **12** |
| 2007-08 | Southend U | 44 | 9 | | |
| 2008-09 | Southend U | 1 | 0 | **45** | **9** |
| 2008-09 | Charlton Ath | 43 | 13 | | |
| 2009-10 | Charlton Ath | 44 | 12 | **87** | **25** |
| 2010-11 | Middlesbrough | 34 | 0 | | |
| 2011-12 | Middlesbrough | 37 | 2 | | |
| 2012-13 | Middlesbrough | 28 | 2 | **99** | **4** |

**BENNETT, Andre (D)**     **0 0**
H: 5 8   W: 10 02   b.Houghton-le-spring
22-10-94

| 2012-13 | Middlesbrough | 0 | 0 | | |
|---|---|---|---|---|---|

**BIKEY, Andre (D)**     **199 11**
H: 6 0   W: 12 08   b.Douala 8-1-85
*Source:* Espanyol, Marco. *Honours:*
Cameroon 25 full caps, 1 goal.

| 2003-04 | Pacos de Ferreira | 2 | 0 | **2** | **0** |
|---|---|---|---|---|---|
| 2004-05 | Dep Aves | 0 | 0 | | |
| 2005 | Shinnik | 11 | 1 | **11** | **1** |
| 2005 | Loko Moscow | 9 | 0 | | |
| 2006 | Loko Moscow | 5 | 0 | **14** | **0** |
| 2006-07 | Reading | 15 | 0 | | |
| 2007-08 | Reading | 22 | 3 | | |
| 2008-09 | Reading | 25 | 3 | | |

| 2009-10 | Reading | 0 | 0 | **62** | **6** |
|---|---|---|---|---|---|
| 2009-10 | Burnley | 28 | 1 | | |
| 2010-11 | Burnley | 28 | 2 | | |
| 2011-12 | Burnley | 14 | 0 | **70** | **3** |
| 2011-12 | *Bristol C* | 7 | 0 | **7** | **0** |
| 2012-13 | Middlesbrough | 33 | 1 | **33** | **1** |

**BROBBEL, Ryan (M)**     **0 0**
b.Hartlepool 5-3-93
*Source:* Scholar. *Honours:* Northern Ireland
Youth.

| 2011-12 | Middlesbrough | 0 | 0 | | |
|---|---|---|---|---|---|
| 2012-13 | Middlesbrough | 0 | 0 | | |

**BURGESS, Christian (D)**     **1 0**
H: 6 5   W: 13 02   b. 7-10-91

| 2012-13 | Middlesbrough | 1 | 0 | **1** | **0** |
|---|---|---|---|---|---|

**CARAYOL, Mustapha (F)**     **101 16**
H: 5 10   W: 11 11   b.Gambia 10-6-89
*Source:* Scholar.

| 2007-08 | Milton Keynes D | 0 | 0 | | |
|---|---|---|---|---|---|
| 2009-10 | Torquay U | 20 | 6 | **20** | **6** |
| 2010-11 | Lincoln C | 33 | 3 | **33** | **3** |
| 2011-12 | Bristol R | 30 | 4 | | |
| 2012-13 | Bristol R | 0 | 0 | **30** | **4** |
| 2012-13 | Middlesbrough | 18 | 3 | **18** | **3** |

**DOLAN, Matthew (M)**     **8 1**
b.Hartlepool 11-2-93
*Source:* Scholar.

| 2010-11 | Middlesbrough | 0 | 0 | | |
|---|---|---|---|---|---|
| 2011-12 | Middlesbrough | 0 | 0 | | |
| 2012-13 | Middlesbrough | 0 | 0 | | |
| 2012-13 | *Yeovil T* | 8 | 1 | **8** | **1** |

**DYER, Kieron (M)**     **329 34**
H: 5 8   W: 10 01   b.Ipswich 29-12-78
*Source:* Trainee. *Honours:* England Youth,
Under-21, B, 33 full caps.

| 1996-97 | Ipswich T | 13 | 0 | | |
|---|---|---|---|---|---|
| 1997-98 | Ipswich T | 41 | 4 | | |
| 1998-99 | Ipswich T | 37 | 5 | | |
| 1999-2000 | Newcastle U | 30 | 3 | | |
| 2000-01 | Newcastle U | 26 | 5 | | |
| 2001-02 | Newcastle U | 18 | 3 | | |
| 2002-03 | Newcastle U | 35 | 2 | | |
| 2003-04 | Newcastle U | 25 | 1 | | |
| 2004-05 | Newcastle U | 23 | 4 | | |
| 2005-06 | Newcastle U | 11 | 0 | | |
| 2006-07 | Newcastle U | 22 | 5 | | |
| 2007-08 | Newcastle U | 0 | 0 | **190** | **23** |
| 2007-08 | West Ham U | 2 | 0 | | |
| 2008-09 | West Ham U | 7 | 0 | | |
| 2009-10 | West Ham U | 10 | 0 | | |
| 2010-11 | West Ham U | 11 | 0 | **30** | **0** |
| 2010-11 | *Ipswich T* | 4 | 0 | **95** | **9** |
| 2011-12 | QPR | 1 | 0 | | |
| 2012-13 | QPR | 4 | 0 | **5** | **0** |
| 2012-13 | Middlesbrough | 9 | 2 | **9** | **2** |

**EMNES, Marvin (F)**     **180 34**
H: 5 11   W: 10 06   b.Rotterdam 27-5-88
*Honours:* Holland Under-21.

| 2005-06 | Sparta Rotterdam | 11 | 1 | | |
|---|---|---|---|---|---|
| 2006-07 | Sparta Rotterdam | 16 | 0 | | |
| 2007-08 | Sparta Rotterdam | 29 | 8 | **56** | **9** |
| 2008-09 | Middlesbrough | 15 | 0 | | |
| 2009-10 | Middlesbrough | 16 | 1 | | |
| 2010-11 | Middlesbrough | 23 | 3 | | |
| 2010-11 | *Swansea C* | 4 | 2 | **4** | **2** |
| 2011-12 | Middlesbrough | 42 | 14 | | |
| 2012-13 | Middlesbrough | 24 | 5 | **120** | **23** |

**FOWLER, Jake (M)**     **0 0**
b.Sunderland 22-9-93
*Source:* Scholar. *Honours:* England Youth.

| 2011-12 | Middlesbrough | 0 | 0 | | |
|---|---|---|---|---|---|
| 2012-13 | Middlesbrough | 0 | 0 | | |

**FRIEND, George (D)**     **133 3**
H: 6 2   W: 13 01   b.Barnstaple 19-10-87

| 2008-09 | Exeter C | 4 | 0 | | |
|---|---|---|---|---|---|
| 2008-09 | Wolverhampton W | 0 | 0 | | |
| 2009-10 | Wolverhampton W | 1 | 0 | **7** | **0** |
| 2009-10 | *Millwall* | 6 | 0 | **6** | **0** |
| 2009-10 | *Southend U* | 6 | 1 | **6** | **1** |
| 2009-10 | *Scunthorpe U* | 4 | 0 | **4** | **0** |
| 2009-10 | *Exeter C* | 13 | 1 | **17** | **1** |
| 2010-11 | Doncaster R | 32 | 1 | | |

| | | | | | |
|---|---|---|---|---|---|
| 2011-12 | Doncaster R | 27 | 0 | | |
| 2012-13 | Doncaster R | 0 | 0 | 59 | 1 |
| 2012-13 | Middlesbrough | 34 | 0 | 34 | 0 |

**GIBSON, Ben (D)**    43   1
H: 6 1   W: 12 04   b.Nunthorpe 15-1-93
*Source:* Scholar. *Honours:* England Youth.

| | | | | | |
|---|---|---|---|---|---|
| 2010-11 | Middlesbrough | 1 | 0 | | |
| 2011-12 | Middlesbrough | 0 | 0 | | |
| 2011-12 | *Plymouth Arg* | 13 | 0 | 13 | 0 |
| 2012-13 | Middlesbrough | 1 | 0 | 2 | 0 |
| 2012-13 | *Tranmere R* | 28 | 1 | 28 | 1 |

**HALLIDAY, Andrew (M)**    83   16
H: 5 8   W: 10 07   b.Glasgow 11-10-91

| | | | | | |
|---|---|---|---|---|---|
| 2008-09 | Livingston | 12 | 1 | | |
| 2009-10 | Livingston | 32 | 14 | 44 | 15 |
| 2010-11 | Middlesbrough | 12 | 1 | | |
| 2011-12 | Middlesbrough | 1 | 0 | | |
| 2011-12 | *Walsall* | 7 | 0 | 7 | 0 |
| 2012-13 | Middlesbrough | 19 | 0 | 32 | 1 |

**HAROUN, Faris (M)**    250   45
H: 6 2   W: 13 00   b.Brussels 22-9-85
*Honours:* Belgium 6 full caps.

| | | | | | |
|---|---|---|---|---|---|
| 2003-04 | Genk | 12 | 3 | | |
| 2004-05 | Genk | 23 | 4 | | |
| 2005-06 | Genk | 20 | 0 | | |
| 2006-07 | Genk | 21 | 5 | | |
| 2007-08 | Genk | 28 | 4 | 104 | 16 |
| 2008-09 | Beerschot | 31 | 8 | | |
| 2009-10 | Beerschot | 31 | 10 | | |
| 2010-11 | Beerschot | 29 | 5 | 91 | 23 |
| 2011-12 | Middlesbrough | 32 | 2 | | |
| 2012-13 | Middlesbrough | 23 | 4 | 55 | 6 |

**HINES, Seb (D)**    66   3
H: 6 1   W: 12 02   b.Wetherby 29-5-88
*Source:* Scholar. *Honours:* England Youth.

| | | | | | |
|---|---|---|---|---|---|
| 2005-06 | Middlesbrough | 0 | 0 | | |
| 2006-07 | Middlesbrough | 0 | 0 | | |
| 2007-08 | Middlesbrough | 1 | 0 | | |
| 2008-09 | Middlesbrough | 1 | 0 | | |
| 2008-09 | *Derby Co* | 0 | 0 | | |
| 2008-09 | *Oldham Ath* | 4 | 0 | 4 | 0 |
| 2009-10 | Middlesbrough | 2 | 0 | | |
| 2010-11 | Middlesbrough | 14 | 1 | | |
| 2011-12 | Middlesbrough | 23 | 1 | | |
| 2012-13 | Middlesbrough | 21 | 1 | 62 | 3 |

**HOYTE, Justin (D)**    200   4
H: 5 11   W: 11 00   b.Waltham Forest 20-11-84
*Source:* Scholar. *Honours:* England Youth, Under-20, Under-21.

| | | | | | |
|---|---|---|---|---|---|
| 2002-03 | Arsenal | 1 | 0 | | |
| 2003-04 | Arsenal | 1 | 0 | | |
| 2004-05 | Arsenal | 5 | 0 | | |
| 2005-06 | Arsenal | 0 | 0 | | |
| 2005-06 | *Sunderland* | 27 | 1 | 27 | 1 |
| 2006-07 | Arsenal | 22 | 1 | | |
| 2007-08 | Arsenal | 5 | 0 | 34 | 1 |
| 2008-09 | Middlesbrough | 22 | 0 | | |
| 2009-10 | Middlesbrough | 30 | 1 | | |
| 2010-11 | Middlesbrough | 17 | 0 | | |
| 2011-12 | Middlesbrough | 39 | 0 | | |
| 2012-13 | Middlesbrough | 31 | 1 | 139 | 2 |

**JACKSON, Adam (D)**    0   0
b.Darlington 18-5-94
*Source:* Scholar. *Honours:* England Youth.

| | | | | |
|---|---|---|---|---|
| 2011-12 | Middlesbrough | 0 | 0 | |
| 2012-13 | Middlesbrough | 0 | 0 | |

**JONES, Jordan (M)**    0   0
H: 5 8   W: 9 07   b.Kettering 24-10-94

| | | | | |
|---|---|---|---|---|
| 2012-13 | Middlesbrough | 0 | 0 | |

**JUTKIEWICZ, Lucas (F)**    192   45
H: 6 1   W: 12 11   b.Southampton 20-3-89
*Source:* Scholar.

| | | | | | |
|---|---|---|---|---|---|
| 2005-06 | Swindon T | 5 | 0 | | |
| 2006-07 | Swindon T | 33 | 5 | 38 | 5 |
| 2006-07 | Everton | 0 | 0 | | |
| 2007-08 | Everton | 0 | 0 | | |
| 2007-08 | *Plymouth Arg* | 3 | 0 | 3 | 0 |
| 2008-09 | Everton | 0 | 0 | | |
| 2008-09 | *Huddersfield T* | 7 | 0 | 7 | 0 |
| 2009-10 | Everton | 0 | 0 | 1 | 0 |
| 2009-10 | *Motherwell* | 33 | 12 | 33 | 12 |

| | | | | | |
|---|---|---|---|---|---|
| 2010-11 | Coventry C | 42 | 9 | | |
| 2011-12 | Coventry C | 25 | 9 | 67 | 18 |
| 2011-12 | Middlesbrough | 19 | 2 | | |
| 2012-13 | Middlesbrough | 24 | 8 | 43 | 10 |

**LEADBITTER, Grant (M)**    274   28
H: 5 9   W: 11 06   b.Chester-le-Street 7-1-86
*Source:* Trainee. *Honours:* FA Schools, England Youth, Under-20, Under-21.

| | | | | | |
|---|---|---|---|---|---|
| 2002-03 | Sunderland | 0 | 0 | | |
| 2003-04 | Sunderland | 0 | 0 | | |
| 2004-05 | Sunderland | 0 | 0 | | |
| 2005-06 | Sunderland | 12 | 0 | | |
| 2005-06 | *Rotherham U* | 5 | 1 | 5 | 1 |
| 2006-07 | Sunderland | 44 | 7 | | |
| 2007-08 | Sunderland | 31 | 2 | | |
| 2008-09 | Sunderland | 23 | 2 | | |
| 2009-10 | Sunderland | 1 | 0 | 111 | 11 |
| 2009-10 | Ipswich T | 38 | 3 | | |
| 2010-11 | Ipswich T | 44 | 5 | | |
| 2011-12 | Ipswich T | 34 | 5 | | |
| 2012-13 | Ipswich T | 0 | 0 | 116 | 13 |
| 2012-13 | Middlesbrough | 42 | 3 | 42 | 3 |

**LEDESMA, Emmanuel (M)**    92   10
H: 5 11   W: 12 02   b.Quilmes 24-5-88

| | | | | | |
|---|---|---|---|---|---|
| 2007-08 | Genoa | 1 | 0 | 1 | 0 |
| 2008-09 | *Salernitana* | 8 | 1 | 8 | 1 |
| 2008-09 | *QPR* | 17 | 1 | 17 | 1 |
| 2009-10 | Novara | 8 | 1 | 8 | 1 |
| 2010-11 | Crotone | 10 | 0 | 10 | 0 |
| 2010-11 | Walsall | 10 | 1 | | |
| 2011-12 | Walsall | 10 | 4 | 20 | 5 |
| 2012-13 | Middlesbrough | 28 | 2 | 28 | 2 |

**LEUTWILER, Jayson (G)**    0   0
H: 6 3   W: 12 07   b.Basel 25-4-89

| | | | | |
|---|---|---|---|---|
| 2012-13 | Middlesbrough | 0 | 0 | |

**MAIN, Curtis (F)**    70   10
H: 5 9   W: 12 02   b.South Shields 20-6-92
*Source:* Scholar.

| | | | | | |
|---|---|---|---|---|---|
| 2007-08 | Darlington | 1 | 0 | | |
| 2008-09 | Darlington | 18 | 2 | | |
| 2009-10 | Darlington | 26 | 3 | | |
| 2010-11 | Darlington | 0 | 0 | 45 | 5 |
| 2011-12 | Middlesbrough | 12 | 2 | | |
| 2012-13 | Middlesbrough | 13 | 3 | 25 | 5 |

**McDONALD, Scott (F)**    340   133
H: 5 7   W: 12 07   b.Melbourne 8-8-83
*Honours:* Australia Youth, Under-20, Under-23, 26 full caps.

| | | | | | |
|---|---|---|---|---|---|
| 1998-99 | Eastern Pride | 3 | 0 | 3 | 0 |
| 1999-2000 | Southampton | 0 | 0 | | |
| 2000-01 | Southampton | 0 | 0 | | |
| 2001-02 | Southampton | 2 | 0 | | |
| 2002-03 | Southampton | 0 | 0 | 2 | 0 |
| 2002-03 | *Huddersfield T* | 13 | 1 | 13 | 1 |
| 2002-03 | *Bournemouth* | 7 | 1 | 7 | 1 |
| 2003-04 | Wimbledon | 2 | 0 | 2 | 0 |
| 2003-04 | Motherwell | 15 | 2 | | |
| 2004-05 | Motherwell | 27 | 15 | | |
| 2005-06 | Motherwell | 35 | 11 | | |
| 2006-07 | Motherwell | 32 | 15 | 109 | 43 |
| 2007-08 | Celtic | 36 | 25 | | |
| 2008-09 | Celtic | 34 | 16 | | |
| 2009-10 | Celtic | 18 | 10 | 88 | 51 |
| 2009-10 | Middlesbrough | 13 | 4 | | |
| 2010-11 | Middlesbrough | 38 | 12 | | |
| 2011-12 | Middlesbrough | 33 | 9 | | |
| 2012-13 | Middlesbrough | 32 | 12 | 116 | 37 |

**McMANUS, Stephen (D)**    238   20
H: 6 2   W: 13 00   b.Lanark 10-9-82
*Honours:* Scotland 26 full caps, 2 goals.

| | | | | | |
|---|---|---|---|---|---|
| 2003-04 | Celtic | 5 | 0 | | |
| 2004-05 | Celtic | 2 | 0 | | |
| 2005-06 | Celtic | 36 | 7 | | |
| 2006-07 | Celtic | 31 | 2 | | |
| 2007-08 | Celtic | 37 | 4 | | |
| 2008-09 | Celtic | 31 | 4 | | |
| 2009-10 | Celtic | 8 | 0 | 150 | 17 |
| 2009-10 | Middlesbrough | 16 | 1 | | |
| 2010-11 | Middlesbrough | 24 | 1 | | |
| 2011-12 | Middlesbrough | 24 | 0 | | |
| 2011-12 | *Bristol C* | 6 | 0 | | |
| 2012-13 | Middlesbrough | 7 | 0 | 71 | 2 |
| 2012-13 | *Bristol C* | 11 | 1 | 17 | 1 |

**MORRIS, Bryn (M)**    1   0
H: 6 0   W: 11 01   b.Hartlepool 25-4-96

| | | | | | |
|---|---|---|---|---|---|
| 2012-13 | Middlesbrough | 1 | 0 | 1 | 0 |

**PARK, Cameron (M)**    7   0
H: 5 10   W: 11 02   b.Marske 6-7-92
*Source:* Scholar. *Honours:* Scotland Youth, Under-21.

| | | | | | |
|---|---|---|---|---|---|
| 2010-11 | Middlesbrough | 4 | 0 | | |
| 2011-12 | Middlesbrough | 0 | 0 | | |
| 2011-12 | *Barnsley* | 3 | 0 | 3 | 0 |
| 2012-13 | Middlesbrough | 0 | 0 | 4 | 0 |

**PARNABY, Stuart (D)**    158   2
H: 5 11   W: 12 00   b.Durham 19-7-82
*Source:* Trainee. *Honours:* England Youth, Under-20, Under-21.

| | | | | | |
|---|---|---|---|---|---|
| 2000-01 | Middlesbrough | 0 | 0 | | |
| 2000-01 | *Halifax T* | 6 | 0 | 6 | 0 |
| 2001-02 | Middlesbrough | 0 | 0 | | |
| 2002-03 | Middlesbrough | 21 | 0 | | |
| 2003-04 | Middlesbrough | 13 | 0 | | |
| 2004-05 | Middlesbrough | 19 | 0 | | |
| 2005-06 | Middlesbrough | 20 | 2 | | |
| 2006-07 | Middlesbrough | 18 | 0 | | |
| 2007-08 | Birmingham C | 13 | 0 | | |
| 2008-09 | Birmingham C | 21 | 0 | | |
| 2009-10 | Birmingham C | 8 | 0 | | |
| 2010-11 | Birmingham C | 5 | 0 | 47 | 0 |
| 2012-13 | Middlesbrough | 14 | 0 | 105 | 2 |

**REACH, Adam (M)**    18   3
H: 6 1   W: 11 07   b.Gateshead 3-2-93
*Source:* Scholar. *Honours:* England Youth.

| | | | | | |
|---|---|---|---|---|---|
| 2010-11 | Middlesbrough | 1 | 1 | | |
| 2011-12 | Middlesbrough | 1 | 0 | | |
| 2012-13 | Middlesbrough | 16 | 2 | 18 | 3 |

**RIPLEY, Connor (G)**    3   0
H: 5 11   W: 11 13   b.Middlesbrough 13-2-93
*Source:* Scholar. *Honours:* England Youth.

| | | | | | |
|---|---|---|---|---|---|
| 2010-11 | Middlesbrough | 1 | 0 | | |
| 2011-12 | Middlesbrough | 1 | 0 | | |
| 2011-12 | *Oxford U* | 1 | 0 | 1 | 0 |
| 2012-13 | Middlesbrough | 0 | 0 | 2 | 0 |

**SMALLWOOD, Richard (M)**    48   3
H: 5 11   W: 11 05   b.Redcar 29-12-90
*Source:* Scholar. *Honours:* England Youth.

| | | | | | |
|---|---|---|---|---|---|
| 2008-09 | Middlesbrough | 0 | 0 | | |
| 2009-10 | Middlesbrough | 0 | 0 | | |
| 2010-11 | Middlesbrough | 13 | 1 | | |
| 2011-12 | Middlesbrough | 13 | 0 | | |
| 2012-13 | Middlesbrough | 22 | 2 | 48 | 3 |

**STEELE, Jason (G)**    128   0
H: 6 2   W: 12 07   b.Newton Aycliffe 18-8-90
*Source:* Scholar. *Honours:* England Youth, Under-21.

| | | | | | |
|---|---|---|---|---|---|
| 2007-08 | Middlesbrough | 0 | 0 | | |
| 2008-09 | Middlesbrough | 0 | 0 | | |
| 2009-10 | Middlesbrough | 0 | 0 | | |
| 2009-10 | *Northampton T* | 13 | 0 | 13 | 0 |
| 2010-11 | Middlesbrough | 35 | 0 | | |
| 2011-12 | Middlesbrough | 34 | 0 | | |
| 2012-13 | Middlesbrough | 46 | 0 | 115 | 0 |

**THOMSON, Kevin (M)**    207   4
H: 6 2   W: 11 05   b.Edinburgh 14-10-84
*Honours:* Scotland 3 full caps.

| | | | | | |
|---|---|---|---|---|---|
| 2003-04 | Hibernian | 23 | 1 | | |
| 2004-05 | Hibernian | 3 | 0 | | |
| 2005-06 | Hibernian | 31 | 0 | | |
| 2006-07 | Hibernian | 23 | 1 | | |
| 2006-07 | Rangers | 9 | 0 | | |
| 2007-08 | Rangers | 26 | 1 | | |
| 2008-09 | Rangers | 11 | 1 | | |
| 2009-10 | Rangers | 25 | 0 | 71 | 2 |
| 2010-11 | Middlesbrough | 19 | 0 | | |
| 2011-12 | Middlesbrough | 22 | 0 | | |
| 2012-13 | Middlesbrough | 9 | 0 | 50 | 0 |
| 2012-13 | *Hibernian* | 6 | 0 | 86 | 2 |

**WILLIAMS, Luke (F)**    21   2
H: 5 11   W: 11 08   b.Middlesbrough 11-6-93
*Source:* Scholar. *Honours:* England Youth.

| | | | | | |
|---|---|---|---|---|---|
| 2009-10 | Middlesbrough | 4 | 0 | | |
| 2010-11 | Middlesbrough | 0 | 0 | | |
| 2011-12 | Middlesbrough | 0 | 0 | | |
| 2012-13 | Middlesbrough | 11 | 2 | 21 | 2 |

## WILLIAMS, Rhys (M)    119   5

H: 6 2   W: 11 05   b.Perth 14-7-88
Source: Scholar. Honours: Wales Under-21. Australia 11 full caps.

|  |  | | | | |
|---|---|---|---|---|---|
| 2006-07 | Middlesbrough | 0 | 0 | | |
| 2007-08 | Middlesbrough | 0 | 0 | | |
| 2008-09 | Middlesbrough | 0 | 0 | | |
| 2008-09 | Burnley | 17 | 0 | 17 | 0 |
| 2009-10 | Middlesbrough | 32 | 2 | | |
| 2010-11 | Middlesbrough | 12 | 1 | | |
| 2011-12 | Middlesbrough | 35 | 2 | | |
| 2012-13 | Middlesbrough | 23 | 0 | 102 | 5 |

## WOODGATE, Jonathan (D)    277   7

H: 6 2   W: 12 06   b.Middlesbrough 22-1-80
Source: Trainee. Honours: England Youth, Under-21, 8 full caps.

|  |  | | | | |
|---|---|---|---|---|---|
| 1996-97 | Leeds U | 0 | 0 | | |
| 1997-98 | Leeds U | 0 | 0 | | |
| 1998-99 | Leeds U | 25 | 2 | | |
| 1999-2000 | Leeds U | 34 | 1 | | |
| 2000-01 | Leeds U | 14 | 1 | | |
| 2001-02 | Leeds U | 13 | 0 | | |
| 2002-03 | Leeds U | 18 | 0 | 104 | 4 |
| 2002-03 | Newcastle U | 10 | 0 | | |
| 2003-04 | Newcastle U | 18 | 0 | 28 | 0 |
| 2004-05 | Real Madrid | 0 | 0 | | |
| 2005-06 | Real Madrid | 9 | 0 | 9 | 0 |
| 2006-07 | Middlesbrough | 30 | 0 | | |
| 2007-08 | Middlesbrough | 16 | 0 | | |
| 2007-08 | Tottenham H | 12 | 1 | | |
| 2008-09 | Tottenham H | 34 | 1 | | |
| 2009-10 | Tottenham H | 3 | 0 | | |
| 2010-11 | Tottenham H | 0 | 0 | 49 | 2 |
| 2011-12 | Stoke C | 17 | 0 | 17 | 0 |
| 2012-13 | Middlesbrough | 24 | 1 | 70 | 1 |

## WYKE, Charlie (F)    25   2

b.Middlesbrough 6-12-92
Source: Scholar.

|  |  | | | | |
|---|---|---|---|---|---|
| 2011-12 | Middlesbrough | 0 | 0 | | |
| 2012-13 | Middlesbrough | 0 | 0 | | |
| 2012-13 | Hartlepool U | 25 | 2 | 25 | 2 |

## ZEMMAMA, Merouane (M)    141   15

H: 5 8   W: 10 05   b.Rabat 7-10-83
Source: Chabab Tabriquet. Honours: Morocco 7 full caps, 1 goal.

|  |  | | | | |
|---|---|---|---|---|---|
| 2003-04 | Raja | 23 | 2 | | |
| 2004-05 | Qatar SC | 0 | 0 | | |
| 2005-06 | Raja | 0 | 0 | 23 | 2 |
| 2006-07 | Hibernian | 23 | 2 | | |
| 2007-08 | Hibernian | 28 | 6 | | |
| 2008-09 | Hibernian | 1 | 0 | | |
| 2008-09 | Al-Sha'ab | 0 | 0 | | |
| 2009-10 | Hibernian | 21 | 2 | | |
| 2010-11 | Hibernian | 4 | 0 | 77 | 10 |
| 2010-11 | Middlesbrough | 9 | 1 | | |
| 2011-12 | Middlesbrough | 15 | 1 | | |
| 2012-13 | Middlesbrough | 17 | 1 | 41 | 3 |

**Players retained or with offer of contract**
Coddington, Luke; Kneeshaw, Wilson Edgar James; Leao, Martins Pereira Rafael – maybe existed previously at Manchester U; Rhoden, Marcos.

**Scholars**
Armstrong, Luke Thomas; Bland, Shane Stephen; Burn, Jonathan David; Coleby, Jonathan James; Fewster, Bradley William; Fryer, Joseph Luke; Garrity, Adam Scott; Griffiths, Priestley David; Kitching, Mark Stephen; Maloney, Lewis Terence James; McAloon, Thomas; McCarthy, Scott; McGlade, Dylan James; McNab, Ross; Montgomery, James Hayden; Morris, Bryn Andrew; Okosieme, Ejiro Onyemachie Denzel; O'Neill, Conor Martin; O'Neill, Stephen Charles; Rivers, Jarrett Anthony; Sirrell, Lewis Jay; Tinkler, Robbie; Warnett, James Peter; Waters, Matthew Charles; Weledji, Kieran Wembanesi.

# MILLWALL (51)

## ABDOU, Nadjim ( )    329   9

H: 5 10   W: 11 02   b.Martigues 13-7-84
Honours: Comoros 4 full caps.

|  |  | | | | |
|---|---|---|---|---|---|
| 2002-03 | Martigues | 26 | 1 | 26 | 1 |
| 2003-04 | Sedan | 17 | 0 | | |
| 2004-05 | Sedan | 32 | 2 | | |
| 2005-06 | Sedan | 0 | 0 | | |
| 2006-07 | Sedan | 17 | 0 | 80 | 2 |
| 2007-08 | Plymouth Arg | 31 | 1 | 31 | 1 |
| 2008-09 | Millwall | 36 | 3 | | |
| 2009-10 | Millwall | 43 | 1 | | |
| 2010-11 | Millwall | 34 | 0 | | |
| 2011-12 | Millwall | 40 | 0 | | |
| 2012-13 | Millwall | 39 | 1 | 192 | 5 |

## BATT, Shaun (M)    102   10

H: 6 3   W: 12 08   b.Harlow 22-2-87
Source: Stevenage B, Dagenham & R, Fisher Ath.

|  |  | | | | |
|---|---|---|---|---|---|
| 2008-09 | Peterborough U | 30 | 2 | | |
| 2009-10 | Peterborough U | 20 | 2 | 50 | 4 |
| 2009-10 | Millwall | 16 | 3 | | |
| 2010-11 | Millwall | 4 | 0 | | |
| 2011-12 | Millwall | 4 | 0 | | |
| 2011-12 | Crawley T | 5 | 0 | 5 | 0 |
| 2012-13 | Millwall | 16 | 1 | 36 | 4 |
| 2012-13 | Leyton Orient | 11 | 2 | 11 | 2 |

## BEEVERS, Mark (D)    189   4

H: 6 4   W: 13 00   b.Barnsley 21-11-89
Source: Scholar. Honours: England Youth.

|  |  | | | | |
|---|---|---|---|---|---|
| 2006-07 | Sheffield W | 2 | 0 | | |
| 2007-08 | Sheffield W | 28 | 0 | | |
| 2008-09 | Sheffield W | 34 | 0 | | |
| 2009-10 | Sheffield W | 35 | 0 | | |
| 2010-11 | Sheffield W | 28 | 2 | | |
| 2011-12 | Sheffield W | 7 | 0 | | |
| 2011-12 | Milton Keynes D | 14 | 1 | 14 | 1 |
| 2012-13 | Sheffield W | 6 | 0 | 140 | 2 |
| 2012-13 | Millwall | 35 | 1 | 35 | 1 |

## BENDER, Tom (M)    3   0

H: 6 3   W: 12 00   b.Harlow 19-1-93
Source: Scholar. Honours: Wales Youth, Under-21.

|  |  | | | | |
|---|---|---|---|---|---|
| 2009-10 | Colchester U | 1 | 0 | | |
| 2010-11 | Colchester U | 0 | 0 | | |
| 2011-12 | Colchester U | 0 | 0 | | |
| 2011-12 | Accrington S | 2 | 0 | 2 | 0 |
| 2012-13 | Colchester U | 0 | 0 | 1 | 0 |
| 2012-13 | Millwall | 0 | 0 | | |

## DUNNE, Alan (D)    273   15

H: 5 10   W: 10 13   b.Dublin 23-8-82
Source: Trainee.

|  |  | | | | |
|---|---|---|---|---|---|
| 1999-2000 | Millwall | 0 | 0 | | |
| 2000-01 | Millwall | 0 | 0 | | |
| 2001-02 | Millwall | 1 | 0 | | |
| 2002-03 | Millwall | 4 | 0 | | |
| 2003-04 | Millwall | 8 | 0 | | |
| 2004-05 | Millwall | 19 | 3 | | |
| 2005-06 | Millwall | 40 | 0 | | |
| 2006-07 | Millwall | 32 | 6 | | |
| 2007-08 | Millwall | 19 | 3 | | |
| 2008-09 | Millwall | 24 | 0 | | |
| 2009-10 | Millwall | 32 | 2 | | |
| 2010-11 | Millwall | 39 | 0 | | |
| 2011-12 | Millwall | 30 | 0 | | |
| 2012-13 | Millwall | 25 | 1 | 273 | 15 |

## FEENEY, Liam (M)    166   17

H: 5 10   W: 12 02   b.Hammersmith 21-1-87
Source: Salisbury C.

|  |  | | | | |
|---|---|---|---|---|---|
| 2008-09 | Southend U | 1 | 0 | 1 | 0 |
| 2008-09 | Bournemouth | 14 | 3 | | |
| 2009-10 | Bournemouth | 44 | 5 | | |
| 2010-11 | Bournemouth | 46 | 4 | | |
| 2011-12 | Bournemouth | 5 | 0 | 109 | 12 |
| 2011-12 | Millwall | 34 | 4 | | |
| 2012-13 | Millwall | 22 | 1 | 56 | 5 |

## FORDE, David (G)    301   0

H: 6 3   W: 13 06   b.Galway 20-12-79
Source: Barry T. Honours: Eire 10 full caps.

|  |  | | | | |
|---|---|---|---|---|---|
| 2001-02 | West Ham U | 0 | 0 | | |
| 2002-03 | West Ham U | 0 | 0 | | |
| 2003-04 | West Ham U | 0 | 0 | | |
| 2004 | Derry C | 11 | 0 | | |
| 2005 | Derry C | 33 | 0 | | |
| 2006 | Derry C | 29 | 0 | 73 | 0 |
| 2006-07 | Cardiff C | 7 | 0 | | |
| 2007-08 | Cardiff C | 0 | 0 | 7 | 0 |
| 2007-08 | Luton T | 5 | 0 | 5 | 0 |
| 2007-08 | Bournemouth | 11 | 0 | 11 | 0 |
| 2008-09 | Millwall | 46 | 0 | | |
| 2009-10 | Millwall | 46 | 0 | | |
| 2010-11 | Millwall | 46 | 0 | | |
| 2011-12 | Millwall | 27 | 0 | | |
| 2012-13 | Millwall | 40 | 0 | 205 | 0 |

## GOODMAN, Jake (D)    0   0

b. 5-8-93

|  |  | | | | |
|---|---|---|---|---|---|
| 2012-13 | Millwall | 0 | 0 | | |

## HENRY, James (M)    166   22

H: 6 1   W: 11 11   b.Reading 10-6-89
Source: Scholar. Honours: England Youth.

|  |  | | | | |
|---|---|---|---|---|---|
| 2006-07 | Reading | 0 | 0 | | |
| 2006-07 | Nottingham F | 1 | 0 | 1 | 0 |
| 2007-08 | Reading | 0 | 0 | | |
| 2007-08 | Bournemouth | 11 | 4 | 11 | 4 |
| 2007-08 | Norwich C | 3 | 0 | 3 | 0 |
| 2008-09 | Reading | 7 | 0 | | |
| 2008-09 | Millwall | 16 | 3 | | |
| 2009-10 | Reading | 3 | 0 | 10 | 0 |
| 2009-10 | Millwall | 9 | 5 | | |
| 2010-11 | Millwall | 42 | 5 | | |
| 2011-12 | Millwall | 39 | 0 | | |
| 2012-13 | Millwall | 35 | 5 | 141 | 18 |

## KEOGH, Andy (F)    320   63

H: 6 0   W: 11 00   b.Dublin 16-5-86
Source: Scholar. Honours: Eire Youth, B, Under-21, 29 full caps, 2 goals.

|  |  | | | | |
|---|---|---|---|---|---|
| 2003-04 | Leeds U | 0 | 0 | | |
| 2004-05 | Leeds U | 0 | 0 | | |
| 2004-05 | Bury | 4 | 2 | 4 | 2 |
| 2004-05 | Scunthorpe U | 25 | 3 | | |
| 2005-06 | Scunthorpe U | 45 | 11 | | |
| 2006-07 | Scunthorpe U | 28 | 7 | 98 | 21 |
| 2006-07 | Wolverhampton W | 17 | 5 | | |
| 2007-08 | Wolverhampton W | 43 | 8 | | |
| 2008-09 | Wolverhampton W | 42 | 5 | | |
| 2009-10 | Wolverhampton W | 13 | 1 | | |
| 2010-11 | Wolverhampton W | 1 | 0 | | |
| 2010-11 | Cardiff C | 16 | 2 | 16 | 2 |
| 2010-11 | Bristol C | 9 | 1 | 9 | 1 |
| 2011-12 | Wolverhampton W | 0 | 0 | 116 | 19 |
| 2011-12 | Leeds U | 22 | 2 | 22 | 2 |
| 2011-12 | Millwall | 18 | 10 | | |
| 2012-13 | Millwall | 37 | 6 | 55 | 16 |

## LOWRY, Shane (D)    102   2

H: 6 1   W: 13 01   b.Perth 12-6-89
Source: Scholar. Honours: Eire Under-21.

|  |  | | | | |
|---|---|---|---|---|---|
| 2007-08 | Aston Villa | 0 | 0 | | |
| 2008-09 | Aston Villa | 0 | 0 | | |
| 2009-10 | Aston Villa | 0 | 0 | | |
| 2009-10 | Plymouth Arg | 13 | 0 | 13 | 0 |
| 2009-10 | Leeds U | 11 | 0 | 11 | 0 |
| 2010-11 | Aston Villa | 0 | 0 | | |
| 2010-11 | Sheffield U | 17 | 0 | 17 | 0 |
| 2011-12 | Aston Villa | 0 | 0 | | |
| 2011-12 | Millwall | 22 | 1 | | |
| 2012-13 | Millwall | 39 | 1 | 61 | 2 |

## MALONE, Scott (D)    93   8

H: 6 2   W: 11 11   b.Rowley Regis 25-3-91
Source: Scholar. Honours: England Youth.

|  |  | | | | |
|---|---|---|---|---|---|
| 2008-09 | Wolverhampton W | 0 | 0 | | |
| 2008-09 | Ujpest | 7 | 1 | 7 | 1 |
| 2009-10 | Wolverhampton W | 0 | 0 | | |
| 2009-10 | Southend U | 17 | 0 | 17 | 0 |
| 2010-11 | Wolverhampton W | 0 | 0 | | |
| 2010-11 | Burton Alb | 22 | 1 | 22 | 1 |
| 2011-12 | Wolverhampton W | 0 | 0 | | |
| 2011-12 | Bournemouth | 32 | 5 | 32 | 5 |
| 2012-13 | Millwall | 15 | 1 | 15 | 1 |

## MARQUIS, John (F)    39   5

H: 6 1   W: 11 03   b.Lewisham 16-5-92
Source: Scholar.

|  |  | | | | |
|---|---|---|---|---|---|
| 2009-10 | Millwall | 1 | 0 | | |
| 2010-11 | Millwall | 11 | 4 | | |
| 2011-12 | Millwall | 17 | 1 | | |
| 2012-13 | Millwall | 10 | 0 | 39 | 5 |

**MKANDAWIRE, Tamika (D)** 219 18
H: 6 1  W: 12 03  b.Malawi 28-5-83
*Source:* Scholar.

| 2002-03 | WBA | 0 | 0 | | |
|---|---|---|---|---|---|
| 2003-04 | WBA | 0 | 0 | | |
| 2006-07 | Hereford U | 39 | 2 | 39 | 2 |
| 2007-08 | Leyton Orient | 35 | 3 | | |
| 2008-09 | Leyton Orient | 36 | 5 | | |
| 2009-10 | Leyton Orient | 43 | 7 | 114 | 15 |
| 2010-11 | Millwall | 35 | 1 | | |
| 2011-12 | Millwall | 13 | 0 | | |
| 2012-13 | Millwall | 0 | 0 | 48 | 1 |
| 2012-13 | *Southend U* | 18 | 0 | 18 | 0 |

**N'GUESSAN, Dany (M)** 190 30
H: 6 0  W: 12 13  b.Paris 11-8-87
*Source:* Auxerre, Rangers.

| 2006-07 | Boston U | 23 | 5 | 23 | 5 |
|---|---|---|---|---|---|
| 2006-07 | Lincoln C | 9 | 0 | | |
| 2007-08 | Lincoln C | 37 | 7 | | |
| 2008-09 | Lincoln C | 45 | 8 | 91 | 15 |
| 2009-10 | Leicester C | 27 | 3 | | |
| 2010-11 | Leicester C | 5 | 0 | 32 | 3 |
| 2010-11 | *Scunthorpe U* | 3 | 1 | 3 | 1 |
| 2010-11 | *Southampton* | 6 | 0 | 6 | 0 |
| 2011-12 | Millwall | 15 | 1 | | |
| 2011-12 | *Charlton Ath* | 7 | 4 | 7 | 4 |
| 2012-13 | Millwall | 13 | 1 | 28 | 2 |

**O'BRIEN, Aiden (F)** 9 0
H: 5 8  W: 10 12  b.Islington 4-10-93
*Source:* Scholar. *Honours:* Eire Youth, Under-21.

| 2010-11 | Millwall | 0 | 0 | | |
|---|---|---|---|---|---|
| 2011-12 | Millwall | 0 | 0 | | |
| 2012-13 | Millwall | 0 | 0 | | |
| 2012-13 | *Crawley T* | 9 | 0 | 9 | 0 |

**OSBORNE, Karleigh (D)** 174 7
H: 6 2  W: 12 04  b.Southall 19-3-88
*Source:* Scholar.

| 2004-05 | Brentford | 1 | 0 | | |
|---|---|---|---|---|---|
| 2005-06 | Brentford | 1 | 0 | | |
| 2006-07 | Brentford | 21 | 0 | | |
| 2007-08 | Brentford | 29 | 1 | | |
| 2008-09 | Brentford | 23 | 4 | | |
| 2009-10 | Brentford | 19 | 0 | | |
| 2010-11 | Brentford | 42 | 1 | | |
| 2011-12 | Brentford | 25 | 0 | 161 | 6 |
| 2012-13 | Millwall | 13 | 1 | 13 | 1 |

**RACON, Therry (M)** 151 10
H: 5 10  W: 10 02  b.Paris 1-5-84

| 2004-05 | Lorient | 28 | 3 | 28 | 3 |
|---|---|---|---|---|---|
| 2005-06 | Guingamp | 0 | 0 | | |
| 2006-07 | Guingamp | 0 | 0 | | |
| 2007-08 | Charlton Ath | 4 | 0 | | |
| 2007-08 | *Brighton & HA* | 8 | 0 | 8 | 0 |
| 2008-09 | Charlton Ath | 19 | 3 | | |
| 2009-10 | Charlton Ath | 36 | 1 | | |
| 2010-11 | Charlton Ath | 39 | 3 | | |
| 2011-12 | Charlton Ath | 0 | 0 | 98 | 7 |
| 2011-12 | Millwall | 0 | 0 | | |
| 2012-13 | Millwall | 1 | 0 | 1 | 0 |
| 2012-13 | *Portsmouth* | 16 | 0 | 16 | 0 |

**ROBINSON, Paul (D)** 291 16
H: 6 1  W: 11 09  b.Barnet 7-1-82
*Source:* Scholar.

| 2000-01 | Millwall | 0 | 0 | | |
|---|---|---|---|---|---|
| 2001-02 | Millwall | 0 | 0 | | |
| 2002-03 | Millwall | 14 | 0 | | |
| 2003-04 | Millwall | 9 | 0 | | |
| 2004-05 | Millwall | 0 | 0 | | |
| 2004-05 | *Torquay U* | 12 | 0 | 12 | 0 |
| 2005-06 | Millwall | 32 | 0 | | |
| 2006-07 | Millwall | 38 | 3 | | |
| 2007-08 | Millwall | 45 | 3 | | |
| 2008-09 | Millwall | 26 | 2 | | |
| 2009-10 | Millwall | 34 | 4 | | |
| 2010-11 | Millwall | 37 | 3 | | |
| 2011-12 | Millwall | 41 | 1 | | |
| 2012-13 | Millwall | 3 | 0 | 279 | 16 |

**SHITTU, Dan (D)** 320 27
H: 6 2  W: 16 03  b.Lagos 2-9-80
*Honours:* Nigeria 32 full caps.

| 1999-2000 | Charlton Ath | 0 | 0 | | |
|---|---|---|---|---|---|
| 2000-01 | Charlton Ath | 0 | 0 | | |
| 2000-01 | *Blackpool* | 17 | 2 | 17 | 2 |
| 2001-02 | Charlton Ath | 0 | 0 | | |
| 2001-02 | QPR | 27 | 2 | | |
| 2002-03 | QPR | 43 | 7 | | |
| 2003-04 | QPR | 20 | 0 | | |
| 2004-05 | QPR | 34 | 4 | | |
| 2005-06 | QPR | 45 | 4 | | |
| 2006-07 | Watford | 30 | 1 | | |
| 2007-08 | Watford | 39 | 7 | 69 | 8 |
| 2008-09 | Bolton W | 10 | 0 | | |
| 2009-10 | Bolton W | 0 | 0 | | |
| 2010-11 | Bolton W | 0 | 0 | 10 | 0 |
| 2010-11 | Millwall | 9 | 0 | | |
| 2010-11 | QPR | 7 | 0 | | |
| 2011-12 | QPR | 0 | 0 | 176 | 17 |
| 2012-13 | Millwall | 39 | 0 | 48 | 0 |

**SMITH, Jack (D)** 253 12
H: 5 11  W: 11 05  b.Hemel Hempstead 14-10-83
*Source:* Scholar.

| 2001-02 | Watford | 0 | 0 | | |
|---|---|---|---|---|---|
| 2002-03 | Watford | 1 | 0 | | |
| 2003-04 | Watford | 17 | 2 | | |
| 2004-05 | Watford | 7 | 0 | 25 | 2 |
| 2005-06 | Swindon T | 38 | 0 | | |
| 2006-07 | Swindon T | 41 | 3 | | |
| 2007-08 | Swindon T | 21 | 1 | | |
| 2008-09 | Swindon T | 38 | 5 | 138 | 9 |
| 2009-10 | Millwall | 31 | 0 | | |
| 2010-11 | Millwall | 9 | 1 | | |
| 2011-12 | Millwall | 33 | 0 | | |
| 2012-13 | Millwall | 17 | 0 | 90 | 1 |

**TAYLOR, Chris (M)** 276 36
H: 5 11  W: 11 00  b.Oldham 20-12-86
*Source:* Scholar.

| 2005-06 | Oldham Ath | 14 | 0 | | |
|---|---|---|---|---|---|
| 2006-07 | Oldham Ath | 44 | 4 | | |
| 2007-08 | Oldham Ath | 42 | 5 | | |
| 2008-09 | Oldham Ath | 42 | 10 | | |
| 2009-10 | Oldham Ath | 32 | 1 | | |
| 2010-11 | Oldham Ath | 42 | 11 | | |
| 2011-12 | Oldham Ath | 38 | 2 | 254 | 33 |
| 2012-13 | Millwall | 22 | 3 | 22 | 3 |

**TAYLOR, Maik (G)** 502 0
H: 6 4  W: 14 02  b.Hildeshein 4-9-71
*Source:* Farnborough T. *Honours:* Northern Ireland Under-21, B, 88 full caps.

| 1995-96 | Barnet | 45 | 0 | | |
|---|---|---|---|---|---|
| 1996-97 | Barnet | 25 | 0 | 70 | 0 |
| 1996-97 | Southampton | 18 | 0 | | |
| 1997-98 | Southampton | 0 | 0 | 18 | 0 |
| 1997-98 | Fulham | 28 | 0 | | |
| 1998-99 | Fulham | 46 | 0 | | |
| 1999-2000 | Fulham | 46 | 0 | | |
| 2000-01 | Fulham | 44 | 0 | | |
| 2001-02 | Fulham | 1 | 0 | | |
| 2002-03 | Fulham | 19 | 0 | | |
| 2003-04 | Fulham | 0 | 0 | 184 | 0 |
| 2003-04 | Birmingham C | 34 | 0 | | |
| 2004-05 | Birmingham C | 38 | 0 | | |
| 2005-06 | Birmingham C | 34 | 0 | | |
| 2006-07 | Birmingham C | 27 | 0 | | |
| 2007-08 | Birmingham C | 34 | 0 | | |
| 2008-09 | Birmingham C | 45 | 0 | | |
| 2009-10 | Birmingham C | 2 | 0 | | |
| 2010-11 | Birmingham C | 0 | 0 | | |
| 2011-12 | Birmingham C | 0 | 0 | 214 | 0 |
| 2011-12 | *Millwall* | 10 | 0 | | |
| 2012-13 | Millwall | 6 | 0 | 16 | 0 |

**TROTTER, Liam (M)** 178 26
H: 6 2  W: 12 02  b.Ipswich 24-8-88
*Source:* Scholar.

| 2005-06 | Ipswich T | 1 | 0 | | |
|---|---|---|---|---|---|
| 2006-07 | Ipswich T | 0 | 0 | | |
| 2006-07 | *Millwall* | 2 | 0 | | |
| 2007-08 | Ipswich T | 7 | 1 | | |
| 2008-09 | Ipswich T | 3 | 1 | | |
| 2008-09 | *Grimsby T* | 15 | 2 | 15 | 2 |
| 2008-09 | *Scunthorpe U* | 12 | 1 | 12 | 1 |
| 2009-10 | Ipswich T | 12 | 0 | 23 | 2 |
| 2009-10 | *Millwall* | 20 | 1 | | |
| 2010-11 | Millwall | 35 | 7 | | |
| 2011-12 | Millwall | 35 | 7 | | |
| 2012-13 | Millwall | 36 | 6 | 128 | 21 |

**WARD, Darren (D)** 466 16
H: 6 3  W: 11 04  b.Harrow 13-9-78
*Source:* Trainee.

| 1995-96 | Watford | 1 | 0 | | |
|---|---|---|---|---|---|
| 1996-97 | Watford | 7 | 0 | | |
| 1997-98 | Watford | 0 | 0 | | |
| 1998-99 | Watford | 1 | 0 | | |
| 1999-2000 | Watford | 9 | 1 | | |
| 1999-2000 | *QPR* | 14 | 0 | 14 | 0 |
| 2000-01 | Watford | 40 | 1 | | |
| 2001-02 | Watford | 1 | 0 | | |
| 2001-02 | Millwall | 14 | 0 | | |
| 2002-03 | Millwall | 39 | 1 | | |
| 2003-04 | Millwall | 46 | 3 | | |
| 2004-05 | Millwall | 43 | 0 | | |
| 2005-06 | Crystal Palace | 43 | 5 | | |
| 2006-07 | Crystal Palace | 20 | 0 | 63 | 5 |
| 2007-08 | Wolverhampton W | 30 | 0 | | |
| 2008-09 | Wolverhampton W | 1 | 0 | | |
| 2008-09 | *Watford* | 9 | 1 | 68 | 0 |
| 2008-09 | *Charlton Ath* | 16 | 0 | 16 | 0 |
| 2009-10 | Wolverhampton W | 0 | 0 | 31 | 0 |
| 2009-10 | Millwall | 31 | 1 | | |
| 2010-11 | Millwall | 31 | 1 | | |
| 2011-12 | Millwall | 30 | 0 | | |
| 2012-13 | Millwall | 1 | 0 | 235 | 6 |
| 2012-13 | *Swindon T* | 39 | 2 | 39 | 2 |

**WOOLFORD, Martyn (M)** 173 20
H: 6 0  W: 11 09  b.Castleford 13-10-85
*Source:* Glasshoughton W, Frickley Ath, York C.

| 2008-09 | Scunthorpe U | 39 | 4 | | |
|---|---|---|---|---|---|
| 2009-10 | Scunthorpe U | 40 | 5 | | |
| 2010-11 | Scunthorpe U | 24 | 6 | 103 | 15 |
| 2010-11 | Bristol C | 15 | 0 | | |
| 2011-12 | Bristol C | 25 | 1 | | |
| 2012-13 | Bristol C | 15 | 3 | 55 | 4 |
| 2012-13 | Millwall | 15 | 1 | 15 | 1 |

**WRIGHT, Josh (M)** 157 2
H: 6 1  W: 11 07  b.Bethnal Green 6-11-89
*Source:* Scholar. *Honours:* England Youth.

| 2007-08 | Charlton Ath | 0 | 0 | | |
|---|---|---|---|---|---|
| 2007-08 | *Barnet* | 32 | 1 | 32 | 1 |
| 2008-09 | Charlton Ath | 2 | 0 | 2 | 0 |
| 2008-09 | *Brentford* | 5 | 0 | 5 | 0 |
| 2008-09 | *Gillingham* | 5 | 0 | 5 | 0 |
| 2009-10 | Scunthorpe U | 35 | 0 | | |
| 2010-11 | Scunthorpe U | 36 | 0 | 71 | 0 |
| 2011-12 | Millwall | 18 | 1 | | |
| 2012-13 | Millwall | 24 | 0 | 42 | 1 |

**Scholars**
Bartlett, Luke Joshua Laurence; Beadle, Tommy; Callaghan, Connor Joseph; Danquah, Richie Kwabena; De Havilland, William Lee; Fitzgerald, Max Raymond; Guinchard, Joe; Hunter, Mitchel Stuart; McManus, Niall Edward; Nelson, Sidney Raymond Kenneth; Newman, Daniel James; Penny, Charlie Phillip; Richards, Dylan Rhys Gus; Sammoutis, Jack Odysseas; Shitta, Touleeb Adedamola Adeleke; Thompson, Ben Rhys; Thongvivat, Nico Joseph; Twum, Jason Benny; Webb, Callum Michael; Wellham, Thomas Ben Francis; Wilkinson, Conor Dominic Geoffrey; Wood, Keaton Matthew Tate.

# MILTON KEYNES D (52)

**ALLI, Bamidele (M)** 0 0
H: 6 1  W: 11 12  b.Watford 11-4-96

| 2012-13 | Milton Keynes D | 0 | 0 | | |
|---|---|---|---|---|---|

**ALLI, Dele (M)** 2 0
H: 6 1  W: 12 00  b. 11-4-96

| 2012-13 | Milton Keynes D | 2 | 0 | 2 | 0 |
|---|---|---|---|---|---|

**BALDOCK, George (M)** 10 0
H: 5 9  W: 10 07  b.Buckingham 26-1-93
*Source:* Youth.

| 2009-10 | Milton Keynes D | 1 | 0 | | |
|---|---|---|---|---|---|
| 2010-11 | Milton Keynes D | 2 | 0 | | |
| 2011-12 | Milton Keynes D | 0 | 0 | | |
| 2011-12 | *Northampton T* | 5 | 0 | 5 | 0 |
| 2012-13 | Milton Keynes D | 2 | 0 | 5 | 0 |

**BOWDITCH, Dean (F)**    272 60
H: 5 11   W: 11 05   b.Bishops Stortford
15-6-86
*Source:* Trainee. *Honours:* FA Schools,
England Youth.

| | | | | |
|---|---|---|---|---|
| 2002-03 | Ipswich T | 5 | 0 | |
| 2003-04 | Ipswich T | 16 | 4 | |
| 2004-05 | Ipswich T | 21 | 3 | |
| 2004-05 | *Burnley* | 10 | 1 | 10   1 |
| 2005-06 | Ipswich T | 21 | 0 | |
| 2005-06 | *Wycombe W* | 11 | 1 | 11   1 |
| 2006-07 | Ipswich T | 9 | 1 | |
| 2006-07 | *Brighton & HA* | 3 | 1 | |
| 2007-08 | Ipswich T | 0 | 0 | |
| 2007-08 | *Northampton T* | 10 | 2 | 10   2 |
| 2007-08 | *Brighton & HA* | 5 | 0 | 8   1 |
| 2008-09 | Ipswich T | 1 | 0 | 73   6 |
| 2008-09 | *Brentford* | 9 | 2 | 9   2 |
| 2009-10 | Yeovil T | 30 | 10 | |
| 2010-11 | Yeovil T | 41 | 15 | 71 25 |
| 2011-12 | Milton Keynes D | 41 | 12 | |
| 2012-13 | Milton Keynes D | 39 | 8 | 80 20 |

**BULLARD, Jimmy (M)**    312 40
H: 5 10   W: 11 05   b.Newham 23-10-78
*Source:* Corinthian, Dartford, Gravesend &
N.

| | | | | |
|---|---|---|---|---|
| 1998-99 | West Ham U | 0 | 0 | |
| 1999-2000 | West Ham U | 0 | 0 | |
| 2000-01 | West Ham U | 0 | 0 | |
| 2001-02 | Peterborough U | 40 | 8 | |
| 2002-03 | Peterborough U | 26 | 3 | 66 11 |
| 2002-03 | Wigan Ath | 17 | 1 | |
| 2003-04 | Wigan Ath | 46 | 2 | |
| 2004-05 | Wigan Ath | 46 | 3 | |
| 2005-06 | Wigan Ath | 36 | 4 | 145 10 |
| 2005-06 | Fulham | 0 | 0 | |
| 2006-07 | Fulham | 4 | 2 | |
| 2007-08 | Fulham | 17 | 2 | |
| 2008-09 | Fulham | 18 | 2 | 39   6 |
| 2008-09 | Hull C | 1 | 0 | |
| 2009-10 | Hull C | 14 | 5 | |
| 2010-11 | Hull C | 8 | 2 | |
| 2010-11 | *Ipswich T* | 16 | 5 | |
| 2011-12 | Hull C | 0 | 0 | 23   7 |
| 2011-12 | Ipswich T | 21 | 1 | |
| 2012-13 | Ipswich T | 0 | 0 | 37   6 |
| 2012-13 | Milton Keynes D | 2 | 0 | 2   0 |

**CHADWICK, Luke (M)**    362 62
H: 5 11   W: 11 08   b.Cambridge 18-11-80
*Source:* Trainee. *Honours:* England Youth,
Under-21.

| | | | | |
|---|---|---|---|---|
| 1998-99 | Manchester U | 0 | 0 | |
| 1999-2000 | Manchester U | 0 | 0 | |
| 2000-01 | Manchester U | 16 | 2 | |
| 2001-02 | Manchester U | 8 | 0 | |
| 2002-03 | Manchester U | 0 | 0 | |
| 2002-03 | *Reading* | 15 | 1 | 15   1 |
| 2003-04 | Manchester U | 0 | 0 | 25   2 |
| 2003-04 | *Burnley* | 36 | 5 | 36   5 |
| 2004-05 | West Ham U | 32 | 1 | |
| 2005-06 | West Ham U | 0 | 0 | 32   1 |
| 2005-06 | Stoke C | 36 | 2 | |
| 2006-07 | Stoke C | 15 | 3 | 51   5 |
| 2006-07 | Norwich C | 4 | 1 | |
| 2007-08 | Norwich C | 13 | 1 | |
| 2008-09 | Norwich C | 0 | 0 | 17   2 |
| 2008-09 | Milton Keynes D | 24 | 6 | |
| 2009-10 | Milton Keynes D | 40 | 2 | |
| 2010-11 | Milton Keynes D | 44 | 0 | |
| 2011-12 | Milton Keynes D | 42 | 2 | |
| 2012-13 | Milton Keynes D | 36 | 6 | 186 16 |

**CHICKSEN, Adam (D)**    76 2
H: 5 8   W: 11 09   b.Milton Keynes 27-9-91
*Source:* Scholar.

| | | | | |
|---|---|---|---|---|
| 2008-09 | Milton Keynes D | 1 | 0 | |
| 2009-10 | Milton Keynes D | 6 | 0 | |
| 2010-11 | Milton Keynes D | 14 | 0 | |
| 2011-12 | Milton Keynes D | 20 | 0 | |
| 2011-12 | *Leyton Orient* | 3 | 0 | 3   0 |
| 2012-13 | Milton Keynes D | 32 | 2 | 73   2 |

**DOUMBE, Stephen (D)**    300 17
H: 6 1   W: 12 05   b.Paris 28-10-79
*Source:* Paris St Germain. *Honours:* France
Youth.

| | | | | |
|---|---|---|---|---|
| 2001-02 | Hibernian | 0 | 0 | |
| 2002-03 | Hibernian | 12 | 0 | |
| 2003-04 | Hibernian | 33 | 2 | 45   2 |
| 2004-05 | Plymouth Arg | 26 | 2 | |
| 2005-06 | Plymouth Arg | 43 | 1 | |
| 2006-07 | Plymouth Arg | 29 | 0 | |
| 2007-08 | Plymouth Arg | 12 | 0 | |
| 2008-09 | Plymouth Arg | 24 | 1 | 134   4 |
| 2009-10 | Milton Keynes D | 33 | 1 | |
| 2010-11 | Milton Keynes D | 54 | 1 | |
| 2011-12 | Milton Keynes D | 20 | 4 | |
| 2012-13 | Milton Keynes D | 24 | 1 | 121 11 |

**FLANAGAN, Tom (D)**    46 4
H: 6 2   W: 11 05   b.Hammersmith 21-10-91
*Source:* Scholar. *Honours:* Northern Ireland
Under-21.

| | | | | |
|---|---|---|---|---|
| 2009-10 | Milton Keynes D | 1 | 0 | |
| 2010-11 | Milton Keynes D | 2 | 0 | |
| 2011-12 | Milton Keynes D | 21 | 3 | |
| 2012-13 | Milton Keynes D | 0 | 0 | 24   3 |
| 2012-13 | *Gillingham* | 13 | 1 | 13   1 |
| 2012-13 | *Barnet* | 9 | 0 | 9   0 |

**GALLOWAY, Brendon (M)**    2 0
H: 6 2   W: 13 10   b.Zimbabwe 17-3-96
*Source:* Schoolboy.

| | | | | |
|---|---|---|---|---|
| 2011-12 | Milton Keynes D | 1 | 0 | |
| 2012-13 | Milton Keynes D | 1 | 0 | 2   0 |

**GLEESON, Stephen (M)**    187 17
H: 6 2   W: 11 00   b.Dublin 3-8-88
*Source:* Scholar. *Honours:* Eire Youth,
Under-21, 2 full caps.

| | | | | |
|---|---|---|---|---|
| 2006-07 | Wolverhampton W | 3 | 0 | |
| 2006-07 | *Stockport Co* | 14 | 2 | |
| 2007-08 | Wolverhampton W | 0 | 0 | |
| 2007-08 | *Hereford U* | 4 | 0 | 4   0 |
| 2007-08 | *Stockport Co* | 6 | 0 | |
| 2008-09 | Wolverhampton W | 0 | 0 | 3   0 |
| 2008-09 | *Stockport Co* | 21 | 2 | 41   4 |
| 2008-09 | *Milton Keynes D* | 5 | 0 | |
| 2009-10 | Milton Keynes D | 29 | 0 | |
| 2010-11 | Milton Keynes D | 36 | 2 | |
| 2011-12 | Milton Keynes D | 39 | 5 | |
| 2012-13 | Milton Keynes D | 30 | 6 | 139 13 |

**KAY, Antony (D)**    384 39
H: 5 11   W: 11 08   b.Barnsley 21-10-82
*Source:* Trainee. *Honours:* England Youth.

| | | | | |
|---|---|---|---|---|
| 1999-2000 | Barnsley | 0 | 0 | |
| 2000-01 | Barnsley | 7 | 0 | |
| 2001-02 | Barnsley | 1 | 0 | |
| 2002-03 | Barnsley | 16 | 0 | |
| 2003-04 | Barnsley | 43 | 3 | |
| 2004-05 | Barnsley | 39 | 6 | |
| 2005-06 | Barnsley | 36 | 1 | |
| 2006-07 | Barnsley | 32 | 1 | 174 11 |
| 2007-08 | Tranmere R | 38 | 6 | |
| 2008-09 | Tranmere R | 44 | 11 | 82 17 |
| 2009-10 | Huddersfield T | 40 | 6 | |
| 2010-11 | Huddersfield T | 37 | 3 | |
| 2011-12 | Huddersfield T | 28 | 1 | |
| 2012-13 | Huddersfield T | 0 | 0 | 95 10 |
| 2012-13 | Milton Keynes D | 33 | 1 | 33   1 |

**LEWINGTON, Dean (D)**    414 15
H: 5 11   W: 11 07   b.Kingston 18-5-84
*Source:* Scholar.

| | | | | |
|---|---|---|---|---|
| 2002-03 | Wimbledon | 1 | 0 | |
| 2003-04 | Wimbledon | 28 | 1 | 29   1 |
| 2004-05 | Milton Keynes D | 43 | 2 | |
| 2005-06 | Milton Keynes D | 44 | 1 | |
| 2006-07 | Milton Keynes D | 45 | 1 | |
| 2007-08 | Milton Keynes D | 45 | 0 | |
| 2008-09 | Milton Keynes D | 40 | 2 | |
| 2009-10 | Milton Keynes D | 42 | 1 | |
| 2010-11 | Milton Keynes D | 42 | 3 | |
| 2011-12 | Milton Keynes D | 46 | 3 | |
| 2012-13 | Milton Keynes D | 38 | 1 | 385 14 |

**LOWE, Ryan (F)**    448 133
H: 5 10   W: 12 08   b.Liverpool 18-9-78
*Source:* Burscough.

| | | | | |
|---|---|---|---|---|
| 2000-01 | Shrewsbury T | 30 | 4 | |

| | | | | | |
|---|---|---|---|---|---|
| 2001-02 | Shrewsbury T | 38 | 7 | | |
| 2002-03 | Shrewsbury T | 39 | 9 | | |
| 2003-04 | Shrewsbury T | 0 | 0 | | |
| 2004-05 | Shrewsbury T | 30 | 3 | 137 23 | |
| 2004-05 | Chester C | 8 | 4 | | |
| 2005-06 | Chester C | 32 | 10 | | |
| 2005-06 | Crewe Alex | 0 | 0 | | |
| 2006-07 | Crewe Alex | 37 | 8 | | |
| 2007-08 | Crewe Alex | 27 | 4 | 64 12 | |
| 2007-08 | *Stockport Co* | 4 | 0 | 4   0 | |
| 2008-09 | Chester C | 45 | 16 | 85 30 | |
| 2009-10 | Bury | 39 | 18 | | |
| 2010-11 | Bury | 46 | 27 | | |
| 2011-12 | Bury | 5 | 4 | 90 49 | |
| 2011-12 | Sheffield W | 26 | 8 | | |
| 2012-13 | Sheffield W | 0 | 0 | 26   8 | |
| 2012-13 | Milton Keynes D | 42 | 11 | 42 11 | |

**MACKENZIE, Gary (D)**    175 7
H: 6 3   W: 13 01   b.Lanark 15-10-85

| | | | | |
|---|---|---|---|---|
| 2003-04 | Rangers | 2 | 0 | |
| 2004-05 | Rangers | 0 | 0 | |
| 2005-06 | Rangers | 0 | 0 | 2   0 |
| 2006-07 | Dundee | 21 | 0 | |
| 2007-08 | Dundee | 33 | 1 | |
| 2008-09 | Dundee | 19 | 0 | |
| 2009-10 | Dundee | 25 | 1 | 98   2 |
| 2010-11 | Milton Keynes D | 26 | 2 | |
| 2011-12 | Milton Keynes D | 26 | 1 | |
| 2012-13 | Milton Keynes D | 11 | 0 | 63   3 |
| 2012-13 | *Blackpool* | 12 | 2 | 12   2 |

**MARTIN, David E (G)**    177 0
H: 6 1   W: 13 04   b.Romford 22-1-86
*Source:* Scholar. *Honours:* England Youth,
Under-20.

| | | | | |
|---|---|---|---|---|
| 2003-04 | Wimbledon | 2 | 0 | 2   0 |
| 2004-05 | Milton Keynes D | 15 | 0 | |
| 2005-06 | Milton Keynes D | 0 | 0 | |
| 2005-06 | Liverpool | 0 | 0 | |
| 2006-07 | Liverpool | 0 | 0 | |
| 2006-07 | *Accrington S* | 10 | 0 | 10   0 |
| 2007-08 | Liverpool | 0 | 0 | |
| 2008-09 | Liverpool | 0 | 0 | |
| 2008-09 | *Leicester C* | 25 | 0 | 25   0 |
| 2009-10 | Liverpool | 0 | 0 | |
| 2009-10 | *Tranmere R* | 3 | 0 | 3   0 |
| 2009-10 | *Leeds U* | 0 | 0 | |
| 2009-10 | *Derby Co* | 2 | 0 | 2   0 |
| 2010-11 | Milton Keynes D | 43 | 0 | |
| 2011-12 | Milton Keynes D | 46 | 0 | |
| 2012-13 | Milton Keynes D | 31 | 0 | 135   0 |

**McLEOD, Izale (F)**    316 106
H: 6 1   W: 11 02   b.Birmingham 15-10-84
*Source:* Scholar. *Honours:* England Under-21.

| | | | | |
|---|---|---|---|---|
| 2002-03 | Derby Co | 29 | 3 | |
| 2003-04 | Derby Co | 10 | 1 | 39   4 |
| 2003-04 | *Sheffield U* | 7 | 0 | 7   0 |
| 2004-05 | Milton Keynes D | 43 | 16 | |
| 2005-06 | Milton Keynes D | 39 | 17 | |
| 2006-07 | Milton Keynes D | 34 | 21 | |
| 2007-08 | Charlton Ath | 18 | 1 | |
| 2007-08 | *Colchester U* | 2 | 0 | 2   0 |
| 2008-09 | Charlton Ath | 2 | 0 | |
| 2008-09 | *Millwall* | 7 | 2 | 7   2 |
| 2009-10 | Charlton Ath | 11 | 2 | |
| 2009-10 | *Peterborough U* | 4 | 0 | 4   0 |
| 2010-11 | Charlton Ath | 0 | 0 | 31   3 |
| 2010-11 | Barnet | 29 | 14 | |
| 2011-12 | Barnet | 44 | 18 | 73 32 |
| 2012-13 | Portsmouth | 24 | 10 | 24 10 |
| 2012-13 | Milton Keynes D | 13 | 1 | 129 55 |

**McLOUGHLIN, Ian (G)**    28 0
H: 6 3   W: 13 08   b.Dublin 9-8-91
*Source:* St Francis. *Honours:* Eire Under-21.

| | | | | |
|---|---|---|---|---|
| 2008-09 | Ipswich T | 0 | 0 | |
| 2009-10 | Ipswich T | 0 | 0 | |
| 2010-11 | Ipswich T | 0 | 0 | |
| 2010-11 | *Stockport Co* | 5 | 0 | 5   0 |
| 2011-12 | Milton Keynes D | 1 | 0 | |
| 2012-13 | Milton Keynes D | 16 | 0 | 17   0 |
| 2012-13 | *Walsall* | 6 | 0 | 6   0 |

**O'SHEA, Jay (M)**    153 29
H: 5 9   W: 12 00   b.Dun Laoghaire 10-8-88
*Honours:* Eire Under-21.

| | | | | |
|---|---|---|---|---|
| 2007 | Bray Wanderers | 27 | 4 | 27   4 |

| 2008 | Galway U | 29 | 8 | | |
|---|---|---|---|---|---|
| 2009 | Galway U | 19 | 3 | 48 | 11 |
| 2009-10 | Birmingham C | 1 | 0 | | |
| 2009-10 | *Middlesbrough* | 2 | 0 | 2 | 0 |
| 2010-11 | Birmingham C | 0 | 0 | 1 | 0 |
| 2010-11 | *Stevenage* | 5 | 0 | 5 | 0 |
| 2010-11 | *Port Vale* | 5 | 1 | 5 | 1 |
| 2011-12 | Milton Keynes D | 28 | 5 | | |
| 2012-13 | Milton Keynes D | 11 | 1 | 39 | 6 |
| 2012-13 | *Chesterfield* | 26 | 7 | 26 | 7 |

**OTSEMOBOR, John (D)**      254   7
H: 5 10   W: 12 07   b.Liverpool 23-3-83
Source: Trainee. Honours: England Youth, Under-20.

| 1999-2000 | Liverpool | 0 | 0 | | |
|---|---|---|---|---|---|
| 2000-01 | Liverpool | 0 | 0 | | |
| 2001-02 | Liverpool | 0 | 0 | | |
| 2002-03 | Liverpool | 0 | 0 | | |
| 2002-03 | *Hull C* | 9 | 3 | 9 | 3 |
| 2003-04 | Liverpool | 4 | 0 | | |
| 2003-04 | *Bolton W* | 1 | 0 | 1 | 0 |
| 2004-05 | Liverpool | 0 | 0 | 4 | 0 |
| 2004-05 | *Crewe Alex* | 14 | 1 | | |
| 2005-06 | Rotherham U | 10 | 0 | 10 | 0 |
| 2005-06 | Crewe Alex | 16 | 0 | | |
| 2006-07 | Crewe Alex | 27 | 0 | 57 | 1 |
| 2007-08 | Norwich C | 43 | 1 | | |
| 2008-09 | Norwich C | 37 | 0 | | |
| 2009-10 | Norwich C | 13 | 1 | 93 | 2 |
| 2009-10 | Southampton | 19 | 0 | 19 | 0 |
| 2010-11 | Sheffield W | 15 | 0 | | |
| 2011-12 | Sheffield W | 11 | 0 | 26 | 0 |
| 2012-13 | Milton Keynes D | 35 | 1 | 35 | 1 |

**POTTER, Darren (M)**      250   14
H: 6 0   W: 10 08   b.Liverpool 21-12-84
Source: Scholar. Honours: Eire Youth, B, Under-21, 5 full caps.

| 2001-02 | Liverpool | 0 | 0 | | |
|---|---|---|---|---|---|
| 2002-03 | Liverpool | 0 | 0 | | |
| 2003-04 | Liverpool | 0 | 0 | | |
| 2004-05 | Liverpool | 2 | 0 | | |
| 2005-06 | Liverpool | 0 | 0 | | |
| 2005-06 | *Southampton* | 10 | 0 | 10 | 0 |
| 2006-07 | Liverpool | 0 | 0 | 2 | 0 |
| 2006-07 | Wolverhampton W | 38 | 0 | | |
| 2007-08 | Wolverhampton W | 18 | 0 | | |
| 2008-09 | Wolverhampton W | 0 | 0 | 56 | 0 |
| 2008-09 | *Sheffield W* | 17 | 2 | | |
| 2009-10 | Sheffield W | 46 | 3 | | |
| 2010-11 | Sheffield W | 33 | 3 | 96 | 8 |
| 2011-12 | Milton Keynes D | 40 | 2 | | |
| 2012-13 | Milton Keynes D | 46 | 4 | 86 | 6 |

**POWELL, Daniel (F)**      115   24
H: 5 11   W: 13 03   b.Luton 12-3-91
Source: Scholar.

| 2008-09 | Milton Keynes D | 7 | 1 | | |
|---|---|---|---|---|---|
| 2009-10 | Milton Keynes D | 2 | 1 | | |
| 2010-11 | Milton Keynes D | 29 | 9 | | |
| 2011-12 | Milton Keynes D | 43 | 6 | | |
| 2012-13 | Milton Keynes D | 34 | 7 | 115 | 24 |

**RASULO, Georgio (M)**      1   0
b.Banbury 23-1-97

| 2012-13 | Milton Keynes D | 1 | 0 | 1 | 0 |
|---|---|---|---|---|---|

**SMITH, Alan (F)**      360   47
H: 5 10   W: 12 04   b.Rothwell 28-10-80
Source: Trainee. Honours: England Youth, Under-21, B, 19 full caps, 1 goal.

| 1997-98 | Leeds U | 0 | 0 | | |
|---|---|---|---|---|---|
| 1998-99 | Leeds U | 22 | 7 | | |
| 1999-2000 | Leeds U | 26 | 4 | | |
| 2000-01 | Leeds U | 33 | 11 | | |
| 2001-02 | Leeds U | 23 | 4 | | |
| 2002-03 | Leeds U | 33 | 3 | | |
| 2003-04 | Leeds U | 35 | 9 | 172 | 38 |
| 2004-05 | Manchester U | 31 | 6 | | |
| 2005-06 | Manchester U | 21 | 1 | | |
| 2006-07 | Manchester U | 9 | 0 | 61 | 7 |
| 2007-08 | Newcastle U | 33 | 0 | | |
| 2008-09 | Newcastle U | 6 | 0 | | |
| 2009-10 | Newcastle U | 32 | 0 | | |
| 2010-11 | Newcastle U | 11 | 0 | | |
| 2011-12 | Newcastle U | 2 | 0 | 84 | 0 |
| 2011-12 | *Milton Keynes D* | 16 | 1 | | |
| 2012-13 | Milton Keynes D | 27 | 1 | 43 | 2 |

**WILLIAMS, Shaun (M)**      166   34
H: 5 9   W: 11 11   b.Dublin 19-10-86
Honours: Eire Under-23.

| 2007 | Drogheda U | 0 | 0 | | |
|---|---|---|---|---|---|
| 2007 | *Dundalk* | 19 | 9 | 19 | 9 |
| 2008 | Drogheda U | 4 | 0 | | |
| 2008 | *Finn Harps* | 14 | 2 | 14 | 2 |
| 2009 | Drogheda U | 1 | 0 | 5 | 0 |
| 2009 | Sporting Fingal | 13 | 7 | | |
| 2010 | Sporting Fingal | 32 | 5 | 45 | 12 |
| 2011-12 | Milton Keynes D | 39 | 8 | | |
| 2012-13 | Milton Keynes D | 44 | 3 | 83 | 11 |

**Scholars**
Ahmed, Mohammed; Alli, Bamidele Jermaine; Burns, Charlie Peter John; Forrester, Remy Lezlee; Galloway, Brendan Joel Zibusiso; Grant, Benjamin Matthew; Hickford, Harry Samuel; Osae, Jonathan Opare; Osei-Addo, Kelvin Kwame; Spence, Mason Kendle; Summerfield, William Oliver.

**Scholars**
Ahmed, Mohammed; Alli, Bamidele Jermaine; Burns, Charlie Peter John; Forrester, Remy Lezlee; Galloway, Brendan Joel Zibusiso; Grant, Benjamin Matthew; Hickford, Harry Samuel; Osae, Jonathan Opare; Osei-Addo, Kelvin Kwame; Spence, Mason Kendle; Summerfield, William Oliver.

# MORECAMBE (53)

**ALESSANDRA, Lewis (F)**      149   15
H: 5 9   W: 11 07   b.Heywood 8-2-89
Source: Scholar.

| 2007-08 | Oldham Ath | 15 | 2 | | |
|---|---|---|---|---|---|
| 2008-09 | Oldham Ath | 32 | 5 | | |
| 2009-10 | Oldham Ath | 1 | 0 | | |
| 2010-11 | Oldham Ath | 19 | 1 | 67 | 8 |
| 2011-12 | Morecambe | 42 | 4 | | |
| 2012-13 | Morecambe | 40 | 3 | 82 | 7 |

**ARESTIDOU, Andreas (G)**      15   0
H: 6 2   W: 13 00   b.Lambeth 6-12-89
Source: Scholar.

| 2007-08 | Blackburn R | 0 | 0 | | |
|---|---|---|---|---|---|
| 2008-09 | Blackburn R | 0 | 0 | | |
| 2009-10 | Shrewsbury T | 2 | 0 | 2 | 0 |
| 2010-11 | Preston NE | 0 | 0 | | |
| 2011-12 | Preston NE | 7 | 0 | 7 | 0 |
| 2012-13 | Morecambe | 6 | 0 | 6 | 0 |

**BURROW, Jordan (F)**      51   5
H: 6 1   W: 11 13   b.Sheffield 12-9-92
Source: Chesterfield Scholar.

| 2011-12 | Morecambe | 19 | 4 | | |
|---|---|---|---|---|---|
| 2012-13 | Morecambe | 32 | 1 | 51 | 5 |

**CARLTON, Danny (F)**      140   21
H: 5 11   W: 12 04   b.Leeds 22-12-83
Source: Morecambe.

| 2007-08 | Carlisle U | 31 | 0 | | |
|---|---|---|---|---|---|
| 2008-09 | Carlisle U | 12 | 3 | 43 | 3 |
| 2008-09 | *Morecambe* | 8 | 2 | | |
| 2008-09 | *Darlington* | 17 | 4 | 17 | 4 |
| 2009-10 | Bury | 7 | 0 | | |
| 2010-11 | Bury | 3 | 0 | 10 | 0 |
| 2010-11 | Morecambe | 16 | 3 | | |
| 2011-12 | Morecambe | 44 | 9 | | |
| 2012-13 | Morecambe | 2 | 0 | 70 | 14 |

**DOYLE, Chris (D)**      4   0

| 2012-13 | Morecambe | 4 | 0 | 4 | 0 |
|---|---|---|---|---|---|

**DRUMMOND, Stuart (M)**      382   53
H: 6 2   W: 13 08   b.Preston 11-12-75
Source: Morecambe.

| 2004-05 | Chester C | 45 | 6 | | |
|---|---|---|---|---|---|
| 2005-06 | Chester C | 42 | 6 | 87 | 12 |
| 2006-07 | Shrewsbury T | 44 | 4 | | |
| 2007-08 | Shrewsbury T | 23 | 3 | 67 | 7 |
| 2007-08 | Morecambe | 18 | 2 | | |
| 2008-09 | Morecambe | 44 | 10 | | |
| 2009-10 | Morecambe | 43 | 9 | | |
| 2010-11 | Morecambe | 41 | 6 | | |
| 2011-12 | Morecambe | 38 | 5 | | |
| 2012-13 | Morecambe | 44 | 2 | 228 | 34 |

**ELLISON, Kevin (M)**      375   74
H: 6 0   W: 12 00   b.Liverpool 23-2-79
Source: Altrincham.

| 2000-01 | Leicester C | 1 | 0 | | |
|---|---|---|---|---|---|
| 2001-02 | Leicester C | 0 | 0 | 1 | 0 |
| 2001-02 | Stockport Co | 11 | 0 | | |
| 2002-03 | Stockport Co | 23 | 1 | | |
| 2003-04 | Stockport Co | 14 | 1 | 48 | 2 |
| 2003-04 | *Lincoln C* | 11 | 0 | 11 | 0 |
| 2004-05 | Chester C | 24 | 9 | | |
| 2004-05 | Hull C | 16 | 1 | | |
| 2005-06 | Hull C | 23 | 1 | 39 | 2 |
| 2006-07 | Tranmere R | 34 | 4 | 34 | 4 |
| 2007-08 | Chester C | 36 | 11 | | |
| 2008-09 | Chester C | 39 | 8 | 99 | 28 |
| 2008-09 | Rotherham U | 39 | 8 | | |
| 2009-10 | Rotherham U | 39 | 8 | | |
| 2010-11 | Rotherham U | 23 | 3 | 62 | 11 |
| 2010-11 | *Bradford C* | 7 | 1 | 7 | 1 |
| 2011-12 | Morecambe | 34 | 15 | | |
| 2012-13 | Morecambe | 40 | 11 | 74 | 26 |

**FENTON, Nick (D)**      524   27
H: 6 0   W: 10 02   b.Preston 23-11-79
Source: Trainee. Honours: England Youth.

| 1996-97 | Manchester C | 0 | 0 | | |
|---|---|---|---|---|---|
| 1997-98 | Manchester C | 0 | 0 | | |
| 1998-99 | Manchester C | 15 | 0 | | |
| 1999-2000 | Manchester C | 0 | 0 | | |
| 1999-2000 | *Notts Co* | 13 | 1 | | |
| 1999-2000 | *Bournemouth* | 8 | 0 | | |
| 2000-01 | Manchester C | 0 | 0 | 15 | 0 |
| 2000-01 | *Bournemouth* | 5 | 0 | 13 | 0 |
| 2000-01 | Notts Co | 30 | 2 | | |
| 2001-02 | Notts Co | 42 | 3 | | |
| 2002-03 | Notts Co | 40 | 3 | | |
| 2003-04 | Notts Co | 43 | 1 | 168 | 10 |
| 2004-05 | Doncaster R | 38 | 1 | | |
| 2005-06 | Doncaster R | 25 | 2 | | |
| 2006-07 | Doncaster R | 0 | 0 | 63 | 3 |
| 2006-07 | Grimsby T | 38 | 4 | | |
| 2007-08 | Grimsby T | 42 | 2 | 80 | 6 |
| 2008-09 | Rotherham U | 45 | 1 | | |
| 2009-10 | Rotherham U | 35 | 0 | | |
| 2010-11 | Rotherham U | 33 | 2 | 112 | 4 |
| 2011-12 | Morecambe | 35 | 3 | | |
| 2012-13 | Morecambe | 38 | 1 | 73 | 4 |

**FLEMING, Andy (M)**      85   9
H: 6 1   W: 12 00   b.Liverpool 18-2-89
Source: Scholar.

| 2006-07 | Wrexham | 2 | 0 | | |
|---|---|---|---|---|---|
| 2007-08 | Wrexham | 4 | 0 | 6 | 0 |
| 2010-11 | Morecambe | 30 | 2 | | |
| 2011-12 | Morecambe | 17 | 2 | | |
| 2012-13 | Morecambe | 32 | 5 | 79 | 9 |

**HAINING, Will (D)**      323   14
H: 6 0   W: 11 02   b.Glasgow 2-10-82
Source: Scholar.

| 2001-02 | Oldham Ath | 4 | 0 | | |
|---|---|---|---|---|---|
| 2002-03 | Oldham Ath | 26 | 2 | | |
| 2003-04 | Oldham Ath | 31 | 2 | | |
| 2004-05 | Oldham Ath | 35 | 5 | | |
| 2005-06 | Oldham Ath | 15 | 0 | | |
| 2006-07 | Oldham Ath | 44 | 2 | 155 | 11 |
| 2007-08 | St Mirren | 29 | 1 | | |
| 2008-09 | St Mirren | 19 | 0 | 48 | 1 |
| 2009-10 | Morecambe | 32 | 1 | | |
| 2010-11 | Morecambe | 12 | 1 | | |
| 2011-12 | Morecambe | 40 | 0 | | |
| 2012-13 | Morecambe | 36 | 0 | 120 | 2 |

**HOLROYD, Chris (F)**      130   14
H: 5 11   W: 12 03   b.Macclesfield 24-10-86
Source: Crewe Alex Scholar.

| 2005-06 | Chester C | 0 | 0 | | |
|---|---|---|---|---|---|
| 2006-07 | Chester C | 22 | 0 | | |
| 2007-08 | Chester C | 25 | 4 | | |
| 2008-09 | Chester C | 0 | 0 | 47 | 4 |

From Cambridge U.

| 2009-10 | Brighton & HA | 13 | 0 | | |
|---|---|---|---|---|---|
| 2010-11 | Brighton & HA | 3 | 0 | 16 | 0 |
| 2010-11 | *Stevenage* | 12 | 6 | 12 | 6 |
| 2010-11 | *Bury* | 4 | 1 | 4 | 1 |
| 2011-12 | Rotherham U | 15 | 1 | 15 | 1 |
| 2011-12 | Preston NE | 20 | 1 | | |
| 2012-13 | Preston NE | 0 | 0 | 20 | 1 |

| | | | | | |
|---|---|---|---|---|---|
| 2012-13 | Macclesfield T | 0 | 0 | | |
| 2012-13 | Morecambe | 16 | 1 | **16** | **1** |

**McCREADY, Chris (D)**     **301** **9**
H: 6 1  W: 12 05  b.Ellesmere Port 5-9-81
*Source:* Scholar.

| | | | | | |
|---|---|---|---|---|---|
| 2000-01 | Crewe Alex | 0 | 0 | | |
| 2001-02 | Crewe Alex | 1 | 0 | | |
| 2002-03 | Crewe Alex | 8 | 0 | | |
| 2003-04 | Crewe Alex | 22 | 0 | | |
| 2004-05 | Crewe Alex | 20 | 0 | | |
| 2005-06 | Crewe Alex | 25 | 0 | | |
| 2006-07 | Tranmere R | 42 | 1 | | |
| 2007-08 | Crewe Alex | 34 | 1 | | |
| 2008-09 | Crewe Alex | 5 | 1 | **115** | **2** |
| 2009-10 | Northampton T | 14 | 0 | **14** | **0** |
| 2009-10 | Tranmere R | 8 | 0 | **50** | **1** |
| 2010-11 | Morecambe | 36 | 4 | | |
| 2011-12 | Morecambe | 46 | 0 | | |
| 2012-13 | Morecambe | 40 | 2 | **122** | **6** |

**McDONALD, Gary (F)**     **346** **36**
H: 6 0  W: 11 06  b.Irvine 10-4-82
*Honours:* Scotland B.

| | | | | | |
|---|---|---|---|---|---|
| 1999-2000 | Kilmarnock | 0 | 0 | | |
| 2000-01 | Kilmarnock | 0 | 0 | | |
| 2001-02 | Kilmarnock | 6 | 0 | | |
| 2002-03 | Kilmarnock | 12 | 2 | | |
| 2003-04 | Kilmarnock | 23 | 3 | | |
| 2004-05 | Kilmarnock | 38 | 3 | | |
| 2005-06 | Kilmarnock | 27 | 3 | **106** | **11** |
| 2006-07 | Oldham Ath | 43 | 7 | | |
| 2007-08 | Oldham Ath | 35 | 4 | **78** | **11** |
| 2008-09 | Aberdeen | 28 | 5 | | |
| 2009-10 | Aberdeen | 24 | 3 | **52** | **8** |
| 2010-11 | Hamilton A | 25 | 0 | **25** | **0** |
| 2011-12 | Morecambe | 42 | 3 | | |
| 2012-13 | Morecambe | 43 | 3 | **85** | **6** |

**McGEE, Joe (M)**     **4** **0**
H: 5 11  W: 10 12  b.Liverpool 6-3-93
*Source:* Youth.

| | | | | | |
|---|---|---|---|---|---|
| 2011-12 | Morecambe | 1 | 0 | | |
| 2012-13 | Morecambe | 3 | 0 | **4** | **0** |

**McGOWAN, Aaron (D)**     **1** **0**

| | | | | | |
|---|---|---|---|---|---|
| 2012-13 | Morecambe | 1 | 0 | **1** | **0** |

**MWASILE, Joe (M)**     **5** **0**
H: 5 8  W: 10 00  b.Zambia 6-7-93

| | | | | | |
|---|---|---|---|---|---|
| 2011-12 | Morecambe | 0 | 0 | | |
| 2012-13 | Morecambe | 5 | 0 | **5** | **0** |

**PARKINSON, Dan (M)**     **6** **0**
H: 5 11  W: 11 02  b.Preston 2-11-92
*Source:* Youth.

| | | | | | |
|---|---|---|---|---|---|
| 2011-12 | Morecambe | 3 | 0 | | |
| 2012-13 | Morecambe | 3 | 0 | **6** | **0** |

**PARRISH, Andy (D)**     **195** **2**
H: 6 0  W: 11 00  b.Bolton 22-6-88
*Source:* Scholar.

| | | | | | |
|---|---|---|---|---|---|
| 2005-06 | Bury | 8 | 0 | | |
| 2006-07 | Bury | 9 | 0 | | |
| 2007-08 | Bury | 26 | 1 | **43** | **1** |
| 2008-09 | Morecambe | 13 | 0 | | |
| 2009-10 | Morecambe | 35 | 0 | | |
| 2010-11 | Morecambe | 41 | 0 | | |
| 2011-12 | Morecambe | 38 | 0 | | |
| 2012-13 | Morecambe | 25 | 1 | **152** | **1** |

**REDSHAW, Jack (F)**     **53** **17**
H: 5 6  W: 10 00  b.Salford 20-11-90
*Source:* Scholar.

| | | | | | |
|---|---|---|---|---|---|
| 2009-10 | Manchester C | 0 | 0 | | |
| 2010-11 | Rochdale | 2 | 0 | **2** | **0** |

From Salford C, Altrincham

| | | | | | |
|---|---|---|---|---|---|
| 2011-12 | Morecambe | 11 | 2 | | |
| 2012-13 | Morecambe | 40 | 15 | **51** | **17** |

**REID, Izak (M)**     **199** **8**
H: 5 5  W: 10 05  b.Stafford 8-7-87
*Source:* Scholar.

| | | | | | |
|---|---|---|---|---|---|
| 2006-07 | Macclesfield T | 8 | 0 | | |
| 2007-08 | Macclesfield T | 25 | 2 | | |
| 2008-09 | Macclesfield T | 38 | 2 | | |
| 2009-10 | Macclesfield T | 37 | 0 | | |
| 2010-11 | Macclesfield T | 37 | 1 | **145** | **6** |
| 2011-12 | Morecambe | 36 | 2 | | |
| 2012-13 | Morecambe | 18 | 1 | **54** | **3** |

**ROCHE, Barry (G)**     **355** **0**
H: 6 5  W: 14 08  b.Dublin 6-4-82
*Source:* Trainee.

| | | | | | |
|---|---|---|---|---|---|
| 1999-2000 | Nottingham F | 0 | 0 | | |
| 2000-01 | Nottingham F | 2 | 0 | | |
| 2001-02 | Nottingham F | 0 | 0 | | |
| 2002-03 | Nottingham F | 1 | 0 | | |
| 2003-04 | Nottingham F | 8 | 0 | | |
| 2004-05 | Nottingham F | 2 | 0 | **13** | **0** |
| 2005-06 | Chesterfield | 41 | 0 | | |
| 2006-07 | Chesterfield | 40 | 0 | | |
| 2007-08 | Chesterfield | 45 | 0 | **126** | **0** |
| 2008-09 | Morecambe | 46 | 0 | | |
| 2009-10 | Morecambe | 42 | 0 | | |
| 2010-11 | Morecambe | 42 | 0 | | |
| 2011-12 | Morecambe | 44 | 0 | | |
| 2012-13 | Morecambe | 42 | 0 | **216** | **0** |

**THRELFALL, Robbie (D)**     **97** **3**
H: 5 11  W: 11 00  b.Liverpool 25-11-88
*Source:* Scholar. *Honours:* England Youth.

| | | | | | |
|---|---|---|---|---|---|
| 2006-07 | Liverpool | 0 | 0 | | |
| 2007-08 | Liverpool | 0 | 0 | | |
| 2007-08 | Hereford U | 9 | 0 | | |
| 2008-09 | Liverpool | 0 | 0 | | |
| 2008-09 | Hereford U | 3 | 0 | **12** | **0** |
| 2008-09 | Stockport Co | 2 | 0 | **2** | **0** |
| 2009-10 | Liverpool | 0 | 0 | | |
| 2009-10 | Northampton T | 4 | 0 | **4** | **0** |
| 2009-10 | Bradford C | 17 | 2 | | |
| 2010-11 | Bradford C | 20 | 0 | | |
| 2011-12 | Bradford C | 17 | 0 | **54** | **2** |
| 2012-13 | Morecambe | 25 | 1 | **25** | **1** |

**WILLIAMS, Ryan (F)**     **16** **2**
H: 5 8  W: 10 09  b.Birkenhead 8-4-91

| | | | | | |
|---|---|---|---|---|---|
| 2012-13 | Morecambe | 16 | 2 | **16** | **2** |

**WRIGHT, Andrew (M)**     **127** **0**
H: 6 1  W: 13 07  b.Formby 15-1-85
*Source:* Liverpool Scholar.
From West Virginia Univ, Cape Cod Crusaders.

| | | | | | |
|---|---|---|---|---|---|
| 2007-08 | Scunthorpe U | 2 | 0 | | |
| 2008-09 | Scunthorpe U | 28 | 0 | | |
| 2009-10 | Scunthorpe U | 19 | 0 | | |
| 2010-11 | Scunthorpe U | 20 | 0 | | |
| 2011-12 | Scunthorpe U | 18 | 0 | **87** | **0** |
| 2012-13 | Morecambe | 40 | 0 | **40** | **0** |

**Scholars**
Dunleavy, Daniel Mark; Lewis, Kyle Francis; McGowan, Aaron Joseph; Naylor, Alexander Ryan; Newton, Michael Callum; Woods, Thomas Andrew.

# NEWCASTLE U (54)

**ABEID, Mehdi (M)**     **31** **3**
H: 6 1  W: 12 08  b.Paris 6-8-92
*Honours:* France Youth, Algeria Under-23.

| | | | | | |
|---|---|---|---|---|---|
| 2008-09 | Lens B | 0 | 0 | | |
| 2009-10 | Lens B | 8 | 0 | | |
| 2010-11 | Lens B | 11 | 3 | **19** | **3** |
| 2011-12 | Newcastle U | 0 | 0 | | |
| 2012-13 | Newcastle U | 0 | 0 | | |
| 2012-13 | St Johnstone | 12 | 0 | **12** | **0** |

**ALNWICK, Jak (G)**     **0** **0**
H: 6 2  W: 12 13  b.Hexham 17-6-93
*Source:* Scholar. *Honours:* England Youth.

| | | | | | |
|---|---|---|---|---|---|
| 2010-11 | Newcastle U | 0 | 0 | | |
| 2011-12 | Newcastle U | 0 | 0 | | |
| 2012-13 | Newcastle U | 0 | 0 | | |

**AMALFITANO, Romain (M)**     **57** **8**
H: 5 9  W: 10 11  b.Nice 27-8-89

| | | | | | |
|---|---|---|---|---|---|
| 2010-11 | Reims | 31 | 5 | | |
| 2011-12 | Reims | 26 | 3 | **57** | **8** |
| 2012-13 | Newcastle U | 0 | 0 | | |

**AMEOBI, Sam (F)**     **28** **1**
H: 6 3  W: 10 04  b.Newcastle 1-5-92
*Source:* Scholar. *Honours:* England Under-21.

| | | | | | |
|---|---|---|---|---|---|
| 2010-11 | Newcastle U | 1 | 0 | | |
| 2011-12 | Newcastle U | 10 | 0 | | |
| 2012-13 | Newcastle U | 8 | 0 | **19** | **0** |
| 2012-13 | Middlesbrough | 9 | 1 | **9** | **1** |

**AMEOBI, Shola (F)**     **292** **51**
H: 6 3  W: 11 13  b.Zaria 12-10-81
*Source:* Trainee. *Honours:* England Under-21. Nigeria 1 full cap.

| | | | | | |
|---|---|---|---|---|---|
| 1998-99 | Newcastle U | 0 | 0 | | |
| 1999-2000 | Newcastle U | 0 | 0 | | |
| 2000-01 | Newcastle U | 20 | 2 | | |
| 2001-02 | Newcastle U | 15 | 0 | | |
| 2002-03 | Newcastle U | 28 | 5 | | |
| 2003-04 | Newcastle U | 26 | 7 | | |
| 2004-05 | Newcastle U | 31 | 2 | | |
| 2005-06 | Newcastle U | 30 | 9 | | |
| 2006-07 | Newcastle U | 12 | 3 | | |
| 2007-08 | Newcastle U | 6 | 0 | | |
| 2007-08 | *Stoke C* | 6 | 0 | **6** | **0** |
| 2008-09 | Newcastle U | 22 | 4 | | |
| 2009-10 | Newcastle U | 18 | 10 | | |
| 2010-11 | Newcastle U | 28 | 6 | | |
| 2011-12 | Newcastle U | 27 | 2 | | |
| 2012-13 | Newcastle U | 23 | 1 | **286** | **51** |

**ANITA, Vurnon (M)**     **134** **5**
H: 5 5  W: 10 04  b.Willemstad 4-4-89
*Honours:* Holland Youth, Under-20, Under-21, 3 full caps.

| | | | | | |
|---|---|---|---|---|---|
| 2005-06 | Ajax | 1 | 0 | | |
| 2006-07 | Ajax | 1 | 0 | | |
| 2007-08 | Ajax | 16 | 0 | | |
| 2008-09 | Ajax | 26 | 0 | | |
| 2009-10 | Ajax | 31 | 3 | | |
| 2010-11 | Ajax | 33 | 2 | | |
| 2011-12 | Ajax | 1 | 0 | **109** | **5** |
| 2012-13 | Newcastle U | 25 | 0 | **25** | **0** |

**BEN ARFA, Hatem (M)**     **208** **35**
H: 5 8  W: 10 08  b.Clamart 7-3-87
*Honours:* France Youth, Under-21, 13 full caps, 2 goals.

| | | | | | |
|---|---|---|---|---|---|
| 2003-04 | Lyon B | 3 | 2 | | |
| 2004-05 | Lyon B | 10 | 3 | | |
| 2004-05 | Lyon | 9 | 0 | | |
| 2005-06 | Lyon | 12 | 0 | | |
| 2005-06 | Lyon B | 10 | 1 | | |
| 2006-07 | Lyon B | 9 | 3 | **32** | **9** |
| 2006-07 | Lyon | 13 | 1 | | |
| 2007-08 | Lyon | 30 | 6 | **64** | **7** |
| 2008-09 | Marseille | 33 | 6 | | |
| 2009-10 | Marseille | 29 | 3 | | |
| 2010-11 | Marseille | 1 | 0 | **63** | **9** |
| 2010-11 | Newcastle U | 4 | 1 | | |
| 2011-12 | Newcastle U | 26 | 5 | | |
| 2012-13 | Newcastle U | 19 | 4 | **49** | **10** |

**BIGIRIMANA, Gael (M)**     **39** **1**
H: 5 9  W: 11 09  b.Burundi 22-10-93
*Source:* Scholar.

| | | | | | |
|---|---|---|---|---|---|
| 2011-12 | Coventry C | 26 | 0 | **26** | **0** |
| 2012-13 | Newcastle U | 13 | 1 | **13** | **1** |

**CABAYE, Yohan (M)**     **251** **41**
H: 5 9  W: 11 05  b.Tourcoing 14-1-86
*Honours:* France Youth, Under-21, 23 full caps, 1 goal.

| | | | | | |
|---|---|---|---|---|---|
| 2004-05 | Lille | 6 | 0 | | |
| 2005-06 | Lille | 27 | 1 | | |
| 2006-07 | Lille | 22 | 3 | | |
| 2007-08 | Lille | 36 | 7 | | |
| 2008-09 | Lille | 32 | 5 | | |
| 2009-10 | Lille | 32 | 13 | | |
| 2010-11 | Lille | 36 | 2 | **191** | **31** |
| 2011-12 | Newcastle U | 34 | 4 | | |
| 2012-13 | Newcastle U | 26 | 6 | **60** | **10** |

**CAMPBELL, Adam (F)**     **3** **0**
H: 5 7  W: 11 07  b.North Shields 1-1-95
*Source:* Wallsend BC. *Honours:* England Youth.

| | | | | | |
|---|---|---|---|---|---|
| 2011-12 | Newcastle U | 0 | 0 | | |
| 2012-13 | Newcastle U | 3 | 0 | **3** | **0** |

**CISSE, Papiss (F)**     **292** **134**
H: 6 0  W: 11 07  b.Dakar 3-6-85
*Honours:* Senegal 26 full caps, 13 goals.

| | | | | | |
|---|---|---|---|---|---|
| 2003-04 | AS Douanes | 26 | 23 | **26** | **23** |
| 2004-05 | Metz B | 10 | 3 | | |
| 2005-06 | Metz B | 3 | 0 | **13** | **3** |
| 2005-06 | Metz | 1 | 0 | | |
| 2005-06 | *Cherbourg* | 28 | 11 | **28** | **11** |
| 2006-07 | Metz | 32 | 12 | | |
| 2007-08 | Metz | 9 | 0 | | |
| 2007-08 | *Chateauroux* | 15 | 4 | **15** | **4** |

| Season | Club | Apps | Gls | Tot | Gls |
|---|---|---|---|---|---|
| 2008-09 | Metz | 37 | 15 | | |
| 2009-10 | Metz | 16 | 8 | 95 | 35 |
| 2009-10 | Freiburg | 16 | 6 | | |
| 2010-11 | Freiburg | 32 | 22 | | |
| 2011-12 | Freiburg | 17 | 9 | 65 | 37 |
| 2011-12 | Newcastle U | 14 | 13 | | |
| 2012-13 | Newcastle U | 36 | 8 | 50 | 21 |

**COLOCCINI, Fabricio (D)**    381 20
H: 6 0   W: 12 04   b.Cordoba 22-1-82
*Honours:* Argentina 36 full caps, 1 goal.

| Season | Club | Apps | Gls | Tot | Gls |
|---|---|---|---|---|---|
| 1998-99 | Boca Juniors | 1 | 1 | | |
| 1999-2000 | Boca Juniors | 1 | 0 | 2 | 1 |
| 1999-2000 | AC Milan | 0 | 0 | | |
| 2000-01 | AC Milan | 0 | 0 | | |
| 2000-01 | San Lorenzo | 19 | 3 | 19 | 3 |
| 2001-02 | Alaves | 33 | 6 | 33 | 6 |
| 2002-03 | Atletico Madrid | 27 | 0 | 27 | 0 |
| 2003-04 | Villarreal | 31 | 1 | 31 | 1 |
| 2004-05 | AC Milan | 1 | 0 | 1 | 0 |
| 2004-05 | La Coruna | 15 | 1 | | |
| 2005-06 | La Coruna | 26 | 0 | | |
| 2006-07 | La Coruna | 26 | 0 | | |
| 2007-08 | La Coruna | 38 | 4 | 105 | 5 |
| 2008-09 | Newcastle U | 34 | 0 | | |
| 2009-10 | Newcastle U | 37 | 2 | | |
| 2010-11 | Newcastle U | 35 | 2 | | |
| 2011-12 | Newcastle U | 35 | 0 | | |
| 2012-13 | Newcastle U | 22 | 0 | 163 | 4 |

**DEBUCHY, Mathieu (D)**    243 16
H: 5 10   W: 12 02   b.Fretin 28-7-85
*Honours:* France Under-21, 14 full caps, 1 goal.

| Season | Club | Apps | Gls | Tot | Gls |
|---|---|---|---|---|---|
| 2003-04 | Lille | 6 | 0 | | |
| 2004-05 | Lille | 16 | 3 | | |
| 2005-06 | Lille | 26 | 4 | | |
| 2006-07 | Lille | 22 | 1 | | |
| 2007-08 | Lille | 16 | 0 | | |
| 2008-09 | Lille | 30 | 0 | | |
| 2009-10 | Lille | 31 | 1 | | |
| 2010-11 | Lille | 35 | 2 | | |
| 2011-12 | Lille | 32 | 5 | | |
| 2012-13 | Lille | 15 | 0 | 229 | 16 |
| 2012-13 | Newcastle U | 14 | 0 | 14 | 0 |

**DUMMETT, Paul (D)**    30 2
H: 5 10   W: 10 02   b.Newcastle 26-9-91
*Source:* Scholar. *Honours:* Wales Under-21.

| Season | Club | Apps | Gls | Tot | Gls |
|---|---|---|---|---|---|
| 2010-11 | Newcastle U | 0 | 0 | | |
| 2011-12 | Newcastle U | 0 | 0 | | |
| 2012-13 | Newcastle U | 0 | 0 | | |
| 2012-13 | *St Mirren* | 30 | 2 | 30 | 2 |

**ELLIOT, Rob (G)**    117 0
H: 6 3   W: 14 10   b.Chatham 30-4-86
*Source:* Scholar.

| Season | Club | Apps | Gls | Tot | Gls |
|---|---|---|---|---|---|
| 2004-05 | Charlton Ath | 0 | 0 | | |
| 2004-05 | Notts Co | 4 | 0 | 4 | 0 |
| 2005-06 | Charlton Ath | 0 | 0 | | |
| 2006-07 | Charlton Ath | 0 | 0 | | |
| 2006-07 | *Accrington S* | 7 | 0 | 7 | 0 |
| 2007-08 | Charlton Ath | 1 | 0 | | |
| 2008-09 | Charlton Ath | 23 | 0 | | |
| 2009-10 | Charlton Ath | 33 | 0 | | |
| 2010-11 | Charlton Ath | 35 | 0 | | |
| 2011-12 | Charlton Ath | 4 | 0 | 96 | 0 |
| 2011-12 | Newcastle U | 0 | 0 | | |
| 2012-13 | Newcastle U | 10 | 0 | 10 | 0 |

**FERGUSON, Shane (D)**    34 1
H: 5 9   W: 10 01   b.Limavady 12-7-91
*Source:* Scholar. *Honours:* Northern Ireland Under-21, B, 8 full caps, 1 goal.

| Season | Club | Apps | Gls | Tot | Gls |
|---|---|---|---|---|---|
| 2008-09 | Newcastle U | 0 | 0 | | |
| 2009-10 | Newcastle U | 0 | 0 | | |
| 2010-11 | Newcastle U | 7 | 0 | | |
| 2011-12 | Newcastle U | 7 | 0 | | |
| 2012-13 | Newcastle U | 9 | 0 | 23 | 0 |
| 2012-13 | *Birmingham C* | 11 | 1 | 11 | 1 |

**GOOD, Curtis (D)**    27 1
H: 6 2   W: 13 05   b.Melbourne 23-3-93

| Season | Club | Apps | Gls | Tot | Gls |
|---|---|---|---|---|---|
| 2011-12 | Melbourne Heart | 24 | 1 | 24 | 1 |
| 2012-13 | Newcastle U | 0 | 0 | | |
| 2012-13 | *Bradford C* | 3 | 0 | 3 | 0 |

**GOSLING, Dan (M)**    60 7
H: 6 0   W: 11 00   b.Brixham 2-2-90
*Source:* Scholar. *Honours:* England Youth, Under-21.

| Season | Club | Apps | Gls | Tot | Gls |
|---|---|---|---|---|---|
| 2006-07 | Plymouth Arg | 12 | 2 | | |
| 2007-08 | Plymouth Arg | 10 | 0 | 22 | 2 |
| 2007-08 | Everton | 0 | 0 | | |
| 2008-09 | Everton | 11 | 2 | | |
| 2009-10 | Everton | 11 | 2 | 22 | 4 |
| 2010-11 | Newcastle U | 1 | 0 | | |
| 2011-12 | Newcastle U | 12 | 1 | | |
| 2012-13 | Newcastle U | 3 | 0 | 16 | 1 |

**GOUFFRAN, Yoan (F)**    264 68
H: 5 9   W: 11 11   b.Villeneuve-Saint-Georges 25-5-86

| Season | Club | Apps | Gls | Tot | Gls |
|---|---|---|---|---|---|
| 2004-05 | Caen | 8 | 0 | | |
| 2005-06 | Caen | 29 | 8 | | |
| 2006-07 | Caen | 37 | 15 | | |
| 2007-08 | Caen | 36 | 10 | 110 | 33 |
| 2008-09 | Bordeaux | 32 | 3 | | |
| 2009-10 | Bordeaux | 32 | 5 | | |
| 2010-11 | Bordeaux | 21 | 2 | | |
| 2011-12 | Bordeaux | 34 | 14 | | |
| 2012-13 | Bordeaux | 20 | 8 | 139 | 32 |
| 2012-13 | Newcastle U | 15 | 3 | 15 | 3 |

**GUTIERREZ, Jonas (M)**    369 16
H: 6 0   W: 11 07   b.Buenos Aires 5-7-82
*Honours:* Argentina 22 full caps, 1 goal.

| Season | Club | Apps | Gls | Tot | Gls |
|---|---|---|---|---|---|
| 2001-02 | Velez Sarsfield | 17 | 0 | | |
| 2002-03 | Velez Sarsfield | 21 | 1 | | |
| 2003-04 | Velez Sarsfield | 27 | 0 | | |
| 2004-05 | Velez Sarsfield | 33 | 0 | 98 | 1 |
| 2005-06 | Mallorca | 30 | 2 | | |
| 2006-07 | Mallorca | 36 | 3 | | |
| 2007-08 | Mallorca | 30 | 0 | 96 | 5 |
| 2008-09 | Newcastle U | 30 | 0 | | |
| 2009-10 | Newcastle U | 37 | 4 | | |
| 2010-11 | Newcastle U | 37 | 3 | | |
| 2011-12 | Newcastle U | 37 | 2 | | |
| 2012-13 | Newcastle U | 34 | 1 | 175 | 10 |

**HAIDARA, Massadio (D)**    48 0
H: 5 11   W: 11 10   b.Trappes 2-12-92

| Season | Club | Apps | Gls | Tot | Gls |
|---|---|---|---|---|---|
| 2010-11 | AS Nancy | 8 | 0 | | |
| 2011-12 | AS Nancy | 19 | 0 | | |
| 2012-13 | AS Nancy | 17 | 0 | 44 | 0 |
| 2012-13 | Newcastle U | 4 | 0 | 4 | 0 |

**HARPER, Steve (G)**    202 0
H: 6 2   W: 13 10   b.Easington 14-3-75
*Source:* Seaham Red Star.

| Season | Club | Apps | Gls | Tot | Gls |
|---|---|---|---|---|---|
| 1993-94 | Newcastle U | 0 | 0 | | |
| 1994-95 | Newcastle U | 0 | 0 | | |
| 1995-96 | Newcastle U | 0 | 0 | | |
| 1995-96 | *Bradford C* | 1 | 0 | 1 | 0 |
| 1996-97 | Newcastle U | 0 | 0 | | |
| 1996-97 | *Stockport Co* | 0 | 0 | | |
| 1997-98 | Newcastle U | 0 | 0 | | |
| 1997-98 | *Hartlepool U* | 15 | 0 | 15 | 0 |
| 1997-98 | *Huddersfield T* | 24 | 0 | 24 | 0 |
| 1998-99 | Newcastle U | 8 | 0 | | |
| 1999-2000 | Newcastle U | 18 | 0 | | |
| 2000-01 | Newcastle U | 5 | 0 | | |
| 2001-02 | Newcastle U | 0 | 0 | | |
| 2002-03 | Newcastle U | 0 | 0 | | |
| 2003-04 | Newcastle U | 0 | 0 | | |
| 2004-05 | Newcastle U | 2 | 0 | | |
| 2005-06 | Newcastle U | 0 | 0 | | |
| 2006-07 | Newcastle U | 18 | 0 | | |
| 2007-08 | Newcastle U | 21 | 0 | | |
| 2008-09 | Newcastle U | 16 | 0 | | |
| 2009-10 | Newcastle U | 45 | 0 | | |
| 2010-11 | Newcastle U | 18 | 0 | | |
| 2011-12 | Newcastle U | 5 | 0 | | |
| 2011-12 | *Brighton & HA* | 5 | 0 | 5 | 0 |
| 2012-13 | Newcastle U | 6 | 0 | 157 | 0 |

**INMAN, Bradden (M)**    21 5
H: 5 9   W: 11 03   b.Adelaide 10-12-91
*Source:* Scholar. *Honours:* Scotland Youth, Under-21.

| Season | Club | Apps | Gls | Tot | Gls |
|---|---|---|---|---|---|
| 2009-10 | Newcastle U | 0 | 0 | | |
| 2010-11 | Newcastle U | 0 | 0 | | |
| 2011-12 | Newcastle U | 0 | 0 | | |
| 2012-13 | Newcastle U | 0 | 0 | | |
| 2012-13 | *Crewe Alex* | 21 | 5 | 21 | 5 |

**KRUL, Tim (G)**    117 0
H: 6 2   W: 11 08   b.Den Haag 3-4-88
*Source:* Academy. *Honours:* Holland Youth, Under-21, 5 full caps.

| Season | Club | Apps | Gls | Tot | Gls |
|---|---|---|---|---|---|
| 2005-06 | Newcastle U | 0 | 0 | | |
| 2006-07 | Newcastle U | 0 | 0 | | |
| 2007-08 | *Falkirk* | 22 | 0 | 22 | 0 |
| 2007-08 | Newcastle U | 0 | 0 | | |
| 2008-09 | Newcastle U | 0 | 0 | | |
| 2008-09 | *Carlisle U* | 9 | 0 | 9 | 0 |
| 2009-10 | Newcastle U | 3 | 0 | | |
| 2010-11 | Newcastle U | 21 | 0 | | |
| 2011-12 | Newcastle U | 38 | 0 | | |
| 2012-13 | Newcastle U | 24 | 0 | 86 | 0 |

**MARVEAUX, Sylvain (M)**    131 17
H: 5 8   W: 10 05   b.Vannes 15-4-86
*Honours:* France Under-21.

| Season | Club | Apps | Gls | Tot | Gls |
|---|---|---|---|---|---|
| 2006-07 | Rennes | 28 | 5 | | |
| 2007-08 | Rennes | 24 | 0 | | |
| 2008-09 | Rennes | 5 | 0 | | |
| 2009-10 | Rennes | 35 | 10 | | |
| 2010-11 | Rennes | 10 | 1 | 102 | 16 |
| 2011-12 | Newcastle U | 7 | 0 | | |
| 2012-13 | Newcastle U | 22 | 1 | 29 | 1 |

**MBABU, Kevin (D)**    1 0
H: 6 0   W: 12 03   b.Zurich 19-4-95

| Season | Club | Apps | Gls | Tot | Gls |
|---|---|---|---|---|---|
| 2012-13 | Servette | 1 | 0 | 1 | 0 |
| 2012-13 | Newcastle U | 0 | 0 | | |

**MIELE, Brandon (M)**    0 0
b.Dublin 28-8-94
*Source:* Scholar.

| Season | Club | Apps | Gls | Tot | Gls |
|---|---|---|---|---|---|
| 2011-12 | Newcastle U | 0 | 0 | | |
| 2012-13 | Newcastle U | 0 | 0 | | |

**NEWTON, Conor (M)**    16 2
H: 5 11   W: 11 00   b.Wickham 17-10-91
*Source:* Scholar.

| Season | Club | Apps | Gls | Tot | Gls |
|---|---|---|---|---|---|
| 2010-11 | Newcastle U | 0 | 0 | | |
| 2011-12 | Newcastle U | 0 | 0 | | |
| 2012-13 | Newcastle U | 0 | 0 | | |
| 2012-13 | *St Mirren* | 16 | 2 | 16 | 2 |

**OBERTAN, Gabriel (F)**    120 5
H: 6 1   W: 12 06   b.Paris 26-2-89
*Honours:* France Youth, Under-21.

| Season | Club | Apps | Gls | Tot | Gls |
|---|---|---|---|---|---|
| 2006-07 | Bordeaux | 17 | 1 | | |
| 2007-08 | Bordeaux | 26 | 2 | | |
| 2008-09 | Bordeaux | 11 | 0 | 54 | 3 |
| 2008-09 | *Lorient* | 15 | 1 | 15 | 1 |
| 2009-10 | Manchester U | 7 | 0 | | |
| 2010-11 | Manchester U | 7 | 0 | 14 | 0 |
| 2011-12 | Newcastle U | 23 | 1 | | |
| 2012-13 | Newcastle U | 14 | 0 | 37 | 1 |

**PERCH, James (D)**    255 13
H: 5 11   W: 11 05   b.Mansfield 29-9-85
*Source:* Scholar.

| Season | Club | Apps | Gls | Tot | Gls |
|---|---|---|---|---|---|
| 2002-03 | Nottingham F | 0 | 0 | | |
| 2003-04 | Nottingham F | 0 | 0 | | |
| 2004-05 | Nottingham F | 22 | 0 | | |
| 2005-06 | Nottingham F | 38 | 3 | | |
| 2006-07 | Nottingham F | 46 | 5 | | |
| 2007-08 | Nottingham F | 30 | 0 | | |
| 2008-09 | Nottingham F | 37 | 3 | | |
| 2009-10 | Nottingham F | 17 | 1 | 190 | 12 |
| 2010-11 | Newcastle U | 13 | 0 | | |
| 2011-12 | Newcastle U | 25 | 0 | | |
| 2012-13 | Newcastle U | 27 | 1 | 65 | 1 |

**RANGER, Nile (F)**    64 4
H: 6 2   W: 13 03   b.Wood Green 11-4-91
*Source:* Southampton Scholar. *Honours:* England Youth.

| Season | Club | Apps | Gls | Tot | Gls |
|---|---|---|---|---|---|
| 2008-09 | Newcastle U | 0 | 0 | | |
| 2009-10 | Newcastle U | 25 | 2 | | |
| 2010-11 | Newcastle U | 24 | 0 | | |
| 2011-12 | Newcastle U | 5 | 0 | | |
| 2011-12 | *Barnsley* | 5 | 0 | 5 | 0 |
| 2011-12 | *Sheffield W* | 8 | 2 | 8 | 2 |
| 2012-13 | Newcastle U | 2 | 0 | 51 | 2 |

**RICHARDSON, Michael (M)**    5 0
H: 5 10   W: 12 02   b.Newcastle 17-3-92
*Source:* Walker Central.

| Season | Club | Apps | Gls | Tot | Gls |
|---|---|---|---|---|---|
| 2010-11 | Newcastle U | 0 | 0 | | |
| 2011-12 | Newcastle U | 0 | 0 | | |
| 2011-12 | *Leyton Orient* | 3 | 0 | 3 | 0 |

| Season | Club | Apps | Gls | Tot | Tot |
|---|---|---|---|---|---|
| 2012-13 | Newcastle U | 0 | 0 | | |
| 2012-13 | *Gillingham* | 2 | 0 | 2 | 0 |

**SANTON, Davide (D)** 106 1
H: 6 2  W: 13 00  b.Portomaggiore 2-1-91
*Honours:* Italy Youth, Under-21, 8 full caps.

| Season | Club | Apps | Gls | Tot | Tot |
|---|---|---|---|---|---|
| 2008-09 | Internazionale | 16 | 0 | | |
| 2009-10 | Internazionale | 12 | 0 | | |
| 2010-11 | Internazionale | 12 | 0 | 40 | 0 |
| 2010-11 | *Cesena* | 11 | 0 | 11 | 0 |
| 2011-12 | Newcastle U | 24 | 0 | | |
| 2012-13 | Newcastle U | 31 | 1 | 55 | 1 |

**SIMPSON, Danny (D)** 160 1
H: 5 9  W: 11 05  b.Eccles 4-1-87
*Source:* Scholar.

| Season | Club | Apps | Gls | Tot | Tot |
|---|---|---|---|---|---|
| 2005-06 | Manchester U | 0 | 0 | | |
| 2006-07 | Manchester U | 0 | 0 | | |
| 2006-07 | *Sunderland* | 14 | 0 | 14 | 0 |
| 2007-08 | Manchester U | 3 | 0 | | |
| 2007-08 | *Ipswich T* | 8 | 0 | 8 | 0 |
| 2008-09 | Manchester U | 0 | 0 | | |
| 2008-09 | *Blackburn R* | 12 | 0 | 12 | 0 |
| 2009-10 | Manchester U | 0 | 0 | 3 | 0 |
| 2009-10 | Newcastle U | 39 | 1 | | |
| 2010-11 | Newcastle U | 30 | 0 | | |
| 2011-12 | Newcastle U | 35 | 0 | | |
| 2012-13 | Newcastle U | 19 | 0 | 123 | 1 |

**SISSOKO, Moussa (M)** 202 23
H: 6 2  W: 13 00  b.Le Blanc Mesnil 16-8-89
*Honours:* France Youth, Under-21, 9 full caps.

| Season | Club | Apps | Gls | Tot | Tot |
|---|---|---|---|---|---|
| 2007-08 | Toulouse | 29 | 1 | | |
| 2008-09 | Toulouse | 35 | 4 | | |
| 2009-10 | Toulouse | 37 | 7 | | |
| 2010-11 | Toulouse | 35 | 5 | | |
| 2011-12 | Toulouse | 35 | 2 | | |
| 2012-13 | Toulouse | 19 | 1 | 190 | 20 |
| 2012-13 | Newcastle U | 12 | 3 | 12 | 3 |

**STREETE, Remie (D)** 0 0
H: 6 2  W: 12 13  b.Boldon 2-11-94
*Source:* Scholar.

| Season | Club | Apps | Gls | Tot | Tot |
|---|---|---|---|---|---|
| 2011-12 | Newcastle U | 0 | 0 | | |
| 2012-13 | Newcastle U | 0 | 0 | | |

**TAVERNIER, James (D)** 31 0
H: 5 9  W: 11 00  b.Bradford 31-10-91
*Source:* Scholar.

| Season | Club | Apps | Gls | Tot | Tot |
|---|---|---|---|---|---|
| 2009-10 | Newcastle U | 0 | 0 | | |
| 2010-11 | Newcastle U | 0 | 0 | | |
| 2011-12 | Newcastle U | 0 | 0 | | |
| 2011-12 | *Carlisle U* | 16 | 0 | 16 | 0 |
| 2011-12 | *Sheffield W* | 6 | 0 | 6 | 0 |
| 2011-12 | *Milton Keynes D* | 7 | 0 | 7 | 0 |
| 2012-13 | Newcastle U | 2 | 0 | 2 | 0 |

**TAYLOR, Ryan (M)** 232 26
H: 5 8  W: 10 04  b.Liverpool 19-8-84
*Source:* Scholar. *Honours:* England Youth, Under-21.

| Season | Club | Apps | Gls | Tot | Tot |
|---|---|---|---|---|---|
| 2001-02 | Tranmere R | 0 | 0 | | |
| 2002-03 | Tranmere R | 25 | 1 | | |
| 2003-04 | Tranmere R | 30 | 5 | | |
| 2004-05 | Tranmere R | 43 | 8 | 98 | 14 |
| 2005-06 | Wigan Ath | 11 | 0 | | |
| 2006-07 | Wigan Ath | 16 | 1 | | |
| 2007-08 | Wigan Ath | 17 | 3 | | |
| 2008-09 | Wigan Ath | 12 | 2 | 56 | 6 |
| 2008-09 | Newcastle U | 10 | 0 | | |
| 2009-10 | Newcastle U | 31 | 4 | | |
| 2010-11 | Newcastle U | 5 | 0 | | |
| 2011-12 | Newcastle U | 31 | 2 | | |
| 2012-13 | Newcastle U | 1 | 0 | 78 | 6 |

**TAYLOR, Steven (D)** 191 11
H: 6 2  W: 13 01  b.Greenwich 23-1-86
*Source:* Trainee. *Honours:* FA Schools, Youth, England Under-20, Under-21, B.

| Season | Club | Apps | Gls | Tot | Tot |
|---|---|---|---|---|---|
| 2002-03 | Newcastle U | 0 | 0 | | |
| 2003-04 | Newcastle U | 1 | 0 | | |
| 2003-04 | *Wycombe W* | 6 | 0 | 6 | 0 |
| 2004-05 | Newcastle U | 13 | 0 | | |
| 2005-06 | Newcastle U | 12 | 0 | | |
| 2006-07 | Newcastle U | 27 | 2 | | |
| 2007-08 | Newcastle U | 31 | 4 | | |
| 2008-09 | Newcastle U | 27 | 4 | | |
| 2009-10 | Newcastle U | 21 | 1 | | |
| 2010-11 | Newcastle U | 14 | 3 | | |
| 2011-12 | Newcastle U | 14 | 0 | | |
| 2012-13 | Newcastle U | 25 | 0 | 185 | 11 |

**TIOTE, Cheik (M)** 162 4
H: 5 11  W: 12 06  b.Yamoussoukro 21-6-86
*Honours:* Ivory Coast 37 full caps, 1 goal.

| Season | Club | Apps | Gls | Tot | Tot |
|---|---|---|---|---|---|
| 2005-06 | Anderlecht | 2 | 0 | | |
| 2006-07 | Anderlecht | 2 | 0 | 4 | 0 |
| 2007-08 | Roda JC | 26 | 2 | 26 | 2 |
| 2008-09 | Twente | 28 | 0 | | |
| 2009-10 | Twente | 28 | 1 | | |
| 2010-11 | Twente | 2 | 0 | 58 | 1 |
| 2010-11 | Newcastle U | 26 | 1 | | |
| 2011-12 | Newcastle U | 24 | 0 | | |
| 2012-13 | Newcastle U | 24 | 0 | 74 | 1 |

**VUCKIC, Haris (F)** 16 1
H: 6 2  W: 12 02  b.Ljubljana 21-8-92
*Source:* Scholar. *Honours:* Slovenia Youth, Under-21, 1 full cap.

| Season | Club | Apps | Gls | Tot | Tot |
|---|---|---|---|---|---|
| 2007-08 | Domzale | 1 | 0 | | |
| 2008-09 | Domzale | 4 | 0 | 5 | 0 |
| 2009-10 | Newcastle U | 2 | 0 | | |
| 2010-11 | Newcastle U | 0 | 0 | | |
| 2011-12 | Newcastle U | 4 | 0 | | |
| 2011-12 | *Cardiff C* | 5 | 1 | 5 | 1 |
| 2012-13 | Newcastle U | 0 | 0 | 6 | 0 |

**WILLIAMSON, Mike (D)** 264 13
H: 6 4  W: 13 03  b.Stoke 8-11-83
*Source:* Trainee.

| Season | Club | Apps | Gls | Tot | Tot |
|---|---|---|---|---|---|
| 2001-02 | Torquay U | 3 | 0 | | |
| 2001-02 | Southampton | 0 | 0 | | |
| 2002-03 | Southampton | 0 | 0 | | |
| 2003-04 | Southampton | 0 | 0 | | |
| 2003-04 | *Torquay U* | 11 | 0 | 14 | 0 |
| 2003-04 | *Doncaster R* | 0 | 0 | | |
| 2004-05 | Southampton | 0 | 0 | | |
| 2004-05 | Wycombe W | 37 | 2 | | |
| 2005-06 | Wycombe W | 39 | 5 | | |
| 2006-07 | Wycombe W | 33 | 1 | | |
| 2007-08 | Wycombe W | 12 | 0 | | |
| 2008-09 | Wycombe W | 22 | 3 | 143 | 11 |
| 2008-09 | Watford | 17 | 1 | | |
| 2009-10 | Watford | 4 | 1 | 21 | 2 |
| 2009-10 | Portsmouth | 0 | 0 | | |
| 2009-10 | Newcastle U | 16 | 0 | | |
| 2010-11 | Newcastle U | 29 | 0 | | |
| 2011-12 | Newcastle U | 22 | 0 | | |
| 2012-13 | Newcastle U | 19 | 0 | 86 | 0 |

**YANGA-MBIWA, Mapou (D)** 199 4
H: 6 0  W: 12 12  b.Bangui 15-5-89
*Honours:* France Under-21, 3 full caps.

| Season | Club | Apps | Gls | Tot | Tot |
|---|---|---|---|---|---|
| 2006-07 | Montpellier | 1 | 0 | | |
| 2007-08 | Montpellier | 33 | 1 | | |
| 2008-09 | Montpellier | 29 | 1 | | |
| 2009-10 | Montpellier | 36 | 0 | | |
| 2010-11 | Montpellier | 36 | 1 | | |
| 2011-12 | Montpellier | 34 | 1 | | |
| 2012-13 | Montpellier | 16 | 0 | 185 | 4 |
| 2012-13 | Newcastle U | 14 | 0 | 14 | 0 |

**Players retained or with offer of contract**
Logan, Steven John.

**Scholars**
Aarons, Rolando; Aird, Lewis Leigh; Booth, Macauley; Gillesphey, Macauley; Gilliead, Alex Nicholas; Heardman, Tom; McKinnon, Ryan; Mitchell, Jonathan Philip; Morgan, James; Olley, Greg Thomas; Quinn, Jonathyn Stephen; Satka, Lubomir; Smith, Liam Phillip; Sterry, Jamie Michael.

# NORTHAMPTON T (55)

**AKINFENWA, Adebayo (F)** 351 119
H: 5 11  W: 13 07  b.Nigeria 10-5-82

| Season | Club | Apps | Gls | Tot | Tot |
|---|---|---|---|---|---|
| 2001 | Atlantas | 19 | 4 | | |
| 2002 | Atlantas | 4 | 1 | 23 | 5 |

From Barry T

| Season | Club | Apps | Gls | Tot | Tot |
|---|---|---|---|---|---|
| 2003-04 | Boston U | 3 | 0 | 3 | 0 |
| 2003-04 | *Leyton Orient* | 1 | 0 | 1 | 0 |
| 2003-04 | *Rushden & D* | 0 | 0 | | |
| 2003-04 | *Doncaster R* | 9 | 4 | 9 | 4 |
| 2004-05 | Torquay U | 37 | 14 | 37 | 14 |
| 2005-06 | Swansea C | 34 | 9 | | |
| 2006-07 | Swansea C | 25 | 5 | | |
| 2007-08 | Swansea C | 0 | 0 | 59 | 14 |
| 2007-08 | Millwall | 7 | 0 | 7 | 0 |
| 2007-08 | Northampton T | 15 | 7 | | |
| 2008-09 | Northampton T | 33 | 13 | | |
| 2009-10 | Northampton T | 40 | 17 | | |
| 2010-11 | Gillingham | 44 | 11 | 44 | 11 |
| 2011-12 | Northampton T | 39 | 18 | | |
| 2012-13 | Northampton T | 41 | 16 | 168 | 71 |

**ARTELL, Dave (D)** 383 35
H: 6 3  W: 14 01  b.Rotherham 22-11-80
*Source:* Trainee.

| Season | Club | Apps | Gls | Tot | Tot |
|---|---|---|---|---|---|
| 1999-2000 | Rotherham U | 1 | 0 | | |
| 2000-01 | Rotherham U | 36 | 4 | | |
| 2001-02 | Rotherham U | 4 | 0 | | |
| 2002-03 | Rotherham U | 0 | 0 | 37 | 4 |
| 2002-03 | *Shrewsbury T* | 28 | 1 | 28 | 1 |
| 2003-04 | Mansfield T | 26 | 3 | | |
| 2004-05 | Mansfield T | 19 | 2 | 45 | 5 |
| 2005-06 | Chester C | 37 | 2 | | |
| 2006-07 | Chester C | 43 | 1 | 80 | 3 |
| 2007-08 | Morecambe | 36 | 3 | | |
| 2008-09 | Morecambe | 37 | 3 | | |
| 2009-10 | Morecambe | 37 | 7 | 110 | 13 |
| 2010-11 | Crewe Alex | 40 | 4 | | |
| 2011-12 | Crewe Alex | 32 | 2 | | |
| 2012-13 | Crewe Alex | 0 | 0 | 72 | 6 |
| 2012-13 | Northampton T | 11 | 3 | 11 | 3 |

**CARLISLE, Clarke (D)** 470 33
H: 6 2  W: 14 11  b.Preston 14-10-79
*Source:* Trainee. *Honours:* England Under-21.

| Season | Club | Apps | Gls | Tot | Tot |
|---|---|---|---|---|---|
| 1997-98 | Blackpool | 11 | 2 | | |
| 1998-99 | Blackpool | 39 | 1 | | |
| 1999-2000 | Blackpool | 43 | 4 | 93 | 7 |
| 2000-01 | QPR | 27 | 3 | | |
| 2001-02 | QPR | 0 | 0 | | |
| 2002-03 | QPR | 36 | 2 | | |
| 2003-04 | QPR | 33 | 1 | 96 | 6 |
| 2004-05 | Leeds U | 35 | 4 | 35 | 4 |
| 2005-06 | Watford | 32 | 3 | | |
| 2006-07 | Watford | 4 | 0 | | |
| 2006-07 | *Luton T* | 5 | 0 | 5 | 0 |
| 2007-08 | Watford | 0 | 0 | 36 | 3 |
| 2007-08 | Burnley | 33 | 2 | | |
| 2008-09 | Burnley | 36 | 3 | | |
| 2009-10 | Burnley | 27 | 0 | | |
| 2010-11 | Burnley | 35 | 1 | | |
| 2011-12 | Burnley | 0 | 0 | 131 | 6 |
| 2011-12 | *Preston NE* | 20 | 3 | 20 | 3 |
| 2011-12 | *Northampton T* | 18 | 1 | | |
| 2012-13 | York C | 10 | 0 | 10 | 0 |
| 2012-13 | Northampton T | 26 | 3 | 44 | 4 |

**COLLINS, Lee (D)** 188 4
H: 6 1  W: 11 10  b.Telford 23-9-83
*Source:* Scholar. *Honours:* England Youth.

| Season | Club | Apps | Gls | Tot | Tot |
|---|---|---|---|---|---|
| 2006-07 | Wolverhampton W | 0 | 0 | | |
| 2007-08 | Wolverhampton W | 0 | 0 | | |
| 2007-08 | *Hereford U* | 16 | 0 | 16 | 0 |
| 2008-09 | Wolverhampton W | 0 | 0 | | |
| 2008-09 | Port Vale | 39 | 1 | | |
| 2009-10 | Port Vale | 45 | 1 | | |
| 2010-11 | Port Vale | 42 | 0 | | |
| 2011-12 | Port Vale | 16 | 0 | 142 | 4 |
| 2011-12 | Barnsley | 7 | 0 | | |
| 2012-13 | Barnsley | 0 | 0 | 7 | 0 |
| 2012-13 | *Shrewsbury T* | 8 | 0 | 8 | 0 |
| 2012-13 | Northampton T | 15 | 0 | 15 | 0 |

**DEMONTAGNAC, Ishmel (F)** 153 15
H: 5 10  W: 11 05  b.Newham 15-6-88
*Source:* Charlton Ath Scholar. *Honours:* England Youth.

| Season | Club | Apps | Gls | Tot | Tot |
|---|---|---|---|---|---|
| 2005-06 | Walsall | 24 | 2 | | |
| 2006-07 | Walsall | 19 | 1 | | |
| 2007-08 | Walsall | 30 | 3 | | |
| 2008-09 | Walsall | 10 | 3 | | |
| 2009-10 | Walsall | 0 | 0 | 83 | 9 |
| 2009-10 | Blackpool | 8 | 0 | | |
| 2009-10 | *Chesterfield* | 10 | 3 | 10 | 3 |
| 2010-11 | Blackpool | 1 | 0 | 9 | 0 |
| 2010-11 | *Stockport Co* | 7 | 2 | 7 | 2 |
| 2011-12 | Notts Co | 17 | 0 | 17 | 0 |
| 2012-13 | Northampton T | 27 | 1 | 27 | 1 |

**DIAS, Claudio (M)** 　1　0
H: 5 10　W: 10 13　b.Milton Keynes 10-11-94

|  |  | | | | |
|---|---|--|--|--|--|
| 2012-13 | Northampton T | 1 | 0 | 1 | 0 |

**GUTTRIDGE, Luke (M)** 　397　45
H: 5 6　W: 9 07　b.Barnstaple 27-3-82
Source: Trainee.

|  |  | | | | |
|---|---|--|--|--|--|
| 1999-2000 | Torquay U | 1 | 0 | | |
| 2000-01 | Torquay U | 0 | 0 | 1 | 0 |
| 2000-01 | Cambridge U | 1 | 1 | | |
| 2001-02 | Cambridge U | 29 | 2 | | |
| 2002-03 | Cambridge U | 43 | 3 | | |
| 2003-04 | Cambridge U | 46 | 11 | | |
| 2004-05 | Cambridge U | 17 | 0 | 136 | 17 |
| 2004-05 | Southend U | 5 | 0 | | |
| 2005-06 | Southend U | 41 | 5 | | |
| 2006-07 | Southend U | 17 | 0 | 63 | 5 |
| 2006-07 | Leyton Orient | 17 | 1 | 17 | 1 |
| 2007-08 | Colchester U | 14 | 0 | 14 | 0 |
| 2008-09 | Northampton T | 25 | 2 | | |
| 2009-10 | Northampton T | 31 | 4 | | |
| 2010-11 | Aldershot T | 41 | 8 | | |
| 2011-12 | Aldershot T | 25 | 4 | 66 | 12 |
| 2011-12 | Northampton T | 19 | 3 | | |
| 2012-13 | Northampton T | 25 | 1 | 100 | 10 |

**HACKETT, Chris (M)** 　301　20
H: 6 0　W: 12 08　b.Oxford 1-3-83
Source: Scholarship.

|  |  | | | | |
|---|---|--|--|--|--|
| 1999-2000 | Oxford U | 2 | 0 | | |
| 2000-01 | Oxford U | 16 | 2 | | |
| 2001-02 | Oxford U | 15 | 0 | | |
| 2002-03 | Oxford U | 12 | 0 | | |
| 2003-04 | Oxford U | 22 | 1 | | |
| 2004-05 | Oxford U | 37 | 4 | | |
| 2005-06 | Oxford U | 21 | 2 | 125 | 9 |
| 2005-06 | Hearts | 2 | 0 | 2 | 0 |
| 2006-07 | Millwall | 33 | 3 | | |
| 2007-08 | Millwall | 6 | 0 | | |
| 2008-09 | Millwall | 22 | 0 | | |
| 2009-10 | Millwall | 40 | 2 | | |
| 2010-11 | Millwall | 16 | 0 | | |
| 2011-12 | Millwall | 3 | 0 | 120 | 1 |
| 2011-12 | *Exeter C* | 5 | 0 | 5 | 0 |
| 2011-12 | *Wycombe W* | 8 | 0 | 8 | 0 |
| 2012-13 | Northampton T | 41 | 6 | 41 | 6 |

**HARDING, Ben (M)** 　209　14
H: 5 10　W: 11 02　b.Carshalton 6-9-84
Source: Scholar.

|  |  | | | | |
|---|---|--|--|--|--|
| 2001-02 | Wimbledon | 0 | 0 | | |
| 2002-03 | Wimbledon | 0 | 0 | | |
| 2003-04 | Wimbledon | 15 | 0 | 15 | 0 |
| 2004-05 | Milton Keynes D | 26 | 4 | | |
| 2005-06 | Milton Keynes D | 10 | 2 | | |
| 2006-07 | Milton Keynes D | 0 | 0 | 36 | 6 |
| 2008-09 | Aldershot T | 29 | 3 | | |
| 2009-10 | Aldershot T | 33 | 1 | | |
| 2010-11 | Aldershot T | 35 | 2 | 97 | 6 |
| 2011-12 | *Wycombe W* | 7 | 0 | 7 | 0 |
| 2011-12 | Northampton T | 19 | 0 | | |
| 2012-13 | Northampton T | 35 | 2 | 54 | 2 |

**HORNBY, Lewis (M)** 　25　0
H: 5 10　W: 10 13　b.Kettering 25-4-94

|  |  | | | | |
|---|---|--|--|--|--|
| 2012-13 | Northampton T | 25 | 0 | 25 | 0 |

**JOHNSON, John (D)** 　144　14
H: 6 0　W: 12 00　b.Middlesbrough 16-9-88
Source: Scholar.

|  |  | | | | |
|---|---|--|--|--|--|
| 2007-08 | Middlesbrough | 0 | 0 | | |
| 2008-09 | Middlesbrough | 1 | 0 | | |
| 2008-09 | *Tranmere R* | 4 | 0 | 4 | 0 |
| 2009-10 | Middlesbrough | 0 | 0 | 1 | 0 |
| 2009-10 | *Northampton T* | 36 | 5 | | |
| 2010-11 | Northampton T | 38 | 7 | | |
| 2011-12 | Northampton T | 45 | 2 | | |
| 2012-13 | Northampton T | 20 | 0 | 139 | 14 |

**LANGMEAD, Kelvin (D)** 　365　35
H: 6 1　W: 12 00　b.Coventry 23-3-85
Source: Scholar.

|  |  | | | | |
|---|---|--|--|--|--|
| 2003-04 | Preston NE | 0 | 0 | | |
| 2003-04 | *Carlisle U* | 11 | 1 | 11 | 1 |
| 2004-05 | Preston NE | 1 | 0 | 1 | 0 |
| 2004-05 | *Kidderminster H* | 10 | 1 | 10 | 1 |
| 2004-05 | Shrewsbury T | 28 | 3 | | |
| 2005-06 | Shrewsbury T | 42 | 9 | | |
| 2006-07 | Shrewsbury T | 45 | 3 | | |
| 2007-08 | Shrewsbury T | 39 | 1 | | |
| 2008-09 | Shrewsbury T | 33 | 0 | | |
| 2009-10 | Shrewsbury T | 44 | 3 | 231 | 19 |
| 2010-11 | Peterborough U | 32 | 3 | | |
| 2011-12 | Peterborough U | 0 | 0 | 32 | 3 |
| 2011-12 | Northampton T | 41 | 4 | | |
| 2012-13 | Northampton T | 39 | 7 | 80 | 11 |

**MOULT, Louis (F)** 　29　2
H: 6 0　W: 13 05　b.Stoke 14-5-92
Source: Scholar.

|  |  | | | | |
|---|---|--|--|--|--|
| 2009-10 | Stoke C | 1 | 0 | | |
| 2010-11 | Stoke C | 0 | 0 | | |
| 2010-11 | *Bradford C* | 11 | 1 | 11 | 1 |
| 2011-12 | Stoke C | 0 | 0 | | |
| 2011-12 | *Accrington S* | 4 | 0 | 4 | 0 |
| 2012-13 | Stoke C | 0 | 0 | 1 | 0 |
| 2012-13 | Northampton T | 13 | 1 | 13 | 1 |

**MOYO, David (F)** 　5　0
b.Harare 17-12-94

|  |  | | | | |
|---|---|--|--|--|--|
| 2012-13 | Northampton T | 5 | 0 | 5 | 0 |

**NICHOLLS, Alex (M)** 　206　31
H: 5 10　W: 11 00　b.Stourbridge 9-12-87
Source: Scholar.

|  |  | | | | |
|---|---|--|--|--|--|
| 2005-06 | Walsall | 8 | 0 | | |
| 2006-07 | Walsall | 0 | 0 | | |
| 2007-08 | Walsall | 19 | 2 | | |
| 2008-09 | Walsall | 45 | 6 | | |
| 2009-10 | Walsall | 37 | 4 | | |
| 2010-11 | Walsall | 37 | 5 | | |
| 2011-12 | Walsall | 45 | 7 | 191 | 24 |
| 2012-13 | Northampton T | 15 | 7 | 15 | 7 |

**O'DONOVAN, Roy (F)** 　180　48
H: 5 10　W: 11 07　b.Cork 10-8-85
Source: Scholar. Honours: Eire Under-21, B.

|  |  | | | | |
|---|---|--|--|--|--|
| 2002-03 | Coventry C | 0 | 0 | | |
| 2003-04 | Coventry C | 0 | 0 | | |
| 2004-05 | Coventry C | 0 | 0 | | |
| 2005 | Cork C | 26 | 6 | | |
| 2006 | Cork C | 29 | 11 | | |
| 2007 | Cork C | 19 | 14 | 74 | 31 |
| 2007-08 | Sunderland | 17 | 0, | | |
| 2008-09 | Sunderland | 0 | 0 | | |
| 2008-09 | *Dundee U* | 11 | 1 | 11 | 1 |
| 2008-09 | *Blackpool* | 12 | 0 | 12 | 0 |
| 2009-10 | Sunderland | 0 | 0 | 17 | 0 |
| 2009-10 | *Southend U* | 4 | 1 | 4 | 1 |
| 2009-10 | *Hartlepool U* | 15 | 9 | 15 | 9 |
| 2010-11 | Coventry C | 2 | 0 | | |
| 2011-12 | Coventry C | 11 | 0 | | |
| 2011-12 | *Hibernian* | 14 | 1 | 14 | 1 |
| 2012-13 | Coventry C | 4 | 0 | 17 | 0 |
| 2012-13 | Northampton T | 16 | 5 | 16 | 5 |

**PLATT, Clive (F)** 　587　107
H: 6 4　W: 12 07　b.Wolverhampton 27-10-77
Source: Trainee.

|  |  | | | | |
|---|---|--|--|--|--|
| 1995-96 | Walsall | 4 | 2 | | |
| 1996-97 | Walsall | 1 | 0 | | |
| 1997-98 | Walsall | 20 | 1 | | |
| 1998-99 | Walsall | 7 | 1 | | |
| 1999-2000 | Walsall | 0 | 0 | 32 | 4 |
| 1999-2000 | Rochdale | 41 | 9 | | |
| 2000-01 | Rochdale | 43 | 8 | | |
| 2001-02 | Rochdale | 43 | 7 | | |
| 2002-03 | Rochdale | 42 | 6 | 169 | 30 |
| 2003-04 | Notts Co | 19 | 3 | 19 | 3 |
| 2003-04 | Peterborough U | 18 | 2 | | |
| 2004-05 | Peterborough U | 19 | 4 | 37 | 6 |
| 2004-05 | Milton Keynes D | 20 | 3 | | |
| 2005-06 | Milton Keynes D | 40 | 6 | | |
| 2006-07 | Milton Keynes D | 42 | 18 | 102 | 27 |
| 2007-08 | Colchester U | 41 | 8 | | |
| 2008-09 | Colchester U | 43 | 10 | | |
| 2009-10 | Colchester U | 41 | 7 | 125 | 25 |
| 2010-11 | Coventry C | 34 | 3 | | |
| 2011-12 | Coventry C | 33 | 4 | 67 | 7 |
| 2012-13 | Northampton T | 36 | 5 | 36 | 5 |

**ROBINSON, Jake (F)** 　277　39
H: 5 7　W: 10 10　b.Brighton 23-10-86
Source: Scholar.

|  |  | | | | |
|---|---|--|--|--|--|
| 2003-04 | Brighton & HA | 9 | 0 | | |
| 2004-05 | Brighton & HA | 10 | 1 | | |
| 2005-06 | Brighton & HA | 27 | 1 | | |
| 2006-07 | Brighton & HA | 38 | 6 | | |
| 2007-08 | Brighton & HA | 34 | 4 | | |
| 2008-09 | Brighton & HA | 5 | 1 | 123 | 13 |
| 2008-09 | *Aldershot T* | 19 | 4 | 19 | 4 |
| 2009-10 | Shrewsbury T | 34 | 3 | | |
| 2010-11 | Shrewsbury T | 22 | 8 | 56 | 11 |
| 2010-11 | *Torquay U* | 22 | 7 | 22 | 7 |
| 2011-12 | Northampton T | 32 | 0 | | |
| 2012-13 | Northampton T | 25 | 4 | 57 | 4 |

**SNEDKER, Dean (G)** 　0　0
H: 6 0　W: 11 13　b.Northampton 17-11-94
Source: Scholar.

|  |  | | | | |
|---|---|--|--|--|--|
| 2011-12 | Northampton T | 0 | 0 | | |
| 2012-13 | Northampton T | 0 | 0 | | |

**TOZER, Ben (D)** 　125　6
H: 6 1　W: 12 11　b.Plymouth 1-3-90
Source: Scholar.

|  |  | | | | |
|---|---|--|--|--|--|
| 2007-08 | Swindon T | 2 | 0 | 2 | 0 |
| 2007-08 | Newcastle U | 0 | 0 | | |
| 2008-09 | Newcastle U | 0 | 0 | | |
| 2009-10 | Newcastle U | 1 | 0 | | |
| 2010-11 | Newcastle U | 0 | 0 | 1 | 0 |
| 2010-11 | *Northampton T* | 31 | 3 | | |
| 2011-12 | Northampton T | 45 | 3 | | |
| 2012-13 | Northampton T | 46 | 0 | 122 | 6 |

**TURNBULL, Paul (M)** 　139　6
H: 6 0　W: 12 07　b.Handforth 23-1-89
Source: Scholar.

|  |  | | | | |
|---|---|--|--|--|--|
| 2004-05 | Stockport Co | 1 | 0 | | |
| 2005-06 | Stockport Co | 0 | 0 | | |
| 2006-07 | Stockport Co | 0 | 0 | | |
| 2007-08 | Stockport Co | 19 | 0 | | |
| 2008-09 | Stockport Co | 34 | 1 | | |
| 2009-10 | Stockport Co | 30 | 0 | | |
| 2010-11 | Stockport Co | 41 | 5 | 125 | 6 |
| 2011-12 | Northampton T | 14 | 0 | | |
| 2012-13 | Northampton T | 0 | 0 | 14 | 0 |

**WIDDOWSON, Joe (D)** 　166　1
H: 6 0　W: 12 00　b.Forest Gate 28-3-89
Source: Scholar.

|  |  | | | | |
|---|---|--|--|--|--|
| 2007-08 | West Ham U | 0 | 0 | | |
| 2007-08 | *Rotherham U* | 3 | 0 | 3 | 0 |
| 2008-09 | West Ham U | 0 | 0 | | |
| 2008-09 | *Grimsby T* | 20 | 1 | | |
| 2009-10 | Grimsby T | 38 | 0 | 58 | 1 |
| 2010-11 | Rochdale | 34 | 0 | | |
| 2011-12 | Rochdale | 32 | 0 | 66 | 0 |
| 2012-13 | Northampton T | 39 | 0 | 39 | 0 |

**WILSON, Lewis (F)** 　8　1
H: 5 10　W: 11 13　b.Milton Keynes 19-2-93
Source: Rushden & D, Newport Pagnell T.

|  |  | | | | |
|---|---|--|--|--|--|
| 2011-12 | Northampton T | 3 | 1 | | |
| 2012-13 | Northampton T | 5 | 0 | 8 | 1 |

**Scholars**
Chambers, Jordan Reece; Craddock, George James; Dias, Claudio Franca; Fitzgerald, Keran Michael; Harmon, Danny Patrick; Heath, Benjamin Michael; Mattock, Harry Raymond; Moyo, David Philani; Powell, Callum James; Reeve, Tyler Lewis; Roberts, Connor Harvey Hugh; Toney, Ivan Benjamin Elijah.

# NORWICH C (56)

**ADEYEMI, Tom (M)** 　111　9
H: 6 1　W: 12 04　b.Milton Keynes 24-10-91
Source: Scholar.

|  |  | | | | |
|---|---|--|--|--|--|
| 2008-09 | Norwich C | 0 | 0 | | |
| 2009-10 | Norwich C | 11 | 0 | | |
| 2010-11 | Norwich C | 0 | 0 | | |
| 2010-11 | *Bradford C* | 34 | 5 | 34 | 5 |
| 2011-12 | Norwich C | 0 | 0 | | |
| 2011-12 | *Oldham Ath* | 36 | 2 | 36 | 2 |
| 2012-13 | Norwich C | 0 | 0 | 11 | 0 |
| 2012-13 | *Brentford* | 30 | 2 | 30 | 2 |

**AYALA, Daniel (M)** 　53　2
H: 6 3　W: 13 03　b.Sevilla 7-11-90
Honours: Spain Under-21.

|  |  | | | | |
|---|---|--|--|--|--|
| 2007-08 | Liverpool | 0 | 0 | | |
| 2008-09 | Liverpool | 0 | 0 | | |
| 2009-10 | Liverpool | 5 | 0 | | |
| 2010-11 | Liverpool | 0 | 0 | 5 | 0 |

| 2010-11 | Hull C | 12 | 1 | 12 | 1 |
|---|---|---|---|---|---|
| 2010-11 | Derby Co | 17 | 0 | 17 | 0 |
| 2011-12 | Norwich C | 7 | 0 | | |
| 2012-13 | Norwich C | 0 | 0 | 7 | 0 |
| 2012-13 | Nottingham F | 12 | 1 | 12 | 1 |

**BARNETT, Leon (D)** 182 8
H: 6 0 W: 12 04 b.Stevenage 30-11-85
*Source:* Scholar.

| 2003-04 | Luton T | 0 | 0 | | |
|---|---|---|---|---|---|
| 2004-05 | Luton T | 0 | 0 | | |
| 2005-06 | Luton T | 20 | 0 | | |
| 2006-07 | Luton T | 39 | 3 | 59 | 3 |
| 2007-08 | WBA | 32 | 3 | | |
| 2008-09 | WBA | 11 | 0 | | |
| 2009-10 | WBA | 2 | 0 | | |
| 2009-10 | Coventry C | 20 | 0 | 20 | 0 |
| 2010-11 | WBA | 0 | 0 | 45 | 3 |
| 2010-11 | Norwich C | 25 | 1 | | |
| 2011-12 | Norwich C | 17 | 1 | | |
| 2012-13 | Norwich C | 8 | 0 | 50 | 2 |
| 2012-13 | Cardiff C | 8 | 0 | 8 | 0 |

**BASSONG, Sebastien (D)** 197 6
H: 6 2 W: 11 07 b.Paris 9-7-86
*Honours:* France Under-21. Cameroon 16 full caps.

| 2005-06 | Metz | 23 | 0 | | |
|---|---|---|---|---|---|
| 2006-07 | Metz | 37 | 1 | | |
| 2007-08 | Metz | 19 | 0 | 79 | 1 |
| 2008-09 | Newcastle U | 30 | 0 | | |
| 2009-10 | Newcastle U | 0 | 0 | 30 | 0 |
| 2009-10 | Tottenham H | 28 | 1 | | |
| 2010-11 | Tottenham H | 12 | 1 | | |
| 2011-12 | Tottenham H | 5 | 0 | | |
| 2011-12 | Wolverhampton W | 9 | 0 | 9 | 0 |
| 2012-13 | Tottenham H | 0 | 0 | 45 | 2 |
| 2012-13 | Norwich C | 34 | 3 | 34 | 3 |

**BECCHIO, Luciano (F)** 298 107
H: 6 2 W: 13 05 b.Cordoba 28-12-83
*Source:* Boca Juniors.

| 2003-04 | Mallorca B | 0 | 0 | | |
|---|---|---|---|---|---|
| 2004-05 | Mallorca B | 0 | 0 | | |
| 2004-05 | Murcia | 16 | 3 | 16 | 3 |
| 2005-06 | Terrassa | 24 | 2 | 24 | 2 |
| 2006-07 | Barcelona Athletic | 10 | 0 | 10 | 0 |
| 2006-07 | Merida | 12 | 5 | | |
| 2007-08 | Merida | 38 | 22 | 50 | 27 |
| 2008-09 | Leeds U | 45 | 15 | | |
| 2009-10 | Leeds U | 37 | 15 | | |
| 2010-11 | Leeds U | 41 | 19 | | |
| 2011-12 | Leeds U | 41 | 11 | | |
| 2012-13 | Leeds U | 26 | 15 | 190 | 75 |
| 2012-13 | Norwich C | 8 | 0 | 8 | 0 |

**BENNETT, Elliott (M)** 220 20
H: 5 9 W: 10 11 b.Telford 18-12-88
*Source:* Scholar.

| 2006-07 | Wolverhampton W | 0 | 0 | | |
|---|---|---|---|---|---|
| 2007-08 | Wolverhampton W | 0 | 0 | | |
| 2007-08 | Crewe Alex | 9 | 1 | 9 | 1 |
| 2007-08 | Bury | 19 | 1 | | |
| 2008-09 | Wolverhampton W | 0 | 0 | | |
| 2008-09 | Bury | 46 | 3 | 65 | 4 |
| 2009-10 | Wolverhampton W | 0 | 0 | | |
| 2009-10 | Brighton & HA | 43 | 7 | | |
| 2010-11 | Brighton & HA | 46 | 6 | 89 | 13 |
| 2011-12 | Norwich C | 33 | 1 | | |
| 2012-13 | Norwich C | 24 | 1 | 57 | 2 |

**BENNETT, Ryan (D)** 214 13
H: 6 2 W: 11 00 b.Thurrock 6-3-90
*Source:* Scholar. *Honours:* England Youth, Under-21.

| 2006-07 | Grimsby T | 13 | 0 | | |
|---|---|---|---|---|---|
| 2007-08 | Grimsby T | 40 | 1 | | |
| 2008-09 | Grimsby T | 45 | 5 | | |
| 2009-10 | Grimsby T | 13 | 0 | 103 | 6 |
| 2009-10 | Peterborough U | 22 | 1 | | |
| 2010-11 | Peterborough U | 34 | 4 | | |
| 2011-12 | Peterborough U | 32 | 1 | 88 | 6 |
| 2011-12 | Norwich C | 8 | 0 | | |
| 2012-13 | Norwich C | 15 | 1 | 23 | 1 |

**BUNN, Mark (G)** 154 0
H: 6 0 W: 12 02 b.Southgate 16-11-84
*Source:* Scholar.

| 2004-05 | Northampton T | 0 | 0 | | |
|---|---|---|---|---|---|
| 2005-06 | Northampton T | 0 | 0 | | |
| 2006-07 | Northampton T | 42 | 0 | | |
| 2007-08 | Northampton T | 45 | 0 | | |
| 2008-09 | Northampton T | 3 | 0 | 90 | 0 |
| 2008-09 | Blackburn R | 0 | 0 | | |
| 2008-09 | Leicester C | 3 | 0 | 3 | 0 |
| 2009-10 | Blackburn R | 0 | 0 | | |
| 2009-10 | Sheffield U | 32 | 0 | 32 | 0 |
| 2010-11 | Blackburn R | 3 | 0 | | |
| 2011-12 | Blackburn R | 3 | 0 | | |
| 2012-13 | Blackburn R | 0 | 0 | 6 | 0 |
| 2012-13 | Norwich C | 23 | 0 | 23 | 0 |

**BUTTERFIELD, Jacob (D)** 107 8
H: 5 10 W: 11 00 b.Bradford 10-6-90
*Source:* Scholar.

| 2007-08 | Barnsley | 3 | 0 | | |
|---|---|---|---|---|---|
| 2008-09 | Barnsley | 3 | 0 | | |
| 2009-10 | Barnsley | 20 | 1 | | |
| 2010-11 | Barnsley | 40 | 2 | | |
| 2011-12 | Barnsley | 24 | 5 | 90 | 8 |
| 2012-13 | Norwich C | 0 | 0 | | |
| 2012-13 | Bolton W | 8 | 0 | 8 | 0 |
| 2012-13 | Crystal Palace | 9 | 0 | 9 | 0 |

**CAMP, Lee (G)** 346 0
H: 5 11 W: 11 11 b.Derby 22-8-84
*Source:* Scholar. *Honours:* England Youth, Under-20, Under-21. Northern Ireland 9 full caps.

| 2002-03 | Derby Co | 1 | 0 | | |
|---|---|---|---|---|---|
| 2003-04 | Derby Co | 0 | 0 | | |
| 2003-04 | QPR | 12 | 0 | | |
| 2004-05 | Derby Co | 45 | 0 | | |
| 2005-06 | Derby Co | 40 | 0 | | |
| 2006-07 | Derby Co | 3 | 0 | 89 | 0 |
| 2006-07 | Norwich C | 11 | 0 | | |
| 2006-07 | QPR | 11 | 0 | | |
| 2007-08 | QPR | 46 | 0 | | |
| 2008-09 | QPR | 4 | 0 | 73 | 0 |
| 2008-09 | Nottingham F | 15 | 0 | | |
| 2009-10 | Nottingham F | 45 | 0 | | |
| 2010-11 | Nottingham F | 46 | 0 | | |
| 2011-12 | Nottingham F | 46 | 0 | | |
| 2012-13 | Nottingham F | 26 | 0 | 178 | 0 |
| 2012-13 | Norwich C | 3 | 0 | 6 | 0 |

**FOX, David (M)** 178 11
H: 5 9 W: 11 08 b.Leek 13-12-83
*Source:* Scholar. *Honours:* England Youth, Under-20.

| 2000-01 | Manchester U | 0 | 0 | | |
|---|---|---|---|---|---|
| 2001-02 | Manchester U | 0 | 0 | | |
| 2002-03 | Manchester U | 0 | 0 | | |
| 2003-04 | Manchester U | 0 | 0 | | |
| 2004-05 | Manchester U | 0 | 0 | | |
| 2004-05 | Shrewsbury T | 4 | 1 | 4 | 1 |
| 2005-06 | Manchester U | 0 | 0 | | |
| 2005-06 | Blackpool | 7 | 1 | | |
| 2006-07 | Blackpool | 37 | 4 | | |
| 2007-08 | Blackpool | 28 | 1 | | |
| 2008-09 | Blackpool | 22 | 0 | 94 | 6 |
| 2009-10 | Colchester U | 18 | 3 | 18 | 3 |
| 2010-11 | Norwich C | 32 | 1 | | |
| 2011-12 | Norwich C | 28 | 0 | | |
| 2012-13 | Norwich C | 2 | 0 | 62 | 1 |

**FRANCOMB, George (D)** 44 0
H: 5 11 W: 11 07 b.Hackney 8-9-91
*Source:* Scholar.

| 2009-10 | Norwich C | 2 | 0 | | |
|---|---|---|---|---|---|
| 2010-11 | Norwich C | 0 | 0 | | |
| 2010-11 | Barnet | 13 | 0 | 13 | 0 |
| 2011-12 | Norwich C | 0 | 0 | | |
| 2011-12 | Hibernian | 14 | 0 | 14 | 0 |
| 2012-13 | Norwich C | 0 | 0 | 2 | 0 |
| 2012-13 | AFC Wimbledon | 15 | 0 | 15 | 0 |

**GARRIDO, Javier (D)** 190 3
H: 5 10 W: 11 12 b.Irun, Spain 15-3-85
*Honours:* Spain Under-21.

| 2004-05 | Real Sociedad | 28 | 0 | | |
|---|---|---|---|---|---|
| 2005-06 | Real Sociedad | 33 | 0 | | |
| 2006-07 | Real Sociedad | 25 | 1 | 86 | 1 |
| 2007-08 | Manchester C | 27 | 0 | | |
| 2008-09 | Manchester C | 13 | 1 | | |
| 2009-10 | Manchester C | 9 | 1 | 49 | 2 |
| 2010-11 | Lazio | 10 | 0 | | |
| 2011-12 | Lazio | 11 | 0 | | |
| 2012-13 | Lazio | 0 | 0 | 21 | 0 |

On loan from Lazio

| 2012-13 | Norwich C | 34 | 0 | 34 | 0 |
|---|---|---|---|---|---|

**HOLT, Grant (F)** 402 147
H: 6 1 W: 14 02 b.Carlisle 12-4-81
*Source:* Workington.

| 1999-2000 | Halifax T | 4 | 0 | | |
|---|---|---|---|---|---|
| 2000-01 | Halifax T | 2 | 0 | 6 | 0 |

From Sengkang,Barrow

| 2002-03 | Sheffield W | 7 | 1 | | |
|---|---|---|---|---|---|
| 2003-04 | Sheffield W | 17 | 2 | 24 | 3 |
| 2003-04 | Rochdale | 14 | 4 | | |
| 2004-05 | Rochdale | 40 | 17 | | |
| 2005-06 | Rochdale | 21 | 14 | 75 | 35 |
| 2005-06 | Nottingham F | 19 | 4 | | |
| 2006-07 | Nottingham F | 45 | 14 | | |
| 2007-08 | Nottingham F | 32 | 3 | 96 | 21 |
| 2007-08 | Blackpool | 4 | 0 | 4 | 0 |
| 2008-09 | Shrewsbury T | 43 | 20 | 43 | 20 |
| 2009-10 | Norwich C | 39 | 24 | | |
| 2010-11 | Norwich C | 45 | 21 | | |
| 2011-12 | Norwich C | 36 | 15 | | |
| 2012-13 | Norwich C | 34 | 8 | 154 | 68 |

**HOOLAHAN, Wes (M)** 382 52
H: 5 6 W: 10 03 b.Dublin 10-8-83
*Honours:* Eire Under-21, 6 full caps, 1 goal.

| 2001-02 | Shelbourne | 20 | 3 | | |
|---|---|---|---|---|---|
| 2002-03 | Shelbourne | 23 | 0 | | |
| 2004 | Shelbourne | 31 | 2 | | |
| 2005 | Shelbourne | 29 | 4 | 103 | 9 |
| 2005-06 | Livingston | 16 | 0 | 16 | 0 |
| 2006-07 | Blackpool | 42 | 8 | | |
| 2007-08 | Blackpool | 45 | 5 | 87 | 13 |
| 2008-09 | Norwich C | 32 | 2 | | |
| 2009-10 | Norwich C | 37 | 11 | | |
| 2010-11 | Norwich C | 41 | 10 | | |
| 2011-12 | Norwich C | 33 | 4 | | |
| 2012-13 | Norwich C | 33 | 3 | 176 | 30 |

**HOWSON, Jonathan (M)** 226 26
H: 5 11 W: 12 01 b.Morley 21-5-88
*Source:* Scholar. *Honours:* England Under-21.

| 2006-07 | Leeds U | 9 | 1 | | |
|---|---|---|---|---|---|
| 2007-08 | Leeds U | 26 | 3 | | |
| 2008-09 | Leeds U | 40 | 4 | | |
| 2009-10 | Leeds U | 45 | 4 | | |
| 2010-11 | Leeds U | 46 | 10 | | |
| 2011-12 | Leeds U | 19 | 1 | 185 | 23 |
| 2011-12 | Norwich C | 11 | 1 | | |
| 2012-13 | Norwich C | 30 | 2 | 41 | 3 |

**JACKSON, Simeon (M)** 191 57
H: 5 10 W: 10 12 b.Kingston, Jamaica 28-3-87
*Source:* Scholar. *Honours:* Canada Youth, 35 full caps, 6 goals.

| 2004-05 | Rushden & D | 3 | 0 | | |
|---|---|---|---|---|---|
| 2005-06 | Rushden & D | 14 | 5 | | |
| 2006-07 | Rushden & D | 0 | 0 | | |
| 2007-08 | Rushden & D | 0 | 0 | 17 | 5 |
| 2007-08 | Gillingham | 18 | 4 | | |
| 2008-09 | Gillingham | 41 | 17 | | |
| 2009-10 | Gillingham | 42 | 14 | 101 | 35 |
| 2010-11 | Norwich C | 38 | 13 | | |
| 2011-12 | Norwich C | 22 | 3 | | |
| 2012-13 | Norwich C | 13 | 1 | 73 | 17 |

**JOHNSON, Brad (M)** 246 30
H: 6 0 W: 12 10 b.Hackney 28-4-87
*Source:* Cambridge U Juniors.

| 2004-05 | Cambridge U | 1 | 0 | 1 | 0 |
|---|---|---|---|---|---|
| 2005-06 | Northampton T | 3 | 0 | | |
| 2006-07 | Northampton T | 27 | 5 | | |
| 2007-08 | Northampton T | 23 | 2 | 53 | 7 |
| 2007-08 | Leeds U | 21 | 3 | | |
| 2008-09 | Leeds U | 15 | 1 | | |
| 2008-09 | Brighton & HA | 10 | 4 | 10 | 4 |
| 2009-10 | Leeds U | 36 | 7 | | |
| 2010-11 | Leeds U | 45 | 5 | 117 | 16 |
| 2011-12 | Norwich C | 28 | 2 | | |
| 2012-13 | Norwich C | 37 | 1 | 65 | 3 |

**KAMARA, Kei (F)** 190 46
H: 6 2 W: 11 10 b.Lawndale 1-9-84
*Honours:* Sierra Leone, 15 full caps, 2 goals.

| 2006 | Columbus Crew | 19 | 3 | | |
|---|---|---|---|---|---|
| 2007 | Columbus Crew | 17 | 2 | 36 | 5 |
| 2008 | San Jose E | 12 | 2 | 12 | 2 |
| 2008 | Houston D | 12 | 3 | | |
| 2009 | Houston D | 22 | 5 | 34 | 8 |

| | | | | | |
|---|---|---|---|---|---|
| 2010 | Sporting Kansas C | 29 | 10 | | |
| 2011 | Sporting Kansas C | 33 | 9 | | |
| 2012 | Sporting Kansas C | 35 | 11 | 97 | 30 |

On loan from Sporting KC

| | | | | | |
|---|---|---|---|---|---|
| 2012-13 | Norwich C | 11 | 1 | 11 | 1 |

**MARTIN, Chris (F)**     193   46
H: 6 2   W: 12 06   b.Beccles 4-11-88
*Source: Scholar. Honours: England Youth.*

| | | | | | |
|---|---|---|---|---|---|
| 2006-07 | Norwich C | 18 | 4 | | |
| 2007-08 | Norwich C | 7 | 0 | | |
| 2008-09 | Norwich C | 0 | 0 | | |
| 2008-09 | *Luton T* | 40 | 11 | 40 | 11 |
| 2009-10 | Norwich C | 42 | 17 | | |
| 2010-11 | Norwich C | 30 | 4 | | |
| 2011-12 | Norwich C | 4 | 0 | | |
| 2011-12 | *Crystal Palace* | 26 | 7 | 26 | 7 |
| 2012-13 | Norwich C | 1 | 0 | 102 | 25 |
| 2012-13 | *Swindon T* | 12 | 1 | 12 | 1 |
| 2012-13 | *Derby Co* | 13 | 2 | 13 | 2 |

**MARTIN, Russell (M)**     308   16
H: 6 0   W: 11 08   b.Brighton 4-1-86
*Source: Lewes. Honours: Scotland 5 full caps.*

| | | | | | |
|---|---|---|---|---|---|
| 2004-05 | Wycombe W | 7 | 0 | | |
| 2005-06 | Wycombe W | 23 | 3 | | |
| 2006-07 | Wycombe W | 42 | 2 | | |
| 2007-08 | Wycombe W | 44 | 0 | 116 | 5 |
| 2008-09 | Peterborough U | 46 | 1 | | |
| 2009-10 | Peterborough U | 10 | 0 | 56 | 1 |
| 2009-10 | Norwich C | 26 | 0 | | |
| 2010-11 | Norwich C | 46 | 5 | | |
| 2011-12 | Norwich C | 33 | 2 | | |
| 2012-13 | Norwich C | 31 | 3 | 136 | 10 |

**MURPHY, Josh (F)**     0   0
H: 5 8   W: 10 07   b.London 24-2-95

| | | | | | |
|---|---|---|---|---|---|
| 2012-13 | Norwich C | 0 | 0 | | |

**PILKINGTON, Anthony (M)**     227   48
H: 5 11   W: 12 00   b.Blackburn 3-11-87
*Source: Atherton Collieries. Honours: Eire Under-21.*

| | | | | | |
|---|---|---|---|---|---|
| 2006-07 | Stockport Co | 24 | 5 | | |
| 2007-08 | Stockport Co | 29 | 6 | | |
| 2008-09 | Stockport Co | 24 | 5 | 77 | 16 |
| 2008-09 | Huddersfield T | 16 | 2 | | |
| 2009-10 | Huddersfield T | 43 | 7 | | |
| 2010-11 | Huddersfield T | 31 | 10 | 90 | 19 |
| 2011-12 | Norwich C | 30 | 8 | | |
| 2012-13 | Norwich C | 30 | 5 | 60 | 13 |

**RUDD, Declan (G)**     24   0
H: 6 3   W: 12 06   b.Diss 16-1-91
*Source: Scholar. Honours: England Youth, Under-20.*

| | | | | | |
|---|---|---|---|---|---|
| 2008-09 | Norwich C | 0 | 0 | | |
| 2009-10 | Norwich C | 7 | 0 | | |
| 2010-11 | Norwich C | 1 | 0 | | |
| 2011-12 | Norwich C | 2 | 0 | | |
| 2012-13 | Norwich C | 0 | 0 | 10 | 0 |
| 2012-13 | *Preston NE* | 14 | 0 | 14 | 0 |

**RUDDY, John (G)**     231   0
H: 6 3   W: 12 07   b.St Ives 24-10-86
*Source: Scholar. Honours: England Youth, 1 full cap.*

| | | | | | |
|---|---|---|---|---|---|
| 2003-04 | Cambridge U | 1 | 0 | | |
| 2004-05 | Cambridge U | 38 | 0 | 39 | 0 |
| 2005-06 | Everton | 1 | 0 | | |
| 2005-06 | *Walsall* | 5 | 0 | 5 | 0 |
| 2005-06 | *Rushden & D* | 3 | 0 | 3 | 0 |
| 2005-06 | *Chester C* | 4 | 0 | 4 | 0 |
| 2006-07 | Everton | 0 | 0 | | |
| 2006-07 | *Stockport Co* | 11 | 0 | | |
| 2006-07 | *Wrexham* | 5 | 0 | 5 | 0 |
| 2006-07 | *Bristol C* | 1 | 0 | 1 | 0 |
| 2007-08 | Everton | 0 | 0 | | |
| 2007-08 | *Stockport Co* | 12 | 0 | 23 | 0 |
| 2008-09 | Everton | 0 | 0 | | |
| 2008-09 | *Crewe Alex* | 19 | 0 | 19 | 0 |
| 2009-10 | Everton | 0 | 0 | 1 | 0 |
| 2009-10 | *Motherwell* | 34 | 0 | 34 | 0 |
| 2010-11 | Norwich C | 45 | 0 | | |
| 2011-12 | Norwich C | 37 | 0 | | |
| 2012-13 | Norwich C | 15 | 0 | 97 | 0 |


**SMITH, Korey (M)**     106   4
H: 5 9   W: 11 01   b.Hatfield 31-1-91
*Source: Scholar.*

| | | | | | |
|---|---|---|---|---|---|
| 2008-09 | Norwich C | 2 | 0 | | |
| 2009-10 | Norwich C | 37 | 4 | | |
| 2010-11 | Norwich C | 28 | 0 | | |
| 2011-12 | Norwich C | 0 | 0 | | |
| 2011-12 | *Barnsley* | 12 | 0 | 12 | 0 |
| 2012-13 | Norwich C | 0 | 0 | 67 | 4 |
| 2012-13 | *Yeovil T* | 17 | 0 | 17 | 0 |
| 2012-13 | *Oldham Ath* | 10 | 0 | 10 | 0 |

**SNODGRASS, Robert (M)**     296   61
H: 6 0   W: 12 02   b.Glasgow 7-9-87
*Honours: Scotland Youth, Under-21, 10 full caps, 2 goals.*

| | | | | | |
|---|---|---|---|---|---|
| 2003-04 | Livingston | 0 | 0 | | |
| 2004-05 | Livingston | 17 | 2 | | |
| 2005-06 | Livingston | 27 | 4 | | |
| 2006-07 | Livingston | 6 | 0 | | |
| 2006-07 | *Stirling A* | 12 | 5 | 12 | 5 |
| 2007-08 | Livingston | 31 | 9 | 81 | 15 |
| 2008-09 | Leeds U | 42 | 9 | | |
| 2009-10 | Leeds U | 44 | 7 | | |
| 2010-11 | Leeds U | 37 | 6 | | |
| 2011-12 | Leeds U | 43 | 13 | 166 | 35 |
| 2012-13 | Norwich C | 37 | 6 | 37 | 6 |

**STEER, Jed (G)**     12   0
H: 6 2   W: 14 00   b.Norwich 23-9-92
*Source: Scholar.*

| | | | | | |
|---|---|---|---|---|---|
| 2009-10 | Norwich C | 0 | 0 | | |
| 2010-11 | Norwich C | 0 | 0 | | |
| 2011-12 | Norwich C | 0 | 0 | | |
| 2011-12 | *Yeovil T* | 12 | 0 | 12 | 0 |
| 2012-13 | Cambridge U | 0 | 0 | | |
| 2012-13 | Norwich C | 0 | 0 | | |

**SURMAN, Andrew (M)**     229   30
H: 5 10   W: 11 06   b.Johannesburg 20-8-86
*Source: Trainee. Honours: England Under-21.*

| | | | | | |
|---|---|---|---|---|---|
| 2003-04 | Southampton | 0 | 0 | | |
| 2004-05 | Southampton | 0 | 0 | | |
| 2004-05 | *Walsall* | 14 | 2 | 14 | 2 |
| 2005-06 | Southampton | 12 | 2 | | |
| 2005-06 | *Bournemouth* | 24 | 6 | 24 | 6 |
| 2006-07 | Southampton | 37 | 4 | | |
| 2007-08 | Southampton | 40 | 2 | | |
| 2008-09 | Southampton | 44 | 7 | | |
| 2009-10 | Southampton | 0 | 0 | 133 | 15 |
| 2009-10 | Wolverhampton W | 7 | 0 | 7 | 0 |
| 2010-11 | Norwich C | 22 | 3 | | |
| 2011-12 | Norwich C | 25 | 4 | | |
| 2012-13 | Norwich C | 4 | 0 | 51 | 7 |

**TETTEY, Alexander (M)**     172   14
H: 5 11   W: 10 09   b.Accra 4-4-86
*Honours: Norway Youth, Under-21, 14 full caps.*

| | | | | | |
|---|---|---|---|---|---|
| 2004-05 | Rosenborg | 0 | 0 | | |
| 2005-06 | Rosenborg | 10 | 1 | | |
| 2006-07 | Rosenborg | 21 | 1 | | |
| 2007-08 | Rosenborg | 25 | 4 | | |
| 2008-09 | Rosenborg | 28 | 6 | | |
| 2009-10 | Rosenborg | 1 | 0 | 85 | 12 |
| 2009-10 | Rennes | 24 | 0 | | |
| 2010-11 | Rennes | 17 | 1 | | |
| 2011-12 | Rennes | 19 | 1 | 60 | 2 |
| 2012-13 | Norwich C | 27 | 0 | 27 | 0 |

**TIERNEY, Marc (D)**     230   2
H: 5 11   W: 11 04   b.Prestwich 23-8-85
*Source: Trainee.*

| | | | | | |
|---|---|---|---|---|---|
| 2003-04 | Oldham Ath | 2 | 0 | | |
| 2004-05 | Oldham Ath | 11 | 0 | | |
| 2005-06 | Oldham Ath | 19 | 0 | | |
| 2006-07 | Oldham Ath | 5 | 0 | 37 | 0 |
| 2007-08 | Shrewsbury T | 18 | 0 | | |
| 2007-08 | Shrewsbury T | 43 | 1 | | |
| 2008-09 | Shrewsbury T | 18 | 0 | 79 | 1 |
| 2008-09 | Colchester U | 26 | 1 | | |
| 2009-10 | Colchester U | 41 | 0 | | |
| 2010-11 | Colchester U | 13 | 0 | 80 | 1 |
| 2010-11 | Norwich C | 16 | 0 | | |
| 2011-12 | Norwich C | 17 | 0 | | |
| 2012-13 | Norwich C | 1 | 0 | 34 | 0 |


**TURNER, Michael (D)**     321   21
H: 6 4   W: 13 05   b.Lewisham 9-11-83
*Source: Scholar.*

| | | | | | |
|---|---|---|---|---|---|
| 2001-02 | Charlton Ath | 0 | 0 | | |
| 2002-03 | Charlton Ath | 0 | 0 | | |
| 2002-03 | *Leyton Orient* | 7 | 1 | 7 | 1 |
| 2003-04 | Charlton Ath | 0 | 0 | | |
| 2004-05 | Charlton Ath | 0 | 0 | | |
| 2004-05 | Brentford | 45 | 1 | | |
| 2005-06 | Brentford | 46 | 2 | 91 | 3 |
| 2006-07 | Hull C | 43 | 3 | | |
| 2007-08 | Hull C | 44 | 5 | | |
| 2008-09 | Hull C | 38 | 4 | | |
| 2009-10 | Hull C | 4 | 0 | 129 | 12 |
| 2009-10 | Sunderland | 29 | 2 | | |
| 2010-11 | Sunderland | 15 | 0 | | |
| 2011-12 | Sunderland | 24 | 0 | | |
| 2012-13 | Sunderland | 0 | 0 | 68 | 2 |
| 2012-13 | Norwich C | 26 | 3 | 26 | 3 |

**VAUGHAN, James (F)**     117   30
H: 5 11   W: 13 00   b.Birmingham 14-7-88
*Source: Scholar. Honours: England Youth, Under-21.*

| | | | | | |
|---|---|---|---|---|---|
| 2004-05 | Everton | 2 | 1 | | |
| 2005-06 | Everton | 1 | 0 | | |
| 2006-07 | Everton | 14 | 4 | | |
| 2007-08 | Everton | 8 | 1 | | |
| 2008-09 | Everton | 13 | 0 | | |
| 2009-10 | Everton | 8 | 1 | | |
| 2009-10 | *Derby Co* | 2 | 0 | 2 | 0 |
| 2010-11 | Everton | 1 | 0 | 47 | 7 |
| 2010-11 | *Crystal Palace* | 30 | 9 | 30 | 9 |
| 2011-12 | Norwich C | 5 | 0 | | |
| 2012-13 | Norwich C | 0 | 0 | 5 | 0 |
| 2012-13 | *Huddersfield T* | 33 | 14 | 33 | 14 |

**WARD, Elliot (D)**     243   20
H: 6 2   W: 13 00   b.Harrow 19-1-85
*Source: Scholar.*

| | | | | | |
|---|---|---|---|---|---|
| 2001-02 | West Ham U | 0 | 0 | | |
| 2002-03 | West Ham U | 0 | 0 | | |
| 2003-04 | West Ham U | 0 | 0 | | |
| 2004-05 | West Ham U | 11 | 0 | | |
| 2004-05 | *Bristol R* | 3 | 0 | 3 | 0 |
| 2005-06 | West Ham U | 4 | 0 | 15 | 0 |
| 2005-06 | *Plymouth Arg* | 16 | 1 | 16 | 1 |
| 2006-07 | Coventry C | 39 | 3 | | |
| 2007-08 | Coventry C | 37 | 6 | | |
| 2008-09 | Coventry C | 33 | 5 | | |
| 2009-10 | Coventry C | 8 | 0 | 117 | 14 |
| 2009-10 | *Doncaster R* | 6 | 1 | 6 | 1 |
| 2009-10 | *Preston NE* | 4 | 0 | 4 | 0 |
| 2010-11 | Norwich C | 39 | 1 | | |
| 2011-12 | Norwich C | 12 | 0 | | |
| 2012-13 | Norwich C | 0 | 0 | 51 | 1 |
| 2012-13 | *Nottingham F* | 31 | 3 | 31 | 3 |

**WHITTAKER, Steven (D)**     304   24
H: 6 1   W: 13 07   b.Edinburgh 16-6-84
*Honours: Scotland Under-21, 18 full caps.*

| | | | | | |
|---|---|---|---|---|---|
| 2001-02 | Hibernian | 1 | 0 | | |
| 2002-03 | Hibernian | 6 | 0 | | |
| 2003-04 | Hibernian | 28 | 1 | | |
| 2004-05 | Hibernian | 37 | 1 | | |
| 2005-06 | Hibernian | 34 | 1 | | |
| 2006-07 | Hibernian | 35 | 1 | 141 | 4 |
| 2007-08 | Rangers | 30 | 4 | | |
| 2008-09 | Rangers | 24 | 2 | | |
| 2009-10 | Rangers | 35 | 7 | | |
| 2010-11 | Rangers | 36 | 4 | | |
| 2011-12 | Rangers | 25 | 2 | 150 | 19 |
| 2012-13 | Norwich C | 13 | 1 | 13 | 1 |

**Players retained or with offer of contract**
Gafaiti, Adel; Loza, Jamar Kasheef; McNeil, Ewan; Murphy, Jacob Kai.

**Scholars**
Barker, Harry Darius; Browne, Stephen
Rhys; Callan-McFadden, Kyle; Hall-Johnson,
Reece; Heath, Harrison; Hodd, Harvey
William; King, Cameron; Lokko, Kevin
Adom; Matthews, Remi Luke; McGeehan,
Cameron Alexander; Morris, Carlton;
Norman, Cameron; Randall, Henry Charles;
Toffolo, Harry; Wyatt, Ben.

# NOTTINGHAM F (57)

**AL-RASHIDI, Khaled (G)**    1   1
H: 6 1   W: 13 01   b. 20-4-87

| | | | | | |
|---|---|---|---|---|---|
| 2011-12 | Al-Arabi | 1 | 1 | 1 | 1 |
| 2012-13 | Nottingham F | 0 | 0 | | |

**BLACKSTOCK, Dexter (F)**    282   74
H: 6 2   W: 13 00   b.Oxford 20-5-86
*Source:* Scholar. *Honours:* England Youth, Under-20, Under-21, Antigua and Barbuda 4 full caps.

| | | | | | |
|---|---|---|---|---|---|
| 2004-05 | Southampton | 9 | 1 | | |
| 2004-05 | *Plymouth Arg* | 14 | 4 | 14 | 4 |
| 2005-06 | Southampton | 19 | 3 | 28 | 4 |
| 2005-06 | *Derby Co* | 9 | 3 | 9 | 3 |
| 2006-07 | QPR | 39 | 13 | | |
| 2007-08 | QPR | 35 | 6 | | |
| 2008-09 | QPR | 36 | 11 | 110 | 30 |
| 2008-09 | *Nottingham F* | 6 | 2 | | |
| 2009-10 | Nottingham F | 39 | 12 | | |
| 2010-11 | Nottingham F | 17 | 5 | | |
| 2011-12 | Nottingham F | 22 | 8 | | |
| 2012-13 | Nottingham F | 37 | 6 | 121 | 33 |

**BLAKE, Jack (M)**    0   0
b.Scotland 22-9-94
*Honours:* Scotland Youth.

| | | | | | |
|---|---|---|---|---|---|
| 2011-12 | Nottingham F | 0 | 0 | | |
| 2012-13 | Nottingham F | 0 | 0 | | |

**COHEN, Chris (M)**    305   18
H: 5 11   W: 10 11   b.Norwich 5-3-87
*Source:* Scholar. *Honours:* England Youth.

| | | | | | |
|---|---|---|---|---|---|
| 2003-04 | West Ham U | 7 | 0 | | |
| 2004-05 | West Ham U | 11 | 0 | | |
| 2005-06 | West Ham U | 0 | 0 | 18 | 0 |
| 2005-06 | Yeovil T | 30 | 1 | | |
| 2006-07 | Yeovil T | 44 | 6 | 74 | 7 |
| 2007-08 | Nottingham F | 41 | 2 | | |
| 2008-09 | Nottingham F | 41 | 2 | | |
| 2009-10 | Nottingham F | 44 | 3 | | |
| 2010-11 | Nottingham F | 42 | 2 | | |
| 2011-12 | Nottingham F | 7 | 0 | | |
| 2012-13 | Nottingham F | 38 | 2 | 213 | 11 |

**COLLINS, Danny (D)**    278   8
H: 6 2   W: 11 13   b.Buckley 6-8-80
*Source:* Buckley T. *Honours:* Wales 12 full caps.

| | | | | | |
|---|---|---|---|---|---|
| 2004-05 | Chester C | 12 | 1 | 12 | 1 |
| 2004-05 | Sunderland | 14 | 0 | | |
| 2005-06 | Sunderland | 23 | 1 | | |
| 2006-07 | Sunderland | 38 | 0 | | |
| 2007-08 | Sunderland | 36 | 1 | | |
| 2008-09 | Sunderland | 35 | 1 | | |
| 2009-10 | Sunderland | 3 | 0 | 149 | 3 |
| 2009-10 | Stoke C | 25 | 0 | | |
| 2010-11 | Stoke C | 25 | 0 | | |
| 2011-12 | Stoke C | 0 | 0 | 50 | 0 |
| 2011-12 | *Ipswich T* | 16 | 3 | 16 | 3 |
| 2011-12 | *West Ham U* | 11 | 1 | 11 | 1 |
| 2012-13 | Nottingham F | 40 | 0 | 40 | 0 |

**COX, Simon (F)**    208   62
H: 5 10   W: 10 12   b.Reading 28-4-87
*Source:* Scholar. *Honours:* Eire 26 full caps, 4 goals.

| | | | | | |
|---|---|---|---|---|---|
| 2005-06 | Reading | 2 | 0 | | |
| 2006-07 | Reading | 0 | 0 | | |
| 2006-07 | *Brentford* | 13 | 0 | 13 | 0 |
| 2006-07 | *Northampton T* | 8 | 3 | 8 | 3 |
| 2007-08 | Reading | 0 | 0 | 2 | 0 |
| 2007-08 | Swindon T | 36 | 15 | | |
| 2008-09 | Swindon T | 45 | 29 | 81 | 44 |
| 2009-10 | WBA | 28 | 9 | | |
| 2010-11 | WBA | 19 | 1 | | |
| 2011-12 | WBA | 18 | 0 | | |
| 2012-13 | WBA | 0 | 0 | 65 | 10 |
| 2012-13 | Nottingham F | 39 | 5 | 39 | 5 |

**DARLOW, Karl (G)**    30   0
H: 6 1   W: 12 05   b.Northampton 8-10-90
*Source:* Scholar.

| | | | | | |
|---|---|---|---|---|---|
| 2009-10 | Nottingham F | 0 | 0 | | |
| 2010-11 | Nottingham F | 1 | 0 | | |
| 2011-12 | Nottingham F | 0 | 0 | | |
| 2012-13 | Nottingham F | 20 | 0 | 21 | 0 |
| 2012-13 | *Walsall* | 9 | 0 | 9 | 0 |

**DERBYSHIRE, Matt (F)**    175   36
H: 5 10   W: 11 01   b.Gt Harwood 14-4-86
*Source:* Gt Harwood T. *Honours:* England Under-21.

| | | | | | |
|---|---|---|---|---|---|
| 2003-04 | Blackburn R | 0 | 0 | | |
| 2004-05 | Blackburn R | 1 | 0 | | |
| 2005-06 | Blackburn R | 0 | 0 | | |
| 2005-06 | *Plymouth Arg* | 12 | 0 | 12 | 0 |
| 2005-06 | *Wrexham* | 16 | 10 | 16 | 10 |
| 2006-07 | Blackburn R | 22 | 5 | | |
| 2007-08 | Blackburn R | 23 | 3 | | |
| 2008-09 | Blackburn R | 17 | 2 | 63 | 10 |
| 2008-09 | *Olympiacos* | 7 | 5 | | |
| 2009-10 | Olympiacos | 19 | 6 | | |
| 2010-11 | Olympiacos | 0 | 0 | 26 | 11 |
| 2010-11 | *Birmingham C* | 13 | 0 | 13 | 0 |
| 2011-12 | Nottingham F | 15 | 1 | | |
| 2012-13 | Nottingham F | 0 | 0 | 15 | 1 |
| 2012-13 | *Oldham Ath* | 18 | 4 | 18 | 4 |
| 2012-13 | *Blackpool* | 12 | 0 | 12 | 0 |

**EVTIMOV, Dimitar (G)**    0   0
H: 6 3   W: 13 00   b.Plevan 7-9-93

| | | | |
|---|---|---|---|
| 2012-13 | Nottingham F | 0 | 0 |

**FINDLEY, Robbie (F)**    154   49
H: 5 9   W: 11 11   b.Phoenix 4-8-85
*Source:* Oregon State Beavers. *Honours:* USA 11 full caps.

| | | | | | |
|---|---|---|---|---|---|
| 2005 | Boulder Rapids | 9 | 10 | | |
| 2006 | Boulder Rapids | 8 | 5 | 17 | 15 |
| 2007 | LA Galaxy | 9 | 2 | 9 | 2 |
| 2007 | Real Salt Lake | 16 | 6 | | |
| 2008 | Real Salt Lake | 29 | 6 | | |
| 2009 | Real Salt Lake | 27 | 12 | | |
| 2010 | Real Salt Lake | 24 | 5 | 96 | 29 |
| 2010-11 | Nottingham F | 2 | 0 | | |
| 2011-12 | Nottingham F | 23 | 3 | | |
| 2012-13 | Nottingham F | 0 | 0 | 25 | 3 |
| 2012-13 | *Gillingham* | 7 | 0 | 7 | 0 |

Transferred to Real Salt Lake January 2013

**GILLETT, Simon (M)**    179   6
H: 5 6   W: 11 07   b.Oxford 6-11-85
*Source:* Trainee.

| | | | | | |
|---|---|---|---|---|---|
| 2003-04 | Southampton | 0 | 0 | | |
| 2004-05 | Southampton | 0 | 0 | | |
| 2005-06 | Southampton | 0 | 0 | | |
| 2005-06 | *Walsall* | 2 | 0 | 2 | 0 |
| 2006-07 | Southampton | 0 | 0 | | |
| 2006-07 | *Blackpool* | 31 | 1 | 31 | 1 |
| 2006-07 | *Bournemouth* | 7 | 1 | 7 | 1 |
| 2007-08 | Southampton | 2 | 0 | | |
| 2007-08 | *Yeovil T* | 4 | 0 | 4 | 0 |
| 2008-09 | Southampton | 27 | 0 | | |
| 2009-10 | Southampton | 2 | 0 | 31 | 0 |
| 2009-10 | *Doncaster R* | 11 | 0 | | |
| 2010-11 | Doncaster R | 22 | 1 | | |
| 2011-12 | Doncaster R | 46 | 3 | | |
| 2012-13 | Doncaster R | 0 | 0 | 79 | 4 |
| 2012-13 | Nottingham F | 25 | 0 | 25 | 0 |

**GREENING, Jonathan (M)**    409   15
H: 5 11   W: 11 00   b.Scarborough 2-1-79
*Source:* Trainee. *Honours:* England Youth, Under-21.

| | | | | | |
|---|---|---|---|---|---|
| 1996-97 | York C | 5 | 0 | | |
| 1997-98 | York C | 20 | 2 | 25 | 2 |
| 1997-98 | Manchester U | 0 | 0 | | |
| 1998-99 | Manchester U | 3 | 0 | | |
| 1999-2000 | Manchester U | 4 | 0 | | |
| 2000-01 | Manchester U | 7 | 0 | 14 | 0 |
| 2001-02 | Middlesbrough | 36 | 1 | | |
| 2002-03 | Middlesbrough | 38 | 2 | | |
| 2003-04 | Middlesbrough | 25 | 1 | 99 | 4 |
| 2004-05 | WBA | 34 | 0 | | |
| 2005-06 | WBA | 38 | 2 | | |
| 2006-07 | WBA | 42 | 2 | | |
| 2007-08 | WBA | 46 | 1 | | |
| 2008-09 | WBA | 34 | 2 | | |
| 2009-10 | WBA | 2 | 0 | 196 | 7 |
| 2009-10 | *Fulham* | 23 | 1 | | |
| 2010-11 | Fulham | 10 | 0 | 33 | 1 |
| 2011-12 | Nottingham F | 31 | 0 | | |
| 2012-13 | Nottingham F | 5 | 0 | 36 | 0 |
| 2012-13 | *Barnsley* | 6 | 1 | 6 | 1 |

**GUEDIOURA, Adlene (M)**    183   17
H: 6 1   W: 12 08   b.La Roche-sur-Yon 12-11-85
*Honours:* Algeria 26 full caps, 1 goal.

| | | | | | |
|---|---|---|---|---|---|
| 2004-05 | Sedan | 0 | 0 | | |
| 2005-06 | Noisy-Le-Sec | 15 | 1 | 15 | 1 |
| 2006-07 | L'Entente | 21 | 3 | 21 | 3 |
| 2007-08 | Creteil | 24 | 6 | 24 | 6 |
| 2008-09 | Kortrijk | 10 | 0 | 10 | 0 |
| 2008-09 | Charleroi | 12 | 0 | | |
| 2009-10 | Charleroi | 13 | 1 | 25 | 1 |
| 2009-10 | Wolverhampton W | 14 | 1 | | |
| 2010-11 | Wolverhampton W | 10 | 1 | | |
| 2011-12 | Wolverhampton W | 10 | 0 | 34 | 2 |
| 2011-12 | *Nottingham F* | 19 | 1 | | |
| 2012-13 | Nottingham F | 35 | 3 | 54 | 4 |

**HALFORD, Greg (D)**    333   39
H: 6 4   W: 12 10   b.Chelmsford 8-12-84
*Source:* Scholar. *Honours:* England Youth, Under-20.

| | | | | | |
|---|---|---|---|---|---|
| 2002-03 | Colchester U | 1 | 0 | | |
| 2003-04 | Colchester U | 18 | 4 | | |
| 2004-05 | Colchester U | 44 | 4 | | |
| 2005-06 | Colchester U | 45 | 7 | | |
| 2006-07 | Colchester U | 28 | 3 | 136 | 18 |
| 2006-07 | Reading | 3 | 0 | 3 | 0 |
| 2007-08 | Sunderland | 8 | 0 | | |
| 2007-08 | *Charlton Ath* | 16 | 2 | 16 | 2 |
| 2008-09 | Sunderland | 0 | 0 | | |
| 2008-09 | *Sheffield U* | 41 | 4 | 41 | 4 |
| 2009-10 | Sunderland | 0 | 0 | 8 | 0 |
| 2009-10 | *Wolverhampton W* | 15 | 0 | | |
| 2010-11 | Wolverhampton W | 2 | 0 | 17 | 0 |
| 2010-11 | *Portsmouth* | 33 | 5 | | |
| 2011-12 | Portsmouth | 42 | 7 | 75 | 12 |
| 2012-13 | Nottingham F | 37 | 3 | 37 | 3 |

**HARDING, Dan (D)**    307   7
H: 6 0   W: 11 11   b.Gloucester 23-12-83
*Source:* Scholar. *Honours:* England Under-21.

| | | | | | |
|---|---|---|---|---|---|
| 2002-03 | Brighton & HA | 0 | 0 | | |
| 2003-04 | Brighton & HA | 23 | 0 | | |
| 2004-05 | Brighton & HA | 43 | 1 | 67 | 1 |
| 2005-06 | Leeds U | 20 | 0 | 20 | 0 |
| 2006-07 | Ipswich T | 42 | 0 | | |
| 2007-08 | Ipswich T | 30 | 1 | | |
| 2008-09 | Ipswich T | 1 | 0 | 73 | 1 |
| 2008-09 | *Southend U* | 19 | 1 | 19 | 1 |
| 2008-09 | *Reading* | 3 | 0 | 3 | 0 |
| 2009-10 | Southampton | 42 | 3 | | |
| 2010-11 | Southampton | 36 | 0 | | |
| 2011-12 | Southampton | 20 | 1 | 98 | 4 |
| 2012-13 | Nottingham F | 27 | 0 | 27 | 0 |

**HENDERSON, Darius (F)**    362   100
H: 6 3   W: 14 03   b.Sutton 7-9-81
*Source:* Trainee.

| | | | | | |
|---|---|---|---|---|---|
| 1999-2000 | Reading | 6 | 0 | | |
| 2000-01 | Reading | 4 | 0 | | |
| 2001-02 | Reading | 38 | 7 | | |
| 2002-03 | Reading | 22 | 4 | | |
| 2003-04 | Reading | 1 | 0 | 71 | 11 |
| 2003-04 | *Brighton & HA* | 10 | 2 | 10 | 2 |
| 2003-04 | *Gillingham* | 4 | 0 | | |
| 2004-05 | Gillingham | 32 | 9 | 36 | 9 |
| 2004-05 | *Swindon T* | 6 | 5 | 6 | 5 |
| 2005-06 | Watford | 30 | 14 | | |
| 2006-07 | Watford | 35 | 3 | | |
| 2007-08 | Watford | 40 | 12 | 105 | 29 |
| 2008-09 | Sheffield U | 32 | 6 | | |
| 2009-10 | Sheffield U | 32 | 12 | | |
| 2010-11 | Sheffield U | 8 | 2 | 72 | 20 |
| 2011-12 | Millwall | 31 | 15 | | |
| 2012-13 | Millwall | 20 | 7 | 51 | 22 |
| 2012-13 | Nottingham F | 11 | 2 | 11 | 2 |

**LANSBURY, Henri (M)**    133   19
H: 6 0   W: 13 06   b.Enfield 12-10-90
*Source:* Scholar. *Honours:* England Youth, Under-21.

| | | | | | |
|---|---|---|---|---|---|
| 2007-08 | Arsenal | 0 | 0 | | |
| 2008-09 | Arsenal | 0 | 0 | | |
| 2008-09 | *Scunthorpe U* | 16 | 4 | 16 | 4 |
| 2009-10 | Arsenal | 1 | 0 | | |
| 2009-10 | *Watford* | 37 | 5 | 37 | 5 |
| 2010-11 | Arsenal | 0 | 0 | | |
| 2010-11 | *Norwich C* | 23 | 4 | 23 | 4 |

| 2011-12 | Arsenal | 2 | 0 | | |
| 2011-12 | *West Ham U* | 22 | 1 | 22 | 1 |
| 2012-13 | Arsenal | 0 | 0 | 3 | 0 |
| 2012-13 | Nottingham F | 32 | 5 | 32 | 5 |

**LASCELLES, Jamaal (D)** 10 1
H: 6 2  W: 13 01  b.Derby 11-11-93
*Source:* Scholar. *Honours:* England Youth.

| 2010-11 | Nottingham F | 0 | 0 | | |
| 2011-12 | Nottingham F | 1 | 0 | | |
| 2011-12 | *Stevenage* | 7 | 1 | 7 | 1 |
| 2012-13 | Nottingham F | 2 | 0 | 3 | 0 |

**MAJEWSKI, Radoslaw (M)** 191 21
H: 5 7  W: 10 06  b.Pruszkow 15-12-86
*Source:* Znicz Pruszkow. *Honours:* Poland Under-21, Under-23, 9 full caps.

| 2006-07 | Groclin | 14 | 0 | | |
| 2007-08 | Groclin | 28 | 4 | 42 | 4 |
| 2008-09 | Polonia Warsaw | 29 | 1 | 29 | 1 |
| 2009-10 | Nottingham F | 35 | 3 | | |
| 2010-11 | Nottingham F | 26 | 2 | | |
| 2011-12 | Nottingham F | 28 | 6 | | |
| 2012-13 | Nottingham F | 31 | 5 | 120 | 16 |

**McGOLDRICK, David (F)** 205 49
H: 6 1  W: 11 10  b.Nottingham 29-11-87
*Source:* Schoolboy.

| 2003-04 | Notts Co | 4 | 0 | | |
| 2004-05 | Notts Co | 0 | 0 | | |
| 2005-06 | Southampton | 1 | 0 | | |
| 2005-06 | *Notts Co* | 6 | 0 | 10 | 0 |
| 2006-07 | Southampton | 9 | 0 | | |
| 2006-07 | *Bournemouth* | 12 | 6 | 12 | 6 |
| 2007-08 | Southampton | 8 | 0 | | |
| 2007-08 | *Port Vale* | 17 | 2 | 17 | 2 |
| 2008-09 | Southampton | 46 | 12 | 64 | 12 |
| 2009-10 | Nottingham F | 33 | 3 | | |
| 2010-11 | Nottingham F | 21 | 5 | | |
| 2011-12 | Nottingham F | 9 | 0 | | |
| 2011-12 | *Sheffield W* | 4 | 1 | 4 | 1 |
| 2012-13 | Nottingham F | 0 | 0 | 63 | 8 |
| 2012-13 | *Coventry C* | 22 | 16 | 22 | 16 |
| 2012-13 | *Ipswich T* | 13 | 4 | 13 | 4 |

**McGUGAN, Lewis (M)** 202 40
H: 5 9  W: 11 06  b.Long Eaton 25-10-88
*Source:* Scholar.

| 2006-07 | Nottingham F | 13 | 2 | | |
| 2007-08 | Nottingham F | 33 | 6 | | |
| 2008-09 | Nottingham F | 33 | 5 | | |
| 2009-10 | Nottingham F | 18 | 3 | | |
| 2010-11 | Nottingham F | 40 | 13 | | |
| 2011-12 | Nottingham F | 35 | 3 | | |
| 2012-13 | Nottingham F | 30 | 8 | 202 | 40 |

**McLAUGHLIN, Stephen (M)** 57 13
H: 5 9  W: 11 12  b.Derry 14-6-90

| 2011 | Derry C | 33 | 3 | | |
| 2012 | Derry C | 24 | 10 | 57 | 13 |
| 2012-13 | Nottingham F | 0 | 0 | | |

**MILLER, Ishmael (F)** 145 23
H: 6 3  W: 14 00  b.Manchester 5-3-87
*Source:* Scholar.

| 2005-06 | Manchester C | 1 | 0 | | |
| 2006-07 | Manchester C | 16 | 0 | | |
| 2007-08 | Manchester C | 0 | 0 | 17 | 0 |
| 2007-08 | WBA | 34 | 9 | | |
| 2008-09 | WBA | 15 | 3 | | |
| 2009-10 | WBA | 15 | 2 | | |
| 2010-11 | WBA | 6 | 0 | 70 | 14 |
| 2010-11 | *QPR* | 12 | 1 | 12 | 1 |
| 2011-12 | Nottingham F | 21 | 3 | | |
| 2012-13 | Nottingham F | 0 | 0 | 21 | 3 |
| 2012-13 | *Middlesbrough* | 25 | 5 | 25 | 5 |

**MORGAN, David (M)** 0 0
b.Northern Ireland 4-7-94
*Source:* Scholar.

| 2011-12 | Nottingham F | 0 | 0 | | |
| 2012-13 | Nottingham F | 0 | 0 | | |

**MOUSSI, Guy (M)** 216 5
H: 6 1  W: 12 11  b.Paris 23-1-85

| 2004-05 | Angers | 15 | 1 | | |
| 2005-06 | Angers | 9 | 0 | | |
| 2006-07 | Angers | 32 | 0 | | |
| 2007-08 | Angers | 35 | 1 | 91 | 2 |
| 2008-09 | Nottingham F | 15 | 0 | | |

| 2009-10 | Nottingham F | 27 | 3 | | |
| 2010-11 | Nottingham F | 31 | 0 | | |
| 2011-12 | Nottingham F | 34 | 0 | | |
| 2012-13 | Nottingham F | 18 | 0 | 125 | 3 |

**OSBORN, Ben (D)** 0 0
b.5-8-94
*Source:* Scholar.

| 2011-12 | Nottingham F | 0 | 0 | | |
| 2012-13 | Nottingham F | 0 | 0 | | |

**REID, Andy (M)** 371 42
H: 5 9  W: 12 08  b.Dublin 29-7-82
*Source:* Trainee. *Honours:* Eire Youth, Under-21, 27 full caps, 4 goals.

| 1999-2000 | Nottingham F | 0 | 0 | | |
| 2000-01 | Nottingham F | 14 | 2 | | |
| 2001-02 | Nottingham F | 29 | 0 | | |
| 2002-03 | Nottingham F | 30 | 1 | | |
| 2003-04 | Nottingham F | 46 | 13 | | |
| 2004-05 | Nottingham F | 25 | 5 | | |
| 2004-05 | Tottenham H | 13 | 1 | | |
| 2005-06 | Tottenham H | 13 | 0 | 26 | 1 |
| 2006-07 | Charlton Ath | 16 | 2 | | |
| 2007-08 | Charlton Ath | 22 | 5 | 38 | 7 |
| 2007-08 | Sunderland | 13 | 1 | | |
| 2008-09 | Sunderland | 32 | 1 | | |
| 2009-10 | Sunderland | 21 | 2 | | |
| 2010-11 | Sunderland | 2 | 0 | 68 | 4 |
| 2010-11 | *Sheffield U* | 9 | 2 | 9 | 2 |
| 2010-11 | *Blackpool* | 5 | 0 | 5 | 0 |
| 2011-12 | Nottingham F | 39 | 2 | | |
| 2012-13 | Nottingham F | 42 | 5 | 225 | 28 |

**TUDGAY, Marcus (F)** 355 81
H: 5 10  W: 12 04  b.Shoreham 3-2-83
*Source:* Trainee.

| 2002-03 | Derby Co | 8 | 0 | | |
| 2003-04 | Derby Co | 29 | 6 | | |
| 2004-05 | Derby Co | 34 | 9 | | |
| 2005-06 | Derby Co | 21 | 2 | 92 | 17 |
| 2005-06 | Sheffield W | 18 | 5 | | |
| 2006-07 | Sheffield W | 40 | 11 | | |
| 2007-08 | Sheffield W | 35 | 7 | | |
| 2008-09 | Sheffield W | 42 | 14 | | |
| 2009-10 | Sheffield W | 43 | 10 | | |
| 2010-11 | Sheffield W | 17 | 2 | 195 | 49 |
| 2010-11 | Nottingham F | 22 | 7 | | |
| 2011-12 | Nottingham F | 34 | 5 | | |
| 2012-13 | Nottingham F | 3 | 0 | 59 | 12 |
| 2012-13 | *Barnsley* | 9 | 3 | 9 | 3 |

**Players retained or with offer of contract**
Ferrier, Morgan James; Gnahore, Wilfried Desire; Grant, Jorge Edward; Otim, Derrick; Polimos, Ilias; Wallace, Kieran Neil.

**Scholars**
Ackroyd, Elliott Richard; Andrews, Jack Shaun; Durrant, Ross Eric; Elliott, Daniel John Eniton Squire; Fenton, Kieran Jetta; Gorman, Lawrence Balfour; Hollingsworth, Michael Paul Teves; Kamaneno, Aristote Amisi; Mulraney, Jake David; Myles, Aaron Jack; Palmer-Samuels, Jordan Ramone; Petravicius, Deimantas; Sebastiao, Eurico Patricio Domingos; Smith, Jordon Clifford; Thomas, Joshua William.

# NOTTS CO (58)

**ARQUIN, Yoann (F)** 41 7
H: 6 2  W: 13 04  b.Le Havre 15-4-88

| 2011-12 | Hereford U | 0 | 0 | | |
| 2012-13 | Notts Co | 41 | 7 | 41 | 7 |

**BENCHERIF, Hamza (D)** 103 19
H: 5 9  W: 12 03  b.Paris 9-2-88
*Source:* Scholar.

| 2006-07 | Nottingham F | 0 | 0 | | |
| 2007-08 | *Lincoln C* | 12 | 1 | 12 | 1 |
| 2008-09 | Nottingham F | 0 | 0 | | |
| 2009-10 | Macclesfield T | 19 | 5 | | |
| 2010-11 | Macclesfield T | 41 | 11 | 60 | 16 |
| 2011-12 | Notts Co | 20 | 2 | | |
| 2012-13 | Notts Co | 11 | 0 | 31 | 2 |

**BIALKOWSKI, Bartosz (G)** 71 0
H: 6 3  W: 12 10  b.Braniewo 6-7-87
*Honours:* Poland Under-20, Under-21.

| 2004-05 | Gornik Zabrze | 7 | 0 | 7 | 0 |
| 2005-06 | Southampton | 5 | 0 | | |
| 2006-07 | Southampton | 8 | 0 | | |
| 2007-08 | Southampton | 1 | 0 | | |
| 2008-09 | Southampton | 0 | 0 | | |
| 2009-10 | Southampton | 7 | 0 | | |
| 2009-10 | *Barnsley* | 2 | 0 | 2 | 0 |
| 2010-11 | Southampton | 0 | 0 | | |
| 2011-12 | Southampton | 1 | 0 | 22 | 0 |
| 2012-13 | Notts Co | 40 | 0 | 40 | 0 |

**BISHOP, Neil (M)** 251 14
H: 6 1  W: 12 10  b.Stockton 7-8-81
*Source:* Billingham T, Gateshead, Spennymoor U, Whitby T, Scarborough, York C.

| 2007-08 | Barnet | 39 | 2 | | |
| 2008-09 | Barnet | 44 | 1 | 83 | 3 |
| 2009-10 | Notts Co | 43 | 1 | | |
| 2010-11 | Notts Co | 43 | 1 | | |
| 2011-12 | Notts Co | 41 | 2 | | |
| 2012-13 | Notts Co | 41 | 7 | 168 | 11 |

**BOUCAUD, Andre (M)** 88 3
H: 5 8  W: 11 01  b.Enfield 10-10-84
*Source:* Scholar. *Honours:* Trinidad & Tobago 8 full caps.

| 2002-03 | Reading | 0 | 0 | | |
| 2002-03 | *Peterborough U* | 6 | 0 | | |
| 2003-04 | Reading | 0 | 0 | | |
| 2003-04 | *Peterborough U* | 8 | 1 | | |
| 2004-05 | Peterborough U | 22 | 1 | | |
| 2005-06 | Peterborough U | 3 | 0 | 39 | 2 |
| From Kettering T | | | | | |
| 2007-08 | Wycombe W | 10 | 0 | 10 | 0 |
| From Kettering T, York C, Luton T | | | | | |
| 2012-13 | Notts Co | 39 | 1 | 39 | 1 |

**CAMPBELL-RYCE, Jamal (M)** 328 27
H: 5 7  W: 12 03  b.Lambeth 6-4-83
*Source:* Scholar. *Honours:* Jamaica 20 full caps.

| 2002-03 | Charlton Ath | 1 | 0 | | |
| 2002-03 | *Leyton Orient* | 17 | 2 | | |
| 2003-04 | Charlton Ath | 2 | 0 | | |
| 2003-04 | *Wimbledon* | 4 | 0 | 4 | 0 |
| 2004-05 | Charlton Ath | 0 | 0 | 3 | 0 |
| 2004-05 | *Chesterfield* | 14 | 0 | 14 | 0 |
| 2004-05 | Rotherham U | 24 | 0 | | |
| 2005-06 | Rotherham U | 7 | 0 | 31 | 0 |
| 2005-06 | *Southend U* | 13 | 0 | | |
| 2005-06 | *Colchester U* | 4 | 0 | 4 | 0 |
| 2006-07 | Southend U | 43 | 2 | | |
| 2007-08 | Southend U | 2 | 0 | 58 | 2 |
| 2007-08 | Barnsley | 37 | 3 | | |
| 2008-09 | Barnsley | 40 | 9 | | |
| 2009-10 | Barnsley | 13 | 0 | 90 | 12 |
| 2009-10 | Bristol C | 14 | 0 | | |
| 2010-11 | Bristol C | 31 | 2 | | |
| 2011-12 | Bristol C | 17 | 0 | 62 | 2 |
| 2011-12 | *Leyton Orient* | 8 | 1 | 25 | 3 |
| 2012-13 | Notts Co | 37 | 8 | 37 | 8 |

**DIXON, Kyle (M)** 0 0
H: 5 9  W: 11 11  b.Nottingham 20-12-94

| 2012-13 | Notts Co | 0 | 0 | | |

**HOLLIS, Haydn (D)** 7 0
H: 6 4  W: 13 01  b.Selston 14-10-92
*Source:* Scholar.

| 2011-12 | Notts Co | 1 | 0 | | |
| 2012-13 | Notts Co | 6 | 0 | 7 | 0 |

**HUGHES, Jeff (D)** 348 58
H: 6 1  W: 11 00  b.Larne 29-5-85
*Source:* Larne Tech Old Boys. *Honours:* Northern Ireland Under-21, 2 full caps.

| 2003-04 | Larne | 21 | 1 | | |
| 2004-05 | Larne | 29 | 0 | 50 | 1 |
| 2005-06 | Lincoln C | 22 | 2 | | |
| 2006-07 | Lincoln C | 41 | 6 | 63 | 8 |
| 2007-08 | Lincoln C | 10 | 0 | 10 | 0 |
| 2007-08 | *Crystal Palace* | 10 | 0 | 10 | 0 |
| 2007-08 | *Peterborough U* | 7 | 1 | 7 | 1 |
| 2008-09 | Bristol R | 43 | 6 | | |
| 2009-10 | Bristol R | 44 | 12 | | |
| 2010-11 | Bristol R | 42 | 10 | 129 | 28 |

| | | | | | |
|---|---|---|---|---|---|
| 2011-12 | Notts Co | 45 | 13 | | |
| 2012-13 | Notts Co | 44 | 7 | 89 | 20 |

**JUDGE, Alan (F)**    155 23
H: 5 6   W: 11 03   b.Dublin 11-11-88
*Honours:* Eire Under-21.

| | | | | | |
|---|---|---|---|---|---|
| 2006-07 | Blackburn R | 0 | 0 | | |
| 2007-08 | Blackburn R | 0 | 0 | | |
| 2008-09 | Blackburn R | 0 | 0 | | |
| 2008-09 | *Plymouth Arg* | 17 | 2 | | |
| 2009-10 | Blackburn R | 0 | 0 | | |
| 2009-10 | *Plymouth Arg* | 37 | 5 | 54 | 7 |
| 2010-11 | Blackburn R | 0 | 0 | | |
| 2010-11 | Notts Co | 19 | 1 | | |
| 2011-12 | Notts Co | 43 | 7 | | |
| 2012-13 | Notts Co | 39 | 8 | 101 | 16 |

**KELLY, Julian (D)**    91 5
H: 5 8   W: 11 04   b.Enfield 6-9-89
*Source:* Arsenal Scholar.

| | | | | | |
|---|---|---|---|---|---|
| 2008-09 | Reading | 7 | 0 | | |
| 2009-10 | Reading | 0 | 0 | | |
| 2009-10 | *Wycombe W* | 9 | 1 | 9 | 1 |
| 2010-11 | Reading | 0 | 0 | 7 | 0 |
| 2010-11 | *Lincoln C* | 21 | 0 | 21 | 0 |
| 2011-12 | Notts Co | 32 | 3 | | |
| 2012-13 | Notts Co | 22 | 1 | 54 | 4 |

**LABADIE, Joss (M)**    126 21
H: 5 7   W: 11 02   b.Croydon 31-8-90

| | | | | | |
|---|---|---|---|---|---|
| 2008-09 | WBA | 0 | 0 | | |
| 2008-09 | *Shrewsbury T* | 1 | 0 | | |
| 2009-10 | WBA | 0 | 0 | | |
| 2009-10 | *Shrewsbury T* | 13 | 5 | 14 | 5 |
| 2009-10 | *Cheltenham T* | 11 | 0 | 11 | 0 |
| 2009-10 | *Tranmere R* | 9 | 3 | | |
| 2010-11 | Tranmere R | 34 | 2 | | |
| 2011-12 | Tranmere R | 27 | 5 | 70 | 10 |
| 2012-13 | Notts Co | 24 | 2 | 24 | 2 |
| 2012-13 | *Torquay U* | 7 | 4 | 7 | 4 |

**LAVELLE-MOORE, Malachi (F)**    0 0
H: 5 11   W: 13 05

| | | | | |
|---|---|---|---|---|
| 2012-13 | Notts Co | 0 | 0 | |

**LEACOCK, Dean (D)**    196 2
H: 6 2   W: 12 04   b.Croydon 10-6-84
*Source:* Trainee. *Honours:* England Youth, Under-20.

| | | | | | |
|---|---|---|---|---|---|
| 2002-03 | Fulham | 0 | 0 | | |
| 2003-04 | Fulham | 4 | 0 | | |
| 2004-05 | Fulham | 0 | 0 | | |
| 2004-05 | *Coventry C* | 13 | 0 | 13 | 0 |
| 2005-06 | Fulham | 5 | 0 | | |
| 2006-07 | Fulham | 0 | 0 | 9 | 0 |
| 2006-07 | Derby Co | 38 | 0 | | |
| 2007-08 | Derby Co | 26 | 0 | | |
| 2008-09 | Derby Co | 11 | 0 | | |
| 2009-10 | Derby Co | 17 | 0 | | |
| 2010-11 | Derby Co | 25 | 1 | | |
| 2011-12 | Derby Co | 0 | 0 | 117 | 1 |
| 2011-12 | *Leyton Orient* | 15 | 0 | 15 | 0 |
| 2012-13 | Notts Co | 42 | 1 | 42 | 1 |

**LIDDLE, Gary (D)**    293 18
H: 6 1   W: 12 06   b.Middlesbrough 15-6-86
*Source:* Trainee. *Honours:* England Youth.

| | | | | | |
|---|---|---|---|---|---|
| 2003-04 | Middlesbrough | 0 | 0 | | |
| 2004-05 | Middlesbrough | 0 | 0 | | |
| 2005-06 | Middlesbrough | 0 | 0 | | |
| 2006-07 | Hartlepool U | 42 | 3 | | |
| 2007-08 | Hartlepool U | 41 | 2 | | |
| 2008-09 | Hartlepool U | 43 | 0 | | |
| 2009-10 | Hartlepool U | 40 | 3 | | |
| 2010-11 | Hartlepool U | 42 | 6 | | |
| 2011-12 | Hartlepool U | 39 | 4 | 247 | 18 |
| 2012-13 | Notts Co | 46 | 0 | 46 | 0 |

**MAHON, Gavin (M)**    451 19
H: 5 11   W: 13 07   b.Birmingham 2-1-77
*Source:* Trainee.

| | | | | | |
|---|---|---|---|---|---|
| 1995-96 | Wolverhampton W | 0 | 0 | | |
| 1996-97 | Hereford U | 11 | 1 | | |
| 1997-98 | Hereford U | 0 | 0 | | |
| 1998-99 | Hereford U | 0 | 0 | 11 | 1 |
| 1998-99 | Brentford | 29 | 4 | | |
| 1999-2000 | Brentford | 37 | 3 | | |
| 2000-01 | Brentford | 40 | 1 | | |
| 2001-02 | Brentford | 35 | 0 | 141 | 8 |
| 2001-02 | Watford | 6 | 0 | | |
| 2002-03 | Watford | 17 | 0 | | |
| 2003-04 | Watford | 32 | 2 | | |
| 2004-05 | Watford | 43 | 0 | | |
| 2005-06 | Watford | 38 | 3 | | |
| 2006-07 | Watford | 34 | 1 | | |
| 2007-08 | Watford | 19 | 0 | 189 | 6 |
| 2007-08 | QPR | 16 | 1 | | |
| 2008-09 | QPR | 35 | 2 | | |
| 2009-10 | QPR | 7 | 1 | | |
| 2010-11 | QPR | 0 | 0 | 58 | 4 |
| 2010-11 | *Crystal Palace* | 0 | 0 | | |
| 2011-12 | Notts Co | 31 | 0 | | |
| 2012-13 | Notts Co | 12 | 0 | 43 | 0 |
| 2012-13 | *Stevenage* | 9 | 0 | 9 | 0 |

**NANGLE, Romello (F)**    7 1
b.Nottingham 20-12-94

| | | | | | |
|---|---|---|---|---|---|
| 2012-13 | Notts Co | 7 | 1 | 7 | 1 |

**PEARCE, Krystian (D)**    135 7
H: 6 1   W: 13 05   b.Birmingham 5-1-90
*Source:* Scholar. *Honours:* England Youth.

| | | | | | |
|---|---|---|---|---|---|
| 2006-07 | Birmingham C | 0 | 0 | | |
| 2007-08 | Birmingham C | 0 | 0 | | |
| 2007-08 | *Port Vale* | 12 | 0 | 12 | 0 |
| 2007-08 | *Notts Co* | 8 | 1 | | |
| 2008-09 | Birmingham C | 0 | 0 | | |
| 2008-09 | *Scunthorpe U* | 39 | 0 | 39 | 0 |
| 2009-10 | Birmingham C | 0 | 0 | | |
| 2009-10 | *Peterborough U* | 2 | 0 | 2 | 0 |
| 2009-10 | *Huddersfield T* | 1 | 0 | 1 | 0 |
| 2010-11 | Notts Co | 27 | 1 | | |
| 2011-12 | Notts Co | 27 | 3 | | |
| 2012-13 | Notts Co | 2 | 1 | 64 | 6 |
| 2012-13 | *Barnet* | 17 | 1 | 17 | 1 |

**PILKINGTON, Kevin (G)**    361 0
H: 6 1   W: 13 08   b.Hitchin 8-3-74
*Source:* Trainee. *Honours:* England Schools.

| | | | | | |
|---|---|---|---|---|---|
| 1992-93 | Manchester U | 0 | 0 | | |
| 1993-94 | Manchester U | 0 | 0 | | |
| 1994-95 | Manchester U | 1 | 0 | | |
| 1995-96 | Manchester U | 3 | 0 | | |
| 1995-96 | *Rochdale* | 6 | 0 | 6 | 0 |
| 1996-97 | Manchester U | 0 | 0 | | |
| 1996-97 | *Rotherham U* | 17 | 0 | 17 | 0 |
| 1997-98 | Manchester U | 2 | 0 | 6 | 0 |
| 1998-99 | Port Vale | 8 | 0 | | |
| 1999-2000 | Port Vale | 15 | 0 | 23 | 0 |
| 2000-01 | Mansfield T | 2 | 0 | | |
| 2001-02 | Mansfield T | 45 | 0 | | |
| 2002-03 | Mansfield T | 32 | 0 | | |
| 2003-04 | Mansfield T | 46 | 0 | | |
| 2004-05 | Mansfield T | 42 | 0 | 167 | 0 |
| 2005-06 | Notts Co | 45 | 0 | | |
| 2006-07 | Notts Co | 39 | 0 | | |
| 2007-08 | Notts Co | 32 | 0 | | |
| 2008-09 | Notts Co | 25 | 0 | | |

From Luton T, Mansfield T

| | | | | | |
|---|---|---|---|---|---|
| 2012-13 | Notts Co | 1 | 0 | 142 | 0 |

**SHEEHAN, Alan (D)**    180 8
H: 5 11   W: 11 02   b.Athlone 14-9-86
*Source:* Scholar. *Honours:* Eire Youth, Under-21.

| | | | | | |
|---|---|---|---|---|---|
| 2004-05 | Leicester C | 1 | 0 | | |
| 2005-06 | Leicester C | 2 | 0 | | |
| 2006-07 | Leicester C | 0 | 0 | | |
| 2006-07 | *Mansfield T* | 10 | 0 | 10 | 0 |
| 2007-08 | Leicester C | 20 | 1 | 23 | 1 |
| 2007-08 | Leeds U | 10 | 1 | | |
| 2008-09 | Leeds U | 11 | 1 | | |
| 2008-09 | *Crewe Alex* | 3 | 0 | 3 | 0 |
| 2009-10 | Leeds U | 0 | 0 | | |
| 2009-10 | *Oldham Ath* | 8 | 1 | 8 | 1 |
| 2009-10 | *Swindon T* | 22 | 1 | | |
| 2010-11 | Leeds U | 0 | 0 | 21 | 2 |
| 2010-11 | Swindon T | 21 | 1 | 43 | 2 |
| 2011-12 | Notts Co | 39 | 2 | | |
| 2012-13 | Notts Co | 33 | 0 | 72 | 2 |

**SHOWUNMI, Enoch (F)**    269 44
H: 6 3   W: 14 11   b.Kilburn 21-4-82
*Source:* Willesden Constantine. *Honours:* Nigeria 2 full caps.

| | | | | | |
|---|---|---|---|---|---|
| 2003-04 | Luton T | 26 | 7 | | |
| 2004-05 | Luton T | 35 | 6 | | |
| 2005-06 | Luton T | 41 | 1 | 102 | 14 |
| 2006-07 | Bristol C | 33 | 10 | | |
| 2007-08 | Bristol C | 17 | 3 | 50 | 13 |
| 2007-08 | *Sheffield W* | 10 | 0 | 10 | 0 |
| 2008-09 | Leeds U | 8 | 2 | | |
| 2009-10 | Leeds U | 7 | 0 | 15 | 2 |
| 2010-11 | Tranmere R | 43 | 11 | | |
| 2011-12 | Tranmere R | 27 | 3 | 70 | 14 |
| 2012-13 | Notts Co | 22 | 1 | 22 | 1 |

**SMITH, Manny (D)**    129 7
H: 6 2   W: 12 03   b.Birmingham 8-11-88
*Source:* Scholar.

| | | | | | |
|---|---|---|---|---|---|
| 2005-06 | Walsall | 0 | 0 | | |
| 2006-07 | Walsall | 3 | 0 | | |
| 2007-08 | Walsall | 4 | 0 | | |
| 2008-09 | Walsall | 26 | 0 | | |
| 2009-10 | Walsall | 33 | 4 | | |
| 2010-11 | Walsall | 25 | 2 | | |
| 2011-12 | Walsall | 33 | 1 | 124 | 7 |
| 2012-13 | Notts Co | 5 | 0 | 5 | 0 |

**SPIESS, Fabian (G)**    7 0
H: 6 2   W: 12 09   b.Germany 30-11-93

| | | | | | |
|---|---|---|---|---|---|
| 2011-12 | Notts Co | 0 | 0 | | |
| 2012-13 | Notts Co | 7 | 0 | 7 | 0 |

**STEWART, Damion (D)**    218 13
H: 6 3   W: 13 10   b.Jamaica 18-8-80
*Source:* Harbour View. *Honours:* Jamaica 56 full caps, 3 goals.

| | | | | | |
|---|---|---|---|---|---|
| 2005-06 | Bradford C | 23 | 1 | 23 | 1 |
| 2006-07 | QPR | 45 | 1 | | |
| 2007-08 | QPR | 39 | 5 | | |
| 2008-09 | QPR | 37 | 2 | | |
| 2009-10 | QPR | 30 | 1 | 151 | 9 |
| 2010-11 | Bristol C | 21 | 1 | | |
| 2011-12 | Bristol C | 3 | 0 | | |
| 2011-12 | *Notts Co* | 17 | 2 | | |
| 2012-13 | Bristol C | 0 | 0 | 24 | 1 |
| 2012-13 | Notts Co | 3 | 0 | 20 | 2 |

Transferred to Pahang April 2013

**TEMPEST, Greg (M)**    3 0
H: 6 0   W: 11 04   b.Nottingham 28-12-95
*Honours:* Northern Ireland Under-21.

| | | | | | |
|---|---|---|---|---|---|
| 2012-13 | Notts Co | 3 | 0 | 3 | 0 |

**THOMPSON, Curtis (M)**    2 0
H: 5 10   W: 12 06   b.Nottingham 2-9-93
*Source:* Scholar.

| | | | | | |
|---|---|---|---|---|---|
| 2011-12 | Notts Co | 0 | 0 | | |
| 2012-13 | Notts Co | 2 | 0 | 2 | 0 |

**WAITE, Tyrell (F)**    8 1
H: 5 11   W: 12 08   b.Derby 1-7-94
*Source:* Ilkeston.

| | | | | | |
|---|---|---|---|---|---|
| 2011-12 | Notts Co | 0 | 0 | | |
| 2012-13 | Notts Co | 8 | 1 | 8 | 1 |

**WHOLEY, Jake (D)**    2 0
H: 5 10   W: 12 04   b.Nottingham 1-12-93
*Source:* Scholar.

| | | | | | |
|---|---|---|---|---|---|
| 2010-11 | Notts Co | 1 | 0 | | |
| 2011-12 | Notts Co | 0 | 0 | | |
| 2012-13 | Notts Co | 1 | 0 | 2 | 0 |

**WILLIAMS, Tom (M)**    1 0
H: 5 11   W: 12 05   b.Carshalton 8-7-80
*Source:* Kettering.

| | | | | | |
|---|---|---|---|---|---|
| 2012-13 | Notts Co | 1 | 0 | 1 | 0 |

**ZOKO, Francois (F)**    351 60
H: 6 0   W: 11 05   b.Daloa 15-9-83

| | | | | | |
|---|---|---|---|---|---|
| 2001-02 | Nancy | 24 | 3 | | |
| 2002-03 | Nancy | 28 | 2 | | |
| 2003-04 | Nancy | 19 | 3 | 71 | 8 |
| 2004-05 | Laval | 27 | 7 | | |
| 2005-06 | Laval | 33 | 2 | 60 | 9 |
| 2006-07 | Mons | 23 | 4 | | |
| 2007-08 | Mons | 32 | 8 | 55 | 12 |
| 2008-09 | Hacettepe | 27 | 1 | 27 | 1 |
| 2009-10 | Ostend | 11 | 4 | 11 | 4 |
| 2010-11 | Carlisle U | 44 | 6 | | |
| 2011-12 | Carlisle U | 45 | 13 | | |
| 2012-13 | Carlisle U | 0 | 0 | 89 | 19 |
| 2012-13 | Notts Co | 38 | 7 | 38 | 7 |

**Players retained or with offer of contract**
Smith, Emmanuele.

**Scholars**
Andrews, Harry Marcus; Bange, Glodi; Campbell, Kameron Lewis; Clarke, Mitchell;

Crust, Matthew James; Dixon, Kyle Antony; Geldenhuys, Kieran; Golding, Jack Callum; Guest, Liam Anthony; Guy, Tyler Richard; Hodge, Elliot Stephen; Lavelle-Moore, Malachi Azar Airto Liam; McGowan, Brad; Nangle, Romello Desmond Camar; Randall, James Elliott.

## OLDHAM ATH (59)

**BAXTER, Jose (F)**     60 16
H: 5 10  W: 11 07  b.Bootle 7-2-92
*Source:* Academy. *Honours:* England Youth.
| | | | | |
|---|---|---|---|---|
| 2008-09 | Everton | 3 | 0 | | |
| 2009-10 | Everton | 2 | 0 | | |
| 2010-11 | Everton | 1 | 0 | | |
| 2011-12 | Everton | 1 | 0 | | |
| 2011-12 | *Tranmere R* | 14 | 3 | 14 | 3 |
| 2012-13 | Everton | 0 | 0 | 7 | 0 |
| 2012-13 | Crystal Palace | 0 | 0 | | |
| 2012-13 | Oldham Ath | 39 | 13 | 39 | 13 |

**BELEZIKA, Glenn (D)**    4 0
H: 5 11  W: 13 01  b.Camden 24-12-94
*Source:* Stalybridge C.
| | | | | |
|---|---|---|---|---|
| 2011-12 | Oldham Ath | 1 | 0 | | |
| 2012-13 | Oldham Ath | 3 | 0 | 4 | 0 |

**BOUZANIS, Dean (G)**    59 0
H: 6 1  W: 13 06  b.Sydney 2-10-90
*Source:* St George Saints, Sydney, Melbourne Vic.
| | | | | |
|---|---|---|---|---|
| 2007-08 | Liverpool | 0 | 0 | | |
| 2008-09 | Liverpool | 0 | 0 | | |
| 2009-10 | Liverpool | 0 | 0 | | |
| 2009-10 | *Accrington S* | 14 | 0 | 14 | 0 |
| 2010-11 | Liverpool | 0 | 0 | | |
| 2011-12 | Oldham Ath | 9 | 0 | | |
| 2012-13 | Oldham Ath | 36 | 0 | 45 | 0 |

**BROWN, Connor (D)**    25 0
H: 5 8  W: 10 12  b.Sheffield 2-10-91
*Source:* Scholar.
| | | | | |
|---|---|---|---|---|
| 2010-11 | Sheffield U | 0 | 0 | | |
| 2011-12 | Sheffield U | 0 | 0 | | |
| 2012-13 | Oldham Ath | 25 | 0 | 25 | 0 |

**BURNS, Ryan (M)**    1 0
H: 6 1  W: 10 07  b.Belfast 8-9-92
*Source:* Scholar.
| | | | | |
|---|---|---|---|---|
| 2010-11 | Oldham Ath | 1 | 0 | | |
| 2011-12 | Oldham Ath | 0 | 0 | | |
| 2012-13 | Oldham Ath | 0 | 0 | 1 | 0 |

**BYRNE, Cliff (D)**    311 10
H: 6 0  W: 12 11  b.Dublin 27-4-82
*Honours:* Eire Youth, Under-21.
| | | | | |
|---|---|---|---|---|
| 1999-2000 | Sunderland | 0 | 0 | | |
| 2000-01 | Sunderland | 0 | 0 | | |
| 2001-02 | Sunderland | 0 | 0 | | |
| 2002-03 | Sunderland | 0 | 0 | | |
| 2002-03 | *Scunthorpe U* | 13 | 0 | | |
| 2003-04 | Scunthorpe U | 39 | 1 | | |
| 2004-05 | Scunthorpe U | 29 | 1 | | |
| 2005-06 | Scunthorpe U | 32 | 1 | | |
| 2006-07 | Scunthorpe U | 24 | 0 | | |
| 2007-08 | Scunthorpe U | 25 | 0 | | |
| 2008-09 | Scunthorpe U | 43 | 2 | | |
| 2009-10 | Scunthorpe U | 36 | 2 | | |
| 2010-11 | Scunthorpe U | 21 | 2 | | |
| 2011-12 | Scunthorpe U | 14 | 0 | 276 | 9 |
| 2012-13 | Oldham Ath | 35 | 1 | 35 | 1 |

**CISAK, Aleksander (G)**    70 0
H: 6 3  W: 14 11  b.Krakow 19-5-89
*Source:* Scholar. *Honours:* Australia Under-20.
| | | | | |
|---|---|---|---|---|
| 2006-07 | Leicester C | 0 | 0 | | |
| 2007-08 | Leicester C | 0 | 0 | | |
| 2008-09 | Leicester C | 0 | 0 | | |
| 2009-10 | Leicester C | 0 | 0 | | |
| 2010-11 | *Accrington S* | 21 | 0 | 21 | 0 |
| 2011-12 | Oldham Ath | 38 | 0 | | |
| 2012-13 | Oldham Ath | 10 | 0 | 48 | 0 |
| 2012-13 | *Portsmouth* | 1 | 0 | 1 | 0 |

**COOPER, Joe (D)**    1 0
b. 25-9-93
| | | | | |
|---|---|---|---|---|
| 2012-13 | Oldham Ath | 1 | 0 | 1 | 0 |

**CROFT, Lee (F)**     244 14
H: 5 11  W: 13 00  b.Wigan 21-6-85
*Source:* Scholar. *Honours:* England Youth, Under-20.
| | | | | |
|---|---|---|---|---|
| 2002-03 | Manchester C | 0 | 0 | | |
| 2003-04 | Manchester C | 0 | 0 | | |
| 2004-05 | Manchester C | 7 | 0 | | |
| 2004-05 | *Oldham Ath* | 12 | 0 | | |
| 2005-06 | Manchester C | 21 | 1 | 28 | 1 |
| 2006-07 | Norwich C | 36 | 3 | | |
| 2007-08 | Norwich C | 41 | 1 | | |
| 2008-09 | Norwich C | 41 | 5 | 118 | 0 |
| 2009-10 | Derby Co | 19 | 1 | | |
| 2010-11 | Derby Co | 0 | 0 | | |
| 2010-11 | *Huddersfield T* | 3 | 0 | 3 | 0 |
| 2011-12 | Derby Co | 8 | 0 | | |
| 2011-12 | *St Johnstone* | 11 | 3 | 11 | 3 |
| 2012-13 | Derby Co | 0 | 0 | 27 | 1 |
| 2012-13 | Oldham Ath | 45 | 0 | 57 | 0 |

**FURMAN, Dean (M)**    172 12
H: 6 0  W: 11 08  b.Cape Town 22-6-88
*Source:* Chelsea Scholar. *Honours:* South Africa 8 full caps.
| | | | | |
|---|---|---|---|---|
| 2007-08 | Rangers | 1 | 0 | 1 | 0 |
| 2008-09 | *Bradford C* | 32 | 4 | 32 | 4 |
| 2009-10 | Oldham Ath | 38 | 0 | | |
| 2010-11 | Oldham Ath | 42 | 5 | | |
| 2011-12 | Oldham Ath | 23 | 1 | | |
| 2012-13 | Oldham Ath | 28 | 2 | 131 | 8 |
| 2012-13 | *Doncaster R* | 8 | 0 | 8 | 0 |

**GOSSET, Danny (M)**    2 0
H: 5 11  W: 11 11  b. 21-2-95
| | | | | |
|---|---|---|---|---|
| 2012-13 | Oldham Ath | 2 | 0 | 2 | 0 |

**GROUNDS, Jonathan (D)**    120 5
H: 6 1  W: 13 10  b.Thornaby 2-2-88
*Source:* Scholar.
| | | | | |
|---|---|---|---|---|
| 2007-08 | Middlesbrough | 5 | 0 | | |
| 2008-09 | Middlesbrough | 2 | 0 | | |
| 2008-09 | *Norwich C* | 16 | 3 | 16 | 3 |
| 2009-10 | Middlesbrough | 20 | 0 | | |
| 2010-11 | Middlesbrough | 6 | 1 | | |
| 2011-12 | Middlesbrough | 0 | 0 | 33 | 1 |
| 2011-12 | *Chesterfield* | 13 | 0 | 13 | 0 |
| 2011-12 | *Yeovil T* | 14 | 0 | 14 | 0 |
| 2012-13 | Oldham Ath | 44 | 1 | 44 | 1 |

**HUGHES, Connor (M)**    7 0
H: 5 11  W: 12 10  b.Bolton 6-5-93
*Source:* Scholar.
| | | | | |
|---|---|---|---|---|
| 2011-12 | Oldham Ath | 4 | 0 | | |
| 2012-13 | Oldham Ath | 3 | 0 | 7 | 0 |

**JACOB, Liam (G)**    1 0
H: 6 3  W: 11 08  b.Sydney 18-8-94
*Source:* Scholar.
| | | | | |
|---|---|---|---|---|
| 2012-13 | Oldham Ath | 1 | 0 | 1 | 0 |

**M'CHANGAMA, Youssouf (M)**    60 6
H: 5 9  W: 11 00  b.Marseille 29-8-90
*Honours:* Comoros 5 full caps.
| | | | | |
|---|---|---|---|---|
| 2009-10 | Sedan B | 10 | 2 | 10 | 2 |
| 2010-11 | Troyes B | 24 | 2 | 24 | 2 |
| 2011-12 | Oldham Ath | 10 | 0 | | |
| 2012-13 | Oldham Ath | 16 | 2 | 26 | 2 |

**MELLOR, David (D)**    26 1
H: 5 9  W: 11 09  b.Oldham 10-7-93
*Source:* Scholar.
| | | | | |
|---|---|---|---|---|
| 2011-12 | Oldham Ath | 21 | 1 | | |
| 2012-13 | Oldham Ath | 5 | 0 | 26 | 1 |

**MILLAR, Kirk (M)**    28 1
H: 5 9  W: 10 07  b.Belfast 7-7-92
*Source:* Scholar. *Honours:* Northern Ireland Under-21.
| | | | | |
|---|---|---|---|---|
| 2008-09 | Linfield | 1 | 0 | 1 | 0 |
| 2009-10 | Oldham Ath | 6 | 0 | | |
| 2010-11 | Oldham Ath | 5 | 0 | | |
| 2011-12 | Oldham Ath | 4 | 0 | | |
| 2012-13 | Oldham Ath | 12 | 1 | 27 | 1 |

**MONTANO, Cristian (F)**    68 11
H: 5 11  W: 12 00  b.Cali 11-12-91
*Source:* Scholar.
| | | | | |
|---|---|---|---|---|
| 2010-11 | West Ham U | 0 | 0 | | |
| 2011-12 | West Ham U | 0 | 0 | | |
| 2011-12 | *Notts Co* | 15 | 4 | 15 | 4 |
| 2011-12 | *Swindon T* | 4 | 1 | 4 | 1 |
| 2011-12 | *Dagenham & R* | 10 | 3 | 10 | 3 |

**MURRAY, Paul (M)**     497 31
H: 5 9  W: 10 08  b.Carlisle 31-8-76
*Source:* Trainee. *Honours:* England Youth, Under-21, B.
| | | | | |
|---|---|---|---|---|
| 1993-94 | Carlisle U | 8 | 0 | | |
| 1994-95 | Carlisle U | 5 | 0 | | |
| 1995-96 | Carlisle U | 28 | 1 | | |
| 1995-96 | QPR | 1 | 0 | | |
| 1996-97 | QPR | 32 | 5 | | |
| 1997-98 | QPR | 32 | 1 | | |
| 1997-98 | QPR | 0 | 0 | | |
| 1998-99 | QPR | 39 | 1 | | |
| 1999-2000 | QPR | 30 | 0 | | |
| 2000-01 | QPR | 6 | 0 | 140 | 7 |
| 2001-02 | Southampton | 1 | 0 | 1 | 0 |
| 2001-02 | Oldham Ath | 24 | 5 | | |
| 2002-03 | Oldham Ath | 30 | 1 | | |
| 2003-04 | Oldham Ath | 41 | 9 | | |
| 2004-05 | Beira Mar | 17 | 2 | | |
| 2005-06 | Beira Mar | 0 | 0 | 17 | 2 |
| 2006-07 | Carlisle U | 14 | 1 | 55 | 2 |
| 2007-08 | Gretna | 32 | 1 | 32 | 1 |
| 2008-09 | Shrewsbury T | 32 | 2 | | |
| 2009-10 | Shrewsbury T | 27 | 0 | 59 | 2 |
| 2010-11 | Hartlepool U | 36 | 1 | | |
| 2011-12 | Hartlepool U | 45 | 1 | | |
| 2012-13 | Hartlepool U | 17 | 0 | 98 | 2 |
| 2012-13 | Oldham Ath | 0 | 0 | 95 | 15 |

**MVOTO, Jean-Yves (D)**    122 8
H: 6 4  W: 14 00  b.Paris 6-9-88
*Source:* Paris St Germain. *Honours:* France Youth.
| | | | | |
|---|---|---|---|---|
| 2007-08 | Sunderland | 0 | 0 | | |
| 2008-09 | Sunderland | 0 | 0 | | |
| 2009-10 | Sunderland | 0 | 0 | | |
| 2009-10 | *Southend U* | 17 | 1 | 17 | 1 |
| 2010-11 | Sunderland | 0 | 0 | | |
| 2010-11 | *Oldham Ath* | 27 | 2 | | |
| 2011-12 | Oldham Ath | 36 | 1 | | |
| 2012-13 | Oldham Ath | 42 | 4 | 105 | 7 |

**SIMPSON, Luke (G)**    0 0
H: 5 10  W: 12 03  b.Bury 23-9-94
| | | | | |
|---|---|---|---|---|
| 2012-13 | Oldham Ath | 0 | 0 | | |

**SIMPSON, Robbie (F)**    167 16
H: 6 1  W: 11 11  b.Poole 15-3-85
*Source:* Cambridge U.
| | | | | |
|---|---|---|---|---|
| 2007-08 | Coventry C | 28 | 1 | | |
| 2008-09 | Coventry C | 33 | 3 | 61 | 4 |
| 2009-10 | Huddersfield T | 13 | 0 | | |
| 2010-11 | Huddersfield T | 0 | 0 | | |
| 2010-11 | *Brentford* | 27 | 4 | 27 | 4 |
| 2011-12 | Huddersfield T | 0 | 0 | 13 | 0 |
| 2011-12 | Oldham Ath | 29 | 6 | | |
| 2012-13 | Oldham Ath | 37 | 2 | 66 | 8 |

**SMITH, Matt (F)**    70 10
H: 6 6  W: 14 00  b.Birmingham 7-6-89
*Source:* Cheltenham T Scholar, Redditch U, Droylsden, Solihull Moors.
| | | | | |
|---|---|---|---|---|
| 2011-12 | Oldham Ath | 28 | 3 | | |
| 2011-12 | *Macclesfield T* | 8 | 1 | 8 | 1 |
| 2012-13 | Oldham Ath | 34 | 6 | 62 | 9 |

**SUTHERLAND, Chris (M)**    10 0
H: 5 11  W: 11 11  b.Middleton 4-8-95
| | | | | |
|---|---|---|---|---|
| 2012-13 | Oldham Ath | 10 | 0 | 10 | 0 |

**TARKOWSKI, James (D)**    46 3
H: 6 1  W: 12 10  b.Manchester 19-11-92
*Source:* Scholar.
| | | | | |
|---|---|---|---|---|
| 2010-11 | Oldham Ath | 9 | 0 | | |
| 2011-12 | Oldham Ath | 16 | 1 | | |
| 2012-13 | Oldham Ath | 21 | 2 | 46 | 3 |

**TAYLOR, Daniel (F)**    8 1
H: 6 0  W: 12 09  b.Newcastle 17-3-93
| | | | | |
|---|---|---|---|---|
| 2012-13 | Oldham Ath | 8 | 1 | 8 | 1 |

**TRUELOVE, Jack (D)**    1 0
| | | | | |
|---|---|---|---|---|
| 2012-13 | Oldham Ath | 1 | 0 | 1 | 0 |

**WESOLOWSKI, James (M)** 173 9
H: 5 8  W: 11 11  b.Sydney 25-8-87
*Source:* Scholar. *Honours:* Australia Youth, Under-20.

| | | | | | |
|---|---|---|---|---|---|
| 2004-05 | Leicester C | 5 | 0 | | |
| 2005-06 | Leicester C | 5 | 0 | | |
| 2006-07 | Leicester C | 19 | 0 | | |
| 2007-08 | Leicester C | 22 | 0 | | |
| 2008-09 | Leicester C | 0 | 0 | | |
| 2008-09 | *Dundee U* | 8 | 0 | 8 | 0 |
| 2008-09 | *Cheltenham T* | 4 | 0 | 4 | 0 |
| 2009-10 | Leicester C | 0 | 0 | | |
| 2009-10 | *Hamilton A* | 29 | 4 | 29 | 4 |
| 2010-11 | Peterborough U | 32 | 2 | 32 | 2 |
| 2011-12 | Oldham Ath | 21 | 3 | | |
| 2012-13 | Oldham Ath | 33 | 0 | 54 | 3 |

**WINCHESTER, Carl (D)** 27 1
H: 5 10  W: 11 08  b.Belfast 12-4-93
*Source:* Scholar. *Honours:* Northern Ireland Under-21, 1 full cap.

| | | | | | |
|---|---|---|---|---|---|
| 2010-11 | Oldham Ath | 6 | 1 | | |
| 2011-12 | Oldham Ath | 12 | 0 | | |
| 2012-13 | Oldham Ath | 9 | 0 | 27 | 1 |

**Scholars**
Bove, Jordon; Brewster, Michael; Clarke, Tomos Allen; Coleman, Joel; Cooper, Joseph Mark; Edwards, Joseph Brian; Foulds, Haydn James; Gosset, Daniel Sion; Hardman, Kyle; Jones, Tomos Emlyn; Kinder, William Michael; McIntosh, Carlton Jordan; Poxon, Jack Elliott; Pritchard, John Vincent; Simpson, Luke Thomas; Sutherland, Christopher Paul; Truelove, Jack Christopher; Wandless, Luke Shaun.

# OXFORD U (60)

**BATT, Damian (D)** 127 2
H: 5 10  W: 11 06  b.Hoddesdon 16-9-84
*Source:* Norwich C Trainee.

| | | | | | |
|---|---|---|---|---|---|
| 2005-06 | Barnet | 22 | 0 | 22 | 0 |

From St Albans C, Stevenage, Woking, Fisher Ath, Grays Ath.

| | | | | | |
|---|---|---|---|---|---|
| 2010-11 | Oxford U | 28 | 0 | | |
| 2011-12 | Oxford U | 40 | 1 | | |
| 2012-13 | Oxford U | 37 | 1 | 105 | 2 |

**BROWN, Wayne (G)** 286 0
H: 6 0  W: 13 11  b.Southampton 14-1-77
*Source:* Supersport U.

| | | | | | |
|---|---|---|---|---|---|
| 1993-94 | Bristol C | 1 | 0 | | |
| 1994-95 | Bristol C | 0 | 0 | | |
| 1995-96 | Bristol C | 0 | 0 | 1 | 0 |

From Weston-S-Mare.

| | | | | | |
|---|---|---|---|---|---|
| 1996-97 | Chester C | 2 | 0 | | |
| 1997-98 | Chester C | 13 | 0 | | |
| 1998-99 | Chester C | 23 | 0 | | |
| 1999-2000 | Chester C | 46 | 0 | | |
| 2000-01 | Chester C | 0 | 0 | | |
| 2001-02 | Chester C | 0 | 0 | | |
| 2004-05 | Chester C | 23 | 0 | | |
| 2005-06 | Chester C | 0 | 0 | 107 | 0 |
| 2006-07 | Hereford U | 39 | 0 | | |
| 2007-08 | Hereford U | 44 | 0 | 83 | 0 |
| 2008-09 | Bury | 35 | 0 | | |
| 2009-10 | Bury | 41 | 0 | 76 | 0 |
| 2010-11 | Supersport U | 13 | 0 | 13 | 0 |
| 2011-12 | Oxford U | 2 | 0 | | |
| 2012-13 | Oxford U | 4 | 0 | 6 | 0 |

**CAPALDI, Tony (D)** 254 12
H: 6 0  W: 11 08  b.Porsgrunn 12-8-81
*Source:* Trainee. *Honours:* Northern Ireland Youth, Under-21, 22 full caps.

| | | | | | |
|---|---|---|---|---|---|
| 1999-2000 | Birmingham C | 0 | 0 | | |
| 2000-01 | Birmingham C | 0 | 0 | | |
| 2001-02 | Birmingham C | 0 | 0 | | |
| 2002-03 | Birmingham C | 1 | 0 | | |
| 2002-03 | Plymouth Arg | 0 | 0 | | |
| 2003-04 | Plymouth Arg | 33 | 7 | | |
| 2004-05 | Plymouth Arg | 45 | 2 | | |
| 2005-06 | Plymouth Arg | 41 | 3 | | |
| 2006-07 | Plymouth Arg | 31 | 0 | 141 | 12 |
| 2007-08 | Cardiff C | 44 | 0 | | |
| 2008-09 | Cardiff C | 3 | 0 | | |
| 2009-10 | Cardiff C | 15 | 0 | 62 | 0 |

| | | | | | |
|---|---|---|---|---|---|
| 2009-10 | *Leeds U* | 3 | 0 | 3 | 0 |
| 2010-11 | *Morecambe* | 18 | 0 | 18 | 0 |
| 2011-12 | Oxford U | 1 | 0 | | |
| 2012-13 | Oxford U | 29 | 0 | 30 | 0 |

**CHAPMAN, Adam (M)** 40 2
H: 5 10  W: 11 00  b.Doncaster 29-11-89
*Source:* Scholar. *Honours:* Northern Ireland Under-21.

| | | | | | |
|---|---|---|---|---|---|
| 2008-09 | Sheffield U | 0 | 0 | | |
| 2009-10 | Sheffield U | 0 | 0 | | |
| 2010-11 | Oxford U | 0 | 0 | | |
| 2011-12 | Oxford U | 14 | 1 | | |
| 2012-13 | Oxford U | 26 | 1 | 40 | 2 |

**CLARKE, Ryan (G)** 186 0
H: 6 3  W: 13 00  b.Bristol 30-4-82
*Source:* Scholar.

| | | | | | |
|---|---|---|---|---|---|
| 2001-02 | Bristol R | 1 | 0 | | |
| 2002-03 | Bristol R | 2 | 0 | | |
| 2003-04 | Bristol R | 2 | 0 | | |
| 2004-05 | Bristol R | 18 | 0 | 23 | 0 |
| 2004-05 | *Southend U* | 1 | 0 | 1 | 0 |
| 2004-05 | *Kidderminster H* | 6 | 0 | 6 | 0 |

From Salisbury C.

| | | | | | |
|---|---|---|---|---|---|
| 2009-10 | Oxford U | 44 | 0 | | |
| 2010-11 | Oxford U | 46 | 0 | | |
| 2011-12 | Oxford U | 42 | 0 | | |
| 2012-13 | Oxford U | 24 | 0 | 156 | 0 |

**CONSTABLE, James (F)** 160 42
H: 6 2  W: 12 12  b.Malmesbury 4-10-84
*Source:* Chippenham T.

| | | | | | |
|---|---|---|---|---|---|
| 2005-06 | Walsall | 17 | 3 | | |
| 2006-07 | Walsall | 6 | 0 | 23 | 3 |

From Kidderminster H.

| | | | | | |
|---|---|---|---|---|---|
| 2007-08 | Shrewsbury T | 14 | 4 | 14 | 4 |
| 2010-11 | Oxford U | 44 | 15 | | |
| 2011-12 | Oxford U | 40 | 11 | | |
| 2012-13 | Oxford U | 39 | 9 | 123 | 35 |

**CRADDOCK, Tom (F)** 162 58
H: 5 11  W: 11 10  b.Durham 14-10-86
*Source:* Scholar.

| | | | | | |
|---|---|---|---|---|---|
| 2005-06 | Middlesbrough | 1 | 0 | | |
| 2006-07 | Middlesbrough | 0 | 0 | | |
| 2006-07 | *Wrexham* | 1 | 1 | 1 | 1 |
| 2007-08 | Middlesbrough | 3 | 0 | | |
| 2007-08 | *Hartlepool U* | 4 | 0 | 4 | 0 |
| 2008-09 | Middlesbrough | 0 | 0 | 4 | 0 |
| 2008-09 | Luton T | 27 | 10 | | |
| 2009-10 | Luton T | 46 | 22 | 73 | 32 |
| 2010-11 | Oxford U | 39 | 14 | | |
| 2011-12 | Oxford U | 9 | 1 | | |
| 2012-13 | Oxford U | 32 | 10 | 80 | 25 |

**CROCOMBE, Max (G)** 4 0
H: 6 4  b.12-8-93

| | | | | | |
|---|---|---|---|---|---|
| 2012-13 | Oxford U | 4 | 0 | 4 | 0 |

**DAVIES, Scott (M)** 119 21
H: 5 11  W: 12 00  b.Aylesbury 10-3-88
*Source:* Scholar. *Honours:* Eire Under-21.

| | | | | | |
|---|---|---|---|---|---|
| 2006-07 | Reading | 0 | 0 | | |
| 2007-08 | Reading | 0 | 0 | | |
| 2008-09 | Reading | 0 | 0 | | |
| 2008-09 | *Aldershot T* | 41 | 13 | | |
| 2009-10 | Reading | 4 | 0 | | |
| 2009-10 | *Wycombe W* | 15 | 3 | | |
| 2009-10 | *Yeovil T* | 4 | 0 | 4 | 0 |
| 2010-11 | Reading | 0 | 0 | 4 | 0 |
| 2010-11 | *Wycombe W* | 8 | 1 | 23 | 4 |
| 2010-11 | *Bristol R* | 7 | 0 | 7 | 0 |
| 2011-12 | Crawley T | 20 | 2 | | |
| 2011-12 | *Aldershot T* | 8 | 1 | 49 | 14 |
| 2012-13 | Crawley T | 0 | 0 | 20 | 2 |
| 2012-13 | Oxford U | 12 | 1 | 12 | 1 |

**DAVIS, Liam (M)** 164 11
H: 5 9  W: 11 07  b.Wandsworth 23-11-86
*Source:* Scholar.

| | | | | | |
|---|---|---|---|---|---|
| 2005-06 | Coventry C | 2 | 0 | | |
| 2006-07 | Coventry C | 3 | 0 | | |
| 2006-07 | *Peterborough U* | 7 | 0 | 7 | 0 |
| 2007-08 | Coventry C | 6 | 0 | 11 | 0 |
| 2008-09 | Northampton T | 29 | 4 | | |
| 2009-10 | Northampton T | 17 | 2 | | |
| 2010-11 | Northampton T | 33 | 2 | 79 | 8 |
| 2011-12 | Oxford U | 44 | 2 | | |
| 2012-13 | Oxford U | 23 | 1 | 67 | 3 |

**DUBERRY, Michael (D)** 409 10
H: 6 1  W: 13 10  b.Enfield 14-10-75
*Source:* Trainee. *Honours:* England Under-21.

| | | | | | |
|---|---|---|---|---|---|
| 1993-94 | Chelsea | 1 | 0 | | |
| 1994-95 | Chelsea | 0 | 0 | | |
| 1995-96 | Chelsea | 22 | 0 | | |
| 1995-96 | *Bournemouth* | 7 | 0 | 7 | 0 |
| 1996-97 | Chelsea | 15 | 1 | | |
| 1997-98 | Chelsea | 23 | 0 | | |
| 1998-99 | Chelsea | 25 | 0 | 86 | 1 |
| 1999-2000 | Leeds U | 13 | 1 | | |
| 2000-01 | Leeds U | 5 | 0 | | |
| 2001-02 | Leeds U | 3 | 0 | | |
| 2002-03 | Leeds U | 14 | 0 | | |
| 2003-04 | Leeds U | 19 | 3 | | |
| 2004-05 | Leeds U | 4 | 0 | 58 | 4 |
| 2004-05 | Stoke C | 25 | 0 | | |
| 2005-06 | Stoke C | 41 | 1 | | |
| 2006-07 | Stoke C | 29 | 0 | 95 | 1 |
| 2006-07 | Reading | 8 | 0 | | |
| 2007-08 | Reading | 13 | 0 | | |
| 2008-09 | Reading | 27 | 0 | 48 | 0 |
| 2009-10 | *Wycombe W* | 18 | 0 | 18 | 0 |
| 2009-10 | St Johnstone | 17 | 1 | | |
| 2010-11 | St Johnstone | 33 | 0 | 50 | 1 |
| 2011-12 | Oxford U | 36 | 3 | | |
| 2012-13 | Oxford U | 11 | 0 | 47 | 3 |

**EVANS, Alex (D)** 1 0
H: 6 1  W: 12 13  b.Treharris 17-9-92
*Source:* Scholar. *Honours:* Wales Youth, Under-21.

| | | | | | |
|---|---|---|---|---|---|
| 2011-12 | Cardiff C | 0 | 0 | | |
| 2012-13 | Cardiff C | 0 | 0 | | |
| 2012-13 | Oxford U | 1 | 0 | 1 | 0 |

**HESLOP, Simon (M)** 100 7
H: 5 11  W: 11 00  b.York 1-5-87
*Source:* Scholar.

| | | | | | |
|---|---|---|---|---|---|
| 2005-06 | Barnsley | 0 | 0 | | |
| 2006-07 | Barnsley | 1 | 0 | | |
| 2007-08 | Barnsley | 0 | 0 | | |
| 2008-09 | Barnsley | 0 | 0 | | |
| 2008-09 | *Grimsby T* | 8 | 0 | 8 | 0 |
| 2009-10 | Barnsley | 0 | 0 | 1 | 0 |
| 2010-11 | Oxford U | 38 | 3 | | |
| 2011-12 | Oxford U | 29 | 3 | | |
| 2012-13 | Oxford U | 24 | 1 | 91 | 7 |

**LEVEN, Peter (M)** 277 43
H: 5 11  W: 12 13  b.Glasgow 27-9-83
*Source:* Rangers.

| | | | | | |
|---|---|---|---|---|---|
| 2004-05 | Kilmarnock | 32 | 4 | | |
| 2005-06 | Kilmarnock | 6 | 0 | | |
| 2006-07 | Kilmarnock | 27 | 1 | 65 | 5 |
| 2007-08 | Chesterfield | 42 | 6 | 42 | 6 |
| 2008-09 | Milton Keynes D | 40 | 10 | | |
| 2009-10 | Milton Keynes D | 31 | 4 | | |
| 2010-11 | Milton Keynes D | 40 | 8 | 111 | 22 |
| 2011-12 | Oxford U | 39 | 6 | | |
| 2012-13 | Oxford U | 20 | 4 | 59 | 10 |

**LONG, Sam (D)** 1 0
b.Oxford 16-1-95

| | | | | | |
|---|---|---|---|---|---|
| 2012-13 | Oxford U | 1 | 0 | 1 | 0 |

**LYNN, David (G)** 0 0
b.Aylesbury 31-1-95

| | | | | | |
|---|---|---|---|---|---|
| 2012-13 | Oxford U | 0 | 0 | | |

**MARSH, Tyrone (F)** 2 0
b. 24-12-93

| | | | | | |
|---|---|---|---|---|---|
| 2012-13 | Oxford U | 2 | 0 | 2 | 0 |

**McCORMICK, Luke (G)** 15 0
H: 6 0  W: 13 12  b.Coventry 15-8-83

| | | | | | |
|---|---|---|---|---|---|
| 2012-13 | Truro City | 0 | 0 | | |
| 2012-13 | Oxford U | 15 | 0 | 15 | 0 |

**O'BRIEN, Luke (D)** 149 2
H: 5 9  W: 12 01  b.Halifax 11-9-88
*Source:* Scholar.

| | | | | | |
|---|---|---|---|---|---|
| 2007-08 | Bradford C | 2 | 0 | | |
| 2008-09 | Bradford C | 35 | 1 | | |
| 2009-10 | Bradford C | 43 | 1 | | |
| 2010-11 | Bradford C | 42 | 0 | | |
| 2011-12 | Bradford C | 9 | 0 | 131 | 2 |
| 2011-12 | *Exeter C* | 3 | 0 | 3 | 0 |
| 2012-13 | Oxford U | 15 | 0 | 15 | 0 |

**O'DOWDA, Callum (M)**    0   0
b.Oxford 23-4-95

| | | | | |
|---|---|---|---|---|
| 2012-13 | Oxford U | 0 | 0 | |

**PARKER, Josh (F)**    45   0
H: 5 11   W: 12 00   b.Slough 1-12-90
*Source:* Scholar. *Honours:* Antigua and Barbuda 7 full caps.

| | | | | | |
|---|---|---|---|---|---|
| 2009-10 | QPR | 4 | 0 | | |
| 2010-11 | QPR | 1 | 0 | 5 | 0 |
| 2010-11 | Northampton T | 3 | 0 | 3 | 0 |
| 2010-11 | Wycombe W | 1 | 0 | 1 | 0 |
| 2011-12 | Oldham Ath | 13 | 0 | 13 | 0 |
| 2011-12 | Dagenham & R | 8 | 0 | 8 | 0 |
| 2012-13 | Oxford U | 15 | 0 | 15 | 0 |

**PITTMAN, Jon-Paul (F)**    123   21
H: 5 9   W: 11 00   b.Oklahoma City 24-10-86
*Source:* Scholar.

| | | | | | |
|---|---|---|---|---|---|
| 2005-06 | Nottingham F | 0 | 0 | | |
| 2005-06 | Hartlepool U | 3 | 0 | 3 | 0 |
| 2006-07 | Bury | 9 | 1 | 9 | 1 |
| 2006-07 | Doncaster R | 0 | 0 | | |
| From Crawley T. | | | | | |
| 2008-09 | Wycombe W | 17 | 3 | | |
| 2009-10 | Wycombe W | 41 | 7 | | |
| 2010-11 | Wycombe W | 19 | 4 | 77 | 14 |
| 2011-12 | Oxford U | 15 | 3 | | |
| 2011-12 | Crawley T | 4 | 1 | 4 | 1 |
| 2012-13 | Oxford U | 15 | 2 | 30 | 5 |

**POTTER, Alfie (M)**    108   14
H: 5 7   W: 9 06   b.Islington 9-1-89
*Source:* Millwall.

| | | | | | |
|---|---|---|---|---|---|
| 2007-08 | Peterborough U | 2 | 0 | 2 | 0 |
| From Kettering T. | | | | | |
| 2010-11 | Oxford U | 38 | 2 | | |
| From Kettering T. | | | | | |
| 2011-12 | Oxford U | 25 | 2 | | |
| 2012-13 | Oxford U | 43 | 10 | 106 | 14 |

**RAYNES, Michael (D)**    245   6
H: 6 4   W: 12 00   b.Wythenshawe 15-10-87
*Source:* Scholar.

| | | | | | |
|---|---|---|---|---|---|
| 2004-05 | Stockport Co | 19 | 0 | | |
| 2005-06 | Stockport Co | 25 | 1 | | |
| 2006-07 | Stockport Co | 9 | 0 | | |
| 2007-08 | Stockport Co | 27 | 0 | | |
| 2008-09 | Stockport Co | 35 | 3 | | |
| 2009-10 | Stockport Co | 25 | 1 | 140 | 4 |
| 2009-10 | Scunthorpe U | 12 | 0 | | |
| 2010-11 | Scunthorpe U | 22 | 0 | 34 | 0 |
| 2011-12 | Rotherham U | 33 | 0 | 33 | 0 |
| 2012-13 | Oxford U | 38 | 1 | 38 | 1 |

**RICHARDS, Justin (F)**    173   37
H: 5 11   W: 11 00   b.Sandwell 16-10-80
*Source:* Trainee.

| | | | | | |
|---|---|---|---|---|---|
| 1998-99 | WBA | 1 | 0 | | |
| 1999-2000 | WBA | 0 | 0 | | |
| 2000-01 | WBA | 0 | 0 | 1 | 0 |
| 2000-01 | Bristol R | 7 | 0 | | |
| 2001-02 | Bristol R | 1 | 0 | | |
| 2002-03 | Bristol R | 8 | 0 | 16 | 0 |
| 2002-03 | Colchester U | 2 | 0 | 2 | 0 |
| From Stevenage B, Woking. | | | | | |
| 2006-07 | Peterborough U | 13 | 1 | 13 | 1 |
| 2006-07 | Boston U | 3 | 0 | 3 | 0 |
| From Kidderminster H. | | | | | |
| 2009-10 | Cheltenham T | 44 | 15 | 44 | 15 |
| 2010-11 | Port Vale | 42 | 9 | 42 | 9 |
| 2011-12 | Burton Alb | 35 | 11 | | |
| 2012-13 | Burton Alb | 13 | 1 | 48 | 12 |
| 2012-13 | Oxford U | 4 | 0 | 4 | 0 |

**RIGG, Sean (F)**    194   23
H: 5 9   W: 12 01   b.Bristol 1-10-88
*Source:* Forest Green R.

| | | | | | |
|---|---|---|---|---|---|
| 2006-07 | Bristol R | 18 | 1 | | |
| 2007-08 | Bristol R | 31 | 1 | | |
| 2008-09 | Bristol R | 8 | 0 | | |
| 2009-10 | Bristol R | 0 | 0 | 57 | 2 |
| 2009-10 | Port Vale | 26 | 3 | | |
| 2010-11 | Port Vale | 25 | 3 | | |
| 2011-12 | Port Vale | 42 | 10 | 93 | 16 |
| 2012-13 | Oxford U | 44 | 5 | 44 | 5 |

**SMALLEY, Deane (M)**    198   28
H: 6 0   W: 11 10   b.Chadderton 5-9-88
*Source:* Scholar.

| | | | | |
|---|---|---|---|---|
| 2006-07 | Oldham Ath | 2 | 0 | |

---

| | | | | | |
|---|---|---|---|---|---|
| 2007-08 | Oldham Ath | 37 | 2 | | |
| 2008-09 | Oldham Ath | 34 | 5 | | |
| 2009-10 | Oldham Ath | 29 | 3 | | |
| 2010-11 | Oldham Ath | 3 | 0 | 105 | 10 |
| 2010-11 | Rochdale | 3 | 0 | 3 | 0 |
| 2010-11 | Chesterfield | 28 | 12 | 28 | 12 |
| 2011-12 | Oxford U | 22 | 1 | | |
| 2011-12 | Bradford C | 13 | 0 | 13 | 0 |
| 2012-13 | Oxford U | 27 | 5 | 49 | 6 |

**WHING, Andrew (D)**    307   6
H: 6 0   W: 12 00   b.Birmingham 20-9-84
*Source:* Scholar.

| | | | | | |
|---|---|---|---|---|---|
| 2002-03 | Coventry C | 14 | 0 | | |
| 2003-04 | Coventry C | 28 | 1 | | |
| 2004-05 | Coventry C | 16 | 1 | | |
| 2005-06 | Coventry C | 32 | 0 | | |
| 2006-07 | Coventry C | 16 | 0 | 106 | 2 |
| 2006-07 | Brighton & HA | 12 | 0 | | |
| 2007-08 | Brighton & HA | 42 | 0 | | |
| 2008-09 | Brighton & HA | 40 | 0 | | |
| 2009-10 | Brighton & HA | 9 | 0 | | |
| 2009-10 | Chesterfield | 11 | 0 | 11 | 0 |
| 2010-11 | Brighton & HA | 0 | 0 | 103 | 0 |
| 2010-11 | Leyton Orient | 24 | 2 | 24 | 2 |
| 2011-12 | Oxford U | 41 | 0 | | |
| 2012-13 | Oxford U | 22 | 2 | 63 | 2 |

**WORLEY, Harry (D)**    106   3
H: 6 3   W: 13 00   b.Warrington 25-11-88
*Source:* Scholar.

| | | | | | |
|---|---|---|---|---|---|
| 2005-06 | Chelsea | 0 | 0 | | |
| 2006-07 | Chelsea | 0 | 0 | | |
| 2006-07 | Doncaster R | 10 | 0 | 10 | 0 |
| 2007-08 | Chelsea | 0 | 0 | | |
| 2007-08 | Carlisle U | 1 | 0 | 1 | 0 |
| 2007-08 | Leicester C | 2 | 0 | | |
| 2008-09 | Leicester C | 0 | 0 | | |
| 2008-09 | Luton T | 8 | 0 | 8 | 0 |
| 2009-10 | Leicester C | 0 | 0 | 2 | 0 |
| 2009-10 | Crewe Alex | 23 | 1 | 23 | 1 |
| 2010-11 | Oxford U | 43 | 1 | | |
| 2011-12 | Oxford U | 10 | 0 | | |
| 2012-13 | Oxford U | 9 | 1 | 62 | 2 |

**WRIGHT, Jake (D)**    127   0
H: 5 10   W: 11 07   b.Keighley 11-3-86
*Source:* Scholar.

| | | | | | |
|---|---|---|---|---|---|
| 2005-06 | Bradford C | 1 | 0 | 1 | 0 |
| From Halifax T, Crawley T. | | | | | |
| 2009-10 | Brighton & HA | 6 | 0 | 6 | 0 |
| 2010-11 | Oxford U | 35 | 0 | | |
| 2011-12 | Oxford U | 43 | 0 | | |
| 2012-13 | Oxford U | 42 | 0 | 120 | 0 |

**Scholars**

Ashby, Joshua James; Clarke, James Moses; Ekpiteta, Marvin Akpereogene Paul Ede; Hackett, Gregory James; Hawtin, Aidan James; Hill, Joshua William Robert; Humphreys, Samuel Aston; Ingram, Conor Patrick; Long, Samuel Patrick Robert; Lynn, David James; Martin, Duran Saul; O'Dowda, Callum Joshua Ryan; Roberts, James Anthony.

---

# PETERBOROUGH U (61)

**AJOSE, Nicholas (F)**    87   20
H: 5 8   W: 11 00   b.Bury 7-10-91
*Source:* Scholar.

| | | | | | |
|---|---|---|---|---|---|
| 2009-10 | Manchester U | 0 | 0 | | |
| 2010-11 | Manchester U | 0 | 0 | | |
| 2010-11 | Bury | 28 | 13 | | |
| 2011-12 | Peterborough U | 2 | 0 | | |
| 2011-12 | Scunthorpe U | 7 | 0 | 7 | 0 |
| 2011-12 | Chesterfield | 12 | 1 | 12 | 1 |
| 2012-13 | Crawley T | 19 | 2 | 19 | 2 |
| 2012-13 | Peterborough U | 0 | 0 | 2 | 0 |
| 2012-13 | Bury | 19 | 4 | 47 | 17 |

**ALCOCK, Craig (D)**    175   3
H: 5 8   W: 11 00   b.Cornwall 8-12-87
*Source:* Youth.

| | | | | |
|---|---|---|---|---|
| 2006-07 | Yeovil T | 1 | 0 | |
| 2007-08 | Yeovil T | 8 | 0 | |
| 2008-09 | Yeovil T | 30 | 1 | |
| 2009-10 | Yeovil T | 42 | 1 | |

---

| | | | | | |
|---|---|---|---|---|---|
| 2010-11 | Yeovil T | 26 | 1 | 107 | 3 |
| 2011-12 | Peterborough U | 41 | 0 | | |
| 2012-13 | Peterborough U | 27 | 0 | 68 | 0 |

**ANDERSON, Jermaine (M)**    1   0
b. 16-5-96

| | | | | | |
|---|---|---|---|---|---|
| 2012-13 | Peterborough U | 1 | 0 | 1 | 0 |

**BARNETT, Tyrone (F)**    105   32
H: 6 3   W: 13 05   b.Stevenage 28-10-85
*Source:* Rushall Olympic, AFC Telford U, Willenhall T, Hednesford T.

| | | | | | |
|---|---|---|---|---|---|
| 2010-11 | Macclesfield T | 45 | 13 | 45 | 13 |
| 2011-12 | Crawley T | 26 | 14 | 26 | 14 |
| 2011-12 | Peterborough U | 13 | 4 | | |
| 2012-13 | Peterborough U | 18 | 1 | 31 | 5 |
| 2012-13 | Ipswich T | 3 | 0 | 3 | 0 |

**BOSTWICK, Michael (D)**    123   14
H: 6 4   W: 14 00   b.Eltham 17-5-88

| | | | | | |
|---|---|---|---|---|---|
| 2006-07 | Millwall | 0 | 0 | | |
| From Rushden & D, Ebbsfleet U. | | | | | |
| 2010-11 | Stevenage | 41 | 2 | | |
| 2011-12 | Stevenage | 43 | 7 | 84 | 9 |
| 2012-13 | Peterborough U | 39 | 5 | 39 | 5 |

**BOYD, George (M)**    282   69
H: 5 10   W: 11 07   b.Chatham 2-10-85
*Source:* Stevenage B. *Honours:* Scotland B, 1 full cap.

| | | | | | |
|---|---|---|---|---|---|
| 2006-07 | Peterborough U | 20 | 6 | | |
| 2007-08 | Peterborough U | 46 | 12 | | |
| 2008-09 | Peterborough U | 46 | 9 | | |
| 2009-10 | Peterborough U | 32 | 9 | | |
| 2009-10 | Nottingham F | 6 | 1 | 6 | 1 |
| 2010-11 | Peterborough U | 43 | 15 | | |
| 2011-12 | Peterborough U | 45 | 7 | | |
| 2012-13 | Peterborough U | 31 | 6 | 263 | 64 |
| 2012-13 | Hull C | 13 | 4 | 13 | 4 |

**BRISLEY, Shaun (M)**    163   6
H: 6 2   W: 12 00   b.Macclesfield 6-5-90
*Source:* Scholar.

| | | | | | |
|---|---|---|---|---|---|
| 2007-08 | Macclesfield T | 10 | 2 | | |
| 2008-09 | Macclesfield T | 38 | 0 | | |
| 2009-10 | Macclesfield T | 33 | 1 | | |
| 2010-11 | Macclesfield T | 14 | 0 | | |
| 2011-12 | Macclesfield T | 29 | 3 | 124 | 6 |
| 2011-12 | Peterborough U | 11 | 0 | | |
| 2012-13 | Peterborough U | 28 | 0 | 39 | 0 |

**CLARKE-HARRIS, Jonson (F)**    15   4
H: 6 0   W: 11 01   b.Leicester 21-7-94

| | | | | | |
|---|---|---|---|---|---|
| 2012-13 | Peterborough U | 0 | 0 | | |
| 2012-13 | Southend U | 3 | 0 | 3 | 0 |
| 2012-13 | Bury | 12 | 4 | 12 | 4 |

**COULSON, Charlie (M)**    1   0
b.Kettering 11-1-96
*Source:* Schoolboy.

| | | | | | |
|---|---|---|---|---|---|
| 2011-12 | Peterborough U | 1 | 0 | | |
| 2012-13 | Peterborough U | 0 | 0 | 1 | 0 |

**DAY, Joe (G)**    0   0
H: 6 1   W: 12 00   b.Brighton 13-8-90
*Source:* Rushden & D.

| | | | | |
|---|---|---|---|---|
| 2011-12 | Peterborough U | 0 | 0 | |
| 2012-13 | Peterborough U | 0 | 0 | |

**FERDINAND, Kane (D)**    93   11
H: 6 1   W: 13 07   b.Newham 7-10-92
*Source:* Scholar. *Honours:* Eire Youth, Under-21.

| | | | | | |
|---|---|---|---|---|---|
| 2010-11 | Southend U | 22 | 2 | | |
| 2011-12 | Southend U | 36 | 7 | | |
| 2012-13 | Southend U | 3 | 1 | 61 | 10 |
| 2012-13 | Peterborough U | 32 | 1 | 32 | 1 |

**FRECKLINGTON, Lee (M)**    248   35
H: 5 8   W: 11 00   b.Lincoln 8-9-85
*Source:* Scholar. *Honours:* Eire B.

| | | | | | |
|---|---|---|---|---|---|
| 2003-04 | Lincoln C | 0 | 0 | | |
| 2004-05 | Lincoln C | 3 | 0 | | |
| 2005-06 | Lincoln C | 18 | 2 | | |
| 2006-07 | Lincoln C | 42 | 8 | | |
| 2007-08 | Lincoln C | 34 | 4 | | |
| 2008-09 | Peterborough U | 27 | 7 | 124 | 21 |
| 2009-10 | Peterborough U | 7 | 0 | | |
| 2009-10 | Peterborough U | 35 | 2 | | |
| 2010-11 | Peterborough U | 9 | 1 | | |
| 2011-12 | Peterborough U | 37 | 5 | | |

2012-13 Peterborough U 5 0 93 8
2012-13 *Rotherham U* 31 6 31 6

**GAYLE, Dwight (F)** 47 20
H: 5 10  W: 11 07  b.Walthamstow 20-10-89
*Source:* Stansted.
2011-12 Dagenham & R 0 0
2012-13 Dagenham & R 18 7 18 7
2012-13 Peterborough U 29 13 29 13

**GORDON, Jaanai (F)** 3 0
H: 5 10  W: 10 02  b.Northampton 7-12-95
2012-13 Peterborough U 3 0 3 0

**GRANT, Peter (M)** 0 0
H: 6 2  W: 11 04  b.Peterborough 3-6-91
2012-13 Peterborough U 0 0

**GRIFFITHS, Scott (D)** 168 1
H: 5 9  W: 11 08  b.Westminster 27-11-85
*Source:* Aveley.
2007-08 Dagenham & R 41 0
2008-09 Dagenham & R 44 0
2009-10 Dagenham & R 13 1 98 1
2009-10 Peterborough U 20 0
2010-11 Peterborough U 0 0
2010-11 *Chesterfield* 29 0
2011-12 Peterborough U 0 0
2011-12 *Crawley T* 6 0 6 0
2011-12 *Chesterfield* 3 0 32 0
2011-12 *Rotherham U* 8 0 8 0
2012-13 Peterborough U 0 0 20 0
2012-13 *Plymouth Arg* 4 0 4 0

**HIBBERT, Dave (F)** 160 34
H: 6 2  W: 12 00  b.Eccleshall 28-1-86
*Source:* Scholar.
2004-05 Port Vale 9 2 9 2
2005-06 Preston NE 10 0
2006-07 Preston NE 0 0 10 0
2006-07 *Rotherham U* 21 2 21 2
2006-07 *Bradford C* 8 0 8 0
2007-08 Shrewsbury T 44 12
2008-09 Shrewsbury T 23 3
2009-10 Shrewsbury T 38 14 105 29
2010-11 Peterborough U 7 1
2011-12 Peterborough U 1 0
2012-13 Peterborough U 0 0 7 1

**KEARNS, Daniel (M)** 89 9
H: 5 10  W: 12 00  b.Belfast 26-8-91
*Source:* West Ham U. *Honours:* Northern Ireland Youth, Eire Youth, Under-21, Under-23.
2010 Dundalk 12 0
2011 Dundalk 37 9 49 9
2011-12 Peterborough U 20 0
2012-13 Peterborough U 1 0 21 0
2012-13 *York C* 9 0 9 0
2012-13 *Rotherham U* 10 0 10 0

**KNIGHT-PERCIVAL, Nathaniel (M)** 31
H: 6 0  W: 11 06  b.Cambridge 31-3-87
*Source:* Histon, Wrexham.
2012-13 Peterborough U 31 0 31 0

**LITTLE, Mark (D)** 184 2
H: 6 1  W: 11 09  b.Worcester 20-8-88
*Source:* Scholar. *Honours:* England Youth.
2005-06 Wolverhampton W 0 0
2006-07 Wolverhampton W 26 0
2007-08 Wolverhampton W 1 0
2007-08 *Northampton T* 17 0
2008-09 Wolverhampton W 0 0
2008-09 *Northampton T* 9 0 26 0
2009-10 Wolverhampton W 0 0 27 0
2009-10 *Chesterfield* 12 0 12 0
2009-10 *Peterborough U* 9 0
2010-11 Peterborough U 35 0
2011-12 Peterborough U 35 1
2012-13 Peterborough U 40 1 119 2

**McCANN, Grant (M)** 458 81
H: 5 10  W: 11 00  b.Belfast 14-4-80
*Source:* Trainee. *Honours:* Northern Ireland Youth, Under-21, 39 full caps, 4 goals.
1998-99 West Ham U 0 0
1999-2000 West Ham U 0 0
2000-01 West Ham U 1 0
2000-01 *Notts Co* 2 0 2 0
2000-01 *Cheltenham T* 30 3

2001-02 West Ham U 3 0
2002-03 West Ham U 0 0 4 0
2002-03 Cheltenham T 27 6
2003-04 Cheltenham T 43 8
2004-05 Cheltenham T 39 4
2005-06 Cheltenham T 39 8
2006-07 Cheltenham T 15 5 193 34
2006-07 Barnsley 22 1
2007-08 Barnsley 19 3 41 4
2007-08 Scunthorpe U 14 1
2008-09 Scunthorpe U 43 9
2009-10 Scunthorpe U 42 8 99 18
2010-11 Peterborough U 38 9
2011-12 Peterborough U 41 8
2012-13 Peterborough U 40 8 119 25

**McDONALD, Shaquille (F)** 0 0
2012-13 Peterborough U 0 0

**MENDEZ-LAING, Nathaniel (M)** 70 9
H: 5 10  W: 11 12  b.Birmingham 15-4-92
*Source:* Scholar.
2009-10 Wolverhampton W 0 0
2010-11 Wolverhampton W 0 0
2010-11 *Peterborough U* 33 5
2011-12 Wolverhampton W 0 0
2011-12 *Sheffield U* 8 1 8 1
2012-13 Peterborough U 21 3 54 8
2012-13 *Portsmouth* 8 0 8 0

**NEWELL, Joe (M)** 46 1
H: 5 11  W: 11 02  b.Tamworth 15-3-93
*Source:* Scholar.
2010-11 Peterborough U 2 0
2011-12 Peterborough U 14 1
2012-13 Peterborough U 30 0 46 1

**NTLHE, Kgosietsile (D)** 14 1
H: 5 9  W: 10 05  b.Pretoria 21-2-94
*Source:* Scholar.
2010-11 Peterborough U 0 0
2011-12 Peterborough U 2 0
2012-13 Peterborough U 12 1 14 1

**OLEJNIK, Robert (G)** 194 0
H: 6 0  W: 15 06  b.Vienna 26-11-86
*Source:* Scholar. *Honours:* Austria Under-21.
2004-05 Aston Villa 0 0
2005-06 Aston Villa 0 0
2006-07 Aston Villa 0 0
2006-07 *Lincoln C* 0 0
2007-08 Falkirk 13 0
2008-09 Falkirk 15 0
2009-10 Falkirk 38 0
2010-11 Falkirk 36 0 102 0
2011-12 Torquay U 46 0 46 0
2012-13 Peterborough U 46 0 46 0

**RICHENS, Michael (D)** 0 0
b.Bedford 28-2-95
2012-13 Peterborough U 0 0

**ROWE, Tommy (M)** 213 29
H: 5 11  W: 12 11  b.Manchester 1-5-89
*Source:* Scholar.
2006-07 Stockport Co 4 0
2007-08 Stockport Co 24 6
2008-09 Stockport Co 44 7 72 13
2008-09 *Peterborough U* 0 0
2009-10 Peterborough U 32 2
2010-11 Peterborough U 35 5
2011-12 Peterborough U 43 4
2012-13 Peterborough U 31 5 141 16

**SAGE, James (D)** 0 0
2011-12 Peterborough U 0 0
2012-13 Peterborough U 0 0

**SINCLAIR, Emile (F)** 169 28
H: 6 0  W: 11 04  b.Leeds 29-12-87
*Source:* Scholar.
2007-08 Nottingham F 12 1
2007-08 *Brentford* 4 0 4 0
2008-09 Nottingham F 3 0 15 1
2008-09 *Macclesfield T* 17 1
2009-10 Macclesfield T 42 7
2010-11 Macclesfield T 31 5
2011-12 Macclesfield T 5 1 95 14
2011-12 *Peterborough U* 35 10
2012-13 Peterborough U 12 3 47 13
2012-13 *Barnsley* 4 0 4 0
2012-13 *Doncaster R* 4 0 4 0

**SWANSON, Danny (M)** 179 18
H: 5 6  W: 9 03  b.Edinburgh 28-12-86
2005-06 Berwick R 27 1
2006-07 Berwick R 3 0
2007-08 Berwick R 14 3 44 4
2007-08 *Dundee U* 12 2
2008-09 Dundee U 30 0
2009-10 Dundee U 31 5
2010-11 Dundee U 21 2
2011-12 Dundee U 14 3 108 12
2012-13 Peterborough U 27 2 27 2

**TOMLIN, Lee (F)** 116 27
H: 5 11  W: 11 09  b.Leicester 1-8-89
*Source:* Leicester C, Rushden & D.
2010-11 Peterborough U 37 8
2011-12 Peterborough U 37 8
2012-13 Peterborough U 42 11 116 27

**ZAKUANI, Gaby (D)** 280 8
H: 6 1  W: 12 13  b.DR Congo 31-5-86
*Source:* Scholar. *Honours:* DR Congo 3 full caps.
2002-03 Leyton Orient 1 0
2003-04 Leyton Orient 10 2
2004-05 Leyton Orient 33 0
2005-06 Leyton Orient 43 1 87 3
2006-07 Fulham 0 0
2006-07 *Stoke C* 9 0
2007-08 Fulham 0 0
2007-08 *Stoke C* 19 0 28 0
2008-09 Fulham 0 0
2008-09 *Peterborough U* 32 1
2009-10 Peterborough U 29 0
2010-11 Peterborough U 30 2
2011-12 Peterborough U 41 1
2012-13 Peterborough U 33 1 165 5

**Players retained or with offer of contract**
Brown, Jevani; Lawlor, Daniel Stephen.

**Scholars**
Anderson, Jermaine Barrington; Burgess, Joe Oliver William; Butt, Charlie Thomas; Carter, Matthew Philip; Carthey, Regan; Cary, Timothy James; Conlon, Tom George Sawyer; Hendry, Jack William; Lynch, Alexander Patrick; O'Reilly, Luke Patrick; Sparrow, Matthew James; Wood, Thomas Michael Ronald; Wright, Levi Mark.

# PLYMOUTH ARG (62)

**BERRY, Durrell (D)** 63 0
H: 5 11  W: 11 11  b.Derby 27-5-92
*Source:* Aston Villa.
2010-11 Aston Villa 0 0
2011-12 Plymouth Arg 35 0
2012-13 Plymouth Arg 28 0 63 0

**BHASERA, Onismor (D)** 223 5
H: 5 9  W: 11 13  b.Mutare 7-12-86
*Honours:* Zimbabwe 19 full caps.
2004 Harare U 0 0
2004-05 Tembisa Classic 14 0 14 0
2005-06 Maritzburg U 27 0
2006-07 Maritzburg U 26 1 53 1
2007-08 Kaizer Chiefs 26 1
2008-09 Kaizer Chiefs 25 0 51 1
2009-10 Plymouth Arg 7 0
2010-11 Plymouth Arg 29 1
2011-12 Plymouth Arg 27 1
2012-13 Plymouth Arg 42 1 105 3

**BLANCHARD, Maximo (D)** 184 5
H: 5 11  W: 11 13  b.Alencon 27-9-86
2006-07 Laval 4 0
2007-08 Laval 22 0 26 0
2008-09 Entente 35 1 35 1
2009-10 Moulins 35 1 35 1
2010-11 Tranmere R 20 0 20 0
2011-12 Plymouth Arg 28 2
2012-13 Plymouth Arg 40 1 68 3

**BRANSTON, Guy (D)** 369 22
H: 6 1  W: 15 01  b.Leicester 9-1-79
*Source:* Trainee.
1997-98 Leicester C 0 0
1997-98 *Colchester U* 12 1

|  |  | | | | |
|---|---|---|---|---|---|
| 1998-99 | Leicester C | 0 | 0 | | |
| 1998-99 | *Colchester U* | 1 | 0 | **13** | **1** |
| 1998-99 | *Plymouth Arg* | 7 | 1 | | |
| 1999-2000 | Leicester C | 0 | 0 | | |
| 1999-2000 | *Lincoln C* | 4 | 0 | **4** | **0** |
| 1999-2000 | Rotherham U | 30 | 4 | | |
| 2000-01 | Rotherham U | 41 | 6 | | |
| 2001-02 | Rotherham U | 10 | 1 | | |
| 2002-03 | Rotherham U | 15 | 2 | | |
| 2003-04 | Rotherham U | 8 | 0 | | |
| 2003-04 | *Wycombe W* | 9 | 0 | **9** | **0** |
| 2003-04 | *Peterborough U* | 14 | 0 | | |
| 2004-05 | Sheffield W | 11 | 0 | **11** | **0** |
| 2004-05 | *Peterborough U* | 4 | 1 | | |
| 2004-05 | Oldham Ath | 7 | 1 | | |
| 2005-06 | Oldham Ath | 38 | 1 | **45** | **2** |
| 2006-07 | Peterborough U | 24 | 0 | | |
| 2007-08 | Peterborough U | 2 | 0 | **44** | **1** |
| 2007-08 | *Rochdale* | 4 | 0 | **4** | **0** |
| 2007-08 | *Northampton T* | 3 | 0 | **3** | **0** |
| 2007-08 | *Notts Co* | 1 | 0 | **1** | **0** |
| 2009-10 | Burton Alb | 19 | 0 | **19** | **0** |
| From Kettering T. | | | | | |
| 2009-10 | *Torquay U* | 16 | 0 | | |
| 2010-11 | Torquay U | 45 | 2 | **61** | **2** |
| 2011-12 | Bradford C | 16 | 1 | **16** | **1** |
| 2011-12 | *Rotherham U* | 2 | 0 | **106** | **13** |
| 2012-13 | Aldershot T | 3 | 0 | **3** | **0** |
| 2012-13 | *Bristol R* | 4 | 1 | **4** | **1** |
| 2012-13 | *Plymouth Arg* | 19 | 0 | **26** | **1** |

**CHADWICK, Nick (F)**    **187 26**
H: 6 0 W: 12 08 b.Market Drayton 26-10-82
*Source:* Scholar.

|  |  | | | | |
|---|---|---|---|---|---|
| 1999-2000 | Everton | 0 | 0 | | |
| 2000-01 | Everton | 0 | 0 | | |
| 2001-02 | Everton | 9 | 3 | | |
| 2002-03 | Everton | 1 | 0 | | |
| 2002-03 | *Derby Co* | 6 | 0 | **6** | **0** |
| 2003-04 | Everton | 3 | 0 | | |
| 2003-04 | *Millwall* | 15 | 4 | **15** | **4** |
| 2004-05 | Everton | 0 | 0 | **14** | **3** |
| 2004-05 | Plymouth Arg | 15 | 1 | | |
| 2005-06 | Plymouth Arg | 37 | 5 | | |
| 2006-07 | Plymouth Arg | 16 | 2 | | |
| 2007-08 | Plymouth Arg | 9 | 2 | | |
| 2008-09 | Plymouth Arg | 0 | 0 | | |
| 2008-09 | *Hereford U* | 10 | 1 | **10** | **1** |
| 2008-09 | *Shrewsbury T* | 15 | 2 | **15** | **2** |
| From Chester C, Barrow. | | | | | |
| 2011-12 | Stockport | 0 | 0 | | |
| 2011-12 | Plymouth Arg | 22 | 5 | | |
| 2012-13 | Plymouth Arg | 28 | 1 | **127** | **16** |

**CHARLES, Anthony (D)**    **201 11**
H: 6 1 W: 12 07 b.Isleworth 11-3-81
*Source:* Brook House.

|  |  | | | | |
|---|---|---|---|---|---|
| 1999-2000 | Crewe Alex | 0 | 0 | | |
| 2000-01 | Crewe Alex | 0 | 0 | | |
| From Hayes, Aldershot T, Farnborough T | | | | | |
| 2004-05 | Barnet | 0 | 0 | | |
| 2005-06 | Barnet | 40 | 0 | | |
| 2006-07 | Barnet | 17 | 0 | **57** | **0** |
| 2008-09 | Aldershot T | 41 | 2 | | |
| 2009-10 | Aldershot T | 33 | 4 | | |
| 2010-11 | Aldershot T | 41 | 5 | **115** | **11** |
| 2011-12 | Northampton T | 9 | 0 | | |
| 2012-13 | Northampton T | 9 | 0 | **18** | **0** |
| 2012-13 | Plymouth Arg | 11 | 0 | **11** | **0** |

**COLE, Jake (G)**    **164 0**
H: 6 2 W: 13 00 b.Hammersmith 11-9-85
*Source:* Scholar.

|  |  | | | | |
|---|---|---|---|---|---|
| 2005-06 | QPR | 3 | 0 | | |
| 2006-07 | QPR | 3 | 0 | | |
| 2007-08 | QPR | 0 | 0 | | |
| 2008-09 | QPR | 0 | 0 | **6** | **0** |
| 2008-09 | *Barnet* | 10 | 0 | | |
| 2009-10 | Barnet | 46 | 0 | | |
| 2010-11 | Barnet | 31 | 0 | **87** | **0** |
| 2011-12 | Plymouth Arg | 37 | 0 | | |
| 2012-13 | Plymouth Arg | 34 | 0 | **71** | **0** |

**COWAN-HALL, Paris (F)**    **44 3**
H: 5 8 W: 11 08 b.Portsmouth 5-10-90

|  |  | | | | |
|---|---|---|---|---|---|
| 2008-09 | Portsmouth | 0 | 0 | | |
| 2009-10 | Portsmouth | 0 | 0 | | |
| 2009-10 | *Grimsby T* | 3 | 0 | **3** | **0** |
| 2010-11 | Portsmouth | 0 | 0 | | |
| 2010-11 | *Scunthorpe U* | 1 | 0 | **1** | **0** |
| 2012-13 | Plymouth Arg | 40 | 3 | **40** | **3** |

**FEENEY, Warren (F)**    **342 75**
H: 5 8 W: 12 04 b.Belfast 17-1-81
*Source:* Trainee. *Honours:* Northern Ireland Schools, Youth, Under-21, 46 full caps, 5 goals.

|  |  | | | | |
|---|---|---|---|---|---|
| 1997-98 | Leeds U | 0 | 0 | | |
| 1998-99 | Leeds U | 0 | 0 | | |
| 1999-2000 | Leeds U | 0 | 0 | | |
| 2000-01 | Leeds U | 0 | 0 | | |
| 2000-01 | *Bournemouth* | 10 | 4 | | |
| 2001-02 | Bournemouth | 37 | 13 | | |
| 2002-03 | Bournemouth | 21 | 7 | | |
| 2003-04 | Bournemouth | 40 | 12 | **108** | **36** |
| 2004-05 | Stockport Co | 31 | 15 | **31** | **15** |
| 2004-05 | Luton T | 6 | 0 | | |
| 2005-06 | Luton T | 42 | 6 | | |
| 2006-07 | Luton T | 29 | 2 | **77** | **8** |
| 2006-07 | *Cardiff C* | 6 | 0 | | |
| 2007-08 | Cardiff C | 5 | 0 | | |
| 2007-08 | *Swansea C* | 10 | 5 | **10** | **5** |
| 2008-09 | *Dundee U* | 23 | 6 | **23** | **6** |
| 2008-09 | Cardiff C | 0 | 0 | | |
| 2009-10 | Cardiff C | 9 | 0 | **20** | **0** |
| 2009-10 | *Sheffield W* | 1 | 0 | **1** | **0** |
| 2010-11 | Oldham Ath | 23 | 0 | **23** | **0** |
| 2011-12 | Plymouth Arg | 28 | 2 | | |
| 2012-13 | Plymouth Arg | 21 | 3 | **49** | **5** |

**GILMARTIN, Rene (G)**    **64 0**
H: 6 5 W: 13 06 b.Dublin 31-5-87
*Source:* St Patrick's BC. *Honours:* Eire Youth, Under-21.

|  |  | | | | |
|---|---|---|---|---|---|
| 2005-06 | Walsall | 2 | 0 | | |
| 2006-07 | Walsall | 0 | 0 | | |
| 2007-08 | Walsall | 0 | 0 | | |
| 2008-09 | Walsall | 11 | 0 | | |
| 2009-10 | Walsall | 22 | 0 | **35** | **0** |
| 2010-11 | Watford | 0 | 0 | | |
| 2011-12 | Watford | 2 | 0 | **2** | **0** |
| 2011-12 | *Yeovil T* | 8 | 0 | **8** | **0** |
| 2011-12 | *Crawley T* | 6 | 0 | **6** | **0** |
| 2012-13 | Plymouth Arg | 13 | 0 | **13** | **0** |

**GRIFFITHS, Rhys (F)**    **222 223**
b. 1-3-80

|  |  | | | | |
|---|---|---|---|---|---|
| 2002-03 | Haverfordwest | 8 | 5 | | |
| 2003-04 | Haverfordwest | 8 | 4 | **16** | **9** |
| 2004-05 | Port Talbot | 5 | 6 | | |
| 2005-06 | Port Talbot | 20 | 28 | **25** | **34** |
| 2006-07 | Llanelli | 19 | 29 | | |
| 2007-08 | Llanelli | 29 | 39 | | |
| 2008-09 | Llanelli | 29 | 30 | | |
| 2009-10 | Llanelli | 33 | 30 | | |
| 2010-11 | Llanelli | 28 | 25 | | |
| 2011-12 | Llanelli | 29 | 24 | **167** | **177** |
| 2012-13 | Plymouth Arg | 14 | 3 | **14** | **3** |

**GURRIERI, Andres (M)**    **83 3**
H: 5 6 W: 10 05 b.Winterthur 3-7-89

|  |  | | | | |
|---|---|---|---|---|---|
| 2007-08 | Ternana | 0 | 0 | | |
| 2008-09 | Ternana | 6 | 0 | | |
| 2008-09 | *Colligiana* | 16 | 2 | **16** | **2** |
| 2009-10 | Ternana | 0 | 0 | **6** | **0** |
| 2010-11 | Sud America | 20 | 0 | **20** | **0** |
| 2011-12 | Burton Alb | 13 | 0 | **13** | **0** |
| 2012-13 | Plymouth Arg | 28 | 1 | **28** | **1** |

**HARVEY, Tyler (F)**    **10 1**
b.Plymouth 29-6-95

|  |  | | | | |
|---|---|---|---|---|---|
| 2012-13 | Plymouth Arg | 10 | 1 | **10** | **1** |

**HOURIHANE, Conor (M)**    **80 7**
H: 5 11 W: 9 11 b.Cork 2-2-91
*Source:* Scholar. *Honours:* Eire Under-21.

|  |  | | | | |
|---|---|---|---|---|---|
| 2008-09 | Sunderland | 0 | 0 | | |
| 2009-10 | Sunderland | 0 | 0 | | |
| 2010-11 | Ipswich T | 0 | 0 | | |
| 2011-12 | Plymouth Arg | 38 | 2 | | |
| 2012-13 | Plymouth Arg | 42 | 5 | **80** | **7** |

**LECOINTE, Matt (F)**    **25 2**
H: 5 10 W: 10 07 b.Plymouth 28-10-94
*Source:* Scholar. *Honours:* England Youth.

|  |  | | | | |
|---|---|---|---|---|---|
| 2011-12 | Plymouth Arg | 19 | 2 | | |
| 2012-13 | Plymouth Arg | 6 | 0 | **25** | **2** |

**LENNOX, Joe (M)**    **19 1**
H: 5 7 W: 11 00 b.Bristol 22-11-91
*Source:* Scholar.

|  |  | | | | |
|---|---|---|---|---|---|
| 2010-11 | Bristol C | 0 | 0 | | |
| 2011-12 | Bristol C | 0 | 0 | | |
| 2011-12 | Plymouth Arg | 8 | 0 | | |
| 2012-13 | Plymouth Arg | 11 | 1 | **19** | **1** |

**LOWRY, Jamie (D)**    **133 11**
H: 6 0 W: 12 00 b.Newquay 18-3-87
*Source:* Scholar.

|  |  | | | | |
|---|---|---|---|---|---|
| 2006-07 | Chesterfield | 8 | 0 | | |
| 2007-08 | Chesterfield | 42 | 6 | | |
| 2008-09 | Chesterfield | 42 | 0 | | |
| 2009-10 | Chesterfield | 13 | 5 | | |
| 2010-11 | Chesterfield | 3 | 0 | | |
| 2011-12 | Chesterfield | 6 | 0 | **114** | **11** |
| 2011-12 | *Crewe Alex* | 10 | 0 | **10** | **0** |
| 2012-13 | Plymouth Arg | 9 | 0 | **9** | **0** |

**NELSON, Curtis (D)**    **79 3**
H: 6 0 W: 11 07 b.Newcastle-u-Lyme 21-5-93
*Source:* Scholar. *Honours:* England Youth.

|  |  | | | | |
|---|---|---|---|---|---|
| 2010-11 | Plymouth Arg | 35 | 0 | | |
| 2011-12 | Plymouth Arg | 17 | 0 | | |
| 2012-13 | Plymouth Arg | 27 | 3 | **79** | **3** |

**RICHARDS, Jamie (D)**    **1 0**
b.Newton Abbot 24-6-94
*Source:* Scholar.

|  |  | | | | |
|---|---|---|---|---|---|
| 2011-12 | Plymouth Arg | 0 | 0 | | |
| 2012-13 | Plymouth Arg | 1 | 0 | **1** | **0** |

**VASSELL, Isaac (F)**    **6 0**
H: 5 7 W: 11 02 b.Newquay 9-9-93
*Source:* Scholar.

|  |  | | | | |
|---|---|---|---|---|---|
| 2011-12 | Plymouth Arg | 6 | 0 | | |
| 2012-13 | Plymouth Arg | 0 | 0 | **6** | **0** |

**WILLIAMS, Robbie (D)**    **225 17**
H: 5 10 W: 11 13 b.Pontefract 2-10-84
*Source:* Scholar.

|  |  | | | | |
|---|---|---|---|---|---|
| 2002-03 | Barnsley | 8 | 0 | | |
| 2003-04 | Barnsley | 4 | 1 | | |
| 2004-05 | Barnsley | 17 | 1 | | |
| 2005-06 | Barnsley | 22 | 2 | | |
| 2006-07 | Barnsley | 15 | 0 | | |
| 2006-07 | *Blackpool* | 9 | 4 | **9** | **4** |
| 2007-08 | Barnsley | 0 | 0 | **66** | **4** |
| 2007-08 | Huddersfield T | 25 | 2 | | |
| 2008-09 | Huddersfield T | 35 | 0 | | |
| 2009-10 | Huddersfield T | 17 | 2 | **77** | **4** |
| 2010-11 | Stockport Co | 22 | 1 | **22** | **1** |
| 2010-11 | Rochdale | 9 | 0 | **9** | **0** |
| 2011-12 | Plymouth Arg | 27 | 2 | | |
| 2012-13 | Plymouth Arg | 15 | 2 | **42** | **4** |

**WOTTON, Paul (D)**    **537 61**
H: 5 11 W: 12 00 b.Plymouth 17-8-77
*Source:* Trainee.

|  |  | | | | |
|---|---|---|---|---|---|
| 1994-95 | Plymouth Arg | 7 | 0 | | |
| 1995-96 | Plymouth Arg | 1 | 0 | | |
| 1996-97 | Plymouth Arg | 9 | 1 | | |
| 1997-98 | Plymouth Arg | 34 | 1 | | |
| 1998-99 | Plymouth Arg | 36 | 1 | | |
| 1999-2000 | Plymouth Arg | 23 | 0 | | |
| 2000-01 | Plymouth Arg | 42 | 4 | | |
| 2001-02 | Plymouth Arg | 46 | 5 | | |
| 2002-03 | Plymouth Arg | 43 | 8 | | |
| 2003-04 | Plymouth Arg | 38 | 9 | | |
| 2004-05 | Plymouth Arg | 40 | 12 | | |
| 2005-06 | Plymouth Arg | 45 | 8 | | |
| 2006-07 | Plymouth Arg | 22 | 4 | | |
| 2007-08 | Plymouth Arg | 8 | 1 | | |
| 2008-09 | Southampton | 29 | 0 | | |
| 2009-10 | Southampton | 26 | 0 | | |
| 2010-11 | Southampton | 2 | 0 | **57** | **0** |
| 2010-11 | *Oxford U* | 4 | 0 | **4** | **0** |
| 2010-11 | *Yeovil T* | 23 | 2 | | |
| 2011-12 | Yeovil T | 22 | 2 | **45** | **4** |
| 2011-12 | *Plymouth Arg* | 18 | 1 | | |
| 2012-13 | Plymouth Arg | 19 | 2 | **431** | **57** |

**YOUNG, Luke (M)**    **65 4**
H: 5 8 W: 11 05 b.Ivybridge 22-2-93
*Source:* Scholar.

|  |  | | | | |
|---|---|---|---|---|---|
| 2010-11 | Plymouth Arg | 5 | 0 | | |
| 2011-12 | Plymouth Arg | 28 | 2 | | |
| 2012-13 | Plymouth Arg | 32 | 2 | **65** | **4** |

**Scholars**

Allen, River Brian Zach; Asumadu-Sakyi, Kieran; Bentley, Aaron Stuart James; Bradley, James; Elcock, Andrew; Harvey, Tyler Marshall; Hutchinson, Joshua; Purrington, Ben; Summers, Nathan Rick Alexander; Watson, Colin Martin; Wheatley, Solomon Patrick.

## PORT VALE (63)

**ANDREW, Calvin (F)**  173  10
H: 6 0  W: 12 11  b.Luton 19-12-86
Source: Scholar.

| | | | | | |
|---|---|---|---|---|---|
| 2004-05 | Luton T | 8 | 0 | | |
| 2005-06 | Luton T | 1 | 1 | | |
| 2005-06 | Grimsby T | 8 | 1 | 8 | 1 |
| 2005-06 | Bristol C | 3 | 0 | 3 | 0 |
| 2006-07 | Luton T | 7 | 1 | | |
| 2007-08 | Luton T | 39 | 2 | 55 | 4 |
| 2008-09 | Crystal Palace | 1 | 0 | | |
| 2008-09 | Brighton & HA | 9 | 2 | 9 | 2 |
| 2009-10 | Crystal Palace | 27 | 1 | | |
| 2010-11 | Crystal Palace | 13 | 0 | | |
| 2010-11 | Millwall | 3 | 0 | 3 | 0 |
| 2010-11 | Swindon T | 10 | 1 | 10 | 1 |
| 2011-12 | Crystal Palace | 6 | 0 | 53 | 1 |
| 2011-12 | Leyton Orient | 10 | 0 | 10 | 0 |
| 2012-13 | Port Vale | 22 | 1 | 22 | 1 |

**BIRCHALL, Chris (M)**  222  12
H: 6 2  W: 12 07  b.Liverpool 5-5-84
Source: Scholar. Honours: Trinidad & Tobago 42 full caps, 4 goals.

| | | | | | |
|---|---|---|---|---|---|
| 2001-02 | Port Vale | 1 | 0 | | |
| 2002-03 | Port Vale | 2 | 0 | | |
| 2003-04 | Port Vale | 10 | 0 | | |
| 2004-05 | Port Vale | 34 | 6 | | |
| 2005-06 | Port Vale | 31 | 1 | | |
| 2006-07 | Coventry C | 28 | 2 | | |
| 2007-08 | Coventry C | 1 | 0 | | |
| 2007-08 | St Mirren | 9 | 0 | 9 | 0 |
| 2008-09 | Coventry C | 0 | 0 | 29 | 2 |
| 2008-09 | Carlisle U | 2 | 0 | 2 | 0 |
| 2008-09 | Brighton & HA | 9 | 0 | 9 | 0 |
| 2009 | LA Galaxy | 11 | 0 | | |
| 2010 | LA Galaxy | 28 | 0 | 39 | 0 |
| 2011 | LA Galaxy | 27 | 1 | 27 | 1 |
| 2012 | Columbus Crew | 18 | 1 | 18 | 1 |
| 2012-13 | Port Vale | 11 | 1 | 89 | 8 |

**BURGE, Ryan (M)**  38  2
H: 5 10  W: 10 03  b.Cheltenham 12-10-88
Source: Scholar.

| | | | | | |
|---|---|---|---|---|---|
| 2005-06 | Birmingham C | 0 | 0 | | |
| 2006-07 | Birmingham C | 0 | 0 | | |
| 2007-08 | Birmingham C | 0 | 0 | | |
| 2008-09 | Barnet | 2 | 0 | 2 | 0 |

From Jerez Industrial.

| | | | | | |
|---|---|---|---|---|---|
| 2010-11 | Doncaster R | 1 | 0 | 1 | 0 |
| 2010-11 | Oxford U | 5 | 0 | 5 | 0 |
| 2011-12 | Port Vale | 0 | 0 | | |
| 2012-13 | Port Vale | 30 | 2 | 30 | 2 |

**DAVIS, Joe (D)**  16  0
H: 6 0  W: 11 07  b.Burnley 10-11-93
Source: Scholar.

| | | | | | |
|---|---|---|---|---|---|
| 2010-11 | Port Vale | 1 | 0 | | |
| 2011-12 | Port Vale | 8 | 0 | | |
| 2012-13 | Port Vale | 7 | 0 | 16 | 0 |

**DODDS, Louis (M)**  239  46
H: 5 10  W: 12 04  b.Sheffield 8-10-86
Source: Scholar.

| | | | | | |
|---|---|---|---|---|---|
| 2005-06 | Leicester C | 0 | 0 | | |
| 2006-07 | Leicester C | 0 | 0 | | |
| 2006-07 | Rochdale | 12 | 2 | 12 | 2 |
| 2007-08 | Leicester C | 0 | 0 | | |
| 2007-08 | Lincoln C | 41 | 9 | 41 | 9 |
| 2008-09 | Port Vale | 44 | 7 | | |
| 2009-10 | Port Vale | 44 | 6 | | |
| 2010-11 | Port Vale | 33 | 9 | | |
| 2011-12 | Port Vale | 35 | 8 | | |
| 2012-13 | Port Vale | 30 | 7 | 186 | 35 |

**DUFFY, Richard (D)**  258  5
H: 5 9  W: 10 03  b.Swansea 30-8-85
Source: Scholar. Honours: Wales Youth, Under-21, 13 full caps.

| | | | | | |
|---|---|---|---|---|---|
| 2002-03 | Swansea C | 0 | 0 | | |
| 2003-04 | Swansea C | 18 | 1 | | |
| 2003-04 | Portsmouth | 1 | 0 | | |
| 2004-05 | Portsmouth | 0 | 0 | | |
| 2004-05 | Burnley | 7 | 1 | 7 | 1 |
| 2004-05 | Coventry C | 14 | 0 | | |
| 2005-06 | Portsmouth | 0 | 0 | | |
| 2005-06 | Coventry C | 32 | 0 | | |
| 2006-07 | Portsmouth | 0 | 0 | | |
| 2006-07 | Coventry C | 13 | 0 | | |
| 2006-07 | Swansea C | 11 | 0 | 29 | 1 |
| 2007-08 | Portsmouth | 0 | 0 | | |
| 2007-08 | Coventry C | 2 | 0 | 61 | 0 |
| 2008-09 | Portsmouth | 0 | 0 | 1 | 0 |
| 2008-09 | Millwall | 12 | 0 | 12 | 0 |
| 2009-10 | Exeter C | 42 | 1 | | |
| 2010-11 | Exeter C | 42 | 2 | | |
| 2011-12 | Exeter C | 28 | 0 | 112 | 3 |
| 2012-13 | Port Vale | 36 | 0 | 36 | 0 |

**GRIFFITH, Anthony (M)**  202  2
H: 6 0  W: 12 00  b.Huddersfield 28-10-86
Source: Glasshoughton W.

| | | | | | |
|---|---|---|---|---|---|
| 2005-06 | Doncaster R | 4 | 0 | | |
| 2005-06 | Oxford U | 0 | 0 | | |
| 2006-07 | Doncaster R | 2 | 0 | | |
| 2006-07 | Darlington | 4 | 0 | 4 | 0 |
| 2007-08 | Doncaster R | 0 | 0 | 6 | 0 |
| 2007-08 | Port Vale | 0 | 0 | | |
| 2008-09 | Port Vale | 38 | 0 | | |
| 2009-10 | Port Vale | 40 | 0 | | |
| 2010-11 | Port Vale | 40 | 1 | | |
| 2011-12 | Port Vale | 43 | 1 | | |
| 2012-13 | Port Vale | 10 | 0 | 171 | 2 |
| 2012-13 | Leyton Orient | 21 | 0 | 21 | 0 |

**HALDANE, Lewis (F)**  210  18
H: 6 0  W: 11 03  b.Trowbridge 13-3-85
Source: Scholar. Honours: Wales Under-21.

| | | | | | |
|---|---|---|---|---|---|
| 2003-04 | Bristol R | 27 | 5 | | |
| 2004-05 | Bristol R | 13 | 0 | | |
| 2005-06 | Bristol R | 30 | 3 | | |
| 2006-07 | Bristol R | 45 | 6 | | |
| 2007-08 | Bristol R | 32 | 1 | | |
| 2008-09 | Bristol R | 0 | 0 | 147 | 15 |
| 2009-10 | Port Vale | 37 | 3 | | |
| 2010-11 | Port Vale | 23 | 0 | | |
| 2011-12 | Port Vale | 3 | 0 | | |
| 2012-13 | Port Vale | 0 | 0 | 63 | 3 |

**HUGHES, Lee (F)**  457  199
H: 5 10  W: 12 00  b.Smethwick 22-5-76
Source: Kidderminster H.

| | | | | | |
|---|---|---|---|---|---|
| 1997-98 | WBA | 37 | 14 | | |
| 1998-99 | WBA | 42 | 31 | | |
| 1999-2000 | WBA | 36 | 12 | | |
| 2000-01 | WBA | 41 | 21 | | |
| 2001-02 | Coventry C | 38 | 14 | | |
| 2002-03 | Coventry C | 4 | 1 | 42 | 15 |
| 2002-03 | WBA | 23 | 0 | | |
| 2003-04 | WBA | 32 | 11 | 211 | 89 |
| 2007-08 | Oldham Ath | 18 | 7 | | |
| 2008-09 | Oldham Ath | 37 | 18 | 55 | 25 |
| 2008-09 | Blackpool | 3 | 1 | 3 | 1 |
| 2009-10 | Notts Co | 39 | 30 | | |
| 2010-11 | Notts Co | 31 | 13 | | |
| 2011-12 | Notts Co | 40 | 10 | | |
| 2012-13 | Notts Co | 18 | 6 | 128 | 59 |
| 2012-13 | Port Vale | 18 | 10 | 18 | 10 |

**JAMES, Kingsley (D)**  11  0
H: 6 1  W: 11 09  b.Rotherham 17-2-92
Source: Scholar.

| | | | | | |
|---|---|---|---|---|---|
| 2010-11 | Sheffield U | 0 | 0 | | |
| 2011-12 | Port Vale | 5 | 0 | | |
| 2012-13 | Port Vale | 6 | 0 | 11 | 0 |

**JOHNSON, Sam (G)**  0  0
H: 6 6  W: 12 04  b.Newcastle-under-Lyme 1-12-92
Source: Scholar.

| | | | |
|---|---|---|---|
| 2011-12 | Port Vale | 0 | 0 |
| 2012-13 | Port Vale | 0 | 0 |

**JONES, Daniel (D)**  143  5
H: 6 2  W: 13 00  b.Rowley Regis 14-7-86
Source: Scholar.

| | | | | | |
|---|---|---|---|---|---|
| 2005-06 | Wolverhampton W | 1 | 0 | | |
| 2006-07 | Wolverhampton W | 8 | 0 | | |
| 2007-08 | Wolverhampton W | 1 | 0 | | |
| 2007-08 | Northampton T | 33 | 3 | 33 | 3 |
| 2008-09 | Wolverhampton W | 0 | 0 | | |
| 2008-09 | Oldham Ath | 23 | 1 | 23 | 1 |
| 2009-10 | Wolverhampton W | 0 | 0 | 10 | 0 |
| 2009-10 | Notts Co | 7 | 0 | 7 | 0 |
| 2009-10 | Bristol R | 17 | 0 | 17 | 0 |
| 2010-11 | Sheffield W | 25 | 0 | | |
| 2011-12 | Sheffield W | 3 | 0 | | |
| 2012-13 | Sheffield W | 9 | 0 | 37 | 0 |
| 2012-13 | Port Vale | 16 | 1 | 16 | 1 |

**LLOYD, Ryan (M)**  9  0
H: 5 10  W: 10 03  b.Newcastle-u-Lyme 1-2-94
Source: Scholar.

| | | | | | |
|---|---|---|---|---|---|
| 2010-11 | Port Vale | 1 | 0 | | |
| 2011-12 | Port Vale | 2 | 0 | | |
| 2012-13 | Port Vale | 6 | 0 | 9 | 0 |

**LOFT, Doug (M)**  187  11
H: 6 0  W: 12 01  b.Maidstone 25-12-86
Source: Hastings U.

| | | | | | |
|---|---|---|---|---|---|
| 2005-06 | Brighton & HA | 3 | 1 | | |
| 2006-07 | Brighton & HA | 11 | 1 | | |
| 2007-08 | Brighton & HA | 13 | 0 | | |
| 2008-09 | Brighton & HA | 12 | 0 | 39 | 2 |
| 2008-09 | Dagenham & R | 11 | 0 | 11 | 0 |
| 2009-10 | Port Vale | 32 | 3 | | |
| 2010-11 | Port Vale | 29 | 1 | | |
| 2011-12 | Port Vale | 44 | 4 | | |
| 2012-13 | Port Vale | 32 | 1 | 137 | 9 |

**McALLISTER, Sean (M)**  112  5
H: 5 8  W: 10 07  b.Bolton 15-8-87
Source: Scholar.

| | | | | | |
|---|---|---|---|---|---|
| 2005-06 | Sheffield W | 2 | 0 | | |
| 2006-07 | Sheffield W | 6 | 1 | | |
| 2007-08 | Sheffield W | 8 | 0 | | |
| 2007-08 | Mansfield T | 7 | 0 | 7 | 0 |
| 2007-08 | Bury | 0 | 0 | | |
| 2008-09 | Sheffield W | 40 | 3 | | |
| 2009-10 | Sheffield W | 12 | 0 | 68 | 4 |
| 2010-11 | Shrewsbury T | 18 | 0 | | |
| 2011-12 | Shrewsbury T | 17 | 1 | 35 | 1 |
| 2012-13 | Port Vale | 2 | 0 | 2 | 0 |

Transferred to Cowdenbeath March 2013

**McCOMBE, John (D)**  226  14
H: 6 2  W: 13 00  b.Pontefract 7-5-85
Source: Scholar.

| | | | | | |
|---|---|---|---|---|---|
| 2002-03 | Huddersfield T | 1 | 0 | | |
| 2003-04 | Huddersfield T | 0 | 0 | | |
| 2004-05 | Huddersfield T | 5 | 0 | | |
| 2005-06 | Huddersfield T | 1 | 0 | | |
| 2005-06 | Torquay U | 0 | 0 | | |
| 2006-07 | Huddersfield T | 7 | 0 | 14 | 0 |
| 2007-08 | Hereford U | 27 | 0 | 27 | 0 |
| 2008-09 | Port Vale | 31 | 2 | | |
| 2009-10 | Port Vale | 40 | 3 | | |
| 2010-11 | Port Vale | 42 | 4 | | |
| 2011-12 | Port Vale | 40 | 4 | | |
| 2012-13 | Port Vale | 32 | 1 | 185 | 14 |

**McDONALD, Clayton (D)**  102  1
H: 6 6  W: 16 05  b.Liverpool 26-12-88
Source: Scholar.

| | | | | | |
|---|---|---|---|---|---|
| 2007-08 | Manchester C | 0 | 0 | | |
| 2007-08 | Manchester C | 0 | 0 | | |
| 2008-09 | Macclesfield T | 2 | 0 | 2 | 0 |
| 2008-09 | Chesterfield | 2 | 0 | 2 | 0 |
| 2009-10 | Manchester C | 0 | 0 | | |
| 2009-10 | Walsall | 26 | 1 | | |
| 2010-11 | Walsall | 14 | 0 | 40 | 1 |
| 2011-12 | Port Vale | 30 | 0 | | |
| 2012-13 | Port Vale | 22 | 0 | 52 | 0 |
| 2012-13 | Bristol R | 6 | 0 | 6 | 0 |

**MORSY, Sam (M)**  71  4
H: 5 9  W: 12 06  b.Wolverhampton 10-9-91
Source: Scholar.

| | | | | | |
|---|---|---|---|---|---|
| 2009-10 | Port Vale | 1 | 0 | | |
| 2010-11 | Port Vale | 16 | 1 | | |
| 2011-12 | Port Vale | 26 | 1 | | |
| 2012-13 | Port Vale | 28 | 2 | 71 | 4 |

**MURPHY, Darren (M)**   118   11
H: 6 0   W: 11 11   b.Cork 28-7-85

| | | | | | |
|---|---|---|---|---|---|
| 2003 | Cobh Ramblers | 26 | 2 | | |
| 2004 | Cobh Ramblers | 23 | 2 | | |
| 2005 | Cobh Ramblers | 5 | 0 | | |
| 2006 | Cobh Ramblers | 21 | 5 | 75 | 9 |
| 2007 | Cork C | 9 | 1 | | |
| 2008 | Cork C | 23 | 1 | 32 | 2 |
| 2010-11 | Stevenage | 5 | 0 | | |
| 2011-12 | Stevenage | 0 | 0 | 5 | 0 |
| 2011-12 | Aldershot T | 3 | 0 | 3 | 0 |
| 2012-13 | Port Vale | 3 | 0 | 3 | 0 |

**MYRIE-WILLIAMS, Jennison (F)**   188   19
H: 5 11   W: 12 08   b.Lambeth 17-5-88
*Source:* Scholar. *Honours:* England Youth.

| | | | | | |
|---|---|---|---|---|---|
| 2005-06 | Bristol C | 1 | 0 | | |
| 2006-07 | Bristol C | 25 | 2 | | |
| 2007-08 | Bristol C | 0 | 0 | | |
| 2007-08 | *Cheltenham T* | 12 | 0 | | |
| 2007-08 | *Tranmere R* | 25 | 3 | 25 | 3 |
| 2008-09 | Bristol C | 0 | 0 | | |
| 2008-09 | *Cheltenham T* | 5 | 1 | 17 | 1 |
| 2008-09 | *Carlisle U* | 8 | 0 | 8 | 0 |
| 2008-09 | *Hereford U* | 15 | 2 | 15 | 2 |
| 2009-10 | Bristol C | 0 | 0 | 26 | 2 |
| 2009-10 | *Dundee U* | 24 | 1 | 24 | 1 |
| 2010-11 | St Johnstone | 6 | 0 | 6 | 0 |
| 2011-12 | *Stevenage* | 17 | 0 | 17 | 0 |
| 2011-12 | Port Vale | 6 | 1 | | |
| 2012-13 | Port Vale | 44 | 9 | 50 | 10 |

**NEAL, Chris (G)**   111   0
H: 6 2   W: 12 04   b.St Albans 23-10-85
*Source:* Scholar.

| | | | | | |
|---|---|---|---|---|---|
| 2004-05 | Preston NE | 1 | 0 | | |
| 2005-06 | Preston NE | 0 | 0 | | |
| 2006-07 | Preston NE | 0 | 0 | | |
| 2006-07 | *Shrewsbury T* | 0 | 0 | | |
| 2007-08 | *Morecambe* | 0 | 0 | | |
| 2007-08 | Preston NE | 0 | 0 | | |
| 2008-09 | Preston NE | 0 | 0 | 1 | 0 |
| 2009-10 | Shrewsbury T | 7 | 0 | | |
| 2010-11 | Shrewsbury T | 22 | 0 | | |
| 2011-12 | Shrewsbury T | 35 | 0 | 64 | 0 |
| 2012-13 | Port Vale | 46 | 0 | 46 | 0 |

**OWEN, Gareth (D)**   255   2
H: 6 1   W: 11 07   b.Cheadle 21-9-82
*Source:* Scholar. *Honours:* Wales Youth.

| | | | | | |
|---|---|---|---|---|---|
| 2001-02 | Stoke C | 0 | 0 | | |
| 2002-03 | Stoke C | 0 | 0 | | |
| 2003-04 | Stoke C | 3 | 0 | | |
| 2003-04 | *Oldham Ath* | 15 | 1 | | |
| 2004-05 | Stoke C | 2 | 0 | 5 | 0 |
| 2004-05 | *Torquay U* | 5 | 0 | 5 | 0 |
| 2004-05 | *Oldham Ath* | 9 | 0 | | |
| 2005-06 | Oldham Ath | 17 | 0 | | |
| 2006-07 | Oldham Ath | 0 | 0 | 41 | 1 |
| 2006-07 | *Stockport Co* | 39 | 0 | | |
| 2007-08 | Stockport Co | 36 | 0 | | |
| 2008-09 | Stockport Co | 8 | 0 | 83 | 0 |
| 2008-09 | *Yeovil T* | 7 | 0 | 7 | 0 |
| 2008-09 | Port Vale | 12 | 0 | | |
| 2009-10 | Port Vale | 40 | 0 | | |
| 2010-11 | Port Vale | 36 | 1 | | |
| 2011-12 | Port Vale | 24 | 0 | | |
| 2012-13 | Port Vale | 2 | 0 | 114 | 1 |

**POPE, Tom (F)**   209   60
H: 6 3   W: 11 03   b.Stoke 27-8-85
*Source:* Biddulph Vic.

| | | | | | |
|---|---|---|---|---|---|
| 2005-06 | Crewe Alex | 0 | 0 | | |
| 2006-07 | Crewe Alex | 4 | 0 | | |
| 2007-08 | Crewe Alex | 26 | 7 | | |
| 2008-09 | Crewe Alex | 26 | 10 | 56 | 17 |
| 2009-10 | Rotherham U | 35 | 3 | | |
| 2010-11 | Rotherham U | 18 | 1 | 53 | 4 |
| 2010-11 | Port Vale | 13 | 3 | | |
| 2011-12 | Port Vale | 41 | 5 | | |
| 2012-13 | Port Vale | 46 | 31 | 100 | 39 |

**PURSE, Darren (D)**   556   34
H: 6 2   W: 12 08   b.Stepney 14-2-77
*Source:* Trainee. *Honours:* England Under-21.

| | | | | | |
|---|---|---|---|---|---|
| 1993-94 | Leyton Orient | 5 | 0 | | |
| 1994-95 | Leyton Orient | 38 | 3 | | |
| 1995-96 | Leyton Orient | 12 | 0 | 55 | 3 |
| 1996-97 | Oxford U | 31 | 1 | | |
| 1997-98 | Oxford U | 28 | 4 | 59 | 5 |
| 1997-98 | Birmingham C | 8 | 0 | | |
| 1998-99 | Birmingham C | 20 | 0 | | |
| 1999-2000 | Birmingham C | 38 | 2 | | |
| 2000-01 | Birmingham C | 37 | 3 | | |
| 2001-02 | Birmingham C | 36 | 3 | | |
| 2002-03 | Birmingham C | 20 | 1 | | |
| 2003-04 | Birmingham C | 9 | 0 | 168 | 9 |
| 2004-05 | WBA | 22 | 0 | 22 | 0 |
| 2005-06 | Cardiff C | 39 | 5 | | |
| 2006-07 | Cardiff C | 31 | 4 | | |
| 2007-08 | Cardiff C | 18 | 1 | | |
| 2008-09 | Cardiff C | 23 | 0 | 111 | 10 |
| 2009-10 | Sheffield W | 39 | 2 | | |
| 2010-11 | Sheffield W | 22 | 0 | 61 | 2 |
| 2010-11 | Millwall | 13 | 1 | | |
| 2011-12 | Millwall | 0 | 0 | 13 | 1 |
| 2011-12 | *Yeovil T* | 5 | 0 | 5 | 0 |
| 2011-12 | Plymouth Arg | 24 | 2 | | |
| 2012-13 | Plymouth Arg | 21 | 0 | 45 | 2 |
| 2012-13 | Port Vale | 17 | 2 | 17 | 2 |

**SHUKER, Chris (M)**   342   37
H: 5 5   W: 9 03   b.Liverpool 9-5-82
*Source:* Scholarship.

| | | | | | |
|---|---|---|---|---|---|
| 1999-2000 | Manchester C | 0 | 0 | | |
| 2000-01 | Manchester C | 0 | 0 | | |
| 2000-01 | *Macclesfield T* | 9 | 1 | 9 | 1 |
| 2001-02 | Manchester C | 2 | 0 | | |
| 2002-03 | Manchester C | 3 | 0 | | |
| 2002-03 | *Walsall* | 5 | 0 | 5 | 0 |
| 2003-04 | Manchester C | 0 | 0 | 5 | 0 |
| 2003-04 | *Rochdale* | 14 | 1 | 14 | 1 |
| 2003-04 | *Hartlepool U* | 14 | 1 | 14 | 1 |
| 2003-04 | Barnsley | 9 | 0 | | |
| 2004-05 | Barnsley | 45 | 7 | | |
| 2005-06 | Barnsley | 46 | 10 | 100 | 17 |
| 2006-07 | Tranmere R | 46 | 6 | | |
| 2007-08 | Tranmere R | 23 | 3 | | |
| 2008-09 | Tranmere R | 28 | 3 | | |
| 2009-10 | Tranmere R | 26 | 2 | 123 | 14 |
| 2010-11 | Morecambe | 27 | 2 | | |
| 2011-12 | Morecambe | 0 | 0 | 27 | 2 |
| 2011-12 | Port Vale | 16 | 1 | | |
| 2012-13 | Port Vale | 29 | 0 | 45 | 1 |

**TAYLOR, Rob (D)**   154   14
H: 6 0   W: 12 08   b.Shrewsbury 16-1-85
*Source:* Ludlow T, Stourport Swifts, Solihull B, Redditch U, Nuneaton B.

| | | | | | |
|---|---|---|---|---|---|
| 2008-09 | Port Vale | 20 | 3 | | |
| 2009-10 | Port Vale | 39 | 8 | | |
| 2010-11 | Port Vale | 36 | 1 | | |
| 2011-12 | Port Vale | 31 | 2 | | |
| 2012-13 | Port Vale | 28 | 0 | 154 | 14 |

**VINCENT, Ashley (M)**   215   25
H: 5 10   W: 11 08   b.Oldbury 26-5-85
*Source:* Wolverhampton W Scholar.

| | | | | | |
|---|---|---|---|---|---|
| 2004-05 | Cheltenham T | 26 | 1 | | |
| 2005-06 | Cheltenham T | 13 | 2 | | |
| 2006-07 | Cheltenham T | 5 | 0 | | |
| 2007-08 | Cheltenham T | 37 | 2 | | |
| 2008-09 | Cheltenham T | 29 | 3 | 110 | 8 |
| 2008-09 | Colchester U | 6 | 1 | | |
| 2009-10 | Colchester U | 19 | 3 | | |
| 2010-11 | Colchester U | 37 | 5 | | |
| 2011-12 | Colchester U | 9 | 1 | 71 | 10 |
| 2012-13 | Port Vale | 34 | 7 | 34 | 7 |

**WILLIAMSON, Ben (F)**   84   19
H: 5 11   W: 11 13   b.Lambeth 25-12-88
*Source:* Worthing.

| | | | | | |
|---|---|---|---|---|---|
| 2010-11 | Jerez Industrial | 12 | 8 | 12 | 8 |
| 2010-11 | Bournemouth | 4 | 0 | | |
| 2011-12 | Bournemouth | 0 | 0 | 4 | 0 |
| 2011-12 | Port Vale | 35 | 3 | | |
| 2012-13 | Port Vale | 33 | 8 | 68 | 11 |

**YATES, Adam (D)**   218   2
H: 5 10   W: 10 07   b.Stoke 28-5-83
*Source:* Scholar.

| | | | | | |
|---|---|---|---|---|---|
| 2000-01 | Crewe Alex | 0 | 0 | | |
| 2001-02 | Crewe Alex | 0 | 0 | | |
| 2002-03 | Crewe Alex | 0 | 0 | | |
| 2003-04 | Crewe Alex | 0 | 0 | | |
| 2004-05 | Crewe Alex | 0 | 0 | | |
| 2005-06 | Crewe Alex | 0 | 0 | | |
| 2006-07 | Crewe Alex | 0 | 0 | | |
| 2007-08 | Morecambe | 44 | 0 | | |
| 2008-09 | Morecambe | 32 | 0 | 76 | 0 |
| 2009-10 | Port Vale | 32 | 0 | | |
| 2010-11 | Port Vale | 46 | 0 | | |
| 2011-12 | Port Vale | 38 | 2 | | |
| 2012-13 | Port Vale | 26 | 0 | 142 | 2 |

**Scholars**
Beesley, Luke Edward; Boot, Ryan Thomas William; Crofts, Joshua William; Davies, Macauley Craid; Evans, Joseph Patrick; Hemmings, Joseph Peter; Lander, David William; Marland, Oliver John; Morris, Thomas Jonathan; Osborne, Elliot James; Price, Douglas William; Pryor, Jack Kieren; Smith, Nathan James; Swaby, Ricardo Nicholas; Warner, Matthew; Whieldon, William George James; Wright, Luke James.

## PORTSMOUTH (64)

**AGYEMANG, Patrick (F)**   414   68
H: 6 1   W: 12 00   b.Walthamstow 29-9-80
*Source:* Trainee. *Honours:* Ghana 3 full caps, 1 goal.

| | | | | | |
|---|---|---|---|---|---|
| 1998-99 | Wimbledon | 0 | 0 | | |
| 1999-2000 | Wimbledon | 0 | 0 | | |
| 1999-2000 | *Brentford* | 12 | 0 | 12 | 0 |
| 2000-01 | Wimbledon | 29 | 4 | | |
| 2001-02 | Wimbledon | 33 | 4 | | |
| 2002-03 | Wimbledon | 33 | 5 | | |
| 2003-04 | Wimbledon | 26 | 7 | 121 | 20 |
| 2003-04 | Gillingham | 20 | 6 | | |
| 2004-05 | Gillingham | 13 | 2 | 33 | 8 |
| 2004-05 | Preston NE | 27 | 4 | | |
| 2005-06 | Preston NE | 42 | 6 | | |
| 2006-07 | Preston NE | 31 | 7 | | |
| 2007-08 | Preston NE | 22 | 4 | 122 | 21 |
| 2007-08 | QPR | 17 | 8 | | |
| 2008-09 | QPR | 20 | 2 | | |
| 2009-10 | QPR | 17 | 3 | | |
| 2009-10 | *Bristol C* | 7 | 0 | 7 | 0 |
| 2010-11 | QPR | 19 | 2 | | |
| 2011-12 | QPR | 2 | 0 | 75 | 15 |
| 2011-12 | *Millwall* | 2 | 0 | 2 | 0 |
| 2011-12 | Stevenage | 13 | 1 | | |
| 2012-13 | Stevenage | 14 | 0 | 27 | 1 |
| 2012-13 | Portsmouth | 15 | 3 | 15 | 3 |

**AKINDE, John (F)**   105   12
H: 6 2   W: 10 01   b.Camberwell 8-7-89
*Source:* Ebbsfleet U.

| | | | | | |
|---|---|---|---|---|---|
| 2008-09 | Bristol C | 7 | 1 | | |
| 2008-09 | *Wycombe W* | 11 | 7 | | |
| 2009-10 | Bristol C | 7 | 0 | | |
| 2009-10 | *Wycombe W* | 6 | 1 | 17 | 8 |
| 2009-10 | *Brentford* | 2 | 0 | 2 | 0 |
| 2010-11 | Bristol C | 2 | 0 | 16 | 1 |
| 2010-11 | *Bristol R* | 14 | 0 | 14 | 0 |
| 2010-11 | *Dagenham & R* | 9 | 2 | | |
| 2011-12 | Crawley T | 25 | 1 | | |
| 2011-12 | *Dagenham & R* | 5 | 0 | 14 | 2 |
| 2012-13 | Crawley T | 6 | 0 | 31 | 1 |
| 2012-13 | Portsmouth | 11 | 0 | 11 | 0 |

**AWFORD, Nick (M)**   1   0

| | | | | | |
|---|---|---|---|---|---|
| 2012-13 | Portsmouth | 1 | 0 | 1 | 0 |

**BUTLER, Dan (D)**   17   0

| | | | | | |
|---|---|---|---|---|---|
| 2012-13 | Portsmouth | 17 | 0 | 17 | 0 |

**BUZSAKY, Akos (M)**   221   31
H: 5 11   W: 11 09   b.Hungary 7-5-82
*Source:* MTK, Porto. *Honours:* Hungary Under-21, 20 full caps, 2 goals.

| | | | | | |
|---|---|---|---|---|---|
| 2004-05 | Plymouth Arg | 15 | 1 | | |
| 2005-06 | Plymouth Arg | 34 | 4 | | |
| 2006-07 | Plymouth Arg | 36 | 3 | | |
| 2007-08 | Plymouth Arg | 11 | 0 | 96 | 8 |
| 2007-08 | QPR | 27 | 10 | | |
| 2008-09 | QPR | 11 | 1 | | |
| 2009-10 | QPR | 39 | 10 | | |
| 2010-11 | QPR | 19 | 0 | | |
| 2011-12 | QPR | 18 | 2 | 114 | 23 |
| 2012-13 | Portsmouth | 6 | 0 | 6 | 0 |
| 2012-13 | *Barnsley* | 5 | 0 | 5 | 0 |

**COMPTON, Jack (M)**    70   3
H: 5 8   W: 10 07   b.Torquay 2-9-88
*Source:* West Bromwich Albion Scholar.

| Season | Club | App | Gls | Tot | Gls |
|---|---|---|---|---|---|
| 2008-09 | Brighton & HA | 0 | 0 | | |

From Havant & Waterloovlle,
Weston-Super-Mare.

| 2010-11 | Falkirk | 24 | 3 | | |
| 2011-12 | Falkirk | 13 | 0 | 37 | 3 |
| 2011-12 | *Bradford C* | 14 | 0 | 14 | 0 |
| 2011-12 | *St Johnstone* | 0 | 0 | | |
| 2012-13 | Portsmouth | 12 | 0 | 12 | 0 |
| 2012-13 | Colchester U | 7 | 0 | 7 | 0 |

**CONNOLLY, David (F)**    402   156
H: 5 9   W: 11 00   b.Willesden 6-6-77
*Source:* Trainee. *Honours:* Eire Under-21, 41 full caps, 9 goals.

| Season | Club | App | Gls | Tot | Gls |
|---|---|---|---|---|---|
| 1994-95 | Watford | 2 | 0 | | |
| 1995-96 | Watford | 11 | 8 | | |
| 1996-97 | Watford | 13 | 2 | 26 | 10 |
| 1997-98 | Feyenoord | 10 | 2 | | |
| 1998-99 | Wolverhampton W | 32 | 6 | 32 | 6 |
| 1999-2000 | *Excelsior* | 32 | 29 | 32 | 29 |
| 2000-01 | Feyenoord | 15 | 5 | 25 | 7 |
| 2001-02 | Wimbledon | 35 | 18 | | |
| 2002-03 | Wimbledon | 28 | 24 | 63 | 42 |
| 2003-04 | West Ham U | 39 | 10 | 39 | 10 |
| 2004-05 | Leicester C | 44 | 13 | | |
| 2005-06 | Leicester C | 5 | 4 | 49 | 17 |
| 2005-06 | Wigan Ath | 17 | 1 | | |
| 2006-07 | Wigan Ath | 2 | 0 | 19 | 1 |
| 2006-07 | Sunderland | 36 | 13 | | |
| 2007-08 | Sunderland | 3 | 0 | | |
| 2008-09 | Sunderland | 0 | 0 | 39 | 13 |
| 2009-10 | Southampton | 20 | 5 | | |
| 2010-11 | Southampton | 15 | 3 | | |
| 2011-12 | Southampton | 26 | 6 | 61 | 14 |
| 2012-13 | Portsmouth | 17 | 7 | 17 | 7 |

**EASTWOOD, Simon (G)**    50   0
H: 6 2   W: 10 13   b.Huddersfield 26-6-89

| Season | Club | App | Gls | Tot | Gls |
|---|---|---|---|---|---|
| 2005-06 | Huddersfield T | 0 | 0 | | |
| 2006-07 | Huddersfield T | 0 | 0 | | |
| 2007-08 | Huddersfield T | 0 | 0 | | |
| 2008-09 | Huddersfield T | 1 | 0 | | |
| 2009-10 | Huddersfield T | 0 | 0 | 1 | 0 |
| 2009-10 | *Bradford C* | 22 | 0 | 22 | 0 |
| 2012-13 | Portsmouth | 27 | 0 | 27 | 0 |

**ERTL, Johannes (D)**    234   6
H: 6 2   W: 12 08   b.Graz 13-11-82
*Honours:* Austria 17 full caps.

| Season | Club | App | Gls | Tot | Gls |
|---|---|---|---|---|---|
| 2003-04 | Kalzdorf | 11 | 3 | 11 | 3 |
| 2004-05 | Sturm Graz | 26 | 0 | | |
| 2005-06 | Sturm Graz | 27 | 0 | | |
| 2006-07 | Sturm Graz | 5 | 0 | 58 | 0 |
| 2006-07 | FK Austria | 24 | 1 | | |
| 2007-08 | FK Austria | 24 | 2 | 48 | 3 |
| 2008-09 | Crystal Palace | 12 | 0 | | |
| 2009-10 | Crystal Palace | 33 | 0 | 45 | 0 |
| 2010-11 | Sheffield U | 28 | 0 | | |
| 2011-12 | Sheffield U | 7 | 0 | | |
| 2012-13 | Sheffield U | 0 | 0 | 35 | 0 |
| 2012-13 | Portsmouth | 37 | 0 | 37 | 0 |

**GYEPES, Gabor (D)**    248   20
H: 6 3   W: 13 00   b.Budapest 26-6-81
*Honours:* Hungary 26 full caps, 1 goal.

| Season | Club | App | Gls | Tot | Gls |
|---|---|---|---|---|---|
| 1999-2000 | Ferencvaros | 2 | 0 | | |
| 2000-01 | Ferencvaros | 29 | 2 | | |
| 2001-02 | Ferencvaros | 33 | 3 | | |
| 2002-03 | Ferencvaros | 17 | 2 | | |
| 2003-04 | Ferencvaros | 7 | 0 | | |
| 2004-05 | Ferencvaros | 26 | 5 | 114 | 12 |
| 2005-06 | Wolverhampton W | 20 | 0 | | |
| 2006-07 | Wolverhampton W | 0 | 0 | 20 | 0 |
| 2007-08 | Northampton T | 13 | 0 | | |
| 2008-09 | Northampton T | 2 | 0 | 15 | 0 |
| 2008-09 | Cardiff C | 27 | 2 | | |
| 2009-10 | Cardiff C | 16 | 1 | | |
| 2010-11 | Cardiff C | 21 | 1 | 64 | 4 |
| 2012-13 | Portsmouth | 35 | 4 | 35 | 4 |

**HARLEY, Jon (D)**    420   15
H: 5 8   W: 10 03   b.Maidstone 26-9-79
*Source:* Trainee. *Honours:* England Under-21.

| Season | Club | App | Gls | Tot | Gls |
|---|---|---|---|---|---|
| 1996-97 | Chelsea | 0 | 0 | | |
| 1997-98 | Chelsea | 3 | 0 | | |
| 1998-99 | Chelsea | 0 | 0 | | |
| 1999-2000 | Chelsea | 17 | 2 | | |
| 2000-01 | Chelsea | 10 | 0 | 30 | 2 |
| 2000-01 | Wimbledon | 6 | 2 | 6 | 2 |
| 2001-02 | Fulham | 10 | 0 | | |
| 2002-03 | Fulham | 11 | 1 | | |
| 2002-03 | *Sheffield U* | 9 | 1 | | |
| 2003-04 | Fulham | 4 | 0 | 25 | 1 |
| 2003-04 | *Sheffield U* | 5 | 0 | | |
| 2003-04 | West Ham U | 15 | 1 | 15 | 1 |
| 2004-05 | Sheffield U | 44 | 2 | | |
| 2005-06 | Sheffield U | 4 | 0 | 62 | 3 |
| 2005-06 | Burnley | 41 | 2 | | |
| 2006-07 | Burnley | 45 | 1 | | |
| 2007-08 | Burnley | 33 | 0 | 119 | 3 |
| 2008-09 | Watford | 37 | 1 | | |
| 2009-10 | Watford | 38 | 1 | 75 | 2 |
| 2010-11 | Notts Co | 39 | 0 | | |
| 2011-12 | Notts Co | 14 | 0 | 53 | 0 |
| 2011-12 | *Rotherham U* | 12 | 0 | 12 | 0 |
| 2012-13 | Portsmouth | 23 | 1 | 23 | 1 |

**HARRIS, Ashley (M)**    31   3
H: 5 8   W: 10 00   b.Waterlooville 9-12-93
*Source:* Scholar.

| Season | Club | App | Gls | Tot | Gls |
|---|---|---|---|---|---|
| 2011-12 | Portsmouth | 5 | 0 | | |
| 2012-13 | Portsmouth | 26 | 3 | 31 | 3 |

**KEENE, James (F)**    155   32
H: 5 11   W: 11 07   b.Wells 26-12-85

| Season | Club | App | Gls | Tot | Gls |
|---|---|---|---|---|---|
| 2004-05 | Portsmouth | 2 | 0 | | |
| 2004-05 | *Kidderminster H* | 5 | 0 | 5 | 0 |
| 2005-06 | Portsmouth | 0 | 0 | | |
| 2005-06 | *Bournemouth* | 11 | 2 | 11 | 2 |
| 2005-06 | *Boston U* | 6 | 1 | 6 | 1 |
| 2006-07 | IF Elfsborg | 11 | 3 | | |
| 2007-08 | IF Elfsborg | 13 | 1 | | |
| 2008-09 | IF Elfsborg | 20 | 6 | | |
| 2009-10 | IF Elfsborg | 27 | 7 | | |
| 2010-11 | IF Elfsborg | 20 | 3 | | |
| 2011-12 | IF Elfsborg | 8 | 0 | | |
| 2011-12 | Fredrikstad | 9 | 2 | 9 | 2 |
| 2011-12 | Djurgarden | 14 | 6 | 14 | 6 |
| 2012-13 | IF Elfsborg | 0 | 0 | 99 | 20 |

On loan from IF Elfsborg

| 2012-13 | Portsmouth | 9 | 1 | 11 | 1 |

**MALONEY, Jack (M)**    9   0

| Season | Club | App | Gls | Tot | Gls |
|---|---|---|---|---|---|
| 2012-13 | Portsmouth | 9 | 0 | 9 | 0 |

**MICHALIK, Lubomir (D)**    173   8
H: 6 4   W: 13 00   b.Cadca 13-8-83
*Source:* Cadca, Martin. *Honours:* Slovakia 7 full caps, 2 goals.

| Season | Club | App | Gls | Tot | Gls |
|---|---|---|---|---|---|
| 2005-06 | Senec | 8 | 1 | | |
| 2006-07 | Senec | 12 | 1 | 20 | 2 |
| 2006-07 | Leeds U | 7 | 1 | | |
| 2006-07 | Bolton W | 4 | 1 | | |
| 2007-08 | Bolton W | 7 | 0 | 11 | 1 |
| 2007-08 | Leeds U | 17 | 0 | | |
| 2008-09 | Leeds U | 19 | 0 | | |
| 2009-10 | Leeds U | 13 | 1 | | |
| 2010-11 | Leeds U | 0 | 0 | 56 | 2 |
| 2010-11 | Carlisle U | 32 | 2 | | |
| 2011-12 | Carlisle U | 36 | 0 | | |
| 2012-13 | Carlisle U | 0 | 0 | 68 | 2 |
| 2012-13 | Portsmouth | 18 | 1 | 18 | 1 |

**MOUTAOUAKIL, Yassin (D)**    82   0
H: 5 11   W: 11 06   b.Nice 18-7-86

| Season | Club | App | Gls | Tot | Gls |
|---|---|---|---|---|---|
| 2005-06 | Chateauroux | 16 | 0 | | |
| 2006-07 | Chateauroux | 13 | 0 | 29 | 0 |
| 2007-08 | Charlton Ath | 10 | 0 | | |
| 2008-09 | Charlton Ath | 11 | 0 | 21 | 0 |
| 2009-10 | *Motherwell* | 13 | 0 | 13 | 0 |
| 2012-13 | Portsmouth | 19 | 0 | 19 | 0 |

**ROCHA, Ricardo (D)**    334   8
H: 6 0   W: 12 08   b.Santo Tirso 3-10-78
*Honours:* Portugal 6 full caps.

| Season | Club | App | Gls | Tot | Gls |
|---|---|---|---|---|---|
| 1998-99 | Famalicao | 28 | 2 | 28 | 2 |
| 1999-2000 | Braga | 25 | 1 | | |
| 2000-01 | Braga | 19 | 0 | | |
| 2000-01 | Braga B | 8 | 0 | 8 | 0 |
| 2001-02 | Braga | 25 | 2 | 69 | 3 |
| 2002-03 | Benfica | 27 | 0 | | |
| 2003-04 | Benfica | 25 | 0 | | |
| 2004-05 | Benfica | 25 | 0 | | |
| 2005-06 | Benfica | 26 | 0 | | |
| 2006-07 | Benfica | 12 | 3 | 115 | 3 |
| 2006-07 | Tottenham H | 9 | 0 | | |
| 2007-08 | Tottenham H | 5 | 0 | | |
| 2008-09 | Tottenham H | 0 | 0 | 14 | 0 |
| 2009-10 | Standard Liege | 7 | 0 | 7 | 0 |
| 2009-10 | Portsmouth | 10 | 0 | | |
| 2010-11 | Portsmouth | 29 | 0 | | |
| 2011-12 | Portsmouth | 33 | 0 | | |
| 2012-13 | Portsmouth | 21 | 0 | 93 | 0 |

**RODGERS, Luke (F)**    364   108
H: 5 8   W: 11 06   b.Birmingham 1-1-82
*Source:* Trainee.

| Season | Club | App | Gls | Tot | Gls |
|---|---|---|---|---|---|
| 1999-2000 | Shrewsbury T | 6 | 1 | | |
| 2000-01 | Shrewsbury T | 26 | 7 | | |
| 2001-02 | Shrewsbury T | 38 | 22 | | |
| 2002-03 | Shrewsbury T | 36 | 16 | | |
| 2004-05 | Shrewsbury T | 36 | 6 | | |
| 2005-06 | Crewe Alex | 26 | 6 | | |
| 2006-07 | Crewe Alex | 12 | 3 | 38 | 9 |
| 2006-07 | Port Vale | 8 | 3 | | |
| 2007-08 | Port Vale | 36 | 9 | | |
| 2008-09 | Port Vale | 15 | 4 | 59 | 16 |
| 2008-09 | Yeovil T | 22 | 3 | 22 | 3 |
| 2009-10 | Notts Co | 42 | 13 | | |
| 2010-11 | Notts Co | 4 | 0 | 46 | 13 |
| 2011 | New York RB | 25 | 10 | 25 | 10 |
| 2012 | Lillestrom | 7 | 1 | 7 | 1 |
| 2012-13 | Portsmouth | 10 | 2 | 10 | 2 |
| 2012-13 | *Shrewsbury T* | 15 | 2 | 157 | 54 |

**RUSSELL, Darel (M)**    470   36
H: 5 10   W: 11 09   b.Mile End 22-10-80
*Source:* Trainee. *Honours:* England Youth.

| Season | Club | App | Gls | Tot | Gls |
|---|---|---|---|---|---|
| 1997-98 | Norwich C | 1 | 0 | | |
| 1998-99 | Norwich C | 13 | 1 | | |
| 1999-2000 | Norwich C | 33 | 4 | | |
| 2000-01 | Norwich C | 41 | 2 | | |
| 2001-02 | Norwich C | 23 | 0 | | |
| 2002-03 | Norwich C | 21 | 0 | | |
| 2003-04 | Stoke C | 46 | 4 | | |
| 2004-05 | Stoke C | 45 | 2 | | |
| 2005-06 | Stoke C | 37 | 3 | | |
| 2006-07 | Stoke C | 43 | 7 | 171 | 16 |
| 2007-08 | Norwich C | 39 | 4 | | |
| 2008-09 | Norwich C | 17 | 0 | | |
| 2009-10 | Norwich C | 35 | 3 | 244 | 18 |
| 2010-11 | Preston NE | 25 | 0 | | |
| 2011-12 | Preston NE | 2 | 0 | 27 | 0 |
| 2011-12 | *Charlton Ath* | 11 | 2 | 11 | 2 |
| 2012-13 | Portsmouth | 17 | 0 | 17 | 0 |

Transferred to Toronto FC February 2013

**SMITH, Phil (G)**    117   0
H: 6 1   W: 13 11   b.Harrow 14-12-79
*Source:* Trainee.

| Season | Club | App | Gls | Tot | Gls |
|---|---|---|---|---|---|
| 1997-98 | Millwall | 0 | 0 | | |
| 1998-99 | Millwall | 5 | 0 | 5 | 0 |

From Folkestone, Dover, Margate, Crawley

| 2006-07 | Swindon T | 31 | 0 | | |
| 2007-08 | Swindon T | 15 | 0 | | |
| 2008-09 | Swindon T | 25 | 0 | | |
| 2009-10 | Swindon T | 6 | 0 | | |
| 2010-11 | Swindon T | 27 | 0 | | |
| 2011-12 | Swindon T | 8 | 0 | 112 | 0 |
| 2012-13 | Portsmouth | 0 | 0 | | |

**SODJE, Sam (D)**    189   21
H: 6 0   W: 12 00   b.Greenwich 29-5-79
*Source:* Stevenage B, Margate. *Honours:* Nigeria 5 full caps.

| Season | Club | App | Gls | Tot | Gls |
|---|---|---|---|---|---|
| 2004-05 | Brentford | 40 | 7 | | |
| 2005-06 | Brentford | 43 | 5 | 83 | 12 |
| 2006-07 | Reading | 3 | 0 | | |
| 2006-07 | WBA | 7 | 1 | 7 | 1 |
| 2007-08 | Reading | 0 | 0 | | |
| 2007-08 | *Charlton Ath* | 27 | 2 | | |
| 2008-09 | Reading | 0 | 0 | | |
| 2008-09 | *Watford* | 1 | 0 | 1 | 0 |
| 2008-09 | *Leeds U* | 5 | 0 | 5 | 0 |
| 2009-10 | *Reading* | 0 | 0 | 3 | 0 |
| 2009-10 | Charlton Ath | 27 | 4 | 54 | 6 |
| 2010-11 | Notts Co | 11 | 0 | | |
| 2011-12 | Notts Co | 16 | 2 | 27 | 2 |
| 2012-13 | Portsmouth | 9 | 0 | 9 | 0 |

**TARBUCK, Bradley (F)**    0   0

| Season | Club | App | Gls | Tot | Gls |
|---|---|---|---|---|---|
| 2012-13 | Portsmouth | 0 | 0 | | |

**THOMPSON, Josh (D)**    83   6
H: 6 4   W: 12 00   b.Bolton 25-2-91
*Source:* Scholar. *Honours:* England Youth.

| | | | | | |
|---|---|---|---|---|---|
| 2008-09 | Stockport Co | 9 | 0 | 9 | 0 |
| 2009-10 | Celtic | 18 | 3 | 18 | 3 |
| 2010-11 | *Rochdale* | 12 | 1 | 12 | 1 |
| 2011-12 | *Chesterfield* | 20 | 1 | 20 | 1 |
| 2012-13 | Portsmouth | 2 | 0 | 2 | 0 |
| 2012-13 | *Colchester U* | 22 | 1 | 22 | 1 |

**WALKER, Liam (M)**    26   2
| | | | | | |
|---|---|---|---|---|---|
| 2012-13 | Portsmouth | 26 | 2 | 26 | 2 |

**WALLACE, Jed (M)**    22   6
b.Reading 15-12-93
*Source:* Lewes.
| | | | | | |
|---|---|---|---|---|---|
| 2011-12 | Portsmouth | 0 | 0 | | |
| 2012-13 | Portsmouth | 22 | 6 | 22 | 6 |

**WEBSTER, Adam (D)**    21   0
H: 6 1   W: 11 11   b.West Wittering 4-1-95
*Source:* Scholar.
| | | | | | |
|---|---|---|---|---|---|
| 2011-12 | Portsmouth | 3 | 0 | | |
| 2012-13 | Portsmouth | 18 | 0 | 21 | 0 |

**Scholars**
Awford, Nicholas Andrew; Branford, George Harry; Close, Ben Easton; Cook, Kane John Messenger; Hartson-Fitzgerald, James Karl; Horsburgh, Lewis David; Kim, Jae Heon; Maloney, Jack Levi; Medway, Harry George; Tarasenko, Nicholas Tarasavich; Tarbuck, Bradley Mark; Triggs, Liam Alexander; Warren, Joshua; Whatmough, Jack David Vincent.

# PRESTON NE (65)

**BEARDSLEY, Chris (F)**    135   15
H: 6 0   W: 12 12   b.Derby 28-2-84
*Source:* Scholar.
| | | | | | |
|---|---|---|---|---|---|
| 2002-03 | Mansfield T | 5 | 0 | | |
| 2003-04 | Mansfield T | 15 | 1 | | |
| 2004-05 | Doncaster R | 4 | 0 | 4 | 0 |
| 2004-05 | Kidderminster H | 25 | 5 | 25 | 5 |
| 2005-06 | Mansfield T | 3 | 0 | | |
| 2006-07 | Mansfield T | 10 | 0 | 33 | 1 |

From Rushden & D, York C, Kettering T.
| | | | | | |
|---|---|---|---|---|---|
| 2010-11 | Stevenage | 23 | 1 | | |
| 2011-12 | Stevenage | 31 | 7 | 54 | 8 |
| 2012-13 | Preston NE | 19 | 1 | 19 | 1 |

**BEAVON, Stuart (F)**    146   34
H: 5 7   W: 10 10   b.Reading 5-5-84
*Source:* Didcot T, Weymouth.
| | | | | | |
|---|---|---|---|---|---|
| 2008-09 | Wycombe W | 8 | 0 | | |
| 2009-10 | Wycombe W | 25 | 3 | | |
| 2010-11 | Wycombe W | 37 | 3 | | |
| 2011-12 | Wycombe W | 43 | 21 | | |
| 2012-13 | Wycombe W | 2 | 1 | 115 | 28 |
| 2012-13 | Preston NE | 31 | 6 | 31 | 6 |

**BUCHANAN, David (M)**    288   2
H: 5 7   W: 11 03   b.Rochdale 6-5-86
*Source:* Scholar. *Honours:* Northern Ireland Youth, Under-21.
| | | | | | |
|---|---|---|---|---|---|
| 2004-05 | Bury | 3 | 0 | | |
| 2005-06 | Bury | 23 | 0 | | |
| 2006-07 | Bury | 41 | 0 | | |
| 2007-08 | Bury | 35 | 0 | | |
| 2008-09 | Bury | 46 | 0 | | |
| 2009-10 | Bury | 38 | 0 | 186 | 0 |
| 2010-11 | Hamilton A | 28 | 1 | 28 | 1 |
| 2011-12 | Tranmere R | 41 | 1 | 41 | 1 |
| 2012-13 | Preston NE | 33 | 0 | 33 | 0 |

**BYROM, Joel (M)**    62   6
H: 6 0   W: 12 04   b.Accrington 14-9-86
*Source:* Scholar.
| | | | | | |
|---|---|---|---|---|---|
| 2004-05 | Blackburn R | 0 | 0 | | |
| 2005-06 | Blackburn R | 0 | 0 | | |
| 2006-07 | Accrington S | 1 | 0 | 1 | 0 |

From Clitheroe, Southport, Clitheroe, Northwich Vic.
| | | | | | |
|---|---|---|---|---|---|
| 2010-11 | Stevenage | 7 | 0 | | |
| 2011-12 | Stevenage | 32 | 4 | 39 | 4 |
| 2012-13 | Preston NE | 22 | 2 | 22 | 2 |

**CANSDELL-SHERRIFF, Shane (D)**    354   23
H: 5 11   W: 11 08   b.Sydney 10-11-82
*Source:* NSW Academy. *Honours:* Australia Youth, Under-23.
| | | | | | |
|---|---|---|---|---|---|
| 1999-2000 | Leeds U | 0 | 0 | | |
| 2000-01 | Leeds U | 0 | 0 | | |
| 2001-02 | Leeds U | 0 | 0 | | |
| 2002-03 | Leeds U | 0 | 0 | | |
| 2002-03 | *Rochdale* | 3 | 0 | | |
| 2003-04 | Aarhus | 29 | 4 | | |
| 2004-05 | Aarhus | 26 | 2 | | |
| 2005-06 | Aarhus | 27 | 1 | 82 | 7 |
| 2006-07 | Tranmere R | 43 | 3 | | |
| 2007-08 | Tranmere R | 44 | 3 | 87 | 6 |
| 2008-09 | Shrewsbury T | 31 | 2 | | |
| 2009-10 | Shrewsbury T | 41 | 1 | | |
| 2010-11 | Shrewsbury T | 41 | 2 | | |
| 2011-12 | Shrewsbury T | 37 | 4 | 150 | 9 |
| 2012-13 | Preston NE | 15 | 1 | 15 | 1 |
| 2012-13 | *Rochdale* | 17 | 0 | 20 | 0 |

**CUMMINS, Graham (F)**    201   80
H: 6 2   W: 11 11   b.Cork 29-12-87
| | | | | | |
|---|---|---|---|---|---|
| 2006 | Cobh Ramblers | 14 | 5 | | |
| 2007 | Cobh Ramblers | 35 | 11 | | |
| 2008 | Cobh Ramblers | 28 | 1 | 77 | 17 |
| 2009 | Waterford U | 28 | 17 | 28 | 17 |
| 2010 | Cork C | 32 | 18 | | |
| 2011 | Cork C | 30 | 24 | 62 | 42 |
| 2011-12 | Preston NE | 15 | 2 | | |
| 2012-13 | Preston NE | 19 | 2 | 34 | 4 |

**DAVIES, Ben (D)**    3   0
| | | | | | |
|---|---|---|---|---|---|
| 2012-13 | Preston NE | 3 | 0 | 3 | 0 |

**FOSTER, Luke (D)**    50   2
H: 6 2   W: 12 08   b.Mexborough 8-9-85
*Source:* Scholar.
| | | | | | |
|---|---|---|---|---|---|
| 2004-05 | Sheffield W | 0 | 0 | | |
| 2005-06 | Lincoln C | 16 | 1 | | |
| 2006-07 | Lincoln C | 0 | 0 | 16 | 1 |

From Stalybridge C, Oxford U, Mansfield T.
| | | | | | |
|---|---|---|---|---|---|
| 2010-11 | Stevenage | 23 | 1 | 23 | 1 |
| 2011-12 | Rotherham U | 5 | 0 | 5 | 0 |
| 2012-13 | Preston NE | 6 | 0 | 6 | 0 |

**GARNER, Joe (F)**    185   42
H: 5 10   W: 11 02   b.Blackburn 12-4-88
*Source:* Scholar. *Honours:* England Schools, Youth.
| | | | | | |
|---|---|---|---|---|---|
| 2004-05 | Blackburn R | 0 | 0 | | |
| 2005-06 | Blackburn R | 0 | 0 | | |
| 2006-07 | Blackburn R | 0 | 0 | | |
| 2006-07 | *Carlisle U* | 18 | 5 | | |
| 2007-08 | *Carlisle U* | 31 | 14 | | |
| 2008-09 | Nottingham F | 28 | 7 | | |
| 2009-10 | Nottingham F | 18 | 2 | | |
| 2010-11 | Nottingham F | 0 | 0 | | |
| 2010-11 | *Huddersfield T* | 16 | 0 | 16 | 0 |
| 2010-11 | *Scunthorpe U* | 18 | 6 | 18 | 6 |
| 2011-12 | Nottingham F | 2 | 0 | 48 | 9 |
| 2011-12 | Watford | 22 | 1 | | |
| 2012-13 | Watford | 2 | 0 | 24 | 1 |
| 2012-13 | *Carlisle U* | 16 | 7 | 65 | 26 |
| 2012-13 | Preston NE | 14 | 0 | 14 | 0 |

**HAYHURST, Will (M)**    23   4
H: 5 10   W: 11 02   b.Longridge 24-2-94
*Source:* Scholar.
| | | | | | |
|---|---|---|---|---|---|
| 2011-12 | Preston NE | 2 | 0 | | |
| 2012-13 | Preston NE | 21 | 4 | 23 | 4 |

**HOLMES, Lee (M)**    170   14
H: 5 8   W: 10 06   b.Mansfield 2-4-87
*Source:* Scholar. *Honours:* FA Schools, England Youth.
| | | | | | |
|---|---|---|---|---|---|
| 2002-03 | Derby Co | 2 | 0 | | |
| 2003-04 | Derby Co | 23 | 2 | | |
| 2004-05 | Derby Co | 3 | 0 | | |
| 2004-05 | *Swindon T* | 15 | 1 | | |
| 2005-06 | Derby Co | 18 | 0 | | |
| 2006-07 | Derby Co | 0 | 0 | | |
| 2006-07 | *Bradford C* | 16 | 0 | 16 | 0 |
| 2007-08 | Derby Co | 0 | 0 | 46 | 2 |
| 2007-08 | *Walsall* | 19 | 4 | 19 | 4 |
| 2008-09 | Southampton | 11 | 0 | | |
| 2009-10 | Southampton | 5 | 0 | | |
| 2010-11 | Southampton | 7 | 0 | | |
| 2011-12 | Southampton | 6 | 1 | 29 | 1 |
| 2011-12 | *Oxford U* | 7 | 2 | 7 | 2 |
| 2011-12 | *Swindon T* | 10 | 1 | 25 | 2 |
| 2012-13 | Preston NE | 28 | 3 | 28 | 3 |

**HUME, Iain (F)**    415   101
H: 5 7   W: 11 02   b.Ontario 31-10-83
*Source:* Juniors. *Honours:* Canada Youth, Under-20, 38 full caps, 6 goals.
| | | | | | |
|---|---|---|---|---|---|
| 1999-2000 | Tranmere R | 3 | 0 | | |
| 2000-01 | Tranmere R | 10 | 0 | | |
| 2001-02 | Tranmere R | 14 | 0 | | |
| 2002-03 | Tranmere R | 35 | 6 | | |
| 2003-04 | Tranmere R | 40 | 10 | | |
| 2004-05 | Tranmere R | 42 | 15 | | |
| 2005-06 | Tranmere R | 6 | 1 | 150 | 32 |
| 2005-06 | Leicester C | 37 | 9 | | |
| 2006-07 | Leicester C | 45 | 13 | | |
| 2007-08 | Leicester C | 40 | 11 | 122 | 33 |
| 2008-09 | Barnsley | 15 | 4 | | |
| 2009-10 | Barnsley | 35 | 5 | | |
| 2010-11 | Barnsley | 1 | 0 | 51 | 9 |
| 2010-11 | Preston NE | 31 | 12 | | |
| 2011-12 | Preston NE | 28 | 9 | | |
| 2012-13 | Preston NE | 0 | 0 | 59 | 21 |
| 2012-13 | *Doncaster R* | 33 | 6 | 33 | 6 |

**HUNTINGTON, Paul (D)**    172   13
H: 6 3   W: 12 08   b.Carlisle 17-9-87
*Source:* Scholar. *Honours:* England Youth.
| | | | | | |
|---|---|---|---|---|---|
| 2005-06 | Newcastle U | 0 | 0 | | |
| 2006-07 | Newcastle U | 11 | 1 | | |
| 2007-08 | Newcastle U | 0 | 0 | 11 | 1 |
| 2007-08 | *Leeds U* | 17 | 2 | | |
| 2008-09 | Leeds U | 4 | 0 | | |
| 2009-10 | Leeds U | 0 | 0 | 21 | 2 |
| 2009-10 | *Stockport Co* | 26 | 0 | 26 | 0 |
| 2010-11 | Yeovil T | 40 | 5 | | |
| 2011-12 | Yeovil T | 37 | 2 | 77 | 7 |
| 2012-13 | Preston NE | 37 | 3 | 37 | 3 |

**JAMES, Steven (G)**    0   0
| | | | | |
|---|---|---|---|---|
| 2012-13 | Preston NE | 0 | 0 | |

**KEANE, Keith (M)**    155   5
H: 5 9   W: 11 01   b.Luton 20-11-86
*Source:* Scholar. *Honours:* Eire Youth, Under-21.
| | | | | | |
|---|---|---|---|---|---|
| 2003-04 | Luton T | 15 | 1 | | |
| 2004-05 | Luton T | 17 | 0 | | |
| 2005-06 | Luton T | 10 | 1 | | |
| 2006-07 | Luton T | 19 | 1 | | |
| 2007-08 | Luton T | 28 | 1 | | |
| 2008-09 | Luton T | 40 | 0 | 129 | 4 |
| 2012-13 | Preston NE | 26 | 1 | 26 | 1 |

**KING, Jack (M)**    36   4
b.Oxford 20-8-85
*Source:* Farnborough T.
| | | | | | |
|---|---|---|---|---|---|
| 2012-13 | Preston NE | 36 | 4 | 36 | 4 |

**LAIRD, Scott (D)**    109   16
H: 5 11   W: 11 05   b.Taunton 15-5-88
*Source:* Scholar.
| | | | | | |
|---|---|---|---|---|---|
| 2006-07 | Plymouth Arg | 0 | 0 | | |
| 2007-08 | Plymouth Arg | 0 | 0 | | |
| 2010-11 | Stevenage | 44 | 4 | | |
| 2011-12 | Stevenage | 46 | 8 | 90 | 12 |
| 2012-13 | Preston NE | 19 | 4 | 19 | 4 |

**MONAKANA, Jeffrey (M)**    38   4
b.Enfield 5-11-93
| | | | | | |
|---|---|---|---|---|---|
| 2012-13 | Preston NE | 38 | 4 | 38 | 4 |

**MOUSINHO, John (M)**    218   16
H: 6 1   W: 12 07   b.Hounslow 30-4-86
*Source:* Univ of Notre Dame.
| | | | | | |
|---|---|---|---|---|---|
| 2005-06 | Brentford | 7 | 0 | | |
| 2006-07 | Brentford | 34 | 0 | | |
| 2007-08 | Brentford | 23 | 2 | 64 | 2 |
| 2008-09 | Wycombe W | 34 | 2 | | |
| 2009-10 | Wycombe W | 39 | 1 | 73 | 3 |
| 2010-11 | Stevenage | 38 | 7 | | |
| 2011-12 | Stevenage | 19 | 3 | 57 | 10 |
| 2012-13 | Preston NE | 24 | 1 | 24 | 1 |

**PROCTER, Andy (M)**    269   29
H: 6 0   W: 12 04   b.Blackburn 13-3-83
*Source:* Great Harwood T.
| | | | | | |
|---|---|---|---|---|---|
| 2006-07 | Accrington S | 43 | 3 | | |
| 2007-08 | Accrington S | 43 | 10 | | |
| 2008-09 | Accrington S | 37 | 3 | | |

| | | | | | |
|---|---|--:|--:|--:|--:|
| 2009-10 | Accrington S | 44 | 5 | | |
| 2010-11 | Accrington S | 43 | 6 | | |
| 2011-12 | Accrington S | 25 | 2 | 235 | 29 |
| 2011-12 | Preston NE | 19 | 0 | | |
| 2012-13 | Preston NE | 15 | 0 | 34 | 0 |

**ROBERTSON, Chris (D)** 162 7
H: 6 3 W: 11 08 b.Dundee 11-10-85
*Source:* Scholar.

| | | | | | |
|---|---|--:|--:|--:|--:|
| 2005-06 | Sheffield U | 0 | 0 | | |
| 2005-06 | *Chester C* | 1 | 0 | 1 | 0 |
| 2006-07 | Sheffield U | 0 | 0 | | |
| 2006-07 | Torquay U | 9 | 1 | | |
| 2009-10 | Torquay U | 45 | 2 | | |
| 2010-11 | Torquay U | 43 | 2 | | |
| 2011-12 | Torquay U | 25 | 1 | 122 | 6 |
| 2011-12 | Preston NE | 18 | 1 | | |
| 2012-13 | Preston NE | 21 | 0 | 39 | 1 |

**SIMONSEN, Steve (G)** 345 0
H: 6 2 W: 12 08 b.South Shields 3-4-79
*Source:* Trainee. *Honours:* England Youth, Under-21.

| | | | | | |
|---|---|--:|--:|--:|--:|
| 1996-97 | Tranmere R | 0 | 0 | | |
| 1997-98 | Tranmere R | 30 | 0 | | |
| 1998-99 | Tranmere R | 5 | 0 | 35 | 0 |
| 1998-99 | Everton | 1 | 0 | | |
| 1999-2000 | Everton | 1 | 0 | | |
| 2000-01 | Everton | 1 | 0 | | |
| 2001-02 | Everton | 25 | 0 | | |
| 2002-03 | Everton | 2 | 0 | | |
| 2003-04 | Everton | 1 | 0 | 30 | 0 |
| 2004-05 | Stoke C | 31 | 0 | | |
| 2005-06 | Stoke C | 45 | 0 | | |
| 2006-07 | Stoke C | 46 | 0 | | |
| 2007-08 | Stoke C | 36 | 0 | | |
| 2008-09 | Stoke C | 5 | 0 | | |
| 2009-10 | Stoke C | 3 | 0 | 166 | 0 |
| 2009-10 | *Sheffield U* | 7 | 0 | | |
| 2010-11 | Sheffield U | 45 | 0 | | |
| 2011-12 | Sheffield U | 44 | 0 | | |
| 2012-13 | Sheffield U | 0 | 0 | 96 | 0 |
| 2012-13 | Preston NE | 10 | 0 | 10 | 0 |
| 2012-13 | Dundee | 8 | 0 | 8 | 0 |

**STUCKMANN, Thorsten (G)** 331 0
H: 6 6 W: 14 11 b.Gutersloh 17-3-81

| | | | | | |
|---|---|--:|--:|--:|--:|
| 2000-01 | Pr Munster | 25 | 0 | | |
| 2001-02 | Pr Munster | 19 | 0 | | |
| 2002-03 | Pr Munster | 30 | 0 | 74 | 0 |
| 2003-04 | E Braunschweig | 21 | 0 | | |
| 2004-05 | E Braunschweig | 36 | 0 | | |
| 2005-06 | E Braunschweig | 34 | 0 | | |
| 2006-07 | E Braunschweig | 34 | 0 | 125 | 0 |
| 2007-08 | A Aachen | 16 | 0 | | |
| 2008-09 | A Aachen | 34 | 0 | | |
| 2009-10 | A Aachen | 31 | 0 | | |
| 2010-11 | A Aachen | 1 | 0 | 82 | 0 |
| 2011-12 | Preston NE | 28 | 0 | | |
| 2012-13 | Preston NE | 22 | 0 | 50 | 0 |

**TRUNDLE, Lee (F)** 322 117
H: 6 0 W: 11 06 b.Liverpool 10-10-76
*Source:* Rhyl.

| | | | | | |
|---|---|--:|--:|--:|--:|
| 2000-01 | Wrexham | 14 | 8 | | |
| 2001-02 | Wrexham | 36 | 8 | | |
| 2002-03 | Wrexham | 44 | 11 | 94 | 27 |
| 2003-04 | Swansea | 31 | 16 | | |
| 2004-05 | Swansea | 42 | 22 | | |
| 2005-06 | Swansea | 36 | 20 | | |
| 2006-07 | Swansea | 34 | 19 | | |
| 2007-08 | Bristol C | 35 | 5 | | |
| 2008-09 | Bristol C | 19 | 2 | | |
| 2008-09 | Leeds U | 10 | 1 | 10 | 1 |
| 2009-10 | Bristol C | 0 | 0 | 54 | 7 |
| 2009-10 | *Swansea* | 20 | 5 | 163 | 82 |
| From Neath | | | | | |
| 2012-13 | Preston NE | 1 | 0 | 1 | 0 |

**WELSH, John (M)** 235 15
H: 5 7 W: 12 02 b.Liverpool 10-1-84
*Source:* Scholar. *Honours:* England Youth, Under-20, Under-21.

| | | | | | |
|---|---|--:|--:|--:|--:|
| 2000-01 | Liverpool | 0 | 0 | | |
| 2001-02 | Liverpool | 0 | 0 | | |
| 2002-03 | Liverpool | 0 | 0 | | |
| 2003-04 | Liverpool | 1 | 0 | | |
| 2004-05 | Liverpool | 3 | 0 | | |
| 2005-06 | Liverpool | 0 | 0 | 4 | 0 |

| | | | | | |
|---|---|--:|--:|--:|--:|
| 2005-06 | Hull C | 32 | 2 | | |
| 2006-07 | Hull C | 18 | 1 | | |
| 2007-08 | Hull C | 0 | 0 | | |
| 2007-08 | *Chester C* | 6 | 0 | 6 | 0 |
| 2008-09 | Hull C | 0 | 0 | 50 | 3 |
| 2008-09 | *Carlisle U* | 4 | 0 | 4 | 0 |
| 2008-09 | *Bury* | 5 | 0 | 5 | 0 |
| 2009-10 | Tranmere R | 45 | 4 | | |
| 2010-11 | Tranmere R | 41 | 4 | | |
| 2011-12 | Tranmere R | 44 | 3 | 130 | 11 |
| 2012-13 | Preston NE | 36 | 1 | 36 | 1 |

**WRIGHT, Bailey (D)** 53 3
H: 5 9 W: 13 05 b.Melbourne 28-7-92
*Source:* Scholar.

| | | | | | |
|---|---|--:|--:|--:|--:|
| 2010-11 | Preston NE | 2 | 0 | | |
| 2011-12 | Preston NE | 13 | 1 | | |
| 2012-13 | Preston NE | 38 | 2 | 53 | 3 |

**WROE, Nicky (M)** 213 28
H: 5 11 W: 10 02 b.Sheffield 28-9-85
*Source:* Scholar.

| | | | | | |
|---|---|--:|--:|--:|--:|
| 2002-03 | Barnsley | 1 | 0 | | |
| 2003-04 | Barnsley | 2 | 1 | | |
| 2004-05 | Barnsley | 31 | 0 | | |
| 2005-06 | Barnsley | 12 | 0 | | |
| 2006-07 | Barnsley | 3 | 0 | 49 | 1 |
| 2006-07 | *Bury* | 5 | 0 | 5 | 0 |
| From York C. | | | | | |
| 2009-10 | Torquay U | 45 | 9 | | |
| 2010-11 | Torquay U | 20 | 3 | 65 | 12 |
| 2010-11 | Shrewsbury T | 18 | 3 | | |
| 2011-12 | Shrewsbury T | 38 | 4 | 56 | 7 |
| 2012-13 | Preston NE | 38 | 8 | 38 | 8 |

**Scholars**
Amis, Joshua Jonathan; Brownhill, Joshua; Croasdale, Ryan Mark; Davies, Benjamin Keith; Forbes, Daniel Jasper; Gray, George Robert; Greenwood, Matthew John; Holmes, Sean Lewis; Hornby-Forbes, Tyler Cecil; James, Steven Paul; Kuba-Kuba, David Elime Nono; Quinn, Thomas Taylor; Ryan, Jack Liam; Scott, Jordan Lee; Scurry, Alan James; Thurston, Adam Timothy; Whittington, Joseph Eric; Wilmer-Anderton, Nicholas Jack; Zibaka, Brandon.

# QPR (66)

**ANDRADE, Bruno (M)** 26 2
H: 5 9 W: 11 09 b.Aveiro 2-10-93
*Source:* Scholar.

| | | | | | |
|---|---|--:|--:|--:|--:|
| 2010-11 | QPR | 1 | 0 | | |
| 2011-12 | QPR | 1 | 0 | | |
| 2011-12 | *Aldershot T* | 1 | 0 | 1 | 0 |
| 2012-13 | QPR | 0 | 0 | 2 | 0 |
| 2012-13 | *Wycombe W* | 23 | 2 | 23 | 2 |

**BALANTA, Angelo (F)** 92 16
H: 5 10 W: 11 11 b.Colombia 1-7-90
*Source:* Scholar.

| | | | | | |
|---|---|--:|--:|--:|--:|
| 2007-08 | QPR | 11 | 1 | | |
| 2008-09 | QPR | 10 | 1 | | |
| 2008-09 | *Wycombe W* | 11 | 3 | 11 | 3 |
| 2009-10 | QPR | 4 | 0 | | |
| 2010-11 | QPR | 0 | 0 | | |
| 2010-11 | *Milton Keynes D* | 18 | 6 | | |
| 2011-12 | QPR | 0 | 0 | | |
| 2011-12 | *Milton Keynes D* | 20 | 4 | | |
| 2012-13 | QPR | 0 | 0 | 25 | 2 |
| 2012-13 | *Milton Keynes D* | 12 | 1 | 50 | 11 |
| 2012-13 | *Yeovil T* | 6 | 0 | 6 | 0 |

**BARTON, Joey (M)** 267 25
H: 5 11 W: 12 05 b.Huyton 2-9-82
*Source:* Scholar. *Honours:* England Under-21, 1 full cap.

| | | | | | |
|---|---|--:|--:|--:|--:|
| 2001-02 | Manchester C | 0 | 0 | | |
| 2002-03 | Manchester C | 7 | 1 | | |
| 2003-04 | Manchester C | 28 | 1 | | |
| 2004-05 | Manchester C | 31 | 1 | | |
| 2005-06 | Manchester C | 31 | 6 | | |
| 2006-07 | Manchester C | 33 | 6 | 130 | 15 |
| 2007-08 | Newcastle U | 23 | 1 | | |
| 2008-09 | Newcastle U | 9 | 1 | | |
| 2009-10 | Newcastle U | 15 | 1 | | |
| 2010-11 | Newcastle U | 32 | 4 | | |

| | | | | | |
|---|---|--:|--:|--:|--:|
| 2011-12 | Newcastle U | 2 | 0 | 81 | 7 |
| 2011-12 | QPR | 31 | 3 | | |
| 2012-13 | QPR | 0 | 0 | 31 | 3 |
| 2012-13 | *Marseille* | 25 | 0 | 25 | 0 |

**BEN HAIM, Tal (D)** 267 3
H: 5 11 W: 11 09 b.Rishon Le Zion 31-3-82
*Source:* Maccabi Tel Aviv. *Honours:* Israel Under-21, 71 full caps, 1 goal.

| | | | | | |
|---|---|--:|--:|--:|--:|
| 2000-01 | Maccabi Tel Aviv | 1 | 0 | | |
| 2001-02 | Maccabi Tel Aviv | 29 | 1 | | |
| 2002-03 | Maccabi Tel Aviv | 30 | 0 | | |
| 2003-04 | Maccabi Tel Aviv | 26 | 1 | 86 | 2 |
| 2004-05 | Bolton W | 21 | 1 | | |
| 2005-06 | Bolton W | 35 | 0 | | |
| 2006-07 | Bolton W | 32 | 0 | 88 | 1 |
| 2007-08 | Chelsea | 13 | 0 | 13 | 0 |
| 2008-09 | Manchester C | 9 | 0 | | |
| 2008-09 | *Sunderland* | 5 | 0 | 5 | 0 |
| 2009-10 | Manchester C | 0 | 0 | 9 | 0 |
| 2009-10 | Portsmouth | 22 | 0 | | |
| 2010-11 | Portsmouth | 0 | 0 | | |
| 2010-11 | *West Ham U* | 8 | 0 | 8 | 0 |
| 2011-12 | Portsmouth | 33 | 0 | | |
| 2012-13 | Portsmouth | 0 | 0 | 55 | 0 |
| 2012-13 | Hapoel Tel-Aviv | 0 | 0 | | |
| 2012-13 | QPR | 3 | 0 | 3 | 0 |

**BOSINGWA, Jose (D)** 271 6
H: 6 0 W: 12 08 b.Kinshasa 24-8-82
*Honours:* Portugal Under-21, 24 full caps.

| | | | | | |
|---|---|--:|--:|--:|--:|
| 2000-01 | Freamunde | 11 | 0 | 11 | 0 |
| 2001-02 | Boavista | 15 | 0 | | |
| 2002-03 | Boavista | 26 | 0 | 41 | 0 |
| 2003-04 | Porto | 13 | 1 | | |
| 2004-05 | Porto | 25 | 1 | | |
| 2005-06 | Porto | 21 | 0 | | |
| 2006-07 | Porto | 25 | 0 | | |
| 2007-08 | Porto | 23 | 1 | 107 | 3 |
| 2008-09 | Chelsea | 34 | 2 | | |
| 2009-10 | Chelsea | 8 | 0 | | |
| 2010-11 | Chelsea | 20 | 0 | | |
| 2011-12 | Chelsea | 27 | 1 | 89 | 3 |
| 2012-13 | QPR | 23 | 0 | 23 | 0 |

**BOTHROYD, Jay (F)** 341 78
H: 6 3 W: 14 13 b.Islington 7-5-82
*Source:* Trainee. *Honours:* England Schools, Youth, Under-20, Under-21, 1 full cap.

| | | | | | |
|---|---|--:|--:|--:|--:|
| 1999-2000 | Arsenal | 0 | 0 | | |
| 2000-01 | Coventry C | 8 | 0 | | |
| 2001-02 | Coventry C | 31 | 6 | | |
| 2002-03 | Coventry C | 33 | 8 | 72 | 14 |
| 2003-04 | *Perugia* | 26 | 4 | 26 | 4 |
| 2004-05 | Blackburn R | 11 | 1 | 11 | 1 |
| 2005-06 | Charlton Ath | 18 | 2 | 18 | 2 |
| 2006-07 | Wolverhampton W | 33 | 9 | | |
| 2007-08 | Wolverhampton W | 22 | 3 | 55 | 12 |
| 2007-08 | *Stoke C* | 4 | 0 | 4 | 0 |
| 2008-09 | Cardiff C | 39 | 12 | | |
| 2009-10 | Cardiff C | 40 | 11 | | |
| 2010-11 | Cardiff C | 37 | 18 | 116 | 41 |
| 2011-12 | QPR | 21 | 2 | | |
| 2012-13 | QPR | 4 | 1 | 25 | 3 |
| 2012-13 | *Sheffield W* | 14 | 1 | 14 | 1 |

**BROWN, Ben (D)** 0 0
*Source:* Scholar.

| | | | | |
|---|---|--:|--:|---|
| 2011-12 | QPR | 0 | 0 | |
| 2012-13 | QPR | 0 | 0 | |

**CAMPBELL, Dudley (F)** 216 67
H: 5 10 W: 11 00 b.Hammersmith 12-11-81
*Source:* Aston Villa Trainee, QPR, Chesham U, Stevenage B, Yeading.

| | | | | | |
|---|---|--:|--:|--:|--:|
| 2005-06 | Brentford | 23 | 9 | 23 | 9 |
| 2005-06 | Birmingham C | 11 | 0 | | |
| 2006-07 | Birmingham C | 32 | 9 | 43 | 9 |
| 2007-08 | Leicester C | 28 | 4 | | |
| 2008-09 | Leicester C | 7 | 0 | | |
| 2008-09 | *Blackpool* | 20 | 9 | | |
| 2009-10 | Leicester C | 3 | 0 | | |
| 2009-10 | *Derby Co* | 8 | 3 | 8 | 3 |
| 2009-10 | *Blackpool* | 15 | 8 | | |
| 2010-11 | Leicester C | 3 | 1 | 41 | 5 |
| 2010-11 | Blackpool | 31 | 13 | 66 | 30 |
| 2011-12 | QPR | 11 | 1 | | |
| 2012-13 | QPR | 0 | 0 | 11 | 1 |
| 2012-13 | *Ipswich T* | 17 | 10 | 17 | 10 |
| 2012-13 | *Blackburn R* | 7 | 0 | 7 | 0 |

**CISSE, Djibril (F)** 375 170
H: 6 0  W: 13 00  b.Arles 12-8-81
Honours: France Under-21, 41 full caps, 9 goals.

| | | | | | |
|---|---|---|---|---|---|
| 1998-99 | Auxerre | 1 | 0 | | |
| 1999-2000 | Auxerre | 2 | 0 | | |
| 2000-01 | Auxerre | 25 | 8 | | |
| 2001-02 | Auxerre | 29 | 22 | | |
| 2002-03 | Auxerre | 33 | 14 | | |
| 2003-04 | Auxerre | 38 | 26 | 128 | 70 |
| 2004-05 | Liverpool | 16 | 4 | | |
| 2005-06 | Liverpool | 33 | 9 | 49 | 13 |
| 2006-07 | Marseille | 21 | 8 | | |
| 2007-08 | Marseille | 35 | 16 | | |
| 2008-09 | Marseille | 2 | 0 | 58 | 24 |
| 2008-09 | Sunderland | 35 | 10 | 35 | 10 |
| 2009-10 | Panathinaikos | 28 | 23 | | |
| 2010-11 | Panathinaikos | 33 | 20 | 61 | 43 |
| 2011-12 | Lazio | 18 | 1 | 18 | 1 |
| 2011-12 | QPR | 8 | 6 | | |
| 2012-13 | QPR | 18 | 3 | 26 | 9 |
| 2012-13 | Al Gharafa | 0 | 0 | | |

**DERRY, Shaun (M)** 568 12
H: 5 10  W: 10 13  b.Nottingham 6-12-77
Source: Trainee.

| | | | | | |
|---|---|---|---|---|---|
| 1995-96 | Notts Co | 12 | 0 | | |
| 1996-97 | Notts Co | 39 | 2 | | |
| 1997-98 | Notts Co | 28 | 2 | 79 | 4 |
| 1997-98 | Sheffield U | 12 | 0 | | |
| 1998-99 | Sheffield U | 26 | 0 | | |
| 1999-2000 | Sheffield U | 34 | 0 | 72 | 0 |
| 1999-2000 | Portsmouth | 9 | 1 | | |
| 2000-01 | Portsmouth | 28 | 0 | | |
| 2001-02 | Portsmouth | 12 | 0 | 49 | 1 |
| 2002-03 | Crystal Palace | 39 | 1 | | |
| 2003-04 | Crystal Palace | 37 | 2 | | |
| 2004-05 | Crystal Palace | 7 | 0 | | |
| 2004-05 | Nottingham F | 7 | 0 | 7 | 0 |
| 2004-05 | Leeds U | 7 | 2 | | |
| 2005-06 | Leeds U | 41 | 0 | | |
| 2006-07 | Leeds U | 23 | 1 | | |
| 2007-08 | Leeds U | 10 | 0 | 71 | 3 |
| 2007-08 | Crystal Palace | 30 | 0 | | |
| 2008-09 | Crystal Palace | 39 | 0 | | |
| 2009-10 | Crystal Palace | 46 | 0 | 198 | 3 |
| 2010-11 | QPR | 45 | 0 | | |
| 2011-12 | QPR | 29 | 1 | | |
| 2012-13 | QPR | 18 | 0 | 92 | 1 |

**DIAKITE, Samba (M)** 118 1
H: 6 1  W: 11 13  b.Montfermeil 24-1-89
Honours: Mali 9 full caps.

| | | | | | |
|---|---|---|---|---|---|
| 2007-08 | Valenciennes B | 7 | 0 | 7 | 0 |
| 2008-09 | Olympique N-le-Sec | 28 | 0 | 28 | 0 |
| 2009-10 | Nancy B | 19 | 0 | 19 | 0 |
| 2009-10 | Nancy | 3 | 0 | | |
| 2010-11 | Nancy | 23 | 0 | | |
| 2011-12 | Nancy | 15 | 0 | 41 | 0 |
| 2011-12 | QPR | 9 | 1 | | |
| 2012-13 | QPR | 14 | 0 | 23 | 1 |

**DOUGHTY, Michael (M)** 26 0
H: 6 1  W: 12 10  b.Westminster 20-11-92
Source: Scholar. Honours: Wales Youth.

| | | | | | |
|---|---|---|---|---|---|
| 2010-11 | QPR | 0 | 0 | | |
| 2011-12 | QPR | 0 | 0 | | |
| 2011-12 | Crawley T | 16 | 0 | 16 | 0 |
| 2011-12 | Aldershot T | 5 | 0 | | |
| 2012-13 | QPR | 0 | 0 | | |
| 2012-13 | Aldershot T | 0 | 0 | 5 | 0 |
| 2012-13 | St Johnstone | 5 | 0 | 5 | 0 |

**EHMER, Max (M)** 66 1
H: 6 2  W: 11 00  b.Frankfurt 3-2-92
Source: Scholar.

| | | | | | |
|---|---|---|---|---|---|
| 2009-10 | QPR | 0 | 0 | | |
| 2010-11 | QPR | 0 | 0 | | |
| 2010-11 | Yeovil T | 27 | 0 | | |
| 2011-12 | QPR | 0 | 0 | | |
| 2011-12 | Yeovil T | 24 | 0 | 51 | 0 |
| 2011-12 | Preston NE | 9 | 0 | 9 | 0 |
| 2012-13 | QPR | 0 | 0 | | |
| 2012-13 | Stevenage | 6 | 1 | 6 | 1 |

**EPHRAIM, Hogan (F)** 153 10
H: 5 9  W: 10 06  b.Islington 31-3-88
Source: Scholar. Honours: England Youth.

| | | | | | |
|---|---|---|---|---|---|
| 2004-05 | West Ham U | 0 | 0 | | |
| 2005-06 | West Ham U | 0 | 0 | | |
| 2006-07 | West Ham U | 0 | 0 | | |
| 2006-07 | Colchester U | 21 | 1 | 21 | 1 |
| 2007-08 | West Ham U | 0 | 0 | | |
| 2007-08 | QPR | 29 | 3 | | |
| 2008-09 | QPR | 27 | 1 | | |
| 2009-10 | QPR | 22 | 0 | | |
| 2009-10 | Leeds U | 3 | 0 | 3 | 0 |
| 2010-11 | QPR | 28 | 3 | | |
| 2011-12 | QPR | 2 | 0 | | |
| 2011-12 | Charlton Ath | 5 | 1 | 5 | 1 |
| 2011-12 | Bristol C | 5 | 1 | 5 | 1 |
| 2012-13 | QPR | 0 | 0 | 108 | 7 |
| 2012-13 | Toronto FC | 11 | 0 | 11 | 0 |

**FAURLIN, Alejandro (M)** 186 13
H: 6 1  W: 12 06  b.Argentina 9-8-86

| | | | | | |
|---|---|---|---|---|---|
| 2004 | Rosario Central | 1 | 0 | | |
| 2005 | Rosario Central | 0 | 0 | | |
| 2006 | Rosario Central | 0 | 0 | 1 | 0 |
| 2007 | Atletico Rafaela | 40 | 1 | 40 | 1 |
| 2008-09 | Instituto | 27 | 7 | 27 | 7 |
| 2009-10 | QPR | 41 | 1 | | |
| 2010-11 | QPR | 40 | 3 | | |
| 2011-12 | QPR | 20 | 1 | | |
| 2012-13 | QPR | 11 | 0 | 112 | 5 |
| 2012-13 | Palermo | 6 | 0 | 6 | 0 |

**FERDINAND, Anton (D)** 274 5
H: 6 2  W: 11 00  b.Peckham 18-2-85
Source: Trainee. Honours: England Youth, Under-20, Under-21.

| | | | | | |
|---|---|---|---|---|---|
| 2002-03 | West Ham U | 0 | 0 | | |
| 2003-04 | West Ham U | 20 | 0 | | |
| 2004-05 | West Ham U | 29 | 1 | | |
| 2005-06 | West Ham U | 33 | 2 | | |
| 2006-07 | West Ham U | 31 | 0 | | |
| 2007-08 | West Ham U | 25 | 2 | | |
| 2008-09 | West Ham U | 0 | 0 | 138 | 5 |
| 2008-09 | Sunderland | 31 | 0 | | |
| 2009-10 | Sunderland | 24 | 0 | | |
| 2010-11 | Sunderland | 27 | 0 | | |
| 2011-12 | Sunderland | 3 | 0 | 85 | 0 |
| 2011-12 | QPR | 31 | 0 | | |
| 2012-13 | QPR | 13 | 0 | 44 | 0 |
| 2012-13 | Bursaspor | 7 | 0 | 7 | 0 |

**FITZPATRICK, David (M)** 0 0
b.Surbiton 10-2-95
Source: Scholar.

| | | | | |
|---|---|---|---|---|
| 2011-12 | QPR | 0 | 0 | |
| 2012-13 | QPR | 0 | 0 | |

**GIBBONS, Jordan (M)** 1 0
H: 5 10  W: 10 12  b. 18-11-93
Source: Scholar.

| | | | | | |
|---|---|---|---|---|---|
| 2011-12 | QPR | 0 | 0 | | |
| 2012-13 | QPR | 0 | 0 | | |
| 2012-13 | Inverness CT | 1 | 0 | 1 | 0 |

**GRANERO, Esteban (M)** 177 17
H: 5 11  W: 11 04  b.Madrid 2-7-87

| | | | | | |
|---|---|---|---|---|---|
| 2005-06 | RM Castilla | 0 | 0 | | |
| 2006-07 | RM Castilla | 23 | 4 | 24 | 4 |
| 2007-08 | Getafe | 27 | 3 | | |
| 2008-09 | Getafe | 35 | 5 | 62 | 8 |
| 2009-10 | Real Madrid | 31 | 3 | | |
| 2010-11 | Real Madrid | 19 | 1 | | |
| 2011-12 | Real Madrid | 17 | 0 | 67 | 4 |
| 2012-13 | QPR | 24 | 1 | 24 | 1 |

**GREEN, Rob (G)** 458 0
H: 6 3  W: 14 09  b.Chertsey 18-1-80
Source: Trainee. Honours: England Youth, B, 12 full caps.

| | | | | | |
|---|---|---|---|---|---|
| 1997-98 | Norwich C | 0 | 0 | | |
| 1998-99 | Norwich C | 2 | 0 | | |
| 1999-2000 | Norwich C | 3 | 0 | | |
| 2000-01 | Norwich C | 5 | 0 | | |
| 2001-02 | Norwich C | 41 | 0 | | |
| 2002-03 | Norwich C | 46 | 0 | | |
| 2003-04 | Norwich C | 46 | 0 | | |
| 2004-05 | Norwich C | 38 | 0 | | |
| 2005-06 | Norwich C | 42 | 0 | 223 | 0 |
| 2006-07 | West Ham U | 26 | 0 | | |
| 2007-08 | West Ham U | 38 | 0 | | |
| 2008-09 | West Ham U | 38 | 0 | | |
| 2009-10 | West Ham U | 38 | 0 | | |
| 2010-11 | West Ham U | 37 | 0 | | |
| 2011-12 | West Ham U | 42 | 0 | 219 | 0 |
| 2012-13 | QPR | 16 | 0 | 16 | 0 |

**HARRIMAN, Michael (D)** 22 0
H: 5 6  W: 11 10  b.Chichester 23-10-92
Source: Scholar. Honours: Eire Youth.

| | | | | | |
|---|---|---|---|---|---|
| 2010-11 | QPR | 0 | 0 | | |
| 2011-12 | QPR | 1 | 0 | | |
| 2012-13 | QPR | 1 | 0 | 2 | 0 |
| 2012-13 | Wycombe W | 20 | 0 | 20 | 0 |

**HEWITT, Troy (F)** 15 2
H: 6 0  W: 12 05  b.Newham 10-2-90
Source: Clapton, Ilford, Harrow B.

| | | | | | |
|---|---|---|---|---|---|
| 2010-11 | QPR | 0 | 0 | | |
| 2011-12 | QPR | 0 | 0 | | |
| 2011-12 | Dagenham & R | 6 | 0 | 6 | 0 |
| 2012-13 | QPR | 0 | 0 | | |
| 2012-13 | Bury | 8 | 2 | 8 | 2 |
| 2012-13 | Colchester U | 1 | 0 | 1 | 0 |

**HILL, Clint (D)** 453 27
H: 6 0  W: 11 06  b.Liverpool 19-10-78
Source: Trainee.

| | | | | | |
|---|---|---|---|---|---|
| 1997-98 | Tranmere R | 14 | 0 | | |
| 1998-99 | Tranmere R | 33 | 4 | | |
| 1999-2000 | Tranmere R | 29 | 5 | | |
| 2000-01 | Tranmere R | 34 | 5 | | |
| 2001-02 | Tranmere R | 30 | 2 | 140 | 16 |
| 2002-03 | Oldham Ath | 17 | 1 | 17 | 1 |
| 2003-04 | Stoke C | 12 | 0 | | |
| 2004-05 | Stoke C | 32 | 1 | | |
| 2005-06 | Stoke C | 13 | 0 | | |
| 2006-07 | Stoke C | 18 | 2 | | |
| 2007-08 | Stoke C | 5 | 0 | 80 | 3 |
| 2007-08 | Crystal Palace | 28 | 3 | | |
| 2008-09 | Crystal Palace | 43 | 1 | | |
| 2009-10 | Crystal Palace | 43 | 1 | 114 | 5 |
| 2010-11 | QPR | 44 | 2 | | |
| 2011-12 | QPR | 22 | 0 | | |
| 2011-12 | Nottingham F | 5 | 0 | 5 | 0 |
| 2012-13 | QPR | 31 | 0 | 97 | 2 |

**HITCHCOCK, Tom (F)** 25 3
H: 5 11  W: 12 08  b.Hemel Hempstead 1-10-92
Source: Scholar.

| | | | | | |
|---|---|---|---|---|---|
| 2009-10 | Blackburn R | 0 | 0 | | |
| 2010-11 | Blackburn R | 0 | 0 | | |
| 2011-12 | Blackburn R | 0 | 0 | | |
| 2011-12 | Plymouth Arg | 8 | 0 | 8 | 0 |
| 2011-12 | QPR | 0 | 0 | | |
| 2012-13 | QPR | 0 | 0 | | |
| 2012-13 | Bristol R | 17 | 3 | 17 | 3 |

**HOILETT, Junior (M)** 140 20
H: 5 8  W: 11 00  b.Ottawa 5-6-90
Source: Scholar.

| | | | | | |
|---|---|---|---|---|---|
| 2007-08 | Blackburn R | 0 | 0 | | |
| 2007-08 | Paderborn | 12 | 1 | 12 | 1 |
| 2008-09 | Blackburn R | 0 | 0 | | |
| 2008-09 | St Pauli | 21 | 6 | 21 | 6 |
| 2009-10 | Blackburn R | 23 | 0 | | |
| 2010-11 | Blackburn R | 24 | 5 | | |
| 2011-12 | Blackburn R | 34 | 7 | 81 | 12 |
| 2012-13 | QPR | 26 | 1 | 26 | 1 |

**HULSE, Rob (F)** 387 115
H: 6 1  W: 12 04  b.Crewe 25-10-79
Source: Trainee.

| | | | | | |
|---|---|---|---|---|---|
| 1998-99 | Crewe Alex | 0 | 0 | | |
| 1999-2000 | Crewe Alex | 4 | 1 | | |
| 2000-01 | Crewe Alex | 33 | 11 | | |
| 2001-02 | Crewe Alex | 41 | 12 | | |
| 2002-03 | Crewe Alex | 38 | 22 | 116 | 46 |
| 2003-04 | WBA | 33 | 10 | | |
| 2004-05 | WBA | 5 | 0 | 38 | 10 |
| 2004-05 | Leeds U | 13 | 6 | | |
| 2005-06 | Leeds U | 39 | 12 | 52 | 18 |
| 2006-07 | Sheffield U | 29 | 8 | | |
| 2007-08 | Sheffield U | 21 | 0 | 50 | 8 |
| 2008-09 | Derby Co | 44 | 15 | | |
| 2009-10 | Derby Co | 37 | 12 | | |
| 2010-11 | Derby Co | 1 | 1 | 82 | 28 |
| 2010-11 | QPR | 21 | 2 | | |
| 2011-12 | QPR | 2 | 0 | | |
| 2012-13 | QPR | 0 | 0 | 23 | 2 |
| 2012-13 | Charlton Ath | 15 | 3 | 15 | 3 |
| 2012-13 | Millwall | 11 | 0 | 11 | 0 |

## JENAS, Jermaine (M) 315 37

H: 5 11 W: 11 00 b.Nottingham 18-2-83
*Source:* Scholar. *Honours:* England Youth, Under-21, B, 21 full caps, 1 goal.

|  |  | | | | |
|---|---|---|---|---|---|
| 1999-2000 | Nottingham F | 0 | 0 | | |
| 2000-01 | Nottingham F | 1 | 0 | | |
| 2001-02 | Nottingham F | 28 | 4 | | |
| 2001-02 | Newcastle U | 12 | 0 | | |
| 2002-03 | Newcastle U | 32 | 6 | | |
| 2003-04 | Newcastle U | 31 | 2 | | |
| 2004-05 | Newcastle U | 31 | 1 | | |
| 2005-06 | Newcastle U | 4 | 0 | 110 | 9 |
| 2005-06 | Tottenham H | 30 | 6 | | |
| 2006-07 | Tottenham H | 25 | 6 | | |
| 2007-08 | Tottenham H | 29 | 4 | | |
| 2008-09 | Tottenham H | 32 | 4 | | |
| 2009-10 | Tottenham H | 19 | 1 | | |
| 2010-11 | Tottenham H | 19 | 0 | | |
| 2011-12 | Tottenham H | 0 | 0 | | |
| 2011-12 | *Aston Villa* | 3 | 0 | 3 | 0 |
| 2012-13 | Tottenham H | 1 | 0 | 155 | 21 |
| 2012-13 | *Nottingham F* | 6 | 1 | 35 | 5 |
| 2012-13 | QPR | 12 | 2 | 12 | 2 |

## JOHNSON, Andy (F) 373 112

H: 5 7 W: 10 09 b.Bedford 10-2-81
*Source:* Trainee. *Honours:* England Youth, Under-20, 8 full caps.

|  |  | | | | |
|---|---|---|---|---|---|
| 1997-98 | Birmingham C | 0 | 0 | | |
| 1998-99 | Birmingham C | 4 | 0 | | |
| 1999-2000 | Birmingham C | 22 | 1 | | |
| 2000-01 | Birmingham C | 34 | 4 | | |
| 2001-02 | Birmingham C | 23 | 3 | 83 | 8 |
| 2002-03 | Crystal Palace | 28 | 11 | | |
| 2003-04 | Crystal Palace | 42 | 27 | | |
| 2004-05 | Crystal Palace | 37 | 21 | | |
| 2005-06 | Crystal Palace | 33 | 15 | 140 | 74 |
| 2006-07 | Everton | 32 | 11 | | |
| 2007-08 | Everton | 29 | 6 | 61 | 17 |
| 2008-09 | Fulham | 31 | 7 | | |
| 2009-10 | Fulham | 8 | 0 | | |
| 2010-11 | Fulham | 27 | 3 | | |
| 2011-12 | Fulham | 20 | 3 | 86 | 13 |
| 2012-13 | QPR | 3 | 0 | 3 | 0 |

## JULIO CESAR, Soares (G) 252 0

H: 6 1 W: 12 05 b.Rio de Janeiro 3-9-79
*Honours:* Brazil 74 full caps.

|  |  | | | | |
|---|---|---|---|---|---|
| 2005-06 | Inter Milan | 29 | 0 | | |
| 2006-07 | Inter Milan | 32 | 0 | | |
| 2007-08 | Inter Milan | 35 | 0 | | |
| 2008-09 | Inter Milan | 36 | 0 | | |
| 2009-10 | Inter Milan | 38 | 0 | | |
| 2010-11 | Inter Milan | 25 | 0 | | |
| 2011-12 | Inter Milan | 33 | 0 | 228 | 0 |
| 2012-13 | QPR | 24 | 0 | 24 | 0 |

## LENNOX, Aaron (G) 0 0

b.Sydney 19-2-93
*Source:* Australia IoS.

|  |  | | |
|---|---|---|---|
| 2011-12 | QPR | 0 | 0 |
| 2012-13 | QPR | 0 | 0 |

## MACKIE, Jamie (F) 199 34

H: 5 8 W: 11 00 b.Dorking 22-9-85
*Source:* Leatherhead. *Honours:* Scotland 9 full caps, 2 goals.

|  |  | | | | |
|---|---|---|---|---|---|
| 2003-04 | Wimbledon | 13 | 0 | 13 | 0 |
| 2004-05 | Milton Keynes D | 3 | 0 | 3 | 0 |
| From Exeter C | | | | | |
| 2007-08 | Plymouth Arg | 13 | 3 | | |
| 2008-09 | Plymouth Arg | 43 | 5 | | |
| 2009-10 | Plymouth Arg | 42 | 8 | 98 | 16 |
| 2010-11 | QPR | 25 | 9 | | |
| 2011-12 | QPR | 31 | 7 | | |
| 2012-13 | QPR | 29 | 2 | 85 | 18 |

## MAGRI, Sam (D)

H: 5 11 W: 11 05 b.Portsmouth 30-3-94
*Source:* Scholar. *Honours:* England Youth.

|  |  | | |
|---|---|---|---|
| 2010-11 | Portsmouth | 0 | 0 |
| 2011-12 | Portsmouth | 0 | 0 |
| 2012-13 | Portsmouth | 0 | 0 |
| 2012-13 | QPR | 0 | 0 |

## MBIA, Stephane (M) 203 10

H: 6 2 W: 12 11 b.Yaounde 20-5-86
*Honours:* Cameroon 46 full caps, 3 goals.

|  |  | | | | |
|---|---|---|---|---|---|
| 2005-06 | Rennes | 22 | 0 | | |
| 2006-07 | Rennes | 31 | 1 | | |
| 2007-08 | Rennes | 25 | 3 | | |
| 2008-09 | Rennes | 27 | 0 | 105 | 4 |
| 2009-10 | Marseille | 27 | 3 | | |
| 2010-11 | Marseille | 26 | 1 | | |
| 2011-12 | Marseille | 15 | 2 | | |
| 2012-13 | Marseille | 1 | 0 | 69 | 6 |
| 2012-13 | QPR | 29 | 0 | 29 | 0 |

## MURPHY, Brian (G) 131 0

H: 6 0 W: 13 00 b.Waterford 7-5-83
*Honours:* Eire Under-21.

|  |  | | | | |
|---|---|---|---|---|---|
| 2000-01 | Manchester C | 0 | 0 | | |
| 2001-02 | Manchester C | 0 | 0 | | |
| 2002-03 | Manchester C | 0 | 0 | | |
| 2002-03 | *Oldham Ath* | 0 | 0 | | |
| 2002-03 | *Peterborough U* | 1 | 0 | 1 | 0 |
| From Waterford | | | | | |
| 2003-04 | Swansea C | 11 | 0 | | |
| 2004-05 | Swansea C | 2 | 0 | | |
| 2005-06 | Swansea C | 0 | 0 | | |
| 2006-07 | Swansea C | 0 | 0 | 13 | 0 |
| 2007 | Bohemians | 29 | 0 | | |
| 2008 | Bohemians | 33 | 0 | | |
| 2009 | Bohemians | 35 | 0 | 97 | 0 |
| 2009-10 | Ipswich T | 16 | 0 | | |
| 2010-11 | Ipswich T | 4 | 0 | | |
| 2011-12 | Ipswich T | 0 | 0 | 20 | 0 |
| 2011-12 | QPR | 0 | 0 | | |
| 2012-13 | QPR | 0 | 0 | | |

## NELSEN, Ryan (D) 279 16

H: 5 11 W: 14 02 b.Christchurch, NZ 18-10-77
*Honours:* New Zealand Under-23, 49 full caps, 7 goals.

|  |  | | | | |
|---|---|---|---|---|---|
| 2001 | DC United | 19 | 0 | | |
| 2002 | DC United | 20 | 4 | | |
| 2003 | DC United | 25 | 1 | | |
| 2004 | DC United | 17 | 2 | 81 | 7 |
| 2004-05 | Blackburn R | 15 | 0 | | |
| 2005-06 | Blackburn R | 31 | 0 | | |
| 2006-07 | Blackburn R | 12 | 0 | | |
| 2007-08 | Blackburn R | 22 | 0 | | |
| 2008-09 | Blackburn R | 35 | 1 | | |
| 2009-10 | Blackburn R | 28 | 4 | | |
| 2010-11 | Blackburn R | 28 | 3 | | |
| 2011-12 | Blackburn R | 1 | 0 | 172 | 8 |
| 2011-12 | Tottenham H | 5 | 0 | 5 | 0 |
| 2012-13 | QPR | 21 | 1 | 21 | 1 |

## ONUOHA, Nedum (D) 165 4

H: 6 2 W: 12 04 b.Warri 12-11-86
*Source:* Scholar. *Honours:* England Youth, Under-20, Under-21.

|  |  | | | | |
|---|---|---|---|---|---|
| 2004-05 | Manchester C | 17 | 0 | | |
| 2005-06 | Manchester C | 10 | 0 | | |
| 2006-07 | Manchester C | 18 | 0 | | |
| 2007-08 | Manchester C | 16 | 1 | | |
| 2008-09 | Manchester C | 23 | 1 | | |
| 2009-10 | Manchester C | 10 | 1 | | |
| 2010-11 | Manchester C | 0 | 0 | | |
| 2010-11 | *Sunderland* | 31 | 1 | 31 | 1 |
| 2011-12 | Manchester C | 1 | 0 | 95 | 3 |
| 2011-12 | QPR | 16 | 0 | | |
| 2012-13 | QPR | 23 | 0 | 39 | 0 |

## PARK, Ji-Sung (M) 293 43

H: 5 9 W: 11 06 b.Seoul 25-2-81
*Honours:* South Korea 101 full caps, 13 goals.

|  |  | | | | |
|---|---|---|---|---|---|
| 2000 | Kyoto Purple S | 13 | 1 | | |
| 2001 | Kyoto Purple S | 38 | 3 | | |
| 2002 | Kyoto Purple S | 25 | 7 | 76 | 11 |
| 2002-03 | PSV Eindhoven | 8 | 0 | | |
| 2003-04 | PSV Eindhoven | 28 | 6 | | |
| 2004-05 | PSV Eindhoven | 28 | 7 | 64 | 13 |
| 2005-06 | Manchester U | 33 | 1 | | |
| 2006-07 | Manchester U | 14 | 5 | | |
| 2007-08 | Manchester U | 12 | 1 | | |
| 2008-09 | Manchester U | 25 | 2 | | |
| 2009-10 | Manchester U | 17 | 3 | | |
| 2010-11 | Manchester U | 15 | 5 | | |
| 2011-12 | Manchester U | 17 | 2 | 133 | 19 |
| 2012-13 | QPR | 20 | 0 | 20 | 0 |

## REMY, Loic (F) 178 61

H: 6 0 W: 11 00 b.Lyon 2-1-87
*Honours:* France Youth, Under-21, 18 full caps, 4 goals.

|  |  | | | | |
|---|---|---|---|---|---|
| 2006-07 | Lyon | 6 | 0 | | |
| 2007-08 | Lyon | 6 | 0 | 12 | 0 |
| 2007-08 | *Lens* | 10 | 3 | 10 | 3 |
| 2008-09 | Nice | 32 | 10 | | |
| 2009-10 | Nice | 34 | 14 | | |
| 2010-11 | Nice | 2 | 1 | 68 | 25 |
| 2010-11 | Marseille | 31 | 15 | | |
| 2011-12 | Marseille | 29 | 11 | | |
| 2012-13 | Marseille | 14 | 1 | 74 | 27 |
| 2012-13 | QPR | 14 | 6 | 14 | 6 |

## SAMBA, Christopher (D) 252 23

H: 6 5 W: 13 03 b.Creteil 28-3-84
*Source:* Issy-les-Moulineaux, Rouen.
*Honours:* Congo Under-20, 26 full caps, 1 goal.

|  |  | | | | |
|---|---|---|---|---|---|
| 2001-02 | Sedan | 1 | 0 | | |
| 2002-03 | Sedan | 0 | 0 | | |
| 2003-04 | Sedan | 3 | 0 | 4 | 0 |
| 2004-05 | Hertha Berlin | 0 | 0 | | |
| 2004-05 | Hertha Berlin II | 16 | 3 | | |
| 2005-06 | Hertha Berlin | 12 | 0 | | |
| 2005-06 | Hertha Berlin II | 12 | 1 | | |
| 2006-07 | Hertha Berlin | 8 | 0 | 20 | 0 |
| 2006-07 | Hertha Berlin II | 2 | 0 | 30 | 4 |
| 2006-07 | Blackburn R | 14 | 2 | | |
| 2007-08 | Blackburn R | 33 | 2 | | |
| 2008-09 | Blackburn R | 35 | 2 | | |
| 2009-10 | Blackburn R | 30 | 4 | | |
| 2010-11 | Blackburn R | 33 | 4 | | |
| 2011-12 | Blackburn R | 16 | 2 | 161 | 16 |
| 2012-13 | Anzhi Makhachkala | 27 | 3 | 27 | 3 |
| 2012-13 | QPR | 10 | 0 | 10 | 0 |

## SENDLES-WHITE, Jamie (D) 0 0

b.Kingston
*Source:* Scholar.

|  |  | | |
|---|---|---|---|
| 2011-12 | QPR | 0 | 0 |
| 2012-13 | QPR | 0 | 0 |

## SHARIFF, Mo (F) 4 0

H: 5 10 b.Newham 5-3-93
*Source:* Slough T Youth.

|  |  | | | | |
|---|---|---|---|---|---|
| 2010-11 | QPR | 0 | 0 | | |
| 2011-12 | QPR | 0 | 0 | | |
| 2012-13 | QPR | 0 | 0 | | |
| 2012-13 | *Dagenham & R* | 4 | 0 | 4 | 0 |

## SKAPETIS, Petros (F) 0 0

*Source:* South Melbourne.

|  |  | | |
|---|---|---|---|
| 2011-12 | QPR | 0 | 0 |
| 2012-13 | QPR | 0 | 0 |

## SUTHERLAND, Frankie (M) 1 0

H: 5 9 W: 10 00 b.Hillingdon 6-12-93
*Source:* Scholar. *Honours:* Eire Youth.

|  |  | | | | |
|---|---|---|---|---|---|
| 2010-11 | QPR | 0 | 0 | | |
| 2011-12 | QPR | 0 | 0 | | |
| 2012-13 | QPR | 0 | 0 | | |
| 2012-13 | *Portsmouth* | 1 | 0 | 1 | 0 |

## TAARABT, Adel (M) 160 34

H: 5 9 W: 10 12 b.Marseille 24-5-89
*Honours:* France Youth. Morocco 16 full caps, 4 goals.

|  |  | | | | |
|---|---|---|---|---|---|
| 2006-07 | Lens | 1 | 0 | 1 | 0 |
| 2006-07 | Tottenham H | 2 | 0 | | |
| 2007-08 | Tottenham H | 6 | 0 | | |
| 2008-09 | Tottenham H | 1 | 0 | | |
| 2008-09 | *QPR* | 7 | 1 | | |
| 2009-10 | Tottenham H | 0 | 0 | 9 | 0 |
| 2009-10 | QPR | 41 | 7 | | |
| 2010-11 | QPR | 44 | 19 | | |
| 2011-12 | QPR | 27 | 2 | | |
| 2012-13 | QPR | 31 | 5 | 150 | 34 |

## TRAORE, Armand (D) 91 1

H: 6 1 W: 12 12 b.Paris 8-10-89
*Source:* Monaco. *Honours:* France Youth. Senegal 3 full caps.

|  |  | | | | |
|---|---|---|---|---|---|
| 2006-07 | Arsenal | 0 | 0 | | |
| 2007-08 | Arsenal | 3 | 0 | | |
| 2008-09 | Arsenal | 0 | 0 | | |
| 2008-09 | *Portsmouth* | 19 | 1 | 19 | 1 |
| 2009-10 | Arsenal | 9 | 0 | | |
| 2010-11 | Arsenal | 0 | 0 | | |
| 2010-11 | *Juventus* | 10 | 0 | 10 | 0 |
| 2011-12 | Arsenal | 1 | 0 | 13 | 0 |
| 2011-12 | QPR | 23 | 0 | | |
| 2012-13 | QPR | 26 | 0 | 49 | 0 |

## WRIGHT-PHILLIPS, Shaun (M) 351 40
H: 5 5  W: 10 01  b.Lewisham 25-10-81
Source: Scholar. Honours: England Under-21, 36 full caps, 6 goals.

|  |  | | | | |
|---|---|---|---|---|---|
| 1998-99 | Manchester C | 0 | 0 | | |
| 1999-2000 | Manchester C | 4 | 0 | | |
| 2000-01 | Manchester C | 15 | 0 | | |
| 2001-02 | Manchester C | 35 | 8 | | |
| 2002-03 | Manchester C | 31 | 1 | | |
| 2003-04 | Manchester C | 34 | 7 | | |
| 2004-05 | Manchester C | 34 | 10 | | |
| 2005-06 | Chelsea | 27 | 0 | | |
| 2006-07 | Chelsea | 27 | 2 | | |
| 2007-08 | Chelsea | 27 | 2 | | |
| 2008-09 | Chelsea | 1 | 0 | 82 | 4 |
| 2008-09 | Manchester C | 27 | 5 | | |
| 2009-10 | Manchester C | 30 | 4 | | |
| 2010-11 | Manchester C | 7 | 0 | | |
| 2011-12 | Manchester C | 0 | 0 | 217 | 35 |
| 2011-12 | QPR | 32 | 0 | | |
| 2012-13 | QPR | 20 | 1 | 52 | 1 |

## YOUNG, Luke (D) 378 9
H: 6 0  W: 12 04  b.Harlow 19-7-79
Source: Trainee. Honours: England Youth, Under-21, 7 full caps.

|  |  | | | | |
|---|---|---|---|---|---|
| 1997-98 | Tottenham H | 0 | 0 | | |
| 1998-99 | Tottenham H | 15 | 0 | | |
| 1999-2000 | Tottenham H | 20 | 0 | | |
| 2000-01 | Tottenham H | 23 | 0 | 58 | 0 |
| 2001-02 | Charlton Ath | 34 | 0 | | |
| 2002-03 | Charlton Ath | 32 | 0 | | |
| 2003-04 | Charlton Ath | 24 | 0 | | |
| 2004-05 | Charlton Ath | 36 | 2 | | |
| 2005-06 | Charlton Ath | 32 | 1 | | |
| 2006-07 | Charlton Ath | 29 | 1 | 187 | 4 |
| 2007-08 | Middlesbrough | 35 | 1 | 35 | 1 |
| 2008-09 | Aston Villa | 34 | 1 | | |
| 2009-10 | Aston Villa | 16 | 0 | | |
| 2010-11 | Aston Villa | 23 | 1 | | |
| 2011-12 | Aston Villa | 2 | 0 | 75 | 2 |
| 2011-12 | QPR | 23 | 2 | | |
| 2012-13 | QPR | 0 | 0 | 23 | 2 |

## YUN, Suk-Young (D) 0 0
H: 6 0  b.Suwon 13-2-90

|  |  | | |
|---|---|---|---|
| 2012-13 | QPR | 0 | 0 |

## ZAMORA, Bobby (F) 401 132
H: 6 1  W: 11 11  b.Barking 16-1-81
Source: Trainee. Honours: England Under-21, 2 full caps.

|  |  | | | | |
|---|---|---|---|---|---|
| 1999-2000 | Bristol R | 4 | 0 | 4 | 0 |
| 1999-2000 | Brighton & HA | 6 | 6 | | |
| 2000-01 | Brighton & HA | 43 | 28 | | |
| 2001-02 | Brighton & HA | 41 | 28 | | |
| 2002-03 | Brighton & HA | 35 | 14 | 125 | 76 |
| 2003-04 | Tottenham H | 16 | 0 | 16 | 0 |
| 2003-04 | West Ham U | 17 | 5 | | |
| 2004-05 | West Ham U | 34 | 7 | | |
| 2005-06 | West Ham U | 34 | 6 | | |
| 2006-07 | West Ham U | 32 | 11 | | |
| 2007-08 | West Ham U | 13 | 1 | 130 | 30 |
| 2008-09 | Fulham | 35 | 2 | | |
| 2009-10 | Fulham | 27 | 8 | | |
| 2010-11 | Fulham | 14 | 5 | | |
| 2011-12 | Fulham | 15 | 5 | 91 | 20 |
| 2011-12 | QPR | 14 | 2 | | |
| 2012-13 | QPR | 21 | 4 | 35 | 6 |

**Players retained or with offer of contract**
Hunt-Laurent, Joshua Ishaele Jacob-Heron; Labao Carreiro, Dylan Jorge Guilherme; Lumley, Joseph Patrick; Nguemkam Monthe, Emmanuel Gaetan; Petrasso, Michael.

**Scholars**
Beckles, Benjamin John; Comley, Brandon; Furlong, Darnell Anthony; Haran, James Darcy; Kpekana, Cole Desmond; Mitchell, Aaron; Page, William Alexander; Smith, Mark David; Wise, Harly John; Young, Ryan Lee.

# READING (67)

## AKPAN, Hope (M) 58 5
H: 6 0  W: 10 08  b.Liverpool 14-8-91
Source: Scholar.

|  |  | | | | |
|---|---|---|---|---|---|
| 2007-08 | Everton | 0 | 0 | | |
| 2008-09 | Everton | 0 | 0 | | |
| 2009-10 | Everton | 0 | 0 | | |
| 2010-11 | Everton | 0 | 0 | | |
| 2010-11 | Hull C | 2 | 0 | 2 | 0 |
| 2011-12 | Crawley T | 26 | 1 | | |
| 2012-13 | Crawley T | 21 | 4 | 47 | 5 |
| 2012-13 | Reading | 9 | 0 | 9 | 0 |

## ANDERSEN, Mikkel (G) 82 0
H: 6 5  W: 12 08  b.Copenhagen 17-12-88
Source: AB Copenhagen. Honours: Denmark Youth, Under-21.

|  |  | | | | |
|---|---|---|---|---|---|
| 2006-07 | Reading | 0 | 0 | | |
| 2007-08 | Reading | 0 | 0 | | |
| 2008-09 | Reading | 0 | 0 | | |
| 2008-09 | Brentford | 1 | 0 | 1 | 0 |
| 2008-09 | Brighton & HA | 5 | 0 | 5 | 0 |
| 2009-10 | Reading | 0 | 0 | | |
| 2009-10 | Bristol R | 39 | 0 | | |
| 2010-11 | Reading | 0 | 0 | | |
| 2010-11 | Bristol R | 19 | 0 | 58 | 0 |
| 2011-12 | Reading | 0 | 0 | | |
| 2012-13 | Reading | 0 | 0 | | |
| 2012-13 | Portsmouth | 18 | 0 | 18 | 0 |

## ARNOLD, Nick (D) 0 0
H: 5 11  W: 12 12  b.Tadley 3-7-93
Source: Scholar.

|  |  | | |
|---|---|---|---|
| 2011-12 | Reading | 0 | 0 |
| 2012-13 | Reading | 0 | 0 |

## BIGNALL, Nicholas (F) 48 4
H: 5 10  W: 11 12  b.Reading 11-7-90
Source: Scholar.

|  |  | | | | |
|---|---|---|---|---|---|
| 2008-09 | Reading | 0 | 0 | | |
| 2008-09 | Northampton T | 5 | 1 | 5 | 1 |
| 2008-09 | Cheltenham T | 13 | 1 | 13 | 1 |
| 2009-10 | Reading | 1 | 0 | | |
| 2009-10 | Stockport Co | 11 | 2 | 11 | 2 |
| 2010-11 | Reading | 0 | 0 | | |
| 2010-11 | Southampton | 3 | 0 | 3 | 0 |
| 2010-11 | Bournemouth | 5 | 0 | 5 | 0 |
| 2010-11 | Brentford | 6 | 0 | 6 | 0 |
| 2011-12 | Reading | 0 | 0 | | |
| 2011-12 | Exeter C | 3 | 0 | 3 | 0 |
| 2011-12 | Wycombe W | 1 | 0 | 1 | 0 |
| 2012-13 | Reading | 0 | 0 | 1 | 0 |

## BLACKMAN, Nick (F) 102 26
H: 6 2  W: 11 08  b.Whitefield 11-11-89
Source: Scholar.

|  |  | | | | |
|---|---|---|---|---|---|
| 2006-07 | Macclesfield T | 1 | 0 | | |
| 2007-08 | Macclesfield T | 11 | 1 | | |
| 2008-09 | Macclesfield T | 0 | 0 | 12 | 1 |
| 2008-09 | Blackburn R | 0 | 0 | | |
| 2008-09 | Blackpool | 5 | 1 | 5 | 1 |
| 2009-10 | Blackburn R | 0 | 0 | | |
| 2009-10 | Oldham Ath | 12 | 1 | 12 | 1 |
| 2010-11 | Blackburn R | 0 | 0 | | |
| 2010-11 | Motherwell | 18 | 10 | 18 | 10 |
| 2010-11 | Aberdeen | 15 | 2 | 15 | 2 |
| 2011-12 | Blackburn R | 1 | 0 | | |
| 2012-13 | Blackburn R | 0 | 0 | 1 | 0 |
| 2012-13 | Sheffield U | 28 | 11 | 28 | 11 |
| 2012-13 | Reading | 0 | 11 | 0 | 11 |

## CARRICO, Daniel (M) 94 2
H: 6 0  W: 11 10  b.Cascais 4-8-88

|  |  | | | | |
|---|---|---|---|---|---|
| 2008-09 | Sporting | 22 | 0 | | |
| 2009-10 | Sporting | 26 | 1 | | |
| 2010-11 | Sporting | 24 | 0 | | |
| 2011-12 | Sporting | 18 | 1 | | |
| 2012-13 | Sporting | 1 | 0 | 91 | 2 |
| 2012-13 | Reading | 3 | 0 | 3 | 0 |

## CHURCH, Simon (F) 151 29
H: 6 0  W: 13 04  b.Amersham 10-12-88
Source: Scholar. Honours: Wales Under-21, 22 full caps, 1 goal.

|  |  | | | | |
|---|---|---|---|---|---|
| 2007-08 | Reading | 0 | 0 | | |
| 2007-08 | Crewe Alex | 12 | 1 | 12 | 1 |
| 2007-08 | Yeovil T | 6 | 0 | 6 | 0 |
| 2008-09 | Reading | 0 | 0 | | |
| 2008-09 | Wycombe W | 9 | 0 | 9 | 0 |
| 2008-09 | Leyton Orient | 13 | 5 | 13 | 5 |
| 2009-10 | Reading | 36 | 10 | | |
| 2010-11 | Reading | 37 | 5 | | |
| 2011-12 | Reading | 31 | 7 | | |
| 2012-13 | Reading | 0 | 0 | 104 | 22 |
| 2012-13 | Huddersfield T | 7 | 1 | 7 | 1 |

## CUMMINGS, Shaun (D) 96 0
H: 6 0  W: 11 10  b.Hammersmith 25-2-89

|  |  | | | | |
|---|---|---|---|---|---|
| 2007-08 | Chelsea | 0 | 0 | | |
| 2008-09 | Chelsea | 0 | 0 | | |
| 2008-09 | Milton Keynes D | 32 | 0 | 32 | 0 |
| 2009-10 | Chelsea | 0 | 0 | | |
| 2009-10 | WBA | 3 | 0 | 3 | 0 |
| 2009-10 | Reading | 8 | 0 | | |
| 2010-11 | Reading | 10 | 0 | | |
| 2011-12 | Reading | 34 | 0 | | |
| 2012-13 | Reading | 9 | 0 | 61 | 0 |

## D'ATH, Lawson (M) 24 3
H: 5 9  W: 12 02  b.Witney 24-12-92
Source: Scholar.

|  |  | | | | |
|---|---|---|---|---|---|
| 2010-11 | Reading | 0 | 0 | | |
| 2011-12 | Reading | 0 | 0 | | |
| 2011-12 | Yeovil T | 14 | 1 | 14 | 1 |
| 2012-13 | Reading | 0 | 0 | | |
| 2012-13 | Cheltenham T | 2 | 1 | 2 | 1 |
| 2012-13 | Exeter C | 8 | 1 | 8 | 1 |

## EDWARDS, Ryan (M) 0 0
H: 5 7  W: 11 07  b.Sydney 17-11-93
Source: Perth Glory. Honours: Australia Under-20.

|  |  | | |
|---|---|---|---|
| 2011-12 | Reading | 0 | 0 |
| 2012-13 | Rochdale | 0 | 0 |

## FEDERICI, Adam (G) 174 1
H: 6 2  W: 14 02  b.Nowra 31-1-85
Honours: Australia Youth, Under-20, Under-21, 6 full caps.

|  |  | | | | |
|---|---|---|---|---|---|
| 2005-06 | Reading | 0 | 0 | | |
| 2006-07 | Reading | 2 | 0 | | |
| 2007-08 | Reading | 0 | 0 | | |
| 2008-09 | Reading | 15 | 1 | | |
| 2008-09 | Southend U | 10 | 0 | 10 | 0 |
| 2009-10 | Reading | 46 | 0 | | |
| 2010-11 | Reading | 34 | 0 | | |
| 2011-12 | Reading | 46 | 0 | | |
| 2012-13 | Reading | 21 | 0 | 164 | 1 |

## GORKSS, Kaspars (D) 346 21
H: 6 3  W: 13 05  b.Riga 6-11-81
Honours: Latvia Under-21, 51 full caps, 5 goals.

|  |  | | | | |
|---|---|---|---|---|---|
| 2002 | Auda Riga | 28 | 0 | 28 | 0 |
| 2003 | Oster | 8 | 0 | | |
| 2004 | Oster | 24 | 1 | 32 | 1 |
| 2005 | Assyriska | 23 | 0 | 23 | 0 |
| 2006 | Ventspils | 28 | 5 | 28 | 5 |
| 2006-07 | Blackpool | 10 | 0 | | |
| 2007-08 | Blackpool | 40 | 5 | 50 | 5 |
| 2008-09 | QPR | 31 | 0 | | |
| 2009-10 | QPR | 41 | 3 | | |
| 2010-11 | QPR | 42 | 3 | | |
| 2011-12 | QPR | 0 | 0 | 114 | 6 |
| 2011-12 | Reading | 42 | 3 | | |
| 2012-13 | Reading | 14 | 1 | 56 | 4 |
| 2012-13 | Wolverhampton W | 15 | 0 | 15 | 0 |

## GUNNARSSON, Brynjar (M) 380 31
H: 6 1  W: 12 01  b.Reykjavik 16-10-75
Honours: Iceland Youth, Under-21, 74 full caps, 4 goals.

|  |  | | | | |
|---|---|---|---|---|---|
| 1995 | KR | 16 | 1 | | |
| 1996 | KR | 18 | 0 | | |
| 1997 | KR | 16 | 0 | 50 | 1 |
| 1998 | Moss | 5 | 2 | 5 | 2 |
| 1999-2000 | Stoke C | 22 | 1 | | |
| 2000-01 | Stoke C | 46 | 5 | | |
| 2001-02 | Stoke C | 23 | 5 | | |
| 2002-03 | Stoke C | 40 | 5 | | |
| 2003-04 | Nottingham F | 13 | 0 | 13 | 0 |
| 2003-04 | Stoke C | 3 | 0 | 134 | 16 |
| 2004-05 | Watford | 36 | 3 | 36 | 3 |
| 2005-06 | Reading | 29 | 4 | | |
| 2006-07 | Reading | 23 | 3 | | |
| 2007-08 | Reading | 20 | 0 | | |

| Season | Club | App | Gls | Tot App | Tot Gls |
|---|---|---|---|---|---|
| 2008-09 | Reading | 27 | 2 | | |
| 2009-10 | Reading | 26 | 0 | | |
| 2010-11 | Reading | 12 | 0 | | |
| 2011-12 | Reading | 5 | 0 | | |
| 2012-13 | Reading | 0 | 0 | 142 | 9 |

**GUNTER, Chris (D)** 194 2
H: 5 11  W: 11 02  b.Newport 21-7-89
*Source:* Scholar. *Honours:* Wales Youth, Under-21, 45 full caps.

| Season | Club | App | Gls | Tot App | Tot Gls |
|---|---|---|---|---|---|
| 2006-07 | Cardiff C | 15 | 0 | | |
| 2007-08 | Cardiff C | 13 | 0 | 28 | 0 |
| 2007-08 | Tottenham H | 2 | 0 | | |
| 2008-09 | Tottenham H | 3 | 0 | 5 | 0 |
| 2008-09 | *Nottingham F* | 8 | 0 | | |
| 2009-10 | Nottingham F | 44 | 1 | | |
| 2010-11 | Nottingham F | 43 | 0 | | |
| 2011-12 | Nottingham F | 46 | 1 | 141 | 2 |
| 2012-13 | Reading | 20 | 0 | 20 | 0 |

**GUTHRIE, Danny (M)** 151 8
H: 5 9  W: 11 06  b.Shrewsbury 18-4-87
*Source:* Scholar. *Honours:* England Schools, Youth.

| Season | Club | App | Gls | Tot App | Tot Gls |
|---|---|---|---|---|---|
| 2004-05 | Liverpool | 0 | 0 | | |
| 2005-06 | Liverpool | 0 | 0 | | |
| 2006-07 | Liverpool | 3 | 0 | | |
| 2006-07 | *Southampton* | 10 | 0 | 10 | 0 |
| 2007-08 | Liverpool | 0 | 0 | 3 | 0 |
| 2007-08 | *Bolton W* | 25 | 0 | 25 | 0 |
| 2008-09 | Newcastle U | 24 | 2 | | |
| 2009-10 | Newcastle U | 38 | 4 | | |
| 2010-11 | Newcastle U | 14 | 0 | | |
| 2011-12 | Newcastle U | 16 | 1 | 92 | 7 |
| 2012-13 | Reading | 21 | 1 | 21 | 1 |

**HARTE, Ian (D)** 395 63
H: 5 11  W: 12 06  b.Drogheda 31-8-77
*Source:* Trainee. *Honours:* Eire 63 full caps, 11 goals.

| Season | Club | App | Gls | Tot App | Tot Gls |
|---|---|---|---|---|---|
| 1995-96 | Leeds U | 4 | 0 | | |
| 1996-97 | Leeds U | 14 | 2 | | |
| 1997-98 | Leeds U | 12 | 0 | | |
| 1998-99 | Leeds U | 35 | 4 | | |
| 1999-2000 | Leeds U | 33 | 6 | | |
| 2000-01 | Leeds U | 29 | 7 | | |
| 2001-02 | Leeds U | 36 | 5 | | |
| 2002-03 | Leeds U | 27 | 3 | | |
| 2003-04 | Leeds U | 23 | 1 | 213 | 28 |
| 2004-05 | Levante | 24 | 1 | | |
| 2005-06 | Levante | 0 | 0 | | |
| 2006-07 | Levante | 6 | 0 | 30 | 1 |
| 2007-08 | Sunderland | 8 | 0 | 8 | 0 |
| 2008-09 | Blackpool | 4 | 0 | 4 | 0 |
| 2008-09 | Carlisle U | 3 | 1 | | |
| 2009-10 | Carlisle U | 45 | 16 | | |
| 2010-11 | Carlisle U | 4 | 2 | 52 | 19 |
| 2010-11 | Reading | 40 | 11 | | |
| 2011-12 | Reading | 32 | 4 | | |
| 2012-13 | Reading | 16 | 0 | 88 | 15 |

**HENLY, Jonathan (G)** 0 0
H: 6 3  W: 13 00  b.Reading 7-6-94

| Season | Club | App | Gls |
|---|---|---|---|
| 2012-13 | Reading | 0 | 0 |

**HUNT, Noel (F)** 289 64
H: 5 8  W: 11 05  b.Waterford 26-12-82
*Honours:* Eire Under-21, B, 3 full caps.

| Season | Club | App | Gls | Tot App | Tot Gls |
|---|---|---|---|---|---|
| 2002-03 | Dunfermline Ath | 12 | 1 | | |
| 2003-04 | Dunfermline Ath | 13 | 2 | | |
| 2004-05 | Dunfermline Ath | 23 | 1 | | |
| 2005-06 | Dunfermline Ath | 32 | 4 | 80 | 8 |
| 2006-07 | Dundee U | 28 | 10 | | |
| 2007-08 | Dundee U | 36 | 13 | 64 | 23 |
| 2008-09 | Reading | 37 | 11 | | |
| 2009-10 | Reading | 10 | 2 | | |
| 2010-11 | Reading | 33 | 10 | | |
| 2011-12 | Reading | 41 | 8 | | |
| 2012-13 | Reading | 24 | 2 | 145 | 33 |

**KARACAN, Jem (M)** 160 9
H: 5 10  W: 11 13  b.Lewisham 21-2-89
*Source:* Scholar. *Honours:* Turkey Youth, Under-21.

| Season | Club | App | Gls | Tot App | Tot Gls |
|---|---|---|---|---|---|
| 2007-08 | Reading | 0 | 0 | | |
| 2007-08 | *Bournemouth* | 13 | 1 | 13 | 1 |
| 2007-08 | *Millwall* | 7 | 0 | 7 | 0 |
| 2008-09 | Reading | 15 | 1 | | |
| 2009-10 | Reading | 27 | 0 | | |
| 2010-11 | Reading | 40 | 3 | | |
| 2011-12 | Reading | 37 | 3 | | |
| 2012-13 | Reading | 21 | 1 | 140 | 8 |

**KEBE, Jimmy (M)** 209 36
H: 6 2  W: 11 07  b.Paris 19-1-84
*Honours:* Mali 8 full caps, 3 goals.

| Season | Club | App | Gls | Tot App | Tot Gls |
|---|---|---|---|---|---|
| 2005-06 | Lens | 0 | 0 | | |
| 2006-07 | *Chateauroux* | 18 | 2 | 18 | 2 |
| 2007-08 | Lens | 0 | 0 | | |
| 2007-08 | *Boulogne* | 16 | 5 | 16 | 5 |
| 2007-08 | Reading | 5 | 0 | | |
| 2008-09 | Reading | 41 | 2 | | |
| 2009-10 | Reading | 42 | 10 | | |
| 2010-11 | Reading | 36 | 9 | | |
| 2011-12 | Reading | 33 | 3 | | |
| 2012-13 | Reading | 18 | 5 | 175 | 29 |

**KELLY, Stephen (D)** 212 2
H: 6 0  W: 12 04  b.Dublin 6-9-83
*Source:* Juniors. *Honours:* Eire Youth, Under-21, 34 full caps.

| Season | Club | App | Gls | Tot App | Tot Gls |
|---|---|---|---|---|---|
| 2000-01 | Tottenham H | 0 | 0 | | |
| 2001-02 | Tottenham H | 0 | 0 | | |
| 2002-03 | Tottenham H | 0 | 0 | | |
| 2002-03 | *Southend U* | 10 | 0 | 10 | 0 |
| 2002-03 | *QPR* | 7 | 0 | 7 | 0 |
| 2003-04 | Tottenham H | 11 | 0 | | |
| 2003-04 | *Watford* | 13 | 0 | 13 | 0 |
| 2004-05 | Tottenham H | 17 | 2 | | |
| 2005-06 | Tottenham H | 9 | 0 | 37 | 2 |
| 2006-07 | Birmingham C | 36 | 0 | | |
| 2007-08 | Birmingham C | 38 | 0 | | |
| 2008-09 | Birmingham C | 5 | 0 | | |
| 2008-09 | *Stoke C* | 6 | 0 | 6 | 0 |
| 2009-10 | Birmingham C | 0 | 0 | 79 | 0 |
| 2009-10 | Fulham | 8 | 0 | | |
| 2010-11 | Fulham | 10 | 0 | | |
| 2011-12 | Fulham | 24 | 0 | | |
| 2012-13 | Fulham | 2 | 0 | 44 | 0 |
| 2012-13 | Reading | 16 | 0 | 16 | 0 |

**LE FONDRE, Adam (F)** 320 131
H: 5 9  W: 11 04  b.Stockport 2-12-86
*Source:* Trainee.

| Season | Club | App | Gls | Tot App | Tot Gls |
|---|---|---|---|---|---|
| 2004-05 | Stockport Co | 20 | 4 | | |
| 2005-06 | Stockport Co | 22 | 6 | | |
| 2006-07 | Stockport Co | 21 | 7 | 63 | 17 |
| 2006-07 | *Rochdale* | 7 | 4 | | |
| 2007-08 | Rochdale | 46 | 16 | | |
| 2008-09 | Rochdale | 44 | 18 | | |
| 2009-10 | Rochdale | 1 | 0 | 98 | 38 |
| 2009-10 | Rotherham U | 44 | 25 | | |
| 2010-11 | Rotherham U | 45 | 23 | | |
| 2011-12 | Rotherham U | 4 | 4 | 93 | 52 |
| 2011-12 | Reading | 32 | 12 | | |
| 2012-13 | Reading | 34 | 12 | 66 | 24 |

**LEIGERTWOOD, Mikele (D)** 368 22
H: 6 1  W: 11 04  b.Enfield 12-11-82
*Source:* Scholar. *Honours:* Antigua and Barbuda 11 full caps, 1 goal.

| Season | Club | App | Gls | Tot App | Tot Gls |
|---|---|---|---|---|---|
| 2001-02 | Wimbledon | 1 | 0 | | |
| 2001-02 | *Leyton Orient* | 8 | 0 | 8 | 0 |
| 2002-03 | Wimbledon | 28 | 0 | | |
| 2003-04 | Wimbledon | 27 | 2 | 56 | 2 |
| 2003-04 | Crystal Palace | 20 | 0 | | |
| 2004-05 | Crystal Palace | 20 | 1 | | |
| 2005-06 | Crystal Palace | 27 | 0 | 59 | 1 |
| 2006-07 | Sheffield U | 19 | 0 | | |
| 2007-08 | Sheffield U | 2 | 0 | 21 | 0 |
| 2007-08 | QPR | 40 | 5 | | |
| 2008-09 | QPR | 42 | 2 | | |
| 2009-10 | QPR | 40 | 5 | | |
| 2009-10 | QPR | 9 | 0 | 131 | 12 |
| 2010-11 | *Reading* | 22 | 1 | | |
| 2011-12 | Reading | 41 | 5 | | |
| 2012-13 | Reading | 30 | 1 | 93 | 7 |

**MACDONALD, Angus (D)** 20 0
H: 6 0  W: 11 00  b.Winchester 15-10-92
*Source:* Scholar.

| Season | Club | App | Gls | Tot App | Tot Gls |
|---|---|---|---|---|---|
| 2011-12 | Reading | 0 | 0 | | |
| 2011-12 | Torquay U | 2 | 0 | | |
| 2012-13 | Reading | 0 | 0 | | |
| 2012-13 | AFC Wimbledon | 4 | 0 | 4 | 0 |
| 2012-13 | Torquay U | 14 | 0 | 16 | 0 |

**MARIAPPA, Adrian (D)** 245 5
H: 5 10  W: 11 12  b.Harrow 3-10-86
*Source:* Scholar. *Honours:* Jamaica 11 full caps.

| Season | Club | App | Gls | Tot App | Tot Gls |
|---|---|---|---|---|---|
| 2005-06 | Watford | 3 | 0 | | |
| 2006-07 | Watford | 19 | 0 | | |
| 2007-08 | Watford | 25 | 0 | | |
| 2008-09 | Watford | 39 | 1 | | |
| 2009-10 | Watford | 46 | 1 | | |
| 2010-11 | Watford | 45 | 1 | | |
| 2011-12 | Watford | 39 | 1 | 216 | 4 |
| 2012-13 | Reading | 29 | 1 | 29 | 1 |

**McANUFF, Jobi (M)** 463 46
H: 5 11  W: 11 05  b.Edmonton 9-11-81
*Source:* Scholar. *Honours:* Jamaica 4 full caps.

| Season | Club | App | Gls | Tot App | Tot Gls |
|---|---|---|---|---|---|
| 2000-01 | Wimbledon | 0 | 0 | | |
| 2001-02 | Wimbledon | 38 | 4 | | |
| 2002-03 | Wimbledon | 31 | 4 | | |
| 2003-04 | Wimbledon | 27 | 5 | 96 | 13 |
| 2003-04 | West Ham U | 12 | 1 | | |
| 2004-05 | West Ham U | 0 | 0 | 13 | 1 |
| 2004-05 | Cardiff C | 43 | 2 | 43 | 2 |
| 2005-06 | Crystal Palace | 41 | 8 | | |
| 2006-07 | Crystal Palace | 34 | 5 | 75 | 13 |
| 2007-08 | Watford | 39 | 2 | | |
| 2008-09 | Watford | 40 | 3 | | |
| 2009-10 | Watford | 3 | 0 | 82 | 5 |
| 2009-10 | Reading | 36 | 3 | | |
| 2010-11 | Reading | 40 | 4 | | |
| 2011-12 | Reading | 40 | 5 | | |
| 2012-13 | Reading | 38 | 0 | 154 | 12 |

**McCARTHY, Alex (G)** 93 0
H: 6 4  W: 11 12  b.Guildford 3-12-89
*Source:* Scholar. *Honours:* England Under-21.

| Season | Club | App | Gls | Tot App | Tot Gls |
|---|---|---|---|---|---|
| 2008-09 | Reading | 0 | 0 | | |
| 2008-09 | *Aldershot T* | 4 | 0 | 4 | 0 |
| 2009-10 | Reading | 0 | 0 | | |
| 2009-10 | *Yeovil T* | 44 | 0 | 44 | 0 |
| 2010-11 | Reading | 13 | 0 | | |
| 2010-11 | *Brentford* | 3 | 0 | 3 | 0 |
| 2011-12 | Reading | 0 | 0 | | |
| 2011-12 | *Leeds U* | 6 | 0 | 6 | 0 |
| 2011-12 | *Ipswich T* | 10 | 0 | 10 | 0 |
| 2012-13 | Reading | 13 | 0 | 26 | 0 |

**McCLEARY, Garath (M)** 142 16
H: 5 10  W: 12 06  b.Oxford 15-5-87
*Source:* Bromley. *Honours:* Jamaica 5 full caps.

| Season | Club | App | Gls | Tot App | Tot Gls |
|---|---|---|---|---|---|
| 2007-08 | Nottingham F | 8 | 1 | | |
| 2008-09 | Nottingham F | 39 | 1 | | |
| 2009-10 | Nottingham F | 24 | 0 | | |
| 2010-11 | Nottingham F | 18 | 2 | | |
| 2011-12 | Nottingham F | 22 | 9 | 111 | 13 |
| 2011-12 | Reading | 0 | 0 | | |
| 2012-13 | Reading | 31 | 3 | 31 | 3 |

**MILLS, Joseph (D)** 83 2
H: 5 9  W: 11 00  b.Swindon 30-10-89
*Source:* Scholar.

| Season | Club | App | Gls | Tot App | Tot Gls |
|---|---|---|---|---|---|
| 2006-07 | Southampton | 0 | 0 | | |
| 2007-08 | Southampton | 0 | 0 | | |
| 2008-09 | Southampton | 8 | 0 | | |
| 2008-09 | *Scunthorpe U* | 14 | 0 | 14 | 0 |
| 2009-10 | Southampton | 16 | 0 | | |
| 2010-11 | Southampton | 2 | 0 | | |
| 2010-11 | *Doncaster R* | 18 | 2 | 18 | 2 |
| 2011-12 | Southampton | 0 | 0 | 26 | 0 |
| 2011-12 | Reading | 15 | 0 | | |
| 2012-13 | Reading | 0 | 0 | 15 | 0 |
| 2012-13 | *Burnley* | 10 | 0 | 10 | 0 |

**MORRISON, Sean (D)** 93 9
H: 6 4  W: 14 00  b.Plymouth 8-1-91
*Source:* Plymouth Arg.

| Season | Club | App | Gls | Tot App | Tot Gls |
|---|---|---|---|---|---|
| 2007-08 | Swindon T | 2 | 0 | | |
| 2008-09 | Swindon T | 20 | 1 | | |
| 2009-10 | Swindon T | 9 | 1 | | |
| 2009-10 | *Southend U* | 8 | 0 | 8 | 0 |
| 2010-11 | Swindon T | 19 | 4 | 50 | 6 |
| 2010-11 | Reading | 0 | 0 | | |
| 2010-11 | *Huddersfield T* | 0 | 0 | | |
| 2011-12 | Reading | 0 | 0 | | |
| 2011-12 | *Huddersfield T* | 19 | 1 | 19 | 1 |
| 2012-13 | Reading | 16 | 2 | 16 | 2 |

**OBITA, Jordan (M)** 27 4
H: 5 11 W: 11 08 b.Oxford 8-12-93
Source: Scholar. Honours: England Youth.

|  |  | | | | |
|---|---|---|---|---|---|
| 2010-11 | Reading | 0 | 0 | | |
| 2011-12 | Reading | 0 | 0 | | |
| 2011-12 | *Barnet* | 5 | 0 | **5** | **0** |
| 2011-12 | *Gillingham* | 6 | 3 | **6** | **3** |
| 2012-13 | Reading | 0 | 0 | | |
| 2012-13 | *Portsmouth* | 8 | 1 | **8** | **1** |
| 2012-13 | *Oldham Ath* | 8 | 0 | **8** | **0** |

**PARTRIDGE, Matt (D)** 0 0
H: 6 3 W: 13 02 b.Reading 24-10-84

| | | | | | |
|---|---|---|---|---|---|
| 2012-13 | Reading | 0 | 0 | | |

**PEARCE, Alex (D)** 173 14
H: 6 0 W: 11 10 b.Wallingford 9-11-88
Source: Scholar. Honours: Scotland Youth, Under-21, 1 full cap, 1 goal.

| | | | | | |
|---|---|---|---|---|---|
| 2006-07 | Reading | 0 | 0 | | |
| 2006-07 | *Northampton T* | 15 | 1 | **15** | **1** |
| 2007-08 | Reading | 0 | 0 | | |
| 2007-08 | *Bournemouth* | 11 | 0 | **11** | **0** |
| 2007-08 | *Norwich C* | 11 | 0 | **11** | **0** |
| 2008-09 | Reading | 16 | 1 | | |
| 2008-09 | *Southampton* | 9 | 2 | **9** | **2** |
| 2009-10 | Reading | 25 | 4 | | |
| 2010-11 | Reading | 21 | 1 | | |
| 2011-12 | Reading | 46 | 5 | | |
| 2012-13 | Reading | 19 | 0 | **127** | **11** |

**POGREBNYAK, Pavel (F)** 286 88
H: 6 2 W: 14 05 b.Moscow 8-11-83
Honours: Russia 33 full caps, 8 goals.

| | | | | | |
|---|---|---|---|---|---|
| 2002 | Spartak Moscow | 2 | 0 | | |
| 2003 | *Baltika* | 40 | 15 | **40** | **15** |
| 2004 | Spartak Moscow | 16 | 2 | **18** | **2** |
| 2004 | *Khimki* | 12 | 6 | **12** | **6** |
| 2005 | *Shinnik* | 23 | 4 | **23** | **4** |
| 2006 | *Tomsk* | 26 | 13 | **26** | **13** |
| 2007 | Zenit | 24 | 11 | | |
| 2008 | Zenit | 19 | 6 | | |
| 2009 | Zenit | 15 | 5 | **58** | **22** |
| 2009-10 | Stuttgart | 28 | 6 | | |
| 2010-11 | Stuttgart | 26 | 8 | | |
| 2011-12 | Stuttgart | 14 | 1 | **68** | **15** |
| 2011-12 | *Fulham* | 12 | 6 | **12** | **6** |
| 2012-13 | Reading | 29 | 5 | **29** | **5** |

**ROBERTS, Jason (F)** 449 137
H: 6 0 W: 14 01 b.Acton 25-1-78
Source: Hayes. Honours: Grenada 22 full caps, 12 goals.

| | | | | | |
|---|---|---|---|---|---|
| 1997-98 | Wolverhampton W | 0 | 0 | | |
| 1997-98 | *Torquay U* | 14 | 6 | **14** | **6** |
| 1997-98 | *Bristol C* | 3 | 1 | **3** | **1** |
| 1998-99 | Bristol R | 37 | 16 | | |
| 1999-2000 | Bristol R | 41 | 22 | **78** | **38** |
| 2000-01 | WBA | 43 | 14 | | |
| 2001-02 | WBA | 14 | 7 | | |
| 2002-03 | WBA | 32 | 3 | | |
| 2003-04 | WBA | 0 | 0 | **89** | **24** |
| 2003-04 | *Portsmouth* | 10 | 1 | **10** | **1** |
| 2003-04 | Wigan Ath | 14 | 8 | | |
| 2004-05 | Wigan Ath | 45 | 21 | | |
| 2005-06 | Wigan Ath | 34 | 8 | **93** | **37** |
| 2006-07 | Blackburn R | 18 | 4 | | |
| 2007-08 | Blackburn R | 26 | 3 | | |
| 2008-09 | Blackburn R | 26 | 7 | | |
| 2009-10 | Blackburn R | 29 | 5 | | |
| 2010-11 | Blackburn R | 25 | 5 | | |
| 2011-12 | Blackburn R | 10 | 0 | **134** | **24** |
| 2011-12 | Reading | 17 | 6 | | |
| 2012-13 | Reading | 11 | 0 | **28** | **6** |

**ROBSON-KANU, Hal (F)** 147 25
H: 5 7 W: 11 08 b.Acton 21-5-89
Honours: England Youth, Under-20. Wales Under-21, 14 full caps, 1 goal.

| | | | | | |
|---|---|---|---|---|---|
| 2007-08 | Reading | 0 | 0 | | |
| 2007-08 | *Southend U* | 8 | 3 | | |
| 2008-09 | Reading | 0 | 0 | | |
| 2008-09 | *Southend U* | 14 | 2 | **22** | **5** |
| 2008-09 | *Swindon T* | 20 | 4 | **20** | **4** |
| 2009-10 | Reading | 17 | 0 | | |
| 2010-11 | Reading | 27 | 5 | | |
| 2011-12 | Reading | 36 | 4 | | |
| 2012-13 | Reading | 25 | 7 | **105** | **16** |

**SAMUEL, Dominic (F)** 3 0
H: 6 0 W: 14 00 b.Southwark 1-4-94
Source: Scholar. Honours: England Youth.

| | | | | | |
|---|---|---|---|---|---|
| 2011-12 | Reading | 0 | 0 | | |
| 2012-13 | Reading | 1 | 0 | **1** | **0** |
| 2012-13 | *Colchester U* | 2 | 0 | **2** | **0** |

**SHEPPARD, Karl (F)** 82 21
H: 5 11 W: 12 08 b.Shelbourne 14-2-91
Source: Scholar. Honours: Eire Under-21.

| | | | | | |
|---|---|---|---|---|---|
| 2007-08 | Everton | 0 | 0 | | |
| 2008-09 | Everton | 0 | 0 | | |
| 2009-10 | Everton | 0 | 0 | | |
| 2010 | Galway U | 33 | 8 | **33** | **8** |
| 2011 | Shamrock R | 24 | 10 | | |
| 2011-12 | Reading | 0 | 0 | | |
| 2012-13 | Reading | 0 | 0 | | |
| 2012-13 | *Accrington S* | 10 | 1 | **10** | **1** |
| 2013 | Shamrock R | 15 | 2 | **39** | **12** |

**SHOREY, Nicky (D)** 394 12
H: 5 9 W: 10 08 b.Romford 19-2-81
Source: Trainee. Honours: England B, 2 full caps.

| | | | | | |
|---|---|---|---|---|---|
| 1999-2000 | Leyton Orient | 7 | 0 | | |
| 2000-01 | Leyton Orient | 8 | 0 | **15** | **0** |
| 2000-01 | Reading | 0 | 0 | | |
| 2001-02 | Reading | 32 | 0 | | |
| 2002-03 | Reading | 43 | 2 | | |
| 2003-04 | Reading | 35 | 2 | | |
| 2004-05 | Reading | 44 | 3 | | |
| 2005-06 | Reading | 40 | 2 | | |
| 2006-07 | Reading | 37 | 1 | | |
| 2007-08 | Reading | 36 | 2 | | |
| 2008-09 | Aston Villa | 34 | 0 | | |
| 2009-10 | Aston Villa | 3 | 0 | **24** | **0** |
| 2009-10 | *Nottingham F* | 9 | 0 | **9** | **0** |
| 2009-10 | *Fulham* | 9 | 0 | **9** | **0** |
| 2010-11 | WBA | 28 | 0 | | |
| 2011-12 | WBA | 25 | 0 | **53** | **0** |
| 2012-13 | Reading | 17 | 0 | **284** | **12** |

**SWEENEY, Pierce (D)** 0 0
H: 5 10 W: 12 07 b. 11-9-94

| | | | | | |
|---|---|---|---|---|---|
| 2012-13 | Reading | 0 | 0 | | |

**TABB, Jay (M)** 321 32
H: 5 7 W: 10 00 b.Tooting 21-2-84
Source: Trainee. Honours: Eire Under-21.

| | | | | | |
|---|---|---|---|---|---|
| 2000-01 | Brentford | 2 | 0 | | |
| 2001-02 | Brentford | 3 | 0 | | |
| 2002-03 | Brentford | 5 | 0 | | |
| 2003-04 | Brentford | 36 | 9 | | |
| 2004-05 | Brentford | 40 | 5 | | |
| 2005-06 | Brentford | 42 | 6 | **128** | **20** |
| 2006-07 | Coventry C | 31 | 3 | | |
| 2007-08 | Coventry C | 42 | 5 | | |
| 2008-09 | Coventry C | 22 | 3 | **95** | **11** |
| 2008-09 | Reading | 9 | 0 | | |
| 2009-10 | Reading | 28 | 0 | | |
| 2010-11 | Reading | 21 | 0 | | |
| 2011-12 | Reading | 19 | 0 | | |
| 2012-13 | Reading | 12 | 0 | **89** | **0** |
| 2012-13 | *Ipswich T* | 9 | 1 | **9** | **1** |

**TANNER, Craig (F)** 0 0
b.Reading 27-10-94
Source: Scholar.

| | | | | | |
|---|---|---|---|---|---|
| 2011-12 | Reading | 0 | 0 | | |
| 2012-13 | Reading | 0 | 0 | | |

**TAYLOR, Jake (M)** 46 4
H: 5 10 W: 12 01 b.Ascot 1-12-91
Source: Scholar. Honours: Wales Under-21.

| | | | | | |
|---|---|---|---|---|---|
| 2010-11 | Reading | 1 | 0 | | |
| 2011-12 | Reading | 0 | 0 | | |
| 2011-12 | *Aldershot T* | 3 | 0 | **3** | **0** |
| 2011-12 | *Exeter C* | 30 | 3 | **30** | **3** |
| 2012-13 | Reading | 0 | 0 | **1** | **0** |
| 2012-13 | *Cheltenham T* | 8 | 1 | **8** | **1** |
| 2012-13 | *Crawley T* | 4 | 0 | **4** | **0** |

**TAYLOR, Stuart (G)** 72 0
H: 6 5 W: 13 07 b.Romford 28-11-80
Source: Trainee. Honours: FA Schools, England Youth, Under-21.

| | | | | | |
|---|---|---|---|---|---|
| 1998-99 | Arsenal | 0 | 0 | | |
| 1999-2000 | Arsenal | 0 | 0 | | |
| 1999-2000 | *Bristol R* | 4 | 0 | **4** | **0** |
| 2000-01 | Arsenal | 0 | 0 | | |
| 2000-01 | *Crystal Palace* | 10 | 0 | **10** | **0** |
| 2000-01 | *Peterborough U* | 6 | 0 | **6** | **0** |
| 2001-02 | Arsenal | 10 | 0 | | |
| 2002-03 | Arsenal | 8 | 0 | | |
| 2003-04 | Arsenal | 0 | 0 | | |
| 2004-05 | Arsenal | 0 | 0 | **18** | **0** |
| 2004-05 | *Leicester C* | 10 | 0 | **10** | **0** |
| 2005-06 | Aston Villa | 2 | 0 | | |
| 2006-07 | Aston Villa | 6 | 0 | | |
| 2007-08 | Aston Villa | 4 | 0 | | |
| 2008-09 | Aston Villa | 0 | 0 | | |
| 2008-09 | *Cardiff C* | 8 | 0 | **8** | **0** |
| 2009-10 | Aston Villa | 0 | 0 | **12** | **0** |
| 2009-10 | Manchester C | 0 | 0 | | |
| 2010-11 | Manchester C | 0 | 0 | | |
| 2011-12 | Manchester C | 0 | 0 | | |
| 2012-13 | Manchester C | 0 | 0 | | |
| 2012-13 | Reading | 4 | 0 | **4** | **0** |

**TSHIBOLA, Aaron (M)** 0 0
H: 6 3 W: 11 01 b.Newham 2-1-95
Source: Scholar.

| | | | | | |
|---|---|---|---|---|---|
| 2011-12 | Reading | 0 | 0 | | |
| 2012-13 | Reading | 0 | 0 | | |

**UGWU, Chigozie (F)** 21 3
H: 6 2 W: 12 00 b.Oxford 22-4-93
Source: Scholar.

| | | | | | |
|---|---|---|---|---|---|
| 2011-12 | Reading | 0 | 0 | | |
| 2012-13 | Reading | 0 | 0 | | |
| 2012-13 | *Yeovil T* | 15 | 3 | **15** | **3** |
| 2012-13 | *Plymouth Arg* | 6 | 0 | **6** | **0** |

**Players retained or with offer of contract**
Fosu, Tariqe Kumahl Malachi Akwesi; Griffin, Shane Anthony; Hector, Michael Anthony James.

**Scholars**
Cooper, Jake Matthew; Dickie, Robert; Hyam, Dominic John; Ikpeazu, Karl Anthony Uchechukwu Mubiru; Ismajli, Shpat; Jeffrey, Jack Len David; Kelly, Liam Anthony; Keown, Niall Martin; Kuhl, Aaron John; Lincoln, Daniel John; Long, Sean Martin; McLennan, George; Moore, Stuart John; Murombedzi, Shepherd Takunda; Ofori, Germaine; Owusu, Nana; Shaughnessy, Conor Glynn; Stacey, Jack William; Taylor-Crossdale, De'juane Ardell Kyle.

# ROCHDALE (68)

**ABADAKI, Godwin (F)** 2 0
H: 5 11 W: 12 04 b.Kwara 21-10-93
Source: Scholar.

| | | | | | |
|---|---|---|---|---|---|
| 2011-12 | Rochdale | 2 | 0 | | |
| 2012-13 | Rochdale | 0 | 0 | **2** | **0** |

**ADEBOLA, Dele (F)** 638 138
H: 6 3 W: 12 08 b.Lagos 23-6-75
Source: Trainee.

| | | | | | |
|---|---|---|---|---|---|
| 1992-93 | Crewe Alex | 6 | 0 | | |
| 1993-94 | Crewe Alex | 0 | 0 | | |
| 1994-95 | Crewe Alex | 30 | 8 | | |
| 1995-96 | Crewe Alex | 29 | 8 | | |
| 1996-97 | Crewe Alex | 32 | 16 | | |
| 1997-98 | Crewe Alex | 27 | 7 | **124** | **39** |
| 1997-98 | Birmingham C | 17 | 7 | | |
| 1998-99 | Birmingham C | 39 | 13 | | |
| 1999-2000 | Birmingham C | 42 | 5 | | |
| 2000-01 | Birmingham C | 31 | 6 | | |
| 2001-02 | Birmingham C | 0 | 0 | **129** | **31** |
| 2001-02 | *Oldham Ath* | 5 | 0 | **5** | **0** |
| 2002-03 | Crystal Palace | 39 | 5 | **39** | **5** |
| 2003-04 | Coventry C | 28 | 2 | | |
| 2003-04 | *Burnley* | 3 | 1 | **3** | **1** |
| 2004-05 | Coventry C | 25 | 5 | | |
| 2004-05 | *Bradford C* | 15 | 3 | **15** | **3** |
| 2005-06 | Coventry C | 44 | 12 | | |
| 2006-07 | Coventry C | 40 | 8 | | |
| 2007-08 | Coventry C | 26 | 4 | **163** | **31** |
| 2007-08 | Bristol C | 17 | 6 | | |
| 2008-09 | Bristol C | 39 | 10 | **56** | **16** |
| 2009-10 | Nottingham F | 33 | 3 | | |
| 2010-11 | Nottingham F | 29 | 2 | **62** | **5** |
| 2011-12 | Hull C | 10 | 0 | **10** | **0** |
| 2011-12 | *Notts Co* | 6 | 1 | **6** | **1** |
| 2012-13 | Rochdale | 26 | 6 | **26** | **6** |

## BARRY-MURPHY, Brian (M) — 454 17
H: 5 10 W: 13 01 b.Cork 27-7-78
Honours: Eire Youth, Under-21.

|  |  | | | | |
|---|---|--:|--:|--:|--:|
| 1995-96 | Cork C | 13 | 0 | | |
| 1996-97 | Cork C | 25 | 0 | | |
| 1997-98 | Cork C | 15 | 1 | | |
| 1998-99 | Cork C | 27 | 1 | 80 | 2 |
| 1999-2000 | Preston NE | 1 | 0 | | |
| 2000-01 | Preston NE | 14 | 0 | | |
| 2001-02 | Preston NE | 4 | 0 | | |
| 2001-02 | *Southend U* | 8 | 1 | 8 | 1 |
| 2002-03 | Preston NE | 2 | 0 | 21 | 0 |
| 2002-03 | *Hartlepool U* | 7 | 0 | 7 | 0 |
| 2002-03 | Sheffield W | 17 | 0 | | |
| 2003-04 | Sheffield W | 41 | 0 | 58 | 0 |
| 2004-05 | Bury | 45 | 6 | | |
| 2005-06 | Bury | 40 | 3 | | |
| 2006-07 | Bury | 14 | 0 | | |
| 2007-08 | Bury | 31 | 1 | | |
| 2008-09 | Bury | 42 | 2 | | |
| 2009-10 | Bury | 46 | 1 | 218 | 13 |
| 2010-11 | Rochdale | 32 | 0 | | |
| 2011-12 | Rochdale | 22 | 1 | | |
| 2012-13 | Rochdale | 8 | 0 | 62 | 1 |

## BENNETT, Rhys (D) — 33 2
H: 6 4 W: 14 05 b.Radcliffe 1-9-91

|  |  | | | | |
|---|---|--:|--:|--:|--:|
| 2011-12 | Falkirk | 0 | 0 | | |
| 2012-13 | Rochdale | 33 | 2 | 33 | 2 |

## BUNNEY, Joe (F) — 1 1
b.Manchester 26-9-93

|  |  | | | | |
|---|---|--:|--:|--:|--:|
| 2012-13 | Rochdale | 1 | 1 | 1 | 1 |

## BYRNE, Neil (D) — 3 0
H: 5 7 W: 8 09 b.Dublin 2-2-93
Source: Scholar. Honours: Eire Youth.

|  |  | | | | |
|---|---|--:|--:|--:|--:|
| 2010-11 | Nottingham F | 0 | 0 | | |
| 2011-12 | Nottingham F | 0 | 0 | | |
| 2011-12 | Rochdale | 3 | 0 | | |
| 2012-13 | Rochdale | 0 | 0 | 3 | 0 |

## CAMPS, Callum (M) — 2 0
b.Stockport 30-11-95

|  |  | | | | |
|---|---|--:|--:|--:|--:|
| 2012-13 | Rochdale | 2 | 0 | 2 | 0 |

## CAVANAGH, Peter (D) — 105 7
H: 5 11 W: 11 08 b.Liverpool 14-10-81
Source: Liverpool Scholar.

|  |  | | | | |
|---|---|--:|--:|--:|--:|
| 2006-07 | Accrington S | 26 | 4 | | |
| 2007-08 | Accrington S | 19 | 1 | | |
| 2008-09 | Accrington S | 29 | 1 | 74 | 6 |

From Fleetwood T

|  |  | | | | |
|---|---|--:|--:|--:|--:|
| 2012-13 | Rochdale | 31 | 1 | 31 | 1 |

## COLLIS, Steve (G) — 88 0
H: 6 3 W: 12 05 b.Harrow 18-3-81
Source: Barnet Juniors.

|  |  | | | | |
|---|---|--:|--:|--:|--:|
| 1999-2000 | Barnet | 0 | 0 | | |
| 2000-01 | Nottingham F | 0 | 0 | | |
| 2001-02 | Nottingham F | 0 | 0 | | |
| 2003-04 | Yeovil T | 11 | 0 | | |
| 2004-05 | Yeovil T | 9 | 0 | | |
| 2005-06 | Yeovil T | 23 | 0 | 43 | 0 |
| 2006-07 | Southend U | 1 | 0 | | |
| 2007-08 | Southend U | 20 | 0 | 21 | 0 |
| 2008-09 | Crewe Alex | 18 | 0 | | |
| 2009-10 | Crewe Alex | 1 | 0 | 19 | 0 |
| 2009-10 | Bristol C | 0 | 0 | | |
| 2009-10 | *Torquay U* | 1 | 0 | 1 | 0 |
| 2010-11 | Peterborough U | 0 | 0 | | |
| 2010-11 | *Northampton T* | 4 | 0 | 4 | 0 |
| 2011-12 | Macclesfield T | 0 | 0 | | |
| 2012-13 | Rochdale | 0 | 0 | | |

## CRANEY, Ian (M) — 182 28
H: 5 10 W: 12 00 b.Liverpool 21-7-82
Source: Runcorn, Altrincham.

|  |  | | | | |
|---|---|--:|--:|--:|--:|
| 2006-07 | Accrington S | 18 | 5 | | |
| 2006-07 | Swansea C | 27 | 0 | | |
| 2007-08 | Swansea C | 1 | 0 | 28 | 0 |
| 2007-08 | Accrington S | 34 | 7 | | |
| 2008-09 | Accrington S | 2 | 1 | | |
| 2008-09 | Huddersfield T | 34 | 5 | | |
| 2009-10 | Huddersfield T | 0 | 0 | 34 | 5 |
| 2009-10 | Morecambe | 16 | 2 | 16 | 2 |

From Fleetwood T.

|  |  | | | | |
|---|---|--:|--:|--:|--:|
| 2010-11 | Accrington S | 22 | 7 | | |
| 2011-12 | Accrington S | 22 | 1 | | |
| 2012-13 | Accrington S | 0 | 0 | 98 | 21 |
| 2012-13 | Rochdale | 6 | 0 | 6 | 0 |

## CURRAN, Craig (F) — 165 23
H: 5 9 W: 11 09 b.Liverpool 23-9-89
Source: Scholar.

|  |  | | | | |
|---|---|--:|--:|--:|--:|
| 2006-07 | Tranmere R | 4 | 4 | | |
| 2007-08 | Tranmere R | 35 | 2 | | |
| 2008-09 | Tranmere R | 15 | 3 | | |
| 2009-10 | Tranmere R | 43 | 5 | 97 | 14 |
| 2010-11 | Carlisle U | 45 | 8 | | |
| 2011-12 | Carlisle U | 12 | 0 | 57 | 8 |
| 2011-12 | *Morecambe* | 7 | 1 | 7 | 1 |
| 2012-13 | Rochdale | 4 | 0 | 4 | 0 |

## DONNELLY, George (F) — 115 26
H: 6 2 W: 13 03 b.Liverpool 28-5-88
Source: Skelmersdale U.

|  |  | | | | |
|---|---|--:|--:|--:|--:|
| 2008-09 | Plymouth Arg | 2 | 0 | | |
| 2009-10 | Plymouth Arg | 0 | 0 | | |
| 2009-10 | *Stockport Co* | 19 | 4 | | |
| 2010-11 | Plymouth Arg | 0 | 0 | 2 | 0 |
| 2010-11 | *Stockport Co* | 23 | 8 | 42 | 12 |

From Fleetwood T

|  |  | | | | |
|---|---|--:|--:|--:|--:|
| 2011-12 | Macclesfield T | 28 | 6 | 28 | 6 |
| 2011-12 | Rochdale | 0 | 0 | | |
| 2012-13 | Rochdale | 43 | 8 | 43 | 8 |

## EDWARDS, Matty (G) — 8 0
H: 6 2 W: 12 11 b.Birkenhead 22-8-90
Source: Leeds U. Honours: Scotland Under-21.

|  |  | | | | |
|---|---|--:|--:|--:|--:|
| 2008-09 | Leeds U | 0 | 0 | | |
| 2009-10 | Rochdale | 0 | 0 | | |
| 2010-11 | Rochdale | 1 | 0 | | |
| 2011-12 | Rochdale | 7 | 0 | | |
| 2012-13 | Rochdale | 0 | 0 | 8 | 0 |

## EDWARDS, Phil (D) — 269 23
H: 5 8 W: 11 03 b.Bootle 8-11-85
Source: Scholar.

|  |  | | | | |
|---|---|--:|--:|--:|--:|
| 2005-06 | Wigan Ath | 0 | 0 | | |
| 2006-07 | Accrington S | 33 | 1 | | |
| 2007-08 | Accrington S | 31 | 1 | | |
| 2008-09 | Accrington S | 46 | 0 | | |
| 2009-10 | Accrington S | 46 | 8 | | |
| 2010-11 | Accrington S | 44 | 13 | 200 | 23 |
| 2011-12 | Stevenage | 22 | 0 | 22 | 0 |
| 2012-13 | Rochdale | 44 | 0 | 47 | 0 |

## GRANT, Robert (M) — 174 42
H: 5 11 W: 12 00 b.Liverpool 1-7-90
Source: Scholar.

|  |  | | | | |
|---|---|--:|--:|--:|--:|
| 2006-07 | Accrington S | 1 | 0 | | |
| 2007-08 | Accrington S | 7 | 0 | | |
| 2008-09 | Accrington S | 15 | 1 | | |
| 2009-10 | Accrington S | 42 | 14 | | |
| 2010-11 | Scunthorpe U | 27 | 0 | | |
| 2010-11 | *Rochdale* | 6 | 2 | | |
| 2011-12 | Scunthorpe U | 29 | 7 | | |
| 2011-12 | *Accrington S* | 8 | 3 | 73 | 18 |
| 2012-13 | Scunthorpe U | 3 | 0 | 59 | 7 |
| 2012-13 | Rochdale | 36 | 15 | 42 | 17 |

## GRAY, Reece (F) — 10 2
H: 5 7 W: 8 08 b.Oldham 1-9-92
Source: Scholar.

|  |  | | | | |
|---|---|--:|--:|--:|--:|
| 2009-10 | Rochdale | 2 | 0 | | |
| 2010-11 | Rochdale | 2 | 1 | | |
| 2011-12 | Rochdale | 4 | 1 | | |
| 2012-13 | Rochdale | 2 | 0 | 10 | 2 |

## GRIMES, Ashley (M) — 126 35
H: 6 0 W: 11 02 b.Swinton 9-12-86
Source: Scholar.

|  |  | | | | |
|---|---|--:|--:|--:|--:|
| 2006-07 | Manchester C | 0 | 0 | | |
| 2006-07 | *Swindon T* | 4 | 0 | 4 | 0 |
| 2007-08 | Manchester C | 0 | 0 | | |
| 2008-09 | Millwall | 17 | 2 | | |
| 2009-10 | Millwall | 4 | 0 | | |
| 2010-11 | Millwall | 0 | 0 | 21 | 2 |
| 2010-11 | *Lincoln C* | 27 | 15 | 27 | 15 |
| 2011-12 | Rochdale | 36 | 8 | | |
| 2012-13 | Rochdale | 38 | 10 | 74 | 18 |

## HAWORTH, Andrew (M) — 67 3
H: 5 11 W: 11 10 b.Lancaster 28-11-88
Source: Scholar.

|  |  | | | | |
|---|---|--:|--:|--:|--:|
| 2007-08 | Blackburn R | 0 | 0 | | |
| 2008-09 | Blackburn R | 0 | 0 | | |
| 2009-10 | Blackburn R | 0 | 0 | | |
| 2009-10 | *Rochdale* | 7 | 0 | | |
| 2010-11 | Bury | 40 | 3 | | |
| 2011-12 | Bury | 6 | 0 | 46 | 3 |
| 2011-12 | *Oxford U* | 4 | 0 | 4 | 0 |
| 2011-12 | *Bradford C* | 3 | 0 | 3 | 0 |
| 2012-13 | Falkirk | 0 | 0 | | |
| 2012-13 | Rochdale | 7 | 0 | 14 | 0 |

## HENDERSON, Ian (F) — 262 35
H: 5 10 W: 11 06 b.Thetford 25-1-85
Source: Scholar. Honours: England Youth, Under-20.

|  |  | | | | |
|---|---|--:|--:|--:|--:|
| 2002-03 | Norwich C | 20 | 1 | | |
| 2003-04 | Norwich C | 19 | 4 | | |
| 2004-05 | Norwich C | 3 | 0 | | |
| 2005-06 | Norwich C | 24 | 1 | | |
| 2006-07 | Norwich C | 2 | 0 | 68 | 6 |
| 2006-07 | *Rotherham U* | 18 | 1 | 18 | 1 |
| 2007-08 | Northampton T | 23 | 0 | | |
| 2008-09 | Northampton T | 3 | 0 | 26 | 0 |
| 2008-09 | *Luton T* | 19 | 1 | 19 | 1 |
| 2009-10 | Colchester U | 13 | 2 | | |
| 2009-10 | *Ankaragucu* | 2 | 0 | 2 | 0 |
| 2010-11 | Colchester U | 36 | 10 | | |
| 2011-12 | Colchester U | 46 | 9 | | |
| 2012-13 | Colchester U | 22 | 3 | 117 | 24 |
| 2012-13 | Rochdale | 12 | 3 | 12 | 3 |

## JONES, Richie (M) — 158 9
H: 6 0 W: 11 00 b.Manchester 26-9-86
Source: Scholar. Honours: England Youth.

|  |  | | | | |
|---|---|--:|--:|--:|--:|
| 2004-05 | Manchester U | 0 | 0 | | |
| 2005-06 | Manchester U | 0 | 0 | | |
| 2006-07 | Manchester U | 0 | 0 | | |
| 2006-07 | *Colchester U* | 6 | 0 | 6 | 0 |
| 2006-07 | *Barnsley* | 4 | 0 | 4 | 0 |
| 2007-08 | Manchester U | 0 | 0 | | |
| 2007-08 | *Yeovil T* | 9 | 0 | 9 | 0 |
| 2008-09 | Hartlepool U | 36 | 3 | | |
| 2009-10 | Hartlepool U | 33 | 4 | 69 | 7 |
| 2010-11 | Oldham Ath | 31 | 1 | 31 | 1 |
| 2011-12 | Bradford C | 32 | 1 | | |
| 2012-13 | Bradford C | 4 | 0 | 36 | 1 |
| 2012-13 | Rochdale | 3 | 0 | 3 | 0 |

## KENNEDY, Jason (M) — 283 22
H: 6 1 W: 13 02 b.Stockton 11-9-86
Source: Scholar.

|  |  | | | | |
|---|---|--:|--:|--:|--:|
| 2004-05 | Middlesbrough | 1 | 0 | | |
| 2005-06 | Middlesbrough | 0 | 0 | | |
| 2006-07 | Middlesbrough | 0 | 0 | | |
| 2006-07 | *Boston U* | 13 | 1 | 13 | 1 |
| 2006-07 | *Bury* | 12 | 0 | 12 | 0 |
| 2007-08 | Middlesbrough | 0 | 0 | 4 | 0 |
| 2007-08 | *Livingston* | 18 | 2 | 18 | 2 |
| 2007-08 | *Darlington* | 13 | 2 | | |
| 2008-09 | Darlington | 46 | 5 | 59 | 7 |
| 2009-10 | Rochdale | 42 | 0 | | |
| 2010-11 | Rochdale | 45 | 4 | | |
| 2011-12 | Rochdale | 44 | 4 | | |
| 2012-13 | Rochdale | 46 | 4 | 177 | 12 |

## LILLIS, Josh (G) — 117 0
H: 6 0 W: 12 08 b.Derby 24-6-87
Source: Scholar.

|  |  | | | | |
|---|---|--:|--:|--:|--:|
| 2006-07 | Scunthorpe U | 1 | 0 | | |
| 2007-08 | Scunthorpe U | 3 | 0 | | |
| 2008-09 | Scunthorpe U | 5 | 0 | | |
| 2008-09 | *Notts Co* | 5 | 0 | 5 | 0 |
| 2009-10 | Scunthorpe U | 8 | 0 | | |
| 2009-10 | *Grimsby T* | 4 | 0 | 4 | 0 |
| 2009-10 | *Rochdale* | 1 | 0 | | |
| 2010-11 | Scunthorpe U | 15 | 0 | | |
| 2010-11 | *Rochdale* | 23 | 0 | | |
| 2011-12 | Scunthorpe U | 6 | 0 | 38 | 0 |
| 2012-13 | Rochdale | 46 | 0 | 70 | 0 |

## LOGAN, Joel (F) — 5 0
b.Manchester 25-1-95

|  |  | | | | |
|---|---|--:|--:|--:|--:|
| 2012-13 | Rochdale | 5 | 0 | 5 | 0 |

## McINTYRE, Kevin (M) — 353 23
H: 6 0 W: 11 10 b.Liverpool 23-12-77
Source: Trainee.

|  |  | | | | |
|---|---|--:|--:|--:|--:|
| 1996-97 | Tranmere R | 0 | 0 | | |
| 1997-98 | Tranmere R | 2 | 0 | | |
| 1998-99 | Tranmere R | 0 | 0 | | |
| 1999-2000 | Tranmere R | 0 | 0 | | |

| Season | Club | App | Gls | Total App | Total Gls |
|---|---|---|---|---|---|
| 2000-01 | Tranmere R | 0 | 0 | | |
| 2001-02 | Tranmere R | 0 | 0 | 2 | 0 |
| 2004-05 | Chester C | 10 | 0 | 10 | 0 |
| 2004-05 | Macclesfield T | 23 | 0 | | |
| 2005-06 | Macclesfield T | 44 | 5 | | |
| 2006-07 | Macclesfield T | 44 | 9 | | |
| 2007-08 | Macclesfield T | 23 | 2 | 134 | 16 |
| 2007-08 | Shrewsbury T | 22 | 2 | | |
| 2008-09 | Shrewsbury T | 26 | 0 | | |
| 2009-10 | Shrewsbury T | 45 | 1 | | |
| 2010-11 | Shrewsbury T | 31 | 1 | 124 | 4 |
| 2011-12 | Accrington S | 45 | 2 | 45 | 2 |
| 2012-13 | Rochdale | 38 | 1 | 38 | 1 |

**MINIHAN, Sam (D)**    1   0
H: 6 1  W: 11 09  b.Rochdale 16-2-94
*Source:* Scholar.

| Season | Club | App | Gls | Total App | Total Gls |
|---|---|---|---|---|---|
| 2011-12 | Rochdale | 1 | 0 | | |
| 2012-13 | Rochdale | 0 | 0 | 1 | 0 |

**O'CONNOR, Darcy (D)**    1   0
b.Oldham

| Season | Club | App | Gls | Total App | Total Gls |
|---|---|---|---|---|---|
| 2012-13 | Rochdale | 1 | 0 | 1 | 0 |

**PEARSON, Matthew (D)**    9   0
H: 6 3  W: 11 05  b.Keighley 3-8-93

| Season | Club | App | Gls | Total App | Total Gls |
|---|---|---|---|---|---|
| 2012-13 | Rochdale | 9 | 0 | 9 | 0 |

**PUTTERILL, Ray (M)**    43   1
H: 5 8  W: 12 02  b.Liverpool 2-3-89
*Source:* Scholar.

| Season | Club | App | Gls | Total App | Total Gls |
|---|---|---|---|---|---|
| 2007-08 | Liverpool | 0 | 0 | | |
| 2008-09 | Liverpool | 0 | 0 | | |
| From Halewood T | | | | | |
| 2010-11 | Accrington S | 25 | 0 | 25 | 0 |
| From Southport | | | | | |
| 2012-13 | Rochdale | 18 | 1 | 18 | 1 |

**RAFFERTY, Joe (D)**    21   0
b. 6-10-93

| Season | Club | App | Gls | Total App | Total Gls |
|---|---|---|---|---|---|
| 2012-13 | Rochdale | 21 | 0 | 21 | 0 |

**TANSER, Scott (D)**    1   0

| Season | Club | App | Gls | Total App | Total Gls |
|---|---|---|---|---|---|
| 2012-13 | Rochdale | 1 | 0 | 1 | 0 |

**THOMAS, Wayne (D)**    456   13
H: 6 1  W: 13 06  b.Gloucester 17-5-79

| Season | Club | App | Gls | Total App | Total Gls |
|---|---|---|---|---|---|
| 1995-96 | Torquay U | 6 | 0 | | |
| 1996-97 | Torquay U | 12 | 0 | | |
| 1997-98 | Torquay U | 21 | 1 | | |
| 1998-99 | Torquay U | 44 | 1 | | |
| 1999-2000 | Torquay U | 40 | 3 | 123 | 5 |
| 2000-01 | Stoke C | 34 | 0 | | |
| 2001-02 | Stoke C | 40 | 2 | | |
| 2002-03 | Stoke C | 41 | 0 | | |
| 2003-04 | Stoke C | 39 | 3 | | |
| 2004-05 | Stoke C | 35 | 2 | 189 | 7 |
| 2005-06 | Burnley | 16 | 1 | | |
| 2006-07 | Burnley | 33 | 0 | | |
| 2007-08 | Burnley | 1 | 0 | 50 | 1 |
| 2007-08 | Southampton | 30 | 0 | | |
| 2009-10 | Southampton | 15 | 0 | 45 | 0 |
| 2010-11 | Doncaster R | 21 | 0 | 21 | 0 |
| 2011-12 | Atromitos | 22 | 0 | 22 | 0 |
| 2012-13 | Veria | 4 | 0 | 4 | 0 |
| 2012-13 | Rochdale | 2 | 0 | 2 | 0 |

**TUTTE, Andrew (M)**    101   10
H: 5 9  W: 10 10  b.Huyton 21-9-90
*Source:* Scholar. *Honours:* England Youth, Under-20.

| Season | Club | App | Gls | Total App | Total Gls |
|---|---|---|---|---|---|
| 2007-08 | Manchester C | 0 | 0 | | |
| 2008-09 | Manchester C | 0 | 0 | | |
| 2009-10 | Manchester C | 0 | 0 | | |
| 2010-11 | Manchester C | 0 | 0 | | |
| 2010-11 | Rochdale | 7 | 0 | | |
| 2010-11 | Shrewsbury T | 2 | 0 | 2 | 0 |
| 2010-11 | Yeovil T | 15 | 2 | 15 | 2 |
| 2011-12 | Rochdale | 40 | 1 | | |
| 2012-13 | Rochdale | 37 | 7 | 84 | 8 |

**Scholars**
Allen, Jamie Paul; Antoine-Clarke, Shaquille Maurice; Ashley, Aaron John; Camps, Callum; Cannon, Andrew Francis; Hill, Callum Paul; Horan, Jack; Leigh, George Vincent; Logan, Joel Alexander; Martin, Connor Jay; Masirika, Kevin Mfumu; O'Connor, D'arcy Christopher; Rabiu, Shamsideen Olalekan Aderoju; Spittle, Jonathan; Tanser, Scott; Tuanzebe, Dimitri Gobula; Whitehall, Daniel.

# ROTHERHAM U (69)

**AGARD, Kieran (F)**    68   13
H: 5 10  W: 10 10  b.Newham 10-10-89
*Source:* Scholar.

| Season | Club | App | Gls | Total App | Total Gls |
|---|---|---|---|---|---|
| 2006-07 | Everton | 0 | 0 | | |
| 2007-08 | Everton | 0 | 0 | | |
| 2008-09 | Everton | 0 | 0 | | |
| 2009-10 | Everton | 1 | 0 | | |
| 2010-11 | Everton | 0 | 0 | 1 | 0 |
| 2010-11 | Kilmarnock | 8 | 1 | 8 | 1 |
| 2010-11 | Peterborough U | 0 | 0 | | |
| 2011-12 | Yeovil T | 29 | 6 | 29 | 6 |
| 2012-13 | Rotherham U | 30 | 6 | 30 | 6 |

**AINSWORTH, Lionel (F)**    171   18
H: 5 9  W: 9 10  b.Nottingham 1-10-87
*Source:* Scholar. *Honours:* England Youth.

| Season | Club | App | Gls | Total App | Total Gls |
|---|---|---|---|---|---|
| 2005-06 | Derby Co | 2 | 0 | | |
| 2006-07 | Derby Co | 0 | 0 | 2 | 0 |
| 2006-07 | Bournemouth | 7 | 0 | 7 | 0 |
| 2006-07 | Wycombe W | 7 | 0 | 7 | 0 |
| 2007-08 | Hereford U | 15 | 4 | | |
| 2007-08 | Watford | 8 | 0 | | |
| 2008-09 | Watford | 7 | 0 | 15 | 0 |
| 2008-09 | Hereford U | 7 | 3 | 22 | 7 |
| 2008-09 | Huddersfield T | 14 | 0 | | |
| 2009-10 | Huddersfield T | 11 | 0 | | |
| 2009-10 | Brentford | 9 | 0 | 9 | 0 |
| 2010-11 | Shrewsbury T | 33 | 9 | | |
| 2010-11 | Huddersfield T | 0 | 0 | 25 | 0 |
| 2011-12 | Shrewsbury T | 21 | 2 | 54 | 11 |
| 2011-12 | Burton Alb | 7 | 0 | 7 | 0 |
| 2012-13 | Rotherham U | 16 | 0 | 16 | 0 |
| 2012-13 | Aldershot T | 7 | 0 | 7 | 0 |

**ARNASON, Kari (M)**    273   14
H: 6 3  W: 13 06  b.Reykjavik 13-10-82
*Honours:* Iceland 25 full caps, 2 goals.

| Season | Club | App | Gls | Total App | Total Gls |
|---|---|---|---|---|---|
| 2001 | Vikingur | 5 | 2 | | |
| 2002 | Vikingur | 5 | 1 | | |
| 2003 | Vikingur | 16 | 0 | | |
| 2004 | Vikingur | 15 | 0 | 41 | 3 |
| 2005 | Djurgarden | 21 | 0 | | |
| 2006 | Djurgarden | 14 | 0 | 35 | 0 |
| 2006-07 | Aarhus | 14 | 2 | | |
| 2007-08 | Aarhus | 25 | 0 | | |
| 2008-09 | Aarhus | 12 | 1 | 51 | 3 |
| 2008-09 | Esbjerg | 8 | 0 | 8 | 0 |
| 2009-10 | Plymouth Arg | 32 | 2 | | |
| 2010-11 | Plymouth Arg | 40 | 1 | 72 | 3 |
| 2011-12 | Aberdeen | 33 | 3 | 33 | 3 |
| 2012-13 | Rotherham U | 33 | 2 | 33 | 2 |

**BRADLEY, Mark (D)**    165   7
H: 6 0  W: 11 05  b.Dudley 14-1-88
*Source:* Scholar. *Honours:* Wales Youth, Under-21, 1 full cap.

| Season | Club | App | Gls | Total App | Total Gls |
|---|---|---|---|---|---|
| 2004-05 | Walsall | 1 | 0 | | |
| 2005-06 | Walsall | 3 | 0 | | |
| 2006-07 | Walsall | 1 | 0 | | |
| 2007-08 | Walsall | 35 | 3 | | |
| 2008-09 | Walsall | 28 | 2 | | |
| 2009-10 | Walsall | 28 | 0 | 96 | 5 |
| 2010-11 | Rotherham U | 21 | 0 | | |
| 2011-12 | Rotherham U | 21 | 1 | | |
| 2012-13 | Rotherham U | 27 | 1 | 69 | 2 |

**DAVIS, Claude (D)**    254   7
H: 6 3  W: 14 04  b.Kingston, Jamaica 6-3-79
*Source:* Portmore U. *Honours:* Jamaica 67 full caps, 2 goals.

| Season | Club | App | Gls | Total App | Total Gls |
|---|---|---|---|---|---|
| 2003-04 | Preston NE | 22 | 1 | | |
| 2004-05 | Preston NE | 32 | 0 | | |
| 2005-06 | Preston NE | 40 | 3 | 94 | 4 |
| 2006-07 | Sheffield U | 21 | .0 | 21 | 0 |
| 2007-08 | Derby Co | 19 | 0 | | |
| 2008-09 | Derby Co | 8 | 0 | | |
| 2008-09 | Crystal Palace | 7 | 0 | | |
| 2009-10 | Derby Co | 0 | 0 | 27 | 0 |
| 2009-10 | Crystal Palace | 21 | 0 | | |
| 2010-11 | Crystal Palace | 24 | 0 | | |
| 2011-12 | Crystal Palace | 0 | 0 | 52 | 0 |
| 2011-12 | Crawley T | 29 | 3 | | |
| 2012-13 | Crawley T | 16 | 0 | 45 | 3 |
| 2012-13 | Rotherham U | 15 | 0 | 15 | 0 |

**DENTON, Alec (F)**    2   0
H: 5 11  W: 12 00  b.Sheffield 30-7-94
*Source:* Scholar.

| Season | Club | App | Gls | Total App | Total Gls |
|---|---|---|---|---|---|
| 2011-12 | Rotherham U | 1 | 0 | | |
| 2012-13 | Rotherham U | 1 | 0 | 2 | 0 |

**MORGAN, Craig (D)**    292   9
H: 6 0  W: 11 04  b.Flint 18-6-85
*Source:* Scholar. *Honours:* Wales Youth, Under-21, 23 full caps.

| Season | Club | App | Gls | Total App | Total Gls |
|---|---|---|---|---|---|
| 2001-02 | Wrexham | 2 | 0 | | |
| 2002-03 | Wrexham | 6 | 1 | | |
| 2003-04 | Wrexham | 18 | 0 | | |
| 2004-05 | Wrexham | 26 | 0 | | |
| 2005-06 | Milton Keynes D | 40 | 0 | | |
| 2005-06 | Milton Keynes D | 3 | 0 | 43 | 0 |
| 2006-07 | Wrexham | 1 | 0 | 53 | 1 |
| 2006-07 | Peterborough U | 23 | 1 | | |
| 2007-08 | Peterborough U | 41 | 2 | | |
| 2008-09 | Peterborough U | 27 | 0 | | |
| 2009-10 | Peterborough U | 34 | 1 | 125 | 4 |
| 2010-11 | Preston NE | 31 | 2 | | |
| 2011-12 | Preston NE | 19 | 1 | | |
| 2012-13 | Preston NE | 0 | 0 | 50 | 3 |
| 2012-13 | Rotherham U | 21 | 1 | 21 | 1 |

**MULLINS, John (D)**    283   19
H: 5 11  W: 12 07  b.Hampstead 6-11-85
*Source:* Scholar.

| Season | Club | App | Gls | Total App | Total Gls |
|---|---|---|---|---|---|
| 2004-05 | Reading | 0 | 0 | | |
| 2004-05 | Kidderminster H | 21 | 2 | 21 | 2 |
| 2005-06 | Reading | 0 | 0 | | |
| 2006-07 | Mansfield T | 43 | 2 | | |
| 2007-08 | Mansfield T | 43 | 2 | 86 | 4 |
| 2008-09 | Stockport Co | 33 | 3 | | |
| 2009-10 | Stockport Co | 36 | 1 | 69 | 4 |
| 2010-11 | Rotherham U | 35 | 1 | | |
| 2011-12 | Rotherham U | 35 | 2 | | |
| 2012-13 | Rotherham U | 29 | 4 | 99 | 7 |
| 2012-13 | Oxford U | 8 | 2 | 8 | 2 |

**NARDIELLO, Daniel (F)**    260   75
H: 5 11  W: 11 04  b.Coventry 22-10-82
*Source:* Trainee. *Honours:* Wales 3 full caps.

| Season | Club | App | Gls | Total App | Total Gls |
|---|---|---|---|---|---|
| 1999-2000 | Manchester U | 0 | 0 | | |
| 2000-01 | Manchester U | 0 | 0 | | |
| 2001-02 | Manchester U | 0 | 0 | | |
| 2002-03 | Manchester U | 0 | 0 | | |
| 2003-04 | Manchester U | 0 | 0 | | |
| 2003-04 | Swansea C | 4 | 0 | 4 | 0 |
| 2003-04 | Barnsley | 16 | 7 | | |
| 2004-05 | Manchester U | 0 | 0 | | |
| 2004-05 | Barnsley | 28 | 7 | | |
| 2005-06 | Barnsley | 34 | 5 | | |
| 2006-07 | Barnsley | 30 | 9 | | |
| 2007-08 | QPR | 8 | 0 | 8 | 0 |
| 2007-08 | Barnsley | 11 | 2 | 119 | 30 |
| 2008-09 | Blackpool | 2 | 0 | | |
| 2008-09 | Hartlepool U | 12 | 3 | 12 | 3 |
| 2009-10 | Blackpool | 5 | 0 | 7 | 0 |
| 2009-10 | Bury | 6 | 4 | 6 | 4 |
| 2009-10 | Oldham Ath | 2 | 0 | 2 | 0 |
| 2010-11 | Exeter C | 30 | 10 | | |
| 2011-12 | Exeter C | 36 | 9 | 66 | 19 |
| 2012-13 | Rotherham U | 36 | 19 | 36 | 19 |

**NOBLE, David (M)**    262   18
H: 6 0  W: 12 04  b.Hitchin 2-2-82
*Source:* Scholar. *Honours:* England Youth, Under-20. Scotland Under-21, B.

| Season | Club | App | Gls | Total App | Total Gls |
|---|---|---|---|---|---|
| 2000-01 | Arsenal | 0 | 0 | | |
| 2001-02 | Arsenal | 0 | 0 | | |
| 2001-02 | Watford | 15 | 1 | 15 | 1 |
| 2002-03 | Arsenal | 0 | 0 | | |
| 2002-03 | West Ham U | 0 | 0 | | |
| 2003-04 | West Ham U | 3 | 0 | 3 | 0 |
| 2003-04 | Boston U | 14 | 2 | | |
| 2004-05 | Boston U | 32 | 3 | | |
| 2005-06 | Boston U | 11 | 0 | 57 | 5 |
| 2005-06 | Bristol C | 24 | 1 | | |
| 2006-07 | Bristol C | 26 | 3 | | |
| 2007-08 | Bristol C | 26 | 2 | | |
| 2008-09 | Bristol C | 9 | 1 | 85 | 7 |
| 2008-09 | Yeovil T | 2 | 0 | 2 | 0 |
| 2009-10 | Exeter C | 0 | 0 | | |
| 2010-11 | Exeter C | 36 | 0 | | |
| 2011-12 | Exeter C | 42 | 2 | 78 | 2 |
| 2012-13 | Rotherham U | 22 | 3 | 22 | 3 |

**O'CONNOR, Michael (M)**    219   21
H: 6 1   W: 11 08   b.Belfast 6-10-87
*Source:* Scholar. *Honours:* Northern Ireland Youth, Under-21, B, 10 full caps.

| 2005-06 | Crewe Alex | 2 | 0 | | |
|---|---|---|---|---|---|
| 2006-07 | Crewe Alex | 29 | 0 | | |
| 2007-08 | Crewe Alex | 23 | 0 | | |
| 2008-09 | Crewe Alex | 23 | 3 | 77 | 3 |
| 2008-09 | Lincoln C | 10 | 1 | 10 | 1 |
| 2009-10 | Scunthorpe U | 32 | 2 | | |
| 2010-11 | Scunthorpe U | 32 | 8 | | |
| 2011-12 | Scunthorpe U | 33 | 1 | 97 | 11 |
| 2012-13 | Rotherham U | 35 | 6 | 35 | 6 |

**ODEJAYI, Kayode (F)**    389   57
H: 6 2   W: 12 02   b.Ibadon 21-2-82
*Source:* Scholar. *Honours:* Nigeria 1 full cap.

| 1999-2000 | Bristol C | 3 | 0 | | |
|---|---|---|---|---|---|
| 2000-01 | Bristol C | 3 | 0 | | |
| 2001-02 | Bristol C | 0 | 0 | | |
| 2002-03 | Bristol C | 0 | 0 | 6 | 0 |
| 2003-04 | Cheltenham T | 30 | 5 | | |
| 2004-05 | Cheltenham T | 32 | 1 | | |
| 2005-06 | Cheltenham T | 41 | 11 | | |
| 2006-07 | Cheltenham T | 45 | 13 | 148 | 30 |
| 2007-08 | Barnsley | 39 | 3 | | |
| 2008-09 | Barnsley | 28 | 1 | | |
| 2008-09 | *Scunthorpe U* | 6 | 1 | 6 | 1 |
| 2009-10 | Barnsley | 5 | 0 | 72 | 4 |
| 2009-10 | Colchester U | 28 | 9 | | |
| 2010-11 | Colchester U | 44 | 4 | | |
| 2011-12 | Colchester U | 43 | 4 | 115 | 17 |
| 2012-13 | Rotherham U | 42 | 5 | 42 | 5 |

**PRINGLE, Ben (M)**    87   11
H: 5 8   W: 11 10   b.Whitley Bay 25-7-88
*Source:* WBA Scholar, Newcastle Blue Star, Morpeth T, Ilkeston T.

| 2009-10 | Derby Co | 5 | 0 | | |
|---|---|---|---|---|---|
| 2010-11 | Derby Co | 15 | 0 | 20 | 0 |
| 2010-11 | *Torquay U* | 5 | 0 | 5 | 0 |
| 2011-12 | Rotherham U | 21 | 4 | | |
| 2012-13 | Rotherham U | 41 | 7 | 62 | 11 |

**REVELL, Alex (F)**    300   59
H: 6 3   W: 13 00   b.Cambridge 7-7-83
*Source:* Scholar.

| 2000-01 | Cambridge U | 4 | 0 | | |
|---|---|---|---|---|---|
| 2001-02 | Cambridge U | 24 | 2 | | |
| 2002-03 | Cambridge U | 9 | 0 | | |
| 2003-04 | Cambridge U | 20 | 3 | 57 | 5 |

From Braintree T.

| 2006-07 | Brighton & HA | 38 | 7 | | |
|---|---|---|---|---|---|
| 2007-08 | Brighton & HA | 21 | 6 | 59 | 13 |
| 2007-08 | Southend U | 8 | 0 | | |
| 2008-09 | Southend U | 23 | 4 | | |
| 2009-10 | Southend U | 3 | 0 | 34 | 4 |
| 2009-10 | *Swindon T* | 10 | 2 | 10 | 2 |
| 2009-10 | Wycombe W | 15 | 6 | 15 | 6 |
| 2010-11 | Leyton Orient | 39 | 13 | | |
| 2011-12 | Leyton Orient | 5 | 0 | 44 | 13 |
| 2011-12 | Rotherham U | 40 | 10 | | |
| 2012-13 | Rotherham U | 41 | 6 | 81 | 16 |

**ROSE, Mitchell (M)**    5   0
H: 5 9   W: 12 03   b.4-7-94

| 2012-13 | Rotherham U | 5 | 0 | 5 | 0 |
|---|---|---|---|---|---|

**SCHOFIELD, Danny (M)**    403   54
H: 5 10   W: 11 02   b.Doncaster 10-4-80
*Source:* Brodsworth MW.

| 1998-99 | Huddersfield T | 1 | 0 | | |
|---|---|---|---|---|---|
| 1999-2000 | Huddersfield T | 2 | 0 | | |
| 2000-01 | Huddersfield T | 1 | 0 | | |
| 2001-02 | Huddersfield T | 40 | 8 | | |
| 2002-03 | Huddersfield T | 30 | 2 | | |
| 2003-04 | Huddersfield T | 40 | 8 | | |
| 2004-05 | Huddersfield T | 33 | 5 | | |
| 2005-06 | Huddersfield T | 41 | 9 | | |
| 2006-07 | Huddersfield T | 35 | 5 | | |
| 2007-08 | Huddersfield T | 25 | 2 | 248 | 39 |
| 2008-09 | Yeovil T | 39 | 4 | | |
| 2009-10 | Yeovil T | 4 | 1 | 43 | 5 |
| 2009-10 | Millwall | 36 | 7 | | |
| 2010-11 | Millwall | 31 | 2 | 67 | 9 |
| 2011-12 | Rotherham U | 37 | 1 | | |
| 2012-13 | Rotherham U | 0 | 0 | 37 | 1 |
| 2012-13 | Accrington S | 8 | 0 | 8 | 0 |

**SHEARER, Scott (G)**    274   0
H: 6 3   W: 12 00   b.Glasgow 15-2-81
*Source:* Tower Hearts. *Honours:* Scotland B.

| 2000-01 | Albion R | 3 | 0 | | |
|---|---|---|---|---|---|
| 2001-02 | Albion R | 10 | 0 | | |
| 2002-03 | Albion R | 36 | 0 | 49 | 0 |
| 2003-04 | Coventry C | 30 | 0 | | |
| 2004-05 | Coventry C | 8 | 0 | 38 | 0 |
| 2004-05 | *Rushden & D* | 13 | 0 | 13 | 0 |
| 2005-06 | Bristol R | 45 | 0 | | |
| 2006-07 | Bristol R | 2 | 0 | 47 | 0 |
| 2006-07 | *Shrewsbury T* | 20 | 0 | 20 | 0 |
| 2007-08 | Wycombe W | 5 | 0 | | |
| 2008-09 | Wycombe W | 29 | 0 | | |
| 2009-10 | Wycombe W | 29 | 0 | | |
| 2010-11 | Wycombe W | 0 | 0 | 63 | 0 |
| 2011-12 | Crawley T | 25 | 0 | 25 | 0 |
| 2012-13 | Rotherham U | 19 | 0 | 19 | 0 |

**SKARZ, Joe (D)**    233   5
H: 5 10   W: 11 04   b.Huddersfield 13-7-89
*Source:* Scholar.

| 2006-07 | Huddersfield T | 17 | 0 | | |
|---|---|---|---|---|---|
| 2007-08 | Huddersfield T | 27 | 0 | | |
| 2008-09 | Huddersfield T | 9 | 1 | | |
| 2008-09 | *Hartlepool U* | 7 | 0 | 7 | 0 |
| 2009-10 | Huddersfield T | 15 | 0 | 68 | 1 |
| 2009-10 | *Shrewsbury T* | 20 | 0 | 20 | 0 |
| 2010-11 | Bury | 46 | 1 | | |
| 2011-12 | Bury | 45 | 1 | | |
| 2012-13 | Bury | 39 | 2 | 130 | 4 |
| 2012-13 | Rotherham U | 8 | 0 | 8 | 0 |

**THOMPSON, Tony (G)**    0   0
b.Liverpool 4-11-94

| 2012-13 | Rotherham U | 0 | 0 | | |
|---|---|---|---|---|---|

**TONGE, Dale (D)**    211   1
H: 5 10   W: 10 06   b.Doncaster 7-5-85
*Source:* Scholar.

| 2003-04 | Barnsley | 1 | 0 | | |
|---|---|---|---|---|---|
| 2004-05 | Barnsley | 14 | 0 | | |
| 2005-06 | Barnsley | 24 | 0 | | |
| 2006-07 | Barnsley | 6 | 0 | 45 | 0 |
| 2006-07 | *Gillingham* | 3 | 0 | 3 | 0 |
| 2007-08 | Rotherham U | 37 | 0 | | |
| 2008-09 | Rotherham U | 39 | 1 | | |
| 2009-10 | Rotherham U | 21 | 0 | | |
| 2010-11 | Rotherham U | 23 | 0 | | |
| 2011-12 | Rotherham U | 32 | 0 | | |
| 2012-13 | Rotherham U | 11 | 0 | 163 | 1 |

**WALKER, Nicky (D)**    2   0
b.Rotherham 8-9-94

| 2012-13 | Rotherham U | 2 | 0 | 2 | 0 |
|---|---|---|---|---|---|

**WARRINGTON, Andy (G)**    372   0
H: 6 3   W: 12 13   b.Sheffield 10-6-76
*Source:* Trainee.

| 1994-95 | York C | 0 | 0 | | |
|---|---|---|---|---|---|
| 1995-96 | York C | 6 | 0 | | |
| 1996-97 | York C | 27 | 0 | | |
| 1997-98 | York C | 17 | 0 | | |
| 1998-99 | York C | 11 | 0 | 61 | 0 |
| 2003-04 | Doncaster R | 46 | 0 | | |
| 2004-05 | Doncaster R | 34 | 0 | | |
| 2005-06 | Doncaster R | 9 | 0 | | |
| 2006-07 | Doncaster R | 0 | 0 | 89 | 0 |
| 2006-07 | Bury | 20 | 0 | 20 | 0 |
| 2007-08 | Rotherham U | 46 | 0 | | |
| 2008-09 | Rotherham U | 38 | 0 | | |
| 2009-10 | Rotherham U | 46 | 0 | | |
| 2010-11 | Rotherham U | 38 | 0 | | |
| 2011-12 | Rotherham U | 7 | 0 | | |
| 2012-13 | Rotherham U | 27 | 0 | 202 | 0 |

**Scholars**
Beedham, Luke David; Bell, Connor Harry James; Bevins, Ayrton Niall; Bryan, Charlie; Cadman, James; Hart, Dominic William James; Johnson, Connor Nichoias; Lucas, Reece; McKay, Laurence George; Rowe, Daniel; Thompson, Anthony; Travis, John Graham Harold; Walker, Nicholas Thomas; Watson, Alistair Clark; Wigley, Harley; Williams, Giorgio Lee; Williamson, Michael; Woods, Philip David.

# SCUNTHORPE U (70)

**ADELAKUN, Hakeeb (F)**    2   0

| 2012-13 | Scunthorpe U | 2 | 0 | 2 | 0 |
|---|---|---|---|---|---|

**BARCHAM, Andy (F)**    199   29
H: 5 8   W: 11 10   b.Basildon 16-12-86
*Source:* Scholar.

| 2005-06 | Tottenham H | 0 | 0 | | |
|---|---|---|---|---|---|
| 2006-07 | Tottenham H | 0 | 0 | | |
| 2007-08 | Tottenham H | 0 | 0 | | |
| 2007-08 | *Leyton Orient* | 25 | 1 | 25 | 1 |
| 2008-09 | Tottenham H | 0 | 0 | | |
| 2008-09 | Gillingham | 33 | 6 | | |
| 2009-10 | Gillingham | 42 | 7 | | |
| 2010-11 | Gillingham | 24 | 6 | 99 | 19 |
| 2011-12 | Scunthorpe U | 41 | 9 | | |
| 2012-13 | Scunthorpe U | 34 | 0 | 75 | 9 |

**CANAVAN, Niall (D)**    70   8
H: 6 3   W: 12 00   b.Guiseley 11-4-91
*Source:* Scholar. *Honours:* Eire Under-21.

| 2009-10 | Scunthorpe U | 7 | 1 | | |
|---|---|---|---|---|---|
| 2010-11 | Scunthorpe U | 8 | 0 | | |
| 2010-11 | *Shrewsbury T* | 3 | 0 | 3 | 0 |
| 2011-12 | Scunthorpe U | 12 | 1 | | |
| 2012-13 | Scunthorpe U | 40 | 6 | 67 | 8 |

**COLLINS, Michael (M)**    235   21
H: 6 0   W: 11 00   b.Halifax 30-4-86
*Source:* Scholar. *Honours:* Eire Youth, Under-21.

| 2004-05 | Huddersfield T | 8 | 0 | | |
|---|---|---|---|---|---|
| 2005-06 | Huddersfield T | 17 | 1 | | |
| 2006-07 | Huddersfield T | 43 | 4 | | |
| 2007-08 | Huddersfield T | 41 | 2 | | |
| 2008-09 | Huddersfield T | 36 | 9 | | |
| 2009-10 | Huddersfield T | 28 | 3 | 173 | 19 |
| 2010-11 | Scunthorpe U | 32 | 1 | | |
| 2011-12 | Scunthorpe U | 1 | 0 | | |
| 2012-13 | Scunthorpe U | 29 | 1 | 62 | 2 |

**DUFFY, Mark (M)**    168   13
H: 5 9   W: 11 05   b.Liverpool 7-10-85
*Source:* Vauxhall M, Prescot C, Southport.

| 2008-09 | Morecambe | 9 | 1 | | |
|---|---|---|---|---|---|
| 2009-10 | Morecambe | 35 | 4 | | |
| 2010-11 | Morecambe | 22 | 0 | 66 | 5 |
| 2010-11 | Scunthorpe U | 22 | 1 | | |
| 2011-12 | Scunthorpe U | 37 | 2 | | |
| 2012-13 | Scunthorpe U | 43 | 5 | 102 | 8 |

**GIBBONS, Robbie (M)**    15   0
H: 5 11   W: 12 00   b.Dublin 8-10-91
*Source:* Scholar.

| 2008-09 | Nottingham F | 0 | 0 | | |
|---|---|---|---|---|---|
| 2009-10 | Nottingham F | 0 | 0 | | |
| 2010-11 | Nottingham F | 0 | 0 | | |
| 2011-12 | Alki | 4 | 0 | 4 | 0 |
| 2011-12 | Ermis | 0 | 0 | | |
| 2011-12 | Alki | 4 | 0 | | |
| 2012-13 | Scunthorpe U | 7 | 0 | 11 | 0 |

**GODDEN, Matthew (F)**    14   0
H: 6 1   W: 12 03   b.Canterbury 29-7-91
*Source:* Scholar.

| 2009-10 | Scunthorpe U | 0 | 0 | | |
|---|---|---|---|---|---|
| 2010-11 | Scunthorpe U | 5 | 0 | | |
| 2011-12 | Scunthorpe U | 1 | 0 | | |
| 2012-13 | Scunthorpe U | 8 | 0 | 14 | 0 |

**GRELLA, Mike (F)**    92   10
H: 5 11   W: 12 02   b.New York 23-1-87
*Source:* Duke University. *Honours:* USA Youth.

| 2008-09 | Leeds U | 11 | 0 | | |
|---|---|---|---|---|---|
| 2009-10 | Leeds U | 17 | 1 | | |
| 2010-11 | Leeds U | 1 | 0 | | |
| 2010-11 | *Carlisle U* | 10 | 3 | 10 | 3 |
| 2010-11 | *Swindon T* | 7 | 1 | 7 | 1 |
| 2011-12 | Leeds U | 0 | 0 | 29 | 1 |
| 2011-12 | Brentford | 11 | 0 | 11 | 0 |
| 2011-12 | Bury | 10 | 4 | 10 | 4 |
| 2012-13 | Scunthorpe U | 25 | 1 | 25 | 1 |

**HAWLEY, Karl (F)**    276   64
H: 5 8   W: 12 02   b.Walsall 6-12-81
*Source:* Scholar.

| 2000-01 | Walsall | 0 | 0 | | |
|---|---|---|---|---|---|

|  |  | | | | |
|---|---|--:|--:|--:|--:|
| 2001-02 | Walsall | 1 | 0 | | |
| 2002-03 | Walsall | 0 | 0 | | |
| 2002-03 | *Raith R* | 17 | 7 | | |
| 2003-04 | Walsall | 0 | 0 | 1 | 0 |
| 2003-04 | *Raith R* | 11 | 2 | 28 | 9 |
| 2004-05 | Carlisle U | 0 | 0 | | |
| 2005-06 | Carlisle U | 46 | 22 | | |
| 2006-07 | Carlisle U | 32 | 12 | 78 | 34 |
| 2007-08 | Preston NE | 25 | 3 | | |
| 2008-09 | Preston NE | 5 | 0 | 30 | 3 |
| 2008-09 | *Northampton T* | 11 | 2 | 11 | 2 |
| 2008-09 | *Colchester U* | 4 | 0 | 4 | 0 |
| 2009-10 | Notts Co | 31 | 3 | | |
| 2010-11 | Notts Co | 24 | 0 | | |
| 2011-12 | Notts Co | 26 | 2 | 81 | 5 |
| 2011-12 | *Crawley T* | 4 | 0 | 4 | 0 |
| 2012-13 | Scunthorpe U | 39 | 11 | 39 | 11 |

**HOLMEN JOHANSEN, Eirik (G)**    8   0
H: 6 6   W: 14 12   b.Oslo 12-7-92

|  |  | | | | |
|---|---|--:|--:|--:|--:|
| 2012-13 | Manchester C | 0 | 0 | | |
| 2012-13 | Scunthorpe U | 8 | 0 | 8 | 0 |

**HORNSEY, Luke (M)**    0   0
H: 5 8   W: 11 01   b.Scunthorpe 15-2-95

|  |  | | |
|---|---|--:|--:|
| 2012-13 | Scunthorpe U | 0 | 0 |

**HOWE, Callum (D)**    0   0
H: 6 0   W: 11 07   b.Doncaster 9-4-94

|  |  | | |
|---|---|--:|--:|
| 2012-13 | Scunthorpe U | 0 | 0 |

**JENNINGS, Connor (F)**    16   0
H: 6 0   W: 12 00   b.Manchester 21-1-91
*Source:* Stalybridge C.

|  |  | | | | |
|---|---|--:|--:|--:|--:|
| 2011-12 | Scunthorpe U | 4 | 0 | | |
| 2012-13 | Scunthorpe U | 12 | 0 | 16 | 0 |

**KEEGAN, Jordan (M)**    3   0
b.Dublin 5-2-92
*Source:* Monaghan U.

|  |  | | | | |
|---|---|--:|--:|--:|--:|
| 2012-13 | Scunthorpe U | 3 | 0 | 3 | 0 |

**KENNEDY, Callum (D)**    58   1
H: 6 1   W: 12 10   b.Chertsey 9-11-89
*Source:* Scholar.

|  |  | | | | |
|---|---|--:|--:|--:|--:|
| 2007-08 | Swindon T | 1 | 0 | | |
| 2008-09 | Swindon T | 4 | 0 | | |
| 2009-10 | Swindon T | 8 | 0 | | |
| 2010-11 | Swindon T | 3 | 0 | | |
| 2010-11 | *Gillingham* | 3 | 0 | 3 | 0 |
| 2010-11 | *Rotherham U* | 5 | 0 | 5 | 0 |
| 2011-12 | Swindon T | 18 | 1 | 33 | 1 |
| 2012-13 | Scunthorpe U | 17 | 0 | 17 | 0 |

**MIRFIN, David (D)**    307   14
H: 6 3   W: 13 00   b.Sheffield 18-4-85
*Source:* Scholar.

|  |  | | | | |
|---|---|--:|--:|--:|--:|
| 2002-03 | Huddersfield T | 1 | 0 | | |
| 2003-04 | Huddersfield T | 21 | 2 | | |
| 2004-05 | Huddersfield T | 41 | 4 | | |
| 2005-06 | Huddersfield T | 31 | 1 | | |
| 2006-07 | Huddersfield T | 38 | 1 | | |
| 2007-08 | Huddersfield T | 29 | 1 | 161 | 9 |
| 2008-09 | Scunthorpe U | 18 | 0 | | |
| 2009-10 | Scunthorpe U | 37 | 1 | | |
| 2010-11 | Scunthorpe U | 23 | 3 | | |
| 2011-12 | *Watford* | 4 | 0 | 4 | 0 |
| 2011-12 | *Scunthorpe U* | 19 | 1 | | |
| 2012-13 | Scunthorpe U | 30 | 0 | 142 | 5 |

**MOZIKA, Damien (M)**    116   9
H: 6 0   W: 11 13   b.Corbeil-Essonnes 15-4-87

|  |  | | | | |
|---|---|--:|--:|--:|--:|
| 2006-07 | Nancy | 0 | 0 | | |
| 2007-08 | Louhans | 28 | 0 | 28 | 0 |
| 2008-09 | Chester C | 22 | 2 | 22 | 2 |

From Tarbiat Yazd.

|  |  | | | | |
|---|---|--:|--:|--:|--:|
| 2010-11 | Bury | 33 | 2 | | |
| 2011-12 | Bury | 4 | 1 | 37 | 3 |
| 2011-12 | *Scunthorpe U* | 18 | 2 | | |
| 2012-13 | Scunthorpe U | 11 | 2 | 29 | 4 |

**NEWEY, Tom (D)**    367   7
H: 5 10   W: 10 02   b.Sheffield 31-10-82
*Source:* Scholar.

|  |  | | | | |
|---|---|--:|--:|--:|--:|
| 2000-01 | Leeds U | 0 | 0 | | |
| 2001-02 | Leeds U | 0 | 0 | | |
| 2002-03 | Leeds U | 0 | 0 | | |
| 2002-03 | *Cambridge U* | 6 | 0 | | |
| 2002-03 | *Darlington* | 7 | 1 | 7 | 1 |
| 2003-04 | Leyton Orient | 34 | 2 | | |
| 2004-05 | Leyton Orient | 20 | 1 | 54 | 3 |
| 2004-05 | *Cambridge U* | 16 | 0 | 22 | 0 |
| 2005-06 | Grimsby T | 38 | 1 | | |
| 2006-07 | Grimsby T | 43 | 1 | | |
| 2007-08 | Grimsby T | 42 | 1 | | |
| 2008-09 | Grimsby T | 24 | 0 | | |
| 2008-09 | *Rochdale* | 2 | 0 | 2 | 0 |
| 2009-10 | Grimsby T | 0 | 0 | 147 | 3 |
| 2009-10 | Bury | 32 | 0 | 32 | 0 |
| 2010-11 | Rotherham U | 38 | 0 | | |
| 2011-12 | Rotherham U | 20 | 0 | 58 | 0 |
| 2012-13 | Scunthorpe U | 45 | 0 | 45 | 0 |

**NOLAN, Eddie (D)**    146   2
H: 6 0   W: 13 05   b.Waterford 5-8-88
*Source:* Scholar. *Honours:* Eire Under-21, 3 full caps.

|  |  | | | | |
|---|---|--:|--:|--:|--:|
| 2005-06 | Blackburn R | 0 | 0 | | |
| 2006-07 | Blackburn R | 0 | 0 | | |
| 2006-07 | *Stockport Co* | 4 | 0 | 4 | 0 |
| 2007-08 | Blackburn R | 0 | 0 | | |
| 2007-08 | *Hartlepool U* | 11 | 0 | 11 | 0 |
| 2008-09 | Blackburn R | 0 | 0 | | |
| 2008-09 | Preston NE | 21 | 0 | | |
| 2009-10 | Preston NE | 19 | 0 | | |
| 2009-10 | *Sheffield W* | 14 | 1 | 14 | 1 |
| 2010-11 | Preston NE | 0 | 0 | 40 | 0 |
| 2010-11 | Scunthorpe U | 35 | 0 | | |
| 2011-12 | Scunthorpe U | 30 | 1 | | |
| 2012-13 | Scunthorpe U | 12 | 0 | 77 | 1 |

**REID, Paul (D)**    317   9
H: 6 2   W: 11 08   b.Carlisle 18-2-82
*Source:* Trainee. *Honours:* England Youth, Under-20.

|  |  | | | | |
|---|---|--:|--:|--:|--:|
| 1998-99 | Carlisle U | 0 | 0 | | |
| 1999-2000 | Carlisle U | 19 | 0 | | |
| 2000-01 | Rangers | 0 | 0 | | |
| 2001-02 | Rangers | 0 | 0 | | |
| 2001-02 | *Preston NE* | 1 | 1 | 1 | 1 |
| 2002-03 | Rangers | 0 | 0 | | |
| 2002-03 | *Northampton T* | 19 | 0 | | |
| 2003-04 | Northampton T | 33 | 2 | 52 | 2 |
| 2004-05 | Barnsley | 41 | 3 | | |
| 2005-06 | Barnsley | 33 | 0 | | |
| 2006-07 | Barnsley | 37 | 0 | | |
| 2007-08 | Barnsley | 3 | 0 | 114 | 3 |
| 2007-08 | *Carlisle U* | 1 | 0 | 20 | 0 |
| 2008-09 | Colchester U | 26 | 1 | | |
| 2009-10 | Colchester U | 12 | 0 | | |
| 2010-11 | Colchester U | 18 | 0 | 56 | 1 |
| 2010-11 | *Scunthorpe U* | 12 | 0 | | |
| 2011-12 | Scunthorpe U | 36 | 1 | | |
| 2012-13 | Scunthorpe U | 26 | 1 | 74 | 2 |

**RIBEIRO, Christian (D)**    66   2
H: 5 8   W: 12 02   b.Neath 14-12-89
*Source:* Scholar. *Honours:* Wales Youth, Under-21, 2 full caps.

|  |  | | | | |
|---|---|--:|--:|--:|--:|
| 2006-07 | Bristol C | 0 | 0 | | |
| 2007-08 | Bristol C | 0 | 0 | | |
| 2008-09 | Bristol C | 0 | 0 | | |
| 2009-10 | Bristol C | 5 | 0 | | |
| 2009-10 | *Stockport Co* | 7 | 0 | 7 | 0 |
| 2009-10 | *Colchester U* | 2 | 0 | 2 | 0 |
| 2010-11 | Bristol C | 9 | 0 | | |
| 2011-12 | Bristol C | 0 | 0 | 14 | 0 |
| 2011-12 | *Carlisle U* | 5 | 0 | 5 | 0 |
| 2011-12 | *Scunthorpe U* | 10 | 0 | | |
| 2012-13 | Scunthorpe U | 28 | 2 | 38 | 2 |

**RYAN, James (M)**    202   26
H: 5 8   W: 11 08   b.Maghull 6-9-88
*Source:* Scholar. *Honours:* Eire Youth, Under-21.

|  |  | | | | |
|---|---|--:|--:|--:|--:|
| 2006-07 | Liverpool | 0 | 0 | | |
| 2007-08 | Liverpool | 0 | 0 | | |
| 2007-08 | *Shrewsbury T* | 4 | 0 | 4 | 0 |
| 2008-09 | Accrington S | 44 | 10 | | |
| 2009-10 | Accrington S | 39 | 3 | | |
| 2010-11 | Accrington S | 46 | 9 | 129 | 22 |
| 2011-12 | Scunthorpe U | 24 | 2 | | |
| 2012-13 | Scunthorpe U | 45 | 2 | 69 | 4 |

**SEDGWICK, Chris (M)**    519   34
H: 5 11   W: 11 10   b.Sheffield 28-4-80
*Source:* Trainee.

|  |  | | | | |
|---|---|--:|--:|--:|--:|
| 1997-98 | Rotherham U | 4 | 0 | | |
| 1998-99 | Rotherham U | 33 | 4 | | |
| 1999-2000 | Rotherham U | 38 | 5 | | |
| 2000-01 | Rotherham U | 21 | 2 | | |
| 2001-02 | Rotherham U | 44 | 1 | | |
| 2002-03 | Rotherham U | 43 | 1 | | |
| 2003-04 | Rotherham U | 40 | 2 | | |
| 2004-05 | Rotherham U | 20 | 2 | 243 | 17 |
| 2004-05 | Preston NE | 24 | 3 | | |
| 2005-06 | Preston NE | 46 | 4 | | |
| 2006-07 | Preston NE | 43 | 1 | | |
| 2007-08 | Preston NE | 42 | 2 | | |
| 2008-09 | Preston NE | 40 | 1 | | |
| 2009-10 | Preston NE | 34 | 1 | 229 | 12 |
| 2010-11 | Sheffield W | 33 | 4 | | |
| 2011-12 | Sheffield W | 10 | 1 | 43 | 5 |
| 2012-13 | Scunthorpe U | 4 | 0 | 4 | 0 |

**SEVERN, James (G)**    2   0
H: 6 4   W: 14 11   b.Nottingham 10-10-91
*Source:* Scholar.

|  |  | | | | |
|---|---|--:|--:|--:|--:|
| 2010-11 | Derby Co | 1 | 0 | | |
| 2011-12 | Derby Co | 0 | 0 | 1 | 0 |
| 2012-13 | Scunthorpe U | 1 | 0 | 1 | 0 |

**SLOCOMBE, Sam (G)**    60   0
H: 6 0   W: 11 11   b.Scunthorpe 5-6-88
*Source:* Bottesford T.

|  |  | | | | |
|---|---|--:|--:|--:|--:|
| 2008-09 | Scunthorpe U | 0 | 0 | | |
| 2009-10 | Scunthorpe U | 1 | 0 | | |
| 2010-11 | Scunthorpe U | 2 | 0 | | |
| 2011-12 | Scunthorpe U | 28 | 0 | | |
| 2012-13 | Scunthorpe U | 29 | 0 | 60 | 0 |

**SODJE, Akpo (F)**    235   55
H: 6 2   W: 12 07   b.London 31-1-80
*Source:* QPR, Stevenage B, Margate, Gravesend & N, Erith & Belvedere.

|  |  | | | | |
|---|---|--:|--:|--:|--:|
| 2004-05 | Huddersfield T | 7 | 0 | 7 | 0 |
| 2004-05 | *Darlington* | 7 | 1 | | |
| 2005-06 | Darlington | 36 | 8 | 43 | 9 |
| 2006-07 | Port Vale | 43 | 14 | | |
| 2007-08 | Port Vale | 3 | 0 | 46 | 14 |
| 2007-08 | *Sheffield W* | 19 | 7 | | |
| 2008-09 | Sheffield W | 11 | 2 | | |
| 2009-10 | Sheffield W | 11 | 0 | 41 | 9 |
| 2009-10 | *Charlton Ath* | 25 | 5 | | |
| 2010-11 | Charlton Ath | 15 | 1 | 40 | 6 |
| 2010-11 | *Hibernian* | 15 | 6 | | |
| 2011-12 | Hibernian | 12 | 0 | 27 | 6 |
| 2011-12 | *Tianjin Taida* | 1 | 1 | 1 | 1 |
| 2012-13 | Preston NE | 14 | 4 | 14 | 4 |
| 2012-13 | Scunthorpe U | 16 | 6 | 16 | 6 |

**WALKER, Josh (M)**    112   7
H: 5 11   W: 11 13   b.Newcastle 21-2-89
*Source:* Scholar. *Honours:* England Schools, Youth, Under-20.

|  |  | | | | |
|---|---|--:|--:|--:|--:|
| 2005-06 | Middlesbrough | 1 | 0 | | |
| 2006-07 | Middlesbrough | 0 | 0 | | |
| 2006-07 | *Bournemouth* | 6 | 0 | 6 | 0 |
| 2007-08 | *Aberdeen* | 8 | 0 | 8 | 0 |
| 2007-08 | *Middlesbrough* | 6 | 0 | | |
| 2008-09 | Middlesbrough | 6 | 0 | | |
| 2009-10 | Middlesbrough | 1 | 0 | 8 | 0 |
| 2009-10 | *Northampton T* | 3 | 0 | | |
| 2009-10 | *Rotherham U* | 15 | 3 | 15 | 3 |
| 2010-11 | Watford | 5 | 0 | | |
| 2010-11 | *Stevenage* | 1 | 0 | | |
| 2010-11 | *Northampton T* | 19 | 0 | 22 | 0 |
| 2011-12 | Watford | 1 | 0 | 6 | 0 |
| 2011-12 | *Stevenage* | 5 | 1 | 6 | 1 |
| 2011-12 | *Scunthorpe U* | 18 | 3 | | |
| 2012-13 | Scunthorpe U | 23 | 0 | 41 | 3 |

**WOOTTON, Jamie (F)**    1   0

|  |  | | | | |
|---|---|--:|--:|--:|--:|
| 2012-13 | Scunthorpe U | 1 | 0 | 1 | 0 |

### Scholars

Adelakun, Hakeeb Adeola Abiola Ayinde; Akeister, Lewis Harry; Bateson, Curtis Devan; Beresford, Billy Jack; Bowskin, Jack Kurtis; Cowling, Zac Christopher; Grayson, George Kevin; Hawley, Ryan Joseph; Hornsey, Luke William; Lacey, Joshua Edward; Megson, Charlie Tony; Smythe, Connor Elliott; Snow, Fabio Jamie; Trice, Lewis Owen; Waring, Daniel Tyler; Wootton, Jamie.

## SHEFFIELD U (71)

**BARRY, Aaron (D)**    0 0

|  |  | | | | |
|---|---|---|---|---|---|
| 2012-13 | Sheffield U | 0 | 0 | | |

**CHAPELL, Jordan (M)**    10 1
H: 5 10 W: 10 09 b.Sheffield 8-9-91

| 2011-12 | Sheffield U | 0 | 0 | | |
| 2012-13 | Sheffield U | 2 | 0 | 2 | 0 |
| 2012-13 | Burton Alb | 2 | 1 | 2 | 1 |
| 2012-13 | Torquay U | 6 | 0 | 6 | 0 |

**COLLINS, Neill (D)**    367 20
H: 6 3 W: 12 07 b.Irvine 2-9-83
*Honours:* Scotland Under-21, B.

| 2000-01 | Queen's Park | 4 | 0 | | |
| 2001-02 | Queen's Park | 28 | 0 | 32 | 0 |
| 2002-03 | Dumbarton | 33 | 2 | | |
| 2003-04 | Dumbarton | 30 | 2 | 63 | 4 |
| 2004-05 | Sunderland | 11 | 0 | | |
| 2005-06 | Sunderland | 0 | 0 | | |
| 2005-06 | Hartlepool U | 22 | 0 | 22 | 0 |
| 2005-06 | Sheffield U | 2 | 0 | | |
| 2006-07 | Sunderland | 7 | 1 | 18 | 1 |
| 2006-07 | Wolverhampton W | 22 | 2 | | |
| 2007-08 | Wolverhampton W | 39 | 3 | | |
| 2008-09 | Wolverhampton W | 23 | 4 | | |
| 2009-10 | Wolverhampton W | 0 | 0 | 84 | 9 |
| 2009-10 | Preston NE | 21 | 1 | 21 | 1 |
| 2009-10 | Leeds U | 9 | 0 | | |
| 2010-11 | Leeds U | 21 | 0 | 30 | 0 |
| 2010-11 | Sheffield U | 14 | 0 | | |
| 2011-12 | Sheffield U | 42 | 2 | | |
| 2012-13 | Sheffield U | 39 | 3 | 97 | 5 |

**COYNE, Danny (G)**    441 0
H: 6 0 W: 13 00 b.Prestatyn 27-8-73
*Source:* Trainee. *Honours:* Wales Schools, Youth, Under-21, B, 16 full caps.

| 1991-92 | Tranmere R | 0 | 0 | | |
| 1992-93 | Tranmere R | 1 | 0 | | |
| 1993-94 | Tranmere R | 5 | 0 | | |
| 1994-95 | Tranmere R | 5 | 0 | | |
| 1995-96 | Tranmere R | 46 | 0 | | |
| 1996-97 | Tranmere R | 21 | 0 | | |
| 1997-98 | Tranmere R | 16 | 0 | | |
| 1998-99 | Tranmere R | 17 | 0 | | |
| 1999-2000 | Grimsby T | 44 | 0 | | |
| 2000-01 | Grimsby T | 46 | 0 | | |
| 2001-02 | Grimsby T | 45 | 0 | | |
| 2002-03 | Grimsby T | 46 | 0 | 181 | 0 |
| 2003-04 | Leicester C | 4 | 0 | 4 | 0 |
| 2004-05 | Burnley | 20 | 0 | | |
| 2005-06 | Burnley | 8 | 0 | | |
| 2006-07 | Burnley | 12 | 0 | 40 | 0 |
| 2007-08 | Tranmere R | 41 | 0 | | |
| 2008-09 | Tranmere R | 39 | 0 | 191 | 0 |
| 2009-10 | Middlesbrough | 23 | 0 | | |
| 2010-11 | Middlesbrough | 1 | 0 | | |
| 2011-12 | Middlesbrough | 1 | 0 | 25 | 0 |
| 2012-13 | Sheffield U | 0 | 0 | | |

**CRESSWELL, Richard (F)**    567 122
H: 6 0 W: 11 08 b.Bridlington 20-9-77
*Source:* Trainee. *Honours:* England Under-21.

| 1995-96 | York C | 16 | 1 | | |
| 1996-97 | York C | 17 | 0 | | |
| 1996-97 | Mansfield T | 5 | 1 | 5 | 1 |
| 1997-98 | York C | 26 | 4 | | |
| 1998-99 | York C | 36 | 16 | | |
| 1998-99 | Sheffield W | 7 | 1 | | |
| 1999-2000 | Sheffield W | 20 | 1 | | |
| 2000-01 | Sheffield W | 4 | 0 | 31 | 2 |
| 2000-01 | Leicester C | 8 | 0 | 8 | 0 |
| 2000-01 | Preston NE | 11 | 2 | | |
| 2001-02 | Preston NE | 40 | 13 | | |
| 2002-03 | Preston NE | 42 | 16 | | |
| 2003-04 | Preston NE | 45 | 2 | | |
| 2004-05 | Preston NE | 46 | 16 | | |
| 2005-06 | Preston NE | 3 | 0 | 187 | 49 |
| 2005-06 | Leeds U | 16 | 5 | | |
| 2006-07 | Leeds U | 22 | 4 | 38 | 9 |
| 2007-08 | Stoke C | 43 | 11 | | |
| 2008-09 | Stoke C | 29 | 0 | | |
| 2009-10 | Stoke C | 2 | 0 | 74 | 11 |
| 2009-10 | Sheffield U | 31 | 12 | | |
| 2010-11 | Sheffield U | 35 | 5 | | |
| 2011-12 | Sheffield U | 42 | 9 | | |
| 2012-13 | Sheffield U | 16 | 1 | 124 | 27 |
| 2012-13 | York C | 5 | 2 | 100 | 23 |

**DE GIROLAMO, Diago (F)**    2 0

| 2012-13 | Sheffield U | 2 | 0 | 2 | 0 |

**DOYLE, Micky (M)**    409 26
H: 5 10 W: 11 00 b.Dublin 8-7-81
*Source:* Celtic. *Honours:* Eire Under-21, 1 full cap.

| 2003-04 | Coventry C | 40 | 5 | | |
| 2004-05 | Coventry C | 44 | 2 | | |
| 2005-06 | Coventry C | 44 | 0 | | |
| 2006-07 | Coventry C | 40 | 3 | | |
| 2007-08 | Coventry C | 42 | 7 | | |
| 2008-09 | Coventry C | 37 | 2 | | |
| 2009-10 | Coventry C | 0 | 0 | | |
| 2009-10 | Leeds U | 42 | 0 | 42 | 0 |
| 2010-11 | Coventry C | 18 | 1 | 265 | 20 |
| 2010-11 | Sheffield U | 16 | 0 | | |
| 2011-12 | Sheffield U | 43 | 3 | | |
| 2012-13 | Sheffield U | 43 | 3 | 102 | 6 |

**FLYNN, Ryan (M)**    131 15
H: 5 8 W: 10 00 b.Falkirk 4-9-88
*Source:* Scholar. *Honours:* Scotland Youth.

| 2006-07 | Liverpool | 0 | 0 | | |
| 2007-08 | Hereford U | 0 | 0 | | |
| 2007-08 | Liverpool | 0 | 0 | | |
| 2008-09 | Liverpool | 0 | 0 | | |
| 2009-10 | Liverpool | 0 | 0 | | |
| 2009-10 | Falkirk | 36 | 5 | | |
| 2010-11 | Falkirk | 33 | 5 | 69 | 10 |
| 2011-12 | Sheffield U | 26 | 2 | | |
| 2012-13 | Sheffield U | 36 | 3 | 62 | 5 |

**HARRIOTT, Matty (M)**    6 0
H: 6 0 W: 12 10 b.Luton 23-9-92
*Source:* Scholar.

| 2010-11 | Sheffield U | 2 | 0 | | |
| 2011-12 | Sheffield U | 4 | 0 | | |
| 2011-12 | Burton Alb | 4 | 0 | 4 | 0 |
| 2012-13 | Sheffield U | 0 | 0 | 2 | 0 |

**HIGGINBOTHAM, Danny (D)**    348 22
H: 6 2 W: 13 01 b.Manchester 29-12-78
*Source:* Trainee.

| 1997-98 | Manchester U | 1 | 0 | | |
| 1998-99 | Manchester U | 0 | 0 | | |
| 1999-2000 | Manchester U | 3 | 0 | 4 | 0 |
| 2000-01 | Derby Co | 26 | 0 | | |
| 2001-02 | Derby Co | 37 | 1 | | |
| 2002-03 | Derby Co | 23 | 2 | 86 | 3 |
| 2002-03 | Southampton | 9 | 0 | | |
| 2003-04 | Southampton | 27 | 0 | | |
| 2004-05 | Southampton | 21 | 1 | | |
| 2005-06 | Southampton | 37 | 3 | 94 | 4 |
| 2006-07 | Stoke C | 44 | 7 | | |
| 2007-08 | Stoke C | 1 | 0 | | |
| 2007-08 | Sunderland | 21 | 3 | | |
| 2008-09 | Sunderland | 1 | 0 | 22 | 3 |
| 2008-09 | Stoke C | 28 | 1 | | |
| 2009-10 | Stoke C | 24 | 1 | | |
| 2010-11 | Stoke C | 10 | 2 | | |
| 2011-12 | Stoke C | 2 | 0 | | |
| 2011-12 | Nottingham F | 6 | 1 | 6 | 1 |
| 2012-13 | Stoke C | 0 | 0 | 109 | 11 |
| 2012-13 | Ipswich T | 12 | 0 | 12 | 0 |
| 2012-13 | Sheffield U | 15 | 0 | 15 | 0 |

**HILL, Matt (D)**    407 8
H: 5 7 W: 12 06 b.Bristol 26-3-81
*Source:* Trainee.

| 1998-99 | Bristol C | 3 | 0 | | |
| 1999-2000 | Bristol C | 14 | 0 | | |
| 2000-01 | Bristol C | 34 | 0 | | |
| 2001-02 | Bristol C | 40 | 1 | | |
| 2002-03 | Bristol C | 42 | 3 | | |
| 2003-04 | Bristol C | 42 | 2 | | |
| 2004-05 | Bristol C | 23 | 0 | 198 | 6 |
| 2004-05 | Preston NE | 14 | 0 | | |
| 2005-06 | Preston NE | 26 | 0 | | |
| 2006-07 | Preston NE | 38 | 0 | | |
| 2007-08 | Preston NE | 26 | 0 | | |
| 2008-09 | Preston NE | 1 | 0 | 105 | 0 |
| 2008-09 | Wolverhampton W | 13 | 0 | | |
| 2009-10 | Wolverhampton W | 2 | 0 | | |
| 2009-10 | QPR | 16 | 0 | 16 | 0 |
| 2010-11 | Wolverhampton W | 0 | 0 | 15 | 0 |
| 2010-11 | Barnsley | 23 | 2 | 23 | 2 |
| 2011-12 | Blackpool | 4 | 0 | 4 | 0 |
| 2011-12 | Sheffield U | 12 | 0 | | |
| 2012-13 | Sheffield U | 34 | 0 | 46 | 0 |

**HOWARD, Mark (G)**    77 0
H: 6 0 W: 11 13 b.Southwark 21-9-86

| 2005-06 | Falkirk | 8 | 0 | 8 | 0 |
| 2006-07 | Cardiff C | 0 | 0 | | |
| 2006-07 | Swansea C | 0 | 0 | | |
| 2007-08 | St Mirren | 10 | 0 | | |
| 2008-09 | St Mirren | 33 | 0 | | |
| 2009-10 | St Mirren | 45 | 0 | 45 | 0 |
| 2010-11 | Aberdeen | 9 | 0 | 9 | 0 |
| 2011-12 | Blackpool | 4 | 0 | 4 | 0 |
| 2011-12 | Sheffield U | 0 | 0 | | |
| 2012-13 | Sheffield U | 11 | 0 | 11 | 0 |

**IRONSIDE, Joe (F)**    12 0

| 2012-13 | Sheffield U | 12 | 0 | 12 | 0 |

**KENNEDY, Terry (D)**    2 0
H: 5 10 W: 12 04 b.Barnsley 14-11-93
*Source:* Scholar.

| 2010-11 | Sheffield U | 1 | 0 | | |
| 2011-12 | Sheffield U | 0 | 0 | | |
| 2012-13 | Sheffield U | 1 | 0 | 2 | 0 |

**KITSON, Dave (F)**    388 125
H: 6 3 W: 12 07 b.Hitchin 21-1-80
*Source:* Arlesey.

| 2000-01 | Cambridge U | 8 | 1 | | |
| 2001-02 | Cambridge U | 33 | 9 | | |
| 2002-03 | Cambridge U | 44 | 20 | | |
| 2003-04 | Cambridge U | 17 | 10 | 102 | 40 |
| 2003-04 | Reading | 17 | 5 | | |
| 2004-05 | Reading | 37 | 19 | | |
| 2005-06 | Reading | 34 | 18 | | |
| 2006-07 | Reading | 13 | 2 | | |
| 2007-08 | Reading | 34 | 10 | | |
| 2008-09 | Stoke C | 16 | 0 | | |
| 2008-09 | Reading | 10 | 2 | 145 | 56 |
| 2009-10 | Stoke C | 18 | 3 | | |
| 2009-10 | Middlesbrough | 6 | 3 | 6 | 3 |
| 2010-11 | Stoke C | 0 | 0 | 34 | 3 |
| 2010-11 | Portsmouth | 35 | 8 | | |
| 2011-12 | Portsmouth | 33 | 4 | | |
| 2012-13 | Portsmouth | 0 | 0 | 68 | 12 |
| 2012-13 | Sheffield U | 33 | 11 | 33 | 11 |

**LONG, George (G)**    39 0
H: 6 0 W: 12 05 b.Sheffield 5-11-93
*Source:* Scholar. *Honours:* England Youth.

| 2010-11 | Sheffield U | 1 | 0 | | |
| 2011-12 | Sheffield U | 2 | 0 | | |
| 2012-13 | Sheffield U | 36 | 0 | 39 | 0 |

**MAGUIRE, Harry (D)**    93 4
H: 6 2 W: 12 06 b.Mosborough 5-3-93
*Source:* Scholar. *Honours:* England Under-21.

| 2010-11 | Sheffield U | 5 | 0 | | |
| 2011-12 | Sheffield U | 44 | 1 | | |
| 2012-13 | Sheffield U | 44 | 3 | 93 | 4 |

**McDONALD, Kevin (M)**    234 21
H: 6 2 W: 13 03 b.Carnoustie 4-11-88
*Honours:* Scotland Youth, Under-21.

| 2005-06 | Dundee | 26 | 3 | | |
| 2006-07 | Dundee | 31 | 2 | | |
| 2007-08 | Dundee | 34 | 9 | 91 | 14 |
| 2008-09 | Burnley | 25 | 1 | | |
| 2009-10 | Burnley | 26 | 1 | | |
| 2010-11 | Burnley | 0 | 0 | 51 | 2 |
| 2010-11 | Scunthorpe U | 5 | 1 | 5 | 1 |
| 2010-11 | Notts Co | 11 | 0 | 11 | 0 |
| 2011-12 | Sheffield U | 31 | 3 | | |
| 2012-13 | Sheffield U | 45 | 1 | 76 | 4 |

**McFADZEAN, Callum (M)**    8 0
b.Sheffield 16-1-94
*Source:* Scholar.

| 2010-11 | Sheffield U | 0 | 0 | | |
| 2011-12 | Sheffield U | 0 | 0 | | |
| 2012-13 | Sheffield U | 8 | 0 | 8 | 0 |

**McMAHON, Tony (D)**    174 6
H: 5 10 W: 11 04 b.Bishop Auckland 24-3-86
*Source:* Scholar. *Honours:* England Youth.

| 2003-04 | Middlesbrough | 0 | 0 | | |

| 2004-05 | Middlesbrough | 13 | 0 | | |
| 2005-06 | Middlesbrough | 3 | 0 | | |
| 2006-07 | Middlesbrough | 0 | 0 | | |
| 2007-08 | Middlesbrough | 1 | 0 | | |
| 2007-08 | *Blackpool* | 2 | 0 | **2** | **0** |
| 2008-09 | Middlesbrough | 13 | 0 | | |
| 2008-09 | *Sheffield W* | 15 | 1 | **15** | **1** |
| 2009-10 | Middlesbrough | 21 | 0 | | |
| 2010-11 | Middlesbrough | 34 | 2 | | |
| 2011-12 | Middlesbrough | 34 | 1 | **119** | **3** |
| 2012-13 | Sheffield U | 38 | 2 | **38** | **2** |

**MILLER, Shaun (F)**  **178 42**
H: 5 10  W: 11 08  b.Alsager 25-9-87
Source: Scholar.

| 2006-07 | Crewe Alex | 7 | 3 | | |
| 2007-08 | Crewe Alex | 15 | 1 | | |
| 2008-09 | Crewe Alex | 33 | 4 | | |
| 2009-10 | Crewe Alex | 33 | 7 | | |
| 2010-11 | Crewe Alex | 42 | 18 | | |
| 2011-12 | Crewe Alex | 33 | 5 | | |
| 2012-13 | Crewe Alex | 0 | 0 | **163** | **38** |
| 2012-13 | Sheffield U | 15 | 4 | **15** | **4** |

**MORGAN, Chris (D)**  **432 20**
H: 6 1  W: 12 03  b.Barnsley 9-11-77
Source: Trainee.

| 1996-97 | Barnsley | 0 | 0 | | |
| 1997-98 | Barnsley | 11 | 0 | | |
| 1998-99 | Barnsley | 19 | 0 | | |
| 1999-2000 | Barnsley | 37 | 0 | | |
| 2000-01 | Barnsley | 40 | 1 | | |
| 2001-02 | Barnsley | 42 | 4 | | |
| 2002-03 | Barnsley | 36 | 2 | **185** | **7** |
| 2003-04 | Sheffield U | 32 | 1 | | |
| 2004-05 | Sheffield U | 41 | 2 | | |
| 2005-06 | Sheffield U | 39 | 3 | | |
| 2006-07 | Sheffield U | 24 | 1 | | |
| 2007-08 | Sheffield U | 25 | 2 | | |
| 2008-09 | Sheffield U | 41 | 2 | | |
| 2009-10 | Sheffield U | 37 | 2 | | |
| 2010-11 | Sheffield U | 8 | 0 | | |
| 2011-12 | Sheffield U | 0 | 0 | | |
| 2012-13 | Sheffield U | 0 | 0 | **247** | **13** |

**MURPHY, Jamie (F)**  **193 36**
H: 6 0  W: 12 00  b. 28-8-89

| 2006-07 | Motherwell | 2 | 0 | | |
| 2007-08 | Motherwell | 16 | 1 | | |
| 2008-09 | Motherwell | 30 | 2 | | |
| 2009-10 | Motherwell | 35 | 6 | | |
| 2010-11 | Motherwell | 35 | 6 | | |
| 2011-12 | Motherwell | 36 | 9 | | |
| 2012-13 | Motherwell | 22 | 10 | **176** | **34** |
| 2012-13 | Sheffield U | 17 | 2 | **17** | **2** |

**PORTER, Chris (F)**  **300 88**
H: 6 1  W: 12 09  b.Wigan 12-12-83
Source: School.

| 2002-03 | Bury | 2 | 0 | | |
| 2003-04 | Bury | 37 | 9 | | |
| 2004-05 | Bury | 32 | 9 | **71** | **18** |
| 2005-06 | Oldham Ath | 31 | 7 | | |
| 2006-07 | Oldham Ath | 35 | 21 | **66** | **28** |
| 2007-08 | Motherwell | 37 | 14 | | |
| 2008-09 | Motherwell | 22 | 9 | **59** | **23** |
| 2008-09 | Derby Co | 5 | 3 | | |
| 2009-10 | Derby Co | 21 | 4 | | |
| 2010-11 | Derby Co | 18 | 2 | **44** | **9** |
| 2011-12 | Sheffield U | 34 | 5 | | |
| 2012-13 | Sheffield U | 21 | 4 | **55** | **9** |
| 2012-13 | *Shrewsbury T* | 5 | 1 | **5** | **1** |

**ROBSON, Barry (M)**  **446 84**
H: 5 11  W: 12 00  b.Inverurie 7-11-78
Honours: Scotland B, 17 full caps.

| 1997-98 | Inverness CT | 23 | 3 | | |
| 1998-99 | Inverness CT | 16 | 0 | | |
| 1999-2000 | Inverness CT | 4 | 0 | | |
| 1999-2000 | *Forfar Ath* | 25 | 9 | **25** | **9** |
| 2000-01 | Inverness CT | 34 | 5 | | |
| 2001-02 | Inverness CT | 24 | 2 | | |
| 2002-03 | Inverness CT | 34 | 10 | **135** | **20** |
| 2003-04 | Dundee U | 28 | 3 | | |
| 2004-05 | Dundee U | 36 | 6 | | |
| 2005-06 | Dundee U | 31 | 1 | | |
| 2006-07 | Dundee U | 29 | 11 | | |
| 2007-08 | Dundee U | 21 | 11 | **145** | **32** |
| 2007-08 | Celtic | 15 | 2 | | |
| 2008-09 | Celtic | 12 | 1 | | |
| 2009-10 | Celtic | 10 | 1 | **37** | **4** |
| 2009-10 | Middlesbrough | 18 | 5 | | |
| 2010-11 | Middlesbrough | 32 | 5 | | |
| 2011-12 | Middlesbrough | 37 | 7 | **87** | **17** |
| 2012-13 | Vancouver W | 0 | 0 | | |
| 2012-13 | Sheffield U | 17 | 2 | **17** | **2** |

**TONNE, Erik (M)**  **18 5**
H: 5 11  W: 12 02  b.Trondheim 7-5-91
Source: Strindheim.

| 2010-11 | Sheffield U | 2 | 0 | | |
| 2011-12 | Sheffield U | 2 | 1 | | |
| 2012-13 | Sheffield U | 0 | 0 | **4** | **1** |
| 2012-13 | *Ham-Kam* | 14 | 4 | **14** | **4** |

**WESTLAKE, Darryl (D)**  **78 1**
H: 5 9  W: 11 00  b.Sutton Coldfield 1-3-91
Source: Scholar.

| 2009-10 | Walsall | 22 | 0 | | |
| 2010-11 | Walsall | 28 | 1 | | |
| 2011-12 | Walsall | 17 | 0 | **67** | **1** |
| 2012-13 | Sheffield U | 11 | 0 | **11** | **0** |

**WHITEHOUSE, Elliott (M)**  **3 0**

| 2012-13 | Sheffield U | 3 | 0 | **3** | **0** |

**WILLIAMS, Marcus (D)**  **214 0**
H: 5 8  W: 10 07  b.Doncaster 8-4-86
Source: Scholar.

| 2003-04 | Scunthorpe U | 1 | 0 | | |
| 2004-05 | Scunthorpe U | 4 | 0 | | |
| 2005-06 | Scunthorpe U | 29 | 0 | | |
| 2006-07 | Scunthorpe U | 35 | 0 | | |
| 2007-08 | Scunthorpe U | 34 | 0 | | |
| 2008-09 | Scunthorpe U | 26 | 0 | | |
| 2009-10 | Scunthorpe U | 37 | 0 | | |
| 2010-11 | Reading | 3 | 0 | | |
| 2010-11 | *Peterborough U* | 3 | 0 | **3** | **0** |
| 2010-11 | *Scunthorpe U* | 5 | 0 | **171** | **0** |
| 2011-12 | Reading | 0 | 0 | **3** | **0** |
| 2011-12 | Sheffield U | 19 | 0 | | |
| 2012-13 | Sheffield U | 18 | 0 | **37** | **0** |

**WILLIS, George (G)**  **0 0**

| 2012-13 | Sheffield U | 0 | 0 | | |

**Scholars**
Banton, Julian Daniel Anthony; Coustrain, Joel; Dimaio, Connor James; Eyre, Jake; Heather, Owen Richard; Hodder, Jordan Paul; Khan, Otis Jan Mohammed; Lynch, Ethan Owen; McDonagh, Jamie-dean Cantona; Owen, Gareth Thomas; Paling, Jason Dean; Pemberton, Max; Ptak, Elliott; Salt, Christopher James; Scarisbrick, Kyle Roy; Smith, Jahmal Beresford; Whitehouse, Elliott Mark; Whiteman, Benjamin; Williams, Joshua David; Williams, Tyler Keaton.

# SHEFFIELD W (72)

**ANTONIO, Michael (M)**  **131 21**
H: 6 0  W: 11 11  b.Wandsworth 28-3-90
Source: Tooting & M.

| 2008-09 | Reading | 0 | 0 | | |
| 2008-09 | *Cheltenham T* | 9 | 0 | **9** | **0** |
| 2009-10 | Reading | 1 | 0 | | |
| 2009-10 | *Southampton* | 28 | 3 | **28** | **3** |
| 2010-11 | Reading | 21 | 1 | | |
| 2011-12 | Reading | 6 | 0 | | |
| 2011-12 | *Colchester U* | 15 | 4 | **15** | **4** |
| 2011-12 | *Sheffield W* | 14 | 5 | | |
| 2012-13 | Reading | 0 | 0 | **28** | **1** |
| 2012-13 | Sheffield W | 37 | 8 | **51** | **13** |

**BENNETT, Julian (D)**  **186 14**
H: 6 1  W: 13 00  b.Nottingham 17-12-84
Source: Scholar.

| 2003-04 | Walsall | 1 | 0 | | |
| 2004-05 | Walsall | 31 | 2 | | |
| 2005-06 | Walsall | 18 | 2 | **51** | **4** |
| 2005-06 | Nottingham F | 18 | 2 | | |
| 2006-07 | Nottingham F | 30 | 2 | | |
| 2007-08 | Nottingham F | 34 | 4 | | |
| 2008-09 | Nottingham F | 12 | 0 | | |
| 2009-10 | Nottingham F | 0 | 0 | | |
| 2010-11 | Nottingham F | 3 | 0 | **97** | **8** |
| 2010-11 | *Crystal Palace* | 13 | 1 | **13** | **1** |
| 2011-12 | Sheffield W | 21 | 2 | | |
| 2012-13 | Sheffield W | 0 | 0 | **21** | **2** |
| 2012-13 | *Shrewsbury T* | 4 | 0 | **4** | **0** |

**BUXTON, Lewis (D)**  **297 4**
H: 6 1  W: 13 11  b.Newport (IW) 10-12-83
Source: School.

| 2000-01 | Portsmouth | 0 | 0 | | |
| 2001-02 | Portsmouth | 29 | 0 | | |
| 2002-03 | Portsmouth | 1 | 0 | | |
| 2002-03 | *Exeter C* | 4 | 0 | **4** | **0** |
| 2002-03 | *Bournemouth* | 17 | 0 | | |
| 2003-04 | Portsmouth | 0 | 0 | | |
| 2003-04 | *Bournemouth* | 26 | 0 | **43** | **0** |
| 2004-05 | Portsmouth | 0 | 0 | **30** | **0** |
| 2004-05 | Stoke C | 16 | 0 | | |
| 2005-06 | Stoke C | 32 | 1 | | |
| 2006-07 | Stoke C | 1 | 0 | | |
| 2007-08 | Stoke C | 4 | 0 | | |
| 2008-09 | Stoke C | 0 | 0 | **53** | **1** |
| 2008-09 | Sheffield W | 32 | 1 | | |
| 2009-10 | Sheffield W | 28 | 0 | | |
| 2010-11 | Sheffield W | 30 | 1 | | |
| 2011-12 | Sheffield W | 37 | 1 | | |
| 2012-13 | Sheffield W | 40 | 0 | **167** | **3** |

**BYWATER, Steve (G)**  **286 0**
H: 6 2  W: 12 10  b.Manchester 7-6-81
Source: Trainee. Honours: England Youth, Under-20, Under-21.

| 1997-98 | Rochdale | 0 | 0 | | |
| 1998-99 | West Ham U | 0 | 0 | | |
| 1999-2000 | West Ham U | 4 | 0 | | |
| 1999-2000 | *Wycombe W* | 2 | 0 | **2** | **0** |
| 1999-2000 | *Hull C* | 4 | 0 | **4** | **0** |
| 2000-01 | West Ham U | 1 | 0 | | |
| 2001-02 | West Ham U | 0 | 0 | | |
| 2001-02 | *Wolverhampton W* | 0 | 0 | | |
| 2001-02 | *Cardiff C* | 0 | 0 | | |
| 2002-03 | West Ham U | 0 | 0 | | |
| 2003-04 | West Ham U | 17 | 0 | | |
| 2004-05 | West Ham U | 36 | 0 | | |
| 2005-06 | West Ham U | 1 | 0 | | |
| 2005-06 | *Coventry C* | 14 | 0 | **14** | **0** |
| 2006-07 | West Ham U | 0 | 0 | **59** | **0** |
| 2006-07 | Derby Co | 37 | 0 | | |
| 2007-08 | Derby Co | 18 | 0 | | |
| 2007-08 | *Ipswich T* | 17 | 0 | **17** | **0** |
| 2008-09 | Derby Co | 31 | 0 | | |
| 2009-10 | Derby Co | 42 | 0 | | |
| 2010-11 | Derby Co | 22 | 0 | | |
| 2010-11 | *Cardiff C* | 8 | 0 | **8** | **0** |
| 2011-12 | Derby Co | 0 | 0 | **150** | **0** |
| 2011-12 | Sheffield W | 32 | 0 | | |
| 2012-13 | Sheffield W | 0 | 0 | **32** | **0** |

**COKE, Giles (M)**  **231 24**
H: 6 0  W: 11 11  b.Westminster 3-6-86
Source: Kingstonian.

| 2004-05 | Mansfield T | 9 | 0 | | |
| 2005-06 | Mansfield T | 40 | 4 | | |
| 2006-07 | Mansfield T | 21 | 1 | **70** | **5** |
| 2007-08 | Northampton T | 20 | 5 | | |
| 2008-09 | Northampton T | 32 | 2 | **52** | **7** |
| 2009-10 | Motherwell | 32 | 2 | **32** | **2** |
| 2010-11 | Sheffield W | 27 | 4 | | |
| 2011-12 | Sheffield W | 0 | 0 | | |
| 2011-12 | *Bury* | 30 | 6 | **30** | **6** |
| 2012-13 | Sheffield W | 16 | 0 | **43** | **4** |
| 2012-13 | *Swindon T* | 4 | 0 | **4** | **0** |

**CORRY, Paul (M)**  **93 7**
H: 6 2  W: 11 12  b.Dublin 3-2-91

| 2010 | UCD | 28 | 4 | | |
| 2011 | UCD | 36 | 2 | | |
| 2012 | UCD | 17 | 1 | **81** | **7** |
| 2012-13 | Sheffield W | 6 | 0 | **6** | **0** |
| 2012-13 | *Tranmere R* | 6 | 0 | **6** | **0** |

**DAVIES, Adam (G)**  **0 0**
b.Rinteln 17-7-92

| 2012-13 | Sheffield W | 0 | 0 | | |

**GARDNER, Anthony (D)**  **280 7**
H: 6 3  W: 14 00  b.Stone 19-9-80
Source: Trainee. Honours: England Under-21, 1 full cap.

| 1998-99 | Port Vale | 15 | 1 | | |
| 1999-2000 | Port Vale | 26 | 3 | **41** | **4** |
| 1999-2000 | Tottenham H | 0 | 0 | | |

|  |  | | | | |
|---|---|---|---|---|---|
| 2000-01 | Tottenham H | 8 | 0 | | |
| 2001-02 | Tottenham H | 15 | 0 | | |
| 2002-03 | Tottenham H | 12 | 1 | | |
| 2003-04 | Tottenham H | 33 | 0 | | |
| 2004-05 | Tottenham H | 17 | 0 | | |
| 2005-06 | Tottenham H | 17 | 0 | | |
| 2006-07 | Tottenham H | 8 | 0 | | |
| 2007-08 | *Everton* | 0 | 0 | | |
| 2007-08 | Tottenham H | 4 | 1 | 114 | 2 |
| 2008-09 | Hull C | 6 | 0 | | |
| 2009-10 | Hull C | 24 | 0 | | |
| 2010-11 | Hull C | 0 | 2 | 32 | 0 |
| 2010-11 | *Crystal Palace* | 28 | 1 | | |
| 2011-12 | *Crystal Palace* | 28 | 0 | 56 | 1 |
| 2012-13 | Sheffield W | 37 | 0 | 37 | 0 |

**HERY, Bastien (M)**   0 0
b.Brou sur Chantereine 23-3-92
| 2012-13 | Sheffield W | 0 | 0 | | |

**JAMESON, Arron (G)**   2 0
H: 6 3  W: 13 01  b.Sheffield 7-11-89
Source: Scholar.
| 2008-09 | Sheffield W | 0 | 0 | | |
| 2009-10 | Sheffield W | 0 | 0 | | |
| 2010-11 | Sheffield W | 2 | 0 | | |
| 2011-12 | Sheffield W | 0 | 0 | | |
| 2012-13 | Sheffield W | 0 | 0 | 2 | 0 |
| 2012-13 | *York C* | 0 | 0 | | |

**JOHNSON, Jermaine (M)**   282 38
H: 5 11  W: 11 05  b.Kingston, Jamaica 25-6-80
Source: Tivoli Gardens. Honours: Jamaica 74 full caps, 9 goals.
| 2001-02 | Bolton W | 10 | 0 | | |
| 2002-03 | Bolton W | 2 | 0 | | |
| 2003-04 | Bolton W | 0 | 0 | 12 | 0 |
| 2003-04 | Oldham Ath | 20 | 5 | | |
| 2004-05 | Oldham Ath | 19 | 4 | | |
| 2005-06 | Oldham Ath | 0 | 0 | 39 | 9 |
| 2006-07 | Bradford C | 27 | 4 | 27 | 4 |
| 2006-07 | Sheffield W | 7 | 2 | | |
| 2007-08 | Sheffield W | 35 | 1 | | |
| 2008-09 | Sheffield W | 37 | 3 | | |
| 2009-10 | Sheffield W | 34 | 5 | | |
| 2010-11 | Sheffield W | 26 | 4 | | |
| 2011-12 | Sheffield W | 24 | 4 | | |
| 2012-13 | Sheffield W | 41 | 6 | 204 | 25 |

**JOHNSON, Reda (D)**   113 18
H: 6 2  W: 13 04  b.Marseille 21-3-88
Honours: Benin 9 full caps.
| 2005-06 | Gueugnon | 0 | 0 | | |
| 2006-07 | Gueugnon | 0 | 0 | | |
| 2007-08 | Amiens | 8 | 0 | | |
| 2008-09 | Amiens | 7 | 0 | 15 | 0 |
| 2009-10 | Plymouth Arg | 25 | 0 | | |
| 2010-11 | Plymouth Arg | 17 | 2 | 42 | 2 |
| 2010-11 | Sheffield W | 16 | 3 | | |
| 2011-12 | Sheffield W | 24 | 7 | | |
| 2012-13 | Sheffield W | 16 | 6 | 56 | 16 |

**KIRKLAND, Chris (G)**   240 0
H: 6 5  W: 14 08  b.Barwell 2-5-81
Source: Trainee. Honours: England Youth, Under-21, 1 full cap.
| 1997-98 | Coventry C | 0 | 0 | | |
| 1998-99 | Coventry C | 0 | 0 | | |
| 1999-2000 | Coventry C | 0 | 0 | | |
| 2000-01 | Coventry C | 23 | 0 | | |
| 2001-02 | Coventry C | 1 | 0 | 24 | 0 |
| 2001-02 | Liverpool | 1 | 0 | | |
| 2002-03 | Liverpool | 8 | 0 | | |
| 2003-04 | Liverpool | 6 | 0 | | |
| 2004-05 | Liverpool | 10 | 0 | | |
| 2005-06 | Liverpool | 0 | 0 | | |
| 2005-06 | *WBA* | 10 | 0 | 10 | 0 |
| 2006-07 | Liverpool | 0 | 0 | 25 | 0 |
| 2006-07 | Wigan Ath | 26 | 0 | | |
| 2007-08 | Wigan Ath | 37 | 0 | | |
| 2008-09 | Wigan Ath | 32 | 0 | | |
| 2009-10 | Wigan Ath | 32 | 0 | | |
| 2010-11 | Wigan Ath | 4 | 0 | | |
| 2010-11 | *Leicester C* | 3 | 0 | 3 | 0 |
| 2011-12 | Wigan Ath | 0 | 0 | 131 | 0 |
| 2011-12 | *Doncaster R* | 1 | 0 | 1 | 0 |
| 2012-13 | Sheffield W | 46 | 0 | 46 | 0 |

**LAVERY, Caolan (F)**   3 0
H: 5 11  W: 11 12  b.Red Deer 22-10-92
| 2012-13 | Sheffield W | 0 | 0 | | |
| 2012-13 | *Southend U* | 3 | 0 | 3 | 0 |

**LEE, Kieran (D)**   148 5
H: 6 1  W: 12 00  b.Stalybridge 22-6-88
Source: Scholar.
| 2006-07 | Manchester U | 1 | 0 | | |
| 2007-08 | Manchester U | 0 | 0 | 1 | 0 |
| 2007-08 | *QPR* | 7 | 0 | 7 | 0 |
| 2008-09 | Oldham Ath | 7 | 0 | | |
| 2009-10 | Oldham Ath | 24 | 1 | | |
| 2010-11 | Oldham Ath | 43 | 2 | | |
| 2011-12 | Oldham Ath | 43 | 2 | 117 | 5 |
| 2012-13 | Sheffield W | 23 | 0 | 23 | 0 |

**LINES, Chris (M)**   231 23
H: 6 2  W: 12 00  b.Bristol 30-11-88
Source: Youth.
| 2005-06 | Bristol R | 4 | 0 | | |
| 2006-07 | Bristol R | 7 | 0 | | |
| 2007-08 | Bristol R | 27 | 3 | | |
| 2008-09 | Bristol R | 45 | 4 | | |
| 2009-10 | Bristol R | 42 | 10 | | |
| 2010-11 | Bristol R | 42 | 3 | | |
| 2011-12 | Bristol R | 1 | 0 | 168 | 20 |
| 2011-12 | Sheffield W | 41 | 3 | | |
| 2012-13 | Sheffield W | 6 | 0 | 47 | 3 |
| 2012-13 | *Milton Keynes D* | 16 | 0 | 16 | 0 |

**LLERA, Miguel (D)**   198 23
H: 6 3  W: 13 12  b.Seville 7-8-79
Source: Recretivo B, San Fernando (loan), Alicante.
| 2005-06 | Gimnastic | 27 | 3 | | |
| 2006-07 | Gimnastic | 12 | 2 | 39 | 5 |
| 2007-08 | Heracles | 13 | 1 | 13 | 1 |
| 2008-09 | Milton Keynes D | 34 | 2 | 34 | 2 |
| 2009-10 | Charlton Ath | 25 | 4 | | |
| 2010-11 | Charlton Ath | 15 | 1 | | |
| 2011-12 | Charlton Ath | 0 | 0 | 40 | 5 |
| 2011-12 | *Brentford* | 0 | 0 | 11 | 0 |
| 2011-12 | Sheffield W | 20 | 4 | | |
| 2012-13 | Sheffield W | 41 | 6 | 61 | 10 |

**MADINE, Gary (F)**   172 39
H: 6 1  W: 12 00  b.Gateshead 24-8-90
Source: Scholar.
| 2007-08 | Carlisle U | 11 | 0 | | |
| 2008-09 | Carlisle U | 14 | 1 | | |
| 2008-09 | *Rochdale* | 3 | 0 | 3 | 0 |
| 2009-10 | Carlisle U | 20 | 4 | | |
| 2009-10 | *Coventry C* | 9 | 0 | 9 | 0 |
| 2009-10 | *Chesterfield* | 4 | 0 | 4 | 0 |
| 2010-11 | Carlisle U | 21 | 8 | 66 | 13 |
| 2010-11 | Sheffield W | 22 | 5 | | |
| 2011-12 | Sheffield W | 38 | 18 | | |
| 2012-13 | Sheffield W | 30 | 3 | 90 | 26 |

**MAGUIRE, Chris (F)**   173 25
H: 5 7  W: 10 05  b.Bellshill 16-1-89
Honours: Scotland Under-21, 2 full caps.
| 2005-06 | Aberdeen | 1 | 0 | | |
| 2006-07 | Aberdeen | 19 | 1 | | |
| 2007-08 | Aberdeen | 28 | 4 | | |
| 2008-09 | Aberdeen | 31 | 3 | | |
| 2009-10 | Aberdeen | 17 | 1 | | |
| 2009-10 | *Kilmarnock* | 14 | 4 | 14 | 4 |
| 2010-11 | Aberdeen | 35 | 7 | 131 | 16 |
| 2011-12 | Derby Co | 7 | 1 | 7 | 1 |
| 2011-12 | *Portsmouth* | 11 | 3 | 11 | 3 |
| 2012-13 | Sheffield W | 10 | 1 | 10 | 1 |

**MATTOCK, Joe (D)**   137 2
H: 5 11  W: 12 05  b.Leicester 15-5-90
Source: Scholar. Honours: England Youth, Under-21.
| 2006-07 | Leicester C | 4 | 0 | | |
| 2007-08 | Leicester C | 31 | 0 | | |
| 2008-09 | Leicester C | 31 | 1 | | |
| 2009-10 | Leicester C | 0 | 0 | 66 | 1 |
| 2009-10 | WBA | 29 | 0 | | |
| 2010-11 | WBA | 0 | 0 | | |
| 2011-12 | WBA | 0 | 0 | 29 | 0 |
| 2011-12 | *Portsmouth* | 7 | 0 | 7 | 0 |
| 2011-12 | *Brighton & HA* | 15 | 1 | 15 | 1 |
| 2012-13 | Sheffield W | 7 | 0 | 7 | 0 |

**MAYOR, Danny (M)**   80 2
H: 6 0  W: 11 12  b.Leyland 18-10-90
Source: Scholar.
| 2008-09 | Preston NE | 0 | 0 | | |
| 2008-09 | *Tranmere R* | 3 | 0 | 3 | 0 |
| 2009-10 | Preston NE | 7 | 0 | | |
| 2010-11 | Preston NE | 21 | 0 | | |
| 2011-12 | Preston NE | 36 | 2 | | |
| 2012-13 | Preston NE | 0 | 0 | 64 | 2 |
| 2012-13 | Sheffield W | 8 | 0 | 8 | 0 |
| 2012-13 | *Southend U* | 5 | 0 | 5 | 0 |

**McCABE, Rhys (M)**   31 1
H: 5 10  W: 11 08  b.Polbeth 24-7-92
Honours: Scotland Under-21.
| 2011-12 | Rangers | 9 | 0 | 9 | 0 |
| 2012-13 | Sheffield W | 22 | 1 | 22 | 1 |

**O'GRADY, Chris (F)**   304 65
H: 6 3  W: 12 04  b.Nottingham 25-1-86
Source: Trainee. Honours: England Youth.
| 2002-03 | Leicester C | 1 | 0 | | |
| 2003-04 | Leicester C | 0 | 0 | | |
| 2004-05 | Leicester C | 0 | 0 | | |
| 2004-05 | *Notts Co* | 9 | 0 | 9 | 0 |
| 2005-06 | Leicester C | 13 | 1 | | |
| 2005-06 | *Rushden & D* | 22 | 4 | 22 | 4 |
| 2006-07 | Leicester C | 10 | 0 | 24 | 1 |
| 2006-07 | Rotherham U | 13 | 4 | | |
| 2007-08 | Rotherham U | 38 | 9 | 51 | 13 |
| 2008-09 | Oldham Ath | 13 | 0 | | |
| 2008-09 | *Bury* | 6 | 0 | 6 | 0 |
| 2008-09 | *Bradford C* | 2 | 0 | 2 | 0 |
| 2008-09 | *Stockport Co* | 18 | 2 | 18 | 2 |
| 2009-10 | Oldham Ath | 0 | 0 | 13 | 0 |
| 2009-10 | Rochdale | 43 | 22 | | |
| 2010-11 | Rochdale | 46 | 9 | | |
| 2011-12 | Rochdale | 1 | 0 | 90 | 31 |
| 2011-12 | Sheffield W | 32 | 5 | | |
| 2012-13 | Sheffield W | 21 | 4 | 53 | 9 |
| 2012-13 | *Barnsley* | 16 | 5 | 16 | 5 |

**PALMER, Liam (M)**   66 1
H: 6 2  W: 12 10  b.Worksop 19-9-91
Source: Scholar. Honours: Scotland Under-21.
| 2010-11 | Sheffield W | 9 | 0 | | |
| 2011-12 | Sheffield W | 14 | 1 | | |
| 2012-13 | Sheffield W | 0 | 0 | 23 | 1 |
| 2012-13 | *Tranmere R* | 43 | 0 | 43 | 0 |

**PECNIK, Nejc (F)**   72 3
H: 6 2  W: 12 09  b.Dravograd 3-1-86
Honours: Slovenia Under-21, 17 full caps, 4 goals.
| 2008-09 | Sparta Prague | 4 | 0 | 4 | 0 |
| 2009-10 | Nacional | 24 | 2 | | |
| 2010-11 | Nacional | 9 | 0 | | |
| 2010-11 | Krylya Sovetov | 13 | 1 | | |
| 2011-12 | Krylya Sovetov | 8 | 0 | 21 | 1 |
| 2011-12 | Nacional | 4 | 0 | 37 | 2 |
| 2012-13 | Sheffield W | 10 | 0 | 10 | 0 |

**PRUTTON, David (M)**   422 24
H: 5 10  W: 13 00  b.Hull 12-9-81
Source: Trainee. Honours: England Youth, Under-21.
| 1998-99 | Nottingham F | 0 | 0 | | |
| 1999-2000 | Nottingham F | 34 | 2 | | |
| 2000-01 | Nottingham F | 42 | 1 | | |
| 2001-02 | Nottingham F | 43 | 3 | | |
| 2002-03 | Nottingham F | 24 | 1 | | |
| 2002-03 | Southampton | 12 | 0 | | |
| 2003-04 | Southampton | 27 | 1 | | |
| 2004-05 | Southampton | 23 | 1 | | |
| 2005-06 | Southampton | 17 | 0 | | |
| 2006-07 | Southampton | 1 | 0 | 82 | 3 |
| 2006-07 | *Nottingham F* | 12 | 2 | 155 | 9 |
| 2007-08 | Leeds U | 43 | 4 | | |
| 2008-09 | Leeds U | 16 | 0 | | |
| 2009-10 | Leeds U | 6 | 0 | 65 | 4 |
| 2009-10 | *Colchester U* | 19 | 3 | 19 | 3 |
| 2010-11 | Swindon T | 41 | 3 | 41 | 3 |
| 2011-12 | Sheffield W | 25 | 2 | | |
| 2012-13 | Sheffield W | 22 | 0 | 47 | 2 |
| 2012-13 | *Scunthorpe U* | 13 | 0 | 13 | 0 |

**RODRI, Lozano (F)**   41 11
H: 5 8  W: 10 00  b.Soria 6-6-90
| 2011-12 | Barcelona B | 18 | 8 | 18 | 8 |
| 2012-13 | Barcelona | 0 | 0 | | |

On loan from Barcelona

| | | | | | |
|---|---|---|---|---|---|
| 2012-13 | Sheffield W | 11 | 1 | **11** | **1** |
| 2012-13 | *Real Zaragoza* | 12 | 2 | **12** | **2** |

**SEMEDO, Jose (D)**      262   5
H: 6 0   W: 12 08   b.Setubal 11-1-85
*Honours:* Portugal Under-21.

| | | | | | |
|---|---|---|---|---|---|
| 2004-05 | Sporting Lisbon | 0 | 0 | | |
| 2004-05 | *Casa Pia* | 34 | 2 | **34** | **2** |
| 2005-06 | *Feirense* | 18 | 0 | **18** | **0** |
| 2006-07 | *Cagliari* | 3 | 0 | **3** | **0** |
| 2007-08 | Charlton Ath | 37 | 0 | | |
| 2008-09 | Charlton Ath | 18 | 0 | | |
| 2009-10 | Charlton Ath | 38 | 1 | | |
| 2010-11 | Charlton Ath | 42 | 1 | **135** | **2** |
| 2011-12 | Sheffield W | 46 | 1 | | |
| 2012-13 | Sheffield W | 26 | 0 | **72** | **1** |

**TAYLOR, Martin (D)**      307   18
H: 6 4   W: 15 00   b.Ashington 9-11-79
*Source:* Trainee. *Honours:* England Youth, Under-21.

| | | | | | |
|---|---|---|---|---|---|
| 1997-98 | Blackburn R | 0 | 0 | | |
| 1998-99 | Blackburn R | 3 | 0 | | |
| 1999-2000 | Blackburn R | 6 | 0 | | |
| 1999-2000 | *Darlington* | 4 | 0 | **4** | **0** |
| 1999-2000 | *Stockport Co* | 7 | 0 | **7** | **0** |
| 2000-01 | Blackburn R | 16 | 3 | | |
| 2001-02 | Blackburn R | 19 | 0 | | |
| 2002-03 | Blackburn R | 33 | 2 | | |
| 2003-04 | Blackburn R | 11 | 0 | **88** | **5** |
| 2003-04 | Birmingham C | 12 | 1 | | |
| 2004-05 | Birmingham C | 7 | 0 | | |
| 2005-06 | Birmingham C | 21 | 0 | | |
| 2006-07 | Birmingham C | 31 | 0 | | |
| 2007-08 | Birmingham C | 4 | 0 | | |
| 2007-08 | *Norwich C* | 8 | 1 | **8** | **1** |
| 2008-09 | Birmingham C | 24 | 1 | | |
| 2009-10 | Birmingham C | 0 | 0 | **99** | **2** |
| 2009-10 | Watford | 19 | 2 | | |
| 2010-11 | Watford | 46 | 6 | | |
| 2011-12 | Watford | 22 | 1 | | |
| 2012-13 | Watford | 3 | 1 | **90** | **10** |
| 2012-13 | Sheffield W | 11 | 0 | **11** | **0** |

**WEAVER, Nick (G)**      316   0
H: 6 4   W: 14 07   b.Sheffield 2-3-79
*Source:* Trainee. *Honours:* England Under-21.

| | | | | | |
|---|---|---|---|---|---|
| 1995-96 | Mansfield T | 1 | 0 | | |
| 1996-97 | Mansfield T | 0 | 0 | **1** | **0** |
| 1996-97 | Manchester C | 0 | 0 | | |
| 1997-98 | Manchester C | 0 | 0 | | |
| 1998-99 | Manchester C | 45 | 0 | | |
| 1999-2000 | Manchester C | 45 | 0 | | |
| 2000-01 | Manchester C | 31 | 0 | | |
| 2001-02 | Manchester C | 25 | 0 | | |
| 2002-03 | Manchester C | 0 | 0 | | |
| 2003-04 | Manchester C | 0 | 0 | | |
| 2004-05 | Manchester C | 1 | 0 | | |
| 2005-06 | Manchester C | 0 | 0 | | |
| 2005-06 | *Sheffield W* | 14 | 0 | | |
| 2006-07 | Manchester C | 25 | 0 | **172** | **0** |
| 2007-08 | Charlton Ath | 45 | 0 | | |
| 2008-09 | Charlton Ath | 22 | 0 | **67** | **0** |
| 2009-10 | *Dundee U* | 18 | 0 | **18** | **0** |
| 2009-10 | Burnley | 0 | 0 | | |
| 2010-11 | Sheffield W | 36 | 0 | | |
| 2011-12 | Sheffield W | 8 | 0 | | |
| 2012-13 | Sheffield W | 0 | 0 | **58** | **0** |

**Players retained or with offer of contract**
Dieseruvwe, Emmanuel Aghohho Oluwafem; Fenwick, Johnny; Jameson, Arron Thomas; McKenzie, Taylor Joshua; Obileye, Stephen Ayomide Oluwagbeng.

**Scholars**
Ayoola, Rasheed Olawale Adetokunbo; Davies, Rhys Calum; Dawes, Charlie; Dawson, Cameron Miles; Harvey, Harry Michael; Hague, Nicholas Luke; Hanna, Simon; Harvey, Adam Dominic; Kingston, Matthew David; Lee, Ryan Simon; Moses, Elias Ashley; Mullan, Sean Francis; Peacock, Marc Douglas; Rudonja, Roy; Smith, Niall; Taylor, Jack Edward; White, Hayden Anthony Roy; Wildsmith, Joseph Charles.

# SHREWSBURY T (73)

**ANYON, Joe (G)**      0   0
H: 6 4   W: 14 01   b.Blackpool 29-12-86

| | | | |
|---|---|---|---|
| 2006-07 | Port Vale | 0 | 0 |
| 2010-11 | Lincoln C | 0 | 0 |
| 2010-11 | Morecambe | 0 | 0 |
| 2012-13 | Shrewsbury T | 0 | 0 |

**BRADSHAW, Tom (F)**      61   10
H: 5 5   W: 11 02   b.Shrewsbury 27-7-92
*Source:* Aberystwyth T. *Honours:* Wales Youth, Under-21.

| | | | | | |
|---|---|---|---|---|---|
| 2009-10 | Shrewsbury T | 6 | 3 | | |
| 2010-11 | Shrewsbury T | 26 | 6 | | |
| 2011-12 | Shrewsbury T | 8 | 1 | | |
| 2012-13 | Shrewsbury T | 21 | 0 | **61** | **10** |

**DOBLE, Ryan (M)**      23   1
H: 6 3   W: 13 00   b.Blaenavon 1-2-91
*Source:* Scholar. *Honours:* Wales Under-21.

| | | | | | |
|---|---|---|---|---|---|
| 2008-09 | Southampton | 0 | 0 | | |
| 2009-10 | Southampton | 0 | 0 | | |
| 2010-11 | Southampton | 0 | 0 | | |
| 2010-11 | *Stockport Co* | 3 | 1 | **3** | **1** |
| 2010-11 | *Oxford U* | 3 | 0 | **3** | **0** |
| 2011-12 | Southampton | 0 | 0 | | |
| 2011-12 | *Bournemouth* | 7 | 0 | **7** | **0** |
| 2011-12 | *Bury* | 5 | 0 | **5** | **0** |
| 2012-13 | Shrewsbury T | 5 | 0 | **5** | **0** |

**GOLDSON, Connor (D)**      24   1
H: 6 3   W: 13 05   b.York 18-12-92
*Source:* Youth.

| | | | | | |
|---|---|---|---|---|---|
| 2010-11 | Shrewsbury T | 3 | 0 | | |
| 2011-12 | Shrewsbury T | 4 | 0 | | |
| 2012-13 | Shrewsbury T | 17 | 1 | **24** | **1** |

**GORNELL, Terry (F)**      163   34
H: 5 11   W: 12 04   b.Liverpool 16-12-89
*Source:* Scholar.

| | | | | | |
|---|---|---|---|---|---|
| 2008-09 | Tranmere R | 10 | 1 | | |
| 2008-09 | *Accrington S* | 11 | 4 | | |
| 2009-10 | Tranmere R | 27 | 2 | | |
| 2010-11 | Tranmere R | 3 | 0 | **40** | **3** |
| 2010-11 | Accrington S | 40 | 13 | **51** | **17** |
| 2011-12 | Shrewsbury T | 41 | 9 | | |
| 2012-13 | Shrewsbury T | 12 | 0 | **53** | **9** |
| 2012-13 | *Rochdale* | 19 | 5 | **19** | **5** |

**GRANDISON, Jermaine (D)**      94   3
H: 6 4   W: 13 03   b.Birmingham 15-12-90
*Source:* Scholar.

| | | | | | |
|---|---|---|---|---|---|
| 2008-09 | Coventry C | 2 | 0 | | |
| 2009-10 | Coventry C | 3 | 0 | | |
| 2010-11 | Coventry C | 0 | 0 | **5** | **0** |
| 2010-11 | *Tranmere R* | 8 | 0 | **8** | **0** |
| 2010-11 | Shrewsbury T | 13 | 0 | | |
| 2011-12 | Shrewsbury T | 38 | 2 | | |
| 2012-13 | Shrewsbury T | 30 | 1 | **81** | **3** |

**HALL, Asa (M)**      208   31
H: 6 2   W: 11 09   b.Sandwell 29-11-86
*Source:* Scholar. *Honours:* England Youth, Under-20.

| | | | | | |
|---|---|---|---|---|---|
| 2004-05 | Birmingham C | 0 | 0 | | |
| 2005-06 | Birmingham C | 0 | 0 | | |
| 2005-06 | *Boston U* | 12 | 0 | **12** | **0** |
| 2006-07 | Birmingham C | 0 | 0 | | |
| 2007-08 | Birmingham C | 0 | 0 | | |
| 2007-08 | *Shrewsbury T* | 15 | 3 | | |
| 2008-09 | Luton T | 42 | 10 | | |
| 2009-10 | Luton T | 33 | 5 | **75** | **15** |
| 2010-11 | Oxford U | 41 | 4 | | |
| 2011-12 | Oxford U | 34 | 7 | **75** | **11** |
| 2012-13 | Shrewsbury T | 15 | 2 | **30** | **5** |
| 2012-13 | *Aldershot T* | 16 | 0 | **16** | **0** |

**HAZELL, Reuben (D)**      359   12
H: 5 11   W: 12 05   b.Birmingham 24-4-79
*Source:* Trainee.

| | | | | | |
|---|---|---|---|---|---|
| 1996-97 | Aston Villa | 0 | 0 | | |
| 1997-98 | Aston Villa | 0 | 0 | | |
| 1998-99 | Aston Villa | 0 | 0 | | |
| 1999-2000 | Tranmere R | 23 | 1 | | |
| 2000-01 | Tranmere R | 13 | 0 | | |
| 2001-02 | Tranmere R | 6 | 0 | **42** | **1** |
| 2001-02 | Torquay U | 19 | 0 | | |
| 2002-03 | Torquay U | 46 | 1 | | |

| | | | | | |
|---|---|---|---|---|---|
| 2003-04 | Torquay U | 19 | 1 | | |
| 2004-05 | Torquay U | 0 | 0 | **84** | **2** |
| 2005-06 | Chesterfield | 33 | 0 | | |
| 2006-07 | Chesterfield | 39 | 2 | | |
| 2007-08 | Chesterfield | 0 | 0 | **72** | **2** |
| 2007-08 | Oldham Ath | 34 | 1 | | |
| 2008-09 | Oldham Ath | 43 | 3 | | |
| 2009-10 | Oldham Ath | 41 | 3 | | |
| 2010-11 | Oldham Ath | 33 | 0 | **151** | **7** |
| 2011-12 | Shrewsbury T | 7 | 0 | | |
| 2012-13 | Shrewsbury T | 3 | 0 | **10** | **0** |

**JACOBSON, Joe (D)**      191   7
H: 5 11   W: 12 06   b.Cardiff 17-11-86
*Source:* Scholar. *Honours:* Wales Under-21.

| | | | | | |
|---|---|---|---|---|---|
| 2005-06 | Cardiff C | 1 | 0 | | |
| 2006-07 | Cardiff C | 0 | 0 | **1** | **0** |
| 2006-07 | *Accrington S* | 6 | 1 | | |
| 2006-07 | *Bristol R* | 11 | 0 | | |
| 2007-08 | Bristol R | 40 | 1 | | |
| 2008-09 | Bristol R | 22 | 0 | **73** | **1** |
| 2009-10 | Oldham Ath | 15 | 0 | | |
| 2010-11 | Oldham Ath | 1 | 0 | **16** | **0** |
| 2010-11 | Accrington S | 26 | 2 | **32** | **3** |
| 2011-12 | Shrewsbury T | 39 | 1 | | |
| 2012-13 | Shrewsbury T | 30 | 2 | **69** | **3** |

**JONES, Darren (D)**      180   6
H: 6 0   W: 14 12   b.Newport 28-8-83
*Source:* Scholar. *Honours:* Wales Schools, Youth.

| | | | | | |
|---|---|---|---|---|---|
| 2000-01 | Bristol C | 0 | 0 | | |
| 2001-02 | Bristol C | 2 | 0 | | |
| 2002-03 | Bristol C | 0 | 0 | | |
| 2003-04 | Bristol C | 0 | 0 | **2** | **0** |
| 2003-04 | *Cheltenham T* | 14 | 1 | **14** | **1** |

From Forest Green R.

| | | | | | |
|---|---|---|---|---|---|
| 2009-10 | Hereford U | 41 | 3 | **41** | **3** |
| 2010-11 | Aldershot T | 43 | 1 | | |
| 2011-12 | Aldershot T | 42 | 0 | **85** | **1** |
| 2012-13 | Shrewsbury T | 38 | 1 | **38** | **1** |

**MAMBO, Yado (D)**      28   1
H: 6 3   W: 13 01   b.Kilburn 22-10-91
*Source:* Scholar.

| | | | | | |
|---|---|---|---|---|---|
| 2009-10 | Charlton Ath | 0 | 0 | | |
| 2010-11 | Charlton Ath | 0 | 0 | | |
| 2011-12 | Charlton Ath | 0 | 0 | | |
| 2012-13 | Charlton Ath | 0 | 0 | | |
| 2012-13 | *AFC Wimbledon* | 13 | 0 | **13** | **0** |
| 2012-13 | Shrewsbury T | 15 | 1 | **15** | **1** |

**McALLISTER, David (M)**      128   29
H: 5 10   W: 11 09   b.Dublin 29-12-88

| | | | | | |
|---|---|---|---|---|---|
| 2008 | Drogheda U | 0 | 0 | | |
| 2008 | *Shelbourne* | 16 | 7 | | |
| 2009 | *Shelbourne* | 30 | 16 | **46** | **23** |
| 2010 | St Patrick's Ath | 32 | 3 | **32** | **3** |
| 2010-11 | Sheffield U | 2 | 1 | | |
| 2011-12 | Sheffield U | 4 | 0 | | |
| 2011-12 | *Shrewsbury T* | 15 | 0 | | |
| 2012-13 | Sheffield U | 14 | 1 | **20** | **2** |
| 2012-13 | Shrewsbury T | 15 | 1 | **30** | **1** |

**McGINN, Stephen (M)**      129   11
H: 5 9   W: 10 01   b.Glasgow 2-12-88
*Honours:* Scotland Under-21.

| | | | | | |
|---|---|---|---|---|---|
| 2006-07 | St Mirren | 4 | 1 | | |
| 2007-08 | St Mirren | 25 | 2 | | |
| 2008-09 | St Mirren | 26 | 1 | | |
| 2009-10 | St Mirren | 18 | 3 | **73** | **7** |
| 2009-10 | Watford | 9 | 0 | | |
| 2010-11 | Watford | 29 | 2 | | |
| 2011-12 | Watford | 0 | 0 | | |
| 2012-13 | Watford | 0 | 0 | **38** | **2** |
| 2012-13 | Shrewsbury T | 18 | 2 | **18** | **2** |

**MORGAN, Marvin (F)**      185   41
H: 6 4   W: 12 08   b.Manchester 13-4-83
*Source:* Wealdstone, Yeading, Woking.

| | | | | | |
|---|---|---|---|---|---|
| 2008-09 | Aldershot T | 32 | 6 | | |
| 2009-10 | Aldershot T | 40 | 15 | | |
| 2010-11 | Aldershot T | 19 | 5 | **91** | **26** |
| 2010-11 | *Dagenham & R* | 12 | 0 | **12** | **0** |
| 2011-12 | Shrewsbury T | 42 | 8 | | |
| 2012-13 | Shrewsbury T | 40 | 7 | **82** | **15** |

**PARRY, Paul (M)**    302 36
H: 5 11  W: 12 12  b.Chepstow 19-8-80
*Source:* Hereford U. *Honours:* Wales 12 full caps, 1 goal.

| | | | |
|---|---|---|---|
| 2003-04 | Cardiff C | 17 | 1 |
| 2004-05 | Cardiff C | 24 | 4 |
| 2005-06 | Cardiff C | 27 | 1 |
| 2006-07 | Cardiff C | 42 | 6 |
| 2007-08 | Cardiff C | 41 | 10 |
| 2008-09 | Cardiff C | 40 | 2 | 191 24 |
| 2009-10 | Preston NE | 17 | 2 |
| 2010-11 | Preston NE | 23 | 0 |
| 2011-12 | Preston NE | 40 | 4 | 80 6 |
| 2012-13 | Shrewsbury T | 31 | 6 | 31 6 |

**PURDIE, Robert (M)**    205 19
H: 5 11 01  b.Wibston 28-9-82
*Source:* Leicester C.

| | | | |
|---|---|---|---|
| 2006-07 | Hereford U | 44 | 6 |
| 2007-08 | Darlington | 39 | 0 |
| 2008-09 | Darlington | 40 | 6 | 79 6 |
| 2009-10 | Oldham Ath | 0 | 0 |
| 2010-11 | Hereford U | 25 | 3 |
| 2011-12 | Hereford U | 34 | 4 | 103 13 |
| 2012-13 | Shrewsbury T | 23 | 0 | 23 0 |

**RICHARDS, Matt (D)**    371 33
H: 5 8  W: 11 00  b.Harlow 26-12-84
*Source:* Scholar. *Honours:* England Under-21.

| | | | |
|---|---|---|---|
| 2001-02 | Ipswich T | 0 | 0 |
| 2002-03 | Ipswich T | 13 | 0 |
| 2003-04 | Ipswich T | 44 | 1 |
| 2004-05 | Ipswich T | 24 | 1 |
| 2005-06 | Ipswich T | 38 | 4 |
| 2006-07 | Ipswich T | 28 | 2 |
| 2007-08 | Ipswich T | 0 | 0 |
| 2007-08 | *Brighton & HA* | 28 | 0 |
| 2008-09 | *Brighton & HA* | 23 | 1 | 51 1 |
| 2008-09 | Wycombe W | 0 | 0 |
| 2008-09 | *Notts Co* | 1 | 0 | 1 0 |
| 2008-09 | Ipswich T | 1 | 0 | 148 8 |
| 2009-10 | Walsall | 40 | 4 |
| 2010-11 | Walsall | 46 | 8 | 86 12 |
| 2011-12 | Shrewsbury T | 42 | 5 |
| 2012-13 | Shrewsbury T | 43 | 7 | 85 12 |

**SUMMERFIELD, Luke (M)**    178 11
H: 6 0  W: 11 00  b.Ivybridge 6-12-87
*Source:* Scholar.

| | | | |
|---|---|---|---|
| 2004-05 | Plymouth Arg | 1 | 0 |
| 2005-06 | Plymouth Arg | 0 | 0 |
| 2006-07 | Plymouth Arg | 23 | 1 |
| 2006-07 | *Bournemouth* | 8 | 1 | 8 1 |
| 2007-08 | Plymouth Arg | 7 | 0 |
| 2008-09 | Plymouth Arg | 29 | 2 |
| 2009-10 | Plymouth Arg | 12 | 0 |
| 2009-10 | *Leyton Orient* | 14 | 0 | 14 0 |
| 2010-11 | Plymouth Arg | 7 | 1 | 79 4 |
| 2011-12 | Cheltenham T | 41 | 4 | 41 4 |
| 2012-13 | Shrewsbury T | 36 | 2 | 36 2 |

**TAYLOR, Jon (M)**    92 13
H: 5 11  W: 12 04  b.Liverpool 23-12-89
*Source:* Youth.

| | | | |
|---|---|---|---|
| 2009-10 | Shrewsbury T | 2 | 0 |
| 2010-11 | Shrewsbury T | 20 | 6 |
| 2011-12 | Shrewsbury T | 33 | 0 |
| 2012-13 | Shrewsbury T | 37 | 7 | 92 13 |

**WEALE, Chris (G)**    243 1
H: 6 2  W: 13 03  b.Chard 9-2-82
*Source:* Juniors.

| | | | |
|---|---|---|---|
| 2003-04 | Yeovil T | 35 | 0 |
| 2004-05 | Yeovil T | 38 | 0 |
| 2005-06 | Yeovil T | 25 | 0 |
| 2006-07 | Bristol C | 1 | 0 |
| 2007-08 | Hereford U | 1 | 0 |
| 2007-08 | Bristol C | 3 | 0 |
| 2008-09 | Bristol C | 5 | 0 | 9 0 |
| 2008-09 | *Hereford U* | 1 | 0 | 2 0 |
| 2008-09 | *Yeovil T* | 10 | 1 | 108 1 |
| 2009-10 | Leicester C | 45 | 0 |
| 2010-11 | Leicester C | 29 | 0 |
| 2011-12 | Leicester C | 1 | 0 | 75 0 |
| 2011-12 | *Northampton T* | 3 | 0 | 3 0 |
| 2012-13 | Shrewsbury T | 46 | 0 | 46 0 |

---

**WILDIG, Aaron (M)**    49 4
H: 5 9  W: 11 02  b.Hereford 15-4-92
*Source:* Scholar. *Honours:* Wales Youth.

| | | | |
|---|---|---|---|
| 2009-10 | Cardiff C | 11 | 1 |
| 2010-11 | Cardiff C | 2 | 0 |
| 2010-11 | *Hamilton A* | 3 | 0 | 3 0 |
| 2011-12 | Cardiff C | 0 | 0 | 13 1 |
| 2011-12 | Shrewsbury T | 12 | 2 |
| 2012-13 | Shrewsbury T | 21 | 1 | 33 3 |

**WOODS, Ryan (M)**    2 0
H: 5 8  b. 13-12-93

| | | | |
|---|---|---|---|
| 2012-13 | Shrewsbury T | 2 | 0 | 2 0 |

**WRIGHT, Mark (M)**    326 52
H: 5 11  W: 11 00  b.Wolverhampton 24-2-82
*Source:* Scholar.

| | | | |
|---|---|---|---|
| 2000-01 | Walsall | 4 | 0 |
| 2001-02 | Walsall | 0 | 0 |
| 2002-03 | Walsall | 5 | 0 |
| 2003-04 | Walsall | 11 | 2 |
| 2004-05 | Walsall | 37 | 2 |
| 2005-06 | Walsall | 30 | 2 |
| 2006-07 | Walsall | 37 | 3 | 124 9 |
| 2007-08 | Milton Keynes D | 34 | 13 |
| 2008-09 | Milton Keynes D | 32 | 5 | 66 18 |
| 2009-10 | Brighton & HA | 4 | 0 | 4 0 |
| 2009-10 | Bristol R | 24 | 0 |
| 2010-11 | Bristol R | 0 | 0 | 24 0 |
| 2010-11 | Shrewsbury T | 45 | 14 |
| 2011-12 | Shrewsbury T | 46 | 10 |
| 2012-13 | Shrewsbury T | 17 | 1 | 108 25 |

**Scholars**
Burton, Callum Alex David; Carpenter, George William; Easthope, David Robert; Evans, Deion Arfon; Gwilliams, Jack Andrew; Holmes, Warren; Jones, Matthew Stephen; Molyneux, Sam Lee; Musselwhite, Charlie; Phillips, Lewis John; Richards, Jack Liam; Roberts, Javia St Michael; Ryan, Scott James; Smith, Dominic James; Stephenson, Dillan O'Neill Raymond; Wearing, Connor; Westray, Sam.

# SOUTHAMPTON (74)

**BARNARD, Lee (F)**    195 68
H: 5 10  W: 10 10  b.Romford 18-7-84
*Source:* Trainee.

| | | | |
|---|---|---|---|
| 2002-03 | Tottenham H | 0 | 0 |
| 2002-03 | *Exeter C* | 3 | 0 | 3 0 |
| 2003-04 | Tottenham H | 0 | 0 |
| 2004-05 | Tottenham H | 0 | 0 |
| 2004-05 | *Leyton Orient* | 8 | 0 | 8 0 |
| 2004-05 | *Northampton T* | 5 | 0 | 5 0 |
| 2005-06 | Tottenham H | 3 | 0 |
| 2006-07 | Tottenham H | 0 | 0 |
| 2007-08 | Tottenham H | 0 | 0 | 3 0 |
| 2007-08 | *Crewe Alex* | 10 | 3 | 10 3 |
| 2007-08 | Southend U | 15 | 9 |
| 2008-09 | Southend U | 35 | 11 |
| 2009-10 | Southend U | 25 | 15 | 75 35 |
| 2009-10 | Southampton | 20 | 9 |
| 2010-11 | Southampton | 36 | 14 |
| 2011-12 | Southampton | 6 | 0 |
| 2012-13 | Southampton | 0 | 0 | 62 23 |
| 2012-13 | *Bournemouth* | 15 | 4 | 15 4 |
| 2012-13 | Oldham Ath | 14 | 3 | 14 3 |

**BORUC, Artur (G)**    244 0
H: 6 4  W: 13 08  b.Siedlce 20-2-80
*Honours:* Poland 51 full caps.

| | | | |
|---|---|---|---|
| 2005-06 | Celtic | 34 | 0 |
| 2006-07 | Celtic | 36 | 0 |
| 2007-08 | Celtic | 30 | 0 |
| 2008-09 | Celtic | 34 | 0 |
| 2009-10 | Celtic | 28 | 0 | 162 0 |
| 2010-11 | Fiorentina | 26 | 0 |
| 2011-12 | Fiorentina | 36 | 0 | 62 0 |
| 2012-13 | Southampton | 20 | 0 | 20 0 |

**BUTTERFIELD, Danny (D)**    418 9
H: 5 10  W: 11 06  b.Boston 21-11-79
*Source:* Trainee. *Honours:* England Youth.

| | | | |
|---|---|---|---|
| 1997-98 | Grimsby T | 7 | 0 |
| 1998-99 | Grimsby T | 12 | 0 |

---

| | | | |
|---|---|---|---|
| 1999-2000 | Grimsby T | 29 | 0 |
| 2000-01 | Grimsby T | 30 | 1 |
| 2001-02 | Grimsby T | 46 | 2 | 124 3 |
| 2002-03 | Crystal Palace | 46 | 1 |
| 2003-04 | Crystal Palace | 45 | 4 |
| 2004-05 | Crystal Palace | 7 | 0 |
| 2005-06 | Crystal Palace | 13 | 0 |
| 2006-07 | Crystal Palace | 28 | 0 |
| 2007-08 | Crystal Palace | 30 | 0 |
| 2008-09 | Crystal Palace | 26 | 1 |
| 2008-09 | *Charlton Ath* | 12 | 0 | 12 0 |
| 2009-10 | Crystal Palace | 37 | 0 | 232 6 |
| 2010-11 | Southampton | 34 | 0 |
| 2011-12 | Southampton | 10 | 0 |
| 2012-13 | Southampton | 0 | 0 | 44 0 |
| 2012-13 | Bolton W | 6 | 0 | 6 0 |

**CHAMBERS, Calum (M)**    0 0
H: 6 0  W: 10 05  b.Petersfield 20-1-95
*Source:* Scholar.

| | | | |
|---|---|---|---|
| 2011-12 | Southampton | 0 | 0 |
| 2012-13 | Southampton | 0 | 0 |

**CHAPLOW, Richard (M)**    253 24
H: 5 9  W: 9 03  b.Accrington 2-2-85
*Source:* Scholar. *Honours:* England Youth, Under-20, Under-21.

| | | | |
|---|---|---|---|
| 2002-03 | Burnley | 5 | 0 |
| 2003-04 | Burnley | 39 | 5 |
| 2004-05 | Burnley | 21 | 2 | 65 7 |
| 2004-05 | WBA | 4 | 0 |
| 2005-06 | WBA | 7 | 0 |
| 2005-06 | *Southampton* | 11 | 1 |
| 2006-07 | WBA | 28 | 1 |
| 2007-08 | WBA | 5 | 0 | 44 1 |
| 2007-08 | Preston NE | 12 | 3 |
| 2008-09 | Preston NE | 25 | 3 |
| 2009-10 | Preston NE | 31 | 2 |
| 2010-11 | Preston NE | 0 | 0 | 68 8 |
| 2010-11 | Southampton | 33 | 4 |
| 2011-12 | Southampton | 25 | 3 |
| 2012-13 | Southampton | 3 | 0 | 72 8 |
| 2012-13 | *Millwall* | 4 | 0 | 4 0 |

**CLYNE, Nathaniel (D)**    156 2
H: 5 9  W: 10 07  b.Stockwell 5-4-91
*Source:* Scholar. *Honours:* England Youth, Under-21.

| | | | |
|---|---|---|---|
| 2008-09 | Crystal Palace | 26 | 0 |
| 2009-10 | Crystal Palace | 22 | 1 |
| 2010-11 | Crystal Palace | 46 | 0 |
| 2011-12 | Crystal Palace | 28 | 0 | 122 1 |
| 2012-13 | Southampton | 34 | 1 | 34 1 |

**CORK, Jack (D)**    229 6
H: 6 0  W: 10 12  b.Carshalton 25-6-89
*Source:* Scholar. *Honours:* England Youth, Under-20, Under-21.

| | | | |
|---|---|---|---|
| 2006-07 | Chelsea | 0 | 0 |
| 2006-07 | *Bournemouth* | 7 | 0 | 7 0 |
| 2007-08 | Chelsea | 0 | 0 |
| 2007-08 | *Scunthorpe U* | 34 | 2 | 34 2 |
| 2008-09 | Chelsea | 0 | 0 |
| 2008-09 | *Southampton* | 23 | 0 |
| 2008-09 | *Watford* | 19 | 0 | 19 0 |
| 2009-10 | Chelsea | 0 | 0 |
| 2009-10 | *Coventry C* | 21 | 0 | 21 0 |
| 2009-10 | *Burnley* | 11 | 1 |
| 2010-11 | Chelsea | 0 | 0 |
| 2010-11 | *Burnley* | 40 | 3 | 51 4 |
| 2011-12 | Southampton | 46 | 0 |
| 2012-13 | Southampton | 28 | 0 | 97 0 |

**CROPPER, Cody (G)**    0 0
H: 6 3  W: 14 05  b.Atlanta 16-2-93
*Source:* Scholar.

| | | | |
|---|---|---|---|
| 2011-12 | Ipswich T | 0 | 0 |
| 2012-13 | Ipswich T | 0 | 0 |
| 2012-13 | Southampton | 0 | 0 |

**DAVIS, Kelvin (G)**    604 0
H: 6 1  W: 11 05  b.Bedford 29-9-76
*Source:* Trainee. *Honours:* England Youth, Under-21.

| | | | |
|---|---|---|---|
| 1993-94 | Luton T | 1 | 0 |
| 1994-95 | Luton T | 9 | 0 |
| 1994-95 | *Torquay U* | 2 | 0 | 2 0 |
| 1995-96 | Luton T | 6 | 0 |
| 1996-97 | Luton T | 0 | 0 |
| 1997-98 | Luton T | 32 | 0 |

| | | | | | |
|---|---|---|---|---|---|
| 1997-98 | Hartlepool U | 2 | 0 | 2 | 0 |
| 1998-99 | Luton T | 44 | 0 | 92 | 0 |
| 1999-2000 | Wimbledon | 0 | 0 | | |
| 2000-01 | Wimbledon | 45 | 0 | | |
| 2001-02 | Wimbledon | 40 | 0 | | |
| 2002-03 | Wimbledon | 46 | 0 | 131 | 0 |
| 2003-04 | Ipswich T | 45 | 0 | | |
| 2004-05 | Ipswich T | 39 | 0 | 84 | 0 |
| 2005-06 | Sunderland | 33 | 0 | 33 | 0 |
| 2006-07 | Southampton | 38 | 0 | | |
| 2007-08 | Southampton | 35 | 0 | | |
| 2008-09 | Southampton | 46 | 0 | | |
| 2009-10 | Southampton | 40 | 0 | | |
| 2010-11 | Southampton | 46 | 0 | | |
| 2011-12 | Southampton | 45 | 0 | | |
| 2012-13 | Southampton | 10 | 0 | 260 | 0 |

**DAVIS, Steven (M)**    297 25
H: 5 8 W: 11 04 b.Ballymena 1-1-85
*Source:* Scholar. *Honours:* Northern Ireland Schools, Youth, Under-21, Under-23, 59 full caps, 4 goals.

| | | | | | |
|---|---|---|---|---|---|
| 2004-05 | Aston Villa | 28 | 1 | | |
| 2005-06 | Aston Villa | 35 | 4 | | |
| 2006-07 | Aston Villa | 28 | 0 | 91 | 5 |
| 2007-08 | Fulham | 22 | 0 | 22 | 0 |
| 2007-08 | *Rangers* | 12 | 0 | | |
| 2008-09 | *Rangers* | 34 | 6 | | |
| 2009-10 | *Rangers* | 36 | 3 | | |
| 2010-11 | *Rangers* | 37 | 4 | | |
| 2011-12 | *Rangers* | 33 | 5 | 152 | 18 |
| 2012-13 | Southampton | 32 | 2 | 32 | 2 |

**DE RIDDER, Steve (F)**    183 37
H: 5 10 W: 11 07 b.Gent 25-2-87

| | | | | | |
|---|---|---|---|---|---|
| 2006-07 | Gent | 1 | 0 | 1 | 0 |
| 2006-07 | Hamme | 16 | 5 | | |
| 2007-08 | Hamme | 34 | 17 | 50 | 22 |
| 2008-09 | De Graafschap | 29 | 0 | | |
| 2009-10 | De Graafschap | 33 | 9 | | |
| 2010-11 | De Graafschap | 31 | 3 | 93 | 12 |
| 2011-12 | Southampton | 32 | 3 | | |
| 2012-13 | Southampton | 4 | 0 | 36 | 3 |
| 2012-13 | *Bolton W* | 3 | 0 | 3 | 0 |

**DICKSON, Ryan (M)**    153 7
H: 5 10 W: 11 05 b.Saltash 14-12-86
*Source:* Scholar.

| | | | | | |
|---|---|---|---|---|---|
| 2004-05 | Plymouth Arg | 3 | 0 | | |
| 2005-06 | Plymouth Arg | 0 | 0 | | |
| 2006-07 | Plymouth Arg | 2 | 0 | | |
| 2006-07 | *Torquay U* | 9 | 1 | 9 | 1 |
| 2007-08 | Plymouth Arg | 0 | 0 | 5 | 0 |
| 2007-08 | Brentford | 31 | 0 | | |
| 2008-09 | Brentford | 39 | 1 | | |
| 2009-10 | Brentford | 27 | 2 | 97 | 3 |
| 2010-11 | Southampton | 23 | 1 | | |
| 2011-12 | Southampton | 0 | 0 | | |
| 2011-12 | *Yeovil T* | 5 | 1 | 5 | 1 |
| 2011-12 | *Leyton Orient* | 9 | 0 | 9 | 0 |
| 2012-13 | Southampton | 0 | 0 | 23 | 1 |
| 2012-13 | *Bradford C* | 5 | 1 | 5 | 1 |

**DO PRADO, Guilherme (F)**    230 49
H: 6 2 W: 12 04 b.Sao Paulo 31-12-81

| | | | | | |
|---|---|---|---|---|---|
| 2002 | Portuguese Santista | 22 | 7 | 22 | 7 |
| 2002-03 | Catania | 6 | 0 | 6 | 0 |
| 2003-04 | Perugia | 17 | 0 | | |
| 2004-05 | Perugia | 17 | 4 | 34 | 4 |
| 2005-06 | Fiorentina | 0 | 0 | | |
| 2006-07 | Fiorentina | 0 | 0 | | |
| 2006-07 | Spezia | 12 | 1 | 12 | 1 |
| 2007-08 | *Mantoba* | 14 | 2 | 14 | 2 |
| 2008-09 | Pro Patria | 14 | 7 | 14 | 7 |
| 2009-10 | Cesena | 34 | 9 | 34 | 9 |
| 2010-11 | Southampton | 34 | 9 | | |
| 2011-12 | Southampton | 42 | 10 | | |
| 2012-13 | Southampton | 18 | 0 | 94 | 19 |

**FONTE, Jose (D)**    295 19
H: 6 2 W: 12 08 b.Penafiel 22-12-83
*Source:* Sporting Lisbon, Salgueiros.
*Honours:* Portugal Under-21.

| | | | | | |
|---|---|---|---|---|---|
| 2004-05 | Felgueiros | 28 | 1 | 28 | 1 |
| 2005-06 | Setubal | 15 | 0 | 15 | 0 |
| 2005-06 | Benfica | 1 | 0 | 1 | 0 |
| 2005-06 | Pacos | 11 | 1 | 11 | 1 |
| 2006-07 | Amadora | 25 | 1 | 25 | 1 |
| 2007-08 | Crystal Palace | 22 | 1 | | |

| | | | | | |
|---|---|---|---|---|---|
| 2008-09 | Crystal Palace | 38 | 4 | | |
| 2009-10 | Crystal Palace | 22 | 1 | 82 | 6 |
| 2009-10 | Southampton | 21 | 0 | | |
| 2010-11 | Southampton | 43 | 7 | | |
| 2011-12 | Southampton | 42 | 1 | | |
| 2012-13 | Southampton | 27 | 2 | 133 | 10 |

**FORECAST, Tommy (G)**    6 0
H: 6 2 W: 11 10 b.Newham 15-10-86
*Source:* Scholar.

| | | | | | |
|---|---|---|---|---|---|
| 2005-06 | Tottenham H | 0 | 0 | | |
| 2006-07 | Tottenham H | 0 | 0 | | |
| 2007-08 | Tottenham H | 0 | 0 | | |
| 2008-09 | Southampton | 0 | 0 | | |
| 2009-10 | Southampton | 0 | 0 | | |
| 2009-10 | *Grimsby T* | 4 | 0 | 4 | 0 |
| 2010-11 | Southampton | 0 | 0 | | |
| 2011-12 | Southampton | 0 | 0 | | |
| 2012-13 | Southampton | 0 | 0 | | |
| 2012-13 | *Gillingham* | 2 | 0 | 2 | 0 |

**FORREN, Vegard (D)**    125 4
H: 6 1 W: 13 04 b.Trondheim 16-2-88
*Honours:* Norway Under-21, Under-7, 7 full caps.

| | | | | | |
|---|---|---|---|---|---|
| 2007-08 | Molde | 12 | 0 | | |
| 2008-09 | Molde | 28 | 1 | | |
| 2009-10 | Molde | 25 | 2 | | |
| 2010-11 | Molde | 26 | 0 | | |
| 2011-12 | Molde | 34 | 1 | 125 | 4 |
| 2012-13 | Southampton | 0 | 0 | | |

**FORTE, Jonathan (M)**    259 42
H: 6 0 W: 12 02 b.Sheffield 25-7-86
*Source:* Scholar. *Honours:* England Youth. Barbados 2 full caps.

| | | | | | |
|---|---|---|---|---|---|
| 2003-04 | Sheffield U | 7 | 0 | | |
| 2004-05 | Sheffield U | 22 | 1 | | |
| 2005-06 | Sheffield U | 1 | 0 | | |
| 2005-06 | *Doncaster R* | 13 | 4 | | |
| 2005-06 | *Rotherham U* | 11 | 4 | 11 | 4 |
| 2006-07 | Sheffield U | 0 | 0 | | |
| 2006-07 | *Doncaster R* | 41 | 5 | 54 | 9 |
| 2007-08 | Scunthorpe U | 38 | 4 | | |
| 2007-08 | Scunthorpe U | 8 | 0 | | |
| 2008-09 | *Notts Co* | 18 | 8 | | |
| 2009-10 | Scunthorpe U | 5 | 0 | | |
| 2010-11 | Scunthorpe U | 24 | 3 | 98 | 9 |
| 2010-11 | Southampton | 10 | 2 | | |
| 2011-12 | Southampton | 1 | 0 | | |
| 2011-12 | *Preston NE* | 3 | 0 | 3 | 0 |
| 2011-12 | *Notts Co* | 10 | 5 | 28 | 13 |
| 2012-13 | Southampton | 0 | 0 | 11 | 2 |
| 2012-13 | *Crawley T* | 12 | 3 | 12 | 3 |
| 2012-13 | *Sheffield U* | 12 | 1 | 42 | 2 |

**FOX, Danny (D)**    293 15
H: 5 11 W: 12 06 b.Winsford 29-5-86
*Source:* Scholar. *Honours:* England Under-21, Scotland 4 full caps.

| | | | | | |
|---|---|---|---|---|---|
| 2004-05 | Everton | 0 | 0 | | |
| 2004-05 | *Stranraer* | 11 | 1 | 11 | 1 |
| 2005-06 | Walsall | 33 | 0 | | |
| 2006-07 | Walsall | 44 | 3 | | |
| 2007-08 | Walsall | 22 | 3 | 99 | 6 |
| 2007-08 | Coventry C | 18 | 1 | | |
| 2008-09 | Coventry C | 39 | 5 | | |
| 2009-10 | Coventry C | 0 | 0 | 57 | 6 |
| 2009-10 | Celtic | 15 | 0 | 15 | 0 |
| 2009-10 | Burnley | 14 | 1 | | |
| 2010-11 | Burnley | 35 | 0 | | |
| 2011-12 | Burnley | 1 | 0 | 50 | 1 |
| 2011-12 | Southampton | 41 | 0 | | |
| 2012-13 | Southampton | 20 | 1 | 61 | 1 |

**GAZZANIGA, Paulo (G)**    29 0
H: 6 5 W: 14 02 b.Santa Fe 2-1-92
*Source:* Valencia Youth.

| | | | | | |
|---|---|---|---|---|---|
| 2011-12 | *Gillingham* | 20 | 0 | 20 | 0 |
| 2012-13 | Southampton | 9 | 0 | 9 | 0 |

**HAMMOND, Dean (M)**    361 38
H: 6 0 W: 11 09 b.Hastings 7-3-83
*Source:* Scholar.

| | | | | | |
|---|---|---|---|---|---|
| 2002-03 | Brighton & HA | 4 | 0 | | |
| 2003-04 | Brighton & HA | 0 | 0 | | |
| 2003-04 | *Leyton Orient* | 8 | 0 | 8 | 0 |
| 2004-05 | Brighton & HA | 30 | 4 | | |
| 2005-06 | Brighton & HA | 41 | 4 | | |
| 2006-07 | Brighton & HA | 37 | 8 | | |

| | | | | | |
|---|---|---|---|---|---|
| 2007-08 | Brighton & HA | 24 | 5 | | |
| 2007-08 | Colchester U | 13 | 0 | | |
| 2008-09 | Colchester U | 41 | 5 | | |
| 2009-10 | Colchester U | 2 | 0 | 56 | 5 |
| 2009-10 | Southampton | 40 | 5 | | |
| 2010-11 | Southampton | 41 | 4 | | |
| 2011-12 | Southampton | 43 | 1 | | |
| 2012-13 | Southampton | 0 | 0 | 124 | 10 |
| 2012-13 | *Brighton & HA* | 37 | 2 | 173 | 23 |

**HOOIVELD, Jos (D)**    222 14
H: 6 3 W: 11 11 b.Zeijen 22-4-83

| | | | | | |
|---|---|---|---|---|---|
| 2002-03 | Heerenveen | 1 | 0 | | |
| 2003-04 | Heerenveen | 12 | 0 | 13 | 0 |
| 2004-05 | Zwolle | 14 | 2 | | |
| 2005-06 | Zwolle | 30 | 1 | 44 | 3 |
| 2006-07 | Kapfenberger | 14 | 0 | 14 | 0 |
| 2007 | Inter Turku | 26 | 4 | | |
| 2008 | Inter Turku | 26 | 4 | 52 | 4 |
| 2009 | AIK Stockholm | 28 | 0 | 28 | 0 |
| 2009-10 | Celtic | 2 | 0 | | |
| 2010-11 | Celtic | 5 | 0 | 7 | 0 |
| 2011-12 | Southampton | 39 | 7 | | |
| 2012-13 | Southampton | 25 | 0 | 64 | 7 |

**HOSKINS, Sam (F)**    22 3
H: 5 8 W: 10 07 b.Dorchester 4-2-93
*Source:* Scholar.

| | | | | | |
|---|---|---|---|---|---|
| 2011-12 | Southampton | 0 | 0 | | |
| 2011-12 | *Preston NE* | 0 | 0 | | |
| 2011-12 | *Rotherham U* | 8 | 2 | 8 | 2 |
| 2012-13 | Southampton | 0 | 0 | | |
| 2012-13 | *Stevenage* | 14 | 1 | 14 | 1 |

**ISGROVE, Lloyd (M)**    0 0
H: 5 10 W: 11 05 b.Yeovil 12-1-93
*Source:* Scholar.

| | | | | | |
|---|---|---|---|---|---|
| 2011-12 | Southampton | 0 | 0 | | |
| 2012-13 | Southampton | 0 | 0 | | |

**LALLANA, Adam (M)**    200 39
H: 5 8 W: 11 06 b.St Albans 10-5-88
*Source:* Scholar. *Honours:* England Youth, Under-21.

| | | | | | |
|---|---|---|---|---|---|
| 2005-06 | Southampton | 0 | 0 | | |
| 2006-07 | Southampton | 1 | 0 | | |
| 2007-08 | Southampton | 5 | 1 | | |
| 2007-08 | *Bournemouth* | 3 | 0 | 3 | 0 |
| 2008-09 | Southampton | 40 | 1 | | |
| 2009-10 | Southampton | 44 | 15 | | |
| 2010-11 | Southampton | 36 | 8 | | |
| 2011-12 | Southampton | 41 | 11 | | |
| 2012-13 | Southampton | 30 | 3 | 197 | 39 |

**LAMBERT, Ricky (F)**    507 199
H: 6 2 W: 14 08 b.Liverpool 16-2-82
*Source:* Trainee.

| | | | | | |
|---|---|---|---|---|---|
| 1999-2000 | Blackpool | 3 | 0 | | |
| 2000-01 | Blackpool | 0 | 0 | 3 | 0 |
| 2000-01 | Macclesfield T | 9 | 0 | | |
| 2001-02 | Macclesfield T | 35 | 8 | 44 | 8 |
| 2001-02 | Stockport Co | 0 | 0 | | |
| 2002-03 | Stockport Co | 29 | 2 | | |
| 2003-04 | Stockport Co | 40 | 12 | | |
| 2004-05 | Stockport Co | 29 | 0 | 98 | 18 |
| 2004-05 | Rochdale | 15 | 6 | | |
| 2005-06 | Rochdale | 46 | 22 | | |
| 2006-07 | Rochdale | 3 | 0 | 64 | 28 |
| 2006-07 | Bristol R | 36 | 8 | | |
| 2007-08 | Bristol R | 46 | 14 | | |
| 2008-09 | Bristol R | 45 | 29 | | |
| 2009-10 | Bristol R | 1 | 1 | 128 | 52 |
| 2009-10 | Southampton | 45 | 30 | | |
| 2010-11 | Southampton | 45 | 21 | | |
| 2011-12 | Southampton | 42 | 27 | | |
| 2012-13 | Southampton | 38 | 15 | 170 | 93 |

**LEE, Tadanari (F)**    198 55
H: 6 0 W: 11 09 b.Tokyo 19-12-85
*Honours:* Japan Under-23, 11 full caps, 2 goals.

| | | | | | |
|---|---|---|---|---|---|
| 2004 | FC Tokyo | 0 | 0 | | |
| 2005 | Kashiwa Reysol | 0 | 0 | | |
| 2006 | Kashiwa Reysol | 31 | 8 | | |
| 2007 | Kashiwa Reysol | 30 | 10 | | |
| 2008 | Kashiwa Reysol | 19 | 4 | | |
| 2009 | Kashiwa Reysol | 20 | 2 | 108 | 24 |
| 2009 | Sanfrecce | 8 | 0 | | |
| 2010 | Sanfrecce | 30 | 11 | | |
| 2011 | Sanfrecce | 32 | 15 | 70 | 26 |

| | | | | | |
|---|---|---|---|---|---|
| 2011-12 | Southampton | 7 | 1 | | |
| 2012-13 | Southampton | 0 | 0 | 7 | 1 |
| 2013 | *FC Tokyo* | 13 | 4 | 13 | 4 |

**MARTIN, Aaron (D)**    36 1
H: 6 3 W: 11 13 b.Newport (IW) 29-9-89
*Source:* Eastleigh.

| | | | | | |
|---|---|---|---|---|---|
| 2009-10 | Southampton | 2 | 0 | | |
| 2010-11 | Southampton | 8 | 0 | | |
| 2011-12 | Southampton | 10 | 1 | | |
| 2012-13 | Southampton | 0 | 0 | 20 | 1 |
| 2012-13 | *Crystal Palace* | 4 | 0 | 4 | 0 |
| 2012-13 | *Coventry C* | 12 | 0 | 12 | 0 |

**MAYUKA, Emmanuel (F)**    72 20
H: 5 9 W: 11 01 b.Kabwe 21-11-90
*Honours:* Zambia 43 full caps, 10 goals.

| | | | | | |
|---|---|---|---|---|---|
| 2010-11 | Young Boys | 27 | 9 | | |
| 2011-12 | Young Boys | 29 | 10 | | |
| 2012-13 | Young Boys | 5 | 1 | 61 | 20 |
| 2012-13 | Southampton | 11 | 0 | 11 | 0 |

**McQUEEN, Sam (M)**    0 0
b.Southampton 6-2-95
*Source:* Scholar.

| | | | |
|---|---|---|---|
| 2011-12 | Southampton | 0 | 0 |
| 2012-13 | Southampton | 0 | 0 |

**MOORE, Corby (M)**    0 0
H: 5 8 W: 10 00 b.Salisbury 21-11-93
*Source:* Scholar.

| | | | |
|---|---|---|---|
| 2011-12 | Southampton | 0 | 0 |
| 2012-13 | Southampton | 0 | 0 |

**PUNCHEON, Jason (M)**    263 44
H: 5 9 W: 12 05 b.Croydon 26-6-86
*Source:* Scholar.

| | | | | | |
|---|---|---|---|---|---|
| 2003-04 | Wimbledon | 8 | 0 | 8 | 0 |
| 2004-05 | Milton Keynes D | 25 | 1 | | |
| 2005-06 | Milton Keynes D | 1 | 0 | | |
| 2006-07 | Barnet | 37 | 5 | | |
| 2007-08 | Barnet | 41 | 10 | 78 | 15 |
| 2008-09 | Plymouth Arg | 6 | 0 | | |
| 2008-09 | *Milton Keynes D* | 27 | 4 | | |
| 2009-10 | Plymouth Arg | 0 | 0 | 6 | 0 |
| 2009-10 | *Milton Keynes D* | 24 | 7 | 77 | 12 |
| 2009-10 | Southampton | 19 | 3 | | |
| 2010-11 | Southampton | 15 | 0 | | |
| 2010-11 | *Millwall* | 7 | 5 | 7 | 5 |
| 2010-11 | *Blackpool* | 11 | 3 | 11 | 3 |
| 2011-12 | Southampton | 8 | 0 | | |
| 2011-12 | *QPR* | 2 | 0 | 2 | 0 |
| 2012-13 | Southampton | 32 | 6 | 74 | 9 |

**RAMIREZ, Gaston (M)**    83 17
H: 6 0 W: 12 00 b.Montevideo 2-12-90
*Honours:* Uruguay Under-20, Under-23, 20 full caps.

| | | | | | |
|---|---|---|---|---|---|
| 2010-11 | Bologna | 24 | 4 | | |
| 2011-12 | Bologna | 33 | 8 | 57 | 12 |
| 2012-13 | Southampton | 26 | 5 | 26 | 5 |

**REED, Harrison (M)**    0 0
b. 27-1-95
*Source:* Scholar.

| | | | |
|---|---|---|---|
| 2011-12 | Southampton | 0 | 0 |
| 2012-13 | Southampton | 0 | 0 |

**REEVES, Ben (D)**    20 1
H: 5 10 W: 10 07 b.Verwood 19-11-91
*Source:* Scholar.

| | | | | | |
|---|---|---|---|---|---|
| 2008-09 | Southampton | 0 | 0 | | |
| 2009-10 | Southampton | 0 | 0 | | |
| 2010-11 | Southampton | 0 | 0 | | |
| 2011-12 | Southampton | 0 | 0 | | |
| 2011-12 | *Dagenham & R* | 5 | 0 | 5 | 0 |
| 2012-13 | Southampton | 3 | 0 | 5 | 0 |
| 2012-13 | *Southend U* | 10 | 1 | 10 | 1 |

**RICHARDSON, Frazer (D)**    260 5
H: 5 11 W: 11 12 b.Rotherham 29-10-82
*Source:* Trainee. *Honours:* England Youth, Under-20.

| | | | | | |
|---|---|---|---|---|---|
| 1999-2000 | Leeds U | 0 | 0 | | |
| 2000-01 | Leeds U | 0 | 0 | | |
| 2001-02 | Leeds U | 0 | 0 | | |
| 2002-03 | Leeds U | 0 | 0 | | |
| 2002-03 | *Stoke C* | 7 | 0 | | |
| 2003-04 | Leeds U | 4 | 0 | | |
| 2003-04 | *Stoke C* | 6 | 1 | 13 | 1 |
| 2004-05 | Leeds U | 38 | 1 | | |
| 2005-06 | Leeds U | 23 | 1 | | |
| 2006-07 | Leeds U | 22 | 0 | | |
| 2007-08 | Leeds U | 39 | 1 | | |
| 2008-09 | Leeds U | 23 | 0 | 149 | 3 |
| 2009-10 | Charlton Ath | 38 | 1 | 38 | 1 |
| 2010-11 | Southampton | 21 | 0 | | |
| 2011-12 | Southampton | 34 | 0 | | |
| 2012-13 | Southampton | 5 | 0 | 60 | 0 |

**RODRIGUEZ, Jay (F)**    157 41
H: 6 0 W: 12 00 b.Burnley 29-7-89
*Source:* Scholar. *Honours:* England Under-21.

| | | | | | |
|---|---|---|---|---|---|
| 2007-08 | Burnley | 1 | 0 | | |
| 2007-08 | *Stirling Alb* | 11 | 3 | 11 | 3 |
| 2008-09 | Burnley | 25 | 2 | | |
| 2009-10 | Burnley | 0 | 0 | | |
| 2009-10 | *Barnsley* | 6 | 1 | 6 | 1 |
| 2010-11 | Burnley | 42 | 14 | | |
| 2011-12 | Burnley | 37 | 15 | 105 | 31 |
| 2012-13 | Southampton | 35 | 6 | 35 | 6 |

**SCHNEIDERLIN, Morgan (M)**    177 8
H: 5 11 W: 11 11 b.Obernai 8-11-89
*Honours:* France Youth.

| | | | | | |
|---|---|---|---|---|---|
| 2007-08 | Strasbourg | 5 | 0 | 5 | 0 |
| 2008-09 | Southampton | 30 | 0 | | |
| 2009-10 | Southampton | 37 | 1 | | |
| 2010-11 | Southampton | 27 | 0 | | |
| 2011-12 | Southampton | 42 | 2 | | |
| 2012-13 | Southampton | 36 | 5 | 172 | 8 |

**SEABORNE, Danny (D)**    116 1
H: 6 0 W: 11 10 b.Barnstaple 5-3-87
*Source:* Scholar.

| | | | | | |
|---|---|---|---|---|---|
| 2008-09 | Exeter C | 33 | 1 | | |
| 2009-10 | Exeter C | 19 | 0 | 52 | 1 |
| 2009-10 | Southampton | 16 | 0 | | |
| 2010-11 | Southampton | 24 | 0 | | |
| 2011-12 | Southampton | 4 | 0 | | |
| 2012-13 | Southampton | 0 | 0 | 44 | 0 |
| 2012-13 | *Charlton Ath* | 7 | 0 | 7 | 0 |
| 2012-13 | *Bournemouth* | 13 | 0 | 13 | 0 |

**SEIDI, Alberto (F)**    1 0
H: 5 10 W: 11 09 b.Guinea-Bissau 20-11-92
*Source:* Scholar.

| | | | | | |
|---|---|---|---|---|---|
| 2011-12 | Southampton | 0 | 0 | | |
| 2011-12 | Southampton | 0 | 0 | | |
| 2012-13 | Southampton | 0 | 0 | | |
| 2012-13 | *Aldershot T* | 1 | 0 | 1 | 0 |

**SHARP, Billy (F)**    289 129
H: 5 9 W: 11 00 b.Sheffield 5-2-86
*Source:* Scholar.

| | | | | | |
|---|---|---|---|---|---|
| 2004-05 | Sheffield U | 2 | 0 | | |
| 2004-05 | *Rushden & D* | 16 | 9 | 16 | 9 |
| 2005-06 | Sheffield U | 0 | 0 | | |
| 2005-06 | Scunthorpe U | 37 | 23 | | |
| 2006-07 | Scunthorpe U | 45 | 30 | 82 | 53 |
| 2007-08 | Sheffield U | 29 | 4 | | |
| 2008-09 | Sheffield U | 22 | 4 | | |
| 2009-10 | Sheffield U | 0 | 0 | 53 | 8 |
| 2009-10 | *Doncaster R* | 33 | 15 | | |
| 2010-11 | Doncaster R | 29 | 15 | | |
| 2011-12 | Doncaster R | 20 | 10 | 82 | 40 |
| 2011-12 | Southampton | 15 | 9 | | |
| 2012-13 | Southampton | 2 | 0 | 17 | 9 |
| 2012-13 | *Nottingham F* | 39 | 10 | 39 | 10 |

**SHAW, Luke (D)**    25 0
H: 6 1 W: 11 11 b.Kingston 12-7-95
*Source:* Scholar.

| | | | | | |
|---|---|---|---|---|---|
| 2011-12 | Southampton | 0 | 0 | | |
| 2012-13 | Southampton | 25 | 0 | 25 | 0 |

**SINCLAIR, Jake (F)**    0 0
H: 5 7 W: 11 00 b.Bath 29-11-94
*Source:* Scholar.

| | | | |
|---|---|---|---|
| 2011-12 | Southampton | 0 | 0 |
| 2012-13 | Southampton | 0 | 0 |

**STEPHENS, Jack (D)**    5 0
H: 6 1 W: 13 03 b.Torpoint 27-1-94
*Source:* Scholar. *Honours:* England Youth.

| | | | | | |
|---|---|---|---|---|---|
| 2010-11 | Plymouth Arg | 5 | 0 | 5 | 0 |
| 2010-11 | Southampton | 0 | 0 | | |
| 2011-12 | Southampton | 0 | 0 | | |
| 2012-13 | Southampton | 0 | 0 | | |

**TURNBULL, Jordan (D)**    0 0
b.Swindon 30-10-94
*Source:* Scholar.

| | | | |
|---|---|---|---|
| 2011-12 | Southampton | 0 | 0 |
| 2012-13 | Southampton | 0 | 0 |

**WARD-PROWSE, James (M)**    15 0
H: 5 8 W: 10 06 b.Portsmouth 1-11-94
*Source:* Scholar. *Honours:* England Youth.

| | | | | | |
|---|---|---|---|---|---|
| 2011-12 | Southampton | 0 | 0 | | |
| 2012-13 | Southampton | 15 | 0 | 15 | 0 |

**YOSHIDA, Maya (D)**    86 5
H: 6 2 W: 12 03 b.Nagasaki 24-8-88
*Honours:* Japan Under-23, 30 full caps, 2 goals.

| | | | | | |
|---|---|---|---|---|---|
| 2010-11 | VVV | 20 | 0 | | |
| 2011-12 | VVV | 32 | 5 | | |
| 2012-13 | VVV | 2 | 0 | 54 | 5 |
| 2012-13 | Southampton | 32 | 0 | 32 | 0 |

**Players retained or with offer of contract**
Curtis, Joe Edward; Gallagher, Samuel James; Gape, Dominic Edwards; Johns, Christopher Patrick Adam; McCarthy, Jason Sean; Mugabi, Bevis Kristofer Kizito; Robinson, Andreas Sonny; Seager, Ryan Paul; Young, Matthew Robert.

**Scholars**
Branker, Jamal Arron Christopher; Britt, William David; Colmer, Fraser William; Flannigan, Jake; Hesketh, Jake Alexander; Higgins, Charlie; Leggett, Thomas Jacob; Nehemie, Isaac; Rowe, Omar Reiss; Targett, Matthew Robert; White, James Steven St John.

## SOUTHEND U (75)

**AUGER, Ryan (M)**    0 0

| | | | |
|---|---|---|---|
| 2012-13 | Southend U | 0 | 0 |

**BARKER, Chris (D)**    510 3
H: 6 2 W: 13 08 b.Sheffield 2-3-80
*Source:* Alfreton.

| | | | | | |
|---|---|---|---|---|---|
| 1998-99 | Barnsley | 0 | 0 | | |
| 1999-2000 | Barnsley | 29 | 0 | | |
| 2000-01 | Barnsley | 40 | 0 | | |
| 2001-02 | Barnsley | 44 | 3 | 113 | 3 |
| 2002-03 | Cardiff C | 40 | 0 | | |
| 2003-04 | Cardiff C | 39 | 0 | | |
| 2004-05 | *Stoke C* | 4 | 0 | 4 | 0 |
| 2004-05 | Cardiff C | 39 | 0 | | |
| 2005-06 | Cardiff C | 41 | 0 | | |
| 2006-07 | Cardiff C | 0 | 0 | 159 | 0 |
| 2006-07 | *Colchester U* | 38 | 0 | 38 | 0 |
| 2007-08 | QPR | 25 | 0 | 25 | 0 |
| 2008-09 | Plymouth Arg | 40 | 0 | | |
| 2009-10 | Plymouth Arg | 14 | 0 | | |
| 2010-11 | Plymouth Arg | 0 | 0 | 54 | 0 |
| 2010-11 | Southend U | 43 | 0 | | |
| 2011-12 | Southend U | 43 | 0 | | |
| 2012-13 | Southend U | 31 | 0 | 117 | 0 |

**BENTLEY, Daniel (G)**    10 0
H: 6 2 W: 11 05 b.Wickford 13-7-93
*Source:* Scholar.

| | | | | | |
|---|---|---|---|---|---|
| 2011-12 | Southend U | 1 | 0 | | |
| 2012-13 | Southend U | 9 | 0 | 10 | 0 |

**BENYON, Elliot (F)**    125 31
H: 5 9 W: 10 01 b.High Wycombe 29-8-87
*Source:* Scholar.

| | | | | | |
|---|---|---|---|---|---|
| 2005-06 | Bristol C | 0 | 0 | | |
| 2006-07 | Bristol C | 0 | 0 | | |
| 2009-10 | Torquay U | 45 | 11 | | |
| 2010-11 | Torquay U | 23 | 13 | | |
| 2010-11 | Swindon T | 12 | 1 | | |
| 2011-12 | Swindon T | 0 | 0 | 12 | 1 |
| 2011-12 | *Wycombe W* | 9 | 0 | 9 | 0 |
| 2011-12 | Southend U | 16 | 2 | | |
| 2012-13 | Southend U | 5 | 0 | 21 | 2 |
| 2012-13 | *Torquay U* | 15 | 4 | 83 | 28 |

**CLOHESSY, Sean (D)**    180 5
H: 5 11 W: 11 07 b.Croydon 12-12-86
*Source:* Arsenal Scholar.

| | | | |
|---|---|---|---|
| 2005-06 | Gillingham | 20 | 1 |
| 2006-07 | Gillingham | 6 | 0 |

| | | | | | | |
|---|---|---|---|---|---|---|
| 2007-08 | Gillingham | 17 | 0 | 43 | 1 | |

From Salisbury C.

| | | | | | | |
|---|---|---|---|---|---|---|
| 2010-11 | Southend U | 46 | 1 | | | |
| 2011-12 | Southend U | 45 | 0 | | | |
| 2012-13 | Southend U | 46 | 3 | 137 | 4 | |

**CORR, Barry (F)**     163 37
H: 6 3   W: 12 07   b.Co Wicklow 2-4-85
*Honours:* Eire Youth.

| | | | | | | |
|---|---|---|---|---|---|---|
| 2001-02 | Leeds U | 0 | 0 | | | |
| 2002-03 | Leeds U | 0 | 0 | | | |
| 2003-04 | Leeds U | 0 | 0 | | | |
| 2004-05 | Leeds U | 0 | 0 | | | |
| 2005-06 | Sheffield W | 16 | 0 | | | |
| 2006-07 | Sheffield W | 1 | 0 | 17 | 0 | |
| 2006-07 | Bristol C | 3 | 0 | 3 | 0 | |
| 2006-07 | Swindon T | 8 | 3 | | | |
| 2007-08 | Swindon T | 17 | 5 | | | |
| 2008-09 | Swindon T | 11 | 2 | 36 | 10 | |
| 2009-10 | Exeter C | 34 | 3 | 34 | 3 | |
| 2010-11 | Southend U | 41 | 18 | | | |
| 2011-12 | Southend U | 0 | 0 | | | |
| 2012-13 | Southend U | 32 | 6 | 73 | 24 | |

**COUGHLAN, Graham (D)**     450 39
H: 6 2   W: 13 07   b.Dublin 18-11-74
*Source:* Bray Wanderers.

| | | | | | | |
|---|---|---|---|---|---|---|
| 1995-96 | Blackburn R | 0 | 0 | | | |
| 1996-97 | Blackburn R | 0 | 0 | | | |
| 1996-97 | Swindon T | 3 | 0 | 3 | 0 | |
| 1997-98 | Blackburn R | 0 | 0 | | | |
| 1998-99 | Livingston | 6 | 0 | | | |
| 1999-2000 | Livingston | 29 | 0 | | | |
| 2000-01 | Livingston | 21 | 2 | 56 | 2 | |
| 2001-02 | Plymouth Arg | 46 | 11 | | | |
| 2002-03 | Plymouth Arg | 42 | 5 | | | |
| 2003-04 | Plymouth Arg | 46 | 0 | | | |
| 2004-05 | Plymouth Arg | 43 | 2 | 177 | 25 | |
| 2005-06 | Sheffield W | 33 | 4 | | | |
| 2006-07 | Sheffield W | 18 | 1 | 51 | 5 | |
| 2006-07 | Burnley | 2 | 0 | 2 | 0 | |
| 2007-08 | Rotherham U | 45 | 1 | 45 | 1 | |
| 2008-09 | Shrewsbury T | 42 | 4 | | | |
| 2009-10 | Shrewsbury T | 36 | 2 | 78 | 6 | |
| 2010-11 | Southend U | 33 | 0 | | | |
| 2011-12 | Southend U | 4 | 0 | | | |
| 2012-13 | Southend U | 1 | 0 | 38 | 0 | |

**CRESSWELL, Ryan (D)**     158 16
H: 5 9   W: 10 05   b.Rotherham 22-12-87
*Source:* Scholar.

| | | | | | | |
|---|---|---|---|---|---|---|
| 2006-07 | Sheffield U | 0 | 0 | | | |
| 2007-08 | Sheffield U | 0 | 0 | | | |
| 2007-08 | Rotherham U | 3 | 0 | | | |
| 2007-08 | Morecambe | 2 | 0 | 2 | 0 | |
| 2007-08 | Macclesfield T | 19 | 1 | 19 | 1 | |
| 2008-09 | Bury | 25 | 1 | | | |
| 2009-10 | Bury | 28 | 0 | 53 | 1 | |
| 2010-11 | Rotherham U | 22 | 4 | | | |
| 2011-12 | Rotherham U | 16 | 4 | 41 | 8 | |
| 2012-13 | Southend U | 43 | 6 | 43 | 6 | |

**EASTWOOD, Freddy (F)**     292 78
H: 5 11   W: 12 04   b.Epsom 29-10-83
*Source:* West Ham U Trainee, Grays Ath.
*Honours:* Wales 11 full caps, 4 goals.

| | | | | | | |
|---|---|---|---|---|---|---|
| 2004-05 | Southend U | 33 | 19 | | | |
| 2005-06 | Southend U | 40 | 23 | | | |
| 2006-07 | Southend U | 42 | 11 | | | |
| 2007-08 | Wolverhampton W | 31 | 3 | 31 | 3 | |
| 2008-09 | Coventry C | 46 | 4 | | | |
| 2009-10 | Coventry C | 36 | 8 | | | |
| 2010-11 | Coventry C | 27 | 5 | | | |
| 2011-12 | Coventry C | 4 | 0 | 113 | 17 | |
| 2011-12 | Southend U | 7 | 2 | | | |
| 2012-13 | Southend U | 26 | 3 | 148 | 58 | |

**HARRIS, Neil (F)**     486 140
H: 5 10   W: 12 08   b.Thurrock 12-7-77
*Source:* Cambridge C.

| | | | | | | |
|---|---|---|---|---|---|---|
| 1997-98 | Millwall | 3 | 0 | | | |
| 1998-99 | Millwall | 39 | 15 | | | |
| 1999-2000 | Millwall | 38 | 25 | | | |
| 2000-01 | Millwall | 42 | 27 | | | |
| 2001-02 | Millwall | 21 | 4 | | | |
| 2002-03 | Millwall | 40 | 12 | | | |
| 2003-04 | Millwall | 38 | 9 | | | |
| 2004-05 | Millwall | 12 | 1 | | | |
| 2004-05 | Cardiff C | 3 | 1 | 3 | 1 | |

| | | | | | | |
|---|---|---|---|---|---|---|
| 2004-05 | Nottingham F | 13 | 0 | | | |
| 2005-06 | Nottingham F | 1 | 0 | | | |
| 2005-06 | Gillingham | 36 | 6 | 36 | 6 | |
| 2006-07 | Nottingham F | 19 | 1 | 33 | 1 | |
| 2006-07 | Millwall | 21 | 5 | | | |
| 2007-08 | Millwall | 27 | 3 | | | |
| 2008-09 | Millwall | 35 | 8 | | | |
| 2009-10 | Millwall | 32 | 13 | | | |
| 2010-11 | Millwall | 26 | 2 | 374 | 124 | |
| 2011-12 | Southend U | 33 | 8 | | | |
| 2012-13 | Southend U | 7 | 0 | 40 | 8 | |

**HURST, Kevan (M)**     284 23
H: 5 10   W: 11 07   b.Chesterfield 27-8-85
*Source:* Sheffield U Scholar.

| | | | | | | |
|---|---|---|---|---|---|---|
| 2003-04 | Boston U | 7 | 1 | 7 | 1 | |
| 2004-05 | Sheffield U | 1 | 0 | | | |
| 2004-05 | Stockport Co | 14 | 1 | 14 | 1 | |
| 2005-06 | Sheffield U | 0 | 0 | | | |
| 2005-06 | Chesterfield | 37 | 4 | | | |
| 2006-07 | Sheffield U | 0 | 0 | 1 | 0 | |
| 2006-07 | Chesterfield | 25 | 3 | 62 | 7 | |
| 2006-07 | Scunthorpe U | 13 | 0 | | | |
| 2007-08 | Scunthorpe U | 3 | 1 | | | |
| 2008-09 | Scunthorpe U | 20 | 2 | 66 | 3 | |
| 2009-10 | Carlisle U | 33 | 2 | | | |
| 2010-11 | Carlisle U | 2 | 0 | 35 | 2 | |
| 2010-11 | Morecambe | 21 | 2 | 21 | 2 | |
| 2011-12 | Walsall | 34 | 2 | 34 | 2 | |
| 2012-13 | Southend U | 44 | 5 | 44 | 5 | |

**LEONARD, Ryan (D)**     40 3
H: 6 0   W: 11 01   b.Plympton 24-5-92
*Source:* Scholar.

| | | | | | | |
|---|---|---|---|---|---|---|
| 2009-10 | Plymouth Arg | 1 | 0 | | | |
| 2010-11 | Plymouth Arg | 0 | 0 | 1 | 0 | |
| 2011-12 | Southend U | 17 | 1 | | | |
| 2012-13 | Southend U | 22 | 2 | 39 | 3 | |

**LUND, Matthew (M)**     48 5
H: 6 0   W: 11 13   b.Manchester 21-11-90
*Source:* Crewe Alex. *Honours:* Northern Ireland Under-21.

| | | | | | | |
|---|---|---|---|---|---|---|
| 2009-10 | Stoke C | 0 | 0 | | | |
| 2010-11 | Stoke C | 0 | 0 | | | |
| 2010-11 | Hereford U | 2 | 0 | 2 | 0 | |
| 2011-12 | Stoke C | 0 | 0 | | | |
| 2011-12 | Oldham Ath | 3 | 0 | 3 | 0 | |
| 2011-12 | Bristol R | 13 | 2 | | | |
| 2012-13 | Stoke C | 0 | 0 | | | |
| 2012-13 | Bristol R | 18 | 2 | 31 | 4 | |
| 2012-13 | Southend U | 12 | 1 | 12 | 1 | |

**MARTIN, David J (M)**     147 14
H: 5 9   W: 10 10   b.Erith 3-6-85
*Source:* Dartford.

| | | | | | | |
|---|---|---|---|---|---|---|
| 2006-07 | Crystal Palace | 5 | 0 | | | |
| 2007-08 | Crystal Palace | 9 | 0 | 14 | 0 | |
| 2007-08 | Millwall | 11 | 2 | | | |
| 2008-09 | Millwall | 44 | 4 | | | |
| 2009-10 | Millwall | 20 | 3 | 75 | 9 | |
| 2009-10 | Derby Co | 11 | 1 | | | |
| 2010-11 | Derby Co | 2 | 0 | | | |
| 2010-11 | Notts Co | 10 | 0 | 10 | 0 | |
| 2011-12 | Derby Co | 0 | 0 | 13 | 1 | |
| 2011-12 | Walsall | 4 | 0 | 4 | 0 | |
| 2011-12 | Southend U | 17 | 3 | | | |
| 2012-13 | Southend U | 14 | 1 | 31 | 4 | |

**MOHSNI, Bilel (D)**     67 18
H: 6 3   W: 11 11   b.Tunisia 21-7-87
*Source:* Les Ulis, Saint-Georges, Sainte Genevieve Sp.

| | | | | | | |
|---|---|---|---|---|---|---|
| 2010-11 | Southend U | 23 | 5 | | | |
| 2011-12 | Southend U | 31 | 13 | | | |
| 2012-13 | Southend U | 8 | 0 | 62 | 18 | |
| 2012-13 | Ipswich T | 5 | 0 | 5 | 0 | |

**NJIE, Seedy (G)**     1 0
b.Birmingham 2-10-81

| | | | | | | |
|---|---|---|---|---|---|---|
| 2012-13 | Southend U | 1 | 0 | 1 | 0 | |

**PAXMAN, Jack (M)**     0 0

| | | | | | | |
|---|---|---|---|---|---|---|
| 2012-13 | Southend U | 0 | 0 | | | |

**PHILLIPS, Mark (D)**     195 12
H: 6 2   W: 11 00   b.Lambeth 27-1-82
*Source:* Scholarship.

| | | | | | | |
|---|---|---|---|---|---|---|
| 1999-2000 | Millwall | 0 | 0 | | | |
| 2000-01 | Millwall | 0 | 0 | | | |

| | | | | | | |
|---|---|---|---|---|---|---|
| 2001-02 | Millwall | 1 | 0 | | | |
| 2002-03 | Millwall | 7 | 0 | | | |
| 2003-04 | Millwall | 0 | 0 | | | |
| 2004-05 | Millwall | 25 | 1 | | | |
| 2005-06 | Millwall | 22 | 0 | | | |
| 2006-07 | Millwall | 12 | 0 | | | |
| 2006-07 | Darlington | 8 | 0 | 8 | 0 | |
| 2007-08 | Millwall | 0 | 0 | 67 | 1 | |
| 2008-09 | Brentford | 33 | 1 | | | |
| 2009-10 | Brentford | 22 | 0 | 55 | 1 | |
| 2010-11 | Southend U | 5 | 0 | | | |
| 2011-12 | Southend U | 39 | 7 | | | |
| 2012-13 | Southend U | 21 | 3 | 65 | 10 | |

**PINNOCK, Mitch (M)**     2 0
H: 5 10   b. 12-12-94

| | | | | | | |
|---|---|---|---|---|---|---|
| 2012-13 | Southend U | 2 | 0 | 2 | 0 | |

**PROSSER, Luke (D)**     96 4
H: 6 2   W: 12 04   b.Waltham Cross 28-5-88
*Source:* Scholar.

| | | | | | | |
|---|---|---|---|---|---|---|
| 2005-06 | Port Vale | 0 | 0 | | | |
| 2006-07 | Port Vale | 0 | 0 | | | |
| 2007-08 | Port Vale | 5 | 0 | | | |
| 2008-09 | Port Vale | 26 | 1 | | | |
| 2009-10 | Port Vale | 2 | 1 | 33 | 2 | |
| 2010-11 | Southend U | 17 | 1 | | | |
| 2011-12 | Southend U | 21 | 1 | | | |
| 2012-13 | Southend U | 25 | 0 | 63 | 2 | |

**SMITH, Paul (G)**     266 0
H: 6 3   W: 14 00   b.Epsom 17-12-79
*Source:* Walton & Hersham.

| | | | | | | |
|---|---|---|---|---|---|---|
| 1998-99 | Charlton Ath | 0 | 0 | | | |
| 1998-99 | Brentford | 0 | 0 | | | |
| 1999-2000 | Charlton Ath | 0 | 0 | | | |

From Carshalton Ath.

| | | | | | | |
|---|---|---|---|---|---|---|
| 2000-01 | Brentford | 2 | 0 | | | |
| 2001-02 | Brentford | 18 | 0 | | | |
| 2002-03 | Brentford | 43 | 0 | | | |
| 2003-04 | Brentford | 24 | 0 | 87 | 0 | |
| 2003-04 | Southampton | 0 | 0 | | | |
| 2004-05 | Southampton | 6 | 0 | | | |
| 2005-06 | Southampton | 9 | 0 | 15 | 0 | |
| 2006-07 | Nottingham F | 45 | 0 | | | |
| 2007-08 | Nottingham F | 46 | 0 | | | |
| 2008-09 | Nottingham F | 28 | 0 | | | |
| 2009-10 | Nottingham F | 1 | 0 | | | |
| 2010-11 | Nottingham F | 0 | 0 | | | |
| 2010-11 | Middlesbrough | 10 | 0 | 10 | 0 | |
| 2011-12 | Nottingham F | 0 | 0 | 120 | 0 | |
| 2012-13 | Southend U | 34 | 0 | 34 | 0 | |

**SPICER, John (M)**     208 14
H: 5 11   W: 11 07   b.Romford 13-9-83
*Source:* Scholar. *Honours:* England Schools, Youth, Under-20.

| | | | | | | |
|---|---|---|---|---|---|---|
| 2001-02 | Arsenal | 0 | 0 | | | |
| 2002-03 | Arsenal | 0 | 0 | | | |
| 2003-04 | Arsenal | 0 | 0 | | | |
| 2004-05 | Arsenal | 0 | 0 | | | |
| 2004-05 | Bournemouth | 39 | 6 | | | |
| 2005-06 | Bournemouth | 4 | 0 | 43 | 6 | |
| 2005-06 | Burnley | 34 | 3 | | | |
| 2006-07 | Burnley | 11 | 1 | | | |
| 2007-08 | Burnley | 24 | 0 | 69 | 4 | |
| 2008-09 | Doncaster R | 30 | 1 | | | |
| 2009-10 | Doncaster R | 20 | 0 | 50 | 1 | |
| 2009-10 | Leyton Orient | 9 | 1 | 9 | 1 | |
| 2010-11 | Notts Co | 23 | 2 | | | |
| 2011-12 | Notts Co | 1 | 0 | 24 | 2 | |
| 2012-13 | Southend U | 13 | 0 | 13 | 0 | |

**SPILLANE, Michael (M)**     152 13
H: 5 9   W: 11 10   b.Jersey 23-3-89
*Source:* Scholar. *Honours:* Eire Youth, Under-21.

| | | | | | | |
|---|---|---|---|---|---|---|
| 2005-06 | Norwich C | 2 | 0 | | | |
| 2006-07 | Norwich C | 5 | 0 | | | |
| 2007-08 | Norwich C | 6 | 0 | | | |
| 2008-09 | Norwich C | 0 | 0 | | | |
| 2008-09 | Luton T | 39 | 3 | 39 | 3 | |
| 2009-10 | Norwich C | 13 | 1 | 26 | 1 | |
| 2010-11 | Brentford | 24 | 1 | | | |
| 2011-12 | Brentford | 0 | 0 | 25 | 1 | |
| 2011-12 | Dagenham & R | 29 | 4 | | | |
| 2012-13 | Dagenham & R | 24 | 4 | 53 | 8 | |
| 2012-13 | Southend U | 9 | 0 | 9 | 0 | |

## STRAKER, Anthony (D) — 183 6
H: 5 9  W: 11 11  b.Ealing 23-9-88
Source: Crystal Palace Scholar. Honours: Grenada 5 full caps.

|  |  | | | | |
|---|---|--:|--:|--:|--:|
| 2008-09 | Aldershot T | 32 | 0 | | |
| 2009-10 | Aldershot T | 37 | 2 | | |
| 2010-11 | Aldershot T | 38 | 2 | | |
| 2010-11 | *Wycombe W* | 4 | 0 | 4 | 0 |
| 2011-12 | Aldershot T | 44 | 2 | 151 | 6 |
| 2012-13 | Southend U | 28 | 0 | 28 | 0 |

## TIMLIN, Michael (M) — 195 11
H: 5 8  W: 11 08  b.New Cross 19-3-85
Source: Trainee. Honours: Eire Youth, Under-21.

|  |  | | | | |
|---|---|--:|--:|--:|--:|
| 2002-03 | Fulham | 0 | 0 | | |
| 2003-04 | Fulham | 0 | 0 | | |
| 2004-05 | Fulham | 0 | 0 | | |
| 2005-06 | Fulham | 0 | 0 | | |
| 2005-06 | *Scunthorpe U* | 1 | 0 | 1 | 0 |
| 2005-06 | *Doncaster R* | 3 | 0 | 3 | 0 |
| 2006-07 | Fulham | 0 | 0 | | |
| 2006-07 | *Swindon T* | 24 | 1 | | |
| 2007-08 | Fulham | 0 | 0 | | |
| 2007-08 | *Swindon T* | 10 | 1 | | |
| 2008-09 | Swindon T | 41 | 2 | | |
| 2009-10 | Swindon T | 21 | 0 | | |
| 2010-11 | Swindon T | 22 | 2 | | |
| 2010-11 | *Southend U* | 8 | 1 | | |
| 2011-12 | Swindon T | 1 | 0 | 119 | 6 |
| 2011-12 | Southend U | 39 | 4 | | |
| 2012-13 | Southend U | 25 | 0 | 72 | 5 |

## TOMLIN, Gavin (F) — 180 39
H: 6 0  W: 12 02  b.Gillingham 13-1-83
Source: Staines T, Yeading.

|  |  | | | | |
|---|---|--:|--:|--:|--:|
| 2006-07 | Brentford | 12 | 0 | | |
| 2007-08 | Brentford | 0 | 0 | 12 | 0 |

From Fisher Ath.

|  |  | | | | |
|---|---|--:|--:|--:|--:|
| 2008-09 | Yeovil T | 42 | 7 | | |
| 2009-10 | Yeovil T | 35 | 7 | 77 | 14 |
| 2010-11 | Dagenham & R | 19 | 2 | | |
| 2010-11 | *Torquay U* | 12 | 4 | 12 | 4 |
| 2011-12 | Dagenham & R | 17 | 0 | 36 | 2 |
| 2011-12 | *Gillingham* | 10 | 6 | 10 | 6 |
| 2012-13 | Southend U | 33 | 13 | 33 | 13 |

## WOODYARD, Alex (M) — 8 0
H: 5 9  W: 10 00  b.Gravesend 3-5-93
Source: Scholar.

|  |  | | | | |
|---|---|--:|--:|--:|--:|
| 2010-11 | Southend U | 3 | 0 | | |
| 2011-12 | Southend U | 0 | 0 | | |
| 2012-13 | Southend U | 5 | 0 | 8 | 0 |

**Players retained or with offer of contract**
Chambers, Luke James.

**Scholars**
Agyakwa, Marlon; Auger, Ryan Scott; Banton, Joshua Jordan Lee-Winston; Barlow, Charlie Harry; Baucutt, Louis James; Bridge, Jack; Coker, Mofopefoluwa Oladipupo; Edwards, Jack; Farrell, Kane Stephen William; Hyams, Robert Edward; Jeffery, Harry George; King, Daniel Charles Lewis; Mullings, Shamir; Njie, Seedy Ishmail; Paxman, Jack Steven; Payne, Jack; Pinnock, James Alexander; Pinnock, Mitchell Bernard; Smith, Edward James; Snook, Daniel John; Tatham, Aaron Jon; Williams, Jason Norrel.

# STEVENAGE (76)

## AKINS, Lucas (F) — 148 18
H: 5 10  W: 11 07  b.Huddersfield 25-2-89
Source: Scholar.

|  |  | | | | |
|---|---|--:|--:|--:|--:|
| 2006-07 | Huddersfield T | 2 | 0 | | |
| 2007-08 | Huddersfield T | 3 | 0 | 5 | 0 |
| 2008-09 | Hamilton A | 11 | 0 | | |
| 2008-09 | *Partick Th* | 9 | 1 | 9 | 1 |
| 2009-10 | Hamilton A | 0 | 0 | 11 | 0 |
| 2010-11 | Tranmere R | 33 | 2 | | |
| 2011-12 | Tranmere R | 44 | 5 | | |
| 2012-13 | Tranmere R | 0 | 0 | 77 | 7 |
| 2012-13 | Stevenage | 46 | 10 | 46 | 10 |

## ARNOLD, Steve (G) — 30 0
H: 6 1  W: 13 02  b.Welham Green 22-8-89
Source: Grays Ath, Hayes & Y.

|  |  | | | | |
|---|---|--:|--:|--:|--:|
| 2012-13 | Stevenage | 30 | 0 | 30 | 0 |

## ASHTON, Jon (D) — 197 3
H: 6 2  W: 13 12  b.Nuneaton 4-10-82
Source: Scholar.

|  |  | | | | |
|---|---|--:|--:|--:|--:|
| 2000-01 | Leicester C | 0 | 0 | | |
| 2001-02 | Leicester C | 7 | 0 | | |
| 2002-03 | *Notts Co* | 4 | 0 | 4 | 0 |
| 2003-04 | Leicester C | 0 | 0 | 7 | 0 |
| 2003-04 | Oxford U | 34 | 0 | | |
| 2004-05 | Oxford U | 30 | 0 | | |
| 2005-06 | Oxford U | 33 | 1 | 97 | 1 |

From Rushden & D, Grays Ath.

|  |  | | | | |
|---|---|--:|--:|--:|--:|
| 2010-11 | Stevenage | 38 | 1 | | |
| 2011-12 | Stevenage | 43 | 1 | | |
| 2012-13 | Stevenage | 8 | 0 | 89 | 2 |

## BALL, Matt (M) — 2 0
H: 5 10  W: 10 10  b.Welwyn Garden City 26-3-93
Source: Scholar. Honours: Northern Ireland Youth, Under-21.

|  |  | | | | |
|---|---|--:|--:|--:|--:|
| 2011-12 | Norwich C | 0 | 0 | | |
| 2011-12 | *Macclesfield T* | 0 | 0 | | |
| 2012-13 | Norwich C | 0 | 0 | | |
| 2012-13 | Stevenage | 2 | 0 | 2 | 0 |

## BELECK, Steve (F) — 18 0
H: 6 3  W: 12 05  b.Yaounde 21-2-92

|  |  | | | | |
|---|---|--:|--:|--:|--:|
| 2012-13 | Udinese | 0 | 0 | | |
| 2012-13 | *Watford* | 5 | 0 | 5 | 0 |

On loan from Udinese

|  |  | | | | |
|---|---|--:|--:|--:|--:|
| 2012-13 | Stevenage | 13 | 0 | 13 | 0 |

## CHARLES, Darius (M) — 130 8
H: 6 1  W: 13 05  b.Ealing 10-12-87
Source: Scholar.

|  |  | | | | |
|---|---|--:|--:|--:|--:|
| 2004-05 | Brentford | 1 | 0 | | |
| 2005-06 | Brentford | 2 | 0 | | |
| 2006-07 | Brentford | 17 | 1 | | |
| 2007-08 | Brentford | 17 | 0 | 37 | 1 |

From Ebbsfleet U.

|  |  | | | | |
|---|---|--:|--:|--:|--:|
| 2010-11 | Stevenage | 28 | 2 | | |
| 2011-12 | Stevenage | 28 | 4 | | |
| 2012-13 | Stevenage | 37 | 1 | 93 | 7 |

## CHORLEY, Ben (D) — 369 15
H: 6 3  W: 13 02  b.Sidcup 30-9-82
Source: Scholar.

|  |  | | | | |
|---|---|--:|--:|--:|--:|
| 2001-02 | Arsenal | 0 | 0 | | |
| 2002-03 | Arsenal | 0 | 0 | | |
| 2002-03 | *Brentford* | 2 | 0 | 2 | 0 |
| 2002-03 | Wimbledon | 10 | 0 | | |
| 2003-04 | Wimbledon | 35 | 2 | 45 | 2 |
| 2004-05 | Milton Keynes D | 41 | 2 | | |
| 2005-06 | Milton Keynes D | 26 | 0 | | |
| 2006-07 | Milton Keynes D | 13 | 1 | 80 | 3 |
| 2006-07 | *Gillingham* | 27 | 1 | 27 | 1 |
| 2007-08 | Tranmere R | 31 | 1 | | |
| 2008-09 | Tranmere R | 45 | 1 | 76 | 2 |
| 2009-10 | Leyton Orient | 42 | 1 | | |
| 2010-11 | Leyton Orient | 29 | 3 | | |
| 2011-12 | Leyton Orient | 32 | 1 | | |
| 2012-13 | Leyton Orient | 28 | 2 | 131 | 7 |
| 2012-13 | Stevenage | 8 | 0 | 8 | 0 |

## COMMINGES, Miguel (D) — 192 0
H: 6 3  W: 12 07  b.Martinique 16-3-82

|  |  | | | | |
|---|---|--:|--:|--:|--:|
| 2002-03 | Amiens | 12 | 0 | 12 | 0 |
| 2003-04 | Reims | 29 | 0 | | |
| 2004-05 | Reims | 21 | 0 | | |
| 2005-06 | Reims | 11 | 0 | | |
| 2006-07 | Reims | 13 | 0 | 74 | 0 |
| 2007-08 | Swindon T | 40 | 0 | 40 | 0 |
| 2008-09 | Cardiff C | 30 | 0 | | |
| 2009-10 | Cardiff C | 1 | 0 | 31 | 0 |
| 2010-11 | Southend U | 7 | 0 | 7 | 0 |
| 2011 | Colorado Rapids | 7 | 0 | 7 | 0 |
| 2012-13 | Stevenage | 21 | 0 | 21 | 0 |

## DAY, Chris (G) — 289 0
H: 6 2  W: 13 07  b.Whipps Cross 28-7-75
Source: Trainee. Honours: England Youth, Under-21.

|  |  | | | | |
|---|---|--:|--:|--:|--:|
| 1992-93 | Tottenham H | 0 | 0 | | |
| 1993-94 | Tottenham H | 0 | 0 | | |
| 1994-95 | Tottenham H | 0 | 0 | | |
| 1995-96 | Tottenham H | 0 | 0 | | |
| 1996-97 | Crystal Palace | 24 | 0 | 24 | 0 |
| 1997-98 | Watford | 0 | 0 | | |
| 1998-99 | Watford | 0 | 0 | | |
| 1999-2000 | Watford | 11 | 0 | | |
| 2000-01 | Watford | 0 | 0 | 11 | 0 |
| 2000-01 | *Lincoln C* | 14 | 0 | 14 | 0 |
| 2001-02 | QPR | 16 | 0 | | |
| 2002-03 | QPR | 12 | 0 | | |
| 2003-04 | QPR | 29 | 0 | | |
| 2004-05 | QPR | 30 | 0 | 87 | 0 |
| 2004-05 | *Preston NE* | 6 | 0 | 6 | 0 |
| 2005-06 | Oldham Ath | 30 | 0 | 30 | 0 |
| 2006-07 | Millwall | 5 | 0 | | |
| 2007-08 | Millwall | 5 | 0 | 10 | 0 |
| 2010-11 | Stevenage | 46 | 0 | | |
| 2011-12 | Stevenage | 44 | 0 | | |
| 2012-13 | Stevenage | 17 | 0 | 107 | 0 |

## DEACON, Roarie (M) — 1 0

|  |  | | | | |
|---|---|--:|--:|--:|--:|
| 2012-13 | Stevenage | 1 | 0 | 1 | 0 |

## DUNNE, James (M) — 152 10
H: 5 11  W: 10 12  b.Bromley 18-9-89
Source: Scholar.

|  |  | | | | |
|---|---|--:|--:|--:|--:|
| 2007-08 | Arsenal | 0 | 0 | | |
| 2008-09 | Arsenal | 0 | 0 | | |
| 2008-09 | *Nottingham F* | 0 | 0 | | |
| 2009-10 | Exeter C | 23 | 3 | | |
| 2010-11 | Exeter C | 42 | 1 | | |
| 2011-12 | Exeter C | 45 | 2 | 110 | 6 |
| 2012-13 | Stevenage | 42 | 4 | 42 | 4 |

## FREEMAN, Luke (F) — 79 11
H: 6 0  W: 10 00  b.Dartford 22-3-92
Source: Scholar.

|  |  | | | | |
|---|---|--:|--:|--:|--:|
| 2007-08 | Gillingham | 1 | 0 | 1 | 0 |
| 2008-09 | Arsenal | 0 | 0 | | |
| 2009-10 | Arsenal | 0 | 0 | | |
| 2010-11 | Arsenal | 0 | 0 | | |
| 2010-11 | *Yeovil T* | 13 | 2 | 13 | 2 |
| 2011-12 | Arsenal | 0 | 0 | | |
| 2011-12 | Stevenage | 26 | 7 | | |
| 2012-13 | Stevenage | 39 | 2 | 65 | 9 |

## FURLONGE, Anthony (D) — 0 0
b. 3-12-94
Honours: Cyprus Under-21.

|  |  | | | | |
|---|---|--:|--:|--:|--:|
| 2012-13 | Stevenage | 0 | 0 | | |

## GRANT, Anthony (M) — 247 10
H: 5 10  W: 11 01  b.Lambeth 4-6-87
Source: Scholar. Honours: England Youth.

|  |  | | | | |
|---|---|--:|--:|--:|--:|
| 2004-05 | Chelsea | 1 | 0 | | |
| 2005-06 | Chelsea | 0 | 0 | | |
| 2005-06 | *Oldham Ath* | 2 | 0 | 2 | 0 |
| 2006-07 | Chelsea | 0 | 0 | | |
| 2006-07 | *Wycombe W* | 40 | 0 | 40 | 0 |
| 2007-08 | Chelsea | 0 | 0 | 1 | 0 |
| 2007-08 | *Luton T* | 4 | 0 | 4 | 0 |
| 2007-08 | *Southend U* | 10 | 0 | | |
| 2008-09 | Southend U | 35 | 1 | | |
| 2009-10 | Southend U | 38 | 0 | | |
| 2010-11 | Southend U | 43 | 8 | | |
| 2011-12 | Southend U | 33 | 1 | 159 | 10 |
| 2012-13 | Southend U | 41 | 0 | 41 | 0 |

## GRAY, David (F) — 114 0
H: 5 11  W: 11 02  b.Edinburgh 4-5-88
Source: Scholar. Honours: Scotland Under-21.

|  |  | | | | |
|---|---|--:|--:|--:|--:|
| 2005-06 | Manchester U | 0 | 0 | | |
| 2006-07 | Manchester U | 0 | 0 | | |
| 2007-08 | Manchester U | 0 | 0 | | |
| 2007-08 | *Crewe Alex* | 1 | 0 | 1 | 0 |
| 2008-09 | Manchester U | 0 | 0 | | |
| 2008-09 | *Plymouth Arg* | 14 | 0 | | |
| 2009-10 | Manchester U | 0 | 0 | | |
| 2009-10 | *Plymouth Arg* | 12 | 0 | 26 | 0 |
| 2010-11 | Preston NE | 22 | 0 | | |
| 2011-12 | Preston NE | 23 | 0 | 45 | 0 |
| 2012-13 | Stevenage | 42 | 0 | 42 | 0 |

## HABER, Marcus (F) — 89 10
H: 6 3  W: 13 04  b.Vancouver 11-1-89
Honours: Canada Youth, Under-23, 7 full caps, 1 goal.

|  |  | | | | |
|---|---|--:|--:|--:|--:|
| 2009-10 | WBA | 0 | 0 | | |
| 2009-10 | *Exeter* | 5 | 0 | 5 | 0 |
| 2010-11 | WBA | 0 | 0 | | |
| 2010-11 | *St Johnstone* | 11 | 1 | | |

| | | | | | |
|---|---|---|---|---|---|
| 2011-12 | St Johnstone | 31 | 2 | 42 | 3 |
| 2012-13 | Stevenage | 42 | 7 | 42 | 7 |

**HILLS, Lee (D)**    68 1
H: 5 10   W: 11 11   b.Croydon 13-4-90
*Source:* Scholar. *Honours:* England Youth.

| | | | | | |
|---|---|---|---|---|---|
| 2007-08 | Crystal Palace | 12 | 1 | | |
| 2008-09 | Crystal Palace | 14 | 0 | | |
| 2008-09 | Colchester U | 2 | 0 | 2 | 0 |
| 2009-10 | Crystal Palace | 19 | 0 | | |
| 2009-10 | Oldham Ath | 3 | 0 | 3 | 0 |
| 2010-11 | Crystal Palace | 0 | 0 | | |
| 2011-12 | Crystal Palace | 0 | 0 | | |
| 2011-12 | Southend U | 7 | 0 | 7 | 0 |
| 2012-13 | Crystal Palace | 0 | 0 | 45 | 1 |
| 2012-13 | Stevenage | 11 | 0 | 11 | 0 |

**IRO, Andy (D)**    84 6
H: 6 5   W: 14 07   b.Liverpool 26-11-84

| | | | | | |
|---|---|---|---|---|---|
| 2008 | Columbus Crew | 21 | 1 | | |
| 2009 | Columbus Crew | 11 | 1 | | |
| 2010 | Columbus Crew | 26 | 3 | | |
| 2011 | Columbus Crew | 4 | 0 | 62 | 5 |
| 2011 | Toronto FC | 13 | 0 | 13 | 0 |
| 2012-13 | Stevenage | 0 | 0 | | |
| 2012-13 | Barnet | 9 | 1 | 9 | 1 |

**JEFFREY, Anthony (M)**    1 0

| | | | | | |
|---|---|---|---|---|---|
| 2012-13 | Stevenage | 1 | 0 | 1 | 0 |

**LOPEZ, Daniel (F)**    27 12
H: 5 9   W: 9 08

| | | | | | |
|---|---|---|---|---|---|
| 2012-13 | Stevenage | 10 | 3 | 10 | 3 |
| 2012-13 | Aldershot T | 12 | 6 | 12 | 6 |
| 2012-13 | Barnet | 5 | 3 | 5 | 3 |

**MORAIS, Filipe (M)**    197 19
H: 5 9   W: 11 10   b.Lisbon 21-11-85
*Source:* Trainee. *Honours:* Portugal Youth, Under-21.

| | | | | | |
|---|---|---|---|---|---|
| 2003-04 | Chelsea | 0 | 0 | | |
| 2004-05 | Chelsea | 0 | 0 | | |
| 2005-06 | Chelsea | 0 | 0 | | |
| 2005-06 | Milton Keynes D | 13 | 0 | 13 | 0 |
| 2006-07 | Millwall | 12 | 1 | 12 | 1 |
| 2006-07 | St Johnstone | 13 | 1 | | |
| 2007-08 | Hibernian | 28 | 1 | | |
| 2008-09 | Hibernian | 2 | 0 | 30 | 1 |
| 2008-09 | Inverness CT | 12 | 3 | 12 | 3 |
| 2009-10 | St Johnstone | 30 | 2 | 43 | 3 |
| 2010-11 | Oldham Ath | 23 | 3 | | |
| 2011-12 | Oldham Ath | 36 | 5 | | |
| 2012-13 | Oldham Ath | 0 | 0 | 59 | 8 |
| 2012-13 | Stevenage | 28 | 3 | 28 | 3 |

**N'GALA, Bondz (D)**    102 3
H: 6 0   W: 12 03   b.Forest Gate 13-9-89
*Source:* Scholar.

| | | | | | |
|---|---|---|---|---|---|
| 2007-08 | West Ham U | 0 | 0 | | |
| 2008-09 | West Ham U | 0 | 0 | | |
| 2008-09 | Milton Keynes D | 3 | 0 | 3 | 0 |
| 2009-10 | West Ham U | 0 | 0 | | |
| 2009-10 | Scunthorpe U | 2 | 0 | 2 | 0 |
| 2009-10 | Plymouth Arg | 9 | 0 | | |
| 2010-11 | Plymouth Arg | 26 | 1 | 35 | 1 |
| 2011-12 | Yeovil T | 31 | 2 | 31 | 2 |
| 2012-13 | Stevenage | 25 | 0 | 25 | 0 |
| 2012-13 | Barnet | 6 | 0 | 6 | 0 |

**N'GUISSAN, Joe (M)**    1 0

| | | | | | |
|---|---|---|---|---|---|
| 2012-13 | Stevenage | 1 | 0 | 1 | 0 |

**ROBERTS, Mark (D)**    173 14
H: 6 1   W: 12 00   b.Northwich 16-10-83
*Source:* Scholar.

| | | | | | |
|---|---|---|---|---|---|
| 2002-03 | Crewe Alex | 0 | 0 | | |
| 2003-04 | Crewe Alex | 0 | 0 | | |
| 2004-05 | Crewe Alex | 6 | 0 | | |
| 2005-06 | Crewe Alex | 0 | 0 | | |
| 2005-06 | Chester C | 1 | 0 | 1 | 0 |
| 2006-07 | Crewe Alex | 0 | 0 | 6 | 0 |
| 2007-08 | Accrington S | 34 | 0 | 34 | 0 |

From Northwich Vic.

| | | | | | |
|---|---|---|---|---|---|
| 2010-11 | Stevenage | 42 | 6 | | |
| 2011-12 | Stevenage | 46 | 6 | | |
| 2012-13 | Stevenage | 44 | 2 | 132 | 14 |

**SHROOT, Robin (M)**    70 10
H: 5 9   W: 11 05   b.Hammersmith 26-3-88
*Source:* Staines T, AFC Wimbledon, Harrow Borough. *Honours:* Northern Ireland Under-21.

| | | | | | |
|---|---|---|---|---|---|
| 2008-09 | Birmingham C | 0 | 0 | | |
| 2008-09 | Walsall | 5 | 0 | 5 | 0 |
| 2009-10 | Birmingham C | 0 | 0 | | |
| 2009-10 | Burton Alb | 7 | 0 | 7 | 0 |
| 2010-11 | Birmingham C | 0 | 0 | | |
| 2010-11 | Cheltenham T | 7 | 1 | 7 | 1 |
| 2011-12 | Stevenage | 25 | 3 | | |
| 2012-13 | Stevenage | 26 | 6 | 51 | 9 |

**SINCLAIR, Robert (M)**    37 2
H: 5 10   W: 11 02   b.Bedford 29-8-89
*Source:* Scholar.

| | | | | | |
|---|---|---|---|---|---|
| 2007-08 | Luton T | 0 | 0 | | |

From Salisbury C.

| | | | | | |
|---|---|---|---|---|---|
| 2010-11 | Stevenage | 27 | 2 | | |
| 2011-12 | Stevenage | 0 | 0 | | |
| 2011-12 | Aldershot T | 4 | 0 | | |
| 2012-13 | Stevenage | 0 | 0 | 27 | 2 |
| 2012-13 | Aldershot T | 6 | 0 | 10 | 0 |

**TANSEY, Greg (M)**    171 23
H: 6 1   W: 12 03   b.Huyton 21-11-88
*Source:* Scholar.

| | | | | | |
|---|---|---|---|---|---|
| 2006-07 | Stockport Co | 3 | 0 | | |
| 2007-08 | Stockport Co | 13 | 0 | | |
| 2008-09 | Stockport Co | 12 | 1 | | |
| 2009-10 | Stockport Co | 32 | 2 | | |
| 2010-11 | Stockport Co | 38 | 10 | 98 | 13 |
| 2011-12 | Inverness CT | 36 | 4 | 36 | 4 |
| 2012-13 | Stevenage | 37 | 6 | 37 | 6 |

**THALASSITIS, Michael (F)**    5 0
H: 6 1   W: 13 00   b.Enfield 19-1-93
*Source:* Youth.

| | | | | | |
|---|---|---|---|---|---|
| 2011-12 | Stevenage | 3 | 0 | | |
| 2012-13 | Stevenage | 2 | 0 | 5 | 0 |

**Scholars**
Allen, George Edward; Carey-Morrell, James Mark; Cathline, Alex Raymond Kwamena; Dhillon, Jhai Singh; Dujon, Brandon Rianan; Gordon, Rohdell Antonio; Hartley, Jimmy; Horlock, Charles Leonard; Joseph, Harold Michael Oluwatimilehin; McCall, Spencer Kennedy; N'Guessan, Joseph David Ruhemann; Okenabirhie, Fejiri Shaun China; Parsons, Jesse Christopher; Perry, Louis George; Pitharas, Christopher Lefteris; Towner, Ryan Alfie; Udoh, Dominic Daniel.

# STOKE C (77)

**ADAM, Charlie (M)**    244 55
H: 6 1   W: 12 00   b.Dundee 10-12-85
*Honours:* Scotland Under-21, B, 23 full caps.

| | | | | | |
|---|---|---|---|---|---|
| 2004-05 | Rangers | 1 | 0 | | |
| 2004-05 | Ross Co | 10 | 2 | 10 | 2 |
| 2005-06 | Rangers | 1 | 0 | | |
| 2005-06 | St Mirren | 29 | 5 | 29 | 5 |
| 2006-07 | Rangers | 32 | 11 | | |
| 2007-08 | Rangers | 16 | 2 | | |
| 2008-09 | Rangers | 9 | 0 | 59 | 13 |
| 2008-09 | Blackpool | 13 | 2 | | |
| 2009-10 | Blackpool | 43 | 16 | | |
| 2010-11 | Blackpool | 35 | 12 | 91 | 30 |
| 2011-12 | Liverpool | 28 | 2 | | |
| 2012-13 | Liverpool | 0 | 0 | 28 | 2 |
| 2012-13 | Stoke C | 27 | 3 | 27 | 3 |

**ALABI, James (F)**    9 1

| | | | | | |
|---|---|---|---|---|---|
| 2012-13 | Stoke C | 0 | 0 | | |
| 2012-13 | Scunthorpe U | 9 | 1 | 9 | 1 |

**BACHMANN, Daniel (G)**    0 0
b.Vienna 9-7-94
*Source:* Scholar.

| | | | | | |
|---|---|---|---|---|---|
| 2011-12 | Stoke C | 0 | 0 | | |
| 2012-13 | Stoke C | 0 | 0 | | |

**BEGOVIC, Asmir (G)**    137 0
H: 6 5   W: 13 01   b.Trebinje 20-6-87
*Source:* La Louviere. *Honours:* Canada Under-20, Bosnia 20 full caps.

| | | | | | |
|---|---|---|---|---|---|
| 2006-07 | Portsmouth | 0 | 0 | | |
| 2006-07 | Macclesfield T | 3 | 0 | 3 | 0 |
| 2007-08 | Portsmouth | 0 | 0 | | |
| 2007-08 | Bournemouth | 8 | 0 | 8 | 0 |
| 2007-08 | Yeovil T | 2 | 0 | | |
| 2008-09 | Portsmouth | 2 | 0 | | |
| 2008-09 | Yeovil T | 14 | 0 | 16 | 0 |
| 2009-10 | Portsmouth | 9 | 0 | 11 | 0 |
| 2009-10 | Ipswich T | 6 | 0 | 6 | 0 |
| 2009-10 | Stoke C | 4 | 0 | | |
| 2010-11 | Stoke C | 28 | 0 | | |
| 2011-12 | Stoke C | 23 | 0 | | |
| 2012-13 | Stoke C | 38 | 0 | 93 | 0 |

**BUTLAND, Jack (G)**    70 0
H: 6 4   W: 12 00   b.Clevedon 10-3-93
*Source:* Scholar. *Honours:* England Youth, Under-20, Under-21, 1 full cap.

| | | | | | |
|---|---|---|---|---|---|
| 2009-10 | Birmingham C | 0 | 0 | | |
| 2010-11 | Birmingham C | 0 | 0 | | |
| 2011-12 | Birmingham C | 0 | 0 | | |
| 2011-12 | Cheltenham T | 24 | 0 | 24 | 0 |
| 2012-13 | Birmingham C | 46 | 0 | 46 | 0 |
| 2012-13 | Stoke C | 0 | 0 | | |

**CAMERON, Geoff (D)**    159 11
H: 6 3   W: 13 02   b.Attleboro 11-7-85
*Honours:* USA 18 full caps, 1 goal.

| | | | | | |
|---|---|---|---|---|---|
| 2008 | Houston D | 24 | 1 | | |
| 2009 | Houston D | 32 | 2 | | |
| 2010 | Houston D | 16 | 3 | | |
| 2011 | Houston D | 37 | 5 | | |
| 2012 | Houston D | 15 | 0 | 124 | 11 |
| 2012-13 | Stoke C | 35 | 0 | 35 | 0 |

**CROUCH, Peter (F)**    420 112
H: 6 7   W: 13 03   b.Macclesfield 30-1-81
*Source:* Trainee. *Honours:* England Youth, Under-20, Under-21, B, 42 full caps, 22 goals.

| | | | | | |
|---|---|---|---|---|---|
| 1998-99 | Tottenham H | 0 | 0 | | |
| 1999-2000 | Tottenham H | 0 | 0 | | |
| 2000-01 | QPR | 42 | 10 | 42 | 10 |
| 2001-02 | Portsmouth | 37 | 18 | | |
| 2001-02 | Aston Villa | 7 | 2 | | |
| 2002-03 | Aston Villa | 14 | 0 | | |
| 2003-04 | Aston Villa | 16 | 4 | 37 | 6 |
| 2003-04 | Norwich C | 15 | 4 | 15 | 4 |
| 2004-05 | Southampton | 27 | 12 | 27 | 12 |
| 2005-06 | Liverpool | 32 | 8 | | |
| 2006-07 | Liverpool | 32 | 9 | | |
| 2007-08 | Liverpool | 21 | 5 | 85 | 22 |
| 2008-09 | Portsmouth | 38 | 11 | | |
| 2009-10 | Portsmouth | 0 | 0 | 75 | 29 |
| 2009-10 | Tottenham H | 38 | 8 | | |
| 2010-11 | Tottenham H | 34 | 4 | | |
| 2011-12 | Tottenham H | 1 | 0 | 73 | 12 |
| 2011-12 | Stoke C | 32 | 10 | | |
| 2012-13 | Stoke C | 34 | 7 | 66 | 17 |

**CUVELIER, Florent (M)**    38 6
H: 6 0   W: 11 05   b.Brussels 12-9-92
*Source:* Scholar. *Honours:* Belgium Youth.

| | | | | | |
|---|---|---|---|---|---|
| 2009-10 | Portsmouth | 0 | 0 | | |
| 2010-11 | Stoke C | 0 | 0 | | |
| 2011-12 | Stoke C | 0 | 0 | | |
| 2011-12 | Walsall | 18 | 4 | | |
| 2012-13 | Stoke C | 0 | 0 | | |
| 2012-13 | Walsall | 19 | 2 | 37 | 6 |
| 2012-13 | Peterborough U | 1 | 0 | 1 | 0 |

**DELAP, Rory (M)**    498 32
H: 6 3   W: 13 00   b.Sutton Coldfield 6-7-76
*Source:* Trainee. *Honours:* Eire Under-21, B, 11 full caps.

| | | | | | |
|---|---|---|---|---|---|
| 1992-93 | Carlisle U | 1 | 0 | | |
| 1993-94 | Carlisle U | 1 | 0 | | |
| 1994-95 | Carlisle U | 3 | 0 | | |
| 1995-96 | Carlisle U | 19 | 3 | | |
| 1996-97 | Carlisle U | 32 | 4 | | |
| 1997-98 | Carlisle U | 9 | 0 | 65 | 7 |
| 1997-98 | Derby Co | 13 | 0 | | |
| 1998-99 | Derby Co | 23 | 0 | | |
| 1999-2000 | Derby Co | 34 | 8 | | |
| 2000-01 | Derby Co | 33 | 3 | 103 | 11 |
| 2001-02 | Southampton | 28 | 2 | | |
| 2002-03 | Southampton | 24 | 0 | | |
| 2003-04 | Southampton | 27 | 1 | | |
| 2004-05 | Southampton | 37 | 2 | | |
| 2005-06 | Southampton | 16 | 0 | 132 | 5 |
| 2005-06 | Sunderland | 6 | 1 | | |

| | | | | |
|---|---|---|---|---|
| 2006-07 | Sunderland | 6 | 0 | 12 1 |
| 2006-07 | Stoke C | 2 | 0 | |
| 2007-08 | Stoke C | 44 | 2 | |
| 2008-09 | Stoke C | 34 | 2 | |
| 2009-10 | Stoke C | 36 | 0 | |
| 2010-11 | Stoke C | 37 | 2 | |
| 2011-12 | Stoke C | 26 | 2 | |
| 2012-13 | Stoke C | 1 | 0 | 180 8 |
| 2012-13 | Barnsley | 6 | 0 | 6 0 |

**EDU, Maurice (M)**    146 15
H: 6 0  W: 12 00  b.Fontana, California 18-4-86
*Honours:* USA 45 full caps, 1 goal.

| | | | | |
|---|---|---|---|---|
| 2007 | Toronto FC | 25 | 4 | |
| 2008 | Toronto FC | 13 | 2 | 38 6 |
| 2008-09 | Rangers | 12 | 2 | |
| 2009-10 | Rangers | 15 | 2 | |
| 2010-11 | Rangers | 33 | 2 | |
| 2011-12 | Rangers | 36 | 3 | 96 9 |
| 2012-13 | Stoke C | 1 | 0 | 1 0 |
| 2012-13 | Bursaspor | 11 | 0 | 11 0 |

**ETHERINGTON, Matthew (M)**    415 37
H: 5 10  W: 10 12  b.Truro 14-8-81
*Source:* School. *Honours:* England Youth, Under-21.

| | | | | |
|---|---|---|---|---|
| 1996-97 | Peterborough U | 1 | 0 | |
| 1997-98 | Peterborough U | 2 | 0 | |
| 1998-99 | Peterborough U | 29 | 3 | |
| 1999-2000 | Peterborough U | 19 | 3 | 51 6 |
| 1999-2000 | Tottenham H | 5 | 0 | |
| 2000-01 | Tottenham H | 6 | 0 | |
| 2001-02 | *Bradford C* | 13 | 1 | 13 1 |
| 2001-02 | Tottenham H | 11 | 0 | |
| 2002-03 | Tottenham H | 23 | 1 | 45 1 |
| 2003-04 | West Ham U | 35 | 5 | |
| 2004-05 | West Ham U | 39 | 4 | |
| 2005-06 | West Ham U | 33 | 2 | |
| 2006-07 | West Ham U | 27 | 0 | |
| 2007-08 | West Ham U | 18 | 3 | |
| 2008-09 | West Ham U | 13 | 2 | 165 16 |
| 2008-09 | Stoke C | 14 | 0 | |
| 2009-10 | Stoke C | 34 | 5 | |
| 2010-11 | Stoke C | 32 | 5 | |
| 2011-12 | Stoke C | 30 | 3 | |
| 2012-13 | Stoke C | 31 | 0 | 141 13 |

**HUTH, Robert (D)**    231 15
H: 6 3  W: 14 07  b.Berlin 18-8-84
*Source:* Scholar. *Honours:* Germany Youth, Under-21, 19 full caps, 2 goals.

| | | | | |
|---|---|---|---|---|
| 2001-02 | Chelsea | 1 | 0 | |
| 2002-03 | Chelsea | 2 | 0 | |
| 2003-04 | Chelsea | 16 | 0 | |
| 2004-05 | Chelsea | 10 | 0 | |
| 2005-06 | Chelsea | 13 | 0 | 42 0 |
| 2006-07 | Middlesbrough | 12 | 1 | |
| 2007-08 | Middlesbrough | 13 | 1 | |
| 2008-09 | Middlesbrough | 24 | 0 | |
| 2009-10 | Middlesbrough | 4 | 0 | 53 2 |
| 2009-10 | Stoke C | 32 | 3 | |
| 2010-11 | Stoke C | 35 | 6 | |
| 2011-12 | Stoke C | 34 | 3 | |
| 2012-13 | Stoke C | 35 | 1 | 136 13 |

**JEROME, Cameron (F)**    303 68
H: 6 1  W: 13 06  b.Huddersfield 14-8-86
*Honours:* England Under-21.

| | | | | |
|---|---|---|---|---|
| 2004-05 | Cardiff C | 29 | 6 | |
| 2005-06 | Cardiff C | 44 | 18 | 73 24 |
| 2005-06 | Birmingham C | 0 | 0 | |
| 2006-07 | Birmingham C | 38 | 7 | |
| 2007-08 | Birmingham C | 33 | 7 | |
| 2008-09 | Birmingham C | 43 | 9 | |
| 2009-10 | Birmingham C | 32 | 11 | |
| 2010-11 | Birmingham C | 34 | 3 | |
| 2011-12 | Birmingham C | 1 | 0 | 181 37 |
| 2011-12 | Stoke C | 23 | 4 | |
| 2012-13 | Stoke C | 26 | 3 | 49 7 |

**JONES, Kenwyne (F)**    266 68
H: 6 2  W: 13 06  b.Trinidad & Tobago 5-10-84
*Source:* W Connection. *Honours:* Trindad & Tobago Youth, Under-23, 51 full caps, 7 goals.

| | | | | |
|---|---|---|---|---|
| 2004-05 | Southampton | 2 | 0 | |
| 2004-05 | *Sheffield W* | 7 | 7 | 7 7 |
| 2004-05 | *Stoke C* | 13 | 3 | |
| 2005-06 | Southampton | 34 | 4 | |
| 2006-07 | Southampton | 34 | 14 | |
| 2007-08 | Southampton | 1 | 1 | 71 19 |
| 2007-08 | Sunderland | 33 | 7 | |
| 2008-09 | Sunderland | 29 | 10 | |
| 2009-10 | Sunderland | 32 | 9 | 94 26 |
| 2010-11 | Stoke C | 34 | 9 | |
| 2011-12 | Stoke C | 21 | 1 | |
| 2012-13 | Stoke C | 26 | 3 | 94 16 |

**KIGHTLY, Michael (F)**    161 29
H: 5 10  W: 10 10  b.Basildon 24-1-86
*Source:* Scholar. *Honours:* England Under-21.

| | | | | |
|---|---|---|---|---|
| 2002-03 | Southend U | 1 | 0 | |
| 2003-04 | Southend U | 11 | 0 | |
| 2004-05 | Southend U | 1 | 0 | 13 0 |

From Grays Ath.

| | | | | |
|---|---|---|---|---|
| 2006-07 | Wolverhampton W | 24 | 8 | |
| 2007-08 | Wolverhampton W | 21 | 4 | |
| 2008-09 | Wolverhampton W | 38 | 8 | |
| 2009-10 | Wolverhampton W | 9 | 0 | |
| 2010-11 | Wolverhampton W | 4 | 0 | |
| 2011-12 | Wolverhampton W | 18 | 3 | |
| 2011-12 | *Watford* | 12 | 3 | 12 3 |
| 2012-13 | Wolverhampton W | 0 | 0 | 114 23 |
| 2012-13 | Stoke C | 22 | 3 | 22 3 |

**NASH, Carlo (G)**    243 0
H: 6 5  W: 14 01  b.Bolton 13-9-73
*Source:* Clitheroe.

| | | | | |
|---|---|---|---|---|
| 1996-97 | Crystal Palace | 21 | 0 | |
| 1997-98 | Crystal Palace | 0 | 0 | 21 0 |
| 1998-99 | Stockport Co | 43 | 0 | |
| 1999-2000 | Stockport Co | 38 | 0 | |
| 2000-01 | Stockport Co | 8 | 0 | 89 0 |
| 2000-01 | Manchester C | 6 | 0 | |
| 2001-02 | Manchester C | 23 | 0 | |
| 2002-03 | Manchester C | 9 | 0 | 38 0 |
| 2003-04 | Middlesbrough | 1 | 0 | |
| 2004-05 | Middlesbrough | 2 | 0 | 3 0 |
| 2004-05 | Preston NE | 7 | 0 | |
| 2005-06 | Preston NE | 46 | 0 | |
| 2006-07 | Preston NE | 29 | 0 | 82 0 |
| 2007-08 | Wigan Ath | 0 | 0 | |
| 2007-08 | *Stoke C* | 10 | 0 | |
| 2008-09 | Wigan Ath | 0 | 0 | |
| 2008-09 | Everton | 0 | 0 | |
| 2009-10 | Everton | 0 | 0 | |
| 2010-11 | Stoke C | 0 | 0 | |
| 2011-12 | Stoke C | 0 | 0 | |
| 2012-13 | Stoke C | 0 | 0 | 10 0 |

**NESS, Jamie (M)**    16 1
H: 6 2  W: 10 13  b.Irvine 2-3-91
*Honours:* Scotland Youth, Under-21.

| | | | | |
|---|---|---|---|---|
| 2010-11 | Rangers | 11 | 0 | |
| 2011-12 | Rangers | 5 | 1 | 16 1 |
| 2012-13 | Stoke C | 0 | 0 | |

**NZONZI, Steven (M)**    158 7
H: 6 3  W: 11 11  b.Paris 15-12-88
*Honours:* France Under-21.

| | | | | |
|---|---|---|---|---|
| 2007-08 | Amiens | 3 | 0 | |
| 2008-09 | Amiens | 34 | 1 | 37 1 |
| 2009-10 | Blackburn R | 33 | 2 | |
| 2010-11 | Blackburn R | 21 | 1 | |
| 2011-12 | Blackburn R | 32 | 2 | 86 5 |
| 2012-13 | Stoke C | 35 | 1 | 35 1 |

**OWEN, Michael (F)**    362 163
H: 5 8  W: 10 12  b.Chester 14-12-79
*Source:* Trainee. *Honours:* England Schools, Youth, Under-21, B, 89 full caps, 40 goals.

| | | | | |
|---|---|---|---|---|
| 1996-97 | Liverpool | 2 | 1 | |
| 1997-98 | Liverpool | 36 | 18 | |
| 1998-99 | Liverpool | 30 | 18 | |
| 1999-2000 | Liverpool | 27 | 11 | |
| 2000-01 | Liverpool | 28 | 16 | |
| 2001-02 | Liverpool | 29 | 19 | |
| 2002-03 | Liverpool | 35 | 19 | |
| 2003-04 | Liverpool | 29 | 16 | 216 118 |
| 2004-05 | Real Madrid | 36 | 13 | 36 13 |
| 2005-06 | Newcastle U | 11 | 7 | |
| 2006-07 | Newcastle U | 3 | 0 | |
| 2007-08 | Newcastle U | 29 | 11 | |
| 2008-09 | Newcastle U | 28 | 8 | |
| 2009-10 | Newcastle U | 0 | 0 | 71 26 |
| 2009-10 | Manchester U | 19 | 3 | |
| 2010-11 | Manchester U | 11 | 2 | |
| 2011-12 | Manchester U | 1 | 0 | 31 5 |
| 2012-13 | Stoke C | 8 | 1 | 8 1 |

**PALACIOS, Wilson (D)**    131 1
H: 5 10  W: 11 11  b.La Ceiba 29-7-84
*Source:* Olimpia. *Honours:* Honduras 84 full caps, 5 goals.

| | | | | |
|---|---|---|---|---|
| 2007-08 | Birmingham C | 7 | 0 | 7 0 |
| 2007-08 | Wigan Ath | 16 | 0 | |
| 2008-09 | Wigan Ath | 21 | 0 | 37 0 |
| 2008-09 | Tottenham H | 11 | 0 | |
| 2009-10 | Tottenham H | 33 | 1 | |
| 2010-11 | Tottenham H | 21 | 0 | |
| 2011-12 | Tottenham H | 0 | 0 | 65 1 |
| 2011-12 | Stoke C | 18 | 0 | |
| 2012-13 | Stoke C | 4 | 0 | 22 0 |

**PENNANT, Jermaine (M)**    284 15
H: 5 9  W: 10 06  b.Nottingham 15-1-83
*Honours:* England Schools, Youth, Under-21.

| | | | | |
|---|---|---|---|---|
| 1998-99 | Notts Co | 0 | 0 | |
| 1998-99 | Arsenal | 0 | 0 | |
| 1999-2000 | Arsenal | 0 | 0 | |
| 2000-01 | Arsenal | 0 | 0 | |
| 2001-02 | Arsenal | 0 | 0 | |
| 2001-02 | *Watford* | 9 | 2 | |
| 2002-03 | Arsenal | 5 | 3 | |
| 2002-03 | *Watford* | 12 | 0 | 21 2 |
| 2003-04 | Arsenal | 0 | 0 | |
| 2003-04 | *Leeds U* | 36 | 2 | 36 2 |
| 2004-05 | Arsenal | 7 | 0 | 12 3 |
| 2004-05 | Birmingham C | 12 | 0 | |
| 2005-06 | Birmingham C | 38 | 2 | 50 2 |
| 2006-07 | Liverpool | 34 | 1 | |
| 2007-08 | Liverpool | 18 | 2 | |
| 2008-09 | Liverpool | 3 | 0 | 55 3 |
| 2008-09 | *Portsmouth* | 13 | 0 | 13 0 |
| 2009-10 | Zaragoza | 25 | 0 | 25 0 |
| 2010-11 | Stoke C | 29 | 3 | |
| 2011-12 | Stoke C | 27 | 0 | |
| 2012-13 | Stoke C | 1 | 0 | 57 3 |
| 2012-13 | *Wolverhampton W* | 15 | 0 | 15 0 |

**ROSSI, Karim (F)**    0 0
b.Zurich 1-5-94
*Source:* Scholar.

| | | | | |
|---|---|---|---|---|
| 2011-12 | Stoke C | 0 | 0 | |
| 2012-13 | Stoke C | 0 | 0 | |

**SHAWCROSS, Ryan (D)**    208 16
H: 6 3  W: 13 13  b.Buckley 4-10-87
*Source:* Scholar. *Honours:* England Under-21, 1 full cap.

| | | | | |
|---|---|---|---|---|
| 2006-07 | Manchester U | 0 | 0 | |
| 2007-08 | Manchester U | 0 | 0 | |
| 2007-08 | Stoke C | 41 | 7 | |
| 2008-09 | Stoke C | 30 | 3 | |
| 2009-10 | Stoke C | 28 | 2 | |
| 2010-11 | Stoke C | 36 | 1 | |
| 2011-12 | Stoke C | 36 | 2 | |
| 2012-13 | Stoke C | 37 | 1 | 208 16 |

**SHEA, Brek (M)**    105 19
H: 6 3  W: 12 11  b.College Station, Texas 28-2-90
*Honours:* USA Youth, Under-20, Under-23, 17 full caps.

| | | | | |
|---|---|---|---|---|
| 2008 | FC Dallas | 2 | 0 | |
| 2009 | FC Dallas | 19 | 0 | |
| 2010 | FC Dallas | 29 | 5 | |
| 2011 | FC Dallas | 32 | 11 | |
| 2012 | FC Dallas | 21 | 3 | 103 19 |
| 2012-13 | Stoke C | 2 | 0 | 2 0 |

**SHOTTON, Ryan (D)**    111 6
H: 6 3  W: 13 05  b.Stoke 30-9-88
*Source:* Scholar.

| | | | | |
|---|---|---|---|---|
| 2006-07 | Stoke C | 0 | 0 | |
| 2007-08 | Stoke C | 0 | 0 | |
| 2008-09 | Stoke C | 0 | 0 | |
| 2008-09 | *Tranmere R* | 33 | 5 | 33 5 |
| 2009-10 | Stoke C | 0 | 0 | |
| 2009-10 | *Barnsley* | 30 | 0 | 30 0 |
| 2010-11 | Stoke C | 2 | 0 | |
| 2011-12 | Stoke C | 23 | 1 | |
| 2012-13 | Stoke C | 23 | 0 | 48 1 |

**SORENSEN, Thomas (G)**    405   0
H: 6 4   W: 13 10   b.Fredericia 12-6-76
*Source:* Odense. *Honours:* Denmark Youth, Under-21, B, 101 full caps.

|  |  | | | | |
|---|---|---|---|---|---|
| 1998-99 | Sunderland | 45 | 0 | | |
| 1999-2000 | Sunderland | 37 | 0 | | |
| 2000-01 | Sunderland | 34 | 0 | | |
| 2001-02 | Sunderland | 34 | 0 | | |
| 2002-03 | Sunderland | 21 | 0 | 171 | 0 |
| 2003-04 | Aston Villa | 38 | 0 | | |
| 2004-05 | Aston Villa | 36 | 0 | | |
| 2005-06 | Aston Villa | 36 | 0 | | |
| 2006-07 | Aston Villa | 29 | 0 | | |
| 2007-08 | Aston Villa | 0 | 0 | 139 | 0 |
| 2008-09 | Stoke C | 36 | 0 | | |
| 2009-10 | Stoke C | 33 | 0 | | |
| 2010-11 | Stoke C | 10 | 0 | | |
| 2011-12 | Stoke C | 16 | 0 | | |
| 2012-13 | Stoke C | 0 | 0 | 95 | 0 |

**UPSON, Matthew (D)**    334   12
H: 6 1   W: 11 04   b.Eye 18-4-79
*Source:* Trainee. *Honours:* England Youth, Under-21, 21 full caps, 2 goals.

|  |  | | | | |
|---|---|---|---|---|---|
| 1995-96 | Luton T | 0 | 0 | | |
| 1996-97 | Luton T | 1 | 0 | 1 | 0 |
| 1996-97 | Arsenal | 0 | 0 | | |
| 1997-98 | Arsenal | 5 | 0 | | |
| 1998-99 | Arsenal | 5 | 0 | | |
| 1999-2000 | Arsenal | 8 | 0 | | |
| 2000-01 | Arsenal | 2 | 0 | | |
| 2000-01 | *Nottingham F* | 1 | 0 | 1 | 0 |
| 2000-01 | *Crystal Palace* | 7 | 0 | 7 | 0 |
| 2001-02 | Arsenal | 14 | 0 | | |
| 2002-03 | Arsenal | 0 | 0 | 34 | 0 |
| 2002-03 | *Reading* | 14 | 0 | 14 | 0 |
| 2002-03 | Birmingham C | 14 | 0 | | |
| 2003-04 | Birmingham C | 30 | 0 | | |
| 2004-05 | Birmingham C | 36 | 2 | | |
| 2005-06 | Birmingham C | 24 | 1 | | |
| 2006-07 | Birmingham C | 9 | 2 | 113 | 5 |
| 2006-07 | West Ham U | 2 | 0 | | |
| 2007-08 | West Ham U | 29 | 1 | | |
| 2008-09 | West Ham U | 37 | 0 | | |
| 2009-10 | West Ham U | 33 | 3 | | |
| 2010-11 | West Ham U | 30 | 0 | 131 | 4 |
| 2011-12 | Stoke C | 14 | 1 | | |
| 2012-13 | Stoke C | 1 | 1 | 15 | 2 |
| 2012-13 | *Brighton & HA* | 18 | 1 | 18 | 1 |

**WALTERS, Jon (F)**    375   72
H: 6 0   W: 12 06   b.Birkenhead 20-9-83
*Source:* Blackburn R Scholar. *Honours:* Eire Youth, Under-21, B, 19 full caps, 4 goals.

|  |  | | | | |
|---|---|---|---|---|---|
| 2001-02 | Bolton W | 0 | 0 | | |
| 2002-03 | Bolton W | 4 | 0 | | |
| 2002-03 | *Hull C* | 11 | 5 | | |
| 2003-04 | Bolton W | 0 | 0 | 4 | 0 |
| 2003-04 | Crewe Alex | 0 | 0 | | |
| 2003-04 | *Barnsley* | 8 | 0 | 8 | 0 |
| 2003-04 | Hull C | 16 | 1 | | |
| 2004-05 | Hull C | 21 | 1 | 48 | 7 |
| 2004-05 | *Scunthorpe U* | 3 | 0 | 3 | 0 |
| 2005-06 | Wrexham | 38 | 5 | 38 | 5 |
| 2006-07 | Chester C | 26 | 9 | 26 | 9 |
| 2006-07 | Ipswich T | 16 | 4 | | |
| 2007-08 | Ipswich T | 40 | 13 | | |
| 2008-09 | Ipswich T | 36 | 5 | | |
| 2009-10 | Ipswich T | 43 | 8 | | |
| 2010-11 | Ipswich T | 1 | 0 | 136 | 30 |
| 2010-11 | Stoke C | 36 | 6 | | |
| 2011-12 | Stoke C | 38 | 7 | | |
| 2012-13 | Stoke C | 38 | 8 | 112 | 21 |

**WHELAN, Glenn (M)**    319   17
H: 5 11   W: 12 07   b.Dublin 13-1-84
*Source:* Scholar. *Honours:* Eire Youth, Under-21, B, 49 full caps, 2 goals.

|  |  | | | | |
|---|---|---|---|---|---|
| 2000-01 | Manchester C | 0 | 0 | | |
| 2001-02 | Manchester C | 0 | 0 | | |
| 2002-03 | Manchester C | 0 | 0 | | |
| 2003-04 | Manchester C | 0 | 0 | | |
| 2003-04 | *Bury* | 13 | 0 | 13 | 0 |
| 2004-05 | Sheffield W | 36 | 2 | | |
| 2005-06 | Sheffield W | 43 | 1 | | |
| 2006-07 | Sheffield W | 38 | 7 | | |
| 2007-08 | Sheffield W | 25 | 2 | 142 | 12 |
| 2007-08 | Stoke C | 14 | 1 | | |

---

|  |  | | | | |
|---|---|---|---|---|---|
| 2008-09 | Stoke C | 26 | 1 | | |
| 2009-10 | Stoke C | 33 | 2 | | |
| 2010-11 | Stoke C | 29 | 0 | | |
| 2011-12 | Stoke C | 30 | 1 | | |
| 2012-13 | Stoke C | 32 | 0 | 164 | 5 |

**WHITEHEAD, Dean (M)**    439   25
H: 5 11   W: 12 06   b.Abingdon 12-1-82
*Source:* Trainee.

|  |  | | | | |
|---|---|---|---|---|---|
| 1999-2000 | Oxford U | 0 | 0 | | |
| 2000-01 | Oxford U | 20 | 0 | | |
| 2001-02 | Oxford U | 40 | 1 | | |
| 2002-03 | Oxford U | 18 | 1 | | |
| 2003-04 | Oxford U | 44 | 7 | 122 | 9 |
| 2004-05 | Sunderland | 42 | 5 | | |
| 2005-06 | Sunderland | 37 | 3 | | |
| 2006-07 | Sunderland | 45 | 4 | | |
| 2007-08 | Sunderland | 27 | 1 | | |
| 2008-09 | Sunderland | 34 | 0 | | |
| 2009-10 | Sunderland | 0 | 0 | 185 | 13 |
| 2009-10 | Stoke C | 36 | 0 | | |
| 2010-11 | Stoke C | 37 | 2 | | |
| 2011-12 | Stoke C | 33 | 0 | | |
| 2012-13 | Stoke C | 26 | 1 | 132 | 3 |

**WILKINSON, Andy (D)**    171   0
H: 5 11   W: 11 00   b.Stone 6-8-84
*Source:* Scholar.

|  |  | | | | |
|---|---|---|---|---|---|
| 2001-02 | Stoke C | 0 | 0 | | |
| 2002-03 | Stoke C | 0 | 0 | | |
| 2003-04 | Stoke C | 3 | 0 | | |
| 2004-05 | Stoke C | 1 | 0 | | |
| 2004-05 | *Shrewsbury T* | 9 | 0 | 9 | 0 |
| 2005-06 | Stoke C | 6 | 0 | | |
| 2006-07 | Stoke C | 4 | 0 | | |
| 2006-07 | *Blackpool* | 7 | 0 | 7 | 0 |
| 2007-08 | Stoke C | 23 | 0 | | |
| 2008-09 | Stoke C | 22 | 0 | | |
| 2009-10 | Stoke C | 25 | 0 | | |
| 2010-11 | Stoke C | 22 | 0 | | |
| 2011-12 | Stoke C | 25 | 0 | | |
| 2012-13 | Stoke C | 24 | 0 | 155 | 0 |

**WILSON, Marc (M)**    149   4
H: 6 2   W: 12 07   b.Lisburn 17-8-87
*Source:* Scholar. *Honours:* Eire Under-21, 7 full caps, 1 goal.

|  |  | | | | |
|---|---|---|---|---|---|
| 2005-06 | Portsmouth | 0 | 0 | | |
| 2005-06 | *Yeovil T* | 2 | 0 | 2 | 0 |
| 2006-07 | Portsmouth | 0 | 0 | | |
| 2006-07 | *Bournemouth* | 19 | 3 | | |
| 2007-08 | Portsmouth | 0 | 0 | | |
| 2007-08 | *Bournemouth* | 7 | 0 | 26 | 3 |
| 2007-08 | *Luton T* | 4 | 0 | 4 | 0 |
| 2008-09 | Portsmouth | 3 | 0 | | |
| 2009-10 | Portsmouth | 28 | 0 | | |
| 2010-11 | Portsmouth | 4 | 0 | 35 | 0 |
| 2010-11 | Stoke C | 28 | 1 | | |
| 2011-12 | Stoke C | 35 | 0 | | |
| 2012-13 | Stoke C | 19 | 0 | 82 | 1 |

**Players retained or with offer of contract**
Brunt, Ryan Samuel; Campbell, James Andrew; Dawson, Lucas Jay; Eve, Dale Donald; Glasgow, Benjamin Luke; Heneghan, Benjamin John; Keane, Jordan Michael; Nardiello, Jack Barrie; O'Reilly, Ryan; Rana-Jerome, Cameron Zishan; Richardson, Jordan; Scott, Kristian Adrian; Thomas, Adam Christopher; Westley, Samuel Edward.

**Scholars**
Barrington, Marcel; Cook, Jake Benjamin; Coulson, Samuel Philip; Hulme, Joseph Andrew; Lecygne, Eddy; Makrillos, Peter; Monlouis, Keiran Dion; Richards, Derice; Ricketts-Hopkinson, Nathan Alton; Sanders, Edward James; Shields, Ryan Joseph; Strong, Curtis; Taylor, Joel; Ward, Charlie.

# SUNDERLAND (78)

**BARDSLEY, Phillip (D)**    196   6
H: 5 11   W: 11 13   b.Salford 28-6-85
*Source:* Trainee. *Honours:* Scotland 12 full caps.

|  |  | | | | |
|---|---|---|---|---|---|
| 2003-04 | Manchester U | 1 | 0 | | |
| 2004-05 | Manchester U | 0 | 0 | | |
| 2005-06 | Manchester U | 8 | 0 | | |

---

|  |  | | | | |
|---|---|---|---|---|---|
| 2005-06 | *Burnley* | 6 | 0 | 6 | 0 |
| 2006-07 | Manchester U | 0 | 0 | | |
| 2006-07 | *Rangers* | 5 | 1 | 5 | 1 |
| 2006-07 | *Aston Villa* | 13 | 0 | 13 | 0 |
| 2007-08 | Manchester U | 0 | 0 | 8 | 0 |
| 2007-08 | *Sheffield U* | 16 | 0 | 16 | 0 |
| 2007-08 | Sunderland | 11 | 0 | | |
| 2008-09 | Sunderland | 28 | 0 | | |
| 2009-10 | Sunderland | 26 | 0 | | |
| 2010-11 | Sunderland | 34 | 3 | | |
| 2011-12 | Sunderland | 31 | 1 | | |
| 2012-13 | Sunderland | 18 | 1 | 148 | 5 |

**BRAMBLE, Titus (D)**    298   10
H: 6 2   W: 13 10   b.Ipswich 31-7-81
*Source:* Trainee. *Honours:* England Under-21.

|  |  | | | | |
|---|---|---|---|---|---|
| 1998-99 | Ipswich T | 4 | 0 | | |
| 1999-2000 | Ipswich T | 0 | 0 | | |
| 1999-2000 | *Colchester U* | 2 | 0 | 2 | 0 |
| 2000-01 | Ipswich T | 26 | 1 | | |
| 2001-02 | Ipswich T | 18 | 0 | 48 | 1 |
| 2002-03 | Newcastle U | 16 | 0 | | |
| 2003-04 | Newcastle U | 29 | 0 | | |
| 2004-05 | Newcastle U | 19 | 1 | | |
| 2005-06 | Newcastle U | 24 | 2 | | |
| 2006-07 | Newcastle U | 17 | 0 | 105 | 3 |
| 2007-08 | Wigan Ath | 26 | 2 | | |
| 2008-09 | Wigan Ath | 35 | 1 | | |
| 2009-10 | Wigan Ath | 35 | 2 | 96 | 5 |
| 2010-11 | Sunderland | 23 | 0 | | |
| 2011-12 | Sunderland | 8 | 1 | | |
| 2012-13 | Sunderland | 16 | 0 | 47 | 1 |

**BROWN, Wes (D)**    252   4
H: 6 1   W: 13 08   b.Manchester 13-10-79
*Source:* Trainee. *Honours:* England Schools, Youth, Under-21, 23 full caps, 1 goal.

|  |  | | | | |
|---|---|---|---|---|---|
| 1996-97 | Manchester U | 0 | 0 | | |
| 1997-98 | Manchester U | 2 | 0 | | |
| 1998-99 | Manchester U | 14 | 0 | | |
| 1999-2000 | Manchester U | 0 | 0 | | |
| 2000-01 | Manchester U | 28 | 0 | | |
| 2001-02 | Manchester U | 17 | 0 | | |
| 2002-03 | Manchester U | 22 | 0 | | |
| 2003-04 | Manchester U | 17 | 0 | | |
| 2004-05 | Manchester U | 21 | 1 | | |
| 2005-06 | Manchester U | 19 | 0 | | |
| 2006-07 | Manchester U | 22 | 0 | | |
| 2007-08 | Manchester U | 36 | 1 | | |
| 2008-09 | Manchester U | 8 | 1 | | |
| 2009-10 | Manchester U | 19 | 0 | | |
| 2010-11 | Manchester U | 7 | 0 | 232 | 3 |
| 2011-12 | Sunderland | 20 | 1 | | |
| 2012-13 | Sunderland | 0 | 0 | 20 | 1 |

**CATTERMOLE, Lee (M)**    180   4
H: 5 10   W: 11 13   b.Stockton 21-3-88
*Source:* Scholar. *Honours:* England Youth, Under-21.

|  |  | | | | |
|---|---|---|---|---|---|
| 2005-06 | Middlesbrough | 14 | 1 | | |
| 2006-07 | Middlesbrough | 31 | 1 | | |
| 2007-08 | Middlesbrough | 24 | 1 | 69 | 3 |
| 2008-09 | Wigan Ath | 33 | 1 | | |
| 2009-10 | Wigan Ath | 0 | 0 | 33 | 1 |
| 2009-10 | Sunderland | 22 | 0 | | |
| 2010-11 | Sunderland | 23 | 0 | | |
| 2011-12 | Sunderland | 23 | 0 | | |
| 2012-13 | Sunderland | 10 | 0 | 78 | 0 |

**COLBACK, Jack (M)**    132   5
H: 5 9   W: 11 05   b.Killingworth 24-10-89
*Source:* Scholar. *Honours:* England Youth.

|  |  | | | | |
|---|---|---|---|---|---|
| 2007-08 | Sunderland | 0 | 0 | | |
| 2008-09 | Sunderland | 0 | 0 | | |
| 2009-10 | Sunderland | 1 | 0 | | |
| 2009-10 | *Ipswich T* | 37 | 4 | | |
| 2010-11 | Sunderland | 11 | 0 | | |
| 2010-11 | *Ipswich T* | 13 | 0 | 50 | 4 |
| 2011-12 | Sunderland | 35 | 1 | | |
| 2012-13 | Sunderland | 35 | 0 | 82 | 1 |

**CUELLAR, Carlos (D)**    316   13
H: 6 3   W: 13 03   b.Madrid 23-8-81
*Source:* Trainee.

|  |  | | | | |
|---|---|---|---|---|---|
| 2000-01 | Calahorra | 27 | 0 | 27 | 0 |
| 2001-02 | Numancia | 23 | 1 | | |
| 2002-03 | Numancia | 39 | 3 | 62 | 4 |
| 2003-04 | Osasuna | 5 | 0 | | |
| 2004-05 | Osasuna | 14 | 0 | | |

| | | | | |
|---|---|---|---|---|
| 2005-06 | Osasuna | 29 | 1 | |
| 2006-07 | Osasuna | 23 | 1 | **71 2** |
| 2007-08 | Rangers | 36 | 4 | **36 4** |
| 2008-09 | Aston Villa | 28 | 0 | |
| 2009-10 | Aston Villa | 36 | 2 | |
| 2010-11 | Aston Villa | 12 | 0 | |
| 2011-12 | Aston Villa | 18 | 0 | **94 2** |
| 2012-13 | Sunderland | 26 | 1 | **26 1** |

**EGAN, John (D)**    **6 0**
H: 6 1 W: 11 11 b.Cork 20-10-92
*Source:* Scholar. *Honours:* Eire Youth, Under-21.

| | | | | |
|---|---|---|---|---|
| 2009-10 | Sunderland | 0 | 0 | |
| 2010-11 | Sunderland | 0 | 0 | |
| 2011-12 | Sunderland | 0 | 0 | |
| 2011-12 | *Crystal Palace* | 1 | 0 | **1 0** |
| 2011-12 | *Sheffield U* | 1 | 0 | **1 0** |
| 2012-13 | Sunderland | 0 | 0 | |
| 2012-13 | *Bradford C* | 4 | 0 | **4 0** |

**ELMOHAMADY, Ahmed (M)**    **172 18**
H: 5 11 W: 12 10 b.El Mahalla El-Kubra 9-9-87
*Honours:* Egypt 64 full caps, 2 goals.

| | | | | |
|---|---|---|---|---|
| 2003-04 | Ghazi Al-Mehalla | 0 | 0 | |
| 2004-05 | Ghazi Al-Mehalla | 14 | 4 | |
| 2005-06 | Ghazi Al-Mehalla | 3 | 0 | **17 4** |
| 2006-07 | ENPPI | 12 | 2 | |
| 2007-08 | ENPPI | 6 | 1 | |
| 2008-09 | ENPPI | 28 | 6 | |
| 2009-10 | ENPPI | 12 | 1 | **58 10** |
| 2010-11 | Sunderland | 36 | 0 | |
| 2011-12 | Sunderland | 18 | 1 | |
| 2012-13 | Sunderland | 0 | 0 | **56 1** |
| 2012-13 | *Hull C* | 41 | 3 | **41 3** |

**FERGUSON, David (D)**    **0 0**
b.Sunderland 7-6-94

| | | | | |
|---|---|---|---|---|
| 2012-13 | Sunderland | 0 | 0 | |

**FLETCHER, Steven (F)**    **280 84**
H: 6 1 W: 12 00 b.Shrewsbury 26-3-87
*Honours:* Scotland Under-20, Under-21, B, 12 full caps, 1 goal.

| | | | | |
|---|---|---|---|---|
| 2003-04 | Hibernian | 5 | 0 | |
| 2004-05 | Hibernian | 20 | 5 | |
| 2005-06 | Hibernian | 34 | 8 | |
| 2006-07 | Hibernian | 31 | 6 | |
| 2007-08 | Hibernian | 32 | 13 | |
| 2008-09 | Hibernian | 34 | 11 | **156 43** |
| 2009-10 | Burnley | 35 | 8 | **35 8** |
| 2010-11 | Wolverhampton W | 29 | 10 | |
| 2011-12 | Wolverhampton W | 32 | 12 | |
| 2012-13 | Wolverhampton W | 0 | 0 | **61 22** |
| 2012-13 | Sunderland | 28 | 11 | **28 11** |

**GARDNER, Craig (M)**    **164 23**
H: 5 10 W: 11 13 b.Solihull 25-11-86
*Source:* Scholar. *Honours:* England Under-21.

| | | | | |
|---|---|---|---|---|
| 2004-05 | Aston Villa | 0 | 0 | |
| 2005-06 | Aston Villa | 8 | 0 | |
| 2006-07 | Aston Villa | 13 | 2 | |
| 2007-08 | Aston Villa | 23 | 3 | |
| 2008-09 | Aston Villa | 14 | 0 | |
| 2009-10 | Aston Villa | 1 | 0 | **59 5** |
| 2009-10 | Birmingham C | 13 | 1 | |
| 2010-11 | Birmingham C | 29 | 8 | **42 9** |
| 2011-12 | Sunderland | 30 | 3 | |
| 2012-13 | Sunderland | 33 | 6 | **63 9** |

**GORRIN, Alejandro (M)**    **0 0**
b.Tenerife 1-8-93
*Source:* Scholar.

| | | | | |
|---|---|---|---|---|
| 2011-12 | Sunderland | 0 | 0 | |
| 2012-13 | Sunderland | 0 | 0 | |

**GRAHAM, Danny (F)**    **303 92**
H: 5 11 W: 12 05 b.Gateshead 12-8-85
*Source:* Trainee. *Honours:* England Youth, Under-20.

| | | | | |
|---|---|---|---|---|
| 2003-04 | Middlesbrough | 0 | 0 | |
| 2003-04 | *Darlington* | 9 | 2 | **9 2** |
| 2004-05 | Middlesbrough | 11 | 1 | |
| 2005-06 | Middlesbrough | 3 | 0 | |
| 2005-06 | *Derby Co* | 14 | 0 | **14 0** |
| 2005-06 | *Leeds U* | 3 | 0 | **3 0** |
| 2006-07 | Middlesbrough | 1 | 0 | **15 1** |
| 2006-07 | *Blackpool* | 4 | 1 | **4 1** |
| 2006-07 | *Carlisle U* | 11 | 7 | |

| | | | | |
|---|---|---|---|---|
| 2007-08 | Carlisle U | 45 | 14 | |
| 2008-09 | Carlisle U | 44 | 15 | **100 36** |
| 2009-10 | Watford | 46 | 14 | |
| 2010-11 | Watford | 45 | 23 | **91 37** |
| 2011-12 | Swansea C | 36 | 12 | |
| 2012-13 | Swansea C | 18 | 3 | **54 15** |
| 2012-13 | Sunderland | 13 | 0 | **13 0** |

**HARRISON, Scott (D)**    **0 0**
b.Middlesbrough 3-9-93

| | | | | |
|---|---|---|---|---|
| 2012-13 | Sunderland | 0 | 0 | |

**JI, Dong-Won (F)**    **69 17**
H: 6 2 W: 12 04 b.Jeju 28-5-91
*Honours:* South Korea Under-23, 21 full caps, 8 goals.

| | | | | |
|---|---|---|---|---|
| 2010 | Chunnam D | 22 | 7 | |
| 2011 | Chunnam D | 11 | 3 | **33 10** |
| 2011-12 | Sunderland | 19 | 2 | |
| 2012-13 | Sunderland | 0 | 0 | **19 2** |
| 2012-13 | *Augsburg* | 17 | 5 | **17 5** |

**JOHNSON, Adam (M)**    **221 34**
H: 5 8 W: 10 00 b.Sunderland 14-7-87
*Source:* Scholar. *Honours:* England Youth, Under-21, 12 full caps, 2 goals.

| | | | | |
|---|---|---|---|---|
| 2004-05 | Middlesbrough | 0 | 0 | |
| 2005-06 | Middlesbrough | 13 | 1 | |
| 2006-07 | Middlesbrough | 12 | 0 | |
| 2006-07 | *Leeds U* | 5 | 0 | **5 0** |
| 2007-08 | Middlesbrough | 19 | 1 | |
| 2007-08 | *Watford* | 12 | 5 | **12 5** |
| 2008-09 | Middlesbrough | 26 | 0 | |
| 2009-10 | Middlesbrough | 26 | 11 | **96 13** |
| 2009-10 | Manchester C | 16 | 1 | |
| 2010-11 | Manchester C | 31 | 4 | |
| 2011-12 | Manchester C | 26 | 6 | |
| 2012-13 | Manchester C | 0 | 0 | **73 11** |
| 2012-13 | Sunderland | 35 | 5 | **35 5** |

**KILGALLON, Matthew (D)**    **227 7**
H: 6 1 W: 12 10 b.York 8-1-84
*Source:* Scholar. *Honours:* England Youth, Under-20, Under-21.

| | | | | |
|---|---|---|---|---|
| 2000-01 | Leeds U | 0 | 0 | |
| 2001-02 | Leeds U | 0 | 0 | |
| 2002-03 | Leeds U | 2 | 0 | |
| 2003-04 | Leeds U | 8 | 2 | |
| 2003-04 | *West Ham U* | 3 | 0 | **3 0** |
| 2004-05 | Leeds U | 26 | 0 | |
| 2005-06 | Leeds U | 25 | 1 | |
| 2006-07 | Leeds U | 19 | 0 | **80 3** |
| 2006-07 | Sheffield U | 6 | 0 | |
| 2007-08 | Sheffield U | 40 | 2 | |
| 2008-09 | Sheffield U | 40 | 1 | |
| 2009-10 | Sheffield U | 21 | 1 | **107 4** |
| 2009-10 | Sunderland | 7 | 0 | |
| 2010-11 | Sunderland | 0 | 0 | |
| 2010-11 | *Middlesbrough* | 2 | 0 | **2 0** |
| 2010-11 | *Doncaster R* | 12 | 0 | **12 0** |
| 2011-12 | Sunderland | 10 | 0 | |
| 2012-13 | Sunderland | 6 | 0 | **23 0** |

**KNOTT, Billy (M)**    **21 3**
H: 5 8 W: 11 02 b.Canvey Island 28-11-92
*Source:* Scholar. *Honours:* England Under-20.

| | | | | |
|---|---|---|---|---|
| 2010-11 | Sunderland | 0 | 0 | |
| 2011-12 | Sunderland | 0 | 0 | |
| 2011-12 | *AFC Wimbledon* | 20 | 3 | **20 3** |
| 2012-13 | Sunderland | 1 | 0 | **1 0** |

**LAIDLER, Jordan (F)**    **0 0**
H: 5 10 W: 11 12 b.North Shields 13-10-93

| | | | | |
|---|---|---|---|---|
| 2012-13 | Sunderland | 0 | 0 | |

**LAING, Louis (D)**    **12 0**
H: 5 11 W: 12 00 b.Newcastle 6-3-93
*Source:* Scholar. *Honours:* England Youth.

| | | | | |
|---|---|---|---|---|
| 2009-10 | Sunderland | 0 | 0 | |
| 2010-11 | Sunderland | 1 | 0 | |
| 2011-12 | Sunderland | 0 | 0 | |
| 2011-12 | *Wycombe W* | 11 | 0 | **11 0** |
| 2012-13 | Sunderland | 0 | 0 | **1 0** |

**LARSSON, Sebastian (M)**    **257 27**
H: 5 11 W: 11 02 b.Eskilstuna 6-6-85
*Source:* Trainee. *Honours:* Sweden Under-21, 54 full caps, 6 goals.

| | | | | |
|---|---|---|---|---|
| 2002-03 | Arsenal | 0 | 0 | |
| 2003-04 | Arsenal | 0 | 0 | |

| | | | | |
|---|---|---|---|---|
| 2004-05 | Arsenal | 0 | 0 | |
| 2005-06 | Arsenal | 3 | 0 | |
| 2006-07 | Arsenal | 0 | 0 | **3 0** |
| 2006-07 | Birmingham C | 43 | 4 | |
| 2007-08 | Birmingham C | 35 | 6 | |
| 2008-09 | Birmingham C | 38 | 1 | |
| 2009-10 | Birmingham C | 33 | 4 | |
| 2010-11 | Birmingham C | 35 | 4 | **184 19** |
| 2011-12 | Sunderland | 32 | 7 | |
| 2012-13 | Sunderland | 38 | 1 | **70 8** |

**LYNCH, Craig (F)**    **8 1**
H: 5 9 W: 10 01 b.Chester-le-Street 25-3-92
*Source:* Scholar.

| | | | | |
|---|---|---|---|---|
| 2010-11 | Sunderland | 2 | 0 | |
| 2011-12 | Sunderland | 0 | 0 | |
| 2012-13 | Sunderland | 0 | 0 | **2 0** |
| 2012-13 | *Hartlepool U* | 6 | 1 | **6 1** |

**MANDRON, Mikael (F)**    **0 0**
H: 6 3 W: 12 13 b.Boulogne 11-10-94
*Source:* Scholar.

| | | | | |
|---|---|---|---|---|
| 2011-12 | Sunderland | 0 | 0 | |
| 2012-13 | Sunderland | 2 | 0 | **2 0** |

**MANGANE, Kader (M)**    **227 23**
H: 6 3 W: 12 07 b.Dakar 23-3-83
*Honours:* Senegal 23 full caps, 1 goal.

| | | | | |
|---|---|---|---|---|
| 2001-02 | Neuchatel Xamax | 1 | 1 | |
| 2003-04 | Neuchatel Xamax | 25 | 1 | |
| 2004-05 | Neuchatel Xamax | 28 | 1 | |
| 2005-06 | Neuchatel Xamax | 26 | 3 | **80 6** |
| 2007-08 | Young Boys | 7 | 1 | **7 1** |
| 2007-08 | Lens | 22 | 5 | |
| 2008-09 | Lens | 1 | 0 | **23 5** |
| 2008-09 | Rennes | 25 | 0 | |
| 2009-10 | Rennes | 34 | 4 | |
| 2010-11 | Rennes | 29 | 3 | |
| 2011-12 | Rennes | 13 | 2 | **101 9** |
| 2012-13 | Al Hilal | 14 | 2 | **14 2** |

On loan from Al Hilal

| | | | | |
|---|---|---|---|---|
| 2012-13 | Sunderland | 2 | 0 | **2 0** |

**MARRS, Liam (D)**    **0 0**
H: 5 9 W: 11 05 b.North Shields 26-11-92
*Source:* Scholar.

| | | | | |
|---|---|---|---|---|
| 2011-12 | Sunderland | 0 | 0 | |
| 2012-13 | Sunderland | 0 | 0 | |

**McCLEAN, James (M)**    **132 25**
H: 5 11 W: 11 00 b.Derry 22-4-89
*Honours:* Northern Ireland Under-21, Eire 13 full caps.

| | | | | |
|---|---|---|---|---|
| 2009 | Derry C | 27 | 1 | |
| 2010 | Derry C | 30 | 10 | |
| 2011 | Derry C | 16 | 7 | **73 18** |
| 2011-12 | Sunderland | 23 | 5 | |
| 2012-13 | Sunderland | 36 | 2 | **59 7** |

**McFADDEN, James (F)**    **277 55**
H: 6 0 W: 12 11 b.Glasgow 14-4-83
*Honours:* Scotland Under-21, B, 48 full caps, 15 goals.

| | | | | |
|---|---|---|---|---|
| 2000-01 | Motherwell | 6 | 0 | |
| 2001-02 | Motherwell | 24 | 10 | |
| 2002-03 | Motherwell | 30 | 13 | |
| 2003-04 | Motherwell | 3 | 3 | |
| 2003-04 | Everton | 23 | 0 | |
| 2004-05 | Everton | 23 | 1 | |
| 2005-06 | Everton | 32 | 6 | |
| 2006-07 | Everton | 19 | 2 | |
| 2007-08 | Everton | 12 | 2 | |
| 2007-08 | Birmingham C | 12 | 4 | |
| 2008-09 | Birmingham C | 30 | 4 | |
| 2009-10 | Birmingham C | 36 | 5 | |
| 2010-11 | Birmingham C | 4 | 0 | **82 13** |
| 2011-12 | Everton | 7 | 0 | |
| 2012-13 | Everton | 0 | 0 | **116 11** |
| 2012-13 | Sunderland | 3 | 0 | **3 0** |
| 2012-13 | Motherwell | 13 | 5 | **76 31** |

**MIGNOLET, Simon (G)**    **212 1**
H: 6 4 W: 13 10 b.St Truiden 6-3-88
*Honours:* Belgium Under-21, 11 full caps.

| | | | | |
|---|---|---|---|---|
| 2006-07 | St Truiden | 2 | 0 | |
| 2007-08 | St Truiden | 25 | 0 | |
| 2008-09 | St Truiden | 35 | 1 | |
| 2009-10 | St Truiden | 37 | 0 | |
| 2010-11 | St Truiden | 23 | 0 | **122 1** |
| 2010-11 | Sunderland | 23 | 0 | |

|  |  | | | | |
|---|---|--|--|--|--|
| 2011-12 | Sunderland | 29 | 0 | | |
| 2012-13 | Sunderland | 38 | 0 | 90 | 0 |

**MITCHELL, Adam (M)**    1   0
b.Barnard Castle 3-4-93
Source: Scholar.

| 2011-12 | Sunderland | 0 | 0 | | |
|---|---|--|--|--|--|
| 2012-13 | Sunderland | 1 | 0 | 1 | 0 |

**N'DIAYE, Alfred (M)**    121   4
H: 6 2   W: 13 08   b.Paris 6-3-90

| 2008-09 | AS Nancy | 24 | 0 | | |
|---|---|--|--|--|--|
| 2009-10 | AS Nancy | 23 | 0 | | |
| 2010-11 | AS Nancy | 13 | 0 | 60 | 0 |
| 2011-12 | Bursaspor | 32 | 3 | | |
| 2012-13 | Bursaspor | 13 | 1 | 45 | 4 |
| 2012-13 | Sunderland | 16 | 0 | 16 | 0 |

**NOBLE, Ryan (F)**    27   3
H: 6 0   W: 11 00   b.Sunderland 6-11-91
Source: Scholar. Honours: England Youth.

| 2009-10 | Sunderland | 0 | 0 | | |
|---|---|--|--|--|--|
| 2009-10 | Watford | 0 | 0 | | |
| 2010-11 | Sunderland | 3 | 0 | | |
| 2010-11 | Derby Co | 1 | 0 | | |
| 2011-12 | Sunderland | 2 | 0 | | |
| 2011-12 | Derby Co | 2 | 0 | 3 | 0 |
| 2011-12 | Hartlepool U | 9 | 2 | | |
| 2012-13 | Sunderland | 0 | 0 | 5 | 0 |
| 2012-13 | Hartlepool U | 10 | 1 | 19 | 3 |

**O'SHEA, John (D)**    329   13
H: 6 3   W: 13 07   b.Waterford 30-4-81
Source: Waterford. Honours: Eire Youth, Under-21, 89 full caps, 1 goal.

| 1998-99 | Manchester U | 0 | 0 | | |
|---|---|--|--|--|--|
| 1999-2000 | Manchester U | 0 | 0 | | |
| 1999-2000 | Bournemouth | 10 | 1 | 10 | 1 |
| 2000-01 | Manchester U | 0 | 0 | | |
| 2001-02 | Manchester U | 9 | 0 | | |
| 2002-03 | Manchester U | 32 | 0 | | |
| 2003-04 | Manchester U | 33 | 2 | | |
| 2004-05 | Manchester U | 23 | 2 | | |
| 2005-06 | Manchester U | 34 | 1 | | |
| 2006-07 | Manchester U | 32 | 4 | | |
| 2007-08 | Manchester U | 28 | 0 | | |
| 2008-09 | Manchester U | 30 | 0 | | |
| 2009-10 | Manchester U | 15 | 1 | | |
| 2010-11 | Manchester U | 20 | 0 | 256 | 10 |
| 2011-12 | Sunderland | 29 | 0 | | |
| 2012-13 | Sunderland | 34 | 2 | 63 | 2 |

**PICKFORD, Jordan (G)**    0   0
b.Washington 7-3-94
Source: Scholar. Honours: England Youth.

| 2010-11 | Sunderland | 0 | 0 | | |
|---|---|--|--|--|--|
| 2011-12 | Sunderland | 0 | 0 | | |
| 2012-13 | Sunderland | 0 | 0 | | |

**REED, Adam (M)**    42   2
H: 5 5   W: 10 03   b.Hartlepool 8-5-91
Source: Scholar.

| 2009-10 | Sunderland | 0 | 0 | | |
|---|---|--|--|--|--|
| 2010-11 | Sunderland | 0 | 0 | | |
| 2010-11 | Brentford | 11 | 0 | 11 | 0 |
| 2011-12 | Sunderland | 0 | 0 | | |
| 2011-12 | Bradford C | 4 | 0 | 4 | 0 |
| 2011-12 | Leyton Orient | 11 | 0 | 11 | 0 |
| 2012-13 | Sunderland | 0 | 0 | | |
| 2012-13 | Portsmouth | 10 | 0 | 10 | 0 |
| 2012-13 | York C | 6 | 2 | 6 | 2 |

**SAHA, Louis (F)**    379   117
H: 6 1   W: 12 08   b.Paris 8-8-78
Honours: France Youth, Under-21, 20 full caps, 4 goals.

| 1997-98 | Metz | 21 | 1 | | |
|---|---|--|--|--|--|
| 1998-99 | Metz | 3 | 0 | | |
| 1998-99 | Newcastle U | 11 | 1 | 11 | 1 |
| 1999-2000 | Metz | 23 | 4 | 47 | 5 |
| 2000-01 | Fulham | 43 | 27 | | |
| 2001-02 | Fulham | 36 | 8 | | |
| 2002-03 | Fulham | 17 | 5 | | |
| 2003-04 | Fulham | 21 | 13 | 117 | 53 |
| 2003-04 | Manchester U | 12 | 7 | | |
| 2004-05 | Manchester U | 14 | 1 | | |
| 2005-06 | Manchester U | 19 | 7 | | |
| 2006-07 | Manchester U | 24 | 8 | | |
| 2007-08 | Manchester U | 17 | 5 | | |
| 2008-09 | Manchester U | 0 | 0 | 86 | 28 |

| 2008-09 | Everton | 24 | 6 | | |
|---|---|--|--|--|--|
| 2009-10 | Everton | 33 | 13 | | |
| 2010-11 | Everton | 22 | 7 | | |
| 2011-12 | Everton | 18 | 1 | 97 | 27 |
| 2011-12 | Tottenham H | 10 | 3 | | |
| 2012-13 | Tottenham H | 0 | 0 | 10 | 3 |
| 2012-13 | Sunderland | 11 | 0 | 11 | 0 |

Transferred to Lazio January 2013

**SESSEGNON, Stephane (M)**    293   41
H: 5 8   W: 11 05   b.Allahe 1-6-84
Honours: Benin 48 full caps, 9 goals.

| 2003-04 | Requins | 2 | 0 | 2 | 0 |
|---|---|--|--|--|--|
| 2004-05 | Creteil | 35 | 5 | | |
| 2005-06 | Creteil | 33 | 5 | 68 | 10 |
| 2006-07 | Le Mans | 31 | 5 | | |
| 2007-08 | Le Mans | 30 | 5 | 61 | 6 |
| 2008-09 | Paris St Germain | 34 | 5 | | |
| 2009-10 | Paris St Germain | 29 | 3 | | |
| 2010-11 | Paris St Germain | 14 | 0 | 77 | 8 |
| 2010-11 | Sunderland | 14 | 3 | | |
| 2011-12 | Sunderland | 36 | 7 | | |
| 2012-13 | Sunderland | 35 | 7 | 85 | 17 |

**VAUGHAN, David (M)**    347   26
H: 5 7   W: 11 00   b.Abergele 18-2-83
Source: Scholar. Honours: Wales Youth, Under-21, 33 full caps, 1 goal.

| 2000-01 | Crewe Alex | 1 | 0 | | |
|---|---|--|--|--|--|
| 2001-02 | Crewe Alex | 13 | 0 | | |
| 2002-03 | Crewe Alex | 32 | 3 | | |
| 2003-04 | Crewe Alex | 31 | 0 | | |
| 2004-05 | Crewe Alex | 44 | 6 | | |
| 2005-06 | Crewe Alex | 34 | 5 | | |
| 2006-07 | Crewe Alex | 29 | 4 | | |
| 2007-08 | Crewe Alex | 1 | 0 | 185 | 18 |
| 2007-08 | Real Sociedad | 7 | 1 | 7 | 1 |
| 2008-09 | Blackpool | 33 | 1 | | |
| 2009-10 | Blackpool | 41 | 1 | | |
| 2010-11 | Blackpool | 35 | 2 | 109 | 4 |
| 2011-12 | Sunderland | 22 | 2 | | |
| 2012-13 | Sunderland | 24 | 1 | 46 | 3 |

**WATSON, Jordan (M)**    0   0
b.Cyprus 7-4-93
Honours: Northern Ireland Youth.

| 2009-10 | Sunderland | 0 | 0 | | |
|---|---|--|--|--|--|
| 2010-11 | Sunderland | 0 | 0 | | |
| 2011-12 | Sunderland | 0 | 0 | | |
| 2012-13 | Sunderland | 0 | 0 | | |

**WESTWOOD, Keiren (G)**    267   0
H: 6 1   W: 13 10   b.Manchester 23-10-84
Source: Scholar. Honours: Eire 15 full caps.

| 2001-02 | Manchester C | 0 | 0 | | |
|---|---|--|--|--|--|
| 2002-03 | Manchester C | 0 | 0 | | |
| 2003-04 | Manchester C | 0 | 0 | | |
| 2003-04 | Oldham Ath | 0 | 0 | | |
| 2004-05 | Manchester C | 0 | 0 | | |
| 2005-06 | Manchester C | 0 | 0 | | |
| 2005-06 | Carlisle U | 35 | 0 | | |
| 2006-07 | Carlisle U | 46 | 0 | | |
| 2007-08 | Carlisle U | 46 | 0 | 127 | 0 |
| 2008-09 | Coventry C | 46 | 0 | | |
| 2009-10 | Coventry C | 44 | 0 | | |
| 2010-11 | Coventry C | 41 | 0 | 131 | 0 |
| 2011-12 | Sunderland | 9 | 0 | | |
| 2012-13 | Sunderland | 0 | 0 | 9 | 0 |

**WICKHAM, Connor (F)**    99   15
H: 6 0   W: 14 01   b.Hereford 31-3-93
Source: School. Honours: England Youth, Under-21.

| 2008-09 | Ipswich T | 2 | 0 | | |
|---|---|--|--|--|--|
| 2009-10 | Ipswich T | 26 | 4 | | |
| 2010-11 | Ipswich T | 37 | 9 | 65 | 13 |
| 2011-12 | Sunderland | 16 | 1 | | |
| 2012-13 | Sunderland | 12 | 0 | 28 | 1 |
| 2012-13 | Sheffield W | 6 | 1 | 6 | 1 |

**Players retained or with offer of contract**
Oliver, Connor; Smith, Martin.

**Scholars**
Agnew, Liam John; Beadling, Thomas; Burke, Peter; Cartwright, Andrew; Dixon, Joel Stephen; Gooch, Lynden Jack; Holland, Ross Kieran; Honeyman, George Christopher; Lawson, Carl; McCarthy, Steven Brian; McNamee, Thomas Gerard; Robson, Thomas; Stinson, James Michael; Stryjek, Maksymilian; Sukar, Jassem Mohamed.

# SWANSEA C (79)

**AGUSTIEN, Kemy (M)**    195   8
H: 5 10   W: 11 05   b.Tilburg 20-8-86
Honours: Holland Under-21.

| 2004-05 | Willem II | 21 | 1 | | |
|---|---|--|--|--|--|
| 2005-06 | Willem II | 34 | 2 | 55 | 3 |
| 2006-07 | Roda JC | 31 | 2 | 31 | 2 |
| 2007-08 | AZ | 25 | 2 | 25 | 2 |
| 2008-09 | Birmingham C | 18 | 0 | 18 | 0 |
| 2009-10 | RKC Waalwijk | 19 | 1 | 19 | 1 |
| 2010-11 | Swansea C | 8 | 0 | | |
| 2010-11 | Crystal Palace | 8 | 0 | 8 | 0 |
| 2011-12 | Swansea C | 13 | 0 | | |
| 2012-13 | Swansea C | 18 | 0 | 39 | 0 |

**ALFEI, Daniel (D)**    1   0
H: 5 11   W: 12 02   b.Swansea 23-2-92
Source: Scholar. Honours: Wales Youth, Under-21.

| 2010-11 | Swansea C | 1 | 0 | | |
|---|---|--|--|--|--|
| 2011-12 | Swansea C | 0 | 0 | | |
| 2012-13 | Swansea C | 0 | 0 | 1 | 0 |

**BARTLEY, Kyle (D)**    61   1
H: 5 11   W: 11 00   b.Stockport 22-5-91
Source: Scholar.

| 2008-09 | Arsenal | 0 | 0 | | |
|---|---|--|--|--|--|
| 2009-10 | Arsenal | 0 | 0 | | |
| 2009-10 | Sheffield U | 14 | 0 | | |
| 2010-11 | Arsenal | 0 | 0 | | |
| 2010-11 | Sheffield U | 21 | 0 | 35 | 0 |
| 2010-11 | Rangers | 5 | 1 | | |
| 2011-12 | Arsenal | 0 | 0 | | |
| 2011-12 | Rangers | 19 | 0 | 24 | 1 |
| 2012-13 | Arsenal | 0 | 0 | | |
| 2012-13 | Swansea C | 2 | 0 | 2 | 0 |

**BRITTON, Leon (M)**    405   11
H: 5 6   W: 10 00   b.Merton 16-9-82
Source: Trainee. Honours: England Youth.

| 1999-2000 | West Ham U | 0 | 0 | | |
|---|---|--|--|--|--|
| 2000-01 | West Ham U | 0 | 0 | | |
| 2001-02 | West Ham U | 0 | 0 | | |
| 2002-03 | West Ham U | 0 | 0 | | |
| 2002-03 | Swansea C | 25 | 0 | | |
| 2003-04 | Swansea C | 42 | 3 | | |
| 2004-05 | Swansea C | 30 | 1 | | |
| 2005-06 | Swansea C | 38 | 4 | | |
| 2006-07 | Swansea C | 41 | 2 | | |
| 2007-08 | Swansea C | 40 | 0 | | |
| 2008-09 | Swansea C | 43 | 0 | | |
| 2009-10 | Swansea C | 36 | 0 | | |
| 2010-11 | Sheffield U | 24 | 0 | 24 | 0 |
| 2010-11 | Swansea C | 17 | 1 | | |
| 2011-12 | Swansea C | 36 | 0 | | |
| 2012-13 | Swansea C | 33 | 0 | 381 | 11 |

**CHICO (D)**    123   1
H: 6 2   W: 11 10   b.Cadiz 6-3-87

| 2006-07 | Cadiz | 1 | 0 | 1 | 0 |
|---|---|--|--|--|--|
| 2008-09 | Almeria | 20 | 1 | | |
| 2009-10 | Almeria | 27 | 0 | 47 | 1 |
| 2010-11 | Genoa | 16 | 0 | 16 | 0 |
| 2011-12 | Mallorca | 33 | 0 | 33 | 0 |
| 2012-13 | Swansea C | 26 | 0 | 26 | 0 |

**CORNELL, David (G)**    25   0
H: 5 11   W: 11 07   b.Gorseinon 28-3-91
Source: Scholar. Honours: Wales Youth, Under-21.

| 2009-10 | Swansea C | 0 | 0 | | |
|---|---|--|--|--|--|
| 2010-11 | Swansea C | 0 | 0 | | |
| 2011-12 | Swansea C | 0 | 0 | | |
| 2011-12 | Hereford U | 25 | 0 | 25 | 0 |
| 2012-13 | Swansea C | 0 | 0 | | |

**DAVIES, Ben (D)**    37   1
H: 5 7   W: 12 00   b.Neath 24-4-93
Source: Scholar. Honours: Wales Youth, 5 full caps.

| 2011-12 | Swansea C | 0 | 0 | | |
|---|---|--|--|--|--|
| 2012-13 | Swansea C | 37 | 1 | 37 | 1 |

**DE GUZMAN, Jonathan (M)    199  33**
H: 5 8   W: 10 02   b.Toronto 13-9-87
Honours: Holland Under-21, 5 full caps.

|  |  | | | | |
|---|---|--:|--:|--:|--:|
| 2005-06 | Feyenoord | 29 | 4 | | |
| 2006-07 | Feyenoord | 32 | 7 | | |
| 2007-08 | Feyenoord | 33 | 8 | | |
| 2008-09 | Feyenoord | 2 | 0 | | |
| 2009-10 | Feyenoord | 13 | 3 | 109 | 22 |
| 2010-11 | Mallorca | 33 | 5 | | |
| 2011-12 | Mallorca | 1 | 1 | 34 | 6 |
| 2011-12 | Villarreal | 19 | 0 | 19 | 0 |
| 2012-13 | Swansea C | 37 | 5 | 37 | 5 |

**DONNELLY, Rory (F)    49  20**
H: 6 2   W: 12 10   b.Belfast 18-2-92

| 2010-11 | Cliftonville | 31 | 7 | | |
|---|---|--:|--:|--:|--:|
| 2011-12 | Cliftonville | 18 | 13 | 49 | 20 |
| 2011-12 | Swansea C | 0 | 0 | | |
| 2012-13 | Swansea C | 0 | 0 | | |

**DYER, Nathan (M)    242  18**
H: 5 5   W: 9 00   b.Trowbridge 29-11-87
Source: Scholar. Honours: England Youth.

| 2005-06 | Southampton | 17 | 0 | | |
|---|---|--:|--:|--:|--:|
| 2005-06 | Burnley | 5 | 2 | 5 | 2 |
| 2006-07 | Southampton | 18 | 0 | | |
| 2007-08 | Southampton | 17 | 1 | | |
| 2008-09 | Southampton | 4 | 0 | 56 | 1 |
| 2008-09 | Sheffield U | 7 | 1 | 7 | 1 |
| 2008-09 | Swansea C | 17 | 2 | | |
| 2009-10 | Swansea C | 40 | 2 | | |
| 2010-11 | Swansea C | 46 | 2 | | |
| 2011-12 | Swansea C | 34 | 5 | | |
| 2012-13 | Swansea C | 37 | 3 | 174 | 14 |

**EDWARDS, Gwion (M)    6  0**
H: 5 9   W: 12 00   b.Carmarthen 1-3-93
Source: Scholar. Honours: Wales Youth.

| 2011-12 | Swansea C | 0 | 0 | | |
|---|---|--:|--:|--:|--:|
| 2012-13 | Swansea C | 0 | 0 | | |
| 2012-13 | St Johnstone | 6 | 0 | 6 | 0 |

**GOWER, Mark (M)    360  40**
H: 5 11   W: 11 12   b.Edmonton 5-10-78
Source: Trainee. Honours: England Schools, Youth.

| 1996-97 | Tottenham H | 0 | 0 | | |
|---|---|--:|--:|--:|--:|
| 1997-98 | Tottenham H | 0 | 0 | | |
| 1998-99 | Tottenham H | 0 | 0 | | |
| 1998-99 | Motherwell | 9 | 1 | 9 | 1 |
| 1999-2000 | Tottenham H | 0 | 0 | | |
| 2000-01 | Barnet | 14 | 1 | | |
| 2001-02 | Barnet | 0 | 0 | | |
| 2002-03 | Barnet | 0 | 0 | 14 | 1 |
| 2003-04 | Southend U | 40 | 6 | | |
| 2004-05 | Southend U | 38 | 6 | | |
| 2005-06 | Southend U | 40 | 6 | | |
| 2006-07 | Southend U | 43 | 8 | | |
| 2007-08 | Southend U | 42 | 9 | 203 | 35 |
| 2008-09 | Swansea C | 36 | 0 | | |
| 2009-10 | Swansea C | 31 | 1 | | |
| 2010-11 | Swansea C | 40 | 2 | | |
| 2011-12 | Swansea C | 20 | 0 | | |
| 2012-13 | Swansea C | 1 | 0 | 128 | 3 |
| 2012-13 | Charlton Ath | 6 | 0 | 6 | 0 |

**HERNANDEZ, Pablo (M)    183  27**
H: 5 8   W: 10 00   b.Castellon 11-4-85
Honours: Spain 4 full caps, 1 goal.

| 2005-06 | Valencia | 1 | 0 | | |
|---|---|--:|--:|--:|--:|
| 2006-07 | Cadiz | 14 | 4 | 14 | 4 |
| 2007-08 | Getafe | 28 | 3 | 28 | 3 |
| 2008-09 | Valencia | 21 | 4 | | |
| 2009-10 | Valencia | 33 | 5 | | |
| 2010-11 | Valencia | 26 | 5 | | |
| 2011-12 | Valencia | 30 | 3 | 111 | 17 |
| 2012-13 | Swansea C | 30 | 3 | 30 | 3 |

**JONES, Henry (M)    0  0**
H: 6 0   W: 13 02   b.Swansea 18-9-93

| 2012-13 | Swansea C | 0 | 0 | | |
|---|---|--:|--:|--:|--:|

**KI, Sung-Yeung (M)    95  9**
H: 6 2   W: 11 10   b.Gwangju 24-1-89
Honours: South Korea Youth, Under-23, 51 full caps, 5 goals.

| 2009-10 | Celtic | 10 | 0 | | |
|---|---|--:|--:|--:|--:|
| 2010-11 | Celtic | 26 | 3 | | |
| 2011-12 | Celtic | 30 | 6 | 66 | 9 |
| 2012-13 | Swansea C | 29 | 0 | 29 | 0 |

**LAMAH, Roland (F)    179  24**
H: 5 11   W: 11 01   b.Leige 31-12-87
Honours: Belgium Youth, Under-21, 4 full caps.

| 2006-07 | Anderlecht | 5 | 0 | 5 | 0 |
|---|---|--:|--:|--:|--:|
| 2007-08 | Roda JC | 32 | 11 | 32 | 11 |
| 2008-09 | Le Mans | 32 | 3 | | |
| 2009-10 | Le Mans | 31 | 4 | | |
| 2010-11 | Le Mans | 25 | 3 | | |
| 2011-12 | Le Mans | 4 | 0 | 92 | 10 |
| 2011-12 | Osasuna | 30 | 1 | | |
| 2012-13 | Osasuna | 15 | 2 | 45 | 3 |

On loan from Osusana

| 2012-13 | Swansea C | 5 | 0 | 5 | 0 |
|---|---|--:|--:|--:|--:|

**LITA, Leroy (F)    313  92**
H: 5 7   W: 11 12   b.DR Congo 28-12-84
Source: Scholar. Honours: England Under-21.

| 2002-03 | Bristol C | 15 | 2 | | |
|---|---|--:|--:|--:|--:|
| 2003-04 | Bristol C | 26 | 5 | | |
| 2004-05 | Bristol C | 44 | 24 | 85 | 31 |
| 2005-06 | Reading | 26 | 11 | | |
| 2006-07 | Reading | 33 | 7 | | |
| 2007-08 | Reading | 14 | 1 | | |
| 2007-08 | Charlton Ath | 8 | 3 | 8 | 3 |
| 2008-09 | Reading | 10 | 1 | 83 | 20 |
| 2008-09 | Norwich C | 16 | 7 | 16 | 7 |
| 2009-10 | Middlesbrough | 40 | 8 | | |
| 2010-11 | Middlesbrough | 38 | 12 | 78 | 20 |
| 2011-12 | Swansea C | 16 | 2 | | |
| 2012-13 | Swansea C | 0 | 0 | 16 | 2 |
| 2012-13 | Birmingham C | 10 | 3 | 10 | 3 |
| 2012-13 | Sheffield W | 17 | 6 | 17 | 6 |

**LOVERIDGE, James (F)    0  0**
H: 6 2   W: 13 04   b.Swansea 16-5-94

| 2012-13 | Swansea C | 0 | 0 | | |
|---|---|--:|--:|--:|--:|

**LUCAS, Lee (M)    2  0**
H: 5 11   W: 11 08   b.Aberdare 10-6-92
Source: Scholar. Honours: Wales Youth, Under-21.

| 2010-11 | Swansea C | 1 | 0 | | |
|---|---|--:|--:|--:|--:|
| 2011-12 | Swansea C | 0 | 0 | | |
| 2011-12 | Burton Alb | 1 | 0 | 1 | 0 |
| 2012-13 | Swansea C | 0 | 0 | 1 | 0 |

**MARCH, Kurtis (M)    0  0**
H: 5 9   W: 11 03   b.Swansea 30-4-93
Source: Scholar. Honours: Wales Youth.

| 2011-12 | Swansea C | 0 | 0 | | |
|---|---|--:|--:|--:|--:|
| 2012-13 | Swansea C | 0 | 0 | | |

**MICHU, Miguel (M)    159  48**
H: 6 1   W: 12 07   b.Oviedo 21-3-86

| 2007-08 | Celta Vigo | 12 | 1 | | |
|---|---|--:|--:|--:|--:|
| 2008-09 | Celta Vigo | 18 | 1 | | |
| 2009-10 | Celta Vigo | 27 | 6 | | |
| 2010-11 | Celta Vigo | 30 | 7 | 87 | 15 |
| 2011-12 | Rayo Vallecano | 37 | 15 | 37 | 15 |
| 2012-13 | Swansea C | 35 | 18 | 35 | 18 |

**MONK, Garry (D)    281  3**
H: 6 0   W: 12 10   b.Bedford 6-3-79
Source: Trainee.

| 1995-96 | Torquay U | 5 | 0 | | |
|---|---|--:|--:|--:|--:|
| 1996-97 | Southampton | 0 | 0 | | |
| 1997-98 | Southampton | 0 | 0 | | |
| 1998-99 | Southampton | 4 | 0 | | |
| 1998-99 | Torquay U | 6 | 0 | 11 | 0 |
| 1999-2000 | Southampton | 2 | 0 | | |
| 1999-2000 | Stockport Co | 2 | 0 | 2 | 0 |
| 2000-01 | Southampton | 2 | 0 | | |
| 2000-01 | Oxford U | 5 | 0 | 5 | 0 |
| 2001-02 | Southampton | 2 | 0 | | |
| 2002-03 | Southampton | 1 | 0 | | |
| 2002-03 | Sheffield W | 15 | 0 | 15 | 0 |
| 2003-04 | Southampton | 0 | 0 | 11 | 0 |
| 2003-04 | Barnsley | 17 | 0 | 17 | 0 |
| 2004-05 | Swansea C | 34 | 0 | | |
| 2005-06 | Swansea C | 33 | 1 | | |
| 2006-07 | Swansea C | 2 | 0 | | |
| 2007-08 | Swansea C | 32 | 1 | | |
| 2008-09 | Swansea C | 40 | 1 | | |
| 2009-10 | Swansea C | 23 | 0 | | |
| 2010-11 | Swansea C | 29 | 0 | | |
| 2011-12 | Swansea C | 16 | 0 | | |
| 2012-13 | Swansea C | 11 | 0 | 220 | 3 |

**MOORE, Luke (F)    215  35**
H: 5 11   W: 11 13   b.Birmingham 13-2-86
Source: Trainee. Honours: FA Schools, England Youth, Under-21.

| 2002-03 | Aston Villa | 0 | 0 | | |
|---|---|--:|--:|--:|--:|
| 2003-04 | Aston Villa | 7 | 0 | | |
| 2003-04 | Wycombe W | 6 | 4 | 6 | 4 |
| 2004-05 | Aston Villa | 25 | 1 | | |
| 2005-06 | Aston Villa | 27 | 8 | | |
| 2006-07 | Aston Villa | 13 | 4 | | |
| 2007-08 | Aston Villa | 10 | 0 | 87 | 14 |
| 2007-08 | WBA | 10 | 0 | | |
| 2008-09 | WBA | 21 | 1 | | |
| 2009-10 | WBA | 26 | 4 | | |
| 2010-11 | WBA | 0 | 0 | 57 | 5 |
| 2010-11 | Derby Co | 13 | 4 | 13 | 4 |
| 2010-11 | Swansea C | 15 | 3 | | |
| 2011-12 | Swansea C | 20 | 2 | | |
| 2012-13 | Swansea C | 17 | 3 | 52 | 8 |

**OBENG, Curtis (D)    9  0**
H: 5 6   W: 10 05   b.Manchester 14-2-89
Honours: England Youth.

| 2007-08 | Manchester C | 0 | 0 | | |
|---|---|--:|--:|--:|--:|
| 2008-09 | Manchester C | 0 | 0 | | |

From Wrexham

| 2011-12 | Swansea C | 0 | 0 | | |
|---|---|--:|--:|--:|--:|
| 2012-13 | Swansea C | 0 | 0 | | |
| 2012-13 | Fleetwood T | 5 | 0 | 5 | 0 |
| 2012-13 | York C | 4 | 0 | 4 | 0 |

**RANGEL, Angel (D)    260  10**
H: 5 11   W: 11 09   b.Barcelona 28-10-82
Source: Tortosa, Reus Deportiu, Girona, Sant Andreu.

| 2006-07 | Terrassa | 34 | 2 | 34 | 2 |
|---|---|--:|--:|--:|--:|
| 2007-08 | Swansea C | 43 | 2 | | |
| 2008-09 | Swansea C | 40 | 1 | | |
| 2009-10 | Swansea C | 38 | 0 | | |
| 2010-11 | Swansea C | 38 | 2 | | |
| 2011-12 | Swansea C | 34 | 0 | | |
| 2012-13 | Swansea C | 33 | 3 | 226 | 8 |

**RICHARDS, Jazz (M)    40  0**
H: 6 1   W: 12 04   b.Swansea 12-4-91
Source: Scholar. Honours: Wales Under-21, 2 full caps.

| 2009-10 | Swansea C | 15 | 0 | | |
|---|---|--:|--:|--:|--:|
| 2010-11 | Swansea C | 6 | 0 | | |
| 2011-12 | Swansea C | 8 | 0 | | |
| 2012-13 | Swansea C | 0 | 0 | 29 | 0 |
| 2012-13 | Crystal Palace | 11 | 0 | 11 | 0 |

**ROUTLEDGE, Wayne (M)    325  29**
H: 5 6   W: 11 02   b.Sidcup 7-1-85
Source: Scholar. Honours: England Youth, Under-20, Under-21.

| 2001-02 | Crystal Palace | 2 | 0 | | |
|---|---|--:|--:|--:|--:|
| 2002-03 | Crystal Palace | 26 | 4 | | |
| 2003-04 | Crystal Palace | 44 | 6 | | |
| 2004-05 | Crystal Palace | 38 | 0 | 110 | 10 |
| 2005-06 | Tottenham H | 3 | 0 | | |
| 2005-06 | Portsmouth | 13 | 0 | 13 | 0 |
| 2006-07 | Tottenham H | 0 | 0 | | |
| 2006-07 | Fulham | 24 | 0 | 24 | 0 |
| 2007-08 | Tottenham H | 2 | 0 | 5 | 0 |
| 2007-08 | Aston Villa | 1 | 0 | | |
| 2008-09 | Aston Villa | 1 | 0 | 2 | 0 |
| 2008-09 | Cardiff C | 9 | 2 | 9 | 2 |
| 2008-09 | QPR | 19 | 1 | | |
| 2009-10 | QPR | 25 | 2 | | |
| 2009-10 | Newcastle U | 17 | 3 | | |
| 2010-11 | Newcastle U | 17 | 0 | 34 | 3 |
| 2010-11 | QPR | 20 | 5 | 64 | 8 |
| 2011-12 | Swansea C | 28 | 1 | | |
| 2012-13 | Swansea C | 36 | 5 | 64 | 6 |

**SHECHTER, Itay (F)    44  8**
H: 5 11   W: 12 00   b.Ramat Yishai 22-2-87
Honours: Israel Youth, Under-21, 18 full caps, 4 goals

| 2010-11 | Hapoel Tel-Aviv | 3 | 4 | 3 | 4 |
|---|---|--:|--:|--:|--:|
| 2011-12 | Kaiserslautern | 23 | 4 | 23 | 3 |

On loan from FC Kaiserslautern

| 2012-13 | Swansea C | 18 | 1 | 18 | 1 |
|---|---|--:|--:|--:|--:|

**SITU, Darnel (D)**                     0   0
H: 6 2   W: 12 02   b.Rouen 18-3-92
*Source:* Lens. *Honours:* France Youth.
2011-12   Swansea C        0   0
2012-13   Swansea C        0   0

**TANCOCK, Scott (D)**                   0   0
H: 6 1   W: 11 10   b.Swansea 29-12-92
*Honours:* Wales Under-21.
2012-13   Swansea C        0   0

**TATE, Alan (D)**                     300   5
H: 6 1   W: 13 05   b.Seaham 2-9-82
*Source:* Scholar.
2000-01   Manchester U     0   0
2001-02   Manchester U     0   0
2002-03   Manchester U     0   0
2002-03   *Swansea C*     27   0
2003-04   Manchester U     0   0
2003-04   Swansea C       26   1
2004-05   Swansea C       23   0
2005-06   Swansea C       43   0
2006-07   Swansea C       38   1
2007-08   Swansea C       21   1
2008-09   Swansea C       25   1
2009-10   Swansea C       39   1
2010-11   Swansea C       40   0
2011-12   Swansea C        5   0
2012-13   Swansea C        3   0   290   5
2012-13   *Leeds U*       10   0    10   0

**TAYLOR, Neil (D)**                    97   0
H: 5 9   W: 10 02   b.Ruthin 7-2-89
*Source:* Scholar. *Honours:* Wales Youth, Under-21, 10 full caps.
2007-08   Wrexham         26   0    26   0
2010-11   Swansea C       29   0
2011-12   Swansea C       36   0
2012-13   Swansea C        6   0    71   0

**TIENDALLI, Dwight (D)**              173   5
H: 5 9   W: 11 08   b.Surinam 21-10-85
*Honours:* Holland Under-21, 2 full caps.
2004-05   FC Utrecht      10   1
2005-06   FC Utrecht      29   2
2006-07   FC Utrecht       1   0    40   3
2006-07   Feyenoord       13   0
2007-08   *Sparta*        13   0    13   0
2008-09   Feyenoord       22   0    35   0
2009-10   FC Twente       26   1
2010-11   FC Twente       18   0
2011-12   FC Twente       27   0    71   1
2012-13   Swansea C       14   1    14   1

**TREMMEL, Gerhard (G)**               108   0
H: 6 3   W: 14 00   b.Munich 16-11-78
2006-07   Energie Cottbus  1   0
2007-08   Energie Cottbus 24   0
2008-09   Energie Cottbus 34   0
2009-10   Energie Cottbus 34   0    93   0
2011-12   Swansea C        1   0
2012-13   Swansea C       14   0    15   0

**VORM, Michel (G)**                   234   0
H: 6 0   W: 13 03   b.Nieuwegein 20-10-83
*Honours:* Holland 10 full caps.
2005-06   Den Bosch       35   0    35   0
2006-07   Utrecht         33   0
2007-08   Utrecht         11   0
2008-09   Utrecht         26   0
2009-10   Utrecht         33   0
2010-11   Utrecht         33   0   136   0
2011-12   Swansea C       37   0
2012-13   Swansea C       26   0    63   0

**WILLIAMS, Ashley (D)**              377  14
H: 6 0   W: 11 02   b.Wolverhampton 23-8-84
*Source:* Hednesford T. *Honours:* Wales 41 full caps, 1 goal.
2003-04   Stockport Co    10   0
2004-05   Stockport Co    44   1
2005-06   Stockport Co    36   1
2006-07   Stockport Co    46   1
2007-08   Stockport Co    26   0   162   3
2007-08   *Swansea C*      3   0
2008-09   Swansea C       46   2
2009-10   Swansea C       46   5
2010-11   Swansea C       46   3
2011-12   Swansea C       37   1
2012-13   Swansea C       37   0   215  11

---

**Players retained or with offer of contract**
Bohari Lita, Leroy Halirou; Sheehan, Joshua Luke.

**Scholars**
Atyeo, Thomas David Benjamin; Bray, Alexander George; Davies, Thomas Oliver; Evans, Samuel; Francis, Corey Benjamin; Jones, Joseph Michael; Llewellyn, Luke; Moore, Lewis Patrick; Peters, Connor Shaquille; Roberts, Connor Richard Jones; Samuel, Alexander Kinloch; Shephard, Liam.

# SWINDON T (80)

**ARCHIBALD-HENVILLE, Troy (D)**120   3
H: 6 2   W: 13 03   b.Newham 4-11-88
*Source:* Scholar.
2007-08   Tottenham H      0   0
2008-09   Tottenham H      0   0
2008-09   *Norwich C*      0   0
2008-09   *Exeter C*      19   0
2009-10   Tottenham H      0   0
2009-10   *Exeter C*      15   0
2010-11   Exeter C        36   1
2011-12   *Exeter C*      45   2   115   3
2012-13   Swindon T        5   0     5   0

**BEDWELL, Leigh (G)**                   1   0
2012-13   Swindon T        1   0     1   0

**BENSON, Paul (F)**                   190  68
H: 6 1   W: 11 01   b.Southend 12-10-79
*Source:* White Notley.
2007-08   Dagenham & R    22   6
2008-09   Dagenham & R    33  17
2009-10   Dagenham & R    45  17
2010-11   Dagenham & R     3   0   103  40
2010-11   Charlton Ath    32  10
2011-12   Charlton Ath     1   0    33  10
2011-12   Swindon T       22  11
2012-13   Swindon T        9   1    31  12
2012-13   *Portsmouth*     7   2     7   2
2012-13   *Cheltenham T*  16   4    16   4

**BESSONE, Fede (D)**                   71   1
H: 5 11   W: 11 13   b.Cordoba 23-1-84
*Source:* Barcelona B, Espanyol B.
2007-08   *Gimnastic*     10   0    10   0
2008-09   Swansea C       15   0
2009-10   Swansea C       21   1
2010-11   Leeds U          6   0
2010-11   *Charlton Ath*  13   0    13   0
2011-12   Leeds U          0   0     6   0
2011-12   Swansea C        1   0
2012-13   Swansea C        0   0    37   1
2012-13   Swindon T        5   0     5   0

**CADDIS, Paul (D)**                   132   5
H: 5 7   W: 10 07   b.Irvine 19-4-88
2007-08   Celtic           2   0
2008-09   Celtic           5   0
2008-09   *Dundee U*      11   0    11   0
2009-10   Celtic          10   0    17   0
2010-11   Swindon T       38   1
2011-12   Swindon T       39   4
2012-13   Swindon T        0   0    77   5
2012-13   *Birmingham C*  27   0    27   0

**COLLINS, James S (F)**               128  43
H: 6 2   W: 13 08   b.Coventry 1-12-90
*Source:* Scholar. *Honours:* Eire Under-21.
2008-09   Aston Villa      0   0
2009-10   Aston Villa      0   0
2009-10   *Darlington*     7   2     7   2
2010-11   Aston Villa      0   0
2010-11   *Burton Alb*    10   4    10   4
2010-11   Shrewsbury T    24   8
2011-12   Shrewsbury T    42  14    66  22
2012-13   Swindon T       45  15    45  15

**COX, Lee (M)**                       100   3
H: 6 1   W: 12 02   b.Leicester 26-6-90
*Source:* Scholar.
2007-08   Leicester C      0   0
2008-09   Leicester C      0   0
2008-09   *Yeovil T*       0   0
2009-10   Inverness CT    35   0
2010-11   Inverness CT    21   1

---

2011-12   Inverness CT     7   0    69   3
2011-12   Swindon T        7   0
2012-13   Swindon T        0   0     7   0
2012-13   *Oxford U*      14   0    14   0
2012-13   *Plymouth Arg*  10   0    10   0

**DE VITA, Raffaele (F)**              141  34
H: 6 0   W: 11 09   b.Rome 23-9-87
*Source:* Scholar.
2005-06   Blackburn R      0   0
2006-07   Blackburn R      0   0
2007-08   Blackburn R      0   0
2008-09   Livingston       7   1
2009-10   Livingston      29   9
2010-11   Livingston      31  12    67  22
2011-12   Swindon T       38   4
2012-13   Swindon T       36   8    74  12

**DEVERA, Joe (D)**                    230   4
H: 6 2   W: 12 00   b.Southgate 6-2-87
2005-06   Barnet           0   0
2006-07   Barnet          26   0
2007-08   Barnet          41   0
2008-09   Barnet          34   1
2009-10   Barnet          33   0
2010-11   Barnet          43   1   177   2
2011-12   Swindon T       28   2
2012-13   Swindon T       25   0    53   2

**FERGUSON, Alex (M)**                   0   0
2012-13   Swindon T        0   0

**FERRY, Simon (M)**                   147   8
H: 5 8   W: 11 00   b.Dundee 11-1-88
2005-06   Celtic           0   0
2006-07   Celtic           0   0
2007-08   Celtic           0   0
2008-09   Celtic           0   0
2009-10   Celtic           0   0
2009-10   Swindon T       40   2
2010-11   Swindon T       21   0
2011-12   Swindon T       44   1
2012-13   Swindon T       42   5   147   8

**FLINT, Aiden (D)**                    64   4
H: 6 2   W: 12 00   b.Pinxton 11-7-89
*Source:* Alfreton T.
2010-11   Swindon T        3   0
2011-12   Swindon T       32   2
2012-13   Swindon T       29   2    64   4

**FODERINGHAM, Wesley (G)**             79   0
H: 6 1   W: 12 00   b.Hammersmith 14-1-91
*Source:* Scholar.
2009-10   Fulham           0   0
2010-11   Crystal Palace   0   0
2011-12   Crystal Palace   0   0
2011-12   Swindon T       33   0
2012-13   Swindon T       46   0    79   0

**FRANCIS, Mark (F)**                    2   0
2012-13   Swindon T        2   0     2   0

**McCORMACK, Alan (M)**                295  23
H: 5 8   W: 11 00   b.Dublin 10-1-84
*Source:* Stella Maris BC.
2002-03   Preston NE       0   0
2003-04   Preston NE       5   0
2003-04   *Leyton Orient* 10   0    10   0
2004-05   Preston NE       3   0
2004-05   *Southend U*     7   2
2005-06   Preston NE       0   0
2005-06   *Motherwell*    24   2    24   2
2006-07   Preston NE       3   0    11   0
2006-07   Southend U      22   3
2007-08   Southend U      42   8
2008-09   Southend U      34   2
2009-10   Southend U      41   3   146  18
2010-11   Charlton Ath    24   1    24   1
2011-12   Swindon T       40   2
2012-13   Swindon T       40   0    80   2

**McEVELEY, James (D)**                238   7
H: 6 1   W: 13 03   b.Liverpool 11-2-85
*Source:* Trainee. *Honours:* England Under-20, Under-21. Scotland B, 3 full caps.
2002-03   Blackburn R      9   0
2003-04   Blackburn R      0   0
2003-04   *Burnley*        4   0     4   0
2004-05   Blackburn R      5   0
2004-05   *Gillingham*    10   1    10   1

|  |  | | | | |
|---|---|--:|--:|--:|--:|
| 2005-06 | Blackburn R | 0 | 0 | | |
| 2005-06 | *Ipswich T* | 19 | 1 | 19 | 1 |
| 2006-07 | Blackburn R | 4 | 0 | 18 | 0 |
| 2006-07 | Derby Co | 15 | 0 | | |
| 2007-08 | Derby Co | 29 | 2 | | |
| 2008-09 | Derby Co | 15 | 0 | | |
| 2008-09 | *Preston NE* | 7 | 0 | 7 | 0 |
| 2008-09 | *Charlton Ath* | 6 | 0 | 6 | 0 |
| 2009-10 | Derby Co | 33 | 2 | 92 | 4 |
| 2010-11 | Barnsley | 17 | 1 | | |
| 2011-12 | Barnsley | 29 | 0 | 46 | 1 |
| 2011-12 | *Swindon T* | 8 | 0 | | |
| 2012-13 | Swindon T | 28 | 0 | 36 | 0 |

**MILLER, Tommy (M)**    477 90
H: 6 0 W: 11 07 b.Shotton 8-1-79
*Source:* Trainee.

|  |  | | | | |
|---|---|--:|--:|--:|--:|
| 1997-98 | Hartlepool U | 13 | 1 | | |
| 1998-99 | Hartlepool U | 34 | 4 | | |
| 1999-2000 | Hartlepool U | 44 | 14 | | |
| 2000-01 | Hartlepool U | 46 | 16 | | |
| 2001-02 | Hartlepool U | 0 | 0 | 137 | 35 |
| 2001-02 | Ipswich T | 8 | 0 | | |
| 2002-03 | Ipswich T | 30 | 6 | | |
| 2003-04 | Ipswich T | 34 | 11 | | |
| 2004-05 | Ipswich T | 45 | 13 | | |
| 2005-06 | Sunderland | 29 | 3 | | |
| 2006-07 | Sunderland | 4 | 0 | 33 | 3 |
| 2006-07 | *Preston NE* | 7 | 0 | 7 | 0 |
| 2007-08 | Ipswich T | 37 | 5 | | |
| 2008-09 | Ipswich T | 32 | 5 | 186 | 40 |
| 2009-10 | Sheffield W | 20 | 1 | | |
| 2010-11 | Sheffield W | 34 | 9 | 54 | 10 |
| 2011-12 | Huddersfield T | 26 | 1 | 26 | 1 |
| 2012-13 | Swindon T | 34 | 1 | 34 | 1 |

**NAVARRO, Alan (M)**    300 10
H: 5 10 W: 11 07 b.Liverpool 31-5-81
*Source:* Trainee.

|  |  | | | | |
|---|---|--:|--:|--:|--:|
| 1998-99 | Liverpool | 0 | 0 | | |
| 1999-2000 | Liverpool | 0 | 0 | | |
| 2000-01 | Liverpool | 0 | 0 | | |
| 2000-01 | *Crewe Alex* | 8 | 1 | | |
| 2001-02 | Liverpool | 0 | 0 | | |
| 2001-02 | *Crewe Alex* | 7 | 0 | 15 | 1 |
| 2002-03 | Tranmere R | 21 | 1 | | |
| 2002-03 | Tranmere R | 5 | 0 | | |
| 2003-04 | Tranmere R | 19 | 0 | | |
| 2004-05 | Tranmere R | 0 | 0 | | |
| 2004-05 | *Chester C* | 3 | 0 | 3 | 0 |
| 2004-05 | *Macclesfield T* | 11 | 1 | | |
| 2005-06 | Tranmere R | 0 | 0 | 45 | 1 |
| From Accrington S. | | | | | |
| 2005-06 | Macclesfield T | 27 | 0 | | |
| 2006-07 | Macclesfield T | 32 | 2 | 70 | 3 |
| 2007-08 | Milton Keynes D | 39 | 3 | | |
| 2008-09 | Milton Keynes D | 38 | 1 | 77 | 4 |
| 2009-10 | Brighton & HA | 36 | 0 | | |
| 2010-11 | Brighton & HA | 6 | 0 | | |
| 2011-12 | Brighton & HA | 33 | 1 | 73 | 1 |
| 2012-13 | Swindon T | 17 | 0 | 17 | 0 |

**OAKLEY, Aaron (D)**    0 0

|  |  | | | | |
|---|---|--:|--:|--:|--:|
| 2012-13 | Swindon T | 0 | 0 | | |

**ROBERTS, Gary (F)**    273 46
H: 5 10 W: 11 09 b.Chester 18-3-84
*Source:* Denbigh T, Bangor C.

|  |  | | | | |
|---|---|--:|--:|--:|--:|
| 2006-07 | Accrington S | 14 | 8 | 14 | 8 |
| 2006-07 | Ipswich T | 33 | 2 | | |
| 2007-08 | Ipswich T | 21 | 1 | 54 | 3 |
| 2007-08 | *Crewe Alex* | 4 | 0 | 4 | 0 |
| 2008-09 | Huddersfield T | 43 | 9 | | |
| 2009-10 | Huddersfield T | 43 | 7 | | |
| 2010-11 | Huddersfield T | 37 | 9 | | |
| 2011-12 | Huddersfield T | 39 | 6 | 162 | 31 |
| 2012-13 | Swindon T | 39 | 4 | 39 | 4 |

**ROONEY, Luke (M)**    90 8
H: 5 8 W: 11 07 b.Southwark 28-12-90
*Source:* Scholar.

|  |  | | | | |
|---|---|--:|--:|--:|--:|
| 2009-10 | Gillingham | 13 | 2 | | |
| 2010-11 | Gillingham | 23 | 1 | | |
| 2011-12 | Gillingham | 17 | 3 | 53 | 6 |
| 2011-12 | *Swindon T* | 20 | 2 | | |
| 2012-13 | Swindon T | 11 | 0 | 31 | 2 |
| 2012-13 | *Burton Alb* | 3 | 0 | 3 | 0 |
| 2012-13 | *Rotherham U* | 3 | 0 | 3 | 0 |

**SMITH, Chris (D)**    1 0
b.Stoke 12-10-90
*Source:* Stone Dominoes.

|  |  | | | | |
|---|---|--:|--:|--:|--:|
| 2011-12 | Swindon T | 1 | 0 | | |
| 2012-13 | Swindon T | 0 | 0 | 1 | 0 |

**STOREY, Miles (F)**    14 1
H: 5 11 W: 11 00 b.West Bromwich 4-1-94
*Source:* Scholar.

|  |  | | | | |
|---|---|--:|--:|--:|--:|
| 2010-11 | Swindon T | 2 | 0 | | |
| 2011-12 | Swindon T | 4 | 0 | | |
| 2012-13 | Swindon T | 8 | 1 | 14 | 1 |

**THOMPSON, Louis (M)**    4 0
H: 5 11 W: 11 10 b.Bristol 19-12-94

|  |  | | | | |
|---|---|--:|--:|--:|--:|
| 2012-13 | Swindon T | 4 | 0 | 4 | 0 |

**THOMPSON, Nathan (D)**    34 0
H: 5 7 W: 11 02 b.Chester 9-11-90
*Source:* Scholar.

|  |  | | | | |
|---|---|--:|--:|--:|--:|
| 2009-10 | Swindon T | 0 | 0 | | |
| 2010-11 | Swindon T | 3 | 0 | | |
| 2011-12 | Swindon T | 5 | 0 | | |
| 2012-13 | Swindon T | 26 | 0 | 34 | 0 |

**WALDON, Connor (F)**    1 0

|  |  | | | | |
|---|---|--:|--:|--:|--:|
| 2012-13 | Swindon T | 1 | 0 | 1 | 0 |

**WILLIAMS, Andy (F)**    267 51
H: 5 11 W: 11 09 b.Hereford 14-8-86
*Source:* Pershore College.

|  |  | | | | |
|---|---|--:|--:|--:|--:|
| 2006-07 | Hereford U | 41 | 8 | | |
| 2007-08 | Bristol R | 41 | 4 | | |
| 2008-09 | Bristol R | 4 | 1 | | |
| 2008-09 | *Hereford U* | 26 | 2 | 67 | 10 |
| 2009-10 | Bristol R | 43 | 3 | 88 | 8 |
| 2010-11 | Yeovil T | 37 | 6 | | |
| 2011-12 | Yeovil T | 35 | 16 | 72 | 22 |
| 2012-13 | Yeovil T | 40 | 11 | 40 | 11 |

**Scholars**
Da-Costa, Curtis; Ferguson, Alexander John; Ferris, Aaron Thomas; Francis, Mark James; Helm, Joshua James; Jones, Mathew Ryan; Kisitu, Salvyn Joshua Kajoba; Murden, Luke Brent; Oakley, Aaron James; Rawlins, Ryan Ayrton; Simpson, Jake Casey; Thompson, Louis Clyde William; Waldon, Connor Mark; Walsh, Liam Thomas.

# TORQUAY U (81)

**BODIN, Billy (M)**    84 13
H: 5 11 W: 11 00 b.Swindon 24-3-92
*Honours:* Wales Youth, Under-21.

|  |  | | | | |
|---|---|--:|--:|--:|--:|
| 2009-10 | Swindon T | 0 | 0 | | |
| 2010-11 | Swindon T | 5 | 0 | | |
| 2011-12 | Swindon T | 11 | 3 | 16 | 3 |
| 2011-12 | *Torquay U* | 17 | 5 | | |
| 2011-12 | *Crewe Alex* | 8 | 0 | 8 | 0 |
| 2012-13 | Torquay U | 43 | 5 | 60 | 10 |

**CRAIG, Nathan (M)**    30 1
H: 5 11 W: 10 11 b.Bangor 25-10-91

|  |  | | | | |
|---|---|--:|--:|--:|--:|
| 2011-12 | *Torquay U* | 30 | 1 | 30 | 1 |

**CRUISE, Thomas (D)**    19 0
H: 5 6 W: 12 07 b.London 9-3-91
*Source:* Scholar. *Honours:* England Youth.

|  |  | | | | |
|---|---|--:|--:|--:|--:|
| 2008-09 | Arsenal | 0 | 0 | | |
| 2009-10 | Arsenal | 0 | 0 | | |
| 2010-11 | Arsenal | 0 | 0 | | |
| 2010-11 | *Carlisle U* | 3 | 0 | 3 | 0 |
| 2012-13 | Torquay U | 16 | 0 | 16 | 0 |

**DOWNES, Aaron (D)**    220 15
H: 6 2 W: 13 02 b.Mudgee 15-5-85
*Honours:* Australia Youth, Under-20, Under-21, Under-23.

|  |  | | | | |
|---|---|--:|--:|--:|--:|
| 2004-05 | Chesterfield | 9 | 2 | | |
| 2005-06 | Chesterfield | 22 | 0 | | |
| 2006-07 | Chesterfield | 45 | 3 | | |
| 2007-08 | Chesterfield | 40 | 2 | | |
| 2008-09 | Chesterfield | 42 | 2 | | |
| 2009-10 | Chesterfield | 7 | 1 | | |
| 2010-11 | Chesterfield | 0 | 0 | | |
| 2011-12 | Chesterfield | 9 | 0 | 174 | 10 |
| 2011-12 | *Bristol R* | 8 | 0 | 8 | 0 |
| 2012-13 | Torquay U | 38 | 5 | 38 | 5 |

**EASTON, Craig (M)**    263 19
H: 5 10 W: 11 01 b.Bellshill 26-2-79
*Source:* Dundee U BC. *Honours:* Scotland Youth, Under-21.

|  |  | | | | |
|---|---|--:|--:|--:|--:|
| 1996-97 | Dundee U | 2 | 0 | | |
| 1997-98 | Dundee U | 29 | 1 | | |
| 1998-99 | Dundee U | 30 | 1 | 61 | 2 |
| 2005-06 | Leyton Orient | 41 | 4 | | |
| 2006-07 | Leyton Orient | 30 | 1 | 71 | 5 |
| 2007-08 | Swindon T | 40 | 6 | | |
| 2008-09 | Swindon T | 23 | 2 | | |
| 2009-10 | Swindon T | 12 | 0 | 75 | 8 |
| 2010-11 | Southend U | 32 | 4 | 32 | 4 |
| 2011-12 | Dunfermline Ath | 3 | 0 | 3 | 0 |
| 2012-13 | Torquay U | 21 | 0 | 21 | 0 |

**HALPIN, Saul (M)**    7 0
H: 6 1 W: 12 00 b.Bodmin 31-5-91
*Source:* Scholar.

|  |  | | | | |
|---|---|--:|--:|--:|--:|
| 2009-10 | Torquay U | 0 | 0 | | |
| 2010-11 | Torquay U | 4 | 0 | | |
| 2011-12 | Torquay U | 1 | 0 | | |
| 2012-13 | Torquay U | 2 | 0 | 7 | 0 |

**HOWE, Rene (F)**    200 56
H: 6 0 W: 14 03 b.Bedford 22-10-86
*Source:* Kettering T.

|  |  | | | | |
|---|---|--:|--:|--:|--:|
| 2007-08 | Peterborough U | 15 | 1 | | |
| 2007-08 | *Rochdale* | 20 | 9 | 20 | 9 |
| 2008-09 | Peterborough U | 0 | 0 | | |
| 2008-09 | *Morecambe* | 37 | 10 | 37 | 10 |
| 2009-10 | Peterborough U | 0 | 0 | | |
| 2009-10 | *Lincoln C* | 17 | 5 | 17 | 5 |
| 2009-10 | *Gillingham* | 18 | 2 | 18 | 2 |
| 2010-11 | Peterborough U | 0 | 0 | 15 | 1 |
| 2010-11 | *Bristol R* | 12 | 1 | 12 | 1 |
| 2011-12 | Torquay U | 39 | 12 | | |
| 2012-13 | Torquay U | 42 | 16 | 81 | 28 |

**JARVIS, Ryan (F)**    233 33
H: 6 1 W: 11 11 b.Fakenham 11-7-86
*Source:* Scholar. *Honours:* FA Schools, England Youth.

|  |  | | | | |
|---|---|--:|--:|--:|--:|
| 2002-03 | Norwich C | 3 | 0 | | |
| 2003-04 | Norwich C | 12 | 1 | | |
| 2004-05 | Norwich C | 4 | 1 | | |
| 2004-05 | *Colchester U* | 6 | 0 | 6 | 0 |
| 2005-06 | Norwich C | 4 | 1 | | |
| 2006-07 | Norwich C | 5 | 0 | | |
| 2006-07 | *Leyton Orient* | 14 | 6 | | |
| 2007-08 | Norwich C | 1 | 0 | 29 | 3 |
| 2007-08 | *Kilmarnock* | 9 | 1 | 9 | 1 |
| 2007-08 | *Notts Co* | 17 | 2 | 17 | 2 |
| 2008-09 | Leyton Orient | 31 | 0 | | |
| 2009-10 | Leyton Orient | 42 | 8 | | |
| 2010-11 | Leyton Orient | 11 | 2 | 98 | 16 |
| 2010-11 | *Northampton T* | 3 | 0 | 3 | 0 |
| 2011-12 | Walsall | 19 | 2 | 19 | 2 |
| 2011-12 | *Torquay U* | 14 | 2 | | |
| 2012-13 | Torquay U | 38 | 7 | 52 | 9 |

**LATHROPE, Damon (M)**    86 0
H: 5 8 W: 10 02 b.Stevenage 28-10-89
*Source:* Scholar.

|  |  | | | | |
|---|---|--:|--:|--:|--:|
| 2007-08 | Norwich C | 0 | 0 | | |
| 2008-09 | Norwich C | 0 | 0 | | |
| 2009-10 | Norwich C | 0 | 0 | | |
| 2010-11 | Torquay U | 18 | 0 | | |
| 2011-12 | Torquay U | 40 | 0 | | |
| 2012-13 | Torquay U | 28 | 0 | 86 | 0 |

**LEADBITTER, Daniel (D)**    15 0
H: 6 0 W: 11 00 b.Newcastle 17-10-90
*Source:* Newcastle U Scholar.

|  |  | | | | |
|---|---|--:|--:|--:|--:|
| 2011-12 | Torquay U | 2 | 0 | | |
| 2012-13 | Torquay U | 13 | 0 | 15 | 0 |

**MACKENZIE, Kirtys (D)**    1 0
b.Newham 17-10-93

|  |  | | | | |
|---|---|--:|--:|--:|--:|
| 2012-13 | *Torquay U* | 1 | 0 | 1 | 0 |

**MACKLIN, Lloyd (M)**    45 0
H: 5 9 W: 12 03 b.Camberley 2-8-91
*Source:* Scholar.

|  |  | | | | |
|---|---|--:|--:|--:|--:|
| 2007-08 | Swindon T | 0 | 0 | | |
| 2008-09 | Swindon T | 2 | 0 | | |
| 2009-10 | Swindon T | 9 | 0 | 11 | 0 |
| 2009-10 | *Torquay U* | 4 | 0 | | |
| 2010-11 | Torquay U | 10 | 0 | | |
| 2011-12 | Torquay U | 4 | 0 | | |
| 2012-13 | Torquay U | 16 | 0 | 34 | 0 |

**MANSELL, Lee (D)**    307 29
H: 5 10   W: 11 10   b.Gloucester 28-10-82
*Source:* Scholar.

| | | | | | |
|---|---|---|---|---|---|
| 2000-01 | Luton T | 18 | 5 | | |
| 2001-02 | Luton T | 11 | 1 | | |
| 2002-03 | Luton T | 1 | 0 | | |
| 2003-04 | Luton T | 16 | 2 | | |
| 2004-05 | Luton T | 1 | 0 | 47 | 8 |
| 2005-06 | Oxford U | 44 | 1 | 44 | 1 |
| 2006-07 | Torquay U | 45 | 4 | | |
| 2009-10 | Torquay U | 39 | 2 | | |
| 2010-11 | Torquay U | 45 | 0 | | |
| 2011-12 | Torquay U | 45 | 12 | | |
| 2012-13 | Torquay U | 42 | 2 | 216 | 20 |

**MORRIS, Ian (D)**    186 14
H: 6 0   W: 11 05   b.Dublin 27-2-87
*Source:* Scholar. *Honours:* Eire Under-21.

| | | | | | |
|---|---|---|---|---|---|
| 2003-04 | Leeds U | 0 | 0 | | |
| 2004-05 | Leeds U | 0 | 0 | | |
| 2005-06 | Leeds U | 0 | 0 | | |
| 2005-06 | *Blackpool* | 30 | 3 | 30 | 3 |
| 2006-07 | Leeds U | 0 | 0 | | |
| 2006-07 | Scunthorpe U | 28 | 3 | | |
| 2007-08 | Scunthorpe U | 25 | 3 | | |
| 2008-09 | Scunthorpe U | 20 | 1 | | |
| 2008-09 | *Carlisle U* | 6 | 0 | 6 | 0 |
| 2009-10 | Scunthorpe U | 3 | 0 | | |
| 2009-10 | *Chesterfield* | 7 | 0 | | |
| 2010-11 | Scunthorpe U | 0 | 0 | 76 | 7 |
| 2010-11 | *Chesterfield* | 19 | 1 | 26 | 1 |
| 2011-12 | Torquay U | 37 | 2 | | |
| 2012-13 | Torquay U | 11 | 1 | 48 | 3 |

**NICHOLSON, Kevin (D)**    262 11
H: 5 8   W: 12 05   b.Derby 2-10-80
*Source:* Trainee. *Honours:* England Schools.

| | | | | | |
|---|---|---|---|---|---|
| 1997-98 | Sheffield W | 0 | 0 | | |
| 1998-99 | Sheffield W | 0 | 0 | | |
| 1999-2000 | Sheffield W | 0 | 0 | | |
| 2000-01 | Sheffield W | 1 | 0 | 1 | 0 |
| *From Forest Green R.* | | | | | |
| 2000-01 | Northampton T | 7 | 0 | 7 | 0 |
| 2000-01 | Notts Co | 11 | 2 | | |
| 2001-02 | Notts Co | 24 | 1 | | |
| 2002-03 | Notts Co | 37 | 0 | | |
| 2003-04 | Notts Co | 23 | 0 | 95 | 3 |
| *From Scarborough, Forest Green R.* | | | | | |
| 2009-10 | Torquay U | 27 | 0 | | |
| 2010-11 | Torquay U | 44 | 3 | | |
| 2011-12 | Torquay U | 46 | 4 | | |
| 2012-13 | Torquay U | 42 | 1 | 159 | 7 |

**OASTLER, Joe (D)**    109 1
H: 5 10   W: 11 03   b.Portsmouth 3-7-90
*Source:* Portsmouth Scholar.

| | | | | | |
|---|---|---|---|---|---|
| 2008-09 | QPR | 0 | 0 | | |
| 2009-10 | QPR | 1 | 0 | | |
| 2010-11 | QPR | 0 | 0 | 1 | 0 |
| 2010-11 | *Torquay U* | 25 | 0 | | |
| 2011-12 | Torquay U | 45 | 0 | | |
| 2012-13 | Torquay U | 38 | 1 | 108 | 1 |

**POKE, Michael (G)**    84 0
H: 6 1   W: 13 12   b.Staines 21-11-85
*Source:* Trainee.

| | | | | | |
|---|---|---|---|---|---|
| 2003-04 | Southampton | 0 | 0 | | |
| 2004-05 | Southampton | 0 | 0 | | |
| 2005-06 | Southampton | 0 | 0 | | |
| 2005-06 | *Oldham Ath* | 0 | 0 | | |
| 2005-06 | *Northampton T* | 0 | 0 | | |
| 2006-07 | Southampton | 0 | 0 | | |
| 2007-08 | Southampton | 4 | 0 | | |
| 2008-09 | Southampton | 0 | 0 | | |
| 2009-10 | Southampton | 0 | 0 | 4 | 0 |
| 2009-10 | *Torquay U* | 29 | 0 | | |
| 2010-11 | Brighton & HA | 0 | 0 | | |
| 2011-12 | Brighton & HA | 0 | 0 | | |
| 2011-12 | *Bristol R* | 8 | 0 | 8 | 0 |
| 2012-13 | Torquay U | 43 | 0 | 72 | 0 |

**RICE, Martin (G)**    5 0
H: 5 11   W: 13 01   b.Exeter 7-3-86
*Source:* Exeter C, Torquay U, Truro C.

| | | | | | |
|---|---|---|---|---|---|
| 2011-12 | Torquay U | 0 | 0 | | |
| 2012-13 | Torquay U | 5 | 0 | 5 | 0 |

**SAAH, Brian (M)**    171 3
H: 6 3   W: 12 03   b.Rush Green 16-12-86
*Source:* Scholar.

| | | | | | |
|---|---|---|---|---|---|
| 2003-04 | Leyton Orient | 6 | 0 | | |
| 2004-05 | Leyton Orient | 12 | 0 | | |
| 2005-06 | Leyton Orient | 3 | 0 | | |
| 2006-07 | Leyton Orient | 32 | 0 | | |
| 2007-08 | Leyton Orient | 25 | 1 | | |
| 2008-09 | Leyton Orient | 15 | 0 | 93 | 1 |
| *From Cambridge U.* | | | | | |
| 2011-12 | Torquay U | 35 | 1 | | |
| 2012-13 | Torquay U | 43 | 1 | 78 | 2 |

**STEVENS, Danny (M)**    129 15
H: 5 5   W: 9 09   b.Enfield 26-11-86
*Source:* Tottenham H Scholar.

| | | | | | |
|---|---|---|---|---|---|
| 2004-05 | Luton T | 0 | 0 | | |
| 2005-06 | Luton T | 1 | 0 | | |
| 2006-07 | Luton T | 0 | 0 | 1 | 0 |
| 2009-10 | Torquay U | 27 | 1 | | |
| 2010-11 | Torquay U | 37 | 3 | | |
| 2011-12 | Torquay U | 41 | 8 | | |
| 2012-13 | Torquay U | 23 | 3 | 128 | 15 |

**THOMPSON, Niall (M)**    18 0
b.Derby 3-9-93

| | | | | | |
|---|---|---|---|---|---|
| 2012-13 | Torquay U | 18 | 0 | 18 | 0 |

**YEOMAN, Ashley (F)**    14 2
H: 5 10   W: 12 01   b.Kingsbridge 25-2-92
*Source:* Scholar.

| | | | | | |
|---|---|---|---|---|---|
| 2010-11 | Torquay U | 0 | 0 | | |
| 2011-12 | Torquay U | 1 | 0 | | |
| 2012-13 | Torquay U | 13 | 2 | 14 | 2 |

**Scholars**
Alexandrou, Jamie Lenos; Avraamides, Alexandros; Beattie, Scott; Berrow, Monty Joshua Hepburn; Campbell, Jordan Michael; Chaney, Sam; Ellacott, Thomas James; Hutchings, Jake Thomas; Mace, Jack; May, Jack Matthew; McCallion, Kevin Patrick; Nardiello, Robert Donato; Palmer, Freddie James; Parcell, Mickey Charles; Shulberg, Sam Oliver Jack; Slatter-Ibbetson, Aaron; Sullivan, Daniel; Thompson, Conor Joseph; Washburn, James.

# TOTTENHAM H (82)

**ADEBAYOR, Emmanuel (F)**    332 121
H: 6 4   W: 11 08   b.Lome 26-2-84
*Source:* Lome. *Honours:* Togo 57 full caps, 27 goals.

| | | | | | |
|---|---|---|---|---|---|
| 2001-02 | Metz | 10 | 2 | | |
| 2002-03 | Metz | 34 | 13 | 44 | 15 |
| 2003-04 | Monaco | 31 | 8 | | |
| 2004-05 | Monaco | 34 | 9 | | |
| 2005-06 | Monaco | 13 | 1 | 78 | 18 |
| 2005-06 | Arsenal | 13 | 4 | | |
| 2006-07 | Arsenal | 29 | 8 | | |
| 2007-08 | Arsenal | 36 | 24 | | |
| 2008-09 | Arsenal | 26 | 10 | 104 | 46 |
| 2009-10 | Manchester C | 26 | 14 | | |
| 2010-11 | Manchester C | 8 | 1 | | |
| 2010-11 | *Real Madrid* | 14 | 5 | 14 | 5 |
| 2011-12 | Manchester C | 0 | 0 | | |
| 2011-12 | *Tottenham H* | 33 | 17 | | |
| 2012-13 | Manchester C | 0 | 0 | 34 | 15 |
| 2012-13 | Tottenham H | 25 | 5 | 58 | 22 |

**ARCHER, Jordan (G)**    27 0
H: 6 1   W: 12 08   b.Walthamstow 12-4-93
*Source:* Brackley T, Thurrock, Margate.
*Honours:* Scotland Youth, Under-21.

| | | | | | |
|---|---|---|---|---|---|
| 2011-12 | Tottenham H | 0 | 0 | | |
| 2012-13 | Tottenham H | 0 | 0 | | |
| 2012-13 | *Wycombe W* | 27 | 0 | 27 | 0 |

**ASSOU-EKOTTO, Benoit (M)**    221 4
H: 5 10   W: 10 12   b.Arras 24-3-84
*Honours:* Cameroon B, 18 full caps.

| | | | | | |
|---|---|---|---|---|---|
| 2003-04 | Lens | 3 | 0 | | |
| 2004-05 | Lens | 29 | 0 | | |
| 2005-06 | Lens | 34 | 0 | 66 | 0 |
| 2006-07 | Tottenham H | 16 | 0 | | |
| 2007-08 | Tottenham H | 1 | 0 | | |
| 2008-09 | Tottenham H | 29 | 0 | | |
| 2009-10 | Tottenham H | 30 | 1 | | |
| 2010-11 | Tottenham H | 30 | 0 | | |
| 2011-12 | Tottenham H | 34 | 2 | | |
| 2012-13 | Tottenham H | 15 | 1 | 155 | 4 |

**BALE, Gareth (D)**    186 47
H: 6 0   W: 11 10   b.Cardiff 16-7-89
*Source:* Scholar. *Honours:* Wales Youth, Under-21, 41 full caps, 9 goals.

| | | | | | |
|---|---|---|---|---|---|
| 2005-06 | Southampton | 2 | 0 | | |
| 2006-07 | Southampton | 38 | 5 | 40 | 5 |
| 2007-08 | Tottenham H | 8 | 2 | | |
| 2008-09 | Tottenham H | 16 | 0 | | |
| 2009-10 | Tottenham H | 23 | 3 | | |
| 2010-11 | Tottenham H | 30 | 7 | | |
| 2011-12 | Tottenham H | 36 | 9 | | |
| 2012-13 | Tottenham H | 33 | 21 | 146 | 42 |

**BENTLEY, David (F)**    201 18
H: 5 10   W: 11 03   b.Peterborough 27-8-84
*Source:* Scholar. *Honours:* England Youth, Under-21, Under-21, B, 7 full caps.

| | | | | | |
|---|---|---|---|---|---|
| 2001-02 | Arsenal | 0 | 0 | | |
| 2002-03 | Arsenal | 0 | 0 | | |
| 2003-04 | Arsenal | 1 | 0 | | |
| 2004-05 | Arsenal | 0 | 0 | | |
| 2004-05 | *Norwich C* | 26 | 2 | 26 | 2 |
| 2005-06 | Arsenal | 0 | 0 | 1 | 0 |
| 2005-06 | Blackburn R | 29 | 3 | | |
| 2006-07 | Blackburn R | 36 | 4 | | |
| 2007-08 | Blackburn R | 37 | 6 | | |
| 2008-09 | Tottenham H | 25 | 1 | | |
| 2009-10 | Tottenham H | 15 | 2 | | |
| 2010-11 | Tottenham H | 2 | 0 | | |
| 2010-11 | *Birmingham C* | 13 | 0 | 13 | 0 |
| 2011-12 | Tottenham H | 0 | 0 | | |
| 2011-12 | *West Ham U* | 5 | 0 | 5 | 0 |
| 2012-13 | Tottenham H | 0 | 0 | 42 | 3 |
| 2012-13 | *Rostov* | 7 | 0 | 7 | 0 |
| 2012-13 | *Blackburn R* | 5 | 0 | 107 | 13 |

**BOSTOCK, John (M)**    46 4
H: 5 10   W: 11 11   b.Camberwell 13-10-91
*Honours:* England Youth.

| | | | | | |
|---|---|---|---|---|---|
| 2007-08 | Crystal Palace | 4 | 0 | 4 | 0 |
| 2008-09 | Tottenham H | 0 | 0 | | |
| 2009-10 | Tottenham H | 0 | 0 | | |
| 2009-10 | *Brentford* | 9 | 2 | 9 | 2 |
| 2010-11 | Tottenham H | 0 | 0 | | |
| 2010-11 | *Hull C* | 11 | 2 | 11 | 2 |
| 2011-12 | Tottenham H | 0 | 0 | | |
| 2011-12 | *Sheffield W* | 4 | 0 | 4 | 0 |
| 2011-12 | *Swindon T* | 3 | 0 | | |
| 2012-13 | Tottenham H | 0 | 0 | | |
| 2012-13 | *Swindon T* | 8 | 0 | 11 | 0 |
| 2013 | *Toronto FC* | 7 | 0 | 7 | 0 |

**BYRNE, Nathan (D)**    39 1
H: 5 10   W: 10 10   b.St Albans 5-6-92
*Source:* Scholar.

| | | | | | |
|---|---|---|---|---|---|
| 2010-11 | Tottenham H | 0 | 0 | | |
| 2010-11 | *Brentford* | 11 | 0 | 11 | 0 |
| 2011-12 | Tottenham H | 0 | 0 | | |
| 2011-12 | *Bournemouth* | 9 | 0 | 9 | 0 |
| 2012-13 | Tottenham H | 0 | 0 | | |
| 2012-13 | *Crawley T* | 12 | 1 | 12 | 1 |
| 2012-13 | *Swindon T* | 7 | 0 | 7 | 0 |

**CARROLL, Tommy (M)**    31 1
H: 5 10   W: 10 00   b.Watford 28-5-92
*Source:* Scholar. *Honours:* England Youth, Under-21.

| | | | | | |
|---|---|---|---|---|---|
| 2010-11 | Tottenham H | 0 | 0 | | |
| 2010-11 | *Leyton Orient* | 12 | 0 | 12 | 0 |
| 2011-12 | Tottenham H | 0 | 0 | | |
| 2011-12 | *Derby Co* | 12 | 1 | 12 | 1 |
| 2012-13 | Tottenham H | 7 | 0 | 7 | 0 |

**CAULKER, Steven (D)**    117 4
H: 6 3   W: 12 00   b.Feltham 29-12-91
*Honours:* England Youth, Under-21, 1 full cap, 1 goal.

| | | | | | |
|---|---|---|---|---|---|
| 2009-10 | Tottenham H | 0 | 0 | | |
| 2009-10 | *Yeovil T* | 44 | 0 | 44 | 0 |
| 2010-11 | Tottenham H | 0 | 0 | | |
| 2010-11 | *Bristol C* | 29 | 2 | 29 | 2 |
| 2011-12 | Tottenham H | 0 | 0 | | |
| 2011-12 | *Swansea C* | 26 | 0 | 26 | 0 |
| 2012-13 | Tottenham H | 18 | 2 | 18 | 2 |

### CEBALLOS, Cristian (M)    0   0
H: 5 8   W: 10 08   b.Barcelona 3-12-92
*Source:* Barcelona Youth.

| | | | | |
|---|---|---|---|---|
| 2011-12 | Tottenham H | 0 | 0 | |
| 2012-13 | Tottenham H | 0 | 0 | |

### COULTHIRST, Shaquile (F)    0   0
b.Hackney 2-1-94

| | | | | |
|---|---|---|---|---|
| 2012-13 | Tottenham H | 0 | 0 | |

### DAWKINS, Simon (F)    70   14
H: 5 10   W: 11 01   b.Edgware 1-12-87
*Source:* Scholar.

| | | | | | |
|---|---|---|---|---|---|
| 2005-06 | Tottenham H | 0 | 0 | | |
| 2006-07 | Tottenham H | 0 | 0 | | |
| 2007-08 | Tottenham H | 0 | 0 | | |
| 2008-09 | Tottenham H | 0 | 0 | | |
| 2008-09 | *Leyton Orient* | 11 | 0 | 11 | 0 |
| 2009-10 | Tottenham H | 0 | 0 | | |
| 2010-11 | Tottenham H | 0 | 0 | | |
| 2011 | *San Jose E* | 26 | 6 | | |
| 2011-12 | Tottenham H | 0 | 0 | | |
| 2012 | *San Jose E* | 29 | 8 | 55 | 14 |
| 2012-13 | Tottenham H | 0 | 0 | | |
| 2012-13 | *Aston Villa* | 4 | 0 | 4 | 0 |

### DAWSON, Michael (D)    287   14
H: 6 2   W: 12 02   b.Leyburn 18-11-83
*Source:* School. *Honours:* England Youth, Under-21, B, 4 full caps.

| | | | | | |
|---|---|---|---|---|---|
| 2000-01 | Nottingham F | 0 | 0 | | |
| 2001-02 | Nottingham F | 1 | 0 | | |
| 2002-03 | Nottingham F | 38 | 5 | | |
| 2003-04 | Nottingham F | 30 | 1 | | |
| 2004-05 | Nottingham F | 14 | 1 | 83 | 7 |
| 2004-05 | Tottenham H | 5 | 0 | | |
| 2005-06 | Tottenham H | 32 | 0 | | |
| 2006-07 | Tottenham H | 37 | 1 | | |
| 2007-08 | Tottenham H | 27 | 1 | | |
| 2008-09 | Tottenham H | 16 | 1 | | |
| 2009-10 | Tottenham H | 29 | 2 | | |
| 2010-11 | Tottenham H | 24 | 1 | | |
| 2011-12 | Tottenham H | 7 | 0 | | |
| 2012-13 | Tottenham H | 27 | 1 | 204 | 7 |

### DEFOE, Jermain (F)    415   152
H: 5 7   W: 10 04   b.Beckton 7-10-82
*Source:* Charlton Ath. *Honours:* England Youth, Under-21, B, 54 full caps, 19 goals.

| | | | | | |
|---|---|---|---|---|---|
| 1999-2000 | West Ham U | 0 | 0 | | |
| 2000-01 | West Ham U | 1 | 0 | | |
| 2000-01 | *Bournemouth* | 29 | 18 | 29 | 18 |
| 2001-02 | West Ham U | 35 | 10 | | |
| 2002-03 | West Ham U | 38 | 8 | | |
| 2003-04 | West Ham U | 19 | 11 | 93 | 29 |
| 2003-04 | Tottenham H | 15 | 7 | | |
| 2004-05 | Tottenham H | 35 | 13 | | |
| 2005-06 | Tottenham H | 36 | 9 | | |
| 2006-07 | Tottenham H | 34 | 10 | | |
| 2007-08 | Tottenham H | 19 | 4 | | |
| 2007-08 | Portsmouth | 12 | 8 | | |
| 2008-09 | Portsmouth | 19 | 7 | 31 | 15 |
| 2008-09 | Tottenham H | 8 | 3 | | |
| 2009-10 | Tottenham H | 34 | 18 | | |
| 2010-11 | Tottenham H | 22 | 4 | | |
| 2011-12 | Tottenham H | 25 | 11 | | |
| 2012-13 | Tottenham H | 34 | 11 | 262 | 90 |

### DEMBELE, Moussa (F)    263   40
H: 5 9   W: 10 01   b.Wilrijk 17-7-87
*Honours:* Belgium Youth, 49 full caps, 5 goals.

| | | | | | |
|---|---|---|---|---|---|
| 2003-04 | Beerschot | 1 | 0 | | |
| 2004-05 | Beerschot | 19 | 1 | 20 | 1 |
| 2005-06 | Willem II | 33 | 9 | 33 | 9 |
| 2006-07 | AZ | 33 | 6 | | |
| 2007-08 | AZ | 33 | 4 | | |
| 2008-09 | AZ | 23 | 10 | | |
| 2009-10 | AZ | 29 | 4 | 118 | 24 |
| 2010-11 | Fulham | 24 | 3 | | |
| 2011-12 | Fulham | 36 | 2 | | |
| 2012-13 | Fulham | 2 | 0 | 62 | 5 |
| 2012-13 | Tottenham H | 30 | 1 | 30 | 1 |

### DEMPSEY, Clint (M)    290   83
H: 6 1   W: 12 02   b.Nacogdoches 9-3-83
*Source:* Furman Univ. *Honours:* USA Under-21, 99 full caps, 35 goals.

| | | | | | |
|---|---|---|---|---|---|
| 2004 | *New England Rev* | 24 | 7 | | |
| 2005 | *New England Rev* | 30 | 11 | | |
| 2006 | *New England Rev* | 23 | 8 | 77 | 26 |
| 2006-07 | Fulham | 10 | 1 | | |
| 2007-08 | Fulham | 36 | 6 | | |
| 2008-09 | Fulham | 35 | 7 | | |
| 2009-10 | Fulham | 29 | 7 | | |
| 2010-11 | Fulham | 37 | 12 | | |
| 2011-12 | Fulham | 37 | 17 | | |
| 2012-13 | Fulham | 0 | 0 | 184 | 50 |
| 2012-13 | Tottenham H | 29 | 7 | 29 | 7 |

### FALQUE, Iago (M)    61   14
H: 5 8   W: 11 00   b.Vigo 4-4-90
*Honours:* Spain Youth, Under-21.

| | | | | | |
|---|---|---|---|---|---|
| 2008-09 | Barcelona B | 1 | 1 | 1 | 1 |
| 2008-09 | *Juventus* | 0 | 0 | | |
| 2009-10 | *Juventus* | 0 | 0 | | |
| 2009-10 | *Bari* | 0 | 0 | | |
| 2010-11 | *Juventus* | 0 | 0 | | |
| 2010-11 | *Villarreal B* | 36 | 11 | 36 | 11 |
| 2011-12 | Tottenham H | 0 | 0 | | |
| 2011-12 | *Southampton* | 1 | 0 | 1 | 0 |
| 2012-13 | Tottenham H | 1 | 0 | 1 | 0 |
| 2012-13 | *Almeria* | 22 | 2 | 22 | 2 |

### FREDERICKS, Ryan (M)    4   0
H: 5 8   W: 11 10   b.Potters Bar 10-10-92
*Source:* Scholar.

| | | | | | |
|---|---|---|---|---|---|
| 2010-11 | Tottenham H | 0 | 0 | | |
| 2011-12 | Tottenham H | 0 | 0 | | |
| 2012-13 | Tottenham H | 0 | 0 | | |
| 2012-13 | *Brentford* | 4 | 0 | 4 | 0 |

### FRIEDEL, Brad (G)    514   1
H: 6 3   W: 14 00   b.Lakewood 18-5-71
*Honours:* USA 82 full caps.

| | | | | | |
|---|---|---|---|---|---|
| 1996 | Columbus Crew | 9 | 0 | | |
| 1997 | Columbus Crew | 29 | 0 | 38 | 0 |
| 1997-98 | Liverpool | 11 | 0 | | |
| 1998-99 | Liverpool | 12 | 0 | | |
| 1999-2000 | Liverpool | 2 | 0 | | |
| 2000-01 | Liverpool | 0 | 0 | 25 | 0 |
| 2000-01 | Blackburn R | 27 | 0 | | |
| 2001-02 | Blackburn R | 36 | 0 | | |
| 2002-03 | Blackburn R | 37 | 0 | | |
| 2003-04 | Blackburn R | 36 | 1 | | |
| 2004-05 | Blackburn R | 38 | 0 | | |
| 2005-06 | Blackburn R | 38 | 0 | | |
| 2006-07 | Blackburn R | 38 | 0 | | |
| 2007-08 | Blackburn R | 38 | 0 | 288 | 1 |
| 2008-09 | Aston Villa | 38 | 0 | | |
| 2009-10 | Aston Villa | 38 | 0 | | |
| 2010-11 | Aston Villa | 38 | 0 | 114 | 0 |
| 2011-12 | Tottenham H | 38 | 0 | | |
| 2012-13 | Tottenham H | 11 | 0 | 49 | 0 |

### FRYERS, Zeki (D)    9   0
H: 6 00   W: 12 00   b.Manchester 9-9-92
*Source:* Scholar. *Honours:* England Youth.

| | | | | | |
|---|---|---|---|---|---|
| 2011-12 | Manchester U | 2 | 0 | | |
| 2012-13 | Manchester U | 0 | 0 | 2 | 0 |
| 2012-13 | *Standard Liege* | 7 | 0 | 7 | 0 |
| 2012-13 | Tottenham H | 0 | 0 | | |

### GALLAS, William (D)    424   27
H: 6 00   W: 12 12   b.Asnieres 17-8-77
*Honours:* France Under-21, 84 full caps, 5 goals.

| | | | | | |
|---|---|---|---|---|---|
| 1996-97 | Caen | 18 | 0 | 18 | 0 |
| 1997-98 | Marseille | 3 | 0 | | |
| 1998-99 | Marseille | 30 | 0 | | |
| 1999-2000 | Marseille | 22 | 0 | | |
| 2000-01 | Marseille | 30 | 2 | 85 | 2 |
| 2001-02 | Chelsea | 30 | 1 | | |
| 2002-03 | Chelsea | 38 | 4 | | |
| 2003-04 | Chelsea | 29 | 0 | | |
| 2004-05 | Chelsea | 28 | 2 | | |
| 2005-06 | Chelsea | 34 | 5 | | |
| 2006-07 | Chelsea | 0 | 0 | 159 | 12 |
| 2006-07 | Arsenal | 21 | 3 | | |
| 2007-08 | Arsenal | 31 | 4 | | |
| 2008-09 | Arsenal | 23 | 2 | | |
| 2009-10 | Arsenal | 26 | 3 | | |
| 2010-11 | Arsenal | 0 | 0 | 101 | 12 |
| 2010-11 | Tottenham H | 27 | 0 | | |
| 2011-12 | Tottenham H | 15 | 0 | | |
| 2012-13 | Tottenham H | 19 | 1 | 61 | 1 |

### GALLIFUOCO, Giancarlo (M)    0   0
b.Sydney 12-1-94
*Source:* Sutherland Sharks.

| | | | | |
|---|---|---|---|---|
| 2011-12 | Tottenham H | 0 | 0 | |
| 2012-13 | Tottenham H | 0 | 0 | |

### GOMES, Heurelho (G)    291   0
H: 6 3   W: 12 13   b.Minas Gerais 15-2-81
*Source:* Democrata. *Honours:* Brazil Under-23, 11 full caps.

| | | | | | |
|---|---|---|---|---|---|
| 2001 | Cruzeiro | 0 | 0 | | |
| 2002 | Cruzeiro | 14 | 0 | | |
| 2003 | Cruzeiro | 40 | 0 | | |
| 2004 | Cruzeiro | 5 | 0 | 59 | 0 |
| 2004-05 | PSV Eindhoven | 30 | 0 | | |
| 2005-06 | PSV Eindhoven | 32 | 0 | | |
| 2006-07 | PSV Eindhoven | 32 | 0 | | |
| 2007-08 | PSV Eindhoven | 34 | 0 | 128 | 0 |
| 2008-09 | Tottenham H | 34 | 0 | | |
| 2009-10 | Tottenham H | 31 | 0 | | |
| 2010-11 | Tottenham H | 30 | 0 | | |
| 2011-12 | Tottenham H | 0 | 0 | | |
| 2012-13 | Tottenham H | 0 | 0 | 95 | 0 |
| 2012-13 | *TSG Hoffenheim* | 9 | 0 | 9 | 0 |

### HALL, Grant (D)    1   0
H: 5 9   W: 11 02   b.Brighton 29-10-91
*Source:* Lewes.

| | | | | | |
|---|---|---|---|---|---|
| 2009-10 | Brighton & HA | 0 | 0 | | |
| 2010-11 | Brighton & HA | 0 | 0 | | |
| 2011-12 | Brighton & HA | 1 | 0 | 1 | 0 |
| 2012-13 | Tottenham H | 0 | 0 | | |

### HOLTBY, Lewis (M)    143   24
H: 5 8   W: 10 04   b.Erkelenz 18-9-90
*Honours:* Germany Youth, Under-21, 3 full caps.

| | | | | | |
|---|---|---|---|---|---|
| 2007-08 | Alemania Aachen | 2 | 0 | | |
| 2008-09 | Alemania Aachen | 31 | 7 | 33 | 7 |
| 2009-10 | Schalke 04 | 9 | 0 | | |
| 2009-10 | *VfL Bochum* | 14 | 2 | 14 | 2 |
| 2010-11 | *Mainz* | 30 | 5 | 30 | 5 |
| 2011-12 | Schalke 04 | 27 | 6 | | |
| 2012-13 | Schalke 04 | 19 | 4 | 55 | 10 |
| 2012-13 | Tottenham H | 11 | 0 | 11 | 0 |

### HUDDLESTONE, Tom (M)    245   9
H: 6 2   W: 11 02   b.Nottingham 28-12-86
*Source:* Scholar. *Honours:* England Youth, Under-20, Under-21, 4 full caps.

| | | | | | |
|---|---|---|---|---|---|
| 2003-04 | Derby Co | 43 | 0 | | |
| 2004-05 | Derby Co | 45 | 0 | 88 | 0 |
| 2005-06 | Tottenham H | 4 | 0 | | |
| 2005-06 | *Wolverhampton W* | 13 | 1 | 13 | 1 |
| 2006-07 | Tottenham H | 21 | 1 | | |
| 2007-08 | Tottenham H | 28 | 3 | | |
| 2008-09 | Tottenham H | 22 | 0 | | |
| 2009-10 | Tottenham H | 33 | 2 | | |
| 2010-11 | Tottenham H | 14 | 2 | | |
| 2011-12 | Tottenham H | 2 | 0 | | |
| 2012-13 | Tottenham H | 20 | 0 | 144 | 8 |

### KABOUL, Younes (D)    177   12
H: 6 2   W: 13 07   b.Annemasse 4-1-86
*Honours:* France Under-21, 5 full caps, 1 goal.

| | | | | | |
|---|---|---|---|---|---|
| 2004-05 | Auxerre | 12 | 1 | | |
| 2005-06 | Auxerre | 9 | 0 | | |
| 2006-07 | Auxerre | 31 | 2 | 52 | 3 |
| 2007-08 | Tottenham H | 21 | 3 | | |
| 2008-09 | Portsmouth | 20 | 1 | | |
| 2009-10 | Portsmouth | 19 | 3 | 39 | 4 |
| 2009-10 | Tottenham H | 10 | 0 | | |
| 2010-11 | Tottenham H | 21 | 1 | | |
| 2011-12 | Tottenham H | 33 | 1 | | |
| 2012-13 | Tottenham H | 1 | 0 | 86 | 5 |

### KANE, Harry (F)    57   14
H: 6 00   W: 10 00   b.Chingford 28-7-93
*Source:* Scholar. *Honours:* England Youth.

| | | | | | |
|---|---|---|---|---|---|
| 2010-11 | Tottenham H | 0 | 0 | | |
| 2010-11 | *Leyton Orient* | 18 | 5 | 18 | 5 |
| 2011-12 | Tottenham H | 0 | 0 | | |
| 2011-12 | *Millwall* | 22 | 7 | 22 | 7 |
| 2012-13 | Tottenham H | 1 | 0 | 1 | 0 |
| 2012-13 | *Norwich C* | 3 | 0 | 3 | 0 |
| 2012-13 | *Leicester C* | 13 | 2 | 13 | 2 |

## LANCASTER, Cameron (F) — 5 0
H: 6 0  W: 11 09  b.Camden 5-11-92
Source: Scholar.

|  |  | | | | |
|---|---|---|---|---|---|
| 2010-11 | Tottenham H | 0 | 0 | | |
| 2010-11 | Dagenham & R | 4 | 0 | 4 | 0 |
| 2011-12 | Tottenham H | 1 | 0 | | |
| 2012-13 | Tottenham H | 0 | 0 | 1 | 0 |

## LENNON, Aaron (M) — 268 26
H: 5 6  W: 10 03  b.Leeds 16-4-87
Source: Trainee. Honours: England Youth, Under-21, B, 21 full caps.

|  |  | | | | |
|---|---|---|---|---|---|
| 2003-04 | Leeds U | 11 | 0 | | |
| 2004-05 | Leeds U | 27 | 1 | 38 | 1 |
| 2005-06 | Tottenham H | 27 | 2 | | |
| 2006-07 | Tottenham H | 26 | 3 | | |
| 2007-08 | Tottenham H | 29 | 2 | | |
| 2008-09 | Tottenham H | 35 | 5 | | |
| 2009-10 | Tottenham H | 22 | 3 | | |
| 2010-11 | Tottenham H | 34 | 3 | | |
| 2011-12 | Tottenham H | 23 | 3 | | |
| 2012-13 | Tottenham H | 34 | 4 | 230 | 25 |

## LIVERMORE, Jake (M) — 83 2
H: 5 9  W: 12 08  b.Enfield 14-11-89
Source: Scholar. Honours: England 1 full cap.

|  |  | | | | |
|---|---|---|---|---|---|
| 2006-07 | Tottenham H | 0 | 0 | | |
| 2007-08 | Tottenham H | 0 | 0 | | |
| 2007-08 | Milton Keynes D | 5 | 0 | 5 | 0 |
| 2008-09 | Tottenham H | 0 | 0 | | |
| 2008-09 | Crewe Alex | 0 | 0 | | |
| 2009-10 | Tottenham H | 1 | 0 | | |
| 2009-10 | Derby Co | 16 | 1 | 16 | 1 |
| 2009-10 | Peterborough U | 9 | 1 | 9 | 1 |
| 2010-11 | Tottenham H | 0 | 0 | | |
| 2010-11 | Ipswich T | 12 | 0 | 12 | 0 |
| 2010-11 | Leeds U | 5 | 0 | 5 | 0 |
| 2011-12 | Tottenham H | 24 | 0 | | |
| 2012-13 | Tottenham H | 11 | 0 | 36 | 0 |

## LLORIS, Hugo (G) — 245 0
H: 6 2  W: 12 03  b.Nice 26-12-86
Honours: France Youth, Under-20, Under-21, 47 full caps.

|  |  | | | | |
|---|---|---|---|---|---|
| 2005-06 | Nice | 5 | 0 | | |
| 2006-07 | Nice | 37 | 0 | | |
| 2007-08 | Nice | 30 | 0 | 72 | 0 |
| 2008-09 | Lyon | 35 | 0 | | |
| 2009-10 | Lyon | 36 | 0 | | |
| 2010-11 | Lyon | 37 | 0 | | |
| 2011-12 | Lyon | 36 | 0 | | |
| 2012-13 | Lyon | 2 | 0 | 146 | 0 |
| 2012-13 | Tottenham H | 27 | 0 | 27 | 0 |

## LUONGO, Massimo (F) — 16 1
H: 5 8  W: 11 10  b.Sydney 25-9-92
Source: Rushden & D.

|  |  | | | | |
|---|---|---|---|---|---|
| 2010-11 | Tottenham H | 0 | 0 | | |
| 2011-12 | Tottenham H | 0 | 0 | | |
| 2012-13 | Tottenham H | 0 | 0 | | |
| 2012-13 | Ipswich T | 9 | 0 | 9 | 0 |
| 2012-13 | Swindon T | 7 | 1 | 7 | 1 |

## MASON, Ryan (F) — 52 6
H: 5 9  W: 10 00  b.Enfield 13-6-91
Source: Scholar. Honours: England Youth.

|  |  | | | | |
|---|---|---|---|---|---|
| 2007-08 | Tottenham H | 0 | 0 | | |
| 2008-09 | Tottenham H | 0 | 0 | | |
| 2009-10 | Tottenham H | 0 | 0 | | |
| 2009-10 | Yeovil T | 28 | 6 | 28 | 6 |
| 2010-11 | Tottenham H | 0 | 0 | | |
| 2010-11 | Doncaster R | 15 | 0 | | |
| 2011-12 | Tottenham H | 0 | 0 | | |
| 2011-12 | Doncaster R | 4 | 0 | 19 | 0 |
| 2011-12 | Millwall | 5 | 0 | 5 | 0 |
| 2012-13 | Tottenham H | 0 | 0 | | |
| 2012-13 | Lorient | 0 | 0 | | |

## MILES, Jonathan (G) — 2 0
b.Colchester

|  |  | | | | |
|---|---|---|---|---|---|
| 2012-13 | Tottenham H | 0 | 0 | | |
| 2012-13 | Dagenham & R | 2 | 0 | 2 | 0 |

## NAUGHTON, Kyle (M) — 154 6
H: 5 11  W: 11 07  b.Sheffield 11-11-88
Honours: England Under-21.

|  |  | | | | |
|---|---|---|---|---|---|
| 2006-07 | Sheffield U | 0 | 0 | | |
| 2007-08 | Gretna | 18 | 0 | 18 | 0 |
| 2007-08 | Sheffield U | 0 | 0 | | |
| 2008-09 | Sheffield U | 40 | 1 | | |
| 2009-10 | Sheffield U | 0 | 0 | 40 | 1 |
| 2009-10 | Tottenham H | 1 | 0 | | |
| 2009-10 | Middlesbrough | 15 | 0 | 15 | 0 |
| 2010-11 | Tottenham H | 0 | 0 | | |
| 2010-11 | Leicester C | 34 | 5 | 34 | 5 |
| 2011-12 | Tottenham H | 0 | 0 | | |
| 2011-12 | Norwich C | 32 | 0 | 32 | 0 |
| 2012-13 | Tottenham H | 14 | 0 | 15 | 0 |

## NICHOLSON, Jake (M) — 2 0
H: 6 0  W: 11 07  b.Harrow 19-7-92
Source: Scholar.

|  |  | | | | |
|---|---|---|---|---|---|
| 2010-11 | Tottenham H | 0 | 0 | | |
| 2010-11 | MyPa | 2 | 0 | 2 | 0 |
| 2011-12 | Tottenham H | 0 | 0 | | |
| 2012-13 | Tottenham H | 0 | 0 | | |

## OBIKA, Jonathan (F) — 105 23
H: 6 0  W: 12 00  b.Enfield 12-9-90
Source: Scholar. Honours: England Youth, Under-20.

|  |  | | | | |
|---|---|---|---|---|---|
| 2008-09 | Tottenham H | 0 | 0 | | |
| 2008-09 | Yeovil T | 10 | 4 | | |
| 2009-10 | Tottenham H | 0 | 0 | | |
| 2009-10 | Yeovil T | 22 | 6 | | |
| 2009-10 | Millwall | 12 | 2 | 12 | 2 |
| 2010-11 | Tottenham H | 0 | 0 | | |
| 2010-11 | Crystal Palace | 7 | 0 | 7 | 0 |
| 2010-11 | Peterborough U | 1 | 1 | 1 | 1 |
| 2010-11 | Swindon T | 5 | 0 | 5 | 0 |
| 2010-11 | Yeovil T | 11 | 3 | | |
| 2011-12 | Tottenham H | 0 | 0 | | |
| 2011-12 | Yeovil T | 27 | 4 | 70 | 17 |
| 2012-13 | Tottenham H | 0 | 0 | | |
| 2012-13 | Charlton Ath | 10 | 3 | 10 | 3 |

## PARKER, Scott (M) — 367 25
H: 5 9  W: 11 10  b.Lambeth 13-10-80
Source: Trainee. Honours: England Schools, Youth, Under-21, 18 full caps.

|  |  | | | | |
|---|---|---|---|---|---|
| 1997-98 | Charlton Ath | 3 | 0 | | |
| 1998-99 | Charlton Ath | 4 | 0 | | |
| 1999-2000 | Charlton Ath | 15 | 1 | | |
| 2000-01 | Charlton Ath | 20 | 1 | | |
| 2000-01 | Norwich C | 6 | 1 | 6 | 1 |
| 2001-02 | Charlton Ath | 38 | 1 | | |
| 2002-03 | Charlton Ath | 28 | 4 | | |
| 2003-04 | Charlton Ath | 20 | 2 | 128 | 9 |
| 2003-04 | Chelsea | 11 | 1 | | |
| 2004-05 | Chelsea | 4 | 0 | 15 | 1 |
| 2005-06 | Newcastle U | 26 | 1 | | |
| 2006-07 | Newcastle U | 29 | 3 | 55 | 4 |
| 2007-08 | West Ham U | 18 | 1 | | |
| 2008-09 | West Ham U | 28 | 1 | | |
| 2009-10 | West Ham U | 31 | 2 | | |
| 2010-11 | West Ham U | 32 | 5 | | |
| 2011-12 | West Ham U | 4 | 1 | 113 | 10 |
| 2011-12 | Tottenham H | 29 | 0 | | |
| 2012-13 | Tottenham H | 21 | 0 | 50 | 0 |

## PARRETT, Dean (M) — 34 3
H: 5 10  W: 11 04  b.Hampstead 16-11-91
Source: Scholar. Honours: England Youth, Under-20.

|  |  | | | | |
|---|---|---|---|---|---|
| 2008-09 | Tottenham H | 0 | 0 | | |
| 2009-10 | Tottenham H | 0 | 0 | | |
| 2009-10 | Aldershot T | 4 | 0 | 4 | 0 |
| 2010-11 | Tottenham H | 0 | 0 | | |
| 2010-11 | Plymouth Arg | 8 | 1 | 8 | 1 |
| 2010-11 | Charlton Ath | 9 | 1 | 9 | 1 |
| 2011-12 | Tottenham H | 0 | 0 | | |
| 2011-12 | Yeovil T | 10 | 1 | 10 | 1 |
| 2012-13 | Tottenham H | 0 | 0 | | |
| 2012-13 | Swindon T | 3 | 0 | 3 | 0 |

## PRITCHARD, Alex (M) — 6 0
H: 5 7  W: 9 11  b.Grays 3-5-93
Source: Scholar.

|  |  | | | | |
|---|---|---|---|---|---|
| 2011-12 | Tottenham H | 0 | 0 | | |
| 2012-13 | Tottenham H | 0 | 0 | | |
| 2012-13 | Peterborough U | 6 | 0 | 6 | 0 |

## ROSE, Danny (M) — 67 2
H: 5 8  W: 11 11  b.Doncaster 2-6-90
Source: Leeds U. Honours: England Youth, Under-21.

|  |  | | | | |
|---|---|---|---|---|---|
| 2007-08 | Tottenham H | 0 | 0 | | |
| 2008-09 | Tottenham H | 0 | 0 | | |
| 2008-09 | Watford | 7 | 0 | 7 | 0 |
| 2009-10 | Tottenham H | 1 | 1 | | |
| 2010-11 | Tottenham H | 4 | 0 | | |
| 2010-11 | Bristol C | 17 | 0 | 17 | 0 |
| 2011-12 | Tottenham H | 11 | 0 | | |
| 2012-13 | Tottenham H | 0 | 0 | 16 | 1 |
| 2012-13 | Sunderland | 27 | 1 | 27 | 1 |

## SANDRO (M) — 107 6
H: 6 2  W: 11 11  b.Riachinho 15-3-89
Honours: Brazil Under-20, Under-23, 17 full caps, 1 goal.

|  |  | | | | |
|---|---|---|---|---|---|
| 2008 | Internacional | 7 | 2 | | |
| 2009 | Internacional | 27 | 1 | | |
| 2010 | Internacional | 9 | 1 | 43 | 4 |
| 2010-11 | Tottenham H | 19 | 1 | | |
| 2011-12 | Tottenham H | 23 | 0 | | |
| 2012-13 | Tottenham H | 22 | 1 | 64 | 2 |

## SIGURDSSON, Gylfi (M) — 147 41
H: 6 1  W: 12 02  b.Reykjavik 9-9-89
Source: Scholar. Honours: Iceland Youth, Under-21, 16 full caps, 4 goals.

|  |  | | | | |
|---|---|---|---|---|---|
| 2007-08 | Reading | 0 | 0 | | |
| 2008-09 | Reading | 0 | 0 | | |
| 2008-09 | Shrewsbury T | 5 | 1 | 5 | 1 |
| 2008-09 | Crewe Alex | 15 | 3 | 15 | 3 |
| 2009-10 | Reading | 38 | 16 | | |
| 2010-11 | Reading | 4 | 2 | 42 | 18 |
| 2010-11 | Hoffenheim | 28 | 9 | | |
| 2011-12 | Hoffenheim | 6 | 0 | 34 | 9 |
| 2011-12 | Swansea C | 18 | 7 | 18 | 7 |
| 2012-13 | Tottenham H | 33 | 3 | 33 | 3 |

## SMITH, Adam (D) — 103 4
H: 5 8  W: 10 07  b.Leytonstone 29-4-91
Source: Scholar. Honours: England Youth, Under-20, Under-21.

|  |  | | | | |
|---|---|---|---|---|---|
| 2007-08 | Tottenham H | 0 | 0 | | |
| 2008-09 | Tottenham H | 0 | 0 | | |
| 2009-10 | Tottenham H | 0 | 0 | | |
| 2009-10 | Wycombe W | 3 | 0 | 3 | 0 |
| 2009-10 | Torquay U | 16 | 0 | 16 | 0 |
| 2010-11 | Tottenham H | 0 | 0 | | |
| 2010-11 | Bournemouth | 38 | 1 | 38 | 1 |
| 2011-12 | Tottenham H | 1 | 0 | | |
| 2011-12 | Milton Keynes D | 17 | 2 | 17 | 2 |
| 2011-12 | Leeds U | 3 | 0 | 3 | 0 |
| 2012-13 | Tottenham H | 0 | 0 | 1 | 0 |
| 2012-13 | Millwall | 25 | 1 | 25 | 1 |

## STEWART, Kevin (D) — 4 0
H: 5 7  W: 11 06  b.Enfield 7-9-93

|  |  | | | | |
|---|---|---|---|---|---|
| 2012-13 | Tottenham H | 0 | 0 | | |
| 2012-13 | Crewe Alex | 4 | 0 | 4 | 0 |

## TOWNSEND, Andros (M) — 106 11
H: 6 0  W: 12 00  b.Chingford 16-7-91
Source: Scholar. Honours: England Youth, Under-21.

|  |  | | | | |
|---|---|---|---|---|---|
| 2008-09 | Tottenham H | 0 | 0 | | |
| 2008-09 | Yeovil T | 10 | 1 | 10 | 1 |
| 2009-10 | Tottenham H | 0 | 0 | | |
| 2009-10 | Leyton Orient | 22 | 2 | 22 | 2 |
| 2009-10 | Milton Keynes D | 9 | 2 | 9 | 2 |
| 2010-11 | Tottenham H | 0 | 0 | | |
| 2010-11 | Ipswich T | 13 | 1 | 13 | 1 |
| 2010-11 | Watford | 3 | 0 | 3 | 0 |
| 2010-11 | Millwall | 11 | 2 | 11 | 2 |
| 2011-12 | Tottenham H | 0 | 0 | | |
| 2011-12 | Leeds U | 6 | 1 | 6 | 1 |
| 2011-12 | Birmingham C | 15 | 0 | 15 | 0 |
| 2012-13 | Tottenham H | 5 | 0 | 5 | 0 |
| 2012-13 | QPR | 12 | 2 | 12 | 2 |

## VAN DER VAART, Rafael (M) — 312 116
H: 5 9  W: 11 09  b.Heemskerk 11-2-83
Honours: Holland 105 full caps, 23 goals.

|  |  | | | | |
|---|---|---|---|---|---|
| 1999-2000 | Ajax | 1 | 0 | | |
| 2000-01 | Ajax | 27 | 7 | | |
| 2001-02 | Ajax | 20 | 14 | | |
| 2002-03 | Ajax | 21 | 18 | | |
| 2003-04 | Ajax | 26 | 7 | | |
| 2004-05 | Ajax | 22 | 6 | 117 | 52 |
| 2005-06 | Hamburg | 19 | 9 | | |
| 2006-07 | Hamburg | 26 | 8 | | |
| 2007-08 | Hamburg | 29 | 12 | 74 | 29 |
| 2008-09 | Real Madrid | 32 | 5 | | |
| 2009-10 | Real Madrid | 26 | 6 | 58 | 11 |
| 2010-11 | Tottenham H | 28 | 13 | | |
| 2011-12 | Tottenham H | 33 | 11 | | |
| 2012-13 | Tottenham H | 2 | 0 | 63 | 24 |

Transferred to Hamburg September 2012

**VERTONGHEN, Jan (D)**    201 30
H: 6 2   W: 12 05   b.Sint-Niklaas 24-4-87
*Honours:* Belgium Youth, Under-21, 49 full caps, 4 goals.

| 2006-07 | Ajax | 3 | 0 | | |
|---|---|---|---|---|---|
| 2006-07 | *RKC* | 12 | 3 | 12 | 3 |
| 2007-08 | Ajax | 31 | 2 | | |
| 2008-09 | Ajax | 26 | 4 | | |
| 2009-10 | Ajax | 32 | 3 | | |
| 2010-11 | Ajax | 32 | 6 | | |
| 2011-12 | Ajax | 31 | 8 | 155 | 23 |
| 2012-13 | Tottenham H | 34 | 4 | 34 | 4 |

**WALKER, Kyle (D)**    148 3
H: 5 10   W: 11 07   b.Sheffield 28-5-90
*Source:* Scholar. *Honours:* England Youth, Under-21, 5 full caps.

| 2008-09 | Sheffield U | 2 | 0 | | |
|---|---|---|---|---|---|
| 2008-09 | *Northampton T* | 9 | 0 | 9 | 0 |
| 2009-10 | Tottenham H | 2 | 0 | | |
| 2009-10 | *Sheffield U* | 26 | 0 | 28 | 0 |
| 2010-11 | Tottenham H | 1 | 0 | | |
| 2010-11 | *QPR* | 20 | 0 | 20 | 0 |
| 2010-11 | *Aston Villa* | 15 | 1 | 15 | 1 |
| 2011-12 | Tottenham H | 37 | 2 | | |
| 2012-13 | Tottenham H | 36 | 0 | 76 | 2 |

**WALLER-LASSEN, Jesse (M)**    0 0
H: 5 8   W: 12 00   b.Crouch End 26-12-92

| 2012-13 | Tottenham H | 0 | 0 | 0 | 0 |
|---|---|---|---|---|---|

**Players retained or with offer of contract**
Bentaleb, Nabil; Coulibaly, Souleymane; Gomelt, Tomislav; Khumalo, Bongani; Michael-Percil, Roman; Vigouroux, Lawrence.

**Scholars**
Akindayini, Daniel Oluwaseun; Ball, Dominic; Brown, Zodel Yeboah; Dombaxe, Laste; Lameiras, Ruben; Lesniak, Filip; McEneff, Aaron; McEvoy, Kenneth; McGee, Luke Paul; McQueen, Alexander Luke; McQueen, Darren; Miller, William; Oduwa, Nathan; Ogilvie, Connor Stuart; Priestley, Liam Joseph; Sonupe, Emmanuel Olukolade; Veljkovic, Milos; Vincent-Young, Kane; Ward, Grant Antony; Winks, Harry.

# TRANMERE R (83)

**AKPA AKPRO, Jean-Louis (F)**    202 32
H: 6 0   W: 10 12   b.Toulouse 4-1-85

| 2004-05 | Toulouse | 13 | 0 | | |
|---|---|---|---|---|---|
| 2005-06 | Toulouse | 14 | 3 | 27 | 3 |
| 2006-07 | Brest | 15 | 2 | 15 | 2 |
| 2007-08 | FC Brussels | 3 | 0 | 3 | 0 |
| 2008-09 | Grimsby T | 20 | 3 | | |
| 2009-10 | Grimsby T | 36 | 5 | 56 | 8 |
| 2010-11 | Rochdale | 32 | 4 | | |
| 2011-12 | Rochdale | 41 | 7 | 73 | 11 |
| 2012-13 | Tranmere R | 28 | 8 | 28 | 8 |

**AMOO, David (F)**    65 6
H: 5 10   W: 12 03   b.Southwark 23-4-91
*Source:* Millwall.

| 2007-08 | Liverpool | 0 | 0 | | |
|---|---|---|---|---|---|
| 2008-09 | Liverpool | 0 | 0 | | |
| 2009-10 | Liverpool | 0 | 0 | | |
| 2010-11 | Liverpool | 0 | 0 | | |
| 2010-11 | *Milton Keynes D* | 3 | 0 | 3 | 0 |
| 2010-11 | *Hull C* | 7 | 1 | 7 | 1 |
| 2011-12 | Liverpool | 0 | 0 | | |
| 2011-12 | *Bury* | 27 | 4 | 27 | 4 |
| 2012-13 | Preston NE | 17 | 0 | 17 | 0 |
| 2012-13 | Tranmere R | 11 | 1 | 11 | 1 |

**BAKAYOGO, Zaoumana (D)**    143 5
H: 5 9   W: 10 08   b.Paris 11-8-86
*Source:* Paris St Germain. *Honours:* Ivory Coast Under-23.

| 2006-07 | Millwall | 5 | 0 | | |
|---|---|---|---|---|---|
| 2007-08 | Millwall | 10 | 0 | 15 | 0 |

From Alfortville.

| 2009-10 | Tranmere R | 29 | 0 | | |
|---|---|---|---|---|---|
| 2010-11 | Tranmere R | 27 | 1 | | |
| 2011-12 | Tranmere R | 26 | 0 | | |
| 2012-13 | Tranmere R | 46 | 4 | 128 | 5 |

**BELL-BAGGIE, Abdulai (F)**    45 1
H: 5 6   W: 10 00   b.London 28-4-92
*Source:* Scholar. *Honours:* England Youth, Sierra Leone 1 full cap.

| 2009-10 | Reading | 0 | 0 | | |
|---|---|---|---|---|---|
| 2009-10 | *Rotherham U* | 11 | 0 | 11 | 0 |
| 2010-11 | Reading | 0 | 0 | | |
| 2010-11 | *Port Vale* | 3 | 0 | 3 | 0 |

From Hayes & Y, Salisbury C

| 2012-13 | Tranmere R | 31 | 1 | 31 | 1 |
|---|---|---|---|---|---|

**BLACK, Paul (D)**    70 1
H: 6 0   W: 12 10   b.Middleton 18-5-90
*Source:* Scholar.

| 2007-08 | Oldham Ath | 2 | 0 | | |
|---|---|---|---|---|---|
| 2008-09 | Oldham Ath | 3 | 0 | | |
| 2009-10 | Oldham Ath | 13 | 1 | | |
| 2010-11 | Oldham Ath | 29 | 0 | | |
| 2011-12 | Oldham Ath | 13 | 0 | 60 | 1 |
| 2012-13 | Tranmere R | 10 | 0 | 10 | 0 |

**BURGESS, Ben (F)**    346 91
H: 6 3   W: 14 04   b.Buxton 9-11-81
*Source:* Trainee. *Honours:* Eire Youth, Under-21.

| 1998-99 | Blackburn R | 0 | 0 | | |
|---|---|---|---|---|---|
| 1999-2000 | Blackburn R | 2 | 0 | | |
| 2000-01 | Blackburn R | 0 | 0 | | |
| 2000-01 | *Northern Spirit* | 27 | 16 | 27 | 16 |
| 2001-02 | Blackburn R | 0 | 0 | | |
| 2001-02 | *Brentford* | 43 | 17 | 43 | 17 |
| 2002-03 | Stockport Co | 19 | 4 | 19 | 4 |
| 2002-03 | *Oldham Ath* | 7 | 0 | 7 | 0 |
| 2002-03 | Hull C | 7 | 4 | | |
| 2003-04 | Hull C | 44 | 18 | | |
| 2004-05 | Hull C | 2 | 0 | | |
| 2005-06 | Hull C | 14 | 2 | | |
| 2006-07 | Hull C | 3 | 0 | 70 | 24 |
| 2006-07 | Blackpool | 27 | 2 | | |
| 2007-08 | Blackpool | 35 | 9 | | |
| 2008-09 | Blackpool | 29 | 6 | | |
| 2009-10 | Blackpool | 35 | 6 | 126 | 23 |
| 2010-11 | Notts Co | 17 | 1 | | |
| 2011-12 | Notts Co | 28 | 4 | 45 | 5 |
| 2011-12 | *Cheltenham T* | 7 | 2 | 7 | 2 |
| 2012-13 | Tranmere R | 9 | 0 | | |

**FON WILLIAMS, Owain (G)**    190 0
H: 6 1   W: 12 09   b.Penygroes 17-3-87
*Source:* Scholar. *Honours:* Wales Youth, Under-21.

| 2005-06 | Crewe Alex | 0 | 0 | | |
|---|---|---|---|---|---|
| 2006-07 | Crewe Alex | 0 | 0 | | |
| 2007-08 | Crewe Alex | 0 | 0 | | |
| 2008-09 | Stockport Co | 33 | 0 | | |
| 2009-10 | Stockport Co | 44 | 0 | | |
| 2010-11 | Stockport Co | 5 | 0 | 82 | 0 |
| 2010-11 | *Bury* | 6 | 0 | 6 | 0 |
| 2010-11 | *Rochdale* | 22 | 0 | 22 | 0 |
| 2011-12 | Tranmere R | 35 | 0 | | |
| 2012-13 | Tranmere R | 45 | 0 | 80 | 0 |

**GOODISON, Ian (D)**    416 12
H: 6 1   W: 13 04   b.St James, Jamaica 21-11-72
*Source:* Olympic Gardens. *Honours:* Jamaica 113 full caps, 9 goals.

| 1999-2000 | Hull C | 18 | 0 | | |
|---|---|---|---|---|---|
| 2000-01 | Hull C | 36 | 1 | | |
| 2001-02 | Hull C | 16 | 0 | | |
| 2002-03 | Hull C | 0 | 0 | 70 | 1 |

From Seba U.

| 2003-04 | Tranmere R | 12 | 0 | | |
|---|---|---|---|---|---|
| 2004-05 | Tranmere R | 44 | 1 | | |
| 2005-06 | Tranmere R | 38 | 1 | | |
| 2006-07 | Tranmere R | 40 | 0 | | |
| 2007-08 | Tranmere R | 42 | 0 | | |
| 2008-09 | Tranmere R | 33 | 1 | | |
| 2009-10 | Tranmere R | 44 | 3 | | |
| 2010-11 | Tranmere R | 40 | 4 | | |
| 2011-12 | Tranmere R | 43 | 1 | | |
| 2012-13 | Tranmere R | 10 | 0 | 346 | 11 |

**HARRISON, Danny (M)**    322 20
H: 5 11   W: 12 04   b.Liverpool 4-11-82
*Source:* Scholar.

| 2001-02 | Tranmere R | 1 | 0 | | |
|---|---|---|---|---|---|
| 2002-03 | Tranmere R | 12 | 0 | | |
| 2003-04 | Tranmere R | 32 | 2 | | |
| 2004-05 | Tranmere R | 32 | 0 | | |
| 2005-06 | Tranmere R | 35 | 2 | | |
| 2006-07 | Tranmere R | 12 | 1 | | |
| 2007-08 | Rotherham U | 44 | 4 | | |
| 2008-09 | Rotherham U | 33 | 1 | | |
| 2009-10 | Rotherham U | 37 | 4 | | |
| 2010-11 | Rotherham U | 30 | 4 | | |
| 2011-12 | Rotherham U | 41 | 2 | 185 | 15 |
| 2012-13 | Tranmere R | 13 | 0 | 137 | 5 |

**HOLMES, Danny (D)**    128 5
H: 6 0   W: 11 13   b.Birkenhead 6-1-89

| 2007-08 | Tranmere R | 0 | 0 | | |
|---|---|---|---|---|---|
| 2008-09 | Tranmere R | 1 | 0 | | |
| 2009-10 | The New Saints | 32 | 0 | | |
| 2010-11 | The New Saints | 26 | 3 | 58 | 3 |
| 2011-12 | Tranmere R | 26 | 0 | | |
| 2012-13 | Tranmere R | 43 | 2 | 70 | 2 |

**KAY, Michael (D)**    34 1
H: 6 0   W: 11 05   b.Consett 12-9-89
*Source:* Scholar.

| 2007-08 | Sunderland | 0 | 0 | | |
|---|---|---|---|---|---|
| 2008-09 | Sunderland | 0 | 0 | | |
| 2009-10 | Sunderland | 0 | 0 | | |
| 2010-11 | Sunderland | 0 | 0 | | |
| 2010-11 | *Tranmere R* | 22 | 1 | | |
| 2011-12 | Tranmere R | 6 | 0 | | |
| 2012-13 | Tranmere R | 6 | 0 | 34 | 1 |

**KIRBY, Jake (M)**    5 0
H: 5 11   W: 12 04   b.Liverpool 9-5-94
*Source:* Scholar.

| 2011-12 | Tranmere R | 1 | 0 | | |
|---|---|---|---|---|---|
| 2012-13 | Tranmere R | 4 | 0 | 5 | 0 |

**McGINTY, Sean (D)**    8 0
H: 6 0   W: 11 09   b.Maidstone 11-8-93
*Source:* Scholar. *Honours:* Eire Youth, Under-21.

| 2010-11 | Manchester U | 0 | 0 | | |
|---|---|---|---|---|---|
| 2011-12 | Manchester U | 0 | 0 | | |
| 2011-12 | *Morecambe* | 4 | 0 | 4 | 0 |
| 2012-13 | Manchester U | 0 | 0 | | |
| 2012-13 | *Oxford U* | 0 | 0 | | |
| 2012-13 | *Carlisle U* | 1 | 0 | 1 | 0 |
| 2012-13 | Tranmere R | 3 | 0 | 3 | 0 |

**McGURK, Adam (F)**    79 10
H: 5 9   W: 12 13   b.Larne 24-1-89
*Source:* Scholar. *Honours:* Northern Ireland Under-21.

| 2005-06 | Aston Villa | 0 | 0 | | |
|---|---|---|---|---|---|
| 2006-07 | Aston Villa | 0 | 0 | | |
| 2007-08 | Aston Villa | 0 | 0 | | |
| 2008-09 | Aston Villa | 0 | 0 | | |
| 2009-10 | Aston Villa | 0 | 0 | | |

From Hednesford T.

| 2010-11 | Tranmere R | 21 | 3 | | |
|---|---|---|---|---|---|
| 2011-12 | Tranmere R | 31 | 4 | | |
| 2012-13 | Tranmere R | 27 | 3 | 79 | 10 |

**MOONEY, Jason (G)**    1 0
H: 6 9   W: 14 00
*Source:* Ards, Bangor, Ards Rangers, Comber Rec.

| 2011-12 | Wycombe W | 0 | 0 | | |
|---|---|---|---|---|---|
| 2012-13 | Tranmere R | 1 | 0 | 1 | 0 |

**POWER, Max (M)**    31 3
H: 5 11   W: 11 13   b.Bebington 27-7-93
*Source:* Scholar.

| 2010-11 | Tranmere R | 0 | 0 | | |
|---|---|---|---|---|---|
| 2011-12 | Tranmere R | 4 | 0 | | |
| 2012-13 | Tranmere R | 27 | 3 | 31 | 3 |

**ROBINSON, Andy (M)**    308 60
H: 5 8   W: 11 04   b.Birkenhead 3-11-79
*Source:* Cammell Laird.

| 2002-03 | Tranmere R | 0 | 0 | | |
|---|---|---|---|---|---|
| 2003-04 | Swansea C | 37 | 8 | | |
| 2004-05 | Swansea C | 37 | 8 | | |
| 2005-06 | Swansea C | 39 | 12 | | |
| 2006-07 | Swansea C | 39 | 7 | | |
| 2007-08 | Swansea C | 40 | 8 | 192 | 43 |
| 2008-09 | Leeds U | 32 | 2 | | |
| 2009-10 | Leeds U | 6 | 0 | | |
| 2009-10 | *Tranmere R* | 5 | | | |
| 2010-11 | Leeds U | | | | |

| 2011-12 | Tranmere R | 25 | 4 | | |
| 2012-13 | Tranmere R | 33 | 10 | 78 | 15 |

**SIDIBE, Mamady (F)** 324 42
H: 6 4   W: 12 02   b.Bamako 18-12-79
*Source:* CA Paris. *Honours:* Mali 14 full caps, 3 goals.

| 2001-02 | Swansea C | 31 | 7 | 31 | 7 |
| 2002-03 | Gillingham | 30 | 3 | | |
| 2003-04 | Gillingham | 41 | 5 | | |
| 2004-05 | Gillingham | 35 | 2 | 106 | 10 |
| 2005-06 | Stoke C | 42 | 6 | | |
| 2006-07 | Stoke C | 43 | 9 | | |
| 2007-08 | Stoke C | 35 | 4 | | |
| 2008-09 | Stoke C | 22 | 3 | | |
| 2009-10 | Stoke C | 24 | 2 | | |
| 2010-11 | Stoke C | 2 | 0 | | |
| 2011-12 | Stoke C | 0 | 0 | | |
| 2012-13 | Stoke C | 0 | 0 | 168 | 24 |
| 2012-13 | Sheffield W | 9 | 1 | 9 | 1 |
| 2012-13 | Tranmere R | 10 | 0 | 10 | 0 |

**STOCKTON, Cole (F)** 32 3
H: 6 1   W: 11 11   b.Huyton 13-3-94
*Source:* Scholar.

| 2011-12 | Tranmere R | 1 | 0 | | |
| 2012-13 | Tranmere R | 31 | 3 | 32 | 3 |

**TAYLOR, Ash (M)** 141 5
H: 6 0   W: 12 00   b.Bromborough 2-9-90
*Source:* Scholar. *Honours:* Wales Youth, Under-21

| 2008-09 | Tranmere R | 1 | 0 | | |
| 2009-10 | Tranmere R | 33 | 1 | | |
| 2010-11 | Tranmere R | 26 | 0 | | |
| 2011-12 | Tranmere R | 37 | 2 | | |
| 2012-13 | Tranmere R | 44 | 2 | 141 | 5 |

**THOMPSON, Joe (M)** 166 16
H: 6 0   W: 9 07   b.Rochdale 5-3-89
*Source:* Scholar.

| 2005-06 | Rochdale | 1 | 0 | | |
| 2006-07 | Rochdale | 13 | 0 | | |
| 2007-08 | Rochdale | 11 | 1 | | |
| 2008-09 | Rochdale | 30 | 5 | | |
| 2009-10 | Rochdale | 36 | 6 | | |
| 2010-11 | Rochdale | 32 | 2 | | |
| 2011-12 | Rochdale | 17 | 1 | | |
| 2012-13 | Tranmere R | 19 | 1 | 19 | 1 |
| 2012-13 | Rochdale | 7 | 0 | 147 | 15 |

**WALLACE, James (M)** 54 5
H: 5 11   W: 12 08   b.Fazakerly 19-12-91
*Source:* Scholar. *Honours:* England Youth, Under-20.

| 2008-09 | Everton | 0 | 0 | | |
| 2009-10 | Everton | 0 | 0 | | |
| 2010-11 | Everton | 0 | 0 | | |
| 2010-11 | Stockport Co | 14 | 1 | 14 | 1 |
| 2010-11 | Bury | 0 | 0 | | |
| 2011-12 | Everton | 0 | 0 | | |
| 2011-12 | Shrewsbury T | 3 | 0 | 3 | 0 |
| 2011-12 | Stevenage | 0 | 0 | | |
| 2011-12 | Tranmere R | 18 | 2 | | |
| 2012-13 | Tranmere R | 19 | 2 | 37 | 4 |

**Scholars**
Beech, Mark Samuel; Davies, Liam; Dunne, Lewis William; Holmes, John Peter; Holmes, Jordan Mark; Jones, Nathan Thomas; Joyce, James Anthony; Lynskey, Christopher; Maher, Benjamin Thomas; Newton, Joseph Luke; Phillips, Jake Terence Kenneth Lee; Ramsbottom, Sam Nicholas; Riley, Leo Paul; Shackleton, Connor Edward; Shaw, Daniel Thomas.

## WALSALL (84)

**BAXENDALE, James (M)** 35 4
H: 5 8   W: 10 03   b.Thorne 16-9-92
*Source:* Leeds U Scholar.

| 2011-12 | Doncaster R | 2 | 0 | | |
| 2011-12 | Hereford U | 1 | 0 | 1 | 0 |
| 2012-13 | Doncaster R | 0 | 0 | 2 | 0 |
| 2012-13 | Walsall | 32 | 4 | 32 | 4 |

**BENNING, Malvind (D)** 10 0
H: 5 10   W: 12 00   b.Sandwell 2-11-93

| 2012-13 | Walsall | 10 | 0 | 10 | 0 |

**BOWERMAN, George (F)** 50 9
H: 5 10   W: 10 07   b.Sedgley 6-11-91
*Source:* Scholar.

| 2010-11 | Walsall | 0 | 0 | | |
| 2011-12 | Walsall | 22 | 3 | | |
| 2012-13 | Walsall | 28 | 6 | 50 | 9 |

**BRANDY, Febian (F)** 98 15
H: 5 6   W: 9 13   b.Manchester 4-2-89

| 2006-07 | Manchester U | 0 | 0 | | |
| 2007-08 | Manchester U | 0 | 0 | | |
| 2007-08 | Swansea C | 19 | 3 | | |
| 2008-09 | Manchester U | 0 | 0 | | |
| 2008-09 | Swansea C | 14 | 0 | 33 | 3 |
| 2008-09 | Hereford U | 15 | 4 | 15 | 4 |
| 2009-10 | Manchester U | 0 | 0 | | |
| 2009-10 | Gillingham | 7 | 1 | 7 | 1 |
| 2010-11 | Notts Co | 9 | 0 | 9 | 0 |
| 2012-13 | Walsall | 34 | 7 | 34 | 7 |

**BUTLER, Andy (D)** 313 32
H: 6 0   W: 13 00   b.Doncaster 4-11-83
*Source:* Scholar.

| 2003-04 | Scunthorpe U | 35 | 2 | | |
| 2004-05 | Scunthorpe U | 37 | 10 | | |
| 2005-06 | Scunthorpe U | 16 | 1 | | |
| 2006-07 | Scunthorpe U | 11 | 1 | | |
| 2006-07 | Grimsby T | 4 | 0 | 4 | 0 |
| 2007-08 | Scunthorpe U | 36 | 2 | 135 | 16 |
| 2008-09 | Huddersfield T | 42 | 4 | | |
| 2009-10 | Huddersfield T | 11 | 0 | 53 | 4 |
| 2009-10 | Blackpool | 7 | 0 | 7 | 0 |
| 2010-11 | Walsall | 31 | 4 | | |
| 2011-12 | Walsall | 42 | 5 | | |
| 2012-13 | Walsall | 41 | 3 | 114 | 12 |

**CHAMBERS, Adam (D)** 309 12
H: 5 10   W: 11 12   b.Sandwell 20-11-80
*Source:* Trainee. *Honours:* England Youth.

| 1998-99 | WBA | 0 | 0 | | |
| 1999-2000 | WBA | 0 | 0 | | |
| 2000-01 | WBA | 11 | 1 | | |
| 2001-02 | WBA | 32 | 0 | | |
| 2002-03 | WBA | 13 | 0 | | |
| 2003-04 | WBA | 0 | 0 | | |
| 2003-04 | Sheffield W | 11 | 0 | 11 | 0 |
| 2004-05 | WBA | 0 | 0 | 56 | 1 |
| 2004-05 | Kidderminster H | 2 | 0 | 2 | 0 |
| 2006-07 | Leyton Orient | 38 | 4 | | |
| 2007-08 | Leyton Orient | 45 | 3 | | |
| 2008-09 | Leyton Orient | 33 | 1 | | |
| 2009-10 | Leyton Orient | 29 | 1 | | |
| 2010-11 | Leyton Orient | 29 | 0 | 174 | 9 |
| 2011-12 | Walsall | 29 | 2 | | |
| 2012-13 | Walsall | 37 | 0 | 66 | 2 |

**CHAMBERS, James (D)** 310 0
H: 5 10   W: 11 11   b.West Bromwich 20-11-80
*Source:* Trainee. *Honours:* England Youth.

| 1998-99 | WBA | 0 | 0 | | |
| 1999-2000 | WBA | 12 | 0 | | |
| 2000-01 | WBA | 31 | 0 | | |
| 2001-02 | WBA | 5 | 0 | | |
| 2002-03 | WBA | 8 | 0 | | |
| 2003-04 | WBA | 17 | 0 | | |
| 2004-05 | WBA | 0 | 0 | 73 | 0 |
| 2004-05 | Watford | 40 | 0 | | |
| 2005-06 | Watford | 38 | 0 | | |
| 2006-07 | Watford | 12 | 0 | 90 | 0 |
| 2006-07 | Cardiff C | 7 | 0 | 7 | 0 |
| 2007-08 | Leicester C | 24 | 0 | 24 | 0 |
| 2008-09 | Doncaster R | 37 | 0 | | |
| 2009-10 | Doncaster R | 43 | 0 | | |
| 2010-11 | Doncaster R | 7 | 0 | | |
| 2011-12 | Doncaster R | 0 | 0 | 87 | 0 |
| 2011-12 | Hereford U | 7 | 0 | 7 | 0 |
| 2012-13 | Walsall | 22 | 0 | 22 | 0 |

**DOWNING, Paul (D)** 63 0
H: 6 1   W: 12 06   b.Taunton 26-10-91
*Source:* Scholar.

| 2009-10 | WBA | 0 | 0 | | |
| 2009-10 | Hereford U | 6 | 0 | | |
| 2010-11 | WBA | 0 | 0 | | |
| 2010-11 | Hereford U | 0 | 0 | 6 | 0 |
| 2010-11 | Swansea C | 0 | 0 | | |
| 2011-12 | WBA | 0 | 0 | | |
| 2011-12 | Barnet | 26 | 0 | 26 | 0 |
| 2012-13 | Walsall | 31 | 1 | 31 | 1 |

**FEATHERSTONE, Nicky (M)** 112 1
H: 5 7   W: 11 02   b.Ferriby 22-9-88

| 2006-07 | Hull C | 2 | 0 | | |
| 2007-08 | Hull C | 6 | 0 | | |
| 2008-09 | Hull C | 0 | 0 | | |
| 2009-10 | Hull C | 0 | 0 | 8 | 0 |
| 2009-10 | Grimsby T | 8 | 0 | 8 | 0 |
| 2010-11 | Hereford U | 27 | 1 | | |
| 2011-12 | Hereford U | 38 | 0 | 65 | 1 |
| 2012-13 | Walsall | 31 | 0 | 31 | 0 |

**GEORGE, Ben (D)** 1 0
H: 5 8   W: 10 13   b. 14-11-93

| 2012-13 | Walsall | 1 | 0 | 1 | 0 |

**GRIGG, Will (M)** 99 27
H: 5 11   W: 11 00   b.Solihull 3-7-91
*Source:* Scholar. *Honours:* Northern Ireland Youth, Under-21, 2 full caps.

| 2008-09 | Walsall | 1 | 0 | | |
| 2009-10 | Walsall | 0 | 0 | | |
| 2010-11 | Walsall | 28 | 4 | | |
| 2011-12 | Walsall | 29 | 4 | | |
| 2012-13 | Walsall | 41 | 19 | 99 | 27 |

**GROF, David (G)** 33 0
H: 6 3   W: 14 02   b.Budapest 17-4-89

| 2008-09 | Hibernian | 0 | 0 | | |
| 2009-10 | Hibernian | 0 | 0 | | |
| 2010-11 | Notts Co | 0 | 0 | | |
| 2011-12 | Walsall | 23 | 0 | | |
| 2012-13 | Walsall | 10 | 0 | 33 | 0 |

**HEMMINGS, Ashley (M)** 63 3
H: 5 8   W: 11 06   b.Lewisham 3-3-91
*Source:* Scholar.

| 2008-09 | Wolverhampton W | 2 | 0 | | |
| 2008-09 | Cheltenham T | 1 | 0 | 1 | 0 |
| 2009-10 | Wolverhampton W | 0 | 0 | | |
| 2010-11 | Wolverhampton W | 0 | 0 | | |
| 2010-11 | Torquay U | 9 | 0 | 9 | 0 |
| 2011-12 | Wolverhampton W | 0 | 0 | | |
| 2011-12 | Plymouth Arg | 23 | 2 | 23 | 2 |
| 2012-13 | Walsall | 28 | 1 | 28 | 1 |

**HOLDEN, Dean (D)** 365 22
H: 6 1   W: 12 04   b.Swinton 15-9-79
*Source:* Trainee. *Honours:* England Youth.

| 1997-98 | Bolton W | 0 | 0 | | |
| 1998-99 | Bolton W | 0 | 0 | | |
| 1999-2000 | Bolton W | 12 | 0 | | |
| 2000-01 | Bolton W | 1 | 1 | 13 | 1 |
| 2001 | Valur | 7 | 0 | 7 | 0 |
| 2001-02 | Oldham Ath | 23 | 2 | | |
| 2002-03 | Oldham Ath | 6 | 0 | | |
| 2003-04 | Oldham Ath | 39 | 4 | | |
| 2004-05 | Oldham Ath | 40 | 2 | 108 | 10 |
| 2005-06 | Peterborough U | 35 | 3 | | |
| 2006-07 | Peterborough U | 21 | 1 | 56 | 4 |
| 2006-07 | Falkirk | 9 | 1 | | |
| 2007-08 | Falkirk | 20 | 0 | | |
| 2008-09 | Falkirk | 19 | 1 | 48 | 2 |
| 2009-10 | Shrewsbury T | 37 | 0 | | |
| 2010-11 | Shrewsbury T | 13 | 0 | 50 | 0 |
| 2010-11 | Rotherham U | 6 | 0 | 6 | 0 |
| 2010-11 | Chesterfield | 17 | 2 | | |
| 2011-12 | Chesterfield | 14 | 1 | 31 | 3 |
| 2011-12 | Rochdale | 21 | 0 | 21 | 0 |
| 2012-13 | Walsall | 25 | 2 | 25 | 2 |

**JONES, Jake (M)** 3 0
H: 5 10   W: 11 09   b.Solihull 6-4-93
*Source:* Scholar.

| 2011-12 | Walsall | 0 | 0 | | |
| 2012-13 | Walsall | 3 | 0 | 3 | 0 |

**JONES, Richard (G)** 0 0
H: 5 8   W: 11 13   b.
| 2012-13 | Walsall | 0 | 0 | | |

**MANTOM, Sam (M)** 48 5
H: 5 9   W: 11 00   b.Stourbridge 20-2-92
*Source:* Scholar.

| 2010-11 | WBA | 0 | 0 | | |
| 2010-11 | Tranmere R | 2 | 0 | 2 | 0 |
| 2010-11 | Oldham Ath | 4 | 0 | 4 | 0 |

| | | | | | |
|---|---|---|---|---|---|
| 2011-12 | WBA | 0 | 0 | | |
| 2011-12 | *Walsall* | 13 | 3 | | |
| 2012-13 | WBA | 0 | 0 | | |
| 2012-13 | Walsall | 29 | 2 | 42 | 5 |

**MORRIS, Kieron (M)**    **0 0**
H: 5 10   W: 11 01

| | | | |
|---|---|---|---|
| 2012-13 | Walsall | 0 | 0 |

**PATERSON, Jamie (F)**    **94 15**
H: 5 9   W: 10 07   b.Coventry 20-12-91
*Source:* Scholar.

| | | | | | |
|---|---|---|---|---|---|
| 2010-11 | Walsall | 14 | 0 | | |
| 2011-12 | Walsall | 34 | 3 | | |
| 2012-13 | Walsall | 46 | 12 | 94 | 15 |

**PURKISS, Ben (D)**    **65 0**
H: 6 2   W: 10 13   b.Sheffield 1-4-84

| | | | | | |
|---|---|---|---|---|---|
| 2001-02 | Sheffield U | 0 | 0 | | |
| 2002-03 | Sheffield U | 0 | 0 | | |

From Gainsborough T, York C

| | | | | | |
|---|---|---|---|---|---|
| 2010-11 | Oxford U | 23 | 0 | 23 | 0 |
| 2011-12 | Hereford U | 15 | 0 | 15 | 0 |
| 2012-13 | Walsall | 27 | 0 | 27 | 0 |

**ROBERTS, Liam (G)**    **0 0**

| | | | |
|---|---|---|---|
| 2012-13 | Walsall | 0 | 0 |

**SAWYERS, Romaine (M)**    **12 0**
H: 5 9   W: 11 00   b.Birmingham 2-11-91
*Source:* Scholar.

| | | | | | |
|---|---|---|---|---|---|
| 2009-10 | WBA | 0 | 0 | | |
| 2010-11 | WBA | 0 | 0 | | |
| 2010-11 | *Port Vale* | 1 | 0 | 1 | 0 |
| 2011-12 | WBA | 0 | 0 | | |
| 2011-12 | *Shrewsbury T* | 7 | 0 | 7 | 0 |
| 2012-13 | WBA | 0 | 0 | | |
| 2012-13 | Walsall | 4 | 0 | 4 | 0 |

**TAUNDRY, Richard (D)**    **169 3**
H: 5 9   W: 12 10   b.Walsall 15-2-89
*Source:* Scholar.

| | | | | | |
|---|---|---|---|---|---|
| 2007-08 | Walsall | 21 | 0 | | |
| 2008-09 | Walsall | 38 | 0 | | |
| 2009-10 | Walsall | 30 | 3 | | |
| 2010-11 | Walsall | 28 | 0 | | |
| 2011-12 | Walsall | 35 | 0 | | |
| 2012-13 | Walsall | 17 | 0 | 169 | 3 |

**TAYLOR, Andy (D)**    **160 3**
H: 5 11   W: 11 07   b.Blackburn 14-3-86
*Source:* Scholar. *Honours:* England Youth, Under-20, Under-21.

| | | | | | |
|---|---|---|---|---|---|
| 2004-05 | Blackburn R | 0 | 0 | | |
| 2005-06 | Blackburn R | 0 | 0 | | |
| 2005-06 | *QPR* | 3 | 0 | 3 | 0 |
| 2005-06 | *Blackpool* | 3 | 0 | 3 | 0 |
| 2006-07 | Blackburn R | 0 | 0 | | |
| 2006-07 | *Crewe Alex* | 4 | 0 | 4 | 0 |
| 2006-07 | *Huddersfield T* | 8 | 0 | 8 | 0 |
| 2007-08 | Blackburn R | 0 | 0 | | |
| 2007-08 | Tranmere R | 30 | 2 | | |
| 2008-09 | Tranmere R | 39 | 1 | 69 | 3 |
| 2009-10 | Sheffield U | 26 | 0 | | |
| 2010-11 | Sheffield U | 9 | 0 | | |
| 2011-12 | Sheffield U | 4 | 0 | | |
| 2012-13 | Sheffield U | 0 | 0 | 39 | 0 |
| 2012-13 | *Nottingham F* | 0 | 0 | | |
| 2012-13 | Walsall | 34 | 0 | 34 | 0 |

**WALKER, Jim (G)**    **482 0**
H: 5 11   W: 13 04   b.Sutton-in-Ashfield 9-7-73
*Source:* Trainee.

| | | | |
|---|---|---|---|
| 1991-92 | Notts Co | 0 | 0 |
| 1992-93 | Notts Co | 0 | 0 |
| 1993-94 | Walsall | 31 | 0 |
| 1994-95 | Walsall | 4 | 0 |
| 1995-96 | Walsall | 26 | 0 |
| 1996-97 | Walsall | 36 | 0 |
| 1997-98 | Walsall | 46 | 0 |
| 1998-99 | Walsall | 46 | 0 |
| 1999-2000 | Walsall | 43 | 0 |
| 2000-01 | Walsall | 44 | 0 |
| 2001-02 | Walsall | 43 | 0 |
| 2002-03 | Walsall | 41 | 0 |
| 2003-04 | Walsall | 43 | 0 |
| 2004-05 | West Ham U | 10 | 0 |
| 2005-06 | West Ham U | 3 | 0 |
| 2006-07 | West Ham U | 0 | 0 |
| 2007-08 | West Ham U | 0 | 0 |
| 2008-09 | West Ham U | 0 | 0 |

| | | | | | |
|---|---|---|---|---|---|
| 2008-09 | *Colchester U* | 16 | 0 | 16 | 0 |
| 2009-10 | West Ham U | 0 | 0 | 13 | 0 |
| 2010-11 | Walsall | 26 | 0 | | |
| 2011-12 | Walsall | 24 | 0 | | |
| 2012-13 | Walsall | 0 | 0 | 453 | 0 |

**WILLIAMS, Aaron (F)**    **6 0**
H: 5 11   W: 12 05   b. 21-10-93

| | | | | | |
|---|---|---|---|---|---|
| 2012-13 | Walsall | 6 | 0 | 6 | 0 |

**Players retained or with offer of contract**
Flanagan, Reece James; Preston, Matthew Eric.

**Scholars**
Ashmore, Jamie Russell; Bakayoko, Amadou; Christophorou, Aris James; Dallison, Alexander Fredrick; Garner, Jordan Craig; Griffiths, Daniel Joseph; Heath, Jake Mitchell; Hobbis, Jacob Nicholas; Jones, Richard James; Kinsella, Liam Mark; McKenzie, Carlton Nesta Coral; Reid, Alex Michael; Roberts, Liam Joseph; Rush, Westleigh Taylor; Sinton, Joseph Christopher; Williams, Callum.

## WATFORD (85)

**ABDI, Almen (M)**    **219 43**
H: 5 11   W: 12 11   b.Prizren 21-10-86
*Honours:* Switzerland, Under-21, 6 full caps.

| | | | | | |
|---|---|---|---|---|---|
| 2003-04 | FC Zurich | 11 | 0 | | |
| 2004-05 | FC Zurich | 5 | 0 | | |
| 2005-06 | FC Zurich | 12 | 0 | | |
| 2006-07 | FC Zurich | 28 | 5 | | |
| 2007-08 | FC Zurich | 31 | 7 | | |
| 2008-09 | FC Zurich | 32 | 19 | | |
| 2009-10 | FC Zurich | 8 | 0 | 127 | 31 |
| 2009-10 | Le Mans | 13 | 0 | 13 | 0 |
| 2010-11 | Udinese | 19 | 0 | | |
| 2011-12 | Udinese | 22 | 0 | 41 | 0 |

On loan from Udinese

| | | | | | |
|---|---|---|---|---|---|
| 2012-13 | Watford | 38 | 12 | 38 | 12 |

**ALMUNIA, Manuel (G)**    **287 0**
H: 6 3   W: 13 00   b.Pamplona 19-5-77

| | | | | | |
|---|---|---|---|---|---|
| 1996-97 | Osasuna B | 2 | 0 | | |
| 1997-98 | Osasuna B | 31 | 0 | | |
| 1998-99 | Osasuna B | 13 | 0 | 46 | 0 |
| 1999-2000 | *Cartagena* | 3 | 0 | 3 | 0 |
| 2000-01 | Sabadell | 25 | 0 | 25 | 0 |
| 2001-02 | Celta Vigo | 0 | 0 | | |
| 2001-02 | Celta Vigo | 0 | 0 | | |
| 2001-02 | *Eibar* | 35 | 0 | 35 | 0 |
| 2002-03 | *Recreativo* | 2 | 0 | 2 | 0 |
| 2003-04 | *Albacete* | 24 | 0 | 24 | 0 |
| 2004-05 | Arsenal | 10 | 0 | | |
| 2005-06 | Arsenal | 0 | 0 | | |
| 2006-07 | Arsenal | 1 | 0 | | |
| 2007-08 | Arsenal | 29 | 0 | | |
| 2008-09 | Arsenal | 32 | 0 | | |
| 2009-10 | Arsenal | 29 | 0 | | |
| 2010-11 | Arsenal | 8 | 0 | | |
| 2011-12 | Arsenal | 0 | 0 | | |
| 2011-12 | *West Ham U* | 4 | 0 | 4 | 0 |
| 2012-13 | Arsenal | 0 | 0 | 109 | 0 |
| 2012-13 | Watford | 39 | 0 | 39 | 0 |

**ANYA, Ikechi (M)**    **58 6**
H: 5 5   W: 11 04   b.Glasgow 3-1-88
*Source:* Scholar.

| | | | | | |
|---|---|---|---|---|---|
| 2004-05 | Wycombe W | 3 | 0 | | |
| 2005-06 | Wycombe W | 2 | 0 | | |
| 2006-07 | Wycombe W | 13 | 0 | | |
| 2007-08 | Wycombe W | 0 | 0 | 18 | 0 |
| 2008-09 | Northampton T | 14 | 3 | 14 | 3 |
| 2010-11 | Celta Vigo | 1 | 0 | 1 | 0 |

From Cadiz

| | | | | | |
|---|---|---|---|---|---|
| 2012-13 | Watford | 25 | 3 | 25 | 3 |

**ASSOMBALONGA, Britt (F)**    **47 15**
H: 5 9   W: 11 13   b.Kinshasa 6-12-92
*Source:* Youth.

| | | | | | |
|---|---|---|---|---|---|
| 2010-11 | Watford | 0 | 0 | | |
| 2011-12 | Watford | 4 | 0 | | |
| 2012-13 | Watford | 0 | 0 | 4 | 0 |
| 2012-13 | *Southend U* | 43 | 15 | 43 | 15 |

**BATTOCCHIO, Cristian (M)**    **28 2**
H: 5 10   W: 10 13   b.Buenos Aires 10-2-92

| | | | | | |
|---|---|---|---|---|---|
| 2010-11 | Udinese | 1 | 0 | | |
| 2011-12 | Udinese | 4 | 0 | | |
| 2012-13 | Udinese | 1 | 0 | 6 | 0 |

On loan from Udinese

| | | | | | |
|---|---|---|---|---|---|
| 2012-13 | Watford | 22 | 2 | 22 | 2 |

**BENNETT, Dale (D)**    **33 1**
H: 5 11   W: 12 02   b.Enfield 6-1-90
*Source:* Scholar.

| | | | | | |
|---|---|---|---|---|---|
| 2008-09 | Watford | 0 | 0 | | |
| 2009-10 | Watford | 10 | 0 | | |
| 2010-11 | Watford | 10 | 0 | | |
| 2011-12 | Watford | 2 | 0 | | |
| 2011-12 | *Brentford* | 5 | 1 | 5 | 1 |
| 2012-13 | Watford | 0 | 0 | 22 | 0 |
| 2012-13 | *AFC Wimbledon* | 5 | 0 | 5 | 0 |
| 2012-13 | *Yeovil T* | 1 | 0 | 1 | 0 |

**BOND, Jonathan (G)**    **20 0**
H: 6 3   W: 13 03   b.Hemel Hempstead 19-5-93
*Source:* Scholar. *Honours:* Wales Youth, Under-21.

| | | | | | |
|---|---|---|---|---|---|
| 2010-11 | Watford | 0 | 0 | | |
| 2011-12 | Watford | 1 | 0 | | |
| 2011-12 | *Dagenham & R* | 5 | 0 | 5 | 0 |
| 2011-12 | *Bury* | 6 | 0 | 6 | 0 |
| 2012-13 | Watford | 8 | 0 | 9 | 0 |

**BONHAM, Jack (G)**    **1 0**
H: 6 4   W: 14 13   b.Stevenage 14-9-93
*Source:* Scholar. *Honours:* Eire Youth.

| | | | | | |
|---|---|---|---|---|---|
| 2010-11 | Watford | 0 | 0 | | |
| 2011-12 | Watford | 0 | 0 | | |
| 2012-13 | Watford | 1 | 0 | 1 | 0 |

**BUABEN, Prince (M)**    **130 8**
H: 6 0   W: 11 09   b.Akosombo 23-4-88
*Honours:* Ghana 2 full caps.

| | | | | | |
|---|---|---|---|---|---|
| 2007-08 | Dundee U | 24 | 3 | | |
| 2008-09 | Dundee U | 22 | 1 | | |
| 2009-10 | Dundee U | 34 | 2 | | |
| 2010-11 | Dundee U | 19 | 1 | 99 | 7 |
| 2011-12 | Watford | 30 | 1 | | |
| 2012-13 | Watford | 1 | 0 | 31 | 1 |

**CASSETTI, Marco (D)**    **390 25**
H: 6 1   W: 12 11   b.Milano 29-5-75
*Honours:* Italy 5 full caps.

| | | | | | |
|---|---|---|---|---|---|
| 1995-96 | Lumezzane | 0 | 0 | | |
| 1996-97 | Montichiari | 1 | 0 | | |
| 1997-98 | Montichiari | 29 | 6 | 30 | 6 |
| 1998-99 | Lumezzane | 19 | 2 | | |
| 1999-2000 | Lumezzane | 31 | 2 | 50 | 4 |
| 2000-01 | Verona | 11 | 0 | | |
| 2001-02 | Verona | 14 | 0 | | |
| 2002-03 | Verona | 11 | 2 | 36 | 2 |
| 2003-04 | Lecce | 30 | 5 | | |
| 2004-05 | Lecce | 34 | 4 | | |
| 2005-06 | Lecce | 29 | 0 | 93 | 9 |
| 2006-07 | Roma | 28 | 2 | | |
| 2007-08 | Roma | 27 | 0 | | |
| 2008-09 | Roma | 20 | 0 | | |
| 2009-10 | Roma | 29 | 2 | | |
| 2010-11 | Roma | 32 | 0 | | |
| 2011-12 | Roma | 7 | 0 | 143 | 4 |
| 2012-13 | Udinese | 0 | 0 | | |

On loan from Udinese

| | | | | | |
|---|---|---|---|---|---|
| 2012-13 | Watford | 38 | 0 | 38 | 0 |

**DEENEY, Troy (F)**    **242 60**
H: 5 11   W: 12 00   b.Solihull 29-6-88
*Source:* Chelmsley T.

| | | | | | |
|---|---|---|---|---|---|
| 2006-07 | Walsall | 1 | 0 | | |
| 2007-08 | Walsall | 35 | 1 | | |
| 2008-09 | Walsall | 45 | 12 | | |
| 2009-10 | Walsall | 42 | 14 | 123 | 27 |
| 2010-11 | Watford | 36 | 3 | | |
| 2011-12 | Watford | 43 | 11 | | |
| 2012-13 | Watford | 40 | 19 | 119 | 33 |

**DICKINSON, Carl (D)**    **184 3**
H: 6 1   W: 12 04   b.Swadlincote 31-3-87
*Source:* Scholar.

| | | | | | |
|---|---|---|---|---|---|
| 2004-05 | Stoke C | 1 | 0 | | |
| 2005-06 | Stoke C | 5 | 0 | | |
| 2006-07 | Stoke C | 13 | 0 | | |
| 2006-07 | *Blackpool* | 7 | 0 | 7 | 0 |
| 2007-08 | Stoke C | 27 | 0 | | |

| Season | Club | App | Gls | Tot App | Tot Gls |
|---|---|---|---|---|---|
| 2008-09 | Stoke C | 5 | 0 | | |
| 2008-09 | *Leeds U* | 7 | 0 | 7 | 0 |
| 2009-10 | Stoke C | 0 | 0 | | |
| 2009-10 | *Barnsley* | 28 | 1 | 28 | 1 |
| 2010-11 | Stoke C | 0 | 0 | 51 | 0 |
| 2010-11 | *Portsmouth* | 36 | 0 | | |
| 2011-12 | Watford | 39 | 2 | | |
| 2012-13 | Watford | 4 | 0 | 43 | 2 |
| 2012-13 | *Portsmouth* | 6 | 0 | 42 | 0 |
| 2012-13 | *Coventry C* | 6 | 0 | 6 | 0 |

**DOYLEY, Lloyd (D)**     365   7
H: 5 10  W: 12 13  b.Whitechapel 1-12-82
*Source:* Scholar. *Honours:* Jamaica 1 full cap.

| Season | Club | App | Gls | Tot App | Tot Gls |
|---|---|---|---|---|---|
| 2000-01 | Watford | 0 | 0 | | |
| 2001-02 | Watford | 20 | 0 | | |
| 2002-03 | Watford | 22 | 0 | | |
| 2003-04 | Watford | 9 | 0 | | |
| 2004-05 | Watford | 29 | 0 | | |
| 2005-06 | Watford | 44 | 0 | | |
| 2006-07 | Watford | 21 | 0 | | |
| 2007-08 | Watford | 36 | 0 | | |
| 2008-09 | Watford | 37 | 0 | | |
| 2009-10 | Watford | 44 | 1 | | |
| 2010-11 | Watford | 36 | 0 | | |
| 2011-12 | Watford | 33 | 0 | | |
| 2012-13 | Watford | 34 | 1 | 365 | 2 |

**EKSTRAND, Joel (D)**     118   2
H: 6 2  W: 12 00  b.Lund 4-2-89

| Season | Club | App | Gls | Tot App | Tot Gls |
|---|---|---|---|---|---|
| 2007-08 | Helsingborgs IF | 12 | 0 | | |
| 2008-09 | Helsingborgs IF | 24 | 0 | | |
| 2009-10 | Helsingborgs IF | 25 | 1 | | |
| 2010-11 | Helsingborgs IF | 12 | 0 | 73 | 1 |
| 2010-11 | Udinese | 1 | 0 | | |
| 2011-12 | Udinese | 12 | 0 | 13 | 0 |
| On loan from Udinese | | | | | |
| 2012-13 | Watford | 32 | 1 | 32 | 1 |

**EUSTACE, John (M)**     346   30
H: 5 11  W: 11 12  b.Solihull 3-11-79
*Source:* Trainee.

| Season | Club | App | Gls | Tot App | Tot Gls |
|---|---|---|---|---|---|
| 1996-97 | Coventry C | 0 | 0 | | |
| 1997-98 | Coventry C | 0 | 0 | | |
| 1998-99 | Coventry C | 0 | 0 | | |
| 1998-99 | *Dundee U* | 11 | 1 | 11 | 1 |
| 1999-2000 | Coventry C | 16 | 1 | | |
| 2000-01 | Coventry C | 32 | 2 | | |
| 2001-02 | Coventry C | 0 | 0 | | |
| 2002-03 | Coventry C | 32 | 4 | 86 | 7 |
| 2002-03 | *Middlesbrough* | 1 | 0 | 1 | 0 |
| 2003-04 | Stoke C | 26 | 5 | | |
| 2004-05 | Stoke C | 7 | 0 | | |
| 2005-06 | Stoke C | 0 | 0 | | |
| 2006-07 | Stoke C | 15 | 0 | | |
| 2006-07 | *Hereford U* | 8 | 0 | 8 | 0 |
| 2007-08 | Stoke C | 26 | 0 | 74 | 5 |
| 2007-08 | Watford | 13 | 0 | | |
| 2008-09 | Watford | 17 | 2 | | |
| 2008-09 | *Derby Co* | 9 | 1 | 9 | 1 |
| 2009-10 | Watford | 42 | 4 | | |
| 2010-11 | Watford | 41 | 6 | | |
| 2011-12 | Watford | 39 | 4 | | |
| 2012-13 | Watford | 5 | 0 | 157 | 16 |

**FANCHONE, Jean Alain (D)**     92   2
H: 5 8  W: 10 13  b.Mulhouse 2-9-88

| Season | Club | App | Gls | Tot App | Tot Gls |
|---|---|---|---|---|---|
| 2008-09 | Strasbourg | 32 | 0 | | |
| 2009-10 | Strasbourg | 26 | 1 | 58 | 1 |
| 2010-11 | Arles | 21 | 0 | 21 | 0 |
| 2012-13 | Udinese | 0 | 0 | | |
| On loan from Udinese | | | | | |
| 2012-13 | Watford | 1 | 0 | 1 | 0 |
| 2012-13 | *Nimes* | 12 | 1 | 12 | 1 |

**FORESTIERI, Fernando (F)**     124   21
H: 5 8  W: 10 07  b.Rosario 16-1-90

| Season | Club | App | Gls | Tot App | Tot Gls |
|---|---|---|---|---|---|
| 2006-07 | Genoa | 1 | 1 | 1 | 1 |
| 2007-08 | Siena | 17 | 1 | | |
| 2008-09 | Siena | 2 | 0 | 19 | 1 |
| 2008-09 | *Vicenza* | 13 | 5 | 13 | 5 |
| 2009-10 | *Malaga* | 19 | 1 | 19 | 1 |
| 2010-11 | *Empoli* | 17 | 3 | 17 | 3 |
| 2011-12 | *Bari* | 27 | 2 | 27 | 2 |
| 2012-13 | Udinese | 0 | 0 | | |
| On loan from Udinese | | | | | |
| 2012-13 | Watford | 28 | 8 | 28 | 8 |

**FORSYTH, Craig (M)**     133   15
H: 6 0  W: 12 00  b.Carnoustie 24-2-89

| Season | Club | App | Gls | Tot App | Tot Gls |
|---|---|---|---|---|---|
| 2006-07 | Dundee | 1 | 0 | | |
| 2007-08 | Dundee | 0 | 0 | | |
| 2007-08 | *Montrose* | 9 | 0 | 9 | 0 |
| 2008-09 | Dundee | 1 | 0 | | |
| 2008-09 | *Arbroath* | 26 | 2 | 26 | 2 |
| 2009-10 | Dundee | 24 | 2 | | |
| 2010-11 | Dundee | 33 | 8 | 59 | 10 |
| 2011-12 | Watford | 20 | 3 | | |
| 2012-13 | Watford | 2 | 0 | 22 | 3 |
| 2012-13 | *Bradford C* | 7 | 0 | 7 | 0 |
| 2012-13 | *Derby Co* | 10 | 0 | 10 | 0 |

**GEIJO, Alexandre (F)**     230   81
H: 6 2  W: 12 09  b.Geneva 5-9-82

| Season | Club | App | Gls | Tot App | Tot Gls |
|---|---|---|---|---|---|
| 2000-01 | Neuchatel Xamax | 1 | 1 | 1 | 1 |
| 2002-03 | Malaga | 1 | 0 | | |
| 2003-04 | Malaga | 1 | 0 | | |
| 2003-04 | Malaga B | 11 | 12 | | |
| 2004-05 | Malaga | 13 | 0 | 15 | 0 |
| 2004-05 | Malaga B | 2 | 2 | | |
| 2005-06 | Malaga B | 1 | 1 | 14 | 15 |
| 2005-06 | Xerez | 36 | 13 | | |
| 2006-07 | Xerez | 21 | 7 | 57 | 20 |
| 2007-08 | Levante | 32 | 5 | | |
| 2008-09 | Levante | 16 | 9 | 48 | 14 |
| 2009-10 | Racing Santander | 19 | 2 | 19 | 2 |
| 2009-10 | Udinese | 4 | 0 | | |
| 2010-11 | *Granada* | 30 | 25 | | |
| 2011-12 | *Granada* | 24 | 2 | | |
| 2012-13 | *Granada* | 0 | 0 | 4 | 0 |
| 2012-13 | *Granada* | 0 | 0 | 54 | 27 |
| On loan from Udinese | | | | | |
| 2012-13 | Watford | 18 | 2 | 18 | 2 |

**HALL, Fitz (D)**     268   12
H: 6 3  W: 13 00  b.Leytonstone 20-12-80
*Source:* Barnet Trainee, Chesham U.

| Season | Club | App | Gls | Tot App | Tot Gls |
|---|---|---|---|---|---|
| 2001-02 | Oldham Ath | 4 | 1 | | |
| 2002-03 | Oldham Ath | 40 | 4 | 44 | 5 |
| 2003-04 | Southampton | 11 | 0 | 11 | 0 |
| 2004-05 | Crystal Palace | 36 | 2 | | |
| 2005-06 | Crystal Palace | 39 | 1 | 75 | 3 |
| 2006-07 | Wigan Ath | 24 | 0 | | |
| 2007-08 | Wigan Ath | 1 | 0 | 25 | 0 |
| 2007-08 | QPR | 14 | 0 | | |
| 2008-09 | QPR | 24 | 2 | | |
| 2009-10 | QPR | 14 | 0 | | |
| 2009-10 | *Newcastle U* | 7 | 0 | 7 | 0 |
| 2010-11 | QPR | 19 | 1 | | |
| 2011-12 | QPR | 14 | 0 | 85 | 3 |
| 2012-13 | Watford | 21 | 1 | 21 | 1 |

**HOBAN, Tommie (D)**     20   2
H: 6 2  W: 11 13  b.Walthamstow 24-1-94
*Source:* Scholar. *Honours:* Eire Youth.

| Season | Club | App | Gls | Tot App | Tot Gls |
|---|---|---|---|---|---|
| 2010-11 | Watford | 1 | 0 | | |
| 2011-12 | Watford | 0 | 0 | | |
| 2012-13 | Watford | 19 | 2 | 20 | 2 |

**HODSON, Lee (D)**     96   1
H: 5 11  W: 11 02  b.Boreham Wood 2-10-91
*Source:* Scholar. *Honours:* Northern Ireland Under-21, 9 full caps.

| Season | Club | App | Gls | Tot App | Tot Gls |
|---|---|---|---|---|---|
| 2008-09 | Watford | 1 | 0 | | |
| 2009-10 | Watford | 31 | 0 | | |
| 2010-11 | Watford | 29 | 1 | | |
| 2011-12 | Watford | 20 | 0 | | |
| 2012-13 | Watford | 2 | 0 | 83 | 1 |
| 2012-13 | *Brentford* | 13 | 0 | 13 | 0 |

**HOGG, Jonathan (M)**     107   1
H: 5 7  W: 10 05  b.Middlesbrough 6-12-88
*Source:* Scholar.

| Season | Club | App | Gls | Tot App | Tot Gls |
|---|---|---|---|---|---|
| 2007-08 | Aston Villa | 0 | 0 | | |
| 2008-09 | Aston Villa | 0 | 0 | | |
| 2009-10 | Aston Villa | 0 | 0 | | |
| 2009-10 | *Darlington* | 5 | 1 | 5 | 1 |
| 2010-11 | Aston Villa | 5 | 0 | | |
| 2010-11 | *Portsmouth* | 19 | 0 | 19 | 0 |
| 2011-12 | Aston Villa | 0 | 0 | 5 | 0 |
| 2011-12 | Watford | 40 | 0 | | |
| 2012-13 | Watford | 38 | 0 | 78 | 0 |

**IWELUMO, Chris (F)**     466   104
H: 6 3  W: 15 03  b.Coatbridge 1-8-78
*Source:* Juniors. *Honours:* Scotland B, 4 full caps.

| Season | Club | App | Gls | Tot App | Tot Gls |
|---|---|---|---|---|---|
| 1996-97 | St Mirren | 14 | 0 | | |
| 1997-98 | St Mirren | 15 | 0 | 26 | 0 |
| 1998-99 | Aarhus Fremad | 27 | 4 | 27 | 4 |
| 1999-2000 | Stoke C | 3 | 0 | | |
| 2000-01 | Stoke C | 2 | 1 | | |
| 2000-01 | *York C* | 12 | 2 | 12 | 2 |
| 2000-01 | *Cheltenham T* | 4 | 1 | 4 | 1 |
| 2001-02 | Stoke C | 38 | 10 | | |
| 2002-03 | Stoke C | 32 | 5 | | |
| 2003-04 | Stoke C | 9 | 0 | 84 | 16 |
| 2003-04 | Brighton & HA | 10 | 4 | 10 | 4 |
| 2004-05 | Aachen | 9 | 0 | 9 | 0 |
| 2005-06 | Colchester U | 46 | 17 | | |
| 2006-07 | Colchester U | 46 | 18 | 92 | 35 |
| 2007-08 | Charlton Ath | 46 | 10 | 46 | 10 |
| 2008-09 | Wolverhampton W | 31 | 14 | | |
| 2009-10 | Wolverhampton W | 15 | 0 | 46 | 14 |
| 2009-10 | *Bristol C* | 7 | 2 | 7 | 2 |
| 2010-11 | Burnley | 45 | 11 | 45 | 11 |
| 2011-12 | Watford | 39 | 4 | | |
| 2012-13 | Watford | 7 | 0 | 46 | 4 |
| 2012-13 | *Notts Co* | 5 | 0 | 5 | 0 |
| 2012-13 | *Oldham Ath* | 7 | 1 | 7 | 1 |

**JENKINS, Ross (M)**     88   4
H: 5 11  W: 12 06  b.Watford 9-11-90
*Source:* Scholar. *Honours:* England Under-20.

| Season | Club | App | Gls | Tot App | Tot Gls |
|---|---|---|---|---|---|
| 2008-09 | Watford | 29 | 1 | | |
| 2009-10 | Watford | 24 | 0 | | |
| 2010-11 | Watford | 19 | 1 | | |
| 2011-12 | Watford | 9 | 0 | | |
| 2012-13 | Watford | 0 | 0 | 81 | 2 |
| 2012-13 | *Plymouth Arg* | 2 | 1 | 2 | 1 |
| 2012-13 | *Barnet* | 5 | 1 | 5 | 1 |

**MENSAH, Bernard (F)**     0   0
b.Hounslow 29-12-94
*Source:* Scholar.

| Season | Club | App | Gls | Tot App | Tot Gls |
|---|---|---|---|---|---|
| 2011-12 | Watford | 0 | 0 | | |
| 2012-13 | Watford | 0 | 0 | | |

**MINGOIA, Piero (M)**     12   1
H: 5 6  W: 10 12  b.Enfield 20-10-91
*Source:* Scholar.

| Season | Club | App | Gls | Tot App | Tot Gls |
|---|---|---|---|---|---|
| 2010-11 | Watford | 5 | 0 | | |
| 2011-12 | Watford | 0 | 0 | | |
| 2011-12 | *Brentford* | 0 | 0 | | |
| 2012-13 | Watford | 0 | 0 | 5 | 0 |
| 2012-13 | *Accrington S* | 7 | 1 | 7 | 1 |

**MUJANGI BIA, Geoffrey (M)**     88   11
H: 5 10  W: 11 11  b.Kinshasa 12-8-89
*Honours:* Belgium Under-21, 2 full caps.

| Season | Club | App | Gls | Tot App | Tot Gls |
|---|---|---|---|---|---|
| 2006-07 | Charleroi | 3 | 0 | | |
| 2007-08 | Charleroi | 17 | 3 | | |
| 2008-09 | Charleroi | 28 | 4 | | |
| 2009-10 | Charleroi | 10 | 2 | 58 | 9 |
| 2009-10 | Wolverhampton W | 3 | 0 | | |
| 2010-11 | Wolverhampton W | 1 | 0 | 4 | 0 |
| 2011-12 | Standard Liege | 22 | 2 | | |
| 2012-13 | Standard Liege | 1 | 0 | 23 | 2 |
| On loan from Standard Liege | | | | | |
| 2012-13 | Watford | 3 | 0 | 3 | 0 |

**MURRAY, Sean (M)**     35   8
H: 5 9  W: 10 10  b.Abbots Langley 11-10-93
*Source:* Scholar. *Honours:* Eire Youth, Under-21.

| Season | Club | App | Gls | Tot App | Tot Gls |
|---|---|---|---|---|---|
| 2010-11 | Watford | 2 | 0 | | |
| 2011-12 | Watford | 18 | 7 | | |
| 2012-13 | Watford | 15 | 1 | 35 | 8 |

**NEUTON, Piccoli (D)**     31   1
H: 6 0  W: 12 05  b.Erechim 14-3-90

| Season | Club | App | Gls | Tot App | Tot Gls |
|---|---|---|---|---|---|
| 2009-10 | Gremio | 1 | 0 | | |
| 2010-11 | Gremio | 15 | 1 | | |
| 2011-12 | Gremio | 4 | 0 | 20 | 1 |
| 2011-12 | Udinese | 3 | 0 | 3 | 0 |
| On loan from Udinese | | | | | |
| 2012-13 | Watford | 8 | 0 | 8 | 0 |

**NOSWORTHY, Nyron (D)**    390   7
H: 6 0   W: 12 08   b.Brixton 11-10-80
*Source:* Trainee. *Honours:* Jamaica 10 full caps, 1 goal.

| Season | Club | Apps | Gls | Tot | Gls |
|---|---|---|---|---|---|
| 1998-99 | Gillingham | 3 | 0 | | |
| 1999-2000 | Gillingham | 29 | 1 | | |
| 2000-01 | Gillingham | 10 | 0 | | |
| 2001-02 | Gillingham | 29 | 0 | | |
| 2002-03 | Gillingham | 39 | 2 | | |
| 2003-04 | Gillingham | 27 | 2 | | |
| 2004-05 | Gillingham | 37 | 0 | 174 | 5 |
| 2005-06 | Sunderland | 30 | 0 | | |
| 2006-07 | Sunderland | 29 | 0 | | |
| 2007-08 | Sunderland | 29 | 0 | | |
| 2008-09 | Sunderland | 16 | 0 | | |
| 2009-10 | Sunderland | 10 | 0 | | |
| 2009-10 | *Sheffield U* | 19 | 0 | | |
| 2010-11 | Sunderland | 0 | 0 | | |
| 2010-11 | *Sheffield U* | 32 | 0 | 51 | 0 |
| 2011-12 | Sunderland | 0 | 0 | 114 | 0 |
| 2011-12 | Watford | 32 | 2 | | |
| 2012-13 | Watford | 19 | 0 | 51 | 2 |

**PUDIL, Daniel (D)**    174   22
H: 6 1   W: 12 11   b.Prague 27-9-85
*Honours:* Czech Republic Youth, Under-21, 23 full caps, 2 goals.

| Season | Club | Apps | Gls | Tot | Gls |
|---|---|---|---|---|---|
| 2003-04 | Blsany | 2 | 2 | 2 | 2 |
| 2005-06 | Liberec | 3 | 4 | | |
| 2006-07 | Liberec | 3 | 3 | 6 | 7 |
| 2007-08 | Slavia Prague | 16 | 6 | 16 | 6 |
| 2008-09 | Genk | 29 | 4 | | |
| 2009-10 | Genk | 27 | 1 | | |
| 2010-11 | Genk | 32 | 0 | | |
| 2011-12 | Genk | 18 | 0 | 106 | 5 |
| 2011-12 | Cesena | 7 | 1 | 7 | 1 |
| 2012-13 | Watford | 37 | 1 | 37 | 1 |

**SMITH, Connor (M)**    7   0
H: 5 11   W: 11 06   b.London 18-2-93

| Season | Club | Apps | Gls | Tot | Gls |
|---|---|---|---|---|---|
| 2012-13 | Watford | 7 | 0 | 7 | 0 |

**THOMPSON, Adam (D)**    37   1
H: 6 2   W: 12 10   b.Harlow 28-9-92
*Source:* Scholar. *Honours:* Northern Ireland Under-21, 2 full caps.

| Season | Club | Apps | Gls | Tot | Gls |
|---|---|---|---|---|---|
| 2010-11 | Watford | 10 | 1 | | |
| 2011-12 | Watford | 0 | 0 | | |
| 2011-12 | *Brentford* | 20 | 0 | 20 | 0 |
| 2012-13 | Watford | 4 | 0 | 14 | 1 |
| 2012-13 | *Wycombe W* | 2 | 0 | 2 | 0 |
| 2012-13 | *Barnet* | 1 | 0 | 1 | 0 |

**VYDRA, Matej (F)**    57   24
H: 5 10   W: 11 09   b.Chotebor 1-5-92
*Honours:* Czech Republic 7 full caps, 2 goals.

| Season | Club | Apps | Gls | Tot | Gls |
|---|---|---|---|---|---|
| 2009-10 | Banik Ostrava | 13 | 4 | 13 | 4 |
| 2010-11 | Udinese | 2 | 0 | | |
| 2011-12 | Club Brugge | 1 | 0 | 1 | 0 |
| 2012-13 | Udinese | 0 | 0 | 2 | 0 |

On loan from Udinese

| Season | Club | Apps | Gls | Tot | Gls |
|---|---|---|---|---|---|
| 2012-13 | Watford | 41 | 20 | 41 | 20 |

**WHICHELOW, Matt (M)**    31   4
H: 5 7   W: 11 10   b.Islington 28-9-91
*Source:* Scholar.

| Season | Club | Apps | Gls | Tot | Gls |
|---|---|---|---|---|---|
| 2010-11 | Watford | 19 | 3 | | |
| 2011-12 | Watford | 2 | 0 | | |
| 2011-12 | *Exeter C* | 2 | 0 | 2 | 0 |
| 2011-12 | *Wycombe W* | 4 | 1 | 4 | 1 |
| 2012-13 | Watford | 0 | 0 | 21 | 3 |
| 2012-13 | *Accrington S* | 4 | 0 | 4 | 0 |

**YEATES, Mark (F)**    282   41
H: 5 8   W: 13 03   b.Dublin 11-1-85
*Source:* Trainee. *Honours:* Eire Youth, Under-21.

| Season | Club | Apps | Gls | Tot | Gls |
|---|---|---|---|---|---|
| 2002-03 | Tottenham H | 0 | 0 | | |
| 2003-04 | Tottenham H | 1 | 0 | | |
| 2003-04 | *Brighton & HA* | 9 | 0 | 9 | 0 |
| 2004-05 | Tottenham H | 2 | 0 | | |
| 2004-05 | *Swindon T* | 4 | 0 | 4 | 0 |
| 2005-06 | Tottenham H | 0 | 0 | | |
| 2005-06 | *Colchester U* | 44 | 5 | | |
| 2006-07 | Tottenham H | 0 | 0 | 3 | 0 |
| 2006-07 | *Hull C* | 5 | 0 | 5 | 0 |
| 2006-07 | *Leicester C* | 9 | 1 | 9 | 1 |
| 2007-08 | Colchester U | 29 | 8 | | |
| 2008-09 | Colchester U | 43 | 12 | 116 | 25 |
| 2009-10 | Middlesbrough | 19 | 1 | 19 | 1 |
| 2009-10 | Sheffield U | 20 | 2 | | |
| 2010-11 | Sheffield U | 35 | 5 | 55 | 7 |
| 2011-12 | Watford | 33 | 3 | | |
| 2012-13 | Watford | 29 | 4 | 62 | 7 |

**Scholars**
Barnum-Bobb, Jazzi; Bawling, Alfred Bobson; Byers, George William; Cox, Ollie Jaspar Charlie; Crowley, Oliver; Cumberbatch, Kurtis Benjamin; Dillon, Christopher; Doherty, Josh; Eaton, Austin Allan; English, Kamaron Javarn Devito; Hope, Ryan Clifford; Jakubiak, Alexander Louis; Johnson, Jorell James; O'Nien, Luke Terry; Westlake, Jack George; Wilks, Daniel John; Willmore, Jordan Alexis Joseph.

# WBA (86)

**ALLAN, Scott (M)**    40   3
H: 5 9   W: 11 00   b.Glasgow 28-11-91
*Honours:* Scotland Youth, Under-21.

| Season | Club | Apps | Gls | Tot | Gls |
|---|---|---|---|---|---|
| 2010-11 | Dundee U | 0 | 0 | | |
| 2010-11 | *Forfar Ath* | 4 | 1 | 4 | 1 |
| 2011-12 | Dundee U | 8 | 0 | 8 | 0 |
| 2011-12 | WBA | 0 | 0 | | |
| 2011-12 | *Portsmouth* | 15 | 1 | | |
| 2012-13 | *Milton Keynes D* | 4 | 0 | 4 | 0 |
| 2012-13 | WBA | 0 | 0 | | |
| 2012-13 | *Portsmouth* | 9 | 1 | 24 | 2 |

**BERAHINO, Saido (F)**    32   12
H: 5 10   W: 11 13   b.Burundi 4-8-93
*Source:* Scholar. *Honours:* England Youth, Under-20.

| Season | Club | Apps | Gls | Tot | Gls |
|---|---|---|---|---|---|
| 2010-11 | WBA | 0 | 0 | | |
| 2011-12 | WBA | 0 | 0 | | |
| 2011-12 | *Northampton T* | 14 | 6 | 14 | 6 |
| 2011-12 | *Brentford* | 8 | 4 | 8 | 4 |
| 2012-13 | WBA | 0 | 0 | | |
| 2012-13 | *Peterborough U* | 10 | 2 | 10 | 2 |

**BROWN, Isaiah (M)**    1   0
H: 6 0   W: 10 13   b.Peterborough 7-1-97

| Season | Club | Apps | Gls | Tot | Gls |
|---|---|---|---|---|---|
| 2012-13 | WBA | 1 | 0 | 1 | 0 |

**BRUNT, Chris (M)**    342   57
H: 6 1   W: 13 04   b.Belfast 14-12-84
*Source:* Trainee. *Honours:* Northern Ireland Under-21, Under-23, 42 full caps, 1 goal.

| Season | Club | Apps | Gls | Tot | Gls |
|---|---|---|---|---|---|
| 2002-03 | Middlesbrough | 0 | 0 | | |
| 2003-04 | Middlesbrough | 0 | 0 | | |
| 2003-04 | Sheffield W | 9 | 2 | | |
| 2004-05 | Sheffield W | 42 | 4 | | |
| 2005-06 | Sheffield W | 44 | 7 | | |
| 2006-07 | Sheffield W | 44 | 11 | | |
| 2007-08 | Sheffield W | 1 | 0 | 140 | 24 |
| 2007-08 | WBA | 34 | 4 | | |
| 2008-09 | WBA | 34 | 8 | | |
| 2009-10 | WBA | 40 | 13 | | |
| 2010-11 | WBA | 34 | 4 | | |
| 2011-12 | WBA | 29 | 2 | | |
| 2012-13 | WBA | 31 | 2 | 202 | 33 |

**DANIELS, Donervorn (D)**    13   1
H: 6 1   W: 14 05   b.Montserrat 24-11-93
*Source:* Scholar.

| Season | Club | Apps | Gls | Tot | Gls |
|---|---|---|---|---|---|
| 2011-12 | WBA | 0 | 0 | | |
| 2012-13 | WBA | 0 | 0 | | |
| 2012-13 | *Tranmere R* | 13 | 1 | 13 | 1 |

**DANIELS, Luke (G)**    96   0
H: 6 1   W: 12 10   b.Bolton 5-1-88
*Source:* Manchester U Scholar. *Honours:* England Youth.

| Season | Club | Apps | Gls | Tot | Gls |
|---|---|---|---|---|---|
| 2006-07 | WBA | 0 | 0 | | |
| 2007-08 | *Motherwell* | 2 | 0 | 2 | 0 |
| 2007-08 | WBA | 0 | 0 | | |
| 2008-09 | WBA | 0 | 0 | | |
| 2008-09 | *Shrewsbury T* | 38 | 0 | 38 | 0 |
| 2009-10 | WBA | 0 | 0 | | |
| 2009-10 | *Tranmere R* | 37 | 0 | 37 | 0 |
| 2010-11 | WBA | 0 | 0 | | |
| 2010-11 | *Charlton Ath* | 0 | 0 | | |
| 2010-11 | *Rochdale* | 1 | 0 | 1 | 0 |
| 2010-11 | *Bristol R* | 9 | 0 | 9 | 0 |
| 2011-12 | WBA | 0 | 0 | | |
| 2011-12 | *Southend U* | 9 | 0 | 9 | 0 |
| 2012-13 | WBA | 0 | 0 | | |

**DAWSON, Craig (D)**    112   23
H: 6 0   W: 12 04   b.Rochdale 6-5-90
*Source:* Radcliffe B. *Honours:* England Under-21.

| Season | Club | Apps | Gls | Tot | Gls |
|---|---|---|---|---|---|
| 2008-09 | Rochdale | 0 | 0 | | |
| 2009-10 | Rochdale | 42 | 9 | | |
| 2010-11 | WBA | 0 | 0 | | |
| 2010-11 | *Rochdale* | 45 | 10 | 87 | 19 |
| 2011-12 | WBA | 8 | 0 | | |
| 2012-13 | WBA | 1 | 0 | 9 | 0 |
| 2012-13 | *Bolton W* | 16 | 4 | 16 | 4 |

**DORRANS, Graham (F)**    222   39
H: 5 9   W: 11 07   b.Glasgow 5-5-87
*Honours:* Scotland Youth, Under-21, 9 full caps.

| Season | Club | Apps | Gls | Tot | Gls |
|---|---|---|---|---|---|
| 2006-07 | Livingston | 8 | 0 | | |
| 2006-07 | *Partick Th* | 15 | 5 | 15 | 5 |
| 2006-07 | Livingston | 34 | 5 | | |
| 2007-08 | Livingston | 34 | 11 | 76 | 16 |
| 2008-09 | WBA | 8 | 0 | | |
| 2009-10 | WBA | 45 | 13 | | |
| 2010-11 | WBA | 21 | 1 | | |
| 2011-12 | WBA | 31 | 3 | | |
| 2012-13 | WBA | 26 | 1 | 131 | 18 |

**FORTUNE, Marc-Antoine (F)**    379   76
H: 6 0   W: 11 13   b.Cayenne 2-7-81

| Season | Club | Apps | Gls | Tot | Gls |
|---|---|---|---|---|---|
| 2000-01 | Angouleme | 18 | 3 | | |
| 2001-02 | Angouleme | 36 | 12 | 54 | 15 |
| 2002-03 | Nancy | 19 | 1 | | |
| 2002-03 | Lille | 15 | 0 | 15 | 0 |
| 2003-04 | Rouen | 34 | 10 | 34 | 10 |
| 2004-05 | Brest | 33 | 10 | 33 | 10 |
| 2005-06 | Utrecht | 31 | 6 | | |
| 2006-07 | Utrecht | 22 | 5 | 53 | 11 |
| 2006-07 | Nancy | 15 | 5 | | |
| 2007-08 | Nancy | 37 | 6 | | |
| 2008-09 | Nancy | 19 | 1 | 90 | 13 |
| 2009-10 | Celtic | 30 | 10 | | |
| 2010-11 | Celtic | 2 | 0 | 32 | 10 |
| 2010-11 | WBA | 25 | 2 | | |
| 2011-12 | WBA | 17 | 2 | | |
| 2011-12 | *Doncaster R* | 5 | 1 | 5 | 1 |
| 2012-13 | WBA | 21 | 2 | 63 | 6 |

**FOSTER, Ben (G)**    209   0
H: 6 2   W: 12 08   b.Leamington Spa 3-4-83
*Source:* Racing Club Warwick. *Honours:* England 6 full caps.

| Season | Club | Apps | Gls | Tot | Gls |
|---|---|---|---|---|---|
| 2000-01 | Stoke C | 0 | 0 | | |
| 2001-02 | Stoke C | 0 | 0 | | |
| 2002-03 | Stoke C | 0 | 0 | | |
| 2003-04 | Stoke C | 0 | 0 | | |
| 2004-05 | Stoke C | 0 | 0 | | |
| 2004-05 | *Kidderminster H* | 2 | 0 | 2 | 0 |
| 2004-05 | *Wrexham* | 17 | 0 | 17 | 0 |
| 2005-06 | Manchester U | 0 | 0 | | |
| 2005-06 | *Watford* | 44 | 0 | | |
| 2006-07 | Manchester U | 0 | 0 | | |
| 2006-07 | *Watford* | 29 | 0 | 73 | 0 |
| 2007-08 | Manchester U | 1 | 0 | | |
| 2008-09 | Manchester U | 2 | 0 | | |
| 2009-10 | Manchester U | 9 | 0 | 12 | 0 |
| 2010-11 | Birmingham C | 38 | 0 | | |
| 2011-12 | Birmingham C | 0 | 0 | 38 | 0 |
| 2011-12 | WBA | 37 | 0 | | |
| 2012-13 | WBA | 30 | 0 | 67 | 0 |

**GARMSTON, Bradley (D)**    13   0
H: 5 9   W: 10 12   b.Greenwich 18-1-94

| Season | Club | Apps | Gls | Tot | Gls |
|---|---|---|---|---|---|
| 2012-13 | WBA | 0 | 0 | | |
| 2012-13 | *Colchester U* | 13 | 0 | 13 | 0 |

**GAYLE, Cameron (D)**    18   1
H: 5 11   W: 11 00   b.Birmingham 22-11-92
*Source:* Scholar.

| Season | Club | Apps | Gls | Tot | Gls |
|---|---|---|---|---|---|
| 2010-11 | WBA | 0 | 0 | | |
| 2011-12 | WBA | 0 | 0 | | |
| 2012-13 | WBA | 0 | 0 | | |
| 2012-13 | *Shrewsbury T* | 18 | 1 | 18 | 1 |

**GERA, Zoltan (M)**    371   66
H: 6 0   W: 11 11   b.Pecs 22-4-79
*Source:* Hakarny. *Honours:* Hungary Under-21, 77 full caps, 23 goals.

| Season | Club | Apps | Gls | Tot | Gls |
|---|---|---|---|---|---|
| 1999-2000 | Pecsi | 15 | 4 | 15 | 4 |
| 2000-01 | Ferencvaros | 32 | 7 | | |
| 2001-02 | Ferencvaros | 27 | 8 | | |

| | | | | |
|---|---|---|---|---|
| 2002-03 | Ferencvaros | 26 | 6 | |
| 2003-04 | Ferencvaros | 30 | 11 | 115 32 |
| 2004-05 | WBA | 38 | 6 | |
| 2005-06 | WBA | 15 | 2 | |
| 2006-07 | WBA | 40 | 5 | |
| 2007-08 | WBA | 43 | 8 | |
| 2008-09 | Fulham | 32 | 2 | |
| 2009-10 | Fulham | 27 | 2 | |
| 2010-11 | Fulham | 27 | 1 | 86 5 |
| 2011-12 | WBA | 3 | 0 | |
| 2012-13 | WBA | 16 | 4 | 155 25 |

**HURST, James (D)**    27 0
H: 5 8 W: 11 11 b.Sutton Coldfield 31-1-92
*Source:* Scholar. *Honours:* England Youth, Under-20.

| | | | | |
|---|---|---|---|---|
| 2008-09 | Portsmouth | 0 | 0 | |
| 2009-10 | Portsmouth | 0 | 0 | |
| 2010-11 | Portsmouth | 0 | 0 | |
| 2010-11 | WBA | 1 | 0 | |
| 2011-12 | WBA | 0 | 0 | |
| 2011-12 | *Blackpool* | 2 | 0 | 2 0 |
| 2011-12 | *Shrewsbury T* | 7 | 0 | |
| 2011-12 | *Chesterfield* | 10 | 0 | 10 0 |
| 2012-13 | WBA | 0 | 1 | 0 |
| 2012-13 | *Birmingham C* | 3 | 0 | 3 0 |
| 2012-13 | *Shrewsbury T* | 4 | 0 | 11 0 |

Transferred to Valur Reykjavik May 2013

**JARA REYES, Gonzalo (D)**    220 5
H: 5 10 W: 12 02 b.Chile 29-8-85
*Honours:* Chile 58 full caps, 3 goals.

| | | | | |
|---|---|---|---|---|
| 2002 | Huachipato | 0 | 0 | |
| 2003 | Huachipato | 17 | 1 | |
| 2004 | Huachipato | 11 | 0 | |
| 2005 | Huachipato | 23 | 0 | |
| 2006 | Huachipato | 18 | 1 | 69 2 |
| 2007 | Colo Colo | 23 | 1 | |
| 2008 | Colo Colo | 25 | 0 | |
| 2009 | Colo Colo | 16 | 0 | 64 1 |
| 2009-10 | WBA | 22 | 1 | |
| 2010-11 | WBA | 29 | 1 | |
| 2011-12 | WBA | 4 | 0 | |
| 2011-12 | *Brighton & HA* | 14 | 0 | 14 0 |
| 2012-13 | WBA | 1 | 0 | 56 2 |
| 2012-13 | *Nottingham F* | 17 | 0 | 17 0 |

**JONES, Billy (M)**    337 22
H: 5 11 W: 13 00 b.Shrewsbury 24-3-87
*Source:* Scholar. *Honours:* England Youth, Under-20.

| | | | | |
|---|---|---|---|---|
| 2003-04 | Crewe Alex | 27 | 1 | |
| 2004-05 | Crewe Alex | 20 | 0 | |
| 2005-06 | Crewe Alex | 44 | 6 | |
| 2006-07 | Crewe Alex | 41 | 1 | 132 8 |
| 2007-08 | Preston NE | 29 | 0 | |
| 2008-09 | Preston NE | 44 | 3 | |
| 2009-10 | Preston NE | 44 | 4 | |
| 2010-11 | Preston NE | 43 | 6 | 160 13 |
| 2011-12 | WBA | 18 | 0 | |
| 2012-13 | WBA | 27 | 1 | 45 1 |

**LONG, Shane (F)**    241 60
H: 5 10 W: 11 02 b.Co. Tipperary 22-1-87
*Honours:* Eire Youth, B, Under-21, 37 full caps, 9 goals.

| | | | | |
|---|---|---|---|---|
| 2005 | Cork C | 1 | 0 | 1 0 |
| 2005-06 | Reading | 11 | 3 | |
| 2006-07 | Reading | 21 | 2 | |
| 2007-08 | Reading | 29 | 3 | |
| 2008-09 | Reading | 37 | 9 | |
| 2009-10 | Reading | 31 | 6 | |
| 2010-11 | Reading | 44 | 21 | |
| 2011-12 | Reading | 1 | 0 | 174 44 |
| 2011-12 | WBA | 32 | 8 | |
| 2012-13 | WBA | 34 | 8 | 66 16 |

**McAULEY, Gareth (D)**    329 25
H: 6 3 W: 13 00 b.Larne 5-12-79
*Source:* Coleraine. *Honours:* Northern Ireland Schools, B, 42 full caps, 2 goals.

| | | | | |
|---|---|---|---|---|
| 2004-05 | Lincoln C | 37 | 3 | |
| 2005-06 | Lincoln C | 35 | 5 | 72 8 |
| 2006-07 | Leicester C | 30 | 3 | |
| 2007-08 | Leicester C | 44 | 2 | 74 5 |
| 2008-09 | Ipswich T | 35 | 0 | |
| 2009-10 | Ipswich T | 41 | 5 | |
| 2010-11 | Ipswich T | 39 | 2 | 115 7 |
| 2011-12 | WBA | 32 | 2 | |
| 2012-13 | WBA | 36 | 3 | 68 5 |

**MORRISON, James (M)**    239 25
H: 5 10 W: 10 06 b.Darlington 25-5-86
*Source:* Trainee. *Honours:* England Youth, Under-20. Scotland 27 full caps, 2 goals.

| | | | | |
|---|---|---|---|---|
| 2003-04 | Middlesbrough | 1 | 0 | |
| 2004-05 | Middlesbrough | 14 | 0 | |
| 2005-06 | Middlesbrough | 24 | 1 | |
| 2006-07 | Middlesbrough | 28 | 2 | 67 3 |
| 2007-08 | WBA | 35 | 4 | |
| 2008-09 | WBA | 30 | 3 | |
| 2009-10 | WBA | 11 | 1 | |
| 2010-11 | WBA | 31 | 4 | |
| 2011-12 | WBA | 30 | 5 | |
| 2012-13 | WBA | 35 | 5 | 172 22 |

**MULUMBU, Youssef (M)**    179 14
H: 5 9 W: 10 03 b.Kinshasa 25-1-87
*Honours:* France Youth, Under-21. DR Congo 14 full caps, 1 goal.

| | | | | |
|---|---|---|---|---|
| 2006-07 | Paris St Germain | 12 | 0 | |
| 2007-08 | Paris St Germain | 1 | 0 | |
| 2007-08 | *Amiens* | 23 | 1 | 23 1 |
| 2008-09 | Paris St Germain | 0 | 0 | 13 0 |
| 2008-09 | WBA | 6 | 0 | |
| 2009-10 | WBA | 40 | 3 | |
| 2010-11 | WBA | 34 | 7 | |
| 2011-12 | WBA | 35 | 1 | |
| 2012-13 | WBA | 28 | 2 | 143 13 |

**MYHILL, Boaz (G)**    332 0
H: 6 3 W: 14 06 b.California 9-11-82
*Source:* Scholar. *Honours:* England Youth, Under-20. Wales 16 full caps.

| | | | | |
|---|---|---|---|---|
| 2000-01 | Aston Villa | 0 | 0 | |
| 2001-02 | Aston Villa | 0 | 0 | |
| 2001-02 | *Stoke C* | 0 | 0 | |
| 2002-03 | Aston Villa | 0 | 0 | |
| 2002-03 | *Bristol C* | 0 | 0 | |
| 2002-03 | *Bradford C* | 2 | 0 | 2 0 |
| 2003-04 | Aston Villa | 0 | 0 | |
| 2003-04 | *Macclesfield T* | 15 | 0 | 15 0 |
| 2003-04 | *Stockport Co* | 2 | 0 | 2 0 |
| 2003-04 | Hull C | 23 | 0 | |
| 2004-05 | Hull C | 45 | 0 | |
| 2005-06 | Hull C | 45 | 0 | |
| 2006-07 | Hull C | 46 | 0 | |
| 2007-08 | Hull C | 43 | 0 | |
| 2008-09 | Hull C | 28 | 0 | |
| 2009-10 | Hull C | 27 | 0 | 257 0 |
| 2010-11 | WBA | 6 | 0 | |
| 2011-12 | WBA | 0 | 0 | |
| 2011-12 | *Birmingham C* | 42 | 0 | 42 0 |
| 2012-13 | WBA | 8 | 0 | 14 0 |

**NABI, Adil (F)**    0 0
H: 5 9 W: 10 10 b.Birmingham 28-2-94
*Source:* Scholar.

| | | | | |
|---|---|---|---|---|
| 2010-11 | WBA | 0 | 0 | |
| 2011-12 | WBA | 0 | 0 | |
| 2012-13 | WBA | 0 | 0 | |

**O'NEIL, Liam (D)**    14 0
H: 6 0 W: 12 06 b.Cambridge 31-7-93
*Source:* Histon.

| | | | | |
|---|---|---|---|---|
| 2011-12 | WBA | 0 | 0 | |
| 2011-12 | *VPS* | 14 | 0 | 14 0 |
| 2012-13 | WBA | 0 | 0 | |

**ODEMWINGIE, Peter (F)**    281 83
H: 6 0 W: 11 09 b.Tashkent 15-7-81
*Honours:* Nigeria 55 full caps, 9 goals.

| | | | | |
|---|---|---|---|---|
| 2002-03 | La Louviere | 14 | 2 | |
| 2003-04 | La Louviere | 27 | 5 | |
| 2004-05 | La Louviere | 3 | 2 | 44 9 |
| 2004-05 | Lille | 20 | 4 | |
| 2005-06 | Lille | 26 | 14 | |
| 2006-07 | Lille | 29 | 5 | 75 23 |
| 2007 | Lok Moscow | 14 | 4 | |
| 2008 | Lok Moscow | 26 | 10 | |
| 2009 | Lok Moscow | 25 | 7 | |
| 2010 | Lok Moscow | 10 | 0 | 75 21 |
| 2010-11 | WBA | 32 | 15 | |
| 2011-12 | WBA | 30 | 10 | |
| 2012-13 | WBA | 25 | 5 | 87 30 |

**OLSSON, Jonas (D)**    313 15
H: 6 4 W: 12 08 b.Landskrona 10-3-83
*Honours:* Sweden Under-21, 21 full caps, 1 goal.

| | | | | |
|---|---|---|---|---|
| 2002 | Landskrona | 0 | 0 | |
| 2003 | Landskrona | 22 | 0 | |
| 2004 | Landskrona | 22 | 1 | |
| 2005 | Landskrona | 12 | 0 | 56 1 |
| 2005-06 | NEC Nijmegen | 34 | 0 | |
| 2006-07 | NEC Nijmegen | 32 | 2 | |
| 2007-08 | NEC Nijmegen | 27 | 3 | 93 5 |
| 2008-09 | WBA | 28 | 2 | |
| 2009-10 | WBA | 43 | 4 | |
| 2010-11 | WBA | 24 | 1 | |
| 2011-12 | WBA | 33 | 2 | |
| 2012-13 | WBA | 36 | 0 | 164 9 |

**POPOV, Goran (D)**    138 5
H: 6 2 W: 12 08 b.Strumica 2-10-84
*Honours:* Macedonia Youth, Under-21, 44 full caps, 2 goals.

| | | | | |
|---|---|---|---|---|
| 2003-04 | AEK Athens | 8 | 0 | 8 0 |
| 2005-06 | Aigaleo | 19 | 0 | |
| 2006-07 | Aigaleo | 25 | 1 | 44 1 |
| 2007-08 | *Levadiakos* | 20 | 0 | 20 0 |
| 2008-09 | Heerenveen | 24 | 1 | |
| 2009-10 | Heerenveen | 27 | 1 | 51 2 |
| 2010-11 | Dynamo Kiev | 1 | 1 | |
| 2011-12 | Dynamo Kiev | 1 | 1 | |
| 2012-13 | Dynamo Kiev | 1 | 0 | 3 2 |

On loan from Dynamo Kiev

| | | | | |
|---|---|---|---|---|
| 2012-13 | WBA | 12 | 0 | 12 0 |

**REID, Steven (M)**    320 27
H: 6 0 W: 12 07 b.Kingston 10-3-81
*Source:* Trainee. *Honours:* England Youth. Eire Under-21, 23 full caps, 2 goals.

| | | | | |
|---|---|---|---|---|
| 1997-98 | Millwall | 1 | 0 | |
| 1998-99 | Millwall | 25 | 0 | |
| 1999-2000 | Millwall | 21 | 0 | |
| 2000-01 | Millwall | 37 | 7 | |
| 2001-02 | Millwall | 35 | 5 | |
| 2002-03 | Millwall | 20 | 6 | 139 18 |
| 2003-04 | Blackburn R | 16 | 0 | |
| 2004-05 | Blackburn R | 28 | 2 | |
| 2005-06 | Blackburn R | 34 | 4 | |
| 2006-07 | Blackburn R | 3 | 0 | |
| 2007-08 | Blackburn R | 24 | 0 | |
| 2008-09 | Blackburn R | 4 | 0 | |
| 2009-10 | Blackburn R | 4 | 0 | 113 6 |
| 2009-10 | *QPR* | 2 | 0 | 2 0 |
| 2009-10 | *WBA* | 10 | 1 | |
| 2010-11 | WBA | 23 | 1 | |
| 2011-12 | WBA | 22 | 1 | |
| 2012-13 | WBA | 11 | 0 | 66 3 |

**RIDGEWELL, Liam (D)**    279 16
H: 5 10 W: 10 03 b.Bexley 21-7-84
*Source:* Scholar. *Honours:* England Youth, Under-20, Under-21.

| | | | | |
|---|---|---|---|---|
| 2001-02 | Aston Villa | 0 | 0 | |
| 2002-03 | Aston Villa | 0 | 0 | |
| 2002-03 | *Bournemouth* | 5 | 0 | 5 0 |
| 2003-04 | Aston Villa | 11 | 0 | |
| 2004-05 | Aston Villa | 15 | 0 | |
| 2005-06 | Aston Villa | 32 | 5 | |
| 2006-07 | Aston Villa | 21 | 1 | 79 6 |
| 2007-08 | Birmingham C | 35 | 1 | |
| 2008-09 | Birmingham C | 36 | 1 | |
| 2009-10 | Birmingham C | 31 | 3 | |
| 2010-11 | Birmingham C | 36 | 4 | |
| 2011-12 | Birmingham C | 14 | 0 | 152 9 |
| 2011-12 | WBA | 13 | 1 | |
| 2012-13 | WBA | 30 | 0 | 43 1 |

**ROOFE, Kemar (M)**    6 0
H: 5 10 W: 11 03 b.Walsall 6-1-93
*Source:* Scholar.

| | | | | |
|---|---|---|---|---|
| 2011-12 | WBA | 0 | 0 | |
| 2012-13 | WBA | 0 | 0 | |
| 2012-13 | *Northampton T* | 6 | 0 | 6 0 |

**ROSENBERG, Markus (F)**    245 84
H: 6 0 W: 12 06 b.Linhamn 27-9-82
*Honours:* Sweden, Under-21, 33 full caps, 6 goals.

| | | | | |
|---|---|---|---|---|
| 2001-02 | Malmo FF | 1 | 1 | |
| 2002-03 | Malmo FF | 2 | 2 | |
| 2003-04 | Malmo FF | 1 | 1 | |
| 2003-04 | Halmstads BK | 3 | 3 | |
| 2004-05 | Halmstads BK | 10 | 11 | 13 14 |

| | | | | | |
|---|---|--:|--:|--:|--:|
| 2004-05 | Malmo FF | 6 | 4 | | |
| 2005-06 | Malmo FF | 4 | 3 | 14 | 11 |
| 2005-06 | Ajax | 30 | 11 | | |
| 2006-07 | Ajax | 8 | 0 | 38 | 11 |
| 2006-07 | Werder Bremen | 14 | 8 | | |
| 2007-08 | Werder Bremen | 30 | 14 | | |
| 2008-09 | Werder Bremen | 29 | 7 | | |
| 2009-10 | Werder Bremen | 17 | 1 | | |
| 2010-11 | *Racing Santander* | 33 | 8 | 33 | 8 |
| 2011-12 | Werder Bremen | 33 | 10 | 123 | 40 |
| 2012-13 | WBA | 24 | 0 | 24 | 0 |

**TAMAS, Gabriel (D)**    262 12
H: 6 2   W: 12 02   b.Brasov 9-11-83
*Honours:* Romania 63 full caps, 3 goals.

| | | | | | |
|---|---|--:|--:|--:|--:|
| 1998-99 | Brasov | 1 | 0 | | |
| 1999-2000 | Brasov | 0 | 0 | 1 | 0 |
| 2000-01 | Tractorul | 15 | 1 | | |
| 2001-02 | Tractorul | 19 | 4 | 34 | 3 |
| 2002-03 | Din Bucharest | 19 | 4 | | |
| 2003-04 | Galatasaray | 6 | 0 | 6 | 0 |
| 2004 | Spartak Moscow | 14 | 0 | | |
| 2004-05 | Din Bucharest | 13 | 0 | | |
| 2005-06 | Din Bucharest | 14 | 1 | | |
| 2006 | Spartak Moscow | 3 | 0 | 17 | 0 |
| 2006-07 | Celta Vigo | 29 | 0 | 29 | 0 |
| 2007-08 | Auxerre | 27 | 0 | 27 | 0 |
| 2008-09 | Din Bucharest | 22 | 0 | | |
| 2009-10 | Din Bucharest | 12 | 2 | 80 | 7 |
| 2009-10 | WBA | 23 | 2 | | |
| 2010-11 | WBA | 26 | 0 | | |
| 2011-12 | WBA | 8 | 0 | | |
| 2012-13 | WBA | 11 | 0 | 68 | 2 |

**THOMAS, Jerome (M)**    221 22
H: 5 9   W: 11 09   b.Wembley 23-3-83
*Source:* Scholar. *Honours:* England Youth, Under-20, Under-21.

| | | | | | |
|---|---|--:|--:|--:|--:|
| 2001-02 | Arsenal | 0 | 0 | | |
| 2001-02 | *QPR* | 4 | 1 | | |
| 2002-03 | Arsenal | 0 | 0 | | |
| 2002-03 | *QPR* | 6 | 2 | 10 | 3 |
| 2003-04 | Arsenal | 0 | 0 | | |
| 2003-04 | Charlton Ath | 1 | 0 | | |
| 2004-05 | Charlton Ath | 24 | 3 | | |
| 2005-06 | Charlton Ath | 25 | 1 | | |
| 2006-07 | Charlton Ath | 20 | 3 | | |
| 2007-08 | Charlton Ath | 32 | 0 | | |
| 2008-09 | Charlton Ath | 1 | 0 | 103 | 7 |
| 2008-09 | Portsmouth | 3 | 0 | | |
| 2009-10 | Portsmouth | 0 | 0 | 3 | 0 |
| 2009-10 | WBA | 27 | 7 | | |
| 2010-11 | WBA | 33 | 3 | | |
| 2011-12 | WBA | 29 | 1 | | |
| 2012-13 | WBA | 10 | 0 | 99 | 11 |
| 2012-13 | *Leeds U* | 6 | 1 | 6 | 1 |

**THORNE, George (M)**    31 1
H: 6 2   W: 13 01   b.Chatham 4-1-93
*Source:* Scholar. *Honours:* England Youth.

| | | | | | |
|---|---|--:|--:|--:|--:|
| 2009-10 | WBA | 1 | 0 | | |
| 2010-11 | WBA | 1 | 0 | | |
| 2011-12 | WBA | 3 | 0 | | |
| 2011-12 | *Portsmouth* | 14 | 0 | 14 | 0 |
| 2012-13 | WBA | 5 | 0 | 10 | 0 |
| 2012-13 | *Peterborough U* | 7 | 1 | 7 | 1 |

**YACOB, Claudio (M)**    155 4
H: 5 11   W: 11 06   b.Carcarana 18-7-87
*Honours:* Argentina, Under-20, 2 full caps, 1 goal.

| | | | | | |
|---|---|--:|--:|--:|--:|
| 2006-07 | Racing Club | 12 | 0 | | |
| 2007-08 | Racing Club | 24 | 0 | | |
| 2008-09 | Racing Club | 25 | 1 | | |
| 2009-10 | Racing Club | 26 | 0 | | |
| 2010-11 | Racing Club | 21 | 2 | | |
| 2011-12 | Racing Club | 17 | 1 | 125 | 4 |
| 2012-13 | WBA | 30 | 0 | 30 | 0 |

**Scholars**
Atkinson, Wesley; Barrow, Daniel; Birch, Aaron; Buchanan, Matthew; Francis, Jordan; Garmston, Bradley; Greenidge, Reiss James; Howkins, Kyle; Jones, Alexander; Jones, Callam; Oldnall, Ged; O'Sullivan, Mani; Pace, Ryan; Palmer, Alexander; Rose, Jack Joseph; Smart, Tom; Wedderburn, Rees.

# WEST HAM U (87)

**CHAMBERS, Leo (D)**    0 0
H: 6 1   W: 13 00   b.London 5-8-95

| | | | |
|---|---|--:|--:|
| 2012-13 | West Ham U | 0 | 0 |

**COLE, Carlton (F)**    287 59
H: 6 3   W: 14 02   b.Croydon 12-11-83
*Source:* Scholar. *Honours:* England Youth, Under-20, Under-21, 7 full caps.

| | | | | | |
|---|---|--:|--:|--:|--:|
| 2000-01 | Chelsea | 0 | 0 | | |
| 2001-02 | Chelsea | 3 | 1 | | |
| 2002-03 | Chelsea | 13 | 3 | | |
| 2002-03 | *Wolverhampton W* | 7 | 1 | 7 | 4 |
| 2003-04 | Chelsea | 0 | 0 | | |
| 2003-04 | *Charlton Ath* | 21 | 4 | 21 | 4 |
| 2004-05 | Chelsea | 0 | 0 | | |
| 2004-05 | *Aston Villa* | 27 | 3 | 27 | 3 |
| 2005-06 | Chelsea | 9 | 0 | 25 | 4 |
| 2006-07 | West Ham U | 17 | 2 | | |
| 2007-08 | West Ham U | 31 | 4 | | |
| 2008-09 | West Ham U | 27 | 10 | | |
| 2009-10 | West Ham U | 30 | 10 | | |
| 2010-11 | West Ham U | 35 | 5 | | |
| 2011-12 | West Ham U | 40 | 14 | | |
| 2012-13 | West Ham U | 27 | 2 | 207 | 47 |

**COLE, Joe (M)**    377 46
H: 5 9   W: 11 09   b.Camden 8-11-81
*Source:* Trainee. *Honours:* England Schools, Youth, Under-21, B, 56 full caps, 10 goals.

| | | | | | |
|---|---|--:|--:|--:|--:|
| 1998-99 | West Ham U | 8 | 0 | | |
| 1999-2000 | West Ham U | 22 | 1 | | |
| 2000-01 | West Ham U | 30 | 5 | | |
| 2001-02 | West Ham U | 30 | 0 | | |
| 2002-03 | West Ham U | 36 | 4 | | |
| 2003-04 | Chelsea | 35 | 1 | | |
| 2004-05 | Chelsea | 28 | 8 | | |
| 2005-06 | Chelsea | 34 | 7 | | |
| 2006-07 | Chelsea | 13 | 0 | | |
| 2007-08 | Chelsea | 33 | 7 | | |
| 2008-09 | Chelsea | 14 | 2 | | |
| 2009-10 | Chelsea | 26 | 2 | 183 | 27 |
| 2010-11 | Liverpool | 20 | 2 | | |
| 2011-12 | Liverpool | 0 | 0 | | |
| 2011-12 | *Lille* | 31 | 4 | 31 | 4 |
| 2012-13 | Liverpool | 6 | 1 | 26 | 3 |
| 2012-13 | West Ham U | 11 | 2 | 137 | 12 |

**COLLINS, James M (D)**    240 10
H: 6 2   W: 14 05   b.Newport 23-8-83
*Source:* Scholar. *Honours:* Wales Youth, Under-21, 41 full caps, 2 goals.

| | | | | | |
|---|---|--:|--:|--:|--:|
| 2000-01 | Cardiff C | 3 | 0 | | |
| 2001-02 | Cardiff C | 7 | 1 | | |
| 2002-03 | Cardiff C | 20 | 1 | | |
| 2003-04 | Cardiff C | 20 | 1 | | |
| 2004-05 | Cardiff C | 34 | 1 | 66 | 3 |
| 2005-06 | West Ham U | 14 | 2 | | |
| 2006-07 | West Ham U | 16 | 0 | | |
| 2007-08 | West Ham U | 3 | 0 | | |
| 2008-09 | West Ham U | 18 | 0 | | |
| 2009-10 | West Ham U | 3 | 0 | | |
| 2009-10 | Aston Villa | 27 | 1 | | |
| 2010-11 | Aston Villa | 32 | 3 | | |
| 2011-12 | Aston Villa | 32 | 1 | 91 | 5 |
| 2012-13 | West Ham U | 29 | 0 | 83 | 2 |

**COLLISON, Jack (M)**    95 11
H: 6 0   W: 13 10   b.Watford 2-10-88
*Source:* Scholar. *Honours:* Wales Under-21, 13 full caps.

| | | | | | |
|---|---|--:|--:|--:|--:|
| 2007-08 | West Ham U | 2 | 0 | | |
| 2008-09 | West Ham U | 20 | 3 | | |
| 2009-10 | West Ham U | 22 | 2 | | |
| 2010-11 | West Ham U | 3 | 0 | | |
| 2011-12 | West Ham U | 31 | 4 | | |
| 2012-13 | West Ham U | 17 | 2 | 95 | 11 |

**DEMEL, Guy (D)**    243 11
H: 6 2   W: 13 12   b.Paris 13-6-81
*Honours:* Ivory Coast 35 full caps.

| | | | | | |
|---|---|--:|--:|--:|--:|
| 1999-2000 | Nimes | 1 | 0 | 1 | 0 |
| 2000-01 | Arsenal | 0 | 0 | | |
| 2001-02 | Bor Dortmund II | 16 | 3 | | |
| 2002-03 | Bor Dortmund II | 24 | 6 | 40 | 9 |
| 2002-03 | Bor Dortmund | 4 | 0 | | |
| 2003-04 | Bor Dortmund | 13 | 0 | | |
| 2004-05 | Bor Dortmund | 16 | 0 | 33 | 0 |
| 2005-06 | Hamburg | 22 | 1 | | |
| 2006-07 | Hamburg | 8 | 0 | | |
| 2007-08 | Hamburg | 26 | 0 | | |
| 2008-09 | Hamburg | 28 | 0 | | |
| 2009-10 | Hamburg | 26 | 1 | | |
| 2010-11 | Hamburg | 21 | 0 | 131 | 2 |
| 2011-12 | West Ham U | 7 | 0 | | |
| 2012-13 | West Ham U | 31 | 0 | 38 | 0 |

**DIAME, Mohamed (M)**    195 11
H: 6 1   W: 11 02   b.Creteil 14-6-87
*Honours:* Senegal 19 full caps.

| | | | | | |
|---|---|--:|--:|--:|--:|
| 2006-07 | Lens | 0 | 0 | | |
| 2007-08 | Linares | 31 | 1 | 31 | 1 |
| 2008-09 | Rayo Vallecano | 35 | 2 | 35 | 2 |
| 2009-10 | Wigan Ath | 34 | 1 | | |
| 2010-11 | Wigan Ath | 36 | 1 | | |
| 2011-12 | Wigan Ath | 26 | 3 | 96 | 5 |
| 2012-13 | West Ham U | 33 | 3 | 33 | 3 |

**DIARRA, Alou (M)**    320 22
H: 6 3   W: 12 05   b.Villepinte 15-7-81
*Source:* Louhans, Bayern Munich.
*Honours:* France Youth, Under-21, 44 full caps.

| | | | | | |
|---|---|--:|--:|--:|--:|
| 2002-03 | Liverpool | 0 | 0 | | |
| 2002-03 | *Le Havre* | 25 | 0 | 25 | 0 |
| 2003-04 | Liverpool | 0 | 0 | | |
| 2003-04 | *Bastia* | 35 | 4 | 35 | 4 |
| 2004-05 | Liverpool | 0 | 0 | | |
| 2004-05 | *Lens* | 34 | 2 | | |
| 2005-06 | Lens | 30 | 2 | 64 | 4 |
| 2006-07 | Lyon | 15 | 1 | 15 | 1 |
| 2007-08 | Bordeaux | 36 | 4 | | |
| 2008-09 | Bordeaux | 35 | 2 | | |
| 2009-10 | Bordeaux | 30 | 1 | | |
| 2010-11 | Bordeaux | 32 | 4 | 133 | 11 |
| 2011-12 | Marseille | 33 | 2 | | |
| 2012-13 | Marseille | 0 | 0 | 33 | 2 |
| 2012-13 | West Ham U | 3 | 0 | 3 | 0 |
| 2012-13 | *Rennes* | 12 | 0 | 12 | 0 |

**DRIVER, Callum (D)**    8 1
H: 5 8   W: 11 11   b.Sidcup 23-10-92
*Source:* Scholar.

| | | | | | |
|---|---|--:|--:|--:|--:|
| 2011-12 | West Ham U | 0 | 0 | | |
| 2011-12 | *Burton Alb* | 8 | 1 | 8 | 1 |
| 2012-13 | West Ham U | 0 | 0 | | |

**FANIMO, Matthias (M)**    0 0
H: 5 8   W: 11 03   b.Lambeth 28-1-94
*Source:* Scholar. *Honours:* England Youth.

| | | | |
|---|---|--:|--:|
| 2011-12 | West Ham U | 0 | 0 |
| 2012-13 | West Ham U | 0 | 0 |

**HALL, Robert (F)**    33 5
H: 6 2   W: 10 05   b.Aylesbury 20-10-93
*Source:* Academy. *Honours:* England Youth.

| | | | | | |
|---|---|--:|--:|--:|--:|
| 2010-11 | West Ham U | 0 | 0 | | |
| 2011-12 | West Ham U | 3 | 0 | | |
| 2011-12 | *Oxford U* | 13 | 5 | 13 | 5 |
| 2011-12 | *Milton Keynes D* | 2 | 0 | 2 | 0 |
| 2012-13 | West Ham U | 1 | 0 | 4 | 0 |
| 2012-13 | *Birmingham C* | 13 | 0 | 13 | 0 |
| 2012-13 | *Bolton W* | 1 | 0 | 1 | 0 |

**HENDERSON, Stephen (G)**    95 0
H: 6 3   W: 11 00   b.Dublin 2-5-88
*Source:* Scholar. *Honours:* Eire Under-21.

| | | | | | |
|---|---|--:|--:|--:|--:|
| 2005-06 | Aston Villa | 0 | 0 | | |
| 2006-07 | Aston Villa | 0 | 0 | | |
| 2007-08 | Bristol C | 1 | 0 | | |
| 2008-09 | Bristol C | 1 | 0 | | |
| 2009-10 | Bristol C | 3 | 0 | | |
| 2009-10 | *Aldershot T* | 8 | 0 | 8 | 0 |
| 2010-11 | Bristol C | 0 | 0 | 5 | 0 |
| 2010-11 | *Yeovil T* | 33 | 0 | 33 | 0 |
| 2011-12 | *Portsmouth* | 25 | 0 | 25 | 0 |
| 2011-12 | West Ham U | 0 | 0 | | |
| 2012-13 | West Ham U | 0 | 0 | | |
| 2012-13 | *Ipswich T* | 24 | 0 | 24 | 0 |

**JAASKELAINEN, Jussi (G)**    630 0
H: 6 3   W: 12 10   b.Vaasa 19-4-75
*Honours:* Finland Youth, Under-21, 56 full caps.

| | | | | | |
|---|---|--:|--:|--:|--:|
| 1992 | MP | 6 | 0 | | |
| 1993 | MP | 6 | 0 | | |
| 1994 | MP | 26 | 0 | | |
| 1995 | MP | 26 | 0 | 64 | 0 |
| 1996 | VPS | 27 | 0 | | |

| | | | | |
|---|---|---|---|---|
| 1997 | VPS | 27 | 0 | 54 0 |
| 1997-98 | Bolton W | 0 | 0 | |
| 1998-99 | Bolton W | 34 | 0 | |
| 1999-2000 | Bolton W | 34 | 0 | |
| 2000-01 | Bolton W | 27 | 0 | |
| 2001-02 | Bolton W | 34 | 0 | |
| 2002-03 | Bolton W | 38 | 0 | |
| 2003-04 | Bolton W | 38 | 0 | |
| 2004-05 | Bolton W | 36 | 0 | |
| 2005-06 | Bolton W | 38 | 0 | |
| 2006-07 | Bolton W | 38 | 0 | |
| 2007-08 | Bolton W | 28 | 0 | |
| 2008-09 | Bolton W | 38 | 0 | |
| 2009-10 | Bolton W | 38 | 0 | |
| 2010-11 | Bolton W | 35 | 0 | |
| 2011-12 | Bolton W | 18 | 0 | 474 0 |
| 2012-13 | West Ham U | 38 | 0 | 38 0 |

**JARVIS, Matthew (M)** 306 33
H: 5 8 W: 11 10 b.Middlesbrough 22-5-86
Source: Scholar. Honours: England 1 full cap.

| | | | | |
|---|---|---|---|---|
| 2003-04 | Gillingham | 10 | 0 | |
| 2004-05 | Gillingham | 30 | 3 | |
| 2005-06 | Gillingham | 35 | 3 | |
| 2006-07 | Gillingham | 35 | 6 | 110 12 |
| 2007-08 | Wolverhampton W | 26 | 1 | |
| 2008-09 | Wolverhampton W | 28 | 3 | |
| 2009-10 | Wolverhampton W | 34 | 3 | |
| 2010-11 | Wolverhampton W | 37 | 4 | |
| 2011-12 | Wolverhampton W | 37 | 8 | |
| 2012-13 | Wolverhampton W | 2 | 0 | 164 19 |
| 2012-13 | West Ham U | 32 | 2 | 32 2 |

**LEE, Elliot (F)** 0 0
H: 5 11 W: 11 05 b.Co. Durham 16-12-94
Source: Scholar.

| | | | |
|---|---|---|---|
| 2011-12 | West Ham U | 0 | 0 |
| 2012-13 | West Ham U | 0 | 0 |

**LLETGET, Sebastian (M)** 0 0
H: 5 10 W: 10 11 b.San Francisco 3-9-92
Honours: USA Youth.

| | | | |
|---|---|---|---|
| 2010-11 | West Ham U | 0 | 0 |
| 2011-12 | West Ham U | 0 | 0 |
| 2012-13 | West Ham U | 0 | 0 |

**MAGUIRE, Sean (F)** 0 0
H: 5 9 W: 11 10 b.Luton 1-5-94
Source: Waterford U.

| | | | |
|---|---|---|---|
| 2012-13 | West Ham U | 0 | 0 |

**MAIGA, Modibo (F)** 164 41
H: 6 1 W: 12 07 b.Bamako 3-9-87
Honours: Mali 40 full caps, 7 goals.

| | | | | |
|---|---|---|---|---|
| 2007-08 | Le Mans | 19 | 0 | |
| 2008-09 | Le Mans | 37 | 8 | |
| 2009-10 | Le Mans | 32 | 7 | 88 15 |
| 2010-11 | Sochaux | 36 | 15 | |
| 2011-12 | Sochaux | 23 | 9 | 59 24 |
| 2012-13 | West Ham U | 17 | 2 | 17 2 |

**McCALLUM, Paul (F)** 18 7
H: 6 3 W: 12 00 b.Streatham 28-7-93
Source: Dulwich Hamlet.

| | | | | |
|---|---|---|---|---|
| 2010-11 | West Ham U | 0 | 0 | |
| 2011-12 | West Ham U | 0 | 0 | |
| 2011-12 | Rochdale | 0 | 0 | |
| 2012-13 | West Ham U | 0 | 0 | |
| 2012-13 | AFC Wimbledon | 9 | 4 | 9 4 |
| 2012-13 | Aldershot T | 9 | 3 | 9 3 |

**McCARTNEY, George (D)** 318 2
H: 5 11 W: 11 02 b.Belfast 29-4-81
Source: Trainee. Honours: Northern Ireland Schools, Youth, Under-21, 34 full caps, 1 goal.

| | | | | |
|---|---|---|---|---|
| 1998-99 | Sunderland | 0 | 0 | |
| 1999-2000 | Sunderland | 0 | 0 | |
| 2000-01 | Sunderland | 2 | 0 | |
| 2001-02 | Sunderland | 18 | 0 | |
| 2002-03 | Sunderland | 24 | 0 | |
| 2003-04 | Sunderland | 41 | 0 | |
| 2004-05 | Sunderland | 36 | 0 | |
| 2005-06 | Sunderland | 13 | 0 | |
| 2006-07 | West Ham U | 22 | 0 | |
| 2007-08 | West Ham U | 38 | 1 | |
| 2008-09 | West Ham U | 1 | 0 | |
| 2008-09 | Sunderland | 16 | 0 | |
| 2009-10 | Sunderland | 25 | 0 | |
| 2010-11 | Sunderland | 0 | 0 | |
| 2010-11 | Leeds U | 32 | 0 | 32 0 |
| 2011-12 | Sunderland | 0 | 0 | 175 0 |
| 2011-12 | West Ham U | 38 | 1 | |
| 2012-13 | West Ham U | 12 | 0 | 111 2 |

**MONCUR, George (M)** 20 2
H: 5 9 W: 10 00 b.Swindon 18-8-93
Source: Scholar. Honours: England Youth.

| | | | | |
|---|---|---|---|---|
| 2010-11 | West Ham U | 0 | 0 | |
| 2011-12 | West Ham U | 0 | 0 | |
| 2011-12 | AFC Wimbledon | 20 | 2 | 20 2 |
| 2012-13 | West Ham U | 0 | 0 | |

**MORRISON, Ravel (M)** 28 3
H: 5 9 W: 11 02 b.Wythenshawe 2-2-93
Source: Scholar. Honours: England Youth.

| | | | | |
|---|---|---|---|---|
| 2009-10 | Manchester U | 0 | 0 | |
| 2010-11 | Manchester U | 0 | 0 | |
| 2011-12 | Manchester U | 0 | 0 | |
| 2011-12 | West Ham U | 1 | 0 | |
| 2012-13 | West Ham U | 0 | 0 | 1 0 |
| 2012-13 | Birmingham C | 27 | 3 | 27 3 |

**NOBLE, Mark (M)** 232 27
H: 5 11 W: 12 00 b.West Ham 8-5-87
Source: Scholar. Honours: England Youth, Under-21.

| | | | | |
|---|---|---|---|---|
| 2004-05 | West Ham U | 13 | 0 | |
| 2005-06 | West Ham U | 5 | 0 | |
| 2005-06 | Hull C | 5 | 0 | 5 0 |
| 2006-07 | West Ham U | 10 | 2 | |
| 2006-07 | Ipswich T | 13 | 1 | 13 1 |
| 2007-08 | West Ham U | 31 | 3 | |
| 2008-09 | West Ham U | 29 | 3 | |
| 2009-10 | West Ham U | 27 | 2 | |
| 2010-11 | West Ham U | 26 | 4 | |
| 2011-12 | West Ham U | 45 | 8 | |
| 2012-13 | West Ham U | 28 | 4 | 214 26 |

**NOLAN, Kevin (M)** 458 91
H: 6 0 W: 14 00 b.Liverpool 24-6-82
Source: Scholar. Honours: England Youth, Under-20, Under-21.

| | | | | |
|---|---|---|---|---|
| 1999-2000 | Bolton W | 4 | 0 | |
| 2000-01 | Bolton W | 31 | 1 | |
| 2001-02 | Bolton W | 35 | 8 | |
| 2002-03 | Bolton W | 33 | 1 | |
| 2003-04 | Bolton W | 37 | 9 | |
| 2004-05 | Bolton W | 36 | 4 | |
| 2005-06 | Bolton W | 36 | 9 | |
| 2006-07 | Bolton W | 31 | 3 | |
| 2007-08 | Bolton W | 33 | 5 | |
| 2008-09 | Bolton W | 20 | 0 | 296 40 |
| 2008-09 | Newcastle U | 11 | 0 | |
| 2009-10 | Newcastle U | 44 | 17 | |
| 2010-11 | Newcastle U | 30 | 12 | 85 29 |
| 2011-12 | West Ham U | 42 | 12 | |
| 2012-13 | West Ham U | 35 | 10 | 77 22 |

**O'BRIEN, Joey (M)** 134 5
H: 5 11 W: 10 13 b.Dublin 17-2-86
Source: Scholar. Honours: Eire Youth, Under-21, 5 full caps.

| | | | | |
|---|---|---|---|---|
| 2004-05 | Bolton W | 1 | 0 | |
| 2004-05 | Sheffield W | 15 | 2 | |
| 2005-06 | Bolton W | 23 | 0 | |
| 2006-07 | Bolton W | 0 | 0 | |
| 2007-08 | Bolton W | 19 | 0 | |
| 2008-09 | Bolton W | 7 | 0 | |
| 2009-10 | Bolton W | 0 | 0 | |
| 2010-11 | Bolton W | 0 | 0 | 50 0 |
| 2010-11 | Sheffield W | 4 | 0 | 19 2 |
| 2011-12 | West Ham U | 32 | 1 | |
| 2012-13 | West Ham U | 33 | 2 | 65 3 |

**O'NEIL, Gary (M)** 348 28
H: 5 10 W: 11 00 b.Beckenham 18-5-83
Source: Scholar. Honours: England Youth, Under-20, Under-21.

| | | | | |
|---|---|---|---|---|
| 1999-2000 | Portsmouth | 1 | 0 | |
| 2000-01 | Portsmouth | 10 | 1 | |
| 2001-02 | Portsmouth | 33 | 1 | |
| 2002-03 | Portsmouth | 31 | 3 | |
| 2003-04 | Portsmouth | 3 | 2 | |
| 2003-04 | Walsall | 7 | 0 | 7 0 |
| 2004-05 | Portsmouth | 24 | 2 | |
| 2004-05 | Cardiff C | 9 | 1 | 9 1 |
| 2005-06 | Portsmouth | 36 | 6 | |
| 2006-07 | Portsmouth | 35 | 1 | |
| 2007-08 | Portsmouth | 2 | 0 | 175 16 |
| 2007-08 | Middlesbrough | 26 | 0 | |
| 2008-09 | Middlesbrough | 29 | 4 | |
| 2009-10 | Middlesbrough | 36 | 4 | |
| 2010-11 | Middlesbrough | 18 | 0 | 109 8 |
| 2010-11 | West Ham U | 8 | 0 | |
| 2011-12 | West Ham U | 16 | 2 | |
| 2012-13 | West Ham U | 24 | 1 | 48 3 |

**POGATETZ, Emanuel (D)** 317 7
H: 6 2 W: 11 12 b.Vienna 16-1-83
Honours: Austria Youth, Under-21, 56 full caps, 2 goals.

| | | | | |
|---|---|---|---|---|
| 1999-2000 | Sturm Graz | 0 | 0 | |
| 2000-01 | Karntern | 33 | 0 | 33 0 |
| 2001-02 | Leverkusen B | 23 | 0 | |
| 2002-03 | Leverkusen B | 3 | 0 | 26 0 |
| 2002-03 | Aarau | 11 | 0 | 11 0 |
| 2003-04 | Graz | 31 | 1 | |
| 2004-05 | Graz | 22 | 1 | 53 2 |
| 2005-06 | Middlesbrough | 24 | 1 | |
| 2006-07 | Middlesbrough | 35 | 2 | |
| 2007-08 | Middlesbrough | 24 | 0 | |
| 2008-09 | Middlesbrough | 27 | 1 | |
| 2009-10 | Middlesbrough | 13 | 0 | 123 4 |
| 2010-11 | Hannover 96 | 28 | 0 | |
| 2011-12 | Hannover 96 | 29 | 1 | 57 1 |
| 2012-13 | Wolfsburg | 8 | 0 | 8 0 |

On loan from Wolfsburg

| | | | | |
|---|---|---|---|---|
| 2012-13 | West Ham U | 6 | 0 | 6 0 |

**POTTS, Danny (D)** 10 0
H: 5 8 W: 11 00 b.Barking 13-4-94
Source: Scholar. Honours: England Youth.

| | | | | |
|---|---|---|---|---|
| 2011-12 | West Ham U | 3 | 0 | |
| 2012-13 | West Ham U | 2 | 0 | 5 0 |
| 2012-13 | Colchester U | 5 | 0 | 5 0 |

**REID, Winston (D)** 154 6
H: 6 3 W: 13 10 b.North Shore 3-7-88
Honours: Denmark Youth, Under-21. New Zealand 14 full caps, 1 goal.

| | | | | |
|---|---|---|---|---|
| 2005-06 | Midtjylland | 9 | 0 | |
| 2006-07 | Midtjylland | 11 | 0 | |
| 2007-08 | Midtjylland | 9 | 0 | |
| 2008-09 | Midtjylland | 25 | 2 | |
| 2009-10 | Midtjylland | 29 | 0 | 83 2 |
| 2010-11 | West Ham U | 7 | 0 | |
| 2011-12 | West Ham U | 28 | 3 | |
| 2012-13 | West Ham U | 36 | 1 | 71 4 |

**SPENCE, Jordan (D)** 57 0
H: 6 2 W: 12 07 b.Woodford 24-5-90
Source: Scholar. Honours: England Youth, Under-21.

| | | | | |
|---|---|---|---|---|
| 2007-08 | West Ham U | 0 | 0 | |
| 2008-09 | West Ham U | 0 | 0 | |
| 2008-09 | Leyton Orient | 20 | 0 | 20 0 |
| 2009-10 | West Ham U | 1 | 0 | |
| 2009-10 | Scunthorpe U | 9 | 0 | 9 0 |
| 2010-11 | West Ham U | 2 | 0 | |
| 2010-11 | Bristol C | 11 | 0 | |
| 2011-12 | West Ham U | 0 | 0 | |
| 2011-12 | Bristol C | 10 | 0 | 21 0 |
| 2012-13 | West Ham U | 4 | 0 | 7 0 |

**SPIEGEL, Raphael (G)** 0 0
H: 6 5 W: 15 00 b.Zurich 19-12-92

| | | | |
|---|---|---|---|
| 2012-13 | Grasshoppers | 0 | 0 |
| 2012-13 | West Ham U | 0 | 0 |

**TAYLOR, Matthew (D)** 487 64
H: 5 11 W: 12 03 b.Oxford 27-11-81
Source: Trainee. Honours: England Youth, Under-21.

| | | | | |
|---|---|---|---|---|
| 1998-99 | Luton T | 0 | 0 | |
| 1999-2000 | Luton T | 41 | 4 | |
| 2000-01 | Luton T | 45 | 1 | |
| 2001-02 | Luton T | 43 | 11 | 129 16 |
| 2002-03 | Portsmouth | 35 | 7 | |
| 2003-04 | Portsmouth | 30 | 0 | |
| 2004-05 | Portsmouth | 32 | 1 | |
| 2005-06 | Portsmouth | 34 | 6 | |
| 2006-07 | Portsmouth | 35 | 8 | |
| 2007-08 | Portsmouth | 13 | 1 | 179 23 |
| 2007-08 | Bolton W | 16 | 3 | |
| 2008-09 | Bolton W | 34 | 10 | |
| 2009-10 | Bolton W | 37 | 8 | |
| 2010-11 | Bolton W | 36 | 2 | 123 23 |
| 2011-12 | West Ham U | 28 | 1 | |
| 2012-13 | West Ham U | 28 | 1 | 56 2 |

## TOMBIDES, Dylan (F) — 0 0
H: 5 11  W: 12 08  b.Perth 8-3-94
*Source:* Scholar.

| Season | Club | Apps | Gls | Tot A | Tot G |
|---|---|---|---|---|---|
| 2011-12 | West Ham U | 0 | 0 | | |
| 2012-13 | West Ham U | 0 | 0 | | |

## TOMKINS, James (D) — 137 7
H: 6 3  W: 11 10  b.Basildon 29-3-89
*Source:* Scholar. *Honours:* England Schools, Youth, Under-21.

| Season | Club | Apps | Gls | Tot A | Tot G |
|---|---|---|---|---|---|
| 2005-06 | West Ham U | 0 | 0 | | |
| 2006-07 | West Ham U | 0 | 0 | | |
| 2007-08 | West Ham U | 6 | 0 | | |
| 2008-09 | West Ham U | 12 | 1 | | |
| 2008-09 | *Derby Co* | 7 | 0 | 7 | 0 |
| 2009-10 | West Ham U | 23 | 0 | | |
| 2010-11 | West Ham U | 19 | 1 | | |
| 2011-12 | West Ham U | 44 | 4 | | |
| 2012-13 | West Ham U | 26 | 1 | 130 | 7 |

## VAZ TE, Ricardo (F) — 125 26
H: 6 2  W: 12 07  b.Lisbon 1-10-86
*Source:* Trainee. *Honours:* Portugal Youth, Under-20, Under-21.

| Season | Club | Apps | Gls | Tot A | Tot G |
|---|---|---|---|---|---|
| 2003-04 | Bolton W | 1 | 0 | | |
| 2004-05 | Bolton W | 7 | 0 | | |
| 2005-06 | Bolton W | 22 | 3 | | |
| 2006-07 | Bolton W | 25 | 0 | | |
| 2006-07 | *Hull C* | 6 | 0 | 6 | 0 |
| 2007-08 | Bolton W | 1 | 0 | | |
| 2008-09 | Bolton W | 2 | 0 | | |
| 2009-10 | Bolton W | 0 | 0 | | |
| 2010-11 | Bolton W | 0 | 0 | 58 | 3 |
| 2011-12 | Barnsley | 22 | 10 | 22 | 10 |
| 2012-13 | West Ham U | 24 | 3 | 39 | 13 |

**Players retained or with offer of contract**
Mpanzu, Pelly Ruddock; Sadlier, Kieran Paul; Turgot, Blair Sebastien.

**Scholars**
Baxter, Samuel James; Boakye-Yiadom, Nana Emeka; Bywater, Kieran; Cullen, Joshua Jon; Girdlestone, Robert; Gogo, Thomas; Guzman, Rosique Gines; Harney, Jamie; Homans, Courtney; Labonne, Dymon Jermaine Kwabena; Makasi, Kusu Moses; Marlow, Ben John; Mavila, Nathan; Miles, Taylor Robert; Nasha, Amos Lawrence; Page, Lewis Robert; Shaw, Frazer Dean; Tombides, Taylor James.

# WIGAN ATH (88)

## AL-HABSI, Ali (G) — 173 0
H: 6 4  W: 12 06  b.Oman 30-12-81
*Source:* Al-Nasser, Al-Mudhaibi. *Honours:* Oman 91 full caps.

| Season | Club | Apps | Gls | Tot A | Tot G |
|---|---|---|---|---|---|
| 2003 | Lyn | 13 | 0 | | |
| 2004 | Lyn | 24 | 0 | | |
| 2005 | Lyn | 25 | 0 | 62 | 0 |
| 2005-06 | Bolton W | 0 | 0 | | |
| 2006-07 | Bolton W | 0 | 0 | | |
| 2007-08 | Bolton W | 10 | 0 | | |
| 2008-09 | Bolton W | 0 | 0 | | |
| 2009-10 | Bolton W | 0 | 0 | | |
| 2010-11 | Bolton W | 0 | 0 | 10 | 0 |
| 2010-11 | *Wigan Ath* | 34 | 0 | | |
| 2011-12 | Wigan Ath | 38 | 0 | | |
| 2012-13 | Wigan Ath | 29 | 0 | 101 | 0 |

## ALCARAZ, Antolin (D) — 249 13
H: 6 0  W: 12 08  b.Roque Gonzalez 30-7-82
*Honours:* Paraguay 24 full caps, 2 goals.

| Season | Club | Apps | Gls | Tot A | Tot G |
|---|---|---|---|---|---|
| 2002-03 | Beira-Mar | 7 | 0 | | |
| 2003-04 | Beira-Mar | 24 | 1 | | |
| 2004-05 | Beira-Mar | 24 | 1 | | |
| 2005-06 | Beira-Mar | 31 | 0 | | |
| 2006-07 | Beira-Mar | 26 | 3 | 112 | 5 |
| 2007-08 | Club Brugge | 10 | 1 | | |
| 2008-09 | Club Brugge | 29 | 3 | | |
| 2009-10 | Club Brugge | 29 | 1 | 68 | 5 |
| 2010-11 | Wigan Ath | 34 | 1 | | |
| 2011-12 | Wigan Ath | 25 | 2 | | |
| 2012-13 | Wigan Ath | 10 | 0 | 69 | 8 |

## ANDRES, Guillermo (F) — 0 0
H: 5 11  W: 10 09  b.Quart De Poblet 13-10-92

| Season | Club | Apps | Gls | Tot A | Tot G |
|---|---|---|---|---|---|
| 2012-13 | Wigan Ath | 0 | 0 | | |

## ANGOY, Jeshua (M) — 0 0
H: 5 11  W: 11 04  b.Barcelona 11-3-93

| Season | Club | Apps | Gls | Tot A | Tot G |
|---|---|---|---|---|---|
| 2012-13 | Wigan Ath | 0 | 0 | | |

## BEAUSEJOUR, Jean (M) — 304 34
H: 5 10  W: 12 08  b.Santiago 1-6-84
*Honours:* Chile 50 full caps, 3 goals.

| Season | Club | Apps | Gls | Tot A | Tot G |
|---|---|---|---|---|---|
| 2002 | Univ Catolica | 1 | 0 | | |
| 2003 | Univ Concepcion | 30 | 3 | 30 | 3 |
| 2004 | Univ Catolica | 15 | 3 | 16 | 3 |
| 2004-05 | Servette | 11 | 1 | 11 | 1 |
| 2005-06 | Gremio | 55 | 7 | 55 | 7 |
| 2006-07 | Gent | 0 | 0 | | |
| 2007-08 | Cobreloa | 22 | 0 | 22 | 0 |
| 2008 | O'Higgins | 34 | 13 | 34 | 13 |
| 2008-09 | America | 17 | 0 | | |
| 2009-10 | America | 28 | 3 | | |
| 2010-11 | America | 2 | 0 | 47 | 3 |
| 2010-11 | Birmingham C | 17 | 2 | | |
| 2011-12 | Birmingham C | 22 | 1 | 39 | 3 |
| 2011-12 | Wigan Ath | 16 | 0 | | |
| 2012-13 | Wigan Ath | 34 | 1 | 50 | 1 |

## BINGHAM, Rakish (F) — 0 0
b.Newham 25-10-93
*Source:* Scholar.

| Season | Club | Apps | Gls | Tot A | Tot G |
|---|---|---|---|---|---|
| 2011-12 | Wigan Ath | 0 | 0 | | |
| 2012-13 | Wigan Ath | 0 | 0 | | |

## BOOTHMAN, Steven (M) — 0 0
H: 5 7  W: 11 00  b.Wigan 18-9-92
*Source:* Scholar.

| Season | Club | Apps | Gls | Tot A | Tot G |
|---|---|---|---|---|---|
| 2011-12 | Wigan Ath | 0 | 0 | | |
| 2012-13 | Wigan Ath | 0 | 0 | | |

## BOSELLI, Mauro (F) — 191 60
H: 6 0  W: 11 11  b.Buenos Aires 22-5-85
*Honours:* Argentina Youth, 4 full caps, 1 goal.

| Season | Club | Apps | Gls | Tot A | Tot G |
|---|---|---|---|---|---|
| 2002-03 | Boca Juniors | 1 | 0 | | |
| 2003-04 | Boca Juniors | 0 | 0 | | |
| 2004-05 | Boca Juniors | 10 | 2 | | |
| 2005-06 | Malaga | 32 | 5 | 32 | 5 |
| 2006-07 | Boca Juniors | 12 | 4 | | |
| 2007-08 | Boca Juniors | 21 | 4 | 44 | 10 |
| 2008-09 | Estudiantes | 25 | 10 | | |
| 2009-10 | Estudiantes | 31 | 22 | | |
| 2010-11 | Wigan Ath | 8 | 0 | | |
| 2010-11 | *Genoa* | 7 | 2 | 7 | 2 |
| 2011-12 | Wigan Ath | 0 | 0 | | |
| 2011-12 | *Estudiantes* | 29 | 11 | 85 | 43 |
| 2012-13 | Wigan Ath | 7 | 0 | 15 | 0 |
| 2012-13 | *Palermo* | 8 | 0 | 8 | 0 |

## BOYCE, Emmerson (D) — 449 21
H: 6 0  W: 12 03  b.Aylesbury 24-9-79
*Source:* Trainee. *Honours:* Barbados 2 full caps.

| Season | Club | Apps | Gls | Tot A | Tot G |
|---|---|---|---|---|---|
| 1997-98 | Luton T | 0 | 0 | | |
| 1998-99 | Luton T | 1 | 0 | | |
| 1999-2000 | Luton T | 30 | 1 | | |
| 2000-01 | Luton T | 42 | 3 | | |
| 2001-02 | Luton T | 37 | 0 | | |
| 2002-03 | Luton T | 34 | 0 | | |
| 2003-04 | Luton T | 42 | 4 | 186 | 8 |
| 2004-05 | Crystal Palace | 27 | 0 | | |
| 2005-06 | Crystal Palace | 42 | 2 | 69 | 2 |
| 2006-07 | Wigan Ath | 34 | 0 | | |
| 2007-08 | Wigan Ath | 25 | 0 | | |
| 2008-09 | Wigan Ath | 27 | 1 | | |
| 2009-10 | Wigan Ath | 24 | 3 | | |
| 2010-11 | Wigan Ath | 22 | 0 | | |
| 2011-12 | Wigan Ath | 26 | 3 | | |
| 2012-13 | Wigan Ath | 36 | 4 | 194 | 11 |

## BUXTON, Adam (D) — 0 0
H: 6 1  W: 12 10  b.Liverpool 12-5-92
*Source:* Scholar.

| Season | Club | Apps | Gls | Tot A | Tot G |
|---|---|---|---|---|---|
| 2010-11 | Wigan Ath | 0 | 0 | | |
| 2011-12 | Wigan Ath | 0 | 0 | | |
| 2012-13 | Wigan Ath | 0 | 0 | | |

## CALDWELL, Gary (D) — 354 16
H: 5 11  W: 11 10  b.Stirling 12-4-82
*Source:* Trainee. *Honours:* Scotland Under-21, 55 full caps, 2 goals.

| Season | Club | Apps | Gls | Tot A | Tot G |
|---|---|---|---|---|---|
| 1998-99 | Newcastle U | 0 | 0 | | |
| 1999-2000 | Newcastle U | 0 | 0 | | |
| 2000-01 | Newcastle U | 0 | 0 | | |
| 2001-02 | Newcastle U | 0 | 0 | | |
| 2001-02 | *Darlington* | 4 | 0 | 4 | 0 |
| 2001-02 | *Hibernian* | 11 | 0 | | |
| 2002-03 | Newcastle U | 0 | 0 | | |
| 2002-03 | *Coventry C* | 36 | 0 | 36 | 0 |
| 2003-04 | Newcastle U | 0 | 0 | | |
| 2003-04 | *Derby Co* | 9 | 0 | 9 | 0 |
| 2003-04 | *Hibernian* | 17 | 1 | | |
| 2004-05 | Hibernian | 37 | 3 | | |
| 2005-06 | Hibernian | 34 | 1 | 99 | 5 |
| 2006-07 | Celtic | 21 | 0 | | |
| 2007-08 | Celtic | 35 | 1 | | |
| 2008-09 | Celtic | 36 | 3 | | |
| 2009-10 | Celtic | 14 | 1 | 106 | 5 |
| 2009-10 | Wigan Ath | 16 | 2 | | |
| 2010-11 | Wigan Ath | 23 | 0 | | |
| 2011-12 | Wigan Ath | 36 | 3 | | |
| 2012-13 | Wigan Ath | 25 | 1 | 100 | 6 |

## CAMPABADAL, Eduard (D) — 1 0
H: 5 10  W: 11 04  b.Tarragona 26-1-93

| Season | Club | Apps | Gls | Tot A | Tot G |
|---|---|---|---|---|---|
| 2012-13 | Wigan Ath | 1 | 0 | 1 | 0 |

## CHOW, Tim (M) — 0 0
W: 11 06  b.Wigan 18-1-94
*Source:* Scholar.

| Season | Club | Apps | Gls | Tot A | Tot G |
|---|---|---|---|---|---|
| 2011-12 | Wigan Ath | 0 | 0 | | |
| 2012-13 | Wigan Ath | 0 | 0 | | |

## CRUSAT, Albert (M) — 259 39
H: 5 5  W: 10 03  b.Barcelona 13-5-82
*Honours:* Spain Youth.

| Season | Club | Apps | Gls | Tot A | Tot G |
|---|---|---|---|---|---|
| 2002-03 | Espanyol | 5 | 0 | | |
| 2003-04 | Rayo Vallecano | 5 | 1 | 5 | 1 |
| 2004-05 | Lleida | 35 | 4 | 35 | 4 |
| 2005-06 | Almeria | 34 | 8 | | |
| 2006-07 | Almeria | 34 | 11 | | |
| 2007-08 | Almeria | 34 | 3 | | |
| 2008-09 | Almeria | 30 | 1 | | |
| 2009-10 | Almeria | 33 | 7 | | |
| 2010-11 | Almeria | 34 | 3 | 199 | 33 |
| 2011-12 | Wigan Ath | 15 | 1 | | |
| 2012-13 | Wigan Ath | 0 | 0 | 15 | 1 |

## DI SANTO, Franco (F) — 177 27
H: 6 4  W: 13 01  b.Mendoza 7-4-89
*Source:* Audax Italiano. *Honours:* Argentina Under-20, 3 full caps.

| Season | Club | Apps | Gls | Tot A | Tot G |
|---|---|---|---|---|---|
| 2006 | Audax Italiano | 18 | 6 | | |
| 2007 | Audax Italiano | 37 | 7 | 55 | 13 |
| 2007-08 | Chelsea | 0 | 0 | | |
| 2008-09 | Chelsea | 8 | 0 | | |
| 2009-10 | Chelsea | 0 | 0 | | |
| 2009-10 | *Blackburn R* | 22 | 1 | 22 | 1 |
| 2010-11 | Chelsea | 0 | 0 | 8 | 0 |
| 2010-11 | Wigan Ath | 25 | 1 | | |
| 2011-12 | Wigan Ath | 32 | 7 | | |
| 2012-13 | Wigan Ath | 35 | 5 | 92 | 13 |

## DICKO, Nouha (M) — 81 22
H: 5 8  W: 11 00  b.Paris 14-5-92

| Season | Club | Apps | Gls | Tot A | Tot G |
|---|---|---|---|---|---|
| 2009-10 | Strasbourg B | 18 | 4 | | |
| 2010-11 | Strasbourg B | 24 | 8 | 42 | 12 |
| 2010-11 | Strasbourg | 3 | 0 | 3 | 0 |
| 2011-12 | Wigan Ath | 0 | 0 | | |
| 2011-12 | *Blackpool* | 10 | 4 | | |
| 2012-13 | Wigan Ath | 0 | 0 | | |
| 2012-13 | *Blackpool* | 22 | 5 | 32 | 9 |
| 2012-13 | *Wolverhampton W* | 4 | 1 | 4 | 1 |

## ESPINOZA, Roger (M) — 126 3
H: 5 10  W: 11 06  b.Puerto Cortes 25-10-86
*Honours:* Honduras 30 full caps, 3 goals.

| Season | Club | Apps | Gls | Tot A | Tot G |
|---|---|---|---|---|---|
| 2008 | Sporting Kansas C | 24 | 1 | | |
| 2009 | Sporting Kansas C | 10 | 0 | | |
| 2010 | Sporting Kansas C | 25 | 0 | | |
| 2011 | Sporting Kansas C | 27 | 1 | | |
| 2012 | Sporting Kansas C | 28 | 0 | 114 | 2 |
| 2012-13 | Wigan Ath | 12 | 1 | 12 | 1 |

**FIGUEROA, Maynor (D)** 203 6
H: 5 11  W: 12 02  b.Jutiapa 2-5-83
Honours: Honduras Under-20, Under-23, 95 full caps, 2 goals.

|  |  | | | | |
|---|---|---|---|---|---|
| 2000-01 | Victoria La Ceiba | 2 | 0 | | |
| 2001-02 | Victoria La Ceiba | 22 | 2 | 24 | 2 |
| 2007-08 | Wigan Ath | 2 | 0 | | |
| 2008-09 | Wigan Ath | 38 | 1 | | |
| 2009-10 | Wigan Ath | 35 | 1 | | |
| 2010-11 | Wigan Ath | 33 | 1 | | |
| 2011-12 | Wigan Ath | 38 | 0 | | |
| 2012-13 | Wigan Ath | 33 | 1 | 179 | 4 |

**FYVIE, Fraser (M)** 59 2
H: 5 8  W: 9 05  b.Aberdeen 27-3-93
Honours: Scotland Youth, Under-21.

| 2009-10 | Aberdeen | 26 | 1 | | |
|---|---|---|---|---|---|
| 2010-11 | Aberdeen | 5 | 0 | | |
| 2011-12 | Aberdeen | 27 | 1 | 58 | 2 |
| 2012-13 | Wigan Ath | 1 | 0 | 1 | 0 |

**GOLOBART, Roman (D)** 26 2
H: 6 4  W: 13 10  b.Barcelona 21-3-92
Source: Espanyol.

| 2010-11 | Wigan Ath | 0 | 0 | | |
|---|---|---|---|---|---|
| 2011-12 | Wigan Ath | 0 | 0 | | |
| 2011-12 | Inverness CT | 22 | 2 | 22 | 2 |
| 2012-13 | Wigan Ath | 3 | 0 | 3 | 0 |
| 2012-13 | Tranmere R | 1 | 0 | 1 | 0 |

**GOMEZ, Jordi (M)** 163 22
H: 5 11  W: 11 09  b.Barcelona 24-5-85

| 2006-07 | Espanyol B | 21 | 0 | 21 | 0 |
|---|---|---|---|---|---|
| 2007-08 | Espanyol | 2 | 0 | 2 | 0 |
| 2008-09 | Swansea C | 44 | 12 | 44 | 12 |
| 2009-10 | Wigan Ath | 23 | 1 | | |
| 2010-11 | Wigan Ath | 13 | 1 | | |
| 2011-12 | Wigan Ath | 28 | 5 | | |
| 2012-13 | Wigan Ath | 32 | 3 | 96 | 10 |

**JONES, David (M)** 190 24
H: 5 11  W: 10 10  b.Southport 4-11-84
Source: Trainee. Honours: England Youth, Under-21.

| 2003-04 | Manchester U | 0 | 0 | | |
|---|---|---|---|---|---|
| 2004-05 | Manchester U | 0 | 0 | | |
| 2005-06 | Manchester U | 0 | 0 | | |
| 2005-06 | Preston NE | 24 | 3 | 24 | 3 |
| 2005-06 | NEC Nijmegen | 17 | 6 | 17 | 6 |
| 2006-07 | Manchester U | 0 | 0 | | |
| 2006-07 | Derby Co | 28 | 6 | | |
| 2007-08 | Derby Co | 14 | 1 | 42 | 7 |
| 2008-09 | Wolverhampton W | 34 | 4 | | |
| 2009-10 | Wolverhampton W | 20 | 1 | | |
| 2010-11 | Wolverhampton W | 12 | 1 | 66 | 6 |
| 2011-12 | Wigan Ath | 16 | 0 | | |
| 2012-13 | Wigan Ath | 13 | 0 | 29 | 0 |
| 2012-13 | Blackburn R | 12 | 2 | 12 | 2 |

**KIERNAN, Rob (D)** 34 0
H: 6 1  W: 11 13  b.Rickmansworth 13-1-91
Source: Scholar. Honours: Eire Under-21.

| 2008-09 | Watford | 0 | 0 | | |
|---|---|---|---|---|---|
| 2009-10 | Watford | 0 | 0 | | |
| 2009-10 | Kilmarnock | 4 | 0 | 4 | 0 |
| 2010-11 | Watford | 0 | 0 | | |
| 2010-11 | Yeovil T | 3 | 0 | 3 | 0 |
| 2010-11 | Bradford C | 8 | 0 | 8 | 0 |
| 2010-11 | Wycombe W | 2 | 0 | 2 | 0 |
| 2011-12 | Wigan Ath | 0 | 0 | | |
| 2011-12 | Accrington S | 3 | 0 | 3 | 0 |
| 2012-13 | Wigan Ath | 0 | 0 | | |
| 2012-13 | Burton Alb | 6 | 0 | 6 | 0 |
| 2012-13 | Brentford | 8 | 0 | 8 | 0 |

**KONE, Arouna (F)** 251 87
H: 6 0  W: 11 08  b.Anyama 11-11-83
Honours: Ivory Coast 39 full caps, 9 goals.

| 2002-03 | Lierse | 21 | 11 | 21 | 11 |
|---|---|---|---|---|---|
| 2003-04 | Roda JC | 28 | 11 | | |
| 2004-05 | Roda JC | 32 | 14 | | |
| 2005-06 | Roda JC | 1 | 1 | 61 | 26 |
| 2005-06 | PSV | 21 | 11 | | |
| 2006-07 | PSV | 31 | 10 | | |
| 2007-08 | PSV | 1 | 0 | 53 | 21 |
| 2007-08 | Sevilla | 21 | 1 | | |
| 2008-09 | Sevilla | 6 | 0 | | |
| 2009-10 | Sevilla | 12 | 0 | | |
| 2009-10 | Hannover 96 | 8 | 2 | 8 | 2 |

| 2010-11 | Sevilla | 1 | 0 | 40 | 1 |
|---|---|---|---|---|---|
| 2011-12 | Levante | 34 | 15 | 34 | 15 |
| 2012-13 | Wigan Ath | 34 | 11 | 34 | 11 |

**LANGLEY, Josh (M)** 0 0
H: 5 11  W: 11 07  b.Warrington 13-8-92
Source: Scholar.

| 2010-11 | Wigan Ath | 0 | 0 | | |
|---|---|---|---|---|---|
| 2011-12 | Wigan Ath | 0 | 0 | | |
| 2012-13 | Wigan Ath | 0 | 0 | | |

**LOPEZ, Adrian (D)** 49 1
H: 6 0  W: 12 00  b.As Pontes 25-2-87

| 2006-07 | La Coruna | 0 | 0 | | |
|---|---|---|---|---|---|
| 2007-08 | La Coruna B | 12 | 0 | 12 | 0 |
| 2007-08 | La Coruna | 15 | 0 | | |
| 2008-09 | La Coruna | 8 | 1 | | |
| 2009-10 | La Coruna | 3 | 0 | 26 | 1 |
| 2010-11 | Wigan Ath | 1 | 0 | | |
| 2011-12 | Wigan Ath | 5 | 0 | | |
| 2012-13 | Wigan Ath | 5 | 0 | 11 | 0 |

**MALONEY, Shaun (M)** 238 53
H: 5 7  W: 10 01  b.Miri 24-1-83
Honours: Scotland Under-20, Under-21, B, 28 full caps, 1 goal.

| 1999-2000 | Celtic | 0 | 0 | | |
|---|---|---|---|---|---|
| 2000-01 | Celtic | 4 | 0 | | |
| 2001-02 | Celtic | 16 | 5 | | |
| 2002-03 | Celtic | 20 | 3 | | |
| 2003-04 | Celtic | 17 | 5 | | |
| 2004-05 | Celtic | 2 | 0 | | |
| 2005-06 | Celtic | 36 | 13 | | |
| 2006-07 | Celtic | 9 | 0 | | |
| 2006-07 | Aston Villa | 8 | 1 | | |
| 2007-08 | Aston Villa | 22 | 4 | 30 | 5 |
| 2008-09 | Celtic | 21 | 4 | | |
| 2009-10 | Celtic | 10 | 4 | | |
| 2010-11 | Celtic | 21 | 5 | | |
| 2011-12 | Celtic | 3 | 0 | 159 | 39 |
| 2011-12 | Wigan Ath | 13 | 3 | | |
| 2012-13 | Wigan Ath | 36 | 6 | 49 | 9 |

**McARTHUR, James (M)** 251 15
H: 5 6  W: 9 13  b.Glasgow 7-10-87
Honours: Scotland Under-21, 12 full caps, 1 goal.

| 2004-05 | Hamilton A | 6 | 0 | | |
|---|---|---|---|---|---|
| 2005-06 | Hamilton A | 20 | 1 | | |
| 2006-07 | Hamilton A | 36 | 1 | | |
| 2007-08 | Hamilton A | 34 | 4 | | |
| 2008-09 | Hamilton A | 37 | 2 | | |
| 2009-10 | Hamilton A | 35 | 1 | 168 | 9 |
| 2010-11 | Wigan Ath | 18 | 0 | | |
| 2011-12 | Wigan Ath | 31 | 3 | | |
| 2012-13 | Wigan Ath | 34 | 3 | 83 | 6 |

**McCARTHY, James (M)** 210 21
H: 5 11  W: 11 05  b.Glasgow 12-11-90
Honours: Eire Youth, Under-21, 15 full caps.

| 2006-07 | Hamilton A | 23 | 1 | | |
|---|---|---|---|---|---|
| 2007-08 | Hamilton A | 35 | 7 | | |
| 2008-09 | Hamilton A | 37 | 6 | 95 | 14 |
| 2009-10 | Wigan Ath | 20 | 1 | | |
| 2010-11 | Wigan Ath | 24 | 3 | | |
| 2011-12 | Wigan Ath | 33 | 0 | | |
| 2012-13 | Wigan Ath | 38 | 3 | 115 | 7 |

**McCORMACK, Jamie (D)** 0 0
H: 5 10  W: 11 09  b.Edinburgh 1-2-92
Source: Hearts Youth.

| 2011-12 | Wigan Ath | 0 | 0 | | |
|---|---|---|---|---|---|
| 2012-13 | Wigan Ath | 0 | 0 | | |

**McMANAMAN, Callum (F)** 40 4
H: 5 9  W: 11 03  b.Huyton 25-4-91
Source: Scholar. Honours: England Youth, Under-20.

| 2008-09 | Wigan Ath | 1 | 0 | | |
|---|---|---|---|---|---|
| 2009-10 | Wigan Ath | 0 | 0 | | |
| 2010-11 | Wigan Ath | 3 | 0 | | |
| 2011-12 | Wigan Ath | 2 | 0 | | |
| 2011-12 | Blackpool | 14 | 2 | 14 | 2 |
| 2012-13 | Wigan Ath | 20 | 2 | 26 | 2 |

**MUSTOE, Jordan (M)** 43 1
H: 5 11  W: 11 11  b.Birkenhead 28-1-91
Source: Scholar.

| 2009-10 | Wigan Ath | 0 | 0 | | |
|---|---|---|---|---|---|
| 2010-11 | Wigan Ath | 0 | 0 | | |

| 2011-12 | Wigan Ath | 0 | 0 | | |
|---|---|---|---|---|---|
| 2011-12 | Barnet | 18 | 0 | 18 | 0 |
| 2012-13 | Wigan Ath | 0 | 0 | | |
| 2012-13 | Morecambe | 11 | 0 | 11 | 0 |
| 2012-13 | Carlisle U | 14 | 1 | 14 | 1 |

**NICHOLLS, Lee (G)** 55 0
H: 6 3  W: 13 05  b.Huyton 5-10-92
Source: Scholar. Honours: England Youth.

| 2009-10 | Wigan Ath | 0 | 0 | | |
|---|---|---|---|---|---|
| 2010-11 | Wigan Ath | 0 | 0 | | |
| 2010-11 | Hartlepool U | 0 | 0 | | |
| 2010-11 | Shrewsbury T | 0 | 0 | | |
| 2010-11 | Sheffield W | 0 | 0 | | |
| 2011-12 | Wigan Ath | 0 | 0 | | |
| 2011-12 | Accrington S | 9 | 0 | 9 | 0 |
| 2012-13 | Wigan Ath | 0 | 0 | | |
| 2012-13 | Northampton T | 46 | 0 | 46 | 0 |

**PHILLIPS, Jack (M)** 0 0
b.Liverpool 15-10-93

| 2012-13 | Wigan Ath | 0 | 0 | | |
|---|---|---|---|---|---|

**POLLITT, Mike (G)** 503 0
H: 6 4  W: 15 03  b.Farnworth 29-2-72
Source: Trainee.

| 1990-91 | Manchester U | 0 | 0 | | |
|---|---|---|---|---|---|
| 1990-91 | Oldham Ath | 0 | 0 | | |
| 1991-92 | Bury | 0 | 0 | | |
| 1992-93 | Lincoln C | 27 | 0 | | |
| 1993-94 | Lincoln C | 30 | 0 | 57 | 0 |
| 1994-95 | Darlington | 40 | 0 | | |
| 1995-96 | Darlington | 15 | 0 | 55 | 0 |
| 1995-96 | Notts Co | 0 | 0 | | |
| 1996-97 | Notts Co | 8 | 0 | | |
| 1997-98 | Notts Co | 2 | 0 | 10 | 0 |
| 1997-98 | Oldham Ath | 16 | 0 | 16 | 0 |
| 1997-98 | Gillingham | 6 | 0 | 6 | 0 |
| 1997-98 | Brentford | 5 | 0 | 5 | 0 |
| 1997-98 | Sunderland | 0 | 0 | | |
| 1998-99 | Rotherham U | 46 | 0 | | |
| 1999-2000 | Rotherham U | 46 | 0 | | |
| 2000-01 | Chesterfield | 46 | 0 | 46 | 0 |
| 2001-02 | Rotherham U | 46 | 0 | | |
| 2002-03 | Rotherham U | 41 | 0 | | |
| 2003-04 | Rotherham U | 43 | 0 | | |
| 2004-05 | Rotherham U | 45 | 0 | 267 | 0 |
| 2005-06 | Wigan Ath | 24 | 0 | | |
| 2006-07 | Wigan Ath | 3 | 0 | | |
| 2006-07 | Ipswich T | 1 | 0 | 1 | 0 |
| 2006-07 | Burnley | 4 | 0 | 4 | 0 |
| 2007-08 | Wigan Ath | 1 | 0 | | |
| 2008-09 | Wigan Ath | 3 | 0 | | |
| 2009-10 | Wigan Ath | 4 | 0 | | |
| 2010-11 | Wigan Ath | 1 | 0 | | |
| 2011-12 | Wigan Ath | 0 | 0 | | |
| 2012-13 | Wigan Ath | 0 | 0 | 36 | 0 |

**RAMIS, Ivan (D)** 207 11
H: 6 2  W: 12 11  b.Sa Pobla 25-10-84

| 2003-04 | Mallorca | 9 | 1 | | |
|---|---|---|---|---|---|
| 2004-05 | Mallorca | 22 | 0 | | |
| 2005-06 | Valladolid | 27 | 0 | 27 | 0 |
| 2006-07 | Mallorca | 7 | 0 | | |
| 2007-08 | Mallorca | 14 | 3 | | |
| 2008-09 | Mallorca | 19 | 0 | | |
| 2009-10 | Mallorca | 26 | 0 | | |
| 2010-11 | Mallorca | 33 | 3 | | |
| 2011-12 | Mallorca | 34 | 2 | 164 | 9 |
| 2012-13 | Wigan Ath | 16 | 2 | 16 | 2 |

**REDMOND, Daniel (D)** 18 5
H: 5 3  W: 10 07  b.Liverpool 2-3-91
Source: Scholar.

| 2009-10 | Wigan Ath | 0 | 0 | | |
|---|---|---|---|---|---|
| 2010-11 | Wigan Ath | 0 | 0 | | |
| 2011-12 | Wigan Ath | 0 | 0 | | |
| 2011-12 | Hamilton A | 18 | 5 | 18 | 5 |
| 2012-13 | Wigan Ath | 0 | 0 | | |

**ROBLES, Joel (G)** 24 0
H: 6 5  W: 13 04  b.Leganes 17-6-90

| 2009-10 | Atletico Madrid | 2 | 0 | | |
|---|---|---|---|---|---|
| 2011-12 | Rayo Vallecano | 13 | 0 | 13 | 0 |
| 2012-13 | Atletico Madrid | 0 | 0 | 2 | 0 |

On loan from Atletico Madrid

| 2012-13 | Wigan Ath | 9 | 0 | 9 | 0 |
|---|---|---|---|---|---|

**SCHARNER, Paul (D)**    359 34
H: 6 3   W: 12 09   b.Scheibbs 11-3-80
*Source:* St Polten. *Honours:* Austria Youth, Under-21, 39 full caps.

| | | | |
|---|---|---|---|
| 1998-99 | FK Austria | 4 | 0 |
| 1999-2000 | FK Austria | 12 | 0 |
| 2000-01 | FK Austria | 14 | 0 |
| 2001-02 | FK Austria | 16 | 1 |
| 2002-03 | FK Austria | 29 | 1 |
| 2003-04 | FK Austria | 9 | 1 | 84 | 3 |
| 2003-04 | Salzburg | 13 | 2 |
| 2004 | Brann | 7 | 1 |
| 2004-05 | Salzburg | 5 | 1 | 18 | 3 |
| 2005 | Brann | 25 | 6 | 32 | 7 |
| 2005-06 | Wigan Ath | 16 | 3 |
| 2006-07 | Wigan Ath | 25 | 3 |
| 2007-08 | Wigan Ath | 37 | 4 |
| 2008-09 | Wigan Ath | 29 | 0 |
| 2009-10 | Wigan Ath | 38 | 4 |
| 2010-11 | Wigan Ath | 0 | 0 |
| 2010-11 | WBA | 33 | 4 |
| 2011-12 | WBA | 29 | 3 | 62 | 7 |
| 2012-13 | Hamburg | 4 | 0 | 4 | 0 |

On loan from Hamburg
| 2012-13 | Wigan Ath | 14 | 0 | 159 | 14 |

**STAM, Ronnie (M)**    240 7
H: 5 9   W: 9 11   b.Breda 18-6-84

| | | | |
|---|---|---|---|
| 2002-03 | NAC Breda | 1 | 0 |
| 2003-04 | NAC Breda | 21 | 1 |
| 2004-05 | NAC Breda | 14 | 0 |
| 2005-06 | NAC Breda | 28 | 1 |
| 2006-07 | NAC Breda | 27 | 2 |
| 2007-08 | NAC Breda | 29 | 0 |
| 2008-09 | NAC Breda | 1 | 0 | 121 | 4 |
| 2008-09 | Twente | 24 | 1 |
| 2009-10 | Twente | 33 | 1 | 57 | 2 |
| 2010-11 | Wigan Ath | 25 | 1 |
| 2011-12 | Wigan Ath | 20 | 0 |
| 2012-13 | Wigan Ath | 17 | 0 | 62 | 1 |

**WATSON, Ben (M)**    269 31
H: 5 10   W: 10 11   b.Camberwell 9-7-85
*Source:* Scholar. *Honours:* England Under-21.

| | | | |
|---|---|---|---|
| 2002-03 | Crystal Palace | 5 | 0 |
| 2003-04 | Crystal Palace | 16 | 1 |
| 2004-05 | Crystal Palace | 21 | 0 |
| 2005-06 | Crystal Palace | 42 | 4 |
| 2006-07 | Crystal Palace | 25 | 3 |
| 2007-08 | Crystal Palace | 42 | 5 |
| 2008-09 | Crystal Palace | 18 | 5 | 169 | 18 |
| 2008-09 | Wigan Ath | 10 | 2 |
| 2009-10 | Wigan Ath | 5 | 1 |
| 2009-10 | QPR | 16 | 2 | 16 | 2 |
| 2009-10 | WBA | 7 | 1 | 7 | 1 |
| 2010-11 | Wigan Ath | 29 | 3 |
| 2011-12 | Wigan Ath | 21 | 3 |
| 2012-13 | Wigan Ath | 12 | 1 | 77 | 10 |

**WATSON, Ryan (M)**    0 0
H: 6 1   W: 11 07   b.Crewe 7-7-93
*Source:* Scholar.

| | | | |
|---|---|---|---|
| 2011-12 | Wigan Ath | 0 | 0 |
| 2012-13 | Wigan Ath | 0 | 0 |
| 2012-13 | Accrington S | 0 | 0 |

**Scholars**
Ainscough, Luke Joseph; Flores, Jordan Michael; Gibbons, Ellis; Hamilton, Matthew Lewis; Jennings, Ryan; Johnson, Joseph; Leigh, Daniel; Mather, Christian; Meadows, Ryan Walter; Thompson, Omar Marquis; Unsworth, Jordan James; Wilson, Michael.

# WOLVERHAMPTON W (89)

**BATTH, Danny (D)**    84 4
H: 6 3   W: 13 05   b.Brierley Hill 21-9-90
*Source:* Scholar.

| | | | |
|---|---|---|---|
| 2009-10 | Wolverhampton W | 0 | 0 |
| 2009-10 | Colchester U | 17 | 1 | 17 | 1 |
| 2010-11 | Wolverhampton W | 0 | 0 |
| 2010-11 | Sheffield U | 1 | 0 | 1 | 0 |
| 2010-11 | Sheffield W | 10 | 0 |
| 2011-12 | Wolverhampton W | 0 | 0 |
| 2011-12 | Sheffield W | 44 | 2 | 54 | 2 |
| 2012-13 | Wolverhampton W | 12 | 1 | 12 | 1 |

**BERRA, Christophe (D)**    264 4
H: 6 1   W: 12 10   b.Edinburgh 31-1-85
*Honours:* Scotland Under-21, B, 27 full caps, 2 goals.

| | | | |
|---|---|---|---|
| 2003-04 | Hearts | 6 | 0 |
| 2004-05 | Hearts | 12 | 0 |
| 2005-06 | Hearts | 12 | 1 |
| 2006-07 | Hearts | 35 | 1 |
| 2007-08 | Hearts | 35 | 2 |
| 2008-09 | Hearts | 23 | 0 | 123 | 4 |
| 2008-09 | Wolverhampton W | 15 | 0 |
| 2009-10 | Wolverhampton W | 32 | 0 |
| 2010-11 | Wolverhampton W | 32 | 0 |
| 2011-12 | Wolverhampton W | 32 | 0 |
| 2012-13 | Wolverhampton W | 30 | 0 | 141 | 0 |

**BOUKARI, Razak (M)**    199 27
H: 6 0   W: 10 13   b.Lome 25-4-87

| | | | |
|---|---|---|---|
| 2004-05 | Chateauroux | 5 | 5 |
| 2005-06 | Chateauroux | 35 | 3 | 40 | 8 |
| 2006-07 | Lens | 29 | 0 |
| 2007-08 | Lens | 18 | 0 |
| 2008-09 | Lens | 26 | 4 |
| 2009-10 | Lens | 27 | 4 |
| 2010-11 | Lens | 17 | 4 | 117 | 12 |
| 2010-11 | Rennes | 18 | 4 |
| 2011-12 | Rennes | 20 | 3 | 38 | 7 |
| 2012-13 | Wolverhampton W | 4 | 0 | 4 | 0 |

**CASSIDY, Jake (F)**    42 16
H: 5 10   W: 11 02   b.Glan Conwy 9-2-93
*Source:* Airbus UK. *Honours:* Wales Youth, Under-21.

| | | | |
|---|---|---|---|
| 2010-11 | Wolverhampton W | 0 | 0 |
| 2011-12 | Wolverhampton W | 0 | 0 |
| 2011-12 | Tranmere R | 10 | 5 |
| 2012-13 | Wolverhampton W | 6 | 0 | 6 | 0 |
| 2012-13 | Tranmere R | 26 | 11 | 36 | 16 |

**COTMAN, Aljaz (G)**    0 0
H: 5 11   b. 26-4-94

| | | | |
|---|---|---|---|
| 2012-13 | Wolverhampton W | 0 | 0 |

**CRADDOCK, Jody (D)**    520 20
H: 6 0   W: 12 04   b.Redditch 25-7-75
*Source:* Christchurch.

| | | | |
|---|---|---|---|
| 1993-94 | Cambridge U | 20 | 0 |
| 1994-95 | Cambridge U | 38 | 0 |
| 1995-96 | Cambridge U | 46 | 3 |
| 1996-97 | Cambridge U | 41 | 1 | 145 | 4 |
| 1997-98 | Sunderland | 32 | 0 |
| 1998-99 | Sunderland | 6 | 0 |
| 1999-2000 | Sunderland | 19 | 0 |
| 1999-2000 | Sheffield U | 10 | 0 | 10 | 0 |
| 2000-01 | Sunderland | 34 | 0 |
| 2001-02 | Sunderland | 30 | 1 |
| 2002-03 | Sunderland | 25 | 1 | 146 | 2 |
| 2003-04 | Wolverhampton W | 32 | 1 |
| 2004-05 | Wolverhampton W | 42 | 1 |
| 2005-06 | Wolverhampton W | 18 | 0 |
| 2006-07 | Wolverhampton W | 34 | 4 |
| 2007-08 | Wolverhampton W | 23 | 1 |
| 2007-08 | Stoke C | 4 | 0 | 4 | 0 |
| 2008-09 | Wolverhampton W | 17 | 1 |
| 2009-10 | Wolverhampton W | 33 | 5 |
| 2010-11 | Wolverhampton W | 15 | 1 |
| 2011-12 | Wolverhampton W | 1 | 0 |
| 2012-13 | Wolverhampton W | 0 | 0 | 215 | 14 |

**CRANSTON, Jordan (D)**    0 0
b. 11-3-93

| | | | |
|---|---|---|---|
| 2012-13 | Wolverhampton W | 0 | 0 |

**DAVIS, David (M)**    75 2
H: 5 8   W: 12 03   b.Smethwick 20-2-91
*Source:* Scholar.

| | | | |
|---|---|---|---|
| 2009-10 | Wolverhampton W | 0 | 0 |
| 2009-10 | Darlington | 5 | 0 | 5 | 0 |
| 2010-11 | Wolverhampton W | 0 | 0 |
| 2010-11 | Walsall | 7 | 0 | 7 | 0 |
| 2010-11 | Shrewsbury T | 19 | 2 | 19 | 2 |
| 2011-12 | Wolverhampton W | 7 | 0 |
| 2011-12 | Chesterfield | 9 | 0 | 9 | 0 |
| 2012-13 | Wolverhampton W | 28 | 0 | 35 | 0 |

**DE VRIES, Dorus (G)**    350
H: 6 1   W: 12 08   b.Bewerwijk 29-12-80

| | | | |
|---|---|---|---|
| 1999-2000 | Telstar | 1 | 0 |
| 2000-01 | Telstar | 27 | 0 |
| 2001-02 | Telstar | 27 | 0 |

| | | | |
|---|---|---|---|
| 2002-03 | Telstar | 26 | 0 | 81 | 0 |
| 2003-04 | Den Haag | 18 | 0 |
| 2004-05 | Den Haag | 32 | 0 |
| 2005-06 | Den Haag | 0 | 0 | 50 | 0 |
| 2006-07 | Dunfermline Ath | 27 | 0 | 27 | 0 |
| 2007-08 | Swansea C | 46 | 0 |
| 2008-09 | Swansea C | 40 | 0 |
| 2009-10 | Swansea C | 46 | 0 |
| 2010-11 | Swansea C | 46 | 0 | 178 | 0 |
| 2011-12 | Wolverhampton W | 4 | 0 |
| 2012-13 | Wolverhampton W | 10 | 0 | 14 | 0 |

**DOHERTY, Matthew (M)**    44 4
H: 6 0   W: 12 08   b.Dublin 17-1-92
*Source:* Bohemians. *Honours:* Eire Youth, Under-21.

| | | | |
|---|---|---|---|
| 2010-11 | Wolverhampton W | 0 | 0 |
| 2011-12 | Wolverhampton W | 1 | 0 |
| 2011-12 | Hibernian | 13 | 2 | 13 | 2 |
| 2012-13 | Wolverhampton W | 13 | 1 | 14 | 1 |
| 2012-13 | Bury | 17 | 1 | 17 | 1 |

**DOUMBIA, Tongo (M)**    81 4
H: 6 3   W: 12 05   b.Vernon 6-8-89

| | | | |
|---|---|---|---|
| 2008-09 | Chateauroux | 1 | 0 | 1 | 0 |
| 2009-10 | Rennes | 3 | 0 |
| 2010-11 | Rennes | 19 | 0 |
| 2011-12 | Rennes | 25 | 2 | 47 | 2 |
| 2012-13 | Wolverhampton W | 33 | 2 | 33 | 2 |

**DOYLE, Kevin (F)**    332 102
H: 5 11   W: 12 06   b.Adamstown 18-9-83
*Source:* Adamstown, Wexford, St Patrick's Ath. *Honours:* Eire Under-21, 53 full caps, 12 goals.

| | | | |
|---|---|---|---|
| 2004 | Cork C | 32 | 13 |
| 2005 | Cork C | 11 | 7 | 43 | 20 |
| 2005-06 | Reading | 45 | 18 |
| 2006-07 | Reading | 32 | 13 |
| 2007-08 | Reading | 36 | 6 |
| 2008-09 | Reading | 41 | 18 | 154 | 55 |
| 2009-10 | Wolverhampton W | 34 | 9 |
| 2010-11 | Wolverhampton W | 26 | 5 |
| 2011-12 | Wolverhampton W | 33 | 4 |
| 2012-13 | Wolverhampton W | 42 | 9 | 135 | 27 |

**EBANKS-BLAKE, Sylvan (F)**    243 82
H: 5 10   W: 13 04   b.Cambridge 29-3-86
*Source:* Scholar. *Honours:* England Under-21.

| | | | |
|---|---|---|---|
| 2004-05 | Manchester U | 0 | 0 |
| 2005-06 | Manchester U | 0 | 0 |
| 2006-07 | Plymouth Arg | 41 | 10 |
| 2007-08 | Plymouth Arg | 25 | 11 | 66 | 21 |
| 2007-08 | Wolverhampton W | 20 | 12 |
| 2008-09 | Wolverhampton W | 41 | 25 |
| 2009-10 | Wolverhampton W | 23 | 2 |
| 2010-11 | Wolverhampton W | 30 | 7 |
| 2011-12 | Wolverhampton W | 23 | 1 |
| 2012-13 | Wolverhampton W | 40 | 14 | 177 | 61 |

**EBANKS-LANDELL, Ethan (M)**    24 0
H: 5 6   W: 11 02   b.Oldbury 16-12-92
*Source:* Scholar.

| | | | |
|---|---|---|---|
| 2009-10 | Wolverhampton W | 0 | 0 |
| 2010-11 | Wolverhampton W | 0 | 0 |
| 2011-12 | Wolverhampton W | 0 | 0 |
| 2012-13 | Wolverhampton W | 0 | 0 |
| 2012-13 | Bury | 24 | 0 | 24 | 0 |

**EDWARDS, Dave (M)**    261 27
H: 5 11   W: 11 04   b.Shrewsbury 3-2-86
*Source:* Scholar. *Honours:* Wales Youth, Under-21, 26 full caps, 3 goals.

| | | | |
|---|---|---|---|
| 2002-03 | Shrewsbury T | 1 | 0 |
| 2003-04 | Shrewsbury T | 27 | 5 |
| 2004-05 | Shrewsbury T | 27 | 5 |
| 2005-06 | Shrewsbury T | 30 | 2 |
| 2006-07 | Shrewsbury T | 45 | 5 | 103 | 12 |
| 2007-08 | Luton T | 19 | 4 | 19 | 4 |
| 2007-08 | Wolverhampton W | 10 | 1 |
| 2008-09 | Wolverhampton W | 44 | 3 |
| 2009-10 | Wolverhampton W | 20 | 1 |
| 2010-11 | Wolverhampton W | 15 | 1 |
| 2011-12 | Wolverhampton W | 26 | 3 |
| 2012-13 | Wolverhampton W | 24 | 2 | 139 | 11 |

**ELOKOBI, George (D)**    136 4
H: 5 10   W: 13 02   b.Cameroon 31-1-86
*Source:* Dulwich Hamlet.

| | | | |
|---|---|---|---|
| 2004-05 | Colchester U | 0 | 0 |

| 2004-05 | Chester C | 5 | 0 | 5 | 0 |
|---|---|---|---|---|---|
| 2005-06 | Colchester U | 12 | 1 | | |
| 2006-07 | Colchester U | 10 | 0 | | |
| 2007-08 | Colchester U | 17 | 1 | 39 | 2 |
| 2007-08 | Wolverhampton W | 15 | 0 | | |
| 2008-09 | Wolverhampton W | 4 | 0 | | |
| 2009-10 | Wolverhampton W | 22 | 0 | | |
| 2010-11 | Wolverhampton W | 27 | 2 | | |
| 2011-12 | Wolverhampton W | 9 | 0 | | |
| 2011-12 | *Nottingham F* | 12 | 0 | 12 | 0 |
| 2012-13 | Wolverhampton W | 2 | 0 | 79 | 2 |
| 2012-13 | *Bristol C* | 1 | 0 | 1 | 0 |

**EVANS, Lee (M)**    **0 0**
*Source:* Newport Co.

| 2012-13 | Wolverhampton W | 0 | 0 | | |
|---|---|---|---|---|---|

**FOLEY, Kevin (D)**    **340 7**
H: 5 9   W: 11 11   b.Luton 1-11-84
*Source:* Scholar. *Honours:* Eire B, Under-21, 8 full caps.

| 2002-03 | Luton T | 2 | 0 | | |
|---|---|---|---|---|---|
| 2003-04 | Luton T | 33 | 1 | | |
| 2004-05 | Luton T | 39 | 2 | | |
| 2005-06 | Luton T | 38 | 0 | | |
| 2006-07 | Luton T | 39 | 0 | | |
| 2007-08 | Luton T | 0 | 0 | 151 | 3 |
| 2007-08 | Wolverhampton W | 44 | 1 | | |
| 2008-09 | Wolverhampton W | 45 | 1 | | |
| 2009-10 | Wolverhampton W | 25 | 0 | | |
| 2010-11 | Wolverhampton W | 33 | 2 | | |
| 2011-12 | Wolverhampton W | 16 | 0 | | |
| 2012-13 | Wolverhampton W | 26 | 0 | 189 | 4 |

**FORDE, Anthony (M)**    **26 0**
H: 5 9   W: 10 10   b.Limerick 16-11-93
*Source:* Scholar. *Honours:* Eire Youth, Under-21.

| 2011-12 | Wolverhampton W | 6 | 0 | | |
|---|---|---|---|---|---|
| 2012-13 | Wolverhampton W | 12 | 0 | 18 | 0 |
| 2012-13 | *Scunthorpe U* | 8 | 0 | 8 | 0 |

**GORMAN, Johnny (M)**    **3 0**
H: 5 9   W: 11 00   b.Sheffield 26-10-92
*Honours:* Northern Ireland Youth, Under-21, 9 full caps.

| 2009-10 | Wolverhampton W | 0 | 0 | | |
|---|---|---|---|---|---|
| 2010-11 | Wolverhampton W | 0 | 0 | | |
| 2011-12 | Wolverhampton W | 1 | 0 | | |
| 2012-13 | Wolverhampton W | 0 | 0 | 1 | 0 |
| 2012-13 | *Plymouth Arg* | 2 | 0 | 2 | 0 |

**GRIFFITHS, Leigh (F)**    **162 75**
H: 5 07   W: 10 01   b.Leith 20-8-90
*Honours:* Scotland Youth, Under-21, B.

| 2006-07 | Livingston | 4 | 1 | | |
|---|---|---|---|---|---|
| 2007-08 | Livingston | 18 | 5 | | |
| 2008-09 | Livingston | 27 | 17 | 49 | 23 |
| 2009-10 | Dundee | 29 | 13 | | |
| 2010-11 | Dundee | 18 | 8 | 47 | 21 |
| 2010-11 | Wolverhampton W | 0 | 0 | | |
| 2011-12 | Wolverhampton W | 0 | 0 | | |
| 2011-12 | *Hibernian* | 30 | 8 | | |
| 2012-13 | Wolverhampton W | 0 | 0 | | |
| 2012-13 | *Hibernian* | 36 | 23 | 66 | 31 |

**HAMMILL, Adam (M)**    **187 17**
H: 5 11   W: 11 07   b.Liverpool 25-1-88
*Source:* Scholar. *Honours:* England Youth, Under-21.

| 2005-06 | Liverpool | 0 | 0 | | |
|---|---|---|---|---|---|
| 2006-07 | Liverpool | 0 | 0 | | |
| 2006-07 | *Dunfermline Ath* | 13 | 1 | 13 | 1 |
| 2007-08 | Liverpool | 0 | 0 | | |
| 2007-08 | *Southampton* | 25 | 0 | 25 | 0 |
| 2008-09 | Liverpool | 0 | 0 | | |
| 2008-09 | *Blackpool* | 22 | 1 | 22 | 1 |
| 2008-09 | *Barnsley* | 14 | 1 | | |
| 2009-10 | Liverpool | 0 | 0 | | |
| 2009-10 | Barnsley | 39 | 4 | | |
| 2010-11 | Barnsley | 25 | 8 | 78 | 13 |
| 2010-11 | Wolverhampton W | 10 | 0 | | |
| 2011-12 | Wolverhampton W | 9 | 0 | | |
| 2011-12 | *Middlesbrough* | 10 | 0 | 10 | 0 |
| 2012-13 | Wolverhampton W | 4 | 0 | 23 | 0 |
| 2012-13 | *Huddersfield T* | 16 | 2 | 16 | 2 |

**HENNESSEY, Wayne (G)**    **167 0**
H: 6 0   W: 11 06   b.Anglesey 24-1-87
*Source:* Scholar. *Honours:* Wales Schools, Youth, Under-21, 38 full caps.

| 2004-05 | Wolverhampton W | 0 | 0 | | |
|---|---|---|---|---|---|
| 2005-06 | Wolverhampton W | 0 | 0 | | |
| 2006-07 | Wolverhampton W | 0 | 0 | | |
| 2006-07 | *Bristol C* | 0 | 0 | | |
| 2006-07 | *Stockport Co* | 15 | 0 | 15 | 0 |
| 2007-08 | Wolverhampton W | 46 | 0 | | |
| 2008-09 | Wolverhampton W | 35 | 0 | | |
| 2009-10 | Wolverhampton W | 13 | 0 | | |
| 2010-11 | Wolverhampton W | 24 | 0 | | |
| 2011-12 | Wolverhampton W | 34 | 0 | | |
| 2012-13 | Wolverhampton W | 0 | 0 | 152 | 0 |

**HENRY, Karl (M)**    **379 8**
H: 6 0   W: 12 00   b.Wolverhampton 26-11-82
*Source:* Trainee. *Honours:* England Youth, Under-20.

| 1999-2000 | Stoke C | 0 | 0 | | |
|---|---|---|---|---|---|
| 2000-01 | Stoke C | 0 | 0 | | |
| 2001-02 | Stoke C | 24 | 0 | | |
| 2002-03 | Stoke C | 18 | 1 | | |
| 2003-04 | Stoke C | 20 | 0 | | |
| 2003-04 | *Cheltenham T* | 9 | 1 | 9 | 1 |
| 2004-05 | Stoke C | 34 | 0 | | |
| 2005-06 | Stoke C | 24 | 0 | 120 | 1 |
| 2006-07 | Wolverhampton W | 34 | 3 | | |
| 2007-08 | Wolverhampton W | 40 | 3 | | |
| 2008-09 | Wolverhampton W | 43 | 0 | | |
| 2009-10 | Wolverhampton W | 34 | 0 | | |
| 2010-11 | Wolverhampton W | 29 | 0 | | |
| 2011-12 | Wolverhampton W | 31 | 0 | | |
| 2012-13 | Wolverhampton W | 39 | 0 | 250 | 6 |

**HUNT, Steve (M)**    **378 55**
H: 5 9   W: 10 10   b.Port Laoise 1-8-80
*Source:* Trainee. *Honours:* Eire Under-21, B, 39 full caps, 1 goal.

| 1999-2000 | Crystal Palace | 3 | 0 | | |
|---|---|---|---|---|---|
| 2000-01 | Crystal Palace | 0 | 0 | 3 | 0 |
| 2001-02 | Brentford | 35 | 4 | | |
| 2002-03 | Brentford | 42 | 7 | | |
| 2003-04 | Brentford | 40 | 11 | | |
| 2004-05 | Brentford | 19 | 3 | 136 | 25 |
| 2005-06 | Reading | 38 | 2 | | |
| 2006-07 | Reading | 35 | 4 | | |
| 2007-08 | Reading | 37 | 5 | | |
| 2008-09 | Reading | 46 | 6 | | |
| 2009-10 | Reading | 0 | 0 | 156 | 17 |
| 2009-10 | *Hull C* | 27 | 6 | 27 | 6 |
| 2010-11 | Wolverhampton W | 20 | 3 | | |
| 2011-12 | Wolverhampton W | 24 | 3 | | |
| 2012-13 | Wolverhampton W | 12 | 1 | 56 | 7 |

**IHIEKWE, Michael (D)**    **0 0**
H: 6 1   W: 12 02   b.Liverpool 20-11-92
*Source:* Scholar.

| 2011-12 | Wolverhampton W | 0 | 0 | | |
|---|---|---|---|---|---|
| 2012-13 | Wolverhampton W | 0 | 0 | | |

**IKEME, Carl (G)**    **114 0**
H: 6 2   W: 13 09   b.Sutton Coldfield 8-6-86
*Source:* Scholar.

| 2005-06 | Wolverhampton W | 0 | 0 | | |
|---|---|---|---|---|---|
| 2005-06 | *Stockport Co* | 9 | 0 | 9 | 0 |
| 2006-07 | Wolverhampton W | 1 | 0 | | |
| 2007-08 | Wolverhampton W | 0 | 0 | | |
| 2008-09 | Wolverhampton W | 12 | 0 | | |
| 2009-10 | Wolverhampton W | 0 | 0 | | |
| 2009-10 | *Charlton Ath* | 4 | 0 | 4 | 0 |
| 2009-10 | *Sheffield U* | 2 | 0 | 2 | 0 |
| 2009-10 | *QPR* | 17 | 0 | 17 | 0 |
| 2010-11 | Wolverhampton W | 0 | 0 | | |
| 2010-11 | *Leicester C* | 5 | 0 | 5 | 0 |
| 2011-12 | Wolverhampton W | 1 | 0 | | |
| 2011-12 | *Middlesbrough* | 10 | 0 | 10 | 0 |
| 2011-12 | *Doncaster R* | 15 | 0 | 15 | 0 |
| 2012-13 | Wolverhampton W | 38 | 0 | 52 | 0 |

**ISMAIL, Zeli (M)**    **7 0**
b.Serbia 12-12-93
*Source:* Scholar.

| 2010-11 | Wolverhampton W | 0 | 0 | | |
|---|---|---|---|---|---|
| 2011-12 | Wolverhampton W | 0 | 0 | | |
| 2012-13 | Wolverhampton W | 0 | 0 | | |
| 2012-13 | *Milton Keynes D* | 7 | 0 | 7 | 0 |

**JAKOBSSON, Tim (M)**    **0 0**
H: 5 11   W: 11 12   b.Taby 19-11-94

| 2012-13 | Wolverhampton W | 0 | 0 | | |
|---|---|---|---|---|---|

**JOHNSON, Roger (D)**    **421 35**
H: 6 3   W: 11 00   b.Ashford (Middlesex) 28-4-83
*Source:* Trainee.

| 1999-2000 | Wycombe W | 1 | 0 | | |
|---|---|---|---|---|---|
| 2000-01 | Wycombe W | 1 | 0 | | |
| 2001-02 | Wycombe W | 7 | 1 | | |
| 2002-03 | Wycombe W | 33 | 3 | | |
| 2003-04 | Wycombe W | 28 | 2 | | |
| 2004-05 | Wycombe W | 42 | 6 | | |
| 2005-06 | Wycombe W | 45 | 7 | 157 | 19 |
| 2006-07 | Cardiff C | 32 | 2 | | |
| 2007-08 | Cardiff C | 42 | 5 | | |
| 2008-09 | Cardiff C | 45 | 5 | 119 | 12 |
| 2009-10 | Birmingham C | 38 | 0 | | |
| 2010-11 | Birmingham C | 38 | 2 | 76 | 2 |
| 2011-12 | Wolverhampton W | 27 | 0 | | |
| 2012-13 | Wolverhampton W | 42 | 2 | 69 | 2 |

**JONSSON, Eggert (D)**    **162 13**
H: 6 2   W: 11 05   b.Reykjavik 18-8-88
*Honours:* Iceland Youth, Under-21, 19 full caps.

| 2005 | Fjaroabyggo | 22 | 5 | 22 | 5 |
|---|---|---|---|---|---|
| 2005-06 | Hearts | 0 | 0 | | |
| 2006-07 | Hearts | 3 | 0 | | |
| 2007-08 | Hearts | 28 | 1 | | |
| 2008-09 | Hearts | 30 | 3 | | |
| 2009-10 | Hearts | 28 | 3 | | |
| 2010-11 | Hearts | 29 | 0 | | |
| 2011-12 | Hearts | 16 | 1 | 134 | 8 |
| 2011-12 | Wolverhampton W | 3 | 0 | | |
| 2012-13 | Wolverhampton W | 1 | 0 | 4 | 0 |
| 2012-13 | *Charlton Ath* | 2 | 0 | 2 | 0 |

**KOSTRNA, Kristian (D)**    **0 0**
H: 5 9   W: 11 05   b.Trnava 15-12-93
*Source:* Scholar. *Honours:* Slovakia Youth.

| 2011-12 | Wolverhampton W | 0 | 0 | | |
|---|---|---|---|---|---|
| 2012-13 | Wolverhampton W | 0 | 0 | | |

**MARGREITTER, Georg (D)**    **84 4**
H: 6 1   W: 12 09   b.Schruns 7-11-88

| 2007-08 | LASK Linz | 7 | 0 | | |
|---|---|---|---|---|---|
| 2009-10 | LASK Linz | 19 | 2 | 26 | 2 |
| 2010-11 | FK Austria | 25 | 1 | | |
| 2011-12 | FK Austria | 29 | 1 | | |
| 2012-13 | FK Austria | 3 | 0 | 57 | 2 |
| 2012-13 | Wolverhampton W | 1 | 0 | 1 | 0 |

**McALINDEN, Liam (F)**    **1 0**
b.Cannock 26-9-93
*Source:* Scholar. *Honours:* Northern Ireland Youth, Under-21.

| 2010-11 | Wolverhampton W | 0 | 0 | | |
|---|---|---|---|---|---|
| 2011-12 | Wolverhampton W | 0 | 0 | | |
| 2012-13 | Wolverhampton W | 1 | 0 | 1 | 0 |

**McCAREY, Aaron (G)**    **14 0**
H: 6 1   W: 11 09   b.Monaghan 14-1-92
*Source:* Monaghan U. *Honours:* Eire Youth, Under-21.

| 2009-10 | Wolverhampton W | 0 | 0 | | |
|---|---|---|---|---|---|
| 2010-11 | Wolverhampton W | 0 | 0 | | |
| 2011-12 | Wolverhampton W | 0 | 0 | | |
| 2012-13 | Wolverhampton W | 0 | 0 | | |
| 2012-13 | *Walsall* | 14 | 0 | 14 | 0 |

**MILIJAS, Nenad (M)**    **288 59**
H: 6 2   W: 13 09   b.Belgrade 30-4-83
*Honours:* Serbia 25 full caps, 4 goals.

| 1999-2000 | Zemun | 2 | 0 | | |
|---|---|---|---|---|---|
| 2000-01 | Zemun | 10 | 0 | | |
| 2001-02 | Zemun | 28 | 1 | | |
| 2002-03 | Zemun | 27 | 2 | | |
| 2003-04 | Zemun | 26 | 3 | | |
| 2004-05 | Zemun | 22 | 3 | | |
| 2005-06 | Zemun | 15 | 9 | 130 | 18 |
| 2005-06 | Red Star Belgrade | 10 | 4 | | |
| 2006-07 | Red Star Belgrade | 25 | 5 | | |
| 2007-08 | Red Star Belgrade | 28 | 10 | | |
| 2008-09 | Red Star Belgrade | 33 | 18 | 96 | 37 |
| 2009-10 | Wolverhampton W | 19 | 2 | | |
| 2010-11 | Wolverhampton W | 23 | 2 | | |
| 2011-12 | Wolverhampton W | 20 | 0 | | |
| 2012-13 | Wolverhampton W | 0 | 0 | 62 | 4 |

**MOLI, David (F)**  0  0
b.Kinshasa 30-11-94
*Source:* Liverpool Scholar.

| Season | Club | Apps | Gls | Tot A | Tot G |
|---|---|---|---|---|---|
| 2011-12 | Wolverhampton W | 0 | 0 | | |
| 2012-13 | Wolverhampton W | 0 | 0 | | |

**MOUYOKOLO, Steven (D)**  64  1
H: 6 3  W: 13 08  b.Melun 24-1-87

| Season | Club | Apps | Gls | Tot A | Tot G |
|---|---|---|---|---|---|
| 2007-08 | Gueugnon | 22 | 0 | 22 | 0 |

From Chateauroux B.

| Season | Club | Apps | Gls | Tot A | Tot G |
|---|---|---|---|---|---|
| 2008-09 | Boulogne | 13 | 0 | 13 | 0 |
| 2009-10 | Hull C | 21 | 1 | 21 | 1 |
| 2010-11 | Wolverhampton W | 4 | 0 | | |
| 2011-12 | Wolverhampton W | 0 | 0 | | |
| 2011-12 | *Sochaux* | 4 | 0 | 4 | 0 |
| 2012-13 | Wolverhampton W | 0 | 0 | 4 | 0 |

**O'HARA, Jamie (M)**  146  16
H: 5 11  W: 12 04  b.Dartford 25-9-86
*Source:* Scholar. *Honours:* England Youth, Under-21.

| Season | Club | Apps | Gls | Tot A | Tot G |
|---|---|---|---|---|---|
| 2004-05 | Tottenham H | 0 | 0 | | |
| 2005-06 | Tottenham H | 0 | 0 | | |
| 2005-06 | *Chesterfield* | 19 | 5 | 19 | 5 |
| 2006-07 | Tottenham H | 0 | 0 | | |
| 2007-08 | Tottenham H | 17 | 1 | | |
| 2007-08 | *Millwall* | 14 | 2 | 14 | 2 |
| 2008-09 | Tottenham H | 15 | 1 | | |
| 2009-10 | Tottenham H | 2 | 0 | | |
| 2009-10 | *Portsmouth* | 26 | 2 | 26 | 2 |
| 2010-11 | Tottenham H | 0 | 0 | 34 | 2 |
| 2010-11 | *Wolverhampton W* | 14 | 3 | | |
| 2011-12 | Wolverhampton W | 19 | 2 | | |
| 2012-13 | Wolverhampton W | 20 | 0 | 53 | 5 |

**PESZKO, Slawomir (M)**  56  2
H: 5 8  W: 10 09  b.Jedlicze 19-2-85
*Honours:* Poland Under-21, 25 full caps, 1 goal.

| Season | Club | Apps | Gls | Tot A | Tot G |
|---|---|---|---|---|---|
| 2010-11 | Cologne | 11 | 0 | | |
| 2011-12 | Cologne | 32 | 2 | 43 | 2 |

On loan from Cologne

| Season | Club | Apps | Gls | Tot A | Tot G |
|---|---|---|---|---|---|
| 2012-13 | Wolverhampton W | 13 | 0 | 13 | 0 |

**PRICE, Jack (M)**  0  0
H: 6 3  W: 13 10  b.Shrewsbury 19-12-92
*Source:* Scholar.

| Season | Club | Apps | Gls | Tot A | Tot G |
|---|---|---|---|---|---|
| 2011-12 | Wolverhampton W | 0 | 0 | | |
| 2012-13 | Wolverhampton W | 0 | 0 | | |

**RECKORD, Jamie (D)**  33  0
H: 5 10  W: 11 11  b.Wolverhampton 9-3-92
*Source:* Scholar.

| Season | Club | Apps | Gls | Tot A | Tot G |
|---|---|---|---|---|---|
| 2010-11 | Wolverhampton W | 0 | 0 | | |
| 2010-11 | *Northampton T* | 7 | 0 | 7 | 0 |
| 2011-12 | Wolverhampton W | 0 | 0 | | |
| 2011-12 | *Scunthorpe U* | 17 | 0 | 17 | 0 |
| 2012-13 | Wolverhampton W | 0 | 0 | | |
| 2012-13 | *Coventry C* | 9 | 0 | 9 | 0 |

**SAKO, Bakary (M)**  207  32
H: 5 11  W: 11 12  b.Ivry Sur Seine 26-4-88

| Season | Club | Apps | Gls | Tot A | Tot G |
|---|---|---|---|---|---|
| 2006-07 | Chateauroux | 17 | 0 | | |
| 2007-08 | Chateauroux | 12 | 1 | | |
| 2008-09 | Chateauroux | 35 | 9 | 64 | 10 |
| 2009-10 | St Etienne | 30 | 1 | | |
| 2010-11 | St Etienne | 38 | 7 | | |
| 2011-12 | St Etienne | 36 | 5 | | |
| 2012-13 | St Etienne | 2 | 0 | 106 | 13 |
| 2012-13 | Wolverhampton W | 37 | 9 | 37 | 9 |

**SIGURDARSON, Bjorn (F)**  107  22
H: 6 1  W: 12 09  b.Akranes 26-12-91
*Honours:* Iceland Youth, Under-21, 1 full cap.

| Season | Club | Apps | Gls | Tot A | Tot G |
|---|---|---|---|---|---|
| 2008-09 | Lillestrom | 5 | 0 | | |
| 2009-10 | Lillestrom | 19 | 4 | | |
| 2010-11 | Lillestrom | 22 | 4 | | |
| 2011-12 | Lillestrom | 24 | 9 | 70 | 17 |
| 2012-13 | Wolverhampton W | 37 | 5 | 37 | 5 |

**STEARMAN, Richard (D)**  257  10
H: 6 2  W: 10 08  b.Wolverhampton 19-8-87
*Source:* Scholar. *Honours:* England Youth, Under-21.

| Season | Club | Apps | Gls | Tot A | Tot G |
|---|---|---|---|---|---|
| 2004-05 | Leicester C | 8 | 1 | | |
| 2005-06 | Leicester C | 34 | 3 | | |
| 2006-07 | Leicester C | 35 | 1 | | |
| 2007-08 | Leicester C | 39 | 2 | 116 | 7 |
| 2008-09 | Wolverhampton W | 37 | 1 | | |
| 2009-10 | Wolverhampton W | 16 | 1 | | |
| 2010-11 | Wolverhampton W | 31 | 0 | | |
| 2011-12 | Wolverhampton W | 30 | 0 | | |
| 2012-13 | Wolverhampton W | 12 | 1 | 126 | 3 |
| 2012-13 | *Ipswich T* | 15 | 0 | 15 | 0 |

**TANK, Jamie (D)**  0  0
H: 6 1  W: 13 02  b.Northampton 29-11-93

| Season | Club | Apps | Gls | Tot A | Tot G |
|---|---|---|---|---|---|
| 2012-13 | Wolverhampton W | 0 | 0 | | |

**WARD, Stephen (D)**  294  20
H: 5 11  W: 12 02  b.Dublin 20-8-85
*Honours:* Eire Youth, Under-21, B, 18 full caps, 2 goals.

| Season | Club | Apps | Gls | Tot A | Tot G |
|---|---|---|---|---|---|
| 2003 | Bohemians | 6 | 0 | | |
| 2004 | Bohemians | 16 | 2 | | |
| 2005 | Bohemians | 29 | 7 | | |
| 2006 | Bohemians | 21 | 2 | 72 | 11 |
| 2006-07 | Wolverhampton W | 18 | 3 | | |
| 2007-08 | Wolverhampton W | 29 | 0 | | |
| 2008-09 | Wolverhampton W | 42 | 0 | | |
| 2009-10 | Wolverhampton W | 22 | 0 | | |
| 2010-11 | Wolverhampton W | 34 | 1 | | |
| 2011-12 | Wolverhampton W | 38 | 3 | | |
| 2012-13 | Wolverhampton W | 39 | 2 | 222 | 9 |

**WHITTALL, Sam (M)**  0  0

| Season | Club | Apps | Gls | Tot A | Tot G |
|---|---|---|---|---|---|
| 2012-13 | Wolverhampton W | 0 | 0 | | |

**WINNALL, Sam (F)**  33  9
H: 5 9  W: 11 04  b.Wolverhampton 19-1-91
*Source:* Scholar.

| Season | Club | Apps | Gls | Tot A | Tot G |
|---|---|---|---|---|---|
| 2009-10 | Wolverhampton W | 0 | 0 | | |
| 2010-11 | Wolverhampton W | 0 | 0 | | |
| 2010-11 | *Burton Alb* | 19 | 7 | 19 | 7 |
| 2011-12 | Wolverhampton W | 0 | 0 | | |
| 2011-12 | *Hereford U* | 8 | 2 | 8 | 2 |
| 2011-12 | *Inverness CT* | 2 | 0 | 2 | 0 |
| 2012-13 | Wolverhampton W | 0 | 0 | | |
| 2012-13 | *Shrewsbury T* | 4 | 0 | 4 | 0 |

**ZUBAR, Ronald (D)**  229  7
H: 6 1  W: 12 08  b.Guadeloupe 20-9-85
*Honours:* France Under-21, Guadeloupe 1 full cap.

| Season | Club | Apps | Gls | Tot A | Tot G |
|---|---|---|---|---|---|
| 2002-03 | Caen | 7 | 0 | | |
| 2003-04 | Caen | 24 | 1 | | |
| 2004-05 | Caen | 34 | 1 | | |
| 2005-06 | Caen | 31 | 0 | 96 | 2 |
| 2006-07 | Marseille | 34 | 0 | | |
| 2007-08 | Marseille | 21 | 1 | | |
| 2008-09 | Marseille | 17 | 1 | 72 | 2 |
| 2009-10 | Wolverhampton W | 23 | 1 | | |
| 2010-11 | Wolverhampton W | 15 | 1 | | |
| 2011-12 | Wolverhampton W | 15 | 1 | | |
| 2012-13 | Wolverhampton W | 8 | 0 | 61 | 3 |

Transferred to Ajaccio January 2013

**Players retained or with offer of contract**
Flatt, Jonathan James Harrison; Iorfa, Dominic; Parry, Robbie Jay.

**Scholars**
Dell, Dominic; Div-Keita, Ibrahim; Dutton, Scott James; Gibson, Jacob; Hill, Thomas Adam; Ifil, Luke Anton; Keane, Cieron Macaully; Kellermann, James Aaron; Murray, Daniel Michael; O'Hanlon, Ben Joseph; O'Neill, Gary; Schofield, Ryan; Smith, Peter Joseph; Streete, Andre Ramone; Stringer-Moth, Dylan Mark; Weeks, Declan Lee.

# WYCOMBE W (90)

**AINSWORTH, Gareth (M)**  539  105
H: 5 10  W: 12 05  b.Blackburn 10-5-73
*Source:* Blackburn R Trainee.

| Season | Club | Apps | Gls | Tot A | Tot G |
|---|---|---|---|---|---|
| 1991-92 | Preston NE | 5 | 0 | | |
| 1992-93 | *Cambridge U* | 4 | 1 | 4 | 1 |
| 1992-93 | Preston NE | 26 | 0 | | |
| 1993-94 | Preston NE | 38 | 11 | | |
| 1994-95 | Preston NE | 16 | 1 | | |
| 1995-96 | Preston NE | 2 | 0 | | |
| 1995-96 | Lincoln C | 31 | 12 | | |
| 1996-97 | Lincoln C | 46 | 22 | | |
| 1997-98 | Lincoln C | 6 | 3 | 83 | 37 |
| 1997-98 | Port Vale | 40 | 5 | | |
| 1998-99 | Port Vale | 15 | 5 | 55 | 10 |
| 1998-99 | Wimbledon | 8 | 0 | | |
| 1999-2000 | Wimbledon | 2 | 2 | | |
| 2000-01 | Wimbledon | 12 | 2 | | |
| 2001-02 | Wimbledon | 2 | 0 | | |
| 2001-02 | *Preston NE* | 5 | 1 | 92 | 13 |
| 2002-03 | Wimbledon | 12 | 2 | 36 | 6 |
| 2002-03 | *Walsall* | 5 | 1 | 5 | 1 |
| 2002-03 | Cardiff C | 9 | 0 | 9 | 0 |
| 2003-04 | QPR | 29 | 6 | | |
| 2004-05 | QPR | 22 | 2 | | |
| 2005-06 | QPR | 43 | 9 | | |
| 2006-07 | QPR | 22 | 1 | | |
| 2007-08 | QPR | 24 | 3 | | |
| 2008-09 | QPR | 0 | 0 | | |
| 2009-10 | QPR | 1 | 0 | 141 | 21 |
| 2009-10 | Wycombe W | 14 | 2 | | |
| 2010-11 | Wycombe W | 43 | 10 | | |
| 2011-12 | Wycombe W | 32 | 2 | | |
| 2012-13 | Wycombe W | 25 | 2 | 114 | 16 |

**ANGOL, Lee (M)**  3  0
H: 5 10  W: 11 04  b. 4-8-94

| Season | Club | Apps | Gls | Tot A | Tot G |
|---|---|---|---|---|---|
| 2012-13 | Wycombe W | 3 | 0 | 3 | 0 |

**BASEY, Grant (D)**  110  5
H: 6 2  W: 13 12  b.Bromley 30-11-88
*Source:* Scholar. *Honours:* Wales Under-21.

| Season | Club | Apps | Gls | Tot A | Tot G |
|---|---|---|---|---|---|
| 2007-08 | Charlton Ath | 8 | 1 | | |
| 2007-08 | *Brentford* | 8 | 0 | 8 | 0 |
| 2008-09 | Charlton Ath | 19 | 0 | | |
| 2009-10 | Charlton Ath | 19 | 0 | | |
| 2010-11 | Charlton Ath | 0 | 0 | 46 | 1 |
| 2010-11 | *Barnet* | 11 | 1 | 11 | 1 |
| 2010-11 | *Peterborough U* | 7 | 1 | | |
| 2011-12 | *Peterborough U* | 3 | 0 | 10 | 1 |
| 2011-12 | Wycombe W | 32 | 2 | | |
| 2012-13 | Wycombe W | 3 | 0 | 35 | 2 |

**BLOOMFIELD, Matt (M)**  254  24
H: 5 9  W: 11 00  b.Felixstowe 8-2-84
*Source:* Scholar. *Honours:* England Youth, Under-20.

| Season | Club | Apps | Gls | Tot A | Tot G |
|---|---|---|---|---|---|
| 2001-02 | Ipswich T | 0 | 0 | | |
| 2002-03 | Ipswich T | 0 | 0 | | |
| 2003-04 | Ipswich T | 0 | 0 | | |
| 2003-04 | Wycombe W | 12 | 1 | | |
| 2004-05 | Wycombe W | 26 | 2 | | |
| 2005-06 | Wycombe W | 39 | 5 | | |
| 2006-07 | Wycombe W | 41 | 4 | | |
| 2007-08 | Wycombe W | 35 | 4 | | |
| 2008-09 | Wycombe W | 20 | 0 | | |
| 2009-10 | Wycombe W | 14 | 2 | | |
| 2010-11 | Wycombe W | 34 | 3 | | |
| 2011-12 | Wycombe W | 31 | 2 | | |
| 2012-13 | Wycombe W | 2 | 1 | 254 | 24 |

**BULL, Nikki (G)**  137  0
H: 6 2  W: 12 08  b.Hastings 2-10-81
*Source:* Scholarship.

| Season | Club | Apps | Gls | Tot A | Tot G |
|---|---|---|---|---|---|
| 1999-2000 | QPR | 0 | 0 | | |
| 2000-01 | QPR | 0 | 0 | | |
| 2001-02 | QPR | 0 | 0 | | |
| 2008-09 | Aldershot T | 30 | 0 | 30 | 0 |
| 2009-10 | Brentford | 6 | 0 | 6 | 0 |
| 2010-11 | Wycombe W | 46 | 0 | | |
| 2011-12 | Wycombe W | 46 | 0 | | |
| 2012-13 | Wycombe W | 9 | 0 | 101 | 0 |

**DOHERTY, Gary (D)**  413  30
H: 6 3  W: 13 13  b.Co. Donegal 31-1-80
*Source:* Trainee. *Honours:* Eire Youth, Under-20, Under-21, 34 full caps, 4 goals.

| Season | Club | Apps | Gls | Tot A | Tot G |
|---|---|---|---|---|---|
| 1997-98 | Luton T | 10 | 0 | | |
| 1998-99 | Luton T | 20 | 6 | | |
| 1999-2000 | Luton T | 40 | 6 | 70 | 12 |
| 1999-2000 | Tottenham H | 2 | 0 | | |
| 2000-01 | Tottenham H | 22 | 3 | | |
| 2001-02 | Tottenham H | 7 | 0 | | |
| 2002-03 | Tottenham H | 15 | 1 | | |
| 2003-04 | Tottenham H | 17 | 0 | | |
| 2004-05 | Tottenham H | 1 | 0 | 64 | 4 |
| 2004-05 | Norwich C | 20 | 2 | | |
| 2005-06 | Norwich C | 42 | 1 | | |
| 2006-07 | Norwich C | 34 | 0 | | |
| 2007-08 | Norwich C | 34 | 0 | | |
| 2008-09 | Norwich C | 34 | 3 | | |
| 2009-10 | Norwich C | 38 | 5 | 202 | 11 |
| 2010-11 | Charlton Ath | 38 | 0 | | |
| 2011-12 | Charlton Ath | 3 | 0 | 41 | 0 |
| 2011-12 | *Wycombe W* | 13 | 1 | | |
| 2012-13 | Wycombe W | 23 | 2 | 36 | 3 |

**DUNNE, Charles (F)**  41  0
H: 5 9  W: 11 09  b.Lambeth 13-2-93
*Source:* Scholar.

| Season | Club | Apps | Gls | Tot A | Tot G |
|---|---|---|---|---|---|
| 2011-12 | Wycombe W | 3 | 0 | | |
| 2012-13 | Wycombe W | 38 | 0 | 41 | 0 |

**EHUI, Georges (M)**  2  0
b. 2-2-94
2012-13  Wycombe W  2  0  2  0

**FOSTER, Danny (D)**  182  4
H: 5 10  W: 12 10  b.Enfield 23-9-84
*Source:* Trainee.
2002-03  Tottenham H  0  0
2003-04  Tottenham H  0  0
2004-05  Tottenham H  0  0
2005-06  Tottenham H  0  0
2006-07  Tottenham H  0  0
2007-08  Dagenham & R  32  1
2008-09  Dagenham & R  38  2  70  3
2009-10  Brentford  36  0  36  0
2010-11  Wycombe W  38  1
2011-12  Wycombe W  29  0
2012-13  Wycombe W  9  0  76  1

**GRANT, Joel (F)**  174  30
H: 6 0  W: 12 01  b.Acton 26-8-87
2005-06  Watford  7  0
2006-07  Watford  0  0  7  0
From Aldershot T.
2008-09  Crewe Alex  28  2
2009-10  Crewe Alex  43  9
2010-11  Crewe Alex  25  5  96  16
2011-12  Wycombe W  30  4
2012-13  Wycombe W  41  10  71  14

**HAUSE, Kortney (D)**  9  1
b. 16-7-95
2012-13  Wycombe W  9  1  9  1

**IGHORAE, Emmanuel (M)**  0  0
b. 10-2-95
2012-13  Wycombe W  0  0

**INGRAM, Matt (G)**  8  0
H: 6 3  W: 12 13  b.Croydon 18-12-93
*Source:* Trainee.
2011-12  Wycombe W  0  0
2012-13  Wycombe W  8  0  8  0

**JOHNSON, Leon (D)**  295  6
H: 6 1  W: 13 05  b.Shoreditch 10-5-81
*Source:* Scholarship.
1999-2000  Southend U  0  0
2000-01  Southend U  20  1
2001-02  Southend U  28  2  48  3
2002-03  Gillingham  18  0
2003-04  Gillingham  20  0
2004-05  Gillingham  8  0
2005-06  Gillingham  28  1
2006-07  Gillingham  24  1  98  2
2007-08  Wycombe W  45  0
2008-09  Wycombe W  29  2
2009-10  Wycombe W  5  0
2010-11  Wycombe W  23  1
2011-12  Wycombe W  27  0
2012-13  Wycombe W  20  0  149  3

**KEWLEY-GRAHAM, Jesse (M)**  8  0
H: 5 10  W: 11 11  b.Hounslow 15-6-93
*Source:* Scholar.
2011-12  Wycombe W  1  0
2012-13  Wycombe W  7  0  8  0

**KRETZSCHMAR, Max (M)**  0  0
b. 12-10-93
*Source:* Scholar.
2011-12  Wycombe W  0  0
2012-13  Wycombe W  0  0

**KUFFOUR, Jo (F)**  434  98
H: 5 8  W: 11 11  b.Edmonton 17-11-81
*Source:* Scholar.
2000-01  Arsenal  0  0
2001-02  Arsenal  0  0
2001-02  *Swindon T*  11  2  11  2
2002-03  Torquay U  30  5
2003-04  Torquay U  41  10
2004-05  Torquay U  34  6
2005-06  Torquay U  43  8  148  29
2006-07  Brentford  39  12  39  12
2007-08  Bournemouth  42  12
2008-09  Bournemouth  2  0  44  12
2008-09  Bristol R  41  11
2009-10  Bristol R  42  14
2010-11  Bristol R  42  6

2011-12  Bristol R  5  1  130  32
2011-12  Gillingham  30  9  30  9
2012-13  Wycombe W  32  2  32  2

**LEWIS, Stuart (M)**  175  6
H: 5 10  W: 11 06  b.Welwyn 15-10-87
*Source:* Scholar. *Honours:* England Youth.
2005-06  Tottenham H  0  0
2006-07  Tottenham H  0  0
2006-07  Barnet  4  0  4  0
From Stevenage B.
2007-08  Gillingham  10  0
2008-09  Gillingham  21  0
2009-10  Gillingham  20  1  51  1
2010-11  Dagenham & R  10  0  10  0
2010-11  Wycombe W  25  2
2011-12  Wycombe W  41  1
2012-13  Wycombe W  44  2  110  5

**LOGAN, Richard (F)**  295  57
H: 6 1  W: 12 05  b.Bury St Edmunds 4-1-82
*Source:* Trainee. *Honours:* England Youth.
1998-99  Ipswich T  2  0
1999-2000  Ipswich T  1  0
2000-01  Ipswich T  0  0
2000-01  *Cambridge U*  5  1  5  1
2001-02  Ipswich T  0  0
2001-02  *Torquay U*  16  4  16  4
2002-03  Ipswich T  0  0  3  0
2002-03  Boston U  27  10
2003-04  Boston U  8  0  35  10
2003-04  Peterborough U  29  7
2004-05  Peterborough U  26  4
2004-05  *Shrewsbury T*  5  1  5  1
2005-06  Peterborough U  28  4  83  15
2005-06  *Lincoln C*  8  2  8  2
From Weymouth.
2008-09  Exeter C  30  4
2009-10  Exeter C  34  4
2010-11  Exeter C  40  11
2011-12  Exeter C  28  5  132  24
2012-13  Wycombe W  8  0  8  0

**McCLURE, Matt (F)**  47  12
H: 5 10  W: 11 00  b.Slough 17-11-91
*Source:* Scholar. *Honours:* Northern Ireland Under-21.
2010-11  Wycombe W  8  0
2011-12  Wycombe W  12  1
2012-13  Wycombe W  27  11  47  12

**McCOY, Marvin (D)**  58  0
H: 5 11  W: 11 00  b.Walthamstow 2-10-88
*Source:* Watford Scholar. *Honours:* Antigua and Barbuda, 6 full caps.
2007-08  Hereford U  0  0
From Leyton, Wealdstone.
2010-11  Wycombe W  21  0
2011-12  Wycombe W  28  0
2012-13  Wycombe W  9  0  58  0

**MORGAN, Dean (M)**  338  43
H: 5 11  W: 13 00  b.Enfield 3-10-83
*Source:* Scholar.
2000-01  Colchester U  4  0
2001-02  Colchester U  30  0
2002-03  Colchester U  37  6
2003-04  Colchester U  0  0  71  6
2003-04  Reading  13  1
2004-05  Reading  18  2  31  3
2005-06  Luton T  36  6
2006-07  Luton T  36  4
2007-08  Luton T  16  1
2007-08  *Southend U*  8  0  8  0
2007-08  *Crewe Alex*  9  1  9  1
2008-09  Luton T  1  0
2008-09  *Leyton Orient*  32  5  32  5
2009-10  Luton T  0  0  88  11
2009-10  *Milton Keynes D*  9  1  9  1
2009-10  *Aldershot T*  9  4  9  4
2010-11  Chesterfield  21  1
2011-12  Chesterfield  17  3  38  4
2011-12  *Oxford U*  10  1  10  1
2012-13  Wycombe W  33  7  33  7

**MORIAS, Junior (F)**  19  0
b. 4-7-95
2012-13  Wycombe W  19  0  19  0

**OLI, Dennis (M)**  171  15
H: 6 0  W: 12 00  b.Newham 28-1-84
2001-02  QPR  2  0
2002-03  QPR  18  0
2003-04  QPR  3  0  23  0
2004-05  Swansea C  1  0  1  0
2004-05  Cambridge U  4  1  4  1
From Grays Ath.
2007-08  Gillingham  22  4
2008-09  Gillingham  31  4
2009-10  Gillingham  36  3
2010-11  Gillingham  21  1
2011-12  Gillingham  23  2  133  14
2012-13  Wycombe W  10  0  10  0

**SCOWEN, Josh (M)**  36  1
H: 5 10  W: 11 09  b.Cheshunt 28-3-93
*Source:* Scholar.
2010-11  Wycombe W  2  0
2011-12  Wycombe W  0  0
2012-13  Wycombe W  34  1  36  1

**SPRING, Matthew (M)**  507  53
H: 5 11  W: 12 05  b.Harlow 17-11-79
*Source:* Trainee.
1997-98  Luton T  12  0
1998-99  Luton T  45  3
1999-2000  Luton T  45  6
2000-01  Luton T  41  4
2001-02  Luton T  42  6
2002-03  Luton T  41  5
2003-04  Luton T  24  1
2004-05  Leeds U  13  1
2005-06  Leeds U  0  0  13  1
2005-06  Watford  39  8
2006-07  Watford  6  0  45  8
2006-07  Luton T  14  1
2007-08  Luton T  44  9
2008-09  Luton T  0  0  308  35
2008-09  *Sheffield U*  11  1  11  1
2008-09  Charlton Ath  13  2
2009-10  Charlton Ath  12  0  25  2
2010-11  Leyton Orient  39  2
2011-12  Leyton Orient  41  4  80  6
2012-13  Wycombe W  25  0  25  0

**STEWART, Anthony (D)**  23  1
H: 5 10  W: 12 03  b.Brixton 18-9-92
*Source:* Scholar.
2011-12  Wycombe W  4  0
2012-13  Wycombe W  19  1  23  1

**TAYLOR, Olly (F)**  6  0
b. 13-12-93
2012-13  Wycombe W  6  0  6  0

**WINFIELD, Dave (D)**  126  8
H: 6 3  W: 13 08  b.Aldershot 24-3-88
*Source:* Youth.
2008-09  Aldershot T  10  0
2009-10  Aldershot T  25  2  35  2
2010-11  Wycombe W  37  2
2011-12  Wycombe W  25  2
2012-13  Wycombe W  29  2  91  6

**WOOD, Sam (M)**  169  8
H: 6 0  W: 11 05  b.Sidcup 9-8-86
*Source:* Cray W, Bromley.
2008-09  Brentford  40  1
2009-10  Brentford  43  2
2010-11  Brentford  20  1
2011-12  Brentford  5  0  108  4
2011-12  *Rotherham U*  26  1  26  1
2012-13  Wycombe W  35  3  35  3

# YEOVIL T (91)

**AYLING, Luke (D)**  124  0
H: 5 11  W: 10 08  b.Lambeth 25-8-91
2009-10  Arsenal  0  0
2009-10  *Yeovil T*  4  0
2010-11  Yeovil T  37  0
2011-12  Yeovil T  44  0
2012-13  Yeovil T  39  0  124  0

**BLIZZARD, Dominic (M)**    196   11
H: 6 2  W: 12 04  b.High Wycombe 2-9-83
*Source:* Scholar.

| Season | Club | App | Gls | Tot | Gls |
|---|---|---|---|---|---|
| 2001-02 | Watford | 0 | 0 | | |
| 2002-03 | Watford | 0 | 0 | | |
| 2003-04 | Watford | 2 | 1 | | |
| 2004-05 | Watford | 17 | 1 | | |
| 2005-06 | Watford | 10 | 0 | | |
| 2006-07 | Watford | 0 | 0 | 29 | 2 |
| 2006-07 | Stockport Co | 7 | 0 | | |
| 2006-07 | Milton Keynes D | 8 | 0 | 8 | 0 |
| 2007-08 | Stockport Co | 27 | 1 | | |
| 2008-09 | Stockport Co | 31 | 3 | 65 | 4 |
| 2009-10 | Bristol R | 34 | 1 | | |
| 2010-11 | Bristol R | 5 | 0 | 39 | 1 |
| 2010-11 | Port Vale | 1 | 0 | 1 | 0 |
| 2011-12 | Yeovil T | 30 | 3 | | |
| 2012-13 | Yeovil T | 24 | 1 | 54 | 4 |

**CHAINEY, Aiden (M)**    0   0
b. 15-9-94

| Season | Club | App | Gls |
|---|---|---|---|
| 2012-13 | Yeovil T | 0 | 0 |

**DAWSON, Kevin (M)**    71   6
H: 5 10  W: 12 08  b.Dublin 30-6-90

| Season | Club | App | Gls | Tot | Gls |
|---|---|---|---|---|---|
| 2011 | Shelbourne | 26 | 2 | | |
| 2012 | Shelbourne | 25 | 2 | 51 | 4 |
| 2012-13 | Yeovil T | 20 | 2 | 20 | 2 |

**EDWARDS, Joe (D)**    43   3
H: 5 8  W: 11 07  b.Gloucester 31-10-90
*Source:* Scholar.

| Season | Club | App | Gls | Tot | Gls |
|---|---|---|---|---|---|
| 2009-10 | Bristol C | 0 | 0 | | |
| 2010-11 | Bristol C | 2 | 0 | | |
| 2011-12 | Bristol C | 2 | 0 | | |
| 2011-12 | Yeovil T | 4 | 1 | | |
| 2012-13 | Bristol C | 0 | 0 | 4 | 0 |
| 2012-13 | Yeovil T | 35 | 2 | 39 | 3 |

**FLETCHER, Wes (F)**    32   5
H: 5 11  W: 12 06  b.Ormskirk 28-2-91
*Source:* Scholar.

| Season | Club | App | Gls | Tot | Gls |
|---|---|---|---|---|---|
| 2009-10 | Burnley | 0 | 0 | | |
| 2009-10 | Grimsby T | 6 | 1 | 6 | 1 |
| 2010-11 | Burnley | 0 | 0 | | |
| 2010-11 | Stockport Co | 9 | 1 | 9 | 1 |
| 2011-12 | Burnley | 0 | 0 | | |
| 2011-12 | Accrington S | 10 | 2 | 10 | 2 |
| 2011-12 | Crewe Alex | 6 | 1 | 6 | 1 |
| 2012-13 | Burnley | 0 | 0 | | |
| 2012-13 | Yeovil T | 1 | 0 | 1 | 0 |

**FOLEY, Sam (M)**    41   5
H: 6 0  W: 11 08  b.St Albans 17-10-86
*Source:* Newport Co.

| Season | Club | App | Gls | Tot | Gls |
|---|---|---|---|---|---|
| 2012-13 | Yeovil T | 41 | 5 | 41 | 5 |

**GORDON, Ben (D)**    40   0
H: 5 11  W: 12 06  b.Bradford 2-3-91
*Source:* Scholar. *Honours:* England Under-20.

| Season | Club | App | Gls | Tot | Gls |
|---|---|---|---|---|---|
| 2008-09 | Chelsea | 0 | 0 | | |
| 2009-10 | Chelsea | 0 | 0 | | |
| 2009-10 | Tranmere R | 4 | 0 | 4 | 0 |
| 2010-11 | Chelsea | 0 | 0 | | |
| 2010-11 | Scunthorpe U | 14 | 0 | 14 | 0 |
| 2011-12 | Chelsea | 0 | 0 | | |
| 2011-12 | Peterborough U | 1 | 0 | 1 | 0 |
| 2011-12 | Kilmarnock | 17 | 0 | 17 | 0 |
| 2012-13 | Chelsea | 0 | 0 | | |
| 2012-13 | Birmingham C | 1 | 0 | 1 | 0 |
| 2012-13 | Yeovil T | 3 | 0 | 3 | 0 |

**HAYNES-BROWN, Curtis (D)**    16   0
H: 6 2  W: 13 00  b.Ipswich 15-4-89
*Source:* Colchester U Scholar, AFC Sudbury, Lowestoft T.

| Season | Club | App | Gls | Tot | Gls |
|---|---|---|---|---|---|
| 2011-12 | Yeovil T | 10 | 0 | | |
| 2012-13 | Yeovil T | 0 | 0 | 10 | 0 |
| 2012-13 | AFC Wimbledon | 6 | 0 | 6 | 0 |

**HAYTER, James (F)**    564   141
H: 5 9  W: 10 13  b.Sandown 9-4-79
*Source:* Trainee.

| Season | Club | App | Gls | Tot | Gls |
|---|---|---|---|---|---|
| 1996-97 | Bournemouth | 2 | 0 | | |
| 1997-98 | Bournemouth | 5 | 0 | | |
| 1998-99 | Bournemouth | 20 | 2 | | |
| 1999-2000 | Bournemouth | 31 | 2 | | |
| 2000-01 | Bournemouth | 40 | 11 | | |
| 2001-02 | Bournemouth | 44 | 7 | | |
| 2002-03 | Bournemouth | 45 | 9 | | |
| 2003-04 | Bournemouth | 44 | 14 | | |
| 2004-05 | Bournemouth | 39 | 19 | | |
| 2005-06 | Bournemouth | 46 | 20 | | |
| 2006-07 | Bournemouth | 42 | 10 | 358 | 94 |
| 2007-08 | Doncaster R | 34 | 7 | | |
| 2008-09 | Doncaster R | 27 | 4 | | |
| 2009-10 | Doncaster R | 38 | 9 | | |
| 2010-11 | Doncaster R | 32 | 9 | | |
| 2011-12 | Doncaster R | 31 | 4 | 162 | 33 |
| 2012-13 | Yeovil T | 44 | 14 | 44 | 14 |

**HINDS, Richard (D)**    295   13
H: 6 2  W: 12 02  b.Sheffield 22-8-80
*Source:* Schoolboy.

| Season | Club | App | Gls | Tot | Gls |
|---|---|---|---|---|---|
| 1998-99 | Tranmere R | 2 | 0 | | |
| 1999-2000 | Tranmere R | 6 | 0 | | |
| 2000-01 | Tranmere R | 29 | 0 | | |
| 2001-02 | Tranmere R | 10 | 0 | | |
| 2002-03 | Tranmere R | 8 | 0 | 55 | 0 |
| 2003-04 | Hull C | 39 | 1 | | |
| 2004-05 | Hull C | 6 | 0 | 45 | 1 |
| 2004-05 | Scunthorpe U | 7 | 0 | | |
| 2005-06 | Scunthorpe U | 42 | 6 | | |
| 2006-07 | Scunthorpe U | 44 | 2 | 93 | 8 |
| 2007-08 | Sheffield W | 38 | 2 | | |
| 2008-09 | Sheffield W | 14 | 0 | | |
| 2009-10 | Sheffield W | 11 | 0 | | |
| 2010-11 | Sheffield W | 4 | 0 | | |
| 2011-12 | Sheffield W | 0 | 0 | 67 | 2 |

From Lincoln C.

| Season | Club | App | Gls | Tot | Gls |
|---|---|---|---|---|---|
| 2011-12 | Yeovil T | 16 | 1 | | |
| 2012-13 | Yeovil T | 19 | 1 | 35 | 2 |

**McALLISTER, Jamie (D)**    472   4
H: 5 10  W: 11 00  b.Glasgow 26-4-78
*Honours:* Scotland 1 full cap.

| Season | Club | App | Gls | Tot | Gls |
|---|---|---|---|---|---|
| 1995-96 | Queen of the S | 2 | 0 | | |
| 1996-97 | Queen of the S | 6 | 0 | | |
| 1997-98 | Queen of the S | 15 | 0 | | |
| 1998-99 | Queen of the S | 27 | 0 | 50 | 0 |
| 1999-2000 | Aberdeen | 34 | 0 | | |
| 2000-01 | Aberdeen | 25 | 0 | | |
| 2001-02 | Aberdeen | 29 | 0 | | |
| 2002-03 | Aberdeen | 29 | 0 | 117 | 0 |
| 2003-04 | Livingston | 34 | 1 | 34 | 1 |
| 2004-05 | Hearts | 30 | 0 | | |
| 2005-06 | Hearts | 17 | 0 | 47 | 0 |
| 2006-07 | Bristol C | 31 | 1 | | |
| 2007-08 | Bristol C | 41 | 0 | | |
| 2008-09 | Bristol C | 35 | 1 | | |
| 2009-10 | Bristol C | 33 | 0 | | |
| 2010-11 | Bristol C | 34 | 1 | | |
| 2011-12 | Bristol C | 12 | 0 | 186 | 3 |
| 2011-12 | Preston NE | 4 | 0 | 4 | 0 |
| 2012-13 | Yeovil T | 34 | 0 | 34 | 0 |

**RALPH, Nathan (D)**    14   1
H: 5 9  W: 11 00  b.Dunmow 14-2-93
*Source:* Scholar.

| Season | Club | App | Gls | Tot | Gls |
|---|---|---|---|---|---|
| 2011-12 | Peterborough U | 0 | 0 | | |
| 2012-13 | Yeovil T | 14 | 1 | 14 | 1 |

**REID, Reuben (F)**    189   38
H: 6 0  W: 12 02  b.Bristol 26-7-88
*Source:* Millfield School.

| Season | Club | App | Gls | Tot | Gls |
|---|---|---|---|---|---|
| 2005-06 | Plymouth Arg | 1 | 0 | | |
| 2006-07 | Plymouth Arg | 6 | 0 | | |
| 2006-07 | Rochdale | 2 | 0 | 2 | 0 |
| 2006-07 | Torquay U | 7 | 2 | 7 | 2 |
| 2007-08 | Plymouth Arg | 0 | 0 | | |
| 2007-08 | Wycombe W | 11 | 1 | 11 | 1 |
| 2007-08 | Brentford | 10 | 1 | 10 | 1 |
| 2008-09 | Rotherham U | 41 | 18 | 41 | 18 |
| 2009-10 | WBA | 4 | 0 | | |
| 2009-10 | Peterborough U | 13 | 0 | 13 | 0 |
| 2010-11 | WBA | 0 | 0 | 4 | 0 |
| 2010-11 | Walsall | 18 | 3 | 18 | 3 |
| 2010-11 | Oldham Ath | 19 | 2 | | |
| 2011-12 | Oldham Ath | 20 | 5 | 39 | 7 |
| 2012-13 | Yeovil T | 19 | 4 | 19 | 4 |
| 2012-13 | Plymouth Arg | 18 | 2 | 25 | 2 |

**STECH, Marek (G)**    56   0
H: 6 3  W: 14 00  b.Prague 28-1-90
*Source:* Sparta Prague, West Ham U Scholar.
*Honours:* Czech Republic Youth, Under-21.

| Season | Club | App | Gls | Tot | Gls |
|---|---|---|---|---|---|
| 2008-09 | West Ham U | 0 | 0 | | |
| 2008-09 | Wycombe W | 2 | 0 | 2 | 0 |
| 2009-10 | West Ham U | 0 | 0 | | |
| 2009-10 | Bournemouth | 1 | 0 | 1 | 0 |
| 2010-11 | West Ham U | 0 | 0 | | |
| 2011-12 | West Ham U | 0 | 0 | | |
| 2011-12 | Yeovil T | 5 | 0 | | |
| 2011-12 | Leyton Orient | 2 | 0 | 2 | 0 |
| 2012-13 | Yeovil T | 46 | 0 | 51 | 0 |

**STEWART, Gareth (G)**    165   0
H: 6 0  W: 12 08  b.Preston 3-2-80
*Source:* Trainee. *Honours:* England Schools, Youth.

| Season | Club | App | Gls | Tot | Gls |
|---|---|---|---|---|---|
| 1996-97 | Blackburn R | 0 | 0 | | |
| 1997-98 | Blackburn R | 0 | 0 | | |
| 1998-99 | Blackburn R | 0 | 0 | | |
| 1999-2000 | Bournemouth | 3 | 0 | | |
| 2000-01 | Bournemouth | 35 | 0 | | |
| 2001-02 | Bournemouth | 45 | 0 | | |
| 2002-03 | Bournemouth | 1 | 0 | | |
| 2003-04 | Bournemouth | 0 | 0 | | |
| 2004-05 | Bournemouth | 0 | 0 | | |
| 2005-06 | Bournemouth | 42 | 0 | | |
| 2006-07 | Bournemouth | 20 | 0 | | |
| 2007-08 | Bournemouth | 18 | 0 | | |
| 2008-09 | Bournemouth | 0 | 0 | 164 | 0 |
| 2011-12 | Yeovil T | 1 | 0 | | |
| 2012-13 | Yeovil T | 0 | 0 | 1 | 0 |

**UPSON, Edward (M)**    114   6
H: 5 10  W: 11 07  b.Bury St Edmunds 21-11-89
*Source:* Scholar. *Honours:* England Youth.

| Season | Club | App | Gls | Tot | Gls |
|---|---|---|---|---|---|
| 2006-07 | Ipswich T | 0 | 0 | | |
| 2007-08 | Ipswich T | 0 | 0 | | |
| 2008-09 | Ipswich T | 0 | 0 | | |
| 2009-10 | Ipswich T | 0 | 0 | | |
| 2009-10 | Barnet | 9 | 1 | 9 | 1 |
| 2010-11 | Yeovil T | 23 | 0 | | |
| 2011-12 | Yeovil T | 41 | 3 | | |
| 2012-13 | Yeovil T | 41 | 2 | 105 | 5 |

**WEBSTER, Byron (D)**    102   9
H: 6 5  W: 12 07  b.Sherburn-in-Elmet 31-3-87
*Source:* York C, Harrogate T, Whitby T.

| Season | Club | App | Gls | Tot | Gls |
|---|---|---|---|---|---|
| 2007-08 | Siad Most | 23 | 4 | | |
| 2008-09 | Siad Most | 0 | 0 | 23 | 4 |
| 2009-10 | Doncaster R | 5 | 0 | | |
| 2010-11 | Doncaster R | 7 | 0 | 12 | 0 |
| 2010-11 | Hereford U | 2 | 0 | 2 | 0 |
| 2010-11 | Northampton T | 8 | 0 | | |
| 2011-12 | Northampton T | 13 | 0 | 21 | 0 |
| 2012-13 | Yeovil T | 44 | 5 | 44 | 5 |

**WILLIAMS, Gavin (M)**    262   33
H: 5 10  W: 11 05  b.Pontypridd 20-6-80
*Source:* Hereford U. *Honours:* Wales 2 full caps.

| Season | Club | App | Gls | Tot | Gls |
|---|---|---|---|---|---|
| 2003-04 | Yeovil T | 42 | 9 | | |
| 2004-05 | Yeovil T | 13 | 2 | | |
| 2004-05 | West Ham U | 10 | 1 | | |
| 2005-06 | West Ham U | 0 | 0 | 10 | 1 |
| 2005-06 | Ipswich T | 12 | 1 | | |
| 2006-07 | Ipswich T | 29 | 2 | | |
| 2007-08 | Ipswich T | 13 | 0 | 54 | 3 |
| 2008-09 | Bristol C | 35 | 3 | | |
| 2009-10 | Bristol C | 14 | 0 | | |
| 2009-10 | Yeovil T | 8 | 5 | | |
| 2010-11 | Bristol C | 3 | 0 | 52 | 3 |
| 2010-11 | Yeovil T | 12 | 1 | | |
| 2011-12 | Bristol R | 19 | 2 | 19 | 2 |
| 2011-12 | Yeovil T | 28 | 4 | | |
| 2012-13 | Yeovil T | 24 | 3 | 127 | 24 |

**YOUNG, Lewis (M)**    71   0
H: 5 10  W: 11 02  b.Stevenage 27-9-89
*Source:* Scholar.

| Season | Club | App | Gls | Tot | Gls |
|---|---|---|---|---|---|
| 2008-09 | Watford | 1 | 0 | | |
| 2009-10 | Watford | 0 | 0 | 1 | 0 |
| 2009-10 | Hereford U | 6 | 0 | 6 | 0 |
| 2010-11 | Burton Alb | 19 | 0 | 19 | 0 |
| 2011-12 | Northampton T | 30 | 0 | 30 | 0 |
| 2012-13 | Yeovil T | 15 | 0 | 15 | 0 |

**Scholars**
Agbo, William David Kwami; Brundle, Mitch Ronnie; Cafer, Matthew Paul; Chainey, Aidan Douglas; Emanuel-Williamson, Melchi Mile; Hansford, Curtis Jake; Jheeta, Taranjeet Singh; MacDevitt, Liam Joshua; Nelson, Elliott Joshua; Smith, Tommy Arthur; Sweet, Lee Robert; Ware, Charlie Peter.

## YORK C (92)

**ALLAN, Tom (D)**     **5**   **0**
b.York 30-10-94

| | | | | | |
|---|---|---|---|---|---|
| 2012-13 | York C | 5 | 0 | 5 | 0 |

**BLAIR, Matty (M)**     **44**   **6**
H: 5 10   W: 11 09   b.Coventry 30-11-87
*Source:* Kidderminster H.

| | | | | | |
|---|---|---|---|---|---|
| 2012-13 | York C | 44 | 6 | 44 | 6 |

**BLANCHETT, Danny (D)**     **77**   **1**
H: 5 11   W: 11 12   b.Wembley 12-3-88
*Source:* Northwood, Hendon, Harrow
Borough, Cambridge C.

| | | | | | |
|---|---|---|---|---|---|
| 2006-07 | Peterborough U | 3 | 1 | | |
| 2007-08 | Peterborough U | 1 | 0 | | |
| 2008-09 | Peterborough U | 3 | 0 | | |
| 2009-10 | Peterborough U | 0 | 0 | 7 | 1 |
| 2009-10 | Hereford U | 13 | 0 | 13 | 0 |
| 2010-11 | Crewe Alex | 39 | 0 | 39 | 0 |
| 2011-12 | Burton Alb | 14 | 0 | 14 | 0 |
| 2012-13 | York C | 4 | 0 | 4 | 0 |

**BULLOCK, Lee (M)**     **406**   **40**
H: 6 0   W: 11 04   b.Stockton 22-5-81
*Source:* Trainee.

| | | | | | |
|---|---|---|---|---|---|
| 1999-2000 | York C | 24 | 0 | | |
| 2000-01 | York C | 33 | 3 | | |
| 2001-02 | York C | 40 | 8 | | |
| 2002-03 | York C | 39 | 6 | | |
| 2003-04 | York C | 35 | 7 | | |
| 2003-04 | Cardiff C | 11 | 3 | | |
| 2004-05 | Cardiff C | 21 | 3 | 32 | 6 |
| 2005-06 | Hartlepool U | 31 | 4 | | |
| 2006-07 | Hartlepool U | 25 | 1 | | |
| 2007-08 | Hartlepool U | 1 | 0 | 57 | 5 |
| 2007-08 | *Mansfield T* | 5 | 0 | 5 | 0 |
| 2007-08 | *Bury* | 8 | 0 | 8 | 0 |
| 2007-08 | Bradford C | 12 | 1 | | |
| 2008-09 | Bradford C | 23 | 3 | | |
| 2009-10 | Bradford C | 41 | 1 | | |
| 2010-11 | Bradford C | 26 | 0 | | |
| 2011-12 | Bradford C | 19 | 0 | 121 | 5 |
| 2012-13 | York C | 12 | 0 | 183 | 24 |

**CHALLINOR, Jon (M)**     **18**   **0**
H: 5 11   b.Northampton 2-12-80

| | | | | | |
|---|---|---|---|---|---|
| 2012-13 | York C | 18 | 0 | 18 | 0 |

**CHAMBERS, Ashley (F)**     **44**   **10**
H: 5 10   W: 11 06   b.Leicester 1-3-90

| | | | | | |
|---|---|---|---|---|---|
| 2005-06 | Leicester C | 0 | 0 | | |
| 2006-07 | Leicester C | 0 | 0 | | |
| 2007-08 | Leicester C | 5 | 0 | | |
| 2008-09 | Leicester C | 1 | 0 | | |
| 2009-10 | Leicester C | 0 | 0 | 6 | 0 |
| 2009-10 | *Wycombe W* | 0 | 0 | | |
| 2009-10 | *Grimsby T* | 0 | 0 | | |
| 2012-13 | York C | 38 | 10 | 38 | 10 |

**COULSON, Michael (F)**     **64**   **9**
H: 5 10   W: 10 00   b.Scarborough 4-4-88
*Source:* Scarborough.

| | | | | | |
|---|---|---|---|---|---|
| 2006-07 | Barnsley | 2 | 0 | | |
| 2007-08 | Barnsley | 12 | 0 | | |
| 2008-09 | Barnsley | 2 | 0 | | |
| 2009-10 | Barnsley | 0 | 0 | 16 | 0 |
| 2009-10 | *Grimsby T* | 29 | 5 | 29 | 5 |
| 2012-13 | York C | 19 | 4 | 19 | 4 |

**DOIG, Chris (D)**     **260**   **5**
H: 6 2   W: 12 06   b.Dumfries 13-2-81
*Source:* Trainee. *Honours:* Scotland Schools,
Youth, Under-21.

| | | | | | |
|---|---|---|---|---|---|
| 1997-98 | Nottingham F | 0 | 0 | | |
| 1998-99 | Nottingham F | 2 | 0 | | |
| 1999-2000 | Nottingham F | 11 | 0 | | |

| | | | | | |
|---|---|---|---|---|---|
| 2000-01 | Nottingham F | 15 | 0 | | |
| 2001-02 | Nottingham F | 8 | 1 | | |
| 2002-03 | Nottingham F | 10 | 0 | | |
| 2003-04 | Nottingham F | 10 | 0 | | |
| 2003-04 | *Northampton T* | 9 | 0 | | |
| 2004-05 | Nottingham F | 21 | 0 | 77 | 1 |
| 2005-06 | Northampton T | 38 | 2 | | |
| 2006-07 | Northampton T | 39 | 0 | | |
| 2007-08 | Northampton T | 15 | 1 | | |
| 2008-09 | Northampton T | 28 | 1 | 129 | 4 |
| 2009-10 | Central Coast M | 26 | 0 | 26 | 0 |
| 2010-11 | Pelita Jaya | 12 | 0 | 12 | 0 |
| 2011-12 | Aldershot T | 2 | 0 | 2 | 0 |
| 2012-13 | York C | 14 | 0 | 14 | 0 |

**EVERSON, Ben (F)**     **11**   **1**
H: 5 10   W: 13 01   b.Middlesbrough 11-2-87

| | | | | | |
|---|---|---|---|---|---|
| 2012-13 | Breidablik | 9 | 1 | 9 | 1 |
| 2012-13 | York C | 2 | 0 | 2 | 0 |

**FYFIELD, Jamal (D)**     **33**   **0**
b.Leyton 17-3-89
*Source:* Maidenhead U.

| | | | | | |
|---|---|---|---|---|---|
| 2012-13 | York C | 33 | 0 | 33 | 0 |

**INGHAM, Michael (G)**     **176**   **0**
H: 6 4   W: 13 08   b.Preston 9-7-80

| | | | | | |
|---|---|---|---|---|---|
| 1998-99 | Cliftonville | 18 | 0 | 18 | 0 |
| 1999-2000 | Sunderland | 0 | 0 | | |
| 1999-2000 | *Carlisle U* | 7 | 0 | 7 | 0 |
| 2000-01 | Sunderland | 0 | 0 | | |
| 2001-02 | Sunderland | 0 | 0 | | |
| 2001-02 | *Stoke C* | 0 | 0 | | |
| 2002-03 | Sunderland | 0 | 0 | | |
| 2002-03 | *Darlington* | 3 | 0 | 3 | 0 |
| 2002-03 | *York C* | 17 | 0 | | |
| 2003-04 | Sunderland | 0 | 0 | | |
| 2003-04 | *Wrexham* | 11 | 0 | | |
| 2004-05 | Sunderland | 2 | 0 | 2 | 0 |
| 2004-05 | *Doncaster R* | 1 | 0 | 1 | 0 |
| 2005-06 | Wrexham | 40 | 0 | | |
| 2006-07 | Wrexham | 31 | 0 | 82 | 0 |
| 2012-13 | York C | 46 | 0 | 63 | 0 |

**JOHNSON, Oli (F)**     **105**   **17**
H: 5 11   W: 12 04   b.Wakefield 6-11-87
*Source:* Nostell MW.

| | | | | | |
|---|---|---|---|---|---|
| 2008-09 | Stockport Co | 24 | 6 | | |
| 2009-10 | Stockport Co | 16 | 1 | 40 | 7 |
| 2009-10 | Norwich C | 17 | 4 | | |
| 2010-11 | Norwich C | 4 | 0 | | |
| 2010-11 | *Yeovil T* | 17 | 3 | | |
| 2011-12 | Norwich C | 0 | 0 | 21 | 4 |
| 2011-12 | *Yeovil T* | 6 | 0 | 23 | 3 |
| 2011-12 | *Oxford U* | 17 | 3 | 17 | 3 |
| 2012-13 | York C | 4 | 0 | 4 | 0 |

**KERR, Scott (M)**     **250**   **8**
H: 5 9   W: 12 09   b.Leeds 11-12-81
*Source:* Scholar.

| | | | | | |
|---|---|---|---|---|---|
| 2000-01 | Bradford C | 1 | 0 | 1 | 0 |
| 2001-02 | Hull C | 0 | 0 | | |
| 2002-03 | Hull C | 0 | 0 | | |
| 2003-04 | Hull C | 0 | 0 | | |
| 2004-05 | Hull C | 0 | 0 | | |

From Scarborough

| | | | | | |
|---|---|---|---|---|---|
| 2005-06 | Lincoln C | 41 | 2 | | |
| 2006-07 | Lincoln C | 44 | 3 | | |
| 2007-08 | Lincoln C | 36 | 1 | | |
| 2008-09 | Lincoln C | 45 | 2 | | |
| 2009-10 | Lincoln C | 39 | 0 | | |
| 2010-11 | Lincoln C | 16 | 0 | 221 | 8 |
| 2012-13 | York C | 28 | 0 | 28 | 0 |

**McDAID, David (M)**     **90**   **21**
H: 5 9   b.Derry 3-12-90

| | | | | | |
|---|---|---|---|---|---|
| 2009 | Derry C | 5 | 3 | | |
| 2010 | Derry C | 28 | 5 | | |
| 2011 | Derry C | 24 | 2 | | |

| | | | | | |
|---|---|---|---|---|---|
| 2012 | Derry C | 29 | 11 | 86 | 21 |
| 2012-13 | York C | 4 | 0 | 4 | 0 |

**McGURK, David (D)**     **67**   **6**
H: 6 0   W: 11 08   b.Middlesbrough 30-9-82
*Source:* Scholar.

| | | | | | |
|---|---|---|---|---|---|
| 2001-02 | Darlington | 12 | 0 | | |
| 2002-03 | Darlington | 4 | 0 | | |
| 2003-04 | Darlington | 27 | 4 | | |
| 2004-05 | Darlington | 10 | 2 | | |
| 2005-06 | Darlington | 3 | 0 | 56 | 6 |
| 2012-13 | York C | 11 | 0 | 11 | 0 |

**McLAUGHLIN, Patrick (M)**     **30**   **3**
H: 6 2   W: 11 09   b.Larne 14-1-91
*Honours:* Northern Ireland Youth, Under-21.

| | | | | | |
|---|---|---|---|---|---|
| 2012-13 | York C | 30 | 3 | 30 | 3 |

**McREADY, John (M)**     **8**   **0**
H: 5 10   W: 11 07   b.South Shields 1-7-92
*Source:* Scholar.

| | | | | | |
|---|---|---|---|---|---|
| 2009-10 | Darlington | 4 | 0 | 4 | 0 |
| 2012-13 | York C | 4 | 0 | 4 | 0 |

**OYEBANJO, Lanre (D)**     **30**   **0**
H: 6 1   W: 11 04   b.Hackney 24-4-90
*Source:* Histon.

| | | | | | |
|---|---|---|---|---|---|
| 2012-13 | York C | 30 | 0 | 30 | 0 |

**PARSLOW, Daniel (D)**     **45**   **1**
H: 5 11   W: 12 05   b.Cardiff 11-9-85

| | | | | | |
|---|---|---|---|---|---|
| 2012-13 | York C | 45 | 1 | 45 | 1 |

**PLATT, Tom (M)**     **7**   **0**
H: 6 1   W: 12 13   b.Pontefract 1-10-93

| | | | | | |
|---|---|---|---|---|---|
| 2012-13 | York C | 7 | 0 | 7 | 0 |

**POTTS, Michael (M)**     **14**   **3**
H: 5 10   W: 13 08   b. 26-11-91

| | | | | | |
|---|---|---|---|---|---|
| 2012-13 | York C | 14 | 3 | 14 | 3 |

**REED, Jamie (F)**     **31**   **1**
H: 5 11   W: 11 07   b.Deeside 13-8-87
*Source:* Scholar.

| | | | | | |
|---|---|---|---|---|---|
| 2005-06 | Wrexham | 3 | 0 | | |
| 2005-06 | *Glentoran* | 7 | 0 | 7 | 0 |
| 2006-07 | Wrexham | 4 | 0 | 7 | 0 |

From Aberystwyth, Rhyl, Bangor C

| | | | | | |
|---|---|---|---|---|---|
| 2012-13 | York C | 17 | 1 | 17 | 1 |

**SMITH, Chris (D)**     **124**   **4**
H: 5 10   W: 12 05   b.Derby 30-6-81

| | | | | | |
|---|---|---|---|---|---|
| 1999-2000 | Reading | 0 | 0 | | |
| 2000-01 | Reading | 0 | 0 | | |
| 2001-02 | York C | 15 | 0 | | |
| 2002-03 | York C | 36 | 0 | | |
| 2003-04 | York C | 28 | 0 | | |

From Tamworth, Mansfield T

| | | | | | |
|---|---|---|---|---|---|
| 2012-13 | York C | 45 | 4 | 124 | 4 |

**SMITH, Jonathan (M)**     **50**   **3**
H: 6 3   W: 11 02   b.Preston 17-10-86
*Source:* Morecambe, Forest Green R, York C.

| | | | | | |
|---|---|---|---|---|---|
| 2011-12 | Swindon T | 38 | 3 | 38 | 3 |
| 2012-13 | York C | 12 | 0 | 12 | 0 |

**WALKER, Jason (F)**     **43**   **9**
H: 5 9   W: 10 13   b.Barrow 21-2-84
*Source:* Morecambe, Barrow, Luton T.

| | | | | | |
|---|---|---|---|---|---|
| 2012-13 | York C | 43 | 9 | 43 | 9 |

**Scholars**
Andrew, Daniel Paul; Archer, Joshua;
Atkinson, Michael Thomas; Banks,
Christopher James; Chamberlain, Thomas
Liam; Coates, Harry Ryan; Dickinson,
Christopher Neil; Green, James; Kelly, Reece
Andrew; Middleton, Benjamin; Middleton,
Daniel; Moncur, Robert; Murray, Cameron
Lochiel; Outerbridge, Jordan Isaiah; Smith,
Oliver Henry Canvin; Tilsley, Niall Joshua;
Weir, Benjamin.

# BLUE SQUARE PREMIER ROLL-CALL

## MANSFIELD TOWN

| Player | H | W | Birthplace | DOB | Source |
|---|---|---|---|---|---|
| Beevers, Lee (D) | 6 2 | 11 07 | Doncaster | 4/12/83 | Colchester U |
| Briscoe, Louis (F) | 6 0 | 13 06 | Burton-on-Trent | 2/4/88 | Ilkeston T |
| Clements, Chris (M) | 5 9 | 10 05 | Birmingham | 6/2/90 | Hednesford T |
| Daniel, Colin (M) | 5 11 | 11 06 | Nottingham | 15/2/88 | Macclesfield T |
| Dempster, John (D) | 6 1 | 11 06 | Kettering | 1/4/83 | Crawley T |
| Dyer, Ross (F) | 6 2 | 13 03 | Stafford | 12/5/88 | Forest Green R |
| Geohaghon, Exodus (D) | 6 5 | 11 10 | Birmingham | 27/2/85 | Kidderminster H |
| Green, Matt (F) | 6 0 | 12 09 | Bath | 22/1/87 | Oxford U |
| Hand, Jamie (M) | 6 0 | 11 08 | Uxbridge | 7/2/84 | Hayes & Yeading U |
| Howell, Anthony (M) | 6 2 | 12 13 | Nottingham | 27/5/86 | Alfreton T |
| Hutchinson, Ben (F) | 5 11 | 12 07 | Nottingham | 27/11/87 | Celtic |
| Jennings, James (D) | 5 10 | 12 00 | Manchester | 2/9/87 | Cambridge U |
| Jones, Luke (D) | 5 9 | 11 09 | Blackburn | 10/4/87 | Kidderminster H |
| Marriott, Alan (G) | 5 11 | 12 05 | Bedford | 3/9/78 | Rushden & D |
| Meikle, Lindon (F) | | | Nottingham | 21/3/88 | Eastwood T |
| Murray, Adam (M) | 5 8 | 10 12 | Birmingham | 30/9/81 | Luton T |
| Pilkington, George (D) | 5 11 | 12 05 | Rugley | 7/11/81 | Luton T |
| Redmond, Shane (G) | 6 0 | 12 10 | Dublin | 23/3/89 | Nottingham F |
| Rhead, Matt (F) | 6 4 | | Stoke | 31/5/84 | Corby T |
| Roberts, Gary (M) | 5 8 | 10 04 | Chester | 2/2/87 | Port Vale |
| Speight, Jake (F) | 5 8 | 12 09 | Sheffield | 28/9/85 | Wrexham |
| Stevenson, Lee (M) | 5 10 | 11 05 | Sheffield | 1/6/84 | Eastwood T |
| Sutton, Ritchie (D) | 6 0 | 11 05 | Stoke | 29/4/86 | Crewe Alex |
| Tafazolli, Ryan (D) | 6 5 | 12 04 | Sutton | 28/9/91 | Southampton |
| Thompson, John (D) | 6 0 | 12 01 | Dublin | 12/10/81 | Oldham Ath |
| Todd, Andrew (M) | 6 0 | 11 03 | Nottingham | 22/2/79 | Eastwood T |
| Tolley, Jamie (M) | 6 1 | 11 03 | Ludlow | 12/5/83 | Wrexham |
| Wright, Nick (M) | 6 2 | 12 00 | Birmingham | 25/11/87 | Kidderminster H |

## NEWPORT COUNTY

| Player | H | W | Birthplace | DOB | Source |
|---|---|---|---|---|---|
| Anthony, Byron (D) | 6 0 | 11 06 | Newport | 20/9/84 | Hereford U |
| Boateng, Michael (D) | | | Peckham | 17/8/91 | Sutton U |
| Crow, Danny (F) | 5 10 | 11 00 | Great Yarmouth | 26/1/86 | Luton T |
| Donnelly, Scott (M) | 5 8 | 11 10 | Hammersmith | 25/12/87 | Farnborough T |
| Flynn, Michael (M) | 5 10 | 13 04 | Newport | 17/10/80 | Bradford C |
| Griffiths, Rhys (F) | 6 3 | 13 12 | Cardiff | 1/3/80 | Plymouth Arg |
| Harris, Jake (M) | 5 8 | 11 03 | Weston-super-Mare | 28/10/90 | Weston-super-Mare |
| Hughes, Andrew (D) | 6 0 | 11 11 | Cardiff | 5/6/92 | Cardiff C |
| James, Tony (D) | 5 10 | 13 06 | Cardiff | 9/10/78 | Burton Alb |
| Louis, Jefferson (F) | 6 2 | 15 00 | Harrow | 22/2/79 | Lincoln C |
| Perry, Joe (G) | 6 0 | 12 07 | Caerphilly | 29/3/92 | Merthyr T |
| Pidgeley, Lenny (G) | 6 4 | 14 09 | Twickenham | 7/2/84 | Exeter C |
| Pipe, David (M) | 5 9 | 12 01 | Caerphilly | 5/11/83 | Bristol R |
| Porter, Max (M) | 5 10 | 12 04 | Hornchurch | 29/6/87 | Barnet |
| Sandell, Andy (D) | 5 11 | 11 09 | Swindon | 8/9/83 | Aldershot T |
| Swallow, Ben (M) | 5 8 | 10 10 | Barry | 20/10/89 | York C |
| Thomson, Jake (M) | 5 11 | 11 04 | Portsmouth | 12/5/89 | Kettering T |
| Washington, Conor (F) | | | Chatham | 18/5/92 | St Ives T |
| Willmott, Robbie (M) | 5 9 | 12 00 | Harlow | 16/5/90 | Cambridge U |
| Yakubu, Ismail (D) | 6 1 | 13 09 | Kano | 8/4/85 | AFC Wimbledon |

# ENGLISH LEAGUE PLAYERS – INDEX

# NATIONAL LIST OF REFEREES FOR SEASON 2013–14

## REFEREES

Adcock, JG (James) – Nottinghamshire
Atkinson, M (Martin) – West Yorkshire
Attwell, SB (Stuart) – Warwickshire
Berry, CJ (Carl) – Surrey
Bond, D (Darren) – Lancashire
Boyeson, C (Carl) – East Yorkshire
Bratt, S (Stephen) – West Midlands
Breakspear, C (Charles) – Surrey
Brown, M (Mark) – East Yorkshire
Bull, M (Michael) – Essex
Clark, R (Richard) – Northumberland
Clattenburg, M (Mark) – County Durham
Collins, LM (Lee) – Surrey
Coote, D (David) – Nottinghamshire
Davies, A (Andy) – Hampshire
Deadman, D (Darren) – Cambridgeshire
Dean, ML (Mike) – Wirral
Dowd, P (Phil) – Staffordshire
Drysdale, D (Darren) – Lincolnshire
Duncan, S (Scott) – Northumberland
D'Urso, AP (Andy) – Essex
East, R (Roger) – Wiltshire
Eltringham, G (Geoff) – County Durham
Foy, CJ (Chris) – Merseyside
Friend, KA (Kevin) – Leicestershire
Gibbs, PN (Phil) – West Midlands
Graham F (Fred) – Essex
Haines, A (Andy) – Tyne & Wear
Harrington, T (Tony) – Cleveland
Haywood, M (Mark) – West Yorkshire
Heywood, M (Mark) – Cheshire
Hill, K (Keith) – Hertfordshire
Hooper, SA (Simon) – Wiltshire
Horwood, G (Graham) – Bedfordshire
Ilderton, EL (Eddie) – Tyne & Wear
Jones, MJ (Michael) – Cheshire
Kettle, TM (Trevor) – Rutland
Langford, O (Oliver) – West Midlands
Lewis, RL (Rob) – Shropshire
Linington, JJ (James) – Isle of Wight
Madley, AJ (Andy) – West Yorkshire
Madley, RJ (Bobby) – West Yorkshire
Malone, BJ (Brendan) – Wiltshire
Marriner, AM (André) – West Midlands
Martin, S (Stephen) – Staffordshire
Mason, LS (Lee) – Lancashire
Mathieson, SW (Scott) – Cheshire
Miller, NS (Nigel) – County Durham
Miller, P (Pat) – Bedfordshire
Mohareb, D (Dean) – Cheshire
Moss, J (Jon) – West Yorkshire
Naylor, MA (Michael) – South Yorkshire
Oliver, M (Michael) – Northumberland
Pawson, CL (Craig) – South Yorkshire
Phillips, DJ (David) –West Sussex
Probert, LW (Lee) – Wiltshire
Robinson, T (Tim) – West Sussex
Rushton, SJ (Steve) – Staffordshire
Russell, MP (Mick) – Hertfordshire
Salisbury, G (Graham) – Lancashire
Sarginson, CD (Chris) – Staffordshire
Scott, GD (Graham) – Oxfordshire
Sheldrake, D (Darren) – Surrey
Shoebridge, RL (Rob) – Derbyshire
Simpson, J (Jeremy) – Lancashire
Stockbridge, S (Seb) – Tyne & Wear
Stroud, KP (Keith) – Hampshire
Sutton, GJ (Gary) – Lincolnshire
Swarbrick, ND (Neil) – Lancashire
Taylor, A (Anthony) – Cheshire
Tierney, P Paul) – Lancashire
Ward, GL (Gavin) – Surrey
Waugh, J (Jock) – South Yorkshire
Webb, D (David) – County Durham
Webb, HM (Howard) – South Yorkshire
Whitestone, D (Dean) – Northamptonshire
Williamson, IG (Iain) – Berkshire
Woolmer, KA (Andy) – Northamptonshire
Wright, KK (Kevin) – Cambridgeshire

## ASSISTANT REFEREES

Akers, C (Chris) – South Yorkshire
Amey, JR (Justin) – Dorset
Amphlett, MJ (Marvyn) – Worcestershire
Astley, MA (Mark) – Manchester
Atkin, R (Robert) – Lincolnshire
Atkin, RT (Ryan) – London
Avent, D (David) – Northamptonshire
Aylott, A (Andrew) – Bedfordshire
Backhouse, A (Anthony) – Cumbria
Bankes, P (Peter) – Merseyside
Barratt, W (Wayne) – Worcestershire
Barrow, SJ (Simon) – Staffordshire
Bartlett, R (Richard) – Cheshire
Beck, SP (Simon) – Bedfordshire
Bennett, A (Andrew) – Devon
Bennett, SP (Simon) – Staffordshire
Benton, DK (David) – South Yorkshire
Beswick, G (Gary) – County Durham
Betts, L (Lee) – Norfolk
Bingham, M (Michael) – Warwickshire
Blackledge, M (Mike) – Cambridgeshire
Blunden, D (Darren) – Kent
Bristow, M (Matthew) – Manchester
Bromley, A (Adam) – Devon
Brook, C (Carl) – East Sussex
Brooks, J (John) – Leicestershire
Brown, S (Simon) – Worcestershire
Bryan, DS (Dave) – Lincolnshire
Bull, W (William) – Hampshire
Buonassisi, M (Mathew) – Northamptonshire
Burt, S (Stuart) – Northamptonshire
Busby, J (John) – Oxfordshire
Bushell, DD (David) – London
Butler, S (Stuart) – Kent
Cann, DJ (Darren) – Norfolk
Child, SA (Stephen) – Kent
Clark, J (Joseph) – West Midlands
Clayton, A (Alan) – Cheshire
Clayton, S (Simon) – County Durham
Coggins, A (Anthony) – Oxfordshire
Collin, J (Jake) – Liverpool
Cook, D (Daniel) – Hampshire
Cook, P (Paul) – East Yorkshire
Cooper, IJ (Ian) – Kent
Cooper, N (Nicholas) – Suffolk
Copeland, SJ (Steven) – Merseyside
Coy, M (Martin) – Durham
Cropp, B (Barry) – Lancashire
Crouch, IJ (Ian) – Kent
Crysell, A (Adam) – Essex
Curry, PE (Paul) – Northumberland
D'Aguilar, M (Michael) – Staffordshire
Dale, A (Alan) – Suffolk
Daly, SDJ (Stephen) – Middlesex
Davies, N (Neil) – Merseyside
Davison, PA (Paul) – Cleveland
Degnarain, A (Ashvin) – London
Denton, MJ (Michael) – Lancashire
Dermott, P (Philip) – Lancashire
Derrien, M (Mark) – Dorset
Dicicco, M (Matthew) – Cleveland
Dudley, IA (Ian) – Nottinghamshire
Duncan, M (Mark) – Cheshire
Dwyer, M (Mark) – West Yorkshire
Eaton, D (Derek) – Gloucestershire
Ellis, R (Rob) – West Midlands
England, DJH (Darren) – South Yorkshire
Evans, K (Karl) – Lancashire
Farries, J (John) – Oxfordshire
Fearn, AE (Amy) – Leicestershire
Finch, S (Steven) – Southampton
Fissenden, I (Ian) – Kent
Fitch, C (Carl) – Suffolk

Flynn, J (John) – Wiltshire
Foley, MJ (Matt) – London
Ford, D (Declan) – Lincolnshire
Fox, A (Andrew) – Warwickshire
Fyvie, G (Graham) – Tyne & Wear
Ganfield, RS (Ron) – Somerset
Garratt, AM (Andy) – West Midlands
Garratt, S (Sarah) – West Midlands
George, M (Mike) – Norfolk
Gibbons, N (Nick) – Lancashire
Gillett, A (Adrian) – Buckinghamshire
Gooch, P (Peter) – Lancashire
Gordon, B (Barry) – County Durham
Graham, P (Paul) – Manchester
Gratton, D (Danny) – Staffordshire
Greenhalgh, N (Nick) – Lancashire
Greenwood, AH (Alf) – North Yorkshire
Griffiths, M (Mark) – South Yorkshire
Grunnill, W (Wayne) – East Yorkshire
Hair, NA (Neil) – Cambridgeshire
Halliday, A (Andy) – North Yorkshire
Handley, D (Darren) – Lancashire
Harris, P (Paul) – Kent
Hart, G (Glen) – County Durham
Hatzidakis, C (Constantine) – Kent
Haycock, KW (Ken) – West Yorkshire
Hendley, AR (Andy) – West Midlands
Hicks, C (Craig) – Surrey
Hillier, J (Jake) – Hertfordshire
Hilton, G (Gary) – Lancashire
Hobbis, N (Nick) – West Midlands
Hobday, P (Paul) – West Midlands
Hodges, R (Robert) – Buckinghamshire
Hodskinson, P (Paul) – Lancashire
Holderness, BC (Barry) – Essex
Holmes, AR (Adrian) – West Yorkshire
Hopkins, AJ (Adam) – Devon
Hopkins, JD (John) – Essex
Howes, M (Mark) – Birmingham
Hudson, S (Shaun) – Tyne & Wear
Hull, J (Joe) – Cheshire
Hulme, R (Richard) – Somerset
Hunt, J (Jonathan) – Liverpool
Hussin, I (Ian) – Liverpool
Hutchinson, AD (Andrew) – Cheshire
Huxtable, B (Brett) – Devon
Hyde, RA (Robert) – London
Ihringova, A (Sasa) – Shropshire
Jerden, GJN (Gary) – Essex
Johnson, KA (Kevin) – Somerset
Johnson, RL (Ryan) – Manchester
Jones, MT (Mark) – Nottinghamshire
Jones, RJ (Robert) – Merseyside
Joyce, R (Ross) – Cleveland
Kane, G (Graham) – East Sussex
Kavanagh, C (Chris) – Lancashire
Kaye, E (Elliott) – Essex

Kelly, P (Paul) – Kent
Kendall, R (Richard) – Bedfordshire
Kettlewell, PT (Paul) – Lancashire
Khatib, B (Billy) – County Durham
Kinseley, N (Nick) – Essex
Kirkup, PJ (Peter) – Northamptonshire
Knapp, SC (Simon) – Bristol
Knowles, CJ (Chris) – Northamptonshire
Laver, AA (Andrew) – Hampshire
Law, GC (Geoff) – Leicestershire
Law, J (John) – Worcestershire
Lawson, KD (Keith) – South Humberside
Leach, D (Daniel) – Oxfordshire
Ledger, S (Scott) – South Yorkshire
Lennard, HW (Harry) – East Sussex
Liddle, G (Geoff) – County Durham
Linden, W (Wes) – Middlesex
Long, SJ (Simon) – Devon
Lucas, S (Simeon) – Lancashire
Lugg, N (Nigel) – Surrey
Lymer, C (Colin) – Hampshire
McCallum, DA (Dave) – Tyne & Wear
McDonough, M (Mick) – Tyne & Wear
McGrath, M (Matt) – East Yorkshire
Mackay, R (Rob) – Bedfordshire
Magill, JP (John) – Essex
Mainwaring, J (James) – Lancashire
Markham, DR (Danny) – Tyne & Wear
Marsden, PR (Paul) – Lancashire
Martin, RJ (Richard) – Weston-super-Mare
Massey, SL (Sian) – West Midlands
Mather, S (Simon) – Manchester
Matthews, A (Adam) – Gloucestershire
Mattocks, KJ (Kevin) – Lancashire
Meeson, DP (Daniel) – Staffordshire
Mellor, JM (Mark) – Hertfordshire
Merchant, R (Rob) – Staffordshire
Meredith, S (Steven) – Nottinghamshire
Metcalfe, RL (Lee) – Lancashire
Muge, G (Gavin) – Bedfordshire
Mullarkey, M (Mike) – Devon
Mulraine, K (Kevin) – Cumbria
Murphy, N (Nigel) – Nottinghamshire
Newbold, AM (Andy) – Leicestershire
Nield, T (Tom) – West Yorkshire
Norcott, WG (Wade) – Essex
Nunn, AJ (Adam) – Wiltshire
O'Brien, J (John) – London
O'Donnell, CJ (Chris) – Bedfordshire
Oldham, SA (Scott) – Lancashire
Parry, MJ (Matthew) – Liverpool
Peart, T (Tony) – North Yorkshire
Perry, MS (Marc) – West Midlands
Plane, S (Steven) – Worcestershire
Plowright, DP (David) – Nottinghamshire
Pollock, R (Bob) – Merseyside
Porter, W (Wayne) – Lincolnshire

Pottage, M (Mark) – Dorset
Powell, CI (Chris) – Dorset
Purkiss, S (Sam) – London
Radford, N (Neil) – Worcestershire
Ramsey, T (Thomas) – Essex
Rathbone, I (Ian) – Northamptonshire
Rees, P (Paul) – Somerset
Richardson, D (David) – West Yorkshire
Robathan, DM (Daniel) – Surrey
Roberts, B (Bob) – Lancashire
Rock, DK (David) – Hertfordshire
Rogers, T (Thomas) – County Durham
Ross, SJ (Stephen) – Lincolnshire
Rubery, SP (Steve) – Essex
Russell, GR (Geoff) – Northamptonshire
Russell, M (Mark) – Somerset
Salisbury, M (Michael) – Lancashire
Saliy, O (Oleksandr) – Middlesex
Sannerude, A (Adrian) – Suffolk
Scholes, MS (Mark) – Buckinghamshire
Scregg, AJ (Andrew) – Liverpool
Sharp, N (Neil) – Cleveland
Siddall, I (Iain) – Lancashire
Slaughter, A (Ashley) – West Sussex
Smallwood, W (William) – Cheshire
Smart, E (Edward) – West Midlands
Smith, M (Michael) – Essex
Smith, N (Nigel) – Derbyshire
Storrie, D (David) – West Yorkshire
Strain, D (Darren) – Cheshire
Street, DR (Duncan) – West Yorkshire
Stretton, GS (Guy) – Leicestershire
Swabey, L (Lee) – Devon
Tankard, A (Anthony) – South Yorkshire
Taylor, G (Grant) – Warwickshire
Thompson, PI (Paul) – Derbyshire
Toner, B (Ben) – Lancashire
Tranter, A (Adrian) – Dorset
Treleaven, D (Dean) – West Sussex
Turner, A (Andrew) – Devon
Tyas, J (Jason) – West Yorkshire
Venamore, L (Lee) – Kent
Webb, MP (Michael) – Surrey
West, RJ (Richard) – East Yorkshire
Whiteley, J (Jason) – West Yorkshire
Whitton, RP (Rob) – Essex
Wigglesworth, RJ (Richard) – South Yorkshire
Wilkes, MJ (Matthew) – West Midlands
Wilson, J (James) – Cheshire
Wilson, M (Marc) – Cambridgeshire
Wood, T (Tim) – Gloucestershire
Woolford, DM (David) – Hampshire
Wootton, R (Ricky) – West Yorkshire
Wright, P (Peter) – Merseyside
Yates, O (Oliver) – Staffordshire
Young, A (Alan) – Cambridgeshire

# TRANSFERS 2012–13

| JUNE 2012 TRANSFERS | From | To | Fee in £ |
|---|---|---|---|
| 18 Ainsworth, Lionel | Shrewsbury T | Rotherham U | Undisclosed |
| 19 Akpro, Jean-Louis A. | Rochdale | Tranmere R | Free |
| 29 Andrews, Keith | WBA | Bolton W | Free |
| 28 Baudry, Mathieu | Bournemouth | Leyton Orient | Free |
| 8 Bean, Marcus | Brentford | Colchester U | Free |
| 15 Bialkowski, Bartosz | Southampton | Notts Co | Free |
| 27 Blake, Robbie | Bolton W | Doncaster R | Free |
| 25 Branston, Guy | Bradford C | Aldershot T | Free |
| 8 Brown, Connor | Sheffield U | Oldham Ath | Free |
| 28 Brown, Jordan | West Ham U | Barnet | Free |
| 14 Brown, Troy | Rotherham U | Aldershot T | Free |
| 7 Bullock, Lee | Bradford C | York C | Free |
| 21 Cadamarteri, Danny | Huddersfield T | Carlisle U | Free |
| 8 Cavanagh, Peter | Fleetwood T | Rochdale | Free |
| 18 Collins, James | Shrewsbury T | Swindon T | Free |
| 27 Cotterill, David | Barnsley | Doncaster R | Free |
| 14 Cowler, Sam | West Ham U | Barnet | Undisclosed |
| 28 Cruise, Tom | Arsenal | Torquay U | Free |
| 20 Diame, Mohamed | Wigan Ath | West Ham U | Free |
| 5 Diamond, Zander | Oldham Ath | Burton Alb | Free |
| 20 Doble, Ryan | Southampton | Shrewsbury T | Free |
| 19 Drury, Adam | Norwich C | Leeds U | Free |
| 11 Edwards, Mike | Notts Co | Carlisle U | Free |
| 27 Ellis, Mark | Torquay U | Crewe Alex | Undisclosed |
| 9 Etuhu, Kelvin | Portsmouth | Barnsley | Free |
| 13 Forbes, Terrell | Leyton Orient | Chesterfield | Free |
| 29 Foster, Benjamin A. | Birmingham C | WBA | Undisclosed |
| 24 Gillespie, Steven | Colchester U | Fleetwood T | Undisclosed |
| 1 Grabban, Lewis | Rotherham U | Bournemouth | Undisclosed |
| 14 Gray, David | Preston NE | Stevenage | Free |
| 29 Guthrie, Danny | Newcastle U | Reading | Free |
| 11 Harris, Louis | Wolverhampton W | AFC Wimbledon | Free |
| 7 Harrison, Danny | Rotherham U | Tranmere R | Free |
| 28 Hayter, James | Doncaster R | Yeovil T | Free |
| 21 Hurst, Kevan | Walsall | Southend U | Free |
| 18 Johnson, Andrew | Fulham | QPR | Free |
| 7 Johnson, Damien | Plymouth Arg | Fleetwood T | Free |
| 26 Johnson, Oli | Oxford U | York C | Free |
| 20 Kennedy, Callum | Swindon T | Scunthorpe U | Free |
| 20 Kuszczak, Tomasz | Manchester U | Brighton & HA | Free |
| 14 Lancashire, Olly | Walsall | Aldershot T | Free |
| 26 Leacock, Dean | Leyton Orient | Notts Co | Free |
| 21 Liddle, Gary | Hartlepool U | Notts Co | Free |
| 11 Long, Stacy | Stevenage | AFC Wimbledon | Free |
| 21 Maguire, Christopher | Derby Co | Sheffield W | Undisclosed |
| 9 Mattock, Joe | WBA | Sheffield W | Free |
| 28 McAllister, Jamie | Bristol C | Yeovil T | Free |
| 27 McCrory, Damien | Dagenham & R | Burton Alb | Free |
| 21 McEveley, Jay | Barnsley | Swindon T | Free |
| 19 Mellis, Jacob | Chelsea | Barnsley | Free |
| 29 Meredith, James | York C | Bradford C | Free |
| 19 Miller, George | Preston NE | Accrington S | Free |
| 21 Miller, Tommy | Huddersfield T | Swindon T | Free |
| 25 Murphy, Danny | Fulham | Blackburn R | Free |
| 22 Mutch, Jordon | Birmingham C | Cardiff C | Undisclosed |
| 21 Navarro, Alan | Brighton & HA | Swindon T | Free |
| 18 Nelsen, Ryan | Tottenham H | QPR | Free |
| 29 Norwood, Oliver | Manchester U | Huddersfield T | Free |
| 22 Nouble, Frank | West Ham U | Wolverhampton W | Free |
| 18 Olejnik, Bobby | Torquay U | Peterborough U | Undisclosed |
| 13 Parkin, Jon | Cardiff C | Fleetwood T | Free |
| 28 Poke, Michael | Brighton & HA | Torquay U | Free |
| 18 Roberts, Gary | Huddersfield T | Swindon T | Free |
| 10 Rodriguez, Jay E. | Burnley | Southampton | Undisclosed |
| 8 Sadler, Mat | Walsall | Crawley T | Free |
| 25 Scannell, Sean | Crystal Palace | Huddersfield T | Undisclosed |
| 12 Showunmi, Enoch | Tranmere R | Notts Co | Free |
| 6 Swanson, Danny | Dundee United | Peterborough U | Free |
| 14 Syers, David | Bradford C | Doncaster R | Free |
| 28 Symes, Michael | Bournemouth | Leyton Orient | Free |
| 22 Tank, Jamie | Walsall | Wolverhampton W | Undisclosed |
| 18 Taylor, Daniel | Newcastle U | Oldham Ath | Free |
| 26 Wallace, James R. | Everton | Tranmere R | Undisclosed |
| 30 Whittaker, Steven | Rangers | Norwich C | Free |
| 18 Williams, Andy | Yeovil T | Swindon T | Free |
| 14 Williams, George | Milton Keynes D | Fulham | Undisclosed |
| 20 Wilson, Laurence | Morecambe | Rotherham U | Free |

## JULY 2012 TRANSFERS

| | | | |
|---|---|---|---|
| 1 Adams, Nicholas | Rochdale | Crawley T | Undisclosed |
| 9 Addison, Miles V.E. | Derby Co | Bournemouth | Undisclosed |
| 27 Agard, Kieran | Yeovil T | Rotherham U | Free |
| 1 Alexander, Gary | Brentford | Crawley T | Undisclosed |
| 20 Allen, Charlie | Notts Co | Gillingham | Free |
| 18 Allsop, Ryan | Millwall | Leyton Orient | Free |
| 30 Almunia, Manuel | Arsenal | Watford | Free |
| 5 Alnwick, Ben | Tottenham H | Barnsley | Free |
| 2 Amankwaah, Kevin | Rochdale | Exeter C | Free |
| 14 Ambrose, Darren | Crystal Palace | Birmingham C | Undisclosed |
| 1 Amoo, David | Liverpool | Preston NE | Free |
| 26 Anderson, Paul | Nottingham F | Bristol C | Free |
| 3 Angol, Lee | Tottenham H | Wycombe W | Undisclosed |
| 6 Anyon, Joe | Lincoln C | Shrewsbury T | Free |
| 1 Archibald-Henville, Troy | Exeter C | Swindon T | Undisclosed |
| 1 Arnason, Kari | Aberdeen | Rotherham U | Free |
| 11 Arquin, Yoann | Hereford | Notts Co | Free |
| 6 Artell, David | Crewe Alex | Port Vale | Free |
| 3 Atkinson, Will | Hull C | Bradford C | Free |
| 2 Baldwin, Pat | Southend U | Exeter C | Free |
| 17 Balkestein, Pim | Brentford | AFC Wimbledon | Free |
| 20 Ball, David M. | Peterborough U | Fleetwood T | Undisclosed |
| 31 Bell, Lee | Crewe Alex | Burton Alb | Free |
| 1 Bennett, Rhys | Bolton W | Rochdale | Free |
| 2 Best, Leon J. | Newcastle U | Blackburn R | 3,000,000 |
| 6 Bigirimana, Gael | Coventry C | Newcastle U | Undisclosed |
| 5 Black, Paul | Oldham Ath | Tranmere R | Free |
| 2 Blanchett, Danny | Burton Alb | York C | Free |
| 5 Bodin, Billy | Swindon T | Torquay U | Undisclosed |
| 6 Bostwick, Michael | Stevenage | Peterborough U | Undisclosed |
| 23 Brito E Silva, Toni | Liverpool | Barnsley | Free |
| 30 Bruce, Alex | Leeds U | Hull C | Free |
| 1 Buchanan, David | Tranmere R | Preston NE | Free |
| 1 Burgess, Ben | Notts Co | Tranmere R | Free |
| 3 Butterfield, Jacob | Barnsley | Norwich C | Tribunal |
| 27 Byrne, Cliff | Scunthorpe U | Oldham Ath | Free |
| 3 Campbell-Ryce, Jamal | Bristol C | Notts Co | Free |
| 1 Cansdell-Sherriff, Shane | Shrewsbury T | Preston NE | Undisclosed |
| 9 Caprice, Jake | Crystal Palace | Blackpool | Free |
| 9 Chambers, Luke | Nottingham F | Ipswich T | Free |
| 26 Chippendale, Aidan | Huddersfield T | Accrington S | Free |
| 5 Clark, Luke | Preston NE | Accrington S | Free |
| 18 Clarke, Nathan | Huddersfield T | Leyton Orient | Free |
| 23 Clarke-Harris, Jonson | Coventry C | Peterborough U | Free |
| 5 Clayton, Adam | Leeds U | Huddersfield T | Undisclosed |
| 5 Clucas, Seanan | Preston NE | Bristol R | Free |
| 19 Clyne, Nathaniel | Crystal Palace | Southampton | Undisclosed |
| 25 Collins, Daniel L. | Stoke C | Nottingham F | Undisclosed |
| 25 Collins, Danny | Stoke C | Nottingham F | Undisclosed |
| 20 Connell, Alan | Swindon T | Bradford C | Free |
| 9 Connolly, Mark | Bolton W | Crawley T | Free |
| 9 Cook, Jordan | Sunderland | Charlton Ath | Free |
| 13 Coutts, Paul | Preston NE | Derby Co | Undisclosed |
| 13 Craig, Tony A. | Millwall | Brentford | Undisclosed |
| 3 Cresswell, Ryan | Rotherham U | Southend U | Free |
| 2 Cuellar, Carlos | Aston Villa | Sunderland | Free |
| 5 Cunningham, Gregory R. | Manchester C | Bristol C | Undisclosed |
| 31 Cureton, Jamie | Leyton Orient | Exeter C | Free |
| 5 Darby, Stephen | Liverpool | Bradford C | Free |
| 1 Davies, Andrew | Stoke C | Bradford C | Free |
| 4 Davies, Arron | Northampton T | Exeter C | Free |
| 6 Davis, Steven | Rangers | Southampton | Free |
| 1 Demontagnac, Ishmel | Notts Co | Northampton T | Free |
| 1 Diame, Mohamed | Wigan Ath | West Ham U | Free |
| 1 Dixon, Paul | Dundee United | Huddersfield T | Free |
| 3 Doherty, Gary | Charlton Ath | Wycombe W | Undisclosed |
| 24 Downes, Aaron | Chesterfield | Torquay U | Free |
| 6 Duffy, Richard | Exeter C | Port Vale | Free |
| 1 Dunne, James | Exeter C | Stevenage | Undisclosed |
| 12 Eastwood, Freddy | Coventry C | Southend U | Free |
| 29 Eckersley, Tom | Bolton W | Accrington S | Free |
| 25 Edgar, Anthony | Yeovil T | Barnet | Free |
| 3 El, Alagui F. | Falkirk | Brentford | Free |
| 4 Elford-Alliyu, Lateef | WBA | Bury | Free |
| 2 Elliott, Stephen | Hearts | Coventry C | Free |
| 20 Faye, Abdoulaye | West Ham U | Hull C | Free |
| 4 Fleck, John | Rangers | Coventry C | Free |
| 26 Fortune, Jonathan | Exeter C | Barnet | Free |
| 27 Friend, George | Doncaster R | Middlesbrough | Undisclosed |
| 17 Futacs, Marko | Portsmouth | Leicester C | Free |
| 1 Gardner, Anthony | Crystal Palace | Sheffield W | Free |
| 19 Gazzaniga, Paulo D. | Gillingham | Southampton | Undisclosed |
| 4 Gilmartin, Rene | Watford | Plymouth Arg | Free |
| 1 Grabban, Lewis | Rotherham U | Bournemouth | Undisclosed |
| 1 Grant, Anthony | Southend U | Stevenage | Free |

| | | | |
|---|---|---|---|
| 24 Gray, Andy | Barnsley | Leeds U | Free |
| 1 Green, Paul | Derby Co | Leeds U | Free |
| 1 Green, Robert | West Ham U | QPR | Free |
| 9 Grella, Mike | Bury | Scunthorpe U | Free |
| 2 Grounds, Jonathan | Middlesbrough | Oldham Ath | Free |
| 23 Guedioura, Adlene | Wolverhampton W | Nottingham F | Undisclosed |
| 17 Gunter, Christopher R. | Nottingham F | Reading | Undisclosed |
| 6 Haber, Marcus | St Johnstone | Stevenage | Undisclosed |
| 3 Hackett, Chris | Millwall | Northampton T | Free |
| 27 Halford, Gregory | Portsmouth | Nottingham F | Undisclosed |
| 1 Hall, Asa | Oxford U | Shrewsbury T | Free |
| 30 Hall, Fitz | QPR | Watford | Free |
| 28 Harding, Daniel A. | Southampton | Nottingham F | Undisclosed |
| 27 Heaton, Tom | Cardiff C | Bristol C | Free |
| 4 Hemmings, Ashley | Wolverhampton W | Walsall | Free |
| 30 Hill, Matt | Blackpool | Sheffield U | Free |
| 18 Hills, Lee | Crystal Palace | Stevenage | Free |
| 1 Hird, Sam | Doncaster R | Chesterfield | Free |
| 27 Hoilett, Junior | Blackburn R | QPR | To be determined |
| 16 Holden, Dean | Rochdale | Walsall | Free |
| 1 Holmes, Lee | Southampton | Preston NE | Free |
| 16 Holness, Marcus | Rochdale | Burton Alb | Free |
| 11 Howard, Steve | Leicester C | Hartlepool U | Free |
| 10 Hoyte, Gavin | Arsenal | Dagenham & R | Free |
| 27 Hyde, Jake | Dundee | Barnet | Free |
| 1 Jaaskelainen, Jussi | Bolton W | West Ham U | Free |
| 1 Jacobs, Michael | Northampton T | Derby Co | Undisclosed |
| 18 James, Lloyd | Colchester U | Leyton Orient | Free |
| 1 Jarvis, Ryan | Walsall | Torquay U | Free |
| 9 Ji-sung, Park | Manchester U | QPR | 2,000,000 |
| 1 Johnson, Andy | Fulham | QPR | Free |
| 11 Jones, Billy | Exeter C | Cheltenham T | Free |
| 1 Jones, Darren | Aldershot T | Shrewsbury T | Free |
| 1 Jones, Gary | Rochdale | Bradford C | Free |
| 1 Jones, Paul | Peterborough U | Crawley T | Free |
| 31 Jones, Rob | Sheffield W | Doncaster R | Free |
| 30 Kenneth, Gary | Dundee United | Bristol R | Free |
| 10 Kenny, Patrick J. | QPR | Leeds U | Undisclosed |
| 19 Keogh, Richard J. | Coventry C | Derby Co | Undisclosed |
| 5 Kilbane, Kevin | Hull C | Coventry C | Free |
| 1 Kirkland, Chris | Wigan Ath | Sheffield W | Free |
| 9 Labadie, Joss | Tranmere R | Notts Co | Free |
| 1 Laird, Scott | Stevenage | Preston NE | Free |
| 1 Leadbitter, Grant | Ipswich T | Middlesbrough | Free |
| 1 Lee, Kieran | Oldham Ath | Sheffield W | Free |
| 1 Lewis, Joe | Peterborough U | Cardiff C | Free |
| 18 Liddle, Michael | Sunderland | Accrington S | Undisclosed |
| 1 Lillis, Josh | Scunthorpe U | Rochdale | Free |
| 19 Loach, Scott J. | Watford | Ipswich T | Undisclosed |
| 4 Lockwood, Adam | Doncaster R | Bury | Free |
| 3 Logan, Richard | Exeter C | Wycombe W | Free |
| 16 Lonergan, Andrew | Leeds U | Bolton W | Undisclosed |
| 9 Lovenkrands, Peter | Newcastle U | Birmingham C | Free |
| 6 Lowton, Matthew | Sheffield U | Aston Villa | Undisclosed |
| 11 Lynch, Joel | Nottingham F | Huddersfield T | Free |
| 17 Mariappa, Adrian J. | Watford | Reading | Undisclosed |
| 4 Marshall, Marcus | Rotherham U | Bury | Free |
| 1 Marsh-Brown, Keanu | Oldham Ath | Yeovil T | Free |
| 27 Mawene, Youl | Aberdeen | Fleetwood T | Free |
| 1 Maxwell, Chris | Wrexham | Fleetwood T | Free |
| 1 McArdle, Rory | Aberdeen | Bradford C | Free |
| 30 McCabe, Rhys | Rangers | Sheffield W | Free |
| 1 McCartney, George | Sunderland | West Ham U | Undisclosed |
| 1 McEveley, James | Barnsley | Swindon T | Free |
| 2 McIntyre, Kevin | Accrington S | Rochdale | Free |
| 21 McLaughlin, Conor | Preston NE | Fleetwood T | Free |
| 30 McMahon, Tony | Middlesbrough | Sheffield U | Free |
| 6 Mendez-Laing, Nathaniel | Wolverhampton W | Peterborough U | Undisclosed |
| 27 Miller, Shaun R. | Crewe Alex | Sheffield U | Undisclosed |
| 3 Mills, Matthew C. | Leicester C | Bolton W | Undisclosed |
| 31 Mirfin, David | Watford | Scunthorpe U | Free |
| 1 Monakana, Jeffrey | Arsenal | Preston NE | Free |
| 26 Mooney, Jason | Wycombe W | Tranmere R | Free |
| 1 Morris, Jody | St Johnstone | Bristol C | Free |
| 16 Morrison, Clinton | Sheffield W | Colchester U | Free |
| 1 Mousinho, John | Stevenage | Preston NE | Free |
| 12 Mullins, Hayden I. | Portsmouth | Birmingham C | Free |
| 2 Murphy, Darren | Stevenage | Port Vale | Free |
| 2 Myrie-Williams, Jennison | Stevenage | Port Vale | Free |
| 4 Naismith, Steven | Rangers | Everton | Free |
| 1 Nardiello, Daniel | Exeter C | Rotherham U | Free |
| 6 Neal, Chris | Shrewsbury T | Port Vale | Free |
| 1 Nelsen, Ryan | Tottenham H | QPR | Free |
| 20 Nelson, Stuart | Notts Co | Gillingham | Free |
| 4 N'Gala, Bondz | Yeovil T | Stevenage | Undisclosed |
| 1 Nicholls, Alex | Walsall | Northampton T | Free |

| | | | |
|---|---|---|---|
| 13 Nicholson, Barry | Preston NE | Fleetwood T | Free |
| 13 Noble, David | Exeter C | Rotherham U | Free |
| 4 Norburn, Oliver | Leicester C | Bristol R | Free |
| 27 Norris, David | Portsmouth | Leeds U | Free |
| 1 Norwood, Oliver J. | Manchester U | Huddersfield T | Undisclosed |
| 19 Nurse, Jon | Dagenham & R | Barnet | Free |
| 31 Oakley, Matt | Leicester C | Exeter C | Free |
| 1 O'Connor, Michael | Scunthorpe U | Rotherham U | Free |
| 1 Odejayi, Kayode | Colchester U | Rotherham U | Free |
| 26 O'Kane, Eunan | Torquay U | Bournemouth | Undisclosed |
| 1 Olejnik, Robert | Torquay U | Peterborough U | Undisclosed |
| 3 Oli, Dennis | Gillingham | Wycombe W | Undisclosed |
| 13 Osborne, Karleigh | Brentford | Millwall | Free |
| 20 Osbourne, Isaiah | Hibernian | Blackpool | Free |
| 5 Otsemobor, Jon | Sheffield W | Milton Keynes D | Free |
| 9 Park, Ji-Sung | Manchester U | QPR | 2,000,000 |
| 2 Parnaby, Stuart | Birmingham C | Middlesbrough | Free |
| 9 Parry, Paul | Preston NE | Shrewsbury T | Free |
| 30 Pearson, Matty | Blackburn R | Rochdale | Free |
| 31 Pienaar, Steven | Tottenham H | Everton | 4,500,000 |
| 1 Platt, Clive | Coventry C | Northampton T | Undisclosed |
| 2 Porter, George | Leyton Orient | Burnley | 90,000 |
| 1 Powell, Nicholas W. | Crewe Alex | Manchester U | Undisclosed |
| 2 Rafferty, Joe | Liverpool | Rochdale | Free |
| 2 Ralph, Nathan | Peterborough U | Yeovil T | Free |
| 24 Reid, Craig | Stevenage | Aldershot T | Undisclosed |
| 1 Reid, Reuben | Oldham Ath | Yeovil T | Free |
| 9 Ribeiro, Christian | Bristol C | Scunthorpe U | Free |
| 1 Richards, Marc | Port Vale | Chesterfield | Free |
| 3 Roberston, Gregor | Chesterfield | Crewe Alex | Free |
| 27 Robertson, Scott | Dundee United | Blackpool | Free |
| 12 Rodallega, Hugo | Wigan Ath | Fulham | Free |
| 4 Sears, Freddie | West Ham U | Colchester U | Free |
| 1 Severn, James | Derby Co | Scunthorpe U | Free |
| 3 Shackell, Jason | Derby Co | Burnley | Undisclosed |
| 1 Sharps, Ian | Shrewsbury T | Rotherham U | Free |
| 1 Shearer, Scott | Crawley T | Rotherham U | Free |
| 10 Shorey, Nicky | WBA | Reading | Free |
| 23 Silva, Toni | Liverpool | Barnsley | Free |
| 10 Smith, Alan | Newcastle U | Milton Keynes D | Free |
| 21 Smith, Jonathan | Swindon T | York C | Undisclosed |
| 9 Smith, Manny | Walsall | Notts Co | Free |
| 26 Snodgrass, Robert | Leeds U | Norwich C | Undisclosed |
| 25 Southern, Keith W. | Blackpool | Huddersfield T | Undisclosed |
| 3 Spring, Matthew | Leyton Orient | Wycombe W | Undisclosed |
| 3 Stanley, Craig | Bristol R | Aldershot T | Free |
| 2 Straker, Anthony | Aldershot T | Southend U | Undisclosed |
| 20 Strevens, Ben | Wycombe W | Gillingham | Free |
| 3 Summerfield, Luke | Cheltenham T | Shrewsbury T | Free |
| 2 Togwell, Sam | Scunthorpe U | Chesterfield | Free |
| 2 Tomlin, Gavin | Dagenham & R | Southend U | Undisclosed |
| 1 Tonkin, Anthony | Oxford U | Aldershot T | Free |
| 27 Turner, Michael | Sunderland | Norwich C | Undisclosed |
| 25 Varney, Luke | Portsmouth | Leeds U | Free |
| 2 Vincent, Ashley | Colchester U | Port Vale | Free |
| 31 Vokes, Samuel M. | Wolverhampton W | Burnley | Undisclosed |
| 6 Walton, Simon | Plymouth Arg | Hartlepool U | Free |
| 6 Weale, Chris | Leicester C | Shrewsbury T | Free |
| 5 Webster, Byron | Northampton T | Yeovil T | Free |
| 1 Welsh, John | Tranmere R | Preston NE | Free |
| 20 Westlake, Darryl | Walsall | Sheffield U | Undisclosed |
| 24 Whitbread, Zak | Norwich C | Leicester C | Free |
| 5 Widdowson, Joe | Rochdale | Northampton T | Undisclosed |
| 4 Wilbraham, Aaron | Norwich C | Crystal Palace | Free |
| 1 Wildig, Aaron | Cardiff C | Shrewsbury T | Free |
| 9 Wilson, Lawrie | Stevenage | Charlton Ath | Undisclosed |
| 3 Wood, Sam | Brentford | Wycombe W | Undisclosed |
| 6 Woodgate, Jonathan | Stoke C | Middlesbrough | Free |
| 9 Woodman, Craig | Brentford | Exeter C | Free |
| 1 Wright, Richard | Ipswich T | Preston NE | Free |
| 1 Wroe, Nicky | Shrewsbury T | Preston NE | Undisclosed |
| 2 Young, Lewis | Northampton T | Yeovil T | Free |

## JULY 2012 TEMPORARY TRANSFERS

23 Amos, Benjamin P. – Manchester U – Hull C; 27 Atkins, Ross – Derby Co – Burton Alb; 19 Ball, Callum – Derby Co – Coventry C; 6 Bridge, Wayne – Manchester C – Brighton & HA; 14 Brodie, Richard J. – Crawley T – Morecambe; 23 Brown, Reece – Manchester U – Coventry C; 16 Brunt, Ryan S. – Stoke C – Leyton Orient; 9 Cofie, John E. – Manchester U – Sheffield U; 20 Cox, Lee D. – Swindon T – Oxford U; 3 Croft, Lee – Derby Co – Oldham Ath; 13 Cuvelier, Florent – Stoke C – Walsall; 2 Edwards, Ryan C. – Blackburn R – Rochdale; 30 Flanagan, Thomas – Milton Keynes D – Gillingham; 20 Forecast, Tommy – Southampton – Gillingham; 6 Forster-Caskey, Jake – Brighton & HA – Oxford U; 24 Hector, Michael – Reading – Shrewsbury T; 13 Ince, Rohan G. – Chelsea – Yeovil T; 13 Lund, Matthew – Stoke C – Bristol R; 24 Luongo, Massimo – Tottenham H – Ipswich T; 27 MacDonald, Angus L. – Reading – AFC Wimbledon; 1 Martin, Aaron – Southampton – Crystal Palace; 17 Mills, Joseph N. – Reading – Burnley; 16 Palmer, Liam J. – Sheffield W – Tranmere R; 1 Da Silva, Fabio – Manchester U – QPR; 19 Ugwu, Chigozie E. – Reading – Yeovil T

## AUGUST 2012 TRANSFERS

| | | | | |
|---|---|---|---|---|
| 31 | Adam, Charles G. | Liverpool | Stoke C | 5,000,000 |
| 21 | Adebayor, Emmanuel | Manchester C | Tottenham H | 5,000,000 |
| 7 | Adebola, Dele | Hull C | Rochdale | Free |
| 31 | Agyemang, Patrick | QPR | Stevenage | Free |
| 2 | Akins, Lucas | Tranmere R | Stevenage | Undisclosed |
| 10 | Allen, Joe | Swansea C | Liverpool | Undisclosed |
| 6 | Antonio, Michail | Reading | Sheffield W | Undisclosed |
| 10 | Arestidou, Andreas | Preston NE | Morecambe | Free |
| 13 | Artell, David | Port Vale | Northampton T | Free |
| 21 | Baldock, Samuel | West Ham U | Bristol C | Undisclosed |
| 17 | Barrett, Adam | Bournemouth | Gillingham | Undisclosed |
| 13 | Barron, Scott | Millwall | Brentford | Undisclosed |
| 17 | Bartley, Kyle | Arsenal | Swansea C | Undisclosed |
| 6 | Barton, Adam | Preston NE | Coventry C | Undisclosed |
| 21 | Bassong, Sebastien | Tottenham H | Norwich C | Undisclosed |
| 11 | Beardsley, Chris | Stevenage | Preston NE | Free |
| 31 | Beavon, Stuart | Wycombe W | Preston NE | Undisclosed |
| 10 | Bellamy, Craig | Liverpool | Cardiff C | Free |
| 29 | Bennett, Joseph | Middlesbrough | Aston Villa | Undisclosed |
| 31 | Berbatov, Dimitar | Manchester U | Fulham | Undisclosed |
| 31 | Bessone, Federico | Swansea C | Swindon T | Free |
| 10 | Blackman, Nicholas | Blackburn R | Sheffield U | Undisclosed |
| 24 | Blake, Darcy | Cardiff C | Crystal Palace | Undisclosed |
| 24 | Bolasie, Yannick | Bristol C | Crystal Palace | Undisclosed |
| 30 | Bowery, Jordan | Chesterfield | Aston Villa | 500,000 |
| 28 | Bullard, Jimmy | Ipswich T | Milton Keynes D | Undisclosed |
| 29 | Bunn, Mark J. | Blackburn R | Norwich C | Undisclosed |
| 28 | Button, David | Tottenham H | Charlton Ath | Undisclosed |
| 22 | Byrne, Shane | Leicester C | Bury | Undisclosed |
| 11 | Byrom, Joel | Stevenage | Preston NE | Free |
| 1 | Carayol, Mustapha | Bristol R | Middlesbrough | Undisclosed |
| 30 | Carlisle, Clarke | Burnley | York C | Free |
| 14 | Caton, James | Bolton W | Blackpool | Free |
| 20 | Chamberlain, Elliott | Leicester C | Exeter C | Free |
| 1 | Collins, James | Aston Villa | West Ham U | 2,500,000 |
| 22 | Connolly, Matthew | QPR | Cardiff C | Undisclosed |
| 24 | Cook, Lee | QPR | Leyton Orient | Free |
| 10 | Cooksley, Harry | Reading | Aldershot T | Free |
| 11 | Cox, Simon | WBA | Nottingham F | Undisclosed |
| 20 | Cranie, Martin | Coventry C | Barnsley | Free |
| 2 | Crofts, Andrew | Norwich C | Brighton & HA | Undisclosed |
| 1 | Curran, Craig | Carlisle U | Rochdale | Free |
| 20 | Davies, Steven G. | Derby Co | Bristol C | Undisclosed |
| 31 | Delaney, Damien | Ipswich T | Crystal Palace | Free |
| 29 | Dembele, Mousa | Fulham | Tottenham H | Undisclosed |
| 31 | Dempsey, Clint | Fulham | Tottenham H | 6,000,000 |
| 11 | Diouf, El Hadji | Doncaster R | Leeds U | Free |
| 31 | Dobbie, Stephen | Swansea C | Brighton & HA | Undisclosed |
| 1 | Downing, Paul | WBA | Walsall | Free |
| 4 | Doyle, Nathan | Barnsley | Bradford C | Free |
| 31 | Eccleston, Nathan G. | Liverpool | Blackpool | Free |
| 13 | Elphick, Tommy | Brighton & HA | Bournemouth | Undisclosed |
| 31 | Ertl, Johnny | Sheffield U | Portsmouth | Free |
| 3 | Etuhu, Dickson P. | Fulham | Blackburn R | Undisclosed |
| 13 | Evans, Alex | Cardiff C | Oxford U | Non-contract |
| 31 | Ferdinand, Kane | Southend U | Peterborough U | 200,000 |
| 24 | Fletcher, Steven K. | Wolverhampton W | Sunderland | 12,000,000 |
| 17 | Freeman, Kieron | Nottingham F | Derby Co | Undisclosed |
| 13 | Fuller, Barry | Gillingham | Barnet | Free |
| 8 | Gerrard, Anthony | Cardiff C | Huddersfield T | Undisclosed |
| 4 | Gillett, Simon | Doncaster R | Nottingham F | Free |
| 16 | Gonzalez, David | Brighton & HA | Barnsley | Free |
| 31 | Grant, Robert | Scunthorpe U | Rochdale | Free |
| 3 | Gurrieri, Andres | Burton Alb | Plymouth Arg | Free |
| 14 | Harewood, Marlon | Nottingham F | Barnsley | Free |
| 17 | Harper, James | Hull C | Doncaster R | Free |
| 20 | Hayes, Paul | Charlton Ath | Brentford | Free |
| 23 | Healy, David | Rangers | Bury | Free |
| 2 | Helguson, Heidar | QPR | Cardiff C | Undisclosed |
| 18 | Hines, Zavon | Burnley | Bradford C | Free |
| 7 | Hoganson, Michael | Newcastle U | Derby Co | Free |
| 16 | Howard, Brian | Reading | Portsmouth | Free |
| 24 | Jarvis, Matthew | Wolverhampton W | West Ham U | 7,500,000 |
| 16 | Jennings, Steve | Motherwell | Coventry C | Free |
| 24 | Johnson, Adam | Manchester C | Sunderland | Undisclosed |
| 31 | Jones, Michael D. | Sheffield W | Crawley T | Undisclosed |
| 10 | Kay, Antony | Huddersfield T | Milton Keynes D | Free |
| 31 | Kennedy, Matthew | Kilmarnock | Everton | Nominal |
| 1 | Kerkar, Salim | Rangers | Charlton Ath | Free |
| 8 | Kightly, Michael J. | Wolverhampton W | Stoke C | Undisclosed |
| 31 | Kitson, Dave | Portsmouth | Sheffield U | Free |
| 28 | Kuffour, Jo | Gillingham | Wycombe W | Free |
| 28 | Lansbury, Henri G. | Arsenal | Nottingham F | Undisclosed |
| 1 | Lowe, Ryan | Sheffield W | Milton Keynes D | Undisclosed |
| 30 | Magri, Sam | Portsmouth | QPR | Free |

| | | | |
|---|---|---|---|
| 21 Massey, Gavin A. | Watford | Colchester U | Free |
| 10 Maybury, Alan | St Johnstone | Birmingham C | Free |
| 31 Maynard, Nicky | West Ham U | Cardiff C | 2,500,000 |
| 16 Mayor, Danny | Preston NE | Sheffield W | Undisclosed |
| 16 McLeod, Izale | Barnet | Portsmouth | Free |
| 17 Montano, Cristian A. | West Ham U | Oldham Ath | Undisclosed |
| 24 Moses, Victor | Wigan Ath | Chelsea | Undisclosed |
| 17 Moult, Louis | Stoke C | Northampton T | Free |
| 13 Newey, Tom | Rotherham U | Scunthorpe U | Free |
| 30 Noone, Craig | Brighton & HA | Cardiff C | 1,000,000 |
| 31 Nzonzi, Steven N.M.C. | Blackburn R | Stoke C | 3,500,000 |
| 1 O'Connor, James F.E. | Doncaster R | Derby Co | Undisclosed |
| 31 Orlandi, Andrea | Swansea C | Brighton & HA | Undisclosed |
| 23 Parkes, Thomas | Leicester C | Bristol R | |
| 15 Paterson, Matt | Southend U | Burton Alb | Free |
| 3 Peltier, Lee A. | Leicester C | Leeds U | Undisclosed |
| 17 Proctor, Jamie | Preston NE | Swansea C | Undisclosed |
| 9 Quinn, Paul | Cardiff C | Doncaster R | Free |
| 31 Quinn, Stephen | Sheffield U | Hull C | Undisclosed |
| 7 Ramage, Peter | QPR | Crystal Palace | Free |
| 8 Regan, Carl | Shrewsbury T | Notts Co | Free |
| 30 Rhodes, Jordan | Huddersfield T | Blackburn R | 8,000,000 |
| 31 Richardson, Kieran E. | Sunderland | Fulham | 2,000,000 |
| 10 Roberts, Connor | Everton | Cheltenham T | Free |
| 13 Rodwell, Jack | Everton | Manchester C | 12,000,000 |
| 31 Russell, Darel | Preston NE | Portsmouth | Free |
| 20 Sammon, Conor | Wigan Ath | Derby Co | Undisclosed |
| 17 Seabright, Jordan | Bournemouth | Dagenham & R | Free |
| 13 Shittu, Danny | QPR | Millwall | Free |
| 17 Simonsen, Steve | Sheffield U | Preston NE | Free |
| 31 Sinclair, Scott | Swansea C | Manchester C | 6,200,000 |
| 10 Smith, Ben | Shrewsbury T | Rochdale | Free |
| 24 Smith, Tommy | QPR | Cardiff C | Undisclosed |
| 23 Stack, Graham | Hibernian | Barnet | Free |
| 31 Stephens, David | Hibernian | Barnet | Free |
| 9 Stock, Brian B. | Doncaster R | Burnley | Undisclosed |
| 10 Straker, Anthony O. | Aldershot T | Southend U | Undisclosed |
| 24 Sung-Yeung, Ki | Celtic | Swansea C | 6,000,000 |
| 28 Taylor, Andy | Sheffield U | Walsall | Free |
| 1 Taylor, Connor | Aston Villa | Walsall | Free |
| 31 Taylor, Martin | Watford | Sheffield W | Undisclosed |
| 30 Taylor, Paul T. | Peterborough U | Ipswich T | Undisclosed |
| 20 Taylor, Stuart | Manchester C | Reading | Free |
| 3 Thompson, Joseph | Rochdale | Tranmere R | Undisclosed |
| 31 Thompson, Josh | Celtic | Portsmouth | Free |
| 17 van Persie, Robin | Arsenal | Manchester U | 24,000,000 |
| 24 Walsh, Joe | Swansea C | Crawley T | Free |
| 13 Weston, Curtis | Gillingham | Barnet | Free |
| 16 Weston, Myles | Brentford | Gillingham | Undisclosed |
| 31 Westwood, Ashley | Crewe Alex | Aston Villa | Undisclosed |
| 16 Williamson, Lee | Sheffield U | Portsmouth | Free |
| 16 Wilson, Mark | Celtic | Bristol C | Free |
| 2 Zebroski, Christopher | Bristol R | Cheltenham T | Undisclosed |
| 3 Zoko, Francois | Carlisle U | Notts Co | Free |

## AUGUST 2012 TEMPORARY TRANSFERS

29 Adeyemi, Thomas – Norwich C – Brentford; 3 Afobe, Benik T. – Arsenal – Bolton W; 30 Ahmed Elmehamady A. – Sunderland – Hull C; 18 Ajose, Nicholas O. – Peterborough U – Crawley T; 17 Ajose, Nicky – Peterborough U – Crawley T; 17 Andersen, Mikkel – Reading – Portsmouth; 16 Anderson, Myles – Blackburn R – Aldershot T; 17 Assombalonga, Britt C. – Watford – Southend U; 1 Atkins, Ross M. – Derby Co – Burton Alb; 7 Ayala, Daniel – Norwich C – Nottingham F; 29 Barkhuizen, Thomas J. – Blackpool – Fleetwood T; 17 Barnard, Lee J. – Southampton – Bournemouth; 14 Belford, Cameron D. – Bury – Southend U; 31 Benayoun, Yossi S. – Chelsea – West Ham U; 31 Bennett, Dale – Watford – AFC Wimbledon; 28 Bidwell, Jake – Everton – Brentford; 28 Boatang, Daniel – Arsenal – Oxford U; 31 Bolger, Cian – Leicester C – Bristol R; 30 Bostock, John – Tottenham H – Swindon T; 31 Bothroyd, Jay – QPR – Sheffield W; 7 Bradley, Sonny – Hull C – Aldershot T; 21 Bunn, Harry C. – Manchester C – Crewe Alex; 31 Caddis, Paul – Swindon T – Birmingham C; 30 Carroll, Andrew T. – Liverpool – West Ham U; 3 Cassidy, Jake A. – Wolverhampton W – Tranmere R; 31 Chalobah, Nathaniel – Chelsea – Watford; 17 Clifford, Conor P. – Chelsea – Portsmouth; 31 Coke, Giles – Sheffield W – Swindon T; 17 Connolly, Paul – Leeds U – Portsmouth; 31 Coppinger, James – Doncaster R – Nottingham F; 7 Cullen, Mark – Hull C – Bury; 31 Delfouneso, Nathan – Aston Villa – Blackpool; 16 Dicko, Nouha – Wigan Ath – Blackpool; 29 East, Daniel – Hull C – Northampton T; 29 Eastham, Ashley – Blackpool – Fleetwood T; 30 Elmohamady, Ahmed – Sunderland – Hull C; 31 Ferdinand, Kane – Southend U – Peterborough U; 13 Forecast, Tommy S. – Southampton – Gillingham; 17 Forte, Jonathan – Southampton – Crawley T; 31 Francomb, George – Norwich C – AFC Wimbledon; 10 Fredericks, Ryan – Tottenham H – Brentford; 14 Gibson, Benjamin J. – Middlesbrough – Tranmere R; 31 Golobet Benet, R. – Wigan Ath – Tranmere R; 31 Goodwillie, David – Blackburn R – Crystal Palace; 10 Gordon, Benjamin L. – Chelsea – Birmingham C; 6 Gorman, Rory J. – Wolverhampton W – Plymouth Arg; 31 Hammill, Adam J. – Wolverhampton W – Huddersfield T; 31 Hammond, Dean – Southampton – Brighton & HA; 3 Harrad, Shaun N. – Bury – Cheltenham T; 24 Haynes-Brown, Curtis L. – Yeovil T – AFC Wimbledon; 31 Hume, Iain – Preston NE – Doncaster R; 16 Hutchinson, Samuel E. – Chelsea – Nottingham F; 22 Jervis, Jake – Birmingham C – Carlisle U; 31 Kane, Harry – Tottenham H – Norwich C; 17 Long, Kevin – Burnley – Portsmouth; 10 Lukaku Bolingoli, R. – Chelsea – WBA; 31 MacDonald, Alexander – Burnley – Plymouth Arg; 16 Marrow, Alex J. – Crystal Palace – Fleetwood T; 20 McEachran, Joshua – Chelsea – Middlesbrough; 3 McGinty, Sean A. – Manchester U – Oxford U; 31 McGoldrick, David J. – Nottingham F – Coventry C; 24 Miller, Ishmael – Nottingham F – Middlesbrough; 11 Miyaichi, Ryo – Arsenal – Wigan Ath; 7 Morrison, Ravel R. – West Ham U – Birmingham C; 6 Mukendi, Henoc – Liverpool – Northampton T; 30 Murphy, Daryl – Celtic – Ipswich; 7 Nicholls, Lee A. – Wigan Ath – Northampton T; 23 Nkumu, Archange – Chelsea – Yeovil T; 21 Obita, Jordan J. – Reading –

Portsmouth; 13 O'Connor, Anthony D. – Blackburn R – Burton Alb; 31 O'Halloran, Michael F. – Bolton W – Carlisle U; 21 Parkes, Thomas – Leicester C – Bristol R; 30 Parsons, Mathew J. – Crystal Palace – Wycombe W; 28 Prutton, David T. – Sheffield W – Scunthorpe U; 24 Ridehalgh, Liam – Huddersfield T – Chesterfield; 31 Risser, Oliver – Swindon T – Stevenage; 23 Rogers, Robert H. – Leeds U – Stevenage; 31 Rooney, Adam – Birmingham C – Swindon T; 31 Rose, Danny – Tottenham H – Sunderland; 7 Sanchez Ayala, D. – Norwich C – Nottingham F; 31 Sharp, William – Southampton – Nottingham F; 6 Sheppard, Karl – Reading – Accrington S; 8 Slew, Jordan – Blackburn R – Oldham Ath; 31 Spearing, Jay F. – Liverpool – Bolton W; 31 Stewart, Cameron R. – Hull C – Burnley; 30 Taylor, Charles J. – Leeds U – York C; 31 Taylor, Martin – Watford – Sheffield W; 30 Thompson, Adam L. – Watford – Wycombe W; 24 Vaughan, James O. – Norwich C – Huddersfield T; 14 Walker, Samuel C. – Chelsea – Bristol R; 30 Ward, Darren P. – Millwall – Swindon T; 10 Watson, Ryan – Wigan Ath – Accrington S

### SEPTEMBER 2012 TRANSFERS

| | | | |
|---|---|---|---|
| 8 Beevers, Mark | Sheffield W | Millwall | Undisclosed |
| 14 Michalik, Lubomir | Carlisle U | Portsmouth | Free |
| 3 Taylor, Martin | Watford | Sheffield W | |

### SEPTEMBER 2012 TEMPORARY TRANSFERS

17 Abadaki, Godwin E. – Rochdale – Huddersfield T; 29 Allan, Scott – WBA – Milton Keynes D; 17 Andersen, Mikkel – Reading – Portsmouth; 19 Anderson, Myles – Blackburn R – Aldershot T; 8 Aneke, Chukwuemeka A.A. – Arsenal – Crewe Alex; 13 Appiah, Kwesi – Crystal Palace – Aldershot T; 26 Archer, Jordan – Tottenham H – Wycombe W; 13 Assombalonga, Britt C. – Watford – Southend U; 12 Atkinson, Christoher – Huddersfield T – Chesterfield; 21 Atkinson, Rob – Fleetwood T – Accrington S; 25 Bailey, James J. – Derby Co – Coventry C; 14 Barkley, Ross – Everton – Sheffield W; 28 Beckford, Jermaine P. – Leicester C – Huddersfield T; 25 Bidwell, Jake – Everton – Brentford; 28 Bond, Andrew M. – Colchester U – Crewe Alex; 25 Burn, Daniel – Fulham – Yeovil T; 8 Clarke, Leon M. – Charlton Ath – Scunthorpe U; 27 Collins, Lee H. – Barnsley – Shrewsbury T; 21 Darlow, Karl – Nottingham F – Walsall; 14 Derbyshire, Matthew – Nottingham F – Oldham Ath; 30 East, Daniel – Hull C – Northampton T; 27 Eastmond, Craig L. – Arsenal – Colchester U; 27 Eaves, Thomas – Bolton W – Bristol R; 21 Edwards, Joseph R. – Bristol C – Yeovil T; 26 Elokobi, George N. – Wolverhampton W – Bristol C; 19 Etheridge, Neil – Fulham – Bristol R; 27 Evans, Micah – Blackburn R – Chesterfield; 21 Findley, Robert – Nottingham F – Gillingham; 13 Gallagher, Paul – Leicester C – Sheffield U; 18 Garner, Joseph A. – Watford – Carlisle U; 14 Gibson, Benjamin J. – Middlesbrough – Tranmere R; 14 Gregory, Steven M. – Bournemouth – AFC Wimbledon; 27 Harris, Robert – Blackpool – Rotherham U; 21 Henderson, Conor A. – Arsenal – Coventry C; 22 Higginbotham, Daniel J. – Stoke C – Ipswich T; 21 Higginbotham, Kallum – Huddersfield T – Carlisle U; 14 Hopper, Thomas – Leicester C – Bury; 27 Ibehre, Jabo O.M. – Milton Keynes D – Colchester U; 28 Jenas, Jermaine – Tottenham H – Nottingham F; 20 Jenkins, Ross A. – Watford – Plymouth Arg; 27 Kiernan, Robert S. – Wigan Ath – Burton Alb; 8 Lita, Leroy – Swansea C – Birmingham C; 8 Lynch, Craig – Sunderland – Hartlepool U; 8 Madjo, Guy B. – Aldershot T – Plymouth Arg; 17 Mingoia, Piero – Watford – Accrington S; 21 Obita, Jordan J. – Reading – Portsmouth; 11 O'Connor, Anthony D. – Blackburn R – Burton Alb; 18 Parish, Elliot – Cardiff C – Wycombe W; 14 Pearce, Krystian M.V. – Notts Co – Barnet; 29 Razak, Abdul – Manchester C – Charlton Ath; 21 Reckord, Jamie – Wolverhampton W – Coventry C; 24 Ridehalgh, Liam – Huddersfield T – Chesterfield; 27 Roofe, Kemar – WBA – Northampton T; 27 Rooney, Luke – Swindon T – Burton Alb; 12 Schofield, Danny – Rotherham U – Accrington S; 14 Smith, Korey – Norwich C – Yeovil T; 30 Taylor, Charles J. – Leeds U – York C; 29 Thomas, Wesley – Bournemouth – Portsmouth; 14 Tonge, Michael W. – Stoke C – Leeds U; 15 Wabara, Reece – Manchester C – Oldham Ath; 21 Warnock, Stephen – Aston Villa – Bolton W; 27 Watt, Herschel O.S. – Arsenal – Colchester U; 12 Whichelow, Matthew – Watford – Accrington S; 12 Wilson, Ben – Sunderland – Chesterfield; 28 Winnall, Sam T – Wolverhampton W – Shrewsbury T; 17 Wood, Christopher – WBA – Millwall; 14 Wright, David – Crystal Palace – Gillingham

### OCTOBER 2012 TEMPORARY TRANSFERS

29 Allan, Scott – WBA – Portsmouth; 19 Andersen, Mikkel – Reading – Portsmouth; 8 Andrade, Bruno M.C. – QPR – Wycombe W; 8 Aneke, Chukwuemeka A.A. – Arsenal – Crewe Alex; 1 Ashton, James – Chelsea – Charlton Ath; 22 Atkinson, Christoher – Huddersfield T – Chesterfield; 23 Balanta, Angelo – QPR – Milton Keynes D; 20 Barkley, Ross – Everton – Sheffield W; 5 Beevers, Mark G. – Sheffield W – Millwall; 3 Bennett, Dale O. – Watford – AFC Wimbledon; 1 Berahino, Saido – WBA – Peterborough U; 28 Bidwell, Jake – Everton – Brentford; 25 Briggs, Matthew – Fulham – Bristol C; 23 Burn, Daniel – Fulham – Yeovil T; 5 Campbell, Dudley J. – QPR – Ipswich T; 23 Chapell, Jordan – Sheffield U – Burton Alb; 12 Clarke-Harris, Jonson S. – Peterborough U – Southend U; 28 Collins, Lee H. – Barnsley – Shrewsbury T; 21 Darlow, Karl – Nottingham F – Walsall; 27 D'Ath, Lawson M. – Reading – Cheltenham T; 31 Derbyshire, Matthew – Nottingham F – Oldham Ath; 22 Dickinson, Carl – Watford – Portsmouth; 4 Doherty, Matthew – Wolverhampton W – Bury; 5 Eastham, Ashley – Blackpool – Notts Co; 25 Eccleston, Nathan G. – Blackpool – Tranmere R; 19 Edwards, Joseph R. – Bristol C – Yeovil T; 10 Edwards, Robert O. – Barnsley – Fleetwood T; 22 Etheridge, Neil – Fulham – Bristol R; 19 Forsyth, Craig – Watford – Bradford C; 3 Francomb, Georgie – Norwich C – AFC Wimbledon; 19 Frecklington, Lee – Peterborough U – Rotherham U; 26 Frei, Kerim – Fulham – Cardiff C; 16 Garner, Joseph A. – Watford – Carlisle U; 9 Griffiths, Scott R. – Peterborough U – Plymouth Arg; 17 Hall, Ryan – Southend U – Leeds U; 1 Haynes-Brown, Curtis L. – Yeovil T – AFC Wimbledon; 25 Helan, Jeremy – Manchester C – Shrewsbury T; 15 Henderson, Stephen – West Ham U – Ipswich T; 22 Hewitt, Troy R. – QPR – Bury; 24 Higginbotham, Daniel J. – Stoke C – Ipswich T; 14 Hopper, Thomas – Leicester C – Bury; 1 Hulse, Robert W. – QPR – Charlton Ath; 1 Hurst, James – WBA – Birmingham C; 11 Huws, Emyr W. – Manchester C – Northampton T; 19 Jervis, Jake – Birmingham C – Tranmere R; 23 Johnson, Daniel A. – Aston Villa – Yeovil T; 5 Kearns, Daniel – Peterborough U – York C; 26 Laird, Marc– Leyton Orient – Southend U; 13 MacDonald, Alexander – Burnley – Plymouth Arg; 5 Madden, Patrick – Carlisle U – Yeovil T; 13 Madjo, Guy B. – Aldershot T – Plymouth Arg; 1 Mambo, Yado M. – Charlton Ath – AFC Wimbledon; 17 McManus, Stephen – Middlesbrough – Bristol C; 5 Mohsni, Bilel – Southend U – Ipswich T; 26 Morris, Josh F – Blackburn R – Rotherham U; 5 Mullins, John – Rotherham U – Oxford U; 19 Munns, Jack – Tottenham H – Aldershot T; 8 Mustoe, Jordan D. – Wigan Ath – Morecambe; 23 Nkumu, Archange – Chelsea – Colchester U; 5 Noble, Ryan A. – Sunderland – Hartlepool U; 25 Obeng, Curtis – Swansea C – Fleetwood T; 26 Osawe, Osayamen – Blackburn R – Accrington S; 26 Oxley, Mark T. – Hull C – Burton Alb; 19 Pennant, Jermaine – Stoke C – Wolverhampton W; 15 Poleon, Dominic – Leeds U – Bury; 26 Proctor, Jamie – Swansea C – Shrewsbury T; 10 Rose, Daniel S. – Fleetwood T – Aldershot T; 15 Spencer, James – Huddersfield T – Brentford; 15 Thompson, Zac J. – Leeds U – Bury; 19 Tonge, Michael W. – Stoke C – Leeds U; 26 Vincelot, Romain – Brighton & HA – Gillingham; 21 Wabara, Reece – Manchester C – Oldham Ath; 12 Wagstaff, Scott A. – Charlton Ath – Leyton Orient; 26 Ward, Elliott L. – Norwich C – Nottingham F; 4 Wellens, Richard P. – Leicester C – Ipswich T; 14 Wilson, Ben – Sunderland – Chesterfield; 9 Wyke, Charles T. – Middlesbrough – Hartlepool U

### NOVEMBER 2012 TRANSFERS

| | | |
|---|---|---|
| 6 Keane, Michael | Manchester U | Leicester C |
| 6 Lingard, Jesse | Manchester U | Leicester C |

### NOVEMBER 2012 TEMPORARY TRANSFERS

15 Adams, Blair V. – Sunderland – Coventry C; 22 Ajala, Ridwan – Bristol C – AFC Wimbledon; 26 Allan, Scott – WBA – Portsmouth; 5 Andrade, Bruno M. – QPR – Wycombe W; 13 Aneke, Chukwuemeka A.A. – Arsenal – Crewe

Alex; 2 Archer, Jordan – Tottenham H – Wycombe W; 21 Azeez, Adebayo – Charlton Ath – Wycombe W; 22 Balanta, Angelo – QPR – Milton Keynes D; 22 Bamford, Patrick J. – Chelsea – Milton Keynes D; 22 Barker, George – Brighton & HA – Barnet; 19 Barnett, Tyrone – Peterborough U – Ipswich T; 4 Beevers, Mark G. – Sheffield W – Millwall; 22 Bennett, Dale O. – Watford – Yeovil T; 2 Bennett, Julian L.L. – Sheffield W – Shrewsbury T; 15 Benson, Paul A. – Swindon T – Portsmouth; 25 Bidwell, Jake – Everton – Brentford; 20 Blyth, Jacob M. – Leicester C – Burton Alb; 6 Brady, Robert – Manchester U – Hull C; 22 Branston, Guy P.B. – Aldershot T – Bristol R; 16 Burn, Daniel – Fulham – Yeovil T; 8 Butterfield, Jacob – Norwich C – Bolton W; 21 Buzsaky, Akos – Portsmouth – Barnsley; 16 Cameron, Courtney – Aston Villa – Rotherham U; 12 Caprice, Jake L. – Blackpool – Dagenham & R; 19 Carlisle, Clarke – York C – Northampton T; 21 Chapell, Jordan – Sheffield U – Burton Alb; 8 Church, Simon R. – Reading – Huddersfield T; 22 Cisak, Aleksander – Oldham Ath – Portsmouth; 21 Clifford, Conor P. – Chelsea – Crawley T; 2 Cooper, Liam D.I. – Hull C – Chesterfield; 5 Dalla Valle, Lauri – Fulham – Crewe Alex; 22 Daniels, Donervon – WBA – Tranmere R; 14 Danns, Neil A. – Leicester C – Bristol C; 25 D'Ath, Lawson M. – Reading – Chesterfield T; 2 Devitt, Jamie M. – Hull C – Rotherham U; 8 Dickenson, Brennan – Brighton & HA – Chesterfield; 22 Djeziri, Adda – Blackpool – Scunthorpe U; 22 Donnelly, Scott P. – Aldershot T – Southend U; 9 Ebanks-Landell, Ethan – Wolverhampton W – Bury; 5 Egan, John – Sunderland – Bradford C; 16 Ellington, Nathan L.F. – Ipswich T – Scunthorpe U; 2 Ferguson, Barry – Blackpool – Fleetwood T; 2 Francomb, Georgie – Norwich C – AFC Wimbledon; 22 Frecklington, Lee – Peterborough U – Rotherham U; 16 Frimpong, Emmanuel Y – Arsenal – Charlton Ath; 21 Garner, Joseph A – Watford – Carlisle U; 22 Gayle, Cameron – WBA – Shrewsbury T; 20 Gayle, Dwight D.B. – Dagenham & R – Peterborough U; 22 Gjokaj, Valentin – Derby Co – Carlisle U; 22 Good, Curtis E. – Newcastle U – Bradford C; 9 Gornell, Terence – Shrewsbury T – Rochdale; 21 Greening, Jonathan – Nottingham F – Barnsley; 2 Griffiths, Scott R. – Peterborough U – Plymouth Arg; 22 Hall, Robert K. D. – West Ham U – Birmingham C; 22 Hector, Michael – Reading – Aldershot T; 22 Helan, Jeremy – Manchester C – Sheffield W; 25 Hewitt, Troy R. – QPR – Bury; 16 Higginbotham, Daniel J. – Stoke C – Ipswich T; 22 Hodson, Lee – Watford – Brentford; 14 Hollands, Daniel T. – Charlton Ath – Swindon T; 22 Hutton, Alan – Aston Villa – Nottingham F; 22 Inman, Bradden – Newcastle U – Crewe Alex; 22 Iro, Andrew – Stevenage – Barnet; 22 Ismail, Zeli – Wolverhampton W – Milton Keynes D; 22 Iwelumo, Christopher – Watford – Notts Co; 22 Jervis, Jake – Birmingham C – Portsmouth; 9 Jonsson, Eggert G. – Wolverhampton W – Charlton Ath; 22 Kane, Todd A.L. – Chelsea – Preston NE; 5 Keane, Michael – Manchester U – Leicester C; 2 Kearns, Daniel – Peterborough U – York C; 15 Kiernan, Robert S. – Wigan Ath – Brentford; 22 King, Joshua C.K. – Manchester U – Blackburn R; 21 Lappin, Simon – Norwich C – Cardiff C; 22 Lee, Hodson J.S. – Watford – Brentford; 5 Lingard, Jesse E. – Manchester U – Leicester C; 9 Lopez Robles, D. – Stevenage – Aldershot T; 21 MacDonald, Angus L. – Reading – Torquay U; 5 Madden, Patrick – Carlisle U – Yeovil T; 16 Madjo, Guy B. – Aldershot T – Plymouth Arg; 9 Mantom, Sam – WBA – Walsall; 15 Martin, Christopher – Norwich C – Swindon T; 22 McCallum, Paul – West Ham U – AFC Wimbledon; 15 McCarey, Aaron – Walsall – Wolverhampton W; 19 McChrystal, Mark T. – Tranmere R – Scunthorpe U; 6 McGinty, Sean – Manchester U – Carlisle U; 5 Meades, Jonathan C.C. – Bournemouth – AFC Wimbledon; 15 Mendez-Laing, Nathaniel – Peterborough U – Portsmouth; 8 Meyler, David – Sunderland – Hull C; 5 Mildenhall, Stephen J. – Millwall – Scunthorpe U; 2 Mkandawire, Tamika – Millwall – Southend U; 22 Molesley, Mark C. – Bournemouth – Plymouth Arg; 19 Mustoe, Jordan D. – Wigan Ath – Morecambe; 16 Naylor, Tom – Derby Co – Bradford C; 6 Nicholls, Lee A. – Wigan Ath – Northampton T; 7 Noble, Ryan A. – Sunderland – Hartlepool U; 22 O'Connell, Jack – Blackburn R – Rotherham U; 22 O'Halloran, Michael F. – Bolton W – Tranmere R; 13 Orr, Bradley J. – Blackburn R – Ipswich T; 20 O'Shea, James – Milton Keynes D – Chesterfield; 19 Pitman, Brett – Bristol C – Bournemouth; 18 Poleon, Dominic – Leeds U – Bury; 22 Potts, Daniel – West Ham U – Colchester U; 5 Reeves, Jake K. – Brentford – AFC Wimbledon; 22 Ridehalgh, Liam – Huddersfield T – Rotherham U; 9 Rodgers, Luke J. – Portsmouth – Shrewsbury T; 8 Rodman, Alexander – Aldershot T – York C; 9 Rooney, Luke – Swindon T – Rotherham U; 9 Seaborne, Daniel A.S. – Southampton – Charlton Ath; 10 Seidi, Alberto A. – Southampton – Aldershot T; 7 Sekajja, Ibra – Crystal Palace – Milton Keynes D; 22 Sidibe, Mamady – Stoke C – Sheffield W; 20 Sinclair, Emile A. – Peterborough U – Barnsley; 6 Sinclair, Robert J. – Stevenage – Aldershot T; 22 Smith, Alex R. – Fulham – Leyton Orient; 22 Smith, Chris – Swindon T – Northampton T; 21 Stockdale, David A. – Fulham – Hull C; 9 Sullivan, John D. – Charlton Ath – Colchester U; 16 Sullivan, Neil – Doncaster R – AFC Wimbledon; 22 Tate, Alan – Swansea C – Leeds U; 22 Taylor, Jake W.T. – Reading – Cheltenham T; 22 Thomas, Jerome – WBA – Leeds U; 22 Thomas, Jerome W. – WBA – Leeds U; 22 Thomas, Wesley – Bournemouth – Blackpool; 9 Thompson, Joshua – Portsmouth – Colchester U; 18 Thompson, Zac J. – Leeds U – Bury; 21 Thorne, George – WBA – Peterborough U; 20 Townsend, Conor – Hull C – Chesterfield; 22 Trotta, Marcello – Fulham – Brentford; 20 Tsend, Conor S. – Hull C – Chesterfield; 14 Tudgay, Marcus – Nottingham F – Barnsley; 22 Turgott, Blair – West Ham U – Bradford C; 22 Wabara, Reece – Manchester C – Oldham Ath; 22 Wakefield, Joshua – Bournemouth – Dagenham & R; 22 Westcarr, Craig N. – Chesterfield – Walsall; 22 Wilson, Daniel – Liverpool – Bristol C; 21 Wood, Christopher – WBA – Millwall; 7 Wyke, Charles T. – Middlesbrough – Hartlepool U; 21 Wylde, Gregg – Bolton W – Bury

## DECEMBER 2012 TRANSFERS

| | | | |
|---|---|---|---|
| 31 Bennett, Ryan | Peterborough U | Norwich C | |
| 24 Gayle, Dwight | Dagenham & R | Peterborough U | 500,000 |

## DECEMBER 2012 TEMPORARY TRANSFERS

26 Allan, Scott – WBA – Portsmouth; 18 Aneke, Chukwuemeka A.A. – Arsenal – Crewe Alex; 29 Belford, Cameron – Bury – Accrington S; 16 Benson, Paul A. – Swindon T – Portsmouth; 3 Brady, Robert – Manchester U – Hull C; 9 Butterfield, Jacob – Norwich C – Bolton W; 13 Caprice, Jake L. – Blackpool – Dagenham & R; 9 Church, Simon R. – Reading – Huddersfield T; 2 Cooper, Liam D.I. – Hull C – Chesterfield; 9 Dalla Valle, L. – Fulham – Crewe Alex; 13 Danns, Neil A. – Leicester C – Bristol C; 22 Gjokaj, Valentin – Derby Co – Carlisle U; 7 Gornell, Terence – Shrewsbury T – Rochdale; 23 Helan, Jeremy – Manchester C – Sheffield W; 22 Jervis, Jake – Birmingham C – Portsmouth; 4 Keane, Michael – Manchester U – Leicester C; 4 Lingard, Jesse E. – Manchester U – Leicester C; 9 Lopez Robles, D. – Stevenage – Aldershot T; 23 McCallum, Paul – West Ham U – AFC Wimbledon; 16 McCarey, Aaron – Wolverhampton W – Walsall; 5 McGinty, Sean – Manchester U – Carlisle U; 15 Mendez-Laing, Nathaniel – Peterborough U – Portsmouth; 9 Mildenhall, Stephen J. – Millwall – Scunthorpe U; 18 Molesley, Mark C. – Bournemouth – Plymouth Arg; 23 Potts, Daniel – West Ham U – Colchester U; 10 Rodgers, Luke J. – Portsmouth – Shrewsbury T; 9 Seaborne, Daniel A.S. – Southampton – Charlton Ath; 23 Sidibe, Mamady – Stoke C – Sheffield W; 4 Sinclair, Robert J. – Stevenage – Aldershot T; 22 Smith, Christopher – Swindon T – Northampton T; 6 Thompson, Joshua – Portsmouth – Colchester U; 22 Townsend, Conor S. – Hull C – Chesterfield; 23 Wakefield, Joshua – Bournemouth – Dagenham & R; 9 Wyke, Charles T. – Middlesbrough – Hartlepool U; 23 Wylde, Gregg – Bolton W – Bury

## JANUARY 2013 TRANSFERS

| | | | |
|---|---|---|---|
| 17 Adams, Blair V. | Sunderland | Coventry C | Undisclosed |
| 21 Ainsworth, Lionel | Rotherham U | Aldershot T | Loan |
| 23 Ajose, Nicky | Peterborough U | Bury | Loan |
| 8 Akpan, Hope | Crawley T | Reading | Undisclosed |
| 31 Aldred, Tom | Colchester U | Accrington S | Free |
| 18 Allsop, Ryan | Leyton Orient | Bournemouth | Free |
| 9 Amoo, David | Preston NE | Tranmere R | Free |
| 7 Anderson, Myles | Blackburn R | Exeter C | Free |
| 3 Ba, Demba | Newcastle U | Chelsea | Undisclosed, reported 7,000,000 |

| | | | | |
|---|---|---|---|---|
| 30 | Becchio, Luciano H. | Leeds U | Norwich C | Undisclosed |
| 1 | Beevers, Mark G. | Sheffield W | Millwall | Undisclosed |
| 30 | Blackman, Nick | Sheffield U | Reading | Undisclosed |
| 30 | Bolger, Cian | Leicester C | Bolton W | Undisclosed |
| 8 | Brady, Robert | Manchester U | Hull C | Undisclosed, reported 2,000,000 |
| 11 | Branston, Guy | Aldershot T | Plymouth Arg | Free |
| 23 | Brunt, Ryan | Stoke C | Bristol R | Undisclosed |
| 31 | Butland, Jack | Birmingham C | Stoke C | 3,500,000 |
| 21 | Campbell, Fraizer | Sunderland | Cardiff C | Undisclosed, reported 650,000 |
| 4 | Carlisle, Clarke | York C | Northampton T | Free |
| 17 | Charles, Anthony | Northampton T | Plymouth Arg | Free |
| 31 | Chorley, Ben | Leyton Orient | Stevenage | Free |
| 7 | Clarke, Leon | Charlton Ath | Coventry C | Free |
| 3 | Cole, Joseph J. | Liverpool | West Ham U | Free |
| 3 | Compton, Jack | Portsmouth | Colchester U | Undisclosed |
| 4 | Cooper, Liam D.I. | Hull C | Chesterfield | Undisclosed |
| 5 | Davies, Craig M. | Barnsley | Bolton W | Undisclosed, reported 300,000 |
| 17 | Edwards, Joseph R. | Bristol C | Yeovil T | Undisclosed |
| 1 | Elford-Alliyu, Lateef | Bury | Crawley T | Free |
| 22 | Essam, Connor | Gillingham | Crawley T | Free |
| 1 | Evans, Gareth | Rotherham U | Fleetwood T | Free |
| 30 | Forrester, Anton | Everton | Blackburn R | Free |
| 4 | Fowler, Lee A. | Fleetwood T | Doncaster R | Undisclosed |
| 18 | Fraser, Ryan | Aberdeen | Bournemouth | Undisclosed, reported 400,000 |
| 2 | Frecklington, Lee | Peterborough U | Rotherham U | Undisclosed |
| 8 | Garner, Joe | Watford | Preston NE | Free |
| 2 | Gayle, Dwight D.B. | Dagenham & R | Peterborough U | Undisclosed |
| 10 | Gornell, Terence | Shrewsbury T | Rochdale | Undisclosed |
| 31 | Graham, Danny | Swansea C | Sunderland | 5,000,000 |
| 9 | Gray, Andy | Leeds U | Bradford C | Free |
| 2 | Hall, Ryan | Southend U | Leeds U | Undisclosed |
| 31 | Harrison, Byron J. | AFC Wimbledon | Cheltenham T | Undisclosed |
| 24 | Henderson, Darius | Millwall | Nottingham F | Undisclosed |
| 3 | Higginbotham, Daniel J. | Stoke C | Sheffield U | Free |
| 8 | Hughes, Lee | Notts Co | Port Vale | Free |
| 10 | Hussey, Chris | Coventry C | AFC Wimbledon | Free |
| 22 | Ibehre, Jabo | Milton Keynes D | Colchester U | Free |
| 31 | Jenas, Jermaine | Tottenham H | QPR | Undisclosed |
| 18 | Jones, Daniel | Sheffield W | Port Vale | Free |
| 11 | Kelly, Liam | Kilmarnock | Bristol C | Undisclosed |
| 11 | Kelly, Stephen M. | Fulham | Reading | Undisclosed |
| 2 | King, Joshua C.K. | Manchester U | Blackburn R | Undisclosed |
| 4 | Laird, Marc | Leyton Orient | Southend U | Free |
| 30 | Legge, Leon | Brentford | Gillingham | Undisclosed |
| 1 | Lucas, David | Birmingham C | Fleetwood T | Undisclosed |
| 11 | MacDonald, Charlie | Milton Keynes D | Leyton Orient | Free |
| 3 | Madden, Patrick | Carlisle U | Yeovil T | Undisclosed |
| 3 | Maguire, Sean | Waterford United | West Ham U | Undisclosed |
| 11 | Mantom, Sam | WBA | Walsall | Free |
| 8 | McAllister, David | Sheffield U | Shrewsbury T | Undisclosed |
| 3 | McChrystal, Mark | Tranmere R | Bristol R | Free |
| 3 | McLeod, Izale | Portsmouth | Milton Keynes D | Free |
| 7 | Meyler, David | Sunderland | Hull C | Undisclosed, reported 1,500,000 |
| 18 | Molesley, Mark | Bournemouth | Exeter C | Free |
| 25 | Moloney, Brendan | Nottingham F | Bristol C | Free |
| 31 | Morison, Steve | Norwich C | Leeds U | Swap |
| 3 | Murphy, Jamie | Motherwell | Sheffield U | Undisclosed |
| 16 | Nelson, Michael | Kilmarnock | Bradford C | Undisclosed, reported 30,000 |
| 7 | Nouble, Frank H.H. | Wolverhampton W | Ipswich T | Undisclosed |
| 31 | O'Donovan, Roy | Coventry C | Northampton T | Free |
| 11 | O'Shea, Jay | Milton Keynes D | Chesterfield | Free |
| 3 | Pitman, Brett | Bristol C | Bournemouth | Undisclosed |
| 16 | Proctor, Jamie | Swansea C | Crawley T | Undisclosed |
| 5 | Purse, Darren | Plymouth Arg | Port Vale | Free |
| 31 | Regan, Carl | Notts Co | Bury | Free |
| 31 | Richards, Justin | Burton Alb | Oxford U | Free |
| 7 | Risser, Oliver | Swindon T | Aldershot T | Free |
| 30 | Ritchie, Matthew T. | Swindon T | Bournemouth | 500,000 |
| 31 | Sainte-Luce, Kevin | Cardiff C | AFC Wimbledon | Free |
| 28 | Scotland, Jason | Ipswich T | Barnsley | Free |
| 10 | Sparrow, Matt | Brighton & HA | Crawley T | Free |
| 17 | Spillane, Michael | Dagenham & R | Southend U | Undisclosed |
| 31 | Stones, John | Barnsley | Everton | reported 3,000,000 |
| 2 | Sturridge, Daniel | Chelsea | Liverpool | 12,000,000 |
| 8 | Sweeney, Peter | Bury | AFC Wimbledon | Free |
| 28 | Taylor, Jason | Rotherham U | Cheltenham T | Free |
| 1 | Thompson, Joshua | Portsmouth | Colchester U | Undisclosed |
| 10 | Tonge, Michael | Stoke C | Leeds U | Undisclosed |
| 11 | Ward, Darren P. | Millwall | Swindon T | Free |
| 31 | Warnock, Stephen | Aston Villa | Leeds U | Free |
| 2 | Wood, Christopher | WBA | Leicester C | Undisclosed, reported 1,000,000 |
| 9 | Woolford, Martyn | Bristol C | Millwall | Undisclosed |
| 30 | Wordsworth, Anthony | Colchester U | Ipswich T | Undisclosed, reported 100,000 |
| 25 | Wright, David | Crystal Palace | Colchester U | Free |
| 25 | Zaha, Wilfried | Crystal Palace | Manchester U | 10,000,000 + 5,000,000 add-ons |

**JANUARY 2013 TEMPORARY TRANSFERS**
15 Abadaki, Godwin E. – Rochdale – Huddersfield T; 6 Adams, Blair V. – Sunderland – Coventry C; 29 Adeyemi, Thomas – Norwich C – Brentford; 31 Ahmed Elmehamady A. – Sunderland – Hull C; 21 Ainsworth, Lionel – Rotherham U – Aldershot T; 6 Ajala, Ridwan – Bristol C – AFC Wimbledon; 23 Ajose, Nicholas O. – Peterborough U – Bury; 31 Alexander, Gary G. – Crawley T – AFC Wimbledon; 17 Andrade, Bruno M.C. – QPR – Wycombe W; 31 Aneke, Chukwuemeka A.A. – Arsenal – Crewe Alex; 28 Appiah, Kwesi – Crystal Palace – Yeovil T; 4 Assombalonga, Britt C. – Watford – Southend U; 18 Azeez, Adebayo – Charlton Ath – Leyton Orient; 1 Bailey, James J. – Derby Co – Coventry C; 31 Bamford, Patrick J. – Chelsea – Milton Keynes D; 31 Banton, Jason S. – Crystal Palace – Plymouth Arg; 11 Barkley, Ross – Everton – Leeds U; 31 Barnard, Lee J.J. – Southampton – Oldham Ath; 31 Batt, Shaun – Millwall – Leyton Orient; 1 Beckford, Jermaine P. – Leicester C – Huddersfield T; 4 Beleck A'Beka, L.S. – Watford – Stevenage; 11 Belford, Cameron – Bury – Accrington S; 29 Benson, Paul A. – Swindon T – Cheltenham T; 6 Bidwell, Jake – Everton – Brentford; 23 Brunt, Ryan S. – Stoke C – Bristol R; 8 Burn, Daniel – Fulham – Yeovil T; 31 Butland, Jack – Stoke C – Birmingham C; 17 Butterfield, Jacob – Norwich C – Crystal Palace; 6 Cameron, Courtney – Aston Villa – Rotherham U; 30 Cansdell-Sheriff, Shane L. – Preston NE – Rochdale; 13 Caprice, Jake L. – Blackpool – Dagenham & R; 3 Chalobah, Nathaniel – Chelsea – Watford; 4 Chamakh, Marouane – Arsenal – West Ham U; 1 Clarke, Leon M. – Charlton Ath – Coventry C; 11 Clifford, Billy – Chelsea – Colchester U; 1 Compton, Jack L.P. – Portsmouth – Colchester U; 15 Connolly, Paul – Leeds U – Preston NE; 26 Cooper, Shaun D. – Crawley T – Portsmouth; 6 Daniels, Donervon – WBA – Tranmere R; 9 Danns, Neil A. – Leicester C – Huddersfield T; 1 Darlow, Karl – Nottingham F – Walsall; 25 Dawson, Craig – WBA – Bolton W; 31 De Ridder, Steve D.M. – Southampton – Bolton W; 31 Delap, Rory J. – Stoke C – Barnsley; 25 Derbyshire, Matthew – Nottingham F – Blackpool; 11 Dickson, Ryan A. – Southampton – Bradford C; 4 Dolan, Matthew – Middlesbrough – Yeovil T; 4 Drury, Adam J. – Manchester C – Burton Alb; 21 Eastham, Ashley – Blackpool – Bury; 4 Ebanks Landell, Ethan – Wolverhampton W – Bury; 31 Edwards, Robert O. – Barnsley – Shrewsbury T; 31 Elmohamady, Ahmed – Sunderland – Hull C; 31 Forte, Jonathan – Southampton – Sheffield U; 25 Frimpong, Emmanuel Y. – Arsenal – Fulham; 11 Gayle, Cameron – WBA – Shrewsbury T; 3 Good, Curtis E. – Newcastle U – Bradford C; 31 Hall, Asa P. – Shrewsbury T – Aldershot T; 13 Hall, Robert K.D. – West Ham U – Birmingham C; 1 Harley, Ryan – Brighton & HA – Milton Keynes D; 1 Harriman, Michael G. – QPR – Wycombe W; 2 Hector, Michael – Reading – Aldershot T; 30 Helan, Jeremy – Manchester C – Sheffield W; 31 Henderson, Stephen – West Ham U – Ipswich T; 2 Henriquez Iturra, A.J. – Manchester U – Wigan Ath; 4 Hewitt, Troy R. – QPR – Bury; 1 Higginbotham, Daniel J. – Stoke C – Sheffield U; 1 Hitchcock, Thomas J. – QPR – Bristol R; 1 Hitchcock, Tom – QPR – Bristol R; 6 Hollands, Daniel T. – Charlton Ath – Swindon T; 4 Hopper, Thomas – Leicester C – Bury; 2 Hoskins, Samuel-Tobias – Southampton – Stevenage; 31 Hughes, Mark – Bury – Accrington S; 29 Hulse, Robert W. – QPR – Millwall; 1 Hume, Iain – Preston NE – Doncaster R; 31 Hunt, Nicky – Rotherham U – Accrington S; 1 Hunt, Nicky – Rotherham U – Accrington S; 3 Inman, Bradden – Newcastle U – Crewe Alex; 6 Iro, Andrew – Stevenage – Barnet; 3 Ismail, Zeli – Wolverhampton W – Milton Keynes D; 30 Iwelumo, Christopher – Watford – Oldham Ath; 10 Jara Reyes, G.A. – WBA – Nottingham F; 10 Jara, Gonzalo – WBA – Nottingham F; 9 Kane, Todd A.L. – Chelsea – Blackburn R; 3 Keane, Michael – Manchester U – Leicester C; 9 Kearns, Daniel – Peterborough U – Rotherham U; 11 Kiernan, Robert S. – Wigan Ath – Brentford; 2 Kisnorbo, Patrick – Leeds U – Ipswich T; 3 Kisnorbo, Patrick – Leeds U – Ipswich T; 24 Lavery, Caolan – Sheffield W – Southend U; 14 Lee, Hodson J.S. – Watford – Brentford; 1 Legge, Leon – Brentford – Gillingham; 23 Lines, Chris – Sheffield W – Milton Keynes D; 25 Lita, Leroy – Swansea C – Sheffield W; 2 Lopez Robles, D. – Swansea – Aldershot T; 31 MacDonald, Alexander – Burnley – Burton Alb; 7 MacDonald, Angus L. – Reading – Torquay U; 29 Maddison, Jonny – Sunderland – Crawley T; 1 Mambo, Yado – Charlton Ath – Shrewsbury T; 1 Mambo, Yado M. – Charlton Ath – Shrewsbury T; 6 Martin, Christopher – Norwich C – Swindon T; 31 Mason, Ryan – Tottenham H – Leyton Orient; 20 McCallum, Paul – West Ham U – AFC Wimbledon; 25 McCullough, Luke – Manchester U – Cheltenham T; 31 McDonald, Alex – Burnley – Burton Alb; 23 McDonald, Clayton – Port Vale – Bristol R; 26 McDonald, Cody D.J. – Coventry C – Gillingham; 4 McGinn, Stephen – Watford – Shrewsbury T; 4 McGoldrick, David J. – Nottingham F – Ipswich T; 25 McKenna, Paul S. – Hull C – Fleetwood T; 4 McLean, Aaron – Hull C – Ipswich T; 13 McLoughlin, Ian – Milton Keynes D – Walsall; 13 Meades, Jonathan C.C. – Bournemouth – AFC Wimbledon; 31 Meades, Jonathan C.C. – Bournemouth – AFC Wimbledon; 1 Mildenhall, Stephen J. – Millwall – Bristol R; 16 Mildenhall, Stephen J. – Millwall – Bristol R; 9 Montrose, Lewis R.E. – Gillingham – Oxford U; 4 Morgan, Adam J. – Liverpool – Rotherham U; 11 Murray, Ronan – Ipswich T – Plymouth Arg; 23 Naylor, Tom – Derby Co – Bradford C; 10 Nimely-Tchuimeni, Alex – Manchester C – Crystal Palace; 30 Obeng, Curtis – Swansea C – York C; 31 Obita, Jordan J. – Reading – Oldham Ath; 24 O'Connell, Jack – Blackburn R – York C; 13 O'Connor, Anthony D. – Blackburn R – Burton Alb; 31 O'Grady, Christopher – Sheffield W – Barnsley; 7 O'Halloran, Michael F. – Bolton W – Tranmere R; 1 O'Toole, John-Joe – Colchester U – Bristol R; 1 O'Toole, John-Joe – Colchester U – Bristol R; 28 Oyeleke, Emmanuel – Brentford – Northampton T; 3 Palmer, Liam J. – Sheffield W – Tranmere R; 26 Payne, Jack – Gillingham – Peterborough U; 9 Petrucci, David – Manchester U – Peterborough U; 9 Petrucci, Davide – Manchester U – Peterborough U; 31 Phillips, Kevin – Blackpool – Crystal Palace; 1 Porter, George – Burnley – Colchester U; 1 Porter, George – Burnley – Colchester U; 31 Pritchard, Alex – Tottenham H – Peterborough U; 25 Pugh, Daniel – Leeds U – Sheffield W; 31 Rachubka, Paul – Leeds U – Accrington S; 26 Reed, Adam – Sunderland – Portsmouth; 31 Reeves, Benjamin N. – Southampton – Southend U; 25 Reid, Reuben – Yeovil T – Plymouth Arg; 25 Richards, Ashley – Swansea C – Crystal Palace; 4 Richards, Justin D. – Burton Alb – Oxford U; 10 Ridehalgh, Liam – Huddersfield T – Rotherham U; 31 Robinson, Anton D. – Huddersfield T – Gillingham; 6 Rodman, Alexander – Aldershot T – York C; 6 Rose, Daniel S. – Fleetwood T – Aldershot T; 29 Rudd, Declan – Norwich C – Preston NE; 3 Samuel, Dominic J. – Reading – Colchester U; 17 Seaborne, Daniel A.S. – Southampton – Bournemouth; 10 Sekajja, Ibra – Crystal Palace – Barnet; 18 Sharps, Ian W. – Rotherham U – Burton Alb; 5 Sinclair, Emile A. – Peterborough U – Doncaster R; 31 Slew, Jordan – Blackburn R – Rotherham U; 25 Spencer, James – Huddersfield T – Crawley T; 29 Stearman, Richard – Wolverhampton W – Ipswich T; 18 Stockdale, David A. – Fulham – Hull C; 17 Sullivan, Neil – Doncaster R – AFC Wimbledon; 15 Sutherland, Frankie J. – QPR – Portsmouth; 31 Symes, Michael – Leyton Orient – Burton Alb; 3 Taylor, Jake W.T. – Reading – Cheltenham T; 31 Thomas, Wesley – Bournemouth – Birmingham C; 3 Thompson, Adam L. – Watford – Barnet; 4 Thompson, Zac J. – Leeds U – Bury; 31 Townsend, Andros – Tottenham H – QPR; 14 Trotta, Marcello – Fulham – Brentford; 25 Tsend, Conor S. – Hull C – Chesterfield; 6 Turgott, Blair – West Ham U – Bradford C; 17 Tyson, Nathan – Derby Co – Millwall; 16 Ugwu, Chigozie E. – Reading – Plymouth Arg; 31 Upson, Matthew – Stoke C – Brighton & HA; 6 Wabara, Reece – Manchester C – Oldham Ath; 14 Walker, Samuel C. – Chelsea – Colchester U; 2 Ward, Darren P. – Millwall – Swindon T; 8 Ward, Elliott L. – Norwich C – Nottingham F; 1 Wood, Christopher – WBA – Leicester C; 9 Wootton, Scott J. – Manchester U – Peterborough U; 10 Wyke, Charles T. – Middlesbrough – Hartlepool U; 26 Zaha, Wilfried – Manchester U – Crystal Palace; 25 Zaha, Wilfried – Manchester U – Crystal Palace; 24 Zubar, Stephane – Bournemouth – Bury

**FEBRUARY 2013 TRANSFERS**

| | | |
|---|---|---|
| 1 Bennett, Alan | Cheltenham T | AFC Wimbledon |
| 1 Croft, Lee | Derby Co | Oldham Ath |
| 14 Garmston, Bradley | WBA | Colchester U |
| 15 Painter, Marcos | Brighton & HA | Bournemouth |

**FEBRUARY 2013 TEMPORARY TRANSFERS**
8 Afobe, Benik T. – Arsenal – Millwall; 8 Agyemang, Patrick – Stevenage – Portsmouth; 21 Alabi, James O. – Stoke C – Scunthorpe U; 25 Ameobi, Samuel – Newcastle U – Middlesbrough; 15 Bentley, David – Tottenham H – Blackburn R;

11 Benyon, Elliott P. – Southend U – Torquay U; 3 Bidwell, Jake – Everton – Brentford; 13 Blyth, Jacob M. – Leicester C – Notts Co; 21 Boyd, George – Peterborough U – Hull C; 28 Briggs, Matthew – Fulham – Watford; 24 Brown, Reece – Manchester U – Ipswich T; 1 Butland, Jack – Stoke C – Birmingham C; 20 Butterfield, Jacob – Norwich C – Crystal Palace; 9 Cameron, Courtney – Aston Villa – Rotherham U; 9 Campbell, Dudley J. – QPR – Blackburn R; 10 Caprice, Jake L. – Blackpool – Dagenham & R; 22 Clark, Jordan – Barnsley – Chesterfield; 15 Clarke-Harris, Jonson S. – Peterborough U – Bury; 12 Clifford, Billy – Chelsea – Colchester U; 8 Cofie, John E. – Manchester U – Notts Co; 26 Cooper, Shaun D. – Crawley T – Portsmouth; 15 Corry, Paul – Sheffield W – Tranmere R; 8 Cox, Lee D. – Swindon T – Plymouth Arg; 7 Daniels, Donervon – WBA – Tranmere R; 21 Darko, Jesse – Cardiff C – AFC Wimbledon; 22 Dickenson, Brennan – Brighton & HA – AFC Wimbledon; 12 Dickinson, Carl – Watford – Coventry C; 3 Dolan, Matthew – Middlesbrough – Yeovil T; 5 Drury, Adam J. – Manchester C – Burton Alb; 21 Eaves, Thomas – Bolton W – Shrewsbury T; 10 Ebanks Landell, E. – Wolverhampton W – Bury; 22 Edwards, Ryan C. – Blackburn R – Fleetwood T; 28 Ferguson, Shane – Newcastle U – Birmingham C; 28 Fletcher, Wesleigh – Burnley – Yeovil T; 26 German, Antonio T. – Brentford – Gillingham; 3 Good, Curtis E. – Newcastle U – Bradford C; 12 Gorkss, Kaspars – Reading – Wolverhampton W; 17 Hall, Robert K.D. – West Ham U – Birmingham C; 27 Hector, Michael – Reading – Cheltenham T; 22 Henshall, Alex – Manchester C – Chesterfield; 21 Howieson, Cameron D.N. – Burnley – Doncaster R; 21 Kane, Harry – Tottenham H – Leicester C; 13 Lopez Robles, D. – Stevenage – Barnet; 14 Lund, Matthew – Stoke C – Southend U; 21 Lundstram, John D. – Everton – Doncaster R; 22 Mahon, Gavin A. – Notts Co – Stevenage; 25 Martin, Aaron – Southampton – Coventry C; 22 Martin, Christopher – Norwich C – Derby Co; 12 Mayor, Danny – Sheffield W – Southend U; 21 McCarey, Aaron – Wolverhampton W – Walsall; 22 McCullough, Luke – Manchester U – Cheltenham T; 11 McGrath, John M. – Burton Alb – York C; 19 Moore, Liam – Leicester C – Brentford; 21 Mustoe, Jordan D. – Wigan Ath – Carlisle U; 13 N'Gala, Bondz – Stevenage – Barnet; 22 Obika, Jonathan – Tottenham H – Charlton Ath; 13 O'Brien, Aiden – Millwall – Crawley T; 25 O'Connell, Jack – Blackburn R – York C; 16 Poleon, Dominic – Leeds U – Sheffield U; 13 Porter, Christopher – Sheffield U – Shrewsbury T; 8 Racon, Therry N. – Millwall – Portsmouth; 12 Rankine, Michael – Aldershot T – York C; 26 Reed, Adam – Sunderland – Portsmouth; 27 Rees, Joshua D. – Arsenal – Brentford; 27 Reid, Reuben – Yeovil T – Plymouth Arg; 15 Rekik, Karim – Manchester C – Blackburn R; 14 Richardson, Michael – Newcastle U – Gillingham; 18 Robinson, Jack – Liverpool – Wolverhampton W; 22 Robinson, Theo – Derby Co – Huddersfield T; 28 Saville, George A. – Chelsea – Millwall; 21 Sidibe, Mamady – Stoke C – Tranmere R; 21 Tunnicliffe, Ryan – Manchester U – Barnsley; 4 Turgott, Blair – West Ham U – Bradford C; 17 Ugwu, Chigozie E. – Reading – Plymouth Arg; 8 Wickham, Connor – Sunderland – Sheffield W; 14 Williams, Ryan – Fulham – Gillingham; 19 Wright-Phillips, Bradley E. – Charlton Ath – Brentford

### MARCH 2013 TRANSFERS

| | | | |
|---|---|---|---|
| 1 Stewart, Jordan | Notts Co | Coventry C | Free |
| 26 Balanta, Angelo | QPR | Yeovil T | Undisclosed |

### MARCH 2013 TEMPORARY TRANSFERS

8 Agyemang, Patrick – Stevenage – Portsmouth; 24 Alabi, James O. – Stoke C – Scunthorpe U; 28 Asante, Akwasi – Birmingham C – Shrewsbury T; 25 Balanta, Angelo – QPR – Yeovil T; 1 Banton, Jason S. – Crystal Palace – Plymouth Arg; 3 Batt, Shaun – Millwall – Leyton Orient; 11 Benyon, Elliott P. – Southend U – Torquay U; 6 Bidwell, Jake – Everton – Brentford; 25 Boyd, George – Peterborough U – Hull C AFC; 1 Briggs, Matthew – Fulham – Watford; 27 Brito E Silva, Toni – Barnsley – Dagenham & R; 12 Bryan, Joseph E. – Bristol C – Plymouth Arg; 27 Burn, Daniel – Fulham – Yeovil T; 28 Butterfield, Daniel – Southampton – Bolton W; 28 Byrne, Nathan – Tottenham H – Swindon T; 26 Cameron, Nathan B. – Coventry C – Northampton T; 14 Carson, Joshua – Ipswich T – York C; 14 Chapell, Jordan – Sheffield U – Torquay U; 15 Chaplow, Richard D. – Southampton – Millwall; 18 Cook, Jordan – Charlton Ath – Yeovil T; 26 Cooper, Shaun D, – Crawley T – Portsmouth; 19 Cresswell, Richard P.W. – Sheffield U – York C; 27 Cuvelier, Florent – Stoke C – Peterborough U; 15 D'Ath, Lawson M. – Reading – Exeter C; 22 De Silva, Kyle M. – Crystal Palace – Barnet; 28 Deaman, Jack – Birmingham C – Cheltenham T; 28 Dicko, Nouha – Wigan Ath – Wolverhampton W; 28 Dobbie, Stephen – Brighton & HA – Crystal Palace; 28 Dolan, Matthew – Middlesbrough – Yeovil T; 7 East, Daniel – Hull C – Gillingham; 15 Easter, Jermaine M. – Crystal Palace – Millwall; 24 Eaves, Thomas – Bolton W – Shrewsbury T; 3 Edwards, Robert O. – Barnsley – Shrewsbury T; 25 Edwards, Ryan C. – Blackburn R – Fleetwood T; 28 Ehmer, Maximilian A. – QPR – Stevenage; 14 Flanagan, Thomas – Milton Keynes D – Barnet; 15 Forde, Anthony – Wolverhampton W – Scunthorpe U; 4 Forsyth, Craig – Watford – Derby Co; 28 Fowler, Lee A. – Doncaster R – Burton Alb; 13 Furman, Dean – Oldham Ath – Doncaster R; 4 Futacs, Marko – Leicester C – Blackpool; 14 Gibson, Benjamin J. – Middlesbrough – Tranmere R; 28 Gilbert, Peter – Lincoln C – Dagenham & R; 14 Gower, Mark – Swansea C – Charlton Ath; 28 Grant, Harry E. – Sheffield W – Gillingham; 4 Griffiths, Anthony J. – Leyton Orient – Port Vale; 28 Hall, Robert K.D. – West Ham U – Bolton W; 11 Hayes, Paul – Brentford – Crawley T; 27 Hector, Michael – Reading – Cheltenham T; 24 Henshall, Alex – Manchester C – Chesterfield; 7 Hewitt, Troy R. – QPR – Colchester U; 28 Holden, Stuart A. – Bolton W – Sheffield W; 28 Howard, Steven J. – Hartlepool U – Sheffield W; 28 Hurst, James – WBA – Shrewsbury T; 7 Jameson, Arron T. – Sheffield W – York C; 1 Jeffrey, Anthony – Arsenal – Stevenage; 6 Jenkins, Ross A. – Watford – Barnet; 7 Johansen, Eirik H. – Manchester C – Scunthorpe U; 19 Johnstone, Samuel L. – Manchester U – Walsall; 2 Jones, David F.L. – Wigan Ath – Blackburn R; 1 Kacaniklic, Alexander – Fulham – Burnley; 15 Kane, Todd A.L. – Chelsea – Blackburn R; 6 Labadie, Joss – Notts Co – Torquay U; 21 Lee, Oliver – Barnet – Birmingham C; 18 Lund, Matthew – Stoke C – Southend U; 24 Lundstram, John D. – Everton – Doncaster R; 28 Luongo, Massimo – Tottenham H – Swindon T; 8 MacDonald, Alexander – Burnley – Burton Alb; 1 MacKenzie, Gary – Milton Keynes D – Blackpool; 18 Maksimenko, Vitalijs – Brighton & HA – Yeovil T; 28 Martin, Christopher – Norwich C – Derby Co; 8 McCallum, Paul – West Ham U – Aldershot T; 28 McGinty, Sean – Manchester U – Tranmere R; 12 McGrath, John M. – Burton Alb – York C; 1 Mersin, Yusuf – Liverpool – Gillingham; 28 Miles, Jonathan – Tottenham H – Dagenham & R; 16 Mkandawire, Tamika – Millwall – Southend U; 3 Obika, Jordan J. – Reading – Oldham Ath; 27 Olofinjana, Seyi G. – Hull C – Sheffield W; 28 Parrett, Dean G. – Tottenham H – Swindon T; 8 Racon, Therry N. – Millwall – Portsmouth; 26 Reed, Adam – Sunderland – York C; 15 Reeves, Benjamin N. – Southampton – Sunderland U; 25 Reid, Bobby – Bristol C – Oldham Ath; 28 Reid, Reuben – Yeovil T – Plymouth Arg; 20 Rodgers, Anton M. – Brighton & HA – Exeter C; 28 Sawyers, Romaine – WBA – Walsall; 28 Shariff, Abdallah M. – QPR – Dagenham & R; 27 Silva, Toni – Barnsley – Dagenham & R; 28 Skarz, Joseph – Bury – Rotherham U; 28 Smith, Alex R. – Fulham – Stevenage; 15 Smith, Korey – Norwich C – Oldham Ath; 8 Smith, Michael – Charlton Ath – Colchester U; 28 St Ledger, Sean – Leicester C – Millwall; 1 Stewart, Cameron – Hull C – Blackburn R; 28 Stewart, Kevin – Tottenham H – Crewe Alex; 8 Sullivan, John – Charlton Ath – AFC Wimbledon; 8 Tabb, Jay – Reading – Ipswich T; 28 Taylor, Cleveland – Burton Alb – Grimsby T; 1 Taylor, Jake W.T. – Reading – Crawley T; 1 Thompson, Joe – Tranmere R – Rochdale; 8 Wilson, Douglas – Hull C – Grimsby T

### APRIL 2013 TEMPORARY TRANSFERS

8 Agyemang, Patrick – Stevenage – Portsmouth; 29 Balanta, Angelo – QPR – Yeovil T; 7 Bidwell, Jake – Everton – Brentford; 14 D'Ath, Lawson M. – Reading – Exeter C; 29 Dolan, Matthew – Middlesbrough – Yeovil T; 2 Ferguson, Shane – Newcastle U – Birmingham C; 2 Forsyth, Craig – Watford – Derby Co; 8 Hayes, Paul – Brentford – Crawley T; 8 Johansen, Eirik H. – Manchester C – Scunthorpe U; 17 Kane, Todd A.L. – Chelsea – Blackburn R; 18 Maksimenko, Vitalijs – Brighton & HA – Yeovil T; 8 McCallum, Paul – West Ham U – Aldershot T; 28 Nicholls, Lee A. – Wigan Ath – Northampton T; 28 O'Connor, Anthony D. – Blackburn R – Burton Alb; 14 Smith, Korey – Norwich C – Oldham Ath; 7 Smith, Michael J. – Charlton Ath – Colchester U; 5 Tabb, Jay A. – Reading – Ipswich T

**MAY 2013 TRANSFERS**

| | | | | |
|---|---|---|---|---|
| 8 | Agyemang, Patrick | Stevenage | Portsmouth | Free |
| 22 | Amorebieta, Fernando | Athletic Bilbao | Fulham | Free |
| 20 | Barcham, Andy | Scunthorpe U | Portsmouth | Free |
| 22 | Black, Paul | Tranmere R | Mansfield T | Free |
| 13 | Blair, Matty | York C | Fleetwood T | Free |
| 22 | Boateng, Derek | Dnipro | Fulham | Free |
| 28 | Boyd, George | Peterborough U | Hull C | Free |
| 9 | Bradley, Sonny | Hull C | Portsmouth | Free |
| 23 | Brindley, Richard | Chesterfield | Rotherham U | Free |
| 22 | Clarke, Tom | Huddersfield T | Preston NE | Free |
| 12 | Clarke-Harris, Jonson | Peterborough U | Oldham Ath | Undisclosed |
| 17 | Clay, Craig | Chesterfield | York C | Free |
| 23 | Collin, Adam | Carlisle U | Rotherham U | Free |
| 12 | Craddock, Tom | Oxford U | Portsmouth | Free |
| 30 | Dawson, Andy | Hull C | Scunthorpe U | Free |
| 20 | Dayton, James | Kilmarnock | Oldham Ath | Free |
| 14 | Devera, Joe | Swindon T | Portsmouth | Free |
| 31 | Doyle, Eoin | Hibernian | Chesterfield | Free |
| 31 | Eardley, Neil | Blackpool | Birmingham C | Free |
| 9 | East, Danny | Hull C | Portsmouth | Free |
| 20 | Eastmond, Craig | Arsenal | Colchester U | Free |
| 28 | Eastwood, Simon | Portsmouth | Blackburn R | Free |
| 28 | Fuller, Barry | Barnet | AFC Wimbledon | Free |
| 14 | Garrido, Javier | Lazio | Norwich C | Undisclosed |
| 17 | Heaton, Tom | Bristol C | Burnley | Free |
| 8 | Hery, Bastien | Sheffield W | Rochdale | Free |
| 21 | Heslop, Simon | Oxford U | Stevenage | Free |
| 22 | Hogan, Liam | FC Halifax | Fleetwood T | Free |
| 22 | Hughes, Jeff | Notts Co | Fleetwood T | Free |
| 17 | Jarvis, Ryan | Torquay U | York C | Free |
| 21 | Jones, Luke | Mansfield T | Stevenage | Free |
| 28 | Judge, Alan | Notts Co | Blackburn R | Free |
| 8 | Lee, Olly | Barnet | Birmingham C | Free |
| 9 | Martin, Chris | Norwich C | Derby Co | Free |
| 9 | McCormick, Luke | Oxford U | Plymouth Arg | Free |
| 31 | McGivern, Ryan | Manchester C | Hibernian | Free |
| 13 | McGuire, Jamie | Fleetwood T | Mansfield T | Free |
| 23 | Meades, Jonathan | Bournemouth | Oxford U | Free |
| 30 | Mildenhall, Steve | Millwall | Bristol R | Free |
| 24 | Mills, Joseph | Reading | Burnley | Free |
| 28 | Murtagh, Keiran | Macclesfield T | Mansfield T | Free |
| 21 | Novak, Lee | Huddersfield | Birmingham C | Free |
| 9 | Padovani, Romain | Monaco | Portsmouth | Free |
| 14 | Randolph, Darren | Motherwell | Birmingham C | Free |
| 21 | Rat, Razvan | Shakhtar Donetsk | West Ham U | Free |
| 21 | Schumacher, Steven | Bury | Fleetwood T | Undisclosed |
| 14 | Skuse, Cole | Bristol C | Ipswich T | Free |
| 16 | Sullivan, John | Charlton Ath | Portsmouth | Free |
| 28 | Taylor, Chris | Millwall | Blackburn R | Free |
| 30 | Tierney, Marc | Norwich C | Bolton W | Free |
| 21 | Tounkara, Oumare | Bristol R | Stevenage | Free |
| 28 | Toure, Kolo | Manchester C | Liverpool | Free |
| 10 | Vincenti, Peter | Aldershot T | Rochdale | Free |
| 24 | Watmore, Duncan | Altrincham | Sunderland | Undisclosed |
| 21 | Wedgbury, Sam | Macclesfield T | Stevenage | Free |
| 27 | Wilson, Danny | Liverpool | Hearts | Free |
| 22 | Wynter, Jordan | Arsenal | Bristol C | Free |

# THE NEW FOREIGN LEGION 2012–13

**JUNE 2012**

| | From | To | Fee in £ |
|---|---|---|---|
| Hazard, Eden | Lille | Chelsea | Undisclosed |
| Mido | Zamalek FC | Barnsley | Free |
| Giroud, Olivier | Montpellier HSC | Arsenal | Undisclosed |
| Saltor, Bruno | Valencia | Brighton & HA | Free |
| Diakite, Samba | Nancy | QPR | Undisclosed |
| Petric, Mladen | Hamburg | Fulham | Free |

**JULY 2012**

| | | | |
|---|---|---|---|
| Kagawa, Shinji | Borussia Dortmund | Manchester U | Undisclosed |
| Sigurdarson, Bjorn | Lillestrom | Wolverhampton W | Undisclosed |
| El Ahmadi, Karim | Feyenoord | Aston Villa | Undisclosed |
| Gomes, Nuno | Sporting Braga | Blackburn R | Free |
| Podolski, Lukas | FC Koln | Arsenal | Undisclosed |
| Sigurdsson, Gylfi | TSG 1899 Hoffenheim | Tottenham H | Undisclosed |
| Nunes, Fabio | Portimonese SC | Blackburn R | Undisclosed |
| Pogrebnyak, Pavel | Stuttgart | Reading | Free |
| Jakupovic, Eldin | Aris FC | Hull C | Free |
| Amado, Diogo | Uniao Leiria | Sheffield W | Free |
| Manuel, Flores Jose | Genoa | Swansea C | 2,000,000 |
| Velikonja, Etien | NK Maribor | Cardiff C | Undisclosed |
| Vertonghen, Jan | Ajax | Tottenham | Undisclosed |
| Borini, Fabio | Roma | Liverpool | Undisclosed |
| Malaga, Kevin | Nice | Coventry C | Free |

| | | | |
|---|---|---|---|
| Pecnik, Nejc | CD Nacional | Sheffield W | Free |
| Maiga, Modibo | Sochaux | West Ham U | 4,700,000 |
| Proschwitz, Nick | SC Paderborn 07 | Hull C | 2,600,000 |
| Cuesta, Miguel Perez | Rayo Vallecano | Swansea C | 2,000,000 |
| Hazard, Thorgan | Lens | Chelsea | Undisclosed |
| Yacob, Claudio | Racing Club | WBA | Free |
| Gomes, Tiago F | Hercules | Blackpool | Free |
| Oscar | Internacional | Chelsea | Undisclosed |
| Bo-Kyung, Kim | Cerezo Osaka | Cardiff C | Undisclosed |
| Good, Curtis | Melbourne Heart | Newcastle U | Undisclosed |
| Edjenguele William | Panetolikos | Coventry C | Free |

### AUGUST 2012

| | | | |
|---|---|---|---|
| Knockaert, Anthony | Guingamp | Leicester C | Undisclosed |
| Vlaar, Ron | Feyenoord | Aston Villa | Undisclosed |
| Ramis, Ivan | Real Mallorca | Wigan Ath | Undisclosed |
| Cazorla, Santi | Malaga | Arsenal | Undisclosed |
| Rosenberg, Markus | Werder Bremen | WBA | Free |
| Cameron, Geoff | Houston Dynamo | Stoke C | Undisclosed |
| Diarra, Alou | Marseille | West Ham U | 2,000,000 |
| Amond, Padraig | Pacos de Ferreira | Accrington S | Free |
| Djeziri, Adda | Viborg FF | Blackpool | Free |
| Kone, Arouna | Levante | Wigan Ath | Undisclosed |
| Noguera, Alberto | Atletico Madrid | Blackpool | Free |
| Anita, Vurnon | Ajax | Newcastle U | Undisclosed |
| Rodgers, Luke | Lillestrom | Portsmouth | Free |
| Assaidi, Oussama | SC Heerenveen | Liverpool | Undisclosed |
| Dervitte, Dorian | Villarreal | Charlton Ath | Free |
| Mirallas, Kevin | Olympiacos | Everton | 6,000,000 |
| Buttner, Alexander | Vitesse | Manchester U | Undisclosed |
| Azpilicueta, Cesar | Marseille | Chelsea | 6,500,000 |
| Moritz, Andre | Mersin Idmanyurdu | Crystal Palace | Free |
| Tettey, Alexander | Rennes | Norwich C | Undisclosed |
| Boukari, Razak | Rennes | Wolverhampton W | Undisclosed |
| Mayuka, Emmanuel | Young Boys | Southampton | Undisclosed |
| Cesar, Julio | Inter Milan | QPR | Undisclosed |
| Sako, Bakary | St Etienne | Wolverhampton W | Undisclosed |
| Yoshida, Maya | VVV-Venlo | Southampton | Undisclosed |
| Benteke, Christian | Racing Genk | Aston Villa | Undisclosed |
| Buchel, Benjamin | USV Eschen/Mauren | Bournemouth | Free |
| Davids, Lorenzo | Augsburg | Bournemouth | Free |
| Dejagah, Ashkan | Wolfsburg | Fulham | Undisclosed |
| Edu, Maurice | Rangers | Stoke C | Undisclosed |
| Garcia, Javi | Benfica | Manchester C | 16,000,000 |
| Granero, Esteban | Real Madrid | QPR | Undisclosed |
| Henrique, Nuno | AD Fafe | Blackburn R | Undisclosed |
| Hernandez, Pablo | Valencia | Swansea C | 5,550,000 |
| Lloris, Hugo | Lyon | Tottenham H | 8,000,000 |
| Lopez, David | Athletic Bilbao | Brighton & HA | Free |
| Maicon | Inter Milan | Manchester C | Undisclosed |
| Mbia, Stephane | Marseille | QPR | Undisclosed |
| Nastasic, Matija | Fiorentina | Manchester C | 10,000,000 |
| Oviedo, Bryan | FC Copenhagen | Everton | 5,000,000 |
| Ramirez, Gaston | Bologna | Southampton | Undisclosed |
| Rosado, Diogo | Sporting Lisbon | Blackburn R | Undisclosed |
| Henriquez, Angelo | Universidad de Chile | Manchester U | Undisclosed |

### JANUARY 2013

| | | | |
|---|---|---|---|
| Wallace | Fluminense | Chelsea | Undisclosed |
| Carrico, Daniel | Sporting Lisbon | Reading | 609,000 |
| Richards, Dane | Vancouver Whitecaps | Burnley | Free |
| Fryers, Zeki | Standard Liege | Tottenham H | 3,000,000 |
| David, Chris | FC Twente | Fulham | Undisclosed |
| Debuchy, Mathieu | Lille | Newcastle U | 5,000,000 |
| Espinoza, Roger | Sporting Kansas City | Wigan Ath | Free |
| N'Diaye, Alfred | Bursaspor | Sunderland | Undisclosed |
| Forestieri, Fernando | Udinese | Watford | Free |
| Remy, Loic | Marseille | QPR | 8,000,000 |
| Ulloa, Leonardo | Almeria | Brighton & HA | 2,000,000 |
| Forren, Vegard | Molde | Southampton | Undisclosed |
| Yanga-Mbiwa, Mapou | Montpellier HSC | Newcastle U | 6,700,000 |
| Gouffran, Yoan | Bordeaux | Newcastle U | Undisclosed |
| Haidara, Massadio | Nancy | Newcastle U | Undisclosed |
| Sissoko, Moussa | Toulouse | Newcastle U | Undisclosed |
| Holtby, Lewis | Schalke 04 | Tottenham H | 1,500,000 |
| Asmundssen, Emil | Fylkir | Brighton & HA | Undisclosed |
| Coutinho, Philippe | Inter Milan | Liverpool | 8,500,000 |
| Suk-Young, Yun | Chunnam Dragons | QPR | Undisclosed |
| Al-Rashidi, Khaled | Al Arabi | Nottingham F | Free |
| Habibou, Habib | Zulte Waregem | Leeds U | Undisclosed |
| Kamara, Mohamed | Partizan Belgrade | Bolton W | Undisclosed |
| Mbabu, Kevin | Servette | Newcastle U | Undisclosed |
| Monreal, Nacho | Malaga | Arsenal | 10,000,000 |
| Samba, Christopher | FC Anzhi Makhachkala | QPR | 12,500,000 |
| Shea, Brek | FC Dallas | Stoke C | 2,500,000 |
| Sylla, Yacouba | Clermont Foot | Aston Villa | 2,000,000 |

# ENGLISH LEAGUE HONOURS 1888–2013

## FA PREMIER LEAGUE

**MAXIMUM POINTS: *a* 126; *b* 114.**
*Won or placed on goal average (ratio), goal difference or most goals scored. ††Not promoted after play-offs.*

| | First | Pts | Second | Pts | Third | Pts |
|---|---|---|---|---|---|---|
| 1992–93a | Manchester U | 84 | Aston Villa | 74 | Norwich C | 72 |
| 1993–94a | Manchester U | 92 | Blackburn R | 84 | Newcastle U | 77 |
| 1994–95a | Blackburn R | 89 | Manchester U | 88 | Nottingham F | 77 |
| 1995–96b | Manchester U | 82 | Newcastle U | 78 | Liverpool | 71 |
| 1996–97b | Manchester U | 75 | Newcastle U* | 68 | Arsenal* | 68 |
| 1997–98b | Arsenal | 78 | Manchester U | 77 | Liverpool | 65 |
| 1998–99b | Manchester U | 79 | Arsenal | 78 | Chelsea | 75 |
| 1999–2000b | Manchester U | 91 | Arsenal | 73 | Leeds U | 69 |
| 2000–01b | Manchester U | 80 | Arsenal | 70 | Liverpool | 69 |
| 2001–02b | Arsenal | 87 | Liverpool | 80 | Manchester U | 77 |
| 2002–03b | Manchester U | 83 | Arsenal | 78 | Newcastle U | 69 |
| 2003–04b | Arsenal | 90 | Chelsea | 79 | Manchester U | 75 |
| 2004–05b | Chelsea | 95 | Arsenal | 83 | Manchester U | 77 |
| 2005–06b | Chelsea | 91 | Manchester U | 83 | Liverpool | 82 |
| 2006–07b | Manchester U | 89 | Chelsea | 83 | Liverpool* | 68 |
| 2007–08b | Manchester U | 87 | Chelsea | 85 | Arsenal | 83 |
| 2008–09b | Manchester U | 90 | Liverpool | 86 | Chelsea | 83 |
| 2009–10b | Chelsea | 86 | Manchester U | 85 | Arsenal | 75 |
| 2010–11b | Manchester U | 80 | Chelsea* | 71 | Manchester C | 71 |
| 2011–12b | Manchester C* | 89 | Manchester U | 89 | Arsenal | 70 |
| 2012–13b | Manchester U | 89 | Manchester C | 78 | Chelsea | 75 |

## FOOTBALL LEAGUE CHAMPIONSHIP

**MAXIMUM POINTS: 138**

| | | | | | | |
|---|---|---|---|---|---|---|
| 2004–05 | Sunderland | 94 | Wigan Ath | 87 | Ipswich T†† | 85 |
| 2005–06 | Reading | 106 | Sheffield U | 90 | Watford | 81 |
| 2006–07 | Sunderland | 88 | Birmingham C | 86 | Derby Co | 84 |
| 2007–08 | WBA | 81 | Stoke C | 79 | Hull C | 75 |
| 2008–09 | Wolverhampton W | 90 | Birmingham C | 83 | Sheffield U†† | 80 |
| 2009–10 | Newcastle U | 102 | WBA | 91 | Nottingham F†† | 79 |
| 2010–11 | QPR | 88 | Norwich C | 84 | Swansea C* | 80 |
| 2011–12 | Reading | 89 | Southampton | 88 | West Ham U | 86 |
| 2012–13 | Cardiff C | 87 | Hull C | 79 | Watford†† | 77 |

## FIRST DIVISION

**MAXIMUM POINTS: 138**

| | | | | | | |
|---|---|---|---|---|---|---|
| 1992–93 | Newcastle U | 96 | West Ham U* | 88 | Portsmouth†† | 88 |
| 1993–94 | Crystal Palace | 90 | Nottingham F | 83 | Millwall†† | 74 |
| 1994–95 | Middlesbrough | 82 | Reading†† | 79 | Bolton W | 77 |
| 1995–96 | Sunderland | 83 | Derby Co | 79 | Crystal Palace†† | 75 |
| 1996–97 | Bolton W | 98 | Barnsley | 80 | Wolverhampton W†† | 76 |
| 1997–98 | Nottingham F | 94 | Middlesbrough | 91 | Sunderland†† | 90 |
| 1998–99 | Sunderland | 105 | Bradford C | 87 | Ipswich T†† | 86 |
| 1999–2000 | Charlton Ath | 91 | Manchester C | 89 | Ipswich T | 87 |
| 2000–01 | Fulham | 101 | Blackburn R | 91 | Bolton W | 87 |
| 2001–02 | Manchester C | 99 | WBA | 89 | Wolverhampton W†† | 86 |
| 2002–03 | Portsmouth | 98 | Leicester C | 92 | Sheffield U†† | 80 |
| 2003–04 | Norwich C | 94 | WBA | 86 | Sunderland†† | 79 |

## FOOTBALL LEAGUE CHAMPIONSHIP 1

**MAXIMUM POINTS: 138**

| | | | | | | |
|---|---|---|---|---|---|---|
| 2004–05 | Luton T | 98 | Hull C | 86 | Tranmere R†† | 79 |
| 2005–06 | Southend U | 82 | Colchester U | 79 | Brentford†† | 76 |
| 2006–07 | Scunthorpe U | 91 | Bristol C | 85 | Blackpool | 83 |
| 2007–08 | Swansea C | 92 | Nottingham F | 82 | Doncaster R | 80 |
| 2008–09 | Leicester C | 96 | Peterborough U | 89 | Milton Keynes D†† | 87 |
| 2009–10 | Norwich C | 95 | Leeds U | 86 | Millwall | 85 |
| 2010–11 | Brighton & HA | 95 | Southampton | 92 | Huddersfield T†† | 87 |
| 2011–12 | Charlton Ath | 101 | Shefield W | 93 | Sheffield U†† | 90 |
| 2012–13 | Doncaster R | 84 | Bournemouth | 83 | Brentford†† | 79 |

## SECOND DIVISION

**MAXIMUM POINTS: 138**

| | | | | | | |
|---|---|---|---|---|---|---|
| 1992–93 | Stoke C | 93 | Bolton W | 90 | Port Vale†† | 89 |
| 1993–94 | Reading | 89 | Port Vale | 88 | Plymouth Arg*†† | 85 |
| 1994–95 | Birmingham C | 89 | Brentford†† | 85 | Crewe Alex†† | 83 |
| 1995–96 | Swindon T | 92 | Oxford U | 83 | Blackpool†† | 82 |
| 1996–97 | Bury | 84 | Stockport Co | 82 | Luton T†† | 78 |
| 1997–98 | Watford | 88 | Bristol C | 85 | Grimsby T | 72 |
| 1998–99 | Fulham | 101 | Walsall | 87 | Manchester C | 82 |
| 1999–2000 | Preston NE | 95 | Burnley | 88 | Gillingham | 85 |
| 2000–01 | Millwall | 93 | Rotherham U | 91 | Reading†† | 86 |
| 2001–02 | Brighton & HA | 90 | Reading | 84 | Brentford*†† | 83 |
| 2002–03 | Wigan Ath | 100 | Crewe Alex | 86 | Bristol C†† | 83 |
| 2003–04 | Plymouth Arg | 90 | QPR | 83 | Bristol C†† | 82 |

## FOOTBALL LEAGUE CHAMPIONSHIP 2

MAXIMUM POINTS: 138

| | First | Pts | Second | Pts | Third | Pts |
|---|---|---|---|---|---|---|
| 2004–05 | Yeovil T | 83 | Scunthorpe U* | 80 | Swansea C | 80 |
| 2005–06 | Carlisle U | 86 | Northampton T | 83 | Leyton Orient | 81 |
| 2006–07 | Walsall | 89 | Hartlepool U | 88 | Swindon T | 85 |
| 2007–08 | Milton Keynes D | 97 | Peterborough U | 92 | Hereford U | 88 |
| 2008–09 | Brentford | 85 | Exeter C | 79 | Wycombe W* | 78 |
| 2009–10 | Notts Co | 93 | Bournemouth | 83 | Rochdale | 82 |
| 2010–11 | Chesterfield | 86 | Bury | 81 | Wycombe W | 80 |
| 2011–12 | Swindon T | 93 | Shrewsbury T | 88 | Crawley T | 84 |
| 2012–13 | Gillingham | 83 | Rotherham U | 79 | Port Vale | 78 |

## THIRD DIVISION

MAXIMUM POINTS: *a* 126; *b* 138.

| | | | | | | |
|---|---|---|---|---|---|---|
| 1992–93*a* | Cardiff C | 83 | Wrexham | 80 | Barnet | 79 |
| 1993–94*a* | Shrewsbury T | 79 | Chester C | 74 | Crewe Alex | 73 |
| 1994–95*a* | Carlisle U | 91 | Walsall | 83 | Chesterfield | 81 |
| 1995–96*b* | Preston NE | 86 | Gillingham | 83 | Bury | 79 |
| 1996–97*b* | Wigan Ath* | 87 | Fulham | 87 | Carlisle U | 84 |
| 1997–98*b* | Notts Co | 99 | Macclesfield T | 82 | Lincoln C | 72 |
| 1998–99*b* | Brentford | 85 | Cambridge U | 81 | Cardiff C | 80 |
| 1999–2000*b* | Swansea C | 85 | Rotherham U | 84 | Northampton T | 82 |
| 2000–01 | Brighton & HA | 92 | Cardiff C | 82 | Chesterfield¶ | 80 |
| 2001–02 | Plymouth Arg | 102 | Luton T | 97 | Mansfield T | 79 |
| 2002–03 | Rushden & D | 87 | Hartlepool U | 85 | Wrexham | 84 |
| 2003–04 | Doncaster R | 92 | Hull C | 88 | Torquay U* | 81 |

¶9pts deducted for irregularities.

## FOOTBALL LEAGUE

MAXIMUM POINTS: *a* 44; *b* 60

| | | | | | | |
|---|---|---|---|---|---|---|
| 1888–89*a* | Preston NE | 40 | Aston Villa | 29 | Wolverhampton W | 28 |
| 1889–90*a* | Preston NE | 33 | Everton | 31 | Blackburn R | 27 |
| 1890–91*a* | Everton | 29 | Preston NE | 27 | Notts Co | 26 |
| 1891–92*b* | Sunderland | 42 | Preston NE | 37 | Bolton W | 36 |

## FIRST DIVISION to 1991–92

MAXIMUM POINTS: *a* 44; *b* 52; *c* 60; *d* 68; *e* 76; *f* 84; *g* 126; *h* 120; *k* 114.

| | | | | | | |
|---|---|---|---|---|---|---|
| 1892–93*c* | Sunderland | 48 | Preston NE | 37 | Everton | 36 |
| 1893–94*c* | Aston Villa | 44 | Sunderland | 38 | Derby Co | 36 |
| 1894–95*c* | Sunderland | 47 | Everton | 42 | Aston Villa | 39 |
| 1895–96*c* | Aston Villa | 45 | Derby Co | 41 | Everton | 39 |
| 1896–97*c* | Aston Villa | 47 | Sheffield U* | 36 | Derby Co | 36 |
| 1897–98*c* | Sheffield U | 42 | Sunderland | 37 | Wolverhampton W* | 35 |
| 1898–99*d* | Aston Villa | 45 | Liverpool | 43 | Burnley | 39 |
| 1899–1900*d* | Aston Villa | 50 | Sheffield U | 48 | Sunderland | 41 |
| 1900–01*d* | Liverpool | 45 | Sunderland | 43 | Notts Co | 40 |
| 1901–02*d* | Sunderland | 44 | Everton | 41 | Newcastle U | 37 |
| 1902–03*d* | The Wednesday | 42 | Aston Villa* | 41 | Sunderland | 41 |
| 1903–04*d* | The Wednesday | 47 | Manchester C | 44 | Everton | 43 |
| 1904–05*d* | Newcastle U | 48 | Everton | 47 | Manchester C | 46 |
| 1905–06*e* | Liverpool | 51 | Preston NE | 47 | The Wednesday | 44 |
| 1906–07*e* | Newcastle U | 51 | Bristol C | 48 | Everton* | 45 |
| 1907–08*e* | Manchester U | 52 | Aston Villa* | 43 | Manchester C | 43 |
| 1908–09*e* | Newcastle U | 53 | Everton | 46 | Sunderland | 44 |
| 1909–10*e* | Aston Villa | 53 | Liverpool | 48 | Blackburn R* | 45 |
| 1910–11*e* | Manchester U | 52 | Aston Villa | 51 | Sunderland* | 45 |
| 1911–12*e* | Blackburn R | 49 | Everton | 46 | Newcastle U | 44 |
| 1912–13*e* | Sunderland | 54 | Aston Villa | 50 | Sheffield W | 49 |
| 1913–14*e* | Blackburn R | 51 | Aston Villa | 44 | Middlesbrough* | 43 |
| 1914–15*e* | Everton | 46 | Oldham Ath | 45 | Blackburn R* | 43 |
| 1919–20*f* | WBA | 60 | Burnley | 51 | Chelsea | 49 |
| 1920–21*f* | Burnley | 59 | Manchester C | 54 | Bolton W | 52 |
| 1921–22*f* | Liverpool | 57 | Tottenham H | 51 | Burnley | 49 |
| 1922–23*f* | Liverpool | 60 | Sunderland | 54 | Huddersfield T | 53 |
| 1923–24*f* | Huddersfield T* | 57 | Cardiff C | 57 | Sunderland | 53 |
| 1924–25*f* | Huddersfield T | 58 | WBA | 56 | Bolton W | 55 |
| 1925–26*f* | Huddersfield T | 57 | Arsenal | 52 | Sunderland | 48 |
| 1926–27*f* | Newcastle U | 56 | Huddersfield T | 51 | Sunderland | 49 |
| 1927–28*f* | Everton | 53 | Huddersfield T | 51 | Leicester C | 48 |
| 1928–29*f* | Sheffield W | 52 | Leicester C | 51 | Aston Villa | 50 |
| 1929–30*f* | Sheffield W | 60 | Derby Co | 50 | Manchester C* | 47 |
| 1930–31*f* | Arsenal | 66 | Aston Villa | 59 | Sheffield W | 52 |
| 1931–32*f* | Everton | 56 | Arsenal | 54 | Sheffield W | 50 |
| 1932–33*f* | Arsenal | 58 | Aston Villa | 54 | Sheffield W | 51 |
| 1933–34*f* | Arsenal | 59 | Huddersfield T | 56 | Tottenham H | 49 |
| 1934–35*f* | Arsenal | 58 | Sunderland | 54 | Sheffield W | 49 |
| 1935–36*f* | Sunderland | 56 | Derby Co* | 48 | Huddersfield T | 48 |
| 1936–37*f* | Manchester C | 57 | Charlton Ath | 54 | Arsenal | 52 |
| 1937–38*f* | Arsenal | 52 | Wolverhampton W | 51 | Preston NE | 49 |
| 1938–39*f* | Everton | 59 | Wolverhampton W | 55 | Charlton Ath | 50 |
| 1946–47*f* | Liverpool | 57 | Manchester U* | 56 | Wolverhampton W | 56 |
| 1947–48*f* | Arsenal | 59 | Manchester U* | 52 | Burnley | 52 |
| 1948–49*f* | Portsmouth | 58 | Manchester U* | 53 | Derby Co | 53 |
| 1949–50*f* | Portsmouth* | 53 | Wolverhampton W | 53 | Sunderland | 52 |
| 1950–51*f* | Tottenham H | 60 | Manchester U | 56 | Blackpool | 50 |

| | First | Pts | Second | Pts | Third | Pts |
|---|---|---|---|---|---|---|
| 1951–52f | Manchester U | 57 | Tottenham H* | 53 | Arsenal | 53 |
| 1952–53f | Arsenal* | 54 | Preston NE | 54 | Wolverhampton W | 51 |
| 1953–54f | Wolverhampton W | 57 | WBA | 53 | Huddersfield T | 51 |
| 1954–55f | Chelsea | 52 | Wolverhampton W* | 48 | Portsmouth* | 48 |
| 1955–56f | Manchester U | 60 | Blackpool* | 49 | Wolverhampton W | 49 |
| 1956–57f | Manchester U | 64 | Tottenham H* | 56 | Preston NE | 56 |
| 1957–58f | Wolverhampton W | 64 | Preston NE | 59 | Tottenham H | 51 |
| 1958–59f | Wolverhampton W | 61 | Manchester U | 55 | Arsenal* | 50 |
| 1959–60f | Burnley | 55 | Wolverhampton W | 54 | Tottenham H | 53 |
| 1960–61f | Tottenham H | 66 | Sheffield W | 58 | Wolverhampton W | 57 |
| 1961–62f | Ipswich T | 56 | Burnley | 53 | Tottenham H | 52 |
| 1962–63f | Everton | 61 | Tottenham H | 55 | Burnley | 54 |
| 1963–64f | Liverpool | 57 | Manchester U | 53 | Everton | 52 |
| 1964–65f | Manchester U* | 61 | Leeds U | 61 | Chelsea | 56 |
| 1965–66f | Liverpool | 61 | Leeds U* | 55 | Burnley | 55 |
| 1966–67f | Manchester U | 60 | Nottingham F* | 56 | Tottenham H | 56 |
| 1967–68f | Manchester C | 58 | Manchester U | 56 | Liverpool | 55 |
| 1968–69f | Leeds U | 67 | Liverpool | 61 | Everton | 57 |
| 1969–70f | Everton | 66 | Leeds U | 57 | Chelsea | 55 |
| 1970–71f | Arsenal | 65 | Leeds U | 64 | Tottenham H* | 52 |
| 1971–72f | Derby Co | 58 | Leeds U* | 57 | Liverpool* | 57 |
| 1972–73f | Liverpool | 60 | Arsenal | 57 | Leeds U | 53 |
| 1973–74f | Leeds U | 62 | Liverpool | 57 | Derby Co | 48 |
| 1974–75f | Derby Co | 53 | Liverpool* | 51 | Ipswich T | 51 |
| 1975–76f | Liverpool | 60 | QPR | 59 | Manchester U | 56 |
| 1976–77f | Liverpool | 57 | Manchester C | 56 | Ipswich T | 52 |
| 1977–78f | Nottingham F | 64 | Liverpool | 57 | Everton | 55 |
| 1978–79f | Liverpool | 68 | Nottingham F | 60 | WBA | 59 |
| 1979–80f | Liverpool | 60 | Manchester U | 58 | Ipswich T | 52 |
| 1980–81f | Aston Villa | 60 | Ipswich T | 56 | Arsenal | 53 |
| 1981–82g | Liverpool | 87 | Ipswich T | 83 | Manchester U | 78 |
| 1982–83g | Liverpool | 82 | Watford | 71 | Manchester U | 70 |
| 1983–84g | Liverpool | 80 | Southampton | 77 | Nottingham F* | 74 |
| 1984–85g | Everton | 90 | Liverpool* | 77 | Tottenham H | 77 |
| 1985–86g | Liverpool | 88 | Everton | 86 | West Ham U | 84 |
| 1986–87g | Everton | 86 | Liverpool | 77 | Tottenham H | 71 |
| 1987–88h | Liverpool | 90 | Manchester U | 81 | Nottingham F | 73 |
| 1988–89k | Arsenal* | 76 | Liverpool | 76 | Nottingham F | 64 |
| 1989–90k | Liverpool | 79 | Aston Villa | 70 | Tottenham H | 63 |
| 1990–91k | Arsenal† | 83 | Liverpool | 76 | Crystal Palace | 69 |
| 1991–92g | Leeds U | 82 | Manchester U | 78 | Sheffield W | 75 |

*No official competition during 1915–19 and 1939–46; Regional Leagues operated.* †2 pts deducted.

## SECOND DIVISION to 1991–92

**MAXIMUM POINTS: *a* 44; *b* 56; *c* 60; *d* 68; *e* 76; *f* 84; *g* 126; *h* 132; *k* 138.**

| | First | Pts | Second | Pts | Third | Pts |
|---|---|---|---|---|---|---|
| 1892–93a | Small Heath | 36 | Sheffield U | 35 | Darwen | 30 |
| 1893–94b | Liverpool | 50 | Small Heath | 42 | Notts Co | 39 |
| 1894–95c | Bury | 48 | Notts Co | 39 | Newton Heath* | 38 |
| 1895–96c | Liverpool* | 46 | Manchester C | 46 | Grimsby T* | 42 |
| 1896–97c | Notts Co | 42 | Newton Heath | 39 | Grimsby T | 38 |
| 1897–98c | Burnley | 48 | Newcastle U | 45 | Manchester C | 39 |
| 1898–99d | Manchester C | 52 | Glossop NE | 46 | Leicester Fosse | 45 |
| 1899–1900d | The Wednesday | 54 | Bolton W | 52 | Small Heath | 46 |
| 1900–01d | Grimsby T | 49 | Small Heath | 48 | Burnley | 44 |
| 1901–02d | WBA | 55 | Middlesbrough | 51 | Preston NE* | 42 |
| 1902–03d | Manchester C | 54 | Small Heath | 51 | Woolwich A | 48 |
| 1903–04d | Preston NE | 50 | Woolwich A | 49 | Manchester U | 48 |
| 1904–05d | Liverpool | 58 | Bolton W | 56 | Manchester U | 53 |
| 1905–06e | Bristol C | 66 | Manchester U | 62 | Chelsea | 53 |
| 1906–07e | Nottingham F | 60 | Chelsea | 57 | Leicester Fosse | 48 |
| 1907–08e | Bradford C | 54 | Leicester Fosse | 52 | Oldham Ath | 50 |
| 1908–09e | Bolton W | 52 | Tottenham H* | 51 | WBA | 51 |
| 1909–10e | Manchester C | 54 | Oldham Ath* | 53 | Hull C* | 53 |
| 1910–11e | WBA | 53 | Bolton W | 51 | Chelsea | 49 |
| 1911–12e | Derby Co* | 54 | Chelsea | 54 | Burnley | 52 |
| 1912–13e | Preston NE | 53 | Burnley | 50 | Birmingham | 46 |
| 1913–14e | Notts Co | 53 | Bradford PA* | 49 | Woolwich A | 49 |
| 1914–15e | Derby Co | 53 | Preston NE | 50 | Barnsley | 47 |
| 1919–20f | Tottenham H | 70 | Huddersfield T | 64 | Birmingham | 56 |
| 1920–21f | Birmingham* | 58 | Cardiff C | 58 | Bristol C | 51 |
| 1921–22f | Nottingham F | 56 | Stoke C* | 52 | Barnsley | 52 |
| 1922–23f | Notts Co | 53 | West Ham U* | 51 | Leicester C | 51 |
| 1923–24f | Leeds U | 54 | Bury* | 51 | Derby Co | 51 |
| 1924–25f | Leicester C | 59 | Manchester U | 57 | Derby Co | 55 |
| 1925–26f | Sheffield W | 60 | Derby Co | 57 | Chelsea | 52 |
| 1926–27f | Middlesbrough | 62 | Portsmouth* | 54 | Manchester C | 54 |
| 1927–28f | Manchester C | 59 | Leeds U | 57 | Chelsea | 54 |
| 1928–29f | Middlesbrough | 55 | Grimsby T | 53 | Bradford PA* | 48 |
| 1929–30f | Blackpool | 58 | Chelsea | 55 | Oldham Ath | 53 |
| 1930–31f | Everton | 61 | WBA | 54 | Tottenham H | 51 |
| 1931–32f | Wolverhampton W | 56 | Leeds U | 54 | Stoke C | 52 |
| 1932–33f | Stoke C | 56 | Tottenham H | 55 | Fulham | 50 |
| 1933–34f | Grimsby T | 59 | Preston NE | 52 | Bolton W* | 51 |
| 1934–35f | Brentford | 61 | Bolton W* | 56 | West Ham U | 56 |

| | First | Pts | Second | Pts | Third | Pts |
|---|---|---|---|---|---|---|
| 1935–36f | Manchester U | 56 | Charlton Ath | 55 | Sheffield U* | 52 |
| 1936–37f | Leicester C | 56 | Blackpool | 55 | Bury | 52 |
| 1937–38f | Aston Villa | 57 | Manchester U* | 53 | Sheffield U | 53 |
| 1938–39f | Blackburn R | 55 | Sheffield U | 54 | Sheffield W | 53 |
| 1946–47f | Manchester C | 62 | Burnley | 58 | Birmingham C | 55 |
| 1947–48f | Birmingham C | 59 | Newcastle U | 56 | Southampton | 52 |
| 1948–49f | Fulham | 57 | WBA | 56 | Southampton | 55 |
| 1949–50f | Tottenham H | 61 | Sheffield W* | 52 | Sheffield U* | 52 |
| 1950–51f | Preston NE | 57 | Manchester C | 52 | Cardiff C | 50 |
| 1951–52f | Sheffield W | 53 | Cardiff C* | 51 | Birmingham C | 51 |
| 1952–53f | Sheffield U | 60 | Huddersfield T | 58 | Luton T | 52 |
| 1953–54f | Leicester C* | 56 | Everton | 56 | Blackburn R | 55 |
| 1954–55f | Birmingham C* | 54 | Luton T* | 54 | Rotherham U | 54 |
| 1955–56f | Sheffield W | 55 | Leeds U | 52 | Liverpool* | 48 |
| 1956–57f | Leicester C | 61 | Nottingham F | 54 | Liverpool | 53 |
| 1957–58f | West Ham U | 57 | Blackburn R | 56 | Charlton Ath | 55 |
| 1958–59f | Sheffield W | 62 | Fulham | 60 | Sheffield U* | 53 |
| 1959–60f | Aston Villa | 59 | Cardiff C | 58 | Liverpool* | 50 |
| 1960–61f | Ipswich T | 59 | Sheffield U | 58 | Liverpool | 52 |
| 1961–62f | Liverpool | 62 | Leyton Orient | 54 | Sunderland | 53 |
| 1962–63f | Stoke C | 53 | Chelsea* | 52 | Sunderland | 52 |
| 1963–64f | Leeds U | 63 | Sunderland | 61 | Preston NE | 56 |
| 1964–65f | Newcastle U | 57 | Northampton T | 56 | Bolton W | 50 |
| 1965–66f | Manchester C | 59 | Southampton | 54 | Coventry C | 53 |
| 1966–67f | Coventry C | 59 | Wolverhampton W | 58 | Carlisle U | 52 |
| 1967–68f | Ipswich T | 59 | QPR* | 58 | Blackpool | 58 |
| 1968–69f | Derby Co | 63 | Crystal Palace | 56 | Charlton Ath | 50 |
| 1969–70f | Huddersfield T | 60 | Blackpool | 53 | Leicester C | 51 |
| 1970–71f | Leicester C | 59 | Sheffield U | 56 | Cardiff C* | 53 |
| 1971–72f | Norwich C | 57 | Birmingham C | 56 | Millwall | 55 |
| 1972–73f | Burnley | 62 | QPR | 61 | Aston Villa | 50 |
| 1973–74f | Middlesbrough | 65 | Luton T | 50 | Carlisle U | 49 |
| 1974–75f | Manchester U | 61 | Aston Villa | 58 | Norwich C | 53 |
| 1975–76f | Sunderland | 56 | Bristol C* | 53 | WBA | 53 |
| 1976–77f | Wolverhampton W | 57 | Chelsea | 55 | Nottingham F | 52 |
| 1977–78f | Bolton W | 58 | Southampton | 57 | Tottenham H* | 56 |
| 1978–79f | Crystal Palace | 57 | Brighton & HA* | 56 | Stoke C | 56 |
| 1979–80f | Leicester C | 55 | Sunderland | 54 | Birmingham C* | 53 |
| 1980–81f | West Ham U | 66 | Notts Co | 53 | Swansea C* | 50 |
| 1981–82g | Luton T | 88 | Watford | 80 | Norwich C | 71 |
| 1982–83g | QPR | 85 | Wolverhampton W | 75 | Leicester C | 70 |
| 1983–84g | Chelsea* | 88 | Sheffield W | 88 | Newcastle U | 80 |
| 1984–85g | Oxford U | 84 | Birmingham C | 82 | Manchester C | 74 |
| 1985–86g | Norwich C | 84 | Charlton Ath | 77 | Wimbledon | 76 |
| 1986–87g | Derby Co | 84 | Portsmouth | 78 | Oldham Ath†† | 75 |
| 1987–88h | Millwall | 82 | Aston Villa* | 78 | Middlesbrough | 78 |
| 1988–89k | Chelsea | 99 | Manchester C | 82 | Crystal Palace | 81 |
| 1989–90k | Leeds U* | 85 | Sheffield U | 85 | Newcastle U†† | 80 |
| 1990–91k | Oldham Ath | 88 | West Ham U | 87 | Sheffield W | 82 |
| 1991–92k | Ipswich T | 84 | Middlesbrough | 80 | Derby Co | 78 |

*No official competition during 1915–19 and 1939–46; Regional Leagues operated.*

## THIRD DIVISION to 1991–92

**MAXIMUM POINTS: 92; 138 FROM 1981–82.**

| | First | Pts | Second | Pts | Third | Pts |
|---|---|---|---|---|---|---|
| 1958–59 | Plymouth Arg | 62 | Hull C | 61 | Brentford* | 57 |
| 1959–60 | Southampton | 61 | Norwich C | 59 | Shrewsbury T* | 52 |
| 1960–61 | Bury | 68 | Walsall | 62 | QPR | 60 |
| 1961–62 | Portsmouth | 65 | Grimsby T | 62 | Bournemouth* | 59 |
| 1962–63 | Northampton T | 62 | Swindon T | 58 | Port Vale | 54 |
| 1963–64 | Coventry C* | 60 | Crystal Palace | 60 | Watford | 58 |
| 1964–65 | Carlisle U | 60 | Bristol C* | 59 | Mansfield T | 59 |
| 1965–66 | Hull C | 69 | Millwall | 65 | QPR | 57 |
| 1966–67 | QPR | 67 | Middlesbrough | 55 | Watford | 54 |
| 1967–68 | Oxford U | 57 | Bury | 56 | Shrewsbury T | 55 |
| 1968–69 | Watford* | 64 | Swindon T | 64 | Luton T | 61 |
| 1969–70 | Orient | 62 | Luton T | 60 | Bristol R | 56 |
| 1970–71 | Preston NE | 61 | Fulham | 60 | Halifax T | 56 |
| 1971–72 | Aston Villa | 70 | Brighton & HA | 65 | Bournemouth* | 62 |
| 1972–73 | Bolton W | 61 | Notts Co | 57 | Blackburn R | 55 |
| 1973–74 | Oldham Ath | 62 | Bristol R* | 61 | York C | 61 |
| 1974–75 | Blackburn R | 60 | Plymouth Arg | 59 | Charlton Ath | 55 |
| 1975–76 | Hereford U | 63 | Cardiff C | 57 | Millwall | 56 |
| 1976–77 | Mansfield T | 64 | Brighton & HA | 61 | Crystal Palace* | 59 |
| 1977–78 | Wrexham | 61 | Cambridge U | 58 | Preston NE* | 56 |
| 1978–79 | Shrewsbury T | 61 | Watford* | 60 | Swansea C | 60 |
| 1979–80 | Grimsby T | 62 | Blackburn R | 59 | Sheffield W | 58 |
| 1980–81 | Rotherham U | 61 | Barnsley* | 59 | Charlton Ath | 59 |
| 1981–82 | Burnley* | 80 | Carlisle U | 80 | Fulham | 78 |
| 1982–83 | Portsmouth | 91 | Cardiff C | 86 | Huddersfield T | 82 |
| 1983–84 | Oxford U | 95 | Wimbledon | 87 | Sheffield U* | 83 |
| 1984–85 | Bradford C | 94 | Millwall | 90 | Hull C | 87 |
| 1985–86 | Reading | 94 | Plymouth Arg | 87 | Derby Co | 84 |
| 1986–87 | Bournemouth | 97 | Middlesbrough | 94 | Swindon T | 87 |
| 1987–88 | Sunderland | 93 | Brighton & HA | 84 | Walsall | 82 |

| | First | Pts | Second | Pts | Third | Pts |
|---|---|---|---|---|---|---|
| 1988–89 | Wolverhampton W | 92 | Sheffield U* | 84 | Port Vale | 84 |
| 1989–90 | Bristol R | 93 | Bristol C | 91 | Notts Co | 87 |
| 1990–91 | Cambridge U | 86 | Southend U | 85 | Grimsby T* | 83 |
| 1991–92 | Brentford | 82 | Birmingham C | 81 | Huddersfield T | 78 |

## FOURTH DIVISION (1958–1992)

**MAXIMUM POINTS: 92; 138 FROM 1981–82.**

| | First | Pts | Second | Pts | Third | Pts | Fourth | Pts |
|---|---|---|---|---|---|---|---|---|
| 1958–59 | Port Vale | 64 | Coventry C* | 60 | York C | 60 | Shrewsbury T | 58 |
| 1959–60 | Walsall | 65 | Notts Co* | 60 | Torquay U | 60 | Watford | 57 |
| 1960–61 | Peterborough U | 66 | Crystal Palace | 64 | Northampton T* | 60 | Bradford PA | 60 |
| 1961–62† | Millwall | 56 | Colchester U | 55 | Wrexham | 53 | Carlisle U | 52 |
| 1962–63 | Brentford | 62 | Oldham Ath* | 59 | Crewe Alex | 59 | Mansfield T* | 57 |
| 1963–64 | Gillingham* | 60 | Carlisle U | 60 | Workington | 59 | Exeter C | 58 |
| 1964–65 | Brighton & HA | 63 | Millwall* | 62 | York C | 62 | Oxford U | 61 |
| 1965–66 | Doncaster R* | 59 | Darlington | 59 | Torquay U | 58 | Colchester U* | 56 |
| 1966–67 | Stockport Co | 64 | Southport* | 59 | Barrow | 59 | Tranmere R | 58 |
| 1967–68 | Luton T | 66 | Barnsley | 61 | Hartlepools U | 60 | Crewe Alex | 58 |
| 1968–69 | Doncaster R | 59 | Halifax T | 57 | Rochdale* | 56 | Bradford C | 56 |
| 1969–70 | Chesterfield | 64 | Wrexham | 61 | Swansea C | 60 | Port Vale | 59 |
| 1970–71 | Notts Co | 69 | Bournemouth | 60 | Oldham Ath | 59 | York C | 56 |
| 1971–72 | Grimsby T | 63 | Southend U | 60 | Brentford | 59 | Scunthorpe U | 57 |
| 1972–73 | Southport | 62 | Hereford U | 58 | Cambridge U | 57 | Aldershot* | 56 |
| 1973–74 | Peterborough U | 65 | Gillingham | 62 | Colchester U | 60 | Bury | 59 |
| 1974–75 | Mansfield T | 68 | Shrewsbury T | 62 | Rotherham U | 59 | Chester* | 57 |
| 1975–76 | Lincoln C | 74 | Northampton T | 68 | Reading | 60 | Tranmere R | 58 |
| 1976–77 | Cambridge U | 65 | Exeter C | 62 | Colchester U* | 59 | Bradford C | 59 |
| 1977–78 | Watford | 71 | Southend U | 60 | Swansea C* | 56 | Brentford | 56 |
| 1978–79 | Reading | 65 | Grimsby T* | 61 | Wimbledon* | 61 | Barnsley | 61 |
| 1979–80 | Huddersfield T | 66 | Walsall | 64 | Newport Co | 61 | Portsmouth* | 60 |
| 1980–81 | Southend U | 67 | Lincoln C | 65 | Doncaster R | 56 | Wimbledon | 55 |
| 1981–82 | Sheffield U | 96 | Bradford C* | 91 | Wigan Ath | 91 | Bournemouth | 88 |
| 1982–83 | Wimbledon | 98 | Hull C | 90 | Port Vale | 88 | Scunthorpe U | 83 |
| 1983–84 | York C | 101 | Doncaster R | 85 | Reading* | 82 | Bristol C | 82 |
| 1984–85 | Chesterfield | 91 | Blackpool | 86 | Darlington | 85 | Bury | 84 |
| 1985–86 | Swindon T | 102 | Chester C | 84 | Mansfield T | 81 | Port Vale | 79 |
| 1986–87 | Northampton T | 99 | Preston NE | 90 | Southend U | 80 | Wolverhampton W†† | 79 |
| 1987–88 | Wolverhampton W | 90 | Cardiff C | 85 | Bolton W | 78 | Scunthorpe U†† | 77 |
| 1988–89 | Rotherham U | 82 | Tranmere R | 80 | Crewe Alex | 78 | Scunthorpe U†† | 77 |
| 1989–90 | Exeter C | 89 | Grimsby T | 79 | Southend U | 75 | Stockport Co†† | 74 |
| 1990–91 | Darlington | 83 | Stockport Co* | 82 | Hartlepool U | 82 | Peterborough U | 80 |
| 1991–92†* | Burnley | 83 | Rotherham U* | 77 | Mansfield T | 77 | Blackpool | 76 |

†*Maximum points:* 88 owing to Accrington Stanley's resignation.
†**Maximum points:* 126 owing to Aldershot being expelled (and only 23 teams started the competition).

## THIRD DIVISION—SOUTH (1920–1958)

**1920–21 SEASON AS THIRD DIVISION. MAXIMUM POINTS: *a* 84; *b* 92.**

| | First | Pts | Second | Pts | Third | Pts |
|---|---|---|---|---|---|---|
| 1920–21*a* | Crystal Palace | 59 | Southampton | 54 | QPR | 53 |
| 1921–22*a* | Southampton* | 61 | Plymouth Arg | 61 | Portsmouth | 53 |
| 1922–23*a* | Bristol C | 59 | Plymouth Arg* | 53 | Swansea T | 53 |
| 1923–24*a* | Portsmouth | 59 | Plymouth Arg | 55 | Millwall | 54 |
| 1924–25*a* | Swansea T | 57 | Plymouth Arg | 56 | Bristol C | 53 |
| 1925–26*a* | Reading | 57 | Plymouth Arg | 56 | Millwall | 53 |
| 1926–27*a* | Bristol C | 62 | Plymouth Arg | 60 | Millwall | 56 |
| 1927–28*a* | Millwall | 65 | Northampton T | 55 | Plymouth Arg | 53 |
| 1928–29*a* | Charlton Ath* | 54 | Crystal Palace | 54 | Northampton T* | 52 |
| 1929–30*a* | Plymouth Arg | 68 | Brentford | 61 | QPR | 51 |
| 1930–31*a* | Notts Co | 59 | Crystal Palace | 51 | Brentford | 50 |
| 1931–32*a* | Fulham | 57 | Reading | 55 | Southend U | 53 |
| 1932–33*a* | Brentford | 62 | Exeter C | 58 | Norwich C | 57 |
| 1933–34*a* | Norwich C | 61 | Coventry C* | 54 | Reading* | 54 |
| 1934–35*a* | Charlton Ath | 61 | Reading | 53 | Coventry C | 51 |
| 1935–36*a* | Coventry C | 57 | Luton T | 56 | Reading | 54 |
| 1936–37*a* | Luton T | 58 | Notts Co | 56 | Brighton & HA | 53 |
| 1937–38*a* | Millwall | 56 | Bristol C | 55 | QPR* | 53 |
| 1938–39*a* | Newport Co | 55 | Crystal Palace | 52 | Brighton & HA | 49 |
| 1939–46 | Competition cancelled owing to war. Regional Leagues operated. | | | | | |
| 1946–47*a* | Cardiff C | 66 | QPR | 57 | Bristol C | 51 |
| 1947–48*a* | QPR | 61 | Bournemouth | 57 | Walsall | 51 |
| 1948–49*a* | Swansea T | 62 | Reading | 55 | Bournemouth | 52 |
| 1949–50*a* | Notts Co | 58 | Northampton T* | 51 | Southend U | 51 |
| 1950–51*b* | Nottingham F | 70 | Norwich C | 64 | Reading* | 57 |
| 1951–52*b* | Plymouth Arg | 66 | Reading* | 61 | Norwich C | 61 |
| 1952–53*b* | Bristol R | 64 | Millwall* | 62 | Northampton T | 62 |
| 1953–54*b* | Ipswich T | 64 | Brighton & HA | 61 | Bristol C | 56 |
| 1954–55*b* | Bristol C | 70 | Leyton Orient | 61 | Southampton | 59 |
| 1955–56*b* | Leyton Orient | 66 | Brighton & HA | 65 | Ipswich T | 64 |
| 1956–57*b* | Ipswich T* | 59 | Torquay U | 59 | Colchester U | 58 |
| 1957–58*b* | Brighton & HA | 60 | Brentford* | 58 | Plymouth Arg | 58 |

## THIRD DIVISION—NORTH (1921–1958)

**MAXIMUM POINTS:** *a* 76; *b* 84; *c* 80; *d* 92.

| | First | Pts | Second | Pts | Third | Pts |
|---|---|---|---|---|---|---|
| 1921–22a | Stockport Co | 56 | Darlington* | 50 | Grimsby T | 50 |
| 1922–23a | Nelson | 51 | Bradford PA | 47 | Walsall | 46 |
| 1923–24b | Wolverhampton W | 63 | Rochdale | 62 | Chesterfield | 54 |
| 1924–25b | Darlington | 58 | Nelson* | 53 | New Brighton | 53 |
| 1925–26b | Grimsby T | 61 | Bradford PA | 60 | Rochdale | 59 |
| 1926–27b | Stoke C | 63 | Rochdale | 58 | Bradford PA | 55 |
| 1927–28b | Bradford PA | 63 | Lincoln C | 55 | Stockport Co | 54 |
| 1928–29b | Bradford C | 63 | Stockport Co | 62 | Wrexham | 52 |
| 1929–30b | Port Vale | 67 | Stockport Co | 63 | Darlington* | 50 |
| 1930–31b | Chesterfield | 58 | Lincoln C | 57 | Wrexham* | 54 |
| 1931–32c | Lincoln C* | 57 | Gateshead | 57 | Chester | 50 |
| 1932–33b | Hull C | 59 | Wrexham | 57 | Stockport Co | 54 |
| 1933–34b | Barnsley | 62 | Chesterfield | 61 | Stockport Co | 59 |
| 1934–35b | Doncaster R | 57 | Halifax T | 55 | Chester | 54 |
| 1935–36b | Chesterfield | 60 | Chester* | 55 | Tranmere R | 55 |
| 1936–37b | Stockport Co | 60 | Lincoln C | 57 | Chester | 53 |
| 1937–38b | Tranmere R | 56 | Doncaster R | 54 | Hull C | 53 |
| 1938–39b | Barnsley | 67 | Doncaster R | 56 | Bradford C | 52 |
| 1939–46 | Competition cancelled owing to war. Regional Leagues operated. | | | | | |
| 1946–47b | Doncaster R | 72 | Rotherham U | 64 | Chester | 56 |
| 1947–48b | Lincoln C | 60 | Rotherham U | 59 | Wrexham | 50 |
| 1948–49b | Hull C | 65 | Rotherham U | 62 | Doncaster R | 50 |
| 1949–50b | Doncaster R | 55 | Gateshead | 53 | Rochdale* | 51 |
| 1950–51d | Rotherham U | 71 | Mansfield T | 64 | Carlisle U | 62 |
| 1951–52d | Lincoln C | 69 | Grimsby T | 66 | Stockport Co | 59 |
| 1952–53d | Oldham Ath | 59 | Port Vale | 58 | Wrexham | 56 |
| 1953–54d | Port Vale | 69 | Barnsley | 58 | Scunthorpe U | 57 |
| 1954–55d | Barnsley | 65 | Accrington S | 61 | Scunthorpe U* | 58 |
| 1955–56d | Grimsby T | 68 | Derby Co | 63 | Accrington S | 59 |
| 1956–57d | Derby Co | 63 | Hartlepools U | 59 | Accrington S* | 58 |
| 1957–58d | Scunthorpe U | 66 | Accrington S | 59 | Bradford C | 57 |

## LEAGUE TITLE WINS

**FA PREMIER LEAGUE** – Manchester U 13, Arsenal 3, Chelsea 3, Blackburn R 1, Manchester C 1.

**FOOTBALL LEAGUE CHAMPIONSHIP** – Reading 2, Sunderland 2, Newcastle U 1, Cardiff C 1, QPR 1, WBA 1, Wolverhampton W 1.

**LEAGUE DIVISION 1** – Liverpool 18, Arsenal 10, Everton 9, Sunderland 8, Aston Villa 7, Manchester U 7, Newcastle U 5, Sheffield W 4, Huddersfield T 3, Leeds U 3, Manchester C 3, Portsmouth 3, Wolverhampton W 3, Blackburn R 2, Burnley 2, Derby Co 2, Nottingham F 2, Preston NE 2, Tottenham H 2; Bolton W, Charlton Ath, Chelsea, Crystal Palace, Fulham, Ipswich T, Middlesbrough, Norwich C, Sheffield U, WBA 1 each.

**FOOTBALL LEAGUE CHAMPIONSHIP 1** – Brighton & HA 1, Charlton Ath 1, Doncaster R 1, Leicester C 1, Luton T 1, Norwich C 1, Southend U 1, Swansea C 1.

**LEAGUE DIVISION 2** – Leicester C 6, Manchester C 6, Birmingham C (one as Small Heath) 5, Sheffield W 5, Derby Co 4, Liverpool 4, Preston NE 4, Ipswich T 3, Leeds U 3, Middlesbrough 3, Notts Co 3, Stoke C 3, Aston Villa 2, Bolton W 2, Burnley 2, Bury 2, Chelsea 2, Fulham 2, Grimsby T 2, Manchester U 2, Millwall 2, Norwich C 2, Nottingham F 2, Tottenham H 2, WBA 2, West Ham U 2, Wolverhampton W 2; Blackburn R, Blackpool, Bradford C, Brentford, Brighton & HA, Bristol C, Coventry C, Crystal Palace, Fulham, Luton T, Newcastle U, QPR, Oldham Ath, Oxford U, Plymouth Arg, Reading, Sheffield U, Sunderland, Swindon T, Watford, Wigan Ath 1 each.

**FOOTBALL LEAGUE CHAMPIONSHIP 2** – Brentford 1, Carlisle U 1, Chesterfield 1, Gillingham 1, Milton Keynes D 1, Notts Co 1, Swindon T 1, Walsall 1, Yeovil T 1.

**LEAGUE DIVISION 3** – Brentford 2, Carlisle U 2, Oxford U 2, Plymouth Arg 2, Portsmouth 2, Preston NE 2, Shrewsbury T 2; Aston Villa, Blackburn R, Bolton W, Bournemouth, Bradford C, Brighton & HA, Bristol R, Burnley, Bury, Cambridge U, Cardiff C, Coventry C, Doncaster R. Grimsby T, Hereford U, Hull C, Leyton Orient, Mansfield T, Northampton T, Notts Co, Oldham Ath, QPR, Reading, Rotherham U, Rushden & D Southampton, Sunderland, Swansea C, Watford, Wigan Ath, Wolverhampton W, Wrexham 1 each.

**LEAGUE DIVISION 4** – Chesterfield 2, Doncaster R 2, Peterborough U 2; Brentford, Brighton & HA, Burnley, Cambridge U, Darlington, Exeter C, Gillingham, Grimsby T, Huddersfield T, Lincoln C, Luton T, Mansfield T, Millwall, Northampton T, Notts Co, Port Vale, Reading, Rotherham U, Sheffield U, Southend U, Southport, Stockport Co, Swindon T, Walsall, Watford, Wimbledon, Wolverhampton W, York C 1 each.

**LEAGUE TITLE WINS TO 1957–58**

DIVISION 3 (South) – Bristol C 3, Charlton Ath 2, Ipswich T 2, Millwall 2, Notts Co 2, Plymouth Arg 2, Swansea T 2; Brentford, Brighton & HA, Bristol R, Cardiff C, Coventry C, Crystal Palace, Fulham, Leyton Orient, Luton T, Newport Co, Norwich C, Nottingham F, Portsmouth, QPR, Reading, Southampton 1 each.

DIVISION 3 (North) – Barnsley 3, Doncaster R 3, Lincoln C 3, Chesterfield 2, Grimsby T 2, Hull C 2, Port Vale 2, Stockport Co 2; Bradford C, Bradford PA, Darlington, Derby Co, Nelson, Oldham Ath, Rotherham U, Scunthorpe U, Stoke C, Tranmere R, Wolverhampton W 1 each.

## PROMOTED AFTER PLAY-OFFS

**(NOT ACCOUNTED FOR IN PREVIOUS SECTION)**

| | |
|---|---|
| 1986–87 | Aldershot to Division 3 |
| 1987–88 | Swansea C to Division 3 |
| 1988–89 | Leyton Orient to Division 3 |
| 1989–90 | Sunderland to Division 1; Notts Co to Division 2; Cambridge U to Division 3 |
| 1990–91 | Notts Co to Division 1; Tranmere R to Division 2; Torquay U to Division 3 |
| 1991–92 | Blackburn R to Premier League; Peterborough U to Division 1 |
| 1992–93 | Swindon T to Premier League; WBA to Division 1; York C to Division 2 |
| 1993–94 | Leicester C to Premier League; Burnley to Division 1; Wycombe W to Division 2 |
| 1994–95 | Huddersfield T to Division 1 |
| 1995–96 | Leicester C to Premier League; Bradford C to Division 1; Plymouth Arg to Division 2 |
| 1996–97 | Crystal Palace to Premier League; Crewe Alex to Division 1; Northampton T to Division 2 |
| 1997–98 | Charlton Ath to Premier League; Colchester U to Division 2 |
| 1998–99 | Watford to Premier League; Scunthorpe U to Division 2 |
| 1999–2000 | Peterborough U to Division 2 |
| 2000–01 | Walsall to Division 1; Blackpool to Division 2 |
| 2001–02 | Birmingham C to Premier League; Stoke C to Division 1; Cheltenham T to Division 2 |
| 2002–03 | Wolverhampton W to Premier League; Cardiff C to Division 1; Bournemouth to Division 2 |
| 2003–04 | Crystal Palace to Premier League; Brighton & HA to Division 1; Huddersfield T to Division 2 |
| 2004–05 | West Ham U to Premier League; Sheffield W to Championship; Southend U to Championship 1 |
| 2005–06 | Watford to Premier League; Barnsley to Championship; Cheltenham T to Championship 1 |
| 2006–07 | Derby Co to Premier League; Blackpool to Championship; Bristol R to Championship 1 |
| 2007–08 | Hull C to Premier League; Doncaster R to Championship; Stockport Co to Championship 1 |
| 2008–09 | Burnley to Premier League; Scunthorpe U to Championship; Gillingham to Championship 1 |
| 2009–10 | Blackpool to Premier League; Millwall to Championship; Dagenham & R to Championship 1 |
| 2010–11 | Swansea C to Premier League; Peterborough U to Championship; Stevenage to Championship 1 |
| 2011–12 | West Ham U to Premier League; Huddersfield T to Championship; Crewe Alex to Championship 1 |
| 2012–13 | Crystal Palace to Premier League; Yeovil T to Championship; Bradford C to Championship 1 |

## RELEGATED CLUBS

1891–92 League extended. Newton Heath, Sheffield W and Nottingham F admitted. *Second Division formed* including Darwen.

1892–93 In Test matches, Sheffield U and Darwen won promotion in place of Notts Co and Accrington S.

1893–94 In Tests, Liverpool and Small Heath won promotion. Newton Heath and Darwen relegated.

1894–95 After Tests, Bury promoted, Liverpool relegated.

1895–96 After Tests, Liverpool promoted, Small Heath relegated.

1896–97 After Tests, Notts Co promoted, Burnley relegated.

1897–98 Test system abolished after success of Stoke C and Burnley. League extended. Blackburn R and Newcastle U elected to First Division. *Automatic promotion and relegation introduced.*

**FA PREMIER LEAGUE TO DIVISION 1**

| | | | |
|---|---|---|---|
| 1992–93 | Crystal Palace, Middlesbrough, Nottingham F | 1998–99 | Charlton Ath, Blackburn R, Nottingham F |
| 1993–94 | Sheffield U, Oldham Ath, Swindon T | 1999–2000 | Wimbledon, Sheffield W, Watford |
| 1994–95 | Crystal Palace, Norwich C, Leicester C, Ipswich T | 2000–01 | Manchester C, Coventry C, Bradford C |
| 1995–96 | Manchester C, QPR, Bolton W | 2001–02 | Ipswich T, Derby Co, Leicester C |
| 1996–97 | Sunderland, Middlesbrough, Nottingham F | 2002–03 | West Ham U, WBA, Sunderland |
| 1997–98 | Bolton W, Barnsley, Crystal Palace | 2003–04 | Leicester C, Leeds U, Wolverhampton W. |

**FA PREMIER LEAGUE TO CHAMPIONSHIP**

| | | | |
|---|---|---|---|
| 2004–05 | Crystal Palace, Norwich C, Southampton | 2009–10 | Burnley, Hull C, Portsmouth |
| 2005–06 | Birmingham C, WBA, Sunderland | 2010–11 | Birmingham C, Blackpool, West Ham U |
| 2006–07 | Sheffield U, Charlton Ath, Watford | 2011–12 | Bolton W, Blackburn R, Wolverhampton W |
| 2007–08 | Reading, Birmingham C, Derby Co | 2012–13 | Wigan Ath, Reading, QPR |
| 2008–09 | Newcastle U, Middlesbrough, WBA | | |

**DIVISION 1 TO DIVISION 2**

| | | | |
|---|---|---|---|
| 1898–99 | Bolton W and Sheffield W | 1928–29 | Bury and Cardiff C |
| 1899–1900 | Burnley and Glossop | 1929–30 | Burnley and Everton |
| 1900–01 | Preston NE and WBA | 1930–31 | Leeds U and Manchester U |
| 1901–02 | Small Heath and Manchester C | 1931–32 | Grimsby T and West Ham U |
| 1902–03 | Grimsby T and Bolton W | 1932–33 | Bolton W and Blackpool |
| 1903–04 | Liverpool and WBA | 1933–34 | Newcastle U and Sheffield U |
| 1904–05 | League extended. Bury and Notts Co, two bottom clubs in First Division, re-elected. | 1934–35 | Leicester C and Tottenham H |
| | | 1935–36 | Aston Villa and Blackburn R |
| 1905–06 | Nottingham F and Wolverhampton W | 1936–37 | Manchester U and Sheffield W |
| 1906–07 | Derby Co and Stoke C | 1937–38 | Manchester C and WBA |
| 1907–08 | Bolton W and Birmingham C | 1938–39 | Birmingham C and Leicester C |
| 1908–09 | Manchester C and Leicester Fosse | 1946–47 | Brentford and Leeds U |
| 1909–10 | Bolton W and Chelsea | 1947–48 | Blackburn R and Grimsby T |
| 1910–11 | Bristol C and Nottingham F | 1948–49 | Preston NE and Sheffield U |
| 1911–12 | Preston NE and Bury | 1949–50 | Manchester C and Birmingham C |
| 1912–13 | Notts Co and Woolwich Arsenal | 1950–51 | Sheffield W and Everton |
| 1913–14 | Preston NE and Derby Co | 1951–52 | Huddersfield T and Fulham |
| 1914–15 | Tottenham H and Chelsea* | 1952–53 | Stoke C and Derby Co |
| 1919–20 | Notts Co and Sheffield W | 1953–54 | Middlesbrough and Liverpool |
| 1920–21 | Derby Co and Bradford PA | 1954–55 | Leicester C and Sheffield W |
| 1921–22 | Bradford C and Manchester U | 1955–56 | Huddersfield T and Sheffield U |
| 1922–23 | Stoke C and Oldham Ath | 1956–57 | Charlton Ath and Cardiff C |
| 1923–24 | Chelsea and Middlesbrough | 1957–58 | Sheffield W and Sunderland |
| 1924–25 | Preston NE and Nottingham F | 1958–59 | Portsmouth and Aston Villa |
| 1925–26 | Manchester C and Notts Co | 1959–60 | Luton T and Leeds U |
| 1926–27 | Leeds U and WBA | 1960–61 | Preston NE and Newcastle U |
| 1927–28 | Tottenham H and Middlesbrough | 1961–62 | Chelsea and Cardiff C |

1962–63 Manchester C and Leyton Orient
1963–64 Bolton W and Ipswich T
1964–65 Wolverhampton W and Birmingham C
1965–66 Northampton T and Blackburn R
1966–67 Aston Villa and Blackpool
1967–68 Fulham and Sheffield U
1968–69 Leicester C and QPR
1969–70 Sunderland and Sheffield W
1970–71 Burnley and Blackpool
1971–72 Huddersfield T and Nottingham F
1972–73 Crystal Palace and WBA
1973–74 Southampton, Manchester U, Norwich C
1974–75 Luton T, Chelsea, Carlisle U
1975–76 Wolverhampton W, Burnley, Sheffield U
1976–77 Sunderland, Stoke C, Tottenham H
1977–78 West Ham U, Newcastle U, Leicester C
1978–79 QPR, Birmingham C, Chelsea
1979–80 Bristol C, Derby Co, Bolton W
1980–81 Norwich C, Leicester C, Crystal Palace
1981–82 Leeds U, Wolverhampton W, Middlesbrough
1982–83 Manchester C, Swansea C, Brighton & HA
1983–84 Birmingham C, Notts Co, Wolverhampton W

1984–85 Norwich C, Sunderland, Stoke C
1985–86 Ipswich T, Birmingham C, WBA
1986–87 Leicester C, Manchester C, Aston Villa
1987–88 Chelsea**, Portsmouth, Watford, Oxford U
1988–89 Middlesbrough, West Ham U, Newcastle U
1989–90 Sheffield W, Charlton Ath, Millwall
1990–91 Sunderland and Derby Co
1991–92 Luton T, Notts Co, West Ham U
1992–93 Brentford, Cambridge U, Bristol R
1993–94 Birmingham C, Oxford U, Peterborough U
1994–95 Swindon T, Burnley, Bristol C, Notts Co
1995–96 Millwall, Watford, Luton T
1996–97 Grimsby T, Oldham Ath, Southend U
1997–98 Manchester C, Stoke C, Reading
1998–99 Bury, Oxford U, Bristol C
1999–2000 Walsall, Port Vale, Swindon T
2000–01 Huddersfield T, QPR, Tranmere R
2001–02 Crewe Alex, Barnsley, Stockport Co
2002–03 Sheffield W, Brighton & HA, Grimsby T
2003–04 Walsall, Bradford C, Wimbledon
**Relegated after play-offs.
*Subsequently re-elected to Division 1 when League was
extended after the War.*

## FOOTBALL LEAGUE CHAMPIONSHIP TO FOOTBALL LEAGUE CHAMPIONSHIP 1

2004–05 Gillingham, Nottingham F, Rotherham U
2005–06 Crewe Alex, Millwall, Brighton & HA
2006–07 Southend U, Luton T, Leeds U
2007–08 Leicester C, Scunthorpe U, Colchester U
2008–09 Norwich C, Southampton, Charlton Ath

2009–10 Sheffield W, Plymouth Arg, Peterborough U
2010–11 Preston NE, Sheffield U, Scunthorpe U
2011–12 Portsmouth, Coventry C, Doncaster R
2012–13 Peterborough U, Wolverhampton W, Bristol C

## DIVISION 2 TO DIVISION 3

1920–21 Stockport Co
1921–22 Bradford PA and Bristol C
1922–23 Rotherham Co and Wolverhampton W
1923–24 Nelson and Bristol C
1924–25 Crystal Palace and Coventry C
1925–26 Stoke C and Stockport Co
1926–27 Darlington and Bradford C
1927–28 Fulham and South Shields
1928–29 Port Vale and Clapton Orient
1929–30 Hull C and Notts Co
1930–31 Reading and Cardiff C
1931–32 Barnsley and Bristol C
1932–33 Chesterfield and Charlton Ath
1933–34 Millwall and Lincoln C
1934–35 Oldham Ath and Notts Co
1935–36 Port Vale and Hull C
1936–37 Doncaster R and Bradford C
1937–38 Barnsley and Stockport Co
1938–39 Norwich C and Tranmere R
1946–47 Swansea T and Newport Co
1947–48 Doncaster R and Millwall
1948–49 Nottingham F and Lincoln C
1949–50 Plymouth Arg and Bradford PA
1950–51 Grimsby T and Chesterfield
1951–52 Coventry C and QPR
1952–53 Southampton and Barnsley
1953–54 Brentford and Oldham Ath
1954–55 Ipswich T and Derby Co
1955–56 Plymouth Arg and Hull C
1956–57 Port Vale and Bury
1957–58 Doncaster R and Notts Co
1958–59 Barnsley and Grimsby T
1959–60 Bristol C and Hull C
1960–61 Lincoln C and Portsmouth
1961–62 Brighton & HA and Bristol R
1962–63 Walsall and Luton T
1963–64 Grimsby T and Scunthorpe U
1964–65 Swindon T and Swansea T
1965–66 Middlesbrough and Leyton Orient
1966–67 Northampton T and Bury
1967–68 Plymouth Arg and Rotherham U

1968–69 Fulham and Bury
1969–70 Preston NE and Aston Villa
1970–71 Blackburn R and Bolton W
1971–72 Charlton Ath and Watford
1972–73 Huddersfield T and Brighton & HA
1973–74 Crystal Palace, Preston NE, Swindon T
1974–75 Millwall, Cardiff C, Sheffield W
1975–76 Oxford U, York C, Portsmouth
1976–77 Carlisle U, Plymouth Arg, Hereford U
1977–78 Blackpool, Mansfield T, Hull C
1978–79 Sheffield U, Millwall, Blackburn R
1979–80 Fulham, Burnley, Charlton Ath
1980–81 Preston NE, Bristol C, Bristol R
1981–82 Cardiff C, Wrexham, Orient
1982–83 Rotherham U, Burnley, Bolton W
1983–84 Derby Co, Swansea C, Cambridge U
1984–85 Notts Co, Cardiff C, Wolverhampton W
1985–86 Carlisle U, Middlesbrough, Fulham
1986–87 Sunderland**, Grimsby T, Brighton & HA
1987–88 Huddersfield T, Reading, Sheffield U**
1988–89 Shrewsbury T, Birmingham C, Walsall
1989–90 Bournemouth, Bradford C, Stoke C
1990–91 WBA and Hull C
1991–92 Plymouth Arg, Brighton & HA, Port Vale
1992–93 Preston NE, Mansfield T, Wigan Ath, Chester C
1993–94 Fulham, Exeter C, Hartlepool U, Barnet
1994–95 Cambridge U, Plymouth Arg, Cardiff C,
Chester C, Leyton Orient
1995–96 Carlisle U, Swansea C, Brighton & HA, Hull C
1996–97 Peterborough U, Shrewsbury T, Rotherham U,
Notts Co
1997–98 Brentford, Plymouth Arg, Carlisle U, Southend U
1998–99 York C, Northampton T, Lincoln C,
Macclesfield T
1999–2000 Cardiff C, Blackpool, Scunthorpe U,
Chesterfield
2000–01 Bristol R, Luton T, Swansea C, Oxford U
2001–02 Bournemouth, Bury, Wrexham, Cambridge U
2002–03 Cheltenham T, Huddersfield T, Mansfield T
Northampton T
2003–04 Grimsby T, Rushden & D, Notts Co, Wycombe W

## FOOTBALL LEAGUE CHAMPIONSHIP 1 TO FOOTBALL LEAGUE CHAMPIONSHIP 2

2004–05 Torquay U, Wrexham, Peterborough U,
Stockport Co
2005–06 Hartlepool U, Milton Keynes D, Swindon T,
Walsall
2006–07 Chesterfield, Bradford C, Rotherham U,
Brentford
2007–08 Bournemouth, Gillingham, Port Vale, Luton T
2008–09 Northampton T, Crewe Alex, Cheltenham T,
Hereford U

2009–10 Gillingham, Wycombe W, Southend U,
Stockport Co
2010–11 Dagenham & R, Bristol R, Plymouth Arg,
Swindon T
2011–12 Wycombe W, Chesterfield, Exeter C, Rochdale
2012–13 Scunthorpe U, Bury, Hartlepool U, Portsmouth

**DIVISION 3 TO DIVISION 4**

1958–59 Stockport Co, Doncaster R, Notts Co, Rochdale
1959–60 York C, Mansfield T, Wrexham, Accrington S
1960–61 Tranmere R, Bradford C, Colchester U, Chesterfield
1961–62 Torquay U, Lincoln C, Brentford, Newport Co
1962–63 Bradford PA, Brighton & HA, Carlisle U, Halifax T
1963–64 Millwall, Crewe Alex, Wrexham, Notts Co
1964–65 Luton T, Port Vale, Colchester U, Barnsley
1965–66 Southend U, Exeter C, Brentford, York C
1966–67 Swansea T, Darlington, Doncaster R, Workington
1967–68 Grimsby T, Colchester U, Scunthorpe U, Peterborough U (demoted)
1968–69 Northampton T, Hartlepool, Crewe Alex, Oldham Ath
1969–70 Bournemouth, Southport, Barrow, Stockport Co
1970–71 Reading, Bury, Doncaster R, Gillingham
1971–72 Mansfield T, Barnsley, Torquay U, Bradford C
1972–73 Rotherham U, Brentford, Swansea C, Scunthorpe U
1973–74 Cambridge U, Shrewsbury T, Southport, Rochdale

1974–75 Bournemouth, Tranmere R, Watford, Huddersfield T
1975–76 Aldershot, Colchester U, Southend U, Halifax T
1976–77 Reading, Northampton T, Grimsby T, York C
1977–78 Port Vale, Bradford C, Hereford U, Portsmouth
1978–79 Peterborough U, Walsall, Tranmere R, Lincoln C
1979–80 Bury, Southend U, Mansfield T, Wimbledon
1980–81 Sheffield U, Colchester U, Blackpool, Hull C
1981–82 Wimbledon, Swindon T, Bristol C, Chester
1982–83 Reading, Wrexham, Doncaster R, Chesterfield
1983–84 Scunthorpe U, Southend U, Port Vale, Exeter C
1984–85 Burnley, Orient, Preston NE, Cambridge U
1985–86 Lincoln C, Cardiff C, Wolverhampton W, Swansea C
1986–87 Bolton W**, Carlisle U, Darlington, Newport Co
1987–88 Rotherham U**, Grimsby T, York C, Doncaster R
1988–89 Southend U, Chesterfield, Gillingham, Aldershot
1989–90 Cardiff C, Northampton T, Blackpool, Walsall
1990–91 Crewe Alex, Rotherham U, Mansfield T
1991–92 Bury, Shrewsbury T, Torquay U, Darlington

** *Relegated after play-offs.*

## APPLICATIONS FOR RE-ELECTION

**FOURTH DIVISION**
**Eleven:** Hartlepool U.
**Seven:** Crewe Alex.
**Six:** Barrow (lost League place to Hereford U 1972), Halifax T, Rochdale, Southport (lost League place to Wigan Ath 1978), York C.
**Five:** Chester C, Darlington, Lincoln C, Stockport Co, Workington (lost League place to Wimbledon 1977).
**Four:** Bradford PA (lost League place to Cambridge U 1970), Newport Co, Northampton T.
**Three:** Doncaster R, Hereford U.
**Two:** Bradford C, Exeter C, Oldham Ath, Scunthorpe U, Torquay U.
**One:** Aldershot, Colchester U, Gateshead (lost League place to Peterborough U 1960), Grimsby T, Swansea C, Tranmere R, Wrexham, Blackpool, Cambridge U, Preston NE.
Accrington S resigned and Oxford U were elected 1962.
Port Vale were forced to re-apply following expulsion in 1968.
Aldershot expelled March 1992. Maidstone U resigned August 1992.

**THIRD DIVISIONS NORTH & SOUTH**
**Seven:** Walsall.
**Six:** Exeter C, Halifax T, Newport Co.
**Five:** Accrington S, Barrow, Gillingham, New Brighton, Southport.
**Four:** Rochdale, Norwich C.
**Three:** Crystal Palace, Crewe Alex, Darlington, Hartlepool U, Merthyr T, Swindon T.
**Two:** Aberdare Ath, Aldershot, Ashington, Bournemouth, Brentford, Chester, Colchester U, Durham C, Millwall, Nelson, QPR, Rotherham U, Southend U, Tranmere R, Watford, Workington.
**One:** Bradford C, Bradford PA, Brighton & HA, Bristol R, Cardiff C, Carlisle U, Charlton Ath, Gateshead, Grimsby T, Mansfield T, Shrewsbury T, Torquay U, York C.

## LEAGUE STATUS FROM 1986–87

**RELEGATED FROM LEAGUE**

| | |
|---|---|
| 1986–87 Lincoln C | 1987–88 Newport Co |
| 1988–89 Darlington | 1989–90 Colchester U |
| 1990–91 — | 1991–92 — |
| 1992–93 Halifax T | 1993–94 — |
| 1994–95 — | 1995–96 — |
| 1996–97 Hereford U | 1997–98 Doncaster R |
| 1998–99 Scarborough | 1999–2000 Chester C |
| 2000–01 Barnet | 2001–02 Halifax T |
| 2002–03 Shrewsbury T, Exeter C | |
| 2003–04 Carlisle U, York C | |
| 2004–05 Kidderminster H, Cambridge U | |
| 2005–06 Oxford U, Rushden & D | |
| 2006–07 Boston U, Torquay U | |
| 2007–08 Mansfield T, Wrexham | |
| 2008–09 Chester C, Luton T | |
| 2009–10 Grimsby T, Darlington | |
| 2010–11 Lincoln C, Stockport Co | |
| 2011–12 Hereford U, Macclesfield T | |
| 2012–13 Barnet, Aldershot T | |

**PROMOTED TO LEAGUE**

| | |
|---|---|
| 1986–87 Scarborough | 1987–88 Lincoln C |
| 1988–89 Maidstone U | 1989–90 Darlington |
| 1990–91 Barnet | 1991–92 Colchester U |
| 1992–93 Wycombe W | 1993–94 — |
| 1994–95 — | 1995–96 — |
| 1996–97 Macclesfield T | 1997–98 Halifax T |
| 1998–99 Cheltenham T | 1999–2000 Kidderminster H |
| 2000–01 Rushden & D | 2001–02 Boston U |
| 2002–03 Yeovil T, Doncaster R | |
| 2003–04 Chester C, Shrewsbury T | |
| 2004–05 Barnet, Carlisle U | |
| 2005–06 Accrington S, Hereford U | |
| 2006–07 Dagenham & R, Morecambe | |
| 2007–08 Aldershot T, Exeter C | |
| 2008–09 Burton Alb, Torquay U | |
| 2009–10 Stevenage B, Oxford U | |
| 2010–11 Crawley T, AFC Wimbledon | |
| 2011–12 Fleetwood T, York C | |
| 2012–13 Mansfield T, Newport Co | |

# LEAGUE ATTENDANCES SINCE 1946–47

| Season | Matches | Total | Div. 1 | Div. 2 | Div. 3 (S) | Div. 3 (N) |
|---|---|---|---|---|---|---|
| 1946–47 | 1848 | 35,604,606 | 15,005,316 | 11,071,572 | 5,664,004 | 3,863,714 |
| 1947–48 | 1848 | 40,259,130 | 16,732,341 | 12,286,350 | 6,653,610 | 4,586,829 |
| 1948–49 | 1848 | 41,271,414 | 17,914,667 | 11,353,237 | 6,998,429 | 5,005,081 |
| 1949–50 | 1848 | 40,517,865 | 17,278,625 | 11,694,158 | 7,104,155 | 4,440,927 |
| 1950–51 | 2028 | 39,584,967 | 16,679,454 | 10,780,580 | 7,367,884 | 4,757,109 |
| 1951–52 | 2028 | 39,015,866 | 16,110,322 | 11,066,189 | 6,958,927 | 4,880,428 |
| 1952–53 | 2028 | 37,149,966 | 16,050,278 | 9,686,654 | 6,704,299 | 4,708,735 |
| 1953–54 | 2028 | 36,174,590 | 16,154,915 | 9,510,053 | 6,311,508 | 4,198,114 |
| 1954–55 | 2028 | 34,133,103 | 15,087,221 | 8,988,794 | 5,996,017 | 4,051,071 |
| 1955–56 | 2028 | 33,150,809 | 14,108,961 | 9,080,002 | 5,692,479 | 4,269,367 |
| 1956–57 | 2028 | 32,744,405 | 13,803,037 | 8,718,162 | 5,622,189 | 4,601,017 |
| 1957–58 | 2028 | 33,562,208 | 14,468,652 | 8,663,712 | 6,097,183 | 4,332,661 |

| Season | Matches | Total | Div. 1 | Div. 2 | Div. 3 | Div. 4 |
|---|---|---|---|---|---|---|
| 1958–59 | 2028 | 33,610,985 | 14,727,691 | 8,641,997 | 5,946,600 | 4,276,697 |
| 1959–60 | 2028 | 32,538,611 | 14,391,227 | 8,399,627 | 5,739,707 | 4,008,050 |
| 1960–61 | 2028 | 28,619,754 | 12,926,948 | 7,033,936 | 4,784,256 | 3,874,614 |
| 1961–62 | 2015 | 27,979,902 | 12,061,194 | 7,453,089 | 5,199,106 | 3,266,513 |
| 1962–63 | 2028 | 28,885,852 | 12,490,239 | 7,792,770 | 5,341,362 | 3,261,481 |
| 1963–64 | 2028 | 28,535,022 | 12,486,626 | 7,594,158 | 5,419,157 | 3,035,081 |
| 1964–65 | 2028 | 27,641,168 | 12,708,752 | 6,984,104 | 4,436,245 | 3,512,067 |
| 1965–66 | 2028 | 27,206,980 | 12,480,644 | 6,914,757 | 4,779,150 | 3,032,429 |
| 1966–67 | 2028 | 28,902,596 | 14,242,957 | 7,253,819 | 4,421,172 | 2,984,648 |
| 1967–68 | 2028 | 30,107,298 | 15,289,410 | 7,450,410 | 4,013,087 | 3,354,391 |
| 1968–69 | 2028 | 29,382,172 | 14,584,851 | 7,382,390 | 4,339,656 | 3,075,275 |
| 1969–70 | 2028 | 29,600,972 | 14,868,754 | 7,581,728 | 4,223,761 | 2,926,729 |
| 1970–71 | 2028 | 28,194,146 | 13,954,337 | 7,098,265 | 4,377,213 | 2,764,331 |
| 1971–72 | 2028 | 28,700,729 | 14,484,603 | 6,769,308 | 4,697,392 | 2,749,426 |
| 1972–73 | 2028 | 25,448,642 | 13,998,154 | 5,631,730 | 3,737,252 | 2,081,506 |
| 1973–74 | 2027 | 24,982,203 | 13,070,991 | 6,326,108 | 3,421,624 | 2,163,480 |
| 1974–75 | 2028 | 25,577,977 | 12,613,178 | 6,955,970 | 4,086,145 | 1,992,684 |
| 1975–76 | 2028 | 24,896,053 | 13,089,861 | 5,798,405 | 3,948,449 | 2,059,338 |
| 1976–77 | 2028 | 26,182,800 | 13,647,585 | 6,250,597 | 4,152,218 | 2,132,400 |
| 1977–78 | 2028 | 25,392,872 | 13,255,677 | 6,474,763 | 3,332,042 | 2,330,390 |
| 1978–79 | 2028 | 24,540,627 | 12,704,549 | 6,153,223 | 3,374,558 | 2,308,297 |
| 1979–80 | 2028 | 24,623,975 | 12,163,002 | 6,112,025 | 3,999,328 | 2,349,620 |
| 1980–81 | 2028 | 21,907,569 | 11,392,894 | 5,175,442 | 3,637,854 | 1,701,379 |
| 1981–82 | 2028 | 20,006,961 | 10,420,793 | 4,750,463 | 2,836,915 | 1,998,790 |
| 1982–83 | 2028 | 18,766,158 | 9,295,613 | 4,974,937 | 2,943,568 | 1,552,040 |
| 1983–84 | 2028 | 18,358,631 | 8,711,448 | 5,359,757 | 2,729,942 | 1,557,484 |
| 1984–85 | 2028 | 17,849,835 | 9,761,404 | 4,030,823 | 2,667,008 | 1,390,600 |
| 1985–86 | 2028 | 16,488,577 | 9,037,854 | 3,551,968 | 2,490,481 | 1,408,274 |
| 1986–87 | 2028 | 17,379,218 | 9,144,676 | 4,168,131 | 2,350,970 | 1,715,441 |
| 1987–88 | 2030 | 17,959,732 | 8,094,571 | 5,341,599 | 2,751,275 | 1,772,287 |
| 1988–89 | 2036 | 18,464,192 | 7,809,993 | 5,887,805 | 3,035,327 | 1,791,067 |
| 1989–90 | 2036 | 19,445,442 | 7,883,039 | 6,867,674 | 2,803,551 | 1,891,178 |
| 1990–91 | 2036 | 19,508,202 | 8,618,709 | 6,285,068 | 2,835,759 | 1,768,666 |
| 1991–92 | 2064* | 20,487,273 | 9,989,160 | 5,809,787 | 2,993,352 | 1,694,974 |

| Season | Matches | Total | FA Premier | Div. 1 | Div. 2 | Div. 3 |
|---|---|---|---|---|---|---|
| 1992–93 | 2028 | 20,657,327 | 9,759,809 | 5,874,017 | 3,483,073 | 1,540,428 |
| 1993–94 | 2028 | 21,683,381 | 10,644,551 | 6,487,104 | 2,972,702 | 1,579,024 |
| 1994–95 | 2028 | 21,856,020 | 11,213,168 | 6,044,293 | 3,037,752 | 1,560,807 |
| 1995–96 | 2036 | 21,844,416 | 10,469,107 | 6,566,349 | 2,843,652 | 1,965,308 |
| 1996–97 | 2036 | 22,783,163 | 10,804,762 | 6,931,539 | 3,195,223 | 1,851,639 |
| 1997–98 | 2036 | 24,692,608 | 11,092,106 | 8,330,018 | 3,503,264 | 1,767,220 |
| 1998–99 | 2036 | 25,435,542 | 11,620,326 | 7,543,369 | 4,169,697 | 2,102,150 |
| 1999–2000 | 2036 | 25,341,090 | 11,668,497 | 7,810,208 | 3,700,433 | 2,161,952 |
| 2000–01 | 2036 | 26,030,167 | 12,472,094 | 7,909,512 | 3,488,166 | 2,160,395 |
| 2001–02 | 2036 | 27,756,977 | 13,043,118 | 8,352,128 | 3,963,153 | 2,398,578 |
| 2002–03 | 2036 | 28,343,386 | 13,468,965 | 8,521,017 | 3,892,469 | 2,460,935 |
| 2003–04 | 2036 | 29,197,510 | 13,303,136 | 8,772,780 | 4,146,495 | 2,975,099 |

| Season | Matches | Total | FA Premier | Championship | League 1 | League 2 |
|---|---|---|---|---|---|---|
| 2004–05 | 2036 | 29,245,870 | 12,878,791 | 9,612,761 | 4,270,674 | 2,483,644 |
| 2005–06 | 2036 | 29,089,084 | 12,871,643 | 9,719,204 | 4,183,011 | 2,315,226 |
| 2006–07 | 2036 | 29,541,949 | 13,058,115 | 10,057,813 | 4,135,599 | 2,290,422 |
| 2007–08 | 2036 | 29,914,212 | 13,708,875 | 9,397,036 | 4,412,023 | 2,396,278 |
| 2008–09 | 2036 | 29,881,966 | 13,527,815 | 9,877,552 | 4,171,834 | 2,304,765 |
| 2009–10 | 2036 | 30,057,892 | 12,977,251 | 9,909,882 | 5,043,099 | 2,127,660 |
| 2010–11 | 2036 | 29,459,105 | 13,406,990 | 9,595,236 | 4,150,547 | 2,306,332 |
| 2011–12 | 2036 | 29,454,401 | 13,148,465 | 9,784,100 | 4,091,897 | 2,429,939 |
| 2012–13 | 2036 | 29,225,443 | 13,653,958 | 9,662,232 | 3,485,290 | 2,423,963 |

*Figures include matches played by Aldershot.
Football League official total for their three divisions in 2001–02 was 14,716,162.

# ENGLISH LEAGUE ATTENDANCES 2012–13

## FA BARCLAYCARD PREMIERSHIP ATTENDANCES

| | Average Gate | | | Season 2012–13 | |
|---|---|---|---|---|---|
| | 2011–13 | 2012–13 | +/–% | Highest | Lowest |
| Arsenal | 60,000 | 60,079 | +0.13 | 60,112 | 59,872 |
| Aston Villa | 33,873 | 35,060 | +3.50 | 42,084 | 28,692 |
| Chelsea | 41,478 | 41,462 | –0.04 | 41,794 | 38,484 |
| Everton | 33,228 | 36,356 | +9.41 | 39,613 | 31,376 |
| Fulham | 25,293 | 25,394 | +0.40 | 25,700 | 24,087 |
| Liverpool | 44,253 | 44,749 | +1.12 | 45,009 | 44,228 |
| Manchester C | 47,044 | 46,974 | –0.15 | 47,386 | 45,579 |
| Manchester U | 75,387 | 75,530 | +0.19 | 75,605 | 75,142 |
| Newcastle U | 49,935 | 50,517 | +1.17 | 52,385 | 43,858 |
| Norwich C | 26,605 | 26,672 | +0.25 | 26,842 | 26,072 |
| QPR | 17,295 | 17,779 | +2.80 | 18,337 | 16,658 |
| Reading | 19,219 | 23,862 | +24.16 | 24,184 | 22,321 |
| Southampton | 26,419 | 30,874 | +16.86 | 32,070 | 28,004 |
| Stoke C | 27,225 | 26,922 | –1.11 | 27,544 | 24,421 |
| Sunderland | 39,095 | 40,544 | +3.71 | 47,456 | 35,628 |
| Swansea C | 19,946 | 20,370 | +2.13 | 20,650 | 19,603 |
| Tottenham H | 36,026 | 36,030 | +0.01 | 36,244 | 35,534 |
| WBA | 24,798 | 25,360 | +2.27 | 26,438 | 23,854 |
| West Ham U | 30,923 | 34,720 | +12.28 | 35,005 | 33,052 |
| Wigan Ath | 18,633 | 19,375 | +3.98 | 23,001 | 15,436 |

TOTAL ATTENDANCES: 13,653,958 (380 games)
Average 35,931 (+3.85%)
HIGHEST: 75,605 Manchester U v Reading
LOWEST: 15,436 Wigan Ath v Reading
HIGHEST AVERAGE: 75,530 Manchester U
LOWEST AVERAGE: 17,779 QPR

## FOOTBALL LEAGUE: CHAMPIONSHIP ATTENDANCES

| | Average Gate | | | Season 2012–13 | |
|---|---|---|---|---|---|
| | 2011–13 | 2012–13 | +/–% | Highest | Lowest |
| Barnsley | 10,331 | 10,207 | –1.20 | 15,744 | 7,844 |
| Birmingham C | 19,126 | 16,703 | –12.67 | 19,630 | 13,532 |
| Blackburn R | 22,551 | 14,997 | –33.50 | 20,735 | 12,230 |
| Blackpool | 12,764 | 13,917 | +9.03 | 15,907 | 12,653 |
| Bolton W | 23,669 | 18,094 | –23.55 | 24,844 | 15,675 |
| Brighton & HA | 20,027 | 26,236 | +31.01 | 30,003 | 23,703 |
| Bristol C | 13,907 | 13,348 | –4.02 | 19,148 | 11,836 |
| Burnley | 14,048 | 12,928 | –7.97 | 21,341 | 10,450 |
| Cardiff C | 22,100 | 22,999 | +4.07 | 26,588 | 20,058 |
| Charlton Ath | 17,401 | 18,500 | +6.32 | 26,185 | 15,585 |
| Crystal Palace | 15,219 | 17,280 | +13.55 | 22,154 | 12,757 |
| Derby Co | 26,020 | 23,228 | –10.73 | 33,010 | 20,063 |
| Huddersfield T | 14,144 | 15,166 | +7.22 | 21,614 | 12,415 |
| Hull C | 18,790 | 17,369 | –7.56 | 23,812 | 14,756 |
| Ipswich T | 18,266 | 17,526 | –4.05 | 21,988 | 15,417 |
| Leeds U | 23,283 | 21,572 | –7.35 | 25,532 | 16,788 |
| Leicester C | 23,036 | 22,054 | –4.26 | 25,913 | 8,585 |
| Middlesbrough | 17,557 | 16,794 | –4.35 | 28,229 | 13,377 |
| Millwall | 11,848 | 10,559 | –10.88 | 18,013 | 8,607 |
| Nottingham F | 21,578 | 23,082 | +6.97 | 28,707 | 18,748 |
| Peterborough U | 9,110 | 8,215 | –9.82 | 13,938 | 5,435 |
| Sheffield W | 21,336 | 24,078 | +12.85 | 31,375 | 18,922 |
| Watford | 12,703 | 13,454 | +5.91 | 16,968 | 11,022 |
| Wolverhampton W | 25,682 | 21,789 | –15.16 | 28,595 | 18,174 |

TOTAL ATTENDANCES: 9,662,232 (552 games)
Average 17,504 (–1.25%)
HIGHEST: 33,010 Derby Co v Nottingham F
LOWEST: 5,435 Peterborough U v Bristol C
HIGHEST AVERAGE: 26,236 Brighton & HA
LOWEST AVERAGE: 8,215 Peterborough U

*Premiership and Football League attendance averages and highest crowd figures for 2012–13 are unofficial.*

## FOOTBALL LEAGUE: DIVISION 1 ATTENDANCES

| | Average Gate | | | Season 2012–13 | |
|---|---|---|---|---|---|
| | 2011–13 | 2012–13 | +/–% | Highest | Lowest |
| Bournemouth | 5,881 | 6,852 | +16.52 | 9,135 | 4,951 |
| Brentford | 5,643 | 6,303 | +11.69 | 12,300 | 4,384 |
| Bury | 3,552 | 2,749 | –22.59 | 5,213 | 1,396 |
| Carlisle U | 5,247 | 4,302 | –18.00 | 5,965 | 3,229 |
| Colchester U | 3,865 | 3,530 | –8.68 | 5,862 | 2,367 |
| Coventry C | 15,118 | 10,864 | –28.14 | 15,185 | 8,862 |
| Crawley T | 3,256 | 3,408 | +4.67 | 5,058 | 2,544 |
| Crewe Alex | 4,124 | 4,903 | +18.89 | 6,547 | 3,770 |
| Doncaster R | 9,341 | 7,239 | –22.50 | 12,785 | 5,411 |
| Hartlepool U | 4,960 | 3,613 | –27.16 | 4,474 | 2,502 |
| Leyton Orient | 4,298 | 4,002 | –6.89 | 5,191 | 2,664 |
| Milton Keynes D | 8,659 | 8,612 | –0.54 | 13,620 | 6,622 |
| Notts Co | 6,807 | 5,522 | –18.88 | 7,608 | 3,409 |
| Oldham Ath | 4,432 | 4,129 | –6.84 | 6,426 | 2,969 |
| Portsmouth | 15,015 | 12,232 | –18.53 | 18,433 | 9,815 |
| Preston NE | 11,820 | 9,263 | –21.64 | 12,014 | 8,013 |
| Scunthorpe U | 4,339 | 3,465 | –20.15 | 6,020 | 2,382 |
| Sheffield U | 18,701 | 18,612 | –0.48 | 23,431 | 15,744 |
| Shrewsbury T | 5,769 | 5,736 | –0.58 | 8,021 | 4,711 |
| Stevenage | 3,558 | 3,170 | –10.91 | 4,518 | 2,374 |
| Swindon T | 8,410 | 8,528 | +1.41 | 11,381 | 7,169 |
| Tranmere R | 5,130 | 6,196 | +20.77 | 10,587 | 4,342 |
| Walsall | 4,274 | 4,234 | –0.93 | 7,504 | 2,787 |
| Yeovil T | 3,984 | 4,072 | +2.21 | 6,006 | 2,900 |

TOTAL ATTENDANCES: 3,485,290 (552 games)
Average 6,314 (–14.39%)
HIGHEST: 23,431 Sheffield U v Brentford
LOWEST: 1,396 Bury v Stevenage
HIGHEST AVERAGE: 18,612 Sheffield U
LOWEST AVERAGE: 2,749 Bury

## FOOTBALL LEAGUE: DIVISION 2 ATTENDANCES

| | Average Gate | | | Season 2012–13 | |
|---|---|---|---|---|---|
| | 2011–13 | 2012–13 | +/–% | Highest | Lowest |
| Accrington S | 1,784 | 1,675 | –6.13 | 3,010 | 1,031 |
| AFC Wimbledon | 4,294 | 4,060 | –5.45 | 4,749 | 3,350 |
| Aldershot T | 2,864 | 2,305 | –19.53 | 3,699 | 1,191 |
| Barnet | 2,265 | 2,440 | +7.71 | 6,001 | 1,483 |
| Bradford C | 10,171 | 10,322 | +1.49 | 13,461 | 8,047 |
| Bristol R | 6,035 | 6,309 | +4.53 | 8,646 | 4,721 |
| Burton Alb | 2,809 | 2,859 | +1.80 | 5,426 | 1,712 |
| Cheltenham T | 3,424 | 3,253 | –5.00 | 5,888 | 2,195 |
| Chesterfield | 6,530 | 5,431 | –16.83 | 7,322 | 3,968 |
| Dagenham & R | 2,090 | 1,903 | –8.95 | 3,781 | 1,227 |
| Exeter C | 4,474 | 4,142 | –7.43 | 6,447 | 3,249 |
| Fleetwood T | 2,264 | 2,856 | +26.13 | 3,705 | 2,019 |
| Gillingham | 5,146 | 6,601 | +28.28 | 11,172 | 4,380 |
| Morecambe | 2,141 | 1,954 | –8.71 | 4,029 | 1,226 |
| Northampton T | 4,808 | 4,785 | –0.47 | 7,471 | 3,541 |
| Oxford U | 7,451 | 5,955 | –20.08 | 7,608 | 4,906 |
| Plymouth Arg | 6,828 | 7,096 | +3.92 | 13,251 | 5,219 |
| Port Vale | 4,819 | 5,727 | +18.85 | 12,496 | 4,139 |
| Rochdale | 3,108 | 2,439 | –21.53 | 5,042 | 1,551 |
| Rotherham U | 3,498 | 7,967 | +127.75 | 11,441 | 5,632 |
| Southend U | 5,999 | 5,003 | –16.60 | 7,498 | 3,908 |
| Torquay U | 2,869 | 2,709 | –5.58 | 5,666 | 1,178 |
| Wycombe W | 4,843 | 3,721 | –23.17 | 7,120 | 2,365 |
| York C | 3,117 | 3,879 | +24.44 | 5,975 | 2,699 |

TOTAL ATTENDANCES: 2,423,963 (552 games)
Average 4,391 (–0.24%)
HIGHEST: 13,461 Bradford C v Rotherham U
LOWEST: 1,031 Accrington S v Dagenham & R
HIGHEST AVERAGE: 10,322 Bradford C
LOWEST AVERAGE: 1,675 Accrington S

# LEAGUE CUP FINALS 1961–2013

*Played as a two-leg final until 1966. All subsequent finals played at Wembley except between 2001 and 2007 (inclusive) which were played at Millennium Stadium, Cardiff.*

| | Year | Winners | Runners-up | Score |
|---|---|---|---|---|
| | 1961 | Aston Villa | Rotherham U | 0-2, 3-0 (aet) |
| | 1962 | Norwich C | Rochdale | 3-0, 1-0 |
| | 1963 | Birmingham C | Aston Villa | 3-1, 0-0 |
| | 1964 | Leicester C | Stoke C | 1-1, 3-2 |
| | 1965 | Chelsea | Leicester C | 3-2, 0-0 |
| | 1966 | WBA | West Ham U | 1-2, 4-1 |
| | 1967 | QPR | WBA | 3-2 |
| | 1968 | Leeds U | Arsenal | 1-0 |
| | 1969 | Swindon T | Arsenal | 3-1 (aet) |
| | 1970 | Manchester C | WBA | 2-1 (aet) |
| | 1971 | Tottenham H | Aston Villa | 2-0 |
| | 1972 | Stoke C | Chelsea | 2-1 |
| | 1973 | Tottenham H | Norwich C | 1-0 |
| | 1974 | Wolverhampton W | Manchester C | 2-1 |
| | 1975 | Aston Villa | Norwich C | 1-0 |
| | 1976 | Manchester C | Newcastle U | 2-1 |
| | 1977 | Aston Villa | Everton | 0-0, 1-1 (aet), 3-2 (aet) |
| | 1978 | Nottingham F | Liverpool | 0-0 (aet), 1-0 |
| | 1979 | Nottingham F | Southampton | 3-2 |
| | 1980 | Wolverhampton W | Nottingham F | 1-0 |
| | 1981 | Liverpool | West Ham U | 1-1 (aet), 2-1 |
| **MILK CUP** | 1982 | Liverpool | Tottenham H | 3-1 (aet) |
| | 1983 | Liverpool | Manchester U | 2-1 (aet) |
| | 1984 | Liverpool | Everton | 0-0 (aet), 1-0 |
| | 1985 | Norwich C | Sunderland | 1-0 |
| | 1986 | Oxford U | QPR | 3-0 |
| **LITTLEWOODS CUP** | 1987 | Arsenal | Liverpool | 2-1 |
| | 1988 | Luton T | Arsenal | 3-2 |
| | 1989 | Nottingham F | Luton T | 3-1 |
| | 1990 | Nottingham F | Oldham Ath | 1-0 |
| **RUMBELOWS LEAGUE CUP** | 1991 | Sheffield W | Manchester U | 1-0 |
| | 1992 | Manchester U | Nottingham F | 1-0 |
| **COCA-COLA CUP** | 1993 | Arsenal | Sheffield W | 2-1 |
| | 1994 | Aston Villa | Manchester U | 3-1 |
| | 1995 | Liverpool | Bolton W | 2-1 |
| | 1996 | Aston Villa | Leeds U | 3-0 |
| | 1997 | Leicester C | Middlesbrough | 1-1 (aet), 1-0 (aet) |
| | 1998 | Chelsea | Middlesbrough | 2-0 (aet) |
| **WORTHINGTON CUP** | 1999 | Tottenham H | Leicester C | 1-0 |
| | 2000 | Leicester C | Tranmere R | 2-1 |
| | 2001 | Liverpool | Birmingham C | 1-1 (aet) |
| | *Liverpool won 5-4 on penalties* | | | |
| | 2002 | Blackburn R | Tottenham H | 2-1 |
| | 2003 | Liverpool | Manchester U | 2-0 |
| **CARLING CUP** | 2004 | Middlesbrough | Bolton W | 2-1 |
| | 2005 | Chelsea | Liverpool | 3-2 (aet) |
| | 2006 | Manchester U | Wigan Ath | 4-0 |
| | 2007 | Chelsea | Arsenal | 2-1 |
| | 2008 | Tottenham H | Chelsea | 2-1 (aet) |
| | 2009 | Manchester U | Tottenham H | 0-0 (aet) |
| | *Manchester U won 4-1 on penalties* | | | |
| | 2010 | Manchester U | Aston Villa | 2-1 |
| | 2011 | Birmingham C | Arsenal | 2-1 |
| | 2012 | Liverpool | Cardiff C | 2-2 (aet) |
| | *Liverpool won 3-2 on penalties.* | | | |
| **CAPITAL ONE CUP** | 2013 | Swansea C | Bradford C | 5-0 |

## LEAGUE CUP WINS
Liverpool 8, Aston Villa 5, Chelsea 4, Manchester U 4, Nottingham F 4, Tottenham H 4, Leicester C 3, Arsenal 2, Birmingham C 2, Manchester C 2, Norwich C 2, Wolverhampton W 2, Blackburn R 1, Leeds U 1, Luton T 1, Middlesbrough 1, Oxford U 1, QPR 1, Sheffield W 1, Stoke C 1, Swansea C 1, Swindon T 1, WBA 1.

## APPEARANCES IN FINALS
Liverpool 11, Aston Villa 8, Manchester U 8, Arsenal 7, Tottenham H 7, Chelsea 6, Nottingham F 6, Leicester C 5, Norwich C 4, Birmingham C 3, Manchester C 3, Middlesbrough 3, WBA 3, Bolton W 2, Everton 2, Leeds U 2, Luton T 2, QPR 2, Sheffield W 2, Stoke C 2, West Ham U 2, Wolverhampton W 2, Blackburn R 1, Bradford C 1, Cardiff C 1, Newcastle U 1, Oldham Ath 1, Oxford U 1, Rochdale 1, Rotherham U 1, Southampton 1, Sunderland 1, Swansea C 1, Swindon T 1, Tranmere R 1, Wigan Ath 1.

## APPEARANCES IN SEMI-FINALS
Arsenal 14, Aston Villa 14, Liverpool 14, Tottenham H 13, Manchester U 12, Chelsea 11, West Ham U 8, Manchester C 7, Blackburn R 6, Nottingham F 6, Birmingham C 5, Leeds U 5, Leicester C 5, Middlesbrough 5, Norwich C 5, Bolton W 4, Burnley 4, Crystal Palace 4, Everton 4, Ipswich T 4, Sheffield W 4, WBA 4, QPR 3, Sunderland 3, Swindon T 3, Wolverhampton W 3, Bristol C 2, Cardiff C 2, Coventry C 2, Derby Co 2, Luton T 2, Oxford U 2, Plymouth Arg 2, Southampton 2, Stoke C 2, Tranmere R 2, Watford 2, Wimbledon 2, Blackpool 1, Bradford C 1, Bury 1, Carlisle U 1, Chester C 1, Huddersfield T 1, Newcastle U 1, Oldham Ath 1, Peterborough U 1, Rochdale 1, Rotherham U 1, Sheffield U 1, Shrewsbury T 1, Stockport Co 1, Swansea C 1, Walsall 1, Wigan Ath 1, Wycombe W 1.

# CAPITAL ONE CUP 2012–13

■ *Denotes player sent off.*

**FIRST ROUND**

Saturday, 11 August 2012

**Bury (0) 1** *(Hughes 64)*
**Middlesbrough (1) 2** *(Emnes 33, Ledesma 61)*     2964
*Bury:* (433) Carson; Jones A, Sodje■, Hughes, Skarz; Sweeney, Schumacher, Carrington (Marshall 64); Worrall, Bishop (John-Lewis 77), Elford-Alliyu (Cullen 68).
*Middlesbrough:* (442) Steele; Hoyte, Williams R, Woodgate, Friend; Bailey, Thomson, Leadbitter, Carayol (Reach 46); Ledesma (Williams L 63), Emnes.

**Carlisle U (1) 1** *(Robson 39)*
**Accrington S (0) 0**     2924
*Carlisle U:* (433) Collin; Potts, Livesey, Edwards, Bugno; Noble, Berrett, Chantler (Thirlwell 90); McGovern (Symington 78), Miller (Beck 83), Robson.
*Accrington S:* (433) Dunbavin; Lindfield, Murphy, Nsiala (Eckersley 77), Liddle; Clark (Dawson 70), Joyce, Miller; Barnett (Hatfield 56), Sheppard, Chippendale.

**Cheltenham T (0) 1** *(Mohamed 58)*
**Milton Keynes D (1) 1** *(Bowditch 45)*     1660
*Cheltenham T:* (4411) Brown; Jombati, Bennett (Lowe 85), Hooman, Jones; McGlashan, Pack, Penn, Mohamed; Deering (Harrad 68); Zebroski (Duffy 84).
*Milton Keynes D:* (442) Martin; Chicksen, MacKenzie, Williams (Kay 29), Lewington; Chadwick (Lowe 71), Potter, Gleeson■, O'Shea (Smith 61); Bowditch, MacDonald.
*aet; Milton Keynes D won on 5-3 on penalties.*

**Crewe Alex (4) 5** *(Leitch-Smith 7, Clayton M 13, 39, Pogba 34, 90)*
**Hartlepool U (0) 0**     2501
*Crewe Alex:* (442) Martin; Davis, Ellis, Dugdale, Robertson; Moore, Westwood, Osman (Murphy 76), Pogba; Clayton M (Turton 84), Leitch-Smith (Daniels 78).
*Hartlepool U:* (442) Flinders; Austin, Collins, Hartley, Horwood; Franks, Walton, Sweeney, Monkhouse; James (Poole 46), Howard.

**Doncaster R (0) 1** *(Brown 74 (pen))*
**York C (0) 1** *(Coulson 65)*     4937
*Doncaster R:* (442) Woods G; Quinn (Wakefield 95), Spurr, Jones R, Husband; Coppinger, Keegan (Syers 57), Woods Martin, Cotterill (Blake 106); Brown, Bennett.
*York C:* (433) Ingham; Parslow, Smith C, Doig, Fyfield; Smith J (Potts 112), Bullock, McLaughlin (Challinor 87); Walker (Blair 78), Coulson, Chambers.
*aet; Doncaster R won on 4-2 on penalties.*

**Hull C (0) 1** *(Mclean 70)*
**Rotherham U (0) 1** *(Ainsworth 52)*     6569
*Hull C:* (442) Amos; Rosenior (Bruce 82), Dudgeon, Chester, Faye (McShane 74); Stewart, Cairney, McKenna (Mclean 66), Koren; Fryatt, Proschwitz.
*Rotherham U:* (442) Shearer; Arnason, Sharps, Mullins, Wilson (Taylor 13); Pringle, Bradley, Noble, Evans (Ainsworth 50); Nardiello (Agard 77), Odejayi.
*aet; Hull C won on 7-6 on penalties.*

**Leeds U (2) 4** *(Becchio 20, Varney 26, Norris 66, McCormack 70 (pen))*
**Shrewsbury T (0) 0**     18,194
*Leeds U:* (442) Kenny; Peltier, Pearce, Austin, White; Byram, Norris, Green (Poleon 77), Varney (Brown 86); Becchio, McCormack (Diouf 76).
*Shrewsbury T:* (442) Weale; Grandison, Hector, Jacobson (Wildig 80), Richards; Wright, Purdie, Summerfield (Hall 79), Parry; Morgan, Gornell (Bradshaw 86).

**Notts Co (0) 0**
**Bradford C (0) 1** *(Hanson 95)*     3460
*Notts Co:* (442) Bialkowski; Regan, Smith (Bencherif 40), Williams, Sheehan; Judge, Bishop, Mahon (Hughes J 79), Arquin; Hughes L, Labadie (Zoko 61).
*Bradford C:* (442) Duke; Darby, Oliver, McArdle, Meredith; Thompson (Baker 74), Jones G, Atkinson, Reid (Doyle 104); Hanson, Connell (Wells 61).
*aet.*

**Rochdale (1) 3** *(Tutte 6, Kennedy 90 (pen), 105 (pen))*
**Barnsley (1) 4** *(Stones 45, Davies 79, Dagnall 95, 105)*     2709
*Rochdale:* (4231) Lillis; Pearson, Edwards Ryan, Edwards P, McIntyre; Cavanagh, Kennedy; Tutte, Donnelly (Putterill 75), Grimes (Curran 85); Adebola (Craney 84).
*Barnsley:* (4231) Alnwick■; Stones (Hassell 85), Foster, McNulty, Wiseman; Mellis, Perkins; O'Brien (Dagnall 18), Etuhu (Cywka 70), Done; Davies.
*aet.*

**Sheffield U (0) 2** *(Blackman 51, Collins 105)*
**Burton Alb (1) 2** *(Yussuf 34, Taylor 97)*     7073
*Sheffield U:* (442) Howard; McMahon, Maguire, Collins, Williams; Flynn (McAllister 90), Doyle, McDonald, Quinn; Porter (Blackman 46), Miller (McFadzean 69).
*Burton Alb:* (442) Atkins; Stanton, Diamond, Holness■, McCrory; Taylor, Weir, Bell, Palmer C (Dyer 68); Yussuf (Webster 79), Kee (Richards 59).
*aet; Burton Alb won on 5-4 on penalties.*

**Walsall (1) 1** *(Hemmings 8)*
**Brentford (0) 0**     2248
*Walsall:* (4411) Grof; Purkiss, Holden, Butler, Taundry; Paterson, Chambers A, Featherstone (Jones 71), Hemmings (Bowerman 67); Cuvelier; Grigg (Brandy 89).
*Brentford:* (442) Moore; O'Connor, Craig, Dean, Weston; Forrester (Forshaw 63), Douglas, Saunders (Diagouraga 46); Logan (Fredericks 71); Reeves■, Donaldson.

**Watford (0) 1** *(Iwelumo 109)*
**Wycombe W (0) 0**     5343
*Watford:* (433) Almunia; Doyley (Hodson 70), Nosworthy, Taylor, Dickinson (Forsyth 77); Eustace, Hogg, Abdi; Yeates, Vydra, Garner (Iwelumo 97).
*Wycombe W:* (451) Bull; McCoy (Johnson 20), Stewart, Doherty, Lewis; Spring, Bloomfield (Angol 100), Wood, Grant, Dunne (Basey 98); Logan.
*aet.*

**Wolverhampton W (0) 1** *(Ebanks-Blake 53)*
**Aldershot T (0) 1** *(Rankine 62)*     11,555
*Wolverhampton W:* (442) Ikeme; Zubar, Johnson, Stearman (Berra 106), Ward; Davis (Hunt 106), Henry, Doumbia, Forde; Doyle (Nouble 91), Ebanks-Blake.
*Aldershot T:* (442) Young; Herd, Lancashire (Payne 8), Bradley, Tonkin; Mekki (Rodman 72), Morris A, Brown, Vincenti (Roberts 91); Rankine, Reid.
*aet; Wolverhampton W won on 7-6 on penalties.*

Sunday, 12 August 2012

**Blackpool (0) 1** *(Baptiste 77)*
**Morecambe (1) 2** *(Alessandra 6, Fleming 56)*     6083
*Blackpool:* (433) Gilks; Eardley, Evatt, Baptiste, Crainey; Sylvestre (Grandin 46), Martinez (Gomes 59), Ferguson; Phillips M, Taylor-Fletcher (Barkhuizen 75), Ince.
*Morecambe:* (433) Roche; Parrish, Haining, McCready, Threlfall (Drummond 82); Fleming, McDonald, Ellison; Wright, Burrow (Brodie 54), Alessandra (Carlton 66).

Monday, 13 August 2012

**Fleetwood T (0) 0**
**Nottingham F (0) 1** *(Blackstock 57)*     3611
*Fleetwood T:* (433) Davies; Beeley, McNulty, Mawene, Howell; McLaughlin (Fowler 69), Nicholson, McGuire; Ball (Gillespie 63), Parkin, Mangan.
*Nottingham F:* (4411) Darlow; Moloney, Ayala, Collins, Harding; Halford, McGugan, Guedioura, Reid; Majewski (Greening 88); Blackstock (Tudgay 81).

**Oldham Ath (2) 2** *(Slew 7, Mvoto 27)*
**Sheffield W (0) 4** *(Johnson J 53, O'Grady 62, 70,*
*Antonio 87)*　　　　　　　　　　　　　　3474
*Oldham Ath:* (442) Cisak; Byrne (Smith 82), Mvoto,
Tarkowski, Grounds; Croft, Wesolowski, Furman,
M'Changama (Hughes 75); Simpson R, Slew.
*Sheffield W:* (442) Kirkland; Buxton, Llera, Gardner,
Johnson R; Antonio, Semedo, Pecnik, Johnson J (Jones
85); Madine (O'Grady 29), Maguire (Coke 39).

**Preston NE (2) 2** *(King 29, Wroe 40)*
**Huddersfield T (0) 0**　　　　　　　　　　5750
*Preston NE:* (442) Stuckmann; Keane, Huntington,
Cansdell-Sherriff, Laird; Wroe (Amoo 80), Mousinho,
Holmes (Buchanan 46), Monakana (Welsh 70); King,
Beardsley.
*Huddersfield T:* (433) Smithies; Hunt, Clarke P, Gerrard
(Clarke T 75), Dixon; Clayton, Gobern, Southern;
Novak, Spencer (Lee 75), Ward (Arfield 46).

Tuesday, 14 August 2012
**Birmingham C (1) 5** *(King 38 (pen), Caldwell 49,*
*Ambrose 54, Lovenkrands 90, Elliott 90)*
**Barnet (1) 1** *(Nurse 31)*　　　　　　　　9905
*Birmingham C:* (442) Lucas; Packwood (Gomis 75),
Davies, Caldwell, Murphy; Burke (Redmond 85),
Mullins, Morrison (Elliott 78), Ambrose; King,
Lovenkrands.
*Barnet:* (4312) O'Brien; Warren, Fortune (Saville 79),
Kamdjo, Brown; Yiadom, Lee (Weston 64), Abdulla;
Holmes; Edgar, Nurse (Hyde 76).

**Bristol C (0) 1** *(Elliott 90)*
**Gillingham (1) 2** *(Kedwell 45 (pen), Strevens 54)*　4339
*Bristol C:* (442) Gerken; Skuse, Fontaine, Nyatanga,
Foster; Adomah, Morris (Bolasie 64), Pearson (Elliott
86), Woolford; Stead, Pitman.
*Gillingham:* (442) Nelson; Fish, Flanagan, Frampton,
Jackman; Whelpdale (Birchall 73), Montrose, Lee, Allen
(Davies 79); Kedwell, Strevens (Dack 65).

**Charlton Ath (1) 1** *(Wagstaff 28)*
**Leyton Orient (1) 1** *(Baudry 45)*　　　　5914
*Charlton Ath:* (442) Hamer; Wilson, Taylor, Cort, Evina;
Green, Kerkar (Pritchard 100), Hollands, Wagstaff; Cook
(Jackson 106), Smith (Wright-Phillips 106).
*Leyton Orient:* (442) Allsop; James, Cuthbert, Clarke
(Chorley 96), Sawyer; Griffith, Baudry, Cox, Smith
Jimmy; Mooney (Symes 64), Lisbie (Brunt 83).
*aet; Leyton Orient won on 4-3 on penalties.*

**Chesterfield (0) 1** *(Lester 109)*
**Tranmere R (0) 2** *(Stockton 93, Bell-Baggie 120)*　3088
*Chesterfield:* (442) Lee; Talbot, Trotman, Hird (Darikwa
76), Smith; Forbes, Allott, Togwell, Whitaker; Richards
(Lester 67), Westcarr (Bowery 54).
*Tranmere R:* (442) Fon Williams; Holmes, Kay, Gibson,
Bakayogo; Thompson, Palmer (Harrison 112), Wallace,
Robinson (Power 112); Stockton, Akpa Akpro (Bell-
Baggie 100).
*aet.*

**Dagenham & R (0) 0**
**Coventry C (0) 1** *(Kilbane 90 (pen))*　　1904
*Dagenham & R:* (433) Lewington; Hoyte, Doe, Spillane,
Ilesanmi; Howell, Ogogo, Bingham; Scott (Reed 66),
Elito, Woodall (Williams 56).
*Coventry C:* (442) Murphy; Clarke J, Brown, Wood,
Hussey; Baker, Daniels, Kilbane, McSheffrey (Elliott 70);
McDonald, Ball (O'Donovan 85).

**Derby Co (3) 5** *(Keogh 30, Buxton 34, 53, Robinson 40,*
*Tyson 83)*
**Scunthorpe U (0) 5** *(Barcham 52, Grella 63, Grant*
*73, 90 (pen), Jennings 90)*　　　　　　4724
*Derby Co:* (442) Fielding; Brayford, Keogh, Buxton,
Roberts (Naylor 62); Hughes (Bennett 87), Bryson
(Davies B 62), Coutts, Jacobs; Robinson, Tyson.
*Scunthorpe U:* (442) Slocombe; Ribeiro, Mirfin, Newey,
Kennedy; Duffy, Walker, Ryan, Barcham (Jennings 84);
Grella, Grant.
*aet; Derby C won on 7-6 on penalties.*

**Exeter C (1) 1** *(O'Flynn 2)*
**Crystal Palace (2) 2** *(Easter 24 (pen), Dikgacoi 43)*　3650
*Exeter C:* (442) Krysiak; Bennett, Baldwin, Coles,
Amankwaah; Moore-Taylor, Sercombe, Davies, Doherty
(Frear 32); O'Flynn (Gow 62), Bauza (Cureton 62).
*Crystal Palace:* (442) Price; Ward, Ramage, Martin,
Moxey; Zaha, Garvan, Dikgacoi, O'Keefe (Wright 78);
Easter (Appiah 87), Murray (Wilbraham 78).

**Ipswich T (1) 3** *(Scotland 40, Smith 56, Cresswell 84)*
**Bristol R (1) 1** *(Smith 26)*　　　　　　8645
*Ipswich T:* (442) Loach; Edwards, Chambers, Smith,
Cresswell; Emmanuel-Thomas, Hyam, Luongo, Martin
(Burke 89); Chopra, Scotland (Stevenson 89).
*Bristol R:* (442) Walker; Smith, Brown L, Virgo,
Paterson; Clarkson, Gill (Lund 61), Brown W, Norburn
(Clucas 63); Harrold, Anyinsah (Clarke 80).

**Millwall (1) 2** *(Ward 23, Batt 85)*
**Crawley T (1) 2** *(Akpan 16, Adams 56)*　　4050
*Millwall:* (442) Taylor M; Smith J, Lowry, Ward, Malone;
Henry (Wright 109), Trotter, Abdou, Feeney (Shittu 61);
Henderson, Taylor C (Batt 61).
*Crawley T:* (442) Jones P; Connolly (Hunt 74),
McFadzean, Davis, Sadler; Simpson, Akpan, Bulman,
Adams (Akinde 100); Clarke (Torres 83), Alexander.
*aet; Crawley T won on 4-1 on penalties.*

**Northampton T (1) 2** *(Artell 37, Nicholls A 48)*
**Cardiff C (1) 1** *(Helguson 4 (pen))*　　　2819
*Northampton T:* (442) Snedker; Johnson, Langmead,
Artell, Widdowson; Guttridge, Harding, Hackett
(Mukendi 56), Tozer; Nicholls A, Platt (Akinfenwa 71).
*Cardiff C:* (442) Lewis; Oshilaja, Keinan, Nugent, John;
Sainte-Luce, McPhail (O'Sullivan 19), Ralls, Conway;
Mason (Mutch 51), Helguson (Jarvis 61).

**Oxford U (0) 0**
**Bournemouth (0) 0**　　　　　　　　　3788
*Oxford U:* (433) Clarke; Batt, Raynes, Wright, Capaldi;
Cox (Smalley 67), Chapman, Forster-Caskey (Heslop
104); Potter, Constable (Craddock 93), Rigg.
*Bournemouth:* (442) Jalal; Francis, Addison, Zubar,
Daniels; Grabban, Partington (McDermott 77), Arter
(Wakefield 98), Pugh; Tubbs (Gregory 61), Thomas.
*aet; Oxford U won on 5-3 on penalties.*

**Peterborough U (3) 4** *(Tomlin 12, Taylor 28, Newell 29,*
*Boyd 58)*
**Southend U (0) 0**　　　　　　　　　　3225
*Peterborough U:* (442) Olejnik; Alcock (Little 61),
Brisley, Zakuani, Ntlhe; Newell (Swanson 68), Tomlin,
Frecklington (McCann 76), Bostwick; Boyd, Taylor.
*Southend U:* (442) Belford; Clohessy, Phillips, Barker,
Prosser; Hall, Ferdinand, Leonard, Straker (Hurst 67);
Harris (Eastwood 40), Benyon (Njie 76).

**Plymouth Arg (1) 3** *(Gorman 45, Cowan-Hall 86,*
*Chadwick 87)*
**Portsmouth (0) 0**　　　　　　　　　　5318
*Plymouth Arg:* (442) Cole; Nelson, Purse, Blanchard,
Bhasera; Gurrieri (Lennox 46), Wotton, Hourihane,
Gorman (Young 74); Chadwick, Lecointe (Cowan-Hall
79).
*Portsmouth:* (442) Eastwood; Webster, Grant, Westwood
(Maloney 34), Butler; Wallace, Magri, Colson, Higgins
(Tarbuck 72); Harris, Thompson.

**Port Vale (1) 1** *(Shuker 9)*
**Burnley (3) 3** *(McCann 11, Austin 29, Marney 42)*　4055
*Port Vale:* (442) Neal; Yates, McCombe, Davis
(McDonald 46), Loft; Myrie-Williams, Morsy, Shuker
(Burge 50), Dodds; Pope, Vincent (Williamson 81).
*Burnley:* (442) Grant; Trippier, Edgar, Shackell, Mills;
Stanislas, Marney, Stock (Duff 86), McCann; Austin,
Wallace.

**Stevenage (3) 3** *(Balkestein 14 (og), Dunne 38, Roberts 45)*
**AFC Wimbledon (1) 1** *(Kiernan 41)*　　2018
*Stevenage:* (442) Day; Gray, Roberts, N'Gala, Charles;
Morais (Akins 71), Dunne, Grant, Freeman; Tansey
(Shroot 70), Haber (Thalassitis 89).

*AFC Wimbledon:* (442) Brown; MacDonald, Cummings, Moore S, Balkestein; Mitchel-King, Long, Kiernan (Harrison 79), Midson; Jolley (Harris 58), Moore L.

**Swindon T (0) 3** *(Benson 53, Navarro 65, 75)*
**Brighton & HA (0) 0**      5737
*Swindon T:* (442) Foderingham; Devera, Archibald-Henville, McCormack, McEveley; Ritchie, Navarro (Ferry 82), Miller, De Vita (Rooney L 87); Benson (Storey 89), Williams.
*Brighton & HA:* (451) Kuszczak; Saltor, Greer, Dunk, Bridge; Noone, Bridcutt, Harley (Calderon 56), Dicker (Agdestein 66), Vicente; Barnes.

**Torquay U (0) 0**
**Leicester C (2) 4** *(Dyer 21, Marshall 36, James 50, Vardy 77)*      3367
*Torquay U:* (4141) Poke; Oastler, Saah, Downes, Nicholson; Lathrope, Mansell, Jarvis (Yeoman 76), Easton (Thompson 63), Morris (Cruise 72); Howe.
*Leicester C:* (442) Schmeichel; De Laet, Morgan, Moore, Konchesky; Marshall, James (King 73), Drinkwater (Danns 78), Dyer (Nugent 66); Beckford, Vardy.

**Yeovil T (2) 3** *(Hinds 4, 45, Marsh-Brown 79)*
**Colchester U (0) 0**      1907
*Yeovil T:* (433) Stech; Ayling, McAllister, Hinds, Webster; Blizzard, Upson, Hayter (Young 70); Reid, Ugwu (Marsh-Brown 70), Foley (Ralph 82).
*Colchester U:* (433) Cousins; Wilson, Eastman, Okuonghae, Rose; Izzet (O'Toole 80), Wordsworth, Bond; Wright Drey (Duguid 58), Henderson, Morrison.

## SECOND ROUND
Tuesday, 28 August 2012
**Aston Villa (1) 3** *(Delph 38, Herd 66, Bent 81)*
**Tranmere R (0) 0**      15,319
*Aston Villa:* (41212) Guzan; Lichaj, Lowton, Baker, Stevens (Holman 67); Herd (Burke 76); Delph, Bannan; Ireland; Weimann (N'Zogbia 71), Bent.
*Tranmere R:* (442) Fon Williams; Holmes, Taylor (Kay 65), Gibson, Bakayogo; Thompson (Bell-Baggie 67), Wallace, Palmer, Robinson (Harrison 76); Cassidy, Akpa Akpro.

**Burnley (1) 1** *(Austin 37)*
**Plymouth Arg (0) 1** *(Williams 90 (pen))*      4119
*Burnley:* (433) Jensen; O'Neill, Mee, Duff, Lafferty; Bartley (Stanislas 98), Hewitt, Stock; MacDonald, Austin (Vokes 54), Treacy (Wallace 46).
*Plymouth Arg:* (442) Cole; Berry, Nelson, Blanchard, Williams; Cowan-Hall, Young, Hourihane, Gorman (Bhasera 67); Sims (Lennox 67), Chadwick (Lecointe 55).
*aet; Burnley won on 3-2 on penalties.*

**Carlisle U (0) 2** *(Beck 90, Symington 99)*
**Ipswich T (1) 1** *(Luongo 24)*      3296
*Carlisle U:* (433) Collin; Potts, Edwards, Murphy, Chantler; Noble, Thirlwell, Berrett (Madden 55); McGovern (Symington 65), Cadamarteri (Beck 78), Robson.
*Ipswich T:* (442) Loach; Edwards (Ainsley 15), Chambers, Smith, Cresswell; Emmanuel-Thomas (Stevenson 77), Luongo, Drury, Carson (Scotland 64); Chopra, Martin.
*aet.*

**Coventry C (2) 3** *(McDonald 20, Kilbane 22, Baker 97)*
**Birmingham C (2) 2** *(Lovenkrands 4, Spector 44)*   10,859
*Coventry C:* (41212) Murphy; Willis (Christie 63), Brown, Edjenguele, Hussey; Jennings; Barton (McSheffrey 80), Kilbane; Baker; McDonald (Ball 90), Elliott.
*Birmingham C:* (442) Doyle; Spector, Caldwell, Davies (Ibanez 71), Gordon (Redmond 66); Burke, Mullins, Gomis, Ambrose; King, Lovenkrands (Rooney 79).
*aet.*

**Crawley T (0) 2** *(Clarke 81, Ajose 90)*
**Bolton W (1) 1** *(Afobe 21)*      2678
*Crawley T:* (451) Jones P; Sadler, McFadzean, Davis, Connolly; Adams, Torres (Bulman 46), Akpan, Ajose, Cooper (Clarke 75); Forte.

*Bolton W:* (451) Lonergan; Alonso, Ream, Knight, Riley; Petrov, Andrews, Davies M (Davies K 72), Vela (Pratley 7), Eagles; Afobe (Sordell 57).

**Doncaster R (1) 3** *(Syers 30, 90, Jones R 57)*
**Hull C (2) 2** *(Mclean 1, Simpson 10)*      4703
*Doncaster R:* (4411) Woods G; Quinn (Cotterill 60), Jones R, McCombe, Spurr; Syers, Harper, Keegan, Husband; Coppinger; Blake (Paynter 68).
*Hull C:* (433) Amos; Dudgeon, Faye (Bruce 87), Chester, Dawson; Evans, Olofinjana, Cairney (McKenna* 37); Stewart, Simpson, Mclean (Aluko 74).

**Gillingham (0) 0**
**Middlesbrough (1) 2** *(Carayol 23, Park 90)*    5146
*Gillingham:* (442) Nelson; Fish (Strevens 71), Davies, Barrett, Martin; Lee (Whelpdale 10), Jackman (Dack 53), Payne, Allen; Kedwell, Burton.
*Middlesbrough:* (343) Steele; Friend, McManus, Hines; Williams R (Haroun 74), Smallwood, Carayol (Zemmama 66), Halliday; Arca, Emnes (Miller 59), Park.

**Leeds U (2) 3** *(Austin 26, Byram 34, Lees 74)*
**Oxford U (0) 0**      13,713
*Leeds U:* (442) Ashdown; Lees, Kisnorbo, Pearce, Drury; Byram (Peltier 90), Brown, Austin (Thompson 83), White; Gray, Diouf (Poleon 76).
*Oxford U:* (433) Clarke; Batt, Raynes, Wright, McGinty; Heslop, Chapman (Boateng 86), Capaldi; Potter (Marsh 81), Constable, Rigg (Pittman 81).

**Leicester C (0) 2** *(Knockaert 60, Futacs 87)*
**Burton Alb (1) 4** *(Palmer C 20, Taylor 53, Weir 64 (pen), Maghoma 68)*      8560
*Leicester C:* (442) Schmeichel; De Laet, St. Ledger, Konchesky, Whitbread; Danns, James, Gallagher (Futacs 56), Knockaert (King 73); Schlupp (Nugent 65), Waghorn.
*Burton Alb:* (442) Atkins; Diamond, Holness, O'Connor, Bell; Taylor (Dyer 62), Weir, Zola (Yussuf 81), McCrory; Palmer C (Kee 86), Maghoma.

**Milton Keynes D (0) 2** *(Chadwick 52, 68)*
**Blackburn R (0) 1** *(Goodwillie 83)*      5873
*Milton Keynes D:* (451) Martin; Otsemobor, MacKenzie, Williams, Chicksen; Powell, Gleeson, Potter, Chadwick (O'Shea 77), Bowditch (Ibehre 90); MacDonald (Lowe 74).
*Blackburn R:* (442) Kean; Orr, Hanley G, Dann, Olsson Marcus; Nunes, Etuhu (Lowe 58), Jorge, Vukcevic; Rochina (Formica 69), Junior (Goodwillie 58).

**Norwich C (1) 2** *(Lappin 32, Hoolahan 56 (pen))*
**Scunthorpe U (1) 1** *(Duffy 34)*      13,116
*Norwich C:* (442) Rudd; Francomb, Turner, Bennett R, Tierney; Fox, Lappin (Pilkington 52), Hoolahan, Surman; Morison (Jackson 80), Martin C.
*Scunthorpe U:* (451) Slocombe; Ribeiro, Mirfin, Canavan, Newey; Duffy, Gibbons, Walker (Prutton 66), Ryan, Barcham (Grant 80); Grella (Jennings 80).

**Nottingham F (0) 1** *(Cox 47)*
**Wigan Ath (3) 4** *(Boselli 25, Figueroa 35, Gomez 44, McManaman 90)*      7545
*Nottingham F:* (442) Camp; Halford (Lascelles 78), Ayala (Moloney 62), Collins, Harding; Cohen (Majewski 66), Gillett, Moussi, Reid; Cox, McGoldrick.
*Wigan Ath:* (343) Al Habsi; Ramis, Alcaraz*, Figueroa; Stam, Jones, Watson B, Beausejour; Crusat (Miyaichi 80), Boselli (Fyvie 83), Gomez (McManaman 72).

**Preston NE (3) 4** *(Wroe 2, 63, Sodje 18, Monakana 41)*
**Crystal Palace (1) 1** *(Wilbraham 37)*      5194
*Preston NE:* (451) Simonsen; Keane (Robertson 46), Huntington, Wright, Laird; Monakana, Wroe, Procter, Welsh, Hayhurst (Buchanan 58); Sodje (Beardsley 68).
*Crystal Palace:* (433) Price; Ward, Martin, Blake, Wright; Williams (Garvan 64), Moxey, O'Keefe; Appiah (Zaha 46), De Silva (Moritz 46), Wilbraham.

**QPR (1) 3** *(Wright-Phillips 29, Zamora 66, Bosingwa 84)*
**Walsall (0) 0**                                     6129
*QPR:* (442) Green; Bosingwa, Nelsen, Ferdinand, Da Silva; Wright-Phillips (Traore 68), Park, Faurlin, Hoilett (Dyer 60); Johnson, Zamora (Cisse 69).
*Walsall:* (442) Grof; Purkiss, Holden, Featherstone, Taylor; Chambers A (Baxendale 37), Butler, Cuvelier, Hemmings (Jones 78); Grigg (Bowerman 70), Paterson.

**Reading (3) 3** *(Pogrebnyak 16, Gunter 19, Knight-Percival 38 (og))*
**Peterborough U (2) 2** *(Taylor 12, Tomlin 17)*     7262
*Reading:* (451) Federici; Gunter, Pearce, Gorkss, Hector; McAnuff, Leigertwood, Karacan (Tabb 72), Guthrie, McCleary (Hunt 62); Pogrebnyak.
*Peterborough U:* (442) Olejnik; Little, Brisley (Newell 26), Knight-Percival, Ntlhe (Sinclair 83); Swanson, Bostwick, McCann, Boyd; Taylor, Tomlin.

**Sheffield W (0) 1** *(Madine 50 (pen))*
**Fulham (0) 0**                                     14,177
*Sheffield W:* (442) Bywater; Buxton, Beevers, Llera, Jones; Antonio, Pecnik, Coke, Semedo; Madine, Maguire (Rodri 69).
*Fulham:* (451) Schwarzer; Kelly (Riether 71), Hangeland, Baird, Kacaniklic; Sidwell, Briggs, Hughes, Kasami (Trotta 63), Duff; Rodallega.

**Stevenage (0) 1** *(Thalassitis 90)*
**Southampton (0) 4** *(Lee 53, Sharp 74, Puncheon 76, Reeves 90)*                                      3062
*Stevenage:* (442) Day; Gray, Ashton, Roberts, Charles; Freeman, Dunne, Tansey (Grant 68), Rogers (Shroot 63); Akins, Haber (Thalassitis 85).
*Southampton:* (451) Gazzaniga; Richardson, Ward-Prowse, Lee, Shaw; Butterfield, Chaplow (Reeves 77), Seaborne, Hammond (Chambers 84), Puncheon; Sharp (Hoskins 85).

**Stoke C (0) 3** *(Jones 63, Walters 86, Crouch 111)*
**Swindon T (2) 4** *(Collins 27, 41, 119, Flint 105)*  9147
*Stoke C:* (442) Sorensen; Shotton (Ness 77), Upson, Huth, Wilson; Pennant, Whitehead, Cameron, Kightly; Jones (Crouch 77), Jerome (Walters 77).
*Swindon T:* (442) Foderingham; Devera, Flint, McCormack, McEveley (Thompson N 98); Ritchie, Miller, Navarro, De Vita (Ferry 73); Williams, Collins.
*aet.*

**Sunderland (1) 2** *(McClean 24, 65)*
**Morecambe (0) 0**                                  22,871
*Sunderland:* (4411) Westwood; Gardner, Bramble, O'Shea, Colback; Johnson, Cattermole (Meyler 78), Larsson, McClean (Campbell 73); Sessegnon; Fletcher (Saha 66).
*Morecambe:* (4141) Roche; Parrish, Haining, Fenton, Threlfall; Wright; Alessandra (Redshaw 72), McDonald, Fleming, Reid (Ellison 60); Brodie (Carlton 60).

**Swansea C (1) 3** *(Graham 24, Moore 59, 88)*
**Barnsley (0) 1** *(Hassell 69)*                    9025
*Swansea C:* (451) Tremmel; Rangel (Dobbie 56), Tate, Davies, Bartley; de Guzman, Agustien, Dyer, Ki (Gower 76), Graham (Richards 56); Moore.
*Barnsley:* (442) Alnwick; Cranie, Wiseman, Stones, Hassell; Golbourne, Dawson, Cywka, Mellis (Clark 63); Davies (Harewood 63), Dagnall.

**Watford (0) 1** *(Anya 71)*
**Bradford C (0) 2** *(Reid 84, Thompson 90)*        5560
*Watford:* (433) Bond; Hodson, Dickinson, Taylor, Thompson; Hogg (Abdi 77), Forsyth, Jenkins; Beleck, Anya (Murray 79), Mujangi Bia (Vydra 57).
*Bradford C:* (433) McLaughlin; Darby, McHugh, Oliver, McArdle; Meredith (Hanson 76), Atkinson, Jones G (Doyle 61); Thompson, Connell, Hines (Reid 59).

**West Ham U (1) 2** *(Maynard 34, Maiga 55)*
**Crewe Alex (0) 0**                                 18,053
*West Ham U:* (433) Henderson; O'Brien, Spence, Diarra, Potts; O'Neil, Nolan (Moncur 84), Taylor (Fanimo 60); Maynard, Maiga, Vaz Te (Hall 73).
*Crewe Alex:* (442) Martin; Mellor, Davis, Ellis (Dugdale 73), Bunn (Osman 62); Murphy, Westwood, Moore, Robertson; Clayton M, Leitch-Smith (Turton 80).

**Yeovil T (1) 2** *(Reid 15, 48)*
**WBA (2) 4** *(Brunt 39, Long 45, 81, El Ghanassy 73)* 6228
*Yeovil T:* (442) Stech; Ayling, Hinds, Webster, McAllister; Marsh-Brown, Blizzard (Ince 79), Upson, Foley; Hayter (Young 76), Reid (Ugwu 80).
*WBA:* (442) Myhill; Jones, Tamas, Dawson, Jara Reyes; Gera (Mulumbu 76), Thorne, Brunt, El Ghanassy; Long (Berahino 84), Rosenberg (Fortune 76).

### Wednesday, 29 August 2012
**Everton (4) 5** *(Mirallas 16, 29, Osman 22, Anichebe 36, Gueye 67)*
**Leyton Orient (0) 0**                              24,124
*Everton:* (442) Mucha; Neville, Jagielka (Garbutt 46), Heitinga, Baines (Duffy 46); Coleman, Osman (Barkley 46), Naismith, Gueye; Mirallas, Anichebe.
*Leyton Orient:* (442) Jones; James (McSweeney 47), Clarke, Chorley, Sawyer; Smith Jimmy, Griffith (Rowlands 56), Baudry, Cox; Odubajo (Cook 74), Lisbie.

### Thursday, 30 August 2012
**Northampton T (1) 1** *(Platt 40)*
**Wolverhampton W (2) 3** *(Batth 16, Nouble 45, Sako 90)*
                                                     3758
*Northampton T:* (442) Snedker; East, Langmead, Artell, Widdowson; Hackett, Guttridge, Tozer (Akinfenwa 57), Harding; Platt (Moult 73), Nicholls A (Mukendi 46).
*Wolverhampton W:* (442) Ikeme; Stearman, Batth, Margreitter, Elokobi; Boukari (Sako 67), Jonsson (Doumbia 67), Davis, Forde (Peszko 83); Sigurdarson, Nouble.

## THIRD ROUND

### Tuesday, 25 September 2012
**Bradford C (0) 3** *(Wells 83, 90, Darby 115)*
**Burton Alb (2) 2** *(Kee 18, Webster 29)*          4178
*Bradford C:* (442) Duke; Darby, Davies, McArdle, Meredith; Hines (Wells 61), Jones G, Ravenhill (Reid 60), Atkinson; Connell (Hanson 61), Thompson.
*Burton Alb:* (442) Tomlinson; O'Connor, Stanton (Corbett 46), Diamond, McCrory; Dyer, Bell, Weir, Webster; Yussuf (Paterson 80), Kee (Taylor 66).
*aet.*

**Chelsea (3) 6** *(Cahill 4, Bertrand 8, Mata 17, Romeu 53 (pen), Torres 58, Moses 71)*
**Wolverhampton W (0) 0**                            32,569
*Chelsea:* (433) Turnbull; Azpilicueta, Cahill, Terry, Bertrand; Ramires (Oscar 59), Romeu, Piazon; Mata (Marin 70), Torres (Hazard 78), Moses.
*Wolverhampton W:* (451) De Vries; Stearman, Margreitter, Batth, Zubar; Peszko (Ismail 83), Edwards, Davis, Hunt (Forde 46), Boukari (Nouble 63); Sigurdarson.

**Crawley T (1) 2** *(Simpson 45, Akpan 62)*
**Swansea C (1) 3** *(Michu 27, Graham 74, Monk 90)*  3963
*Crawley T:* (442) Jones P; Sadler, Davis, Walsh, Byrne; Adams, Bulman, Akpan, Simpson; Clarke (Ajose 85), Forte (Alexander 85).
*Swansea C:* (442) Tremmel; Davies, Ki, Monk, Tiendalli; Britton, Gower, Michu (Donnelly 58); Routledge, Moore, Richards (Graham 67).

**Leeds U (1) 2** *(White 4, Austin 70)*
**Everton (0) 1** *(Distin 81)*                      21,164
*Leeds U:* (433) Ashdown; Byram, Lees, Pearce, White; Austin, Tonge, Brown; Pugh, Diouf, Becchio.
*Everton:* (442) Mucha; Coleman, Heitinga, Distin, Oviedo; Naismith (Jelavic 65), Fellaini, Junior (Neville 46), Gueye (Pienaar 46); Mirallas, Anichebe.

**Manchester C (1) 2** *(Balotelli 27, Kolarov 64)*
**Aston Villa (0) 4** *(Barry 59 (og), Agbonlahor 70, 113, N'Zogbia 96)*                                   28,015
*Manchester C:* (343) Pantilimon; Nastasic, Toure K, Lescott (Dzeko 74); Milner, Barry, Kolarov, Razak (Helan 106); Tevez, Balotelli, Suarez (Sinclair 62).
*Aston Villa:* (4231) Given; Lowton, Vlaar, Clark, Bennett (Lichaj 86); Delph, El Ahmadi (Herd 72); N'Zogbia, Weimann (Albrighton 66), Agbonlahor; Benteke.
*aet.*

**Milton Keynes D (0) 0**
**Sunderland (0) 2** *(Gardner 54, McClean 82)*    10,489
*Milton Keynes D:* (451) McLoughlin; Chicksen, Kay, Williams, Lewington; Powell (O'Shea 77), Gleeson, Potter, Chadwick (Lowe 62), Bowditch; Smith (MacDonald 62).
*Sunderland:* (442) Westwood; Gardner, Meyler, Kilgallon, Rose; Colback, Cattermole■, Vaughan, McClean; Saha, Sessegnon (Johnson 85).

**Preston NE (1) 1** *(King 40)*
**Middlesbrough (2) 3** *(Ledesma 13, Zemmama 18,*
*Smallwood 61)*    4959
*Preston NE:* (442) Simonsen; Mousinho (Procter 86), Huntington, Cansdell-Sherriff, Laird; Monakana (Hayhurst 79), Wroe, King (Cummins 79), Amoo; Beavon, Byrom.
*Middlesbrough:* (442) Leutwiler; Parnaby, Hines, McManus, Halliday; Bailey, Smallwood, Arca (Thomson 86), Zemmama (Emnes 62); Williams L, Ledesma (Haroun 63).

**Southampton (1) 2** *(Rodriguez 30, 78 (pen))*
**Sheffield W (0) 0**    9890
*Southampton:* (433) Gazzaniga; Richardson, Yoshida, Hooiveld, Seaborne; Chaplow, Ward-Prowse, Cork (Robinson 81); Do Prado (Reeves 71), De Ridder, Rodriguez (Hoskins 85).
*Sheffield W:* (442) Bywater; Lee (Mattock 46), Llera, Beevers, Jones; Pecnik, Semedo, Corry (Johnson 66), Antonio; Madine, Maguire (O'Grady 66).

**Swindon T (2) 3** *(Benson 19, Williams 42,*
*Archibald-Henville 83)*
**Burnley (0) 1** *(Austin 74)*    7353
*Swindon T:* (442) Foderingham; Thompson N, McCormack, Archibald-Henville (Flint 84), McEveley; Ritchie, Navarro (Ferry 81), Miller, Roberts; Williams, Benson (Collins 87).
*Burnley:* (532) Jensen; Trippier, Edgar, Duff, Mee, Mills (Vokes 46); Bartley, McCann, Stock (Marney 56); Wallace, Austin.

**West Ham U (1) 1** *(Maiga 7)*
**Wigan Ath (3) 4** *(Boselli 14, Ramis 38, Boselli 41,*
*Gomez 84 (pen))*    25,934
*West Ham U:* (433) Henderson; Spence, Tomkins, McCartney, Potts; Vaz Te (Fanimo 62), Noble (Taylor 72), O'Neil (Tombides 84); Hall, Maiga, Jarvis.
*Wigan Ath:* (343) Al Habsi; Ramis, Lopez, Caldwell; Stam, Jones, McArthur (Fyvie 85), Figueroa; Boselli (Orsula 90), Miyaichi, McManaman (Gomez 74).

**Wednesday, 26 September 2012**
**Arsenal (1) 6** *(Giroud 39, Oxlade-Chamberlain 57,*
*Arshavin 63, Walcott 74, 90, Miquel 80)*
**Coventry C (0) 1** *(Ball 78)*    58,351
*Arsenal:* (4132) Martinez; Yennaris, Djourou, Miquel, Andre Santos; Angha; Walcott, Coquelin (Frimpong 72), Oxlade-Chamberlain (Gnabry 72); Giroud (Chamakh 72), Arshavin.
*Coventry C:* (451) Murphy; Clarke J, Wood, Brown, Reckord; Bailey, Barton, McSheffrey, Moussa (Fleck 60), Baker; Elliott (Ball 69).

**Carlisle U (0) 0**
**Tottenham H (1) 3** *(Vertonghen 37, Townsend 53,*
*Sigurdsson 89)*    12,625
*Carlisle U:* (442) Gillespie; Simek, Livesey, Murphy, Chantler; McGovern (Symington 61), Thirlwell (Noble 61), Berrett, Robson; Higginbotham (Beck 60), Cadamarteri.
*Tottenham H:* (442) Cudicini; Smith, Dawson, Caulker, Vertonghen (Walker 65); Townsend, Huddlestone, Sigurdsson, Falque; Dempsey (Obika 75), Mason (Carroll 70).

**Manchester U (1) 2** *(Anderson 44, Cleverley 58)*
**Newcastle U (0) 1** *(Cisse 62)*    46,358
*Manchester U:* (433) De Gea; Vermijl (Tunnicliffe 77), Wootton, Keane, Buttner (Brady 86); Cleverley, Fletcher, Anderson; Rooney (Powell 77), Welbeck, Hernandez.
*Newcastle U:* (4411) Elliot; Perch, Williamson, Coloccini (Ferguson 61), Tavernier; Obertan, Tiote (Bigirimana 71), Gosling, Marveaux; Vuckic (Cisse 61); Ameobi Shola.

**Norwich C (1) 1** *(Tettey 26)*
**Doncaster R (0) 0**    13,902
*Norwich C:* (433) Bunn; Bennett E, Ward, Bennett R, Tierney; Butterfield, Fox, Martin (Hoolahan 71); Tettey, Holt, Kane (Jackson 50).
*Doncaster R:* (442) Woods G; Quinn, Martis, McCombe, Spurr (Bennett 61); Cotterill, Woods Martin (Syers 50), Harper, Husband; Blake (Brown 57), Hume.

**QPR (1) 2** *(Hoilett 14, Cisse 71)*
**Reading (1) 3** *(Gorkss 16, Shorey 76, Pogrebnyak 81)*
    11,562
*QPR:* (442) Julio Cesar; Dyer (Nelsen 65), Mbia, Hill, Onuoha; Park (Zamora 67), Faurlin (Diakite 87), Granero, Hoilett; Cisse, Mackie.
*Reading:* (442) McCarthy; Cummings, Mariappa (Morrison 79), Gorkss, Shorey; Kebe (McCleary 69), Karacan, Tabb, Robson-Kanu; Pogrebnyak, Hunt.

**WBA (1) 1** *(Tamas 3)*
**Liverpool (1) 2** *(Sahin 17, 82)*    21,164
*WBA:* (433) Foster; Jones, Olsson, Tamas, Ridgewell (Dawson 22); Mulumbu, Dorrans, Thorne; Rosenberg, Fortune (El Ghanassy 87), Lukaku (Long 70).
*Liverpool:* (433) Jones; Wisdom, Carragher, Coates, Robinson; Henderson, Sahin, Downing; Pacheco (Suso 81), Yesil (Sinclair 81), Assaidi.

**FOURTH ROUND**

**Tuesday, 30 October 2012**
**Leeds U (1) 3** *(Tonge 35, Diouf 88, Becchio 90 (pen))*
**Southampton (0) 0**    17,002
*Leeds U:* (442) Ashdown; Peltier (Pugh 90), Lees, Pearce, White; Byram, Austin, Brown, Tonge; Varney (Becchio 90), Diouf (Gray 90).
*Southampton:* (433) Davis K; Butterfield, Hooiveld, Seaborne, Reeves; Mayuka, Chaplow, De Ridder (Isgrove 67); Ward-Prowse, Lee (Shaw 67), Do Prado.

**Reading (4) 5** *(Roberts 12, Koscielny 18 (og),*
*Leigertwood 20, Hunt 37, Pogrebnyak 116)*
**Arsenal (1) 7** *(Walcott 45, 90, 120, Giroud 64,*
*Koscielny 89, Chamakh 103, 120)*    23,980
*Reading:* (442) Federici; Gunter, Gorkss, Morrison, Shorey; Tabb, McCleary (McAnuff 73), Leigertwood, Robson-Kanu; Roberts (Church 90), Hunt (Pogrebnyak 73).
*Arsenal:* (433) Martinez; Jenkinson, Koscielny, Djourou, Miquel (Meade 105); Arshavin, Frimpong (Giroud 62), Coquelin; Walcott, Chamakh, Gnabry (Eisfeld 62).
*aet.*

**Sunderland (0) 0**
**Middlesbrough (1) 1** *(McDonald 39)*    32,535
*Sunderland:* (442) Westwood; Bardsley, O'Shea, Cuellar, Colback; Johnson (Campbell 82), Cattermole, Vaughan, Sessegnon; Fletcher, Saha (McClean 59).
*Middlesbrough:* (442) Steele; Hoyte, Hines (Parnaby 65), Bikey, Friend; Ledesma (Reach 79), Leadbitter, Bailey, Haroun; Miller (Smallwood 90), McDonald.

**Swindon T (0) 2** *(Storey 78, 81)*
**Aston Villa (2) 3** *(Benteke 30, 90, Agbonlahor 39)*   14,434
*Swindon T:* (442) Foderingham; Devera, McCormack, Flint, McEveley; Ritchie, Miller, Ferry, Roberts (Thompson L 69); Benson (Williams 51), Collins (Storey 75).
*Aston Villa:* (442) Given; Lowton, Herd (Stevens 30), Vlaar, Lichaj; Weimann, Ireland (Bent 83), El Ahmadi, Bannan (Delph 82); Agbonlahor, Benteke.

**Wigan Ath (0) 0**
**Bradford C (0) 0**    11,777
*Wigan Ath:* (343) Al Habsi; Ramis, Watson B, Lopez; Stam (Orsula 120), Fyvie, Jones, Redmond (Beausejour 77); Gomez, Boselli, McManaman (Maloney 77).
*Bradford C:* (442) Duke; Darby, McHugh, McArdle, Meredith; Hines (Baker 101), Thompson (Jones G 56), Doyle, Atkinson; Wells (Connell 65), Hanson.
*aet; Bradford C won on 4-2 on penalties.*

Michu slots home Swansea City's second goal in his side's 5-0 thrashing of League Two's Bradford City in the Capital One Cup Final in February. Bradford returned to Wembley later in the season to clinch promotion to League One. (Action Images)

Wednesday, 31 October 2012

**Chelsea (1) 5** *(Luiz 31 (pen), Cahill 52, Hazard 90 (pen), Sturridge 97, Ramires 116)*
**Manchester U (2) 4** *(Giggs 22, 120 (pen), Hernandez 43, Nani 59)*         41,126
*Chelsea:* (4231) Cech; Azpilicueta, Cahill, Luiz, Bertrand; Romeu (Oscar 71), Mikel (Ramires 46); Moses, Mata, Piazon (Hazard 55); Sturridge.
*Manchester U:* (433) Lindegaard; Da Silva, Wootton, Keane, Buttner (Powell 46); Anderson (Tunnicliffe 81), Giggs, Fletcher; Nani, Hernandez, Welbeck (Macheda 99).
*aet.*

**Liverpool (0) 1** *(Suarez 76)*
**Swansea C (1) 3** *(Chico 34, Dyer 72, de Guzman 90)*         37,521
*Liverpool:* (4231) Jones; Henderson, Carragher, Coates, Robinson; Allen, Shelvey; Downing, Cole (Gerrard 46), Assaidi (Sterling 65); Yesil (Suarez 46).
*Swansea C:* (4411) Tremmel; Chico (Monk 58), Richards, Williams, Tiendalli; Hernandez (Routledge 75), Britton, Ki, Dyer; de Guzman; Michu.

**Norwich C (0) 2** *(Vertonghen 84 (og), Jackson 87)*
**Tottenham H (0) 1** *(Bale 66)*         16,465
*Norwich C:* (4411) Bunn; Whittaker, Turner, Bennett R, Tierney; Snodgrass, Fox (Tettey 68), Butterfield (Jackson 68), Surman (Holt 82); Howson; Morison.
*Tottenham H:* (4411) Lloris; Walker (Defoe 90), Dawson, Caulker, Naughton; Sigurdsson, Livermore (Huddlestone 46), Carroll (Vertonghen 79), Falque; Bale; Dempsey.

## QUARTER-FINALS

Tuesday, 11 December 2012

**Bradford C (1) 1** *(Thompson 16)*
**Arsenal (0) 1** *(Vermaelen 88)*         23,971
*Bradford C:* (442) Duke; Darby, McHugh, McArdle, Meredith; Thompson (Jones R 72), Doyle, Jones G, Atkinson (Turgott 92); Hanson, Wells (Connell 74).
*Arsenal:* (4141) Szczesny; Sagna, Mertesacker, Vermaelen, Gibbs; Cazorla; Ramsey (Rosicky 69), Wilshere, Podolski (Oxlade-Chamberlain 69), Coquelin (Chamakh 60); Gervinho.
*aet; Bradford C won on 3-2 on penalties.*

**Norwich C (1) 1** *(Morison 19)*
**Aston Villa (1) 4** *(Holman 21, Weimann 79, 85, Benteke 90)*         26,142
*Norwich C:* (442) Bunn; Martin R, Barnett, Bassong, Tierney; Snodgrass, Howson (Bennett E 87), Johnson, Pilkington; Holt, Morison (Jackson 80).
*Aston Villa:* (352) Given; Clark, Herd, Baker; Lowton, El Ahmadi, Delph, Holman (N'Zogbia 73), Lichaj; Benteke, Bent (Weimann 35).

Wednesday, 12 December 2012

**Swansea C (0) 1** *(Hines 81 (og))*
**Middlesbrough (0) 0**         15,048
*Swansea C:* (451) Tremmel; Tiendalli, Chico, Monk, Davies; Dyer, Britton, de Guzman, Shechter (Moore 55), Routledge (Ki 65); Michu.
*Middlesbrough:* (442) Steele; Hoyte, Bikey (Halliday 64), Hines, Friend; Haroun (Smallwood 65), Leadbitter (Miller 82), Bailey, Ledesma; Jutkiewicz, McDonald.

Wednesday, 19 December 2012

**Leeds U (1) 1** *(Becchio 37)*
**Chelsea (0) 5** *(Mata 47, Ivanovic 64, Moses 66, Hazard 81, Torres 84)*         33,816
*Leeds U:* (442) Ashdown; Byram, Lees, Pearce, Peltier; Green, Brown (Norris 72), Tonge, Thomas (White 68); Diouf (McCormack 72), Becchio.
*Chelsea:* (4231) Cech; Azpilicueta, Ivanovic, Luiz, Bertrand (Cole 74); Lampard, Oscar; Marin (Hazard 60), Mata (Ferreira 86), Moses; Torres.

**SEMI-FINALS FIRST LEG**

Tuesday, 8 January 2013

**Bradford C (1) 3** *(Wells 19, McArdle 77, McHugh 88)*

**Aston Villa (0) 1** *(Weimann 82)* 22,245

*Bradford C:* (442) Duke; Darby, McArdle, McHugh, Good; Hines (Turgott 65), Jones G, Doyle, Atkinson; Wells, Hanson.
*Aston Villa:* (442) Given; Lowton, Clark, Baker, Bennett; Agbonlahor (Bent 57 (Burke 85)), Delph, Bannan, N'Zogbia; Benteke, Weimann.

Wednesday, 9 January 2013

**Chelsea (0) 0**

**Swansea C (1) 2** *(Michu 39, Graham 90)* 40,172

*Chelsea:* (4231) Turnbull; Azpilicueta, Ivanovic, Cahill, Cole; Luiz, Ramires (Lampard 71); Hazard, Oscar (Marin 83), Mata; Torres (Ba 81).
*Swansea C:* (433) Tremmel; Rangel, Chico, Williams, Davies; Britton, de Guzman, Ki; Routledge (Tiendalli 62), Hernandez, Michu (Graham 83).

**SEMI-FINALS SECOND LEG**

Tuesday, 22 January 2013

**Aston Villa (1) 2** *(Benteke 24, Weimann 89)*

**Bradford C (0) 1** *(Hanson 55)* 40,193

*Aston Villa:* (4312) Given; Lowton, Vlaar, Clark, Bennett (Weimann 70); Ireland, Delph, Bannan (Bent 62); N'Zogbia; Benteke, Agbonlahor.
*Bradford C:* (442) Duke; Darby, McHugh, McArdle, Good; Hines (Thompson 71), Jones G, Doyle, Atkinson; Hanson, Wells (Turgott 87).

Wednesday, 23 January 2013

**Swansea C (0) 0**

**Chelsea (0) 0** 19,506

*Swansea C:* (433) Tremmel; Rangel, Chico, Williams, Davies; Britton, de Guzman, Ki; Hernandez, Michu, Routledge (Dyer 65).
*Chelsea:* (433) Cech; Azpilicueta, Cahill, Ivanovic (Luiz 68), Cole (Bertrand 86); Ramires, Oscar (Torres 81), Lampard; Hazard■, Ba, Mata.

**CAPITAL ONE CUP FINAL**

Sunday, 24 February 2013

**Swansea C (2) 5      Bradford C (0) 0**

(at Wembley Stadium, attendance 82,597)

*Swansea C:* (451) Tremmel; Rangel, Williams, Ki (Monk 62), Davies (Tiendalli 84); Dyer (Lamah 77), Britton, de Guzman, Routledge, Hernandez; Ki.
*Scorers:* Dyer 16, 48, Michu 40, de Guzman 59 (pen), 90).

*Bradford C:* (442) Duke■; Darby, McHugh, McArdle, Good (Davies 46); Atkinson, Jones G, Doyle, Thompson (Hines 73); Wells (McLaughlin 57), Hanson.

*Referee:* Kevin Friend.

# LEAGUE CUP ATTENDANCES

| Season | Attendances | Games | Average |
|---|---|---|---|
| 1960–61 | 1,204,580 | 112 | 10,755 |
| 1961–62 | 1,030,534 | 104 | 9,909 |
| 1962–63 | 1,029,893 | 102 | 10,097 |
| 1963–64 | 945,265 | 104 | 9,089 |
| 1964–65 | 962,802 | 98 | 9,825 |
| 1965–66 | 1,205,876 | 106 | 11,376 |
| 1966–67 | 1,394,553 | 118 | 11,818 |
| 1967–68 | 1,671,326 | 110 | 15,194 |
| 1968–69 | 2,064,647 | 118 | 17,497 |
| 1969–70 | 2,299,819 | 122 | 18,851 |
| 1970–71 | 2,035,315 | 116 | 17,546 |
| 1971–72 | 2,397,154 | 123 | 19,489 |
| 1972–73 | 1,935,474 | 120 | 16,129 |
| 1973–74 | 1,722,629 | 132 | 13,050 |
| 1974–75 | 1,901,094 | 127 | 14,969 |
| 1975–76 | 1,841,735 | 140 | 13,155 |
| 1976–77 | 2,236,636 | 147 | 15,215 |
| 1977–78 | 2,038,295 | 148 | 13,772 |
| 1978–79 | 1,825,643 | 139 | 13,134 |
| 1979–80 | 2,322,866 | 169 | 13,745 |
| 1980–81 | 2,051,576 | 161 | 12,743 |
| 1981–82 | 1,880,682 | 161 | 11,681 |
| 1982–83 | 1,679,756 | 160 | 10,498 |
| 1983–84 | 1,900,491 | 168 | 11,312 |
| 1984–85 | 1,876,429 | 167 | 11,236 |
| 1985–86 | 1,579,916 | 163 | 9,693 |
| 1986–87 | 1,531,498 | 157 | 9,755 |
| 1987–88 | 1,539,253 | 158 | 9,742 |
| 1988–89 | 1,552,780 | 162 | 9,585 |
| 1989–90 | 1,836,916 | 168 | 10,934 |
| 1990–91 | 1,675,496 | 159 | 10,538 |
| 1991–92 | 1,622,337 | 164 | 9,892 |
| 1992–93 | 1,558,031 | 161 | 9,677 |
| 1993–94 | 1,744,120 | 163 | 10,700 |
| 1994–95 | 1,530,478 | 157 | 9,748 |
| 1995–96 | 1,776,060 | 162 | 10,963 |
| 1996–97 | 1,529,321 | 163 | 9,382 |
| 1997–98 | 1,484,297 | 153 | 9,701 |
| 1998–99 | 1,555,856 | 153 | 10,169 |
| 1999–2000 | 1,354,233 | 153 | 8,851 |
| 2000–01 | 1,501,304 | 154 | 9,749 |
| 2001–02 | 1,076,390 | 93 | 11,574 |
| 2002–03 | 1,242,478 | 92 | 13,505 |
| 2003–04 | 1,267,729 | 93 | 13,631 |
| 2004–05 | 1,313,693 | 93 | 14,216 |
| 2005–06 | 1,072,362 | 93 | 11,531 |
| 2006–07 | 1,098,403 | 93 | 11,811 |
| 2007–08 | 1,332,841 | 94 | 14,179 |
| 2008–09 | 1,329,753 | 93 | 14,298 |
| 2009–10 | 1,376,405 | 93 | 14,800 |
| 2010–11 | 1,197,917 | 93 | 12,881 |
| 2011–12 | 1,209,684 | 93 | 13,007 |
| 2012–13 | 1,210,031 | 93 | 13,011 |

### CAPITAL ONE CUP 2012–13

| Round | Aggregate | Games | Average |
|---|---|---|---|
| One | 169,508 | 35 | 4,843 |
| Two | 229,517 | 25 | 9,181 |
| Three | 312,476 | 16 | 19,530 |
| Four | 194,840 | 8 | 24,355 |
| Quarter-finals | 98,977 | 4 | 24,744 |
| Semi-finals | 122,116 | 4 | 30,529 |
| Final | 82,597 | 1 | 82,597 |
| Total | 1,210,031 | 93 | 13,011 |

# FOOTBALL LEAGUE TROPHY
# FINALS 1984–2013

*The 1984 final was played at Boothferry Park, Hull. All subsequent finals played at Wembley except between 2001 and 2007 (inclusive) which were played at Millennium Stadium, Cardiff.*

| | *Year* | *Winners* | *Runners-up* | *Score* |
|---|---|---|---|---|
| **ASSOCIATE MEMBERS' CUP** | 1984 | Bournemouth | Hull C | 2-1 |
| **FREIGHT ROVER TROPHY** | 1985 | Wigan Ath | Brentford | 3-1 |
| | 1986 | Bristol C | Bolton W | 3-0 |
| | 1987 | Mansfield T | Bristol C | 1-1 (aet) |
| | *Mansfield T won 5-4 on penalties* | | | |
| **SHERPA VANS TROPHY** | 1988 | Wolverhampton W | Burnley | 2-0 |
| | 1989 | Bolton W | Torquay U | 4-1 |
| **LEYLAND DAF CUP** | 1990 | Tranmere R | Bristol R | 2-1 |
| | 1991 | Birmingham C | Tranmere R | 3-2 |
| **AUTOGLASS TROPHY** | 1992 | Stoke C | Stockport Co | 1-0 |
| | 1993 | Port Vale | Stockport Co | 2-1 |
| | 1994 | Swansea C | Huddersfield T | 1-1 (aet) |
| | *Swansea C won 3-1 on penalties* | | | |
| **AUTO WINDSCREENS SHIELD** | 1995 | Birmingham C | Carlisle U | 1-0 (aet) |
| | 1996 | Rotherham U | Shrewsbury T | 2-1 |
| | 1997 | Carlisle U | Colchester U | 0-0 (aet) |
| | *Carlisle U won 4-3 on penalties* | | | |
| | 1998 | Grimsby T | Bournemouth | 2-1 |
| | 1999 | Wigan Ath | Millwall | 1-0 |
| | 2000 | Stoke C | Bristol C | 2-1 |
| **LDV VANS TROPHY** | 2001 | Port Vale | Brentford | 2-1 |
| | 2002 | Blackpool | Cambridge U | 4-1 |
| | 2003 | Bristol C | Carlisle U | 2-0 |
| | 2004 | Blackpool | Southend U | 2-0 |
| | 2005 | Wrexham | Southend U | 2-0 (aet) |
| **FOOTBALL LEAGUE TROPHY** | 2006 | Swansea C | Carlisle U | 2-1 |
| **JOHNSTONE'S PAINT TROPHY** | 2007 | Doncaster R | Bristol R | 3-2 (aet) |
| | 2008 | Milton Keynes D | Grimsby T | 2-0 |
| | 2009 | Luton T | Scunthorpe U | 3-2 (aet) |
| | 2010 | Southampton | Carlisle U | 4-1 |
| | 2011 | Carlisle U | Brentford | 1-0 |
| | 2012 | Chesterfield | Swindon T | 2-0 |
| | 2013 | Crewe Alex | Southend U | 2-0 |

**FOOTBALL LEAGUE TROPHY WINS**

Birmingham C 2, Blackpool 2, Bristol C 2, Carlisle U 2, Port Vale 2, Stoke C 2, Swansea C 2, Wigan Ath 2, Bolton W 1, Bournemouth 1, Chesterfield 1, Crewe Alex 1, Doncaster R 1, Grimsby T 1, Luton T 1, Mansfield T 1, Milton Keynes D 1, Rotherham U 1, Southampton 1, Tranmere R 1, Wolverhampton W 1, Wrexham 1.

**APPEARANCES IN FINALS**

Carlisle U 6, Bristol C 4, Brentford 3, Birmingham C 2, Blackpool 2, Bolton W 2, Bournemouth 2, Bristol R 2, Grimsby T 2, Port Vale 2, Southend U 2, Stockport Co 2, Stoke C 2, Swansea C 2, Tranmere R 2, Wigan Ath 2, Burnley 1, Cambridge U 1, Chesterfield 1, Colchester U 1, Crewe Alex 1, Doncaster R 1, Huddersfield T 1, Hull C 1, Luton T 1, Mansfield T 1, Millwall 1, Milton Keynes D 1, Rotherham U 1, Scunthorpe U 1, Shrewsbury T 1, Southampton 1, Southend U 1, Swindon T 1, Torquay U 1, Wolverhampton W 1, Wrexham 1.

# JOHNSTONE'S PAINT TROPHY 2012–13

**  Denotes player sent off.**

## NORTHERN SECTION FIRST ROUND

Tuesday, 4 September 2012

**Accrington S (0) 0**
**Morecambe (1) 2** *(Redshaw 31, Ellison 63)*      1049
*Accrington S:* (4231) Dawber; Lindfield, Eckersley, Murphy, Molyneux; Barnett, Watson; Gray, Clark, Chippendale; Sheppard (Dixon 54).
*Morecambe:* (433) Arestidou; Reid, McCready, Fenton, Wright; Drummond, McGee (Alessandra 62), Fleming; Redshaw, Burrow (Brodie 67), Ellison (Mwasile 87).

**Carlisle U (0) 1** *(McGovern 68)*
**Preston NE (1) 1** *(Beardsley 3)*      3471
*Carlisle U:* (442) Gillespie; Simek, Edwards, Murphy, Chantler; McGovern, Noble■, Berrett, Robson (Potts 90); Jervis, Madden.
*Preston NE:* (442) Simonsen; Keane, Robertson, Wright, Buchanan; Amoo, Procter, King, Hayhurst (Monakana 64); Cummins (Wroe 53), Beardsley (Sodje 79).
*Preston NE won on 3-1 on penalties.*

**Chesterfield (0) 2** *(Whitaker 48, Smith M 90 (og))*
**Oldham Ath (1) 1** *(Smith M 23)*      2384
*Chesterfield:* (442) Lee (O'Donnell 89); Forbes, Trotman, Hird, Ridehalgh; Talbot, Togwell, Randall (Clay 90), Whitaker; Richards, Boden (Hazel 64).
*Oldham Ath:* (442) Bouzanis; Byrne, Mvoto, Tarkowski, Grounds; Croft (Millar 70), Winchester (Mellor 71), M'Changama, Montano; Simpson R (Hughes 65), Smith M.

**Coventry C (0) 0**
**Burton Alb (0) 0**      5437
*Coventry C:* (41212) Murphy; Christie, Brown, Wood, Hussey; Jennings (Daniels 85); Baker, Kilbane; McSheffrey; McDonald (Elliott 46), McGoldrick.
*Burton Alb:* (442) Atkins (Lyness 46); Corbett, Holness, Webster, McCrory; Taylor, Bell, Dyer, Palmer C; Paterson (Richards 69), Kee (Yussuf 58).
*Coventry C won on 10-9 on penalties.*

**Port Vale (0) 2** *(Myrie-Williams 57, 75 (pen))*
**Tranmere R (0) 0**      2702
*Port Vale:* (442) Neal; Duffy (Yates 70), McCombe, McDonald, Loft; Myrie-Williams, Morsy (Burge 56), Shuker, Vincent; Dodds (Williamson 70), Pope.
*Tranmere R:* (442) Fon Williams; Holmes (Kay 46), Gibson, Golobart, Bakayogo; McGurk, Harrison, Power (Kirby 75), Bell-Baggie; Thompson (Stockton 64), Cassidy.

**Rochdale (1) 2** *(Grant 26 (pen), Putterill 58)*
**Fleetwood T (0) 2** *(McGuire 64, 72)*      1256
*Rochdale:* (4231) Smith; Pearson, Bennett, Edwards P, McIntyre; Craney, Barry-Murphy (Rafferty 82); Tutte, Donnelly, Putterill; Grant.
*Fleetwood T:* (433) Davies; Beeley, Atkinson, Eastham, Goodall; Nicholson, Marrow (Milligan 56), McGuire; Ball, Gillespie (Titchiner 62), Mangan.
*Rochdale won on 4-2 on penalties.*

**Rotherham U (0) 0**
**York C (0) 1** *(Blair 80)*      3975
*Rotherham U:* (442) Warrington; Bradley (Noble 23), Mullins, Sharps, Wilson; Ainsworth (Nardiello 78), O'Connor (Pringle 46), Taylor, Evans; Revell, Agard.
*York C:* (433) Oyebanjo, Smith C, Carlisle, Taylor; Blair, Parslow, Smith J; Coulson, Walker (Challinor 90), McLaughlin.

**Scunthorpe U (1) 1** *(Duffy 11)*
**Notts Co (1) 2** *(Showunmi 41, Regan 58)*      1153
*Scunthorpe U:* (4141) Slocombe; Ribeiro, Mirfin, Canavan, Newey; Prutton; Jennings, Keegan (Barcham 68), Gibbons (Hughes 82), Duffy (Ryan 68); Grella.

*Notts Co:* (442) Bialkowski; Regan, Leacock, Liddle, Sheehan; Labadie (Dixon 90), Arquin, Bencherif, Zoko (Wholey 90); Showunmi, Boucaud.

## SOUTHERN SECTION FIRST ROUND

Tuesday, 4 September 2012

**Bristol R (0) 0**
**Yeovil T (0) 3** *(Upson 71, 86, Foley 90)*      2810
*Bristol R:* (532) Walker; Smith (Broghammer 76), Parkes, Bolger, Virgo, Paterson; Gill, Brown W, Brown L; Clarkson, Richards.
*Yeovil T:* (442) Stech; Ayling, McAllister■, Hinds, Webster (Ince 62); Blizzard, Marsh-Brown (Ralph 76), Upson, Foley; Hayter (Ugwu 59), Reid.

**Crawley T (1) 3** *(Walsh 40, Clarke 47, Neilson 86)*
**Gillingham (1) 2** *(Dack 22, Montrose 49)*      1249
*Crawley T:* (442) Jones P; Hunt, Connolly, Cooper, Walsh; Simpson, Bulman, Jones M (Davies 72), Adams (Neilson 63); Clarke, Forte (Akinde 78).
*Gillingham:* (442) Forecast; Fish (Evans 13), Martin, Flanagan, Frampton; Montrose, Jackman, Allen, Whelpdale (Birchall 66); Dack, Strevens.

**Dagenham & R (3) 3** *(Woodall 12, Scott 31, Spillane 35 (pen))*
**Stevenage (1) 2** *(Roberts 26, Shroot 73)*      981
*Dagenham & R:* (433) Lewington; Hoyte, Wilkinson, Doe, Ilesanmi; Spillane, Ogogo, Howell (Bingham 78); Woodall, Scott, Green Dominic (Green Danny J 78).
*Stevenage:* (451) Arnold; Gray, N'Gala, Roberts, Charles; Rogers (Shroot 62), Grant (Haber 46), Risser, Tansey, Morais; Agyemang (Freeman 62).

**Exeter C (0) 0**
**Aldershot T (0) 0**      1944
*Exeter C:* (433) Krysiak; Tully, Baldwin (Frear 56), Moore-Taylor, Woodman; Sercombe, Doherty, Bennett; O'Flynn, Gow (Keohane 82), Bauza (Chamberlain 74).
*Aldershot T:* (442) Morris G; Herd, Lancashire, Bradley, Anderson; Mekki (Branston 88), Morris A, Brown (Rankine 30), Roberts (Rodman 77); Vincenti, Reid.
*Aldershot T won on 4-3 on penalties.*

**Northampton T (1) 1** *(Robinson 11)*
**Milton Keynes D (0) 0**      3444
*Northampton T:* (442) Nicholls L; East, Langmead, Charles, Widdowson; Robinson (Turnbull 75), Tozer, Mukendi, Demontagnac (Wilson 70); Akinfenwa, Moult (Nicholls A 82).
*Milton Keynes D:* (433) Martin; Spence (Ibehre 69), Williams, Kay, Chicksen; Smith (O'Shea 69), Gleeson, Bullard (Chadwick 56); Powell, MacDonald, Bowditch.

**Portsmouth (1) 2** *(Rodgers 45, Howard 67)*
**Bournemouth (1) 2** *(MacDonald 5, 59)*      5979
*Portsmouth:* (442) Andersen; Connolly (Clifford 76), Long, Thompson (Williamson 46), Harley; Dumbuya, Russell, Howard, Harris; McLeod (Walker 63), Rodgers.
*Bournemouth:* (4411) Jalal; Francis, Addison, Elphick, Cook; Fogden (Pugh 85), MacDonald, Hughes (Partington 88), Arter; McQuoid (Barnard 68); Grabban.
*Portsmouth won on 4-3 on penalties.*

**Southend U (0) 2** *(Tomlin 59 (pen), Cresswell 90)*
**AFC Wimbledon (1) 1** *(Merrifield 39)*      1925
*Southend U:* (442) Smith; Clohessy, Phillips, Cresswell, Prosser; Leonard, Spicer, Timlin, Straker (Benyon 70); Assombalonga (Harris 70), Tomlin (Barker 79).
*AFC Wimbledon:* (442) Jaimez-Ruiz; Francomb, MacDonald (Balkestein 71), Bennett D, Fenlon (Jolley 78); Kiernan (Long 65), Moore S, Merrifield, Johnson; Harrison, Midson.

Wednesday, 5 September 2012
**Oxford U (0) 1** *(Potter 88)*
**Swindon T (0) 0**                                7746
*Oxford U:* (433) Clarke; Batt, Wright, Raynes, Capaldi; Chapman, Boateng (Potter 52), Forster-Caskey; Craddock (McGinty 90), Constable, Pittman.
*Swindon T:* (442) Foderingham; Devera, Ward, McCormack, Bessone; De Vita, Ferry (Miller 66), Coke (Flint 81), Rooney A; Benson (Bostock 66), Williams.

## NORTHERN SECTION SECOND ROUND

Tuesday, 9 October 2012
**Doncaster R (0) 1** *(Ball 83)*
**Chesterfield (0) 0**                              4030
*Doncaster R:* (442) Woods G; Keegan, Jones R, Spurr, Husband; Cotterill, Syers, Woods Martin, Bennett; Blake (Ball 82), Paynter (Brown 46).
*Chesterfield:* (442) O'Donnell; Forbes, Trotman, Darikwa (Boden 86), Ridehalgh; Evans (Lester 76), Clay (Randall 76), Togwell, Atkinson; Westcarr, Talbot.

**Hartlepool U (0) 0**
**Bradford C (0) 0**                                1777
*Hartlepool U:* (442) Flinders; Holden, Baldwin, Hartley, Austin; Horwood, Walton (Sweeney 62), Humphreys, Franks; Wyke, Noble.
*Bradford C:* (433) McLaughlin; Darby, McArdle, Davies, McHugh (Meredith 72); Jones R (Doyle 70), Ravenhill, Atkinson; Connell, Hanson (Wells 69), Thompson.
*Bradford C won on 3-2 on penalties.*

**Morecambe (1) 2** *(Mustoe 21, Brodie 78 (pen))*
**Preston NE (0) 4** *(Cummins 56, Sodje 75, 90,*
*Huntington 81)*                                    2577
*Morecambe:* (433) Arestidou; Haining, McCready, Fenton, Mustoe (Redshaw 83); Reid, Fleming, McGee (Drummond 77); McDonald, Burrow (Alessandra 77), Brodie.
*Preston NE:* (433) Simonsen; Keane, Huntington, Robertson, Laird; Procter, Welsh, Wroe; Amoo (King 74), Cummins (Sodje 74), Hayhurst (Monakana 65).

**Rochdale (1) 1** *(Grimes 18)*
**Bury (0) 1** *(Schumacher 52)*                    2826
*Rochdale:* (442) Smith; Rafferty, Edwards Ryan (Pearson 7), Bennett, McIntyre; Grimes, Cavanagh, Edwards P, Putterill (Tutte 12); Donnelly, Curran■.
*Bury:* (442) Carson; Doherty, Lockwood, Hughes, Skarz; Marshall, Byrne (Sweeney 83), Schumacher, Hopper; Healy (Cullen 61), Bishop.
*Bury won on 5-4 on penalties.*

**Shrewsbury T (0) 1** *(Hall 61)*
**Crewe Alex (1) 2** *(Murphy 9, Clayton M 57)*     2063
*Shrewsbury T:* (442) Anyon (Weale 20); Grandison, Jones, Collins, Richards; Wright (Hall 58), Wildig, Summerfield, Taylor; Parry, Morgan.
*Crewe Alex:* (442) Martin; Mellor, Ellis, Davis, Tootle; Pogba, Murphy, Bond, Aneke (Daniels 79); Leitch-Smith, Clayton M.

**Walsall (1) 2** *(Cuvelier 26 (pen), Grigg 47)*
**Port Vale (0) 2** *(Burge 49, Pope 61)*           2845
*Walsall:* (4411) Darlow; Taundry, Butler, Downing, Taylor; Baxendale (Jones 78), Cuvelier, Featherstone, Hemmings (Brandy 77); Paterson; Grigg (Bowerman 85).
*Port Vale:* (442) Johnson; Yates, Duffy (Davis 77), McCombe, Taylor; Myrie-Williams, Shuker, Burge, Vincent (Lloyd 64); Pope, Williamson (Dodds 82).
*Port Vale won on 7-5 on penalties.*

**York C (0) 0**
**Coventry C (0) 4** *(McGoldrick 58, 81, Ball 72, Hussey 90)*
                                                    2771
*York C:* (442) Ingham; Challinor, Smith C, Doig (Carlisle 51), Fyfield; Johnson (Parslow 68), Kerr (Reed J 75), Blair, Kearns; Chambers, Walker.
*Coventry C:* (442) Murphy; Clarke J, Cameron, Wood (Christie 31), Reckord; Baker, Moussa (Hussey 76), Bailey, Fleck (Jennings 74); Ball, McGoldrick.

Wednesday, 17 October 2012
**Notts Co (0) 1** *(Stewart 75)*
**Sheffield U (2) 4** *(Miller 24, 52, Maguire 45, 54)*   2082
*Notts Co:* (433) Bialkowski; Stewart, Liddle, Bencherif, Sheehan; Mahon (Campbell-Ryce 46), Boucaud, Hughes J; Zoko, Shownumi (Hughes L 46), Arquin (Nangle 76).
*Sheffield U:* (442) Long; Westlake, Maguire, Hill, Williams; Flynn, Doyle, Miller (Philliskirk 81), Chapell (Jean-Francois 76); Porter (Ironside 89), Harriott.

## SOUTHERN SECTION SECOND ROUND

Tuesday, 9 October 2012
**Brentford (0) 1** *(Saunders 73)*
**Crawley T (0) 0**                                 2739
*Brentford:* (442) Lee; Legge, Dean, Craig, Barron (Dallas 75); Adeyemi, O'Connor, Diagouraga, Forrester (Saunders 46); Hayes, Donaldson (German 58).
*Crawley T:* (442) Jones P; Hunt, McFadzean, Walsh, Byrne; Jones M (Akpan 77), Bulman (Ajose 77), Connolly, Torres; Forte (Alexander 75), Clarke.

**Cheltenham T (2) 2** *(Duffy 31, Lowe 45)*
**Oxford U (1) 4** *(Craddock 35, Worley 67, Constable 71,*
*Leven 81 (pen))*                                   1236
*Cheltenham T:* (433) Brown; Lowe, Hooman (Jombati 75), Elliott, Jones; Pack, Deering (Carter 80), Penn; Duffy, Harrad (Mohamed 80), Goulding.
*Oxford U:* (442) Clarke; Boateng (Whing 61), Worley, Capaldi, O'Brien; Heslop, Chapman, Leven, Forster-Caskey (Rigg 81); Constable, Craddock (Marsh 90).

**Leyton Orient (1) 1** *(Odubajo 25)*
**Barnet (0) 0**                                    1404
*Leyton Orient:* (442) Allsop; James (Laird 82), Baudry, Clarke, Sawyer; Odubajo, Smith Jimmy, Griffith, Cox (McSweeney 65); Symes, Mooney (Obafemi 65).
*Barnet:* (442) Stack; Fuller (Nurse 69), Stephens, Pearce, Brown (Saville 90); Yiadom, Kamdjo, Byrne, Lowe (Edgar 75); Holmes, Hyde.

**Northampton T (0) 2** *(Akinfenwa 52 (pen), Mukendi 54)*
**Colchester U (1) 1** *(Sears 31)*                 1561
*Northampton T:* (442) Higgs (Snedker 43); Hackett, Langmead, Artell, Widdowson; Demontagnac (Wilson 74), Mukendi, Tozer, Roofe (Hornby 61); Nicholls A, Akinfenwa.
*Colchester U:* (433) Cousins; White, Okuonghae (Eastman 46), Heath, Coker; Duguid, Bean (Gilbey 46), Wordsworth (Wright Drey 69); Sears, Morrison■, Henderson.

**Plymouth Arg (2) 2** *(Cowan-Hall 1, Gurrieri 30)*
**Aldershot T (1) 1** *(Reid 12)*                   2580
*Plymouth Arg:* (451) Gilmartin; Berry, Nelson, Richards, Griffiths S; Cowan-Hall (Sims 46), Young, Gurrieri, Hourihane, Lennox; Chadwick (Griffiths R 73).
*Aldershot T:* (4231) Morris G; Herd, Brown, Branston, Anderson (Tonkin 32); Vincenti, Morris A; Cadogan (Mekki 56), Donnelly (Lancashire 86), Hylton; Reid.

**Portsmouth (1) 1** *(McLeod 45)*
**Wycombe W (2) 3** *(Grant 1, Morgan 8, 56)*       7292
*Portsmouth:* (442) Eastwood; Webster, Gyepes, Michalik (Harris 60), Harley; Williamson, Howard, Ertl, Buzsaky (Rodgers 78); Thomas, McLeod.
*Wycombe W:* (442) Bull; Foster, Winfield, Stewart, Dunne; Andrade, Scowen, Spring, Grant; Kuffour (Morias 81), Morgan.

**Southend U (1) 2** *(Cresswell 17, Assombalonga 62)*
**Dagenham & R (0) 0**                              2965
*Southend U:* (442) Smith; Clohessy, Cresswell, Prosser, Barker; Hurst, Woodyard, Timlin, Martin; Assombalonga, Tomlin.
*Dagenham & R:* (442) Lewington; Hoyte, Wilkinson, Doe, Ilesanmi; Elito, Howell, Saunders, Green Danny J (Green Dominic 63); Reed (Williams 63), Woodall (Gayle 63).

**Tuesday, 16 October 2012**

**Torquay U (1) 2** *(Jarvis 25, 57)*

**Yeovil T (1) 2** *(Hayter 38, 90)* 1280

*Torquay U:* (433) Poke; Leadbitter, Downes, Saah, Cruise; Mansell, Easton (Howe 90), Craig; Jarvis (Thompson 73), Bodin, Stevens (Oastler 82).

*Yeovil T:* (442) Stech; Blizzard, Hinds (Webster 71), Burn, McAllister; Marsh-Brown, Upson, Foley, Smith; Hayter, Reid (Williams 71).

*Yeovil T won on 5-4 on penalties.*

## NORTHERN SECTION QUARTER-FINALS

**Tuesday, 4 December 2012**

**Coventry C (0) 1** *(Maguire 58 (og))*

**Sheffield U (0) 1** *(McAllister 81)* 10,162

*Coventry C:* (451) Murphy; Christie, Wood, Edjenguele, Adams; Baker, Jennings, Bailey, Moussa (Fleck 76), McSheffrey; McGoldrick.

*Sheffield U:* (442) Long; Westlake, Maguire, Hill, Williams; Flynn, McAllister, Doyle, McFadzean (Chapell 66); Cresswell (Ironside 71), Cofie (De Girolamo 72).

*Coventry C won on 4-2 on penalties.*

**Crewe Alex (1) 1** *(Pogba 45)*

**Doncaster R (0) 1** *(Brown 90)* 1892

*Crewe Alex:* (442) Phillips, Tootle■, Davis, Dugdale, Robertson; Pogba, Osman, Inman (Moore 88), Clayton M (Colclough 82); Aneke (Turton 76), Dalla Valle.

*Doncaster R:* (442) Woods G; Griffin (Quinn 65), Martis, Wakefield, Husband (Finnigan 54); Cotterill (Hume 54), Clingan, Meade, Middleton; Brown, Blake.

*Crewe Alex won on 5-3 on penalties.*

**Port Vale (0) 0**

**Bradford C (0) 2** *(Jones R 46, Forsyth 55)* 2786

*Port Vale:* (442) Neal; Yates, McCombe, Chilvers, Loft; Myrie-Williams, Morsy, McAllister (Taylor 58), Vincent; Williamson (Dodds 46), Andrew (Shuker 58).

*Bradford C:* (442) McLaughlin; Darby (Doyle 61), Good, Naylor, McHugh; Turgott (Jones G 62), Jones R, Ravenhill, Forsyth; Thompson (Hanson 72), Connell.

**Tuesday, 18 December 2012**

**Bury (0) 3** *(Skarz 62, Doherty 84, Schumacher 90)*

**Preston NE (1) 3** *(King 25, Procter 68, Beavon 90)* 2023

*Bury:* (442) Carson; Doherty, Sodje, Hughes, Skarz; Worrall (Jones C 91), Schumacher, Thompson, Wylde; Healy (Hewitt 75), Hopper (John-Lewis 75).

*Preston NE:* (433) Stuckmann; King, Wright, Foster, Cansdell-Sherriff■; Byrom, Procter, Mousinho; Cummins, Beavon, Monakana (Holmes 45 (Amoo 88)).

*Preston NE won on 5-4 on penalties.*

## SOUTHERN SECTION QUARTER-FINALS

**Tuesday, 4 December 2012**

**Plymouth Arg (1) 1** *(MacDonald 20)*

**Oxford U (0) 1** *(Constable 62)* 2383

*Plymouth Arg:* (4411) Gilmartin; Berry■, Nelson, Blanchard, Bhasera; Molesley (Lowry 83), Hourihane, Gurrieri, MacDonald; Cowan-Hall (Harvey 90); Chadwick (Griffiths R 68).

*Oxford U:* (442) Clarke; Batt, Raynes, Wright, Davis; Cox (Constable 54), Chapman, Rigg, Forster-Caskey; Marsh (Heslop 54), Potter.

*Oxford U won on 4-1 on penalties.*

**Southend U (2) 2** *(Mkandawire 27, Hurst 39)*

**Brentford (0) 1** *(Hayes 85)* 3052

*Southend U:* (442) Smith; Clohessy, Cresswell, Prosser, Barker; Hurst, Mkandawire, Timlin, Martin (Straker 80); Corr, Assombalonga.

*Brentford:* (442) Moore; Hodson, Dean, Kiernan, Bidwell (Pierre 46); Saunders, Diagouraga (Legge 62), Reeves, Barron; Forrester (German 30), Hayes.

**Yeovil T (2) 2** *(Upson 32, Foley 45)*

**Wycombe W (0) 0** 1771

*Yeovil T:* (442) Stech; Ayling (Marsh-Brown 70), Webster, Burn, McAllister; Edwards, Smith (Reid 46), Upson, Foley; Hayter, Williams.

*Wycombe W:* (442) Archer; McCoy, Dunne, Winfield, Wood (Ehui 78); Morias (Hause 47), Kewley-Graham, Spring■, Andrade; Morgan, Azeez (McClure 25).

**Wednesday, 5 December 2012**

**Northampton T (0) 0**

**Leyton Orient (0) 3** *(Mooney 57, 65, Symes 73 (pen))* 1752

*Northampton T:* (442) Nicholls; East, Widdowson, Langmead, Tozer; Robinson (Hackett 69), Harding, Huws, Demontagnac (Mukendi 78); Moult (Akinfenwa 69), Platt.

*Leyton Orient:* (442) Jones; McSweeney, Sawyer, Cuthbert, Baudry; Odubajo, Griffith (Smith Jimmy J 50), James (Smith A 82), Cox; Brunt, Mooney (Symes 66).

## NORTHERN SECTION SEMI-FINALS

**Thursday, 10 January 2013**

**Coventry C (1) 3** *(Jennings 41, Baker 90, Clarke L 90)*

**Preston NE (0) 2** *(Foster 67, Beavon 80)* 12,655

*Coventry C:* (451) Murphy; Clarke J, Wood, Edjenguele, Adams; Baker, Jennings (Moussa 75), Bailey (Thomas 53), Fleck, McSheffrey (Elliott 86); Clarke L.

*Preston NE:* (442) Simonsen; King, Foster, Cansdell-Sherriff (Robertson 18), Buchanan; Holmes, Wroe, Welsh, Byrom (Monakana 56); Garner, Beavon (Procter 82).

**Tuesday, 15 January 2013**

**Crewe Alex (1) 4** *(Doyle 44 (og), Clayton M 77, Inman 89, Aneke 90)*

**Bradford C (1) 1** *(Reid 18)* 2935

*Crewe Alex:* (442) Martin (Phillips 46); Mellor, Dugdale, Davis, Tootle; Moore, Murphy, Osman, Inman; Pogba (Aneke 71), Leitch-Smith (Clayton M 64).

*Bradford C:* (442) McLaughlin; Doyle, Naylor, Good, Dickson (McHugh 84); Turgott, Ravenhill, Jones R, Reid; Gray (Hines 66), Connell (Wells 66).

## SOUTHERN SECTION SEMI-FINALS

**Tuesday, 8 January 2013**

**Leyton Orient (0) 1** *(Mooney 90)*

**Yeovil T (0) 0** 2755

*Leyton Orient:* (442) Jones; Odubajo, Cuthbert, Chorley, Sawyer (Cook 74); Griffith■, James, Baudry, Cox; Lisbie (Symes 61), Mooney.

*Yeovil T:* (442) Stech; Ayling, Hinds, Webster, Burn; Williams (Ralph 78), Blizzard, Upson (Dolan 49), McAllister; Hayter, Foley (Dawson 74).

**Oxford U (2) 3** *(Marsh 14, Craddock 31, Rigg 89)*

**Southend U (1) 3** *(Corr 6, 59, Clohessy 54)* 2882

*Oxford U:* (442) Clarke; Batt, Raynes, Wright, O'Brien (Davis 67); Heslop (Worley 81), Capaldi, Rigg, Potter; Marsh (Parker 67), Craddock.

*Southend U:* (442) Smith (Bentley 90); Clohessy, Phillips, Barker, Straker; Hurst, Cresswell, Timlin, Woodyard (Prosser 86); Corr (Benyon 86), Tomlin.

*Southend U won 5-4 on penalties.*

**NORTHERN AREA FINAL**

Tuesday, 5 February 2013

**Coventry C (0) 0**

**Crewe Alex (0) 3** *(Inman 52, 78, Leitch-Smith 85)* 31,054

*Coventry C:* (442) Murphy (Dunn 46); Christie, Wood, Edjenguele, Adams; Baker, Jennings, Moussa, McSheffrey (Bailey 81); Elliott (Ball 74), Clarke L.
*Crewe Alex:* (442) Phillips; Mellor, Ellis, Dugdale, Tootle; Moore, Murphy, Osman, Inman (Robertson 82); Leitch-Smith, Aneke.

Wednesday, 20 February 2013

**Crewe Alex (0) 0**

**Coventry C (0) 2** *(Clarke L 90, Ellis 90 (og))* 8325

*Crewe Alex:* (442) Phillips; Mellor, Dugdale, Ellis, Robertson; Pogba, Murphy, Osman, Inman; Aneke, Leitch-Smith.
*Coventry C:* (442) Murphy; Christie, Cameron, Wood (Clarke J 58), Dickinson; Baker, Jennings, Bailey (Fleck 74), McSheffrey; Clarke L, Elliott (Wilson 67).

**SOUTHERN AREA FINAL**

Tuesday, 5 February 2013

**Leyton Orient (0) 0**

**Southend U (0) 1** *(Leonard 57)* 5359

*Leyton Orient:* (442) Jones; Odubajo, Cuthbert, Baudry, Sawyer; Cox, Rowlands (Smith Jimmy 75), James, Cook; Batt (Obafemi 87), Mooney.
*Southend U:* (442) Smith; Clohessy, Phillips, Cresswell, Barker; Hurst, Woodyard, Timlin (Spicer 87), Leonard; Assombalonga (Corr 88), Reeves (Lavery 90).

Wednesday, 20 February 2013

**Southend U (0) 2** *(Corr 61, Reeves 90)*

**Leyton Orient (1) 2** *(Batt 8, Mooney 72)* 9421

*Southend U:* (442) Smith; Clohessy, Phillips, Prosser, Barker; Hurst, Lund, Woodyard (Corr 35), Leonard; Assombalonga.
*Leyton Orient:* (442) Jones; Odubajo, Cuthbert, Baudry, McSweeney; Cox, Rowlands (Griffith 74), James, Cook; Batt, Mooney.

**JOHNSTONE'S PAINT TROPHY FINAL**

Sunday, 7 April 2013

(at Wembley Stadium, attendance 43,842)

**Crewe Alex (1) 2     Southend U (0) 0**

*Crewe Alex:* (442) Phillips; Mellor, Davis, Ellis, Tootle; Moore, Murphy, Osman, Inman (Colclough 69); Clayton M (Leitch-Smith 83), Aneke (Ray 90).
*Scorers:* Murphy 6, Clayton M 49.

*Southend U:* (442) Smith; Clohessy, Cresswell, Prosser, Barker (Corr 57); Hurst, Mkandawire (Eastwood 77), Mohsni (Reeves 57), Straker; Tomlin, Assombalonga.

*Referee:* Nigel Miller.

# JOHNSTONE'S PAINT TROPHY ATTENDANCES 2012–13

| Round | Aggregate | Games | Average |
|---|---|---|---|
| One | 47,505 | 16 | 2,969 |
| Two | 42,028 | 16 | 2,627 |
| Area Quarter-finals | 25,821 | 8 | 3,228 |
| Area Semi-finals | 21,227 | 4 | 5,307 |
| Area Finals | 54,159 | 4 | 13,540 |
| Final | 43,842 | 1 | 43,842 |
| Total | 234,582 | 49 | 4,787 |

# FA CUP FINALS 1872–2013

| | | | |
|---|---|---|---|
| 1872 and 1874–92 | Kennington Oval | 1911 | Replay at Old Trafford |
| 1873 | Lillie Bridge | 1912 | Replay at Bramall Lane |
| 1886 | Replay at Derby (Racecourse Ground) | 1915 | Old Trafford, Manchester |
| 1893 | Fallowfield, Manchester | 1920–22 | Stamford Bridge |
| 1894 | Everton | 1923–2000 | Wembley |
| 1895–1914 | Crystal Palace | 1970 | Replay at Old Trafford |
| 1901 | Replay at Bolton | 2001–2006 | Millennium Stadium, Cardiff |
| 1910 | Replay at Everton | 2007 to date | Wembley |

| Year | Winners | Runners-up | Score |
|---|---|---|---|
| 1872 | Wanderers | Royal Engineers | 1-0 |
| 1873 | Wanderers | Oxford University | 2-0 |
| 1874 | Oxford University | Royal Engineers | 2-0 |
| 1875 | Royal Engineers | Old Etonians | 2-0 (after 1-1 draw aet) |
| 1876 | Wanderers | Old Etonians | 3-0 (after 1-1 draw aet) |
| 1877 | Wanderers | Oxford University | 2-1 (aet) |
| 1878 | Wanderers* | Royal Engineers | 3-1 |
| 1879 | Old Etonians | Clapham R | 1-0 |
| 1880 | Clapham R | Oxford University | 1-0 |
| 1881 | Old Carthusians | Old Etonians | 3-0 |
| 1882 | Old Etonians | Blackburn R | 1-0 |
| 1883 | Blackburn Olympic | Old Etonians | 2-1 (aet) |
| 1884 | Blackburn R | Queen's Park, Glasgow | 2-1 |
| 1885 | Blackburn R | Queen's Park, Glasgow | 2-0 |
| 1886 | Blackburn R† | WBA | 2-0 (after 0-0 draw) |
| 1887 | Aston Villa | WBA | 2-0 |
| 1888 | WBA | Preston NE | 2-1 |
| 1889 | Preston NE | Wolverhampton W | 3-0 |
| 1890 | Blackburn R | The Wednesday | 6-1 |
| 1891 | Blackburn R | Notts Co | 3-1 |
| 1892 | WBA | Aston Villa | 3-0 |
| 1893 | Wolverhampton W | Everton | 1-0 |
| 1894 | Notts Co | Bolton W | 4-1 |
| 1895 | Aston Villa | WBA | 1-0 |
| 1896 | The Wednesday | Wolverhampton W | 2-1 |
| 1897 | Aston Villa | Everton | 3-2 |
| 1898 | Nottingham F | Derby Co | 3-1 |
| 1899 | Sheffield U | Derby Co | 4-1 |
| 1900 | Bury | Southampton | 4-0 |
| 1901 | Tottenham H | Sheffield U | 3-1 (after 2-2 draw) |
| 1902 | Sheffield U | Southampton | 2-1 (after 1-1 draw) |
| 1903 | Bury | Derby Co | 6-0 |
| 1904 | Manchester C | Bolton W | 1-0 |
| 1905 | Aston Villa | Newcastle U | 2-0 |
| 1906 | Everton | Newcastle U | 1-0 |
| 1907 | The Wednesday | Everton | 2-1 |
| 1908 | Wolverhampton W | Newcastle U | 3-1 |
| 1909 | Manchester U | Bristol C | 1-0 |
| 1910 | Newcastle U | Barnsley | 2-0 (after 1-1 draw) |
| 1911 | Bradford C | Newcastle U | 1-0 (after 0-0 draw) |
| 1912 | Barnsley | WBA | 1-0 (aet, after 0-0 draw) |
| 1913 | Aston Villa | Sunderland | 1-0 |
| 1914 | Burnley | Liverpool | 1-0 |
| 1915 | Sheffield U | Chelsea | 3-0 |
| 1920 | Aston Villa | Huddersfield T | 1-0 (aet) |
| 1921 | Tottenham H | Wolverhampton W | 1-0 |
| 1922 | Huddersfield T | Preston NE | 1-0 |
| 1923 | Bolton W | West Ham U | 2-0 |
| 1924 | Newcastle U | Aston Villa | 2-0 |
| 1925 | Sheffield U | Cardiff C | 1-0 |
| 1926 | Bolton W | Manchester C | 1-0 |
| 1927 | Cardiff C | Arsenal | 1-0 |
| 1928 | Blackburn R | Huddersfield T | 3-1 |
| 1929 | Bolton W | Portsmouth | 2-0 |
| 1930 | Arsenal | Huddersfield T | 2-0 |
| 1931 | WBA | Birmingham | 2-1 |
| 1932 | Newcastle U | Arsenal | 2-1 |
| 1933 | Everton | Manchester C | 3-0 |
| 1934 | Manchester C | Portsmouth | 2-1 |
| 1935 | Sheffield W | WBA | 4-2 |
| 1936 | Arsenal | Sheffield U | 1-0 |
| 1937 | Sunderland | Preston NE | 3-1 |
| 1938 | Preston NE | Huddersfield T | 1-0 (aet) |
| 1939 | Portsmouth | Wolverhampton W | 4-1 |
| 1946 | Derby Co | Charlton Ath | 4-1 (aet) |

| Year | Winners | Runners-up | Score |
|------|---------|-----------|-------|
| 1947 | Charlton Ath | Burnley | 1-0 (aet) |
| 1948 | Manchester U | Blackpool | 4-2 |
| 1949 | Wolverhampton W | Leicester C | 3-1 |
| 1950 | Arsenal | Liverpool | 2-0 |
| 1951 | Newcastle U | Blackpool | 2-0 |
| 1952 | Newcastle U | Arsenal | 1-0 |
| 1953 | Blackpool | Bolton W | 4-3 |
| 1954 | WBA | Preston NE | 3-2 |
| 1955 | Newcastle U | Manchester C | 3-1 |
| 1956 | Manchester C | Birmingham C | 3-1 |
| 1957 | Aston Villa | Manchester U | 2-1 |
| 1958 | Bolton W | Manchester U | 2-0 |
| 1959 | Nottingham F | Luton T | 2-1 |
| 1960 | Wolverhampton W | Blackburn R | 3-0 |
| 1961 | Tottenham H | Leicester C | 2-0 |
| 1962 | Tottenham H | Burnley | 3-1 |
| 1963 | Manchester U | Leicester C | 3-1 |
| 1964 | West Ham U | Preston NE | 3-2 |
| 1965 | Liverpool | Leeds U | 2-1 (aet) |
| 1966 | Everton | Sheffield W | 3-2 |
| 1967 | Tottenham H | Chelsea | 2-1 |
| 1968 | WBA | Everton | 1-0 (aet) |
| 1969 | Manchester C | Leicester C | 1-0 |
| 1970 | Chelsea | Leeds U | 2-1 (aet) |
| | *(after 2-2 draw, after extra time)* | | |
| 1971 | Arsenal | Liverpool | 2-1 (aet) |
| 1972 | Leeds U | Arsenal | 1-0 |
| 1973 | Sunderland | Leeds U | 1-0 |
| 1974 | Liverpool | Newcastle U | 3-0 |
| 1975 | West Ham U | Fulham | 2-0 |
| 1976 | Southampton | Manchester U | 1-0 |
| 1977 | Manchester U | Liverpool | 2-1 |
| 1978 | Ipswich T | Arsenal | 1-0 |
| 1979 | Arsenal | Manchester U | 3-2 |
| 1980 | West Ham U | Arsenal | 1-0 |
| 1981 | Tottenham H | Manchester C | 3-2 |
| | *(after 1-1 draw, after extra time)* | | |
| 1982 | Tottenham H | QPR | 1-0 |
| | *(after 1-1 draw, after extra time)* | | |
| 1983 | Manchester U | Brighton & HA | 4-0 |
| | *(after 2-2 draw, after extra time)* | | |
| 1984 | Everton | Watford | 2-0 |
| 1985 | Manchester U | Everton | 1-0 (aet) |
| 1986 | Liverpool | Everton | 3-1 |
| 1987 | Coventry C | Tottenham H | 3-2 (aet) |
| 1988 | Wimbledon | Liverpool | 1-0 |
| 1989 | Liverpool | Everton | 3-2 (aet) |
| 1990 | Manchester U | Crystal Palace | 1-0 |
| | *(after 3-3 draw, after extra time)* | | |
| 1991 | Tottenham H | Nottingham F | 2-1 (aet) |
| 1992 | Liverpool | Sunderland | 2-0 |
| 1993 | Arsenal | Sheffield W | 2-1 (aet) |
| | *(after 1-1 draw, after extra time)* | | |
| 1994 | Manchester U | Chelsea | 4-0 |
| 1995 | Everton | Manchester U | 1-0 |
| 1996 | Manchester U | Liverpool | 1-0 |
| 1997 | Chelsea | Middlesbrough | 2-0 |
| 1998 | Arsenal | Newcastle U | 2-0 |
| 1999 | Manchester U | Newcastle U | 2-0 |
| 2000 | Chelsea | Aston Villa | 1-0 |
| 2001 | Liverpool | Arsenal | 2-1 |
| 2002 | Arsenal | Chelsea | 2-0 |
| 2003 | Arsenal | Southampton | 1-0 |
| 2004 | Manchester U | Millwall | 3-0 |
| 2005 | Arsenal | Manchester U | 0-0 (aet) |
| | *(Arsenal won 5-4 on penalties)* | | |
| 2006 | Liverpool | West Ham U | 3-3 (aet) |
| | *(Liverpool won 3-1 on penalties)* | | |
| 2007 | Chelsea | Manchester U | 1-0 (aet) |
| 2008 | Portsmouth | Cardiff C | 1-0 |
| 2009 | Chelsea | Everton | 2-1 |
| 2010 | Chelsea | Portsmouth | 1-0 |
| 2011 | Manchester C | Stoke C | 1-0 |
| 2012 | Chelsea | Liverpool | 2-1 |
| 2013 | Wigan Ath | Manchester C | 1-0 |

\* *Won outright, but restored to the Football Association.* † *A special trophy was awarded for third consecutive win.*

## FA CUP WINS

Manchester U 11, Arsenal 10, Tottenham H 8, Aston Villa 7, Chelsea 7, Liverpool 7, Blackburn R 6, Newcastle U 6, Everton 5, Manchester C 5, The Wanderers 5, WBA 5, Bolton W 4, Sheffield U 4, Wolverhampton W 4, Sheffield W 3, West Ham U 3, Bury 2, Nottingham F 2, Old Etonians 2, Portsmouth 2, Preston NE 2, Sunderland 2, Barnsley 1, Blackburn Olympic 1, Blackpool 1, Bradford C 1, Burnley 1, Cardiff C 1, Charlton Ath 1, Clapham R 1, Coventry C 1, Derby Co 1, Huddersfield T 1, Ipswich T 1, Leeds U 1, Notts Co 1, Old Carthusians 1, Oxford University 1, Royal Engineers 1, Southampton 1, Wigan Ath 1, Wimbledon 1.

## APPEARANCES IN FINALS

Manchester U 18, Arsenal 17, Liverpool 14, Everton 13, Newcastle U 13, Chelsea 11, Aston Villa 10, Manchester C 10, WBA 10, Tottenham H 9, Blackburn R 8, Wolverhampton W 8, Bolton W 7, Preston NE 7, Old Etonians 6, Sheffield U 6, Sheffield W 6, Huddersfield T 5, Portsmouth 5, *The Wanderers 5, West Ham U 5, Derby Co 4, Leeds U 4, Leicester C 4, Oxford University 4, Royal Engineers 4, Southampton 4, Sunderland 4, Blackpool 3, Bradford 3, Burnley 3, Cardiff C 3, Nottingham F 3, Barnsley 2, Birmingham C 2, *Bury 2, Charlton Ath 2, Clapham R 2, Notts Co 2, Queen's Park (Glasgow) 2, *Blackburn Olympic 1, *Bradford C 1, Brighton & HA 1, Bristol C 1, *Coventry C 1, Crystal Palace 1, Fulham 1, *Ipswich T 1, Luton T 1, Middlesbrough 1, Millwall 1, *Old Carthusians 1, QPR 1, Stoke C 1, Watford 1, *Wigan Ath 1, *Wimbledon 1.
* *Denotes undefeated.*

## APPEARANCES IN SEMI-FINALS

Manchester U 27, Arsenal 26, Everton 25, Liverpool 23, Chelsea 21, Aston Villa 20, WBA 20, Tottenham H 19, Blackburn R 18, Newcastle U 17, Sheffield W 16, Bolton W 14, Wolverhampton W 14, Derby Co 13, Sheffield U 13, Manchester C 12, Nottingham F 12, Sunderland 12, Southampton 11, Preston NE 10, Birmingham C 9, Burnley 8, Leeds U 8, Leicester C 8, Huddersfield T 7, Portsmouth 7, West Ham U 7, Old Etonians 6, Fulham 6, Oxford University 6, Millwall 5, Notts Co 5, The Wanderers 5, Watford 5, Cardiff C 4, Luton T 4, Queen's Park (Glasgow) 4, Royal Engineers 4, Stoke C 4, Barnsley 3, Blackpool 3, Clapham R 3, Crystal Palace (professional club) 3, Ipswich T 3, Middlesbrough 3, Norwich C 3, Old Carthusians 3, Oldham Ath 3, The Swifts 3, Blackburn Olympic 2, Bristol C 2, Bury 2, Charlton Ath 2, Grimsby T 2, Swansea T 2, Swindon T 2, Wimbledon 2, Bradford C 1, Brighton & HA 1, Cambridge University 1, Chesterfield 1, Coventry C 1, Crewe Alex 1, Crystal Palace (amateur club) 1, Darwen 1, Derby Junction 1, Glasgow R 1, Hull C 1, Marlow 1, Old Harrovians 1, Orient 1, Plymouth Arg 1, Port Vale 1, QPR 1, Reading 1, Shropshire W 1, Wigan Ath 1, Wycombe W 1, York C 1.

# FA CUP ATTENDANCES 1969–2013

| | 1st Round | 2nd Round | 3rd Round | 4th Round | 5th Round | 6th Round | Semi-finals & Final | Total | No. of matches | Average per match |
|---|---|---|---|---|---|---|---|---|---|---|
| 2012–13 | 135,642 | 115,965 | 645,676 | 373,892 | 288,509 | 221,216 | 234,210 | 2,015,110 | 156 | 12,917 |
| 2011–12 | 155,858 | 92,267 | 640,700 | 391,214 | 250,666 | 194,971 | 262,064 | 1,987,740 | 151 | 13,164 |
| 2010–11 | 169,259 | 101,291 | 637,202 | 390,524 | 284,311 | 164,092 | 250,256 | 1,996,935 | 150 | 13,313 |
| 2009–10 | 147,078 | 100,476 | 613,113 | 335,426 | 288,604 | 144,918 | 254,806 | 1,884,421 | 151 | 12,480 |
| 2008–09 | 161,526 | 96,923 | 631,070 | 529,585 | 297,364 | 149,566 | 264,635 | 2,131,669 | 163 | 13,078 |
| 2007–08 | 175,195 | 99,528 | 704,300 | 356,404 | 276,903 | 142,780 | 256,210 | 2,011,320 | 152 | 13,232 |
| 2006–07 | 168,884 | 113,924 | 708,628 | 478,924 | 340,612 | 230,064 | 177,810 | 2,218,846 | 158 | 14,043 |
| 2005–06 | 188,876 | 107,456 | 654,570 | 388,339 | 286,225 | 163,449 | 177,723 | 1,966,638 | 160 | 12,291 |
| 2004–05 | 161,197 | 98,702 | 602,152 | 477,472 | 339,082 | 127,914 | 193,233 | 1,999,752 | 146 | 13,697 |
| 2003–04 | 162,738 | 117,967 | 624,732 | 347,964 | 292,521 | 156,780 | 167,401 | 1,870,103 | 149 | 12,551 |
| 2002–03 | 189,905 | 104,103 | 577,494 | 404,599 | 242,483 | 156,244 | 175,498 | 1,850,326 | 150 | 12,336 |
| 2001–02 | 198,369 | 119,781 | 566,284 | 330,434 | 249,190 | 173,757 | 171,278 | 1,809,093 | 148 | 12,224 |
| 2000–01 | 171,689 | 122,061 | 577,204 | 398,241 | 256,899 | 100,663 | 177,778 | 1,804,535 | 151 | 11,951 |
| 1999–2000 | 181,485 | 127,728 | 514,030 | 374,795 | 182,511 | 105,443 | 214,921 | 1,700,913 | 158 | 10,765 |
| 1998–99 | 191,954 | 132,341 | 609,486 | 431,613 | 359,398 | 181,005 | 202,150 | 2,107,947 | 155 | 13,599 |
| 1997–98 | 204,803 | 130,261 | 629,127 | 455,557 | 341,290 | 192,651 | 172,007 | 2,125,696 | 165 | 12,883 |
| 1996–97 | 209,521 | 122,324 | 651,139 | 402,293 | 199,873 | 67,035 | 191,813 | 1,843,998 | 151 | 12,211 |
| 1995–96 | 185,538 | 115,669 | 748,997 | 391,218 | 274,055 | 174,142 | 156,500 | 2,046,199 | 167 | 12,252 |
| 1994–95 | 219,511 | 125,629 | 640,017 | 438,596 | 257,650 | 159,787 | 174,059 | 2,015,249 | 161 | 12,517 |
| 1993–94 | 190,683 | 118,031 | 691,064 | 430,234 | 172,196 | 134,705 | 228,233 | 1,965,146 | 159 | 12,359 |
| 1992–93 | 241,968 | 174,702 | 612,494 | 377,211 | 198,379 | 149,675 | 293,241 | 2,047,670 | 161 | 12,718 |
| 1991–92 | 231,940 | 117,078 | 586,014 | 372,576 | 270,537 | 155,603 | 201,592 | 1,935,340 | 160 | 12,095 |
| 1990–91 | 194,195 | 121,450 | 594,592 | 530,279 | 276,112 | 124,826 | 196,434 | 2,038,518 | 162 | 12,583 |
| 1989–90 | 209,542 | 133,483 | 683,047 | 412,483 | 351,423 | 165,205 | 277,420 | 2,190,463 | 170 | 12,885 |
| 1988–89 | 212,775 | 121,326 | 690,199 | 421,255 | 206,781 | 176,629 | 167,353 | 1,966,318 | 164 | 12,173 |
| 1987–88 | 204,411 | 104,561 | 720,121 | 443,133 | 281,461 | 119,313 | 177,585 | 2,050,585 | 155 | 13,229 |
| 1986–87 | 209,290 | 146,761 | 593,520 | 349,342 | 263,550 | 119,396 | 195,533 | 1,877,400 | 165 | 11,378 |
| 1985–86 | 171,142 | 130,034 | 486,838 | 495,526 | 311,833 | 184,262 | 192,316 | 1,971,951 | 168 | 11,738 |
| 1984–85 | 174,604 | 137,078 | 616,229 | 320,772 | 269,232 | 148,690 | 242,754 | 1,909,359 | 157 | 12,162 |
| 1983–84 | 192,276 | 151,647 | 625,965 | 417,298 | 181,832 | 185,382 | 187,000 | 1,941,400 | 166 | 11,695 |
| 1982–83 | 191,312 | 150,046 | 670,503 | 452,688 | 260,069 | 193,845 | 291,162 | 2,209,625 | 154 | 14,348 |
| 1981–82 | 236,220 | 127,300 | 513,185 | 356,987 | 203,334 | 124,308 | 279,621 | 1,840,955 | 160 | 11,506 |
| 1980–81 | 246,824 | 194,502 | 832,578 | 534,402 | 320,530 | 288,714 | 339,250 | 2,756,800 | 169 | 16,312 |
| 1979–80 | 267,121 | 204,759 | 804,701 | 507,725 | 364,039 | 157,530 | 355,541 | 2,661,416 | 163 | 16,328 |
| 1978–79 | 243,773 | 185,343 | 880,345 | 537,748 | 243,683 | 263,213 | 249,897 | 2,604,002 | 166 | 15,687 |
| 1977–78 | 258,248 | 178,930 | 881,406 | 540,164 | 400,751 | 137,059 | 198,020 | 2,594,578 | 160 | 16,216 |
| 1976–77 | 379,230 | 192,159 | 942,523 | 631,265 | 373,330 | 205,379 | 258,216 | 2,982,102 | 174 | 17,139 |
| 1975–76 | 255,533 | 178,099 | 867,880 | 573,843 | 417,925 | 206,851 | 205,810 | 2,759,941 | 161 | 17,142 |
| 1974–75 | 283,956 | 170,466 | 914,994 | 646,434 | 393,323 | 268,361 | 291,369 | 2,968,903 | 172 | 17,261 |
| 1973–74 | 214,236 | 125,295 | 840,142 | 747,909 | 346,012 | 233,307 | 273,051 | 2,779,952 | 167 | 16,646 |
| 1972–73 | 259,432 | 169,114 | 938,741 | 735,825 | 357,386 | 241,934 | 226,543 | 2,928,975 | 160 | 18,306 |
| 1971–72 | 277,726 | 236,127 | 986,094 | 711,399 | 486,378 | 230,292 | 248,546 | 3,158,562 | 160 | 19,741 |
| 1970–71 | 329,687 | 230,942 | 956,683 | 757,852 | 360,687 | 304,937 | 279,644 | 3,220,432 | 162 | 19,879 |
| 1969–70 | 345,229 | 195,102 | 925,930 | 651,374 | 319,893 | 198,537 | 390,700 | 3,026,765 | 170 | 17,805 |

# THE BUDWEISER FA CUP 2012–13
## PRELIMINARY AND QUALIFYING ROUNDS

**EXTRA PRELIMINARY ROUND**

| | |
|---|---|
| Dunston UTS v Armthorpe Wel | 2-0 |
| Liversedge v West Auckland T | 2-4 |
| Crook T v Penrith | 2-1 |
| Thackley v Hebburn T | 1-3 |
| Jarrow Roofing Boldon CA v Pickering T | 1-1, 4-2 |
| Newton Aycliffe v Holker OB | 1-1, 0-3 |
| Tadcaster Alb v Consett | 1-1, 3-2 |
| *aet.* | |
| Ashington v Sunderland RCA | 1-1, 2-1 |
| Chester-le-Street T v Billingham T | 0-0, 0-1 |
| South Shields v Darlington Railway Ath | 0-0, 6-5 |
| Northallerton T v Guisborough T | 4-5 |
| Billingham Synthonia v Celtic Nation | 0-1 |
| Marske U v Stokesley Sports Club | 1-0 |
| North Shields v Birtley T | 1-1, 0-2 |
| Durham C v Newcastle Benfield | 2-1 |
| Washington v Esh Winning | 0-3 |
| Tow Law T v Bishop Auckland | 0-2 |
| Eccleshill U v Glasshoughton Wel | 4-2 |
| Spennymoor T v Scarborough Ath | 1-0 |
| Bedlington Terriers v Morpeth T | 2-1 |
| Pontefract Coll v Norton & Stockton A | 2-2, 2-5 |
| *aet.* | |
| Silsden v Brighouse T | 2-3 |
| Whitehaven v Shildon | 0-3 |
| West Allotment Celtic v Selby T | 2-1 |
| Bridlington T v Whitley Bay | 1-2 |
| Daisy Hill v Formby | 0-5 |
| AFC Blackpool v AFC Liverpool | 3-6 |
| Dinnington T v Atherton Coll | 0-2 |
| Irlam v Hallam | 5-3 |
| Bootle v Alsager T | 4-1 |
| Maine Road v Squires Gate | 3-0 |
| Atherton LR v Rossington Main | 4-2 |
| St Helens T v Abbey Hey | 1-5 |
| Padiham v Wigan Robin Park | 1-0 |
| Hemsworth MW v Runcorn Linnets | 1-1, 2-2 |
| *aet; Hemsworth MW won 4-3 on penalties.* | |
| Colne v Congleton T | 0-0, 2-5 |
| Stockport Sports v Ashton Ath | 0-0, 1-2 |
| Cheadle T v Maltby Main | 1-1, 0-1 |
| Parkgate v Runcorn T | 2-3 |
| AFC Emley v Chadderton | 0-2 |
| Staveley MW v Hall Road Rangers | 2-1 |
| Nostell MW v Winsford U | 0-1 |
| Barton T OB v Barnoldswick T | 2-0 |
| Winterton Rangers v Bacup Bor | 0-3 |
| Shepshed Dyn v Heanor T | 0-3 |
| Long Eaton U v Dunkirk | 0-1 |
| Blackstones v Barrow T | 5-1 |
| Spalding U v Blaby & Whetstone Ath | 1-2 |
| Arnold T v Holbeach U | 0-2 |
| Shirebrook T v Kirby Muxloe | 0-1 |
| Boston T v Quorn | 0-2 |
| Glossop NE v Louth T | 0-0, 2-1 |
| *aet.* | |
| Retford U v Bardon Hill | 2-1 |
| Oadby T v Anstey Nomads | 3-1 |
| Holbrook Sports v Deeping Rangers | 3-1 |
| Thurnby Nirvana v Lincoln Moorlands R | 4-2 |
| St Andrews v Borrowash Vic | 1-2 |
| Sleaford T v Holwell Sports | 2-0 |
| Teversal v Loughborough Univ | 1-2 |
| Causeway U v Continental Star | 1-1, 0-3 |
| Norton U v Alvechurch | 2-2, 2-1 |
| Highgate U v Wellington | 1-1, 3-3 |
| *aet; Wellington won 7-6 on penalties.* | |
| Coleshill T v AFC Wulfrunians | 1-1, 2-3 |
| *aet.* | |
| Bloxwich U v Studley | 2-3 |
| Brocton v Bewdley T | 2-2, 0-1 |
| Dudley Sports v Heath Hayes | 2-2, 1-2 |
| *aet.* | |
| Boldmere St M v Bridgnorth T | 1-3 |
| Pilkington XXX v Atherstone T | 5-4 |
| Stone Dominoes v Rocester | 0-3 |
| Dudley T v Southam U | 4-1 |
| Eccleshall v Stourport Swifts | 0-1 |
| Lye T v Bartley Green | 2-2, 2-1 |

| | |
|---|---|
| Cradley T v Shifnal T | 3-0 |
| Tipton T v Wolverhampton Cas | 0-1 |
| Ellesmere Rangers v Coventry Sphinx | 0-4 |
| Gornal Ath v Malvern T | 4-0 |
| Earlswood T v Nuneaton Griff | 3-3, 1-3 |
| Shawbury U v Westfields | 2-4 |
| Pegasus Juniors v Long Buckby | 2-1 |
| Tividale v Stratford T | 5-2 |
| Willenhall T v Sporting Khalsa | 1-1, 2-3 |
| Godmanchester R v Thetford T | 2-1 |
| Irchester U v Huntingdon T | 0-1 |
| Ely C v Rothwell Corinthians | 7-1 |
| Peterborough Northern Star v Wellingborough | |
| Whitworths | 5-1 |
| Dereham T v Stewarts & Lloyds Corby | 3-1 |
| Rushden & Higham U v Bugbrooke St M | 1-3 |
| Fakenham T v St Ives T | 0-1 |
| Thrapston T v Cogenhoe U | 2-0 |
| Wellingborough T v March T U | 2-1 |
| Wisbech T v Desborough T | 1-1, 5-2 |
| Northampton Spencer v Yaxley | 1-1, 1-3 |
| Brantham Ath v Mildenhall T | 1-0 |
| Wivenhoe T v Haverhill R | 1-1, 0-2 |
| FC Clacton v Halstead T | 1-3 |
| Felixstowe & Walton U v Team Bury | 3-1 |
| Walsham-le-Willows v Burnham Ramblers | 1-3 |
| Barkingside v Great Yarmouth T | 1-1, 0-3 |
| Kirkley & Pakefield v Sawbridgeworth T | 1-1, 7-3 |
| Stansted v Norwich U | 1-2 |
| Gorleston v Stanway R | 3-1 |
| Takeley v Newmarket T | 2-1 |
| London APSA v Long Melford | 3-1 |
| Basildon U v Diss T | 1-0 |
| Debenham LC v Whitton U | 0-2 |
| Southend Manor v Hullbridge Sports | 1-0 |
| Woodbridge T v Great Wakering R | 1-2 |
| Bowers & Pitsea v Eton Manor | 1-3 |
| Ipswich W v Hadleigh U | 0-3 |
| AFC Dunstable v Ampthill T | 4-1 |
| Hanworth Villa v Bethnal Green U | 2-2, 5-1 |
| Hoddesdon T v Berkhamsted | 1-1, 1-2 |
| Wodson Park v Colney Heath | 0-4 |
| Bedfont Sports v Tring Ath | 0-1 |
| Haringey Bor v AFC Kempston R | 1-3 |
| Staines Lammas v Barking | 4-4, 1-0 |
| Wembley v Langford | 3-2 |
| Biggleswade U v Cranfield U | 2-0 |
| Broxbourne Bor V&E removed v Dunstable T w/o | |
| Hadley v Hertford T | 2-0 |
| Hanwell T v Haringey & Waltham Dev | 1-3 |
| Harefield U v Hillingdon Bor | 3-0 |
| Crawley Green v Stotfold | 1-2 |
| London Colney v Hatfield T | 3-0 |
| Kings Langley v St Margaretsbury | 1-1, 2-3 |
| Aylesbury U v Enfield 1893 | 4-0 |
| London Maccabi Lions v Clapton | 4-0 |
| Sporting Bengal U v Cockfosters | 1-3 |
| Oxhey Jets v Leverstock Green | 5-2 |
| Ardley U v Holyport | 4-2 |
| Kidlington v Shrivenham | 2-2, 3-6 |
| Cove v Slimbridge | 2-0 |
| Reading T v Newport Pagnell T | 1-6 |
| Hartley Wintney v Holmer Green | 2-1 |
| Old Woodstock T v Wantage T | 1-4 |
| Bracknell T v Binfield | 2-1 |
| Ascot U v Sandhurst T | 6-1 |
| Thame U v Newbury | 1-0 |
| Witney T v Marlow | 1-1, 3-4 |
| Wokingham & Emmbrook v Camberley T | 0-2 |
| Abingdon T v Fairford T | 1-0 |
| Flackwell Heath v Windsor | 0-1 |
| Erith T v Ringmer | 2-4 |
| Littlehampton T v Molesey | 4-0 |
| Tunbridge Wells v Beckenham T | 1-4 |
| Peacehaven & Telscombe v Banstead Ath | 2-1 |
| Chessington & Hook U v Warlingham | 2-2, 3-2 |
| Cobham v South Park | 1-1, 0-3 |
| Pagham v Sevenoaks T | 2-1 |
| Arundel v Epsom & Ewell | 1-2 |
| Lordswood v Erith & Belvedere | 3-2 |

| | |
|---|---|
| Dorking v VCD Ath | 3-4 |
| Redhill v Whyteleafe | 1-0 |
| Deal T v Ashford U | 1-2 |
| Lingfield v AFC Uckfield | 4-2 |
| Hailsham T v Greenwich Bor | 2-4 |
| Fisher v East Preston | 1-1, 0-1 |
| Mole Valley SCR v Badshot Lea | 1-1, 1-4 |
| Horley T v Holmesdale | 5-1 |
| Lancing v Selsey | 6-1 |
| Egham T v Westfield | 4-0 |
| Chichester C v Crowborough Ath | 2-5 |
| Shoreham v Colliers Wood U | 2-2, 1-4 |
| St Francis Rangers v Rye U | 0-1 |
| Corinthian v Croydon | 3-2 |
| Hassocks v Sidley U | 0-1 |
| Raynes Park Vale v Horsham YMCA | 8-0 |
| Bitton v Bristol Manor Farm | 3-1 |
| Bemerton HH v Hamworthy U | 1-2 |
| Winterbourne U v Moneyfields | 1-2 |
| Hallen v Fawley | 4-0 |
| Farnham T v Alresford T | 0-3 |
| Highworth T v Corsham T | 3-1 |
| GE Hamble v Whitchurch U | 2-0 |
| Almondsbury UWE v Petersfield T | 1-1, 3-2 |
| *aet.* | |
| East Cowes Vic Ath v Verwood T | 3-2 |
| Downton v Ash U | 4-1 |
| Hayling U v Fareham T | 0-3 |
| Wootton Bassett T v Calne T | 4-2 |
| Horndean v Brockenhurst | 2-0 |
| Fleet Spurs v Totton & Eling | 2-3 |
| Alton T v Bradford T | 3-0 |
| Ringwood T v Cadbury Heath | 1-5 |
| Longwell Green Sports v Melksham T | 0-0, 1-3 |
| Christchurch v Cowes Sports | 2-1 |
| Romsey T v Lymington T | 4-0 |
| New Milton T v Newport (IW) | 0-2 |
| Blackfield & Langley v AFC Portchester | 6-1 |
| Bournemouth v Pewsey Vale | 0-1 |
| Plymouth Parkway v Welton R | 3-1 |
| Gillingham T v Tavistock | 5-0 |
| Bodmin T v Brislington | 3-1 |
| Bishop Sutton v Radstock T | 5-2 |
| Street v Hengrove Ath | 1-3 |
| Chard T v Ilfracombe T | 1-0 |
| Wells C v Barnstaple T | 3-2 |
| Larkhall Ath v Willand R | 2-1 |
| Odd Down v Saltash U | 3-1 |
| Buckland Ath v Bridport | 2-1 |
| Sherborne T v Elmore | 3-1 |

**PRELIMINARY ROUND**

| | |
|---|---|
| Harrogate Railway Ath v South Shields | 1-1, 0-1 |
| Birtley T v West Auckland T | 1-4 |
| Jarrow Roofing Boldon CA v Farsley | 2-3 |
| Shildon v Guisborough T | 1-1, 6-0 |
| Bishop Auckland v Esh Winning | 7-1 |
| Ossett T v Goole | 1-0 |
| Garforth T v Wakefield | 1-4 |
| Tadcaster Alb v Norton & Stockton A | 3-0 |
| Brighouse T v Eccleshill U | 1-2 |
| Hebburn T v Ossett Alb | 1-3 |
| Celtic Nation v Dunston UTS | 1-2 |
| *Tie awarded to Dunston UTS; Celtic Nation fielded an ineligible player.* | |
| Crook v Holker OB | 4-4, 1-3 |
| Marske U v Ashington | 1-4 |
| Spennymoor T v West Allotment Celtic | 3-0 |
| Whitley Bay v Bedlington Terriers | 0-3 |
| Durham C v Billingham T | 1-2 |
| Staveley MW v Bamber Bridge | 3-3, 2-5 |
| Chadderton v Maltby Main | 0-1 |
| Ashton Ath v Lancaster C | 2-2, 1-4 |
| Padiham v Burscough | 0-0, 1-2 |
| *aet.* | |
| Mossley v Bootle | 0-3 |
| Maine Road v Bacup Bor | 2-1 |
| Barton T OB v Cammell Laird | 1-2 |
| Atherton Coll v Congleton T | 2-1 |
| Ramsbottom U v Brigg T | 3-0 |
| Winsford U v Trafford | 0-2 |
| AFC Liverpool v Prescot Cables | 0-1 |
| Irlam v Runcorn T | 1-2 |
| Atherton LR v Warrington T | 0-3 |
| Formby v Skelmersdale U | 1-3 |
| Northwich Vic v Curzon Ashton | 0-0, 2-2 |
| *aet; Curzon Ashton won 4-2 on penalties.* | |

| | |
|---|---|
| Sheffield v Abbey Hey | 1-2 |
| Clitheroe v Radcliffe Bor | 2-2, 1-0 |
| Salford C v Hemsworth MW | 5-1 |
| Loughborough Dyn v Glossop NE | 3-0 |
| Lincoln U v Thurnby Nirvana | 1-0 |
| New Mills v Mickleover Sports | 2-2, 1-1 |
| *aet; New Mills won 6-5 on penalties.* | |
| Holbrook Sports v Belper T | 1-6 |
| Coalville T v Loughborough Univ | 5-3 |
| Stamford v Borrowash Vic | 1-0 |
| Kirby Muxloe v Holbeach U | 0-2 |
| Blaby & Whetstone Ath v Heanor T | 2-1 |
| Carlton T v Oadby T | 3-2 |
| Hucknall T v Retford U | 0-1 |
| Sleaford T v Rainworth MW | 1-2 |
| Blackstones v Gresley | 1-3 |
| Quorn v Dunkirk | 2-1 |
| Chasetown v Rocester | 2-1 |
| Cradley T v Norton U | 4-4, 0-5 |
| Studley v Rugby T | 1-4 |
| Halesowen T v Dudley T | 1-2 |
| Gornal Ath v Coventry Sphinx | 6-0 |
| Leek T v Evesham U | 2-1 |
| Market Drayton T v Newcastle T | 2-1 |
| Heath Hayes v Tividale | 3-4 |
| Sporting Khalsa v Nuneaton Griff | 1-1, 1-5 |
| AFC Wulfrunians v Kidsgrove Ath | 1-0 |
| Stourport Swifts v Continental Star | 1-1, 3-1 |
| Wellington v Bewdley T | 3-5 |
| Lye T v Bridgnorth T | 0-1 |
| Westfields v Romulus | 2-1 |
| Sutton Coldfield T v Pegasus Juniors | 2-1 |
| Wolverhampton Cas v Pilkington XXX | 2-0 |
| Godmanchester R v Daventry T | 3-4 |
| Peterborough Northern Star v Thrapston T | 3-1 |
| Bugbrooke St M v Ely C | 2-2, 3-1 |
| Huntingdon T v St Ives T | 3-2 |
| Dereham T v Woodford U | 3-0 |
| *Original match abandoned after 23 minutes due to waterlogged pitch with score at 2-0.* | |
| Wisbech T v Yaxley | 3-0 |
| Wellingborough T v King's Lynn T | 1-3 |
| Soham T Rangers v Burnham Ramblers | 5-1 |
| Great Yarmouth T v Witham T | 1-8 |
| Grays Ath v Takeley | 1-0 |
| Tilbury v Brantham Ath | 5-1 |
| AFC Sudbury v Ilford | 5-0 |
| Kirkley & Pakefield v Southend Manor | 0-2 |
| Harlow T v Hadleigh U | 1-2 |
| Halstead T v Brentwood T | 0-6 |
| Needham Market v Gorleston | 6-2 |
| Eton Manor v Norwich U | 0-2 |
| Felixstowe & Walton U v Heybridge Swifts | 1-1, 0-4 |
| Whitton U v Aveley | 0-3 |
| Basildon U v Haverhill R | 1-0 |
| Maldon & Tiptree v London APSA | 9-1 |
| Wroxham v Great Wakering R | 2-0 |
| St Margaretsbury v Leighton T | 0-0, 3-2 |
| London Colney v Harefield U | 1-2 |
| Haringey & Waltham Dev v Waltham Abbey | 1-2 |
| Biggleswade U v Ware | 0-1 |
| Ashford T (Middlesex) v Tring Ath | 2-2, 2-0 |
| AFC Kempston R v Cockfosters | 3-1 |
| London Maccabi Lions v Oxhey Jets | 3-1 |
| Berkhamsted v Hadley | 3-1 |
| Cheshunt v Potters Bar T | 2-2, 1-3 |
| Aylesbury U v Northwood | 2-5 |
| Hanworth Villa v Royston T | 1-2 |
| Colney Heath v Stotfold | 1-1, 7-3 |
| Staines Lammas v Barton R | 0-2 |
| AFC Dunstable v Redbridge | 5-0 |
| Biggleswade T v AFC Hayes | 3-0 |
| Uxbridge v Wembley | 2-2, 5-0 |
| Romford v Waltham Forest | 1-4 |
| North Greenford U v Dunstable T | 2-4 |
| Bishop's Cleeve v Ascot U | 2-1 |
| *Original match abandoned after 81 minutes due to waterlogged pitch with score at 2-2.* | |
| Cinderford T v Abingdon T | 5-0 |
| Didcot T v Abingdon U | 2-1 |
| Camberley T v Chalfont St Peter | 0-5 |
| Hungerford T v Beaconsfield SYCOB | 5-2 |
| Aylesbury v Windsor | 0-2 |
| Wantage T v Hartley Wintney | 4-1 |
| Newport Pagnell T v Ardley U | 6-2 |
| Fleet T v Marlow | 0-2 |
| North Leigh v Thame U | 6-0 |

| | |
|---|---|
| Cirencester T v Merthyr T | 0-1 |
| Cove v Thatcham T | 2-5 |
| Bracknell T v Shrivenham | 2-0 |
| Lordswood v Pagham | 0-0, 1-1 |
| *aet; Pagham won 4-2 on penalties.* | |
| Chertsey T v Beckenham T | 1-4 |
| Horley T v Leatherhead | 1-1, 0-3 |
| Lancing v South Park | 0-1 |
| Epsom & Ewell v Three Bridges | 2-1 |
| Badshot Lea v Egham T | 2-1 |
| Chipstead v Crowborough Ath | 5-2 |
| Sittingbourne v Burnham | 2-1 |
| Faversham T v Ringmer | 2-1 |
| Chatham T v Peacehaven & Telscombe | 2-1 |
| Crawley Down Gatwick v Tooting & Mitcham U | 1-3 |
| Slough T v Corinthian | 4-2 |
| Horsham v Raynes Park Vale | 2-2, 3-1 |
| Merstham v Walton & Hersham | 1-5 |
| VCD Ath v Whitstable T | 2-1 |
| Burgess Hill T v Littlehampton T | 0-3 |
| Redhill v Corinthian Cas | 3-0 |
| Godalming T v Ramsgate | 5-2 |
| Herne Bay v Folkestone Invicta | 1-3 |
| Dulwich Hamlet v Hythe T | 1-0 |
| Maidstone U v Colliers Wood U | 4-1 |
| Guildford C v East Preston | 5-3 |
| Eastbourne T v Chessington & Hook U | 2-0 |
| Walton Casuals v Thamesmead T | 1-2 |
| *Original match abandoned after 45 minutes due to* | |
| *waterlogged pitch with score at 0-2.* | |
| Ashford U v Lingfield | 1-3 |
| Worthing v Rye U | 5-1 |
| Greenwich Bor v Sidley U | 2-2, 1-0 |
| Christchurch v Alresford T | 2-1 |
| Highworth T v Shortwood U | 1-0 |
| Blackfield & Langley v Downton | 1-0 |
| Mangotsfield U v Bitton | 2-0 |
| Yate T v Poole T | 5-0 |
| GE Hamble v Totton & Eling | 0-1 |
| Pewsey Vale v Melksham T | 2-3 |
| Moneyfields v Newport (IW) | 0-1 |
| Sholing v East Cowes Vic Ath | 4-0 |
| Cadbury Heath v Almondsbury UWE | 2-3 |
| Hallen v Swindon Supermarine | 1-4 |
| Horndean v Romsey T | 2-0 |
| Wootton Bassett T v Hamworthy U | 1-0 |
| Wimborne T v Fareham T | 0-1 |
| Winchester C v Alton T | 3-0 |
| Gillingham T v Bishop Sutton | 3-3, 3-2 |
| Wells C v Bodmin T | 0-4 |
| Clevedon T v Tiverton T | 2-0 |
| Buckland Ath v Hengrove Ath | 5-0 |
| Sherborne T v Odd Down | 2-0 |
| Larkhall Ath v Bridgwater T | 3-2 |
| Paulton R v Taunton T | 1-1, 2-3 |
| Chard T v Plymouth Parkway | 1-4 |

**FIRST QUALIFYING ROUND**

| | |
|---|---|
| Spennymoor T v South Shields | 2-0 |
| Tadcaster Alb v Holker OB | 3-0 |
| Durham C v Shildon | 1-3 |
| Farsley v Ossett Alb | 1-1, 0-1 |
| Ossett T v Whitby T | 1-1, 0-1 |
| Bedlington Terriers v Bishop Auckland | 0-1 |
| Dunston UTS v Kendal T | 3-3, 2-4 |
| *aet.* | |
| Ashington v West Auckland T | 2-3 |
| Eccleshill U v North Ferriby U | 0-2 |
| Blyth Spartans v Garforth T | 1-0 |
| Abbey Hey v Atherton Coll | 2-1 |
| Warrington T v Maine Road | 1-0 |
| Burscough v Witton Alb | 2-4 |
| Worksop T v Frickley Ath | 0-2 |
| Skelmersdale U v Clitheroe | 1-0 |
| Lancaster C v Salford C | 0-4 |
| Chorley v Nantwich T | 2-0 |
| Bootle v Bamber Bridge | 1-2 |
| Prescot Cables v Ashton U | 1-3 |
| Stocksbridge PS v Marine | 0-3 |
| FC United of Manchester v Cammell Laird | 5-0 |
| Runcorn T v Trafford | 0-4 |
| Curzon Ashton v Maltby Main | 8-1 |
| AFC Fylde v Ramsbottom U | 3-1 |
| Retford U v New Mills | 1-2 |
| Matlock T v Belper T | 2-2, 0-3 |
| Holbeach U v Stamford | 1-2 |
| Eastwood T v Blaby & Whetstone Ath | 1-1, 3-1 |

| | |
|---|---|
| Quorn v Buxton | 1-2 |
| Thurnby Nirvana v Gresley | 2-2, 1-4 |
| Loughborough Dyn v Grantham T | 2-2, 1-3 |
| Rainworth MW v Carlton T | 2-2, 1-3 |
| Coalville T v Ilkeston | 0-1 |
| Dudley T v Nuneaton Griff | 0-1 |
| Rugby T v Bedworth U | 1-1, 0-1 |
| *aet.* | |
| Chasetown v Market Drayton T | 1-1, 2-1 |
| *aet.* | |
| Redditch U v Hednesford T | 0-3 |
| Norton U v Westfields | 2-5 |
| Barwell v AFC Wulfrunians | 3-0 |
| Bridgnorth T v Rushall Olympic | 3-1 |
| Leamington v Stourbridge | 2-2, 2-1 |
| Sutton Coldfield T v Gornal Ath | 0-3 |
| Stourport Swifts v Stafford Rangers | 1-1, 1-2 |
| *aet.* | |
| Wolverhampton Cas v Tividale | 1-1, 2-4 |
| Leek T v Bewdley T | 5-1 |
| Cambridge C v Huntingdon T | 7-0 |
| Daventry T v King's Lynn T | 1-1, 3-2 |
| *aet.* | |
| St Neots T v Peterborough Northern Star | 5-0 |
| Wisbech T v Kettering T | 0-0, 0-3 |
| Bugbrooke St M v Dereham T | 1-4 |
| Tilbury v Lowestoft T | 0-2 |
| Heybridge Swifts v AFC Sudbury | 4-1 |
| Soham T Rangers v Maldon & Tiptree | 0-2 |
| Basildon U v Thurrock | 0-3 |
| Bury T v Canvey Island | 3-0 |
| Wroxham v Brentwood T | 0-5 |
| Leiston v Southend Manor | 5-1 |
| Concord Rangers v Needham Market | 1-0 |
| East Thurrock U v Witham T | 2-0 |
| Grays Ath v Norwich U | 2-1 |
| Aveley v Hadleigh U | 6-1 |
| Dunstable T v Ashford T (Middlesex) | 2-2, 0-3 |
| AFC Kempston R v Hampton & Richmond Bor | 0-3 |
| Chesham U v Northwood | 0-1 |
| Enfield T v St Margaretsbury | 2-0 |
| Harrow Bor v St Albans C | 1-3 |
| London Maccabi Lions v AFC Dunstable | 2-4 |
| Hemel Hempstead T v Waltham Forest | 2-5 |
| Waltham Abbey v Bedford T | 1-0 |
| Hendon v Potters Bar T | 1-1, 3-0 |
| Uxbridge v Berkhamsted | 3-4 |
| Ware v Hitchin T | 0-5 |
| Barton R v Arlesey T | 0-1 |
| Colney Heath v Harefield U | 1-2 |
| Wingate & Finchley v Royston T | 1-1, 3-2 |
| Wealdstone v Biggleswade T | 2-0 |
| Bishop's Cleeve v Bracknell T | 6-0 |
| Chalfont St Peter v Newport Pagnell T | 3-2 |
| Windsor v Didcot T | 0-1 |
| Cinderford T v Merthyr T | 1-1, 0-3 |
| Hungerford T v Banbury U | 1-1, 2-0 |
| North Leigh v Wantage T | 6-1 |
| Marlow v Thatcham T | 1-3 |
| Littlehampton T v Eastbourne T | 0-1 |
| VCD Ath v Horsham | 0-1 |
| Slough T v Lingfield | 4-1 |
| Faversham T v Margate | 2-2, 0-3 |
| Bognor Regis T v Epsom & Ewell | 4-0 |
| Badshot Lea v Walton & Hersham | 3-2 |
| Godalming T v Dulwich Hamlet | 2-2, 2-2 |
| *aet; Dulwich Hamlet won 3-1 on penalties.* | |
| Leatherhead v Tooting & Mitcham U | 3-1 |
| Greenwich Bor v Cray W | 0-1 |
| Redhill v Lewes | 1-3 |
| Beckenham T v Metropolitan Police | 1-7 |
| South Park v Walton & Hersham | 1-1, 1-0 |
| Chipstead v Maidstone U | 0-4 |
| Pagham v Carshalton Ath | 0-0, 0-3 |
| Guildford C v Kingstonian | 0-3 |
| Whitehawk v Sittingbourne | 5-0 |
| Thamesmead T v Worthing | 2-0 |
| Hastings U v Chatham T | 3-1 |
| Fareham T v Christchurch | 2-1 |
| Newport (IW) v Horndean | 2-0 |
| Chippenham T v Mangotsfield U | 3-1 |
| Blackfield & Langley v Almondsbury UWE | 4-0 |
| Totton & Eling v Weymouth | 2-2, 0-3 |
| Winchester C v Yate T | 1-2 |
| Swindon Supermarine v AFC Totton | 0-6 |
| Wootton Bassett T v Highworth T | 3-1 |
| Sholing v Melksham T | 4-0 |

Bashley v Gosport Bor ... 1-1, 2-3
Plymouth Parkway v Buckland Ath ... 1-1, 1-5
Gillingham T v Taunton T ... 0-0, 3-1
Bideford v Bodmin T ... 2-2, 3-2
*aet.*
Larkhall Ath v Frome T ... 0-0, 0-4
Clevedon T v Sherborne T ... 5-0

## SECOND QUALIFYING ROUND
Bishop Auckland v AFC Fylde ... 1-2
Halifax T v Abbey Hey ... 6-0
Curzon Ashton v Bradford PA ... 1-3
Blyth Spartans v Workington ... 1-1, 0-1
Shildon v Altrincham ... 0-3
Ashton U v Marine ... 0-2
Salford C v FC United of Manchester ... 2-3
Trafford v Spennymoor T ... 5-3
Stalybridge Celtic v Vauxhall Motors ... 1-0
Bamber Bridge v Guiseley ... 0-1
Kendal T v Witton Alb ... 4-2
Colwyn Bay v Warrington T ... 3-2
Gainsborough Trinity v Chester ... 1-1, 1-2
*aet.*
Tadcaster Alb v Skelmersdale U ... 4-1
Whitby T v Droylsden ... 4-3
North Ferriby U v Ossett Alb ... 1-2
West Auckland T v Harrogate T ... 2-2, 1-5
Chorley v Frickley Ath ... 1-3
Gornal Ath v Worcester C ... 0-4
Boston U v Kettering T ... 1-0
Solihull Moors v Westfields ... 1-1, 2-1
Hinckley U v Tividale ... 5-3
Cambridge C v Grantham T ... 3-1
Eastwood T v Histon ... 3-5
Nuneaton Griff v Hednesford T ... 2-3
Gresley v Stafford Rangers ... 3-2
Carlton T v New Mills ... 4-3
Brackley T v Daventry T ... 4-0
Dereham T v Chasetown ... 2-1
Ilkeston v Belper T ... 2-2, 5-1
Stamford v Buxton ... 1-3
Leek T v Bridgnorth T ... 3-0
Barwell v Bedworth U ... 3-2
Corby T v Leamington ... 3-2
Northwood v AFC Dunstable ... 1-1, 3-0
Wealdstone v Lowestoft T ... 1-2
Ashford T (Middlesex) v St Albans C ... 2-6
Hayes & Yeading U v Heybridge Swifts ... 3-2
Carshalton Ath v Chalfont St Peter ... 0-1
Hendon v Lewes ... 3-0
St Neots T v Boreham Wood ... 1-2
Chelmsford C v Leatherhead ... 2-1
Dover Ath v Tonbridge Angels ... 2-1
Brentwood T v Maldon & Tiptree ... 1-1, 1-1
*aet; Brentwood T won 9-8 on penalties.*
Badshot Lea v Leiston ... 4-2
Aveley v Margate ... 1-4
Waltham Abbey v Eastbourne Bor ... 2-4
Billericay T v AFC Hornchurch ... 3-1
Concord Rangers v Welling U ... 1-1, 1-2
Enfield T v Bishop's Stortford ... 1-4
Cray W v Thamesmead T ... 3-1
Waltham Forest v Hampton & Richmond Bor ... 1-0
Whitehawk v Hitchin T ... 1-1, 0-5
South Park v Harefield U ... 0-0, 4-1
Arlesey T v Dulwich Hamlet ... 1-0
Staines T v Hastings U ... 2-3
Berkhamsted v Metropolitan Police ... 0-3
Slough T v Eastbourne T ... 5-1
Bury T v Wingate & Finchley ... 2-1
Horsham v Thurrock ... 1-2
Sutton U v Bromley ... 0-1
Grays Ath v Maidstone U ... 0-5
Kingstonian v East Thurrock U ... 2-3
Bishop's Cleeve v Chippenham T ... 1-2
Truro C v AFC Totton ... 2-3
Dorchester T v Wootton Bassett T ... 4-0
Buckland Ath v Bath C ... 1-2
Gloucester C v Thatcham T ... 2-1
Gillingham T v Sholing ... 1-3
North Leigh v Havant & Waterlooville ... 1-0
Basingstoke T v Weymouth ... 3-1
Merthyr T v Hungerford T ... 0-0, 1-1
*aet; Merthyr T won 5-4 on penalties.*
Frome T v Weston Super Mare ... 0-2
Didcot T v Clevedon T ... 3-1
Newport (IW) v Salisbury C ... 0-3

Gosport Bor v Bideford ... 2-0
Fareham T v Blackfield & Langley ... 0-2
Farnborough v Eastleigh ... 1-2
Maidenhead U v Bognor Regis T ... 4-2
Yate T v Oxford C ... 2-1

## THIRD QUALIFYING ROUND
Ilkeston v Gresley ... 4-2
Chester v Halifax T ... 1-1, 1-3
Hednesford T v Buxton ... 2-2, 1-2
AFC Fylde v Solihull Moors ... 4-1
Carlton T v Bradford PA ... 1-3
Colwyn Bay v Guiseley ... 1-1, 1-3
Stalybridge Celtic v Whitby T ... 3-1
Barwell v Workington ... 1-1, 0-2
Hinckley U v Ossett Alb ... 2-2, 0-1
FC United of Manchester v Kendal T ... 3-1
Leek T v Altrincham ... 0-2
Trafford v Marine ... 1-3
Harrogate T v Frickley Ath ... 3-2
Tadcaster Alb v Boston U ... 0-2
Hastings U v Hitchin T ... 2-2, 2-1
Histon v Corby T ... 1-1, 1-2
Cambridge C v Billericay T ... 1-1, 4-2
Margate v Slough T ... 0-1
Dereham T v Metropolitan Police ... 1-1, 0-2
South Park v Brentwood T ... 3-1
Chalfont St Peter v Bishop's Stortford ... 1-1, 1-3
Cray W v Chelmsford C ... 1-2
Dover Ath v Bromley ... 1-2
Northwood v Boreham Wood ... 0-4
East Thurrock U v Maidstone U ... 3-0
Bury T v Hampton & Richmond Bor ... 4-0
St Albans C v Lowestoft T ... 0-1
Eastbourne Bor v Hendon ... 2-2, 1-2
Arlesey T v Brackley T ... 4-3
Welling U v Thurrock ... 1-1, 3-1
Weston Super Mare v Worcester C ... 1-1, 0-1
Dorchester T v Basingstoke T ... 1-0
Yate T v North Leigh ... 2-1
Gloucester C v Eastleigh ... 1-0
Chippenham T v Badshot Lea ... 3-1
Didcot T v Maidenhead U ... 1-0
AFC Totton v Merthyr T ... 3-2
Bath C v Gosport Bor ... 1-1, 1-3
Sholing v Blackfield & Langley ... 1-3
Hayes & Yeading U v Salisbury C ... 2-1

## FOURTH QUALIFYING ROUND
Alfreton T v Gateshead ... 2-0
Hyde v Harrogate T ... 1-1, 0-1
FC United of Manchester v Hereford U ... 0-2
Barrow v Tamworth ... 2-0
Guiseley v Buxton ... 2-0
Grimsby v Kidderminster H ... 2-4
Bradford PA v Ossett Alb ... 4-1
Wrexham v Southport ... 2-0
AFC Fylde v Ilkeston ... 1-1, 1-0
Boston U v Altrincham ... 1-3
Lincoln C v Halifax T ... 0-0, 2-0
Macclesfield T v Marine ... 3-1
Workington v Mansfield T ... 1-2
Stockport Co v Stalybridge Celtic ... 5-3
AFC Telford U v Nuneaton T ... 2-2, 0-1
*aet.*
South Park v Metropolitan Police ... 0-3
Didcot T v Arlesey T ... 0-1
Forest Green R v Dartford ... 1-1, 4-1
Yate T v Newport Co ... 3-3, 3-1
*aet.*
Slough T v Gosport Bor ... 0-0, 2-1
Hastings U v Blackfield & Langley ... 3-0
Bromley v Worcester C ... 2-1
Chelmsford C v East Thurrock U ... 2-2, 4-4
*aet; Chelmsford C won 5-3 on penalties.*
Hayes & Yeading U v Boreham Wood ... 2-3
AFC Totton v Cambridge C ... 2-3
Welling U v Bishop's Stortford ... 1-3
Braintree T v Lowestoft T ... 3-2
Dorchester T v Bury T ... 3-1
Cambridge U v Luton T ... 0-2
Gloucester C v Chippenham T ... 1-0
Corby T v Hendon ... 1-2
Woking v Ebbsfleet U ... 0-1

# THE BUDWEISER FA CUP 2012–13
## COMPETITION PROPER

**\*** *Denotes player sent off.*

**FIRST ROUND**

Friday, 2 November 2012

**Cambridge City (0) 0**
**Milton Keynes D (0) 0**      1564
*Cambridge C:* (442) Barrett; Pepper, Theobald, Chaffey, Brighton; Allen, Cambridge, Prada, Abbs (Marriott 60); Hammond, Bryant (Lester 79).
*Milton Keynes D:* (4231) Martin; Otsemobor, Williams, Kay, Lewington; Gleeson, Potter; O'Shea (Alli 64), Chicksen, Chadwick (Smith 86); Lowe.

Saturday, 3 November 2012

**AFC Fylde (0) 1** *(Farrell 90)*
**Accrington S (2) 4** *(Hatfield 32, 45, 77, 86)*    1213
*AFC Fylde:* (433) Hinchliffe; Haslam, Hughes, Steel (Winter 46), Sumner; Dorney (Dean 46), Booth, Taylor; Barnes (Jarvis 46), Farrell, Allen.
*Accrington S:* (4231) Dunbavin; Winnard, Murphy, Molyneux (Osawe 90), Liddle; Joyce, Atkinson; Miller, Hatfield (Barnett 87), Boco; Amond (Sampson 82).

**Aldershot T (0) 2** *(Hylton 57, 85)*
**Hendon (1) 1** *(Cracknell 29)*      1822
*Aldershot T:* (442) Morris G; Herd, Brown, Bradley, Tonkin; Rose, Cadogan (Morris A 90), Vincenti, Hylton; Rankine (Payne 46), Reid (Donnelly 86).
*Hendon:* (4141) Laurencin; Wharton, Fisher, Brathwaite, McCluskey; MacLaren K (Rankin 86); Cracknell, Murray, Aite-Ouakrim (Mazzoney 76), MacLaren C; Ngoyi (Gambin 63).

**Barnet (0) 0**
**Oxford U (0) 2** *(Constable 56, Rigg 80)*    2346
*Barnet:* (442) Cowler; Fuller, Stephens, Fortune, Brown; Yiadom, Kamdjo, Lee (Davids 73), Byrne; Weston (Allen 73), John (Lowe 60).
*Oxford U:* (442) Clarke; Capaldi, Wright, Raynes, Whing; Rigg, Leven, Chapman, Potter; Constable, Pittman (Cox 63).

**Bishop's Stortford (1) 1** *(Johnson 7)*
**Hastings U (0) 2** *(Ray 70, Attwood 88)*    1212
*Bishop's Stortford:* (451) Chambers; Sinclair-Furlonge, Anderson, Francis, Herd; Waller-Lassen (Sturrock 78), Johnson (Webb 84), Cawley, Prestedge, Greeen (Abdullahi 81); Sappleton.
*Hastings U:* (433) Armstrong-Ford; Cox, Ray, Jirbandey, Richardson; Carey, Manning, Crellin; Ellis, Attwood, Goldburg.

**Boreham Wood (0) 0**
**Brentford (2) 2** *(Donaldson 16, Forrester 44)*    1495
*Boreham Wood:* (442) Russell; Nunn, Jefford, Reynolds, Jones; Vilhete, Isaac, Montgomery, Hutton (Morgan 63); Akurang, Riza (Effiong 67).
*Brentford:* (442) Lee; O'Connor, Craig, Bidwell, Forshaw; Legge (Dean 84), Adeyemi, Douglas, Forrester (Dallas 75); Hayes (Saunders 81), Donaldson.

**Bournemouth (1) 4** *(McQuoid 30, 79, Pugh 59, Fogden 90)*
**Dagenham & R (0) 0**      5827
*Bournemouth:* (442) Jalal; Francis, Cook, Elphick, Daniels; Grabban (Fogden 82), MacDonald, Arter (O'Kane 82), Pugh; McQuoid, Tubbs (McDermott 72).
*Dagenham & R:* (442) Lewington (Seabright 46); Ogogo, Doe, Wilkinson, Ilesanmi; Spillane (Woodall 27), Saunders, Howell (Hoyte 72), Elito; Williams, Gayle.

**Bristol R (1) 1** *(Clarkson 5)*
**Sheffield U (0) 2** *(Blackman 53, Porter 62)*    4712
*Bristol R:* (442) Walker; Smith, Paterson, Kenneth, Brown L; Clucas (Brown W 74), Clarkson, Lund, Broghammer (Richards 74); Eaves (Norburn 74), Riordan.
*Sheffield U:* (442) Long; Maguire, Hill, Collins, McMahon; Miller, Flynn, Doyle, McDonald; Porter (Cresswell 78), Blackman (Williams 71).

**Bury (1) 1** *(Sodje 35)*
**Exeter C (0) 0**      1821
*Bury:* (442) Carson; Skarz, Lockwood, Sodje**\***, Doherty; Poleon, Schumacher, Sweeney, Worrall; Hewitt, Healy (Hughes 62).
*Exeter C:* (3511) Krysiak; Baldwin, Coles, Amankwaah (Dawson 86); Tully (O'Flynn 46), Oakley, Bennett, Sercombe, Woodman; Gow; Cureton.

**Carlisle U (1) 4** *(Symington 45, Noble 61, Berrett 81, Garner 87)*
**Ebbsfleet U (0) 2** *(Elder 58, Howe 90)*    2373
*Carlisle U:* (433) Collin; Simek, Livesey, Edwards, Chantler (Bugno 86); Noble, Murphy, Berrett; Symington (Welsh 84), Garner, Cadamarteri (McGovern 71).
*Ebbsfleet U:* (433) Edwards; Stone, Ada, Walsh (Elder 56), Lorraine; Phipp, Howe, Barrett (Soares 77); Bellamy, Azeez, Enver-Marum (Ashikodi 67).

**Chelmsford (1) 3** *(Simmonds 23, 63, Slabber 89)*
**Colchester U (0) 1** *(Rose 70)*    3016
*Chelmsford:* (442) Searle; Brindley, Miller, Clark, Palmer; Cook, Cornhill, Rainford, Slabber; Simmonds, Welsh (Corcoran 74).
*Colchester U:* (433) Cousins; White, Okuonghae, Eastman, Rose; Bean, Wordsworth, Eastmond (Morrison 68); Henderson (Massey 68), Watt (Sears 60), Ibehre.

**Cheltenham T (1) 3** *(Thomas 3 (og), Mohamed 65, Zebroski 90)*
**Yate T (0) 0**      3055
*Cheltenham T:* (442) Brown; Jombati, Bennett, Lowe, Jones; Deering, Penn, D'Ath (Pack 46), Mohamed; Duffy (Goulding 61), Harrad (Zebroski 61).
*Yate T:* (442) Dempsey; Warren, Thomas, Vahid, Cox; Harmer (Meaker 73), Wring, Groves, Purnell (Bryant 88); Page (Hiroli 88), Knigton.

**Chesterfield (3) 6** *(Boden 16, Randall 29, Clay 42, Forbes 54, Lester 79, Westcarr 90)*
**Hartlepool U (0) 1** *(Sweeney 78)*    3083
*Chesterfield:* (4411) O'Donnell; Talbot, Forbes, Cooper (Westcarr 77), Smith; Whitaker, Clay, Togwell, Randall (Broadhead 90); Darikwa; Boden (Lester 70).
*Hartlepool U:* (433) Flinders; Austin, Hartley, Baldwin (Collins 56), Horwood; Walton, Sweeney, Murray (Franks 56); Humphreys (Poole 58), Howard, Noble.

**Coventry C (1) 3** *(Ball 28, Christie 63, Jennings 89)*
**Arlesey T (0) 0**      6594
*Coventry C:* (442) Murphy; Clarke J, Christie, Edjenguele, Reckord (Willis 72); Baker, Jennings, Moussa, Fleck; McSheffrey (McDonald 56), Ball (O'Donovan 79).
*Arlesey T:* (442) Abbey N; Thurlbourne, Blackett, Frater, Davis (Patrick 87); Goss, Farrell (Abbey Z 79), Hatch, Marsh (Prosper 56); Dillon, Roberts.

**Crewe Alex (2) 4** *(Pogba 19, Ellis 40, Aneke 62, Murphy 77)*
**Wycombe W (1) 1** *(Spring 13)*    2417
*Crewe Alex:* (4411) Martin; Mellor, Ellis, Davis, Tootle; West (Daniels 66), Murphy, Osman (Turton 72), Moore; Aneke (Robertson 82); Pogba.
*Wycombe W:* (4141) Archer; Stewart (Hause 41), Winfield, Doherty (Logan 9); Dunne; Spring; Andrade, Scowen, Wood, Grant; Morias (Kewley-Graham 58).

**Doncaster R (2) 3** *(Woods Martin 27, Hume 36, Brown 76)*
**Bradford PA (0) 1** *(Marshall 56)*      4602
*Doncaster R:* (442) Woods G; Griffin, Jones R, Spurr, Husband; Syers (Blake 42), Keegan, Woods Martin, Clingan; Paynter (Brown 57), Hume (Woods Michael 89).
*Bradford PA:* (433) Deasy (Higginson 82); Duckworth, Knowles, Hotte, Drury; Marshall, O'Brien (Holland 54), Deacey; Davidson, James (Greaves 70), Walker.

**Fleetwood T (3) 3** *(Ball 11, Parkin 17 (pen), 34 (pen))*
**Bromley (0) 0**      1696
*Fleetwood T:* (442) Davies; McLaughlin, Edwards (McNulty 31), Mawene, Howell; Obeng, Ferguson (Milligan 81), Fowler, Brown (McGuire 68); Ball, Parkin.
*Bromley:* (433) Welch; Ming (Malcolm 79), Harwood, Sobers, Patterson; Waldren (Rhule 80), Fuseini, Buchanan; Finn, Pacquette, Joseph-Dubois (Chaaban 63).

**Forest Green R (1) 2** *(Norwood 34, Oshodi 49)*
**Port Vale (2) 3** *(Vincent 7, McDonald 12, Williamson 80)*      1753
*Forest Green R:* (433) Russell; Turley, Oshodi, Racine, Stokes (Brogan 46); Klukowski, Bangura, Asafu-Adjaye; Styche (Taylor 46), Vieira (Koroma 83), Norwood.
*Port Vale:* (442) Neal; Yates, Davis, McDonald, Taylor (Loft 71); Vincent, Morsy, Burge, Myrie-Williams (Shuker 85); Dodds (Williamson 72), Pope.

**Gillingham (0) 4** *(Fish 59, Burton 65, Kedwell 76 (pen), Birchall 90)*
**Scunthorpe U (0) 0**      4017
*Gillingham:* (442) Nelson; Fish, Vincelot, Jackman, Davies; Payne, Barrett, Dack (Lee 21), Whelpdale; Weston (Birchall 79), Burton (Kedwell 71).
*Scunthorpe U:* (442) Slocombe; Ribeiro, Newey, Mirfin, Reid; Walker, Collins (Mozika 70), Duffy, Barcham (Ryan 78); Hawley, Grella (Jennings 78).

**Guiseley (2) 2** *(Brooksby 14, Boshell D 35)*
**Barrow (1) 2** *(Boyes 44, Hunter 48)*      1605
*Guiseley:* (433) Drench; Meynell, Ellis, Bower, Holdsworth; Boshell D, Rea, Brooksby (Wilson J 62); Holsgrave (Dale 90), Boshell N (Walshaw 62), Rothery.
*Barrow:* (433) Hurst; Flynn, Pearson M, Anderson, Hessey; Harvey, Bake, Hunter; Rutherford, Boyes, Almond (Rowe Danny M 86).

**Hereford U (2) 3** *(Evans 3, Bowman 12, 73 (pen))*
**Shrewsbury T (1) 1** *(Summerfield 30)*      3251
*Hereford U:* (451) Bittner; Gallinagh, Stam, Todd, Heath; McQuilkin (Smikle 67), Evans, O'Keefe (Graham 87), Pell, Clucas (Clist 90); Bowman.
*Shrewsbury T:* (442) Weale; Grandison, Jones, Collins, Purdie; Taylor, Summerfield, Hall (Wildig 85), Helan (Proctor 69); Parry, Morgan.

**Kidderminster H (0) 0**
**Oldham Ath (0) 2** *(Montano 52, Baxter 65)*      2888
*Kidderminster H:* (433) Vaughan N; Vaughan L, Dunkley, Gowling, Williams (Demetriou 66); Vincent, Storer, Briggs (Pilkington 83); Rowe, Malbon, Blissett (Johnson 64).
*Oldham Ath:* (442) Bouzanis; Wabara, Byrne (Brown 58), Tarkowski, Grounds; Croft (Sutherland 90), Wesolowski, Simpson R, Montano (Furman 84); Derbyshire, Baxter.

**Lincoln C (1) 1** *(Taylor 45)*
**Walsall (0) 1** *(Bowerman 87)*      2032
*Lincoln C:* (451) Farman; Gray, Boyce, Miller, Gilbert; Smith A (Larkin 78), Fofana, Mills, Power (Nicolau 78), Sheridan; Taylor J (Oliver 84).
*Walsall:* (352) Grof; Purkiss, Butler, Holden; Chambers J, Bowerman, Chambers A, Featherstone, Hemmings (Jones 58); Grigg (Williams 70), Paterson (Taundry 80).

**Luton T (0) 1** *(Rendell 84)*
**Nuneaton T (1) 1** *(Waite 20)*      3089
*Luton T:* (451) Brill; Henry, Kovacs, Rowe-Turner (Robinson J 70), Howells; Fleetwood (Watkins 83), O'Donnell, Rendell, Mendy, Gray; Walker.
*Nuneaton T:* (352) McNamara; Malaga, Dean, Cowan; McNamee (Armson 46), Sleath, Forsdick, Walker, James; Brown, Waite (Taylor 71).

**Mansfield T (0) 0**
**Slough T (0) 0**      1686
*Mansfield T:* (442) Redmond; Beevers, Geohaghon, Dempster, Sutton; Meikle, Clements, Howell, Briscoe; Hutchinson (Wright 66), Green.
*Slough T:* (352) Warrington; Brown, Bowden-Haase, Woozley; Rhone, Swift (Logie 84), Deeney D, Burgess, Fraser; Smith, Burnell (Sonner 79).

**Met Police (0) 1** *(Tait 83)*
**Crawley T (1) 2** *(Simpson 36, Clarke 69)*      1485
*Met Police:* (4411) Butler; Lovett, Crook (Taylor 75), Dolan (Palmer 76); Bourne; Sutherland, Smart, Brown; Smith; Tait; Newton.
*Crawley T:* (442) Jones P; Byrne (Sadler 27), Connolly, McFadzean, Walsh; Jones M (Akinde 80), Simpson, Bulman, Torres (Adams 64); Clarke, Alexander.

**Morecambe (1) 1** *(Fleming 12)*
**Rochdale (0) 1** *(Kennedy 72)*      1839
*Morecambe:* (433) Roche; Parrish, Fenton, Haining, Wright; McDonald, Drummond, Ellison; Redshaw, Alessandra (Parkinson 78), Fleming.
*Rochdale:* (433) Lillis; Edwards P, Bennett, Edwards Ryan, McIntyre; Tutte, Kennedy, Cavanagh; Grant, Adebola, Donnelly.

**Northampton T (0) 0** *(Moult 61)*
**Bradford C (1) 1** *(Atkinson 32)*      2512
*Northampton T:* (442) Higgs; Johnson, Langmead, Charles (Moyo 72), Widdowson; East, Huws, Tozer, Hackett; Moult (Platt 80), Akinfenwa.
*Bradford C:* (41212) Duke; Darby, Doyle, McHugh, Meredith; Brown; Atkinson, Jones R; Jones G (McArdle 81); Connell (Wells 76), Thompson (Hanson 76).

**Portsmouth (0) 0**
**Notts Co (1) 2** *(Zoko 45, Arquin 56)*      7560
*Portsmouth:* (442) Eastwood; Dumbuya, Michalik, Gyepes, Webster; Buzsaky (Harley 85), Ertl (Compton 59), Howard (Walker 85), Rodgers; Allan*, McLeod.
*Notts Co:* (451) Bialkowski; Liddle, Stewart, Leacock, Hughes J; Campbell-Ryce, Judge (Williams 90), Bishop, Boucaud (Labadie 81), Zoko; Arquin (Showunmi 90).

**Preston NE (2) 3** *(Byrom 38, Amoo 41, Robertson 70)*
**Yeovil T (0) 0**      4757
*Preston NE:* (442) Simonsen; Keane, Robertson, Huntington, Cansdell-Sherriff (Amoo 10); Monakana (Holmes 71), Wroe, Byrom (Procter 71), Laird; Beavon, King.
*Yeovil T:* (442) Stech; Blizzard, Hinds (Haynes-Brown 88), Burn, McAllister; Marsh-Brown (Reid 61), Upson*, Foley, Williams; Madden, Hayter.

**Rotherham U (1) 3** *(Bradley 30, Frecklington 53, 56)*
**Stevenage (0) 2** *(Dunne 58, Morais 73)*      4324
*Rotherham U:* (442) Warrington; Bradley, Sharps, Morgan C, Morris; Devitt (O'Connor 78), Arnason, Frecklington, Pringle (Agard 83); Revell (Taylor 90), Odejayi.
*Stevenage:* (4231) Arnold; Gray (Lopez 86), N'Gala, Roberts, Charles; Grant, Dunne; Akins (Rogers 89), Morais, Freeman (Agyemang 46); Haber.

**Southend U (1) 3** *(Corr 33, Laird 85, Eastwood 88)*
**Stockport Co (0) 0**      3084
*Southend U:* (433) Smith; Clohessy, Phillips, Cresswell (Prosser 23), Barker; Woodyard, Laird, Timlin; Hurst (Leonard 77), Corr (Eastwood 76), Tomlin.
*Stockport Co:* (4231) Ormson; Halls (Rowe 65), Fagbola, Tunnicliffe, Newton; Turnbull (Hattersley 39), Connor; Collins (Whitehead 60), Kenyon, Mainwaring; Hobson.

**Swindon T (0) 0**
**Macclesfield T (0) 2** *(Diagne 63, Thompson L 90 (og))*
6408
*Swindon T:* (442) Foderingham; Thompson N, Flint■,
Ward, McEveley; De Vita (Ritchie 49), Ferry, Archibald-
Henville (Thompson L 72), Roberts; Williams, Rooney A
(Collins 46).
*Macclesfield T:* (442) Cronin; Jackson, Diagne, Martin,
Braham-Barrett; McNamee (Mackreth 55), Murtagh,
Wedgbury, Kissock (Mills P 81); Barnes-Homer
(Fairhurst 90), Morgan-Smith.

**Torquay U (0) 0**
**Harrogate T (1) 1** *(Chilaka 20)*
1817
*Torquay U:* (4141) Poke; Leadbitter, Saah, Downes,
Nicholson (Yeoman 79); Lathrope; Mansell, Craig, Bodin
(Jarvis 59), Stevens (Thompson 60); Howe.
*Harrogate T:* (433) MacGillivray; Samuels, White,
Killock, Merris; Bolder, Dean, Platt; Forrest (Clayton
57), Beesley (Allan 71), Chilaka.

**Wrexham (1) 2** *(Ashton 2 (pen), Wright D 85)*
**Alfreton T (1) 4** *(Clayton 27, Bradley 60 (pen),*
*Tomlinson 79, 90)*
2409
*Wrexham:* (433) Mayebi■; Wright S (Rushton 77),
Westwood, Devine, Ashton; Harris, Keates, Hunt;
Cieslewicz (Coughlin 59), Morrell (Ogleby 77), Wright D.
*Alfreton T:* (442) Stewart; Law, Franks, Streete,
Meadows; Brown, Killock, Bradley■, Arnold; Clayton
(Quinn 88), Tomlinson■.

**York C (0) 1** *(Reed J 62)*
**AFC Wimbledon (0) 1** *(Strutton 80)*
2752
*York C:* (433) Ingham; Parslow, Smith C, Carlisle,
Fyfield; Kearns, Kerr, McLaughlin (Reed J 59); Blair,
Walker, Chambers (Johnson 90).
*AFC Wimbledon:* (4411) Brown; Fenlon (Osano 73),
Antwi, Mambo, Cummings; Yussuff, Gregory, Harris
(Harrison 46), Jolley; Moore L (Strutton 74); Midson.

Sunday, 4 November 2012
**Burton Alb (0) 3** *(Diamond 53, Maghoma 77, Zola 90)*
**Altrincham (2) 3** *(Rodgers 29, Stanton 34 (og),*
*McCrory 85 (og))*
1989
*Burton Alb:* (442) Oxley; O'Connor, Diamond, Stanton,
McCrory; Chapell, Bell, Weir, Maghoma; Kee (Paterson
69), Zola.
*Altrincham:* (442) Coburn; Densmore, Hall, Leather,
Doughty; Richman, Moult, Rodgers, Clee (Watmore 81);
Lawrie, Reeves (Brooke 88).

**Dorchester T (0) 1** *(Gosling 49)*
**Plymouth Arg (0) 0**
3196
*Dorchester T:* (451) Matthews; Jermyn, Walker, Clough,
Smeeton; Gosling, Nicholls, Gleeson (Symes 86), Garcia,
Martin; Watson.
*Plymouth Arg:* (4411) Gilmartin; Berry, Nelson,
Blanchard, Griffiths S; Lennox (Young 58), Hourihane■,
Lowry (Feeney 67), Bhasera; Gurrieri; Griffiths R
(Cowan-Hall 74).

Tuesday, 13 November 2012
**Braintree T (0) 0**
**Tranmere R (1) 3** *(Thompson 24, Stockton 53, Power 90)*
1503
*Braintree T:* (442) Naisbitt; O'Connor, Paine, Wells
(Bailey-Dennis 38), Habergham; Mulley (Daley 29),
Davis, Quinton, Sparkes; Marks (Sheppard 67), Holman.
*Tranmere R:* (442) Fon Williams; Holmes, Taylor
(Goodison 57), Gibson, Bakayogo; Thompson (Kirby
43), Wallace (Power 77), Robinson, Harrison; Stockton,
Jervis.

Wednesday, 14 November 2012
**Gloucester C (0) 0**
**Leyton Orient (0) 2** *(Mooney 87, Cox 88)*
1381
*Gloucester C:* (352) Green Mike; Hamblin, Coupe,
Holland; Green Michael, Webb, Hogg, Goddard (Davies
59), Harris (Tillson 89); Edwards, Harding (Morford 54).
*Leyton Orient:* (442) Allsop; Odubajo (McSweeney 57),
Clarke, Baudry, Sawyer; Smith Jimmy (Rowlands 86),
Griffith, James, Cox; Mooney, Brunt (Lisbie 60).

## FIRST ROUND REPLAYS

Monday, 12 November 2012
**AFC Wimbledon (1) 4** *(Strutton 34, 78, Harrison 97,*
*Midson 99)*
**York C (1) 3** *(Brown 22 (og), Reed J 90, 119)* 1954
*AFC Wimbledon:* (4312) Brown; Fenlon (Osano 62),
Mambo, Mitchel-King, Cummings; Jolley, Gregory,
Johnson (Harrison 61); Yussuff (Long 42); Midson,
Strutton.
*York C:* (442) Ingham; Oyebanjo, Carlisle, Smith C,
Fyfield; Chambers, Kerr■, Parslow (Reed J 89), Kearns;
Blair, Walker (Johnson 84).
*aet.*

Tuesday, 13 November 2012
**Barrow (0) 1** *(Hunter 90)*
**Guiseley (0) 0**
1372
*Barrow:* (433) Hurst; Flynn, Pearson M, Aldred, Hessey;
Hunter, Baker, Harvey; Jackson, Boyes, Almond
(Rutherford 90).
*Guiseley:* (4231) Drench; Holdsworth, Ellis, Bower,
Meynell; Rea, Boshell D; Brooksby, Walshaw (Wilson J
85), Rothery; Holsgrave (Boshell N 75).

**Bradford C (1) 3** *(Atkinson 35, Wells 90 (pen),*
*McHugh 120)*
**Northampton T (1) 3** *(Demontagnac 43 (pen), Platt 90,*
*Langmead 109)*
2951
*Bradford C:* (442) McLaughlin; Darby, McArdle,
McHugh, Meredith; Atkinson, Ravenhill, Brown (Jones
G 63), Hines (Baker 29); Connell (Wells 73), Hanson.
*Northampton T:* (442) Higgs; East, Tozer, Langmead,
Widdowson; Mukendi, Huws, Hornby, Demontagnac
(Akinfenwa 81); Platt, Wilson (Toney 91).
*aet; Bradford C won 4-2 on penalties.*

**Milton Keynes D (3) 6** *(Williams 12, 74 (pen), O'Shea 43,*
*Bowditch 45, Alli 75, Chicksen 77)*
**Cambridge C (0) 1** *(Theobald 60)*
4126
*Milton Keynes D:* (442) Martin; Doumbe, Kay, Williams,
Lewington; Bowditch (Chicksen 61), Gleeson, Alli
(Galloway 79), O'Shea; Lowe (Rasulo 67), MacDonald.
*Cambridge C:* (442) Barrett; Pepper, Theobald, Chaffey,
Brighton; Allen (Abbs 69), Prada (Lester 69), Cambridge
(Nightingale 63), Bryant; Hammond, Marriott.

**Nuneaton T (0) 0**
**Luton T (1) 2** *(Rendell 22, 72 (pen))*
1596
*Nuneaton T:* (352) McNamara; Malaga, Cowan, Dean;
Forsdick, Armson (Taylor 77), Sleath, Walker, James;
Brown, Waite (York 65).
*Luton T:* (442) Tyler; Henry, Rowe-Turner, Kovacs,
Howells; Walker (Robinson M 55), Lawless, Mendy,
O'Donnell (Dance 90); Rendell, Gray (Woolley 90).

**Rochdale (0) 0**
**Morecambe (1) 1** *(McDonald 44)*
1675
*Rochdale:* (433) Lillis; Bennett (Byrne 45), Pearson,
Edwards P, McIntyre; Tutte, Cavanagh, Kennedy
(Craney 73); Grimes (Putterill 62), Adebola, Donnelly.
*Morecambe:* (433) Roche; Parrish, McCready, Fenton,
Wright; McDonald, Drummond, Fleming; Reid,
Alessandra (Parkinson 90), Ellison.

**Slough T (0) 1** *(Bowden-Haase 66)*
**Mansfield T (1) 1** *(Woozley 45 (og))*
1593
*Slough T:* (352) Warrington; Brown, Bowden-Haase,
Woozley; Fraser, Burgess, Deeney D (Logie 35), Swift,
Rhone (Sinclair 62); Burnell (Sonner 81), Smith.
*Mansfield T:* (442) Redmond; Sutton, Geohaghon,
Dempster■, Beevers; Meikle (Daniel 106), Clements,
Howell, Briscoe; Hutchinson (Rhead 81), Wright
(Speight 57).
*aet; Mansfield T won 4-1 on penalties.*

**Walsall (0) 2** *(Taundry 81, Paterson 120)*
**Lincoln C (0) 3** *(Power 50, Oliver 102, 118)*        1762
*Walsall:* (442) Grof; Chambers J, Holden, Butler, Benning; Taundry (Jones 111), Chambers A, Featherstone, Paterson; Bowerman (Williams 70), Brandy (Hemmings 79).
*Lincoln C:* (4411) Farman; Gray (Bore 84), Boyce, Miller, Gilbert; Sheridan, Mills, Fofana, Smith A (Oliver 80); Power (Nutter 111); Taylor J.

Thursday, 15 November 2012
**Altrincham (0) 0**
**Burton Alb (0) 2** *(Palmer C 65, Zola 75)*        2428
*Altrincham:* (442) Coburn; Leather, Doughty, Havern, Hall; Watmore (Brooke 79), Moult, Richman, Clee (Lacey 79); Lawrie, Reeves.
*Burton Alb:* (433) Oxley; O'Connor, McCrory, Diamond, Holness; Bell, Weir (McGrath 84), Palmer C; Maghoma (Palmer M 90), Zola (Kee 84), Taylor.

## SECOND ROUND

Friday, 30 November 2012
**Bradford C (0) 1** *(Hanson 70)*
**Brentford (1) 1** *(Donaldson 43)*        3620
*Bradford C:* (442) Duke; Darby, Good, McArdle, Meredith; Turgott, Ravenhill (Jones G 61), Doyle, Thompson (Atkinson 61); Hanson, Connell (Wells 61).
*Brentford:* (442) Lee; Logan, Craig, Dean, Bidwell; Saunders (Barron 71), Forshaw, Diagouraga, Forrester (Dallas 76); Donaldson, Hayes (German 82).

Saturday, 1 December 2012
**Accrington S (1) 3** *(Lindfield 25, Beattie 80, Molyneux 90)*
**Oxford U (1) 3** *(Pittman 12, Constable 86, Raynes 90)*        1195
*Accrington S:* (442) Rachubka; Winnard, Murphy, Nsiala, Liddle; Lindfield (Mingoia 90), Joyce, Miller, Boco; Beattie (Gray 84), Amond (Molyneux 68).
*Oxford U:* (442) Clarke; Whing (Chapman 49), Raynes, Wright, Capaldi; Potter, Cox (Batt 46), Leven, Rigg; Constable, Pittman (Davis 45).

**Bury (1) 1** *(Doherty 33 (pen))*
**Southend U (1) 1** *(Tomlin 41)*        2391
*Bury:* (442) Carson; Doherty, Hughes, Ebanks-Landell, Skarz; Worrall, Thompson, Sweeney, Wylde; Hewitt (Carole 86), John-Lewis.
*Southend U:* (442) Smith; Clohessy, Cresswell, Phillips, Barker; Hurst, Timlin, Laird, Martin (Corr 78); Eastwood (Benyon 67), Tomlin.

**Carlisle U (0) 1** *(Beck 72)*
**Bournemouth (2) 3** *(Fogden 30, O'Kane 36, Pugh 90)*        2980
*Carlisle U:* (442) Collin; Simek (Gjokaj 46), Livesey, Edwards, Chantler; Symington (McGovern 46), Thirlwell, Potts, Robson (Welsh 56); Beck, Garner.
*Bournemouth:* (442) Jalal; Francis, Cook, Elphick, Daniels; Pugh, MacDonald (McQuoid 57), O'Kane, Fogden; Pitman (Partington 82), Grabban (Fletcher 90).

**Coventry C (1) 2** *(McSheffrey 38 (pen), Baker 46)*
**Morecambe (0) 1** *(Ellison 77)*        6339
*Coventry C:* (451) Dunn; Christie (Clarke J 86), Wood, Edjenguele, Adams; Baker, Jennings, Barton, Moussa, McSheffrey; O'Donovan.
*Morecambe:* (433) Roche; Wright, Fenton, McCready, Threlfall (Haining 88); McDonald (Reid 68), Drummond, Fleming; Alessandra, Redshaw (Parkinson 80), Ellison.

**Crawley T (2) 3** *(Adams 23, Clarke 41, Alexander 89 (pen))*
**Chelmsford (0) 0**        3012
*Crawley T:* (442) Jones P; Sadler, Connolly, Davis, Hunt; Torres, Akpan (Bulman 82), Simpson, Adams (Jones M 80); Clarke (Akinde 71), Alexander.
*Chelmsford:* (433) Searle; Brindley (Hamilton 77), Miller, Haines, Palmer; Cornhill, Rainford, Cook; Simmonds■, Slabber (Edmans 71), Welsh (Corcoran 68).

**Crewe Alex (0) 0**
**Burton Alb (1) 1** *(Zola 5)*        3065
*Crewe Alex:* (442) Martin; Tootle, Ellis, Robertson, Davis; Moore (Colclough 74), Murphy, Aneke (Clayton M 74), Osman; Pogba, Dalla Valle.
*Burton Alb:* (451) Lyness; McCrory, O'Connor, Holness, Webster; Maghoma (Taylor 81), Weir, Bell, Chapell (Dyer 75), Palmer C (McGrath 46); Zola.

**Fleetwood T (1) 2** *(Brown 11, Ball 88)*
**Aldershot T (2) 3** *(Hylton 19, 75, Vincenti 45)*        1757
*Fleetwood T:* (442) Davies; Beeley, McNulty (Howell 78), Marrow, Goodall; Johnson (Milligan 46), Ferguson, Nicholson (Gillespie 58), Brown; Ball, Barkhuizen.
*Aldershot T:* (442) Young; Herd, Brown, Bradley, Tonkin; Cadogan (Sinclair 81), Morris A, Hector, Vincenti; Reid (Payne 70), Hylton (Bergqvist 90).

**Harrogate T (1) 1** *(Platt 41)*
**Hastings U (0) 1** *(Crellin 61)*        2986
*Harrogate T:* (433) MacGillivray; Samuels, White, Killock, Merris; Platt, Bolder, Dean (Clayton 77); Chilaka, Beesley (Allan 77), Forrest (Elam 68).
*Hastings U:* (433) Armstrong-Ford; Cox, Ray, Jirbandey, Whitehead; Dixon, Carey, Crellin, Okojie (Ellis 51), Attwood, Goldburg.

**Lincoln C (1) 3** *(Power 45, 66, Taylor 47)*
**Mansfield T (1) 3** *(Green 21, Briscoe 53, Rhead 90)*        4414
*Lincoln C:* (4411) Farman; Gray, Boyce, Miller, Gilbert; Smith A (Oliver 87), Mills, Fofana, Sheridan; Power; Taylor J.
*Mansfield T:* (442) Redmond; Thompson, Dempster, Geohaghon, Beevers; Briscoe, Murray, Clements, Meikle (Rhead 84); Green, Hutchinson (Speight 72).

**Luton T (1) 2** *(Gray 30, Lawless 68)*
**Dorchester T (0) 1** *(Pugh 71)*        3287
*Luton T:* (442) Tyler; Henry, Beckwith (Lacey 64), Kovacs, Rowe-Turner; Lawless, O'Donnell (Mendy 89), Smith, Howells; Rendell, Gray (Fleetwood 80).
*Dorchester T:* (442) Matthews; Walker, Clough, Pugh, Jermyn (Thomson 71); Gosling, Gleeson, Nicholls, Martin; Choper-Nagarcia (Malsom 46), Watson.

**Oldham Ath (1) 3** *(Wabara 45, Derbyshire 70, 77)*
**Doncaster R (1) 1** *(Blake 4)*        2783
*Oldham Ath:* (442) Cisak; Brown, Mvoto, Wabara, Grounds; Croft, Furman, Wesolowski, Montano; Derbyshire, Baxter.
*Doncaster R:* (442) Woods G; Quinn, Jones R, Martis, Spurr; Syers (Woods Michael 88), Keegan, Clingan, Husband; Brown, Blake.

**Preston NE (2) 2** *(Monakana 12, Beavon 38)*
**Gillingham (0) 0**        5271
*Preston NE:* (442) Stuckmann; Kane, Robertson, Huntington, Cansdell-Sherriff; Monakana (Trundle 90), Wroe (King 46), Welsh, Holmes; Beavon, Mousinho (Procter 74).
*Gillingham:* (442) Forecast; Fish, Davies (Whelpdale 48), Barrett, Martin (Lee 46); Allen, Montrose, Weston, Vincelot; Birchall, Burton (Kedwell 68).

**Rotherham U (1) 1** *(Pringle 42)*
**Notts Co (1) 1** *(Arquin 32)*        7903
*Rotherham U:* (4231) Warrington; Bradley, Sharps, Mullins, Cameron; Taylor, O'Connor; Pringle, Frecklington, Nardiello; Revell.
*Notts Co:* (4141) Bialkowski; Kelly, Liddle, Bencherif, Sheehan; Mahon (Labadie 76); Hughes J, Bishop, Judge, Zoko; Arquin.

**Sheffield U (0) 2** *(Miller 90, 90)*
**Port Vale (1) 1** *(Pope 33)*        10,215
*Sheffield U:* (442) Long; Westlake, Maguire, Collins (Williams 46), Hill; Flynn, McAllister (Cofie 66), Doyle, Blackman; Miller, Porter (Cresswell 87).
*Port Vale:* (442) Neal; Duffy, McCombe, McDonald, Yates; Myrie-Williams (Dodds 75), Burge, James, Vincent (Taylor 85); Williamson (Andrew 75), Pope.

**Tranmere R (1) 2** *(Stockton 42, McGurk 57)*
**Chesterfield (1) 1** *(Cooper 31)* 3781
*Tranmere R:* (442) Fon Williams; Holmes, Goodison, Gibson, Bakayogo; McGurk, Wallace (Power 11), Harrison, Robinson (Thompson 77); Stockton, O'Halloran.
*Chesterfield:* (4411) Lee; Talbot, Hird, Cooper, Smith; Darikwa, Togwell, Clay (Randall 62), Boa Morte; Whitaker (Lester 62); Richards.

**Sunday, 2 December 2012**
**Alfreton T (1) 2** *(Clayton 4, Tomlinson 52)*
**Leyton Orient (3) 4** *(Cox 25, 86, Mooney 30, 36)* 1104
*Alfreton T:* (442) Stewart; Law, Kempson, Killock, Franklin; Meadows (Emerton 90), Bradley, Streete, Arnold; Clayton (Worsfold 90), Tomlinson (Denton 82).
*Leyton Orient:* (442) Allsop; Odubajo, Chorley, Baudry, Smith A (Cuthbert 87); Cox, Rowlands, James, Cook (Smith Jimmy 79); Lisbie (Brunt 90), Mooney.

**Milton Keynes D (1) 2** *(Gleeson 45, Otsemobor 90)*
**AFC Wimbledon (0) 1** *(Midson 59)* 16,459
*Milton Keynes D:* (4231) Martin; Otsemobor, Kay, Williams, Lewington; Gleeson, Potter; Bowditch, Chadwick (Doumbe 90), Balanta (Ismail 66); Lowe (Smith 80).
*AFC Wimbledon:* (442) Sullivan; Osano, Fenlon (Balkestein 90), Antwi, Mambo; Moore L (Johnson 80), Gregory, Long, Ajala; Harrison (Strutton 71), Midson.

**Monday, 3 December 2012**
**Cheltenham T (1) 1** *(Harrad 16)*
**Hereford U (1) 1** *(O'Keefe 20)* 5070
*Cheltenham T:* (4231) Brown; Lowe, Bennett, Elliott, Jones; Pack, Carter; McGlashan (Deering 78), Taylor Jake (Goulding 59), Mohamed; Harrad (Penn 59).
*Hereford U:* (451) Bittner; Gallinagh, Graham, Stam, Heath; Smikle (Marsh 78), Pell, Evans, O'Keefe, Clucas; Bowman.

**Tuesday, 18 December 2012**
**Barrow (1) 1** *(Baker 29)*
**Macclesfield T (1) 1** *(Charnock 19)* 1179
*Barrow:* (433) Hurst; Flynn, Hessey, Pearson M, Skelton; Owen, Harvey, Baker; Rutherford, McConville (Rowe Danny M 87), Boyes.
*Macclesfield T:* (442) Cronin; Jackson, Brown N, Charnock, Braham-Barrett; Mackreth (Mills P 73), Murtagh, Wedgbury, Kissock (Winn 88); Barnes-Homer (Morgan-Smith 82), Holroyd.

**SECOND ROUND REPLAYS**

**Tuesday, 11 December 2012**
**Hereford U (0) 1** *(Clucas 74)*
**Cheltenham T (1) 2** *(Harrad 45 (pen), Mohamed 114)* 5026
*Hereford U:* (451) Bittner; Gallinagh (Perry 115), Graham, Stam, Heath; Smikle, Pell, O'Keefe, Evans (Watkins 60), Clucas; Bowman (Marsh 16).
*Cheltenham T:* (442) Brown; Jombati, Bennett, Elliott, Jones; McGlashan (Pack 68), Penn (Mohamed 81), Carter, Zebroski; Harrad (Duffy 72), Taylor Jake.
*aet.*

**Southend U (0) 1** *(Tomlin 63)*
**Bury (0) 1** *(Thompson 59)* 3043
*Southend U:* (442) Bentley; Clohessy, Cresswell, Prosser, Barker; Hurst, Laird, Timlin, Martin (Eastwood 73); Tomlin, Corr (Benyon 116).
*Bury:* (541) Carson; Doherty, Sodje, Ebanks-Landell (Sweeney 77), Hughes, Skarz; Worrall, Schumacher, Thompson, Soares (Wylde 83); Bishop (Hewitt 65).
*aet; Southend U won 3-2 on penalties.*

**Wednesday, 12 December 2012**
**Mansfield T (1) 2** *(Farman 14 (og), Briscoe 77)*
**Lincoln C (1) 1** *(Smith 41)* 5304
*Mansfield T:* (442) Marriott; Beevers, Geohaghon, Dempster, Thompson (Sutton 46); Meikle, Howell, Clements, Briscoe; Green, Hutchinson (Rhead 61).

**Lincoln C:** (442) Farman; Gilbert, Boyce, Miller, Gray; Smith (Larkin 81), Mills (Oliver 80), Fofana, Sheridan (Robinson 86); Power, Taylor J.

**Thursday, 13 December 2012**
**Hastings U (0) 1** *(Carey 47 (pen))*
**Harrogate T (0) 1** *(Platt 90)* 4028
*Hastings U:* (442) Armstrong-Ford; Cox, Dixon, Ray, Jirbandey; Whitehead, Ellis, Carey, Goldburg (Okojie 82); Attwood, Vickers (Manning 72).
*Harrogate T:* (442) MacGillivray; Samuels, Killock, Bloomer, Merris; Bolder, Platt, Dean, Forrest (Elam 68); Chilaka (Hardy 61), Beesley (Allan 71).
*aet; Hastings U won 5-4 on penalties.*

**Tuesday, 18 December 2012**
**Brentford (1) 4** *(Trotta 45 (pen), 102, Donaldson 103, Forrester 106)*
**Bradford C (1) 2** *(Reid 34, Connell 94 (pen))* 2643
*Brentford:* (442) Gounet; Logan, Craig, Legge, Bidwell; Dallas (Donaldson 78), Douglas, Adeyemi (Diagouraga 64), Saunders (Forrester 71); Hayes, Trotta.
*Bradford C:* (442) McLaughlin; Jones R, McArdle, McHugh, Bass (Curtis 106); Turgott, Ravenhill, Brown, Reid (Thompson 56); Hines (Baker 67), Connell.
*aet.*

**Notts Co (0) 0**
**Rotherham U (3) 3** *(Pringle 9, Bradley 22, Nardiello 41)* 2990
*Notts Co:* (433) Mitchell; Kelly, Liddle, Stewart[■], Sheehan; Bishop, Boucaud (Labadie 46); Hughes J (Zoko 46); Campbell-Ryce, Arquin (Showunmi 46), Judge.
*Rotherham U:* (442) Warrington; Bradley, Mullins, Arnason, O'Connell (Cameron 74); Frecklington, Taylor (Rose 86), O'Connor, Pringle; Revell, Nardiello (Walker 90).

**Oxford U (0) 2** *(Constable 66, Leven 79)*
**Accrington S (0) 0** 2566
*Oxford U:* (442) Clarke; Batt, Wright, Raynes, Davis; Potter, Chapman (Cox 16), Leven, Rigg (Duberry 90); Constable, Craddock (Capaldi 80).
*Accrington S:* (442) Rachubka; Nsiala, Winnard (Amond 46), Murphy (Dixon 54), Liddle; Lindfield, Clark, Joyce, Molyneux; Beattie (Mingoia 62), Boco.

**Saturday, 29 December 2012**
**Macclesfield T (2) 4** *(Kissock 7, Holroyd 16, 69, Barnes-Homer 67)*
**Barrow (1) 1** *(Boyes 17)* 1554
*Macclesfield T:* (442) Cronin; Jackson, Brown N, Martin, Braham-Barrett; Mackreth (Winn 72), Murtagh, Wedgbury, Kissock; Barnes-Homer (Henry 85), Holroyd (Morgan-Smith 80).
*Barrow:* (442) Hurst; Flynn (Jackson 77), Hessey, Pearson M, Skelton; Rutherford, Owen, Harvey, McConville (Rowe 73); Almond, Boyes.

**THIRD ROUND**

**Saturday, 5 January 2013**
**Aldershot T (2) 3** *(Hylton 6, 23, 62)*
**Rotherham U (0) 1** *(Frecklington 71 (pen))* 2992
*Aldershot T:* (4141) Young; Herd, Brown, Hector, Tonkin; Morris A; Cadogan (Mekki 83), Rose, Bradley, Vincenti; Hylton[■].
*Rotherham U:* (4231) Warrington; Bradley, Arnason[■], Mullins, O'Connell; Pringle, Taylor; O'Connor (Morgan A 46), Frecklington, Nardiello (Cameron 46); Revell (Odejayi 60).

**Aston Villa (0) 2** *(Bent 46, Weimann 83)*
**Ipswich T (1) 1** *(Chopra 31)* 24,854
*Aston Villa:* (442) Given; Lichaj, Clark, Baker, Bennett; Albrighton (Weimann 43), Bannan, Delph, N'Zogbia (Ireland 70); Bowery (Agbonlahor 62), Bent.
*Ipswich T:* (442) Loach; Hewitt, Kisnorbo, Smith, Cresswell; Martin, Reo-Coker, Hyam, Emmanuel-Thomas (McGoldrick 60); Chopra (Mclean 74), Murphy (Edwards 70).

**Barnsley (0) 1** *(Rose 85)*
**Burnley (0) 0**      5091
*Barnsley:* (442) Steele; Stones, Cranie, McNulty, Kennedy (Cywka 68); O'Brien, Dawson, Perkins, Golbourne; Harewood (Noble-Lazarus 85), Dagnall (Rose 82).
*Burnley:* (4411) Jensen; Trippier, Duff (Bartley 83), Shackell, Lafferty; Ings, Marney, Stock■, Treacy (Edgar 46); Wallace (Richards 69); Vokes.

**Blackburn R (1) 2** *(Murphy 7, Hanley G 58)*
**Bristol C (0) 0**      5504
*Blackburn R:* (442) Kean; Henley (Vukcevic 35), Hanley G, Dann, Olsson Martin; Rosado (King 77), Lowe (Pedersen 63), Murphy, Rochina; Rhodes, Kazim-Richards.
*Bristol C:* (352) Heaton; Wilson J, Carey, Fontaine; Wilson M (Reid 63), Cunningham (Woolford 70), Skuse, Pearson, Anderson; Stead (Davies 59), Taylor.

**Bolton W (1) 2** *(Lee 12, Sordell 49)*
**Sunderland (0) 2** *(Wickham 60, Gardner 75)*      12,204
*Bolton W:* (442) Lonergan; Riley (Mears 36), Knight, Ricketts, Alonso; Lee, Pratley, Andrews, Petrov; Ngog (Eagles 81), Sordell (Davies K 64).
*Sunderland:* (451) Mignolet; Bardsley, Bramble, Cuellar (Wickham 57), Rose (Colback 20); Johnson, Larsson, Gardner, Vaughan, McClean; Fletcher.

**Brighton & HA (1) 2** *(Orlandi 33, Hoskins 87)*
**Newcastle U (0) 0**      21,740
*Brighton & HA:* (433) Ankergren; Lopez, Greer, El-Abd, Bridge; Bridcutt, Hammond (Crofts 83), Orlandi (LuaLua 60); Barnes, Mackail-Smith (Hoskins 71), Dicker.
*Newcastle U:* (433) Elliot; Tavernier, Perch (Dummett 46), Williamson, Santon; Anita, Abeid (Ranger 46), Bigirimana; Obertan (Marveaux 71), Ameobi Shola■, Ameobi Sam.

**Charlton Ath (0) 0**
**Huddersfield T (1) 1** *(Beckford 11)*      6657
*Charlton Ath:* (442) Button; Wilson, Dervite■, Taylor, Evina; Cook (Morrison 59), Stephens, Pritchard, Kerkar (Jackson 78); Kermorgant, Wright-Phillips (Azeez 78).
*Huddersfield T:* (442) Smithies; Hunt, Clarke P, Gerrard, Dixon; Arfield, Norwood, Clayton, Scannell; Vaughan, Beckford (Novak 83).

**Crawley T (1) 1** *(Adams 1)*
**Reading (2) 3** *(Le Fondre 13, 49 (pen), Hunt 44)*      5880
*Crawley T:* (442) Jones P; Sadler, Walsh, Connolly, Hunt (Akinde 82); Adams, Simpson, Akpan, Jones M (Elford-Alliyu 68); Clarke, Alexander.
*Reading:* (442) Federici; Cummings, Pearce, Morrison, Harte; McCleary (Gunter 85), Karacan (Guthrie 59), Tabb, Robson-Kanu; Hunt, Le Fondre.

**Crystal Palace (0) 0**
**Stoke C (0) 0**      13,693
*Crystal Palace:* (442) Price; Parr, Ramage, Delaney, Moxey; Zaha (Williams 55), Jedinak, O'Keefe, Bolasie (Banton 68); Moritz, Easter (Appiah 66).
*Stoke C:* (442) Sorensen; Shotton, Huth, Shawcross, Cameron; Kightly (Jerome 54), Walters, Whitehead, Nzonzi; Crouch (Jones 74), Owen (Adam 53).

**Derby Co (1) 5** *(Davies B 42, Sammon 54, Brayford 63, Hendrick 72, Bennett 87)*
**Tranmere R (0) 0**      11,740
*Derby Co:* (442) Legzdins; Brayford, O'Brien, Keogh, Roberts (Freeman 74); Coutts (Doyle 79), Hughes, Hendrick, Davies B (Bennett 84); Jacobs, Sammon.
*Tranmere R:* (442) Fon Williams; Holmes, Taylor, Daniels, Bakayogo; McGurk, Palmer, Power, Robinson (Black 74); O'Halloran, Stockton.

**Fulham (0) 1** *(Karagounis 80)*
**Blackpool (0) 1** *(Sylvestre 60)*      14,473
*Fulham:* (4411) Stockdale; Riether, Hughes, Hangeland, Briggs (Frei 72); Dejagah (Rodallega 54), Karagounis, Sidwell, Kacaniklic (Richardson 70); Ruiz; Berbatov.

*Blackpool:* (433) Gilks; Eardley, Baptiste, Broadfoot, Harris (Crainey 82); Basham, Osbourne, Sylvestre; Ince, Phillips K (Eccleston 90), Delfouneso.

**Hull C (0) 1** *(Proschwitz 90)*
**Leyton Orient (0) 1** *(Mooney 78)*      8585
*Hull C:* (442) Jakupovic; Rosenior, McShane, Bruce, Dawson; Stewart (Cullen 90), McKenna (Wilson 76), Olofinjana, Cairney; Simpson, Proschwitz.
*Leyton Orient:* (442) Jones; McSweeney, Chorley, Baudry, Cox (Smith Jimmy 88); Odubajo, Rowlands, James, Cook; Lisbie, Mooney.

**Leeds U (0) 1** *(Becchio 60)*
**Birmingham C (1) 1** *(Elliott 33)*      11,447
*Leeds U:* (442) Ashdown; Lees, Pearce, Tate (Somma 79), Drury; Hall (Byram 46), Brown, Norris, White (Diouf 46); McCormack, Becchio.
*Birmingham C:* (442) Doyle; Packwood (Hancox 66), Caldwell, Davies, Robinson; Burke, Gomis, Reilly, Elliott; Morrison (Hales 85), Redmond.

**Leicester C (2) 2** *(Wood 3, De Laet 21)*
**Burton Alb (0) 0**      14,463
*Leicester C:* (442) Schmeichel; De Laet, Morgan, Keane, Konchesky; Marshall (Knockaert 62), King, James, Dyer; Futacs (Waghorn 75), Wood (Nugent 63).
*Burton Alb:* (442) Lyness; Stanton, Holness, Webster, McCrory; Drury (Phillips 73), Weir, Bell, McGrath (Taylor 62); Maghoma, Zola (Kee 73).

**Luton T (0) 1** *(Lawless 46)*
**Wolverhampton W (0) 0**      9638
*Luton T:* (442) Tyler; Henry, Taylor, Kovacs, Rowe-Turner; Lawless, Mendy, Smith, O'Donnell (Fleetwood 77); Shaw, Gray (Rendell 90).
*Wolverhampton W:* (442) Ikeme; Foley (Davis 75), Forde (Peszko 67), Johnson, Berra; Sako, Henry, O'Hara, Ward; Doyle (Cassidy 68), Ebanks-Blake.

**Macclesfield T (0) 2** *(Barnes-Homer 85, 88 (pen))*
**Cardiff C (0) 1** *(Jarvis 57)*      3165
*Macclesfield T:* (442) Cronin; Martin (Winn 66), Brown N, Mills P, Braham-Barrett; Henry (Mackreth 61), Murtagh, Wedgbury, Kissock; Barnes-Homer, Morgan-Smith (Fairhurst 71).
*Cardiff C:* (442) Lewis; McNaughton (Coulson 58), Oshilaja, Nugent, John; Harris (O'Sullivan 64), Kiss (Wharton 72), McPhail, Ralls; Velikonja, Jarvis.

**Manchester C (2) 3** *(Tevez 25, Barry 44, Lopes 90)*
**Watford (0) 0**      46,821
*Manchester C:* (433) Pantilimon; Zabaleta, Kompany, Lescott, Clichy; Milner, Javi Garcia (Sinclair 74), Barry; Silva (Lopes 88), Dzeko (Balotelli 70), Tevez.
*Watford:* (451) Bond; Doyley, Nosworthy, Ekstrand, Cassetti; Forestieri (Mujangi Bia 63), Eustace (Battocchio 85), Chalobah, Pudil (Neuton 46), Vydra; Deeney.

**Middlesbrough (1) 4** *(Zemmama 22, Halliday 47, Zemmama 68, Miller 85)*
**Hastings U (0) 1** *(Goldburg 69)*      12,579
*Middlesbrough:* (442) Steele; Halliday, Williams R, Bailey, Parnaby (Haroun 73); Zemmama (Morris 82), Smallwood, Thomson, Reach; Miller, Williams L (Jones 61).
*Hastings U:* (442) O'Brien; Whitehead, Vickers (Ellis 52), Ray, Cox (Manning 72); Carey, Jirbandey, Crellin, Dixon (Okojie 77); Camara, Goldburg.

**Millwall (1) 1** *(Feeney 31)*
**Preston NE (0) 0**      5364
*Millwall:* (442) Forde; Smith A, Osborne, Beevers, Lowry; Henry, Wright, Abdou, Feeney (Batt 46); N'Guessan, Henderson (Smith J 87).
*Preston NE:* (451) Simonsen; Robertson, Huntington, Cansdell-Sherriff (Byrom 46), Buchanan; Kane (Amoo 46), Wroe, Welsh, Mousinho (Cummins 81), King; Beavon.

**Nottingham F (1) 2** *(Smith 13 (og), Sharp 90)*
**Oldham Ath (0) 3** *(Simpson R 54, 58, Baxter 61)*    11,293
*Nottingham F:* (442) Camp; Moloney, Halford, Collins■,
Harding; Cohen, Gillett, Majewski (Sharp 66), Reid
(McGugan 37); Blackstock, Cox.
*Oldham Ath:* (442) Bouzanis; Wabara, Byrne, Mvoto,
Grounds; Croft (Millar 90), Furman, Simpson R (Taylor
81), M'Changama; Baxter, Smith M.

**Oxford U (0) 0**
**Sheffield U (1) 3** *(McMahon 17, Kitson 68, Blackman 87)*
                                            7079
*Oxford U:* (442) Clarke; Batt, Duberry, Wright, O'Brien
(Rigg 67); Potter, Heslop, Leven, Capaldi; Craddock,
Richards.
*Sheffield U:* (451) Long; McMahon, Maguire,
Higginbotham, Hill (Williams 12); Blackman, Doyle,
McDonald, Murphy (Cresswell 88), Flynn; Kitson
(Ironside 76).

**Peterborough U (0) 0**
**Norwich C (2) 3** *(Bennett E 30, Jackson 41, Snodgrass 70)*
                                    13,198
*Peterborough U:* (352) Olejnik; Alcock (Gordon 34),
Brisley, Knight-Percival (Ajose 46); Little, Ferdinand,
Bostwick, Newell, Rowe; Swanson (McCann 54), Boyd.
*Norwich C:* (442) Rudd; Martin R, Barnett, Bennett R,
Tierney; Bennett E, Fox, Johnson, Lappin; Snodgrass
(Butterfield 72), Jackson.

**QPR (0) 1** *(Dyer 90)*
**WBA (0) 1** *(Long 79)*                        8984
*QPR:* (4231) Julio Cesar; Dyer, Ben Haim, Nelsen
(Onuoha 71), Hill; Mbia, Granero (Bothroyd 46);
Mackie, Taarabt, Park; Campbell.
*WBA:* (4411) Myhill; Jones, Tamas, McAuley, Ridgewell;
Gera (Fortune 21 (Thomas 45)), Thorne, Brunt,
Morrison; Long; Lukaku (Dawson 88).

**Sheffield W (0) 0**
**Milton Keynes D (0) 0**                      11,462
*Sheffield W:* (442) Bywater; Buxton, Taylor, Llera,
Mattock; Lee, McCabe (Semedo 87), Prutton, Antonio;
Maguire (Johnson J 68), Sidibe (Madine 55).
*Milton Keynes D:* (4231) Martin; Doumbe, Williams,
Kay, Lewington; Potter, Harley, Ismail (Alli 67), Smith
(MacKenzie 71), Chicksen; Lowe (Rasulo 90).

**Southampton (1) 1** *(Rodriguez 22)*
**Chelsea (2) 5** *(Ba 35, 61, Moses 45, Ivanovic 52,*
*Lampard 83 (pen))*                      27,813
*Southampton:* (451) Boruc; Cork, Fonte (Hooiveld 63),
Yoshida, Shaw; Puncheon (Lee 78), Davis S, Schneiderlin
(De Ridder 54), Ward-Prowse, Do Prado; Rodriguez.
*Chelsea:* (451) Turnbull; Azpilicueta, Ivanovic (Lampard
65), Cahill, Cole; Ramires, Luiz, Mata (Oscar 79),
Hazard, Moses (Marin 73); Ba.

**Southend U (1) 2** *(Corr 39, 54)*
**Brentford (2) 2** *(Adeyemi 29, Cresswell 38 (og))*    5540
*Southend U:* (442) Smith; Clohessy, Phillips, Cresswell,
Prosser; Hurst, Woodyard, Laird, Timlin; Tomlin, Corr
(Benyon 78).
*Brentford:* (442) Moore; Hodson, Craig, Dean, Bidwell;
Saunders (Forrester 68), Adeyemi (Reeves 78), Douglas,
Forshaw; Donaldson, Hayes (Trotta 71).

**Tottenham H (3) 3** *(Dempsey 14, 37, Bale 33)*
**Coventry C (0) 0**                         35,766
*Tottenham H:* (433) Friedel; Naughton, Dawson,
Caulker, Assou-Ekotto; Huddlestone, Parker (Dembele
80), Sigurdsson (Carroll 79); Dempsey, Adebayor, Bale
(Townsend 70).
*Coventry C:* (4411) Murphy; Adams, Edjenguele, Wood,
Clarke J; Baker, Jennings (Fleck 71), Bailey (Thomas
59), McSheffrey, Moussa (Barton 50); Clarke L.

**West Ham U (1) 2** *(Collins 27, 59)*
**Manchester U (1) 2** *(Cleverley 23, van Persie 90)*    32,922
*West Ham U:* (433) Jaaskelainen; Demel, Collins,

Tomkins, Potts; Cole J (Taylor 78), Collison, Nolan; Vaz
Te (Jarvis 61), Cole C, Diarra (Noble 73).
*Manchester U:* (442) De Gea; Smalling (Giggs 78), Evans,
Vidic, Buttner; Da Silva, Scholes (Valencia 68),
Cleverley, Kagawa; Hernandez (van Persie 68), Welbeck.

**Wigan Ath (0) 1** *(Gomez 70)*
**Bournemouth (1) 1** *(O'Kane 41)*            8199
*Wigan Ath:* (343) Pollitt; Boyce, Golobart, Figueroa;
Stam, Fyvie (McArthur 79), Jones (Dicko 79), Redmond
(Henriquez 46); Gomez, Boselli, McManaman.
*Bournemouth:* (442) Jalal; Francis, Elphick, Cook,
Daniels; McQuoid (Pitman 88), O'Kane, Arter, Pugh;
Tubbs (Fogden 66), Hughes (Partington 90).

### Sunday, 6 January 2013
**Mansfield T (0) 1** *(Green 79)*
**Liverpool (1) 2** *(Sturridge 7, Suarez 59)*       7574
*Mansfield T:* (451) Marriott; Thompson, Dempster,
Geohaghon, Beevers; Meikle, Clements (Rhead 81),
Murray, Howell, Briscoe (Daniel 64); Green.
*Liverpool:* (433) Jones; Wisdom (Flanagan 79), Coates,
Carragher, Robinson; Lucas, Allen, Shelvey; Suso
(Henderson 55), Sturridge (Suarez 55), Downing.

**Swansea C (0) 2** *(Michu 58, Graham 87)*
**Arsenal (0) 2** *(Podolski 81, Gibbs 83)*      18,848
*Swansea C:* (451) Vorm; Tiendalli, Chico, Bartley,
Davies; Dyer, Britton (Agustien 69), de Guzman (Michu
56), Ki, Routledge (Hernandez 56); Graham.
*Arsenal:* (433) Szczesny; Sagna, Mertesacker, Koscielny,
Gibbs; Arteta, Wilshere, Ramsey (Podolski 72); Walcott,
Giroud, Cazorla.

### Monday, 7 January 2013
**Cheltenham T (0) 1** *(Penn 51)*
**Everton (2) 5** *(Jelavic 12, Baines 21 (pen), Osman 49,*
*Coleman 58, Fellaini 89)*                 6891
*Cheltenham T:* (4411) Brown; Jombati, Bennett, Elliott,
Jones; McGlashan (Deering 80), Pack, Carter (Taylor
Jake 66), Mohamed; Penn; Goulding (Duffy 66).
*Everton:* (4231) Howard; Coleman, Jagielka, Distin,
Baines (Gueye 63); Neville, Osman (Naismith 68);
Anichebe, Fellaini, Oviedo; Jelavic (Hitzlsperger 80).

---

### THIRD ROUND REPLAYS

### Tuesday, 15 January 2013
**Birmingham C (1) 1** *(Elliott 36)*
**Leeds U (0) 2** *(McCormack 70, Diouf 76 (pen))*    8962
*Birmingham C:* (442) Doyle; Caddis, Caldwell, Davies,
Robinson; Burke, Morrison (Lovenkrands 77), Gomis,
Elliott; Redmond (Zigic 83), King.
*Leeds U:* (442) Ashdown; Byram, Peltier, Lees, Drury
(White 11); Green, Austin, Brown, Varney; Diouf
(Pearce 90), McCormack.

**Blackpool (0) 1** *(Delfouneso 82)*
**Fulham (0) 2** *(Richardson 90, Hangeland 116)*    8706
*Blackpool:* (433) Gilks; Eardley, Broadfoot, Baptiste,
Crainey; Osbourne (Sylvestre 78), Basham (Cathcart 89),
Taylor-Fletcher; Ince, Delfouneso, Eccleston (Gomes
65).
*Fulham:* (442) Schwarzer; Riether, Hangeland, Senderos
(Hughes 71), Briggs; Kacaniklic (Richardson 87),
Karagounis, Baird, Dejagah; Petric (Duff 79), Rodallega.
*aet.*

**Bournemouth (0) 0**
**Wigan Ath (1) 1** *(Boselli 18)*             8890
*Bournemouth:* (4141) Jalal; Francis, Elphick, Cook,
Daniels; Hughes (Tubbs 80); McQuoid (Fogden 66),
O'Kane, Arter, Grabban (Pugh 34); Thomas.
*Wigan Ath:* (433) Pollitt (Al Habsi 46); Stam, Boyce,
Golobart, Figueroa; Fyvie, Gomez, Espinoza;
McManaman (Dicko 60), Boselli (Mustoe 90),
Henriquez.

**Brentford (1) 2** *(Hayes 26, Donaldson 76)*
**Southend U (0) 1** *(Corr 69)*    6526
*Brentford:* (433) Moore; Hodson, Craig, Dean, Bidwell; Diagouraga, Douglas, Forshaw (Saunders 90); Donaldson, Hayes (Trotta 75), Forrester (Barron 79).
*Southend U:* (442) Smith; Clohessy, Cresswell (Woodyard 48), Phillips, Barker; Hurst (Leonard 68), Timlin, Prosser, Straker (Harris 89); Corr, Tomlin.

**Leyton Orient (0) 1** *(Cox 87)*
**Hull C (1) 2** *(Proschwitz 41, Cairney 117)*   3601
*Leyton Orient:* (451) Jones; Odubajo, Chorley, Baudry (Cuthbert 46), Sawyer; Smith Jimmy (Symes 59), Rowlands, James, Cook (McSweeney 79), Cox; Mooney.
*Hull C:* (352) Jakupovic; Chester, Bruce, McShane; Rosenior, Cairney, Evans, Quinn (Stewart 78), Dawson (Olofinjana 83); Simpson, Proschwitz.
*aet.*

**Milton Keynes D (1) 2** *(Williams 28 (pen), Bowditch 75)*
**Sheffield W (0) 0**    6786
*Milton Keynes D:* (451) Martin; Otsemobor, MacKenzie (Doumbe 72), Kay, Lewington; Powell (Alli 88), Smith, Potter, Williams, Bowditch (Chicksen 78); Lowe.
*Sheffield W:* (442) Bywater; Buxton, Llera, Taylor, Mattock; Lee (Antonio 62), Semedo, Corry, Pecnik (O'Grady 54); Madine, Johnson J (Mayor 13).

**Stoke C (0) 4** *(Jones 69, Walters 95, 110, Jerome 120)*
**Crystal Palace (0) 1** *(Murray 87 (pen))*   11,617
*Stoke C:* (442) Sorensen; Cameron, Shawcross, Huth, Wilkinson (Whelan 37); Kightly (Jerome 55), Whitehead, Nzonzi, Etherington; Walters, Crouch (Jones 63).
*Crystal Palace:* (451) Price; Ramage, Delaney, Gabbidon (Murray 79), Parsons; Zaha (Bolasie 46), Jedinak, Williams, Boateng (Moritz 65), Easter; Wilbraham.
*aet.*

**Sunderland (0) 0**
**Bolton W (0) 2** *(Sordell 64 (pen), 73)*   17,505
*Sunderland:* (4411) Mignolet; Bardsley, Kilgallon, Bramble, Colback (Cattermole 76); Johnson (Larsson 71), Vaughan, Gardner, McClean; Sessegnon; Wickham (Campbell 71).
*Bolton W:* (4231) Lonergan; Mears, Knight, Ricketts, Alonso; Vela (Holden 74), Spearing; Afobe (Lee 70), Pratley, Eagles; Sordell (Davies K 85).

**WBA (0) 0**
**QPR (0) 1** *(Bothroyd 75)*   11,184
*WBA:* (442) Myhill; Jones, McAuley, Tamas (El Ghanassy 81), Popov; Dorrans, Morrison (Reid 90), Thorne, Thomas (Odemwingie 71); Lukaku, Rosenberg.
*QPR:* (442) Green; Onuoha, Hill, Ferdinand, Ben Haim; Mackie (Taarabt 90), Park, Derry, Faurlin; Bothroyd (Mbia 80), Cisse (Wright-Phillips 46).

Wednesday, 16 January 2013

**Arsenal (0) 1** *(Wilshere 86)*
**Swansea C (0) 0**    58,359
*Arsenal:* (4231) Szczesny; Sagna, Mertesacker, Vermaelen, Gibbs; Diaby (Ramsey 82), Coquelin; Walcott, Wilshere, Cazorla; Giroud.
*Swansea C:* (4231) Vorm; Bartley, Richards, Chico, Tiendalli; Agustien (Hernandez 59), Britton; Routledge, de Guzman (Ki 60), Dyer; Graham (Michu 71).

**Manchester U (1) 1** *(Rooney 9)*
**West Ham U (0) 0**    71,081
*Manchester U:* (442) Lindegaard; Da Silva, Jones, Smalling, Buttner; Valencia, Anderson (Carrick 67), Giggs, Nani (Scholes 77); Rooney, Hernandez.
*West Ham U:* (442) Jaaskelainen; Spence, Reid, Tomkins, Potts; O'Neil, Diarra, Diame (Collison 65), Taylor; Vaz Te (Lee 78), Cole C (Nolan 65).

## FOURTH ROUND

Friday, 25 January 2013

**Millwall (1) 2** *(Shittu 27, Marquis 89)*
**Aston Villa (1) 1** *(Bent 22)*    15,007
*Millwall:* (442) Forde; Smith A, Shittu, Osborne, Beevers; Henry, Trotter, Abdou, Feeney; Marquis (Smith J 90), Keogh (N'Guessan 82).
*Aston Villa:* (352) Given; Vlaar, Clark, Lichaj; Lowton, Westwood, Delph (Bannan 39), N'Zogbia, Bennett; Bent, Weimann (Bowery 81).

Saturday, 26 January 2013

**Bolton W (1) 1** *(Sordell 27)*
**Everton (1) 2** *(Pienaar 18, Heitinga 90)*   18,760
*Bolton W:* (4231) Lonergan; Ricketts, Knight, Ream, Alonso; Spearing, Vela (Holden 81); Lee, Pratley, Eagles (Afobe 74); Sordell (Ngog 85).
*Everton:* (4312) Howard; Neville, Jagielka, Distin, Baines; Mirallas (Gueye 17), Osman, Pienaar; Fellaini; Jelavic (Heitinga 80), Anichebe.

**Brighton & HA (1) 2** *(Barnes 33, Ulloa 62)*
**Arsenal (1) 3** *(Giroud 16, 56, Walcott 85)*   27,113
*Brighton & HA:* (433) Ankergren; Calderon, El-Abd, Bridge, Greer (Dicker 37); Lopez, Bridcutt, Hammond; Barnes, Ulloa (Mackail-Smith 73), Buckley (LuaLua 46).
*Arsenal:* (433) Szczesny; Jenkinson, Mertesacker, Andre Santos (Gibbs 78), Koscielny; Diaby, Rosicky (Wilshere 68), Ramsey; Oxlade-Chamberlain (Walcott 68), Giroud, Podolski.

**Derby Co (0) 0**
**Blackburn R (1) 3** *(Kazim-Richards 44, Dann 66, Rhodes 71)*   14,013
*Derby Co:* (442) Legzdins; Brayford, Roberts, Bryson, Keogh; Coutts, Hendrick, Ward (Jacobs 73), O'Brien (O'Connor 82); Hughes (Davies B 75), Sammon.
*Blackburn R:* (451) Kean; Olsson Martin, Dann, Hanley G, Lowe; Pedersen, Murphy, Olsson Marcus (Dunn 83), Kazim-Richards, King (Rochina 10); Rhodes.

**Huddersfield T (0) 1** *(Novak 74 (pen))*
**Leicester C (0) 1** *(Wood 82)*    11,945
*Huddersfield T:* (442) Smithies; Hunt, Clarke P, Gerrard, Woods; Clayton, Norwood, Sinnott (Scannell 66), Arfield; Novak (Lee 81), Vaughan.
*Leicester C:* (442) Schmeichel; De Laet, Morgan, Keane, Konchesky; Marshall, King, Wellens (Drinkwater 69), Dyer; Waghorn (Wood 60), Vardy (Nugent 60).

**Hull C (0) 0**
**Barnsley (0) 1** *(Dagnall 70)*    9932
*Hull C:* (352) Jakupovic; Chester, Bruce (Stewart 72), McShane; Rosenior, Olofinjana (Simpson 60), Meyler, Quinn, Brady; Koren, Proschwitz.
*Barnsley:* (352) Steele; Hassell, Cranie, Kennedy; Wiseman (Stones 65), Perkins, Mellis (O'Brien 58), Etuhu, Golbourne; Dagnall (Foster 75), Harewood.

**Macclesfield T (0) 0**
**Wigan Ath (1) 1** *(Gomez 7 (pen))*    5849
*Macclesfield T:* (442) Anyon; Jackson, Brown N, Audel, Braham-Barrett; Mackreth, Murtagh, Wedgbury, Kissock (Winn 78); Fairhurst (McDonald 76), Barnes-Homer.
*Wigan Ath:* (4231) Robles; Stam, Figueroa, Golobart, Mustoe; Espinoza, Fyvie (Jones 53); Dicko (Lopez 66), Gomez, McManaman; Henriquez.

**Manchester U (1) 4** *(Giggs 3 (pen), Rooney 50, Hernandez 52, 66)*
**Fulham (0) 1** *(Hughes 77)*    72,596
*Manchester U:* (4411) De Gea; Da Silva, Jones, Smalling, Evra; Nani, Anderson (Kagawa 71), Carrick (Scholes 61), Giggs (Valencia 71); Rooney; Hernandez.
*Fulham:* (4411) Schwarzer; Riether, Hughes, Hangeland, Riise; Kacaniklic, Sidwell, Baird (Karagounis 46), Duff (Rodallega 61); Ruiz (Dejagah 70); Berbatov.

**Middlesbrough (0) 2** *(Jutkiewicz 83, 90)*
**Aldershot T (0) 1** *(Hylton 89)*      12,684
*Middlesbrough:* (352) Steele; Bikey, Williams R, Hines (Leadbitter 78); Parnaby, Reach, Zemmama, Bailey, Smallwood (Halliday 61); Emnes (Ledesma 61), Jutkiewicz.
*Aldershot T:* (442) Young; Herd, Brown, Bradley, Morris A; Cadogan (Mekki 78), Hector (Rankine 87), Rose, Vincenti; Hylton, Reid (Risser 69).

**Norwich C (0) 0**
**Luton T (0) 1** *(Rendell 80)*      26,521
*Norwich C:* (442) Rudd; Martin R, Barnett, Bennett R, Garrido; Bennett E (Pilkington 73), Fox, Howson, Surman (Hoolahan 72); Jackson, Kane (Holt 46).
*Luton T:* (442) Tyler; Henry, Kovacs, Rowe-Turner, Taylor; Lawless, Mendy (O'Donnell 68), Smith, Howells; Shaw (Rendell 74), Gray (Fleetwood 75).

**QPR (0) 2** *(Bothroyd 83, Da Silva 90)*
**Milton Keynes D (2) 4** *(Traore 4 (og), Lowe 40,*
*Harley 50, Potter 56)*      17,081
*QPR:* (442) Green; Da Silva, Ben Haim, Ferdinand, Traore; Mackie, Faurlin, Granero, Park (Zamora 67); Bothroyd, Campbell.
*Milton Keynes D:* (4231) Martin; Otsemobor, MacKenzie (Harley 20), Kay, Lewington; Williams, Potter; Chicksen, Smith (Lines 75), Bowditch (Alli 90); Lowe.

**Reading (2) 4** *(Hunt 6, 50, Leigertwood 40, McCleary 54)*
**Sheffield U (0) 0**      14,715
*Reading:* (442) Federici; Kelly, Mariappa, Morrison, Shorey; McCleary, Leigertwood (Guthrie 84), Karacan, Robson-Kanu; Hunt, Le Fondre.
*Sheffield U:* (442) Long; Westlake (Collins 76), Higginbotham, Maguire, McMahon; Blackman, McDonald (Whitehouse 69), Doyle, Murphy; Porter (Flynn 60), Kitson.

**Stoke C (0) 0**
**Manchester C (0) 1** *(Zabaleta 85)*      19,814
*Stoke C:* (442) Sorensen; Shotton, Shawcross, Huth, Wilkinson (Whitehead 73); Kightly (Jerome 67), Whelan, Nzonzi, Etherington; Walters, Jones (Crouch 73).
*Manchester C:* (442) Pantilimon; Zabaleta, Kompany (Clichy 40), Lescott, Kolarov (Aguero 62); Milner, Barry, Javi Garcia, Silva; Tevez (Rodwell 87), Dzeko.

Sunday, 27 January 2013

**Brentford (1) 2** *(Trotta 42, Forrester 73 (pen))*
**Chelsea (0) 2** *(Oscar 55, Torres 83)*      12,146
*Brentford:* (433) Moore; Hodson, Craig, Dean, Logan; Forshaw (Saunders 84), Douglas, Diagouraga; Donaldson, Trotta (Adeyemi 70), Forrester (Barron 80).
*Chelsea:* (4231) Turnbull; Ivanovic (Azpilicueta 79), Cahill, Terry, Cole; Ramires, Lampard, Marin (Mata 46), Oscar, Bertrand (Ba 82); Torres.

**Leeds U (1) 2** *(Varney 15, McCormack 50)*
**Tottenham H (0) 1** *(Dempsey 58)*      29,943
*Leeds U:* (442) Ashdown; Byram, Lees, Peltier, White; Green, Austin, Brown, Varney; Diouf (Pearce 90), McCormack (Somma 90).
*Tottenham H:* (4231) Friedel; Naughton (Walker 66), Caulker, Vertonghen, Assou-Ekotto; Huddlestone (Dembele 59), Lennon; Parker, Sigurdsson (Obika 59), Bale; Dempsey.

**Oldham Ath (2) 3** *(Smith M 2, 45, Wabara 48)*
**Liverpool (1) 2** *(Suarez 17, Allen 79)*      10,295
*Oldham Ath:* (4411) Bouzanis; Wabara, Mvoto, Byrne, Grounds; Croft, Wesolowski, M'Changama (Winchester 10), Simpson R (Taylor 77); Baxter; Smith M (Mellor 84).
*Liverpool:* (4231) Jones; Wisdom (Gerrard 55), Skrtel, Coates, Robinson; Henderson, Allen; Sterling (Shelvey 72), Suarez, Borini (Downing 55); Sturridge.

**FOURTH ROUND REPLAYS**

Tuesday, 12 February 2013

**Leicester C (1) 1** *(Keane 7)*
**Huddersfield T (1) 2** *(Clayton 5, Scannell 75)*      14,517
*Leicester C:* (442) Schmeichel; De Laet, Keane, Morgan, Konchesky; James, Gallagher, Wellens (Dyer 81), Knockaert; Futacs (Waghorn 74), Nugent (Vardy 74).
*Huddersfield T:* (442) Bennett; Dixon, Wallace, Gerrard, Woods; Sinnott (Norwood 65), Arfield, Atkinson (Gobern 83), Clayton; Scannell, Lee (Vaughan 70).

Sunday, 17 February 2013

**Chelsea (0) 4** *(Mata 54, Oscar 68, Lampard 71, Terry 81)*
**Brentford (0) 0**      40,961
*Chelsea:* (4231) Cech; Ivanovic, Cahill, Terry, Cole; Luiz, Lampard (Bertrand 80); Oscar, Mata (Benayoun 76), Moses (Hazard 65); Ba.
*Brentford:* (442) Moore; Logan, Craig, Dean, Bidwell; Adeyemi, Diagouraga (Reeves 73), Douglas, Forshaw (Saunders 78); Donaldson, Trotta (Forrester 56).

**FIFTH ROUND**

Saturday, 16 February 2013

**Arsenal (0) 0**
**Blackburn R (0) 1** *(Kazim-Richards 72)*      60,070
*Arsenal:* (4231) Szczesny; Coquelin, Vermaelen, Koscielny, Monreal; Diaby, Rosicky (Wilshere 70); Arteta, Gervinho (Walcott 70), Oxlade-Chamberlain (Cazorla 70); Giroud.
*Blackburn R:* (4411) Kean; Orr, Dann, Hanley G, Olsson Martin; Pedersen, Williamson, Lowe, Olsson Marcus (Bentley 63); Kazim-Richards; Rhodes (Goodwillie 82).

**Luton T (0) 0**
**Millwall (2) 3** *(Henry 12, Hulse 36, N'Guessan 86)*      9768
*Luton T:* (442) Tyler; Taylor, Henry, Kovacs, Howells; Lawless, Smith, Mendy (Shaw 69), O'Donnell (Fleetwood 64); Rendell, Gray.
*Millwall:* (442) Forde; Dunne, Beevers, Osborne, Lowry; Henry (Smith A 89), Trotter, Abdou, Feeney (N'Guessan 62); Hulse (Marquis 70), Keogh.

**Milton Keynes D (0) 1** *(Bowditch 61)*
**Barnsley (2) 3** *(Dagnall 3, 90, Harewood 19)*      14,475
*Milton Keynes D:* (4231) Martin; Otsemobor, MacKenzie, Williams, Lewington; Potter, Harley (Chicksen 46); Bowditch (Lines 67), Chadwick, Powell; Smith**.
*Barnsley:* (352) Steele; Wiseman, Cranie, Kennedy; Hassell (Delap 70), Etuhu (O'Brien 57), Perkins, Mellis, Golbourne; Dagnall, Harewood (Scotland 46).

**Oldham Ath (1) 2** *(Obita 13, Smith M 90)*
**Everton (1) 2** *(Anichebe 24, Jagielka 48)*      9473
*Oldham Ath:* (442) Bouzanis; Brown, Mvoto, Tarkowski, Grounds; Croft, Wesolowski (Furman 66), Baxter, Obita (Simpson R 77); Iwelumo (Smith M 61), Barnard.
*Everton:* (442) Howard; Neville, Jagielka, Distin, Baines; Osman, Gibson, Fellaini, Pienaar (Oviedo 79); Anichebe (Mirallas 46), Jelavic (Duffy 90).

Sunday, 17 February 2013

**Huddersfield T (0) 1** *(Novak 62)*
**Wigan Ath (2) 4** *(McManaman 31, Kone 40, 89,*
*McArthur 56)*      12,117
*Huddersfield T:* (433) Smithies; Hunt, Gerrard, Clarke P, Woods; Danns, Atkinson (Novak 46), Clayton; Scannell (Norwood 65), Lee (Vaughan 46), Arfield.
*Wigan Ath:* (352) Robles; Golobart, Scharner, Figueroa; Stam, Gomez (Beausejour 74), McArthur (McCarthy 90), Espinoza (Maloney 57), Fyvie; Kone, McManaman.

**Manchester C (2) 4** *(Toure 5, Aguero 15 (pen), 74, Tevez 52)*
**Leeds U (0) 0**      46,849
*Manchester C:* (4132) Pantilimon; Zabaleta, Toure K, Nastasic, Kolarov; Milner, Toure Y, Javi Garcia (Rodwell 60), Silva; Aguero (Dzeko 81), Tevez (Maicon 64).
*Leeds U:* (442) Ashdown; Byram, Lees, Peltier, Warnock; White, Austin (Tonge 77), Brown (Norris 46), Varney; Diouf, McCormack (Morison 46).

Monday, 18 February 2013
**Manchester U (0) 2** *(Nani 69, Hernandez 72)*
**Reading (0) 1** *(McAnuff 81)*                    75,213
*Manchester U:* (442) De Gea; Smalling, Jones (Nani 42),
Vidic, Buttner; Valencia, Cleverley, Anderson (Carrick
83), Young (van Persie 64); Welbeck, Hernandez.
*Reading:* (442) Federici; Kelly, Mariappa, Morrison,
Shorey; McCleary (Robson-Kanu 70), Leigertwood
(Guthrie 63), Karacan, McAnuff; Hunt, Le Fondre.

Wednesday, 27 February 2013
**Middlesbrough (0) 0**
**Chelsea (0) 2** *(Torres 51, Moses 73)*                    27,856
*Middlesbrough:* (442) Steele; Bailey, McManus, Bikey
(Hines 35), Friend; Carayol (Zemmama 74), Leadbitter,
Williams R, Haroun; Main (Miller 62); McDonald.
*Chelsea:* (4231) Cech; Ferreira, Ivanovic, Terry, Bertrand;
Ake, Ramires; Moses (Luiz 76), Oscar (Marin 79),
Benayoun (Hazard 58); Torres.

## FIFTH ROUND REPLAY

Tuesday, 26 February 2013
**Everton (2) 3** *(Mirallas 15, Baines 34 (pen), Osman 62)*
**Oldham Ath (0) 1** *(Smith M 64)*                    32,688
*Everton:* (4411) Howard; Coleman, Jagielka, Distin,
Baines; Mirallas (Naismith 84), Neville, Gibson, Pienaar
(Hitzlsperger 89); Osman; Jelavic.
*Oldham Ath:* (442) Bouzanis; Brown (Wesolowski 76),
Mvoto, Tarkowski, Grounds; Croft, Furman, Baxter,
Obita (Simpson R 55); Iwelumo (Smith M 55), Barnard.

## SIXTH ROUND

Saturday, 9 March 2013
**Everton (0) 0**
**Wigan Ath (3) 3** *(Figueroa 30, McManaman 31,
Gomez 33)*                    35,068
*Everton:* (4411) Mucha; Coleman, Heitinga, Distin,
Baines; Mirallas (Barkley 79), Neville (Anichebe 46),
Osman, Pienaar; Fellaini (Gibson 67); Jelavic.
*Wigan Ath:* (343) Robles; Scharner, Alcaraz (Golobart
90), Figueroa; Boyce, McCarthy, Gomez, Beausejour;
McManaman (Miyaichi 40 (McArthur 72)), Kone,
Maloney.

**Manchester C (3) 5** *(Tevez 11, 31, 50, Kolarov 27, Silva 65)*
**Barnsley (0) 0**                    46,728
*Manchester C:* (442) Pantilimon; Zabaleta, Toure K,
Lescott, Kolarov; Nasri (Sinclair 52), Toure Y, Barry,
Silva (Razak 66); Dzeko, Tevez (Milner 76).
*Barnsley:* (442) Steele; Wiseman, Cranie, Kennedy,
Foster; Etuhu (O'Brien 52), Tunnicliffe, Perkins, Cywka
(Mellis 52); Dagnall (Scotland 52), Harewood.

Sunday, 10 March 2013
**Manchester U (2) 2** *(Hernandez 5, Rooney 11)*
**Chelsea (0) 2** *(Hazard 59, Ramires 68)*                    75,196
*Manchester U:* (442) De Gea; Da Silva, Evans,
Ferdinand, Evra; Carrick, Cleverley, Nani (Valencia 45),
Kagawa (Welbeck 76); Rooney, Hernandez (van Persie
62).
*Chelsea:* (4231) Cech; Azpilicueta, Luiz, Cahill, Cole;
Ramires, Lampard (Mikel 52); Moses (Hazard 52), Mata,
Oscar; Ba (Torres 77).

**Millwall (0) 0**
**Blackburn R (0) 0**                    14,885
*Millwall:* (433) Forde; Dunne, Shittu, Beevers, Lowry;
Smith J, Trotter, Taylor C; N'Guessan, Hulse, Keogh.
*Blackburn R:* (442) Kean; Henley (Orr 36 (Dunn 48)),
Dann, Hanley G, Olsson Marcus; Bentley, Lowe, King
(Nuno Gomes 87), Pedersen; Rhodes, Best.

## SIXTH ROUND REPLAYS

Wednesday, 13 March 2013
**Blackburn R (0) 0**
**Millwall (1) 1** *(Shittu 42)*                    8635
*Blackburn R:* (442) Kean; Lowe, Dann, Hanley G,
Olsson Marcus (Nuno Gomes 46); Best, Rhodes.
*Millwall:* (433) Forde; Dunne, Shittu, Beevers, Lowry;
Taylor C, Trotter, Smith J; N'Guessan (Abdou 66), Hulse
(Marquis 85), Keogh.

Monday, 1 April 2013
**Chelsea (0) 1** *(Ba 49)*
**Manchester U (0) 0**                    40,704
*Chelsea:* (451) Cech; Azpilicueta, Ivanovic, Luiz, Cole
(Bertrand 21); Ramires, Mikel, Hazard, Oscar (Moses
90), Mata; Ba (Torres 90).
*Manchester U:* (442) De Gea; Jones, Smalling, Ferdinand,
Evra; Valencia, Carrick, Cleverley (van Persie 61), Nani
(Giggs 65); Welbeck (Young 80), Hernandez.

## SEMI-FINALS

Saturday, 13 April 2013
**Millwall (0) 0**
**Wigan Ath (1) 2** *(Maloney 25, McManaman 78)*    62,335
*Millwall:* (433) Forde; Dunne, Shittu, Beevers, Lowry;
Smith J (Hulse 67), Abdou (Trotter 72), St. Ledger;
Henry, Keogh (Batt 89), Taylor C.
*Wigan Ath:* (442) Al Habsi; Beausejour (McArthur 60),
Alcaraz, Boyce, Figueroa; McManaman (Henriquez 89),
McCarthy, Scharner, Maloney; Kone, Gomez.

Sunday, 14 April 2013
**Chelsea (0) 1** *(Ba 66)*
**Manchester C (1) 2** *(Nasri 35, Aguero 47)*                    85,621
*Chelsea:* (433) Cech; Azpilicueta, Ivanovic, Luiz,
Bertrand; Ramires, Mikel (Torres 66), Hazard; Mata, Ba,
Oscar.
*Manchester C:* (442) Pantilimon; Zabaleta, Kompany,
Nastasic, Clichy; Milner, Toure Y, Barry, Nasri (Lescott
86); Tevez (Javi Garcia 72), Aguero.

**THE FA CUP FINAL**

Saturday, 11 May 2013

(at Wembley Stadium, attendance 86,254)

**Manchester C (0) 0     Wigan Ath (0) 1**

*Manchester C:* (442) Hart; Zabaleta■, Kompany, Nastasic, Clichy; Silva, Toure Y, Barry (Dzeko 90), Nasri (Milner 54); Aguero, Tevez (Rodwell 69).

*Wigan Ath:* (442) Robles; Boyce, Scharner, Alcaraz, Espinoza; McCarthy, McArthur, Gomez (Watson B 81), McManaman; Kone, Maloney.
*Scorer:* Watson B 90.

*Referee:* Andre Marriner.

On the final whistle, Wigan Athletic's players rush to congratulate team-mate Ben Watson who scored a late winner in the club's surprise 1-0 win over Manchester City in the FA Cup Final. (Action Images)

# BLUE SQUARE PREMIER 2012–13

(P) *Promoted into division at end of 2011–12 season.*    (R) *Relegated into division at end of 2011–12 season.*

| | | | Total | | | | Home | | | | Away | | | | | | |
|---|---|---|---|---|---|---|---|---|---|---|---|---|---|---|---|---|---|
| | | P | W | D | L | F | A | W | D | L | F | A | W | D | L | F | A | GD | Pts |
| 1 | Mansfield T | 46 | 30 | 5 | 11 | 92 | 52 | 17 | 3 | 3 | 53 | 17 | 13 | 2 | 8 | 39 | 35 | 40 | 95 |
| 2 | Kidderminster H | 46 | 28 | 9 | 9 | 82 | 40 | 15 | 4 | 4 | 49 | 22 | 13 | 5 | 5 | 33 | 18 | 42 | 93 |
| 3 | Newport Co¶ | 46 | 25 | 10 | 11 | 85 | 60 | 13 | 5 | 5 | 43 | 27 | 12 | 5 | 6 | 42 | 33 | 25 | 85 |
| 4 | Grimsby T | 46 | 23 | 14 | 9 | 70 | 38 | 13 | 5 | 5 | 42 | 19 | 10 | 9 | 4 | 28 | 19 | 32 | 83 |
| 5 | Wrexham | 46 | 22 | 14 | 10 | 74 | 45 | 11 | 9 | 3 | 45 | 24 | 11 | 5 | 7 | 29 | 21 | 29 | 80 |
| 6 | Hereford U (R) | 46 | 19 | 13 | 14 | 73 | 63 | 9 | 6 | 8 | 37 | 33 | 10 | 7 | 6 | 36 | 30 | 10 | 70 |
| 7 | Luton T | 46 | 18 | 13 | 15 | 70 | 62 | 10 | 7 | 6 | 43 | 26 | 8 | 6 | 9 | 27 | 36 | 8 | 67 |
| 8 | Dartford (P) | 46 | 19 | 9 | 18 | 67 | 63 | 12 | 4 | 7 | 41 | 26 | 7 | 5 | 11 | 26 | 37 | 4 | 66 |
| 9 | Braintree T | 46 | 19 | 9 | 18 | 63 | 72 | 9 | 5 | 9 | 32 | 40 | 10 | 4 | 9 | 31 | 32 | −9 | 66 |
| 10 | Forest Green R | 46 | 18 | 11 | 17 | 63 | 49 | 8 | 6 | 9 | 33 | 24 | 10 | 5 | 8 | 30 | 25 | 14 | 65 |
| 11 | Macclesfield T (R) | 46 | 17 | 12 | 17 | 65 | 70 | 10 | 6 | 7 | 29 | 28 | 7 | 6 | 10 | 36 | 42 | −5 | 63 |
| 12 | Woking (P) | 46 | 18 | 8 | 20 | 73 | 81 | 13 | 3 | 7 | 47 | 34 | 5 | 5 | 13 | 26 | 47 | −8 | 62 |
| 13 | Alfreton T | 46 | 16 | 12 | 18 | 69 | 74 | 9 | 5 | 9 | 41 | 39 | 7 | 7 | 9 | 28 | 35 | −5 | 60 |
| 14 | Cambridge U | 46 | 15 | 14 | 17 | 68 | 69 | 9 | 7 | 7 | 33 | 30 | 6 | 7 | 10 | 35 | 39 | −1 | 59 |
| 15 | Nuneaton T (P) | 46 | 14 | 15 | 17 | 55 | 63 | 8 | 9 | 6 | 29 | 25 | 6 | 6 | 11 | 26 | 38 | −8 | 57 |
| 16 | Lincoln C | 46 | 15 | 11 | 20 | 66 | 73 | 9 | 5 | 9 | 34 | 36 | 6 | 6 | 11 | 32 | 37 | −7 | 56 |
| 17 | Gateshead | 46 | 13 | 16 | 17 | 58 | 61 | 9 | 9 | 5 | 35 | 22 | 4 | 7 | 12 | 23 | 39 | −3 | 55 |
| 18 | Hyde U (P) | 46 | 16 | 7 | 23 | 63 | 75 | 9 | 5 | 9 | 35 | 31 | 7 | 2 | 14 | 28 | 44 | −12 | 55 |
| 19 | Tamworth | 46 | 15 | 10 | 21 | 55 | 69 | 9 | 4 | 10 | 25 | 27 | 6 | 6 | 11 | 30 | 42 | −14 | 55 |
| 20 | Southport | 46 | 14 | 12 | 20 | 72 | 86 | 7 | 4 | 12 | 32 | 44 | 7 | 8 | 8 | 40 | 42 | −14 | 54 |
| 21 | Stockport Co | 46 | 13 | 11 | 22 | 57 | 76 | 8 | 2 | 13 | 34 | 39 | 5 | 9 | 9 | 23 | 37 | −19 | 50 |
| 22 | Barrow | 46 | 11 | 13 | 22 | 45 | 83 | 5 | 7 | 11 | 20 | 35 | 6 | 6 | 11 | 25 | 48 | −38 | 46 |
| 23 | Ebbsfleet U | 46 | 8 | 15 | 23 | 55 | 89 | 5 | 11 | 7 | 31 | 37 | 3 | 4 | 16 | 24 | 52 | −34 | 39 |
| 24 | AFC Telford U | 46 | 6 | 17 | 23 | 52 | 79 | 2 | 9 | 12 | 22 | 42 | 4 | 8 | 11 | 30 | 37 | −27 | 35 |

¶*Newport Co promoted via play-offs.*

## BLUE SQUARE PREMIER LEADING GOALSCORERS 2012–13

| Player | Club | League | FA Cup | FA Trophy | Play-Offs | Total |
|---|---|---|---|---|---|---|
| Matt Green | Mansfield T | 25 | 2 | 0 | | 27 |
| Adam Cunnington | Tamworth | 21 | 0 | 0 | | 21 |
| Matthew Barnes-Homer | Macclesfield T | 18 | 3 | 0 | | 21 |
| Andy Brown | Nuneaton T | 19 | 0 | 0 | | 19 |
| Anthony Malbon | Kidderminster H | 19 | 0 | 0 | 0 | 19 |
| Aaron O'Connor | Newport Co | 18 | 0 | 0 | 1 | 19 |
| Paul Clayton | Alfreton T | 17 | 2 | 0 | | 19 |
| Andre Gray | Luton T | 17 | 1 | 1 | | 19 |
| Bradley Bubb | Woking | 18 | 0 | 0 | | 18 |
| Danny Wright | Wrexham | 15 | 1 | 2 | 0 | 18 |
| Ryan Bowman | Hereford U | 15 | 2 | 0 | | 17 |
| Adam Boyes | Barrow | 13 | 2 | 2 | | 17 |
| Tom Elliott | Cambridge U | 15 | 0 | 1 | | 16 |
| James Norwood | Forest Green R | 15 | 1 | 0 | | 16 |
| Nathan Elder | Ebbsfleet U | 15 | 1 | 0 | | 16 |
| Andy Cook | Grimsby T | 11 | 0 | 5 | 0 | 16 |
| Josh Gillies | Gateshead | 15 | 0 | 0 | | 15 |
| Phil Jevons | Hyde U | 15 | 0 | 0 | | 15 |
| Harry Crawford | Dartford | 13 | 0 | 2 | | 15 |
| Christian Jolley | Newport Co | 13 | 0 | 0 | 2 | 15 |

## BLUE SQUARE PREMIER PLAY-OFFS

■ *Denotes player sent off.*

### SEMI-FINAL FIRST LEG

Tuesday, 23 April 2013

**Wrexham (1) 2** *(Artell 45, Ashton 85 (pen))*
**Kidderminster H (0) 1** *(Gash 57 (pen))*     6315
*Wrexham:* (433) Maxwell; Wright S, Artell, Riley, Ashton; Harris, Keates, Clarke; Ormerod, Morrell (Adebola 73), Hunt.
*Kidderminster H:* (433) Lewis; Vaughan L, Gowling, Dunkley, Demetriou; Storer, Vincent (Briggs 39), Jackman; Johnson (Devaney 61), Gash, Malbon.

Wednesday, 24 April 2013

**Grimsby T (0) 0**
**Newport Co (0) 1** *(Yakubu 89)*     5414
*Grimsby T:* (442) McKeown; Hatton, Pearson S, Miller, Thomas; Taylor (Marshall 72), Disley, Naylor, Devitt (Thanoj 58); Hearn, Cook.
*Newport Co:* (352) Pidgeley; James, Yakubu, Anthony; Pipe, Sandell, Gilbey (Donnelly 86), Minshull, Flynn; Crow (Washington 65), Jolley (Willmott 88).

### SEMI-FINAL SECOND LEG

Sunday, 28 April 2013

**Kidderminster H (0) 1** *(Dunkley 64)*
**Wrexham (1) 3** *(Ormerod 30; Clarke 69, Ashton 85 (pen))*
    6202
*Kidderminster H:* (442) Lewis; Vaughan L, Gowling, Dunkley, Williams (Gittings 77); Devaney, Storer, Jackman, Pilkington (Johnson 62); Malbon, Gash (Rowe 69).
*Wrexham:* (433) Maxwell; Wright S, Artell, Riley, Ashton; Hunt, Harris, Keates (Little 86); Ormerod (Cieslewicz 61), Morrell (Adebola 69), Clarke.

**Newport Co (1) 1** *(Jolley 31)*
**Grimsby T (0) 0**     6615
*Newport Co:* (541) Pidgeley; Pipe, James, Yakubu, Anthony, Sandell; Jolley (Willmott 86), Minshull, Flynn, Gilbey; Crow (O'Connor 72).
*Grimsby T:* (541) McKeown; Hatton (Southwell 68), Pearson S (Cook 46), Miller, Naylor, Thomas; Colbeck, Disley, Thanoj, Marshall; Hearn (Hannah 64).

### FINAL (at Wembley)

Sunday, 5 May 2013

**Wrexham (0) 0**
**Newport Co (0) 2** *(Jolley 86, O'Connor 90)*     16,346
*Wrexham:* (442) Maxwell; Wright S, Riley, Artell, Ashton; Hunt, Harris (Adebola 88), Keates (Little 80), Clarke; Ormerod, Morrell (Cieslewicz 68).
*Newport Co:* (442) Pidgeley; Pipe, James, Yakubu, Anthony; Gilbey, Minshull, Flynn (Donnelly 74), Sandell; Crow (O'Connor 62), Jolley.
*Referee:* Michael Ball.

## BLUE SQUARE PREMIER ATTENDANCES BY CLUB 2012–13

|  | Aggregate 2012–13 | Average 2012–13 | Highest Attendance 2012–13 |
|---|---|---|---|
| Luton T | 135,443 | 5,889 | 6,744  v. Woking |
| Grimsby T | 87,706 | 3,813 | 7,405  v. Lincoln C |
| Wrexham | 80,968 | 3,520 | 4,378  v. Mansfield T |
| Stockport Co | 80,036 | 3,480 | 6,113  v. Dartford |
| Mansfield T | 63,432 | 2,758 | 6,394  v. Wrexham |
| Newport Co | 54,522 | 2,371 | 4,365  v. Hereford U |
| Cambridge U | 51,474 | 2,238 | 3,217  v. Luton T |
| Kidderminster H | 50,538 | 2,197 | 6,453  v. Stockport Co |
| Lincoln C | 50,169 | 2,181 | 5,702  v. Grimsby T |
| Hereford U | 40,295 | 1,752 | 2,902  v. Kidderminster H |
| AFC Telford U | 39,783 | 1,730 | 2,931  v. Wrexham |
| Macclesfield T | 38,418 | 1,670 | 4,027  v. Stockport Co |
| Woking | 36,815 | 1,601 | 2,961  v. Luton T |
| Dartford | 31,409 | 1,366 | 3,116  v. Ebbsfleet U |
| Forest Green R | 27,124 | 1,179 | 2,332  v. Newport Co |
| Tamworth | 23,417 | 1,018 | 1,968  v. Mansfield T |
| Nuneaton T | 22,896 | 995 | 1,543  v. Wrexham |
| Southport | 22,030 | 958 | 1,743  v. Grimsby T |
| Barrow | 21,124 | 918 | 1,278  v. Dartford |
| Ebbsfleet U | 20,183 | 878 | 2,242  v. Dartford |
| Hyde | 18,609 | 809 | 2,540  v. Stockport Co |
| Alfreton T | 17,172 | 747 | 1,537  v. Mansfield T |
| Braintree T | 15,431 | 671 | 1,755  v. Mansfield T |
| Gateshead | 11,552 | 502 | 803  v. Lincoln C |

# BLUE SQUARE NORTH 2012–13

(P) *Promoted into division at end of 2011–12 season.*  (R) *Relegated into division at end of 2011–12 season.*

| | | | | | Total | | Home | | | | | Away | | | | | | | |
|---|---|---|---|---|---|---|---|---|---|---|---|---|---|---|---|---|---|---|---|
| | | P | W | D | L | F | A | W | D | L | F | A | W | D | L | F | A | GD | Pts |
| 1 | Chester (P) | 42 | 34 | 5 | 3 | 103 | 32 | 18 | 2 | 1 | 48 | 11 | 16 | 3 | 2 | 55 | 21 | 71 | 107 |
| 2 | Guiseley | 42 | 28 | 7 | 7 | 83 | 45 | 14 | 4 | 3 | 40 | 22 | 14 | 3 | 4 | 43 | 23 | 38 | 91 |
| 3 | Brackley T (P) | 42 | 26 | 7 | 9 | 76 | 44 | 12 | 3 | 6 | 36 | 24 | 14 | 4 | 3 | 40 | 20 | 32 | 85 |
| 4 | Altrincham | 42 | 24 | 8 | 10 | 100 | 51 | 15 | 1 | 5 | 56 | 22 | 9 | 7 | 5 | 44 | 29 | 49 | 80 |
| 5 | FC Halifax T¶ | 42 | 21 | 12 | 9 | 86 | 38 | 9 | 7 | 5 | 49 | 20 | 12 | 5 | 4 | 37 | 18 | 48 | 75 |
| 6 | Harrogate T | 42 | 20 | 9 | 13 | 72 | 50 | 9 | 6 | 6 | 45 | 28 | 11 | 3 | 7 | 27 | 22 | 22 | 69 |
| 7 | Bradford Park Avenue (P) | 42 | 19 | 9 | 14 | 75 | 52 | 10 | 5 | 6 | 31 | 22 | 9 | 4 | 8 | 44 | 30 | 23 | 66 |
| 8 | Gainsborough Trinity | 42 | 18 | 12 | 12 | 68 | 45 | 7 | 7 | 7 | 33 | 26 | 11 | 5 | 5 | 35 | 19 | 23 | 66 |
| 9 | Solihull Moors‡ | 42 | 17 | 9 | 16 | 58 | 54 | 10 | 2 | 9 | 27 | 25 | 7 | 7 | 7 | 31 | 29 | 4 | 56 |
| 10 | Oxford C (P) | 42 | 13 | 16 | 13 | 62 | 57 | 5 | 11 | 5 | 34 | 27 | 8 | 5 | 8 | 28 | 30 | 5 | 55 |
| 11 | Gloucester C | 42 | 16 | 6 | 20 | 54 | 63 | 7 | 6 | 8 | 33 | 28 | 9 | 0 | 12 | 21 | 35 | –9 | 54 |
| 12 | Vauxhall Motors | 42 | 15 | 8 | 19 | 58 | 64 | 9 | 4 | 8 | 30 | 27 | 6 | 4 | 11 | 28 | 37 | –6 | 53 |
| 13 | Stalybridge Celtic | 42 | 13 | 13 | 16 | 55 | 62 | 7 | 6 | 8 | 30 | 33 | 6 | 7 | 8 | 25 | 29 | –7 | 52 |
| 14 | Workington* | 42 | 16 | 8 | 18 | 60 | 68 | 7 | 4 | 10 | 28 | 34 | 9 | 4 | 8 | 32 | 34 | –8 | 52 |
| 15 | Worcester C | 42 | 14 | 8 | 20 | 57 | 62 | 7 | 4 | 10 | 29 | 30 | 7 | 4 | 10 | 28 | 32 | –5 | 50 |
| 16 | Boston U | 42 | 14 | 7 | 21 | 68 | 73 | 7 | 4 | 10 | 41 | 37 | 7 | 3 | 11 | 27 | 36 | –5 | 49 |
| 17 | Bishop's Stortford | 42 | 12 | 13 | 17 | 58 | 74 | 6 | 6 | 9 | 27 | 36 | 6 | 7 | 8 | 31 | 38 | –16 | 49 |
| 18 | Colwyn Bay | 42 | 14 | 7 | 21 | 57 | 78 | 7 | 1 | 13 | 27 | 44 | 7 | 6 | 8 | 30 | 34 | –21 | 49 |
| 19 | Histon | 42 | 11 | 11 | 20 | 48 | 73 | 9 | 4 | 8 | 30 | 31 | 2 | 7 | 12 | 18 | 42 | –25 | 44 |
| 20 | Corby T | 42 | 12 | 8 | 22 | 66 | 92 | 7 | 4 | 10 | 36 | 43 | 5 | 4 | 12 | 30 | 49 | –26 | 44 |
| 21 | Droylsden | 42 | 5 | 7 | 30 | 43 | 124 | 4 | 3 | 14 | 25 | 56 | 1 | 4 | 16 | 18 | 68 | –81 | 22 |
| 22 | Hinckley U† | 42 | 3 | 4 | 35 | 37 | 143 | 1 | 3 | 17 | 16 | 67 | 2 | 1 | 18 | 21 | 76 | –106 | 7 |

*Workington deducted 4 points. †Hinckley U deducted 6 points. ‡Solihull Moors deducted 4 points.
¶FC Halifax T promoted via play-offs.

## BLUE SQUARE NORTH PLAY-OFFS 2012–13

**SEMI-FINALS FIRST LEG**
Tuesday 30 April 2013
**FC Halifax T (1) 1** *(Gardner 15)*
**Guiseley (0) 1** *(Ellis 58)*                    2367
*FC Halifax T:* Glennon; Lowe, McManus, Toulson, Hogan, Pearson, Worsley (Worthington 55), Williams, Gardner (Seddon 84), Gregory (Needham 84), Johnson.
*Guiseley:* Drench; Wilson M, Ellis, McWilliams, Hardy, Wilson J, Holdsworth, Carole (Mullen 90), Rothery (Pearson 84), Rea, Walshaw.
*Referee:* A. Holmes.

Tuesday 30 April 2013
**Altrincham (0) 2** *(Richman 78, Moult 90)*
**Brackley T (0) 1** *(Louis 70)*                    1618
*Altrincham:* Coburn; Havern, Doughty, Leather, Clee, Boshell (Lacey 79), Richman, Densmore, Reeves, Lawrie (Moult 76), Watmore (Brooke 84).
*Brackley T:* Turley; Austin, Sharpe, Odhiambo, Clifton, McDonald (Nisevic 89), Solkhon, Reid, Walker, Story (Mulligan 79), Robinson (Louis 59).
*Referee:* A. Miller.

**SEMI-FINALS SECOND LEG**
Saturday 4 May 2013
**Guiseley (0) 0**
**FC Halifax T (0) 2** *(Gardner 50, Gregory 81)*    2424
*Guiseley:* Drench; Meynell, Wilson M, Ellis (Carole 75), Hardy, Wilson J, Holdsworth, Rothery, Rea, Walshaw, Pearson.
*FC Halifax T:* Glennon; Lowe, McManus, Toulson, Hogan, Pearson, Williams, Needham, Gardner (Seddon 71), Gregory, Johnson.
*Referee:* R. Wigglesworth.

Saturday 4 May 2013
**Brackley T (2) 3** *(Louis 4, Reid 24, Walker 53)*
**Altrincham (0) 0**                                1353
*Brackley T:* Turley; Austin, Sharpe, Odhiambo, McDonald, Solkhon, Reid, Winters (Nisevic 57), Walker, Louis (Diggin 74), Mulligan (Robinson 65).
*Altrincham:* Coburn; Havern, Doughty (Lacey 68), Leather, Rodgers, Clee, Richman, Densmore, Reeves, Lawrie, Watmore (Moult 52).
*Referee:* S. Plane.

**FINAL**
Sunday 12 May 2013
**Brackley T (0) 0**
**FC Halifax T (0) 1** *(Gregory 74)*                2604
*Brackley T:* Turley; Austin, Sharpe, Odhiambo (Story 84), McDonald, Solkhon, Reid, Winters, Walker, Louis (Robinson 78), Mulligan (Diggin 78).
*FC Halifax T:* Glennon; Lowe, McManus, Toulson (Bolton 46), Hogan, Pearson, Williams, Needham, Gardner, Gregory, Johnson (Moke 73).
*Referee:* D. England.

# BLUE SQUARE SOUTH 2012–13

(P) *Promoted into division at end of 2011–12 season.*    (R) *Relegated into division at end of 2011–12 season.*

| | | P | W | D | L | F | A | W | D | L | F | A | W | D | L | F | A | GD | Pts |
|---|---|---|---|---|---|---|---|---|---|---|---|---|---|---|---|---|---|---|---|
| | | | | | | *Total* | | | | *Home* | | | | | *Away* | | | | |
| 1 | Welling U | 42 | 26 | 8 | 8 | 90 | 44 | 16 | 5 | 0 | 55 | 20 | 10 | 3 | 8 | 35 | 24 | 46 | 86 |
| 2 | Salisbury C*¶ | 42 | 25 | 8 | 9 | 80 | 47 | 16 | 4 | 1 | 48 | 22 | 9 | 4 | 8 | 32 | 25 | 33 | 82 |
| 3 | Dover Ath | 42 | 22 | 10 | 10 | 69 | 44 | 9 | 5 | 7 | 27 | 24 | 13 | 5 | 3 | 42 | 20 | 25 | 76 |
| 4 | Eastleigh | 42 | 22 | 6 | 14 | 79 | 61 | 16 | 3 | 2 | 49 | 21 | 6 | 3 | 12 | 30 | 40 | 18 | 72 |
| 5 | Chelmsford C | 42 | 22 | 6 | 14 | 70 | 56 | 14 | 3 | 4 | 46 | 27 | 8 | 3 | 10 | 24 | 29 | 14 | 72 |
| 6 | Sutton U | 42 | 20 | 10 | 12 | 66 | 49 | 11 | 4 | 6 | 37 | 27 | 9 | 6 | 6 | 29 | 22 | 17 | 70 |
| 7 | Weston-super-Mare | 42 | 19 | 10 | 13 | 61 | 55 | 10 | 5 | 6 | 34 | 30 | 9 | 5 | 7 | 27 | 25 | 6 | 67 |
| 8 | Dorchester T | 42 | 19 | 8 | 15 | 59 | 62 | 12 | 5 | 4 | 35 | 24 | 7 | 3 | 11 | 24 | 38 | −3 | 65 |
| 9 | Boreham Wood | 42 | 15 | 17 | 10 | 59 | 46 | 10 | 7 | 4 | 33 | 17 | 5 | 10 | 6 | 26 | 29 | 13 | 62 |
| 10 | Havant & Waterlooville | 42 | 14 | 16 | 12 | 68 | 60 | 10 | 5 | 6 | 41 | 27 | 4 | 11 | 6 | 27 | 33 | 8 | 58 |
| 11 | Bath C (R) | 42 | 15 | 10 | 17 | 60 | 58 | 7 | 7 | 7 | 30 | 29 | 8 | 3 | 10 | 30 | 29 | 2 | 55 |
| 12 | Eastbourne Borough | 42 | 14 | 9 | 19 | 42 | 52 | 7 | 3 | 11 | 17 | 26 | 7 | 6 | 8 | 25 | 26 | −10 | 51 |
| 13 | Farnborough† | 42 | 19 | 7 | 16 | 76 | 75 | 13 | 3 | 5 | 47 | 30 | 6 | 4 | 11 | 29 | 45 | 1 | 50 |
| 14 | Basingstoke T | 42 | 12 | 12 | 18 | 63 | 73 | 8 | 4 | 9 | 34 | 37 | 4 | 8 | 9 | 29 | 36 | −10 | 48 |
| 15 | Bromley | 42 | 14 | 6 | 22 | 54 | 69 | 7 | 4 | 10 | 25 | 30 | 7 | 2 | 12 | 29 | 39 | −15 | 48 |
| 16 | Tonbridge Angels | 42 | 12 | 12 | 18 | 56 | 77 | 8 | 7 | 6 | 29 | 31 | 4 | 5 | 12 | 27 | 46 | −21 | 48 |
| 17 | Hayes & Yeading U (R) | 42 | 13 | 9 | 20 | 64 | 89 | 9 | 5 | 7 | 38 | 35 | 4 | 4 | 13 | 26 | 54 | −25 | 48 |
| 18 | Staines T | 42 | 13 | 8 | 21 | 61 | 78 | 7 | 4 | 10 | 33 | 42 | 6 | 4 | 11 | 28 | 36 | −17 | 47 |
| 19 | Maidenhead U | 42 | 13 | 6 | 23 | 64 | 68 | 9 | 2 | 10 | 37 | 31 | 4 | 4 | 13 | 27 | 37 | −4 | 45 |
| 20 | AFC Hornchurch (P) | 42 | 11 | 11 | 20 | 47 | 64 | 7 | 8 | 6 | 21 | 21 | 4 | 3 | 14 | 26 | 43 | −17 | 44 |
| 21 | Billericay T (P) | 42 | 11 | 7 | 24 | 62 | 90 | 8 | 4 | 9 | 37 | 32 | 3 | 3 | 15 | 25 | 58 | −28 | 40 |
| 22 | Truro C‡ | 42 | 9 | 8 | 25 | 57 | 90 | 5 | 5 | 11 | 30 | 41 | 4 | 3 | 14 | 27 | 49 | −33 | 25 |

*Salisbury C deducted 1 point. †Farnborough deducted 14 points. ‡Truro C deducted 10 points.
¶Salisbury C promoted via play-offs.

## BLUE SQUARE SOUTH PLAY-OFFS 2012–13

**SEMI-FINALS FIRST LEG**
Tuesday 30 April 2013
**Chelmsford C (0) 1** *(Cook 89 (pen))*
**Salisbury C (0) 0**                          1248
*Chelmsford C:* St Louis-Hamilton; Clark, Haines, Palmer, Miller, Ainsley, Bridges, Cook, Bakare (Simmonds 87), Cornhill, Slabber (Edmans 67).
*Salisbury C:* Puddy; Wilson, Clarke (Lewis 87), Dutton, Hart, McPhee, Wellard, Sinclair S, Sinclair R (Fitchett 61), Matthews, White.
*Referee:* P. Harris.

Tuesday 30 April 2013
**Eastleigh (0) 1** *(Zebroski 66)*
**Dover Ath (2) 3** *(Ademola 1, May 18, McMahon 90)*  915
*Eastleigh:* Flitney, Todd, Beckwith, Green, Nelson, Binns (Lacey 36), Reason, Hughes (Watkins 72), Southam, Scannell (Zebroski 36), McAllister.
*Dover Ath:* Walker; Simpemba, Wynter, Kamara, McMahon, Rance, Sterling, May, Ademola, Modeste, Ottaway.
*Referee:* D. Cook.

**SEMI-FINALS SECOND LEG**
Saturday 4 May 2013
**Salisbury C (1) 2** *(White 45, Sinclair S 90)*
**Chelmsford C (0) 0**                          1554
*Salisbury C:* Puddy; Wilson, Dutton, Hart, Brett, McPhee, Wellard, Frear (Lewis 46), Sinclair S, White (Matthews 90), Fitchett.
*Chelmsford C:* St Louis-Hamilton (Searle 38), Clark, Haines, Palmer, Miller, Ainsley, Bridges (Rainford 78), Cook, Cornhill, Simmonds, Edmans (Vassell 61).
*Referee:* D. Rock.

Saturday 4 May 2013
**Dover Ath (0) 0**
**Eastleigh (0) 2** *(Southam 49, Zebroski 89)*  1662
*aet; Dover Ath won 4-2 on penalties.*
*Dover Ath:* Walker; Simpemba, Wynter, Kamara, McMahon, Rance, Sterling, May (Willock 95), Ademola (Bricknell 71), Modeste (Sessegnon 78), Ottaway.
*Eastleigh:* Flitney; Todd, Beckwith, Nelson, Lacey, Reason (Binns 108), Hughes, Southam, Forbes (Scannell 60), Zebroski, McAllister (Peacock 75).
*Referee:* C. Hicks.

**FINAL**
Saturday 12 May 2013
**Salisbury C (0) 3** *(Wellard 48, Sinclair S 98, White 111)*
**Dover Ath (0) 2** *(Simpemba 88, Bricknell 118)*  3408
*aet.*
*Salisbury C:* Puddy; Wilson, Clarke, Dutton, Hart, McPhee, Wellard (Brett 52), Sinclair S, Sinclair R (Matthews 86), White, Lewis (Fitchett 78).
*Dover Ath:* Walker, Simpemba, Wynter, Kamara, McMahon, Rance, Sterling, May (Bricknell 65), Ademola (Harrington 73), Modeste, Ottaway (Willock 65).
*Referee:* A. Hopkins.

# AFC TELFORD UNITED

*Ground:* The New Bucks Head Stadium, Watling Street, Wellington, Telford, Shropshire TF1 2TU.
*Tel:* (01952) 640 064.   *Fax:* (01952) 640 021.   *Website:* www.telfordutd.co.uk.   *Year Formed:* 2004.
*Record Gate:* 5,710 (2007 v Burscough).   *Nickname:* 'The Bucks' or 'Lillywhites'.   *Manager:* Liam Watson.
*Secretary:* Sharon Bowyer. *Colours:* White shirts with black trim, black shorts, white and black socks.

## AFC TELFORD UNITED – BLUE SQUARE PREMIER 2012–13 LEAGUE RECORD

| Match No. | Date | Venue | Opponents | Result | H/T Score | Lg Pos. | Goalscorers | Attendance |
|---|---|---|---|---|---|---|---|---|
| 1 | Aug 11 | A | Barrow | D 0-0 | 0-0 | 16 | | 1041 |
| 2 | 14 | H | Forest Green R | L 1-2 | 0-2 | 20 | Rooney [60] | 1582 |
| 3 | 18 | H | Braintree T | W 3-0 | 2-0 | 11 | Spray [15], St Aimie [18], Rooney (pen) [83] | 1524 |
| 4 | 25 | A | Luton T | W 1-0 | 1-0 | 8 | St Aimie [42] | 5970 |
| 5 | 27 | H | Stockport Co | D 2-2 | 0-1 | 8 | St Aimie [56], Valentine [65] | 2079 |
| 6 | Sept 1 | A | Southport | W 3-0 | 1-0 | 6 | Jones [25], Grand (og) [49], St Aimie [57] | 1005 |
| 7 | 4 | A | Nuneaton T | L 1-3 | 1-1 | 10 | Rooney (pen) [37] | 992 |
| 8 | 8 | H | Lincoln C | D 1-1 | 0-1 | 9 | Trainer [87] | 1794 |
| 9 | 15 | A | Cambridge U | D 3-3 | 0-0 | 10 | Jones [57], Davies [83], Spray [87] | 1962 |
| 10 | 22 | H | Mansfield T | D 2-2 | 2-2 | 13 | Tafazolli (og) [15], Davies [34] | 1736 |
| 11 | 25 | A | Newport Co | L 2-4 | 1-1 | 13 | St Aimie [27], Sandell (og) [81] | 1503 |
| 12 | 29 | A | Gateshead | D 1-1 | 0-1 | 13 | Leslie [64] | 524 |
| 13 | Oct 6 | H | Woking | W 1-0 | 1-0 | 10 | Byfield (pen) [7] | 1584 |
| 14 | 9 | A | Dartford | W 4-1 | 2-0 | 8 | Jones 2 [35, 37], Hubbins [55], Trainer [69] | 1359 |
| 15 | 13 | A | Grimsby T | L 1-2 | 1-2 | 9 | Jones [21] | 2349 |
| 16 | 27 | A | Alfreton T | D 1-1 | 0-1 | 9 | Sharp [69] | 572 |
| 17 | Nov 6 | H | Ebbsfleet U | D 2-2 | 2-1 | 19 | Jones 2 [6, 26] | 1542 |
| 18 | 10 | A | Tamworth | D 0-0 | 0-0 | 11 | | 935 |
| 19 | 17 | H | Kidderminster H | L 0-2 | 0-0 | 12 | | 2160 |
| 20 | Dec 4 | H | Barrow | D 1-1 | 1-0 | 15 | Leslie [44] | 1333 |
| 21 | 8 | A | Hyde | L 1-2 | 1-0 | 17 | Leslie [35] | 523 |
| 22 | 26 | A | Wrexham | L 1-4 | 0-1 | 20 | Reid [73] | 4330 |
| 23 | 29 | A | Stockport Co | D 2-2 | 0-0 | 29 | Trainer [68], Hubbins [79] | 2791 |
| 24 | Jan 1 | H | Wrexham | L 0-2 | 0-1 | 20 | | 2931 |
| 25 | 5 | H | Southport | L 1-3 | 0-0 | 21 | Reid [88] | 1643 |
| 26 | 8 | A | Hereford U | D 1-1 | 0-1 | 21 | Kinsella [90] | 1490 |
| 27 | 12 | A | Braintree T | L 2-3 | 0-1 | 21 | Rooney 2 [66, 90] | 507 |
| 28 | 15 | H | Luton T | D 0-0 | 0-0 | 21 | | 1606 |
| 29 | 19 | H | Alfreton T | D 0-0 | 0-0 | 21 | | 1291 |
| 30 | 29 | A | Kidderminster H | L 0-1 | 0-1 | 21 | | 1785 |
| 31 | Feb 2 | H | Cambridge U | L 1-2 | 1-1 | 21 | Reid [30] | 1788 |
| 32 | 9 | A | Grimsby T | L 0-1 | 0-0 | 21 | | 4462 |
| 33 | 12 | H | Hyde | L 1-3 | 0-1 | 21 | Peniket [66] | 1394 |
| 34 | 16 | H | Tamworth | D 3-3 | 1-2 | 22 | Craney [30], Trainer [73], Reid [85] | 1747 |
| 35 | 23 | A | Newport Co | L 1-2 | 0-0 | 24 | Trainer [90] | 1761 |
| 36 | Mar 2 | A | Mansfield T | L 0-1 | 0-0 | 24 | | 2725 |
| 37 | 9 | H | Macclesfield T | L 0-2 | 0-1 | 24 | | 1567 |
| 38 | 13 | H | Gateshead | D 0-0 | 0-0 | 24 | | 1260 |
| 39 | 16 | A | Woking | L 2-5 | 0-3 | 24 | Jones [54], Williams [81] | 1320 |
| 40 | 19 | A | Macclesfield T | L 1-2 | 1-1 | 24 | Jones [34] | 1381 |
| 41 | 23 | A | Lincoln C | L 2-3 | 1-1 | 24 | Jones [39], Leslie [53] | 1724 |
| 42 | 30 | H | Nuneaton T | L 0-3 | 0-1 | 24 | | 1893 |
| 43 | Apr 1 | A | Forest Green R | D 0-0 | 0-0 | 24 | | 1061 |
| 44 | 6 | H | Dartford | L 0-2 | 0-1 | 24 | | 1375 |
| 45 | 13 | A | Ebbsfleet U | W 3-1 | 3-1 | 24 | Williams 3 [18, 28, 35] | 686 |
| 46 | 20 | H | Hereford U | L 0-4 | 0-1 | 24 | | 2102 |

**Final League Position: 24 – Relegated to Conference North**

## GOALSCORERS

*League (52):* Jones 10, Rooney 5 (2 pens), St Aimie 5, Trainer 5, Leslie 4, Reid 4, Williams 4, Davies 2, Hubbins 2, Spray 2, Byfield 1 (1 pen), Craney 1, Kinsella 1, Peniket 1, Sharp 1, Valentine 1, own goals 3.
*FA Cup (2):* Jones 1, Valentine 1.
*FA Trophy (2):* Leslie 1, Taylor 1.

Column notes above table: **Bennett 2 + 2**, **Bradley — + 3**

| Young 46 | Salmon 43 | Preston 23+1 | Blackburn 3 | Valentine 33 | Jones 26+4 | Rooney 24+12 | Trainer 46 | Leslie 37+2 | Reid 16+4 | St Aimie 18+7 | Hubbins 15+11 | Spray 20+17 | Taylor 16+7 | Rose 34 | Brown 6+12 | Briscoe 8+1 | Davies 9+4 | Byfield 2+5 | Chilvers 8 | Sharp 5+3 | Roberts —+1 | Wylde 1+1 | Kinsella 7 | Lamplough —+1 | Peniket 1+5 | Watson 5 | Craney 10+1 | Graham 4+2 | Henry 4+1 | Smith J 3+1 | Rodney —+3 | Ford 5+1 | Williams 10 | Adaggio 4+2 | Meechan 2+5 | Smith C 6 | O'Neil 4+2 | Match No. |
|---|---|---|---|---|---|---|---|---|---|---|---|---|---|---|---|---|---|---|---|---|---|---|---|---|---|---|---|---|---|---|---|---|---|---|---|---|---|---|
| 1 | 2 | 3 | 4 | 5 | 6 | 7 | 8 | 9 | 10² | 11¹ | 12 | 13 | | | | | | | | | | | | | | | | | | | | | | | | | | 1 |
| 1 | 2 | 4 | 3 | 5 | 9 | 6³ | 7² | 8 | 10¹ | 11 | 12 | 14 | 13 | | | | | | | | | | | | | | | | | | | | | | | | | 2 |
| 1 | 2 | 4 | | 5 | | 7³ | 8 | 9 | 13 | 10 | 6¹ | 11² | 14 | 3 | 12 | | | | | | | | | | | | | | | | | | | | | | | 3 |
| 1 | 2 | 4■ | 3 | | 7 | 8 | 9 | 14■ | 10³ | 6¹ | 11² | 13 | 5 | 12 | | | | | | | | | | | | | | | | | | | | | | | | 4 |
| 1 | 2 | | 4 | 3 | 12 | 7 | 8 | 11 | | 9 | 5² | 10¹ | | 6 | 13 | | | | | | | | | | | | | | | | | | | | | | | 5 |
| 1 | 2 | | | 5 | 10² | 7 | 8 | 9 | | 11 | 6¹ | | 13 | 4 | 12 | | 3³ | 14 | | | | | | | | | | | | | | | | | | | | 6 |
| 1 | 2 | | | 5 | 10 | 8 | 7 | 9 | | 11 | | 12 | | 4 | 6¹ | 3 | | | | | | | | | | | | | | | | | | | | | | 7 |
| 1 | 2 | | | 5² | 6 | 7³ | 8 | 9 | | 10 | | 12 | | 4 | 13 | 3¹ | 14 | 11 | | | | | | | | | | | | | | | | | | | | 8 |
| 1 | 2 | | | | 10² | 12 | 8 | 9¹ | | 11³ | | 13 | 5 | 3 | 6 | | 7 | 14 | 4 | | | | | | | | | | | | | | | | | | | 9 |
| 1 | 2 | | | | 6² | 13 | 8 | 9 | | 10³ | | 11¹ | 5 | 4 | 12 | | 7 | 14 | 3■ | | | | | | | | | | | | | | | | | | | 10 |
| 1 | 2 | 3■ | | | 6¹ | 13 | 8 | 9 | | 10■ | 12 | 11³ | 5 | 4 | | | 7² | 14 | | | | | | | | | | | | | | | | | | | | 11 |
| 1 | 2 | | | | | 7² | 9 | 10 | | 12 | 11 | 5 | 3 | 6¹ | | 8 | 13 | 4 | | | | | | | | | | | | | | | | | | | | 12 |
| 1 | 2 | | | | 12 | | 8 | 9 | | 6¹ | 11 | 5 | 4 | 13 | | 7³ | 10² | 3 | 14 | | | | | | | | | | | | | | | | | | | 13 |
| 1 | 2 | | | | 10 | | 7 | 9³ | | 6¹ | 11² | 5 | 4 | 12 | | 8 | | 3 | 13 | 14 | | | | | | | | | | | | | | | | | | 14 |
| 1 | 2 | | | | 10 | 12 | 8 | 9 | | 11 | 6 | 13 | 5² | 4 | | 7¹ | | 3 | | | | | | | | | | | | | | | | | | | | 15 |
| 1 | | | | | 2 | 10 | | 7 | 9 | | 13 | 6² | 11¹ | 5 | 3 | 8 | | 4 | 12 | | | | | | | | | | | | | | | | | | | 16 |
| 1 | 2 | 12 | | | 5 | 6 | | 7 | 9 | | 10² | 13 | 14 | 8 | 4 | | 3¹ | 11³ | | | | | | | | | | | | | | | | | | | | 17 |
| 1 | 2 | 3 | | | 5 | 6■ | | 7 | 9³ | | 10¹ | 12 | 13 | 8 | 4 | | 11² | | | | | | | | | | | | | | | | | | | | | 18 |
| 1 | 2 | 3 | | | 5 | | 14 | 7 | 9 | | 10² | 13 | 8³ | 4 | 6 | | 12 | | | | | | | | | | | | | | | | | | | | | 19 |
| 1 | 2 | 3 | | | 5 | | 7² | 8 | 9 | | 14 | 6¹ | 11 | 4 | 12 | 13 | | 10³ | | | | | | | | | | | | | | | | | | | | 20 |
| 1 | 2 | 3 | | | 5 | 6 | 8² | 7¹ | 9 | | 13 | | 10 | 4 | 12 | 14 | | 11³ | | | | | | | | | | | | | | | | | | | | 21 |
| 1 | 2 | 3 | | | 5 | | 7 | 8 | 10³ | 13 | 11 | 6² | 14 | 4¹ | | | 9 | | | 12 | | | | | | | | | | | | | | | | | | 22 |
| 1 | 2 | 3 | | | 5 | 12 | 8 | 9 | 10 | 11³ | 14 | 6² | | 13 | 7¹ | | 4 | | | | | | | | | | | | | | | | | | | | | 23 |
| 1 | 2 | 3 | | | 5 | 14 | 7 | 9¹ | 11 | 10² | 6³ | 13 | 12 | 4 | 8 | | | | | | | | | | | | | | | | | | | | | | | 24 |
| 1 | 2 | 3 | | | 5 | 13 | 7² | 9³ | 10 | 12 | 6 | 11¹ | 4 | | | | | | | | | | 8 | 14 | | | | | | | | | | | | | 25 |
| 1 | 2 | 4 | | | 5 | 6 | 13 | 8 | 9 | 11¹ | 12 | 10² | 3 | | | | | | | | | | 7 | | | | | | | | | | | | | | | 26 |
| 1 | 2 | 3 | | | 5² | 10 | 6 | 7 | 9² | 13 | 12 | 11¹ | 14 | 4 | | | | | | | | | 8 | | | | | | | | | | | | | | | 27 |
| 1 | 2 | 3 | | | 10² | 8 | 7 | 9 | 11¹ | 12 | 13 | 5 | 4 | | | | | | | | | | 6¹ | | | | | | | | | | | | | | | 28 |
| 1 | 2 | 3 | | | 10² | 8 | 7 | 9 | | 11 | 12 | 13 | 5 | 4 | | | | | | | | | 6¹ | | | | | | | | | | | | | | | 29 |
| 1 | 2 | 3 | | | 10 | 7¹ | 8 | 9² | 11³ | 13 | 14 | 5 | 4 | | | | | | | | | | 6 | 12 | | | | | | | | | | | | | | 30 |
| 1 | 2 | 3 | | | 9 | 10 | 13 | 7 | | 11 | 6¹ | 5 | 4 | | | | | | | | | | 8² | 12 | | | | | | | | | | | | | | 31 |
| 1 | 2 | | | | 6 | 11¹ | 7 | 10 | | 5² | 3 | | | | | | | | | | | | | 14 | 4 | 8 | 9³ | 12 | 13 | | | | | | | | | 32 |
| 1 | 2¹ | | | | 5 | | 7 | 14 | 11 | 12 | 4 | | | | | | | | | | | | 13 | 3 | 10 | 9³ | 6 | 8² | | | | | | | | | | 33 |
| 1 | | | | | 5 | | 7 | 11 | | 2 | | | | 4 | | | | | | | | | 13 | 3 | 10 | 9² | 6 | 8¹ | 12 | | | | | | | | | 34 |
| 1 | | | | | 2 | | 6 | 10² | | 7 | | | | 4 | | | | | | | | | 11 | 3 | 5 | 12 | 9 | 8¹ | 13 | | | | | | | | 35 |
| 1 | 5 | | | | 2 | 10¹ | 8 | 11 | | 7 | | | | | | | | | | | | | 4■ | 9 | 12 | 6² | | 13 | 3 | | | | | | | | 36 |
| 1 | 2¹ | 10 | | | 4 | 12 | 14 | 9 | | 11 | 13 | | 6 | | | | | | | | | | | 5³ | 7² | | | | | 3 | 8 | | | | | | 37 |
| 1 | 2 | 3 | | | 5 | 11¹ | 8 | 7 | 9 | | 12 | | | | | | | | | | | | | 6² | | | | | | 4 | 10 | 13 | | | | | 38 |
| 1 | 2 | 3¹ | | | 5 | 10 | 6 | 7 | 9³ | | 13 | | | 12 | | | | | | | | | | 8² | | | | | | 4 | 11 | | 14 | | | | 39 |
| 1 | 2 | | | | 5 | 6³ | 9¹ | 8 | | | 10² | | | 4 | | | | | | | | | | 12 | | | | | | 3 | 11 | | 13 | 7 | 14 | 40 |
| 1 | 2 | | | | 5 | 11² | 6¹ | 8 | 12 | | 9³ | | | 3 | | | | | | | | | | 4 | | | | | | 10 | 13 | 14 | 7 | | | 41 |
| 1 | 2 | | | | 5 | 12 | 7 | 9² | | 10 | | | 4 | 14 | | | | | | | | | | 8¹ | | | | | | 6³ | 11 | 3 | 13 | | 42 |
| 1 | 2 | | | | | 3¹ | 6 | 9 | | 7 | | | 4 | 14 | | | | 12 | | | | | | | | | | | | 10³ | 11 | 13 | 5 | 8² | | 43 |
| 1 | 5 | | | | | 8 | 7 | 9² | | 11¹ | | | 3³ | | | | | 13 | | | | | | | | | | | 14 | 6 | 2 | 12 | 4 | 10 | | 44 |
| 1 | 5 | | | | | 9 | 8 | 10 | | 12 | | | | 3 | | | | 13 | | | | | | | | | | | | 11 | 2 | 7¹ | 4■ | 6 | | 45 |
| 1 | 3 | 4³ | | | 5 | 12 | 8² | 7 | 9 | | 14 | | | 6¹ | | | | 13 | | | | | | | | | | | | 10 | 2 | | | 11 | | 46 |

---

**FA Cup**

| | | | |
|---|---|---|---|
| Fourth Qualifying | Nuneaton T | (h) | 2-2 |
| *Replay* | Nuneaton T | (a) | 0-1 |

*aet.*

**FA Trophy**

| | | | |
|---|---|---|---|
| First Round | Nuneaton T | (h) | 1-0 |
| Second Round | King's Lynn T | (a) | 1-3 |

# ALFRETON TOWN

*Ground:* The Impact Arena, North Street, Alfreton, Derbyshire DE55 7FZ. *Tel:* (01773) 830 277.
*Fax:* (01773) 836 164. *Website:* www.alfretontownfc.com. *Year Formed:* 1959.
*Record Gate:* 5,023 (1960 v Matlock T). *Nickname:* 'The Reds'. *Manager:* Nicky Law.
*Secretary:* Bryan Rudkin. *Colours:* All red.

## ALFRETON TOWN – BLUE SQUARE PREMIER 2012–13 LEAGUE RECORD

| Match No. | Date | Venue | Opponents | Result | H/T Score | Lg Pos. | Goalscorers | Attendance |
|---|---|---|---|---|---|---|---|---|
| 1 | Aug 11 | A | Stockport Co | L | 0-1 | 0-1 | 22 | | 3448 |
| 2 | 14 | H | Southport | D | 3-3 | 1-1 | 18 | Clayton 2 [6, 85], Tomlinson (pen) [61] | 562 |
| 3 | 18 | H | Hereford U | L | 0-3 | 0-0 | 21 | | 690 |
| 4 | 25 | A | Barrow | W | 3-1 | 1-0 | 15 | Clayton 2 [28, 71], Tomlinson [51] | 798 |
| 5 | 27 | H | Nuneaton T | L | 0-3 | 0-0 | 21 | | 680 |
| 6 | Sept 1 | A | Dartford | L | 1-5 | 0-3 | 21 | Meadows [80] | 1145 |
| 7 | 4 | A | Lincoln C | W | 2-1 | 0-1 | 18 | Wilson, A [64], Kempson [80] | 1566 |
| 8 | 8 | H | Luton T | W | 3-0 | 2-0 | 14 | Wilson, A 2 [2, 66], Bradley (pen) [23] | 1392 |
| 9 | 15 | A | Forest Green R | D | 1-1 | 0-1 | 16 | Bradley (pen) [90] | 1072 |
| 10 | 22 | H | Kidderminster H | D | 1-1 | 1-0 | 15 | Bradley [29] | 659 |
| 11 | 29 | H | Braintree T | D | 1-1 | 1-0 | 17 | Bradley (pen) [44] | 496 |
| 12 | Oct 6 | A | Macclesfield T | W | 2-1 | 1-1 | 16 | Bradley [1], Arnold [87] | 1437 |
| 13 | 9 | H | Grimsby T | L | 0-2 | 0-1 | 18 | | 1192 |
| 14 | 13 | A | Ebbsfleet U | D | 0-0 | 0-0 | 18 | | 804 |
| 15 | 27 | H | AFC Telford U | D | 1-1 | 1-0 | 16 | Tomlinson [45] | 572 |
| 16 | Nov 6 | A | Gateshead | L | 0-2 | 0-2 | 17 | | 475 |
| 17 | 9 | H | Newport Co | W | 4-3 | 3-1 | 15 | Arnold [6], Clayton 2 [17, 70], Bradley (pen) [45] | 663 |
| 18 | 17 | A | Woking | W | 2-1 | 1-1 | 15 | Clayton 2 [26, 54] | 1537 |
| 19 | 20 | A | Hyde | D | 1-1 | 1-1 | 12 | Franks [39] | 444 |
| 20 | Dec 8 | A | Luton T | L | 0-3 | 0-0 | 18 | | 5648 |
| 21 | 18 | H | Cambridge U | D | 1-1 | 1-0 | 17 | Law [27] | 534 |
| 22 | 26 | A | Mansfield T | W | 2-1 | 1-1 | 15 | Clayton [37], Tomlinson [57] | 4186 |
| 23 | Jan 1 | H | Mansfield T | L | 0-3 | 0-1 | 16 | | 1537 |
| 24 | 5 | H | Dartford | W | 3-2 | 1-1 | 14 | Meadows 2 [45, 89], Brown [75] | 522 |
| 25 | 8 | H | Wrexham | L | 1-2 | 1-1 | 16 | Tomlinson [33] | 628 |
| 26 | 12 | A | Hereford U | D | 3-3 | 1-2 | 13 | Clayton [37], Arnold [57], Franklin [63] | 1565 |
| 27 | 19 | A | AFC Telford U | D | 0-0 | 0-0 | 14 | | 1291 |
| 28 | Feb 2 | A | Grimsby T | L | 2-4 | 1-2 | 17 | Bradley (pen) [27], Clayton [71] | 3868 |
| 29 | 9 | H | Woking | L | 0-3 | 0-0 | 18 | | 606 |
| 30 | 12 | A | Cambridge U | W | 3-0 | 0-0 | 15 | Franks [52], Arnold [89], Clayton [90] | 1779 |
| 31 | 16 | H | Macclesfield T | L | 1-2 | 1-1 | 16 | Clayton [36] | 740 |
| 32 | 19 | A | Nuneaton T | L | 0-1 | 0-0 | 17 | | 781 |
| 33 | 23 | A | Kidderminster H | L | 1-3 | 1-3 | 17 | Tomlinson [29] | 2209 |
| 34 | 26 | H | Hyde | W | 5-1 | 2-0 | 16 | Tomlinson 3 (1 pen) [5, 15, 48 (p)], Clayton [69], Boden [90] | 476 |
| 35 | Mar 2 | A | Wrexham | D | 1-1 | 0-1 | 16 | Boden [57] | 3706 |
| 36 | 9 | A | Tamworth | D | 1-1 | 1-0 | 16 | Soares [79] | 703 |
| 37 | 12 | H | Ebbsfleet U | W | 3-0 | 2-0 | 14 | Bradley (pen) [14], Tomlinson [29], Rose [71] | 459 |
| 38 | 16 | H | Gateshead | W | 3-2 | 0-2 | 13 | Tomlinson [77], Hewitt [78], Boden [90] | 566 |
| 39 | 28 | A | Braintree T | L | 1-2 | 0-1 | 16 | Soares [90] | 409 |
| 40 | 30 | H | Lincoln C | L | 0-2 | 0-1 | 17 | | 1189 |
| 41 | Apr 1 | A | Southport | W | 2-0 | 2-0 | 15 | Brown [2], Meadows [37] | 830 |
| 42 | 6 | H | Stockport Co | L | 2-3 | 1-1 | 15 | Meadows [21], Arnold [90] | 1157 |
| 43 | 9 | H | Barrow | W | 4-0 | 0-0 | 15 | Clayton 2 [47, 54], Arnold 2 [69, 81] | 525 |
| 44 | 11 | H | Tamworth | W | 3-0 | 2-0 | 13 | Bradley (pen) [20], Clayton [32], Arnold [62] | 568 |
| 45 | 13 | A | Newport Co | L | 0-2 | 0-1 | 14 | | 2138 |
| 46 | 20 | H | Forest Green R | W | 2-1 | 2-0 | 13 | Law [9], Arnold [37] | 759 |

**Final League Position: 13**

### GOALSCORERS

*League (69):* Clayton 17, Tomlinson 11 (2 pens), Arnold 9, Bradley 9 (7 pens), Meadows 5, Boden 3, Wilson, A 3,
Brown 2, Franks 2, Law 2, Soares 2, Franklin 1, Hewitt 1, Kempson 1, Rose 1.
*FA Cup (8):* Tomlinson 4, Clayton 2, Arnold 1, Bradley 1.
*FA Trophy (1):* Bradley 1.

| Barnes 18 | Law 42+2 | Kempson 33 | Franks 27+3 | Franklin 35+1 | Russell 8+7 | Bradley 41+2 | Brown 26+4 | Arnold 37+8 | Tomlinson 29+10 | Christie 1 | Streete 34+3 | Clayton 32+10 | Denton —+3 | Quinn 17+2 | Taylor 4+7 | Meadows 26+13 | Wilson A 8+2 | Stewart 16 | Worsfold 1+8 | Killock 14+1 | Harriott 9+1 | Wilson M —+1 | Emerton —+2 | Soares 10+8 | Boden 6+7 | Hewitt 11+4 | Pickford 12 | Rose 9 | Match No. |
|---|---|---|---|---|---|---|---|---|---|---|---|---|---|---|---|---|---|---|---|---|---|---|---|---|---|---|---|---|---|
| 1 | 2 | 3 | 4 | 5 | 6 | 7 | 8² | 9 | 10³ | 11¹ | 12 | 13 | 14 | | | | | | | | | | | | | | | | 1 |
| 1 | 2 | 4 | 3 | | 6 | 8 | 5 | 9 | 10 | | 7 | 11 | | | | | | | | | | | | | | | | | 2 |
| 1 | 6 | | 3 | 5 | 9¹ | 8 | 7 | 11 | 12 | | 2 | 10² | 13⁸ | 4 | | | | | | | | | | | | | | | 3 |
| 1 | 2 | 3 | | 5 | 6 | 8 | 9 | | 10 | | 4 | 11¹ | | | 7² | 12 | 13 | | | | | | | | | | | | 4 |
| 1 | 2 | 3 | | 5 | 6² | 8 | 7 | 12 | 11 | | 4³ | 10 | | | | 9¹ | 14 | 13 | | | | | | | | | | | 5 |
| | 2 | 3 | 5 | | 9 | 7 | 8 | 13 | 11² | | | 10³ | | 4 | 6¹ | 12 | 14 | | | 1 | | | | | | | | | 6 |
| | 2 | 3 | 4 | 5 | | 8 | 9 | 11 | | | 7 | 12 | | | 6 | 10¹ | | | | 1 | | | | | | | | | 7 |
| | 2 | 3 | 6 | 5 | 13 | 7 | 8 | 11³ | 14 | | 4 | 12 | | | | 9² | 10¹ | | | 1 | | | | | | | | | 8 |
| | 2² | 8 | 3 | 12 | 7 | 6 | 10 | 13 | | | 5 | | | 4 | | 9¹ | 11³ | | 14 | 1 | | | | | | | | | 9 |
| | 2² | 6 | 5 | 12 | 7³ | 8 | 10 | 13 | | | 4 | 3 | | | 14 | 9¹ | 11 | | | 1 | | | | | | | | | 10 |
| | 2 | 3 | 6 | 5 | 12 | 8 | 9¹ | 11 | 14 | | 4 | 13 | | | | 7² | 10³ | | | 1 | | | | | | | | | 11 |
| | 2 | 4 | | 5 | | 7 | 9 | 10¹ | | | 3 | 12 | | | | 13 | 6² | 11 | | 1 | 8 | | | | | | | | 12 |
| | 2 | 4 | | 5 | 13 | 8 | | 11 | 9¹ | | 7 | 12 | | | | 6² | 10 | | | 1 | 3 | | | | | | | | 13 |
| | 2 | 3 | | 5 | | 7 | | 11 | 12 | | 8 | 9² | | | 6 | 10¹ | | | | 1 | 13 | 4 | | | | | | | 14 |
| | 2 | 3 | | 5 | | 6 | 12 | 7 | 11 | | 8 | 10¹ | | | | 9 | | | | 1 | 4 | | | | | | | | 15 |
| | 2 | | 4 | 3¹ | 12 | | 6 | 8 | | | 7 | 9² | | 14 | 13 | 10 | | | | 1 | 11³ | 5 | | | | | | | 16 |
| | 2 | | 4 | 5¹ | | 6 | 12 | 9 | 10 | | 7 | 11 | | | | 8 | | | | 1 | 3 | | | | | | | | 17 |
| | 2 | | 4 | 5 | | 9 | 12 | 11 | | | 7 | 10 | | | 13 | 6² | | | | 1 | 3 | | 8¹ | | | | | | 18 |
| | | 5 | 4² | 2 | 12 | 8 | 14 | 11 | 9¹ | | 7 | 10 | | | 13 | | | | | 1 | 3 | | 6³ | | | | | | 19 |
| | 2 | 5 | 9¹ | 3 | | 8³ | | 11 | 6 | | 10² | 13 | 4 | | | | | | | 1 | 12 | 7 | | | | | | | 20 |
| | 2 | 3¹ | 12 | 5 | | 7 | 9 | 11 | 8⁸ | | 10 | | | | | | | | | 1 | 4 | 6 | | | | | | | 21 |
| 1 | | 5 | | 7 | | 2 | 8 | 6 | 9² | 10¹ | | 11 | | 3 | | 4 | | | | | 12 | 13 | | | | | | | 22 |
| 1 | 2 | 4 | | 6² | 7³ | 8 | 9 | 11 | 10¹ | | 3 | 13 | 12 | | | 5 | | | 14 | | | | | | | | | | 23 |
| 1 | 2 | 3 | | 5¹ | 6³ | 8 | 11 | 10² | | | 7 | 13 | | | | 9 | | | | | | 14 | 4 | 12 | | | | | 24 |
| 1 | 2³ | 3 | | 14 | | 8 | 9 | 10¹ | | | 4 | 11 | | | | 13 | 6 | | | | | | | 12 | 5 | 7² | | | 25 |
| 1 | 2 | 3 | 4 | 5 | | 7 | 10¹ | | 8 | | 11 | | | | | 6 | | | | | | | | 12 | | 9 | | | 26 |
| 1 | 6 | 3 | 4 | 5 | 13 | | 9 | 10¹ | | | 2 | 11 | | | | 8² | | | | | 7 | | | 12 | | | | | 27 |
| 1 | 2 | 3 | | 5 | 6 | 11³ | 9² | | | | 7 | 12 | | | | 14 | 4 | 8 | | | | | | 10¹ | 13 | | | | 28 |
| 1 | 2² | 4 | 3 | 5 | | 7¹ | | 9 | | | 8 | 11 | 13 | | | 6 | | | | | 12 | | | 10³ | | 14 | | | 29 |
| 1 | 6 | 4 | 3 | 5 | | 7 | | 11 | | | 2 | 10 | | | | 8 | | | | | | | | 9 | | | | | 30 |
| 1 | 2 | 3 | 4 | 5 | | 8 | | 10 | 14 | | 6² | 11¹ | | | | 7³ | | | | | | | | 13 | 12 | 9 | | | 31 |
| 1 | 2 | 3 | 4 | 5 | | 7 | | 9² | 11 | | 12 | 10³ | | | | 6 | | | | | | | | 13 | 14 | 8¹ | | | 32 |
| 1¹ | 2 | 4 | 7 | 5 | | 9 | | 12 | 11³ | | 8⁸ | 10² | | | | 3 | | | | | | | | 6 | | 14 | 13 | | 33 |
| | 2 | 3 | 12 | 5 | | 7 | 8 | 9 | 11³ | | | 10 | | 4¹ | | 13 | | | | | | | | 6² | 14 | | 1 | | 34 |
| | 13 | 4 | 2 | 5 | | 8 | 6 | 12 | 11¹ | | 3 | | | 14 | | | | | | | | | | 7² | 10³ | 9 | 1 | | 35 |
| | 2 | 4¹ | 12 | 5 | | 7 | 6 | 9 | 11² | | 3 | | | 13 | | 14 | 8 | | | | | | | | 10³ | | 1 | | 36 |
| | 2 | | | 5 | | 8³ | 7 | 12 | 10² | | 11 | | | 4 | | 14 | | | | | | | | 6¹ | 13 | 9 | 1 | 3 | 37 |
| | 2 | | | 5 | | 8³ | 9 | 13 | 10 | | 11¹ | | | 3 | | 14 | | | | | | | | 7² | 12 | 6 | 1 | 4 | 38 |
| | 2¹ | | | 5 | | 8³ | 7 | 13 | 10 | | 12 | | | 3 | | 14 | | | | | | | | 9 | 11² | 6 | 1 | 4 | 39 |
| | 3 | 2 | | 5⁸ | | 7 | 13 | 11³ | | | 8 | 10¹ | | 4 | | 12 | | | | | | | | 6 | 14 | 9² | 1 | | 40 |
| | 4 | | | | 6 | 8 | 10 | | | | 2 | 3 | | | | 7 | | | | | 9 | | | 11 | | | 1 | 5 | 41 |
| 1 | 12 | 3 | | | | 7 | 8¹ | 10 | 13 | | 5 | 11 | | 4 | | 9 | | | | | | | | 6² | 14 | | | 2³ | 42 |
| | 2 | 3 | | | | 7 | | 9 | 11² | | 4 | 10¹ | | | | 8 | | | | | | | 12 | 13 | 6 | | 1 | 5 | 43 |
| | 2 | 3 | | | | 7 | | 11 | 12 | | 4 | 10² | | | | 13 | 8 | | | | | | | 6¹ | 9 | | 1 | 5 | 44 |
| | 2 | 3 | 14 | | | 7 | | 6 | 11² | | 4 | 10¹ | | | | 13 | 9 | | | | | | | 12 | 8³ | | 1 | 5 | 45 |
| | 6 | 3 | | 5 | | 8 | | 11 | 12 | | 7 | 10² | | 4¹ | | 9³ | | | | | | | | 13 | 14 | | 1 | 2 | 46 |

**FA Cup**

| | | | |
|---|---|---|---|
| Fourth Qualifying | Gateshead | (h) | 2-0 |
| First Round | Wrexham | (a) | 4-2 |
| Second Round | Leyton Orient | (h) | 2-4 |

**FA Trophy**

| | | | |
|---|---|---|---|
| First Round | Kidderminster H | (h) | 1-3 |

# BARROW

*Ground:* Furness Building Society Stadium, Wilkie Road, Barrow-in-Furness, Cumbria LA14 5UW.
*Tel:* (01229) 823 061.  *Website:* www.barrowafc.com.  *Year Formed:* 1901.
*Record Gate:* 16,854 (1954 v Swansea T, FA Cup 3rd rd).  *Nickname:* 'The Bluebirds'.
*Manager:* Dave Bayliss.  *Colours:* White shirts, blue shorts, white socks.

## BARROW – BLUE SQUARE PREMIER 2012–13 LEAGUE RECORD

| Match No. | Date | Venue | Opponents | Result | H/T Score | Lg Pos. | Goalscorers | Attendance |
|---|---|---|---|---|---|---|---|---|
| 1 | Aug 11 | H | AFC Telford U | D | 0-0 | 0-0 | 17 | | 1041 |
| 2 | 14 | A | Hyde | D | 0-0 | 0-0 | 17 | | 798 |
| 3 | 18 | A | Woking | L | 1-3 | 1-1 | 20 | Hunter [15] | 1373 |
| 4 | 25 | H | Alfreton T | L | 1-3 | 0-1 | 21 | Boyes [77] | 798 |
| 5 | 27 | A | Macclesfield T | L | 0-2 | 0-1 | 23 | | 1711 |
| 6 | Sept 1 | H | Kidderminster H | D | 1-1 | 0-1 | 22 | Baker [77] | 716 |
| 7 | 4 | H | Grimsby T | D | 2-2 | 1-0 | 22 | Baker (pen) [45], Jackson [60] | 966 |
| 8 | 8 | A | Tamworth | W | 3-1 | 1-1 | 21 | Jackson [19], Boyes 2 [79, 90] | 892 |
| 9 | 15 | H | Newport Co | L | 0-3 | 0-1 | 22 | | 802 |
| 10 | 22 | A | Ebbsfleet U | W | 4-2 | 3-0 | 19 | Baker 3 (1 pen) [20, 36 (p), 63], Rutherford [25] | 780 |
| 11 | 25 | A | Wrexham | L | 0-3 | 0-1 | 21 | | 2881 |
| 12 | 29 | H | Cambridge U | L | 1-4 | 0-2 | 22 | Skelton [54] | 904 |
| 13 | Oct 6 | A | Braintree T | W | 3-2 | 1-2 | 19 | Almond 2 [42, 81], Rowe, Danny M [90] | 608 |
| 14 | 9 | H | Southport | W | 3-2 | 0-1 | 19 | Boyes 2 [73, 84], Baker [86] | 924 |
| 15 | 13 | H | Dartford | D | 0-0 | 0-0 | 19 | | 1278 |
| 16 | 27 | A | Nuneaton T | D | 1-1 | 0-0 | 17 | Rowe, Danny M [64] | 844 |
| 17 | Nov 6 | A | Stockport Co | L | 1-3 | 0-1 | 18 | Rowe, Danny M [64] | 2805 |
| 18 | 10 | H | Lincoln C | L | 1-2 | 0-1 | 22 | Baker (pen) [85] | 987 |
| 19 | 17 | H | Forest Green R | D | 2-2 | 1-1 | 23 | Boyes [45], Flynn [61] | 853 |
| 20 | Dec 4 | A | AFC Telford U | D | 1-1 | 0-1 | 23 | Jackson [90] | 1333 |
| 21 | 7 | H | Hereford U | L | 0-2 | 0-1 | 24 | | 867 |
| 22 | 26 | H | Gateshead | L | 0-2 | 0-1 | 24 | | 1135 |
| 23 | Jan 1 | A | Gateshead | W | 1-0 | 1-0 | 24 | Boyes [1] | 610 |
| 24 | 5 | A | Kidderminster H | L | 0-2 | 0-1 | 24 | | 1703 |
| 25 | 8 | A | Luton T | L | 1-6 | 0-3 | 24 | Boyes [68] | 5165 |
| 26 | 19 | A | Newport Co | W | 2-0 | 1-0 | 23 | Flynn [41], Rowe, Danny L [62] | 2107 |
| 27 | Feb 2 | H | Luton T | W | 1-0 | 1-0 | 22 | Boyes [5] | 1188 |
| 28 | 9 | A | Mansfield T | L | 1-8 | 1-5 | 22 | Rowe, Danny L (pen) [17] | 2226 |
| 29 | 12 | A | Southport | L | 2-5 | 1-0 | 22 | Flynn [6], Boyes (pen) [83] | 806 |
| 30 | 16 | H | Nuneaton T | L | 1-2 | 0-0 | 23 | Boyes [48] | 998 |
| 31 | 19 | H | Woking | W | 2-0 | 1-0 | 21 | Rowe, Danny M [9], Rowe, Danny L [53] | 624 |
| 32 | 23 | A | Lincoln C | D | 0-0 | 0-0 | 22 | | 1830 |
| 33 | 26 | H | Wrexham | L | 0-1 | 0-0 | 22 | | 889 |
| 34 | Mar 2 | H | Tamworth | W | 2-0 | 1-0 | 20 | Rowe, Danny L [15], Harvey [90] | 896 |
| 35 | 9 | A | Forest Green R | D | 1-1 | 0-1 | 20 | Baker [63] | 904 |
| 36 | 12 | H | Stockport Co | L | 0-2 | 0-0 | 21 | | 803 |
| 37 | 16 | A | Hereford U | L | 1-2 | 1-1 | 22 | Boyes [22] | 1273 |
| 38 | 19 | A | Dartford | W | 1-0 | 0-0 | 22 | Baker (pen) [74] | 908 |
| 39 | 27 | H | Macclesfield T | W | 1-0 | 0-0 | 22 | Harvey [59] | 716 |
| 40 | 30 | A | Grimsby T | D | 0-0 | 0-0 | 22 | | 3532 |
| 41 | Apr 1 | H | Hyde | D | 1-1 | 1-1 | 22 | Pearson, M [22] | 1001 |
| 42 | 3 | H | Ebbsfleet U | D | 1-1 | 0-1 | 22 | Boyes [77] | 844 |
| 43 | 6 | H | Mansfield T | L | 0-4 | 0-2 | 22 | | 1114 |
| 44 | 9 | A | Alfreton T | L | 0-4 | 0-0 | 22 | | 525 |
| 45 | 13 | A | Cambridge U | L | 1-2 | 1-2 | 22 | Baker (pen) [45] | 2758 |
| 46 | 20 | H | Braintree T | L | 0-1 | 0-0 | 22 | | 780 |

**Final League Position: 22 – Relegated to Conference North**

### GOALSCORERS

*League (45):* Boyes 13 (1 pen), Baker 10 (5 pens), Rowe, Danny L 4 (1 pen), Rowe, Danny M 4, Flynn 3, Jackson 3, Almond 2, Harvey 2, Hunter 1, Pearson, M 1, Rutherford 1, Skelton 1.
*FA Cup (7):* Boyes 3, Hunter 2, Almond 1, Baker 1.
*FA Trophy (10):* Baker 3 (2 pens), Boyes 2, Flynn 2, McConville 1, Rowe, Danny M 1, own goal 1.

| Hurst 45 | Pearson M 42+1 | Hessey 25+5 | Anderson 17+1 | Skelton 38+1 | Rutherford 40+4 | Owen 25+2 | Hunter 39 | Rowe Danny M 21+12 | Boyes 41+2 | Jackson 8+15 | Mukendi 1+3 | Cole —+3 | Baker 36+2 | Anoruo —+2 | Aldred 11 | Moore 1+4 | Hulbert 1 | McConville 14+11 | Flynn 19+3 | Almond 10+1 | Harvey 28+2 | Byrne 1 | Pearson S 1+1 | Rowe Danny L 19+2 | O'Donnell 5+1 | McEvilly —+6 | Eckersley 1 | Sodje 9 | Williams 3 | Dawson 5+4 | Match No. |
|---|---|---|---|---|---|---|---|---|---|---|---|---|---|---|---|---|---|---|---|---|---|---|---|---|---|---|---|---|---|---|---|
| 1 | 2 | 3 | 4 | 5 | 6 | 7 | 8 | 9 | 10 | 11$^1$ | 12 | 13 | | | | | | | | | | | | | | | | | | | 1 |
| 1 | 2 | 4 | 5 | 3 | 6 | 7 | 8 | 9 | 11 | 13 | | 12 | 10$^1$ | | | | | | | | | | | | | | | | | | 2 |
| 1 | 2 | 3 | 4 | 5 | 6$^3$ | 7 | 8 | 9 | 10$^1$ | 11$^2$ | 12 | 14 | 13 | | | | | | | | | | | | | | | | | | 3 |
| 1 | 2 | 3 | 4 | 5 | 9 | 6$^1$ | 8 | 11$^2$ | 10 | 12 | 13 | | 7 | | | | | | | | | | | | | | | | | | 4 |
| 1 | 3 | | 2 | 5$^3$ | 6 | 7$^1$ | 8 | 14 | 10 | 13 | 11$^2$ | | 12 | | 4 | 9 | | | | | | | | | | | | | | | 5 |
| 1 | 2 | | 3 | 5 | 6 | | 8 | 9$^1$ | 10 | 11$^2$ | | | 7 | 13 | 4 | 12 | | | | | | | | | | | | | | | 6 |
| 1 | 2 | | 3 | 5 | 6 | | 8 | 9$^1$ | 10 | 11 | | | 7 | | 4 | 12 | | | | | | | | | | | | | | | 7 |
| 1 | 2 | 14 | 3 | 5 | 6 | 13 | | 9$^2$ | 10 | 11$^1$ | | | 7 | | 4 | 12 | | 8$^3$ | | | | | | | | | | | | | 8 |
| 1 | 2 | 12 | 3$^1$ | 5$^3$ | 6 | | 8 | 9 | 10 | 11$^2$ | | | 7 | | 4 | 14 | | 13 | | | | | | | | | | | | | 9 |
| 1 | 3 | 5$^4$ | | 12 | 10 | 7 | 9 | | 11$^2$ | 13 | | | 8 | | 4 | | | 6$^1$ | 2 | | | | | | | | | | | | 10 |
| 1 | 3 | | | 5 | 6 | 8 | 9$^1$ | 13 | 10 | 12 | | | 7 | | 4 | | | 11$^2$ | 2 | | | | | | | | | | | | 11 |
| 1$^1$ | 3 | 12 | | 5$^3$ | 6 | 7$^4$ | | 13 | 10 | 14 | | | 8 | | 4 | | | 9$^2$ | 2 | 11 | | | | | | | | | | | 12 |
| 1 | 5 | | 3 | 8 | 11 | | 6 | 12 | 10$^2$ | 13 | | | 7 | | 4$^1$ | | | 2 | 9 | | | | | | | | | | | | 13 |
| 1 | 3 | 14 | 4 | 5$^3$ | 6 | | 8$^2$ | 9$^1$ | 10 | 12 | | | 7 | | | | | 2 | 11 | 13 | | | | | | | | | | | 14 |
| 1 | 4 | 5 | 3 | 9 | | | 8 | 12 | 10 | 13 | | | 6 | | | | | 2 | 11$^2$ | 7$^1$ | | | | | | | | | | | 15 |
| 1 | 3 | 5 | 4 | 6 | | 8 | 13 | 10 | 12 | | | | | | | | | 9$^2$ | 2 | 11$^1$ | 7 | | | | | | | | | | 16 |
| 1 | 5 | 3 | 4 | 9 | | 6$^2$ | 12 | 10 | 13 | | | | 8 | | | | | 2 | 11 | 7$^1$ | | | | | | | | | | | 17 |
| 1 | 3 | 5 | | 6 | | 8$^2$ | 9$^1$ | 12 | 10 | | | | 7 | | 4 | | | 14 | 2$^3$ | 11 | 13 | | | | | | | | | | 18 |
| 1 | 4 | 3 | | 12 | | 6 | | 10 | 11 | | | | 8 | | 5 | | | 2 | 9$^1$ | 7 | | | | | | | | | | | 19 |
| 1 | 3 | 5 | 4 | 9 | | 6$^1$ | | 10$^2$ | 13 | | | | 7 | | | | | 12 | 2 | 11 | 8 | | | | | | | | | | 20 |
| 1$^1$ | 3 | 5 | | 6 | | 7 | | 10 | 13 | | | | 8 | | | | | 14 | 2 | 11$^3$ | 9 | 4$^2$ | 12 | | | | | | | | 21 |
| 1 | 4 | 3 | | 5 | 6 | | 9 | 13 | 11$^3$ | 14 | | | 7$^1$ | | | | | 10$^2$ | 2 | 12 | 8 | | | | | | | | | | 22 |
| 1 | 5 | 3 | 4 | 2 | 6 | 7 | 9 | | 11 | | | | | | | | | 10 | | 8 | | | | | | | | | | | 23 |
| 1 | 5 | 3 | 4 | 2 | 6 | 7$^1$ | 10 | 12 | 8 | 13 | | | | | | | | 11$^2$ | | 9 | | | | | | | | | | | 24 |
| 1 | 4 | 5 | 3 | 6 | 12 | 7$^1$ | 9 | 11 | 10 | | | | | | | | | 10 | 2 | 8 | | | | | | | | | | | 25 |
| 1 | 4 | 3 | | 5 | 6 | 7 | | 10 | | | | | 8 | | | | | 9 | 2 | | | | | 11 | | | | | | | 26 |
| 1 | 4 | 12 | | 5 | 6 | 7 | | 9$^2$ | 10 | | | | 8 | | | | | 13 | 2 | | | | | 11$^3$ | 3$^1$ | 14 | | | | | 27 |
| | 3 | | | 2 | 9 | 7 | | 6$^1$ | 11$^2$ | 10 | | | 12 | | 5 | | | | 8 | | | 1 | | 10 | 13 | 4 | | | | | 28 |
| 1 | 3 | | | 5 | 6 | 8$^4$ | 9 | 12 | 10 | | | | | | | | | | 2 | 7 | | | | 11$^1$ | | 4 | | | | | 29 |
| 1 | 3 | | | 5 | 6 | | 2 | 9$^1$ | 10 | | | | 7 | | | | | 13 | | 8 | | | | 11$^2$ | 12 | 4 | | | | | 30 |
| 1 | 3 | | | 5 | 6$^1$ | | 2 | 9 | 11$^2$ | | | | 7 | | | | | 12 | | 8 | | | | 10 | 13 | 4 | | | | | 31 |
| 1 | 3 | | | 5 | 6 | 7 | 2 | 10 | | | | | 8 | | | | | | | 9 | | | | 11 | | 4 | | | | | 32 |
| 1 | 3 | | | 5 | 6 | 7$^1$ | 2 | 10 | | | | | 8 | | | | | | | 9 | | | | 11 | 12 | 4 | | | | | 33 |
| 1 | 3 | 12 | | 5 | 6 | | 2 | 9$^1$ | | | | | 7 | | | | | 11$^2$ | | 8 | | | | 10 | 13 | 4 | | | | | 34 |
| 1 | 3 | | 2 | 6 | | | 5 | 8 | 13 | | | | 7 | | | | | 10 | | 9 | | | | 11$^2$ | 12 | 4$^1$ | | | | | 35 |
| 1 | 3 | | | 5 | 6 | | 2 | 9$^1$ | 10 | | | | 7 | | | | | 12 | | 8 | | | | 11 | | 4 | | | | | 36 |
| 1 | 2 | 4 | | 5 | | | 6 | | 11 | | | | 7 | | | | | 9$^4$ | | 8 | | | | 10 | | 3 | | | | | 37 |
| 1 | | 3 | | 5 | | | 8 | 2 | | | | | 10 | | | | | | | 7 | | | | 12 | 9 | 11 | | | 4 | 6$^1$ | 38 |
| 1 | | 3 | | 5 | 12 | | 7 | 2 | | | | | 10 | | | | | | | 6 | | | | 8 | 11 | | | | 4 | 9$^1$ | 39 |
| 1 | 12 | 3 | | 5 | 14 | | 7 | 2 | 13$^3$ | 9 | | | 6 | | | | | | | 10 | | | | 8 | | | | | 4$^1$ | 11$^2$ | 40 |
| 1 | 4 | 3 | | 5 | 9 | 7$^1$ | 2 | | | | | | 10 | | | | | | | 8 | | | | 11 | | | | | 12 | | 41 |
| 1 | 3 | 4 | | 5 | 13 | 6$^1$ | 2 | | 10 | | | | 7 | | | | | 9 | | 8 | | | | 12 | | | | | 11$^2$ | | 42 |
| 1 | 3 | | | 5 | 6$^1$ | 7 | 2 | | 11 | | | | 8 | | | | | 9 | | | | | | 10 | 4 | | | | 12 | | 43 |
| 1 | 3 | 5$^1$ | | 9 | 6 | | 2$^3$ | 11 | | | | | 7 | | | | | 12 | 13 | 8 | | | | 10$^2$ | 4 | | | | 14 | | 44 |
| 1 | 3 | | | 5 | 6$^2$ | 7 | | 12 | 10 | | | | 8 | | | | | 14 | 2 | 9$^1$ | | | | 11$^3$ | 4 | | | | 13 | | 45 |
| 1 | 3$^1$ | | | 5 | 6$^2$ | 7 | 2 | 10 | 11$^3$ | | | | 14 | | | | | 12 | | 8 | | | | 13 | 4 | | | 9 | | | 46 |

**FA Cup**

| | | | |
|---|---|---|---|
| Fourth Qualifying | Tamworth | (h) | 2-0 |
| First Round | Guiseley | (a) | 2-2 |
| *Replay* | Guiseley | (h) | 1-0 |
| Second Round | Macclesfield T | (h) | 1-1 |
| *Replay* | Macclesfield T | (a) | 1-4 |

**FA Trophy**

| | | | |
|---|---|---|---|
| First Round | Hyde | (a) | 1-1 |
| *Replay* | Hyde | (h) | 1-0 |
| Second Round | Chesham U | (a) | 5-1 |
| Third Round | Gateshead | (h) | 3-2 |
| Quarter-Finals | Gainsborough Trinity | (a) | 0-2 |

# BRAINTREE TOWN

*Ground:* The Amlin Stadium, Clockhouse Way, Braintree, Essex CM7 3RD.   *Tel:* (01376) 345 617.   *Fax:* (01376) 330 976.
*Website:* www.braintreetownfc.org.uk   *Year Formed:* 1898.   *Record Gate:* 2,029 (2002 v Cambridge U).
*Nickname:* 'The Iron'.   *Manager:* Alan Devonshire.   *Colours:* Orange shirts, blue shorts, blue socks.

## BRAINTREE TOWN – BLUE SQUARE PREMIER 2012–13 LEAGUE RECORD

| Match No. | Date | Venue | Opponents | Result | H/T Score | Lg Pos. | Goalscorers | Attendance |
|---|---|---|---|---|---|---|---|---|
| 1 | Aug 11 | H | Hyde | D | 2-2 | 0-2 | 8 | Sheppard [47], Quinton [90] | 598 |
| 2 | 14 | A | Ebbsfleet U | W | 1-0 | 0-0 | 7 | Davis [70] | 857 |
| 3 | 18 | A | AFC Telford U | L | 0-3 | 0-2 | 14 | | 1524 |
| 4 | 25 | H | Newport Co | L | 1-2 | 0-0 | 16 | Quinton [53] | 611 |
| 5 | 28 | A | Woking | W | 4-1 | 1-1 | 11 | Holman 2 [16, 64], Cestor (og) [51], Symons [54] | 1588 |
| 6 | Sept 1 | H | Tamworth | W | 2-1 | 1-1 | 10 | Gash [21], Holman (pen) [60] | 501 |
| 7 | 4 | H | Kidderminster H | D | 1-1 | 1-0 | 11 | Holman [17] | 579 |
| 8 | 8 | A | Macclesfield T | L | 1-2 | 1-1 | 12 | Quinton (pen) [21] | 1509 |
| 9 | 15 | A | Mansfield T | L | 0-2 | 0-1 | 15 | | 2049 |
| 10 | 22 | H | Stockport Co | D | 0-0 | 0-0 | 14 | | 653 |
| 11 | 25 | H | Dartford | L | 0-2 | 0-2 | 16 | | 721 |
| 12 | 29 | A | Alfreton T | D | 1-1 | 0-1 | 16 | Davis (pen) [80] | 496 |
| 13 | Oct 6 | H | Barrow | L | 2-3 | 2-1 | 18 | Marks [8], Holman [12] | 608 |
| 14 | 9 | A | Luton T | W | 3-2 | 2-1 | 16 | Holman [6], Marks [32], Paine [67] | 5523 |
| 15 | 13 | A | Hereford U | D | 0-0 | 0-0 | 17 | | 1537 |
| 16 | Nov 6 | A | Lincoln C | L | 0-3 | 0-1 | 21 | | 1455 |
| 17 | 10 | H | Gateshead | W | 2-1 | 1-1 | 19 | Marks [6], Wells [55] | 678 |
| 18 | 17 | H | Grimsby T | L | 0-3 | 0-1 | 21 | | 3722 |
| 19 | 20 | H | Wrexham | L | 1-5 | 1-3 | 22 | Sheppard [18] | 508 |
| 20 | Dec 8 | A | Southport | W | 2-0 | 2-0 | 21 | Marks 2 [16, 20] | 803 |
| 21 | 18 | H | Forest Green R | W | 3-1 | 1-0 | 18 | Marks [29], Daley [71], Davis (pen) [82] | 480 |
| 22 | 26 | H | Cambridge U | L | 0-3 | 0-1 | 19 | | 1133 |
| 23 | Jan 1 | A | Cambridge U | L | 0-1 | 0-0 | 21 | | 2406 |
| 24 | 5 | A | Tamworth | W | 4-1 | 2-0 | 19 | Holman [17], Paine [20], Daley [61], Davis (pen) [88] | 763 |
| 25 | 8 | A | Macclesfield T | L | 0-3 | 0-1 | 19 | | 502 |
| 26 | 12 | H | AFC Telford U | W | 3-2 | 1-0 | 17 | Marks [6], Daley [51], Davis (pen) [80] | 507 |
| 27 | 26 | A | Nuneaton T | W | 4-2 | 1-1 | 13 | Mulley [17], Holman [48], Wells [67], Dack [87] | 761 |
| 28 | Feb 9 | H | Hereford U | L | 0-2 | 0-1 | 16 | | 658 |
| 29 | 12 | A | Forest Green R | L | 1-4 | 1-2 | 19 | Daley [42] | 918 |
| 30 | 19 | H | Grimsby T | W | 2-0 | 1-0 | 16 | Daley 2 [27, 76] | 880 |
| 31 | 26 | H | Luton T | W | 2-0 | 1-0 | 15 | Marks [42], Davis [49] | 1003 |
| 32 | Mar 2 | A | Gateshead | W | 2-1 | 1-0 | 13 | Wells [10], Marks [86] | 327 |
| 33 | 16 | A | Stockport Co | W | 3-1 | 0-0 | 14 | Holman [47], Davis 2 (1 pen) [53, 60 (p)] | 3250 |
| 34 | 19 | A | Woking | D | 1-1 | 0-1 | 13 | Holman [84] | 506 |
| 35 | 21 | H | Nuneaton T | D | 2-2 | 2-2 | 13 | Sparkes [16], Marks [32] | 421 |
| 36 | 26 | H | Lincoln C | L | 0-3 | 0-1 | 13 | | 447 |
| 37 | 28 | H | Alfreton T | W | 2-1 | 1-0 | 13 | Marks [1], Davis (pen) [85] | 409 |
| 38 | 30 | A | Kidderminster H | L | 1-2 | 1-0 | 13 | Davis [44] | 2266 |
| 39 | Apr 1 | H | Ebbsfleet U | W | 3-1 | 2-1 | 13 | Daley [12], Mulley [41], Davis (pen) [65] | 822 |
| 40 | 3 | H | Southport | L | 1-3 | 0-1 | 13 | Marks [61] | 451 |
| 41 | 6 | A | Hyde | W | 2-1 | 2-0 | 11 | Mulley [42], Wright [45] | 509 |
| 42 | 9 | A | Newport Co | L | 0-1 | 0-0 | 12 | | 1864 |
| 43 | 11 | A | Dartford | D | 0-0 | 0-0 | 12 | | 1051 |
| 44 | 13 | H | Mansfield T | W | 2-1 | 0-1 | 10 | Paine [60], Sheppard [71] | 1755 |
| 45 | 16 | A | Wrexham | D | 1-1 | 1-1 | 9 | Wright [18] | 2312 |
| 46 | 20 | A | Barrow | W | 1-0 | 0-0 | 9 | Holman [86] | 780 |

**Final League Position: 9**

### GOALSCORERS
*League (63):* Marks 12, Davis 11 (7 pens), Holman 11 (1 pen), Daley 7, Mulley 3, Paine 3, Quinton 3 (1 pen), Sheppard 3, Wells 3, Wright 2, Dack 1, Gash 1, Sparkes 1, Symons 1, own goal 1.
*FA Cup (3):* Marks 2, O'Connor 1.
*FA Trophy (1):* Holman 1.

| Naisbitt 24 | Peters 29+2 | Paine 32+5 | Wells 42 | Habergham 37+2 | McNish 1 | Symons 30+5 | Davis 39 | Sparkes 22+17 | Marks 34+4 | Dawkin 4+8 | Sheppard 7+17 | Mulley 33+6 | Quinton 12+4 | Bailey-Dennis 11+2 | Gash 6 | Holman 29+5 | O'Connor 11+3 | Daley 24+6 | Massey 29 | Hunt 1+3 | Cowan 1 | Watts 4+7 | McDonald 22 | Dack —+4 | Walker 2+2 | Wickham 1+5 | Cox —+3 | Woodyard 5+7 | Wright 9+1 | Smith 5+1 | Match No. |
|---|---|---|---|---|---|---|---|---|---|---|---|---|---|---|---|---|---|---|---|---|---|---|---|---|---|---|---|---|---|---|---|
| 1 | 2 | 3 | 4 | 5 | $6^1$ | $7^3$ | 8 | 9 | 10 | $11^2$ | 12 | 13 | 14 | | | | | | | | | | | | | | | | | | 1 |
| 1 | | 2 | 4 | 5 | | $7^1$ | 8 | 9 | $10^8$ | $11^2$ | 13 | 6 | 12 | 3 | | | | | | | | | | | | | | | | | 2 |
| 1 | 12 | 8 | 3 | 2 | | $6^1$ | 7 | 5 | | $10^3$ | 14 | $9^2$ | 13 | | 4 | 11 | | | | | | | | | | | | | | | 3 |
| 1 | 2 | 7 | 4 | 5 | | | 8 | 9 | $10^1$ | | 12 | 13 | $6^2$ | | 3 | 11 | | | | | | | | | | | | | | | 4 |
| 1 | 2 | 14 | 4 | 5 | | 7 | $8^3$ | $6^2$ | | | 12 | 13 | 9 | | 3 | 10 | $11^1$ | | | | | | | | | | | | | | 5 |
| 1 | 2 | | 4 | 5 | | 6 | 7 | $9^1$ | 14 | 12 | | 13 | $8^2$ | | 3 | $10^3$ | 11 | | | | | | | | | | | | | | 6 |
| 1 | $2^1$ | 12 | 4 | 5 | | 6 | 7 | $9^2$ | 14 | 13 | | 8 | | | 3 | 10 | $11^3$ | | | | | | | | | | | | | | 7 |
| 1 | 2 | | 4 | 5 | | 8 | | $9^1$ | 14 | 12 | | | $6^3$ | $7^2$ | 3 | 10 | 11 | 13 | | | | | | | | | | | | | 8 |
| 1 | 5 | 3 | 4 | | | 8 | | $6^1$ | 10 | 12 | | $9^2$ | 7 | 2 | | 11 | 13 | | | | | | | | | | | | | | 9 |
| 1 | 2 | 13 | 4 | | | 7 | | 9 | 10 | | 12 | 6 | 8 | 3 | | 11 | $5^2$ | | | | | | | | | | | | | | 10 |
| 1 | $2^2$ | 13 | 4 | | | 8 | | 9 | $10^3$ | 12 | 14 | 6 | 7 | $3^1$ | | 11 | 5 | | | | | | | | | | | | | | 11 |
| 1 | | 3 | 4 | 5 | | 7 | 8 | $9^2$ | 10 | 12 | 13 | 6 | | | | $11^1$ | 2 | | | | | | | | | | | | | | 12 |
| 1 | | 4 | $3^1$ | 5 | | 7 | 8 | | 10 | $9^2$ | | $6^3$ | 13 | 12 | | 11 | 2 | 14 | | | | | | | | | | | | | 13 |
| 1 | | 4 | | 3 | | $7^1$ | 8 | 12 | 10 | | 13 | 6 | 9 | 5 | | $11^7$ | 2 | | | | | | | | | | | | | | 14 |
| 1 | | 4 | | $5^1$ | | 7 | 8 | 12 | 11 | | 13 | 6 | 9 | | | $10^2$ | 2 | | | | | | | 3 | | | | | | | 15 |
| 1 | 14 | 3 | 2 | | | $7^1$ | $8^3$ | 12 | $10^2$ | | 13 | 9 | 6 | | | 11 | 5 | 4 | | | | | | | | | | | | | 16 |
| 1 | | 3 | 4 | 12 | | | 8 | $9^1$ | 10 | | $11^2$ | 6 | 7 | | | 13 | 2 | | 5 | | | | | | | | | | | | 17 |
| 1 | $2^3$ | | 4 | $5^1$ | | 6 | 8 | $9^2$ | | | 13 | | | 12 | | 10 | 3 | 11 | 7 | 14 | | | | | | | | | | | 18 |
| 1 | | 3 | 4 | 14 | | 13 | 7 | 12 | | | $11^1$ | $9^3$ | | | | 10 | 2 | 6 | 5 | $8^2$ | | | | | | | | | | | 19 |
| 1 | 2 | | 4 | 5 | | 8 | 7 | 13 | 10 | | 9 | | | | | 12 | $6^1$ | 3 | | $11^2$ | | | | | | | | | | | 20 |
| 1 | $2^8$ | 7 | 3 | 5 | | | 8 | | $11^3$ | | 14 | $9^2$ | | | | $10^1$ | 12 | 6 | 4 | | | 13 | | | | | | | | | 21 |
| 1 | | 7 | 3 | 5 | | $8^3$ | | 12 | 11 | | 13 | $9^2$ | | | | $10^1$ | 2 | 6 | 4 | 14 | | | | | | | | | | | 22 |
| 1 | 2 | 7 | 3 | $5^1$ | | | $10^2$ | 13 | 11 | | 12 | | | | | 9 | 6 | 4 | | 8 | | | | | | | | | | | 23 |
| | 2 | 8 | 3 | | | 7 | | 11 | | | 14 | $9^3$ | | | | $10^1$ | $6^2$ | 4 | 12 | | | 5 | 1 | 13 | | | | | | | 24 |
| | 2 | | 3 | | | 8 | 7 | $9^1$ | 11 | | 14 | $6^3$ | | | | $10^2$ | 12 | 4 | | | | 5 | 1 | 13 | | | | | | | 25 |
| | 2 | 7 | 3 | 5 | | 13 | 8 | | 10 | | | 6 | | | | $11^1$ | $9^2$ | 4 | | | | | 1 | 12 | | | | | | | 26 |
| | 2 | 7 | 3 | 5 | | | 8 | 13 | | | | 9 | | | | 10 | $6^2$ | 4 | | | | | 1 | 12 | $11^1$ | | | | | | 27 |
| | 2 | $7^3$ | 3 | 5 | | | $8^2$ | 14 | 10 | | | 6 | | | | 11 | | 12 | 4 | | | | 1 | | $9^1$ | 13 | | | | | 28 |
| | 2 | $6^1$ | 5 | 3 | | | 12 | | 14 | 10 | | 8 | | | | $11^3$ | | 7 | 4 | | | | 1 | | 13 | $9^2$ | | | | | 29 |
| | 2 | 8 | 3 | 5 | | | 7 | | 10 | | | 6 | | | | $11^1$ | 9 | 4 | | | | | 1 | 12 | | | | | | | 30 |
| | 2 | $7^8$ | 4 | 5 | | 12 | 8 | 13 | 10 | | | $9^3$ | | | | $11^2$ | $6^1$ | 3 | | | | 14 | 1 | | | | | | | | 31 |
| | 2 | | 4 | 5 | | 7 | 8 | 14 | 11 | | | $9^2$ | | | | $10^1$ | $6^3$ | 3 | | | | 13 | 1 | | 12 | | | | | | 32 |
| | 2 | | 4 | 5 | | 7 | 8 | 14 | 11 | | | $9^1$ | | | | $10^3$ | $6^2$ | 3 | | | | 12 | 1 | | 13 | | | | | | 33 |
| | 2 | | 3 | 5 | | 7 | 8 | 9 | 10 | | | 11 | | | | | $6^1$ | 4 | | | | 1 | | | 12 | | | | | | 34 |
| | $2^2$ | 8 | 3 | 5 | | 7 | | 9 | 10 | | | $11^1$ | | | | 6 | 4 | | | | | 1 | | | 13 | 12 | | | | | 35 |
| | 2 | 3 | $5^2$ | | | $7^3$ | 8 | 9 | 10 | | $11^1$ | | | | | 6 | 4 | | | | | 13 | 1 | | 14 | 12 | | | | | 36 |
| | 2 | 3 | 5 | | | 8 | 7 | $9^2$ | 10 | | 12 | | | | | 14 | 4 | | | | | 13 | 1 | | | $6^3$ | $11^1$ | | | | 37 |
| | 4 | 2 | $5^1$ | | | 14 | 7 | 12 | | | $6^2$ | | | | | $8^3$ | | | | | | 11 | 1 | | 13 | 3 | 10 | 9 | | | 38 |
| | 2 | 3 | | $7^2$ | | 8 | 14 | 11 | | | 9 | | | | | 6 | $5^1$ | | | | | 12 | 1 | | 13 | $10^3$ | 4 | | | | 39 |
| 1 | $2^1$ | 7 | 3 | 5 | | $8^2$ | 9 | 10 | | | 6 | | | | | 13 | | | | | | 14 | 12 | $11^3$ | 4 | | | | | | 40 |
| | 2 | 3 | | 5 | | 7 | 12 | 11 | | | 9 | | | | | $6^2$ | 4 | | | | | 8 | 1 | | $10^1$ | 13 | | | | | 41 |
| | 2 | 4 | | 5 | | 6² | 13 | | $10^1$ | 8 | | | | | | 7 | 3 | | | | | 1 | | 9 | 12 | 11 | | | | | 42 |
| 12 | 2 | 3 | 5 | | | $8^1$ | 7 | | 10 | | | 13 | 6 | | | $9^3$ | | | | | | 1 | | 14 | $11^2$ | 4 | | | | | 43 |
| | 2 | 4 | 5 | | | 6 | 9 | 14 | | | $11^3$ | 7 | | 13 | | $8^1$ | 3 | | | | | 1 | | 12 | $10^2$ | | | | | | 44 |
| | 2 | | 3 | 5 | | 6 | 7 | $10^2$ | | | $9^1$ | 13 | | 12 | | 14 | 4 | | | | | 1 | | 8 | $11^3$ | | | | | | 45 |
| | 2 | 3 | | 5 | | 9 | $7^2$ | 10 | | | 13 | $6^3$ | | 12 | | 8 | 4 | | | | | 1 | | 14 | $11^1$ | | | | | | 46 |

**FA Cup**
Fourth Qualifying   Lowestoft T                     (h)   3-2
First Round          Tranmere R                      (h)   0-3

**FA Trophy**
First Round          Havant & Waterlooville   (h)   1-2

# CAMBRIDGE UNITED

*Ground:* R Costings Abbey Stadium, Newmarket Road, Cambridge CB5 8LN.   *Tel:* (01223) 566 500.
*Fax:* (01223) 729 220.   *Website:* www.cambridge-united.co.uk   *Year Formed:* 1912.
*Record Gate:* 14,000 (1970 v Chelsea, Friendly).   *Nickname:* 'The U's'.   *Head Coach:* Richard Money.
*Secretary:* Claire Osbourn.   *Colours:* Amber shirts with black trim, black shorts, black socks with amber trim.

## CAMBRIDGE UNITED – BLUE SQUARE PREMIER 2012–13 LEAGUE RECORD

| Match No. | Date | Venue | Opponents | Result | H/T Score | Lg Pos. | Goalscorers | Attendance |
|---|---|---|---|---|---|---|---|---|
| 1 | Aug 11 | A | Forest Green R | D | 1-1 | 1-0 | 12 | Elliott [33] | 1128 |
| 2 | 14 | H | Lincoln C | W | 2-1 | 1-1 | 8 | Elliott [3], Moke [81] | 2546 |
| 3 | 18 | H | Southport | W | 2-0 | 0-0 | 4 | Elliott 2 [52, 55] | 2004 |
| 4 | 25 | A | Nuneaton T | D | 2-2 | 0-0 | 6 | Elliott [52], Jennings [90] | 1175 |
| 5 | 27 | H | Dartford | L | 1-2 | 0-0 | 9 | Jennings (pen) [85] | 2691 |
| 6 | Sept 1 | A | Stockport Co | D | 1-1 | 1-1 | 13 | Berry [37] | 3060 |
| 7 | 4 | A | Luton T | L | 2-3 | 1-1 | 14 | Wellard [13], McAuley [88] | 6742 |
| 8 | 8 | H | Wrexham | L | 1-4 | 0-1 | 16 | Coulson [84] | 2304 |
| 9 | 15 | H | AFC Telford U | D | 3-3 | 0-0 | 17 | Pugh [70], Gash [75], Shaw [90] | 1962 |
| 10 | 22 | A | Hereford U | L | 2-4 | 1-1 | 18 | Gash 2 [14, 47] | 1677 |
| 11 | 25 | H | Kidderminster H | L | 1-3 | 0-0 | 19 | Coulson [50] | 1815 |
| 12 | 29 | A | Barrow | W | 4-1 | 2-0 | 15 | Gash (pen) [5], Flynn (og) [8], Pugh [52], Shaw [72] | 904 |
| 13 | Oct 6 | H | Mansfield T | W | 4-1 | 1-0 | 14 | Gash [9], Berry [49], Elliott [51], Jarvis [58] | 2545 |
| 14 | 9 | A | Woking | L | 1-2 | 0-1 | 15 | Willmott [64] | 1420 |
| 15 | 13 | A | Gateshead | D | 0-0 | 0-0 | 16 | | 768 |
| 16 | 27 | H | Hyde | L | 0-1 | 0-0 | 18 | | 1779 |
| 17 | Nov 6 | A | Newport Co | L | 2-6 | 1-3 | 20 | Elliott [28], Berry [69] | 1787 |
| 18 | 10 | H | Macclesfield T | W | 2-0 | 0-0 | 18 | Willmott [55], Elliott [58] | 1821 |
| 19 | 17 | H | Tamworth | D | 1-1 | 0-0 | 18 | Dunk [76] | 3003 |
| 20 | Dec 4 | A | Ebbsfleet U | W | 4-2 | 1-1 | 17 | Elliott 3 [1, 64, 76], Smith [65] | 842 |
| 21 | 8 | H | Gateshead | W | 3-0 | 1-0 | 13 | Shaw [15], Coulson [47], Jennings [61] | 1840 |
| 22 | 18 | A | Alfreton T | D | 1-1 | 0-1 | 13 | Gash (pen) [90] | 534 |
| 23 | 26 | A | Braintree T | W | 3-0 | 1-0 | 10 | Gash [25], Smith [59], Pugh [62] | 1133 |
| 24 | 29 | A | Dartford | D | 1-1 | 1-1 | 8 | Gash [45] | 1716 |
| 25 | Jan 1 | H | Braintree T | W | 1-0 | 0-0 | 8 | Gash [74] | 2406 |
| 26 | 5 | H | Stockport Co | W | 4-1 | 2-1 | 7 | Hughes 2 [19, 55], Coulson [42], Elliott [70] | 2305 |
| 27 | 15 | A | Nuneaton T | L | 1-3 | 0-1 | 8 | Gash [88] | 1740 |
| 28 | 26 | H | Grimsby T | D | 0-0 | 0-0 | 9 | | 2764 |
| 29 | Feb 2 | A | AFC Telford U | W | 2-1 | 1-1 | 8 | Pugh [17], Gash [74] | 1788 |
| 30 | 9 | A | Kidderminster H | L | 2-3 | 1-2 | 9 | Gowling (og) [43], Gash [89] | 1949 |
| 31 | 12 | H | Alfreton T | L | 0-3 | 0-0 | 10 | | 1779 |
| 32 | 16 | A | Mansfield T | L | 1-3 | 1-2 | 10 | Hughes [31] | 2508 |
| 33 | 23 | H | Hereford U | L | 1-3 | 0-1 | 13 | Shaw [51] | 2171 |
| 34 | 26 | A | Tamworth | W | 2-1 | 1-0 | 11 | Elliott [9], Gash (pen) [64] | 668 |
| 35 | Mar 2 | H | Forest Green R | D | 0-0 | 0-0 | 11 | | 2221 |
| 36 | 5 | H | Southport | L | 1-2 | 1-0 | 12 | Blissett [1] | 615 |
| 37 | 9 | H | Woking | W | 1-0 | 0-0 | 11 | Shaw [90] | 2054 |
| 38 | 16 | A | Grimsby T | W | 1-0 | 1-0 | 9 | Naylor (og) [27] | 3516 |
| 39 | 19 | H | Ebbsfleet U | D | 1-1 | 0-0 | 10 | Dunk [80] | 1737 |
| 40 | 26 | A | Hyde | L | 1-2 | 1-1 | 11 | Hughes [15] | 404 |
| 41 | 30 | H | Luton T | D | 2-2 | 1-0 | 11 | Shaw [20], Blissett [61] | 3217 |
| 42 | Apr 1 | A | Lincoln C | D | 0-0 | 0-0 | 12 | | 2721 |
| 43 | 5 | H | Newport Co | D | 0-0 | 0-0 | 11 | | 2012 |
| 44 | 9 | A | Wrexham | L | 0-1 | 0-1 | 13 | | 2574 |
| 45 | 13 | H | Barrow | W | 2-1 | 2-1 | 13 | Smith [26], Elliott [45] | 2758 |
| 46 | 20 | A | Macclesfield T | L | 1-2 | 1-2 | 14 | Elliott [15] | 1987 |

**Final League Position: 14**

## GOALSCORERS

*League (68):* Elliott 15, Gash 13 (3 pens), Shaw 6, Coulson 4, Hughes 4, Pugh 4, Berry 3, Jennings 3 (1 pen), Smith 3, Blissett 2, Dunk 2, Willmott 2, Jarvis 1, McAuley 1, Moke 1, Wellard 1, own goals 3.
*FA Cup (0).*
*FA Trophy (3):* Gash 2, Elliott 1.

| Hedge 18 | Roberts 26 + 2 | Coulson 39 | Garner 5 | Jennings 21 + 1 | Willmott 15 + 5 | Wellard 8 + 9 | Jarvis 38 + 3 | Dunk 30 + 2 | Elliott 31 + 1 | Berry 23 + 5 | Hughes 29 + 7 | Moke 2 + 10 | Smith 11 + 9 | McAuley 40 + 2 | Shaw 32 + 5 | Pugh 17 + 9 | Hudson 2 + 4 | Ross 15 | Gibson 2 + 3 | Gorman — + 2 | Wylde 5 + 1 | Thorpe 8 + 4 | Andrew 6 | Gash 27 | Marriott — + 2 | Thalassitis — + 2 | Eades — + 1 | Steer 4 | Haynes-Brown 12 + 6 | Hurst — + 1 | Wassmer 17 | Fletcher 1 + 1 | Brighton — + 5 | Anderson 4 + 1 | Reed 6 + 1 | Taylor — + 1 | Blissett 3 + 4 | Pope 9 | Match No. |
|---|---|---|---|---|---|---|---|---|---|---|---|---|---|---|---|---|---|---|---|---|---|---|---|---|---|---|---|---|---|---|---|---|---|---|---|---|---|---|---|
| 1 | 2 | 3 | 4 | 5 | 6 | 7 | 8 | $9^2$ | $10^3$ | $11^1$ | 12 | 13 | 14 |  |  |  |  |  |  |  |  |  |  |  |  |  |  |  |  |  |  |  |  |  |  |  |  |  | 1 |
| 1 |  | 3 | 4 | 5 | 6 |  | 8 | $9^3$ | $10^1$ |  |  | 13 | 12 | 2 | 7 | $11^2$ | 14 |  |  |  |  |  |  |  |  |  |  |  |  |  |  |  |  |  |  |  |  |  | 2 |
| 1 |  | 3 | 4 | 5 | 6 | 13 | 8 | $9^2$ | 11 | 10 |  | 12 |  | 2 | $7^1$ |  |  |  |  |  |  |  |  |  |  |  |  |  |  |  |  |  |  |  |  |  |  |  | 3 |
| 1 |  | 4 | 3 | 5 | 6 |  | 8 | 9 | $11^2$ | 10 |  | 13 | 12 | 2 | $7^1$ |  |  |  |  |  |  |  |  |  |  |  |  |  |  |  |  |  |  |  |  |  |  |  | 4 |
|  |  |  | $3^2$ | 5 | 6 | 8 |  | $9^3$ | 10 | 7 | 13 | $11^1$ | 12 | 2 |  |  |  | 4 | 1 |  | 14 |  |  |  |  |  |  |  |  |  |  |  |  |  |  |  |  |  | 5 |
| 1 |  | 3 |  | 5 | 6 | 7 | 8 |  | $11^1$ | 10 | $9^3$ | 14 | 12 | 2 | 13 | $4^2$ |  |  |  |  |  |  |  |  |  |  |  |  |  |  |  |  |  |  |  |  |  |  | 6 |
| 1 |  | 4 |  | 5 | $9^2$ | 8 | 7 |  | 11 | $10^1$ | 6 | 12 |  | 2 | 13 | 3 |  |  |  |  |  |  |  |  |  |  |  |  |  |  |  |  |  |  |  |  |  |  | 7 |
| 1 |  | 3 |  | 5 | $6^1$ | 8 | 7 |  | $10^2$ | 12 | $11^3$ | 9 | 13 | 2 | 14 | 4 |  |  |  |  |  |  |  |  |  |  |  |  |  |  |  |  |  |  |  |  |  |  | 8 |
| 1 |  | 4 |  |  | $9^1$ |  | 7 | $6^3$ |  | 14 | 3 | 8 | 10 |  | 13 | $2^2$ |  |  |  |  | 5 | 11 | 12 |  |  |  |  |  |  |  |  |  |  |  |  |  |  |  | 9 |
| 1 |  | 4 |  |  | $9^2$ |  | 8 | 6 |  | 3 | $7^3$ | $10^1$ |  | 2 | 5 | 11 |  |  |  |  | 14 | 12 | 13 |  |  |  |  |  |  |  |  |  |  |  |  |  |  |  | 10 |
| 1 |  | 3 | 5 |  | 13 |  | 14 | $8^1$ | $6^3$ | 12 | 4 | $7^2$ | 11 | 2 | $9^1$ | 10 |  |  |  |  |  |  |  |  |  |  |  |  |  |  |  |  |  |  |  |  |  | 11 |
| 1 |  | 3 |  | $9^2$ | 7 |  | $6^1$ | 12 | 4 | 8 | 10 |  | 2 | 5 | 11 | 13 |  |  |  |  |  |  |  |  |  |  |  |  |  |  |  |  |  |  |  |  |  |  | 12 |
| 1 |  | 3 |  | $6^2$ | 12 | $8^1$ | 11 | 9 |  | 13 | 4 | 7 | 14 | 2 | 5 | $10^3$ |  |  |  |  |  |  |  |  |  |  |  |  |  |  |  |  |  |  |  |  |  | 13 |
| 1 |  | 4 |  | 9 | 13 | $6^1$ | $11^3$ | 8 |  | 12 | 3 | $7^2$ | 14 | 2 | 5 | 10 |  |  |  |  |  |  |  |  |  |  |  |  |  |  |  |  |  |  |  |  |  |  | 14 |
| 1 |  | 3 | 5 | 13 |  | 6 | $11^3$ | 8 | 14 |  | $10^2$ | 4 | $7^1$ | 12 | 2 | 9 |  |  |  |  |  |  |  |  |  |  |  |  |  |  |  |  |  |  |  |  |  |  | 15 |
| 1 |  | 4 | 14 | 9 |  | $2^2$ | 13 | $11^1$ | 7 | 6 |  | $3^3$ | 8 | 12 | 5 |  |  |  |  |  | $9^3$ |  |  |  |  |  |  |  |  |  |  |  |  |  |  |  |  |  | 16 |
| 1 |  | 3 | 5 |  | $7^2$ |  | 12 | 10 | 8 | 14 | $11^1$ | 2 | 6 | 13 | 4 |  |  |  |  |  | $9^3$ |  |  |  |  |  |  |  |  |  |  |  |  |  |  |  |  |  | 17 |
|  | 2 | 3 |  | 5 | 6 |  | 7 | $9^1$ | $11^2$ | 8 | 12 |  | 4 | 13 |  |  |  |  |  |  |  | 10 |  |  |  |  |  | 1 |  |  |  |  |  |  |  |  |  |  | 18 |
|  | 2 | 3 |  | 5 | 6 |  | 8 | $9^1$ | 11 | 7 |  |  | 4 |  |  |  |  |  |  |  |  | 10 |  |  |  |  |  | 1 |  |  |  |  |  |  |  |  |  |  | 19 |
|  | 2 | 3 |  | 5 | 12 |  | 8 | $9^2$ | $11^3$ |  |  | 13 | 4 | 7 | $6^4$ |  |  |  |  |  |  | 14 | $10^1$ |  |  |  |  | 1 |  |  |  |  |  |  |  |  |  |  | 20 |
|  | $2^3$ | 3 |  | $5^2$ | 6 |  | 8 | 9 | $11^1$ |  |  |  | 12 | 4 | 7 |  |  |  |  |  |  | 14 | 10 |  |  |  |  | 1 | 13 |  |  |  |  |  |  |  |  |  | 21 |
|  | 2 | 3 |  | 5 | 12 | 13 | $8^2$ | 9 | $11^3$ |  |  |  | 4 | 7 | $6^1$ | 1 |  |  |  |  | 14 | 10 |  |  |  |  |  |  |  |  |  |  |  |  |  |  |  | 22 |
|  | 2 | 3 |  | 5 |  |  | 8 | $9^2$ |  |  | 12 | $11^1$ | 4 | $7^4$ | 6 | 1 |  |  |  |  |  | 10 |  |  |  |  |  | 13 |  |  |  |  |  |  |  |  |  | 23 |
| 1 | 2 | 3 |  | 12 | 13 | $8^1$ |  | 7 |  | $11^1$ | 4 | 6 |  |  |  | 1 |  |  |  |  |  | 10 |  |  |  |  |  | 5 |  |  |  |  |  |  |  |  |  | 24 |
|  | 2 | 3 |  | 5 | 12 | 14 | 7 | $9^2$ |  | 8 | $11^1$ | 4 | $6^3$ | 1 |  |  |  |  |  |  |  | 10 |  |  |  |  |  | 13 |  |  |  |  |  |  |  |  |  | 25 |
|  | 2 | 3 |  | 5 | 13 | 7 | $9^3$ | $11^2$ |  | 8 | 4 |  | $6^1$ | 14 | 1 |  |  |  |  |  | 10 |  |  |  |  |  | 12 |  |  |  |  |  |  |  |  |  |  | 26 |
|  |  | 3 |  | 5 | 13 | 7 |  | 11 | 4 | $7^2$ | 9 | 1 | $6^1$ | $2^2$ |  |  |  |  |  |  |  | 10 |  |  |  |  |  | 12 | 14 |  |  |  |  |  |  |  |  |  | 27 |
|  |  | 3 |  | 5 | 12 | 7 |  | 4 | 13 | 6 | 8 | 1 |  |  |  | 10 |  |  |  |  |  |  |  |  |  |  |  | $9^2$ | 2 | $11^1$ |  |  |  |  |  |  |  |  | 28 |
| 14 |  | 3 |  | 8 | $9^2$ |  | 11 |  | 4 | $7^1$ | $6^3$ | 1 |  |  |  | 10 |  |  |  |  |  |  |  |  |  |  |  | 5 | 2 | 12 | 13 |  |  |  |  |  |  |  | 29 |
|  | 2 | 3 |  | $6^2$ | 5 |  | 9 | 11 |  | 4 | $7^1$ | 12 | 1 |  |  | 10 |  |  |  |  |  |  |  |  |  |  |  | 8 | 13 |  |  |  |  |  |  |  |  |  | 30 |
|  | 2 | 3 |  | $6^1$ |  |  | 9 | 8 |  | 4 | 12 | 14 | 1 | 11 |  |  |  |  |  |  |  |  |  |  |  |  |  | $7^2$ | 13 | 5 | $10^3$ |  |  |  |  |  |  |  | 31 |
| 1 | 5 | 3 |  | 7 |  |  | 9 | $6^2$ |  | 2 | $8^1$ |  |  |  |  | 10 |  |  |  |  |  |  |  |  |  |  |  | 4 | 12 | 13 | $11^3$ | 14 |  |  |  |  |  |  | 32 |
|  | 2 | 3 |  | 7 | 9 | $11^2$ | $6^3$ | 8 |  | 4 | 12 |  | 1 |  |  | 10 |  |  |  |  |  |  |  |  |  |  |  |  | 13 | $5^1$ | 14 |  |  |  |  |  |  |  | 33 |
| 12 | 3 |  |  | 9 | $11^3$ | 14 | $8^1$ |  | 4 | 7 | 13 | 1 |  |  |  | 10 |  |  |  |  |  |  |  |  |  |  |  | 5 | 2 |  | $6^2$ |  |  |  |  |  |  |  | 34 |
|  | 2 |  |  | 8 | 9 | 11 |  | 12 | 4 | 7 |  | 1 |  |  |  | 10 |  |  |  |  |  |  |  |  |  |  |  | 5 | 3 |  | $6^1$ |  |  |  |  |  |  |  | 35 |
|  | 3 |  |  | 12 | 11 |  | $7^1$ | 6 | 4 | 8 |  | 1 |  |  |  |  |  |  |  |  |  |  |  |  |  |  | 5 | 2 |  | 10 | 9 |  |  |  |  |  |  | 36 |
|  | 2 |  |  | 7 | $9^2$ |  | $10^1$ | 4 | 8 | 12 |  | [ ] |  |  |  |  |  |  |  |  |  |  |  | 13 | 3 |  | 5 | 6 | 11 | 1 |  |  |  |  |  |  | 37 |
|  | 2 | 3 |  | 7 | 9 | $10^1$ | 11 |  | 8 | 6 |  |  |  |  |  |  |  |  |  |  |  |  |  | 5 | 4 |  |  |  |  | 12 | 1 |  |  |  |  |  |  | 38 |
|  | 2 | 3 |  | $8^2$ | 9 | 10 | 13 | $11^3$ |  | 7 | $6^1$ |  |  |  |  | 12 |  |  |  |  |  |  | 5 | 4 |  |  |  |  | 14 | 1 |  |  |  |  |  |  | 39 |
|  | 2 |  |  | 8 | 9 | 11 | $6^1$ | 10 |  | 3 | 7 |  |  |  |  |  |  |  |  |  |  |  | 5 | 4 |  |  |  |  |  | 1 |  |  |  |  |  |  | 40 |
|  | 2 | $3^1$ |  | 8 | 9 | 10 | 6 | $11^2$ | 12 | 7 |  |  |  |  |  |  |  |  |  |  |  |  | 5 | 4 |  |  |  |  | 13 | 1 |  |  |  |  |  |  | 41 |
|  | 2 |  |  | 8 | 9 | 10 | 6 | 11 | 4 | 5 |  |  |  |  |  |  |  |  |  |  |  |  | 3 |  |  |  |  |  | 7 | 1 |  |  |  |  |  |  | 42 |
|  | 2 |  |  | 8 | 9 | 10 | $6^2$ | $11^1$ | 3 | 7 | 12 |  |  |  |  |  |  |  |  |  |  |  | 4 |  |  |  |  |  | 5 | 13 | 1 |  |  |  |  |  | 43 |
|  | 2 | 4 |  | $8^3$ | 9 | 11 | 14 | $6^2$ | $10^1$ | 5 | 7 | 13 | [ ] | 12 |  |  |  |  |  |  |  | 3 |  |  |  |  |  |  | 1 |  |  |  |  |  |  | 44 |
|  | 2 | 3 |  | 8 | 5 | 10 | 12 | $11^1$ | 13 | $7^2$ | 6 | [ ] |  |  |  |  |  |  |  |  |  | 9 | 4 |  |  |  |  |  | 1 |  |  |  |  |  |  | 45 |
|  | 2 | 3 |  | 13 | 9 | $10^1$ | 8 | $7^2$ | 11 |  | 12 | 6 | 4 | 1 |  |  |  |  |  |  |  | 5 |  |  |  |  |  |  |  |  |  |  |  |  |  |  | 46 |

**FA Cup**

| | | | | |
|---|---|---|---|---|
| Fourth Qualifying | Luton T | (h) | 0-2 | |

**FA Trophy**

| | | | |
|---|---|---|---|
| First Round | Billericay T | (a) | 3-0 |
| Second Round | Gateshead | (h) | 0-1 |

# DARTFORD

*Ground:* Princes Park, Grassbanks, Darenth Road, Dartford DA1 1RT
*Tel:* (01322) 299 990.   *Website:* www.dartfordfc.co.uk.   *Year Formed:* 1888.   *Record Gate:* 4,097 (2006 v Horsham
YMCA, Ryman League).   *Nickname:* 'The Darts'.   *Manager:* Tony Burman.   *Secretary:* Peter Martin.
*Colours:* White shirts with black trim, black shorts, white socks.

## DARTFORD – BLUE SQUARE PREMIER 2012–13 LEAGUE RECORD

| Match No. | Date | Venue | Opponents | Result | H/T Score | Lg Pos. | Goalscorers | Attendance |
|---|---|---|---|---|---|---|---|---|
| 1 | Aug 11 | H | Tamworth | L | 2-3 | 1-2 | 20 | Bradbrook 45, Crawford 79 | 1370 |
| 2 | 14 | A | Woking | L | 0-1 | 0-0 | 21 | | 1846 |
| 3 | 18 | A | Macclesfield T | L | 0-2 | 0-1 | 23 | | 1420 |
| 4 | 25 | H | Kidderminster H | W | 1-0 | 1-0 | 19 | Burns 36 | 1068 |
| 5 | 27 | A | Cambridge U | W | 2-1 | 0-0 | 14 | Harris 48, Collier 88 | 2691 |
| 6 | Sept 1 | H | Alfreton T | W | 5-1 | 3-0 | 12 | Crawford 3 11, 48, 82, Erskine 37, Bradbrook 45 | 1145 |
| 7 | 4 | H | Newport Co | W | 2-1 | 0-0 | 8 | Crawford 49, Rose 90 | 1446 |
| 8 | 8 | A | Gateshead | L | 0-2 | 0-1 | 10 | | 758 |
| 9 | 15 | H | Hereford U | W | 4-0 | 1-0 | 7 | Hayes 6, Rogers 47, Harris 76, Wallis 89 | 1601 |
| 10 | 22 | A | Wrexham | D | 2-2 | 1-2 | 8 | Harris 4, Noble 90 | 3772 |
| 11 | 25 | A | Braintree T | W | 2-0 | 2-0 | 6 | Bonner 17, Erskine 34 | 721 |
| 12 | 29 | H | Hyde | W | 2-1 | 0-1 | 5 | Crawford 85, Rose 90 | 1338 |
| 13 | Oct 6 | A | Grimsby T | W | 2-0 | 0-0 | 5 | Champion 52, Birchall 85 | 4009 |
| 14 | 9 | A | AFC Telford U | L | 1-4 | 0-2 | 5 | Bradbrook 76 | 1359 |
| 15 | 13 | A | Barrow | D | 0-0 | 0-0 | 6 | | 1278 |
| 16 | 26 | H | Mansfield T | W | 2-0 | 2-0 | 3 | Hayes 45, Bradbrook 45 | 1737 |
| 17 | Nov 6 | H | Forest Green R | L | 0-1 | 0-1 | 6 | | 915 |
| 18 | 10 | A | Luton T | W | 2-0 | 2-0 | 5 | Noble 6, Bonner 41 | 6567 |
| 19 | 17 | H | Southport | D | 2-2 | 2-1 | 5 | Bradbrook 2 (1 pen) 17, 33 (p) | 1506 |
| 20 | Dec 1 | A | Tamworth | L | 2-3 | 1-0 | 5 | Ajayi 16, Harris 70 | 832 |
| 21 | 4 | A | Nuneaton T | L | 0-1 | 0-1 | 5 | | 651 |
| 22 | 8 | H | Lincoln C | L | 2-4 | 0-4 | 6 | Crawford 2 49, 71 | 1466 |
| 23 | 22 | A | Kidderminster H | L | 1-5 | 1-2 | 7 | Erskine 9 | 1779 |
| 24 | 26 | H | Ebbsfleet U | W | 3-1 | 0-0 | 7 | Crawford 2 52, 68, Bradbrook 80 | 3116 |
| 25 | 29 | H | Cambridge U | D | 1-1 | 1-1 | 7 | Crawford 23 | 1716 |
| 26 | Jan 1 | A | Ebbsfleet U | D | 2-2 | 1-0 | 7 | Wallis 12, Crawford 48 | 2242 |
| 27 | 5 | A | Alfreton T | L | 2-3 | 1-1 | 8 | Hayes 3, Collier 59 | 522 |
| 28 | 15 | H | Macclesfield T | W | 2-0 | 1-0 | 7 | Wallis 14, Noble 82 | 821 |
| 29 | Feb 2 | A | Mansfield T | L | 0-5 | 0-1 | 10 | | 2598 |
| 30 | 9 | A | Lincoln C | L | 1-2 | 0-1 | 10 | Noble 76 | 1789 |
| 31 | 12 | H | Luton T | W | 1-0 | 0-0 | 9 | Hayes 72 | 1802 |
| 32 | Mar 2 | A | Southport | D | 2-2 | 1-1 | 12 | Crawford 29, Bonner 59 | 823 |
| 33 | 5 | H | Stockport Co | D | 1-1 | 0-1 | 11 | Harris 70 | 757 |
| 34 | 9 | A | Wrexham | W | 2-1 | 0-1 | 10 | Evans 74, Bradbrook 90 | 815 |
| 35 | 16 | A | Hyde | L | 0-3 | 0-1 | 12 | | 475 |
| 36 | 19 | H | Barrow | L | 0-1 | 0-0 | 12 | | 908 |
| 37 | 23 | H | Gateshead | W | 3-0 | 0-0 | 12 | Hayes 2 66, 72, Sheringham 86 | 1020 |
| 38 | 26 | A | Hereford U | L | 0-1 | 0-1 | 12 | | 662 |
| 39 | 30 | A | Newport Co | D | 0-0 | 0-0 | 12 | | 2111 |
| 40 | Apr 1 | H | Woking | W | 4-1 | 2-1 | 10 | Collier 7, Noble 2 45, 90, Sheringham 60 | 1407 |
| 41 | 6 | A | AFC Telford U | W | 2-0 | 1-0 | 9 | Prior 11, Sheringham 49 | 1375 |
| 42 | 9 | H | Grimsby T | L | 1-2 | 1-0 | 10 | Evans 26 | 1201 |
| 43 | 11 | H | Braintree T | D | 0-0 | 0-0 | 8 | | 1051 |
| 44 | 13 | A | Stockport Co | W | 1-0 | 0-0 | 8 | Sheringham 72 | 6113 |
| 45 | 16 | A | Forest Green R | W | 3-2 | 2-0 | 7 | Harris 8, Bradbrook 2 (1 pen) 25 (p), 52 | 575 |
| 46 | 20 | H | Nuneaton T | L | 0-1 | 0-0 | 8 | | 1844 |

**Final League Position: 8**

## GOALSCORERS

*League (67):* Crawford 13, Bradbrook 10 (2 pens), Harris 6, Hayes 6, Noble 6, Sheringham 4, Bonner 3, Collier 3,
Erskine 3, Wallis 3, Evans 2, Rose 2, Ajayi 1, Birchall 1, Burns 1, Champion 1, Prior 1, Rogers 1.
*FA Cup (2):* Crawford 1, Erskine 1.
*FA Trophy (15):* Bradbrook 3 (1 pen), Crawford 2, Green D 2, Harris 2, Burns 1, Collier 1, Erskine 1, Hayes 1, Noble 1,
Wallis 1.

| Wells 3 | Burns 43+1 | Bonner 44 | Arber 37+1 | Green A 17+1 | Noble 23+13 | Champion 42 | Bradbrook 41 | Rogers 23+13 | Erskine 23+14 | Harris 28+11 | Crawford 17+9 | Hayes 35+7 | Wallis 19+14 | Collier 8+24 | Rose 33+3 | Bettinelli 35 | Birchall 4+2 | Ajayi 3 | Eisa —+1 | Monger —+1 | Green D 1+2 | Evans 6+9 | Prior 5+4 | Sheringham 8+2 | Somogyi 8 | Match No. |
|---|---|---|---|---|---|---|---|---|---|---|---|---|---|---|---|---|---|---|---|---|---|---|---|---|---|---|
| 1 | 2 | 3 | 4 | 5 | $6^3$ | 7 | 8 | $9^2$ | $10^1$ | 11 | 12 | 13 | 14 | | | | | | | | | | | | | 1 |
| 1 | 2 | 3 | 5 | 4 | $6^1$ | 7 | 8 | $9^3$ | $10^1$ | $11^2$ | 12 | | | | 13 | 14 | | | | | | | | | | 2 |
| | $6^2$ | 3 | 7 | 5 | | 4 | 8 | $9^3$ | $11^1$ | 12 | 10 | 13 | 14 | | 2 | 1 | | | | | | | | | | 3 |
| 12 | 3 | 4 | $5^1$ | 13 | | 7 | 8 | 9 | | 10 | 11 | $6^2$ | | | 2 | 1 | | | | | | | | | | 4 |
| | 2 | 3 | 4 | | 13 | 8 | 11 | | $10^3$ | 9 | 14 | $6^1$ | $7^2$ | 12 | 5 | 1 | | | | | | | | | | 5 |
| | 2 | 3 | 4 | | 13 | 7 | $8^3$ | 9 | $10^2$ | | 11 | $6^1$ | 14 | 12 | 5 | 1 | | | | | | | | | | 6 |
| | 2 | 3 | 4 | | 13 | 7 | 8 | 9 | 10 | $12^3$ | $11^1$ | $6^2$ | 14 | | 5 | 1 | | | | | | | | | | 7 |
| | 2 | 3 | 4 | | 12 | 7 | 8 | $9^2$ | 11 | | $10^1$ | $6^3$ | 13 | 14 | 5 | 1 | | | | | | | | | | 8 |
| | 2 | 3 | 4 | | 14 | 8 | $7^2$ | 9 | 10 | 12 | $11^1$ | $6^3$ | 13 | | 5 | 1 | | | | | | | | | | 9 |
| | 5 | 4 | 3 | | 13 | 7 | 8 | | $11^1$ | 10 | 12 | $6^2$ | $9^3$ | 14 | 2 | 1 | | | | | | | | | | 10 |
| | 2 | 3 | 4 | | | 8 | 9 | 12 | $10^3$ | $11^1$ | 13 | 6 | $7^2$ | | 5 | 1 | 14 | | | | | | | | | 11 |
| | 2 | 3 | 4 | | 13 | 8 | | 9 | $10^3$ | 14 | 12 | 6 | $7^2$ | · | 5 | 1 | $11^1$ | | | | | | | | | 12 |
| | 2 | 4 | 3 | | | 8 | 7 | 6 | | 12 | $11^1$ | | 13 | 9 | 5 | 1 | $10^2$ | | | | | | | | | 13 |
| | 2 | 3 | 4 | | 9 | $7^3$ | 8 | | 13 | 12 | $11^2$ | 6 | 14 | | 5 | 1 | $10^1$ | | | | | | | | | 14 |
| 9 | 3 | 4 | | 8 | | 6 | $10^3$ | $11^1$ | 14 | 13 | 7 | $5^2$ | 2 | 1 | 12 | | | | | | | | | | | 15 |
| | 2 | 3 | 4 | | 9 | | 8 | 13 | 12 | $10^3$ | | $6^2$ | 7 | 14 | 5 | 1 | $11^1$ | | | | | | | | | 16 |
| | 2 | 3 | 4 | 14 | 9 | $7^2$ | 8 | | 12 | 11 | $10^▪$ | $6^1$ | | 13 | $5^3$ | 1 | | | | | | | | | | 17 |
| | 2 | 4 | 3 | | 9 | 7 | 8 | 13 | 10 | $11^2$ | | $6^1$ | | 12 | 5 | 1 | | | | | | | | | | 18 |
| | 2 | 3 | 4 | | $9^2$ | 7 | 8 | 13 | $11^3$ | 10 | | $6^1$ | 12 | 14 | 5 | 1 | | | | | | | | | | 19 |
| | 3 | $5^▪$ | | | $6^3$ | 8 | 7 | 14 | $10^2$ | 11 | 13 | $9^1$ | | 12 | 2 | 1 | | 4 | | | | | | | | 20 |
| | 2 | | | | $10^2$ | | 3 | | 8 | 11 | 9 | 12 | $6^1$ | 7 | 13 | 5 | 1 | 4 | | | | | | | | 21 |
| | 2 | 4 | | | | 6 | 7 | 8 | $9^2$ | 12 | $11^1$ | 10 | 13 | 14 | 5 | 1 | $3^3$ | | | | | | | | | 22 |
| | 2 | 4 | 14 | | 13 | 3 | 7 | $9^3$ | 10 | 12 | $11^1$ | 6 | $8^2$ | | 5 | 1 | | | | | | | | | | 23 |
| | 2 | 3 | 4 | | $9^1$ | 7 | 8 | 12 | $10^2$ | $13^3$ | 6 | | 14 | | 5 | 1 | | | | | | | | | | 24 |
| | 3 | 4 | | | $9^1$ | 7 | 8 | 5 | $10^2$ | 12 | 11 | 6 | | 13 | 2 | 1 | | | | | | | | | | 25 |
| | 2 | 3 | 4 | | | 7 | 8 | 12 | 13 | $10^1$ | 11 | $6^3$ | $9^2$ | 14 | 5 | 1 | | | | | | | | | | 26 |
| | 2 | | 3 | | | 8 | $4^3$ | $9^2$ | $11^1$ | | 10 | 6 | 7 | 12 | 5 | 1 | | | 13 | 14 | | | | | | 27 |
| 6 | 3 | 5 | 13 | 4 | | | 14 | 12 | $11^3$ | $10^2$ | 7 | $8^1$ | 2 | 1 | | | | | | | 9 | | | | | 28 |
| 10 | 8 | 3 | 4 | 7 | 2 | | $6^2$ | 12 | $9^3$ | | 14 | $11^1$ | | | | | | | | | 13 | 5 | | | | 29 |
| | 5 | 4 | 7 | | 10 | 3 | $8^2$ | | $11^1$ | 9 | | $6^3$ | | 12 | 2 | 1 | | | | | 13 | 14 | | | | 30 |
| | 3 | 4 | 5 | 9 | 7 | 8 | 12 | 14 | $10^1$ | | $6^2$ | 13 | $11^3$ | 2 | 1 | | | | | | | | | | | 31 |
| | 5 | 4 | | 2 | | 3 | 8 | 6 | 12 | $7^1$ | 11 | 10 | $9^2$ | | | 1 | | | | | 13 | | | | | 32 |
| | 2 | 3 | | 5 | 4 | 8 | $9^1$ | 13 | $11^3$ | 10 | 6 | $7^2$ | 14 | | 13 | 1 | | | | | 12 | | | | | 33 |
| 7 | 4 | 5 | 2 | | 3 | 8 | $6^1$ | 10 | $11^3$ | | $9^2$ | 14 | | 13 | | 1 | | | | | 12 | | | | | 34 |
| | 2 | 3 | 4 | 5 | 14 | 8 | 7 | $9^3$ | $10^1$ | 11 | | $6^2$ | | 12 | | 1 | | | | | 13 | | | | | 35 |
| | 2 | 3 | 4 | | 13 | 7 | 8 | | 12 | 10 | | $6^2$ | | 14 | 5 | 1 | | | | | $9^3$ | $11^1$ | | | | 36 |
| | 2 | 3 | 4 | 5 | $9^2$ | 7 | 8 | 14 | | $10^1$ | 13 | | | | | 1 | | | | | $6^3$ | 12 | 11 | | | 37 |
| 1 | 2 | 3 | $4^▪$ | | 6 | 7 | 8 | 9 | 13 | | 14 | | | 12 | $5^3$ | | | | | | | $11^2$ | $10^1$ | | | 38 |
| | 5 | 3 | | 2 | 9 | 6 | 8 | | 14 | | $4^2$ | 7 | | 13 | | 1 | | | | | $10^1$ | $11^3$ | 12 | 1 | | 39 |
| | 2 | 3 | 4 | 5 | 9 | 7 | 8 | | | | | $6^3$ | 14 | $11^2$ | | 1 | | | | | 13 | 12 | $10^1$ | 1 | | 40 |
| | 2 | 3 | 4 | | $9^2$ | | 8 | 13 | | $6^3$ | 7 | 12 | 5 | | | 1 | | | | | 14 | 11 | $10^1$ | 1 | | 41 |
| | 2 | 3 | 4 | 5 | 12 | 8 | 9 | | 13 | | | $7^1$ | $10^2$ | | | 1 | | | | | 6 | 14 | $11^3$ | 1 | | 42 |
| | 2 | 4 | | $5^2$ | 9 | 7 | 8 | 13 | | $10^3$ | | 6 | | 14 | 3 | | | | | | | $11^1$ | 12 | 1 | | 43 |
| | 2 | 4 | | | | 3 | 7 | 9 | | 14 | | 12 | 8 | $11^1$ | 5 | | | | | | $6^3$ | 13 | $10^2$ | 1 | | 44 |
| 6 | $4^1$ | 5 | 2 | | 3 | 9 | 12 | | 10 | | | $7^3$ | $8^2$ | 14 | | | | | | | 13 | | 11 | 1 | | 45 |
| | 2 | 3 | 4 | 5 | | 7 | 10 | 12 | | $9^2$ | | $6^3$ | $8^1$ | 13 | | | | | | | 14 | | 11 | 1 | | 46 |

**FA Cup**

| | | | |
|---|---|---|---|
| Fourth Qualifying | Forest Green R | (a) | 1-1 |
| *Replay* | Forest Green R | (h) | 1-4 |

**FA Trophy**

| | | | |
|---|---|---|---|
| First Round | Kingstonian | (a) | 4-0 |
| Second Round | Tonbridge Angels | (h) | 3-0 |
| Third Round | Bromley | (h) | 4-2 |
| Quarter-Finals | FC Halifax T | (a) | 1-1 |
| *Replay* | FC Halifax T | (h) | 3-2 |
| Semi-Finals | Grimsby T | (a) | 0-3 |
| | Grimsby T | (h) | 0-0 |

# EBBSFLEET UNITED

*Ground:* Stonebridge Road, Northfleet, Kent DA11 9GN. *Tel:* (01474) 533 796. *Fax:* (01474) 324 754.
*Website:* www.ebbsfleetunited.co.uk *Year Formed:* 1946. *Record Gate:* 12,032 (1963 v Sunderland, FA Cup 4th rd).
*Nickname:* 'The Fleet'. *Manager:* Liam Daish. *Secretary:* Peter Danzey. *Colours:* Red shirts with white trim, white shorts, red socks.

## EBBSFLEET UNITED – BLUE SQUARE PREMIER 2012–13 LEAGUE RECORD

| Match No. | Date | Venue | Opponents | Result | H/T Score | Lg Pos. | Goalscorers | Attendance |
|---|---|---|---|---|---|---|---|---|
| 1 | Aug 11 | A | Nuneaton T | W 5-4 | 3-2 | 2 | Phipp 2 [20, 88], Elder [23], Ashikodi [32], Enver-Marum [50] | 1088 |
| 2 | 14 | H | Braintree T | L 0-1 | 0-0 | 11 | | 857 |
| 3 | 18 | H | Wrexham | D 1-1 | 0-0 | 12 | Enver-Marum [70] | 843 |
| 4 | 25 | A | Hereford U | L 2-4 | 0-2 | 14 | Ashikodi [50], Howe [90] | 1906 |
| 5 | 27 | H | Luton T | L 1-3 | 0-2 | 20 | Elder [86] | 1701 |
| 6 | Sept 1 | A | Lincoln C | D 1-1 | 0-1 | 19 | Bellamy [62] | 1682 |
| 7 | 4 | A | Forest Green R | L 1-4 | 1-4 | 21 | Walsh [12] | 914 |
| 8 | 8 | H | Mansfield T | W 3-1 | 0-1 | 19 | Elder [58], Walsh [60], Enver-Marum (pen) [81] | 828 |
| 9 | 15 | A | Southport | L 0-1 | 0-0 | 21 | | 872 |
| 10 | 22 | H | Barrow | L 2-4 | 0-3 | 22 | Phipp [46], Elder [49] | 780 |
| 11 | 25 | H | Woking | D 2-2 | 1-2 | 22· | Howe [8], Walsh [75] | 738 |
| 12 | 29 | A | Stockport Co | L 1-3 | 0-0 | 23 | Elder (pen) [61] | 4641 |
| 13 | Oct 6 | H | Kidderminster H | D 1-1 | 1-1 | 23 | Elder [35] | 726 |
| 14 | 9 | A | Newport Co | L 0-1 | 0-1 | 23 | | 2453 |
| 15 | 13 | H | Alfreton T | D 0-0 | 0-0 | 23 | | 804 |
| 16 | 27 | A | Tamworth | W 1-0 | 1-0 | 22 | Phipp [45] | 838 |
| 17 | Nov 6 | A | AFC Telford U | D 2-2 | 1-2 | 23 | Elder 2 (1 pen) [8, 54 (p)] | 1542 |
| 18 | 10 | H | Hyde | W 3-2 | 1-2 | 21 | Barrett [35], Elder [72], Godden [79] | 779 |
| 19 | 17 | A | Macclesfield T | W 2-1 | 0-1 | 19 | Walsh [57], Elder (pen) [86] | 1896 |
| 20 | Dec 1 | H | Grimsby T | D 1-1 | 1-1 | 20 | Godden [42] | 1164 |
| 21 | 4 | H | Cambridge U | L 2-4 | 1-1 | 21 | Enver-Marum [13], Godden [49] | 842 |
| 22 | 8 | H | Mansfield T | L 1-4 | 1-2 | 22 | Enver-Marum [23] | 1845 |
| 23 | 26 | A | Dartford | L 1-3 | 0-0 | 23 | Enver-Marum [48] | 3116 |
| 24 | Jan 1 | H | Dartford | D 2-2 | 0-1 | 23 | Elder 2 [50, 90] | 2242 |
| 25 | 5 | H | Lincoln C | D 1-1 | 1-0 | 22 | Phipp [36] | 889 |
| 26 | 13 | A | Woking | L 0-1 | 0-0 | 23 | | 1419 |
| 27 | Feb 1 | H | Macclesfield T | L 0-4 | 0-1 | 24 | | 799 |
| 28 | 9 | H | Gateshead | W 3-1 | 2-1 | 24 | Scott 2 [3, 38], Enver-Marum [67] | 636 |
| 29 | 16 | H | Stockport Co | D 0-0 | 0-0 | 24 | | 912 |
| 30 | 19 | H | Hereford U | W 1-0 | 1-0 | 23 | Scott [37] | 614 |
| 31 | 26 | A | Grimsby T | L 1-3 | 0-2 | 23 | Enver-Marum [74] | 3129 |
| 32 | Mar 2 | A | Kidderminster H | L 2-3 | 1-1 | 23 | Shitta [13], Elder (pen) [90] | 2048 |
| 33 | 5 | A | Wrexham | L 1-4 | 0-4 | 23 | Elder [77] | 2390 |
| 34 | 9 | H | Newport Co | D 1-1 | 0-1 | 23 | Enver-Marum [55] | 808 |
| 35 | 12 | A | Alfreton T | L 0-3 | 0-2 | 23 | | 459 |
| 36 | 16 | H | Southport | W 4-1 | 4-0 | 23 | Bellamy [6], Payne [12], Elder [14], Godden [29] | 603 |
| 37 | 19 | A | Cambridge U | D 1-1 | 0-0 | 23 | Godden [70] | 1737 |
| 38 | 30 | H | Forest Green R | L 0-2 | 0-1 | 23 | | 749 |
| 39 | Apr 1 | A | Braintree T | L 1-3 | 1-2 | 23 | Enver-Marum [36] | 822 |
| 40 | 3 | A | Barrow | D 1-1 | 1-0 | 23 | Walsh [41] | 844 |
| 41 | 6 | H | Nuneaton T | D 1-1 | 1-0 | 23 | Phipp [34] | 695 |
| 42 | 9 | A | Hyde | L 0-1 | 0-1 | 23 | | 385 |
| 43 | 13 | H | AFC Telford U | L 1-3 | 1-3 | 23 | Payne [16] | 686 |
| 44 | 16 | H | Tamworth | D 1-1 | 0-0 | 23 | Enver-Marum [80] | 488 |
| 45 | 18 | A | Luton T | L 0-2 | 0-1 | 23 | | 5934 |
| 46 | 20 | A | Gateshead | L 0-2 | 0-0 | 23 | | 532 |

**Final League Position: 23 – Relegated to Conference South**

### GOALSCORERS

*League (55):* Elder 15 (4 pens), Enver-Marum 11 (1 pen), Phipp 6, Godden 5, Walsh 5, Scott 3, Ashikodi 2, Bellamy 2, Howe 2, Payne 2, Barrett 1, Shitta 1.
*FA Cup (3):* Ashikodi 1, Elder 1, Howe 1.
*FA Trophy (0).*

| Edwards 43 | Howe 43 + 1 | Ada 19 | Lorraine 39 | Blake 6 + 2 | Barrett 41 + 1 | Bellamy 21 + 17 | Phipp 40 + 2 | Enver-Marum 34 + 12 | Elder 32 + 10 | Ashikodi 15 + 8 | Walsh 27 + 8 | Folkes 4 + 3 | Greenhalgh 1 + 9 | Stone 26 + 2 | Azeez 11 + 19 | Marwa 7 | Williams —+ 3 | Soares 7 + 1 | Carew 27 | Godden 9 + 1 | Menz 3 + 1 | Saville 13 + 2 | Gwillim 14 | Scott 6 | Payne 12 + 1 | Shitta 2 + 1 | Alabi 1 + 5 | Luzardo 2 + 1 | Azin 1 + 1 | Match No. |
|---|---|---|---|---|---|---|---|---|---|---|---|---|---|---|---|---|---|---|---|---|---|---|---|---|---|---|---|---|---|---|
| 1 | 2 | 3 | 4 | 5 | 6 | 7 | 8 | $9^2$ | $10^1$ | 11 | 12 | 13 | | | | | | | | | | | | | | | | | | 1 |
| 1 | 2 | $3^4$ | 4 | 5 | 6 | $7^2$ | 8 | 9 | $10^1$ | 11 | 12 | | | 13 | | | | | | | | | | | | | | | | 2 |
| 1 | 5 | 3 | 4 | | 6 | $7^1$ | 8 | 9 | $10^1$ | 11 | 12 | | | | 2 | 13 | | | | | | | | | | | | | | 3 |
| 1 | 3 | 4 | 5 | | 7 | 6 | 8 | $11^1$ | 10 | $9^2$ | 12 | | | 13 | $2^3$ | 14 | | | | | | | | | | | | | | 4 |
| 1 | 5 | 3 | 4 | | $6^2$ | 8 | 7 | 13 | 10 | 11 | 12 | | | | 2 | $9^1$ | | | | | | | | | | | | | | 5 |
| 1 | 5 | 6 | 4 | | $8^2$ | 13 | 7 | $10^1$ | 12 | $11^3$ | 3 | | 14 | 2 | 9 | | | | | | | | | | | | | | | 6 |
| 1 | 5 | $3^1$ | 4 | | 8 | 13 | 9 | 12 | 10 | $11^3$ | 7 | | 14 | 2 | $6^2$ | | | | | | | | | | | | | | | 7 |
| 1 | 2 | 7 | 3 | 5 | 6 | $9^1$ | 13 | 11 | $10^3$ | 4 | 12 | | | | | $8^2$ | 14 | | | | | | | | | | | | | 8 |
| 1 | 5 | $4^4$ | 3 | | 7 | 12 | $2^1$ | $6^2$ | 10 | 13 | 11 | | $9^3$ | 14 | | | 8 | | | | | | | | | | | | | 9 |
| 1 | 5 | 3 | | | 6 | | 9 | 12 | 10 | 11 | 4 | | $8^1$ | 2 | | 7 | | | | | | | | | | | | | | 10 |
| 1 | 5 | 2 | 3 | | 6 | | 8 | $9^1$ | 10 | 11 | 4 | | 12 | | | 7 | | | | | | | | | | | | | | 11 |
| 1 | 2 | 5 | 4 | | $6^1$ | 12 | 8 | 13 | 10 | 11 | 3 | | | | | | $7^2$ | | | 9 | | | | | | | | | | 12 |
| 1 | 5 | 3 | 4 | | $8^2$ | | 9 | 12 | 10 | $11^3$ | 13 | | 14 | 2 | | | $7^1$ | 6 | | | | | | | | | | | | 13 |
| 1 | 5 | 3 | 4 | | 12 | | 8 | $7^2$ | 13 | $10^3$ | 11 | | 14 | 2 | | | $6^1$ | 9 | | | | | | | | | | | | 14 |
| 1 | 5 | 3 | 4 | | 6 | | $8^1$ | 12 | 9 | $10^2$ | 13 | | | 2 | 14 | | | | | | $11^3$ | 7 | | | | | | | | 15 |
| 1 | 2 | 5 | 4 | | 8 | | 9 | $11^3$ | 13 | 14 | $10^2$ | 3 | 12 | | | | $6^1$ | 7 | | | | | | | | | | | | 16 |
| 1 | 5 | 4 | 3 | | 7 | | 8 | 12 | 10 | $11^1$ | 2 | | | $6^2$ | | | 13 | 9 | | | | | | | | | | | | 17 |
| 1 | 5 | 3 | 4 | | 7 | | 8 | $11^2$ | 10 | | | | $2^1$ | 12 | 13 | | $6^3$ | 9 | 14 | | | | | | | | | | | 18 |
| 1 | 5 | 4 | | | $8^1$ | | 12 | 9 | 14 | 11 | | 3 | 13 | 2 | $10^2$ | | $6^3$ | 7 | | | | | | | | | | | | 19 |
| 1 | 5 | 3 | | | 8 | | 13 | 9 | $10^1$ | 12 | 4 | | | 2 | $6^2$ | | | 7 | 11 | | | | | | | | | | | 20 |
| 1 | 5 | 4 | | | 8 | | 12 | $9^1$ | 10 | | 3 | | | 2 | 6 | | | 7 | 11 | | | | | | | | | | | 21 |
| $1^2$ | 2 | | 4 | | 7 | | $9^1$ | 8 | | $11^3$ | 14 | 3 | 5 | 12 | | | | | 6 | 10 | 13 | | | | | | | | | 22 |
| 1 | 5 | | 4 | | 8 | 7 | | 9 | 10 | $11^1$ | | 3 | 12 | 2 | 6 | | | | | | | | | | | | | | | 23 |
| 1 | 5 | 4 | | 13 | 8 | | | $9^3$ | 10 | 11 | | $3^2$ | $6^1$ | 2 | | 12 | 14 | 7 | | | | | | | | | | | | 24 |
| 1 | 5 | 4 | | | 8 | | 12 | 9 | 10 | 11 | | 3 | | 2 | 6 | | | $7^1$ | | | | | | | | | | | | 25 |
| 1 | 5 | 3 | | | $7^3$ | | 12 | 8 | 10 | $11^2$ | 13 | | | 2 | $6^1$ | 14 | | 9 | 4 | | | | | | | | | | | 26 |
| 1 | 8 | 4 | | | 6 | | $7^1$ | 14 | 9 | | | | | 2 | | | | | | | | 3 | 5 | $10^2$ | $11^3$ | 12 | 13 | | | 27 |
| 1 | $9^1$ | 4 | | | 7 | | 12 | 8 | $10^3$ | 13 | | | | 2 | | | | | | | | 4 | 5 | $11^2$ | 6 | | 14 | | | 28 |
| 1 | 9 | 3 | | | 7 | | 12 | 8 | $10^2$ | 13 | | | | 2 | | | | | | | | 4 | $5^1$ | 11 | $6^3$ | | 14 | | | 29 |
| 1 | $9^2$ | 3 | | | 8 | | 13 | | $10^1$ | 14 | | | | 2 | 12 | | | | 7 | | | 4 | 5 | 11 | $6^3$ | | | | | 30 |
| 1 | 2 | 4 | | | $8^3$ | | 12 | | 9 | 14 | | | | $7^1$ | 13 | | | | | 6 | | 3 | 5 | 10 | $11^2$ | | | | | 31 |
| 1 | 2 | 4 | | | 8 | | 13 | | $9^2$ | 12 | | | | 14 | | | | | | 6 | | 3 | 5 | 10 | | $7^2$ | $11^1$ | | | 32 |
| 1 | | 4 | 3 | 13 | | | 9 | $6^1$ | 10 | 11 | | | 12 | | | | | | | 7 | | $5^1$ | 2 | | | $8^2$ | 14 | | | 33 |
| 1 | | 3 | | | | | 9 | 8 | 2 | $6^1$ | 11 | | 4 | | | | | | | 12 | | 7 | 10 | | 5 | | | | | 34 |
| 1 | 2 | 4 | | | $6^2$ | 7 | | $9^1$ | 10 | 3 | | | | | 13 | | | | | 8 | 11 | 5 | | 12 | | | | | | 35 |
| 1 | 5 | 3 | | | | | 9 | 8 | 2 | 12 | 11 | | 7 | | 13 | | | | | 4 | $10^1$ | $6^2$ | | | | | | | | 36 |
| 1 | 5 | 3 | | | | | 9 | 8 | 2 | 13 | $10^2$ | | 4 | | 12 | | | | | 7 | 11 | $6^1$ | | | | | | | | 37 |
| 1 | $2^1$ | 3 | | | $7^3$ | 14 | 8 | 13 | $10^2$ | 4 | 12 | | | | | | | | | 9 | 11 | 5 | 6 | | | | | | | 38 |
| 1 | 2 | $4^2$ | | | | | 8 | 10 | 9 | 12 | | | | 14 | | | | | | $7^1$ | $11^3$ | 13 | 5 | 6 | | | | | | 39 |
| 1 | 2 | | | | $7^1$ | | 8 | 9 | 10 | 11 | 12 | | 3 | | | | | | | 6 | | 4 | 5 | | | | | | | 40 |
| 1 | 9 | | | | $8^1$ | 7 | 2 | | 10 | 11 | | | 3 | 12 | | | | | | 6 | | $4^2$ | 5 | | | | 13 | | | 41 |
| 1 | 12 | | | | 7 | | 8 | 9 | 10 | $11^2$ | 13 | | 3 | $2^1$ | | | | | | 6 | | 4 | $5^3$ | | | | | 14 | | 42 |
| | 2 | 3 | 5 | | $8^3$ | 7 | | | $10^1$ | 13 | $11^2$ | | | 12 | | | | | 9 | 1 | | 4 | | 6 | | | | 14 | | 43 |
| | 5 | 3 | | 13 | | | 8 | 12 | 10 | | | | | 2 | $9^1$ | | | | $7^2$ | 1 | | 6 | | | | | | 4 | 11 | 44 |
| 1 | 5 | $4^1$ | 3 | | 7 | | 9 | | 2 | 10 | $11^2$ | | 13 | | | | | | | | | 12 | | 6 | | | 8 | | | 45 |
| | 7 | 14 | 8 | $5^3$ | 6 | | | 10 | $9^2$ | 13 | 3 | | | 2 | 12 | | | $11^1$ | | 1 | 4 | | | | | | | | | 46 |

**FA Cup**

| | | | | |
|---|---|---|---|---|
| Fourth Qualifying | Woking | (a) | 1-0 | |
| First Round | Carlisle U | (a) | 2-4 | |

**FA Trophy**

| | | | | |
|---|---|---|---|---|
| First Round | Hereford U | (h) | 0-1 | |

# FOREST GREEN ROVERS

*Ground:* The New Lawn, Another Way, Nailsworth, Gloucestershire GL6 0FG.   *Tel:* (01453) 834 860.
*Fax:* (01453) 835 291.   *Website:* www.forestgreenroversfc.com   *Year Formed:* 1890.
*Record Gate:* 4,836 (2009 v Derby Co, FA Cup 3rd rd)   *Nickname:* 'The Rovers'.   *Manager:* David Hockaday.
*Secretary:* Michelle McDonald.   *Colours:* Black and white striped shirts, black shorts, black socks.

## FOREST GREEN ROVERS – BLUE SQUARE PREMIER 2012–13 LEAGUE RECORD

| Match No. | Date | Venue | Opponents | Result | H/T Score | Lg Pos. | Goalscorers | Attendance |
|---|---|---|---|---|---|---|---|---|
| 1 | Aug 11 | H | Cambridge U | D 1-1 | 0-1 | 13 | Klukowski (pen) 90 | 1128 |
| 2 | 14 | A | AFC Telford U | W 2-1 | 2-0 | 9 | Racine 5, Blackburn (og) 40 | 1582 |
| 3 | 18 | A | Gateshead | D 1-1 | 0-0 | 10 | Styche (pen) 90 | 531 |
| 4 | 25 | H | Woking | W 3-1 | 0-1 | 7 | Vieira 62, Taylor 2 90, 90 | 979 |
| 5 | 27 | A | Kidderminster H | W 1-0 | 0-0 | 3 | Norwood 81 | 1742 |
| 6 | Sept 1 | H | Hyde | W 3-1 | 2-0 | 2 | Styche 12, Turley 18, Wright, B 90 | 768 |
| 7 | 4 | H | Ebbsfleet U | W 4-1 | 4-1 | 1 | Klukowski 18, Wright, B 27, Taylor 30, Oshodi 41 | 914 |
| 8 | 8 | A | Grimsby T | L 0-1 | 0-0 | 2 | | 3270 |
| 9 | 15 | H | Alfreton T | D 1-1 | 1-0 | 3 | Klukowski 10 | 1072 |
| 10 | 22 | A | Macclesfield T | W 2-1 | 1-0 | 2 | Taylor 35, Brogan 90 | 1729 |
| 11 | 25 | A | Hereford U | W 2-1 | 2-1 | 2 | Wright, B 16, Klukowski 32 | 1656 |
| 12 | 28 | H | Lincoln C | W 3-0 | 1-0 | 1 | Taylor 2 16, 51, Vieira 63 | 1395 |
| 13 | Oct 6 | A | Wrexham | L 1-2 | 0-0 | 2 | Norwood 90 | 4053 |
| 14 | 9 | H | Tamworth | L 1-2 | 0-2 | 2 | Collins 61 | 1022 |
| 15 | 13 | A | Mansfield T | L 0-1 | 0-0 | 5 | | 2019 |
| 16 | 27 | H | Luton T | L 1-2 | 0-0 | 6 | Klukowski 47 | 2112 |
| 17 | Nov 6 | A | Dartford | W 1-0 | 1-0 | 5 | Klukowski 11 | 915 |
| 18 | 10 | H | Stockport Co | W 4-1 | 3-0 | 3 | Klukowski 5, Hobson (og) 15, Norwood 25, Styche 87 | 1176 |
| 19 | 17 | A | Barrow | D 2-2 | 1-1 | 3 | Norwood 15, Taylor 88 | 853 |
| 20 | Dec 1 | H | Nuneaton T | W 1-0 | 0-0 | 2 | Norwood 52 | 948 |
| 21 | 8 | H | Macclesfield T | D 1-1 | 0-1 | 4 | Stokes 85 | 901 |
| 22 | 18 | A | Braintree T | L 1-3 | 0-1 | 4 | Stokes 74 | 480 |
| 23 | 26 | H | Newport Co | L 1-2 | 0-0 | 4 | Brogan 47 | 2332 |
| 24 | Jan 1 | A | Newport Co | W 5-0 | 2-0 | 4 | Norwood 3 38, 68, 78, Klukowski 45, Styche 74 | 2787 |
| 25 | 5 | A | Hyde | W 1-0 | 0-0 | 4 | Norwood 46 | 553 |
| 26 | 12 | A | Nuneaton T | D 1-1 | 0-0 | 4 | Taylor 57 | 910 |
| 27 | 19 | A | Stockport Co | L 1-2 | 0-1 | 4 | Styche 63 | 2802 |
| 28 | 26 | A | Lincoln C | W 2-1 | 2-0 | 4 | Klukowski 7, Stokes 45 | 1663 |
| 29 | Feb 2 | H | Wrexham | D 0-0 | 0-0 | 3 | | 1840 |
| 30 | 9 | A | Luton T | D 1-1 | 1-1 | 3 | Taylor 14 | 6374 |
| 31 | 12 | H | Braintree T | W 4-1 | 2-1 | 3 | Norwood 3 19, 27, 64, Klukowski 53 | 918 |
| 32 | 16 | A | Gateshead | W 1-0 | 0-0 | 3 | Vieira 60 | 1139 |
| 33 | 19 | H | Kidderminster H | L 0-1 | 0-1 | 4 | | 1449 |
| 34 | 26 | A | Woking | L 0-2 | 0-0 | 6 | | 1105 |
| 35 | Mar 2 | A | Cambridge U | D 0-0 | 0-0 | 6 | | 2221 |
| 36 | 5 | H | Grimsby T | L 0-1 | 0-0 | 6 | | 744 |
| 37 | 9 | H | Barrow | D 1-1 | 1-0 | 6 | Norwood 9 | 904 |
| 38 | 12 | A | Southport | W 2-1 | 0-1 | 6 | Odubade 87, Burns 90 | 632 |
| 39 | 15 | H | Mansfield T | L 1-2 | 0-1 | 6 | Norwood 87 | 1109 |
| 40 | 30 | A | Ebbsfleet U | W 2-0 | 1-0 | 6 | Norwood 38, Connolly 82 | 749 |
| 41 | Apr 1 | H | AFC Telford U | D 0-0 | 0-0 | 6 | | 1061 |
| 42 | 6 | A | Tamworth | L 1-2 | 0-2 | 6 | Klukowski 48 | 773 |
| 43 | 9 | H | Hereford U | L 0-1 | 0-0 | 7 | | 1142 |
| 44 | 13 | A | Southport | L 0-1 | 0-0 | 7 | | 1496 |
| 45 | 16 | H | Dartford | L 2-3 | 0-2 | 8 | Stokes 48, Turley 79 | 575 |
| 46 | 20 | A | Alfreton T | L 1-2 | 0-2 | 10 | Turley 56 | 759 |

**Final League Position: 10**

### GOALSCORERS

*League (63):* Norwood 15, Klukowski 11 (1 pen), Taylor 9, Styche 5 (1 pen), Stokes 4, Turley 3, Vieira 3, Wright, B 3, Brogan 2, Burns 1, Collins 1, Connolly 1, Oshodi 1, Racine 1, own goals 2.
*FA Cup (7):* Klukowski 2, Norwood 2, Oshodi 1, Taylor 1, Viera 1.
*FA Trophy (3):* Stokes 1, Styche 1, Taylor 1.

| Russell 46 | Turley 35+2 | Collins 17+4 | Oshodi 39+2 | Asafu-Adjaye 22+2 | Norwood 38+3 | Klukowski 35+5 | Forbes 27+6 | Bangura 29+4 | Taylor 33+9 | Vieira 21+13 | Rowe 7+7 | Wright B 10+8 | Styche 8+16 | Racine 23 | Marsh 2+3 | Green 21 | Koroma 5+10 | Stokes 35+1 | Brogan 7+6 | Hodgkiss 24+2 | Jarvis 1+1 | Odubade 3+11 | Bennett 5+2 | Williams —+3 | Fowler 3+2 | Burns 5+1 | Connolly 5+2 | Match No. |
|---|---|---|---|---|---|---|---|---|---|---|---|---|---|---|---|---|---|---|---|---|---|---|---|---|---|---|---|---|
| 1 | 2 | 3 | 4 | 5 | 6 | 7 | 8 | $9^1$ | $10^3$ | $11^2$ | 12 | 13 | 14 | | | | | | | | | | | | | | | 1 |
| 1 | 2 | 7 | 4 | 5 | 9 | | $6^3$ | 14 | 12 | | 8 | 11 | $10^1$ | 3 | 13 | | | | | | | | | | | | | 2 |
| 1 | 2 | 6 | 4 | 5 | 12 | | $7^3$ | 14 | $9^2$ | 8 | $11^1$ | 10 | | 3 | 13 | | | | | | | | | | | | | 3 |
| 1 | 2 | 6 | 3 | 5 | 8 | | 12 | | 14 | $10^2$ | 7 | $11^1$ | $9^3$ | 4 | 13 | | | | | | | | | | | | | 4 |
| 1 | 2 | 7 | 4 | 5 | 9 | | 12 | | $10^3$ | 13 | $8^2$ | | 14 | | | $11^1$ | 3 | $6^8$ | | | | | | | | | | 5 |
| 1 | 2 | 6 | 3 | 5 | 9 | 12 | 7 | | 13 | $10^2$ | | 14 | $11^3$ | 4 | $8^1$ | | | | | | | | | | | | | 6 |
| 1 | 2 | $8^1$ | 3 | 5 | $11^3$ | 7 | 6 | 12 | 10 | | | $9^2$ | 14 | 4 | | 13 | | | | | | | | | | | | 7 |
| 1 | 2 | 8 | 3 | 5 | 9 | | 6 | $7^3$ | 12 | | 14 | $11^2$ | $10^1$ | 4 | | 13 | | | | | | | | | | | | 8 |
| 1 | 2 | 6 | 3 | 5 | 11 | 7 | | 13 | $10^1$ | $9^3$ | $8^2$ | | 12 | 4 | | 14 | | | | | | | | | | | | 9 |
| 1 | 3 | 6 | 4 | 2 | | 12 | $8^3$ | 7 | 11 | $10^2$ | | | $9^1$ | 14 | | | | 5 | 13 | | | | | | | | | 10 |
| 1 | 3 | 8 | 4 | 2 | | $6^2$ | 13 | 7 | 11 | $10^1$ | | | $9^3$ | 12 | | | | 5 | 14 | | | | | | | | | 11 |
| 1 | 2 | 9 | 3 | 4 | | $7^2$ | 8 | $6^1$ | 10 | 12 | | | $11^3$ | | | | 14 | 5 | 13 | | | | | | | | | 12 |
| 1 | 4 | 6 | 3 | 2 | 13 | | 8 | $7^1$ | 11 | $10^3$ | | | $9^2$ | $14^8$ | | | | 5 | 12 | | | | | | | | | 13 |
| 1 | 3 | 7 | | 2 | 11 | 12 | $6^3$ | | 10 | 13 | | | $9^2$ | | | | 4 | 14 | 5 | $8^1$ | | | | | | | | 14 |
| 1 | 4 | | 5 | $9^3$ | 11 | 6 | | 10 | 12 | | 13 | | 3 | | | | $7^1$ | 14 | $8^2$ | 2 | | | | | | | | 15 |
| 1 | 3 | | 4 | | 8 | 6 | 12 | 9 | 11 | | | | $10^1$ | 5 | | $7^8$ | | 2 | | | | | | | | | | 16 |
| 1 | $2^8$ | | 3 | 5 | $11^3$ | 9 | | 7 | $10^2$ | 13 | | | | 4 | | 6 | 14 | 12 | $8^1$ | 2 | | | | | | | | 17 |
| 1 | | | 3 | 2 | $9^2$ | 7 | | 6 | 10 | $11^1$ | | | | 13 | 4 | | 8 | 12 | 5 | | | | | | | | | 18 |
| 1 | | 4 | | | 11 | $8^3$ | | $7^2$ | 10 | 14 | | | | 12 | 3 | | 6 | $9^1$ | 5 | 13 | 2 | | | | | | | 19 |
| 1 | 2 | | 4 | 12 | 8 | | | 7 | 11 | $9^2$ | | | | 13 | 3 | | | $10^1$ | 5 | 6 | | | | | | | | 20 |
| 1 | 2 | | 3 | | $11^3$ | 6 | | 7 | $10^1$ | 13 | | | | 12 | 4 | | $9^2$ | 5 | 8 | | 14 | | | | | | | 21 |
| 1 | 2 | 7 | $3^2$ | | 11 | $6^3$ | | | 13 | | | | | | 4 | | 8 | $9^8$ | 5 | 14 | 12 | $10^1$ | | | | | | 22 |
| 1 | $3^8$ | 6 | | | $11^3$ | $9^1$ | | 13 | 10 | 14 | | | | 12 | 4 | | $7^2$ | 5 | 8 | 2 | | | | | | | | 23 |
| 1 | | 3 | 14 | 11 | 9 | | $7^2$ | 6 | 10 | | 13 | | | 12 | 4 | | $5^3$ | $8^1$ | 2 | | | | | | | | | 24 |
| 1 | | | 4 | | 10 | 8 | 6 | 7 | 11 | | | $9^1$ | | 12 | 5 | | 3 | | 2 | | | | | | | | | 25 |
| 1 | 14 | | $3^2$ | | 11 | 8 | $6^3$ | 7 | 10 | $9^1$ | 13 | | | 12 | 4 | | 5 | | 2 | | | | | | | | | 26 |
| 1 | 3 | 13 | 4 | | $11^3$ | 8 | $6^2$ | 7 | 10 | $9^1$ | | | | 12 | | | 5 | | 2 | 14 | | | | | | | | 27 |
| 1 | 3 | 7 | 4 | 13 | $11^1$ | 8 | 6 | | 9 | 12 | | | | $10^2$ | | | 5 | | 2 | | | | | | | | | 28 |
| 1 | 4 | 13 | 5 | | $11^3$ | 7 | $8^2$ | 6 | 10 | 12 | | | | $9^1$ | | | 3 | | 2 | 14 | | | | | | | | 29 |
| 1 | 4 | | $5^2$ | 10 | 8 | | $7^8$ | 11 | $9^3$ | | | | | | 6 | | 3 | | 2 | 12 | 13 | | | | | | | 30 |
| 1 | 5 | 12 | | 11 | 6 | $7^3$ | | 10 | $9^2$ | 14 | | | | $8^1$ | | | 3 | | 2 | 13 | 4 | | | | | | | 31 |
| 1 | 4 | 13 | 3 | 10 | 7 | | $11^2$ | $9^3$ | $8^1$ | 14 | | | | 6 | | | 5 | | 2 | 12 | | | | | | | | 32 |
| 1 | 4 | $8^1$ | 3 | $11^2$ | 6 | | 10 | 9 | 13 | | | | | 7 | | | 5 | | 2 | 12 | | | | | | | | 33 |
| 1 | 3 | $6^1$ | 4 | $9^2$ | 8 | | 10 | 11 | 14 | | | | | $7^3$ | | | 5 | | 2 | 13 | | 12 | | | | | | 34 |
| 1 | 3 | | 10 | 9 | $8^1$ | | $12^3$ | 11 | | 13 | | | 4 | 6 | | | 5 | | 2 | 14 | | $7^2$ | | | | | | 35 |
| 1 | 4 | 5 | 11 | 7 | 12 | $6^2$ | $10^3$ | 9 | | 14 | | | | 3 | | | | | 2 | 13 | | $8^1$ | | | | | | 36 |
| 1 | | 4 | 11 | 7 | 8 | 6 | 10 | 12 | | 5 | | | | 3 | | | | | 2 | | | $9^1$ | | | | | | 37 |
| 1 | | 4 | 2 | 11 | $9^2$ | 8 | 7 | $10^1$ | | 3 | | | | 6 | | | 5 | | | 13 | | | 12 | | | | | 38 |
| 1 | | 4 | | 11 | 13 | 6 | $7^2$ | 12 | | 3 | | | | 8 | | | 5 | | 2 | $10^1$ | | 14 | $9^3$ | | | | | 39 |
| 1 | | 3 | | $9^3$ | 13 | 8 | 7 | $10^1$ | | | | | | 6 | 14 | | 5 | | 2 | | | 4 | | $11^2$ | 12 | | | 40 |
| 1 | | 5 | | 10 | $7^2$ | 13 | 6 | $9^1$ | | | | | | 8 | 14 | | 3 | | 2 | | | 4 | | $11^3$ | 12 | | | 41 |
| 1 | 13 | 12 | 4 | | 10 | 6 | 9 | $7^2$ | | | | | | 8 | | | 5 | | 2 | | | $3^1$ | | 11 | | | | 42 |
| 1 | 3 | 14 | 4 | | $10^3$ | 8 | 6 | | 12 | | | | | $7^3$ | | | 5 | | 2 | 13 | | | | $9^1$ | 11 | | | 43 |
| 1 | 4 | 5 | 2 | | 7 | 8 | 6 | | 13 | | | | | $3^3$ | | | 14 | | $9^1$ | 12 | | | | $10^2$ | 11 | | | 44 |
| 1 | 5 | $4^8$ | 10 | $7^1$ | 8 | 6 | | $9^3$ | 13 | | | | | 3 | | | 2 | | 14 | 12 | | | | $11^2$ | | | | 45 |
| 1 | 3 | | 11 | $8^3$ | 7 | | 12 | $6^1$ | 13 | | | | | 5 | | | 2 | | $9^2$ | 4 | 14 | | | 10 | | | | 46 |

**FA Cup**

| | | | | |
|---|---|---|---|---|
| Fourth Qualifying | Dartford | (h) | 1-1 | |
| *Replay* | Dartford | (a) | 4-1 | |
| First Round | Port Vale | (h) | 2-3 | |

**FA Trophy**

| | | | | |
|---|---|---|---|---|
| First Round | AFC Totton | (h) | 2-1 | |
| Second Round | Gainsborough Trinity | (h) | 1-2 | |

# GATESHEAD

*Ground:* Gateshead International Stadium, Neilson Road, Gateshead NE10 0EF. *Tel:* (0191) 478 3883.
*Fax:* (0191) 440 0404. *Website:* www.gateshead-fc.com *Year Formed:* 1889 (Reformed 1977).
*Record Gate:* 20,752 (1937 v Lincoln C, Division 3N (at Redheugh Park). *Nickname:* 'The Tynesiders', 'The Heed'.
*Manager:* Anth Smith. *Colours:* White shirts, black shorts and socks.

## GATESHEAD – BLUE SQUARE PREMIER 2012–13 LEAGUE RECORD

| Match No. | Date | Venue | Opponents | Result | H/T Score | Lg Pos. | Goalscorers | Attendance |
|---|---|---|---|---|---|---|---|---|
| 1 | Aug 11 | A | Luton T | D | 2-2 | 2-0 | 9 | Hatch [25], Odubade [35] | 6743 |
| 2 | 14 | H | Mansfield T | W | 4-1 | 1-1 | 3 | Hatch [11], Fisher 2 [56, 86], Bush [71] | 801 |
| 3 | 18 | H | Forest Green R | D | 1-1 | 0-0 | 9 | Fisher [53] | 531 |
| 4 | 24 | A | Stockport Co | W | 2-1 | 0-1 | 2 | Donaldson [55], Cummins [66] | 3213 |
| 5 | 27 | H | Lincoln C | D | 1-1 | 1-0 | 7 | Marwood [45] | 803 |
| 6 | Sept 1 | A | Nuneaton T | W | 1-0 | 0-0 | 4 | Odubade [63] | 835 |
| 7 | 4 | A | Southport | L | 1-2 | 0-0 | 2 | Gillies [74] | 686 |
| 8 | 8 | H | Dartford | W | 2-0 | 1-0 | 4 | Cummins [40], Gillies [63] | 758 |
| 9 | 15 | H | Tamworth | L | 0-2 | 0-1 | 1 | | 622 |
| 10 | 22 | A | Woking | L | 1-2 | 0-2 | 5 | Turnbull [68] | 1609 |
| 11 | 25 | A | Grimsby T | L | 0-3 | 0-2 | 5 | | 3202 |
| 12 | 29 | H | AFC Telford U | D | 1-1 | 1-0 | 8 | McGorrigan [31] | 524 |
| 13 | Oct 6 | A | Hyde | D | 1-1 | 1-1 | 9 | Gillies [35] | 470 |
| 14 | 9 | H | Macclesfield T | D | 2-2 | 1-0 | 7 | Chandler [37], Curtis [63] | 557 |
| 15 | 13 | H | Cambridge U | D | 0-0 | 0-0 | 9 | | 768 |
| 16 | 27 | A | Kidderminster H | D | 1-1 | 0-0 | 8 | Clark [90] | 1639 |
| 17 | Nov 3 | H | Woking | W | 2-1 | 2-1 | 8 | Gillies [32], Hatch [45] | 473 |
| 18 | 6 | H | Alfreton T | W | 2-0 | 2-0 | 8 | Hatch [5], Gillies [36] | 475 |
| 19 | 10 | A | Braintree T | L | 1-2 | 1-1 | 8 | Donaldson [29] | 678 |
| 20 | 17 | A | Wrexham | D | 1-1 | 0-1 | 7 | Donaldson [63] | 3011 |
| 21 | Dec 1 | A | Newport Co | L | 1-3 | 0-1 | 8 | Odubade [70] | 1473 |
| 22 | 8 | A | Cambridge U | L | 0-3 | 0-1 | 14 | | 1840 |
| 23 | 26 | A | Barrow | W | 2-0 | 1-0 | 11 | Gillies 2 [42, 85] | 1135 |
| 24 | 29 | A | Lincoln C | D | 1-1 | 0-0 | 12 | Gillies (pen) [61] | 1906 |
| 25 | Jan 1 | H | Barrow | L | 0-1 | 0-1 | 15 | | 610 |
| 26 | Feb 2 | A | Tamworth | L | 0-2 | 0-0 | 20 | | 618 |
| 27 | 9 | A | Ebbsfleet U | L | 1-3 | 1-2 | 20 | Gillies [27] | 636 |
| 28 | 16 | A | Forest Green R | L | 0-1 | 0-0 | 20 | | 1139 |
| 29 | 19 | H | Wrexham | L | 0-1 | 0-0 | 22 | | 513 |
| 30 | 22 | A | Macclesfield T | W | 4-0 | 4-0 | 20 | Chandler 2 [2, 45], Brown [18], Donaldson [20] | 1467 |
| 31 | Mar 2 | H | Braintree T | L | 1-2 | 0-1 | 22 | Everson [85] | 327 |
| 32 | 5 | H | Kidderminster H | W | 2-0 | 0-0 | 18 | Chandler [71], Hatch [90] | 273 |
| 33 | 9 | H | Hyde | W | 3-0 | 1-0 | 17 | Brown [4], Donaldson (pen) [83], Everson [88] | 371 |
| 34 | 13 | A | AFC Telford U | D | 0-0 | 0-0 | 18 | | 1260 |
| 35 | 16 | A | Alfreton T | L | 2-3 | 2-0 | 19 | Brown (og) [20], Gillies (pen) [40] | 566 |
| 36 | 19 | H | Hereford U | W | 3-2 | 2-1 | 17 | Donaldson [19], Brown 2 [43, 55] | 259 |
| 37 | 23 | A | Dartford | L | 0-3 | 0-0 | 19 | | 1020 |
| 38 | 26 | H | Grimsby T | D | 1-1 | 0-0 | 19 | Gillies [79] | 351 |
| 39 | 28 | H | Newport Co | D | 0-0 | 0-0 | 17 | | 227 |
| 40 | 30 | H | Southport | D | 2-2 | 0-0 | 18 | Cummins [90], Gillies [90] | 406 |
| 41 | Apr 1 | A | Mansfield T | L | 0-4 | 0-1 | 18 | | 3472 |
| 42 | 6 | H | Luton T | W | 5-1 | 3-1 | 18 | Donaldson 2 [12, 66], Gillies 2 (1 pen) [16, 45 (p)], Hatch [90] | 382 |
| 43 | 9 | A | Nuneaton T | L | 0-2 | 0-2 | 19 | | 304 |
| 44 | 13 | A | Hereford U | D | 1-1 | 1-0 | 19 | Magnay [24] | 1599 |
| 45 | 16 | A | Stockport Co | D | 1-1 | 0-0 | 19 | Gillies [56] | 685 |
| 46 | 20 | H | Ebbsfleet U | W | 2-0 | 0-0 | 17 | Hatch [49], Henderson [90] | 532 |

**Final League Position: 17**

## GOALSCORERS

*League (58):* Gillies 15 (3 pens), Donaldson 8 (1 pen), Hatch 7, Brown 4, Chandler 4, Cummins 3, Fisher 3, Odubade 3, Everson 2, Bush 1, Clark 1, Curtis 1, Henderson 1, Magnay 1, Marwood 1, McGorrigan 1, Turnbull 1, own goal 1.
*FA Cup (0).*
*FA Trophy (5):* Bullock 1, Clark 1, Magnay 1, Odubade 1, own goal 1.

| Bartlett 46 | Magnay 32 + 1 | Bush 15 + 5 | Curtis 40 | Clark 32 + 1 | Gillies 45 | Turnbull 45 + 1 | Chandler 35 + 2 | Cummins 24 + 15 | Hatch 20 + 9 | Odubade 14 + 8 | Marwood 12 + 17 | Fisher 10 + 13 | Boyle 33 + 4 | Wilson 5 + 4 | McGorrigan 2 + 10 | Donaldson 38 + 1 | Carr — + 2 | McGlen 2 + 1 | Brown 24 + 5 | Bullock 7 | Henderson 5 + 6 | Galpin 8 | Bore 9 + 1 | Everson 2 + 9 | Fowler 1 + 3 | Match No. |
|---|---|---|---|---|---|---|---|---|---|---|---|---|---|---|---|---|---|---|---|---|---|---|---|---|---|---|
| 1 | 2 | 3 | 4 | 5 | 6[1] | 7 | 8 | 9[3] | 10 | 11[2] | 12 | 13 | 14 |  |  |  |  |  |  |  |  |  |  |  |  | 1 |
| 1 | 2[2] | 5 | 3 | 4 |  | 7 | 8 | 6 | 10[3] |  | 12 | 11 | 14 |  | 9[1] | 13 |  |  |  |  |  |  |  |  |  | 2 |
| 1 | 2 | 5[3] | 3 | 4 |  | 7 | 8 | 6 | 10 | 11[2] | 12 |  | 14 |  | 9[1] | 13 |  |  |  |  |  |  |  |  |  | 3 |
| 1 | 2 | 4 |  | 3 | 9 | 7 |  | 6[1] | 10[2] | 14 | 12 | 11[3] | 5 | 13 |  | 8 |  |  |  |  |  |  |  |  |  | 4 |
| 1 | 2 | 4 | 3 | 5 | 6 | 7[2] | 8 | 9 | 10[3] | 11[1] | 12 | 13 | 14 |  |  |  |  |  |  |  |  |  |  |  |  | 5 |
| 1 | 2 | 8 | 4 |  | 6 | 7 | 3 | 9[1] | 10[2] | 11[3] | 12 | 13 | 5 | 14 |  |  |  |  |  |  |  |  |  |  |  | 6 |
| 1 | 2 | 4 | 3 |  | 6 | 7 | 8 | 9[2] | 10[1] | 11 | 12 |  | 5 | 13 |  |  |  |  |  |  |  |  |  |  |  | 7 |
| 1 | 2 | 4 | 3 | 9[3] | 7 | 8 | 6 | 11[1] | 13 | 14 | 12 | 10[2] | 5 |  |  |  |  |  |  |  |  |  |  |  |  | 8 |
| 1 | 2 | 5 | 4 | 11 | 7 | 6 | 8[1] | 10[3] | 12[4] | 13 | 3[2] | 14 | 9 |  |  |  |  |  |  |  |  |  |  |  |  | 9 |
| 1 | 2 | 5[4] | 3 |  | 8 | 7 | 9[1] | 10[2] | 11 | 4 | 12 | 6 | 13 |  |  |  |  |  |  |  |  |  |  |  |  | 10 |
| 1 | 2 |  | 6[3] | 7 | 8 | 9[1] | 11 | 12 | 4 | 5[2] | 14 | 10 | 13 |  |  |  |  |  |  |  |  |  |  |  |  | 11 |
| 1 | 2[1] | 4 | 3 | 6 | 7 | 8 | 14 | 9[2] | 13 | 5[3] | 12 | 11 | 10 |  |  |  |  |  |  |  |  |  |  |  |  | 12 |
| 1 |  | 5 | 4 | 9 | 7 | 6 | 13 | 8 | 14 | 3[2] | 2 | 11[1] | 10[3] |  |  | 12 |  |  |  |  |  |  |  |  |  | 13 |
| 1 |  | 4 | 5 | 3 | 6[2] | 7 | 8 | 14 | 9[3] | 13 | 12 | 10 |  |  | 2 | 11[1] |  |  |  |  |  |  |  |  |  | 14 |
| 1 |  | 3 | 2 | 4 | 11 | 8 | 7 | 10[1] | 12 | 13 | 6 |  | 5 | 9[2] |  |  |  |  |  |  |  |  |  |  |  | 15 |
| 1 | 2 | 14 | 3 | 4 | 6 | 7[3] | 13 | 10[2] | 12 | 5 | 9 |  |  |  |  | 11[1] | 8 |  |  |  |  |  |  |  |  | 16 |
| 1 | 5 | 13 | 3 | 4 | 8[2] | 7 | 14 | 10[3] | 12 | 2 | 9 |  |  |  |  | 11[1] | 6 |  |  |  |  |  |  |  |  | 17 |
| 1 | 2 | 14 | 4 | 5 | 6[3] | 7 | 13 | 9[2] | 12 | 3 | 10 |  |  |  |  | 11[1] | 8 |  |  |  |  |  |  |  |  | 18 |
| 1 | 2 | 14 | 3 | 4 | 8 | 6[2] | 9[1] | 11 | 13 | 5[3] | 10 | 12 | 7 |  |  |  |  |  |  |  |  |  |  |  |  | 19 |
| 1 |  | 3 | 4 | 6 | 7 | 12 | 10[3] | 13 | 11[2] | 5 | 2 | 9 | 8[1] |  |  |  |  |  |  |  |  |  |  |  |  | 20 |
| 1 | 14 | 3 | 4 | 6 | 7[1] | 12 | 10 | 13 | 11[2] | 2 | 5[3] | 8 |  |  |  | 9 |  |  |  |  |  |  |  |  |  | 21 |
| 1 | 2 | 14 | 3[4] | 4 | 8[3] | 13 | 6 | 9[1] | 11 | 12 | 5 | 10 |  |  |  | 7[2] |  |  |  |  |  |  |  |  |  | 22 |
| 1 | 2 | 3 | 4 | 6 | 8 | 7 | 11[1] | 12 | 5 | 10 |  |  |  |  |  | 9[2] |  |  | 13 |  |  |  |  |  |  | 23 |
| 1 | 2 | 3 | 4 | 6 | 8 | 7 | 12 | 9[1] | 5 | 10 |  |  |  |  |  | 11 |  |  |  |  |  |  |  |  |  | 24 |
| 1 | 3 | 10[3] | 2 | 4 | 5 | 6 | 7 | 12 | 13 | 9[1] | 8 |  |  |  |  | 14 |  |  | 11[2] |  |  |  |  |  |  | 25 |
| 1 |  | 3 | 4 | 5 | 6 | 2 | 7 | 12 |  |  |  | 13 |  |  | 8 | 14 |  |  | 10[1] | 9[3] | 11[2] |  |  |  |  | 26 |
| 1 |  | 4 | 3 | 8[2] | 7 | 6 | 13 | 11 |  |  | 10 |  |  |  |  | 9[1] |  | 12 |  |  | 5 | 2 |  |  |  | 27 |
| 1 |  | 3 | 6 | 8 | 7 |  | 10 |  |  | 12 | 11[1] |  |  |  |  | 9 |  |  | 4 |  | 5 | 2 |  |  |  | 28 |
| 1 |  | 3 | 12 | 6 | 7 | 8 |  | 4 |  |  | 9[1] |  | 13 |  |  | 10 |  |  | 11 |  | 5[2] | 2 |  |  |  | 29 |
| 1 | 2 | 3 | 4 | 6[1] | 7[3] | 8 | 14 |  |  |  | 12 |  | 5 |  |  | 9 |  |  | 10[2] |  |  | 11 | 13 |  |  | 30 |
| 1 | 2 | 3 | 4 | 6[1] | 7 | 8 | 14 | 12 |  |  | 9[2] |  | 5[3] |  |  | 10 |  |  | 11 |  |  |  | 13 |  |  | 31 |
| 1 | 2 | 3 | 4 | 6 | 8 | 7 |  | 13 |  | 10[3] |  |  | 5 | 14 | 11[1] | 9[2] |  |  |  |  |  | 12 |  |  |  | 32 |
| 1 | 2 | 3 | 4 | 6[1] | 7 | 8 | 14 | 13 |  |  | 9[3] |  | 5 |  |  | 11 |  |  | 10[2] |  |  | 12 |  |  |  | 33 |
| 1 | 2[2] | 3 | 4 | 7[1] | 8 | 6 | 12 | 14 |  |  | 10 |  | 5 |  |  | 11 |  |  | 9[3] |  |  | 13 |  |  |  | 34 |
| 1 |  | 3 | 4 | 6 | 7 | 8 | 2 | 12[4] |  |  | 9[3] |  | 5 |  | 11[1] | 10[2] |  |  |  |  |  |  | 13 | 14 |  | 35 |
| 1 |  | 3 | 4 | 6 | 7 | 8 | 12 |  |  |  | 9 |  | 5 |  | 11 | 10 |  |  |  |  |  | 2[1] |  |  |  | 36 |
| 1 |  | 3 | 4 | 10 | 7 | 8 | 2 |  |  |  | 9[1] |  | 5 | 6 | 11 |  |  |  | 12 |  |  |  |  |  |  | 37 |
| 1 |  | 3 | 4 | 6 | 7 | 8 | 2 |  |  |  | 5 | 13 | 11 | 10[1] | 12 |  |  |  |  |  |  |  | 9[2] |  |  | 38 |
| 1 |  | 3 | 4 | 5 | 7 | 2 | 9 | 12 |  |  |  | 8 |  |  |  |  |  |  | 10[1] | 6 | 11 |  |  |  |  | 39 |
| 1 |  | 3 | 4[1] | 9 | 7 | 8 | 5 | 12 |  |  |  | 6 |  |  |  | 11 |  |  | 13 | 2 | 10[2] |  |  |  |  | 40 |
| 1 |  | 3 | 5[2] | 6 | 4 | 9 | 11 | 2 | 7 | 8[1] | 10[3] |  |  |  |  | 12 | 14 | 13 |  |  |  |  |  |  |  | 41 |
| 1 | 2 | 3 | 9[3] | 4 | 7 | 8 | 12 |  |  |  | 5 |  | 11[2] | 10[1] |  |  |  |  | 6 | 13 | 14 |  |  |  |  | 42 |
| 1 | 4 | 3 | 6[2] | 7 | 12 | 8[1] | 11 | 13 |  |  | 5 |  | 9 |  |  | 10[3] |  |  |  |  |  | 2 | 14 |  |  | 43 |
| 1 | 4 | 3 | 6 | 5 | 8 | 7 | 10[2] |  |  |  | 12 | 13 |  |  |  | 9[1] |  |  | 11 |  |  | 2 |  |  |  | 44 |
| 1 | 4 | 3 | 9 | 7 | 8 | 2[1] | 10 |  |  |  | 12 | 13 |  |  |  | 11 | 14 | 5[2] | 6[3] |  |  |  |  |  |  | 45 |
| 1 | 2 | 4 | 6 | 7 | 3 | 9 | 11[2] | 8 |  |  | 12 | 5 |  |  |  | 10[1] | 13 |  |  |  |  |  |  |  |  | 46 |

**FA Cup**
Fourth Qualifying   Alfreton T   (a)   0-2

**FA Trophy**
First Round   Macclesfield T   (h)   2-0
Second Round   Cambridge U   (a)   1-0
Third Round   Barrow   (a)   2-3

# GRIMSBY TOWN

*Ground:* Blundell Park, Cleethorpes, NE Lincolnshire DN35 7PY. *Tel:* (01472) 605 050. *Fax:* (01472) 693 665.
*Website:* www.grimsby-townfc.co.uk *Year Formed:* 1878. *Record Gate:* 31,651 (1937 v Wolverhampton W, FA Cup
5th rd). *Nickname:* 'The Mariners'. *Team Managers:* Rob Scott & Paul Hurst. *Secretary:* Ian Fleming.
*Colours:* Black and white striped shirts, black shorts, white socks.

## GRIMSBY TOWN – BLUE SQUARE PREMIER 2012–13 LEAGUE RECORD

| Match No. | Date | Venue | Opponents | Result | H/T Score | Lg Pos. | Goalscorers | Attendance |
|---|---|---|---|---|---|---|---|---|
| 1 | Aug 11 | A | Southport | D | 1-1 | 0-0 | 14 | Disley [74] | 1743 |
| 2 | 14 | H | Stockport Co | L | 1-2 | 0-0 | 19 | Pond [69] | 3670 |
| 3 | 18 | H | Nuneaton T | D | 0-0 | 0-0 | 18 | | 3095 |
| 4 | 25 | A | Wrexham | D | 0-0 | 0-0 | 17 | | 3127 |
| 5 | 27 | H | Mansfield T | W | 4-1 | 2-0 | 12 | Artus [35], Pearson, G 2 (1 pen) [45 (p), 76], Colbeck [61] | 3397 |
| 6 | Sept 1 | A | Hereford U | W | 2-0 | 2-0 | 11 | Southwell [40], Pearson, S [44] | 2059 |
| 7 | 4 | A | Barrow | D | 2-2 | 0-1 | 12 | Elding 2 (1 pen) [67, 83 (p)] | 966 |
| 8 | 8 | H | Forest Green R | W | 1-0 | 0-0 | 7 | Pond [63] | 3270 |
| 9 | 15 | A | Kidderminster H | D | 0-0 | 0-0 | 9 | | 1811 |
| 10 | 21 | H | Luton T | W | 4-1 | 3-0 | 6 | Colbeck [8], Cook [40], Hannah [43], Beckwith (og) [71] | 4074 |
| 11 | 25 | H | Gateshead | W | 3-0 | 2-0 | 4 | Niven [13], Pond [20], Hannah [70] | 3202 |
| 12 | 29 | A | Newport Co | D | 0-0 | 0-0 | 6 | | 2968 |
| 13 | Oct 6 | H | Dartford | L | 0-2 | 0-0 | 6 | | 4009 |
| 14 | 9 | A | Alfreton T | W | 2-0 | 1-0 | 6 | Neilson [39], Hannah [88] | 1192 |
| 15 | 13 | A | AFC Telford U | W | 2-1 | 2-1 | 4 | Pond [12], Miller [39] | 2349 |
| 16 | 27 | H | Macclesfield T | L | 0-1 | 0-0 | 5 | | 3014 |
| 17 | Nov 3 | A | Tamworth | W | 1-0 | 0-0 | 3 | Cook [63] | 1042 |
| 18 | 6 | A | Hyde | L | 2-3 | 1-2 | 4 | Hannah 2 [45, 53] | 822 |
| 19 | 10 | H | Woking | W | 5-1 | 3-1 | 2 | Hatton 2 [11, 76], Disley [18], Thanoj [34], Cook [91] | 3418 |
| 20 | 17 | H | Braintree T | W | 3-0 | 1-0 | 1 | Hannah 2 [43, 65], Disley [52] | 3722 |
| 21 | Dec 1 | A | Ebbsfleet U | D | 1-1 | 1-1 | 2 | Marshall [3] | 1164 |
| 22 | 8 | H | Tamworth | W | 2-0 | 1-0 | 1 | Disley [7], Hannah [51] | 3109 |
| 23 | 21 | H | Wrexham | W | 1-0 | 0-0 | 1 | Hannah [77] | 4302 |
| 24 | 26 | A | Lincoln C | W | 4-1 | 2-0 | 1 | Cook [37], Boyce (og) [43], Disley [58], Colbeck [66] | 5702 |
| 25 | Jan 1 | H | Lincoln C | D | 1-1 | 1-1 | 1 | Miller [22] | 7405 |
| 26 | 5 | H | Hereford U | D | 1-1 | 1-1 | 1 | Pond [2] | 3793 |
| 27 | 22 | H | Hyde | W | 2-0 | 0-0 | 1 | Cook 2 [84, 90] | 2755 |
| 28 | 26 | A | Cambridge U | D | 0-0 | 0-0 | 1 | | 2764 |
| 29 | Feb 2 | H | Alfreton T | W | 4-2 | 2-1 | 1 | Devitt (pen) [41], Brodie [45], Cook [58], Disley [81] | 3868 |
| 30 | 9 | H | AFC Telford U | W | 1-0 | 0-0 | 1 | Brodie [48] | 4462 |
| 31 | 19 | A | Braintree T | L | 0-2 | 0-1 | 2 | | 880 |
| 32 | 26 | H | Ebbsfleet U | W | 3-1 | 2-0 | 3 | Marshall [1], Cook [38], Disley [87] | 3129 |
| 33 | Mar 5 | A | Forest Green R | W | 1-0 | 0-0 | 4 | Naylor [74] | 744 |
| 34 | 9 | H | Kidderminster H | L | 1-3 | 0-2 | 5 | Miller [50] | 4629 |
| 35 | 12 | A | Mansfield T | L | 0-2 | 0-0 | 5 | | 3896 |
| 36 | 16 | H | Cambridge U | L | 0-1 | 0-1 | 5 | | 3516 |
| 37 | 19 | A | Nuneaton T | L | 0-1 | 0-1 | 5 | | 964 |
| 38 | 26 | A | Gateshead | D | 1-1 | 0-0 | 5 | Thanoj [47] | 351 |
| 39 | 30 | H | Barrow | D | 0-0 | 0-0 | 5 | | 3532 |
| 40 | Apr 1 | A | Stockport Co | W | 2-1 | 0-0 | 5 | Hannah [48], Hatton [57] | 3804 |
| 41 | 3 | A | Macclesfield T | W | 3-1 | 2-1 | 5 | Cook [13], Pearson, S [37], Artus [71] | 1776 |
| 42 | 6 | H | Southport | D | 2-2 | 1-2 | 5 | Cook [35], Taylor [90] | 3780 |
| 43 | 9 | A | Dartford | W | 2-1 | 0-1 | 5 | Cook [79], Thomas [88] | 1201 |
| 44 | 12 | A | Luton T | D | 1-1 | 0-0 | 5 | Southwell [54] | 5662 |
| 45 | 16 | A | Woking | W | 1-0 | 0-0 | 5 | John-Lewis [75] | 1570 |
| 46 | 20 | H | Newport Co | W | 3-0 | 3-0 | 4 | Devitt [18], Thanoj [24], Hearn [44] | 4555 |

**Final League Position: 4**

## GOALSCORERS

*League (70):* Cook 11, Hannah 10, Disley 7, Pond 5, Colbeck 3, Hatton 3, Miller 3, Thanoj 3, Artus 2, Brodie 2, Devitt 2 (1 pen), Elding 2 (1 pen), Marshall 2, Pearson, G 2 (1 pen), Pearson, S 2, Southwell 2, Hearn 1, John-Lewis 1, Naylor 1, Neilson 1, Niven 1, Taylor 1, Thomas 1, own goals 2.
*FA Cup (2):* Neilsen 1, Niven 1.
*FA Trophy (14):* Cook 5, Devitt 2 (1 pen), Disley 2, Marshall 2, Pearson G 1, Pearson S 1, Miller 1.
*Blue Square Premier Play-Offs (0).*

| McKeown 43 | Wood 28 + 2 | Pond 26 | Pearson S 34 | Thomas 39 + 2 | Colbeck 31 + 8 | Niven 30 + 4 | Disley 40 | Artus 14 + 8 | Pearson G 7 + 5 | Cook 35 + 8 | Elding 8 + 8 | Soares 1 + 3 | Hearn 2 + 3 | Hatton 25 + 4 | Thanoj 10 + 10 | Southwell 5 + 25 | Neilson 10 | Hannah 24 + 4 | Miller 25 + 1 | Marshall 22 + 3 | Rankine — + 3 | Brodie 6 + 4 | Devitt 11 + 3 | Fleming 3 | John-Lewis 6 + 9 | Naylor 13 + 1 | Wilson 1 + 2 | Taylor 5 + 2 | Ford 2 | Match No. |
|---|---|---|---|---|---|---|---|---|---|---|---|---|---|---|---|---|---|---|---|---|---|---|---|---|---|---|---|---|---|---|
| 1 | 2 | 3 | 4 | 5 | 6 | 7 | 8 | 9 | $10^2$ | $11^1$ | 12 | 13 | | | | | | | | | | | | | | | | | | 1 |
| 1 | 2 | 4 | 3 | 5 | 6 | 7 | 8 | $9^3$ | $10^1$ | $11^2$ | 12 | 14 | 13 | | | | | | | | | | | | | | | | | 2 |
| 1 | | 4 | 3 | 5 | 6 | | 7 | 14 | 13 | $11^1$ | $10^2$ | $9^3$ | | 2 | 8 | 12 | | | | | | | | | | | | | | 3 |
| 1 | | 3 | 4 | 5 | 6 | 8 | 7 | $9^2$ | $10^1$ | 12 | $11^3$ | | | 2 | 13 | 14 | | | | | | | | | | | | | | 4 |
| 1 | 2 | 4 | 3 | 5 | 6 | 8 | 7 | 9 | 10 | $11^1$ | 12 | | | | | | | | | | | | | | | | | | | 5 |
| 1 | 2 | 4 | 3 | 5 | 6 | 8 | 7 | 9 | $10^1$ | $11^2$ | 13 | | | | | | | | | | | | | | | | | | | 6 |
| 1 | 2 | 4 | 3 | 5 | 6 | $8^1$ | 7 | $9^3$ | | $10^2$ | 13 | 14 | | 12 | 11 | | | | | | | | | | | | | | | 7 |
| 1 | $2^2$ | 4 | 3 | 5 | 6 | 8 | 7 | $9^3$ | | $10^1$ | 11 | | | 13 | 14 | 12 | | | | | | | | | | | | | | 8 |
| 1 | $2^1$ | 4 | 3 | 5 | 6 | 7 | 8 | 9 | $13^3$ | $10^2$ | 11 | | | 12 | 14 | | | | | | | | | | | | | | | 9 |
| 1 | 2 | 4 | 3 | 5 | 6 | 8 | 7 | 12 | | 10 | | | | | 13 | | | $9^1$ | $11^2$ | | | | | | | | | | | 10 |
| 1 | 2 | 4 | 3 | 5 | 6 | $8^3$ | 7 | 14 | | $10^1$ | 12 | | | | 13 | | | 9 | $11^1$ | | | | | | | | | | | 11 |
| 1 | 2 | 4 | 3 | 5 | 6 | | 7 | 8 | | $10^1$ | 12 | | | | 13 | 14 | | $9^3$ | $11^2$ | | | | | | | | | | | 12 |
| 1 | 2 | 4 | 3 | 5 | 6 | $8^1$ | 7 | 12 | | $10^2$ | | | | | 13 | 14 | | 9 | $11^3$ | | | | | | | | | | | 13 |
| 1 | 2 | 4 | 3 | 5 | 6 | 8 | 7 | | | | 12 | $11^1$ | | | | | | 9 | 10 | | | | | | | | | | | 14 |
| 1 | 2 | 3 | | 5 | 6 | 7 | 8 | 13 | | | 12 | $11^3$ | | | 14 | | 4 | $9^2$ | $10^1$ | | | | | | | | | | | 15 |
| 1 | 2 | 4 | 3 | 5 | $6^2$ | $8^3$ | 7 | 14 | | 10 | | | | | 12 | 13 | | $9^4$ | $11^1$ | | | | | | | | | | | 16 |
| 1 | 2 | 4 | | 5 | 6 | 8 | 7 | 14 | | | 12 | $11^1$ | | | | 13 | | $10^2$ | 3 | $9^3$ | | | | | | | | | | 17 |
| 1 | $2^3$ | 5 | 4 | 3 | 6 | $8^1$ | 7 | 13 | $10^2$ | | | | | | 12 | 14 | | 11 | 9 | | | | | | | | | | | 18 |
| 1 | | 4 | 3 | 5 | $6^1$ | 12 | 7 | | | 10 | | | | 2 | 8 | 13 | | | $11^2$ | 9 | | | | | | | | | | 19 |
| 1 | | 4 | 3 | 5 | 14 | $7^3$ | 13 | | | 10 | | | | 2 | 8 | 12 | | $9^1$ | 11 | 6 | | | | | | | | | | 20 |
| 1 | | 4 | 3 | 5 | 12 | 6 | 7 | | | | | | | 2 | 8 | 11 | | | $10^1$ | $9^2$ | | 13 | | | | | | | | 21 |
| 1 | | 4 | 3 | 5 | 12 | 7 | 8 | 13 | | 10 | | | | 2 | | 14 | | $9^1$ | $11^2$ | $6^3$ | | | | | | | | | | 22 |
| 1 | | 4 | | 5 | | 7 | 8 | | | | | 11 | | 2 | | 12 | | $9^1$ | 10 | 3 | | 6 | | | | | | | | 23 |
| 1 | 14 | 4 | | 5 | 6 | 8 | 7 | | | | | $11^1$ | | $2^3$ | | | | $10^2$ | 9 | 3 | | 12 | | | | | | | | 24 |
| 1 | 13 | | 3 | $5^4$ | $6^2$ | 7 | 8 | | | | | $11^1$ | | 2 | | 12 | 4 | $10^3$ | 9 | | | 14 | | | | | | | | 25 |
| 1 | | 5 | 3 | | $6^1$ | 7 | 8 | | | | | $11^2$ | | 2 | 13 | | 4 | | 9 | | | 10 | 12 | | | | | | | 26 |
| | | 5 | 3 | | 6 | 7 | $8^2$ | | | | | 13 | | 2 | | 12 | 4 | | 9 | $11^3$ | | $10^1$ | | 1 | | | | | | 27 |
| 1 | | | 3 | 5 | | 7 | 8 | 13 | | | | $10^1$ | | 2 | | 11 | 4 | | 9 | | | 12 | $6^2$ | | | | | | | 28 |
| 1 | | | 3 | 5 | 12 | 14 | 7 | | | | | 11 | | 2 | $8^3$ | | 4 | | 6 | | | $10^2$ | $9^1$ | | | 13 | | | | 29 |
| 1 | | | 3 | 5 | 6 | 8 | 7 | | | | | 10 | | 2 | | 13 | 4 | | $9^2$ | | | $11^1$ | 12 | | | | | | | 30 |
| 1 | | 3 | | $5^3$ | 8 | 6 | 7 | | | | | $10^2$ | | 2 | | 12 | 4 | | $9^1$ | | | 13 | 14 | | 11 | | | | | 31 |
| 1 | 5 | 3 | | | 12 | 8 | 7 | | | | | 10 | | 2 | | $11^2$ | 4 | | $6^1$ | | | $9^3$ | 13 | | 14 | | | | | 32 |
| 1 | 2 | $3^3$ | | | 6 | $8^1$ | 7 | 10 | | | | 14 | | | | 12 | 4 | | 9 | $11^2$ | | | 13 | | 5 | | | | | 33 |
| 1 | 2 | | 4 | | $6^1$ | 7 | 10 | 8 | | | | $11^2$ | | 5 | | | | | $9^3$ | 14 | | 12 | 13 | | 3 | | | | | 34 |
| 1 | 2 | 3 | | | | $7^1$ | 10 | 13 | | | | | | 5 | | 12 | 4 | | $11^3$ | $6^2$ | | 14 | 9 | | 8 | | | | | 35 |
| 1 | | $3^3$ | 5 | | 12 | | 8 | | | | | 10 | | 13 | 2 | | 4 | | $6^1$ | $11^2$ | | 9 | | | 7 | | 14 | | | 36 |
| 1 | $5^3$ | 3 | | | 14 | 6 | 7 | 13 | | | | | | 2 | | 12 | 4 | $10^2$ | | | | $9^1$ | 11 | | | 8 | | | | 37 |
| 1 | 2 | 3 | | 5 | 6 | | | 13 | | | | | | | | 12 | 4 | | | $9^2$ | | $10^1$ | | | | 11 | 7 | 8 | | 38 |
| 1 | 2 | 3 | | 5 | | | 7 | | | | | 11 | 14 | | | | 4 | | $9^2$ | | | 12 | 8 | | | | 13 | $6^3$ | | 39 |
| 1 | 5 | 3 | | | 6 | | 7 | | | | | $10^3$ | | 2 | | 13 | 4 | | $11^2$ | $9^1$ | | | | | | 14 | 8 | 12 | | 40 |
| 1 | | 3 | 5 | | 12 | | 7 | $9^3$ | | | | $10^2$ | | 2 | 14 | | 4 | | $11^1$ | | | 13 | 8 | | | | | 6 | | 41 |
| 1 | | 3 | 5 | | $6^3$ | 8 | | | | | | 11 | 13 | 2 | | | 4 | $10^2$ | | $9^1$ | | 14 | 7 | | | | | 12 | | 42 |
| 1 | 5 | | | | 12 | $9^4$ | $8^3$ | 7 | 14 | 10 | | | | 2 | | 13 | | | | $3^1$ | | | 11 | 4 | | | | $6^2$ | | 43 |
| 1 | 2 | | | | $3^1$ | | 12 | 8 | | | | 11 | 13 | 7 | | 9 | 4 | | | | | | 10 | | | | | $6^2$ | 5 | 44 |
| | 5 | | | | | | 7 | 14 | | | | | | 2 | 8 | 13 | 4 | $10^2$ | 12 | 9 | | $6^3$ | 1 | | 11 | 4 | | $3^1$ | | 45 |
| | 5 | | | | $6^2$ | 8 | | | | $10^1$ | | | | 2 | 7 | 13 | 4 | 12 | 3 | 14 | | 11 | 1 | | | 4 | | $9^3$ | | 46 |

**FA Cup**

| | | | |
|---|---|---|---|
| Fourth Qualifying | Kidderminster H | (h) | 2-4 |

**Blue Square Premier Play-Offs**

| | | | |
|---|---|---|---|
| Semi-Finals | Newport | (h) | 0-1 |
| | Newport | (a) | 0-1 |

**FA Trophy**

| | | | |
|---|---|---|---|
| First Round | Buxton | (h) | 0-0 |
| *Replay* | Buxton | (a) | 1-0 |
| Second Round | Havant & Waterlooville | (h) | 4-0 |
| Third Round | Welling U | (a) | 2-1 |
| Quarter-Finals | Luton T | (h) | 3-0 |
| Semi-Finals | Dartford | (h) | 3-0 |
| | Dartford | (a) | 0-0 |
| Final (Wembley) | Wrexham | (a) | 1-1 |

# HEREFORD UNITED

*Ground:* Edgar Street Athletic Ground, Blackfriars Street, Hereford HR4 9JU
*Tel:* (08442) 761 939.  *Fax:* (08442) 761 982.  *Website:* www.herefordunited.co.uk  *Year Formed:* 1924.
*Record Gate:* 18,114 (1958 v Sheffield W, FA Cup 3rd rd). *Nickname:* 'The Bulls'.  *Manager:* Martin Foyle.
*Secretary:* Lee Symonds.  *Colours:* White shirts with black trim, black shorts, white socks.

## HEREFORD UNITED – BLUE SQUARE PREMIER 2012–13 LEAGUE RECORD

| Match No. | Date | Venue | Opponents | Result | H/T Score | Lg Pos. | Goalscorers | Attendance |
|---|---|---|---|---|---|---|---|---|
| 1 | Aug 10 | H | Macclesfield T | W 2-1 | 1-0 | 1 | Canham [15], Jackson [66] | 2139 |
| 2 | 14 | A | Tamworth | D 2-2 | 2-0 | 6 | Watkins [9], Pell (pen) [35] | 1265 |
| 3 | 18 | A | Alfreton T | W 3-0 | 0-0 | 2 | Watkins [55], Canham [64], Nichols [68] | 690 |
| 4 | 25 | H | Ebbsfleet U | W 4-2 | 2-0 | 2 | Watkins [27], Canham [37], Carruthers [49], Bowman [89] | 1906 |
| 5 | 28 | A | Newport Co | L 0-2 | 0-0 | 4 | | 4365 |
| 6 | Sept 1 | H | Grimsby T | L 0-2 | 0-2 | 9 | | 2059 |
| 7 | 4 | H | Woking | W 2-1 | 2-0 | 7 | Sammons [5], Clucas [44] | 1481 |
| 8 | 8 | A | Hyde | L 2-5 | 1-1 | 8 | Bowman 2 [5, 77] | 688 |
| 9 | 15 | A | Dartford | L 0-4 | 0-1 | 12 | | 1601 |
| 10 | 22 | H | Cambridge U | W 4-2 | 1-1 | 11 | Bowman [35], Clucas [48], Jackson 2 [51, 53] | 1677 |
| 11 | 25 | H | Forest Green R | L 1-2 | 1-2 | 12 | Stam [7] | 1656 |
| 12 | 29 | A | Mansfield T | D 1-1 | 1-1 | 11 | Jackson [22] | 2248 |
| 13 | Oct 6 | H | Stockport Co | L 1-2 | 0-2 | 12 | Marsh [77] | 1889 |
| 14 | 9 | A | Nuneaton T | D 0-0 | 0-0 | 12 | | 969 |
| 15 | 13 | H | Braintree T | D 0-0 | 0-0 | 14 | | 1537 |
| 16 | 27 | A | Southport | D 2-2 | 2-2 | 14 | Clucas [6], Bowman (pen) [14] | 1028 |
| 17 | Nov 6 | H | Luton T | W 1-0 | 0-0 | 12 | McQuilkin [55] | 2108 |
| 18 | 10 | A | Wrexham | W 2-1 | 1-0 | 9 | Todd [8], Graham [90] | 3620 |
| 19 | 17 | A | Lincoln C | L 2-3 | 0-1 | 10 | Bowman [55], Evans [82] | 2233 |
| 20 | Dec 7 | A | Barrow | W 2-0 | 1-0 | 9 | O'Keefe [45], Bowman [78] | 867 |
| 21 | 26 | H | Kidderminster H | L 0-1 | 0-1 | 14 | | 2902 |
| 22 | Jan 1 | A | Kidderminster H | W 1-0 | 1-0 | 12 | O'Keefe (pen) [13] | 3674 |
| 23 | 5 | A | Grimsby T | D 1-1 | 1-1 | 10 | Bowman [42] | 3793 |
| 24 | 8 | H | AFC Telford U | D 1-1 | 1-0 | 11 | Watkins [2] | 1490 |
| 25 | 12 | H | Alfreton T | D 3-3 | 2-1 | 11 | Bowman 2 [20, 48], Stam [45] | 1565 |
| 26 | Feb 2 | H | Southport | D 2-2 | 0-1 | 12 | Bowman [75], O'Keefe [84] | 1513 |
| 27 | 9 | A | Braintree T | W 2-0 | 1-0 | 12 | Sharp [20], Watkins [58] | 658 |
| 28 | 12 | H | Wrexham | L 0-1 | 0-1 | 13 | | 1781 |
| 29 | 16 | H | Lincoln C | W 3-2 | 1-2 | 11 | Stam [13], Sharp 2 [57, 62] | 1914 |
| 30 | 19 | A | Ebbsfleet U | L 0-1 | 0-1 | 11 | | 614 |
| 31 | 23 | A | Cambridge U | W 3-1 | 1-0 | 9 | Bowman 2 (2 pens) [40, 75], Jarvis (og) [71] | 2171 |
| 32 | 26 | A | Stockport Co | W 3-2 | 1-1 | 7 | Graham [29], Bowman [54], O'Keefe [81] | 2618 |
| 33 | Mar 2 | H | Nuneaton T | D 0-0 | 0-0 | 7 | | 1908 |
| 34 | 5 | H | Newport Co | L 2-3 | 1-0 | 8 | O'Keefe 2 (2 pens) [42, 75] | 2519 |
| 35 | 9 | A | Luton T | D 1-1 | 1-0 | 9 | Jackson [23] | 6001 |
| 36 | 16 | H | Barrow | W 2-1 | 1-1 | 8 | O'Keefe (pen) [36], Smikle [90] | 1273 |
| 37 | 19 | A | Gateshead | L 2-3 | 1-2 | 9 | Sharp [17], Jackson [50] | 259 |
| 38 | 23 | H | Hyde | L 1-2 | 1-0 | 10 | O'Keefe [25] | 1152 |
| 39 | 26 | H | Dartford | W 1-0 | 1-0 | 8 | O'Keefe [38] | 662 |
| 40 | 30 | A | Woking | D 1-1 | 1-0 | 8 | McNerney (og) [44] | 2303 |
| 41 | Apr 1 | H | Tamworth | W 5-2 | 3-0 | 7 | O'Keefe 2 (2 pens) [17, 45], McDonald [29], Clucas [50], James [67] | 1424 |
| 42 | 6 | A | Macclesfield T | W 1-0 | 1-0 | 7 | Clucas [3] | 1687 |
| 43 | 9 | A | Forest Green R | W 1-0 | 0-0 | 6 | McDonald [56] | 1142 |
| 44 | 13 | H | Gateshead | D 1-1 | 0-1 | 6 | Clucas [65] | 1599 |
| 45 | 16 | H | Mansfield T | L 1-2 | 1-1 | 6 | Bowman [8] | 2141 |
| 46 | 20 | A | AFC Telford U | W 4-0 | 1-0 | 6 | Clucas 2 [39, 47], Jackson [62], O'Keefe [73] | 2102 |

**Final League Position: 6**

## GOALSCORERS

*League (73):* Bowman 15 (3 pens), O'Keefe 12 (6 pens), Clucas 8, Jackson 7, Watkins 5, Sharp 4, Canham 3, Stam 3, Graham 2, McDonald 2, Carruthers 1, Evans 1, James 1, Marsh 1, McQuilkin 1, Nichols 1, Pell 1 (1 pen), Sammons 1, Smikle 1, Todd 1, own goals 2.
*FA Cup (7):* Bowman 4 (1 pen), Clucas 1, Evans 1, O'Keefe 1.
*FA Trophy (1):* O'Keefe 1.

| Hanford 12 | Gallinagh 26 + 1 | Townsend 7 | Graham 42 + 1 | Carruthers 18 + 3 | Watkins 34 | Clist 12 + 4 | Pell 22 + 1 | Clucas 41 | Jackson 12 + 13 | Canham 8 + 2 | Nichols 4 + 5 | Sammons 5 + 4 | McQuilkin 4 + 5 | Stam 35 + 2 | Evans 10 + 6 | Bowman 30 + 9 | Smikle 6 + 18 | Plummer — + 3 | Anthony 2 | Heath 12 + 8 | Bittner 34 | O'Keefe 30 + 3 | Marsh 4 + 3 | Todd 5 | Perry 2 + 6 | Hackney 1 | Corbett 5 | Sharp 25 | Musa 15 | James 21 | McDonald 5 + 6 | Connor 11 + 2 | Jones — + 2 | Bush 6 | Match No. |
|---|---|---|---|---|---|---|---|---|---|---|---|---|---|---|---|---|---|---|---|---|---|---|---|---|---|---|---|---|---|---|---|---|---|---|---|
| 1 | 2 | 3 | 4 | 5 | 6 | 7[2] | 8 | 9 | 10[3] | 11[1] | 12 | 13 | 14 | | | | | | | | | | | | | | | | | | | | | | 1 |
| 1 | 2 | 4[3] | 3 | 5 | 6 | 8[2] | 7 | 9 | 10[8] | 11[1] | 12 | 14 | | 13 | | | | | | | | | | | | | | | | | | | | | 2 |
| 1 | 2 | 3 | | 5 | 6 | 14 | 8 | 9[2] | 11 | 10[3] | 7[1] | 13 | 4 | 12 | | | | | | | | | | | | | | | | | | | | | 3 |
| 1 | 2 | 3 | 4 | 5 | 6[2] | 8 | 7 | 9[3] | | 11 | 10[1] | | | | 13 | 12 | 14 | | | | | | | | | | | | | | | | | | 4 |
| 1 | 2 | 3 | 4 | 5[2] | 7 | 8 | 6 | 9 | 10[1] | 11 | | | | | 12 | 13 | | | | | | | | | | | | | | | | | | | 5 |
| 1 | 2 | 3 | 4 | 5 | | 8[3] | 7 | 9 | 10[2] | 11 | 14 | | | | 13 | 6[1] | 12 | | | | | | | | | | | | | | | | | | 6 |
| 1 | 2 | | 4 | 5 | | 7 | | 9 | 11 | 13 | 8[1] | | | 3 | 12 | 10[2] | 6[3] | 14 | | | | | | | | | | | | | | | | | 7 |
| 1 | 2 | | 4 | 3 | | 8 | 7 | | 10[1] | 13 | 9[3] | | | 5 | 12 | 11 | 6[2] | 14 | | | | | | | | | | | | | | | | | 8 |
| 1 | 2 | | 4 | 7[2] | 6 | 9[1] | 8[3] | 10 | | | 12 | 14 | | | 13 | 11 | | | 3 | 5 | | | | | | | | | | | | | | | 9 |
| | 2 | | 4 | | 6[3] | | 10 | 8 | 9[2] | 13 | | | 7[1] | 3 | 12 | 11 | | 5[1] | 14 | 1 | | | | | | | | | | | | | | | 10 |
| | 2 | | 4 | 5 | 6 | | 7 | 9 | 11 | | | | 8[1] | 3 | | 10 | | | | 1 | 12 | | | | | | | | | | | | | | 11 |
| | 2 | | 4 | 5 | 6 | 7 | 10 | 9 | 11[1] | 12 | | | | 3 | | | | | | 1 | 8 | | | | | | | | | | | | | | 12 |
| | 2 | | 3 | 5 | 6 | | 7 | 9 | 10[2] | | | 13 | | 4[1] | 8 | 12 | | | | 1 | | 11 | | | | | | | | | | | | | 13 |
| | 2 | | 3[1] | 5[2] | 6[3] | 14 | 7 | 9 | | | | | 12 | 8 | 11 | | | | 13 | 1 | | 10 | 4 | | | | | | | | | | | | 14 |
| | 2 | | | 8[2] | 6 | 9 | | | | 14 | 3 | 7[3] | 10 | 12 | | 5 | 1 | | | 11[1] | 4 | 13 | | | | | | | | | | | | | 15 |
| | 2 | | | | 8[3] | 9 | | | | 6[1] | 4 | 7 | 10 | 14 | | 5 | 1 | 13 | 11[2] | 3 | 12 | | | | | | | | | | | | | | 16 |
| | 2 | 14 | | | 7[3] | 10 | | | | 6[2] | 3 | 9 | 11[1] | 13 | | 5 | 1 | 8 | | 4 | 12 | | | | | | | | | | | | | | 17 |
| | | 3 | | 10 | 12 | 6 | | | | 8[1] | 2 | 7[2] | 11 | 13 | | 5 | 1 | 9 | | 4 | | | | | | | | | | | | | | | 18 |
| | 2 | | 4 | | 9[3] | 10 | | | | 6[2] | 3 | 8 | 11[1] | 13 | | 5 | 1 | 7 | 14 | 12 | | | | | | | | | | | | | | | 19 |
| | 2 | | 4 | | 5 | 8 | | | | 12 | 3 | 7 | 11 | 6[2] | | 1 | 9[3] | 13 | 14 | 10[1] | | | | | | | | | | | | | | | 20 |
| 13[3] | 3[2] | 2 | | 11 | | 7 | 9 | | | | 4 | 8 | | 6 | | 5 | 1 | 12 | 14 | 10[1] | | | | | | | | | | | | | | | 21 |
| | | 3 | | 6 | 12 | 7 | | | | 4 | | 13 | 9[2] | | | 5 | 1 | 8 | | 10[1] | | 2 | 11 | | | | | | | | | | | | 22 |
| | | 3 | | 6 | | 7 | | | | 4 | | 10 | | | | 5 | 1 | 8 | | | | 2 | 11 | 9 | | | | | | | | | | | 23 |
| | | 3 | | 6 | 13 | 7 | | | | 4 | | 10[3] | 14 | | | 5 | 1 | 8 | | 12 | | 2 | 11 | 9[2] | | | | | | | | | | | 24 |
| | | 3 | | 6 | | 7 | | | | 4 | | 9[1] | 10 | 13 | | 12 | 1 | 8 | | | | 2 | 11 | 5[2] | | | | | | | | | | | 25 |
| 1 | | | 3 | | 6[3] | | | 9 | 13 | | | 4[2] | | | | 11 | 12 | | | 8 | | | 2 | 10[1] | 5 | 7 | 14 | | | | | | | | 26 |
| 1 | 2 | | 4 | | 6 | | | 9 | 12 | | | 3 | | | | 11[1] | | | | 7 | | | 10[2] | 5 | 8 | 13 | | | | | | | | | 27 |
| 1 | 2[2] | | 3 | | 6 | | | 9 | 12 | | | 4 | | | | 10 | 13 | | | 7 | | | 11[1] | 5 | 8 | | | | | | | | | | 28 |
| | 2 | | 3 | | 6 | | | 9 | 12 | | | 4 | | | | 10[1] | | | | 7 | | | 11 | 5 | 8 | | | | | | | | | | 29 |
| | 2 | | 3 | 14 | 6 | | | 9 | 12 | | | 4 | | | | 10 | 13 | | | 1 | 7 | | | 11[2] | 5[1] | 8[1] | | | | | | | | | 30 |
| | 2 | | 3 | | 6[2] | | | 9 | 12 | | | 4 | | | | 11 | | | | 1 | 8 | | | 10[1] | 5 | 7 | 13 | | | | | | | | 31 |
| | 2 | | 4 | | 9[3] | | | 6 | 12 | | | 3 | | | | 11 | | | 13 | 1 | 8 | | | 10[2] | 5[1] | 7 | 14 | | | | | | | | 32 |
| | 2[1] | | 3 | 14 | 6 | | | 9[3] | 13 | | | 4 | | | | 10 | | | | 1 | 7 | | | 11[2] | 5 | 8 | | 12 | | | | | | | 33 |
| | | 3 | 13 | 6[1] | | | | 9 | 11[2] | | | 4 | | | 12 | | | | | 1 | 8 | | | 10 | 5 | 7 | | 2 | | | | | | | 34 |
| | | 5 | 8[1] | | | | | 11 | 10 | | | 4 | | | 13 | | | | 12 | 1 | 6 | | | 9[3] | 3 | 7 | | 2 | | | | | | | 35 |
| | | 3 | 6[2] | | | | | 9 | 10 | | | 4 | | | 13 | 12 | | | 14 | 1 | 8 | | | 11[1] | 5[3] | 7 | | 2 | | | | | | | 36 |
| | | 3 | 8 | | | | | 11 | 10 | | | 12 | | | | | | | | 1 | 7[1] | | | 9 | 2 | 6 | 4 | 5 | | | | | | | 37 |
| | | 3 | 5 | 6 | | | | 9 | 10[1] | | | 4 | 12 | 13 | | | | | | 1 | 7[3] | | | 11 | | 8 | | 2[2] | 14 | | | | | | 38 |
| | | 3 | 5[1] | 6 | | | | 9 | | | | 4 | 10 | | | | 2 | | | 1 | 7 | | | 11 | | 8 | | 12 | | | | | | | 39 |
| | | 3 | | 6 | | | | 9 | 10 | | | 4 | 12 | | | | 2 | | | 1 | 8 | | | 11[1] | | 7 | 13 | | | | | | 5[2] | | 40 |
| | | 3 | | 6[1] | | | | 9[2] | 12 | | | | 10 | 13 | | | | | | 12[1] | 7[3] | | | 11 | | 8 | 4 | 2 | 14 | 5 | | | | | 41 |
| | | 3 | | 6 | | | | 9 | 13 | | | 4 | 10 | | | | 12[1] | | | | 8 | | | 11[2] | | 2 | | 5[1] | | | | | | | 42 |
| | | 3 | | 6 | | | | 9 | | | | 4 | 11 | | | | | | | 1 | 8 | | | 10 | | 7 | 4 | 2 | 5 | | | | | | 43 |
| | | 3 | | 6 | | | | 9 | 12 | | | 4 | 10 | | | | | | | 1 | 7 | | | 11[1] | | 8 | 5 | 2 | | | | | | | 44 |
| | | 3 | | 6 | | | | 9 | 12 | | | 4 | 10[2] | | | | | | | 1 | 7 | | | 11[1] | | 8 | 13 | 2 | 5 | | | | | | 45 |
| | | 4 | | 6[2] | | | | 9 | 12 | | | | 10[1] | 13 | | | | | | 14 | 1 | 8 | | | 11[3] | | 7 | 3 | 2 | 5 | | | | | 46 |

**FA Cup**

| Fourth Qualifying | FC United of Manchester | (a) | 2-0 |
|---|---|---|---|
| First Round | Shrewsbury T | (h) | 3-1 |
| Second Round | Cheltenham T | (a) | 1-1 |
| *Replay* | Cheltenham T | (h) | 1-2 |
| *aet.* | | | |

**FA Trophy**

| First Round | Ebbsfleet U | (a) | 1-0 |
|---|---|---|---|
| Second Round | Chelmsford C | (h) | 0-3 |

# HYDE

*Ground:* Ewen Fields, Walker Lane, Hyde, Cheshire SK14 5PL.
*Tel:* (0161) 367 7273.   *Fax:* (0161) 367 7273.   *Website:* www.hydefc.co.uk   *Year Formed:* 1885.
*Record Gate:* 9,500 (1952 v Nelson, FA Cup).   *Nickname:* 'The Tigers'.   *Manager:* Scott McGivern.
*Secretary:* Andy McAnulty.   *Colours:* Red shirts, navy shorts, navy socks.

## HYDE – BLUE SQUARE PREMIER 2012–13 LEAGUE RECORD

| Match No. | Date | Venue | Opponents | Result | H/T Score | Lg Pos. | Goalscorers | Attendance |
|---|---|---|---|---|---|---|---|---|
| 1 | Aug 11 | A | Braintree T | D 2-2 | 2-0 | 10 | Spencer, S 2 (1 pen) [23, 36 (p)] | 598 |
| 2 | 14 | H | Barrow | D 0-0 | 0-0 | 16 | | 798 |
| 3 | 17 | H | Luton T | L 1-2 | 0-0 | 17 | Blinkhorn [55] | 1141 |
| 4 | 25 | A | Mansfield T | L 0-1 | 0-1 | 20 | | 2203 |
| 5 | 27 | H | Southport | L 0-2 | 0-1 | 22 | | 734 |
| 6 | Sept 1 | A | Forest Green R | L 1-3 | 0-2 | 23 | Crowther [56] | 768 |
| 7 | 4 | A | Wrexham | L 0-2 | 0-0 | 24 | | 3176 |
| 8 | 8 | H | Hereford U | W 5-2 | 1-1 | 23 | Spencer, S [39], Brown [52], Jevons 3 [72, 80, 84] | 688 |
| 9 | 15 | A | Lincoln C | L 2-3 | 0-1 | 23 | Spencer, S (pen) [64], Jevons [70] | 1745 |
| 10 | 22 | H | Nuneaton T | D 2-2 | 1-0 | 23 | Griffin [19], Jevons [65] | 585 |
| 11 | 29 | A | Dartford | L 1-2 | 1-0 | 24 | Brown [28] | 1338 |
| 12 | Oct 6 | H | Gateshead | D 1-1 | 1-1 | 24 | Spencer, S [6] | 470 |
| 13 | 9 | A | Kidderminster H | L 0-3 | 0-2 | 24 | | 1457 |
| 14 | 13 | H | Tamworth | W 2-1 | 0-1 | 24 | Jevons 2 (1 pen) [54, 75 (p)] | 657 |
| 15 | 27 | A | Cambridge U | W 1-0 | 0-0 | 23 | Crowther [84] | 1779 |
| 16 | Nov 6 | H | Grimsby T | W 3-2 | 2-1 | 22 | Brown 2 [4, 68], Crowther [17] | 822 |
| 17 | 10 | A | Ebbsfleet U | L 2-3 | 2-1 | 23 | Crowther [4], Blinkhorn [11] | 779 |
| 18 | 17 | A | Newport Co | W 3-1 | 1-0 | 22 | Jevons (pen) [29], Ashworth [76], Spencer, S [90] | 2096 |
| 19 | 20 | H | Alfreton T | D 1-1 | 1-1 | 21 | Jevons [42] | 444 |
| 20 | Dec 1 | H | Woking | W 7-0 | 1-0 | 18 | Jevons 4 [44, 61, 89, 90], Spencer, S [51], Harris [79], Poole [86] | 429 |
| 21 | 4 | A | Macclesfield T | L 2-3 | 2-0 | 20 | Brown [4], Jevons (pen) [45] | 1124 |
| 22 | 8 | H | AFC Telford U | W 2-1 | 0-1 | 16 | Poole [55], Spencer, S [66] | 523 |
| 23 | 26 | A | Stockport Co | W 2-0 | 2-0 | 12 | Griffin [10], Sedgwick [20] | 3963 |
| 24 | 29 | H | Southport | W 1-0 | 1-0 | 9 | Griffin [21] | 1068 |
| 25 | Jan 1 | H | Stockport Co | L 0-1 | 0-0 | 11 | | 2540 |
| 26 | 5 | H | Forest Green R | L 0-1 | 0-0 | 12 | | 553 |
| 27 | 22 | A | Grimsby T | L 0-2 | 0-0 | 15 | | 2755 |
| 28 | Feb 2 | A | Woking | L 1-2 | 1-1 | 18 | Blinkhorn [20] | 1236 |
| 29 | 9 | H | Macclesfield T | D 1-1 | 0-1 | 19 | Spencer, S [90] | 1184 |
| 30 | 12 | A | AFC Telford U | W 3-1 | 1-0 | 16 | Blinkhorn [35], Spencer, S [60], Jevons (pen) [79] | 1394 |
| 31 | 16 | H | Kidderminster H | L 0-4 | 0-1 | 17 | | 717 |
| 32 | 19 | H | Mansfield T | L 0-1 | 0-0 | 18 | | 675 |
| 33 | 23 | A | Tamworth | L 0-2 | 0-0 | 18 | | 746 |
| 34 | 26 | A | Alfreton T | L 1-5 | 0-2 | 18 | Broadbent [79] | 476 |
| 35 | Mar 2 | H | Newport Co | L 0-1 | 0-1 | 19 | | 640 |
| 36 | 9 | A | Gateshead | L 0-3 | 0-1 | 21 | | 371 |
| 37 | 12 | A | Luton T | W 2-1 | 1-1 | 20 | Almond [19], Milligan (pen) [70] | 4847 |
| 38 | 16 | H | Dartford | W 3-0 | 1-0 | 17 | Hogan [26], Blinkhorn [69], Almond [83] | 475 |
| 39 | 23 | A | Hereford U | W 2-1 | 0-1 | 17 | Brown [63], Almond [74] | 1152 |
| 40 | 26 | H | Cambridge U | W 2-1 | 1-1 | 14 | Blinkhorn [3], Brizell [81] | 404 |
| 41 | 30 | H | Wrexham | W 2-0 | 1-0 | 14 | Hogan [31], McCartan [90] | 1846 |
| 42 | Apr 1 | A | Barrow | D 1-1 | 1-1 | 14 | Hogan [2] | 1001 |
| 43 | 6 | H | Braintree T | L 1-2 | 0-2 | 14 | Milligan [83] | 509 |
| 44 | 9 | H | Ebbsfleet U | W 1-0 | 1-0 | 14 | Blinkhorn [43] | 385 |
| 45 | 13 | A | Nuneaton T | L 1-3 | 0-1 | 15 | Almond [90] | 1158 |
| 46 | 20 | H | Lincoln C | L 1-5 | 0-2 | 18 | Ashworth [50] | 1390 |

**Final League Position: 18**

## GOALSCORERS
*League (63):* Jevons 15 (4 pens), Spencer, S 10 (2 pens), Blinkhorn 7, Brown 6, Almond 4, Crowther 4, Griffin 3, Hogan 3, Ashworth 2, Milligan 2 (1 pen), Poole 2, Brizell 1, Broadbent 1, Harris 1, McCartan 1, Sedgwick 1.
*FA Cup (1):* Jevons 1.
*FA Trophy (1):* Brown 1.

| Carnell 31 | Brizell 37 + 3 | Ashworth 45 | Pearson 7 + 2 | Griffin 38 + 1 | Brown 35 + 2 | Byrne 9 + 3 | Moses 8 + 17 | Poole 16 + 12 | Jevons 26 + 9 | Spencer S 29 + 6 | Cox 3 + 10 | Williams R 5 + 5 | Douglas-Pringle — + 4 | Lomax 26 + 3 | Spencer G 1 + 7 | Cassidy 11 + 2 | Blinkhorn 25 + 5 | McNiven — + 3 | Frith 4 | Tomsett 38 + 1 | Crowther 15 + 3 | Dennis 22 + 1 | Dilo 11 | Sedgwick 15 + 3 | Harris — + 4 | Allott 5 | Putterill — + 1 | McCartan 5 + 11 | Osawe — + 2 | Anderson 3 + 1 | Almond 13 | Broadbent — + 2 | Milligan 12 | Hogan 10 + 1 | Fitzgerald 1 | *Match No.* |
|---|---|---|---|---|---|---|---|---|---|---|---|---|---|---|---|---|---|---|---|---|---|---|---|---|---|---|---|---|---|---|---|---|---|---|---|---|
| 1 | 2 | 3 | 4■ | 5 | 6 | 7 | 8 | $9^{1}$ | $10^{2}$ | $11^{3}$ | 12 | 13 | 14 | | | | | | | | | | | | | | | | | | | | | | | 1 |
| 1 | 2 | 4 | | 3 | $6^{3}$ | 7 | $9^{1}$ | | 11 | 10 | $8^{2}$ | 5 | 13 | 12 | 14 | | | | | | | | | | | | | | | | | | | | | 2 |
| 1 | 2 | 3 | | 5 | $8^{1}$ | $7^{3}$ | | | $9^{2}$ | 10 | | 4 | | 14 | 12 | 6 | 11 | 13 | | | | | | | | | | | | | | | | | | 3 |
| | 5 | 4 | | 2 | $8^{2}$ | $6^{3}$ | | | 10 | 9 | | 3 | 13 | | 14 | $7^{1}$ | 11 | | 1 | 12 | | | | | | | | | | | | | | | | 4 |
| 1 | 5 | 3 | 2 | 9■ | $6^{1}$ | 8 | | | 11 | 10 | | $4^{2}$ | 12 | 13 | | | | | | 7 | | | | | | | | | | | | | | | | 5 |
| 1 | 2 | 4 | $3^{1}$ | | $6^{2}$ | 13 | | | $11^{3}$ | 10 | | 12 | | 5 | | 7 | | 14 | | 8 | 9 | | | | | | | | | | | | | | | 6 |
| 1 | 2 | 4 | 3 | | 6 | | | | 10 | 9 | 12 | | | 5 | | $7^{1}$ | | | | 8■ | 11 | | | | | | | | | | | | | | | 7 |
| 1 | 2 | 5 | 4 | | 7 | $8^{3}$ | 14 | 13 | $11^{2}$ | 10 | 12 | | | 3 | | 6 | | | | | $9^{1}$ | | | | | | | | | | | | | | | 8 |
| 1 | 2 | 4 | 3 | 13 | 8 | | | 12 | 11 | 10 | 9 | | | $5^{2}$ | | $7^{1}$ | | | | 6 | | | | | | | | | | | | | | | | 9 |
| 1 | 2 | $5^{2}$ | 4 | 3 | 7 | | | 12 | 11 | 10 | 9 | | | | | | | | | 8 | $6^{1}$ | 13 | | | | | | | | | | | | | | 10 |
| 1 | 2 | | | 5 | $7^{3}$ | 8 | | $9^{1}$ | $11^{2}$ | 10 | 14 | 13 | | 4 | | | | | | 6 | 12 | 3 | | | | | | | | | | | | | | 11 |
| | 2 | 5 | 14 | | 6 | $8^{1}$ | | 7 | $11^{2}$ | 10 | 13 | | | 3 | | | | | 1 | 9 | 12 | $4^{3}$ | | | | | | | | | | | | | | 12 |
| | 2 | 4 | 12 | | | $8^{2}$ | $6^{3}$ | 7 | 14 | 10 | 13 | | | 5 | | | | | 1 | 9 | 11 | $3^{1}$ | | | | | | | | | | | | | | 13 |
| 1 | 2 | 4 | | 5 | 8 | | 13 | $6^{2}$ | $11^{1}$ | 10 | | | | 3 | | | 12 | | | 7 | 9 | | | | | | | | | | | | | | | 14 |
| 1 | | 4 | | 3 | $6^{1}$ | | 13 | 12 | $9^{2}$ | 10 | | | | 2 | | 7 | | | | 8 | 11 | 5 | | | | | | | | | | | | | | 15 |
| | 2 | 5 | | 3 | 6 | | 13 | 12 | | $10^{3}$ | 14 | | | | | $8^{2}$ | $11^{1}$ | | 1 | 7 | 9 | 4 | | | | | | | | | | | | | | 16 |
| | 2 | 3 | | 5 | $6^{3}$ | | 12 | | 13 | 10 | 14 | | | | | $8^{1}$ | $11^{2}$ | | | 7 | 9 | 4 | 1 | | | | | | | | | | | | | 17 |
| | | 3 | | 5 | | | 13 | $6^{2}$ | $11^{1}$ | 10 | | | | 2 | | | 12 | | | 7 | 8 | 4 | 1 | 9 | | | | | | | | | | | | 18 |
| | 2 | 4 | | 5 | 7 | | 14 | 13 | $11^{3}$ | | | 12 | | | | | 10 | | | 8 | 9 | $3^{1}$ | 1 | $6^{2}$ | | | | | | | | | | | | 19 |
| | 13 | 4 | | $5^{2}$ | 8 | | 12 | 6 | 11 | $10^{3}$ | | | | 2 | | | | | | 7 | | 3 | 1 | $9^{1}$ | 14 | | | | | | | | | | | 20 |
| | | 4 | | 5 | $7^{3}$ | | 14 | | $10^{2}$ | 9 | 12 | | | 2 | | | 13 | | | 6 | $11^{1}$ | 3 | 1 | 8 | | | | | | | | | | | | 21 |
| 1 | 12 | 4 | | 5 | 6 | | 14 | $9^{2}$ | | 10 | | | | 2 | | | $11^{3}$ | | | 8 | 13 | $3^{1}$ | | 7 | | | | | | | | | | | | 22 |
| 1 | 2 | 4 | | 5 | 12 | 14 | 13 | $6^{1}$ | | 10 | | | | 3 | | | $11^{2}$ | | | 7 | $9^{3}$ | | | 8 | | | | | | | | | | | | 23 |
| 1 | 2 | 4 | | 5 | 6 | | $7^{3}$ | 12 | | $10^{2}$ | | | | 3 | | | $11^{1}$ | | | 8 | 9 | | | 14 | 13 | | | | | | | | | | | 24 |
| 1 | 2 | 5 | | 3 | 6 | 14 | | 12 | 13 | 10 | | | | 4 | | | $11^{2}$ | | | 7 | $9^{1}$ | | | $8^{3}$ | | | | | | | | | | | | 25 |
| 1 | $2^{3}$ | 5 | | 3 | | | | 6 | $11^{2}$ | 10 | 14 | | | 4 | | $9^{1}$ | 12 | | | 8 | | | | | 13 | 7 | | | | | | | | | | 26 |
| 1 | $2^{3}$ | 3 | | 5 | | | | $6^{2}$ | $11^{1}$ | 10 | | | | 4 | | | 12 | | | 9 | | | | 7 | 14 | 8 | 13 | | | | | | | | | 27 |
| | 2 | 4 | | 5 | | | | $9^{2}$ | | 10 | | | | 3 | | 14 | 11 | | | 7 | | | 1 | $6^{3}$ | | $8^{1}$ | | 12 | 13 | | | | | | | 28 |
| | 2 | 3 | | 5 | | | 13 | 9 | $10^{1}$ | 12 | | | | 4 | | | 11 | | | 8 | | | 1 | $7^{2}$ | | | | $6^{3}$ | 14 | | | | | | | 29 |
| | 2 | 4 | | 5 | | | 13 | 14 | 10 | 12 | | | | 3 | | | $11^{1}$ | | | 7 | | | 1 | 6 | | $8^{2}$ | | $9^{3}$ | | | | | | | | 30 |
| | $2^{3}$ | 5 | | 3 | 12 | | $6^{2}$ | | 10 | | | | | 4 | 13 | | | | | 8 | | | 1 | 9 | | $7^{1}$ | | 11 | | 14 | | | | | | 31 |
| | 14 | 5 | | 3 | $6^{2}$ | | | | 13 | $10^{3}$ | | | | 2 | 12 | 8 | | | | | | | 1 | 7 | | | | $9^{1}$ | | 4 | 11 | | | | | 32 |
| | 2 | 5 | | 3 | 6 | | 14 | | | | | | | $7^{1}$ | 12 | | | 13 | | $9^{3}$ | | | 1 | 8■ | | | | 10 | | 4 | $11^{2}$ | | | | | 33 |
| 1 | 2 | 3 | | 5 | 6 | | $7^{2}$ | | | | | | | 8 | 9 | 14 | 11 | | | $10^{3}$ | | | | | | | | 12 | | $4^{1}$ | | 13 | | | | 34 |
| 1 | 2 | 3 | | $5^{3}$ | 6 | | | | $11^{2}$ | | | | | 4 | 13 | | 10 | | | 7 | | | | $8^{1}$ | | | | 12 | | | | 14 | 9 | | | 35 |
| 1 | 2 | 3 | | 5 | 6 | | | | | 10 | | | | | | | 11 | | | $7^{2}$ | | 4 | | | | | | 13 | | | $9^{1}$ | | 8 | 12 | | 36 |
| 1 | 2 | 3 | | 5 | 7 | | | | | | | | | | | | 11 | | | 8 | | 4 | | 13 | | | | 12 | | | 10 | | $9^{2}$ | $6^{1}$ | | 37 |
| 1 | 2 | 4 | | 5 | $9^{1}$ | | 12 | 13 | | | | | | | | | 11 | | | 7 | | 3 | | | | | | 14 | | | 10 | | $8^{3}$ | $6^{2}$ | | 38 |
| 1 | 2 | 3 | | 5 | 9 | | 14 | 13 | 12 | | | | | | | | $11^{1}$ | | | 8 | | 4 | | | | | | | | | $10^{3}$ | | 7 | $6^{2}$ | | 39 |
| 1 | 2 | 4 | | 5 | 7 | | | 13 | 14 | | | 12 | | | | | $11^{3}$ | | | 9 | | $3^{1}$ | | | | | | | | | 10 | | 8 | $6^{2}$ | | 40 |
| 1 | 2 | 4 | | 5 | $8^{1}$ | | 12 | | 14 | | | | | | | | 11 | | | 7 | | 3 | | | | | | 13 | | | $10^{3}$ | | 9 | $6^{2}$ | | 41 |
| 1 | 2■ | 4 | | 5 | | | 7 | | | | | | | | | | $11^{1}$ | | | 8 | | 3 | | | | | | 12 | | | 10 | | 9 | 6 | | 42 |
| 1 | | 4 | | 5 | | | $7^{1}$ | $2^{3}$ | 13 | 12 | | | | | | | $10^{2}$ | | | 6 | | 3 | | | | | | 14 | | | 11 | | 8 | 9 | | 43 |
| 1 | | 4 | | 5■ | 7 | | | 6 | 11 | 12 | | | | | | | $10^{1}$ | | | | | 3 | | | | | | | | | 9 | | 8 | 2 | | 44 |
| 1 | | 3 | | | 7 | | | $6^{3}$ | 10 | 13 | | $4^{2}$ | | | | | $11^{1}$ | | | | | 5 | | 12 | | | | 14 | | | 9 | | 8 | 2 | | 45 |
| 1 | 2 | 4 | | | 6 | | | | 13 | 12 | | | | | | | $10^{3}$ | | | 7 | | 3 | | | | | | 14 | | | $11^{1}$ | | $8^{2}$ | 9 | 5 | 46 |

**FA Cup**

| | | | |
|---|---|---|---|
| Fourth Qualifying | Harrogate T | (h) | 1-1 |
| *Replay* | Harrogate T | (a) | 0-1 |

**FA Trophy**

| | | | |
|---|---|---|---|
| First Round | Barrow | (h) | 1-1 |
| *Replay* | Barrow | (a) | 0-1 |

# KIDDERMINSTER HARRIERS

*Ground:* Aggborough Stadium, Hoo Road, Kidderminster DY10 1NB. *Tel:* (01562) 823 931. *Fax:* (01562) 827 329.
*Website:* www.harriers.co.uk *Year Formed:* 1886. *Record Gate:* 9,155 (1948 v Hereford U). *Nickname:* 'The Harriers'.
*Manager:* Steve Burr. *Secretary:* Graham Hill. *Colours:* Red shirts, white shorts, red socks.

## KIDDERMINSTER HARRIERS – BLUE SQUARE PREMIER 2012–13 LEAGUE RECORD

| Match No. | Date | Venue | Opponents | Result | | H/T Score | Lg Pos. | Goalscorers | Attendance |
|---|---|---|---|---|---|---|---|---|---|
| 1 | Aug 11 | A | Lincoln C | L | 0-1 | 0-1 | 23 | | 2112 |
| 2 | 14 | H | Luton T | L | 0-2 | 0-2 | 22 | | 2275 |
| 3 | 18 | H | Mansfield T | L | 2-3 | 1-1 | 24 | Byrne [8], Johnson [52] | 1770 |
| 4 | 25 | A | Dartford | L | 0-1 | 0-1 | 24 | | 1068 |
| 5 | 27 | H | Forest Green R | L | 0-1 | 0-0 | 24 | | 1742 |
| 6 | Sept 1 | A | Barrow | D | 1-1 | 1-0 | 24 | Pilkington [8] | 716 |
| 7 | 4 | A | Braintree T | D | 1-1 | 1-0 | 23 | Demetriou [89] | 579 |
| 8 | 8 | H | Southport | D | 2-2 | 1-0 | 24 | Storer [17], Malbon [88] | 1650 |
| 9 | 15 | H | Grimsby T | D | 0-0 | 0-0 | 24 | | 1811 |
| 10 | 22 | A | Alfreton T | D | 1-1 | 0-1 | 24 | Malbon [65] | 659 |
| 11 | 25 | A | Cambridge U | W | 3-1 | 0-0 | 23 | Rowe 3 [60, 69, 85] | 1815 |
| 12 | 29 | H | Macclesfield T | W | 3-0 | 1-0 | 20 | Dunkley [43], Rowe [50], Johnson [73] | 1654 |
| 13 | Oct 6 | A | Ebbsfleet U | D | 1-1 | 1-1 | 20 | Malbon [28] | 726 |
| 14 | 9 | H | Hyde | W | 3-0 | 2-0 | 20 | Vincent [16], Rowe 2 [23, 90] | 1457 |
| 15 | 13 | A | Stockport Co | L | 0-1 | 0-1 | 21 | | 3426 |
| 16 | 27 | H | Gateshead | D | 1-1 | 0-0 | 21 | Malbon [46] | 1639 |
| 17 | Nov 6 | A | Woking | D | 2-2 | 2-1 | 19 | Blissett 2 [16, 42] | 1168 |
| 18 | 10 | H | Nuneaton T | W | 1-0 | 0-0 | 17 | Gowling [89] | 1592 |
| 19 | 17 | A | AFC Telford U | W | 2-0 | 0-0 | 16 | Johnson [82], Rowe [90] | 2160 |
| 20 | Dec 1 | H | Wrexham | W | 2-0 | 0-0 | 11 | Matt [57], Blissett [90] | 2378 |
| 21 | 4 | A | Tamworth | W | 1-0 | 0-0 | 8 | Rowe [90] | 1031 |
| 22 | 8 | H | Newport Co | W | 3-2 | 1-2 | 7 | Matt 3 [23, 58, 78] | 1951 |
| 23 | 22 | H | Dartford | W | 5-1 | 2-1 | 6 | Dunkley [4], Matt 2 [32, 69], Williams [76], Vaughan, L [90] | 1779 |
| 24 | 26 | A | Hereford U | W | 1-0 | 1-0 | 5 | Matt [6] | 2902 |
| 25 | Jan 1 | H | Hereford U | L | 0-1 | 0-1 | 6 | | 3674 |
| 26 | 5 | H | Barrow | W | 2-0 | 1-0 | 5 | Rowe [3], Matt [83] | 1703 |
| 27 | 12 | A | Mansfield T | W | 2-0 | 2-0 | 5 | Demetriou [22], Vaughan, L [25] | 2405 |
| 28 | 19 | A | Macclesfield T | L | 0-1 | 0-0 | 5 | | 1342 |
| 29 | 29 | H | AFC Telford U | W | 1-0 | 1-0 | 5 | Johnson [37] | 1785 |
| 30 | Feb 9 | H | Cambridge U | W | 3-2 | 2-1 | 4 | Dunkley [27], Johnson [42], Malbon [51] | 1949 |
| 31 | 16 | A | Hyde | W | 4-0 | 1-0 | 5 | Malbon 2 [20, 58], Johnson [55], Pearson [67] | 717 |
| 32 | 19 | A | Forest Green R | W | 1-0 | 1-0 | 3 | Malbon [26] | 1449 |
| 33 | 23 | H | Alfreton T | W | 3-1 | 3-1 | 2 | Morgan-Smith [1], Gowling [38], Malbon [45] | 2209 |
| 34 | 26 | A | Nuneaton T | W | 1-0 | 0-0 | 2 | Malbon [71] | 1087 |
| 35 | Mar 2 | H | Ebbsfleet U | W | 3-2 | 1-1 | 2 | Vincent [14], Malbon [61], Gittings [88] | 2048 |
| 36 | 5 | A | Gateshead | L | 0-2 | 0-0 | 2 | | 273 |
| 37 | 9 | H | Grimsby T | W | 3-1 | 2-0 | 2 | Malbon 2 [32, 77], Gash [45] | 4629 |
| 38 | 16 | H | Tamworth | W | 4-1 | 2-1 | 3 | Briggs [37], Pilkington [45], Gash 2 [58, 84] | 2392 |
| 39 | 19 | A | Newport Co | W | 2-1 | 1-1 | 1 | Gash [27], Dunkley [90] | 2652 |
| 40 | 23 | A | Southport | W | 3-1 | 1-0 | 1 | Gash [43], Malbon [86], Rowe [90] | 946 |
| 41 | 26 | H | Woking | D | 2-2 | 1-1 | 1 | Gowling [13], Malbon [55] | 2035 |
| 42 | 30 | H | Braintree T | W | 2-1 | 0-1 | 1 | Malbon [60], Wells (og) [63] | 2266 |
| 43 | Apr 1 | A | Luton T | W | 2-1 | 2-0 | 1 | Gowling [13], Malbon [36] | 6108 |
| 44 | 6 | H | Lincoln C | W | 3-0 | 1-0 | 1 | Jackman [27], Storer [80], Vaughan, L [89] | 2326 |
| 45 | 13 | A | Wrexham | W | 2-1 | 1-0 | 1 | Vincent [19], Gash [71] | 4013 |
| 46 | 20 | H | Stockport Co | W | 4-0 | 0-0 | 2 | Malbon 2 [51, 53], Dunkley [57], Devaney [75] | 6453 |

**Final League Position: 2**

### GOALSCORERS
*League (82):* Malbon 19, Rowe 10, Matt 8, Gash 6, Johnson 6, Dunkley 5, Gowling 4, Blissett 3, Vaughan, L 3, Vincent 3, Demetriou 2, Pilkington 2, Storer 2, Briggs 1, Byrne 1, Devaney 1, Gittings 1, Jackman 1, Morgan-Smith 1, Pearson 1, Williams 1, own goal 1.
*FA Cup (4):* Dunkley 1, Johnson 1, Malbon 1, Vaughan L 1.
*FA Trophy (3):* Dunkley 1, Pilkington 1, Rowe 1.
*Blue Square Premier Play-Offs (2):* Dunkley 1, Gash 1 (1 pen).

| Lewis 33 | Austin 5 | Geohaghon 3 | Williams 6 + 4 | Demetriou 42 + 1 | Vincent 33 + 6 | Briggs 30 + 3 | Gittings 17 + 9 | Shakes 8 + 9 | Rowe 14 + 22 | Pilkington 15 + 10 | Byrne 3 + 1 | Johnson 21 + 18 | Malbon 43 + 3 | Storer 34 + 2 | Blissett 15 + 10 | Dunkley 43 | Vaughan N 13 | Vaughan L 40 | Guinan — + 5 | Peniket 5 + 6 | Panther — + 2 | Gowling 40 | Watkins 3 + 1 | Matt 7 + 1 | Clancy — + 3 | Jackman 14 + 2 | Morgan-Smith 5 | Jarvis — + 1 | Pearson 2 + 4 | Devaney 2 + 6 | Gash 10 + 1 | Match No. |
|---|---|---|---|---|---|---|---|---|---|---|---|---|---|---|---|---|---|---|---|---|---|---|---|---|---|---|---|---|---|---|---|---|
| 1 | 2 | 3 | 4 | 5¹ | 6 | 7 | 8² | 9³ | 10 | 11 | 12 | 13 | 14 | | | | | | | | | | | | | | | | | | | 1 |
| 1 | 4 | 3 | 5 | | 6 | 2 | 12 | 10¹ | 13 | 8 | | 9² | 11 | 7 | | | | | | | | | | | | | | | | | | 2 |
| 1 | 5 | 3 | 4 | | 7 | 8 | 13 | 9¹ | 14 | 6 | | 11³ | 10 | 2² | 12 | | | | | | | | | | | | | | | | | 3 |
| 1 | 3 | | 5 | 12 | 7 | 2² | 6 | 10 | 14 | 8 | | 9³ | 11¹ | 13 | 4 | | | | | | | | | | | | | | | | | 4 |
| | | 4 | 5 | 8 | 6 | 14 | 9² | 13 | 10³ | 7 | 11² | 3 | 1 | 2 | 12 | | | | | | | | | | | | | | | | | 5 |
| 3 | | | 5 | 8 | 9³ | 6¹ | 12 | 10 | 7 | 11² | 4 | 1 | 2 | 13 | 14 | | | | | | | | | | | | | | | | | 6 |
| | | 5 | 13 | 7² | 6 | 9 | 11¹ | 8 | 12 | 3 | 1 | 2 | 14 | 10³ | 4 | | | | | | | | | | | | | | | | | 7 |
| | | 5 | 8 | 9³ | 6 | 13 | 7¹ | 10² | 4 | 1 | 2 | 14 | 11 | 12 | 3 | | | | | | | | | | | | | | | | | 8 |
| | | 5 | 6 | 7 | 8 | 13 | 11¹ | 12 | 9³ | 4 | 1 | 2 | 14 | 10² | 3 | | | | | | | | | | | | | | | | | 9 |
| | | 5 | 6 | 7 | 8² | 13 | 12 | 11 | 9 | 4 | 1 | 2 | 10¹ | 3 | | | | | | | | | | | | | | | | | | 10 |
| | | 5 | 6 | 7 | 8² | 14 | 12 | 13 | 11³ | 9 | 4 | 1 | 2 | 10¹ | 3 | | | | | | | | | | | | | | | | | 11 |
| | | 5 | 6 | 7 | 8¹ | 14 | 9² | 13 | 11³ | 10 | 4 | 1 | 2 | 3 | 12 | | | | | | | | | | | | | | | | | 12 |
| | | 5 | 6 | 7 | 13 | 14 | 9³ | 11 | 10¹ | 4 | 1 | 2 | 12 | 3 | 8² | | | | | | | | | | | | | | | | | 13 |
| | 13 | 5 | 6³ | 7 | 9 | 12 | 10¹ | 14 | 11 | 3 | 1 | 2 | 4² | 8 | | | | | | | | | | | | | | | | | | 14 |
| | | 5 | 8 | 7² | 9³ | 13 | 10 | 12 | 11 | 4 | 1 | 2 | 14 | 3 | 6¹ | | | | | | | | | | | | | | | | | 15 |
| | 5 | | 8 | 7 | 11¹ | 12 | 9² | 6 | 10 | 4 | 1 | 2 | 13 | 3 | | | | | | | | | | | | | | | | | | 16 |
| | | 5 | 7 | 8¹ | 12 | 9² | 13 | 10³ | 6 | 11 | 3 | 1 | 2 | 14 | 4 | | | | | | | | | | | | | | | | | 17 |
| 1 | | 5 | 8 | 7³ | 10² | 14 | 13 | 9 | 6 | 11¹ | 4 | 2 | 12 | 3 | | | | | | | | | | | | | | | | | | 18 |
| 1 | | 5 | 14 | 8 | 13 | 6¹ | 9 | 10² | 7 | 11¹ | 3 | 2 | 4 | 12 | | | | | | | | | | | | | | | | | | 19 |
| 1 | | 5 | 13 | 8 | 6² | 12 | 9 | 10¹ | 7 | 14 | 3 | 2 | 3 | 11³ | | | | | | | | | | | | | | | | | | 20 |
| 1 | | 5 | 7 | 13 | 12 | 11² | 8 | 6 | 9¹ | 4 | 2 | 14 | 3 | 10³ | | | | | | | | | | | | | | | | | | 21 |
| 1 | | 5 | 13 | 8 | 6 | 12 | 9² | 11¹ | 7 | 14 | 4 | 2 | 3 | 10³ | | | | | | | | | | | | | | | | | | 22 |
| 1 | 13 | 5 | 7 | 8 | 9³ | 12 | 11¹ | 6 | 3 | 2 | 4² | 10 | 14 | | | | | | | | | | | | | | | | | | | 23 |
| 1 | | 5 | 6 | 7 | 9³ | 13 | 11² | 8 | 12 | 4 | 2 | 3 | 10¹ | 14 | | | | | | | | | | | | | | | | | | 24 |
| 1 | | 5 | 7 | 8 | 9 | 12 | 10 | 6¹ | 13 | 4 | 2 | 3 | 11² | | | | | | | | | | | | | | | | | | | 25 |
| 1 | 14 | 5 | 8 | 7 | 9³ | 6¹ | 10² | 12 | 13 | 3 | 2 | 4 | 11 | | | | | | | | | | | | | | | | | | | 26 |
| 1 | | 2 | 7 | 8 | 14 | 10² | 9¹ | 11³ | 6 | 13 | 3 | 5 | 4 | 12⁸ | | | | | | | | | | | | | | | | | | 27 |
| 1 | | 5 | 7² | 8¹ | 10 | 13 | 11 | 9 | 6 | 12 | 3 | 2 | 4 | | | | | | | | | | | | | | | | | | | 28 |
| 1 | | 5 | 13 | 14 | 12 | 9² | 11 | 8¹ | 7 | 10 | 4 | 2 | 3 | 6³ | | | | | | | | | | | | | | | | | | 29 |
| 1 | | 5 | 6 | | 14 | 12 | 9³ | 11 | 7 | 3 | 2 | 4 | 8¹ | 10² | 13 | | | | | | | | | | | | | | | | | 30 |
| 1 | | 3 | 6 | 8 | 13 | 14 | 9 | 11² | 7³ | 4 | 2 | 5 | 10¹ | 12 | | | | | | | | | | | | | | | | | | 31 |
| 1 | | 5 | 2² | 10 | 14 | 7¹ | 9 | 8 | 6 | 4 | 3 | 12 | 11³ | 13 | | | | | | | | | | | | | | | | | | 32 |
| 1 | | 5 | 8³ | 2 | 11² | 9 | 6 | 12 | 4 | 3 | 7 | 10¹ | 14 | 13 | | | | | | | | | | | | | | | | | | 33 |
| 1 | | 5 | 6 | 12 | 11² | 9³ | 7 | 3 | 2 | 4 | 8 | 10¹ | 14 | 13 | | | | | | | | | | | | | | | | | | 34 |
| 1 | | 5 | 6 | 7¹ | 12 | 13 | 9 | 10³ | 8 | 3 | 2 | 4 | 11² | 14 | | | | | | | | | | | | | | | | | | 35 |
| 1 | | 5 | 6 | 8² | 10 | 9 | 7 | 3 | 2 | 4 | 13 | 11¹ | 12 | | | | | | | | | | | | | | | | | | | 36 |
| 1 | | 5 | 12 | 9¹ | 14 | 13 | 11³ | 6 | 4 | 2 | 3 | 7 | 8² | 10 | | | | | | | | | | | | | | | | | | 37 |
| 1 | 14 | 5 | 6 | 7 | 12 | 11¹² | 13 | 9¹ | 3 | 2 | 4 | 8³ | 10 | | | | | | | | | | | | | | | | | | | 38 |
| 1 | | 5 | 6 | 8¹ | 13 | 11¹² | 12 | 9 | 3 | 2 | 4 | 7 | 10 | | | | | | | | | | | | | | | | | | | 39 |
| 1 | | 5 | 13 | 8¹ | 14 | 12 | 11 | 6 | 3 | 2 | 4 | 7³ | 9² | 10 | | | | | | | | | | | | | | | | | | 40 |
| 1 | | 5 | 7 | 13 | 14 | 12 | 11³ | 9 | 6² | 3 | 2 | 8¹ | 10 | | | | | | | | | | | | | | | | | | | 41 |
| 1 | | 5 | 8 | 13 | 11¹² | 12 | 9 | 6 | 3 | 2 | 4 | 7¹ | 10 | | | | | | | | | | | | | | | | | | | 42 |
| 1 | | 5 | 12 | 7¹ | 14 | 9² | 13 | 11³ | 6 | 3 | 2 | 4 | 8 | 10 | | | | | | | | | | | | | | | | | | 43 |
| 1 | | 3 | 9² | 14 | 6¹ | 13 | 11³ | 8 | 4 | 2 | 5 | 7 | 12 | 10 | | | | | | | | | | | | | | | | | | 44 |
| 1 | | 5 | 8 | 12 | 13 | 11³ | 10² | 6 | 4 | 2 | 3 | 7¹ | 14 | 9 | | | | | | | | | | | | | | | | | | 45 |
| 1 | | 5 | 8 | 13 | 12 | 11 | 9³ | 6² | 4 | 2 | 3 | 7 | 14 | 10¹ | | | | | | | | | | | | | | | | | | 46 |

**FA Cup**

| | | | | |
|---|---|---|---|---|
| Fourth Qualifying | Grimsby T | (a) | 4-2 |
| First Round | Oldham Ath | (h) | 0-2 |

**FA Trophy**

| | | | |
|---|---|---|---|
| First Round | Alfreton T | (a) | 3-1 |
| Second Round | Bromley | (a) | 0-1 |

**Blue Square Premier Play-Offs**

| | | | |
|---|---|---|---|
| Semi-Finals | Wrexham | (a) | 1-2 |
| | Wrexham | (h) | 1-3 |

# LINCOLN CITY

*Ground:* Sincil Bank Stadium, Sincil Bank, Lincoln LN5 8LD.   *Tel:* (01522) 880 011.   *Fax:* (01522) 880 020.
*Website:* www.redimps.com   *Year Formed:* 1884.   *Record Gate:* 23,196 (1967 v Derby Co, League Cup 4th rd).
*Nickname:* 'The Red Imps'.   *Manager:* Gary Simpson.   *Colours:* Red and white striped shirts, black shorts, red socks
with white trim.

## LINCOLN CITY – BLUE SQUARE PREMIER 2012–13 LEAGUE RECORD

| Match No. | Date | Venue | Opponents | Result | H/T Score | Lg Pos. | Goalscorers | Attendance |
|---|---|---|---|---|---|---|---|---|
| 1 | Aug 11 | H | Kidderminster H | W 1-0 | 1-0 | 4 | Taylor, J [39] | 2112 |
| 2 | 14 | A | Cambridge U | L 1-2 | 1-1 | 13 | Boyce [39] | 2546 |
| 3 | 18 | A | Newport Co | L 1-2 | 0-2 | 15 | Taylor, J [51] | 3024 |
| 4 | 25 | H | Macclesfield T | L 2-3 | 1-1 | 18 | Taylor, J [31], Boyce [89] | 2009 |
| 5 | 27 | A | Gateshead | D 1-1 | 0-1 | 18 | Robinson [89] | 803 |
| 6 | Sept 1 | H | Ebbsfleet U | D 1-1 | 1-0 | 17 | Nicolau [3] | 1682 |
| 7 | 4 | H | Alfreton T | L 1-2 | 1-0 | 20 | Nicolau [27] | 1566 |
| 8 | 8 | A | AFC Telford U | D 1-1 | 1-0 | 22 | Oliver [43] | 1794 |
| 9 | 15 | H | Hyde | W 3-2 | 1-0 | 18 | Larkin 2 (2 pens) [43, 67], Oliver [88] | 1745 |
| 10 | 22 | A | Tamworth | L 0-1 | 0-1 | 21 | | 1042 |
| 11 | 25 | H | Nuneaton T | W 2-1 | 0-1 | 15 | Nicolau [75], Miller [83] | 1579 |
| 12 | 28 | A | Forest Green R | L 0-3 | 0-1 | 17 | | 1395 |
| 13 | Oct 6 | H | Luton T | L 1-2 | 0-1 | 21 | Taylor, J [58] | 2970 |
| 14 | 9 | A | Mansfield T | D 0-0 | 0-0 | 21 | | 2325 |
| 15 | 13 | A | Wrexham | W 4-2 | 1-0 | 20 | Nicolau [20], Taylor, J [56], Robinson [69], Larkin [88] | 3809 |
| 16 | 27 | H | Stockport Co | D 3-3 | 1-0 | 19 | Taylor, J 2 [30, 90], Nutter [66] | 1873 |
| 17 | Nov 6 | H | Braintree T | W 3-0 | 1-0 | 15 | Sheridan [5], Boyce [47], Taylor, J [49] | 1455 |
| 18 | 10 | A | Barrow | W 2-1 | 1-0 | 13 | Power [40], Oliver [64] | 987 |
| 19 | 17 | H | Hereford U | W 3-2 | 1-0 | 9 | Taylor, J [45], Heath (og) [71], Larkin (pen) [81] | 2233 |
| 20 | Dec 4 | A | Woking | L 0-2 | 0-1 | 12 | | 2526 |
| 21 | 8 | A | Dartford | W 4-2 | 4-0 | 10 | Gray [7], Larkin 3 [24, 32, 45] | 1466 |
| 22 | 26 | H | Grimsby T | L 1-4 | 0-2 | 13 | Power (pen) [53] | 5702 |
| 23 | 29 | H | Gateshead | D 1-1 | 0-0 | 13 | Robinson [63] | 1906 |
| 24 | Jan 1 | A | Grimsby T | D 1-1 | 1-1 | 14 | Power [9] | 7405 |
| 25 | 5 | A | Ebbsfleet U | D 1-1 | 0-1 | 13 | Robinson [90] | 889 |
| 26 | 8 | A | Southport | L 2-4 | 1-3 | 14 | Taylor, J [37], Oliver [80] | 815 |
| 27 | 12 | H | Newport Co | L 2-4 | 1-4 | 15 | Oliver [44], Bush [78] | 1970 |
| 28 | 26 | H | Forest Green R | L 1-2 | 0-2 | 17 | Smith, A (pen) [86] | 1663 |
| 29 | Feb 9 | H | Dartford | W 2-1 | 1-0 | 14 | Oliver [6], Larkin (pen) [89] | 1789 |
| 30 | 12 | A | Stockport Co | L 0-2 | 0-0 | 18 | | 2769 |
| 31 | 16 | A | Hereford U | L 2-3 | 2-1 | 18 | Musa (og) [9], Power (pen) [38] | 1914 |
| 32 | 23 | H | Barrow | D 0-0 | 0-0 | 19 | | 1830 |
| 33 | 26 | H | Mansfield T | L 0-1 | 0-0 | 19 | | 2734 |
| 34 | Mar 2 | A | Woking | D 1-1 | 1-1 | 18 | Oliver [25] | 1766 |
| 35 | 6 | A | Macclesfield T | L 1-2 | 1-0 | 19 | Power (pen) [23] | 1557 |
| 36 | 9 | H | Southport | W 1-0 | 1-0 | 18 | Power (pen) [14] | 1827 |
| 37 | 12 | H | Wrexham | L 1-2 | 1-0 | 19 | Westwood (og) [34] | 1379 |
| 38 | 16 | A | Nuneaton T | L 0-1 | 0-0 | 20 | | 1122 |
| 39 | 23 | H | AFC Telford U | W 3-2 | 1-1 | 20 | Jordan [12], Taylor, J 2 [77, 88] | 1724 |
| 40 | 26 | A | Braintree T | W 3-0 | 1-0 | 17 | Diagne 2 [26, 74], Boyce [79] | 447 |
| 41 | 30 | A | Alfreton T | W 2-0 | 1-0 | 17 | Hobson [41], Oliver [81] | 1189 |
| 42 | Apr 1 | H | Cambridge U | D 0-0 | 0-0 | 16 | | 2721 |
| 43 | 6 | A | Kidderminster H | L 0-3 | 0-1 | 19 | | 2326 |
| 44 | 9 | A | Luton T | L 0-3 | 0-2 | 20 | | 5393 |
| 45 | 13 | H | Tamworth | W 2-1 | 0-1 | 18 | Taylor, J [67], Power (pen) [83] | 3174 |
| 46 | 20 | A | Hyde | W 5-1 | 2-0 | 16 | Power (pen) [27], Fofana [45], Oliver 3 [48, 62, 86] | 1390 |

**Final League Position: 16**

### GOALSCORERS

*League (66):* Taylor, J 13, Oliver 11, Larkin 8 (4 pens), Power 8 (6 pens), Boyce 4, Nicolau 4, Robinson 4, Diagne 2, Bush 1, Fofana 1, Gray 1, Hobson 1, Jordan 1, Miller 1, Nutter 1, Sheridan 1, Smith, A 1 (1 pen), own goals 3.
*FA Cup (10):* Power 3, Taylor J 3, Oliver 2, Sheridan 1, Smith A 1.
*FA Trophy (1):* Power 1.

| Farman 39 + 1 | Gray 31 + 4 | Miller 38 | Boyce 41 | Nutter 12 | Daley 4 + 1 | Mills 17 + 1 | Power 34 + 3 | Smith A 19 + 11 | Duffy 3 | Taylor J 33 + 8 | Sheridan 30 + 10 | Oliver 22 + 15 | Nicolau 18 + 8 | McCammon 1 + 1 | Hutchison 7 | Larkin 13 + 16 | Robson 10 + 1 | Robinson 5 + 13 | Bore 5 + 2 | Fofana 25 + 2 | Morgan 6 + 2 | Gilbert 14 | Garner 12 + 3 | Bassele 1 + 1 | Preece 7 + 1 | Thomson 3 | Barraclough — + 1 | Bush 2 + 1 | Platt — + 1 | Turnbull 14 + 1 | Jones 7 + 6 | Hobson 5 + 7 | Brown 10 | Diagne 7 | Jordan 10 + 2 | Dali 1 + 3 | Match No. |
|---|---|---|---|---|---|---|---|---|---|---|---|---|---|---|---|---|---|---|---|---|---|---|---|---|---|---|---|---|---|---|---|---|---|---|---|---|---|
| 1 | 2 | 3 | 4 | 5 | $6^2$ | 7 | 8 | $9^1$ | $10^3$ | 11 | 12 | 13 | 14 | | | | | | | | | | | | | | | | | | | | | | | | 1 |
| 1 | 2 | 4 | 3 | $5^2$ | $6^1$ | 7 | 8 | $9^2$ | 10 | 11 | 13 | 12 | 14 | | | | | | | | | | | | | | | | | | | | | | | | 2 |
| 1 | 3 | 8 | 4 | 5 | $2^3$ | 6 | 7 | $9^2$ | $10^1$ | 11 | 13 | | 14 | 12 | | | | | | | | | | | | | | | | | | | | | | | 3 |
| 1 | 2 | | 3 | 5 | $6^1$ | 7 | 8 | | | 11 | | $9^3$ | 13 | 14 | $10^2$ | 4 | 12 | | | | | | | | | | | | | | | | | | | | 4 |
| 1 | 3 | 5 | 12 | | | 7 | 8 | | | 11 | | $6^3$ | 14 | | $9^1$ | 4 | 10 | $2^2$ | 13 | | | | | | | | | | | | | | | | | | 5 |
| 1 | 2 | 4 | 5 | | | $7^1$ | 8 | | | 11 | | 6 | 14 | | $9^3$ | 3 | $10^2$ | 12 | 13 | | | | | | | | | | | | | | | | | | 6 |
| 1 | 7 | $4^2$ | 5 | 12 | | | $8^1$ | | | 11 | | 13 | 14 | | 9 | 3 | 10 | $2^3$ | 6 | | | | | | | | | | | | | | | | | | 7 |
| 1 | 2 | 3 | 5 | | | 7 | | | | $10^1$ | $6^2$ | 11 | 9 | | 4 | 12 | | | 13 | 8 | | | | | | | | | | | | | | | | | 8 |
| 1 | 2 | 3 | 5 | | | 6 | | | | | | $9^1$ | 11 | $8^3$ | | 4 | $10^2$ | | 13 | 12 | 7 | 14 | | | | | | | | | | | | | | | 9 |
| 1 | 2 | 3 | 5 | | | 7 | | | | | 13 | 12 | $10^1$ | 11 | | $4^3$ | | | | 14 | $6^2$ | 8 | 9 | | | | | | | | | | | | | | 10 |
| 1 | 2 | 4 | 3 | 5 | | | | | | | | $6^3$ | 14 | | | $9^2$ | 10 | 12 | | 13 | | $11^1$ | 7 | 8 | | | | | | | | | | | | | 11 |
| 1 | 4 | 3 | 2 | | | | | | | | | $6^3$ | 12 | 14 | 10 | $7^2$ | | | | $11^1$ | 5 | 13 | 9 | 8 | | | | | | | | | | | | | 12 |
| 1 | 2 | $4^3$ | 3 | | | | 7 | | | | | 11 | 14 | | 9 | | | | 12 | 13 | $8^2$ | $6^1$ | 10 | 5 | | | | | | | | | | | | | 13 |
| 1 | 5 | 4 | 3 | | | | 6 | | | | | 11 | 12 | | 7 | | $10^2$ | | | 13 | $9^1$ | 8 | 2 | | | | | | | | | | | | | | 14 |
| 1 | 2 | 5 | 3 | | | | | | | 8 | 14 | $9^1$ | | | $11^2$ | 12 | | 7 | | 13 | $10^3$ | 6 | 4 | | | | | | | | | | | | | | 15 |
| 1 | 8 | 4 | 3 | 5 | | | | | | | 9 | $6^2$ | | | 11 | $10^3$ | 13 | 14 | | 12 | $2^1$ | | 7 | | | | | | | | | | | | | | 16 |
| 1 | 2 | 4 | 3 | | | | | | | 6 | $9^1$ | $7^3$ | | | $11^2$ | 10 | 12 | | | 13 | | 8 | 14 | 5 | | | | | | | | | | | | | 17 |
| 1 | 2 | 4 | 3 | | | | | | | 8 | $10^3$ | $6^1$ | | | $11^2$ | 9 | 12 | | | 13 | | 7 | | | 5 | 14 | | | | | | | | | | | 18 |
| 1 | 2 | 4 | 3 | | | 7 | | | | | $10^1$ | $6^2$ | | | $11^2$ | 9 | 13 | | | 12 | | 8 | | | 5 | 14 | | | | | | | | | | | 19 |
| 1 | 2 | | 3 | | | | | | | 6 | 10 | 14 | | | 11 | $9^3$ | 12 | | | 13 | | $7^2$ | 5 | 4 | $8^1$ | | | | | | | | | | | | 20 |
| | 8 | 4 | | 3 | | | | | | | | $6^1$ | | | 11 | 9 | | | | 10 | 2 | 12 | 7 | | 5 | | | | | 1 | | | | | | | 21 |
| 1 | $2^1$ | 4 | 3 | | | 7 | 8 | 13 | | | 10 | $6^3$ | 11 | $9^2$ | | 14 | | | | 5 | 12 | | | | | | | | | | | | | | | | 22 |
| | | 4 | 3 | | | | $6^2$ | 9 | | | 14 | 8 | 11 | | $10^3$ | 2 | 13 | | | 7 | $5^1$ | 12 | | | | | | | | 1 | | | | | | | 23 |
| 12 | 7 | 2 | 3 | | | | 8 | $14$ | | | 10 | $6^3$ | 11 | | $9^7$ | 13 | 5 | | | 4 | $1^1$ | | | | | | | | | | | | | | | | 24 |
| 1 | 7 | 2 | 3 | | | | 10 | | | | 11 | $6^1$ | | | $9^3$ | 12 | 5 | 14 | | $4^2$ | | 8 | 13 | | | | | | | | | | | | | | 25 |
| 1 | 4 | 2 | 3 | | | | 8 | | | | $10^1$ | 11 | $9^3$ | | 12 | $5^2$ | 6 | | | 7 | | 13 | 14 | | | | | | | | | | | | | | 26 |
| 1 | 6 | 4 | $3^1$ | | | | 7 | | | | 9 | 8 | 10 | 12 | 11 | $2^2$ | 13 | | | 5 | | | | | | | | | | | | | | | | | 27 |
| | 2 | 4 | | | | | | 13 | | | $11^1$ | $6^2$ | 12 | | $9^3$ | 10 | | | | 3 | | 1 | 7 | | 5 | | | 8 | 14 | | | | | | | | 28 |
| 14 | 2 | 3 | | | | | 7 | $6^1$ | | | $9^4$ | $10^2$ | | | $11^3$ | | | | | 5 | 4 | 1 | | | | | | 8 | 12 | 13 | | | | | | | 29 |
| | 2 | 3 | | | | | 7 | $6^2$ | | | 12 | | 10 | 14 | $11^1$ | 13 | | | | 5 | 4 | 1 | | | | | | 8 | $9^3$ | | | | | | | | 30 |
| | 2 | 4 | | | | | 9 | | | | 13 | | $11^1$ | | 14 | $8^2$ | | 7 | | $5^3$ | 3 | 1 | | | | | | 6 | $10^3$ | 12 | | | | | | | 31 |
| 1 | 2 | 3 | | | | | 9 | 13 | | | $10^1$ | | 12 | 5 | $11^3$ | 14 | | $7^2$ | | 4 | | | | | | | | 8 | 6 | | | | | | | | 32 |
| 1 | $12^2$ | 2 | 3 | | | | 10 | 13 | | | 6 | | 11 | 5 | 14 | | | $7^1$ | | 4 | | | | | | | | $8^3$ | $9^2$ | | | | | | | | 33 |
| 1 | 2 | 3 | | | | | 10 | 6 | | | 9 | | 11 | | 8 | | | | | 7 | | | | | | | | | 4 | 5 | | | | | | | 34 |
| 1 | 2 | 3 | | | | | 10 | 9 | | | 12 | $6^1$ | 11 | | 8 | | | | | $5^3$ | 4 | | | | | | | $7^2$ | 13 | | | | 14 | | | | 35 |
| 1 | 2 | 3 | | | | | $7^3$ | 13 | | | $9^1$ | 12 | $10^4$ | | 6 | | | | | 4 | | | | | | | | $11^2$ | 14 | | 5 | 8 | | | | | 36 |
| 1 | 14 | 2 | 3 | | | | 9 | 12 | | | 10 | | | | 6 | | | | | $4^3$ | | | | | | | | $8^1$ | $11^2$ | | 5 | 7 | 13 | | | | 37 |
| 1 | 2 | 3 | | | | | 10 | $9^2$ | | | $6^1$ | 12 | | | 7 | | | | | 13 | 11 | | | | | | | 4 | 5 | 8 | | | | | | 38 |
| 1 | 2 | 3 | | | | | 9 | | | | 10 | 8 | | | $7^2$ | | | | | 14 | 13 | $11^1$ | | | | | | 4 | 5 | $6^3$ | 12 | | | | | | 39 |
| 1 | 13 | 2 | 3 | | | | 12 | 14 | | | 10 | $5^3$ | | | $8^1$ | | | | | 7 | | | | | | | | 4 | $9^2$ | 6 | $11^4$ | | | | | | 40 |
| 1 | $2^1$ | 5 | 3 | | | | 7 | 12 | | | $10^3$ | 9 | 13 | | 6 | 14 | $11^2$ | 4 | | 8 | | | | | | | | | | | | | | | | | 41 |
| 1 | 2 | 3 | | | | | $9^1$ | | | | 10 | 8 | 11 | | 13 | | | | | $6^2$ | 12 | 4 | 5 | 7 | | | | | | | | | | | | | 42 |
| 1 | 5 | 4 | | | | | 6 | $10^1$ | | | 11 | 8 | 9 | | 7 | | | | | 12 | 2 | | 3 | | | | | | | | | | | | | | 43 |
| 1 | 2 | 3 | 4 | | | | 12 | | | | $11^3$ | 9 | 13 | | 7 | | | | | 6 | $10^2$ | 5 | | $8^1$ | 14 | | | | | | | | | | | | 44 |
| 1 | 2 | 3 | | | | | 9 | | | | $11^3$ | 8 | 10 | $5^2$ | 14 | | | | | 6 | 12 | 13 | 4 | | $7^1$ | | | | | | | | | | | | 45 |
| $1^3$ | 2 | 4 | | | | | 9 | | | | 13 | $8^2$ | 11 | 5 | 7 | | | | | 14 | | | 6 | $10^1$ | | 3 | | | 12 | | | | | | | | 46 |

**FA Cup**

| | | | |
|---|---|---|---|
| Fourth Qualifying | Halifax T | (h) | 0-0 |
| *Replay* | Halifax T | (a) | 2-0 |
| First Round | Walsall | (h) | 1-1 |
| *Replay* | Walsall | (a) | 3-2 |
| Second Round | Mansfield T | (h) | 3-3 |
| *Replay* | Mansfield T | (a) | 1-2 |

**FA Trophy**

| | | | |
|---|---|---|---|
| First Round | Tamworth | (a) | 1-3 |

# LUTON TOWN

*Ground:* Kenilworth Road Stadium, 1 Maple Road, Luton, Bedfordshire LU4 8AW.   *Tel:* (01582) 411 622.
*Fax:* (01582) 405 070.   *Website:* www.lutontown.co.uk   *Year Formed:* 1885.   *Record Gate:* 30,869 (1959 v Blackpool,
FA Cup 6th rd replay).   *Nickname:* 'The Hatters'.   *Manager:* John Still.   *Colours:* Orange shirts, black shorts, white
socks with orange trim.

## LUTON TOWN – BLUE SQUARE PREMIER 2012–13 LEAGUE RECORD

| Match No. | Date | Venue | Opponents | Result | H/T Score | Lg Pos. | Goalscorers | Attendance |
|---|---|---|---|---|---|---|---|---|
| 1 | Aug 11 | H | Gateshead | D | 2-2 | 0-2 | 11 | Shaw [61], Fleetwood [71] | 6743 |
| 2 | 14 | A | Kidderminster H | W | 2-0 | 2-0 | 4 | Fleetwood 2 [22, 30] | 2275 |
| 3 | 17 | A | Hyde | W | 2-1 | 0-0 | 1 | O'Donnell [69], Fleetwood [78] | 1141 |
| 4 | 25 | H | AFC Telford U | L | 0-1 | 0-1 | 9 | | 5970 |
| 5 | 27 | A | Ebbsfleet U | W | 3-1 | 2-0 | 5 | Fleetwood 2 [10, 73], Rendell [19] | 1701 |
| 6 | Sept 1 | H | Macclesfield T | W | 4-1 | 2-0 | 3 | Howells [1], Gray [17], Rendell [82], Fleetwood [90] | 5803 |
| 7 | 4 | H | Cambridge U | W | 3-2 | 1-1 | 2 | Kovacs [18], Gray [53], Beckwith [61] | 6742 |
| 8 | 8 | A | Alfreton T | L | 0-3 | 0-2 | 6 | | 1392 |
| 9 | 15 | H | Wrexham | D | 0-0 | 0-0 | 6 | | 6675 |
| 10 | 21 | A | Grimsby T | L | 1-4 | 0-3 | 7 | Rendell [76] | 4074 |
| 11 | 25 | A | Tamworth | W | 2-1 | 0-1 | 5 | Kasim [63], Fleetwood [66] | 1137 |
| 12 | 29 | H | Southport | W | 3-1 | 1-1 | 4 | Fleetwood [4], Rendell 2 (1 pen) [47, 51 (p)] | 5696 |
| 13 | Oct 6 | A | Lincoln C | W | 2-1 | 1-0 | 4 | Farman (og) [28], Shaw [48] | 2970 |
| 14 | 9 | H | Braintree T | L | 2-3 | 1-2 | 4 | Ainge [37], Walker [58] | 5523 |
| 15 | 13 | H | Nuneaton T | W | 2-0 | 0-0 | 3 | Lawless 2 [86, 90] | 6148 |
| 16 | 27 | A | Forest Green R | W | 2-1 | 0-0 | 2 | Fleetwood [75], Rendell (pen) [90] | 2112 |
| 17 | Nov 6 | A | Hereford U | L | 0-1 | 0-0 | 3 | | 2108 |
| 18 | 10 | H | Dartford | L | 0-2 | 0-2 | 6 | | 6567 |
| 19 | 18 | A | Mansfield T | D | 2-2 | 1-1 | 6 | Gray 2 [26, 67] | 2619 |
| 20 | Dec 8 | H | Alfreton T | W | 3-0 | 0-0 | 5 | O'Donnell [53], Smith [56], Gray [58] | 5648 |
| 21 | 11 | A | Newport Co | L | 2-5 | 1-3 | 5 | Gray [16], Shaw [61] | 2247 |
| 22 | 26 | H | Woking | W | 3-1 | 2-0 | 4 | Kovacs [15], Shaw [37], Rendell (pen) [82] | 6744 |
| 23 | Jan 1 | A | Woking | L | 1-3 | 1-1 | 5 | Gray [8] | 2961 |
| 24 | 8 | H | Barrow | W | 6-1 | 3-0 | 5 | Neilson [2], Kovacs [27], Shaw 3 [29, 59, 64], Gray [72] | 5165 |
| 25 | 15 | A | AFC Telford U | D | 0-0 | 0-0 | 6 | | 1606 |
| 26 | Feb 2 | A | Barrow | L | 0-1 | 0-1 | 7 | | 1188 |
| 27 | 9 | H | Forest Green R | D | 1-1 | 1-1 | 7 | Gray [5] | 6374 |
| 28 | 12 | A | Dartford | L | 0-1 | 0-0 | 7 | | 1802 |
| 29 | 19 | A | Macclesfield T | D | 1-1 | 1-0 | 8 | Gray [15] | 1984 |
| 30 | 23 | H | Mansfield T | L | 2-3 | 1-2 | 8 | Rendell [37], Gray [47] | 5968 |
| 31 | 26 | A | Braintree T | L | 0-2 | 0-1 | 10 | | 1003 |
| 32 | Mar 2 | A | Stockport Co | W | 1-0 | 1-0 | 8 | Howells [45] | 4074 |
| 33 | 5 | A | Nuneaton T | D | 0-0 | 0-0 | 7 | | 1173 |
| 34 | 9 | H | Hereford U | D | 1-1 | 0-1 | 8 | Martin [87] | 6001 |
| 35 | 12 | H | Hyde | L | 1-2 | 1-1 | 8 | Howells [37] | 4847 |
| 36 | 16 | A | Wrexham | D | 0-0 | 0-0 | 11 | | 3907 |
| 37 | 19 | H | Stockport Co | W | 1-0 | 1-0 | 8 | McNulty [44] | 5106 |
| 38 | 23 | H | Tamworth | D | 0-0 | 0-0 | 8 | | 5501 |
| 39 | 30 | A | Cambridge U | D | 2-2 | 0-1 | 9 | Shaw [53], Taiwo (pen) [65] | 3217 |
| 40 | Apr 1 | H | Kidderminster H | L | 1-2 | 0-2 | 9 | Gray [83] | 6108 |
| 41 | 6 | A | Gateshead | L | 1-5 | 1-3 | 9 | Walker [35] | 382 |
| 42 | 9 | H | Lincoln C | W | 3-0 | 2-0 | 9 | Martin 2 [41, 72], Gray [43] | 5393 |
| 43 | 12 | H | Grimsby T | D | 1-1 | 0-0 | 8 | Lawless [76] | 5662 |
| 44 | 16 | H | Newport Co | D | 2-2 | 1-0 | 11 | Gray 2 [12, 79] | 5125 |
| 45 | 18 | H | Ebbsfleet U | W | 2-0 | 1-0 | 9 | Wall 2 [4, 77] | 5934 |
| 46 | 20 | A | Southport | W | 3-1 | 2-1 | 7 | Robinson, M [30], Gray 2 [34, 82] | 1406 |

**Final League Position: 7**

## GOALSCORERS

*League (70):* Gray 17, Fleetwood 10, Rendell 8 (3 pens), Shaw 8, Howells 3, Kovacs 3, Lawless 3, Martin 3, O'Donnell 2,
Walker 2, Wall 2, Ainge 1, Beckwith 1, Kasim 1, McNulty 1, Neilson 1, Robinson, M 1, Smith 1, Taiwo 1 (1 pen),
own goal 1.
*FA Cup (9):* Rendell 4 (1 pen), Gray 2, Lawless 2, Shaw 1.
*FA Trophy (9):* Walker 2, Ainge 1, Fleetwood 1, Gray 1, O'Donnell 1, Shaw 1, Watkins 1, own goal 1.

| Tyler 39 | Rowe-Turner 32 + 5 | Taylor 13 + 4 | Kovacs 19 + 1 | Henry 33 | O'Donnell 20 + 8 | Kasim 5 + 6 | Howells 34 + 7 | Rendell 28 + 8 | Fleetwood 19 + 11 | Gray 39 + 5 | Shaw 26 + 5 | Lawless 35 + 2 | Watkins 2 + 3 | Robinson M 6 + 4 | Beckwith 8 | Woolley — + 4 | Essam 5 + 4 | Robinson J 3 + 4 | Walker 2 + 10 | Ainge 19 + 3 | Brill 7 | Mendy 16 + 2 | Smith 26 + 2 | Neilson 6 + 2 | McNulty 20 | Martin 14 + 2 | Thomas 2 | Goodman 11 | Wall 5 + 7 | Taiwo 8 + 1 | Griffiths 4 + 2 | Match No. |
|---|---|---|---|---|---|---|---|---|---|---|---|---|---|---|---|---|---|---|---|---|---|---|---|---|---|---|---|---|---|---|---|---|
| 1 | 2 | 3² | 4 | 5 | 6 | 7¹ | 8 | 9 | 10 | 11³ | 12 | 13 | 14 | | | | | | | | | | | | | | | | | | | 1 |
| 1 | 5 | 2 | 3 | 4 | 6 | 7 | | 9 | 10¹ | 12 | 11² | 8 | 13 | | | | | | | | | | | | | | | | | | | 2 |
| 1 | 3 | 5¹ | 4 | 2 | 8 | 6² | 12 | 9 | 11³ | 13 | 10 | 7 | | 14 | | | | | | | | | | | | | | | | | | 3 |
| 1 | 5 | 12 | | 4⁸ | 8 | 7¹ | 3 | 9 | 10 | 13 | 11 | 2 | 6² | | | | | | | | | | | | | | | | | | | 4 |
| 1 | 4 | 5 | | | 6² | | 8 | 7 | 11 | 9¹ | 10 | 2 | 13 | | | | 3 | 12 | | | | | | | | | | | | | | 5 |
| 1 | 2¹ | 5 | 4³ | | 9 | | 8 | 7 | 10 | 11² | | 6 | 12 | | | | 3 | 13 | 14 | | | | | | | | | | | | | 6 |
| 1 | 2 | 5 | 3 | | 6 | | 8 | 10¹ | 11² | 9 | | 7 | | | | | 4 | 13 | 12 | | | | | | | | | | | | | 7 |
| 1 | | 2² | 4¹ | 5 | 8 | 13 | 9 | | 14 | 11 | | 6 | 7³ | | | | 3 | | 12 | 10 | | | | | | | | | | | | 8 |
| 1 | 12 | | 4 | 2 | 8 | 14 | 5¹ | 7 | 10² | 11³ | 9 | 6 | | | | | 3 | | | 13 | | | | | | | | | | | | 9 |
| 1 | | | 4¹ | 5² | 7 | 13 | 2 | 8 | 11³ | 9 | 10 | 6 | | | | | 3 | 12 | 14 | | | | | | | | | | | | | 10 |
| 1 | 5¹ | | | 2³ | 7 | 13 | 8 | 9 | 14 | 11 | 10² | 6 | | | | | 3 | 4 | 12 | | | | | | | | | | | | | 11 |
| 1 | 12 | | | 2 | 8 | 7¹ | 5 | 10³ | 9² | 11 | 13 | 6 | | | | | 3 | 14 | | 4 | | | | | | | | | | | | 12 |
| 1 | 12 | | | 2 | 7 | 14 | 5 | 10¹ | 11 | 9³ | 13 | 8 | | | | | | 4 | 6² | 3 | | | | | | | | | | | | 13 |
| 1 | | | | 2 | 8 | 12 | 3 | | 11⁸ | 6 | 10 | 7 | | | | | | 4² | 9¹ | 13 | 5 | | | | | | | | | | | 14 |
| 1 | 5 | | 13 | 2 | 7 | | 9 | 8 | | 11² | 10 | 6 | | | | | | 4¹ | | 12 | 3 | | | | | | | | | | | 15 |
| | 2 | | 3 | 5 | 12 | | 8 | 9 | 11¹ | 6 | 10 | | | | | | | | | 4 | 1 | 7 | | | | | | | | | | 16 |
| | 5³ | | 3¹ | 2 | 14 | | 8 | 10 | 11 | 9² | | 13 | | | | | | | 12 | 4 | 1 | 7 | 6 | | | | | | | | | 17 |
| | | | 3 | 7 | | | 5 | 10 | 11 | 9 | | 2 | | | | | | | 12 | 4 | 1 | 6¹ | 8 | | | | | | | | | 18 |
| 1 | 5 | | 3 | 2 | | | 9 | 11 | 12 | 10¹ | | 6 | | | | | | | | 4 | | 7 | 8 | | | | | | | | | 19 |
| 1 | 4 | | 3 | 2 | 9³ | | 8 | 10 | 12 | 11¹ | 13 | 6 | | | | | | | 14 | 5 | | | 7 | | | | | | | | | 20 |
| 1 | 2 | | 4 | 9² | | | 6 | 10 | 13 | 11 | 12 | 7 | | | 3 | | | | | 5 | | 8¹ | | | | | | | | | | 21 |
| 1 | | | 3 | 2 | 12 | | 5 | 10 | 8¹ | 11² | 9 | 6 | 13 | | | | | | | 4 | | 7 | | | | | | | | | | 22 |
| 1 | 14 | | 3 | 2 | | | 5³ | 11 | 12 | 8 | 10² | 6 | | | | | | | | 4 | | 7¹ | 13 | 9 | | | | | | | | 23 |
| 1 | 5 | 3 | 4 | 2 | | | 12 | 13 | 14 | 10³ | 11² | 6 | | | | | | | | | | 8 | 9¹ | 7 | | | | | | | | 24 |
| 1 | 3 | 5 | 4 | 2 | | | 12 | | 13 | 11² | 10 | 6 | | | | | | | | | | 7 | 8 | 9¹ | | | | | | | | 25 |
| 1 | 3⁸ | 5³ | | 2 | | | 14 | 13 | | 11 | 10² | 6 | | | | | | | | | | 7¹ | 8 | 12 | 4 | 9 | | | | | | 26 |
| 1 | | | 5 | 2 | 13 | | 3 | | 14 | 11³ | 10 | 7⁸ | | | | | | | | | | 12 | 8 | 6¹ | 4 | 9² | | | | | | 27 |
| 1 | | 14 | 3 | 2 | 13 | | 5 | 12 | | 11 | 10¹ | | | | | | | | | | | 8³ | 7 | 6 | 4 | 9² | | | | | | 28 |
| 1 | 4 | 5³ | | 2 | 12 | | 9 | 10¹ | 14 | 6 | 11 | 8 | | | | | | | | | | 13 | 7² | | 3 | | | | | | | 29 |
| 1 | 3 | | | 2 | | | 13 | 11 | 12 | 10 | 8 | | | | | | | | | | | 9 | 6² | 4 | 7¹ | 5 | | | | | | 30 |
| 1 | 5¹ | 12 | | 2 | | | 9² | 10 | 11 | | 6 | | | | | | | | 14 | | | 7³ | 8 | 13 | 3 | 4⁸ | | | | | | 31 |
| 1 | 4 | 12 | 6¹ | 2 | | | 5 | 13 | 10² | 11³ | 7 | | | | | | | | 14 | | | 8 | 9 | | 3 | | | | | | | 32 |
| 1 | 4 | | | 2 | 12 | | 9 | 13 | 10³ | 11² | 6 | | | | | | | | | | | 7¹ | 8 | 3 | | | | | | 5 | 14 | 33 |
| 1 | | 3³ | | 2 | 14 | | 9 | 10¹ | | 11 | 6 | | | | | | | | | | | 7² | 8 | | 4 | 13 | | | | 5 | 12 | 34 |
| 1 | 14 | 5³ | | 2 | 8 | | 9 | | | 11² | | 6¹ | | | | | | | 12 | | | 7 | | | 3 | 13 | | | 4 | 10 | | 35 |
| 1 | 9 | | | | | | 5 | 10¹ | | | | | | | | | | | 13 | 2 | | 7 | 6 | | 3 | 8 | | 4 | 11² | 12 | | 36 |
| 1 | 5 | | | | | | 6 | | | 11¹ | 10 | | | | | | | | 12 | 2 | | 7 | | | 3 | 9 | | 4 | | 8 | | 37 |
| 1 | 5 | | | | | | 6 | 13 | | 12 | 10² | | | | | | | | 2 | | | 7 | | | 3 | 9 | | 4 | 11¹ | 8 | | 38 |
| 1 | 5 | | | | | | 9 | | | 11 | 10 | | | | | | | | 2 | | | 7 | | | 3 | 6¹ | | 4 | 12 | 8 | | 39 |
| 1 | 5 | | | | | | 6 | 11³ | | 14 | 10 | | 7 | | | | | | 2 | | | 13 | | | 3¹ | 9² | | 4 | | 8 | 12 | 40 |
| | 5 | | | | | | | 13 | | 11 | | | 12 | | | | | 6 | 2 | 1 | | 7 | | | 3 | 9 | | 4 | 10² | 8¹ | | 41 |
| | | | 2 | | | | | 12 | | 11³ | 10² | | 6¹ | 8 | | | | | 14 | 4 | 1 | | 7 | | | 3 | 9 | | 13 | 5 | | 42 |
| | 5 | | | | | | | | | 6 | 11¹ | | 2 | 9 | | | | | | 1 | | 8 | | | 4 | 10 | | 12 | 7 | 3 | | 43 |
| | 3 | | | | | | | 12 | | 11 | 10² | 9¹ | 6 | | | | | | | 1 | | 2 | | | 4 | 8 | | 13 | 7 | 5 | | 44 |
| 1 | 3 | | | | | 7 | | 10² | 8 | | | | 9³ | 13 | | | | | 6 | 14 | | 2 | | | 4¹ | | | 5 | 11 | 12 | | 45 |
| 1 | 4¹ | | | | | | | 13 | | 9 | 10 | 7 | 6 | | | | | | 12 | | | 2 | | | 11² | | 3 | 14 | 8⁸ | 5 | | 46 |

**FA Cup**

| | | | |
|---|---|---|---|
| Fourth Qualifying | Cambridge U | (a) | 2-0 |
| First Round | Nuneaton T | (h) | 1-1 |
| Replay | Nuneaton T | (a) | 2-0 |
| Second Round | Dorchester T | (h) | 2-1 |
| Third Round | Wolverhampton W | (h) | 1-0 |
| Fourth Round | Norwich C | (a) | 1-0 |
| Fifth Round | Millwall | (h) | 0-3 |

**FA Trophy**

| | | | |
|---|---|---|---|
| First Round | Dorchester T | (a) | 2-2 |
| Replay | Dorchester T | (h) | 3-1 |
| Second Round | Skelmersdale U | (h) | 2-0 |
| Third Round | Matlock T | (a) | 2-1 |
| Quarter-Finals | Grimsby T | (a) | 0-3 |

# MACCLESFIELD TOWN

*Ground:* Moss Rose Stadium, London Road, Macclesfield, Cheshire SK11 7SP.   *Tel:* (01625) 264 686.
*Fax:* (01625) 264 692.   *Website:* www.mtfc.co.uk   *Year Formed:* 1874.   *Record Gate:* 9,008 (1948 v Winsford U,
Cheshire Senior Cup 2nd rd).   *Nickname:* 'The Silkmen'.   *Manager:* John Askey.   *Colours:* Blue shirts with white
trim, white shorts, blue socks.

## MACCLESFIELD TOWN – BLUE SQUARE PREMIER 2012–13 LEAGUE RECORD

| Match No. | Date | Venue | Opponents | Result | H/T Score | Lg Pos. | Goalscorers | Attendance |
|---|---|---|---|---|---|---|---|---|
| 1 | Aug 10 | A | Hereford U | L | 1-2 | 0-1 | 24 | Barnes-Homer (pen) [59] | 2139 |
| 2 | 14 | H | Wrexham | W | 2-0 | 1-0 | 10 | Fairhurst [10], Mendy [76] | 2368 |
| 3 | 18 | H | Dartford | W | 2-0 | 1-0 | 6 | Champion (og) [34], Henry (pen) [89] | 1420 |
| 4 | 25 | A | Lincoln C | W | 3-2 | 1-1 | 4 | Fairhurst [12], Barnes-Homer [77], Holroyd [87] | 2009 |
| 5 | 27 | H | Barrow | W | 2-0 | 1-0 | 2 | Barnes-Homer 2 [16, 90] | 1711 |
| 6 | Sept 1 | A | Luton T | L | 1-4 | 0-2 | 5 | Brown, N [51] | 5803 |
| 7 | 4 | A | Stockport Co | W | 4-3 | 2-2 | 5 | Holroyd 3 [27, 35, 51], Tunnicliffe (og) [82] | 4208 |
| 8 | 8 | H | Braintree T | W | 2-1 | 1-1 | 2 | Kissock [26], Barnes-Homer (pen) [85] | 1509 |
| 9 | 15 | A | Nuneaton T | D | 3-3 | 0-2 | 2 | Murtagh [70], Mendy [90], Barnes-Homer [90] | 939 |
| 10 | 22 | H | Forest Green R | L | 1-2 | 0-1 | 4 | Barnes-Homer [64] | 1729 |
| 11 | 29 | A | Kidderminster H | L | 0-3 | 0-1 | 8 | | 1654 |
| 12 | Oct 6 | H | Alfreton T | L | 1-2 | 1-1 | 9 | Barnes-Homer (pen) [26] | 1437 |
| 13 | 9 | A | Gateshead | D | 2-2 | 0-1 | 10 | Barnes-Homer [71], Holroyd [84] | 557 |
| 14 | 13 | H | Newport Co | D | 1-1 | 0-1 | 11 | Barnes-Homer [81] | 1544 |
| 15 | 27 | A | Grimsby T | W | 1-0 | 0-0 | 7 | Barnes-Homer (pen) [83] | 3014 |
| 16 | Nov 6 | H | Tamworth | W | 2-0 | 1-0 | 7 | Morgan-Smith [14], Jackson [79] | 1089 |
| 17 | 10 | A | Cambridge U | L | 0-2 | 0-0 | 7 | | 1821 |
| 18 | 17 | H | Ebbsfleet U | L | 1-2 | 1-0 | 8 | Holroyd [45] | 1896 |
| 19 | 20 | H | Mansfield T | L | 0-3 | 0-1 | 9 | | 1272 |
| 20 | Dec 4 | H | Hyde | W | 3-2 | 0-2 | 7 | Barnes-Homer [56], Brown, N [82], Holroyd [90] | 1124 |
| 21 | 8 | A | Forest Green R | D | 1-1 | 1-0 | 9 | Fairhurst [24] | 901 |
| 22 | 15 | H | Nuneaton T | D | 0-0 | 0-0 | 9 | | 1280 |
| 23 | 26 | A | Southport | L | 2-3 | 0-2 | 9 | Mackreth [55], Barnes-Homer [70] | 1173 |
| 24 | Jan 1 | H | Southport | D | 2-2 | 0-2 | 10 | Barnes-Homer 2 [80, 84] | 1481 |
| 25 | 8 | A | Braintree T | W | 3-0 | 1-0 | 9 | Morgan-Smith [32], Fairhurst 2 [67, 80] | 502 |
| 26 | 15 | A | Dartford | L | 0-2 | 0-1 | 10 | | 821 |
| 27 | 19 | H | Kidderminster H | W | 1-0 | 0-0 | 9 | Fairhurst [56] | 1342 |
| 28 | Feb 2 | A | Ebbsfleet U | W | 4-0 | 1-0 | 7 | Murtagh [2], Fairhurst [58], Mackreth 2 [62, 89] | 799 |
| 29 | 9 | A | Hyde | D | 1-1 | 1-0 | 8 | Fairhurst [22] | 1184 |
| 30 | 12 | A | Tamworth | D | 0-0 | 0-0 | 8 | | 670 |
| 31 | 16 | A | Alfreton T | W | 2-1 | 1-1 | 7 | Audel [31], Fairhurst [58] | 740 |
| 32 | 19 | H | Luton T | D | 1-1 | 0-1 | 7 | Fairhurst [76] | 1984 |
| 33 | 22 | H | Gateshead | L | 0-4 | 0-4 | 7 | | 1467 |
| 34 | Mar 6 | H | Lincoln C | W | 2-1 | 0-1 | 7 | Garner (og) [47], Barnes-Homer [55] | 1557 |
| 35 | 9 | A | AFC Telford U | W | 2-0 | 1-0 | 7 | Morgan-Smith 2 [30, 54] | 1567 |
| 36 | 12 | H | Woking | D | 0-0 | 0-0 | 7 | | 1350 |
| 37 | 19 | H | AFC Telford U | W | 2-1 | 1-1 | 7 | Fairhurst [3], Barnes-Homer [90] | 1381 |
| 38 | 27 | A | Barrow | L | 0-1 | 0-0 | 7 | | 716 |
| 39 | 30 | H | Stockport Co | D | 1-1 | 0-0 | 7 | Barnes-Homer [63] | 4027 |
| 40 | Apr 1 | A | Wrexham | D | 0-0 | 0-0 | 8 | | 4351 |
| 41 | 3 | H | Grimsby T | L | 1-3 | 1-2 | 8 | Mills, P [26] | 1776 |
| 42 | 6 | H | Hereford U | L | 0-1 | 0-1 | 8 | | 1687 |
| 43 | 9 | A | Mansfield T | L | 1-3 | 0-2 | 8 | Mills, P [89] | 3694 |
| 44 | 11 | A | Newport Co | L | 1-4 | 1-3 | 9 | Burgess [3] | 1606 |
| 45 | 13 | A | Woking | L | 4-5 | 0-5 | 12 | Fairhurst 2 [60, 83], Madjo [71], Gnahoua [90] | 1543 |
| 46 | 20 | H | Cambridge U | W | 2-1 | 2-1 | 11 | Mills, P [39], Madjo [45] | 1987 |

**Final League Position: 11**

## GOALSCORERS

*League (65):* Barnes-Homer 18 (4 pens), Fairhurst 13, Holroyd 7, Morgan-Smith 4, Mackreth 3, Mills, P 3, Brown, N 2,
Madjo 2, Mendy 2, Murtagh 2, Audel 1, Burgess 1, Gnahoua 1, Henry 1 (1 pen), Jackson 1, Kissock 1, own goals 3.
*FA Cup (12):* Barnes-Homer 5 (1 pen), Holroyd 2, Diagne 1, Charnock 1, Kissock 1, Morgan-Smith 1, own goal 1.
*FA Trophy (0).*

| Cronin 28 | Jackson 36 | Charnock 13 | Brown N 22 | Braham-Barrett 40 | Henry 11 + 4 | Mendy 12 + 2 | Murtagh 39 | Winn 17 + 13 | Barnes-Homer 34 + 3 | Wedgbury 37 + 1 | Edmans — + 3 | Brown S — + 1 | Kissock 37 + 3 | Fairhurst 28 + 12 | Mackreth 18 + 17 | Diagne 7 + 9 | Holroyd 13 + 6 | Martin 13 + 1 | Morgan-Smith 14 + 10 | McNamee 3 + 1 | Mills P 28 + 2 | Mills Andy — + 1 | Payne — + 1 | Audel 19 | Taylor 18 | McDonald 3 + 7 | Kasim 5 | Evans 1 + 1 | Gorman — + 1 | Da Costa — + 1 | Madjo 5 + 3 | Fermino 4 | Gnahoua — + 3 | Burgess 1 | Match No. |
|---|---|---|---|---|---|---|---|---|---|---|---|---|---|---|---|---|---|---|---|---|---|---|---|---|---|---|---|---|---|---|---|---|---|---|---|
| 1 | 2 | 3 | 4 | 5 | 6 | 7 | 8¹ | 9 | 10 | 11² | 12 | 13 | | | | | | | | | | | | | | | | | | | | | | | 1 |
| 1 | 2 | 4 | 3 | 5 | 6¹ | 13 | 8 | 10³ | 7 | 14 | | | 9 | 11² | 12 | | | | | | | | | | | | | | | | | | | | 2 |
| 1 | 2 | 4 | 3 | 5 | 6 | 13 | 8 | 10³ | 7 | 14 | | | 9¹ | 11² | 12 | | | | | | | | | | | | | | | | | | | | 3 |
| 1 | 2¹ | 4 | 3 | 5 | 6 | 8 | 7 | 13 | 10 | 9² | | | 11³ | 12 | 14 | | | | | | | | | | | | | | | | | | | | 4 |
| 1 | | 4 | 3 | 5 | 13 | 8 | 7 | 14 | 11 | 2 | | | 6¹ | 9² | 12 | 10³ | | | | | | | | | | | | | | | | | | | 5 |
| 1 | | 4 | 3 | 5 | 7¹ | 8 | 9 | 10 | 13 | 6 | | | 14 | 11² | 2³ | 12 | | | | | | | | | | | | | | | | | | | 6 |
| 1 | 4 | 3 | 2 | 8¹ | 7 | 5 | 10 | 9 | 6² | | | | 12 | 13 | 14 | | | | | | | | | | | | | | | | | | | | 7 |
| 1 | 2 | 4 | 3 | 5 | 6¹ | 8 | 14 | 10 | 9³ | 13 | | | 11² | 12 | 7 | | | | | | | | | | | | | | | | | | | | 8 |
| 1 | 2 | 3 | | 8 | | 7 | 10 | | 6² | | | | 12 | 11 | 13 | 9¹ | 4 | | | | | | | | | | | | | | | | | | 9 |
| 1 | 2 | 3 | | 5 | | 8 | 7 | 10 | 9⁸ | 11² | 12 | | 4 | 13 | | 6¹ | | | | | | | | | | | | | | | | | | | 10 |
| 1 | 2 | 4 | | 5 | 6¹ | 8 | 7 | 9² | 11 | 10 | | | 13 | 12 | 3 | | | | | | | | | | | | | | | | | | | | 11 |
| 1 | 2 | 3 | | 5 | 8² | 7 | 10 | 13 | 12 | 14 | | | 6³ | 11 | 9¹ | 4 | | | | | | | | | | | | | | | | | | | 12 |
| 1 | 2 | 3 | 4 | 8 | 7 | 10 | 6² | 9³ | 14 | 13 | | | 12 | 5 | 11¹ | | | | | | | | | | | | | | | | | | | | 13 |
| 1 | 2 | 3 | | 5 | 6 | 9 | 10 | 7 | 8² | 13 | | | 11¹ | 4 | | 12 | | | | | | | | | | | | | | | | | | | 14 |
| 1 | 2¹ | | | 12 | | 7 | 9 | 10 | 8 | 6² | | | 13 | 14 | 5 | 3 | 11³ | 4 | | | | | | | | | | | | | | | | | 15 |
| 1 | 2 | | | 5 | | 7 | 12 | 10 | 8 | 9² | | | 6¹ | 4 | 3 | 11 | 13 | | | | | | | | | | | | | | | | | | 16 |
| 1 | 2 | | | 5 | | 8 | 10 | 7 | 9 | 13 | | | 6² | 3 | 12 | 4 | 11¹ | | | | | | | | | | | | | | | | | | 17 |
| 1 | 2 | | | 5 | 9³ | 7 | 12 | 8 | 6 | 10¹ | | | 13 | 4 | 11² | 3 | 14 | | | | | | | | | | | | | | | | | | 18 |
| 1 | 2 | 4 | | 5 | 6¹ | 8 | 10² | 7 | 9 | | | | 12 | 11 | 3 | 13 | | | | | | | | | | | | | | | | | | | 19 |
| 1 | 2 | 4 | 3 | 5 | 14 | 7 | 6² | 10 | 8 | 9¹ | | | 13 | 12 | | | | | | | | | | | | | | | | | | | | | 20 |
| 1 | | 4 | 3 | 5¹ | | 8 | 12 | 10² | 6 | 11³ | | | 14 | 9 | 2 | 13 | 7 | | | | | | | | | | | | | | | | | | 21 |
| 1 | | 3 | 4 | 5 | 6 | | 10 | 8 | 13 | 9¹ | | | 12 | 11 | 2 | 7² | | | | | | | | | | | | | | | | | | | 22 |
| 1 | | 3 | 5 | 13 | | 7 | 12 | 9² | 10¹ | 6 | | | 4 | 14 | 2 | 11³ | 8 | | | | | | | | | | | | | | | | | | 23 |
| 1 | 2⁸ | 3 | | 5 | | 7 | 14 | 10³ | 8 | 9² | | | 13 | 6¹ | 11 | 4 | 12 | | | | | | | | | | | | | | | | | | 24 |
| 1 | | 4 | 2 | 9 | | 7 | 5 | | 8 | 11 | | | 6 | | 10 | 3 | | | | | | | | | | | | | | | | | | | 25 |
| 1 | | 3 | 2 | 8¹ | | 7 | 9 | | 4 | 11 | | | 6 | 12 | 10² | 5 | 13 | | | | | | | | | | | | | | | | | | 26 |
| 1 | | 4 | | 5 | | 8 | 12 | 11 | 7 | 9¹ | | | 10 | 6² | 13 | | | | 3⁸ | 2 | | | | | | | | | | | | | | | 27 |
| | 2 | 3¹ | | 5 | | | 11 | | | | | | 8 | 9 | 10² | | | | 6 | | 12 | | | 1 | 4 | 13 | | | | | | | | | 28 |
| | 2 | | | 5 | | | 10 | | | | | | 7 | 9 | 11¹ | | | | 6 | | 3 | | | 1 | 4 | 12 | 8 | | | | | | | | 29 |
| | 2 | | | 5 | | | 11 | | | | | | 7 | 9³ | 10² | | | | 6¹ | | 4 | | 3 | 1 | 13 | 8 | 12 | 14 | | | | | | | 30 |
| | 2 | | | | | | 8 | 13 | 12 | | | | 6 | 9¹ | 10⁸ | | | | 14 | | | | 3 | 1 | 4 | 11² | 7 | | | | | | | | 31 |
| | 2 | | | 5 | | | 8² | 12 | 10 | | | | 6 | 9 | 11 | | | | 13 | | | | 3 | 1⁸ | 4 | 7¹ | | | | | | | | | 32 |
| 1 | 2 | | | 5 | | | 12 | 10² | 7 | | | | 9¹ | 11 | 14 | | | | 4 | | | | 3 | | | 13 | | | | | 8³ | 6 | | | 33 |
| | 2 | | | 5 | | | 7 | 12 | 10 | 6 | | | 8² | 9³ | 13 | | | | 11¹ | | | | 3 | 1 | 4 | | | | 14 | | | | | | 34 |
| | 2 | | | 5 | | | 7 | 13 | 10 | 6 | | | 8² | 9¹ | 14 | | | | 11³ | | | | 3 | 1 | 4 | | 12 | | | | | | | | 35 |
| | 2¹ | | | 5 | | | 7 | 12 | 10 | 6 | | | 8³ | 11² | 13 | | | | 9 | | | | 3 | 1 | 4 | | 14 | | | | | | | | 36 |
| | 2 | | | 5 | | | 7³ | 5 | 11 | 8 | | | 12 | 6¹ | 13 | | | | 9 | | | | 3 | 1 | 4 | 10² | | | | | 14 | | | | 37 |
| | 2 | | | 5 | | | 7 | | 6 | | | | 8 | 9 | 13 | | | | 12 | | | | 3 | 1 | 4 | 10² | 11¹ | | | | | | | | 38 |
| | 2 | | | 5 | | | 7 | 10 | 8 | | | | 9 | 12 | 6 | | | | 11¹ | | | | 3 | 1 | 4 | 3 | 1 | | | | | | | | 39 |
| | 2 | 3 | | 5 | | | 6¹ | 10 | 9 | 8 | | | 7 | 12 | | | | | 11 | | | | | 1 | 4 | 5 | 1 | | | | 8 | | | | 40 |
| | 2 | | | 5 | | | 9 | 8 | 7 | | | | 11 | 10¹ | | | | | 4 | | | | 3 | 1 | | 12 | | | | | 13 | 6² | | | 41 |
| | 2 | | | 5 | | | 9 | 8 | 7² | 10 | | | 12 | | | | | | 4 | | | | 3 | 1 | | | | | | 11 | 6¹ | 13 | | 42 |
| | 5 | | | 2 | | | 8 | 6¹ | 7 | | | | 10 | 11 | 9 | | | | 4 | | | | 3 | 1 | | | | | | 12 | | | | 43 |
| | 2 | | | | | | 7 | 10 | 8 | | | | 6 | 12 | 13 | | | | | | | | 3 | 1 | 4 | | | | | 11² | 9 | | 5¹ | 44 |
| | 2 | | | 5 | | | 7 | 5 | 8¹ | | | | 9 | 10 | 6 | | | | | | | | 3 | 1 | 4 | | | | | 11 | 12 | | | 45 |
| | 2 | | | 5 | | | 7 | 5 | 8 | | | | 9 | 10 | 6¹ | | | | | | | | 3 | 1 | 4 | | | | | 11 | 12 | | | 46 |

**FA Cup**

| | | | |
|---|---|---|---|
| Fourth Qualifying | Marine | (h) | 3-1 |
| First Round | Swindon T | (a) | 2-0 |
| Second Round | Barrow | (a) | 1-1 |
| *Replay* | Barrow | (h) | 4-1 |
| Third Round | Cardiff C | (h) | 2-1 |
| Fourth Round | Wigan Ath | (h) | 0-1 |

**FA Trophy**

| | | | |
|---|---|---|---|
| First Round | Gateshead | (a) | 0-2 |

# MANSFIELD TOWN

*Ground:* One Call Stadium, Quarry Lane, Mansfield, Nottinghamshire NG18 5DA.   *Tel:* (01623) 482 482.
*Fax:* (01623) 482 495. *Website:* www.mansfieldtown.net   *Year Formed:* 1897.   *Record Gate:* 24,467 (1953 v Nottingham F,
FA Cup 3rd rd). *Nickname:* 'The Stags'.   *Manager:* Paul Cox.   *Secretary:* Keith Burnand.   *Colours:* Yellow and blue
striped shirts, blue shorts, yellow socks with blue trim.

## MANSFIELD TOWN – BLUE SQUARE PREMIER 2012–13 LEAGUE RECORD

| Match No. | Date | Venue | Opponents | Result | H/T Score | Lg Pos. | Goalscorers | Attendance |
|---|---|---|---|---|---|---|---|---|
| 1 | Aug 11 | H | Newport Co | L | 3-4 | 0-2 | 19 | Speight 2 [48, 89], Green [50] | 2924 |
| 2 | 14 | A | Gateshead | L | 1-4 | 1-1 | 23 | Jones [18] | 801 |
| 3 | 18 | A | Kidderminster H | W | 3-2 | 1-1 | 16 | Green [45], Meikle 2 [60, 79] | 1770 |
| 4 | 25 | H | Hyde | W | 1-0 | 1-0 | 12 | Green [7] | 2203 |
| 5 | 27 | A | Grimsby T | L | 1-4 | 0-2 | 15 | Rhead [86] | 3397 |
| 6 | Sept 1 | H | Woking | W | 3-1 | 2-0 | 14 | Briscoe [10], Rhead [45], Speight [90] | 2061 |
| 7 | 4 | H | Tamworth | W | 2-0 | 1-0 | 9 | Green (pen) [45], Jones [62] | 2105 |
| 8 | 8 | A | Ebbsfleet U | L | 1-3 | 1-0 | 11 | Briscoe (pen) [42] | 828 |
| 9 | 15 | H | Braintree T | W | 2-0 | 1-0 | 8 | Stevenson [42], Speight [86] | 2049 |
| 10 | 22 | A | AFC Telford U | D | 2-2 | 2-2 | 10 | Beevers [12], Speight (pen) [39] | 1736 |
| 11 | 29 | H | Hereford U | D | 1-1 | 1-1 | 10 | Geohaghon [45] | 2248 |
| 12 | Oct 6 | A | Cambridge U | L | 1-4 | 0-1 | 13 | Speight [71] | 2545 |
| 13 | 9 | H | Lincoln C | D | 0-0 | 0-0 | 13 | | 2325 |
| 14 | 13 | H | Forest Green R | W | 1-0 | 0-0 | 11 | Rhead [89] | 2019 |
| 15 | 26 | A | Dartford | L | 0-2 | 0-2 | 11 | | 1737 |
| 16 | Nov 6 | A | Nuneaton T | D | 1-1 | 0-0 | 14 | Wright [60] | 838 |
| 17 | 10 | A | Southport | W | 1-0 | 1-0 | 10 | Hutchinson [2] | 1918 |
| 18 | 18 | H | Luton T | D | 2-2 | 1-1 | 11 | Hutchinson [8], Green [85] | 2619 |
| 19 | 20 | A | Macclesfield T | W | 3-0 | 1-0 | 7 | Green [40], Meikle [66], Jones [88] | 1272 |
| 20 | Dec 8 | H | Ebbsfleet U | W | 4-1 | 2-1 | 8 | Hutchinson [15], Stone (og) [37], Howell [70], Green (pen) [78] | 1845 |
| 21 | 26 | H | Alfreton T | L | 1-2 | 1-1 | 8 | Dempster [35] | 4186 |
| 22 | Jan 1 | A | Alfreton T | W | 3-0 | 1-0 | 9 | Geohaghon [43], Daniel [57], Dempster [72] | 1537 |
| 23 | 12 | H | Kidderminster H | L | 0-2 | 0-2 | 10 | | 2405 |
| 24 | 15 | A | Stockport Co | W | 3-1 | 3-0 | 9 | Daniel [38], Stevenson [40], Green (pen) [45] | 2647 |
| 25 | 19 | A | Southport | W | 2-1 | 1-1 | 8 | Murray [19], Stevenson [54] | 804 |
| 26 | Feb 2 | H | Dartford | W | 5-0 | 1-0 | 6 | Murray [5], Howell [54], Jones [66], Green [79], Stevenson (pen) [85] | 2598 |
| 27 | 9 | H | Barrow | W | 8-1 | 5-1 | 6 | Stevenson 2 [8, 68], Green 3 (2 pens) [23 (p), 32, 52 (p)], Daniel [30], Murray [43], Howell [70] | 2226 |
| 28 | 12 | A | Newport Co | L | 0-2 | 0-0 | 6 | | 1902 |
| 29 | 16 | A | Cambridge U | W | 3-1 | 2-1 | 6 | Stevenson [11], Jones [39], Daniel [71] | 2508 |
| 30 | 19 | A | Hyde | W | 1-0 | 0-0 | 6 | Briscoe [46] | 675 |
| 31 | 23 | A | Luton T | W | 3-2 | 2-1 | 6 | Green (pen) [32], Daniel [44], Meikle [90] | 5968 |
| 32 | 26 | A | Lincoln C | W | 1-0 | 0-0 | 4 | Green [90] | 2734 |
| 33 | Mar 2 | H | AFC Telford U | W | 1-0 | 0-0 | 3 | Green [49] | 2725 |
| 34 | 6 | A | Woking | W | 2-1 | 1-0 | 3 | Briscoe [33], Jones [77] | 1179 |
| 35 | 9 | H | Stockport Co | W | 4-1 | 2-0 | 3 | Chapman 3 [13, 20, 77], Green [57] | 2628 |
| 36 | 12 | H | Grimsby T | W | 2-0 | 0-0 | 2 | Rhead [64], Chapman [82] | 3896 |
| 37 | 15 | A | Forest Green R | W | 2-1 | 1-0 | 1 | Oshodi (og) [30], Stevenson [47] | 1109 |
| 38 | 26 | H | Nuneaton T | W | 1-0 | 0-0 | 2 | Briscoe [67] | 2384 |
| 39 | 30 | A | Tamworth | W | 1-0 | 0-0 | 2 | Jones [61] | 1968 |
| 40 | Apr 1 | H | Gateshead | W | 4-0 | 1-0 | 2 | Howell [21], Briscoe [73], Green [77], Hutchinson (pen) [90] | 3472 |
| 41 | 4 | A | Wrexham | L | 1-2 | 0-0 | 2 | Green [53] | 4378 |
| 42 | 6 | A | Barrow | W | 4-0 | 2-0 | 2 | Green 2 (1 pen) [29, 42 (p)], Stevenson 2 [60, 90] | 1114 |
| 43 | 9 | H | Macclesfield T | W | 3-1 | 2-0 | 1 | Green [17], Jones [41], Stevenson [51] | 3694 |
| 44 | 13 | A | Braintree T | L | 1-2 | 1-0 | 2 | Green [8] | 1755 |
| 45 | 16 | A | Hereford U | W | 2-1 | 1-1 | 1 | Green 2 [37, 90] | 2141 |
| 46 | 20 | H | Wrexham | W | 1-0 | 1-0 | 1 | Green (pen) [40] | 6394 |

**Final League Position: 1 – Promoted to Football League Two**

### GOALSCORERS

*League (92):* Green 25 (8 pens), Stevenson 11 (1 pen), Jones 8, Briscoe 6 (1 pen), Speight 6 (1 pen), Daniel 5,
Chapman 4, Howell 4, Hutchinson 4 (1 pen), Meikle 4, Rhead 4, Murray 3, Dempster 2, Geohaghon 2, Beevers 1,
Wright 1, own goals 2.
*FA Cup (9):* Briscoe 2, Green 2, Speight 2, Rhead 1, own goals 2.
*FA Trophy (2):* Daniel 1, Murray 1.

| Marriott 37 | Owens 2 | Jones 32 | Pilkington 4 | Beevers 35+1 | Roberts 8+2 | Howell 30+6 | Tolley 2 | Meikle 29+14 | Green 40+2 | Dyer 1 | Speight 8+11 | Wright 4+13 | Daniel 34+7 | Thompson 7+1 | Rhead 10+23 | Sutton 20+5 | Dempster 33 | Todd 4+1 | Briscoe 26+13 | Hand —+1 | Clements 14+3 | Geoghaghon 17 | Murray 35+1 | Tafazolli 4+1 | Stevenson 24+3 | Redmond 6 | Taiwo 1 | Mitchell 3 | Hutchinson 6+4 | Jennings 13 | Chapman 9+2 | Taylor 8 | Match No. |
|---|---|---|---|---|---|---|---|---|---|---|---|---|---|---|---|---|---|---|---|---|---|---|---|---|---|---|---|---|---|---|---|---|---|
| 1 | 2 | 3 | 4 | 5 | 6 | 7 | $8^2$ | 9 | 10 | $11^1$ | 12 | 13 | | | | | | | | | | | | | | | | | | | | | 1 |
| 1 | $5^3$ | 3 | $4^2$ | $2^4$ | 8 | 6 | $7^1$ | 9 | 10 | | 12 | | 11 | 13 | 14 | | | | | | | | | | | | | | | | | | 2 |
| 1 | | | 4 | | 8 | 7 | | 9 | $11^1$ | | 12 | 5 | 10 | 2 | 3 | 6 | | | | | | | | | | | | | | | | | 3 |
| 1 | | 3 | | | 8 | 7 | | 6 | $10^9$ | | 12 | 14 | 2 | $11^1$ | 5 | 4 | | | $9^2$ | 13 | | | | | | | | | | | | | 4 |
| 1 | | | 4 | 13 | $6^8$ | 8 | | 9 | 10 | | $11^2$ | | $5^3$ | 12 | 2 | 3 | | | 14 | | $7^1$ | | | | | | | | | | | | 5 |
| 1 | | 3 | | | | 7 | | 6 | $10^9$ | | 12 | 14 | 2 | $11^2$ | 5 | | | | $9^1$ | | 13 | 4 | 8 | | | | | | | | | | 6 |
| 1 | | 3 | | | 12 | 7 | | $9^3$ | $10^2$ | | 13 | | 5 | 11 | 2 | | | | $6^1$ | | 14 | 4 | 8 | | | | | | | | | | 7 |
| 1 | | 3 | | | 12 | 7 | | $9^1$ | $10^8$ | | 13 | 14 | 5 | 11 | 2 | | | | $6^3$ | | | 4 | 8 | | | | | | | | | | 8 |
| 1 | | | 8 | | 12 | | | 13 | | | $10^2$ | | 5 | $11^1$ | 4 | | | | 6 | 3 | 7 | 2 | 9 | | | | | | | | | | 9 |
| 1 | | | 5 | | 13 | | | 12 | | | 11 | | 8 | $10^2$ | $2^3$ | | | | 14 | 7 | 3 | 6 | 4 | $9^1$ | | | | | | | | | 10 |
| | | | 4 | | | 7 | | $10^2$ | | | 9 | $11^1$ | 8 | 2 | 12 | 5 | | | 13 | | 3 | 6 | | | 1 | | | | | | | | 11 |
| | | | 4 | | | 8 | | 9 | 10 | | 11 | | 12 | $2^1$ | 5 | | | | 14 | | $3^2$ | 7 | 13 | | 1 | $6^3$ | | | | | | | 12 |
| | | | 6 | | | | | 10 | | | 9 | | 5 | 11 | 4 | 3 | 8 | | | | 7 | 2 | | | 1 | | | | | | | | 13 |
| | | | 6 | | | | | 12 | $10^1$ | | 8 | | 5 | 11 | 4 | 3 | $9^2$ | 13 | | | 2 | 7 | | | 1 | | | | | | | | 14 |
| | | | 6 | 8 | | | | 13 | 10 | | 7 | | $9^3$ | $11^2$ | 12 | 4 | 5 | 14 | | | 3 | | $2^1$ | | 1 | | | | | | | | 15 |
| | | | 5 | | | 7 | | 11 | 13 | | $10^2$ | 12 | | 2 | 4 | | $8^1$ | | 6 | 3 | | | 1 | | 9 | | | | | | | | 16 |
| | | | 5 | | | 8 | | 9 | | | 12 | $10^1$ | | 2 | 4 | | 6 | | $7^2$ | 3 | 13 | | 1 | | 11 | | | | | | | | 17 |
| | | | 5 | | | 7 | | $6^3$ | 12 | | 13 | $11^1$ | | 2 | 14 | 4 | | | 9 | 8 | 3 | | 1 | | $10^2$ | | | | | | | | 18 |
| | | 3 | 5 | | | | | 6 | $11^1$ | | 12 | | 14 | 2 | | 4 | | | $9^3$ | 7 | | 8 | 13 | 1 | $10^2$ | | | | | | | | 19 |
| 1 | | | 2 | | 8 | | | $6^1$ | $11^2$ | | 13 | 14 | 5 | | | 4 | | | $9^3$ | | 7 | 3 | | 12 | $10^1$ | | | | | | | | 20 |
| 1 | | | 2 | | 8 | | | 6 | 11 | | 13 | | | 12 | 5 | 4 | | | $9^2$ | | $7^3$ | 3 | 14 | | $10^1$ | | | | | | | | 21 |
| 1 | | | 5 | | | 7 | | 9 | 10 | | | 11 | 2 | | | 3 | | | | | $8^1$ | 4 | 6 | | 12 | | | | | | | | 22 |
| 1 | | $2^3$ | | | 7 | | | 9 | 10 | | | 13 | $5^2$ | 14 | 12 | 3 | | | $11^1$ | | 8 | 4 | 6 | | | | | | | | | | 23 |
| 1 | | 3 | 5 | | 8 | | | $9^1$ | 10 | | | 11 | | | 2 | 4 | | | 12 | | | 7 | 6 | | | | | | | | | | 24 |
| 1 | | 4 | 5 | | 8 | | | 6 | 11 | | | $9^1$ | | | 2 | 3 | | | 12 | | | 7 | 10 | | | | | | | | | | 25 |
| 1 | | 3 | 5 | | 8 | | | $9^1$ | $11^3$ | | 14 | $6^2$ | 13 | | 4 | | | | 12 | | | 7 | 10 | | | | | | 2 | | | | 26 |
| 1 | | 4 | 5 | | 8 | | | $11^1$ | | | 13 | $6^2$ | 12 | | 3 | 9 | | | 14 | | $7^3$ | | 10 | | | | | | 2 | | | | 27 |
| 1 | | 4 | 2 | | 7 | | | 11 | | | 9 | | | 3 | | $6^1$ | | | 8 | | | | 10 | | | | | | 5 | | | | 28 |
| 1 | | 4 | 5 | | 8 | | | 12 | 11 | | 6 | | | 3 | | $9^1$ | | | 7 | | | | 10 | | | | | | 2 | | | | 29 |
| 1 | | 3 | 2 | | 7 | | | 12 | $11^2$ | | 13 | $9^1$ | | | 4 | 6 | | | 8 | | | | 10 | | | | | | 5 | | | | 30 |
| 1 | | 4 | 2 | | | | | 13 | $10^3$ | | 14 | 9 | | | | 5 | | | $6^2$ | 7 | | 8 | $11^1$ | | | | | | 12 | 3 | | | 31 |
| 1 | | 4 | 2 | | | | | 13 | $11^3$ | | | 9 | 12 | | 3 | $6^2$ | | | 8 | 7 | | 8 | $10^1$ | | | | | | 14 | 5 | | | 32 |
| 1 | | 3 | 5 | | | | | 12 | 11 | | 13 | $6^2$ | | 4 | | $9^1$ | | | 8 | 7 | | | 10 | | | | | | 2 | | | | 33 |
| 1 | | 3 | 2 | | | | | 12 | $10^3$ | | 14 | 9 | 13 | | | $6^1$ | | | 4 | 7 | | | $11^2$ | | | | | | 5 | 8 | | | 34 |
| 1 | | 4 | 5 | | | | | 9 | $11^2$ | | 12 | $6^1$ | 13 | 14 | 3 | | | | 7 | | | | 10 | | | | | | $2^3$ | 8 | | | 35 |
| 1 | | 4 | 5 | | 14 | | | $9^2$ | $11^3$ | | 6 | 12 | 3 | | 13 | | | | 7 | | | | $10^1$ | | | | | | 2 | 8 | | | 36 |
| 1 | | 3 | 2 | | 13 | | | 6 | $11^3$ | | $9^1$ | 14 | 4 | | 12 | | | | 7 | | | | $10^1$ | | | | | | 5 | 8 | | | 37 |
| 1 | | 4 | 5 | | | | | 9 | 11 | | $6^2$ | 14 | 12 | 3 | 13 | | | | 7 | | | | $10^3$ | | | | | | $2^1$ | 8 | | | 38 |
| 1 | | 4 | 2 | | 14 | | | 6 | $11^3$ | | 12 | 13 | 3 | | $9^1$ | | | | 8 | | | | $10^2$ | | | | | | | 7 | 5 | | 39 |
| 1 | | 4 | 2 | | 7 | | | 13 | $10^3$ | | $9^2$ | 12 | 3 | | 6 | | | | 8 | | | | $11^1$ | | 14 | | | | | 5 | | | 40 |
| 1 | | 3 | 2 | | 8 | | | 6 | 11 | | $9^1$ | 13 | 4 | | 12 | | | | 7 | | | | | | | | | | $10^2$ | 5 | | | 41 |
| 1 | | 3 | 2 | | 6 | | | 13 | $10^1$ | | $11^3$ | 12 | 4 | 14 | $9^2$ | | | | 7 | 8 | | | | | | | | | | 5 | | | 42 |
| 1 | | 4 | 5 | | $8^3$ | | | 12 | $11^2$ | | 6 | 13 | 3 | | $9^1$ | | | | 7 | 10 | | | | | | | | | 14 | 2 | | | 43 |
| 1 | | 5 | 2 | | $6^3$ | | | 13 | 10 | | 11 | 12 | 4 | | $9^2$ | | | | 7 | $8^1$ | | | | | | | | | 14 | 3 | | | 44 |
| 1 | | 3 | $2^1$ | | | | | 11 | 10 | | 14 | 13 | 12 | 4 | $9^3$ | | | | 6 | $8^2$ | | | | | | | | | 7 | 5 | | | 45 |
| 1 | | 3 | 2 | | 13 | | | $9^1$ | $11^3$ | | 12 | 14 | 4 | | 6 | | | | 7 | $10^2$ | | | | | | | | | 8 | 5 | | | 46 |

**FA Cup**

| | | | | |
|---|---|---|---|---|
| Fourth Qualifying | Workington | (a) | 2-1 |
| First Round | Slough T | (h) | 0-0 |
| *Replay* | Slough T | (a) | 1-1 |

*aet; Mansfield won 4-1 on penalties.*

| | | | |
|---|---|---|---|
| Second Round | Lincoln C | (a) | 3-3 |
| *Replay* | Lincoln C | (h) | 2-1 |
| Third Round | Liverpool | (h) | 1-2 |

**FA Trophy**

| | | | |
|---|---|---|---|
| First Round | Matlock T | (h) | 1-1 |
| *Replay* | Matlock T | (a) | 1-2 |

# NEWPORT COUNTY

*Ground:* Rodney Parade, Rodney Road, Newport, South Wales NP19 OUU.   *Tel:* (01633) 670 690.
*Website:* www.newport-county.co.uk   *Year Formed:* 1912.   *Record Gate:* 4,616 (at Newport Stadium 2006 v Swansea
C).   *Nickname:* 'The Exiles'.   *Manager:* Justin Edinburgh.   *Secretary:* Mike Everett.   *Colours:* Amber shirts with
black trim, black shorts, amber socks with black trim.

## NEWPORT COUNTY – BLUE SQUARE PREMIER 2012–13 LEAGUE RECORD

| Match No. | Date | Venue | Opponents | Result | H/T Score | Lg Pos. | Goalscorers | Atten- dance |
|---|---|---|---|---|---|---|---|---|
| 1 | Aug 11 | A | Mansfield T | W 4-3 | 2-0 | 3 | Yakubu [10], James [13], O'Connor [56], Louis [66] | 2924 |
| 2 | 14 | H | Nuneaton T | W 4-0 | 2-0 | 1 | O'Connor 2 [13, 52], Louis [20], Evans, L [86] | 2646 |
| 3 | 18 | H | Lincoln C | W 2-1 | 2-0 | 1 | O'Connor 2 [7, 27] | 3024 |
| 4 | 25 | A | Braintree T | W 2-1 | 0-0 | 1 | Porter [69], Yakubu [84] | 611 |
| 5 | 28 | H | Hereford U | W 2-0 | 0-0 | 1 | Sandell [75], O'Connor [90] | 4365 |
| 6 | Sept 1 | A | Wrexham | L 0-2 | 0-1 | 1 | | 3820 |
| 7 | 4 | A | Dartford | L 1-2 | 0-0 | 3 | O'Connor [54] | 1446 |
| 8 | 8 | H | Stockport Co | D 0-0 | 0-0 | 5 | | 2306 |
| 9 | 15 | A | Barrow | W 3-0 | 1-0 | 1 | Evans, L [44], Crow 2 [70, 77] | 802 |
| 10 | 22 | H | Southport | W 2-1 | 0-1 | 1 | O'Connor [76], Swallow [90] | 2802 |
| 11 | 25 | A | AFC Telford U | W 4-2 | 1-1 | 1 | O'Connor [45], Preston (og) [49], Yakubu [72], Sandell [78] | 1503 |
| 12 | 29 | H | Grimsby T | D 0-0 | 0-0 | 2 | | 2968 |
| 13 | Oct 6 | A | Tamworth | W 2-1 | 1-0 | 1 | Yakubu [45], O'Connor [63] | 1201 |
| 14 | 9 | H | Ebbsfleet U | W 1-0 | 1-0 | 1 | Yakubu [30] | 2453 |
| 15 | 13 | A | Macclesfield T | D 1-1 | 1-0 | 1 | James [43] | 1544 |
| 16 | 27 | A | Woking | L 2-3 | 1-2 | 1 | Sandell [45], Flynn [89] | 2088 |
| 17 | Nov 6 | H | Cambridge U | W 6-2 | 3-1 | 1 | Minshull [16], Flynn [17], Sandell [30], O'Connor 2 [62, 70], Smith [90] | 1787 |
| 18 | 9 | A | Alfreton T | L 3-4 | 1-3 | 1 | Smith [35], O'Connor 2 [60, 89] | 663 |
| 19 | 17 | H | Hyde | L 1-3 | 0-1 | 2 | Jolley [55] | 2096 |
| 20 | Dec 1 | H | Gateshead | W 3-1 | 1-0 | 1 | Jolley 2 [38, 56], Smith [53] | 1473 |
| 21 | 8 | A | Kidderminster H | L 2-3 | 2-1 | 3 | Smith [31], Evans, L [37] | 1951 |
| 22 | 11 | H | Luton T | W 5-2 | 3-1 | 1 | O'Connor [12], Jolley 2 [23, 67], Henry (og) [38], Sandell [64] | 2247 |
| 23 | 26 | A | Forest Green R | W 2-1 | 0-0 | 2 | Swallow [70], Charles [74] | 2332 |
| 24 | Jan 1 | A | Forest Green R | L 0-5 | 0-2 | 3 | | 2787 |
| 25 | 4 | A | Wrexham | D 1-1 | 0-1 | 3 | Porter [56] | 3627 |
| 26 | 12 | A | Lincoln C | W 4-2 | 4-1 | 2 | O'Connor 2 [22, 37], Willmott 2 [40, 45] | 1970 |
| 27 | 19 | H | Barrow | L 0-2 | 0-1 | 2 | | 2107 |
| 28 | Feb 9 | H | Tamworth | D 2-2 | 2-0 | 5 | Donnelly [1], Anthony [30] | 1712 |
| 29 | 12 | H | Mansfield T | W 2-0 | 0-0 | 4 | Sandell (pen) [67], Jolley [78] | 1902 |
| 30 | 16 | A | Woking | W 3-1 | 3-0 | 4 | Minshull 2 [19, 34], Anthony [37] | 2116 |
| 31 | 23 | H | AFC Telford U | W 2-1 | 0-0 | 3 | Jolley [55], Crow [75] | 1761 |
| 32 | Mar 2 | A | Hyde | W 1-0 | 1-0 | 4 | Jolley [10] | 640 |
| 33 | 5 | A | Hereford U | W 3-2 | 0-1 | 3 | Minshull 2 [72, 81], Willmott [90] | 2519 |
| 34 | 9 | A | Ebbsfleet U | D 1-1 | 1-0 | 4 | Minshull [44] | 808 |
| 35 | 19 | H | Kidderminster H | L 1-2 | 1-1 | 4 | Sandell [30] | 2652 |
| 36 | 23 | A | Stockport Co | L 0-1 | 0-0 | 4 | | 3154 |
| 37 | 26 | A | Southport | W 2-0 | 2-0 | 4 | O'Connor [10], Jolley [34] | 606 |
| 38 | 28 | A | Gateshead | D 0-0 | 0-0 | 4 | | 227 |
| 39 | 30 | H | Dartford | D 0-0 | 0-0 | 4 | | 2111 |
| 40 | Apr 1 | A | Nuneaton T | W 2-1 | 0-1 | 3 | Willmott [58], Armson (og) [77] | 1068 |
| 41 | 5 | A | Cambridge U | D 0-0 | 0-0 | 3 | | 2012 |
| 42 | 9 | H | Braintree T | W 1-0 | 0-0 | 4 | Washington [48] | 1864 |
| 43 | 11 | H | Macclesfield T | W 4-1 | 3-1 | 3 | Jolley [24], Sandell (pen) [41], Willmott 2 [45, 65] | 1606 |
| 44 | 13 | H | Alfreton T | W 2-0 | 1-0 | 3 | Jolley [45], Anthony [67] | 2138 |
| 45 | 16 | A | Luton T | D 2-2 | 0-1 | 3 | Jolley 2 [52, 84] | 5125 |
| 46 | 20 | A | Grimsby T | L 0-3 | 0-3 | 3 | | 4555 |

**Final League Position: 3 – Promoted to Football League Two via play-offs**

### GOALSCORERS

*League (85):* O'Connor 18, Jolley 13, Sandell 8 (2 pens), Minshull 6, Willmott 6, Yakubu 5, Smith 4, Anthony 3, Crow 3,
Evans, L 3, Flynn 2, James 2, Louis 2, Porter 2, Swallow 2, Charles 1, Donnelly 1, Washington 1, own goals 3.
*FA Cup (4):* O'Connor 2, James 1, Louis 1.
*FA Trophy (0).*
*Blue Square Premier Play-Offs (2):* Jolley 2, O'Connor 1, Yakubu 1.

| Pidgeley 36 | Sandell 42 | James 41 | Yakubu 35+1 | Pipe 41 | Thomson 12+10 | Evans L 18+4 | Porter 26 | Crow 20+5 | Louis 11+6 | O'Connor 36+3 | Minshull 28+9 | Charles 2+9 | Hughes 18+8 | Flynn 28+11 | Harris —+5 | Swallow 7+13 | Washington 5+10 | Smith 9 | Julian 10+1 | Jolley 22+2 | Anthony 19+2 | Willmott 10+9 | Donnelly 16+2 | Griffiths 4+6 | Boateng 3 | Evans W 3+3 | Gilbey 4+1 | Match No. |
|---|---|---|---|---|---|---|---|---|---|---|---|---|---|---|---|---|---|---|---|---|---|---|---|---|---|---|---|---|
| 1 | 2 | 3 | 4 | 5 | 6 | $7^3$ | 8 | $9^1$ | 10 | $11^2$ | 12 | 13 | 14 | | | | | | | | | | | | | | | 1 |
| 1 | 5 | $3^1$ | 4 | 2 | $7^2$ | 8 | 6 | 10 | 11 | $9^3$ | | | 12 | 13 | 14 | | | | | | | | | | | | | 2 |
| 1 | 5 | 3 | 4 | 2 | 7 | $8^1$ | 6 | 10 | $11^3$ | $9^2$ | | | 13 | 12 | 14 | | | | | | | | | | | | | 3 |
| 1 | 5 | 3 | 4 | 2 | $8^1$ | 12 | $6^2$ | $11^3$ | 10 | 9 | | | 13 | 14 | 7 | | | | | | | | | | | | | 4 |
| 1 | 6 | 4 | 5 | 2 | 12 | $7^1$ | 3 | 9 | $10^2$ | 11 | | | 13 | 8 | | | | | | | | | | | | | | 5 |
| 1 | 5 | 4 | 3 | 2 | $6^1$ | 12 | 8 | $9^2$ | 10 | 14 | 11 | $7^3$ | 13 | | | | | | | | | | | | | | | 6 |
| 1 | 5 | 3 | 4 | 2 | 6 | 8 | 9 | $10^1$ | 11 | $7^2$ | | | 13 | 12 | | | | | | | | | | | | | | 7 |
| 1 | 5 | 4 | | 2 | 7 | 6 | 10 | $11^2$ | 9 | 13 | 3 | $8^1$ | 12 | | | | | | | | | | | | | | | 8 |
| 1 | 5 | 3 | $4^3$ | 2 | 8 | 6 | 11 | 12 | $10^1$ | $7^2$ | 14 | 9 | 13 | | | | | | | | | | | | | | | 9 |
| 1 | 5 | 4 | 2 | 13 | 9 | $6^1$ | 11 | 12 | $10^3$ | 7 | 3 | $8^2$ | 14 | | | | | | | | | | | | | | | 10 |
| 1 | 5 | $3^3$ | 4 | 2 | 12 | $8^1$ | 6 | $11^2$ | 10 | 9 | 7 | 13 | 14 | | | | | | | | | | | | | | | 11 |
| 1 | 5 | 3 | 4 | 2 | 8 | 6 | 10 | $11^1$ | 9 | 7 | | 13 | 12 | | | | | | | | | | | | | | | 12 |
| 1 | 5 | $3^2$ | 4 | 2 | 8 | 6 | 11 | 12 | $10^1$ | $7^3$ | 13 | 14 | 9 | | | | | | | | | | | | | | | 13 |
| 1 | 5 | 3 | 4 | 2 | $9^3$ | 6 | $11^1$ | 12 | 10 | 7 | 13 | 14 | $8^2$ | | | | | | | | | | | | | | | 14 |
| 1 | 5 | 3 | $4^2$ | $2^3$ | 6 | 7 | 11 | 10 | 12 | 14 | 13 | 8 | $9^1$ | | | | | | | | | | | | | | | 15 |
| 1 | 5 | 4 | | $8^1$ | $7^2$ | 2 | 10 | 12 | 11 | 6 | 3 | 14 | $9^2$ | 13 | | | | | | | | | | | | | | 16 |
| 1 | 5 | 3 | $4^2$ | 2 | 14 | 13 | 6 | $10^3$ | 7 | 9 | $8^1$ | 12 | 11 | | | | | | | | | | | | | | | 17 |
| 1 | 5 | 3 | 4 | 2 | 12 | 13 | 6 | 14 | 10 | $7^1$ | $8^2$ | $9^3$ | 11 | | | | | | | | | | | | | | | 18 |
| | 5 | 4 | | 2 | $8^1$ | 6 | 10 | $7^1$ | 3 | 12 | | 13 | 14 | $11^2$ | | 13 | 14 | 1 | 9 | | | | | | | | | 19 |
| | 5 | 3 | 4 | 2 | $7^1$ | 6 | | $9^2$ | 12 | 8 | | | | | | 13 | 10 | 1 | 11 | | | | | | | | | 20 |
| | 5 | 3 | 4 | 2 | 7 | $6^3$ | 10 | 14 | $8^2$ | 13 | | | 12 | $11^1$ | | 1 | 9 | | | | | | | | | | | 21 |
| | 5 | $3^1$ | 4 | $2^3$ | 7 | 6 | 10 | 13 | 14 | 12 | 8 | | $11^1$ | | | 1 | $9^3$ | | | | | | | | | | | 22 |
| | 3 | 4 | $2^3$ | 7 | 6 | | 11 | | 12 | 5 | 8 | 13 | $9^1$ | $10^2$ | 1 | | 14 | | | | | | | | | | | 23 |
| | 5 | 3 | 4 | | $7^2$ | 6 | | 10 | 14 | 12 | 8 | | $9^3$ | 13 | $11^1$ | 1 | | 2 | | | | | | | | | | 24 |
| | 5 | 3 | $4^1$ | 2 | 8 | 6 | 13 | | 10 | | | $7^2$ | 12 | 9 | | 11 | 1 | | | | | | | | | | | 25 |
| | 5 | 3 | | 2 | | $7^2$ | $6^1$ | 13 | | 11 | 12 | | | 4 | 8 | 14 | | | 1 | 10 | $9^3$ | | | | | | | | 26 |
| | 5 | 4 | | $2^3$ | 8 | | 12 | | $9^1$ | $6^2$ | | 3 | 7 | 14 | 13 | | | 1 | 11 | 10 | | | | | | | | 27 |
| $1^1$ | 4 | | 3 | 2 | | | | | 10 | | 6 | | | 7 | | 13 | 14 | | 12 | $11^3$ | 5 | 8 | $9^2$ | | | | | 28 |
| 1 | 6 | 2 | 3 | 5 | | | | | $10^1$ | | | | | 7 | | | 8 | | 12 | 11 | 4 | | 9 | | | | | 29 |
| 1 | 9 | 2 | 3 | 5 | 12 | | | | 11 | | | | | 6 | | | 7 | | $10^2$ | | 4 | 13 | $8^1$ | | | | | 30 |
| 1 | 7 | 2 | 3 | 5 | 13 | | | | $10^2$ | | | | | 6 | | | 8 | | $11^3$ | | 4 | 14 | $9^1$ | 12 | | | | 31 |
| 1 | 9 | 2 | 3 | 5 | 12 | | | | $10^3$ | | | | | 6 | | | 7 | | 11 | | 4 | | $8^1$ | 13 | | | | 32 |
| 1 | 8 | 2 | 3 | 5 | | | | | $9^2$ | | | | | 6 | | | 7 | | 11 | | 4 | 13 | 12 | $10^1$ | | | | 33 |
| 1 | 9 | 3 | 2 | 5 | 14 | | | | 12 | | | | | 8 | | | 7 | | $11^2$ | | 4 | 13 | $6^3$ | $10^1$ | | | | 34 |
| 1 | 6 | 3 | 4 | 2 | 12 | | | | $11^2$ | | | | | 8 | | | $9^1$ | | 10 | | 5 | 13 | 7 | | | | | 35 |
| 1 | 9 | $3^1$ | | 8 | | | | | 11 | | | 7 | | 4 | $10^2$ | 2 | 13 | | 6 | 14 | $5^3$ | 12 | | | | | | 36 |
| 1 | 6 | 3 | | 5 | | | | | $10^2$ | | 8 | | | 4 | | | $11^1$ | | 2 | 12 | 9 | 13 | | 7 | | | | 37 |
| 1 | 7 | 4 | | 2 | | | | | 5 | | 6 | | | 3 | | | $9^1$ | | 8 | 12 | 10 | | | 11 | | | | 38 |
| 1 | 7 | $4^2$ | 13 | 2 | | | | | 10 | | 6 | | | 3 | | | 12 | | 5 | 11 | 8 | | | $9^1$ | | | | 39 |
| 1 | 9 | 3 | | 5 | | | | | $10^2$ | | 6 | | | 2 | | | 11 | | 4 | 12 | 8 | 13 | | $7^1$ | | | | 40 |
| 1 | | 3 | 4 | 5 | | | | | $10^2$ | | 7 | | | 9 | | | 12 | | $11^1$ | 2 | 6 | 8 | 13 | | | | | 41 |
| 1 | | 4 | 2 | | | | | | 9 | | $6^3$ | | | 12 | | | 7 | | $10^1$ | 5 | 11 | $8^2$ | | | | 14 | 13 | 42 |
| 1 | 6 | 4 | | | 12 | | | | 7 | | 3 | 14 | 13 | $9^1$ | | | 5 | | 10 | $11^2$ | $8^3$ | | | 2 | | | | 43 |
| 1 | 6 | 4 | $5^1$ | 2 | | | | | 13 | | | 3 | 8 | | 11 | | | | $7^2$ | 12 | 10 | 14 | | $9^3$ | | | | 44 |
| 1 | 8 | 3 | | 2 | | | | | 14 | | $9^1$ | 6 | | 5 | 13 | | $10^1$ | | 12 | 4 | 11 | $7^2$ | | | | | | 45 |
| | 4 | | | | | | | | 12 | | | 5 | 8 | 13 | $10^2$ | 1 | | 3 | 11 | $7^3$ | $9^1$ | 2 | 14 | 6 | | | | 46 |

**FA Cup**

| | | | |
|---|---|---|---|
| Fourth Qualifying | Yate T | (a) | 3-3 |
| *Replay* | Yate T | (h) | 1-3 |

**FA Trophy**

| | | | |
|---|---|---|---|
| First Round | Welling U | (a) | 0-2 |

**Blue Square Premier Play-offs**

| | | | |
|---|---|---|---|
| Semi-Finals | Grimsby T | (a) | 1-0 |
| | Grimsby T | (h) | 1-0 |
| Final (Wembley) | Wrexham | | 2-0 |

# NUNEATON TOWN

*Ground:* Triton Showers Community Arena, Liberty Way, Nuneaton, Warwickshire CV11 6RR.
*Tel:* (0247) 638 5738.   *Fax:* (0247) 637 2995.   *Website:* nuneatontownfc.com   *Year Formed:* 1889.
*Record Gate:* 3,111 (2009 v Chasetown, Southern League Division 1 Play-Off Final).   *Nickname:* 'Boro'.
*Manager:* Kevin Wilkin.   *Secretary:* Richard Dean.   *Colours:* Blue and white striped shirts, white shorts, white socks.

## NUNEATON TOWN – BLUE SQUARE PREMIER 2012–13 LEAGUE RECORD

| Match No. | Date | Venue | Opponents | Result | H/T Score | Lg Pos. | Goalscorers | Attendance |
|---|---|---|---|---|---|---|---|---|
| 1 | Aug 11 | H | Ebbsfleet U | L | 4-5 | 2-3 | 18 | Brown 2 [8, 90], Walker [17], Thompson-Brown [56] | 1088 |
| 2 | 14 | A | Newport Co | L | 0-4 | 0-2 | 24 | | 2646 |
| 3 | 18 | A | Grimsby T | D | 0-0 | 0-0 | 22 | | 3095 |
| 4 | 25 | H | Cambridge U | D | 2-2 | 0-0 | 22 | Walker [53], Armson (pen) [90] | 1175 |
| 5 | 27 | A | Alfreton T | W | 3-0 | 0-0 | 16 | Walker 3 [53, 79, 90] | 680 |
| 6 | Sept 1 | H | Gateshead | L | 0-1 | 0-0 | 18 | | 835 |
| 7 | 4 | H | AFC Telford U | W | 3-1 | 1-1 | 15 | Walker [13], Armson (pen) [74], Brown [87] | 992 |
| 8 | 8 | A | Woking | L | 1-6 | 0-2 | 20 | Brown [90] | 1512 |
| 9 | 15 | H | Macclesfield T | D | 3-3 | 2-0 | 20 | Brown [6], Armson (pen) [13], Sleath [77] | 939 |
| 10 | 22 | A | Hyde | D | 2-2 | 0-1 | 20 | York 2 [74, 75] | 585 |
| 11 | 25 | A | Lincoln C | L | 1-2 | 1-0 | 20 | Armson [3] | 1579 |
| 12 | 29 | H | Wrexham | D | 0-0 | 0-0 | 21 | | 1543 |
| 13 | Oct 6 | A | Southport | L | 1-3 | 0-2 | 22 | Walker [75] | 1302 |
| 14 | 9 | H | Hereford U | D | 0-0 | 0-0 | 22 | | 969 |
| 15 | 13 | A | Luton T | L | 0-2 | 0-0 | 22 | | 6148 |
| 16 | 27 | H | Barrow | D | 1-1 | 0-0 | 24 | Brown [90] | 844 |
| 17 | Nov 6 | H | Mansfield T | D | 1-1 | 0-0 | 24 | Taylor [50] | 838 |
| 18 | 10 | A | Kidderminster H | L | 0-1 | 0-0 | 24 | | 1592 |
| 19 | 17 | H | Stockport Co | W | 2-0 | 1-0 | 24 | Brown [45], Walker (pen) [82] | 1221 |
| 20 | Dec 1 | A | Forest Green R | L | 0-1 | 0-0 | 24 | | 948 |
| 21 | 4 | H | Dartford | W | 1-0 | 1-0 | 22 | Brown [45] | 651 |
| 22 | 8 | A | Wrexham | L | 1-6 | 0-3 | 24 | York [89] | 2739 |
| 23 | 15 | A | Macclesfield T | D | 0-0 | 0-0 | 23 | | 1280 |
| 24 | 26 | H | Tamworth | W | 2-1 | 0-1 | 22 | Brown [84], Armson (pen) [89] | 1389 |
| 25 | Jan 2 | A | Tamworth | L | 1-2 | 1-1 | 22 | Forsdick [18] | 1516 |
| 26 | 12 | H | Forest Green R | D | 1-1 | 0-0 | 22 | Gordon [82] | 910 |
| 27 | 15 | A | Cambridge U | W | 3-1 | 1-0 | 22 | Armson 2 [14, 60], Brown [64] | 1740 |
| 28 | 26 | H | Braintree T | L | 2-4 | 1-1 | 22 | Forsdick [41], Gordon [77] | 761 |
| 29 | Feb 2 | A | Stockport Co | L | 2-3 | 2-2 | 23 | Brown 2 [14, 19] | 4133 |
| 30 | 9 | H | Southport | L | 0-1 | 0-1 | 23 | | 779 |
| 31 | 16 | A | Barrow | W | 2-1 | 0-0 | 21 | Brown [89], Dance [90] | 998 |
| 32 | 19 | H | Alfreton T | W | 1-0 | 0-0 | 20 | Dance (pen) [90] | 781 |
| 33 | 26 | H | Kidderminster H | L | 0-1 | 0-0 | 21 | | 1087 |
| 34 | Mar 2 | A | Hereford U | D | 0-0 | 0-0 | 21 | | 1908 |
| 35 | 5 | H | Luton T | D | 0-0 | 0-0 | 21 | | 1173 |
| 36 | 16 | H | Lincoln C | W | 1-0 | 0-0 | 21 | York [90] | 1122 |
| 37 | 19 | H | Grimsby T | W | 1-0 | 1-0 | 19 | Brown [17] | 964 |
| 38 | 21 | A | Braintree T | D | 2-2 | 2-2 | 18 | York [20], Armson [44] | 421 |
| 39 | 26 | A | Mansfield T | L | 0-1 | 0-0 | 21 | | 2384 |
| 40 | 28 | H | Woking | D | 0-0 | 0-0 | 21 | | 609 |
| 41 | 30 | A | AFC Telford U | W | 3-0 | 1-0 | 19 | Phillips [34], Brown 2 [49, 73] | 1893 |
| 42 | Apr 1 | H | Newport Co | L | 1-2 | 1-0 | 19 | Forsdick [15] | 1068 |
| 43 | 6 | A | Ebbsfleet U | D | 1-1 | 0-1 | 21 | Brown [90] | 695 |
| 44 | 9 | A | Gateshead | W | 2-0 | 2-0 | 16 | York [11], Brown [36] | 304 |
| 45 | 13 | H | Hyde | W | 3-1 | 1-0 | 16 | Brown [34], Forsdick [55], Moult [69] | 1158 |
| 46 | 20 | A | Dartford | W | 1-0 | 0-0 | 15 | York [81] | 1844 |

**Final League Position: 15**

### GOALSCORERS

*League (55):* Brown 19, Armson 8 (4 pens), Walker 8 (1 pen), York 7, Forsdick 4, Dance 2 (1 pen), Gordon 2, Moult 1, Phillips 1, Sleath 1, Taylor 1, Thompson-Brown 1.
*FA Cup (4):* Waite 2, Armson 1, Forsdick 1.
*FA Trophy (0).*

| McNamara 15 | Cartwright 14 + 2 | Cowan 37 | Gordon 28 + 2 | O'Halloran 33 + 4 | Thompson-Brown 3 + 9 | Armson 36 + 4 | Sleath 22 + 7 | Walker 35 + 8 | James 9 + 5 | Brown 45 + 1 | York 32 + 14 | Patterson 2 + 6 | Collett 7 | Dean 40 | Perry 4 + 8 | Parry 1 | Adams 15 + 5 | Forsdick 35 + 1 | Ford 3 + 1 | McNamee 7 + 3 | Smith 7 | Taylor 11 + 7 | Waite 2 + 3 | Malaga 3 | Newton 5 + 4 | Burge 17 | Phillips 17 | Dance 5 + 10 | Moult 16 + 1 | Match No. |
|---|---|---|---|---|---|---|---|---|---|---|---|---|---|---|---|---|---|---|---|---|---|---|---|---|---|---|---|---|---|---|
| 1 | 2 | 3 | 4 | 5 | 6 | 7² | 8 | 9 | 10¹ | 11 | 12 | 13 | | | | | | | | | | | | | | | | | | 1 |
| | 2 | 11 | 9 | 8¹ | 6 | 7 | 4³ | 5² | | 10 | 13 | 12 | 1 | 3 | 14 | | | | | | | | | | | | | | | 2 |
| | 5 | 2 | 4 | 9 | | 8 | 7 | 6 | | 11¹ | 10 | | 1 | 3 | 12 | | | | | | | | | | | | | | | 3 |
| | | | 4 | 2 | 9 | 5¹ | 7 | 6 | 8 | 11 | 10 | 12 | 1 | 3 | | | | | | | | | | | | | | | | 4 |
| | | 3 | 2 | 5 | 12 | 7 | 8 | 6 | 10 | 11¹ | 9 | | 1 | 4 | | | | | | | | | | | | | | | | 5 |
| 1 | | 3 | 2 | 5 | 13 | 6² | 7 | 8 | | 11 | 10 | 9¹ | | 4 | 12 | | | | | | | | | | | | | | | 6 |
| 1 | | 4 | 2 | 5 | | 7 | 8 | 6 | | 11 | 10¹ | | | 3 | 9 | | 12 | | | | | | | | | | | | | 7 |
| 1 | | 3 | 2 | 5 | 12 | 8¹ | 6 | 7 | | 10 | 9² | 13 | | 4 | 11³ | | 14 | | | | | | | | | | | | | 8 |
| | | 4 | 2 | 12 | | 6 | 8 | 7 | | 11 | 13 | | 1 | 3 | 10² | | 9 | 5¹ | | | | | | | | | | | | 9 |
| | | 4 | 3 | | | 7 | 8³ | 6 | | 11 | 13 | 12² | 1 | 2 | 10 | | 5¹ | 9 | 14 | | | | | | | | | | | 10 |
| | | 3 | 2 | 12 | 14 | 5 | 6 | 7 | | 11³ | 10¹ | | 1 | 4 | 13 | | | 9⁴ | 8² | | | | | | | | | | | 11 |
| 1 | | 4 | 2 | 5 | 12 | 9 | 7 | 8 | | 11 | 10² | | | 3 | 13 | | | 6¹ | | | | | | | | | | | | 12 |
| 1 | | 4 | 2 | 3¹ | 12 | 7 | 8² | 9 | | 10 | 11 | | | 5 | 13 | | | 14 | 6¹ | | | | | | | | | | | 13 |
| 1 | | 4 | 2 | 13 | 14 | 7¹ | 12 | 8 | | 11 | 10³ | | | 3 | | | 9 | 5² | 6 | | | | | | | | | | | 14 |
| 1 | | 3 | 2 | | 12 | 7 | 8 | 9 | | 10 | 11¹ | | | 4 | | | 6 | 5 | | | | | | | | | | | | 15 |
| | | 4 | 2² | 14 | | 7 | 9 | 13 | 10 | 12 | | | | 5 | | | 5 | 8 | 1 | 6¹ | 11³ | | | | | | | | | 16 |
| 1 | | 4 | | | | 6 | 7 | 8 | 3 | 9 | 12 | | | 5 | | | 2 | | | 10¹ | 11 | | | | | | | | | 17 |
| | | 4 | | 7¹ | | 12 | 6 | 8 | 9 | 11³ | 13 | | | 3 | | | 5 | | | 1 | 10² | 14 | 2 | | | | | | | 18 |
| | | 3 | | 5 | | | 6 | 8 | 10 | 9² | 12 | | | 4 | | | 7 | | | 1 | 13 | 11¹ | 2 | | | | | | | 19 |
| 2 | 3⁴ | 5 | | 12 | | 7 | 9 | 10 | 13 | | | | | 4 | | | 14 | 8³ | | 1 | 6² | | 11¹ | | | | | | | 20 |
| 2 | | 3 | 5 | | | 7 | 9¹ | 10 | 12 | | | | | 4 | | | 8 | | | 1 | 6 | | 11 | | | | | | | 21 |
| 2 | | 4 | 5 | | | 8 | 9¹ | 11 | 14 | | | | | 3 | | | 12 | 7 | | 1 | 6² | 13 | 10³ | | | | | | | 22 |
| 2 | | 3¹ | 5 | | | 9 | 14 | 10 | 12 | | | | | 4 | | | 7 | 8 | | 1 | 6³ | 13 | 11² | | | | | | | 23 |
| 1 | 2 | 4 | 3 | 5 | | 9² | 14 | 9 | 5 | 10 | 11² | | | | | | 7 | 8 | | | 6¹ | | 11¹ | | | | | | | 24 |
| 1 | 2 | 4⁴ | 12 | | | 14 | | 9 | 5 | 10 | 11² | | | 3 | | | 7³ | 8 | | | 6¹ | | 13 | | | | | | | 25 |
| 1 | 2² | 3 | 5³ | | | 6 | | 9 | | 11 | 10 | | | 4 | | | 8¹ | 7 | 13 | | 14 | | 12 | | | | | | | 26 |
| 1 | 2 | 4 | 5 | | | 6 | | 9 | | 11 | 10¹ | | | 3 | | | 7 | 8² | 13 | | 12 | | | | | | | | | 27 |
| 1 | 2 | 3 | 5¹ | | | 6 | | 9 | | 11 | 10 | | | 4 | 13 | | 7² | 8 | | | | | 12 | | | | | | | 28 |
| | | 4 | | | | 6 | | 9 | | 11 | 10³ | | | 5 | 14 | | 8² | 3 | 7¹ | | | 13 | 1 | 2 | 12 | | | | | 29 |
| 1 | | 3 | 5² | | | 9 | | 8 | | 10 | 12 | | | 4 | | | 7 | | | 13 | | | | | 2 | 6¹ | 11 | | | 30 |
| | | 4 | | | | 7 | 13 | 9¹ | | 11 | 6³ | | | 3 | | | 8 | 5² | 12 | | | | | | 1 | 2 | 14 | 10 | | 31 |
| | | 3 | | | | 7¹ | 14 | 9 | | 10 | 6 | | | 4 | | | 8 | 5³ | 12 | | | | | | 1 | 2 | 13 | 11² | | 32 |
| | | 4 | | | | 7 | 13 | 9¹ | | 10 | 6 | | | 3 | | | 8 | 5 | 12 | | | | | | 1 | 2 | | 11² | | 33 |
| | | 4 | | 5 | | 7 | 14 | 12 | 13 | 11 | 6 | | | 3 | | | 8³ | | | | 9¹ | | | | 1 | 2 | | 10² | | 34 |
| | | 4 | | 5 | | 7 | 13 | 12 | | 10 | 6 | | | 3 | | | 8 | | | | 9² | | | | 1 | 2 | | 11¹ | | 35 |
| 13 | | 3 | | 5 | | 6 | 7 | | | 10 | 9 | | | 4 | | | 8¹ | | | | | | | | 1 | 2 | 12 | 11² | | 36 |
| | | 4 | | 5 | | 6 | 9¹ | | | 10 | 6 | | | 3 | | | 7 | | | | | | | | 1 | 2 | 12 | 11 | | 37 |
| | | 3 | | 5 | | 7 | 8¹ | 14 | | 10 | 6 | | | 4 | | | 9² | 13 | | | | | | | 1 | 2 | 12 | 11³ | | 38 |
| | 2 | 3 | 7 | 8 | | | 6 | 4² | 13 | 12 | | | | 5 | | | | 9 | | | | | | | 1 | | 10 | 11¹ | | 39 |
| | | 4 | | 5 | | 7 | 8² | 9¹ | | 11 | 10 | | | 3 | | | 6 | | | | | | | | 1 | 2 | 13 | 12 | | 40 |
| 13 | | 3 | | 5 | | 7³ | 12 | 14 | | 10 | 9 | | | 4 | | | 8¹ | | | | | | | | 1 | 2 | 6 | 11² | | 41 |
| 5³ | 4 | | 12 | | | 7 | | 14 | | 10 | 6 | | | 3 | | | 13 | 8 | | | | | | | 1 | 2 | 9¹ | 11² | | 42 |
| | 4 | 3 | 5 | | | 7 | | 13 | 12 | 10 | 6 | | | | | | 8 | | | | | | | | 1 | 2 | 9² | 11¹ | | 43 |
| | 3 | 4 | 5 | | | 7 | | | | 10 | 6 | | | 8 | | | 9 | | | | | | | | 1 | 2 | 12 | 11¹ | | 44 |
| | 4 | | 5 | | | 7 | | 13 | | 10 | 6 | | | 3 | | | 9 | 8² | | | | | | | 1 | 2 | 12 | 11¹ | | 45 |
| | 3 | 14 | 5¹ | 8 | | | | 13 | | 10 | 6 | | | 4³ | | | 7 | 9 | | | | | | | 1 | 2 | 12 | 11² | | 46 |

**FA Cup**

| | | | |
|---|---|---|---|
| Fourth Qualifying | AFC Telford U | (a) | 2-2 |
| *Replay* | AFC Telford U | (h) | 1-0 |
| First Round | Luton T | (a) | 1-1 |
| *Replay* | Luton T | (h) | 0-2 |

**FA Trophy**

| | | | |
|---|---|---|---|
| First Round | AFC Telford | (a) | 0-1 |

# SOUTHPORT

*Ground:* Merseyrail Community Stadium, Haig Avenue, Southport PR8 6JZ.   *Tel:* (01704) 533 422.
*Website:* southportfc.net   *Year Formed:* 1881.   *Record Gate:* 20,010 (1932 v Newcastle U).
*Nickname:* 'The Sandgrounders'.   *Manager:* Alan Wright.   *Secretary:* Ken Hilton.   *Colours:* Yellow and black striped
shirts, yellow shorts, yellow socks.

## SOUTHPORT – BLUE SQUARE PREMIER 2012–13 LEAGUE RECORD

| Match No. | Date | Venue | Opponents | Result | H/T Score | Lg Pos. | Goalscorers | Attendance |
|---|---|---|---|---|---|---|---|---|
| 1 | Aug 11 | H | Grimsby T | D | 1-1 | 0-0 | 15 | Grand [87] | 1743 |
| 2 | 14 | A | Alfreton T | D | 3-3 | 1-1 | 15 | Whalley [31], Almond [68], Tames [90] | 562 |
| 3 | 18 | A | Cambridge U | L | 0-2 | 0-0 | 19 | | 2004 |
| 4 | 25 | H | Tamworth | L | 0-3 | 0-2 | 23 | | 1014 |
| 5 | 27 | A | Hyde | W | 2-0 | 1-0 | 17 | Almond [12], Tames [50] | 734 |
| 6 | Sept 1 | H | AFC Telford U | L | 0-3 | 0-1 | 20 | | 1005 |
| 7 | 4 | H | Gateshead | W | 2-1 | 0-0 | 17 | Whalley [70], Ledsham [87] | 686 |
| 8 | 8 | A | Kidderminster H | D | 2-2 | 0-1 | 18 | Ledsham [59], Gray (pen) [65] | 1650 |
| 9 | 15 | H | Ebbsfleet U | W | 1-0 | 0-0 | 14 | Lever (pen) [90] | 872 |
| 10 | 22 | A | Newport Co | L | 1-2 | 1-0 | 16 | Lever (pen) [18] | 2802 |
| 11 | 25 | H | Stockport Co | D | 1-1 | 0-1 | 14 | Newton (og) [85] | 818 |
| 12 | 29 | A | Luton T | L | 1-3 | 1-1 | 18 | Parry [45] | 5696 |
| 13 | Oct 6 | H | Nuneaton T | W | 3-1 | 2-0 | 17 | Lever (pen) [19], Grand [24], Almond [68] | 1302 |
| 14 | 9 | A | Barrow | L | 2-3 | 1-0 | 17 | Lynch [28], Anderson (og) [56] | 924 |
| 15 | 13 | A | Woking | W | 3-2 | 1-1 | 15 | Parry [40], Lynch [56], Lever (pen) [82] | 1739 |
| 16 | 27 | H | Hereford U | D | 2-2 | 2-2 | 15 | Ledsham [33], Lever (pen) [38] | 1028 |
| 17 | Nov 6 | H | Wrexham | L | 1-4 | 1-0 | 16 | Tames [37] | 1324 |
| 18 | 10 | A | Mansfield T | L | 0-1 | 0-1 | 20 | | 1918 |
| 19 | 17 | A | Dartford | D | 2-2 | 1-2 | 20 | Akrigg [21], Ledsham [90] | 1506 |
| 20 | Dec 1 | A | Stockport Co | W | 4-3 | 3-2 | 17 | Almond [6], Akrigg [8], Owens [34], Rowe (og) [89] | 3445 |
| 21 | 8 | H | Braintree T | L | 0-2 | 0-2 | 20 | | 803 |
| 22 | 26 | A | Macclesfield T | W | 3-2 | 2-0 | 18 | Willis [24], Almond [29], Whalley [77] | 1173 |
| 23 | 29 | H | Hyde | L | 0-1 | 0-1 | 18 | | 1068 |
| 24 | Jan 1 | A | Macclesfield T | D | 2-2 | 2-0 | 19 | Lever 2 (1 pen) [8 (pl, 11] | 1481 |
| 25 | 5 | A | AFC Telford U | W | 3-1 | 0-0 | 17 | Grand 2 [65, 69], Almond [77] | 1643 |
| 26 | 8 | H | Lincoln C | W | 4-2 | 3-1 | 12 | Grand 2 [18, 25], Owens [32], Ledsham [77] | 815 |
| 27 | 19 | H | Mansfield T | L | 1-2 | 1-1 | 13 | Whalley [6] | 804 |
| 28 | 29 | A | Wrexham | D | 2-2 | 1-1 | 12 | Ledsham [13], Owens [81] | 3002 |
| 29 | Feb 2 | A | Hereford U | D | 2-2 | 1-0 | 13 | Whalley [32], Byrne [68] | 1513 |
| 30 | 9 | A | Nuneaton T | W | 1-0 | 1-0 | 13 | O'Halloran (og) [15] | 779 |
| 31 | 12 | H | Barrow | W | 5-2 | 0-1 | 11 | Willis [49], Ledsham 2 [57, 73], Almond [65], Owens [78] | 806 |
| 32 | 23 | H | Woking | L | 1-2 | 0-1 | 14 | Chalmers [61] | 911 |
| 33 | Mar 2 | H | Dartford | D | 2-2 | 1-1 | 14 | Owens [40], Whalley (pen) [83] | 823 |
| 34 | 5 | H | Cambridge U | W | 2-1 | 0-1 | 13 | Byrne [54], Whalley (pen) [60] | 615 |
| 35 | 9 | A | Lincoln C | L | 0-1 | 0-1 | 13 | | 1827 |
| 36 | 12 | H | Forest Green R | L | 1-2 | 1-0 | 13 | Whalley (pen) [30] | 632 |
| 37 | 16 | A | Ebbsfleet U | L | 1-4 | 0-4 | 15 | Almond [48] | 603 |
| 38 | 19 | A | Tamworth | L | 1-2 | 1-0 | 16 | Chalmers [40] | 565 |
| 39 | 23 | H | Kidderminster H | L | 1-3 | 0-1 | 16 | Hattersley [58] | 946 |
| 40 | 26 | H | Newport Co | L | 0-2 | 0-2 | 18 | | 606 |
| 41 | 30 | A | Gateshead | D | 2-2 | 0-0 | 20 | Almond [58], Whalley [64] | 406 |
| 42 | Apr 1 | H | Alfreton T | L | 0-2 | 0-2 | 20 | | 830 |
| 43 | 3 | A | Braintree T | W | 3-1 | 1-0 | 17 | Almond 2 [9, 62], Grand [50] | 451 |
| 44 | 6 | A | Grimsby T | D | 2-2 | 2-1 | 17 | Ledsham 2 [19, 45] | 3780 |
| 45 | 13 | A | Forest Green R | W | 1-0 | 0-0 | 17 | Stokes (og) [77] | 1496 |
| 46 | 20 | H | Luton T | L | 1-3 | 1-2 | 20 | Clancy [2] | 1406 |

**Final League Position: 20**

## GOALSCORERS

*League (72):* Almond 11, Ledsham 10, Whalley 9 (3 pens), Grand 7, Lever 7 (6 pens), Owens 5, Tames 3, Akrigg 2, Byrne 2, Chalmers 2, Lynch 2, Parry 2, Willis 2, Clancy 1, Gray 1 (1 pen), Hattersley 1, own goals 5.
*FA Cup (0).*
*FA Trophy (11):* Tames 3, Almond 2, Ledsham 2, Whalley 2 (2 pens), Owens 1, Parry 1.

| McMillan 38 | Smith J 41+2 | Akrigg 11 | Grand 41 | Lever 27+4 | Whalley 42+1 | Parry 35+3 | Moogan 24 | Benjamin 16+11 | Gray 7 | Bakare 7+14 | Ledsham 38+5 | Almond 22+15 | Chalmers 18+11 | Tames 9+18 | Stephenson 3+4 | Barnes 1+3 | Lynch 19+5 | Poku 30+2 | Willis 10+8 | Ellison 3 | Joyce —+7 | Owens 22 | Byrne 10 | Kay 14+2 | Clancy 4+5 | Hattersley 6+2 | Hibbert 1+2 | Smith B 2 | Hedge 5 | Match No. |
|---|---|---|---|---|---|---|---|---|---|---|---|---|---|---|---|---|---|---|---|---|---|---|---|---|---|---|---|---|---|---|
| 1 | 2 | 3 | 4 | 5 | 6 | 7 | 8[3] | 9[1] | 10[2] | 11 | 12 | 13 | 14 | | | | | | | | | | | | | | | | | 1 |
| 1 | 4 | 5 | 3 | 6 | 11[1] | 2 | 8 | 7[2] | 10[3] | 9 | 12 | 13 | 14 | | | | | | | | | | | | | | | | | 2 |
| 1 | 2 | 3 | 4 | 5 | | 7 | 8 | 11[2] | 10[3] | 9 | 6[1] | 12 | 13 | 14 | | | | | | | | | | | | | | | | 3 |
| 1 | 2 | 3[2] | 4 | | 8 | | | 12 | 10[3] | 11 | 9 | 7 | 6[1] | | 14 | 5 | 13 | | | | | | | | | | | | | 4 |
| 1 | 2 | | 5 | 3 | | 8 | 7[1] | 9 | 10[3] | 12 | | 6[1] | 13 | 11[2] | | 14 | 4 | | | | | | | | | | | | | 5 |
| 1 | 2 | 4[3] | 5 | 9 | 8 | | 6[1] | 11 | 13 | 12 | | 14 | 10[2] | | | 3 | 7 | | | | | | | | | | | | | 6 |
| 1 | 2 | | 5 | 3 | 6[1] | | 8 | 13 | 10[2] | 9[3] | 11 | 12 | | | | 4 | 7 | 14 | | | | | | | | | | | | 7 |
| 1 | 4 | | 5 | 6 | 7[2] | 2 | | 13 | 11[3] | 10[1] | 9 | 14 | 12 | | | 3 | 8 | | | | | | | | | | | | | 8 |
| 1 | 2 | | 4 | 5 | 6 | 7[1] | 8 | 11[2] | 13 | 10[3] | 14 | 12 | | | | 3 | 9 | | | | | | | | | | | | | 9 |
| 1 | 2 | 3 | 5 | 7[3] | 6 | | 10 | 13 | 12 | 8 | 9[1] | 14 | | | | 4 | 11[2] | | | | | | | | | | | | | 10 |
| 1 | 2 | | 4 | 5 | 6 | 8[2] | 9 | 13 | 10 | 11[1] | | 14 | | | | 3[3] | 7 | 14 | | | | | | | | | | | | 11 |
| 1 | 4[1] | | 5 | 6 | 7 | 2 | | 8[2] | 14 | | 11 | 10[3] | | | | 3 | 9 | 13 | | | | | | | | | | | | 12 |
| 1 | | 4 | 5 | 3[1] | 6 | 2 | | 8[3] | 14 | | 9 | 11[2] | 13 | | | 7 | 12 | 10 | | | | | | | | | | | | 13 |
| 1 | 13 | 4 | 3 | | 8 | 2 | 9 | | | 11[1] | | 12 | | | | 5 | 7 | 6 | 10[2] | | | | | | | | | | | 14 |
| 1 | | | 3 | 5 | 6 | 2 | | 8 | | | | 13 | 11[2] | | | 4 | 7 | 9[8] | 10[1] | 12 | | | | | | | | | | 15 |
| 1 | 12 | | 4 | 5[8] | 9 | 2 | 7 | | | 6 | 13 | | 11 | 10[2] | | 3[1] | 8 | 14 | | | | | | | | | | | | 16 |
| 1 | 2[2] | | 5 | | 6 | 4 | 8 | 12 | | 11 | | 10[1] | 9[3] | | | 13 | 7[3] | 3 | 14 | | | | | | | | | | | 17 |
| 1 | 4 | | 5 | 6 | 7 | 3 | 9[3] | 8[1] | | | 10[2] | 12 | 14 | 11 | 13 | 2 | | | | | | | | | | | | | | 18 |
| 1 | 2 | 3[3] | 4 | 5 | 9 | | 7 | | | 6 | 10 | 13 | 11[12] | 12 | | 14 | 8[1] | | | | | | | | | | | | | 19 |
| 1 | 2 | 3 | 4[2] | 5 | 10[3] | | 8 | | | 6 | 13 | | | | | 14 | 7 | | | | | 11 | | | | | | | | 20 |
| 1 | 2 | 3[1] | | 5 | 6 | | 8 | | | 14 | 12 | 9 | 13 | 11[3] | | 4 | 7 | | | | | 10[2] | | | | | | | | 21 |
| 1 | 3 | | 4 | 10[1] | 5 | | 6 | | | 12 | 9 | 11[2] | | | | 2 | 7 | 8 | 13 | | | | | | | | | | | 22 |
| 1 | 3 | | 4 | 10 | 5 | | 7[2] | | | 13 | 8 | 11[1] | 12 | | | 2 | 6[3] | 9 | 14 | | | | | | | | | | | 23 |
| 1 | 3 | | 4 | 5 | 6[2] | | 7 | 8 | | 12 | 10 | 13 | | | | 2 | | 9 | | | | 11[1] | | | | | | | | 24 |
| 1 | 3 | | 4 | 5 | .7[3] | 2 | 8[1] | 11[2] | | 14 | 9 | 12 | | | | 6 | 13 | | | | | 10 | | | | | | | | 25 |
| 1 | 3 | | 4 | 6 | 9[3] | 2 | | 14 | | 7 | 11[2] | | 12 | | | 5 | 8 | | | | | 13 | 10[1] | | | | | | | 26 |
| 1 | 2 | 3 | 4 | | 10 | 5 | 7[3] | 8 | | 12 | 6 | | 14 | 11[2] | | | 9[1] | 13 | | | | 14 | 10 | | | | | | | 27 |
| 1 | 2 | 3[1] | 4 | | 9 | | 8 | 11 | | 13 | 6 | | 12 | | | 5[2] | 7[3] | | | | | 14 | 10 | | | | | | | 28 |
| 1 | 4 | | 5 | | 10 | 12 | | 8[1] | | 7 | | 2 | | | | | | 9 | | | | 6 | 3 | 11 | | | | | | 29 |
| 1 | 2 | | 3 | | 9[2] | | 7[1] | | | 6 | 12 | 5 | 13 | | | | 8 | | | | | 11 | 4 | 10 | | | | | | 30 |
| 1 | 3 | | 4[1] | | 10 | 12 | | 7 | | 11[3] | 5 | 14 | | | | | 8 | 13 | | | | 9 | 2[2] | 6 | | | | | | 31 |
| 1 | 2 | | 5[8] | | 7 | 12 | | 10[1] | | 11 | 3[2] | 13 | | | | | 8 | 14 | | | | 6 | 4[3] | 9 | | | | | | 32 |
| 1 | 3 | | | | 10 | 6 | | 8 | | 12 | 2[2] | | | | | | 7 | 11[1] | | | | 5 | 4 | 9 | 13 | | | | | 33 |
| 1 | 3 | | | | 10 | 4 | | 14 | | 8[3] | 13 | 5 | | | | | 6[2] | 9[1] | | | | 11 | 2 | 7 | 12 | | | | | 34 |
| 1 | 2 | | | | 9 | 3 | | | | 10 | 12 | 7[2] | 14 | | | | 6 | 13 | | | | 11 | 4[8] | 5[1] | 8[3] | | | | | 35 |
| 1 | 5 | 4 | 12 | 6 | 3 | | 7 | | | 11 | 10[2] | 2[1] | | | | | 13 | | | | | | 8 | 9 | | | | | | 36 |
| 1 | 5 | 4[2] | 13 | 6 | 3 | | 7[1] | | | 12 | 11 | 2 | 14 | | | | 8 | | | | | | 9 | 10[3] | | | | | | 37 |
| 1[8] | 5 | | 4 | 13 | 6 | 3 | | 7 | | 14 | 2[1] | | | | | | 9 | | | | | 11[3] | 8 | 10[2] | 12 | | | | | 38 |
| | | 3 | 5 | 6[3] | 4 | 7[2] | | 9[1] | 12 | | 2 | 8 | | | | | 11 | | | 13 | 14 | 10 | | | 1 | | | | | 39 |
| 2 | | 4 | 5 | 6 | 3 | 8[3] | | 9 | 14 | | 7[1] | | | | | | 11 | | | 12 | | 10 | 13 | 12 | | 1[2] | | | | 40 |
| | 5 | 3 | 13 | 6[2] | 7 | | | 9 | 12 | 2[8] | 11 | | | | | 4 | 8 | | | | | 10[1] | | | | 1 | | | | 41 |
| | 3 | 4 | 5 | 11 | 6 | | 13 | | | 8[2] | 10 | 9 | | | | | 2 | 7[1] | 12 | | | | | | | 1 | | | | 42 |
| | 3 | 4 | 6 | 7[2] | 9 | | 13 | 8 | | 10 | 2[1] | | | | | | 11 | 5 | | | | | | 12 | | 1 | | | | 43 |
| | 6 | 5 | 4 | 7 | 8 | | 13 | 9 | | 10[3] | 2 | | | | | | 11[1] | | | | | 3[2] | 14 | 12 | | 1 | | | | 44 |
| | 2 | 4 | | 7 | 3 | | | 8 | | 9 | 6 | | | | | 12 | | | | | | 5 | 10[1] | 11 | | 1 | | | | 45 |
| | 3 | | 4 | 14 | | 6[2] | | 13 | | 11[1] | 2 | 9 | | 12 | 7[3] | 5 | | 10 | | | | 8 | | 1 | | | | | | 46 |

**FA Cup**

| | | | |
|---|---|---|---|
| Fourth Qualifying | Wrexham | (a) | 0-2 |

**FA Trophy**

| | | | |
|---|---|---|---|
| First Round | Stafford Rangers | (a) | 4-0 |
| Second Round | Stockport Co | (a) | 1-1 |
| *Replay* | Stockport Co | (h) | 3-1 |
| Third Round | King's Lynn T | (a) | 2-0 |
| Quarter-Finals | Wrexham | (h) | 1-3 |

# STOCKPORT COUNTY

*Ground:* Edgeley Park, Hardcastle Road, Edgeley, Stockport, Cheshire SK3 9DD.   *Tel:* (0161) 286 8888 (ext 257).
*Fax:* (0161) 429 7392.   *Website:* stockportcounty.com   *Year Formed:* 1883.   *Record Gate:* 27,833 (1950 v Liverpool, FA Cup 5th rd).   *Nickname:* 'County' or 'The Hatters'.   *Manager:* Ian Bogie.   *Secretary:* Tony Whiteside.
*Colours:* Reflex blue shirts with one broad white band, reflex blue shorts, white socks.

## STOCKPORT COUNTY – BLUE SQUARE PREMIER 2012–13 LEAGUE RECORD

| Match No. | Date | Venue | Opponents | Result | H/T Score | Lg Pos. | Goalscorers | Atten-dance |
|---|---|---|---|---|---|---|---|---|
| 1 | Aug 11 | H | Alfreton T | W 1-0 | 1-0 | 7 | Hattersley [36] | 3448 |
| 2 | 14 | A | Grimsby T | W 2-1 | 0-0 | 2 | Rowe [81], Whitehead [90] | 3670 |
| 3 | 18 | A | Tamworth | L 0-1 | 0-1 | 8 | | 1270 |
| 4 | 24 | H | Gateshead | L 1-2 | 1-0 | 9 | Connor [34] | 3213 |
| 5 | 27 | A | AFC Telford U | D 2-2 | 1-0 | 11 | Whitehead 2 [42, 61] | 2079 |
| 6 | Sept 1 | H | Cambridge U | D 1-1 | 1-1 | 15 | Newton (pen) [30] | 3060 |
| 7 | 4 | H | Macclesfield T | L 3-4 | 2-2 | 16 | Hattersley [24], Whitehead [29], O'Donnell, D [62] | 4208 |
| 8 | 8 | A | Newport Co | D 0-0 | 0-0 | 15 | | 2306 |
| 9 | 15 | H | Woking | L 1-2 | 1-1 | 19 | Kenyon [15] | 3151 |
| 10 | 22 | A | Braintree T | D 0-0 | 0-0 | 17 | | 653 |
| 11 | 25 | A | Southport | D 1-1 | 1-0 | 18 | Hattersley [40] | 818 |
| 12 | 29 | H | Ebbsfleet U | W 3-1 | 0-0 | 14 | Hobson 2 [51, 53], Collins [57] | 4641 |
| 13 | Oct 6 | A | Hereford U | W 2-1 | 2-0 | 11 | Hobson 2 [18, 42] | 1889 |
| 14 | 10 | H | Wrexham | L 2-3 | 1-2 | 14 | Hattersley 2 [23, 84] | 3789 |
| 15 | 13 | H | Kidderminster H | W 1-0 | 1-0 | 12 | Newton (pen) [44] | 3426 |
| 16 | 27 | A | Lincoln C | D 3-3 | 0-1 | 12 | Fagbola [46], Hobson [62], Turnbull [75] | 1873 |
| 17 | Nov 6 | H | Barrow | W 3-1 | 1-0 | 9 | Hattersley 2 [36, 49], Mainwaring [58] | 2805 |
| 18 | 10 | A | Forest Green R | L 1-4 | 0-3 | 12 | Newton (pen) [76] | 1176 |
| 19 | 17 | A | Nuneaton T | L 0-2 | 0-1 | 13 | | 1221 |
| 20 | Dec 1 | H | Southport | L 3-4 | 2-3 | 16 | Turnbull [42], Hattersley (pen) [44], Halls [58] | 3445 |
| 21 | 8 | A | Woking | L 0-1 | 0-0 | 19 | | 1520 |
| 22 | 26 | H | Hyde | L 0-2 | 0-2 | 21 | | 3963 |
| 23 | 29 | H | AFC Telford U | D 2-2 | 0-0 | 21 | Jennings [70], Hobson [90] | 2791 |
| 24 | Jan 1 | H | Hyde | W 1-0 | 0-0 | 17 | Jennings [60] | 2540 |
| 25 | 5 | A | Cambridge U | L 1-4 | 1-2 | 20 | Whitehead [20] | 2305 |
| 26 | 15 | H | Mansfield T | L 1-3 | 0-3 | 21 | Meaney [81] | 2647 |
| 27 | 19 | H | Forest Green R | W 2-1 | 1-0 | 20 | Newton [40], Nolan [49] | 2802 |
| 28 | Feb 2 | H | Nuneaton T | W 3-2 | 2-2 | 16 | Jennings [4], Hattersley [11], Nolan [67] | 4133 |
| 29 | 9 | A | Wrexham | L 1-3 | 0-1 | 17 | Jennings [90] | 4206 |
| 30 | 12 | H | Lincoln C | W 2-0 | 0-0 | 14 | Hattersley [57], Newton [63] | 2769 |
| 31 | 16 | A | Ebbsfleet U | D 0-0 | 0-0 | 14 | | 912 |
| 32 | 19 | H | Tamworth | L 0-1 | 0-1 | 15 | | 2732 |
| 33 | 26 | H | Hereford U | L 2-3 | 1-1 | 17 | Cirak [17], Tunnicliffe [63] | 2618 |
| 34 | Mar 2 | H | Luton T | L 0-1 | 0-1 | 17 | | 4074 |
| 35 | 5 | A | Dartford | D 1-1 | 1-0 | 17 | Cullen [11] | 757 |
| 36 | 9 | A | Mansfield T | L 1-4 | 0-2 | 19 | Marshall [69] | 2628 |
| 37 | 12 | A | Barrow | W 2-0 | 0-0 | 17 | Cullen 2 [76, 81] | 803 |
| 38 | 16 | H | Braintree T | L 1-3 | 0-0 | 18 | Kenyon [84] | 3250 |
| 39 | 19 | A | Luton T | L 0-1 | 0-1 | 20 | | 5106 |
| 40 | 23 | H | Newport Co | W 1-0 | 0-0 | 18 | Minshull (og) [60] | 3154 |
| 41 | 30 | A | Macclesfield T | D 1-1 | 0-0 | 21 | Macken [75] | 4027 |
| 42 | Apr 1 | H | Grimsby T | L 1-2 | 0-0 | 21 | Kenyon [61] | 3804 |
| 43 | 6 | A | Alfreton T | W 3-2 | 1-1 | 20 | Tunnicliffe [40], Cullen [49], Nolan [61] | 1157 |
| 44 | 13 | H | Dartford | L 0-1 | 0-0 | 21 | | 6113 |
| 45 | 16 | A | Gateshead | D 1-1 | 0-0 | 21 | Cirak [90] | 685 |
| 46 | 20 | A | Kidderminster H | L 0-4 | 0-0 | 21 | | 6453 |

**Final League Position: 21 – Relegated to Conference North**

### GOALSCORERS

*League (57):* Hattersley 10 (1 pen), Hobson 6, Newton 5 (3 pens), Whitehead 5, Cullen 4, Jennings 4, Kenyon 3, Nolan 3, Cirak 2, Tunnicliffe 2, Turnbull 2, Collins 1, Connor 1, Fagbola 1, Halls 1, Macken 1, Mainwaring 1, Marshall 1, Meaney 1, O'Donnell, D 1, Rowe 1, own goal 1.
*FA Cup (5):* Hobson 1, Newton 1, Rowe 1, Sheridan 1, Whitehead 1.
*FA Trophy (7):* Jennings 4, Hattersley 2, Rose 1.

| Ormson 20+1 | Halls 32+2 | O'Donnell D 7+3 | Tunnicliffe 43+2 | Newton 42+1 | Sheridan 20+8 | Connor 21+2 | Nolan 24+7 | Kenyon 35+4 | Hattersley 26+3 | Hobson 17+8 | Whitehead 28+14 | Rowe 5+8 | Fagbola 35+3 | Piergianni 1+2 | Darkwah 2+3 | Collins 8+10 | Meaney —+4 | Mainwaring 27+5 | King 6 | Turnbull 12 | Eckersley —+2 | Jennings 13 | Bunney —+1 | Holden 1 | Brownhill 3 | O'Donnell R 20 | Cullen 15+1 | Macken 5+8 | Cirak 6+5 | Hammar 5+1 | Hackney 2+8 | Marshall 4+7 | Vidal 4 | Charnock 5 | Bullock 9 | Schofield 3+2 | Windsor —+3 | Match No. |
|---|---|---|---|---|---|---|---|---|---|---|---|---|---|---|---|---|---|---|---|---|---|---|---|---|---|---|---|---|---|---|---|---|---|---|---|---|---|---|
| 1 | 2 | 3 | 4 | 5 | $6^1$ | 7 | 8 | $9^2$ | 10 | 11 | $12^3$ | 13 | 14 | | | | | | | | | | | | | | | | | | | | | | | | | 1 |
| 1 | 2 | 3 | 4 | 5 | | 7 | 6 | 9 | $10^2$ | $11^1$ | 13 | $8^3$ | | | 12 | 14 | | | | | | | | | | | | | | | | | | | | | | 2 |
| 1 | $2^2$ | 3 | 4 | 5 | | 6 | 7 | 8 | $10^3$ | $11^1$ | 12 | 9 | | | 13 | | | 14 | | | | | | | | | | | | | | | | | | | | 3 |
| 1 | $2^2$ | 3 | 4 | 5 | $6^1$ | 8 | 7 | 9 | 10 | 11 | 12 | 13 | | | | | | | | | | | | | | | | | | | | | | | | | | 4 |
| 1 | 13 | $5^2$ | 2 | $8^1$ | 6 | 12 | $7^3$ | 10 | 14 | 9 | 11 | 3 | 4 | | | | | | | | | | | | | | | | | | | | | | | | | 5 |
| 1 | 13 | 3 | 4 | 5 | 9 | 7 | 10 | 11 | $8^1$ | 12 | $2^2$ | $6^3$ | 14 | | | | | | | | | | | | | | | | | | | | | | | | | 6 |
| 1 | | 3 | 4 | 5 | $7^1$ | 8 | 12 | 9 | 11 | 13 | $10^3$ | 2 | $6^2$ | | | 14 | | | | | | | | | | | | | | | | | | | | | | 7 |
| 1 | 14 | 3 | 2 | 9 | 6 | $4^1$ | 8 | $10^2$ | $11^3$ | 7 | 5 | 12 | | | 13 | | | | | | | | | | | | | | | | | | | | | | | 8 |
| 1 | | 4 | 5 | $7^3$ | 3 | $14^4$ | 9 | 10 | 12 | 8 | $11^2$ | 2 | | | | 13 | | $6^1$ | | | | | | | | | | | | | | | | | | | | 9 |
| | 2 | 4 | 5 | $8^1$ | 3 | $10^2$ | $11^3$ | 12 | 9 | 14 | 6 | | | | | 13 | 1 | 7 | | | | | | | | | | | | | | | | | | | | 10 |
| | 6 | 3 | 5 | 14 | $4^3$ | 8 | $10^1$ | 11 | $9^2$ | 2 | | | 13 | | | 12 | 1 | 7 | | | | | | | | | | | | | | | | | | | | 11 |
| | 5 | 2 | 8 | 14 | $3^2$ | 6 | 9 | $11^3$ | $10^1$ | 4 | | | 12 | | | 13 | 1 | 7 | | | | | | | | | | | | | | | | | | | | 12 |
| | 2 | 4 | $5^2$ | 6 | | 12 | 11 | $9^3$ | | 14 | 3 | | $10^1$ | | | 8 | 1 | 7 | 13 | | | | | | | | | | | | | | | | | | | 13 |
| | 2 | 3 | 5 | | | | 10 | 11 | $6^2$ | 13 | 4 | | $8^1$ | 12 | | 9 | 1 | 7 | | | | | | | | | | | | | | | | | | | | 14 |
| 1 | 2 | 4 | 5 | 14 | 13 | | 12 | 10 | $11^2$ | $6^3$ | 3 | | $8^1$ | | | 9 | | 7 | | | | | | | | | | | | | | | | | | | | 15 |
| 1 | $2^2$ | 3 | 5 | $11^1$ | 13 | | 7 | | 10 | $6^3$ | 4 | | 12 | | | 9 | 8 | | 9 | 14 | | | | | | | | | | | | | | | | | | 16 |
| 1 | 2 | | 4 | 5 | 13 | 8 | | | $10^3$ | $11^1$ | 6 | 14 | 3 | | | $12^2$ | 9 | 7 | | | | | | | | | | | | | | | | | | | | 17 |
| 1 | $2^2$ | | 4 | 5 | | 7 | | 12 | 10 | 11 | $9^3$ | 14 | $3^1$ | | | 13 | 8 | 6 | | | | | | | | | | | | | | | | | | | | 18 |
| 1 | | | 4 | 5 | 13 | 3 | | 8 | 14 | 11 | $12^2$ | | 2 | | | $6^1$ | 9 | $7^3$ | 10 | | | | | | | | | | | | | | | | | | | 19 |
| 12 | 2 | 13 | 4 | 5 | | 3 | | | $10^3$ | $11^2$ | 14 | 8 | | | | 9 | $11^1$ | 7 | 6 | | | | | | | | | | | | | | | | | | | 20 |
| 1 | $2^3$ | 4 | 3 | 5 | 8 | 7 | | | | $11^2$ | | 14 | 12 | | | 10 | | $9^1$ | | 6 | 13 | | | | | | | | | | | | | | | | | 21 |
| 1 | $2^1$ | 4 | | | 8 | 12 | 7 | | | 11 | 13 | 5 | | | 6 | | 9 | | | 10 | | $3^2$ | | | | | | | | | | | | | | | | 22 |
| 1 | $2^1$ | 12 | 3 | | | 6 | 7 | | | 13 | 11 | | $4^3$ | 14 | $9^2$ | 8 | | | | 10 | | | 5 | | | | | | | | | | | | | | | 23 |
| 1 | | 3 | | 12 | 7 | 6 | 2 | | | 13 | $11^2$ | | 4 | | $9^1$ | 8 | | | | 10 | | | 5 | | | | | | | | | | | | | | | 24 |
| 1 | | 4 | 13 | | $3^3$ | 8 | 7 | 14 | 12 | 10 | | | 2 | | | $6^1$ | 9 | | | 11 | | | $5^2$ | | | | | | | | | | | | | | | 25 |
| | $2^1$ | | 3 | 5 | | 7 | $8^3$ | 9 | $11^2$ | | 6 | | 4 | | | 12 | 14 | 13 | | 10 | | | | | 1 | | | | | | | | | | | | | 26 |
| | 2 | | 4 | 5 | $6^2$ | | 7 | 8 | $10^1$ | 12 | 9 | | 3 | | | 13 | | | | 11 | | | | | 1 | | | | | | | | | | | | | 27 |
| | 2 | | 4 | 5 | | 8 | 7 | $11^1$ | | $6^2$ | 3 | | | | | 9 | | | | 10 | | | | | 1 | 12 | 13 | | | | | | | | | | | 28 |
| | 2 | | 4 | 5 | | 7 | 8 | $6^2$ | | 12 | 3 | | | | | 9 | | | | 10 | | | | | 1 | $11^1$ | 13 | | | | | | | | | | | 29 |
| | 2 | | 4 | 5 | 13 | | 8 | 7 | $11^1$ | 14 | 3 | | | | | 9 | | | | $6^2$ | | | | | 1 | $10^3$ | | 12 | | | | | | | | | | 30 |
| | 2 | | 4 | 5 | | | 8 | $7^4$ | $11^1$ | 13 | 3 | | | | | 9 | | | | 6 | | | | | 1 | | $10^2$ | 12 | | | | | | | | | | 31 |
| | 2 | | $5^3$ | 3 | 6 | | 8 | $10^1$ | | | 4 | | | | | $9^2$ | | | | | | | | | 1 | 11 | 14 | 13 | 7 | 12 | | | | | | | | 32 |
| | 5 | | 4 | 2 | $7^1$ | | 8 | 13 | 14 | | | | | | | 9 | | | | | | | | | 1 | $10^3$ | | $11^2$ | 3 | 6 | 12 | | | | | | | 33 |
| | $2^3$ | | 4 | 5 | 7 | | 8 | 10 | | 12 | | | | | | $9^2$ | | | | | | | | | 1 | $11^1$ | | 14 | 3 | 13 | 6 | | | | | | | 34 |
| | 2 | | 4 | 5 | | | 8 | 7 | | $6^1$ | | | | | | 9 | | | | | | | | | 1 | $10^2$ | 13 | 11 | 3 | 12 | | | | | | | | 35 |
| | 5 | | 4 | 2 | | | 8 | 7 | | 9 | | | 14 | | | $6^1$ | | | | | | | | | 1 | 11 | 13 | $10^2$ | $3^3$ | | 12 | | | | | | | 36 |
| | 2 | | 3 | 5 | 7 | | $8^3$ | 6 | | $10^1$ | | 4 | | | | | | | | | | | | | 1 | $11^2$ | 12 | 14 | | 13 | 9 | | | | | | | 37 |
| | | | $4^3$ | 5 | | | $8^1$ | 12 | | 7 | | | | | | | | | | | | | | | 1 | 11 | 14 | | 13 | $9^2$ | 2 | 3 | 6 | 10 | | | | 38 |
| | | | 12 | 5 | | | 9 | | | | | | 3 | | | $10^3$ | | | | | | | | | 1 | 11 | 13 | 14 | | 7 | | $2^1$ | 4 | 6 | $8^2$ | | | 39 |
| | 2 | | | 5 | $9^1$ | | 12 | 7 | | $6^2$ | | | 3 | | | | | | | | | | | | 1 | $10^3$ | 11 | | 14 | | | 4 | 8 | 13 | | | 40 |
| | 2 | | 12 | 5 | $9^2$ | | $8^3$ | | | 7 | | | 3 | | | | | | | | | | | | 1 | 10 | 11 | | 14 | | $4^1$ | 6 | 13 | | | | 41 |
| | $2^4$ | | 4 | 5 | 13 | | 12 | $8^3$ | | $11^1$ | | | 3 | | | | | | | | | | | | 1 | 9 | 10 | | 14 | | 7 | $6^2$ | | | | | 42 |
| | | | 3 | 5 | 6 | | 8 | 4 | | | | | 2 | | | $11^2$ | | | | | | | | | 1 | $9^1$ | 10 | | 12 | | 7 | | | 13 | | | 43 |
| | | | 3 | 5 | 6 | | $9^3$ | 8 | | 12 | | | 2 | | | 13 | | | | | | | | | 1 | $11^2$ | 10 | | 14 | | $4^1$ | 7 | | | | | 44 |
| | | | 4 | 5 | | | 12 | 7 | | $11^3$ | | | 3 | | | 9 | | | | | | | | | 1 | | 10 | 13 | $6^2$ | $2^1$ | | 8 | | 14 | | | 45 |
| 1 | | | 4 | 5 | 6 | | 8 | | | 10 | | | 3 | | | $9^2$ | | | | | | | | | | | $11^3$ | 13 | $12^2$ | 2 | | $7^1$ | | 14 | | | 46 |

**FA Cup**
Fourth Qualifying   Stalybridge Celtic   (h)   5-3
First Round   Southend U   (a)   0-3

**FA Trophy**
First Round   Ossett T   (h)   6-0
Second Round   Southport   (h)   1-1

# TAMWORTH

*Ground:* The Lamb Ground, Kettlebrook, Tamworth, Staffordshire B77 1AA.   *Tel:* (01827) 65798.
*Fax:* (01827) 62236.   *Website:* thelambs.co.uk   *Year Formed:* 1933.   *Record Gate:* 4,920 (1948 v Atherstone T).
*Nickname:* 'The Lambs'.   *Caretake manager:* Dale Belford.   *Secretary:* Rod Hadley.   *Colours:* Red shirts with white
trim, white shorts, red socks.

## TAMWORTH – BLUE SQUARE PREMIER 2012–13 LEAGUE RECORD

| Match No. | Date | Venue | Opponents | Result | H/T Score | Lg Pos. | Goalscorers | Attendance |
|---|---|---|---|---|---|---|---|---|
| 1 | Aug 11 | A | Dartford | W 3-2 | 2-1 | 4 | Till [27], Cunnington 2 [40, 76] | 1370 |
| 2 | 14 | H | Hereford U | D 2-2 | 0-2 | 5 | Wright [48], Cunnington [88] | 1265 |
| 3 | 18 | H | Stockport Co | W 1-0 | 1-0 | 5 | Oji [45] | 1270 |
| 4 | 25 | A | Southport | W 3-0 | 2-0 | 3 | Cunnington (pen) [36], Collins [45], Wright [49] | 1014 |
| 5 | 27 | H | Wrexham | L 0-1 | 0-1 | 6 | | 1433 |
| 6 | Sept 1 | A | Braintree T | L 1-2 | 1-1 | 8 | Cunnington [35] | 501 |
| 7 | 4 | A | Mansfield T | L 0-2 | 0-1 | 13 | | 2105 |
| 8 | 8 | H | Barrow | L 1-3 | 1-1 | 13 | Cunnington (pen) [44] | 892 |
| 9 | 15 | A | Gateshead | W 2-0 | 1-0 | 11 | Cunnington (pen) [36], Marshall [51] | 622 |
| 10 | 22 | H | Lincoln C | W 1-0 | 1-0 | 9 | Kerry [1] | 1042 |
| 11 | 25 | H | Luton T | L 1-2 | 1-0 | 9 | Dempster [22] | 1137 |
| 12 | 29 | A | Woking | W 3-2 | 2-0 | 7 | Wright [8], Cunnington [23], Baldock [70] | 1467 |
| 13 | Oct 6 | H | Newport Co | L 1-2 | 0-1 | 8 | Cunnington [61] | 1201 |
| 14 | 9 | A | Forest Green R | W 2-1 | 2-0 | 7 | Cunnington 2 (1 pen) [22, 25 (p)] | 1022 |
| 15 | 13 | A | Hyde | L 1-2 | 1-0 | 7 | Kelly [31] | 657 |
| 16 | 27 | H | Ebbsfleet U | L 0-1 | 0-1 | 10 | | 838 |
| 17 | Nov 3 | H | Grimsby T | L 0-1 | 0-0 | 10 | | 1042 |
| 18 | 6 | A | Macclesfield T | L 0-2 | 0-1 | 13 | | 1089 |
| 19 | 10 | H | AFC Telford U | D 0-0 | 0-0 | 14 | | 935 |
| 20 | 17 | A | Cambridge U | D 1-1 | 0-0 | 14 | Cunnington [77] | 3003 |
| 21 | Dec 1 | A | Dartford | W 3-2 | 0-1 | 9 | Barrow 2 (2 pens) [56, 85], Hendrie, L [88] | 832 |
| 22 | 4 | H | Kidderminster H | L 0-1 | 0-0 | 11 | | 1031 |
| 23 | 8 | A | Grimsby T | L 0-2 | 0-1 | 15 | | 3109 |
| 24 | 26 | A | Nuneaton T | L 1-2 | 1-0 | 17 | Wright [34] | 1389 |
| 25 | 29 | H | Wrexham | D 2-2 | 1-1 | 17 | Gudger [29], Barrow [85] | 3703 |
| 26 | Jan 2 | H | Nuneaton T | W 2-1 | 1-1 | 16 | Barrow [44], Tait [76] | 1516 |
| 27 | 5 | H | Braintree T | L 1-4 | 0-2 | 18 | Cunnington [72] | 763 |
| 28 | Feb 2 | H | Gateshead | W 2-0 | 0-0 | 15 | Lloyd [80], Cunnington (pen) [90] | 618 |
| 29 | 9 | A | Newport Co | D 2-2 | 0-2 | 15 | Hendrie, L [74], Cunnington (pen) [90] | 1712 |
| 30 | 12 | H | Macclesfield T | D 0-0 | 0-0 | 17 | | 670 |
| 31 | 16 | A | AFC Telford U | D 3-3 | 2-1 | 15 | Wright 3 [18, 41, 77] | 1747 |
| 32 | 19 | A | Stockport Co | W 1-0 | 1-0 | 14 | Cunnington (pen) [16] | 2732 |
| 33 | 23 | H | Hyde | W 2-0 | 0-0 | 12 | Oji [51], Wright [57] | 746 |
| 34 | 26 | H | Cambridge U | L 1-2 | 0-1 | 13 | Cunnington [89] | 668 |
| 35 | Mar 2 | A | Barrow | L 0-2 | 0-1 | 15 | | 896 |
| 36 | 9 | H | Alfreton T | D 1-1 | 0-1 | 14 | Byfield [65] | 703 |
| 37 | 16 | A | Kidderminster H | L 1-4 | 1-2 | 16 | Cunnington [5] | 2392 |
| 38 | 19 | H | Southport | W 2-1 | 0-1 | 15 | Lloyd [83], Byfield [90] | 565 |
| 39 | 23 | A | Luton T | D 0-0 | 0-0 | 14 | | 5501 |
| 40 | 30 | H | Mansfield T | L 0-1 | 0-0 | 16 | | 1968 |
| 41 | Apr 1 | A | Hereford U | L 2-5 | 0-3 | 17 | Connor (og) [74], Hendrie, L [88] | 1424 |
| 42 | 6 | H | Forest Green R | W 2-1 | 2-0 | 16 | Cunnington 2 [6, 42] | 773 |
| 43 | 11 | A | Alfreton T | L 0-3 | 0-2 | 18 | | 568 |
| 44 | 13 | A | Lincoln C | L 1-2 | 1-0 | 20 | Gray (og) [7] | 3174 |
| 45 | 16 | A | Ebbsfleet U | D 1-1 | 0-0 | 20 | Wylde [72] | 488 |
| 46 | 20 | H | Woking | W 2-1 | 1-1 | 19 | Marshall [36], Cunnington (pen) [60] | 1509 |

**Final League Position: 19**

## GOALSCORERS

*League (55):* Cunnington 21 (8 pens), Wright 8, Barrow 4 (2 pens), Hendrie, L 3, Byfield 2, Lloyd 2, Marshall 2, Oji 2, Baldock 1, Collins 1, Dempster 1, Gudger 1, Kelly 1, Kerry 1, Tait 1, Till 1, Wylde 1, own goals 2.
*FA Cup (0).*
*FA Trophy (9):* Kelly 3, Baldock 2, Wright 2, Courtney 1, Turner 1.

| Breedon 39 | Tait 31+3 | Oji 23+3 | Marshall 35+2 | Barrow 22+2 | Kelly 33+2 | Till 24+7 | Kerry 25+2 | Marna 3+1 | Wright 32+9 | Cunnington 42+3 | Gudger 26+7 | Llado 1+7 | Collins 3+11 | Courtney 38+1 | Ivey-Ward —+5 | Bottomer —+2 | Mitchell 4 | Jeffers 6 | Mukendi 1 | Baldock 14+1 | Harrop 1+1 | Girvan —+1 | Dempster 6 | Johnson —+1 | Taylor G 10 | Hendrie L 24+3 | Moke 4+5 | Severn 3 | Regan 4+1 | Healy —+2 | Roberts-Nurse 1 | Turner —+1 | Thorpe 13 | Lloyd 8+7 | Byfield 10+8 | Perry 3+9 | Hessenthaler 5+1 | Hendrie S 2+3 | Wylde 10 | Match No. |
|---|---|---|---|---|---|---|---|---|---|---|---|---|---|---|---|---|---|---|---|---|---|---|---|---|---|---|---|---|---|---|---|---|---|---|---|---|---|---|---|---|
| 1 | 2 | 3 | 4 | 5 | 6¹ | 7 | 8 |  | 9² | 10 | 11 | 12 | 13 |  |  |  |  |  |  |  |  |  |  |  |  |  |  |  |  |  |  |  |  |  |  |  |  |  |  | 1 |
| 1 | 2 | 4 | 3 | 9 |  | 6 | 7 | 8 | 11 | 10 | 5¹ |  | 12 |  |  |  |  |  |  |  |  |  |  |  |  |  |  |  |  |  |  |  |  |  |  |  |  |  |  | 2 |
| 1 | 2 | 3 | 4 | 9 | 6² | 7 |  | 8¹ | 11 | 10 | 5 |  | 13 | 12 |  |  |  |  |  |  |  |  |  |  |  |  |  |  |  |  |  |  |  |  |  |  |  |  |  | 3 |
| 1 | 2 |  | 4 | 9 | 6¹ |  | 8 |  | 11² | 10³ | 5 | 12 | 7 | 3 | 13 | 14 |  |  |  |  |  |  |  |  |  |  |  |  |  |  |  |  |  |  |  |  |  |  |  | 4 |
| 1 | 2 | 4 |  | 9 | 6 |  |  |  | 10⁸ | 11 | 5 | 8² | 7¹ | 3 | 12 | 13 |  |  |  |  |  |  |  |  |  |  |  |  |  |  |  |  |  |  |  |  |  |  |  | 5 |
| 1 | 2 | 4³ | 3 | 9 | 6² |  | 8 |  | 10 |  | 5 |  |  | 14 | 12 | 13 |  |  |  | 7 | 11¹ |  |  |  |  |  |  |  |  |  |  |  |  |  |  |  |  |  |  | 6 |
| 1 | 2 | 3¹ |  | 9 | 7 |  |  |  | 11 |  | 5 | 13 | 8² | 4 | 12 |  |  |  |  | 10 |  |  | 6³ | 14 |  |  |  |  |  |  |  |  |  |  |  |  |  |  |  | 7 |
| 1 | 2 |  |  | 9 | 6³ | 7 |  |  | 10 |  | 5¹ |  | 12 | 4 | 14 |  |  |  | 11² | 8 |  | 3 | 13 |  |  |  |  |  |  |  |  |  |  |  |  |  |  |  |  | 8 |
| 1 | 2 | 3 | 5 |  | 8² | 7 |  |  | 11³ | 10 | 12 | 14 | 13 |  |  |  |  |  | 9¹ | 6 |  | 4 |  |  |  |  |  |  |  |  |  |  |  |  |  |  |  |  |  | 9 |
| 1 | 2⁴ | 4 | 5³ | 6 | 7 |  |  |  | 11² | 10 | 12 |  |  | 13 |  | 14 |  |  | 9¹ | 8 |  | 3 |  |  |  |  |  |  |  |  |  |  |  |  |  |  |  |  |  | 10 |
| 1 |  |  | 4 | 5¹ | 6 | 7 |  |  |  | 11 | 10 | 12 |  | 13 |  | 2 |  |  | 9² | 8 |  | 3 |  |  |  |  |  |  |  |  |  |  |  |  |  |  |  |  |  | 11 |
| 1 |  |  | 4 | 9¹ | 12 | 6² | 7 |  | 11 | 10³ |  |  | 13 | 14 | 2 |  |  |  |  | 8 |  | 3 |  |  | 5 |  |  |  |  |  |  |  |  |  |  |  |  |  |  | 12 |
| 1 |  | 3 |  | 8² | 6³ | 9 | 14 |  | 10 | 11 |  |  |  | 13 | 2 |  |  |  |  |  |  |  | 7¹ | 4 | 5 | 12 |  |  |  |  |  |  |  |  |  |  |  |  |  | 13 |
| 1 | 2 | 13 | 4 | 8¹ | 12 | 9 |  |  | 11 | 10 |  |  |  | 5 |  |  |  |  |  |  |  |  | 6 |  | 3 | 7² |  |  |  |  |  |  |  |  |  |  |  |  |  | 14 |
| 1 | 2 | 7 | 4 | 12 | 9 | 6 |  |  | 11 | 10 |  |  |  | 3 |  |  |  |  |  |  |  |  |  |  | 5¹ | 8 |  |  |  |  |  |  |  |  |  |  |  |  |  | 15 |
| 1 | 2 | 4 | 14 | 8¹ | 12 | 9 |  |  | 10³ | 11 |  |  |  | 5 |  |  |  |  |  |  |  |  | 6² |  | 3 | 7 | 13 |  |  |  |  |  |  |  |  |  |  |  |  | 16 |
| 1 | 14 | 3¹ | 4 | 9 | 12 | 6³ | 7 |  | 11 | 10² |  |  |  | 2 |  |  |  |  |  |  |  |  |  |  | 5 | 8¹ | 13 |  |  |  |  |  |  |  |  |  |  |  |  | 17 |
| 1 | 2 | 3 | 8¹ | 6³ | 9 |  |  |  | 13 | 11 | 14 |  |  | 12 | 4 |  |  |  |  |  |  |  |  |  | 5 | 7 | 10² |  |  |  |  |  |  |  |  |  |  |  |  | 18 |
| 1 | 2 | 4 | 5 | 8 | 6 |  |  |  | 10 | 11 |  |  |  | 3 |  |  |  |  |  |  |  |  |  |  | 9 | 7¹ | 12 |  |  |  |  |  |  |  |  |  |  |  |  | 19 |
| 1 | 2 | 3 | 9 | 8 | 6³ | 12 |  |  | 11² | 10 |  |  |  | 13 | 4 |  |  |  |  | 14 |  |  |  |  | 5 | 7¹ |  |  |  |  |  |  |  |  |  |  |  |  |  | 20 |
|  | 2 |  | 4 | 9 | 8 | 13 | 7³ |  | 12 | 11¹ |  |  |  | 3 |  |  |  |  |  | 10 |  |  |  |  | 5² | 14 | 6 | 1 |  |  |  |  |  |  |  |  |  |  |  | 21 |
|  | 2² |  | 4 | 5 | 7 | 6 |  |  | 9 | 12 | 10¹ |  |  | 14 |  |  |  |  |  | 3 |  |  | 8 |  |  |  |  |  |  |  | 1 |  | 13 | 11³ |  |  |  |  |  | 22 |
|  | 3 |  | 4 | 5 | 12 | 8 |  |  | 10 | 9 |  |  |  | 2 |  |  |  |  |  | 7 |  |  |  |  |  |  |  |  |  |  | 1 |  |  | 11 | 6¹ |  |  |  |  | 23 |
| 1 | 2 |  | 5³ | 9 | 14 | 8² |  |  | 11 | 10¹ |  |  |  | 4 |  |  |  |  |  | 6 |  |  |  |  |  | 7 |  |  |  |  |  |  |  | 12 | 3 | 13 |  |  |  | 24 |
| 1 | 2 | 14 | 6 | 5 | 9¹ |  |  |  | 10 | 13 | 11² |  |  | 4 |  |  |  |  |  |  |  |  | 7³ |  |  | 8 |  |  |  |  |  |  |  | 12 | 3 |  |  |  |  | 25 |
| 1 | 2 | 3 | 13 | 9 | 8³ | 6 |  |  |  | 11² |  |  |  | 5 |  |  |  |  |  |  |  |  |  |  |  | 7 |  |  | 4 | 12 | 10¹ | 14 |  |  |  |  |  |  |  | 26 |
| 1 | 2 | 4 | 3 | 5 | 8¹ | 6² | 9 |  | 10 | 12 | 13 |  |  | 11 |  |  |  |  |  |  |  |  |  |  |  | 7 |  |  |  |  |  |  |  |  |  |  |  |  |  | 27 |
| 1 | 12 | 3 | 5¹ | 8 | 6² |  |  |  | 10 | 11 | 14 |  |  | 9³ | 4 |  |  |  |  |  |  |  |  |  |  | 7 |  |  |  |  |  |  | 2 | 13 |  |  |  |  |  | 28 |
| 1 | 12 | 2 |  | 6 | 8² |  |  |  | 11 | 10 |  |  |  | 4 |  |  |  |  |  |  |  |  |  |  |  | 7 |  |  |  |  |  |  | 5¹ | 9³ | 13 | 14 |  |  |  | 29 |
| 1 | 14 | 4 | 3 | 8 |  |  |  |  | 11² | 9¹ | 5 |  |  | 7 |  |  |  |  |  |  |  |  |  |  |  | 6 |  |  |  |  |  |  | 2 | 13 | 10³ | 12 |  |  |  | 30 |
| 1 |  | 4 | 3 | 8 |  |  |  |  | 11 | 10² | 6 |  |  | 5 |  |  |  |  |  |  |  |  |  |  |  | 7 |  |  |  |  |  |  | 2 | 12 | 9¹ | 13 |  |  |  | 31 |
| 1 |  | 4 | 3 | 8¹ |  |  |  |  | 11¹ | 10 | 9 |  |  | 2 |  |  |  |  |  |  |  |  |  |  |  | 5 |  |  |  |  |  |  | 6 | 12 | 7 | 13 |  |  |  | 32 |
| 1 |  | 3 | 4 | 8¹ |  |  |  |  | 10 | 11² |  |  |  | 5 |  |  |  |  |  |  |  |  |  |  |  | 6 |  |  |  |  |  |  | 2 | 9 | 12 |  | 7 | 13 |  | 33 |
| 1 | 2³ | 3 | 4 | 6 |  |  |  |  | 11¹ | 10 |  |  |  | 5 |  |  |  |  |  |  |  |  |  |  |  | 13 |  |  |  |  |  |  |  | 9² | 14 | 12 | 8 |  |  | 34 |
| 1 |  | 4 | 3 | 8 |  |  |  |  | 11 | 6 |  |  |  | 5 |  |  |  |  |  |  |  |  |  |  |  | 7 |  |  |  |  |  |  | 2 | 9¹ | 12 | 10 | 7² |  |  | 35 |
| 1 | 2 | 4 | 3 | 8 |  |  |  |  | 11¹ | 10 |  |  |  | 5 |  |  |  |  |  |  |  |  |  |  |  |  |  |  |  |  |  |  | 6 | 13 | 9 | 12 | 7² |  |  | 36 |
| 1 |  |  | 4 | 7 |  |  |  |  | 11² | 9 | 5 |  |  | 6 |  |  |  |  |  |  |  |  |  |  |  |  |  |  |  |  |  |  | 2 | 13 | 8¹ | 10 | 12 | 3 |  | 37 |
|  | 4 |  |  | 8 |  |  |  |  | 11² | 9 | 5 |  |  | 6 |  |  |  | 1 |  |  |  |  |  |  |  | 7 |  |  |  |  |  |  | 2 | 12 | 13 | 10¹ | 3 |  |  | 38 |
|  | 12 |  | 4 | 6 |  |  |  |  | 13 | 10³ | 5 |  |  | 7 |  |  |  | 1 |  |  |  |  |  |  |  | 8 |  |  |  |  |  |  | 2¹ | 9² | 11 | 14 | 3 |  |  | 39 |
|  | 5 |  | 8 | 6 |  |  |  |  | 12 | 10 | 2³ |  |  | 3 |  |  |  | 1 |  |  |  |  |  |  |  | 7 |  |  |  |  |  |  |  | 9² | 11¹ | 14 | 13 | 4 | 40 |
|  | 2 |  | 4 | 7 |  |  |  |  | 13 | 10² | 6 |  |  | 5 |  |  |  | 1 |  |  |  |  |  |  |  | 8 |  |  |  |  |  |  |  | 9¹ | 11³ | 12 | 14 | 3 | 41 |
| 1 | 5 |  | 4 | 8 | 12 |  |  |  | 10² | 9 | 6 |  |  |  |  |  |  |  |  |  |  |  |  |  |  | 7 |  |  |  |  |  |  | 2 |  | 13 | 11¹ |  |  | 3 | 42 |
| 1 | 2 | 3 | 6 | 12 | 9 |  |  |  | 11 | 10³ |  |  |  |  |  |  |  |  |  | 13 |  |  |  |  |  | 8² |  |  |  |  |  |  | 5 |  | 14 | 7¹ |  | 4 | 43 |
| 1 | 5 | 3 | 8 | 6³ | 12 |  |  |  | 13 | 11 |  |  |  | 9 |  |  |  |  |  | 2¹ |  |  |  |  |  | 7 |  |  |  |  |  |  |  |  | 14 | 10² |  | 4 | 44 |
| 1 | 5 | 3 | 7 | 6¹ | 12 |  |  |  | 10 | 2 |  |  |  | 9 |  |  |  |  |  |  |  |  |  |  |  | 8 |  |  |  |  |  |  |  |  | 11 |  |  | 4 | 45 |
| 1 | 2 | 4 | 8 | 11 |  |  |  |  | 13 | 9² | 5 |  |  | 6 |  |  |  |  |  |  |  |  |  |  |  | 7 |  |  |  |  |  |  |  |  | 10¹ | 12 |  | 3 | 46 |

**FA Cup**

| | | | |
|---|---|---|---|
| Fourth Qualifying | Barrow | (a) | 0-2 |

**FA Trophy**

| | | | |
|---|---|---|---|
| First Round | Lincoln C | (h) | 3-1 |
| Second Round | Corby T | (h) | 1-1 |
| *Replay* | Corby T | (a) | 4-2 |
| Third Round | Gainsborough Trinity | (a) | 1-2 |

# WOKING

*Ground:* Kingfield Stadium, Kingfield, Woking, Surrey GU22 9AA.  *Tel:* (01483) 722 470.  *Fax:* (01483) 888 423.
*Website:* wokingfc.co.uk  *Year Formed:* 1889.  *Record Gate:* 6,064 (1997 v Coventry C, FA Cup 3rd rd).
*Nickname:* 'The Cardinals'.  *Manager:* Gary Hill.  *Secretary:* Derek Powell.  *Colours:* Red shirts with white trim,
black shorts, white socks with black and red trim.

## WOKING – BLUE SQUARE PREMIER 2012–13 LEAGUE RECORD

| Match No. | Date | | Venue | Opponents | Result | H/T Score | Lg Pos. | Goalscorers | Attendance |
|---|---|---|---|---|---|---|---|---|---|
| 1 | Aug | 11 | A | Wrexham | L 1-3 | 0-2 | 24 | Bubb [66] | 4088 |
| 2 | | 14 | H | Dartford | W 1-0 | 0-0 | 14 | Sole (pen) [82] | 1846 |
| 3 | | 18 | H | Barrow | W 3-1 | 1-1 | 7 | McNerney [20], Bubb [57], Pires [79] | 1373 |
| 4 | | 25 | A | Forest Green R | L 1-3 | 1-0 | 11 | Betsy (pen) [43] | 979 |
| 5 | | 28 | H | Braintree T | L 1-4 | 1-1 | 15 | Williams [45] | 1588 |
| 6 | Sept | 1 | A | Mansfield T | L 1-3 | 0-2 | 16 | McNerney [84] | 2061 |
| 7 | | 4 | A | Hereford U | L 1-2 | 0-2 | 16 | Betsy [82] | 1481 |
| 8 | | 8 | H | Nuneaton T | W 6-1 | 2-0 | 19 | McCallum [25], Sawyer [45], Bubb 4 [48, 55, 68, 70] | 1512 |
| 9 | | 15 | A | Stockport Co | W 2-1 | 1-1 | 17 | McCallum [24], Pires [65] | 3151 |
| 10 | | 22 | H | Gateshead | W 2-1 | 2-0 | 14 | Parkinson [6], McCallum [26] | 1609 |
| 11 | | 25 | A | Ebbsfleet U | D 2-2 | 2-1 | 13 | Parkinson [16], Johnson [22] | 738 |
| 12 | | 29 | H | Tamworth | L 2-3 | 0-2 | 10 | Betsy [69], Cestor [90] | 1467 |
| 13 | Oct | 6 | A | AFC Telford U | L 0-1 | 0-1 | 12 | | 1584 |
| 14 | | 9 | H | Cambridge U | W 2-1 | 1-0 | 15 | Bubb [19], Betsy [60] | 1420 |
| 15 | | 13 | H | Southport | L 2-3 | 1-1 | 11 | Betsy [11], McCallum [73] | 1739 |
| 16 | | 27 | A | Newport Co | W 3-2 | 2-1 | 13 | Betsy 2 [6, 15], Bubb [67] | 2088 |
| 17 | Nov | 3 | A | Gateshead | L 1-2 | 1-2 | 11 | Parkinson [6] | 473 |
| 18 | | 6 | H | Kidderminster H | D 2-2 | 1-2 | 11 | Sawyer [3], Bubb [65] | 1168 |
| 19 | | 10 | A | Grimsby T | L 1-5 | 1-3 | 15 | Sinclair [2] | 3418 |
| 20 | | 17 | H | Alfreton T | L 1-2 | 1-1 | 17 | Williams [39] | 1537 |
| 21 | Dec | 1 | A | Hyde | L 0-7 | 0-1 | 19 | | 429 |
| 22 | | 4 | A | Lincoln C | W 2-0 | 1-0 | 14 | Betsy (pen) [6], Bubb [67] | 2526 |
| 23 | | 8 | H | Stockport Co | W 1-0 | 0-0 | 12 | Doyle [85] | 1520 |
| 24 | | 26 | A | Luton T | L 1-3 | 0-2 | 16 | McNerney [71] | 6744 |
| 25 | Jan | 1 | H | Luton T | W 3-1 | 1-1 | 14 | Knott 2 [3, 74], Stockley [78] | 2961 |
| 26 | | 13 | H | Ebbsfleet U | W 1-0 | 0-0 | 12 | Stockley [89] | 1419 |
| 27 | Feb | 2 | H | Hyde | W 2-1 | 1-1 | 11 | Knott 2 [10, 47] | 1236 |
| 28 | | 9 | A | Alfreton T | W 3-0 | 0-0 | 11 | Bubb [67], Betsy [72], Knott [83] | 606 |
| 29 | | 16 | A | Newport Co | L 1-3 | 0-3 | 13 | McCallum [90] | 2116 |
| 30 | | 19 | A | Barrow | L 0-2 | 0-1 | 13 | | 624 |
| 31 | | 23 | A | Southport | W 2-1 | 1-0 | 11 | Bubb 2 [42, 69] | 911 |
| 32 | | 26 | H | Forest Green R | W 2-0 | 0-0 | 9 | Betsy [51], Parkinson [78] | 1105 |
| 33 | Mar | 2 | H | Lincoln C | D 1-1 | 1-1 | 10 | Johnson [2] | 1766 |
| 34 | | 6 | H | Mansfield T | L 1-2 | 0-1 | 10 | Bubb (pen) [69] | 1179 |
| 35 | | 9 | A | Cambridge U | L 0-1 | 0-0 | 12 | | 2054 |
| 36 | | 12 | A | Macclesfield T | D 0-0 | 0-0 | 12 | | 1350 |
| 37 | | 16 | H | AFC Telford U | W 5-2 | 3-0 | 10 | Bubb 3 (1 pen) [4, 43, 89 (p)], Stockley [13], Betsy [90] | 1320 |
| 38 | | 19 | A | Braintree T | D 1-1 | 1-0 | 11 | Stockley [22] | 506 |
| 39 | | 26 | A | Kidderminster H | D 2-2 | 1-1 | 10 | Bubb (pen) [22], Knott [56] | 2035 |
| 40 | | 28 | A | Nuneaton T | D 0-0 | 0-0 | 10 | | 609 |
| 41 | | 30 | H | Hereford U | D 1-1 | 0-1 | 10 | Betsy [52] | 2303 |
| 42 | Apr | 1 | A | Dartford | L 1-4 | 1-2 | 11 | Stockley [34] | 1407 |
| 43 | | 6 | H | Wrexham | W 2-0 | 0-0 | 10 | Stockley 2 [60, 68] | 1518 |
| 44 | | 13 | H | Macclesfield T | W 5-4 | 5-0 | 9 | Knott 2 [4, 33], Betsy [7], Stockley 2 (1 pen) [23 (p), 28] | 1543 |
| 45 | | 16 | H | Grimsby T | L 0-1 | 0-0 | 10 | | 1570 |
| 46 | | 23 | A | Tamworth | L 1-2 | 1-1 | 12 | Stockley [21] | 1509 |

**Final League Position: 12**

## GOALSCORERS

*League (73):* Bubb 18 (3 pens), Betsy 13 (2 pens), Stockley 10 (1 pen), Knott 8, McCallum 5, Parkinson 4, McNerney 3,
Johnson 2, Pires 2, Sawyer 2, Williams 2, Cestor 1, Doyle 1, Sinclair 1, Sole 1 (1 pen).
*FA Cup (0).*
*FA Trophy (7):* Knott 2, Stockley 2, Betsy 1, McCallum 1, Williams 1.

| Howe 28 | Newton 43 | McNerney 43 + 2 | Johnson 35 + 1 | Cestor 26 + 11 | Ricketts 44 + 1 | Sawyer 33 + 1 | Betsy 46 | Pires 12 + 11 | McCallum 23 + 20 | Williams 9 + 17 | Bubb 33 + 3 | Sole — + 2 | Sinclair 5 + 15 | Parkinson 36 + 5 | Davies 1 + 1 | Doyle 12 + 8 | Frith — + 12 | Beasant 2 + 1 | Knott 20 | Nutter 19 + 3 | Stockley 20 + 6 | Putnis 3 + 1 | Brown 13 | Francis — + 3 | Simmonds — + 2 | Match No. |
|---|---|---|---|---|---|---|---|---|---|---|---|---|---|---|---|---|---|---|---|---|---|---|---|---|---|---|
| 1 | 2 | 3 | 4 | 5 | $6^3$ | 7 | 8 | $9^1$ | 10 | $11^2$ | 12 | 13 | 14 | | | | | | | | | | | | | 1 |
| 1 | 2 | 5 | 4 | 3 | $6^3$ | 7 | 8 | 9 | 12 | $11^1$ | $10^2$ | 13 | 14 | | | | | | | | | | | | | 2 |
| 1 | 2 | 3 | $4^3$ | 5 | 7 | 6 | 8 | 11 | 12 | $10^1$ | $9^2$ | | | 13 | 14 | | | | | | | | | | | 3 |
| 1 | 2 | 4 | 9 | 3 | 6 | 8 | $7^3$ | 10 | 14 | 12 | $11^2$ | | 13 | $5^1$ | | | | | | | | | | | | 4 |
| 1 | 2 | $4^3$ | 3 | 5 | $7^1$ | 6 | 8 | $10^2$ | 13 | 11 | 9 | | | 12 | | 14 | | | | | | | | | | 5 |
| 1 | 2 | 3 | $4^3$ | 5 | $6^1$ | 7 | 9 | $10^2$ | 11 | 12 | | | 13 | 8 | | 14 | | | | | | | | | | 6 |
| 1 | 2 | 3 | 4 | $5^1$ | $8^3$ | 7 | 10 | $11^2$ | 6 | | | | 13 | 9 | 12 | 14 | | | | | | | | | | 7 |
| 1 | 2 | 3 | 5 | | | | $7^2$ | 9 | 14 | 11 | 12 | $10^3$ | $6^1$ | 8 | | 4 | 13 | | | | | | | | | 8 |
| 1 | 2 | 3 | 4 | 14 | $6^1$ | 8 | 9 | 13 | $11^2$ | | | $10^3$ | | 12 | 7 | 5 | | | | | | | | | | 9 |
| 1 | 2 | 3 | 4 | 13 | 7 | $9^2$ | 6 | | $10^3$ | 12 | $11^1$ | | | 14 | 8 | 5 | | | | | | | | | | 10 |
| 1 | $2^3$ | 3 | 4 | 13 | 7 | 9 | 6 | 12 | $10^1$ | | 11 | | | 14 | 8 | $5^2$ | | | | | | | | | | 11 |
| 1 | 2 | 3 | 4 | 14 | 7 | | | 11 | 12 | 10 | 13 | $9^3$ | | 6 | $8^1$ | $5^2$ | | | | | | | | | | 12 |
| $1^1$ | $2^2$ | 3 | | 5 | 7 | 6 | 8 | $10^1$ | $11^1$ | | 9 | | 14 | 13 | | 4 | | 12 | | | | | | | | 13 |
| | | 3 | 4 | 5 | 2 | 7 | 6 | | $9^3$ | 13 | $10^2$ | | | | 12 | 8 | | 14 | 1 | $11^1$ | | | | | | 14 |
| | | $3^1$ | 4 | $5^2$ | 2 | 8 | 11 | 12 | 9 | 13 | 10 | | | $7^1$ | 6 | | | 1 | | | | | | | | 15 |
| 1 | 2 | 3 | 6 | 5 | 9 | 8 | 7 | $10^1$ | $11^2$ | | | 12 | | | | 4 | 13 | | | | | | | | | 16 |
| 1 | 2 | 3 | 4 | 5 | $6^3$ | 8 | 9 | $10^1$ | $11^2$ | 14 | 13 | | | | | 7 | 12 | | | | | | | | | 17 |
| 1 | 2 | 3 | 4 | 13 | 6 | 7 | 9 | 14 | 11 | | | $10^3$ | | | 12 | $8^1$ | $5^2$ | | | | | | | | | 18 |
| 1 | 2 | 3 | $4^1$ | 5 | $9^3$ | $8^1$ | 10 | 12 | 6 | | | $11^2$ | | | 7 | 14 | 13 | | | | | | | | | 19 |
| 1 | 2 | 3 | 13 | | | | 8 | 12 | $4^1$ | 11 | | | 9 | $6^2$ | | | | | | 5 | 10 | | | | | 20 |
| 1 | 2 | 3 | $4^1$ | 14 | 7 | $8^3$ | 6 | | 13 | $11^2$ | | | 12 | | | | | | $9^1$ | 5 | 10 | | | | | 21 |
| 1 | 2 | 3 | | 5 | 6 | $7^3$ | 8 | | 13 | $10^1$ | $11^2$ | | 14 | | | 4 | | | | 9 | 12 | | | | | 22 |
| 1 | 2 | 3 | | $5^1$ | 8 | | 6 | 13 | | $10^2$ | 11 | | $9^3$ | 14 | | 4 | | | | 7 | 12 | | | | | 23 |
| 1 | 2 | 3 | | 14 | $6^2$ | | 9 | 12 | 10 | 13 | 7 | | | | | 4 | | | | 8 | $5^1$ | $11^1$ | | | | 24 |
| 1 | 2 | $3^1$ | | | | | 8 | 6 | $10^2$ | 13 | | 11 | 14 | 9 | | 4 | | | | $7^3$ | 5 | 12 | | | | 25 |
| 1 | 2 | 4 | | 14 | 8 | | 6 | $7^2$ | 13 | | 11 | | 9 | $5^1$ | | | | | | 10 | $3^3$ | 12 | | | | 26 |
| 1 | | 4 | 3 | 14 | 2 | $8^2$ | 6 | | 13 | 12 | | $10^3$ | | | 7 | | | | | 9 | 5 | $11^1$ | | | | 27 |
| $1^1$ | 2 | 6 | 3 | | 8 | $9^2$ | 10 | | 13 | | $11^3$ | | | | | 4 | | | | 7 | 5 | 14 | 12 | | | 28 |
| | 2 | 10 | 4 | | 8 | $7^2$ | 11 | 12 | 14 | $9^3$ | | 3 | | | | | | | | $6^1$ | 5 | 13 | 1 | | | 29 |
| | 2 | $4^2$ | 5 | 7 | $8^4$ | 6 | 14 | 9 | $11^1$ | | | 3 | 13 | 12 | | | | | | | $10^3$ | | 1 | | | 30 |
| | 2 | 4 | 3 | $5^2$ | 7 | | | 11 | 13 | 12 | 9 | | | 8 | | | | | | 6 | $10^1$ | | 1 | | | 31 |
| | 2 | 3 | 4 | $5^2$ | 7 | | 6 | | 13 | 12 | | $10^3$ | | 8 | | 14 | | | | 9 | $11^1$ | | 1 | | | 32 |
| | 2 | 3 | $4^1$ | 9 | 7 | | 6 | 12 | 13 | 10 | | | | 8 | | 14 | | | | 5 | $11^2$ | | 1 | | | 33 |
| | $2^3$ | 3 | 4 | $9^1$ | 7 | | 6 | 12 | 10 | | | | | 8 | | 14 | | | | $5^2$ | 11 | | 1 | 13 | | 34 |
| | $2^1$ | 3 | 4 | | 8 | 9 | 10 | | 13 | | | | $6^2$ | | | 7 | | | 12 | 5 | 11 | | 1 | | | 35 |
| | 2 | 3 | 4 | 12 | 6 | $9^1$ | 10 | | | | | | | 8 | | 7 | | | | 5 | 11 | | 1 | | | 36 |
| | 2 | 3 | 4 | | | | 7 | | 10 | 12 | | | $6^3$ | 8 | | 14 | | | $9^1$ | 5 | $11^2$ | | 1 | 13 | | 37 |
| | 2 | 4 | 3 | 5 | 8 | | 10 | | | | | | 6 | | | 7 | | | 12 | $9^1$ | 11 | | 1 | | | 38 |
| | 2 | 3 | 4 | 13 | 7 | $8^2$ | 9 | 12 | | | | | $6^1$ | | | 14 | | | $10^3$ | 5 | 11 | | 1 | | | 39 |
| | 2 | 3 | | 5 | 6 | 9 | 10 | 12 | | | | | $7^2$ | | 4 | 14 | | | $8^3$ | | $11^1$ | | 1 | 13 | | 40 |
| | 2 | 3 | 4 | $9^1$ | 14 | 12 | 6 | 11 | $10^2$ | | | | | | | 8 | | | | 5 | 13 | | 1 | | | 41 |
| | 2 | 13 | $4^3$ | $6^2$ | 9 | 10 | | 12 | | | | | $7^1$ | | 3 | 8 | | | | 5 | 11 | | 1 | | | 42 |
| | 2 | 3 | | 5 | $9^3$ | 7 | 6 | $11^2$ | 13 | | | | | | 4 | | | | $8^1$ | 12 | 10 | | 1 | | 14 | 43 |
| | 2 | 6 | | 5 | $4^1$ | 7 | 9 | 8 | 14 | | | | | | $3^2$ | | | | 10 | 13 | $11^3$ | | 1 | 12 | | 44 |
| 1 | 2 | 12 | 4 | | $8^1$ | 7 | 6 | 9 | 13 | | | | | | 5 | | | | | 11 | 3 | $10^2$ | | | | 45 |
| 1 | 2 | 4 | | 5 | 7 | $6^2$ | 9 | 11 | 13 | | | | | | 3 | 12 | | | | $8^1$ | 10 | | | | | 46 |

**FA Cup**
Fourth Qualifying   Ebbsfleet U    (h)   0-1

**FA Trophy**
First Round   Farnborough    (h)   7-0
Second Round   Welling U    (h)   0-1

# WREXHAM

*Ground:* Racecourse Ground, Mold Road, Wrexham LL11 2AH.   *Tel:* (01978) 262 129.   *Fax:* (01978) 357 821.
*Website:* wrexhamafc.co.uk   *Year Formed:* 1872.   *Record Gate:* 34,445 (1957 v Manchester U, FA Cup 4th rd).
*Nickname:* 'Red Dragons'.   *Manager:* Andy Morrell.   *Secretary:* Geraint Parry.   *Colours:* Red shirts, white shorts,
red socks.

## WREXHAM – BLUE SQUARE PREMIER 2012–13 LEAGUE RECORD

| Match No. | Date | Venue | Opponents | Result | H/T Score | Lg Pos. | Goalscorers | Attendance |
|---|---|---|---|---|---|---|---|---|
| 1 | Aug 11 | H | Woking | W 3-1 | 2-0 | 1 | Ogleby [18], Keates [41], Creighton [74] | 4088 |
| 2 | 14 | A | Macclesfield T | L 0-2 | 0-1 | 12 | | 2368 |
| 3 | 18 | A | Ebbsfleet U | D 1-1 | 0-0 | 13 | Hunt [49] | 843 |
| 4 | 25 | H | Grimsby T | D 0-0 | 0-0 | 13 | | 3127 |
| 5 | 27 | A | Tamworth | W 1-0 | 1-0 | 10 | Courtney (og) [8] | 1433 |
| 6 | Sept 1 | H | Newport Co | W 2-0 | 1-0 | 7 | Cieslewicz [24], Wright, D [82] | 3820 |
| 7 | 4 | H | Hyde | W 2-0 | 0-0 | 6 | Little (pen) [78], Harris [90] | 3176 |
| 8 | 8 | A | Cambridge U | W 4-1 | 1-0 | 4 | Morrell 2 [34, 56], Wright, D 2 [48, 86] | 2304 |
| 9 | 15 | A | Luton T | D 0-0 | 0-0 | 4 | | 6675 |
| 10 | 22 | H | Dartford | D 2-2 | 2-1 | 3 | Wright, D [16], Bishop [42] | 3772 |
| 11 | 25 | H | Barrow | W 3-0 | 1-0 | 3 | Harris [18], Bishop [71], Ogleby [83] | 2881 |
| 12 | 29 | A | Nuneaton T | D 0-0 | 0-0 | 3 | | 1543 |
| 13 | Oct 6 | H | Forest Green R | W 2-1 | 0-0 | 3 | Cieslewicz 2 [57, 73] | 4053 |
| 14 | 10 | A | Stockport Co | W 3-2 | 2-1 | 2 | Hobson (og) [25], Ashton 2 (2 pens) [37, 82] | 3789 |
| 15 | 13 | H | Lincoln C | L 2-4 | 0-1 | 2 | Colbeck [79], Clarke [90] | 3809 |
| 16 | Nov 6 | A | Southport | W 4-1 | 1-0 | 2 | Harris [56], Lynch (og) [78], Ogleby [81], Westwood [86] | 1324 |
| 17 | 10 | H | Hereford U | L 1-2 | 0-1 | 4 | Wright, S [58] | 3620 |
| 18 | 17 | H | Gateshead | D 1-1 | 1-0 | 4 | Rushton [37] | 3011 |
| 19 | 20 | A | Braintree T | W 5-1 | 3-1 | 2 | Wright, D 2 [9, 65], Ormerod [16], Rushton [39], Cieslewicz [79] | 508 |
| 20 | Dec 1 | A | Kidderminster H | L 0-2 | 0-0 | 4 | | 2378 |
| 21 | 8 | A | Nuneaton T | W 6-1 | 3-0 | 2 | Hunt [20], Morrell [31], Ashton (1 pen) [45, 90 (p)], Ogleby [73], Cieslewicz [83] | 2739 |
| 22 | 21 | A | Grimsby T | L 0-1 | 0-0 | 3 | | 4302 |
| 23 | 26 | H | AFC Telford U | W 4-1 | 1-0 | 3 | Ormerod 2 [2, 71], Rushton [60], Wright, D [69] | 4330 |
| 24 | 29 | H | Tamworth | D 2-2 | 1-1 | 3 | Ormerod [26], Wright, D [74] | 3703 |
| 25 | Jan 1 | A | AFC Telford U | W 2-0 | 1-0 | 2 | Wright, D [24], Cieslewicz [85] | 2931 |
| 26 | 4 | A | Newport Co | D 1-1 | 1-0 | 1 | Wright, D [34] | 3627 |
| 27 | 8 | A | Alfreton T | W 2-1 | 1-1 | 1 | Ashton [17], Clarke [75] | 628 |
| 28 | 29 | H | Southport | D 2-2 | 1-1 | 2 | Wright, D [7], Clarke [70] | 3002 |
| 29 | Feb 2 | A | Forest Green R | D 0-0 | 0-0 | 2 | | 1840 |
| 30 | 9 | H | Stockport Co | W 3-1 | 1-0 | 2 | Clarke [8], Wright, D [82], Ogleby [88] | 4206 |
| 31 | 12 | A | Hereford U | W 1-0 | 1-0 | 2 | Harris [32] | 1781 |
| 32 | 19 | A | Gateshead | W 1-0 | 0-0 | 1 | Ormerod [60] | 513 |
| 33 | 26 | A | Barrow | W 1-0 | 0-0 | 1 | Thornton [84] | 889 |
| 34 | Mar 2 | H | Alfreton T | D 1-1 | 1-0 | 1 | Thornton [9] | 3706 |
| 35 | 5 | H | Ebbsfleet U | W 4-1 | 4-0 | 1 | Adebola [3], Ormerod [11], Thornton [29], Ogleby [45] | 2390 |
| 36 | 9 | A | Dartford | L 1-2 | 1-0 | 1 | Wright, D [26] | 815 |
| 37 | 12 | A | Lincoln C | W 2-1 | 0-1 | 1 | Ormerod [61], Adebola [66] | 1379 |
| 38 | 16 | H | Luton T | D 0-0 | 0-0 | 1 | | 3907 |
| 39 | 30 | A | Hyde | L 0-2 | 0-1 | 3 | | 1846 |
| 40 | Apr 1 | H | Macclesfield T | D 0-0 | 0-0 | 4 | | 4351 |
| 41 | 4 | H | Mansfield T | W 2-1 | 0-0 | 3 | Keates [68], Wright, D [78] | 4378 |
| 42 | 6 | A | Woking | L 0-2 | 0-0 | 3 | | 1518 |
| 43 | 9 | A | Cambridge U | W 1-0 | 1-0 | 3 | Colbeck [5] | 2574 |
| 44 | 13 | H | Kidderminster H | L 1-2 | 0-1 | 4 | Wright, D [62] | 4013 |
| 45 | 16 | H | Braintree T | D 1-1 | 1-1 | 4 | Morrell [3] | 2312 |
| 46 | 20 | A | Mansfield T | L 0-1 | 0-1 | 5 | | 6394 |

**Final League Position: 5**

## GOALSCORERS

*League (74):* Wright, D 15, Ormerod 7, Cieslewicz 6, Ogleby 6, Ashton 5 (3 pens), Clarke 4, Harris 4, Morrell 4, Rushton 3, Thornton 3, Adebola 2, Bishop 2, Colbeck 2, Hunt 2, Keates 2, Creighton 1, Little 1 (1 pen), Westwood 1, Wright, S 1, own goals 3.
*FA Cup (4):* Ashton 1 (pen), Keates 1, Ormerod 1, Wright D 1.
*FA Trophy (21):* Cieslewicz 3, Morrell 3, Clarke 2, Thornton 2 (1 pen), Wright D 2, Ashton 1, Harris 1, Hunt 1, Keates 1 (1 pen), Ogleby 1, Ormerod 1, Rushton 1, Walker 1, Westwood 1.
*Blue Square Premier Play-Offs (5):* Ashton 2 (2 pens), Artell 1, Clarke 1, Ormerod 1.

| Mayebi 23 | Walker 16+5 | Creighton 3+1 | Westwood 36 | Ashton 38+1 | Keates 38 | Harris 37 | Hunt 37+2 | Omnerod 29+10 | Ogleby 9+17 | Wright D 37+4 | Morrell 13+11 | Clarke 29+5 | Cieslewicz 18+20 | Riley 32+2 | Little 1+17 | Wright S 23+2 | Bishop 4 | Colbeck 2+5 | Rushton 11+6 | Coughlin 6 | Devine 4 | Alfei 11 | Reid —+4 | Maxwell 17 | Thornton 7+3 | Artell 8 | Adebola 10+3 | Clowes 4 | Evans 3+1 | Royle —+1 | Match No. |
|---|---|---|---|---|---|---|---|---|---|---|---|---|---|---|---|---|---|---|---|---|---|---|---|---|---|---|---|---|---|---|---|
| 1 | 2 | 3 | 4 | 5 | 6 | 7 | $8^2$ | $9^1$ | $10^3$ | 11 | 12 | 13 | 14 | | | | | | | | | | | | | | | | | | 1 |
| 1 | 2 | 3 | 4 | 5 | 7 | 6 | 8 | 11 | $9^1$ | $10^2$ | 12 | 13 | | | | | | | | | | | | | | | | | | | 2 |
| 1 | 2 | $3^1$ | 4 | 5 | 7 | 6 | 8 | 11 | $9^3$ | $10^2$ | 13 | 14 | 12 | | | | | | | | | | | | | | | | | | 3 |
| 1 | 2 | | 3 | 5 | 7 | $6^4$ | $8^2$ | 11 | 14 | 12 | $10^1$ | | $9^3$ | 4 | | 13 | | | | | | | | | | | | | | | 4 |
| 1 | 2 | | 3 | 5 | 7 | | 8 | 12 | $10^3$ | 13 | $11^2$ | 6 | $9^1$ | 4 | | 14 | | | | | | | | | | | | | | | 5 |
| 1 | 2 | | $3^1$ | 5 | 7 | 6 | 8 | $10^3$ | 11 | 13 | 14 | | $9^2$ | 4 | | | 12 | | | | | | | | | | | | | | 6 |
| 1 | 2 | | | 5 | 7 | 6 | 8 | $10^3$ | $11^1$ | 12 | 13 | | $9^2$ | 4 | | 14 | 3 | | | | | | | | | | | | | | 7 |
| 1 | 2 | | | 5 | 7 | 6 | $8^3$ | 13 | 12 | 10 | $11^1$ | | $9^2$ | 4 | | 14 | 3 | | | | | | | | | | | | | | 8 |
| 1 | 2 | | | 5 | 7 | 6 | 8 | 13 | 12 | $10^2$ | | | $9^1$ | 4 | | | 3 | | 11 | | | | | | | | | | | | 9 |
| 1 | 2 | | | 5 | 7 | 6 | 8 | 13 | | 11 | 14 | | $9^2$ | 4 | | 12 | | $3^1$ | $10^3$ | | | | | | | | | | | | 10 |
| 1 | 2 | | 4 | 5 | 7 | 6 | | 13 | 12 | 10 | $8^3$ | | $9^1$ | | | | 3 | | $11^{12}$ | 14 | | | | | | | | | | | 11 |
| 1 | 2 | | 4 | 5 | 7 | 6 | 8 | | $10^2$ | 12 | | 13 | $9^1$ | | 14 | | 3 | | $11^3$ | | | | | | | | | | | | 12 |
| 1 | | | 4 | 5 | 7 | $6^2$ | 8 | 12 | 11 | $10^1$ | 13 | | $9^3$ | 3 | | 2 | | | | | 14 | | | | | | | | | | 13 |
| | | | 4 | $5^4$ | 7 | 6 | 8 | 13 | 10 | $11^{12}$ | 12 | | $9^1$ | 3 | | 2 | | | | | | | 1 | | | | | | | | 14 |
| | $12^3$ | 3 | | 5 | 7 | | 8 | 11 | 9 | $10^2$ | | 6 | | $4^1$ | | 2 | | 13 | | 14 | | | 1 | | | | | | | | 15 |
| | | 3 | | 5 | 6 | | $7^3$ | 12 | 10 | $9^1$ | 8 | | | 13 | | 2 | 4 | | 14 | | | $11^{12}$ | 1 | | | | | | | | 16 |
| | | 3 | | 5 | 7 | 6 | 8 | 13 | $11^2$ | $10^1$ | | 12 | | | | 2 | 4 | | | | | 9 | 1 | | | | | | | | 17 |
| | | 3 | | 5 | 7 | 6 | 8 | $10^1$ | 13 | 11 | | 12 | | 4 | | 2 | | | | | | $9^2$ | 1 | | | | | | | | 18 |
| 1 | | | 4 | 5 | | $6^3$ | 8 | $11^2$ | 12 | 10 | 7 | | | 13 | | 3 | | | 14 | | | $9^1$ | | 2 | | | | | | | 19 |
| 1 | | 3 | | 5 | | 6 | 8 | 12 | 10 | $11^3$ | 14 | 7 | | 13 | | 4 | | | | | | $9^2$ | | 2 | | | | | | | 20 |
| 1 | 13 | $3^2$ | | 5 | 7 | 6 | 8 | 10 | 12 | $11^1$ | 14 | | $9^3$ | 4 | | | | | | | 2 | | | | | | | | | | 21 |
| 1 | 2 | | | 5 | 7 | $6^2$ | 8 | $9^3$ | 10 | $11^1$ | 13 | 12 | | 4 | | 3 | | | | 14 | | | | | | | | | | | 22 |
| 1 | 3 | | | 5 | 7 | $6^3$ | 8 | | 11 | $10^2$ | | | $9^1$ | 4 | | | | | 14 | 12 | | | | | 2 | 13 | | | | | 23 |
| 1 | 13 | 3 | | 5 | $7^4$ | 6 | 8 | 12 | $10^2$ | 11 | | | $9^1$ | 4 | | | | | 2 | | | | | | | | | | | | 24 |
| 1 | | 3 | | 5 | 7 | 6 | 8 | $11^1$ | 10 | 12 | 13 | | $9^2$ | 4 | | | | | 2 | | | | | | | | | | | | 25 |
| 1 | | | 4 | 5 | 7 | $6^1$ | 8 | 9 | 12 | 10 | $11^2$ | | | 3 | | 2 | | | 13 | | | | | | | | | | | | 26 |
| 1 | | | 4 | 5 | 7 | 6 | 8 | $11^1$ | $10^4$ | 12 | | | $9^2$ | 3 | | 2 | | | 13 | | | | | | | | | | | | 27 |
| 1 | | 3 | | 5 | 7 | 6 | 8 | $11^1$ | 10 | 13 | 12 | | $9^2$ | 4 | | | | | 2 | | | | | | | | | | | | 28 |
| | 2 | $3^1$ | | 5 | 7 | 6 | 8 | $9^2$ | 10 | $11^3$ | 14 | 13 | | 4 | | | | | 12 | | | | | 1 | 3¹ | | | | | | 29 |
| | | 3 | | 5 | 7 | 6 | 8 | $11^1$ | $10^2$ | 13 | 12 | | 9 | 4 | | 2 | | | | | | | | 1 | | | | | | | 30 |
| | | 3 | | 5 | 7 | 6 | 8 | $11^2$ | $10^1$ | 12 | 13 | | 9 | 4 | | 2 | | | | | | | | 1 | | | | | | | 31 |
| | | 3 | | 5 | 6 | 7 | 8 | $11^2$ | 10 | 12 | 13 | | $9^1$ | 4 | | 2 | | | | | | | | 1 | | | | | | | 32 |
| | | | 4 | 5 | $7^1$ | $6^4$ | 8 | $11^2$ | $10^3$ | 12 | | | 9 | 3 | | 2 | | | 14 | | | | | 1 | 13 | | | | | | 33 |
| | | 3 | | 5 | 7 | | 8 | 11 | | 13 | 12 | | $9^2$ | | | 2 | | | | | | | | 1 | $6^1$ | 4 | 10 | | | | 34 |
| | | 3 | | 5 | $7^3$ | | 8 | 12 | | $11^2$ | 13 | | 9 | | | 2 | | | 14 | | | | | 1 | 6 | 4 | $10^1$ | | | | 35 |
| | | 3 | | 5 | 7 | 6 | | 12 | $10^1$ | 13 | | | 9 | | | 2 | | | | | | | | 1 | 8 | 4 | $11^2$ | | | | 36 |
| | 13 | 3 | | $5^1$ | 6 | | 8 | 11 | | 12 | | | 9 | | | 2 | | | | | | | | 1 | 7 | $4^2$ | 10 | | | | 37 |
| | | 3 | | 5 | 7 | $6^2$ | 8 | 11 | | 13 | 12 | | $9^1$ | 4 | | 2 | | | | | | | | 1 | 8 | | 10 | | | | 38 |
| | | 3 | | 5 | $7^2$ | 6 | | 11 | | 13 | 12 | | $9^3$ | 4 | | 2 | | | 14 | | | | | 1 | $8^1$ | | 10 | | | | 39 |
| | | 3 | | 5 | 7 | 6 | 8 | 12 | $10^2$ | $11^1$ | | | $9^3$ | 4 | | 2 | | | | | | | | 1 | 14 | | 13 | | | | 40 |
| 12 | | $3^1$ | | 5 | 7 | 6 | 8 | $11^2$ | 10 | | | | $9^3$ | 4 | | 2 | | | 14 | | | | | 1 | | | 13 | | | | 41 |
| 2 | 14 | | | 5 | $7^1$ | 6 | 8 | 12 | $10^2$ | | | | 9 | $4^3$ | | 3 | | | | | | | | 1 | 13 | | 11 | | | | 42 |
| 2 | | | | 5 | 7 | 6 | | $9^2$ | | 13 | 14 | | | | | | | | $11^3$ | | | | | 1 | $8^1$ | 4 | 10 | 3 | 12 | | 43 |
| 2 | | | | 5 | 7 | 6 | $8^2$ | 11 | | 13 | 14 | | $9^1$ | | | | | | | | | | 12 | 1 | | 4 | $10^3$ | 3 | 6 | | 44 |
| | | | | 5 | 6 | | 8 | $11^1$ | 10 | | | | $9^2$ | | | 2 | | | | | | | 12 | 1 | | 4 | 13 | 3 | 7 | | 45 |
| 2 | 13 | | | 5 | $6^1$ | | 8 | $11^1$ | | | | | $9^2$ | | | | | | | | | | | 1 | 12 | $3^4$ | 10 | 4 | 7 | 14 | 46 |

## FA Cup

| | | | |
|---|---|---|---|
| Fourth Qualifying | Southport | (h) | 2-0 |
| First Round | Alfreton T | (h) | 2-4 |

## Blue Square Premier Play-offs

| | | | |
|---|---|---|---|
| Semi-Finals | Kidderminster H | (h) | 2-1 |
| | Kidderminster H | (a) | 3-1 |
| Final (Wembley) | Newport Co | | 0-2 |

## FA Trophy

| | | | |
|---|---|---|---|
| First Round | Rushall Olympic | (h) | 5-0 |
| Second Round | Solihull Moors | (h) | 3-2 |
| Third Round | Sutton U | (a) | 5-0 |
| Quarter-Finals | Southport | (a) | 3-1 |
| Semi-Finals | Gainsborough Trinity | (h) | 3-1 |
| | Gainsborough Trinity | (a) | 1-2 |
| Final (Wembley) | Grimsby T | (h) | 1-1 |

# SCOTTISH LEAGUE TABLES 2012-13

(P) *Promoted into division at end of 2011–12 season.*   (R) *Relegated into division at end of 2011–12 season.*

## CLYDESDALE BANK SCOTTISH PREMIER LEAGUE 2012-13

| | | | | Total | | | Home | | | | Away | | | | | | |
|---|---|---|---|---|---|---|---|---|---|---|---|---|---|---|---|---|---|
| | | P | W | D | L | F | A | W | D | L | F | A | W | D | L | F | A | GD | Pts |
| 1 | Celtic | 38 | 24 | 7 | 7 | 92 | 35 | 15 | 2 | 2 | 52 | 14 | 9 | 5 | 5 | 40 | 21 | 57 | 79 |
| 2 | Motherwell | 38 | 18 | 9 | 11 | 67 | 51 | 9 | 6 | 4 | 35 | 24 | 9 | 3 | 7 | 32 | 27 | 16 | 63 |
| 3 | St Johnstone | 38 | 14 | 14 | 10 | 45 | 44 | 9 | 7 | 3 | 25 | 17 | 5 | 7 | 7 | 20 | 27 | 1 | 56 |
| 4 | Inverness CT | 38 | 13 | 15 | 10 | 64 | 60 | 7 | 8 | 4 | 35 | 27 | 6 | 7 | 6 | 29 | 33 | 4 | 54 |
| 5 | Ross Co (P) | 38 | 13 | 14 | 11 | 47 | 48 | 8 | 8 | 3 | 22 | 15 | 5 | 6 | 8 | 25 | 33 | -1 | 53 |
| 6 | Dundee U | 38 | 11 | 14 | 13 | 51 | 62 | 4 | 9 | 6 | 30 | 33 | 7 | 5 | 7 | 21 | 29 | -11 | 47 |
| 7 | Hibernian | 38 | 13 | 12 | 13 | 49 | 52 | 7 | 7 | 5 | 26 | 22 | 6 | 5 | 8 | 23 | 30 | -3 | 51 |
| 8 | Aberdeen | 38 | 11 | 15 | 12 | 41 | 43 | 6 | 9 | 4 | 18 | 15 | 5 | 6 | 8 | 23 | 28 | -2 | 48 |
| 9 | Kilmarnock | 38 | 11 | 12 | 15 | 52 | 53 | 5 | 4 | 10 | 25 | 29 | 6 | 8 | 5 | 27 | 24 | -1 | 45 |
| 10 | Hearts | 38 | 11 | 11 | 16 | 40 | 49 | 9 | 3 | 7 | 27 | 25 | 2 | 8 | 9 | 13 | 24 | -9 | 44 |
| 11 | St Mirren | 38 | 9 | 14 | 15 | 47 | 60 | 6 | 6 | 7 | 25 | 31 | 3 | 8 | 8 | 22 | 29 | -13 | 41 |
| 12 | Dundee (P)* | 38 | 7 | 9 | 22 | 28 | 66 | 4 | 4 | 11 | 17 | 34 | 3 | 5 | 11 | 11 | 32 | -38 | 30 |

*Top 6 teams split after 33 games. *Promoted due to Rangers demotion to Third Division.*

## IRN-BRU SCOTTISH FOOTBALL LEAGUE FIRST DIVISION 2012-13

| | | | | Total | | | Home | | | | Away | | | | | | |
|---|---|---|---|---|---|---|---|---|---|---|---|---|---|---|---|---|---|
| | | P | W | D | L | F | A | W | D | L | F | A | W | D | L | F | A | GD | Pts |
| 1 | Partick Th | 36 | 23 | 9 | 4 | 76 | 28 | 15 | 2 | 1 | 51 | 13 | 8 | 7 | 3 | 25 | 15 | 48 | 78 |
| 2 | Greenock Morton | 36 | 20 | 7 | 9 | 73 | 47 | 11 | 2 | 5 | 33 | 21 | 9 | 5 | 4 | 40 | 26 | 26 | 67 |
| 3 | Falkirk | 36 | 15 | 8 | 13 | 52 | 48 | 7 | 4 | 7 | 28 | 25 | 8 | 4 | 6 | 24 | 23 | 4 | 53 |
| 4 | Livingston | 36 | 14 | 10 | 12 | 58 | 56 | 6 | 5 | 7 | 31 | 28 | 8 | 5 | 5 | 27 | 28 | 2 | 52 |
| 5 | Hamilton A | 36 | 14 | 9 | 13 | 52 | 45 | 7 | 4 | 7 | 26 | 23 | 7 | 5 | 6 | 26 | 22 | 7 | 51 |
| 6 | Raith R | 36 | 11 | 13 | 12 | 45 | 48 | 6 | 8 | 4 | 23 | 21 | 5 | 5 | 8 | 22 | 27 | -3 | 46 |
| 7 | Dumbarton (P) | 36 | 13 | 4 | 19 | 58 | 83 | 4 | 3 | 11 | 26 | 40 | 9 | 1 | 8 | 32 | 43 | -25 | 43 |
| 8 | Cowdenbeath (P) | 36 | 8 | 12 | 16 | 51 | 65 | 4 | 8 | 6 | 30 | 34 | 4 | 4 | 10 | 21 | 31 | -14 | 36 |
| 9 | Dunfermline Ath (R) | 36 | 14 | 7 | 15 | 62 | 59 | 6 | 2 | 10 | 27 | 29 | 8 | 5 | 5 | 35 | 30 | 3 | 34 |
| 10 | Airdrie U | 36 | 5 | 7 | 24 | 41 | 89 | 1 | 5 | 12 | 19 | 40 | 4 | 2 | 12 | 22 | 49 | -48 | 22 |

*Dunfermline Ath deducted 15 points and relegated after play-offs.*

## IRN-BRU SCOTTISH FOOTBALL LEAGUE SECOND DIVISION 2012-13

| | | | | Total | | | Home | | | | Away | | | | | | |
|---|---|---|---|---|---|---|---|---|---|---|---|---|---|---|---|---|---|
| | | P | W | D | L | F | A | W | D | L | F | A | W | D | L | F | A | GD | Pts |
| 1 | Queen of the S (R) | 36 | 29 | 5 | 2 | 92 | 23 | 15 | 3 | 0 | 41 | 9 | 14 | 2 | 2 | 51 | 14 | 69 | 92 |
| 2 | Alloa Ath (P) | 36 | 20 | 7 | 9 | 62 | 35 | 9 | 4 | 5 | 31 | 19 | 11 | 3 | 4 | 31 | 16 | 27 | 67 |
| 3 | Brechin C | 36 | 19 | 4 | 13 | 72 | 59 | 12 | 1 | 5 | 44 | 30 | 7 | 3 | 8 | 28 | 29 | 13 | 61 |
| 4 | Forfar Ath | 36 | 17 | 3 | 16 | 67 | 74 | 10 | 2 | 6 | 39 | 38 | 7 | 1 | 10 | 28 | 36 | -7 | 54 |
| 5 | Arbroath | 36 | 15 | 7 | 14 | 47 | 57 | 9 | 4 | 5 | 28 | 22 | 6 | 3 | 9 | 19 | 35 | -10 | 52 |
| 6 | Stenhousemuir | 36 | 12 | 13 | 11 | 59 | 59 | 8 | 5 | 5 | 27 | 22 | 4 | 8 | 6 | 32 | 37 | 0 | 49 |
| 7 | Ayr U (R) | 36 | 12 | 5 | 19 | 53 | 65 | 8 | 2 | 8 | 30 | 30 | 4 | 3 | 11 | 23 | 35 | -12 | 41 |
| 8 | Stranraer (P) | 36 | 10 | 7 | 19 | 43 | 71 | 7 | 4 | 7 | 27 | 33 | 3 | 3 | 12 | 16 | 38 | -28 | 37 |
| 9 | East Fife | 36 | 8 | 8 | 20 | 50 | 65 | 5 | 4 | 9 | 25 | 28 | 3 | 4 | 11 | 25 | 37 | -15 | 32 |
| 10 | Albion R (P) | 36 | 7 | 3 | 26 | 45 | 82 | 5 | 2 | 11 | 28 | 39 | 2 | 1 | 15 | 17 | 43 | -37 | 24 |

*East Fife not relegated after play-offs.*
*Alloa Ath promoted via play-offs.*

## IRN-BRU SCOTTISH FOOTBALL LEAGUE THIRD DIVISION 2012-13

| | | | | Total | | | Home | | | | Away | | | | | | |
|---|---|---|---|---|---|---|---|---|---|---|---|---|---|---|---|---|---|
| | | P | W | D | L | F | A | W | D | L | F | A | W | D | L | F | A | GD | Pts |
| 1 | Rangers (R)* | 36 | 25 | 8 | 3 | 87 | 29 | 13 | 3 | 2 | 44 | 12 | 12 | 5 | 1 | 43 | 17 | 58 | 83 |
| 2 | Peterhead | 36 | 17 | 8 | 11 | 52 | 28 | 9 | 5 | 4 | 26 | 11 | 8 | 3 | 7 | 26 | 17 | 24 | 59 |
| 3 | Queen's Park | 36 | 16 | 8 | 12 | 60 | 54 | 5 | 7 | 6 | 27 | 27 | 11 | 1 | 6 | 33 | 27 | 6 | 56 |
| 4 | Berwick Rangers | 36 | 14 | 7 | 15 | 59 | 55 | 10 | 4 | 4 | 34 | 21 | 4 | 3 | 11 | 25 | 34 | 4 | 49 |
| 5 | Elgin C | 36 | 13 | 10 | 13 | 67 | 69 | 9 | 1 | 8 | 41 | 40 | 4 | 9 | 5 | 26 | 29 | -2 | 49 |
| 6 | Montrose | 36 | 12 | 11 | 13 | 60 | 68 | 6 | 7 | 5 | 34 | 32 | 6 | 4 | 8 | 26 | 36 | -8 | 47 |
| 7 | Stirling Alb (R) | 36 | 12 | 9 | 15 | 59 | 58 | 9 | 3 | 6 | 38 | 24 | 3 | 6 | 9 | 21 | 34 | 1 | 45 |
| 8 | Annan Ath | 36 | 11 | 10 | 15 | 54 | 65 | 7 | 5 | 6 | 31 | 26 | 4 | 5 | 9 | 23 | 39 | -11 | 43 |
| 9 | Clyde | 36 | 12 | 4 | 20 | 42 | 66 | 8 | 2 | 8 | 25 | 29 | 4 | 2 | 12 | 17 | 37 | -24 | 40 |
| 10 | East Stirlingshire | 36 | 8 | 5 | 23 | 49 | 97 | 5 | 3 | 10 | 28 | 39 | 3 | 2 | 13 | 21 | 58 | -48 | 29 |

*Demoted from SPL for financial irregularities; 3 teams promoted to Second Division in 2011–12.*

# SCOTTISH LEAGUE ATTENDANCES 2012–13

### CLYDESDALE BANK SCOTTISH PREMIER LEAGUE ATTENDANCES

| | Average Gate | | | Season 2012–13 | |
|---|---|---|---|---|---|
| | 2012–13 | 2011–12 | +/–% | Highest | Lowest |
| Aberdeen | 9,611 | 9,296 | +3.39 | 18,000 | 6,334 |
| Celtic | 46,917 | 50,283 | –6.69 | 57,000 | 39,959 |
| Dundee | 5,943 | 4,223 | +40.73 | 11,419 | 3,674 |
| Dundee U | 7,547 | 7,481 | +0.88 | 13,538 | 5,117 |
| Hearts | 13,163 | 13,381 | –1.63 | 17,062 | 10,080 |
| Hibernian | 10,489 | 9,909 | +5.85 | 16,805 | 8,121 |
| Inverness CT | 4,038 | 4,181 | –3.42 | 6,766 | 2,529 |
| Kilmarnock | 4,647 | 5,537 | –16.07 | 6,523 | 3,198 |
| Motherwell | 5,362 | 5,946 | –9.82 | 10,496 | 3,649 |
| Ross Co | 4,430 | 2,873 | +54.19 | 6,110 | 2,837 |
| St Johnstone | 3,712 | 4,169 | –10.96 | 6,700 | 2,167 |
| St Mirren | 4,389 | 4,492 | –2.29 | 6,347 | 3,065 |

### IRN BRU SCOTTISH FIRST DIVISION ATTENDANCES

| | Average Gate | | | Season 2012–13 | |
|---|---|---|---|---|---|
| | 2012–13 | 2011–12 | +/–% | Highest | Lowest |
| Airdrie U | 936 | 833 | +12.36 | 1,648 | 554 |
| Cowdenbeath | 791 | 469 | +68.66 | 2,507 | 370 |
| Dumbarton | 927 | 630 | +47.14 | 1,530 | 483 |
| Dunfermline Ath | 3,796 | 4,799 | –20.90 | 5,835 | 2,461 |
| Falkirk | 3,102 | 3,187 | –2.67 | 4,804 | 2,288 |
| Greenock Morton | 2,137 | 1,814 | +17.81 | 5,647 | 1,302 |
| Hamilton A | 1,231 | 1,764 | –30.22 | 2,450 | 775 |
| Livingston | 1,308 | 1,774 | –26.27 | 1,762 | 787 |
| Partick Th | 3,614 | 2,344 | +54.18 | 8,875 | 2,046 |
| Raith R | 1,829 | 1,932 | –5.33 | 4,294 | 1,117 |

### IRN BRU SCOTTISH SECOND DIVISION ATTENDANCES

| | Average Gate | | | Season 2012–13 | |
|---|---|---|---|---|---|
| | 2012–13 | 2011–12 | +/–% | Highest | Lowest |
| Albion R | 387 | 462 | –16.23 | 853 | 206 |
| Alloa Ath | 551 | 672 | –18.01 | 1,224 | 382 |
| Arbroath | 684 | 803 | –14.82 | 940 | 387 |
| Ayr U | 1,007 | 1,500 | –32.87 | 1,373 | 631 |
| Brechin C | 549 | 516 | +6.40 | 978 | 401 |
| East Fife | 526 | 599 | –12.19 | 753 | 408 |
| Forfar Ath | 539 | 512 | +5.27 | 903 | 293 |
| Queen of S | 1,659 | 1,550 | +7.03 | 2,568 | 1,247 |
| Stenhousemuir | 543 | 594 | –8.59 | 818 | 360 |
| Stranraer | 426 | 354 | +20.34 | 1,015 | 169 |

### IRN BRU SCOTTISH THIRD DIVISION ATTENDANCES

| | Average Gate | | | Season 2012–13 | |
|---|---|---|---|---|---|
| | 2012–13 | 2011–12 | +/–% | Highest | Lowest |
| Annan Ath | 641 | 472 | +35.81 | 2,517 | 242 |
| Berwick R | 917 | 396 | +131.57 | 4,476 | 382 |
| Clyde | 1,313 | 566 | +131.98 | 7,600 | 401 |
| East Stirling | 612 | 321 | +90.65 | 2,854 | 192 |
| Elgin C | 1,030 | 627 | +64.27 | 3,663 | 352 |
| Montrose | 831 | 334 | +148.80 | 4,686 | 244 |
| Peterhead | 938 | 487 | +92.61 | 4,855 | 225 |
| Queen's Park | 2,803 | 519 | +440.08 | 30,117 | 374 |
| Rangers | 45,744 | 46,324 | –1.25 | 50,048 | 34,441 |
| Stirling Alb | 897 | 572 | +56.82 | 3,751 | 327 |

# ABERDEEN

*Year Formed:* 1903. *Ground & Address:* Pittodrie Stadium, Pittodrie St, Aberdeen AB24 5QH. *Telephone:* 01224 650400. *Fax:* 01224 644173. *E-mail:* feedback@afc.co.uk *Website:* www.afc.co.uk
*Ground Capacity:* all seated: 21,421. *Size of Pitch:* 115yd × 72yd.
*Chairman:* Stewart Milne. *Secretary:* David Johnston.
*Manager:* Derek McInnes. *Assistant Manager:* Archie Knox. *U-19 Coach:* Neil Cooper.
*Club Nicknames:* 'The Dons', 'The Reds', 'The Dandies'.
*Previous Grounds:* None.
*Record Attendance:* 45,061 v Hearts, Scottish Cup 4th rd, 13 Mar 1954.
*Record Transfer Fee received:* £1.75 million for Eoin Jess to Coventry City (February 1996).
*Record Transfer Fee paid:* £1m+ for Paul Bernard from Oldham Athletic (September 1995).
*Record Victory:* 13-0 v Peterhead, Scottish Cup 3rd rd, 10 Feb 1923.
*Record Defeat:* 0-9 v Celtic, Premier League, 6 Nov 2010.
*Most Capped Player:* Alex McLeish, 77 (Scotland).
*Most League Appearances:* 556: Willie Miller, 1973-90.
*Most League Goals in Season (Individual):* 38: Benny Yorston, Division I, 1929-30.
*Most Goals Overall (Individual):* 199: Joe Harper, 1969-72; 1976-81.

## ABERDEEN – SCOTTISH PREMIER LEAGUE 2012–13 LEAGUE RECORD

| Match No. | Date | Venue | Opponents | Result | H/T Score | Lg Pos. | Goalscorers | Attendance |
|---|---|---|---|---|---|---|---|---|
| 1 | Aug 4 | A | Celtic | L 0-1 | 0-0 | 11 | | 48,251 |
| 2 | 11 | H | Ross Co | D 0-0 | 0-0 | 9 | | 14,010 |
| 3 | 18 | A | St Johnstone | W 2-1 | 1-0 | 5 | Osbourne [16], Hayes [47] | 4857 |
| 4 | 26 | H | Hearts | D 0-0 | 0-0 | 9 | | 11,971 |
| 5 | Sept 1 | H | St Mirren | D 0-0 | 0-0 | 9 | | 9288 |
| 6 | 15 | A | Inverness CT | D 1-1 | 0-0 | 7 | Smith [84] | 4499 |
| 7 | 23 | H | Motherwell | D 3-3 | 1-1 | 8 | Rae [6], McGinn [84], Magennis [90] | 8577 |
| 8 | 29 | H | Hibernian | W 2-1 | 1-1 | 6 | McGinn [4], Rae [71] | 8282 |
| 9 | Oct 6 | A | Kilmarnock | W 3-1 | 0-1 | 3 | Rae [46], McGinn [55], Vernon [90] | 5540 |
| 10 | 20 | A | Dundee U | D 1-1 | 0-1 | 3 | McGinn [53] | 9858 |
| 11 | 27 | H | Dundee | W 2-0 | 1-0 | 3 | McGinn [14], Hayes [74] | 10,425 |
| 12 | Nov 3 | A | Ross Co | L 1-2 | 0-1 | 4 | McGinn [77] | 6064 |
| 13 | 10 | A | St Mirren | W 4-1 | 2-0 | 3 | Hayes [10], McGinn [45], Clark [86], Reynolds [87] | 4486 |
| 14 | 17 | H | Celtic | L 0-2 | 0-0 | 3 | | 18,000 |
| 15 | 24 | H | Hibernian | W 1-0 | 0-0 | 2 | McGinn [77] | 12,007 |
| 16 | 27 | H | Inverness CT | L 2-3 | 1-1 | 4 | Magennis 2 [45, 50] | 9193 |
| 17 | Dec 8 | A | Hearts | L 0-2 | 0-1 | 5 | | 14,410 |
| 18 | 15 | H | Kilmarnock | L 0-2 | 0-1 | 7 | | 8790 |
| 19 | 22 | H | St Johnstone | W 2-0 | 0-0 | 4 | McGinn 2 [63, 81] | 7051 |
| 20 | 26 | A | Motherwell | L 1-4 | 1-3 | 5 | Hayes [34] | 5093 |
| 21 | 29 | A | Dundee | W 3-1 | 0-0 | 5 | McGinn 3 [46, 69, 89] | 9013 |
| 22 | Jan 2 | H | Dundee U | D 2-2 | 1-2 | 5 | Vernon [11], McGinn [53] | 13,176 |
| 23 | 19 | A | Inverness CT | L 0-3 | 0-0 | 5 | | 4734 |
| 24 | 27 | H | Hibernian | D 0-0 | 0-0 | 5 | | 7184 |
| 25 | 30 | A | St Johnstone | L 1-3 | 1-1 | 6 | McGinn [44] | 2167 |
| 26 | Feb 9 | H | St Mirren | D 0-0 | 0-0 | 7 | | 7240 |
| 27 | 15 | H | Dundee | W 1-0 | 1-0 | 5 | McGinn [18] | 7841 |
| 28 | 23 | A | Kilmarnock | D 1-1 | 1-1 | 8 | Fallon [7] | 4390 |
| 29 | 26 | A | Ross Co | L 0-1 | 0-0 | 8 | | 6394 |
| 30 | Mar 9 | H | Motherwell | D 0-0 | 0-0 | 9 | | 8210 |
| 31 | 16 | A | Celtic | L 3-4 | 1-1 | 9 | Vernon [45], Magennis 2 [53, 60] | 46,395 |
| 32 | 30 | H | Hearts | W 2-0 | 1-0 | 7 | McGinn 2 [10, 55] | 10,175 |
| 33 | Apr 6 | A | Dundee U | L 0-1 | 0-0 | 8 | | 8577 |
| 34 | 22 | A | Hibernian | D 0-0 | 0-0 | 8 | | 8326 |
| 35 | 27 | H | Kilmarnock | W 1-0 | 1-0 | 7 | McGinn [4] | 6334 |
| 36 | May 5 | A | Dundee | D 1-1 | 0-1 | 7 | McGinn (pen) [70] | 6441 |
| 37 | 11 | A | St Mirren | D 0-0 | 0-0 | 7 | | 4292 |
| 38 | 18 | H | Hearts | D 1-1 | 0-0 | 8 | Hamill (og) [78] | 10,465 |

**Final League Position: 8**

**Honours**
*League Champions:* Division I 1954-55. Premier Division 1979-80, 1983-84, 1984-85; *Runners-up:* Division I 1910-11, 1936-37, 1955-56, 1970-71, 1971-72. Premier Division 1977-78, 1980-81, 1981-82, 1988-89, 1989-90, 1990-91, 1992-93, 1993-94.
*Scottish Cup Winners:* 1947, 1970, 1982, 1983, 1984, 1986, 1990; *Runners-up:* 1937, 1953, 1954, 1959, 1967, 1978, 1993, 2000.
*League Cup Winners:* 1955-56, 1976-77, 1985-86, 1989-90, 1995-96; *Runners-up:* 1946-47, 1978-79, 1979-80, 1987-88, 1988-89, 1992-93, 1999-2000.
*Drybrough Cup Winners:* 1971, 1980.

**European:** *European Cup:* 12 matches (1980-81, 1984-85, 1985-86); *Cup Winners' Cup:* 39 matches (1967-68, 1970-71, 1978-79, 1982-83 winners, 1983-84 semi-finals, 1986-87, 1990-91, 1993-94); *UEFA Cup:* 56 matches (*Fairs Cup:* 1968-69. *UEFA Cup:* 1971-72, 1972-73, 1973-74, 1977-78, 1979-80, 1981-82, 1987-88, 1988-89, 1989-90, 1991-92, 1994-95, 1996-97, 2000-01, 2002-03, 2007-08). *Europa League:* 2 matches (2009–10).

**Club colours:** All red with white trim.

**Goalscorers:** *League (41):* McGinn 20 (1 pen), Magennis 5, Hayes 4, Rae 3, Vernon 3, Clark 1, Fallon 1, Osbourne 1, Reynolds 1, Smith 1, own goal 1.
*William Hill Scottish FA Cup (3):* Fallon 1, McGinn 1, Shaughnessy 1.
*Scottish Communities League Cup (5):* Vernon 3, Magennis 1, Rae 1.

| Langfield J 37 | Jack R 18 | Anderson R 30+1 | Considine A 17+1 | Naysmith G 7+2 | Osbourne I 21+2 | Hughes S 22+1 | Rae G 34+1 | Hayes J 29+6 | McGinn N 33+2 | Vernon S 29+6 | Clark C 6+4 | Fraser R 13+3 | Magennis J 18+17 | Pawlett P 4+8 | Reynolds M 34+1 | Megginson M 1+2 | Fallon R 8+7 | Smith C 7+11 | Milsom R 3+10 | Brown Jordon —+2 | Robertson C 21+2 | McManus D —+7 | Shaughnessy J 22+1 | Masson J 1+6 | Brown Jason 1+1 | Murray C —+1 | Low N 1+4 | Storie C 1 | Match No. |
|---|---|---|---|---|---|---|---|---|---|---|---|---|---|---|---|---|---|---|---|---|---|---|---|---|---|---|---|---|---|
| 1 | 2 | 3 | 4 | 5¹ | 6 | 7 | 8 | 9² | 10³ | 11 | 12 | 13 | 14 | | | | | | | | | | | | | | | | 1 |
| 1 | 2² | 3 | 4 | 5 | 7 | 9 | 8 | 6³ | 11¹ | 10 | | 12 | 13 | 14 | | | | | | | | | | | | | | | 2 |
| 1 | 2 | 3¹ | 4 | 5 | 6 | 8 | 7 | 10³ | | 11 | | 9² | 14 | | 12 | 13 | | | | | | | | | | | | | 3 |
| 1 | 6 | 2 | 3 | 8¹ | 5 | | 7 | 11 | | 10³ | 12 | 9² | 14 | | 4 | | 13 | | | | | | | | | | | | 4 |
| 1 | | 3 | 5 | | 7 | 6¹ | 8 | 9 | | 10 | 12 | 11² | 2 | | 4 | | 13 | | | | | | | | | | | | 5 |
| 1 | 2² | 4⁸ | 3 | | 6 | 8 | 9 | 12 | 11¹ | | | 7³ | 10 | | 5 | 14 | 13 | | | | | | | | | | | | 6 |
| 1 | 6³ | 3 | 5 | | 12 | 8 | 7² | 11 | 13 | 10¹ | | 9 | 2 | | 4 | | 14 | | | | | | | | | | | | 7 |
| 1 | 2 | 3 | 5 | | 6 | 8 | 7 | | 11 | 9² | | 10¹ | 12 | | 4 | | | 13 | | | | | | | | | | | 8 |
| 1 | 2 | 3 | 5 | | 7 | 6 | 8² | 12 | 10³ | 11 | | 9¹ | 13 | | 4 | | | | 14 | | | | | | | | | | 9 |
| 1 | | 3 | | | 2³ | 6 | 7¹ | 13 | 11 | 10 | 8 | 9² | 14 | | 4 | | | 12 | 5 | | | | | | | | | | 10 |
| 1 | | 3 | | | 2 | 6² | 7 | 12 | 11 | 10 | 8¹ | 9³ | 13 | | 4 | | | 14 | 5 | | | | | | | | | | 11 |
| 1 | | 2 | 3¹ | 5 | 8 | 6³ | 7 | 14 | 11 | 10² | 12 | 9 | | | 4 | | | 13 | | | | | | | | | | | 12 |
| 1 | | 2 | 3 | | 6 | | | 9 | 10³ | 12 | 7 | 11¹ | 5² | | 4 | | | | | | 8 | 13 | 14 | | | | | | 13 |
| 1 | | 4 | 3 | | 7 | | 6¹ | 11³ | 10 | 13 | 8 | 9² | 5 | | 2 | | 14 | | | | 12 | | | | | | | | 14 |
| 1 | | 2 | 4 | | 6² | | | 9 | 8 | 10 | 7 | | 5 | | 3 | | 12 | 11¹ | | | | | 13 | | | | | | 15 |
| 1 | | 2 | 4 | | | | | 9³ | 8 | 11 | 7¹ | | 5 | | 3 | | 10 | 13 | | | | 14 | 6 | 12² | | | | | 16 |
| 1 | | 3¹ | 5 | | | | 8 | 6 | 10 | 11³ | | | 2 | | 4 | | 13 | 7² | | | | 14 | 9 | 12 | | | | | 17 |
| 1⁸ | | 4² | | | | | 6 | 8 | 7 | 11 | | | 5 | | 2 | | 10¹ | | | | 3 | 14 | 9³ | 13 | 12 | | | | 18 |
| 1 | | 3 | | | | | 7 | | 10 | 8 | | | 9² | | 4 | | 6¹ | 11³ | | | 13 | 5 | | 2 | 12 | 1 | 14 | | 19 |
| 1 | | 3² | 13 | | | | 6 | 11 | 9 | 7 | | | 2 | | 4 | | 10³ | 12 | | | 5 | 14 | 8¹ | | | | | | 20 |
| 1 | | 12 | 3¹ | | | | 7 | 9 | 10 | 8 | | 13 | 14 | | 4 | | 6 | | | | 5³ | 2 | 11² | | | | | | 21 |
| 1 | | 3 | | | | | 12 | 6 | 9 | 8 | 11 | | 7¹ | | 4 | | 10² | 13 | | | 5 | 2 | | | | | | | 22 |
| 1 | | 4³ | | | | | 12 | 10 | 6 | 7 | 11 | 9² | | | 13 | | 5 | | | | 8 | 14 | 3 | 2¹ | | | | | 23 |
| 1 | | 3 | | | | | 8 | 7 | 11³ | 10 | 12 | | 14 | 6¹ | 4 | | 13 | 9² | | | 5 | 2 | | | | | | | 24 |
| 1 | | | | | | | 4³ | 8 | 9 | 12 | 10 | | 7¹ | | 6 | 13 | 3 | | | 11² | 14 | 5 | 2 | | | | | | 25 |
| 1 | | 3 | | | | | 7 | 9² | 8 | 11 | 10 | 13 | | | 12 | | 6³ | 4⁸ | | | 14 | | 5¹ | 2 | | | | | 26 |
| 1 | | 3 | | | | 12 | 2 | 8 | 7 | 9 | 10 | 11 | | | 14 | | 6² | | | | 13 | | 5¹ | 4³ | | | | | 27 |
| 1 | 6³ | 3 | | 5¹ | | | 7 | 8 | 13 | 10 | | | 14 | | 4 | | 11 | 9² | | 12 | 2 | | | | | | | | 28 |
| 1 | 6 | 3 | | | | | 8² | 7 | 9³ | 11 | | | 2 | 12 | 4 | | 10¹ | 13 | | 5 | 14 | | | | | | | | 29 |
| 1 | 6³ | 3 | | 12 | | | 8 | 7 | 9² | 10 | 11 | | 13 | | 4 | | 14 | | | | 5¹ | 2 | | | | | | | 30 |
| 1 | 6 | 3 | | | | | 8² | 7 | 9¹ | 11 | 10 | | 2 | 12 | 5 | | | 13 | | | | 4 | | | | | | | 31 |
| 1 | 6³ | 3 | | | | | 7 | 9¹ | 11 | 10 | | 8² | 12 | 4 | | | 14 | | | 5 | 2 | | | | | 13 | | | 32 |
| 1 | 7 | 3 | | 5 | | | 8 | 6¹ | 9 | 10 | | 11² | 14 | | 4 | | 13 | | | | | 2³ | | | 12 | | | | 33 |
| 1 | 6 | 3 | | | | | 7 | 9³ | 10 | 12 | | 11² | 13 | | 4 | | 14 | 8¹ | | 5 | 2 | | | | | | | | 34 |
| 1 | 6 | | | 3 | | | 8² | 12 | 11 | 9 | 10³ | | 13 | | 4 | | | 14 | | | 5 | 2 | | | | | 7¹ | | 35 |
| 1 | 8 | | | 2 | | | 6¹ | 7 | | 11³ | | 13 | 9² | 4 | 10⁸ | 14 | | | | | 5 | 3 | | | 12 | | | | 36 |
| 1 | 7 | | | 3 | | | 8² | 6 | 9 | 10³ | | 14 | | 4 | 11¹ | 12 | | | | | 5 | 2 | | | 13 | | | | 37 |
| 1 | | | | 3 | | | 8³ | 9 | 10 | 13 | | 6² | | 4 | 11¹ | | | | | | 2 | 12 | 5 | 14 | 7 | | | | 38 |

# AIRDRIEONIANS

*Year Formed:* 2002. *Ground & Address:* Excelsior Stadium, New Broomfield, Craigneuk Avenue, Airdrie ML6 8QZ.
*Telephone:* (Stadium) 01236 622000. *Fax:* 01236 626002. *Postal Address:* 60 St Enoch Square, Glasgow G1 4AG.
*E-mail:* annmarie@ballantyneand.co.uk *Website:* www.airdriefc.com
*Ground Capacity:* 10,171 (all seated). *Size of Pitch:* 105m × 67m.
*Chairman:* Jim Ballantyne. *Secretary:* Ann Marie Ballantyne.
*Manager:* Jimmy Boyle. *First Team Coach:* Paul Lovering.
*Club Nickname:* 'The Diamonds'.
*Record Attendance:* 5924 v Motherwell, Scottish Cup 3rd rd, 6 Jan 2007.
*Record Victory:* 11-0 v Gala Fairydean, Scottish Cup 3rd rd, 19 Nov 2011.
*Record Defeat:* 1-6 v Greenock Morton, Second Division, 1 Nov 2003.
*Most League Appearances:* 222, Paul Lovering 2004-12.
*Most League Goals in Season (Individual):* 19: Alan Russell, 2007-08.
*Most Goals Overall (Individual):* 33: Stephen McKeown, 2002-08.

## AIRDRIE UNITED – SCOTTISH FIRST DIVISION 2012–13 LEAGUE RECORD

| Match No. | Date | Venue | Opponents | Result | H/T Score | Lg Pos. | Goalscorers | Attendance |
|---|---|---|---|---|---|---|---|---|
| 1 | Aug 11 | H | Dumbarton | W 4-1 | 3-0 | 2 | Boyle, John 3 [14, 25, 31], Di Giacomo [88] | 897 |
| 2 | 18 | A | Livingston | W 2-0 | 0-0 | 1 | Boyle, John [48], Bain [70] | 1170 |
| 3 | 25 | H | Dunfermline Ath | L 1-2 | 1-0 | 3 | Boyle, John [26] | 1229 |
| 4 | Sept 1 | H | Cowdenbeath | L 0-3 | 0-1 | 5 | | 816 |
| 5 | 15 | A | Raith R | L 0-2 | 0-1 | 6 | | 1481 |
| 6 | 22 | A | Falkirk | D 1-1 | 0-1 | 6 | Cook [68] | 2951 |
| 7 | 29 | H | Greenock Morton | L 2-3 | 1-0 | 7 | Boyle, John 2 [37, 80] | 1054 |
| 8 | Oct 6 | H | Hamilton A | L 0-4 | 0-0 | 8 | | 868 |
| 9 | 20 | A | Partick Th | L 0-7 | 0-5 | 8 | | 2545 |
| 10 | 27 | A | Dumbarton | W 4-3 | 0-2 | 8 | Stallard [65], Watt, J [68], Forsyth (og) [89], Blockley [90] | 774 |
| 11 | Nov 9 | H | Livingston | L 1-3 | 1-1 | 8 | Di Giacomo [20] | 1003 |
| 12 | 17 | A | Cowdenbeath | D 1-1 | 0-0 | 9 | Buchanan, G [77] | 423 |
| 13 | 24 | H | Raith R | D 0-0 | 0-0 | 9 | | 747 |
| 14 | Dec 15 | A | Greenock Morton | L 0-2 | 0-1 | 9 | | 1302 |
| 15 | 22 | H | Falkirk | L 1-4 | 0-1 | 9 | Donnelly [56] | 914 |
| 16 | 26 | A | Hamilton A | L 0-3 | 0-2 | 9 | | 1179 |
| 17 | 29 | H | Partick Th | D 1-1 | 1-0 | 9 | Boyle, John [41] | 1617 |
| 18 | Jan 2 | H | Cowdenbeath | D 1-1 | 0-1 | 9 | Donnelly [68] | 776 |
| 19 | 5 | A | Raith R | L 0-2 | 0-1 | 9 | | 1270 |
| 20 | 12 | A | Dunfermline Ath | W 3-1 | 1-1 | 9 | Donnelly 2 [4, 59], Di Giacomo (pen) [83] | 2823 |
| 21 | 19 | H | Dumbarton | L 1-2 | 1-2 | 9 | Donnelly [11] | 844 |
| 22 | 26 | A | Falkirk | L 3-4 | 0-3 | 10 | Di Giacomo (pen) [57], McLaren [88], Boyle, John [90] | 2715 |
| 23 | Feb 9 | H | Greenock Morton | L 0-4 | 0-2 | 10 | | 984 |
| 24 | 16 | A | Hamilton A | D 2-2 | 0-0 | 10 | Moore (pen) [64], Bain [90] | 755 |
| 25 | 23 | A | Partick Th | L 0-1 | 0-0 | 10 | | 3021 |
| 26 | Mar 2 | A | Livingston | L 1-4 | 0-3 | 10 | Boyle, John [90] | 1132 |
| 27 | 9 | H | Dunfermline Ath | D 3-3 | 1-1 | 10 | Blockley [11], Donnelly [53], McLaren [85] | 702 |
| 28 | 16 | A | Cowdenbeath | L 2-3 | 1-1 | 10 | Moore [12], Kirkpatrick [82] | 407 |
| 29 | 23 | H | Raith R | L 1-2 | 1-1 | 10 | Bain [7] | 554 |
| 30 | 30 | H | Falkirk | L 0-1 | 0-0 | 10 | | 790 |
| 31 | Apr 6 | A | Greenock Morton | L 2-5 | 0-2 | 10 | Lynch [70], Cook [73] | 1772 |
| 32 | 9 | A | Hamilton A | L 0-5 | 0-3 | 10 | | 850 |
| 33 | 13 | H | Partick Th | L 1-2 | 1-0 | 10 | Watt, L [35] | 1648 |
| 34 | 20 | A | Dumbarton | L 1-4 | 0-2 | 10 | Coogans [64] | 828 |
| 35 | 27 | H | Livingston | L 0-2 | 0-1 | 10 | | 650 |
| 36 | May 4 | A | Dunfermline Ath | W 2-1 | 0-0 | 10 | Coogans [46], McLaren [62] | 4624 |

**Final League Position: 10 – Relegated to Scottish Second Division**

**Honours**
*League Champions:* Second Division 2003-04; *Runners-up:* Second Division 2007-08.
*League Challenge Cup Winners:* 2008-09; *Runners-up:* 2003-04.

**Club colours:** Shirt: White with red trim. Shorts: Red. Socks: Red.

**Goalscorers:** *League (41):* Boyle, John 10, Donnelly 6, Di Giacomo 4 (2 pens), Bain 3, McLaren 3, Blockley 2, Coogans 2, Cook 2, Moore 2 (1 pen), Buchanan G 1, Kirkpatrick 1, Lynch 1, Stallard 1, Watt J 1, Watt L 1, own goal 1.
*William Hill Scottish FA Cup (5):* Buchanan G 1, Di Giacomo 1 (1 pen), Griffin 1, Watt J 1, own goal 1.
*Scottish Communities League Cup (2):* Blockley 1, Cook 1.
*Ramsdens Cup (1):* McLaren 1.

| Arthur K 16+2 | Hart M 9 | MacDonald C 7 | Lilley D 16+5 | Warren M 24+3 | Bain J 25+6 | Barclay J 6+6 | Cook A 9+2 | Boyle John 23+2 | McLaren W 17+10 | Donnelly R 21+11 | Griffin G 3+6 | Di Giacomo P 5+12 | Buchanan G 26+2 | Lynch S 15+4 | Blockley N 25+1 | Boyle Jack 9+4 | Wright J —+1 | Stallard K 5 | Evans G 15+3 | Brown L —+1 | Watt L 11+2 | McKenna C —+1 | Watt J 8+3 | Sally S —+1 | Allan J —+1 | O'Neil C 23+1 | Adam G 8 | Haggarty J —+1 | Buchanan L 5+1 | Duncan A 1 | Ronald O —+2 | Lamie R 17 | Davidson R 5 | Kirkpatrick J 2+3 | Hetherington S 14 | Thomson R 11 | Moore J 6+3 | Drummond G 4+1 | Coogans L 5+2 | Match No. |
|---|---|---|---|---|---|---|---|---|---|---|---|---|---|---|---|---|---|---|---|---|---|---|---|---|---|---|---|---|---|---|---|---|---|---|---|---|---|---|---|---|
| 1 | 2 | 3 | 4 | 5² | 6 | 7 | 8¹ | 9 | 10 | 11³ | 12 | 13 | 14 | | | | | | | | | | | | | | | | | | | | | | | | | | | 1 |
| 1 | 2 | 3 | 4 | 5 | 6 | 13 | 8 | 9¹ | 10³ | 11² | 12 | | 14 | | 7 | | | | | | | | | | | | | | | | | | | | | | | | | 2 |
| 1 | 2 | 3 | 4 | 5 | 6 | 13 | 8 | 9² | 10¹ | 11³ | 12 | 13 | 14 | | 7 | | | | | | | | | | | | | | | | | | | | | | | | | 3 |
| 1 | 2 | 3 | | 5⁴ | 6 | 7² | 8 | 9¹ | 10 | 11³ | 12 | 13 | 14 | | | | | | 4 | | | | | | | | | | | | | | | | | | | | | 4 |
| 1 | 2 | 3 | 4 | 5 | 6² | 7³ | 8 | 9¹ | 10 | 11 | 12 | 13 | 14 | | | | | | | | | | | | | | | | | | | | | | | | | | | 5 |
| 1 | 2 | 3 | 4 | 5 | 6 | 7 | 8 | 9³ | 10¹ | 11² | 12 | 13 | 14 | | | | | | | | | | | | | | | | | | | | | | | | | | | 6 |
| 1 | 2 | 4¹ | 3⁴ | 5 | 6 | 7 | 8 | 9³ | 10 | 11² | 12 | 13 | 14 | | | | | | | | | | | | | | | | | | | | | | | | | | | 7 |
| 1 | 2 | 3 | 4 | 5 | 6² | 7 | 8³ | 9 | 10¹ | 11 | 12 | 13 | 14 | | | | | | | | | | | | | | | | | | | | | | | | | | | 8 |
| 1 | 2 | 3 | 4 | 5¹ | 6² | 7 | 8 | 9 | 10 | 11³ | 12 | 13 | 14⁴ | | | | | | | | | | | | | | | | | | | | | | | | | | | 9 |
| 1 | 2 | 3¹ | 4³ | 5 | 6 | 7² | 8 | 9 | 10 | 11 | 12 | 13 | 14 | | | | | | | | | | | | | | | | | | | | | | | | | | | 10 |
| 1 | 2 | 3 | 4¹ | 5 | 6 | | 8 | 9³ | 10 | 11² | | 13 | 14 | | | | | | | | | | | | | | | | | | | | | | | | | | | 11 |
| | | 3 | 4 | 5 | 6³ | 7 | 8 | 9² | 10¹ | 11 | 12 | 13 | 14 | | | | | | | | | | | | | 1 | | | | | | 2 | | | | | | | | 12 |
| | | 3 | 4 | 5 | 6 | 7 | 8⁴ | 9³ | 10¹ | 11² | 12 | 13 | 14 | | | | | | | | | | | | | 1 | | | | | | 2 | | | | | | | | 13 |
| | | 3 | 4 | 5 | 6¹ | 7 | 8 | 9² | 10 | 11 | 12 | 13 | 14 | | | | | | | | | | | | | 1 | | | | | | 2³ | | | | | | | | 14 |
| | | 3 | 4 | 5 | 6 | 7⁴ | 8¹ | 9² | 10 | 11 | 12 | 13 | | | | | | | | | | | | | | 1 | | | | | | 2 | | | | | | | | 15 |
| | | 3 | 4 | 5 | 6¹ | 7³ | 8 | 9² | 10 | 11 | 12 | 13 | 14 | | | | | | | | | | | | | 1 | | | | | | 2 | | | | | | | | 16 |
| 14 | | 3 | 4 | 5³ | 6 | 7 | 8 | 9² | 10¹ | 11 | 12 | 13 | | | | | | | | | | | | | | 1 | | | | | | 2 | | | | | | | | 17 |
| 12 | | 3¹ | 4 | 5 | 6 | 7³ | 8 | 9 | 10 | 11² | | 13 | 14 | | | | | | | | | | | | | 1 | | | | | | 2 | | | | | | | | 18 |
| | | 3¹ | 4 | 5 | 6 | 7 | 8 | 9 | 10² | 11³ | 12 | 13 | 14 | | | | | | | | | | | | | 1 | | | | | | 2 | | | | | | | | 19 |
| 14 | | 3 | 4 | 5 | 6³ | 7 | 8 | 9 | 10¹ | 11² | 12 | 13 | | | | | | | | | | | | | | 1 | | | | | | 2 | | | | | | | | 20 |
| 1 | | 3 | 4 | 5 | 6² | 7³ | 8¹ | 9 | 10 | 11 | 12 | 13 | 14 | | | | | | | | | | | | | | | | | | | 2 | | | | | | | | 21 |
| 1 | | 3 | 4 | 5 | 6 | 7 | 8 | 9 | 10 | 11¹ | 12 | 13 | | | | | | | | | | | | | | | | | | | | 2² | | | | | | | | 22 |
| 1 | | | 4 | 5⁴ | | 7 | 8 | 10 | | 11¹ | 12 | 13 | 14 | | | | | | | | | | | | | | | | | | | 2 | | 3⁴ | | | 6³ | 9² | | 23 |
| | | | 4 | | 6 | 7 | | | 10³ | | 12 | 13 | 14 | | | | | | | | 5 | | 9² | | | 1 | | | | | | 2 | | 3¹ | 11 | | 8 | | | 24 |
| | | | 4 | | 6 | 7 | | 9³ | 10 | | 12 | 13 | | | | | | | | | 5¹ | | | | | 1 | | | | | | 2 | | 3 | | 11² | 8 | | | 25 |
| | | | 4 | | 6 | 7 | | 9³ | 10¹ | 11 | 12 | | 14 | | | | | | 13⁴ | | 5² | | | | | 1 | | | | | | 2 | | 3 | | | 8 | | | 26 |
| | | | 4 | | 6 | 7 | | 9 | 10¹ | 11 | 12 | 13 | 14 | | | | | | | | 5² | | | | | 1 | | | | | | 2³ | | 3 | | | 8 | | | 27 |
| | | | 4 | 5 | 6 | 7 | | 9 | 10¹ | 11² | 12 | 13 | 14 | | | | | | | | | | | | | 1 | | | | | | 2 | | 3 | | | 8 | | | 28 |
| | | | 4 | 5 | 6 | 7² | | 9 | 10 | 11³ | 12 | 13 | 14 | | | | | | | | | | | | | 1 | | | | | | 2¹ | | 3 | | | 8 | | | 29 |
| | | | 4 | 5 | 6³ | 7 | | 9¹ | 10² | 11 | 12 | 13 | 14 | | | | | | | | | | | | | 1 | | | | | | 2 | | 3 | | | 8 | | | 30 |
| | | | 4 | 5⁴ | 6¹ | 7 | | 9 | 10 | 11 | 12 | 13 | | | | | | | | | | | | | | 1 | | | | | | 2 | | 3² | | | | | | 31 |
| | | | 4¹ | 5 | 6³ | 7 | | 9 | 10² | 11 | 12 | 13 | 14 | | | | | | | | | | | | | 1 | | | | | | 2 | | 3 | | | 8 | | | 32 |
| | | | 4 | 5 | 6 | 7 | | 9 | 10 | 11 | 12 | 13 | | | | | | | | | | | | | | 1 | | | | | | 2¹ | | 3 | | | 8 | | | 33 |
| 12 | | | 4 | 5 | 6 | 7 | | 9³ | 10 | 11¹ | | 13 | 14 | | | | | | | | | | | | | | | | | | | 2 | | 3 | | | 8 | 1² | | 34 |
| 1 | | | 4 | 5³ | 6² | 7 | | 9 | | | 12 | 13 | 14 | | | | | | | | | | | | | | | | | | | 2 | | 3 | 11 | | 8 | 10¹ | | 35 |
| 1 | | | 4 | 5 | 6² | 7³ | | 9 | | | 12 | 13 | 14 | | | | | | | | | | | | | | | | | | | 2 | | 3 | 11 | | 8 | 10¹ | | 36 |

# ALBION ROVERS

*Year Formed:* 1882. *Ground & Address:* Cliftonhill Stadium, Main St, Coatbridge ML5 3RB. *Telephone/Fax:* 01236 606334.
*E-mail:* info@albionroversfc.com *Website:* albionroversfc.com
*Ground capacity:* 1,249 (seated: 489). *Size of Pitch:* 101m × 66m.
*Chairman* Robert Watt. *Secretary:* Frank Meade.
*Manager:* James Ward. *Assistant Manager:* Mark Cameron. *Physio:* John McMenamy.
*Club Nickname:* 'The Wee Rovers'.
*Previous Grounds:* Cowheath Park, Meadow Park, Whifflet.
*Record Attendance:* 27,381 v Rangers, Scottish Cup 2nd rd, 8 Feb 1936.
*Record Transfer Fee received:* £40,000 from Motherwell for Bruce Cleland.
*Record Transfer Fee paid:* £7000 for Gerry McTeague to Stirling Albion, September 1989.
*Record Victory:* 12-0 v Airdriehill, Scottish Cup 1st rd, 3 Sept 1887.
*Record Defeat:* 1-11 v Partick Th, League Cup 2nd rd, 11 Aug 1993.
*Most Capped Player:* Jock White, 1 (2), Scotland.
*Most League Appearances:* 399: Murdy Walls, 1921-36.
*Most League Goals in Season (Individual):* 41: Jim Renwick, Division II, 1932-33.
*Most Goals Overall (Individual):* 105: Bunty Weir, 1928-31.

## ALBION ROVERS – SCOTTISH SECOND DIVISION 2012–13 LEAGUE RECORD

| Match No. | Date | Venue | Opponents | Result | H/T Score | Lg Pos. | Goalscorers | Atten- dance |
|---|---|---|---|---|---|---|---|---|
| 1 | Aug 11 | A | Brechin C | L | 0-1 | 0-1 | 9 | | 413 |
| 2 | 18 | H | Alloa Ath | L | 0-3 | 0-1 | 10 | | 393 |
| 3 | 25 | A | Queen of the S | L | 0-1 | 0-1 | 10 | | 1426 |
| 4 | Sept 1 | A | East Fife | W | 2-1 | 1-1 | 8 | Forster (og) 44, Brannan 63 | 514 |
| 5 | 15 | H | Stranraer | W | 2-1 | 0-0 | 7 | Crooks 49, McGuigan 80 | 376 |
| 6 | 22 | H | Stenhousemuir | D | 4-4 | 1-2 | 6 | Crawford 2 13, 84, McGuigan 49, Phillips 82 | 389 |
| 7 | 29 | A | Forfar Ath | L | 2-4 | 0-2 | 7 | McGuigan 71, Crawford (pen) 81 | 452 |
| 8 | Oct 6 | A | Ayr U | L | 1-2 | 1-1 | 7 | Howarth 45 | 1023 |
| 9 | 20 | H | Arbroath | W | 4-0 | 1-0 | 6 | Crawford 2 16, 90, Howarth 72, Stevenson, A (pen) 77 | 313 |
| 10 | 27 | A | Alloa Ath | L | 1-5 | 0-2 | 8 | Crawford 48 | 467 |
| 11 | Nov 17 | H | East Fife | L | 0-3 | 0-1 | 9 | | 338 |
| 12 | 20 | A | Brechin C | L | 1-2 | 1-0 | 9 | Phillips 30 | 220 |
| 13 | 24 | A | Stranraer | D | 1-1 | 1-0 | 9 | Crawford 39 | 298 |
| 14 | Dec 15 | A | Stenhousemuir | L | 0-1 | 0-0 | 10 | | 396 |
| 15 | 18 | H | Forfar Ath | L | 2-3 | 2-2 | 10 | Boyle 35, Howarth 40 | 249 |
| 16 | 26 | H | Ayr U | W | 2-0 | 1-0 | 10 | Stevenson, A 24, Elliot 69 | 509 |
| 17 | 29 | A | Arbroath | L | 1-2 | 1-1 | 10 | Donnelly, C 27 | 569 |
| 18 | Jan 2 | H | Stranraer | L | 2-3 | 0-2 | 10 | Howarth 55, Stevenson, A 87 | 367 |
| 19 | 5 | A | East Fife | L | 0-2 | 0-1 | 10 | | 486 |
| 20 | 12 | H | Queen of the S | L | 0-3 | 0-1 | 10 | | 810 |
| 21 | Feb 9 | H | Arbroath | L | 0-1 | 0-1 | 10 | | 346 |
| 22 | 16 | A | Ayr U | L | 2-5 | 1-2 | 10 | Winters 2 42, 84 | 1064 |
| 23 | 23 | A | Queen of the S | L | 0-3 | 0-1 | 10 | | 1520 |
| 24 | 26 | A | Forfar Ath | L | 2-4 | 1-1 | 10 | Walker 12, Andrews 65 | 293 |
| 25 | Mar 2 | H | Alloa Ath | L | 1-5 | 0-3 | 10 | Andrews 46 | 319 |
| 26 | 5 | H | Stenhousemuir | W | 4-3 | 2-0 | 10 | Dallas 8, Crawford 19, Reid 50, Sally 69 | 206 |
| 27 | 9 | A | Stranraer | L | 2-3 | 2-1 | 10 | Crawford 6, Walker 27 | 266 |
| 28 | 19 | H | East Fife | D | 1-1 | 1-1 | 10 | Dallas 31 | 206 |
| 29 | 30 | A | Stenhousemuir | W | 1-0 | 1-0 | 10 | Dallas 1 | 360 |
| 30 | Apr 2 | H | Forfar Ath | L | 1-2 | 1-1 | 10 | Dallas 7 | 220 |
| 31 | 6 | A | Arbroath | L | 1-2 | 0-0 | 10 | Walker 55 | 555 |
| 32 | 13 | H | Ayr U | L | 1-3 | 0-2 | 10 | Dallas 57 | 475 |
| 33 | 20 | H | Brechin C | W | 3-1 | 1-0 | 10 | Green 29, Dallas 65, Crawford (pen) 90 | 378 |
| 34 | 27 | A | Alloa Ath | L | 1-4 | 1-3 | 10 | Walker 18 | 1224 |
| 35 | 30 | A | Brechin C | L | 0-2 | 0-1 | 10 | | 402 |
| 36 | May 4 | H | Queen of the S | L | 0-1 | 0-0 | 10 | | 853 |

**Final League Position: 10 – Relegated to Scottish Third Division**

**Honours**
*League Champions:* Division II 1933-34, Second Division 1988-89; *Runners-up:* Division II 1913-14, 1937-38, 1947-48.
*Promoted to Second Division:* 2010-11 (play-offs).
*Scottish Cup Runners-up:* 1920.

**Club colours:** All red with yellow trim.

**Goalscorers:** *League (45):* Crawford 10 (2 pens), Dallas 6, Howarth 4, Walker 4, McGuigan 3, Stevenson A 3 (1 pen), Andrews 2, Phillips 2, Winters 2, Boyle 1, Brannan 1, Crooks 1, Donnelly C 1, Elliot 1, Green 1, Reid 1, Sally 1, own goal 1.
*William Hill Scottish FA Cup (1):* Stevenson A 1.
*Scottish Communities League Cup (0).*
*Ramsdens Cup (0).*

| McCluskey C 4 | Reid A 31 | Russell B 26+1 | Dick G 2+2 | O'Byrne M 8+1 | Donnelly C 35+1 | Stevenson C 5+5 | Innes P 19+1 | Phillips G 32+4 | Crooks J 8+6 | Howarth S 11+11 | Crawford D 30+3 | Gilmartin J 1+2 | Brannan K 5+5 | Boyle C 14+12 | Marriott S 21+5 | McWilliams R 4 | Stevenson A 18+1 | McGuigan M 5+1 | McGinley M 20+1 | Tiffney R 2+9 | Green K 12+3 | Halsman B 5+2 | Elliot C 6 | Dallas C 16+1 | Andrews M 16+1 | Scully R 6 | Ronald O —+1 | Sally S 12+3 | Walker P 11+4 | Winters R 2+1 | Thomson G 7+3 | Shepherd G 2 | Ferry D —+1 | Match No. |
|---|---|---|---|---|---|---|---|---|---|---|---|---|---|---|---|---|---|---|---|---|---|---|---|---|---|---|---|---|---|---|---|---|---|---|
| 1 | 2 | 3 | 4 | 5 | 6 | 7¹ | 8 | 9² | 10 | 11³ | 12 | 13 | 14 | | | | | | | | | | | | | | | | | | | | | 1 |
| 1 | 2 | 5¹ | 8³ | 3 | 4 | 6 | 7 | 9 | 10 | 11² | 14 | 13 | | 12 | | | | | | | | | | | | | | | | | | | | 2 |
| 1 | 5 | 9 | | 4 | 3 | | 7 | 13 | 10¹ | | 6⁷ | 11 | 8 | 12 | 2 | | | | | | | | | | | | | | | | | | | 3 |
| | 2² | 5 | | | 4 | 13 | 8 | 12 | 10³ | 14 | 6 | | | 9¹ | 11 | | 3 | 1 | 7 | | | | | | | | | | | | | | | 4 |
| | 2² | 5 | | | 4 | 13 | 8 | 14 | 11 | | 6 | | | 9³ | 10¹ | | 3 | 1 | 7 | 12 | | | | | | | | | | | | | | 5 |
| | 5 | 14 | | | 4 | 2² | 8 | 12 | 10³ | 13 | 6 | | | 9¹ | | | 3 | 1 | 7 | 11 | | | | | | | | | | | | | | 6 |
| | 5 | 13 | | | 4 | 7 | 2 | 9¹ | 10² | 14 | 6 | | | 12 | | | 3 | 1 | 8 | 11³ | | | | | | | | | | | | | | 7 |
| 2 | 5¹ | 3 | 4 | | | | | 9¹ | 13 | 10² | 6 | | | 12 | | | 8 | | 7 | 11 | 1 | | | | | | | | | | | | | 8 |
| 2 | | 3 | 4 | | | | | 9 | | 10¹ | 6 | | | | 5 | 7 | 8 | | 11 | 1 | 12 | | | | | | | | | | | | | 9 |
| 2 | 12 | 3 | 4 | | | | | 9 | 13 | 10³ | 6 | | | 14 | 5¹ | 7 | 8 | | 11² | 1 | | | | | | | | | | | | | | 10 |
| 2 | 5 | 3 | 4 | | | 7¹ | | 9 | 13 | 11² | 6 | | | 10³ | 12 | | 8 | | 1 | 14 | | | | | | | | | | | | | | 11 |
| 2 | 5 | 4 | | | | | 13 | 11 | | 10¹ | 6 | | | 9 | 12 | | 8² | 7 | 1 | | 3 | | | | | | | | | | | | | 12 |
| 1 | 2 | 5¹ | 13 | 4 | | 7 | | 9 | | | 6 | | | | 12 | 11 | | | | | 3 | | | 8² | 10 | | | | | | | | | 13 |
| 2 | 5 | 4¹ | 12 | | | | | 9 | 13 | | 6 | | | 14 | | | 7⁴ | 8³ | 1 | | 3 | | | 11² | 10 | | | | | | | | | 14 |
| 2 | 5 | 4 | 13 | | | | | 9 | | | | | | 7 | 11 | | 8¹ | | 1 | 12 | 3 | | | 6² | 10 | | | | | | | | | 15 |
| 2 | 5 | 4 | | | | | | 9 | 13 | 11¹ | 6³ | | | 14 | 12 | | 8² | | 1 | | 3 | | | 7 | 10⁸ | | | | | | | | | 16 |
| 2 | 3 | 5 | | | | | | 9 | 13 | 11² | 6 | | | 10³ | 12 | | 7 | | 1 | 14 | | | | 4¹ | 8 | | | | | | | | | 17 |
| 2 | 5⁴ | 4 | | | | | | 9 | 12 | 10¹ | 6 | | | 7 | 3 | | 8 | | 1 | | | | | | 11 | | | | | | | | | 18 |
| 2 | | 4 | 13 | | | | | 9 | | | 6¹ | | | 12 | 5 | | 7² | | 8 | | 1 | | | 10 | 11 | 3 | | | | | | | | 19 |
| 2 | 5 | 3 | | | | | | 9¹ | | | 6² | | | 8 | | | 7 | | | | 2 | | | 12 | 11 | 10 | 4 | 1 | 13 | | | | | 20 |
| | | 4 | | | | | | 9 | | | 6 | | | | 5 | | 8¹ | | 7 | | 2 | | | 10² | 3 | 1 | | 11 | 12 | 13 | | | | 21 |
| 7 | 5 | 3 | | | | | | 9 | | | 6³ | | | | | | 8² | | | | 2 | | 13 | 14 | 4 | 1 | | 11¹ | 12 | 10 | | | | 22 |
| 2 | 5 | 7 | | | 4² | | | 9 | | | | | | 14 | | | 8 | | | | 1 | | | 6 | 3 | | | 11¹ | 13 | 10³ | 12 | | | 23 |
| 2 | 5 | 3 | | | 8⁴ | | | 9 | | | | | | 12 | | | 7¹ | | | | 1 | 13 | | | 4 | | | 11 | 10² | 6 | | | | 24 |
| 2 | 5 | 3 | 6 | | | | | 11 | | | 12³ | 13 | | 14 | | | | | | | 1 | | | 9² | 4 | | | 8 | 10 | 7¹ | | | | 25 |
| 2 | 5¹ | | | | 4 | 13 | 8 | 9 | | | 6 | | | 12 | | | | | | | 3 | | | | 11 | 1 | | | 7² | 10 | | | | 26 |
| 2 | 5 | 8 | | | 4 | | | 9 | 13 | | 6 | | | | | | | | | | 3⁴ | | | | 11 | 1 | | | 12 | 10² | 7¹ | | | 27 |
| 2 | 5 | 4 | | | | | | 9 | 13 | | | | | 12 | | | 7² | | | | 3 | | | | 11 | 1 | | | 8³ | 10 | | | | 28 |
| 2 | | 4 | | | | 7 | 8 | | | | 6 | | | 12 | 5 | | | | | 14 | 3 | | | | | 1 | | 11¹ | 9³ | | 10² | | | 29 |
| 2 | 5 | 4 | | | | 7¹ | | 9 | 13 | | 6 | | | 12 | | | | | | | 3 | | | | | 1 | | 8 | 11 | 10² | | | | 30 |
| 2 | 5⁴ | 4 | | | | 7 | | | 10 | | 6 | | | 12 | | | | | | 14 | 3 | | | | | 1 | | 9² | 8³ | 11¹ | 13 | | | 31 |
| 2 | | 4 | | | | | 8 | 9 | | | 6 | | | | 5 | | | | | 14 | 3 | | 13 | | | 1 | | 11¹ | | 12 | 7³ | | | 32 |
| | | 4 | | | | 7 | | 9 | | | 6 | | | 12 | 5 | | 8 | | | | 3 | | 13 | | | 1 | | 11 | | 2¹ | 10² | | | 33 |
| | | 4 | | | | 7¹ | 8 | | | | 6 | | | 9 | 2 | | | | | 14 | 3 | | 12 | | | 1 | | 13 | 5 | 11² | 10³ | | | 34 |
| 2 | | 4 | | | | 6² | 9 | | | | | | | 7 | 5 | | | | | 12 | 3 | | 14 | | | 11 | | 13 | | 6⁸ | 10¹ | | i | 35 |
| 2 | | 4 | | | | | 5 | | | | 6 | | | 9 | 8 | | 3³ | | | 14 | | | 12 | | | 10² | | 11¹ | 7 | 1 | | | 13 | 36 |

# ALLOA ATHLETIC

*Year Formed:* 1878. *Ground & Address:* Recreation Park, Clackmannan Rd, Alloa FK10 1RY. *Telephone:* 01259 722695. *Fax:* 01259 210886. *E-mail:* fcadmin@alloaatheltic.co.uk *Website:* www.alloaathletic.co.uk
*Ground Capacity:* 3,100 (seated: 919). *Size of Pitch:* 102m × 69m.
*Honorary President:* George Ormiston. *Chairman:* Mike Mulraney. *Secretary:* Ewen G. Cameron.
*Manager:* Paul Hartley. *Assistant Manager:* Paddy Connolly. *Coach:* Malky Boyle. *Physio:* Niam Mohammed.
*Club Nicknames:* 'The Wasps', 'The Hornets'.
*Previous Grounds:* West End Public Park, Gabberston Park, Bellevue Park.
*Record Attendance:* 13,000 v Dunfermline Athletic, Scottish Cup 3rd rd replay, 26 Feb 1939.
*Record Transfer Fee received:* £100,000 for Martin Cameron to Bristol Rovers.
*Record Transfer Fee paid:* £26,000 for Ross Hamilton from Stenhousemuir.
*Record Victory:* 9-0 v Selkirk, Scottish Cup First Round, 28 November 2005.
*Record Defeat:* 0-10 v Dundee, Division II, 8 Mar 1947 v Third Lanark, League Cup, 8 Aug 1953.
*Most Capped Player:* Jock Hepburn, 1, Scotland.
*Most League Goals in Season (Individual):* 49: 'Wee' Willie Crilley, Division II, 1921-22.
*Most Goals Overall (Individual):* 19: Willie Irvine, 1996-2001.

## ALLOA ATHLETIC – SCOTTISH SECOND DIVISION 2012–13 LEAGUE RECORD

| Match No. | Date | Venue | Opponents | Result | H/T Score | Lg Pos. | Goalscorers | Atten- dance |
|---|---|---|---|---|---|---|---|---|
| 1 | Aug 11 | H | East Fife | D 1-1 | 0-1 | 3 | Simmons [74] | 625 |
| 2 | 18 | A | Albion R | W 3-0 | 1-0 | 1 | Grehan [14], Thomson 2 [79, 83] | 393 |
| 3 | 25 | H | Arbroath | L 2-3 | 2-1 | 6 | Cawley 2 [18, 32] | 575 |
| 4 | Sept 1 | A | Brechin C | W 3-1 | 0-0 | 3 | Thomson [65], Cawley [74], Grehan [88] | 491 |
| 5 | 15 | H | Stenhousemuir | L 0-2 | 0-0 | 5 | | 509 |
| 6 | 22 | H | Stranraer | W 3-0 | 2-0 | 4 | Cawley [21], Grehan (pen) [45], Holmes [90] | 429 |
| 7 | 29 | A | Queen of the S | L 0-1 | 0-0 | 4 | | 1370 |
| 8 | Oct 6 | A | Forfar Ath | W 3-2 | 2-1 | 4 | McCord, Ryan (pen) [7], Marr [22], Gordon [83] | 487 |
| 9 | 20 | H | Ayr U | W 1-0 | 1-0 | 3 | Gordon [45] | 595 |
| 10 | 27 | H | Albion R | W 5-1 | 2-0 | 2 | Grehan 3 [20, 57, 64], Marriott (og) [42], Megginson [82] | 467 |
| 11 | Nov 10 | A | East Fife | W 1-0 | 1-0 | 2 | Holmes [32] | 515 |
| 12 | 17 | A | Brechin C | D 2-2 | 1-0 | 2 | Cawley [43], Grehan [62] | 501 |
| 13 | 24 | A | Stenhousemuir | W 2-0 | 2-0 | 2 | Cawley [24], Simmons [36] | 671 |
| 14 | Dec 11 | H | Queen of the S | W 1-0 | 0-0 | 2 | McCord, Ryan (pen) [58] | 475 |
| 15 | 15 | A | Stranraer | L 2-3 | 0-1 | 2 | Holmes [61], Thomson [81] | 245 |
| 16 | 22 | H | Forfar Ath | W 2-1 | 2-1 | 2 | McCord, Ryan 2 [4, 20] | 401 |
| 17 | 29 | A | Ayr U | D 0-0 | 0-0 | 2 | | 927 |
| 18 | Jan 2 | H | Stenhousemuir | W 1-0 | 1-0 | 2 | McCord, Ryan [17] | 603 |
| 19 | 5 | A | Brechin C | L 2-3 | 2-1 | 2 | Cawley [17], McCord, Ryan (pen) [38] | 602 |
| 20 | 19 | H | East Fife | D 1-1 | 1-1 | 2 | Marr [34] | 551 |
| 21 | 26 | H | Stranraer | W 4-1 | 1-0 | 2 | McCord, Ryan [32], Megginson [60], Holmes 2 [67, 73] | 451 |
| 22 | Feb 2 | A | Queen of the S | D 0-0 | 0-0 | 2 | | 1738 |
| 23 | 9 | H | Ayr U | D 2-2 | 0-1 | 2 | Megginson [63], Gordon [90] | 521 |
| 24 | 16 | A | Forfar Ath | W 1-0 | 0-0 | 2 | Gordon [89] | 511 |
| 25 | 23 | H | Arbroath | L 0-1 | 0-1 | 2 | | 451 |
| 26 | 27 | A | Arbroath | W 2-1 | 1-0 | 2 | McCord, Ryan (pen) [19], Cawley [89] | 471 |
| 27 | Mar 2 | A | Albion R | W 5-1 | 3-0 | 2 | Grehan [9], Elliot 2 [31, 39], Holmes [78], Cawley [85] | 319 |
| 28 | 9 | A | Stenhousemuir | D 1-1 | 1-0 | 2 | McCord, Ryan (pen) [22] | 513 |
| 29 | 16 | H | Brechin C | L 0-1 | 0-0 | 2 | | 382 |
| 30 | 23 | H | Queen of the S | L 1-2 | 0-1 | 2 | Cawley [56] | 647 |
| 31 | 30 | A | Stranraer | W 2-1 | 0-0 | 2 | Holmes [55], McCord, Ryan [68] | 322 |
| 32 | Apr 6 | A | Ayr U | W 2-0 | 1-0 | 2 | McCord, Ryan [27], Holmes [90] | 898 |
| 33 | 13 | H | Forfar Ath | W 1-0 | 0-0 | 2 | Cawley [47] | 507 |
| 34 | 20 | A | East Fife | L 1-2 | 0-1 | 2 | Tiffoney [84] | 497 |
| 35 | 27 | H | Albion R | W 4-1 | 3-1 | 2 | Cawley 2 [4, 88], Simmons [22], Tiffoney [31] | 1224 |
| 36 | May 4 | A | Arbroath | W 1-0 | 0-0 | 2 | Hynd [89] | 901 |

**Final League Position: 2 – Promoted to Scottish First Division after play-offs**

**Honours**
*League Champions:* Division II 1921-22; Third Division 1997-98, 2011-12. *Runners-up:* Division II 1938-39.
Second Division 1976-77, 1981-82, 1984-85, 1988-89, 1999-2000, 2001-02, 2009-10, 2012-13 (promoted via play-offs).
*League Challenge Cup Winners:* 1999-2000; *Runners-up:* 2001-02.

**Club colours:** Shirt: Gold with black trim. Shorts: Black. Socks: Black.

**Goalscorers:** *League (62):* Cawley 13, McCord, Ryan 11 (5 pens), Grehan 8 (1 pen), Holmes 8, Gordon 4, Thomson 4, Megginson 3, Simmons 3, Elliot 2, Marr 2, Tiffoney 2, Hynd 1, own goal 1.
*William Hill Scottish FA Cup (0).*
*Scottish Communities League Cup (2):* Gordon 1, Grehan 1.
*Ramsdens Cup (1):* Gordon 1.
*Play-Offs (7):* Elliot 2 (1 pen), Moon 2, Cawley 1, McCord, Ryan 1, Tiffoney 1.

| Bain S 35 | Doyle J 27 | Simmons S 29 + 2 | Marr J 32 | Meggatt D 30 | Holmes G 31 + 2 | Young D 20 + 1 | Cawley K 25 + 9 | Docherty M 17 + 11 | Grehan M 21 + 10 | Cox D 2 | Thomson R 4 + 10 | McCord Ross 3 + 12 | Gordon B 33 | McCord Ryan 30 + 1 | Ferns E 3 + 17 | Megginson M 10 + 2 | Low N 9 + 1 | Tapping C 1 + 3 | Bonar L — + 3 | Stokes G 1 + 2 | Tiffoney J 6 + 1 | Gallagher C 5 + 4 | Moon K 11 | Elliot C 10 | Hardie M — + 1 | Hynd S — + 2 | McDowall C 1 | McLelland L — + 1 | Match No. |
|---|---|---|---|---|---|---|---|---|---|---|---|---|---|---|---|---|---|---|---|---|---|---|---|---|---|---|---|---|---|
| 1 | 2 | 3 | 4 | 5 | 6 | 7 | 8 | 9[1] | 10 | 11[2] | 12 | 13 | | | | | | | | | | | | | | | | | 1 |
| 1 | 2 | 6[3] | 4 | 5 | 8[2] | 7 | 11 | 14 | 10[1] | | 12 | 13 | 3 | 9 | | | | | | | | | | | | | | | 2 |
| 1 | 2 | 8[1] | 4 | 5 | 6[2] | 7 | 11 | | 10 | | 12 | 13 | 3 | 9 | | | | | | | | | | | | | | | 3 |
| 1 | 2 | 6[3] | 3 | 5 | 10 | 8 | 9 | 13 | 14 | 11[2] | 12 | | 4 | 7[1] | | | | | | | | | | | | | | | 4 |
| 1 | 2 | 8[3] | 4 | 5 | 12 | 7 | 10 | | 11[2] | | | 13 | 6[1] | 3 | 9 | 14 | | | | | | | | | | | | | 5 |
| 1 | 2 | 8[3] | 4 | 5 | 6 | 7 | 10[2] | 13 | 11 | | | | 9[1] | 12 | 14 | 3 | | | | | | | | | | | | | 6 |
| 1 | 2 | 7 | 4 | 5 | 11 | 6[1] | 9 | 12 | 10[2] | | | 13 | 3 | 8 | | | | | | | | | | | | | | | 7 |
| 1 | 2[3] | 6 | 4 | 5 | 9 | 7 | 12 | | | | 10[1] | 14 | 3 | 8 | 13 | 11[2] | | | | | | | | | | | | | 8 |
| 1 | 2 | | 4 | 5 | 9 | 7 | 11[3] | 13 | 12 | | 10[2] | 14 | 3 | 6 | | 8[1] | | | | | | | | | | | | | 9 |
| 1 | 2 | 7 | 4 | 5 | 9[1] | | | 13 | 14 | | 10[3] | 12 | 3 | 6 | 11 | 8[2] | | | | | | | | | | | | | 10 |
| 1 | | 9 | 4 | 5 | 7 | 8 | 12 | 2[3] | 11 | | | | 3 | 6 | 13 | 10[1] | | | | | | | | | | | | | 11 |
| 1 | | 4 | 2 | 5 | 9[3] | 7 | 11 | 8[2] | 10[1] | | 12 | | 3 | 6 | 14 | 13 | | | | | | | | | | | | | 12 |
| 1 | 2 | 7[2] | 4 | 5 | 9 | 8 | 6 | | | | 11[1] | 14 | 3 | 12 | 10[3] | 13 | | | | | | | | | | | | | 13 |
| 1 | 2 | | 4 | 5 | 9[1] | 7 | 11 | | 10[2] | | | 13 | 3 | 6 | 8 | 12 | | | | | | | | | | | | | 14 |
| 1 | 2 | 10[1] | 4 | | 11[3] | | 12 | 5 | 14 | | | 13 | 3 | 9 | 7 | 6 | 8[2] | | | | | | | | | | | | 15 |
| 1 | 2[3] | 14 | 4 | 5 | 9[4] | 7 | 11 | | 10[1] | | 12 | 13 | 3 | 6 | 8[2] | | | | | | | | | | | | | | 16 |
| 1 | 2 | 7 | 4 | 5 | | | 10 | | | 11[1] | | 8[2] | 3 | 6 | 13 | | 9 | 12 | | | | | | | | | | | 17 |
| 1 | 2 | 7 | 4 | 5 | 9 | | 10[1] | | | | | 8[2] | 3 | 6 | 13 | | 11 | 12 | | | | | | | | | | | 18 |
| 1 | 2[1] | 6 | 4 | | 8[3] | | 10 | 5 | | | | 13 | 3 | 7 | 11 | | 9[2] | 12 | 14 | | | | | | | | | | 19 |
| 1 | | 8[1] | 4 | 5 | 9[3] | 7 | | 13 | 12 | | | | 3 | 6 | 14 | 11[2] | | | | | 2 | 10 | | | | | | | 20 |
| 1 | | 8 | 4 | 5 | 9[3] | 7 | | | 12 | | | 14 | 3 | 6 | 13 | 11[2] | | | | | 2 | 10[1] | | | | | | | 21 |
| 1 | | 7 | 3 | 5 | 10[1] | 8 | 11[2] | | 12 | | | | 4 | 6 | 14 | 9[3] | | | | | 2 | 13 | | | | | | | 22 |
| 1 | | 8 | 3 | 5 | 14 | 7 | 11 | | 13 | | | | 4 | 9[3] | 12 | 10[2] | | | | | 2 | 6[1] | | | | | | | 23 |
| 1 | 2 | | | 5 | 8 | 7[1] | 9 | 3 | 10[2] | | | | 4 | 6 | 14 | 11[3] | | | | | 12 | 13 | | | | | | | 24 |
| 1 | 2 | 13 | 4 | 5 | 9 | | 10 | | 12 | | | | 3 | 8 | 14 | 11[1] | | | | | 7[2] | 6[3] | | | | | | | 25 |
| 1 | 2 | 7[1] | 4 | 5 | 9 | | 12 | | 11 | | | | 3 | 8 | 13 | | | | | | | | 6[2] | 10 | | | | | 26 |
| 1 | 2 | 7 | 3 | 5 | 9 | | 12 | | 11[3] | | | | 4 | 8[2] | 13 | | | | | | 14 | | 6[1] | 10 | | | | | 27 |
| 1 | 2 | 8 | 3 | 4 | 11 | | 12 | 5 | 9[1] | | | | 7 | 13 | 14 | | | | | | | | 6[2] | 10[3] | | | | | 28 |
| 1 | 2 | 4[1] | | 5 | | 7 | 12 | | 14 | | | | 3 | 8 | 13 | 11 | | | | | | 9[2] | 6[3] | 10 | | | | | 29 |
| 1 | 2 | 7[1] | 4 | 5 | 8 | | 9 | | 11 | | | | 3 | 12 | | | | | | | | | 6 | 10 | | | | | 30 |
| 1 | 2 | 7 | 4 | 5 | 8 | | 9 | | 11[1] | | | | 3 | 12 | 13 | | | | | | | | 6[2] | 10 | | | | | 31 |
| 1 | 2 | 7 | 4 | 5 | 9 | | 11[1] | | 12 | | | | 3 | 8 | | | | | | | | | 6 | 10 | | | | | 32 |
| 1 | 2 | 7[1] | 4 | 5 | 8[3] | 12 | 11 | 14 | 13 | | | | 3 | 9[2] | | | | | | | | | 6 | 10 | | | | | 33 |
| 1 | 2 | 8 | 3 | 5 | 10 | | 9 | 13 | 12 | | | | 4 | 6[3] | | | | | | | 14 | | 7[2] | 11[1] | | | | | 34 |
| 1 | 7 | 4[3] | 6 | 5 | 11 | | 10[1] | | | | | | 3 | 12 | | | | | | | 2 | 9[2] | 8 | | 13 | 14 | | | 35 |
| | 3 | | 4 | 5 | 9 | 7 | 12 | | 10[3] | | | | 8[2] | 6 | | | | | | | 2 | 11[1] | | | | 14 | 1 | 13 | 36 |

# ANNAN ATHLETIC

*Year Formed:* 1942. *Ground & Address:* Galabank, North Street, Annan DG12 5DQ. *Téléphone:* 01461 204108.
*E-mail:* annanathleticfc@aol.com *Website:* www.annanathleticfc.com
*Ground capacity:* 2,517 (seated: 500). *Size of Pitch:* 100m × 62m.
*Chairman:* Henry McLelland.
*Secretary:* Alan Irving.
*Manager:* Jim Chapman.
*Assistant Manager:* John Joyce.
*Coaches:* Bill Bentley.
*Club Nicknames:* 'Galabankies', 'Black and Golds'.
*Most League Appearances:* 128: Steven Sloan, 2008-13.
*Most League Goals in Season (Individual):* 15: Mike Jack, 2008-09.
*Most Goals Overall (Individual):* 23: Graeme Bell, 2008-13.

## ANNAN ATHLETIC – SCOTTISH THIRD DIVISION 2012–13 LEAGUE RECORD

| Match No. | Date | Venue | Opponents | Result | H/T Score | Lg Pos. | Goalscorers | Atten- dance |
|---|---|---|---|---|---|---|---|---|
| 1 | Aug 11 | A | Stirling A | L 1-5 | 0-4 | 10 | Bell [72] | 646 |
| 2 | 18 | H | Berwick R | W 3-2 | 0-2 | 7 | Chaplain 2 (1 pen) [56 (p), 59], Love [61] | 512 |
| 3 | 25 | A | Montrose | D 0-0 | 0-0 | 6 | | 267 |
| 4 | Sept 1 | A | Clyde | L 1-2 | 0-1 | 7 | Thorburn [55] | 505 |
| 5 | 15 | H | Rangers | D 0-0 | 0-0 | 8 | | 2517 |
| 6 | 22 | H | Peterhead | W 2-1 | 1-0 | 7 | Ramage [2], Daly [56] | 484 |
| 7 | Oct 13 | A | Queen's Park | D 2-2 | 1-1 | 5 | Ramage [20], McGowan [70] | 626 |
| 8 | 20 | A | Elgin C | D 2-2 | 1-2 | 7 | Hopkirk 2 [34, 46] | 734 |
| 9 | 27 | H | East Stirling | W 5-2 | 2-0 | 5 | Hopkirk 3 [42, 68, 90], Love [45], Chaplain (pen) [79] | 374 |
| 10 | Nov 10 | H | Stirling A | W 5-2 | 2-0 | 3 | Love 2 [30, 89], Chaplain [37], McGachie [67], Daly [85] | 508 |
| 11 | 17 | A | Berwick R | L 1-3 | 0-2 | 5 | Ramage [90] | 460 |
| 12 | 24 | H | Clyde | L 1-3 | 0-2 | 6 | Chaplain (pen) [79] | 489 |
| 13 | Dec 8 | H | Queen's Park | L 2-3 | 0-1 | 7 | Donley [89], Daly [90] | 453 |
| 14 | 15 | A | Peterhead | L 0-2 | 0-0 | 7 | | 378 |
| 15 | 18 | A | Rangers | L 0-3 | 0-1 | 8 | | 42,135 |
| 16 | 22 | A | East Stirling | D 2-2 | 2-1 | 7 | Ramage [17], Love [39] | 192 |
| 17 | 29 | H | Elgin C | W 2-0 | 1-0 | 6 | Ramage [11], Chaplain (pen) [80] | 356 |
| 18 | Jan 2 | H | Rangers | L 1-3 | 1-1 | 7 | Love [35] | 2441 |
| 19 | 5 | A | Clyde | W 3-2 | 2-0 | 7 | Chaplain [14], Daly 2 [15, 47] | 524 |
| 20 | 12 | H | Montrose | W 2-1 | 0-0 | 6 | Hopkirk [62], Love [69] | 352 |
| 21 | 29 | A | Peterhead | D 0-0 | 0-0 | 6 | | 309 |
| 22 | Feb 2 | A | Queen's Park | D 2-2 | 1-0 | 6 | McNiff [21], Love [83] | 558 |
| 23 | 9 | A | Elgin C | L 1-3 | 0-3 | 6 | Daly [54] | 550 |
| 24 | 16 | H | East Stirling | L 1-2 | 0-0 | 6 | Orsi [79] | 349 |
| 25 | 19 | H | Stirling A | L 1-2 | 1-1 | 6 | Chaplain [15] | 327 |
| 26 | 23 | A | Montrose | L 1-5 | 0-4 | 7 | Love [81] | 425 |
| 27 | Mar 2 | H | Berwick R | D 2-2 | 0-1 | 8 | Love [62], Chaplain [70] | 427 |
| 28 | 9 | A | Rangers | W 2-1 | 0-0 | 8 | Love [48], Hopkirk [55] | 34,441 |
| 29 | 16 | H | Clyde | L 0-1 | 0-1 | 8 | | 464 |
| 30 | 30 | A | Peterhead | L 0-2 | 0-0 | 9 | | 483 |
| 31 | Apr 6 | H | Elgin C | D 2-2 | 0-0 | 9 | Chisholm [69], Hopkirk [90] | 379 |
| 32 | 10 | H | Queen's Park | W 2-0 | 1-0 | 9 | Chaplain [28], Hopkirk [84] | 242 |
| 33 | 13 | A | East Stirling | W 2-1 | 1-1 | 7 | Hopkirk [25], Love [78] | 288 |
| 34 | 20 | A | Stirling A | L 0-1 | 0-1 | 9 | | 488 |
| 35 | 27 | A | Berwick R | W 2-0 | 1-0 | 8 | Chaplain [45], McNiff [90] | 627 |
| 36 | May 4 | H | Montrose | D 1-1 | 0-1 | 8 | Daly [58] | 386 |

**Final League Position: 8**

**Honours**
*East of Scotland Premier League:* Winners (4).
*East of Scotland League Cup:* Winners (1).
*East of Scotland Div 1:* Winners (1).
*South of Scotland League:* Winners (2).
*South of Scotland League Cup:* Winners (4).
*Scottish Challenge Cup South:* Winners (1).
*Scottish Qualifying Cup South:* Winners (1).

**Club colours:** Shirt: Gold with black trim. Shorts: Black. Socks: Gold.

**Goalscorers:** *League (54):* Love 12, Chaplain 11 (4 pens), Hopkirk 10, Daly 7, Ramage 5, McNiff 2, Bell 1, Chisholm 1, Donley 1, McGachie 1, McGowan 1, Orsi 1, Thorburn 1.
*William Hill Scottish FA Cup (1):* Chaplain 1.
*Scottish Communities League Cup (0).*
*Ramsdens Cup (1):* Bell 1.

| Mitchell A 34 | Blake J 23 | McGowan M 36 | Chaplain S 35 + 1 | Thorburn G 7 + 5 | Sloan S 20 + 9 | McKechnie J 10 + 11 | Swinglehurst S 29 | Love A 20 + 10 | Daly M 23 + 7 | Ramage G 14 + 1 | Steele J 13 + 2 | Bell G — + 1 | McGachie K 8 + 4 | Jardine C 28 + 3 | Donley A 3 + 9 | Watson P 17 + 3 | Murray D 7 + 7 | Hopkirk D 19 + 2 | Watson J 1 + 2 | Summersgill C 2 | Monaghan H 11 + 4 | McNiff M 15 + 1 | Orsi D 7 | Hawke L 2 + 4 | Chisholm I 11 | Black S 1 + 2 | Match No. |
|---|---|---|---|---|---|---|---|---|---|---|---|---|---|---|---|---|---|---|---|---|---|---|---|---|---|---|---|
| 1 | 2 | 3 | 4 | 5 | 6 | $7^2$ | 8 | $9^1$ | $10^3$ | $11^1$ | 12 | | 13 | 14 | | | | | | | | | | | | | 1 |
| 1 | 2 | 4 | 7 | 5 | 6 | | 3 | 9 | $11^1$ | | 10 | | | | 8 | 12 | | | | | | | | | | | 2 |
| 1 | 2 | 4 | 8 | $5^1$ | $6^9$ | 13 | 3 | $9^2$ | 10 | 14 | | | 11 | 7 | 12 | | | | | | | | | | | | 3 |
| 1 | 2 | 3 | 6 | 13 | | 4 | | 7 | | | $11^2$ | 10 | $8^1$ | 12 | 5 | 9 | | | | | | | | | | | 4 |
| 1 | 2 | 5 | 8 | | 13 | 14 | 4 | $11^1$ | $9^2$ | | $6^3$ | 12 | 7 | | 3 | 10 | | | | | | | | | | | 5 |
| 1 | 2 | 5 | 10 | | 6 | | 4 | 11 | $8^1$ | | 12 | 7 | | | 3 | 9 | | | | | | | | | | | 6 |
| 1 | $2^1$ | 5 | 8 | 9 | | 4 | 12 | 6 | | 11 | | | 3 | $10^1$ | 7 | 13 | | | | | | | | | | | 7 |
| 1 | 2 | 5 | 8 | $9^1$ | | 13 | 3 | $6^3$ | $7^2$ | | 10 | 12 | 4 | 14 | 11 | | | | | | | | | | | | 8 |
| 1 | 2 | 5 | 7 | | 12 | | 9 | 14 | $6^1$ | 13 | $10^3$ | $8^2$ | 4 | | 11 | 3 | | | | | | | | | | | 9 |
| 1 | 2 | 3 | $9^2$ | 14 | 12 | 5 | | 7 | 13 | $10^1$ | 6 | 11 | $8^3$ | 4 | | | | | | | | | | | | | 10 |
| 1 | 2 | 4 | $8^3$ | 14 | 12 | $5^2$ | | $9^1$ | 13 | 10 | 6 | 11 | 7 | 3 | | | | | | | | | | | | | 11 |
| | 2 | 4 | 14 | 7 | | $5^1$ | $3^8$ | 12 | $10^3$ | | 6 | 11 | 8 | 13 | $9^2$ | | 1 | | | | | | | | | | 12 |
| 1 | 2 | 4 | 7 | 5 | | $9^2$ | 13 | $10^1$ | 6 | $11^2$ | 8 | 12 | 3 | 14 | | | | | | | | | | | | | 13 |
| 1 | 2 | 5 | 8 | | 14 | 13 | 3 | 9 | 10 | | $6^3$ | 12 | $7^2$ | $11^1$ | 4 | | | | | | | | | | | | 14 |
| 1 | 2 | 5 | 9 | 12 | 13 | | 4 | 6 | $10^2$ | $11^1$ | | | $7^3$ | 8 | 14 | 3 | | | | | | | | | | | 15 |
| 1 | 2 | 5 | 8 | | 12 | 14 | 4 | $6^3$ | 13 | $11^1$ | 9 | | 7 | $10^2$ | $3^8$ | | | | | | | | | | | | 16 |
| 1 | 2 | 5 | 8 | | 13 | 14 | 4 | $9^3$ | 12 | $10^1$ | 6 | | 7 | $11^2$ | | 3 | | | | | | | | | | | 17 |
| 1 | 2 | 5 | 10 | | $7^3$ | 13 | 4 | $9^1$ | 11 | | $6^2$ | | 8 | 14 | | 12 | | 3 | | | | | | | | | 18 |
| 1 | 2 | 5 | 8 | 12 | 9 | $7^2$ | $4^3$ | $6^1$ | 11 | | | | 14 | | 10 | 13 | | 3 | | | | | | | | | 19 |
| 1 | 2 | 5 | 7 | | 9 | | 4 | 6 | $10^1$ | | 8 | 12 | | 11 | | 3 | | | | | | | | | | | 20 |
| 1 | 2 | 5 | 8 | | 9 | | 4 | $6^2$ | 11 | | $7^1$ | | 13 | 10 | | 3 | 12 | | | | | | | | | | 21 |
| 1 | 2 | 5 | 7 | | $6^2$ | | 4 | 13 | $10^1$ | | | | 11 | | 3 | 8 | 9 | 12 | | | | | | | | | 22 |
| 1 | $2^1$ | 5 | 7 | | 6 | | 4 | | 10 | | 12 | | 13 | 11 | | $3^2$ | 8 | 9 | | | | | | | | | 23 |
| 1 | | $5^3$ | $8^2$ | | 2 | 13 | 4 | 12 | 10 | | 7 | | | 11 | | $3^1$ | 6 | 9 | 14 | | | | | | | | 24 |
| 1 | | 5 | 8 | | 2 | 13 | $4^3$ | 12 | 11 | | 14 | | | 10 | | $9^1$ | $7^2$ | 6 | | 3 | | | | | | | 25 |
| | 2 | 8 | | 6 | | 4 | 12 | $10^2$ | | | $7^3$ | | | 13 | 11 | 1 | $9^1$ | 5 | | 14 | 3 | | | | | | 26 |
| 1 | | 5 | 8 | $6^1$ | | 3 | 9 | | | 7 | | | 12 | 11 | | 4 | 10 | | 2 | | | | | | | | 27 |
| 1 | | 5 | 7 | 12 | | $4^3$ | 9 | 14 | | 8 | | | $6^1$ | 11 | | 3 | $10^2$ | | 2 | 13 | | | | | | | 28 |
| 1 | | 5 | 8 | 13 | | 4 | 9 | | $7^2$ | | | | $11^1$ | 10 | | 3 | 6 | 12 | $2^3$ | 14 | | | | | | | 29 |
| 1 | | 5 | 8 | $9^2$ | | 4 | $6^1$ | 10 | | 7 | 13 | | | 11 | | 12 | 3 | | 2 | | | | | | | | 30 |
| 1 | | 5 | 8 | 6 | | 9 | $4^1$ | 10 | | 7 | | | 12 | 11 | | 3 | | | 2 | | | | | | | | 31 |
| 1 | | 5 | $8^2$ | 6 | | 9 | | 13 | 10 | | 7 | 4 | | 11 | | 12 | 3 | | $2^1$ | | | | | | | | 32 |
| 1 | | 5 | $7^2$ | 8 | | $9^1$ | | 12 | 10 | | 6 | 4 | | 11 | | 13 | 3 | | 2 | | | | | | | | 33 |
| 1 | | 5 | 8 | $6^1$ | | $9^2$ | | 12 | 10 | | 7 | 14 | 3 | $11^3$ | | 13 | 4 | | 2 | | | | | | | | 34 |
| 1 | | 5 | 8 | | $7^2$ | 13 | 4 | | 10 | | 3 | | 12 | | | 6 | 9 | | $11^1$ | 2 | | | | | | | 35 |
| 1 | | 5 | 8 | | 7 | | 4 | 13 | $10^1$ | | 6 | | | 3 | 12 | | | $9^2$ | 11 | 2 | | | | | | | 36 |

# ARBROATH

*Year Formed:* 1878. *Ground & Address:* Gayfield Park, Arbroath DD11 1QB. *Telephone:* 01241 872157. *Fax:* 01241 431125. *E-mail:* afc@gayfield.fsnet.co.uk *Website:* www.arbroathfc.co.uk
*Ground Capacity:* 4,165 (seated: 860). *Size of Pitch:* 105m × 65m.
*Chairman:* John Christison. *Secretary:* Dr Gary Callon. *Administrator:* Mike Cargill.
*Player-Manager:* Paul Sheerin. *Assistant Manager:* Stewart Petrie. *Physio:* Kris Robertson.
*Club Nickname:* 'The Red Lichties'.
*Previous Grounds:* Lesser Gayfield.
*Record Attendance:* 13,510 v Rangers, Scottish Cup 3rd rd, 23 Feb 1952.
*Record Transfer Fee received:* £120,000 for Paul Tosh to Dundee (Aug 1993).
*Record Transfer Fee paid:* £20,000 for Douglas Robb from Montrose (1981).
*Record Victory:* 36-0 v Bon Accord, Scottish Cup 1st rd, 12 Sept 1885.
*Record Defeat:* 1-9 v Celtic, League Cup 3rd rd, 25 Aug 1993.
*Most Capped Player:* Ned Doig, 2 (5), Scotland.
*Most League Appearances:* 445: Tom Cargill, 1966-81.
*Most League Goals in Season (Individual):* 45: Dave Easson, Division II, 1958-59.
*Most Goals Overall (Individual):* 120: Jimmy Jack, 1966-71.

## ARBROATH – SCOTTISH SECOND DIVISION 2012–13 LEAGUE RECORD

| Match No. | Date | Venue | Opponents | Result | H/T Score | Lg Pos. | Goalscorers | Attendance |
|---|---|---|---|---|---|---|---|---|
| 1 | Aug 11 | A | Stranraer | D 1-1 | 0-1 | 4 | Gribben 46 | 290 |
| 2 | 18 | H | Ayr U | W 4-2 | 1-1 | 2 | Holmes 45, Kerr 47, Gribben 72, Rennie 83 | 714 |
| 3 | 25 | A | Alloa Ath | W 3-2 | 1-2 | 1 | Holmes 45, Currie 54, Travis 63 | 575 |
| 4 | Sept 1 | A | Queen of the S | L 0-6 | 0-2 | 4 | | 1554 |
| 5 | 15 | H | East Fife | W 2-0 | 2-0 | 3 | Doris 26, Holmes 28 | 624 |
| 6 | 22 | H | Forfar Ath | D 1-1 | 0-1 | 3 | Doris (pen) 52 | 940 |
| 7 | 29 | A | Stenhousemuir | D 2-2 | 0-0 | 3 | Sibanda 61, Currie 90 | 633 |
| 8 | Oct 6 | H | Brechin C | W 3-1 | 1-0 | 3 | Keddie 24, Currie 75, Holmes 86 | 854 |
| 9 | 20 | A | Albion R | L 0-4 | 0-1 | 4 | | 313 |
| 10 | 27 | A | Ayr U | L 0-2 | 0-1 | 4 | | 1062 |
| 11 | Nov 17 | A | Queen of the S | L 2-3 | 1-2 | 6 | Doris 2 (2 pens) 45, 90 | 691 |
| 12 | 21 | H | Stranraer | W 2-1 | 1-0 | 4 | Currie 23, Doris 90 | 387 |
| 13 | 24 | A | East Fife | L 1-2 | 1-1 | 5 | Currie 43 | 570 |
| 14 | Dec 8 | H | Stenhousemuir | D 2-2 | 1-1 | 5 | Doris 10, Malcolm 51 | 647 |
| 15 | 15 | A | Forfar Ath | D 1-1 | 0-0 | 4 | Holmes 90 | 719 |
| 16 | 26 | A | Brechin C | L 2-3 | 0-2 | 6 | Sheerin 2, Doris (pen) 64 | 978 |
| 17 | 29 | H | Albion R | W 2-1 | 1-1 | 5 | Holmes 19, Doris (pen) 90 | 569 |
| 18 | Jan 2 | H | East Fife | W 1-0 | 0-0 | 5 | Sheerin 53 | 813 |
| 19 | 5 | A | Queen of the S | L 1-5 | 1-0 | 5 | Doris 18 | 1693 |
| 20 | 26 | H | Forfar Ath | W 3-1 | 2-0 | 4 | Sibanda 8, Bayne 2 17, 56 | 843 |
| 21 | Feb 2 | A | Stenhousemuir | L 0-1 | 0-1 | 4 | | 459 |
| 22 | 9 | A | Albion R | W 1-0 | 1-0 | 4 | Hamilton 35 | 346 |
| 23 | 16 | H | Brechin C | L 0-1 | 0-0 | 4 | | 904 |
| 24 | 19 | A | Stranraer | L 0-2 | 0-1 | 5 | | 169 |
| 25 | 23 | A | Alloa Ath | W 1-0 | 1-0 | 4 | Holmes 41 | 451 |
| 26 | 27 | H | Alloa Ath | L 1-2 | 0-1 | 5 | Malcolm 64 | 471 |
| 27 | Mar 2 | A | Ayr U | L 1-4 | 1-2 | 5 | Holmes 2 | 651 |
| 28 | 9 | A | East Fife | W 1-0 | 0-0 | 5 | Bayne 85 | 426 |
| 29 | 16 | H | Queen of the S | D 1-1 | 0-0 | 5 | Smith, E 83 | 656 |
| 30 | 30 | A | Forfar Ath | W 4-2 | 1-1 | 4 | Doris 7, Hamilton 56, Travis 73, Sheerin 89 | 770 |
| 31 | Apr 3 | H | Stenhousemuir | D 0-0 | 0-0 | 4 | | 532 |
| 32 | 6 | H | Albion R | W 2-1 | 0-0 | 4 | Doris (pen) 83, Keddie 89 | 555 |
| 33 | 13 | A | Brechin C | L 0-2 | 0-0 | 5 | | 747 |
| 34 | 20 | H | Stranraer | W 1-0 | 1-0 | 4 | Sheerin 25 | 562 |
| 35 | 27 | A | Ayr U | W 1-0 | 0-0 | 4 | Smith, E 60 | 834 |
| 36 | May 4 | H | Alloa Ath | L 0-1 | 0-0 | 5 | | 901 |

**Final League Position: 5**

**Honours**
*League Champions:* Third Division 2010-11. *League Runners-up:* Division II 1934-35, 1958-59, 1967-68, 1971-72; Second Division 2000-01; Third Division 1997-98, 2007-08. *Promoted to Second Division:* 2007-08 (play-offs).
*Scottish Cup:* Quarter-finals 1993.

**Club colours:** Shirt: Maroon with white trim. Shorts: White. Socks: White.

**Goalscorers:** *League (47):* Doris 11 (6 pens), Holmes 8, Currie 5, Sheerin 4, Bayne 3, Gribben 2, Hamilton 2, Keddie 2, Malcolm 2, Sibanda 2, Smith E 2, Travis 2, Kerr 1, Rennie 1.
*William Hill Scottish FA Cup (7):* Doris 3 (1 pen), Currie 1, Gribben 1, Holmes 1, Kerr 1.
*Scottish Communities League Cup (1):* Currie 1.
*Ramsdens Cup (12):* Gribben 5 (1 pen), Sibanda 3, Currie 1, Doris 1, Keddie 1, Robertson 1.

| Hill D 5 | Baxter M 31 | Keddie A 36 | Travis M 19 | Brennan K 2 | Sibanda L 16+12 | Currie P 12+6 | Kerr B 28+1 | Sheerin P 30+2 | Doris S 32 | Gribben D 10+7 | Holmes D 19+13 | Banjo D 5+5 | Mair J 1+2 | Hamilton C 32 | Rennie D 6+17 | Bullock A 9+1 | Malcolm S 16+5 | Morrison S 22 | Robertson S 24+2 | Birse C 3+5 | Chisholm R 17 | Bayne G 10+6 | Smith E 9+5 | Watt M 1 | Adams S 1+2 | Robertson D —+1 | Smith P —+1 | Match No. |
|---|---|---|---|---|---|---|---|---|---|---|---|---|---|---|---|---|---|---|---|---|---|---|---|---|---|---|---|---|
| 1 | 2 | 3 | 4 | 5 | $6^1$ | 7 | $8^2$ | 9 | 10 | $11^3$ | 12 | 13 | 14 | | | | | | | | | | | | | | | 1 |
| $1^2$ | 2 | 5 | 4 | | 14 | 8 | 7 | $9^3$ | $10^1$ | 11 | 12 | | | 3 | 6 | 13 | | | | | | | | | | | | 2 |
| | | 4 | 2 | | $6^1$ | 8 | 7 | 9 | | $11^2$ | $10^3$ | 14 | 13 | 5 | $12^2$ | 1 | 3 | | | | | | | | | | | 3 |
| | 2 | $4^3$ | 3 | | 13 | $8^2$ | 7 | 12 | 6 | 11 | 10 | | | $9^1$ | 5 | | 1 | 14 | | | | | | | | | | 4 |
| | 2 | 5 | | | 13 | $7^2$ | $9^3$ | 11 | 12 | $10^2$ | | | | 3 | $6^3$ | | 4 | 1 | $8^1$ | 14 | | | | | | | | 5 |
| | 2 | 5 | | | 13 | $7^2$ | $9^3$ | 11 | 12 | $10^1$ | | | | 3 | 6 | | 4 | 1 | $8^1$ | 14 | | | | | | | | 6 |
| | 2 | 3 | | | 11 | 12 | 7 | | 10 | 6 | | 13 | | 5 | | | 4 | 1 | $8^2$ | $9^1$ | | | | | | | | 7 |
| | 2 | 4 | | | $6^1$ | 9 | 8 | | $11^2$ | 10 | 13 | 14 | | 5 | 12 | | 3 | 1 | $7^3$ | | | | | | | | | 8 |
| | 2 | 5 | | | 13 | $10^4$ | 8 | $9^2$ | 11 | | 12 | $7^1$ | | 6 | | | 4 | 1 | 3 | | | | | | | | | 9 |
| | 2 | 7 | | 5 | 13 | | 8 | 9 | 10 | 12 | 11 | | | $6^1$ | | 1 | 3 | $4^2$ | | | | | | | | | | 10 |
| | 2 | 4 | | | 12 | $6^2$ | 7 | 8 | 10 | $9^1$ | 11 | | 5 | 13 | | | 1 | 3 | | | | | | | | | | 11 |
| | 2 | 4 | | | $6^1$ | 8 | 7 | $9^3$ | 10 | 13 | $11^2$ | | 5 | 12 | 14 | 1 | 3 | | | | | | | | | | | 12 |
| | | 3 | | | $6^1$ | 8 | 7 | $9^2$ | 11 | 12 | 10 | 2 | 5 | 13 | | 1 | 4 | | | | | | | | | | | 13 |
| | 2 | 4 | | | 14 | 7 | $9^3$ | $10^2$ | 12 | 11 | | | 5 | 13 | 3 | 1 | 8 | $6^1$ | | | | | | | | | | 14 |
| | 2 | 4 | | | 6 | $8^2$ | 13 | 11 | $9^3$ | 14 | | 5 | 12 | 1 | 3 | 7 | $10^1$ | | | | | | | | | | | 15 |
| | 2 | 4 | | | 6 | 7 | $9^3$ | 10 | 11 | 12 | 5 | 1 | 3 | $8^1$ | 13 | | | | | | | | | | | | | 16 |
| 1 | 2 | 5 | | | $6^1$ | 14 | $7^3$ | 9 | 10 | 13 | $11^2$ | 3 | 12 | 4 | 8 | | | | | | | | | | | | | 17 |
| 1 | 2 | 5 | | | 12 | 6 | 8 | $9^3$ | 10 | $11^2$ | 3 | 13 | $4^1$ | 7 | 14 | | | | | | | | | | | | | 18 |
| 1 | 2 | 4 | | | 13 | 6 | 7 | $9^1$ | 10 | $11^2$ | 12 | 5 | 3 | 8 | | | | | | | | | | | | | | 19 |
| | $2^1$ | 4 | | | 6 | 13 | 8 | 9 | 10 | 14 | | | | 5 | | 1 | 3 | | 12 | | $7^2$ | $11^3$ | | | | | | 20 |
| | 2 | 4 | | | $6^1$ | 7 | $9^3$ | $10^2$ | 13 | | | | 5 | 3 | 1 | 14 | | 8 | 11 | 12 | | | | | | | | 21 |
| | 2 | 4 | 3 | | $6^1$ | 7 | 10 | | | | | | 5 | | 1 | 8 | | 9 | 11 | 12 | | | | | | | | 22 |
| | 2 | 4 | 3 | | 7 | 12 | 10 | 14 | | | | | $5^3$ | 13 | 1 | $8^1$ | | 9 | 11 | $6^2$ | | | | | | | | 23 |
| | 2 | 4 | $3^3$ | | 13 | 7 | 9 | 10 | | | | | 5 | 12 | 1 | $8^2$ | | 6 | $11^1$ | 14 | | | | | | | | 24 |
| | 2 | 4 | $3^3$ | | 8 | $10^2$ | 9 | $11^1$ | | | | | 5 | 13 | 14 | 1 | 7 | 12 | 6 | | | | | | | | | 25 |
| | 4 | 2 | | | 12 | 7 | $9^3$ | $10^1$ | $11^2$ | | | | 5 | 14 | | 3 | 1 | 8 | 13 | 6 | | | | | | | | 26 |
| | 4 | $2^1$ | | | 6 | $8^4$ | 10 | 11 | | | | | 5 | | | 1 | 3 | 9 | $7^2$ | | | | 12 | 13 | | | | 27 |
| 5 | 4 | 3 | | | | 8 | 7 | $10^1$ | 9 | | | | | | | 1 | 2 | 11 | 12 | $6^2$ | | | 13 | | | | | 28 |
| | 2 | 5 | 4 | | | 11 | 7 | 9 | | | | | | | | 1 | 3 | 8 | 12 | 6 | | $10^1$ | | | | | | 29 |
| | 2 | 4 | 3 | | | $7^1$ | 9 | 11 | | | | | 5 | 13 | | 1 | | 12 | 8 | 14 | $6^2$ | $10^3$ | | | | | | 30 |
| | 2 | 5 | 4 | | 12 | | 9 | 11 | 13 | | | | 3 | | | 1 | 7 | 8 | $10^2$ | $6^1$ | | | | | | | | 31 |
| | 2 | 4 | $3^2$ | | | 9 | 11 | $10^3$ | | | | | 5 | 12 | 14 | 1 | 8 | 7 | 13 | $6^1$ | | | | | | | | 32 |
| | 2 | 5 | $4^3$ | | 13 | | 9 | 11 | 12 | | | | 3 | $6^2$ | | 1 | 8 | 7 | $10^1$ | 14 | | | | | | | | 33 |
| 5 | 4 | 3 | | | 12 | | 9 | 11 | 13 | 2 | | | | 1 | 14 | $8^3$ | | 7 | $10^2$ | $6^1$ | | | | | | | | 34 |
| | 4 | 3 | $7^2$ | | | 9 | $11^1$ | 13 | 2 | | | | 5 | 12 | 1 | 8 | | $10^3$ | 6 | | | | | | | 14 | | 35 |
| | 2 | 4 | 3 | | | 8 | 9 | $11^1$ | 6 | | | | 5 | 13 | 1 | $7^2$ | 10 | 12 | | | | | | | | | | 36 |

# AYR UNITED

*Year Formed:* 1910. *Ground & Address:* Somerset Park, Tryfield Place, Ayr KA8 9NB. *Telephone:* 01292 263435.
*Fax:* 01292 281314. *E-mail:* info@ayrunitedfc.co.uk *Website:* ayrunitedfc.co.uk
*Ground Capacity:* 10,185 (seated: 1,597). *Size of Pitch:* 101m × 66m.
*Chairman:* Lachlan Cameron.
*Managing Director:* Lewis Grant.
*Manager:* Mark Roberts. *Assistant Manager:* David White. *Physio:* Ryan MacLeod.
*Club Nickname:* 'The Honest Men'.
*Previous Grounds:* None.
*Record Attendance:* 25,225 v Rangers, Division I, 13 Sept 1969.
*Record Transfer Fee received:* £300,000 for Steven Nicol to Liverpool (Oct 1981).
*Record Transfer Fee paid:* £90,000 for Mark Campbell from Stranraer (March 1999).
*Record Victory:* 11-1 v Dumbarton, League Cup, 13 Aug 1952.
*Record Defeat:* 0-9 in Division I v Rangers (1929); v Hearts (1931); B Division v Third Lanark (1954).
*Most Capped Player:* Jim Nisbet, 3, Scotland.
*Most League Appearances:* 459: John Murphy, 1963-78.
*Most League League and Cup Goals in Season (Individual):* 66: Jimmy Smith, 1927-28.
*Most League and Cup Goals Overall (Individual):* 213: Peter Price, 1955-61.

## AYR UNITED – SCOTTISH SECOND DIVISION 2012–13 LEAGUE RECORD

| Match No. | Date | | Venue | Opponents | Result | | H/T Score | Lg Pos. | Goalscorers | Attendance |
|---|---|---|---|---|---|---|---|---|---|---|
| 1 | Aug | 11 | H | Stenhousemuir | D | 1-1 | 1-0 | 5 | Winters [19] | 1248 |
| 2 | | 18 | A | Arbroath | L | 2-4 | 1-1 | 8 | Sinclair [22], Holmes (og) [67] | 714 |
| 3 | | 25 | H | Forfar Ath | L | 2-3 | 1-1 | 9 | Sinclair 2 [6, 52] | 1094 |
| 4 | Sept | 1 | A | Stranraer | L | 0-2 | 0-2 | 10 | | 772 |
| 5 | | 15 | H | Queen of the S | L | 2-4 | 2-2 | 10 | Mackinnon 2 [9, 19] | 1373 |
| 6 | | 22 | A | East Fife | W | 3-2 | 2-1 | 9 | Sinclair 2 [9, 35], McAusland [88] | 575 |
| 7 | | 29 | H | Brechin C | W | 3-0 | 1-0 | 6 | Moffat [26], Twaddle [53], Sinclair [68] | 993 |
| 8 | Oct | 6 | H | Albion R | W | 2-1 | 1-1 | 6 | Moffat 2 (2 pens) [2, 90] | 1023 |
| 9 | | 20 | A | Alloa Ath | L | 0-1 | 0-1 | 7 | | 595 |
| 10 | | 27 | A | Arbroath | W | 2-0 | 1-0 | 6 | Mackinnon [16], Moffat [90] | 1062 |
| 11 | Nov | 10 | A | Stenhousemuir | D | 1-1 | 0-0 | 6 | Moffat [68] | 586 |
| 12 | | 17 | H | Stranraer | W | 2-1 | 0-1 | 4 | Moffat 2 (1 pen) [57 (p), 90] | 1006 |
| 13 | | 24 | A | Queen of the S | L | 0-2 | 0-1 | 6 | | 1953 |
| 14 | Dec | 15 | H | East Fife | L | 2-3 | 2-0 | 8 | White (og) [3], McAusland [17] | 943 |
| 15 | | 26 | A | Albion R | L | 0-2 | 0-1 | 8 | | 509 |
| 16 | | 29 | H | Alloa Ath | D | 0-0 | 0-0 | 8 | | 927 |
| 17 | Jan | 2 | H | Queen of the S | L | 1-5 | 1-2 | 8 | Winters [30] | 1216 |
| 18 | | 5 | A | Stranraer | W | 1-0 | 1-0 | 8 | Winters [38] | 803 |
| 19 | | 12 | A | Forfar Ath | L | 1-2 | 0-1 | 8 | Sinclair [48] | 479 |
| 20 | | 26 | A | East Fife | D | 3-3 | 2-3 | 8 | Moffat [5], McAusland [17], McDonald [85] | 514 |
| 21 | Feb | 9 | A | Alloa Ath | D | 2-2 | 1-0 | 8 | Buchanan [36], McGregor [57] | 521 |
| 22 | | 16 | H | Albion R | W | 5-2 | 2-1 | 8 | Donald 2 [18, 56], Moffat 3 (1 pen) [25 (p), 59, 67] | 1064 |
| 23 | | 19 | A | Brechin C | L | 1-2 | 0-1 | 8 | Moyes (og) [56] | 412 |
| 24 | | 23 | H | Forfar Ath | W | 2-1 | 1-0 | 7 | Buchanan [19], Donald [69] | 1008 |
| 25 | | 26 | A | Stenhousemuir | L | 1-2 | 1-0 | 7 | Winters [33] | 821 |
| 26 | Mar | 2 | A | Arbroath | W | 4-1 | 2-1 | 7 | Moffat 4 (2 pens) [41 (p), 43, 72 (p), 75] | 651 |
| 27 | | 5 | H | Brechin C | L | 1-2 | 0-1 | 7 | Buchanan [50] | 631 |
| 28 | | 9 | A | Queen of the S | L | 0-2 | 0-1 | 7 | | 1471 |
| 29 | | 16 | H | Stranraer | W | 2-1 | 2-0 | 7 | Hunter [8], Donald [11] | 1022 |
| 30 | | 23 | A | Brechin C | L | 1-2 | 0-2 | 7 | Buchanan [61] | 427 |
| 31 | | 30 | H | East Fife | W | 2-1 | 0-1 | 6 | Buchanan [79], Winters [87] | 956 |
| 32 | Apr | 6 | H | Alloa Ath | L | 0-2 | 0-1 | 6 | | 898 |
| 33 | | 13 | A | Albion R | W | 3-1 | 2-0 | 6 | Moffat [31], Buchanan [41], McLaughlin [84] | 475 |
| 34 | | 20 | A | Stenhousemuir | L | 0-4 | 0-3 | 7 | | 497 |
| 35 | | 27 | H | Arbroath | L | 0-1 | 0-0 | 7 | | 834 |
| 36 | May | 4 | A | Forfar Ath | L | 1-2 | 1-2 | 7 | Bolochoweckyj (og) [36] | 622 |

**Final League Position: 7**

**Honours**
*League Champions:* Division II 1911-12, 1912-13, 1927-28, 1936-37, 1958-59, 1965-66. Second Division 1987-88, 1996-97; *Runners-up:* Division II 1910-11, 1955-56, 1968-69. Second Divison 2008-09. *Promoted to First Division:* 2008-09 (play-offs). *Promoted to First Division:* 2010-11 (play-offs).
*Scottish Cup:* Semi-finals 2002.
*League Cup: Runners-up:* 2001-02.
*B&Q Cup Runners-up:* 1990-91, 1991-92.

**Club colours:** All white.

**Goalscorers:** *League (53):* Moffat 16 (6 pens), Sinclair 7, Buchanan 6, Winters 5, Donald 4, Mackinnon 3, McAusland 3, Hunter 1, McDonald 1, McGregor 1, McLaughlin 1, Twaddle 1, own goals 4.
*William Hill Scottish FA Cup (3):* Moffat 2 (1 pen), Sinclair 1.
*Scottish Communities League Cup (7):* Moffat 3 (1 pen), Sinclair 2, Tiffoney 1, Winters 1.
*Ramsdens Cup (1):* Shankland 1.

| Brown A 18 | Hunter A 23+3 | Robertson J 19+1 | Campbell M 2 | Brownlie D 15+1 | Sinclair D 26+1 | Winters D 16+17 | McStay R 13+6 | Moffat M 34 | Shankland M 5+9 | Marenghi A 8+5 | Roberts M 6+9 | Crawford R 33+2 | Longridge J 2+1 | McCann A 30 | Robertson R 3+10 | McGowan M 1+2 | Twaddle M 16+1 | Martin D 2 | McAusland K 24+1 | Mackinnon D 8 | Wyllie A 5+4 | McGill D 2+1 | Donald M 19+1 | Bain E 1 | McDonald C 1 | Buchanan L 14 | McGregor N 14 | Smith Christopher 13+1 | Smith G 15 | McLaughlin S 8 | Nisbet R —+1 | Wardrobe M —+2 | Match No. |
|---|---|---|---|---|---|---|---|---|---|---|---|---|---|---|---|---|---|---|---|---|---|---|---|---|---|---|---|---|---|---|---|---|---|
| 1 | 2 | 3³ | 4 | 5 | 6 | 7 | 8² | 9 | 10¹ | 11 | 12 | 13 | 14 | | | | | | | | | | | | | | | | | | | | 1 |
| 1 | 6 | 2 | 4² | 5 | 7 | 11 | 8¹ | 9 | 14 | 12 | | | | | 3 | 10³ | 13 | | | | | | | | | | | | | | | | 2 |
| 1 | 2 | 4¹ | | 5 | 6 | 10² | | 9 | 14 | 11³ | 8 | 3 | 13 | 7 | 12 | | | | | | | | | | | | | | | | | | 3 |
| | 6⁸ | | | 3 | 7 | 12 | | 10 | 14 | 9¹ | 11 | 8 | | 4 | 2² | 13³ | 5 | 1 | | | | | | | | | | | | | | | 4 |
| | 3 | | | 6 | 12 | 8 | 11 | | | | 7 | 4 | 9¹ | | 5 | 1 | 2 | 10 | | | | | | | | | | | | | | | 5 |
| 1 | 9³ | 3 | | 7 | 13 | 8¹ | 10 | 14 | | 6 | | 4 | 12 | | 5 | | 2 | 11² | | | | | | | | | | | | | | | 6 |
| 1 | 9 | 3 | | 7² | 10¹ | 8 | 11³ | 12 | | 14 | 6 | 4⁸ | 13 | | 5 | | 2 | | | | | | | | | | | | | | | | 7 |
| 1 | 2 | 3 | | 7 | 13 | 8² | 10 | 9¹ | | 14 | 6 | | 12 | | 5 | 4 | 11³ | | | | | | | | | | | | | | | | 8 |
| 1 | 7 | 3 | | | 9¹ | 8³ | 10 | | | 13 | 6 | 4 | 12 | | 5 | | 2 | 11² | 14 | | | | | | | | | | | | | | 9 |
| 1 | 7 | 3 | | | 12 | 8² | 10 | | | 11¹ | 6 | 4 | | | 5 | | 2 | 9 | 13 | | | | | | | | | | | | | | 10 |
| 1 | 2¹ | | | | 13 | 7 | 9 | | | 10² | 6 | 4 | | | 5 | 3 | 11 | 8 | | | | | | | | | | | | | | | 11 |
| 1 | 2 | | | 8 | 13 | 7⁸ | 9 | 12 | | 10² | 6 | 4 | | | 5 | 3 | 11¹ | | | | | | | | | | | | | | | | 12 |
| 1 | 2 | | | 6 | 12 | | 9 | 13 | | 11 | 7 | 4 | | | 5 | 3 | 10¹ | 8² | | | | | | | | | | | | | | | 13 |
| 1 | 8 | 3 | 4 | 7 | 10² | 12 | 11 | | 9¹ | 13 | 6 | | | | 5 | 2 | | | | | | | | | | | | | | | | | 14 |
| 1 | 8 | | 3² | 7 | 10 | | 11 | 13 | 9¹ | | 6 | 4 | | | 5 | 2 | | 12 | | | | | | | | | | | | | | | 15 |
| 1 | | 3 | 7 | 11² | 8 | 10 | 13 | | | 6 | 4 | 12 | | | 5 | 2 | | 9¹ | | | | | | | | | | | | | | | 16 |
| 1 | 13 | 3 | 7 | 10³ | 8² | 11 | | | | 6 | 4 | 14 | | | 5 | 2 | | 9¹ | 12 | | | | | | | | | | | | | | 17 |
| | 2 | 3 | 8 | 11¹ | 12 | 10 | | | | 7² | 4 | 13 | | | 5 | 6 | | | 9 | 1 | | | | | | | | | | | | | 18 |
| 1 | 12 | 2² | 3 | 7 | 11 | | | 10³ | 13 | | 8¹ | 4 | 14 | | 5 | 6 | | | 9 | | | | | | | | | | | | | | 19 |
| 1 | 6¹ | 4 | 7 | 12 | 11 | | 13 | | 8 | 5 | | | | 2 | | | 9 | | | 3² | 10 | | | | | | | | | | | | 20 |
| 1 | 6 | | 7 | 12 | 11¹ | | | 8 | | 5 | | | | 2 | | | 9 | | | 10⁸ | 3 | 4 | | | | | | | | | | | 21 |
| | 6 | | 7 | 11 | 13 | 10 | | 12 | | 8¹ | | | | 5 | | | 2 | | | 9² | | 3 | 4 | 1 | | | | | | | | | 22 |
| | 6¹ | | 7 | 12 | | 10 | | | | 8 | | | | 5 | | | 2 | | | 9 | 11 | 3 | 4 | 1 | | | | | | | | | 23 |
| | 12 | | 7¹ | 6 | | 11 | | | | 8 | | | | 5 | | | 2 | | | 9 | 10 | 4 | 3 | 1 | | | | | | | | | 24 |
| | 2 | 5 | 7 | 6¹ | | 10 | | | | 8 | | | | | | | 12 | | | 9 | 11 | 3 | 4 | 1 | | | | | | | | | 25 |
| | 2 | 4¹ | 12 | 6 | 9² | 13 | 10 | | | 14 | 7 | | | 5 | | | 8 | | | 11³ | 3 | | 1 | | | | | | | | | | 26 |
| | 13 | 2² | | 7 | 6¹ | 12 | 10 | | | 14 | 8³ | | | 5 | | | 9 | | | 11 | 3 | 4 | 1 | | | | | | | | | | 27 |
| | 2 | | | 7¹ | 12 | 8² | | | | 13 | 11 | 6 | | 5 | | | 9 | | | 10 | 3 | 4 | 1 | | | | | | | | | | 28 |
| | 6 | 2 | | 7 | 12 | 10 | | | | | 5 | | | | | | 9 | | | 11¹ | 3 | 4 | 1 | 8 | | | | | | | | | 29 |
| | 2 | | | 12 | | 10 | 6¹ | | | 8 | 5 | | | | | | 9 | | | 11 | 3⁸ | 4 | 1 | 7 | | | | | | | | | 30 |
| | 2 | 3 | | 12 | | 10 | 6¹ | | | 8 | 5 | | | | | | 9 | | | 11 | | 4 | 1 | 7 | | | | | | | | | 31 |
| | 2² | | 3 | 12 | 14 | 10 | 6¹ | | | 8 | 5 | | | 13 | | | 9 | | | 11³ | | 4 | 1 | 7 | | | | | | | | | 32 |
| 7 | | | | 12 | | 10² | 13 | | | 6³ | 3 | | | 5 | 14 | | 9 | | | 11² | 2 | 4 | 1 | 8 | | | | | | | | | 33 |
| | | | | 12 | 10² | 13 | | | | 7 | 8 | | | 2 | 6 | | 5 | | | 11¹ | 3 | 4⁸ | 1 | 9 | | | | | | | | | 34 |
| | | 4 | | 10¹ | 11² | 13 | 9 | | | 8 | 2 | | | 6³ | 9 | | 3 | | | | 1 | 7 | 12 | 14 | | | | | | | | | 35 |
| | | 4⁸ | | 10 | 11¹ | 8² | 5 | | | 2 | 7 | | | 9 | | | 3 | | | 12 | 1 | 6 | 13 | | | | | | | | | | 36 |

# BERWICK RANGERS

*Year Formed:* 1884. *Ground & Address:* Shielfield Park, Tweedmouth, Berwick-upon-Tweed TD15 2EF. *Telephone:* 01289 307424. *Fax:* 01289 309424. *Email:* club@berwickrangersfc.co.uk *Website:* berwickrangersfc.co.uk
*Ground Capacity:* 4,131 (seated: 1,366). *Size of Pitch:* 101m × 64m.
*Chairman:* Brian Porteous. *Vice-Chairman:* John Bell. *Football Secretary:* Dennis McCleary.
*Manager:* Ian Little. *Assistant Manager:* Robbie Horn. *Physio:* Richard Walker.
*Club Nicknames:* 'The Borderers', 'Black and Gold', 'The Wee Gers'.
*Previous Grounds:* Bull Stob Close, Pier Field, Meadow Field, Union Park, Old Shielfield.
*Record Transfer Fee received:* £80,000 for John Hughes to Swansea City (Nov 1989).
*Record Transfer Fee paid:* £27,000 for Sandy Ross from Cowdenbeath (Mar 1991).
*Record Attendance:* 13,283 v Rangers, Scottish Cup 1st rd, 28 Jan 1967.
*Record Victory:* 8-1 v Forfar Ath, Division II, 25 Dec 1965; v Vale of Leithen, Scottish Cup, Dec 1966.
*Record Defeat:* 1-9 v Hamilton A, First Division, 9 Aug 1980.
*Most League Appearances:* 439: Eric Tait, 1970-87.
*Most League Goals in Season (Individual):* 33: Ken Bowron, Division II, 1963-64.
*Most Goals Overall (Individual):* 114: Eric Tait, 1970-87.

## BERWICK RANGERS – SCOTTISH THIRD DIVISION 2012–13 LEAGUE RECORD

| Match No. | Date | Venue | Opponents | Result | H/T Score | Lg Pos. | Goalscorers | Atten-dance |
|---|---|---|---|---|---|---|---|---|
| 1 | Aug 11 | H | Elgin C | D 0-0 | 0-0 | 6 | | 539 |
| 2 | 18 | A | Annan Ath | L 2-3 | 2-0 | 9 | Addison [14], McLaren [25] | 512 |
| 3 | 26 | H | Rangers | D 1-1 | 0-1 | 9 | McLaren [62] | 4140 |
| 4 | Sept 1 | H | East Stirling | W 3-0 | 2-0 | 6 | Lavery [11], McLaren [39], Hoskins [80] | 520 |
| 5 | 15 | A | Montrose | L 1-3 | 1-2 | 6 | Lavery [45] | 258 |
| 6 | 22 | H | Stirling A | W 4-1 | 2-0 | 6 | Currie, L [17], Lavery [45], Ferguson 2 [62, 88] | 544 |
| 7 | Oct 6 | A | Peterhead | L 0-1 | 0-0 | 6 | | 455 |
| 8 | 20 | H | Clyde | W 2-1 | 1-1 | 5 | Hoskins [44], Notman [77] | 546 |
| 9 | 27 | A | Queen's Park | D 1-1 | 1-1 | 6 | Lavery [32] | 487 |
| 10 | Nov 10 | A | Elgin C | L 1-3 | 1-2 | 7 | Gray, R [19] | 790 |
| 11 | 17 | H | Annan Ath | W 3-1 | 2-0 | 7 | Lavery [24], Gray, R [44], Hoskins [54] | 460 |
| 12 | 25 | A | East Stirling | W 1-0 | 1-0 | 5 | Gray, R [22] | 327 |
| 13 | Dec 1 | H | Montrose | L 1-4 | 1-2 | 5 | Lavery [9] | 484 |
| 14 | 8 | H | Peterhead | D 1-1 | 0-1 | 5 | Lavery [58] | 396 |
| 15 | 15 | A | Stirling A | L 3-6 | 2-4 | 6 | Lavery [24], Currie, L 2 [30, 58] | 427 |
| 16 | 29 | A | Clyde | L 1-2 | 1-0 | 7 | Carse [3] | 427 |
| 17 | Jan 2 | A | Montrose | W 3-1 | 1-1 | 6 | Lavery [25], McLaren [74], McDonald [90] | 434 |
| 18 | 5 | A | East Stirling | W 2-0 | 2-0 | 6 | Lavery [10], Easton [17] | 473 |
| 19 | 12 | A | Rangers | L 2-4 | 0-1 | 7 | Gray, R [65], McLaren [73] | 44,976 |
| 20 | Feb 2 | A | Peterhead | D 1-1 | 1-1 | 7 | Lavery [6] | 432 |
| 21 | 9 | H | Clyde | D 3-3 | 0-1 | 7 | Lavery 2 [47, 63], McLaren [49] | 507 |
| 22 | 16 | A | Queen's Park | L 1-2 | 1-1 | 7 | Lavery [8] | 462 |
| 23 | 23 | H | Rangers | L 1-3 | 1-2 | 8 | Argyriou (og) [6] | 4476 |
| 24 | 26 | H | Elgin C | W 2-1 | 0-1 | 6 | Lavery [59], Dalziel [74] | 382 |
| 25 | Mar 2 | A | Annan Ath | D 2-2 | 1-0 | 6 | Dalziel [14], McLaren [67] | 427 |
| 26 | 5 | H | Stirling A | W 1-0 | 0-0 | 5 | Currie, L [87] | 402 |
| 27 | 9 | H | Montrose | W 4-0 | 1-0 | 4 | McLaren 3 [12, 52, 70], Carse [90] | 478 |
| 28 | 12 | H | Queen's Park | W 2-0 | 0-0 | 4 | Easton [60], Janczyk [76] | 456 |
| 29 | 16 | A | East Stirling | W 3-0 | 2-0 | 3 | Miller (og) [23], Dalziel [38], McDonald [72] | 248 |
| 30 | 23 | H | Peterhead | L 0-2 | 0-0 | 4 | | 454 |
| 31 | 30 | A | Stirling A | L 0-1 | 0-0 | 5 | | 601 |
| 32 | Apr 6 | A | Clyde | L 1-2 | 0-1 | 5 | Notman [53] | 472 |
| 33 | 13 | A | Queen's Park | W 4-1 | 3-1 | 4 | Notman 2 [10, 50], Lavery [13], Currie, L [25] | 623 |
| 34 | 20 | A | Elgin C | W 2-1 | 0-1 | 4 | Lavery [65], McDonald [75] | 870 |
| 35 | 27 | H | Annan Ath | L 0-2 | 0-1 | 4 | | 627 |
| 36 | May 4 | A | Rangers | L 0-1 | 0-1 | 4 | | 50,048 |

**Final League Position: 4**

**Honours**
*League Champions:* Second Division 1978-79. Third Division 2006-07;
*Runners-up:* Second Division 1993-94. Third Division 1999-2000, 2005-06 (not promoted).
*Scottish Cup:* Quarter-finals 1953-54, 1979-80.
*League Cup:* Semi-finals 1963-64.
*League Challenge Cup:* Quarter-finals 2004-05.

**Club colours:** Shirt: Black with gold vertical stripes. Shorts: Black. Socks: Black.

**Goalscorers:** *League (59):* Lavery 17, McLaren 10, Currie L 5, Gray R 4, Notman 4, Dalziel 3, Hoskins 3, McDonald 3, Carse 2, Easton 2, Ferguson 2, Addison 1, Janczyk 1, own goals 2.
*William Hill Scottish FA Cup (4):* Currie 3 (2 pens), Lavery 1.
*Scottish Communities League Cup (3):* Currie L 2, Addison 1.
*Ramsdens Cup (2):* Janczyk 1, McDonald 1.
*Play-Offs (2):* Lavery 2 (1 pen).

| Bejaoui Y 12 | Jacobs D 30+4 | Brydon D 28+1 | Townsley C 30 | Lancaster M 2 | McDonald K 27+5 | Janczyk N 27+3 | Currie L 32+1 | Giefty D 24+6 | McLaren F 24+7 | Addison P 5+10 | Ferguson J 5+5 | Lavery D 29+6 | Droudge D 4 | Pownsley C 2 | Stevenson C —+2 | Smith G —+1 | Hoskins D 19+1 | Notman S 24+3 | Noble S 2+5 | McLean A 13+3 | Morris J —+7 | Gray R 7+2 | McCaldon I 7 | O'Brien K —+4 | Carse D 2+10 | Easton D 13+3 | Currie D —+1 | McCallum M 17 | Dalziel S 11+6 | Match No. |
|---|---|---|---|---|---|---|---|---|---|---|---|---|---|---|---|---|---|---|---|---|---|---|---|---|---|---|---|---|---|---|
| 1 | 2 | 3 | 4 | 5 | 6 | 7 | 8 | 9¹ | 10 | 11² | 12 | 13 | | | | | | | | | | | | | | | | | | 1 |
| 1 | 13 | 4 | 5 | | 9 | 8³ | 7 | | 10² | 6¹ | | 11 | | | 2 | 3 | 12 | 14 | | | | | | | | | | | | 2 |
| 1 | | 4 | 3 | | 9 | 7¹ | 8 | 12 | 13 | 11 | | 10² | | | | | 5 | 6 | | | | | | | | | | | | 3 |
| 1 | 14 | 5 | 4 | | 9³ | 7¹ | 8 | 11 | 12 | 13 | | 10² | 2 | | | | 3 | 6 | | | | | | | | | | | | 4 |
| 1 | 12 | 3 | 4 | | 9 | | 8 | | 11 | 7² | 14 | 10 | 2¹ | | 13 | | | 5 | 6³ | | | | | | | | | | | 5 |
| 1 | 2 | 4 | | | 11 | 7 | 6³ | 13 | 9² | 14 | 12 | 10¹ | | 3 | | | 5 | 8 | | | | | | | | | | | | 6 |
| 1 | 2 | 4 | 3 | | 6 | 8 | 7³ | 14 | 12 | 11² | | 13 | | | | | 5 | 9 | 10¹ | | | | | | | | | | | 7 |
| 1 | 2 | 4 | | | 9 | 8 | 13 | 10² | 6³ | | | 11¹ | | | | | 5 | 7 | 12 | 3 | 14 | | | | | | | | | 8 |
| 1 | 2 | 7 | | | 9 | 6¹ | 8 | | 11² | 14 | | 10³ | | | | | 5 | 4 | 13 | 3 | | 12 | | | | | | | | 9 |
| 1 | 2 | 3 | | | 8¹ | 12 | 9 | | | 13 | 10 | | | | | | 5 | 6 | 11² | 4 | | 7 | | | | | | | | 10 |
| | 2 | 4 | 3³ | | 9 | | 8 | 13 | 12 | | | 11¹ | 10 | | | | 5 | 7 | | | 14 | | 6² | 1 | | | | | | 11 |
| | 2 | 3 | 4 | | 8 | | 7 | 12 | | | | 11¹ | 10 | | | | 5 | 6⁸ | | | | | 9 | 1 | | | | | | 12 |
| | 2 | 4 | 3 | | 6 | 7¹ | 8 | 9 | | 13 | | 11² | 10 | | | | 5³ | | | 12 | | | 1 | 14 | | | | | | 13 |
| 1 | 2 | 4 | 3 | | 9 | 8 | | | 12 | | | 11¹ | 10³ | | | | 5 | 7 | | | 13 | 6² | 14 | | | | | | | 14 |
| 1 | 2¹ | 4 | 3 | | 7 | | 8 | | 14 | | | 11² | 10³ | | | | 5 | 6 | 12 | | 9 | | 13 | | | | | | | 15 |
| | | 4 | 3³ | | 6 | 7 | 8 | 5 | 12 | 14 | | 10² | | | | | | 13 | 2 | | 9 | 1 | 11¹ | | | | | | | 16 |
| | 2 | 4 | 3 | | 10 | 7 | 8 | 5 | 6 | | | 11² | | | | | | 13 | | | 9¹ | 1 | | 12 | | | | | | 17 |
| | 2 | 4 | 3 | | 9 | 7 | 8 | 5 | 6² | 14 | | 11¹ | | | | | | 13 | | | | 1 | 12 | 10³ | | | | | | 18 |
| | 2 | | 3 | | 9 | 8³ | 7 | 5 | 6 | | | 11² | | | | | 14 | | 4 | | 12 | 1 | 10¹ | 13 | | | | | | 19 |
| | 2 | 3 | 6 | | 8 | 7² | 4 | 5 | 9 | | | 10³ | | | | | 13 | | | | 14 | 11¹ | 1 | 12 | | | | | | 20 |
| | 2 | 3 | 4 | | 9 | 7¹ | 8 | 5 | 6² | | | 10 | | | | | 12 | | | | | 11 | 1 | 13 | | | | | | 21 |
| 12 | | 3 | 4 | | 9⁸ | 7¹ | 8 | 5 | 6³ | | | 10² | | | | | 2⁸ | | | | | 14 | 11 | 1 | 13 | | | | | 22 |
| | 2 | 3 | 4 | | | 7 | 8 | 9 | 12 | | | 11² | | | 5 | | | | | | 14 | 13 | 6¹ | 1 | 10³ | | | | | 23 |
| | 2 | 3 | 4 | | 13 | 8 | 9 | 6 | | | | 11² | | | 5¹ | 7 | | | | | | 12 | 1 | 10 | | | | | | 24 |
| | 2 | 3 | 4 | | 13 | 8² | 7 | 9 | 6³ | | | 10¹ | | | 5 | | | | | | 14 | 12 | 1 | 11 | | | | | | 25 |
| | 2 | 3 | 4 | | 6² | 14 | 8 | 5 | 9 | 13 | | 12 | | | 7 | | | | | | | 11¹ | 1 | 10³ | | | | — | | 26 |
| | 2 | 3 | 4 | | | 7 | | 5 | 6¹ | 12 | | 10² | | 14 | 8 | | | | | | 13 | 9 | 1 | 11³ | | | | | | 27 |
| | 2 | 4 | | | 13 | 7 | 9 | 5 | 6¹ | 12 | | | | 8 | | | 3 | 14 | | | | 10² | 1 | 11³ | | | | | | 28 |
| | 2 | 4¹ | 3 | | 13 | 7² | 8 | 5 | 10 | | | 14 | | 6 | | | 12 | | | | 9 | | 1 | 11³ | | | | | | 29 |
| | 2 | | 4 | | 6² | 8¹ | 9 | 5 | | 13 | | 12 | | 7 | 3 | | | | | | 10 | | 1 | 11 | | | | | | 30 |
| | 2 | 3 | | | 12 | | 8 | 9 | 6 | | | 10¹ | | 5 | 7 | 4 | | | | | 13 | | 1 | 11² | | | | | | 31 |
| | 2 | 3 | | | 7² | 8 | 13 | 6 | | 10 | | | | 5 | 9 | 4 | | | | | 12 | | 1 | 11¹ | | | | | | 32 |
| | 2 | 4 | | | 13 | 9 | 5 | 6³ | | 11¹ | | | | 7 | 3 | 14 | | | | | 10² | | 1 | 12 | | | | | | 33 |
| | 2 | 3 | | | 10 | 7 | 8 | 5 | 6¹ | | | 11² | | | | | 4 | 13 | | | 9 | | 1 | 12 | | | | | | 34 |
| | 2 | 3 | | | 10² | 8 | 7⁸ | 5 | | 11¹ | | | | 6 | | 4 | 13 | | | | 14 | 9³ | 1 | 12 | | | | | | 35 |
| | 2 | 14 | 4 | | 9 | 7 | | | 10 | 8¹ | | 13 | | 5 | 6³ | 3 | | | | | 12 | | 1 | 11² | | | | | | 36 |

# BRECHIN CITY

*Year Formed:* 1906. *Ground & Address:* Glebe Park, Trinity Rd, Brechin, Angus DD9 6BJ. *Telephone:* 01356 622856.
*Fax:* 01382 206331. *E-mail:* secretary@brechincityfc.com *Website:* www.brechincity.com
*Ground Capacity:* 3,960 (seated: 1,519). *Size of Pitch:* 101m × 61m.
*Chairman:* Kenneth Ferguson. *Vice-Chairman:* Martin Smith. *Secretary:* Gus Fairlie.
*Manager:* Ray McKinnon. *Assistant Manager:* Kevin McGowne. *Physio:* Tom Gilmartin.
*Club Nicknames:* 'The City', 'The Hedgemen'.
*Previous Grounds:* Nursery Park.
*Record Attendance:* 8122 v Aberdeen, Scottish Cup 3rd rd, 3 Feb 1973.
*Record Transfer Fee received:* £100,000 for Scott Thomson to Aberdeen (1991) and Chris Templeman to Morton (2004).
*Record Transfer Fee paid:* £16,000 for Sandy Ross from Berwick Rangers (1991).
*Record Victory:* 12-1 v Thornhill, Scottish Cup 1st rd, 28 Jan 1926.
*Record Defeat:* 0-10 v Airdrieonians, Albion R and Cowdenbeath, all in Division II, 1937-38.
*Most League Appearances:* 459: David Watt, 1975-89.
*Most League Goals in Season (Individual):* 26: Ronald McIntosh, Division II, 1959-60.
*Most Goals Overall (Individual):* 131: Ian Campbell, 1977-85.

## BRECHIN CITY – SCOTTISH SECOND DIVISION 2012–13 LEAGUE RECORD

| Match No. | Date | Venue | Opponents | Result | H/T Score | Lg Pos. | Goalscorers | Attendance |
|---|---|---|---|---|---|---|---|---|
| 1 | Aug 11 | H | Albion R | W 1-0 | 1-0 | 2 | Jackson [16] | 413 |
| 2 | 18 | A | Stenhousemuir | L 1-3 | 0-1 | 6 | Jackson [58] | 522 |
| 3 | 25 | H | East Fife | W 2-1 | 2-0 | 4 | Jackson 2 [11; 13] | 588 |
| 4 | Sept 1 | H | Alloa Ath | L 1-3 | 0-0 | 5 | Jackson [51] | 491 |
| 5 | 15 | A | Forfar Ath | L 0-1 | 0-1 | 6 |  | 708 |
| 6 | 22 | H | Queen of the S | L 0-3 | 0-2 | 7 |  | 538 |
| 7 | 29 | A | Ayr U | L 0-3 | 0-1 | 8 |  | 993 |
| 8 | Oct 6 | A | Arbroath | L 1-3 | 0-1 | 8 | McKenna [51] | 854 |
| 9 | 20 | H | Stranraer | W 3-0 | 2-0 | 8 | Jackson 2 [27, 31], McKenna [65] | 485 |
| 10 | 27 | H | Stenhousemuir | W 7-2 | 3-1 | 7 | Byrne [9], Trouten 3 [31, 42, 63], McKenna (pen) [69], Carcary 2 [82, 84] | 542 |
| 11 | Nov 17 | A | Alloa Ath | D 2-2 | 0-1 | 7 | Brown [69], Jackson [83] | 501 |
| 12 | 20 | A | Albion R | W 2-1 | 0-1 | 5 | Jackson [47], Carcary [72] | 220 |
| 13 | 24 | H | Forfar Ath | W 4-1 | 1-0 | 3 | Brown [15], Byrne (pen) [52], Jackson 2 [61, 90] | 702 |
| 14 | Dec 15 | A | Queen of the S | L 0-1 | 0-1 | 5 |  | 1419 |
| 15 | 26 | H | Arbroath | W 3-2 | 2-0 | 4 | Malcolm (og) [8], McLean, P [36], Trouten [61] | 978 |
| 16 | 29 | A | Stranraer | W 2-0 | 1-0 | 4 | Trouten (pen) [12], Carcary [62] | 326 |
| 17 | Jan 2 | A | Forfar Ath | W 4-1 | 0-0 | 3 | McKenna [47], Brown [58], Carcary [64], Dalziel [81] | 903 |
| 18 | 5 | H | Alloa Ath | W 3-2 | 1-2 | 3 | McKenna [4], Trouten [50], Jackson [83] | 602 |
| 19 | 12 | A | East Fife | D 2-2 | 2-2 | 3 | Trouten [6], Carcary [30] | 578 |
| 20 | Feb 16 | A | Arbroath | W 1-0 | 0-0 | 3 | Trouten [87] | 904 |
| 21 | 19 | H | Ayr U | W 2-1 | 1-0 | 3 | McLauchlan 2 [40, 59] | 412 |
| 22 | Mar 2 | A | Stenhousemuir | D 3-3 | 1-1 | 3 | Trouten [6], Moyes [70], McKenna [77] | 504 |
| 23 | 5 | A | Ayr U | W 2-1 | 1-0 | 3 | Moyes [25], Hay [75] | 631 |
| 24 | 16 | A | Alloa Ath | W 1-0 | 0-0 | 3 | Trouten [53] | 382 |
| 25 | 23 | H | Ayr U | W 2-1 | 2-0 | 3 | Carcary [15], Trouten [19] | 427 |
| 26 | 27 | H | Queen of the S | L 0-6 | 0-5 | 3 |  | 627 |
| 27 | 30 | A | Queen of the S | L 1-2 | 0-1 | 3 | Trouten (pen) [75] | 2026 |
| 28 | Apr 2 | H | East Fife | W 6-0 | 4-0 | 3 | Carcary 2 [8, 36], Jackson 2 [15, 47], McLean, P [19], Ferguson [70] | 471 |
| 29 | 6 | A | Stranraer | L 2-3 | 2-1 | 3 | Carcary [35], McLean, P [39] | 299 |
| 30 | 9 | H | Forfar Ath | L 3-4 | 0-2 | 3 | Hay [57], Trouten 2 [76, 87] | 581 |
| 31 | 13 | H | Arbroath | W 2-0 | 0-0 | 3 | Jackson [64], McLauchlan [86] | 747 |
| 32 | 20 | A | Albion R | L 1-3 | 0-1 | 3 | Trouten (pen) [84] | 378 |
| 33 | 23 | H | Stranraer | D 2-2 | 0-1 | 3 | Jackson [57], Trouten [83] | 401 |
| 34 | 27 | A | Stenhousemuir | L 1-2 | 0-2 | 3 | Trouten [75] | 474 |
| 35 | 30 | H | Albion R | W 2-0 | 1-0 | 3 | Carcary 2 [19, 69] | 402 |
| 36 | May 4 | A | East Fife | W 3-0 | 0-0 | 3 | McKenna [70], Brown 2 [80, 85] | 753 |

**Final League Position: 3**

**Honours**
*League Champions:* Second Division 1982-83, 1989-90, 2004-05. Third Division 2001-02. C Division 1953-54.
*Runners-up:* Second Division 1992-93, 2002-03. Third Division 1995-96.
*League Challenge Cup Runners-up* 2002-03.

**Club colours:** Shirt: Red with white trim. Shorts: White. Socks: Red.

**Goalscorers:** *League (72):* Trouten 17 (3 pens), Jackson 16, Carcary 12, McKenna 7 (1 pen), Brown 5, McLauchlan 3, McLean P 3, Byrne 2 (1 pen), Hay 2, Moyes 2, Dalziel 1, Ferguson 1, own goal 1.
*William Hill Scottish FA Cup (8):* Byrne 2, Trouten 2, Brown 1, Carcary 1, Jackson 1, own goal 1.
*Scottish Communities League Cup (0).*
*Ramsdens Cup (1):* Jackson 1.
*Play-Offs (3):* Jackson 2, Trouten 1 (pen).

| Andrews M 29 | McLean P 32 + 1 | Brown J 19 + 4 | McLauchlan G 27 | Moyes E 27 | Stewart J 21 + 10 | Brady G 17 + 8 | Molloy C 14 | McKenna D 22 + 11 | Jackson A 35 | Dalziel S 6 + 8 | Fusco G 25 + 4 | Stewart R 11 + 12 | Carcary D 15 + 12 | Murray J 1 | Trouten A 25 + 3 | Lowdon J 1 + 2 | Smith A — + 3 | Fisher R 1 | Byrne K 10 | Nelson C 7 | Hay G 23 | Murdoch A 1 + 1 | Cameron G 3 + 5 | Pursehouse A 10 + 2 | Rodger G 3 | Longridge B 3 + 1 | Ferguson R 8 + 2 | Match No. |
|---|---|---|---|---|---|---|---|---|---|---|---|---|---|---|---|---|---|---|---|---|---|---|---|---|---|---|---|---|
| 1 | 2 | 3 | 4 | 5 | 6 | 7 | 8 | 9 | 10 | 11 | | | | | | | | | | | | | | | | | | 1 |
| 1 | 2 | 5 | 3 | 4 | 6² | 8 | 7 | 12 | 10 | 11 | | 9¹ | 13 | | | | | | | | | | | | | | | 2 |
| 1 | | 3 | 4 | 5 | 2 | 7¹ | 8 | 9² | 10 | 11 | 12 | 6 | 13 | | | | | | | | | | | | | | | 3 |
| 1 | | 5 | | 3 | 2 | 7 | 8² | 9¹ | 10 | 11³ | 14 | 6 | 13 | 4 | 12 | | | | | | | | | | | | | 4 |
| 1 | 13 | 5 | 3 | 4 | 2 | 7 | 8¹ | 14 | 10 | 11³ | | 6² | 12 | | 9 | | | | | | | | | | | | | 5 |
| 1 | 3 | 5 | | 4 | 2 | 8 | | 9 | 10 | 11 | 7 | | | | | 6¹ | 12 | | | | | | | | | | | 6 |
| 1 | 2 | 5 | | 3² | 6 | 8 | | 13 | 10³ | 12 | 7 | | | 9 | | 14 | 4 | 11¹ | | | | | | | | | | 7 |
| | 3 | 5 | | 4 | 2³ | 7 | | 9 | 10¹ | 12 | 8 | | 13 | | 6² | 14 | | 11 | 1 | | | | | | | | | 8 |
| | 2 | 5 | 4 | 3 | | 7 | 8¹ | 9 | 10 | 14 | 12 | | 13 | | 6³ | | | 11² | 1 | | | | | | | | | 9 |
| | 2 | 3 | 5 | 4 | 14 | 7¹ | 8³ | 9 | 10 | | 12 | | 13 | | 6 | | | 11² | 1 | | | | | | | | | 10 |
| | 2 | 5 | | 4 | 13 | | 7 | 12 | 11 | | 8² | | 9¹ | | 6 | | | 10 | 1 | 3 | | | | | | | | 11 |
| | 2 | 5 | | 3 | | | 7 | 9¹ | 11 | | 8 | | 12 | | 6 | | | 10 | 1 | 4 | | | | | | | | 12 |
| | 2 | 5 | | 4 | 14 | 7² | 9 | 13 | 10 | | 8 | | | | 6¹ | 12³ | | 11 | 1 | 3 | | | | | | | | 13 |
| 1 | 5 | | 2 | 3 | 9² | | 7¹ | 12 | 10 | 14 | 8 | | 13 | | 6 | | | 11³ | | 4 | | | | | | | | 14 |
| 1 | 5 | | 2 | 4 | 13 | | 8 | 12 | 10 | | 7 | | 9² | | 6 | | | 11¹ | | 3 | | | | | | | | 15 |
| 1 | 5 | | 2 | 4 | 12 | | 8 | 14 | 10³ | 13 | 7 | | 9² | | 6¹ | | | 11 | | 3 | | | | | | | | 16 |
| 1 | 2 | 5 | 7 | 4 | | 12 | 8¹ | 9³ | 10 | 13 | 6 | 14 | 11² | | | | | | | 3 | | | | | | | | 17 |
| 1 | 5 | 9 | 2¹ | 4 | 14 | 8 | | 6² | 10 | 13 | 7 | | 11³ | | 12 | | | | | 3 | | | | | | | | 18 |
| 1 | 2 | 5 | 4 | | 13 | 8 | | 10¹ | 11 | 12 | 7² | 14 | 9³ | | 6 | | | | | 3 | | | | | | | | 19 |
| 1 | 2 | | 5 | 4 | 8² | 13 | | 11 | 10¹ | | 7 | 12 | 9³ | | 6 | 14 | | | | 3 | | | | | | | | 20 |
| 1 | 5 | 14 | 2 | 4 | 8² | 13 | | 9³ | 10 | | 7 | 12 | 11¹ | | 6 | | | | | 3 | | | | | | | | 21 |
| 1 | 5 | | 2 | 4 | 8 | 13 | | 11² | 10 | | 7⁸ | 12 | 9¹ | | 6 | | | | | 3 | | | | | | | | 22 |
| 1 | 2 | 6 | 5 | 4² | 9 | 8 | | 7³ | 10 | | | 11¹ | 12 | | | | | | | 3 | 13 | 14 | | | | | | 23 |
| 1 | 5 | | 4 | 6 | 9² | 13 | | 10¹ | 11³ | | 8 | 14 | 12 | | 7 | | | | | 3 | | | 2 | | | | | 24 |
| 1 | 5 | | 2 | 4 | 8 | | | 9² | 11 | | 7 | 13 | 10¹ | | 6 | | | | | 3 | | | 12 | | | | | 25 |
| 1 | 5 | | 2⁴ | 4¹ | 13 | 7 | | 9² | 10 | | 8 | 14 | 11³ | | 6 | | | | | 3 | | | 12 | | | | | 26 |
| 1 | 5 | | | 7 | | | | 11 | | | 10³ | 12 | 8 | | | | | | | 4 | 6¹ | 14 | 2 | 3 | 9² | 13 | | 27 |
| 1 | 5 | | | | 13 | | | 10 | | | 7² | 9¹ | 11 | | 6 | | | | | 3 | 12 | 2 | 4 | | 8 | | | 28 |
| 1 | 5 | | 3 | | 7³ | 14 | | 9¹ | 10 | | | 12 | 11 | | 6 | | | | | 4 | 13 | 2 | | | 8² | | | 29 |
| 1 | 5 | | 4 | | 13 | | | 12 | 10 | | 7 | 9² | 11¹ | | 6 | | | | | 3 | | 2 | | | 8 | | | 30 |
| 1 | 3 | 12 | 5 | | 8 | | | 13 | 10 | | 7 | 9³ | | | | | | | | 4¹ | | 14 | 2 | | 11² | 6 | | 31 |
| 1⁸ | 5 | 13 | 3 | | 14 | | | 9 | 10 | | 8² | 12 | | | 6 | | | | | 4 | | 7¹ | 2³ | | | 11 | | 32 |
| | 2 | 5 | 3 | 4 | 8² | 13 | | 12 | 10 | | 7¹ | 9 | | | 6 | | | | 1 | | | | | | | 11 | | 33 |
| 1 | 5 | | 4¹ | | | 8 | | 9³ | 11 | | | 10 | 12 | | 13 | | | | | 3 | | 6² | 2 | 7 | | 14 | | 34 |
| 1 | | 5 | 3 | 4 | 6 | | | 10² | | | 7 | 12 | 11 | | 9 | | | | | | | 2 | | | 13 | 8¹ | | 35 |
| 1 | 3 | 12 | 4 | | 7 | 8 | | 11 | | | | 10 | | | | | | | | | 6 | 5 | | | 9¹ | 2 | | 36 |

# CELTIC

*Year Formed:* 1888. *Ground & Address:* Celtic Park, Glasgow G40 3RE. *Telephone:* 0871 226 1888. *Fax:* 0141 551 4223.
*E-mail:* customerservices@celticfc.co.uk *Website:* www.celticfc.net
*Ground Capacity:* 60,355 (all seated). *Size of Pitch:* 105m × 68m.
*Chairman:* Ian Bankier. *Chief Executive:* Peter Lawwell. *Secretary:* Michael Nicholson.
*Manager:* Neil Lennon. *Assistant Manager:* Johan Mjallby. *First Team Coach:* Garry Parker. *Physio:* Graham Parsons.
*Club Nicknames:* 'The Bhoys', 'The Hoops', 'The Celts'. *Previous Grounds:* None.
*Record Attendance:* 92,000 v Rangers, Division I, 1 Jan 1938.
*Record Transfer Fee received:* £6,500,000 for Stilian Petrov to Aston Villa (August 2007).
*Record Transfer Fee paid:* £6,000,000 for Chris Sutton from Chelsea (July 2000).
*Record Victory:* 11-0 Dundee, Division I, 26 Oct 1895.
*Record Defeat:* 0-8 v Motherwell, Division I, 30 Apr 1937.
*Most Capped Player:* Pat Bonner 80, Republic of Ireland.
*Most League Appearances:* 486: Billy McNeill, 1957-75.
*Most League Goals in Season (Individual):* 50: James McGrory, Division I, 1935-36.
*Most Goals Overall (Individual):* 397: James McGrory, 1922-39.

**Honours**
*League Champions:* (44 times) Division I 1892-93, 1893-94, 1895-96, 1897-98, 1904-05, 1905-06, 1906-07, 1907-08, 1908-09, 1909-10, 1913-14, 1914-15, 1915-16, 1916-17, 1918-19, 1921-22, 1925-26, 1935-36, 1937-38, 1953-54, 1965-66, 1966-67, 1967-68, 1968-69, 1969-70, 1970-71, 1971-72, 1972-73, 1973-74. Premier Division 1976-77, 1978-79, 1980-81, 1981-82, 1985-86, 1987-88, 1997-98, 2000-01, 2001-02, 2003-04, 2005-06, 2006-07, 2007-08, 2011-12, 2012-13. *Runners-up:* 31 times.
*Scottish Cup Winners:* (36 times) 1892, 1899, 1900, 1904, 1907, 1908, 1911, 1912, 1914, 1923, 1925, 1927, 1931, 1933, 1937, 1951, 1954, 1965, 1967, 1969, 1971, 1972, 1974, 1975, 1977, 1980, 1985, 1988, 1989, 1995, 2001, 2004, 2005, 2007, 2011, 2013.
*Runners-up:* 18 times.

## CELTIC – SCOTTISH PREMIER LEAGUE 2012–13 LEAGUE RECORD

| Match No. | Date | Venue | Opponents | Result | H/T Score | Lg Pos. | Goalscorers | Attendance |
|---|---|---|---|---|---|---|---|---|
| 1 | Aug 4 | H | Aberdeen | W 1-0 | 0-0 | 2 | Commons [79] | 48,251 |
| 2 | 18 | A | Ross Co | D 1-1 | 0-0 | 4 | Commons [90] | 6110 |
| 3 | 25 | A | Inverness CT | W 4-2 | 2-0 | 1 | Wanyama [4], Watt 2 [25, 64], Mulgrew [48] | 6100 |
| 4 | Sept 1 | H | Hibernian | D 2-2 | 1-0 | 1 | Lustig [10], McPake (og) [69] | 45,867 |
| 5 | 15 | A | St Johnstone | L 1-2 | 1-1 | 5 | Commons [4] | 6700 |
| 6 | 22 | H | Dundee | W 2-0 | 1-0 | 3 | Hooper [43], Wanyama [49] | 41,073 |
| 7 | 29 | A | Motherwell | W 2-0 | 2-0 | 1 | Hooper [32], Cummins (og) [35] | 10,496 |
| 8 | Oct 7 | H | Hearts | W 1-0 | 1-0 | 1 | Samaras [34] | 46,204 |
| 9 | 20 | A | St Mirren | W 5-0 | 4-0 | 1 | Hooper [15], Ambrose [18], Wanyama 2 [32, 38], Watt [86] | 6008 |
| 10 | 27 | H | Kilmarnock | L 0-2 | 0-1 | 1 | | 47,971 |
| 11 | Nov 4 | A | Dundee U | D 2-2 | 0-0 | 1 | Miku [69], Watt [80] | 10,521 |
| 12 | 11 | H | St Johnstone | D 1-1 | 0-0 | 2 | Watt [51] | 43,804 |
| 13 | 17 | A | Aberdeen | W 2-0 | 0-0 | 1 | Nouioui [73], Mulgrew [77] | 18,000 |
| 14 | 24 | H | Inverness CT | L 0-1 | 0-0 | 1 | | 44,379 |
| 15 | 28 | A | Hearts | W 4-0 | 3-0 | 1 | Nouioui [10], Lustig [22], Stevenson (og) [30], Hooper [83] | 15,264 |
| 16 | Dec 8 | A | Kilmarnock | W 3-1 | 1-0 | 1 | Brown [27], Ledley [65], Samaras [74] | 6501 |
| 17 | 15 | H | St Mirren | W 2-0 | 1-0 | 1 | Wanyama [15], Hooper [83] | 47,790 |
| 18 | 22 | A | Ross Co | W 4-0 | 0-0 | 1 | Brown [46], Hooper 2 [53, 64], Forrest [70] | 49,428 |
| 19 | 26 | A | Dundee | W 2-0 | 1-0 | 1 | Samaras [16], Hooper [71] | 9276 |
| 20 | 29 | A | Hibernian | L 0-1 | 0-1 | 1 | | 16,805 |
| 21 | Jan 2 | H | Motherwell | W 1-0 | 0-0 | 1 | Hooper [79] | 48,002 |
| 22 | 19 | H | Hearts | W 4-1 | 2-0 | 1 | Hooper 2 [2, 85], Samaras [12], Nouioui [90] | 48,374 |
| 23 | 22 | H | Dundee U | W 4-0 | 2-0 | 1 | Hooper 2 [19, 80], Wanyama [33], Brown [84] | 42,596 |
| 24 | 30 | H | Kilmarnock | W 4-1 | 1-0 | 1 | Ledley [41], Matthews 2 [50, 83], Stokes [78] | 43,652 |
| 25 | Feb 9 | A | Inverness CT | W 3-1 | 1-1 | 1 | Commons [20], Gershon [48], Miku [82] | 6175 |
| 26 | 16 | H | Dundee U | W 6-2 | 3-1 | 1 | Ambrose [11], Commons 2 (1 pen) [22, 55 (o)], Ledley [37], Stokes 2 [70, 82] | 46,496 |
| 27 | 19 | A | St Johnstone | D 1-1 | 1-0 | 1 | Ambrose [37] | 5352 |
| 28 | 24 | H | Dundee | W 5-0 | 1-0 | 1 | Ledley 2 [13, 73], Forrest (pen) [50], McGeouch [57], Hooper [83] | 39,959 |
| 29 | 27 | A | Motherwell | L 1-2 | 0-1 | 1 | Samaras [63] | 8641 |
| 30 | Mar 9 | A | Ross Co | L 2-3 | 2-2 | 1 | Mulgrew [15], Hooper [21] | 6031 |
| 31 | 16 | H | Aberdeen | W 4-3 | 1-1 | 1 | Commons [1], Mulgrew [68], Hooper [87], Samaras [90] | 46,395 |
| 32 | 31 | A | St Mirren | D 1-1 | 1-0 | 1 | Commons [6] | 6066 |
| 33 | Apr 6 | H | Hibernian | W 3-0 | 1-0 | 1 | Commons 2 [16, 52], Lustig [61] | 49,174 |
| 34 | 21 | H | Inverness CT | W 4-1 | 0-0 | 1 | Hooper 2 [61, 73], Ledley [66], Samaras [88] | 55,000 |
| 35 | 28 | A | Motherwell | L 1-3 | 1-1 | 1 | Hooper [40] | 7503 |
| 36 | May 5 | A | Ross Co | D 1-1 | 1-1 | 1 | Stokes [4] | 5873 |
| 37 | 11 | H | St Johnstone | W 4-0 | 2-0 | 1 | Ledley [2], Mulgrew [36], Forrest [52], Wright (og) [90] | 57,000 |
| 38 | 19 | A | Dundee U | W 4-0 | 3-0 | 1 | Commons [11], Samaras 2 [17, 27], Stokes [85] | 8717 |

**Final League Position: 1 – Scottish Premier League Champions**

*League Cup Winners:* (14 times) 1956-57, 1957-58, 1965-66, 1966-67, 1967-68, 1968-69, 1969-70, 1974-75, 1982-83, 1997-98, 1999-2000, 2000-01, 2005-06, 2008-09; *Runners-up:* 15 times.

**European:** *European Cup/Champions League:* 152 matches (1966-67 winners, 1967-68, 1968-69, 1969-70 runners-up, 1970-71, 1971-72, 1972-73, 1973-74 semi-finals, 1974-75, 1977-78, 1979-80, 1981-82, 1982-83, 1986-87, 1988-89, 1998-99, 2001-02, 2002-03, 2003-04, 2004-05, 2005-06, 2006-07, 2007-08, 2008-09, 2009-10, 2010-11, 2012-13). *Cup Winners' Cup:* 28 matches (1963-64 semi-finals, 1965-66 semi-finals, 1975-76, 1980-81, 1984-85, 1985-86, 1989-90, 1995-96). *UEFA Cup:* 75 matches (*Fairs Cup:* 1962-63, 1964-65. *UEFA Cup:* 1976-77, 1983-84, 1987-88, 1991-92, 1992-93, 1993-94, 1996-97, 1997-98, 1998-99, 1999-2000, 2000-01, 2001-02, 2002-03 runners-up, 2003-04 quarter-finals). *Europa League:* 16 matches (2009-10, 2010-11, 2011-12).

**Club colours:** Shirt: Green and white hoops. Shorts: White. Socks: White.

**Goalscorers:** *League (92):* Hooper 19, Commons 11 (1 pen), Samaras 9, Ledley 7, Wanyama 6, Mulgrew 5, Stokes 5, Watt 5, Ambrose 3, Brown 3, Forrest 3 (1 pen), Lustig 3, Nouioui 3, Matthews 2, Miku 2, Gershon 1, McGeouch 1, own goals 4.
*William Hill Scottish FA Cup (14):* Commons 3 (1 pen), Hooper 2, Ledley 2, Stokes 2, Forrest 1, Matthews 1, Mulgrew 1, Wanyama 1, own goal 1.
*Scottish Communities League Cup (11):* Hooper 6, Commons 3 (1 pen), Mulgrew 2.
*UEFA Champions League (17):* Samaras 5, Commons 3 (1 pen), Hooper 3, Wanyama 2, Ledley 1, Mulgrew 1, Watt 1, own goal 1.

| Forster F 34 | Matthews A 19+3 | Wanyama V 31+1 | Rogne T 8+5 | Izaguirre E 29+3 | Commons K 25+2 | Kayal B 19+8 | Ledley J 21+4 | Samaras G 18+7 | Stokes A 11+6 | Hooper G 30+2 | Wilson K 31+1 | McCourt P 4+11 | Murphy D —+1 | Mulgrew C 30 | Lustig M 21+2 | Watt T 9+11 | Slane P —+1 | Twardzik F 2 | Forrest J 10+5 | Bangura M —+1 | Chalmers J —+2 | Irvine J —+1 | Brown S 14+3 | Miku N 5+6 | Nouioui L 8+6 | McGeouch D 4+8 | Ambrose E 24+3 | Herron J —+1 | Zaluska L 4 | Gershon R 3 | Fraser M 1 | Rojic T 3+5 | Atajic B —+1 | Match No. |
|---|---|---|---|---|---|---|---|---|---|---|---|---|---|---|---|---|---|---|---|---|---|---|---|---|---|---|---|---|---|---|---|---|---|---|
| 1 | 2 | 3 | 4 | 5 | 6 | 7² | 8 | 9¹ | 10³ | 11 | 12 | 13 | 14 | | | | | | | | | | | | | | | | | | | | | 1 |
| 1 | 2 | 11 | | 3 | 6 | 10 | 7 | 5 | | | 4² | | | 8 | 9¹ | 12 | 13 | | | | | | | | | | | | | | | | | 2 |
| 1 | 2² | 7 | | | 5² | | | | | 10¹ | 3 | 9 | | 4 | 6 | 11 | | | 8 | 12 | 13 | 14 | | | | | | | | | | | | 3 |
| 1 | 2 | 8¹ | | 5 | 13 | | | | | 10 | 3 | 9² | | 7 | 11 | | | | 4 | 6 | | | 12 | | | | | | | | | | | 4 |
| 1 | | 8 | 13 | | 5² | 9 | | | | 10 | 3 | | | 4 | 2 | 12 | | | 6 | | | | 7³ | 11¹ | 14 | | | | | | | | | 5 |
| 1 | 2 | 8 | | | 5 | 9² | | | | 11 | 3 | | | 4 | 12 | | | | 6 | | | | 7³ | | 10¹ | 13 | 14 | | | | | | | 6 |
| 1 | | 8 | | 5 | 10² | | 14 | 12 | | 11 | 3 | | | 9 | 2³ | | | | 6 | | | | 7¹ | 13 | | | 4 | | | | | | | 7 |
| 1 | | 7 | | 5 | 10 | 13 | 12 | 9 | | 11² | 4 | | | 8¹ | 2³ | | | | 6 | | | | | 14 | | | 3 | | | | | | | 8 |
| 1 | 2³ | 6 | | | 12 | | | 8 | 7 | 10 | 3¹ | | | 4 | 14 | 11 | | | | | | | 13 | 9² | | | 5 | | | | | | | 9 |
| 1 | 2 | | | 5 | 10² | 7¹ | 8 | | | 12 | 4 | 13 | | 9 | 14 | | | | | | | | 11³ | | | | 3 | | | | | | | 10 |
| 1 | 2 | 7 | 3¹ | 5² | 10³ | | | 8 | | | 4 | 14 | | 9 | 11 | | | | 6 | 13 | | | | | | | 12 | | | | | | | 11 |
| 1 | 2 | 7 | | | 9 | 13 | 8² | 11 | | 4 | | | | 5 | 12 | | | | 6 | 10¹ | 14 | 3³ | | | | | | | | | | | | 12 |
| 1 | 2 | 7 | | | 9¹ | 8 | 10² | | | 4 | | | | 5 | 6 | 11 | | | | 12 | 13 | 3 | | | | | | | | | | | | 13 |
| 1 | 5² | 7 | | | 6 | 8 | 9 | | 11³ | | 12 | | | 4 | 2 | 10¹ | | | | 13 | 14 | 3 | | | | | | | | | | | | 14 |
| 1 | 12 | 8 | | | 6 | 7 | 9² | 14 | 11 | 4 | | | | 5 | 2¹ | | | | 13 | 10³ | 3 | | | | | | | | | | | | | 15 |
| 1 | 2 | 7 | | | 5² | 13 | 8 | 12 | 10³ | 4 | | | | 9 | | | | | 6 | 14 | 11¹ | 3 | | | | | | | | | | | | 16 |
| 1 | 5 | 8 | | | 12 | | 7³ | | 10² | 11 | 4 | 14 | | 9 | 2 | | | | 6 | 13 | 3¹ | | | | | | | | | | | | | 17 |
| 1 | 6 | | | 5 | | 7¹ | | 9³ | 10 | 3 | | | | 4 | | 13 | | | 12 | 6 | 11² | | 2 | 14 | | | | | | | | | | 18 |
| 1 | 6 | 5 | | | 8² | | 10 | | 9 | 3 | 14 | | | 4¹ | 12 | 11³ | | | 13 | 7 | | | 2 | | | | | | | | | | | 19 |
| 1 | 8 | 4² | 5 | | 13 | | 10 | 11 | 3 | 12 | | | | 2 | | | | | 7 | | 9¹ | 14 | 6³ | | | | | | | | | | | 20 |
| 1 | 2 | 8 | 14 | 5 | 6² | 7¹ | | 10 | 11 | 4 | | | | 9 | 12 | | | | | | 13 | 3² | | | | | | | | | | | | 21 |
| | 2² | 8 | 14 | 5 | 6³ | 12 | 9¹ | 10 | | 11 | | | | 4 | 3 | | | | | 7 | 13 | | | | | | 1 | | | | | | | 22 |
| | 13 | 7 | 3 | 5 | | 6¹ | 8 | 9 | 14 | 10 | | | | 4 | 2² | | | | | 12 | 11³ | | | | | | 1 | | | | | | | 23 |
| | 5 | 7 | | 8¹ | 9 | 12 | 11² | 14 | 10 | 3 | | | | 4 | 2 | 13 | | | 6 | | | | | | | | 1 | | | | | | | 24 |
| 1 | 13 | | 4 | | 7¹ | 6 | | 11 | | | 9³ | | | | 14 | | | | 12 | | 10 | 5 | | | | | 2² | 3 | 8 | | | | | 25 |
| 1 | 2 | 7³ | | 5 | 6² | 12 | 8 | | 10 | 11 | 4 | | | 9 | | | | | 14 | | | 3¹ | | | | | | | | | 13 | | | 26 |
| 1 | 2² | 7 | 13 | 5 | 11³ | | 8 | | 14 | 10 | 3 | | | 4 | | | | | 12 | | 9³ | 6 | | | | | | | | | | | | 27 |
| 1 | 12 | 3 | | 5² | | 7 | 8 | | 10 | 11 | 4 | | | | | | | | 9³ | | 14 | 6 | 2¹ | | | | | | | | 13 | | | 28 |
| 1 | 2 | 4 | 3 | 5 | 6 | | 7² | 12 | 10 | 11³ | 14 | | | 4 | | | | | 9 | | | 13 | | | | | 8¹ | | | | | | | 29 |
| 1 | | 13 | | 12 | 7 | 6 | | 9³ | 11 | 3 | | | | 8 | 14 | | | | | | 10 | 5² | 2 | | 4¹ | | | | | | | | | 30 |
| 1 | | | 5 | 9 | 6¹ | 8 | 12 | 10² | 11 | 4 | | | | 7 | 2 | | | | | | | 13 | 3 | | | | | | | | | | | 31 |
| 1 | 3⁴ | | 5 | 8¹ | 6 | 7 | 11³ | 12 | 10² | 4 | | | | 9 | | 14 | | | | | | 13 | 2 | | | | | | | | | | | 32 |
| 1 | 7 | | 5 | 6² | | 8 | 12 | 10 | 11³ | 4 | 14 | | | 9 | 2¹ | | | | | | | 3 | | | | | | | | | 13 | | | 33 |
| 1 | 7 | | 12 | 9 | | 8 | 13 | 11² | 10 | 4 | 14 | | | 5 | 2³ | | | | 6¹ | | | 3 | | | | | | | | | | | | 34 |
| 1 | 8 | 3¹ | 5 | | 7 | | 10³ | 14 | 11 | | 12 | | | 4 | 2 | 9 | | | | | | 13 | | | | | | | | | 6² | | | 35 |
| | | 5 | 9¹ | 14 | 8 | | 11 | | | 3 | 13 | | | 2 | 10 | | | | | | | 6² | 7³ | 1 | 4 | 12 | | | | | | | | 36 |
| 1 | 7 | | 5³ | | 14 | 8 | 12 | 10 | 11 | 3 | | | | 4 | 2 | | | | | 9² | | 6¹ | 13 | | | | | | | | | | | 37 |
| 1 | | 5 | 9¹ | | 8 | 10³ | 13 | 11 | 3 | 6² | | | | 2 | | | | | | | 7 | | 4 | | | | | | | | | 12 | 14 | 38 |

# CLYDE

*Year Formed:* 1877. *Ground & Address:* Broadwood Stadium, Cumbernauld, G68 9NE. *Telephone:* 01236 451511.
*Fax:* 01236 733490. *E-mail:* info@clydefc.co.uk *Website:* www.clydefc.co.uk
*Ground Capacity:* 8,006 (all seated). *Size of Pitch:* 100m × 68m.
*Chairman:* John Alexander. *Secretary:* John Taylor.
*Manager:* Jim Duffy. *Assistant Manager:* Chic Charnley. *Physio:* Iain McKinlay.
*Club Nickname:* 'The Bully Wee'.
*Previous Grounds:* Barrowfield Park 1877-98, Shawfield Stadium 1898-1986, Firhill Stadium 1986-91, Douglas Park 1991-94.
*Record Attendance:* 52,000 v Rangers, Division I, 21 Nov 1908.
*Record Transfer Fee received:* £200,000 from Blackburn R for Gordon Greer (May 2001).
*Record Transfer Fee paid:* £14,000 for Harry Hood from Sunderland (1966).
*Record Victory:* 11-1 v Cowdenbeath, Division II, 6 Oct 1951.
*Record Defeat:* 0-11 v Dumbarton, Scottish Cup 4th rd, 22 Nov, 1879; v Rangers, Scottish Cup 4th rd, 13 Nov 1880.
*Most Capped Player:* Tommy Ring, 12, Scotland.
*Most League Appearances:* 420: Brian Ahern, 1971-81; 1987-88.
*Most League Goals in Season (Individual):* 32: Bill Boyd, 1932-33.
*Most Goals Overall (Individual):* 124: Tommy Ring, 1950-60.

## CLYDE – SCOTTISH THIRD DIVISION 2012–13 LEAGUE RECORD

| Match No. | Date | Venue | Opponents | Result | H/T Score | Lg Pos. | Goalscorers | Attendance |
|---|---|---|---|---|---|---|---|---|
| 1 | Aug 11 | A | Montrose | W 3-2 | 0-2 | 3 | Gilfillan [56], Neill [60], McColm [81] | 333 |
| 2 | 18 | H | Peterhead | L 0-2 | 0-2 | 6 | | 401 |
| 3 | 25 | A | Stirling A | W 1-0 | 1-0 | 3 | Watt [24] | 855 |
| 4 | Sept 1 | H | Annan Ath | W 2-1 | 1-0 | 2 | Watt [26], Chaplain (og) [58] | 505 |
| 5 | 15 | A | Queen's Park | L 0-1 | 0-1 | 5 | | 907 |
| 6 | 22 | A | East Stirling | L 0-3 | 0-2 | 5 | | 467 |
| 7 | Oct 17 | H | Elgin C | D 2-2 | 1-2 | 5 | McColm [42], Sweeney (pen) [55] | 458 |
| 8 | 20 | A | Berwick R | L 1-2 | 1-1 | 8 | Watt [41] | 546 |
| 9 | 28 | H | Rangers | L 0-2 | 0-1 | 8 | | 7500 |
| 10 | Nov 10 | H | Montrose | L 1-2 | 0-0 | 8 | Scullion [78] | 496 |
| 11 | 17 | A | Peterhead | L 0-1 | 0-1 | 9 | | 514 |
| 12 | 24 | A | Annan Ath | W 3-1 | 2-0 | 8 | Gilfillan 2 [12, 49], Marsh [16] | 489 |
| 13 | Dec 8 | A | Elgin C | L 1-2 | 1-1 | 8 | Nicolson (og) [30] | 665 |
| 14 | 15 | H | East Stirling | W 2-1 | 1-1 | 8 | Scullion [20], Watt [52] | 428 |
| 15 | 26 | A | Rangers | L 0-3 | 0-2 | 8 | | 47,463 |
| 16 | 29 | H | Berwick R | W 2-1 | 0-1 | 8 | Brydon (og) [50], Watt [89] | 427 |
| 17 | Jan 2 | A | Queen's Park | L 1-4 | 1-3 | 8 | Watt [23] | 842 |
| 18 | 5 | H | Annan Ath | L 2-3 | 0-2 | 8 | Sweeney [60], Graham [78] | 524 |
| 19 | 12 | H | Stirling A | W 2-1 | 1-0 | 8 | McCluskey, S [21], Sweeney [64] | 912 |
| 20 | 19 | A | Montrose | D 1-1 | 1-0 | 8 | Sweeney (pen) [8] | 336 |
| 21 | Feb 2 | H | Elgin C | D 1-1 | 1-0 | 8 | McCluskey, S [45] | 492 |
| 22 | 9 | A | Berwick R | D 3-3 | 1-0 | 8 | Sharp [27], Sweeney [58], Scullion [79] | 507 |
| 23 | 16 | H | Rangers | L 1-4 | 0-3 | 8 | Watt [47] | 7600 |
| 24 | 19 | A | East Stirling | L 0-3 | 0-1 | 9 | | 301 |
| 25 | 23 | A | Stirling A | L 0-2 | 0-2 | 10 | | 604 |
| 26 | 26 | H | Queen's Park | L 0-3 | 0-1 | 10 | | 451 |
| 27 | Mar 2 | H | Peterhead | W 2-0 | 0-0 | 10 | Watt [65], Sweeney (pen) [84] | 558 |
| 28 | 9 | H | Queen's Park | L 2-3 | 1-0 | 10 | McColm 2 [12, 51] | 631 |
| 29 | 16 | A | Annan Ath | W 1-0 | 1-0 | 9 | Sweeney (pen) [45] | 464 |
| 30 | 30 | H | East Stirling | W 2-0 | 1-0 | 8 | Scullion [18], Sweeney [90] | 508 |
| 31 | Apr 2 | A | Elgin C | L 2-4 | 1-1 | 8 | McGachie 2 [23, 82] | 494 |
| 32 | 6 | H | Berwick R | W 2-1 | 1-0 | 8 | Watt [39], Sweeney [86] | 472 |
| 33 | 13 | A | Rangers | L 0-2 | 0-0 | 9 | | 44,453 |
| 34 | 20 | H | Montrose | W 1-0 | 0-0 | 8 | Scullion [66] | 523 |
| 35 | 27 | A | Peterhead | L 0-3 | 0-1 | 9 | | 560 |
| 36 | May 4 | H | Stirling A | L 1-2 | 1-0 | 9 | McCluskey, S [5] | 745 |

**Final League Position: 9**

**Honours**
*League Champions:* Division II 1904-05, 1951-52, 1956-57, 1961-62, 1972-73. Second Division 1977-78, 1981-82, 1992-93, 1999-2000.
*Runners-up:* Division II 1903-04, 1905-06, 1925-26, 1963-64. First Division 2002-03, 2003-04.
*Scottish Cup Winners:* 1939, 1955, 1958; *Runners-up:* 1910, 1912, 1949.
*League Challenge Cup Runners-up:* 2006-07.

**Club colours:** Shirt: Red and white stripes. Shorts: Black. Socks: Red.

**Goalscorers:** *League (42):* Sweeney 9 (4 pens), Watt 9, Scullion 5, McColm 4, Gilfillan 3, McCluskey S 3, McGachie 2, Graham 1, Marsh 1, Neill 1, Sharp 1, own goals 3.
*William Hill Scottish FA Cup (5):* McCluskey S 2, Gilfillan 1, Sweeney 1 (1 pen), Watt 1.
*Scottish Communities League Cup (1):* Neill 1.
*Ramsdens Cup (0).*

| Barclay J 36 | Kane J 17+4 | Gray I 29 | Marsh D 13+1 | Sharp L 11+3 | Neill J 8+4 | Masterton S 5+2 | Sweeney J 28+6 | Gilfillan B 16+1 | McCluskey S 24+8 | McColm S 27+2 | Watt K 28+7 | Graham G —+9 | Brown G 15+1 | MacBeth R 5+5 | Hay P 28 | Scullion P 14+9 | Wedderburn C 3 | Kane A 1 | Trialist A —+1 | Oliver M 12+1 | Fitzharris S 12+8 | Lanie R 4 | McDonald K 12+4 | Traynor G 1 | Lyden J 13+1 | Nicoll K 10 | Fitzpatrick D 6+7 | McGachie K 6+9 | Fordyce C 6 | McCusker M 3+4 | Bronsky S 1 | Orrick P 2 | Match No. |
|---|---|---|---|---|---|---|---|---|---|---|---|---|---|---|---|---|---|---|---|---|---|---|---|---|---|---|---|---|---|---|---|---|---|
| 1 | 2 | 3 | 4 | 5 | 6 | $7^1$ | 8 | 9 | $10^2$ | 11 | 12 | 13 | | | | | | | | | | | | | | | | | | | | | 1 |
| 1 | 2 | 3 | 4 | $5^1$ | 6 | $7^2$ | 8 | $11^3$ | 10 | 9 | 13 | | | | 12 | 14 | | | | | | | | | | | | | | | | | 2 |
| 1 | 5 | 3 | 4 | | 7 | $6^2$ | 13 | | 11 | $9^1$ | 10 | | | | 2 | | 8 | 12 | | | | | | | | | | | | | | | 3 |
| 1 | | 5 | 3 | 7 | $8^2$ | 12 | $11^1$ | | 9 | 10 | | | | 2 | 13 | 6 | | 4 | | | | | | | | | | | | | | | 4 |
| 1 | | 3 | | $6^2$ | $7^3$ | 13 | $11^1$ | 12 | 9 | 10 | | | | 2 | | 8 | | 4 | 5 | 14 | | | | | | | | | | | | | 5 |
| 1 | 5 | | 4 | | 13 | 12 | 7 | $8^3$ | 11 | $9^2$ | 10 | 14 | 2 | | $6^1$ | | 3 | | | | | | | | | | | | | | | | 6 |
| 1 | | 4 | | 3 | | 7 | 11 | | $9^2$ | $10^2$ | 13 | | 2 | | 8 | 12 | | 5 | 6 | | | | | | | | | | | | | | 7 |
| 1 | 12 | $4^4$ | | 5 | 8 | 13 | | $9^1$ | 14 | | 10 | | 2 | $6^3$ | 7 | $11^2$ | | 3 | | | | | | | | | | | | | | | 8 |
| 1 | 12 | | 3 | 5 | $6^5$ | | 7 | $10^1$ | $11^2$ | 9 | 13 | | 2 | | $8^3$ | | | 4 | 14 | | | | | | | | | | | | | | 9 |
| 1 | | 4 | 5 | | $8^2$ | 7 | 11 | $9^3$ | 10 | | 2 | 14 | $6^1$ | 13 | | | | 3 | 12 | | | | | | | | | | | | | | 10 |
| 1 | 2 | 3 | 4 | | $8^3$ | 6 | 12 | 9 | $11^1$ | | 14 | 7 | $10^2$ | | | | | 5 | 13 | | | | | | | | | | | | | | 11 |
| 1 | 2 | 8 | $4^4$ | 5 | 12 | | $11^2$ | 10 | $9^3$ | 13 | | 7 | 14 | | | | | $6^1$ | 3 | | | | | | | | | | | | | | 12 |
| 1 | 2 | 3 | | 12 | | 13 | 10 | | 9 | 11 | $5^1$ | $7^2$ | 8 | | | | | 6 | 4 | | | | | | | | | | | | | | 13 |
| 1 | 2 | 4 | | | 13 | $11^3$ | | 9 | 10 | 14 | $5^1$ | $7^2$ | 9 | | | | | 12 | 6 | 3 | | | | | | | | | | | | | 14 |
| 1 | 2 | 3 | | 13 | | 12 | $10^3$ | 14 | 9 | 11 | 5 | $7^2$ | 8 | | | | | $6^1$ | 4 | | | | | | | | | | | | | | 15 |
| 1 | 2 | | 3 | 5 | | 7 | $10^3$ | 12 | $9^2$ | 11 | | $8^1$ | 14 | | | | | 4 | 6 | 13 | | | | | | | | | | | | | 16 |
| 1 | 2 | | 3 | 5 | 6 | | 7 | 14 | 12 | $11^2$ | 10 | | $8^3$ | | | | | 4 | $9^1$ | 13 | | | | | | | | | | | | | 17 |
| 1 | 2 | | 3 | | 14 | 8 | $9^2$ | 11 | 12 | 10 | 13 | | 7 | | | | | 4 | $6^1$ | | $5^3$ | | | | | | | | | | | | 18 |
| 1 | 3 | 12 | | 8 | | 11 | $9^3$ | $10^2$ | 13 | 2 | 6 | | | | 5 | | | 14 | | 4 | $7^1$ | | | | | | | | | | | | 19 |
| 1 | | 4 | | 8 | | 11 | 9 | $10^2$ | 13 | 2 | 6 | $7^1$ | | | 5 | | | 12 | 3 | | | | | | | | | | | | | | 20 |
| 1 | 14 | $7^3$ | | 8 | | 11 | 9 | $10^2$ | | 2 | | | | | 5 | 13 | | | 3 | $4^1$ | 6 | 12 | | | | | | | | | | | 21 |
| 1 | 2 | 3 | | 5 | | 7 | | 6 | 9 | $11^2$ | | 13 | | | $8^1$ | | | 4 | | 10 | 12 | | | | | | | | | | | | 22 |
| 1 | 5 | 4 | 13 | | 8 | | 9 | 11 | 10 | | $2^2$ | $3^1$ | 14 | | | | | 7 | | $6^3$ | 12 | | | | | | | | | | | | 23 |
| 1 | 2 | 3 | | 5 | | 8 | | 11 | 13 | $10^3$ | 14 | 12 | | | | | | $7^2$ | | 4 | 6 | $9^1$ | | | | | | | | | | | 24 |
| 1 | 2 | $3^1$ | | | $7^3$ | | $11^2$ | 10 | | 14 | 8 | 12 | | | 5 | | | 4 | 6 | 13 | 9 | | | | | | | | | | | | 25 |
| 1 | $2^1$ | 3 | | | 8 | | 11 | $9^3$ | 12 | 13 | 6 | 7 | | | 5 | | | 4 | | 14 | $10^2$ | | | | | | | | | | | | 26 |
| 1 | | 4 | | | 7 | | $11^2$ | 9 | $10^1$ | | 8 | 2 | | | 12 | | | 5 | | 3 | $6^3$ | 14 | 13 | | | | | | | | | | 27 |
| 1 | 13 | 4 | | | 8 | | 6 | 9 | $10^1$ | 7 | 11 | | | | $5^2$ | | | 3 | 2 | | 12 | | | | | | | | | | | | 28 |
| 1 | | 3 | | | 8 | | $11^2$ | 9 | $10^1$ | 7 | 2 | | | | 13 | | | 5 | | | 4 | 6 | 14 | 12 | 4 | | | | | | | | 29 |
| 1 | | 3 | | | 8 | | 11 | 9 | $10^2$ | 7 | $2^1$ | | | | 5 | | | 6 | 12 | | 4 | 13 | | | | | | | | | | | 30 |
| 1 | | 3 | | | 7 | | 12 | | | 8 | 2 | | | | 6 | 5 | | 9 | | 11 | 4 | $10^1$ | | | | | | | | | | | 31 |
| 1 | | 7 | | | 8 | | $11^2$ | 10 | | 4 | $2^1$ | | | | $9^3$ | 5 | | 6 | 14 | 12 | 3 | 13 | | | | | | | | | | | 32 |
| 1 | | 3 | | | 7 | | $9^2$ | 12 | | 8 | $2^3$ | | | | 13 | 5 | | 14 | 6 | $10^1$ | 4 | 11 | | | | | | | | | | | 33 |
| 1 | | 4 | | | 8 | | 13 | 10 | | 2 | 12 | | | | $6^2$ | 5 | | 7 | | $9^1$ | 14 | 3 | $11^3$ | | | | | | | | | | 34 |
| 1 | 3 | 14 | | | 8 | | 6 | $10^2$ | | 7 | | | | | 5 | 4 | | 13 | $11^1$ | | 12 | $2^5$ | $9^1$ | | | | | | | | | | 35 |
| 1 | $4^5$ | | | | 7 | | 11 | $10^1$ | 14 | 8 | 2 | | | | 5 | 3 | | $9^3$ | 12 | | 13 | | $6^2$ | | | | | | | | | | 36 |

# COWDENBEATH

*Year Formed:* 1882. *Ground & Address:* Central Park, Cowdenbeath KY4 9QQ. *Telephone:* 01383 610166. *Fax:* 01383 512132.
*E-mail:* office@cowdenbeathfc.com *Website:* www.cowdenbeathfc.com
*Ground Capacity:* 4,370 (seated: 1,431). *Size of Pitch:* 98m × 59m.
*Chairman:* Donald Findlay QC. *Vice Chairman:* John Lints. *Operations:* John Cameron.
*Club Nicknames:* 'The Blue Brazil', 'Cowden', 'The Miners'.
*Manager:* Colin Cameron. *Assistant Manager:* Lee Makel.
*Previous Grounds:* North End Park.
*Record Attendance:* 25,586 v Rangers, League Cup quarter-final, 21 Sept 1949.
*Record Transfer Fee received:* £30,000 for Nicky Henderson to Falkirk (March 1994).
*Record Victory:* 12-0 v Johnstone, Scottish Cup 1st rd, 21 Jan 1928.
*Record Defeat:* 1-11 v Clyde, Division II, 6 Oct 1951.
*Most Capped Player:* Jim Paterson, 3, Scotland.
*Most League and Cup Appearances:* 491, Ray Allan 1972-75, 1979-89.
*Most League Goals in Season (Individual):* 54, Rab Walls, Division II, 1938-39.
*Most Goals Overall (Individual):* 127, Willie Devlin, 1922-26, 1929-30.

## COWDENBEATH – SCOTTISH FIRST DIVISION 2012–13 LEAGUE RECORD

| Match No. | Date | Venue | Opponents | Result | H/T Score | Lg Pos. | Goalscorers | Atten-dance |
|---|---|---|---|---|---|---|---|---|
| 1 | Aug 11 | H | Dunfermline Ath | L 0-4 | 0-1 | 10 | | 2507 |
| 2 | 18 | A | Dumbarton | W 3-0 | 2-0 | 5 | Coult [9], Stewart, G [17], McKenzie (pen) [82] | 695 |
| 3 | 25 | H | Hamilton A | W 1-0 | 1-0 | 5 | Miller [12] | 525 |
| 4 | Sept 1 | A | Airdrie U | W 3-0 | 1-0 | 3 | Miller [5], Coult [76], McKenzie [85] | 816 |
| 5 | 15 | H | Greenock Morton | L 3-4 | 1-2 | 4 | Armstrong [40], Ramsay [82], Stevenson [90] | 611 |
| 6 | 22 | A | Partick Th | L 1-2 | 0-1 | 5 | Stevenson [49] | 2510 |
| 7 | 29 | H | Falkirk | D 1-1 | 1-1 | 5 | Coult [18] | 699 |
| 8 | Oct 6 | A | Livingston | D 1-1 | 0-0 | 5 | Milne [90] | 1203 |
| 9 | 20 | H | Raith R | D 4-4 | 2-2 | 5 | Miller [6], Stevenson [24], Coult 2 [78, 80] | 1209 |
| 10 | 27 | A | Dunfermline Ath | L 0-3 | 0-1 | 6 | | 3353 |
| 11 | Nov 10 | H | Dumbarton | L 0-1 | 0-1 | 6 | | 415 |
| 12 | 17 | H | Airdrie U | D 1-1 | 0-0 | 6 | Stewart, G [70] | 423 |
| 13 | 24 | A | Greenock Morton | L 0-1 | 0-0 | 7 | | 1526 |
| 14 | Dec 15 | A | Falkirk | L 0-2 | 0-2 | 7 | | 2647 |
| 15 | 22 | H | Livingston | D 1-1 | 1-0 | 7 | McKenzie [1] | 409 |
| 16 | 29 | H | Raith R | D 2-2 | 2-0 | 8 | Milne [9], Stevenson (pen) [42] | 1877 |
| 17 | Jan 2 | A | Airdrie U | D 1-1 | 1-0 | 8 | Brett [3] | 776 |
| 18 | 5 | A | Greenock Morton | D 1-1 | 1-0 | 8 | Caddis [37] | 647 |
| 19 | 12 | A | Hamilton A | L 1-2 | 1-0 | 8 | Hemmings [24] | 1021 |
| 20 | 26 | A | Partick Th | L 1-2 | 1-2 | 9 | Hemmings [9] | 2543 |
| 21 | Feb 9 | H | Falkirk | W 4-1 | 2-1 | 9 | Armstrong 2 [35, 73], Hemmings [38], Stevenson [90] | 566 |
| 22 | 12 | H | Dunfermline Ath | W 4-2 | 1-0 | 7 | Milne [33], Linton 2 [75, 88], Hemmings [81] | 1330 |
| 23 | 16 | A | Livingston | L 0-3 | 0-3 | 8 | | 1112 |
| 24 | 23 | H | Raith R | D 1-1 | 0-0 | 8 | Stewart, G [81] | 1078 |
| 25 | Mar 2 | A | Dumbarton | D 2-2 | 1-0 | 8 | Stevenson [11], Moore [90] | 742 |
| 26 | 9 | H | Hamilton A | D 1-1 | 1-1 | 8 | Moore [38] | 370 |
| 27 | 16 | H | Airdrie U | W 3-2 | 1-1 | 7 | McKenzie [13], Stewart, G [68], Moore [88] | 407 |
| 28 | 23 | A | Greenock Morton | L 2-4 | 2-0 | 8 | Moore [13], Stevenson [40] | 1533 |
| 29 | 27 | H | Partick Th | L 0-3 | 0-2 | 9 | | 716 |
| 30 | 30 | H | Partick Th | L 1-2 | 1-1 | 9 | Moore [31] | 1214 |
| 31 | Apr 6 | A | Falkirk | L 0-4 | 0-0 | 9 | | 2539 |
| 32 | 9 | H | Livingston | D 2-2 | 1-1 | 8 | Stewart, G [35], McKenzie [90] | 455 |
| 33 | 13 | A | Raith R | W 1-0 | 1-0 | 8 | Stevenson [41] | 1574 |
| 34 | 20 | A | Dunfermline Ath | L 0-1 | 0-0 | 9 | | 4879 |
| 35 | 27 | H | Dumbarton | L 2-3 | 1-3 | 9 | Moore [15], Miller [88] | 659 |
| 36 | May 4 | A | Hamilton A | W 3-1 | 0-1 | 8 | Linton [48], Moore [72], McKenzie [84] | 1434 |

**Final League Position: 8**

**Honours**

*League Champions:* Division II 1913-14, 1914-15, 1938-39. Second Division 2011-12. Third Division 2005-06. *Runners-up:* Division II 1921-22, 1923-24, 1969-70. Second Division 1991-92. Third Division 2000-01, 2008-09. *Promoted to First Division:* 2009-10 (play-offs).
*Scottish Cup:* Quarter-finals 1931.
*League Cup:* Semi-finals 1959-60, 1970-71.

**Club colours:** Shirt: Royal blue. Shorts: White. Socks: Red.

**Goalscorers:** *League (51):* Stevenson 8 (1 pen), Moore 7, McKenzie 6 (1 pen), Coult 5, Stewart G 5, Hemmings 4, Miller 4, Armstrong 3, Linton 3, Milne 3, Brett 1, Caddis 1, Ramsay 1.
*William Hill Scottish FA Cup (8):* Stewart G 3, Coult 2, McKenzie 1, Ramsey 1, Stephenson 1.
*Scottish Communities League Cup (1):* McKenzie 1.
*Ramsdens Cup (6):* Stephenson 2, Adamson 1, Coult 1, McKenzie 1, Miller 1.

| Flynn T 30 | Brett D 23+5 | Armstrong J 35 | Mbu J 11+2 | Adamson K 32 | McKenzie M 26+7 | Cameron C 19+2 | Ramsay M 10+10 | Linton S 22+3 | Stevenson J 32+3 | Coult L 18+10 | Stewart G 17+8 | Miller K 16+11 | Milne L 12+7 | O'Brien T 23+7 | Callaghan L —+1 | Bennett S 1 | Thomas Z 1+4 | Cowan D 18 | Toult L 1 | Garcia-Rey R 1+2 | Wight C —+2 | Puigdollers A 3 | Navas P —+3 | Stanton S 2 | Caddis L 3 | Hemmings K 7 | Robertson J 4 | Moore C 11+1 | Stewart C 5 | Naismith J 3+2 | Wilson L 1 | McAllister S 9 | Match No. |
|---|---|---|---|---|---|---|---|---|---|---|---|---|---|---|---|---|---|---|---|---|---|---|---|---|---|---|---|---|---|---|---|---|---|
| 1 | 2 | 3 |  | 4 | 5 | 6 | 7 | $8^2$ | 9 | $10^1$ | 11 | 12 | 13 |  |  |  |  |  |  |  |  |  |  |  |  |  |  |  |  |  |  |  | 1 |
| 1 | 2 | 3 |  | 4 | $6^3$ | $7^2$ |  | 5 | 9 | $11^1$ | 10 | 8 | 12 | 13 | 14 |  |  |  |  |  |  |  |  |  |  |  |  |  |  |  |  |  | 2 |
| 1 |  | 3 |  | 4 | 6 | $7^3$ |  | 5 | $9^2$ | 11 | $10^1$ | 8 | 13 | 14 |  | 2 | 12 |  |  |  |  |  |  |  |  |  |  |  |  |  |  |  | 3 |
| 1 | 2 | 3 |  | 4 | 6 | $8^2$ |  | 5 | $9^3$ | 11 | $10^1$ | 7 | 13 | 12 |  |  | 14 |  |  |  |  |  |  |  |  |  |  |  |  |  |  |  | 4 |
| 1 | 2 | 5 |  | 3 | 6 | 8 | 13 | 4 | 10 | $11^1$ |  | 7 |  | $9^2$ |  |  | 12 |  |  |  |  |  |  |  |  |  |  |  |  |  |  |  | 5 |
| 1 | 13 | 3 |  | 4 | 6 | $7^3$ | 8 | 5 | $9^2$ |  | $10^1$ | 12 | 14 |  |  | 11 | 2 |  |  |  |  |  |  |  |  |  |  |  |  |  |  |  | 6 |
| 1 |  | $4^1$ |  | 3 | $6^3$ | 8 | 11 | 5 | 9 | 10 | 13 | 14 | $7^2$ | 12 |  |  | 2 |  |  |  |  |  |  |  |  |  |  |  |  |  |  |  | 7 |
| 1 |  | $4^4$ |  | 8 | $6^3$ | $3^2$ | 7 | 5 | 9 |  | $10^1$ | 13 | 14 |  |  | 2 | 11 | 12 |  |  |  |  |  |  |  |  |  |  |  |  |  |  | 8 |
| 1 | 2 |  |  | 4 | 5 | 6 | 8 | 13 |  | 10 | 12 | 11 | $9^1$ | 7 |  |  | $3^2$ |  |  |  |  |  |  |  |  |  |  |  |  |  |  |  | 9 |
| $1^1$ |  | 3 | 4 | 5 | 6 | 7 |  | 9 | 11 | 10 | 13 |  | $8^2$ |  |  | 2 |  |  |  | 12 |  |  |  |  |  |  |  |  |  |  |  |  | 10 |
| 1 |  | 3 | 4 | 5 | 6 | 12 | $8^1$ | 9 | 11 | 10 |  |  |  |  |  | 2 |  |  |  |  |  | 7 |  |  |  |  |  |  |  |  |  |  | 11 |
| 1 | $6^1$ | 3 | 4 | 5 |  | 7 |  | 9 | 11 | 10 | 13 | . |  |  |  | 2 |  |  |  |  |  | $8^2$ | 12 |  |  |  |  |  |  |  |  |  | 12 |
| 1 | 12 | 4 |  | 5 | 6 |  | 10 |  | 9 | $11^2$ | $13^3$ | 8 |  | 3 |  |  | 2 |  |  |  |  | $7^1$ | 14 |  |  |  |  |  |  |  |  |  | 13 |
| 1 | 12 | 3 | 14 | 5 | $6^1$ | $7^3$ | 8 |  | 10 | $11^2$ |  | 9 |  | 4 |  | 13 | 2 |  |  |  |  |  |  |  |  |  |  |  |  |  |  |  | 14 |
| 1 | $11^2$ | 3 | 4 | 5 | 6 | $7^1$ |  | 13 | 9 |  | 10 | 12 | $8^3$ |  |  | 2 | 14 |  |  |  |  |  |  |  |  |  |  |  |  |  |  |  | 15 |
| 1 | 10 | 3 | 4 |  | 6 | 12 |  | 9 | $11^2$ |  | 5 | 8 | $7^1$ |  |  | 2 |  |  |  |  |  |  |  | 13 |  |  |  |  |  |  |  |  | 16 |
| 1 | 10 | 3 | 4 | 5 | 6 |  |  | 12 | 11 |  | $9^1$ | 8 | 7 |  |  | 2 |  |  |  |  |  |  |  |  |  |  |  |  |  |  |  |  | 17 |
| 1 | $6^2$ | 4 | 3 | $5^3$ | 13 | $7^1$ |  | 12 |  | 14 |  | 8 |  |  |  | 2 |  |  |  |  |  |  |  |  |  | 9 | 10 | 11 |  |  |  |  | 18 |
| 1 | $8^3$ | 3 | 4 |  | 13 | $6^2$ |  | 5 | 14 |  | 12 |  | $7^1$ |  |  | 2 |  |  |  |  |  |  |  |  |  | 10 | 9 | 11 |  |  |  |  | 19 |
| 1 | 2 | 3 | 4 | 5 | 12 |  | 9 | 8 | $11^1$ |  | 13 |  | $7^2$ |  |  |  |  |  |  |  |  |  |  |  |  |  | 6 | 10 |  |  |  |  | 20 |
| 1 | 2 | 3 |  | 5 | 13 |  | 9 | 6 | $10^1$ | 12 |  | 8 | 4 |  |  |  |  |  |  |  |  |  |  |  |  |  |  | $11^2$ | 7 |  |  |  | 21 |
| 1 | 2 | 3 |  | 5 |  |  | 9 | $6^2$ | $10^1$ | 12 | 13 | 7 | 4 |  |  |  |  |  |  |  |  |  |  |  |  |  |  | 11 | 8 |  |  |  | 22 |
| 1 | 2 | 3 | 13 | 5 | 14 |  | 9 | 6 | $11^1$ | 12 | 8 | 4 | $7^2$ |  |  |  |  |  |  |  |  |  |  |  |  |  |  | $10^3$ |  |  |  |  | 23 |
| 1 | $2^3$ | 3 |  | 5 |  |  | 9 | 6 | $10^2$ | 13 | 14 | 7 | 4 |  |  |  |  |  |  |  |  |  |  |  |  |  |  | $11^1$ | 8 | 12 |  |  | 24 |
| $1^1$ | $2^2$ | 3 |  | 4 | 9 |  | 5 | 6 | 13 | 11 |  |  | 12 |  |  |  |  |  |  |  |  |  |  |  |  |  |  | 7 | 10 |  |  |  | 25 |
|  | 2 | 3 |  | 5 | 6 |  | 12 | 8 | $9^2$ | 13 | 11 |  | 7 | $4^1$ |  |  |  |  |  |  |  |  |  |  |  |  |  | 10 | 1 |  |  |  | 26 |
|  | 2 | 4 |  | 5 | 9 |  | 13 | $8^2$ | 6 | 12 | $11^1$ |  | 3 | 7 |  |  |  |  |  |  |  |  |  |  |  |  |  | $10^3$ | 1 | 14 |  |  | 27 |
|  | 2 | 3 |  | 5 | 6 |  | 14 | $7^1$ | 9 | 13 | 10 |  | 12 |  |  |  |  |  |  |  |  |  |  |  |  |  |  | $11^2$ | 4 | 1 |  | $8^3$ | 28 |
|  | 2 | 3 |  | 5 | 6 |  | 13 |  | 9 | 14 | $11^3$ |  | $8^2$ | 12 |  |  |  |  |  |  |  |  |  |  |  |  |  | 10 | 1 | $4^1$ |  | 7 | 29 |
|  |  | 3 |  | 4 | $6^1$ |  | $7^3$ | 5 | 9 | 14 | 13 | $10^2$ | 12 |  |  |  | 2 |  |  |  |  |  |  |  |  |  |  | 11 | 1 |  |  | 8 | 30 |
|  |  | 4 |  | 12 |  | $10^1$ | 5 | 6 | 13 | 8 |  | 7 |  | 2 |  |  |  |  |  |  |  |  |  |  |  |  |  | 11 | 1 | $3^2$ |  | 9 | 31 |
| 1 |  | 3 |  | 6 | 7 | 13 | $5^1$ | 9 |  | 11 | 12 |  | 4 |  |  |  | 2 |  |  |  |  |  |  |  |  |  |  | $10^2$ |  |  |  | 8 | 32 |
| 1 | 13 | 3 |  | 5 | 6 | $7^1$ | 12 |  | $9^2$ |  | 11 | 10 |  | 4 |  |  | 2 |  |  |  |  |  |  |  |  |  |  |  |  | 14 |  | 8 | 33 |
| 1 | 13 | 3 |  | 5 | 7 | $6^1$ | 14 |  | 8 |  | $11^3$ | 12 |  | 4 |  |  | $2^2$ |  |  |  |  |  |  |  |  |  |  | 10 |  |  |  | 9 | 34 |
| 1 | 2 | 4 |  | $5^1$ | 7 | $6^2$ | 13 | 12 | 8 |  |  | 10 |  | 3 |  |  |  |  |  |  |  |  |  |  |  |  |  | 11 |  |  |  | 9 | 35 |
| 1 | 2 | 3 |  | 5 | 13 |  | $9^3$ | 10 | 14 | 12 |  | $8^2$ | $6^1$ | 4 |  |  |  |  |  |  |  |  |  |  |  |  |  | 11 |  |  |  | 7 | 36 |

# DUMBARTON

*Year Formed:* 1872. *Ground:* Bet Butler Stadium, Castle Road, Dumbarton G82 1JJ. *Telephone/Fax:* 01389 762569.
*E-mail:* enquiries@dumbartonfc.com *Website:* www.dumbartonfootballclub.com
*Ground Capacity:* total: 2,025. *Size of Pitch:* 104m × 69m.
*Chairman:* Alan Jardine. *Club Secretary:* David Prophet. *Chief Executive Officer:* Gilbert Lawrie.
*Player-Manager:* Ian Murray. *Assistant Manager:* Jack Ross. *Physio:* Ahmed Habib.
*Club Nickname:* 'The Sons'.
*Previous Grounds:* Broadmeadow, Ropework Lane, Townend Ground, Boghead Park, Cliftonhill Stadium.
*Record Attendance:* 18,000 v Raith Rovers, Scottish Cup, 2 Mar 1957.
*Record Transfer Fee received:* £125,000 for Graeme Sharp to Everton (March 1982).
*Record Transfer Fee paid:* £50,000 for Charlie Gibson from Stirling Albion (1989).
*Record Victory:* 13-1 v Kirkintilloch Central, Scottish Cup 1st rd, 1 Sept 1888.
*Record Defeat:* 1-11 v Albion Rovers, Division II, 30 Jan 1926: v Ayr United, League Cup, 13 Aug 1952.
*Most Capped Player:* James McAulay, 9, Scotland.
*Most League Appearances:* 297: Andy Jardine, 1957-67.
*Most Goals in Season (Individual):* 38: Kenny Wilson, Division II, 1971-72. *(League and Cup):* 46 Hughie Gallacher, 1955-56.
*Most Goals Overall (Individual):* 202: Hughie Gallacher, 1954-62

## DUMBARTON – SCOTTISH FIRST DIVISION 2012–13 LEAGUE RECORD

| Match No. | Date | Venue | Opponents | Result | H/T Score | Lg Pos. | Goalscorers | Attendance |
|---|---|---|---|---|---|---|---|---|
| 1 | Aug 11 | A | Airdrie U | L 1-4 | 0-3 | 9 | Lister [62] | 897 |
| 2 | 18 | H | Cowdenbeath | L 0-3 | 0-2 | 10 | | 695 |
| 3 | 25 | A | Partick Th | L 0-3 | 0-1 | 10 | | 2944 |
| 4 | Sept 1 | A | Greenock Morton | L 0-3 | 0-1 | 10 | | 1602 |
| 5 | 15 | H | Dunfermline Ath | L 0-2 | 0-1 | 10 | | 1021 |
| 6 | 22 | H | Hamilton A | D 3-3 | 1-1 | 10 | Kilday (og) [34], Lister [73], Prunty [77] | 695 |
| 7 | 29 | A | Livingston | L 0-5 | 0-3 | 10 | | 1021 |
| 8 | Oct 6 | A | Raith R | D 2-2 | 0-1 | 10 | Lister [52], Prunty [90] | 1425 |
| 9 | 20 | H | Falkirk | L 0-2 | 0-2 | 10 | | 1041 |
| 10 | 27 | H | Airdrie U | L 3-4 | 2-0 | 10 | Prunty [23], Lister [27], McDougall [75] | 774 |
| 11 | Nov 10 | A | Cowdenbeath | W 1-0 | 1-0 | 10 | Gilhaney [29] | 415 |
| 12 | 17 | H | Greenock Morton | L 1-5 | 0-3 | 10 | Prunty [84] | 1188 |
| 13 | 24 | A | Dunfermline Ath | L 0-4 | 0-2 | 10 | | 3565 |
| 14 | Dec 29 | A | Falkirk | W 4-3 | 1-1 | 10 | Lister 2 [45, 79], Agnew 2 (1 pen) [67 (p), 76] | 3097 |
| 15 | Jan 2 | A | Greenock Morton | W 3-0 | 2-0 | 10 | Fleming [32], Agnew [39], Prunty [79] | 2414 |
| 16 | 5 | H | Dunfermline Ath | L 0-1 | 0-1 | 10 | | 1043 |
| 17 | 12 | H | Partick Th | W 2-0 | 1-0 | 10 | Balatoni (og) [21], Prunty [63] | 1530 |
| 18 | 19 | A | Airdrie U | W 2-1 | 2-1 | 10 | McCusker [24], Lister [33] | 844 |
| 19 | 26 | A | Hamilton A | W 3-1 | 1-0 | 8 | Turner [34], Gilhaney [56], Page (og) [90] | 878 |
| 20 | Feb 2 | H | Livingston | L 3-4 | 0-1 | 8 | Gilhaney [71], Lithgow [90], Prunty [90] | 744 |
| 21 | 9 | A | Livingston | W 3-2 | 2-2 | 8 | Prunty [4], Graham, Andrew [23], Agnew (pen) [69] | 1170 |
| 22 | 16 | A | Raith R | L 2-3 | 1-1 | 9 | Prunty 2 [45, 58] | 1304 |
| 23 | 23 | H | Falkirk | L 0-2 | 0-2 | 9 | | 997 |
| 24 | Mar 2 | H | Cowdenbeath | D 2-2 | 0-1 | 9 | Prunty [66], Agnew [84] | 742 |
| 25 | 9 | A | Partick Th | L 0-3 | 0-1 | 9 | | 2715 |
| 26 | 16 | H | Greenock Morton | L 0-3 | 0-2 | 9 | | 1241 |
| 27 | 23 | A | Dunfermline Ath | W 4-3 | 0-1 | 9 | McDougall 2 [51, 84], Turner [59], Agnew [65] | 3409 |
| 28 | 27 | H | Raith R | W 4-2 | 1-2 | 8 | Lister 3 [36, 64, 84], Agnew (pen) [70] | 483 |
| 29 | 30 | A | Hamilton A | W 3-2 | 1-0 | 7 | McDougall [24], Agnew [48], McGinn [84] | 943 |
| 30 | Apr 2 | A | Hamilton A | L 1-2 | 1-0 | 8 | Lister [12] | 775 |
| 31 | 6 | H | Livingston | L 0-3 | 0-1 | 8 | | 705 |
| 32 | 9 | H | Raith R | L 1-2 | 0-1 | 7 | Gilhaney [70] | 553 |
| 33 | 16 | A | Falkirk | W 3-1 | 2-1 | 7 | Gilhaney [19], Fleming 2 [21, 65] | 2288 |
| 34 | 20 | H | Airdrie U | W 4-1 | 2-0 | 7 | Graham, Andrew [6], McGinn [43], McDougall [48], Agnew [74] | 828 |
| 35 | 27 | A | Cowdenbeath | W 3-2 | 3-1 | 7 | Agnew 2 (1 pen) [35, 44 (p)], Lister [39] | 659 |
| 36 | May 4 | H | Partick Th | D 0-0 | 0-0 | 7 | | 1528 |

**Final League Position: 7**

**Honours**

*League Champions:* Division I 1890-91 (shared with Rangers), 1891-92. Division II 1910-11, 1971-72. Second Division 1991-92. Third Division 2008-09;
*Runners-up:* First Division 1983-84. Division II 1907-08. Second Division 1994-95. Third Division 2001-02.
*Scottish Cup Winners:* 1883; *Runners-up:* 1881, 1882, 1887, 1891, 1897.

**Club colours:** Shirt: White with yellow and black horizontal stripe. Shorts: White. Socks: White.

**Goalscorers:** *League (58):* Lister 12, Agnew 11 (4 pens), Prunty 11, Gilhaney 5, McDougall 5, Fleming 3, Graham, Andrew 2, McGinn 2, Turner 2, Lithgow 1, McCusker 1, own goals 3.
*William Hill Scottish FA Cup (5):* Graham, Andrew 1, Lister 1, Lithgow 1, Prunty 1, Turner 1.
*Scottish Communities League Cup (4):* Lister 2, Gilhaney 1, Prunty 1.
*Ramsdens Cup (0).*

| Grindlay S 22+2 | Graham Andrew 30 | Lithgow A 29+2 | Creaney J 18+6 | McNiff M 8+1 | Johnston P 4+6 | Fleming G 26+2 | Agnew S 33+3 | McDougall S 24+6 | Prunty B 22+12 | Lister J 30+4 | Gilhaney M 30+3 | Lamont M 11+12 | Devlin N 15+1 | Forsyth R 9+6 | Forbes R 1 | Metcalf R —+2 | Turner C 28 | Ewings J 14+1 | Lyden J —+1 | McCusker M 1+8 | Smith S 19 | Thomson G —+1 | McGinn P 14 | Urquhart S 3 | Phinn N 3+3 | Ronald O —+6 | Winters R 1+2 | Asghar A 1+2 | Horne J —+1 | Match No. |
|---|---|---|---|---|---|---|---|---|---|---|---|---|---|---|---|---|---|---|---|---|---|---|---|---|---|---|---|---|---|---|
| 1 | 2 | 3 | 4 | 5 | $6^2$ | 7 | 8 | 9 | $10^1$ | 11 | 12 | 13 | | | | | | | | | | | | | | | | | | 1 |
| 1 | 4 | 3 | | 13 | | 7 | 8 | 11 | 12 | $10^1$ | 6 | $9^2$ | 2 | 5 | | | | | | | | | | | | | | | | 2 |
| 1 | 3 | 4 | 14 | | 12 | 6 | 13 | 8 | $11^1$ | 7 | $10^2$ | | 2 | $5^3$ | 9 | | | | | | | | | | | | | | | 3 |
| 1 | 4 | 3 | 5 | 12 | 14 | $6^1$ | 8 | $9^3$ | 11 | 10 | $7^2$ | 13 | 2 | | | | | | | | | | | | | | | | | 4 |
| 1 | | 3 | $5^3$ | 4 | 13 | 7 | $8^1$ | 9 | 11 | 10 | $6^2$ | 12 | 2 | 14 | | | | | | | | | | | | | | | | 5 |
| 1 | 4 | 3 | $10^1$ | | | $7^2$ | 8 | 12 | 13 | $11^3$ | 9 | 6 | 2 | 5 | | 14 | | | | | | | | | | | | | | 6 |
| 1 | | 3 | 13 | $5^2$ | 12 | 6 | 8 | 14 | $10^1$ | 11 | | $9^3$ | 2 | 4 | | | 7 | | | | | | | | | | | | | 7 |
| | 2 | 3 | | $4^2$ | 6 | 10 | 8 | | 13 | 11 | 12 | $9^1$ | | 5 | | | 7 | 1 | | | | | | | | | | | | 8 |
| | 2 | 3 | | $4^2$ | $6^1$ | 10 | 8 | | 13 | 11 | 12 | 9 | | 5 | | | 7 | 1 | | | | | | | | | | | | 9 |
| | 2 | 4 | $5^3$ | | 6 | 7 | 12 | $10^2$ | 11 | 9 | 13 | 14 | 3 | | | | $8^1$ | 1 | | | | | | | | | | | | 10 |
| | 3 | | 5 | 4 | | 7 | $9^1$ | $11^2$ | 10 | 6 | 12 | 2 | | | | | 8 | 1 | 13 | | | | | | | | | | | 11 |
| | 3 | | 5 | 4 | 13 | $6^3$ | 7 | $10^1$ | 9 | $11^2$ | 8 | 12 | 2 | 14 | | | | 1 | | | | | | | | | | | | 12 |
| $1^4$ | 4 | 3 | $5^2$ | | 8 | 12 | 9 | $11^3$ | $6^1$ | 10 | 2 | 13 | | | | | 7 | 14 | | | | | | | | | | | | 13 |
| | 3 | 4 | $5^4$ | | 7 | $7^1$ | 8 | $11^2$ | 12 | $10^3$ | 9 | | 2 | 13 | | | 6 | 1 | | 14 | | | | | | | | | | 14 |
| | 3 | 4 | $10^1$ | | 8 | 9 | 12 | $11^2$ | $6^3$ | 14 | 2 | | | 5 | | | 7 | 1 | | 13 | | | | | | | | | | 15 |
| | 3 | 4 | $10^1$ | | 8 | $9^3$ | 13 | 11 | 6 | 2 | 5 | | | | | | 7 | 1 | | 12 | | | | | | | | | | 16 |
| 12 | 3 | 4 | 13 | | 8 | 9 | $10^3$ | $11^2$ | 6 | 2 | | | | | | | 7 | $1^1$ | | 14 | 5 | | | | | | | | | 17 |
| | 3 | 4 | 9 | | 8 | 12 | 10 | 6 | 2 | 13 | | | | | | | 7 | 1 | | $11^1$ | $5^2$ | | | | | | | | | 18 |
| | 3 | 4 | $9^2$ | | 8 | 10 | $11^1$ | 6 | 12 | 2 | 13 | | | | | | $7^3$ | 1 | | | 5 | 14 | | | | | | | | 19 |
| | 3 | 4 | 12 | | 8 | 11 | 10 | 6 | $9^1$ | 2 | | | | | | | $7^2$ | 1 | | 13 | 5 | 2 | | | | | | | | 20 |
| 14 | 4 | 3 | 13 | | 11 | 8 | $10^2$ | 12 | $6^4$ | $9^1$ | | | | | | | 7 | $1^3$ | | | 5 | 2 | | | | | | | | 21 |
| 1 | | 3 | $6^2$ | 8 | 12 | 11 | 10 | $9^1$ | 14 | | | | | | | | | | | 14 | 5 | | 2 | 4 | $7^3$ | 13 | | | | 22 |
| 1 | $3^2$ | 14 | $10^1$ | 8 | $9^3$ | 11 | 6 | 7 | 13 | | | | | | | | | | | 13 | 5 | | 2 | 4 | 12 | | 13 | | | 23 |
| 1 | | 4 | 7 | $9^1$ | $11^2$ | 10 | 6 | 8 | | | | | | | | | 8 | | | | 5 | | 2 | 3 | 12 | | | $11^1$ | | 24 |
| 1 | 3 | 4 | $5^2$ | $7^3$ | 12 | 10 | 13 | 6 | | | | | | | | | 8 | | | 14 | 9 | | 2 | | 13 | | 12 | | | 25 |
| 1 | 3 | 4 | | 11 | 8 | 9 | $10^1$ | 6 | | | | | | | | | $7^2$ | | | | 5 | | 2 | | 13 | | 12 | | | 26 |
| 1 | 3 | | 5 | | 7 | 9 | $11^2$ | 12 | 6 | 13 | | | | | | | 8 | | | | 4 | | 2 | | $10^1$ | | | | | 27 |
| 1 | 3 | 12 | 5 | | 8 | $9^3$ | $10^1$ | $11^3$ | 6 | 13 | | | | | | | 7 | | | | 4 | | 2 | | | 14 | | | | 28 |
| 1 | 4 | | 5 | | 7 | $9^2$ | 12 | 10 | 6 | | | | | | | | 8 | | | | 3 | | 2 | | $11^1$ | 13 | | | | 29 |
| 1 | 3 | 12 | 5 | | 8 | $9^1$ | $10^3$ | 11 | 6 | | | | | | | | 7 | | | | 4 | | $2^2$ | | 13 | | 14 | | | 30 |
| 1 | 3 | 4 | $5^2$ | | 8 | $11^1$ | 12 | $10^2$ | 6 | 9 | | 14 | | | | | 7 | | | | | | 2 | | | | 2 | 13 | | 31 |
| 1 | 3 | 4 | $5^2$ | | $8^1$ | 6 | 12 | 11 | 10 | 9 | | | | | | | 7 | | | | 2 | | | | 13 | | | | | 32 |
| 1 | 3 | 4 | 5 | | $8^2$ | 6 | $11^1$ | 12 | 10 | 9 | 13 | | | | | | 7 | | | | 2 | | | | | | | | | 33 |
| 1 | 3 | $4^3$ | 14 | | $10^1$ | 8 | 9 | 12 | 11 | $6^2$ | 13 | | | | | | 7 | | | | 5 | | 2 | | | | | | | 34 |
| 1 | 3 | $4^2$ | 13 | | $10^1$ | 8 | 9 | 12 | 11 | 6 | | | | | | | 7 | | | | 5 | | 2 | | | | | | | 35 |
| | $3^1$ | | 5 | | $11^2$ | 8 | 9 | 10 | 13 | 6 | | | | | | | $7^3$ | 1 | | | 4 | | 2 | | 12 | | 14 | | | 36 |

# DUNDEE

*Year Formed:* 1893. *Ground & Address:* Dens Park Stadium, Sandeman St, Dundee DD3 7JY. *Telephone:* 01382 889966.
*Fax:* 01382 832284. *E-mail:* laura@dundeefc.co.uk *Website:* www.dundeefc.co.uk
*Ground Capacity:* 12,085 (all seated). *Size of Pitch:* 101m × 66m.
*Chief Executive:* Scot Gardiner. *Club Secretary:* Laura Hayes.
*Manager:* John Brown. *Assistant Manager:* Ray Farningham. *Youth Development Coach:* Gordon Wallace.
*Physio:* Karen Gibson.
*Club Nicknames:* 'The Dark Blues' or 'The Dee'.
*Previous Grounds:* Carolina Port 1893-98.
*Record Attendance:* 43,024 v Rangers, Scottish Cup 2nd rd, 7 Feb 1953.
*Record Transfer Fee received:* £1,200,000 for Robert Douglas to Celtic (2000).
*Record Transfer Fee paid:* £600,000 for Fabian Caballero from Sol de América (Paraguay) (July 2000).
*Record Victory:* 10-0 Division II v Alloa, 9 Mar 1947 and v Dunfermline Ath, 22 Mar 1947.
*Record Defeat:* 0-11 v Celtic, Division I, 26 Oct 1895.
*Most Capped Player:* Alex Hamilton, 24, Scotland.
*Most League Appearances:* 400: Barry Smith, 1995-2006.
*Most League Goals in Season (Individual):* 52: Alan Gilzean, 1960-64.
*Most Goals Overall (Individual):* 113: Alan Gilzean 1960-64.

## DUNDEE – SCOTTISH PREMIER LEAGUE 2012–13 LEAGUE RECORD

| Match No. | Date | | Venue | Opponents | Result | | H/T Score | Lg Pos. | Goalscorers | Atten- dance |
|---|---|---|---|---|---|---|---|---|---|---|
| 1 | Aug | 4 | A | Kilmarnock | D | 0-0 | 0-0 | 5 | | 6523 |
| 2 | | 11 | H | St Mirren | L | 0-2 | 0-1 | 11 | | 5984 |
| 3 | | 19 | A | Dundee U | L | 0-3 | 0-3 | 12 | | 13,538 |
| 4 | | 25 | H | Ross Co | L | 0-1 | 0-0 | 12 | | 4905 |
| 5 | Sept | 2 | A | Hearts | W | 1-0 | 1-0 | 10 | Conroy (pen) [3] | 12,446 |
| 6 | | 15 | H | Motherwell | L | 1-2 | 1-0 | 12 | Nish [20] | 5176 |
| 7 | | 22 | A | Celtic | L | 0-2 | 0-1 | 12 | | 41,073 |
| 8 | | 29 | H | St Johnstone | L | 1-3 | 1-2 | 12 | Conroy (pen) [22] | 6158 |
| 9 | Oct | 6 | A | Hibernian | L | 0-3 | 0-1 | 12 | | 10,163 |
| 10 | | 19 | H | Inverness CT | L | 1-4 | 1-2 | 12 | Nish [13] | 5006 |
| 11 | | 27 | A | Aberdeen | L | 0-2 | 0-1 | 12 | | 10,425 |
| 12 | Nov | 3 | H | Hearts | W | 1-0 | 1-0 | 12 | Lockwood [22] | 5344 |
| 13 | | 10 | A | Motherwell | D | 1-1 | 1-1 | 12 | Riley [28] | 4318 |
| 14 | | 17 | H | Hibernian | W | 3-1 | 1-0 | 12 | Benedictus [21], Milne [47], McBride (pen) [52] | 6743 |
| 15 | | 24 | A | St Mirren | L | 1-3 | 0-1 | 12 | Conroy (pen) [64] | 4825 |
| 16 | Dec | 9 | H | Dundee U | L | 0-3 | 0-1 | 12 | | 11,419 |
| 17 | | 15 | A | Ross Co | D | 1-1 | 1-0 | 12 | Davidson [37] | 3129 |
| 18 | | 22 | A | Inverness CT | L | 1-4 | 1-2 | 12 | Riley [19] | 3003 |
| 19 | | 26 | H | Celtic | L | 0-2 | 0-1 | 12 | | 9276 |
| 20 | | 29 | H | Aberdeen | L | 1-3 | 0-0 | 12 | Stewart [82] | 9013 |
| 21 | Jan | 2 | A | St Johnstone | L | 0-1 | 0-1 | 12 | | 5055 |
| 22 | | 19 | A | Hibernian | D | 1-1 | 1-0 | 12 | Baird, J [8] | 10,386 |
| 23 | | 27 | H | Kilmarnock | D | 0-0 | 0-0 | 12 | | 4782 |
| 24 | | 30 | A | Hearts | L | 0-1 | 0-0 | 12 | | 11,284 |
| 25 | Feb | 8 | H | Ross Co | L | 0-2 | 0-0 | 12 | | 4726 |
| 26 | | 15 | A | Aberdeen | L | 0-1 | 0-1 | 12 | | 7841 |
| 27 | | 24 | A | Celtic | L | 0-5 | 0-1 | 12 | | 39,959 |
| 28 | | 27 | H | St Johnstone | D | 2-2 | 1-1 | 12 | Baird, J [42], Stewart [89] | 5224 |
| 29 | Mar | 6 | H | St Mirren | W | 2-1 | 0-1 | 12 | Baird, J [68], McAlister [78] | 3674 |
| 30 | | 9 | H | Inverness CT | D | 1-1 | 1-0 | 12 | Baird, J [13] | 4114 |
| 31 | | 17 | A | Dundee U | D | 1-1 | 0-0 | 12 | Conroy [67] | 10,731 |
| 32 | | 30 | H | Motherwell | L | 0-3 | 0-1 | 12 | | 4838 |
| 33 | Apr. | 6 | A | Kilmarnock | W | 2-1 | 1-0 | 12 | Harkins 2 [6, 77] | 4966 |
| 34 | | 20 | A | St Mirren | W | 2-1 | 1-0 | 12 | McAlister [40], Finnigan [82] | 4002 |
| 35 | | 27 | H | Hearts | W | 1-0 | 0-0 | 12 | Conroy [82] | 5896 |
| 36 | May | 5 | H | Aberdeen | D | 1-1 | 1-0 | 12 | McAlister [20] | 6441 |
| 37 | | 11 | A | Kilmarnock | L | 2-3 | 1-1 | 12 | Conroy [19], Stewart [83] | 4190 |
| 38 | | 18 | A | Hibernian | L | 0-1 | 0-0 | 12 | | 9522 |

**Final League Position: 12 – Relegated to Scottish First Division**

**Honours**
*League Champions:* Division I 1961-62. First Division 1978-79, 1991-92, 1997-98. Division II 1946-47;
*Runners-up:* Division I 1902-03, 1906-07, 1908-09, 1948-49. First Division 1980-81, 2007-08, 2009-10, 2011-12.
*Scottish Cup Winners:* 1910; *Runners-up:* 1925, 1952, 1964, 2003.
*League Cup Winners:* 1951-52, 1952-53, 1973-74; *Runners-up:* 1967-68, 1980-81, 1995-96.
*League Challenge Cup Winners:* 1990–91, 2009-10.
*B&Q (Centenary) Cup Winners:* 1990-91; *Runners-up:* 1994-95.

**European:** *European Cup:* 8 matches (1962-63 semi-finals). *Cup Winners' Cup:* 2 matches: (1964-65).
*UEFA Cup:* 22 matches: (*Fairs Cup:* 1967-68 semi-finals. *UEFA Cup:* 1971-72, 1973-74, 1974-75, 2003-04).

**Club colours:** Shirt: Navy blue with one white and one red band. Shorts: White. Socks: Navy blue.

**Goalscorers:** *League (28):* Conroy 6 (3 pens), Baird J 4, McAlister 3, Stewart 3, Harkins 2, Nish 2, Riley 2, Benedictus 1, Davidson 1, Finnigan 1, Lockwood 1, McBride 1 (1 pen), Milne 1.
*William Hill Scottish FA Cup (8):* McAlister 2, Baird J 1, Conroy 1 (1 pen), Gallagher 1, Milne 1, Nish 1, Toshney 1.
*Scottish Communities League Cup (1):* Milne 1.

| Douglas R 30 | Irvine G 34 | Benedictus K 24+3 | McGregor N 5 | Lockwood M 21+2 | McAlister J 38 | Davidson J 35+1 | McBride K 20+4 | Conroy R 19+14 | Baird J 29+8 | Stewart M 5+10 | Webster G —+3 | Grassi D 10+1 | O'Donnell S 6 | McIntosh L —+1 | Riley N 19+9 | Boyle M 1+8 | Nish C 21+3 | Toshney L 20+3 | Milne S 11+13 | Kerr M 6+2 | Easton B 17 | Gallagher D 24 | Harkins G 14 | Morgan D —+1 | Finnigan C 1+7 | Simonsen S 8 | Cowan D —+2 | Barrowman A —+1 | Thomson J —+1 | Match No. |
|---|---|---|---|---|---|---|---|---|---|---|---|---|---|---|---|---|---|---|---|---|---|---|---|---|---|---|---|---|---|---|
| 1 | 2 | 3 | 4 | 5 | 6 | 7 | 8¹ | 9 | 10 | 11 | 12 | | | | | | | | | | | | | | | | | | | 1 |
| 1 | 2 | 4 | | 3 | 6 | 8 | | 9 | 10 | 11¹ | 13 | 5 | 7² | 12 | | | | | | | | | | | | | | | | 2 |
| 1 | 2 | 4 | | 5 | 6² | 8 | | 9 | 10¹ | 12 | 14 | 3 | 7⁸ | | 11³ | 13 | | | | | | | | | | | | | | 3 |
| 1 | 2 | 3¹ | 4 | | 7 | 9 | | 6 | 14 | 11² | | 5 | 8 | | | 13 | 10 | 12³ | | | | | | | | | | | | 4 |
| 1 | 2 | | 3 | 5 | 8 | 7 | | 9 | 10 | | | 4 | | | | 11¹ | 6 | 12 | | | | | | | | | | | | 5 |
| 1 | 2 | 12 | 3 | 5 | 6 | 8¹ | | 9 | 11² | 13 | | | | | 14 | 10 | 4 | | 7³ | | | | | | | | | | | 6 |
| 1 | 2 | 3 | | 5 | 7 | 4 | | 9 | 10² | | | | | 13 | 12 | 11 | | 6¹ | 8 | | | | | | | | | | | 7 |
| 1 | 2 | 13 | | 4 | 6 | 8 | | 5 | 11¹ | | | | | 12 | 9 | 10 | 3² | | 7 | | | | | | | | | | | 8 |
| 1 | 2 | 4 | | 6 | 9³ | 7¹ | 10 | | | 3 | | | | 12 | 14 | 11² | | 13 | 8 | 5 | | | | | | | | | | 9 |
| 1 | 2 | | 3 | 5² | 9 | 7 | | 13 | 12 | | 4 | | | 6 | | 10 | | 11¹ | 8 | | | | | | | | | | | 10 |
| 1 | 2 | 3 | | 12 | 11 | 7 | 8 | 9 | 14 | | | | | 6³ | | 10² | | 13 | | 5¹ | 4 | | | | | | | | | 11 |
| 1 | 2 | 5 | | 3 | 9 | 8 | 7 | 13 | 12 | | | | | 6 | | 11¹ | | 10² | | | 4 | | | | | | | | | 12 |
| 1 | 2 | 4 | | 5 | 9 | 8 | 7 | 12 | 13 | | | | | 6¹ | | 10 | | 11² | | | 3 | | | | | | | | | 13 |
| 1 | 2 | 4 | | 5 | 9 | 8 | 7 | 13 | 12 | | | | | 6² | | 11³ | 14 | 10¹ | | | 3 | | | | | | | | | 14 |
| 1 | 2 | 4 | | | 9 | 7 | 8 | 5 | 12 | | | | | 6² | 13 | 10⁸ | | 11¹ | | | 3 | | | | | | | | | 15 |
| 1 | 2 | 3 | | 5 | 9 | 7 | 8 | | 11 | | | | | 6 | 12 | | | 10¹ | | | 4 | | | | | | | | | 16 |
| 1 | 2 | 3¹ | | 5 | 6 | 8 | 7 | 13 | 10³ | 14 | | | | 9² | | 11 | 12 | | | | 4 | | | | | | | | | 17 |
| 1 | 2 | 4 | | 3 | 9 | 7 | 8 | 13 | 11¹ | 12 | | | | 6² | | 10 | | | | | 5 | | | | | | | | | 18 |
| 1 | 2 | 4 | | 3 | 6 | | 8 | 9 | 10¹ | 12 | | 7² | | | 13 | 11 | | | | | 5 | | | | | | | | | 19 |
| 1 | 2 | 3 | | 5 | 9 | 12 | 8² | 13 | 11 | 14 | | 7¹ | | 6³ | | 10 | | | | | 4 | | | | | | | | | 20 |
| 1 | 2 | | | 9 | 8 | 12 | | 14 | 13 | | | 7¹ | | 6 | | 10² | 5 | 11³ | | 4 | 3 | | | | | | | | | 21 |
| 1 | 2 | | | 7 | 8 | | 12 | 6 | 10 | | | | | | 11 | 3 | 9¹ | | | 5 | 4 | | | | | | | | | 22 |
| 1 | 2 | | | 8 | 7 | | | 13 | 9 | 6² | | | | 12 | | 11 | 3 | 10¹ | | | 5 | 4 | | | | | | | | 23 |
| 1 | 2 | | | 9 | 7 | 12 | | 10 | | | | | | 6¹ | | 11 | 3 | | | | 5 | 4 | 8 | | | | | | | 24 |
| 1 | 2 | | | 10 | 6 | 7² | | 9 | 13 | | | | | 12 | | 11¹ | 3 | | | | 5 | 4 | 8 | | | | | | | 25 |
| 1 | 2 | | | 10 | 7 | | | 9¹ | 11 | | | | | 6 | | 12 | 3 | | | | 5 | 4 | 8 | | | | | | | 26 |
| 1 | 2 | 3 | | 12⁸ | 7 | 8 | 13 | 9 | 11 | | | | | 6³ | | | | | | | 5¹ | 4 | 10² | 14 | | | | | | 27 |
| 1 | 2 | 3 | | | 7 | 8 | | 9 | 11² | 13 | | 12 | | 6¹ | | 14 | 5 | | | | 4⁸ | 10³ | | | | | | | | 28 |
| 1 | 2 | | | 10 | 6 | 7¹ | 13 | 9³ | | 4 | | | | 12 | | | 3 | 11² | | 5 | | 8 | 14 | | | | | | | 29 |
| 1 | 2 | | | 8 | 7 | | 9 | 11 | | 4 | | | | 6 | | | 3 | | | 5 | | 10¹ | 12 | | | | | | | 30 |
| | | 2⁸ | 12 | | 8 | 7² | 13 | 9 | 11 | | | 4 | | 6¹ | | | 3 | | | 5 | | 10³ | | | 1 | 14 | | | | 31 |
| | 2 | | | 8 | 7 | | | 9¹ | 11² | | | 3 | | 6 | | | 4 | | | 5 | | 10 | | 12 | 1 | 13 | | | | 32 |
| | 2 | 5 | | 8 | 7 | 6 | | | 11¹ | | | | | | | 3 | | 13 | 9 | 4 | 10² | | | 1 | | 12 | | | 33 |
| | 2 | | | 3² | 8 | 7³ | 6 | 14 | 11¹ | | | | | 13 | | | 5 | | | 9 | 4 | 10 | | 12 | 1 | | | | 34 |
| | 3 | | | 2¹ | 7 | 9² | 8 | 12 | 11³ | | | | | | 14² | 13 | 5 | | | 6 | 4 | | | 10 | 1 | | | | 35 |
| | 2³ | | | 4¹ | 9 | 7 | 8 | 13 | 11² | | | | | | | 5 | | 14 | 6 | 3 | 10 | | | 12 | 1 | | | | 36 |
| | 2 | 3 | | | 6 | 7 | 8 | 9 | 11³ | 12 | | | | | | 5³ | | | | 4 | 10² | | 13 | 1 | | | 14 | | 37 |
| | 2 | 9 | | 5 | 6 | | 8 | 12 | 11 | | | | | 13 | | | 3² | | 7¹ | | 4³ | 10 | | 14 | 1 | | | | 38 |

# DUNDEE UNITED

*Year Formed:* 1909 (1923). *Ground & Address:* Tannadice Park, Tannadice St, Dundee DD3 7JW. *Telephone:* 01382 833166. *Fax:* 01382 889398. *E-mail:* enquiries@dundeeunited.co.uk *Website:* www.dundeeunitedfc.co.uk
*Ground Capacity:* 14,223 (all seated). *Size of Pitch:* 100m × 66m.
*Chairman:* Stephen Thompson, OBE. *Vice-Chair:* Cath Thompson. *Secretary:* Spence Anderson.
*Manager:* Jackie McNamara. *Assistant Manager:* Simon Donnelly. *First Team Coach:* Darren Jackson. *Physio:* Jeff Clarke.
*Club Nicknames:* 'The Terrors', 'The Arabs'.
*Previous Grounds:* None.
*Record Attendance:* 28,000 v Barcelona, Fairs Cup, 16 Nov 1966.
*Record Transfer Fee received:* £4,000,000 for Duncan Ferguson from Rangers (July 1993).
*Record Transfer Fee paid:* £750,000 for Steven Pressley from Coventry C (July 1995).
*Record Victory:* 14-0 v Nithsdale Wanderers, Scottish Cup 1st rd, 17 Jan 1931.
*Record Defeat:* 1-12 v Motherwell, Division II, 23 Jan 1954.
*Most Capped Player:* Maurice Malpas, 55, Scotland.
*Most League Appearances:* 618, Maurice Malpas, 1980-2000.
*Most Appearances in European Matches:* 76, Dave Narey (record for Scottish player).
*Most League Goals in Season (Individual):* 40: John Coyle, Division II, 1955-56.
*Most Goals Overall (Individual):* 199: Peter McKay, 1947-54.

## DUNDEE UNITED – SCOTTISH PREMIER LEAGUE 2012–13 LEAGUE RECORD

| Match No. | Date | Venue | Opponents | Result | H/T Score | Lg Pos. | Goalscorers | Attendance |
|---|---|---|---|---|---|---|---|---|
| 1 | Aug 5 | H | Hibernian | W 3-0 | 1-0 | 1 | Russell [3], Daly [74], Gardyne [90] | 7267 |
| 2 | 19 | H | Dundee | W 3-0 | 3-0 | 1 | Gunning [14], Russell 2 [35, 38] | 13,538 |
| 3 | 25 | A | Kilmarnock | L 1-3 | 0-0 | 3 | Daly [79] | 4516 |
| 4 | Sept 1 | A | St Johnstone | D 0-0 | 0-0 | 3 | | 5014 |
| 5 | 14 | H | Ross Co | D 0-0 | 0-0 | 2 | | 6892 |
| 6 | 22 | H | Hearts | L 0-3 | 0-2 | 7 | | 6597 |
| 7 | 29 | A | Inverness CT | L 0-4 | 0-2 | 11 | | 3059 |
| 8 | Oct 20 | H | Aberdeen | D 1-1 | 1-0 | 11 | Rankin [22] | 9858 |
| 9 | 27 | A | St Mirren | W 1-0 | 0-0 | 10 | Russell (pen) [69] | 4333 |
| 10 | Nov 4 | H | Celtic | D 2-2 | 0-0 | 10 | Mackay-Steven [89], Ambrose (og) [90] | 10,521 |
| 11 | 7 | A | Motherwell | W 1-0 | 0-0 | 7 | Russell [84] | 3941 |
| 12 | 11 | H | Hibernian | L 1-2 | 0-1 | 6 | Mackay-Steven [53] | 10,596 |
| 13 | 16 | H | Kilmarnock | D 3-3 | 0-2 | 8 | Mackay-Steven [48], Daly 2 [56, 90] | 6287 |
| 14 | 24 | A | Ross Co | W 2-1 | 0-0 | 7 | Russell [52], Armstrong [64] | 3930 |
| 15 | 27 | A | Motherwell | L 1-2 | 1-2 | 7 | Daly [37] | 5289 |
| 16 | Dec 9 | A | Dundee | W 3-0 | 1-0 | 7 | Watson [17], Daly (pen) [71], Flood [88] | 11,419 |
| 17 | 15 | H | Inverness CT | D 4-4 | 3-2 | 6 | Meekings (og) [5], Daly 2 (1 pen) [6, 90 (p)], Skacel [8] | 5483 |
| 18 | 23 | A | Hearts | L 1-2 | 0-2 | 8 | Watson [57] | 13,603 |
| 19 | 26 | H | St Johnstone | D 1-1 | 1-0 | 8 | Gunning [2] | 7063 |
| 20 | 30 | H | St Mirren | L 3-4 | 2-1 | 8 | Daly (pen) [43], Armstrong [45], Douglas [90] | 6386 |
| 21 | Jan 2 | A | Aberdeen | D 2-2 | 2-1 | 8 | Gunning [20], Langfield (og) [34] | 13,176 |
| 22 | 19 | A | Kilmarnock | W 3-2 | 1-1 | 7 | Russell 3 [43, 63, 88] | 4112 |
| 23 | 22 | A | Celtic | L 0-4 | 0-2 | 7 | | 42,596 |
| 24 | 26 | H | Ross Co | D 1-1 | 0-0 | 7 | Mackay-Steven [52] | 5117 |
| 25 | Feb 9 | H | Hearts | W 3-1 | 1-0 | 6 | Russell [2], Flood [62], Gardyne [89] | 6842 |
| 26 | 16 | A | Celtic | L 2-6 | 1-3 | 9 | Armstrong [10], Russell [90] | 46,496 |
| 27 | 19 | A | Motherwell | W 1-0 | 1-0 | 8 | Russell [17] | 4633 |
| 28 | 24 | H | Hibernian | D 2-2 | 1-1 | 9 | Rankin [6], Russell (pen) [86] | 6160 |
| 29 | 27 | A | Inverness CT | D 0-0 | 0-0 | 8 | | 3413 |
| 30 | Mar 9 | A | St Mirren | D 0-0 | 0-0 | 7 | | 3394 |
| 31 | 17 | H | Dundee | D 1-1 | 0-0 | 7 | Gardyne [89] | 10,731 |
| 32 | Apr 1 | A | St Johnstone | D 1-1 | 1-0 | 8 | Gauld [24] | 4613 |
| 33 | 6 | H | Aberdeen | W 1-0 | 0-0 | 6 | Boulding [90] | 8577 |
| 34 | 19 | H | Motherwell | L 1-3 | 0-2 | 6 | Daly [69] | 5634 |
| 35 | 26 | A | Ross Co | L 0-1 | 0-0 | 6 | | 3183 |
| 36 | May 4 | H | St Johnstone | L 0-1 | 0-1 | 6 | | 6437 |
| 37 | 11 | A | Inverness CT | W 2-1 | 0-1 | 6 | Dow [50], Mackay-Steven [90] | 3728 |
| 38 | 19 | H | Celtic | L 0-4 | 0-3 | 6 | | 8717 |

**Final League Position: 6**

**Honours**
*League Champions:* Premier Division 1982-83.
Division II 1924-25, 1928-29.
*Runners-up:* Division II 1930-31, 1959-60. First Division 1995-96. *Scottish Cup Winners:* 1994, 2010; *Runners-up:* 1974, 1981, 1985, 1987, 1988, 1991, 2005.
*League Cup Winners:* 1979-80, 1980-81; *Runners-up:* 1981-82, 1984-85, 1997-98, 2007-08.
*League Challenge Cup Runners-up:* 1995-96.

**European:** *European Cup:* 8 matches (1983-84, semi-finals). *Cup Winners' Cup:* 10 matches (1974-75, 1988-89, 1994-95). *UEFA Cup:* 86 matches (*Fairs Cup:* 1966-67, 1969-70, 1970-71. *UEFA Cup:* 1975-76, 1977-78, 1978-79, 1979-80, 1980-81, 1981-82, 1982-83, 1984-85, 1985-86, 1986-87 runners-up, 1987-88, 1989-90, 1990-91, 1993-94, 1997-98, 2005-06). *Europa League:* 6 matches (2010-2011, 2011-12, 2012-13).

**Club colours:** Shirt: Tangerine with black trim. Shorts: Black. Socks: Tangerine with black hoop.

**Goalscorers:** *League (51):* Russell 13 (2 pens), Daly 10 (3 pens), Mackay-Steven 5, Armstrong 3, Gardyne 3, Gunning 3, Flood 2, Rankin 2, Watson 2, Boulding 1, Douglas 1, Dow 1, Gauld 1, Skacel 1, own goals 3.
*William Hill Scottish FA Cup (13):* Daly 5, Russell 5, Mackay-Steven 2, McLean 1.
*Scottish Communities League Cup (2):* Russell 2.
*Europa League (2):* Flood 1, Gunning 1.

| Cierzniak R 38 | Watson K 29 | Dillon S 31 | Gunning G 25 | Douglas B 27 + 1 | Flood W 37 | Ryan R 12 + 10 | Rankin J 35 | Mackay-Steven G 19 + 4 | Daly J 35 + 1 | Russell J 30 + 2 | McLean B 25 + 4 | Gardyne M 10 + 20 | Armstrong S 30 + 6 | Dow R 3 + 9 | Gauld R 5 + 5 | Millar M 11 + 7 | Hilson D — + 1 | Skacel R 5 + 9 | Lecny M — + 2 | Souttar J 7 + 1 | Petrie D — + 1 | Boulding R 3 + 5 | Tornstrand M — + 1 | Thomson R — + 2 | Johnston L 1 + 1 | Match No. |
|---|---|---|---|---|---|---|---|---|---|---|---|---|---|---|---|---|---|---|---|---|---|---|---|---|---|---|
| 1 | 2 | $3^1$ | 4 | 5 | 6 | 7 | 8 | $9^3$ | 10 | $11^2$ | 12 | 13 | 14 | | | | | | | | | | | | | 1 |
| 1 | 2 | 3 | $4^2$ | 5 | 6 | 7 | 8 | | 11 | $10^4$ | 13 | $9^1$ | 12 | | | | | | | | | | | | | 2 |
| 1 | 3 | 2 | 4 | 5 | $7^3$ | $6^2$ | 8 | $9^1$ | 10 | 11 | 13 | 12 | 14 | | | | | | | | | | | | | 3 |
| 1 | $2^1$ | 3 | 4 | 5 | 6 | $8^2$ | 7 | | $10^3$ | 11 | 12 | 14 | 9 | 13 | | | | | | | | | | | | 4 |
| 1 | 5 | 2 | 4 | | 6 | | 8 | | 10 | 3 | 9 | 7 | $11^1$ | 12 | | | | | | | | | | | | 5 |
| 1 | 2 | 5 | 4 | | 6 | | 7 | 13 | 10 | 3 | $11^2$ | 8 | $9^1$ | 12 | | | | | | | | | | | | 6 |
| 1 | 5 | 3 | 4 | | 6 | $7^3$ | $8^1$ | 11 | 10 | 2 | 9 | 13 | 12 | 14 | | | | | | | | | | | | 7 |
| 1 | 4 | 2 | 3 | 5 | 13 | 7 | | | 10 | 11 | | $9^1$ | $8^3$ | 14 | $6^2$ | 12 | | | | | | | | | | 8 |
| 1 | 2 | 3 | 5 | | 7 | 12 | | 9 | 4 | 10 | $11^2$ | $8^3$ | 14 | | $6^1$ | | | 13 | | | | | | | | 9 |
| 1 | 2 | 3 | 4 | 5 | 6 | $7^1$ | 8 | 12 | 10 | $11^3$ | | $9^2$ | | | 14 | | | 13 | | | | | | | | 10 |
| 1 | 4 | 2 | 5 | | 6 | $8^1$ | $7^2$ | 12 | 11 | $10^3$ | 3 | 9 | | | 14 | | | 13 | | | | | | | | 11 |
| 1 | 2 | 3 | 4 | | 6 | | 8 | 12 | 11 | 10 | 5 | $9^2$ | | | $7^1$ | | | 13 | | | | | | | | 12 |
| 1 | | 3 | 4 | 5 | 7 | | $8^1$ | 9 | 11 | 10 | 2 | | 6 | | | 12 | | | | | | | | | | 13 |
| 1 | | 3 | 4 | 5 | 8 | 13 | $7^1$ | $9^2$ | 11 | $6^3$ | 2 | 14 | 10 | | | 12 | | | | | | | | | | 14 |
| 1 | | 3 | 4 | 5 | $8^2$ | 13 | $7^1$ | | 10 | 11 | 2 | 12 | 6 | | 9 | | | | | | | | | | | 15 |
| 1 | 2 | | 4 | 5 | 6 | 12 | 7 | | 10 | $11^2$ | 3 | 13 | 9 | | $8^1$ | | | | | | | | | | | 16 |
| 1 | 2 | | 4 | 5 | 7 | | 8 | | 10 | 11 | 3 | 12 | $6^1$ | | $9^2$ | 13 | | | | | | | | | | 17 |
| 1 | 2 | | 4 | 5 | 6 | | 8 | | 11 | 10 | 3 | | $7^2$ | 13 | $9^1$ | 12 | | | | | | | | | | 18 |
| 1 | $2^1$ | | 4 | 5 | 6 | 13 | 7 | | 11 | 10 | 3 | 12 | $8^3$ | | 14 | $9^2$ | | | | | | | | | | 19 |
| 1 | $2^2$ | | 4 | 5 | $7^1$ | 13 | 8 | | 10 | 11 | $3^4$ | 12 | 6 | | $9^3$ | 14 | | | | | | | | | | 20 |
| 1 | | 3 | 4 | 5 | 7 | 9 | 8 | | | 10 | $11^2$ | | 13 | 6 | | | | | | $2^1$ | 12 | | | | | 21 |
| 1 | 2 | 3 | 4 | 5 | 6 | | 8 | $11^1$ | 10 | $9^2$ | | 13 | | | 7 | 12 | | | | | | | | | | 22 |
| 1 | 2 | 3 | 4 | 5 | 6 | | 8 | $9^2$ | 11 | 10 | | 12 | | | $7^1$ | 13 | | | | | | | | | | 23 |
| 1 | 2 | 3 | 4 | 5 | 7 | 13 | 8 | $9^1$ | 10 | $11^3$ | | 14 | $6^2$ | | | 12 | | | | | | | | | | 24 |
| 1 | 2 | 4 | $3^1$ | 5 | 6 | | 8 | $9^2$ | 11 | 10 | 12 | 13 | 7 | | | | | | | | | | | | | 25 |
| 1 | 2 | 3 | | 5 | $7^1$ | 12 | 8 | 9 | $11^2$ | 10 | 4 | 13 | 6 | | | | | | | | | | | | | 26 |
| 1 | 2 | 4 | | $5^1$ | 8 | 6 | 11 | 10 | 9 | 3 | | 7 | | | 12 | | | | | | | | | | | 27 |
| 1 | 2 | 5 | | 12 | 6 | $7^1$ | 8 | 11 | 4 | 10 | 3 | 13 | $9^2$ | | | | | | | | | | | | | 28 |
| 1 | 2 | 4 | | 3 | 7 | | 8 | 9 | 10 | $11^1$ | 5 | | 6 | | 12 | | | | | | | | | | | 29 |
| 1 | 2 | 3 | | 5 | 6 | $8^2$ | $7^1$ | 11 | $4^1$ | 13 | 9 | | | | | | | | | | | $10^3$ | 12 | 14 | | 30 |
| 1 | 2 | 4 | | 5 | | $8^1$ | | $9^3$ | 10 | 3 | 13 | 6 | | | 12 | 7 | | | | | | $11^2$ | | 14 | | 31 |
| 1 | 2 | 4 | | 5 | 7 | 12 | | 11 | $3^3$ | $6^2$ | $10^4$ | 13 | $9^1$ | 8 | | | | | 14 | | | | | | | 32 |
| 1 | 2 | 3 | | 5 | 7 | | $8^2$ | 12 | 11 | $9^1$ | | 10 | 6 | | | | | | | 4 | 13 | | | | | 33 |
| 1 | | 4 | 5 | 7 | | $9^1$ | $10^3$ | 11 | 2 | 13 | 8 | 12 | $6^2$ | | | | | | | 3 | 14 | | | | | 34 |
| 1 | 2 | $3^4$ | 6 | | $9^2$ | $10^3$ | 11 | 4 | 14 | 8 | $7^1$ | | 5 | | | | | | | 5 | 12 | | | 13 | | 35 |
| 1 | 2 | | 7 | | 9 | 11 | 12 | 3 | $6^2$ | 10 | 14 | $8^3$ | | 4 | | | | | | 4 | 13 | | | $5^1$ | | 36 |
| 1 | | 6 | | 7 | 10 | 3 | $11^3$ | 2 | 13 | 8 | $5^1$ | $9^2$ | 12 | | | | | | | 4 | 14 | | | | | 37 |
| 1 | | 8 | 7 | $5^1$ | $10^3$ | 4 | 13 | 3 | 9 | 14 | 12 | 6 | 2 | | | | | | | | $11^2$ | | | | | 38 |

# DUNFERMLINE ATHLETIC

*Year Formed:* 1885. *Ground & Address:* East End Park, Halbeath Road, Dunfermline KY12 7RB.
*Telephone:* 01383 724295. *Fax:* 01383 745 959. *E-mail:* enquiries@dafc.co.uk
*Website:* www.dafc.co.uk
*Ground Capacity:* 11,380 (all seated). *Size of Pitch:* 105m × 65m.
*Chairman:* John Yorkston. *Deputy Chairman:* Rodney Shearer.
*Manager:* Jim Jefferies. *Physio:* Kenny Murray. *Head of Youth Development:* Steven Wright.
*Club Nickname:* 'The Pars'.
*Previous Grounds:* None.
*Record Attendance:* 27,816 v Celtic, Division I, 30 Apr 1968.
*Record Transfer Fee received:* £650,000 for Jackie McNamara to Celtic (Oct 1995).
*Record Transfer Fee paid:* £540,000 for Istvan Kozma from Bordeaux (Sept 1989).
*Record Victory:* 11-2 v Stenhousemuir, Division II, 27 Sept 1930.
*Record Defeat:* 1-13 v St. Bernard's, Scottish Cup, 1st rd; 15 Sept 1883.
*Most Capped Player:* Colin Miller 16 (61), Canada.
*Most League Appearances:* 497: Norrie McCathie, 1981-96.
*Most League Goals in Season (Individual):* 53: Bobby Skinner, Division II, 1925-26.
*Most Goals Overall (Individual):* 212: Charles Dickson, 1954-64.

## DUNFERMLINE ATHLETIC – SCOTTISH FIRST DIVISION 2012–13 LEAGUE RECORD

| Match No. | Date | Venue | Opponents | Result | H/T Score | Lg Pos. | Goalscorers | Attendance |
|---|---|---|---|---|---|---|---|---|
| 1 | Aug 11 | A | Cowdenbeath | W 4-0 | 1-0 | 1 | Barrowman [44], Thomson 2 [49, 79], Falkingham [83] | 2507 |
| 2 | 18 | H | Partick Th | L 0-1 | 0-1 | 4 | | 3540 |
| 3 | 25 | A | Airdrie U | W 2-1 | 0-1 | 4 | Dowie [80], Husband [84] | 1229 |
| 4 | Sept 1 | H | Raith R | W 3-1 | 2-0 | 2 | Wallace [25], Falkingham [33], Barrowman [56] | 5634 |
| 5 | 15 | A | Dumbarton | W 2-0 | 1-0 | 2 | Kirk [41], Jordan [52] | 1021 |
| 6 | 22 | H | Livingston | W 4-0 | 2-0 | 2 | Barrowman 2 [26, 65], McMillan [30], Thomson [61] | 2958 |
| 7 | 29 | A | Hamilton A | W 3-0 | 0-0 | 2 | Wallace 2 [47, 70], Thomson [89] | 1330 |
| 8 | Oct 6 | A | Falkirk | D 2-2 | 0-1 | 1 | Barrowman [79], Thomson [82] | 4691 |
| 9 | 20 | H | Greenock Morton | D 2-2 | 0-1 | 2 | Husband (pen) [83], Wallace [87] | 3511 |
| 10 | 27 | H | Cowdenbeath | W 3-0 | 1-0 | 1 | Cardle [28], Armstrong (og) [77], Dargo [84] | 3353 |
| 11 | Nov 10 | A | Partick Th | L 1-5 | 1-3 | 2 | Muirhead (og) [24] | 5268 |
| 12 | 17 | A | Raith R | W 3-1 | 1-1 | 2 | Husband 2 [37, 88], Cardle [47] | 4294 |
| 13 | 24 | H | Dumbarton | W 4-0 | 2-0 | 2 | Falkingham [31], Graham, Andrew (og) [37], Wallace (pen) [69], Cardle [90] | 3565 |
| 14 | Dec 8 | A | Livingston | L 1-2 | 0-0 | 2 | Barrowman (pen) [90] | 1495 |
| 15 | 15 | H | Hamilton A | D 1-1 | 1-1 | 2 | Barrowman [33] | 2864 |
| 16 | 26 | H | Falkirk | L 0-1 | 0-0 | 3 | | 5746 |
| 17 | 29 | A | Greenock Morton | L 2-4 | 1-1 | 3 | Morris [9], Wallace [77] | 3076 |
| 18 | Jan 2 | H | Raith R | W 1-0 | 0-0 | 3 | Geggan [71] | 5835 |
| 19 | 5 | A | Dumbarton | W 1-0 | 1-0 | 1 | Barrowman [1] | 1043 |
| 20 | 12 | H | Airdrie U | L 1-3 | 1-1 | 2 | Wallace [13] | 2823 |
| 21 | 26 | H | Livingston | L 0-1 | 0-1 | 3 | | 2461 |
| 22 | Feb 9 | A | Hamilton A | W 2-1 | 1-0 | 3 | Kirk [37], Kane [64] | 1248 |
| 23 | 12 | A | Cowdenbeath | L 2-4 | 0-1 | 3 | Dowie [70], Kirk [71] | 1330 |
| 24 | 16 | A | Falkirk | L 0-1 | 0-0 | 3 | | 3680 |
| 25 | 23 | H | Greenock Morton | L 1-4 | 0-1 | 3 | Morris [83] | 2720 |
| 26 | Mar 2 | H | Partick Th | L 0-4 | 0-4 | 4 | | 2822 |
| 27 | 9 | A | Airdrie U | D 3-3 | 1-1 | 4 | Husband [22], Wallace [86], Kirk [90] | 702 |
| 28 | 16 | A | Raith R | D 1-1 | 0-1 | 4 | Geggan [58] | 3733 |
| 29 | 23 | H | Dumbarton | L 3-4 | 1-0 | 4 | Wallace [41], Barrowman 2 [49, 56] | 3409 |
| 30 | 27 | H | Falkirk | L 0-2 | 0-1 | 4 | | 2879 |
| 31 | 30 | A | Livingston | D 2-2 | 1-0 | 5 | Thomson [22], Husband (pen) [90] | 1465 |
| 32 | Apr 6 | H | Hamilton A | L 2-3 | 1-1 | 5 | Thomson [36], Husband (pen) [66] | 4697 |
| 33 | 13 | A | Greenock Morton | W 1-0 | 1-0 | 9 | Thomson [10] | 1634 |
| 34 | 20 | H | Cowdenbeath | W 1-0 | 0-0 | 8 | Husband (pen) [67] | 4879 |
| 35 | 27 | A | Partick Th | D 3-3 | 0-1 | 8 | Wallace [65], Geggan [72], Thomson [80] | 5663 |
| 36 | May 4 | H | Airdrie U | L 1-2 | 0-0 | 9 | Thomson [58] | 4624 |

**Final League Position: 9 – Relegated to Scottish Second Division after play-offs. Deducted 15 points.**

**Honours**
*League Champions:* First Division 1988-89, 1995-96, 2010-11. Division II 1925-26. Second Division 1985-86; *Runners-up:* First Division 1986-87, 1993-94, 1994-95, 1999-2000. Division II 1912-13, 1933-34, 1954-55, 1957-58, 1972-73. Second Division 1978-79.
*Scottish Cup Winners:* 1961, 1968; *Runners-up:* 1965, 2004, 2007.
*League Cup Runners-up:* 1949-50, 1991-92, 2005-06.
*League Challenge Cup Runners-up:* 2007-08.

**European**: *Cup Winners' Cup:* 14 matches (1961-62, 1968-69 semi-finals). *UEFA Cup:* 32 matches (*Fairs Cup:* 1962-63, 1964-65, 1965-66, 1966-67, 1969-70. *UEFA Cup:* 2004-05, 2007-08).

**Club colours:** Shirt: Black and white stripes. Shorts: White. Socks: White.

**Goalscorers:** *League (62):* Barrowman 10 (1 pen), Thomson 10, Wallace 10 (1 pen), Husband 8 (4 pens), Kirk 4, Cardle 3, Falkingham 3, Geggan 3, Dowie 2, Morris 2, Dargo 1, Jordan 1, Kane 1, McMillan 1, own goals 3.
*William Hill Scottish FA Cup (1):* Barrowman 1.
*Scottish Communities League Cup (3):* Barrowman 2, Wallace 1.
*Ramsdens Cup (2):* Barrowman 1, Wallace 1.
*Play-Offs (8):* Husband 3, Smith 2, Millen 1 (pen), Thompson 1, own goal 1.

| Gallacher P 28 | Geggan A 27+1 | Dowie A 30 | Potter J 11+1 | Jordan S 20 | McMillan J 27 | Willis P 2 | Thomson R 23+10 | Falkingham J 29+1 | Whittle A 11+13 | Barrowman A 20+2 | Kirk A 10+16 | Burns P —+1 | Dargo C 9+16 | Cardle J 20+5 | Husband S 26+4 | Wallace R 27+4 | Morris C 26 | Kane C 10+4 | D'Angelo I —+1 | Byrne S 10+4 | Drummond R —+3 | Hrivnak M 8 | Millen R 9+2 | El Bakhtaoui F —+1 | Smith A 5+5 | Young K 7 | Munro G 1+1 | Henderson B —+1 | Martin L —+1 | Match No. |
|---|---|---|---|---|---|---|---|---|---|---|---|---|---|---|---|---|---|---|---|---|---|---|---|---|---|---|---|---|---|---|
| 1 | 2 | 3 | 4 | 5 | 6 | 7 | 8 | $9^3$ | $10^2$ | $11^1$ | 12 | 13 | 14 | | | | | | | | | | | | | | | | | 1 |
| 1 | 2 | 3 | 4 | 5 | $8^1$ | $9^3$ | 7 | $11^{12}$ | 14 | 10 | 13 | | | | 6 | 12 | | | | | | | | | | | | | | 2 |
| 1 | 2 | 7 | 3 | 5 | 4 | | $9^2$ | 14 | 10 | $11^1$ | | | | 13 | $6^3$ | 8 | 12 | | | | | | | | | | | | | 3 |
| 1 | 7 | 3 | | 5 | 2 | | $8^3$ | | 10 | 13 | | | 14 | $11^2$ | $6^1$ | 9 | 4 | 12 | | | | | | | | | | | | 4 |
| 1 | 7 | 3 | | 5 | 2 | | 9 | $6^1$ | 10 | | 12 | | | $8^2$ | $11^3$ | 4 | | 13 | 14 | | | | | | | | | | | 5 |
| 1 | 7 | 3 | | 5 | 2 | | 12 | | 14 | $10^2$ | 13 | | $11^1$ | $6^3$ | 8 | 9 | 4 | | | | | | | | | | | | | 6 |
| 1 | 8 | 3 | | 5 | 2 | | 13 | $6^2$ | | $10^1$ | 12 | | | 9 | 7 | 11 | 4 | | | | | | | | | | | | | 7 |
| 1 | 7 | 3 | | 5 | 2 | | 12 | $9^1$ | | 11 | 13 | | | $10^2$ | 6 | 8 | 4 | | | | | | | | | | | | | 8 |
| 1 | 7 | 3 | | | 2 | | 5 | 9 | | $11^2$ | 12 | | 13 | $10^1$ | 6 | 8 | 4 | | | | | | | | | | | | | 9 |
| 1 | 2 | 3 | | 5 | | | 7 | 6 | | $10^1$ | 12 | | 13 | $9^3$ | 8 | $11^2$ | 4 | | | 14 | | | | | | | | | | 10 |
| 1 | 6 | 3 | | 2 | | | 9 | 8 | 14 | 11 | 12 | | | 13 | $7^3$ | $10^2$ | 4 | $5^1$ | | | | | | | | | | | | 11 |
| 1 | 2 | 3 | | 5 | | | $7^1$ | 9 | 14 | $10^3$ | 13 | | | 12 | 6 | 8 | $11^2$ | 4 | | | | | | | | | | | | 12 |
| 1 | 2 | 3 | | 5 | | | 7 | $6^2$ | | 14 | $11^3$ | | | 12 | 9 | 8 | $10^1$ | 4 | | 13 | | | | | | | | | | 13 |
| | 7 | $3^9$ | | 5 | 2 | | 12 | 6 | 14 | 11 | | | | $10^2$ | $9^1$ | 8 | 13 | $4^*$ | | | | i | | | | | | | | 14 |
| | 8 | 3 | 4 | 5 | 2 | | $9^2$ | 6 | 13 | $10^3$ | 14 | | | $11^1$ | 7 | 12 | | | | | 1 | | | | | | | | | 15 |
| 1 | 8 | 3 | 4 | 5 | $2^*$ | | 12 | 6 | | $10^2$ | 13 | | | 7 | $9^1$ | $11^3$ | | | | | | | | | | | | | | 16 |
| 1 | 2 | 3 | | 5 | | | 8 | 6 | 14 | $11^3$ | 13 | | | $10^2$ | 12 | $7^1$ | 9 | 4 | | | | | | | | | | | | 17 |
| 1 | 2 | 3 | | 5 | | | 8 | 6 | | 12 | $11^1$ | | | 14 | $9^3$ | 13 | 10 | 4 | | | $7^2$ | | | | | | | | | 18 |
| 1 | 7 | 3 | | 5 | $2^1$ | | 12 | 6 | $9^2$ | 10 | | | | 13 | | 11 | 4 | | | 8 | | | | | | | | | | 19 |
| 1 | $8^2$ | 3 | | 5 | 2 | | 6 | | $9^3$ | $10^1$ | 12 | | 14 | 13 | 7 | 11 | 4 | | | | | | | | | | | | | 20 |
| 1 | $7^1$ | 3 | 4 | 5 | 2 | | 12 | 6 | | 11 | | | 13 | 9 | | $10^2$ | | | | 8 | | | | | | | | | | 21 |
| 1 | | 3 | | $5^1$ | 2 | | 13 | 6 | 14 | 10 | | | | $9^3$ | $11^2$ | 4 | 7 | | | 8 | | 12 | | | | | | | | 22 |
| 1 | | 3 | | 5 | | | 12 | 6 | 14 | 10 | | | 13 | $11^2$ | 9 | 4 | $7^3$ | | | $8^1$ | | 2 | | | | | | | | 23 |
| 1 | | 3 | | 5 | | | 8 | $9^1$ | 12 | 11 | | | $10^2$ | 13 | 7 | 6 | 4 | | | | | 2 | | | | | | | | 24 |
| 1 | 2 | 3 | | 5 | | | 8 | | | 11 | | | $10^2$ | 9 | 12 | 6 | 4 | $7^1$ | | | | | 13 | | | | | | | 25 |
| 1 | 2 | 3 | | 5 | | | 8 | | | $9^1$ | | | $11^3$ | $10^2$ | 12 | 6 | 4 | 7 | | | | 14 | 13 | | | | | | | 26 |
| 1 | | 4 | 5 | | | | 6 | 9 | | 12 | | | $11^1$ | 13 | 8 | 10 | 3 | $7^3$ | | | | $2^2$ | 14 | | | | | | | 27 |
| 1 | 6 | 3 | | 5 | 2 | | $8^1$ | 14 | | $11^2$ | | | | $9^3$ | 7 | 10 | 4 | 12 | | | | | 13 | | | | | | | 28 |
| 1 | $6^3$ | 3 | 4 | 5 | 2 | | $8^1$ | 12 | | 10 | 13 | | | 14 | $9^2$ | 7 | 11 | | | | | | | | | | | | | 29 |
| 1 | | 3 | | 5 | 2 | | 12 | $8^3$ | 14 | 10 | | | | 7 | 11 | $6^1$ | $9^2$ | | | | | 13 | 4 | | | | | | | 30 |
| | | $4^2$ | | | | | 8 | 9 | 5 | | | | $11^3$ | 7 | $10^1$ | 6 | 13 | | 1 | 2 | | 12 | 3 | 14 | | | | | | 31 |
| $8^1$ | | | | | | | 9 | 11 | 5 | | | | | $7^2$ | 4 | 12 | 6 | | 1 | 2 | | 10 | 3 | 13 | | | | | | 32 |
| | | 3 | | | | | 11 | 7 | $9^1$ | | | | | | 6 | 8 | 12 | 1 | 5 | | | $10^2$ | 2 | 4 | 13 | | | | | 33 |
| | | 12 | | | | | 11 | 9 | 5 | | | | 7 | | 4 | 6 | $8^1$ | 1 | 2 | | | 10 | 3 | | | | | | | 34 |
| 13 | | $4^1$ | | | | | $11^3$ | 9 | 5 | | | | 7 | 12 | 3 | | $6^2$ | 14 | 1 | 2 | | 10 | 6 | | | | | | | 35 |
| 6 | | | | | | | 11 | 8 | 5 | | | | 14 | 7 | 9 | 4 | $12^2$ | 13 | | 1 | $2^3$ | 10 | 3 | | | | | | | 36 |

# EAST FIFE

*Year Formed:* 1903. *Ground & Address:* Bayview Stadium, Harbour View, Methil, Fife KY8 3RW. *Telephone:* 01333 426323. *Fax:* 01333 426376. *E-mail:* office@eastfife.org. *Website:* www.eastfifefc.info
*Ground Capacity:* 1,992. *Size of Pitch:* 105m × 65m.
*Chairman:* Sid Columbine. *Managing Director:* Lee Murray. *Secretary:* Jim Stevenson.
*Manager:* Willie Aitchison. *Assistant Manager:* Robert Malcolm. *Physio:* Brian McNeill.
*Club Nickname:* 'The Fifers'.
*Previous Ground:* Bayview Park.
*Record Attendance:* 22,515 v Raith Rovers, Division I, 2 Jan 1950.
*Record Transfer Fee received:* £150,000 for Paul Hunter from Hull C (March 1990).
*Record Transfer Fee paid:* £70,000 for John Sludden from Kilmarnock (July 1991).
*Record Victory:* 13-2 v Edinburgh City, Division II, 11 Dec 1937.
*Record Defeat:* 0-9 v Hearts, Division I, 5 Oct 1957.
*Most Capped Player:* George Aitken, 5 (8), Scotland.
*Most League Appearances:* 517: David Clarke, 1968-86.
*Most League Goals in Season (Individual):* 41: Jock Wood, Division II; 1926-27 and Henry Morris, Division II, 1947-48.
*Most Goals Overall (Individual):* 225: Phil Weir, 1922-35.

## EAST FIFE – SCOTTISH SECOND DIVISION 2012–13 LEAGUE RECORD

| Match No. | Date | Venue | Opponents | Result | H/T Score | Lg Pos. | Goalscorers | Attendance |
|---|---|---|---|---|---|---|---|---|
| 1 | Aug 11 | A | Alloa Ath | D 1-1 | 1-0 | 6 | McCormack [30] | 625 |
| 2 | 18 | H | Queen of the S | D 0-0 | 0-0 | 7 | | 628 |
| 3 | 25 | A | Brechin C | L 1-2 | 0-2 | 7 | Wardlaw [78] | 588 |
| 4 | Sept 1 | H | Albion R | L 1-2 | 1-1 | 9 | McBride [2] | 514 |
| 5 | 15 | A | Arbroath | L 0-2 | 0-2 | 9 | | 624 |
| 6 | 22 | H | Ayr U | L 2-3 | 1-2 | 10 | Pollock [5], Barr, R [83] | 575 |
| 7 | 29 | A | Stranraer | W 6-2 | 3-1 | 9 | Barr, R [23], McManus, P [33], Wardlaw 2 [42, 71], Pollock 2 [57, 66] | 475 |
| 8 | Oct 6 | A | Stenhousemuir | L 0-3 | 0-0 | 9 | | 589 |
| 9 | 20 | H | Forfar Ath | W 3-0 | 1-0 | 9 | Muir [38], Smith, S [89], McManus, P [90] | 541 |
| 10 | 28 | A | Queen of the S | L 0-1 | 0-1 | 9 | | 1577 |
| 11 | Nov 10 | H | Alloa Ath | L 0-1 | 0-1 | 9 | | 515 |
| 12 | 17 | A | Albion R | W 3-0 | 1-0 | 8 | Gormley [11], Barr, R [69], McBride [86] | 338 |
| 13 | 24 | H | Arbroath | W 2-1 | 1-1 | 8 | Jamieson [13], McBride [47] | 570 |
| 14 | Dec 15 | A | Ayr U | W 3-2 | 0-2 | 7 | White [89], McBride 2 (1 pen) [56, 65 (p)] | 943 |
| 15 | 18 | H | Stranraer | L 0-1 | 0-1 | 7 | | 441 |
| 16 | 22 | H | Stenhousemuir | W 3-2 | 2-0 | 4 | Barr, R [5], Campbell [32], McBride [71] | 408 |
| 17 | 29 | A | Forfar Ath | L 2-3 | 2-1 | 6 | Johnstone [7], Willis [21] | 619 |
| 18 | Jan 2 | A | Arbroath | L 0-1 | 0-0 | 6 | | 813 |
| 19 | 5 | H | Albion R | W 2-0 | 1-0 | 6 | Samuel 2 [12, 46] | 486 |
| 20 | 12 | H | Brechin C | D 2-2 | 2-2 | 6 | Samuel [28], Barr, R [37] | 578 |
| 21 | 19 | A | Alloa Ath | D 1-1 | 1-1 | 6 | McManus, P [23] | 551 |
| 22 | 26 | H | Ayr U | D 3-3 | 3-2 | 6 | White [26], McManus, P 2 [34, 45] | 514 |
| 23 | Feb 2 | A | Stranraer | L 1-3 | 0-2 | 6 | Willis [53] | 254 |
| 24 | 9 | H | Forfar Ath | L 1-2 | 0-1 | 6 | McBride (pen) [88] | 502 |
| 25 | 16 | A | Stenhousemuir | L 1-2 | 0-0 | 7 | McBride [55] | 476 |
| 26 | Mar 2 | H | Queen of the S | L 2-3 | 0-1 | 8 | McManus, P [64], Gormley [96] | 627 |
| 27 | 9 | H | Arbroath | L 0-1 | 0-0 | 9 | | 426 |
| 28 | 19 | A | Albion R | D 1-1 | 1-1 | 9 | Willis [44] | 206 |
| 29 | 30 | A | Ayr U | L 1-2 | 1-0 | 9 | Durie [15] | 956 |
| 30 | Apr 2 | A | Brechin C | L 0-6 | 0-4 | 9 | | 471 |
| 31 | 6 | A | Forfar Ath | L 2-3 | 1-1 | 9 | Sloan, R [45], McBride [80] | 471 |
| 32 | 9 | H | Stranraer | D 1-1 | 0-0 | 9 | McBride (pen) [90] | 426 |
| 33 | 13 | H | Stenhousemuir | L 1-2 | 0-1 | 9 | McBride [67] | 461 |
| 34 | 20 | H | Alloa Ath | W 2-1 | 1-0 | 9 | Barr, R [39], Willis [56] | 497 |
| 35 | 27 | A | Queen of the S | D 2-2 | 1-0 | 9 | Campbell [36], Wardlaw [76] | 2568 |
| 36 | May 4 | H | Brechin C | L 0-3 | 0-0 | 9 | | 753 |

**Final League Position: 9 – Remain in Scottish Second Division after play-offs**

**Honours**
*League Champions:* Division II 1947-48. Third Division 2007-08.
*Runners-up:* Division II 1929-30, 1970-71. Second Division 1983-84, 1995-96. Third Division 2002-03.
*Scottish Cup Winners:* 1938; *Runners-up:* 1927, 1950.
*League Cup Winners:* 1947-48, 1949-50, 1953-54.

**Club colours:** Shirt: Black with gold sleeves. Shorts: Black with gold trim. Socks: Black.

**Goalscorers:** *League (50):* McBride 11 (3 pens), Barr R 6, McManus P 6, Wardlaw 4, Willis 4, Pollock 3, Samuel 3, Campbell 2, Gormley 2, White 2, Durie 1, Jamieson 1, Johnstone 1, McCormack 1, Muir 1, Sloan R 1, Smith S 1.
*William Hill Scottish FA Cup (1):* Muir 1.
*Scottish Communities League Cup (0).*
*Ramsdens Cup (2):* McBride 1, Samuel 1.
*Play-Offs (4):* Muir 2, Gormley 1, own goal 1.

| Brown M 9+1 | McCormack D 21 | Campbell S 27 | Wedderburn C 3 | Cook A 4 | Durie S 32 | Muir D 27+3 | Sloan R 11+13 | McBride S 22+7 | Wardlaw G 12+2 | McManus P 22+3 | Jamieson S 5+12 | Malcolm R 2+1 | Smith Darren 21+1 | Doris S 1 | Forster J 12 | Smith S 4+2 | Willis P 32 | White D 18+2 | Brown R —+1 | Pollock J 7+6 | Collier A 2 | Barr R 30 | Antell C 25 | Johnstone C 21+2 | Gormley L 4+11 | Samuel C 17+5 | Keenan D 5+3 | Match No. |
|---|---|---|---|---|---|---|---|---|---|---|---|---|---|---|---|---|---|---|---|---|---|---|---|---|---|---|---|---|
| 1 | 2 | 3¹ | 4 | 5 | 6 | 7 | 8 | 9 | 10 | 11² | 12 | 13 | | | | | | | | | | | | | | | | 1 |
| 1 | 3 | 2 | 4 | 5 | 6 | 7 | 9¹ | 12 | 11 | 10² | 13 | | 8 | | | | | | | | | | | | | | | 2 |
| 1 | 3¹ | | 4 | 5 | 2 | 7 | 9 | 12 | 11 | 10 | | | 8 | 6 | | | | | | | | | | | | | | 3 |
| 1 | 3² | | | | 2 | | 8 | 9 | 11 | 10¹ | 12 | | 7³ | | 4 | 5 | 6 | 13 | 14 | | | | | | | | | 4 |
| 1 | | | | | 2 | | 8 | 13 | 12 | 11² | 10 | | 7 | | 5 | 3 | 6 | 4 | | 9¹ | | | | | | | | 5 |
| | 3 | | | 5³ | 2 | 12 | 14 | 13 | 10² | 11 | | | 7 | | 4 | | 6 | | | | | 8¹ | 1 | 9 | | | | 6 |
| | 2 | 3 | | | | 7 | | | 11 | 10 | | | | | 4 | 5 | 6 | | | | | 8 | 1 | 9 | | | | 7 |
| | 2 | 3 | | | | 7 | 13 | 12 | 10² | 11 | | | | | 4 | 5 | 6 | | | | | 8¹ | 1 | 9 | | | | 8 |
| 5 | 3 | | | | 2 | 7 | 12 | | 10 | | | | 8 | | 4 | 13 | 6² | | | | | 11 | 1 | 9¹ | | | | 9 |
| 5¹ | 3 | | | | 2 | 7 | 9³ | | 14 | 11 | | | | | 4 | 13 | 6 | 8² | | | | 10 | 1 | 12 | | | | 10 |
| | | | | | | 7 | 2 | 3 | 8² | 10¹ | 12 | | 11 | | | | 6 | 4 | 13 | | | 9 | 1 | 5 | | | | 11 |
| | | | | | | 7 | 2 | | 12 | 3 | | | 10 | | 8¹ | | 9 | 4 | 13 | | | 6 | 1 | 5 | | 11² | | 12 |
| | | | | | | | 2 | 13 | 14 | 7 | | | 10³ | | 9 | 3 | 8 | 4 | | | | 6 | 1 | 5² | | 11¹ | 12 | 13 |
| | | | | | | | 2 | 7 | 13 | 11 | | | 10² | | 8 | 4 | 9³ | 3 | 14 | | | 6 | 1 | 5¹ | | 12 | | 14 |
| | | | | | | | 2 | 4 | 5³ | 9 | | | 12 | | 8² | 3 | 7 | | 13 | | | 6 | 1 | 14 | | 11¹ | 10 | 15 |
| 4 | | | | | | | 2 | 7 | 12 | 10 | | | | | 8 | 3 | 9 | | | | | 6¹ | 1 | 5 | | 11 | | 16 |
| | 3⁸ | | | | | | 2 | 7 | 6² | | 12 | | 9 | | | | 8 | | | | | 11 | 1 | 5 | 13 | 10¹ | | 17 |
| | | | | | | 7 | 2 | 8 | | 13 | | | 9¹ | | 4 | | 10 | 3 | 12 | | | 6³ | 1 | 5⁴ | 14 | 11² | | 18 |
| 5² | 4 | | | | | | 2 | 7 | 13 | 10¹ | | | 8³ | | | 3 | 6 | | 12 | | | 9 | 1 | | 14 | 11 | | 19 |
| 5 | | | 4 | | 2 | | | 9 | 11² | 12 | | | 7 | | | | 8 | 3 | | | | 6 | 1 | | 13 | 10¹ | | 20 |
| | 3 | | | | | 7 | | 2 | | | 12 | | | | 8 | | 6 | 4 | | | | 9 | 1 | 5 | | 10¹ | | 21 |
| | 3 | | | | | 7 | 2 | 8 | 11 | 10 | | | | | | | 4 | | | | | 6 | 1 | 5 | | | | 22 |
| | 3 | | | | | 7 | 2 | 14 | 12 | 11 | | | | | 8 | 4³ | | 13 | | | | 6 | 1 | 5¹ | | 10² | 9 | 23 |
| | 3 | | 4 | | 2 | 7 | | | | | 12 | | 10¹ | | 8 | | 9 | | | | | 6 | 1 | 5² | 13 | 11³ | 14 | 24 |
| | | | 4 | | 2 | | 3 | | 11 | 10 | | | | | 8 | | 7 | | | | | 6 | 1 | 5 | | 12 | 9¹ | 25 |
| | | | | | 2 | | 3 | 9 | 10³ | | 14 | | 7² | | | | 8 | 4 | | | | 6 | 1 | 5 | 12 | 11¹ | 13 | 26 |
| 1 | | 5 | 4 | | 2 | | | | | 10² | 12 | | 7 | | | | 6 | 3 | | | | 9 | | | 11¹ | 13 | 8 | 27 |
| 1 | | 5 | 4 | | 2 | | | | 12 | 11¹ | | | 10 | | 6 | | 8 | 3 | | | | 7 | | 9 | | | | 28 |
| 1 | 6 | 3 | | | 2 | | 5 | 8 | 9¹ | 13 | | | | | 7 | 4 | | | | | | 11 | | | | 12 | 10² | 29 |
| 1 | 7 | 3 | | | 2 | 4 | | 8 | 9¹ | | | | | | 6 | | | | | | | 11 | | 5 | | 10 | 12 | 30 |
| | | | 4 | | 2 | 7 | 5¹ | 9 | | | | | 13 | | 3² | | 8 | | | | | 6 | 1 | | 12 | 10 | 11 | 31 |
| 12 | 4² | | | | 2 | | 3 | 9 | | 10 | | | 7³ | | | | 8 | 13 | | | | 6 | 1¹ | 5 | 14 | 11 | | 32 |
| | 4⁸ | | | | 2 | | 3 | 14 | 10 | 11³ | 7¹ | | | | | | 8 | | | | | 6 | 1 | 5 | 13 | 12 | 9² | 33 |
| | 4 | | | | 2 | | 8 | 13 | 9 | 11¹ | 12 | | 7 | | | | | 3 | | | | 6² | 1 | 5 | | | 10 | 34 |
| | 8¹ | | | | 2 | | 3 | | 7 | 11² | 13 | | 12 | | | | 6 | 4 | | | | 9 | 1 | 5 | | | 10 | 35 |
| | 3 | | | | 2 | 7 | | 9 | 11 | 12 | | | 8 | | | | | 4¹ | | | | 6 | 1 | 5 | 13 | | 10² | 36 |

# EAST STIRLINGSHIRE

*Year Formed:* 1880. *Grounds:* Ochilview Park (with Stenhousemuir). *Contact address:* 81d Main Street, Bainsford, Falkirk
FK2 7NZ. *Telephone/Fax:* 01324 629 942.
*E-mail:* fceaststirlingshire@gmail.com *Website:* www.eaststirlingshirefc.com
*Ground Capacity:* 3,776 (626 seated). *Size of Pitch:* 100m × 66m.
*Chairman:* Tony Ford. *Secretary:* Tadek Kopszywa.
*Head Coach:* John Coughlin. *Assistant Manager:* Matthew Kerr.
*Club Nickname:* 'The Shire'.
*Previous Grounds:* Burnhouse, Randyford Park, Merchiston Park, New Kilbowie Park, Firs Park.
*Record Attendance:* 12,000 v Partick Th, *Scottish Cup* 3rd rd, 21 Feb 1921.
*Record Transfer Fee received:* £35,000 for Jim Docherty to Chelsea (1978).
*Record Transfer Fee paid:* £6,000 for Colin McKinnon from Falkirk (March 1991).
*Record Victory:* 11-2 v Vale of Bannock, *Scottish Cup* 2nd rd, 22 Sept 1888.
*Record Defeat:* 1-12 v Dundee United, Division II, 13 Apr 1936.
*Most Capped Player:* Humphrey Jones, 5 (14), Wales.
*Most League Appearances:* 415: Gordon Russell, 1983-2001.
*Most League Goals in Season (Individual):* 36: Malcolm Morrison, Division II, 1938-39.

## EAST STIRLINGSHIRE – SCOTTISH THIRD DIVISION 2012–13 LEAGUE RECORD

| Match No. | Date | Venue | Opponents | Result | H/T Score | Lg Pos. | Goalscorers | Atten- dance |
|---|---|---|---|---|---|---|---|---|
| 1 | Aug 11 | H | Queen's Park | L 0-2 | 0-0 | 9 | | 430 |
| 2 | 18 | A | Rangers | L 1-5 | 1-2 | 10 | Quinn (pen) [3] | 49,118 |
| 3 | 25 | H | Elgin C | L 1-4 | 0-3 | 10 | Turner [60] | 257 |
| 4 | Sept 1 | A | Berwick R | L 0-3 | 0-2 | 10 | | 520 |
| 5 | 15 | H | Stirling A | W 3-1 | 0-0 | 10 | Maxwell [70], Greenhill [81], Shepherd [90] | 487 |
| 6 | 22 | H | Clyde | W 3-0 | 2-0 | 8 | Turner [25], Quinn [39], Savage [90] | 467 |
| 7 | Oct 6 | A | Montrose | L 1-3 | 0-3 | 10 | Hume [86] | 244 |
| 8 | 20 | H | Peterhead | W 2-1 | 1-1 | 9 | Turner 2 [32, 51] | 296 |
| 9 | 27 | A | Annan Ath | L 2-5 | 0-2 | 9 | Quinn [60], Shepherd [90] | 374 |
| 10 | Nov 13 | A | Queen's Park | W 2-1 | 1-1 | 8 | Greenhill [45], Quinn (pen) [73] | 374 |
| 11 | 17 | H | Rangers | L 2-6 | 1-2 | 8 | Turner [41], Quinn (pen) [58] | 2854 |
| 12 | 25 | H | Berwick R | L 0-1 | 0-1 | 9 | | 327 |
| 13 | Dec 15 | A | Clyde | L 1-2 | 1-1 | 9 | Quinn (pen) [33] | 428 |
| 14 | 19 | H | Montrose | D 2-2 | 2-1 | 9 | Turner 2 [25, 45] | 211 |
| 15 | 22 | H | Annan Ath | D 2-2 | 1-2 | 9 | Stirling 2 (1 pen) [37, 47 (p)] | 192 |
| 16 | 29 | A | Peterhead | L 0-2 | 0-1 | 9 | | 446 |
| 17 | Jan 2 | H | Stirling A | D 1-1 | 1-1 | 9 | Holt [45] | 621 |
| 18 | 5 | A | Berwick R | L 0-2 | 0-2 | 9 | | 473 |
| 19 | 12 | A | Elgin C | W 4-3 | 3-2 | 9 | Hunter 2 [7, 14], Turner (pen) [44], Glasgow [57] | 697 |
| 20 | 19 | H | Queen's Park | L 0-2 | 0-1 | 9 | | 415 |
| 21 | Feb 2 | A | Montrose | D 2-2 | 2-1 | 9 | Greenhill 2 [18, 23] | 327 |
| 22 | 9 | H | Peterhead | L 2-4 | 0-4 | 9 | Jackson [88], Glasgow [90] | 278 |
| 23 | 12 | A | Stirling A | D 1-1 | 0-0 | 9 | Turner (pen) [55] | 376 |
| 24 | 16 | A | Annan Ath | W 2-1 | 0-0 | 9 | Glasgow [49], Holt [57] | 349 |
| 25 | 19 | H | Clyde | W 3-0 | 1-0 | 8 | Herd [18], Quinn (pen) [57], Stirling [63] | 301 |
| 26 | 23 | H | Elgin C | W 3-2 | 1-1 | 6 | Quinn (pen) [40], Herd [47], Maxwell [84] | 277 |
| 27 | Mar 2 | A | Rangers | L 1-3 | 1-0 | 9 | Stirling [40] | 44,534 |
| 28 | 9 | A | Stirling A | L 1-9 | 0-3 | 9 | Wright [56] | 563 |
| 29 | 16 | H | Berwick R | L 0-3 | 0-2 | 10 | | 248 |
| 30 | 23 | H | Montrose | L 1-2 | 1-1 | 10 | Wright [43] | 261 |
| 31 | 30 | A | Clyde | L 0-2 | 0-1 | 10 | | 508 |
| 32 | Apr 6 | A | Peterhead | L 0-6 | 0-5 | 10 | | 456 |
| 33 | 13 | H | Annan Ath | L 1-2 | 1-1 | 10 | Wright [17] | 288 |
| 34 | 20 | A | Queen's Park | L 1-5 | 1-2 | 10 | Glasgow [37] | 485 |
| 35 | 27 | H | Rangers | L 2-4 | 1-2 | 10 | Quinn 2 (1 pen) [22 (p), 50] | 2805 |
| 36 | May 4 | A | Elgin C | L 2-3 | 2-2 | 10 | Glasgow [17], Quinn [43] | 786 |

**Final League Position: 10**

**Honours**
*League Champions:* Division II 1931-32; C Division 1947-48.
*Runners-up:* Division II 1962-63. Second Division 1979-80. Division Three 1923-24.

**Club colours:** Shirt: Black and white hoops. Shorts: Black. Socks: Black and white hoops.

**Goalscorers:** *League (49):* Quinn 11 (7 pens), Turner 9 (2 pens), Glasgow 5, Greenhill 4, Stirling 4 (1 pen), Wright 3, Herd 2, Holt 2, Hunter 2, Maxwell 2, Shepherd 2, Hume 1, Jackson 1, Savage 1.
*William Hill Scottish FA Cup (3):* Greenhill 2, Turner 1.
*Scottish Communities League Cup (1):* Herd 1.
*Ramsdens Cup (7):* Herd 3, Maxwell 2, Kelly 1, Turner 1.

| McWilliams R 3 | Hume C 9+1 | Miller R 29+2 | Jackson S 32+1 | Shepherd N 12+6 | Greenhill D 30+4 | Begg M 11+7 | Devlin R 6 | Maxwell S 31+2 | Turner K 27+1 | Herd M 17+4 | Quinn P 20+5 | Hunter M 26+6 | Benton J —+5 | Kelly S 8+1 | Glasgow J 11+10 | Hay G 31 | Donaldson C —+1 | Dunlop M 1 | Gillespie K 2+4 | Savage J —+2 | Zofle P 8+5 | McKernon J 13 | Lurinsky A —+1 | Holt J 9 | Trialist A 1 | Buchanan R 12 | Stirling A 20 | Kelly C —+8 | McCaughie D —+2 | Wright M 9+7 | Anderson C —+2 | Hamilton J 4+1 | Moffat C 6 | McGregor G 6 | Gordon C 2 | Match No. |
|---|---|---|---|---|---|---|---|---|---|---|---|---|---|---|---|---|---|---|---|---|---|---|---|---|---|---|---|---|---|---|---|---|---|---|---|---|
| 2³ | 3 | 4 | 5 | 6¹ | 7² | 8 | 9 | 10 | 11 | 12 | 13 | 14 | | | | | | | | | | | | | | | | | | | | | | | | 1 |
| 1 | 9 | 3¹ | 2 | 5 | 6¹ | 12 | 4 | 10² | 11 | 8 | 7 | | 14 | 13 | | | | | | | | | | | | | | | | | | | | | | 2 |
| 1 | 7¹ | 4 | 3 | 5² | 6 | 9 | 8 | | 10 | | 11 | 12 | | 2 | 13 | | | | | | | | | | | | | | | | | | | | | 3 |
| | 2¹ | 3 | 13 | 10 | 8 | 7³ | 5² | 9 | 11 | 12 | | 6 | | 4 | | 1 | 14 | | | | | | | | | | | | | | | | | | | 4 |
| 14 | 3¹ | 2 | 12 | 11 | 13 | 7³ | 9 | 10 | 6² | | 8 | | 5 | | 1 | | 4 | | | | | | | | | | | | | | | | | | | 5 |
| 6 | 8 | 3 | 5¹ | 10 | 7 | 2¹ | 9 | 11³ | | 12 | 4 | | | 1 | | 13 | 14 | | | | | | | | | | | | | | | | | | | 6 |
| 2 | 7 | 4 | 12 | 6 | 8¹ | | 9 | 11 | | 10³ | 5² | | 3 | 1 | | 14 | 13 | | | | | | | | | | | | | | | | | | | 7 |
| 2 | 3 | 4 | 5 | 12 | 13 | | 9 | 10² | | 11¹ | 7 | | 8 | 1 | | | 6 | | | | | | | | | | | | | | | | | | | 8 |
| 2 | 3⁴ | 4¹ | 5 | 12 | | | 9 | 10³ | | 11 | 8² | | 7 | 1 | | 13 | 6 | 14 | | | | | | | | | | | | | | | | | | 9 |
| 2 | | 3 | 5 | 10 | 13 | | 9 | 12 | 11² | 7 | 4 | | 1 | | | 8¹ | 6 | | | | | | | | | | | | | | | | | | | 10 |
| 3 | 2 | 5 | 6² | 14 | | | 9¹ | 10 | 12 | 11³ | 13 | | 4 | | | 7⁸ | 8 | | | | | | | | | | | | | | | | | | | 11 |
| 3 | 2 | 5 | 9 | 7² | | | 12 | 8 | 10¹ | 11 | 13 | | | 1 | | | 6 | 4 | | | | | | | | | | | | | | | | | | 12 |
| 4 | 2 | 5¹ | 6 | | | | 12 | 10 | 9³ | 11² | 13 | | 14 | 1 | | | 7 | 3 | 8 | | | | | | | | | | | | | | | | | 13 |
| 3 | 2 | | | | | | 10 | 11 | 6 | | 5¹ | | | 1 | | | 9 | 7 | | | 4 | 8 | 12 | | | | | | | | | | | | | 14 |
| 7 | 2 | 6² | | | | | 5 | 10 | | 13 | 4 | | | 1 | | | 9¹ | 8 | | 3 | 11 | 12 | | | | | | | | | | | | | | 15 |
| | 2 | | 6³ | 9 | | | 5 | 10¹ | 11² | 13 | | | 12 | 1 | | | 8 | | 3 | 4 | 7 | 14 | | | | | | | | | | | | | | 16 |
| | 2 | | 12 | 9¹ | | | 5 | 10 | 6 | | 13 | | | 1 | | | 7 | 8 | | 3 | 4 | 11² | | | | | | | | | | | | | | 17 |
| | 2 | | 12 | 8 | | | 5 | | 9¹ | 10² | 6 | | | 1 | | | 13 | 7 | | 4 | 3 | 11³ | 14 | | | | | | | | | | | | | 18 |
| 13 | | | 8 | 10¹ | | | 5 | 11 | 2 | | 9 | | | 1 | | | | 7 | 3⁹ | 4 | 6² | | 14 | | | | | | | | | | | | | 19 |
| 3 | 4 | | 6³ | 9² | | | 5 | 11 | 2¹ | | 7 | | 14 | 1 | | 12 | 13 | 8 | | | 10 | | | | | | | | | | | | | | | 20 |
| 3 | 2 | | 7 | | | | 5 | 11 | 9 | | 8 | | | 10¹ | 1 | | | | | | 4 | 6 | | 12 | | | | | | | | | | | | 21 |
| 7 | 2 | | 6 | | | | 5 | 11² | 8¹ | | 4 | | | 9 | 1 | | | | | | 3 | 10 | 13 | 12 | | | | | | | | | | | | 22 |
| 3 | 2 | 13 | 6 | | | | | 10 | 8 | | 7 | | | 9¹ | 1 | | | | | 5 | 4 | 11² | | 12 | | | | | | | | | | | | 23 |
| 3 | 2 | 12 | 6 | | | | | 8² | 10 | | 7 | | | 9¹ | 1 | | | | | 5 | 4 | 11 | | 13 | | | | | | | | | | | | 24 |
| 7 | 2 | 12 | 6 | | | | 5 | | 8³ | 10¹ | 4 | | | 11² | 1 | | | | | | 3 | 9 | 13 | 14 | | | | | | | | | | | | 25 |
| 3 | 2 | 12 | 6 | | | | 5 | 13 | 8² | 11 | 7 | | | 9¹ | 1 | | | | | | 4 | 10³ | | 14 | | | | | | | | | | | | 26 |
| 3 | 2² | 7 | | 5 | 6 | | | 10³ | 8 | | 11¹ | | | 1 | | 13 | 14 | | | | 4 | 9 | | 12 | | | | | | | | | | | | 27 |
| 4 | 3⁴ | 6 | 12 | 5 | | | 10³ | 11 | | 7 | | | | 1 | | 2 | 8¹ | | | | 7 | | 9 | | | | | | | | | | | | | 28 |
| 3 | | 6 | 13 | 5 | | | 10¹ | 11 | | | 9² | | | 1 | | 2 | 4 | | | | 7 | | 8 | 12 | | | | | | | | | | | | 29 |
| 3 | 4 | 6 | | 5 | | | 12² | 10 | 8 | | 13 | | | 1 | | | 11¹ | | | | 7 | | 9 | 2 | | | | | | | | | | | | 30 |
| 13 | 4 | | | 5 | | | | 11¹ | 7 | | 9² | | | 1 | | | | | | | 10 | | 12 | 8 | | 2 | 3 | 6 | | | | | | | | 31 |
| 3 | 2 | 6 | | 9 | | | | | 7 | | 13 | | | 1 | | 12 | | | | | 11³ | 14 | 10² | 5¹ | 4 | 8 | | | | | | | | | | 32 |
| 3 | 2 | 6 | | 5 | 10 | | | | 7¹ | | | | | 12 | 1 | | | | | | 8 | | 9 | | 4 | 11 | | | | | | | | | | 33 |
| 2 | 3 | 7 | | 5 | 10³ | | | 13 | 8¹ | 14 | | | | 6 | | | | | | | | 11 | | 12 | 4 | 9² | 1 | | | | | | | | | 34 |
| 3 | 2 | 6 | | 5 | 10⁴ | | | 11 | 6 | | | | | 12 | 1 | | | | | | | 9 | | | 4 | 7¹ | | | | | | | | | | 35 |
| | 3 | 6 | | 5 | | | | 11² | 8 | 13 | | | | 10³ | | | | | | | 12 | | 9¹ | 14 | 2 | 4 | 7 | 1 | | | | | | | | 36 |

# ELGIN CITY

*Year Formed:* 1893. *Ground and Address:* Borough Briggs, Borough Briggs Road, Elgin IV30 1AP.
*Telephone:* 01343 551114. *Fax:* 01343 547921. *E-mail:* accountsecfc@btconnect.com *Website:* www.elgincity.com
*Ground Capacity:* 3,927 (seated: 478). *Size of pitch:* 102m × 68m.
*Chairman:* Graham Tatters. *Secretary:* Kate Taylor.
*Manager:* Ross Jack. *Physio:* Kerry Hendry.
*Previous names:* 1893-1900 Elgin City, 1900–03 Elgin City United, 1903– Elgin City.
*Club Nicknames:* 'City', 'The Black & Whites'.
*Previous Grounds:* Association Park 1893-95; Milnfield Park 1895-1909; Station Park 1909-19; Cooper Park 1919-21.
*Record Attendance:* 12,608 v Arbroath, Scottish Cup, 17 Feb 1968.
*Record Transfer Fee received:* £32,000 for Michael Teasdale to Dundee (Jan 1994).
*Record Transfer Fee paid:* £10,000 for Russell McBride from Fraserburgh (July 2001).
*Record Victory:* 18-1 v Brora Rangers, North of Scotland Cup, 6 Feb 1960.
*Record Defeat:* 1-14 v Hearts, Scottish Cup, 4 Feb 1939.
*Most League Appearances:* 224: David Hind, 2001-09.
*Most League Goals in Season (Individual):* 19: Martin Johnston, 2005-06.
*Most Goals Overall (Individual):* 72: Craig Gunn, 2009–13.

### ELGIN CITY – SCOTTISH THIRD DIVISION 2012–13 LEAGUE RECORD

| Match No. | Date | Venue | Opponents | Result | H/T Score | Lg Pos. | Goalscorers | Atten- dance |
|---|---|---|---|---|---|---|---|---|
| 1 | Aug 11 | A | Berwick R | D 0-0 | 0-0 | 7 | | 539 |
| 2 | 18 | H | Stirling A | W 3-1 | 1-1 | 4 | Gunn [17], Nicolson [55], Wyness [80] | 631 |
| 3 | 25 | A | East Stirling | W 4-1 | 3-0 | 1 | Cameron [7], Gunn [16], O'Donoghue [39], Wyness [59] | 257 |
| 4 | Sept 2 | A | Rangers | L 1-5 | 1-3 | 5 | Duff [15] | 46,015 |
| 5 | 15 | H | Peterhead | W 2-0 | 0-0 | 1 | Moore 2 (2 pens) [58, 66] | 945 |
| 6 | 22 | H | Queen's Park | L 0-4 | 0-2 | 3 | | 855 |
| 7 | Oct 13 | H | Montrose | W 6-1 | 3-0 | 2 | Leslie 3 [22, 45, 70], Moore [35], Nicolson [60], McLean [80] | 725 |
| 8 | 17 | A | Clyde | D 2-2 | 2-1 | 2 | Duff [8], Niven [35] | 458 |
| 9 | 20 | H | Annan Ath | D 2-2 | 2-1 | 2 | Duff [30], Gunn [38] | 734 |
| 10 | 27 | A | Montrose | D 2-2 | 2-0 | 1 | Leslie [21], Moore (pen) [33] | 346 |
| 11 | Nov 10 | H | Berwick R | W 3-1 | 2-1 | 2 | Nicolson [16], Leslie [25], Wyness [90] | 790 |
| 12 | 17 | A | Stirling A | W 4-1 | 4-1 | 2 | Gunn 3 [6, 27, 31], Leslie [35] | 454 |
| 13 | Dec 5 | H | Peterhead | D 1-1 | 0-1 | 2 | Leslie [60] | 225 |
| 14 | 8 | H | Clyde | W 2-1 | 1-1 | 2 | Leslie 2 [35, 81] | 665 |
| 15 | 15 | A | Queen's Park | D 1-1 | 1-1 | 2 | Leslie [6] | 466 |
| 16 | 22 | H | Rangers | L 2-6 | 2-3 | 2 | Moore [18], Nicolson [32] | 3448 |
| 17 | 29 | A | Annan Ath | L 0-2 | 0-1 | 2 | | 356 |
| 18 | Jan 2 | H | Peterhead | L 0-3 | 0-2 | 3 | | 880 |
| 19 | 5 | A | Rangers | D 1-1 | 0-1 | 5 | Alexander (og) [87] | 46,406 |
| 20 | 12 | H | East Stirling | L 3-4 | 2-3 | 5 | Hunter (og) [41], Leslie [45], Gunn [65] | 697 |
| 21 | Feb 2 | A | Clyde | D 1-1 | 0-1 | 5 | Millar [79] | 492 |
| 22 | 9 | A | Annan Ath | W 3-1 | 3-0 | 4 | Moore [14], Harkins [23], Gunn [43] | 550 |
| 23 | 16 | A | Montrose | L 1-4 | 0-3 | 5 | Millar [80] | 432 |
| 24 | 23 | A | East Stirling | L 2-3 | 1-1 | 5 | McDonald [15], Gunn [52] | 277 |
| 25 | 26 | A | Berwick R | L 1-2 | 1-0 | 5 | Gunn [3] | 382 |
| 26 | Mar 2 | H | Stirling A | L 1-2 | 1-2 | 5 | Leslie [23] | 681 |
| 27 | 5 | H | Queen's Park | L 3-5 | 0-3 | 6 | Millar [69], Gunn [80], Cameron [90] | 352 |
| 28 | 9 | A | Peterhead | W 1-0 | 1-0 | 6 | Moore [9] | 496 |
| 29 | 16 | H | Rangers | L 0-1 | 0-0 | 6 | | 3663 |
| 30 | 30 | A | Queen's Park | W 1-0 | 0-0 | 6 | Leslie (pen) [57] | 557 |
| 31 | Apr 2 | H | Clyde | W 4-2 | 1-1 | 6 | Millar 2 [30, 75], Gunn [54], Gray (og) [57] | 494 |
| 32 | 6 | A | Annan Ath | D 2-2 | 0-0 | 6 | Morrison [77], Wyness [90] | 379 |
| 33 | 13 | H | Montrose | W 3-2 | 1-1 | 6 | McMullan [43], Harkins 2 (1 pen) [62, 88 (p)] | 777 |
| 34 | 20 | H | Berwick R | L 1-2 | 1-0 | 6 | Leslie (pen) [7] | 870 |
| 35 | 27 | A | Stirling A | D 1-1 | 1-0 | 5 | Gunn [12] | 528 |
| 36 | May 4 | H | East Stirling | W 3-2 | 2-2 | 5 | Duff [16], Leslie [39], McLean [89] | 786 |

**Final League Position: 5**

**Honours**
*Scottish Cup:* Quarter-finals 1968.
*Highland League Champions:* winners 15 times.
*Scottish Qualifying Cup (North):* winners 7 times.
*North of Scotland Cup:* winners 17 times.
*Highland League Cup:* winners 5 times.
*Inverness Cup:* winners twice.

**Club colours:** Shirt: Black and white stripes. Shorts: Black. Socks: Red.

**Goalscorers:** *League (67):* Leslie 15 (2 pens), Gunn 13, Moore 7 (3 pens), Millar 5, Duff 4, Nicolson 4, Wyness 4, Harkins 3 (1 pen), Cameron 2, McLean 2, McDonald 1, McMullan 1, Morrison 1, Niven 1, O'Donoghue 1, own goals 3.
*William Hill Scottish FA Cup (8):* Gunn 2, Leslie 2, Cameron 1, Harkins 1, Moore 1 (1 pen), Nicolson 1.
*Scottish Communities League Cup (0).*
*Ramsdens Cup (5):* Leslie 2, Gunn 1, Moore 1, Wyness 1.

| Gibson J 17 | Niven D 27 | Crighton S 35 | Nicolson M 33 | Cameron B 36 | Moore D 33 | O'Donoghue R 20+3 | Wyness D 13+8 | McMullan P 26+4 | Leslie S 30+1 | Gunn C 30+3 | Duff J 28 | Beveridge G 13+10 | Harkins P 14+12 | Millar P 6+19 | McLean C 2+13 | Forbes F —+2 | MacLeod A —+1 | McHardy D —+3 | Malin J 19 | Morrison G 12+4 | McDonald C 2 | McKinnon R —+2 | Match No. |
|---|---|---|---|---|---|---|---|---|---|---|---|---|---|---|---|---|---|---|---|---|---|---|---|
| 1 | 2 | 3 | 4 | 5 | $6^8$ | 7 | 8 | 9 | 10 | 11 | | | | | | | | | | | | | 1 |
| 1 | 7 | 2 | 4 | 6 | | | $8^3$ | $11^2$ | 5 | 10 | 3 | $9^1$ | 12 | 13 | 14 | | | | | | | | 2 |
| 1 | 8 | 3 | 6 | $11^1$ | | | 7 | $9^3$ | 5 | $10^2$ | 4 | 2 | 12 | 13 | 14 | | | | | | | | 3 |
| 1 | 2 | 5 | 4 | 7 | 10 | 8 | $9^2$ | $6^1$ | 12 | $11^3$ | 3 | | 14 | 13 | | | | | | | | | 4 |
| 1 | 2 | 5 | 4 | 6 | 9 | $7^2$ | $11^1$ | 13 | 8 | 10 | 3 | 12 | | | | | | | | | | | 5 |
| 1 | 5 | 3 | $8^3$ | 6 | $9^2$ | 14 | 7 | 11 | 4 | 2 | 12 | $10^1$ | 13 | | | | | | | | | | 6 |
| 1 | $2^3$ | 3 | 8 | $6^2$ | 9 | 5 | $11^1$ | 10 | 4 | 7 | 13 | 14 | 12 | | | | | | | | | | 7 |
| 1 | 6 | 4 | 7 | 9 | 10 | 12 | 11 | $8^2$ | 5 | 3 | 13 | $2^1$ | | | | | | | | | | | 8 |
| 1 | $7^1$ | 3 | 8 | 6 | 9 | $5^2$ | 11 | 10 | 4 | 2 | 13 | 12 | | | | | | | | | | | 9 |
| 1 | | 3 | 8 | 6 | 9 | 7 | | 5 | $11^1$ | 10 | 4 | 2 | 12 | | | | | | | | | | 10 |
| 1 | | 3 | 8 | 6 | 9 | 7 | 12 | 5 | 11 | $10^1$ | 4 | $2^2$ | 13 | | | | | | | | | | 11 |
| 1 | 2 | 3 | 11 | $9^1$ | $8^3$ | 13 | 5 | 7 | $10^2$ | 4 | 6 | 12 | 14 | | | | | | | | | | 12 |
| 1 | 2 | 4 | 8 | $6^2$ | 9 | 7 | 12 | $5^3$ | 10 | $11^1$ | 3 | 13 | 14 | | | | | | | | | | 13 |
| 1 | $2^8$ | 3 | 8 | 6 | 9 | 7 | $10^1$ | 11 | 12 | 4 | 5 | | | | | | | | | | | | 14 |
| 1 | 4 | 2 | 8 | 7 | $10^2$ | 11 | 6 | 3 | 12 | $5^1$ | 13 | | | | | | | | | | | | 15 |
| 1 | 2 | 3 | 4 | 6 | 9 | 7 | $10^1$ | 14 | 11 | $5^2$ | 12 | $8^3$ | 13 | | | | | | | | | | 16 |
| 1 | 2 | 3 | 7 | 11 | 9 | 8 | $6^2$ | $5^3$ | 10 | $4^1$ | 13 | 12 | 14 | | | | | | | | | | 17 |
| | 2 | 3 | 8 | 6 | 9 | 7 | $10^2$ | $5^1$ | 11 | $4^3$ | 12 | 13 | 14 | | | | | | 1 | | | | 18 |
| | 6 | 3 | 2 | 7 | 10 | $8^2$ | 13 | 11 | 4 | $5^1$ | $9^8$ | | | | | | | | 1 | | | | 19 |
| | 2 | 3 | $8^1$ | 6 | 9 | $7^3$ | $10^2$ | $11^8$ | 12 | 4 | 5 | 13 | 14 | | | | | | 1 | | | | 20 |
| | 2 | 7 | 11 | $6^2$ | 9 | 8 | $10^1$ | 4 | 5 | 13 | 12 | | | | | | | | 1 | 3 | | | 21 |
| | $5^1$ | 2 | 4 | 6 | 10 | 7 | 12 | $11^3$ | 3 | 14 | $9^2$ | 13 | | | | | | | 1 | 8 | | | 22 |
| | $3^8$ | 8 | 6 | 9 | $7^2$ | $5^1$ | 11 | 10 | 4 | 12 | 13 | | | | | | | | 1 | 2 | | | 23 |
| | | 8 | 6 | 9 | 12 | 3 | 11 | $10^2$ | 7 | $5^1$ | 13 | | | | | | | | 1 | 2 | | 4 | 24 |
| | 3 | 7 | 8 | 5 | 11 | 10 | 12 | $6^3$ | 13 | $2^2$ | 14 | | | | | | | | 1 | 9 | | $4^1$ | 25 |
| | 4 | $8^3$ | 6 | 9 | 13 | $5^2$ | 11 | 10 | 3 | 2 | 14 | 12 | | | | | | | 1 | $7^1$ | | | 26 |
| | 3 | 4 | 6 | 9 | $8^2$ | 5 | $11^3$ | 10 | 2 | 12 | 13 | 14 | | | | | | | 1 | $7^1$ | | | 27 |
| | $2^1$ | 4 | 8 | 6 | 9 | 5 | 7 | 11 | 3 | 10 | | | | | | | | | 1 | 12 | | | 28 |
| | 2 | 3 | 8 | $6^2$ | 9 | $5^3$ | 7 | 10 | 4 | 14 | 12 | $11^1$ | | | | | | | 1 | 13 | | | 29 |
| | 2 | 3 | 8 | 7 | $9^1$ | $5^2$ | 11 | 6 | 4 | 13 | 10 | | | | | | | | 1 | 12 | | | 30 |
| | $2^1$ | 3 | 9 | 7 | $10^2$ | 5 | $8^2$ | 6 | 4 | 14 | 12 | 11 | | | | | | | 1 | 13 | | | 31 |
| | 2 | 4 | 6 | 9 | 13 | $5^1$ | 10 | 11 | 3 | $7^2$ | | | | | | | | | 1 | 8 | 12 | | 32 |
| | 2 | 3 | 7 | 10 | 12 | 5 | $11^1$ | 6 | 4 | 9 | | | | | | | | | 1 | 8 | | | 33 |
| | 2 | 4 | 9 | 6 | 10 | 14 | $5^3$ | 11 | 13 | 3 | 12 | $7^2$ | | | | | | | 1 | $8^1$ | | | 34 |
| | $2^1$ | 3 | 7 | 6 | 9 | 13 | 5 | 10 | 4 | 12 | $11^2$ | 14 | | | | | | | 1 | $0^3$ | | | 35 |
| | 2 | 3 | 5 | 8 | 10 | 11 | 9 | 4 | $7^1$ | 13 | | | | | | | | | 1 | $6^2$ | 12 | | 36 |

# FALKIRK

*Year Formed:* 1876. *Ground & Address:* The Falkirk Stadium, Westfield, Falkirk FK2 9DX. *Telephone:* 01324 624121.
*Fax:* 01324 612418. *Email:* post@falkirkfc.co.uk *Website:* www.falkirkfc.co.uk
*Ground Capacity:* 8,750 (all seated). *Size of Pitch:* 105m × 68m.
*Chairman:* Martin Ritchie. *Secretary:* Robert Bateman.
*Manager:* Gary Holt.
*Club Nickname:* 'The Bairns'.
*Previous Grounds:* Randyford 1876-81; Blinkbonny Grounds 1881-83; Brockville Park 1883-2003.
*Record Attendance:* 23,100 v Celtic, Scottish Cup 3rd rd, 21 Feb 1953.
*Record Transfer Fee received:* £380,000 for John Hughes to Celtic (Aug 1995).
*Record Transfer Fee paid:* £225,000 to Chelsea for Kevin McAllister (Aug 1991).
*Record Victory:* 11-1 v Tillicoultry, Scottish Cup 1st rd, 7 Sep 1889.
*Record Defeat:* 1-11 v Airdrieonians, Division I, 28 Apr 1951.
*Most Capped Player:* Alex Parker, 14 (15), Scotland.
*Most League Appearances:* 451: Tom Ferguson, 1919-32.
*Most League Goals in Season (Individual):* 43: Evelyn Morrison, Division I, 1928-29.
*Most Goals Overall (Individual):* 154: Kenneth Dawson, 1935-51.

## FALKIRK – SCOTTISH FIRST DIVISION 2012–13 LEAGUE RECORD

| Match No. | Date | Venue | Opponents | Result | | H/T Score | Lg Pos. | Goalscorers | Attendance |
|---|---|---|---|---|---|---|---|---|---|
| 1 | Aug 11 | A | Partick Th | L | 1-3 | 0-2 | 7 | Taylor [53] | 3487 |
| 2 | 18 | H | Raith R | L | 0-2 | 0-1 | 9 | | 3064 |
| 3 | 25 | A | Greenock Morton | W | 2-1 | 2-1 | 6 | Fulton, J [9], Taylor [39] | 1756 |
| 4 | Sept 2 | H | Livingston | L | 1-2 | 1-1 | 8 | Murdoch (pen) [34] | 2974 |
| 5 | 15 | A | Hamilton A | D | 1-1 | 1-1 | 8 | Taylor [5] | 1174 |
| 6 | 22 | H | Airdrie U | D | 1-1 | 1-0 | 7 | Murdoch (pen) [35] | 2951 |
| 7 | 29 | A | Cowdenbeath | D | 1-1 | 1-1 | 8 | Weatherston [3] | 699 |
| 8 | Oct 6 | H | Dunfermline Ath | D | 2-2 | 1-0 | 7 | Taylor 2 [30, 55] | 4691 |
| 9 | 20 | A | Dumbarton | W | 2-0 | 2-0 | 7 | Taylor [16], Weatherston [32] | 1041 |
| 10 | 27 | H | Partick Th | D | 0-0 | 0-0 | 7 | | 3818 |
| 11 | Nov 10 | A | Raith R | L | 1-2 | 1-0 | 7 | Leahy [43] | 1986 |
| 12 | 17 | A | Livingston | L | 1-2 | 0-1 | 8 | McGrandles [84] | 1471 |
| 13 | 24 | H | Hamilton A | W | 2-1 | 0-0 | 6 | McGrandles [83], Small [90] | 2682 |
| 14 | Dec 15 | H | Cowdenbeath | W | 2-0 | 2-0 | 6 | Murdoch (pen) [33], Taylor [42] | 2647 |
| 15 | 22 | A | Airdrie U | W | 4-1 | 1-0 | 6 | Fulton, J [43], Taylor 3 [67, 80, 90] | 914 |
| 16 | 26 | A | Dunfermline Ath | W | 1-0 | 0-0 | 4 | Alston [90] | 5746 |
| 17 | 29 | H | Dumbarton | L | 3-4 | 1-1 | 4 | Taylor 3 [43, 86, 89] | 3097 |
| 18 | Jan 5 | A | Hamilton A | D | 1-1 | 1-0 | 5 | Taylor [13] | 1423 |
| 19 | 12 | H | Greenock Morton | L | 0-1 | 0-0 | 6 | | 3078 |
| 20 | 19 | A | Partick Th | L | 1-4 | 1-2 | 6 | Taylor [18] | 3280 |
| 21 | 26 | H | Airdrie U | W | 4-3 | 3-0 | 5 | Taylor 2 [9, 35], Murdoch [24], Dods [73] | 2715 |
| 22 | Feb 9 | A | Cowdenbeath | L | 1-4 | 1-2 | 5 | Taylor [2] | 566 |
| 23 | 16 | H | Dunfermline Ath | W | 1-0 | 0-0 | 5 | Weatherston [87] | 3680 |
| 24 | 19 | H | Livingston | W | 2-0 | 1-0 | 5 | Taylor 2 [39, 63] | 2583 |
| 25 | 23 | A | Dumbarton | W | 2-0 | 2-0 | 5 | Grant [25], Weatherston [30] | 997 |
| 26 | Mar 5 | H | Raith R | D | 1-1 | 0-1 | 5 | Murdoch [90] | 2428 |
| 27 | 9 | A | Greenock Morton | L | 0-2 | 0-2 | 5 | | 1962 |
| 28 | 23 | H | Hamilton A | L | 0-2 | 0-2 | 5 | | 2616 |
| 29 | 27 | A | Dunfermline Ath | W | 2-0 | 1-0 | 5 | Taylor [10], Alston [88] | 2879 |
| 30 | 30 | A | Airdrie U | W | 1-0 | 0-0 | 4 | Taylor [58] | 790 |
| 31 | Apr 2 | A | Livingston | W | 2-1 | 0-1 | 3 | Higgins [62], Talbot (og) [73] | 1100 |
| 32 | 6 | H | Cowdenbeath | W | 4-0 | 0-0 | 3 | Dods [69], Sibbald [78], Higgins 2 (1 pen) [87 (p), 89] | 2539 |
| 33 | 16 | H | Dumbarton | L | 1-3 | 1-2 | 4 | Taylor [33] | 2288 |
| 34 | 20 | H | Partick Th | L | 0-2 | 0-0 | 4 | | 4804 |
| 35 | 27 | A | Raith R | D | 0-0 | 0-0 | 5 | | 1406 |
| 36 | May 4 | H | Greenock Morton | W | 4-1 | 0-1 | 3 | Sibbald [60], Taylor (pen) [64], Duffie [79], Higgins [89] | 3179 |

**Final League Position: 3**

**Honours**
*League Champions:* Division II 1935-36, 1969-70, 1974-75. First Division 1990-91, 1993-94, 2002-03, 2004-05. Second Division 1979-80;
*Runners-up:* Division I 1907-08, 1909-10. First Division 1985-86, 1988-89, 1997-98, 1998-99. Division II 1904-05, 1951-52, 1960-61.
*Scottish Cup Winners:* 1913, 1957; *Runners-up:* 1997, 2009. *League Cup Runners-up:* 1947-48. *B&Q Cup Winners:* 1993-94. *League Challenge Cup Winners:* 1997-98, 2004-05, 2011-12.

**European:** *Europa League:* 2 matches (2009-10).

**Club colours:** Shirt: Navy blue with white seams. Shorts: White. Socks: Red.

**Goalscorers:** *League (52):* Taylor 24 (1 pen), Murdoch 5 (3 pens), Higgins 4 (1 pen), Weatherston 4, Alston 2, Dods 2, Fulton J 2, McGrandles 2, Sibbald 2, Duffie 1, Grant 1, Leahy 1, Small 1, own goal 1.
*William Hill Scottish FA Cup (10):* Alston 3, Taylor 2, Duffie 1, Fulton J 1, Murdoch 1, Sibbald 1, Weatherston 1.
*Scottish Communities League Cup (2):* Kingsley 1, Taylor 1.
*Ramsdens Cup (3):* Taylor 2, Duffie 1.

| McGovern M 35 | Duffie K 28+1 | Flynn J 33 | Smith C 4+2 | Kingsley S 35 | Fulton J 23+5 | Murdoch S 32 | Fulton D 5+3 | Alston B 27+7 | Haworth A 7+5 | Taylor L 34 | Sibbald C 11+9 | Weatherston D 16+8 | White J —+3 | Dods D 27 | Higgins S 14+11 | Faulds K 1+1 | McGrandles C 23+3 | Small L —+11 | Leahy L 5+3 | Neilson R 3 | McGeever R 6+1 | Grant T 15+8 | Dick L 3 | Vaulks W 4+2 | Bowman G 1 | Rowan L 2 | Flannigan I 2+1 | Match No. |
|---|---|---|---|---|---|---|---|---|---|---|---|---|---|---|---|---|---|---|---|---|---|---|---|---|---|---|---|---|
| 1 | 2 | 3 | 4 | 5 | 6 | 7 | 8¹ | 9 | 10 | 11 | 12 | | | | | | | | | | | | | | | | | 1 |
| 1 | 2 | 3 | 4 | 5 | 7 | 8 | | 6 | 11² | 10 | 13 | 9¹ | 12 | | | | | | | | | | | | | | | 2 |
| 1 | 2 | 3 | 4 | 5 | 7 | 8 | | 9 | 12 | 11 | 10² | 6¹ | 13 | | | | | | | | | | | | | | | 3 |
| 1 | 2 | | 4 | 5 | 7¹ | 8 | 12 | 6² | 13 | 11 | 14 | 9³ | | 3 | 10 | | | | | | | | | | | | | 4 |
| 1 | 12 | 3 | 4 | 5 | | 7 | | 6¹ | 9 | 11 | 8 | 2² | 13 | | 10² | 14 | | | | | | | | | | | | 5 |
| 1 | 2 | | 4 | 5 | | 8 | | 12 | 6 | 10 | | 9¹ | | 3 | 11 | 7 | | | | | | | | | | | | 6 |
| 1 | 2 | | 4 | 5 | | 7 | | 12 | 9² | 10 | | 8¹ | | 3 | 11³ | | 6 | 13 | 14 | | | | | | | | | 7 |
| 1 | 6 | 4 | 14 | 5 | 7 | 9 | 13 | 11 | 12 | | | | | 3 | 10¹ | | | | | | 8² | 2³ | | | | | | 8 |
| 1 | 6 | 2 | 12 | 5¹ | 7 | 8 | 14 | 10³ | 11² | | | | | 3 | | | | 13 | | | 9 | 4 | | | | | | 9 |
| 1 | 6 | 2 | | 5 | 13 | 7 | | 8² | 12 | 10 | 11¹ | | | 3 | | | | | | | 9 | 4 | | | | | | 10 |
| 1 | 2² | | | 5 | 6 | 7 | 8 | 10 | 11 | | | | | 3 | 12 | | | | | | 9¹ | 4 | 13 | | | | | 11 |
| 1 | 2² | | | 5 | 7¹ | 8 | | 9 | 10 | 11 | 13 | | | 3 | 12 | | 6 | | | | | 4 | | | | | | 12 |
| 1 | 2 | | 4 | 5 | 10¹ | 7 | | 12 | 11 | | 8 | | | 3 | 9 | | | 13 | | | | 6² | | | | | | 13 |
| 1 | 2 | | 4 | 5 | 8¹ | 7 | | 13 | 11³ | 6 | | | | 3 | 12 | | 10 | 14 | | | | 9² | | | | | | 14 |
| 1 | 2 | | 4 | 5 | 11 | 6 | | 12 | 10 | 7¹ | | | | 3 | 13 | | 9 | | | | | 8² | | | | | | 15 |
| 1 | 2 | 3 | | 5 | 10 | 8 | | 7 | 11 | 4 | | | | 12 | 9 | | 6¹ | | | | | | | | | | | 16 |
| 1 | | | 4 | 5 | 13 | 7 | | 6 | 10 | 8³ | | 2² | | 3 | 11¹ | | 9 | 14 | 12 | | | | | | | | | 17 |
| 1 | 2 | | 4 | 5 | 10² | 6 | | 8 | 11 | | | | | | 7 | 13 | 12 | | | | 3 | 9¹ | | | | | | 18 |
| 1 | 2 | 4 | | | 10 | 6² | | 9 | 11 | 12 | | | | 3 | 7 | 13 | | | | | | 8¹ | 5 | | | | | 19 |
| 1 | 2 | | | 5 | 10 | 6 | | 9 | 11 | | 4 | 12 | | 3 | 7 | | | | | | | 8¹ | | | | | | 20 |
| 1 | 2 | 3 | | 5 | 8² | 6 | | 7 | 11 | 12 | | | | | 4 | | 10¹ | | | | | 9 | 13 | | | | | 21 |
| 1 | 2 | | | 5 | 6 | 7 | 12¹ | 8 | 11 | 13 | | | | 3 | 10 | | | | | | 9³ | 4² | 14 | | | | | 22 |
| 1 | 2 | | 4 | 5 | 8¹ | 7 | | 6 | 11 | 13 | | | | 3 | 12 | | | | | | 9 | 10² | | | | | | 23 |
| 1 | 2 | | 4 | 5 | 13 | 6 | | 9² | 11 | 12 | | 10 | | 3 | 7 | | | | | | | 8¹ | | | | | | 24 |
| 1 | 2 | | 4 | 5 | 8 | 6 | | 11² | 10 | | | | | 3 | 12 | | | | 13 | | 9 | 7¹ | | | | | | 25 |
| 1 | 2 | | 4 | 5 | 8 | | 14 | 9 | 11¹ | 10 | | | | 3 | 7² | | 6³ | 12 | | | | 13 | | | | | | 26 |
| 1 | 2 | | 4 | | 7² | 6 | | 9 | 11 | 8³ | | 12 | | | 13 | 14 | | | | | | 10¹ | 5 | 3 | | | | 27 |
| | | | 4 | 5 | 13 | 7¹ | | | 11² | 10³ | 12 | 9 | | 3 | | | 8 | 6 | 14 | | | | | | 2 | 1 | | 28 |
| 1 | 2 | 3 | | 5 | 9² | 8 | | 7³ | 11 | 13 | 12 | | | | 4 | | 10 | 14 | | | | 6¹ | | | | | | 29 |
| 1 | 2 | | 4 | 5 | 9³ | 6 | | 10¹ | 11 | 14 | | 12 | | 3 | 13 | | 7 | | | | | 8² | | | | | | 30 |
| 1 | 2 | 3 | | 5 | 8 | 7 | | | | 9 | | 10¹ | | 4 | 11 | | 6 | | | | | 12 | | | | | | 31 |
| 1 | | | 4 | | | 6 | | 8 | | 10 | | | | 3 | 11 | | 9¹ | 12 | | | | 7² | 5 | 14 | 2 | 13 | | 32 |
| 1 | | 3 | | 5 | | | | 7³ | 9² | 11 | | 14 | | | 13 | | 6 | 10¹ | | | | 12 | | 4 | 2 | 8 | | 33 |
| 1 | 2 | | 4 | 5 | 7² | 8 | | 9¹ | 11 | 6 | | | | 3 | 12 | | 10 | | | | | 13 | | | | | | 34 |
| 1 | 2 | | 4 | 5 | 13 | 8³ | 12 | 11 | 9 | 6 | | 14 | | | 10¹ | | | | | | | | 3 | | | 7² | | 35 |
| 1 | 2 | | 4 | 5 | 8² | 7 | | 13 | 10 | 6 | | 12 | | 3 | 11 | | | | | | | 9¹ | | 14 | | | | 36 |

# FORFAR ATHLETIC

*Year Formed:* 1885. *Ground & Address:* Station Park, Carseview Road, Forfar DD8 3BT. *Telephone:* 01307 463576.
*Fax:* 01307 466956. *E-mail:* pat@ramsayladders.co.uk *Website:* www.forfarathletic.co.uk
*Ground Capacity:* 4,602 (seated: 739). *Size of Pitch:* 103m × 64m.
*Chairman:* Alastair Donald. *Vice Chairman:* Jim Farquhar. *Secretary:* David McGregor.
*Manager:* Dick Campbell. *Assistant Manager:* Ian Campbell. *Physios:* Duncan Sangster and Donald Ritchie.
*Club Nicknames:* 'The Loons', 'The Sky Blues'.
*Previous Grounds:* None.
*Record Attendance:* 10,780 v Rangers, Scottish Cup 2nd rd, 2 Feb 1970.
*Record Transfer Fee received:* £65,000 for David Bingham to Dunfermline Ath (September 1995).
*Record Transfer Fee paid:* £50,000 for Ian McPhee from Airdrieonians (1991).
*Record Victory:* 14-1 v Lindertis, Scottish Cup 1st rd, 1 Sept 1888.
*Record Defeat:* 2-12 v King's Park, Division II, 2 Jan 1930.
*Most League Appearances:* 463: Ian McPhee, 1978-88 and 1991-98.
*Most League Goals in Season (Individual):* 46: Dave Kilgour, Division II, 1929-30.
*Most Goals Overall:* 125: John Clark, 1978-91.

## FORFAR ATHLETIC – SCOTTISH SECOND DIVISION 2012–13 LEAGUE RECORD

| Match No. | Date | Venue | Opponents | Result | | H/T Score | Lg Pos. | Goalscorers | Attendance |
|---|---|---|---|---|---|---|---|---|---|
| 1 | Aug 11 | A | Queen of the S | L | 0-2 | 0-1 | 10 | | 1247 |
| 2 | 18 | H | Stranraer | W | 4-0 | 1-0 | 5 | Swankie [8], Denholm [50], Staunton (og) [52], Fotheringham, M [67] | 449 |
| 3 | 25 | A | Ayr U | W | 3-2 | 1-1 | 3 | Campbell, I (pen) [45], Swankie [59], Fotheringham, M [89] | 1094 |
| 4 | Sept 1 | A | Stenhousemuir | W | 4-0 | 2-0 | 2 | Tulloch [37], Campbell, I (pen) [45], Denholm [62], Templeman [89] | 673 |
| 5 | 15 | H | Brechin C | W | 1-0 | 1-0 | 2 | Fotheringham, M [22] | 708 |
| 6 | 22 | A | Arbroath | D | 1-1 | 1-0 | 2 | Bolochoweckyj [4] | 940 |
| 7 | 29 | H | Albion R | W | 4-2 | 2-0 | 2 | Campbell, R 3 [13, 19, 55], Templeman (pen) [62] | 452 |
| 8 | Oct 6 | A | Alloa Ath | L | 2-3 | 1-2 | 2 | Denholm 2 [8, 79] | 487 |
| 9 | 20 | A | East Fife | L | 0-3 | 0-1 | 2 | | 541 |
| 10 | 27 | A | Stranraer | L | 1-4 | 1-2 | 3 | Denholm [28] | 258 |
| 11 | Nov 17 | H | Stenhousemuir | W | 3-2 | 2-1 | 3 | Swankie 2 [5, 23], Motion [74] | 432 |
| 12 | 20 | H | Queen of the S | L | 1-5 | 1-3 | 3 | Swankie [25] | 391 |
| 13 | 24 | A | Brechin C | L | 1-4 | 0-1 | 4 | Campbell, R [69] | 702 |
| 14 | Dec 15 | H | Arbroath | D | 1-1 | 0-0 | 3 | Hilson [74] | 719 |
| 15 | 18 | A | Albion R | W | 3-2 | 2-2 | 3 | Craigen 2 [1, 24], Sellars [90] | 249 |
| 16 | 22 | H | Alloa Ath | L | 1-2 | 1-2 | 3 | Templeman [36] | 401 |
| 17 | 29 | H | East Fife | W | 3-2 | 1-2 | 3 | Campbell, I (pen) [33], Denholm [57], Swankie [58] | 619 |
| 18 | Jan 2 | H | Brechin C | L | 1-4 | 0-0 | 4 | Swankie [80] | 903 |
| 19 | 5 | A | Stenhousemuir | L | 0-2 | 0-0 | 4 | | 461 |
| 20 | 12 | H | Ayr U | W | 2-1 | 1-0 | 4 | Robertson, J (og) [9], Swankie [52] | 479 |
| 21 | 19 | A | Queen of the S | L | 1-3 | 1-2 | 4 | Bolochoweckyj [15] | 1481 |
| 22 | 26 | A | Arbroath | L | 1-3 | 0-2 | 5 | Campbell, I (pen) [72] | 843 |
| 23 | Feb 9 | A | East Fife | W | 2-1 | 1-0 | 5 | Templeman 2 [33, 71] | 502 |
| 24 | 16 | H | Alloa Ath | L | 0-1 | 0-0 | 5 | | 511 |
| 25 | 23 | A | Ayr U | L | 1-2 | 0-1 | 5 | Campbell, I (pen) [74] | 1008 |
| 26 | 26 | H | Albion R | W | 4-2 | 1-1 | 4 | Denholm [42], Fotheringham, M [50], Hilson [52], Malin [83] | 293 |
| 27 | Mar 2 | H | Stranraer | W | 3-1 | 3-0 | 4 | Malin [18], Kader [44], Templeman [45] | 448 |
| 28 | 16 | A | Stenhousemuir | D | 3-3 | 2-3 | 4 | Kader [10], Campbell, I (pen) [37], Denholm [77] | 395 |
| 29 | 30 | H | Arbroath | L | 2-4 | 1-1 | 5 | Denholm [30], Templeman [55] | 770 |
| 30 | Apr 2 | A | Albion R | W | 2-1 | 1-1 | 4 | Campbell, I [45], Templeman [70] | 220 |
| 31 | 6 | H | East Fife | W | 3-2 | 1-1 | 5 | Malin 2 [20, 51], Swankie [82] | 471 |
| 32 | 9 | A | Brechin C | W | 4-3 | 2-0 | 4 | Hilson [13], Bolochoweckyj [33], Malin [47], Swankie [84] | 581 |
| 33 | 13 | A | Alloa Ath | L | 0-1 | 0-0 | 4 | | 507 |
| 34 | 20 | H | Queen of the S | L | 0-4 | 0-1 | 5 | | 555 |
| 35 | 27 | A | Stranraer | W | 3-0 | 2-0 | 5 | Dunlop (og) [10], Templeman [28], Kader [69] | 422 |
| 36 | May 4 | H | Ayr U | W | 2-1 | 2-1 | 4 | Templeman [12], Campbell, I (pen) [45] | 622 |

**Final League Position: 4**

**Honours**
*League Champions:* Second Division 1983-84. Third Division 1994-95; C Division 1948-49.
*Runners-up: Third Division* 1996-97, 2009-10. *Promoted to Second Division:* 2009-10 (play-offs).
*Scottish Cup:* Semi-finals 1982.
*League Cup:* Semi-finals 1977-78.
*League Challenge Cup:* Semi-finals 2004-05.

**Club colours:** Shirt: Sky blue and navy stripes. Shorts: Navy. Socks: Navy.

**Goalscorers:** *League (67):* Swankie 10, Templeman 10 (1 pen), Denholm 9, Campbell I 8 (7 pens), Malin 5, Campbell R 4, Fotheringham M 4, Bolochoweckyj 3, Hilson 3, Kader 3, Craigen 2, Motion 1, Sellars 1, Tulloch 1, own goals 3.
*William Hill Scottish FA Cup (9):* Campbell R 2, Swankie 2, Campbell I 1 (1 pen), King 1, Robertson 1, Templeman 1, Tulloch 1.
*Scottish Communities League Cup (0).*
*Ramsdens Cup (5):* Swankie 2, Denholm 1, Gibson 1, Kader 1.
*Play-Offs (4):* Templeman 2, Campbell I 1, Robertson 1.

| Seutar D 10 | McCulloch M 34 | Tulloch S 16+4 | Bolochoweckyj M 26+1 | Campbell I 34+1 | Campbell R 21+8 | Motion K 7+7 | Gibson K 4 | Denholm D 25+3 | Templeman C 34+1 | Swankie G 31+1 | Dunlop M 11+4 | King C 1+19 | Kader O 8+17 | Fotheringham M 19+7 | Gibson G 1 | Sellars B 5+9 | Faeroe O 11 | Webster S —+1 | Smith A —+1 | Craigen J 10 | Gray C —+1 | Keiller L —+1 | Scott D 3 | Thomson G —+1 | Hamilton J 8 | Robertson W 14+6 | Hilson D 19+1 | Bishop J 2 | Malin G 15+5 | Hill D 15 | Brown J 9+6 | Fotheringham G 3 | Match No. |
|---|---|---|---|---|---|---|---|---|---|---|---|---|---|---|---|---|---|---|---|---|---|---|---|---|---|---|---|---|---|---|---|---|---|
| 1 | 2 | 3 | 4 | 5 | $6^2$ | 7 | $8^1$ | $9^2$ | 10 | 11 | 12 | 13 | 14 | | | | | | | | | | | | | | | | | | | | 1 |
| 1 | 2 | 5 | 4 | 3 | $6^3$ | 14 | $8^1$ | $9^2$ | 11 | 10 | | 12 | 13 | 7 | | | | | | | | | | | | | | | | | | | 2 |
| 1 | 2 | 5 | 4 | 3 | $7^2$ | 13 | $11^1$ | $6^3$ | 9 | | | 12 | 8 | 10 | 14 | | | | | | | | | | | | | | | | | | 3 |
| 1 | 2 | 3 | 8 | 5 | 6 | 13 | $11^2$ | $9^1$ | 4 | 10 | | 12 | $7^3$ | 14 | | | | | | | | | | | | | | | | | | | 4 |
| 1 | | 4 | 2 | 5 | 6 | 12 | 7 | $9^2$ | 8 | 10 | | 13 | $11^1$ | 14 | | | | | $3^3$ | | | | | | | | | | | | | | 5 |
| 1 | 2 | $7^4$ | $4^8$ | 3 | 6 | 14 | | $9^1$ | $11^2$ | 10 | | 12 | $8^3$ | 13 | | 5 | | | | | | | | | | | | | | | | | 6 |
| 1 | 3 | | | $6^3$ | 5 | $10^1$ | | 8 | 11 | 12 | | 9 | 7 | 2 | | $4^2$ | 13 | 14 | | | | | | | | | | | | | | | 7 |
| 1 | 2 | 4 | | 12 | 6 | 5 | $11^3$ | $8^2$ | 10 | | | 13 | $9^1$ | 7 | | 14 | 3 | | | | | | | | | | | | | | | | 8 |
| | $2^4$ | 14 | 3 | 5 | 6 | 7 | $10^2$ | 12 | | | | $4^3$ | 13 | $9^1$ | | $11^8$ | | | | 8 | | | | | | | | | | | | | 9 |
| 1 | 2 | 12 | 3 | $5^3$ | $7^1$ | 8 | 11 | 10 | 4 | $9^2$ | | 6 | 13 | 14 | | | | | | | | | | | | | | | | | | | 10 |
| | 2 | 4 | 5 | $6^2$ | $9^1$ | | 8 | 11 | 3 | 13 | | 7 | 12 | | | 10 | | | | 1 | | | | | | | | | | | | | 11 |
| | 2 | 3 | 5 | $10^2$ | $8^1$ | | 11 | $4^8$ | 12 | 6 | | 7 | 13 | | | | $9^1$ | | | 1 | | | 14 | | | | | | | | | | 12 |
| | $2^4$ | 3 | 5 | 6 | 12 | | $9^1$ | $10^3$ | $11^2$ | | | 13 | 14 | 7 | | 4 | 8 | | | 1 | | | | | | | | | | | | | 13 |
| | 4 | 3 | 5 | $6^2$ | | | 10 | 11 | 13 | 14 | | | 12 | | | $2^2$ | | | | $7^1$ | | | | | | 1 | 8 | 9 | | | | | 14 |
| 4 | 2 | $3^1$ | 5 | $6^3$ | | | 10 | 11 | | | | 14 | 13 | 12 | | | | | | 7 | | | | | | 1 | $8^2$ | 9 | | | | | 15 |
| 3 | $7^4$ | | 5 | $6^1$ | 14 | | $11^3$ | 12 | | | | 13 | 9 | 2 | | $4^2$ | | | | | | | | | | 1 | 8 | 10 | | | | | 16 |
| | 2 | 4 | 5 | 14 | | | 9 | $10^3$ | 11 | | | 13 | | 8 | | | | | | | | | | | | 1 | $7^1$ | | $6^2$ | 3 | 12 | | 17 |
| 7 | | 4 | 5 | | | | 9 | $10^3$ | 11 | 14 | | | 13 | $8^2$ | | | | | | | | | | | | 1 | $2^1$ | | 6 | 3 | 12 | | 18 |
| | 2 | | 5 | 13 | | | $9^1$ | $10^3$ | 11 | 4 | 12 | | 14 | $7^2$ | | | | | | | | | | | | 1 | 8 | | 6 | 3 | | | 19 |
| | 4 | 12 | 5 | 14 | | | $9^3$ | 10 | 11 | 3 | | 13 | | $2^1$ | | | | | | | | | | | | 1 | 7 | | $6^2$ | 8 | | | 20 |
| | 2 | 4 | 5 | 14 | | | $9^1$ | $10^3$ | 11 | | | 13 | 12 | 3 | | | | | | | | | | | | 1 | $8^2$ | | 6 | 7 | | | 21 |
| 3 | 12 | | 5 | 13 | | | $9^1$ | $10^2$ | 11 | | | | $7^3$ | 4 | | | | | | $2^8$ | | | | | | 6 | | | 14 | 1 | 8 | | 22 |
| | 2 | 3 | 5 | $6^2$ | | | $10^3$ | 11 | 4 | 13 | 14 | 12 | | | | 7 | | | | | | | | | | | | | 1 | | $8^1$ | 9 | 23 |
| | 2 | 4 | 3 | $7^2$ | | | $10^3$ | 11 | 5 | 14 | | 12 | | 13 | | | | | | | | | | | | | 13 | | 8 | 1 | 9 | $6^1$ | 24 |
| | 2 | 12 | 3 | 5 | 6 | 13 | 10 | 11 | $4^1$ | | | | $7^3$ | 9 | | 14 | | | | | | | | | | $7^3$ | 9 | | 14 | 1 | $8^2$ | | 25 |
| | 2 | 4 | 3 | 5 | | | $9^8$ | 10 | 11 | 14 | 12 | | $7^3$ | | | | | | | | | | | | | | $6^1$ | | $8^2$ | 1 | 13 | | 26 |
| | 2 | 4 | $3^8$ | $5^1$ | 14 | | 11 | 10 | | $9^2$ | $6^3$ | 8 | | | | | | | | | | | | | | 12 | | | 7 | 1 | 13 | | 27 |
| 3 | 4 | | 5 | | | | 12 | 10 | 11 | | | $6^1$ | 8 | | | | | | | | | | | | 2 | | 9 | | $7^2$ | 1 | 13 | | 28 |
| | 2 | 4 | | 5 | | | 9 | 10 | 11 | 14 | $6^1$ | $8^2$ | | 3 | | | | | | | | | | | | | 13 | | $7^3$ | 1 | 12 | | 29 |
| | 2 | 4 | | 5 | | | 12 | 9 | $10^3$ | 3 | 14 | | | $6^2$ | 11 | | | | | | | | | | | $6^2$ | 11 | | 13 | 1 | 8 | $7^1$ | 30 |
| | 2 | $4^3$ | | 5 | | | 9 | 10 | 11 | | | 13 | $8^1$ | | | 3 | | | | | | | | | | 14 | $6^2$ | | 7 | 1 | 12 | | 31 |
| | 2 | | 3 | 5 | | | 9 | 10 | 11 | | | 13 | $8^2$ | | | $4^3$ | | | | | | | | | | 14 | $6^1$ | | 7 | 1 | 12 | | 32 |
| | 2 | | 3 | 5 | 14 | | 9 | $10^1$ | 11 | | | 12 | | 4 | | | | | | | | | | | | 13 | 6 | | 7 | 1 | $8^2$ | | 33 |
| | 2 | | 3 | $5^2$ | 14 | | 9 | $10^1$ | 11 | 13 | | 12 | | 4 | | | | | | | | | | | | 4 | $6^3$ | | 8 | 1 | 7 | | 34 |
| 4 | | 3 | 5 | $11^3$ | | | 6 | 10 | | $2^1$ | 14 | 13 | | 12 | | 9 | | | | | | | | | | 12 | 9 | | $7^2$ | 1 | 8 | | 35 |
| 4 | | $3^1$ | 5 | 11 | | | $9^2$ | 10 | | 12 | | | 13 | | | 2 | | | | | | | | | | 2 | 6 | | 8 | 1 | 7 | | 36 |

# GREENOCK MORTON

*Year Formed:* 1874. *Ground & Address:* Cappielow Park, Sinclair St, Greenock PA15 2TY. *Telephone:* 01475 723571.
*Fax:* 01475 781084. *E-mail:* info@gmfc.net *Website:* www.gmfc.net
*Ground Capacity:* 11,612 (seated: 6,062). *Size of Pitch:* 100m × 65m.
*Chairman:* Douglas Rae. *Chief Executive:* Gillian Donaldson. *Company Secretary:* Mary Davidson.
*Manager:* Allan Moore. *Assistant Manager:* Mark McNally. *Physio:* Alyson Hendry.
*Club Nickname:* 'The Ton'.
*Previous Grounds:* Grant Street 1874, Garvel Park 1875, Cappielow Park 1879, Ladyburn Park 1882, Cappielow Park 1883.
*Record Attendance:* 23,500 v Celtic, 29 April 1922.
*Record Transfer Fee received:* £500,000 for Derek Lilley to Leeds United (March 1997).
*Record Transfer Fee paid:* £250,000 for Janne Lindberg and Marko Rajamäki from MyPa, Finland (Nov 1994).
*Record Victory:* 11-0 v Carfin Shamrock, Scottish Cup 4th rd, 13 Nov 1886.
*Record Defeat:* 1-10 v Port Glasgow Ath, Division II, 5 May, 1894 and v St Bernards, Division II, 14 Oct 1933.
*Most Capped Player:* Jimmy Cowan, 25, Scotland.
*Most League Appearances:* 534: Derek Collins, 1987-98, 2001-05.
*Most League Goals in Season (Individual):* 58: Allan McGraw, Division II, 1963-64.
*Most Goals Overall (Individual):* 136: Andy Ritchie, 1976-83.

## GREENOCK MORTON – SCOTTISH FIRST DIVISION 2012–13 LEAGUE RECORD

| Match No. | Date | Venue | Opponents | Result | H/T Score | Lg Pos. | Goalscorers | Attendance |
|---|---|---|---|---|---|---|---|---|
| 1 | Aug 11 | H | Livingston | D 2-2 | 1-2 | 6 | Weatherson [7], Wallace [80] | 1898 |
| 2 | 18 | A | Hamilton A | D 1-1 | 1-0 | 6 | O'Brien [15] | 1572 |
| 3 | 25 | H | Falkirk | L 1-2 | 1-2 | 7 | Campbell [31] | 1756 |
| 4 | Sept 1 | H | Dumbarton | W 3-0 | 1-0 | 6 | Campbell 3 (1 pen) [43, 54 (p), 76] | 1602 |
| 5 | 15 | A | Cowdenbeath | W 4-3 | 2-1 | 5 | Weatherson 2 [12, 25], Campbell [46], O'Brien [54] | 611 |
| 6 | 22 | H | Raith R | W 1-0 | 0-0 | 3 | Stirling [67] | 1628 |
| 7 | 29 | A | Airdrie U | W 3-2 | 0-1 | 3 | Campbell 2 [49, 79], O'Brien [68] | 1054 |
| 8 | Oct 6 | H | Partick Th | W 3-1 | 2-1 | 3 | Rutkiewicz [14], McLaughlin, M [39], O'Brien [86] | 3445 |
| 9 | 20 | A | Dunfermline Ath | D 2-2 | 1-0 | 3 | Campbell 2 [40, 76] | 3511 |
| 10 | 27 | A | Livingston | D 2-2 | 0-1 | 3 | Campbell 2 [50, 55] | 1417 |
| 11 | Nov 10 | H | Hamilton A | L 0-1 | 0-1 | 3 | | 1815 |
| 12 | 17 | A | Dumbarton | W 5-1 | 3-0 | 3 | Hardie 2 (1 pen) [3 (p), 17], Weatherson 2 [37, 61], Graham [54] | 1188 |
| 13 | 24 | H | Cowdenbeath | W 1-0 | 0-0 | 3 | Hawke [88] | 1526 |
| 14 | Dec 8 | A | Raith R | D 3-3 | 1-1 | 3 | Rutkiewicz [8], O'Brien [65], Hardie [88] | 1375 |
| 15 | 15 | H | Airdrie U | W 2-0 | 1-0 | 3 | Graham [43], Hardie [83] | 1302 |
| 16 | 26 | A | Partick Th | W 2-1 | 0-1 | 2 | Hardie [64], Taggart [84] | 4955 |
| 17 | 29 | H | Dunfermline Ath | W 4-2 | 1-1 | 2 | Bachirou [44], Tidser 2 [56, 89], Weatherson [61] | 3076 |
| 18 | Jan 2 | H | Dumbarton | L 0-3 | 0-2 | 1 | | 2414 |
| 19 | 5 | A | Cowdenbeath | D 1-1 | 0-1 | 2 | MacDonald [51] | 647 |
| 20 | 12 | A | Falkirk | W 1-0 | 0-0 | 1 | Hardie [64] | 3078 |
| 21 | 19 | H | Livingston | W 2-1 | 1-0 | 1 | Hardie [15], MacDonald [68] | 1913 |
| 22 | 26 | H | Raith R | W 1-0 | 0-0 | 1 | Tidser [53] | 2006 |
| 23 | Feb 9 | A | Airdrie U | W 4-0 | 2-0 | 1 | O'Brien [24], McMenamin [44], MacDonald [52], Wilkie [60] | 984 |
| 24 | 16 | H | Partick Th | D 2-2 | 0-1 | 1 | MacDonald 2 (1 pen) [57, 81 (p)] | 5647 |
| 25 | 23 | A | Dunfermline Ath | W 4-1 | 1-0 | 1 | MacDonald 2 (1 pen) [31 (p), 50], Tidser 2 [46, 64] | 2720 |
| 26 | Mar 5 | A | Hamilton A | L 1-2 | 1-1 | 1 | O'Brien [8] | 1009 |
| 27 | 9 | H | Falkirk | W 2-0 | 2-0 | 1 | Campbell [30], MacDonald [44] | 1962 |
| 28 | 16 | A | Dumbarton | W 3-0 | 2-0 | 1 | Tidser [32], Hardie [38], MacDonald [81] | 1241 |
| 29 | 23 | H | Cowdenbeath | W 4-2 | 0-2 | 1 | MacDonald 2 (1 pen) [51 (p), 54], Taggart [63], Hardie [71] | 1533 |
| 30 | 30 | A | Raith R | L 1-2 | 0-2 | 2 | Wilkie [72] | 1529 |
| 31 | Apr 6 | H | Airdrie U | W 5-2 | 2-0 | 2 | MacDonald 3 [5, 22, 60], McMenamin (pen) [69], Warren (og) [85] | 1772 |
| 32 | 10 | A | Partick Th | L 0-1 | 0-1 | 2 | | 8875 |
| 33 | 13 | H | Dunfermline Ath | L 0-1 | 0-1 | 2 | | 1634 |
| 34 | 20 | A | Livingston | W 2-0 | 1-0 | 2 | Campbell [43], Wilkie [55] | 1158 |
| 35 | 27 | H | Hamilton A | L 0-2 | 0-1 | 2 | | 1541 |
| 36 | May 4 | A | Falkirk | L 1-4 | 1-0 | 2 | McLaughlin, M [27] | 3179 |

**Final League Position: 2**

**Honours**
*League Champions:* First Division 1977-78, 1983-84, 1986-87. Division II 1949-50, 1963-64, 1966-67. Second Division 1994-95, 2006-07. Third Division 2002-03.
*Runners-up:* Division 1 1916-17. First Division 2012-13. Division II 1899-1900, 1928-29, 1936-37.
*Scottish Cup Winners:* 1922; *Runners-up:* 1948. *League Cup Runners-up:* 1963-64.
*B&Q Cup Runners-up:* 1992-93.

**European:** *UEFA Cup:* 2 matches (*Fairs Cup:* 1968-69).

**Club colours:** Shirt: Blue and white hoops. Shorts: White with blue trim. Socks: White.

**Goalscorers:** *League (73):* MacDonald 14 (3 pens), Campbell 13 (1 pen), Hardie 9 (1 pen), O'Brien 7, Tidser 6, Weatherson 6, Wilkie 3, Graham 2, McLaughlin M 2, McMenamin 2 (1 pen), Rutkiewicz 2, Taggart 2, Bachirou 1, Hawke 1, Stirling 1, Wallace 1, own goal 1.
*William Hill Scottish FA Cup (12):* Tidser 5 (1 pen), Weatherson 5, Hardie 1, MacDonald 1.
*Scottish Communities League Cup (5):* McLaughlin M 1, Stirling 1, Tidser 1, Wallace 1, Weatherson 1.
*Ramsdens Cup (3):* O'Brien 1, Tidser 1, Wallace 1.

| Gaston D 33 | Taggart S 29+4 | Naismith J 3+1 | Rutkiewicz K 25 | Halsman J 5+5 | Reid C 30 | Wallace A 10+10 | Stirling S 6+1 | Tidser M 31 | O'Brien D 31+2 | Weatherson P 18+10 | Graham D 16+8 | Mensing S 1 | Dyer W 23+1 | O'Ware T 10+4 | Bachirou F 31+2 | Campbell A 15+8 | Wilkie K 10+12 | Hawke L —+5 | McLaughlin M 21 | Gormley L —+1 | Hardie M 19+4 | MacDonald P 14+7 | McLaughlin D 1+1 | McMenamin C 11+4 | McDaid D —+1 | Fulton A —+2 | Hutton D 3 | McLean E —+1 | Match No. |
|---|---|---|---|---|---|---|---|---|---|---|---|---|---|---|---|---|---|---|---|---|---|---|---|---|---|---|---|---|---|
| 1 | 2 | 3¹ | 4 | 5 | 6 | 7 | 8 | 9 | 10 | 11 | 12 | | | | | | | | | | | | | | | | | | 1 |
| 1 | 2 | | 3¹ | 8² | 7 | 9⁸ | 10 | 11³ | 6 | 4 | 5 | 12 | 13 | 14 | | | | | | | | | | | | | | | 2 |
| 1 | 2 | 4 | 3 | 6¹ | 7² | 9³ | 12 | 11 | 5 | 8 | 10 | 13 | 14 | | | | | | | | | | | | | | | | 3 |
| 1 | 2 | | 3 | 14 | 8 | 9 | 10² | 6³ | 5 | 7¹ | 11 | 12 | 13 | 4 | | | | | | | | | | | | | | | 4 |
| 1 | 6 | | 3 | 12 | 13 | 8 | 9 | 10¹ | 5 | 2 | 7 | 11² | 4 | | | | | | | | | | | | | | | | 5 |
| 1 | 2 | | 3 | | 6 | 8 | | 10 | 9 | 5 | 7 | 11¹ | 4 | 12 | | | | | | | | | | | | | | | 6 |
| 1 | 2 | 4 | 3 | | 6 | 8¹ | 9 | 10 | 12 | 5 | 7 | 11 | | | | | | | | | | | | | | | | | 7 |
| 1 | 14 | 3 | 2 | | 6¹ | 8 | 9 | 10² | 12 | 5 | 7 | 11 | 4³ | 13 | | | | | | | | | | | | | | | 8 |
| 1 | 13 | 3 | 2² | 14 | 8 | 9 | 10¹ | 6 | 5 | 7 | 11 | 4 | 12³ | | | | | | | | | | | | | | | | 9 |
| 1 | | 3 | 2 | 12 | 8² | 9 | 10 | 6¹ | 5 | 7 | 11 | 13 | 4 | | | | | | | | | | | | | | | | 10 |
| 1 | 2 | 3 | | 6² | 8 | 9 | 10 | 13 | 5 | 11 | 7¹ | 4 | 12 | | | | | | | | | | | | | | | | 11 |
| 1 | 2 | 4 | 12 | 3 | 8 | 11 | 10³ | 9 | 5¹ | 6² | 13 | 14 | 7 | | | | | | | | | | | | | | | | 12 |
| 1 | 2 | 4 | 3 | | 8 | 11 | 10 | 9 | 5¹ | 6 | 12² | 13 | 7 | | | | | | | | | | | | | | | | 13 |
| 1 | 2 | 3 | | | 8 | 11 | 10² | 9 | 5³ | 12 | 6 | 13 | 4¹ | 7 | 14 | | | | | | | | | | | | | | 14 |
| 1 | 2 | 3¹ | | 13 | 8 | 10 | 11² | 9³ | 5 | 12 | 6 | 4 | 7 | 14 | | | | | | | | | | | | | | | 15 |
| 1 | 14 | 3 | 2 | 12 | 8 | 10² | 9¹ | 5³ | 6 | 4 | 7 | 13 | | | | | | | | | | | | | | | | | 16 |
| 1 | 13 | 3 | 2 | 9² | 8 | 11 | 10¹ | 5 | 6 | 7 | 12 | 4 | | | | | | | | | | | | | | | | | 17 |
| 1 | 9 | 3 | 2³ | 13 | 8 | 11 | 10¹ | 5 | 14 | 6 | 4² | 7 | 12 | | | | | | | | | | | | | | | | 18 |
| 1 | 2 | 3 | 13 | 4 | 6¹ | 8 | 9² | 10³ | 5 | 7 | 12 | 14 | 11 | | | | | | | | | | | | | | | | 19 |
| 1 | | 3 | 2 | 8 | 11 | 12 | 9² | 5 | 6 | 13 | 4 | 7 | 10¹ | | | | | | | | | | | | | | | | 20 |
| 1 | 2 | 3 | 5 | 8 | 11 | 13 | 9¹ | 6 | 12 | 4 | 7 | 10² | | | | | | | | | | | | | | | | | 21 |
| 1 | 2 | 3³ | 5 | 8 | 11 | 13 | 9¹ | 14 | 6 | 4 | 7 | 10² | 12 | | | | | | | | | | | | | | | | 22 |
| 1 | 2 | 3 | 13 | 7 | 9² | 12 | 14 | 5 | 4 | 8³ | 6 | 10¹ | 11 | | | | | | | | | | | | | | | | 23 |
| 1 | 2 | 3 | | 7 | 9 | 14 | 13 | 5 | 4 | 8² | 6¹ | 12 | 10 | 11³ | | | | | | | | | | | | | | | 24 |
| 1 | 2 | 3 | 4 | 7 | 9 | 12 | 14 | 5 | 8 | 13 | 11³ | 10¹ | 6² | | | | | | | | | | | | | | | | 25 |
| 1 | 2 | 3 | | 8 | 11 | 12 | 9³ | 5 | 4 | 6 | 13 | 14 | 7¹ | 10² | | | | | | | | | | | | | | | 26 |
| 1 | 2 | 3 | 4 | | 8 | 9 | | 5 | 6 | 10¹ | 13 | 7² | 11 | 12 | | | | | | | | | | | | | | | 27 |
| 1 | 2 | 3 | 13 | 4 | 14 | 8³ | 5 | 6 | 10¹ | 9² | 7 | 11 | 12 | | | | | | | | | | | | | | | | 28 |
| 1 | 2 | 3 | 13 | 4 | 14 | 8 | 5 | 6 | 11¹ | 9³ | 7² | 10 | 12 | | | | | | | | | | | | | | | | 29 |
| 1 | 2 | 3 | | 8 | 9¹ | 14 | 5 | 6 | 12 | 13 | 4³ | 7 | 11 | 10² | | | | | | | | | | | | | | | 30 |
| 1 | 2 | 5 | 3¹ | 13 | 8 | 9 | 7 | 12 | 6³ | 4 | 10¹ | 11 | 14 | | | | | | | | | | | | | | | | 31 |
| 1 | 12 | 3 | 5 | 8 | 9 | 2¹ | 6 | 13 | 14 | 4³ | 7 | 11 | 10² | | | | | | | | | | | | | | | | 32 |
| 1 | 2 | 5³ | 3 | 6 | 9² | 12 | 8¹ | 14 | 7 | 4 | 10 | 11 | 13 | | | | | | | | | | | | | | | | 33 |
| 5 | 2 | 8 | 4 | 9 | 14 | 13 | 11¹ | 6³ | 3 | 7² | 12 | 10 | | | | | | | | | | | | | 1 | | | | 34 |
| 5 | 9 | 2 | 6³ | 14 | 13 | 4 | 11¹ | 8 | 3 | 7 | 12 | 10² | | | | | | | | | | | | | 1 | | | | 35 |
| 2 | 7³ | 3¹ | 9 | 5 | 8 | 11 | 6 | 4 | 13 | 10² | 12 | | | | | | | | | | | | | 13 | 10² | 12 | 1 | 14 | 36 |

# HAMILTON ACADEMICAL

*Year Formed:* 1874. *Ground:* New Douglas Park, Cadzow Avenue, Hamilton ML3 0FT. *Telephone:* 01698 368652.
*Fax:* 01698 285422. *E-mail:* scott@acciesfc.co.uk *Website:* www.acciesfc.co.uk
*Ground Capacity:* 6,078 (all seated). *Size of Pitch:* 105m × 68m.
*Chairman:* Les Gray. *Secretary:* Scott Struthers.
*Player Manager:* Alex Neil. *Physio:* Pauline Robertson.
*Club Nickname:* 'The Accies'.
*Previous Grounds:* Bent Farm, South Avenue, South Haugh, Douglas Park, Cliftonhill Stadium, Firhill Stadium.
*Record Attendance:* 28,690 v Hearts, Scottish Cup 3rd rd, 3 Mar 1937 (at Douglas Park); 5,895 v Rangers, 28 Feb 2009 (at New Douglas Park).
*Record Transfer Fee received:* £1,200,000 for James McCarthy to Wigan Ath (July 2009).
*Record Transfer Fee paid:* £180,000 for Tomas Cerny from Sigma Olomouc (July 2009).
*Record Victory:* 9-0 v Gala Fairydean, Scottish Cup 1st rd, 28 Jan 1922.
*Record Defeat:* 1-11 v Hibernian, Division I, 6 Nov 1965.
*Most Capped Player:* Colin Miller, 29 (61), Canada, 1988-94.
*Most League Appearances:* 452: Rikki Ferguson, 1974-88.
*Most League Goals in Season (Individual):* 35: David Wilson, Division I; 1936-37.
*Most Goals Overall (Individual):* 246: David Wilson, 1928-39.

## HAMILTON ACADEMICAL – SCOTTISH FIRST DIVISION 2012–13 LEAGUE RECORD

| Match No. | Date | Venue | Opponents | Result | H/T Score | Lg Pos. | Goalscorers | Atten- dance |
|---|---|---|---|---|---|---|---|---|
| 1 | Aug 11 | A | Raith R | L 0-2 | 0-0 | 8 | | 1868 |
| 2 | 18 | H | Greenock Morton | D 1-1 | 0-1 | 8 | Crawford [81] | 1572 |
| 3 | 25 | A | Cowdenbeath | L 0-1 | 0-1 | 9 | | 525 |
| 4 | Sept 1 | A | Partick Th | L 0-4 | 0-1 | 9 | | 2603 |
| 5 | 15 | H | Falkirk | D 1-1 | 1-1 | 9 | Routledge [42] | 1174 |
| 6 | 22 | A | Dumbarton | D 3-3 | 1-1 | 9 | Crawford [21], Keatings 2 [88, 90] | 695 |
| 7 | 29 | H | Dunfermline Ath | L 0-3 | 0-0 | 9 | | 1330 |
| 8 | Oct 6 | A | Airdrie U | W 4-0 | 0-0 | 9 | Crawford [67], Longridge [72], May 2 (1 pen) [82, 88 (p)] | 868 |
| 9 | 20 | H | Livingston | L 1-2 | 1-2 | 9 | May [1] | 943 |
| 10 | 27 | H | Raith R | L 0-1 | 0-1 | 9 | | 1079 |
| 11 | Nov 10 | A | Greenock Morton | W 1-0 | 1-0 | 9 | May [21] | 1815 |
| 12 | 16 | H | Partick Th | W 1-0 | 1-0 | 7 | Smith (og) [41] | 2450 |
| 13 | 24 | A | Falkirk | L 1-2 | 0-0 | 8 | Page [58] | 2682 |
| 14 | Dec 15 | A | Dunfermline Ath | D 1-1 | 1-1 | 8 | May [17] | 2864 |
| 15 | 26 | H | Airdrie U | W 3-0 | 2-0 | 7 | Longridge [15], Neil [23], Page [55] | 1179 |
| 16 | Jan 5 | H | Falkirk | D 1-1 | 0-1 | 7 | Mackinnon [80] | 1423 |
| 17 | 12 | H | Cowdenbeath | W 2-1 | 0-1 | 7 | Page [61], May [65] | 1021 |
| 18 | 19 | A | Raith R | W 2-0 | 0-0 | 7 | Ellis (og) [89], May [90] | 1194 |
| 19 | 26 | A | Dumbarton | L 1-3 | 0-1 | 7 | May [60] | 878 |
| 20 | Feb 9 | H | Dunfermline Ath | L 1-2 | 0-1 | 7 | Gillespie [66] | 1248 |
| 21 | 16 | A | Airdrie U | D 2-2 | 0-0 | 7 | May 2 [61, 90] | 755 |
| 22 | 19 | A | Partick Th | L 0-1 | 0-0 | 7 | | 2046 |
| 23 | 23 | H | Livingston | D 1-1 | 0-0 | 7 | May [90] | 914 |
| 24 | Mar 5 | H | Greenock Morton | W 2-1 | 1-1 | 7 | Gaston (og) [35], Gordon [58] | 1009 |
| 25 | 9 | A | Cowdenbeath | D 1-1 | 1-1 | 7 | May [32] | 370 |
| 26 | 16 | H | Partick Th | L 0-2 | 0-0 | 8 | | 1852 |
| 27 | 23 | A | Falkirk | W 2-0 | 2-0 | 7 | Routledge [14], Longridge [26] | 2616 |
| 28 | 30 | H | Dumbarton | L 2-3 | 0-1 | 8 | Ryan [63], May [87] | 943 |
| 29 | Apr 2 | H | Dumbarton | W 2-1 | 0-1 | 7 | May 2 [79, 85] | 775 |
| 30 | 6 | A | Dunfermline Ath | W 3-2 | 1-1 | 7 | McShane [2], Devlin [57], Canning [77] | 4697 |
| 31 | 9 | H | Airdrie U | W 5-0 | 3-0 | 7 | May 3 (1 pen) [9 (p), 37, 74], McShane [22], Brophy [87] | 850 |
| 32 | 13 | A | Livingston | W 3-0 | 2-0 | 5 | May 3 (1 pen) [41 (p), 43, 84] | 1607 |
| 33 | 16 | A | Livingston | D 0-0 | 0-0 | 5 | | 787 |
| 34 | 20 | H | Raith R | W 2-0 | 0-0 | 5 | May [52], Ryan [90] | 969 |
| 35 | 27 | A | Greenock Morton | W 2-0 | 1-0 | 4 | May 2 [39, 55] | 1541 |
| 36 | May 4 | H | Cowdenbeath | L 1-3 | 1-0 | 5 | May [27] | 1434 |

**Final League Position: 5**

**Honours**
*League Champions:* Division II 1903-04. First Division 1985-86, 1987-88, 2007-08; Third Division 2000-01.
*Runners-up:* Division II 1952-53, 1964-65; Second Division 1996-97, 2003-04.
*Scottish Cup Runners-up:* 1911, 1935. *League Cup:* Semi-finalists three times. *League Challenge Cup Runners-up:* 2005-06, 2011-12. *B&Q Cup Winners:* 1991-92, 1992-93.

**Club colours:** Shirt: Red and white hoops. Shorts: White. Socks: White.

**Goalscorers:** *League (52):* May 25 (3 pens), Crawford 3, Longridge 3, Page 3, Keatings 2, McShane 2, Routledge 2, Ryan 2, Brophy 1, Canning 1, Devlin 1, Gillespie 1, Gordon 1, Mackinnon 1, Neil 1, own goals 3.
*William Hill Scottish FA Cup (6):* Crawford 1, Devlin 1, Gillespie 1, May 1, Routledge 1, Ryan 1.
*Scottish Communities League Cup (3):* Crawford 1, Mackinnon 1, Routledge 1.
*Ramsdens Cup (0).*

| Cuthbert K 36 | McGlinchey C 11 | Canning M 33 | Devlin M 17+5 | Hendrie S 20+3 | Neil A 21 | Gillespie G 24+8 | Routledge J 34 | Fraser G 5+6 | Crawford A 30+3 | McShane J 9+6 | Ryan A 3+24 | Kirkpatrick J —+2 | Mackinnon D 17+7 | Fisher G 18+10 | Longridge L 22+10 | Gordon Z 31+1 | Kilday L 4+1 | Keatings J 2+6 | May S 33 | Page J 21+1 | Finnie R 4 | Brophy E —+1 | McMann S 1 | Match No. |
|---|---|---|---|---|---|---|---|---|---|---|---|---|---|---|---|---|---|---|---|---|---|---|---|---|
| 1 | 2 | 3 | 4 | 5 | 6 | 7[1] | 8 |  | 9[2] | 10[3] | 11 | 12 | 13 | 14 |  |  |  |  |  |  |  |  |  | 1 |
| 1 | 2[2] | 3[1] | 4 | 5 | 6[8] | 13 | 7 | 14 | 9 | 10 |  |  | 8[3] | 11 | 12 |  |  |  |  |  |  |  |  | 2 |
| 1 |  | 3 | 5 |  |  |  |  |  | 4[1] | 8 | 11 | 10 | 12 | 9[2] | 6[8] | 14 | 7 | 2 | 13 |  |  |  |  | 3 |
| 1 |  | 3 | 10 | 12 | 6 |  | 11 |  | 9[3] | 13 |  |  |  | 4[1] | 7[2] | 2 | 5 | 14 | 8 |  |  |  |  | 4 |
| 1 |  | 5 | 3 | 14 | 8 | 7[1] | 12 | 13 | 9[3] | 11 |  |  |  |  |  | 2 | 4 | 6[2] | 10 |  |  |  |  | 5 |
| 1 |  | 4 | 12 | 3 | 10 | 6 | 7 |  |  |  |  |  |  | 8[2] | 11 | 2 | 5[1] | 13 | 9 |  |  |  |  | 6 |
| 1 | 2 | 8 | 3 | 5 | 6 | 14 | 11[3] | 12 | 7[2] | 13 |  |  |  | 10[1] |  |  |  |  | 9 | 4 |  |  |  | 7 |
| 1 |  | 3 | 5 | 7[2] | 2 | 8 | 6[1] |  | 9 | 13 | 12 |  |  | 10[3] | 14 |  |  |  | 11 | 4 |  |  |  | 8 |
| 1 |  | 3 | 5 | 8[8] | 2 | 6 | 9[2] |  | 10 | 14 | 12[3] |  |  | 7[1] | 13 |  |  |  | 11 | 4 |  |  |  | 9 |
| 1 |  | 3 | 12 | 5[1] | 8 | 6 | 11 | 13 | 7[3] | 9[2] |  |  |  |  |  | 2 | 14 |  | 10 | 4 |  |  |  | 10 |
| 1 |  | 5 | 3 |  | 6 | 13 | 9 |  | 8 | 12 |  |  |  | 10[1] |  | 2 |  |  | 11 | 4 | 7[2] |  |  | 11 |
| 1 |  | 5[2] | 3 |  | 6 | 12 | 9 | 14 | 8 | 13 |  |  |  | 7[1] |  | 2 |  |  | 11 | 4 | 10[3] |  |  | 12 |
| 1 |  | 5[1] | 3 |  | 8 | 6 | 7 | 13 | 9 | 12 |  |  |  |  |  | 2 |  |  | 11 | 4 | 10[2] |  |  | 13 |
| 1 |  | 5[1] | 3 | 12 | 8 | 7 | 14 |  | 10 | 13 |  |  |  | 9[3] | 6 | 2 |  |  | 11[2] | 4 |  |  |  | 14 |
| 1 |  | 5 | 3 | 7 | 12 | 6 | 9[3] |  | 13 | 14 |  |  |  | 8[2] | 11[1] | 2 |  |  | 10 | 4 |  |  |  | 15 |
| 1 |  | 5[2] | 3 | 7 | 12 | 6 | 9 |  | 13 | 14 |  |  |  | 8 | 11[3] | 2[1] |  |  | 10 | 4 |  |  |  | 16 |
| 1 |  | 5[2] | 3 | 7[8] | 13 | 6 | 8[1] |  | 9 | 12 |  |  |  | 14 | 11[3] | 2 |  |  | 10 | 4 |  |  |  | 17 |
| 1 |  | 5 | 3 |  | 6[2] | 8[1] | 9 |  | 7 | 13 |  |  |  | 12 | 10 | 2 |  |  | 11 | 4 |  |  |  | 18 |
| 1 |  | 5[3] | 3 |  | 6[1] | 9 | 8 |  | 10 | 14 |  |  | 13 | 12 | 7[2] | 2 |  |  | 11 | 4 |  |  |  | 19 |
| 1 |  | 3 | 14 | 5[3] | 8 | 6 | 10[2] | 12 | 9[1] | 13 |  |  |  | 7 |  | 2 |  |  | 11 | 4 |  |  |  | 20 |
| 1 |  | 3 | 6 | 5 | 8 |  | 10[1] | 13 | 14 | 12 |  |  |  | 9[2] | 7 | 2[3] |  |  | 11 | 4 |  |  |  | 21 |
| 1 |  | 3 | 5 | 7[1] | 9 | 8 | 14 | 13 | 10 | 12 |  |  |  | 6[2] |  | 2[3] |  |  | 11 | 4 |  |  |  | 22 |
| 1 |  | 3 | 5 | 9 | 7 | 13 | 11 |  | 8 | 6[1] |  |  |  | 12 |  | 2[2] |  |  | 10 | 4 |  |  |  | 23 |
| 1 |  | 3 | 4 | 6 | 5 | 9 | 12 |  | 7[1] | 8 |  |  |  | 10 |  | 2 |  |  | 11 |  |  |  |  | 24 |
| 1 |  | 3[3] | 4 | 6 | 5 | 8 | 13 |  | 10[2] | 7[1] |  |  |  | 9 | 12 | 2 |  | 14 | 11 |  |  |  |  | 25 |
| 1 |  | 3 | 4 | 14 | 6[1] | 5[3] | 9 | 12 | 13 | 7[2] |  |  |  | 8 | 10 | 2 |  |  | 11 |  |  |  |  | 26 |
| 1 |  | 3 | 5 | 11 | 7 | 12 | 9 |  | 8[1] |  |  |  |  | 6 |  | 2 |  |  | 10 | 4 |  |  |  | 27 |
| 1 |  | 4 | 5 | 7[1] | 9 | 13 | 12 |  | 10 | 8[8] |  |  |  | 6 |  | 2[2] |  |  | 11 | 3 |  |  |  | 28 |
| 1 |  | 3 | 12 |  | 9 | 7 | 6 | 14 | 10[2] | 8 |  |  |  | 13 |  | 2 |  |  | 11 | 4[1] | 5[3] |  |  | 29 |
| 1 |  | 4 | 3 | 5[1] | 9 | 7 | 6 |  | 11[2] | 13 |  |  |  | 8 | 12 | 2 |  |  | 10 |  |  |  |  | 30 |
| 1 |  | 3 | 4[8] | 5 | 8[2] | 7 | 9 |  | 11[1] | 12 |  |  |  | 6 |  | 2 |  |  | 10[3] | 13 |  |  | 14 | 31 |
| 1 |  | 3 | 13 | 7[1] | 2 | 9 | 6 |  | 11[2] | 14 |  |  |  | 8 | 12 | 5 |  |  | 10[3] | 4[8] |  |  |  | 32 |
| 1 |  | 3 | 4 | 12 | 5 | 9 | 6 |  | 8 | 7[1] |  |  |  | 13 |  | 2[2] |  |  | 10 |  |  | 11 |  | 33 |
| 1 |  | 4 | 3 | 5 | 6[2] | 8 | 9[3] |  | 11[1] | 12 |  |  |  | 7 | 14 | 13 |  | 2[2] | 10 |  |  |  |  | 34 |
| 1 |  | 3 | 4 | 5 | 6[2] | 7 | 9[3] |  | 11[1] | 12 |  |  |  | 8 | 14 | 13 |  | 2 | 10 |  |  |  |  | 35 |
| 1 |  | 3 | 4 | 5 | 7[1] | 6 | 8 |  | 11[8] | 9 |  |  |  | 12 |  | 2 |  |  | 10 |  |  |  |  | 36 |

# HEART OF MIDLOTHIAN

*Year Formed:* 1874. *Ground & Address:* Tynecastle Stadium, McLeod Street, Edinburgh EH11 2NL. *Telephone:* 0871 663 1874. *Fax:* 0131 200 7222. *E-mail:* hearts@homplc.co.uk *Website:* www.heartsfc.co.uk
*Ground Capacity:* 17,402. *Size of Pitch:* 100m × 64m.
*Administrators:* Bryan Jackson, James Stephen and Trevor Birch.
*Manager:* Gary Locke. *Assistant Manager:* Billy Brown. *Physio:* Rob Marshall.
*Club Nicknames:* 'Hearts', 'Jambos'.
*Previous Grounds:* The Meadows 1874, Powderhall 1878, Old Tynecastle 1881 Tynecastle Park, 1886.
*Record Attendance:* 53,396 v Rangers, Scottish Cup 3rd rd, 13 Feb 1932 (57,857 v Barcelona, 28 July 2007 at Murrayfield).
*Record Transfer Fee received:* £9,000,000 for Craig Gordon to Sunderland (August 2008).
*Record of Transfer paid:* £850,000 for Mirsad Beslija to Genk (January 2006).
*Record Victory:* 15-0 v King's Park, Scottish Cup 2nd rd, 13 Feb 1937 (21-0 v Anchor, EFA Cup, 30 Oct 1880).
*Record Defeat:* 1-8 v Vale of Leven, Scottish Cup 3rd rd, 1883.
*Most Capped Player:* Steven Pressley, 32, Scotland.
*Most League Appearances:* 515: Gary Mackay, 1980-97.
*Most League Goals in Season (Individual):* 44: Barney Battles, 1930-31.
*Most Goals Overall (Individual):* 214: John Robertson, 1983-98.

## HEART OF MIDLOTHIAN – SCOTTISH PREMIER LEAGUE 2012–13 LEAGUE RECORD

| Match No. | Date | | Venue | Opponents | Result | H/T Score | Lg Pos. | Goalscorers | Atten-dance |
|---|---|---|---|---|---|---|---|---|---|
| 1 | Aug | 4 | H | St Johnstone | W 2-0 | 1-0 | 1 | Sutton (pen) [30], Templeton [82] | 13,022 |
| 2 | | 12 | A | Hibernian | D 1-1 | 1-1 | 2 | Driver [29] | 12,887 |
| 3 | | 18 | H | Inverness CT | D 2-2 | 2-0 | 1 | Novikovas [15], Sutton (pen) [41] | 11,512 |
| 4 | | 26 | A | Aberdeen | D 0-0 | 0-0 | 4 | | 11,971 |
| 5 | Sept | 2 | H | Dundee | L 0-1 | 0-1 | 7 | | 12,446 |
| 6 | | 15 | A | St Mirren | L 0-2 | 0-1 | 9 | | 4307 |
| 7 | | 22 | A | Dundee U | W 3-0 | 2-0 | 5 | Paterson 2 [28, 61], Novikovas [30] | 6597 |
| 8 | | 29 | H | Kilmarnock | L 1-3 | 0-1 | 8 | Zaliukas [88] | 11,847 |
| 9 | Oct | 7 | A | Celtic | L 0-1 | 0-1 | 9 | | 46,204 |
| 10 | | 21 | H | Motherwell | W 1-0 | 1-0 | 8 | Grainger [14] | 11,572 |
| 11 | | 27 | H | Ross Co | D 2-2 | 1-0 | 7 | Novikovas [40], Sutton [90] | 12,139 |
| 12 | Nov | 3 | A | Dundee | L 0-1 | 0-1 | 9 | | 5344 |
| 13 | | 10 | A | Inverness CT | D 1-1 | 0-1 | 10 | Zaliukas (pen) [90] | 3332 |
| 14 | | 17 | H | St Mirren | W 1-0 | 0-0 | 7 | Grainger [64] | 16,443 |
| 15 | | 24 | A | Motherwell | D 0-0 | 0-0 | 9 | | 4147 |
| 16 | | 28 | H | Celtic | L 0-4 | 0-3 | 9 | | 15,264 |
| 17 | Dec | 8 | H | Aberdeen | W 2-0 | 1-0 | 7 | Stevenson (pen) [32], Paterson [54] | 14,410 |
| 18 | | 15 | A | St Johnstone | D 2-2 | 2-1 | 9 | Sutton [15], Driver [38] | 2974 |
| 19 | | 23 | H | Dundee U | W 2-1 | 2-0 | 6 | Stevenson 2 (1 pen) [15, 31 (p)] | 13,603 |
| 20 | | 26 | A | Kilmarnock | L 0-1 | 0-1 | 9 | | 5163 |
| 21 | Jan | 3 | H | Hibernian | D 0-0 | 0-0 | 9 | | 17,062 |
| 22 | | 19 | A | Celtic | L 1-4 | 0-2 | 9 | Holt [69] | 48,374 |
| 23 | | 30 | H | Dundee | W 1-0 | 0-0 | 9 | Sutton [86] | 11,284 |
| 24 | Feb | 2 | A | Ross Co | D 2-2 | 1-1 | 8 | Ngoo [31], Walker [63] | 3903 |
| 25 | | 9 | A | Dundee U | L 1-3 | 0-1 | 10 | Ngoo [76] | 6842 |
| 26 | | 16 | H | Kilmarnock | L 0-3 | 0-1 | 10 | | 14,280 |
| 27 | | 23 | H | Inverness CT | L 2-3 | 0-1 | 10 | Holt [55], Webster [74] | 11,325 |
| 28 | | 27 | A | St Mirren | L 0-2 | 0-2 | 11 | | 3369 |
| 29 | Mar | 2 | A | Motherwell | L 1-2 | 0-2 | 11 | Sutton [59] | 11,048 |
| 30 | | 5 | H | St Johnstone | W 2-0 | 1-0 | 10 | Stevenson [33], Sutton [83] | 10,080 |
| 31 | | 10 | A | Hibernian | D 0-0 | 0-0 | 10 | | 15,007 |
| 32 | | 30 | A | Aberdeen | L 0-2 | 0-1 | 10 | | 10,175 |
| 33 | Apr | 6 | H | Ross Co | W 4-2 | 0-1 | 10 | Ngoo 2 [49, 84], Holt [79], Ikonomou (og) [80] | 10,456 |
| 34 | | 20 | A | Kilmarnock | W 1-0 | 1-0 | 10 | Sutton [4] | 3572 |
| 35 | | 27 | A | Dundee | L 0-1 | 0-0 | 10 | | 5896 |
| 36 | May | 4 | H | St Mirren | W 3-0 | 2-0 | 8 | Walker [14], McHattie [43], Hamill (pen) [54] | 16,312 |
| 37 | | 12 | H | Hibernian | L 1-2 | 1-0 | 10 | Barr [45] | 15,994 |
| 38 | | 18 | A | Aberdeen | D 1-1 | 0-0 | 10 | Stevenson [62] | 10,465 |

**Final League Position: 10**

**Honours**
*League Champions:* Division I 1894-95, 1896-97, 1957-58, 1959-60. First Division 1979-80;
*Runners-up:* Division I 1893-94, 1898-99, 1903-04, 1905-06, 1914-15, 1937-38, 1953-54, 1956-57, 1958-59, 1964-65. Premier Division 1985-86, 1987-88, 1991-92, 2005-06. First Division 1977-78, 1982-83.
*Scottish Cup Winners:* 1891, 1896, 1901, 1906, 1956, 1998, 2006, 2012; *Runners-up:* 1903, 1907, 1968, 1976, 1986, 1996.
*League Cup Winners:* 1954-55, 1958-59, 1959-60, 1962-63; *Runners-up:* 1961-62, 1996-97, 2012-13.

**European:** *European Cup:* 8 matches (1958-59, 1960-61, 2006-07). *Cup Winners' Cup:* 10 matches (1976-77, 1996-97, 1998-99). *UEFA Cup:* 47 matches (*Fairs Cup:* 1961-62, 1963-64, 1965-66. *UEFA Cup:* 1984-85, 1986-87, 1988-89, 1990-91, 1992-93, 1993-94, 2000-01, 2003-04, 2004-05, 2006-07). *Europa League:* 8 matches (2010-11, 2011-12, 2012-13).

**Club colours:** Shirt: Maroon with white trim. Shorts: White with maroon trim. Socks: Maroon with white tops.

**Goalscorers:** *League (40):* Sutton 8 (2 pens), Stevenson 5 (2 pens), Ngoo 4, Holt 3, Novikovas 3, Paterson 3, Driver 2, Grainger 2, Walker 2, Zaliukas 2 (1 pen), Barr 1, Hamill 1 (1 pen), McHattie 1, Templeton 1, Webster 1, own goal 1.
*William Hill Scottish FA Cup (0).*
*Scottish Communities League Cup (7):* Stevenson 2, Zaliukas 2, Grainger 1, Ngoo 1, Paterson 1.
*Europa League (1):* Templeton 1.

| MacDonald J 38 | Paterson C 18 + 4 | Webster A 33 | Zaliukas M 24 + 1 | McHattie K 21 | Barr D 30 + 2 | McGowan R 20 | Robinson S 7 + 6 | Templeton D 2 | Sutton J 20 + 15 | Driver A 15 + 7 | Taouil M 23 + 8 | Novikovas A 16 + 14 | Carrick D 5 + 11 | Grainger D 13 | Walker J 16 + 8 | Prychynenko D 1 + 3 | Holt J 16 + 5 | Stevenson R 28 + 1 | McGowan D 11 + 8 | Enckelman P — + 1 | Smith G 4 + 5 | Wilson D 13 | Tapping C 10 + 1 | Mullen F 7 + 1 | King B 4 + 4 | Ngoo M 15 | McKay B 1 + 1 | Hamill J 6 + 1 | Smith D 1 + 2 | McGhee J — + 1 | Match No. |
|---|---|---|---|---|---|---|---|---|---|---|---|---|---|---|---|---|---|---|---|---|---|---|---|---|---|---|---|---|---|---|---|
| 1 | 2 | 3 | 4 | 5 | $6^3$ | 7 | $8^1$ | 9 | 10 | $11^2$ | 12 | 13 | 14 | | | | | | | | | | | | | | | | | | 1 |
| 1 | 2 | 3 | 4 | 5 | 8 | 7 | $6^1$ | 9 | 10 | $11^2$ | 12 | 13 | | | | | | | | | | | | | | | | | | | 2 |
| 1 | 2 | 3 | $4^1$ | | 7 | 6 | 12 | | 10 | $9^2$ | $8^3$ | 11 | | | 5 | | 13 | 14 | | | | | | | | | | | | | 3 |
| 1 | $7^3$ | 3 | $4^1$ | | 8 | 2 | | | 11 | 6 | 9 | $10^2$ | 14 | | 5 | | 12 | 13 | | | | | | | | | | | | | 4 |
| 1 | 7 | 3 | 4 | | $6^3$ | 2 | | | $11^1$ | 13 | 8 | 10 | $9^2$ | | 5 | | 14 | | | | 12 | | | | | | | | | | 5 |
| 1 | 9 | 4 | 3 | | $8^1$ | 2 | | | 12 | $6^2$ | 7 | 10 | 13 | | 5 | | 11 | | | | | | | | | | | | | | 6 |
| 1 | $11^2$ | | 4 | | 3 | 2 | 6 | | 13 | 12 | $7^3$ | 10 | $8^1$ | | 5 | | 9 | 14 | | | | | | | | | | | | | 7 |
| 1 | 11 | | 4 | | 3 | 2 | $8^1$ | | 12 | $10^2$ | 7 | 6 | 13 | | 5 | | 9 | | | | | | | | | | | | | | 8 |
| 1 | $11^2$ | 3 | 4 | | 6 | 2 | 14 | | 13 | 9 | 7 | $10^3$ | | | 5 | | 8 | 12 | | | | | | | | | | | | | 9 |
| 1 | 7 | 3 | 4 | | $6^2$ | 2 | 13 | | 12 | 8 | $10^3$ | $11^1$ | | | 5 | | 9 | 14 | | | | | | | | | | | | | 10 |
| 1 | $6^2$ | 3 | 4 | | 8 | 2 | | | 12 | 10 | 9 | $11^1$ | | | 5 | | | 7 | | | | 13 | | | | | | | | | 11 |
| 1 | 10 | 4 | 5 | | 7 | 2 | $8^1$ | | $11^2$ | 12 | 6 | $9^3$ | | | 3 | | 14 | 13 | | | | | | | | | | | | | 12 |
| 1 | 10 | 3 | 4 | | $7^3$ | 2 | | | 14 | 12 | $8^2$ | $11^1$ | | | 5 | | 6 | 9 | 13 | | | | | | | | | | | | 13 |
| 1 | $6^1$ | 3 | 4 | | 7 | 2 | | | | | | 13 | 14 | 12 | 5 | | $9^2$ | $10^3$ | 11 | | 8 | | | | | | | | | | 14 |
| 1 | 8 | 4 | 3 | | 6 | 2 | | | | | | 14 | 12 | 13 | $5^1$ | | $10^2$ | $9^3$ | 11 | | 7 | | | | | | | | | | 15 |
| 1 | 6 | 3 | 4 | 5 | 8 | 2 | | | | | | 13 | 14 | 12 | | | $9^3$ | $10^1$ | 11 | | $7^2$ | | | | | | | | | | 16 |
| 1 | 12 | 3 | 4 | 5 | 7 | 2 | | | 10 | 9 | $6^3$ | 13 | | | 14 | | $8^1$ | $11^2$ | | | | | | | | | | | | | 17 |
| 1 | $11^3$ | 3 | 4 | 5 | $7^1$ | 2 | | | 10 | 8 | | 14 | 13 | | | | 6 | 12 | | | $9^2$ | | | | | | | | | | 18 |
| 1 | 13 | 3 | 4 | 5 | 7 | 2 | | | 11 | $9^1$ | 12 | 14 | | | | | 6 | $8^1$ | | | $10^2$ | | | | | | | | | | 19 |
| 1 | 12 | 3 | 4 | 5 | $8^2$ | 2 | 14 | | 11 | 9 | $7^3$ | 13 | | | | | 6 | | | | $10^1$ | | | | | | | | | | 20 |
| 1 | 13 | 3 | 4 | | | 2 | | $8^1$ | 11 | $6^3$ | 9 | $10^2$ | | | 14 | | | 12 | | | | | 7 | 3 | | | | | | | 21 |
| 1 | $10^1$ | 3 | | 5 | | 2 | | | 11 | 9 | $8^3$ | | 14 | 12 | | | 6 | $7^2$ | | | | | 4 | 13 | | | | | | | 22 |
| 1 | | 3 | 4 | | | | | | | | | 13 | 14 | 12 | $6^3$ | | $7^2$ | 8 | | | | | 5 | 9 | 2 | $10^1$ | 11 | | | | 23 |
| 1 | | 3 | 4 | | | | | | | | | | 13 | 12 | $6^2$ | | $8^1$ | 9 | 14 | | | | 5 | $7^3$ | 2 | 10 | 11 | | | | 24 |
| 1 | | 3 | $4^1$ | | | | | | | | | 14 | 13 | 12 | $6^2$ | | 7 | 8 | | | | | 2 | 9 | 5 | $10^3$ | 11 | | | | 25 |
| 1 | | 3 | $4^1$ | | 8 | | | | | | | | 13 | | 14 | | 10 | $7^2$ | 12 | | | | 5 | 9 | 2 | $6^3$ | 11 | | | | 26 |
| 1 | | 3 | | 5 | 8 | | | | | | | | | 12 | | | $10^2$ | $6^3$ | 7 | | 14 | | 4 | 9 | $2^1$ | 13 | 11 | | | | 27 |
| 1 | | 3 | $2^2$ | 5 | | | | | | | | | 14 | 12 | | | $8^1$ | 10 | $6^3$ | | 9 | 13 | 4 | 7 | | | 11 | | | | 28 |
| 1 | | 3 | 10 | 5 | 8 | | | | | | 12 | | | | $9^3$ | $6^3$ | | $2^2$ | | | | 13 | 4 | $7^1$ | 13 | 14 | 11 | | | | 29 |
| 1 | | 3 | 8 | 5 | | | | | $10^3$ | | $7^2$ | $9^1$ | 12 | | 13 | | 6 | | 14 | | | | 4 | 7 | $2^1$ | 11 | | | | | 30 |
| 1 | | 3 | 11 | 5 | | | | | | | 8 | $9^2$ | 13 | 14 | $6^3$ | | | | | | | | 4 | 7 | $2^1$ | 10 | 12 | | | | 31 |
| 1 | | 3 | $11^3$ | 5 | | | | | | | 7 | 13 | 14 | 9 | 6 | | | | | | | | 4 | $8^2$ | | 10 | 12 | | | | 32 |
| 1 | | | 14 | 5 | $8^1$ | | | | | | 13 | $11^3$ | | 9 | 12 | | 6 | | | | | | 4 | $7^2$ | | 10 | 3 | 2 | | | 33 |
| 1 | | 3 | $8^3$ | 5 | | | | | | | 13 | 12 | | 11 | $9^2$ | | 6 | 7 | 14 | | | | 4 | | | $10^1$ | 2 | | | | 34 |
| 1 | $3^4$ | | 4 | 5 | | | | | 10 | | 12 | 13 | | | $9^2$ | | $8^3$ | 6 | 2 | | | | 14 | $11^1$ | | 7 | | | | | 35 |
| 1 | | | 4 | 5 | | | | | 10 | | $7^3$ | $11^1$ | | $9^2$ | 6 | | 8 | | 3 | | | | 13 | | | 2 | 12 | 14 | | | 36 |
| 1 | 4 | | 5 | 3 | | | | | 11 | | $8^2$ | 12 | | 9 | $6^3$ | | 7 | | 14 | | | | $10^1$ | 2 | 13 | | | | | | 37 |
| 1 | 4 | 13 | 5 | | | | | | 14 | | 8 | $9^1$ | 12 | 6 | $7^2$ | 3 | | | | | | $11^3$ | 2 | 10 | | | | | | | 38 |

# HIBERNIAN

*Year Formed:* 1875. *Ground & Address:* Easter Road Stadium, 12 Albion Place, Edinburgh EH7 5QG. *Telephone:* 0131 661 2159. *Fax:* 0131 659 6488. *E-mail:* club@hibernianfc.co.uk *Website:* www.hibernianfc.co.uk
*Ground Capacity:* 20,421 (all seated). *Size of Pitch:* 102m × 67m.
*Chairman:* Rod Petrie. *Club Secretary:* Garry O'Hagan.
*Manager:* Pat Fenlon. *First Team Coach:* Liam O'Brien. *Physio:* Calum Rea.
*Club Nickname:* 'Hibs', 'Hibees'.
*Previous Grounds:* Meadows 1875-78, Powderhall 1878-79, Mayfield 1879-80, First Easter Road 1880-92, Second Easter Road 1892-.
*Record Attendance:* 65,860 v Hearts, Division I, 2 Jan 1950.
*Record Transfer Fee received:* £4,400,000 for Scott Brown from Celtic (2007).
*Record of Transfer paid:* £700,000 for Ulises de la Cruz to LDU Quito (2001).
*Record Victory:* 15-1 v Pebbles Rovers, Scottish Cup 2nd rd, 11 Feb 1961.
*Record Defeat:* 0-10 v Rangers, Division I, 24 Dec 1898.
*Most Capped Player:* Lawrie Reilly, 38, Scotland.
*Most League Appearances:* 446: Arthur Duncan.
*Most League Goals in Season (Individual):* 42: Joe Baker, 1959-60.
*Most Goals Overall (Individual):* 233: Lawrie Reilly, 1945-58.

## HIBERNIAN – SCOTTISH PREMIER LEAGUE 2012–13 LEAGUE RECORD

| Match No. | Date | Venue | Opponents | Result | H/T Score | Lg Pos. | Goalscorers | Attendance |
|---|---|---|---|---|---|---|---|---|
| 1 | Aug 5 | A | Dundee U | L 0-3 | 0-1 | 12 | | 7267 |
| 2 | 12 | H | Hearts | D 1-1 | 1-1 | 12 | Griffiths [45] | 12,887 |
| 3 | 18 | A | St Mirren | W 2-1 | 1-0 | 6 | Griffiths 2 [15, 61] | 5039 |
| 4 | 25 | H | St Johnstone | W 2-0 | 1-0 | 2 | Hanlon [45], Doyle [53] | 9639 |
| 5 | Sept 1 | A | Celtic | D 2-2 | 0-1 | 2 | Clancy [53], Cairney [73] | 45,867 |
| 6 | 15 | H | Kilmarnock | W 2-1 | 2-1 | 2 | Griffiths 2 (1 pen) [14, 45 (p)] | 9723 |
| 7 | 22 | H | Inverness CT | D 2-2 | 2-1 | 2 | Doyle [23], Wotherspoon [31] | 9908 |
| 8 | 29 | A | Aberdeen | L 1-2 | 1-1 | 5 | Doyle [33] | 8282 |
| 9 | Oct 6 | H | Dundee | W 3-0 | 1-0 | 1 | Doyle [29], Griffiths (pen) [51], Wotherspoon [74] | 10,163 |
| 10 | 20 | A | Ross Co | L 2-3 | 2-2 | 4 | Griffiths [6], McPake [45] | 4070 |
| 11 | 26 | A | Motherwell | W 4-0 | 1-0 | 2 | Wotherspoon [28], Griffiths 2 (2 pens) [64, 74], Handling [90] | 5301 |
| 12 | Nov 3 | H | St Mirren | W 2-1 | 1-1 | 1 | Griffiths 2 [37, 65] | 10,358 |
| 13 | 11 | H | Dundee U | W 2-1 | 1-0 | 1 | Griffiths [19], Doyle [51] | 10,596 |
| 14 | 17 | A | Dundee | L 1-3 | 0-1 | 2 | Griffiths [90] | 6743 |
| 15 | 24 | H | Aberdeen | L 0-1 | 0-0 | 3 | | 12,007 |
| 16 | 28 | A | St Johnstone | W 1-0 | 0-0 | 2 | Cairney [82] | 3266 |
| 17 | Dec 8 | A | Inverness CT | L 0-3 | 0-1 | 4 | | 3422 |
| 18 | 15 | H | Motherwell | L 2-3 | 1-0 | 4 | Doyle 2 [41, 55] | 8817 |
| 19 | 23 | A | Kilmarnock | D 1-1 | 1-1 | 4 | Doyle [26] | 4028 |
| 20 | 26 | H | Ross Co | L 0-1 | 0-0 | 4 | | 8980 |
| 21 | 29 | H | Celtic | W 1-0 | 1-0 | 4 | Griffiths [9] | 16,805 |
| 22 | Jan 3 | A | Hearts | D 0-0 | 0-0 | 4 | | 17,062 |
| 23 | 19 | H | Dundee | D 1-1 | 0-1 | 4 | Griffiths [49] | 10,386 |
| 24 | 27 | A | Aberdeen | D 0-0 | 0-0 | 4 | | 7184 |
| 25 | 30 | A | Ross Co | L 0-1 | 0-1 | 4 | | 3055 |
| 26 | Feb 11 | H | St Johnstone | L 1-3 | 0-2 | 5 | Griffiths [82] | 8735 |
| 27 | 16 | A | St Mirren | W 1-0 | 0-0 | 4 | Griffiths (pen) [72] | 4524 |
| 28 | 24 | A | Dundee U | D 2-2 | 1-1 | 6 | McPake [27], Griffiths [51] | 6160 |
| 29 | 27 | H | Kilmarnock | D 2-2 | 0-0 | 6 | McGivern [85], Griffiths [88] | 8121 |
| 30 | Mar 10 | H | Hearts | D 0-0 | 0-0 | 6 | | 15,007 |
| 31 | 15 | A | Motherwell | L 1-4 | 1-0 | 6 | Taiwo [23] | 5108 |
| 32 | 30 | H | Inverness CT | L 1-2 | 0-0 | 8 | Griffiths [59] | 10,055 |
| 33 | Apr 6 | A | Celtic | L 0-3 | 0-1 | 9 | | 49,174 |
| 34 | 22 | H | Aberdeen | D 0-0 | 0-0 | 9 | | 8326 |
| 35 | 27 | H | St Mirren | D 3-3 | 1-0 | 9 | Griffiths 2 [31, 86], Caldwell [67] | 9264 |
| 36 | May 12 | A | Hearts | W 2-1 | 0-1 | 9 | Griffiths [48], Caldwell [90] | 15,994 |
| 37 | 15 | A | Kilmarnock | W 3-1 | 1-0 | 7 | Robertson [10], Doyle 2 [86, 90] | 3198 |
| 38 | 18 | H | Dundee | W 1-0 | 0-0 | 7 | Wotherspoon [79] | 9522 |

**Final League Position: 7**

**Honours**
*League Champions:* Division I 1902-03, 1947-48, 1950-51, 1951-52. First Division 1980-81, 1998-99. Division II 1893-94, 1894-95, 1932-33; *Runners-up:* Division I 1896-97, 1946-47, 1949-50, 1952-53, 1973-74, 1974-75.
*Scottish Cup Winners:* 1887, 1902; *Runners-up:* 1896, 1914, 1923, 1924, 1947, 1958, 1972, 1979, 2001, 2012, 2013.
*League Cup Winners:* 1972-73, 1991-92, 2006-07; *Runners-up:* 1950-51, 1968-69, 1974-75, 1985-86, 1993-94, 2003-04.
*Drybrough Cup Winners:* 1972-73, 1973-74.

**European:** *European Cup:* 6 matches (1955-56 semi-finals). *Cup Winners' Cup:* 6 matches (1972-73). *UEFA Cup:* 64 matches (*Fairs Cup:* 1960-61 semi-finals, 1961-62, 1962-63, 1965-66, 1967-68, 1968-69, 1970-71. *UEFA Cup:* 1973-74, 1974-75, 1975-76, 1976-77, 1978-79, 1989-90, 1992-93, 2001-02, 2005-06. *Europa League:* 2 matches 2010-11).

**Club colours:** Shirt: Green with white sleeves. Shorts: White. Socks: Green.

**Goalscorers:** *League (49):* Griffiths 23 (5 pens), Doyle 10, Wotherspoon 4, Cairney 2, Caldwell 2, McPake 2, Clancy 1, Handling 1, Hanlon 1, McGivern 1, Robertson 1, Taiwo 1.
*William Hill Scottish FA Cup (10):* Griffiths 5 (1 pen), Deegan 1, Done 1, Doyle 1, Harris 1, own goal 1.
*Scottish Communities League Cup: (0).*

| Williams B 37 | Clancy T 19 | McPake J 29 | Stephens D 1 | Hanlon P 34 | Cairney P 26+3 | Stevenson L 22+7 | Doyle E 28+8 | Wotherspoon D 26+8 | Sproule 12+8 | Griffiths L 36 | Handling D 4+11 | Caldwell R 3+14 | O'Hanlon S —+1 | Maybury A 24+3 | Deegan G 19+1 | Claros J 29+5 | Kuqi S 1+12 | McGivern R 25+2 | Taiwo T 24+2 | Harris A 6+5 | Stanton S —+1 | Robertson S 8+4 | Done M 6+1 | Thomson K 5+1 | Forster J 3 | Murdoch S 1 | Horribine D —+1 | Match No. |
|---|---|---|---|---|---|---|---|---|---|---|---|---|---|---|---|---|---|---|---|---|---|---|---|---|---|---|---|---|
| 1 | 2 | 3[3] | 4 | 5 | 6 | 7[1] | 8 | 9 | 10[2] | 11 | 12 | 13 | 14 |  |  |  |  |  |  |  |  |  |  |  |  |  |  | 1 |
| 1 | 2 | 3 |  | 4 | 10 | 7[1] | 9[2] | 8 |  | 11[3] | 14 | 13 |  | 5 | 6 | 12 |  |  |  |  |  |  |  |  |  |  |  | 2 |
| 1 | 2 | 4 | 3 | 9[1] | 10[2] | 8 |  | 12 |  | 11[3] |  |  | 14 | 5 | 6 | 7 | 13 |  |  |  |  |  |  |  |  |  |  | 3 |
| 1 | 2 | 3 |  | 4 | 9 | 11[1] | 6 | 10[2] |  | 12 |  |  |  | 5 | 8 | 7 | 13 |  |  |  |  |  |  |  |  |  |  | 4 |
| 1 | 2 | 3 |  | 4 | 9 | 12 | 11 | 6[2] |  | 13 | 10 |  |  | 5 | 7[1] | 8 |  |  |  |  |  |  |  |  |  |  |  | 5 |
| 1 | 2 | 3 |  | 4 | 8 | 12 | 11[3] | 9[1] | 14 | 10[2] |  | 13 |  | 5 | 6 | 7 |  |  |  |  |  |  |  |  |  |  |  | 6 |
| 1 | 2 | 3 |  | 4 | 9[1] | 10 | 6 | 12 |  | 11 |  |  |  | 5 | 7 | 8 |  |  |  |  |  |  |  |  |  |  |  | 7 |
| 1 | 2 | 3 |  | 4 | 9[3] | 10 | 6[2] |  |  | 11 |  | 13 |  | 5[1] | 7 | 8 | 14 | 12 |  |  |  |  |  |  |  |  |  | 8 |
| 1 | 2 | 3 |  | 4 | 9[3] | 10 | 6 |  |  | 11[2] |  |  |  | 8[1] | 7 | 13 | 5 | 12 | 14 |  |  |  |  |  |  |  |  | 9 |
| 1 |  | 3 | 4 | 9[2] | 11[1] | 7 | 10 |  |  | 13 |  |  |  | 2 | 8 | 12 | 5 | 6 |  |  |  |  |  |  |  |  |  | 10 |
| 1 | 2[1] | 4 | 3 | 9[3] | 13 | 10 | 6 |  |  | 11[2] | 14 |  |  | 12 | 7 | 5 | 8 |  |  |  |  |  |  |  |  |  |  | 11 |
| 1 |  | 3 |  | 4 | 9 | 12 | 11[1] | 6 |  | 10 |  |  |  | 2 | 7 | 5 | 8 |  |  |  |  |  |  |  |  |  |  | 12 |
| 1 |  |  |  | 4 | 9 | 8 | 11[3] | 6[2] | 13 | 10[1] |  |  |  | 2 | 7 | 12 | 5 | 3 | 14 |  |  |  |  |  |  |  |  | 13 |
| 1 |  | 3 |  | 9 | 5 | 11[1] | 6 | 13 |  | 10 |  | 14 |  | 2 | 8[2] | 12 | 4 | 7 |  |  |  |  |  |  |  |  |  | 14 |
| 1 |  | 3 |  | 9 | 5 | 11[1] | 6[2] |  |  | 10 | 12 |  |  | 2 | 7 | 13 | 4 | 8 |  |  |  |  |  |  |  |  |  | 15 |
| 1 |  | 3 |  | 9[2] | 5 | 11[1] | 6 | 13 |  | 10[3] | 12 |  |  | 2 | 8 | 14 | 4 | 7 |  |  |  |  |  |  |  |  |  | 16 |
| 1 |  | 3 |  | 9[1] | 5 | 12 | 8[2] | 10 |  | 11 |  |  |  | 2 | 6 | 13 | 4 | 7 |  |  |  |  |  |  |  |  |  | 17 |
| 1 | 3 |  | 4 | 9[3] | 10[2] | 6 | 11[1] | 14 |  | 13 |  |  |  | 2 | 12 | 8 | 5 | 7 |  |  |  |  |  |  |  |  |  | 18 |
| 1 |  |  |  | 4 | 9 | 5 | 11[3] | 6 |  | 12 | 10 |  |  | 2 | 7 | 13 | 14 | 3 | 8[2] |  |  |  |  |  |  |  |  | 19 |
| 1 | 2[3] | 3 |  | 4 | 9 | 11 | 6[2] | 10 |  | 12 |  |  |  | 8 | 13 | 14 | 5 | 7[1] |  |  |  |  |  |  |  |  |  | 20 |
| 1 | 2[1] | 3 |  | 4 | 9 | 5 | 10 | 13 |  | 11[2] | 14 |  |  | 12 | 6 | 8 |  |  | 7[3] |  |  |  |  |  |  |  |  | 21 |
| 1 | 2 | 3 |  | 4 | 9[1] | 13 | 10 | 12 |  | 11 |  |  |  |  | 6 | 8 |  | 5 | 7[2] |  |  |  |  |  |  |  |  | 22 |
| 1 | 2 | 3 |  | 4 |  | 9[1] | 11 | 6 |  | 10 | 12 |  |  |  | 7[2] | 8 |  | 5 | 13 |  |  |  |  |  |  |  |  | 23 |
| 1 | 2 | 3 |  | 4 | 9[3] | 12 | 13 | 6 |  | 10 | 14 |  |  |  | 7 |  |  | 11[2] | 5[1] | 8 |  |  |  |  |  |  |  | 24 |
| 1 | 2[1] | 4 | 3 |  | 5 |  | 10[2] | 14 |  | 11 | 9 | 13 |  | 12 | 6[3] | 7 |  |  |  |  |  | 8 |  |  |  |  |  | 25 |
| 1 |  | 3 | 4 | 12 | 9 | 11[3] |  |  |  | 10 | 14 |  |  | 2[2] | 7[1] | 13 | 5 |  |  |  |  | 8 | 6 |  |  |  |  | 26 |
| 1 |  | 3 | 4 | 9[2] | 2 | 13 | 12 |  |  | 11[3] |  | 14 |  |  | 7 |  | 5 | 8 |  |  |  | 10 | 6[1] |  |  |  |  | 27 |
| 1 |  | 3 | 4 | 10 | 2 | 12 |  |  |  | 11[1] |  | 13 |  |  | 7 |  | 5 | 8 |  |  |  | 9 | 6[2] |  |  |  |  | 28 |
| 1 |  | 3 |  | 10[2] | 5 | 14 | 12 |  |  | 11 |  |  |  | 2 | 8 |  | 4 | 9[3] | 13 |  |  | 7 | 6[1] |  |  |  |  | 29 |
| 1 |  | 3 |  | 5 | 13 | 10[2] |  |  |  | 11 |  |  |  | 2 | 8 |  | 4 | 9[3] | 12 |  |  | 7 | 6[1] | 14 |  |  |  | 30 |
| 1 |  | 3 |  | 5 | 12 | 9 |  |  |  | 11 |  |  |  | 2 | 7 |  | 4 | 8 | 13 |  |  |  | 6[2] | 10[1] |  |  |  | 31 |
| 1 | 2 | 3 |  | 12 | 5[3] | 10 | 14 |  |  | 11 |  |  |  |  | 6[2] |  | 4 | 7[1] | 9 |  |  |  | 13 | 8 |  |  |  | 32 |
| 1 | 2 | 3 | 4 | 12 | 14 |  | 6[1] |  |  | 11 |  |  |  |  | 7[3] |  | 9 | 5 |  |  |  | 10 | 13 | 8[2] |  |  |  | 33 |
| 1 | 2 | 3 | 4 |  | 5 | 11[1] |  |  |  | 10 | 6[3] | 12 |  |  |  | 13 |  | 7[2] | 9 |  |  | 14 | 8 |  |  |  |  | 34 |
| 1 |  | 3 | 4 |  |  | 10[1] |  | 13 |  | 11 | 6[3] | 12 |  | 2 | 8 |  | 5 | 7 | 9 |  |  |  |  |  |  |  |  | 35 |
| 1 |  |  | 4 |  | 5 |  |  |  |  | 11 |  | 6 |  | 2 | 9 |  |  | 7 | 10 |  |  | 12 |  | 8[1] | 3 |  |  | 36 |
| 1 |  |  | 4 |  | 5 | 10 | 8[2] | 6 |  |  |  |  |  | 2 | 11[3] |  |  |  | 14 |  |  | 13 | 9 | 7[1] | 3 | 1 | 12 | 37 |
| 1 |  |  | 4 |  | 9 | 12 | 13 |  |  | 11[1] | 10 |  |  | 2 | 8 |  | 5 | 7[3] | 6[2] |  |  | 14 |  |  | 3 |  |  | 38 |

# INVERNESS CALEDONIAN THISTLE

*Year Formed:* 1994. *Ground & Address:* Tulloch Caledonian Stadium, Stadium Road, Inverness IV1 1FF. *Telephone:* 01463 222880. *Fax:* 01463 227479. *E-mail:* jim.falconer@ictfc.co.uk *Website:* www.ictfc.co.uk
*Ground Capacity:* 7,780 (all seated). *Size of Pitch:* 105m × 68m.
*Chairman:* Kenny Cameron. *Vice Chairman:* Graeme Bennett. *Club Secretary:* Ian MacDonald.
*Club Nicknames:* 'Caley Thistle', 'Caley Jags', 'ICT'.
*Manager:* Terry Butcher. *Assistant Manager:* Maurice Malpas. *Physios:* John McCreadie and Fiona Hogg.
*Record Attendance:* 7753 v Rangers, SPL, 20 January 2008.
*Record Transfer Fee received:* £400,000 for Marius Niculae to Dinamo Bucharest (July 2008).
*Record of Transfer paid:* £65,000 for John Rankin from Ross County (July 2006).
*Record Victory:* 8-1 v Annan Ath, Scottish Cup 3rd rd, 24 January 1998.
*Record Defeats:* 0-6 v Airdrieonians, First Division, 21 Sep 2000 and 0-6 v Celtic, League Cup 3rd rd, 22 Sep 2010.
*Most Capped Player:* Richard Hastings, 38 (59), Canada.
*Most League Appearances:* 490: Ross Tokely, 1995-2012.
*Most League Goals in Season:* 27: Iain Stewart, 1996-97; Denis Wyness, 2002-03.
*Most Goals Overall (Individual):* 118: Denis Wyness, 2000-03, 2005-08.

## INVERNESS CALEDONIAN THISTLE –
## SCOTTISH PREMIER LEAGUE 2012–13 LEAGUE RECORD

| Match No. | Date | Venue | Opponents | Result | H/T Score | Lg Pos. | Goalscorers | Attendance |
|---|---|---|---|---|---|---|---|---|
| 1 | Aug 4 | A | St Mirren | D 2-2 | 0-1 | 2 | Ross [70], McKay [76] | 4104 |
| 2 | 11 | H | Kilmarnock | D 1-1 | 1-1 | 5 | Shinnie, A [8] | 3012 |
| 3 | 18 | A | Hearts | D 2-2 | 0-2 | 8 | Shinnie, A (pen) [58], Pepper [90] | 11,512 |
| 4 | 25 | H | Celtic | L 2-4 | 0-2 | 10 | Draper 2 [82, 87] | 6100 |
| 5 | Sept 2 | A | Motherwell | L 1-4 | 1-2 | 11 | Foran [28] | 4031 |
| 6 | 15 | H | Aberdeen | D 1-1 | 0-0 | 11 | Foran (pen) [67] | 4499 |
| 7 | 22 | A | Hibernian | D 2-2 | 1-2 | 11 | Pepper [39], Foran [81] | 9908 |
| 8 | 29 | H | Dundee U | W 4-0 | 2-0 | 9 | Foran 2 [31, 35], Shinnie, A [70], Roberts [73] | 3059 |
| 9 | Oct 5 | H | Ross Co | W 3-1 | 2-0 | 6 | Draper [9], Shinnie, A [28], Doran [87] | 6766 |
| 10 | 19 | A | Dundee | W 4-1 | 2-1 | 3 | McKay 2 [4, 85], Warren [7], Shinnie, A (pen) [81] | 5006 |
| 11 | 27 | H | St Johnstone | D 1-1 | 0-0 | 5 | McKay [73] | 3154 |
| 12 | Nov 3 | A | Kilmarnock | W 2-1 | 1-0 | 3 | Shinnie, A [22], McKay (pen) [77] | 4541 |
| 13 | 10 | H | Hearts | D 1-1 | 1-0 | 4 | Tudur Jones [19] | 3332 |
| 14 | 18 | H | Motherwell | L 1-5 | 0-2 | 7 | Foran [47] | 2948 |
| 15 | 24 | A | Celtic | W 1-0 | 0-0 | 5 | McKay [65] | 44,379 |
| 16 | 27 | A | Aberdeen | W 3-2 | 1-1 | 2 | McKay 2 [36, 82], Warren [58] | 9193 |
| 17 | Dec 8 | H | Hibernian | W 3-0 | 1-0 | 2 | Draper [13], Foran [76], McKay [87] | 3422 |
| 18 | 15 | H | Dundee U | D 4-4 | 2-3 | 3 | McKay 3 (1 pen) [26, 28, 62 (p)], Warren [86] | 5483 |
| 19 | 22 | H | Dundee | W 4-1 | 2-1 | 2 | McKay 2 (1 pen) [12 (p), 48], Tudur Jones [24], Shinnie, A [70] | 3003 |
| 20 | 26 | H | St Mirren | D 2-2 | 1-1 | 2 | Shinnie, A [38], Foran [67] | 3506 |
| 21 | 29 | A | St Johnstone | D 0-0 | 0-0 | 2 | | 2975 |
| 22 | Jan 19 | A | Aberdeen | W 3-0 | 0-0 | 2 | Shinnie, A [53], McKay 2 [61, 78] | 4734 |
| 23 | 30 | A | St Mirren | L 1-2 | 1-1 | 2 | McKay (pen) [45] | 3065 |
| 24 | Feb 9 | H | Celtic | L 1-3 | 1-1 | 2 | Ross [9] | 6175 |
| 25 | 13 | H | Kilmarnock | D 1-1 | 1-0 | 2 | Ross [21] | 2529 |
| 26 | 16 | A | Motherwell | L 0-3 | 0-1 | 3 | | 4179 |
| 27 | 23 | A | Hearts | W 3-2 | 1-0 | 2 | Warren 2 [15, 77], McKay [62] | 11,325 |
| 28 | 27 | H | Dundee U | D 0-0 | 0-0 | 3 | | 3413 |
| 29 | Mar 2 | A | Ross Co | D 0-0 | 0-0 | 3 | | 5959 |
| 30 | 9 | A | Dundee | D 1-1 | 0-1 | 4 | McKay [83] | 4114 |
| 31 | 16 | H | Ross Co | W 2-1 | 1-1 | 3 | Shinnie, A [5], McKay (pen) [59] | 5750 |
| 32 | 30 | A | Hibernian | W 2-1 | 0-0 | 3 | Draper [48], Shinnie, A [65] | 10,055 |
| 33 | Apr 5 | H | St Johnstone | D 0-0 | 0-0 | 3 | | 3744 |
| 34 | 21 | A | Celtic | L 1-4 | 0-0 | 3 | Doran [90] | 55,000 |
| 35 | 27 | A | St Johnstone | L 0-1 | 0-0 | 3 | | 2368 |
| 36 | May 4 | H | Motherwell | W 4-3 | 3-1 | 3 | McKay 3 [3, 27, 84], Shinnie, A [25] | 3857 |
| 37 | 11 | H | Dundee U | L 1-2 | 1-0 | 3 | Doran [42] | 3728 |
| 38 | 19 | A | Ross Co | L 0-1 | 0-1 | 4 | | 6002 |

**Final League Position: 4**

**Honours**
*League Champions:* First Division 2003-04, 2009-10. Third Division 1996-97.
*Scottish Cup:* Semi-finals 2003, 2004; Quarter-finals 1996.
*Runners-up:* Second Division 1998-99.
*League Cup:* Semi-finals 2012-13.
*League Challenge Cup Winners:* 2003-04. *Runners-up:* 1999-2000, 2009-10.

**Club colours:** Shirt: Blue with red trim. Shorts: Blue. Socks: Blue.

**Goalscorers:** *League (64):* McKay 23 (5 pens), Shinnie A 12 (2 pens), Foran 8 (1 pen), Draper 5, Warren 5, Doran 3, Ross 3, Pepper 2, Tudur Jones 2, Roberts 1.
*William Hill Scottish FA Cup (5):* McKay 3 (1 pen), Foran 2.
*Scottish Communities League Cup (7):* Shinnie A 4, McKay 1, Shinnie G 1 (1 pen), Warren 1.

| Esson R 15 | Raven D 36 | Warren G 31 | King S 4 | Shinnie G 37 | Tudur Jones O 31+2 | Draper R 33+1 | Sutherland S 5+16 | Shinnie A 37+1 | Doran A 38 | McKay B 33+5 | Meekings J 31+3 | Ross N 8+13 | Polworth L —+3 | Morrison G 2+7 | Oswell J —+2 | Foran R 25+3 | Pepper C 2+10 | Blackman A 2 | Roberts P 8+9 | Reguero A 23+1 | Cooper M 2+1 | Devine D 8+2 | Gibbons J —+1 | Taylor C 4+3 | Hogg C 3 | Match No. |
|---|---|---|---|---|---|---|---|---|---|---|---|---|---|---|---|---|---|---|---|---|---|---|---|---|---|---|
| 1 | $2^1$ | 3 | 4 | 5 | 6 | 7 | $8^2$ | $9^3$ | 10 | 11 | 12 | 13 | 14 | | | | | | | | | | | | | 1 |
| 1 | 2 | 4 | 5 | 3 | $6^4$ | 7 | $10^3$ | $8^2$ | 9 | $11^1$ | | 12 | | 13 | 14 | | | | | | | | | | | 2 |
| 1 | $2^1$ | 3 | 4 | 5 | 6 | 8 | | 11 | $10^2$ | $9^2$ | 12 | 13 | | | | $7^1$ | 14 | | | | | | | | | 3 |
| 1 | $2^2$ | 4 | 5 | 3 | 6 | $11^1$ | 7 | 10 | 9 | 13 | $8^3$ | | | | | 12 | 14 | | | | | | | | | 4 |
| 1 | 3 | 4 | | 5 | $6^1$ | 7 | $8^2$ | $11^3$ | 10 | 13 | 2 | | | | | 12 | 9 | 14 | | | | | | | | 5 |
| 1 | 2 | 4 | 5 | | $7^1$ | 6 | $12^3$ | $8^1$ | $10^2$ | 13 | 3 | | | | | 11 | 14 | 9 | | | | | | | | 6 |
| 1 | 2 | 4 | 5 | | 6 | | $8^2$ | 10 | 13 | 3 | | 12 | | | | 11 | $7^3$ | $9^1$ | 14 | | | | | | | 7 |
| | 2 | 4 | 5 | | 8 | | $10^1$ | 9 | 14 | 3 | | | 7 | 13 | | $6^2$ | 12 | | $11^3$ | 1 | | | | | | 8 |
| | 2 | 4 | 5 | 7 | 8 | | $11^2$ | 6 | 14 | 3 | | 13 | | | | $10^1$ | 12 | | $9^3$ | 1 | | | | | | 9 |
| | 2 | 4 | 5 | 7 | 8 | 12 | 10 | 6 | 11 | 3 | | | | | | | | | $9^1$ | 1 | | | | | | 10 |
| | 2 | 5 | 3 | 4 | 7 | 12 | $8^2$ | 10 | 6 | 9 | | 13 | | | | | | | $11^1$ | 1 | | | | | | 11 |
| | 2 | 3 | 5 | 7 | 8 | 12 | $10^2$ | 6 | 11 | 4 | | | | | | 13 | | | $9^1$ | 1 | | | | | | 12 |
| | 2 | 3 | 5 | 7 | | 12 | $11^2$ | 6 | 10 | 4 | | 13 | | | | 8 | | | $9^1$ | 1 | | | | | | 13 |
| | 2 | 3 | 5 | 8 | | 12 | 11 | 6 | $10^1$ | 4 | | | | | | $7^2$ | 9 | 13 | | 1 | | | | | | 14 |
| | 2 | 4 | 5 | 6 | | 12 | 9 | 8 | $11^1$ | 3 | | | | | | 7 | 13 | | $10^2$ | 1 | | | | | | 15 |
| | 2 | 4 | 5 | 7 | 12 | | 8 | 6 | 11 | 3 | | | | | | 9 | | | $10^1$ | 1 | | | | | | 16 |
| | 2 | 3 | 5 | 8 | 7 | 12 | 9 | 6 | 11 | 4 | | | | | | $10^1$ | | | | 1 | | | | | | 17 |
| | 2 | 3 | 5 | 8 | $7^1$ | 12 | $9^3$ | 6 | $10^2$ | 4 | | 14 | | | | 11 | | | 13 | 1 | | | | | | 18 |
| | 2 | 4 | 3 | 8 | 7 | | 9 | $6^3$ | $10^2$ | $5^1$ | | | | | | 11 | 14 | | 13 | 1 | 12 | | | | | 19 |
| | 2 | 5 | 3 | 9 | 8 | 7 | | 6 | $11^1$ | | | | | | | 10 | | | 12 | 1 | 4 | | | | | 20 |
| | 2 | 5 | 3 | 9 | 8 | $7^2$ | | 6 | $11^3$ | 14 | | | | | | $10^1$ | 12 | | 13 | 1 | 4 | | | | | 21 |
| | 2 | 4 | 3 | 8 | 7 | | $10^1$ | $6^2$ | 11 | 5 | 13 | | | | | 9 | | | 12 | 1 | | | | | | 22 |
| | 3 | | 5 | 6 | $7^1$ | 9 | $8^3$ | 11 | 4 | 12 | | $10^2$ | | | | 14 | | | 1 | 2 | | 13 | | | | 23 |
| 1 | 2 | 3 | 5 | 7 | 8 | 13 | 10 | $6^2$ | 11 | 4 | | 9 | $9^1$ | | | 12 | | | | | | | | | | 24 |
| 1 | 2 | 4 | 3 | 8 | 9 | 13 | $10^1$ | $6^2$ | 11 | 5 | 7 | | | | | | | | 12 | | | | | | | 25 |
| 1 | 2 | 4 | 5 | 7 | $8^3$ | 12 | 11 | $6^2$ | $10^1$ | 3 | 9 | 14 | | | | | 13 | | | | | | | | | 26 |
| 1 | 2 | 3 | 5 | 7 | 6 | 12 | 9 | $10^2$ | $11^1$ | 8 | 4 | | | | | 13 | | | | | | 4 | 13 | | | 27 |
| 1 | 2 | | 3 | 8 | 7 | 12 | 10 | 6 | $11^2$ | 5 | $9^1$ | | | | | 13 | | | | | | 4 | | | | 28 |
| 1 | 2 | 4 | 3 | 8 | 7 | | 10 | $6^1$ | 11 | 5 | 12 | | | | | $9^2$ | | | | | | | 13 | | | 29 |
| 1 | 2 | 3 | | 9 | 7 | 8 | 10 | $6^2$ | 11 | 4 | 12 | | | | | 13 | | | | | | | $5^1$ | | | 30 |
| $1^1$ | 2 | 5 | | 10 | 9 | | $7^2$ | 8 | 11 | 4 | 13 | | | | | 6 | | | 12 | | | | 3 | | | 31 |
| | 2 | | 5 | 8 | 7 | | $10^1$ | 6 | 11 | 3 | 12 | | | | | 9 | | | 1 | 4 | | | | | | 32 |
| | 2 | 3 | 9 | 8 | | $10^1$ | 6 | 11 | 5 | 12 | 7 | | | | | | | | 1 | 4 | | | | | | 33 |
| | 2 | $3^1$ | 5 | 6 | 7 | | $10^2$ | 8 | 11 | 4 | 9 | | | | | | 1 | | 12 | 13 | | | | | | 34 |
| | $2^8$ | | 5 | $7^2$ | 9 | 13 | 6 | $11^1$ | 4 | 12 | 8 | | | | | | 1 | | 3 | 10 | | | | | | 35 |
| | | 3 | 12 | 8 | $10^1$ | 6 | 11 | 2 | 7 | 9 | | | | | | | 1 | | 5 | | | 4 | | | | 36 |
| | 2 | 3 | 12 | $9^1$ | 13 | 10 | 6 | 11 | 4 | $7^2$ | 8 | | | | | 1 | | 5 | | | | | | | | 37 |
| | 2 | 3 | | | 13 | 10 | 7 | 11 | 5 | 12 | | | | | | $6^1$ | 1 | | 8 | $9^2$ | 4 | | | | | 38 |

# KILMARNOCK

*Year Formed:* 1869. *Ground & Address:* Rugby Park, Kilmarnock KA1 2DP. *Telephone:* 01563 545300. *Fax:* 01563 522181. *Email:* kirstencallaghan@kilmarnockfc.co.uk *Website:* www.kilmarnockfc.co.uk
*Ground Capacity:* 18,128 (all seated). *Size of Pitch:* 102m × 67m.
*Chairman:* Michael Johnston. *Secretary:* Kirsten Callaghan.
*Manager:* Allan Johnston. *Assistant Manager:* Sandy Clark.
*Club Nickname:* 'Killie'.
*Previous Grounds:* Rugby Park (Dundonald Road); The Grange; Holm Quarry; Rugby Park 1899.
*Record Attendance:* 35,995 v Rangers, Scottish Cup Quarter-final, 10 Mar 1962.
*Record Transfer Fee received:* £1,900,000 for Stephen Naismith to Rangers (2007).
*Record Transfer Fee paid:* £340,000 for Paul Wright from St Johnstone (1995).
*Record Victory:* 11-1 v Paisley Academical, Scottish Cup 1st rd, 18 Jan 1930.
*Record Defeat:* 1-9 v Celtic, Division I, 13 Aug 1938.
*Most Capped Player:* Joe Nibloe, 11, Scotland.
*Most League Appearances:* 481: Alan Robertson, 1972-88.
*Most League Goals in Season (Individual):* 34: Harry 'Peerie' Cunningham 1927-28; Andy Kerr 1960-61.
*Most Goals Overall (Individual):* 148: Willy Culley, 1912-23.

## KILMARNOCK – SCOTTISH PREMIER LEAGUE 2012–13 LEAGUE RECORD

| Match No. | Date | Venue | Opponents | Result | H/T Score | Lg Pos. | Goalscorers | Attendance |
|---|---|---|---|---|---|---|---|---|
| 1 | Aug 4 | H | Dundee | D 0-0 | 0-0 | 6 | | 6523 |
| 2 | 11 | A | Inverness CT | D 1-1 | 1-1 | 6 | Pascali [45] | 3012 |
| 3 | 18 | H | Motherwell | L 1-2 | 1-2 | 10 | Harkins [30] | 4969 |
| 4 | 25 | H | Dundee U | W 3-1 | 0-0 | 6 | McKenzie [47], Perez (pen) [50], Winchester [56] | 4516 |
| 5 | Sept 1 | A | Ross Co | D 0-0 | 0-0 | 7 | | 4006 |
| 6 | 15 | A | Hibernian | L 1-2 | 1-2 | 8 | Racchi [32] | 9723 |
| 7 | 22 | H | St Mirren | W 3-1 | 1-0 | 4 | Sheridan [26], Fowler [57], Dayton [61] | 4879 |
| 8 | 29 | A | Hearts | W 3-1 | 1-0 | 3 | Sheridan 3 [32, 51, 62] | 11,847 |
| 9 | Oct 6 | H | Aberdeen | L 1-3 | 1-0 | 6 | O'Leary [3] | 5540 |
| 10 | 20 | A | St Johnstone | L 1-2 | 0-1 | 7 | Fowler [90] | 3113 |
| 11 | 27 | A | Celtic | W 2-0 | 1-0 | 6 | Sheridan [43], Kelly (pen) [62] | 47,971 |
| 12 | Nov 3 | H | Inverness CT | L 1-2 | 0-1 | 7 | Kelly [56] | 4541 |
| 13 | 10 | H | Ross Co | W 3-0 | 0-0 | 5 | Heffernan 2 [67, 82], Harkins [77] | 4012 |
| 14 | 16 | A | Dundee U | D 3-3 | 2-0 | 5 | Sheridan 2 [9, 30], Heffernan [53] | 6287 |
| 15 | 24 | H | St Johnstone | L 1-2 | 0-1 | 8 | Nelson [85] | 4208 |
| 16 | Dec 8 | H | Celtic | L 1-3 | 0-1 | 9 | Sheridan [90] | 6501 |
| 17 | 15 | A | Aberdeen | W 2-0 | 1-0 | 8 | Kelly 2 (1 pen) [45 (p), 86] | 8790 |
| 18 | 23 | H | Hibernian | D 1-1 | 1-1 | 9 | Heffernan [6] | 4028 |
| 19 | 26 | H | Hearts | W 1-0 | 1-0 | 6 | Kelly (pen) [27] | 5163 |
| 20 | 29 | A | Motherwell | D 2-2 | 1-0 | 6 | Perez [13], Heffernan [62] | 4903 |
| 21 | Jan 2 | A | St Mirren | D 1-1 | 1-0 | 7 | Kelly (pen) [5] | 6347 |
| 22 | 19 | H | Dundee U | L 2-3 | 1-1 | 8 | Pascali 2 [18, 90] | 4112 |
| 23 | 27 | A | Dundee | D 0-0 | 0-0 | 8 | | 4782 |
| 24 | 30 | A | Celtic | L 1-4 | 0-1 | 8 | Sheridan [48] | 43,652 |
| 25 | Feb 9 | H | Motherwell | W 2-0 | 1-0 | 8 | Hammell (og) [13], Gros [71] | 4246 |
| 26 | 13 | A | Inverness CT | D 1-1 | 0-1 | 6 | Perez [90] | 2529 |
| 27 | 16 | A | Hearts | W 3-0 | 1-0 | 5 | Heffernan 3 [42, 65, 71] | 14,280 |
| 28 | 23 | H | Aberdeen | D 1-1 | 1-1 | 6 | Heffernan [40] | 4390 |
| 29 | 27 | A | Hibernian | D 2-2 | 0-0 | 7 | Clingan [46], Winchester [86] | 8121 |
| 30 | Mar 9 | A | St Johnstone | L 0-2 | 0-0 | 8 | | 2425 |
| 31 | 30 | A | Ross Co | W 1-0 | 1-0 | 6 | Fowler [2] | 3782 |
| 32 | Apr 3 | H | St Mirren | D 1-1 | 0-1 | 6 | Boyd [47] | 4494 |
| 33 | 6 | H | Dundee | L 1-2 | 0-1 | 7 | Boyd [74] | 4966 |
| 34 | 20 | H | Hearts | L 0-1 | 0-1 | 7 | | 3572 |
| 35 | 27 | A | Aberdeen | L 0-1 | 0-1 | 8 | | 6334 |
| 36 | May 11 | A | Dundee | W 3-2 | 1-1 | 8 | McKenzie [4], Johnston [58], Clingan [73] | 4190 |
| 37 | 15 | H | Hibernian | L 1-3 | 0-1 | 9 | Ashcroft [57] | 3198 |
| 38 | 18 | H | St Mirren | L 1-3 | 1-1 | 9 | Boyd [25] | 4428 |

**Final League Position: 9**

**Honours**
*League Champions:* Division I 1964-65. Division II 1897-98, 1898-99; *Runners-up:* Division I 1959-60, 1960-61, 1962-63, 1963-64. First Division 1975-76, 1978-79, 1981-82, 1992-93. Division II 1953-54, 1973-74. Second Division 1989-90.
*Scottish Cup Winners:* 1920, 1929, 1997; *Runners-up:* 1898, 1932, 1938, 1957, 1960.
*League Cup Winners:* 2011-12; *Runners-up:* 1952-53, 1960-61, 1962-63, 2000-01, 2006-07.

**European:** *European Cup:* 4 matches (1965-66). *Cup Winners' Cup:* 4 matches (1997-98). *UEFA Cup:* 32 matches (*Fairs Cup:* 1964-65, 1966-67 semi-finals, 1969-70, 1970-71. *UEFA Cup:* 1998-99, 1999-2000, 2001-02).

**Club colours:** Shirts: White and dark blue stripes. Shorts: Dark blue. Socks: Dark blue with yellow tops.

**Goalscorers:** *League (52):* Heffernan 9, Sheridan 9, Kelly 6 (4 pens), Boyd 3, Fowler 3, Pascali 3, Perez 3 (1 pen), Clingan 2, Harkins 2, McKenzie 2, Winchester 2, Ashcroft 1, Dayton 1, Gros 1, Johnston 1, Nelson 1, O'Leary 1, Racchi 1, own goal 1.
*William Hill Scottish FA Cup (6):* Heffernan 3 (1 pen), Borja 1, Dayton 1, Sheridan 1.
*Scottish Communities League Cup (1):* Nelson 1.

| Bell C 30 | O'Leary R 22+6 | Pascali M 24 | Nelson M 21 | Tesselaar J 25+1 | Kelly L 19 | Johnson L 7+4 | Harkins G 14+2 | Kennedy M 3 | Fowler J 33+1 | Dayton J 23+4 | Racchi D 8+8 | Boulding R 1+3 | McKenzie R 8+14 | Perez B 19+6 | Letheren K 8+1 | Winchester J 5+3 | Gros W 9+8 | McKeown R 16 | Sheridan C 19+7 | Johnston C 4+7 | Pursehouse A 1 | Heffernan P 22+5 | O'Hara M 13+4 | Sissoko M 18+2 | Slater C 1+1 | Barbour R 16 | Hay G 4+4 | Ibrahim R 2+4 | Clingan S 13+1 | Boyd K 6+2 | Davidson R 2 | Ashcroft L 2+1 | Muirhead R —+1 | Kiltie G —+1 | Match No. |
|---|---|---|---|---|---|---|---|---|---|---|---|---|---|---|---|---|---|---|---|---|---|---|---|---|---|---|---|---|---|---|---|---|---|---|---|
| 1 | 2 | 3 | 4 | 5 | 6 | 7² | 8 | 9³ | 10 | 11¹ | 12 | 13 | 14 | | | | | | | | | | | | | | | | | | | | | | 1 |
| 1 | 4 | 10 | 5 | 2 | 6 | 9 | 8² | 11³ | 3 | 7¹ | 12 | 14 | 13 | | | | | | | | | | | | | | | | | | | | | | 2 |
| 1 | 2³ | 3 | 4 | 5 | 7 | 6¹ | 9 | 11² | 8 | 14 | 12 | 10 | | 13 | | | | | | | | | | | | | | | | | | | | | 3 |
| | 2 | 4 | 3 | 5 | 7 | 13 | 11¹ | | 8 | | | | 9 | 10³ | 6² | | | 1 | 12 | 14 | | | | | | | | | | | | | | | 4 |
| | 4 | 11 | 3 | | 8 | | | | 2 | 6 | 7² | 13 | 10 | 9¹ | 1 | | | 12 | 5 | | | | | | | | | | | | | | | | 5 |
| | 3 | 7 | 4 | | 9 | | 14 | | 2 | 6³ | 8² | | 11¹ | 1 | | | | 12 | 5 | 10 | 13 | | | | | | | | | | | | | | | 6 |
| | 2 | 4 | 3 | | 7 | | 11² | | 5 | 8¹ | 9 | | 13 | 1 | | | | 6 | 10 | 12 | | | | | | | | | | | | | | | 7 |
| | 3 | 7 | 4 | | 8² | | 14 | 10 | 2 | 6¹ | 9³ | | | 1 | 13 | | | 5 | 11 | 12 | | | | | | | | | | | | | | | 8 |
| | 2 | 3 | 4 | | 8 | | 10² | | 7 | 9³ | 6¹ | | 13 | 1 | | | 14 | 5 | 11 | 12 | | | | | | | | | | | | | | | 9 |
| 1 | 2 | 3 | 4 | | 9 | | 7³ | | 8 | 10¹ | | | 13 | | | | 14 | 5 | 11 | 6² | 12 | | | | | | | | | | | | | | 10 |
| 1 | 4 | 6 | 3 | 14 | 7 | 8 | | | 10³ | | | 5² | | 13 | 2 | 11¹ | | | 12 | 9 | | | | | | | | | | | | | | | 11 |
| 1* | 3 | 8 | 4 | | 9 | 7³ | 13 | | 10² | | 6 | | 14 | 5 | 11¹ | | | 12 | 2 | | | | | | | | | | | | | | | | 12 |
| 1 | 3 | 9¹ | 4 | 5 | 7 | | 8 | | 2 | | | | | 6 | | | 11 | | 10 | 12 | | | | | | | | | | | | | | | 13 |
| 1 | 3 | 9 | 4 | 5 | 7 | 12 | 8 | | 2 | | | | | 6¹ | | | 10 | | 11 | | | | | | | | | | | | | | | | 14 |
| 1 | 3 | 7* | 4 | 5³ | | 8¹ | 9 | | 2 | 14 | 13 | | | 6² | | | 10 | | 11 | 12 | | | | | | | | | | | | | | | 15 |
| 1 | 4 | | 3 | 5 | 6 | | 9² | | 2 | | 7¹ | | 14 | 8³ | | | 11 | | 10 | 13 | 12 | | | | | | | | | | | | | | 16 |
| 1 | 12 | 8 | 4 | 5 | 6 | | 9 | | 2 | 14 | | | 13 | 7³ | | | 10 | | 11² | | 3¹ | | | | | | | | | | | | | | 17 |
| 1 | 14 | 4 | 5 | 2 | | | 7¹ | | 9 | 6 | | | 12 | 8³ | | | 10 | 13 | 11² | | 3 | | | | | | | | | | | | | | 18 |
| 1 | 14 | 6 | 3 | | 8 | 12 | | | 2 | 9² | | | 13 | 7¹ | | | 5 | 11 | 10³ | 4 | | | | | | | | | | | | | | | 19 |
| 1 | 4 | | 3 | | 8 | 7² | | | 2 | 9 | | | 6¹ | | | | 5 | 10 | 11 | 12 | 13 | | | | | | | | | | | | | | 20 |
| 1 | 3 | 8¹ | 4 | | 7 | | | | 2 | 9 | | | 13 | 6² | | | 5 | 10 | 11 | 12 | | | | | | | | | | | | | | | 21 |
| 1 | 3 | 8 | | | | | | | 2 | 9 | 6¹ | | 13 | 12 | 14 | | 5 | 11² | 10 | 4 | 7³ | | | | | | | | | | | | | | 22 |
| 1 | | 4 | 2 | | | | | | 7 | 14 | | | 11³ | 8¹ | | | 9 | 13 | 10² | 3 | 6 | 5 | 12 | | | | | | | | | | | | 23 |
| 1 | 13 | | 4 | | | | | | 8 | 9 | 12 | | | 6¹ | 10³ | 5² | 11 | | 14 | 7 | 3 | 2 | | | | | | | | | | | | | 24 |
| | 8 | | 4¹ | | | | | | 2 | 9 | 14 | | | 7² | 1 | | 11 | | 10 | 6 | 3 | 5¹ | 13 | 12 | | | | | | | | | | | 25 |
| | 5 | | 3 | | | | | | 9 | 12 | | | 14 | 13 | 1 | | 11 | | 10 | 7³ | 4 | 2 | 8¹ | 6² | | | | | | | | | | | 26 |
| 1 | 13 | 3² | 5 | | | | | | 7 | 10¹ | 12 | | 14 | 6 | | | 9 | | 11 | 4 | 2 | | 8³ | | | | | | | | | | | | 27 |
| 1 | 4 | | 5 | | | | | | 6 | 11 | | | | 8¹ | | | 9² | 13 | 10 | 3 | | 2 | 12 | 7 | | | | | | | | | | | 28 |
| 1 | | | 5 | | | | | | 7 | 9 | | | 6 | 11 | 3 | 12 | | | 10 | 4 | | 2 | 8 | | | | | | | | | | | | 29 |
| 1 | 4 | | 5² | | | | | | 7 | 9 | | | 6¹ | 11³ | 12 | | | 10 | | 3 | 2 | 13 | 8 | 14 | | | | | | | | | | | 30 |
| 1 | 14 | | 5 | | | | | | 8 | 10¹ | | 7 | 13 | | 9 | 12 | | | | 3 | 4 | 2³ | 6 | 11² | | | | | | | | | | | 31 |
| 1 | | | 5 | | | | | | 7 | | | 13 | 8¹ | | | 11² | 3 | 4 | | 2 | 9 | 12 | 6 | 10 | | | | | | | | | | | 32 |
| 1 | | | 5¹ | | | | | | 7 | | | | 6² | 13 | | 12 | 11² | 8 | 4 | | 2 | 8 | 14 | 9 | 10 | | | | | | | | | | 33 |
| 1 | 3³ | | 5¹ | | | | | | 7 | | | 13 | | 14 | | 12 | 11 | 8 | 4 | | 2 | 9² | 6 | 10 | | | | | | | | | | | 34 |
| 1 | | | 4² | | | | | | 5 | | | | 7 | 9¹ | 13 | 10 | 11 | 8 | 3 | | 2 | 6 | 12 | | | | | | | | | | | | 35 |
| 1 | | 2 | | | | | | | 9 | | | | 7¹ | | | 8 | 13 | 5 | 4³ | 3 | | 12 | 6 | 10² | 11 | 14 | | | | | | | | | 36 |
| 1 | | 4 | | | | | | | 12 | 6 | 13 | | | 14 | 9 | | 10 | 3 | | 5³ | 2¹ | 11² | 7 | | | 8 | | | | | | | | | 37 |
| 1 | | | | | | | | | 2 | | | | 7² | | | 5³ | 11¹ | 8 | | 3 | | | 14 | | 6 | 10 | 9 | 4 | 12 | 13 | | | | | 38 |

# LIVINGSTON

*Year Formed:* 1974. *Ground:* The Braidwood Motor Company Stadium, Almondvale Stadium, Alderstone Road, Livingston EH54 7DN. *Telephone:* 01506 417000. *Fax:* 01506 429 948.
*Email:* lfcreception@livingstonfc.co.uk *Website:* www.livingstonfc.co.uk
*Ground Capacity:* 10,005 (all seated). *Size of Pitch:* 98m × 69m.
*Chairman:* Gordon McDougall. *Vice Chairman:* Robert Wilson.
*Manager:* Richie Burke. *Assistant Manager:* Mark Burchill. *Physio:* Andy Mackenzie.
*Club Nickname:* 'Livi Lions'.
*Previous Grounds:* Meadowbank Stadium (as Meadowbank Thistle).
*Record Attendance:* 10,024 v Celtic, Premier League, 18 Aug 2001.
*Record Transfer Fee received:* £1,000,000 for David Fernandez to Celtic (June 2002).
*Record Transfer Fee paid:* £120,000 for Wes Hoolahan from Shelbourne (December 2005).
*Record Victory:* 7-0 v Queen of the South, Scottish Cup, 29 Jan 2000.
*Record Defeat:* 0-8 v Hamilton A. Division II, 14 Dec 1974.
*Most Capped Player (under 18):* Ian Little.
*Most League Appearances:* 446: Walter Boyd, 1979-89.
*Most League Goals in Season (Individual):* 22: Leigh Griffiths, 2008-09; Iain Russell, 2010-11.
*Most Goals Overall (Individual):* 64: David Roseburgh, 1986-93.

## LIVINGSTON – SCOTTISH FIRST DIVISION 2012–13 LEAGUE RECORD

| Match No. | Date | Venue | Opponents | Result | H/T Score | Lg Pos. | Goalscorers | Atten- dance |
|---|---|---|---|---|---|---|---|---|
| 1 | Aug 11 | A | Greenock Morton | D 2-2 | 2-1 | 5 | Russell, I [25], Scougall [39] | 1898 |
| 2 | 18 | H | Airdrie U | L 0-2 | 0-0 | 7 | | 1170 |
| 3 | 25 | A | Raith R | D 0-0 | 0-0 | 8 | | 1774 |
| 4 | Sept 2 | A | Falkirk | W 2-1 | 1-1 | 7 | Fordyce [39], Andreu [90] | 2974 |
| 5 | 15 | H | Partick Th | L 1-2 | 0-1 | 7 | Morton [59] | 1745 |
| 6 | 22 | A | Dunfermline Ath | L 0-4 | 0-2 | 8 | | 2958 |
| 7 | 29 | H | Dumbarton | W 5-0 | 3-0 | 6 | McNulty 2 [9, 36], Barr, C [12], Booth [65], Jacobs, Keaghan [77] | 1021 |
| 8 | Oct 6 | H | Cowdenbeath | D 1-1 | 0-0 | 6 | Jacobs, Keaghan [71] | 1203 |
| 9 | 20 | A | Hamilton A | W 2-1 | 2-1 | 6 | Scougall [3], McNulty [9] | 943 |
| 10 | 27 | H | Greenock Morton | D 2-2 | 1-0 | 5 | Russell, I 2 (1 pen) [8, 79 (p)] | 1417 |
| 11 | Nov 9 | A | Airdrie U | W 3-1 | 1-1 | 5 | McNulty [25], Fox [63], Russell, I (pen) [87] | 1003 |
| 12 | 17 | H | Falkirk | W 2-1 | 1-0 | 4 | McNulty [23], Jacobs, Keaghan [65] | 1471 |
| 13 | 24 | A | Partick Th | L 0-2 | 0-0 | 5 | | 2508 |
| 14 | Dec 8 | H | Dunfermline Ath | W 2-1 | 0-0 | 4 | Garcia Tena [65], Mullen [90] | 1495 |
| 15 | 22 | A | Cowdenbeath | D 1-1 | 0-1 | 4 | Scougall [70] | 409 |
| 16 | Jan 5 | H | Partick Th | D 2-2 | 1-2 | 6 | Andreu [29], McNulty [90] | 1762 |
| 17 | 12 | H | Raith R | W 2-1 | 1-1 | 4 | Russell, I [29], Barr, C [49] | 1424 |
| 18 | 19 | A | Greenock Morton | L 1-2 | 0-1 | 4 | Russell, I [53] | 1913 |
| 19 | 26 | A | Dunfermline Ath | W 1-0 | 1-0 | 4 | Andreu [21] | 2461 |
| 20 | Feb 2 | A | Dumbarton | W 4-3 | 1-0 | 4 | Russell, I 2 [43, 82], Scougall [47], Morton [86] | 744 |
| 21 | 9 | H | Dumbarton | L 2-3 | 2-2 | 4 | Morton [22], Russell, I (pen) [45] | 1170 |
| 22 | 16 | H | Cowdenbeath | W 3-0 | 3-0 | 4 | Russell, I [27], Andreu [39], Garcia Tena [44] | 1112 |
| 23 | 19 | A | Falkirk | L 0-2 | 0-1 | 4 | | 2583 |
| 24 | 23 | A | Hamilton A | D 1-1 | 0-0 | 4 | Russell, I [77] | 914 |
| 25 | Mar 2 | H | Airdrie U | W 4-1 | 3-0 | 3 | Andreu 2 [21, 39], Russell, I [44], Scougall [77] | 1132 |
| 26 | 9 | A | Raith R | W 2-0 | 2-0 | 3 | Russell, I (pen) [20], Scougall [35] | 1117 |
| 27 | 23 | A | Partick Th | L 1-6 | 0-4 | 3 | Watson [46] | 2897 |
| 28 | 30 | H | Dunfermline Ath | D 2-2 | 0-1 | 3 | Andreu [54], McNulty [68] | 1465 |
| 29 | Apr 2 | H | Falkirk | L 1-2 | 1-0 | 4 | Russell, I (pen) [26] | 1100 |
| 30 | 6 | A | Dumbarton | W 3-0 | 1-0 | 4 | Lander [32], Watson [47], Mullen [77] | 705 |
| 31 | 9 | A | Cowdenbeath | D 2-2 | 1-1 | 4 | Watson [7], Barr, C [71] | 455 |
| 32 | 13 | H | Hamilton A | L 0-3 | 0-2 | 4 | | 1607 |
| 33 | 16 | H | Hamilton A | D 0-0 | 0-0 | 3 | | 787 |
| 34 | 20 | H | Greenock Morton | L 0-2 | 0-1 | 3 | | 1158 |
| 35 | 27 | A | Airdrie U | W 2-0 | 1-0 | 3 | Barr, C [26], Garcia Tena [80] | 650 |
| 36 | May 4 | H | Raith R | L 2-3 | 1-1 | 4 | Fox (pen) [45], Russell, I [90] | 1302 |

**Final League Position: 4**

**Honours**
*League Champions:* First Division 2000-01. Second Division 1986-87, 1998-99, 2010-11. Third Division 1995-96, 2009-10;
*Runners-up:* Second Division 1982-83. First Division 1987-88.
*Scottish Cup:* Semi-finals 2001, 2004.
*League Cup Winners:* 2003-04. Semi-finals 1984-85. *B&Q Cup:* Semi-finals 1992-93, 1993-94, 2001.
*League Challenge Cup Runners-up:* 2000-01.

**European:** *UEFA Cup:* 4 matches (2002-03).

**Club colours:** Shirt: Yellow. Shorts: Black. Socks: Yellow.

**Goalscorers:** *League (58):* Russell I 15 (5 pens), Andreu 7, McNulty 7, Scougall 6, Barr C 4, Garcia Tena 3, Jacobs, Keaghan 3, Morton 3, Watson 3, Fox 2 (1 pen), Mullen 2, Booth 1, Fordyce 1, Lander 1.
*William Hill Scottish FA Cup (0).*
*Scottish Communities League Cup (12):* McNulty 4, Russell I 3 (1 pen), Morton 2, Barr R 1, Easton 1, McCann 1.
*Ramsdens Cup (0).*

| McNeil A 33 | McCann K 28+1 | Barr C 32 | Watson P 17+1 | Fordyce C 8+4 | Andreu A 33 | Docherty R 9+1 | Scougall S 27+1 | McNulty M 20+6 | Morton J 11+13 | Russell I 28+5 | Barr R 4+1 | Jacobs Keaghan 10+1 | McDonald C 1+4 | Mullen D 2+21 | Booth C 22+9 | Garcia Tena J 29 | Easton D —+4 | Gray R —+6 | Fox I 27 | Jacobs Kyle 14+4 | O'Brien B 23 | Talbot J 8+4 | Donaldson C 3+2 | Lander K 4+2 | Downie J —+3 | Jemieson D 3 | Match No. |
|---|---|---|---|---|---|---|---|---|---|---|---|---|---|---|---|---|---|---|---|---|---|---|---|---|---|---|---|
| 1 | 2 | 3 | 4 | 5 | 6³ | 7 | 8 | 9 | 10² | 11¹ | 12 | 13 | 14 | | | | | | | | | | | | | | 1 |
| 1 | 2 | 4 | 3 | 5¹ | 9 | 7² | 8 | 11 | | 10 | 6 | | | 12 | 13 | | | | | | | | | | | | 2 |
| 1 | 2 | | 3 | 4 | 9 | 7 | 8 | 10 | | 11 | 6 | | | 5 | | | | | | | | | | | | | 3 |
| 1 | | 4 | 3⁴ | 2 | 8 | 6 | 7 | 13 | 10¹ | 11 | 9² | | | 12 | | 5 | | | | | | | | | | | 4 |
| 1 | | 4 | | 2² | 7 | 6 | 9¹ | 12 | 10 | 11 | 8 | | | | 5 | 3 | 13 | | | | | | | | | | 5 |
| 1 | | 4 | | 2 | 6 | 7 | 11 | 10 | 12 | 9² | | 8¹ | | | 5 | 3 | | 13 | | | | | | | | | 6 |
| 1 | | 4 | 3 | | 7 | 2 | 10¹ | 11 | 8² | 9³ | | 6 | | | 12 | 5 | 13 | 14 | | | | | | | | | 7 |
| 1 | | 4 | 3¹ | | 6 | 2² | 11³ | 10 | 9 | 7 | | 8 | | | 12 | 5 | 14 | 13 | | | | | | | | | 8 |
| 1 | 2⁴ | 4 | | 13 | 6 | | 9 | 11¹ | | 12 | | 10 | | | 5 | 3 | | | 7 | 8² | | | | | | | 9 |
| 1 | | 4 | | 2 | 6 | | 11¹ | 10 | | 9 | | 7 | | | 13 | 5 | 3 | 12 | 8² | | | | | | | | 10 |
| 1 | 2 | 4 | | 13 | 6 | | 10 | 12 | 9¹ | 11 | | | | | 8 | 5 | 3² | | 7 | | | | | | | | 11 |
| 1 | 2 | 3 | | 14 | 6³ | | 8¹ | 10 | 12² | 9 | | | | | 13 | 5 | 4 | | 7 | | 11 | | | | | | 12 |
| 1 | 2² | 3 | | 14 | 8¹ | | 9 | 11 | | 10 | | | | | 12 | 5 | 4 | | 6 | 13 | 7³ | | | | | | 13 |
| 1 | 5 | 4⁴ | | | 6 | | 10³ | 11 | 12 | | | 9 | | | 14 | 13 | 3 | | 7¹ | 2² | 8 | | | | | | 14 |
| 1 | 4 | | | 2¹ | 6 | | 11 | 10 | 12 | 13 | | 9 | | | 5 | 3 | | | 7² | | 8 | | | | | | 15 |
| 1 | 2 | 3 | | | 6 | | 11 | 10 | 12 | 9¹ | | | | | 13 | 5 | 4 | | 8² | | 7 | | | | | | 16 |
| 1 | 2 | 3 | | | 6 | | 9 | 10³ | 12 | 11¹ | | | | | 14 | 5² | 4 | | 8 | 13 | 7 | | | | | | 17 |
| 1 | 5³ | 4 | | | 6 | | 11 | 10 | 12 | 9¹ | | | | | 13 | 14 | 3 | | 8² | 2 | 7 | | | | | | 18 |
| 1 | 5 | 4 | | | 6¹ | | 10 | 9 | 12 | 11² | | | | | 13 | 14 | 4 | | 8 | 2³ | 7 | | | | | | 19 |
| 1 | 5 | 3 | 12 | | 9 | | 10³ | 11² | 13 | 6 | | | | | 14 | 4¹ | | | 8 | 2 | 7 | | | | | | 20 |
| 1 | 2 | 4 | | | 8 | | 9 | | 11² | 10 | | | | | 12 | 5 | 3 | 13 | | 6¹ | 7 | | | | | | 21 |
| 1 | 5 | 3¹ | 2 | | 6 | | 9³ | | 11 | 10 | | | | | 13 | | 4 | 14 | 8² | 12 | 7 | | | | | | 22 |
| 1 | 5 | 4 | 2¹ | | 6 | | 9 | | 10² | 11 | | | | | 13 | 14 | 3 | | 7³ | 12 | 8 | | | | | | 23 |
| 1 | 2 | 3 | | | 10 | | 9 | 12 | | 11 | | | | | 13 | 5 | 4 | | 8² | 6¹ | 7 | | | | | | 24 |
| 1 | 2 | 3 | | | 11¹ | | 7 | 12 | 13 | 10² | | | | | 5³ | 4 | | | 9 | 6 | 8 | 14 | | | | | 25 |
| 1 | 2 | 4 | 3 | | 10 | | 11³ | 12 | | 9² | | | | | 13 | 5 | | | 7 | 6¹ | 8 | 14 | | | | | 26 |
| 1 | 2 | 4 | 3³ | | 9² | | | 10 | 13 | 11¹ | | | | | 12 | 5 | | | 7 | 6 | 8 | 14 | | | | | 27 |
| 1 | 2¹ | 4 | | | 10 | | 9² | 12 | | 11 | | | | | 13 | 3 | | | 6³ | 8 | 7 | 5 | 14 | | | | 28 |
| 1 | 2 | | | | | | 11¹ | 9² | 10⁴ | | | 14 | 12 | 4³ | 3 | | 13 | 6 | 8 | 7 | 5 | | | | | | 29 |
| 1 | 5³ | 2 | 4 | | | | | | | 12 | 9² | 3 | | | 11 | 6 | 7 | 8 | 14 | 10¹ | 13 | | | | | | 30 |
| 1 | 2 | 4 | 5 | | | | 13 | 12 | | | | 14 | 6² | 3 | | 9 | 7¹ | 8 | 10 | | 11³ | | | | | | 31 |
| 1 | 2 | | 3 | | 10³ | 4² | 12 | | 8 | 9 | | 13 | 14 | | 6 | | | | | 5 | 7 | 11¹ | | | | | 32 |
| 14 | 3 | 7 | | 11 | 12⁴ | 9¹ | | 13 | | 10² | 5³ | 4 | | | 6 | | | | 8 | 2 | | | 1 | | | | 33 |
| | 3 | 2 | | | 8 | | | 10 | | 12 | 9³ | 4 | | | 6 | | | | 7 | 14 | 5¹ | 11² | 13 | | 1 | | 34 |
| | 2 | 4 | 9 | | 6 | | | 10¹ | 11² | | | 13 | 3 | | 7³ | | | | 8 | 5 | | 12 | 14 | 1 | | | 35 |
| 1 | 5² | 3 | 2 | | 10 | | | 12 | 11 | | | 9¹ | 4 | | 6 | | | | 7 | 8 | | 13 | | | | | 36 |

# MONTROSE

*Year Formed:* 1879. *Ground & Address:* Links Park, Wellington St, Montrose DD10 8QD. *Telephone:* 01674 673200.
*Fax:* 01674 677311. *E-mail:* glynis@montrosefc.co.uk *Website:* www.montrosefc.co.uk
*Ground Capacity:* total: 3,292, (seated: 1,338). *Size of Pitch:* 100m × 64m.
*Chairman:* Derek Sim. *Vice-Chairman:* John Crawford. *Secretary:* Malcolm J. Watters.
*Manager:* Stuart Garden. *Assistant Manager:* Lee Wilkie. *Physio:* Scott McCreadie.
*Club Nickname:* 'The Gable Endies'.
*Previous Grounds:* None.
*Record Attendance:* 8,983 v Dundee, Scottish Cup 3rd rd, 17 Mar 1973.
*Record Transfer Fee received:* £50,000 for Gary Murray to Hibernian (Dec 1980).
*Record Transfer Fee paid:* £17,500 for Jim Smith from Airdrieonians (Feb 1992).
*Record Victory:* 12-0 v Vale of Leithen, Scottish Cup 2nd rd, 4 Jan 1975.
*Record Defeat:* 0-13 v Aberdeen, 17 Mar 1951.
*Most Capped Player:* Alexander Keillor, 2 (6), Scotland.
*Most League Appearances:* 432: David Larter, 1987-98.
*Most League Goals in Season (Individual):* 28: Brian Third, Division II, 1972-73.

## MONTROSE – SCOTTISH THIRD DIVISION 2012–13 LEAGUE RECORD

| Match No. | Date | Venue | Opponents | Result | H/T Score | Lg Pos. | Goalscorers | Attendance |
|---|---|---|---|---|---|---|---|---|
| 1 | Aug 11 | H | Clyde | L 2-3 | 2-0 | 8 | Young, L [11], Watson [25] | 333 |
| 2 | 18 | A | Queen's Park | D 2-2 | 1-0 | 8 | Young, L [28], Johnston [64] | 498 |
| 3 | 25 | H | Annan Ath | D 0-0 | 0-0 | 8 | | 267 |
| 4 | Sept 1 | A | Peterhead | L 0-2 | 0-0 | 9 | | 509 |
| 5 | 15 | H | Berwick R | W 3-1 | 2-1 | 7 | McIntosh, L 2 [29,77], Gray, D (pen) [31] | 258 |
| 6 | 23 | A | Rangers | L 1-4 | 1-1 | 9 | Argyriou (og) [35] | 45,081 |
| 7 | Oct 6 | H | East Stirling | W 3-1 | 3-0 | 7 | McIntosh, L [16], Gray, D (pen) [21], Masson [33] | 244 |
| 8 | 13 | A | Elgin C | L 1-6 | 0-3 | 8 | Gray, D (pen) [58] | 725 |
| 9 | 20 | A | Stirling A | W 3-1 | 3-1 | 6 | McAnespie (og) [10], McIntosh, L [31], Morton [45] | 527 |
| 10 | 27 | H | Elgin C | D 2-2 | 0-2 | 7 | Wood, G [74], Winter [90] | 346 |
| 11 | Nov 3 | A | Clyde | W 2-1 | 0-0 | 5 | McLeish [66], Winter [81] | 496 |
| 12 | 17 | H | Queen's Park | D 1-1 | 1-0 | 6 | Young, L [1] | 415 |
| 13 | 24 | H | Peterhead | W 2-0 | 2-0 | 4 | Wood, G [4], Masson [15] | 479 |
| 14 | Dec 1 | A | Berwick R | W 4-1 | 2-1 | 3 | McIntosh, L [11], Winter [22], Johnston [80], Young, L [84] | 484 |
| 15 | 15 | H | Rangers | L 2-4 | 1-1 | 5 | Young, L [16], Gray, D [76] | 4205 |
| 16 | 19 | A | East Stirling | D 2-2 | 1-2 | 4 | Young, L [13], Wood, G [63] | 211 |
| 17 | 29 | H | Stirling A | W 3-2 | 2-2 | 3 | Winter [24], Wood, G [35], McIntosh, L [60] | 336 |
| 18 | Jan 2 | H | Berwick R | L 1-3 | 1-1 | 5 | Young, L [39] | 434 |
| 19 | 5 | A | Peterhead | W 1-0 | 1-0 | 3 | Johnston [3] | 594 |
| 20 | 12 | A | Annan Ath | L 1-2 | 0-0 | 4 | Wood, G [89] | 352 |
| 21 | 19 | H | Clyde | D 1-1 | 0-1 | 3 | Johnston [59] | 336 |
| 22 | 26 | A | Rangers | D 1-1 | 0-1 | 3 | Gray, D [89] | 46,273 |
| 23 | Feb 2 | H | East Stirling | D 2-2 | 1-2 | 3 | Boyle [37], Gray, D [83] | 327 |
| 24 | 9 | A | Stirling A | L 1-3 | 1-2 | 5 | McNally [26] | 472 |
| 25 | 16 | H | Elgin C | W 4-1 | 3-0 | 4 | Wood, G [7], McNally [17], Boyle [31], McIntosh, R [63] | 432 |
| 26 | 23 | A | Annan Ath | W 5-1 | 4-0 | 3 | Boyle 4 [11,15,35,47], Winter (pen) [26] | 425 |
| 27 | Mar 2 | A | Queen's Park | W 2-1 | 0-1 | 3 | McIntosh, L [73], Boyle [76] | 482 |
| 28 | 9 | A | Berwick R | L 0-4 | 0-1 | 3 | | 478 |
| 29 | 16 | H | Peterhead | L 0-6 | 0-3 | 4 | | 444 |
| 30 | 23 | A | East Stirling | W 2-1 | 1-1 | 3 | Watson 2 [31,90] | 261 |
| 31 | 30 | H | Rangers | D 0-0 | 0-0 | 3 | | 4686 |
| 32 | Apr 6 | H | Stirling A | D 2-2 | 1-1 | 4 | Boyle [36], McIntosh, R [66] | 448 |
| 33 | 13 | A | Elgin C | L 2-3 | 1-1 | 5 | Masson [28], Johnston [51] | 777 |
| 34 | 20 | A | Clyde | L 0-1 | 0-0 | 5 | | 523 |
| 35 | 27 | H | Queen's Park | L 1-2 | 0-1 | 6 | Boyle [60] | 538 |
| 36 | May 4 | A | Annan Ath | D 1-1 | 1-0 | 6 | Johnston [24] | 386 |

**Final League Position: 6**

**Honours**
*League Champions:* Second Division 1984-85; *Runners-up:* Second Division 1990-91. Third Division 1994-95.
*Scottish Cup:* Quarter-finals 1973, 1976.
*League Cup:* Semi-finals 1975-76.
*B&Q Cup:* Semi-finals 1992-93.
*League Challenge Cup:* Semi-finals 1996-97.

**Club colours:** Shirt: Blue with white trim. Shorts: White with blue trim. Socks: Blue with white trim.

**Goalscorers:** *League (60):* Boyle 9, McIntosh L 7, Young L 7, Gray D 6 (3 pens), Johnston 6, Wood G 6, Winter 5 (1 pen), Masson 3, Watson 3, McIntosh R 2, McNally 2, McLeish 1, Morton 1, own goals 2.
*William Hill Scottish FA Cup (1):* Lunan 1,
*Scottish Communities League Cup (2):* Boyle 1, Watson 1.
*Ramsdens Cup (6):* Masson 2, Boyle 1, Watson 1 (1 pen), Wood G 1, Young L 1.

| Wood S 17 + 1 | McNally S 32 | Campbell A 30 | Wood G 33 + 2 | Watson P 23 + 2 | Gray D 16 + 11 | Masson T 31 + 1 | McLeish C 12 + 4 | Young L 25 + 6 | Boyle M 15 | Johnston S 20 + 12 | Crawford D 8 + 1 | Lunan P 18 + 1 | Mosson G — + 1 | Crawford J 25 + 1 | McIntosh L 19 + 10 | Norton S 4 + 11 | McIntosh R 28 + 2 | McGuire P — + 2 | Winter J 22 + 2 | Gibson J 11 | McCord R 6 + 6 | McDonald C 1 | Gordon S — + 1 | Sturrock K — + 1 | | Match No. |
|---|---|---|---|---|---|---|---|---|---|---|---|---|---|---|---|---|---|---|---|---|---|---|---|---|---|---|
| 1 | 2 | 3 | 4 | 5 | 6 | 7 | 8 | 9 | 10 | 11 | | | | | | | | | | | | | | | | 1 |
| | 2 | 4 | 11 | 5 | 8³ | 6 | 7² | 9¹ | | 10 | 1 | 3 | 12 | 13 | 14 | | | | | | | | | | | 2 |
| | 2 | 3 | 11 | 5 | 6² | 7 | 14 | 9³ | | 10¹ | 1 | 4 | | 8 | 12 | 13 | | | | | | | | | | 3 |
| | 2 | 4 | 11 | | 6 | 7 | 8 | | | 9 | 1 | 3 | | | 10 | | 5 | | | | | | | | | 4 |
| | 2 | 4 | 11 | | 6 | 8 | | 9¹ | | 12 | 1 | 3 | | 7 | 10 | | 5 | | | | | | | | | 5 |
| | 2 | 4 | 11 | | 6³ | 8 | | 9 | | 12 | 1 | 3 | | 7 | 10¹ | | 5² | 13 | 14 | | | | | | | 6 |
| | 2 | | 10¹ | | 6² | 8 | 7 | 9 | | 12 | 1 | 4 | | 5 | 11³ | 14 | 3 | | 13 | | | | | | | 7 |
| | 2 | | 11 | | 6 | 7 | 9² | 8 | | | 1 | 4¹ | | 3 | 10 | 13 | 5 | 12 | | | | | | | | 8 |
| 1 | 2⁴ | | 12 | | 13 | 6 | 7 | 14 | | 9 | | 3 | | 4 | 10¹ | 11² | 5 | | 8³ | | | | | | | 9 |
| 1⁴ | | 3 | 13 | | | 7³ | 6² | 14 | | 9 | 12 | 4 | | 2 | 10 | 11¹ | 5 | | 8 | | | | | | | 10 |
| | | 2 | 5 | 12 | 6¹ | | 8 | 9 | | 11 | 1 | | | 4 | | 10 | 3 | | 7 | | | | | | | 11 |
| 1 | 2 | 5 | 10 | | 13 | 12 | 8¹ | 6 | | 9² | | | | 3 | | 11 | 4 | | 7 | | | | | | | 12 |
| 1 | 2 | 4 | 11 | 5 | | 8 | | 6 | | 12 | | | | 3 | 10¹ | | 9 | | 7 | | | | | | | 13 |
| 1 | 2 | 4 | 11 | 5 | | 7 | | 6 | | 12 | | | | 3 | 10¹ | | 9 | | 8 | | | | | | | 14 |
| 1 | 2 | 4 | 11 | 5 | 12 | 8² | | 6³ | | 14 | | | | 3 | 10 | 13 | 9¹ | | 7 | | | | | | | 15 |
| 1 | 2 | 4 | 11 | 5 | 13 | 7 | | 6 | | 12 | | | | 3 | 10¹ | | 9² | | 8 | | | | | | | 16 |
| 1 | 2 | 4 | 11 | 5 | 12 | 8 | | 6¹ | | 13 | | | | 3 | 10³ | 14 | 9² | | 7 | | | | | | | 17 |
| 1 | 2 | 4 | 10 | 5² | | 8 | | 6 | | 13 | | | | 3¹ | 11 | 12 | 9 | | 7 | | | | | | | 18 |
| 1 | 2 | 4 | 10 | | | 8 | 12 | 6¹ | | 9 | | | | 3 | 11 | | 5 | | 7 | | | | | | | 19 |
| 1 | 2 | 3 | 11 | 12 | 13 | 7² | 8¹ | 6 | | 9 | | | | 4 | 10 | | 5 | | | | | | | | | 20 |
| 1 | 2⁴ | 4 | 10 | 5 | 6 | 7 | | | | 9 | | | | 3 | 11 | | 8 | | | | | | | | | 21 |
| | | 4 | 10 | 5 | 12 | 2 | | | 6 | 9² | | | | 3 | 11¹ | 13 | 8 | | 7 | 1 | | | | | 22 |
| | | 5 | 11 | 3 | 12 | 2 | | | 6 | 9³ | | | | 4 | 10¹ | 14 | 8 | | 7² | 1 | 13 | | | | 23 |
| | 2³ | 4 | 11 | | 6² | 8 | 14 | | | 10 | 9¹ | | | 3 | 13 | | 5 | | 7 | 1 | 12 | | | | 24 |
| | 2¹ | 4 | 11 | 5² | 6 | 7 | | 14 | 10³ | | | | | 3 | 13 | | 9 | | 8 | 1 | 12 | | | | 25 |
| | 2 | 4 | 11² | 5 | 7 | 6³ | | 14 | 10 | | | 12 | | 3¹ | 13 | | 9 | | 8 | 1 | | | | | 26 |
| | 2 | 3¹ | 11 | 5 | 6⁴ | | | 9² | 10 | 13 | | 4 | | | 12 | | | | 7 | 1 | 8 | | | | 27 |
| | 2 | | 11 | 5 | | | 14 | 6 | | 13 | | 4 | | 3⁴ | 10³ | 12 | 9² | | 7¹ | 1 | 8 | | | | 28 |
| | 3 | | 11 | 5 | 13 | 2 | | 6² | 10 | 14 | | 4 | | | 12 | | 9¹ | | 7 | 1 | 8³ | | | | 29 |
| 1 | 2 | | 11 | 5 | 8³ | 6 | 7² | 13 | 10 | 9 | | 4⁴ | | 3¹ | 12 | | | | | | 14 | | | | 30 |
| | 2 | 3 | 11 | 5 | 7¹ | 6 | | 12 | 10 | 9 | | | | | 14 | | 13 | | 8² | 1 | | | 4² | | 31 |
| | 2 | 4 | | 5 | | 8 | | 6 | 10 | 11 | | 3 | | | | 9 | | | 7¹ | 1 | 12 | | | | 32 |
| 13 | 2 | 3 | 11 | 5 | | 8 | | 6 | 10³ | 9 | | 4 | | | 14 | | | | 7¹ | 1² | 12 | | | | 33 |
| 1 | 2 | 4 | 10 | 5² | 14 | 8 | | 6³ | 11 | 9¹ | | 3 | | | | 13 | | | 7 | | 12 | | | | 34 |
| 1 | 2 | 3 | 11 | 5² | 13⁴ | 7 | | 6 | 10 | | | 4 | | | | 12 | 9 | | | 8¹ | | | | | 35 |
| 1 | 2 | 4 | 11 | | | 8 | | 6¹ | 10² | 9 | | 3 | | | | 12 | 5 | | | 7 | | | 13 | | 36 |

# MOTHERWELL

*Year Formed:* 1886. *Ground & Address:* Fir Park Stadium, Motherwell ML1 2QN. *Telephone:* 01698 333333. *Fax:* 01698 338001.
*E-mail:* mfcenquiries@motherwellfc.co.uk *Website:* www.motherwellfc.co.uk
*Ground Capacity:* 13,742 (all seated). *Size of Pitch:* 100m × 68m.
*Manager:* Stuart McCall. *Assistant Manager:* Kenny Black. *Physio:* John Porteous.
*Club Nicknames:* 'The Well', 'The Steelmen'.
*Previous Grounds:* The Meadows, Dalziel Park.
*Record Attendance:* 35,632 v Rangers, Scottish Cup 4th rd replay, 12 Mar 1952.
*Record Transfer Fee received:* £1,750,000 for Phil O'Donnell to Celtic (September 1994).
*Record Transfer Fee paid:* £500,000 for John Spencer from Everton (Jan 1999).
*Record Victory:* 12-1 v Dundee U, Division II, 23 Jan 1954.
*Record Defeat:* 0-8 v Aberdeen, Premier Division, 26 Mar 1979.
*Most Capped Player:* Stephen Craigan, 54, Northern Ireland.
*Most League Appearances:* 626: Bobby Ferrier, 1918-37.
*Most League Goals in Season (Individual):* 52: Willie McFadyen, Division I, 1931-32.
*Most Goals Overall (Individual):* 283: Hugh Ferguson, 1916-25.

## MOTHERWELL – SCOTTISH PREMIER LEAGUE 2012–13 LEAGUE RECORD

| Match No. | Date | Venue | Opponents | Result | H/T Score | Lg Pos. | Goalscorers | Attendance |
|---|---|---|---|---|---|---|---|---|
| 1 | Aug 4 | A | Ross Co | D 0-0 | 0-0 | 7 | | 4828 |
| 2 | 11 | H | St Johnstone | D 1-1 | 0-0 | 7 | McHugh [78] | 4490 |
| 3 | 18 | A | Kilmarnock | W 2-1 | 2-1 | 2 | Murphy 2 [12, 37] | 4969 |
| 4 | 26 | H | St Mirren | D 1-1 | 1-0 | 5 | Higdon [2] | 4559 |
| 5 | Sept 2 | H | Inverness CT | W 4-1 | 2-1 | 1 | Hateley [11], Higdon 3 [12, 72, 79] | 4031 |
| 6 | 15 | A | Dundee | W 2-1 | 0-1 | 1 | Higdon 2 [75, 85] | 5176 |
| 7 | 23 | A | Aberdeen | D 3-3 | 1-1 | 1 | Higdon [42], Hutchinson [48], Law [82] | 8577 |
| 8 | 29 | H | Celtic | L 0-2 | 0-2 | 2 | | 10,496 |
| 9 | Oct 21 | A | Hearts | L 0-1 | 0-1 | 6 | | 11,572 |
| 10 | 26 | H | Hibernian | L 0-4 | 0-1 | 6 | | 5301 |
| 11 | Nov 3 | A | St Johnstone | W 3-1 | 2-0 | 6 | Murphy 2 [1, 38], Law [73] | 3112 |
| 12 | 7 | H | Dundee U | L 0-1 | 0-0 | 6 | | 3941 |
| 13 | 10 | H | Dundee | D 1-1 | 1-1 | 7 | Higdon [45] | 4318 |
| 14 | 18 | A | Inverness CT | W 5-1 | 2-0 | 4 | Higdon [18], Murphy [21], Cummins [52], Ojamaa [72], Daley [89] | 2948 |
| 15 | 24 | H | Hearts | D 0-0 | 0-0 | 6 | | 4147 |
| 16 | 27 | A | Dundee U | W 2-1 | 2-1 | 5 | Higdon [7], Humphrey [10] | 5289 |
| 17 | Dec 8 | H | Ross Co | W 3-2 | 1-1 | 3 | Higdon [25], Law [46], Lasley [82] | 3739 |
| 18 | 15 | A | Hibernian | W 3-2 | 0-1 | 2 | Murphy 2 [64, 80], McHugh [88] | 8817 |
| 19 | 21 | A | St Mirren | L 1-2 | 0-2 | 2 | McHugh [77] | 4023 |
| 20 | 26 | H | Aberdeen | W 4-1 | 3-1 | 3 | Hateley [9], Murphy 2 [31, 45], Higdon [55] | 5093 |
| 21 | 29 | H | Kilmarnock | D 2-2 | 0-1 | 2 | Murphy [71], Ojamaa [74] | 4903 |
| 22 | Jan 2 | A | Celtic | L 0-1 | 0-0 | 3 | | 48,002 |
| 23 | 20 | H | St Johnstone | W 3-2 | 2-0 | 3 | Higdon 3 [8, 20, 69] | 3649 |
| 24 | Feb 9 | A | Kilmarnock | L 0-2 | 0-1 | 3 | | 4246 |
| 25 | 16 | H | Inverness CT | W 3-0 | 1-0 | 2 | Higdon 2 [30, 56], Law [52] | 4179 |
| 26 | 19 | H | Dundee U | L 0-1 | 0-1 | 2 | | 4633 |
| 27 | 23 | A | Ross Co | L 0-3 | 0-1 | 3 | | 3797 |
| 28 | 27 | H | Celtic | W 2-1 | 1-0 | 2 | Humphrey [31], Higdon [73] | 8641 |
| 29 | Mar 2 | A | Hearts | W 2-1 | 2-0 | 2 | Higdon [3], McGowan, D (og) [8] | 11,048 |
| 30 | 9 | A | Aberdeen | D 0-0 | 0-0 | 2 | | 8210 |
| 31 | 15 | H | Hibernian | W 4-1 | 0-1 | 2 | Higdon [48], McFadden [54], Higginbotham [67], Hateley [84] | 5108 |
| 32 | 30 | A | Dundee | W 3-0 | 1-0 | 2 | Higdon [9], Law 2 [63, 79] | 4838 |
| 33 | Apr 6 | H | St Mirren | D 2-2 | 1-1 | 2 | Higdon [34], McFadden [84] | 5414 |
| 34 | 19 | A | Dundee U | W 3-1 | 2-0 | 2 | Higdon 2 [3, 55], Ojamaa [8] | 5634 |
| 35 | 28 | H | Celtic | W 3-1 | 1-1 | 2 | Ojamaa [45], Higdon (pen) [50], Forster (og) [55] | 7503 |
| 36 | May 4 | A | Inverness CT | L 3-4 | 1-3 | 2 | McFadden 2 [36, 64], Higdon (pen) [49] | 3857 |
| 37 | 12 | H | Ross Co | W 2-0 | 2-0 | 2 | McFadden [8], Humphrey [45] | 7734 |
| 38 | 19 | A | St Johnstone | L 0-2 | 0-1 | 2 | | 5025 |

**Final League Position: 2**

**Honours**
*League Champions:* Division I 1931-32. First Division 1981-82, 1984-85. Division II 1953-54, 1968-69.
*Runners-up:* Premier Division 1994-95, 2012-13. Division I 1926-27, 1929-30, 1932-33, 1933-34. Division II 1894-95, 1902-03.
*Scottish Cup:* 1952, 1991; *Runners-up:* 1931, 1933, 1939, 1951, 2011.
*League Cup Winners:* 1950-51; *Runners-up:* 1954-55, 2004-05.

**European:** *Champions League:* 2 matches (2012–13). *Cup Winners' Cup:* 2 matches (1991-92). *UEFA Cup:* 8 matches (1994-95, 1995-96, 2008-09). *Europa League:* 14 matches (2009-10, 2010-11, 2012–13).

**Club colours:** Shirt: Amber with maroon band. Shorts: Amber. Socks: Amber.

**Goalscorers:** *League (67):* Higdon 26 (2 pens), Murphy 10, Law 6, McFadden 5, Ojamaa 4, Hateley 3, Humphrey 3, McHugh 3, Cummins 1, Daley 1, Higginbotham 1, Hutchinson 1, Lasley 1, own goals 2.
*William Hill Scottish FA Cup (2):* Higdon 1 (1 pen), Murphy 1.
*Scottish Communities League Cup (0).*
*UEFA Champions League (0).*
*Europa League (0).*

| Randolph D 36 | Hammell S 31 | Law N 38 | Hutchinson S 31 | Hateley T 34 | Humphrey C 32 + 1 | Higdon M 37 | Murphy J 20 + 2 | Lasley K 36 | Ramsden S 28 + 1 | Daley O 2 + 12 | Ojamaa H 32 + 5 | McHugh R 2 + 23 | Francis-Angol Z 8 + 14 | Hetherington S 1 + 2 | Cummins A 17 + 5 | Kerr F 9 + 5 | Carswell S 7 + 16 | Page J 1 | Hollis L 2 + 1 | Higginbotham K 3 + 7 | McFadden J 11 + 2 | Saunders S — + 1 | Stewart R — + 1 | Match No. |
|---|---|---|---|---|---|---|---|---|---|---|---|---|---|---|---|---|---|---|---|---|---|---|---|---|
| 1 | 2 | 3 | 4 | 5 | 6¹ | 7 | 8 | 9 | 10 | 11² | 12 | 13 | | | | | | | | | | | | 1 |
| 1 | 5⁵ | 8 | 3 | 2 | | 10 | 9 | 7³ | 4 | 6¹ | 11² | 12 | 13 | 14 | | | | | | | | | | 2 |
| 1 | | 7² | 3 | 2 | 6³ | 11 | 9 | 8 | 4¹ | | 10 | | 5 | 13 | 12 | 14 | | | | | | | | 3 |
| 1 | 5 | 8² | 4⁴ | | 12 | 11 | 9¹ | 7 | | | 10³ | | 14 | 6 | 3 | 2 | 13 | | | | | | | 4 |
| 1 | 8¹ | | 9 | 6³ | 10 | 12 | 7 | | | 13 | 11² | 5 | | 4 | 2 | 14 | 3 | | | | | | | 5 |
| 1 | 5 | 8 | 4 | 6 | 9 | 10 | 11¹ | 7 | | 13 | 12 | | | | 3² | 2 | | | | | | | | 6 |
| 1 | 5 | 8 | 4 | 6 | 9 | 10 | 12 | 7 | | | 11¹ | | | | 3 | 2 | | | | | | | | 7 |
| 1 | 9¹ | 3 | 7 | 6² | 10 | 11³ | 8 | 2 | 13 | 14 | | 5 | | 4⁴ | 12 | | | | | | | | | 8 |
| 1 | 5 | 9³ | 3¹ | 7 | 6 | 11 | 10² | 8 | 2 | 14 | 13 | | | 4 | 12 | | | | | | | | | 9 |
| 1 | 5 | 8³ | | 2 | 6 | 10² | 9 | 7 | 4 | 12 | 11¹ | 13 | | 3 | 14 | | | | | | | | | 10 |
| 1 | 5¹ | 8 | | 2 | 6³ | 10 | 9 | 7 | 4 | | 11² | 12 | 13 | 3 | 14 | | | | | | | | | 11 |
| 1 | 5 | 8 | | 2 | 6² | 11 | 9 | 7 | 3 | 13 | 10¹ | 12 | | 4 | | | | | | | | | | 12 |
| 1 | 5¹ | 8 | | 2 | 6³ | 10 | 9² | 7 | 4 | 13 | 11 | 14 | 12 | 3 | | | | | | | | | | 13 |
| 1 | 5 | 8 | 3 | 2 | 6² | 10 | 9³ | 7 | | 13 | 11¹ | 12 | | 4 | 14 | | | | | | | | | 14 |
| 1 | 5¹ | 8 | 3 | 2 | 6 | 10 | 9 | 7 | | | 11 | | | 12 | 4 | | | | | | | | | 15 |
| 1 | | 8 | 3 | 2 | 6 | 11 | 9 | 7 | | | 10¹ | | 5 | | 4 | 12 | | | | | | | | 16 |
| | 5 | 8² | 3 | 2 | 6 | 11³ | 9 | 7 | | | 10¹ | 12 | 14 | | 4 | 13 | 1 | | | | | | | 17 |
| 1 | 5 | 8 | 3 | 2 | 6 | 11 | 9 | 7² | 13 | | 10³ | 12 | 14 | | 4¹ | | | | | | | | | 18 |
| 1 | 5² | 8 | 3 | 2 | 6 | 11 | 9 | 7 | 4 | 14 | 10 | 12 | 13 | | | | | | | | | | | 19 |
| 1 | 8³ | 3 | 7 | | 10 | 9 | 6 | 2¹ | | 11² | 14 | 5 | | 12 | 4 | 13 | | | | | | | | 20 |
| 1 | 5 | 8 | 3¹ | 2 | 6 | 10 | 9 | 7 | 4 | | 11 | 13 | | 12² | | | | | | | | | | 21 |
| 1 | 5 | 7 | | 2 | 6 | | 11 | 8 | 4 | 12 | 10² | 13 | 9¹ | | 3 | | | | | | | | | 22 |
| 1² | 5 | 8 | 3 | 2 | 6 | 10 | | 7 | 4 | | 9³ | 11¹ | 12 | | | 14 | 13 | | | | | | | 23 |
| 1 | 5 | 8 | 3 | 9³ | 6 | 10 | | 7¹ | 2² | | 11 | 13 | | 14⁴ | 4¹ | | 12 | | | | | | | 24 |
| 1 | 5 | 8 | 3 | 2 | 6 | 10 | | | 4¹ | | 11³ | 13 | 12 | 12 | 7 | | 9² | | | | | | | 25 |
| 1 | 5¹ | 8 | 3 | 2 | 6 | 10 | | | 4 | | 11³ | 13 | 12 | | 7 | | 9² | 14 | | | | | | 26 |
| 1 | | 6 | 4 | | 7³ | 11 | | 8 | 2 | 14 | 10 | 13 | 3² | | 5 | 9¹ | | 12 | | | | | | 27 |
| 1 | 5 | 8 | 3 | | 6 | 10³ | | 7 | 2 | | 11² | 14 | | | 4 | 14 | 13 | 9¹ | | | | | | 28 |
| 1 | 5 | 8 | 4 | 2 | 6¹ | 11 | | 7 | | 12 | 10² | 13 | | | 3 | 14 | | 9³ | | | | | | 29 |
| 1 | 5 | 7³ | | 2 | | 11 | | 8 | 4 | | 10² | 13 | | 3 | 6 | | 12 | 9¹ | 14 | | | | | 30 |
| 1 | 5 | 8³ | 3 | 2 | | 10 | | 7¹ | 4 | | 11 | 14 | 13 | | 12 | | 9³ | 6 | | | | | | 31 |
| 1 | 5 | 7 | 4 | 2 | 6¹ | 10² | | 8³ | 3 | | 11 | 13 | | | 14 | | 12 | 9 | | | | | | 32 |
| 1 | | 8 | 3 | 2 | 6 | 10 | | 7 | 4 | | 11 | | 5 | | | | 9 | | | | | | | 33 |
| 1 | 5 | 9 | 3 | 2 | 7² | 11 | | 8 | 4 | | 6 | | | 13 | 12 | | 10¹ | | | | | | | 34 |
| 1 | 5 | 8³ | 3 | 2 | 6 | 11 | | 7 | 4 | | 10² | 13 | | | 12 | | 14 | 9¹ | | | | | | 35 |
| 1 | 3 | 8 | 4 | 2 | 6¹ | 11 | | 9 | 5² | | 10⁸ | 13 | | 12 | | | 7 | | | | | | | 36 |
| 1³ | 5 | 8³ | 3 | 2 | 6 | 10¹ | | 7 | 4 | | | 12 | | | 9 | | 13 | 11 | 14 | | | | | 37 |
| | 5 | 8 | 3 | | | 10 | | 7 | 4 | 14 | 11³ | 12 | | | 2 | 9¹ | 1 | 13 | 6² | | | | | 38 |

# PARTICK THISTLE

*Year Formed:* 1876. *Ground & Address:* Firhill Stadium, 80 Firhill Rd, Glasgow G20 7AL. *Telephone:* 0141 579 1971.
*Fax:* 0141 945 1525. *E-mail:* mail@ptfc.co.uk *Website:* www.ptfc.co.uk
*Ground Capacity:* 13,141 (seated: 10,921). *Size of Pitch:* 105m × 69m.
*Chairman:* David Beattie. *General Manager:* Ian Maxwell.
*Manager:* Alan Archibald. *Assistant Manager:* Scott Paterson. *Head of Youth Development:* Gerry Britton.
*Physio:* Kenny Crichton.
*Club Nickname:* 'The Jags'.
*Previous Grounds:* Overnewton Park; Jordanvale Park; Muirpark; Inchview; Meadowside Park.
*Record Attendance:* 49,838 v Rangers, Division I, 18 Feb 1922. *Ground Record:* 54,728, Scotland v Ireland, 25 Feb 1928.
*Record Transfer Fee received:* £200,000 for Mo Johnston to Watford (July 1981).
*Record Transfer Fee paid:* £85,000 for Andy Murdoch from Celtic (Feb 1991).
*Record Victory:* 16-0 v Royal Albert, Scottish Cup 1st rd, 17 Jan 1931.
*Record Defeat:* 0-10 v Queen's Park, Scottish Cup 5th rd, 3 Dec 1881.
*Most Capped Player:* Alan Rough, 51 (53), Scotland.
*Most League Appearances:* 410: Alan Rough, 1969-82.
*Most League Goals in Season (Individual):* 41: Alex Hair, Division I, 1926-27.
*Most Goals Overall (Individual):* 229: Willie Sharp, 1939-57.

## PARTICK THISTLE – SCOTTISH FIRST DIVISION 2012–13 LEAGUE RECORD

| Match No. | Date | Venue | Opponents | Result | H/T Score | Lg Pos. | Goalscorers | Attendance |
|---|---|---|---|---|---|---|---|---|
| 1 | Aug 11 | H | Falkirk | W 3-1 | 2-0 | 3 | Lawless [4], Doolan 2 [7, 57] | 3487 |
| 2 | 18 | A | Dunfermline Ath | W 1-0 | 1-0 | 3 | Lawless [24] | 3540 |
| 3 | 25 | H | Dumbarton | W 3-0 | 1-0 | 1 | Doolan [16], Erskine [63], Bannigan [70] | 2944 |
| 4 | Sept 1 | H | Hamilton A | W 4-0 | 1-0 | 1 | Welsh [41], Craig 2 [59, 86], Lawless [64] | 2603 |
| 5 | 15 | A | Livingston | W 2-1 | 1-0 | 1 | Lawless 2 [36, 48] | 1745 |
| 6 | 22 | H | Cowdenbeath | W 2-1 | 1-0 | 1 | Muirhead (pen) [25], Linton (og) [70] | 2510 |
| 7 | 29 | A | Raith R | D 1-1 | 0-0 | 1 | Doolan [90] | 1957 |
| 8 | Oct 6 | A | Greenock Morton | L 1-3 | 1-2 | 2 | Craig [20] | 3445 |
| 9 | 20 | H | Airdrie U | W 7-0 | 5-0 | 1 | Erskine 2 [4, 45], Muirhead (pen) [11], Lawless [30], Welsh [47], Doolan [57], Forbes [80] | 2545 |
| 10 | 27 | A | Falkirk | D 0-0 | 0-0 | 2 | | 3818 |
| 11 | Nov 10 | H | Dunfermline Ath | W 5-1 | 3-1 | 1 | Lawless 2 [5, 75], Balatoni [34], O'Donnell, S [39], Forbes [56] | 5268 |
| 12 | 16 | A | Hamilton A | L 0-1 | 0-1 | 1 | | 2450 |
| 13 | 24 | H | Livingston | W 2-0 | 0-0 | 1 | Sinclair [54], Bannigan [64] | 2508 |
| 14 | Dec 15 | H | Raith R | W 3-2 | 2-1 | 1 | Bannigan [21], Lawless [32], Craig [87] | 2221 |
| 15 | 26 | H | Greenock Morton | L 1-2 | 1-0 | 1 | Craig [28] | 4955 |
| 16 | 29 | A | Airdrie U | D 1-1 | 0-1 | 2 | Erskine [79] | 1617 |
| 17 | Jan 5 | A | Livingston | D 2-2 | 2-1 | 3 | Doolan [25], Craig [32] | 1762 |
| 18 | 12 | A | Dumbarton | L 0-2 | 0-1 | 3 | | 1530 |
| 19 | 19 | H | Falkirk | W 4-1 | 2-1 | 2 | Balatoni 2 [4, 62], Erskine 2 [20, 64] | 3280 |
| 20 | 26 | H | Cowdenbeath | W 2-1 | 2-1 | 2 | Craig [25], Balatoni [44] | 2543 |
| 21 | Feb 16 | A | Greenock Morton | D 2-2 | 1-0 | 2 | Erskine [9], Craig [47] | 5647 |
| 22 | 19 | H | Hamilton A | W 1-0 | 0-0 | 2 | Muirhead (pen) [55] | 2046 |
| 23 | 23 | H | Airdrie U | W 1-0 | 0-0 | 2 | Erskine [76] | 3021 |
| 24 | Mar 2 | A | Dunfermline Ath | W 4-0 | 4-0 | 2 | Craig 3 [4, 22, 33], Forbes [15] | 2822 |
| 25 | 9 | H | Dumbarton | W 3-0 | 1-0 | 2 | Lawless 2 [9, 74], Doolan [81] | 2715 |
| 26 | 16 | A | Hamilton A | W 2-0 | 1-0 | 2 | Balatoni [44], Elliot [84] | 1852 |
| 27 | 23 | H | Livingston | W 6-1 | 4-0 | 2 | Muirhead (pen) [19], Craig [22], Craigen [36], Lawless [43], Erskine [57], Doolan [69] | 2897 |
| 28 | 27 | A | Cowdenbeath | W 3-0 | 2-0 | 1 | O'Donnell, S [24], Doolan 2 [30, 79] | 716 |
| 29 | 30 | A | Cowdenbeath | W 2-1 | 1-1 | 1 | Doolan 2 [12, 62] | 1214 |
| 30 | Apr 2 | A | Raith R | D 0-0 | 0-0 | 1 | | 1761 |
| 31 | 10 | H | Greenock Morton | W 1-0 | 1-0 | 1 | Craigen [41] | 8875 |
| 32 | 13 | A | Airdrie U | W 2-1 | 0-1 | 1 | Balatoni [89], Elliot [90] | 1648 |
| 33 | 16 | H | Raith R | D 0-0 | 0-0 | 1 | | 4963 |
| 34 | 20 | A | Falkirk | D 2-0 | 0-0 | 1 | Dowie [50], Erskine [78] | 4804 |
| 35 | 27 | H | Dunfermline Ath | D 3-3 | 1-0 | 1 | McMillan [27], Erskine [84], Lawless [90] | 5663 |
| 36 | May 4 | A | Dumbarton | D 0-0 | 0-0 | 1 | | 1528 |

**Final League Position: 1 – Promoted to Scottish Premier League**

**Honours**
*League Champions:* First Division 1975-76, 2001-02, 2012-13; Division II 1896-97, 1899-1900, 1970-71; Second Division 2000-01; *Runners-up:* First Division 1991-92, 2008-09. Division II 1901-02. *Promoted to First Division:* 2005-06 (play-offs).
*Scottish Cup Winners:* 1921; *Runners-up:* 1930.
*League Cup Winners:* 1971-72; *Runners-up:* 1953-54, 1956-57, 1958-59.
*League Challenge Cup Runners-up:* 2012-13.

**European:** *Fairs Cup:* 4 matches (1963-64). *UEFA Cup:* 2 matches (1972-73). *Intertoto Cup:* 4 matches (1995-96).

**Club colours:** Shirt: Yellow with thin red stripes and trim. Shorts: Black. Socks: Black.

**Goalscorers:** *League (76):* Lawless 13, Craig 12, Doolan 12, Erskine 11, Balatoni 6, Muirhead 4 (4 pens), Bannigan 3, Forbes 3, Craigen 2, Elliot 2, O'Donnell S 2, Welsh 2, Dowie 1, McMillan 1, Sinclair 1, own goal 1.
*William Hill Scottish FA Cup (2):* Forbes 1, own goal 1.
*Scottish Communities League Cup (2):* Erskine 1, Lawless 1.
*Ramsdens Cup (11):* Erskine 4, Craig 2, Doohlan 2, Bannigan 1, Elliot 1, Sinclair 1.

| Fox S 29 | O'Donnell S 26+3 | Muirhead A 29+1 | Archibald A 17 | Bannigan S 32+1 | Paton P 24 | Murray H 12 | Welsh S 22+3 | Erskine C 31+3 | Lawless S 30+5 | Doolan K 18+15 | Elliot C 4+18 | Sinclair A 27+5 | Craigen J 10+8 | Craig S 18+7 | Balatoni C 28+1 | Forbes R 22+5 | Sekhon A 1 | Slane P —+2 | Scully R —+1 | McGuigan M 1+11 | Smith G 6 | Black J —+1 | Wilson D —+1 | McMillan J 2+1 | Dowie A 5 | Daniels G 1 | Lindsay L 1 | Leyden J —+1 | Match No. |
|---|---|---|---|---|---|---|---|---|---|---|---|---|---|---|---|---|---|---|---|---|---|---|---|---|---|---|---|---|---|
| 1 | 2 | 3 | 4 | $5^3$ | 6 | 7 | 8 | $9^2$ | $10^1$ | 11 | 12 | 13 | 14 | | | | | | | | | | | | | | | | 1 |
| 1 | 2 | 3 | 4 | 5 | 7 | 8 | 9 | $11^2$ | 6 | $10^1$ | 12 | | | | | | | | | | | | | | | | | | 2 |
| 1 | 2 | 3 | 4 | 5 | 6 | 7 | $8^1$ | 11 | $9^3$ | $10^1$ | 13 | 12 | 14 | | | | | | | | | | | | | | | | 3 |
| 1 | 2 | 3 | $4^2$ | 5 | 7 | 11 | 8 | $9^3$ | 6 | $10^1$ | 14 | | | 12 | 13 | | | | | | | | | | | | | | 4 |
| 1 | 2 | 3 | 4 | 5 | 6 | 7 | 8 | 10 | $9^2$ | | | 12 | 13 | | $11^1$ | | | | | | | | | | | | | | 5 |
| 1 | 2 | 3 | 4 | 8 | 6 | 7 | | 11 | 9 | 12 | $10^1$ | $5^2$ | | | 13 | | | | | | | | | | | | | | 6 |
| 1 | 2 | 3 | 4 | 8 | 6 | $7^2$ | | 10 | 9 | 12 | $11^1$ | | 14 | | 13 | $5^3$ | | | | | | | | | | | | | 7 |
| 1 | 2 | 3 | 4 | 5 | 6 | 7 | | $11^1$ | $9^2$ | 12 | | 10 | | | $8^3$ | 13 | | | | | | | | | | | | | 8 |
| 1 | 2 | 3 | | 5 | 7 | | | 9 | $11^3$ | $6^2$ | 12 | 14 | | $10^1$ | 4 | 8 | 13 | | | | | | | | | | | | 9 |
| 1 | 2 | 3 | | $5^1$ | 7 | | | 9 | 10 | $6^3$ | 13 | 14 | 12 | 11 | 4 | $8^2$ | | | | | | | | | | | | | 10 |
| $1^1$ | $6^3$ | 2 | 3 | | 8 | | | 11 | 9 | $10^2$ | | | 14 | 5 | 4 | 7 | | | 12 | 13 | | | | | | | | | 11 |
| | 2 | 3 | 4 | | $6▪$ | | | 11 | $9^1$ | 10 | | | | 5 | 7 | 8 | | | | 12 | 1 | | | | | | | | 12 |
| | 2 | 3 | | 8 | 7 | | | $11^3$ | $9^2$ | $10^1$ | | | | 5 | 4 | 6 | | | | 12 | 1 | 13 | 14 | | | | | | 13 |
| | | 2 | | 4 | 8 | 7 | | $10^1$ | 6 | | | | | 5 | 11 | 3 | | 9 | | 12 | 1 | | | | | | | | 14 |
| 12 | 2 | 4 | 9 | 6 | | 13 | $10^1$ | $8^2$ | | 5 | 11 | 3 | $7▪$ | | | | | | | 1 | | | | | | | | | 15 |
| | 2 | 4 | 8 | 7 | | | $11^1$ | 9 | 6 | 12 | | | | 5 | 10 | 3 | | | | 1 | | | | | | | | | 16 |
| | 2 | 4 | 8 | 7 | | | $10▪$ | 12 | 14 | $9^1$ | | | | 5 | $11^2$ | 3 | $6^3$ | | | 13 | 1 | | | | | | | | 17 |
| 1 | $2^1$ | 4 | 9 | 7 | $8^3$ | | 6 | $11^2$ | | | | | 5 | 14 | 10 | 3 | 12 | | | 13 | | | | | | | | | 18 |
| 1 | | 4 | 8 | 2 | $6^2$ | 12 | 11 | | $9^1$ | 14 | | | 5 | 13 | $10^3$ | 3 | 7 | | | | | | | | | | | | 19 |
| 1 | 14 | 4 | 8 | 6 | | 2 | 11 | | 12 | 13 | | 5 | $9^2$ | $10^1$ | 3 | $7^3$ | | | | | | | | | | | | | 20 |
| 1 | 14 | 4 | | 9 | 7 | $6▪$ | 2 | $11^2$ | 12 | 13 | | | 5 | $10^3$ | 8 | $8^1$ | | | | | | | | | | | | | 21 |
| 1 | 2 | 3 | | 8 | 7 | | 6 | 11 | $9^2$ | 12 | | 5 | $10^1$ | 4 | 13 | | | | | | | | | | | | | | 22 |
| 1 | 2 | 3 | | 8 | $6^3$ | | 12 | 11 | $9^1$ | 10 | | 5 | 14 | 13 | 4 | $7^2$ | | | | | | | | | | | | | 23 |
| 1 | 2 | 3 | | $8^1$ | | | 7 | 11 | $9^3$ | 13 | | 5 | 12 | $10^2$ | 4 | 6 | | | | 14 | | | | | | | | | 24 |
| 1 | 2 | $11^3$ | | 8 | | | 13 | 12 | | 5 | 6 | $10^2$ | 4 | $7^1$ | | | | | | 14 | | | | | | | | | 25 |
| 1 | 2 | 3 | | 8 | | | 6 | $11^2$ | 9 | 14 | 13 | 5 | 12 | $10^3$ | 4 | $7^1$ | | | | | | | | | | | | | 26 |
| 1 | 2 | 3 | | | 6 | | $9^3$ | $10^2$ | 8 | 12 | 13 | 5 | 7 | $11^1$ | 4 | 14 | | | | | | | | | | | | | 27 |
| 1 | 2 | 3 | 12 | $7^1$ | | 6 | 11 | $9^2$ | $10^3$ | 13 | 5 | 8 | | 4 | | 14 | | | | | | | | | | | | | 28 |
| 1 | 2 | 3 | 6 | | | 9 | 10 | $8^1$ | $11^2$ | 12 | 5 | 7 | 13 | 4 | | | | | | | | | | | | | | | 29 |
| 1 | 2 | $3▪$ | | 7 | | | 6 | 10 | $8^1$ | $11^2$ | 5 | 9 | 13 | 4 | | | | | | 12 | | | | | | | | | 30 |
| 1 | 2 | | | 8 | | | 7 | $11^2$ | 12 | 10 | 13 | 5 | 6 | 3 | $9^1$ | | | | | | | | | | 4 | | | | 31 |
| 1 | 2 | | | 7 | | | 6 | 12 | 13 | 11 | 14 | 4 | $9^3$ | $10^1$ | 5 | $8^2$ | | | | | | | | | 3 | | | | 32 |
| 1 | 2 | | | 8 | | | 6 | 11 | 12 | $10^3$ | 13 | 5 | $9^2$ | 14 | 4 | $7^1$ | | | | | | | | | 3 | | | | 33 |
| 1 | 2 | | | 8 | | | $10^2$ | 7 | $11^3$ | 12 | 5 | 9 | 13 | 4 | $6^1$ | | | | | 14 | | | | | 3 | | | | 34 |
| 1 | 12 | | | 8 | | | 11 | 9 | 13 | $6^1$ | 5 | 14 | 4 | $7^3$ | | | | | | $10^2$ | | | | | 2 | 3 | | | 35 |
| | 2 | | | 7 | | | 12 | $9^2$ | $10^3$ | $11^1$ | 8 | | 3 | 6 | | | | | 14 | | | | | 5 | | 1 | 4 | 13 | 36 |

# PETERHEAD

*Year Formed:* 1891. *Ground and Address:* Balmoor Stadium, Balmoor Terrace, Peterhead AB42 1EQ.
*Telephone:* 01779 478256. *Fax:* 01779 490682. *E-mail:* office@peterheadfc.co.uk *Website:* www.peterheadfc.co.uk
*Ground Capacity:* 4,000 (seated: 1,000). *Size of Pitch:* 101m × 64m.
*Chairman:* Rodger Morrison. *Vice-Chairman:* Ian Grant. *Secretary:* Brian McCombie.
*Manager:* Jim McInally. *Assistant coaches:* David Nicholls and Craig Tully. *Physio:* Greig Smith.
*Club Nickname:* 'Blue Toon'.
*Previous Ground:* Recreation Park.
*Record Attendance:* 8,643 v Raith R, Scottish Cup 4th rd replay, 25 Feb 1987 (Recreation Park); 4,855 v Rangers, Third
Division, 19 Jan 2013 (at Balmoor).
*Record Victory:* 8-0 v Forfar Athletic, Second Division, 30 Sep 2006.
*Record Defeat:* 0-13 v Aberdeen, Scottish Cup 3rd rd, 10 Feb 1923.
*Most League Appearances:* 275: Martin Bavidge, 2003-13.
*Most League Goals in Season (Individual):* 21: Iain Stewart, 2002-03; Scott Michie, 2004-05; Rory McAllister, 2012-13.
*Most Goals Overall (Individual):* 98: Martin Bavidge, 2003-13.

## PETERHEAD – SCOTTISH THIRD DIVISION 2012–13 LEAGUE RECORD

| Match No. | Date | Venue | Opponents | Result | H/T Score | Lg Pos. | Goalscorers | Attendance |
|---|---|---|---|---|---|---|---|---|
| 1 | Aug 11 | H | Rangers | D 2-2 | 0-1 | 4 | McAllister [64], McLaughlin [82] | 4485 |
| 2 | 18 | A | Clyde | W 2-0 | 2-0 | 2 | Winters [20], McAllister (pen) [29] | 401 |
| 3 | 25 | H | Queen's Park | W 1-0 | 0-0 | 2 | McAllister (pen) [82] | 539 |
| 4 | Sept 1 | H | Montrose | W 2-0 | 0-0 | 1 | McAllister 2 [52, 72] | 509 |
| 5 | 15 | A | Elgin C | L 0-2 | 0-0 | 2 | | 945 |
| 6 | 22 | A | Annan Ath | L 1-2 | 0-1 | 2 | Bavidge [85] | 484 |
| 7 | Oct 6 | H | Berwick R | W 1-0 | 0-0 | 2 | Maguire [77] | 455 |
| 8 | 20 | A | East Stirling | L 1-2 | 1-1 | 4 | McAllister (pen) [2] | 296 |
| 9 | 27 | H | Stirling A | D 2-2 | 2-1 | 4 | Bavidge [10], Smith, R [28] | 508 |
| 10 | Nov 10 | A | Rangers | L 0-2 | 0-1 | 6 | | 48,407 |
| 11 | 17 | H | Clyde | W 1-0 | 1-0 | 3 | Winters [45] | 514 |
| 12 | 24 | A | Montrose | L 0-2 | 0-2 | 5 | | 479 |
| 13 | Dec 5 | H | Elgin C | D 1-1 | 1-0 | 6 | Cox [23] | 225 |
| 14 | 8 | A | Berwick R | D 1-1 | 1-0 | 6 | McLaughlin [26] | 396 |
| 15 | 15 | A | Annan Ath | W 2-0 | 0-0 | 4 | McAllister [58], Bavidge [84] | 378 |
| 16 | 22 | A | Stirling A | L 0-1 | 0-0 | 5 | | 416 |
| 17 | 29 | H | East Stirling | W 2-0 | 1-0 | 4 | Bavidge [6], Cox [73] | 446 |
| 18 | Jan 2 | A | Elgin C | W 3-0 | 2-0 | 2 | Cox [19], Strachan [38], Winters [75] | 880 |
| 19 | 5 | H | Montrose | L 0-1 | 0-1 | 4 | | 594 |
| 20 | 12 | A | Queen's Park | D 0-0 | 0-0 | 3 | | 584 |
| 21 | 20 | H | Rangers | L 0-1 | 0-1 | 4 | | 4855 |
| 22 | 29 | A | Annan Ath | D 0-0 | 0-0 | 4 | | 309 |
| 23 | Feb 2 | H | Berwick R | D 1-1 | 1-1 | 4 | McAllister [5] | 432 |
| 24 | 9 | A | East Stirling | W 4-2 | 4-0 | 3 | McAllister 2 [22, 25], Rodgers [29], McLaughlin [31] | 278 |
| 25 | 16 | A | Stirling A | D 0-0 | 0-0 | 3 | | 466 |
| 26 | 23 | H | Queen's Park | L 0-2 | 0-1 | 4 | | 479 |
| 27 | Mar 2 | A | Clyde | L 0-2 | 0-0 | 4 | | 558 |
| 28 | 9 | H | Elgin C | L 0-1 | 0-1 | 5 | | 496 |
| 29 | 16 | A | Montrose | W 6-0 | 3-0 | 5 | McCann [7], McAllister 3 [18, 31, 88], Rodgers 2 [86, 90] | 444 |
| 30 | 23 | A | Berwick R | W 2-0 | 0-0 | 5 | McCann [51], McAllister [84] | 454 |
| 31 | 30 | H | Annan Ath | W 2-0 | 0-0 | 4 | McAllister 2 [70, 90] | 483 |
| 32 | Apr 6 | H | East Stirling | W 6-0 | 5-0 | 3 | McAllister 2 [3, 40], Bavidge [16], Redman 2 [17, 57], Cowie [39] | 456 |
| 33 | 13 | A | Stirling A | W 1-0 | 1-0 | 2 | McAllister [34] | 502 |
| 34 | 20 | A | Rangers | W 2-1 | 1-1 | 2 | Ross [23], McAllister [56] | 43,961 |
| 35 | 27 | H | Clyde | W 3-0 | 1-0 | 2 | Rodgers 2 [44, 48], McAllister (pen) [69] | 560 |
| 36 | May 4 | A | Queen's Park | W 3-0 | 1-0 | 2 | Gilfillan [21], Rodgers [52], Cowie [79] | 462 |

**Final League Position: 2**

**Honours**
*Third Division Runners up:* 2004-05, 2012-13.
*Scottish Cup:* Quarter-finals 2001.

**Club colours:** Shirt: Royal blue shirts with two white stripes. Shorts: White. Socks: Royal blue.

**Goalscorers:** *League (52):* McAllister 21 (4 pens), Rodgers 6, Bavidge 5, Cox 3, McLaughlin 3, Winters 3, Cowie 2, McCann 2, Redman 2, Gilfillan 1, Maguire 1, Ross 1, Smith R 1, Strachan 1.
*William Hill Scottish FA Cup (2):* Deasley 1, Smith R 1.
*Scottish Communities League Cup (0).*
*Ramsdens Cup (1):* McAllister 1.
*Play-Offs (4):* Cox 2, McAllister 1, Rogers 1 (pen).

| Jarvie P 6 | Ross 28 | Strachan R 29+3 | MacDonald C 6 | Sharp G 15+9 | Redman J 34 | Cowie D 33+1 | McLaughlin S 26 | Noble S 35 | Winters R 10+10 | McAllister R 31+3 | Bavidge M 14+15 | Maguire S 4+12 | Deasley B 2+11 | Smith R 29+2 | McCallum M 5+1 | McBain R 1+1 | Harding R 3 | Kelly D —+4 | Ross D 2 | Cox D 26+1 | Smith G 25 | McCann R 13+7 | Tully C —+3 | Rodgers A 9+5 | Gilfillan B 7+5 | McGlinchey C 3+7 | Alexander G —+1 | Fitzgerald J —+1 | Match No. |
|---|---|---|---|---|---|---|---|---|---|---|---|---|---|---|---|---|---|---|---|---|---|---|---|---|---|---|---|---|---|
| 1 | 2 | 3 | 4 | 5 | 6 | $7^3$ | 8 | 9 | $10^1$ | $11^2$ | 12 | 13 | 14 | | | | | | | | | | | | | | | | 1 |
| 1 | 3 | 6 | 4 | | 7 | $8^3$ | 9 | 5 | $11^1$ | $10^2$ | 12 | 13 | 14 | 2 | | | | | | | | | | | | | | | 2 |
| 1 | 2 | 3 | 4 | 5 | 6 | $7^1$ | 8 | 9 | $11^2$ | $10^3$ | 12 | 13 | 14 | | | | | | | | | | | | | | | | 3 |
| | 2 | 3 | 4 | 5 | 6 | $7^2$ | 8 | 9 | | $11^3$ | 12 | 13 | 14 | | | 1 | | | | | | | | | | | | | 4 |
| $3^4$ | 7 | $4^4$ | $2^1$ | 8 | 6 | | 9 | 5 | $10^3$ | $11^2$ | 13 | | | 12 | 1 | 14 | | | | | | | | | | | | | 5 |
| | 2 | | | 8 | 7 | 9 | | $6^1$ | 10 | 11 | 12 | | | 3 | 1 | $5^2$ | 4 | 13 | | | | | | | | | | | 6 |
| 1 | 8 | 7 | 4 | | 6 | 9 | 5 | $11^2$ | $10^1$ | | | 13 | 12 | $2^1$ | | | 3 | 14 | | | | | | | | | | | 7 |
| 1 | $4^4$ | 6 | | 2 | $7^1$ | | 9 | 5 | $10^3$ | 12 | $11^2$ | 8 | 13 | | | 3 | 14 | | | | | | | | | | | | 8 |
| $1^1$ | 4 | $7^3$ | 2 | | 14 | 9 | 5 | 13 | 10 | 11 | | 8 | 3 | 12 | | | | | | $6^2$ | | | | | | | | | 9 |
| | 2 | 3 | | $6^2$ | $7^1$ | 5 | 9 | 14 | 11 | 13 | | 12 | 4 | 1 | | | | | 10 | $8^3$ | | | | | | | | | 10 |
| | 4 | 3 | | | 7 | 5 | 8 | 9 | $10^1$ | 14 | $11^3$ | 13 | 2 | 1 | | | | 12 | | $6^2$ | | | | | | | | | 11 |
| | 4 | 7 | | | 8 | $2^1$ | 9 | 5 | $10^2$ | 12 | 11 | | 13 | 2 | | | | | | 6 | 1 | | | | | | | | 12 |
| | 4 | 3 | | | 5 | 7 | 8 | 9 | $11^1$ | 10 | 12 | | 13 | 2 | | | | | | $6^2$ | 1 | | | | | | | | 13 |
| | 4 | 3 | | | 5 | 6 | 8 | 9 | 13 | $10^1$ | $11^1$ | | 2 | | | | | | | 7 | 1 | 12 | | | | | | | 14 |
| | 2 | 3 | | | 5 | 7 | 8 | 9 | 14 | $10^1$ | $11^2$ | 13 | 4 | | | | | | | $6^3$ | 1 | 12 | | | | | | | 15 |
| $3^4$ | 8 | 12 | 7 | 2 | 9 | 5 | 13 | $10^3$ | $11^1$ | 14 | | 4 | | | | | | | | $6^2$ | 1 | | | | | | | | 16 |
| | 3 | 13 | 5 | 6 | 8 | 9 | 12 | $10^1$ | $11^3$ | 14 | | 4 | | | | | | | | 7 | 1 | $2^2$ | | | | | | | 17 |
| | 8 | 12 | $7^1$ | 2 | 9 | 5 | 13 | $10^2$ | 11 | 14 | | 4 | | | | | | | | $6^3$ | 1 | 3 | | | | | | | 18 |
| | 4 | $2^2$ | | $7^3$ | 8 | 5 | 12 | $9^1$ | 11 | 13 | | 3 | | | | | | | | 10 | 1 | 6 | 14 | | | | | | 19 |
| 3 | 7 | 14 | 8 | $2^1$ | 9 | 5 | $11^2$ | 12 | $10^1$ | | | 4 | | | | | | | | 13 | 1 | 6 | | | | | | | 20 |
| 2 | $3^2$ | 13 | 5 | $7^3$ | 8 | 9 | 14 | $10^4$ | 12 | | | 4 | | | | | | | | 11 | 1 | $6^1$ | | | | | | | 21 |
| $3^1$ | | 8 | 7 | | 5 | 13 | | 9 | $11^2$ | | $4^4$ | | | | | | | | | 6 | 1 | 2 | 12 | 10 | | | | | 22 |
| 3 | | 8 | 7 | 9 | 5 | | 10 | 13 | $4^1$ | 14 | | 4 | | | | | | | | $6^3$ | 1 | 2 | | $11^2$ | 12 | | | | 23 |
| | 13 | 7 | $3^1$ | 11 | 5 | | 9 | 12 | | 14 | 4 | | 4 | | | | | | | 6 | 1 | 2 | | $10^3$ | | $8^2$ | | | 24 |
| $3^2$ | 14 | | 8 | 7 | 9 | 5 | | 10 | 12 | | | 4 | | | | | | | | $6^3$ | 1 | 2 | | $11^1$ | 13 | | | | 25 |
| | 4 | 13 | $6^3$ | 7 | 8 | 5 | | 9 | | | 3 | | | | | | | | | 10 | 1 | $2^1$ | | $11^2$ | 12 | 14 | | | 26 |
| | $4^4$ | 12 | $7^2$ | $8^3$ | 11 | 5 | | 10 | | | 3 | | | | | | | | | 6 | 1 | 14 | | 13 | $9^1$ | 2 | | | 27 |
| | | 2 | 7 | 8 | | 5 | | 10 | $6^1$ | | 4 | | | | | | | | | 9 | 1 | 13 | | $11^2$ | 3 | 12 | | | 28 |
| 3 | 12 | | 2 | 8 | 7 | | 5 | 9 | 13 | | 4 | | | | | | | | | $6^1$ | 1 | $11^2$ | | 14 | $10^3$ | | | | 29 |
| 3 | 14 | | 2 | 8 | 7 | | 5 | $10^2$ | 12 | | 4 | | | | | | | | | $6^3$ | 1 | $11^1$ | | 13 | 9 | | | | 30 |
| 3 | 8 | | 2 | $6^3$ | $7^1$ | | 5 | 9 | 12 | | 4 | | | | | | | | | $11^2$ | 1 | | | 13 | 10 | 14 | | | 31 |
| 3 | 9 | | 2 | $6^2$ | 8 | | 5 | 10 | 12 | | 4 | | | | | | | | | $11^3$ | 1 | | | $7^1$ | 13 | 14 | | | 32 |
| 3 | 9 | | 2 | 7 | 8 | | 5 | $10^2$ | $11^1$ | | 4 | | | | | | | | | $6^3$ | 1 | 13 | | $10^3$ | 12 | 14 | | | 33 |
| 3 | 9 | | 2 | 8 | $7^1$ | | 5 | 11 | | | 4 | | | | | | | | | $6^2$ | 1 | 13 | | $10^3$ | 12 | 14 | | | 34 |
| 3 | $9^2$ | | 2 | 8 | 7 | | 5 | $10^3$ | | | 4 | | | | | | | | | $6^1$ | 1 | 12 | | 11 | 13 | 14 | | | 35 |
| 3 | 4 | | 12 | 7 | 6 | | $5^1$ | | | | | | | | | | | | | $9^2$ | 1 | 11 | 14 | $10^3$ | 8 | 2 | | 13 | 36 |

# QUEEN OF THE SOUTH

*Year Formed:* 1919. *Ground & Address:* Palmerston Park, Dumfries DG2 9BA. *Telephone:* 01387 254853.
*Fax:* 01387 240470. *E-mail:* admin@qosfc.com *Website:* www.qosfc.com
*Ground Capacity:* 6,412 (seated: 3,509) *Size of Pitch:* 102m × 66m.
*Chairman:* Billy Hewitson. *Vice-Chairman:* Craig Paterson. *Assistant Club Secretary:* Susan Grierson.
*Manager:* Jim McIntyre. *Assistant Manager:* Gerry McCabe. *Physio:* Crawford Quinn.
*Club Nickname:* 'The Doonhamers'.
*Previous Grounds:* None.
*Record Attendance:* 26,552 v Hearts, Scottish Cup 3rd rd, 23 Feb 1952.
*Record Transfer Fee received:* £250,000 for Andy Thomson to Southend U (July 1994).
*Record Transfer Fee paid:* £30,000 for Jim Butter from Alloa Athletic (1995).
*Record Victory:* 11-1 v Stranraer, Scottish Cup 1st rd, 16 Jan 1932.
*Record Defeat:* 2-10 v Dundee, Division I, 1 Dec 1962.
*Most Capped Player:* Billy Houliston, 3, Scotland.
*Most League Appearances:* 731: Allan Ball, 1963-82.
*Most League Goals in Season (Individual):* 37: Jimmy Gray, Division II, 1927-28.
*Most Goals in Season:* 41: Jimmy Rutherford, 1931-32; Nicky Clark, 2012-13.
*Most Goals Overall (Individual):* 251: Jim Patterson, 1949-63.

## QUEEN OF THE SOUTH – SCOTTISH SECOND DIVISION 2012-13 LEAGUE RECORD

| Match No. | Date | Venue | Opponents | Result | H/T Score | Lg Pos. | Goalscorers | Attendance |
|---|---|---|---|---|---|---|---|---|
| 1 | Aug 11 | H | Forfar Ath | W 2-0 | 1-0 | 1 | Lyle [32], Reilly [89] | 1247 |
| 2 | 18 | A | East Fife | D 0-0 | 0-0 | 4 | | 628 |
| 3 | 25 | A | Albion R | W 1-0 | 1-0 | 2 | Lyle [21] | 1426 |
| 4 | Sept 1 | H | Arbroath | W 6-0 | 2-0 | 1 | Gibson [17], Clark [37], Reilly 3 [53, 64, 90], Smith [87] | 1554 |
| 5 | 15 | A | Ayr U | W 4-2 | 2-2 | 1 | Clark [16], Burns [31], Reilly 2 [62, 69] | 1373 |
| 6 | 22 | A | Brechin C | W 3-0 | 2-0 | 1 | Higgins [7], Lyle [40], Gibson (pen) [53] | 538 |
| 7 | 29 | H | Alloa Ath | W 1-0 | 0-0 | 1 | Clark [67] | 1370 |
| 8 | Oct 6 | A | Stranraer | W 2-0 | 1-0 | 1 | Reilly [28], Clark [90] | 1015 |
| 9 | 20 | H | Stenhousemuir | D 2-2 | 1-0 | 1 | Durnan [2], Clark [48] | 1531 |
| 10 | 28 | H | East Fife | W 1-0 | 1-0 | 1 | Lyle [4] | 1577 |
| 11 | Nov 17 | A | Arbroath | W 3-2 | 2-1 | 1 | Clark [22], Higgins [28], Durnan [60] | 691 |
| 12 | 20 | A | Forfar Ath | W 5-1 | 3-1 | 1 | Clark 2 [5, 49], McGuffie (pen) [22], Durnan [27], Hopkirk [81] | 391 |
| 13 | 24 | H | Ayr U | W 2-0 | 1-0 | 1 | McGuffie [16], Clark [55] | 1953 |
| 14 | Dec 11 | A | Alloa Ath | L 0-1 | 0-0 | 1 | | 475 |
| 15 | 15 | H | Brechin C | W 1-0 | 1-0 | 1 | Carmichael [21] | 1419 |
| 16 | 26 | H | Stranraer | W 4-1 | 1-1 | 1 | Clark 3 [31, 63, 70], Smith [84] | 2122 |
| 17 | 29 | A | Stenhousemuir | W 3-1 | 1-0 | 1 | Reilly 2 [32, 69], Clark [55] | 632 |
| 18 | Jan 2 | A | Ayr U | W 5-1 | 2-1 | 1 | McStay (og) [32], Clark [43], Carmichael [47], McCann (og) [69], Lyle [72] | 1216 |
| 19 | 5 | H | Arbroath | W 5-1 | 0-1 | 1 | Lyle [54], Clark 2 [58, 84], Carmichael [65], McKenna [81] | 1693 |
| 20 | 12 | A | Albion R | W 3-0 | 1-0 | 1 | Clark [41], Lyle [68], Young [76] | 810 |
| 21 | 19 | H | Forfar Ath | W 3-1 | 2-1 | 1 | McGuffie [11], Lyle [19], Clark [70] | 1481 |
| 22 | Feb 2 | H | Alloa Ath | D 0-0 | 0-0 | 1 | | 1738 |
| 23 | 9 | H | Stenhousemuir | W 2-1 | 2-0 | 1 | Young [34], Mitchell [45] | 1354 |
| 24 | 16 | A | Stranraer | W 5-0 | 3-0 | 1 | Burns [17], McGuffie (pen) [24], Lyle 2 [39, 71], Clark [59] | 810 |
| 25 | 23 | H | Albion R | W 3-0 | 1-0 | 1 | Lyle [43], Clark [76], Durnan [81] | 1520 |
| 26 | Mar 2 | A | East Fife | W 3-2 | 1-0 | 1 | Reilly [15], Clark [66], Durnan [70] | 627 |
| 27 | 9 | H | Ayr U | W 2-0 | 1-0 | 1 | Lyle [45], Reilly [60] | 1471 |
| 28 | 16 | A | Arbroath | D 1-1 | 0-0 | 1 | Clark [90] | 656 |
| 29 | 23 | A | Alloa Ath | W 2-1 | 1-0 | 1 | Clark [40], McGuffie (pen) [85] | 647 |
| 30 | 27 | A | Brechin C | W 6-0 | 5-0 | 1 | Clark 2 [1, 42], Paton 2 [3, 36], Moyes (og) [18], Reilly [57] | 627 |
| 31 | 30 | H | Brechin C | W 2-1 | 1-0 | 1 | Durnan [16], Lyle [73] | 2026 |
| 32 | Apr 13 | H | Stranraer | W 2-0 | 1-0 | 1 | Holt [31], Clark [76] | 1806 |
| 33 | 16 | A | Stenhousemuir | L 1-2 | 1-1 | 1 | Mitchell [44] | 504 |
| 34 | 20 | A | Forfar Ath | W 4-0 | 1-0 | 1 | Paton [33], Clark 3 [54, 56, 85] | 555 |
| 35 | 27 | H | East Fife | D 2-2 | 0-1 | 1 | Clark 2 [87, 90] | 2568 |
| 36 | May 4 | A | Albion R | W 1-0 | 0-0 | 1 | Clark [71] | 853 |

**Final League Position: 1 – Promoted to Scottish First Division**

**Honours**
*League Champions:* Division II 1950-51. Second Division 2001-02, 2012-13.
*Runners-up:* Division II 1932-33, 1961-62, 1974-75. Second Division 1980-81, 1985-86.
*Scottish Cup Runners-up:* 2007-08.
*League Cup:* semi-finals 1950-51, 1960-61.
*League Challenge Cup Winners:* 2002-03, 2012–13; *Runners-up:* 1997-98, 2010-11. *B&Q Cup:* semi-finals 1991-92.

**European:** *UEFA Cup:* 2 matches (2008-09).

**Club colours:** Shirt: Royal blue with white trim. Shorts: Royal blue. Socks: Royal blue.

**Goalscorers:** *League (92):* Clark 32, Lyle 13, Reilly 12, Durnan 6, McGuffie 5 (3 pens), Carmichael 3, Paton 3, Burns 2, Gibson 2 (1 pen), Higgins 2, Mitchell 2, Smith 2, Young 2, Holt 1, Hopkirk 1, McKenna 1, own goals 3.
*William Hill Scottish FA Cup (3):* Clark 2, Reilly 1.
*Scottish Communities League Cup (7):* Clark 3, Higgins 1, Lyle 1, Mitchell 1, Reilly 1.
*Ramsdens Cup (8):* Clark 4, Durnan 1, McGuffie 1, Reilly 1, Young 1.

| Robinson L 36 | McGuffie R 23+5 | Durnan M 32 | Higgins C 32 | Holt K 25+3 | McKenna S 28+3 | Mitchell C 33 | Orsi D 4+9 | Carmichael D 34 | Lyle D 23+6 | Clark N 36 | Reilly G 17+13 | Johnston A 1+3 | Hopkirk D —+5 | Young D 22+4 | Gibson W 11+6 | Black S 4+7 | Smith K —+18 | Burns P 23+1 | Johnson L —+1 | Paton M 6+4 | Fitzpatrick M 3+1 | Slattery P 3+1 | Atkinson J —+1 | Match No. |
|---|---|---|---|---|---|---|---|---|---|---|---|---|---|---|---|---|---|---|---|---|---|---|---|---|
| 1 | 2 | 3 | 4 | 5 | 6 | 7 | 8 | 9 | 10[1] | 11 | 12 | | | | | | | | | | | | | 1 |
| 1 | 2 | 3 | 4 | 5 | 7 | 6 | | 9[1] | 11[3] | 10[2] | 12 | 8[4] | 13 | 14 | | | | | | | | | | 2 |
| 1 | 2[1] | 3 | 4 | 5 | 7 | 6 | | 9 | 10[3] | 11 | 14 | | | 9[2] | 12 | 13 | | | | | | | | 3 |
| 1 | | 3 | 4 | 5 | 8[3] | 2 | 13 | 9 | 11[1] | 10 | 7 | | | 6[2] | 14 | 12 | | | | | | | | 4 |
| 1 | 14 | 4 | 3 | 5 | 8 | 2 | 12 | 11 | 13 | 9[2] | 10[2] | | | 6[1] | 7 | | | | | | | | | 5 |
| 1 | | 3 | 4 | 5 | 8 | 2 | 13 | 6[2] | 10 | 11[1] | 12 | | | 9[3] | 7 | 14 | | | | | | | | 6 |
| 1 | | 3 | 4 | 5 | | 2 | 12 | 6 | 11 | 10 | | | | 9[1] | 7 | | | | | | | | | 7 |
| 1 | 12 | 3 | 4 | 5 | 13 | 2 | 6 | 11 | 10[2] | 8 | 9 | | | 7[1] | | | | | | | | | | 8 |
| 1 | | 3 | 4 | 5[8] | 12 | 2 | 13 | 6 | 14 | 11[3] | 10[2] | 8[8] | | 9[1] | 7 | | | | | | | | | 9 |
| 1 | 2 | | 4 | 6 | 5 | 8 | | 10[2] | 9[1] | 11 | 13 | 12 | | 3 | 7 | | | | | | | | | 10 |
| 1 | 5 | 3 | 4 | 8 | 2 | | 6[1] | 11 | 10 | 9[2] | 13 | 14 | 12 | 7[3] | | | | | | | | | | 11 |
| 1 | 5 | 3 | 4 | 8 | 2 | | 9[1] | 10[2] | 11[3] | 12 | 14 | 7 | 6 | 13 | | | | | | | | | | 12 |
| 1 | 2 | 3 | 4 | | 7 | 5 | 14 | 9[1] | 10[3] | 11[2] | 13 | 12 | 8 | | 6 | | | | | | | | | 13 |
| 1 | 5 | 3 | 4 | 12 | 7 | 2 | | 9 | 11 | 10[3] | 14 | | 6[2] | 13 | 8[1] | | | | | | | | | 14 |
| 1 | 2 | 3 | 4 | 13 | 7[2] | 5 | | 6 | 10[1] | 11 | 12 | | | 8 | 9 | | | | | | | | | 15 |
| 1 | 2 | 3 | 4 | 5 | 7 | | 12 | 6[3] | 11[2] | 10 | 14 | | | 8 | 9[1] | 13 | | | | | | | | 16 |
| 1 | 2 | 3 | 4 | 5 | 12 | 7 | 6[1] | 9 | 10[3] | 11 | 13 | | | 8[2] | | 14 | | | | | | | | 17 |
| 1 | 2[2] | 4 | 3 | 5 | 8 | 6 | | 9 | 12 | 11 | 10[3] | 7[1] | 13 | 14 | | | | | | | | | | 18 |
| 1 | 2 | 3[8] | 4 | 5 | 8 | 7 | | 6 | 9[2] | 11 | 10[1] | 12 | | | 13 | | | | | | | | | 19 |
| 1 | | 3 | 4 | 5 | 8 | 2 | 13 | 9 | 10[3] | 11[2] | | 7[1] | 14 | 12 | 6 | | | | | | | | | 20 |
| 1 | | 4 | 3 | 5 | 7 | 2 | | 9 | 10[2] | 11[1] | 12 | | | 8 | 13 | 6 | | | | | | | | 21 |
| 1 | 2 | 3 | 4 | | 7 | 5 | | 6 | 11[1] | 10 | 12 | | | 8 | 9 | | | | | | | | | 22 |
| 1 | | 3 | 4 | 5 | 8 | 2 | | 9 | 11[1] | 10[2] | 12 | | | 7 | 13 | 6 | | | | | | | | 23 |
| 1 | | 4 | 3 | 5[8] | 8 | 2 | | 9 | 10[3] | 11 | 14 | 7[1] | 13 | 12 | 6 | | | | | | | | | 24 |
| 1 | 13 | 3 | 4 | 5 | 7 | 2 | | 9 | 10[1] | 11[3] | 12 | 8[2] | | 14 | 6 | | | | | | | | | 25 |
| 1 | 5 | 3 | 4 | 8 | 2 | | 6[2] | | 10 | 11[3] | 7 | 13 | | 14 | 9[1] | 12 | | | | | | | | 26 |
| 1 | 2 | 3 | 4 | 5 | | 6 | | 9 | 8 | 11 | 10 | | | 7 | | | | | | | | | | 27 |
| 1 | 4 | 3 | | 12 | 7 | 2 | | 11 | 8[3] | 10 | 9[2] | | | 14 | 6 | 13 | 5[1] | | | | | | | 28 |
| 1 | 12 | 3[1] | 4 | 8 | 2 | | 9 | | 10[3] | 11 | 14 | | 7 | 6[2] | | 13 | 5 | | | | | | | 29 |
| 1 | 12 | 3[1] | 4 | 5 | 7 | 2 | | 9[2] | 14 | 11[3] | 10 | | 13 | | 6 | 8 | | | | | | | | 30 |
| 1 | | 3 | 4 | | 7 | 2 | | 6[2] | 12 | 11[1] | 10[3] | 8 | 13 | | 14 | 9 | 5 | | | | | | | 31 |
| 1 | 2 | 3 | | 5 | | 9 | | 12 | 11[2] | 8[1] | | 4 | 13 | 7 | | 10[3] | 14 | 6 | | | | | | 32 |
| 1 | | 3 | 5 | 8 | 2 | | 6[1] | | 10 | 11 | | 4 | 12 | | 9 | | 7 | | | | | | | 33 |
| 1 | | 3 | 4 | 5 | 8[3] | 2 | 12 | | 9[2] | 10 | 7 | | 13 | 6 | 11[1] | | 14 | | | | | | | 34 |
| 1 | 2 | 3[8] | 4 | 5 | 7 | | | 6 | 10[3] | 11 | | 12 | 14 | 13 | 8[1] | 9 | | | | | | | | 35 |
| 1[3] | 2 | | 4 | 5 | | 6[2] | 9 | 11 | 10 | | | 3 | 13 | 7 | | 12 | | 8[1] | 14 | | | | | 36 |

# QUEEN'S PARK

*Year Formed:* 1867. *Ground & Address:* Hampden Park, Mount Florida, Glasgow G42 9BA. *Telephone:* 0141 632 1275.
*Fax:* 0141 636 1612. *E-mail:* secretary@queensparkfc.co.uk *Website:* queensparkfc.co.uk
*Ground Capacity:* 52,025 (all seated). *Size of Pitch:* 105m × 68m.
*President:* Ross Craven. *Secretary:* Christine Wright. *Treasurer:* David Gordon.
*Head Coach:* Gardner Spiers.
*Club Nickname:* 'The Spiders'.
*Previous Grounds:* 1st Hampden (Recreation Ground); (Titwood Park was used as an interim measure between 1st &
2nd Hampdens); 2nd Hampden (Cathkin); 3rd Hampden.
*Record Attendance:* 95,772 v Rangers, Scottish Cup 1st rd, 18 Jan 1930.
*Record for Ground:* 149,547 Scotland v England, 1937.
*Record Transfer Fee received:* Not applicable due to amateur status.
*Record Transfer Fee paid:* Not applicable due to amateur status.
*Record Victory:* 16-0 v St. Peter's, Scottish Cup 1st rd, 12 Sep 1885.
*Record Defeat:* 0-9 v Motherwell, Division I, 26 Apr 1930.
*Most Capped Player:* Walter Arnott, 14, Scotland.
*Most League Appearances:* 532: Ross Caven, 1982-2002.
*Most League Goals in Season (Individual):* 30: William Martin, Division I, 1937-38.
*Most Goals Overall (Individual):* 163: James B. McAlpine, 1919-33.

## QUEEN'S PARK – SCOTTISH THIRD DIVISION 2012–13 LEAGUE RECORD

| Match No. | Date | Venue | Opponents | Result | H/T Score | Lg Pos. | Goalscorers | Attendance |
|---|---|---|---|---|---|---|---|---|
| 1 | Aug 11 | A | East Stirling | W 2-0 | 0-0 | 2 | Shankland 2 [48, 68] | 430 |
| 2 | 18 | H | Montrose | D 2-2 | 0-1 | 3 | Longworth [86], Smith [90] | 498 |
| 3 | 25 | A | Peterhead | L 0-1 | 0-0 | 5 | | 539 |
| 4 | Sept 1 | A | Stirling A | W 2-1 | 1-1 | 4 | Brough [21], Longworth [83] | 740 |
| 5 | 15 | H | Clyde | W 1-0 | 1-0 | 3 | Watt [27] | 907 |
| 6 | 22 | A | Elgin C | W 4-0 | 2-0 | 1 | Shankland [29], Quinn [32], Longworth 2 [73, 89] | 855 |
| 7 | Oct 13 | A | Annan Ath | D 2-2 | 1-1 | 1 | Shankland 2 [37, 48] | 626 |
| 8 | 20 | A | Rangers | L 0-2 | 0-0 | 3 | | 49,463 |
| 9 | 27 | H | Berwick R | D 1-1 | 1-1 | 3 | Quinn [34] | 487 |
| 10 | Nov 13 | H | East Stirling | L 1-2 | 1-1 | 4 | Robertson [35] | 374 |
| 11 | 17 | A | Montrose | D 1-1 | 0-1 | 4 | Gallacher [60] | 415 |
| 12 | 23 | H | Stirling A | W 2-1 | 0-0 | 3 | Connolly [48], Quinn (pen) [89] | 557 |
| 13 | Dec 8 | A | Annan Ath | W 3-2 | 1-0 | 3 | Quinn (pen) [25], McParland [48], Connolly [68] | 453 |
| 14 | 15 | H | Elgin C | D 1-1 | 1-1 | 3 | Robertson [41] | 466 |
| 15 | 29 | H | Rangers | L 0-1 | 0-0 | 5 | | 30,117 |
| 16 | Jan 2 | H | Clyde | W 4-1 | 3-1 | 4 | Keenan 2 [2, 77], Burns [6], Scullion (og) [45] | 842 |
| 17 | 5 | A | Stirling A | W 3-2 | 1-0 | 2 | Connolly [29], McGinn [53], McParland [66] | 657 |
| 18 | 12 | H | Peterhead | D 0-0 | 0-0 | 2 | | 584 |
| 19 | 19 | A | East Stirling | W 2-0 | 1-0 | 2 | Quinn [38], Miller (og) [71] | 415 |
| 20 | Feb 2 | A | Annan Ath | D 2-2 | 0-1 | 2 | Longworth 2 [59, 85] | 558 |
| 21 | 9 | A | Rangers | L 0-4 | 0-0 | 2 | | 46,104 |
| 22 | 16 | H | Berwick R | W 2-1 | 1-1 | 2 | Longworth [24], McParland [61] | 462 |
| 23 | 23 | A | Peterhead | W 2-0 | 1-0 | 2 | Noble (og) [12], Shankland [50] | 479 |
| 24 | 26 | A | Clyde | W 3-0 | 1-0 | 2 | Connolly [15], Shankland 2 [53, 83] | 451 |
| 25 | Mar 2 | H | Montrose | L 1-2 | 1-0 | 2 | Keenan [39] | 482 |
| 26 | 5 | A | Elgin C | W 5-3 | 3-0 | 2 | Burns 2 [12, 66], Shankland [14], Spittal [32], Keenan [58] | 352 |
| 27 | 9 | A | Clyde | W 3-2 | 0-1 | 2 | Keenan [52], McParland [58], Shankland [60] | 631 |
| 28 | 12 | A | Berwick R | L 0-2 | 0-0 | 2 | | 456 |
| 29 | 30 | H | Elgin C | L 0-1 | 0-0 | 2 | | 557 |
| 30 | Apr 2 | H | Stirling A | D 2-2 | 0-1 | 2 | Anderson [57], Connolly [77] | 494 |
| 31 | 7 | H | Rangers | L 1-4 | 0-2 | 2 | Shankland [87] | 11,492 |
| 32 | 10 | A | Annan Ath | L 0-2 | 0-1 | 2 | | 242 |
| 33 | 13 | A | Berwick R | L 1-4 | 1-3 | 3 | Urquhart [4] | 623 |
| 34 | 20 | H | East Stirling | W 5-1 | 2-1 | 3 | Anderson [17], Longworth 2 [44, 53], Burns [81], Connolly [90] | 485 |
| 35 | 27 | A | Montrose | W 2-1 | 1-0 | 3 | Quinn [43], Gibson [75] | 538 |
| 36 | May 4 | H | Peterhead | L 0-3 | 0-1 | 3 | | 462 |

**Final League Position: 3**

## Scottish League Clubs – Queen's Park

**Honours**
*League Champions:* Division II 1922-23. B Division 1955-56. Second Division 1980-81. Third Division 1999-2000.
*Runners-up:* Third Divsion 2011-12. *Promoted to Second Division:* 2006-07 (play-offs).
*Scottish Cup Winners:* 1874, 1875, 1876, 1880, 1881, 1882, 1884, 1886, 1890, 1893; *Runners-up:* 1892, 1900.
*FA Cup Runners-up:* 1884, 1885.

**Club colours:** Shirt: Black and white thin hoops. Shorts: White. Socks: White.

**Goalscorers:** *League (60):* Shankland 11, Longworth 9, Connolly 6, Quinn 6 (2 pens), Keenan 5, Burns 4, McParland 4, Anderson 2, Robertson 2, Brough 1, Gallacher 1, Gibson 1, McGinn 1, Smith 1, Spittal 1, Urquhart 1, Watt 1, own goals 3.
*William Hill Scottish FA Cup (4):* Anderson 1, Longworth 1 (1 pen), Quinn 1, Shankland 1.
*Scottish Communities League Cup (6):* Brough 2, Burns 1, Keenan 1, Longworth 1 (1 pen), Shankland 1.
*Ramsdens Cup (6):* Quinn 3, Little 1, Longworth 1, Shankland 1.
*Play-Offs (1):* Shankland 1.

| Parry N 32 | Little R 31 | Bradley P 21+4 | Brough J 18 | Robertson A 34 | Ronald O 2+2 | Capuano G 9+4 | Keenan M 29+3 | Burns S 21+6 | Quinn A 20+5 | Longworth J 28+3 | Shankland L 19+14 | Watt I 4+11 | Gallacher P 24+1 | Anderson D 27 | Smith C 1+10 | Lochhead B 4+1 | Gibson S 4+1 | Urquhart A 5+3 | Spittal B 14+2 | McGinn P 8 | McParland A 22+1 | Connolly A 17+6 | McVey C —+2 | Davison L 1+4 | McKenna M 1 | Coll B —+1 | Gebbie K —+1 | Match No. |
|---|---|---|---|---|---|---|---|---|---|---|---|---|---|---|---|---|---|---|---|---|---|---|---|---|---|---|---|---|
| 1 | 2 | 3 | 4 | 5 | 6$^2$ | 7 | 8 | 9$^1$ | 10 | 11 | 12 | 13 |  |  |  |  |  |  |  |  |  |  |  |  |  |  |  | 1 |
| 1 | 2 | 4 | 3 | 5 | 6$^1$ | 7 | 8 | 14 | 10$^2$ | 11$^3$ | 12 |  | 13 | 9 |  |  |  |  |  |  |  |  |  |  |  |  |  | 2 |
| 1 | 2 | 4 | 3 | 5 | 6$^1$ | 7$^2$ | 14 | 9 | 10$^3$ | 11 | 12 | 8 | 13 |  |  |  |  |  |  |  |  |  |  |  |  |  |  | 3 |
| 1 | 2 | 4 | 3 | 5 | 6$^1$ | 7 | 8 | 9 | 11$^2$ | 10 | 12 | 13 |  |  |  |  |  |  |  |  |  |  |  |  |  |  |  | 4 |
| 1 | 2 | 4 | 3 | 5 | 6$^2$ | 7 | 13 | 11$^1$ | 10 | 8 | 12 | 14 | 9$^3$ |  |  |  |  |  |  |  |  |  |  |  |  |  |  | 5 |
| 1 | 2 | 3 |  | 5 | 6$^3$ | 12 | 14 | 7 | 8$^1$ | 10$^2$ | 11 | 9 | 4 | 13 |  |  |  |  |  |  |  |  |  |  |  |  |  | 6 |
| 1 | 3 | 5 | 4 |  | 6 | 11$^2$ | 10$^1$ | 7 | 9 | 13 | 2 | 8 | 12 |  |  |  |  |  |  |  |  |  |  |  |  |  |  | 7 |
| 1 | 3 | 5 | 4 | 8$^1$ | 6$^3$ | 11$^2$ | 13 | 10 | 9 | 12 | 2 | 7 | 14 |  |  |  |  |  |  |  |  |  |  |  |  |  |  | 8 |
| 1 | 2 | 5$^1$ | 3 | 8 | 7 | 9$^2$ | 11 | 10 | 12 | 4 | 6 | 13 |  |  |  |  |  |  |  |  |  |  |  |  |  |  |  | 9 |
| 1$^1$ | 3 | 4 | 5 | 9$^2$ | 6 | 8 | 11$^1$ | 7$^3$ | 10 | 13 | 2 | 12 | 14 |  |  |  |  |  |  |  |  |  |  |  |  |  |  | 10 |
| 2 | 8 | 6 | 3 | 10 | 11$^2$ | 12 | 5 | 9$^1$ | 1 | 4 | 7 | 13 |  |  |  |  |  |  |  |  |  |  |  |  |  |  |  | 11 |
| 1 | 4 | 5 | 6 | 13 | 10 | 7$^1$ | 9$^2$ | 12 | 3 |  |  |  |  |  |  |  |  |  |  |  | 2 | 8 | 11 |  |  |  |  |  | 12 |
| 1 | 4 | 5 | 11$^1$ | 7$^3$ | 10 | 12 | 13 | 3 | 8 | 14 |  |  |  |  |  |  |  |  |  |  | 2 | 6 | 9$^2$ |  |  |  |  |  | 13 |
| 1 | 3 | 5$^1$ | 11 | 6 | 10$^2$ | 13 | 12 | 4 | 7$^3$ | 14 |  |  |  |  |  |  |  |  |  | 2 | 8 | 9 |  |  |  |  |  |  | 14 |
| 1 | 3 | 4$^1$ | 5 | 8 | 10 | 11$^2$ | 9$^1$ | 6 | 7 |  |  |  |  |  |  |  |  |  |  | 2 | 13 | 12 |  |  |  |  |  |  | 15 |
| 1 | 3 | 5 | 14 | 8$^2$ | 11$^1$ | 10 | 13 | 12 | 4 | 7$^3$ |  |  |  |  |  |  |  |  |  | 2 | 6 | 9 |  |  |  |  |  |  | 16 |
| 1 | 3$^1$ | 12 | 5 | 9 | 11 | 10$^2$ | 13 | 4 | 7 |  |  |  |  |  |  |  |  |  |  | 2 | 8 | 6 |  |  |  |  |  |  | 17 |
| 1 | 3 | 5 | 8$^1$ | 11$^2$ | 10 | 13 | 12 | 4 | 7 |  |  |  |  |  |  |  |  |  |  | 2 | 6 | 9 |  |  |  |  |  |  | 18 |
| 1 | 3 | 4 | 5 | 13 | 9$^1$ | 11 | 10 | 12 | 8 |  |  |  |  |  |  |  |  |  |  | 2 | 7$^2$ | 6 |  |  |  |  |  |  | 19 |
| 1 | 3 | 12 | 4 | 5 | 10$^2$ | 11$^3$ | 13 | 7 | 14 | 2$^1$ | 6 |  |  |  |  |  |  |  |  | 8 | 9 |  |  |  |  |  |  |  | 20 |
| 1 | 2 | 3 | 5 | 4$^2$ | 13 | 6$^3$ | 11 | 14 | 8 |  |  |  |  |  |  |  |  |  | 12 | 10$^1$ | 9 | 7 |  |  |  |  |  |  | 21 |
| 1 | 3 | 4 | 5 | 10$^1$ | 11$^1$ | 7 | 9 | 8 |  |  |  |  |  |  |  |  |  |  |  | 2 | 6 | 12 |  |  |  |  |  |  | 22 |
| 1 | 3 | 4 | 5 | 8 | 9 | 10 | 11$^1$ |  |  |  |  |  |  |  |  |  | 6 | 2 |  |  |  |  | 7 | 12 |  |  |  |  | 23 |
| 1 | 3 | 4 | 5 | 12 | 11 | 7 | 10 |  |  |  |  |  |  |  |  |  | 6 | 2 |  |  |  |  | 8 | 9$^1$ |  |  |  |  | 24 |
| 1 | 3 | 4 | 5 | 10 | 11$^1$ | 7 | 9 | 12 | 8 |  |  |  |  |  |  |  |  |  |  | 2 | 6 |  |  |  |  |  |  |  | 25 |
| 1 | 3 | 13 | 4 | 5 | 11 | 9 | 10$^3$ | 2$^2$ | 7 |  |  |  |  |  |  |  |  | 6$^1$ |  |  | 8 |  | 14 | 12 |  |  |  |  | 26 |
| 1 | 4 | 3 | 5 | 12 | 9 | 11 | 10 | 7 |  |  |  |  |  |  |  |  |  | 2 |  |  | 8 | 6$^1$ |  |  |  |  |  |  | 27 |
| 1 | 4 | 3 | 5 | 11 | 9$^1$ | 10 | 6$^2$ | 2 | 7 |  |  |  |  |  |  |  |  | 12 |  |  | 8 | 13 |  |  |  |  |  |  | 28 |
| 1 | 4 | 3 | 5 | 12 | 7 | 10$^1$ | 2 | 8 |  |  |  |  |  |  |  |  | 9 |  |  |  | 6 | 11$^2$ | 13 |  |  |  |  |  | 29 |
| 1 | 3 | 4 | 5 | 10$^2$ | 7 | 13 | 2$^1$ | 6 |  |  |  |  |  |  |  |  | 11 |  |  |  | 8 | 9 | 12 |  |  |  |  |  | 30 |
| 1 | 3 | 4 | 5 | 10$^3$ | 12 | 14 | 7 | 13 | 2 | 6 |  |  |  |  |  |  | 11$^2$ |  |  |  | 8 | 9$^1$ |  |  |  |  |  |  | 31 |
| 1 | 2 | 4 | 5 | 7 | 12 | 10$^1$ | 6$^2$ | 3 | 8 |  |  |  |  |  |  |  | 14 | 11 |  |  | 9$^3$ | 13 |  |  |  |  |  |  | 32 |
| 1 | 3 | 4$^2$ | 5 | 8 | 7 | 13 | 11 | 10 |  |  |  |  |  | 12 | 9$^3$ | 2 |  |  | 14 |  |  |  | 6$^1$ |  |  |  |  |  | 33 |
|  |  |  | 5 | 9$^3$ | 10 | 14 | 7 | 8$^1$ | 4 | 6$^2$ | 1 | 3 | 13 | 11 |  |  | 2 | 12 |  |  |  |  |  |  |  |  |  | 34 |
| 12 |  | 5$^1$ | 8$^4$ | 9$^2$ | 10 | 11 | 13 | 4 |  |  | 1 | 3 | 2 |  |  | 7 | 6$^2$ | 14 |  |  |  |  |  |  |  |  |  | 35 |
| 4$^2$ | 3$^1$ |  | 7$^3$ | 10 | 14 | 2 | 1 | 5 | 6 |  |  |  | 8 | 11 | 9 | 12 | 13 |  |  |  |  |  |  |  |  |  |  | 36 |

# RAITH ROVERS

*Year Formed:* 1883. *Ground & Address:* Stark's Park, Pratt St, Kirkcaldy KY1 1SA. *Telephone:* 01592 263514. *Fax:* 01592 642833. *E-mail:* info@raithrovers.net *Website:* www.raithrovers.net
*Ground Capacity:* 10,104 (all seated). *Size of Pitch:* 103m × 64m.
*Chairman:* Turnbull Hutton. *Secretary:* Eric Drysdale.
*Manager:* Grant Murray. *Assistant Manager:* Paul Smith.
*Club Nickname:* 'Rovers'.
*Previous Grounds:* Robbie's Park.
*Record Attendance:* 31,306 v Hearts, Scottish Cup 2nd rd, 7 Feb 1953.
*Record Transfer Fee received:* £900,000 for Steve McAnespie to Bolton Wanderers (Sept 1995).
*Record Transfer Fee paid:* £225,000 for Paul Harvey from Airdrieonians (July 1996).
*Record Victory:* 10-1 v Coldstream, Scottish Cup 2nd rd, 13 Feb 1954.
*Record Defeat:* 2-11 v Morton, Division II, 18 Mar 1936.
*Most Capped Player:* David Morris, 6, Scotland.
*Most League Appearances:* 430: Willie McNaught, 1946-51.
*Most League Goals in Season (Individual):* 38: Norman Haywood, Division II, 1937-38.
*Most Goals Overall (Individual):* 154: Gordon Dalziel (League), 1987-94.

## RAITH ROVERS – SCOTTISH FIRST DIVISION 2012–13 LEAGUE RECORD

| Match No. | Date | Venue | Opponents | Result | H/T Score | Lg Pos. | Goalscorers | Atten- dance |
|---|---|---|---|---|---|---|---|---|
| 1 | Aug 11 | H | Hamilton A | W 2-0 | 0-0 | 4 | Graham 2 (1 pen) 63 (p), 86 | 1868 |
| 2 | 18 | A | Falkirk | W 2-0 | 1-0 | 2 | Walker 45, Clarke 47 | 3064 |
| 3 | 25 | H | Livingston | D 0-0 | 0-0 | 2 | | 1774 |
| 4 | Sept 1 | A | Dunfermline Ath | L 1-3 | 0-2 | 4 | Graham 51 | 5634 |
| 5 | 15 | H | Airdrie U | W 2-0 | 1-0 | 3 | Graham 37, Spence 83 | 1481 |
| 6 | 22 | A | Greenock Morton | L 0-1 | 0-0 | 4 | | 1628 |
| 7 | 29 | H | Partick Th | D 1-1 | 0-0 | 4 | Spence 67 | 1957 |
| 8 | Oct 6 | H | Dumbarton | D 2-2 | 1-0 | 4 | Graham 23, Spence 69 | 1425 |
| 9 | 20 | A | Cowdenbeath | D 4-4 | 2-2 | 4 | Graham, B 36, Spence 45, Clarke 81, Mensing 90 | 1209 |
| 10 | 27 | A | Hamilton A | W 1-0 | 1-0 | 4 | Walker 45 | 1079 |
| 11 | Nov 10 | H | Falkirk | W 2-1 | 0-1 | 4 | Smith 56, Anderson, G 85 | 1986 |
| 12 | 17 | H | Dunfermline Ath | L 1-3 | 1-1 | 5 | Clarke 24 | 4294 |
| 13 | 24 | A | Airdrie U | D 0-0 | 0-0 | 4 | | 747 |
| 14 | Dec 8 | H | Greenock Morton | D 3-3 | 1-1 | 5 | Graham 2 23, 71, Spence 85 | 1375 |
| 15 | 15 | A | Partick Th | L 2-3 | 1-2 | 5 | Spence 13, Graham 81 | 2221 |
| 16 | 29 | H | Cowdenbeath | D 2-2 | 0-2 | 6 | Hill 50, Spence 53 | 1877 |
| 17 | Jan 2 | A | Dunfermline Ath | L 0-1 | 0-0 | 6 | | 5835 |
| 18 | 5 | H | Airdrie U | W 2-0 | 1-0 | 4 | Graham 35, Clarke 61 | 1270 |
| 19 | 12 | A | Livingston | L 1-2 | 1-1 | 5 | Graham 34 | 1424 |
| 20 | 19 | A | Hamilton A | L 0-2 | 0-0 | 5 | | 1194 |
| 21 | 26 | A | Greenock Morton | L 0-1 | 0-0 | 6 | | 2006 |
| 22 | Feb 16 | H | Dumbarton | W 3-2 | 1-1 | 6 | Walker 39, Clarke 52, Graham 90 | 1304 |
| 23 | 23 | A | Cowdenbeath | D 1-1 | 0-0 | 6 | Graham 48 | 1078 |
| 24 | Mar 5 | A | Falkirk | D 1-1 | 1-0 | 6 | Graham 30 | 2428 |
| 25 | 9 | H | Livingston | L 0-2 | 0-2 | 6 | | 1117 |
| 26 | 16 | H | Dunfermline Ath | D 1-1 | 1-0 | 6 | Spence 39 | 3733 |
| 27 | 23 | A | Airdrie U | W 2-1 | 1-1 | 6 | Spence 44, Anderson, G 78 | 554 |
| 28 | 27 | A | Dumbarton | L 2-4 | 2-1 | 6 | Spence 4, Anderson, G 25 | 483 |
| 29 | 30 | H | Greenock Morton | W 2-1 | 2-0 | 6 | Graham 12, Tidser (og) 38 | 1529 |
| 30 | Apr 2 | H | Partick Th | D 0-0 | 0-0 | 6 | | 1761 |
| 31 | 9 | A | Dumbarton | W 2-1 | 1-0 | 6 | Spence 14, Graham 75 | 553 |
| 32 | 13 | H | Cowdenbeath | L 0-1 | 0-1 | 6 | | 1574 |
| 33 | 16 | A | Partick Th | D 0-0 | 0-0 | 6 | | 4963 |
| 34 | 20 | A | Hamilton A | L 0-2 | 0-0 | 6 | | 969 |
| 35 | 27 | H | Falkirk | D 0-0 | 0-0 | 6 | | 1406 |
| 36 | May 4 | A | Livingston | W 3-2 | 1-1 | 6 | Anderson, G 21, Graham 2 82, 90 | 1302 |

**Final League Position: 6**

**Honours**
*League Champions:* First Division 1992-93, 1994-95. Second Division 2002-03, 2008-09. Division II 1907-08, 1909-10 (shared), 1937-38, 1948-49; *Runners-up:* Division II 1908-09, 1926-27, 1966-67. Second Division 1975-76, 1977-78, 1986-87.
*Scottish Cup Runners-up:* 1913.
*League Cup Winners:* 1994-95. *Runners-up:* 1948-49.

**European:** *UEFA Cup:* 6 matches (1995-96).

**Club colours:** Shirt: Navy blue with white trim. Shorts: White. Socks: White.

**Goalscorers:** *League (45):* Graham 18 (1 pen), Spence 11, Clarke 5, Anderson G 4, Walker 3, Hill 1, Mensing 1, Smith 1, own goal 1.
*William Hill Scottish FA Cup (8):* Graham 2, Spence 2, Anderson G 1, Hill 1, Mensing 1, Walker 1 (1 pen).
*Scottish Communities League Cup (9):* Graham 4, Hill 2, Clarke 1, Spence 1, Walker 1.
*Ramsdens Cup (9):* Graham 3, Clarke 2, Anderson G 1, Hill 1, Spence 1, Walker 1.

| McGurn D 27 | Thomson J 35 | Hill D 23+2 | Ellis L 23+2 | Malone E 30+4 | Anderson G 27+6 | Anderson S 26+6 | Walker A 35 | Hamill J 23+4 | Clarke P 17+10 | Graham B 33+1 | Callachan R 4+6 | Spence G 22+10 | Wilson C 1 | Murray G 9+1 | Smith D 16+3 | Mensing S 27 | Laidlaw R 9+1 | Donaldson R 2+5 | Watt J 3+3 | Vaughan L —+3 | Cardle J 4+3 | Match No. |
|---|---|---|---|---|---|---|---|---|---|---|---|---|---|---|---|---|---|---|---|---|---|---|
| 1 | 2 | 3 | 4 | 5 | 6[1] | 7 | 8 | 9 | 10 | 11 | 12 | | | | | | | | | | | 1 |
| 1 | 2 | 4 | 3 | 5 | 11[1] | 6 | 9 | 8 | 7 | 10 | 12 | | | | | | | | | | | 2 |
| 1 | 2 | 4 | 3 | 5 | 6[1] | 7 | 8 | 9 | 11 | 10 | | 12 | | | | | | | | | | 3 |
| 1 | 2 | 4 | | 5 | 6[2] | 7 | 8 | 9 | 11[3] | 10 | | 14 | 3[1] | 12 | 13 | | | | | | | 4 |
| 1 | 2 | 4 | | 5 | 13 | 7 | 8 | 9 | 11[1] | 10 | | 12 | | | 6[2] | 3 | | | | | | 5 |
| 1 | 2 | 4 | | 5 | 12 | 7 | 8 | 9[1] | 10 | 11 | | | | | 6 | 3 | | | | | | 6 |
| 1 | 2 | 4 | | 5 | 6[1] | 7 | 8 | 12 | | 10 | 13 | 11[2] | | | 9 | 3 | | | | | | 7 |
| 1 | 2 | 4 | | 5 | 6 | 7 | 8 | | 10 | | | 11 | | | 9 | 3 | | | | | | 8 |
| 1 | 2 | 4[2] | 13 | 5 | | 7 | 8 | 9 | 12 | 10 | | 11 | | | 6[1] | 3 | | | | | | 9 |
| 1[1] | 2 | 4[2] | 3 | 5 | | 6 | 8 | 13 | 11 | 10 | | 9[3] | | 14 | 7 | 12 | | | | | | 10 |
| | 2 | 4 | 8 | 5 | 6 | 12 | 7 | | 11 | | | 10[1] | | 9 | 3 | | 1 | | | | | 11 |
| | 2 | 4[a] | 3 | 5 | 6[2] | 12 | 8[a] | | 11 | 13 | | 10[1] | | 9 | 7 | | 1 | | | | | 12 |
| | 2 | 4[1] | | 5 | 6 | 7 | | 8 | 11[2] | 10 | | 13 | | 9 | | 3 | 1 | | 12 | | | 13 |
| | 2 | 4 | 3 | 5 | 6[2] | 8 | 7 | | 9[1] | 13 | | 10 | | 12 | 11 | | 1 | | | | | 14 |
| | 2 | 5 | 3 | 4 | 6 | | 8 | 7 | 12 | 10 | | 11 | | | 9[1] | | 1 | | | | | 15 |
| | | 4[3] | 3 | 5 | 6 | 13 | 7 | 8[2] | 12 | 10 | | 11[1] | | 9 | 2 | | 1 | 14 | | | | 16 |
| | 2 | 4 | | 5[1] | 6[2] | | 7 | 8 | 13 | 10 | | 11 | | | 9 | 3 | 1 | 12 | | | | 17 |
| 1 | 2 | 4 | | 5[1] | 6 | 7 | 8 | | 11 | 10 | | | | | 9 | 3 | 12 | | | | | 18 |
| 1 | 2 | 4 | | 5 | 6 | 8[2] | 7 | 13 | 11[1] | 10 | | 12 | | | 9 | 3 | | | | | | 19 |
| 1 | 2 | 4[a] | 3 | 5 | 6 | 7 | 8 | | 12 | 10 | | 11[1] | | 9[2] | | | 13 | | | | | 20 |
| 1 | 2 | | | 4 | 5 | | 8[1] | 7 | 9 | 11 | 10 | | | 12 | 6 | 3 | | | | | | 21 |
| 1 | 2 | | | 4 | 5 | 6[1] | 7 | 8 | 9[2] | 11 | 10 | | | 13 | 12 | 3 | | | | | | 22 |
| 1 | 2 | | | 4 | 5 | 6 | 7 | 8 | 9[1] | 11 | 10 | | | 12 | | 3 | | | | | | 23 |
| 1 | 2 | | | 4 | 5 | 6[1] | 3 | 8 | 9 | 11 | 10 | | 7 | | | | | 12 | | | | 24 |
| 1 | 2 | 14 | | 4 | 5 | 6[1] | 7 | 8 | 9 | 11[2] | 10 | | | 12 | 3[3] | | | | 13 | | | 25 |
| 1 | 2 | | | 4 | 5 | 12 | 7 | 6 | 13 | 10 | | 11[2] | | | 3 | 8 | | | 9[1] | | | 26 |
| 1 | 2 | 4 | | 5 | 12 | 7[1] | 6 | | 10 | | | 11 | | | 3 | 8 | | | 9 | | | 27 |
| 1 | 2 | 4[2] | | 5 | 6[3] | 13 | 8 | 12 | 14 | 10 | | 11 | | | 3 | 7 | | | 9[1] | | | 28 |
| 1 | 2 | 5[1] | 12 | | 6[2] | 7 | 8 | 9 | | 10 | 13 | 11[3] | | 4 | 3 | | | | | 14 | | 29 |
| 1 | 2 | | | 5 | 13 | 6 | 7 | 8 | 9[2] | 10 | | 11 | | 4[1] | 3 | | | | | 12 | | 30 |
| 1 | | 5 | | 4 | 13 | 9[3] | 7 | 6 | 8[2] | 11 | 14 | 10 | | | 3[1] | 2 | | | | 12 | | 31 |
| 1 | 2 | | | 5 | 14 | 6 | 7[2] | 8 | 9[3] | 10 | 13 | 11 | | 4[1] | 3 | | | | | 12 | | 32 |
| 1 | | 5 | 12 | 3[1] | 4 | 14 | 13 | 6[2] | 8 | | | 11 | | 7 | 10 | 2 | | | | | 9[3] | 33 |
| 1 | 2 | | | 4 | | 5 | 12 | 14 | 6[3] | 8[1] | | 11 | | 7 | 10[2] | 3 | | | 13 | | 9 | 34 |
| | 2 | 4[3] | | | | 14 | 6[2] | | 8 | | 13 | 10 | | 7 | 11[1] | 3 | | 1 | 5 | 12 | 9 | 35 |
| | 2 | 4 | | | | 7[2] | | 8 | | | | 12 | 10 | 6 | 9[1] | 3 | | 1 | 5 | 13 | 11 | 36 |

# RANGERS

*Year Formed:* 1873. *Ground & Address:* Ibrox Stadium, 150 Edmiston Drive, Glasgow G51 2XD.
*Telephone:* 0871 702 1972. *Fax:* 0870 600 1978. *Website:* www.rangers.co.uk
*Ground Capacity:* 51,082 (all seated). *Size of Pitch:* 105m × 68m.
*Manager:* Ally McCoist. *Assistant Manager:* Kenny McDowall. *Coach:* Ian Durrant. *Head of Football Administration:* Andrew Dickson.
*Club Nickname:* 'The Gers', 'The Teddy Bears'.
*Previous Grounds:* Flesher's Haugh, Burnbank, Kinning Park, Old Ibrox.
*Record Attendance:* 118,567 v Celtic, Division I, 2 Jan 1939.
*Record Transfer Fee received:* £8,500,000 for Giovanni van Bronckhorst to Arsenal (July 2001).
*Record Transfer Fee paid:* £12,000,000 for Tore Andre Flo from Chelsea (November 2000).
*Record Victory:* 14-2 v Blairgowrie, Scottish Cup 1st rd, 20 Jan, 1934.
*Record Defeat:* 1-7 v Celtic, League Cup Final, 19 Oct 1957.
*Most Capped Player:* Ally McCoist, 60, Scotland.
*Most League Appearances:* 496: John Greig, 1962-78.
*Most League Goals in Season (Individual):* 44: Sam English, Division I, 1931-32.
*Most Goals Overall (Individual):* 355: Ally McCoist; 1985-98.

**Honours**
*League Champions:* (54 times) Division I 1890-91 (shared), 1898-99, 1899-1900, 1900-01, 1901-02, 1910-11, 1911-12, 1912-13, 1917-18, 1919-20, 1920-21, 1922-23, 1923-24, 1924-25, 1926-27, 1927-28, 1928-29, 1929-30, 1930-31, 1932-33, 1933-34, 1934-35, 1936-37, 1938-39, 1946-47, 1948-49, 1949-50, 1952-53, 1955-56, 1956-57, 1958-59, 1960-61, 1962-63, 1963-64, 1974-75. Premier Division: 1975-76, 1977-78, 1986-87, 1988-89, 1989-90, 1990-91, 1991-92, 1992-93, 1993-94, 1994-95, 1995-96, 1996-97, 1998-99, 1999-2000, 2002-03, 2004-05, 2008-09, 2009-10, 2010-11. *Runners-up:* 30 times. Third Division 2012-13.

## RANGERS – SCOTTISH THIRD DIVISION 2012–13 LEAGUE RECORD

| Match No. | Date | Venue | Opponents | Result | H/T Score | Lg Pos. | Goalscorers | Attendance |
|---|---|---|---|---|---|---|---|---|
| 1 | Aug 11 | A | Peterhead | D | 2-2 | 1-0 | 5 | McKay [27], Little [90] | 4485 |
| 2 | 18 | H | East Stirling | W | 5-1 | 2-1 | 1 | Little 3 [15, 41, 74], Sandaza [64], McCulloch [90] | 49,118 |
| 3 | 26 | A | Berwick R | D | 1-1 | 1-0 | 4 | Little [45] | 4140 |
| 4 | Sept 2 | H | Elgin C | W | 5-1 | 3-1 | 3 | Shiels [24], Templeton 2 [29, 49], McCulloch 2 [45, 59] | 46,015 |
| 5 | 15 | A | Annan Ath | D | 0-0 | 0-0 | 4 | | 2517 |
| 6 | 23 | H | Montrose | W | 4-1 | 1-1 | 2 | Shiels [27], Macleod [55], McCulloch [60], Crawford [82] | 45,081 |
| 7 | Oct 6 | A | Stirling A | L | 0-1 | 0-1 | 3 | | 3751 |
| 8 | 20 | H | Queen's Park | W | 2-0 | 0-0 | 1 | McCulloch 2 [57, 90] | 49,463 |
| 9 | 28 | A | Clyde | W | 2-0 | 1-0 | 1 | Shiels [17], McCulloch [80] | 7500 |
| 10 | Nov 10 | H | Peterhead | W | 2-0 | 1-0 | 1 | McCulloch [43], Wallace [66] | 48,407 |
| 11 | 17 | A | East Stirling | W | 6-2 | 2-1 | 1 | McCulloch 2 (2 pens) [12, 82], Little [39], Wallace [49], Kyle [63], Naismith [71] | 2854 |
| 12 | Dec 8 | H | Stirling A | W | 2-0 | 0-0 | 1 | Templeton [59], Little [90] | 49,913 |
| 13 | 15 | A | Montrose | W | 4-2 | 1-1 | 1 | McCulloch (pen) [23], Kyle [67], Shiels [69], Crawford [90] | 4205 |
| 14 | 18 | H | Annan Ath | W | 3-0 | 1-0 | 1 | Templeton 2 [29, 70], Little [64] | 42,135 |
| 15 | 22 | A | Elgin C | W | 6-2 | 3-2 | 1 | Little 2 [5, 24], McCulloch 2 [41, 60], Macleod [64], Hutton [83] | 3448 |
| 16 | 26 | H | Clyde | W | 3-0 | 2-0 | 1 | Wallace [21], Templeton [38], Shiels [76] | 47,463 |
| 17 | 29 | A | Queen's Park | W | 1-0 | 0-0 | 1 | Aird [90] | 30,117 |
| 18 | Jan 2 | A | Annan Ath | W | 3-1 | 1-1 | 1 | Templeton 2 [26, 83], Crawford [63] | 2441 |
| 19 | 5 | H | Elgin C | D | 1-1 | 1-0 | 1 | Macleod [9] | 46,406 |
| 20 | 12 | H | Berwick R | W | 4-2 | 1-0 | 1 | Little 3 [9, 47, 74], Templeton [53] | 44,976 |
| 21 | 20 | A | Peterhead | W | 1-0 | 1-0 | 1 | Sandaza [30] | 4855 |
| 22 | 26 | H | Montrose | D | 1-1 | 1-0 | 1 | Crawford, J (og) [45] | 46,273 |
| 23 | Feb 9 | H | Queen's Park | W | 4-0 | 0-0 | 1 | Black [51], Little 2 [63, 89], Shiels [78] | 46,104 |
| 24 | 16 | A | Clyde | W | 4-1 | 3-0 | 1 | Little 2 [8, 24], Templeton 2 [44, 54] | 7600 |
| 25 | 23 | A | Berwick R | W | 3-1 | 2-1 | 1 | Shiels (pen) [9], Little [45], Faure [66] | 4476 |
| 26 | 26 | A | Stirling A | D | 1-1 | 1-0 | 1 | Little [16] | 3707 |
| 27 | Mar 2 | H | East Stirling | W | 3-1 | 0-1 | 1 | Little 2 [51, 63], McCulloch [62] | 44,534 |
| 28 | 9 | H | Annan Ath | L | 1-2 | 0-0 | 1 | Little [59] | 34,441 |
| 29 | 16 | A | Elgin C | W | 1-0 | 0-0 | 1 | McCulloch (pen) [73] | 3663 |
| 30 | 23 | H | Stirling A | D | 0-0 | 0-0 | 1 | | 44,608 |
| 31 | 30 | A | Montrose | D | 0-0 | 0-0 | 1 | | 4686 |
| 32 | Apr 7 | H | Queen's Park | W | 4-1 | 2-0 | 1 | Templeton 2 [18, 86], Aird [35], Hemmings [68] | 11,492 |
| 33 | 13 | H | Clyde | W | 2-0 | 0-0 | 1 | McCulloch [55], Hutton [89] | 44,453 |
| 34 | 20 | H | Peterhead | L | 1-2 | 1-1 | 1 | McCulloch [12] | 43,961 |
| 35 | 27 | A | East Stirling | W | 4-2 | 2-1 | 1 | Crawford [6], Templeton 2 [45, 79], Black [65] | 2805 |
| 36 | May 4 | H | Berwick R | W | 1-0 | 1-0 | 1 | Aird [32] | 50,048 |

**Final League Position: 1 – Promoted to Scottish Second Division**

*Scottish Cup Winners:* (33 times) 1894, 1897, 1898, 1903, 1928, 1930, 1932, 1934, 1935, 1936, 1948, 1949, 1950, 1953, 1960, 1962, 1963, 1964, 1966, 1973, 1976, 1978, 1979, 1981, 1992, 1993, 1996, 1999, 2000, 2002, 2003, 2008, 2009; *Runners-up:* 17 times.
*League Cup Winners:* (27 times) 1946-47, 1948-49, 1960-61, 1961-62, 1963-64, 1964-65, 1970-71, 1975-76, 1977-78, 1978-79, 1981-82, 1983-84, 1984-85, 1986-87, 1987-88, 1988-89, 1990-91, 1992-93, 1993-94, 1996-97, 1998-99, 2001-02, 2002-03, 2004-05, 2007-08, 2009-10, 2010-11; *Runners-up:* 7 times.

**European:** *European Cup:* 161 matches (1956-57, 1957-58, 1959-60 semi-finals, 1961-62, 1963-64, 1964-65, 1975-76, 1976-77, 1978-79, 1987-88, 1989-90, 1990-91, 1991-92, 1992-93 final pool, 1993-94, 1994-95, 1995-96; 1996-97, 1997-98, 1999-2000, 2000-01, 2001-02, 2003-04, 2004-05, 2005-06, 2007-08, 2008-09, 2009-10, 2010-11, 2011-12).
*Cup Winners' Cup:* 54 matches (1960-61 runners-up, 1962-63, 1966-67 runners-up, 1969-70, 1971-72 winners, 1973-74, 1977-78, 1979-80, 1981-82, 1983-84).
*UEFA Cup:* 88 matches (*Fairs Cup:* 1967-68, 1968-69 semi-finals, 1970-71. *UEFA Cup:* 1982-83, 1984-85, 1985-86, 1986-87, 1988-89, 1997-98, 1998-99, 1999-2000, 2000-01, 2001-02, 2002-03, 2004-05, 2006-07, 2007-08 runners-up). *Europa League:* 6 matches (2010-11, 2011-12).

**Club colours:** Shirt: Royal blue. Shorts: White. Socks: Red with white tops.

**Goalscorers:** *League (87):* Little 22, McCulloch 17 (4 pens), Templeton 15, Shiels 7 (1 pen), Crawford 4, Aird 3, Macleod 3, Wallace 3, Black 2, Hutton 2, Kyle 2, Sandaza 2, Faure 1, Hemmings 1, McKay 1, Naismith 1, own goal 1.
*William Hill Scottish FA Cup (11):* Shiels 3, McCulloch 2, McKay 2, Naismith 2, Crawford 1, Kyle 1.
*Scottish Communities League Cup (9):* McCulloch 5, Shiels 2, Little 1, Wallace 1.
*Ramsdens Cup (5):* Little 2, McCulloch 2 (1 pen), McKay 1.

| Alexander N 35 | Broadfoot K 2 | Goian D 2 | Bocanegra C 3 | Little A 26 + 2 | Black I 28 + 1 | Macleod L 21 | Wallace L 33 | McCulloch L 28 | Shiels D 19 + 2 | McKay B 15 + 16 | Sandaza F 8 + 6 | Kyle K 3 + 5 | Emilson Cribari S 25 + 1 | Perry R 15 + 2 | Argyriou A 17 + 3 | Crawford R 9 + 12 | Naismith K 4 + 13 | Templeton D 24 | Faure S 12 + 6 | Aird F 9 + 11 | Hutton K 26 + 1 | Hegarty C 24 | Walsh T — + 1 | Stella F — + 1 | Cole D 1 + 2 | Mitchell A 4 + 3 | Hemmings K 2 + 3 | Gasparotto L 1 + 3 | Stoney D — + 3 | Smith A — + 1 | Match No. |
|---|---|---|---|---|---|---|---|---|---|---|---|---|---|---|---|---|---|---|---|---|---|---|---|---|---|---|---|---|---|---|---|
| 1 | 2 | 3 | 4 | 5 | 6 | $7^2$ | 8 | 9 | 10 | $11^1$ | 12 | 13 | | | | | | | | | | | | | | | | | | | 1 |
| 1 | 2 | 3 | 4 | $5^3$ | 6 | | 8 | $9^2$ | 10 | $7^1$ | 12 | 11 | 14 | 13 | | | | | | | | | | | | | | | | | 2 |
| 1 | | | 4 | 6 | 9 | $8^3$ | | 7 | | $10^1$ | $11^2$ | 12 | 3 | 2 | 5 | 13 | 14 | | | | | | | | | | | | | | 3 |
| 1 | | | | $11^1$ | $7^2$ | 6 | 5 | 10 | 8 | 12 | | | 14 | 4 | 3 | 2 | | $9^3$ | 13 | | | | | | | | | | | | 4 |
| 1 | | | | 7 | 9 | 5 | 11 | $10^1$ | 8 | 12 | | | 4 | 3 | 13 | | | $6^2$ | 2 | | | | | | | | | | | | 5 |
| 1 | | | | $8^2$ | 7 | | 5 | 11 | $10^3$ | $9^1$ | 13 | | 4 | 3 | 6 | 14 | | 2 | 12 | | | | | | | | | | | | 6 |
| 1 | | | | $7^3$ | 8 | | 5 | 11 | 10 | 12 | 13 | | 4 | $2^1$ | 14 | 6 | | $9^2$ | | | | | | | | | | | | | 7 |
| 1 | | | | 12 | 7 | | 8 | 5 | 10 | $9^2$ | 13 | | 4 | 3 | 2 | $11^1$ | | 6 | | | | | | | | | | | | | 8 |
| 1 | | | | $11^3$ | 8 | 9 | 5 | 10 | | $6^1$ | 12 | | $4^2$ | 3 | 13 | 14 | | 7 | 2 | | | | | | | | | | | | 9 |
| 1 | | | | $10^1$ | $8^2$ | 4 | 5 | 9 | | 11 | 6 | | 2 | $7^3$ | 12 | 14 | | 13 | 3 | | | | | | | | | | | | 10 |
| 1 | | | | $6^2$ | 7 | $8^3$ | 5 | 3 | | $10^1$ | 9 | 11 | 2 | 14 | 12 | 13 | | 4 | | | | | | | | | | | | | 11 |
| 1 | | | | 13 | 8 | | 5 | 4 | $10^2$ | 9 | $11^3$ | | 2 | 12 | $6^3$ | 7 | | 3 | 14 | | | | | | | | | | | | 12 |
| 1 | | | | 6 | 7 | | 5 | 3 | $10^2$ | 12 | $11^3$ | | 2 | 14 | 13 | $9^1$ | | 8 | 4 | | | | | | | | | | | | 13 |
| 1 | | | | $7^3$ | 9 | | $5^8$ | 8 | $10^2$ | $11^1$ | 12 | | 2 | 14 | 6 | 13 | | 4 | 3 | | | | | | | | | | | | 14 |
| 1 | | | | 6 | $8^3$ | | 5 | 10 | | 11 | | | 4 | 12 | $2^1$ | 13 | $9^1$ | 1 | 7 | 3 | 14 | | | | | | | | | | 15 |
| 1 | | | | $6^1$ | 8 | | 5 | 11 | | 12 | 9 | | $4^2$ | 3 | 14 | $10^3$ | | 7 | 2 | 13 | | | | | | | | | | | 16 |
| 1 | | | | $7^1$ | | | 5 | 10 | | 9 | 13 | | 4 | 3 | 6 | 11 | | 12 | $8^2$ | 2 | | | | | | | | | | | 17 |
| 1 | | | | 10 | 7 | | 5 | 13 | | 11 | | | 4 | 8 | $9^2$ | 12 | | 6 | 3 | $2^1$ | | | | | | | | | | | 18 |
| 1 | | | | 8 | 7 | $9^1$ | 5 | 11 | | 13 | 12 | | 4 | $3^3$ | 10 | 14 | | $6^2$ | 2 | | | | | | | | | | | | 19 |
| 1 | | | | 6 | 8 | | 5 | $10^2$ | | 11 | | | 4 | 3 | 12 | $9^3$ | | 12 | 13 | 7 | $2^1$ | | | | | | | | | | 20 |
| 1 | | | | 11 | $8^1$ | 6 | 5 | 13 | | $10^2$ | | | 4 | 3 | 12 | 9 | | 7 | 2 | | | | | | | | | | | | 21 |
| 1 | | | | 6 | 12 | $7^1$ | 5 | $11^3$ | | 14 | 10 | | 4 | 3 | 9 | 13 | | 8 | $2^2$ | | | | | | | | | | | | 22 |
| 1 | | | | 10 | 7 | | 5 | $11^2$ | | $6^1$ | | | 4 | 2 | 13 | $9^3$ | | 12 | 8 | 3 | | | | | | 14 | | | | | 23 |
| 1 | | | | 11 | $7^1$ | | 5 | $9^3$ | | 8 | | | 3 | 2 | 12 | $10^2$ | | 13 | 6 | 4 | | | | | | 14 | | | | | 24 |
| 1 | | | | 11 | 7 | | 5 | 9 | | $8^1$ | | | $3^2$ | 2 | 12 | $10^3$ | | 13 | 14 | 6 | 4 | | | | | | | | | | 25 |
| 1 | | | | 9 | 6 | | 5 | $10^2$ | | 12 | 13 | | 4 | 2 | 7 | $11^1$ | | 8 | 3 | | | | | | | | | | | | 26 |
| 1 | | | | 10 | 7 | | 5 | $11^2$ | | 12 | | | 4 | 2 | $6^1$ | $9^3$ | | 14 | 8 | 3 | | | | | | 13 | | | | | 27 |
| 1 | | | | 6 | 8 | | 5 | 11 | $10^1$ | 12 | 13 | | 4 | 2 | $9^2$ | | | 7 | 3 | | | | | | | | | | | | 28 |
| 1 | | | | $6^2$ | 7* | | 5 | 10 | | 12 | | | $11^1$ | 13 | 8 | 4 | | 9 | 2 | | | | | | | | | | | | 29 |
| 1 | | | | | | | 5 | 3 | | $8^1$ | | | 4 | 13 | 9 | 12 | | 7 | $10^2$ | 6 | 2 | | | | | 14 | $11^3$ | | | | 30 |
| 1 | | | | 8 | | | 5 | 4 | | 12 | | | 3 | $7^1$ | 13 | 10 | | 6 | 9 | 2 | | | | | | $11^2$ | | | | | 31 |
| 1 | | | | 8 | | | 5 | 10 | | 13 | | | 4 | $2^1$ | $6^2$ | 14 | 11 | 3 | 9 | 7 | | | | | | $12^3$ | | | | | 32 |
| 1 | | | | 8 | | | 5 | 10 | | | | | $4^1$ | | $6^2$ | 13 | 11 | 3 | $9^3$ | 7 | 2 | | | | | | 12 | 14 | | | 33 |
| 1 | | | | 10 | 7 | | 5 | 11 | | 12 | | | $6^2$ | 3 | $9^1$ | 8 | | $4^3$ | | | 2 | | | | | | 14 | 13 | | | 34 |
| 1 | | | | $10^2$ | 6 | | | 7 | | | | | 3 | | 8 | $11^1$ | 9 | 5 | $4^3$ | | 2 | | | | | | 12 | 13 | 14 | | 35 |
| 1 | | | | $11^1$ | 8 | $9^3$ | | 4 | | | | | | | 14 | 7 | $10^2$ | | 6 | | 2 | | | | | | 12 | 5 | 13 | 3 | 36 |

# ROSS COUNTY

*Year Formed:* 1929. *Ground & Address:* The Global Energy Stadium, Victoria Park, Dingwall IV15 9QZ. *Telephone:*
01349 860860. *Fax:* 01349 866277. *E-mail:* donnie.macbean@rosscountyfootballclub.co.uk
*Website:* www.rosscountyfootballclub.co.uk
*Ground Capacity:* 6,700 (all seated). *Size of Ground:* 105 × 68m.
*Chairman:* Rory MacGregor. *Secretary:* Donnie MacBean.
*Manager:* Derek Adams. *Assistant Manager:* Neale Cooper. *Director of Football:* George Adams.
*Club Nickname:* 'The Staggies'.
*Record Attendance:* 6,110 v Celtic, Premier League, 18 August 2012.
*Record Transfer Fee received:* £200,000 for Neil Tarrant to Aston Villa (April 1999).
*Record Transfer Fee paid:* £50,000 for Derek Holmes from Hearts (1999).
*Record Victory:* 11-0 v St Cuthbert Wanderers, Scottish Cup 1st rd, 11 Dec 1993.
*Record Defeat:* 0-7 v Kilmarnock, Scottish Cup 3rd rd, 17 Feb 1962.
*Most League Appearances:* 230: Mark McCulloch, 2002-2009.
*Most League Goals in Season:* 24: Andrew Barrowman, 2007-08.
*Most League Goals (Overall):* 47: Sean Higgins, 2002-09.

## ROSS COUNTY – SCOTTISH PREMIER LEAGUE 2012–13 LEAGUE RECORD

| Match No. | Date | | Venue | Opponents | Result | | H/T Score | Lg Pos. | Goalscorers | Atten-dance |
|---|---|---|---|---|---|---|---|---|---|---|
| 1 | Aug | 4 | H | Motherwell | D | 0-0 | 0-0 | 8 | | 4828 |
| 2 | | 11 | A | Aberdeen | D | 0-0 | 0-0 | 8 | | 14,010 |
| 3 | | 18 | H | Celtic | D | 1-1 | 0-0 | 9 | Brittain [49] | 6110 |
| 4 | | 25 | A | Dundee | W | 1-0 | 0-0 | 4 | Brittain (pen) [72] | 4905 |
| 5 | Sept | 1 | H | Kilmarnock | D | 0-0 | 0-0 | 4 | | 4006 |
| 6 | | 14 | A | Dundee U | D | 0-0 | 0-0 | 4 | | 6892 |
| 7 | | 22 | H | St Johnstone | L | 1-2 | 0-1 | 8 | Morrow [68] | 4094 |
| 8 | | 29 | A | St Mirren | L | 4-5 | 2-1 | 10 | Vigurs [11], Munro [45], Quinn 2 [79, 80] | 3706 |
| 9 | Oct | 5 | A | Inverness CT | L | 1-3 | 0-2 | 10 | Vigurs [48] | 6766 |
| 10 | | 20 | H | Hibernian | W | 3-2 | 2-2 | 9 | Kettlewell [9], Vigurs [34], McMenamin [83] | 4070 |
| 11 | | 27 | A | Hearts | D | 2-2 | 0-1 | 9 | Brittain (pen) [55], Kettlewell [77] | 12,139 |
| 12 | Nov | 3 | H | Aberdeen | W | 2-1 | 1-0 | 8 | Reynolds (og) [37], Ross [49] | 6064 |
| 13 | | 10 | A | Kilmarnock | L | 0-3 | 0-0 | 9 | | 4012 |
| 14 | | 17 | A | St Johnstone | D | 1-1 | 0-0 | 10 | Craig (og) [70] | 3037 |
| 15 | | 24 | H | Dundee U | L | 1-2 | 0-0 | 10 | Vigurs [49] | 3930 |
| 16 | | 27 | H | St Mirren | D | 0-0 | 0-0 | 10 | | 2837 |
| 17 | Dec | 8 | A | Motherwell | L | 2-3 | 1-1 | 10 | Quinn 2 [17, 70] | 3739 |
| 18 | | 15 | H | Dundee | D | 1-1 | 0-1 | 10 | Glen [74] | 3129 |
| 19 | | 22 | A | Celtic | L | 0-4 | 0-0 | 11 | | 49,428 |
| 20 | | 26 | A | Hibernian | W | 1-0 | 0-0 | 11 | Brittain [57] | 8980 |
| 21 | Jan | 19 | A | St Mirren | W | 4-1 | 1-0 | 11 | Brittain [22], Morrow [67], Sproule 2 [71, 74] | 3802 |
| 22 | | 26 | A | Dundee U | D | 1-1 | 0-0 | 10 | Brittain [82] | 5117 |
| 23 | | 30 | H | Hibernian | W | 1-0 | 1-0 | 10 | Sproule [36] | 3055 |
| 24 | Feb | 2 | H | Hearts | D | 2-2 | 1-1 | 10 | Quinn [20], Vigurs [90] | 3903 |
| 25 | | 8 | A | Dundee | W | 2-0 | 0-0 | 7 | Lawson [80], Glen [90] | 4726 |
| 26 | | 16 | H | St Johnstone | W | 1-0 | 1-0 | 8 | Sproule [11] | 3516 |
| 27 | | 23 | H | Motherwell | W | 3-0 | 1-0 | 5 | Sproule [34], Brittain [71], Vigurs [89] | 3797 |
| 28 | | 26 | A | Aberdeen | W | 1-0 | 0-0 | 3 | Glen [81] | 6394 |
| 29 | Mar | 2 | H | Inverness CT | D | 0-0 | 0-0 | 4 | | 5959 |
| 30 | | 9 | H | Celtic | W | 3-2 | 2-2 | 3 | Munro [30], Morrow [36], Wohlfarth [90] | 6031 |
| 31 | | 16 | H | Inverness CT | L | 1-2 | 1-1 | 4 | Lawson [35] | 5750 |
| 32 | | 30 | H | Kilmarnock | L | 0-1 | 0-1 | 4 | | 3782 |
| 33 | Apr | 6 | A | Hearts | L | 2-4 | 1-0 | 5 | Wohlfarth 2 [22, 54] | 10,456 |
| 34 | | 21 | A | St Johnstone | D | 2-2 | 1-2 | 5 | Brittain 2 (2 pens) [15, 76] | 2444 |
| 35 | | 26 | H | Dundee U | W | 1-0 | 0-0 | 4 | Sproule [54] | 3183 |
| 36 | May | 5 | H | Celtic | D | 1-1 | 1-1 | 5 | Vigurs [41] | 5873 |
| 37 | | 12 | A | Motherwell | L | 0-2 | 0-2 | 5 | | 7734 |
| 38 | | 19 | H | Inverness CT | W | 1-0 | 1-0 | 5 | Hainault [44] | 6002 |

**Final League Position: 5**

**Honours**
*League Champions:* First Division 2011-12. Second Division 2007-08. Third Division 1998-99.
*Scottish Cup Runners-up:* 2009-10.
*League Challenge Cup Winners:* 2006-07, 2010-11; *Runners-up:* 2004-05, 2008-09.

**Club colours:** Shirt: Navy blue with red and white trim. Shorts: Navy blue. Socks: Navy blue with white tops.

**Goalscorers:** *League (47):* Brittain 9 (4 pens), Vigurs 7, Sproule 6, Quinn 5, Glen 3, Morrow 3, Wohlfarth 3, Kettlewell 2, Lawson 2, Munro 2, Hainault 1, McMenamin 1, Ross 1, own goals 2.
*William Hill Scottish FA Cup (4):* Vigurs 2, Brittain 1, Quinn 1.
*Scottish Communities League Cup (1):* Duncan 1.

| Fraser M 24 | Fitzpatrick M 18 + 2 | Munro G 36 + 1 | Boyd S 34 + 1 | Tokely R 13 + 4 | Lawson P 20 + 2 | McMenamin C 10 + 9 | Brittain R 34 | Vigurs I 37 | Scott M 8 + 7 | Duncan R 1 + 2 | Corcoran M 2 + 3 | Morrow S 17 + 6 | Kettlewell S 19 + 6 | Quinn R 31 | Cooper A 7 + 8 | Glen G 6 + 20 | Kovacevic M 28 + 2 | Fotheringham M 12 + 2 | Ross S 4 + 6 | Brown M 13 | Ikonomou E 18 | Sproule I 14 | Wohlfarth S 6 + 10 | Hainault A 5 + 3 | Micic B — + 1 | Gallacher P 1 | Match No. |
|---|---|---|---|---|---|---|---|---|---|---|---|---|---|---|---|---|---|---|---|---|---|---|---|---|---|---|---|
| 1 | 2 | 3 | 4 | 5 | 6 | 7 | 8 | 9 | 10² | 11¹ | 12 | 13 |  |  |  |  |  |  |  |  |  |  |  |  |  |  | 1 |
| 1 | 2 | 3 | 4 | 5 | 6¹ | 7 | 8 | 9 | 10 | 12 | 13 |  | 11² |  |  |  |  |  |  |  |  |  |  |  |  |  | 2 |
| 1 | 2 | 3 | 4 | 5 |  |  | 11 | 7 | 8 |  |  |  |  | 10 | 6 | 9 |  |  |  |  |  |  |  |  |  |  | 3 |
| 1 | 2 | 3 | 4 | 5 | 10¹ |  |  | 7 | 8 |  |  | 13 | 11² | 12 | 6 | 9 |  |  |  |  |  |  |  |  |  |  | 4 |
| 1 | 5 | 3 | 4 | 2 | 10 |  | 8² | 9 | 13 |  |  |  |  | 12 | 7 | 6 | 11¹ |  |  |  |  |  |  |  |  |  | 5 |
| 1 | 5 | 3 | 4 | 2² | 10¹ |  | 8 | 9 | 14 |  |  |  |  | 12 | 7 | 6 | 11³ | 13 |  |  |  |  |  |  |  |  | 6 |
| 1 | 2³ | 3 | 4 | 5¹ |  | 13 | 7 | 8 | 14 |  |  |  |  | 10 | 6 | 9 | 11² | 12 |  |  |  |  |  |  |  |  | 7 |
| 1 | 5 | 4 | 3 | 2 |  | 13 | 10¹ | 7 |  |  |  |  | 11² | 9¹ | 6 | 12 | 8 | 14 |  |  |  |  |  |  |  |  | 8 |
| 1 | 3 | 5 | 4 | 2 |  | 11 | 8 | 7 | 9¹ |  |  |  |  | 12 | 6 | 13 | 10² |  |  |  |  |  |  |  |  |  | 9 |
| 1 | 5 | 3 | 2 | 14 |  | 12 | 7 | 9 |  |  |  |  |  | 6 | 8 | 13³ | 4 | 10¹ | 11² |  |  |  |  |  |  |  | 10 |
| 1 | 5 | 3 | 4 | 14 |  | 12 | 6 | 10³ | 13 |  |  |  |  | 8 | 7¹ | 11² | 2 | 9 |  |  |  |  |  |  |  |  | 11 |
| 1 | 5 | 4 | 3 |  |  | 12 | 6 | 11² |  |  |  |  |  | 7 | 9 | 13 | 2 | 8 | 10¹ |  |  |  |  |  |  |  | 12 |
| 1 | 2 | 4 | 3 |  |  | 12 | 7 | 6 |  |  |  |  |  | 9¹ | 8¹ | 13 | 14 | 5 | 10 | 11² |  |  |  |  |  |  | 13 |
| 1 | 5¹ | 4 | 3 | 12 |  | 13 | 7 | 6 |  |  |  |  |  | 11³ | 8 |  | 14 | 2 | 9 | 10¹ |  |  |  |  |  |  | 14 |
| 1 |  | 5 | 3 | 4 |  | 12 | 6 | 10 |  |  |  |  |  | 11² | 7¹ | 9 |  | 2 | 8 | 13 |  |  |  |  |  |  | 15 |
| 12 | 5¹ | 4 | 3 |  |  | 13 | 6 | 10 |  |  |  |  |  | 11² | 8 | 9 | 14 | 2 | 7³ | 1 |  |  |  |  |  |  | 16 |
| 5 | 12 | 4 | 3 |  |  | 10 | 6² | 8 |  |  |  |  |  | 13 | 9 | 14 | 11³ | 2¹ | 7 | 1 |  |  |  |  |  |  | 17 |
| 5 | 4 | 3 | 2 |  |  | 11 | 6 | 10 |  |  |  |  |  | 7 |  | 9 | 12 | 8¹ |  | 1 |  |  |  |  |  |  | 18 |
| 2 | 3 | 4 | 13 | 11 |  | 8 | 9 |  |  | 12 |  | 6³ | 7² | 10¹ | 14 | 5 |  |  |  | 1 |  |  |  |  |  |  | 19 |
| 2 | 4 | 3 | 13 | 12 |  | 8 | 9 | 14 |  |  |  | 6¹ | 7 | 10 | 11³ | 5² |  |  |  | 1 |  |  |  |  |  |  | 20 |
|  | 4 | 3 | 7 |  |  | 8 | 9³ |  |  | 12 |  | 10 | 14 | 11¹ | 2 |  | 13 | 1 | 5 | 6² |  |  |  |  |  |  | 21 |
| 13 | 4 | 3 | 7² |  |  | 8 | 9 |  |  | 11 |  | 10¹ | 12 | 2 |  | 1 | 5 | 6 |  |  |  |  |  |  |  |  | 22 |
|  | 4 | 3 | 8 |  |  | 7 | 10 |  |  | 11² |  | 9 | 13 | 2 |  | 1 | 5 | 6¹ | 12 |  |  |  |  |  |  |  | 23 |
|  | 4 | 3 | 7 |  |  | 8 | 10 |  |  | 11¹ |  | 6 | 9² | 12 | 2 | 1 | 5 | 12 |  |  |  |  |  |  |  |  | 24 |
|  | 3 | 4 | 8 |  |  | 7 | 9³ | 11² | 14 |  |  | 10 | 6¹ | 13 | 2 | 1 | 5 | 12 |  |  |  |  |  |  |  |  | 25 |
|  | 5 | 4 | 8 |  |  | 7 | 11² | 14 | 10 |  |  | 9¹ | 12 | 2 |  | 1 | 3 | 6³ | 13 |  |  |  |  |  |  |  | 26 |
|  | 5 | 4 | 8³ |  |  | 9 | 7 | 11² | 10 |  |  | 12 | 2 |  |  | 1 | 3 | 6¹ | 13 | 14 |  |  |  |  |  |  | 27 |
|  | 4 | 3 | 8 |  |  | 7 | 9 | 11¹ | 6 |  |  | 13 | 2 |  |  | 1 | 5 | 10² | 12 |  |  |  |  |  |  |  | 28 |
| 1 | 5 | 4 | 8 |  |  | 7 | 10 | 11¹ | 9 |  |  | 12 | 2 |  |  | 3 | 6 | 13 |  |  |  |  |  |  |  |  | 29 |
| 1 | 5 | 4 | 6 |  |  | 9 | 8 | 11¹ | 7 | 10² |  | 2 |  |  |  | 3 | 12 | 13 |  |  |  |  |  |  |  |  | 30 |
| 1 | 4³ | 5 | 6 |  |  | 10 | 11 | 8² | 7 | 13 | 14 | 2 |  |  |  | 3 | 9¹ | 12 |  |  |  |  |  |  |  |  | 31 |
| 1 | 5 | 4 | 8³ |  |  | 7 | 9¹ | 10² | 11 | 6 | 13 | 2 | 14 |  |  | 3 | 12 |  |  |  |  |  |  |  |  |  | 32 |
| 1 | 3 | 4² | 8³ |  |  | 7 | 9 | 12 | 10¹ |  |  | 13 | 2 |  |  | 5 | 6 | 11 | 14 |  |  |  |  |  |  |  | 33 |
| 1 | 3 |  | 8 |  |  | 7 | 9 | 14 | 10 |  |  | 2 | 13 |  |  | 5¹ | 6 | 11³ | 4 | 12² |  |  |  |  |  |  | 34 |
| 1 | 4 |  | 6 |  |  | 8 | 10 | 14 | 13 |  |  | 9¹ | 2 | 12 |  | 5 | 7² | 11² | 3 |  |  |  |  |  |  |  | 35 |
| 1 | 4 | 12 | 7 |  |  | 8 | 10 | 9 |  |  |  | 2¹ | 13 |  |  | 5 | 6² | 11 | 3 |  |  |  |  |  |  |  | 36 |
| 1 | 4 |  | 6³ |  |  | 8¹ | 9 | 10² | 14 |  |  | 13 | 2 | 12 |  | 5 | 7 | 11 | 3 |  |  |  |  |  |  |  | 37 |
|  | 4 |  | 6 |  |  | 8 | 13 | 9 | 14 |  | 12 | 2 | 10² | 3 |  | 7³ | 11¹ | 5 |  |  |  |  |  | 1 |  |  | 38 |

# ST JOHNSTONE

*Year Formed:* 1884. *Ground & Address:* McDiarmid Park, Crieff Road, Perth PH1 2SJ. *Telephone:* 01738 459090. *Fax:* 01738 625 771. *Email:* karin@perthsaints.co.uk *Website:* www.perthstjohnstonefc.co.uk
*Ground Capacity:* 10,673 (all seated). *Size of Pitch:* 105m × 68m.
*Chairman:* Steve Brown.
*Manager:* Tommy Wright. *Assistant Manager:* Callum Davidson. *Youth Coach:* Tommy Campbell. *Physio:* John Kerr.
*Club Nickname:* 'Saints'.
*Previous Grounds:* Recreation Grounds, Muirton Park.
*Record Attendance:* 29,972 v Dundee, Scottish Cup 2nd rd, 10 Feb 1951 (Muirton Park): 10,545 v Dundee, Premier Division, 23 May 1999 (McDiarmid Park).
*Record Transfer Fee received:* £1,750,000 for Callum Davidson to Blackburn R (March 1998).
*Record Transfer Fee paid:* £400,000 for Billy Dodds from Dundee (1994).
*Record Victory:* 9-0 v Albion R, League Cup, 9 Mar 1946.
*Record Defeat:* 1-10 v Third Lanark, Scottish Cup 1st rd, 24 Jan 1903.
*Most Capped Player:* Nick Dasovic, 26, Canada.
*Most League Appearances:* 298: Drew Rutherford, 1976-85.
*Most League Goals in Season (Individual):* 36: Jimmy Benson, Division II, 1931-32.
*Most Goals Overall (Individual):* 140: John Brogan, 1977-83.

## ST JOHNSTONE – SCOTTISH PREMIER LEAGUE 2012–13 LEAGUE RECORD

| Match No. | Date | | Venue | Opponents | Result | | H/T Score | Lg Pos. | Goalscorers | Attendance |
|---|---|---|---|---|---|---|---|---|---|---|
| 1 | Aug | 4 | A | Hearts | L | 0-2 | 0-1 | 12 | | 13,022 |
| 2 | | 11 | A | Motherwell | D | 1-1 | 0-0 | 10 | Davidson, M 58 | 4490 |
| 3 | | 18 | H | Aberdeen | L | 1-2 | 0-1 | 12 | Hasselbaink 83 | 4857 |
| 4 | | 25 | A | Hibernian | L | 0-2 | 0-1 | 11 | | 9639 |
| 5 | Sept | 1 | H | Dundee U | D | 0-0 | 0-0 | 11 | | 5014 |
| 6 | | 15 | H | Celtic | W | 2-1 | 1-1 | 10 | Tade 18, Vine 80 | 6700 |
| 7 | | 22 | A | Ross Co | W | 2-1 | 1-0 | 9 | Craig 30, Wright 86 | 4094 |
| 8 | | 29 | A | Dundee | W | 3-1 | 2-1 | 7 | Tade 16, Craig 27, MacLean 52 | 6158 |
| 9 | Oct | 6 | H | St Mirren | W | 2-1 | 2-0 | 4 | Hasselbaink 22, Davidson, M 37 | 3223 |
| 10 | | 20 | H | Kilmarnock | W | 2-1 | 1-0 | 2 | Davidson, M 30, Hasselbaink 90 | 3113 |
| 11 | | 27 | A | Inverness CT | D | 1-1 | 0-0 | 4 | Robertson 90 | 3154 |
| 12 | Nov | 3 | H | Motherwell | L | 1-3 | 0-2 | 5 | Robertson 88 | 3112 |
| 13 | | 11 | A | Celtic | D | 1-1 | 0-0 | 5 | Hasselbaink 77 | 43,804 |
| 14 | | 17 | H | Ross Co | D | 1-1 | 0-0 | 4 | MacKay 51 | 3037 |
| 15 | | 24 | A | Kilmarnock | W | 2-1 | 1-0 | 4 | Davidson, M 31, Vine 89 | 4208 |
| 16 | | 28 | H | Hibernian | L | 0-1 | 0-0 | 6 | | 3266 |
| 17 | Dec | 8 | A | St Mirren | D | 1-1 | 1-0 | 6 | Davidson, M 15 | 3702 |
| 18 | | 15 | H | Hearts | D | 2-2 | 1-2 | 5 | Vine 16, MacLean 60 | 2974 |
| 19 | | 22 | A | Aberdeen | L | 0-2 | 0-0 | 6 | | 7051 |
| 20 | | 26 | A | Dundee U | D | 1-1 | 0-1 | 7 | McLean (og) 47 | 7063 |
| 21 | | 29 | H | Inverness CT | D | 0-0 | 0-0 | 7 | | 2975 |
| 22 | Jan | 2 | H | Dundee | W | 1-0 | 1-0 | 6 | Craig 33 | 5055 |
| 23 | | 20 | A | Motherwell | L | 2-3 | 0-2 | 6 | Hasselbaink 77, Craig 79 | 3649 |
| 24 | | 30 | H | Aberdeen | W | 3-1 | 1-1 | 5 | Tade 33, Vine 68, MacKay 70 | 2167 |
| 25 | Feb | 11 | A | Hibernian | W | 3-1 | 2-0 | 4 | Vine 2 23, 26, Cregg 58 | 8735 |
| 26 | | 16 | A | Ross Co | L | 0-1 | 0-1 | 6 | | 3516 |
| 27 | | 19 | H | Celtic | D | 1-1 | 0-1 | 5 | Hasselbaink 82 | 5352 |
| 28 | | 23 | H | St Mirren | W | 1-0 | 0-0 | 4 | Vine 52 | 2816 |
| 29 | | 27 | A | Dundee | D | 2-2 | 1-1 | 5 | MacLean 36, MacKay 68 | 5224 |
| 30 | Mar | 5 | A | Hearts | L | 0-2 | 0-1 | 5 | | 10,080 |
| 31 | | 9 | H | Kilmarnock | W | 2-0 | 0-0 | 5 | Davidson, M 58, Tade 85 | 2425 |
| 32 | Apr | 1 | H | Dundee U | D | 1-1 | 0-1 | 5 | Craig 90 | 4613 |
| 33 | | 5 | A | Inverness CT | D | 0-0 | 0-0 | 4 | | 3744 |
| 34 | | 21 | H | Ross Co | D | 2-2 | 2-1 | 4 | MacLean 6, Davidson, M 25 | 2444 |
| 35 | | 27 | H | Inverness CT | W | 1-0 | 0-0 | 4 | MacLean 77 | 2368 |
| 36 | May | 4 | A | Dundee U | W | 1-0 | 1-0 | 4 | Craig 38 | 6437 |
| 37 | | 11 | A | Celtic | L | 0-4 | 0-2 | 4 | | 57,000 |
| 38 | | 19 | H | Motherwell | W | 2-0 | 1-0 | 3 | Craig 36, Hasselbaink 47 | 5025 |

**Final League Position: 3**

## Honours

*League Champions:* First Division 1982-83, 1989-90, 1996-97, 2008-09. Division II 1923-24, 1959-60, 1962-63;
*Runners-up:* Division II 1931-32. First Division 2005-06, 2006-07. Second Division 1987-88.
*Scottish Cup:* Semi-finals 1934, 1968, 1989, 1991, 2007, 2008.
*League Cup Runners-up:* 1969-70, 1998-99.
*League Challenge Cup Winners:* 2007-08; *Runners-up:* 1996-97.

**European:** *UEFA Cup:* 12 matches (1971-72, 1999-2000, 2012-13).

**Club colours:** Shirt: Blue. Short: White. Socks: Blue and white hoops.

**Goalscorers:** *League (45):* Craig 7, Davidson M 7, Hasselbaink 7, Vine 7, MacLean 5, Tade 4, MacKay 3, Robertson 2, Cregg 1, Wright 1, own goal 1.
*William Hill Scottish FA Cup (3):* MacLean 1 (1 pen), McCracken 1, Tade 1.
*Scottish Communities League Cup (4):* MacLean 2, Craig 1, Davidson M 1.
*Europa League (1):* Tade 1.

| Mannus A 38 | MacKay D 32 | McCracken D 15+1 | Wright F 35 | Davidson C 20+1 | Miller C 25+1 | Davidson M 31+1 | Cregg P 19+5 | Craig L 37 | Hasselbaink N 15+21 | Tade G 25+11 | Vine R 28+7 | Adams J —+4 | May S —+3 | Anderson S 28+2 | Higgins S 1+2 | Scobbie T 11+7 | Miller G 13+4 | Pawlett P 7+2 | MacLean S 27+4 | Beattie C —+2 | Robertson D 1+6 | Moon K —+1 | Caddis L —+2 | Doughty M 1+4 | Abeid M 9+3 | Edwards G —+6 | Match No. |
|---|---|---|---|---|---|---|---|---|---|---|---|---|---|---|---|---|---|---|---|---|---|---|---|---|---|---|---|
| 1 | 2 | 3 | 4 | 5 | 6² | 7 | 8¹ | 9 | 10³ | 11 | 12 | 13 | 14 | | | | | | | | | | | | | | 1 |
| 1 | 4 | | 3 | 5 | 6 | 8¹ | 7² | 9 | 10 | 11 | | 13 | | 2 | 12 | | | | | | | | | | | | 2 |
| 1 | 2 | | 4 | | 6¹ | 8² | 7 | 9 | 10 | | 12 | 14 | | 3 | 11 | 5³ | 13 | | | | | | | | | | 3 |
| 1 | 2 | | 4 | 5 | | 8 | 7¹ | 9 | 6² | 10³ | 11 | 14 | | 3 | 13 | | | | 12 | | | | | | | | 4 |
| 1 | 5 | | 4 | | | 8 | 7² | 9 | 12 | 10 | 11 | 13 | | 3 | | | 2 | | 6¹ | | | | | | | | 5 |
| 1 | 5 | | 4 | | 12 | 8¹ | 7 | 9 | 13 | 11 | 10³ | | | 3 | | | 2 | | 6² | | 14 | | | | | | 6 |
| 1 | 7 | 14 | 4 | | 10 | 12 | 9² | 11 | 8¹ | 5³ | 6 | | | 3 | | | 2 | | 13 | | | | | | | | 7 |
| 1 | 5 | | 4 | | 6 | 8 | 7¹ | 9 | 12 | 10 | | | | 3 | | | 2 | | 11² | 13 | | | | | | | 8 |
| 1 | 2 | | 4 | | 7 | 8 | | 9 | 11¹ | 10² | | | | 3 | 5 | 6 | | | 13 | 12 | | | | | | | 9 |
| 1 | 5 | | 4 | | 7³ | 8 | | 9 | 6 | 11 | 10² | | | 3 | | 12 | 2¹ | | 13 | 14 | | | | | | | 10 |
| 1 | 2 | 3¹ | | 5 | 6 | | 8 | 9² | 7³ | 11 | | 4 | | 12 | | | 10 | | 13 | 14 | | | | | | | 11 |
| 1 | 5 | | 4 | | 6 | 7 | | 8² | 11 | 10¹ | 12 | | | 3 | | | 2 | | 9 | 13 | | | | | | | 12 |
| 1 | 2 | 3¹ | 4 | 5 | 6 | 7 | | 9 | 10³ | 13 | 14 | | | | 12 | | 11 | 8² | | | | | | | | | 13 |
| 1 | 2 | | 4 | 5 | 7 | 8 | | 9 | 6 | 11¹¹ | 12 | | | 3 | | | 10 | | | | | | | | | | 14 |
| 1 | 2 | | 4 | 5 | 7 | 8 | | 9³ | 6¹ | 11² | 12 | | | 3 | | 13 | 10 | 14 | | | | | | | | | 15 |
| 1 | 5 | | 4 | | 7 | 8 | | 9 | 12 | 11² | 6¹ | | | 3 | | | 2 | | 10 | 13³ | 14 | | | | | | 16 |
| 1 | | 3 | 5 | 7 | 8 | 14 | 9 | | 11² | 6¹ | | 4 | | 12 | 2 | 13 | 10³ | | | | | | | | | | 17 |
| 1 | 4 | | 5 | | 8 | 7 | 9 | 13 | 12 | 11² | | | | 3 | 2 | 6¹ | 10 | | | | | | | | | | 18 |
| 1 | 6 | | 3 | 5 | 7¹ | 8 | 12 | 9 | 14 | 13 | 10² | | | 4 | | | 2³ | | 11 | | | | | | | | 19 |
| 1 | 2 | 4 | 3 | | 8 | 7 | 9 | | 10 | 12 | | | | 5 | | | 6¹ | | 11 | | | | | | | | 20 |
| 1 | 2 | 3 | 4 | 5 | | 8 | 7² | 9 | 13 | 11 | 12 | | | | | | 6 | | 10¹ | | | | | | | | 21 |
| 1 | 2 | 3 | 4 | 5¹ | 7 | 8 | | 9 | 14 | 10² | 11³ | | | 12 | | | 6 | | 13 | | | | | | | | 22 |
| 1 | 2 | 3 | 4 | 5 | 6³ | | 14 | 7 | 12 | 10² | 11 | | | 13 | | 8¹ | 9 | | | | | | | | | | 23 |
| 1 | 2 | 3 | 4 | 5 | | | 7 | 8 | 6¹ | 11 | 9² | | | 13 | | | 10 | | | | 12 | | | | | | 24 |
| 1 | | 3 | 4 | 5 | | 8 | 7 | 9 | 13 | 12 | 6² | 2 | | | | | 11¹ | | | | 14 | 10³ | | | | | 25 |
| 1 | | 4 | 5 | 3 | | 7¹ | 6² | 10 | 14 | 13 | 9³ | 2 | | | | | 11 | | | | 12 | 8 | | | | | 26 |
| 1 | | 3 | 4 | | | 7 | 9 | 13 | 12 | 11² | | 2 | 5 | | | | 10³ | | | | 8¹ | 6 | 14 | | | | 27 |
| 1 | | 3 | 4 | 5 | | 8 | 7 | 9 | 13 | 12 | 11 | 2 | | | | | 10² | | | | 6¹ | | | | | | 28 |
| 1 | 2 | 3 | 4 | | 8³ | | 7 | 9 | 13 | 12 | 11² | 14 | 5 | | | | 10 | | | | 6¹ | | | | | | 29 |
| 1 | 2 | 4 | 3² | 5 | | 8 | 7 | 9 | 14 | 12 | 10³ | 13 | | | | | 11 | | | | 6¹ | | | | | | 30 |
| 1 | 2 | 4 | | 5 | 7 | 8 | | 9 | 6² | 12 | 11¹ | 3 | | | | | 10³ | | | | 13 | 14 | | | | | 31 |
| 1 | 2 | | 4 | | 7 | 8 | | 9 | 12 | 10¹ | 6² | 3 | | | | | 11 | | | | 14 | 13 | | | | | 32 |
| 1 | 2 | | 4 | 3¹ | 8 | | 9 | 14 | 6² | 10³ | | 5 | 12 | | | | 11 | | | | 7 | 13 | | | | | 33 |
| 1 | 2 | | 4 | | 8 | 7 | | 13 | 6² | 9¹ | | 3 | 5 | | | | 10 | | | | 11 | 12 | | | | | 34 |
| 1 | 2 | | 4 | | 7 | | 14 | 8 | 13 | 6² | 9³ | 3 | 5 | | | | 11 | | | | 10¹ | 12 | | | | | 35 |
| 1 | 2 | | 4 | | 6¹ | 7 | 12 | 8³ | 13 | 11 | 10² | 3 | 5 | | | | 9 | | | | 14 | | | | | | 36 |
| 1 | 2 | | 4 | 12 | | 7 | 6 | 8 | 13 | 11 | 10² | 3 | 5¹ | | | | 9³ | | 14 | | | | | | | | 37 |
| 1 | 4 | | | 5 | 7 | 8 | | 9 | 6² | 13 | 10¹ | 3 | 14 | 2³ | 11 | | | | 12 | | | | | | | | 38 |

# ST MIRREN

*Year Formed:* 1877. *Ground & Address:* St Mirren Park, Greenhill Road, Paisley PA3 1RU. *Telephone:* 0141 889 2558.
*Fax:* 0141 848 6444. *E-mail:* info@saintmirren.net *Website:* www.saintmirren.net
*Ground Capacity:* 8,023 (all seated). *Size of Pitch:* 100m × 64m.
*Chairman:* Stewart Gilmour. *Vice-Chairman:* George Campbell. *Secretary:* Chris Stewart.
*Manager:* Danny Lennon. *First Team Coach:* Tommy Craig. *Youth Development Officer:* David Longwell. *Physio:*
Gerry Docherty.
*Club Nickname:* 'The Buddies'.
*Previous Grounds:* Shortroods 1877-79, Thistle Park Greenhill 1879-83, Westmarch 1883-94, Love Street 1894-2009.
*Record Attendance:* 47,438 v Celtic, League Cup, 20 Aug 1949.
*Record Transfer Fee received:* £850,000 for Ian Ferguson to Rangers (Feb 1988).
*Record Transfer Fee paid:* £400,000 for Thomas Stickroth from Bayer Uerdingen (March 1990).
*Record Victory:* 15-0 v Glasgow University, Scottish Cup 1st rd, 30 Jan 1960.
*Record Defeat:* 0-9 v Rangers, Division I, 4 Dec 1897.
*Most Capped Player:* Godmundor Torfason, 29, Iceland.
*Most League Appearances:* 399: Hugh Murray, 1997-2012.
*Most League Goals in Season (Individual):* 45: Dunky Walker, Division I, 1921-22.
*Most Goals Overall (Individual):* 221: David McCrae, 1923-34.

## ST MIRREN – SCOTTISH PREMIER LEAGUE 2012–13 LEAGUE RECORD

| Match No. | Date | Venue | Opponents | Result | H/T Score | Lg Pos. | Goalscorers | Attendance |
|---|---|---|---|---|---|---|---|---|
| 1 | Aug 4 | H | Inverness CT | D 2-2 | 1-0 | 4 | Guy [32], McGregor [90] | 4104 |
| 2 | 11 | A | Dundee | W 2-0 | 1-0 | 1 | McLean [39], Parkin [63] | 5984 |
| 3 | 18 | H | Hibernian | L 1-2 | 0-1 | 3 | Thompson [63] | 5039 |
| 4 | 26 | A | Motherwell | D 1-1 | 0-1 | 7 | Reilly [90] | 4559 |
| 5 | Sept 1 | A | Aberdeen | D 0-0 | 0-0 | 6 | | 9288 |
| 6 | 15 | H | Hearts | W 2-0 | 1-0 | 3 | Goodwin [38], Guy [48] | 4307 |
| 7 | 22 | A | Kilmarnock | L 1-3 | 0-1 | 6 | McGowan [83] | 4879 |
| 8 | 29 | H | Ross Co | W 5-4 | 1-2 | 4 | Thompson 2 [39, 89], Guy (pen) [55], Parkin [59], McLean [64] | 3706 |
| 9 | Oct 6 | A | St Johnstone | L 1-2 | 0-2 | 7 | Guy [49] | 3223 |
| 10 | 20 | H | Celtic | L 0-5 | 0-4 | 8 | | 6008 |
| 11 | 27 | H | Dundee U | L 0-1 | 0-0 | 11 | | 4333 |
| 12 | Nov 3 | A | Hibernian | L 1-2 | 1-1 | 11 | McLean [32] | 10,358 |
| 13 | 10 | H | Aberdeen | L 1-4 | 0-2 | 11 | Thompson [88] | 4486 |
| 14 | 17 | A | Hearts | L 0-1 | 0-0 | 11 | | 16,443 |
| 15 | 24 | H | Dundee | W 3-1 | 1-0 | 11 | Thompson 2 [31, 72], Imrie [87] | 4825 |
| 16 | 27 | A | Ross Co | D 0-0 | 0-0 | 11 | | 2837 |
| 17 | Dec 8 | H | St Johnstone | D 1-1 | 0-1 | 11 | Dummett [69] | 3702 |
| 18 | 15 | A | Celtic | L 0-2 | 0-1 | 11 | | 47,790 |
| 19 | 21 | A | Motherwell | W 2-1 | 2-0 | 10 | Thompson 2 [39, 42] | 4023 |
| 20 | 26 | A | Inverness CT | D 2-2 | 1-1 | 10 | Imrie [2], Thompson [55] | 3506 |
| 21 | 30 | A | Dundee U | W 4-3 | 1-2 | 10 | Dummett [16], Thompson [50], McAusland [66], van Zanten [78] | 6386 |
| 22 | Jan 2 | H | Kilmarnock | D 1-1 | 0-1 | 10 | McGowan (pen) [68] | 6347 |
| 23 | 19 | H | Ross Co | L 1-4 | 0-1 | 10 | Thompson [50] | 3802 |
| 24 | 30 | A | Inverness CT | W 2-1 | 1-1 | 11 | Goncalves [26], Thompson [82] | 3065 |
| 25 | Feb 9 | A | Aberdeen | D 0-0 | 0-0 | 11 | | 7240 |
| 26 | 16 | H | Hibernian | L 0-1 | 0-0 | 11 | | 4524 |
| 27 | 23 | A | St Johnstone | L 0-1 | 0-0 | 11 | | 2816 |
| 28 | 27 | H | Hearts | W 2-0 | 2-0 | 10 | McGowan (pen) [4], Carey [45] | 3369 |
| 29 | Mar 6 | A | Dundee | L 1-2 | 1-0 | 11 | Imrie [20] | 3674 |
| 30 | 9 | H | Dundee U | D 0-0 | 0-0 | 10 | | 3394 |
| 31 | 31 | H | Celtic | D 1-1 | 0-1 | 10 | McGowan (pen) [81] | 6066 |
| 32 | Apr 3 | A | Kilmarnock | D 1-1 | 1-0 | 10 | Goncalves [36] | 4494 |
| 33 | 6 | A | Motherwell | D 2-2 | 1-1 | 11 | Newton [41], Guy [75] | 5414 |
| 34 | 20 | H | Dundee | L 1-2 | 0-1 | 11 | Thompson [52] | 4002 |
| 35 | 27 | A | Hibernian | D 3-3 | 0-1 | 11 | Goncalves [60], McAusland 2 [78, 82] | 9264 |
| 36 | May 4 | A | Hearts | L 0-3 | 0-2 | 11 | | 16,312 |
| 37 | 11 | H | Aberdeen | D 0-0 | 0-0 | 11 | | 4292 |
| 38 | 18 | A | Kilmarnock | W 3-1 | 1-1 | 11 | McGinn, J [20], McGowan (pen) [75], Newton [88] | 4428 |

**Final League Position: 11**

**Honours**
*League Champions:* First Division 1976-77, 1999-2000, 2005-06. Division II 1967-68;
*Runners-up:* First Division 2004-05; Division II 1935-36.
*Scottish Cup Winners:* 1926, 1959, 1987; *Runners-up:* 1908, 1934, 1962.
*League Cup Winners:* 2012-13; *Runners-up:* 1955-56, 2009-10.
*League Challenge Cup Winners:* 2005-06.
*B&Q Cup Runners-up:* 1993-94. *Anglo-Scottish Cup:* 1979-80.

**European:** *Cup Winners' Cup:* 4 matches (1987-88). *UEFA Cup:* 10 matches (1980-81, 1983-84, 1985-86).

**Club colours:** Shirt: Black and white vertical stripes. Shorts: White. Socks: White.

**Goalscorers:** *League (47):* Thompson 13, Guy 5 (1 pen), McGowan 5 (4 pens), Goncalves 3, Imrie 3, McAusland 3, McLean 3, Dummett 2, Newton 2, Parkin 2, Carey 1, Goodwin 1, McGinn 1, McGregor 1, Reilly 1, van Zanten 1.
*William Hill Scottish FA Cup (5):* Goncalves 3, McLean 1, Robertson 1.
*Scottish Communities League Cup (14):* Thompson 3, Goncalves 2, McGowan 2 (1 pen), McLean 2 (1 pen), Guy 1, Mair 1, Newton 1, Parkin 1, Teale 1.

| Samson C 38 | van Zanten D 32+2 | McGregor D 3 | Mair L 21+3 | Barron D 8+4 | Teale G 23+7 | McGowan P 25 | McLean K 26+3 | Imrie D 13+14 | Parkin S 12+15 | Guy L 17+12 | Robertson J 11+8 | Reilly T 2+7 | Carey G 18+8 | Thompson S 33+1 | McAusland M 35+1 | Goodwin J 29 | Dummett P 29+1 | McGinn J 15+7 | Newton C 16 | Goncalves E 11+1 | Puri S 1+2 | Smith J —+2 | Brady A —+1 | Yaqub M —+1 | Match No. |
|---|---|---|---|---|---|---|---|---|---|---|---|---|---|---|---|---|---|---|---|---|---|---|---|---|---|
| 1 | 2 | 3 | 4 | 5 | 6¹ | 7 | 8 | 9² | 10 | 11* | 12 | 13 | | | | | | | | | | | | | 1 |
| 1 | 2 | 3 | 4 | | 14 | 6 | 7 | 9² | 11 | | 5³ | 12 | 8 | 10¹ | 13 | | | | | | | | | | 2 |
| 1 | | 4³ | 5 | 14 | 13 | 6 | 7 | 10 | 9 | | 12 | | 3¹ | 8 | 2 | 11² | | | | | | | | | 3 |
| 1 | 2 | | 4 | | 12 | 8³ | 6 | 9¹ | 11² | 14 | 13 | | 5 | 10 | 3 | 7 | | | | | | | | | 4 |
| 1 | 2¹ | | 4 | 12 | 6² | 7 | 8 | 13 | | 11³ | 14 | | 5 | 10 | 3 | 9 | | | | | | | | | 5 |
| 1 | 2 | | 4 | 12 | 6 | 8² | 13 | 14 | 11 | | 5¹ | 10³ | 3 | 7 | 9 | | | | | | | | | | 6 |
| 1 | 2¹ | | 4 | 13 | 6 | 8 | 9² | 14 | 12 | 11 | | 10³ | 3 | 7 | 5 | | | | | | | | | | 7 |
| 1 | 2 | | 4 | | 14 | | 13 | 6¹ | 12 | 11² | 7¹ | | 9 | 10 | 3 | 8 | 5 | | | | | | | | 8 |
| 1 | 2 | 3 | | | 6² | 12 | 9¹ | 11³ | 14 | 13 | 8 | 10 | 4 | 7 | 5 | | | | | | | | | | 9 |
| 1 | 2 | | 4 | 10¹ | | 9 | 12 | 6 | | 6 | | | 7 | 11 | 3 | 8² | 5 | 13 | | | | | | | 10 |
| 1 | 2 | | 4 | 13 | | 6³ | 12 | 11¹ | 7² | 14 | 9 | 10 | 3 | 8 | 5 | | | | | | | | | | 11 |
| 1 | 2 | | 4 | 13 | 9 | 7³ | 11¹ | 12 | | 6² | 14 | 10 | 3 | 8⁴ | 5 | | | | | | | | | | 12 |
| 1 | 2 | | 4 | 6 | 9³ | 10² | 13 | 7¹ | 12 | 14 | 11 | 3 | | 5 | | | | | | | | | | | 13 |
| 1 | 2 | 4³ | 6 | 9 | 13 | 12 | 14 | 10¹ | 8² | 11 | 3 | 7 | 5 | | | | | | | | | | | | 14 |
| 1 | 2 | 4 | 7 | 8 | 13 | 12 | 11² | | | 10 | 3 | 6 | 5 | 9¹ | | | | | | | | | | | 15 |
| 1 | 2 | 3 | 7 | 8 | 13 | 12 | 11² | 10¹ | 4 | 6 | 5 | 9 | | | | | | | | | | | | | 16 |
| 1 | 2 | 3 | 9³ | 6 | 12 | 13 | 11² | 14 | 10 | 4¹ | 7 | 5 | 8 | | | | | | | | | | | | 17 |
| 1 | 2 | | 6 | 9 | 10 | 12 | 13 | 8² | 11¹ | 3 | 4 | 5 | 7 | | | | | | | | | | | | 18 |
| 1 | 13 | 12 | 2³ | 6¹ | 8 | 11 | 7 | 14 | 10 | 3 | 4 | 5² | 9 | | | | | | | | | | | | 19 |
| 1 | 4 | 5 | 2 | 7 | 10¹ | 6 | 12 | 8 | 9 | 11 | 3 | | | | | | | | | | | | | | 20 |
| 1 | 2 | 12 | 7 | 8 | | 13 | 10 | 6¹ | 14 | 11² | 3 | 4 | 5 | 9³ | | | | | | | | | | | 21 |
| 1 | 2 | 6 | 7 | | 12 | 13 | 10² | 8 | 11 | 3 | 4 | 5 | 9¹ | | | | | | | | | | | | 22 |
| 1 | 2 | 6 | 9³ | 12 | 10² | 13 | 7 | 5 | 11 | 3 | 4 | 14 | 8¹ | | | | | | | | | | | | 23 |
| 1 | 2 | 12 | 7 | 8 | 9³ | 13 | 5 | 11 | 3¹ | 4 | 14 | 6 | 10² | | | | | | | | | | | | 24 |
| 1 | | 4 | 11 | 7 | 5¹ | 12 | 10 | 2 | 3 | 9 | 6 | 8 | | | | | | | | | | | | | 25 |
| 1 | 2 | 7 | 6¹ | 14 | 13 | 9² | 11 | 3 | 4 | 5 | 12 | 8³ | 10 | | | | | | | | | | | | 26 |
| 1 | 2¹ | 7 | 6 | 12 | 13 | 10 | 3 | 4 | 5 | 9² | 8 | 11 | | | | | | | | | | | | | 27 |
| 1 | 13 | 4 | 2³ | 6² | 14 | 12 | 11 | 10⁵ | 9 | 3 | 5 | 8 | 7 | | | | | | | | | | | | 28 |
| 1 | 2 | 4³ | 8 | 9 | 7 | 10² | 11¹ | 5 | 12 | 3 | 14 | 6 | 13 | | | | | | | | | | | | 29 |
| 1 | 2 | 7 | 8³ | 13 | 14 | 12 | 5 | 11² | 3 | 4 | 9 | 6¹ | 10 | | | | | | | | | | | | 30 |
| 1 | 2 | 6 | 7 | 12 | 10 | 3 | 4 | 5 | 9¹ | 8 | 11²¹ | 13 | | | | | | | | | | | | | 31 |
| 1 | 2 | 6³ | 7 | 12 | 13 | 10 | 3 | 4 | 5 | 9¹ | 8 | 11²¹ | 14 | | | | | | | | | | | | 32 |
| 1 | 2 | 10 | 8 | 6² | 14 | 12 | 11¹³ | 3 | 4 | 5 | 13 | 7 | 9¹ | | | | | | | | | | | | 33 |
| 1 | 2 | 14 | 6 | 8¹ | 9² | 11³ | 13 | 10 | 3 | 4⁴ | 5 | 12 | 7 | | | | | | | | | | | | 34 |
| 1 | 2 | 6 | 8 | 12 | | 5 | 10 | 3 | 4 | 9¹ | 7 | 11 | | | | | | | | | | | | | 35 |
| 1 | 2¹ | 4 | 6 | 8 | 9⁴ | 12 | 14 | 13 | 11³ | 3 | 5 | 7 | 10² | | | | | | | | | | | | 36 |
| 1 | 2 | 6 | 9 | 11 | 12³ | 8² | 3 | 4 | 5 | 13 | 7 | 10¹ | 14 | | | | | | | | | | | | 37 |
| 1 | 2 | 8² | 6 | 10 | 3 | 4 | 5 | 9¹ | 7 | 11¹ | 14 | 12 | 13 | | | | | | | | | | | | 38 |

# STENHOUSEMUIR

*Year Formed:* 1884. *Ground & Address:* Ochilview Park, Gladstone Rd, Stenhousemuir FK5 4QL. *Telephone:* 01324 562992. *Fax:* 01324 562980. *E-mail:* info@stenhousemuirfc.com *Website:* www.stenhousemuirfc.com
*Ground Capacity:* 3,776 (seated: 626). *Size of Pitch:* 101m × 66m.
*Chairman:* Bill Darroch. *Vice-Chairman:* Gordon Thompson. *Secretary/General Manager:* Margaret Kilpatrick.
*Manager:* Martyn Corrigan. *Assistant Manager:* Kevin McGoldrick. *Physio:* Laura Chimimba.
*Club Nickname:* 'The Warriors'.
*Previous Grounds:* Tryst Ground 1884-86, Goschen Park 1886-90.
*Record Attendance:* 12,500 v East Fife, Scottish Cup Quarter-final, 11 Mar 1950.
*Record Transfer Fee received:* £70,000 for Euan Donaldson to St Johnstone (May 1995).
*Record Transfer Fee paid:* £20,000 to Livingston for Ian Little (June 1995); £20,000 to East Fife for Paul Hunter (September 1995).
*Record Victory:* 9-2 v Dundee U, Division II, 16 Apr 1937.
*Record Defeat:* 2-11 v Dunfermline Ath, Division II, 27 Sept 1930.
*Most League Appearances:* 434: Jimmy Richardson, 1957-73.
*Most League Goals in Season (Individual):* 32: Robert Taylor, Division II, 1925-26.

## STENHOUSEMUIR – SCOTTISH SECOND DIVISION 2012–13 LEAGUE RECORD

| Match No. | Date | Venue | Opponents | Result | H/T Score | Lg Pos. | Goalscorers | Attendance |
|---|---|---|---|---|---|---|---|---|
| 1 | Aug 11 | A | Ayr U | D 1-1 | 0-1 | 7 | McMillan [90] | 1248 |
| 2 | 18 | H | Brechin C | W 3-1 | 1-0 | 3 | Gemmell 3 [21, 73, 90] | 522 |
| 3 | 25 | A | Stranraer | D 1-1 | 1-0 | 5 | McMillan [19] | 290 |
| 4 | Sept 1 | H | Forfar Ath | L 0-4 | 0-2 | 6 | | 673 |
| 5 | 15 | A | Alloa Ath | W 2-0 | 0-0 | 4 | Smith, D [67], Ferguson (pen) [90] | 509 |
| 6 | 22 | H | Albion R | D 4-4 | 2-1 | 5 | Kean 3 [26, 32, 90], Rodgers [56] | 389 |
| 7 | 29 | H | Arbroath | D 2-2 | 0-0 | 5 | Gemmell [46], McKinlay [90] | 633 |
| 8 | Oct 6 | H | East Fife | W 3-0 | 0-0 | 5 | Gemmell 2 [66, 69], Kean [72] | 589 |
| 9 | 20 | A | Queen of the S | D 2-2 | 0-1 | 5 | Gemmell [68], Ferguson (pen) [71] | 1531 |
| 10 | 27 | A | Brechin C | L 2-7 | 1-3 | 5 | Gemmell [29], Dickson [55] | 542 |
| 11 | Nov 10 | H | Ayr U | D 1-1 | 0-0 | 4 | Smith, D [84] | 586 |
| 12 | 17 | A | Forfar Ath | L 2-3 | 1-2 | 5 | McMillan [35], Rodgers (pen) [58] | 432 |
| 13 | 24 | H | Alloa Ath | L 0-2 | 0-2 | 7 | | 671 |
| 14 | Dec 8 | A | Arbroath | D 2-2 | 1-1 | 7 | Smith, D [3], Kean [90] | 647 |
| 15 | 15 | H | Albion R | W 1-0 | 0-0 | 6 | Smith, D [53] | 396 |
| 16 | 22 | A | East Fife | L 2-3 | 0-2 | 7 | Kean [57], Rodgers [69] | 408 |
| 17 | 29 | H | Queen of the S | L 1-3 | 0-1 | 7 | Kean [90] | 632 |
| 18 | Jan 2 | A | Alloa Ath | L 0-1 | 0-1 | 7 | | 603 |
| 19 | 5 | H | Forfar Ath | W 2-0 | 0-0 | 7 | Dickson [65], Smith, D [67] | 461 |
| 20 | 12 | A | Stranraer | D 0-0 | 0-0 | 7 | | 484 |
| 21 | Feb 2 | H | Arbroath | W 1-0 | 1-0 | 7 | Gemmell [45] | 459 |
| 22 | 9 | A | Queen of the S | L 1-2 | 0-2 | 7 | Corcoran [47] | 1354 |
| 23 | 16 | H | East Fife | W 2-1 | 0-0 | 6 | Hodge 2 [60, 85] | 476 |
| 24 | 23 | A | Stranraer | D 1-1 | 1-1 | 6 | McKinlay [22] | 346 |
| 25 | 26 | A | Ayr U | W 2-1 | 0-1 | 6 | Dickson [60], Corcoran [90] | 821 |
| 26 | Mar 2 | H | Brechin C | D 3-3 | 1-1 | 6 | Smith, D [20], Hay (og) [55], Gemmell [63] | 504 |
| 27 | 5 | A | Albion R | L 3-4 | 0-2 | 6 | Gemmell 2 (1 pen) [53 (p), 85], Reid [90] | 206 |
| 28 | 9 | H | Alloa Ath | D 1-1 | 0-1 | 6 | Smith, D [69] | 513 |
| 29 | 16 | A | Forfar Ath | D 3-3 | 3-2 | 6 | Kean [5], Gemmell 2 [31, 35] | 395 |
| 30 | 30 | H | Albion R | L 0-1 | 0-1 | 7 | | 360 |
| 31 | Apr 3 | A | Arbroath | D 0-0 | 0-0 | 7 | | 532 |
| 32 | 13 | A | East Fife | W 2-1 | 1-0 | 7 | Buist [43], Gemmell [52] | 461 |
| 33 | 16 | H | Queen of the S | W 2-1 | 1-1 | 6 | Smith, D [28], Dickson [72] | 504 |
| 34 | 20 | H | Ayr U | W 4-0 | 3-0 | 6 | Dickson [5], Gemmell 2 (1 pen) [20, 42 (p)], Smith, D [56] | 497 |
| 35 | 27 | A | Brechin C | W 2-1 | 2-0 | 6 | Rowson [8], Reid [34] | 474 |
| 36 | May 4 | H | Stranraer | L 1-2 | 1-2 | 6 | Gemmell [22] | 818 |

**Final League Position: 6**

**Honours**
*League Champions:* Third Division runners-up: 1998-99. *Promoted to Second Division:* 2008-09 (play-offs).
*Scottish Cup:* Semi-finals 1902-03. Quarter-finals 1948-49, 1949-50, 1994-95.
*League Cup:* Quarter-finals 1947-48, 1960-61, 1975-76.
*League Challenge Cup Winners:* 1995-96.

**Club colours:** Shirt: Maroon with white trim. Shorts: White. Socks: Maroon.

**Goalscorers:** *League (59):* Gemmell 18 (2 pens), Smith D 9, Kean 8, Dickson 5, McMillan 3, Rodgers 3 (1 pen), Corcoran 2, Ferguson 2 (2 pens), Hodge 2, McKinlay 2, Reid 2, Buist 1, Rowson 1, own goal 1.
*William Hill Scottish FA Cup (6):* Kean 3, Smith D 2, Gemmell 1.
*Scottish Communities League Cup (7):* Ferguson 2 (2 pens), Gemmell 2, Smith D 2, Kean 1 (1 pen).
*Ramsdens Cup (5):* Dickson 1, Ferguson 1, Gemmell 1, Kean 1, Rodgers 1.

| Reidford C 22 | Ross G 32+1 | McKinlay K 25+1 | Thomson I 18+11 | McMillan R 27+1 | Hodge B 35 | Smith D 29+3 | Rodgers A 9+7 | Kean S 26+3 | Anderson C 12+8 | Dickson S 29+5 | Brash R 1+4 | Buist S 20 | Gemmell J 23+1 | Love S —+4 | Ferguson B 16+5 | Lawson A 1+1 | Thomson R 7 | Kilday L 3 | Paton E 3+3 | McKay B 3+1 | Phinn N —+1 | Exposito-Hepburn D —+1 | Duncan R 1+1 | Anderson K —+1 | Ronald O —+1 | Rowson D 18 | Reid J 8+5 | Corcoran M 9+5 | Shaw D —+1 | Mbu J 5 | Devlin N 7+1 | Smith C 7 | Kouider-Aisser S —+7 | Summers C —+1 | Match No. |
|---|---|---|---|---|---|---|---|---|---|---|---|---|---|---|---|---|---|---|---|---|---|---|---|---|---|---|---|---|---|---|---|---|---|---|---|
| 1 | 2 | 3 | 4 | 5 | 6 | 7 | 8¹ | 9 | 10 | 11 | 12 | | | | | | | | | | | | | | | | | | | | | | | | 1 |
| 1 | 2 | | 12 | 4 | 7 | 8 | 9¹ | 11² | 6³ | 5 | 13 | 3 | 10 | 14 | | | | | | | | | | | | | | | | | | | | | 2 |
| 1 | 2 | | 9 | 4¹ | 6 | 7² | 11 | 10 | 5 | 13 | | 3 | 8 | | 12 | | | | | | | | | | | | | | | | | | | | 3 |
| 1 | 2³ | 5¹ | 7 | 4 | 8 | 12 | 14 | 9² | 13 | 11 | | 3 | 10 | | 6 | | | | | | | | | | | | | | | | | | | | 4 |
| 1 | 5 | | 4 | | 7¹ | 9 | 10 | 11³ | 6 | 8 | 12 | 3² | | 14 | 2 | 13 | | | | | | | | | | | | | | | | | | | 5 |
| 1 | 5 | 12 | 8 | 3 | 4 | 6 | 10 | 11 | 7 | 9 | | | 2¹ | | | | | | | | | | | | | | | | | | | | | | 6 |
| | 2 | 5 | | 3 | 7 | 9 | 6 | 11 | 8 | | | 10 | | 4 | 1 | | | | | | | | | | | | | | | | | | | | 7 |
| | 2 | 5 | 13 | 4 | 7 | 6 | 10¹ | 11³ | 8² | 9 | | 12 | | | 1 | 3 | 14 | | | | | | | | | | | | | | | | | | 8 |
| | 2 | 5 | 7² | 8 | | 11¹ | 9 | 6 | 12 | | | 10 | | 3 | 1 | 4 | 13 | | | | | | | | | | | | | | | | | | 9 |
| | 2 | 3 | 12 | 8 | | 13 | 11 | 6² | 9 | | | 10 | 4⁸ | | 1 | 5¹ | 7 | | | | | | | | | | | | | | | | | | 10 |
| | 2 | 5 | 7¹ | 4 | 8 | 6 | 13 | 11 | 12 | 9² | | 10 | | | 1 | | 3 | | | | | | | | | | | | | | | | | | 11 |
| | 2 | 5 | 7³ | 4 | 8 | | 12 | 11 | 13 | 9 | | 10¹ | | 6² | 1 | | 3 | 14 | | | | | | | | | | | | | | | | | 12 |
| | 2 | 5 | | 4 | 8 | 6 | 10² | 11 | 7¹ | 9 | | | 1 | | 12 | 3 | 13 | | | | | | | | | | | | | | | | | | 13 |
| 1 | 2 | 5 | 8² | 4 | 9 | 11 | | 10 | | 12 | | 3 | | | 6¹ | | | 7 | 13 | | | | | | | | | | | | | | | | 14 |
| 1 | 2 | 5⁸ | 7 | 3 | 8 | 11² | | 10 | | 12 | | 4 | 13 | 6 | | | | | 9¹ | | | | | | | | | | | | | | | | 15 |
| 1 | 2¹ | | 4 | | 7 | 10 | 12 | 11 | 9³ | 5 | 8 | 3 | | | 6² | | | | | | | | | 13 | 14 | | | | | | | | | | 16 |
| 1 | 2 | 5 | 3 | 4 | 7 | 8¹ | | 11 | 9 | 10² | | | 12 | 6 | | | | | | | | | | | 13 | | | | | | | | | | 17 |
| 1 | | 5 | 9¹ | 4 | 8 | 11 | | 10 | 13 | 12 | | 3 | | | 6² | | | | | | | | | | 2 | 7 | | | | | | | | | 18 |
| 1 | 2 | 5 | 14 | 4 | 8 | 11² | 13 | 10 | 12 | 9³ | | 3 | | | 6¹ | | | | | | | | | | | 7 | | | | | | | | | 19 |
| 1 | 2 | 5 | | 4 | 6 | 10³ | 14 | 11 | 12 | 9² | | 3 | | | 8¹ | | | | | | | | | | | 7 | 13 | | | | | | | | 20 |
| 1 | 2 | 5 | | 4 | 7 | 8² | | 9¹ | | 10³ | | 3 | 11 | 14 | | | | | | | | | | | | 6 | 13 | 12 | | | | | | | 21 |
| 1 | 2 | 5 | | 4 | 8 | 9 | | | 12 | 6¹ | | 3 | 11 | | | | | | | | | | | | | 7 | | 10 | | | | | | | 22 |
| 1² | | 5 | 12 | 4 | 8 | 9³ | | 14 | 6¹ | | | 3 | 11 | 2 | | | | | | | | | | | | 7 | | 10 | 13 | | | | | | 23 |
| 1 | 14 | 5 | 12 | 4³ | 8 | 9 | | | 6² | | | 3 | 10 | | | | | | | | | | | | | 7 | 13 | 11¹ | | | | | | | 24 |
| 1 | 2 | 5 | | 4 | 6 | 9 | | 8¹ | | | | 3 | 11 | 12 | | | | | | | | | | | | 7 | | 10 | | | | | | | 25 |
| 1 | 2 | 5¹ | 12 | | 6³ | 9 | | 14 | | 8 | | 3 | 10⁸ | 13 | | | | | | | | | | | | 7 | | 11² | | 4 | | | | | 26 |
| 1 | 2 | | 6 | | 8 | 9 | | 13 | | 5³ | | 3 | 10 | 14 | | | | | | | | | | | | 7¹ | 12 | 11² | | 4 | | | | | 27 |
| 1 | 5 | | 8 | | 7¹ | 9 | | 11 | | | | 3 | 10 | 2 | | | | | | | | | | | | | 12 | 6 | | 4 | | | | | 28 |
| 1 | 5 | | 13 | 12 | 6³ | 11 | | 14 | | 3⁸ | | | 10 | | | | | | | | | | | | | 8 | 7 | 9² | | 4¹ | 2 | | | | 29 |
| | 2³ | | 14 | 4 | 6 | 9 | | 11 | | 5² | | | 10 | | | | | | | | | | | | | 7 | 8¹ | | | 3 | 12 | 1 | 13 | | 30 |
| | | | 8 | 4 | 5 | 12 | | 11¹ | | 3 | | | 10 | | | | | | | | | | | | | 7 | 9 | 6² | | | 2 | 1 | 13 | | 31 |
| | 5 | | 9 | 4 | 7 | 12 | | | | 6 | | | 3¹ | 11³ | | | | | | | | | | | | 8 | 10² | 13 | | | 2 | 1 | 14 | | 32 |
| | 5 | 3 | | 4 | 7 | 9 | | 10¹ | | | | | 11 | | | | | | | | | | | | | 8 | 6² | 13 | | | 2 | 1 | 12 | | 33 |
| | 3 | 5 | | 4 | 6 | 11² | | 8 | | 10¹ | | | 7³ | 9 | | | | | | | | | | | | 7 | 9 | 13 | | | 2 | 1 | 12 | 14 | 34 |
| | 5 | 3² | 13 | 4 | 8 | 11 | | 10¹ | | 9 | | | 7 | | | | | | | | | | | | | 7 | 6³ | 14 | | | 2 | 1 | 12 | | 35 |
| | 5⁸ | 3 | 14 | 4 | 8 | 11² | | 12 | | 9 | | | 10 | | | | | | | | | | | | | 7¹ | 6³ | | | | 2 | 1 | 13 | | 36 |

# STIRLING ALBION

*Year Formed:* 1945. *Ground & Address:* Forthbank Stadium, Springkerse, Stirling FK7 7UJ. *Telephone:* 01786 450399.
*Fax:* 01786 448592. *Email:* admin@stirlingalbionfc.co.uk *Website:* www.stirlingalbionfc.co.uk
*Ground Capacity:* 3,808 (seated: 2,508). *Size of Pitch:* 101m × 68m.
*Chair:* Stuart Brown.
*Manager:* Greig McDonald. *Assistant Manager:* Marc McCulloch.
*Club Nickname:* 'The Binos'.
*Previous Grounds:* Annfield 1945-92.
*Record Attendance:* 26,400 v Celtic, Scottish Cup 4th rd, 14 Mar 1959 (Annfield); 3808 v Aberdeen, Scottish Cup 4th rd,
15 February 1996 (Forthbank).
*Record Transfer Fee received:* £90,000 for Stephen Nicholas to Motherwell (Mar 1999).
*Record Transfer Fee paid:* £25,000 for Craig Taggart from Falkirk (Aug 1994).
*Record Victory:* 20-0 v Selkirk, Scottish Cup 1st rd, 8 Dec 1984.
*Record Defeat:* 0-9 v Dundee U, Division I, 30 Dec 1967; 0-9 v Ross Co Scottish Cup 5th rd, 6 Feb 2010.
*Most League Appearances:* 504: Matt McPhee, 1967-81.
*Most League Goals in Season (Individual):* 27: Joe Hughes, Division II, 1969-70.
*Most Goals Overall (Individual):* 129: Billy Steele, 1971-83.

## STIRLING ALBION – SCOTTISH THIRD DIVISION 2012–13 LEAGUE RECORD

| Match No. | Date | Venue | Opponents | Result | H/T Score | Lg Pos. | Goalscorers | Atten- dance |
|---|---|---|---|---|---|---|---|---|
| 1 | Aug 11 | H | Annan Ath | W 5-1 | 4-0 | 1 | Davidson 16, Weir, G 31, Ashe 37, Clark 42, Macpherson 67 | 646 |
| 2 | 18 | A | Elgin C | L 1-3 | 1-1 | 5 | Davidson 4 | 631 |
| 3 | 25 | H | Clyde | L 0-1 | 0-1 | 7 | | 855 |
| 4 | Sept 1 | H | Queen's Park | L 1-2 | 1-1 | 8 | Flood 10 | 740 |
| 5 | 15 | A | East Stirling | L 1-3 | 0-0 | 9 | Ferry 55 | 487 |
| 6 | 22 | A | Berwick R | L 1-4 | 0-2 | 10 | White 75 | 544 |
| 7 | Oct 6 | H | Rangers | W 1-0 | 1-0 | 9 | Allison 9 | 3751 |
| 8 | 20 | A | Montrose | L 1-3 | 1-3 | 10 | Thom 7 | 527 |
| 9 | 27 | A | Peterhead | D 2-2 | 1-2 | 10 | White 31, Flood 84 | 508 |
| 10 | Nov 10 | A | Annan Ath | L 2-5 | 0-2 | 10 | Weir, G 60, Day 73 | 508 |
| 11 | 17 | H | Elgin C | L 1-4 | 1-4 | 10 | Weir, G 38 | 454 |
| 12 | 23 | A | Queen's Park | L 1-2 | 0-0 | 10 | Davidson 58 | 557 |
| 13 | Dec 8 | A | Rangers | L 0-2 | 0-0 | 10 | | 49,913 |
| 14 | 15 | H | Berwick R | W 6-3 | 4-2 | 10 | Day 17, Thom 26, White 2 (1 pen) 37, 80 (p), Ferry 45, Weir, S 83 | 427 |
| 15 | 22 | H | Peterhead | W 1-0 | 0-0 | 10 | White (pen) 67 | 416 |
| 16 | 29 | H | Montrose | L 2-3 | 2-2 | 10 | Davidson 2 27, 44 | 336 |
| 17 | Jan 2 | A | East Stirling | D 1-1 | 1-1 | 10 | Thom 24 | 621 |
| 18 | 5 | H | Queen's Park | L 2-3 | 0-1 | 10 | Ferry 2 58, 75 | 657 |
| 19 | 12 | A | Clyde | L 1-2 | 0-1 | 10 | White 61 | 912 |
| 20 | Feb 9 | H | Montrose | W 3-1 | 2-1 | 10 | White 37, Ferry 43, Day 87 | 472 |
| 21 | 12 | A | East Stirling | D 1-1 | 0-0 | 10 | Weir, G 47 | 376 |
| 22 | 16 | A | Peterhead | D 0-0 | 0-0 | 10 | | 466 |
| 23 | 19 | H | Annan Ath | W 2-1 | 1-1 | 10 | Weir, G 21, White 50 | 327 |
| 24 | 23 | H | Clyde | W 2-0 | 2-0 | 9 | McAnespie 5, Ferry 32 | 604 |
| 25 | 26 | H | Rangers | D 1-1 | 0-1 | 9 | Forsyth 51 | 3707 |
| 26 | Mar 2 | A | Elgin C | W 2-1 | 2-1 | 7 | McAnespie 2 7, 37 | 681 |
| 27 | 5 | A | Berwick R | L 0-1 | 0-0 | 7 | | 402 |
| 28 | 9 | H | East Stirling | W 9-1 | 3-0 | 7 | Gillespie (og) 28, White 4 (2 pens) 38, 42 (p), 80 (p), 90, Ferry 2 53, 70, Johnston 66, Flood 72 | 563 |
| 29 | 23 | A | Rangers | D 0-0 | 0-0 | 7 | | 44,608 |
| 30 | 30 | H | Berwick R | W 1-0 | 0-0 | 7 | Ferry 87 | 601 |
| 31 | Apr 2 | A | Queen's Park | D 2-2 | 1-0 | 7 | Thom 12, Davidson 55 | 494 |
| 32 | 6 | A | Montrose | D 2-2 | 1-1 | 7 | Ferry 7, Flood 87 | 448 |
| 33 | 13 | H | Peterhead | L 0-1 | 0-1 | 8 | | 502 |
| 34 | 20 | A | Annan Ath | W 1-0 | 1-0 | 7 | Day 2 | 488 |
| 35 | 27 | H | Elgin C | D 1-1 | 0-1 | 7 | Day 57 | 528 |
| 36 | May 4 | A | Clyde | W 2-1 | 0-1 | 7 | White (pen) 55, McGeachie 80 | 745 |

**Final League Position: 7**

**Honours**
*League Champions:* Division II 1952-53, 1957-58, 1960-61, 1964-65. Second Division 1976-77, 1990-91, 1995-96, 2009-10; *Runners-up:* Division II 1948-49, 1950-51. Second Division 2006-07. Third Division 2003-04. *Promoted to First Division:* 2006-07 (play-offs).
*League Cup:* Semi-finals 1961-62.

**Club colours:** All red with white trim.

**Goalscorers:** *League (59):* White 13 (5 pens), Ferry 10, Davidson 6, Day 5, Weir G 5, Flood 4, Thom 4, McAnespie 3, Allison 1, Ashe 1, Clark 1, Forsyth 1, Johnston 1, Macpherson 1, McGeachie 1, Weir S 1, own goal 1.
*William Hill Scottish FA Cup (5):* Weir S 2 (1 pen), McDonald 1, White 1.
*Scottish Communities League Cup (1):* Ferry 1 (1 pen).
*Ramsdens Cup (0).*

| Filler S 14 | McGeachie R 13+2 | Clark J 8+1 | Allison B 21 | Ashe D 8+11 | McCunnie J 24+4 | Macpherson G 2 | Ferry M 35+1 | Weir G 25+4 | Coyne B 1 | Davidson S 23+7 | Brass G 1+4 | McSorley D 10+4 | McClune D 29+2 | Peat M 13+2 | McAnespie K 26+2 | Flood J 10+17 | Thom G 22+1 | Weir S 4+5 | McCulloch M 9 | Day S 16+7 | White J 28+1 | McDonald Greig 1+1 | Bishop J 15 | Johnston P 17+3 | Cunningham A 2+13 | Stickler J —+1 | Crawford D 9 | Forsyth R 10+1 | Hamilton L —+1 | Forbes S —+1 | Match No. |
|---|---|---|---|---|---|---|---|---|---|---|---|---|---|---|---|---|---|---|---|---|---|---|---|---|---|---|---|---|---|---|---|
| 1 | $2^2$ | 3 | 4 | 5 | 6 | | $7^3$ | 8 | 9 | $10^1$ | 11 | 12 | 13 | 14 | | | | | | | | | | | | | | | | | 1 |
| | $2^1$ | 3 | 4 | 5 | $6^3$ | | $7^2$ | 8 | 10 | 9 | 11 | | 13 | 1 | 12 | 14 | | | | | | | | | | | | | | | 2 |
| 13 | | | $4^2$ | 5 | $7^1$ | | 8 | 10 | | 6 | | 12 | 2 | 1 | $9^3$ | 14 | 3 | 11 | | | | | | | | | | | | | 3 |
| | | | 4 | 12 | | | 9 | 11 | | 13 | | 7 | 2 | 1 | $5^3$ | $6^2$ | 3 | 14 | $8^1$ | 10 | | | | | | | | | | | 4 |
| | 2 | | 4 | 5 | 13 | | 9 | $10^3$ | | $11$ | | 8 | | 1 | | $6^1$ | 3 | 14 | $7^2$ | 12 | | | | | | | | | | | 5 |
| 1 | | | 4 | 12 | 2 | | 8 | $11^2$ | | 7 | | | | | $6^1$ | 3 | 13 | 5 | 9 | 10 | | | | | | | | | | | 6 |
| 11 | | | 4 | | | | 9 | 6 | | $7^2$ | 2 | 12 | 5 | 14 | 3 | $10^3$ | 8 | 13 | 11 | | | | | | | | | | | | 7 |
| 1 | | | 4 | 12 | | | $9^3$ | 6 | | 14 | | 7 | 2 | | 5 | $3^2$ | $10^4$ | $8^1$ | 13 | 11 | | | | | | | | | | | 8 |
| 1 | $2^1$ | | 5 | | | | 13 | 7 | | 10 | | 8 | $6^2$ | | 4 | 12 | 3 | | 9 | 11 | | | | | | | | | | | 9 |
| $1^4$ | | | 4 | | $5^1$ | | 9 | $10^2$ | | 7 | 2 | 12 | | | 13 | $8^2$ | 3 | $6^3$ | 11 | | | | | | | | | | | | 10 |
| | $5^2$ | $12^3$ | 4 | 3 | | | 7 | 10 | | 13 | | | $2^1$ | 1 | | 9 | 14 | 8 | 6 | 11 | | | | | | | | | | | 11 |
| | 12 | | | $2^2$ | | | 8 | 9 | | 11 | 14 | 13 | | 1 | | $6^1$ | | 5 | 7 | $10^3$ | 3 | 4 | | | | | | | | | 12 |
| $8^1$ | | | | | | | 9 | 11 | | 13 | | $7^4$ | 2 | 1 | 5 | 12 | $3^3$ | | $6^2$ | 10 | 14 | 4 | | | | | | | | | 13 |
| 2 | | | | | | | 8 | 7 | | $11^1$ | 14 | 6 | 1 | 5 | 12 | 3 | 13 | | $9^1$ | $10^3$ | 4 | | | | | | | | | | 14 |
| 2 | 4 | | | | | | 7 | 6 | | $11^1$ | 12 | 8 | 1 | 5 | 3 | | | 9 | $10^4$ | | | | | | | | | | | | 15 |
| 2 | $7^1$ | 12 | | | | | 8 | 6 | | 11 | 14 | 3 | 1 | 5 | 13 | 4 | $10^3$ | $9^2$ | | | | | | | | | | | | | 16 |
| | $4^2$ | 13 | | | | | 8 | 11 | | $10^3$ | 2 | $6^1$ | 1 | 5 | | $3^4$ | | 9 | | 12 | | 7 | 14 | | | | | | | | 17 |
| 2 | 3 | | $5^3$ | | | | 7 | | | $11^1$ | 8 | 1 | 4 | 13 | | 9 | 10 | | $6^2$ | 12 | 14 | | | | | | | | | | 18 |
| 2 | 8 | 4 | 14 | | | | 7 | 12 | | $11^2$ | $3^1$ | 1 | 5 | $9^3$ | 10 | 6 | 13 | | | | | | | | | | | | | | 19 |
| | 4 | | 2 | | | | 7 | 9 | | $11^1$ | 8 | 5 | 12 | 10 | 3 | 6 | 1 | | | | | | | | | | | | | | 20 |
| | 4 | | | $2^2$ | | | 6 | 9 | | $11^1$ | 7 | $5^3$ | 12 | 10 | 3 | 8 | 14 | 1 | 13 | | | | | | | | | | | | 21 |
| | $7^4$ | 2 | | | | | 8 | 11 | | 3 | 9 | 12 | 10 | 4 | $6^1$ | 1 | 5 | | | | | | | | | | | | | | 22 |
| | 2 | | | | | | 8 | $6^3$ | 12 | 7 | 14 | 13 | 4 | 10 | 3 | $9^2$ | $11^1$ | 1 | 5 | | | | | | | | | | | | 23 |
| | 2 | | | | | | 8 | $11^1$ | 13 | 7 | 6 | 14 | 3 | 10 | 4 | $9^1$ | $12^2$ | 1 | 5 | | | | | | | | | | | | 24 |
| | 3 | 12 | 2 | 8 | | | 6 | 9 | | $7^1$ | | $11^2$ | 4 | 10 | 13 | 1 | 5 | | | | | | | | | | | | | | 25 |
| 1 | $3^1$ | 13 | 2 | 7 | | | $11^2$ | 8 | | 6 | 14 | 12 | 10 | 4 | $9^3$ | | 5 | | | | | | | | | | | | | | 26 |
| 1 | 3 | | 2 | 8 | | | 11 | $7^2$ | | 6 | 12 | 13 | 10 | 4 | $9^1$ | 5 | | | | | | | | | | | | | | | 27 |
| 1 | | 4 | 14 | 2 | 7 | | $11^1$ | 6 | | $8^2$ | 13 | 10 | 3 | $9^3$ | 12 | 5 | | | | | | | | | | | | | | | 28 |
| 1 | 3 | | 8 | 12 | | | $11^1$ | 7 | | $6^2$ | 3 | 10 | 4 | $9^3$ | 14 | 5 | | | | | | | | | | | | | | | 29 |
| 1 | $3^3$ | 14 | 2 | 7 | 12 | | 11 | 8 | | 5 | $6^1$ | 4 | 10 | $9^2$ | 13 | | | | | | | | | | | | | | | | 30 |
| 1 | | 13 | 2 | 9 | $8^2$ | | $11^2$ | 7 | | 5 | $6^1$ | 3 | 10 | 12 | 14 | 4 | | | | | | | | | | | | | | | 31 |
| 1 | | 12 | 2 | 10 | $8^2$ | | 13 | 9 | | 7 | 14 | 4 | 11 | 3 | $6^2$ | $5^1$ | | | | | | | | | | | | | | | 32 |
| 1 | | | $2^2$ | 8 | 6 | | $11^1$ | 7 | | 5 | 14 | 3 | 13 | 10 | 4 | $9^3$ | 12 | | | | | | | | | | | | | | 33 |
| | 7 | | 5 | 2 | 8 | | 12 | $11^1$ | | 3 | $6^2$ | 4 | 9 | $10^3$ | | 13 | 14 | 1 | | | | | | | | | | | | | 34 |
| | $2^2$ | 11 | $4^3$ | 13 | 6 | | 5 | | | 7 | | 3 | 8 | 10 | $9^1$ | 14 | 1 | 12 | | | | | | | | | | | | | 35 |
| | 2 | 7 | 5 | 3 | 8 | | | $4^1$ | 9 | 6 | 10 | | $11^2$ | 12 | 1 | 13 | | | | | | | | | | | | | | | 36 |

# STRANRAER

*Year Formed:* 1870. *Ground & Address:* Stair Park, London Rd, Stranraer DG9 8BS. *Telephone and Fax:* 01776 703271.
*E-mail:* secretary@stranraerfc.org *Website:* www.stranraerfc.org
*Ground Capacity:* 6,250 (seated: 1,830). *Size of Pitch:* 103m × 64m.
*Chairman:* Robert Rice. *Vice-Chairman:* Iain Dougan. *Secretary:* Hilde Law.
*Manager:* Stephen Aitken. *Assistant Manager:* Stephen Farrell. *Physio:* Walter Cannon.
*Club Nicknames:* 'The Blues', 'The Clayholers'.
*Previous Grounds:* None.
*Record Attendance:* 6500 v Rangers, Scottish Cup 1st rd, 24 Jan 1948.
*Record Transfer Fee received:* £90,000 for Mark Campbell to Ayr U (1999).
*Record Transfer Fee paid:* £35,000 for Michael Moore from St Johnstone (Mar 2005).
*Record Victory:* 9-0 v St Cuthbert Wanderers, Scottish Cup 2nd rd, 23 Oct 2010; 9-0 v Wigtown & Bladnoch, Scottish Cup 2nd rd, 22 Oct 2011.
*Record Defeat:* 1-11 v Queen of the South, Scottish Cup 1st rd, 16 Jan 1932.
*Most League Appearances:* 301: Keith Knox, 1986-90; 1999-2001.
*Most League Goals in Season (Individual):* 27: Derek Frye, 1977-78.
*Most Goals Overall (Individual):* 115: Jim Campbell, 1965-75.

## STRANRAER – SCOTTISH SECOND DIVISION 2012–13 LEAGUE RECORD

| Match No. | Date | Venue | Opponents | Result | | H/T Score | Lg Pos. | Goalscorers | Attendance |
|---|---|---|---|---|---|---|---|---|---|
| 1 | Aug 11 | H | Arbroath | D | 1-1 | 1-0 | 8 | Moore [22] | 290 |
| 2 | 18 | A | Forfar Ath | L | 0-4 | 0-1 | 9 | | 449 |
| 3 | 25 | H | Stenhousemuir | D | 1-1 | 0-1 | 8 | Borris [59] | 290 |
| 4 | Sept 1 | H | Ayr U | W | 2-0 | 2-0 | 7 | Malcolm 2 [34, 38] | 772 |
| 5 | 15 | A | Albion R | L | 1-2 | 0-0 | 8 | Aitken [60] | 376 |
| 6 | 22 | A | Alloa Ath | L | 0-3 | 0-2 | 8 | | 429 |
| 7 | 29 | H | East Fife | L | 2-6 | 1-3 | 10 | Borris [44], Malcolm [78] | 475 |
| 8 | Oct 6 | H | Queen of the S | L | 0-2 | 0-1 | 10 | | 1015 |
| 9 | 20 | A | Brechin C | L | 0-3 | 0-2 | 10 | | 485 |
| 10 | 27 | H | Forfar Ath | W | 4-1 | 2-1 | 10 | Malcolm 2 [4, 73], Aitken [40], McKeown [90] | 258 |
| 11 | Nov 17 | A | Ayr U | L | 1-2 | 1-0 | 10 | Moore [31] | 1006 |
| 12 | 21 | A | Arbroath | L | 1-2 | 0-1 | 10 | Love [47] | 387 |
| 13 | 24 | H | Albion R | D | 1-1 | 0-1 | 10 | Malcolm (pen) [90] | 298 |
| 14 | Dec 15 | H | Alloa Ath | W | 3-2 | 1-0 | 9 | Dunlop [44], Malcolm [56], Love [79] | 245 |
| 15 | 18 | A | East Fife | W | 1-0 | 1-0 | 9 | Malcolm [34] | 441 |
| 16 | 26 | A | Queen of the S | L | 1-4 | 1-1 | 9 | McKeown [20] | 2122 |
| 17 | 29 | H | Brechin C | L | 0-2 | 0-1 | 9 | | 326 |
| 18 | Jan 2 | A | Albion R | W | 3-2 | 2-0 | 9 | Aitken 2 (1 pen) [14, 86 (p)], Borris [20] | 367 |
| 19 | 5 | H | Ayr U | L | 0-1 | 0-1 | 9 | | 803 |
| 20 | 12 | A | Stenhousemuir | D | 0-0 | 0-0 | 9 | | 484 |
| 21 | 26 | A | Alloa Ath | L | 1-4 | 0-1 | 9 | Gallagher [59] | 451 |
| 22 | Feb 2 | H | East Fife | W | 3-1 | 2-0 | 9 | Gribben 2 [9, 29], Winter [58] | 254 |
| 23 | 16 | H | Queen of the S | L | 0-5 | 0-3 | 9 | | 810 |
| 24 | 19 | H | Arbroath | W | 2-0 | 1-0 | 9 | Morrison (og) [21], Love [58] | 169 |
| 25 | 23 | H | Stenhousemuir | D | 1-1 | 1-1 | 9 | Gribben [3] | 346 |
| 26 | Mar 2 | A | Forfar Ath | L | 1-3 | 0-3 | 9 | Malcolm [63] | 448 |
| 27 | 9 | H | Albion R | W | 3-2 | 1-2 | 8 | Malcolm 3 [40, 56, 74] | 266 |
| 28 | 16 | A | Ayr U | L | 1-2 | 0-2 | 8 | Malcolm [68] | 1022 |
| 29 | 30 | H | Alloa Ath | L | 1-2 | 0-0 | 8 | Love [87] | 322 |
| 30 | Apr 6 | H | Brechin C | W | 3-2 | 1-2 | 8 | Malcolm 2 (1 pen) [28 (p), 71], Aitken [77] | 299 |
| 31 | 9 | A | East Fife | D | 1-1 | 0-0 | 8 | Gribben [62] | 426 |
| 32 | 13 | A | Queen of the S | L | 0-2 | 0-1 | 8 | | 1806 |
| 33 | 20 | A | Arbroath | L | 0-1 | 0-1 | 8 | | 562 |
| 34 | 23 | A | Brechin C | D | 2-2 | 1-0 | 8 | One [44], Malcolm [86] | 401 |
| 35 | 27 | H | Forfar Ath | L | 0-3 | 0-2 | 8 | | 422 |
| 36 | May 4 | A | Stenhousemuir | W | 2-1 | 2-1 | 8 | Malcolm 2 (1 pen) [4, 44 (p)] | 818 |

**Final League Position: 8**

**Honours**
*League Champions:* Second Division 1993-94, 1997-98. Third Division 2003-04.
*Runners-up:* Second Division 2004-05, Third Division 2007-08. Promoted to Second Division 2011-12 (play-offs).
*Scottish Cup:* Quarter-finals 2003
*League Challenge Cup Winners:* 1996-97.
*Qualifying Cup Winners:* 1937.

**Club colours:** Shirt: Royal blue with black trim. Shorts: White with black trim. Socks: Royal blue.

**Goalscorers:** *League (43):* Malcolm 18 (3 pens), Aitken 5 (1 pen), Gribben 4, Love 4, Borris 3, McKeown 2, Moore 2, Dunlop 1, Gallagher 1, One 1, Winter 1, own goal 1.
*William Hill Scottish FA Cup (5):* Winter 3, Aitken 1, Malcolm 1.
*Scottish Communities League Cup (0).*
*Ramsdens Cup (1):* Winter 1.

| Mitchell D 32 | McKeown F 36 | Staunton M 29+1 | Dunlop M 35 | Winter S 32+2 | Gallagher G 36 | Aitken C 33 | Borris R 25+6 | Malcolm C 36 | Love R 19+14 | Moore M 13+17 | Kinnaird Lloyd 25+5 | Agnew D 2+7 | Forde A —+3 | Wright M 2+11 | Wood K —+1 | Cadwell R 1+2 | One A 6+10 | MacGregor D 13+1 | Phinn N 4+2 | Campbell J 2+8 | Gribben D 12+3 | Stewart C 3 | Match No. |
|---|---|---|---|---|---|---|---|---|---|---|---|---|---|---|---|---|---|---|---|---|---|---|---|
| 1 | 2 | 3 | $4^1$ | 5 | 6 | 7 | $8^2$ | 9 | 10 | $11^3$ | 12 | 13 | 14 | | | | | | | | | | 1 |
| 1 | 4 | 2 | 3 | 6 | 7 | 8 | $9^2$ | $11^3$ | 5 | $10^1$ | 13 | | | 12 | 14 | | | | | | | | 2 |
| 1 | 4 | 3 | 5 | 6 | 7 | 8 | $9^2$ | 11 | $10^1$ | | | 2 | 13 | 12 | | | | | | | | | 3 |
| 1 | 4 | 3 | 5 | 6 | 7 | 8 | $10^2$ | $11^3$ | $9^1$ | | | 2 | 13 | 14 | 12 | | | | | | | | 4 |
| 1 | 4 | 3 | $5^3$ | $9^1$ | 8 | 7 | $6^2$ | 11 | 10 | | | 2 | 13 | 12 | 14 | | | | | | | | 5 |
| $1^4$ | 4 | 3 | 5 | $6^3$ | 8 | 7 | $9^2$ | 11 | $10^1$ | 13 | | 2 | | 14 | 12 | | | | | | | | 6 |
| | 3 | 4 | 5 | 6 | 7 | 8 | 11 | 10 | | 2 | | 9 | | | 1 | | | | | | | | 7 |
| 1 | 3 | $2^3$ | 4 | 7 | 5 | $8^1$ | 10 | 11 | 9 | 12 | 14 | $6^2$ | 13 | | | | | | | | | | 8 |
| 1 | 4 | 2 | 3 | 6 | 5 | 7 | 11 | $10^2$ | $9^2$ | 12 | 14 | $8^1$ | 13 | | | | | | | | | | 9 |
| 1 | 3 | 2 | 4 | $9^3$ | 8 | $7^4$ | $6^1$ | 11 | 14 | $10^2$ | 5 | | | | | | | 13 | | | | | 10 |
| 1 | 3 | 2 | 4 | 7 | 8 | 11 | 9 | $10^1$ | 6 | | | | | | | | | 12 | 5 | | | | 11 |
| 1 | 4 | 2 | 5 | 6 | 7 | 11 | 9 | $10^2$ | | | | 12 | | | | | | 13 | 3 | $8^1$ | | | 12 |
| 1 | 3 | 2 | 4 | 6 | 7 | 11 | 9 | 10 | | | | 12 | | | | | | 5 | | $8^1$ | | | 13 |
| 1 | 3 | 2 | 4 | 9 | 6 | 8 | $11^3$ | 12 | 13 | | | 14 | | | | | | $10^2$ | 5 | $7^1$ | | | 14 |
| 1 | 3 | 2 | 4 | 6 | $8^3$ | 7 | 13 | 11 | $9^2$ | 12 | | | | | | | | $10^1$ | 5 | 14 | | | 15 |
| 1 | 4 | $2^1$ | 3 | $6^3$ | 7 | 8 | 13 | 11 | 9 | $10^2$ | | | | | | | 14 | 5 | | 12 | | | 16 |
| 1 | 3 | 4 | 6 | 2 | 8 | 9 | $11^3$ | 12 | 13 | | | 14 | | | | | | $10^2$ | 5 | $7^1$ | | | 17 |
| 1 | 4 | 14 | 3 | 6 | 7 | $8^3$ | $9^2$ | $11^1$ | 12 | 10 | | 2 | 13 | | | | | 5 | | | | | 18 |
| 1 | 3 | | 4 | 6 | 7 | 8 | $9^2$ | 11 | 12 | $10^1$ | | 2 | 13 | | | | | 5 | | | | | 19 |
| 1 | 3 | | 4 | $6^2$ | 8 | 7 | $9^3$ | 11 | 13 | $10^1$ | | 2 | | | | | | 12 | 5 | | 14 | | 20 |
| 1 | 3 | | 4 | 9 | 8 | 7 | 12 | 11 | 13 | | | 2 | | | | | | $10^2$ | 5 | | $6^1$ | | 21 |
| 1 | 3 | | 4 | $6^3$ | 7 | 8 | 9 | 10 | 14 | 13 | | 2 | | | | | | $5^1$ | | 12 | $11^2$ | | 22 |
| $1^4$ | 3 | 5 | 4 | 6 | 7 | 8 | $9^3$ | 11 | 13 | | | $2^1$ | | | | | | 12 | | 14 | $10^2$ | | 23 |
| | 3 | 5 | 4 | $6^2$ | $7^1$ | 8 | 9 | 11 | 13 | 14 | | 2 | | | | | | | | 12 | $10^3$ | 1 | 24 |
| | 3 | 5 | 4 | | 7 | 8 | 9 | 10 | 12 | $11^2$ | | 2 | | | | | | | 13 | | $6^1$ | 1 | 25 |
| | 3 | $5^3$ | 4 | 6 | 7 | 8 | $9^1$ | 11 | 13 | 10 | | $2^2$ | | | | | | | | 14 | 12 | 1 | 26 |
| 1 | 3 | 5 | 4 | 6 | 7 | $8^3$ | 12 | 11 | $9^1$ | 13 | | 2 | | | | | | | | 14 | $10^2$ | | 27 |
| 1 | 3 | 5 | 4 | 6 | 8 | 7 | 13 | 11 | $9^1$ | 12 | | $2^2$ | | | | | | | | | 10 | | 28 |
| 1 | 3 | | 4 | $9^2$ | 7 | 8 | 12 | 6 | 13 | $10^1$ | | 2 | | | | | | 14 | | $5^3$ | 11 | | 29 |
| 1 | 3 | 5 | 4 | 7 | 8 | 9 | 10 | $6^1$ | 13 | | | 2 | | | | | | | | 12 | $11^2$ | | 30 |
| 1 | 3 | 5 | 4 | 13 | 7 | 8 | $9^3$ | 11 | $6^2$ | 12 | | 2 | | | | | | | | 14 | $10^1$ | | 31 |
| 1 | 4 | 5 | 3 | 13 | 8 | 7 | 9 | 11 | $6^2$ | 12 | | 2 | | | | | | | | | $10^1$ | | 32 |
| 1 | 3 | 5 | 4 | $6^1$ | 8 | 7 | $9^2$ | 11 | 12 | 13 | | 2 | | | | | | | | 14 | $10^3$ | | 33 |
| 1 | 3 | 5 | 4 | $6^1$ | 8 | 7 | 11 | $9^3$ | 13 | | | 2 | | | | | | $10^2$ | | 14 | 12 | | 34 |
| 1 | 3 | 5 | $4^1$ | $6^2$ | 7 | 8 | 9 | 11 | 13 | | | 2 | | | | | | $10^3$ | 12 | | 14 | | 35 |
| 1 | 3 | 5 | | $6^1$ | 7 | 8 | 9 | $11^3$ | 12 | 13 | | 2 | | | | | | 14 | | 4 | $10^2$ | | 36 |

# SCOTTISH LEAGUE HONOURS 1890–2013

*On goal average (ratio)/difference.   †Held jointly after indecisive play-off.   ‡Won on deciding match.
¶Two points deducted for fielding ineligible player. Competition suspended 1940–45 during war;
Regional Leagues operating.   ‡‡Two points deducted for registration irregularities.
§Not promoted after play-offs.   §§Ten points deducted for entering administration.

## PREMIER LEAGUE
*Maximum points: 108*

|  | First | Pts | Second | Pts | Third | Pts |
|---|---|---|---|---|---|---|
| 1998–99 | Rangers | 77 | Celtic | 71 | St Johnstone | 57 |
| 1999–2000 | Rangers | 90 | Celtic | 69 | Hearts | 54 |

*Maximum points: 114*

|  | First | Pts | Second | Pts | Third | Pts |
|---|---|---|---|---|---|---|
| 2000–01 | Celtic | 97 | Rangers | 82 | Hibernian | 66 |
| 2001–02 | Celtic | 103 | Rangers | 85 | Livingston | 58 |
| 2002–03 | Rangers* | 97 | Celtic | 97 | Hearts | 63 |
| 2003–04 | Celtic | 98 | Rangers | 81 | Hearts | 68 |
| 2004–05 | Rangers | 93 | Celtic | 92 | Hibernian* | 61 |
| 2005–06 | Celtic | 91 | Hearts | 74 | Rangers | 73 |
| 2006–07 | Celtic | 84 | Rangers | 72 | Aberdeen | 65 |
| 2007–08 | Celtic | 89 | Rangers | 86 | Motherwell | 60 |
| 2008–09 | Rangers | 86 | Celtic | 82 | Hearts | 59 |
| 2009–10 | Rangers | 87 | Celtic | 81 | Dundee U | 63 |
| 2010–11 | Rangers | 93 | Celtic | 92 | Hearts | 63 |
| 2011–12 | Celtic | 93 | Rangers§§ | 73 | Motherwell | 62 |
| 2012–13 | Celtic | 79 | Motherwell | 63 | St Johnstone | 56 |

## PREMIER DIVISION
*Maximum points: 72*

|  | First | Pts | Second | Pts | Third | Pts |
|---|---|---|---|---|---|---|
| 1975–76 | Rangers | 54 | Celtic | 48 | Hibernian | 43 |
| 1976–77 | Celtic | 55 | Rangers | 46 | Aberdeen | 43 |
| 1977–78 | Rangers | 55 | Aberdeen | 53 | Dundee U | 40 |
| 1978–79 | Celtic | 48 | Rangers | 45 | Dundee U | 44 |
| 1979–80 | Aberdeen | 48 | Celtic | 47 | St Mirren | 42 |
| 1980–81 | Celtic | 56 | Aberdeen | 49 | Rangers* | 44 |
| 1981–82 | Celtic | 55 | Aberdeen | 53 | Rangers | 43 |
| 1982–83 | Dundee U | 56 | Celtic* | 55 | Aberdeen | 55 |
| 1983–84 | Aberdeen | 57 | Celtic | 50 | Dundee U | 47 |
| 1984–85 | Aberdeen | 59 | Celtic | 52 | Dundee U | 47 |
| 1985–86 | Celtic* | 50 | Hearts | 50 | Dundee U | 47 |

*Maximum points: 88*

|  | First | Pts | Second | Pts | Third | Pts |
|---|---|---|---|---|---|---|
| 1986–87 | Rangers | 69 | Celtic | 63 | Dundee U | 60 |
| 1987–88 | Celtic | 72 | Hearts | 62 | Rangers | 60 |

*Maximum points: 72*

|  | First | Pts | Second | Pts | Third | Pts |
|---|---|---|---|---|---|---|
| 1988–89 | Rangers | 56 | Aberdeen | 50 | Celtic | 46 |
| 1989–90 | Rangers | 51 | Aberdeen* | 44 | Hearts | 44 |
| 1990–91 | Rangers | 55 | Aberdeen | 53 | Celtic* | 41 |

*Maximum points: 88*

|  | First | Pts | Second | Pts | Third | Pts |
|---|---|---|---|---|---|---|
| 1991–92 | Rangers | 72 | Hearts | 63 | Celtic | 62 |
| 1992–93 | Rangers | 73 | Aberdeen | 64 | Celtic | 60 |
| 1993–94 | Rangers | 58 | Aberdeen | 55 | Motherwell | 54 |

*Maximum points: 108*

|  | First | Pts | Second | Pts | Third | Pts |
|---|---|---|---|---|---|---|
| 1994–95 | Rangers | 69 | Motherwell | 54 | Hibernian | 53 |
| 1995–96 | Rangers | 87 | Celtic | 83 | Aberdeen* | 55 |
| 1996–97 | Rangers | 80 | Celtic | 75 | Dundee U | 60 |
| 1997–98 | Celtic | 74 | Rangers | 72 | Hearts | 67 |

## FIRST DIVISION
*Maximum points: 52*

|  | First | Pts | Second | Pts | Third | Pts |
|---|---|---|---|---|---|---|
| 1975–76 | Partick Th | 41 | Kilmarnock | 35 | Montrose | 30 |

*Maximum points: 78*

|  | First | Pts | Second | Pts | Third | Pts |
|---|---|---|---|---|---|---|
| 1976–77 | St Mirren | 62 | Clydebank | 58 | Dundee | 51 |
| 1977–78 | Morton* | 58 | Hearts | 58 | Dundee | 57 |
| 1978–79 | Dundee | 55 | Kilmarnock* | 54 | Clydebank | 54 |
| 1979–80 | Hearts | 53 | Airdrieonians | 51 | Ayr U* | 44 |
| 1980–81 | Hibernian | 57 | Dundee | 52 | St Johnstone | 51 |
| 1981–82 | Motherwell | 61 | Kilmarnock | 51 | Hearts | 50 |
| 1982–83 | St Johnstone | 55 | Hearts | 54 | Clydebank | 50 |
| 1983–84 | Morton | 54 | Dumbarton | 51 | Partick Th | 46 |
| 1984–85 | Motherwell | 50 | Clydebank | 48 | Falkirk | 45 |
| 1985–86 | Hamilton A | 56 | Falkirk | 45 | Kilmarnock | 44 |

*Maximum points: 88*

|  | First | Pts | Second | Pts | Third | Pts |
|---|---|---|---|---|---|---|
| 1986–87 | Morton | 57 | Dunfermline Ath | 56 | Dumbarton | 53 |
| 1987–88 | Hamilton A | 56 | Meadowbank Th | 52 | Clydebank | 49 |

|  | First | Pts | Second | Pts | Third | Pts |
|---|---|---|---|---|---|---|
| | | | *Maximum points: 78* | | | |
| 1988–89 | Dunfermline Ath | 54 | Falkirk | 52 | Clydebank | 48 |
| 1989–90 | St Johnstone | 58 | Airdrieonians | 54 | Clydebank | 44 |
| 1990–91 | Falkirk | 54 | Airdrieonians | 53 | Dundee | 52 |
| | | | *Maximum points: 88* | | | |
| 1991–92 | Dundee | 58 | Partick Th* | 57 | Hamilton A | 57 |
| 1992–93 | Raith R | 65 | Kilmarnock | 54 | Dunfermline Ath | 52 |
| 1993–94 | Falkirk | 66 | Dunfermline Ath | 65 | Airdrieonians | 54 |
| | | | *Maximum points: 108* | | | |
| 1994–95 | Raith R | 69 | Dunfermline Ath* | 68 | Dundee | 68 |
| 1995–96 | Dunfermline Ath | 71 | Dundee U* | 67 | Greenock Morton | 67 |
| 1996–97 | St Johnstone | 80 | Airdieonians | 60 | Dundee* | 58 |
| 1997–98 | Dundee | 70 | Falkirk | 65 | Raith R* | 60 |
| 1998–99 | Hibernian | 89 | Falkirk | 66 | Ayr U | 62 |
| 1999–2000 | St Mirren | 76 | Dunfermline Ath | 71 | Falkirk | 68 |
| 2000–01 | Livingston | 76 | Ayr U | 69 | Falkirk | 56 |
| 2001–02 | Partick Th | 66 | Airdrieonians | 56 | Ayr U | 52 |
| 2002–03 | Falkirk | 81 | Clyde | 72 | St Johnstone | 67 |
| 2003–04 | Inverness CT | 70 | Clyde | 69 | St Johnstone | 57 |
| 2004–05 | Falkirk | 75 | St Mirren* | 60 | Clyde | 60 |
| 2005–06 | St Mirren | 76 | St Johnstone | 66 | Hamilton A | 59 |
| 2006–07 | Gretna | 66 | St Johnstone | 65 | Dundee* | 53 |
| 2007–08 | Hamilton A | 76 | Dundee | 69 | St Johnstone | 58 |
| 2008–09 | St Johnstone | 65 | Partick Th | 55 | Dunfermline Ath | 51 |
| 2009–10 | Inverness CT | 73 | Dundee | 61 | Dunfermline Ath | 58 |
| 2010–11 | Dunfermline Ath | 70 | Raith R | 60 | Falkirk | 58 |
| 2011–12 | Ross Co | 79 | Dundee | 55 | Falkirk | 52 |
| 2012–13 | Partick Th | 78 | Greenock Morton | 67 | Falkirk | 53 |

## SECOND DIVISION

|  | First | Pts | Second | Pts | Third | Pts |
|---|---|---|---|---|---|---|
| | | | *Maximum points: 52* | | | |
| 1975–76 | Clydebank* | 40 | Raith R | 40 | Alloa Ath | 35 |
| | | | *Maximum points: 78* | | | |
| 1976–77 | Stirling Alb | 55 | Alloa Ath | 51 | Dunfermline Ath | 50 |
| 1977–78 | Clyde* | 53 | Raith R | 53 | Dunfermline Ath | 48 |
| 1978–79 | Berwick R | 54 | Dunfermline Ath | 52 | Falkirk | 50 |
| 1979–80 | Falkirk | 50 | East Stirling | 49 | Forfar Ath | 46 |
| 1980–81 | Queen's Park | 50 | Queen of the S | 46 | Cowdenbeath | 45 |
| 1981–82 | Clyde | 59 | Alloa Ath* | 50 | Arbroath | 50 |
| 1982–83 | Brechin C | 55 | Meadowbank Th | 54 | Arbroath | 49 |
| 1983–84 | Forfar Ath | 63 | East Fife | 47 | Berwick R | 43 |
| 1984–85 | Montrose | 53 | Alloa Ath | 50 | Dunfermline Ath | 49 |
| 1985–86 | Dunfermline Ath | 57 | Queen of the S | 55 | Meadowbank Th | 49 |
| 1986–87 | Meadowbank Th | 55 | Raith R* | 52 | Stirling Alb* | 52 |
| 1987–88 | Ayr U | 61 | St Johnstone | 59 | Queen's Park | 51 |
| 1988–89 | Albion R | 50 | Alloa Ath | 45 | Brechin C | 43 |
| 1989–90 | Brechin C | 49 | Kilmarnock | 48 | Stirling Alb | 47 |
| 1990–91 | Stirling Alb | 54 | Montrose | 46 | Cowdenbeath | 45 |
| 1991–92 | Dumbarton | 52 | Cowdenbeath | 51 | Alloa Ath | 50 |
| 1992–93 | Clyde | 54 | Brechin C* | 53 | Stranraer | 53 |
| 1993–94 | Stranraer | 56 | Berwick R | 48 | Stenhousemuir* | 47 |
| | | | *Maximum points: 108* | | | |
| 1994–95 | Greenock Morton | 64 | Dumbarton | 60 | Stirling Alb | 58 |
| 1995–96 | Stirling Alb | 81 | East Fife | 67 | Berwick R | 60 |
| 1996–97 | Ayr U | 77 | Hamilton A | 74 | Livingston | 64 |
| 1997–98 | Stranraer | 61 | Clydebank | 60 | Livingston | 59 |
| 1998–99 | Livingston | 77 | Inverness CT | 72 | Clyde | 53 |
| 1999–2000 | Clyde | 65 | Alloa Ath | 64 | Ross Co | 62 |
| 2000–01 | Partick Th | 75 | Arbroath | 58 | Berwick R* | 54 |
| 2001–02 | Queen of the S | 67 | Alloa Ath | 59 | Forfar Ath | 53 |
| 2002–03 | Raith R | 59 | Brechin C | 55 | Airdrie U | 54 |
| 2003–04 | Airdrie U | 70 | Hamilton A | 62 | Dumbarton | 60 |
| 2004–05 | Brechin C | 72 | Stranraer | 63 | Greenock Morton | 62 |
| 2005–06 | Gretna | 88 | Greenock Morton§ | 70 | Peterhead*§ | 57 |
| 2006–07 | Greenock Morton | 77 | Stirling Alb | 69 | Raith R§ | 62 |
| 2007–08 | Ross Co | 73 | Airdrie U | 66 | Raith R§ | 60 |
| 2008–09 | Raith R | 76 | Ayr U | 74 | Brechin C§ | 62 |
| 2009–10 | Stirling Alb* | 65 | Alloa Ath§ | 65 | Cowdenbeath | 54 |
| 2010–11 | Livingston | 82 | Ayr U* | 59 | Forfar Ath§ | 59 |
| 2011–12 | Cowdenbeath | 71 | Arbroath§ | 63 | Dumbarton | 58 |
| 2012–13 | Queen of the S | 92 | Alloa Ath | 67 | Brechin C | 61 |

## THIRD DIVISION
*Maximum points: 108*

| | First | Pts | Second | Pts | Third | Pts |
|---|---|---|---|---|---|---|
| 1994–95 | Forfar Ath | 80 | Montrose | 67 | Ross Co | 60 |
| 1995–96 | Livingston | 72 | Brechin C | 63 | Inverness CT | 57 |
| 1996–97 | Inverness CT | 76 | Forfar Ath* | 67 | Ross Co | 67 |
| 1997–98 | Alloa Ath | 76 | Arbroath | 68 | Ross Co* | 67 |
| 1998–99 | Ross Co | 77 | Stenhousemuir | 64 | Brechin C | 59 |
| 1999–2000 | Queen's Park | 69 | Berwick R | 66 | Forfar Ath | 61 |
| 2000–01 | Hamilton A* | 76 | Cowdenbeath | 76 | Brechin C | 72 |
| 2001–02 | Brechin C | 73 | Dumbarton | 61 | Albion R | 59 |
| 2002–03 | Greenock Morton | 72 | East Fife | 71 | Albion R | 70 |
| 2003–04 | Stranraer | 79 | Stirling Alb | 77 | Gretna | 68 |
| 2004–05 | Gretna | 98 | Peterhead | 78 | Cowdenbeath | 51 |
| 2005–06 | Cowdenbeath* | 76 | Berwick R§ | 76 | Stenhousemuir§ | 73 |
| 2006–07 | Berwick R | 75 | Arbroath§ | 70 | Queen's Park | 68 |
| 2007–08 | East Fife | 88 | Stranraer | 65 | Montrose§ | 59 |
| 2008–09 | Dumbarton | 67 | Cowdenbeath§ | 63 | East Stirling§ | 61 |
| 2009–10 | Livingston | 78 | Forfar Ath | 63 | East Stirling§ | 61 |
| 2010–11 | Arbroath | 66 | Albion R | 61 | Queen's Park*§ | 59 |
| 2011–12 | Alloa Ath | 77 | Queen's Park§ | 63 | Stranraer§ | 58 |
| 2012–13 | Rangers | 83 | Peterhead§ | 59 | Queen's Park§ | 56 |

## DIVISION I to 1974–75
*Maximum points: a 36; b 44; c 40; d 52; e 60; f 68; g 76; h 84.*

| | First | Pts | Second | Pts | Third | Pts |
|---|---|---|---|---|---|---|
| 1890–91a | Dumbarton† | 29 | Rangers† | 29 | Celtic | 21 |
| 1891–92b | Dumbarton | 37 | Celtic | 35 | Hearts | 34 |
| 1892–93a | Celtic | 29 | Rangers | 28 | St Mirren | 20 |
| 1893–94a | Celtic | 29 | Hearts | 26 | St Bernard's | 23 |
| 1894–95a | Hearts | 31 | Celtic | 26 | Rangers | 22 |
| 1895–96a | Celtic | 30 | Rangers | 26 | Hibernian | 24 |
| 1896–97a | Hearts | 28 | Hibernian | 26 | Rangers | 25 |
| 1897–98a | Celtic | 33 | Rangers | 29 | Hibernian | 22 |
| 1898–99a | Rangers | 36 | Hearts | 26 | Celtic | 24 |
| 1899–1900a | Rangers | 32 | Celtic | 25 | Hibernian | 24 |
| 1900–01c | Rangers | 35 | Celtic | 29 | Hibernian | 25 |
| 1901–02a | Rangers | 28 | Celtic | 26 | Hearts | 22 |
| 1902–03b | Hibernian | 37 | Dundee | 31 | Rangers | 29 |
| 1903–04d | Third Lanark | 43 | Hearts | 39 | Celtic* | 38 |
| 1904–05d | Celtic‡ | 41 | Rangers | 41 | Third Lanark | 35 |
| 1905–06e | Celtic | 49 | Hearts | 43 | Airdrieonians | 38 |
| 1906–07f | Celtic | 55 | Dundee | 48 | Rangers | 45 |
| 1907–08f | Celtic | 55 | Falkirk | 51 | Rangers | 50 |
| 1908–09f | Celtic | 51 | Dundee | 50 | Clyde | 48 |
| 1909–10f | Celtic | 54 | Falkirk | 52 | Rangers | 46 |
| 1910–11f | Rangers | 52 | Aberdeen | 48 | Falkirk | 44 |
| 1911–12f | Rangers | 51 | Celtic | 45 | Clyde | 42 |
| 1912–13f | Rangers | 53 | Celtic | 49 | Hearts* | 41 |
| 1913–14g | Celtic | 65 | Rangers | 59 | Hearts* | 54 |
| 1914–15g | Celtic | 65 | Hearts | 61 | Rangers | 50 |
| 1915–16g | Celtic | 67 | Rangers | 56 | Morton | 51 |
| 1916–17g | Celtic | 64 | Morton | 54 | Rangers | 53 |
| 1917–18f | Rangers | 56 | Celtic | 55 | Kilmarnock* | 43 |
| 1918–19f | Celtic | 58 | Rangers | 57 | Morton | 47 |
| 1919–20h | Rangers | 71 | Celtic | 68 | Motherwell | 57 |
| 1920–21h | Rangers | 76 | Celtic | 66 | Hearts | 50 |
| 1921–22h | Celtic | 67 | Rangers | 66 | Raith R | 51 |
| 1922–23g | Rangers | 55 | Airdrieonians | 50 | Celtic | 46 |
| 1923–24g | Rangers | 59 | Airdrieonians | 50 | Celtic | 46 |
| 1924–25g | Rangers | 60 | Airdrieonians | 57 | Hibernian | 52 |
| 1925–26g | Celtic | 58 | Airdrieonians* | 50 | Hearts | 50 |
| 1926–27g | Rangers | 56 | Motherwell | 51 | Celtic | 49 |
| 1927–28g | Rangers | 60 | Celtic* | 55 | Motherwell | 55 |
| 1928–29g | Rangers | 67 | Celtic | 51 | Motherwell | 50 |
| 1929–30g | Rangers | 60 | Motherwell | 55 | Aberdeen | 53 |
| 1930–31g | Rangers | 60 | Celtic | 58 | Motherwell | 56 |
| 1931–32g | Motherwell | 66 | Rangers | 61 | Celtic | 48 |
| 1932–33g | Rangers | 62 | Motherwell | 59 | Hearts | 50 |
| 1933–34g | Rangers | 66 | Motherwell | 62 | Celtic | 47 |
| 1934–35g | Rangers | 55 | Celtic | 52 | Hearts | 50 |
| 1935–36g | Celtic | 66 | Rangers* | 61 | Aberdeen | 61 |
| 1936–37g | Rangers | 61 | Aberdeen | 54 | Celtic | 52 |
| 1937–38g | Celtic | 61 | Hearts | 58 | Rangers | 49 |
| 1938–39g | Rangers | 59 | Celtic | 48 | Aberdeen | 46 |
| 1946–47e | Rangers | 46 | Hibernian | 44 | Aberdeen | 39 |

| | First | Pts | Second | Pts | Third | Pts |
|---|---|---|---|---|---|---|
| 1947–48e | Hibernian | 48 | Rangers | 46 | Partick Th | 36 |
| 1948–49e | Rangers | 46 | Dundee | 45 | Hibernian | 39 |
| 1949–50e | Rangers | 50 | Hibernian | 49 | Hearts | 43 |
| 1950–51e | Hibernian | 48 | Rangers* | 38 | Dundee | 38 |
| 1951–52e | Hibernian | 45 | Rangers | 41 | East Fife | 37 |
| 1952–53e | Rangers* | 43 | Hibernian | 43 | East Fife | 39 |
| 1953–54e | Celtic | 43 | Hearts | 38 | Partick Th | 35 |
| 1954–55e | Aberdeen | 49 | Celtic | 46 | Rangers | 41 |
| 1955–56f | Rangers | 52 | Aberdeen | 46 | Hearts* | 45 |
| 1956–57f | Rangers | 55 | Hearts | 53 | Kilmarnock | 42 |
| 1957–58f | Hearts | 62 | Rangers | 49 | Celtic | 46 |
| 1958–59f | Rangers | 50 | Hearts | 48 | Motherwell | 44 |
| 1959–60f | Hearts | 54 | Kilmarnock | 50 | Rangers* | 42 |
| 1960–61f | Rangers | 51 | Kilmarnock | 50 | Third Lanark | 42 |
| 1961–62f | Dundee | 54 | Rangers | 51 | Celtic | 46 |
| 1962–63f | Rangers | 57 | Kilmarnock | 48 | Partick Th | 46 |
| 1963–64f | Rangers | 55 | Kilmarnock | 49 | Celtic* | 47 |
| 1964–65f | Kilmarnock* | 50 | Hearts | 50 | Dunfermline Ath | 49 |
| 1965–66f | Celtic | 57 | Rangers | 55 | Kilmarnock | 45 |
| 1966–67f | Celtic | 58 | Rangers | 55 | Clyde | 46 |
| 1967–68f | Celtic | 63 | Rangers | 61 | Hibernian | 45 |
| 1968–69f | Celtic | 54 | Rangers | 49 | Dunfermline Ath | 45 |
| 1969–70f | Celtic | 57 | Rangers | 45 | Hibernian | 44 |
| 1970–71f | Celtic | 56 | Aberdeen | 54 | St Johnstone | 44 |
| 1971–72f | Celtic | 60 | Aberdeen | 50 | Rangers | 44 |
| 1972–73f | Celtic | 57 | Rangers | 56 | Hibernian | 45 |
| 1973–74f | Celtic | 53 | Hibernian | 49 | Rangers | 48 |
| 1974–75f | Rangers | 56 | Hibernian | 49 | Celtic | 45 |

## DIVISION II to 1974–75

*Maximum points: a 76; b 72; c 68; d 52; e 60; f 36; g 44.*

| | First | Pts | Second | Pts | Third | Pts |
|---|---|---|---|---|---|---|
| 1893–94f | Hibernian | 29 | Cowlairs | 27 | Clyde | 24 |
| 1894–95f | Hibernian | 30 | Motherwell | 22 | Port Glasgow | 20 |
| 1895–96f | Abercorn | 27 | Leith Ath | 23 | Renton | 21 |
| 1896–97f | Partick Th | 31 | Leith Ath | 27 | Kilmarnock* | 21 |
| 1897–98f | Kilmarnock | 29 | Port Glasgow | 25 | Morton | 22 |
| 1898–99f | Kilmarnock | 32 | Leith Ath | 27 | Port Glasgow | 25 |
| 1899–1900f | Partick Th | 29 | Morton | 28 | Port Glasgow | 20 |
| 1900–01f | St Bernard's | 25 | Airdrieonians | 23 | Abercorn | 21 |
| 1901–02g | Port Glasgow | 32 | Partick Th | 31 | Motherwell | 26 |
| 1902–03g | Airdrieonians | 35 | Motherwell | 28 | Ayr U* | 27 |
| 1903–04g | Hamilton A | 37 | Clyde | 29 | Ayr U | 28 |
| 1904–05g | Clyde | 32 | Falkirk | 28 | Hamilton A | 27 |
| 1905–06g | Leith Ath | 34 | Clyde | 31 | Albion R | 27 |
| 1906–07g | St Bernard's | 32 | Vale of Leven* | 27 | Arthurlie | 27 |
| 1907–08g | Raith R | 30 | Dumbarton*‡‡ | 27 | Ayr U | 27 |
| 1908–09g | Abercorn | 31 | Raith R* | 28 | Vale of Leven | 28 |
| 1909–10g | Leith Ath‡ | 33 | Raith R | 33 | St Bernard's | 27 |
| 1910–11g | Dumbarton | 31 | Ayr U | 27 | Albion R | 25 |
| 1911–12g | Ayr U | 35 | Abercorn | 30 | Dumbarton | 27 |
| 1912–13d | Ayr U | 34 | Dunfermline Ath | 33 | East Stirling | 32 |
| 1913–14g | Cowdenbeath | 31 | Albion R | 27 | Dunfermline Ath* | 26 |
| 1914–15d | Cowdenbeath* | 37 | St Bernard's* | 37 | Leith Ath | 37 |
| 1921–22a | Alloa Ath | 60 | Cowdenbeath | 47 | Armadale | 45 |
| 1922–23a | Queen's Park | 57 | Clydebank¶ | 50 | St Johnstone¶ | 45 |
| 1923–24a | St Johnstone | 56 | Cowdenbeath | 55 | Bathgate | 44 |
| 1924–25a | Dundee U | 50 | Clydebank | 48 | Clyde | 47 |
| 1925–26a | Dunfermline Ath | 59 | Clyde | 53 | Ayr U | 52 |
| 1926–27a | Bo'ness | 56 | Raith R | 49 | Clydebank | 45 |
| 1927–28a | Ayr U | 54 | Third Lanark | 45 | King's Park | 44 |
| 1928–29b | Dundee U | 51 | Morton | 50 | Arbroath | 47 |
| 1929–30a | Leith Ath* | 57 | East Fife | 57 | Albion R | 54 |
| 1930–31a | Third Lanark | 61 | Dundee U | 50 | Dunfermline Ath | 47 |
| 1931–32a | East Stirling* | 55 | St Johnstone | 55 | Raith R* | 46 |
| 1932–33c | Hibernian | 54 | Queen of the S | 49 | Dunfermline Ath | 47 |
| 1933–34c | Albion R | 45 | Dunfermline Ath* | 44 | Arbroath | 44 |
| 1934–35c | Third Lanark | 52 | Arbroath | 50 | St Bernard's | 47 |
| 1935–36c | Falkirk | 59 | St Mirren | 52 | Morton | 48 |
| 1936–37c | Ayr U | 54 | Morton | 51 | St Bernard's | 48 |
| 1937–38c | Raith R | 59 | Albion R | 48 | Airdrieonians | 47 |
| 1938–39c | Cowdenbeath | 60 | Alloa Ath* | 48 | East Fife | 48 |
| 1946–47d | Dundee | 45 | Airdrieonians | 42 | East Fife | 31 |
| 1947–48e | East Fife | 53 | Albion R | 42 | Hamilton A | 40 |
| 1948–49e | Raith R* | 42 | Stirling Alb | 42 | Airdrieonians* | 41 |
| 1949–50e | Morton | 47 | Airdrieonians | 44 | Dunfermline Ath* | 36 |

| | First | Pts | Second | Pts | Third | Pts |
|---|---|---|---|---|---|---|
| 1950–51e | Queen of the S* | 45 | Stirling Alb | 45 | Ayr U* | 36 |
| 1951–52e | Clyde | 44 | Falkirk | 43 | Ayr U | 39 |
| 1952–53e | Stirling Alb | 44 | Hamilton A | 43 | Queen's Park | 37 |
| 1953–54e | Motherwell | 45 | Kilmarnock | 42 | Third Lanark* | 36 |
| 1954–55e | Airdrieonians | 46 | Dunfermline Ath | 42 | Hamilton A | 39 |
| 1955–56b | Queen's Park | 54 | Ayr U | 51 | St Johnstone | 49 |
| 1956–57b | Clyde | 64 | Third Lanark | 51 | Cowdenbeath | 45 |
| 1957–58b | Stirling Alb | 55 | Dunfermline Ath | 53 | Arbroath | 47 |
| 1958–59b | Ayr U | 60 | Arbroath | 51 | Stenhousemuir | 46 |
| 1959–60b | St Johnstone | 53 | Dundee U | 50 | Queen of the S | 49 |
| 1960–61b | Stirling Alb | 55 | Falkirk | 54 | Stenhousemuir | 50 |
| 1961–62b | Clyde | 54 | Queen of the S | 53 | Morton | 44 |
| 1962–63b | St Johnstone | 55 | East Stirling | 49 | Morton | 48 |
| 1963–64b | Morton | 67 | Clyde | 53 | Arbroath | 46 |
| 1964–65b | Stirling Alb | 59 | Hamilton A | 50 | Queen of the S | 45 |
| 1965–66b | Ayr U | 53 | Airdrieonians | 50 | Queen of the S | 47 |
| 1966–67a | Morton | 69 | Raith R | 58 | Arbroath | 57 |
| 1967–68b | St Mirren | 62 | Arbroath | 53 | East Fife | 49 |
| 1968–69b | Motherwell | 64 | Ayr U | 53 | East Fife* | 48 |
| 1969–70b | Falkirk | 56 | Cowdenbeath | 55 | Queen of the S | 50 |
| 1970–71b | Partick Th | 56 | East Fife | 51 | Arbroath | 46 |
| 1971–72b | Dumbarton* | 52 | Arbroath | 52 | Stirling Alb | 50 |
| 1972–73b | Clyde | 56 | Dumfermline Ath | 52 | Raith R* | 47 |
| 1973–74b | Airdrieonians | 60 | Kilmarnock | 58 | Hamilton A | 55 |
| 1974–75a | Falkirk | 54 | Queen of the S* | 53 | Montrose | 53 |

Elected to First Division: 1894 Clyde; 1895 Hibernian; 1896 Abercorn; 1897 Partick Th; 1899 Kilmarnock; 1900 Morton and Partick Th; 1902 Port Glasgow and Partick Th; 1903 Airdrieonians and Motherwell; 1905 Falkirk and Aberdeen; 1906 Clyde and Hamilton A; 1910 Raith R; 1913 Ayr U and Dumbarton.

## RELEGATED FROM PREMIER LEAGUE

| | |
|---|---|
| 1998–99 Dunfermline Ath | 2006–07 Dunfermline Ath |
| 1999–2000 *No relegation due to League reorganization* | 2007–08 Gretna |
| 2000–01 St Mirren | 2008–09 Inverness CT |
| 2001–02 St Johnstone | 2009–10 Falkirk |
| 2002–03 *No relegated team* | 2010–11 Hamilton A |
| 2003–04 Partick Th | 2011–12 Dunfermline Ath, Rangers (demoted) |
| 2004–05 Dundee | 2012–13 Dundee |
| 2005–06 Livingston | |

## RELEGATED FROM PREMIER DIVISION

| | |
|---|---|
| 1974–75 *No relegation due to League reorganization* | 1986–87 Clydebank, Hamilton A |
| 1975–76 Dundee, St Johnstone | 1987–88 Falkirk, Dunfermline Ath, Morton |
| 1976–77 Hearts, Kilmarnock | 1988–89 Hamilton A |
| 1977–78 Ayr U, Clydebank | 1989–90 Dundee |
| 1978–79 Hearts, Motherwell | 1990–91 *None* |
| 1979–80 Dundee, Hibernian | 1991–92 St Mirren, Dunfermline Ath |
| 1980–81 Kilmarnock, Hearts | 1992–93 Falkirk, Airdrieonians |
| 1981–82 Partick Th, Airdrieonians | 1993–94 *See footnote* |
| 1982–83 Morton, Kilmarnock | 1994–95 Dundee U |
| 1983–84 St Johnstone, Motherwell | 1995–96 Partick Th, Falkirk |
| 1984–85 Dumbarton, Morton | 1996–97 Raith R |
| 1985–86 *No relegation due to League reorganization* | 1997–98 Hibernian |

## RELEGATED FROM FIRST DIVISION

| | |
|---|---|
| 1975–76 Dunfermline Ath, Clyde | 1980–81 Stirling Alb, Berwick R |
| 1976–77 Raith R, Falkirk | 1996–97 Clydebank, East Fife |
| 1977–78 Alloa Ath, East Fife | 1997–98 Partick Th, Stirling Alb |
| 1981–82 East Stirling, Queen of the S | 1998–99 Hamilton A, Stranraer |
| 1982–83 Dunfermline Ath, Queen's Park | 1999–2000 Clydebank |
| 1983–84 Raith R, Alloa Ath | 2000–01 Morton, Alloa Ath |
| 1984–85 Meadowbank Th, St Johnstone | 2001–02 Raith R |
| 1985–86 Ayr U, Alloa Ath | 2002–03 Alloa Ath, Arbroath |
| 1986–87 Brechin C, Montrose | 2003–04 Ayr U, Brechin C |
| 1987–88 East Fife, Dumbarton | 2004–05 Partick Th, Raith R |
| 1988–89 Kilmarnock, Queen of the S | 2005–06 Stranraer, Brechin C |
| 1989–90 Albion R, Alloa Ath | 2006–07 Airdrie U, Ross Co |
| 1990–91 Clyde, Brechin C | 2007–08 Stirling Alb |
| 1992–93 Meadowbank Th, Cowdenbeath | 2008–09 Clyde |
| 1993–94 *See footnote* | 2009–10 Airdrie U, Ayr U |
| 1994–95 Ayr U, Stranraer | 2010–11 Cowdenbeath, Stirling Alb |
| 1995–96 Hamilton A, Dumbarton | 2011–12 Ayr U, Queen of the S |
| 1978–79 Montrose, Queen of the S | 2012–13 Dunfermline Ath, Airdrie U |
| 1979–80 Arbroath, Clyde | |

## RELEGATED FROM SECOND DIVISION

| | | | |
|---|---|---|---|
| 1994–95 | Meadowbank Th, Brechin C | 2004–05 | Arbroath, Berwick R |
| 1995–96 | Forfar Ath, Montrose | 2005–06 | Dumbarton |
| 1996–97 | Dumbarton, Berwick R | 2006–07 | Stranraer, Forfar Ath |
| 1997–98 | Stenhousemuir, Brechin C | 2007–08 | Cowdenbeath, Berwick R |
| 1998–99 | East Fife, Forfar Ath | 2008–09 | Stranraer, Queen's Park |
| 1999–2000 | Hamilton A** | 2009–10 | Arbroath, Clyde |
| 2000–01 | Queen's Park, Stirling Alb | 2010–11 | Alloa Ath, Peterhead |
| 2001–02 | Morton | 2011–12 | Stirling Alb |
| 2002–03 | Stranraer, Cowdenbeath | 2012–13 | Albion R |
| 2003–04 | East Fife, Stenhousemuir | | |

## RELEGATED FROM DIVISION I (TO 1973–74)

| | | | |
|---|---|---|---|
| 1921–22 | *Queen's Park, Dumbarton, Clydebank | 1951–52 | Morton, Stirling Alb |
| 1922–23 | Albion R, Alloa Ath | 1952–53 | Motherwell, Third Lanark |
| 1923–24 | Clyde, Clydebank | 1953–54 | Airdrieonians, Hamilton A |
| 1924–25 | Third Lanark, Ayr U | 1954–55 | *No clubs relegated* |
| 1925–26 | Raith R, Clydebank | 1955–56 | Stirling Alb, Clyde |
| 1926–27 | Morton, Dundee U | 1956–57 | Dunfermline Ath, Ayr U |
| 1927–28 | Dunfermline Ath, Bo'ness | 1957–58 | East Fife, Queen's Park |
| 1928–29 | Third Lanark, Raith R | 1958–59 | Queen of the S, Falkirk |
| 1929–30 | St Johnstone, Dundee U | 1959–60 | Arbroath, Stirling Alb |
| 1930–31 | Hibernian, East Fife | 1960–61 | Ayr U, Clyde |
| 1931–32 | Dundee U, Leith Ath | 1961–62 | St Johnstone, Stirling Alb |
| 1932–33 | Morton, East Stirling | 1962–63 | Clyde, Raith R |
| 1933–34 | Third Lanark, Cowdenbeath | 1963–64 | Queen of the S, East Stirling |
| 1934–35 | St Mirren, Falkirk | 1964–65 | Airdrieonians, Third Lanark |
| 1935–36 | Airdrieonians, Ayr U | 1965–66 | Morton, Hamilton A |
| 1936–37 | Dunfermline Ath, Albion R | 1966–67 | St Mirren, Ayr U |
| 1937–38 | Dundee, Morton | 1967–68 | Motherwell, Stirling Alb |
| 1938–39 | Queen's Park, Raith R | 1968–69 | Falkirk, Arbroath |
| 1946–47 | Kilmarnock, Hamilton A | 1969–70 | Raith R, Partick Th |
| 1947–48 | Airdrieonians, Queen's Park | 1970–71 | St Mirren, Cowdenbeath |
| 1948–49 | Morton, Albion R | 1971–72 | Clyde, Dunfermline Ath |
| 1949–50 | Queen of the S, Stirling Alb | 1972–73 | Kilmarnock, Airdrieonians |
| 1950–51 | Clyde, Falkirk | 1973–74 | East Fife, Falkirk |

*Season 1921–22 – only 1 club promoted, 3 clubs relegated. **15pts deducted for failing to field a team.*

**Scottish League Championship wins:** Rangers 54, Celtic 44, Aberdeen 4, Hearts 4, Hibernian 4, Dumbarton 2, Dundee 1, Dundee U 1, Kilmarnock 1, Motherwell 1, Third Lanark 1.

*From 1946–47 to 1955–56 the two divisions were known as A and B. A division 3 had existed for three years from 1923–24 and was revived for three more seasons from 1946–47 as Division C when it included reserve teams.*

*At the end of the 1993–94 season four divisions were created assisted by the admission of two new clubs Ross County and Inverness Caledonian Thistle. Only one club was promoted from Division 1 and Division 2. The three relegated from the Premier joined with teams finishing second to seventh in Division 1 to form the new First Division. Five relegated from Division 1 combined with those who finished second to sixth to form a new Second Division and the bottom eight in Division 2 linked with the two newcomers to form a new Third Division.*

*At the end of the 1997–98 season the nine clubs remaining in the Premier Division plus the promoted team from the First Division formed a breakaway Premier League.*

*At the end of the 1999–2000 season two teams were added to the Scottish League. There was no relegation from the Premier League but two promoted from the First Division and three from each of the Second and Third Divisions. One team was relegated from the First Division and one from the Second Division, leaving 12 teams in each division. In season 2002–03, Falkirk were not promoted to the Premier League due to the failure of their ground to meet League rules. Inverness Caledonian Thistle were promoted after a previous refusal in 2003–04 because of ground sharing.*

*At the end of 2005–06 the Scottish League introduced play-offs for the team finishing second from the bottom of the First Division against the second, third and fourth finishing teams in the Second Division and with a similar procedure for the Second Division and the Third Division.*

# SCOTTISH LEAGUE PLAY-OFFS 2012–13

**■** *Denotes player sent off.*

## DIVISION 1 SEMI-FINALS FIRST LEG

Wednesday, 8 May 2013

**Brechin C (0) 0**

**Alloa Ath (1) 2** *(McCord Ryan 40, Moon 56)*    582

*Brechin C:* (433) Andrews; Pursehouse, Hay (McLauchlan 65), Moyes, Brown (Brady 69); Cameron, Stewart J, Ferguson; Trouten, Jackson, Carcary (McKenna 59).
*Alloa Ath:* (442) Bain; Doyle, Gordon, Marr (Docherty 59), Meggatt; Moon, Simmons, McCord Ryan (Grehan 86), Holmes; Elliot (Young 81), Cawley.

**Forfar Ath (3) 3** *(Robertson 34, Templeman 38, 45)*

**Dunfermline Ath (0) 1** *(Husband 84)*    1562

*Forfar Ath:* (442) Hill; Dunlop, McCulloch, Bolochoweckyj, Campbell I; Campbell R (Kader 72), Robertson, Malin (Brown 82), Hilson (King 86); Templeman, Swankie.
*Dunfermline Ath:* (442) Hrivnak; Geggan, Young, Potter (Millen 79), Whittle; Falkingham, Husband, Byrne, Kane (Dargo 63); Smith, Thomson.

## DIVISION 1 SEMI-FINALS SECOND LEG

Saturday, 11 May 2013

**Alloa Ath (1) 2** *(Cawley 36, Elliot 68 (pen))*

**Brechin C (1) 3** *(Jackson 4, Trouten 52 (pen), Jackson 90)*    856

*Alloa Ath:* (442) Bain; Tiffoney, Gordon, Doyle, Meggatt; Moon, McCord Ryan (Young 65), Simmons, Holmes; Elliot (Ferns 87), Cawley.
*Brechin C:* (433) Andrews; McLean P, Hay, Moyes, McLauchlan; Stewart R (Stewart J 72), Rodger (Pursehouse 53), Ferguson (McKenna 66); Trouten, Carcary, Jackson.

**Dunfermline Ath (1) 6** *(Dunlop 36 (og), Thomson 62, Millen 83 (pen), Smith 102, Husband 110, 118)*

**Forfar Ath (1) 1** *(Campbell I 6)*    4252

*Dunfermline Ath:* (442) Hrivnak; Millen, Young, Potter, Whittle (Kane 111); Geggan (Byrne 91), Husband, Falkingham, Wallace (Dargo 11); Smith, Thomson.
*Forfar Ath:* (442) Hill; Dunlop■, McCulloch■, Bolochoweckyj, Campbell I■; Hilson (Sellars 93), Robertson, Malin (Brown 71), Campbell R (Kader 46); Templeman, Swankie.
*aet.*

## DIVISION 1 FINAL FIRST LEG

Wednesday, 15 May 2013

**Alloa Ath (2) 3** *(Tiffoney 27, Elliot 45, Moon 90)*

**Dunfermline Ath (0) 0**    2765

*Alloa Ath:* (442) Bain; Tiffoney (Docherty 71), Doyle, Gordon, Meggatt; Moon, McCord Ryan (Young 60), Simmons, Holmes; Elliot, Cawley.
*Dunfermline Ath:* (442) Hrivnak; Millen, Young, Potter, Whittle; Byrne, Husband, Falkingham, Thomson; Smith (El Bakhtaoui 82), Dargo (Drummond 63).

## DIVISION 1 FINAL SECOND LEG

Sunday, 19 May 2013

**Dunfermline Ath (0) 1** *(Smith 72)*

**Alloa Ath (0) 0**    5110

*Dunfermline Ath:* (442) Hrivnak; Millen, Young, Potter (Dargo 46), Whittle; Geggan, Kane, Husband■, Falkingham; Smith, Thomson.
*Alloa Ath:* (442) Bain; Doyle, Gordon, Marr, Meggatt; Moon, Simmons, McCord Ryan (Young 59), Holmes; Elliot, Cawley.

## DIVISION 2 SEMI-FINALS FIRST LEG

Wednesday, 8 May 2013

**Berwick R (0) 1** *(Lavery 72)*

**East Fife (1) 1** *(Muir 44)*    732

*Berwick R:* (442) McCallum; Jacobs, McLean, Townsley, Gielty; Notman, Janczyk, Currie (Lavery 62), McDonald (Easton 70); McLaren, Dalziel (Morris 84).
*East Fife:* (442) Antell; Durie, Campbell, White, Johnstone; Barr R, Muir, Willis, McBride; Samuel (Wardlaw 88), McManus P.

**Queen's Park (0) 0**

**Peterhead (0) 1** *(Rodgers 90 (pen))*    651

*Queen's Park:* (433) Parry; Spittal, Gallacher, Brough, Robertson; Anderson, Longworth, McParland; Connolly, Keenan (Quinn 75), Burns (Shankland 81).
*Peterhead:* (4411) Smith G; Sharp, Ross, Smith R, Noble; Redman, Cowie, Strachan (McCann 73), Cox; Gilfillan; McAllister (Rodgers 61).

## DIVISION 2 SEMI-FINALS SECOND LEG

Saturday, 11 May 2013

**East Fife (0) 2** *(McDonald 78 (og), Gormley 119)*

**Berwick R (0) 1** *(Lavery 61 (pen))*    856

*East Fife:* (442) Antell; Durie, White, Campbell, Johnstone; McBride, Muir, Willis, Barr R; McManus P (Gormley 86), Samuel (Wardlaw 65).
*Berwick R:* (442) McCallum; Jacobs, McLean, Hoskins, Gielty; Easton (McDonald 69), Notman, Janczyk, Lavery (Addison 90); Dalziel, McLaren (Currie 82).
*aet.*

**Peterhead (2) 3** *(Cox 4, 10, McAllister 64)*

**Queen's Park (0) 1** *(Shankland 87)*    954

*Peterhead:* (442) Smith G; Ross, Smith R, Gilfillan, Sharp; Noble, Redman, Cowie (Strachan■ 66), Cox (McGlinchey 75); McAllister, Rodgers (McCann 66).
*Queen's Park:* (442) Parry; Gallacher, Brough, Robertson, Capuano (McParland 46); Anderson, Connolly, Quinn (Longworth 75), Spittal; Watt (Burns 46), Shankland.

## DIVISION 2 FINAL FIRST LEG

Wednesday, 15 May 2013

**East Fife (0) 0**

**Peterhead (0) 0**    826

*East Fife:* (451) Antell; Durie, Campbell, White, Johnstone; Muir, Willis, Smith Darren, Barr R (Gormley 77), McBride; Wardlaw (Samuel 48).
*Peterhead:* (442) Smith G; Sharp, Ross, Smith R, Noble; Cox, Cowie, Redman, Gilfillan; McAllister, Rodgers (McCann 83).

## DIVISION 2 FINAL SECOND LEG

Sunday, 19 May 2013

**Peterhead (0) 0**

**East Fife (0) 1** *(Muir 48)*    1855

*Peterhead:* (442) Smith G; Sharp, Ross, Smith R, Noble; Redman, Cowie, Gilfillan (Bavidge 81), Cox; McAllister, Rodgers.
*East Fife:* (442) Antell; Durie, Campbell, White, Johnstone; Willis, Muir, Smith Darren, McBride; Samuel; McManus (Barr R 74).

# SCOTTISH LEAGUE CUP FINALS 1946–2013

| Season | Winners | Runners-up | Score |
|---|---|---|---|
| 1946–47 | Rangers | Aberdeen | 4-0 |
| 1947–48 | East Fife | Falkirk | 4-1 after 0-0 draw (*aet.*) |
| 1948–49 | Rangers | Raith R | 2-0 |
| 1949–50 | East Fife | Dunfermline Ath | 3-0 |
| 1950–51 | Motherwell | Hibernian | 3-0 |
| 1951–52 | Dundee | Rangers | 3-2 |
| 1952–53 | Dundee | Kilmarnock | 2-0 |
| 1953–54 | East Fife | Partick Th | 3-2 |
| 1954–55 | Hearts | Motherwell | 4-2 |
| 1955–56 | Aberdeen | St Mirren | 2-1 |
| 1956–57 | Celtic | Partick Th | 3-0 after 0-0 draw |
| 1957–58 | Celtic | Rangers | 7-1 |
| 1958–59 | Hearts | Partick Th | 5-1 |
| 1959–60 | Hearts | Third Lanark | 2-1 |
| 1960–61 | Rangers | Kilmarnock | 2-0 |
| 1961–62 | Rangers | Hearts | 3-1 after 1-1 draw |
| 1962–63 | Hearts | Kilmarnock | 1-0 |
| 1963–64 | Rangers | Morton | 5-0 |
| 1964–65 | Rangers | Celtic | 2-1 |
| 1965–66 | Celtic | Rangers | 2-1 |
| 1966–67 | Celtic | Rangers | 1-0 |
| 1967–68 | Celtic | Dundee | 5-3 |
| 1968–69 | Celtic | Hibernian | 6-2 |
| 1969–70 | Celtic | St Johnstone | 1-0 |
| 1970–71 | Rangers | Celtic | 1-0 |
| 1971–72 | Partick Th | Celtic | 4-1 |
| 1972–73 | Hibernian | Celtic | 2-1 |
| 1973–74 | Dundee | Celtic | 1-0 |
| 1974–75 | Celtic | Hibernian | 6-3 |
| 1975–76 | Rangers | Celtic | 1-0 |
| 1976–77 | Aberdeen | Celtic | 2-1 |
| 1977–78 | Rangers | Celtic | 2-1 (*aet.*) |
| 1978–79 | Rangers | Aberdeen | 2-1 |
| 1979–80 | Dundee U | Aberdeen | 3-0 after 0-0 draw (*aet.*) |
| 1980–81 | Dundee U | Dundee | 3-0 |
| 1981–82 | Rangers | Dundee U | 2-1 |
| 1982–83 | Celtic | Rangers | 2-1 |
| 1983–84 | Rangers | Celtic | 3-2 |
| 1984–85 | Rangers | Dundee U | 1-0 |
| 1985–86 | Aberdeen | Hibernian | 3-0 |
| 1986–87 | Rangers | Celtic | 2-1 |
| 1987–88 | Rangers | Aberdeen | 3-3 |
| | | *(aet; Rangers won 5-3 on penalties)* | |
| 1988–89 | Rangers | Aberdeen | 3-2 (*aet.*) |
| 1989–90 | Aberdeen | Rangers | 2-1 |
| 1990–91 | Rangers | Celtic | 2-1 |
| 1991–92 | Hibernian | Dunfermline Ath | 2-0 |
| 1992–93 | Rangers | Aberdeen | 2-1 (*aet.*) |
| 1993–94 | Rangers | Hibernian | 2-1 |
| 1994–95 | Raith R | Celtic | 2-2 |
| | | *(aet; Raith R won 6-5 on penalties)* | |
| 1995–96 | Aberdeen | Dundee | 2-0 |
| 1996–97 | Rangers | Hearts | 4-3 |
| 1997–98 | Celtic | Dundee U | 3-0 |
| 1998–99 | Rangers | St Johnstone | 2-1 |
| 1999–2000 | Celtic | Aberdeen | 2-0 |
| 2000–01 | Celtic | Kilmarnock | 3-0 |
| 2001–02 | Rangers | Ayr U | 4-0 |
| 2002–03 | Rangers | Celtic | 2-1 |
| 2003–04 | Livingston | Hibernian | 2-0 |
| 2004–05 | Rangers | Motherwell | 5-1 |
| 2005–06 | Celtic | Dunfermline Ath | 3-0 |
| 2006–07 | Hibernian | Kilmarnock | 5-1 |
| 2007–08 | Rangers | Dundee U | 2-2 |
| | | *(aet; Rangers won 3-2 on penalties)* | |
| 2008–09 | Celtic | Rangers | 2-0 (*aet.*) |
| 2009–10 | Rangers | St Mirren | 1-0 |
| 2010–11 | Rangers | Celtic | 2-1 (*aet.*) |
| 2011–12 | Kilmarnock | Celtic | 1-0 |
| 2012–13 | St Mirren | Hearts | 3-2 |

## SCOTTISH LEAGUE CUP WINS

Rangers 27, Celtic 14, Aberdeen 5, Hearts 4, Dundee 3, East Fife 3, Hibernian 3, Dundee U 2, Kilmarnock 1, Livingston 1, Motherwell 1, Partick Th 1, Raith R 1, St Mirren 1.

## APPEARANCES IN FINALS

Rangers 34, Celtic 29, Aberdeen 12, Hibernian 9, Hearts 7, Dundee 6, Dundee U 6, Kilmarnock 6, Partick Th 4, Dunfermline Ath 3, East Fife 3, Motherwell 3, St Mirren 3, Raith R 2, St Johnstone 2, Ayr U 1, Falkirk 1, Livingston 1, Morton 1, Third Lanark 1.

# SCOTTISH COMMUNITIES
# LEAGUE CUP 2012–13

**■** *Denotes player sent off.*

**FIRST ROUND**

Tuesday, 31 July 2012

**Peterhead (0) 0**
**Dundee (0) 0**                                                     844
*Peterhead:* (352) Jarvie; Ross, Strachan, McDonald; Sharp, Redman (Maguire 102), Cowie (McBain 94), McLaughlin, Noble; Winters (Deasley 69), McAllister.
*Dundee:* (352) Douglas; McGregor, Benedictus, Gallagher; Irvine, Webster (Reid 110), McBride, Conroy, Lockwood; Baird, McIntosh
*aet; Dundee won 4-1 on penalties.*

Saturday, 4 August 2012

**Arbroath (0) 1** *(Currie 83)*
**Stirling A (1) 1** *(Ferry 42 (pen))*                              579
*Arbroath:* (442) Hill; Baxter, Brennan, Robertson (Travis 46), Keddie; Sibanda (Rennie 69), Currie, Banjo, Sheerin; Doris, Gribben (Holmes 62).
*Stirling A:* (442) Crawford; Ashe, McAnespie (McGeachie 88), McCunnie, Clark; Davidson, Allison, Macpherson (McSorley 91), Ferry; Weir, Coyne (Brass 84).
*aet; Arbroath won 3-2 on penalties.*

**Ayr U (0) 6** *(Winters 48, Moffat 59, 90 (pen), Tiffoney 63, Sinclair 68, 90)*
**Clyde (0) 1** *(Neill 82)*                                        1022
*Ayr U:* (442) Brown; Tiffoney, Campbell, Brownlie, McCann; McGowan (Winters 34), Sinclair, McStay, Moffat; Shankland, Marenghi.
*Clyde:* (433) Barclay; Brown (Graham 63), Gray, Marsh, Sharp; Oliver, Hay (Neill 53), Sweeney; McColm, Scullion (MacBeth 73), McCluskey S.

**Dumbarton (1) 2** *(Prunty 45, Lister 84)*
**Albion R (0) 0**                                                   479
*Dumbarton:* (442) Grindlay; Lyden, Lithgow, Graham, Creaney; Johnston, Fleming, Agnew (Gilhaney 72), McDougall; Lister, Prunty.
*Albion R:* (442) McCluskey; Reid, O'Byrne, Donnelly, Russell; Stevenson, Innes, Dick, Phillips (Boyle 85); Crooks (Gilmartin 78), Howarth (Pierce 67).

**Falkirk (0) 2** *(Kingsley 67, Taylor 89)*
**Elgin C (0) 0**                                                   1549
*Falkirk:* (4321) McGovern; Duffie, Dods (Smith 18), Flynn, Kingsley; Fulton J (Fulton D 80), Sibbald, Murdoch; Haworth, Leahy (Alston 46); Taylor.
*Elgin C:* (442) Gibson; Niven, Cameron (McLean 90), Crighton, McMullan; O'Donoghue (Beveridge 70), Wyness (Hallford 76), Moore, Nicolson; Leslie, Gunn.

**Forfar Ath (0) 0**
**Partick Th (2) 2** *(Erskine 18, Lawless 37)*                      693
*Forfar Ath:* (442) Scott; McCulloch, Bolochoweckyj, Dunlop, Campbell I; Gibson, Denholm, King (Fotheringham M 57), Swankie; Kader (Campbell R 46), Templeman (Motion 64).
*Partick Th:* (442) Fox; O'Donnell S, Muirhead, Archibald, Sinclair; Bannigan, Welsh, Murray■, Erskine (Craigen 66); Doolan (McGuigan 73), Lawless (Halsman 90).

**Hamilton A (0) 2** *(Routledge 66, Mackinnon 80)*
**Annan Ath (0) 0**                                                  620
*Hamilton A:* (442) Cuthbert; McGlinchey, Canning, Devlin, Hendrie; Fraser (Neil 73), Routledge, Gillespie (Kirkpatrick 83), Crawford; McShane, Ryan (Mackinnon 78).
*Annan Ath:* (442) Summersgill; Blake, Swinglehurst, McGowan, Thorburn; Steele, Jardine (McKechnie 58), Chaplain, Murray (Love 46); Daly, Bell (Ramage 70).

**Montrose (2) 2** *(Boyle 31, Watson 43)*
**Cowdenbeath (0) 1** *(McKenzie 90)*                                312
*Montrose:* (442) Wood S; McNally, Lunan, Campbell, Watson; Gray D, Masson, McLeish, Johnston; Boyle, Wood G (Crawford 80).
*Cowdenbeath:* (442) Flynn; Brett (Milne 67), Armstrong, Mbu, Linton; McKenzie, Garcia-Rey (Miller 46), Cameron, O'Brien; Coult, Stevenson.

**Queen of the S (1) 5** *(Mitchell 9, Higgins 67, Clark 83, 86, Lyle 89)*
**Alloa Ath (0) 2** *(Gordon 64, Grehan 78)*                        967
*Queen of the S:* (352) Robinson; McGuffie, Durnan, Higgins; Mitchell, Young (Black 90), McKenna, Orsi (McShane 90), Holt; Clark (Reilly 88), Lyle.
*Alloa Ath:* (433) Bain; Doyle, Gordon, Harding, Docherty; Young, Simmons (Cawley 56), McCord Ryan (McCord Ross 72); Holmes, Grehan, Cox.

**Queen's Park (0) 3** *(Brough 60, 104, Shankland 88)*
**Airdrie U (0) 2** *(Blockley 47, Cook 66)*                         622
*Queen's Park:* (433) Parry; Monaghan (Burns 69), Little, Brough, Bradley; Keenan, Longworth, Anderson (Capuano 118); Ronald (Shankland 78), Quinn, Robertson.
*Airdrie U:* (442) Arthur; Hart, Lilley, MacDonald, Warren; McLaren (Gilchrist 82), Blockley, Lynch, Griffin (Cook 61); Di Giacomo (Donnelly 65), Boyle John.
*aet.*

**Raith R (1) 4** *(Graham 25, 73, Hill 58, Clarke 85)*
**Berwick R (1) 3** *(Currie L 9, 65, Addison 50)*                  1071
*Raith R:* (442) McGurn; Thomson, Ellis, Hill (Donaldson 87), Malone; Anderson G (Spence 71), Anderson S, Walker, Hamill; Graham, Clarke.
*Berwick R:* (451) Bejaoui; Jacobs, McLean, Brydon, Lancaster; McDonald, Janczyk, Gielty (Stevenson 87), Currie L, Addison (Miller 79); McLaren.

**Stenhousemuir (1) 4** *(Gemmell 1, Smith D 76, 90, Kean 88 (pen))*
**Brechin C (0) 0**                                                  282
*Stenhousemuir:* (442) Reidford; Ross, McMillan, Thomson I, McKinlay; Ferguson (Smith D 59), Hodge (Brash 88), Anderson, Dickson; Gemmell (Kean 80), Rodgers.
*Brechin C:* (442) Andrews; McLean, McLauchlan■, Moyes, Brown; Stewart R (Stewart J 59), Brady (Fusco 69), Molloy, Carcary (Dalziel 51); Jackson, McKenna.

**Stranraer (0) 0**
**Livingston (3) 8** *(Morton 17, 87, McNulty 23, 66, 83, Russell I 39, 80, McCann 62)*                               284
*Stranraer:* (442) Mitchell; Kinnaird, Staunton, McKeown, Dunlop; Winter, Gallagher, Aitken, Borris (Moore 57); Malcolm (Agnew 72), Love (Forde 72).
*Livingston:* (442) McNeil; McCann, Watson, Barr C, Fordyce, McDonald 78); Docherty (Beaumont 79), Andreu (Barr R 65), Russell I, Morton; McNulty, Scougall.

Sunday, 5 August 2012

**East Stirling (1) 1** *(Herd 34)*
**Morton (3) 5** *(McLaughlin M 1, Weatherson 11, Stirling 37, Wallace 67, Tidser 86)*                                  581
*East Stirling:* (4141) McWilliams; Hume, Jackson, Miller, Shepherd; Devlin, Herd (Turner 46), Begg, Hunter (Benton 76), Maxwell; Greenhill.
*Morton:* (4141) Gaston; Taggart, Rutkiewicz, McLaughlin M (Naismith 60), Halsman; Reid; Wallace (Graham 68), Stirling, Tidser, O'Brien; Weatherson (Campbell 71).

Tuesday, 7 August 2012

**Rangers (2) 4** *(McCulloch 16, 62, Shiels 34, Wallace 47)*
**East Fife (0) 0**                                               38,160
*Rangers:* (343) Alexander; Broadfoot, Goian, Bocanegra; Little, Macleod (Sandaza 67), Black (Hutton 81), Wallace; McCulloch, Shiels, McKay (Kyle 81).
*East Fife:* (442) Brown M; Durie, Campbell, McCormack, Cook; Johnstone (Brown R 81), Muir, Smith Darren, McBride (Sloan R 61); Wardlaw, McQuade (Jamieson 61).

**SECOND ROUND**

Wednesday, 22 August 2012

**Morton (0) 0**
**Aberdeen (0) 2** *(Rae 109, Vernon 115)*                          2817
*Morton:* (4141) Gaston; Taggart, Reid, McLaughlin M (Naismith 86), Dyer; Bachirou; Graham, Stirling (Wallace 60), Tidser, O'Brien; Weatherson (Campbell 73).
*Aberdeen:* (433) Langfield; Osbourne, Considine, Reynolds, Naysmith (Magennis 116); Rae, Hughes (Clark 43); Jack; Hayes, Vernon, Fraser (Pawlett 86).
*aet.*

**Tuesday, 28 August 2012**
**Dunfermline Ath (2) 3** *(Barrowman 4, 64, Wallace 41)*
**Montrose (0) 0** 903
*Dunfermline Ath:* (433) Gallacher; McMillan, Dowie, Morris, Jordan; Husband, Geggan, Falkingham (Dargo 68); Wallace (Byrne 75), Barrowman, Whittle (D'Angelo 46).
*Montrose:* (442) Wood S; McNally, Lunan, Campbell, Watson (Mosson 6 (Reid 46)); Masson, Gray D, Crawford, McLeish; Wood G, Johnston.

**Hamilton A (0) 1** *(Crawford 107)*
**Partick Th (0) 0** 1268
*Hamilton A:* (4411) Cuthbert; Gordon, Neil, Kilday, Hendrie; Longridge, Fisher (Fraser 91), Crawford, Kirkpatrick (Keatings 51); Routledge; McShane (Ryan 100).
*Partick Th:* (433) Fox; O'Donnell S, Muirhead, Archibald, Sinclair; Welsh (McGuigan 109), Paton, Bannigan; Lawless (Elliot 60), Doolan, Erskine (Craigen 70).
*aet.*

**Kilmarnock (0) 1** *(Nelson 90)*
**Stenhousemuir (2) 2** *(Ferguson 20 (pen), Gemmell 43)*
2538
*Kilmarnock:* (4231) Letheren; Fowler, O'Leary, Nelson, Tesselaar (O'Hara 14); Johnson (Dayton 46), Pascali; Racchi, Perez (Gros 59), Winchester; McKenzie.
*Stenhousemuir:* (4411) Reidford; Ross, Buist, McMillan, McKinlay; Ferguson (Smith D 82), Thomson I (Anderson 73), Hodge, Dickson (Rodgers 89); Kean; Gemmell.

**Livingston (1) 3** *(Russell I 39 (pen), Barr R 96, Easton 102)*
**Dumbarton (1) 2** *(Lister 36, Gilhaney 110)* 493
*Livingston:* (442) McNeil; Cummings, Andreu, Fordyce, McDonald; Barr R (Downie 104), Docherty, Scougall, Morton (Easton 77); Russell I (Gray 90), McNulty.
*Dumbarton:* (442) Grindlay; Devlin, Lithgow, Graham, Creaney (Johnston 98); Gilhaney, Fleming, Agnew, McDougall (Lamont 103); Prunty, Lister (McNiff 109).
*aet.*

**Queen of the S (2) 2** *(Clark 13, Reilly 42)*
**Hibernian (0) 0** 2658
*Queen of the S:* (442) Robinson; Mitchell, Durnan, Higgins, Holt; Carmichael, McKenna, Young, Orsi; Lyle (Reilly 22), Clark (Gibson 76).
*Hibernian:* (442) Williams; Clancy, O'Hanlon, Hanlon, Kujabi (Wotherspoon 46); Cairney, Deegan, Claros, Booth (Maybury 46); Griffiths, Kuqi (Doyle 69).

**Ross Co (0) 1** *(Duncan 84)*
**Raith R (2) 4** *(Spence 25, Graham 41, 63, Hill 51)* 1147
*Ross Co:* (433) Brown; Bateson, Kovacevic, Boyd, Fitzpatrick; Lawson, Scott, Morrow; Duncan, Byrne, Glen.
*Raith R:* (442) McGurn; Thomson, Ellis (Wilson 30), Malone, Hill; Spence (Anderson G 78), Anderson S, Walker, Hamill (Callachan 83); Clarke, Graham.

**Wednesday, 29 August 2012**
**Arbroath (0) 0**
**Inverness CT (1) 2** *(Shinnie A 7, 71)* 672
*Arbroath:* (442) Bullock; Baxter (Malcolm 64), Travis (Banjo 72), Keddie, Hamilton; Doris, Kerr, Currie, Sheerin; Holmes (Sibanda 30), Gribben.
*Inverness CT:* (442) Esson; Meekings, Warren, King (Raven 58), Shinnie G; Sutherland, Tudur Jones, Draper, Doran; Shinnie A (Morrison 89), McKay (Pepper 81).

**Queen's Park (1) 2** *(Longworth 24 (pen), Burns 76)*
**Dundee (1) 1** *(Milne 5)* 707
*Queen's Park:* (433) Parry; Little, Brough, Bradley, Robertson; Capuano, Anderson, Keenan; Watt (Shankland 63), Longworth, Burns (Ronald 85).
*Dundee:* (442) Douglas; Irvine, McGregor■, Grassi, Lockwood; McAlister, Davidson, Webster (Gallagher 25); Conroy; Baird J, Milne (O'Donnell 63).

**St Mirren (4) 5** *(Guy 16, Thompson 24, McGowan 30, McLean 38 (pen), Teale 58)*
**Ayr U (1) 1** *(Moffat 39)* 2306
*St Mirren:* (352) Samson; McAusland (van Zanten 57), Mair, Barron; Teale, McLean, Goodwin (Robertson 63), McGowan, Carey; Thompson, Guy (Parkin 63).
*Ayr U:* (442) Brown; Hunter, Campbell (Twaddle 10), Brownlie, McCann; McGowan (Robertson R 46), Sinclair, Crawford, Marenghi; Moffat, Winters (Shankland 67).

**Thursday, 30 August 2012**
**Rangers (2) 3** *(McCulloch 18, Little 32, McCulloch 52)*
**Falkirk (0) 0** 26,450
*Rangers:* (442) Alexander; Argyriou, Emilson Cribari, Bocanegra, Wallace; Faure (Kyle 77), Black, Shiels (McKay 63), Macleod (Crawford 77); Little, McCulloch.
*Falkirk:* (442) McGovern; Duffie, Smith, Flynn, Kingsley; Weatherston (Fulton D 86), Fulton J, Murdoch, Alston; Sibbald (Haworth 70), Taylor.

**THIRD ROUND**
**Tuesday, 25 September 2012**
**Celtic (2) 4** *(Hooper 12, 37, 58, 60)*
**Raith R (1) 1** *(Walker 28)* 14,737
*Celtic:* (442) Zaluska; Matthews, Rogne, Wilson, Mulgrew; McGeouch, Ambrose, Kayal (Ledley 61), Forrest (Commons 82); Watt (McCourt 71), Hooper.
*Raith R:* (442) McGurn; Thomson, Mensing, Hill, Malone (Ellis 89); Anderson G (Smith 68), Anderson S, Walker, Hamill; Spence (Callachan 68), Graham.

**Hearts (1) 3** *(Grainger 45, Zaliukas 70, 74)*
**Livingston (0) 1** *(McNulty 56)* 6322
*Hearts:* (4231) MacDonald; McGowan R, Barr, Zaliukas, Grainger; Stevenson, Taouil; Driver (Carrick 83), Robinson, Novikovas; Paterson (Sutton 81).
*Livingston:* (442) McNeil; Docherty, Watson, Barr C, Garcia Tena (Fordyce 76); Andreu, Scougall, Jacobs Keaghan, Russell (Easton 85); McNulty, Morton (Gray 83).

**Queen of the S (0) 0**
**Dundee U (1) 1** *(Russell 28)* 2374
*Queen of the S:* (442) Robinson; Mitchell, Durnan, Higgins, Holt; Carmichael, McKenna (Burns 46), Young, Gibson; Reilly (Lyle 82), Clark.
*Dundee U:* (442) Cierzniak; Watson, Dillon, Gunning, McLean; Gardyne, Ryan (Armstrong 66), Rankin, Flood (Millar 78); Russell, Daly.

**St Johnstone (2) 4** *(MacLean 18, 40, Davidson 76, Craig 85)*
**Queen's Park (1) 1** *(Keenan 30)* 1304
*St Johnstone:* (442) Tuffey; Miller, Anderson, McCracken, Scobbie; Hasselbaink (Craig 78), Robertson, Davidson M (Caddis 78), Moon; Tade (Beattie 78), MacLean.
*Queen's Park:* (442) Parry; Little, Bradley, Brough, Robertson■; Shankland (Gallacher 78), Keenan, Anderson, Burns (Watt 72); Longworth, Quinn (Smith 82).

**St Mirren (0) 1** *(Mair 90)*
**Hamilton A (0) 0** 1914
*St Mirren:* (3142) Samson; McAusland, Mair, Dummett; Goodwin; Imrie, McGowan, McLean (van Zanten 46), Carey; Parkin, Guy (Thompson 35).
*Hamilton A:* (541) Cuthbert; Gillespie, Canning, Neil, Devlin, Hendrie; Longridge, Fisher (Gordon 61), Routledge, Crawford; Keatings (Ryan 85).

**Stenhousemuir (1) 1** *(Ferguson 40 (pen))*
**Inverness CT (1) 1** *(McKay 23)* 705
*Stenhousemuir:* (442) Thomson R; Ross, Buist (Rodgers 96), McMillan, McKinlay; Ferguson, Thomson I (Anderson 103), Hodge, Dickson (Smith D 69); Gemmell, Kean.
*Inverness CT:* (433) Esson; Raven, Shinnie G, Warren, Meekings; Doran, Draper, Shinnie A; McKay (Roberts 102), Foran, Pepper (Morrison 79).
*aet; Inverness CT won 6-5 on penalties.*

Wednesday, 26 September 2012
**Dunfermline Ath (0) 0**
**Aberdeen (0) 1** *(Vernon 90)*     3057
*Dunfermline Ath:* (442) Gallacher; McMillan, Dowie, Morris, Jordan; Cardle, Geggan (Kirk 87), Husband, Falkingham (Thomson 80); Barrowman, Wallace.
*Aberdeen:* (433) Langfield; Magennis (Anderson 67), Reynolds, Considine, Robertson (Hughes 75); Osbourne, Rae, Clark; McGinn, Hayes (Vernon 61), Smith.

**Rangers (0) 2** *(McCulloch 50, Shiels 56)*
**Motherwell (0) 0**     29,413
*Rangers:* (442) Alexander; Faure, Perry, Emilson Cribari, Wallace; Argyriou, McCulloch, Macleod, Aird (McKay 81); Sandaza (Hutton 24), Shiels (Crawford 75).
*Motherwell:* (4411) Randolph; Kerr, Hutchinson, Cummins, Hammell (Francis-Angol 65); Humphrey (Daley 72), Hateley (Murphy 64), Lasley, Law; Ojamaa; Higdon.

## QUARTER-FINALS

Tuesday, 30 October 2012
**Aberdeen (1) 2** *(Vernon 22, Magennis 90)*
**St Mirren (1) 2** *(Parkin 6, McLean 69)*     7610
*Aberdeen:* (442) Langfield; Reynolds, Anderson, Osbourne, Robertson (Smith 83); Hughes, Rae, McGinn, Hayes; Magennis (Naysmith 106), Vernon (Fraser 78).
*St Mirren:* (442) Samson; van Zanten, McAusland, Mair, Dummett; Imrie (Carey 87), Goodwin, McLean, Teale; Parkin (Guy 93), Thompson.
*aet; St Mirren won 4-2 on penalties.*

**Celtic (3) 5** *(Commons 28, 32, 57 (pen), Hooper 38, Mulgrew 61)*
**St Johnstone (0) 0**     14,399
*Celtic:* (4312) Forster; Lustig, Ambrose (McCourt 71), Wilson, Izaguirre; Commons, Brown (Matthews 64), Wanyama; Ledley; Hooper (Mulgrew 46), Watt.
*St Johnstone:* (442) Mannus; Miller, Anderson, McCracken, MacKay; Millar, Davidson M (Robertson 64), Moon, Craig; Vine (MacLean 46), Tade (Hasselbaink 74).

Wednesday, 31 October 2012
**Dundee U (1) 1** *(Russell 35)*
**Hearts (1) 1** *(Paterson 21)*     3789
*Dundee U:* (442) Cierzniak; Watson, Dillon, Daly (McLean 107), Gunning; Flood, Ryan (Skacel 95), Rankin, Armstrong; Gardyne (Mackay-Steven 66), Russell.
*Hearts:* (433) MacDonald; McGowan R, Webster, Zaliukas, Grainger; Stevenson (Robinson 54), Barr[■], Taouil (McGowan D 109); Paterson, Sutton, Novikovas (Driver 97).
*aet; Hearts won 5-4 on penalties.*

**Rangers (0) 0**
**Inverness CT (1) 3** *(Shinnie A 27, Warren 59, Shinnie G 79 (pen))*     28,033
*Rangers:* (433) Alexander; Hegarty, Perry (Argyriou 46), Emilson Cribari, Wallace; Hutton (Kyle 62), Black, Macleod; Little, McCulloch, Shiels (McKay 62).
*Inverness CT:* (4411) Reguero; Raven, Warren, Meekings, Shinnie G; Doran, Tudur Jones, Draper, Roberts (Sutherland 82); Shinnie A (Foran 88); McKay (Pepper 90).

## SEMI-FINALS

Saturday, 26 January 2013
**Inverness CT (0) 1** *(Shinnie A 49)*
**Hearts (0) 1** *(Ngoo 66)*     16,336
*Inverness CT:* (451) Reguero; Raven, Warren, Meekings, Shinnie G; Doran (Roberts 89), Draper, Tudur Jones, Shinnie A, Foran (Sutherland 97); McKay.
*Hearts:* (451) MacDonald; Mullen, Webster, Zaliukas, Wilson; Holt, Walker (McGowan D 112), Robinson[■], Tapping (Taouil 97), Driver (Novikovas 67); Ngoo.
*aet; Hearts won 5-4 on penalties.*

Sunday, 27 January 2013
**St Mirren (1) 3** *(Goncalves 8, McGowan 64 (pen), Thompson 69)*
**Celtic (1) 2** *(Hooper 45, Mulgrew 90)*     24,417
*St Mirren:* (4231) Samson; van Zanten, Goodwin, McAusland, Carey; Newton, McGinn (Barron 76); Teale, McGowan (Mair 90), Goncalves (Guy 90); Thompson.
*Celtic:* (4132) Zaluska; Matthews, Wilson, Mulgrew, Izaguirre; Wanyama (Lustig 74); Brown, Hooper, Ledley; Nouioui (Commons 64), Samaras (Stokes 74).

### SCOTTISH COMMUNITIES CUP FINAL
Sunday, 17 March 2013
(at Hampden Park, attendance 44,036)
**St Mirren (1) 3     Hearts (1) 2**

*St Mirren:* (4231) Samson; van Zanten, McAusland, Goodwin, Dummett; Newton, McGinn (Carey 81); Teale, McGowan, Goncalves (Mair 90); Thompson (Parkin 77).
*Scorers:* Goncalves 37, Thompson 46, Newton 66.
*Hearts:* (442) MacDonald; McGowan D, Webster, Wilson, McHattie; Stevenson, Taouil (Carrick 80), Barr (Holt 70), Walker (Novikovas 64); Sutton, Ngoo.
*Scorer:* Stevenson 10, 85.
*Referee:* Craig Thomson.

St Mirren's Conor Newton scores in the Scottish League Cup Final as Hearts are beaten 3-2 at Hampden in March.
It was the Paisley club's first major honour since the 1987 Scottish Cup. (PA)

# RAMSDENS LEAGUE CHALLENGE CUP 2012–13

■ *Denotes player sent off.*

**FIRST ROUND NORTH-EAST**

Saturday, 28 July 2012
**Cowdenbeath (1) 1** *(Coult 2)*
**Alloa Ath (1) 1** *(Gordon 20)*          323
*Cowdenbeath:* (4141) Flynn; Cowan (Linton 90), Armstrong, Mbu, Adamson; Garcia-Rey (O'Brien 45); McKenzie, Milne (Stewart 67), Ramsay, Stevenson; Coult.
*Alloa Ath:* (442) Bain; Doyle, Gordon, Harding, Docherty; Cawley (McCord Ross 81), Young, McCord Ryan, Holmes; Grehan, Cox.
*aet; Cowdenbeath won 3-1 on penalties.*

**Elgin C (1) 5** *(Gunn 19, Leslie 50, 89, Moore 52, Wyness 87)*
**Arbroath (5) 7** *(Sibanda 16, 28, 43, Doris 21, Gribben 45, 66, 71 (pen))*          561
*Elgin C:* (442) Duffy; Niven, Crighton, Duff, McMullan (Wyness 72); Cameron, O'Donoghue (Hallford 72), McLean (Beveridge 45); Moore; Gunn, Leslie.
*Arbroath:* (442) Hill; Baxter, Brennan, Kerr, Robertson; Sheerin, Keddie (Travis 49), Sibanda (Rennie 63); Currie; Doris (Holmes 72), Gribben.

**Falkirk (1) 3** *(Duffie 34, Taylor 51, 57)*
**Stirling A (0) 0**          1532
*Falkirk:* (4411) McGovern; Duffie, Dods, Flynn, Kingsley; Sibbald (Dick 82), Fulton J (Fulton D 77), Murdoch, Leahy (White 78); Taylor; Haworth.
*Stirling A:* (442) Filler; Thom, McDonald, Allison, Ashe; McSorley, Macpherson (Davidson 59), McCunnie (86), Ferry; Weir (Brass 74), Coyne.

**Forfar Ath (1) 3** *(Kader 13, Denholm 53, Swankie 66)*
**Dunfermline Ath (2) 2** *(Wallace 16, Barrowman 35)*          840
*Forfar Ath:* (442) Soutar; McCulloch, Dunlop, Campbell I, Bolochoweckyj; King (Motion 72), Kader (Campbell R 80), Gibson, Denholm; Templeman (Fotheringham M 72), Swankie.
*Dunfermline Ath:* (442) Gallacher; Geggan, Potter, Dowie, McMillan; Husband (Kane 67), Thomson (Whittle 77), Falkingham, Cardle; Barrowman, Wallace (Kirk 67).

**Montrose (1) 4** *(Watson 28, Boyle 60, Wood G 66, Masson 81)*
**Inverurie Loco Works (1) 2** *(Mackay 16, Souter 88)*          401
*Montrose:* (442) Wood S; McNally, Lunan, Campbell, Watson; Masson, Young L (Clark 82), McLeish, Johnston (Gray 80); Boyle, Wood G.
*Inverurie Loco Works:* (442) Gray; Park, Bain (Young 71), Adams, Scott; Broadhurst, McLean (Strachan 62), Stewart, Maitland; Bagshaw (Souter 64), Mackay.

**Peterhead (0) 1** *(McAllister 75)*
**East Fife (1) 2** *(McBride 10 (pen), Samuel 54)*          520
*Peterhead:* (433) Jarvie; Sharp, Ross, MacDonald, Noble; Strachan, McLaughlin, Cowie; Redman (Bavidge 58), McAllister, Deasley (Winters 58).
*East Fife:* (442) Brown M; Durie, Campbell, McCormack, Johnstone; Jamieson, Smith Darren, Muir, McBride; Wardlaw (Brown R 28), Samuel (Malcolm 84).

**Wick Academy (0) 2** *(Geruzel 51, Allan D 61)*
**Raith R (1) 4** *(Graham 39, Hill 57, Anderson G 71, Clarke 83)*          980
*Wick Academy:* (4231) Gray; Cunningham, Steven, Farquhar (Ross 82), Allan R; Manson (Weir 86), Shearer; Mackay, Geruzel, Allan D; Macadie.
*Raith R:* (442) McGurn; Thomson, Murray, Hill (Ellis 76), Malone; Anderson G (Callachan 85), Anderson S, Walker, Hamill; Graham, Clarke.

Sunday, 29 July 2012
**Brechin C (1) 1** *(Jackson 43)*
**Rangers (1) 2** *(Little 4, McCulloch 102)*          4123
*Brechin C:* (442) Andrews; McLean P, Moyes, McLauchlan, Brown; Stewart R (Stewart J 82), Brady, Molloy, Carcary (Dalziel 62); McKenna (Fusco 111), Jackson.
*Rangers:* (442) Alexander; Goian, Bocanegra, Broadfoot, Wallace; McKay (Naismith 96), Black, Hutton, Macleod; Little (Crawford 111), McCulloch.
*aet.*

**FIRST ROUND SOUTH-WEST**

Saturday, 28 July 2012
**Annan Ath (0) 1** *(Bell 74)*
**Livingston (0) 0**          572
*Annan Ath:* (442) Mitchell; Blake, McGowan, Swinglehurst, Thorburn; Love (Bell 62), Chaplain, McKechnie, Murray; Daly (McGachie 76), Ramage (Steele 62).
*Livingston:* (442) McNeil; McCann, Watson, Fordyce, McDonald; Barr R (Downie 78), Andreu, Jacobs Keaghan (Russell I 24), Scougall; McNulty, Morton (Beaumont 75).

**Berwick R (0) 2** *(Janczyk 76, McDonald 113)*
**Queen's Park (0) 2** *(Quinn 54, 101)*          372
*Berwick R:* (433) Bejaoui; Jacobs, McLean, Brydon, Gielty; McDonald, Janczyk (Stevenson 105), Currie L; McLaren, Ferguson (Addison 65), Lavery (Miller 70).
*Queen's Park:* (4411) Parry; Monaghan, Little, Keenan, Bradley; Ronald (Shankland 119), Urquhart (Gallacher 90), Longworth, Robertson; Capuano; Quinn.
*aet; Queen's Park won 3-2 on penalties.*

**Clyde (0) 0**
**Partick Th (0) 1** *(Doolan 73)*          1065
*Clyde:* (442) Barclay; Brown (Graham 86), Gray, Marsh, Sharp; Oliver, Sweeney, Hay, Fitzpatrick (Watt 38); Scullion, McColm (McCluskey S 86).
*Partick Th:* (451) Fox; O'Donnell, Muirhead, Archibald, Bannigan; Lawless, Welsh, Murray, Paton, Erskine (Craigen 81); Elliot (Doolan 68).

**Dumbarton (0) 0**
**Queen of the S (0) 1** *(Clark 69)*          684
*Dumbarton:* (442) Grindlay; Marr, Lithgow, Graham, Creaney; Gilhaney (Johnston 73), Fleming, Agnew, McDougall; Lister, Prunty (Lamont 73).
*Queen of the S:* (442) Robinson; McGuffie, Durnan, Higgins, Holt; Carmichael, McKenna, Young, Gibson (Lyle 79); Smith (Reilly 63), Clark.

**East Stirling (2) 3** *(Herd 28, 42, Maxwell 86)*
**Ayr U (0) 1** *(Shankland 51)*          493
*East Stirling:* (442) Hay; Hume, Jackson, Hunter, Shepherd; Greenhill, Miller, Begg (Gillespie 75), Maxwell; Herd, Devlin.
*Ayr U:* (442) Brown; Tiffoney, Brownlie, Robertson J, McCann; Marenghi (Crawford 52), McStay, Sinclair, Robertson R (Roberts 60); Moffat, Shankland.

**Hamilton A (0) 0**
**Airdrie U (0) 1** *(McLaren 85)*          1005
*Hamilton A:* (442) Cuthbert; McGlinchey (Mackinnon 88), Canning, Devlin, Hendrie; Fraser, Crawford, Gillespie, Martin; Ryan (Longridge 66), McShane.
*Airdrie U:* (442) Arthur; Hart, Lilley, MacDonald, Warren; Evans (Stallard 73), Blockley, Lynch, Griffin; Di Giacomo (Donnelly 60), Boyle John (McLaren 82).

**Morton (0) 2** *(Wallace 48, O'Brien 59)*
**Albion R (0) 0**          1269
*Morton:* (4141) Gaston; Taggart, Rutkiewicz, McLaughlin M (Naismith 71), Dyer; Reid; Wallace (Graham 77), Stirling, Tidser, O'Brien; Weatherson (Campbell 73).

*Albion R:* (4411) McCluskey; Reid, O'Byrne, Donnelly, Russell; Stevenson C, Innes, Stevenson A■, Phillips; Dick (Marriott 59); Crooks (Howarth 70).

**Stranraer (0) 1** *(Winter 71)*
**Stenhousemuir (1) 2** *(Gemmell 36, Ferguson 86)*        306
*Stranraer:* (442) Mitchell; Kinnaird, McKeown, Staunton, Dunlop; Winter, Gallagher, Aitken, Borris; Malcolm (Moore 68), Love.
*Stenhousemuir:* (4231) Reidford; Ross, McMillan, Buist, McKinlay; Hodge, Paton; Ferguson, Rodgers (Smith D 76), Dickson; Gemmell.

### SECOND ROUND NORTH-EAST

Tuesday, 14 August 2012

**Arbroath (3) 3** *(Currie 22, Gribben 35, 38)*
**Forfar Ath (2) 2** *(Swankie 30, Gibson 44)*        732
*Arbroath:* (442) Hill; Baxter, Travis, Keddie, Brennan; Rennie, Kerr (Sheerin 73), Currie (Sibanda 51), Mair; Holmes, Gribben (Doris 77).
*Forfar Ath:* (442) Soutar; McCulloch, Bolochoweckyj, Tulloch, Campbell I■; Campbell R (Motion 73), Gibson, Denholm (Dunlop 83), Fotheringham M; Swankie, King (Templeman 73).

**Cowdenbeath (1) 3** *(Stevenson 44, 73, Miller 67)*
**East Fife (0) 0**        466
*Cowdenbeath:* (442) Flynn; Brett, Armstrong, Adamson, McKenzie (Callaghan 82); Milne (O'Brien 68), Miller, Stevenson, Linton; Stewart, Coult (Nicholson 77).
*East Fife:* (442) Brown M; Durie, White, McCormack, Cook (Brewster 86); Sloan R, Brown R (Smith Darren 70), Muir, McBride; Wardlaw, McManus P.

**Raith R (3) 5** *(Walker 7, Graham 32, 54, Clarke 42, Spence 90)*
**Montrose (1) 2** *(Watson 45 (pen), Young L 77)*        773
*Raith R:* (442) McGurn■; Thomson, Ellis, Hill, Malone; Anderson G (Callachan 59), Anderson S, Walker, Hamill; Graham (Spence 85), Clarke (Laidlaw 44).
*Montrose:* (442) Wood S; McNally, Campbell, Lunan, Watson; Gray, Masson, McLeish (Young L 57), Johnston; Boyle, Wood G.

Tuesday, 21 August 2012
**Falkirk (0) 0**
**Rangers (1) 1** *(Little 45)*        6747
*Falkirk:* (4411) McGovern; Duffie, Flynn, Smith, Kingsley; Alston, Murdoch, Fulton J, Weatherston (Haworth 75); Sibbald (White 83); Taylor.
*Rangers:* (352) Alexander; Broadfoot, Emilson Cribari, Bocanegra; Hegarty (Crawford 84), McKay (Naismith 70), McCulloch, Black, Macleod; Little, Sandaza (Kyle 70).

### SECOND ROUND SOUTH-WEST

Tuesday, 14 August 2012
**Annan Ath (0) 0**
**Stenhousemuir (2) 3** *(Kean 25, Dickson 31, Rodgers 60)*
        449
*Annan Ath:* (442) Mitchell; Blake, McGowan, Swinglehurst, Thorburn; Sloan, Jardine, Daly (McGachie 62), Love; Steele, Chaplain (Watson 83).
*Stenhousemuir:* (442) Reidford; Ross, Buist, McMillan, Dickson; Anderson (Thomson I 62), Hodge (Brash 79), Rodgers, Smith D (Love 82); Kean, Gemmell.

**East Stirling (2) 3** *(Maxwell 23, Turner 36, Herd 89)*
**Airdrie U (0) 0**        383
*East Stirling:* (442) McWilliams; Hume, Jackson, Miller, Shepherd; Greenhill, Devlin, Hunter (Benton 87), Maxwell; Turner (Herd 81), Quinn.
*Airdrie U:* (442) Arthur; Hart, Lilley, MacDonald, Griffin; Bain (Buchanan G 74), Lynch (Boyle Jack 46), Blockley, McLaren; Cook (Di Giacomo 46), Boyle John.

**Morton (1) 1** *(Tidser 38)*
**Queen of the S (0) 2** *(Durnan 66, Clark 105)*        1178
*Morton:* (4141) Gaston; Taggart, Rutkiewicz, McLaughlin M, Halsman (Wilkie 113); Reid (Graham 71); Wallace, Stirling (Campbell 78), Tidser, O'Brien; Weatherson.
*Queen of the S:* (4132) Robinson; McGuffie, Durnan, Higgins, Holt; McKenna; Mitchell, Johnston (Orsi 105), Carmichael; Reilly (Lyle 67), Clark (Hopkirk 119).
*aet.*

**Queen's Park (1) 4** *(Shankland 18, Longworth 54, Quinn 81, Little 86)*
**Partick Th (2) 5** *(Sinclair 34, Elliot 40, Erskine 65, 90, Bannigan 90)*        1605
*Queen's Park:* (433) Parry; Little, Brough, Bradley, Robertson; Capuano (Smith 80), Longworth, Keenan; Ronald (Burns 46), Quinn, Shankland.
*Partick Th:* (433) Scully; O'Donnell S, Muirhead, Balatoni, Sinclair; Paton, Craigen, Welsh (Erskine 8); McGuigan (Lawless 56), Elliot (Doolan 83), Bannigan.

### QUARTER-FINALS

Sunday, 9 September 2012
**Arbroath (1) 1** *(Robertson 34)*
**Stenhousemuir (0) 0**        623
*Arbroath:* (442) Morrison; Baxter, Malcolm, Keddie, Hamilton; Rennie (Sibanda 74), Kerr, Robertson (Birse 82), Sheerin; Holmes, Doris (Gribben 74).
*Stenhousemuir:* (442) Reidford; Ross, Buist (Rodgers 82), McMillan, Dickson; Ferguson (Anderson 72), Hodge, Thomson I, Smith D; Gemmell■, Kean.

**East Stirling (1) 1** *(Kelly 24)*
**Cowdenbeath (2) 2** *(McKenzie 10, Adamson 40)*        414
*East Stirling:* (4411) Hay; Jackson, Miller, Kelly, Shepherd; Herd (Donaldson 85), Devlin (Begg 78), Hunter, Maxwell; Greenhill (Glasgow 87); Turner.
*Cowdenbeath:* (442) Flynn; Brett, Armstrong, Adamson, Linton; McKenzie, Miller, Cameron (O'Brien 46 (Navas 78)), Milne (Ramsay 55); Stevenson, Coult.

**Partick Th (0) 3** *(Erskine 50, 58, Craig 53)*
**Raith R (0) 0**        1807
*Partick Th:* (433) Fox; O'Donnell S, Muirhead, Archibald (Balatoni 65), Bannigan; Paton, Murray (Sinclair 66), Welsh; Lawless, Craig (Elliot 70), Erskine.
*Raith R:* (442) Fleming; Thomson, Murray, Malone, Donaldson; Anderson G (Smith 66), Anderson S (Callachan 73), Walker, Hamill; Graham, Clarke (Spence 76).

Tuesday, 18 September 2012
**Rangers (0) 2** *(McKay 55, McCulloch 72 (pen))*
**Queen of the S (0) 2** *(Clark 49, Reilly 90)*        23,932
*Rangers:* (442) Alexander; Argyriou, Perry, Emilson Cribari, Wallace; McKay (Faure 79), McCulloch, Black, Macleod (Naismith 79); Shiels, Sandaza (Kyle■ 54).
*Queen of the S:* (4231) Robinson; McGuffie, Higgins, Durnan, Holt; Mitchell (Lyle 84), Young; Carmichael (Orsi 97), Reilly, Gibson■; Clark.
*aet; Queen of the S won 4-3 on penalties.*

### SEMI-FINALS

Sunday, 14 October 2012
**Cowdenbeath (0) 0**
**Partick Th (0) 1** *(Craig 74)*        1159
*Cowdenbeath:* (4411) Flynn; Cowan, Garcia-Rey, Adamson, Linton (Mbu 83); McKenzie, O'Brien, Miller, Stevenson; Ramsay (Coult 77); Stewart.
*Partick Th:* (4411) Fox; O'Donnell S, Muirhead, Balatoni, Bannigan; Lawless, Paton, Forbes (Slane 61), Welsh; Erskine (Doolan 77); Craig (Elliot 89).

**Queen of the S (1) 2** *(Young 9, McGuffie 117)*
**Arbroath (0) 1** *(Keddie 58)*        2310
*Queen of the S:* (442) Robinson; Mitchell, McGuffie, Durnan, Holt; Carmichael, McKenna, Young, Orsi (Lyle 69); Reilly (Johnston 103), Clark (Black 120).
*Arbroath:* (451) Morrison; Baxter, Malcolm, Keddie, Hamilton (Banjo 46); Sibanda (Holmes 109), Robertson, Kerr, Currie, Rennie (Gribben 89); Doris.
*aet.*

**RAMSDENS CUP FINAL**

Sunday, 7 April 2013

(at Livingston, attendance 9452)

**Queen of the S (0) 1     Partick Th (0) 1**

*Queen of the S:* (442) Robinson; Mitchell, Durnan, Higgins, Fitzpatrick; Carmichael, McKenna, Young, Paton (Black 115); Lyle (Reilly 78), Clark (Smith 101).
*Scorer:* Clark 101.

*Partick Th:* (433) Fox; O'Donnell S, Muirhead■, Balatoni, Sinclair; Welsh, Craigen, Bannigan (Forbes 94); Lawless (Elliot 60), Craig (Doolan 66), Erskine.
*Scorer:* Doolan 120.

*Referee:* Allan Crawford.

*aet; Queen of the S won 6-5 on penalties.*

# LEAGUE CHALLENGE FINALS 1991–2013

| Season | Winners | Runners-up | Score |
|---|---|---|---|
| 1990–91 | Dundee | Ayr U | 3-2 |
| 1991–92 | Hamilton A | Ayr U | 1-0 |
| 1992–93 | Hamilton A | Morton | 3-2 |
| 1993–94 | Falkirk | St Mirren | 3-0 |
| 1994–95 | Airdrieonians | Dundee | 3-2 |
| 1995–96 | Stenhousemuir | Dundee U | 0-0 |
| | *(aet; Stenhousemuir won 5-4 on penalties)* | | |
| 1996–97 | Stranraer | St Johnstone | 1-0 |
| 1997–98 | Falkirk | Queen of the S | 1-0 |
| 1998–99 | no competition | | |
| 1999–2000 | Alloa Ath | Inverness CT | 4-4 |
| | *(aet; Alloa Ath won 5-4 on penalties)* | | |
| 2000–01 | Airdrieonians | Livingston | 2-2 |
| | *(aet; Airdrieonians won 3-2 on penalties)* | | |
| 2001–02 | Airdrieonians | Alloa Ath | 2-1 |
| 2002–03 | Queen of the S | Brechin C | 2-0 |
| 2003–04 | Inverness CT | Airdrie U | 2-0 |
| 2004–05 | Falkirk | Ross Co | 2-1 |
| 2005–06 | St Mirren | Hamilton A | 2-1 |
| 2006–07 | Ross Co | Clyde | 1-1 |
| | *(aet; Ross Co won 5-4 on penalties)* | | |
| 2007–08 | St Johnstone | Dunfermline Ath | 3-2 |
| 2008–09 | Airdrie U | Ross Co | 2-2 |
| | *(aet; Airdrie U won 3-2 on penalties)* | | |
| 2009–10 | Dundee | Inverness CT | 3-2 |
| 2010–11 | Ross Co | Queen of the S | 2-0 |
| 2011–12 | Falkirk | Hamilton A | 1-0 |
| 2012–13 | Queen of the S | Partick Th | 1-1 |
| | *(aet; Queen of the S won 6-5 on penalties)* | | |

# SCOTTISH CUP FINALS 1874–2013

| Year | Winners | Runners-up | Score |
|------|---------|-----------|-------|
| 1874 | Queen's Park | Clydesdale | 2-0 |
| 1875 | Queen's Park | Renton | 3-0 |
| 1876 | Queen's Park | Third Lanark | 2-0 after 1-1 draw |
| 1877 | Vale of Leven | Rangers | 3-2 after 0-0 and 1-1 draws |
| 1878 | Vale of Leven | Third Lanark | 1-0 |
| 1879 | Vale of Leven* | Rangers | |
| 1880 | Queen's Park | Thornlibank | 3-0 |
| 1881 | Queen's Park† | Dumbarton | 3-1 |
| 1882 | Queen's Park | Dumbarton | 4-1 after 2-2 draw |
| 1883 | Dumbarton | Vale of Leven | 2-1 after 2-2 draw |
| 1884 | Queen's Park‡ | Vale of Leven | |
| 1885 | Renton | Vale of Leven | 3-1 after 0-0 draw |
| 1886 | Queen's Park | Renton | 3-1 |
| 1887 | Hibernian | Dumbarton | 2-1 |
| 1888 | Renton | Cambuslang | 6-1 |
| 1889 | Third Lanark§ | Celtic | 2-1 |
| 1890 | Queen's Park | Vale of Leven | 2-1 after 1-1 draw |
| 1891 | Hearts | Dumbarton | 1-0 |
| 1892 | Celtic¶ | Queen's Park | 5-1 |
| 1893 | Queen's Park | Celtic | 2-1 |
| 1894 | Rangers | Celtic | 3-1 |
| 1895 | St Bernard's | Renton | 2-1 |
| 1896 | Hearts | Hibernian | 3-1 |
| 1897 | Rangers | Dumbarton | 5-1 |
| 1898 | Rangers | Kilmarnock | 2-0 |
| 1899 | Celtic | Rangers | 2-0 |
| 1900 | Celtic | Queen's Park | 4-3 |
| 1901 | Hearts | Celtic | 4-3 |
| 1902 | Hibernian | Celtic | 1-0 |
| 1903 | Rangers | Hearts | 2-0 after 1-1 and 0-0 draws |
| 1904 | Celtic | Rangers | 3-2 |
| 1905 | Third Lanark | Rangers | 3-1 after 0-0 draw |
| 1906 | Hearts | Third Lanark | 1-0 |
| 1907 | Celtic | Hearts | 3-0 |
| 1908 | Celtic | St Mirren | 5-1 |
| 1909 | •• | | |
| 1910 | Dundee | Clyde | 2-1 after 2-2 and 0-0 draws |
| 1911 | Celtic | Hamilton A | 2-0 after 0-0 draw |
| 1912 | Celtic | Clyde | 2-0 |
| 1913 | Falkirk | Raith R | 2-0 |
| 1914 | Celtic | Hibernian | 4-1 after 0-0 draw |
| 1920 | Kilmarnock | Albion R | 3-2 |
| 1921 | Partick Th | Rangers | 1-0 |
| 1922 | Morton | Rangers | 1-0 |
| 1923 | Celtic | Hibernian | 1-0 |
| 1924 | Airdrieonians | Hibernian | 2-0 |
| 1925 | Celtic | Dundee | 2-1 |
| 1926 | St Mirren | Celtic | 2-0 |
| 1927 | Celtic | East Fife | 3-1 |
| 1928 | Rangers | Celtic | 4-0 |
| 1929 | Kilmarnock | Rangers | 2-0 |
| 1930 | Rangers | Partick Th | 2-1 after 0-0 draw |
| 1931 | Celtic | Motherwell | 4-2 after 2-2 draw |
| 1932 | Rangers | Kilmarnock | 3-0 after 1-1 draw |
| 1933 | Celtic | Motherwell | 1-0 |
| 1934 | Rangers | St Mirren | 5-0 |
| 1935 | Rangers | Hamilton A | 2-1 |
| 1936 | Rangers | Third Lanark | 1-0 |
| 1937 | Celtic | Aberdeen | 2-1 |
| 1938 | East Fife | Kilmarnock | 4-2 after 1-1 draw |
| 1939 | Clyde | Motherwell | 4-0 |
| 1947 | Aberdeen | Hibernian | 2-1 |
| 1948 | Rangers | Morton | 1-0 after 1-1 draw |
| 1949 | Rangers | Clyde | 4-1 |
| 1950 | Rangers | East Fife | 3-0 |
| 1951 | Celtic | Motherwell | 1-0 |
| 1952 | Motherwell | Dundee | 4-0 |
| 1953 | Rangers | Aberdeen | 1-0 after 1-1 draw |
| 1954 | Celtic | Aberdeen | 2-1 |
| 1955 | Clyde | Celtic | 1-0 after 1-1 draw |
| 1956 | Hearts | Celtic | 3-1 |
| 1957 | Falkirk | Kilmarnock | 2-1 after 1-1 draw |
| 1958 | Clyde | Hibernian | 1-0 |
| 1959 | St Mirren | Aberdeen | 3-1 |
| 1960 | Rangers | Kilmarnock | 2-0 |

| Year | Winners | Runners-up | Score |
|------|---------|-----------|-------|
| 1961 | Dunfermline Ath | Celtic | 2-0 after 0-0 draw |
| 1962 | Rangers | St Mirren | 2-0 |
| 1963 | Rangers | Celtic | 3-0 after 1-1 draw |
| 1964 | Rangers | Dundee | 3-1 |
| 1965 | Celtic | Dunfermline Ath | 3-2 |
| 1966 | Rangers | Celtic | 1-0 after 0-0 draw |
| 1967 | Celtic | Aberdeen | 2-0 |
| 1968 | Dunfermline Ath | Hearts | 3-1 |
| 1969 | Celtic | Rangers | 4-0 |
| 1970 | Aberdeen | Celtic | 3-1 |
| 1971 | Celtic | Rangers | 2-1 after 1-1 draw |
| 1972 | Celtic | Hibernian | 6-1 |
| 1973 | Rangers | Celtic | 3-2 |
| 1974 | Celtic | Dundee U | 3-0 |
| 1975 | Celtic | Airdrieonians | 3-1 |
| 1976 | Rangers | Hearts | 3-1 |
| 1977 | Celtic | Rangers | 1-0 |
| 1978 | Rangers | Aberdeen | 2-1 |
| 1979 | Rangers | Hibernian | 3-2 after 0-0 and 0-0 draws |
| 1980 | Celtic | Rangers | 1-0 |
| 1981 | Rangers | Dundee U | 4-1 after 0-0 draw |
| 1982 | Aberdeen | Rangers | 4-1 (aet) |
| 1983 | Aberdeen | Rangers | 1-0 (aet) |
| 1984 | Aberdeen | Celtic | 2-1 (aet) |
| 1985 | Celtic | Dundee U | 2-1 |
| 1986 | Aberdeen | Hearts | 3-0 |
| 1987 | St Mirren | Dundee U | 1-0 (aet) |
| 1988 | Celtic | Dundee U | 2-1 |
| 1989 | Celtic | Rangers | 1-0 |
| 1990 | Aberdeen | Celtic | 0-0 (aet) |
|      | | *(Aberdeen won 9-8 on penalties)* | |
| 1991 | Motherwell | Dundee U | 4-3 (aet) |
| 1992 | Rangers | Airdrieonians | 2-1 |
| 1993 | Rangers | Aberdeen | 2-1 |
| 1994 | Dundee U | Rangers | 1-0 |
| 1995 | Celtic | Airdrieonians | 1-0 |
| 1996 | Rangers | Hearts | 5-1 |
| 1997 | Kilmarnock | Falkirk | 1-0 |
| 1998 | Hearts | Rangers | 2-1 |
| 1999 | Rangers | Celtic | 1-0 |
| 2000 | Rangers | Aberdeen | 4-0 |
| 2001 | Celtic | Hibernian | 3-0 |
| 2002 | Rangers | Celtic | 3-2 |
| 2003 | Rangers | Dundee | 1-0 |
| 2004 | Celtic | Dunfermline Ath | 3-1 |
| 2005 | Celtic | Dundee U | 1-0 |
| 2006 | Hearts | Gretna | 1-1 (aet) |
|      | | *(Hearts won 4-2 on penalties)* | |
| 2007 | Celtic | Dunfermline Ath | 1-0 |
| 2008 | Rangers | Queen of the S | 3-2 |
| 2009 | Rangers | Falkirk | 1-0 |
| 2010 | Dundee U | Ross Co | 3-0 |
| 2011 | Celtic | Motherwell | 3-0 |
| 2012 | Hearts | Hibernian | 5-1 |
| 2013 | Celtic | Hibernian | 3-0 |

*Vale of Leven awarded cup, Rangers failing to appear for replay after 1-1 draw.
†After Dumbarton protested the first game, which Queen's Park won 2-1.
‡Queen's Park awarded cup, Vale of Leven failing to appear.
§Replay by order of Scottish FA because of playing conditions in first match, won 3-0 by Third Lanark.
¶After mutually protested game which Celtic won 1-0.
••Owing to riot, the cup was withheld after two drawn games between Celtic and Rangers 2-2 and 1-1.

### SCOTTISH CUP WINS

Celtic 36, Rangers 33, Queen's Park 10, Hearts 8, Aberdeen 7, Clyde 3, Kilmarnock 3, St Mirren 3, Vale of Leven 3, Dundee U 2, Dunfermline Ath 2, Falkirk 2, Hibernian 2, Motherwell 2, Renton 2, Third Lanark 2, Airdrieonians 1, Dumbarton 1, Dundee 1, East Fife 1, Morton 1, Partick Th 1, St Bernard's 1.

### APPEARANCES IN FINAL

Celtic 54, Rangers 50, Aberdeen 15, Hearts 14, Hibernian 13, Queen's Park 12, Dundee U 9, Kilmarnock 8, Motherwell 7, Vale of Leven 7, Clyde 6, Dumbarton 6, St Mirren 6, Third Lanark 6, Dundee 5, Dunfermline Ath 5, Renton 5, Airdrieonians 4, Falkirk 4, East Fife 3, Hamilton A 2, Morton 2, Partick Th 2, Albion R 1, Cambuslang 1, Clydesdale 1, Gretna 1, Queen of the S 1, Raith R 1, Ross Co 1, St Bernard's 1, Thornliebank 1.

# WILLIAM HILL SCOTTISH CUP 2012–13

■ *Denotes player sent off.*

**PRELIMINARY ROUND**

| | |
|---|---|
| Fort William v Preston Ath | 1-3 |
| Keith v St Cuthbert W | 0-1 |

**FIRST ROUND**

| | |
|---|---|
| Bonnyrigg Rose v Girvan | 2-1 |
| Buckie Th v Rothes | 0-0, 4-0 |
| Civil Service Strollers v Newton Stewart | 4-0 |
| Clachnacuddin v Lossiemouth | 2-1 |
| Edinburgh Univ v St Cuthbert W | 1-2 |
| Formartine U v Brora Rangers | 3-2 |
| Fraserburgh v Coldstream | 4-0 |
| Glasgow University v Selkirk | 0-2 |
| Hawick Royal Albert v Golspie Sutherland | 1-4 |
| Hermes v Deveronvale | 1-4 |
| Huntly v Wigtown & Bladnoch | 2-2, 2-0 |
| Irvine Meadow v Gala Fairydean | 4-0 |
| Preston Ath v Nairn Co | 0-2 |
| Shotts Bon Accord v Edinburgh C | 1-1, 1-4 |
| Spartans v Wick Academy | 0-2 |
| Threave R v Vale of Leithen | 0-1 |
| Turriff U v Burntisland Shipyard | 6-1 |
| Whitehill Welfare v Inverurie Loco Works | 2-4 |

**SECOND ROUND**

| | |
|---|---|
| Berwick R v Wick Academy | 1-0 |
| Buckie Th v Annan Ath | 0-0, 2-1 |
| Civil Service Strollers v Turriff U | 1-2 |
| Clachnacuddin v Formartine U | 4-2 |
| Clyde v Nairn Co | 3-3, 2-3 |
| Cove Rangers v Golspie Sutherland | 7-0 |
| Dalbeattie Star v Stirling A | 0-5 |
| Deveronvale v Peterhead | 3-2 |
| Elgin C v St Cuthbert W | 3-1 |
| Forres Mechanics v Rangers | 0-1 |
| Fraserburgh v East Stirling | 1-2 |
| Inverurie Loco Works v Huntly | 4-3 |
| Montrose v Edinburgh C | 1-3 |
| Queen's Park v Irvine Meadow | 3-0 |
| Selkirk v Vale of Leithen | 1-1, 1-5 |
| Stirling University v Bonnyrigg Rose Ath | 0-1 |

**THIRD ROUND**

Saturday, 3 November 2012

**Airdrie U (1) 2** *(Griffin 28, Thomson 78 (og))*
**Raith R (1) 2** *(Mensing 13, Spence 90)*            854
*Airdrie U:* (442) Arthur; Hart, Evans, Buchanan G, Griffin; Bain, Stallard, Blockley, Watt J (McLaren 69); Di Giacomo (Donnelly 79), Boyle John.
*Raith R:* (433) Laidlaw; Thomson, Ellis, Hill, Donaldson; Mensing, Walker, Anderson S (Anderson G 80); Spence, Graham, Clarke (Smith 46).

**Albion R (1) 1** *(Stevenson 45)*
**Morton (0) 1** *(Weatherson 58)*            656
*Albion R:* (442) McGinley; Reid, Stevenson, O'Byrne, Russell; Crawford, Donnelly, Marriott (Innes 61), Phillips; Boyle (Brannan 70), Howarth (Crooks 75).
*Morton:* (442) Gaston (Hutton 76); Taggart, Rutkiewicz, McLaughlin M (O'Ware 67), Dyer; Graham, Wilkie (Wallace 57), Tidser, O'Brien; Weatherson, Campbell.

**Ayr U (0) 2** *(Moffat 50, 60 (pen))*
**Clachnacuddin (1) 1** *(Graham 14)*            1032
*Ayr U:* (433) Brown; Hunter, Robertson J (Robertson R 22), McCann, Twaddle; Wyllie, Crawford, McStay; Shankland (Winters 55), Roberts (Brownlie 67), Moffat.
*Clachnacuddin:* (4231) Campbell; Scott-Woodhouse, Milne, Williamson, Tatters; Finnis, Callum (Brindle 67); Ross, Pollock, Graham (Morrison 76); Ellis (Urquhart 53).

**Brechin C (0) 2** *(Jackson 61, Dunn 78 (og))*
**Bonnyrigg Rose Ath (1) 2** *(Grady 21, Renton 58)*            602
*Brechin C:* (442) Nelson; McLean, Hay, Moyes, Brown; Trouten, Brady (Stewart R 87), Molloy (Stewart J 62), McKenna (Carcary 55); Jackson, Byrne.
*Bonnyrigg Rose Ath:* (352) Burgess; Archibald; Dunn, Woodburn; McLeish, McKenna; Burrell, King, Roseburgh; Renton, Grady.

**Buckie Th (0) 0**
**Turriff U (1) 1** *(Harris 14)*            800
*Buckie Th:* (442) Main; Wood, Angus, Wood, Shewan (Carrol 87); Napier (Sutherland 78), Munro, Davidson, Sutherland; Smith (Gardiner 83), Clark.
*Turriff U:* (451) Coutts; Davidson, Anderson, Simpson, Bowden; Ligertwood, Mackenzie, Davidson (Fraser 61), Young, Gauld (Henderson 74); Harris ( 87).

**Cowdenbeath (3) 8** *(Stewart G 25, 31, 41, Coult 47, 51, McKenzie 49, Ramsay 64, Stevenson 78)*
**Vale of Leithen (1) 1** *(Moffat 2)*            309
*Cowdenbeath:* (442) Wight; Brett, Armstrong, Mbu, Adamson (Miller 60); McKenzie, Ramsay (Cameron 68), Puigdollers, Stevenson; Stewart G (Thomas 65), Coult.
*Vale of Leithen:* (442) Hudson; Gordon, McKenzie, Blakie, Draper (Paterson 68); Sproule, Dodds■, Devlin, Inglis; Moffat (Smith 77), Noon (Cairney 68).

**Dumbarton (2) 4** *(Graham 13, Lister 45, Prunty 76, Lithgow 89)*
**East Stirling (1) 1** *(Greenhill 44)*            446
*Dumbarton:* (442) Ewings; Devlin, Lithgow, Graham Andrew, Forsyth; Fleming (Johnston 83), Turner, Agnew, Gilhaney (McDougall 65); Lister, Prunty (Lamont 77).
*East Stirling:* (4141) Hay; Jackson, Miller, Kelly, Shepherd; McKernon; Turner, Zufle, Greenhill, Maxwell (Herd 52); Quinn.

**Edinburgh C (0) 0**
**Queen of the S (1) 2** *(Clark 42, Reilly G 65)*            1038
*Edinburgh C:* (541) Stobie; Harrison, Fusco, Scott, McLean (Devlin 71), Dingwall; Gair, Vanson (Clapperton 80), Torrance, Howat; Guthrie (Elliott 79).
*Queen of the S:* (433) Robinson; Mitchell, Black, Higgins, McGuffie; Burns (McShane 79), Carmichael (Gibson 68), McKenna; Clark, Reilly, Lyle.

**Elgin C (2) 5** *(Leslie 27, Gunn 32, Moore 55 (pen), Nicolson 67, Harkins 73)*
**East Fife (0) 1** *(Muir 78)*            748
*Elgin C:* (442) Gibson; Beveridge, Crighton, Duff, McMullan; Cameron, O'Donoghue, Nicolson (Harkins 70), Moore; Gunn (Wyness 74), Leslie (Millar 74).
*East Fife:* (451) Antell; Durie, Campbell, White, Sloan R (Gordon 69); Smith Darren, Johnstone, Muir, Pollock (Jamieson 57); McBride; McManus P.

**Forfar Ath (3) 3** *(Templeman 11, Swankie 26, Tulloch 39)*
**Nairn Co (0) 3** *(Macdonald 57, Naismith R 72, MacMillan 90)*            546
*Forfar Ath:* (442) Soutar; McCulloch, Bolochoweckyj, Tulloch, Campbell I; Campbell R (Sellars 73), Motion, Templeman, Denholm (Reid 89); Swankie, King (Kader 59).
*Nairn Co:* (442) Donaldson; Webb, Morrison, Macdonald, Neill; Main, Watson, Ellis (MacMillan 53), Main; Gethins, Cameron (Mendes 30 (Naismith R 53)).

**Inverurie Loco Works (0) 3** *(Bain 67, Gauld 86, 90)*
**Arbroath (2) 3** *(Doris 5 (pen), Currie 23, Gribben 58)* 732
*Inverurie Loco Works:* (433) Reid; Michie, Park, Broadhurst, McLean; Souter (Begg 84), Stewart, Bain; Mckay, Gauld, Low (Ross 69).
*Arbroath:* (433) Morrison; Baxter, Malcolm, Keddie, Brennan; Currie, Kerr, Sheerin (Robertson 89); Doris, Holmes (Rennie D 76), Gribben (Sibanda 73).

**Partick Th (2) 2** *(Forbes 13, Redford 38 (og))*
**Cove Rangers (0) 1** *(Milne 86)* 1957
*Partick Th:* (433) Fox; O'Donnell S, Muirhead, Balatoni, Sinclair; Craig■, Paton, Forbes; Lawless (Elliot 62), Doolan (Slane 62), Erskine (Rowson 81).
*Cove Rangers:* (442) McKenzie; Yule, Redford, Watson, Lawrie; Singer (McCulloch 46), Emslie, Beagrie, Scully (Stott 69); Johnston, Leyden (Milne 58).

**Rangers (3) 7** *(Shiels 2, 21, McCulloch 33, 72, Crawford 73, McKay 82, 89)*
**Alloa Ath (0) 0** 25,478
*Rangers:* (442) Alexander; Argyriou (Crawford 54), Perry, Emilson Cribari (Naismith 72), Hegarty; Little, Black, Macleod, Aird (McKay 61); Shiels, McCulloch.
*Alloa Ath:* (451) Bain; Doyle■, Gordon, Marr, Meggatt; Simmons (Grehan 55), McCord Ryan, Young, Holmes, Low (Docherty 74); Cawley (Thomson 79).

**Stenhousemuir (0) 1** *(Kean 78)*
**Berwick R (1) 1** *(Currie 32)* 439
*Stenhousemuir:* (4231) Thomson R; Ross, O'Grady, McKinlay■, Dickson (Rodgers 58); Paton (Smith D 46), Anderson (Thomson I 53); Ferguson, Hodge, Kean; Gemmell.
*Berwick R:* (442) Bejaoui; Jacobs, Townsley, Brydon, Hoskins; Notman, Gray R, Currie L, McDonald; Lavery (Ferguson 84), McLaren (Noble 45).

**Stirling A (0) 0**
**Deveronvale (0) 1** *(Cowie 57)* 688
*Stirling A:* (3412) Filler; McCunnie, Thom, Allison; McGeachie (Flood 74), McSorley (Ferry 61), McClune, Day; Weir G; Davidson (Cunningham 67), White.
*Deveronvale:* (442) McConnachie; Rennie, Henry, Fraser, Adams; Rodger, Lombardi (Barclay 89), Cowie (Urquhart 78), Watt; Morrison (Duncan 72), Blackhall.

**Stranraer (0) 1** *(Malcolm 72)*
**Queen's Park (0) 1** *(Anderson 52)* 344
*Stranraer:* (442) Mitchell; Staunton, Dunlop, McKeown, Kinnaird (MacGregor 75); Winter, Gallagher, Aitken, Wright (Love 62); Moore, Malcolm.
*Queen's Park:* (433) Parry; Gallacher, Brough, Little, Robertson; Capuano, Keenan, Anderson (Quinn 65); Shankland, Longworth, Burns (McParland 83).

**THIRD ROUND REPLAYS**

Saturday, 10 November 2012
**Arbroath (2) 3** *(Kerr 36, Holmes 38, Doris 47)*
**Inverurie Loco Works (0) 1** *(Gauld 90)* 1108
*Arbroath:* (442) Morrison; Baxter, Hamilton, Robertson, Keddie; Gribben (Rennie 82), Kerr, Currie, Sheerin (Banjo 90); Doris (Sibanda 73), Holmes.
*Inverurie Loco Works:* (433) Reid; Michie, McLean■, Broadhurst, Park; Souter (Begg 46), Stewart, Bain; Mackay (Adams 77), Gauld, Maitland (Ross 54).

**Bonnyrigg Rose Ath (0) 0**
**Brechin C (4) 6** *(Byrne 11, 53, Brown 16, Trouten 19, 33, Carcary 71)* 1082
*Bonnyrigg Rose Ath:* (352) Burgess (Ellison 48); Archibald, Dunn, Woodburn; McLeish, King (Thomson 36), Burrell (Hamilton 66), McKenna■, Roseburgh; Renton, Grady.
*Brechin C:* (442) Nelson; McLean, Moyes, Hay, Brown; Trouten, Fusco (Stewart J 67), Molloy, Carcary (Stewart R 77); Byrne, Jackson (Dalziel 63).

**Nairn Co (0) 2** *(Gethins 79, Cameron 88)*
**Forfar Ath (1) 3** *(Campbell R 41, 58, Swankie 54)* 578
*Nairn Co:* (352) Donaldson; Webb, Macdonald, Morrison; Main, Ellis (Cameron 75), Mackintosh, Main, Neill; Gethins, Duncanson.
*Forfar Ath:* (442) Soutar; McCulloch, Bolochoweckyj, Dunlop, Campbell I; Campbell R, Tulloch (Sellars 65), Templeman, Motion; Swankie (Bishop 90), Fotheringham M (King 76).

**Queen's Park (0) 0**
**Stranraer (1) 4** *(Winter 16, 63, Aitken 70, Winter 77)* 551
*Queen's Park:* (433) Parry; Gallacher, Little, Brough■, Robertson; Capuano■, Longworth, Keenan (Bradley 86); Ronald (McParland 72), Quinn (Smith 66), Shankland.
*Stranraer:* (442) Mitchell; Staunton, McKeown, Dunlop, MacGregor; Winter (Agnew 80), Aitken (Rafferty 86), Gallagher, Love; Moore (Wright 72), Malcolm.

Tuesday, 13 November 2012
**Berwick R (1) 2** *(Currie L 11 (pen), Lavery 66)*
**Stenhousemuir (1) 5** *(Smith D 39, Gemmell 48, Kean 52, 56, Smith 86)* 402
*Berwick R:* (433) Bejaoui; Jacobs (Gielty 82), Townsley, Brydon, Hoskins; Notman, Janczyk (Ferguson 57), Currie L■; Lavery, Noble (McDonald 57), Gray.
*Stenhousemuir:* (433) Thomson R; Ferguson, Thomson I, McMillan R, Ross; Anderson, Smith D (O'Grady 87), Hodge (Brash 90); Gemmell (Rodgers 61), Kean, Dickson.

**Morton (0) 3** *(Hardie 51, Tidser 53, 73)*
**Albion R (0) 0** 746
*Morton:* (433) Gaston; Taggart, Reid, Rutkiewicz, Dyer (Halsman 82); Hardie, Bachirou (Wilkie 83), Tidser; Graham, Weatherson (Hawke 78), O'Brien.
*Albion R:* (442) McGinley; Reid, O'Byrne, Donnelly, Russell; Crawford, Stevenson, Innes, Phillips (Tiffeny 87); Howarth (Crooks 69), Boyle (Brannan 61).

**Raith R (2) 4** *(Spence 5, Walker 21 (pen), Anderson G 55, Hill 99)*
**Airdrie U (2) 3** *(Watt J 3, Di Giacomo 45 (pen), Buchanan G 86)* 935
*Raith R:* (442) Laidlaw; Thomson, Ellis, Hill, Malone; Anderson G (Callachan 114), Mensing, Walker, Hamill (Anderson S 76); Spence, Clarke.
*Airdrie U:* (442) Arthur (Duncan 32); Evans, Buchanan G, Lilley, Warren; Bain (Boyle Jack 62), Stallard, Blockley, Watt J; Di Giacomo (McLaren 76), Donnelly.
*aet.*

**FOURTH ROUND**

Saturday, 1 December 2012
**Aberdeen (0) 1** *(McGinn 90)*
**Motherwell (0) 1** *(Murphy 80)* 6061
*Aberdeen:* (352) Langfield; Anderson (Smith 88), Reynolds, Considine; McGinn, Vernon, Rae, Shaughnessy, Hayes; Fallon, Magennis.
*Motherwell:* (442) Hollis; Hateley, Kerr, Cummins, Hammell; Humphrey, Lasley, Law, Murphy; Ojamaa, Higdon.

**Celtic (1) 1** *(Keddie 36 (og))*
**Arbroath (0) 1** *(Doris 87)* 15,000
*Celtic:* (442) Zaluska; Matthews, Ambrose, Rogne, Chalmers (Izaguirre 54); McGeouch, Brown (Kayal 64), Wanyama, Ibrahim; Lustig (Nouioui 79), Miku.
*Arbroath:* (541) Morrison; Baxter, Malcolm, Robertson, Keddie, Hamilton; Currie (Rennie 64), Doris, Kerr, Sheerin (Birse 75); Holmes (Gribben 90).

**Forfar Ath (0) 2** *(Robertson 59, King 74)*
**Ayr U (1) 1** *(Sinclair 16)* 505
*Forfar Ath:* (442) Hamilton; McCulloch, Bolochoweckyj, Campbell I, Tulloch (Dunlop 88); Fotheringham M (Motion 46), Campbell R (King 65), Robertson, Craigen; Templeman, Swankie.
*Ayr U:* (433) Brown; McAusland, Robertson J, McCann, Twaddle; Sinclair, Crawford (Marenghi 83), Hunter; Moffat, Roberts (Robertson R 68), Winters.

**Kilmarnock (1) 2** *(Sheridan 8, Perez 69)*
**Queen of the S (0) 1** *(Clark 77)* 4295
*Kilmarnock:* (4132) Bell; Fowler, O'Leary, Nelson, Tesselaar; Johnson; Racchi (McKenzie 70), Perez (Dayton 81), Harkins; Sheridan, Heffernan (Davidson 86).
*Queen of the S:* (4231) Robinson; McGuffie (Holt 87), Durnan, Higgins, Mitchell; Young, McKenna■; Burns, Lyle (Gibson 90), Carmichael (Reilly 90); Clark.

**Livingston (0) 0**

**Dundee (2) 2** *(Milne 9, Conroy 17 (pen))* 1432
*Livingston:* (442) McNeil; Jacobs Kyle, Barr, Garcia Tena, Booth; Andreu (Morton 71), Fox (Mullen 63), O'Brien, Jacobs Keaghan; McNulty, Scougall.
*Dundee:* (442) Douglas; Irvine, Benedictus, Gallagher, Lockwood; Conroy, McBride, Davidson, McAlister; Milne (Boyle 46), Baird J (Toshney 86).

**Partick Th (0) 0**

**Dunfermline Ath (1) 1** *(Barrowman 35)* 3197
*Partick Th:* (433) Smith; O'Donnell S, Muirhead▪, Balatoni, Sinclair; Murray (Craig 70), Forbes, Bannigan; Lawless (Archibald 30), Doolan (McGuigan 56), Erskine.
*Dunfermline Ath:* (433) Gallacher; McMillan, Dowie, Morris, Jordan; Husband (Byrne 82), Thomson, Geggan; Falkingham (Cardle 42), Barrowman▪, Dargo (Wallace 70).

**Raith R (0) 2** *(Graham 55, 89)*

**Deveronvale (0) 1** *(Fraser 58 (pen))* 1439
*Raith R:* (442) Laidlaw; Thomson, Mensing (Ellis 28), Hill▪, Malone; Anderson G (Spence 84), Anderson S, Hamill, Smith; Graham, Clarke (Donaldson 58).
*Deveronvale:* (442) McConnachie; Rae, Henry, Fraser, Adams; Rennie (Noble 74), Cowie, Rodger, Barclay (Urquhart 88); Duncan (Morrison 83), Blackhall.

**Ross Co (0) 3** *(Quinn 49, Vigurs 86, Brittain 90)*

**Inverness CT (1) 3** *(McKay 30, Foran 74, 90)* 5077
*Ross Co:* (442) Brown; Kovacevic, Tokely, Boyd, Fitzpatrick; Brittain, Kettlewell (Fotheringham 81), Vigurs, Quinn; Morrow (Ross 79), Glen.
*Inverness CT:* (4411) Reguero; Raven, Warren, Meekings, Shinnie G; Shinnie A, Draper, Tudur Jones, Doran; McKay (Roberts 90); Foran.

**St Mirren (2) 2** *(McLean 32, Robertson 42)*

**Brechin C (0) 0** 2363
*St Mirren:* (442) Samson; van Zanten, Mair, McAusland, Dummett; Teale, Robertson, McLean (Barron 86), McGinn (Imrie 32); Parkin, Guy (Reilly 83).
*Brechin C:* (442) Nelson; McLean, Moyes, McLauchlan, Brown (Stewart J 35); Carcary (Stewart R 62), Hay, Molloy, Fusco; Jackson, Byrne (McKenna 75).

**Stenhousemuir (0) 0**

**Falkirk (1) 1** *(Duffie 9)* 1758
*Stenhousemuir:* (442) Reidford; Ross, Buist, McMillan, McKinlay; Dickson (Paton 88), Thomson I (Anderson 84), Hodge, Smith; Rodgers, Kean.
*Falkirk:* (4411) McGovern; Duffie, Dods, Flynn (McGeever 46), Kingsley; McGrandles, Grant, Murdoch, Sibbald; Fulton J (Alston 36); Taylor (Higgins 90).

**Stranraer (0) 0**

**Dundee U (3) 5** *(Russell 13, 27, Daly 40, 61, Russell 69)* 1089
*Stranraer:* (442) Mitchell; Staunton, McKeown, Dunlop, MacGregor; Winter, Phinn (Aitken 79), Gallagher, Love (Agnew 79); Moore (One 68), Malcolm.
*Dundee U:* (442) Cierzniak; McLean, Watson, Gunning, Douglas; Armstrong (Dow 71), Rankin, Flood (Ryan 62), Skacel (Gardyne 65); Russell, Daly.

**Turriff U (1) 1** *(Simpson 40)*

**Morton (1) 1** *(Weatherson 45)* 824
*Turriff U:* (4411) Coutts; Davidson, Anderson, Simpson, Bowden▪; Young, Davidson, Herd, Gauld (Chalmers 83); Henderson (Gray 62); Harris ( 90).
*Morton:* (433) Gaston; Taggart, Reid▪, Rutkiewicz, Dyer; Bachirou (McLaughlin M 90), Hardie, Tidser; Graham, Weatherson (Hawke 74), O'Brien.

**Sunday, 2 December 2012**

**Hibernian (0) 1** *(Zaliukas 84 (og))*

**Hearts (0) 0** 17,052
*Hibernian:* (442) Williams; Maybury, Hanlon, McGivern, Stevenson; Wotherspoon, Taiwo, Claros, Cairney; Griffiths (Caldwell 54), Doyle (Sproule 71).
*Hearts:* (451) MacDonald; McGowan R, Zaliukas, Webster, McHattie; Walker (Sutton 74), Barr (Robinson 59), Taouil, Stevenson, Novikovas (Driver 46); Paterson.

**Rangers (1) 3** *(Shiels 43, Kyle 68, Naismith 85)*

**Elgin C (0) 0** 23,195
*Rangers:* (442) Alexander; Argyriou, Hegarty, McCulloch, Wallace; Little (Templeton 73), Black (Cole 59), Macleod, McKay; Kyle (Naismith 83), Shiels.
*Elgin C:* (4411) Gibson; Beveridge, Crighton, Duff, Niven; Cameron, Nicolson (Wyness 77), O'Donoghue (Harkins 73), Moore; Leslie; Gunn (Millar 89).

**Monday, 17 December 2012**

**Cowdenbeath (0) 0**

**St Johnstone (0) 3** *(McCracken 54, MacLean 76 (pen), Tade 87)* 809
*Cowdenbeath:* (4411) Flynn; Cowan, Armstrong, Mbu (Cameron 64), Adamson; McKenzie, O'Brien, Milne, Brett; Miller (Navas 72); Coult (Thomas 80).
*St Johnstone:* (442) Mannus; MacKay, McCracken, Anderson, Scobbie; Millar (Cregg 84), Davidson M, Craig, Hasselbaink (Beattie 69); MacLean (Caddis 78), Tade.

**Dumbarton (0) 1** *(Turner 58)*

**Hamilton A (2) 3** *(Crawford 24, Devlin 41, Gillespie 75)* 469
*Dumbarton:* (4132) Grindlay; Devlin, Graham, Lithgow, McNiff; Turner▪; Fleming (Gilhaney 46), Agnew, Lamont; Lister, Prunty (McDougall 71).
*Hamilton A:* (4141) Cuthbert; Gordon, Canning, Devlin, McGlinchey; Neil (Fraser 81); Crawford, Fisher (Gillespie 69), Routledge, Longridge; Mackinnon (Ryan 84).

## FOURTH ROUND REPLAYS

**Tuesday, 11 December 2012**

**Inverness CT (1) 2** *(McKay 9 (pen), 54)*

**Ross Co (1) 1** *(Vigurs 41)* 4135
*Inverness CT:* (4411) Reguero; Raven, Shinnie G, Warren, Meekings; Doran, Draper, Tudur Jones, Foran; Shinnie A (Sutherland 75); McKay (Roberts 88).
*Ross Co:* (4411) Brown; Kovacevic, Tokely (Munro 46), Boyd, Fitzpatrick; Brittain, Kettlewell, Fotheringham (Cooper 65), Quinn (Ross 78); Vigurs; McMenamin.

**Motherwell (0) 1** *(Higdon 90 (pen))*

**Aberdeen (0) 2** *(Fallon 51, Shaughnessy 61)* 4516
*Motherwell:* (442) Randolph; Hateley (Kerr 85), Hutchinson, Cummins (Francis-Angol 73), Hammell; Humphrey, Lasley, Carswell, Murphy; Higdon, Ojamaa (McHugh 73).
*Aberdeen:* (442) Langfield; Magennis, Reynolds, Robertson, Shaughnessy; Rae, Considine, Fallon, Hayes; Vernon, McGinn.

**Wednesday, 12 December 2012**

**Arbroath (0) 0**

**Celtic (1) 1** *(Matthews 18)* 4127
*Arbroath:* (451) Morrison; Baxter, Hamilton, Malcolm, Keddie; Sibanda (Rennie 73), Kerr (Birse 76), Currie, Robertson, Sheerin (Holmes 76); Doris.
*Celtic:* (352) Forster; Ambrose; Wilson, Mulgrew; Matthews (McGeouch 90), Izaguirre (Wanyama 65); Brown, Kayal, Samaras; Nouioui (Hooper 65), Lustig.

Monday, 17 December 2012

**Morton (2) 6** *(Weatherson 37, 82, 84, Tidser 45 (pen), 63, MacDonald 77)*

**Turriff U (0) 0**                                                   915

*Morton:* (442) Gaston; Taggart, Reid, McLaughlin M, Dyer; Graham (Wallace 69), Bachirou (Wilkie 74), Tidser, O'Brien; Weatherson, Campbell (MacDonald 60).
*Turriff U:* (442) Coutts; Davidson (Chalmers 64), Anderson R, Simpson, Herd; Young, Davidson, Ligertwood (Fraser 75), Gray; Harris ( 46), Henderson.

## FIFTH ROUND

Saturday, 2 February 2013

**Dundee U (2) 3** *(Russell 1, 79, Daly 36)*

**Rangers (0) 0**                                                   9564

*Dundee U:* (442) Cierzniak; Watson, Dillon, Gunning, Douglas; Armstrong (Ryan 67), Flood, Rankin, Mackay-Steven (Gardyne 67); Russell, Daly.
*Rangers:* (442) Alexander; Faure, Perry (Hegarty 41), Emilson Cribari, Wallace; Little, Hutton, Black▪, Templeton; Sandaza (Naismith▪ 46), Shiels (McKay 73).

**Dunfermline Ath (0) 0**

**Hamilton A (0) 2** *(May 51, Routledge 61)*                       2588

*Dunfermline Ath:* (442) Gallacher; Millen (Thomson 69), Dowie, Morris, McMillan; Husband, Byrne (Whittle 55), Falkingham, Cardle; Wallace (Dargo 82), Kirk.
*Hamilton A:* (4141) Cuthbert; Gordon, Canning, Page, Hendrie; Neil; Crawford, Routledge, Mackinnon, Longridge; May (Ryan 87).

**Falkirk (1) 4** *(Taylor 19, 83, Murdoch 68, Weatherston 75)*

**Forfar Ath (1) 1** *(Campbell I 21 (pen))*                        1967

*Falkirk:* (451) McGovern; Duffie, Dods, Flynn, Kingsley; Fulton J (Fulton D 87), Alston, Murdoch, Higgins (Grant T 87), McGrandles (Weatherston 66); Taylor.
*Forfar Ath:* (442) Hill; McCulloch, Bolochoweckyj, Tulloch, Campbell I; Campbell R, Hilson (Denholm 74), Faeroe (Fotheringham M 80), Malin (Brown 77); Templeman, Swankie.

**Kilmarnock (0) 2** *(Heffernan 58, 85)*

**Inverness CT (0) 0**                                              3172

*Kilmarnock:* (4231) Bell; Barbour, Sissoko, Tesselaar, McKeown; Fowler, O'Hara; Dayton (Hay 70), Perez, Gros; Sheridan (Heffernan 45).
*Inverness CT:* (4411) Esson; Raven, Meekings, Warren, Shinnie G; Doran, Tudur Jones, Foran (Roberts 16), Ross (Gibbons 81); Shinnie A (Taylor 31); McKay.

**St Mirren (0) 2** *(Goncalves 49, 56)*

**St Johnstone (0) 0**                                              3507

*St Mirren:* (442) Samson; van Zanten, McAusland, Goodwin, Carey; Teale, McGinn, Newton, Goncalves; Thompson (Guy 81), McGowan (Dummett 66).
*St Johnstone:* (442) Mannus; MacKay, McCracken, Wright, Scobbie; Vine, Cregg (Edwards 72), Doughty (Abeid 59), Craig; Tade (Hasselbaink 57), MacLean.

Sunday, 3 February 2013

**Dundee (1) 5** *(McAlister 29, Toshney 65, Nish 71, Baird J 74, Gallagher 82)*

**Morton (1) 1** *(Tidser 31)*                                     3336

*Dundee:* (4411) Douglas; Irvine, Toshney, Gallagher, Easton; Riley, McBride (Conroy 86), Davidson, McAlister; Baird J (Stewart 86); Nish (Milne 80).
*Morton:* (433) Gaston; Taggart, Reid, Rutkiewicz, Dyer; Bachirou, Hardie (Wilkie 72), Tidser; Graham (Weatherson 72), MacDonald, O'Brien.

**Hibernian (0) 1** *(Deegan 49)*

**Aberdeen (0) 0**                                                 11,877

*Hibernian:* (451) Williams; Maybury, McPake, Hanlon, McGivern; Wotherspoon (Done 71), Cairney, Claros, Deegan (Robertson 86), Stevenson; Griffiths (Handling 89).
*Aberdeen:* (451) Langfield; Shaughnessy, Anderson, Reynolds, Robertson; Hayes, Hughes, Rae (Vernon 75),

Osbourne, Milsom (Pawlett 59); McGinn.

**Raith R (0) 0**

**Celtic (0) 3** *(Commons 56 (pen), Forrest 83, Mulgrew 86)*      7144

*Raith R:* (442) McGurn; Thomson, Mensing, Ellis, Malone; Smith (Anderson G 65), Anderson S (Spence 74), Walker, Hamill (Callachan 90); Graham, Clarke.
*Celtic:* (442) Zaluska; Matthews, Lustig, Wilson, Mulgrew; Commons (Stokes 75), Ledley, Wanyama, Kayal (Brown 60); Watt (Forrest 60), Hooper.

## QUARTER-FINALS

Saturday, 2 March 2013

**Hamilton A (0) 1** *(Ryan 74)*

**Falkirk (1) 2** *(Alston 44, 71)*                                3452

*Hamilton A:* (4141) Cuthbert; Fisher, Canning, Page▪, Devlin; Neil (Crawford 62); Gillespie (Ryan 72), Mackinnon, Routledge, Longridge (Hendrie 86); May.
*Falkirk:* (4141) McGovern; Duffie, Flynn, Dods, Kingsley (Dick 41); Murdoch; Weatherston, Grant (Higgins 46), McGrandles, Alston; Taylor (Small 90).

**St Mirren (1) 1** *(Goncalves 13)*

**Celtic (2) 2** *(Ledley 5, Stokes 21)*                           5572

*St Mirren:* (4231) Samson; van Zanten, McAusland, Mair, Dummett (Parkin 86); McGinn, Newton; Teale, McGowan (Carey 73), Goncalves; Thompson.
*Celtic:* (343) Forster; Rogne (Kayal 81), Ambrose, Wilson; Matthews, Wanyama, Ledley, Izaguirre; Forrest, Hooper (Commons 90), Stokes (Samaras 71).

Sunday, 3 March 2013

**Dundee (1) 1** *(McAlister 19)*

**Dundee U (2) 2** *(McLean 11, Mackay-Steven 35)*                 10,191

*Dundee:* (442) Douglas; Irvine, Toshney, Grassi, Easton; Riley (Stewart 72), McAlister, Davidson, Conroy; Milne (Nish 80), Baird J.
*Dundee U:* (4411) Cierzniak; Watson, McLean, Dillon, Douglas; Armstrong, Flood, Rankin, Gardyne (Ryan 65); Mackay-Steven; Daly.

**Kilmarnock (1) 2** *(Dayton 26, Heffernan 72 (pen))*

**Hibernian (2) 4** *(Griffiths 15, Done 39,*
*Griffiths 82, 89 (pen))*                                         7272

*Kilmarnock:* (4411) Bell; Barbour▪, Sissoko, Tesselaar (Boyd 84), McKeown (Sheridan 65); Winchester (O'Hara 79), Fowler, Clingan, Dayton; Gros; Heffernan.
*Hibernian:* (451) Williams; Maybury, McPake, McGivern, Stevenson; Done (Doyle 79), Robertson, Taiwo (Deegan 79), Claros, Wotherspoon; Griffiths (Harris 90).

## SEMI-FINALS

Saturday, 13 April 2013

**Hibernian (0) 4** *(Harris 51, Griffiths 78, Doyle 83, Griffiths 115)*

**Falkirk (3) 3** *(Sibbald 6, Fulton J 18, Alston 30)*           22,410

*Hibernian:* (433) Williams; Clancy, McPake, Hanlon, McGivern; Robertson (Handling 32), Claros,. Thomson (Taiwo 64); Cairney (Doyle 46), Griffiths, Harris.
*Falkirk:* (4231) McGovern; Duffie, Dods, Flynn, Kingsley; Murdoch, Sibbald; Fulton J (Weatherston 73), McGrandles (Higgins 79), Alston (Grant 64); Taylor.
*aet.*

Sunday, 14 April 2013

**Dundee U (2) 3** *(Mackay-Steven 24, Daly 30, 71)*

**Celtic (2) 4** *(Commons 2, Wanyama 31, Commons 60, Stokes 104)*                                                24,828

*Dundee U:* (451) Cierzniak; Watson, Souttar, Dillon, Douglas; Gauld (Gardyne 84), Flood, Millar (Armstrong 63), Rankin (Boulding 107), Mackay-Steven; Daly.
*Celtic:* (442) Forster; Lustig (Stokes 77), Ambrose, Wilson, Izaguirre; Forrest, Wanyama (Kayal 77), Ledley, Mulgrew; Commons (Samaras 103), Hooper.
*aet.*

### WILLIAM HILL SCOTTISH CUP FINAL

Sunday, 26 May 2013

(at Hampden Park, attendance 51,254)

**Hibernian (0) 0    Celtic (2) 3**

*Hibernian:* (451) Williams; Maybury, Forster, Hanlon, McGivern; Harris, Taiwo, Claros, Thomson (Caldwell 76), Griffiths (Stevenson 84); Doyle (Handling 71).

*Celtic:* (442) Forster; Lustig, Wilson, Mulgrew, Izaguirre; Forrest (McCourt 88), Brown (Ambrose 81), Ledley, Commons (Samaras 76); Stokes, Hooper.
*Scorers:* Hooper 8, 31, Ledley 80.

*Referee:* William Collum.

Celtic skipper Scott Brown lifts the Scottish FA Cup trophy following his side's 3-0 defeat of Hibernian.
(Action Images)

# SCOTTISH JUNIOR FOOTBALL 2012–13

## PRESS & JOURNAL HIGHLAND LEAGUE

| | P | W | D | L | F | A | GD | Pts |
|---|---|---|---|---|---|---|---|---|
| Cove Rangers | 34 | 25 | 5 | 4 | 101 | 26 | 75 | 80 |
| Formartine U | 34 | 25 | 3 | 6 | 106 | 39 | 67 | 78 |
| Wick Academy | 34 | 25 | 1 | 8 | 101 | 48 | 53 | 76 |
| Nairn Co | 34 | 22 | 5 | 7 | 80 | 43 | 37 | 71 |
| Clachnacuddin | 34 | 21 | 3 | 10 | 68 | 49 | 19 | 66 |
| Fraserburgh | 34 | 18 | 5 | 11 | 83 | 47 | 36 | 59 |
| Deveronvale | 34 | 17 | 7 | 10 | 66 | 45 | 21 | 58 |
| Brora Rangers | 34 | 17 | 4 | 13 | 83 | 52 | 31 | 55 |
| Forres Mechanics | 34 | 16 | 7 | 11 | 78 | 49 | 29 | 55 |
| Inverurie Loco Works | 34 | 16 | 5 | 13 | 71 | 60 | 11 | 53 |
| Turriff U | 34 | 16 | 4 | 14 | 68 | 67 | 1 | 52 |
| Buckie Th | 34 | 13 | 7 | 14 | 58 | 62 | –4 | 46 |
| Huntly | 34 | 14 | 3 | 17 | 66 | 68 | –2 | 45 |
| Keith | 34 | 12 | 7 | 15 | 56 | 65 | –9 | 43 |
| Strathspey Th | 34 | 5 | 0 | 29 | 23 | 112 | –89 | 15 |
| Rothes | 34 | 4 | 2 | 28 | 29 | 126 | –97 | 14 |
| Lossiemouth | 34 | 3 | 1 | 30 | 35 | 108 | –73 | 10 |
| Fort William | 34 | 1 | 3 | 30 | 20 | 126 | –106 | 6 |

## EAST OF SCOTLAND PREMIER DIVISION

| | P | W | D | L | F | A | GD | Pts |
|---|---|---|---|---|---|---|---|---|
| Whitehill Welfare | 22 | 18 | 1 | 3 | 53 | 21 | 32 | 55 |
| Stirling University | 22 | 15 | 2 | 5 | 54 | 22 | 32 | 47 |
| Spartans | 22 | 14 | 4 | 4 | 44 | 23 | 21 | 46 |
| Gretna 2008 | 22 | 9 | 7 | 6 | 34 | 25 | 9 | 34 |
| Edinburgh City | 22 | 9 | 3 | 10 | 31 | 32 | –1 | 30 |
| Lothian Th | 22 | 8 | 3 | 11 | 35 | 38 | –3 | 27 |
| Hutchison Vale | | | | | | | | |
| Preston Ath | 22 | 7 | 3 | 12 | 41 | 55 | –14 | 24 |
| Civil Service Strollers | 22 | 7 | 3 | 12 | 30 | 56 | –26 | 24 |
| Vale of Leithen | 22 | 5 | 8 | 9 | 41 | 49 | –8 | 23 |
| Heriot–Watt University | 22 | 6 | 5 | 11 | 21 | 37 | –16 | 23 |
| Edinburgh University | 22 | 4 | 8 | 10 | 26 | 40 | –14 | 20 |
| Tynecastle | 22 | 5 | 3 | 14 | 41 | 53 | –12 | 18 |

## SOUTH OF SCOTLAND LEAGUE

| | P | W | D | L | F | A | GD | Pts |
|---|---|---|---|---|---|---|---|---|
| Dalbeattie Star | 22 | 18 | 2 | 2 | 93 | 17 | 76 | 56 |
| St Cuthbert W | 22 | 16 | 2 | 4 | 67 | 30 | 37 | 50 |
| Wigtown & Bladnoch | 22 | 15 | 2 | 5 | 62 | 30 | 32 | 47 |
| Threave R | 22 | 15 | 1 | 6 | 76 | 27 | 49 | 46 |
| Heston R | 22 | 12 | 1 | 9 | 59 | 42 | 17 | 37 |
| Newton Stewart | 22 | 11 | 1 | 10 | 62 | 44 | 18 | 34 |
| Abbey Vale | 22 | 10 | 1 | 11 | 48 | 52 | –4 | 31 |
| Nithsdale W | 22 | 10 | 1 | 11 | 52 | 57 | –5 | 31 |
| Crichton | 22 | 8 | 2 | 12 | 52 | 56 | –4 | 26 |
| Mid Annandale | 22 | 7 | 0 | 15 | 36 | 59 | –23 | 21 |
| Creetown | 22 | 2 | 1 | 19 | 21 | 80 | –59 | 7 |
| Fleet Star | 22 | 1 | 0 | 21 | 13 | 147 | –134 | 3 |

## STAGECOACH WEST OF SCOTLAND LEAGUE
## SUPER LEAGUE PREMIER DIVISION

| | P | W | D | L | F | A | GD | Pts |
|---|---|---|---|---|---|---|---|---|
| Auchinleck Talbot | 22 | 20 | 2 | 0 | 62 | 14 | 48 | 62 |
| Petershill | 22 | 11 | 6 | 5 | 41 | 23 | 18 | 39 |
| Clydebank | 22 | 11 | 3 | 8 | 34 | 32 | 2 | 36 |
| Glenafton Ath | 22 | 10 | 2 | 10 | 26 | 37 | –11 | 32 |
| Irvine Meadow | 22 | 9 | 3 | 10 | 36 | 37 | –1 | 30 |
| Arthurlie | 22 | 8 | 5 | 9 | 40 | 40 | 0 | 29 |
| Kirkintilloch Rob Roy | 22 | 8 | 5 | 9 | 49 | 50 | –1 | 29 |
| Pollok | 22 | 7 | 6 | 9 | 25 | 35 | –10 | 27 |
| Cumnock Juniors | 22 | 7 | 4 | 11 | 36 | 40 | –4 | 25 |
| Ashfield | 22 | 7 | 4 | 11 | 35 | 40 | –5 | 25 |
| Beith Juniors | 22 | 7 | 3 | 12 | 36 | 50 | –14 | 24 |
| Shotts Bon Accord | 22 | 2 | 7 | 13 | 23 | 45 | –22 | 13 |

## NORTH REGION JUNIOR FOOTBALL
## PMAC GROUP FIRST DIVISION

| | P | W | D | L | F | A | GD | Pts |
|---|---|---|---|---|---|---|---|---|
| Culter | 26 | 21 | 1 | 4 | 92 | 29 | 63 | 64 |
| Dyce Juniors | 26 | 17 | 3 | 6 | 60 | 38 | 22 | 54 |
| Hermes | 26 | 15 | 2 | 9 | 63 | 43 | 20 | 47 |
| Banks o' Dee | 26 | 13 | 5 | 8 | 58 | 38 | 20 | 44 |
| Deveronside | 26 | 13 | 3 | 10 | 42 | 50 | –8 | 42 |
| FC Stoneywood | 26 | 12 | 5 | 9 | 63 | 44 | 19 | 41 |
| Stonehaven | 26 | 10 | 7 | 9 | 64 | 47 | 17 | 37 |
| Maud | 26 | 11 | 4 | 11 | 55 | 52 | 3 | 37 |
| Ellon U | 26 | 9 | 8 | 9 | 39 | 40 | –1 | 35 |
| Banchory St Ternan | 26 | 10 | 2 | 14 | 43 | 69 | –26 | 32 |
| Longside | 26 | 9 | 2 | 15 | 46 | 61 | –15 | 29 |
| Hall Russell U | 26 | 6 | 9 | 11 | 36 | 50 | –14 | 27 |
| Lewis U | 26 | 5 | 3 | 18 | 35 | 73 | –38 | 18 |
| Fraserburgh U | 26 | 4 | 0 | 22 | 24 | 86 | –62 | 12 |

## EAST REGION JUNIOR FOOTBALL
## McBOOKIE.COM EAST SUPERLEAGUE

| | P | W | D | L | F | A | GD | Pts |
|---|---|---|---|---|---|---|---|---|
| Linlithgow Rose | 22 | 19 | 3 | 0 | 59 | 15 | 44 | 60 |
| Bonnyrigg Rose Ath | 22 | 12 | 5 | 5 | 58 | 36 | 22 | 41 |
| Camelon Juniors | 22 | 12 | 3 | 7 | 50 | 39 | 11 | 39 |
| Bo'ness U | 22 | 11 | 5 | 6 | 44 | 32 | 12 | 38 |
| Kelty Hearts | 22 | 8 | 4 | 10 | 33 | 33 | 0 | 28 |
| Broxburn Ath | 22 | 8 | 4 | 10 | 31 | 32 | –1 | 28 |
| Musselburgh Ath | 22 | 8 | 3 | 11 | 32 | 37 | –5 | 27 |
| Hill of Beath Hawthorn | 22 | 7 | 5 | 10 | 38 | 38 | 0 | 26 |
| Carnoustie Panmure | 22 | 8 | 2 | 12 | 33 | 52 | –19 | 26 |
| Lochee U | 22 | 7 | 4 | 11 | 33 | 51 | –18 | 25 |
| Sauchie Juniors | 22 | 6 | 6 | 10 | 28 | 32 | –4 | 24 |
| St Andrews U | 22 | 3 | 2 | 17 | 24 | 66 | –42 | 11 |

# WELSH FOOTBALL 2012–13

## CORBETT SPORTS WELSH PREMIER LEAGUE 2012–13

| | | | Total | | | | Home | | | | | Away | | | | | | |
|---|---|---|---|---|---|---|---|---|---|---|---|---|---|---|---|---|---|---|
| | | P | W | D | L | F | A | W | D | L | F | A | W | D | L | F | A | GD | Pts |
| 1 | The New Saints | 32 | 24 | 4 | 4 | 86 | 22 | 13 | 1 | 2 | 45 | 9 | 11 | 3 | 2 | 41 | 13 | 64 | 76 |
| 2 | Airbus UK Broughton | 32 | 17 | 3 | 12 | 76 | 42 | 11 | 2 | 3 | 40 | 15 | 6 | 1 | 9 | 36 | 27 | 34 | 54 |
| 3 | Bangor C | 32 | 14 | 9 | 9 | 65 | 53 | 8 | 5 | 3 | 42 | 23 | 6 | 4 | 6 | 23 | 30 | 12 | 51 |
| 4 | Port Talbot T | 32 | 13 | 8 | 11 | 51 | 52 | 9 | 3 | 4 | 34 | 23 | 4 | 5 | 7 | 17 | 29 | −1 | 47 |
| 5 | Prestatyn T | 32 | 11 | 7 | 14 | 62 | 79 | 8 | 2 | 6 | 33 | 34 | 3 | 5 | 8 | 29 | 45 | −17 | 40 |
| 6 | Carmarthen T | 32 | 10 | 7 | 15 | 36 | 50 | 7 | 5 | 4 | 20 | 16 | 3 | 2 | 11 | 16 | 34 | −14 | 37 |
| 7 | Bala T | 32 | 17 | 5 | 10 | 62 | 41 | 10 | 2 | 4 | 37 | 24 | 7 | 3 | 6 | 25 | 17 | 21 | 56 |
| 8 | Gap Connah's Quay | 32 | 12 | 5 | 15 | 62 | 69 | 7 | 3 | 6 | 33 | 33 | 5 | 2 | 9 | 29 | 36 | −7 | 40 |
| 9 | Newtown | 32 | 10 | 7 | 15 | 44 | 54 | 3 | 5 | 8 | 17 | 29 | 7 | 2 | 7 | 27 | 25 | −10 | 37 |
| 10 | Aberystwyth T | 32 | 9 | 10 | 13 | 40 | 59 | 7 | 4 | 5 | 23 | 25 | 2 | 6 | 8 | 17 | 34 | −19 | 37 |
| 11 | Llanelli | 32 | 10 | 6 | 16 | 41 | 68 | 3 | 3 | 10 | 20 | 44 | 7 | 3 | 6 | 21 | 24 | −27 | 36 |
| 12 | Afan Lido | 32 | 8 | 3 | 21 | 43 | 79 | 5 | 2 | 9 | 18 | 31 | 3 | 1 | 12 | 25 | 48 | −36 | 27 |

*Gap Connah's Quay deducted 1 point. Top 6 teams split after 22 games.*

## PREVIOUS WELSH LEAGUE WINNERS

| | | | | | |
|---|---|---|---|---|---|
| 1993 | Cwmbran Town | 1999 | Barry Town | 2005 | TNS |
| 1994 | Bangor City | 2000 | TNS | 2006 | TNS |
| 1995 | Bangor City | 2001 | Barry Town | 2007 | TNS |
| 1996 | Barry Town | 2002 | Barry Town | 2008 | Llanelli |
| 1997 | Barry Town | 2003 | Barry Town | 2009 | Rhyl |
| 1998 | Barry Town | 2004 | Rhyl | 2010 | The New Saints |
| | | | | 2011 | Bangor C |
| | | | | 2012 | The New Saints |
| | | | | 2013 | The New Saints |

## MACWHIRTER WELSH LEAGUE 2012–13

| | | | | | Total | | | | Home | | | | | Away | | | | | |
|---|---|---|---|---|---|---|---|---|---|---|---|---|---|---|---|---|---|---|---|
| | | P | W | D | L | F | A | W | D | L | F | A | W | D | L | F | A | GD | Pts |
| 1 | West End | 28 | 18 | 4 | 6 | 64 | 29 | 8 | 2 | 4 | 30 | 15 | 10 | 2 | 2 | 34 | 14 | 35 | 58 |
| 2 | Cambrian & Clydach | 28 | 17 | 5 | 6 | 56 | 26 | 11 | 1 | 2 | 33 | 8 | 6 | 4 | 4 | 23 | 18 | 30 | 56 |
| 3 | Taffs Well | 28 | 14 | 7 | 7 | 57 | 39 | 8 | 4 | 2 | 33 | 18 | 6 | 3 | 5 | 24 | 21 | 18 | 49 |
| 4 | Haverfordwest Co | 28 | 13 | 8 | 7 | 63 | 46 | 6 | 3 | 5 | 31 | 19 | 7 | 5 | 2 | 32 | 16 | 28 | 47 |
| 5 | Aberdare T | 28 | 13 | 8 | 7 | 45 | 35 | 5 | 6 | 3 | 20 | 18 | 8 | 2 | 4 | 25 | 17 | 10 | 47 |
| 6 | AFC Porth | 28 | 13 | 7 | 8 | 39 | 34 | 5 | 5 | 4 | 21 | 17 | 8 | 2 | 4 | 18 | 17 | 5 | 46 |
| 7 | Monmouth T | 28 | 13 | 6 | 9 | 54 | 43 | 7 | 3 | 4 | 26 | 18 | 6 | 3 | 5 | 28 | 25 | 11 | 42 |
| 8 | Bryntirion Ath | 28 | 10 | 9 | 9 | 38 | 40 | 4 | 4 | 6 | 19 | 26 | 6 | 5 | 3 | 19 | 14 | −2 | 39 |
| 9 | Ton Pentre | 28 | 9 | 9 | 10 | 39 | 39 | 6 | 3 | 5 | 22 | 17 | 3 | 6 | 5 | 17 | 22 | 0 | 36 |
| 10 | Pontardawe T | 28 | 10 | 5 | 13 | 34 | 39 | 6 | 2 | 6 | 20 | 18 | 4 | 3 | 7 | 14 | 21 | −5 | 35 |
| 11 | Goytre U | 28 | 10 | 4 | 14 | 33 | 51 | 6 | 2 | 6 | 15 | 22 | 4 | 2 | 8 | 18 | 29 | −18 | 34 |
| 12 | Cwmbran Celtic | 28 | 9 | 5 | 14 | 41 | 52 | 7 | 2 | 5 | 26 | 24 | 2 | 3 | 9 | 15 | 28 | −11 | 32 |
| 13 | Bridgend T | 28 | 8 | 7 | 13 | 28 | 51 | 2 | 5 | 7 | 12 | 22 | 6 | 2 | 6 | 16 | 29 | −23 | 31 |
| 14 | Tata Steel | 28 | 5 | 6 | 17 | 28 | 61 | 3 | 1 | 10 | 13 | 33 | 2 | 5 | 7 | 15 | 28 | −33 | 21 |
| 15 | Caerleon | 28 | 1 | 4 | 23 | 18 | 63 | 0 | 4 | 10 | 11 | 30 | 1 | 0 | 13 | 7 | 33 | −45 | 7 |

*Monmouth Town deducted 3 points. Barry T withdrew from league – record expunged.*

## HUWS GRAY CYMRU ALLIANCE LEAGUE 2012–13

| | | | | | Total | | | | Home | | | | | Away | | | | | |
|---|---|---|---|---|---|---|---|---|---|---|---|---|---|---|---|---|---|---|---|
| | | P | W | D | L | F | A | W | D | L | F | A | W | D | L | F | A | GD | Pts |
| 1 | Rhyl | 30 | 24 | 6 | 0 | 100 | 24 | 11 | 4 | 0 | 53 | 13 | 13 | 2 | 0 | 47 | 11 | 76 | 78 |
| 2 | Cefn Druids | 30 | 22 | 3 | 5 | 79 | 32 | 12 | 1 | 2 | 42 | 13 | 10 | 2 | 3 | 37 | 19 | 47 | 69 |
| 3 | Conwy Borough | 30 | 18 | 7 | 5 | 57 | 37 | 11 | 3 | 1 | 31 | 16 | 7 | 4 | 4 | 26 | 21 | 20 | 61 |
| 4 | Caersws | 30 | 18 | 3 | 9 | 90 | 42 | 9 | 1 | 5 | 53 | 19 | 9 | 2 | 4 | 37 | 23 | 48 | 57 |
| 5 | Buckley T | 30 | 13 | 10 | 7 | 60 | 35 | 7 | 6 | 2 | 36 | 17 | 6 | 4 | 5 | 24 | 18 | 25 | 49 |
| 6 | Flint Town U | 30 | 14 | 6 | 10 | 61 | 51 | 9 | 1 | 5 | 35 | 24 | 5 | 5 | 5 | 26 | 27 | 10 | 48 |
| 7 | Holyhead Hotspur | 30 | 13 | 4 | 13 | 51 | 55 | 10 | 1 | 4 | 31 | 20 | 3 | 3 | 9 | 20 | 35 | −4 | 43 |
| 8 | Guilsfield | 30 | 12 | 6 | 12 | 61 | 54 | 7 | 4 | 4 | 36 | 23 | 5 | 2 | 8 | 25 | 31 | 7 | 42 |
| 9 | CPD Porthmadog | 30 | 11 | 5 | 14 | 48 | 52 | 6 | 2 | 7 | 25 | 31 | 5 | 3 | 7 | 23 | 21 | −4 | 38 |
| 10 | Penrhyncoch | 30 | 9 | 7 | 14 | 50 | 63 | 5 | 2 | 8 | 25 | 35 | 4 | 5 | 6 | 25 | 28 | −13 | 34 |
| 11 | Rhayader T | 30 | 9 | 6 | 15 | 44 | 66 | 6 | 3 | 6 | 29 | 27 | 3 | 3 | 9 | 15 | 39 | −22 | 33 |
| 12 | Llandudno | 30 | 8 | 8 | 14 | 36 | 59 | 4 | 7 | 4 | 24 | 26 | 4 | 1 | 10 | 12 | 33 | −23 | 32 |
| 13 | Penycae | 30 | 7 | 5 | 18 | 49 | 84 | 6 | 3 | 6 | 32 | 36 | 1 | 2 | 12 | 17 | 48 | −35 | 26 |
| 14 | Rhydymwyn | 30 | 6 | 8 | 16 | 49 | 96 | 5 | 2 | 8 | 21 | 42 | 1 | 6 | 8 | 28 | 54 | −47 | 26 |
| 15 | Llanrhaeadr YM | 30 | 4 | 7 | 19 | 29 | 87 | 1 | 6 | 8 | 18 | 33 | 3 | 1 | 11 | 11 | 54 | −58 | 19 |
| 16 | Ruthin T | 30 | 3 | 7 | 20 | 47 | 74 | 1 | 3 | 11 | 17 | 28 | 2 | 4 | 9 | 30 | 46 | −27 | 16 |

## WELSH CUP 2012–13

### FIRST QUALIFYING ROUND – NORTH

| | |
|---|---|
| Amlwch T v Corwen | 0-3 |
| Connah's Quay T v Flint Mountain | 4-0 |
| FC Nomads of Connah's Quay v Kinmel Bay Sports | 3-1 |
| Greenfield w.o. v West Shore withdrew | |
| Gresford Ath v New Brighton Villa | 2-1 |
| Halkyn U w.o. v Caernarfon W withdrew | |
| Johnstown Youth v Llanuwchllyn | 0-6 |
| Knighton T v Gaerwen | 4-1 |
| Lex XI v Machynlleth | 3-1 |
| Llandyrnog U v Bodedern Ath | 3-4 |
| Llanfairpwll v Dyffryn Nantlle Vale | 3-1 |
| Llanfyllin T v Bethel | 2-6 |
| Llanllyfni v Castell Alun Colts | 4-3 |
| Llanystumdwy v Caerwys | 0-2 |
| Montgomery T v Blaenau Amateur | 7-1 |
| Pen Y Ffordd v Penmaenmawr Phoenix | 1-0 |
| Penrhyndeudraeth w.o. v Acton Village withdrew | |
| Presteigne St Andrews v Kerry | 4-1 |
| Trearddur Bay U w.o. v Penley withdrew | |

### FIRST QUALIFYING ROUND – SOUTH

| | |
|---|---|
| AFC Llwydcoed v Cwmbran T | 8-2 |
| Cardiff Hibernian v Aber Valley YMCA | 0-1 |
| Cardiff Metropolitan v Splott Alb | 1-2 |
| Carnetown v Aberfan | 2-5 |
| Ely Valley v Kenfig Hill | 3-5 |
| Fleur de Lys Welfare v Bridgend Street | 1-2 |
| Garw v Llantwit Major | 0-2 |
| Llanharry v Treforest | 0-5 |
| Llanwern v Tonyrefail Welfare | 3-1 |
| Merthyr Saints v Cwmamman U | 0-2 |
| Nelson Cavaliers v Pontyclun | 1-3 |
| Newcastle Emlyn v Chepstow T | 1-3 |
| Newport Civil Service v Cardiff Grange Harlequins | 3-4 |
| Penrhiwceiber Constitutional Ath v Abertillery Bluebirds | 1-9 |
| Perthcelyn U v Tredegar Ath | 4-0 |
| Pontypridd T v Graig y Rhacca | 5-0 |
| Porthcawl T Ath v Brecon Corinthians | 1-2 |
| Rhydyfelin v Llantwit Fardre | 1-4 |
| STM Sports v Ton & Gelli | 0-4 |
| Tredegar T v Llandrindod Wells | 5-1 |
| Trefelin v Risca U | 2-3 |
| Treharris Ath Western v Baglan Dragons | 3-2 |
| Treowen Stars v Trethomas Bluebirds | 5-1 |

### SECOND QUALIFYING ROUND – NORTH

| | |
|---|---|
| Berriew v Caernarfon T | 3-4 |
| Bethel v Llanrug U | 1-2 |
| Bethesda Ath v Corwen | 0-3 |
| Bodedern Ath v Lex XI | 4-2 |
| Brickfield Rangers v Dolgellau Ath Amateur | 3-1 |
| Brymbo v Caerwys | 6-0 |
| Coedpoeth U v Trearddur Bay U | 3-2 |
| Connah's Quay T v Gwalchmai | 0-7 |
| FC Cefn withdrew v Greenfield w.o. | |
| FC Nomads of Connah's Quay v Llanidloes T | 1-4 |
| Gresford Ath v Denbigh T | 0-7 |
| Holywell T v Llanfairpwll | 3-0 |
| Knighton T v Four Crosses | 2-4 |
| Llanberis v Pen Y Ffordd | 1-0 |
| Llandudno Junction v Llangollen T | 3-0 |
| Llangefni T v Waterloo R | 0-4 |
| Llanllyfni v Barmouth & Dyffryn U | 2-1 |
| Llanrwst U v Pwllheli | 1-3 |
| Llansantffraid Village v Bow Street | 1-0 |
| Llanuwchllyn v Nefyn U | 2-0 |
| Montgomery T v Chirk AAA | 6-2 |
| Penrhyndeudraeth v Halkyn U | 2-3 |
| Presteigne St Andrews v Glantraeth | 3-2 |
| Rhos Aelwyd v Glan Conwy | 0-4 |
| Tywyn Bryncrug v Mold Alexandra | 0-3 |
| Venture Community v Overton Recreational | 2-0 |
| Welshpool T v Carno | 1-2 |

### SECOND QUALIFYING ROUND – SOUTH

| | |
|---|---|
| Aberbargoed Buds v Perthcelyn U | 3-0 |
| Ammanford v Kenfig Hill | 5-1 |
| Bettws v Pontyclun | 2-2 |
| *Pontyclun won 3-1 on penalties.* | |
| Brecon Corinthians v Aberaeron | 4-1 |
| Bridgend Street v Aberfan | 1-0 |
| Briton Ferry Llansawel v Pontypridd T | 1-3 |
| Builth Wells v AFC Llwydcoed | 0-4 |
| Caldicot T v Treforest | 1-2 |
| Cardiff Corinthians v Caerau | 0-5 |
| Cardiff Grange Harlequins v Treharris Ath Western | 3-0 |
| Chepstow T v Ton & Gelli | 2-1 |
| Croesyceiliog v Treowen Stars | 4-0 |
| Cwmaman Institute v Newbridge on Wye | 4-6 |
| Garden Village v Ely Rangers | 1-4 |
| Goytre (Gwent) v Abertillery Bluebirds | 3-0 |
| Llantwit Fardre v Aber Valley YMCA | 1-0 |
| Llantwit Major v Caerau Ely | 1-2 |
| Penrhiwceiber Rangers v Dinas Powys | 1-3 |
| Risca U v Newport YMCA | 2-1 |
| Splott Alb v Cwmamman U | 2-6 |
| Tredegar T v Llanwern | 1-2 |

### FIRST ROUND – NORTH

| | |
|---|---|
| Brickfield Rangers v Pwllheli | 2-5 |
| Brymbo v Penycae | 1-1 |
| *aet; Brymbo won 3-0 on penalties.* | |
| Cefn Druids v Llanberis | 7-1 |
| Coedpoeth U v Caersws | 1-2 |
| Corwen v Ruthin T | 2-1 |
| *aet.* | |
| CPD Porthmadog v Llandudno | 2-3 |
| Flint Town U v Guilsfield Ath | 3-2 |
| Four Crosses v Llanrug U | 1-2 |
| Gwalchmai v Carno | 4-1 |
| Halkyn U v Llanidloes T | 1-6 |
| Holyhead Hotspur v Llansantffraid Village | 6-2 |
| Holywell T v Denbigh T | 3-1 |
| Llandudno Junction v Mold Alexandra | 4-2 |
| Llanllyfni v Greenfield | 0-4 |
| Llanrhaeadr Ym Mochant v Glan Conwy | 2-1 |
| *aet.* | |
| Llanuwchllyn v Buckley T | 3-6 |
| *aet.* | |
| Rhyl v Bodedern Ath | 7-0 |
| Venture Community v Montgomery T | 2-5 |
| *aet.* | |
| Waterloo R v Rhydymwyn | 5-1 |
| Caernarfon T v Conwy Bor | 0-0 |
| *aet; Conwy Bor won 4-3 on penalties.* | |

### FIRST ROUND – SOUTH

| | |
|---|---|
| Aberbargoed Buds v Treforest | 2-1 |
| AFC Porth v Monmouth T | 0-0 |
| *aet; Monmouth T won 6-5 on penalties.* | |
| Ammanford v Chepstow T | 1-2 |
| Brecon Corinthians v Haverfordwest Co | 2-5 |
| Caerau v Llantwit Fardre | 8-0 |
| Caerleon v Barry T | 2-5 |
| Cardiff Grange Harlequins v Llanwern | 4-3 |
| Croesyceiliog v Caerau Ely | 3-7 |
| Cwmamman U v Newbridge on Wye | 1-5 |
| Cwmbran Celtic v Cambrian & Clydach Vale | 0-1 |
| Dinas Powys v Ton Pentre | 1-3 |
| Ely Rangers v Bryntirion Ath | 3-1 |
| Goytre (Gwent) v AFC Llwydcoed | 3-0 |
| Goytre U v Pontyclun | 6-0 |
| Pontypridd T v Aberdare T | 0-0 |
| *aet; Aberdare T won 3-0 on penalties.* | |
| Presteigne St Andrews v Penrhyncoch | 0-2 |
| Rhayader T v Risca U | 2-0 |
| Tata Steel v Bridgend Street | 7-4 |
| West End v Taffs Well | 4-0 |
| Bridgend T v Pontardawe T | 0-1 |

## SECOND ROUND – NORTH

| | |
|---|---|
| Brymbo v Cefn Druids | 1-3 |
| Conwy Bor v Buckley T | 1-1 |

*aet; Conwy Bor won 4-3 on penalties.*

| | |
|---|---|
| Corwen v Gwalchmai | 1-2 |

*aet.*

| | |
|---|---|
| Flint Town U v Greenfield | 3-0 |
| Holywell T v Llandudno | 5-3 |

*aet.*

| | |
|---|---|
| Llanidloes T v Caersws | 3-2 |
| Llanrhaeadr Ym Mochant v Llanrug U | 2-3 |
| Montgomery T v Llandudno Junction | 1-3 |
| Waterloo R v Rhyl | 0-5 |
| Holyhead Hotspur v Pwllheli | 5-2 |

## SECOND ROUND – SOUTH

| | |
|---|---|
| Caerau v Goytre (Gwent) | 1-3 |
| Goytre U v Caerau Ely | 2-4 |
| Pontardawe T v Ton Pentre | 2-0 |
| Aberdare T v Tata Steel | 2-1 |
| Cambrian & Clydach Vale v Haverfordwest Co | 0-1 |
| Chepstow T v Cardiff Grange Harlequins | 4-1 |
| Ely Rangers v Aberbargoed Buds | 6-1 |
| Newbridge on Wye v Monmouth T | 1-5 |
| Penrhyncoch v Barry T | 1-2 |
| West End v Rhayader T | 2-0 |

## THIRD ROUND

| | |
|---|---|
| Aberystwyth T v Rhyl | 2-5 |
| Afan Lido v Prestatyn T | 3-4 |
| Airbus UK Broughton v Port Talbot T | 3-0 |
| Bangor C v Aberdare T | 4-1 |
| Barry T v Ely Rangers | 3-1 |

*aet.*

| | |
|---|---|
| Flint Town U v Llanidloes T | 1-0 |
| Gap Connah's Quay v Llanelli | 4-2 |
| Gwalchmai v Chepstow T | 0-2 |
| Holyhead Hotspur v Carmarthen T | 1-2 |
| Holywell T v Caerau Ely | 0-2 |
| Llandudno Junction v Haverfordwest Co | 2-3 |
| Llanrug U v West End | 0-5 |
| Monmouth T v Bala T | 2-3 |

| | |
|---|---|
| Newtown v Cefn Druids | 2-0 |
| Pontardawe T v Goytre (Gwent) | 2-0 |
| The New Saints v Conwy Bor | 3-1 |

## FOURTH ROUND

| | |
|---|---|
| Newtown v Airbus UK Broughton | 1-1 |

*aet; Airbus UK Broughton won 5-4 on penalties.*

| | |
|---|---|
| The New Saints v Rhyl | 5-1 |
| Flint Town U v Caerau Ely | 3-1 |
| Barry T v Pontardawe T | 2-1 |
| Carmarthen T v Bala T | 3-2 |

*aet.*

| | |
|---|---|
| Chepstow T v Haverfordwest Co | 3-4 |
| Gap Connah's Quay v Bangor C | 0-2 |
| Prestatyn T v West End | 2-0 |

## QUARTER-FINALS

| | |
|---|---|
| Bangor C v Airbus UK Broughton | 1-0 |
| Carmarthen T v Prestatyn T | 2-3 |

*aet.*

| | |
|---|---|
| Flint Town U v Barry T | 0-2 |
| Haverfordwest Co v The New Saints | 0-1 |

## SEMI-FINALS

| | |
|---|---|
| Bangor C v The New Saints | 1-0 |
| Barry T v Prestatyn T | 1-2 |

## FINAL (at Racecourse Ground, Wrexham)

Saturday 6 May 2013

**Prestatyn T (1) 3** *(Price 2, 111, Parkinson 103)*

**Bangor C (0) 1** *(Simm 60)*      1732

*aet.*

*Prestatyn T:* Hill-Dunt; Davies, Stephens, Hayes, Stones, Wilson, Parker, Gibson (Owen 106), Parkinson, Price (France 119), Stephens.

*Bangor C:* Idzi; Edwards, Roberts, Morley (Booth 65), Brewerton, Johnston■, Jones Chris (Edwards 59), Brownhill (Hay 105), Davies, Simm, Allen.

*Referee:* Kevin Morgan (Cardiff).

## PREVIOUS WELSH CUP WINNERS

| | | | | | | | |
|---|---|---|---|---|---|---|---|
| 1878 | Wrexham | 1910 | Wrexham | 1952 | Rhyl | 1984 | Shrewsbury Town |
| 1879 | Newtown White Star | 1911 | Wrexham | 1953 | Rhyl | 1985 | Shrewsbury Town |
| 1880 | Druids | 1912 | Cardiff City | 1954 | Flint Town United | 1986 | Wrexham |
| 1881 | Druids | 1913 | Swansea Town | 1955 | Barry Town | 1987 | Merthyr Tydfil |
| 1882 | Druids | 1914 | Wrexham | 1956 | Cardiff City | 1988 | Cardiff City |
| 1883 | Wrexham | 1915 | Wrexham | 1957 | Wrexham | 1989 | Swansea City |
| 1884 | Oswestry White Stars | 1920 | Cardiff City | 1958 | Wrexham | 1990 | Hereford United |
| 1885 | Druids | 1921 | Wrexham | 1959 | Cardiff City | 1991 | Swansea City |
| 1886 | Druids | 1922 | Cardiff City | 1960 | Wrexham | 1992 | Cardiff City |
| 1887 | Chirk | 1923 | Cardiff City | 1961 | Swansea Town | 1993 | Cardiff City |
| 1888 | Chirk | 1924 | Wrexham | 1962 | Bangor City | 1994 | Barry Town |
| 1889 | Bangor | 1925 | Wrexham | 1963 | Borough United | 1995 | Wrexham |
| 1890 | Chirk | 1926 | Ebbw Vale | 1964 | Cardiff City | 1996 | TNS |
| 1891 | Shrewsbury Town | 1927 | Cardiff City | 1965 | Cardiff City | 1997 | Barry Town |
| 1892 | Chirk | 1928 | Cardiff City | 1966 | Swansea Town | 1998 | Bangor City |
| 1893 | Wrexham | 1929 | Connah's Quay | 1967 | Cardiff City | 1999 | Inter Cable-Tel |
| 1894 | Chirk | 1930 | Cardiff City | 1968 | Cardiff City | 2000 | Bangor City |
| 1895 | Newtown | 1931 | Wrexham | 1969 | Cardiff City | 2001 | Barry Town |
| 1896 | Bangor | 1932 | Swansea Town | 1970 | Cardiff City | 2002 | Barry Town |
| 1897 | Wrexham | 1933 | Chester | 1971 | Cardiff City | 2003 | Barry Town |
| 1898 | Druids | 1934 | Bristol City | 1972 | Wrexham | 2004 | Rhyl |
| 1899 | Druids | 1935 | Tranmere Rovers | 1973 | Cardiff City | 2005 | TNS |
| 1900 | Aberystwyth Town | 1936 | Crewe Alexandra | 1974 | Cardiff City | 2006 | Rhyl |
| 1901 | Oswestry United | 1937 | Crewe Alexandra | 1975 | Wrexham | 2007 | Carmarthen Town |
| 1902 | Wellington Town | 1938 | Shrewsbury Town | 1976 | Cardiff City | 2008 | Bangor C |
| 1903 | Wrexham | 1939 | South Liverpool | 1977 | Shrewsbury Town | 2009 | Bangor C |
| 1904 | Druids | 1940 | Wellington Town | 1978 | Wrexham | 2010 | Bangor C |
| 1905 | Wrexham | 1947 | Chester | 1979 | Shrewsbury Town | 2011 | Llanelli |
| 1906 | Wellington Town | 1948 | Lovell's Athletic | 1980 | Newport County | 2012 | The New Saints |
| 1907 | Oswestry United | 1949 | Merthyr Tydfil | 1981 | Swansea City | 2013 | Prestatyn T |
| 1908 | Chester | 1950 | Swansea Town | 1982 | Swansea City | | |
| 1909 | Wrexham | 1951 | Merthyr Tydfil | 1983 | Swansea City | | |

## THE WELSH LEAGUE CUP 2012–13

**FIRST ROUND**

| | |
|---|---|
| Buckley Town v Penrhyncoch | 1-2 |
| Cambrian & Clydach Vale v Haverfordwest County | 0-4 |
| Rhyl v CPD Porthmadog | 2-0 |
| Taffs Well v Bryntirion Athletic | 2-2 |

*aet; Bryntirion Athletic won 3-2 on penalties.*

**SECOND ROUND**

| | |
|---|---|
| Bala Town v Bangor City | 6-1 |
| Bryntirion Athletic v Carmarthen Town | 1-2 |
| Haverfordwest County v Llanelli | 3-5 |
| Newtown v Afan Lido | 4-5 |
| Penrhyncoch v Airbus UK Broughton | 0-1 |
| Port Talbot Town v Aberystwyth Town | 2-2 |

*aet; Port Talbot Town won 5-4 on penalties.*

| | |
|---|---|
| Prestatyn Town v The New Saints | 0-2 |
| Rhyl v Gap Connah's Quay | 1-3 |

**THIRD ROUND**

| | |
|---|---|
| Llanelli v Afan Lido | 6-3 |
| Bala Town v The New Saints | 2-3 |
| Carmarthen Town v Port Talbot Town | 3-2 |
| Gap Connah's Quay v Airbus UK Broughton | 1-3 |

**SEMI-FINALS**

| | |
|---|---|
| Carmarthen Town v Llanelli | 2-1 |
| The New Saints v Airbus UK Broughton | 5-2 |

**FINAL (at Latham Park, Newtown)**

Saturday 12 January 2013

**Carmarthen Town (1) 3** *(Hughes 42, Corey Thomas 60, 67)*

**The New Saints (1) 3** *(Evans 7, Finley 58, Wilde 85)*

*aet; Carmarthen Town won 3-1 on penalties.*

*Carmarthen Town:* Cann; Hillier, Hanford, Rees, Hicks, Cummings, Fowler (Corey Thomas 22) , Palmer, Hughes (Doidge 81), Liam Thomas, Casey Thomas (Hood 108).

*The New Saints:* Harrison; Spender (Jones 70), Marriott, Evans, Rawlinson, Edwards, Seargeant, Finley (Fraughan 82), Wilde, Draper (Darlington 72), Edwards.

*Referee:* Nick Pratt.

## THE FAW TROPHY 2012–13

**ROUND 3 NORTH**

| | |
|---|---|
| Gwalchmai v Bodedern Ath | 2-1 |
| Borras Park Alb v Presteigne St. Andrews | 5-3 |
| Bow Street FC v Glan Conwy | 0-1 |
| Caernarfon T v Meliden | 2-1 |
| Chirk AAA v Johnstown Youth | 7-0 |
| Denbigh T v Tywyn Bryncrug | 3-2 |
| FC Nomads of Connah's Quay v Gresford Ath | 2-1 |
| Greenfield v Pwllheli | 2-3 |
| Llanberis v Argoed U | 5-1 |
| Llandudno Junction v Holywell T | 1-3 |
| Llanfairpwll v Llanfair U | 1-2 |
| Llangollen T v Nefyn U | 4-0 |
| Llanrug U v Brymbo | 1-2 |
| Llanrwst U v Pen Y Ffordd | 3-1 |
| Machynlleth v Amlwch T | 3-1 |
| Montgomery T v Llandrindod Wells | 5-2 |
| Overton Recreational v Llandyrnog U | 2-2 |

*Overton Recreational won 9-8 on penalties.*

| | |
|---|---|
| Penley v Hawarden Rangers | 1-3 |

**ROUND 3 SOUTH**

| | |
|---|---|
| Aber Valley YMCA v Ragged School | 3-5 |
| Baglan Dragons v Llanharry | 1-6 |
| Bryn Rovers v Blaenavon Blues | 2-3 |
| Cwm & Llantwit Welfare v Blaenrhondda | 7-1 |
| Fleur de Lys Welfare v Aberbargoed Buds walkover |  |

*Fleur de Lys withdrew.*

| | |
|---|---|
| Kilvey Fords FC v Cowbridge T | 5-1 |
| Llangynwydd Rangers v Ton & Gelli | 1-4 |
| Penlan v Pentwynmawr Ath | 4-2 |
| Perthcelyn U v Dafen Welfare | 1-4 |
| STM Sports v Morriston Olympic | 4-4 |

*aet; STM Sports won 4-2 on penalties.*

| | |
|---|---|
| Sully Sports v Kenfig Hill | 5-2 |
| Tongwynlais v Creigiau | 1-2 |

*aet.*

| | |
|---|---|
| Trelewis Welfare v Albion Rovers | 1-3 |

*aet.*

| | |
|---|---|
| Treowen Stars v Abertillery Excelsiors | 5-3 |

**ROUND 4 NORTH**

| | |
|---|---|
| Borras Park Alb v Pwllheli | 1-0 |
| Denbigh T v Montgomery T | 4-2 |
| Glan Conwy v Llangollen T | 4-3 |
| Holywell T v Chirk AAA | 4-2 |
| Llanfair U v Llanberis | 2-3 |

*aet.*

| | |
|---|---|
| Llanrwst U v Brymbo | 2-4 |
| Machynlleth v Hawarden Rangers | 5-4 |

*aet.*

| | |
|---|---|
| Overton Recreational v FC Nomads of Connah's Quay | 0-1 |
| Caernarfon T v Gwalchmai | 2-0 |

**ROUND 4 SOUTH**

| | |
|---|---|
| Aberbargoed Buds v STM Sports | 4-4 |

*aet; STM Sports won 9-8 on penalties.*

| | |
|---|---|
| Blaenavon Blues v Dafen Welfare | 0-2 |
| Creigiau v Treowen Stars | 0-2 |
| Llanharry v Cwm & Llantwit Welfare | 0-2 |
| Penlan v Ragged School | 3-4 |

*aet.*

| | |
|---|---|
| Sully Sports v Kilvey Fords | 2-3 |
| Ton & Gelli v Albion Rovers | 3-1 |

**ROUND 5 NORTH**

| | |
|---|---|
| Holywell T v Brymbo | 1-0 |
| FC Nomads of Connah's Quay v Borras Park Alb | 1-3 |
| Glan Conwy v Denbigh T | 3-2 |

*aet.*

| | |
|---|---|
| Llanberis v Caernarfon T | 0-2 |

**ROUND 5 SOUTH**

| | |
|---|---|
| Cwm & Llantwit Welfare FC v Machynlleth | 4-2 |
| Ragged School v Kilvey Fords | 0-2 |
| STM Sports v Dafen Welfare | 2-3 |
| Ton & Gelli v Treowen Stars | 1-2 |

**QUARTER-FINALS**

| | |
|---|---|
| Caernarfon T v Glan Conwy | 1-0 |
| Cwm & Llantwit Welfare v Holywell T | 2-6 |
| Kilvey Fords FC v Dafen Welfare | 4-1 |
| Treowen Stars v Borras Park Alb | 3-1 |

*aet.*

**SEMI-FINALS**

| | |
|---|---|
| Holywell T v Caernarfon T | 1-3 |
| Kilvey Fords v Treowen Stars | 1-0 |

**FINAL**

| | |
|---|---|
| Kilvey Fords v Caernarfon T | 0-6 |

*at Latham Park, Newtown.*

# NORTHERN IRISH FOOTBALL 2012–13

## NORTHERN IRISH DANSKE BANK PREMIER LEAGUE 2012–13

| | | | | Total | | | | Home | | | | | Away | | | | | | |
|---|---|---|---|---|---|---|---|---|---|---|---|---|---|---|---|---|---|---|---|---|
| | | P | W | D | L | F | A | W | D | L | F | A | W | D | L | F | A | GD | Pts |
| 1 | Cliftonville | 38 | 29 | 4 | 5 | 95 | 38 | 18 | 1 | 1 | 56 | 15 | 11 | 3 | 4 | 39 | 23 | 57 | 91 |
| 2 | Crusaders | 38 | 26 | 5 | 7 | 82 | 41 | 15 | 4 | 0 | 45 | 14 | 11 | 1 | 7 | 37 | 27 | 41 | 83 |
| 3 | Linfield | 38 | 17 | 11 | 10 | 69 | 48 | 10 | 4 | 5 | 34 | 20 | 7 | 7 | 5 | 35 | 28 | 21 | 62 |
| 4 | Glentoran | 38 | 15 | 12 | 11 | 63 | 44 | 9 | 6 | 4 | 37 | 21 | 6 | 6 | 7 | 26 | 23 | 19 | 57 |
| 5 | Ballinamallard U | 38 | 15 | 8 | 15 | 49 | 43 | 6 | 6 | 7 | 21 | 22 | 9 | 2 | 8 | 28 | 21 | 6 | 53 |
| 6 | Coleraine | 38 | 13 | 14 | 11 | 50 | 57 | 8 | 5 | 5 | 26 | 27 | 5 | 9 | 6 | 24 | 30 | −7 | 53 |
| 7 | Portadown | 38 | 15 | 10 | 13 | 55 | 55 | 9 | 5 | 5 | 32 | 27 | 6 | 5 | 8 | 23 | 28 | 0 | 55 |
| 8 | Ballymena U | 38 | 11 | 13 | 14 | 54 | 68 | 6 | 7 | 6 | 30 | 31 | 5 | 6 | 8 | 24 | 37 | −14 | 46 |
| 9 | Glenavon | 38 | 12 | 6 | 20 | 64 | 62 | 8 | 4 | 8 | 44 | 30 | 4 | 2 | 12 | 20 | 32 | 2 | 42 |
| 10 | Dungannon Swifts | 38 | 9 | 13 | 16 | 42 | 58 | 5 | 7 | 6 | 21 | 23 | 4 | 6 | 10 | 21 | 35 | −16 | 40 |
| 11 | Donegal Celtic | 38 | 6 | 9 | 23 | 32 | 80 | 5 | 3 | 11 | 16 | 39 | 1 | 6 | 12 | 16 | 41 | −48 | 27 |
| 12 | Lisburn Distillery | 38 | 4 | 7 | 27 | 29 | 90 | 2 | 4 | 13 | 12 | 41 | 2 | 3 | 14 | 17 | 49 | −61 | 19 |

*Lisburn Distillery relegated. Top 6 split after 33 games.*

### PROMOTION / RELEGATION PLAY OFF

**FIRST LEG**

Warrenpoint T v Donegal Celtic — 1-0

**SECOND LEG**

Donegal Celtic v Warrenpoint T — 2-1

*Warrenpoint T won on away goals and promoted to Premier League.*

## LEADING GOALSCORERS (League Goals only)

| | | | | |
|---|---|---|---|---|
| Liam Boyce *(Cliftonville)* | 29 | Mark Farren *(Glenavon)* | 10 |
| Andrew Waterworth *(Glentoran)* | 20 | Jason McCartney *(Ballinamallard U)* | 10 |
| Darren Murray *(Portadown)* | 18 | George McMullan *(Cliftonville)* | 10 |
| Curtis Allen *(Coleraine)* | 17 | Stephen Garrett *(Cliftonville)* | 9 |
| Joe Gormley *(Cliftonville)* | 17 | Ciaran Martyn *(Glenavon)* | 9 |
| Jordan Owens *(Crusaders)* | 16 | Ryan Campbell *(Ballinamallard U)* | 8 |
| Timmy Adamson *(Crusaders)* | 15 | Paul Heatley *(Crusaders)* | 8 |
| Gary McCutcheon *(Crusaders)* | 13 | Stephen Lowry *(Coleraine)* | 8 |
| David Cushley *(Ballymena U)* | 11 | David Rainey *(Crusaders)* | 8 |
| Brian McCaul *(Linfield)* | 11 | Matt Tipton *(Linfield)* | 8 |
| Guy Bates *(Glenavon)* | 10 | Kevin Braniff *(Portadown)* | 7 |
| Joshua Cahoon *(Dungannon Swifts)* | 10 | Michael Carvill *(Linfield)* | 7 |
| Richard Clarke *(Glentoran)* | 10 | | |

## IRISH LEAGUE CHAMPIONSHIP WINNERS

| | | | | | | | | | |
|---|---|---|---|---|---|---|---|---|---|
| 1891 | Linfield | 1913 | Glentoran | 1940 | Belfast Celtic | 1970 | Glentoran | 1993 | Linfield |
| 1892 | Linfield | 1914 | Linfield | 1948 | Belfast Celtic | 1971 | Linfield | 1994 | Linfield |
| 1893 | Linfield | 1915 | Belfast Celtic | 1949 | Linfield | 1972 | Glentoran | 1995 | Crusaders |
| 1894 | Glentoran | 1920 | Belfast Celtic | 1950 | Linfield | 1973 | Crusaders | 1996 | Portadown |
| 1895 | Linfield | 1921 | Glentoran | 1951 | Glentoran | 1974 | Coleraine | 1997 | Crusaders |
| 1896 | Distillery | 1922 | Linfield | 1952 | Glenavon | 1975 | Linfield | 1998 | Cliftonville |
| 1897 | Glentoran | 1923 | Linfield | 1953 | Glentoran | 1976 | Crusaders | 1999 | Glentoran |
| 1898 | Linfield | 1924 | Queen's Island | 1954 | Linfield | 1977 | Glentoran | 2000 | Linfield |
| 1899 | Distillery | 1925 | Glentoran | 1955 | Linfield | 1978 | Linfield | 2001 | Linfield |
| 1900 | Belfast Celtic | 1926 | Belfast Celtic | 1956 | Linfield | 1979 | Linfield | 2002 | Portadown |
| 1901 | Distillery | 1927 | Belfast Celtic | 1957 | Glentoran | 1980 | Linfield | 2003 | Glentoran |
| 1902 | Linfield | 1928 | Belfast Celtic | 1958 | Ards | 1981 | Glentoran | 2004 | Linfield |
| 1903 | Distillery | 1929 | Belfast Celtic | 1959 | Linfield | 1982 | Linfield | 2005 | Glentoran |
| 1904 | Linfield | 1930 | Linfield | 1960 | Glenavon | 1983 | Linfield | 2006 | Linfield |
| 1905 | Glentoran | 1931 | Glentoran | 1961 | Linfield | 1984 | Linfield | 2007 | Linfield |
| 1906 | Cliftonville | 1932 | Linfield | 1962 | Linfield | 1985 | Linfield | 2008 | Linfield |
| | Distillery | 1933 | Belfast Celtic | 1963 | Distillery | 1986 | Linfield | 2009 | Glentoran |
| 1907 | Linfield | 1934 | Linfield | 1964 | Glentoran | 1987 | Linfield | 2010 | Linfield |
| 1908 | Linfield | 1935 | Linfield | 1965 | Derry City | 1988 | Glentoran | 2011 | Linfield |
| 1909 | Linfield | 1936 | Belfast Celtic | 1966 | Linfield | 1989 | Linfield | 2012 | Linfield |
| 1910 | Cliftonville | 1937 | Belfast Celtic | 1967 | Glentoran | 1990 | Portadown | 2013 | Cliftonville |
| 1911 | Linfield | 1938 | Belfast Celtic | 1968 | Glentoran | 1991 | Portadown | | |
| 1912 | Glentoran | 1939 | Belfast Celtic | 1969 | Linfield | 1992 | Glentoran | | |

## BELFAST TELEGRAPH CHAMPIONSHIP ONE 2012–13

| | | P | W | D | L | F | A | W | D | L | F | A | W | D | L | F | A | GD | Pts |
|---|---|---|---|---|---|---|---|---|---|---|---|---|---|---|---|---|---|---|---|
| | | | | *Total* | | | | | *Home* | | | | | *Away* | | | | | |
| 1 | Ards | 24 | 18 | 5 | 1 | 56 | 19 | 11 | 1 | 0 | 27 | 7 | 7 | 4 | 1 | 29 | 12 | 37 | 59 |
| 2 | Warrenpoint T* | 24 | 15 | 5 | 4 | 46 | 23 | 8 | 3 | 1 | 24 | 12 | 7 | 2 | 3 | 22 | 11 | 23 | 50 |
| 3 | Institute | 24 | 14 | 5 | 5 | 50 | 23 | 7 | 2 | 3 | 22 | 10 | 7 | 3 | 2 | 28 | 13 | 27 | 47 |
| 4 | Dundela | 24 | 13 | 4 | 7 | 62 | 51 | 6 | 3 | 3 | 31 | 24 | 7 | 1 | 4 | 31 | 27 | 11 | 43 |
| 5 | Carrick Rangers | 24 | 11 | 6 | 7 | 48 | 32 | 7 | 4 | 1 | 26 | 7 | 4 | 2 | 6 | 22 | 25 | 16 | 39 |
| 6 | H&W Welders | 24 | 10 | 4 | 10 | 37 | 35 | 5 | 2 | 5 | 22 | 17 | 5 | 2 | 5 | 15 | 18 | 2 | 34 |
| 7 | Dergview | 24 | 7 | 6 | 11 | 27 | 39 | 4 | 5 | 3 | 16 | 14 | 3 | 1 | 8 | 11 | 25 | −12 | 27 |
| 8 | Larne | 24 | 5 | 9 | 10 | 24 | 40 | 2 | 5 | 5 | 10 | 21 | 3 | 4 | 5 | 14 | 19 | −16 | 24 |
| 9 | Coagh U | 24 | 6 | 5 | 13 | 35 | 51 | 3 | 2 | 7 | 20 | 27 | 3 | 3 | 6 | 15 | 24 | −16 | 23 |
| 10 | Bangor | 24 | 6 | 5 | 13 | 23 | 42 | 4 | 1 | 7 | 13 | 20 | 2 | 4 | 6 | 10 | 22 | −19 | 23 |
| 11 | Loughgall | 24 | 6 | 5 | 13 | 27 | 48 | 4 | 2 | 6 | 16 | 26 | 2 | 3 | 7 | 11 | 22 | −21 | 23 |
| 12 | Limavady U | 24 | 5 | 6 | 13 | 34 | 49 | 4 | 1 | 7 | 18 | 22 | 1 | 5 | 6 | 16 | 27 | −15 | 21 |
| 13 | Tobermore U | 24 | 6 | 3 | 15 | 38 | 55 | 4 | 3 | 5 | 27 | 28 | 2 | 0 | 10 | 11 | 27 | −17 | 21 |
| 14 | Newry C† | 0 | 0 | 0 | 0 | 0 | 0 | 0 | 0 | 0 | 0 | 0 | 0 | 0 | 0 | 0 | 0 | 0 | 0 |

*Warrenpoint T promoted via play-offs. †Newry C dissolved, record expunged.

## BELFAST TELEGRAPH CHAMPIONSHIP (Previously First Division)

| 1996 | Coleraine | 2002 | Lisburn Distillery | 2008 | Loughgall |
|---|---|---|---|---|---|
| 1997 | Ballymena United | 2003 | Dungannon Swifts | 2009 | Portadown |
| 1998 | Newry Town | 2004 | Loughgall | 2010 | Loughgall |
| 1999 | Distillery | 2005 | Armagh City | 2011 | Carrick Rangers |
| 2000 | Omagh Town | 2006 | Crusaders | 2012 | Ballinamallard U |
| 2001 | Ards | 2007 | Institute | 2013 | Ards |

## BELFAST TELEGRAPH CHAMPIONSHIP TWO 2012–13

| | | P | W | D | L | F | A | W | D | L | F | A | W | D | L | F | A | GD | Pts |
|---|---|---|---|---|---|---|---|---|---|---|---|---|---|---|---|---|---|---|---|
| | | | | *Total* | | | | | *Home* | | | | | *Away* | | | | | |
| 1 | Knockbreda | 30 | 25 | 2 | 3 | 106 | 25 | 14 | 0 | 1 | 63 | 10 | 11 | 2 | 2 | 43 | 13 | 81 | 77 |
| 2 | Ballyclare Comrades | 30 | 23 | 2 | 5 | 77 | 28 | 12 | 1 | 2 | 32 | 11 | 11 | 1 | 3 | 45 | 17 | 49 | 71 |
| 3 | Armagh C | 30 | 21 | 3 | 6 | 81 | 34 | 13 | 0 | 2 | 49 | 16 | 8 | 3 | 4 | 32 | 18 | 47 | 66 |
| 4 | Lurgan Celtic | 30 | 20 | 3 | 7 | 71 | 43 | 12 | 1 | 2 | 38 | 18 | 8 | 2 | 5 | 33 | 25 | 28 | 63 |
| 5 | Glebe Rangers | 30 | 15 | 7 | 8 | 58 | 41 | 7 | 5 | 3 | 33 | 23 | 8 | 2 | 5 | 25 | 18 | 17 | 52 |
| 6 | Wakehurst | 30 | 16 | 4 | 10 | 61 | 50 | 8 | 3 | 4 | 28 | 24 | 8 | 1 | 6 | 33 | 26 | 11 | 52 |
| 7 | Queen's University | 30 | 13 | 6 | 11 | 65 | 43 | 7 | 2 | 6 | 33 | 20 | 6 | 4 | 5 | 32 | 23 | 22 | 45 |
| 8 | PSNI | 30 | 14 | 1 | 15 | 60 | 48 | 6 | 0 | 9 | 30 | 27 | 8 | 1 | 6 | 30 | 21 | 12 | 43 |
| 9 | Banbridge T | 30 | 11 | 7 | 12 | 57 | 58 | 6 | 3 | 6 | 32 | 28 | 5 | 4 | 6 | 25 | 30 | −1 | 40 |
| 10 | Ballymoney U | 30 | 10 | 7 | 13 | 53 | 67 | 5 | 4 | 6 | 26 | 30 | 5 | 3 | 7 | 27 | 37 | −14 | 37 |
| 11 | Annagh U | 30 | 9 | 7 | 14 | 39 | 53 | 2 | 5 | 8 | 14 | 27 | 7 | 2 | 6 | 25 | 26 | −14 | 34 |
| 12 | Moyola Park | 30 | 6 | 10 | 14 | 35 | 51 | 3 | 5 | 7 | 20 | 25 | 3 | 5 | 7 | 15 | 26 | −16 | 28 |
| 13 | Portstewart | 30 | 5 | 7 | 18 | 37 | 70 | 3 | 5 | 7 | 20 | 24 | 2 | 2 | 11 | 17 | 46 | −33 | 22 |
| 14 | Sport & Leisure Swifts | 30 | 5 | 5 | 20 | 41 | 101 | 3 | 2 | 10 | 20 | 49 | 2 | 3 | 10 | 21 | 52 | −60 | 20 |
| 15 | Killymoon Rangers | 30 | 4 | 7 | 19 | 38 | 85 | 4 | 4 | 7 | 26 | 41 | 0 | 3 | 12 | 12 | 44 | −47 | 19 |
| 16 | Chimney Corner | 30 | 3 | 2 | 25 | 26 | 108 | 3 | 0 | 12 | 14 | 52 | 0 | 2 | 13 | 12 | 56 | −82 | 11 |

## IFA YOUTH LEAGUE 2012–13

### SECTION A

| | P | W | D | L | F | A | GD | Pts |
|---|---|---|---|---|---|---|---|---|
| Glentoran Colts | 22 | 14 | 6 | 2 | 64 | 32 | 48 | — |
| Linfield Rangers | 22 | 14 | 5 | 3 | 80 | 30 | 50 | 47 |
| Cliftonville Strollers | 22 | 13 | 7 | 2 | 50 | 25 | 25 | 46 |
| Ballinamallard U III | 22 | 9 | 5 | 8 | 46 | 42 | 4 | 32 |
| Lisburn Distillery III | 22 | 9 | 5 | 8 | 38 | 35 | 3 | 32 |
| Glenavon III | 22 | 8 | 7 | 7 | 48 | 41 | 7 | 31 |
| Carrick Rangers Colts | 22 | 8 | 5 | 9 | 63 | 61 | 2 | 29 |
| Dungannon Swifts Youth | 22 | 7 | 5 | 10 | 33 | 45 | −12 | 26 |
| Newington YC U18 | 22 | 6 | 5 | 11 | 49 | 63 | −14 | 23 |
| Donegal Celtic Youth | 22 | 5 | 7 | 10 | 35 | 66 | −31 | 22 |
| Ballymena U III | 22 | 5 | 0 | 17 | 37 | 66 | −29 | 15 |
| Newry C Wanderers | 22 | 4 | 3 | 15 | 30 | 67 | −37 | 15 |

### SECTION B

| | P | W | D | L | F | A | GD | Pts |
|---|---|---|---|---|---|---|---|---|
| Dungannon Swifts | 18 | 15 | 1 | 2 | 88 | 24 | 64 | 46 |
| Limavady U | 18 | 13 | 3 | 2 | 65 | 17 | 48 | 42 |
| Portadown III | 18 | 10 | 2 | 6 | 41 | 29 | 12 | 32 |
| Institute Colts | 18 | 10 | 1 | 7 | 40 | 28 | 12 | 31 |
| Ballyclare Comrades Colts | 18 | 9 | 2 | 7 | 41 | 38 | 3 | 29 |
| Ards Youth | 18 | 9 | 0 | 9 | 45 | 36 | 9 | 27 |
| St Oliver Plunkett | 18 | 8 | 2 | 8 | 32 | 34 | −2 | 26 |
| Sport & Leisure Swifts | 18 | 6 | 2 | 10 | 38 | 49 | −11 | 20 |
| Ballymoney U Colts | 18 | 2 | 1 | 15 | 23 | 86 | −63 | 7 |
| Larne U18 | 18 | 1 | 0 | 17 | 16 | 88 | −72 | 3 |

## IFA RESERVE LEAGUE 2012–13

| | P | W | D | L | F | A | GD | Pts |
|---|---|---|---|---|---|---|---|---|
| Ballinamallard U II | 33 | 25 | 4 | 4 | 96 | 37 | 59 | 79 |
| Cliftonville Olympic | 33 | 22 | 4 | 7 | 93 | 44 | 49 | 70 |
| Linfield Swifts | 33 | 19 | 5 | 9 | 77 | 54 | 23 | 62 |
| Glentoran II | 33 | 18 | 6 | 9 | 85 | 58 | 27 | 60 |
| Crusaders Reserves | 33 | 17 | 6 | 10 | 77 | 53 | 24 | 57 |
| Ballymena U Reserves | 33 | 11 | 8 | 14 | 72 | 67 | 5 | 41 |
| Coleraine Reserves | 33 | 11 | 8 | 14 | 69 | 80 | −11 | 41 |
| Glenavon Reserves | 33 | 11 | 7 | 15 | 62 | 75 | −13 | 40 |
| Lisburn Distillery II | 33 | 12 | 4 | 17 | 54 | 71 | −17 | 40 |
| Donegal Celtic Reserves | 33 | 9 | 2 | 22 | 46 | 74 | −28 | 29 |
| Dungannon Swifts Reserves | 33 | 6 | 4 | 23 | 54 | 116 | −62 | 22 |
| Portadown Reserves | 33 | 5 | 6 | 22 | 57 | 113 | −56 | 21 |

## MARIE CURIE IRISH CUP 2012–13

**ROUND 1**

| | |
|---|---|
| 18th Newtownabbey v Camlough R | 0-2 |
| Abbey Villa v Shorts | 5-1 |
| Ballywalter Rec v Bangor Swifts | 0-5 |
| Bangor Rangers v UUJ | 0-1 |
| Bloomfield v Laurelvale | 2-1 |
| Bryansburn Rangers v Crumlin Star | 0-1 |
| Carniny Amateur & Youth v Ardstraw | 3-3 |
| Desertmartin v Rathfriland Rangers | 0-4 |
| Dollingstown v Dunmurry YM | 3-2 |
| Downshire YM v Crewe U | 3-1 |
| Draperstown Celtic v Drumaness Mills | 2-6 |
| Dungiven v Dromore Amateurs | 0-2 |
| East Belfast v Comber Rec | 1-5 |
| Fivemiletown U v Shankill U | 0-1 |
| Groomsport v Ards Rangers | 0-3 |
| Holywood v Ballynure OB | 0-2 |
| Kilmore Rec v Lurgan T Boys | 5-0 |
| Kilroot Rec v Seagoe | 1-2 |
| Larne Tech. OB v Islandmagee | 1-2 |
| Lisanally R v Dromara Village | 0-3 |
| Lisburn R v Grove U | 2-1 |
| Lower Maze v Iveagh U | 5-2 |
| Malachians v Newington YC | 4-6 |
| Markethill Swifts v Immaculata | 1-6 |
| Newcastle v Ballymacash Rangers | 1-1 |
| Newtowne v Moneyslane | 5-1 |
| Nortel v Mossley YM | 3-1 |
| Oxford Sunnyside v 1st Bangor | 3-3 |
| Oxford U Stars v Brantwood | 3-2 |
| Rathfern Rangers v Banbridge Rangers | 2-2 |
| Richhill v Barn U | 1-3 |
| Roe R v Rosario YC | 1-3 |
| Sirocco Works v Raceview | 2-1 |
| Tandragee Rovers v Derriaghy CC | 1-0 |
| Wellington Rec v FC Ballynure | 8-0 |

*Wellington Rec ejected for fielding ineligible players.*

**ROUND 2**

| | |
|---|---|
| Bangor Amateurs v Newcastle | 2-3 |
| Barn U v Crumlin Star | 1-2 |
| FC Ballynure v Mountjoy U | 1-3 |
| Ards Rangers v Lower Maze | 6-0 |
| Ballynahinch U v Dromore Amateurs | 2-1 |
| Ballynure OB v Carniny Amateur & Youth | 3-2 |
| Bloomfield v Rathfriland Rangers | 1-3 |
| Comber Rec v Camlough R. | 4-1 |

*Comber Rec ejected for fielding ineligible players.*

| | |
|---|---|
| Dollingstown v Oxford U Stars | 1-2 |
| Downshire YM v Sirocco Works | 1-3 |
| Dromara Village v Killyleagh YC | 0-2 |

*Killyleagh YC ejected for fielding ineligible players.*

| | |
|---|---|
| Drumaness Mills v Saintfield U | 4-2 |
| Dunmurry Rec v Bangor Swifts | 4-2 |
| Immaculata v Newbuildings U | 4-1 |
| Islandmagee v Shankill U | 7-0 |
| Nortel v Kilmore Rec | 0-3 |
| Oxford Sunnyside v Crumlin U | 2-3 |
| Rathfern Rangers v Abbey Villa | 2-1 |
| Rosario YC v Magherafelt Sky Blues | 2-0 |
| Seagoe v Malachians | 3-4 |
| Tandragee Rovers v Newtowne | 3-1 |
| UUJ v Lisburn Rangers | 1-2 |

**ROUND 3**

| | |
|---|---|
| Ballynure OB v Rathfern Rangers | 2-1 |
| Camlough R v Ards Rangers | 2-3 |
| Crumlin U v Dromara Village | 1-2 |
| Drumaness Mills v Islandmagee | 8-1 |
| Immaculata v Dunmurry Rec | 8-1 |
| Kilmore Rec v Malachians | 4-3 |
| Lisburn Rangers v Ballynahinch U | 1-3 |
| Newcastle v Crumlin U | 0-3 |
| Sirocco Works v Mountjoy U | 0-1 |
| Tandragee Rovers v Rosario YC | 0-2 |

**ROUND 4**

| | |
|---|---|
| Annagh U v Rosario YC | 3-3 |
| Ards Rangers v Immaculata | 3-5 |
| Armagh City v Ards | 2-2 |
| Ballyclare Comrades v Portstewart | 3-2 |
| Ballymoney U v Ballynahinch U | 1-1 |
| Bangor v Crumlin U | 3-0 |
| Chimney Corner v Loughgall | 0-2 |
| Dundela v Glebe Rangers | 1-0 |
| H&W Welders v Oxford U Stars | 2-0 |
| Institute v Dergview | 1-0 |
| Killymoon Rangers v Dromara Village | 4-2 |
| Kilmore Rec w.o. v Drumaness Mills *disqualified* | |
| Larne v Wakehurst | 3-2 |
| Limavady U v Knockbreda | 0-3 |
| Lurgan Celtic v Carrick Rangers | 1-0 |
| Moyola Park v Coagh U | 0-2 |
| Queen's University v Banbridge Rangers | 3-1 |
| Rathfriland Rangers v Ballynure OB | 1-0 |
| Tobermore U v Mountjoy U | 7-1 |
| Warrenpoint T v Sport & Leisure Swifts | 4-2 |

**ROUND 5**

| | |
|---|---|
| Ards v Immaculata | 4-0 |
| Ballyclare Comrades v Bangor | 2-3 |
| Ballymena U v Warrenpoint T | 2-1 |
| Cliftonville v Ballinamallard U | 4-2 |
| Coleraine v Ballynahinch U | 7-0 |
| Dundela v Queen's University | 4-3 |
| Glenavon v H&W Welders | 5-1 |
| Institute v Rathfriland Rangers | 2-1 |
| Killymoon Rangers v Glentoran | 1-4 |
| Knockbreda v Rosario YC | 5-1 |
| Larne v Lurgan Celtic | 1-1, 1-4 |
| Linfield v Crusaders | 2-2, 1-2 |
| Lisburn Distillery v Coagh U | 5-1 |
| Loughgall v Donegal Celtic | 1-3 |
| Portadown v Dungannon Swifts | 2-1 |
| Tobermore U v Kilmore Rec | 2-2, 0-1 |

**ROUND 6**

| | |
|---|---|
| Lisburn Distillery v Dundela | 2-1 |
| Ballymena U v Coleraine | 2-3 |
| Bangor v Glentoran | 2-5 |
| Cliftonville v Donegal Celtic | 2-0 |
| Crusaders v Glenavon | 4-1 |
| Institute v Kilmore Rec | 0-2 |
| Lurgan Celtic v Knockbreda | 0-3 |
| Portadown v Ards | 1-0 |

**QUARTER-FINALS**

| | |
|---|---|
| Cliftonville v Kilmore Rec | 2-0 |
| Coleraine v Portadown | 0-3 |
| Crusaders v Lisburn Distillery | 1-1, 1-1 |

*Crusaders won 4-3 on penalties.*

| | |
|---|---|
| Knockbreda v Glentoran | 1-3 |

**SEMI-FINALS**

| | |
|---|---|
| Crusaders v Cliftonville | 0-2 |
| Portadown v Glentoran | 0-1 |

**FINAL**

Saturday 4 May 2013
*(at Windsor Park, Belfast)*

**Cliftonville (0) 1** *(Gormley 34)*

**Glentoran (0) 3** *(Waterworth 64, 101, Callacher 99)*

*aet.*

*Cliftonville:* Devlin; Seydak, McGovern (O'Carroll 60), Smyth, Johnston, Caldwell■, McMullan, Catney, Garrett (Cosgrove 82), Boyce, Gormley (Donnelly 82).

*Glentoran:* Morris; Hill (Nixon 109), Magee, Ward, Callacher, McAlorum (Kane 100), Clarke M (O'Hanlon 70), Carson, Howland, Clarke R■, Waterworth.

*Referee:* Arnold Hunter.

Replays only used in Rounds 5 and 6 and Quarter-finals; otherwise extra-time and penalties decided drawn games.

## IRISH CUP FINALS (from 1946–47)

| | |
|---|---|
| 1946–47 Belfast Celtic 1, Glentoran 0 | 1982–83 Glentoran 1:2, Linfield 1:1 |
| 1947–48 Linfield 3, Coleraine 0 | 1983–84 Ballymena U 4, |
| 1948–49 Derry City 3, Glentoran 1 | Carrick Rangers 1 |
| 1949–50 Linfield 2, Distillery 1 | 1984–85 Glentoran 1:1, Linfield 1:0 |
| 1950–51 Glentoran 3, Ballymena U 1 | 1985–86 Glentoran 2, Coleraine 1 |
| 1951–52 Ards 1, Glentoran 0 | 1986–87 Glentoran 1, Larne 0 |
| 1952–53 Linfield 5, Coleraine 0 | 1987–88 Glentoran 1, Glenavon 0 |
| 1953–54 Derry City 1, Glentoran 0 | 1988–89 Ballymena U 1, Larne 0 |
| 1954–55 Dundela 3, Glenavon 0 | 1989–90 Glentoran 3, Portadown 0 |
| 1955–56 Distillery 1, Glentoran 0 | 1990–91 Portadown 2, Glenavon 1 |
| 1956–57 Glenavon 2, Derry City 0 | 1991–92 Glenavon 2, Linfield 1 |
| 1957–58 Ballymena U 2, Linfield 0 | 1992–93 Bangor 1:1:1, Ards 1:1:0 |
| 1958–59 Glenavon 2, Ballymena U 0 | 1993–94 Linfield 2, Bangor 0 |
| 1959–60 Linfield 5, Ards 1 | 1994–95 Linfield 3, Carrick Rangers 1 |
| 1960–61 Glenavon 5, Linfield 1 | 1995–96 Glentoran 1, Glenavon 0 |
| 1961–62 Linfield 4, Portadown 0 | 1996–97 Glentoran 1, Cliftonville 0 |
| 1962–63 Linfield 2, Distillery 1 | 1997–98 Glentoran 1, Glenavon 0 |
| 1963–64 Derry City 2, Glentoran 0 | 1998–99 *Portadown awarded trophy after Cliftonville* |
| 1964–65 Coleraine 2, Glenavon 1 | *were eliminated for using an ineligible player in* |
| 1965–66 Glentoran 2, Linfield 0 | *semi-final.* |
| 1966–67 Crusaders 3, Glentoran 1 | |
| 1967–68 Crusaders 2, Linfield 0 | 1999–2000 Glentoran 1, Portadown 0 |
| 1968–69 Ards 4, Distillery 2 | 2000–01 Glentoran 1, Linfield 0 |
| 1969–70 Linfield 2, Ballymena U 1 | 2001–02 Linfield 2, Portadown 1 |
| 1970–71 Distillery 3, Derry City | 2002–03 Coleraine 1, Glentoran 0 |
| 1971–72 Coleraine 2, Portadown 1 | 2003–04 Glentoran 1, Coleraine 0 |
| 1972–73 Glentoran 3, Linfield 2 | 2004–05 Portadown 5, Larne 1 |
| 1973–74 Ards 2, Ballymena U 1 | 2005–06 Linfield 2, Glentoran 1 |
| 1974–75 Coleraine 1:0:1, Linfield 1:0:0 | 2006–07 Linfield 2, Dungannon Swifts 2 |
| 1975–76 Carrick Rangers 2, Linfield 1 | *(aet; Linfield won 3-2 on penalties).* |
| 1976–77 Coleraine 4, Linfield 1 | 2007–08 Linfield 2, Coleraine 1 |
| 1977–78 Linfield 3, Ballymena U 1 | 2008–09 Crusaders 1, Cliftonville 0 |
| 1978–79 Cliftonville 3, Portadown 2 | 2009–10 Linfield 2, Portadown 1 |
| 1979–80 Linfield 2, Crusaders 0 | 2010–11 Linfield 2, Crusaders 1 |
| 1980–81 Ballymena U 1, Glenavon 0 | 2011–12 Linfield 4, Crusaders 1 |
| 1981–82 Linfield 2, Coleraine 1 | 2012–13 Glentoran 3, Cliftonville 1 |

## SETANTA SPORTS CUP 2012–13

**FIRST ROUND – FIRST LEG**

| | |
|---|---|
| Cork City v Cliftonville | 4-0 |
| Drogheda U v Portadown | 3-2 |
| St Patrick's Ath v Glentoran | 0-0 |
| Shamrock R v Coleraine | 0-1 |

**FIRST ROUND – SECOND LEG**

| | |
|---|---|
| Cliftonville v Cork C | 2-2 (2-6) |
| Glentoran v St Patrick's Ath | 1-0 (1-0) |
| Portadown v Drogheda U | 0-5 (2-7) |
| Coleraine v Shamrock R | 0-2 (1-2) |

**QUARTER-FINALS – FIRST LEG**

| | |
|---|---|
| Sligo R v Glentoran | 5-0 |
| Cork C v Crusaders | 1-0 |
| Derry City v Drogheda U | 1-1 |
| Shamrock R v Linfield | 4-1 |

**QUARTER-FINALS – SECOND LEG**

| | |
|---|---|
| Glentoran v Sligo R | 0-3 (0-8) |
| Crusaders v Cork C | 1-3 (1-4) |
| Drogheda U v Derry C | 2-1 (3-2) |
| Linfield v Shamrock R | 1-3 (2-7) |

**SEMI-FINALS – FIRST LEG**

| | |
|---|---|
| Shamrock R v Cork C | 1-1 |
| Drogheda U v Sligo R | 2-0 |

**SEMI-FINALS –SECOND LEG**

| | |
|---|---|
| Cork C v Shamrock R | 2-2 (3-3) |
| *Shamrock R won on away goals.* | |
| Sligo R v Drogheda U | 1-0 (1-2) |

**FINAL**

Saturday 11 May 2013
*(at Tallaght Stadium, Dublin)*

**Shamrock R (3) 7** *(Chambers 11, O'Connor 13, Sheppard 45, Finn 55, 56, Dennehy 75, 88)*

**Drogheda U (0) 1** *(O'Neil 65)*      4022

*Shamrock R:* Murphy; Sullivan, Foran, McGuinness, Ledwith, O'Connor (Kilduff 71), Finn, Rice, Chambers, Dennehy, Sheppard (Quigley 60) (McCabe 77).
*Drogheda U:* Sava; Grimes, Prendergast, Gannon (McNally 72), Byrne, Rusk (O'Brien 60), Brennan R, Daly (O'Conor 60), Cassidy, Brennan G, O'Neill.
*Referee:* Rob Rogers.

## SETANTA SPORTS CUP WINNERS

| | | |
|---|---|---|
| 2004–05 Linfield | 2007–08 Cork C | 2011–12 Crusaders |
| 2005–06 Drogheda U | 2009–10 Bohemians | 2012–13 Shamrock R |
| 2006–07 Drogheda U | 2010–11 Shamrock R | |

## ULSTER CUP WINNERS

| | | | |
|---|---|---|---|
| 1949 Linfield | 1962 Linfield | 1975 Coleraine | 1988 Glentoran | 2001 *No competition* |
| 1950 Larne | 1963 Crusaders | 1976 Glentoran | 1989 Glentoran | 2002 *No competition* |
| 1951 Glentoran | 1964 Linfield | 1977 Linfield | 1990 Portadown | 2003 Dungannon Swifts |
| 1952 *No competition* | 1965 Coleraine | 1978 Linfield | 1991 Bangor | *(Confined to* |
| 1953 Glentoran | 1966 Glentoran | 1979 Linfield | 1992 Linfield | *First Division clubs)* |
| 1954 Crusaders | 1967 Linfield | 1980 Ballymena U | 1993 Crusaders | 2004–2013 *No competition* |
| 1955 Glenavon | 1968 Coleraine | 1981 Glentoran | 1994 Bangor | |
| 1956 Linfield | 1969 Coleraine | 1982 Glentoran | 1995 Portadown | |
| 1957 Linfield | 1970 Linfield | 1983 Glentoran | 1996 Portadown | |
| 1958 Distillery | 1971 Linfield | 1984 Linfield | 1997 Coleraine | |
| 1959 Glenavon | 1972 Coleraine | 1985 Coleraine | 1998 Ballyclare Comrades | |
| 1960 Linfield | 1973 Ards | 1986 Coleraine | 1999 Distillery | |
| 1961 Ballymena U | 1974 Linfield | 1987 Larne | 2000 *No competition* | |

## ROLL OF HONOUR SEASON 2012–13

| Competition | Winner | Runner-up |
|---|---|---|
| Carling Irish Premiership | Cliftonville | Crusaders |
| Marie Curie Irish Cup | Glentoran | Cliftonville |
| Irish Championship Division One | Ards | Warrenpoint T |
| Irish Championship Division Two | Knockbreda | Ballyclare Comrades |
| Irn Bru League Cup | Cliftonville | Crusaders |
| County Antrim Shield | Ballymena U | Linfield |
| Steel & Sons Cup | Glentoran II | Ards |
| *Cup withheld – Glentoran II disqualified for fielding an illegible player.* | | |
| Co Antrim Junior Shield | Portaferry R | Woodvale |
| Setanta Sports Cup | Shamrock R | Drogheda U |
| Coca-Cola Irish Junior Cup | Strathroy Harps | Harryville Homers |
| Mid Ulster Cup (Senior) | Dungannon Swifts | Banbridge T |
| Harry Cavan Youth Cup | Linfield Rangers | Ballinamallard U |
| George Wilson Memorial Cup | Cliftonville Olympic | Crusaders Reserves |
| North West Senior Cup | Coleraine | Institute |
| The Fermanagh Mulhern Cup | Enniskillen Town U | Tummery Ath |
| Britton Rose Bowl | Northern Irish AFL | Scottish Amateur FA |
| Coca-Cola Intermediate Cup | Institute | Ards Rangers |

## NORTHERN IRELAND FOOTBALL WRITERS ASSOCIATION AWARDS

**MANAGER OF THE YEAR**
Tommy Breslin (Cliftonville)

**HALL OF FAME**
Malcolm Brodie and Alan McDonald

**PLAYER OF THE YEAR**
Liam Boyce (Cliftonville)

**TEAM OF THE SEASON**
Conor Devlin (Cliftonville)
George McMullan (Cliftonville)
David Magowan (Crusaders)
Marc Smyth (Cliftonville)
Craig McClean (Crusaders)
Declan Caddell (Crusaders)
Barry Johnston (Cliftonville)
Ryan Catney (Cliftonville)
Paul Heatley (Crusaders)
Liam Boyce (Cliftonville)
Joe Gormley (Cliftonville).

**YOUNG PLAYER OF THE YEAR**
Conor Devlin (Cliftonville)

**INTERNATIONAL PERSONALITY OF THE YEAR**
Roy Carroll (Olympiakos)

**JUNIOR TEAM OF THE YEAR**
Ards

**CHAMPIONSHIP PLAYER OF THE YEAR**
James Cully (Ards)

**MERIT AWARD**
Bob Ramsey (Northern Ireland Schools FA)

## CARLING PLAYER OF THE MONTH

| Month | Player | Team |
|---|---|---|
| August | Jamie Mulgrew | Linfield |
| September | Matthew Tipton | Portadown |
| October | Gary Hamilton | Glentoran |
| November | Barry Johnston | Cliftonville |
| December | William Murphy | Linfield |
| January | Chris Morrow | Crusaders |
| February | Niall Morgan | Dungannon Swifts |
| March | Peter Thompson | Linfield |
| April | James Costello | Ballymena U |

## CHAMPIONSHIP PLAYER OF THE MONTH

| Month | Player | Team |
|---|---|---|
| August | Nathan McConnell | Ards |
| September | Ricky Copeland | Newry C |
| October | Andy Crawford | Ballinamallard U |
| November | Ben Browne | Bangor |
| December | Keith Johnston | Warrenpoint T |
| January | Gary Workman | Larne |
| February | Marty Havern | Newry C |
| March | David Kee | Ballinamallard U |
| April | Darragh Hanaphy | Newry C |

## CARLING MANAGER OF THE MONTH

| Month | Manager | Team |
|---|---|---|
| August | Ronnie McFall | Portadown |
| September | Ronnie McFall | Portadown |
| October | Scott Young | Glentoran |
| November | Tommy Breslin | Cliftonville |
| December | Oran Kearney | Coleraine |
| January | Stephen Baxter | Crusaders |
| February | David Jeffrey | Linfield |
| March | Stephen Baxter | Crusaders |
| April | Glenn Ferguson | Ballymena U |

# EUROPEAN CUP FINALS

## EUROPEAN CUP FINALS 1956–1992

| Year | Winners | | Runners-up | | Venue | Attendance | Referee |
|---|---|---|---|---|---|---|---|
| 1956 | Real Madrid | 4 | Reims | 3 | Paris | 38,000 | Ellis (E) |
| 1957 | Real Madrid | 2 | Fiorentina | 0 | Madrid | 124,000 | Horn (Ho) |
| 1958 | Real Madrid | 3 | AC Milan | 2 (aet) | Brussels | 67,000 | Alsteen (Bel) |
| 1959 | Real Madrid | 2 | Reims | 0 | Stuttgart | 80,000 | Dutsch (WG) |
| 1960 | Real Madrid | 7 | Eintracht Frankfurt | 3 | Glasgow | 135,000 | Mowat (S) |
| 1961 | Benfica | 3 | Barcelona | 2 | Berne | 28,000 | Dienst (Sw) |
| 1962 | Benfica | 5 | Real Madrid | 3 | Amsterdam | 65,000 | Horn (Ho) |
| 1963 | AC Milan | 2 | Benfica | 1 | Wembley | 45,000 | Holland (E) |
| 1964 | Internazionale | 3 | Real Madrid | 1 | Vienna | 74,000 | Stoll (A) |
| 1965 | Internazionale | 1 | Benfica | 0 | Milan | 80,000 | Dienst (Sw) |
| 1966 | Real Madrid | 2 | Partizan Belgrade | 1 | Brussels | 55,000 | Kreitlein (WG) |
| 1967 | Celtic | 2 | Internazionale | 1 | Lisbon | 56,000 | Tschenscher (WG) |
| 1968 | Manchester U | 4 | Benfica | 1 (aet) | Wembley | 100,000 | Lo Bello (I) |
| 1969 | AC Milan | 4 | Ajax | 1 | Madrid | 50,000 | Ortiz (Sp) |
| 1970 | Feyenoord | 2 | Celtic | 1 (aet) | Milan | 50,000 | Lo Bello (I) |
| 1971 | Ajax | 2 | Panathinaikos | 0 | Wembley | 90,000 | Taylor (E) |
| 1972 | Ajax | 2 | Internazionale | 0 | Rotterdam | 67,000 | Helies (F) |
| 1973 | Ajax | 1 | Juventus | 0 | Belgrade | 93,500 | Guglovic (Y) |
| 1974 | Bayern Munich | 1 | Atletico Madrid | 1 | Brussels | 49,000 | Loraux (Bel) |
| Replay | Bayern Munich | 4 | Atletico Madrid | 0 | Brussels | 23,000 | Delcourt (Bel) |
| 1975 | Bayern Munich | 2 | Leeds U | 0 | Paris | 50,000 | Kitabdjian (F) |
| 1976 | Bayern Munich | 1 | St Etienne | 0 | Glasgow | 54,864 | Palotai (H) |
| 1977 | Liverpool | 3 | Moenchengladbach | 1 | Rome | 57,000 | Wurtz (F) |
| 1978 | Liverpool | 1 | FC Brugge | 0 | Wembley | 92,000 | Corver (Ho) |
| 1979 | Nottingham F | 1 | Malmo | 0 | Munich | 57,500 | Linemayr (A) |
| 1980 | Nottingham F | 1 | Hamburg | 0 | Madrid | 50,000 | Garrido (P) |
| 1981 | Liverpool | 1 | Real Madrid | 0 | Paris | 48,360 | Palotai (H) |
| 1982 | Aston Villa | 1 | Bayern Munich | 0 | Rotterdam | 46,000 | Konrath (F) |
| 1983 | Hamburg | 1 | Juventus | 0 | Athens | 80,000 | Rainea (R) |
| 1984 | Liverpool | 1 | Roma | 1 | Rome | 69,693 | Fredriksson (Se) |
| | (aet; Liverpool won 4-2 on penalties) | | | | | | |
| 1985 | Juventus | 1 | Liverpool | 0 | Brussels | 58,000 | Daina (Sw) |
| 1986 | Steaua Bucharest | 0 | Barcelona | 0 | Seville | 70,000 | Vautrot (F) |
| | (aet; Steaua won 2-0 on penalties) | | | | | | |
| 1987 | Porto | 2 | Bayern Munich | 1 | Vienna | 59,000 | Ponnet (Bel) |
| 1988 | PSV Eindhoven | 0 | Benfica | 0 | Stuttgart | 70,000 | Agnolin (I) |
| | (aet; PSV won 6-5 on penalties) | | | | | | |
| 1989 | AC Milan | 4 | Steaua Bucharest | 0 | Barcelona | 97,000 | Tritschler (WG) |
| 1990 | AC Milan | 1 | Benfica | 0 | Vienna | 57,500 | Kohl (A) |
| 1991 | Red Star Belgrade | 0 | Marseille | 0 | Bari | 56,000 | Lanese (I) |
| | (aet; Red Star won 5-3 on penalties) | | | | | | |
| 1992 | Barcelona | 1 | Sampdoria | 0 (aet) | Wembley | 70,827 | Schmidhuber (G) |

## UEFA CHAMPIONS LEAGUE FINALS 1993–2013

| Year | Winners | | Runners-up | | Venue | Attendance | Referee |
|---|---|---|---|---|---|---|---|
| 1993 | Marseille* | 1 | AC Milan | 0 | Munich | 64,400 | Rothlisberger (Sw) |
| 1994 | AC Milan | 4 | Barcelona | 0 | Athens | 70,000 | Don (E) |
| 1995 | Ajax | 1 | AC Milan | 0 | Vienna | 49,730 | Craciunescu (R) |
| 1996 | Juventus | 1 | Ajax | 1 | Rome | 67,000 | Vega (Sp) |
| | (aet; Juventus won 4-2 on penalties) | | | | | | |
| 1997 | Borussia Dortmund | 3 | Juventus | 1 | Munich | 59,000 | Puhl (H) |
| 1998 | Real Madrid | 1 | Juventus | 0 | Amsterdam | 47,500 | Krug (G) |
| 1999 | Manchester U | 2 | Bayern Munich | 1 | Barcelona | 90,000 | Collina (I) |
| 2000 | Real Madrid | 3 | Valencia | 0 | Paris | 78,759 | Braschi (I) |
| 2001 | Bayern Munich | 1 | Valencia | 1 | Milan | 71,500 | Jol (Ho) |
| | (aet; Bayern Munich won 5-4 on penalties) | | | | | | |
| 2002 | Real Madrid | 2 | Leverkusen | 1 | Glasgow | 52,000 | Meier (Sw) |
| 2003 | AC Milan | 0 | Juventus | 0 | Manchester | 63,215 | Merk (G) |
| | (aet; AC Milan won 3-2 on penalties) | | | | | | |
| 2004 | Porto | 3 | Monaco | 0 | Gelsenkirchen | 52,000 | Nielsen (D) |
| 2005 | Liverpool | 3 | AC Milan | 3 | Istanbul | 65,000 | González (Sp) |
| | (aet; Liverpool won 3-2 on penalties) | | | | | | |
| 2006 | Barcelona | 2 | Arsenal | 1 | Paris | 79,500 | Hauge (N) |
| 2007 | AC Milan | 2 | Liverpool | 1 | Athens | 74,000 | Fandel (G) |
| 2008 | Manchester U | 1 | Chelsea | 1 | Moscow | 69,552 | Michel (Slo) |
| | (aet; Manchester U won 6-5 on penalties) | | | | | | |
| 2009 | Barcelona | 2 | Manchester U | 0 | Rome | 62,467 | Busacca (Sw) |
| 2010 | Internazionale | 2 | Bayern Munich | 0 | Madrid | 74,954 | Webb (E) |
| 2011 | Barcelona | 3 | Manchester U | 1 | Wembley | 87,695 | Kassai (H) |
| 2012 | Chelsea | 1 | Bayern Munich | 1 | Munich | 69,901 | Proença (P) |
| | (aet; Chelsea won 4-3 on penalties) | | | | | | |
| 2013 | Bayern Munich | 2 | Borussia Dortmund | 1 | Wembley | 86,298 | Rizzoli (I) |

*Subsequently stripped of title.

# UEFA CHAMPIONS LEAGUE 2012-13

■ *Denotes player sent off.*

**FIRST QUALIFYING ROUND FIRST LEG**

Tuesday, 3 July 2012

**F91 Dudelange (2) 7** *(Melisse 25, Benzouien 29, 53, Legros 47, Joachim 51, 90, DiOrsi 78 (og))*

**Tre Penne (0) 0**                                          1070

*F91 Dudelange:* (4132) Joubert; Martino (Zeghdane 65), Prempeh, Tournut, Melisse; Payal (Hug 57); Benzouien, Steinmetz, Legros; Kitenge (Gomez 57), Joachim.
*Tre Penne:* (4141) Valentini; Bonini, Tamburini (Nanni L 85), D'Orsi, Baschetti; Cardini; Cibelli, Gasperoni (Rossi 76), Chiaruzzi, Marani; Pignieri (Valli 57).

**Linfield (0) 0**

**B36 Torshavn (0) 0**                                      1341

*Linfield:* (442) Glendinning; Ervin, Douglas, Watson (Armstrong 46), Curran; Fordyce, Garrett, Mulgrew, McCaul (Carvill 65); McAllister, Thompson (Tipton 75).
*B36 Torshavn:* (442) Joensen; Eysturoy, Rasmussen, Faero, Joensen S; Olsen B (Skorini 84), Danielsen, Olsen S, Jacobsen; Borg (Sorensen 67), Cieslewicz (Matras 92).

**Valletta (6) 8** *(Caruana 4, Mifsud 10, 18, 45, 70, Jhonnattann 17, 23, Agius E 72)*

**Lusitans (0) 0**                                          1136

*Valletta:* (4321) Krul; Borg, Caruana, Jusselio Donizete, Azzopardi (Falzon 69); Riccardo Rocha (Fenech 46), Briffa, Denni; Jhonnattann (Agius E 81), William Barbosa; Mifsud.
*Lusitans:* (4141) Benitez; Maciel (Meza 85), Fontan, Brito, Veloso (Goncalves 52); Atabu; Bruninho, Escaleira, Soares (Miguel 23), Bertran; Reis.

**FIRST QUALIFYING ROUND SECOND LEG**

Tuesday, 10 July 2012

**B36 Torshavn (0) 0**

**Linfield (0) 0**                                          1422

*B36 Torshavn:* (4231) Joensen M; Eysturoy, Rasmussen, Faero, Joensen S; Olsen B (Matras 100), Danielsen, Jacobsen, Borg (Sorensen 74 (Olsen D 109)), Olsen S; Cieslewicz.
*Linfield:* (442) Glendinning; Ervin, Armstrong, Douglas, Curran; Fordyce (McCaul 65), Garrett, Mulgrew, Carvill; Thompson (Browne 77), McAllister.
*aet; Linfield won 4-3 on penalties.*

**Lusitans (0) 0**

**Valletta (1) 1** *(Jhonnattann 16)*                       517

*Lusitans:* (4231) Fernandez; Maciel, Fontan, Brito, Goncalves; Alberto (Soares 90), Zarioh; Bruninho, Escaleira (Atabu 72), Moreira; Miguel (Reis 65).
*Valletta:* (4321) Krul; Borg, Jusselio Donizete (Fenech 61), Caruana, Azzopardi (Falzon 59); Riccardo Rocha, Briffa (c), Denni; Jhonnattann (Agius E 67), William Barbosa; Mifsud.

**Tre Penne (0) 0**

**F91 Dudelange (4) 4** *(Joachim 28, 34, Benzouien 41, Gomez 45)*                                            455

*Tre Penne:* (532) Valentini; Bonini, Tamburini (Nanni L 50), D'Orsi, Mikhaylovskiy, Baschetti; Gasperoni, Cardini (Rossi 35), Cibelli; Valli (Nanni F 69), Pignieri.
*F91 Dudelange:* (442) Joubert; Martino (Prempeh 62), Caillet, Beltorangal, Melisse; Benzouien (Touray 62), Haddadji, Legros, da Mota; Gomez, Joachim (Kitenge 62).

**SECOND QUALIFYING ROUND FIRST LEG**

Tuesday, 17 July 2012

**F91 Dudelange (0) 1** *(Joachim 75)*

**SV Red Bull Salzbug (0) 0**                               1600

*F91 Dudelange:* (4231) Joubert; Prempeh, Tournut, Caillet, Melisse; Payal, Legros; Joachim (Kitenge 87), Steinmetz (Haddadji 88), Benzouien (Zeghdane 92); da Mota.
*SV Red Bull Salzbug:* (4231) Walke; Schwegler, Sekagya, Hinteregger, Ulmer; Leitgeb, Mendes; Zarate (Soriano■ 53), Cristiano (Lindgren 74), Svento (Klein 6); Maierhofer.

**Flora Tallinn (0) 0**

**FC Basel (0) 2** *(Frei A 64, 87 (pen))*                  3123

*Flora Tallinn:* (4132) Pedok; Baranov, Palatu, Mets, Jurgenson; Minkenen; Alliku (Masitsev 71), Frolov, Luigend (Peitre 76); Mool (Luts 71), Beglarishvili.
*FC Basel:* (442) Sommer; Degen P, Sauro, Dragovic, Joo-Ho Park; Degen D (Vuleta 73), Yapi Yapo, Diaz, Zoua (Stocker 62); Frei A (Andrist 87), Streller (c).

**HJK Helsinki (2) 7** *(Makela 14, 79, 84, Vayrynen 21 (pen), Pohjanpalo 49, Schuller 58, Pohjanpalo 68)*

**KR Reykjavik (0) 0**                                      6327

*HJK Helsinki:* (442) Wallen; Hakanpaa (Lindstrom 47), Fowler, Mannstrom, Vayrynen (Okkonen 63); Sumusalo, Savage, Sorsa, Schuller (Perovuo 76); Makela, Pohjanpalo.
*KR Reykjavik:* (442) Halldorsson; Weston, Snorrason (Atlason 47), Gunnarsson, Sigurdsson G; Gudjonsson (Sigurjonsson 59), Sigurdsson B, Hauksson O, Arnarsson (Jonsson E 67); Ragnarsson, Ludviksson.

**Neftchi (2) 3** *(Imamverdiyev 22, Wobay 24, Canales 63)*

**Zestafoni (0) 0**                                         5233

*Neftchi:* (4231) Mehdiyev; Melikov, Mitreski, Yunuszade (Yunisoglu 70), Bruno; Sadygov, Ramos; Wobay, Imamverdiyev (Seyidov 77), Flavinho (Abdullayev A); Canales.
*Zestafoni:* (4132) Kvaskhvadze; Gongadze, Sadjaia, Kobakhidze, Eliava (Grigalashvili Tornike 77); Sharikadze; Menteshashvili, Aptsiauri (Guguchia 66), Gorgiashvili; Dvali, Owonikoko (Mujiri 59).

**Shamrock R (0) 0**

**Ekranas (0) 0**                                           4800

*Shamrock R:* (442) Jansson; Powell, Sives, Oman, Rice; Kavanagh (Dennehy 70), McCabe (Turner 75), Twigg, Brennan (OfDonnell 83); Finn, Sullivan.
*Ekranas:* (442) Zubas; Urdinov, Luksa, Kucys, Kymantas; Varnas, Dedura, Andjelkovic (Norvilas 90), Vertelis; Tomkevicius, Samusiovas.

**Skenderbeu (0) 1** *(Plaku 65)*

**Derbrecen (0) 0**                                         7000

*Skenderbeu:* (442) Shehi; Fagu, Radas, Arapi, Gvozdenovic; Allmuca, Orelesi, Vucaj, Muzaka; Plaku (Bicaj 90), Xhafaj (Kuli 90).
*Derbrecen:* (442) Novakovic; Nagy, Meszaros, Simac, Korhut; Bodi, Varga, Szakaly, Rezes (Mate 90); Coulibaly, Kulcsar (Luis Ramos 72).

**Slovan Liberec (1) 1** *(Hadascok 24)*

**Shakhtyor Karagandy (0) 0**                               5500

*Slovan Liberec:* (442) Bicik; Kelic, Janu, Novak, Bosancic; Kusnir, Fleisman, Nezmar, Hadascok (Delarge 79); Stajner, Blazek (Sural 61).
*Shakhtyor Karagandy:* (442) Mokin; Poryvaev, Dzidic, Vasiljevic, Kirov; Vicius (Canas 67), Kukeyev (Visnakovs 80), Bayzhanov (Tarasov 76), Arsenijevic; Gridin, Finonchenko.

**The New Saints (0) 0**
**Helsingborg (0) 0** 1408
*The New Saints:* (442) Harrison; Spender, Marriott, Baker, Evans; Draper (Ward 90), Seargeant (Finley 69), Jones C, Jones C (Ruscoe 87); Darlington, Edwards A.
*Helsingborg:* (442) Hansson; Sadiku, Atta, Mahlangu, Gashi; Sorum (Sundin 80), Bouaouzan (Nordmark 47), Edman, Finnbogason; Andersson C, Hanstveit.

**Ulisses (0) 0**
**Sheriff (0) 1** *(Gheorghiev 60)* 3165
*Ulisses:* (4231) Hovhannisyan; Sahakyan, Ugrekhelidze, Simonyan, Grigoryan N; Grigoryan D, Grigoryan A; Ngavouka-Tseke, Aragoney (Bareghamyan 66), Jikia; Balabekyan (Adamyan 66 Hakhnazaryan 78)).
*Sheriff:* (4231) Stoyanov; Metoua, Samardzic, Pereira, Apatic; Onica, Marjanovic; Gheorghiev (Pajovic 87), Stanojevic, Dedov (Zamaliev 79); Rios Pinto (Dima 69).

**Valletta (0) 1** *(Mifsud 66)*
**Partizan Belgrade (3) 4** *(Tomic 6, Ivanov 33,*
*Scepovic M 42, Ostojic 71)* 1200
*Valletta:* (442) Krul; Briffa, Caruana, Borg (Agius E 80), Azzopardi (Gabriel 46); Denni, Falzon, Riccardo Rocha, Fenech (Jhonnattann 66); Mifsud, William Barbosa.
*Partizan Belgrade:* (4141) Stojkovic; Aksentijevic, Ivanov, Ostojic, Volkov; Markovic S; Tomic (Zubya 76), Lovre (Ilic 39), Babovic, Markovic L (Ninkovic 57); Scepovic M.

**Zilina (0) 1** *(Piacek 83)*
**Hapoel Kiryat Shmona (0) 0** 4281
*Zilina:* (442) Dubravka; Leitner, Piacek, Mabouka, Nunes; Barcik (Angelovic 90), Pecovsky, Sulek, Pich; Ceesay (Deza 71), Guima (Majtan 59).
*Hapoel Kiryat Shmona:* (442) Amos; Tzedek, Gabai, Matovic, Hasarma; Gerzycich, Tasevski (Gazal 84), Rochet, Badash (Abed 78); Abuhatzira, Solari (Marisat 90).

**Wednesday, 18 July 2012**

**AEL Limassol (2) 3** *(Vouho 17, Ouon 31, Dickson 55)*
**Linfield (0) 0** 5904
*AEL Limassol:* (442) Degra; Airosa, Carlitos, Ouon, Junior; Bebe (Rui Miguel 60), Gilberto, Dede (Nicolaou 76), Monteiro (Paulo Sergio 55); Dickson, Vouho.
*Linfield:* (442) Blayney; Douglas, Armstrong, Burns, Ervin; Curran, Garrett, Mulgrew (Henderson 78), Thompson (McCaul 74); Carvill, McAllister (Browne 80).

**BATE Borisov (1) 3** *(Mozolevski 42, Rodionov 90, 90)*
**Vardar (0) 2** *(Kostovski 55, Stepanovik 63)* 4900
*BATE Borisov:* (4312) Gorbunov; Polyakov, Radkov, Simic, Bordachev; Volodko, Likhtarovich (Rudik 71), Olekhnovich; Mozolevski; Pavlov (Kontsevoy 71), Rodionov.
*Vardar:* (442) Zahov; Ilievski, Tanevski, Vajs, Alechenwu; Randjelovic (Manevski 87), Stojakovic (Guobadia 84), Stepanovik, Temelkov; Kostovski, Georgiev (Petrov 60).

**Buducnost Podgorica (0) 0**
**Slask Wroclaw (1) 2** *(Elsner 19, Mila 49 (pen))* 5500
*Buducnost Podgorica:* (442) Agovic; Kamberovic, Djikanovic, Pekovic, Radunovic; Kalezic, Vukcevic N (Beck 75); Golubovic, Boskovic (Radonjic 59), Kurbegovic; Adrovic (Vukcevic M 85).
*Slask Wroclaw:* (4231) Kelemen; Socha, Kowalczyk, Pawelec, Mraz; Kazmierczak, Elsner; Cetnarski (Patejuk 71), Mila, Sobota (Stevanovic 89); Gikiewicz L (Diaz 82).

**Ludogorets Razgrad (0) 1** *(Marcelinho 68)*
**Dinamo Zagreb (0) 1** *(Rukavina 90)* 5500
*Ludogorets Razgrad:* (4231) Golubovic; Minev, Barthe, Guldan, Junior Caicara; Genchev, Dyakov (Moti 84); Stoyanov (Guela 91), Ivanov (Aleksandrov 87), Marcelinho; Gargorov.
*Dinamo Zagreb:* (4231) Kelava; Vrsaljko, Vida, Tonel, Pivaric (Beqiraj 57); Tomecak (Rukavina 89), Kovacic; Badelj, Sammir, Ibanez; Cop (Alispahic 74).

**Maribor (0) 4** *(Beric 47, 76, Mezga 67 (pen),*
*Marcos Tavares 90)*
**Zeljeznicar (1) 1** *(Adilovic 15)* 10,000
*Maribor:* (4231) Handanovic; Mejac, Arghus, Rajcevic, Trajkovski; Mertelj (Filipovic 72), Cvijanovic; Mezga (Lesjak 81), Marcos Tavares, Ibraimi; Beric (Velikonja 90).
*Zeljeznicar:* (4231) Antolovic; Colic, Kerla, Bogicevic, Kvesic; Zolotic, Jamak (Stanic 81); Selimovic (Beslija 71), Svraka, Zeba; Adilovic.

**Molde (0) 3** *(Angan 54, 84, Forren 75 (pen))*
**FK Ventspils (0) 0** 7428
*Molde:* (4231) Pettersen; Linnes, Hovland, Forren, Rindaroy; Eikrem, Hoseth (Berg Hestad 43); Mostrom (Chukwa 75), Berget (Tripic 83), Gatt; Angan.
*FK Ventspils:* (4231) Uvarenko; Timofejev, Smirnovs, Badyautdinov (Barinovs 79), Kurakins; Paulius, Gilmanov; Saito, Kozlovs (Zatkins 82), Turkovs; Martinez.

---

**SECOND QUALIFYING ROUND SECOND LEG**

**Tuesday, 24 July 2012**

**Debrecen (1) 3** *(Coulibaly 12, 87, Varga 58)*
**Skenderbeu (0) 0** 8399
*Debrecen:* (4231) Novakovic; Nikolov, Meszaros, Simac, Korhut; Varga, Luis Ramos (Mate 89); Bodi (Lucas Marcolini 82), Szakaly, Yannick (Rezes 74); Coulibaly.
*Skenderbeu:* (442) Shehi; Fagu (Kuli 85), Radas, Arapi, Gvozdenovic; Allmuca (Kerciku 66), Orelesi, Vucaj (Bicaj 89), Muzaka; Plaku, Xhafaj.

**Ekranas (1) 2** *(Andjelkovic 46, Kymantas 64)*
**Shamrock R (0) 1** *(McCabe 90 (pen))* 350
*Ekranas:* (361) Zubas; Urdinov, Dedura, Samusiovas; Luksa (Kavaliauskas 91), Kucys, Andjelkovic, Vertelis (Umeh 81), Tomkevicius, Kymantas; Varnas.
*Shamrock R:* (451) Jansson; Powell, Sives, Oman, Rice (Kavanagh 74); Sullivan, Brennan (Turner 66), Dennehy (Kilduff 80), Finn, McCabe; Twigg.

**FC Basel (2) 3** *(Zoua 9, 31, Diaz 63)*
**Flora Tallinn (0) 0** 20,467
*FC Basel:* (442) Vailati; Steinhofer (Andrist 67), Sauro, Dragovic, Voser; Degen D, Cabral, Diaz (Grether 80), Vuleta; Zoua, Streller (Frei A 73).
*Flora Tallinn:* (442) Pedok; Baranov, Palatu, Mets, Peitre; Alliku, Laabus (Beglarishvili 76), Frolov, Luigend (Minkenen 86); Prosa (Mool 70), Luts.

**FK Ventspils (1) 1** *(Kurakins 24)*
**Molde (1) 1** *(Eikrem 37)* 3000
*FK Ventspils:* (4231) Uvarenko; Timofejevs, Badyautdinov, Smirnovs, Kurakins; Gilmanov, Paulius; Saito, Turkovs (Zatkins 68), Kozlovs (Agoh 88); Martinez.
*Molde:* (442) Pettersen; Linnes, Vatshaug, Hovland, Rindaroy; Mostrom (Tripic 59), Berg Hestad, Eikrem (Camara 74); Stamnestro; Chima, Angan (Dantas 72).

**Hapoel Kiryat Shmona (0) 2** *(Abed 71, Abuhatzira 78)*
**Zilina (0) 0** 4200
*Hapoel Kiryat Shmona:* (442) Amos; Matovic, Tzedek, Gabai, Hasarma; Gerzycich, Tasevski (Gazal 61), Rochet (Abed 70), Badash (Vahaba 87); Abuhatzira, Solari.
*Zilina:* (442) Dubravka; Angelovic, Leitner, Piacek, Mabouka; Barcik, Pecovsky, Sulek (Paur 82), Majtan (Deza 67); Pich, Ceesay (Guima 47).

**KR Reykjavik (0) 0** *(Atlason 74)*
**HJK Helsinki (0) 2** *(Saik 66, Lindstrom 72)* 562
*KR Reykjavik:* (4132) Thorgeirsson; Hauksson H (Luthviksson 89), Josepsson, Sigurdarson G, Gunnarsson; Snorrason; Sigurjonsson, Sigurdsson B (Gudjonsson B 70), Jonsson E; Jonsson B (Ragnarsson 66), Atlason.
*HJK Helsinki:* (442) Wallen; Kansikas, Lindstrom, Lahti, Sumusalo; Sorsa (Pelvas 70), Perovuo, Okkonen (Schuller 26 (Lod 59), Alho; Sadik, Makela.

**Partizan Belgrade (1) 3** *(Tomic 10, 67, Mitrovic 73)*
**Valletta (0) 1** *(Mifsud 60)*                    10,000
*Partizan Belgrade:* (4231) Petrovic; Aksentijevic, Ostojic, Ivanov, Volkov; Markovic S, Ilic S; Markovic L, Babovic (Vukic 66), Tomic (Ninkovic 77); Scepovic S (Mitrovic 64).
*Valletta:* (4411) Krul; Borg, Riccardo Rocha, Caruana (Agius E 46), Azzopardi; Denni (Fenech 51), Gabriel, Briffa, Falzon (Agius G 85); William Barbosa; Mifsud.

**Shakhtyor Karagandy (1) 1** *(Kukeyev 41 (pen))*
**Slovan Liberec (0) 1** *(Blazek 120)*            17,000
*Shakhtyor Karagandy:* (442) Mokin; Poryvaev, Dzidic, Vasiljevic, Kirov; Vicius, Kukeyev, Arsenijevic (Visnakovs 120), Canas; Gridin (Bayzhanov 77), Finonchenko (Tarasov 114).
*Slovan Liberec:* (442) Bicik; Kelic, Janu, Vacha, Breznanik; Kusnir, Fleisman, Nezmar, Hadascok (Bosancic 64); Sural, Stajner (Blazek 86).
*aet.*

**Sheriff (0) 1** *(Samardizic 66 (pen))*
**Ulisses (0) 0**                                   6755
*Sheriff:* (4231) Stoyanov; Metoua, Samardzic, Pereira, Apatic; Onica, Marjanovic; Gheorghiev (Balima 76), Stanojevic (Rouamba 59), Dedov; Pesic (Dima 90).
*Ulisses:* (4231) Hovhannisyan; Sahakyan, Ugrekhelidze, Simonyan (Hakhnazaryan 81), Grigoryan N; Grigoryan D (Balabekyan 63), Grigoryan A; Ngavouka-Tseke, Aragoney (Machkalyan 85), Bareghamyan; Jikia.

**SV Red Bull Salzburg (2) 4** *(Jantscher 29, Hinteregger 38, Da Silva 82 (pen), Zarate 83)*
**F91 Dudelange (1) 3** *(Steinmetz 27, 58, Joachim 49)* 6600
*SV Red Bull Salzburg:* (433) Walke; Schwegler (Klein 75), Ulmer, Hinteregger, Mendes Da Silva; Jantscher, Ilsanker, Hierlander; Leitgeb (Zarate 60), Teigl, Maierhofer (Da Silva 47).
*F91 Dudelange:* (433) Joubert; Benzouien■, Prempeh, Tournut, Caillet; Payal (Zeghdane 90), Melisse, Legros; Steinmetz (Haddadji 80), Joachim, Da Mota Alves (Beltorangal 88).

**Zeljeznicar (0) 1** *(Kvesic 59)*
**Maribor (1) 2** *(Ibraimi 20, Tavares 86)*        10,236
*Zeljeznicar:* (4231) Antolovic; Colic■, Kerla, Bogicevic, Kvesic; Svraka■, Zolotic, Beslija (Stanic■ 56), Jamak (Vasilic 65), Zeba (Bekric 46); Adilovic.
*Maribor:* (4231) Handanovic; Potokar (Trajkovski 78), Rajcevic, Arghus, Mejac; Mertelj (Lesjak 87), Filipovic; Cvijanovic, Marcos Tavares, Ibraimi (Mezga 45); Beric.

**Zestafoni (2) 2** *(Mujiri 16, Dvali 19)*
**Neftchi (1) 2** *(Wobay 22, Sadygov 52 (pen))*   4500
*Zestafoni:* (442) Kvaskhvadze; Gongadze (Eliava 69), Grigalashvili Tedore, Kobakhidze, Grigalashvili Tornike (Aptsiauri 63); Owonikoko (Benashvili 55), Sharikadze, Menteshashvili, Gorgiashvili; Mujiri, Dvali.
*Neftchi:* (4231) Mehdiyev; Melikov, Yunuszade, Mitreski, Bruno; Sadygov (Mehtiyev 82), Ramos; Wobay (Abdullayev A 75), Imamverdiyev (Seyidov 69), Flavinho; Canales.

**Wednesday, 25 July 2012**
**Dinamo Zagreb (1) 3** *(Rukavina 34, 61, Vida 90)*
**Ludogorets (2) 2** *(Gargorov 13, Marcelinho 36)* 25,000
*Dinamo Zagreb:* (442) Kelava; Ibanez (Alispahic 47), Tonel, Vida, Vrsaljko; Calello (Cop 63), Kovacic, Sammir, Badelj; Beqiraj (Peko 71), Rukavina.
*Ludogorets:* (442) Golubovic; Barthe, Minev, Guldan, Junior Caicara; Genchev, Ivanov (Moti 89), Dyakov, Stoyanov (Guela 74); Marcelinho■, Gargorov (Bakalov 77).

**Helsingborg (2) 3** *(Atta 9, Sorum 28, Dos Santos 90)*
**The New Saints (0) 0**                            5613
*Helsingborg:* (442) Hansson; Sadiku, Atta, Nordmark, Mahlangu; Lindstrom, Gashi (Wahlstedt 86), Sorum (Sundin 46), Finnbogason (Dos Santos 71); Andersson C, Uronen.

*The New Saints:* (442) Harrison; Spender, Marriott, Baker, Evans; Draper (Fraughan 76), Seargeant (Finley 70), Jones C, Jones C; Darlington (Edwards K 87), Edwards A.

**Linfield (0) 0**
**AEL Limassol (0) 0**                              995
*Linfield:* (442) Blayney; Douglas, Murphy, Armstrong, Thompson; Burns, Garrett (Fordyce 84), Ervin, Mulgrew; Henderson (Carvill 78), McAllister (Browne 85).
*AEL Limassol:* (442) Degra; Junior, Maykon, Rui Miguel (Dede 71), Edmar (Dickson 61); Nicolaou (Konstantinou 78), Paulo Sergio, Bebe, Carlitos; Ouon, Vouho.

**Slask Wroclaw (0) 0**
**Buducnost Podgorica (1) 1** *(Vukcevic N 8)*     18,222
*Slask Wroclaw:* (4231) Kelemen; Kowalczyk, Grodzicki, Pawelec, Spahic; Elsner, Kazmierczak; Cetnarski (Sobota 46), Mila, Mraz (Patejuk 38); Gikiewicz L.
*Buducnost Podgorica:* (4231) Agovic; Kamberovic, Djikanovic (Nikac 86), Pekovic, Radunovic; Kalezic (Mugosa 79), Vukcevic N; Vukcevic M, Boskovic, Kurbegovic (Golubovic 70); Adrovic.

**Vardar (0) 0**
**BATE Borisov (0) 0**                              34,000
*Vardar:* (442) Zahov; Tanevski, Vajs, Gimenez (Stojakovic 47), Cikarski; Randelovic (Bojovic 90), Ilievski, Temelkov, Stepanovik (Manevski 76); Georgiev, Kostovski.
*BATE Borisov:* (442) Gorbunov; Yurevich, Radkov, Bordachev, Simic; Likhtarovich (Rudik 74), Volodko, Olekhnovich, Kontsevoy; Mozolevski (Pavlov 80), Rodionov.

### THIRD QUALIFYING ROUND FIRST LEG

**Tuesday, 31 July 2012**
**Dynamo Kiev (0) 2** *(Immers 57 (og), Ideye B 70)*
**Feyenoord (0) 1** *(Schaken 50)*                 53,612
*Dynamo Kiev:* (451) Koval; Danilo Silva, Betao, Mykhalyk, Popov; Vukojevic (Milevskiy 56), Veloso, Yarmolenko, Kranjcar (Gusev 47), Ninkovic; Ideye B.
*Feyenoord:* (4132) Mulder; Janmaat (Singh 35), De Vrij, Martins Indi, Nelom; Vormer (Vilhena 72); Leerdam, Clasie (Kongolo 90), Immers; Cisse, Schaken.

**Motherwell (0) 0**
**Panathinaikos (1) 2** *(Christodoulopoulos 13, Mavrias 76)*
                                                    9035
*Motherwell:* (442) Randolph; Hateley, Hutchinson, Ramsden, Hammell; Humphrey, Law, Lasley, Murphy; Ojamaa (Daley 79), Higdon.
*Panathinaikos:* (451) Karnezis; Velazquez, Boumsong, Vyntra, Spyropoulos; Zeca, Marinos (Katsouranis 67), Sissoko, Vitolo, Christodoulopoulos (Fornaroli 85); Toche (Mavrias 75).

**Wednesday, 1 August 2012**
**AEL Limassol (1) 1** *(Vouho 14)*
**Partizan Belgrade (0) 0**                        8000
*AEL Limassol:* (433) Degra; Airosa, Carlitos, Ouon, Junior; Bebe (Rui Miguel 61), Gilberto, Dede; Monteiro (Edmar 67), Vouho (Nicolaou 82), Dickson.
*Partizan Belgrade:* (541) Stojkovic; Volkov, Ivanov, Ostojic, Aksentijevic, Markovic S; Tomic (Markovic L 86), Lovre, Ilic S (Vukic 75), Babovic; Scepovic (Zubya 71).

**Anderlecht (3) 5** *(De Sutter 3, Kanu 22, Mbokani 42, 53, Jovanovic 87)*
**Ekranas (0) 0**                                   12,203
*Anderlecht:* (442) Proto; Deschacht, Odoi, Safari, Wasilewski; Biglia, Gillet (Canesin 69), Kanu (Kljestan 62), Jovanovic; De Sutter (Yakovenko 81), Mbokani.
*Ekranas:* (442) Zubas; Urdinov, Dedura, Samusiovas, Luksa; Kucys, Andjelkovic, Vertelis (Kavaliauskas 84), Tomkevicius (Gleveckas 90); Kymantas (Buinickij 61), Varnas.

**BATE Borisov (0) 1** *(Sidibe 90 (og))*
**Debrecen (0) 1** *(Sidibe 68)*     5170

*BATE Borisov:* (433) Gorbunov; Yurevich, Radkov, Bordachev, Simic; Likhtarovich (Rudik 57), Volodko, Hleb (Vasilyuk 75); Kontsevoy (Pavlov 57), Mozolevski, Rodionov.
*Debrecen:* (442) Verpecz; Simac, Nikolov, Meszaros, Korhut; Ramos (Sidibe 59), Bodi, Varga, Szakaly; Rezes (Yannick 79), Coulibaly (Mate 87).

**Celtic (0) 2** *(Hooper 54, Mulgrew 61)*
**HJK Helsinki (0) 1** *(Schuller 47)*     52,849

*Celtic:* (442) Forster; Matthews, Wanyama, Mulgrew, Izaguirre; Forrest, Brown, Ledley, Samaras (Lustig 87); Commons (Stokes 65), Hooper (McCourt 87).
*HJK Helsinki:* (451) Wallen; Sorsa, Lahti, Lindstrom, Sumusalo; Vayrynen (Okkonen 74), Perovuo; Mannstrom, Schuller (Pohjanpalo 84), Savage; Makela (Sadik 60).

**CFR Cluj (0) 1** *(Cadu 54 (pen))*
**Slovan Liberec (0) 0**     8000

*CFR Cluj:* (4231) Mario Felgueiras; Ivo Pinto, Cadu, Rada, Muresan (Sare 47); Camora, Vass (Edimar 78); Bastos (Diogo Valente 81), Deac, Sougou; Kapetanos.
*Slovan Liberec:* (4231) Bicik; Kelic, Toth, Fleisman, Kusnir (Lyulka 47); Bosancic, Vacha; Breznanik, Hadascok (Blazek 68), Stajner (Morozenko 90); Sural.

**FC Copenhagen (0) 0**
**Club Brugge (0) 0**     14,023

*FC Copenhagen:* (442) Wiland; Jacobsen, Ottesen, Sigurdsson, Oviedo; Jorgensen, Kristensen, Bolanos (Vingaard 71); Claudemir; Santin, Cornelius.
*Club Brugge:* (442) Kujovic; Hoefkens, Larsen, Donk, Jordi; Odjija Ofoe, Zimling (Van Acker 68), Rafaelov, Blondel; Tchite (Akpala 75), Meunier.

**Fenerbahce (0) 1** *(Irtegun 90)*
**Vaslui (0) 1** *(Antal 76)*     42,000

*Fenerbahce:* (442) Demirel; Korkmaz, Ali Kaldirim, Gonul, Irtegun; Topal (Sow 79), Alex, Baroni, Stoch (Erkin 62); Kuyt, Senturk (Topuz 47).
*Vaslui:* (442) Coman; Varela, Milanov, Charalambous, Antal (Buhaescu 89); Stanciu (Sburlea 61), Caue, Sanmartean, N'Doye; Salageanu, Niculae (Costin 82).

**Hapoel Kiryat Shmona (1) 4** *(Badash 43 (pen), Abuhatzira 53, Gerzycich 71, 76)*
**Neftchi (0) 0**     2500

*Hapoel Kiryat Shmona:* (442) Amos; Tzedek, Gabai, Hasarma, Matovic; Gerzycich, Tasevski (Abed 65), Rochet, Badash (Lencse 77); Abuhatzira, Solari (Gazal 21).
*Neftchi:* (442) Mehdiev; Melikov, Mitreski, Bertucci, Yunuszade; Sadygov, Flavinho (Abdullayev A 81), Wobay, Ramos; Imamverdiyev (Seyidov 60), Canales.

**Maribor (2) 4** *(Mezga 14, 48, Tavares 39, Beric 78)*
**F91 Dudelange (0) 1** *(Joachim 90)*     12,500

*Maribor:* (442) Handanovic; Mejac (Potokar 59), Trajkovski, Rajcevic, Arghus; Mezga, Ibraimi (Filipovic 68), Cvijanovic, Mertelj; Tavares, Beric (Komazec 86).
*F91 Dudelange:* (442) Joubert; Prempeh, Tournut, Caillet, Payal (Hug 66); Legros, Steinmetz (Kitenge 74), Joachim, Da Mota Alves; Idazza (Beltorangal 66), Melisse.

**Molde (0) 0**
**FC Basel (0) 1** *(Zoua 80)*     6564

*Molde:* (442) Pettersen; Vatshaug, Hovland, Forren, Rindaroy; Linnes (Simonsen 65), Berg Hestad (Hoseth 80), Eikrem, Mostrom; Angan▪, Chukwa.
*FC Basel:* (451) Sommer; Park, Dragovic, Sauro, Steinhofer; Degen D (Zoua 62), Yapi Yapo, Stocker, Diaz, Cabral; Streller.

**Sheriff (0) 0**
**Dinamo Zagreb (1) 1** *(Beqiraj 15)*     9000

*Sheriff:* (442) Stoyanov; Joao Pereira, Metoua, Apatic (Luvannor 61), Samardzic; Onica (Cheptine 80), Gheorghiev (Balima 59), Marjanovic (Ivanov 71), Stanojevic; Dedov, Pesic.
*Dinamo Zagreb:* (442) Kelava; Simunic, Tonel, Vida, Pivaric; Leko, Sammir (Calello 70), Badelj, Pokrivac; Rukavina (Alispahic 83), Beqiraj (Cop 63).

**Slask Wroclaw (0) 0**
**Helsingborg (1) 3** *(Finnbogason 37, Andersson C 73, Nordmark 86)*     10,000

*Slask Wroclaw:* (442) Kelemen; Kowalcyzk, Grodzicki, Pawelec, Elsner▪; Spahic, Sobota, Mila, Kazmierczak (Stevanovic 76); Patejuk (Gikiewicz L 76), Voskamp (Diaz 67).
*Helsingborg:* (442) Hansson; Atta, Mahlangu, Wahlstedt (Nordmark 82), Uronen; Sadiku, Lindstrom, Gashi, Andersson C; Sorum (Dos Santos 67), Finnbogason (Sundin 90).

**THIRD QUALIFYING ROUND SECOND LEG**

Tuesday, 7 August 2012

**Debrecen (0) 0**
**BATE Borisov (1) 2** *(Mozolevski 26, Volodko 60)*     10,500

*Debrecen:* (442) Verpecz; Korhut, Simac (Mate 85), Nikolov▪, Meszaros; Nagy (Sidibe 47), Ramos, Bodi, Szakaly; Yannick (Rezes 66), Coulibaly.
*BATE Borisov:* (442) Gorbunov; Radkov, Bordachev, Simic, Polyakov; Volodko (Rudik 84), Hleb, Olekhnovich, Baga (Yurevich 47); Mozolevski, Rodionov (Pavlov 65).

**Feyenoord (0) 0**
**Dynamo Kiev (0) 1** *(Ideye B 90)*     48,000

*Feyenoord:* (442) Mulder; Leerdam, Nelom (Singh 87), Janmaat (Vormer 77), De Vrij; Martins Indi, Clasie, Immers, Cisse; Fernandez (Cabral 68), Schaken.
*Dynamo Kiev:* (442) Koval; Popov, Danilo Silva, Betao, Veloso; Vukojevic, Mykhalyk, Gusev (Milevskiy 83), Ninkovic (Garmash 90); Yarmolenko, Ideye B.

Wednesday, 8 August 2012

**Club Brugge (1) 2** *(Jordi 25, Odjija Ofoe 67)*
**FC Copenhagen (0) 3** *(Jorgensen 62, Bolanos 79, Santin 90)*     16,500

*Club Brugge:* (442) Kujovic; Hoefkens (Akpala 82), Larsen, Donk, Jordi; Odjija Ofoe, Zimling (Vazquez 85), Rafaelov (Lestienne 91); Blondel; Tchite, Meunier.
*FC Copenhagen:* (442) Wiland; Jacobsen, Ottesen, Sigurdsson, Jorgensen (Grindheim 86); Oviedo, Claudemir, Kristensen, Vingaard (Cornelius 72); Bolanos (Bengtsson 91), Santin.

**Dinamo Zagreb (2) 4** *(Vida 17, Beqiraj 35, Cop 79, Ibanez 88)*
**Sheriff (0) 0**     28,000

*Dinamo Zagreb:* (442) Kelava; Pivaric, Simunic, Tonel, Vida; Ademi, Leko, Badelj, Alispahic (Peko 65); Beqiraj (Cop 75), Rukavina (Ibanez 86).
*Sheriff:* (442) Stoyanov; Joao Pereira (Pajovic 37), Metoua, Apatic, Samardzic; Luvannor (Balima 47), Onica, Gheorghiev, Marjanovic (Ivanov 66); Stanojevic, Pesic.

**Ekranas (0) 0**
**Anderlecht (3) 6** *(Kljestan 10, Praet 32, Yakovenko 46, De Sutter 48, Molins 63, Canesin 88)*     4225

*Ekranas:* (442) Zubas▪; Urdinov (Umeh 70), Dedura, Samusiovas, Luksa; Kucys, Andjelkovic, Vertelis, Buinickij (Kauneckas 28); Kymantas (Kavaliauskas 60), Varnas.
*Anderlecht:* (442) Proto; Deschacht, Odoi, Safari, Biglia (Marecek 46); Mbenza, Kljestan, Praet, Gillet (Mollins 46); Yakovenko, De Sutter (Canesin 59).

**F91 Dudelange (0) 0**
**Maribor (0) 1** *(Mertelj 80)*                                     1236
*F91 Dudelange:* (4231) Joubert; Benzouien (Idazza 34),
Tournut, Caillet, Melisse; Legros, Hug (Kitenge 68);
Zeghdane (Beltorangal 76), Da Mota Alves, Steinmetz;
Joachim.
*Maribor:* (4231) Handanovic; Mejac, Rajcevic, Arghus,
Potokar; Mertelj (Dodlek 90), Cvijanovic (Ibraimi 67);
Filipovic, Mezga, Tavares; Beric (Komazec 79).

**FC Basel (0) 1** *(Degen D 76)*
**Molde (1) 1** *(Berget 33)*                                     18,567
*FC Basel:* (442) Sommer; Park, Sauro, Steinhofer,
Dragovic; Degen D (Frei F 90), Yapi Yapo (Salah 75),
Stocker (Zoua 85), Diaz; Cabral, Streller.
*Molde:* (442) Pettersen; Vatshaug, Hovland (Simonsen
27), Rindaroy (Hoseth 58), Forren; Berg Hestad, Eikrem
(Stamnesstro 71), Mostrom, Linnes; Berget, Chukwa.

**Helsingborg (1) 3** *(Sorum 44, 52, 70)*
**Slask Wroclaw (1) 1** *(Diaz 31)*                                     4836
*Helsingborg:* (442) Hansson; Wahlstedt (Bergholtz 87),
Sadiku, Atta, Uronen; Lindstrom (Nordmark 29),
Mahlangu, Gashi, Andersson C; Sorum (Dos Santos 73),
Finnbogason.
*Slask Wroclaw:* (442) Kelemen; Stevanovic, Pawelec,
Kowalcyzk, Jodlowiec (Voskamp 76); Mraz, Sobota,
Mila, Kazmierczak; Patejuk (Cetnarski 76), Diaz
(Gikiewicz L 76).

**HJK Helsinki (0) 0**
**Celtic (0) 2** *(Ledley 67, Samaras 86)*                                     10,269
*HJK Helsinki:* (4411) Wallen; Sorsa, Lahti, Lindstrom,
Sumusalo; Mannstrom (Zeneli 74), Vayrynen, Perovuo
(Sadik 69), Savage; Schuller; Pohjanpalo (Pelvas 78).
*Celtic:* (442) Forster; Matthews, Wanyama■, Rogne,
Mulgrew; Brown, Commons (Forrest 74), Ledley,
Izaguirre; Samaras (Murphy 88), Hooper (Kayal 74).

**Neftchi (1) 2** *(Wobay 32, Imamverdiyev 77)*
**Hapoel Kiryat Shmona (0) 2** *(Badash 51, Lencse 90)* 2355
*Neftchi:* (442) Stamenkovic; Yunisoglu, Bertucci,
Yunuszade, Sadygov; Flavinho, Wobay, Ramos, Seyidov
(Imanverdiyev 63); Canales, Mehdiyev (Abdullayev A 79).
*Hapoel Kiryat Shmona:* (442) Amos; Tzedek, Gabai,
Hasarma, Matovic; Gazal, Gerzycich (Abed 57), Tasevski
(Elisha 79), Rochet; Badash (Lencse 65), Abuhatzira.

**Panathinaikos (0) 3** *(Christodoulopoulos 51, Mavrias 75,*
*Sissoko 83)*
**Motherwell (0) 0**                                     27,000
*Panathinaikos:* (451) Karnezis; Vyntra, Velazquez,
Boumsong, Spyropoulos; Christodoulopoulos
(Petropoulos 78), Marinos (Katsouranis 71), Vitolo,
Zeca, Sissoko; Toche (Mavrias 71).
*Motherwell:* (442) Randolph; Hateley, Ramsden,
Hutchinson, Hammell; Daley (Higdon 76), Cummins
(Francis-Angol 76), Lasley, Law; Murphy, Ojamaa.

**Partizan Belgrade (0) 0**
**AEL Limassol (1) 1** *(Junior 24)*                                     21,000
*Partizan Belgrade:* (442) Stojkovic; Volkov, Ivanov,
Ostojic, Tomic; Aksentijevic, Markovic S, Ilic S (Zubya
63), Babovic (Ninkovic 47); Markovic L, Scepovic.
*AEL Limassol:* (442) Degra; Nicolaou, Airosa, Carlitos,
Ouon; Junior, Edmar (Paulo Sergio 86), Bebe (Gilberto
61), Dede; Monteiro■, Vouho (Dickson 73).

**Slovan Liberec (0) 1** *(Sural 59)*
**CFR Cluj (1) 2** *(Kapetanos 45, Sougou 90)*                                     5537
*Slovan Liberec:* (442) Bicik; Kelic, Karisik (Nezmar 77),
Janu (Morozenko 55), Lyulka; Vacha, Bosancic,
Breznanik, Fleisman; Blazek (Hadascok 67), Sural.
*CFR Cluj:* (442) Mario Felgueiras; Ivo Pinto, Cadu,
Edimar (Nicoara 84), Rada; Camora, Sare, Bastos
(Muresan 62), Vass (Ronny 79); Kapetanos, Sougou.

**Vaslui (1) 1** *(Niculae 15)*
**Fenerbahce (1) 4** *(Erkin 13, Kuyt 72, 77, Sow 90)*   16,000
*Vaslui:* (361) Coman; Varela, Milanov, Charalambous;
Salageanu, Stanciu, Antal (Zsiga 84), Caue (Sburlea 75),
Sanmartean, N'Doye (Costin 80); Niculae.
*Fenerbahce:* (361) Demirel; Korkmaz, Ali Kaldirim,
Gonul; Irtegun, Alex (Topal 82), Baroni, Sahin, Topuz,
Erkin (Stoch 62); Kuyt (Sow 87).

## PLAY-OFF ROUND FIRST LEG

Tuesday, 21 August 2012
**Borussia Moenchengladbach (1) 1** *(Ring 14)*
**Dynamo Kiev (2) 3** *(Mykhalyk 29, Yarmolenko 37,*
*De Jong 82 (og))*                             .             46,279
*Borussia Moenchengladbach:* (442) ter Stegen; Jantschke,
Stranzl, Dominguez, Daems; Ring (Herrmann 70),
Nordtveit (Cigerci 75), Xhaka, Arango; De Camargo
(Hanke 70), De Jong.
*Dynamo Kiev:* (4141) Koval; Danilo Silva, Betao,
Mykhalyk, Taiwo; Veloso; Ninkovic (Raffael 79),
Kranjcar (Vukojevic 66), Garmash, Yarmolenko; Ideye
(Mehmedi 90).

**FC Basel (1) 1** *(Streller 45)*
**CFR Cluj (0) 2** *(Sougou 66, 71)*                                     13,000
*FC Basel:* (4411) Sommer; Steinhofer, Sauro (Kovac 87),
Dragovic, Park; Degen D (Frei F 73), Cabral, Diaz,
Stocker (Frei A 80); Salah; Streller.
*CFR Cluj:* (442) Mario Felgueiras; Ivo Pinto, Cadu,
Rada, Camora; Sougou, Rui Pedro (Nicoara 73), Bastos,
Sare; Godemeche (Muresan 68), Kapetanos (Ronny 51).

**FC Copenhagen (1) 1** *(Santin 39)*
**Lille (0) 0**                                     15,654
*FC Copenhagen:* (442) Wiland; Jacobsen, Sigurdsson,
Stadsgaard, Bengtsson; Bolanos (Vingaard 87),
Kristensen, Claudemir, Oviedo (Delaney 80); Santin
(Cornelius 66), Jorgensen.
*Lille:* (4231) Landreau; Beria, Rozehnal, Chedjou, Digne
(Roux 63); Balmont (Gueye 47), Mavuba; Kalou, Martin
(Pedretti 90), Payet; De Melo.

**Helsingborg (0) 0**
**Celtic (1) 2** *(Commons 2, Samaras 75)*                                     12,200
*Helsingborg:* (442) Hansson; Atta, Andersson C,
Wahlstedt (Accam 63), Uronen; Sadiku, Mahlangu,
Gashi, Bedoya; Sorum (Dos Santos 65), Djurdjic.
*Celtic:* (442) Forster; Matthews, Izaguirre, Mulgrew,
Rogne; Brown, Commons (Watt 89), Ledley (Wilson 65),
Kayal (Forrest 46); Samaras, Hooper.

**Spartak Moscow (0) 2** *(Emenike 60, Kombarov 70)*
**Fenerbahce (0) 1** *(Kuyt 66)*                                     30,000
*Spartak Moscow:* (4411) Dykan; Makeev, Pareja, Suchy,
Kombarov; McGeady, Rafael Carioca, Romulo (De Zeeuw
44), Bilyaletdinov; Ari (Dzjuba 78); Emenike (Welliton 73).
*Fenerbahce:* (442) Gunok; Gonul, Yobo, Korkmaz, Ali
Kaldirim; Topuz (Erkin 88), Sahin, Topal (Bienvenu 84),
Baroni; Sow (Krasic 78), Kuyt.

Wednesday, 22 August 2012
**AEL Limassol (1) 2** *(Junior 35, Rui Miguel 74)*
**Anderlecht (0) 1** *(Mbokani 63)*                                     10,000
*AEL Limassol:* (4231) Degra; Airosa, Ouon, Junior,
Carlitos; Dede, Nicolaou; Paulo Sergio (Dickson 66),
Bebe (Rui Miguel 50), Edmar (Gilberto 85); Vouho.
*Anderlecht:* (4231) Proto; Odoi, Wasilewski, Kouyate,
Safari; Biglia, Kljestan; Gillet, Kanu, Jovanovic■
(Yakovenko 76); Mbokani.

**BATE Borisov (1) 2** *(Rodionov 30, 79)*
**Hapoel Kiryat Shmona (0) 0**                                     12,000
*BATE Borisov:* (442) Gorbunov; Radkov, Bordachev,
Simic, Polyakov; Likhtarovich (Pavlov 63), Volodko,
Bressan (Silvakov 84), Hleb; Mozolevski (Vasilyuk 63),
Rodionov.
*Hapoel Kiryat Shmona:* (442) Amos; Vahaba (Abed 54),
Tzedek, Gabai, Matovic■; Hasarma, Gazal (Badash 69),
Tasevski, Rochet; Abuhatzira, Lencse (Levi 75).

**Braga (0) 1** *(Ismaily 69)*
**Udinese (1) 1** *(Basta 24)* 20,000
*Braga:* (4411) Beto; Leandro Salino, Douglao, Paulo Vinicius, Ismaily; Alan (Ewerton 85), Hugo Viana, Custodio, Helder Barbosa (Ruben Micael 59); Mossoro (Ze Luis 88); Lima.
*Udinese:* (352) Brkic; Benatia, Danilo, Domizzi; Basta, Pinzi, Willians, Pereyra (Agyemang-Badu 74), Armero (Pasquale 86); Fabbrini (Maicosuel 73), Di Natale.

**Dinamo Zagreb (1) 2** *(Cop 11, Badelj 75)*
**Maribor (1) 1** *(Badelj 40 (og))* 30,000
*Dinamo Zagreb:* (442) Kelava; Pivaric, Tonel, Simunic, Vida; Leko (Peko 47), Sammir (Vrsaljko 89), Badelj, Ademi; Cop, Rukavina (Beqiraj 58).
*Maribor:* (442) Handanovic; Mejac, Arghus, Rajcevic, Potokar; Mertelj, Ibraimi, Filipovic (Mezga 80), Cvijanovic; Tavares, Beric (Komazec 83).

**Malaga (2) 2** *(Demichelis 18, Eliseu 35)*
**Panathinaikos (0) 0** 28,000
*Malaga:* (442) Willy; Jesus Gamez, Demichelis, Weligton, Monreal; Isco, Toulalan, Maresca (Camacho 71), Eliseu (Duda 79); Joaquin, Fabrice (Buonanotte 71).
*Panathinaikos:* (4321) Karnezis; Vyntra, Boumsong (Andre Pinto 65), Velazquez, Spyropoulos; Katsouranis, Vitolo, Zeca (Christodoulopoulos 40); Mavrias, Sissoko; Fornaroli (Toche 70).

---

**PLAY-OFF ROUND SECOND LEG**

Tuesday, 28 August 2012
**Anderlecht (0) 2** *(Mbokani 82, Yakovenko 90)*
**AEL Limassol (0) 0** 21,000
*Anderlecht:* (442) Proto; Odoi (Juhasz 81), Wasilewski, Kouyate, Deschacht; Biglia, Gillet (Bruno 75), Kljestan, Kanu; Mbokani, De Sutter (Yakovenko 66).
*AEL Limassol:* (442) Degra; Airosa, Ouon, Junior, Carlitos; Nicolaou, Dede, Monteiro (Gilberto 38), Rui Miguel (Maykon 80); Edmar (Dickson 63), Vouho.

**Hapoel Kiryat Shmona (0) 1** *(Lencse 68)*
**BATE Borisov (0) 1** *(Pavlov 90)* 4000
*Hapoel Kiryat Shmona:* (433) Amos; Tzedek, Gazal, Gabai, Hasarma; Abuhatzira, Levi, Tasevski (Elisha 64); Rochet (Badash 57), Sallalich (Abed 62), Lencse.
*BATE Borisov:* (442) Gorbunov; Likhtarovich (Yurevich 61), Volodko, Mozolevski, Radkov; Hleb (Pavlov 64), Bordachev, Rodionov, Simic; Silvakov (Olekhnovich 84), Polyakov.

**Maribor (0) 0**
**Dinamo Zagreb (1) 1** *(Tonel 13)* 13,000
*Maribor:* (442) Handanovic; Milec, Rajcevic, Arghus■, Mejac; Filipovic (Mezga 47), Mertelj, Cvijanovic, Ibraimi (Komazec 71); Tavares, Beric.
*Dinamo Zagreb:* (442) Kelava; Vida, Tonel, Simunic, Pivaric; Badelj, Ademi (Calello 47), Ibanez, Cop; Sammir (Krstanovic 84), Beqiraj (Leko 47).

**Panathinaikos (0) 0**
**Malaga (0) 0** 27,719
*Panathinaikos:* (433) Karnezis; Vyntra, Velazquez, Andre Pinto, Spyropoulos; Katsouranis (Marinos 72), Vitolo, Zeca (Mavrias 47); Christodoulopoulos, Fornaroli (Toche 74), Sissoko.
*Malaga:* (4231) Willy; Jesus Gamez, Demichelis, Weligton, Monreal; Toulalan, Camacho; Eliseu (Duda 89), Isco, Joaquin (Portillo 91); Fabrice (Juanmi 64).

**Udinese (1) 1** *(Armero 26)*
**Braga (0) 1** *(Ruben Micael 73)* 30,000
*Udinese:* (352) Brkic; Benatia, Danilo, Domizzi; Basta, Pinzi, Willians (Agyemang-Badu 47), Pereyra (Pasquale 69), Armero; Fabbrini (Maicosuel 82), Di Natale.
*Braga:* (4231) Beto; Leandro Salino, Douglao, Paulo Vinicius, Ismaily; Custodio, Hugo Viana; Alan (Paulo Cesar 95), Ruben Amorim (Ruben Micael 61), Mossoro (Eder 108); Lima.
*aet; Braga won 5-4 on penalties.*

Wednesday, 29 August 2012
**Celtic (1) 2** *(Hooper 30, Wanyama 88)*
**Helsingborg (0) 0** 51,566
*Celtic:* (4411) Forster; Matthews (Lustig 76), Wilson, Mulgrew, Izaguirre; Forrest, Brown, Wanyama, Samaras (Watt 69); Commons; Hooper (McCourt 90).
*Helsingborg:* (442) Hansson; Wahlstedt (Lindstrom 75), Baffo, Atta (Nordmark 81), Uronen; Bedoya, Gashi, Mahlangu, Andersson C; Sorum (Accam 61), Djurdjic.

**CFR Cluj (1) 1** *(Kapetanos 21)*
**FC Basel (0) 0** 17,000
*CFR Cluj:* (442) Mario Felgueiras; Ivo Pinto, Rada, Cadu, Camora; Sougou, Diogo Valente (Nicoara 74), Muresan, Sare (Godemeche 52); Bastos, Kapetanos (Nicoara 83).
*FC Basel:* (442) Sommer; Steinhofer, Sauro, Dragovic (Zoua 47), Park (Schar 86); Frei F, Diaz (Andrist 70), Cabral, Degen D; Frei A, Streller.

**Dynamo Kiev (0) 1** *(Ideye 89)*
**Borussia Moenchengladbach (0) 2** *(Khacheridi 71 (og), Arango 79)* 66,872
*Dynamo Kiev:* (4141) Koval; Danilo Silva, Betao, Khacheridi, Taiwo; Veloso; Gusev, Ninkovic (Vukojevic 47), Garmash, Yarmolenko; Ideye (Ruben 90).
*Borussia Moenchengladbach:* (442) ter Stegen; Jantschke, Stranzl, Brouwers, Daems; Herrmann (Ring 64), Nordtveit, Xhaka, Arango; Hanke (Hrgota 60), De Jong (De Camargo 73).

**Fenerbahce (0) 1** *(Sow 70)*
**Spartak Moscow (1) 1** *(Ari 7)* 47,000
*Fenerbahce:* (442) Gunok; Gonul, Yobo, Korkmaz, Ali Kaldirim; Topuz (Baroni 80), Sahin (Alex 60), Topal, Krasic (Stoch 17); Kuyt, Sow.
*Spartak Moscow:* (4231) Dykan; Makeev, Insaurralde, Suchy, Kombarov D; Romulo, De Zeeuw■; Kombarov K (Bilyaletdinov 67), Ari (Rafael Carioca 52), McGeady; Emenike (Dzjuba 75).

**Lille (1) 2** *(Digne 44, De Melo 106)*
**FC Copenhagen (0) 0** 47,500
*Lille:* (4231) Landreau; Beria, Basa, Chedjou, Digne; Balmont (Gueye 106), Mavuba; Kalou, Martin (Pedretti 83), Payet (Roux 92); De Melo.
*FC Copenhagen:* (4411) Wiland; Jacobsen, Sigurdsson, Stadsgaard, Bengtsson; Bolanos (Vetokele 86), Claudemir, Kristensen, Oviedo (Delaney 115); Jorgensen; Santin (Cornelius 61).
*aet.*

# GROUP STAGE

## GROUP A

**Tuesday, 18 September 2012**
**Dinamo Zagreb (0) 0**
**FC Porto (1) 2** *(Gonzalez 41, Defour 90)*          15,000
*Dinamo Zagreb:* (4321) Kelava; Vida, Tonel, Simunic, Pivaric; Ademi (Beqiraj 58), Calello (Kovacic 79), Brozovic; Rukavina (Carrasco 67), Sammir; Cop.
*FC Porto:* (433) Helton; Miguel Lopes, Maicon, Otamendi, Alex Sandro L; Gonzalez, Defour, Joao Moutinho; Varela (Atsu 72), Rodriguez (Mangala 88), Martinez (Kleber 77).

**Paris St Germain (3) 4** *(Ibrahimovic 19 (pen), Thiago Silva 29, Alex 32, Pastore 90)*
**Dynamo Kiev (0) 1** *(Veloso 86)*          48,000
*Paris St Germain:* (4321) Sirigu; Jallet, Alex, Thiago Silva (Camara 81), Maxwell; Chantome, Verratti, Matuidi; Menez (Nene 77), Pastore; Ibrahimovic (Lavezzi 72).
*Dynamo Kiev:* (4231) Koval; Danilo Silva, Khacheridi, Mykhalyk (Betao 46), Taiwo; Garmash (Vukojevic 52), Veloso; Yarmolenko, Kranjcar (Gusev 76), Raffael; Ideye B.

**Wednesday, 3 October 2012**
**Dynamo Kiev (2) 2** *(Gusev 3, Pivaric 34 (og))*
**Dinamo Zagreb (0) 0**          55,898
*Dynamo Kiev:* (4231) Shovkovskiy; Danilo Silva, Mykhalyk, Khacheridi, Taiwo; Veloso, Vukojevic; Yarmolenko (Mehmedi 80), Kranjcar (Garmash 46), Gusev (Raffael 82); Ideye B.
*Dinamo Zagreb:* (4231) Kelava; Vida, Tonel, Simunic, Pivaric; Calello (Cop 46), Ademi; Brozovic, Sammir (Carrasco 78), Kovacic; Beqiraj (Rukavina 58).

**FC Porto (0) 1** *(Rodriguez 83)*
**Paris St Germain (0) 0**          40,000
*FC Porto:* (433) Helton; Danilo, Maicon, Otamendi, Alex Sandro L; Gonzalez (Defour 81), Fernando, Joao Moutinho; Varela (Atsu 73), Martinez, Rodriguez (Mangala 90).
*Paris St Germain:* (4312) Sirigu; Van Der Wiel (Jallet 62), Thiago Silva, Sakho, Maxwell; Chantome, Verratti, Matuidi; Nene; Menez (Lavezzi 73 (Pastore 81)), Ibrahimovic.

**Wednesday, 24 October 2012**
**Dinamo Zagreb (0) 0**
**Paris St Germain (2) 2** *(Ibrahimovic 32, Menez 43)* 10,000
*Dinamo Zagreb:* (433) Kelava; Vrsaljko S, Puljic, Simunic, Pivaric; Brozovic, Vida, Kovacic (Halilovic 90); Ibanez (Calello 46), Sammir, Cop (Rukavina 70).
*Paris St Germain:* (41212) Sirigu; Jallet, Alex (Camara 46), Thiago Silva, Maxwell; Bodmer (Sissoko M 60); Verratti, Matuidi; Menez (Hoarau 77); Pastore, Ibrahimovic.

**FC Porto (2) 3** *(Varela 15, Martinez 36, 78)*
**Dynamo Kiev (1) 2** *(Gusev 21, Ideye B 72)*          41,000
*FC Porto:* (433) Helton; Danilo, Maicon, Otamendi, Mangala; Gonzalez, Fernando, Joao Moutinho (Defour 75); Varela (Atsu 64), Martinez, Rodriguez (Miguel Lopes 90).
*Dynamo Kiev:* (433) Shovkovskiy; Betao, Mykhalyk, Khacheridi, Taiwo; Garmash, Vukojevic (Kranjcar 84), Veloso; Yarmolenko, Ideye B, Gusev.

**Tuesday, 6 November 2012**
**Dynamo Kiev (0) 0**
**FC Porto (0) 0**          52,000
*Dynamo Kiev:* (4231) Koval; Betao, Mykhalyk, Khacheridi, Taiwo; Veloso, Vukojevic (Kranjcar 87); Yarmolenko, Milevskiy (Haruna 58), Gusev; Ruben (Ideye B 66).
*FC Porto:* (433) Helton; Danilo, Otamendi, Ba, Mangala; Gonzalez, Defour (Andre Castro 80), Joao Moutinho; Rodriguez (Kleber 90), Martinez, Varela (Atsu 75).

**Paris St Germain (1) 4** *(Alex 17, Matuidi 61, Menez 65, Hoarau 80)*
**Dinamo Zagreb (0) 0**          47,000
*Paris St Germain:* (433) Sirigu; Jallet, Alex, Thiago Silva, Maxwell; Sissoko M (Verratti 46), Matuidi, Rabiot; Menez (Hoarau 76), Ibrahimovic, Lavezzi (Pastore 68).
*Dinamo Zagreb:* (532) Kelava; Vrsaljko S, Vida, Simunic, Puljic, Pivaric; Kovacic (Halilovic 85), Ademi, Brozovic; Sammir, Rukavina (Calello 73).

**Wednesday, 21 November 2012**
**Dynamo Kiev (0) 0**
**Paris St Germain (1) 2** *(Lavezzi 45, 52)*          50,000
*Dynamo Kiev:* (4231) Koval; Danilo Silva, Betao, Khacheridi, Taiwo; Garmash (Bohdanov 78), Veloso; Dudu Rodrigues, Haruna (Milevskiy 66), Gusev (Yarmolenko 66); Ideye B.
*Paris St Germain:* (433) Sirigu; Van Der Wiel, Alex, Thiago Silva, Maxwell; Sissoko M (Chantome 67), Verratti (Armand 78), Matuidi; Lavezzi, Ibrahimovic, Nene (Pastore 87).

**FC Porto (1) 3** *(Gonzalez 20, Joao Moutinho 67, Varela 85)*
**Dinamo Zagreb (0) 0**          10,000
*FC Porto:* (433) Helton; Danilo, Ba (Alex Sandro L 67), Otamendi, Mangala; Gonzalez (Atsu 75), Defour (Fernando 66), Joao Moutinho; Rodriguez, Martinez, Varela.
*Dinamo Zagreb:* (433) Kelava; Vrsaljko S, Vida, Simunic, Pivaric; Kovacic, Ademi, Brozovic; Beqiraj (Krstanovic 86), Sammir (Puljic 76), Cop (Halilovic 84).

**Tuesday, 4 December 2012**
**Dinamo Zagreb (0) 1** *(Krstanovic 90 (pen))*
**Dynamo Kiev (1) 1** *(Yarmolenko 45)*          3500
*Dinamo Zagreb:* (4231) Kelava; Vrsaljko S, Vida, Simunic, Ibanez; Ademi, Kovacic; Brozovic (Pivaric 73), Sammir, Cop (Krstanovic 61); Beqiraj .
*Dynamo Kiev:* (4231) Koval; Betao, Vukojevic, Mykhalyk, Taiwo; Garmash, Veloso; Yarmolenko, Haruna (Bohdanov 90), Dudu Rodrigues (Mehmedi 84); Ideye B (Ruben 77).

**Paris St Germain (1) 2** *(Thiago Silva 29, Lavezzi 61)*
**FC Porto (1) 1** *(Martinez 33)*          40,000
*Paris St Germain:* (433) Sirigu; Van Der Wiel, Alex, Thiago Silva, Maxwell; Chantome, Matuidi, Pastore (Nene 88); Menez (Jallet 85), Ibrahimovic, Lavezzi (Verratti 77).
*FC Porto:* (433) Helton; Danilo, Otamendi, Mangala, Alex Sandro L (Ba 85); Gonzalez, Fernando (Defour 71), Joao Moutinho; Rodriguez, Martinez, Varela (Atsu 85).

| Group A Table | P | W | D | L | F | A | GD | Pts |
|---|---|---|---|---|---|---|---|---|
| Paris St Germain | 6 | 5 | 0 | 1 | 14 | 3 | 11 | 15 |
| FC Porto | 6 | 4 | 1 | 1 | 10 | 4 | 6 | 13 |
| Dynamo Kiev | 6 | 1 | 2 | 3 | 6 | 10 | −4 | 5 |
| Dinamo Zagreb | 6 | 0 | 1 | 5 | 1 | 14 | −13 | 1 |

## GROUP B

**Tuesday, 18 September 2012**
**Montpellier (1) 1** *(Belhanda 9 (pen))*
**Arsenal (2) 2** *(Podolski 16, Gervinho 18)*          30,000
*Montpellier:* (4231) Jourdren; Bocaly, Yanga-Mbiwa, Hilton, Bedimo; Estrada (Herrera 78), Saihi; Mounier (Ait-Fana 67), Belhanda, Cabella; Camara (Stambouli 78).
*Arsenal:* (4231) Mannone; Jenkinson, Mertesacker, Vermaelen, Gibbs; Diaby, Arteta; Gervinho, Cazorla (Coquelin 90), Podolski (Walcott 90); Giroud (Ramsey 76).

**Olympiakos (0) 1** *(Abdoun 58)*
**Schalke 04 (1) 2** *(Howedes 41, Huntelaar 59)*       28,000
*Olympiakos:* (4231) Megyeri; Torosidis, Contreras, Manolas, Holebas; Maniatis, Modesto (Greco 69); Paulo Machado, David Fuster (Ibagaza 58), Abdoun (Mitroglou 69); Djebbour.
*Schalke 04:* (442) Unnerstall; Howedes, Papadopoulos, Matip, Fuchs C; Neustadter, Jones (Hoger 90), Barnetta (Afellay 79), Holtby; Farfan (Draxler 90), Huntelaar.

**Wednesday, 3 October 2012**
**Arsenal (1) 3** *(Gervinho 42, Podolski 56, Ramsey 90)*
**Olympiakos (1) 1** *(Mitroglou 45)*       60,034
*Arsenal:* (4231) Mannone; Jenkinson, Koscielny, Vermaelen, Gibbs; Arteta, Cazorla; Coquelin, Oxlade-Chamberlain (Walcott 70), Gervinho (Giroud 79); Podolski (Ramsey 79).
*Olympiakos:* (4231) Megyeri; Diakite (Ibagaza 72), Manolas, Contreras, Holebas; Siovas, Maniatis; Greco (Abdoun 67), David Fuster, Paulo Machado (Pantelic 79); Mitroglou.

**Schalke 04 (1) 2** *(Draxler 26, Huntelaar 53 (pen))*
**Montpellier (1) 2** *(Ait-Fana 13, Camara 90)*       59,000
*Schalke 04:* (433) Unnerstall; Uchida, Papadopoulos, Howedes, Fuchs C; Draxler (Afellay 54), Neustadter, Hoger; Holtby (Barnetta 83), Huntelaar, Pukki (Farfan 66).
*Montpellier:* (433) Jourdren; Bocaly■, Yanga-Mbiwa, Hilton, Stambouli; Belhanda (Tinhan 68), Saihi, Estrada (Marveaux J 68); Cabella, Camara, Ait-Fana (Congre 54).

**Wednesday, 24 October 2012**
**Arsenal (0) 0**
**Schalke 04 (0) 2** *(Huntelaar 76, Afellay 86)*       60,049
*Arsenal:* (442) Mannone; Jenkinson (Gnabry 82), Mertesacker, Vermaelen, Andre Santos; Ramsey, Coquelin, Arteta, Podolski (Arshavin 82); Cazorla, Gervinho (Giroud 75).
*Schalke 04:* (442) Unnerstall; Uchida, Howedes, Matip, Fuchs C; Hoger (Jones 46), Neustadter, Holtby (Barnetta 65), Afellay; Farfan, Huntelaar (Marica 87).

**Montpellier (0) 1** *(Charbonnier 49)*
**Olympiakos (0) 2** *(Torosidis 73, Mitroglou 90)*       27,000
*Montpellier:* (4231) Pionnier; Stambouli, Yanga-Mbiwa, Hilton, Bedimo; Saihi (Marveaux J 85), Cabella; Mounier (Estrada 62), Belhanda, Utaka; Charbonnier (Camara 68).
*Olympiakos:* (4231) Carroll; Torosidis, Manolas, Contreras, Holebas; Modesto, Maniatis; Greco (Abdoun 60), David Fuster (Lykogiannis 88), Paulo Machado; Djebbour (Mitroglou 70).

**Tuesday, 6 November 2012**
**Olympiakos (1) 3** *(Paulo Machado 4, Greco 80, Mitroglou 82)*
**Montpellier (0) 1** *(Belhanda 67 (pen))*       25,000
*Olympiakos:* (4231) Carroll; Torosidis, Manolas, Siovas, Holebas; Modesto (David Fuster 74), Maniatis; Abdoun, Paulo Machado (Fejsa L 87); Greco; Mitroglou (Lykogiannis 90).
*Montpellier:* (433) Jourdren; Bocaly, Yanga-Mbiwa, Hilton (Congre 79); Bedimo; Saihi, Cabella (Charbonnier 46), Belhanda; Marveaux J, Camara, Mounier (Tinhan 62).

**Schalke 04 (1) 2** *(Huntelaar 45, Farfan 67)*
**Arsenal (2) 2** *(Walcott 18, Giroud 26)*       50,000
*Schalke 04:* (4231) Unnerstall; Uchida (Hoger 25 (Papadopoulos 66)), Howedes, Matip, Fuchs C; Jones, Neustadter; Farfan, Holtby (Barnetta 90), Afellay; Huntelaar.
*Arsenal:* (4231) Mannone; Sagna, Koscielny, Mertesacker, Vermaelen; Arteta, Wilshere; Walcott, Cazorla (Coquelin 90), Podolski (Andre Santos 90); Giroud.

**Wednesday, 21 November 2012**
**Arsenal (0) 2** *(Wilshere 49, Podolski 63)*
**Montpellier (0) 0**       59,760
*Arsenal:* (433) Szczesny; Sagna, Mertesacker, Vermaelen; Arteta, Cazorla (Coquelin 84), Wilshere; Oxlade-Chamberlain (Ramsey 69), Giroud (Gervinho 84), Podolski.
*Montpellier:* (4231) Jourdren; Deplagne, Congre, El Kaoutari, Bedimo; Yanga-Mbiwa, Estrada (Marveaux J 79); Cabella (Herrera 68), Belhanda, Mounier; Charbonnier (Martin 68).

**Schalke 04 (0) 1** *(Fuchs C 77)*
**Olympiakos (0) 0**       52,000
*Schalke 04:* (4231) Unnerstall; Howedes, Papadopoulos, Matip, Fuchs C; Jones, Neustadter; Farfan, Holtby (Pukki 71), Draxler (Barnetta 88); Huntelaar (Marica 90).
*Olympiakos:* (433) Carroll; Torosidis, Manolas, Siovas, Holebas; Maniatis, Modesto (Ibagaza 81), Greco (David Fuster 65); Abdoun, Mitroglou (Djebbour 74), Paulo Machado.

**Tuesday, 4 December 2012**
**Montpellier (0) 1** *(Herrera 59)*
**Schalke 04 (0) 1** *(Howedes 56)*       23,142
*Montpellier:* (4231) Ligali; Congre, Yanga-Mbiwa, Hilton, Bedimo; Stambouli (Pitau 46), Estrada; Mounier (Belhanda 67), Cabella, Camara (Utaka 67); Herrera.
*Schalke 04:* (4231) Hildebrand; Uchida, Howedes, Metzelder, Kolasinac; Holtby, Neustadter; Pukki (Obasi Ogbuke 84), Barnetta (Jones 72), Draxler; Marica (Huntelaar 77).

**Olympiakos (0) 2** *(Maniatis 65, Mitroglou 73)*
**Arsenal (1) 1** *(Rosicky 38)*       30,000
*Olympiakos:* (433) Carroll; Diakite, Manolas, Contreras, Torosidis; Paulo Machado, Maniatis, Fejsa (David Fuster 60); Greco, Djebbour (Ibagaza 82), Abdoun (Mitroglou 72).
*Arsenal:* (433) Szczesny; Jenkinson, Squillaci, Vermaelen, Meade (Angha 83); Coquelin, Rosicky (Arshavin 46), Ramsey; Oxlade-Chamberlain, Chamakh, Gervinho.

| Group B Table | P | W | D | L | F | A | GD | Pts |
|---|---|---|---|---|---|---|---|---|
| Schalke 04 | 6 | 3 | 3 | 0 | 10 | 6 | 4 | 12 |
| Arsenal | 6 | 3 | 1 | 2 | 10 | 8 | 2 | 10 |
| Olympiakos | 6 | 3 | 0 | 3 | 9 | 9 | 0 | 9 |
| Montpellier | 6 | 0 | 2 | 4 | 6 | 12 | –6 | 2 |

## GROUP C

**Tuesday, 18 September 2012**
**AC Milan (0) 0**
**Anderlecht (0) 0**       20,000
*AC Milan:* (433) Abbiati; De Sciglio, Bonera (Yepes 74), Mexes, Antonini; Flamini, De Jong, Nocerino; Boateng (El Shaarawy 60), Emanuelson (Constant 79), Pazzini.
*Anderlecht:* (4411) Proto; Gillet, Wasilewski, Nuytinck, Deschacht; Bruno (Juhasz 78), Biglia, Kouyate (Praet 79), Kljestan; Kanu (Yakovenko 88); Mbokani.

**Malaga (2) 3** *(Isco 3, Saviola 13, Isco 76)*
**Zenit St Petersburg (0) 0**       28,000
*Malaga:* (4132) Willy; Jesus Gamez, Demichelis, Weligton, Monreal; Camacho; Joaquin (Duda 84), Portillo (Iturra 46); Eliseu; Isco, Saviola (Santa Cruz 62).
*Zenit St Petersburg:* (433) Malafeev; Aniukov, Bruno Alves, Lombaerts, Lukovic (Bystrov 40); Shirokov (Lumb 86), Denisov, Zyryanov (Djordjevic 75); Faitzulin, Kerzhakov, Hulk.

**Wednesday, 3 October 2012**
**Anderlecht (0) 0**
**Malaga (1) 3** *(Eliseu 45, 64, Joaquin 57 (pen))*       18,000
*Anderlecht:* (4231) Proto; Gillet, Wasilewski, Nuytinck, Deschacht; Biglia, Kouyate; Bruno (Kljestan 47), Kanu, Jovanovic (Yakovenko 59); Mbokani.
*Malaga:* (442) Willy; Sergio Sanchez, Demichelis, Weligton, Monreal; Joaquin (Duda 74), Iturra, Camacho, Eliseu; Saviola (Santa Cruz 66), Isco (Fernandez 81).

**Zenit St Petersburg (1) 2** *(Hulk 45, Shirokov 49)*
**AC Milan (2) 3** *(Emanuelson 13, El Shaarawy 16,*
*Hubocan 76 (og))* 18,000
*Zenit St Petersburg:* (442) Malafeev; Aniukov, Hubocan, Lombaerts (Bukharov 89), Criscito; Faitzulin (Kanunnikov 79), Witsel, Shirokov, Bystrov (Zyryanov 72); Hulk, Kerzhakov.
*AC Milan:* (451) Abbiati; Abate I, Bonera, Zapata, Antonini; De Jong, Montolivo, Emanuelson (Nocerino 64), Boateng (Yepes 80), El Shaarawy; Bojan (Pazzini 52).

**Wednesday, 24 October 2012**
**Malaga (0) 1** *(Joaquin 64)*
**AC Milan (0) 0** 23,807
*Malaga:* (4411) Willy; Jesus Gamez, Demichelis, Weligton, Eliseu; Portillo (Onyewu 90), Camacho, Iturra, Isco; Joaquin (Duda 85); Saviola (Santa Cruz 70).
*AC Milan:* (451) Amelia; Bonera, Mexes, Acerbi (Bojan 79), De Sciglio; Emanuelson, Ambrosini, Constant (Alexandre Pato 69), Montolivo, El Shaarawy; Pazzini.

**Zenit St Petersburg (0) 1** *(Kerzhakov 72 (pen))*
**Anderlecht (0) 0** 18,000
*Zenit St Petersburg:* (433) Malafeev; Aniukov, Hubocan, Lombaerts, Criscito; Witsel, Semak S (Zyryanov 66), Shirokov (Bruno Alves 75); Faitzulin (Bystrov 58), Kerzhakov, Hulk.
*Anderlecht:* (451) Proto; Wasilewski (Molins 83), Kouyate, Nuytinck, Deschacht; Gillet, Biglia, Praet (Yakovenko 74), Kanu, Jovanovic; De Sutter.

**Tuesday, 6 November 2012**
**AC Milan (0) 1** *(Alexandre Pato 73)*
**Malaga (1) 1** *(Eliseu 40)* 20,000
*AC Milan:* (4411) Abbiati; Abate I (De Sciglio 6), Bonera, Mexes, Constant; Emanuelson (Robinho 80), De Jong, Montolivo, El Shaarawy (Boateng 62); Bojan; Alexandre Pato.
*Malaga:* (4231) Willy; Jesus Gamez, Demichelis, Weligton, Sergio Sanchez; Camacho, Iturra (Toulalan 74); Joaquin (Fernandez 81), Isco, Eliseu; Saviola (Santa Cruz 68).

**Anderlecht (1) 1** *(Mbokani 17)*
**Zenit St Petersburg (0) 0** 19,000
*Anderlecht:* (4231) Proto; Safari B, Nuytinck, Kouyate, Gillet; Kljestan, Biglia, Jovanovic, Praet (Kanu 79), Bruno (Yakovenko 72); Mbokani.
*Zenit St Petersburg:* (433) Malafeev; Aniukov, Hubocan, Lombaerts (Bruno Alves 69), Criscito; Shirokov, Witsel, Denisov; Bystrov (Kanunnikov 77), Kerzhakov, Semak (Danny 46).

**Wednesday, 21 November 2012**
**Anderlecht (0) 1** *(De Sutter 79)*
**AC Milan (0) 3** *(El Shaarawy 47, Mexes 72,*
*Alexandre Pato 90)* 25,000
*Anderlecht:* (4231) Proto; Gillet, Kouyate, Nuytinck■, Deschacht; Kljestan, Biglia; Bruno (Yakovenko 66), Praet (De Sutter 76), Jovanovic (Canesin 78); Mbokani.
*AC Milan:* (433) Abbiati; De Sciglio, Mexes (Zapata 80), Yepes, Constant (Emanuelson 75); Montolivo, De Jong, Nocerino; Boateng, Bojan (Alexandre Pato 68), El Shaarawy.

**Zenit St Petersburg (0) 2** *(Danny 49, Faitzulin 87)*
**Malaga (2) 2** *(Buonanotte 8, Fernandez 9)* 45,000
*Zenit St Petersburg:* (4321) Malafeev; Aniukov (Bystrov 81), Bruno Alves, Lombaerts, Hubocan; Witsel, Denisov, Shirokov (Faitzulin 72); Hulk, Danny; Kerzhakov.
*Malaga:* (442) Willy; Jesus Gamez, Demichelis (Weligton 46), Onyewu, Eliseu; Fernandez (Juanmi 76), Toulalan, Camacho, Duda (Portillo 62); Buonanotte, Santa Cruz.

**Tuesday, 4 December 2012**
**AC Milan (0) 0**
**Zenit St Petersburg (1) 1** *(Danny 35)* 49,000
*AC Milan:* (4312) Abbiati; De Sciglio, Zapata, Acerbi, Mesbah (Robinho 65); Flamini (El Shaarawy 80), Ambrosini, Emanuelson; Bojan (Petagna 90); Pazzini, Boateng.
*Zenit St Petersburg:* (4321) Malafeev; Hubocan, Lombaerts, Bruno Alves, Aniukov; Shirokov (Kanunnikov 88), Denisov, Witsel; Danny, Semak; Hulk (Zyryanov 79).

**Malaga (1) 2** *(Duda 45, 61)*
**Anderlecht (0) 2** *(Jovanovic 50, Mbokani 89)* 25,000
*Malaga:* (442) Kameni; Sergio Sanchez, Onyewu, Weligton (Jesus Gamez 54), Eliseu; Fernandez, Toulalan (Camacho 17), Iturra, Duda (Portillo 80); Buonanotte, Santa Cruz.
*Anderlecht:* (4231) Proto; Gillet, Kouyate, Deschacht, Safari B; Biglia, Kljestan; Bruno, Praet (De Sutter 71), Jovanovic (Vargas 85); Mbokani.

| Group C Table | P | W | D | L | F | A | GD | Pts |
|---|---|---|---|---|---|---|---|---|
| Malaga | 6 | 3 | 3 | 0 | 12 | 5 | 7 | 12 |
| AC Milan | 6 | 2 | 2 | 2 | 7 | 6 | 1 | 8 |
| Zenit St Petersburg | 6 | 2 | 1 | 3 | 6 | 9 | –3 | 7 |
| Anderlecht | 6 | 1 | 2 | 3 | 4 | 9 | –5 | 5 |

## GROUP D

**Tuesday, 18 September 2012**
**Borussia Dortmund (0) 1** *(Lewandowski 87)*
**Ajax (0) 0** 80,500
*Borussia Dortmund:* (4231) Weidenfeller; Piszczek, Subotic N, Hummels, Schmelzer; Gundogan (Leitner 89), Kehl; Blaszczykowski (Perisic 73), Gotze (Schieber 88), Reus; Lewandowski.
*Ajax:* (433) Vermeer; Van Rhijn, Alderweireld, Moisander, Blind; De Jong, Poulsen, Eriksen; Sana (Sulejmani 89), Babel (Schone 79), Boerrigter.

**Real Madrid (0) 3** *(Marcelo 76, Benzema 87, Ronaldo 90)*
**Manchester C (0) 2** *(Dzeko 69, Kolarov 85)* 67,000
*Real Madrid:* (4231) Casillas; Arbeloa, Pepe, Varane, Marcelo; Khedira (Modric 73), Alonso; Di Maria, Essien (Ozil 65), Ronaldo; Higuain (Benzema 73).
*Manchester C:* (451) Hart; Maicon (Zabaleta 74), Kompany, Nastasic, Clichy; Javi Garcia, Silva (Dzeko 63), Toure Y, Barry, Nasri (Kolarov 36); Tevez.

**Wednesday, 3 October 2012**
**Ajax (0) 1** *(Moisander 56)*
**Real Madrid (1) 4** *(Ronaldo 42, 79, 81, Benzema 48)* 45,000
*Ajax:* (433) Vermeer; Van Rhijn, Alderweireld, Moisander, Blind; De Jong, Poulsen (Sporkslede 69), Eriksen; Sana (Hoesen 66), Babel R (Lukoki 81), Boerrigter.
*Real Madrid:* (433) Casillas; Arbeloa, Sergio Ramos, Pepe, Marcelo; Alonso, Essien (Khedira 78), Kaka R (Ozil 75); Callejon (Di Maria 61), Benzema, Ronaldo.

**Manchester C (0) 1** *(Balotelli 90 (pen))*
**Borussia Dortmund (0) 1** *(Reus 62)* 43,607
*Manchester C:* (442) Hart; Zabaleta, Kompany, Nastasic, Clichy (Balotelli 81); Silva, Javi Garcia (Rodwell 34), Toure Y, Nasri (Kolarov 56); Dzeko, Aguero.
*Borussia Dortmund:* (4231) Weidenfeller; Piszczek, Subotic N, Hummels (Felipe Santana 74), Schmelzer; Gundogan (Grosskreutz 82), Bender; Blaszczykowski, Gotze (Kehl 88), Reus; Lewandowski.

**Wednesday, 24 October 2012**
**Ajax (1) 3** *(De Jong 45, Moisander 57, Eriksen 68)*
**Manchester C (1) 1** *(Nasri 22)* 45,743
*Ajax:* (433) Vermeer; Van Rhijn, Alderweireld, Moisander, Blind; Schone (Boerrigter 89), Poulsen, Eriksen; Sana (Enoh 74), De Jong, Babel R.
*Manchester C:* (4231) Hart; Richards, Kompany, Lescott (Kolarov 63), Clichy; Toure Y, Barry (Tevez 71); Milner (Balotelli 77), Aguero, Nasri; Dzeko.

**Borussia Dortmund (1) 2** *(Lewandowski 36, Schmelzer 64)*
**Real Madrid (1) 1** *(Ronaldo 38)* 65,829
*Borussia Dortmund:* (4231) Weidenfeller; Piszczek,
Subotic N, Hummels, Schmelzer; Bender (Gundogan 67),
Kehl; Reus (Perisic 90), Gotze (Schieber 87),
Grosskreutz; Lewandowski.
*Real Madrid:* (4231) Casillas; Sergio Ramos, Varane,
Pepe, Essien; Alonso, Khedira (Modric 20); Di Maria,
Ozil, Ronaldo; Benzema (Higuain 73).

Tuesday, 6 November 2012
**Manchester C (1) 2** *(Toure Y 22, Aguero 74)*
**Ajax (2) 2** *(De Jong 10, 17)* 40,222
*Manchester C:* (4231) Hart; Zabaleta, Kompany,
Nastasic, Clichy; Javi Garcia (Balotelli 46), Barry
(Kolarov 85); Nasri, Toure Y, Aguero; Tevez (Dzeko 66).
*Ajax:* (433) Vermeer; Van Rhijn, Alderweireld,
Moisander, Blind; De Jong, Poulsen (Fischer 87), Schone
(Enoh 78); Boerrigter (Sana 90), Eriksen, Babel.

**Real Madrid (1) 2** *(Pepe 34, Ozil 89)*
**Borussia Dortmund (2) 2** *(Reus 28, Arbeloa 45 (og))*
65,000
*Real Madrid:* (4231) Casillas; Sergio Ramos, Varane,
Pepe, Arbeloa (Kaka R 78); Alonso, Modric (Essien 46);
Di Maria, Ozil, Ronaldo; Higuain (Callejon 46).
*Borussia Dortmund:* (4231) Weidenfeller; Piszczek,
Subotic N, Hummels, Schmelzer; Gundogan (Perisic 81),
Kehl; Reus (Bender 74), Gotze (Leitner 90),
Grosskreutz; Lewandowski.

Wednesday, 21 November 2012
**Ajax (0) 1** *(Hoesen 86)*
**Borussia Dortmund (3) 4** *(Reus 8, Gotze 36,
Lewandowski 41, 67)* 48,913
*Ajax:* (433) Vermeer; Van Rhijn, Alderweireld,
Moisander, Blind; Enoh (Hoesen 63), Poulsen (Schone
46), Eriksen; Lukoki, De Jong, Boerrigter (Fischer 73).
*Borussia Dortmund:* (4231) Weidenfeller; Piszczek,
Subotic N, Hummels, Schmelzer; Bender (Perisic 63),
Gundogan; Gotze (Blaszczykowski 70), Reus (Schieber
79), Grosskreutz; Lewandowski.

**Manchester C (0) 1** *(Aguero 74 (pen))*
**Real Madrid (1) 1** *(Benzema 10)* 45,740
*Manchester C:* (352) Hart; Zabaleta, Kompany, Nastasic;
Maicon, Kolarov (Javi Garcia 46), Nasri (Tevez 60),
Toure Y, Silva; Dzeko, Aguero (Milner 88).
*Real Madrid:* (4231) Casillas; Arbeloa⁸, Sergio Ramos,
Pepe, Fabio Coentrao; Khedira, Alonso; Di Maria
(Albiol 90), Modric (Callejon 68), Ronaldo; Benzema
(Varane 74).

Tuesday, 4 December 2012
**Borussia Dortmund (0) 1** *(Schieber 57)*
**Manchester C (0) 0** 62,000
*Borussia Dortmund:* (4321) Weidenfeller; Kirch
(Bittencourt 88), Hummels, Felipe Santana, Schmelzer;
Grosskreutz, Gundogan, Leitner; Reus (Blaszczykowski
46), Perisic; Schieber (Lewandowski 77).
*Manchester C:* (4231) Hart; Maicon, Kompany, Lescott,
Nastasic; Barry, Javi Garcia; Nasri (Zabaleta 68), Tevez,
Sinclair (Aguero 57); Dzeko (Balotelli 65).

**Real Madrid (2) 4** *(Ronaldo 13, Callejon 28, Kaka R 49,
Callejon 88)*
**Ajax (0) 1** *(Boerrigter 60)* 51,000
*Real Madrid:* (4231) Adan; Nacho, Carvalho, Varane,
Fabio Coentrao (Pepe 23); Khedira, Modric; Callejon,
Kaka R (Jose Rodriguez 72), Ronaldo; Benzema
(Morata 80).
*Ajax:* (433) Vermeer; Van Rhijn, Alderweireld,
Moisander, Blind; De Jong, Poulsen (Schone 40),
Eriksen; Boerrigter, Hoesen (Enoh 77), Fischer (Sana
78).

| Group D Table | P | W | D | L | F | A | GD | Pts |
|---|---|---|---|---|---|---|---|---|
| Borussia Dortmund | 6 | 4 | 2 | 0 | 11 | 5 | 6 | 14 |
| Real Madrid | 6 | 3 | 2 | 1 | 15 | 9 | 6 | 11 |
| Ajax | 6 | 1 | 1 | 4 | 8 | 16 | –8 | 4 |
| Manchester C | 6 | 0 | 3 | 3 | 7 | 11 | –4 | 3 |

## GROUP E

Wednesday, 19 September 2012
**Chelsea (2) 2** *(Oscar 31, 33)*
**Juventus (1) 2** *(Vidal 38, Quagliarella 80)* 40,918
*Chelsea:* (4231) Cech; Ivanovic, Luiz, Terry, Cole; Mikel,
Lampard; Ramires (Bertrand 69), Hazard E, Oscar
(Mata 74); Torres.
*Juventus:* (352) Buffon; Barzagli, Bonucci, Chiellini;
Lichtsteiner (Isla 77), Vidal, Pirlo, Marchisio, Asamoah;
Giovinco (Quagliarella 75), Vucinic (Matri A 88).

**Shakhtar Donetsk (1) 2** *(Mkhitaryan 44, 76)*
**Nordsjaelland (0) 0** 51,624
*Shakhtar Donetsk:* (451) Pyatov; Srna, Kucher, Rakitskiy,
Rat; Ilsinho (Alex Teixeira 70), Fernandinho,
Hubschman, Willian (Douglas Costa 81), Mkhitaryan;
Luiz Adriano (Devic 75).
*Nordsjaelland:* (451) Hansen; Parkhurst, Okore, Runje,
Mtiliga; Lorentzen (Nordstrand M 72), Adu, Stokholm,
John (Laudrup 81), Christensen (Christiansen 62);
Beckmann.

Tuesday, 2 October 2012
**Juventus (1) 1** *(Bonucci 25)*
**Shakhtar Donetsk (1) 1** *(Alex Teixeira 23)* 45,000
*Juventus:* (352) Buffon; Barzagli, Bonucci, Chiellini;
Lichtsteiner, Vidal (Pogba 85), Pirlo, Marchisio,
Asamoah; Matri A (Quagliarella 65), Vucinic (Giovino
58).
*Shakhtar Donetsk:* (4231) Pyatov; Srna, Kucher,
Rakitskiy, Rat; Fernandinho, Hubschman; Mkhitaryan,
Willian, Alex Teixeira (Ilsinho 84); Luiz Adriano.

**Nordsjaelland (0) 0**
**Chelsea (1) 4** *(Mata 33, 82, Luiz 79, Ramires 89)* 42,000
*Nordsjaelland:* (4231) Hansen; Parkhurst, Okore, Runje,
Mtiliga; Adu, Stokholm; Lorentzen (Laudrup 84),
Nordstrand (Ticinovic 65), John; Beckmann (Christensen
75).
*Chelsea:* (4231) Cech; Ivanovic, Luiz, Cahill, Cole;
Ramires, Lampard; Moses (Hazard E 65), Oscar, Mata
(Mikel 83); Torres.

Tuesday, 23 October 2012
**Nordsjaelland (0) 1** *(Beckmann 50)*
**Juventus (0) 1** *(Vucinic 81)* 10,100
*Nordsjaelland:* (4231) Hansen; Parkhurst, Okore, Runje,
Mtiliga; Adu, Stokholm; Laudrup (Christensen 70),
Lorentzen (Christiansen 88), John; Beckmann
(Nordstrand M 67).
*Juventus:* (352) Buffon; Lucio (Bendtner 76), Bonucci,
Chiellini, Isla, Vidal (Giaccherini 83), Pirlo, Marchisio,
De Ceglie; Matri A (Vucinic 69), Giovinco.

**Shakhtar Donetsk (1) 2** *(Alex Teixeira 3, Fernandinho 52)*
**Chelsea (0) 1** *(Oscar 88)* 50,000
*Shakhtar Donetsk:* (4231) Pyatov; Srna, Kucher,
Rakitskiy, Rat; Hubschman, Fernandinho; Alex Teixeira
(Ilsinho 82), Mkhitaryan, Willian (Douglas Costa 88);
Luiz Adriano.
*Chelsea:* (451) Cech; Ivanovic, Terry, Luiz, Cole; Oscar,
Ramires, Mikel, Lampard (Hazard E 18), Mata; Torres
(Sturridge 70).

Wednesday, 7 November 2012
**Chelsea (2) 3** *(Torres 6, Oscar 40, Moses 90)*
**Shakhtar Donetsk (1) 2** *(Willian 9, 47)* 41,067
*Chelsea:* (4231) Cech; Ivanovic, Luiz, Cahill, Bertrand;
Ramires, Mikel; Hazard, Mata, Oscar (Moses 80); Torres
(Sturridge 90).
*Shakhtar Donetsk:* (4231) Pyatov; Srna, Kucher,
Rakitskiy, Rat; Hubschman, Fernandinho; Alex Teixeira
(Ilsinho 78), Mkhitaryan, Willian; Luiz Adriano.

**Juventus (3) 4** *(Marchisio 6, Vidal 23, Giovinco 37,*
*Quagliarella 75)*
**Nordsjaelland (0) 0**                                          37,165
*Juventus:* (352) Buffon; Barzagli, Bonucci, Chiellini
(Lucio 69); Isla, Vidal (Pogba 53), Pirlo, Marchisio,
Asamoah; Giovinco (Quagliarella 60), Matri A.
*Nordsjaelland:* (4231) Hansen; Parkhurst, Okore, Runje,
Mtiliga; Adu (Christiansen 46), Stokholm; Lorentzen,
Laudrup (Christensen 47), John; Beckmann (Nordstrand
M 72).

Tuesday, 20 November 2012
**Juventus (1) 3** *(Quagliarella 38, Vidal 61, Giovinco 90)*
**Chelsea (0) 0**                                               40,000
*Juventus:* (352) Buffon; Barzagli, Bonucci, Chiellini;
Lichtsteiner, Vidal, Pirlo, Marchisio,
Asamoah; Quagliarella (Pogba 89), Vucinic (Giovinco
83).
*Chelsea:* (523) Cech; Azpilicueta (Moses 60), Luiz, Cahill,
Ivanovic, Cole; Ramires, Mikel (Torres 71); Hazard E,
Mata, Oscar.

**Nordsjaelland (2) 2** *(Nordstrand M 24, Lorentzen 30)*
**Shakhtar Donetsk (2) 5** *(Luiz Adriano 26, 53, 82,*
*Willian 45, 50)*                                               23,000
*Nordsjaelland:* (4231) Hansen; Parkhurst, Okore, Runje,
Mtiliga; Adu, Stokholm; Lorentzen, Christensen
(Christiansen 58), John (Aynaoglu 82); Nordstrand M
(Ticinovic 75).
*Shakhtar Donetsk:* (4231) Pyatov; Srna, Kucher,
Rakitskiy, Rat; Stepanenko, Fernandinho; Alex Teixeira
(Douglas Costa 78), Mkhitaryan, Willian (Ilsinho 86);
Luiz Adriano (Eduardo 82).

Wednesday, 5 December 2012
**Chelsea (2) 6** *(Luiz 39 (pen), Torres 45, 56, Cahill 51,*
*Mata 63, Oscar 71)*
**Nordsjaelland (0) 1** *(John 46)*                             40,084
*Chelsea:* (4231) Cech; Ivanovic, Luiz, Cahill, Cole
(Bertrand 60); Romeu, Ramires (Oscar 65); Hazard E,
Mata (Ferreira 74), Moses; Torres.
*Nordsjaelland:* (451) Hansen; Ticinovic (Issah 64),
Parkhurst, Runje (Beckmann 10), Mtiliga; Gundelach,
Stokholm, Adu, Christiansen (Kildentoft 61), John;
Lorentzen.

**Shakhtar Donetsk (0) 0**
**Juventus (0) 1** *(Kucher 56 (og))*                           48,000
*Shakhtar Donetsk:* (4231) Pyatov; Srna, Kucher,
Rakitskiy, Rat; Stepanenko, Fernandinho; Alex Teixeira
(Ilsinho 65), Mkhitaryan, Willian; Eduardo (Devic 46).
*Juventus:* (352) Buffon; Barzagli, Bonucci, Chiellini;
Lichtsteiner, Vidal, Pirlo, Pogba, Asamoah; Giovinco
(Giaccherini 90), Vucinic (Matri A 88).

| Group E Table | P | W | D | L | F | A | GD | Pts |
|---|---|---|---|---|---|---|---|---|
| Juventus | 6 | 3 | 3 | 0 | 12 | 4 | 8 | 12 |
| Shakhtar Donetsk | 6 | 3 | 1 | 2 | 12 | 8 | 4 | 10 |
| Chelsea | 6 | 3 | 1 | 2 | 16 | 10 | 6 | 10 |
| Nordsjaelland | 6 | 0 | 1 | 5 | 4 | 22 | –18 | 1 |

## GROUP F

Wednesday, 19 September 2012
**Bayern Munich (1) 2** *(Schweinsteiger 38, Kroos 76)*
**Valencia (0) 1** *(Haedo Valdez 90)*                          65,374
*Bayern Munich:* (4231) Neuer; Lahm, Boateng, Dante,
Badstuber; Javi Martinez (Gustavo L 69),
Schweinsteiger; Robben, Kroos, Ribery (Muller 46);
Pizarro (Mandzukic 63).
*Valencia:* (442) Diego Alves; Joao Pereira, Ricardo
Costa, Rami■, Cissokho; Feghouli, Parejo, Tino Costa,
Guardado (Viera J 71); Jonas (Haedo Valdez 63),
Soldado (Barragan 88).

**Lille (0) 1** *(Chedjou 60)*
**BATE Borisov (3) 3** *(Volodko 6, Rodionov 20,*
*Olekhnovich E 43)*                                             43,215
*Lille:* (352) Landreau; Debuchy (Sidibe 85), Basa,
Chedjou; Digne, Balmont, Mavuba A, Kalou, Martin
(Roux 46); Payet, De Melo (Ryan Mendes 46).
*BATE Borisov:* (451) Gorbunov; Volodko, Radkov,
Simic, Polyakov; Bordachev, Olekhnovich, Likhtarovich
(Silvakov 66), Pavlov (Bressan 80), Hleb; Rodionov
(Mozolevski 89).

Tuesday, 2 October 2012
**BATE Borisov (1) 3** *(Pavlov 23, Rodionov 78, Bressan 90)*
**Bayern Munich (0) 1** *(Ribery 90)*                           16,000
*BATE Borisov:* (3421) Gorbunov; Polyakov, Simic,
Filipenko; Bordachev, Olekhnovich, Likhtarovich
(Silvakov 65), Volodko; Pavlov (Bressan 84), Hleb;
Rodionov (Mozolevski 87).
*Bayern Munich:* (4231) Neuer; Lahm, Boateng, Dante,
Badstuber (Schweinsteiger 77); Javi Martinez (Shaqiri
58), Gustavo L; Muller, Kroos, Ribery; Mandzukic
(Pizarro 75).

**Valencia (1) 2** *(Jonas 38, 74)*
**Lille (0) 0**                                                 36,000
*Valencia:* (4231) Guaita; Barragan, Carlos Delgado,
Victor Ruiz, Cissokho; Tino Costa, Gago; Feghouli (Joao
Pereira 87), Jonas (Parejo 81), Guardado; Soldado
(Haedo Valdez 84).
*Lille:* (433) Landreau; Debuchy■, Basa, Chedjou (Digne
82), Beria; Balmont, Gueye, Pedretti; Payet, Roux (De
Melo 64), Ryan Mendes (Rodelin R 73).

Tuesday, 23 October 2012
**BATE Borisov (0) 0**
**Valencia (1) 3** *(Soldado 45 (pen), 55, 69)*                 17,000
*BATE Borisov:* (4321) Gorbunov; Polyakov, Filipenko,
Simic, Bordachev; Volodko (Bressan 75), Likhtarovich
(Silvakov 53), Olekhnovich; Pavlov (Mozolevski 66),
Hleb; Rodionov.
*Valencia:* (4231) Diego Alves; Joao Pereira, Rami,
Ricardo Costa, Cissokho; Albelda (Ever 72), Gago;
Feghouli (Barragan 82), Tino Costa, Guardado; Soldado
(Jonas 77).

**Lille (0) 0**
**Bayern Munich (1) 1** *(Muller 20 (pen))*                     50,000
*Lille:* (433) Landreau; Sidibe, Beria, Chedjou, Digne;
Balmont, Pedretti (Rozehnal 90), Martin; Kalou (Payet
56), De Melo, Roux (Ryan Mendes 77).
*Bayern Munich:* (4231) Neuer; Lahm, Boateng, Dante,
Badstuber; Schweinsteiger, Javi Martinez; Muller (Alaba
84), Kroos (Gustavo L 81), Ribery (Shaqiri 46);
Mandzukic.

Wednesday, 7 November 2012
**Bayern Munich (5) 6** *(Schweinsteiger 5, Pizarro 18, 28, 33,*
*Robben 23, Kroos 66)*
**Lille (0) 1** *(Kalou 57)*                                    64,500
*Bayern Munich:* (4231) Neuer; Lahm, Boateng, Dante,
Alaba; Javi Martinez, Schweinsteiger (Tymoschuk 67);
Robben, Muller (Kroos 60), Ribery (Shaqiri 72); Pizarro.
*Lille:* (433) Landreau; Debuchy, Basa, Chedjou, Beria;
Rozehnal (Mavuba 46), Balmont, Pedretti; Kalou
(Martin 72); Payet (De Melo 46), Roux.

**Valencia (2) 4** *(Jonas 26, Soldado 29 (pen), Feghouli 51, 86)*
**BATE Borisov (0) 2** *(Bressan 54, Mozolevski 83)*            38,000
*Valencia:* (4411) Guaita; Joao Pereira, Rami, Ricardo
Costa, Cissokho; Feghouli, Tino Costa, Gago, Guardado
(Albelda 88); Jonas (Ever 67); Soldado (Haedo Valdez
79).
*BATE Borisov:* (4141) Gorbunov; Polyakov, Filipenko,
Radkov, Bordachev; Likhtarovich (Silvakov 55);
Volodko, Bressan (Kontsevoy 88), Hleb (Mozolevski 77),
Baga; Rodionov.

Tuesday, 20 November 2012
**BATE Borisov (0) 0**
**Lille (2) 2** *(Sidibe 14, Bruno 31)* 21,000
*BATE Borisov:* (433) Gorbunov; Polyakov, Radkov,
Filipenko, Bordachev; Volodko (Kontsevoy 46), Baga,
Olekhnovich (Vasilyuk 84); Hleb (Silvakov 77),
Rodionov, Bressan.
*Lille:* (433) Elana; Sidibe■, Basa, Rozehnal, Digne;
Gueye, Pedretti, Martin (Bonnart 77); Bruno (Roux 64),
Rodelin R, Kalou (Payet 69).

**Valencia (0) 1** *(Feghouli 77)*
**Bayern Munich (0) 1** *(Muller 82)* 28,000
*Valencia:* (4411) Guaita; Barragan■, Rami, Ricardo
Costa, Cissokho; Feghouli, Tino Costa, Parejo (Jonas 75),
Guardado (Haedo Valdez 86); Ever (Albelda 80);
Soldado.
*Bayern Munich:* (4231) Neuer; Lahm, Dante, Badstuber,
Alaba; Javi Martinez, Schweinsteiger; Muller, Kroos
(Shaqiri 66), Ribery (Gomez 79); Pizarro (Mandzukic
66).

Wednesday, 5 December 2012
**Bayern Munich (1) 4** *(Gomez 21, Muller 54, Shaqiri 66,*
*Alaba 83)*
**BATE Borisov (0) 1** *(Filipenko 89)* 68,138
*Bayern Munich:* (4231) Neuer; Rafinha, Van Buyten,
Boateng■, Contento; Tymoschuk, Schweinsteiger (Ribery
72); Muller (Dante 54), Kroos (Alaba 64), Shaqiri;
Gomez.
*BATE Borisov:* (433) Gorbunov; Polyakov■, Radkov,
Filipenko, Bordachev (Yurevich 84); Olekhnovich, Baga,
Volodko; Kontsevoy (Bressan 58), Rodionov (Vasilyuk
67), Hleb.

**Lille (0) 0**
**Valencia (1) 1** *(Jonas 36 (pen))* 35,000
*Lille:* (4321) Elana; Beria, Basa, Chedjou, Digne; Gueye,
Mavuba (Martin 56), Balmont (Payet 70); Kalou,
Rodelin; Bruno (Roux 77).
*Valencia:* (4231) Guaita; Ricardo Costa, Rami, Salva
Ruiz (Viera J 83), Cissokho; Tino Costa, Albelda (Gago
74); Feghouli (Piatti 61), Jonas, Guardado; Haedo
Valdez.

| Group F Table | P | W | D | L | F | A | GD | Pts |
| --- | --- | --- | --- | --- | --- | --- | --- | --- |
| Bayern Munich | 6 | 4 | 1 | 1 | 15 | 7 | 8 | 13 |
| Valencia | 6 | 4 | 1 | 1 | 12 | 5 | 7 | 13 |
| BATE Borisov | 6 | 2 | 0 | 4 | 9 | 15 | –6 | 6 |
| Lille | 6 | 1 | 0 | 5 | 4 | 13 | –9 | 3 |

## GROUP G

Wednesday, 19 September 2012
**Barcelona (1) 3** *(Tello 14, Messi 71, 80)*
**Spartak Moscow (1) 2** *(Dani Alves 30 (og), Romulo 58)*
82,241
*Barcelona:* (433) Valdes V; Dani Alves (Sanchez 64),
Pique (Song 12), Mascherano, Adriano; Xavi, Busquets,
Fabregas; Pedro, Messi, Tello (Villa 76).
*Spartak Moscow:* (4231) Dykan; Kombarov K (Makeev
46), Insaurralde, Suchy, Kombarov D; Kallstrom (Jurado
79), Rafael Carioca P; McGeady, Romulo, Ari (Dzjuba
83); Emenike.

**Celtic (0) 0**
**Benfica (0) 0** 57,795
*Celtic:* (4411) Forster; Matthews, Lustig (Rogne 63),
Wilson, Izaguirre (Hooper 66); Forrest, Brown,
Wanyama, Mulgrew; Commons; Miku.
*Benfica:* (4132) Artur Moraes; Almeida A, Garay, Jardel,
Melgarejo; Matic; Salvio, Perez, Gaitan (Nolito 82);
Aimar (Cardozo 63), Rodrigo (Bruno Cesar 70).

Tuesday, 2 October 2012
**Benfica (0) 0**
**Barcelona (1) 2** *(Sanchez 6, Fabregas 55)* 65,000
*Benfica:* (433) Artur Moraes; Maxi Pereira, Jardel, Garay,
Melgarejo; Salvio, Matic, Gaitan (Nolito 75); Perez
(Aimar 61), Lima, Bruno Cesar (Carlos Martins 46).

*Barcelona:* (433) Valdes V; Dani Alves, Puyol (Song 78),
Mascherano, Jordi Alba; Xavi, Busquets■, Fabregas
(Iniesta 72); Pedro (Villa 82), Messi, Sanchez.

**Spartak Moscow (1) 2** *(Emenike 41, 48)*
**Celtic (1) 3** *(Hooper 12, Kombarov D 71 (og),*
*Samaras 90)* 31,000
*Spartak Moscow:* (451) Pesiakov; Makeev, Insaurralde■,
Pareja, Kombarov D; Ari (Kozlov 85), Kallstrom, Rafael
Carioca P, De Zeeuw (Bryzgalov 65), McGeady (Dzjuba
76); Emenike.
*Celtic:* (442) Forster; Ambrose, Wilson, Wanyama
(Forrest 70), Izaguirre; Lustig, Brown, Commons,
Mulgrew (Ledley 80); Samaras, Hooper.

Tuesday, 23 October 2012
**Barcelona (1) 2** *(Iniesta 45, Jordi Alba 90)*
**Celtic (1) 1** *(Samaras 18)* 75,000
*Barcelona:* (433) Valdes V; Adriano, Bartra,
Mascherano, Jordi Alba; Xavi, Song, Iniesta; Sanchez
(Villa 80), Messi, Pedro (Tello 76).
*Celtic:* (451) Forster; Lustig, Wilson, Ambrose, Izaguirre;
Samaras (Forrest 44), Brown (Commons 63), Wanyama,
Ledley, Mulgrew (Kayal 76); Hooper.

**Spartak Moscow (2) 2** *(Rafael Carioca P 3, Jardel 43 (og))*
**Benfica (1) 1** *(Lima 33)* 30,000
*Spartak Moscow:* (4231) Rebrov; Makeev, Pareja, Suchy,
Kombarov D; Rafael Carioca P, Kallstrom (Bryzgalov
79); Jurado, Ananidze (Kombarov 57), Bilyaletdinov
(Welliton 73); Ari.
*Benfica:* (433) Artur Moraes; Maxi Pereira, Jardel,
Garay, Melgarejo; Perez, Matic (John 89), Salvio; Lima,
Rodrigo (Cardozo 64), Bruno Cesar (Gaitan 65).

Wednesday, 7 November 2012
**Benfica (0) 2** *(Cardozo 55, 69)*
**Spartak Moscow (0) 0** 35,675
*Benfica:* (433) Artur Moraes; Almeida A, Jardel, Garay,
Melgarejo; Maxi Pereira (Gomes 82), Perez, Rodrigo
(Cardozo 46); John, Lima (Bruno Cesar 74), Salvio.
*Spartak Moscow:* (4231) Rebrov; Kombarov K
(Ananidze 62), Pareja■, Insaurralde, Makeev; Rafael
Carioca P, Kallstrom (Dzjuba 71); Bilyaletdinov (Suchy
79), Jurado, Kombarov D; Ari.

**Celtic (1) 2** *(Wanyama 21, Watt 83)*
**Barcelona (0) 1** *(Messi 90)* 55,283
*Celtic:* (4411) Forster; Lustig (Watt 72), Ambrose,
Wilson, Matthews; Commons, Wanyama, Ledley,
Mulgrew; Samaras (Kayal 79); Miku.
*Barcelona:* (433) Valdes V; Dani Alves, Bartra (Pique
71), Mascherano, Jordi Alba; Xavi, Song (Fabregas 71),
Iniesta; Pedro, Messi, Sanchez (Villa 67).

Tuesday, 20 November 2012
**Benfica (1) 2** *(John 7, Garay 71)*
**Celtic (1) 1** *(Samaras 32)* 49,000
*Benfica:* (433) Artur Moraes; Almeida, Luisao, Garay,
Melgarejo; John, Matic (Maxi Pereira 78), Lima (Gaitan
75); Perez, Cardozo, Salvio (Jardel 90).
*Celtic:* (442) Forster; Lustig, Wilson, Ambrose,
Matthews; Brown (Commons 64), Ledley (Watt 80),
Wanyama, Mulgrew (Kayal 46); Samaras, Hooper.

**Spartak Moscow (0) 0**
**Barcelona (3) 3** *(Dani Alves 16, Messi 27, 39)* 69,500
*Spartak Moscow:* (4231) Dykan; Makeev, Insaurralde,
Suchy, Kombarov D; Rafael Carioca P (Bryzgalov 75),
Kallstrom; Kombarov K (Welliton 63), Jurado, Ari;
Emenike (Ananidze 63).
*Barcelona:* (433) Valdes V; Dani Alves, Pique,
Mascherano, Jordi Alba (Montoya 87); Fabregas, Xavi
(Song 82), Busquets; Pedro (Deulofeu 85), Messi,
Iniesta.

Wednesday, 5 December 2012
**Barcelona (0) 0**
**Benfica (0) 0**                                    75,000
*Barcelona:* (433) Pinto; Montoya, Puyol, Adriano (Pique 66), Planas; Thiago, Song, Sergi Roberto; Tello (Deulofeu 79), Rafinha (Messi 58), Villa.
*Benfica:* (433) Artur Moraes; Maxi Pereira, Luisao, Garay, Melgarejo; Gomes, Matic, Nolito (Bruno Cesar 63); John, Lima (Cardozo 74), Rodrigo (Almeida A 74).

**Celtic (1) 2** *(Hooper 21, Commons 82 (pen))*
**Spartak Moscow (1) 1** *(Ari 39)*                  60,000
*Celtic:* (4411) Forster; Lustig (Matthews 71), Wilson, Ambrose, Izaguirre; Mulgrew, Brown (Ledley 84), Kayal (Nouioui 73), Commons; Samaras; Hooper.
*Spartak Moscow:* (4231) Pesiakov; Kombarov K, Insaurralde, Suchy, Kombarov D; Rafael Carioca P, Kallstrom■; Jurado, Dzjuba, Ari (McGeady 61); Emenike.

| Group G Table | P | W | D | L | F | A | GD | Pts |
|---|---|---|---|---|---|---|---|---|
| Barcelona | 6 | 4 | 1 | 1 | 11 | 5 | 6 | 13 |
| Celtic | 6 | 3 | 1 | 2 | 9 | 8 | 1 | 10 |
| Benfica | 6 | 2 | 2 | 2 | 5 | 5 | 0 | 8 |
| Spartak Moscow | 6 | 1 | 0 | 5 | 7 | 14 | −7 | 3 |

## GROUP H

Wednesday, 19 September 2012
**Braga (0) 0**
**CFR Cluj (2) 2** *(Bastos 19, 34)*                24,000
*Braga:* (4231) Beto; Leandro Salino (Paulo Cesar 71), Nuno Andre, Paulo Vinicius, Ismaily; Custodio, Hugo Viana (Ze Luis 64); Alan (Helder Barbosa 46), Mossoro, Ruben Micael; Eder.
*CFR Cluj:* (442) Mario Felgueiras; Ivo Pinto, Cadu R, Rada, Camora; Muresan, Luis Alberto (Godemeche 65), Sougou (Aguirregaray 46), Sepsi; Bastos (Rui Pedro 79), Kapetanos.

**Manchester U (1) 1** *(Carrick 7)*
**Galatasaray (0) 0**                               74,653
*Manchester U:* (4411) De Gea; Da Silva, Vidic, Evans, Evra; Valencia A, Carrick, Scholes (Fletcher D 79), Nani; Kagawa (Welbeck 84); van Persie (Hernandez 81).
*Galatasaray:* (442) Muslera; Eboue, Nounkeu, Kaya, Balta; Altintop, Felipe Melo (Yilmaz A 79), Inan, Amrabat (Colak 63); Yilmaz B, Bulut (Elmander 15).

Tuesday, 2 October 2012
**CFR Cluj (1) 1** *(Kapetanos 14)*
**Manchester U (1) 2** *(van Persie 29, 49)*        24,000
*CFR Cluj:* (442) Mario Felgueiras; Sepsi, Cadu R, Rada, Ivo Pinto; Sougou (Luis Alberto 23), Aguirregaray (Nicoara 80), Muresan, Camora; Bastos, Kapetanos (Bjelanovic 61).
*Manchester U:* (442) De Gea; Da Silva, Ferdinand, Evans (Wootton 79), Evra; Cleverley, Anderson, Fletcher D, Rooney; Hernandez (Welbeck 83), van Persie.

**Galatasaray (0) 0**
**Braga (1) 2** *(Ruben Micael 27, Alan 90)*        52,000
*Galatasaray:* (442) Muslera; Eboue, Kaya, Nounkeu, Riera; Inan S, Felipe Melo (Yilmaz A 46), Amrabat (Yilmaz A 46), Colak (Kurtulus 78); Bulut, Yilmaz B.
*Braga:* (4231) Beto; Leandro Salino, Douglao, Paulo Vinicius, Ismaily (Helder Barbosa 84); Custodio, Hugo Viana (Djamal B 79); Ruben Amorim, Alan, Ruben Micael (Nuno Andre 90); Eder.

Tuesday, 23 October 2012
**Galatasaray (0) 1** *(Yilmaz 77)*
**CFR Cluj (1) 1** *(Nounkeu 19 (og))*              46,000
*Galatasaray:* (442) Muslera; Eboue (Sarioglu 68), Nounkeu, Kaya, Riera; Altintop (Yilmaz B 39), Inan S, Felipe Melo, Amrabat; Bulut, Elmander (Colak 42).
*CFR Cluj:* (442) Mario Felgueiras; Sepsi (Rada 53), Cadu R, Piccolo, Ivo Pinto; Luis Alberto, Aguirregaray■, Godemeche, Camora; Bastos (Nicoara 71), Kapetanos (Muresan 78).

**Manchester U (1) 3** *(Hernandez 25, Evans 62, Hernandez 75)*
**Braga (2) 2** *(Alan 2, 20)*                      73,195
*Manchester U:* (4312) De Gea; Da Silva, Carrick, Evans, Buttner; Kagawa (Nani 46), Fletcher D, Cleverley; Rooney; Hernandez (Giggs 79), van Persie.
*Braga:* (4231) Beto; Leandro Salino, Nuno Andre, Paulo Vinicius, Echijile; Custodio, Hugo Viana; Ruben Amorim (Helder Barbosa 80), Alan (Mossoro 86), Ruben Micael (Ze Luis 88); Eder.

Wednesday, 7 November 2012
**Braga (0) 1** *(Alan 49 (pen))*
**Manchester U (0) 3** *(van Persie 80, Rooney 85 (pen), Hernandez 90)*                         19,015
*Braga:* (4231) Beto; Leandro Salino, Nuno Andre, Douglao, Echijile (Ze Luis 90); Custodio, Hugo Viana (Mossoro 86); Alan, Ruben Micael, Ruben Amorim (Helder Barbosa 80); Eder.
*Manchester U:* (4312) De Gea; Valencia A, Smalling, Evans (Ferdinand 58), Evra; Nani (Da Silva 73), Anderson, Giggs; Rooney; Hernandez, Welbeck (van Persie 64).

**CFR Cluj (0) 1** *(Sougou 53)*
**Galatasaray (1) 3** *(Yilmaz B 18, 61, 74)*       19,520
*CFR Cluj:* (4411) Mario Felgueiras; Ivo Pinto, Sepsi (Bastos 31), Piccolo, Cadu R; Camora, Muresan, Godemeche (Bjelanovic 46), Luis Alberto; Kapetanos (Diogo Valente 76); Sougou.
*Galatasaray:* (442) Muslera; Cris, Nounkeu, Eboue, Altintop (Kaya 90); Inan S, Riera, Kurtulus (Sarioglu 89), Colak; Yilmaz B, Bulut (Amrabat 76).

Tuesday, 20 November 2012
**CFR Cluj (3) 3** *(Rui Pedro 7, 15, 33)*
**Braga (1) 1** *(Alan 17)*                         13,000
*CFR Cluj:* (4231) Mario Felgueiras; Ivo Pinto, Cadu R, Piccolo, Rada; Luis Alberto, Muresan; Sougou (Aguirregaray 74), Rui Pedro (Kapetanos 81), Camora; Bastos (Godemeche 82).
*Braga:* (433) Beto; Leandro Salino (Helder Barbosa 33), Douglao■, Nuno Andre, Ismaily; Ruben Micael, Custodio, Hugo Viana (Mossoro 69); Alan, Eder (Ze Luis 57), Ruben Amorim.

**Galatasaray (0) 1** *(Yilmaz B 54)*
**Manchester U (0) 0**                              43,000
*Galatasaray:* (442) Muslera; Eboue, Kaya, Nounkeu, Riera; Altintop, Inan S, Felipe Melo, Amrabat (Colak 81); Yilmaz B (Bulut 90), Elmander (Baytar 63).
*Manchester U:* (4231) Lindegaard; Da Silva, Jones, Carrick, Buttner; Anderson (Young 74), Fletcher D; Cleverley, Powell (Macheda 74), Welbeck (King 85); Hernandez.

Wednesday, 5 December 2012
**Braga (1) 1** *(Mossoro 32)*
**Galatasaray (0) 2** *(Yilmaz B 58, Yilmaz A 79)*  13,000
*Braga:* (4231) Quim; Leandro Salino, Nuno Andre, Paulo Vinicius, Echijile; Custodio (Hugo Viana 80), Ruben Amorim; Alan, Mossoro, Ismaily; Eder (Carlao 86).
*Galatasaray:* (442) Muslera; Eboue, Nounkeu, Riera; Altintop (Yilmaz A 46), Felipe Melo, Inan S, Colak (Bulut 69); Yilmaz B, Elmander (Amrabat 46).

**Manchester U (0) 0**
**CFR Cluj (0) 1** *(Luis Alberto 56)*              71,521
*Manchester U:* (433) De Gea; Jones, Wootton, Smalling, Buttner; Powell (Macheda 73), Cleverley (Scholes 45); Giggs (Fletcher D 86); Welbeck, Rooney, Hernandez.
*CFR Cluj:* (442) Mario Felgueiras; Ivo Pinto, Cadu R, Piccolo, Rada; Muresan, Luis Alberto, Rui Pedro (Aguirregaray 71), Camora; Sougou (Kapetanos 90), Bastos (Maftei 78).

| Group H Table | P | W | D | L | F | A | GD | Pts |
|---|---|---|---|---|---|---|---|---|
| Manchester U | 6 | 4 | 0 | 2 | 9 | 6 | 3 | 12 |
| Galatasaray | 6 | 3 | 1 | 2 | 7 | 6 | 1 | 10 |
| CFR Cluj | 6 | 3 | 1 | 2 | 9 | 7 | 2 | 10 |
| Braga | 6 | 1 | 0 | 5 | 7 | 13 | −6 | 3 |

## KNOCK-OUT STAGE

**ROUND OF 16 FIRST LEG**

Tuesday, 12 February 2013

**Celtic (0) 0**
**Juventus (1) 3** *(Matri 3, Marchisio 77, Vucinic 83)*   57,917
*Celtic:* (4411) Forster; Lustig (Matthews 58), Wilson, Ambrose, Izaguirre; Forrest, Brown (Kayal 80), Wanyama, Mulgrew; Commons (Watt 73); Hooper.
*Juventus:* (352) Buffon; Barzagli, Bonucci, Caceres; Lichtsteiner, Vidal, Pirlo, Marchisio, Peluso (Padoin 69); Matri (Pogba 80), Vucinic (Anelka 85).

**Valencia (0) 1** *(Rami 90)*
**Paris St Germain (2) 2** *(Lavezzi 10, Pastore 43)*   55,000
*Valencia:* (451) Guaita; Joao Pereira, Rami, Ricardo Costa, Guardado; Feghouli (Viera J 83), Ever (Canales 46), Parejo, Tino Costa, Jonas (Haedo Valdez 46); Soldado.
*Paris St Germain:* (442) Sirigu; Jallet, Alex, Sakho, Maxwell; Lucas Moura (Chantome 53), Matuidi, Verratti, Pastore (Armand 88); Ibrahimovic Z■, Lavezzi (Menez 76).

Wednesday, 13 February 2013

**Real Madrid (1) 1** *(Ronaldo 30)*
**Manchester U (1) 1** *(Welbeck 20)*   85,454
*Real Madrid:* (4231) Diego Lopez; Arbeloa, Sergio Ramos, Varane, Fabio Coentrao; Khedira, Alonso (Pepe 83); Di Maria (Modric 75), Ozil, Ronaldo; Benzema (Higuain 64).
*Manchester U:* (4411) De Gea; Da Silva, Ferdinand, Evans, Evra; Welbeck (Valencia A 73), Carrick, Jones, Kagawa (Giggs 64); Rooney (Anderson 84); van Persie.

**Shakhtar Donetsk (1) 1** *(Srna 31, Douglas Costa 68)*
**Borussia Dortmund (1) 2** *(Lewandowski 41, Hummels 87)*   52,000
*Shakhtar Donetsk:* (4231) Pyatov; Srna, Rakitskiy, Chygrynskiy, Rat; Fernandinho, Hubschman; Alex Teixeira (Eduardo 83), Mkhitaryan, Taison (Douglas Costa 62); Luiz Adriano.
*Borussia Dortmund:* (4231) Weidenfeller; Piszczek, Felipe Santana, Hummels, Schmelzer; Kehl, Bender; Blaszczykowski (Leitner 80), Gotze, Reus (Schieber 90); Lewandowski.

Tuesday, 19 February 2013

**Arsenal (0) 1** *(Podolski 55)*
**Bayern Munich (2) 3** *(Kroos 7, Muller 21, Mandzukic 77)*   59,974
*Arsenal:* (4231) Szczesny; Sagna, Mertesacker, Koscielny, Vermaelen; Arteta, Wilshere; Ramsey (Rosicky 71), Cazorla, Podolski (Giroud 71); Walcott.
*Bayern Munich:* (4231) Neuer; Lahm, Van Buyten, Dante, Alaba; Javi Martinez, Schweinsteiger; Muller, Kroos (Gustavo L 73), Ribery (Robben 63); Mandzukic (Gomez 78).

**FC Porto (0) 1** *(Joao Moutinho 56)*
**Malaga (0) 0**   26,000
*FC Porto:* (433) Helton; Danilo, Otamendi, Mangala, Alex Sandro L; Gonzalez (Andre Castro 90), Fernando, Joao Moutinho; Izmailov (Atsu 70), Martinez, Varela (Rodriguez 58).
*Malaga:* (442) Willy; Sergio Sanchez, Demichelis, Weligton, Antunes; Toulalan, Iturra (Camacho 78), Joaquin (Portillo 63), Isco; Julio Baptista (Piazon 78), Santa Cruz.

Wednesday, 20 February 2013

**AC Milan (0) 2** *(Boateng 57, Muntari 81)*
**Barcelona (0) 0**   75,000
*AC Milan:* (433) Abbiati; Abate, Mexes, Zapata, Constant; Ambrosini, Montolivo, Muntari; Boateng, Pazzini (Niang 75), El Shaarawy (Traore 88).
*Barcelona:* (433) Valdes V; Dani Alves, Pique, Puyol (Mascherano 88), Jordi Alba; Xavi, Busquets, Fabregas (Sanchez 62); Pedro, Messi, Iniesta.

**Galatasaray (1) 1** *(Yilmaz B 12)*
**Schalke 04 (1) 1** *(Jones 45)*   45,000
*Galatasaray:* (442) Muslera; Sarioglu (Bulut 84), Kaya, Nounkeu, Riera; Altintop (Eboue 66), Felipe Melo, Inan S, Sneijder (Amrabat 46); Yilmaz B, Drogba.
*Schalke 04:* (442) Hildebrand; Hoger, Howedes, Matip, Kolasinac; Draxler (Barnetta 84), Jones, Neustadter, Michel Bastos; Farfan, Huntelaar (Pukki 75).

**ROUND OF 16 SECOND LEG**

Tuesday, 5 March 2013

**Borussia Dortmund (2) 3** *(Felipe Santana 31, Gotze 37, Blaszczykowski 59)*
**Shakhtar Donetsk (0) 0**   80,645
*Borussia Dortmund:* (4231) Weidenfeller; Piszczek, Subotic N, Felipe Santana, Schmelzer; Gundogan (Sahin 82), Bender (Kehl 46); Blaszczykowski (Grosskreutz 69), Gotze, Reus; Lewandowski.
*Shakhtar Donetsk:* (4231) Pyatov; Srna, Rakitskiy, Kucher, Rat; Fernandinho, Hubschman (Stepanenko 82); Alex Teixeira, Mkhitaryan, Taison (Douglas Costa 46); Luiz Adriano.

**Manchester U (0) 1** *(Sergio Ramos 48 (og))*
**Real Madrid (0) 2** *(Modric 66, Ronaldo 69)*   74,959
*Manchester U:* (4231) De Gea; Da Silva (Valencia A 87), Vidic, Ferdinand, Evra; Carrick, Cleverley (Rooney 73); Nani■, Welbeck (Young 80), Giggs; van Persie.
*Real Madrid:* (4231) Diego Lopez; Arbeloa (Modric 59), Varane, Sergio Ramos, Fabio Coentrao; Khedira, Alonso; Di Maria (Kaka R 45), Ozil (Pepe 71), Ronaldo; Higuain.

Wednesday, 6 March 2013

**Juventus (1) 2** *(Matri 24, Quagliarella 65)*
**Celtic (0) 0**   35,000
*Juventus:* (352) Buffon; Barzagli, Marrone, Bonucci, Padoin, Vidal (Isla 67), Pirlo (Giaccherini 69), Pogba, Peluso (Asamoah 59); Quagliarella, Matri.
*Celtic:* (451) Forster; Matthews (Forrest 52), Wilson, Kayal, Izaguirre; Commons (Nouioui 73), Wanyama (Ambrose 46), Ledley, Mulgrew, Samaras; Hooper.

**Paris St Germain (0) 1** *(Lavezzi 66)*
**Valencia (0) 1** *(Jonas 55)*   43,000
*Paris St Germain:* (442) Sirigu; Jallet (Van Der Wiel 27), Thiago Silva, Alex, Maxwell; Chantome, Thiago Motta (Gameiro 58), Matuidi, Pastore; Lucas Moura (Sakho 83), Lavezzi.
*Valencia:* (4231) Guaita; Barragan, Mathieu, Victor Ruiz, Cissokho; Parejo, Albelda (Ever 46); Feghouli (Piatti 63), Tino Costa, Jonas (Haedo Valdez 76); Soldado.

Tuesday, 12 March 2013

**Barcelona (2) 4** *(Messi 5, 40, Villa 55, Jordi Alba 90)*
**AC Milan (0) 0**   96,000
*Barcelona:* (433) Valdes V; Dani Alves, Pique, Mascherano (Puyol 77), Jordi Alba; Xavi, Busquets, Iniesta; Pedro (Adriano 83), Messi, Villa (Sanchez 74).
*AC Milan:* (433) Abbiati; Abate I, Mexes, Zapata, Constant; Montolivo, Ambrosini (Muntari 60), Flamini (Bojan 75); Niang (Robinho 60), Boateng, El Shaarawy.

**Schalke 04 (1) 2** *(Neustadter 17, Michel Bastos 63)*
**Galatasaray (2) 3** *(Altintop 37, Yilmaz B 42,‾ Bulut 90)*   52,000
*Schalke 04:* (4231) Hildebrand; Uchida, Howedes, Matip, Kolasinac; Hoger (Meyer 86), Neustadter (Fuchs C 46); Farfan, Draxler, Michel Bastos; Pukki (Obasi Ogbuke 85).
*Galatasaray:* (4132) Muslera; Eboue, Kaya (Zan 78), Nounkeu, Riera; Felipe Melo; Altintop, Sneijder (Amrabat 70), Inan S; Drogba, Yilmaz B (Bulut 86).

Wednesday, 13 March 2013
**Bayern Munich (0) 0**
**Arsenal (1) 2** *(Giroud 3, Koscielny 86)* 66,000
*Bayern Munich:* (4231) Neuer; Lahm, Van Buyten, Dante, Alaba; Javi Martinez, Gustavo L; Muller, Kroos (Tymoschuk 81), Robben; Mandzukic (Gomez 73).
*Arsenal:* (433) Fabianski; Jenkinson, Mertesacker, Koscielny, Gibbs; Arteta, Rosicky, Ramsey (Gervinho 72); Walcott (Oxlade-Chamberlain 72), Giroud, Cazorla.

**Malaga (1) 2** *(Isco 43, Santa Cruz 77)*
**FC Porto (0) 0** 35,000
*Malaga:* (442) Willy; Jesus Gamez, Demichelis, Weligton, Antunes; Joaquin (Camacho 88), Toulalan, Iturra, Isco; Julio Baptista (Santa Cruz 73), Saviola (Piazon 79).
*FC Porto:* (433) Helton; Danilo, Otamendi, Mangala, Alex Sandro (Atsu 70); Joao Moutinho (Rodriguez 46), Fernando, Gonzalez; Varela (Maicon 58), Martinez, Defour■.

### QUARTER-FINALS FIRST LEG

Tuesday, 2 April 2013
**Bayern Munich (1) 2** *(Alaba 1, Muller 63)*
**Juventus (0) 0** 66,000
*Bayern Munich:* (4231) Neuer; Lahm, Van Buyten, Dante, Alaba; Schweinsteiger, Gustavo L; Muller, Kroos (Robben 16), Ribery (Shaqiri 90); Mandzukic (Gomez 90).
*Juventus:* (352) Buffon; Barzagli, Bonucci, Chiellini; Lichtsteiner, Vidal, Pirlo, Marchisio, Peluso (Pogba 75); Matri A (Vucinic 65), Quagliarella (Giovinco 65).

**Paris St Germain (0) 2** *(Ibrahimovic 79, Matuidi 90)*
**Barcelona (1) 2** *(Messi 38, Xavi 89 (pen))* 45,000
*Paris St Germain:* (442) Sirigu; Jallet, Alex, Thiago Silva, Maxwell; Beckham (Verratti 70), Matuidi, Lucas Moura, Pastore (Gameiro 76); Ibrahimovic, Lavezzi (Menez 66).
*Barcelona:* (433) Valdes V; Dani Alves, Pique, Mascherano (Bartra 84), Jordi Alba; Xavi, Busquets, Iniesta; Sanchez, Messi (Fabregas 46), Villa (Tello 81).

Wednesday, 3 April 2013
**Malaga (0) 0**
**Borussia Dortmund (0) 0** 28,963
*Malaga:* (4231) Willy; Jesus Gamez, Demichelis, Weligton, Antunes; Toulalan, Iturra; Joaquin, Saviola (Portillo 67), Isco (Duda 87); Julio Baptista (Santa Cruz 76).
*Borussia Dortmund:* (4231) Weidenfeller; Piszczek, Subotic N, Felipe Santana, Schmelzer; Gundogan, Kehl (Bender 79); Reus (Schieber 69), Gotze (Kirch 90), Grosskreutz; Lewandowski.

**Real Madrid (2) 3** *(Ronaldo 9, Benzema 29, Higuain 73)*
**Galatasaray (0) 0** 80,000
*Real Madrid:* (4231) Diego Lopez; Essien, Sergio Ramos, Varane, Fabio Coentrao; Alonso, Khedira; Di Maria (Pepe 86), Ozil (Modric 80), Ronaldo; Benzema (Higuain 65).
*Galatasaray:* (442) Muslera; Eboue, Kaya, Nounkeu, Riera (Amrabat 83); Altintop (Bulut 78), Felipe Melo, Sneijder (Zan 46), Inan S; Yilmaz B, Drogba.

### QUARTER-FINALS SECOND LEG

Tuesday, 9 April 2013
**Borussia Dortmund (1) 3** *(Lewandowski 40, Reus 90, Felipe Santana 90)*
**Malaga (1) 2** *(Joaquin 25, Eliseu 82)* 65,000
*Borussia Dortmund:* (4231) Weidenfeller; Piszczek, Subotic N, Felipe Santana, Schmelzer; Gundogan (Hummels 86), Bender (Sahin 72); Blaszczykowski (Schieber 72), Gotze, Reus; Lewandowski.
*Malaga:* (4411) Willy; Jesus Gamez, Demichelis, Sergio Sanchez, Antunes; Joaquin (Portillo 87), Toulalan, Camacho, Duda (Eliseu 74); Isco; Julio Baptista (Santa Cruz 83).

**Galatasaray (0) 3** *(Eboue 57, Sneijder 71, Drogba 72)*
**Real Madrid (1) 2** *(Ronaldo 8, 90)* 52,000
*Galatasaray:* (4312) Muslera; Eboue (Elmander 80), Zan, Kaya, Riera; Altintop (Amrabat 46), Felipe Melo, Inan S; Sneijder; Bulut (Sarioglu 63), Drogba.
*Real Madrid:* (4231) Diego Lopez; Essien (Arbeloa■ 31), Pepe, Varane, Fabio Coentrao; Khedira, Modric; Di Maria, Ozil (Albiol 81), Ronaldo; Higuain (Benzema 73).

Wednesday, 10 April 2013
**Barcelona (0) 1** *(Pedro 71)*
**Paris St Germain (0) 1** *(Pastore 50)* 78,000
*Barcelona:* (433) Valdes V; Dani Alves, Pique, Adriano (Bartra 62), Jordi Alba; Xavi, Busquets, Iniesta; Pedro, Fabregas (Messi 62), Villa (Song 83).
*Paris St Germain:* (442) Sirigu; Jallet (Van Der Wiel 88), Alex, Thiago Silva, Maxwell; Lucas Moura, Verratti (Beckham 83), Thiago Motta, Pastore; Ibrahimovic, Lavezzi (Gameiro 81).

**Juventus (0) 0**
**Bayern Munich (0) 2** *(Mandzukic 64, Pizarro 90)* 38,000
*Juventus:* (352) Buffon; Barzagli, Bonucci, Chiellini; Padoin (Isla 69), Pogba, Pirlo, Marchisio (Giaccherini 79), Asamoah; Quagliarella (Matri A 66), Vucinic.
*Bayern Munich:* (4231) Neuer; Lahm, Van Buyten (Boateng 35), Dante, Alaba; Javi Martinez, Schweinsteiger; Robben, Muller, Ribery (Gustavo L 80); Mandzukic (Pizarro 83).

### SEMI-FINALS FIRST LEG

Tuesday, 23 April 2013
**Bayern Munich (1) 4** *(Muller 25, 82, Gomez 49, Robben 73)*
**Barcelona (0) 0** 68,000
*Bayern Munich:* (4231) Neuer; Lahm, Boateng, Dante, Alaba; Javi Martinez, Schweinsteiger; Robben, Muller (Pizarro 83), Ribery (Shaqiri 88); Gomez (Gustavo L 71).
*Barcelona:* (433) Valdes V; Dani Alves, Pique, Bartra, Jordi Alba; Xavi, Busquets, Iniesta; Sanchez, Messi, Pedro (Villa 83).

Wednesday, 24 April 2013
**Borussia Dortmund (1) 4** *(Lewandowski 8, 50, 55, 67 (pen))*
**Real Madrid (1) 1** *(Ronaldo 43)* 65,829
*Borussia Dortmund:* (4231) Weidenfeller; Piszczek (Grosskreutz 83), Subotic N, Hummels, Schmelzer; Bender, Gundogan (Schieber 90); Blaszczykowski (Kehl 82), Gotze, Reus; Lewandowski.
*Real Madrid:* (4231) Diego Lopez; Sergio Ramos, Varane, Pepe, Fabio Coentrao; Khedira, Alonso (Kaka R 80); Ozil, Modric (Di Maria 68), Ronaldo; Higuain (Benzema 68).

### SEMI-FINALS SECOND LEG

Tuesday, 30 April 2013
**Real Madrid (0) 2** *(Benzema 82, Sergio Ramos 88)*
**Borussia Dortmund (0) 0** 76,000
*Real Madrid:* (4231) Diego Lopez; Essien, Varane, Sergio Ramos, Fabio Coentrao (Kaka R 57); Modric, Alonso (Khedira 67); Di Maria, Ozil, Ronaldo; Higuain (Benzema 67).
*Borussia Dortmund:* (4231) Weidenfeller; Piszczek, Subotic N, Hummels, Schmelzer; Gundogan, Bender (Felipe Santana 90); Blaszczykowski, Gotze (Grosskreutz 14), Reus; Lewandowski (Kehl 87).

Wednesday, 1 May 2013
**Barcelona (0) 0**
**Bayern Munich (0) 3** *(Robben 48, Pique 72 (og), Muller 76)* 90,000
*Barcelona:* (433) Valdes V; Dani Alves, Pique, Bartra (Montoya 87), Adriano; Xavi (Sanchez 55), Song, Iniesta (Thiago 65); Villa, Fabregas, Pedro.
*Bayern Munich:* (4231) Neuer; Lahm (Rafinha 77), Boateng, Van Buyten, Alaba; Javi Martinez (Tymoschuk 74), Schweinsteiger (Gustavo L 66); Robben, Muller, Ribery; Mandzukic.

### CHAMPIONS LEAGUE FINAL
Saturday, 25 May 2013

(at Wembley, 86,298)

**Borussia Dortmund (0) 1** *(Gundogan 67 (pen))*     **Bayern Munich (0) 2** *(Mandzukic 60, Robben 89)*

*Borussia Dortmund:* (4231) Weidenfeller; Piszczek, Subotic N, Hummels, Schmelzer; Bender (Sahin 90), Gundogan; Blaszczykowski (Schieber 90), Reus, Grosskreutz; Lewandowski.

*Bayern Munich:* (4231) Neuer; Lahm, Boateng, Dante, Alaba; Javi Martinez, Schweinsteiger; Robben, Muller, Ribery (Gustavo L 90); Mandzukic (Gomez 90).

*Referee:* Nicola Rizzoli.

Bayern Munich's Dutch winger Arjen Robben skips past Borussia Dortmund's Mats Hummels before scoring the winning goal in Munich's 2-1 Champions League Final victory over their German rivals at Wembley. (Action Images)

# EUROPEAN CUP-WINNERS' CUP
# FINALS 1961–99

| Year | Winners | | Runners-up | | Venue | Attendance | Referee |
|------|---------|---|-----------|---|-------|-----------|---------|
| 1961 | Fiorentina | 2 | Rangers | 0 *(1st Leg)* | Glasgow | 80,000 | Steiner (A) |
| | Fiorentina | 2 | Rangers | 1 *(2nd Leg)* | Florence | 50,000 | Hernadi (H) |
| 1962 | Atletico Madrid | 1 | Fiorentina | 1 | Glasgow | 27,389 | Wharton (S) |
| *Replay* | Atletico Madrid | 3 | Fiorentina | 0 | Stuttgart | 38,000 | Tschenscher (WG) |
| 1963 | Tottenham Hotspur | 5 | Atletico Madrid | 1 | Rotterdam | 49,000 | Van Leuwen (Ho) |
| 1964 | Sporting Lisbon | 3 | MTK Budapest | 3 *(aet)* | Brussels | 3000 | Van Nuffel (Bel) |
| *Replay* | Sporting Lisbon | 1 | MTK Budapest | 0 | Antwerp | 19,000 | Versyp (Bel) |
| 1965 | West Ham U | 2 | Munich 1860 | 0 | Wembley | 100,000 | Szolt (H) |
| 1966 | Borussia Dortmund | 2 | Liverpool | 1 *(aet)* | Glasgow | 41,657 | Schwinte (F) |
| 1967 | Bayern Munich | 1 | Rangers | 0 *(aet)* | Nuremberg | 69,480 | Lo Bello (I) |
| 1968 | AC Milan | 2 | Hamburg | 0 | Rotterdam | 53,000 | Ortiz (Sp) |
| 1969 | Slovan Bratislava | 3 | Barcelona | 2 | Basle | 19,000 | Van Ravens (Ho) |
| 1970 | Manchester C | 2 | Gornik Zabrze | 1 | Vienna | 8,000 | Schiller (A) |
| 1971 | Chelsea | 1 | Real Madrid | 1 *(aet)* | Athens | 42,000 | Scheurer (Sw) |
| *Replay* | Chelsea | 2 | Real Madrid | 1 *(aet)* | Athens | 35,000 | Bucheli (Sw) |
| 1972 | Rangers | 3 | Moscow Dynamo | 2 | Barcelona | 24,000 | Ortiz (Sp) |
| 1973 | AC Milan | 1 | Leeds U | 0 | Salonika | 45,000 | Mihas (Gr) |
| 1974 | Magdeburg | 2 | AC Milan | 0 | Rotterdam | 4000 | Van Gemert (Ho) |
| 1975 | Dynamo Kiev | 3 | Ferencvaros | 0 | Basle | 13,000 | Davidson (S) |
| 1976 | Anderlecht | 4 | West Ham U | 2 | Brussels | 58,000 | Wurtz (F) |
| 1977 | Hamburg | 2 | Anderlecht | 0 | Amsterdam | 65,000 | Partridge (E) |
| 1978 | Anderlecht | 4 | Austria/WAC | 0 | Paris | 48,679 | Adlinger (WG) |
| 1979 | Barcelona | 4 | Fortuna Dusseldorf | 3 *(aet)* | Basle | 58,000 | Palotai (H) |
| 1980 | Valencia | 0 | Arsenal | 0 | Brussels | 36,000 | Christov (Cz) |
| | *(aet; Valencia won 5-4 on penalties)* | | | | | | |
| 1981 | Dynamo Tbilisi | 2 | Carl Zeiss Jena | 1 | Dusseldorf | 9000 | Lattanzi (I) |
| 1982 | Barcelona | 2 | Standard Liege | 1 | Barcelona | 100,000 | Eschweiler (WG) |
| 1983 | Aberdeen | 2 | Real Madrid | 1 *(aet)* | Gothenburg | 17,804 | Menegali (I) |
| 1984 | Juventus | 2 | Porto | 1 | Basle | 60,000 | Prokop (EG) |
| 1985 | Everton | 3 | Rapid Vienna | 1 | Rotterdam | 50,000 | Casarin (I) |
| 1986 | Dynamo Kiev | 3 | Atletico Madrid | 0 | Lyon | 39,300 | Wohrer (A) |
| 1987 | Ajax | 1 | Lokomotiv Leipzig | 0 | Athens | 35,000 | Agnolin (I) |
| 1988 | Mechelen | 1 | Ajax | 0 | Strasbourg | 39,446 | Pauly (WG) |
| 1989 | Barcelona | 2 | Sampdoria | 0 | Berne | 45,000 | Courtney (E) |
| 1990 | Sampdoria | 2 | Anderlecht | 0 | Gothenburg | 20,103 | Galler (Sw) |
| 1991 | Manchester U | 2 | Barcelona | 1 | Rotterdam | 42,000 | Karlsson (Se) |
| 1992 | Werder Bremen | 2 | Monaco | 0 | Lisbon | 16,000 | D'Elia (I) |
| 1993 | Parma | 3 | Antwerp | 1 | Wembley | 37,393 | Assenmacher (G) |
| 1994 | Arsenal | 1 | Parma | 0 | Copenhagen | 33,765 | Krondl (CzR) |
| 1995 | Zaragoza | 2 | Arsenal | 1 | Paris | 42,424 | Ceccarini (I) |
| 1996 | Paris St Germain | 1 | Rapid Vienna | 0 | Brussels | 37,500 | Pairetto (I) |
| 1997 | Barcelona | 1 | Paris St Germain | 0 | Rotterdam | 45,000 | Merk (G) |
| 1998 | Chelsea | 1 | Stuttgart | 0 | Stockholm | 30,216 | Braschi (I) |
| 1999 | Lazio | 2 | Mallorca | 1 | Villa Park | 33,021 | Benko (A) |

# INTER-CITIES FAIRS CUP FINALS 1958–71

*(Winners in italics)*

| Year | First Leg | Attendance | Second Leg | Attendance |
|------|-----------|-----------|------------|-----------|
| 1958 | London 2 Barcelona 2 | 45,466 | *Barcelona* 6 London 0 | 62,000 |
| 1960 | Birmingham C 0 Barcelona 0 | 40,500 | *Barcelona* 4 Birmingham C 1 | 70,000 |
| 1961 | Birmingham C 2 Roma 2 | 21,005 | *Roma* 2 Birmingham C 0 | 60,000 |
| 1962 | Valencia 6 Barcelona 2 | 65,000 | Barcelona 1 *Valencia* 1 | 60,000 |
| 1963 | Dynamo Zagreb 1 Valencia 2 | 40,000 | *Valencia* 2 Dynamo Zagreb 0 | 55,000 |
| 1964 | *Zaragoza* 2 Valencia 1 | 50,000 | (in Barcelona) | |
| 1965 | *Ferencvaros* 1 Juventus 0 | 25,000 | (in Turin) | |
| 1966 | Barcelona 0 Zaragoza 1 | 70,000 | Zaragoza 2 *Barcelona* 4 | 70,000 |
| 1967 | Dynamo Zagreb 2 Leeds U 0 | 40,000 | Leeds U 0 *Dynamo Zagreb* 0 | 35,604 |
| 1968 | Leeds U 1 Ferencvaros 0 | 25,368 | Ferencvaros 0 *Leeds U* 0 | 70,000 |
| 1969 | Newcastle U 3 Ujpest Dozsa 0 | 60,000 | Ujpest Dozsa 2 *Newcastle U* 3 | 37,000 |
| 1970 | Anderlecht 3 Arsenal 1 | 37,000 | *Arsenal* 3 Anderlecht 0 | 51,612 |
| 1971 | Juventus 0 Leeds U 0 *(abandoned 51 minutes)* | 42,000 | | |
| | Juventus 2 Leeds U 2 | 42,000 | *Leeds U* 1* Juventus 1 | 42,483 |

# UEFA CUP FINALS 1972–97

*(Winners in italics)*

| Year | First Leg | Attendance | Second Leg | Attendance |
|---|---|---|---|---|
| 1972 | Wolverhampton W 1 Tottenham H 2 | 45,000 | *Tottenham H* 1 Wolverhampton W 1 | 48,000 |
| 1973 | Liverpool 0 Moenchengladbach 0 *(abandoned 27 minutes)* | 44,967 | | |
| | Liverpool 3 Moenchengladbach 0 | 41,169 | Moenchengladbach 2 *Liverpool* 0 | 35,000 |
| 1974 | Tottenham H 2 Feyenoord 2 | 46,281 | *Feyenoord* 2 Tottenham H 0 | 68,000 |
| 1975 | Moenchengladbach 0 Twente 0 | 45,000 | Twente 1 *Moenchengladbach* 5 | 24,500 |
| 1976 | Liverpool 3 FC Brugge 2 | 56,000 | FC Brugge 1 *Liverpool* 1 | 32,000 |
| 1977 | Juventus 1 Athletic Bilbao 0 | 75,000 | Athletic Bilbao 2 *Juventus* 1* | 43,000 |
| 1978 | Bastia 0 PSV Eindhoven 0 | 15,000 | *PSV Eindhoven* 3 Bastia 0 | 27,000 |
| 1979 | Red Star Belgrade 1 Moenchengladbach 1 | 87,500 | *Moenchengladbach* 1 Red Star Belgrade 0 | 45,000 |
| 1980 | Moenchengladbach 3 Eintracht Frankfurt 2 | 25,000 | *Eintracht Frankfurt* 1* Moenchengladbach 0 | 60,000 |
| 1981 | Ipswich T 3 AZ 67 Alkmaar 0 | 27,532 | AZ 67 Alkmaar 4 *Ipswich T* 2 | 28,500 |
| 1982 | Gothenburg 1 Hamburg 0 | 42,548 | Hamburg 0 *Gothenburg* 3 | 60,000 |
| 1983 | Anderlecht 1 Benfica 0 | 45,000 | Benfica 1 *Anderlecht* 1 | 80,000 |
| 1984 | Anderlecht 1 Tottenham H 1 | 40,000 | *Tottenham H* 1[1] Anderlecht 1 | 46,258 |
| 1985 | Videoton 0 Real Madrid 3 | 30,000 | *Real Madrid* 0 Videoton 1 | 98,300 |
| 1986 | Real Madrid 5 Cologne 1 | 80,000 | Cologne 2 *Real Madrid* 0 | 15,000 |
| 1987 | Gothenburg 1 Dundee U 0 | 50,023 | Dundee U 1 *Gothenburg* 1 | 20,911 |
| 1988 | Espanol 3 Bayer Leverkusen 0 | 42,000 | *Bayer Leverkusen* 3[2] Espanol 0 | 22,000 |
| 1989 | Napoli 2 Stuttgart 1 | 83,000 | Stuttgart 3 *Napoli* 3 | 67,000 |
| 1990 | Juventus 3 Fiorentina 1 | 45,000 | Fiorentina 0 *Juventus* 0 | 32,000 |
| 1991 | Internazionale 2 Roma 0 | 68,887 | Roma 1 *Internazionale* 0 | 70,901 |
| 1992 | Torino 2 Ajax 2 | 65,377 | *Ajax* 0* Torino 0 | 40,000 |
| 1993 | Borussia Dortmund 1 Juventus 3 | 37,000 | *Juventus* 3 Borussia Dortmund 0 | 62,781 |
| 1994 | Salzburg 0 Internazionale 1 | 47,500 | *Internazionale* 1 Salzburg 0 | 80,326 |
| 1995 | Parma 1 Juventus 0 | 23,000 | Juventus 1 *Parma* 1 | 80,750 |
| 1996 | Bayern Munich 2 Bordeaux 0 | 62,000 | Bordeaux 1 *Bayern Munich* 3 | 36,000 |
| 1997 | Schalke 1 Internazionale 0 | 56,824 | Internazionale 1 *Schalke* 0[3] | 81,670 |

*\*won on away goals*    [1]*aet; Tottenham H won 4-3 on penalties*    [2]*aet; Bayer Leverkusen won 3-2 on penalties*
[3]*aet; Schalke won 4-1 on penalties*

# UEFA CUP FINALS 1998–2009

| Year | Winners | | Runners-up | | Venue | Attendance | Referee |
|---|---|---|---|---|---|---|---|
| 1998 | Internazionale | 3 | Lazio | 0 | Paris | 42,938 | Nieto (Sp) |
| 1999 | Parma | 3 | Marseille | 0 | Moscow | 61,000 | Dallas (S) |
| 2000 | Galatasaray | 0 | Arsenal | 0 | Copenhagen | 38,919 | Nieto (Sp) |
| | *(aet; Galatasaray won 4-1 on penalties)* | | | | | | |
| 2001 | Liverpool | 5 | Alaves | 4 | Dortmund | 65,000 | Veissiere (F) |
| | *(aet; Liverpool won on sudden death)* | | | | | | |
| 2002 | Feyenoord | 3 | Borussia Dortmund | 2 | Rotterdam | 45,000 | Pereira (P) |
| 2003 | Porto | 3 | Celtic | 2 | Seville | 52,972 | Michel (Slo) |
| | *(aet)* | | | | | | |
| 2004 | Valencia | 2 | Marseille | 0 | Gothenburg | 40,000 | Collina (I) |
| 2005 | CSKA Moscow | 3 | Sporting Lisbon | 1 | Lisbon | 48,000 | Poll (E) |
| 2006 | Sevilla | 4 | Middlesbrough | 0 | Eindhoven | 36,500 | Fandel (G) |
| 2007 | Sevilla | 2 | Espanyol | 2 | Glasgow | 50,670 | Busacca (Sw) |
| | *(aet; Sevilla won 3-1 on penalties)* | | | | | | |
| 2008 | Zenit St Petersburg | 2 | Rangers | 0 | Manchester | 43,878 | Fröjdfeldt (Se) |
| 2009 | Shakhtar Donetsk | 2 | Werder Bremen | 1 | Istanbul | 40,000 | Chantalejo (Sp) |
| | *(aet)* | | | | | | |

# UEFA EUROPA LEAGUE FINALS 2010–13

| Year | Winners | | Runners-up | | Venue | Attendance | Referee |
|---|---|---|---|---|---|---|---|
| 2010 | Atletico Madrid | 2 | Fulham | 1 | Hamburg | 49,000 | Rizzoli (I) |
| | *(aet)* | | | | | | |
| 2011 | Porto | 1 | Braga | 0 | Dublin | 45,391 | Carballo (Sp) |
| 2012 | Atletico Madrid | 3 | Athletic Bilbao | 0 | Bucharest | 52,347 | Stark (G) |
| 2013 | Chelsea | 2 | Benfica | 1 | Amsterdam | 53,000 | Kuipers (H) |

# UEFA EUROPA LEAGUE 2012–13

■ *Denotes player sent off.*

**FIRST QUALIFYING ROUND FIRST LEG**

**Tuesday, 3 July 2012**

**Skendija 79 (0) 0**

**Portadown (0) 0** 1324

*Skendija 79:* (4231) Nikov; Elmazovski (Aliji 56), Neziri, Berisha, Cuculi; Mustafi, Demiri; Selmani, Emini (Hasan 76), Taipi; Ejupi (Redzepi 84).
*Portadown:* (442) Miskelly; Casement, Gartland, Breen, Redman; Mackle, McCafferty, McNeill, Tomelty (Lecky 30); Murray, Braniff.

**Vikingur (0) 0**

**Gomel (0) 6** *(Hleb 53, 55, Voronkov 57, Aleksiyevich 58, Kashewski 69, Lyavitski 80)* 450

*Vikingur:* (4141) Turi; Gregersen, Lambanum, Hansen B, Jacobsen E (Ble 51); Niclasen (Hansen Hedin 62); Jacobsen H, Vatinhammar, Djurhuus (Bassene 70), Bartalstovu; Hansen Hjartvard.
*Gomel:* (4231) Ostojic; Kashevsky, Kuzmenok, Kirilchik, Klimovich; Matveychik (Timoshenko 68), Nowak (Levitskiy 46); Voronkov, Aleksievich, Demidovich (Platonov 58); Hleb.

**Thursday, 5 July 2012**

**Bangor C (0) 0**

**Zimbru Chisinau (0) 0** 1022

*Bangor C:* (451) Idzi; Brownhill, Brewerton, Johnston, Roberts; Edwards (Jones 68), Allen, Garside, Smyth (Morley 77), Davies; Simm (Bull 68).
*Zimbru Chisinau:* (4141) Calancea; Balasa, Cuznetov, Derkach A, Zastavnyi; Tumbasevic (Iavorschi 46); Gorceac, Barakhoev (Slivca 77), Korgalidze (Shishkin 70), Catan; Molla.

**Birkirkara (0) 2** *(Jou Silva 53, Triganza 87)*

**Metalurg Skopje (1) 2** *(Nestorovski 2, Curlinov 55)* 610

*Birkirkara:* (4321) Gauci; Camenzuli, Vukanac, Pereira, Zerafa; Scicluna (Zammit 89), Muscat, Fenech; Jou Silva, Joselito dos Reis (Triganza 76); Shodiya.
*Metalurg Skopje:* (442) Pacovski; Petkovski, Krstev, Kralevski, Ljamcevski B; Ljamcevski P (Tenekedziev 52), Stevanovic, Dimoski, Alomerovic; Nestorovski (Naumovski 65), Curlinov (Peev 81).

**Bohemians (0) 0**

**Thor Akureyri (0) 0** 1253

*Bohemians:* (4141) McNulty; Heary, McMillan, Feely, Byrne; McEvoy; Buckley, Mulcahy (Traynor 84), Ward, McMahon (Scully 58); Wilson (Moore 77).
*Thor Akureyri:* (442) Rajkovic; Albertsson Andri (Stromberg 76), Albertsson Atli, Vrenko, Funicello; Jonsson, Kristjansson, Hjaltalin (Aevarsson 66), Hjaltason; Hilmarsson I, Hannesson J (Bjornsson 76).

**Borac Banja Luka (2) 2** *(Stokic 39, Dugic 42)*

**Celik Niksic (1) 2** *(Bojic 36 (pen), Agovic 83)* 5000

*Borac Banja Luka:* (451) Avdukic; Stupar (Zizovic 30), Milic, Markovic, Zaric; Stokic (Radulovic O 64), Krunic, Grahovac, Zivkovic (Dujakovic Sinisa■ 78), Kantar■; Dugic.
*Celik Niksic:* (4231) Banovic; Bojic, Bulatovic, Radovic, Dubljevic; Adrovic, Bulajic; Zoric D (Nikolic 92), Ivanovic, Simic (Agovic 63); Jovovic (Brnovic 46).

**Cefn Druids (0) 0**

**MYPA (0) 0** 813

*Cefn Druids:* (541) Mullock; Harris, Hesp, James, Edwards G, Darlington; Dures (Price 74), Hughes, Quinn, Burke (Duckett 89); Jones S (Cann 80).
*MYPA:* (433) Kuismala; Koskinen, Nongatamba, Aho (Vuorinen 37), Vesala; Gela, Ramadingaye, Saxman (O'Shaughnessy 78); Oksanen, O'Neill, Kukka (Sihvola 62).

**Cliftonville (0) 1** *(Boyce 71)*

**Kalmar (0) 0** 1106

*Cliftonville:* (4231) Brown R; McGovern, Cosgrove, Smyth, Scannell R; Caldwell (O'Carroll 69), Catney; Garrett (Lynch 90), McMullan, Donnelly; Gormley (Boyce 69).
*Kalmar:* (442) Berisha; Ohman, Arajuuri, Thorthevic, Skjelvik; Diouf, Rydstrom, Thorbjornsson (Hallberg 79), Israelsson; McDonald (Andersson 70), Dauda (Soderqvist 70).

**Crusaders (0) 0**

**Rosenborg (1) 3** *(Dorsin 19, 76, Dockal 71)* 862

*Crusaders:* (442) O'Neill; McKeown, Leeman, Magowan, McBride; Owens (McAllister 83), Caddell■, Watson, Heatley (McClean 72); Adamson, Rainey (Snoddy 86).
*Rosenborg:* (4411) Orlund; Ankersen, Vagan, Wangberg (Hoiland 68), Dorsin; Dockal, Issah, Henriksen, Svensson; Chibuike (Midtsjo 77); Iversen (Prica 55).

**Dacia Chisinau (1) 1** *(Sow 42)*

**Celje (0) 0** 4052

*Dacia Chisinau:* (4231) Matiughin; Dimovski, Popovici, Celio Santos, Mamah; Krkotic, Cojocari; Mihailov (Stjepanovic 81), Guira, Caraus (Orbu■ 61); Sow (Sali 90).
*Celje:* (442) Kotnik; Zitko, Krajcer, Gaber, Gobec (Centrih 76); Mocic, Kolsi, Vrhovec, Bajde (Romih 59); Bezjak, Mocivnik (Verbic 43).

**Differdange 03 (2) 3** *(Kettenmeyer 31, Bettmer 41, Er Rafik 47)*

**NSI Runavik (0) 0** 820

*Differdange 03:* (442) Weber; Franzoni, Bukvic, Siebenaler (Ribeiro PA 71), Rodrigues; Bastos, Kettenmeyer, Lebresne (Janisch 53), Bettmer; Er Rafik, Caron (Piskor 80).
*NSI Runavik:* (433) Joensen K; Jacobsen M, Joensen J, Joensen P, Jacobsen S; Frederiksberg Andras, Arge, Mortensen; Olsen M (Liknargotu 82), Olsen K, Frederiksberg Arni.

**EB/Streymur (3) 3** *(Hanssen L 9 (pen), 33 (pen), Samuelson 25)*

**Gandzasar Kapan (0) 1** *(Correia 72)* 523

*EB/Streymur:* (433) Torgard; Hansen G, Olsen A, Hansen P, Danielsen; Hanssen L, Dam (Olsen B 68), Samuelsen; Frederiksberg, Hansen Arnbjorn, Niclasen.
*Gandzasar Kapan:* (352) Khachatryan; Avagyan A, Tatintsyan, Obradovic; Diakaridia (Sargsyan 62), Vukomanovic (Seedorf 54), Kasule, Krasovski, Diego Lomba; Keita (Nasibyan 75), Correia.

**FC Santa Coloma (0) 0**

**Osijek (0) 1** *(Milicevic 77)* 400

*FC Santa Coloma:* (4231) Eloy Casals; Fite, Ribolleda, Sonejee, Sanchez Javier (Jimenez 70); Pousa, Rebes; Romero (Garcia 63), Sanchez Juli, Mota (Mercade 60); Urbani.
*Osijek:* (4231) Vargic; Ibriks, Vrgoc, Smoje, Leskovic; Pusic, Kurtovic; Kvrzic (Misic M 89), Jugovic, Petrovic (Milicevic 41); Perosevic (Zulim 81).

**FC Twente (2) 6** *(Schilder 28, 29, Tadic 63, John 71, Plet 77, 79)*

**UE Santa Coloma (0) 0** 18,000

*FC Twente:* (433) Boschker; Breukers, Roseler, Wisgerhof, Kuiper (Fer 64); Brama, Janssen (Tadic 46), Schilder; Verhoek (Chadli 46), Plet, John.
*UE Santa Coloma:* (4231) Perianes; Lopez (Pedescoll 94), Gutierrez, Orosa, Rubio; Rodriguez V, Sirvan; Salvat■, Codina (Alonso 77), Bernat; Riera (Vall 69).

**FH Hafnarfijordur (1) 2** *(Ingason 44, Bjornsson 81)*

**USV Eschen-Mauren (0) 1** *(Fassler 48)* 1290

*FH Hafnarfijordur:* (4231) Gunnleifsson; Antoniusson, Bjarnason, Vidarsson, Thomas (Gudmundsson 72); Runarsson, Gunnlaugsson (Ingvarsson 80); Palsson (Bjornsson 62), Sverrisson, Gudnason; Ingason.
*USV Eschen-Mauren:* (4231) Buchel; Fisch, Simma, Manojlovic, Barandun; Fassler, Batir; Huber (Giger 46), Christen, Istrefi (Ospelt 90); Dulundu (Kuster 88).

**FK Baku (0) 0**

**Mura 05 (0) 0** 3024

*FK Baku:* (442) Mammadov A; Rodriguez, Ivanovs, Kargbo, Maharramov; Cesnauskis, Horvat (Mammadov E 61), Kovacevic, Solic (Hajiyev 55); Verpakovskis (Parks 69), Juninho.
*Mura 05:* (4231) Luk; Kramar, Marusko, Cipot, Janza; Horvat, Sres; Bohar, Eterovic, Fajic; Jelic (Gruskovnjak 77).

**Flamurtari (0) 0**

**Budapest Honved (0) 1** *(Vernes 46)* 6000

*Flamurtari:* (4411) Koliqi; Arberi, Veliu, Brahja, Mici; Progmi (Kuqi 61), Pezo, Lena, Telushi; Sosa (Memelli 61); Pejic.
*Budapest Honved:* (4231) Kemenes; Lovric, Debreceni, Ignjatovic, Vidovic; Hidi (Diarra 69), Tchami (Barath 85); Vernes (Diaby 58), Johnson, Ivancsics; Delczeg.

**IF Elfsborg (5) 8** *(Hult 5, 24, 26 (pen), Jawo 10, Nilsson 37, Claesson 51, Frick 54, Larsson 62)*

**Floriana (0) 0** 2653

*IF Elfsborg:* (442) Ellegaard; Larsson, Jorgensen, Jonsson, Klarstrom (Wede 58); Claesson, Rohden, Svensson, Hult (Holmen 66); Nilsson (Frick 46), Jawo.
*Floriana:* (442) Borg Jurgen; Pisani, Borg M, Farrugia T■, Micallef; Borg Joseph (Borg S 17), Borg C, Farrugia B, Paris; Caruana (Brincat 84), Woods (Darmanin 78).

**Jagodina (0) 0**

**Ordabasy Shymkent (0) 1** *(Mansour 85)* 4000

*Jagodina:* (442) Bondzulic; Dukic, Tomic, Zivanovic, Projic; Djenic (Nikodijevic 71), Gogic, Stojkov, Stojkovic (Milenkovic 83); Stojanovic, Mudrinski (Kostic 68).
*Ordabasy Shymkent:* (4231) Bekbaev; Adyrbekov, Trajkovic, Mwesigwa, Larbi Arouri; Karpovich, Kasyanov; Mansour, Ashirbeko (Beysenov 73), Pakholyuk (Thilas 84); Tazhimbetov (Babatunde 66).

**JJK Jyvaskyla (1) 2** *(Gruborovics 16, Wusu 66)*

**Stabaek (0) 0** 1817

*JJK Jyvaskyla:* (4411) Korhonen; Markkula (Turpeenniemi 66), Pasoja, Reintam, van Gelderen; Manninen (Hilska 91), Poutiainen, Gruborovics, Innanen; Virtanen (Tuomanen 55); Wusu.
*Stabaek:* (442) Sayouba; Hedenstad, Cunningham, Hammer, Eiriksson; Brustad, Kleiven, Clark (Sortevik 79), Haugsdal; Haidar (Stengel 68), Boli (Stokkelien 83).

**KF Tirana (2) 2** *(Mucollari 40, Ferraj 45)*

**Grevenmacher (0) 0** 3000

*KF Tirana:* (4231) Lika I; Kalari, Pisha, Pashaj, Ahmataj; Duro (Cota 66), Mucollari; Lika G, Taku, Ferraj (Tushe 65); Balaj (Morina 89).
*Grevenmacher:* (4231) Schaab; Battaglia, Heinz, Brzyski, Hoffmann; Bechtold, Furst; Schiltz (Herres 86), Steffen (Goncalo Almeida 38), Louadj; Huss (Gaspar 69).

**KuPS Kuopio (2) 2** *(Joenmaki 5 (pen), Purje 19)*

**Llanelli (1) 1** *(Bowen J 45)* 1870

*KuPS Kuopio:* (433) Hilander; Karkkainen, Tabe, Nissinen, Berg (Venalainen 62); Hynynen, Joenmaki, Obiefule; Ilo, James (Puri 46), Purje (Voutilainen 85).
*Llanelli:* (442) Morris; Thomas, Surman, Venables, Grist; Bowen J, Corbisiero, Evans A, Kellaway (Williams 55); Bowen L (Evans S 90), Rose.

**La Fiorita (0) 0**

**Liepajas Metalurgs (1) 2** *(Leliuga 40, Solonicins 90)* 416

*La Fiorita:* (4132) Montanari; Bucchi, Enakarhire, Bollini G, Mazzola; Confalone; Cavalli, Bollini F (Bellocchi 53), Perrotta; Guidi (Fucili 68), Parma (Forcellini 69).
*Liepajas Metalurgs:* (4231) Steinbors; Zirnis (Leliuga 34), Baguzis, Mihadjuks, Surnins; Krjauklis, Klava; Afanasjevs (Sadcins 90), Savalnieks, Solonicins; Kamess (Gucs 75).

**Lech Poznan (0) 2** *(Murawski 61, Lovrencsics 65)*

**Zhetysu Taldykorgan (0) 0** 23,108

*Lech Poznan:* (4231) Kotorowski; Mozdzen, Wolakiewicz, Kaminski, Henriquez; Tralka (Murawski 54), Drewniak; Lovrencsics, Krivets (Ubiparip 46), Tonev (Kielb 85); Slusarski.

*Zhetysu Taldykorgan:* (433) Loginovskiy; Mukanov, Mihajlov, Dautov, Djalovic; Kostic, Dobrasinovic, Skoryh (Spanov 81); Junuzovic (Shchetkin 70), Belic, Muzhikov (Kumisbekov 70).

**Levadia Tallinn (0) 1** *(Juvenal (og))*

**Siauliai (0) 0** 850

*Levadia Tallinn:* (442) Smishko; Kulinits, Artjunin, Morozov, Podholjuzin; Pebre (Toomet 84), Kaljumae, Antonov, Subbotin; Hunt, Taar.
*Siauliai:* (4141) Jurevicius; Bartkus, Rimavicius, Lunskis, Juvenal; Kirhners; Kozlovs, Vezevicius (Jasaitis 83), Eliosius (Hvorostianov 69), Cesanelli; Rimkevicius.

**MTK Budapest (1) 1** *(Lazok 30)*

**FK Senica (0) 1** *(Blackburn 58)* 800

*MTK Budapest:* (4231) Hegedus; Wolfe, Kalnoki-Kis■, Kelemen, Hidvegi; Zsidai, Vukmir; Csiki (Nikhazi 60), Kanta, Racz (Vass 81); Lazok (Tischler 83).
*FK Senica:* (433) Kamesch; Krizko, Brabec, Pavlik, Kalabiska; Kona, Wijlaars, Durica (Ventura 92); Divis (Bolinha 75), Hosek (Janso 90), Blackburn.

**Olimpija Ljubljana (0) 3** *(Ivelja 53, Franklin 76, 90)*

**Jeunesse Esch (0) 0** 2000

*Olimpija Ljubljana:* (433) Dzafic; Delamea-Mlinar (Jovic 46), Sretenovic, Zarifovic, Salkic; Trifkovic, Ivelja, Radujko; Sporar, Nikezic (Valencic 84), Skerjanc (Franklin 52).
*Jeunesse Esch:* (442) Oberweis; Moreira, Hoffmann, Portier, Collette; Benichou (Ibrahimovic 64), Miceli, Agovic D, Benajiba (Agovic E 87); Quere, Ndongala (Ramdedovic 82).

**Pyunik (0) 0**

**Zeta (0) 3** *(Vujacic 61, Pelicic Z 81, Orlandic 90)* 2545

*Pyunik:* (4231) Ohanyan; Hovsepyan, Voskanyan, Hovhannisyan G, Hovhannisyan A; Poghosyan Gagik (Malakyan 75), Yuspashyan; Hovhannisyan K, Bakalyan (Hovhannisyan H53), Poghosyan Ghukas (Minasyan 57); Ayvazyan.
*Zeta:* (442) Bulatovic; Radulovic MM, Vujacic, Radulovic MB, Novovic; Doslak, Zlaticanin, Burzanovic, Bozovic (Kalacevic 89); Boljevic (Pelicic Z 80), Orlandic.

**Renova (2) 4** *(Bajrami 10 (pen), 14 (pen), 83, Skenderi 60)*

**Libertas (0) 0** 612

*Renova:* (4321) Zendeli; Siljanovski, Ristov, Stepanovski, Simovski; Nuhiu, Emini (Skenderi 55), Bajrami; Gafuri, Pandev (Fetai 85); Andonov (Ismaili 50).
*Libertas:* (532) Ceccoli; Molinari (Vagnetti 65), Mastronicola, Torelli, Simoncini D, Benvenuti; Facondini, Rocchi, Antonelli; Fantini (Zennaro 76), de Luigi (Morelli 61).

**Rudar Pljevlja (0) 0**

**Shirak (0) 1** *(Ly 71)* 400

*Rudar Pljevlja:* (442) Vuklis; Nestorovic, Adzic, Ivanovic, Igumanovic (Bakoc 80); Kalutherovic, Alic, Vlahovic, Jovanovic M; Jovanovic I, Stojanovic (Neric 64).
*Shirak:* (4231) Harutyunyan; Grigoryan, Mkoyan, Kadio, Hovhannisyan; Maradyan (Tigranyan 71), Davtyan T; Diop (Mkrtchyan 80), Barikyan, Ly; Fofana (Hakobyan 88).

**Sarajevo (2) 5** *(Suljic 2, Torlak 45, Karamatic 54 (pen), Hadzic 79, Tatomirovic 90)*

**Hibernians (2) 2** *(Farrugia 20, Soares 33)* 7000

*Sarajevo:* (433) Adilovic; Gujic, Tatomirovic, Torlak, Tadejevic (Karamatic 46); Comor (Hadzic 68), Sesar, Zlatkovic; Suljic, Haskic, Husejinovic (Sunjevaric 82).
*Hibernians:* (4141) Muscat M; Pulis, Vandelannoite, Camilleri, Rodolfo Soares■; Kristensen; Herrera, Jackson, Cohen (Caruana 85), Marcelo (Pisani 77); Farrugia.

**St Patrick's Ath (1) 1** *(Fagan 39)*

**IBV Vestmannaeyjar (0) 0** 1652

*St Patrick's Ath:* (4141) Clarke; O'Brien, Browne, Kenna, Bermingham; Chambers; O'Connor (Flood 87), Bolger, Russell, Meenan; Fagan (Kelly D 48).
*IBV Vestmannaeyjar:* (4411) Dhaira; Baldock, Guthjonsson, Christiansen, Garner; Mawejje (Olafsson Arnor 83), Thorarinsson, Jeffs (Thorvardarson 89), Valdimarsson; Guthmundsson T; Olsen (Spear 43).

**Suduva (0) 0**
**FC Daugava (0) 1** *(Kovaljovs 87)* 15,500
*Suduva:* (4231) Davidovs; Borovskij, Lohinov, Radzius, Slavickas; Leimonas, Chvedukas; Urbsys (Soblinskas 68), Rafael Gaucho, Eliosius; Luksys (Beniusis 61).
*FC Daugava:* (442) Ikstens; Sokolovs, Tsintsadze, Mihalj, Polovinchuk; Kovaljovs (Silagailis 88), Mamaev (Yashin 59), Logins, Zizilevs; Gongadze (Volkovs 67), Ibe.

**Teuta (0) 0**
**Metalurgi Rustavi (0) 3** *(Tatanashvili 77, Kvaratskhelia 84, 90 (pen))* 850
*Teuta:* (442) Rizvani; Jakupi, Sheta, Osmani (Bakiasi 70), Buiu; Deliallisi, Hoxha A, Veliaj, Nika; Dosti (Eminhaziri 72), Mancaku (Pajaziti 63).
*Metalurgi Rustavi:* (451) Bediashvili; Kakushadze (Tekturmanidze 46), Kvaratskhelia, Makhviladze, Sukhiashvili; Japaridze, Maisuradze, Razmadze, Dobrovolski (Mikaberidze 60), Getsadze; Sikharulidze (Tatanashvili 75).

**Torpedo Kutaisi (0) 1** *(Sabanadze 62)*
**Aktobe (0) 1** *(Bikmaev 82)* 5160
*Torpedo Kutaisi:* (4231) Migineishvili; Rigvava, Kvakhadze, Gamezardashvili, Guruli; Datunaishvili, Digmelashvili; Dolidze (Ioseliani 75), Kukhianidze (Pantsulaia 81), Sabanadze; Gotsiridze (Bolkvadze 58).
*Aktobe:* (4411) Narzikulov; Klimavicius (Badlo 76), Smakov, Logvinenko, Kenzhisariev; Bajer (Lisenkov 90), Kapadze, Covalciuc, Bikmaev; Khayrullin; Geynrikh (Zemlianukhin 28).

**Trans Narva (0) 0**
**Inter Baku (2) 5** *(Tskhadadze 11, 35, Mammadov 62, Adamia 70, Hajiyev 76 (pen))* 300
*Trans Narva:* (442) Malkov; Kazakov, Kitto, Abramenko, Grigorjev; Leontovits (Borisovs 63), Kuplovs-Oginskis, Gruznov (Kutuzov 61), Medeckis; Gussev (Skinjov 85), Alekseev.
*Inter Baku:* (4231) Lomaia; Abdoulaye, Abramidze, Levin, Kandelaki; Georgievski, Dashdemirov; Tskhadadze (Tales 73), Niasse, Mammadov (Hajiyev 67); Adamia (Genov 82).

**Xazar Lankaran (2) 2** *(Subasic 7, Scarlatache 30)*
**Nomme Kalju (1) 2** *(Wakui 5, Puri 70)* 15,500
*Xazar Lankaran:* (442) Agayev; Bonfim, Scarlatache, Abishov, Allahverdiyev; Pit, Alviz, Amirguliyev, Tounkara (Vilana 71); Subasic, Brenes.
*Nomme Kalju:* (442) Teles; Sisov, Barengrub, Rodrigues, Kallaste; Konsa (Melts 85), Ceesay, Puri, Quintieri (Jevdokimov 87); Viikmae, Wakui.

**FIRST QUALIFYING ROUND SECOND LEG**
Tuesday, 10 July 2012
**Floriana (0) 0**
**IF Elfsborg (1) 4** *(Moback 19, Hiljemark 50, Frick 67, Claesson 77)* 266
*Floriana:* (442) Borg Jurgen; Paris, Borg S, Pisani, Farrugia B; Borg C, Micallef, Caruana (Brincat 72), Woods; Borg M, Darmanin.
*IF Elfsborg:* (442) Andersson A; Moback, Holmen. S, Andersson M, Wede; Rohden (Claesson 68), Hiljemark (Ishizaki 65), Hedlund, Jawo; Frick, Abdulrahman.

**Grevenmacher (0) 0**
**KF Tirana (0) 0** 546
*Grevenmacher:* (433) Schaab; Braun, Brzyski, Henry, Hoffmann; Battaglia (Huss 67), Bechtold, Furst; Goncalo Almeida (Brandao 79), Schiltz (Gaspar 83), Louadj.
*KF Tirana:* (4321) Lika I; Kalari, Pisha■, Pashaj, Ahmataj (Dabulla 93); Taku, Karabeci, Mucollari; Lika G, Ferraj (Tushe 51 (Cota 70)); Balaj.

**Nomme Kalju (0) 0**
**Xazar Lankaran (1) 2** *(Abishov 41, Subasic 85)* 1281
*Nomme Kalju:* (442) Teles; Sisov, Barengrub, Rodrigues, Kallaste; Konsa, Ceesay, Puri (Jevdokimov 80), Quintieri; Viikmae, Wakui.

**Xazar Lankaran:** (4231) Agayev; Bonfim, Scarlatache, Allahverdiyev, Todorov; Abishov, Amirguliyev; Tounkara (Brenes 84), Alviz, Pit (Abdullayev 92); Subasic (Vilana 88).

**Portadown (0) 2** *(Lecky 45, Redman 80)*
**Skendija 79 (1) 1** *(Cuculi 4)* 1029
*Portadown:* (442) Miskelly; Casement, Gartland, Breen, Redman; Mackle (O'Hara 84), McCafferty, McNeill, Lecky; Murray, Braniff.
*Skendija 79:* (4231) Velii; Berisha (Hasan 84), Neziri, Miskovski, Cuculi; Mustafi, Demiri; Selmani, Taipi, Aliji (Redzepi 80); Ejupi (Emini 61).

Thursday, 12 July 2012
**Aktobe (0) 1** *(Bikmaev 75)*
**Torpedo Kutaisi (0) 0** 12,632
*Aktobe:* (4141) Sidelnikov; Badlo, Smakov, Primus, Kenzhisariev; Logvinenko; Bajer (Klimavicius 90), Kapadze, Covalciuc, Bikmaev (Lisenkov 87); Khayrullin (Zemlianukhin 90).
*Torpedo Kutaisi:* (4231) Migineishvili; Rigvava, Kvakhadze, Gamezardashvili, Guruli; Datunaishvili, Digmelashvili (Pirtskhalava 57); Dolidze (Grigalashvili 63), Bolkvadze, Sabanadze; Gotsiridze (Tugushi 79).

**Budapest Honved (1) 2** *(Vernes 45, Tchami 57)*
**Flamurtari (0) 0** 1877
*Budapest Honved:* (4231) Kemenes; Lovric, Debreceni, Ignjatovic, Vidovic; Hidi, Johnson; Vernes (Diaby 71), Ivancsics (Diarra 84), Tchami (Faggyas 84); Delczeg.
*Flamurtari:* (4123) Koliqi; Arberi, Veliu, Rajovic, Mici; Pezo; Telushi (Cela 73), Lena; Sosa (Pepa 70), Pejic (Kuqi 84), Memelli.

**Celik Niksic (0) 1** *(Milic (og) 54)*
**Borac Banja Luka (0) 1** *(Grahovac 58)* 2684
*Celik Niksic:* (4321) Banovic; Dubljevic, Bojic, Radovic, Bulatovic; Zoric (Nikolic 91), Adrovic, Bulajic; Ivanovic, Kasapi (Simic 65); Jovovic (Agovic 46).
*Borac Banja Luka:* (442) Avdukic; Zivkovic■, Markovic, Milic, Zaric; Krunic, Zizovic (Radulovic O 56), Grahovac, Radulovic A (Kunic 81); Dugic (Dujakovic Stefan 36), Stokic.

**Celje (0) 0**
**Dacia Chisinau (1) 1** *(Mihailov 32 (pen))* 3065
*Celje:* (4231) Kotnik; Krajcer, Centrih (Gaber 60), Zitko, Gobec; Romih (Verbic 46), Kolsi; Mocic, Vrhovec, Bajde (Mocivnik 70); Bezjak.
*Dacia Chisinau:* (4231) Gaiduchevici; Dimovski, Popovici, Celio Santos, Mamah; Krkotic, Cojocari; Mihailov, Guira (Grosu 66), Josan (Stjepanovic 80); Sow (Sali■ 59).

**FC Daugava (0) 2** *(Ibe 52, 54)*
**Suduva (2) 3** *(Soblinskas 8, Rafael Gaucho 45, 84)* 1034
*FC Daugava:* (442) Ikstens; Sokolovs, Tsintsadze, Mihalj, Polovinchuk; Kovaljovs, Mamaev (Yashin 56), Logins, Zizilevs (Gongadze 87); Volkovs (Ulyanov 86), Ibe.
*Suduva:* (4231) Davidovs; Soblinskas, Lohinov, Urba (Luksys 78), Slavickas; Leimonas, Chvedukas; Urbsys, Rafael Gaucho (Lasevicius 90), Eliosius (Breive 83); Beniusis.

**FK Senica (0) 2** *(Blackburn 72, Kalabiska 72)*
**MTK Budapest (0) 1** *(Kanta 51 (pen))* 2788
*FK Senica:* (433) Kamesch; Krizko, Brabec, Pavlik, Kalabiska; Kona, Wyljaars, Durica (Janso 90); Divis (Bolinha 90), Hosek (Diarrassouba 60), Blackburn.
*MTK Budapest:* (4231) Hegedus; Wolfe, Vukmir, Kelemen, Hidvegi; Zsidai, Vadnai■; Konyves, Kanta, Racz (Csiki 46); Lazok (Nikhazi 74).

**Gandzasar Kapan (0) 2** *(Avagyan H 67, Lomba 72)*
**EB/Streymur (0) 0** 2156
*Gandzasar Kapan:* (4231) Beglaryan; Manucharyan (Seedorf R 51), Obradovic, Tatintsyan, Avagyan A; Kasule, Vukomanovic (Sargsyan 65); Nasibyan (Avagyan H 61), Correia, Diego Lomba; Keita.

*EB/Streymur:* (433) Torgard; Frederiksberg, Olsen A, Hansen G, Niclasen (Hansen Arnbjorn 90); Hansen P, Dam (Hansen Johannes 80), Danielsen (Olsen B 74); Anghel, Samuelsen, Hanssen L.

**Gomel (0) 4** *(Demidovich 49, 56, Kashevsky 71, Timoshenko 88)*

**Vikingur (0) 0**                    7234

*Gomel:* (4231) Sakovich; Evseenko (Matveychik 46), Tsyenchen, Kirilchik, Kashevsky; Kozeka, Levitskiy; Timoshenko, Demidovich, Nowak (Hleb 46 (Yakhno 64)); Platonov.

*Vikingur:* (4231) Turi; Hansen Bardur, Gregersen, Jacobsen E, Jacobsen H; Niclasen (Lambanum 46), Vatinhammar; Bartalstovu, Ble, Djurhuus (Sorensen 81); Hansen Hjartvard (Lervig 90).

**Hibernians (4) 4** *(Dias 22, 35, Farrugia 40, 44)*

**Sarajevo (3) 4** *(Hadzic 13, 27, Suljic 23, Sunjevaric 90)* 722

*Hibernians:* (4132) Muscat M; Herrera, Pulis, Camilleri, Vandelannoite; Kristensen; Cohen, Jackson, Pisani (Bezzina 74); Dias, Farrugia.

*Sarajevo:* (433) Adilovic; Gujic, Tatomirovic, Torlak, Belosevic (Karamatic 46); Suljic, Sesar, Comor; Hadzic (Haskic 82), Husejinovic (Sunjevaric 67), Zlatkovic.

**IBV Vestmannaeyjar (0) 2** *(Garner 83, Birgisson 98)*

**St Patrick's Ath (0) 1** *(O'Flynn 99)*        866

*IBV Vestmannaeyjar:* (4411) Dhaira; Olafsson Arnor (Guthmundsson T 52), Guthjonsson, Christiansen, Garner; Mawejje, Thorarinsson, Jeffs (Gudmundsson G 65), Valdimarsson; Baldock; Olsen (Birgisson 81).

*St Patrick's Ath:* (4141) Clarke; O'Brien, Kenna, Browne, Bermingham; Chambers; O'Connor Sean, Forrester (Carroll 81), Bolger, Meenan (Kelly J 58); Flood (O'Flynn 68).

*aet.*

**Inter Baku (1) 2** *(Georgievski 21, Hajiyev 86)*

**Trans Narva (0) 0**                   994

*Inter Baku:* (451) Tevdoradze; Dashdemirov, Abdoulaye, Abramidze, Levin; Amirdzhanov, Adamia (Hajiyev 77), Georgievski, Niasse, Mammadov (Genov 86); Tskhadadze (Tales 60).

*Trans Narva:* (4231) Malkov; Kuplovs-Oginskis, Kitto, Abramenko, Grigorjev; Kazakov, Medeckis; Leontovits (Kutuzov 88), Alekseev, Gussev (Ovsjannikov 84); Gruznov (Borisovs 57).

**Jeunesse Esch (0) 0**

**Olimpija Ljubljana (2) 3** *(Besic 25, Sretenovic 38, Omladic 66)*                   988

*Jeunesse Esch:* (442) Oberweis; Moreira, Hoffmann, Portier, Collette (Vitali 46); Ramdedovic (Delgado 46), Miceli (Quere 61), Agovic D, Benajiba; Ibrahimovic, Ndongala.

*Olimpija Ljubljana:* (433) Seliga; Jovic, Sretenovic, Zarifovic, Salkic; Trifkovic, Radujko (Bozic 46), Lovrecic; Franklin, Besic A (Sporar 75), Valencic (Omladic 64).

**Kalmar (3) 4** *(Israelsson 10, Thorthevic 16, Dauda 38, Berisha 90 (pen))*

**Cliftonville (0) 0**                   3824

*Kalmar:* (442) Berisha; Nouri, Thorthevic, Arajuuri, Skjelvik; Hallberg, Rydstrom, Gutu (Thorbjornsson 85), Israelsson; Soderqvist (Mendes 91), Dauda (Andersson 46).

*Cliftonville:* (4231) Brown R; McGovern, Cosgrove, Smyth, Scannell R; Caldwell, Catney; Garrett (Boyce 59), McMullan, Donnelly (Gormley 78); O'Carroll (Scannell C 65).

**Libertas (0) 0**

**Renova (1) 4** *(Nuhiu 16, Jancevski 61, 64 (pen), Ismaili 87)*                   288

*Libertas:* (532) Simoncini A; Molinari, Mastronicola, Torelli, Simoncini D, Polidori (Angeli 85); Facondini (Santarini 78), Rocchi, Antonelli; Morelli, Zennaro (Fantini 65).

*Renova:* (4321) Zendeli; Velija, Stepanovski, Ristov (Asani 67), Simovski; Siljanovski, Bajrami, Nuhiu; Gafuri (Skenderi 65), Pandev (Ismaili 59); Jancevski.

**Liepajas Metalurgs (1) 4** *(Kamess 1, Afanasjevs 72, Solonicins 82 (pen), Askerov 85)*

**La Fiorita (0) 0**                   1226

*Liepajas Metalurgs:* (4231) Steinbors; Solonicins, Baguzis, Mihadjuks, Surnins; Krjauklis, Klava; Savalnieks (Hmizs 86), Afanasjevs, Leliuga (Sadcins 66); Kamess (Askerov 79).

*La Fiorita:* (4132) Montanari; Bucchi, Enakarhire, Bollini G, Mazzola; Confalone; Cavalli, Bollini F (Bellocchi[■] 63), Perrotta; Parma (Zanotti 88), Rinaldi (Fucili 82).

**Llanelli (0) 1** *(Bowen L 50 (pen))*

**KuPS Kuopio (0) 1** *(Paananen 59)*        534

*Llanelli:* (442) Morris; Thomas, Surman, Venables, Grist; Bowen J, Corbisiero, Evans A, Williams (Evans S 71); Bowen L (Kellaway 64), Rose.

*KuPS Kuopio:* (433) Hilander; Nissinen, Tabe, Joenmaki, Venalainen; Hynynen, Karkkainen, Obiefule; Ilo, James (Paananen 46), Purje.

**Metalurg Skopje (0) 0**

**Birkirkara (0) 0**                   382

*Metalurg Skopje:* (4132) Pavlovic; Petkovski, Kralevski, Dragovic, Ljamcevski B; Krstev; Dimoski (Dodevski 86), Alomerovic (Memedi 80), Stevanovic; Curlinov, Nestorovski (Naumovski 59).

*Birkirkara:* (4321) Gauci; Camenzuli (Sciberras 56), Vukanac (Triganza 77), Pereira, Zerafa; Sicluna (Camilleri 87), Muscat, Fenech; Jou Silva, Joselito dos Reis; Shodiya.

**Metalurgi Rustavi (3) 6** *(Tekturmanidze 14, 19, Tatanashvili 37, 69, Getsadze 59, Mikaberidze 73)*

**Teuta (0) 1** *(Deliallisi 65)*              995

*Metalurgi Rustavi:* (451) Bediashvili; Japaridze, Kvaratskhelia (Gavashelishvili 46), Makhviladze, Sukhiashvili (Dobrovolski 54); Tekturmanidze, Mikaberidze, Razmadze (Kavtaradze 46), Maisuradze, Getsadze; Tatanashvili.

*Teuta:* (442) Rizvani; Jakupi, Hoxha R, Sheta, Buiu; Deliallisi, Osmani, Veliaj (Hoxha A 38), Nika (Pajaziti 46); Dosti (Devolli 57), Mancaku.

**Mura 05 (1) 2** *(Eterovic 26, Fajic 83)*

**FK Baku (0) 0**                   2537

*Mura 05:* (442) Drakovic; Kramar, Marusko, Cipot, Janza; Bohar, Horvat, Kouter (Bohan 92), Sres (Gruskovnjak 80); Eterovic, Jelic (Fajic 50).

*FK Baku:* (4141) Mammadov A; Rodriguez, Ivanovs, Kargbo, Popkhadze; Kovacevic; Cesnauskis, Juninho (Novruzov 79), Hajiyev (Solic 29), Mammadov E (Verpakovskis 72); Parks.

**MYPA (3) 5** *(A Lody 25, Saxman 37, Williams 44, O'Neill 47, Opoku 70)*

**Cefn Druids (0) 0**                   1820

*MYPA:* (442) Kuismala; Vesala, Koskinen, Nongatamba (Vuorinen 60), Kukka; Opoku, Ramadingaye (O'Shaughnessy 67), Saxman, Sesay; Williams, O'Neill (Selin 67).

*Cefn Druids:* (433) Mullock; Harris, Hesp (Duckett 73), Edwards G, Darlington; Quinn (Price 60), James, Hughes; Burke, Jones S, Dures (McElmeel 56).

**NSI Runavik (0) 0**

**Differdange 03 (2) 3** *(Er Rafik 14, 45, Albanese 73)* 345

*NSI Runavik:* (433) Joensen K (Hoj 35); Jacobsen M, Joensen J, Joensen P, Jacobsen S; Frederiksberg Andras, Olsen Ma, Arge (Ellingsgaard 83); Frederiksberg Arni, Olsen K (Liknargotu 66), Mortensen.

*Differdange 03:* (442) Weber; Franzoni (Afoun 76), Bukvic, Siebenaler, Rodrigues (Meligner 69); Lebresne (Ribeiro PA 76), Bettmer, Albanese, Janisch; Piskor, Er Rafik.

**Ordabasy Shymkent (0) 0**

**Jagodina (0) 0**                  15,523

*Ordabasy Shymkent:* (442) Bekbaev; Adyrbekov, Trajkovic, Mwesigwa, Larbi Arouri; Pakholyuk, Kasyanov, Karpovich, Mansour (Kozhabaev 90); Babatunde (Thilas 84), Tazhimbetov (Beysenov 78).

*Jagodina:* (442) Bondzulic; Dukic (Nikodijevic 87), Tomic, Zivanovic[■], Projic; Stojkovic (Vukmirovic 88), Gogic, Stojkov, Djenic (Kostic 74); Stojanovic, Mudrinski.

**Osijek (1) 3** *(Kvrzic 28, Perosevic 56, Jugovic 70)*
**FC Santa Coloma (0) 1** *(Bousenine 81)* 1497
*Osijek:* (4132) Vargic; Ibriks, Vrgoc, Smoje, Leskovic; Kurtovic (Zulim 75); Kvrzic (Misic M 46), Jugovic, Petrovic; Milicevic (Novakovic S 88), Perosevic.
*FC Santa Coloma:* (4231) Eloy Casals; Fite, Ribolleda, Sanchez G, Sanchez Javier; Pousa, Rebes (Garcia 46); Bousenine, Urbani (Mota 70), Mercade; Romero (Abdian 80).

**Rosenborg (0) 1** *(Ankersen 81)*
**Crusaders (0) 0** 3688
*Rosenborg:* (442) Orlund; Hoiland, Wangberg, Vagan, Ankersen; Berntsen, Henriksen (Strandberg 46), Issah (Svensson 61), Midtsjo; Prica, Fredheim (Chibuike 70).
*Crusaders:* (4141) O'Neill; Magowan, Gibson, Coates, McClean; Watson (Snoddy 81); Owens, Adamson, Rainey, Heatley (Gargan 75); McCutcheon (McAllister 76).

**Shirak (1) 1** *(Diop D 14)*
**Rudar Pljevlja (1) 1** *(Mkoyan 11 (og))* 2655
*Shirak:* (4411) Harutyunyan; Grigoryan, Kadio, Mkoyan, Hovhannisyan; Diop, Muradyan, Davtyan T, Ly (Mkrtchyan 91); Barikyan (Tigranyan 63); Fofana (Hakobyan 82).
*Rudar Pljevlja:* (433) Vuklis; Nestorovic, Adzic, Ivanovic, Igumanovic (Rustemovic 85); Alic, Vlahovic, Popovic; Kalutherovic (Stojanovic 46), Jovanovic I (Bakoc 78), Brnovic.

**Siauliai (1) 2** *(Rimkevicius 40 (pen), Kozlovs 80)*
**Levadia Tallinn (0) 1** *(Rattel 76)* 1487
*Siauliai:* (4141) Jurevicius; Kirhners, Rimavicius, Lunskis, Juvenal (Urbelis 87); Bartkus; Kozlovs, Vezevicius (Jasaitis 83), Birskys (Eliosius 67), Cesanelli; Rimkevicius.
*Levadia Tallinn:* (442) Smishko; Kulinits, Artjunin, Morozov, Podholjuzin; Subbotin (Leitan 88), Kaljumae, Antonov, Pebre (Toomet 59); Hunt (Rattel 54), Taar.

**Stabaek (2) 3** *(Kleiven 37, Stokkelien 45 (pen), Haugsdal 64)*
**JJK Jyvaskyla (1) 2** *(van Gelderen 45, Innanen 51)* 3291
*Stabaek:* (4411) Sayouba; Hedenstad, Cunningham, Hammer, Eiriksson; Brustad, Clark (Haidar 42), Kleiven, Stengel (Hansen 59); Haugsdal; Stokkelien (Boli 78).
*JJK Jyvaskyla:* (4231) Korhonen; Markkula, Reintam, Pasoja, van Gelderen; Poutiainen, Tuomanen; Innanen (Hilska 87), Gruborovics, Virtanen (Turpeenniemi 63); Wusu.

**Thor Akureyri (2) 5** *(Kristjansson 36, 73, 90, Hjaltalin 39, Feely 50 (og))*
**Bohemians (1) 1** *(Scully 23)* 934
*Thor Akureyri:* (433) Rajkovic; Albertsson Andri, Vrenko, Albertsson Alti (Olafsson 76), Funicello; Aevarsson (Stromberg 79), Hjaltalin, Kristjansson; Jonsson, Hannesson J (Rosbergsson 88), Hjaltason.
*Bohemians:* (4141) McNulty; Feely, Feely, McMillan, Byrne; McEvoy; Buckley (Wilson 60), Martin, Ward (Moore 67), McMahon (Traynor 61); Scully.

**UE Santa Coloma (0) 0**
**FC Twente (3) 3** *(Janssen 19 (pen), Wisgerhof 29, Plet 34)* 1497
*UE Santa Coloma:* (4231) Rivas; Pedescoll, Gutierrez, Orosa, Rubio; Rodriguez V, Sirvan; Vall (Blazquez 46), Codina, Bernat (Rodriguez A 64); Riera (Jimenez 69).
*FC Twente:* (433) Boschker; Breukers, Roseler, Wisgerhof (Gortemaker 71), Kuiper; Promes, Brama (Holscher 62), Janssen; Verhoek, Plet (Born 46), John.

**USV Eschen-Mauren (0) 0**
**FH Hafnarfjordur (1) 1** *(Gudnason 12)* 510
*USV Eschen-Mauren:* (4231) Buchel; Fisch (Huber 73), Simma, Manojlovic, Barandun; Fassler, Batir; Giger, Christen, Istrefi; Dulundu.

**FH Hafnarfjordur:** (4231) Gunnleifsson; Antoniusson, Thorisson, Bjarnason, Thomas; Vidarsson, Gunnlaugsson; Runarsson (Ingvarsson 90), Sverrisson (Palsson 90), Gudnason; Ingason (Bjornsson 69).

**Zeta (1) 1** *(Radulovic MB 16)*
**Pyunik (1) 2** *(Tatoyan 19, Poghosyan Gagik 88)* 1055
*Zeta:* (4141) Bulatovic; Radulovic MM, Radulovic MB, Vujacic, Novovic; Zlaticanin (Pelicic Z 60); Doslak, Boljevic, Burzanovic, Bozovic (Kalacevic 77); Knezevic (Orlandic 68).
*Pyunik:* (4231) Ohanyan; Tatoyan (Grigoryan 46), Hovsepyan, Hovhannisyan G, Hovhannisyan A; Poghosyan Gagik, Yuspashyan; Hovhannisyan K, Bakalyan (Melkonyan 84), Voskanyan; Hovhannisyan H (Ayvazyan 58).

**Zhetysu Taldykorgan (1) 1** *(Muzhikov 44)*
**Lech Poznan (1) 1** *(Slusarski 13)* 3476
*Zhetysu Taldykorgan:* (4411) Loginovskiy; Mihajlov, Dobrasinovic, Dyakov, Mukanov (Korobov 87); Spanov (Kumisbekov 84), Kostic, Skoryh, Muzhikov; Belic (Shchetkin 67); Junuzovic.
*Lech Poznan:* (4132) Kotorowski; Mozdzen, Wolakiewicz, Kaminski, Henriquez; Drewniak; Lovrencsics (Kielb 66), Murawski, Thurthevic (Tonev 79); Ubiparip, Slusarski (Kedziora 90).

**Zimbru Chisinau (2) 2** *(Molla 29, 31)*
**Bangor C (1) 1** *(Smyth 44)* 4075
*Zimbru Chisinau:* (442) Calancea; Balasa, Cuznetov, Derkach A, Zastavnyi (Tumbasevic 55); Gorceac, Barakhoev, Shishkin (Korgalidze 71), Catan; Nikolaev (Gafina 82), Molla.
*Bangor C:* (451) Idzi; Brownhill, Brewerton, Johnston, Roberts; Jones (Simm 60), Allen, Garside (Morley 66), Edwards (Bull 55), Smyth; Davies.

## SECOND QUALIFYING ROUND FIRST LEG

Thursday, 19 July 2012
**AGF Aarhus (1) 1** *(Kure 3)*
**Dila Gori (1) 2** *(Vatsadze 34, Aladashvili 84)* 9030
*AGF Aarhus:* (442) Rasmussen; Sorin, Haland, Kure, Eckersley; Petersen, Jorgensen, Norregaard, Akharraz (Berg 75); Johannsson (Skhirtladze 75), Graulund (Devdariani 59).
*Dila Gori:* (442) Skender; Shashiashvili, Salukvadze, Tomashvili (Oniani 46), Kvirkvelia; Aladashvili, Bechvaia (Kashia 53), Arziani, Gogua; Guruli, Vatsadze (Modebadze 72).

**AIK Solna (0) 1** *(Lundberg 56)*
**FH Hafnarfjordur (1) 1** *(Gudnason 40)* 5840
*AIK Solna:* (4132) Turina; Lorentzson, Ahman-Persson, Backman, Johansson; Danielsson; Gustavsson, Quaison (Kamara 80), Lalawele (Kayongo 72); Borges, Lundberg.
*FH Hafnarfjordur:* (4231) Gunnleifsson; Antoniusson, Vidarsson, Thorisson, Thomas; Runarsson, Gunnlaugsson; Palsson (Snorrason 74), Sverrisson, Gudnason; Ingason (Bjornsson 80).

**Anzhi Makhachkala (1) 1** *(Jucilei 22)*
**Budapest Honved (0) 0** 6554
*Anzhi Makhachkala:* (442) Gaboulov V; Logashov, Samba, Joao Carlos, Zhirkov (Tagirbekov 77); Boussoufa, Ahmedov, Jucilei, Shatov (Lakhiyalov 69); Traore (Smolov 83), Eto'o.
*Budapest Honved:* (4231) Kemenes; Lovric, Ignjatovic, Debreceni, Vidovic; Hidi (Vecsei 61), Johnson; Diaby (Vernes 56), Ivancsics (Diarra 82), Tchami; Delczeg.

**APOEL Nicosia (2) 2** *(Ailton 33, Alexandrou 40)*
**FK Senica (0) 0** 16,332
*APOEL Nicosia:* (4231) Chiotis; Mario Sergio, Borda, Zuela, Alexandrou; Nuno Morais, Helio Pinto; Charalambides (Aloneftis 77), Ben Achour (Helder Sousa 76), Manduca (Adorno 90); Ailton.
*FK Senica:* (442) Svenger; Krizko (Babic 84), Brabec, Koutny, Krajcik; Divis (Blackburn 59), Wijlaars, Kona, Kalabiska (Frydek 65); Masaryk, Varadi.

**Bnei Yehuda Tel Aviv (0) 2** *(Ndlovu 82, Galvan 90)*
**Shirak (0) 0** 1894
*Bnei Yehuda Tel Aviv:* (442) Aiyenugba; Azuz, Cohen, Haddad■, Edri; Ivaskevicius, Galvan, Abu Zaid (Nachum 63); Menashe (Mori 46); Marinkovic (Agajev 77), Ndlovu.
*Shirak:* (4231) Harutyunyan; Paltajyan, Mkoyan, Kadio, Hovhannisyan; Muradyan, Tigranyan (Davtyan T 71); Diop, Hakobyan (Barikyan■ 60), Ly Y; Fofana (Mkrtchyan 83).

**Dacia Chisinau (1) 1** *(Mihailov 32)*
**IF Elfsborg (0) 0** 5405
*Dacia Chisinau:* (4231) Matiughin; Dimovski, Ilescu, Lucas, Mamah; Krkotic, Cojocari; Mihailov, Guira, Josan (Stjepanovic 61); Sow (Cairo 90).
*IF Elfsborg:* (4231) Ellegaard; Larsson, Jonsson, Jorgensen, Klarstrom; Svensson, Hiljemark; Claesson (Elm 76), Ishizaki, Hult; Nilsson.

**Differdange 03 (0) 0**
**KAA Gent (1) 1** *(Arzo 27)* 1194
*Differdange 03:* (4231) Weber; Franzoni, Bukvic, Siebenaler, Rodrigues; Lebresne, Kettenmeyer■; Ribeiro PA (Meligner 69), Bettmer (Caron 57), Janisch (May 71); Er Rafik.
*KAA Gent:* (4141) Padt; Baric, Corstjens, Melli, Mareval; Arzo; Messoudi (Foket 79), Conte, Van der Bruggen, Bruls; Kola (Arbeitman 71).

**Eskisehirspor (1) 2** *(Potuk 41, Wright 65 (og))*
**St Johnstone (0) 0** 12,675
*Eskisehirspor:* (442) Boffin; Sari, Diego Angelo, Cetin, Dede; Malecki (Eser 78), Gucer, Potuk, Zengin (Nuhiu 85); Karadeniz (Tello 69), Kamara.
*St Johnstone:* (4231) Mannus; Miller, Wright, McCracken, Davidson C; Cregg (Moon 85), Adams (May 78); Millar, Davidson M, Craig; Higgins (Hasselbaink 69).

**FC Twente (0) 1** *(Tadic 66)*
**Inter Turku (1) 1** *(Bouwman 38)* 18,100
*FC Twente:* (433) Mihaylov; Rosales, Douglas, Wisgerhof, Bengtsson (Brama 46); Fer, Schilder, Tadic; Chadli, Plet, Gyasi (Janssen 62).
*Inter Turku:* (433) Reponen; Nyman, Aho, Diallo, Lehtonen; Antunez, Bouwman (Asis 90), Paajanen (Kauppi 85); Ojala (Gnabouyou 81), Kauko, Sirbiladze.

**Hajduk Split (1) 2** *(Vukusic 34, Trebotic 58)*
**Skonto (0) 0** 22,545
*Hajduk Split:* (4141) Blazevic; Vrsajevic, Maloca, Jonjic, Jozinovic; Radosevic; Susic (Ozobic 66), Andrijasevic (Stojanovic 88), Trebotic (Kukoc 78), Caktas; Vukusic.
*Skonto:* (4411) Malins; Gjorgjievski, Savcenkovs, Maksimenko, Amirkhanov; Segundo, Fertovs, Ibragimov (Rode 72), Sinelnikovs; Blanks (Sabala 49); Labukas.

**Inter Baku (0) 1** *(Tales 45)*
**Asteras Tripolis (0) 1** *(Perrone 54)* 1000
*Inter Baku:* (541) Lomaia; Amirdzhanov, Abramidze, Abdoulaye, Levin, Kandelaki; Mammadov (Hajiyev 46), Niasse (Zlatinov 71), Georgievski, Adamia (Genov 89); Tales.
*Asteras Tripolis:* (4222) Bantis; Tsambouris, Juanito, Bartolini, Formica; Alvarez, Usero; Ximo Navarro, Fragoulakis (Bakasetas 53); Perrone (Kourbelis 91), Rayo (Pipinis 87).

**JJK Jyvaskyla (2) 3** *(Gruborovics 27 (pen), 43, 47)*
**Zeta (2) 2** *(Doslak 17, Radulovic MB 38)* 1837
*JJK Jyvaskyla:* (442) Korhonen; Markkula, Reintam, Pasoja, van Gelderen; Virtanen (Hilska 25), Tuomanen, Poutiainen, Innanen (Turpeenniemi 86); Gruborovics, Wusu (Markkanen 90).
*Zeta:* (433) Bulatovic; Radulovic MM, Vujacic, Radulovic MB, Novovic; Pelicic Z (Zlaticanin 68), Burzanovic, Bozovic (Kalacevic 90); Doslak (Dabic 70), Korac, Boljevic.

**KF Tirana (1) 1** *(Cota 38)*
**Aalesund (0) 1** *(Stewart 57)* 2310
*KF Tirana:* (4321) Lika I; Sina, Pashaj, Dushku, Ahmataj; Taku, Karabeci, Mucollari (Tushe 76); Lika G, Ferraj (Morina 76); Cota.
*Aalesund:* (451) Grytebust; Wembangomo, Tollas, Arnefjord, Matland; Stewart, Morrison, Skiri (Ulvestad 34), Carlsen (Barrantes 68), Fuhre; Skagestad (Sellin 87).

**Levadia Tallinn (0) 1** *(Morozov 82)*
**Anorthosis Famagusta (1) 3** *(Spadacio 45 (pen),*
*Laborde 55, Toni Calvo 62)* 2250
*Levadia Tallinn:* (442) Smishko; Kulinits, Artjunin, Morozov, Podholjuzin; Subbotin, Kaljumae, Antonov, Pebre (Toomet 57); Hunt (Teever 74), Taar (Rattel 61).
*Anorthosis Famagusta:* (4231) Blazic; Ilic, Colin, Paulo Jorge, Boaventura; Alexa, Laban (Ohayon 65); Toni Calvo, Juliano Spadacio, Laborde (Andic 80); Okkas (Rezek 70).

**Levski Sofia (0) 1** *(Raykov 72)*
**Sarajevo (0) 0** 12,552
*Levski Sofia:* (4231) Iliev; Mulder, Ivanov, Elie, Starokin (Prochazka 71); Angelov, Gadzhev; Cristovao, Marcinho (Joao Silva 82), Yovov (Raykov 60); Basile de Carvalho.
*Sarajevo:* (4231) Adilovic; Tatomirovic, Dupovac, Torlak, Belosevic (Tadejevic 76); Comor (Sunjevaric 76), Sesar; Suljic, Husejinovic (Karamatic 90), Zlatkovic; Hadzic.

**Liepajas Metalurgs (1) 2** *(Leliuga 43, Klava 49)*
**Legia Warsaw (1) 2** *(Kucharczyk 20, Kosecki 47)* 3106
*Liepajas Metalurgs:* (4231) Dorosevs; Zirnis■, Baguzis, Mihadjuks, Surnins (Leliuga 34); Tamosauskas, Klava; Afanasjevs (Mezs 70), Solonicins, Savalnieks; Kamess (Hmizs 90).
*Legia Warsaw:* (4141) Kuciak; Jedrzejczyk, Inaki Astiz, Zewlakow, Wawrzyniak; Lukasik (Furman 90); Kosecki, Gol (Ljuboja 76), Radovic, Zyro (Saganowski 69); Kucharczyk.

**Lokomotiv Plovdiv (1) 4** *(Todorov 24, Lazarov 49, 64,*
*Tassio 90)*
**Vitesse (2) 4** *(Reis 23, Ginkel 30, 77, Bony 53)* 1500
*Lokomotiv Plovdiv:* (4231) Gospodinov; Rodrigues, Salamastrakis, Bengelloun, Venkov; Georgiev V, Todorov; Georgiev D (Tassio 57), Zlatinski (Kiriakidis 85), Serginho (Eli Marques 72); Lazarov.
*Vitesse:* (4123) Velthuizen; Yasuda, Kalas, Kashia, van Aanholt (van der Struijk 70); van der Heijden; Hofs (Propper 62), van Ginkel; Ibarra (Chanturia 80), Bony, Reis.

**Maccabi Netanya (0) 1** *(Shivhon 75)*
**KuPS Kuopio (2) 2** *(Paananen 36, 45)* 4010
*Maccabi Netanya:* (442) Cennamo; Pinas, Krupnik, Pietrasiak, Shitrit; Tchalisher, Tamir (Sarhan 71), Manzur (Shivhon 46), Peretz; Shriki (Akel 70), Sabaa.
*KuPS Kuopio:* (433) Hilander; Karkkainen, Tabe, Nissinen, Joenmaki; Taipale, Obiefule, Paananen (James 76); Hynynen, Purje (Zahovaiko 86), Ilo (Puri 68).

**Metalurgi Rustavi (1) 1** *(Tatanashvili 29)*
**Viktoria Plzen (2) 3** *(Horvath 14, 59, Kolar 32)* 3166
*Metalurgi Rustavi:* (4231) Bediashvili; Japaridze, Gavashelishvili, Makhviladze, Sukhiashvili; Razmadze, Maisuradze; Kavtaradze (Dobrovolski 46), Mikaberidze (Sikharulidze 67), Getsadze; Tatanashvili (Janelidze 67).
*Viktoria Plzen:* (4231) Bolek; Rajtoral, Sevinsky, Prochazka, Limbersky; Horvath, Darida; Fillo (Stipek 85), Kolar (Hanousek 88), Malakyan (Zeman 65); Duris.

**Metalurh Donetsk (2) 7** *(Makrides 17, 49,*
*Ghazaryan 36, 61, 86, Danilo 51, Junior Moraes 78)*
**Celik Niksic (0) 0** 3224
*Metalurh Donetsk:* (4231) Bandura; Morozyuk, Checher, Volovik, Golaydo; Lazic, Priyma (Hryshchenko 76); Danilo (Junior Moraes 54), Makrides, Ze Soares (Nelson 64); Ghazaryan.
*Celik Niksic:* (4231) Banovic; Nikolic, Radovic, Dubljevic, Videkanic (Drincic 88); Adrovic, Bulajic; Zoric, Simic (Brnovic 86), Ivanovic (Agovic 64); Jovovic.

**Milsami-Ursidos (2) 4** *(Boghiu 16, 51,*
*Rafael Wellington 33, Gheti 87)*
**Aktobe (1) 2** *(Kapadze 8, Smakov 56)* 3000
*Milsami-Ursidos:* (4231) Negai; Rassulov, Sosnovsky,
Rafael Wellington, Bruno Simao; Elias (Gheti 68),
Casabella; Stoleru (Nurudeen 59), Boghiu, Garla;
Guilherme.
*Aktobe:* (4411) Sidelnikov; Badlo, Smakov, Logvinenko
(Primus 46), Kenzhisariev; Bajer, Kapadze, Covalciuc,
Bikmaev; Khayrullin; Geynrikh.

**Mlada Boleslav (2) 3** *(Magera 33, 43, Scuk 79)*
**Thor Akureyri (0) 0** 3867
*Mlada Boleslav:* (442) Seda; Boril, Rolko, Smejkal, Sirl;
Sivric (Ondrejka 66), Kudela, Scuk, Mares (Nespor 79);
Chramosta, Magera.
*Thor Akureyri:* (4231) Rajkovic; Albertsson Andri,
Vrenko, Albertsson Alti (Hilmarsson 46), Funicello;
Aevarsson, Hjaltalin; Jonsson (Olafsson 86),
Kristjansson, Hjaltason (Bjornsson 59); Hannesson J.

**Mura 05 (0) 0**
**CSKA Sofia (0) 0** 2500
*Mura 05:* (442) Drakovic; Majer, Kramar, Cipot,
Marusko; Bohar (Kouter 94), Jelic, Horvat■, Janza; Fajic,
Eterovic (Sres 54).
*CSKA Sofia:* (442) Cerny; Bandalovski, Popov,
Krachunov, Nilson; Njongo Priso (Karachanakov 71),
Yanev K (Sasha 80), Yanchev, Yanev H (Yovchev 84);
Andrianantenaina, Sheridan■.

**Naftan Novopolotsk (0) 3** *(Gavryushko 47 (pen), 67,*
*Zhukovskiy 76)*
**Red Star Belgrade (3) 4** *(Kasalica 9, 69, Milunovic 18, 34)*
4500
*Naftan Novopolotsk:* (4231) Dovgyallo; Gorbachyov,
Berezovskyi, Naumov, Zyulev (Obrazov 27); Bukatkin,
Trukhov; Sorokin, Cernych, Kobets (Zhukovskiy 73);
Kovalenko (Gavryushko 46).
*Red Star Belgrade:* (433) Bajkovic; Mikic, Maksimovic,
Krneta, Mladenovic; Dimitrijevic, Milivojevic, Evandro
(Cadu 71); Lazovic, Kasalica, Milunovic (Vesovic 77).

**Olimpija Ljubljana (0) 0**
**Tromso (0) 0** 2600
*Olimpija Ljubljana:* (433) Dzafic; Jovic, Sretenovic,
Zarifovic, Sarasola; Trifkovic, Radujko, Lovrecic (Salkic
90); Omladic (Valencic 62), Sporar (Nikezic 81),
Franklin.
*Tromso:* (442) Sahlman; Norbye, Bjorck, Koppinen,
Yndestad; Andersen, Johansen, Yttergard, Drage
(Nystrom 79 (Kristiansen R 88)); Ondrasek (Arst 88),
Bendiksen.

**Osijek (1) 1** *(Milicevic 5)*
**Kalmar (1) 3** *(Mendes 34, Dauda 66, Gutu 68)* 2655
*Osijek:* (4231) Vargic; Ibriks, Vrgoc, Smoje, Leskovic■;
Jugovic, Kurtovic; Milicevic (Aleksic I 66), Kvrzic
(Dugandzic 79), Petrovic (Misic J 72); Perosevic.
*Kalmar:* (442) Berisha; Nouri, Arajuuri, Thorthevic,
Skjelvik; Mendes (Hallberg 77), Rydstrom,
Thorbjornsson (Israelsson 46), Diouf (Gutu 46);
Andersson, Dauda.

**Rapid Bucharest (3) 3** *(Filipe Teixeira 8, Grigore 40,*
*Pancu 45)*
**MYPA (1) 1** *(Williams 26)* 7343
*Rapid Bucharest:* (4141) Albut; Rui Duarte, Abrudan,
Oros, Milisavljevic; Grigore; Roman (Goga 57), Grigorie
(Ilijoski 46), Filipe Teixeira (Voicu 72), Surdu; Pancu.
*MYPA:* (343) Kuismala; Aho, Koskinen, Nongatamba;
Vesala, Gela (Selin 81), Saxman (Ramadingaye 72),
Sesay (Kukka 66); Oksanen, Williams, O'Neill.

**Renova (0) 0**
**Gomel (2) 2** *(Demidovich 20, Nowak 39)* 833
*Renova:* (4321) Zendeli; Siljanovski, Ristov (Asani 46),
Stepanovski, Simovski; Nuhiu, Bajrami, Skenderi; Gafuri,
Pandev (Ismaili 46); Jancevski (Andonov 63).
*Gomel:* (4231) Ostojic; Matveychik, Kashevsky, Kirilchik,
Klimovich; Kozeka, Voronkov (Evseenko 70);
Demidovich (Yakhno 84), Levitskiy, Nowak
(Timoshenko 68); Platonov.

**Rosenborg (2) 2** *(Dockal 33, 47 (pen))*
**Ordabasy Shymkent (0) 2** *(Pakholyuk 75, Mansour 90)*
3709
*Rosenborg:* (4411) Orlund; Ankersen, Vagan,
Strandberg, Dorsin; Dockal, Issah, Henriksen, Svensson
(Iversen 70); Chibuike (Fredheim 46); Prica.
*Ordabasy Shymkent:* (4231) Bekbaev; Mwesigwa,
Trajkovic, Mukhtarov, Larbi Arouri; Karpovich,
Beysenov (Pakholyuk 46); Mansour, Kasyanov,
Babatunde (Adyrbekov 83); Tazhimbetov (Thilas 68).

**Ruch Chorzow (0) 3** *(Piech 74, 83, Starzynski 90)*
**Metalurg Skopje (0) 1** *(Memedi 69)* 3000
*Ruch Chorzow:* (442) Peskovic; Djokic, Stawarczyk,
Sadlok, Szyndrowski; Zienczuk, Malinowski, Straka
(Starzynski 57), Janoszka (Sultes 63); Jankowski (Kuswik
78), Piech.
*Metalurg Skopje:* (4411) Pavlovic; Petkovski, Kralevski,
Dragovic, Ljamcevski B; Dimoski (Dalceski 90), Krstev,
Stevanovic, Memedi; Alomerovic (Nestorovski 50);
Curlinov (Dodevski 86).

**Servette (0) 2** *(Karanovic 48, Gissi 79)*
**Gandzasar Kapan (0) 0** 5830
*Servette:* (4231) Gonzalez; Ruefli, Mfuyi, Schneider,
Moubandje; Pizzinat (Pasche 46), Kouassi; Lang (Gissi
74), Marcos de Azevedo (Moutinho 63), Treand;
Karanovic.
*Gandzasar Kapan:* (4231) Beglaryan; Krasovski
(Manucharyan 53), Tatintsyan, Obradovic, Avagyan A;
Kasule, Voukumanovic; Diego Lomba, Correia, Nasibyan
(Grigoryan 64); Keita (Seedorf 58).

**Shakhtyor Soligorsk (1) 1** *(Osipenko 63)*
**Ried (0) 1** *(Hadzic 70 (pen))* 3370
*Shakhtyor Soligorsk:* (4411) Tsygalko; Rozhkov,
Postnikov, Yanushkevich, Kolomyts; Balanovich (Tsevan
84), Grenkov, Khachaturyan, Sitko (Rios 80);
Komarovsky; Osipenko (Leonchik 88).
*Ried:* (3331) Gebauer; Reifeltshammer, Reiter, Riegler;
Hinum, Ziegl (Zulj 80), Schicker; Nacho Rodriguez
(Walch 86), Hadzic, Meilinger; Gartler (Guillem 90).

**Siroki Brijeg (0) 1** *(Wagner 90)*
**St Patrick's Ath (1) 1** *(Fagan 12)* 3629
*Siroki Brijeg:* (4231) Bilobrk; Jurcevic■, Dzidic D, Jese,
Bertosa; Serdarusic (Dzidic I 46), Zlomislic (Ricardo
Baiano 67); Coric, Wagner, Bloudek; Roskam (Kordic
55).
*St Patrick's Ath:* (4141) Clarke; O'Brien, Browne, Kenna,
Bermingham; Chambers; O'Connor (Meenan 75),
Bolger, Russell, Forrester (Kelly J 86); Fagan.

**Slaven Koprivnica (3) 6** *(Breen 1 (og), Busic 14, 33,*
*Rak 56, 72, 80)*
**Portadown (0) 0** 2000
*Slaven Koprivnica:* (4231) Rodic; Puric, Bubnjic
(Pilipovic 72), Kokalovic, Maras; Batarelo, Brlek; Rak,
Vugrinec (Grgic 64), Delic; Busic (Saban 58).
*Portadown:* (4312) McArdle; Mackle, Gartland, Breen
(Burns 78), Redman; McNeill, Casement, McCafferty;
Braniff; Lecky, Murray (O'Hara 64).

**Slovan Bratislava (1) 1** *(Sebo 26)*
**Videoton (1) 1** *(Oliveira 30)* 6218
*Slovan Bratislava:* (433) Kovac; Bagayoko, Kladrubsky
(Sabo 67), Gorosito, Pauschek; Milinkovic, Grendel
(Meszaros 78), Luksik; Sebo, Halenar (Szarka 87),
Peltier.
*Videoton:* (4231) Bozovic; Brachi, Souza, Caneira,
Stopira; Mitrovic, Toth (Szekeres 88); Gyurcso
(Fernandez 80), Sandor, Oliveira; Nikolic N (Torghelle
75).

**Spartak Trnava (3) 3** *(Karhan 38, Mikovic 44, 45)*
**Sligo R (0) 1** *(Peers 68)* 6832
*Spartak Trnava:* (4141) Filipko; Habanek, Janecka,
Cvirik, Stozicky; Gross; Gasparik, Bicak (Koubsky 84),
Karhan, Mikovic (Schranz 70); Tomacek (Pavelka 60).
*Sligo R:* (4231) Rogers; Conneely, Peers, McGuinness,
Gaynor (Henderson 90); Ventre, Cawley; Cretaro
(Milien 77), Ndo, Boco; North.

**Vojvodina (0) 1** *(Oumarou 90)*
**Suduva (0) 1** *(Beniusis 56)* 6103
*Vojvodina:* (4231) Supic; Vulicevic (Smiljanic 87), Djuric, Trajkovic, Pavlovic; Mitosevic, Ajuru (Bojovic 60); Stevanovic, Almami Moreira, Bilbija (Skuletic 71); Oumarou.
*Suduva:* (4231) Davidovs; Soblinskas, Lohinov, Radzius (Urba 79), Slavickas; Leimonas, Chvedukas; Luksys, Rafael Gaucho, Eliosius (Urbsys 68); Beniusis (Borovskij 71).

**Xazar Lankaran (1) 1** *(Subasic 4)*
**Lech Poznan (1) 1** *(Mozdzen 19)* 15,000
*Xazar Lankaran:* (4231) Agayev; Bonfim, Scarlatache, Allahverdiyev, Todorov; Abishov, Amirguliyev; Tounkara, Alviz (Brenes 46), Pit (Vilana 80); Subasic.
*Lech Poznan:* (4141) Buric; Mozdzen, Kaminski, Arboleda, Henriquez; Wolakiewicz; Ubiparip (Lovrencsics 87), Murawski, Drewniak■, Tonev (Wilk 73); Slusarski (Thurthevic 60).

**Young Boys (0) 1** *(Frey 53)*
**Zimbru Chisinau (0) 0** 9117
*Young Boys:* (4132) Wolfli; Sutter, Nef, Ojala, Spycher; Silberbauer; Gonzalez (Frey 46), Farnerud (Costanzo 72), Raimondi (Nuzzolo 63); Vitkieviez, Mayuka.
*Zimbru Chisinau:* (4141) Calancea; Balasa, Cuznetov, Derkach A, Zastavnyi; Tumbasevic (Anton 82); Gorceac, Barakhoev, Shishkin (Iavorschi 57), Catan (Cucu 65); Molla.

**Zalgiris Vilnius (0) 1** *(Radavicius 72)*
**Admira Wacker Modling (1) 1** *(Hosiner 12)* 2473
*Zalgiris Vilnius:* (4231) Vitkauskas; Vaitkunas, Skerla, Peric, Radavicius; Nagumanov (Grgurovic 83), Kuklys; Svrljuga (Bilinski 46), Pek, Silenas (Komolov 84); Elliot.
*Admira Wacker Modling:* (4231) Tischler; Plassnegger, Windbichler, Drescher, Palla (Schrott 84); Mevoungou, Toth; Sabitzer, Schwab (Thurauer 81), Jezek; Hosiner (Ouedraogo 65).

## SECOND QUALIFYING ROUND SECOND LEG

Thursday, 26 July 2012
**Aalesund (1) 5** *(Barrantes 45, Tollas 48, James 64, 77, Stewart 83)*
**KF Tirana (0) 0** 4225
*Aalesund:* (4231) Grytebust; Wembangomo, Tollas, Arnefjord, Matland (Skagestad 67); Ulvestad, Carlsen; Stewart, Barrantes, Fuhre (Myklebust 68); Post (James 46).
*KF Tirana:* (4321) Lika I; Sina (Morina 53), Dushku, Pisha, Ahmataj; Ferraj (Peposhi 58), Taku, Pashaj; Karabeci (Mucollari 69), Lika G; Cota.

**Admira Wacker Modling (3) 5** *(Schwab 4, Jezek 14 (pen), 52, Ouedraogo 31, Hosiner 70)*
**Zalgiris Vilnius (1) 1** *(Kuklys 22)* 4000
*Admira Wacker Modling:* (4231) Tischler; Plassnegger, Windbichler, Drescher, Weber; Mevoungou, Toth; Sabitzer (Seebacher 82), Schwab (Hosiner 56), Jezek (Schick T 62); Ouedraogo.
*Zalgiris Vilnius:* (442) Vitkauskas; Freidgeimas, Jankauskas, Skerla, Vaitkunas (Svrljuga 42); Pek, Peric, Kuklys (Nagumanov 57), Radavicius; Elliot, Bilinski (Komolov 74).

**Aktobe (1) 3** *(Khayrullin 39, Geynrikh 50, Simao 90 (og))*
**Milsami-Ursidos (0) 0** 11,300
*Aktobe:* (4411) Sidelnikov; Badlo, Smakov, Logvinenko (Primus 46), Kenzhisariev; Bajer, Kapadze, Covalciuc, Bikmaev (Lisenkov 71); Khayrullin; Geynrikh (Klimavicius 78).
*Milsami-Ursidos:* (4141) Negai; Rassulov, Sosnovsky, Rafael Wellington, Bruno Simao; Nurudeen; Casabella (Furdui 56), Stoleru (Guilherme 47), Garla, Elias; Boghiu (Traore 72).

**Anorthosis Famagusta (2) 3** *(Toni Calvo 13, Okkas 41, Laborde 62)*
**Levadia Tallinn (0) 0** 6892
*Anorthosis Famagusta:* (4231) Blazic; Ilic, Colin, Paulo Jorge, Boaventura; Alexa, Laban (Roncatto 74); Toni Calvo (Ohayon 56), Juliano Spadacio, Laborde; Okkas (Rezek 56).

**Levadia Tallinn:** (442) Smishko; Kulinits, Artjunin (Pikk 68), Morozov, Podholjuzin; Subbotin (Toomet 63), Kaljumae, Antonov, Pebre; Taar (Hunt 80), Rattel.

**Asteras Tripolis (0) 1** *(Ximo Navarro 68)*
**Inter Baku (0) 1** *(Tales 88)* 2661
*Asteras Tripolis:* (4231) Bantis; Tsambouris, Bartolini (Kourbelis 61), Juanito, Pipinis (Gialousis 76); Usero, Alvarez; Ximo Navarro, Rayo, Formica (Bakasetas 57); Perrone.
*Inter Baku:* (343) Lomaia; Barmettler, Abdoulaye, Levin (Tskhadadze 71); Dashdemirov, Zlatinov, Georgievski, Kandelaki; Hajiyev (Mammadov 67), Tales, Adamia (Genov 61).
*aet; Asteras Tripolis won 4-2 on penalties.*

**Budapest Honved (0) 0**
**Anzhi Makhachkala (1) 4** *(Eto'o 7, 81, Traore 53, Shatov 68)* 5100
*Budapest Honved:* (433) Kemenes; Lovric, Debreceni, Ignjatovic, Vidovic; Ivancsics (Diarra 70), Johnson, Hidi (Faggyas 58); Tchami, Delczeg (Diaby 46), Vernes■.
*Anzhi Makhachkala:* (442) Gaboulov V; Logashov, Samba (Gaboulov G 66), Joao Carlos, Tagirbekov; Shatov, Ahmedov, Jucilei, Boussoufa (Zhirkov 54); Eto'o, Traore (Smolov 73).

**Celik Niksic (1) 2** *(Jovovic 23, Zoric 50 (pen))*
**Metalurh Donetsk (1) 4** *(Danilo 15, Junior Moraes 53, Volovik 72, Ze Soares 84)* 1480
*Celik Niksic:* (442) Banovic; Nikolic, Dubljevic, Radovic, Bulatovic (Videkanic 60); Simic (Kasapi 60), Adrovic, Zoric, Bulajic; Ivanovic (Agovic 80), Jovovic.
*Metalurh Donetsk:* (4231) Bandura; Yedigaryan, Checher, Volovik, Golaydo (Morozyuk 46); Lazic (Makrides 72), Danilo; Nelson, Dimitrov, Ghazaryan (Ze Soares 60); Junior Moraes.

**CSKA Sofia (1) 1** *(Popov 18)*
**Mura 05 (0) 1** *(Fajic 76)* 5800
*CSKA Sofia:* (442) Cerny; Sasha, Popov, Krachunov, Nilson; Njongo Priso, Yanev K (Yovchev 88), Yanchev, Karachanakov (Granchov 78); Yanev H, Andrianantenaina.
*Mura 05:* (442) Drakovic; Janza, Kramar, Cipot, Majer; Jelic, Marusko, Sres (Gruskovnjak 90), Bohar; Eterovic (Kouter 75), Fajic.

**Dila Gori (0) 3** *(Vatsadze 62, 83, Shashiashvili 74)*
**AGF Aarhus (1) 1** *(Skender 34 (og))* 5810
*Dila Gori:* (442) Skender; Shashiashvili, Salukvadze, Oniani, Kvirkvelia; Aladashvili (Akhalkatsi 57), Kashia (Bechvaia 27), Grigalashvili, Gogua (Modebadze 77); Guruli, Vatsadze.
*AGF Aarhus:* (442) Rasmussen; Kirkeskov, Sorin, Haland, Eckersley; Sloth, Jorgensen, Norregaard, Akharraz (Petersen 64); Devdariani (Larsen 71), Johannsson (Graulund 43).

**FH Hafnarfijordur (0) 0**
**AIK Solna (1) 1** *(Lorentzson 40)* 2198
*FH Hafnarfijordur:* (4231) Gunnleifsson; Antoniusson, Vidarsson, Thorisson, Thomas; Runarsson (Snorrason 82), Gunnlaugsson; Palsson (Bjornsson 64), Sverrisson, Gudnason; Ingason (Bjarnason 89).
*AIK Solna:* (442) Turina; Lorentzson, Eriksson, Backman, Johansson; Gustavsson, Danielsson, Ahman-Persson, Lalawele (Kayongo 62); Borges, Lundberg.

**FK Senica (0) 0**
**Apoel Nicosia (0) 1** *(Helio Pinto 73)* 3069
*FK Senica:* (433) Svenger; Krajcik, Koutny, Brabec, Kalabiska; Kona, Babic (Varadi 74), Krizko (Stepanek 81); Divis (Frydek 78), Masaryk, Blackburn.
*Apoel Nicosia:* (4231) Chiotis; Mario Sergio, Borda, Zuela, Alexandrou; Nuno Morais, Helio Pinto (Charalampous 88); Charalambides (Aloneftis 74), Ben Achour (Helder Sousa 63), Manduca; Ailton.

**Gandzasar Kapan (0) 1** *(Avagyan H 90)*
**Servette (0) 3** *(Marcos de Azevedo 47, Pont 64, 68)* 1488
*Gandzasar Kapan:* (4231) Beglaryan; Manucharyan, Tatintsyan (Diakaridia 55), Obradovic, Avagyan A; Kasule, Vukomanovic; Correia (Avagyan H 63), Seedorf, Diego Lomba; Keita (Nasibyan 73).
*Servette:* (4231) Barroca; Pont, Mfuyi (Gissi 73), Moubandje, Schneider; Kouassi, Pizzinat (Poceiro 67); Lang (Moutinho 75), Pasche, Marcos de Azevedo; Karanovic.

**Gomel (0) 0**
**Renova (0) 1** *(Asani 56)* 10,250
*Gomel:* (4231) Bushma; Matveychik (Evseenko 92), Kirilchik, Kashevsky, Klimovich; Kozeka, Voronkov; Nowak, Levitskiy, Platonov; Demidovich (Timoshenko 77).
*Renova:* (4321) Zendeli; Velija Bilal, Stepanovski, Asani, Simovski (Fetai 85); Siljanovski, Bajrami, Nuhiu; Gafuri (Ismaili 77), Emini (Skenderi 56); Andonov.

**IF Elfsborg (2) 2** *(Nilsson 9, 40)*
**Dacia Chisinau (0) 0** 3181
*IF Elfsborg:* (442) Ellegaard; Larsson, Jonsson, Moback, Klarstrom; Ishizaki, Hiljemark (Rohden 68), Svensson, Hult; Nilsson (Claesson 83), Elm.
*Dacia Chisinau:* (4231) Gaiduchevici; Dimovski (Pavlov 83), Ilescu, Lucas, Mamah; Guira, Cojocari; Mihailov (Orbu 22), Josan (Cairo 46), Krkotic; Sow.

**Inter Turku (0) 0**
**FC Twente (3) 5** *(Fer 4, 37, Plet 7, Chadli 77, 89)* 7610
*Inter Turku:* (4231) Reponen; Nyman (Nikkari 46), Aho, Diallo, Antunez; Bouwman, Paajanen; Ojala (Duah 74), Kauko, Gnabouyou (Asis 46); Sirbiladze.
*FC Twente:* (433) Mihaylov; Rosales, Douglas, Wisgerhof (Bjelland 78), Schilder (Breukers 72); Janssen, Fer, Brama; Tadic, Plet (Verhoek 76), Chadli.

**KAA Gent (1) 3** *(Melli 41, Conte 63, Kola 74)*
**Differdange 03 (2) 2** *(Er Rafik 24, Bettmer 37)* 6504
*KAA Gent:* (4141) Boeckx; Baric, Corstjens, Melli, Wallace; Arzo (N Diaye 74); Messoudi (Arbeitman 85), Conte, Van der Bruggen (Raman 80), Bruls; Kola.
*Differdange 03:* (442) Weber; Franzoni, Bukvic, Siebenaler, Janisch; Bettmer, May, Afoun (Bastos 74), Meligner; Er Rafik (Piskor 77), Caron (Albanese 79).

**Kalmar (2) 3** *(Dauda 25, Ibriks 45 (og), Nouri 90)*
**Osijek (0) 0** 4653
*Kalmar:* (442) Berisha; Ohman, Arajuuri, Thorthevic, Nouri; Mendes (Diouf 75), Rydstrom, Gutu, Israelsson (McDonald 85); Andersson, Dauda (Soderqvist 72).
*Osijek:* (442) Vargic; Ibriks, Smoje, Leko, Vrgoc; Kvrzic■, Jugovic, Kurtovic (Misic J 67), Perosevic; Dugandzic (Pavic 83), Milicevic (Pongracic 58).

**KuPS Kuopio (0) 0**
**Maccabi Netanya (1) 1** *(Sabaa 40)* 3018
*KuPS Kuopio:* (433) Hilander; Karkkainen, Nissinen, Tabe, Joenmaki; Taipale, Obiefule, Paananen (James 90); Hynynen (Puri 86), Purje, Ilo (Venalainen 75).
*Maccabi Netanya:* (433) Cennamo; Shitrit, Levy, Pietrasiak, Pinas; Shivhon, Tchalisher (Sarhan 85), El Khatib; Shriki (Tamir 74), Sabaa, Peretz (Akel 64).

**Lech Poznan (1) 1** *(Tonev 16)*
**Xazar Lankaran (0) 0** 25,840
*Lech Poznan:* (4141) Buric; Mozdzen, Kaminski, Arboleda, Henriquez; Wolakiewicz; Ubiparip (Lovrencsics 63), Tralka (Thurthevic 93), Murawski, Tonev; Slusarski (Bereszynski 87).
*Xazar Lankaran:* (4231) Agayev; Bonfim, Scarlatache, Allahverdiyev, Todorov (Vilana 80); Abishov, Amirguliyev■; Tounkara (Brenes 65), Alviz, Pit; Subasic.

**Legia Warsaw (2) 5** *(Saganowski 4, 39, 79, Gol 57, Zyro 61)*
**Liepajas Metalurgs (1) 1** *(Kamess 45)* 12,300
*Legia Warsaw:* (4141) Kuciak; Jedrzejczyk, Zewlakow (Suler 78), Inaki Astiz, Wawrzyniak; Lukasik (Furman 64); Kucharczyk (Zyro 61), Gol, Radovic, Kosecki; Saganowski.

*Liepajas Metalurgs:* (442) Dorosevs; Hmizs (Ikaunieks 88), Baguzis, Mezs, Savalnieks; Solonicins■, Tamosauskas, Mihadjuks, Leliuga (Flaksis 81); Kamess, Afanasjevs (Sadcins 67).

**Metalurg Skopje (0) 0**
**Ruch Chorzow (2) 3** *(Janoszka 9, Straka 15, Piech 63)* 755
*Metalurg Skopje:* (442) Pavlovic; Petkovski, Kralevski, Dragovic■, Ljamcevski B; Dimoski (Ljamcevski P 46), Krstev, Stevanovic, Memedi (Alomerovic 58); Curlinov, Ristovski (Nestorovski 65).
*Ruch Chorzow:* (442) Peskovic; Djokic (Lewczuk 53), Stawarczyk, Sadlok, Szyndrowski; Zienczuk, Malinowski (Lisowski 65), Straka, Janoszka (Starzynski 76); Jankowski, Piech.

**MYPA (0) 0**
**Rapid Bucharest (2) 2** *(Surdu 19, Ilijoski 42)* 1282
*MYPA:* (4141) Kuismala; Oksanen, Nongatamba (Sihvola 46), Aho, Vesala; Koskinen; Sesay, Saxman, Gela, Selin (Anttilainen 46); Williams (Kukka 67).
*Rapid Bucharest:* (442) Albut; Rui Duarte (Coman A 73), Abrudan, Oros, Voicu; Milisavljevic, Grigorie, Filipe Teixeira (Ciolacu 66), Goga; Ilijoski (Bozovic 46), Surdu.

**Ordabasy Shymkent (1) 1** *(Mansour 32)*
**Rosenborg (0) 2** *(Holm 67, Dockal 90)* 22,000
*Ordabasy Shymkent:* (4411) Bekbaev; Mwesigwa, Trajkovic, Mukhtarov, Larbi Arouri; Mansour, Karpovich, Pakholyuk (Thilas 93); Babatunde (Adyrbekov 84); Kasyanov; Tazhimbetov (Beysenov 75).
*Rosenborg:* (442) Orlund; Ankersen (Wangberg■ 46), Strandberg, Vagan, Dorsin; Dockal, Henriksen, Issah (Selnaes 67), Svensson; Prica (Iversen 82), Holm.

**Portadown (1) 2** *(Lecky 45, McCafferty 67 (pen))*
**Slaven Koprivnica (2) 4** *(Bubnjic 10, Brlek 14, Saban 62, 64)* 393
*Portadown:* (442) Miskelly; Casement, Gartland, Breen, O'Hara; Mackle, McCafferty, McNeill, Redman; Lecky (Murray 81), Braniff.
*Slaven Koprivnica:* (433) Rodic; Maras, Grgic, Sestak, Bubnjic (Kokalovic 62); Batarelo (Canathija 46), Takac, Kupresak; Brlek, Saban, Delic (Busic 68).

**Red Star Belgrade (2) 3** *(Kasalica 9, Dimitrijevic 15, Vesovic 90)*
**Naftan Novopolotsk (1) 3** *(Sorokin 21, Naumov 58, Kovalenko 82)* 27,500
*Red Star Belgrade:* (433) Bajkovic; Mikic, Maksimovic, Krneta, Mladenovic; Milivojevic (Mijailovic 62), Dimitrijevic (Cadu 78), Evandro; Lazovic, Kasalica, Milunovic (Vesovic 85).
*Naftan Novopolotsk:* (4231) Dovgyallo; Gorbachyov, Naumov, Berezovskyi, Obrazov; Trukhov, Bukatkin■; Cernych, Kobets (Zhukovskiy 83), Sorokin; Gavryushko (Kovalenko 59).

**Ried (0) 0**
**Shakhtyor Soligorsk (0) 0** 4100
*Ried:* (3331) Gebauer; Reifeltshammer, Reiter, Riegler; Hinum, Hadzic, Schicker; Nacho Rodriguez, Zulj (Ziegl 46), Meilinger (Schreiner 88); Guillem (Carril 59).
*Shakhtyor Soligorsk:* (4411) Tsygalko; Rozhkov, Postnikov, Yanushkevich, Kolomyts; Balanovich, Khachaturyan, Grenkov, Sitko (Rios 80); Komarovsky (Leonchik 79); Osipenko.

**Sarajevo (2) 3** *(Husejinovic 12, 62, Suljic 14)*
**Levski Sofia (1) 1** *(Basile de Carvalho 34 (pen))* 11,122
*Sarajevo:* (4231) Adilovic; Tatomirovic, Dupovac, Torlak, Belosevic; Sunjevaric, Sesar; Suljic (Karamatic 78), Husejinovic (Comor 69), Zlatkovic (Tadejevic 30); Hadzic.
*Levski Sofia:* (4231) Iliev; Mulder, Ivanov, Angelov, Starokin; Prochazka, Gadzhev; Agyemang (Joao Silva 71), Marcinho (Tonev 82), Raykov; Basile de Carvalho.

**Shirak (0) 0**
**Bnei Yehuda Tel Aviv (1) 1** *(Menashe 31)*     2517
*Shirak:* (4231) Harutyunyan; Mkrtchyan (Hakobyan 65), Mkoyan, Kadio, Hovhannisyan (Davoyan 67); Tigranyan, Davtyan T (Nalbandyan 57); Diop, Muradyan, Ly; Fofana.
*Bnei Yehuda Tel Aviv:* (442) Aiyenugba; Bargig, Cohen, Mori, Edri; Ivaskevicius, Galvan (Agajev 71), Abu Zaid, Menashe (Nachum 54); Marinkovic (Nash 87), Ndlovu.

**Skonto (0) 1** *(Sinelnikovs 90)*
**Hajduk Split (0) 0**     3112
*Skonto:* (442) Malins; Ibragimov, Savcenkovs, Maksimenko, Kukanos; Mingazov, Fertovs, Rode, Segundo (Sinelnikovs 87); Sabala, Labukas (Blanks 62).
*Hajduk Split:* (442) Blazevic; Vrsajevic, Maloca, Milovic, Stojanovic; Oremus (Tomas 94), Radosevic, Lustica, Caktas (Vukovic 77); Maglica (Ozobic 61), Vukusic .

**Sligo R (0) 1** *(McGuinness 90)*
**Spartak Trnava (0) 1** *(Cvirik 70)*     3754
*Sligo R:* (4411) Rogers; Conneely, Peers, McGuinness, Gaynor; Milien (Connolly 77), Cawley, Ventre (Lynch 72), Boco; Ndo; North (Quigley 50).
*Spartak Trnava:* (442) Filipko; Stozicky, Janecka, Cvirik, Hanzel; Mikovic (Gasparik 67), Gross, Karhan, Bicak; Vyskocil (Carnota 62), Schranz (Koubsky 85).

**St Johnstone (1) 1** *(Tade 35)*
**Eskisehirspor (0) 1** *(Sari 52)*     6023
*St Johnstone:* (442) Mannus; Miller (Mackay 60), Wright, McCracken, Davidson C; Millar, Davidson M, Cregg, Craig; Tade (Higgins 67), Hasselbaink (May 84).
*Eskisehirspor:* (442) Boffin; Sari, Cetin, Diego Angelo, Dede; Eser (Nuhiu 73), Gucer (Guven 81), Potuk, Tello; Zengin (Malecki 61), Kamara.

**St Patrick's Ath (1) 2** *(Russell 39, Fagan 105)*
**Siroki Brijeg (0) 1** *(Dzidic I 65)*     1805
*St Patrick's Ath:* (4141) Clarke; O'Brien, Browne, Kenna, Bermingham; Chambers; O'Connor (Meenan 89), Russell, Bolger, Forrester (Kelly J 106); Fagan (Flood 111).
*Siroki Brijeg:* (4231) Bilobrk; Coric, Dzidic I (Dzidic D 85), Jese, Bertosa; Wagner, Zlomislic; Bloudek (Roskam 63), Ricardo Baiano (Ivankovic 85), Silic; Kordic.
*aet.*

**Suduva (0) 0**
**Vojvodina (3) 4** *(Moreira 4, Skuletic 37, Stevanovic 40, Oumarou 48)*     2000
*Suduva:* (433) Davidovs; Chvedukas, Borovskij (Breive 83), Radzius, Slavickas; Urba (Beniusis 55), Leimonas, Lohinov; Luksys, Rafael Gaucho, Eliosius (Soblinskas 46).
*Vojvodina:* (4231) Supic; Vulicevic, Djuric, Trajkovic[*], Pavlovic; Mitosevic (Ajuru 31), Poletanovic (Bilbija 81); Stevanovic, Almami Moreira, Skuletic; Oumarou (Bojovic 63).

**Thor Akureyri (0) 0**
**Mlada Boleslav (1) 1** *(Magera 31)*     798
*Thor Akureyri:* (4231) Wicks; Albertsson Andri, Vrenko, Albertsson Alti (Hannesson K 80), Funicello; Aevarsson (Hjaltason 73), Hjaltalin; Bjornsson (Hilmarsson 73), Kristjansson, Jonsson; Hannesson J[*].
*Mlada Boleslav:* (4231) Seda; Kysela (Brunclik 46), Rolko, Smejkal (Johana 80), Boril; Kudela, Scuk; Sivric, Magera, Mares; Nespor (Ondrejka 63).

**Tromso (0) 1** *(Koppinen 108)*
**Olimpija Ljubljana (0) 0**     2297
*Tromso:* (442) Sahlman; Norbye (Kristiansen R 45), Bjorck, Koppinen, Yndestad; Andersen, Johansen, Yttergard, Drage (Lysvoll 100); Bendiksen (Arst 74), Ondrasek.
*Olimpija Ljubljana:* (433) Dzafic; Jovic, Sretenovic, Zarifovic, Fink Matic; Trifkovic, Radujko[*], Lovrecic; Franklin (Nikezic 105), Sporar, Skerjanc (Omladic 78).
*aet.*

**Videoton (0) 0**
**Slovan Bratislava (0) 0**     8028
*Videoton:* (4231) Bozovic; Szolnoki, Caneira, Souza, Stopira; Mitrovic, Toth (Kovacs 67); Gyurcso (Torghelle 86), Sandor, Oliveira (Fernandez 81); Nikolic N.
*Slovan Bratislava:* (433) Putnocky; Bagayoko (Janosik 88), Gorosito, Pauschek, Luksik; Grendel (Szarka 83), Kopunek, Milinkovic; Peltier, Halenar (Hlohovsky 78), Sebo .

**Viktoria Plzen (2) 2** *(Duris 7, Darida 10)*
**Metalurgi Rustavi (0) 0**     11,446
*Viktoria Plzen:* (4231) Bolek; Rajtoral, Sevinsky, Prochazka, Limbersky; Horvath, Darida; Fillo (Hora 63), Kolar (Hanousek 83), Malakyan (Reznik 77); Duris.
*Metalurgi Rustavi:* (442) Bediashvili; Kakushadze (Lobjanidze 46), Intskirveli, Makhviladze, Sukhiashvili; Japaridze, Mikaberidze, Maisuradze, Dobrovolski; Tatanashvili (Sikharulidze 61), Getsadze (Kavtaradze 74).

**Vitesse (2) 3** *(van Ginkel 25, van Aanholt 45, Bony 48)*
**Lokomotiv Plovdiv (0) 1** *(Zlatinski 80 (pen))*     13,469
*Vitesse:* (4123) Velthuizen; van der Struijk, Kalas[*], Kashia, van Aanholt; van der Heijden; Hofs (Propper 77), van Ginkel; Ibarra (Chanturia 73), Bony (Havenaar 69), Reis.
*Lokomotiv Plovdiv:* (4141) Kunchev; Eli Marques (Timonov 72), Salamastrakis, Georgiev V, Venkov; Kiriakidis; Todorov, Georgiev D (Yordanov 56), Zlatinski, Lazarov; Tassio (Malamov 58).

**Zeta (1) 1** *(Doslak 82)*
**JJK Jyvaskyla (0) 0**     3000
*Zeta:* (433) Brnovic; Radulovic MM (Knezevic 67), Vujacic (Pelicic V 58), Radulovic MB, Novovic; Doslak, Burzanovic, Zlaticanin (Pelicic Z 46); Bozovic, Korac, Boljevic.
*JJK Jyvaskyla:* (442) Korhonen; Markkula, Pasoja, Reintam, van Gelderen; Innanen (Hilska 86), Tuomanen (Linjala 85), Gruborovics, Poutiainen; Wusu, Markkanen (Turpeenniemi 59).

**Zimbru Chisinau (1) 1** *(Barakhoev 42)*
**Young Boys (0) 0**     4000
*Zimbru Chisinau:* (442) Caiancea; Balasa, Derkach A, Cuznetsov, Zastavnyi; Korgalidze, Tumbasevic, Shishkin (Anton 75), Catan; Barakhoev (Spataru 83), Molla.
*Young Boys:* (4312) Wolfli; Sutter, Nef, Veskovac, Lecjaks; Vitkieviez (Schneuwly 75), Silberbauer (Gonzalez 67), Spycher; Farnerud; Mayuka, Frey (Costanzo M 91).
*aet; Young Boys won 4-1 on penalties.*

**THIRD QUALIFYING ROUND FIRST LEG**

Thursday, 2 August 2012

**AC Horsens (0) 1** *(Fagerberg 90 (pen))*
**IF Elfsborg (0) 1** *(Nilsson 65)*     3552
*AC Horsens:* (4411) Ronnow; Juel Andersen, Agesen, Rasmussen M, Kortegaard; Kryger (Toft 67), Kielstrup, Drachmann, Mehl (Klove 62); Spelmann; Fagerberg.
*IF Elfsborg:* (442) Ellegaard; Larsson, Moback, Jonsson, Klarstrom; Ishizaki, Hiljemark, Svensson, Hult (Claesson 80); Nilsson (Jawo 74 (Augustsson 86)), Elm.

**Admira Wacker Modling (0) 0**
**Sparta Prague (1) 2** *(Mevoungou 29 (og), Kweuke 58)*     5345
*Admira Wacker Modling:* (442) Tischler; Plassnegger (Schick 77), Windbichler, Drescher, Weber; Sabitzer, Schachner, Mevoungou, Jezek (Seebacher 71); Ouedraogo (Hosiner 60), Schwab.
*Sparta Prague:* (442) Vaclik; Vidlicka, Svejdik, Jarosik, Pamic; Kaderabek (Prikryl 80), Husbauer, Holek, Krejci (Zapotocny 89); Kweuke, Keric (Kadlec 54).

**AIK Solna (0) 3** *(Lorentzson 60, Borges 78, Lundberg 86)*
**Lech Poznan (0) 0** 10,658
*AIK Solna:* (442) Turina; Lorentzson, Eriksson, Backman, Johansson; Gustavsson (Lalawele 79), Tjernstrom, Ahman-Persson (Danielsson 79), Kayongo; Borges, Lundberg.
*Lech Poznan:* (4141) Buric; Mozdzen (Ubiparip 72), Kaminski, Arboleda, Henriquez; Wolakiewicz (Drewniak 83); Lovrencsics, Tralka, Murawski, Tonev (Bereszynski 85); Slusarski.

**Anzhi Makhachkala (0) 2** *(Shatov 63, Smolov 74)*
**Vitesse (0) 0** 5000
*Anzhi Makhachkala:* (442) Gaboulov V; Logashov, Samba, Joao Carlos (Gadzhibekov 15), Tagirbekov; Shatov (Carcela Gonzalez 88), Ahmedov (Gaboulov G 19), Jucilei, Boussoufa; Eto'o, Smolov.
*Vitesse:* (4123) Velthuizen; Yasuda, van der Struijk, Kashia, van Aanholt; van der Heijden (Cziommer 78); Propper (Havenaar 71), van Ginkel; Ibarra, Bony, Reis.

**APOEL Nicosia (1) 2** *(Mario Sergio 34, Aloneftis 890)*
**Aalesund (1) 1** *(Stewart 16)* 16,708
*APOEL Nicosia:* (4231) Chiotis; Mario Sergio, Borda, Zuela, Alexandrou; Nuno Morais, Helio Pinto; Charalambides (Aloneftis 64), Ben Achour (Helder Sousa 83); Manduca; Adorno (Budimir 56).
*Aalesund:* (451) Grytebust; Wembangomo, Tollas, Arnefjord, Jaager; Stewart, Ulvestad, Morrison, Carlsen (Skagestad 90), Fuhre (Matland 70); James (Sellin 79).

**Arsenal Kyiv (1) 3** *(Mazilu 6, Kovpak 61, Matoukou 83)*
**Mura 05 (0) 0** 3200
*Arsenal Kyiv:* (4231) Borovyk; Leandro, Hitchenko, Matoukou, Polivoy; Maksymov, Shakhov (Stargorodsky 67); Adiyiah (Kovpak 57), Shatskikh, Kobakhidze (Mikoliunas 77); Mazilu.
*Mura 05:* (442) Drakovic; Majer, Cipot, Kramar, Janza; Bohar (Gruskovnjak 91), Marusko, Kouter (Buzeti 62), Sres (Vas 84); Eterovic, Jelic.
*Match awarded to Mura 3-0, Arsenal Kyiv fielded an ineligible player.*

**Asteras Tripolis (0) 1** *(Rayo 48)*
**Maritimo (0) 1** *(Fidelis 71)* 2000
*Asteras Tripolis:* (4231) Bantis; Tsambouris, Juanito, Kourbelis (Hegon 68), Pipinis; Usero (Bakasetas 86), Alvarez; Ximo Navarro, Rayo, Fragoulakis (Sankare 46); Perrone.
*Maritimo:* (4231) Salin; Briguel, Joao Guilherme, Roberge, Ruben Ferreira; Joao Luiz, Rafael Miranda; Danilo (Igor Rossi 87), Heldon (Rodrigo Antonio 74), Sami; Fidelis (Adilson 85).

**Athletic Bilbao (2) 3** *(Isma Lopez 16, 20, 68)*
**Slaven Koprivnica (1) 1** *(Delic 19)* 28,000
*Athletic Bilbao:* (4231) Iraizoz; Iraola, Gurpegui, Jonas Ramalho (Ekiza 46), Perez; Iturraspe, De Marcos; Ibai Gomez (Llorente 46), Toquero (Ruiz de Galarreta 63), Isma Lopez; Susaeta.
*Slaven Koprivnica:* (4231) Rodic; Puric, Kokalovic, Bubnjic, Maras; Batarelo, Grgic; Rak (Pilipovic 81), Canathija, Delic (Glavica 59); Busic (Saban 53).

**Bnei Yehuda Tel Aviv (0) 0**
**PAOK Salonika (0) 2** *(Georgiadis 62, Athanasiadis 72)* 2000
*Bnei Yehuda Tel Aviv:* (442) Aiyenugba; Azuz, Cohen, Mori, Edri; Nachum (Agajev 66), Ivaskevicius, Galvan (Levi 82), Menashe (Abu Zaid 46); Marinkovic, Ndlovu.
*PAOK Salonika:* (442) Glikos; Etto, Khumalo, Katsikas, Lino; Georgiadis (Salpingidis 82), Lazar (Kace 75), Garcia, Robert; Giannou (Pelkas 71), Athanasiadis.

**Dila Gori (0) 0**
**Anorthosis Famagusta (0) 1** *(Okkas 69)* 7500
*Dila Gori:* (442) Skender; Shashiashvili, Salukvadze, Oniani, Kvirkvelia; Guruli, Grigalashvili (Aladashvili 46), Bechvaia (Katsitadze 77), Gogua■; Vatsadze, Modebadze (Gvalia 62).
*Anorthosis Famagusta:* (4231) Blazic; Ilic B, Colin, Paulo Jorge, Boaventura; Alexa, Laban (Roncatto 65); Toni Calvo (Ohayon 78), Juliano Spadacio, Laborde; Okkas (Rezek 75).

**Dundee U (1) 2** *(Flood 36, Watson 76)*
**Dynamo Moscow (0) 2** *(Semshov 50, Kokorin 90)* 10,500
*Dundee U:* (4321) Cierzniak; Watson, Dillon, Gunning, Douglas; Flood, Rankin, Ryan; Russell, MacKay-Steven; Daly.
*Dynamo Moscow:* (4231) Shunin; Wilkshire, Schildenfeld, Rykov, Lomic; Yusupov (Sapeta 90), Semshov; Dzsudzsak, Kokorin, Misimovic; Kuranyi .

**Eskiesehirspor (0) 1** *(Nuhiu 62)*
**Marseille (0) 1** *(Gignac 49)* 12,780
*Eskiesehirspor:* (4123) Boffin; Sari (Albayrak 81), Cetin, Diego Angelo, Dede; Gucer; Potuk, Zengin (Guven 46); Kamara, Nuhiu, Malecki (Eser 68).
*Marseille:* (4231) Mandanda; Fanni, N'Koulou, Mbia, Morel; Kabore, Cheyrou; Amalfitano, Valbuena (Raspentino 87), Ayew A; Gignac (Ayew J 72).

**FC Twente (0) 2** *(Fer 52, Chadli 58)*
**Mlada Boleslav (0) 0** 18,500
*FC Twente:* (433) Mihaylov; Rosales, Douglas, Bjelland, Schilder; Janssen (Gutierrez 73), Brama, Fer; Tadic, Plet (Bulykin 46), Chadli.
*Mlada Boleslav:* (4231) Seda; Kysela, Kudela, Johana, Boril; Brunclik (Taborsky 84), Scuk; Sivric, Magera (Zbrozek 62), Mares; Nespor (Ondrejka 69).

**Gomel (0) 0**
**Liverpool (0) 1** *(Downing 67)* 12,220
*Gomel:* (4231) Bushma; Matveychik, Kirilchik, Kashevsky, Klimovich; Voronkov, Levitskiy (Demidovich 84); Nowak (Lipatkin 74), Kozeka (Timoshenko 90), Platonov; Alumona.
*Liverpool:* (433) Jones; Johnson (Kelly 46), Skrtel, Carragher, Jose Enrique; Gerrard, Spearing, Henderson (Lucas Leiva 65); Downing, Borini, Cole (Sterling 23).

**Hajduk Split (0) 0**
**Internazionale (2) 3** *(Sneijder 18, Nagatomo 44, Coutinho 73)* 33,000
*Hajduk Split:* (4231) Blazevic; Vrsajevic, Maloca, Milovic, Jozinovic; Andrijasevic (Milic A 57), Radosevic; Oremus (Tomas 78), Ozobic (Maglica 46), Caktas; Vukusic.
*Internazionale:* (4321) Handanovic; Moreira, Silvestre, Chivu (Samuel 46), Nagatomo; Zanetti, Cambiasso, Guarin; Palacio, Sneijder (Coutinho 65); Milito (Livaja 77).

**Heerenveen (1) 4** *(Djuricic 9, 64, de Roon 69, Fazli 89)*
**Rapid Bucharest (0) 0** 18,000
*Heerenveen:* (433) Nordfeldt; Zuiverloon, Gouweleeuw, Zomer, Raitala; de Roon, Kums, Ziyech (van Anholt 53); van La Parra, Djuricic (Fazli 86), Tannane (Valpoort 71).
*Rapid Bucharest:* (442) Albut; Rui Duarte, Oros, Constantin, Bozovic; Roman (Ciolacu 76), Grigore, Grigorie, Milisavljevic (Filipe Teixeira 58); Ilijoski (Goga 63), Surdu.

**Kalmar (1) 1** *(Andersson 18)*
**Young Boys (0) 0** 3681
*Kalmar:* (442) Berisha; Nouri, Arajuuri, Thorthevic, Skjelvik; Diouf (Ohman 86), Rydstrom, Gutu, Israelsson; Andersson (McDonald 90), Soderqvist (Dauda 46).
*Young Boys:* (4141) Wolfli; Sutter, Nef, Ojala, Raimondi; Spycher; Schneuwly, Farnerud, Costanzo (Frey 68), Nuzzolo (Gonzalez 81); Mayuka (Bobadilla 46).

**KRC Genk (2) 2** *(Vossen 18 (pen), Monrose 44)*
**Aktobe (1) 1** *(Badlo 25)* 15,350
*KRC Genk:* (442) Koteles; Dani Fernandez (Nwanganga 84), Ngcongca, Nadson, Katuka; Buffel (Limbombe 46), Gorius, Hyland, Monrose; Vossen (Barda 76), Benteke.
*Aktobe:* (4411) Sidelnikov; Badlo■, Smakov, Primus, Kenzhisariev; Bikmaev (Lisenko 89), Kapadze, Covalciuc, Bajer; Khayrullin; Geynrikh (Klimavicius 82).

**KuPS Kuopio (0) 1** *(Puri 73)*
**Bursaspor (0) 0** 3045
*KuPS Kuopio:* (433) Hilander; Karkkainen, Nissinen, Tabe, Joenmaki; Taipale, Obiefule, Paananen (James 91); Hynynen, Puri, Ilo (Venalainen 81).
*Bursaspor:* (4411) Carson; Chretien, Ozturk, Aziz, Aslantas; Odabasi (Bahadir 60), N'Diaye, Cagiran (Kocak 88), Ipek (Kiraz 60); Batalla; Pinto.

**Red Star Belgrade (0) 0**
**Omonia (0) 0** 26,930
*Red Star Belgrade:* (433) Bajkovic; Vesovic■, Maksimovic, Jovanovic, Mladenovic; Mijailovic, Dimitrijevic (Cadu 88), Evandro; Lazovic (Milivojevic 80), Kasalica, Milunovic.
*Omonia:* (451) Leoni; Danielson, Pavicevic, Scaramozzino, Shpungin; Christofi, Margaca (Freddy 78), Nuno Assis (Bruno Aguiar 69), Marco Soares, Leandro; Alves A (Alves J 89).

**Ried (0) 2** *(Gartler 52, Hadzic 62 (pen))*
**Legia Warsaw (0) 1** *(Ljuboja 85)* 4200
*Ried:* (3331) Gebauer; Reifeltshammer, Reiter, Riegler; Hinum, Ziegl, Schicker; Grossinger (Nacho Rodriguez 60), Hadzic, Meilinger (Guillem 79); Gartler (Zulj 71).
*Legia Warsaw:* (4141) Kuciak; Jedrzejczyk, Inaki Astiz, Zewlakow, Wawrzyniak■; Lukasik (Vrdoljak 72); Kucharczyk (Rzezniczak 64), Gol (Saganowski 46), Radovic, Kosecki; Ljuboja.

**Ruch Chorzow (0) 0**
**Viktoria Plzen (0) 2** *(Stipek 79, Duris 85)* 3824
*Ruch Chorzow:* (442) Peskovic; Djokic, Stawarczyk, Sadlok, Szyndrowski; Zienczuk, Malinowski, Straka (Lisowski 57), Janoszka (Starzynski 61); Jankowski, Piech (Niedzielan 81).
*Viktoria Plzen:* (4231) Bolek; Rajtoral, Sevinsky, Prochazka, Limbersky; Horvath, Darida; Fillo, Kolar (Hanousek 88), Hora (Stipek 74); Duris (Hejda 90).

**Sarajevo (2) 2** *(Suljic 17, Belosevic 43)*
**Zeta (1) 1** *(Bozovic 45)* 12,259
*Sarajevo:* (4231) Bandovic; Tatomirovic, Dupovac, Torlak, Belosevic; Sunjevaric (Comor 75), Sesar (Haskic 85); Suljic (Karamatic 64), Husejinovic, Zlatkovic; Hadzic.
*Zeta:* (433) Brnovic; Radulovic MM, Pelicic V■, Radulovic MB, Novovic; Burzanovic, Zlaticanin, Bozovic (Kalacevic 81); Doslak, Korac, Boljevic (Dabic 53).

**Servette (0) 1** *(Schneider 69)*
**Rosenborg (0) 1** *(Dockal 81)* 5722
*Servette:* (4231) Barroca; Gomes, Kouassi, Schneider, Moubandje (Pont 84); Pizzinat, Grippo; Marcos de Azevedo, Pasche (Gissi 82), Lang (Poceiro 58); Karanovic.
*Rosenborg:* (4411) Orlund; Hoiland, Strandberg, Vagan, Dorsin; Dockal, Issah, Svensson, Fredheim (Selnaes 77); Henriksen; Chibuike (Alas J 93).

**St Patrick's Ath (0) 0**
**Hannover 96 (1) 3** *(Andreasen 6, Pander 67, Ya Konan 80)* 5500
*St Patrick's Ath:* (4141) Clarke; O'Brien, Kenna, Browne, Bermingham; Chambers; Forrester (Carroll J 87), Russell, Bolger (Flood 83), O'Connor (Meenan 79); Fagan.
*Hannover 96:* (442) Zieler; Cherundolo, Haggui, Eggimann, Pander; Stindl, Sergio Pinto, Andreasen (Schmiedebach 72), Huszti (Rausch 57); Ya Konan, Schlaudraff (Abdellaoue 79).

**Steaua Bucharest (0) 0**
**Spartak Trnava (1) 1** *(Mikovic 6)* 20,000
*Steaua Bucharest:* (442) Tatarusanu; Georgievski (Balan 62), Gardos, Chiriches, Latovlevici (Costea 46); Chipciu, Bourceanu, Pintilii, Tanase■; Rusescu, Nikolic (Adi 46).
*Spartak Trnava:* (4141) Filipko; Stozicky, Janecka, Cvirik, Hanzel; Gross; Sabo, Carnota (Tomacek 61), Karhan, Bicak (Kascak 79); Mikovic (Gasparik 87).

**Tromso (1) 1** *(Ondrasek 43)*
**Metalurh Donetsk (0) 1** *(Bjorck 88 (og))* 2276
*Tromso:* (442) Sahlman; Norbye, Bjorck, Koppinen, Kristiansen R; Andersen, Bendiksen, Yttergard, Drage (Yndestad 79); Ondrasek, Arst (Lysvoll V 66).
*Metalurh Donetsk:* (4231) Bandura; Morozyuk, Volovik, Checher, Yedigaryan; Lazic, Priyma; Makrides (Nelson 66), Dimitrov, Ghazaryan; Junior Moraes (Danilo 75).

**Videoton (0) 1** *(Nikolic N 78)*
**KAA Gent (0) 0** 5900
*Videoton:* (4231) Bozovic M; Brachi (Szolnoki 75), Caneira, Souza, Stopira; Mitrovic, Toth (Renato Neto 87); Gyurcso, Sandor (Kovacs 61), Oliveira; Nikolic N.
*KAA Gent:* (4141) Padt; Rafinha, Arzo, Melli, Mareval; N'Diaye; Messoudi (Remacle 72), Conte, Van der Bruggen, Bruls (Soumahoro Y 82); Arbeitman.

**Vojvodina (0) 2** *(Oumarou 75, Bojovic 90)*
**Rapid Vienna (0) 1** *(Alar 90)* 9735
*Vojvodina:* (4231) Supic; Vulicevic, Djuric, Jokic, Pavlovic; Greene, Poletanovic (Ajuru 84); Skuletic (Bilbija 66), Almami Moreira, Stevanovic; Oumarou (Bojovic 89).
*Rapid Vienna:* (4231) Konigshofer; Schimpelsberger, Sonnleitner, Pichler, Katzer; Kulovits, Heikkinen; Burgstaller (Alar 79), Hofmann, Drazan (Trimmel 68); Boyd.

## THIRD QUALIFYING ROUND SECOND LEG

Thursday, 9 August 2012

**Aalesund (0) 0**
**APOEL Nicosia (1) 1** *(Adorno 36)* 5057
*Aalesund:* (4231) Grytebust; Jaager, Tollas, Arnefjord, Matland; Carlsen (Wembangomo 46), Morrison; Stewart, Barrantes, Fuhre (Post 46); James.
*APOEL Nicosia:* (451) Chiotis; Mario Sergio, Borda, Zuela, Alexandrou; Manduca, Helio Pinto, Nuno Morais, Ben Achour (Helder Sousa 89), Charalambides (Aloneftis 78); Adorno (Budimir 83).

**Aktobe (1) 1** *(Kenzhisariev 30)*
**KRC Genk (1) 2** *(Nadson 36, Buffel 51)* 12,805
*Aktobe:* (4312) Sidelnikov; Klimavicius, Smakov, Primus, Kenzhisariev; Geynrikh (Zemlianukhin■ 76), Kapadze, Covalciuc; Khayrullin; Bikmaev (Lisenkov 81), Bajer.
*KRC Genk:* (442) Koteles; Dani Fernandez, Nadson, Ngcongca, Katuka; Buffel (Nwanganga 83), Gorius, Hyland, Barda (Monrose 42); Vossen (Camus 88), Benteke.

**Anorthosis Famagusta (0) 0**
**Dila Gori (0) 3** *(Vatsadze 54, 80, Salukvadze 78)* 9782
*Anorthosis Famagusta:* (4231) Blazic; Ilic, Colin, Paulo Jorge, Boaventura; Alexa, Laban■; Ohayon (Rezek 57), Juliano Spadacio, Laborde; Okkas (Roncatto 67).
*Dila Gori:* (4231) Skender; Shashiashvili, Salukvadze, Oniani, Kvirkvelia; Grigalashvili, Bechvaia; Kakhelishvili (Akhalkatsi 46), Guruli, Gvalia; Vatsadze.
*Match abandoned after 82 minutes due to crowd disturbance. Result stands at 0-3.*

**Bursaspor (3) 6** *(Ozturk 23, Pinto 28, 49, Batalla 36, N'Diaye 47, Tufan 72)*
**KuPS Kuopio (0) 0** 19,052
*Bursaspor:* (442) Carson; Chretien, Ozturk, Aziz, Aslantas (Tufan 63); Sestak (Odabasi 73), N'Diaye, Cagiran, Ipek; Batalla, Pinto (Bangura 76).
*KuPS Kuopio:* (433) Hilander; Karkkainen, Tabe, Nissinen, Joenmaki (Puri 41); Taipale (Hoivala 78), Obiefule, Paananen; Hynynen, Purje, Ilo (Venalainen 46).

**Dynamo Moscow (3) 5** *(Semshov 2, Kokorin 22, Yusupov 40, Sapeta 83, 89)*
**Dundee U (0) 0** 9063
*Dynamo Moscow:* (442) Berezovsky; Wilkshire, Rykov (Schildenfeld 63), Fernandez, Lomic; Misimovic, Yusupov (Sapeta 63), Semshov, Dzsudzsak (Bakkal 63); Kuranyi, Kokorin.
*Dundee U:* (442) Cierzniak; Watson, McLean, Gunning, Douglas; Flood, Ryan, Rankin (Armstrong 59), MacKay-Steven (Dow 85); Daly, Russell (Gardyne 78).

**Hannover 96 (1) 2** *(Haggui 32, Eggimann 47)*
**St Patrick's Ath (0) 0** 24,500
*Hannover 96:* (442) Zieler; Cherundolo, Haggui, Schulz (Eggimann 39), Rausch; Stindl, Sergio Pinto (Schmiedebach 64), Andreasen, Huszti; Ya Konan (Sobiech 46), Abdellaoue.
*St Patrick's Ath:* (4141) Clarke; O'Brien, Kenna, Browne, Bermingham; Chambers; Forrester (Meenan 58), Russell (Carroll J 64), Bolger, O'Connor; Fagan (Flood 79).

**IF Elfsborg (2) 2** *(Nilsson 6, Elm 18)*
**AC Horsens (3) 3** *(Kryger 4, Kortegaard 13, 36)* 3467
*IF Elfsborg:* (442) Ellegaard; Larsson, Jonsson (Augustsson 69), Moback, Klarstrom; Claesson, Svensson, Hiljemark (Ishizaki 61), Hult; Nilsson, Elm.
*AC Horsens:* (442) Ronnow; Juel Andersen, Agesen, Rasmussen M, Kortegaard; Kryger, Kielstrup, Drachmann, Klove (Nohr 90); Spelmann, Fagerberg (Toft 82).

**Internazionale (0) 0**
**Hajduk Split (1) 2** *(Vukusic 23 (pen), 58)* 44,154
*Internazionale:* (4321) Handanovic; Moreira, Ranocchia, Samuel, Mbaye (Nagatomo 55); Zanetti, Cambiasso, Guarin; Sneijder (Silvestre 84), Coutinho (Longo 64); Milito D.
*Hajduk Split:* (442) Blazevic; Vrsajevic, Maloca (Jonjic 10), Milovic, Jozinovic; Oremus, Radosevic, Milic A, Andrijasevic (Caktas 59); Vukovic (Lustica 83), Vukusic .

**KAA Gent (0) 0**
**Videoton (1) 3** *(Oliveira 13, Nikolic N 68, 71)* 5829
*KAA Gent:* (4123) Padt; Baric (Kola 60), Melli, Arzo, Mareval (Wallace 69); Gecov (Messoudi[■] 60); N'Diaye, Bruls[■]; Conte, Arbeitman, Remacle.
*Videoton:* (4231) Bozovic; Brachi, Caneira, Souza, Stopira; Mitrovic N, Toth (Kovacs 69); Gyurcso, Sandor, Oliveira (Neto 73); Nikolic N (Torghelle 79).

**Lech Poznan (0) 1** *(Mozdzen 72)*
**AIK Solna (0) 0** 12,220
*Lech Poznan:* (4231) Buric; Ceesay, Wolakiewicz, Arboleda, Henriquez; Tralka (Bereszynski 60), Murawski; Mozdzen, Drewniak, Tonev (Ubiparip 60); Lovrencsics (Wilk 85).
*AIK Solna:* (442) Turina; Lorentzson, Eriksson, Backman, Johansson; Lalawele, Ahman-Persson, Danielsson, Kayongo (Tjernstrom 81); Lundberg (Karikari 72), Borges.

**Legia Warsaw (1) 3** *(Saganowski 41, Radovic 55, Ljuboja 63)*
**Ried (0) 1** *(Zulj 76)* 15,028
*Legia Warsaw:* (4141) Kuciak; Jedrzejczyk, Zewlakow (Suler 12), Inaki Astiz, Rzezniczak; Lukasik (Gol 59); Vrdoljak[■], Radovic, Ljuboja (Zyro 79), Kosecki; Saganowski.
*Ried:* (4141) Gebauer; Hinum, Reifeltshammer, Riegler, Schicker; Ziegl (Carril 58); Hadzic (Zulj 73), Nacho Rodriguez (Grossinger 56), Reiter, Meilinger; Gartler.

**Liverpool (2) 3** *(Borini 21, Gerrard 41, Johnson 72)*
**Gomel (0) 0** 43,256
*Liverpool:* (433) Reina; Johnson, Skrtel (Carragher 77), Agger, Jose Enrique; Lucas Leiva (Spearing 86), Gerrard, Shelvey (Adam 76); Downing, Suarez, Borini.
*Gomel:* (4231) Bushma; Matveychik, Kashevsky, Kuzmenok, Klimovich (Evseenko 86); Voronkov, Kozeka (Kirilchik 75); Nowak (Lipatkin 63), Aleksievich, Platonov; Alumona.

**Maritimo (0) 0**
**Asteras Tripolis (0) 0** 3915
*Maritimo:* (4231) Salin; Briguel, Joao Guilherme, Roberge, Ruben Ferreira[■]; Joao Luiz, Rafael Miranda; Danilo (Rodrigo Antonio 61), Heldon (Igor Rossi 73), Sami; Fidelis (Adilson 77).
*Asteras Tripolis:* (4231) Fulop; Tsambouris, Sankare, Bartolini, Pipinis; Juanito, Alvarez (Bakasetas 62); Ximo Navarro, Usero (Fragoulakis 74), Rayo; Perrone.

**Marseille (2) 3** *(Ayew A 7, 66, Gignac 36)*
**Eskiesehirspor (0) 0** 5432
*Marseille:* (4231) Mandanda; Fanni, N'Koulou, Mbia (Azpilicueta 82), Morel; Kabore, Cheyrou[■]; Amalfitano, Valbuena (Ayew J 73), Ayew A; Gignac (Abdullah 79).
*Eskiesehirspor:* (4141) Boffin; Sari, Cetin, Diego Angelo, Dede; Gucer; Guven (Tello 46), Kamara, Potuk, Zengin (Malecki 46); Nuhiu.

**Metalurh Donetsk (0) 0**
**Tromso (1) 1** *(Prijovic 9)* 2885
*Metalurh Donetsk:* (4231) Bandura; Morozyuk, Checher, Volovik, Yedigaryan; Priyma (Dimitrov 72), Lazic; Ze Soares (Nelson 46), Makrides, Ghazaryan; Junior Moraes (Traore 58).
*Tromso:* (442) Sahlman; Yndestad, Bjorck, Koppinen, Kristiansen R; Bendiksen, Kara, Yttergard, Drage (Andersen 81); Prijovic (Arst 62), Ondrasek (Ciss 86).

**Mlada Boleslav (0) 0**
**FC Twente (2) 2** *(Chadli 9, Fer 31)* 3077
*Mlada Boleslav:* (343) Seda; Kysela, Johana, Zbrozek; Boril, Kudela, Brunclik (Opiela 79), Sirl; Sivric, Magera (Ondrejka 22), Mares (Nespor 60).
*FC Twente:* (433) Fernandes; Rosales, Douglas, Bjelland, Schilder (Wisgerhof 77); Janssen, Brama, Fer; Tadic (Gutierrez 60), Bulykin (Verhoek 64), Chadli.

**Mura 05 (0) 0**
**Arsenal Kyiv (1) 2** *(Kobakhidze 2, Homenyuk 61)* 4525
*Mura 05:* (4231) Drakovic; Majer, Cipot, Kramar, Janza; Marusko, Horvat; Jelic (Kouter 90), Eterovic (Vas 66), Bohar (Sres 71); Fajic.
*Arsenal Kyiv:* (4231) Pankiv; Mikoliunas, Hitchenko, Symonenko[■], Polivoy; Maksymov, Shakhov[■]; Adiyiah (Simovic 35), Shatskikh, Kobakhidze (Kovpak 81); Mazilu (Homenyuk 61).

**Omonia (0) 0**
**Red Star Belgrade (0) 0** 13,977
*Omonia:* (4231) Leoni; Shpungin, Pavicevic, Danielson, Scaramozzino; Marco Soares, Leandro (Margaca 95); Christofi, Nuno Assis (Bruno Aguiar 73), Avraam (Alves J 83); Freddy.
*Red Star Belgrade:* (4132) Bajkovic; Mikic, Maksimovic, Jovanovic, Mladenovic; Mijailovic; Dimitrijevic, Milivojevic, Lazovic (Milunovic 102); Evandro (Miric 119), Kasalica.
*aet; Red Star Belgrade won 6-5 on penalties.*

**PAOK Salonika (0) 4** *(Athanasiadis 48, 52, Robert 79, Pelkas 90)*
**Bnei Yehuda Tel Aviv (1) 1** *(Marinkovic 7)* 9544
*PAOK Salonika:* (442) Glikos; Etto, Khumalo, Katsikas (Intzidis 37), Lino; Georgiadis, Fotakis (Kace 46), Lazar, Robert; Salpingidis (Pelkas 71), Athanasiadis.
*Bnei Yehuda Tel Aviv:* (442) Aiyenugba; Azuz, Cohen, Haddad, Edri; Ivaskevicius, Galvan (Nachum 56), Abu Zaid, Menashe[■]; Marinkovic, Ndlovu.

**Rapid Bucharest (1) 1** *(Herea 20 (pen))*
**Heerenveen (0) 0** 2410
*Rapid Bucharest:* (442) Albut; Rui Duarte (Goga 48), Oros, Glauber, Bozovic; Roman, Grigorie, Filipe Teixeira, Herea (Milisavljevic 73); Surdu, Ciolacu (Ilijoski 46).
*Heerenveen:* (433) Nordfeldt; Zuiverloon, Gouweleeuw, Zomer, Raitala; Kums, Ziyech (van Anholt 46), de Roon; Tannane, Djuricic (El Akchaoui 74), van La Parra (Assaidi 46).

**Rapid Vienna (0) 2** *(Alar 90 (pen), Boyd 90)*
**Vojvodina (0) 0** 15,834
*Rapid Vienna:* (4231) Konigshofer; Trimmel, Sonnleitner, Gerson, Katzer; Prager (Alar 71), Heikkinen; Hofmann, Burgstaller (Kulovits 94), Drazan; Boyd.
*Vojvodina:* (433) Supic; Vulicevic, Djuric, Trajkovic, Pavlovic[■]; Ajuru (Mitosevic 73), Greene (Jokic 87), Poletanovic (Bojovic 93); Stevanovic, Oumarou, Almami Moreira.

**Rosenborg (0) 0**
**Servette (0) 0** 6725
*Rosenborg:* (4231) Orlund; Hoiland, Vagan, Strandberg, Dorsin; Svensson, Issah; Dockal, Henriksen, Fredheim (Selnaes 85); Prica.
*Servette:* (451) Barroca; Gomes, Kouassi, Schneider, Moubandje (Ruefli 83); Grippo, Pizzinat, Pasche (de Azevedo[■] 71), Paratte (Lang 63), Moutinho; Karanovic.

**Slaven Koprivnica (1) 2** *(Maras 28, Gregurina 68)*
**Athletic Bilbao (0) 1** *(Muniain 47)* 3047
*Slaven Koprivnica:* (3412) Rodic; Kokalovic, Maras, Bubnjic; Puric, Canathija (Grgic 74), Batarelo (Gregurina 66), Delic (Vugrinec 59); Glavica; Rak, Busic.
*Athletic Bilbao:* (4231) Iraizoz; Iraola, Gurpegui, Ekiza (Muniain 46), Perez Inigo; Iturraspe, De Marcos; Ibai Gomez (Ruiz de Galarreta 46), Toquero (Llorente 46), Isma Lopez; Susaeta.

**Sparta Prague (2) 2** *(Kweuke 36, 39)*
**Admira Wacker Modling (1) 2** *(Thurauer 19,*
*Sulimani 69)* 8732
*Sparta Prague:* (442) Vaclik; Vidlicka, Svejdik, Jarosik, Pamic; Kaderabek (Grajciar 81), Husbauer, Holek, Prikryl (Skalak 50); Kweuke, Kadlec (Keric 89).
*Admira Wacker Modling:* (442) Tischler; Plassnegger, Pollhuber, Schrott, Weber; Seebacher, Thurauer, Mevoungou (Schachner 62), Sabitzer; Sulimani (Schicker 80), Schwab (Hosiner 64).

**Spartak Trnava (0) 0**
**Steaua Bucharest (1) 3** *(Adi 8, Rusescu 77, Nikolic 84)*
16,175
*Spartak Trnava:* (4231) Filipko; Stozicky, Janecka, Cvirik (Tomacek 24), Hanzel; Gross, Karhan; Sabo, Carnota (Mikinic 82), Bicak (Koubsky 87); Mikovic.
*Steaua Bucharest:* (4231) Stanca; Georgievski, Gardos, Chiriches, Parvulescu; Bourceanu, Pintilii; Chipciu, Rusescu (Balan 89), Costea (Latovlevici 80); Adi (Nikolic 60).

**Viktoria Plzen (3) 5** *(Duris 21, 12, 28, Bakos 54, 87)*
**Ruch Chorzow (0) 0** 11,651
*Viktoria Plzen:* (442) Bolek; Rajtoral, Sevinsky, Prochazka, Limbersky (Reznik 71); Fillo (Stipek 60), Darida, Horvath (Hanousek 76), Kolar; Bakos, Duris.
*Ruch Chorzow:* (442) Peskovic; Djokic, Stawarczyk, Sadlok, Szyndrowski; Zienczuk, Malinowski, Panka, Lisowski (Lewczuk 81); Jankowski (Janoszka 64), Piech (Kuswik 78).

**Vitesse (0) 0**
**Anzhi Makhachkala (0) 2** *(Eto'o 48, 84 (pen))* 13,392
*Vitesse:* (4123) Velthuizen; Yasuda, Kalas, Kashia, van Aanholt; van der Heijden (Propper 78); Cziommer*, van Ginkel; Ibarra (Chanturia 74), Bony, Reis (Havenaar 74).
*Anzhi Makhachkala:* (4141) Gaboulov V; Agalarov, Samba, Joao Carlos, Tagirbekov; Jucilei; Carcela Gonzalez, Boussoufa (Lakhiyalov 77), Gaboulov G, Zhirkov (Shatov 74); Eto'o (Smolov 85).

**Young Boys (1) 3** *(Mayuka 7, Raimondi 69, Bobadilla 82)*
**Kalmar (0) 0** 10,124
*Young Boys:* (4141) Wolfli; Sutter, Nef, Ojala, Raimondi; Spycher; Mayuka (Gonzalez 89), Farnerud, Schneuwly, Nuzzolo (Costanzo 81); Bobadilla (Frey 83).
*Kalmar:* (442) Berisha; Ohman (Skjelvik 46), Arajuuri, Thorthevic, Nouri; Diouf, Rydstrom, Gutu (Eriksson 56), Israelsson; Andersson (McDonald 79), Dauda.

**Zeta (1) 1** *(Burzanovic 9)*
**Sarajevo (0) 0** 5879
*Zeta:* (433) Bulatovic; Radulovic MM, Radulovic MB, Kaludjerovic, Novovic; Bozovic (Ajkovic 60), Burzanovic, Zlaticanin; Doslak, Korac (Knezevic 80), Boljevic (Dabic 73).
*Sarajevo:* (4231) Bandovic; Tatomirovic, Dupovac, Torlak, Belosevic (Karamatic 58); Sunjevaric (Comor 58), Sesar; Suljic, Husejinovic, Zlatkovic; Hadzic.

**PLAY-OFF ROUND FIRST LEG**
Wednesday, 22 August 2012
**VfB Stuttgart (0) 2** *(Ibisevic 72, 90)*
**Dinamo Moscow (0) 0** 20,400
*VfB Stuttgart:* (4231) Ulreich; Hoogland, Tasci, Rodriguez, Boka; Kvist Jorgensen, Gentner; Harnik (Torun 62), Hajnai (Cacau 78), Okazaki (Traore 62); Ibisevic.
*Dinamo Moscow:* (4231) Shunin; Wilkshire, Schildenfeld, Fernandez, Lomic; Yusupov, Noboa; Nyakhaychyk (Granat 86), Misimovic Z (Semshov 39), Dzsudzsak; Kuranyi (Panyukov 76).

Thursday, 23 August 2012
**AC Horsens (1) 1** *(Spelmann 16)*
**Sporting Lisbon (0) 1** *(Carrillo 80)* 4000
*AC Horsens:* (442) Ronnow; Nohr, Rasmussen M, Agesen, Kortegaard; Drachmann J, Kielstrup, Retov, Klove (Bjerregaard 87); Fagerberg (Hajdarevic 76), Spelmann.
*Sporting Lisbon:* (442) Rui Patricio; Cedric, Boulahrouz, Rojo, Insua; Carrillo, Elias (Andre Martins 79), Adrien Silva, Schaars (Labyad 59); van Wolfswinkel R, Jeffren (Diego Capel 67).

**AIK Solna (0) 0**
**CSKA Moscow (0) 1** *(Honda 62)* 16,889
*AIK Solna:* (442) Turina; Backman, Karlsson, Johansson N, Danielsson (Moro 80); Mutumba-Kayongo, Borges, Gustafsson, Lorentzson; Karikari (Tjernstrom 63), Lundberg.
*CSKA Moscow:* (433) Akinfeev; Ignashevich, Mario Fernandes (Nababkin 72), Berezutsky, Shchennikov; Honda, Dzagoev, Musa; Cauna (Wernbloom 67), Elm, Tosic (Gonzalez 78).

**Anzhi Makhachkala (0) 1** *(Traore 52)*
**AZ Alkmaar (0) 0** 7000
*Anzhi Makhachkala:* (4411) Gabulov; Agalarov, Samba, Joao Carlos, Tagirbekov; Carcela-Gonzalez, Jucilei, Boussoufa, Shatov; Eto'o; Traore (Smolov 79).
*AZ Alkmaar:* (433) Alvarado; Marcellis, Viergever, Gorter, Reijnen; Falkenburg, Maher, Elm; Beerens (Berghuis 75), Altidore, Martens.

**Athletic Bilbao (3) 6** *(Aduriz 25, Susaeta 31,*
*Inigo Perez 43, Aduriz 52, Susaeta 58, Iraola 85)*
**HJK Helsinki (0) 0** 40,000
*Athletic Bilbao:* (433) Iraizoz; Iraola, Gurpegui, San Jose, Inigo Perez; Aduriz (Ibai 60), Iturraspe, De Marcos; Susaeta (Muniain 70), Ander Herrera (Ruiz de Galarreta 75), Lopez.
*HJK Helsinki:* (4231) Wallen; Sorsa, Lindstrom, Lahti, Sumusalo; Schuller (Mattila 47), Perovuo; Mannstrom, Vayrynen (Zeneli 66), Savage; Sadik (Makela 72).

**Atromitos (1) 1** *(Epstein 24)*
**Newcastle U (1) 1** *(Taylor R 45)* 4872
*Atromitos:* (433) Itandje; Skondras, Fitanidis, Lazaridis, Giannoulis (Karagounis 86); Dimoutsos, Iglesias, Brito; Beljic (Chumbinho 61), Kuqi (Karamanos 60), Epstein.
*Newcastle U:* (442) Harper; Tavernier, Williamson, Perch, Taylor R; Gosling (Amalfitano 64), Bigirimana, Anita, Marveaux (Gutierrez 70); Cisse (Campbell 77), Obertan.

**Bursaspor (1) 3** *(Batalla 41, 83, Sestak 54)*
**FC Twente (1) 1** *(Chadli 32)* 24,000
*Bursaspor:* (442) Carson; Chretien M, Aziz (Erdogan 11), Ozturk, Wederson; N'Diaye, Cagiran, Ipek, Batalla (Kiraz 91); Sestak (Forsell 70), Pinto.
*FC Twente:* (433) Mihailov; Bjelland, Rosales, Douglas, Schilder; Brama (Gutierrez 63), Fer, Janssen; Tadic, Chadli (Bulykin 81), Castaignos (Verhoek 73).

**Crvena Zvezda (0) 0**
**Bordeaux (0) 0** 39,000
*Crvena Zvezda:* (442) Bajkovic; Maksimovic, Jovanovic (Spajic 86), Mladenovic, Mijailovic; Dimitrijevic, Mikic, Lazovic (Asamoah 80), Milivojevic; Vesovic (Miric 70), Milunovic.
*Bordeaux:* (442) Carasso; Ciani, Mariano, Planus, Tremoulinas; Sane, Sertic, Ben Khalfallah (Diabate 54), Obraniak; Maurice-Belay (Jussie 83), Gouffran (N'Guemo 90).

**Debrecen (0) 0**
**Club Brugge (0) 3** *(Blondel 59, Rafaelov 78, Bacca 90)*
8000
*Debrecen:* (4132) Poleksic; Simac, Meszaros, Nagy (Marcolini 88), Mohl; Ramos*; Rezes (Kulcsar 80), Varga, Szakaly; Sidibe (Bodi 67), Coulibaly.
*Club Brugge:* (442) Jorgacevic; Hoefkens, Larsen, Donk, Odjija Ofoe (Jorgensen 91); Jordi, Zimling (Vazquez 86), Rafaelov, Blondel; Tchite (Bacca 67), Meunier T.

**Dinamo Bucurest (0) 0**
**Metalist Kharkiv (1) 2** *(Cleiton Xavier 10, Cristaldo 57)*
18,000
*Dinamo Bucurest:* (442) Balgradean; Luchin, Grigore, Koulibaly, Pulhac; Matei, Ba (Galchev 60), Munteanu (Axente 78), Mansaly; Alexe (Curtean 66), Tucudean.
*Metalist Kharkiv:* (4141) Goryainov; Obradovic, Gueye, Torsiglieri, Fininho**; Torres; Edmar, Willian (Blanco 58), Cleiton Xavier (Marlos 83), Sosa; Cristaldo (Rebenok 69).

**F91 Dudelange (1) 1** *(Joachim 21)*
**Hapoel Tel Aviv (3) 3** *(Caillet 5 (og), Ben Haim 20 (pen), Cohen 28)* 937
*F91 Dudelange:* (4231) Joubert; Prempeh, Tournut (Da Mota Alves 47), Caillet, Melisse; Hug, Payal (Zeghdane 47); Idazza (Kitenge 76), Steinmetz, Legros; Joachim.
*Hapoel Tel Aviv:* (4411) Apoula; Pantsil, Haimovich, Badir, Antebi; Toama (Bruno Coutinho 64), Igiebor, Djemba-Djemba, Cohen; Ben Haim (Maman 81); Damari (Merey 47).

**FC Lucerne (1) 2** *(Rangelov 8, Winter 72)*
**KRC Genk (1) 1** *(Vossen 13)* 10,000
*FC Lucerne:* (442) Zibung; Puljic, Lustenberger, Stahel, Sarr; Winter (Hochstrasser 90), Wiss, Gygax, Muntwiler; Lezcano (Kryeziu 84), Rangelov.
*KRC Genk:* (442) Koteles; Ngcongca, Nadson, Dani Fernandez, Hyland; Gorius (Koulibaly 47), Buffel (Nwanganga 85), Monrose (Limbombe 85), Tshimanga; Vossen, Benteke.

**Midtjylland (0) 0**
**Young Boys (1) 3** *(Bobadilla 43, Farnerud 85, Costanzo 90)* 4522
*Midtjylland:* (4411) Lossl; Villafane (Afriyie 78), Juelsgaard, Sviatchenko, Bak Nielsen; Olsen, Albaek, Hassan, Uzochukwu; Igboun Emeka; Nworuh (Rasmussen** 60).
*Young Boys:* (442) Wolfli; Ojala, Nef, Zverotic, Spycher; Farnerud (Silberbauer 86), Schneuwly (Costanzo 74); Raimondi, Nuzzolo R; Bobadilla, Mayuka (Frey 85).

**Feyenoord (0) 2** *(Nelom 61, Achahbar 90)*
**Sparta Prague (2) 2** *(Kadlec 24, 28)* 45,000
*Feyenoord:* (433) Mulder; Janmaat, Mathijsen, Martins Indi, Nelom; Clasie, Leerdam (Vormer 64), Immers; Fernandez (Achahbar 82), Cisse (Elabdellaoui 64), Schaken.
*Sparta Prague:* (442) Vaclik; Vidlicka, Svejdik, Jarosik, Pamic; Kaderabek (Prikryl 70), Husbauer, Matejovsky (Holek 84), Skalak J; Kweuke, Kadlec (Pavelka 87).

**FK Ekranas (0) 0**
**Steaua Bucharest (1) 2** *(Martinovic 37, Popa 77)* 5500
*FK Ekranas:* (451) Kauneckas; Samusiovas, Dedura, Urdinov, Luksa; Kucys (Girdvainis 79), Kymantas (Norvilas 77), Andjelkovic, Vertelis, Tomkevicius; Buinickij (Varnas 64).
*Steaua Bucharest:* (442) Stanca; Chiriches, Popa, Pintilii, Latovlevici; Georgievski, Martinovic, Chipciu A (Rusescu 58), Bourceanu (Filip 54); Nikolic (Adi 63), Costea.

**Hearts (0) 0**
**Liverpool (0) 1** *(Webster 78 (og))* 15,965
*Hearts:* (4411) MacDonald; McGowan, Webster, Zaliukas, Grainger; Paterson, Barr (Robinson 87), Taouil, Novikovas (Carrick 84); Templeton (Driver 79); Sutton.
*Liverpool:* (433) Reina; Kelly, Carragher, Agger, Robinson (Downing 62); Henderson, Adam, Spearing (Allen 67); Shelvey, Borini (Morgan 90), Sterling.

**Legia Warsaw (1) 1** *(Kosecki 43)*
**Rosenborg (0) 1** *(Dockal 81)* 25,000
*Legia Warsaw:* (433) Vasile; Jedrzejczyk, Wawrzyniak, Astiz, Rzezniczak; Radovic, Lukasik (Furman 91), Kosecki; Ljuboja, Saganowski, Kucharczyk (Zyro 77).
*Rosenborg:* (442) Orlund; Dorsin, Reginiussen, Hoiland, Strandberg; Dockal, Henriksen, Svensson, Diskerud M; Elyounoussi, Fredheim Holm (Prica 75).

**Liberec (0) 2** *(Breznanik 63, Vacha 91 (pen))*
**Dnipro Dnipropetrovsk (1) 2** *(Konoplianka 44, Matheus 50)* 4226
*Liberec:* (442) Bicik; Kelic, Janu (Morozenko 84), Lyulka, Kusnir (Hadascok 61); Vacha, Bosancic (Maicon 47), Breznanik, Fleisman; Nezmar, Sural.
*Dnipro Dnipropetrovsk:* (433) Lastuvka; Cheberyachko, Mazuch, Mandzyuk, Strinic; Giuliano, Rotan, Aliev (Odibe 75); Zozulya, Matheus, Konoplianka (Oliynyk 66).

**Lokeren (1) 2** *(Harbaoui 11, Maric 91 (pen))*
**Viktoria Plzen (1) 1** *(Bakos 30)* 6000
*Lokeren:* (433) Barry; Galitsios, Maric, Taravel, De Bock; Persoons, Overmeire, Leko (Maric 87); De Ceulaer (De Pauw 81), Harbaoui, Patosi (Mokulu 76).
*Viktoria Plzen:* (4231) Kozacik; Rajtoral, Prochazka, Sevinsky**, Limbersky; Horvath, Darida; Fillo (Hora 56), Hanousek (Hejda 90), Duris (Reznik 86); Bakos.

**Maritimo (0) 1** *(Fidelis 65)*
**Dila Gori (0) 0** 4000
*Maritimo:* (4231) Salin; Briguel, Joao Guilherme, Roberge, Luis Olim; Joao Luiz (Rodrigo Antonio 82), Rafael Miranda; Nhuck (Danilo Dias 56), David Simao, Sami; Adilson (Fidelis 55).
*Dila Gori:* (4231) Skender; Shashiashvili, Salukvadze, Oniani, Kvirkvelia; Grigalashvili (Akhalkatsi 71), Gogua; Bechvaia, Klimiashvili (Kakhelishvili 57), Guruli (Iluridze 63); Gvalia .

**Molde (1) 2** *(Eikrem 32, Mostrom 91)*
**Heerenveen (0) 0** 4656
*Molde:* (433) Pettersen; Linnes, Vatshaug, Forren, Rindaroy; Eikrem, Berg Hestad (Diouf 70), Mostrom; Gatt (Simonsen 82), Berget J (Hussain 70), Chukwa.
*Heerenveen:* (433) Nordfeldt; Zuiverloon, Gouweleeuw, Zomer (Kruiswijk 59), El Akchaoui; van Anholt, Kums, de Roon; Van La Parra (Fazli 86), Djuricic, Tannane (Valpoort 46).

**Motherwell (0) 0**
**Levante (1) 2** *(Juanlu 42, El Zhar 62)* 6286
*Motherwell:* (4411) Randolph; Hateley, Hutchinson**, Cummins, Hammell; Humphrey (McHugh 68), Lasley, Law (Carswell 86), Murphy; Ojamaa (Kerr 68); Higdon.
*Levante:* (4411) Navas; Lell, Ballesteros, Navarro, Karabelas (El Zhar 40); Pedro Lopez, Michel (Pallardo 66), Iborra, Juanlu (Oscar Serrano 76); Barkero; Gekas.

**Mura 05 (0) 0**
**Lazio (1) 2** *(Hernanes 32, Klose 60)* 5000
*Mura 05:* (352) Drakovic; Travner, Marusko, Kramer (Sres 63); Buzeti, Horvat, Janza, Eterovic (Kouter 79), Vas; Bohar (Majer 87), Fajic.
*Lazio:* (433) Marchetti; Konko, Biava, Dias, Cavanda; Hernanes (Lulic 60), Ledesma, Onazi; Candreva, Klose (Floccari 83), Mauri (Sres 72).

**Neftchi (0) 1** *(Shukurov 82 (pen))*
**APOEL Nicosia (0) 1** *(Benachour 84)* 8000
*Neftchi:* (4231) Stamenkovic; Shukurov, Yunuszade, Mitreski, Bertucci; Ramos, Sadygov; Wobay (Abdullayev A 77), Imamverdiyev (Seyidov 66), Flavinho; Canales.
*APOEL Nicosia:* (4231) Chiotis; Mario Sergio, Borda, Zuela, Alexandrou; Morais, Pinto; Aloneftis, Helder Sousa (Benachour 47), Charalambidis (Adorno 59); Budimir (Solomou 89).

**PAOK Salonika (0) 2** *(Athanasiadis 70, Katsikas 84)*
**Rapid Vienna (1) 1** *(Alar 26)* 20,000
*PAOK Salonika:* (442) Glykos; Katsikas, Lino, Khumalo, Georgiadis (Lawrence 69); Robert (Fotakis 47), Lazar**, Kace, Etto; Athanasiadis, Giannou (Salpingidis 47).
*Rapid Vienna:* (4411) Konigshofer; Schimpelsberger, Sonnleitner, Ferreira, Katzer; Burgstaller, Heikkinen, Ildiz, Grozurek (Schrammel 66); Hoffmann (Kulovits 78); Alar (Boyd T 83).

**Sheriff (1) 1** *(Pajovic 27)*
**Marseille (1) 2** *(Ayew J 19, Gignac 54)* 13,000
*Sheriff:* (4231) Stoyanov; Metoua, Samardzic, Pajovic, Morales; Rouamba, Onica (Ivanov 76); Balima, Stanojevic (Pascenco 72), Dedov (Luvannor 80); Pesic.
*Marseille:* (4231) Mandanda; Fanni, N'Koulou, Mbia, Morel; Kabore, Abdullah; Valbuena (Raspentino 63), Amalfitano, Ayew J (Omrani 89); Gignac (Remy 75).

**Slask Wroclaw (1) 3** *(Jodlowiec 35, Patejuk 55, Kazmierczak 62)*
**Hannover 96 (3) 5** *(Andreasen 8, 83, Schlaudraff 26, Stindl 41, Schmiedebach 86)* 15,000
*Slask Wroclaw:* (442) Gikiewicz; Pawelec, Kowalcyzk, Elsner (Patejuk 47), Jodlowiec; Mraz, Sobota, Mila, Stevanovic; Kazmierczak, Gikiewicz (Voskamp 47).
*Hannover 96:* (442) Zieler; Haggui, Cherundolo, Felipe, Pander; Huszti (Schmiedebach 67), Andreasen, Stindl, Pinto; Konan D (Sobiech 76), Schlaudraff (Nikci 86).

**Trabzonspor (0) 0**
**Videoton (0) 0** 21,000
*Trabzonspor:* (4231) Kivrak; Balci, Kacar (Yumlu 75), Bamba, Celustka; Colman (Alanzinho 47), Zokora; Sen (Oztekin 43), Sapara, Adin; Altintop.
*Videoton:* (4231) Bozovic; Brachi, Caneira, Vinicius, Stopira; Toth, Mitrovic; Walter, Sandor (Renato Neto 81), Oliveira (Nikolic 87); Torghelle (Nikolic 75).

**Tromso (1) 3** *(Prijovic 38, Bjorck 78, Mbodji 83)*
**Partizan Belgrade (1) 2** *(Markovic 44, Mitrovic 85)* 3386
*Tromso:* (442) Sahlman; Kristiansen R, Bjorck, Koppinen, Ciss (Yndestad 79); Andersen (Bendiksen 73), Mbodji, Jenssen, Drage T; Ondrasek, Prijovic (Johansen 64).
*Partizan Belgrade:* (4141) Stojkovic; Aksentijevic, Miljkovic A, Ivanov, Volkov; Markovic (Smiljanic 90); Tomic, Babovic (Ilic 82), Medo, Markovic; Scepovic (Mitrovic 59).

**Vaslui (0) 0**
**Internazionale (1) 2** *(Cambiasso 24, Palacio R 74)* 15,000
*Vaslui:* (4132) Coman; Milanov, Celeban (Caue 74), Charalambous, Salageanu; Varela; Antal, N'Doye, Sanmartean; Stanciu (Varga 47), Niculae (Sburlea 62).
*Internazionale:* (433) Castellazzi; Zanetti, Ranocchia, Silvestre, Maicon; Guarin, Cambiasso, Mudingayi (Nagatomo 72); Milito (Coutinho 73), Sneijder (Juan 83), Palacio R.

**Zeta (0) 0**
**PSV Eindhoven (1) 5** *(Toivonen 3, Matavz 75, Strootman 78, Lens 84, Van Bommel 91)* 7000
*Zeta:* (4231) Bulatovic; Radulovic MM, Radulovic MB, Vujacic, Novovic; Zlaticanin (Pelicic Z 82), Bozovic (Ajkovic 47); Dosljak, Burzanovic, Boljevic; Korac.
*PSV Eindhoven:* (433) Tyton; Hutchinson, Marcelo, Derijck, Ritzmaier; Van Bommel, Toivonen, Strootman; Lens, Matavz, Mertens.

**PLAY-OFF ROUND SECOND LEG**

Tuesday, 28 August 2012
**Dinamo Moscow (0) 1** *(Kokorin 79)*
**VfB Stuttgart (0) 1** *(Ibisevic 65)* 9000
*Dinamo Moscow:* (442) Shunin; Chicherin, Fernandez, Schildenfeld, Granat; Dzsudzsak (Nyakhaychyk 69), Sapeta (Semshov 62), Noboa, Lomic; Kuranyi (Misimovic Z 69), Kokorin.
*VfB Stuttgart:* (433) Ulreich; Sakai, Rodriguez, Tasci, Boka (Molinaro C 75); Gentner, Hajnal, Kvist Jorgensen; Harnik (Torun 69), Ibisevic (Cacau 79), Okazaki.

Thursday, 30 August 2012
**APOEL Nicosia (1) 1** *(Benachour 45)*
**Neftchi (2) 3** *(Imamverdiyev 23, Wobay 31, Flavinho 61)* 20,000
*APOEL Nicosia:* (4411) Chiotis; Mario Sergio, Klukowski (Charalambidis 64), Borda, Alexandrou; Aloneftis, Pinto, Morais, Manduca (Abdullayev 82); Benachour (Helder Sousa 73); Budimir.

**Neftchi:** (442) Stamenkovic; Shukurov, Yunuszade[■], Mitreski, Bertucci; Wobay (Abdullayev A 77), Ramos, Sadygov, Flavinho; Canales (Guliyev T 86), Imamverdiyev (Seyidov 73).

**AZ Alkmaar (0) 0**
**Anzhi Makhachkala (2) 5** *(Boussoufa 18, Eto'o 45, Traore 80, Carcela-Gonzalez 84, Lakhiyalov 90)* 13,000
*AZ Alkmaar:* (433) Alvarado; Marcellis, Reijnen, Viergever, Gorter; Falkenburg, Maher, Elm; Beerens (Rosheuvel 73), Altidore (Boymans 61), Martens (Gudmundsson 42).
*Anzhi Makhachkala:* (4231) Gabulov; Agalarov, Samba, Joao Carlos, Logashov (Zhirkov 55); Shatov (Smolov 73), Jucilei; Carcela-Gonzalez, Eto'o (Lakhiyalov 86), Boussoufa; Traore.

**Bordeaux (0) 3** *(Gouffran 54, Jussie 73, Gouffran 90 (pen))*
**Crvena Zvezda (1) 2** *(Mladenovic 45, Mikic 90)* 21,789
*Bordeaux:* (4231) Carrasso; Henrique (Plasil 71), Sane, Mariano, Planus (Saivet 72); Tremoulinas, Gouffran; Sertic, Obraniak, Jussie (Marange 74); Maurice-Belay[■].
*Crvena Zvezda:* (442) Bajkovic; Mikic, Maksimovic, Jovanovic (Babalj 86), Mladenovic; Lazovic, Mijailovic, Dimitrijevic, Vesovic (Asamoah 77); Milunovic (Miric 64), Kasalica.

**Club Brugge (1) 4** *(Larsen 26, Vazquez 49, Tchite 51, Bacca 67)*
**Debrecen (1) 1** *(Szakaly 35)* 20,500
*Club Brugge:* (442) Jorgacevic; Hoefkens, Larsen (Almeback 55), Donk, Jordi; Meunier T (Jorgensen 47), Vazquez, Blondel (Van Acker 62), Rafaelov; Bacca, Tchite.
*Debrecen:* (442) Verpecz; Nagy, Simac, Meszaros, Mohl; Bodi (Kulcsar 72), Szakaly (Spitzmuller 81), Varga, Rezes[■]; Sidibe (Korhut 55), Coulibaly.

**CSKA Moscow (0) 0**
**AIK Solna (1) 2** *(Karikari 7, Lorentzson 90)* 14,000
*CSKA Moscow:* (4411) Akinfeev; Mario Fernandes, Berezutsky, Ignashevich, Nababkin; Tosic, Elm, Cauna, Dzagoev; Honda; Musa.
*AIK Solna:* (442) Turina; Lorentzson, Karlsson, Backman, Johansson; Lalawele, Danielsson, Borges, Mutumba-Kayongo (Tjernstrom 69); Quasion (Lundberg 69), Karikari.

**Dila Gori (0) 0**
**Maritimo (1) 2** *(Nhuck 42, Danilo Dias 90)* 15,000
*Dila Gori:* (442) Skender; Kashia (Kakhelishvili 64), Salukvadze (Tomashvili 18), Oniani, Kvirkvelia; Guruli, Bechvaia, Grigalashvili, Gogua; Iluridze (Akhalkatsi 47), Vatsadze.
*Maritimo:* (4411) Salin; Briguel, Joao Guilherme, Roberge, Luis Olim; Nhuck (Igor Rossi 68), Rafael Miranda, Rodrigo Antonio[■], Sami (Danilo Dias 74); David Simao (Marcio Rosario 59); Fidelis.

**Dnipro Dnipropetrovsk (1) 4** *(Aliev 13 (pen), 60 (pen), Konoplianka 76, Kalinic 88)*
**Liberec (0) 2** *(Breznanik 62, Kelic 73)* 27,076
*Dnipro Dnipropetrovsk:* (442) Lastuvka; Mazuch, Strinic, Odibe, Cheberyachko; Giuliano, Rotan, Aliev (Mandzyuk 89), Konoplianka; Zozulya (Kravchenko 73), Matheus (Kalinic 58).
*Liberec:* (442) Bicik; Kelic, Janu, Lyulka, Kusnir (Rabusic 80); Vacha, Bosancic (Karisik 29), Breznanik, Fleisman; Nezmar[■], Hadascok (Blazek 63).

**FC Twente (1) 4** *(Fer 27 (pen), 117, Schilder 62, Gutierrez 63)*
**Bursaspor (1) 1** *(Pinto 45)* 30,206
*FC Twente:* (433) Mihailov; Rosales, Wisgerhof, Douglas, Schilder; Fer, Brama, Janssen (Gutierrez 61); Tadic, Bulykin (Verhoek 60), Castaignos (Landzaat 119).
*Bursaspor:* (4231) Carson; Sestak, Ozturk, Erdogan, Wederson; Cagiran, N'Diaye (Kocak 83), Chretien M[■], Batalla (Kiraz 113), Ipek (Aslantas 41); Pinto.
*aet.*

**Hannover 96 (2) 5** *(Abdellaoui 23 (pen), Huszti 36, 89, Sobiech 69, 85)*
**Slask Wroclaw (1) 1** *(Kazmierczak 11)*      30,000
*Hannover 96:* (442) Zieler; Cherundolo (Sakai 71), Eggiman, Haggui, Schulz (Rausch 40); Stindl, Schmiedebach, Andreasen, Huszti; Schlaudraff (Sobiech 64), Abdellaoui.
*Slask Wroclaw:* (4231) Kelemen; Socha, Kowalcyzk, Jodlowiec■, Spahic; Elsner (Stevanovic 82), Kazmierczak; Sobota, Mila, Patejuk (Voskamp 66); Diaz (Pawelec 47).

**Hapoel Tel Aviv (0) 4** *(Maman 69, 85, Merey 80, Toama 89)*
**F91 Dudelange (0) 0**      5500
*Hapoel Tel Aviv:* (442) Apoula; Pantsil, Badir, Shushan M, Antebi; Bruno Coutinho (Toama 58), Djemba-Djemba, Ben Haim (Atadjanov 80), Cohen (Maman 58); Damari, Merey.
*F91 Dudelange:* (442) Joubert; Martino, Prempeh, Caillet, Melisse; Payal (Malget 89), Legros, Hug (Touray 86), Benzouien; Da Mota Alves, Kitenge (Pedro 74).

**Heerenveen (0) 1** *(Valpoort 90)*
**Molde (0) 2** *(Berget 55, Diouf 74)*      18,000
*Heerenveen:* (433) Nordfeldt; Zuiverloon, Kruiswijk, Zomer, El Akchaoui (Raitala 72); Kums, de Roon, van Anholt (Gouweleeuw 61); Van La Parra (De Ridder 76), Djuricic, Valpoort.
*Molde:* (433) Pettersen; Linnes, Vatshaug, Forren, Rindaroy; Eikrem (Hoseth 76), Berg Hestad, Mostrom; Gatt (Hussain 75), Berget (Chukwa 58), Diouf.

**HJK Helsinki (1) 3** *(Schuller 26, Perovuo 63, Pohjanpalo 71)*
**Athletic Bilbao (0) 3** *(San Jose 67, Toquero 78, Igor Martinez 89)*      5580
*HJK Helsinki:* (442) Wallen; Sorsa (Okkonen 56), Lahti, Moren (Savage 77), Kansikas; Mannstrom, Schuller (Hakanpaa 66), Perovuo, Zeneli; Pohjanpalo, Pelvas■.
*Athletic Bilbao:* (433) Raul; Ruiz de Galarreta, Ekiza, San Jose, Castillo; De Marcos (Ramalho 47), Iturraspe (Inigo Perez 47), Muniain; Susaeta (Igor Martinez 47), Toquero, Ibai.

**Internazionale (0) 2** *(Palacio R 77, Guarin 91)*
**Vaslui (1) 2** *(Stanciu 36 (pen), Varela 80)*      41,000
*Internazionale:* (442) Castellazzi■; Zanetti, Samuel (Guarin 47), Juan, Jonathan (Ranocchia 83); Nagatomo, Silvestre, Cambiasso, Coutinho; Palacio R, Cassano (Belec 35).
*Vaslui:* (442) Straton; Cordos, Varela, Antal, Salageanu; Stanciu, Caue (Sanmartean 61), Tukura, N'Doye; Celeban, Sburlea.

**KRC Genk (0) 2** *(Dani Fernandez 58, Masika 89)*
**FC Lucerne (0) 0**      12,134
*KRC Genk:* (442) Koteles; Dani Fernandez, Nadson, Koulibaly, Ngcongca (Croux 85); Buffel, Hyland, Gorius, Nwanganga (Masika 87); Monrose, Vossen (Hubert 90).
*FC Lucerne:* (442) Zibung; Sarr, Stahel (Hochstrasser 80), Puljic, Lustenberger; Gygax (Pacar 74), Wiss, Muntwiler, Winter; Rangelov■, Lezcano (Hyka 40).

**Lazio (2) 3** *(Kozak 31, 55, Zarate 42)*
**Mura 05 (0) 1** *(Travner 88)*      15,000
*Lazio:* (442) Bizzarri; Dias, Scaloni, Biava, Cavanda; Lulic (Candreva 70), Hernanes (Konko 79), Gonzalez (Rozzi 62), Onazi; Zarate, Kozak.
*Mura 05:* (442) Drakovic; Majer, Kramer, Travner, Janza; Horvat (Kouter 84), Vas (Kozar 88), Marusko, Bohar (Buzeti 47); Fajic, Eterovic.

**Levante (0) 1** *(Gekas 72)*
**Motherwell (0) 0**      13,398
*Levante:* (4141) Navas; Juanfran, Ballesteros (Hector 76), Navarro, Pedro Lopez; Diop P; El Zhar, Iborra (Pallardo 79), Barkero (Michel 61), Juanlu; Gekas.
*Motherwell:* (4411) Randolph; Kerr, Cummins, Page, Hammell (Francis-Angol 74); Murphy, Lasley, Carswell (Humphrey 68), Hetherington; Ojamaa (McHugh 67); Higdon.

**Liverpool (0) 1** *(Suarez 88)*
**Hearts (0) 1** *(Templeton 85)*      44,361
*Liverpool:* (433) Reina; Kelly, Carragher, Skrtel, Downing; Henderson (Borini 76), Allen, Shelvey; Gerrard, Morgan (Sterling 62), Suarez.
*Hearts:* (4411) MacDonald; McGowan, Webster, Zaliukas, Grainger; Novikovas (Carrick 75), Barr, Taouil, Paterson; Templeton; Sutton (Driver 66).

**Marseille (0) 0**
**Sheriff (0) 0**      9783
*Marseille:* (4231) Mandanda; Mango, Kabore, N'Koulou, Morel;- Abdullah, Cheyrou; Amalfitano (Valbuena 80), Ayew, Ayew J; Remy (Gignac 68).
*Sheriff:* (433) Stoyanov; Morales, Samardzic, Pajovic, Metoua; Stanojevic (Ivanov 70), Rouamba, Onica; Dedov (Luvannor 86), Pesic (Dadu 77), Balima.

**Metalist Kharkiv (1) 2** *(Blanco 30, Cristaldo 62)*
**Dinamo Bucurest (0) 1** *(Curtean 53)*      33,417
*Metalist Kharkiv:* (4231) Goryainov; Obradovic, Gueye, Torsiglieri, Barvinko; Torres, Cleiton Xavier; Sosa (Willian 78), Blanco (Edmar 58), Marlos (Taison 58); Cristaldo.
*Dinamo Bucurest:* (442) Balgradean; Luchin, Grigore, Koulibaly, Nica; Matei, Galchev (Filip■ 47), Munteanu, Curtean; Mansaly (Danciulescu 73), Tucudean (Alexe 47).

**Newcastle U (1) 1** *(Vuckic 21)*
**Atromitos (0) 0**      29,242
*Newcastle U:* (4411) Krul; Simpson, Coloccini, Williamson, Taylor R (Vuckic 11); Obertan, Bigirimana, Perch (Tavernier 59), Marveaux (Amalfitano 90); Gosling; Ba.
*Atromitos:* (4231) Itandje; Skondras, Fitanidis, Lazaridis, Giannoulis; Iglesias, Brito (Kuqi 88); Dimoutsos (Garcia 85), Chumbinho (Beljic 75), Epstein; Karamanos.

**Partizan Belgrade (0) 1** *(Ivanov 76)*
**Tromso (0) 0**      21,000
*Partizan Belgrade:* (442) Stojkovic; Miljkovic A, Volkov, Ivanov, Ostojic; Medo, Tomic, Markovic (Smiljanic 79), Ilic (Ninkovic 73); Markovic (Zubya 47), Mitrovic.
*Tromso:* (442) Lekstrom; Mbodji, Kristiansen R, Bjorck, Koppinen; Ciss, Drage T, Jenssen, Bendiksen (Norbye 79); Ondrasek (Aarst 79), Prijovic (Andersen 60).

**PSV Einhoven (5) 9** *(Jorgensen 6, van Ooijen 13, 75, Matavz 16, 28, 64, Wijnaldum 40, 67, 84)*
**Zeta (0) 0**      22,000
*PSV Einhoven:* (442) Waterman; Jorgensen, Willems (Ritzmaier 47), Derijck, Manolev; Engelaar, van Ooijen, Wijnaldum, Narsingh; Depay, Matavz.
*Zeta:* (442) Bulatovic; Radulovic MM, Kaluderovic, Novovic, Radulovic MB (Vujacic 30); Bozovic (Zlaticanin 72), Dosljak, Burzanovic, Boljevic; Korac, Pelicic Z (Ajkovic 47).

**Rapid Vienna (1) 3** *(Alar 32, Boyd T 49, Hoffmann 90)*
**PAOK Salonika (0) 0**      16,000
*Rapid Vienna:* (451) Konigshofer; Trimmel (Schrammel 86), Sonnleitner, Ferreira, Katzer; Alar, Heikkinen (Prager 70), Hoffmann, Ildiz, Burgstaller; Boyd T.
*PAOK Salonika:* (442) Glykos; Etto, Khumalo, Vivian, Lino; Georgiadis, Pablo Garcia, Kace (Pelkas 71), Robert (Fotakis 47); Athanasiadis, Giannou (Lawrence 47).

**Rosenborg (0) 2** *(Reginiussen 70, Diskerud 88)*
**Legia Warsaw (1) 1** *(Ljuboja 37)*      4500
*Rosenborg:* (4411) Orlund; Hoiland, Reginiussen, Ronning, Dorsin; Dockal, Svensson, Diskerud, Fredheim Holm; Prica; Elyounoussi.
*Legia Warsaw:* (4141) Kuciak; Rzezniczak, Astiz, Zewlakow, Wawrzyniak; Lukasik; Radovic (Zyro 73), Gol, Ljuboja, Kosecki; Saganowski.

**Sparta Prague (0) 2** *(Kadlec 62 (pen), Jarosik 70)*
**Feyenoord (0) 0**      17,036
*Sparta Prague:* (442) Vaclik; Jarosik, Svejdik, Vidlicka, Pamic (Pavelka 19); Matejovsky (Holek 78), Kaderabek (Skalak 89), Husbauer, Prikryl (Krejci 68); Kweuke, Kadlec.
*Feyenoord:* (442) Mulder; Leerdam (Fernandez 74), Janmaat, De Vrij, Mathijsen; Martins Indi, Clasie, Vormer, Immers; Cisse, Schaken.

**Sporting Lisbon (2) 5** *(van Wolfswinkel R 9, 55,*
*Kortegaard 24 (og), Carrillo 58, Elias 64)*
**AC Horsens (0) 0** 25,000
*Sporting Lisbon:* (433) Rui Patricio; Cedric, Boulahrouz,
Rojo, Pranjic; Adrien Silva (Andre Martins 67),
Fernandes (Carrico 74), Elias; Carrillo (Jeffren 67), van
Wolfswinkel R, Diego Capel.
*AC Horsens:* (442) Ronnow; Andersen, Rasmussen M,
Aslam, Kortegaard; Drachmann J, Retov (Nohr 71),
Kielstrup, Klove; Spelmann (Hajdarevic 63), Fagerberg
(Bjerregaard 47).

**Steaua Bucharest (2) 3** *(Adi 21, 87, Dumitras 31)*
**FK Ekranas (0) 0** 15,500
*Steaua Bucharest:* (4231) Tatarusanu; Dumitras, Gardos,
Martinovic (Puscas 58), Latovlevici; Filip, Pintilii;
Chipciu A (Prepelita 47), Rusescu (Costea 47), Popa;
Adi.
*FK Ekranas:* (4231) Zubas; Tomkevicius, Dedura,
Girdvainis, Urdinov; Kucys, Andjelkovic; Luksa, Varnas
(Buinickij 90), Vertelis (Kavaliauskas 71); Kymantas
(Markevicius 78).

**Videoton (0) 0**
**Trabzonspor (0) 0** 10,000
*Videoton:* (4231) Bozovic; Brachi, Caneira, Vinicius,
Stopira; Toth, Mitrovic N; Oliveira (Gyurcso 78), Sandor,
Walter (Kovacs 103); Nikolic (Torghelle 71).
*Trabzonspor:* (4231) Kivrak; Balci, Yumlu■, Bamba,
Celustka; Aydogdu, Zokora; Sen (Altintop 61),
Alanzinho (Sapara 112), Oztekin (Vittek 84); Paulo
Henrique.
*aet; Videoton won 4-2 on penalties.*

**Viktoria Plzen (1) 1** *(Bakos 38)*
**Lokeren (0) 0** 11,700
*Viktoria Plzen:* (4231) Kozacik; Reznik, Prochazka,
Cisovsky, Limbersky; Rajtoral (Malakjan 90), Horvath;
Darida, Duris (Hora 78), Hanousek (Fillo 89); Bakos.
*Lokeren:* (4231) Barry; Galitsios, Maric, Taravel, De
Bock; Persoons, Leko (Maric 74); Overmeire, Patosi
(Mokulu 81), Harbaoui; De Ceulaer (De Pauw 81).

**Young Boys (0) 0**
**Midtjylland (0) 2** *(Igboun Emeka 76 (pen), Bak Nielsen*
*90)* 9327
*Young Boys:* (442) Wolfli; Ojala, Nef■, Spycher
(Silberbauer 67), Sutter; Nuzzolo, Farnerud, Schneuwly,
Raimondi (Lecjaks 35); Vitkieviez (Zverotic 86),
Bobadilla.
*Midtjylland:* (442) Lossl; Villafane, Ojuola, Juelsgaard,
Sviatchenko; Albaek, Larsen (Nworuh 69), Hassan
(Christensen 77), Uzochukwu; Igboun Emeka,
Andersson (Bak Nielsen 84).

## GROUP STAGE

### GROUP A

**Thursday, 20 September 2012**
**Udinese (0) 1** *(Di Natale 90)*
**Anzhi Makhachkala (1) 1** *(Padelli 45 (og))* 6500
*Udinese:* (3511) Padelli; Benatia, Danilo, Domizzi;
Faraoni, Agyemang-Badu (Di Natale 58), Willians (Basta
59), Lazzari, Armero; Pereyra (Pinzi 76); Ranegie.
*Anzhi Makhachkala:* (4231) Pomæzan; Agalarov, Joao
Carlos, Samba, Zhirkov; Jucilei, Boussoufa; Diarra,
Eto'o, Shatov; Traore (Carcela-Gonzalez 60).

**Young Boys (1) 3** *(Nuzzolo 38, Ojala 53, Zarate 63)*
**Liverpool (2) 5** *(Ojala 4 (og), Wisdom 40, Coates 67,*
*Shelvey 76, 88)* 31,120
*Young Boys:* (4231) Wolfli; Sutter, Veskovac, Ojala,
Raimondi; Zverotic (Frey 81), Spycher; Zarate
(Gonzalez 65), Farnerud, Nuzzolo (Schneuwly 69);
Bobadilla.
*Liverpool:* (4321) Jones; Wisdom, Carragher, Coates,
Jose Enrique; Henderson, Sahin, Suso; Assaidi O
(Shelvey 66), Downing (Sterling 77); Pacheco (Borini
61).

**Thursday, 4 October 2012**
**Anzhi Makhachkala (0) 2** *(Eto'o 62 (pen), 90)*
**Young Boys (0) 0** 14,000
*Anzhi Makhachkala:* (4231) Gabulov V; Agalarov,
Samba, Joao Carlos (Gabulov G 78), Tagirbekov
(Zhirkov 17); Jucilei, Diarra; Shatov, Eto'o, Boussoufa;
Traore (Carcela-Gonzalez 63).
*Young Boys:* (4231) Wolfli; Nef, Ojala, Veskovac,
Lecjaks; Zverotic, Costanzo; Schneuwly (Frey 66), Zarate
(Nuzzolo R 66), Vitkieviez (Gonzalez 77); Bobadilla.

**Liverpool (1) 2** *(Shelvey 23, Suarez 75)*
**Udinese (0) 3** *(Di Natale 46, Coates 70 (og), Pasquale 72)*
40,092
*Liverpool:* (433) Reina; Johnson, Coates, Carragher,
Robinson; Henderson (Gerrard 65), Allen, Shelvey;
Downing, Borini (Sterling 79), Assaidi O (Suarez 65).
*Udinese:* (343) Brkic; Benatia, Danilo, Domizzi; Faraoni,
Agyemang-Badu, Pinzi (Willians 70), Pasquale; Pereyra,
Di Natale (Ranegie 85), Armero (Lazzari 46).

**Thursday, 25 October 2012**
**Liverpool (0) 1** *(Downing 53)*
**Anzhi Makhachkala (0) 0** 39,358
*Liverpool:* (433) Jones; Wisdom, Skrtel, Agger, Johnson
(Sterling 46); Gerrard, Sahin, Shelvey (Allen 80);
Downing, Suarez, Assaidi.
*Anzhi Makhachkala:* (433) Gabulov V; Agalarov
(Logashov 61), Samba, Joao Carlos, Zhirkov; Shatov,
Gabulov G, Boussoufa (Lakhiyalov 77); Carcela-
Gonzalez, Eto'o, Smolov (Traore 64).

**Young Boys (1) 3** *(Bobadilla 4, 72, 82 (pen))*
**Udinese (0) 1** *(Coda 75)* 20,143
*Young Boys:* (4231) Wolfli; Sutter, Nef, Ojala, Raimondi;
Costanzo (Schneuwly 71), Zverotic; Zarate (Gonzalez
79), Farnerud (Veskovac 87), Nuzzolo; Bobadilla.
*Udinese:* (352) Brkic; Benatia, Danilo, Coda; Faraoni,
Agyemang-Badu (Pereyra 46), Lazzari (Domizzi 71),
Willians F, Armero; Fabbrini, Ranegie (Di Natale 46).

**Thursday, 8 November 2012**
**Anzhi Makhachkala (1) 1** *(Traore 45)*
**Liverpool (0) 0** 15,000
*Anzhi Makhachkala:* (4231) Gabulov; Logashov, Samba,
Joao Carlos, Tagirbekov; Ahmedov (Carcela-Gonzalez
29 (Lakhiyalov 90)), Jucilei; Zhirkov, Eto'o, Boussoufa;
Traore (Smolov 80).
*Liverpool:* (4231) Jones; Wisdom, Carragher, Coates,
Flanagan; Henderson, Coady (Suso 61); Cole (Assaidi
77), Shelvey, Downing, Morgan (Pacheco 61).

**Udinese (0) 2** *(Di Natale 47, Fabbrini 83)*
**Young Boys (1) 3** *(Bobadilla 27, Farnerud 65,*
*Nuzzolo R 73)* 12,000
*Udinese:* (352) Brkic; Coda, Danilo, Domizzi; Basta,
Pereyra (Faraoni 64), Willians (Fabbrini 53), Lazzari,
Armero; Di Natale, Ranegie.
*Young Boys:* (4231) Wolfli; Sutter, Nef, Veskovac,
Raimondi; Zverotic, Schneuwly (Doubai 74); Zarate
(Gonzalez 81), Farnerud, Nuzzolo R; Bobadilla (Frey
88).

Thursday, 22 November 2012
**Anzhi Makhachkala (0) 2** *(Samba 72, Eto'o 75)*
**Udinese (0) 0** 7500
*Anzhi Makhachkala:* (4231) Gabulov; Logashov, Samba (Lakhiyalov 86), Joao Carlos, Tagirbekov; Shatov, Jucilei; Carcela-Gonzalez (Traore 67), Boussoufa, Zhirkov; Eto'o.
*Udinese:* (3142) Brkic; Heurtaux, Danilo, Domizzi; Willians■; Faraoni (Basta 56 (Ranegie 76)), Agyemang-Badu, Pereyra, Armero (Pasquale 71); Fabbrini, Di Natale.

**Liverpool (1) 2** *(Shelvey 33, Cole 72)*
**Young Boys (0) 2** *(Bobadilla 52, Zverotic 88)* 37,810
*Liverpool:* (433) Reina; Wisdom (Gerrard 31), Skrtel, Carragher, Downing; Suso (Suarez 64), Sahin, Henderson; Cole (Sterling 75), Shelvey, Assaidi O.
*Young Boys:* (4231) Wolfli; Sutter, Nef, Veskovac (Ojala 23), Lecjaks; Zverotic, Farnerud; Zarate, Schneuwly (Vitkieviez 82), Nuzzolo (Frey 77); Bobadilla.

Thursday, 6 December 2012
**Udinese (0) 0**
**Liverpool (1) 1** *(Henderson 23)* 12,000
*Udinese:* (442) Padelli; Faraoni, Heurtaux, Danilo, Pasquale■; Pereyra, Agyemang-Badu, Pinzi (Benatia 46 (Reinthaler 65)), Armero; Fabbrini, Ranegie (Di Natale 85).
*Liverpool:* (433) Reina; Johnson, Skrtel, Carragher, Jose Enrique; Henderson, Allen, Sahin (Shelvey 12); Suso (Sterling 71), Suarez, Downing.

**Young Boys (1) 3** *(Zarate 37, Costanzo 52, Gonzalez 90)*
**Anzhi Makhachkala (1) 1** *(Ahmedov 45)* 17,132
*Young Boys:* (433) Wolfli; Sutter, Nef, Ojala, Raimondi; Schneuwly, Farnerud, Costanzo (Doubai 73); Zarate (Gonzalez 77), Bobadilla (Frey 88), Nuzzolo R.
*Anzhi Makhachkala:* (4411) Gabulov V; Logashov, Samba (Agalarov 46), Joao Carlos, Tagirbekov; Ahmedov (Carcela-Gonzalez 80), Jucilei, Diarra (Lakhiyalov 85), Shatov; Eto'o; Traore■.

| Group A Table | P | W | D | L | F | A | GD | Pts |
|---|---|---|---|---|---|---|---|---|
| Liverpool | 6 | 3 | 1 | 2 | 11 | 9 | 2 | 10 |
| Anzhi Makhachkala | 6 | 3 | 1 | 2 | 7 | 5 | 2 | 10 |
| Young Boys | 6 | 3 | 1 | 2 | 14 | 13 | 1 | 10 |
| Udinese | 6 | 1 | 1 | 4 | 7 | 12 | -5 | 4 |

**GROUP B**

Thursday, 20 September 2012
**Hapoel Tel Aviv (0) 0**
**Atletico Madrid (2) 3** *(Rodriguez 37, Diego Costa 40, Raul Garcia 63)* 12,000
*Hapoel Tel Aviv:* (4231) Apoula; Pantsil, Shushan M, Badir, Antebi; Djemba-Djemba, Bruno Coutinho (Toama 58); Maman, Vermouth (Cohen 75), Ben Haim; Tamuz (Merey 69).
*Atletico Madrid:* (442) Sergio Asenjo; Silvio, Miranda, Cata Diaz, Cisma; Raul Garcia, Mario Suarez, Emre, Rodriguez (Juanfran 74); Adrian (Koke 68), Diego Costa (Saul 78).

**Viktoria Plzen (0) 3** *(Horvath 47, Duris 58, Rajtoral 80)*
**Academica de Coimbra (1) 1** *(Wilson Eduardo 19)* 10,848
*Viktoria Plzen:* (4141) Kozacik; Reznik, Prochazka, Cisovsky, Limbersky; Horvath; Rajtoral (Malakjan 90), Darida, Hanousek, Hora (Zeman 60); Duris (Fillo 75).
*Academica de Coimbra:* (433) Ricardo; Rodrigo Galo, Halliche (Bruno China 48), Reiner Ferreira, Nivaldo; Makelele (Edinho 73), Flavio Ferreira, Keita (Ogu 63); Marinho, Cisse, Wilson Eduardo.

Thursday, 4 October 2012
**Academica de Coimbra (0) 1** *(Cisse 47)*
**Hapoel Tel Aviv (0) 1** *(Damari 90)* 5667
*Academica de Coimbra:* (433) Ricardo; Joao Dias, Flavio Ferreira, Reiner Ferreira, Helder Cabral; Cleyton (Makelele 69), Bruno China, Ogu; Marinho (Afonso 85), Cisse (Edinho 58), Wilson Eduardo.
*Hapoel Tel Aviv:* (4231) Apoula; Pantsil, Badir, Haimovich, Antebi; Djemba-Djemba, Gordana (Maman 61); Cohen (Damari 61), Vermouth, Ben Haim (Toama 66); Tamuz.

**Atletico Madrid (0) 1** *(Rodriguez 90)*
**Viktoria Plzen (0) 0** 20,000
*Atletico Madrid:* (442) Sergio Asenjo; Kader (Saul 85), Pulido, Cata Diaz, Cisma; Koke (Tiago 63), Gabi, Emre, Rodriguez; Adrian, Diego Costa (Raul Garcia 61).
*Viktoria Plzen:* (4231) Kozacik; Reznik, Sevinsky, Cisovsky, Limbersky; Darida (Hejda 90), Prochazka; Rajtoral (Hora 89), Hanousek, Duris; Bakos ( 90).

Thursday, 25 October 2012
**Atletico Madrid (0) 2** *(Diego Costa 48, Emre 68)*
**Academica de Coimbra (0) 1** *(Cisse 85)* 10,000
*Atletico Madrid:* (451) Sergio Asenjo; Silvio, Cata Diaz, Pulido, Filipe Luis; Koke (Rodriguez 61), Gabi, Tiago, Emre (Raul Garcia 76), Adrian (Saul 82); Diego Costa.
*Academica de Coimbra:* (442) Ricardo; Joao Dias, Flavio Ferreira, Halliche (Junior Lopes 22), Nivaldo; Marinho, Makelele (Cisse 60), Bruno China, Ogu (Cleyton 61); Edinho, Wilson Eduardo B.

**Hapoel Tel Aviv (1) 1** *(Maman 19)*
**Viktoria Plzen (1) 2** *(Horvath 45, Rajtoral 55)* 14,500
*Hapoel Tel Aviv:* (442) Apoula; Khutaba■, Danin, Haimovich, Badir; Maman, Djemba-Djemba (Cohen 75), Gordana (Toama 59), Tamuz (Pantsil 69); Damari, Ben Haim.
*Viktoria Plzen:* (4411) Kozacik; Cisovsky, Sevinsky, Reznik, Limbersky; Horvath, Duris (Zeman 74), Darida, Kolar (Hora 82); Rajtoral; Bakos (Hejda 88).

Thursday, 8 November 2012
**Academica de Coimbra (1) 2** *(Wilson Eduardo B 29, 70 (pen))*
**Atletico Madrid (0) 0** 3000
*Academica de Coimbra:* (442) Ricardo; Joao Dias, Flavio Ferreira, Joao Real, Nivaldo; Cleyton, Keita (Bruno China 79), Makelele, Marinho (Afonso 70); Cisse (Edinho 84), Wilson Eduardo B.
*Atletico Madrid:* (451) Sergio Asenjo; Silvio, Cata Diaz, Pulido, Filipe Luis; Koke, Mario Suarez (Emre 58), Tiago (Kader 71), Saul (Martin P 46), Adrian; Raul Garcia.

**Viktoria Plzen (2) 4** *(Kolar 23, 76, Stipek D 40, Bakos 84)*
**Hapoel Tel Aviv (0) 0** 11,389
*Viktoria Plzen:* (4231) Kozacik; Reznik, Prochazka, Cisovsky, Limbersky; Darida, Horvath (Zeman 80); Stipek D (Hora 67), Kolar, Duris; Bakos (Malakjan 85).
*Hapoel Tel Aviv:* (4231) Apoula; Pantsil, Shushan M, Petkovic, Antebi (Badir 46); Djemba-Djemba■, Gordana (Merey 74); Cohen (Maman 60), Toama, Danin; Tamuz.

Thursday, 22 November 2012
**Academica de Coimbra (0) 1** *(Edinho 89 (pen))*
**Viktoria Plzen (0) 1** *(Horvath 57 (pen))* 3717
*Academica de Coimbra:* (433) Ricardo; Joao Dias, Flavio Ferreira, Keita, Joao Real; Cleyton, Ogu (Cisse 70), Marinho; Wilson Eduardo B (Afonso 81), Reiner Ferreira, Edinho.
*Viktoria Plzen:* (433) Kozacik; Reznik, Prochazka, Cisovsky, Limbersky; Horvath, Duris (Malakjan 84), Darida; Stipek D (Zeman 73), Bakos, Hora (Sevinsky 89).

**Atletico Madrid (1) 1** *(Raul Garcia 7)*
**Hapoel Tel Aviv (0) 0** 10,000
*Atletico Madrid:* (4141) Sergio Asenjo; Silvio, Pulido, Cata Diaz, Cisma; Mario Suarez; Rodriguez (Martin P 87), Raul Garcia, Emre, Adrian; Diego Costa (Koke 58).
*Hapoel Tel Aviv:* (343) Apoula; Shushan M, Haimovich, Petkovic; Pantsil, Maman, Gordana (Mare 77), Danin; Vermouth (Toama 62), Damari, Ben Haim.

Thursday, 6 December 2012
**Hapoel Tel Aviv (0) 2** *(Mare 57, Maman 80)*
**Academica de Coimbra (0) 0** 12,000
*Hapoel Tel Aviv:* (541) Apoula; Khutaba, Shushan M, Haimovich, Petkovic, Danin; Vermouth (Maman 69), Izenstein, Toama, Ben Haim (Lax 86); Tamuz (Mare 46).
*Academica de Coimbra:* (433) Peiser; Joao Dias, Joao Real, Flavio Ferreira, Nivaldo (Cisse 71); Cleyton, Keita, Ogu (Makelele 70); Wilson Eduardo B, Edinho, Marinho (Afonso 82).

**Viktoria Plzen (1) 1** *(Prochazka 27)*
**Atletico Madrid (0) 0** 11,067
*Viktoria Plzen:* (4231) Kozacik; Reznik, Prochazka, Cisovsky, Limbersky; Horvath (Sevinsky 90), Darida; Rajtoral (Zeman 74), Kolar ( 89), Duris; Bakos.
*Atletico Madrid:* (442) Sergio Asenjo; Cisma (Saul 86), Miranda, Pulido, Juanfran (Koke 59); Raul Garcia, Emre, Tiago, Manquillo (Martin P 88); Diego Costa*, Adrian.

| Group B Table | P | W | D | L | F | A | GD | Pts |
|---|---|---|---|---|---|---|---|---|
| Viktoria Plzen | 6 | 4 | 1 | 1 | 11 | 4 | 7 | 13 |
| Atletico Madrid | 6 | 4 | 0 | 2 | 7 | 4 | 3 | 12 |
| Academica de Coimbra | 6 | 1 | 2 | 3 | 6 | 9 | –3 | 5 |
| Hapoel Tel Aviv | 6 | 1 | 1 | 4 | 4 | 11 | –7 | 4 |

## GROUP C

Thursday, 20 September 2012
**AEL Limassol (0) 0**
**Borussia Moenchengladbach (0) 0** 8500
*AEL Limassol:* (4321) Degra; Airosa, Junior, Parpas, Maykon (Bebe 76); Dede, Rui Miguel, Nicolaou; Edmar (Paulo Sergio G 71), Gilberto; Vouho (Orlando Sa 58).
*Borussia Moenchengladbach:* (4231) ter Stegen; Jantschke, Brouwers, Dominguez, Wendt; Nordtveit, Cigerci T; Herrmann, Ring (Rupp 79), Hrgota (Xhaka 46); Hanke (De Camargo 82).

**Fenerbahce (1) 2** *(Erkin 28, Alex 57)*
**Marseille (0) 2** *(Valbuena 83, Ayew A 90)* 47,000
*Fenerbahce:* (4231) Demirel; Ali Kaldirim, Irtegun, Yobo, Gonul; Topal, Meireles; Erkin (Stoch 87), Alex (Baroni 67), Topuz; Sow (Bienvenu 74).
*Marseille:* (433) Mandanda; Fanni, N'Diaye (Cheyrou 42), N'Koulou, Morel; Kabore, Barton (Ayew J 72), Amalfitano; Ayew A, Remy (Gignac 63), Valbuena.

Thursday, 4 October 2012
**Borussia Moenchengladbach (1) 2** *(De Jong 18, De Camargo 74)*
**Fenerbahce (2) 4** *(Baroni 25, 87, Meireles 40, Kuyt 71)* 46,279
*Borussia Moenchengladbach:* (4231) ter Stegen; Nordtveit, Stranzl, Brouwers, Daems; Cigerci T (De Camargo 62), Marx; Ring (Hrgota 46), Xhaka (Mlapa 86), Arango; De Jong.
*Fenerbahce:* (433) Demirel; Gonul, Irtegun, Korkmaz, Ali Kaldirim; Meireles, Baroni, Topal; Kuyt (Sahin S 90), Sow (Krasic 78), Erkin.

**Marseille (1) 5** *(Fanni 42, Lucas Mendes 61, Remy 77, 90, Gignac 90)*
**AEL Limassol (1) 1** *(Ouon 22)* 7500
*Marseille:* (4231) Mandanda; Aloe, N'Koulou (M'Bow 83); Fanni, Lucas Mendes; Kabore, Abdullah (Valbuena 53); Ayew J, Barton, Raspentino (Gignac 69); Remy.
*AEL Limassol:* (4231) Degra; Theophilou, Ouon, Junior, Carlitos (Parpas 78); Nicolaou (Konstantinou 77), Dede; Monteiro, Bebe, Paulo Sergio; Vouho (Orlando Sa 89).

Thursday, 25 October 2012
**AEL Limassol (0) 0**
**Fenerbahce (0) 1** *(Korkmaz 72)* 8000
*AEL Limassol:* (433) Degra; Junior, Nicolaou (Bebe 78), Airosa, Carlitos; Ouon, Rui Miguel, Dede; Monteiro, Paulo Sergio G (Gilberto 70), Vouho (Orlando Sa 73).
*Fenerbahce:* (442) Demirel; Korkmaz, Ali Kaldirim, Irtegun, Gonul; Topal, Baroni, Sahin S, Erkin (Krasic 68); Sow (Kesimal 90), Kuyt (Stoch 85).

**Borussia Moenchengladbach (1) 2** *(Daems F 33 (pen), Mlapa 67)*
**Marseille (0) 0** 45,000
*Borussia Moenchengladbach:* (442) ter Stegen; Jantschke (Brouwers 34), Stranzl, Dominguez, Daems F; Rupp, Marx, Nordtveit, Arango; Herrmann (Hanke 80), De Jong (Mlapa 65).
*Marseille:* (4231) Mandanda; Abdallah K (Cheyrou 83), Fanni, N'Koulou, Lucas Mendes; Kabore, Barton; Amalfitano, Valbuena (Raspentino 77), Ayew J; Remy (Ayew 65).

Thursday, 8 November 2012
**Fenerbahce (2) 2** *(Kuyt 11, Sow 41)*
**AEL Limassol (0) 0** 45,000
*Fenerbahce:* (4231) Demirel; Gonul, Yobo, Irtegun, Ali Kaldirim (Erkin 72); Meireles (Niyaz 83), Topal; Kuyt, Baroni (Sahin S 72), Stoch; Sow.
*AEL Limassol:* (433) Degra; Parpas, Dede, Ouon*, Carlitos; Bebe, Nicolaou, Rui Miguel; Monteiro (Edmar 60), Konstantinou (Vouho 73), Paulo Sergio G (Dickson 60).

**Marseille (0) 2** *(Barton 54, Ayew J 67)*
**Borussia Moenchengladbach (1) 2** *(Hanke 19, Arango 90)* 15,000
*Marseille:* (433) Mandanda; Fanni, Diawara (Kabore 82), Lucas Mendes, Morel; Amalfitano (Valbuena 68), Cheyrou, Barton; Ayew J (Abdallah K 87), Remy, Ayew A.
*Borussia Moenchengladbach:* (442) ter Stegen; Jantschke, Brouwers, Dominguez, Wendt; Rupp, Marx (Xhaka 74), Nordtveit, Arango; Herrmann (Mlapa 71), Hanke (De Camargo 73).

Thursday, 22 November 2012
**Borussia Moenchengladbach (0) 2** *(De Camargo 79, 90)*
**AEL Limassol (0) 0** 49,000
*Borussia Moenchengladbach:* (442) ter Stegen; Jantschke, Stranzl, Dominguez, Wendt; Ring (Mlapa 63), Nordtveit, Marx (Xhaka 72), Arango; Herrmann, Hanke (De Camargo 74).
*AEL Limassol:* (433) Degra; Airosa, Parpas (Dickson 69), Junior, Carlitos; Bebe*, Dede, Nicolaou; Rui Miguel (Konstantinou 84), Orlando Sa, Edmar.

**Marseille (0) 0**
**Fenerbahce (1) 1** *(Irtegun 40)* 15,000
*Marseille:* (4231) Mandanda; Abdallah K, Fanni, Lucas Mendes, Morel; Abdullah, Barton (Jobello 85); Raspentino (Cheyrou 69), Amalfitano, Ayew A; Ayew J.
*Fenerbahce:* (4231) Demirel; Gonul, Irtegun, Yobo, Ali Kaldirim; Meireles, Topal; Kuyt, Baroni (Sahin S 89), Erkin (Stoch 85); Sow (Topuz 79).

Thursday, 6 December 2012
**AEL Limassol (1) 3** *(Orlando Sa 41, Edmar 79, Junior 82)*
**Marseille (0) 0** 3500
*AEL Limassol:* (433) Degra; Parpas (Theophilou 84), Ouon, Junior (Kyriakou 90), Carlitos; Dede, Paulo Sergio, Nicolaou; Dickson, Orlando Sa (Vouho 72), Edmar.
*Marseille:* (433) Bracigliano; Abdallah K (Azouni 74), Fanni, N'Diaye, Lucas Mendes; M'Bow, Raspentino, Abdullah; Jobello (Osei 78), Omrani (Santiago 63), Remy.

**Fenerbahce (0) 0**
**Borussia Moenchengladbach (2) 3** *(Cigerci T 23, Hanke 29 (pen), De Jong 79)* 19,000
*Fenerbahce:* (4231) Gunok; Sam, Kesimal, Korkmaz, Cek; Sahin, Topal (Erkin 76); Krasic, Niyaz (Baroni 59), Stoch (Kuyt 59); Bienvenu.
*Borussia Moenchengladbach:* (442) Heimeroth; Korb, Brouwers, Dominguez, Wendt; Hrgota, Ring, Xhaka, Cigerci T (Younes 72); Mlapa (Zimmermann 80), Hanke (De Jong 67).

| Group C Table | P | W | D | L | F | A | GD | Pts |
|---|---|---|---|---|---|---|---|---|
| Fenerbahce | 6 | 4 | 1 | 1 | 10 | 7 | 3 | 13 |
| Borussia M'gladbach | 6 | 3 | 2 | 1 | 11 | 6 | 5 | 11 |
| Marseille | 6 | 1 | 2 | 3 | 9 | 11 | –2 | 5 |
| AEL Limassol | 6 | 1 | 1 | 4 | 4 | 10 | –6 | 4 |

## GROUP D

Thursday, 20 September 2012
**Bordeaux (2) 4** *(Sane 13, Gouffran 27, Engels 47 (og), Jussie 66)*
**Club Brugge (0) 0** 13,609
*Bordeaux:* (433) Carasso; Mariano, Henrique, Planus, Tremoulinas (Marange 67); Plasil, Sane, Saivet (Sacko 75); Diabate C, Jussie, Gouffran (Sertic 61).
*Club Brugge:* (4132) Jorgacevic; Hoefkens, Almeback, Jordi, Hogli (Lestienne 73); Jorgensen; Van Acker T (Engels 46), Vazquez, Blondel (Odjija Ofoe 74); Bacca, Tchite.

**Maritimo (0) 0**
**Newcastle U (0) 0** 4000
*Maritimo:* (4231) Salin; Briguel, Joao Guilherme, Roberge, Luis Olim; Rafael Miranda, Joao Luiz; Nhuck (Fidelis 54), David Simao (Goncalo Abreu 75), Sami; Danilo Dias (Adilson G 82).
*Newcastle U:* (442) Elliot; Perch, Williamson, Taylor S, Santon; Obertan (Marveaux 80), Bigirimana, Gosling, Amalfitano (Ferguson 76); Ameobi Shola, Vuckic (Ameobi Sam 53).

Thursday, 4 October 2012
**Club Brugge (0) 2** *(Bacca 57, Vleminckx 70)*
**Maritimo (0) 0** 16,000
*Club Brugge:* (433) Jorgacevic; Hoefkens, Almeback, Buysse, Jordi; Odjija Ofoe, Blondel, Vazquez; Vleminckx, Bacca, Lestienne (Trickovski 89).
*Maritimo:* (433) Salin; Briguel, Joao Guilherme, Roberge, Ruben Ferreira; Rafael Miranda, Joao Luiz (Adilson G 85), Rodrigo Antonio (Danilo Dias 66); Nhuck (David Simao 80), Fidelis, Sami.

**Newcastle U (2) 3** *(Ameobi Shola 16, Henrique 40 (og), Cisse 49)*
**Bordeaux (0) 0** 30,987
*Newcastle U:* (433) Elliot (Harper 46); Simpson, Williamson, Perch, Ferguson; Anita, Cabaye (Bigirimana 61), Tiote (Gosling 71); Cisse, Ameobi Shola, Obertan.
*Bordeaux:* (442) Carasso; Mariano, Henrique, Planus, Tremoulinas; Saivet, Sane, Plasil (N'Guemo 46), Obraniak (Diabate 46); Jussie, Gouffran (Bellion 67).

Thursday, 25 October 2012
**Maritimo (1) 1** *(Roberge 36)*
**Bordeaux (1) 1** *(Gouffran 30)* 3000
*Maritimo:* (433) Salin; Briguel, Ruben Ferreira, Roberge, Joao Guilherme; Rafael Miranda, Joao Luiz (David Simao 76), Nhuck (Rodrigo Antonio 58); Fidelis (Ibrahim 73), Sami, Danilo Dias.
*Bordeaux:* (433) Olimpa; Henrique, Mariano, Planus, Tremoulinas; N'Guemo, Plasil, Obraniak (Saivet 76); Gouffran, Jussie (Sertic 65), Maurice-Belay (Sacko 80).

**Newcastle U (0) 1** *(Obertan 48)*
**Club Brugge (0) 0** 33,124
*Newcastle U:* (442) Harper; Perch, Santon, Taylor S, Ferguson (Cabaye 80); Obertan, Tiote, Bigirimana, Anita (Ameobi Shola 46); Ameobi Sam (Coloccini 73), Cisse.
*Club Brugge:* (433) Jorgacevic; Hogli, Hoefkens, Buysse, Jordi; Odjija Ofoe, Jorgensen, Blondel (Van Acker 83); Rafaelov (Trickovski 55), Bacca, Lestienne.

Thursday, 8 November 2012
**Bordeaux (1) 1** *(Bellion 16)*
**Maritimo (0) 0** 13,392
*Bordeaux:* (442) Carasso; Mariano, Henrique, Sane, Tremoulinas; Sertic, Plasil, Ben Khalfallah (Marange 77), Maurice-Belay; Bellion (Sacko 63), Diabate C (N'Guemo 63).
*Maritimo:* (532) Salin; Briguel, Joao Guilherme (Nhuck 56), Marcio Rosario, Roberge, Ruben Ferreira; Olberdam (David Simao 67), Rafael Miranda, Joao Luiz (Danilo Dias 80); Sami, Fidelis.

**Club Brugge (2) 2** *(Trickovski 14, Jorgensen 19)*
**Newcastle U (2) 2** *(Anita 41, Ameobi Shola 43)* 18,000
*Club Brugge:* (4231) Jorgacevic; Hogli, Hoefkens, Almeback, Jordi; Donk, Odjija Ofoe (Lagrou 81); Lestienne, Jorgensen, Trickovski (Tchite 46); Bacca.
*Newcastle U:* (4141) Krul; Anita, Williamson (Taylor S 58), Coloccini, Tavernier; Tiote; Ameobi Sam (Amalfitano 83), Marveaux, Bigirimana (Cabaye 72), Obertan; Ameobi Shola.

Thursday, 22 November 2012
**Club Brugge (0) 1** *(Lestienne 85)*
**Bordeaux (2) 2** *(Jussie 3, 40)* 16,500
*Club Brugge:* (433) Kujovic; Hoefkens, Almeback (Blondel 46), Jordi, Buysse; Jorgensen, Donk, Odjija Ofoe; Rafaelov (Vleminckx 46), Bacca (Meunier T 60), Lestienne.

*Bordeaux:* (4231) Carasso; Sane, Henrique, Planus, Tremoulinas; Plasil (Ben Khalfallah 79), N'Guemo; Mariano, Sertic, Jussie (Bellion 73); Maurice-Belay (Diabate 46).

**Newcastle U (1) 1** *(Marveaux 23)*
**Maritimo (0) 1** *(Fidelis 79)* 21,632
*Newcastle U:* (4411) Krul; Simpson, Taylor S, Coloccini, Santon; Marveaux, Bigirimana, Anita, Ameobi Sam (Abeid 76); Ben Arfa (Ba D 40); Cisse (Amalfitano 50).
*Maritimo:* (433) Salin; Joao Diogo, Roberge, Marcio Rosario, Ruben Ferreira; Joao Luiz, Rafael Miranda, David Simao (Ruben Brigido 73); Danilo Dias, Adilson G (Fidelis 59), Sami.

Thursday, 6 December 2012
**Bordeaux (1) 2** *(Diabate 29, 72)*
**Newcastle U (0) 0** 20,000
*Bordeaux:* (442) Olimpa; Chalme, Planus, Marange, Poundje; Ben Khalfallah, Biyogo Poko, Sertic, Saivet; Bellion, Diabate (Sacko 88).
*Newcastle U:* (4231) Elliot; Tavernier, Williamson (Coloccini 74), Perch, Ferguson; Abeid, Bigirimana; Ranger, Marveaux, Ameobi Sam (Anita 46); Ameobi Shola (Cisse 80).

**Maritimo (1) 2** *(Goncalo Abreu 19, Nhuck 87)*
**Club Brugge (0) 1** *(Rafaelov 86 (pen))* 10,000
*Maritimo:* (433) Salin; Briguel, Joao Guilherme, Igor Rossi, Goncalo Abreu (Nhuck 54); Semedo, Rodrigo Antonio, Luis Olim; Ruben Brigido (Danilo Dias 75), Adilson G, Sami (Rafael Miranda 63).
*Club Brugge:* (433) Jorgacevic; Hogli, Almeback, Jordi, Blondel (Odjija Ofoe 70); Meunier T, Van Acker (Lestienne 74), Verstraete; Tchite (Donk 74), Rafaelov, Vleminckx.

| Group D Table | P | W | D | L | F | A | GD | Pts |
|---|---|---|---|---|---|---|---|---|
| Bordeaux | 6 | 4 | 1 | 1 | 10 | 5 | 5 | 13 |
| Newcastle U | 6 | 2 | 3 | 1 | 7 | 5 | 2 | 9 |
| Maritimo | 6 | 1 | 3 | 2 | 4 | 6 | -2 | 6 |
| Club Brugge | 6 | 1 | 1 | 4 | 6 | 11 | -5 | 4 |

## GROUP E

Thursday, 20 September 2012
**FC Copenhagen (1) 2** *(Claudemir 20, Cornelius 74)*
**Molde (1) 1** *(Diouf 45)* 11,633
*FC Copenhagen:* (442) Christensen; Stadsgaard, Sigurdsson, Jacobsen, Bengtsson; Kristensen, Claudemir, Bolanos (Delaney 82), Jorgensen (Vingaard 25); Cornelius, Santin (Vetokele 65).
*Molde:* (433) Pettersen; Vatshaug, Forren, Linnes, Rindaroy; Hoseth (Hussain 41), Berget J (Ekpo 82), Berg Hestad; Diouf, Angan (Chukwa 83), Mostrom.

**VfB Stuttgart (1) 2** *(Ibisevic V 6, Niedermaier 85)*
**Steaua Bucharest (1) 2** *(Chipciu A 7, Rusescu 80 (pen))* 17,000
*VfB Stuttgart:* (4321) Ulreich; Niedermaier, Rodriguez, Sakai, Boka; Kvist Jorgensen (Harnik 82), Gentner, Torun (Okazaki 62); Hajnal (Traore 82), Cacau; Ibisevic V.
*Steaua Bucharest:* (433) Tatarusanu; Szukala, Chiriches, Georgievski, Parvulescu (Latovlevici 81); Prepelita (Rusescu 46), Bourceanu, Filip (Pintilii 46); Popa, Nikolic, Chipciu A.

Thursday, 4 October 2012
**Molde (0) 2** *(Berget J 58, Chukwa 88)*
**VfB Stuttgart (0) 0** 6000
*Molde:* (433) Pettersen; Linnes, Steenslid, Forren, Simonsen; Berg Hestad, Hussain (Gatt 81), Eikrem; Stamnesstro (Mostrom 46), Chukwa, Diouf (Berget J 30).
*VfB Stuttgart:* (433) Ulreich; Rudiger (Boka 82), Tasci, Niedermaier, Molinaro; Gentner, Kuzmanovic, Hajnal (Holzhauser 67); Harnik, Ibisevic, Traore (Cacau 67).

**Steaua Bucharest (1) 1** *(Sigurdsson 83 (og))*
**FC Copenhagen (0) 0** 50,000
*Steaua Bucharest:* (442) Tatarusanu; Matei (Rusescu 64), Gardos, Chiriches, Parvulescu; Popa, Pintilii, Bourceanu, Tanase; Prepelita (Chipciu A 46), Adi ( 46).

*FC Copenhagen:* (442) Wiland; Jacobsen, Sigurdsson, Stadsgaard, Bengtsson (Santin 86); Gislason (Vingaard 73), Kristensen, Claudemir, Delaney; Jorgensen, Cornelius.

**Thursday, 25 October 2012**
**Steaua Bucharest (2) 2** *(Chiriches 30, Rusescu 32)*
**Molde (0) 0** 45,000
*Steaua Bucharest:* (442) Tatarusanu; Georgievski, Szukala, Chiriches, Latovlevici; Chipciu A, Bourceanu, Pintilii (Balan 63), Tanase; Rusescu (Popa 46), Adi (Costea 55).
*Molde:* (433) Soderberg; Johansen, Steenslid, Odegard, Simonsen; Hussain (Furu 90), Stamnesstro, Ekpo; Gatt (Hestad 69), Angan, Hollingen (Camara 46).

**VfB Stuttgart (0) 0**
**FC Copenhagen (0) 0** 15,300
*VfB Stuttgart:* (451) Ulreich; Sakai (Hajnal 83), Tasci, Niedermaier, Molinaro; Harnik, Gentner, Kvist Jorgensen, Holzhauser (Torun 46), Traore (Okazaki 61); Ibisevic V.
*FC Copenhagen:* (4231) Wiland; Jacobsen, Stadsgaard, Sigurdsson, Bengtsson; Kristensen, Delaney; Bolanos, Claudemir, Gislason (Grindheim C 79); Santin (Cornelius 84).

**Thursday, 8 November 2012**
**FC Copenhagen (0) 0**
**VfB Stuttgart (0) 2** *(Ibisevic V 75, Harnik 90)* 24,681
*FC Copenhagen:* (442) Christensen; Jacobsen, Sigurdsson, Stadsgaard, Bengtsson; Claudemir, Grindheim C (Jorgensen 57), Kristensen (Bolanos 81), Delaney; Santin, Cornelius.
*VfB Stuttgart:* (433) Ulreich; Molinaro, Niedermaier, Tasci, Sakai; Traore (Boka 63), Kvist Jorgensen, Gentner; Harnik, Ibisevic V, Okazaki (Kuzmanovic 86).

**Molde (0) 1** *(Chukwa 56)*
**Steaua Bucharest (2) 2** *(Chipciu A 21, Latovlevici 37)* 5239
*Molde:* (4411) Soderberg; Linnes, Vatshaug, Forren, Simonsen; Gatt (Mostrom 46), Eikrem, Berg Hestad, Diouf (Berget J 46); Hussain (Angan 77); Chukwa.
*Steaua Bucharest:* (343) Tatarusanu; Szukala, Chiriches, Gardos; Chipciu A, Bourceanu, Prepelita (Pintilii 69), Parvulescu (Latovlevici 16); Tanase, Adi ( 56), Costea.

**Thursday, 22 November 2012**
**Molde (0) 1** *(Chukwa 62)*
**FC Copenhagen (1) 2** *(Santin 21 (pen), Gislason 76)* 5740
*Molde:* (442) Pettersen; Linnes, Vatshaug, Forren, Rindaroy; Gatt, Eikrem (Angan 85), Berg Hestad (Hussain 46), Mostrom; Berget J (Diouf 55), Chukwa.
*FC Copenhagen:* (442) Christensen; Jacobsen, Sigurdsson, Stadsgaard, Bengtsson; Gislason, Kristensen, Claudemir, Delaney; Santin (Amankwaa 87), Cornelius (Bolanos 80).

**Steaua Bucharest (0) 1** *(Costea 83)*
**VfB Stuttgart (4) 5** *(Tasci 5, Harnik 19, Sakai 23, Okazaki 32, 55)* 50,000
*Steaua Bucharest:* (343) Tatarusanu; Szukala, Chiriches, Gardos (Costea 32); Chipciu A, Bourceanu, Pintilii (Prepelita 57), Latovlevici; Popa, Rusescu, Tanase (Adi 62).
*VfB Stuttgart:* (442) Ulreich; Sakai (Rudiger 70), Tasci, Rodriguez, Molinaro; Harnik (Traore 61), Kvist Jorgensen, Kuzmanovic, Okazaki; Gentner (Hajnal 46), Ibisevic V.

**Thursday, 6 December 2012**
**FC Copenhagen (0) 1** *(Vetokele 87)*
**Steaua Bucharest (0) 1** *(Rusescu 73)* 3400
*FC Copenhagen:* (442) Christensen; Jacobsen, Sigurdsson, Stadsgaard, Bengtsson; Gislason (Santin 74), Claudemir (Vetokele 65), Kristensen, Delaney; Jorgensen, Cornelius.
*Steaua Bucharest:* (4231) Tatarusanu; Chipciu A, Gardos, Chiriches, Latovlevici; Pintilii, Bourceanu; Popa (Prepelita 88), Rusescu (Filip 85), Tanase[■]; Nikolic (Martinovic 62).

**VfB Stuttgart (0) 0**
**Molde (1) 1** *(Angan 45)* 15,000
*VfB Stuttgart:* (4231) Ulreich; Sakai, Rodriguez, Niedermaier, Molinaro; Hajnal (Rocker 88), Gentner; Okazaki (Holzhauser 70), Torun (Harnik 29), Traore; Ibisevic V.
*Molde:* (4231) Pettersen; Linnes, Odegard, Forren, Rindaroy; Eikrem, Mostrom; Gatt (Hussain 68), Berget J (Simonsen 79), Diouf; Angan (Chukwa 64).

**Group E Table**

| | P | W | D | L | F | A | GD | Pts |
|---|---|---|---|---|---|---|---|---|
| Steaua Bucharest | 6 | 3 | 2 | 1 | 9 | 9 | 0 | 11 |
| VfB Stuttgart | 6 | 2 | 2 | 2 | 9 | 6 | 3 | 8 |
| FC Copenhagen | 6 | 2 | 2 | 2 | 5 | 6 | −1 | 8 |
| Molde | 6 | 2 | 0 | 4 | 6 | 8 | −2 | 6 |

**GROUP F**
**Thursday, 20 September 2012**
**Dnipro Dnipropetrovsk (0) 2** *(Matheus 50, Hutchinson 58 (og))*
**PSV Eindhoven (0) 0** 31,003
*Dnipro Dnipropetrovsk:* (4132) Lastuvka; Mandzyuk V, Mazuch, Cheberyachko, Strinic; Rotan; Matheus (Odibe 90), Giuliano, Konoplianka (Denisov 84); Zozulya (Kankava 84), Seleznyov.
*PSV Eindhoven:* (4231) Waterman; Hutchinson, Marcelo, Derijck, Willems (Engelaar 46); Van Bommel, Strootman; Narsingh (Matavz 74), Toivonen, Mertens (Depay 74); Lens.

**Napoli (1) 4** *(Vargas 6, 46, 69, Dzemaili 90)*
**AIK Solna (0) 0** 35,000
*Napoli:* (3142) Rosati; Gamberini, Fernandez, Aronica; Donadel (Dzemaili 56); Mesto, Behrami, El Kaddouri (Hamsik[■] 46), Dossena; Insigne L, Vargas (Zuniga 80).
*AIK Solna:* (442) Turina; Lorentzson, Karlsson, Majstorovic, Johansson N; Lalawele, Borges, Danielsson (Lundberg 81), Mutumba-Kayongo (Quasion 70); Karikari (Goitom 76), Bangura.

**Thursday, 4 October 2012**
**AIK Solna (2) 2** *(Danielsson 5, Goitom 45)*
**Dnipro Dnipropetrovsk (1) 3** *(Kalinic 41, Mandzyuk V 75, Seleznyov 83)* 10,091
*AIK Solna:* (442) Turina; Lorentzson, Karlsson, Backman, Johansson N; Lalawele, Moro, Danielsson, Gustafsson (Mutumba-Kayongo 65); Goitom (Borges 65), Karikari (Bangura 75).
*Dnipro Dnipropetrovsk:* (442) Lastuvka; Mandzyuk V, Mazuch (Matheus 65), Cheberyachko (Fedetskiy 46), Strinic; Aliev (Kravchenko 78), Rotan, Giuliano, Konoplianka; Kalinic, Seleznyov.

**PSV Eindhoven (2) 3** *(Lens 19, Mertens 41, Marcelo 53)*
**Napoli (0) 0** 23,000
*PSV Eindhoven:* (433) Waterman; Hutchinson, Derijck, Marcelo, Bouma; Van Bommel, Toivonen, Strootman; Narsingh, Lens, Mertens.
*Napoli:* (3511) Rosati; Cannavaro, Fernandez, Aronica; Mesto, Dzemaili, El Kaddouri (Cavani 46), Donadel, Dossena (Zuniga 72); Insigne L (Pandev 62); Vargas.

**Thursday, 25 October 2012**
**Dnipro Dnipropetrovsk (2) 3** *(Fedetskiy 2, Matheus 42, Giuliano 64)*
**Napoli (0) 1** *(Cavani 75 (pen))* 29,000
*Dnipro Dnipropetrovsk:* (442) Lastuvka; Mandzyuk V, Mazuch, Cheberyachko, Strinic; Fedetskiy (Denisov 82), Rotan, Giuliano, Matheus; Seleznyov (Kalinic 58), Zozulya (Kankava 37).
*Napoli:* (352) Rosati; Gamberini (Inler 79), Fernandez, Aronica; Mesto, Donadel, Dzemaili, Dossena (Pandev 52), Zuniga; Insigne L, Vargas (Cavani 52).

**PSV Eindhoven (0) 1** *(Lens 80)*
**AIK Solna (0) 1** *(Karikari 60)* 14,400
*PSV Eindhoven:* (433) Waterman (Tyton 57); Hutchinson, Derijck, Marcelo, Willems; van Ooijen (Narsingh 56), Wijnaldum, Strootman; Lens, Matavz, Mertens.
*AIK Solna:* (442) Turina; Lorentzson, Karlsson, Majstorovic, Johansson N; Lalawele (Gustafsson 46), Danielsson, Borges, Mutumba-Kayongo (Lundberg 71); Quasion (Bangura 64), Karikari.

**Thursday, 8 November 2012**

**AIK Solna (1) 1** *(Bangura 12)*

**PSV Eindhoven (0) 0**                    12,360

*AIK Solna:* (343) Turina; Lorentzson, Karlsson, Backman; Johansson N, Gustafsson (Tjernstrom 75), Danielsson, Moro; Quasion (Lundberg 69), Bangura, Borges.
*PSV Eindhoven:* (433) Waterman; Manolev (Depay 75), Derijck, Marcelo, Willems; Engelaar, Wijnaldum, Hutchinson; Narsingh (Locadia J 64), Matavz, Mertens.

**Napoli (1) 4** *(Cavani 7, 77, 88, 90)*

**Dnipro Dnipropetrovsk (1) 2** *(Fedetskiy 34, Zozulya 52)*
                                                         25,000
*Napoli:* (352) Rosati; Fernandez, Aronica (Pandev 72), Britos; Mesto, Donadel (Hamsik 55), Inler, Dossena, Dzemaili; Cavani, Vargas (Insigne L 55).
*Dnipro Dnipropetrovsk:* (4231) Lastuvka; Mazuch, Odibe, Mandzyuk V, Denisov; Rotan, Kankava; Fedetskiy (Matheus 86), Konoplianka (Cheberyachko 81), Aliev (Giuliano 55); Zozulya.

**Thursday, 22 November 2012**

**AIK Solna (1) 1** *(Danielsson 35)*

**Napoli (1) 2** *(Dzemaili 19, Cavani 90 (pen))*        28,556

*AIK Solna:* (442) Turina; Lorentzson, Karlsson, Backman, Johansson N; Lundberg, Danielsson, Moro; Quasion (Karikari 76); Bangura, Borges.
*Napoli:* (352) Rosati; Gamberini, Aronica[#], Britos; Mesto (Zuniga 64), Donadel (Inler 62), Dzemaili (Hamsik 73), Behrami, Dossena; Cavani, Vargas.

**PSV Einhoven (1) 1** *(Wijnaldum 18)*

**Dnipro Dnipropetrovsk (1) 2** *(Seleznyov 24,
Konoplianka 74)*                                        25,000

*PSV Einhoven:* (433) Waterman; Manolev (Locadia J 87), Derijck, Marcelo, Bouma; Hutchinson, Wijnaldum, Engelaar (Depay 67); Lens, Matavz, Mertens.
*Dnipro Dnipropetrovsk:* (4411) Lastuvka; Mandzyuk V, Mazuch, Cheberyachko, Strinic (Denisov 69); Matheus, Rotan, Kankava[#], Konoplianka (Fedetskiy 85); Giuliano; Seleznyov (Zozulya 77).

**Thursday, 6 December 2012**

**Dnipro Dnipropetrovsk (2) 4** *(Kalinic 20 (pen),
Zozulya 39, 52, Kravchenko 86)*

**AIK Solna (0) 0**                                       25,000

*Dnipro Dnipropetrovsk:* (442) Lastuvka; Mandzyuk V, Mazuch (Fedetskiy 46), Cheberyachko, Strinic (Denisov 57); Giuliano, Rotan, Kravchenko, Konoplianka; Kalinic (Aliev 57), Zozulya.
*AIK Solna:* (442) Turina; Lorentzson, Karlsson, Backman, Johansson N; Lundberg (Gustafsson 65), Danielsson, Moro (Karikari 65), Quasion (Ahman-Persson 90); Borges, Bangura.

**Napoli (1) 1** *(Cavani 18)*

**PSV Eindhoven (2) 3** *(Matavz 30, 42, 60)*           15,000

*Napoli:* (433) Rosati; Campagnaro, Fernandez, Bruno Uvini, Dossena; Donadel, Inler (Pandev 57), Maggio (Mesto 69); Vargas, El Kaddouri, Cavani (Insigne 66).
*PSV Eindhoven:* (343) Waterman; Manolev, Jorgensen, Marcelo; Bouma, van Ooijen (Brenet 87), Engelaar, Lens; Wijnaldum, Depay, Lens.

| Group F Table | P | W | D | L | F | A | GD | Pts |
|---|---|---|---|---|---|---|---|---|
| Dnipro Dnipropetrovsk | 6 | 5 | 0 | 1 | 16 | 8 | 8 | 15 |
| Napoli | 6 | 3 | 0 | 3 | 12 | 12 | 0 | 9 |
| PSV Eindhoven | 6 | 2 | 1 | 3 | 8 | 7 | 1 | 7 |
| AIK Solna | 6 | 1 | 1 | 4 | 5 | 14 | –9 | 4 |

## GROUP G

**Thursday, 20 September 2012**

**KRC Genk (1) 3** *(Vossen 22, Buffel 78, De Ceulaer 90)*

**Videoton (0) 0**                                       10,000

*KRC Genk:* (352) Van Hout; Dani Fernandez A ( 77), Simaeys, Koulibaly; Hamalainen, Buffel, Gorius, Hyland, Monrose (Plet 81); De Ceulaer, Vossen (Kumordzi 72).
*Videoton:* (451) Bozovic; Brachi, Caneira, Vinicius, Stopira; Toth (Kovacs 66), Mitrovic N, Oliveira (Gyurcso 58), Sandor, Walter; Torghelle (Nikolic 72).

**Sporting Lisbon (0) 0**

**FC Basel (0) 0**                                       22,325

*Sporting Lisbon:* (442) Rui Patricio; Cedric, Xandao[#], Rojo, Pranjic; Izmailov (Andre Martins 67), Fernandes, Elias (Carrico 56), Carrillo (Labyad 76); van Wolfswinkel R, Diego Capel.
*FC Basel:* (442) Sommer; Steinhofer, Dragovic, Sauro, Park; Salah (Zoua 74), Diaz (Frei F 83), Cabral, Stocker (Degen 90); Streller, Frei A.

**Thursday, 4 October 2012**

**FC Basel (0) 2** *(Streller 70 (pen), 84)*

**KRC Genk (2) 2** *(De Ceulaer 10, Vossen 38)*         14,023

*FC Basel:* (442) Sommer; Degen P, Sauro, Dragovic (Schar 53), Park; Salah M, Diaz (Frei F 70), Cabral, Stocker; Frei A (Zoua 46), Streller.
*KRC Genk:* (4141) Van Hout; Dani Fernandez A, Nadson, Koulibaly, Tshimanga; Buffel (Nwanganga 67); Kumordzi (Plet 86), De Ceulaer (Hamalainen 76), Gorius, Vossen; Ngcongca.

**Videoton (3) 3** *(Vinicius 16, Oliveira 21, Nikolic 35)*

**Sporting Lisbon (0) 0**                                8000

*Videoton:* (4231) Bozovic; Brachi, Caneira, Vinicius, Stopira (Renato Neto 89); Toth, Mitrovic N; Walter (Gyurcso 68), Sandor, Oliveira; Nikolic (Torghelle 78).
*Sporting Lisbon:* (442) Rui Patricio; Rinaudo (van Wolfswinkel R 30), Rojo, Boulahrouz (Adrien Silva 71), Pranjic; Izmailov, Fernandes, Andre Martins, Jeffren; Labyad (Schaars 46), Viola.

**Thursday, 25 October 2012**

**KRC Genk (1) 2** *(De Ceulaer 25, Barda 87)*

**Sporting Lisbon (1) 1** *(Schaars 8)*                 14,000

*KRC Genk:* (442) Van Hout; Dani Fernandez A, Koulibaly, Nadson, Hamalainen; Monrose (Barda 84), Ngcongca, Gorius, Buffel; De Ceulaer (Plet 62), Vossen (Kumordzi 90).
*Sporting Lisbon:* (442) Rui Patricio; Cedric, Rojo, Boulahrouz[#], Pranjic (Diego Capel 58); Adrien Silva (Xandao 79), Rinaudo, Schaars, Insua; Jeffren (Viola 61), van Wolfswinkel R.

**Videoton (2) 2** *(Schar 3 (og), Caneira 33)*

**FC Basel (0) 1** *(Schar 90)*                         11,000

*Videoton:* (4231) Bozovic; Brachi, Caneira, Vinicius, Szolnoki; Renato Neto, Mitrovic N; Walter (Torghelle 86), Sandor (Toth 73), Gyurcso (Oliveira 79); Nikolic.
*FC Basel:* (4231) Sommer; Steinhofer, Schar, Dragovic, Park (Voser 46); Cabral; Degen D (Frei F 72), Diaz, Stocker, Salah M (Pak 57); Streller.

**Thursday, 8 November 2012**

**FC Basel (0) 1** *(Streller 80)*

**Videoton (0) 0**                                       12,000

*FC Basel:* (442) Sommer; Degen P, Schar, Dragovic, Steinhofer; Degen D (Zoua 90), Diaz (Frei F 75), Cabral, Stocker; Streller, Frei A (Salah 66).
*Videoton:* (4231) Bozovic; Brachi, Caneira, Vinicius, Szolnoki; Mitrovic N, Renato Neto; Oliveira, Sandor (Kovacs 90), Gyurcso (Walter 83); Torghelle (Nikolic 69).

**Sporting Lisbon (0) 1** *(van Wolfswinkel R 65)*

**KRC Genk (0) 1** *(Plet 90)*                          25,000

*Sporting Lisbon:* (4231) Rui Patricio; Cedric, Xandao, Rojo, Insua; Elias, Schaars[#]; Labyad (Tiago Ilori 83), Viola (Fernandes 63), Diego Capel (Carrillo 87); van Wolfswinkel R.
*KRC Genk:* (4231) Van Hout; Dani Fernandez A, Koulibaly, Nadson, Tshimanga; Ngcongca, Hyland (Plet 67); Buffel, Gorius, Monrose (Masika 77); Vossen.

**Thursday, 22 November 2012**

**FC Basel (1) 3** *(Schar 23, Stocker 67, Degen D 72)*

**Sporting Lisbon (0) 0**                               13,066

*FC Basel:* (442) Sommer; Degen P, Schar, Dragovic, Steinhofer; Degen D, Cabral[#], Stocker (Zoua 80), Diaz; Frei F (Ajeti 89), Frei A (Salah 65).
*Sporting Lisbon:* (451) Rui Patricio; Cedric, Xandao, Rojo, Insua; Fernandes (Betinho 69), Elias, Diego Capel, Pranjic, Labyad (Carrillo 60); van Wolfswinkel R.

**Videoton (0) 0**
**KRC Genk (1) 1** *(Barda 19)* 11,000
*Videoton:* (4231) Bozovic; Brachi, Kaka (Walter 81), Vinicius, Szolnoki; Renato Neto, Mitrovic N; Gyurcso, Sandor (Torghelle 75), Oliveira (Kovacs 46); Nikolic.
*KRC Genk:* (4231) Van Hout; Dani Fernandez A, Ngcongca, Nadson, Tshimanga; Hyland, Gorius; Buffel, Monrose (Masika 75), Barda (Plet 70); Vossen (Kumordzi 90).

**Thursday, 6 December 2012**
**KRC Genk (0) 0**
**FC Basel (0) 0** 12,500
*KRC Genk:* (433) Koteles; Koulibaly, Hubert, Dani Fernandez A, Hamalainen; Ngcongca, Hyland, Limbombe (Schrijvers 88); Barda (Monrose 68), De Ceulaer (Masika 58), Plet.
*FC Basel:* (442) Sommer; Dragovic, Steinhofer, Schar, Degen P; Degen D (Salah 68), Yapi Yapo, Frei F, Diaz; Stocker, Streller.

**Friday, 7 December 2012**
**Sporting Lisbon (0) 2** *(Labyad 65, Viola 83)*
**Videoton (0) 1** *(Sandor 80 (pen))* 8080
*Sporting Lisbon:* (433) Marcelo; Cedric, Boulahrouz, Xandao, Insua; Fernandes, Rinaudo, Esgaio; Labyad, Viola, Diego Capel (Pranjic 86).
*Videoton:* (4231) Tujvel; Brachi, Caneira, Vinicius, Szolnoki; Renato Neto, Toth (Kovacs 73); Oliveira (Gyurcso 57), Sandor■, Walter; Nikolic N (Paraiba 73).

| Group G Table | P | W | D | L | F | A | GD | Pts |
|---|---|---|---|---|---|---|---|---|
| KRC Genk | 6 | 3 | 3 | 0 | 9 | 4 | 5 | 12 |
| FC Basel | 6 | 2 | 3 | 1 | 7 | 4 | 3 | 9 |
| Videoton | 6 | 2 | 0 | 4 | 6 | 8 | -2 | 6 |
| Sporting Lisbon | 6 | 1 | 2 | 3 | 4 | 10 | -6 | 5 |

## GROUP H

**Thursday, 20 September 2012**
**Internazionale (1) 2** *(Livaja 39, Nagatomo 90)*
**Rubin Kazan (1) 2** *(Ryazantsev 17, Rondon 84)* 28,472
*Internazionale:* (532) Handanovic; Jonathan M (Guarin 46), Ranocchia, Zanetti, Samuel, Nagatomo; Gargano, Coutinho, Cambiasso; Livaja (Milito 61), Cassano (Pereira 67).
*Rubin Kazan:* (4411) Ryzhikov; Kuzmin, Sharonov, Cesar Navas, Marcano; Ryazantsev (Orbaiz 69), Natcho, Bocchetti (Kaleshin 81), Karadeniz (Kasaev 85); Eremenko; Rondon.

**Partizan Belgrade (0) 0**
**Neftchi (0) 0** 18,000
*Partizan Belgrade:* (442) Stojkovic; Miljkovic A, Ivanov, Lazevski, Ostojic; Medo, Tomic, Markovic S (Jojic 63), Ilic; Markovic L, Mitrovic (Scepovic 73).
*Neftchi:* (541) Stamenkovic; Guliyev T, Mitreski, Bertucci, Shukurov, Sadygov; Flavinho (Abdullayev A 77), Wobay (Mehdiyev 87), Ramos, Imamverdiyev (Seyidov 58); Canales.

**Thursday, 4 October 2012**
**Neftchi (0) 1** *(Canales 53)*
**Internazionale (3) 3** *(Coutinho 10, Obi 30, Livaja 42)* 30,000
*Neftchi:* (4231) Stamenkovic; Shukurov, Yunuszade, Mitreski, Bertucci; Ramos, Sadygov; Wobay, Nurahmadov (Seyidov 46), Flavinho; Canales.
*Internazionale:* (352) Handanovic; Silvestre, Cambiasso, Juan; Jonathan, Guarin (Gargano 82), Mudingayi, Obi (Ranocchia 64), Pereira; Coutinho (Garritano 75), Livaja.

**Rubin Kazan (1) 2** *(Karadeniz 45, Ryazantsev 48)*
**Partizan Belgrade (0) 0** 9000
*Rubin Kazan:* (451) Ryzhikov; Kuzmin, Bocchetti, Cesar Navas, Marcano; Ryazantsev (Carlos Eduardo 83), Eremenko R, Orbaiz, Natcho, Karadeniz (Kasaev 77); Rondon (Davydov 82).
*Partizan Belgrade:* (4312) Stojkovic; Miljkovic A, Ostojic, Ivanov, Volkov; Markovic S, Medo, Jojic, Ilic (Scepovic 74); Markovic L, Ninkovic (Mitrovic 62).

**Thursday, 25 October 2012**
**Internazionale (0) 1** *(Palacio R 88)*
**Partizan Belgrade (0) 0** 18,626
*Internazionale:* (3412) Handanovic; Silvestre, Cambiasso, Juan; Jonathan, Guarin, Mudingayi, Pereira; Coutinho (Palacio R 31); Livaja (Zanetti 52), Cassano (Milito 76).
*Partizan Belgrade:* (4231) Petrovic; Miljkovic A, Ostojic, Ivanov, Volkov; Medo, Smiljanic; Tomic (Markovic 80), Ilic S (Jojic 75), Markovic L; Mitrovic (Scepovic M 68).

**Rubin Kazan (1) 1** *(Kasaev 16)*
**Neftchi (0) 0** 15,000
*Rubin Kazan:* (4231) Ryzhikov; Kuzmin, Marcano, Cesar Navas, Kaleshin; Natcho, Orbaiz; Kasaev, Karadeniz (Dyadyun 70), Ansaldi; Rondon.
*Neftchi:* (4411) Stamenkovic; Shukurov, Guliyev T, Mitreski, Bertucci; Wobay, Ramos, Sadygov, Flavinho; Seyidov (Abdullayev A 50); Canales.

**Thursday, 8 November 2012**
**Neftchi (0) 0**
**Rubin Kazan (1) 1** *(Dyadyun 16)* 17,000
*Neftchi:* (4231) Stamenkovic; Shukurov (Musazade 89), Mitreski, Guliyev T, Bertucci; Sadygov (Seyidov 57); Ramos; Wobay, Flavinho, Mehdiyev (Abdullayev A 53); Canales.
*Rubin Kazan:* (4231) Ryzhikov; Kaleshin, Marcano, Cesar Navas, Ansaldi; Orbaiz, Natcho; Kasaev (Tore 84), Dyadyun (Davydov 77), Karadeniz; Rondon (Eremenko 80).

**Partizan Belgrade (0) 1** *(Tomic 90)*
**Internazionale (0) 3** *(Palacio R 51, 75, Guarin 87)* 21,000
*Partizan Belgrade:* (4411) Petrovic; Miljkovic A, Ostojic, Ivanov, Lazevski; Tomic, Medo (Scepovic M 55), Smiljanic, Markovic; Ilic S (Jojic 30); Scepovic S (Mitrovic 69).
*Internazionale:* (451) Handanovic; Jonathan, Silvestre, Juan, Nagatomo (Palacio R 46); Zanetti, Guarin, Mudingayi (Gargano 14), Cambiasso, Pereira; Livaja (Cassano 76).

**Thursday, 22 November 2012**
**Neftchi (1) 1** *(Flavinho 10)*
**Partizan Belgrade (0) 1** *(Mitrovic 67)* 10,000
*Neftchi:* (4231) Stamenkovic; Mehdiyev, Yunuszade, Mitreski, Bertucci; Sadygov, Guliyev T; Wobay, Imamverdiyev (Abdullayev A 62), Flavinho; Canales.
*Partizan Belgrade:* (4231) Petrovic; Miljkovic A, Ostojic, Ivanov, Volkov; Jojic (Markovic 83), Smiljanic; Tomic, Ilic S, Markovic L (Mitrovic■ 46); Scepovic S (Scepovic M 66).

**Rubin Kazan (1) 3** *(Karadeniz 1, Rondon 87, 90)*
**Internazionale (0) 0** 18,000
*Rubin Kazan:* (442) Ryzhikov; Kuzmin, Sharonov, Bocchetti, Ansaldi; Karadeniz, Orbaiz, Natcho, Kasaev (Tore 61); Eremenko (Carlos Eduardo 8), Dyadyun (Rondon 59).
*Internazionale:* (4411) Belec; Silvestre, Pereira, Ranocchia (Donkor 73), Juan; Jonathan, Benassi, Gargano, Romano (Zanetti 46); Coutinho; Livaja (Palacio R 46).

**Thursday, 6 December 2012**
**Internazionale (1) 2** *(Livaja 9, 54)*
**Neftchi (0) 2** *(Sadygov 52, Canales 89)* 9000
*Internazionale:* (4231) Belec; Jonathan M (Bandini 62), Cambiasso, Samuel (Cassano 46), Pereira; Romano, Benassi; Pasa, Garritano (Nagatomo 53), Coutinho; Livaja.
*Neftchi:* (4411) Stamenkovic; Shukurov (Mehdiyev 46), Mitreski, Guliyev T, Bertucci; Wobay, Sadygov (Seyidov 77), Ramos, Flavinho; Imamverdiyev (Abdullayev A 90); Canales.

**Partizan Belgrade (0) 1** *(Markovic S 54)*
**Rubin Kazan (0) 1** *(Rondon 59)* 8000
*Partizan Belgrade:* (4231) Petrovic; Miljkovic A, Ostojic, Ivanov, Volkov; Smiljanic, Markovic S; Tomic (Jojic 74), Ilic S, Markovic L (Knezevic 90); Scepovic S (Scepovic M 72).
*Rubin Kazan:* (4231) Arlauskis; Ansaldi, Marcano, Sharonov, Kuzmin; Orbaiz, Bocchetti; Kasaev (Davydov 62), Carlos Eduardo (Eremenko 75), Karadeniz; Rondon.

**Group H Table**

| | P | W | D | L | F | A | GD | Pts |
|---|---|---|---|---|---|---|---|---|
| Rubin Kazan | 6 | 4 | 2 | 0 | 10 | 3 | 7 | 14 |
| Internazionale | 6 | 3 | 2 | 1 | 11 | 9 | 2 | 11 |
| Partizan Belgrade | 6 | 0 | 3 | 3 | 3 | 8 | −5 | 3 |
| Neftchi | 6 | 0 | 3 | 3 | 4 | 8 | −4 | 3 |

## GROUP I

Thursday, 20 September 2012

**Athletic Bilbao (1) 1** *(Susaeta 40)*

**Hapoel Kiryat Shmona (1) 1** *(Rochet 13)*          30,000

*Athletic Bilbao:* (4321) Iraizoz; Iraola, Gurpegi, Amorebieta, Castillo (Ruiz de Galarreta 82); Muniain, Iturraspe, De Marcos; Susaeta, Lopez (Llorente 47); Aduriz (Ibai 59).
*Hapoel Kiryat Shmona:* (442) Amos; Gabai E, Tzedek, Hasarma, Matovic; Tasevski, Rochet (Elisha 74), Gazal, Einbinder (Vahaba 90); Abuhatzira (Porokara 80), Lencse.

**Lyon (0) 2** *(Gomis 59, Lopez L 61)*

**Sparta Prague (0) 1** *(Krejci 77)*          42,000

*Lyon:* (433) Vercoutre; Reveillere, Kone, Bisevac, Dabo (Umtiti 43); Malbranque (Fofana 83), Gonalons, Grenier; Lacazette, Gomis, Lopez L (Monzon 68).
*Sparta Prague:* (4231) Vaclik; Vidlicka, Svejdik, Jarosik, Pamic; Pavelka (Holek 58), Husbauer (Balaj 85); Kaderabek, Kadlec, Prikryl (Krejci 71); Kweuke.

Thursday, 4 October 2012

**Hapoel Kiryat Shmona (1) 3** *(Abuhatzira 8, 66 (pen), Levi 51*

**Lyon (3) 4** *(Fofana 17, 90, Monzon 22, Reveillere 32)* 5000

*Hapoel Kiryat Shmona:* (442) Amos; Gabai E, Hasarma (Cohen 46), Tzedek, Levi; Gerzycich, Elisha (Gazal 88), Rochet, Einbinder; Lencse (Abed 46), Abuhatzira.
*Lyon:* (433) Vercoutre; Reveillere, Lovren, Kone, Monzon; Gonalons, Fofana, Ghezzal (Malbranque 63); Briand, Grenier (Benzia 54), Lopez L.

**Sparta Prague (2) 3** *(Zapotocny 25, Balaj 41, Husbauer 56 (pen))*

**Athletic Bilbao (0) 1** *(De Marcos 73)*          13,750

*Sparta Prague:* (4231) Vaclik; Svejdik, Jarosik, Zapotocny, Pamic; Holek, Husbauer, Kadlec (Prikryl 87), Matejovsky (Pavelka 79), Krejci (Skalak 72); Balaj.
*Athletic Bilbao:* (4141) Iraizoz; Iraola, Gurpegi, Amorebieta, Castillo (Ander Herrera 62); Iturraspe; Susaeta, Muniain, De Marcos, Ibai (Lopez 57); Aduriz (Llorente 64).

Thursday, 25 October 2012

**Lyon (0) 2** *(Lopez L 54, Briand 86)*

**Athletic Bilbao (0) 1** *(Ibai 78)*          30,587

*Lyon:* (433) Vercoutre; Reveillere, Lovren, Kone, Umtiti; Fofana, Gonalons, Malbranque (Lacazette 65); Briand, Lopez L (Gomis 65), Monzon.
*Athletic Bilbao:* (433) Iraizoz; Iraola, Gurpegi, Amorebieta, Aurtenetxe; Iturraspe, Ander Herrera, De Marcos; Susaeta, Aduriz (Llorente 60), Muniain (Ibai 66).

**Sparta Prague (3) 3** *(Krejci 7, Kadlec 10, Svejdik 44)*

**Hapoel Kiryat Shmona (0) 1** *(Abuhatzira 76)*          10,324

*Sparta Prague:* (4141) Vaclik T; Zapotocny, Svejdik, Jarosik, Pamic; Holek; Kadlec (Prikryl 68), Husbauer, Matejovsky, Krejci (Kaderabek 80); Kweuke (Balaj 62).
*Hapoel Kiryat Shmona:* (451) Amos; Matovic, Cohen, Tzedek, Gabai E; Einbinder (Elisha 46), Rochet, Gerzycich (Tasevski 77), Gazal (Abed 46), Abuhatzira; Lencse.

Thursday, 8 November 2012

**Athletic Bilbao (0) 2** *(Ander Herrera 48, Aduriz 55 (pen))*

**Lyon (2) 3** *(Gomis 22, Gourcuff 45, Lacazette 63)* 35,000

*Athletic Bilbao:* (433) Iraizoz; Iraola, Gurpegi, Amorebieta, Aurtenetxe (Ibai 46); De Marcos, Iturraspe, Ander Herrera; Susaeta, Aduriz (Llorente 70), Muniain (Lopez 85).
*Lyon:* (4231) Vercoutre; Reveillere, Bisevac, Lovren, Umtiti; Fofana, Gonalons; Lacazette (Ferri 81), Gourcuff, Monzon (Malbranque 68); Gomis (Lopez L 73).

**Hapoel Kiryat Shmona (1) 1** *(Tasevski 3)*

**Sparta Prague (1) 1** *(Kweuke 24)*          800

*Hapoel Kiryat Shmona:* (4141) Amos; Levi, Hasarma (Vahaba 58), Cohen, Matovic; Gerzycich; Tasevski, Sallalich, Einbinder, Gazal (Abuhatzira 61); Lencse (Rochet 82).
*Sparta Prague:* (442) Vaclik; Zapotocny, Svejdik, Jarosik, Hybs; Kaderabek (Skalak 73), Holek, Husbauer, Krejci (Prikryl 63); Matejovsky, Kweuke (Balaj 79).

Thursday, 22 November 2012

**Sparta Prague (0) 1** *(Husbauer 53)*

**Lyon (0) 1** *(Benzia 46)*          17,121

*Sparta Prague:* (4231) Vaclik; Zapotocny, Svejdik, Jarosik, Pamic; Holek, Matejovsky (Jirasek 89); Kaderabek (Prikryl 53), Husbauer, Krejci (Skalak 90); Kweuke.
*Lyon:* (4231) Vercoutre; Monzon, Umtiti, Kone, Reveillere; Grenier, Fofana; Ghezzal, Gourcuff (Plea 69), Ferri; Benzia (Novillo 71).

Wednesday, 28 November 2012

**Hapoel Kiryat Shmona (0) 0**

**Athletic Bilbao (1) 2** *(Llorente 35, Toquero 77)* 150

*Hapoel Kiryat Shmona:* (4231) Amos; Gabai E, Tzedek, Vahaba, Levi; Einbinder, Elisha; Sallalich (Marisat 71), Tasevski (Mizrachi 57), Porokara (Abuhatzira 46); Abed.
*Athletic Bilbao:* (433) Raul; Ramalho, San Jose, Laporte, Castillo; Toquero, Moran, Pena (Jonxa 85); Igor Martinez (Undabarrena 77), Llorente, Lopez (Ibai 65).

Thursday, 6 December 2012

**Athletic Bilbao (0) 0**

**Sparta Prague (0) 0**          30,000

*Athletic Bilbao:* (4231) Raul; Toquero (Moran 46), Ramalho, Laporte, Castillo; San Jose, Iturraspe; Igor Martinez C, Muniain (Pena 46), Lopez; Llorente (Aduriz 46).
*Sparta Prague:* (4231) Cech; Vidlicka, Zapotocny, Svejdik, Hybs; Holek, Matejovsky (Janos 87); Kaderabek (Kadlec 69), Husbauer, Skalak J; Kweuke (Balaj 82).

**Lyon (1) 2** *(Sarr 15, Benzia 58)*

**Hapoel Kiryat Shmona (0) 0**          29,087

*Lyon:* (4231) Lopes; Zeffane, Kone B, Sarr, Monzon; Ferri, Fofana; Plea (Novillo 70), Gourcuff (Kone S 46); Michel Bastos; Benzia (Martial 79).
*Hapoel Kiryat Shmona:* (433) Amos; Gabai, Tzedek, Vahaba, Levi; Einbinder, Rochet, Tasevski (Gazal 63); Sallalich, Abuhatzira (Marisat 72), Abed (Mizrachi 61).

**Group I Table**

| | P | W | D | L | F | A | GD | Pts |
|---|---|---|---|---|---|---|---|---|
| Lyon | 6 | 5 | 1 | 0 | 14 | 8 | 6 | 16 |
| Sparta Prague | 6 | 2 | 3 | 1 | 9 | 6 | 3 | 9 |
| Athletic Bilbao | 6 | 1 | 2 | 3 | 7 | 9 | −2 | 5 |
| Hapoel Kiryat Shmona | 6 | 0 | 2 | 4 | 6 | 13 | −7 | 2 |

## GROUP J

Thursday, 20 September 2012

**Maribor (1) 3** *(Beric 25, Ibraimi 62, Tavares 88 (pen))*

**Panathinaikos (0) 0**          11,000

*Maribor:* (4231) Handanovic; Milec, Rajcevic, Potokar (Vidovic 80), Mejac; Mertelj, Cvijanovic G; Mezga (Dodlek 85), Tavares (Filipovic 90), Ibraimi; Beric.
*Panathinaikos:* (433) Karnezis; Vyntra, Boumsong, Velazquez, Spyropoulos[■]; Zeca, Vitolo, Katsouranis; Sissoko, Christodoulopoulos (Fornaroli 56), Owusu-Abeyie (Mavrias 74).

**Tottenham H (0) 0**

**Lazio (0) 0**          25,030

*Tottenham H:* (4231) Lloris; Walker, Caulker, Vertonghen, Naughton; Sandro, Dembele (Mason 90); Lennon (Townsend 81), Dempsey (Sigurdsson 76), Bale; Defoe.
*Lazio:* (4141) Marchetti; Lulic, Dias, Biava, Cavanda; Ledesma; Onazi (Zarate 80), Gonzalez, Hernanes (Ciani 90), Mauri (Ederson 90); Klose.

**Thursday, 4 October 2012**
**Lazio (0) 1** *(Ederson 62)*
**Maribor (0) 0** 15,000
*Lazio:* (4411) Bizzarri; Ciani, Dias, Cavanda, Konko; Ederson (Onazi 69), Hernanes, Gonzalez (Zarate 84), Cana; Candreva; Floccari (Kozak 90).
*Maribor:* (433) Handanovic; Vidovic■, Rajcevic, Mejac, Filipovic; Milec, Cvijanovic G (Komazec 86), Mertelj; Ibraimi, Tavares (Mezga 61), Beric.

**Panathinaikos (0) 1** *(Toche 77)*
**Tottenham H (1) 1** *(Dawson 35)* 23,000
*Panathinaikos:* (451) Karnezis; Seitaridis, Triantafyllopoulos, Andre Pinto A, Vyntra; Christodoulopoulos (Mavrias 85), Zeca, Vitolo, Marinos (Sissoko 46), Owusu-Abeyie (Chouchoumis 90); Toche.
*Tottenham H:* (4231) Lloris; Walker, Dawson, Caulker, Vertonghen; Huddlestone (Sandro 81), Dembele; Lennon (Townsend 75), Dempsey (Sigurdsson 66), Bale; Defoe.

**Thursday, 25 October 2012**
**Maribor (1) 1** *(Beric 42)*
**Tottenham H (0) 1** *(Sigurdsson 58)* 13,000
*Maribor:* (4231) Handanovic; Milec, Rajcevic, Arghus, Mejac; Mertelj, Cvijanovic G; Mezga (Filipovic 73), Tavares (Komazec 90), Ibraimi; Beric.
*Tottenham H:* (4231) Lloris; Walker, Caulker, Vertonghen, Naughton; Sandro (Livermore 84), Huddlestone; Lennon, Sigurdsson (Dempsey 75), Townsend (Falque 46); Defoe.

**Panathinaikos (0) 1** *(Toche 90)*
**Lazio (1) 1** *(Seitaridis 25 (og))* 17,000
*Panathinaikos:* (433) Karnezis; Seitaridis, Andre Pinto A, Velazquez, Spyropoulos; Zeca, Vitolo, Fourlanos (Owusu-Abeyie 67); Sissoko (Mavrias 79), Fornaroli (Toche 75), Christodoulopoulos.
*Lazio:* (433) Bizzarri; Konko, Ciani, Dias, Cavanda; Gonzalez (Cana 86), Ledesma, Hernanes (Onazi 78); Candreva, Floccari, Mauri (Zarate 46).

**Thursday, 8 November 2012**
**Lazio (2) 3** *(Kozak 22, 40, Floccari 59)*
**Panathinaikos (0) 0** 8500
*Lazio:* (433) Marchetti; Scaloni, Ciani, Cana, Radu; Gonzalez (Hernanes 67), Ledesma (Lulic 80), Onazi; Floccari, Zarate M, Kozak (Klose 76).
*Panathinaikos:* (433) Karnezis; Seitaridis, Velazquez, Vyntra, Spyropoulos; Zeca (Lagos 78), Vitolo, Chouchoumis (Mavrias 59); Christodoulopoulos, Toche J (Petropoulos 24), Owusu-Abeyie.

**Tottenham H (1) 3** *(Defoe 22, 49, 77)*
**Maribor (1) 1** *(Beric 40)* 27,089
*Tottenham H:* (442) Lloris; Walker, Dawson, Vertonghen, Naughton; Lennon (Falque 90), Huddlestone, Carroll, Bale (Mason 86); Defoe (Dempsey 82), Adebayor.
*Maribor:* (4411) Handanovic; Milec, Rajcevic, Arghus, Mejac; Cvijanovic G (Mezga 69), Mertelj (Dodlek 89), Filipovic, Ibraimi; Tavares (Komazec 76); Beric.

**Thursday, 22 November 2012**
**Lazio (0) 0**
**Tottenham H (0) 0** 20,000
*Lazio:* (451) Marchetti; Cavanda, Biava, Ciani, Radu; Mauri, Gonzalez, Ledesma, Hernanes (Ederson 69), Lulic (Candreva 78); Kozak (Floccari 78).
*Tottenham H:* (442) Lloris; Walker, Caulker, Vertonghen, Naughton; Sigurdsson (Lennon 63), Sandro, Carroll (Dembele 76), Bale; Dempsey (Defoe 63), Adebayor.

**Panathinaikos (0) 1** *(Vitolo 67 (pen))*
**Maribor (0) 0** 12,000
*Panathinaikos:* (433) Karnezis; Seitaridis, Vyntra, Spyropoulos, Velazquez; Sissoko (Marinos 81), Vitolo, Mavrias; Zeca, Toche (Petropoulos 72), Owusu-Abeyie (Fornaroli 35).

*Maribor:* (4231) Handanovic; Mejac■, Rajcevic, Arghus, Filipovic; Milec (Viler M 69), Ibraimi; Cvijanovic (Potokar 46), Mertelj, Tavares (Dodlek 77); Beric.

**Thursday, 6 December 2012**
**Maribor (0) 1** *(Tavares 84)*
**Lazio (3) 4** *(Kozak 16, Radu 32, Floccari 38, 51)* 12,000
*Maribor:* (4231) Handanovic; Mertelj, Rajcevic, Potokar, Trajkovski; Filipovic (Dodlek 57), Cvijanovic G (Arghus 80); Mezga (Crnic 80), Tavares, Ibraimi; Beric.
*Lazio:* (442) Bizzarri; Cavanda, Cana, Ciani, Radu (Scaloni 56); Ederson, Onazi, Hernanes (Gonzalez 56), Lulic; Kozak (Rozzi 78), Floccari.

**Tottenham H (1) 3** *(Adebayor 29, Karnezis 76 (og), Defoe 83)*
**Panathinaikos (0) 1** *(Zeca 54)* 32,554
*Tottenham H:* (442) Friedel; Walker, Caulker, Vertonghen, Naughton; Lennon (Livermore 87), Sandro, Carroll (Dembele 75), Dempsey (Sigurdsson 80); Defoe, Adebayor.
*Panathinaikos:* (433) Karnezis; Seitaridis, Triantafyllopoulos, Vyntra, Spyropoulos; Vitolo, Sow (Christodoulopoulos 60), Sissoko; Zeca, Mavrias (Fornaroli 83), Toche J (Petropoulos 78).

| Group J Table | P | W | D | L | F | A | GD | Pts |
|---|---|---|---|---|---|---|---|---|
| Lazio | 6 | 3 | 3 | 0 | 9 | 2 | 7 | 12 |
| Tottenham H | 6 | 2 | 4 | 0 | 8 | 4 | 4 | 10 |
| Panathinaikos | 6 | 1 | 2 | 3 | 4 | 11 | –7 | 5 |
| Maribor | 6 | 1 | 1 | 4 | 6 | 10 | –4 | 4 |

**GROUP K**
**Thursday, 20 September 2012**
**Bayer Leverkusen (0) 0**
**Metalist Kharkiv (0) 0** 15,322
*Bayer Leverkusen:* (433) Leno; Schwaab, Toprak O, Wollscheid, Hosogai; Reinartz, Rolfes, Bender (Schurrle 63); Renato Augusto (Castro 62), Kiessling (Fernandes 76), Bellarabi.
*Metalist Kharkiv:* (4231) Goryainov; Villagra, Gueye, Torsiglieri, Fininho; Torres, Edmar; Taison (Willian 64), Cleiton Xavier, Sosa J (Pshenichnikh 88); Cristaldo (Marlos 76).

**Rapid Vienna (0) 1** *(Katzer 66)*
**Rosenborg (1) 2** *(Elyounoussi 18, Dorsin 60)* 800
*Rapid Vienna:* (4231) Konigshofer; Trimmel, Sonnleitner, Ferreira, Katzer; Heikkinen, Ildiz (Prager 70); Alar, Hoffmann, Boyd T; Burgstaller (Grozurek 85).
*Rosenborg:* (4231) Orlund; Gamboa, Reginiussen, Ronning, Dorsin; Svensson, Diskerud M (Iversen 90); Dockal, Elyounoussi, Fredheim Holm (Selnaes 81); Prica.

**Thursday, 4 October 2012**
**Metalist Kharkiv (0) 2** *(Edmar 67, Cleiton Xavier 80)*
**Rapid Vienna (0) 0** 40,003
*Metalist Kharkiv:* (4231) Goryainov; Villagra, Gueye, Torsiglieri, Fininho; Torres, Cleiton Xavier; Sosa J (Marlos 83), Blanco (Edmar 51), Taison; Cristaldo (Willian 73).
*Rapid Vienna:* (4231) Konigshofer; Trimmel, Sonnleitner, Ferreira, Katzer; Heikkinen, Ildiz; Prager, Hoffmann (Kulovits 87), Burgstaller■; Alar (Grozurek 76).

**Rosenborg (0) 0**
**Bayer Leverkusen (0) 1** *(Kiessling 76)* 12,587
*Rosenborg:* (4231) Orlund; Gamboa, Strandberg, Ronning, Dorsin; Svensson, Selnaes (Iversen 88); Dockal (Chibuike 79), Elyounoussi, Fredheim Holm (Issah 69); Prica.
*Bayer Leverkusen:* (442) Leno; Schwaab, Friedrich (Toprak O 46), Wollscheid, Kadlec; Castro, Renato Augusto, Rolfes, Bender; Fernandes (Kiessling 75), Schurrle (Sam 64).

Thursday, 25 October 2012
**Rapid Vienna (0) 0**
**Bayer Leverkusen (1) 4** *(Wollscheid 37, Castro 56, 90, Bellarabi 58)* 44,000
*Rapid Vienna:* (4231) Konigshofer; Trimmel, Sonnleitner, Ferreira, Katzer; Heikkinen (Boyd T 46), Kulovits; Prager, Ildiz (Schimpelsberger 63), Drazan; Alar (Schrammel 78).
*Bayer Leverkusen:* (433) Leno; Schwaab, Wollscheid, Friedrich, Kadlec (Bender 10); Hosogai, Rolfes, Castro; Bellarabi, Kiessling (Fernandes 70), Schurrle (Hegeler 61).

**Rosenborg (0) 1** *(Elyounoussi 46)*
**Metalist Kharkiv (0) 2** *(Marlos 80, Cleiton Xavier 89)*
10,985
*Rosenborg:* (4231) Orlund; Gamboa, Strandberg, Reginiussen, Dorsin; Svensson, Diskerud M; Dockal, Elyounoussi, Chibuike (Fredheim Holm 77); Prica.
*Metalist Kharkiv:* (4141) Goryainov; Villagra, Torsiglieri, Gueye, Fininho; Torres; Marlos (Rebenok 90), Cleiton Xavier, Blanco (Edmar 72), Taison; Willian (Cristaldo 46).

Thursday, 8 November 2012
**Bayer Leverkusen (1) 3** *(Hegeler 4, Schurrle 53, Friedrich 66)*
**Rapid Vienna (0) 0** 19,000
*Bayer Leverkusen:* (433) Rensing; Carvajal (Carlinhos 74), Friedrich, Toprak O, Hosogai; Reinartz, Hegeler, Rolfes; Schurrle (Renato Augusto 61), Fernandes, Sam (Castro 46).
*Rapid Vienna:* (4231) Konigshofer; Schimpelsberger, Sonnleitner, Ferreira, Schrammel; Pichler, Kulovits; Trimmel, Wydra, Grozurek; Boyd T (Prokopic 86).

**Metalist Kharkiv (1) 3** *(Taison 4, Cleiton Xavier 70, Torres 90)*
**Rosenborg (1) 1** *(Dockal 42)* 34,235
*Metalist Kharkiv:* (4321) Disljenkovic (Goryainov 46); Villagra, Gueye, Torsiglieri, Fininho; Edmar, Torres, Marlos; Cleiton Xavier, Taison (Blanco 82); Cristaldo (Willian 75).
*Rosenborg:* (4231) Hansen; Gamboa, Strandberg (Ronning 79), Reginiussen, Dorsin; Svensson, Issah; Dockal, Iversen (Hoiland 84), Selnaes (Diskerud 63); Fredheim Holm.

Thursday, 22 November 2012
**Metalist Kharkiv (0) 2** *(Cristaldo 46, Cleiton Xavier 85)*
**Bayer Leverkusen (0) 0** 31,218
*Metalist Kharkiv:* (4231) Goryainov; Villagra, Gueye, Torsiglieri, Fininho; Edmar, Torres; Willian (Marlos 72), Cleiton Xavier, Taison (Sharpar V 88); Cristaldo (Blanco 83).
*Bayer Leverkusen:* (4231) Leno; Carlinhos, Friedrich, Wollscheid, Pusch; Hegeler, Reinartz (Meffert 65); Kohr, Renato Augusto, Steffen (Aydin 46); Fernandes (Kiessling 78).

**Rosenborg (1) 3** *(Chibuike 28, Elyounoussi 77, Prica 80)*
**Rapid Vienna (0) 2** *(Schrammel 54, Boyd T 67)* 8320
*Rosenborg:* (4411) Hansen; Gamboa, Strandberg, Reginiussen, Dorsin; Dockal (Iversen 75), Diskerud M, Fredheim Holm (Selnaes 60), Svensson; Elyounoussi; Chibuike (Prica 75).
*Rapid Vienna:* (4231) Novota; Schimpelsberger (Grozurek 86), Sonnleitner, Ferreira, Schrammel; Heikkinen, Pichler (Wydra 83); Trimmel, Alar (Drazan 51), Burgstaller; Boyd T.

Thursday, 6 December 2012
**Bayer Leverkusen (0) 1** *(Riedel 65)*
**Rosenborg (0) 0** 10,000
*Bayer Leverkusen:* (442) Lomb; Riedel, Wollscheid, Friedrich, Carlinhos; Renato Augusto (Sam 46), Hegeler, Reinartz (Rolfes 46), Kohr; Fernandes, Steffen (Aydin 75).
*Rosenborg:* (442) Hansen; Gamboa, Dorsin, Reginiussen, Ronning; Chibuike, Selnaes (Iversen 72), Svensson (Alas 83), Diskerud M; Prica (Issah 46), Elyounoussi.

**Rapid Vienna (1) 1** *(Alar 13)*
**Metalist Kharkiv (0) 0** 29,400
*Rapid Vienna:* (442) Konigshofer; Schrammel, Sonnleitner, Pichler■, Ferreira; Schimpelsberger, Heikkinen, Wydra (Kulovits 46), Trimmel (Drazan 63); Alar (Boyd T 75), Burgstaller.
*Metalist Kharkiv:* (442) Goryainov; Villagra, Torsiglieri, Fininho (Edmar 72), Sosa; Torres, Blanco, Marlos, Gueye; Willian, Cristaldo.

| Group K Table | P | W | D | L | F | A | GD | Pts |
|---|---|---|---|---|---|---|---|---|
| Metalist Kharkiv | 6 | 4 | 1 | 1 | 9 | 3 | 6 | 13 |
| Bayer Leverkusen | 6 | 4 | 1 | 1 | 9 | 2 | 7 | 13 |
| Rosenborg | 6 | 2 | 0 | 4 | 7 | 10 | –3 | 6 |
| Rapid Vienna | 6 | 1 | 0 | 5 | 4 | 14 | –10 | 3 |

## GROUP L

Thursday, 20 September 2012
**FC Twente (1) 2** *(Janssen 7, Chadli 54)*
**Hannover 96 (0) 2** *(Sobiech 68, Wisgerhof 72 (og))* 22,500
*FC Twente:* (433) Mihailov; Rosales, Douglas, Wisgerhof, Braafheid (Boyata 50); Janssen, Brama, Schilder R (Landzaat 46); Tadic, Castaignos, Chadli (Gutierrez 77).
*Hannover 96:* (442) Zieler; Cherundolo, Felipe, Eggiman, Rausch; Stindl, Pinto (Nikci 31), Andreasen (Schmiedebach 75), Huszti; Schlaudraff, Abdellaoui (Sobiech 46).

**Levante (1) 1** *(Juanfran 40)*
**Helsingborg (0) 0** 14,000
*Levante:* (442) Navas; Navarro, Juanfran, Ballesteros, Pedro Lopez; Pedro Rios (Pallardo 86), Juanlu, Michel (Barkero 59), Diop P; Angel (Ruben 71), Iborra.
*Helsingborg:* (541) Hansson; Baffo, Uronen, Mahlangu (Dos Santos 84), Larsson, Lindstrom (Bouaouzan 73); Andersson C, Gashi, Bedoya, Accam D (Sorum 64); Djurdjic.

Thursday, 4 October 2012
**Hannover 96 (1) 2** *(Huszti 21 (pen), Konan D 49)*
**Levante (1) 1** *(Michel 10 (pen))* 37,000
*Hannover 96:* (4312) Zieler; Cherundolo, Haggui■, Eggiman, Rausch; Stindl, Pinto, Huszti (Schmiedebach 84); Schlaudraff (Felipe 11); Konan D, Sobiech (Diouf 76).
*Levante:* (433) Navas; Lell (El Zhar 33), Ballesteros, Hector, Karabelas; Iborra, Dudka (Angel 69), Pedro Lopez; Pedro Rios M, Gekas (Ruben 69), Michel.

**Helsingborg (2) 2** *(Djurdjic 7, 43)*
**FC Twente (0) 2** *(Bengtsson 74, Douglas 88)* 5578
*Helsingborg:* (442) Hansson; Andersson C, Atta, Larsson (Baffo 46), Uronen; Lindstrom (Wahlstedt 78), Mahlangu, Gashi, Bouaouzan; Djurdjic, Bedoya (Accam D 41).
*FC Twente:* (433) Mihailov; Rosales (Bengtsson 62), Boyata, Douglas, Braafheid (Landzaat 83); Schilder R, Gutierrez (Cabral 62), Brama; Chadli, Castaignos, Tadic.

Thursday, 25 October 2012
**Helsingborg (0) 1** *(Dos Santos 90)*
**Hannover 96 (1) 2** *(Diouf 12, Konan D 90)* 8338
*Helsingborg:* (442) Hansson; Andersson C, Atta, Larsson, Uronen; Lindstrom (Accam D 46), Mahlangu, Gashi, Bouaouzan (Dos Santos 66); Bedoya, Djurdjic.
*Hannover 96:* (4141) Zieler; Cherundolo, Eggiman, Schulz, Rausch; Stindl; Konan D, Pinto, Huszti (Pander 88), Abdellaoui (Sobiech 46); Diouf (Schmiedebach 75).

**Levante (0) 3** *(Michel 59 (pen), Pedro Rios 78, 88)*
**FC Twente (0) 0** 8505
*Levante:* (451) Navas; Lell, Ballesteros, Hector, Karabelas; Pedro Rios, Diop P, Michel (Barkero 87), Iborra, Juanlu (Ruben 83); Gekas (Angel 62).
*FC Twente:* (433) Mihailov; Rosales, Douglas, Bengtsson, Braafheid (Cabral 62); Brama, Gutierrez (Schilder R 61), Landzaat (Janssen 69); Tadic, Castaignos, Chadli.

Thursday, 8 November 2012
**FC Twente (0) 0**
**Levante (0) 0** 19,500
*FC Twente:* (433) Mihailov; Rosales, Bengtsson, Douglas, Braafheid; Janssen, Brama, Schilder (Bulykin 62); Cabral (Gutierrez 76), Castaignos, Tadic.
*Levante:* (4231) Navas; Lell, Hector, Ballesteros, Karabelas; Iborra, Diop P; Pedro Rios, Michel (Barkero 84), Ruben (Juanlu 77); Gekas (Angel 74).

**Hannover 96 (1) 3** *(Diouf 3, 50, Huszti 90 (pen))*
**Helsingborg (0) 2** *(Djurdjic 59, Bedoya 68)* 45,566
*Hannover 96:* (442) Zieler; Cherundolo, Eggiman, Haggui, Rausch (Pander 73); Stindl, Schmiedebach, Schulz, Huszti; Konan D (Schlaudraff 71), Diouf (Sobiech 87).
*Helsingborg:* (442) Hansson; Andersson C, Larsson■, Atta■, Uronen (Hanstveit 84); Lindstrom (Accam D 90), Mahlangu, Gashi, Bouaouzan (Dos Santos 46); Djurdjic, Bedoya.

Thursday, 22 November 2012
**Hannover 96 (0) 0**
**FC Twente (0) 0** 35,800
*Hannover 96:* (442) Zieler; Cherundolo, Eggiman, Haggui, Pander; Nikci (Schmiedebach 70), Schulz, Pinto, Huszti (Rausch 77); Schlaudraff (Konan D 61), Sobiech.
*FC Twente:* (433) Boschker; Rosales (Breukers 76), Douglas, Bengtsson■, Braafheid; Janssen, Brama, Pelupessy (Fer 63); Gutierrez, Bulykin (Castaignos 70), Tadic.

**Helsingborg (0) 1** *(Sorum 89)*
**Levante (2) 3** *(Angel 8, Diop P 37, Iborra 81)* 4453
*Helsingborg:* (442) Hansson; Andersson C (Krafth 25), Hanstveit, Baffo, Uronen; Lindstrom (Accam D 68), Mahlangu, Gashi, Bedoya; Djurdjic, Dos Santos (Sorum 77).
*Levante:* (433) Navas; Karabelas, Ballesteros, Lell, Hector; Diop P, Iborra (Pallardo 83), Michel (Pedro Lopez 86); Pedro Rios, Angel, Ruben (Barkero 73).

Thursday, 6 December 2012
**FC Twente (0) 1** *(Tadic 74)*
**Helsingborg (2) 3** *(Djurdjic 6, Bedoya 21, Sorum 67)*
21,000
*FC Twente:* (433) Bednarek; Breukers, Wisgerhof, Boyata, Braafheid; Pelupessy J, Landzaat (Brama 73), Holscher; Born (Tadic 72), Castaignos, Chadli (Bulykin 60).
*Helsingborg:* (442) Hansson; Krafth, Larsson, Hanstveit, Edman (Wahlstedt 75); Bedoya, Gashi, Mahlangu, Bouaouzan (Accam D 84); Djurdjic, Sorum (Dos Santos 75).

**Levante (0) 2** *(Angel 50, Iborra 90)*
**Hannover 96 (2) 2** *(Stindl 18, Konan D 26)* 18,000
*Levante:* (433) Navas; Navarro, Hector, Karabelas, Pedro Lopez; Michel, Diop P (Pallardo 74), Ruben (Barkero 59); Angel, Iborra, El Zhar (Juanlu 59).
*Hannover 96:* (442) Zieler; Haggui, Sakai, Schulz, Pinto; Schmiedebach, Huszti (Cherundolo 70), Stindl (Nikci 38), Rausch; Konan D (Abdellaoui 89), Diouf.

| Group L Table | P | W | D | L | F | A | GD | Pts |
|---|---|---|---|---|---|---|---|---|
| Hannover 96 | 6 | 3 | 3 | 0 | 11 | 8 | 3 | 12 |
| Levante | 6 | 3 | 2 | 1 | 10 | 5 | 5 | 11 |
| Helsingborg | 6 | 1 | 1 | 4 | 9 | 12 | –3 | 4 |
| FC Twente | 6 | 0 | 4 | 2 | 5 | 10 | –5 | 4 |

## KNOCK-OUT STAGE

**SECOND ROUND FIRST LEG**

Thursday, 14 February 2013
**Ajax (1) 2** *(Alderweireld 28, Van Rhijn 49)*
**Steaua Bucharest (0) 0** 48,000
*Ajax:* (433) Vermeer (Cillessen 46); Van Rhijn, Alderweireld, Moisander, Blind; De Jong, Schone, Eriksen; Cuenca (Poulsen 73), Sigthorsson (Boerrigter 82), Fischer.
*Steaua Bucharest:* (4231) Tatarusanu; Rapa, Chiriches, Gardos, Latovlevici; Pintilii■, Bourceanu; Chipciu A, Rusescu (Adi 71), Popa (Costea 82); Nikolic (Tatu 53).

**Anzhi Makhachkala (1) 3** *(Eto'o 34, Ahmedov 48, Boussoufa 64)*
**Hannover 96 (1) 1** *(Huszti 22)* 12,000
*Anzhi Makhachkala:* (433) Gabulov; Yeschenko, Joao Carlos, Ewerton, Zhirkov; Diarra, Jucilei, Ahmedov; Boussoufa, Eto'o, Willian (Carcela-Gonzalez 85).
*Hannover 96:* (442) Zieler; Chahed, Djourou, Schulz, Pocognoli (Pander 79); Schlaudraff (Abdellaoui 66), Schmiedebach, Pinto, Huszti; Konan D, Diouf (Sobiech 71).

**Atletico Madrid (0) 0**
**Rubin Kazan (1) 2** *(Karadeniz 6, Orbaiz 90)* 20,000
*Atletico Madrid:* (442) Sergio Asenjo; Juanfran, Godin, Cata Diaz (Raul Garcia 60), Filipe Luis (Saul 66); Rodriguez, Mario Suarez (Koke 46), Tiago, Turan; Adrian, Falcao.
*Rubin Kazan:* (4231) Ryzhikov; Ansaldi, Sharonov■, Cesar Navas, Marcano; Natcho, Orbaiz, Kisliak, Eremenko, Karadeniz (Kuzmin 88); Rondon (Dyadyun 86).

**FC Basel (1) 2** *(Stocker 23, Streller 68)*
**Dnipro Dnipropetrovsk (0) 0** 8314
*FC Basel:* (4141) Sommer; Degen P (Salah 68), Schar, Dragovic, Park; Cabral; Degen D, Die, Frei (El-Nenny 78), Stocker (Zoua 88); Streller.
*Dnipro Dnipropetrovsk:* (442) Lastuvka; Mandzyuk V, Mazuch, Cheberyachko, Strinic; Giuliano, Rotan, Kravchenko (Matheus 53), Konoplianka; Zozulya (Kankava 69), Kalinic (Seleznyov 53).

**BATE Borisov (0) 0**
**Fenerbahce (0) 0** 6500
*BATE Borisov:* (4141) Gorbunov; Yurevich, Radkov, Filipenko, Bordachev; Rudik (Pavlov 46); Olekhnovich, Baga (Mozolevski 64), Hleb (Kurlovich 79), Volodko A; Rodionov.
*Fenerbahce:* (433) Demirel; Gonul, Irtegun, Korkmaz, Ziegler; Baroni (Sahin S 85), Topal, Meireles■; Sow (Ucan 90), Webo (Erkin 71), Kuyt.

**Bayer Leverkusen (0) 0**
**Benfica (0) 1** *(Cardozo 61)* 36,000
*Bayer Leverkusen:* (4321) Leno; Hosogai (Boenisch 82), Wollscheid, Schwaab, Kadlec; Bender, Rolfes, Hegeler; Castro (Milik 70), Schurrle (Sam 46); Kiessling.
*Benfica:* (433) Artur Moraes; Almeida A, Luisao, Garay, Melgarejo; Gaitan, Matic, Gomes (Perez 42); Urreta (Salvio 57), Cardozo (Lima 72), John.

**Borussia Moenchengladbach (1) 3** *(Stranzl 17 (pen),*
*Marx 84 (pen), Arango 88)*
**Lazio (0) 3** *(Floccari 57, Kozak 64, 90)*          46,279
*Borussia Moenchengladbach:* (442) ter Stegen; Stranzl,
Brouwers, Dominguez, Wendt; Cigerci (Xhaka 75),
Jantschke (Hanke 75), Nordtveit (Marx 72), Arango;
Herrmann, De Jong.
*Lazio:* (4321) Marchetti; Konko, Dias■, Biava, Radu;
Lulic (Ciani 87), Ledesma (Kozak 46), Gonzalez;
Candreva (Cana 71), Hernanes; Floccari.

**Dynamo Kiev (1) 1** *(Haruna 20)*
**Bordeaux (1) 1** *(Obraniak 23)*          35,000
*Dynamo Kiev:* (4231) Koval; Mykhalyk, Taiwo,
Khacheridi, Vida; Haruna, Veloso; Kranjcar (Gusev 61),
Bezus (Garmash 69), Yarmolenko; Mehmedi (Ruben
79).
*Bordeaux:* (334) Carasso; Henrique, Planus, Sane;
Faubert, Tremoulinas, Sertic; Plasil (Biyogo Poko 90),
Obraniak, Maurice-Belay (Rolan 66), Bellion (Saivet 61).

**Internazionale (1) 2** *(Palacio R 20, 86)*
**CFR Cluj (0) 0**          14,790
*Internazionale:* (433) Handanovic; Nagatomo, Silvestre,
Ranocchia, Pereira; Guarin, Cambiasso, Kovacic
(Jonathan 88); Gargano, Milito (Palacio R 10), Cassano
(Alvarez 73).
*CFR Cluj:* (442) Mario Felgueiras; Ivo Pinto, Piccolo,
Cadu, Camora; Muresan, Rada, Godemeche (Maftei 39),
Sepsi; Rui Pedro (Bjelanovic 84), Maah (Hora 78).

**Levante (2) 3** *(Pedro Rios 10, Barkero 40 (pen),*
*Martins 56)*
**Olympiakos (0) 0**          17,000
*Levante:* (4231) Navas; Pedro Lopez, Navarro, Hector,
Juanfran; Diop P (Michel 60), Iborra; Pedro Rios (Valdo
67), Barkero, Ruben; Martins (Acquafresca 82).
*Olympiakos:* (4231) Megyeri; Maniatis, Manolas,
Contreras, Holebas; Modesto (Greco 46), Fejsa;
Abdoun■, Paulo Machado (Fetfatzidis 75), Vlachodimos
(Mitroglou 59); Djebbour.

**Napoli (0) 0**
**Viktoria Plzen (1) 3** *(Darida 28, Rajtoral 79, Tecl 89)*
          15,000
*Napoli:* (343) De Sanctis; Gamberini (Hamsik 46),
Rolando, Britos; Maggio, Donadel (Inler 72), Dzemaili,
Zuniga; El Kaddouri (Calaio 59), Pandev, Cavani.
*Viktoria Plzen:* (4231) Kozacik; Reznik, Cisovsky,
Prochazka, Limbersky; Darida, Horvath; Rajtoral (Fillo
85), Kolar (Hejda 90), Kovarik J; Bakos (Tecl 59).

**Newcastle U (0) 0**
**Metalist Kharkiv (0) 0**          30,157
*Newcastle U:* (4411) Krul; Yanga-Mbiwa, Taylor S,
Coloccini, Santon; Obertan (Marveaux 62), Tiote
(Ameobi Shola 79), Cabaye, Gutierrez; Sissoko; Cisse.
*Metalist Kharkiv:* (4141) Goryainov; Villagra, Gueye,
Torsiglieri, Fininho; Torres; Marlos (Willian 73), Edmar,
Cleiton Xavier, Sosa J; Cristaldo (Jakson 81).

**Sparta Prague (0) 0**
**Chelsea (0) 1** *(Oscar 82)*          18,952
*Sparta Prague:* (433) Vaclik T; Zapotocny, Svejdik,
Holek, Hybs; Husbauer (Bednar 85), Vacha, Matejovsky;
Kadlec, Lafata ( 76), Krejci (Pamic 81).
*Chelsea:* (4231) Cech; Azpilicueta, Ivanovic, Cahill,
Bertrand; Lampard, Ramires; Marin (Benayoun 68),
Mata (Oscar 82), Hazard; Torres.

**Tottenham H (1) 2** *(Bale 45, 90)*
**Lyon (0) 1** *(Umtiti 55)*          31,762
*Tottenham H:* (4231) Friedel; Walker, Gallas,
Vertonghen, Assou-Ekotto; Dembele, Parker
(Livermore 90); Lennon (Sigurdsson 79), Dempsey
(Holtby 67), Bale; Adebayor.
*Lyon:* (4231) Vercoutre; Reveillere, Lovren, Bisevac,
Umtiti; Gonalons, Fofana; Lacazette, Malbranque
(Grenier 82), Lopez (Ghezzal 88); Gomis.

**VfB Stuttgart (1) 1** *(Gentner 42)*
**KRC Genk (0) 1** *(Plet 90)*          15,200
*VfB Stuttgart:* (4231) Ulreich; Sakai, Tasci, Niedermaier,
Boka; Kvist Jorgensen, Gentner; Harnik (Okazaki 57),
Torun (Holzhauser 46), Traore (Maxim 74); Ibisevic V.
*KRC Genk:* (442) Koteles; Ngcongca, Simaeys,
Koulibaly, Tshimanga; Buffel, Kumordzi (Gorius 74),
Hyland, De Ceulaer (Monrose 83); Vossen (Plet 68),
Barda.

**Zenit St Petersburg (0) 2** *(Hulk 70, Semak 72)*
**Liverpool (0) 0**          21,000
*Zenit St Petersburg:* (433) Malafeev; Aniukov, Luis Neto,
Lombaerts, Hubocan; Shirokov, Denisov, Witsel; Hulk,
Kerzhakov (Faitzulin 82), Danny (Semak 54).
*Liverpool:* (433) Reina; Johnson, Skrtel, Carragher, Jose
Enrique; Gerrard, Allen, Henderson; Downing, Suarez,
Sterling (Lucas 78).

## SECOND ROUND SECOND LEG

Thursday, 21 February 2013
**Benfica (0) 2** *(John 60, Matic 77)*
**Bayer Leverkusen (0) 1** *(Schurrle 75)*          35,000
*Benfica:* (433) Artur Moraes; Almeida A, Luisao, Garay,
Melgarejo; Carlos Martins (Salvio 53), Matic, Gaitan;
Perez, Cardozo (Lima 64), John (Jardel 90).
*Bayer Leverkusen:* (433) Leno; Carvajal, Wollscheid,
Toprak O, Boenisch; Reinartz (Milik 73), Rolfes, Bender
(Hegeler 57); Castro, Kiessling, Schurrle.

**Bordeaux (1) 1** *(Diabate C 41)*
**Dynamo Kiev (0) 0**          11,889
*Bordeaux:* (3142) Carasso; Biyogo Poko, Planus,
Marange; Sertic; Faubert, Obraniak (Plasil 84),
Tremoulinas (Maurice-Belay 85), Poundje; Saivet,
Diabate C.
*Dynamo Kiev:* (433) Koval; Vida, Khacheridi, Mykhalyk,
Taiwo; Haruna, Kranjcar (Garmash 80), Veloso; Bezus
(Gusev 46), Mehmedi (Ideye B 46), Yarmolenko.

**CFR Cluj (0) 0**
**Internazionale (2) 3** *(Guarin 22, 45, Benassi 88)*          6000
*CFR Cluj:* (352) Mario Felgueiras; Cadu, Piccolo, Rada
(Kapetanos 36); Ivo Pinto, Sepsi, Muresan (Hora 9),
Godemeche, Camora■; Rui Pedro (Diogo Valente 71),
Maah.
*Internazionale:* (442) Handanovic; Zanetti, Ranocchia,
Juan, Pereira; Guarin (Mbaye 66), Cambiasso, Kovacic,
Alvarez (Pasa 54); Cassano, Palacio R (Benassi 46).

**Chelsea (0) 1** *(Hazard E 90)*
**Sparta Prague (1) 1** *(Lafata 17)*          38,642
*Chelsea:* (433) Cech; Azpilicueta, Terry, Cahill, Bertrand;
Ramires, Mikel, Moses; Mata, Torres, Oscar (Hazard E
67).
*Sparta Prague:* (433) Vaclik; Zapotocny, Holek, Svejdik,
Hybs; Prikryl, Vacha, Krejci; Matejovsky, Lafata ( 82),
Kadlec (Bednar 90).

**Dnipro Dnipropetrovsk (0) 1** *(Seleznyov 77 (pen))*
**FC Basel (0) 1** *(Schar 81 (pen))*          28,000
*Dnipro Dnipropetrovsk:* (442) Lastuvka; Mandzyuk V,
Douglas (Kalinic■ 53), Cheberyachko, Strinic; Fedetskiy
(Konoplianka 31), Giuliano, Rotan, Matheus
(Kravchenko 54); Zozulya, Seleznyov.
*FC Basel:* (442) Sommer; Steinhofer, Schar, Dragovic,
Park; Degen (Zoua 82), Cabral, Die, Stocker; Salah M
(El-Nenny 89), Frei■.

**Fenerbahce (1) 1** *(Baroni 45 (pen))*
**BATE Borisov (0) 0**          Behind closed doors
*Fenerbahce:* (433) Demirel; Gonul, Yobo, Korkmaz,
Ziegler; Baroni, Ucan (Sahin S 62), Topal; Kuyt, Webo
(Senturk 77), Sow (Erkin 85).
*BATE Borisov:* (4321) Gorbunov; Yurevich (Aleksievich
75), Gayduchlik, Filipenko, Bordachev (Mozolevski 84);
Volodko A (Pavlov 65), Olekhnovich, Rudik, Baga■,
Hleb; Rodionov.

**Hannover 96 (0) 1** *(Pinto 70)*
**Anzhi Makhachkala (0) 1** *(Traore 90)*    40,000
*Hannover 96:* (442) Zieler; Sakai (Sobiech 83), Djourou, Schulz, Pocognoli (Rausch 71); Konan D, Schmiedebach (Schlaudraff 61), Pinto, Huszti; Abdellaoui, Diouf.
*Anzhi Makhachkala:* (4231) Gabulov; Logashov, Joao Carlos, Ewerton, Yeschenko; Jucilei, Diarra; Boussoufa (Carcela-Gonzalez 78), Ahmedov (Shatov 90), Willian (Traore 67); Eto'o.

**KRC Genk (0) 0**
**VfB Stuttgart (1) 2** *(Boka 45, Gentner 58)*    16,000
*KRC Genk:* (442) Koteles; Ngcongca, Simaeys, Koulibaly, Tshimanga; Hyland, Kumordzi (Barda 61), Gorius, Buffel (Ojo 77); Plet, De Ceulaer (Monrose 71).
*VfB Stuttgart:* (442) Ulreich; Sakai, Tasci, Rudiger, Boka; Kvist Jorgensen, Gentner, Harnik, Okazaki (Holzhauser 77); Traore (Maxim 75), Ibisevic (Macheda 83).

**Lazio (2) 2** *(Candreva 10, Gonzalez 33)*
**Borussia Moenchengladbach (0) 0**    25,000
*Lazio:* (4411) Marchetti; Biava, Radu, Konko, Lulic; Hernanes, Gonzalez (Onazi 69), Ledesma, Cana; Candreva (Bruno Pereirinha M 82); Floccari (Kozak 78).
*Borussia Moenchengladbach:* (4411) ter Stegen; Dominguez, Wendt, Jantschke, Stranzl; Cigerci (Hanke 69), Marx (Xhaka 81), Nordtveit, Arango (Younes 52); Herrmann; De Jong.

**Liverpool (2) 3** *(Suarez 28, Allen 43, Suarez 59)*
**Zenit St Petersburg (1) 1** *(Hulk 19)*    43,026
*Liverpool:* (4231) Reina; Johnson, Carragher, Agger, Jose Enrique; Lucas, Allen (Shelvey 59); Downing (Sterling 84), Gerrard, Henderson (Assaidi 59); Suarez.
*Zenit St Petersburg:* (433) Malafeev; Aniukov, Luis Neto, Lombaerts (Criscito 46), Hubocan; Witsel, Denisov, Shirokov, Danny (Faitzulin 46), Hulk, Semak S (Rodic 84).

**Lyon (1) 1** *(Gonalons 17)*
**Tottenham H (0) 1** *(Dembele 90)*    38,761
*Lyon:* (433) Vercoutre; Reveillere, Bisevac, Lovren, Umtiti; Fofana, Grenier, Gonalons; Lacazette (Malbranque 65), Gomis (Briand 82), Lopez (Ghezzal 73).
*Tottenham H:* (4231) Friedel; Walker, Gallas W, Vertonghen, Assou-Ekotto; Dembele, Parker (Livermore 84); Lennon (Dempsey 66), Holtby (Sigurdsson 74), Bale; Adebayor.

**Metalist Kharkiv (0) 0**
**Newcastle U (0) 1** *(Ameobi Shola 64 (pen))*    39,973
*Metalist Kharkiv:* (4231) Goryainov; Villagra, Gueye, Torsiglieri, Fininho; Torres (Willian 66), Edmar (Blanco 82); Marlos (Jakson 67), Cleiton Xavier, Sosa J; Cristaldo.
*Newcastle U:* (442) Krul; Simpson, Yanga-Mbiwa, Coloccini, Haidara; Sissoko, Anita (Perch 76), Cabaye (Bigirimana 87), Marveaux; Ameobi Shola, Cisse (Gutierrez 75).

**Olympiakos (0) 0**
**Levante (1) 1** *(Martins 9)*    30,000
*Olympiakos:* (433) Carroll; Maniatis, Contreras, Siovas, Lykogiannis (Holebas 46); Paulo Machado, Fejsa, Greco (Fetfatzidis 46); Vlachodimos, Mitroglou (Ibagaza 76), Djebbour.
*Levante:* (4231) Navas; Hector, Ballesteros, Navarro, Juanfran; Michel (Dudka 86), Iborra; Pedro Rios M (Valdo 68), Barkero, Ruben; Martins (Acquafresca 83).

**Rubin Kazan (0) 0**
**Atletico Madrid (0) 1** *(Falcao 84)*    3000
*Rubin Kazan:* (4231) Ryzhikov; Kuzmin, Cesar Navas■, Marcano, Ansaldi; Orbaiz, Natcho (Ryazantsev A 87); Karadeniz, Eremenko R, Kisliak (Kaleshin 77); Rondon.
*Atletico Madrid:* (4231) Sergio Asenjo; Manquillo, Miranda, Cata Diaz, Cisma; Mario Suarez, Raul Garcia; Rodriguez, Saul, Adrian; Falcao.

**Steaua Bucharest (1) 2** *(Latovlevici 38, Chiriches 76)*
**Ajax (0) 0**    40,000
*Steaua Bucharest:* (433) Tatarusanu; Rapa, Gardos, Chiriches, Latovlevici; Tatu (Parvulescu 77), Prepelita (Filip 46), Tanase ( 66); Popa, Rusescu, Chipciu A.
*Ajax:* (433) Vermeer; Van Rhijn, Alderweireld, Moisander, Blind; Poulsen, De Jong, Eriksen; Cuenca (Boerrigter 70), Sigthorsson (Schone 70), Fischer (Serero 81).
*aet; Steaua Bucharest won 4-2 on penalties.*

**Viktoria Plzen (0) 2** *(Kovarik J 50, Tecl 74)*
**Napoli (0) 0**    11,067
*Viktoria Plzen:* (4231) Kozacik; Reznik, Cisovsky, Prochazka, Limbersky; Darida, Horvath; Rajtoral (Fillo 83), Kolar ( 89), Kovarik J; Bakos (Tecl 57).
*Napoli:* (433) De Sanctis; Maggio, Gamberini (Cannavaro 65), Rolando, Zuniga; Dzemaili, Donadel (Cavani 46), Behrami (Inler 46); Pandev, Calaio, Insigne.

## THIRD ROUND FIRST LEG

Thursday, 7 March 2013
**Anzhi Makhachkala (0) 0**
**Newcastle U (0) 0**    5000
*Anzhi Makhachkala:* (4231) Gabulov; Yeschenko (Logashov 90), Joao Carlos, Ewerton, Zhirkov; Jucilei, Diarra; Ahmedov, Willian (Traore 22), Shatov (Carcela-Gonzalez 84); Eto'o.
*Newcastle U:* (4231) Elliot; Simpson, Yanga-Mbiwa, Perch, Haidara; Cabaye (Tiote 84), Anita (Taylor S 75); Ben Arfa (Ameobi Shola 64), Marveaux, Obertan; Sissoko.

**FC Basel (0) 2** *(Diaz 82, Frei 90 (pen))*
**Zenit St Petersburg (0) 0**    12,000
*FC Basel:* (4231) Sommer; Degen P, Schar, Dragovic, Park; Cabral, Die (El-Nenny 69); Degen D (Steinhofer 61), Diaz, Salah M; Zoua (Frei A 79).
*Zenit St Petersburg:* (433) Malafeev; Hubocan, Luis Neto■, Lombaerts, Rodic; Witsel, Denisov, Shirokov, Danny (Kerzhakov 82); Hulk, Semak S (Faitzulin 46).

**Benfica (1) 1** *(Carasso 21 (og))*
**Bordeaux (0) 0**    43,248
*Benfica:* (433) Artur Moraes; Almeida A, Luisao, Garay, Melgarejo; Gaitan, Roderick Miranda, Carlos Martins (Perez 63); Rodrigo, Cardozo (Salvio 63), John (Lima 74).
*Bordeaux:* (442) Carasso; Mariano, Sane, Henrique, Tremoulinas; Faubert (Traore 43), Plasil, Sertic, Obraniak; Maurice-Belay (Ben Khalfallah 79), Rolan (Bellion 66).

**Levante (0) 0**
**Rubin Kazan (0) 0**    13,000
*Levante:* (4411) Navas; Pedro Lopez, Navarro, Ballesteros, Juanfran; Barkero, Iborra, Diop P (Pedro Rios 68), Michel■; Ruben (Juanlu 80); Martins.
*Rubin Kazan:* (4411) Ryzhikov; Kuzmin, Sharonov, Ansaldi■, Marcano; Karadeniz, Natcho, Orbaiz, Kasaev (Kaleshin 54); Eremenko R; Rondon (Dyadyun 85).

**Steaua Bucharest (1) 1** *(Rusescu 34 (pen))*
**Chelsea (0) 0**    45,000
*Steaua Bucharest:* (4231) Tatarusanu; Rapa, Szukala, Chiriches, Latovlevici; Bourceanu, Pintilii (Prepelita 58); Popa, Chipciu A, Tanase (Tatu 82); Rusescu (Gardos 90).
*Chelsea:* (4231) Cech; Ivanovic, Luiz, Terry, Bertrand; Lampard, Mikel; Benayoun (Mata 64), Oscar, Hazard E (Marin 75); Torres.

**Tottenham H (2) 3** *(Bale 6, Sigurdsson 18, Vertonghen 53)*
**Internazionale (0) 0**    34,353
*Tottenham H:* (4231) Friedel; Walker, Gallas W, Vertonghen, Assou-Ekotto; Parker, Dembele (Livermore 64); Lennon (Naughton 81), Sigurdsson (Holtby 70), Bale; Defoe.
*Internazionale:* (4231) Handanovic; Zanetti, Ranocchia, Chivu, Juan (Palacio R 46); Gargano, Cambiasso; Alvarez (Jonathan 67), Kovacic (Guarin 55), Pereira; Cassano.

**VfB Stuttgart (0) 0**
**Lazio (1) 2** *(Ederson 21, Onazi 56)*          28,750
*VfB Stuttgart:* (4231) Ulreich; Sakai, Tasci, Rudiger, Boka; Kvist Jorgensen (Harnik 55), Gentner; Okazaki, Maxim (Hajnal 41), Traore; Macheda (Holzhauser 90).
*Lazio:* (4141) Marchetti; Bruno Pereirinha M, Cana, Ciani, Radu; Hernanes (Gonzalez 72); Candreva, Onazi, Ederson (Ledesma 64), Lulic; Kozak (Floccari 84).

**Viktoria Plzen (0) 0**
**Fenerbahce (0) 1** *(Webo 81)*          11,701
*Viktoria Plzen:* (4231) Kozacik; Rajtoral, Cisovsky, Prochazka, Reznik; Darida, Horvath; Duris (Fillo 69), Kolar (Hejda 89), Kovarik J; Bakos (Tecl 60).
*Fenerbahce:* (4231) Demirel; Gonul, Irtegun, Yobo, Ziegler; Topal, Sahin, Kuyt, Baroni, Sow (Erkin 83); Webo (Topuz 85).

**THIRD ROUND SECOND LEG**

Thursday, 14 March 2013
**Bordeaux (0) 2** *(Diabate C 74, Jardel 90 (og))*
**Benfica (1) 3** *(Jardel 30, Cardozo 75, 90)*          30,000
*Bordeaux:* (4231) Carrasso; Mariano (Ben Khalfallah 72), Sane, Henrique, Tremoulinas; Plasil, Sertic (Biyogo Poko 68); Obraniak, Saivet, Diabate C; Maurice-Belay (Sacko 77).
*Benfica:* (433) Artur Moraes; Almeida A, Jardel, Roderick Miranda, Melgarejo; Gaitan, Matic, Salvio (Maxi Pereira 88); Perez, Rodrigo (Cardozo 66), John (Carlos Martins 83).

**Chelsea (1) 3** *(Mata 33, Terry 58, Torres 71)*
**Steaua Bucharest (1) 1** *(Chiriches 46)*          28,817
*Chelsea:* (4231) Cech; Azpilicueta, Terry, Luiz, Cole; Ramires, Mikel; Hazard (Benayoun 90), Mata (Moses 90), Oscar; Torres.
*Steaua Bucharest:* (4231) Tatarusanu; Rapa (Adi 83), Szukala, Chiriches, Latovlevici; Bourceanu, Pintilii; Popa, Chipciu A, Tanase (Tatu 78); Rusescu.

**Fenerbahce (1) 1** *(Ucan 44)*
**Viktoria Plzen (0) 1** *(Darida 61)*          Behind closed doors
*Fenerbahce:* (4231) Demirel; Gonul, Yobo, Irtegun, Ziegler; Sahin S, Topal (Ucan 35); Kuyt, Baroni (Korkmaz 90), Erkin; Sow (Topuz 82).
*Viktoria Plzen:* (4231) Kozacik; Reznik, Cisovsky, Prochazka, Limbersky; Horvath ( 72), Darida; Rajtoral (Fillo 88), Kolar, Kovarik J; Bakos (Tecl 65).

**Internazionale (1) 4** *(Cassano 20, Palacio R 52, Gallas W 75 (og), Alvarez 110)*
**Tottenham H (0) 1** *(Adebayor 96)*          18,241
*Internazionale:* (4312) Handanovic; Jonathan (Ranocchia 108), Juan, Chivu, Zanetti; Gargano, Kovacic (Benassi 79), Cambiasso; Guarin (Alvarez 71); Palacio R, Cassano.
*Tottenham H:* (442) Friedel; Walker, Gallas W, Vertonghen, Naughton (Caulker 104); Dembele, Livermore (Lennon 70), Parker, Sigurdsson; Defoe (Holtby 56), Adebayor.
*aet.*

**Lazio (2) 3** *(Kozak 6, 8, 87)*
**VfB Stuttgart (0) 1** *(Hajnal 62)*          Behind closed doors
*Lazio:* (442) Marchetti (Bizzarri 43); Bruno Pereirinha M, Biava, Ciani, Radu; Candreva, Onazi, Hernanes (Ederson 73), Lulic; Mauri (Ledesma 66), Kozak.
*VfB Stuttgart:* (4231) Ulreich; Sakai, Tasci, Niedermaier, Molinaro; Gentner, Holzhauser; Okazaki, Hajnal (Harnik 74), Macheda (Traore 64); Ibisevic.

**Newcastle U (0) 1** *(Cisse 90)*
**Anzhi Makhachkala (0) 0**          45,487
*Newcastle U:* (4141) Elliot; Santon, Taylor S, Yanga-Mbiwa, Haidara; Tiote; Sissoko, Cabaye (Gutierrez 37), Anita (Campbell 71), Marveaux; Cisse.
*Anzhi Makhachkala:* (433) Gabulov; Yeschenko, Ewerton, Joao Carlos, Zhirkov; Jucilei, Ahmedov, Diarra (Shatov 74); Boussoufa, Eto'o, Carcela-Gonzalez■.

**Rubin Kazan (0) 2** *(Rondon 99, Dyadyun 112)*
**Levante (0) 0**          1000
*Rubin Kazan:* (4231) Ryzhikov; Kuzmin, Marcano, Sharonov, Kaleshin; Orbaiz, Natcho; Karadeniz (Kisliak 116), Eremenko R, Kasaev (Dyadyun 101); Rondon.
*Levante:* (4231) Navas; Lell, Ballesteros, Navarro, Juanfran; Iborra, Diop; El Zhar (Pedro Rios 76), Barkero, Ruben (Juanlu 90); Acquafresca (Valdo 65).
*aet.*

**Zenit St Petersburg (1) 1** *(Witsel 30)*
**FC Basel (0) 0**          20,000
*Zenit St Petersburg:* (433) Zhevnov; Aniukov, Bruno Alves (Bystrov 73), Lombaerts, Hubocan; Witsel (Bukharov 90), Denisov, Shirokov; Hulk, Kerzhakov, Danny (Faitzulin 84).
*FC Basel:* (4231) Sommer; Degen (Steinhofer 90), Schar, Dragovic, Park; El-Nenny, Cabral; Salah M, Diaz■, Stocker (Frei F 18); Streller (Sauro 65).

**QUARTER-FINALS FIRST LEG**

Thursday, 4 April 2013
**Benfica (1) 3** *(Rodrigo 25, Lima 65, Cardozo 71 (pen))*
**Newcastle U (1) 1** *(Cisse 12)*          44,133
*Benfica:* (433) Artur Moraes; Almeida A, Luisao, Garay, Melgarejo; John, Matic, Gomes (Perez 61); Rodrigo (Lima 61), Cardozo (Maxi Pereira 77), Gaitan.
*Newcastle U:* (4231) Krul; Simpson (Gosling 83), Taylor S, Yanga-Mbiwa, Santon; Perch (Anita 62), Cabaye; Gutierrez, Sissoko, Marveaux (Ameobi Shola 80); Cisse.

**Chelsea (2) 3** *(Torres 16, Moses 32, Torres 70)*
**Rubin Kazan (1) 1** *(Natcho 41 (pen))*          32,994
*Chelsea:* (4231) Cech; Azpilicueta, Terry, Luiz, Bertrand; Ramires, Lampard; Moses (Hazard E 65), Benayoun (Marin 83), Mata (Oscar 78); Torres.
*Rubin Kazan:* (4411) Ryzhikov; Cesar Navas, Kuzmin (Kasaev 82), Kaleshin, Ansaldi; Sharonov, Orbaiz, Eremenko, Karadeniz; Natcho; Dyadyun (Rondon 64).

**Fenerbahce (0) 2** *(Webo 79 (pen), Kuyt 90)*
**Lazio (0) 0**          51,000
*Fenerbahce:* (4231) Demirel; Gonul, Yobo, Korkmaz, Ziegler; Topal (Erkin 71), Meireles; Kuyt, Baroni (Ucan 76), Sow (Topuz 86); Webo.
*Lazio:* (361) Marchetti; Ciani, Cana, Radu; Gonzalez, Candreva, Onazi■, Ederson (Ledesma 63), Hernanes (Mauri 86), Lulic; Kozak (Klose 72).

**Tottenham H (1) 2** *(Adebayor 40, Sigurdsson 58)*
**FC Basel (2) 2** *(Stocker 30, Frei F 35)*          32,136
*Tottenham H:* (4231) Friedel; Naughton, Gallas W, Vertonghen, Assou-Ekotto (Dawson 57); Dembele, Parker; Lennon (Sigurdsson 24), Bale, Holtby (Dempsey 63); Adebayor.
*FC Basel:* (4231) Sommer; Steinhofer, Schar, Dragovic, Voser; El-Nenny, Die (Cabral 66); Salah (Degen 84), Frei F, Stocker; Streller (Zoua 71).

**QUARTER-FINALS SECOND LEG**

Thursday, 11 April 2013
**FC Basel (1) 2** *(Salah M 27, Dragovic 49)*
**Tottenham H (1) 2** *(Dempsey 23, 82)*          40,000
*FC Basel:* (4321) Sommer; Degen P, Schar, Dragovic, Park; El-Nenny, Frei F, Die (Diaz 58); Salah M (Frei A 111), Stocker (Steinhofer 70); Streller.
*Tottenham H:* (4231) Friedel; Walker, Dawson, Vertonghen■, Naughton (Assou-Ekotto 78); Dembele (Carroll 59), Parker (Huddlestone 77); Holtby, Dempsey, Sigurdsson; Adebayor.
*aet; FC Basel won 4-1 on penalties.*

**Lazio (0) 1** *(Lulic 61)*
**Fenerbahce (0) 1** *(Erkin 73)*          1000
*Lazio:* (4321) Marchetti; Biava (Klose 56), Ciani, Cana, Radu; Hernanes, Ledesma, Lulic; Candreva, Ederson (Floccari 73); Kozak (Rozzi 77).
*Fenerbahce:* (4231) Demirel; Gonul, Yobo, Korkmaz, Ziegler; Meireles, Sahin S; Kuyt, Baroni (Ucan 73), Erkin (Krasic 87); Webo (Topuz 80).

**Newcastle U (0) 1** *(Cisse 71)*

**Benfica (0) 1** *(Salvio 90)*                    52,157

*Newcastle U:* (4411) Krul; Simpson, Williamson, Yanga-Mbiwa, Haidara (Marveaux 67); Anita (Ben Arfa 63), Bigirimana (Ameobi Shola 46), Cabaye, Gutierrez; Sissoko; Cisse.

*Benfica:* (433) Artur Moraes; Almeida, Luisao, Garay, Melgarejo; Salvio (Jardel 90), Matic, Perez; John (Rodrigo 76), Lima (Cardozo 72), Gaitan.

**Rubin Kazan (0) 3** *(Marcano 51, Karadeniz 62, Natcho 75 (pen))*

**Chelsea (1) 2** *(Torres 5, Moses 55)*            25,000

*Rubin Kazan:* (442) Ryzhikov; Kuzmin (Kaleshin 46), Marcano, Cesar Navas, Ansaldi; Karadeniz, Orbaiz (Dyadyun 66), Natcho, Kasaev (Ryazantsev A 72); Eremenko, Rondon.

*Chelsea:* (442) Cech; Azpilicueta, Terry, Luiz, Ferreira; Ramires (Mikel 60), Ake N, Moses, Lampard (Ivanovic 90); Benayoun (Oscar 77), Torres.

## SEMI-FINALS FIRST LEG

Thursday, 25 April 2013

**FC Basel (0) 1** *(Schar 87 (pen))*

**Chelsea (1) 2** *(Moses 12, Luiz 90)*            36,000

*FC Basel:* (4141) Sommer; Degen P, Schar, Dragovic, Park; Frei; Salah M (Degen 78), El-Nenny (Zoua 65), Die (Diaz 61), Stocker; Streller.

*Chelsea:* (4141) Cech; Azpilicueta, Ivanovic, Terry, Cole; Luiz; Hazard E (Mata 71), Ramires, Lampard (Oscar 80), Moses; Torres.

**Fenerbahce (0) 1** *(Korkmaz 72)*

**Benfica (0) 0**                    51,000

*Fenerbahce:* (4231) Demirel; Gonul, Yobo, Korkmaz, Ziegler; Meireles (Ucan 64), Topal; Kuyt, Baroni (Sahin S 86), Sow (Krasic 87); Webo.

*Benfica:* (433) Artur Moraes; Maxi Pereira, Jardel, Garay, Melgarejo; Gomes (Carlos Martins 81), Aimar (Gaitan 46), Matic; John (Rodrigo 64), Cardozo, Salvio.

## SEMI-FINALS SECOND LEG

Thursday, 2 May 2013

**Benfica (2) 3** *(Gaitan 9, Cardozo 35, 66)*

**Fenerbahce (1) 1** *(Kuyt 23 (pen))*            55,402

*Benfica:* (433) Artur Moraes; Maxi Pereira, Luisao, Garay, Almeida; Perez, Matic, Gaitan (Roderick Miranda 90); Lima, Cardozo (Urreta 87), Salvio.

*Fenerbahce:* (433) Demirel; Gonul (Irtegun 61), Yobo (Stoch 75), Korkmaz, Ziegler; Sahin S (Topuz 44), Baroni, Erkin; Kuyt, Sow, Ucan.

**Chelsea (0) 3** *(Torres 50, Moses 52, Luiz 59)*

**FC Basel (1) 1** *(Salah 45)*            39,403

*Chelsea:* (4231) Cech; Azpilicueta, Ivanovic, Cahill, Bertrand; Lampard, Luiz (Ake 81); Ramires (Oscar 66), Hazard (Mata 75), Moses; Torres.

*FC Basel:* (433) Sommer; Steinhofer, Schar, Sauro, Voser; El-Nenny, Frei (Diaz 75), Die; Salah, Streller (Zoua 62), Stocker (Degen 62).

## UEFA EUROPA LEAGUE FINAL

Wednesday, 15 May 2013

(in Amsterdam, 53,000)

**Benfica (0) 1** *(Cardozo 68 (pen))*     **Chelsea (0) 2** *(Torres 59, Ivanovic 90)*

*Benfica:* (433) Artur Moraes; Almeida A, Luisao, Garay (Jardel 78), Melgarejo (John 66); Perez, Matic, Rodrigo (Lima 65); Gaitan, Cardozo, Salvio.

*Chelsea:* (4231) Cech; Azpilicueta, Ivanovic, Cahill, Cole; Lampard, Luiz; Ramires, Mata, Oscar; Torres.

*Referee:* Bjorn Kuipers.

Benfica goalkeeper Guilherme Artur Moraes is beaten by Chelsea striker Fernando Torres as the Spaniard scores his club's first goal in their 2-1 victory in the Europa League Final at the Amsterdam Arena. (PA)

# UEFA CHAMPIONS LEAGUE 2013–14

## PARTICIPATING CLUBS
*The list below is provisional and is subject to pending legal proceedings and final confirmation from UEFA.*

### UEFA CHAMPIONS LEAGUE GROUP STAGE
Bayern Munich (GER) – holders
Barcelona (ESP)
Chelsea (ENG)
Real Madrid (ESP)
Manchester U (ENG)
FC Porto (POR)
Benfica (POR)
Atletico Madrid (ESP)
Shakhtar Donetsk (UKR)
Marseille (FRA)
CSKA Moscow (RUS)
Paris Saint-Germain (FRA)
Juventus (ITA)
Manchester C (ENG)
Ajax (NED)
Borussia Dortmund (GER)
Olympiacos (GRE)
Galatasaray (TUR)
Bayer Leverkusen (GER)
FC Copenhagen (DEN)
Napoli (ITA)
Anderlecht (BEL)

### UEFA CHAMPIONS LEAGUE PLAY-OFF – LEAGUE ROUTE
Arsenal (ENG)
AC Milan (ITA)
Schalke 04 (GER)
Real Sociedad (ESP)
Pacos de Ferreira (POR)

### UEFA CHAMPIONS LEAGUE THIRD QUALIFYING ROUND – LEAGUE ROUTE
Olympique Lyonnais (FRA)
Zenit St Petersburg (RUS)
PSV Eindhoven (NED)
Metalist Kharkiv (UKR)
Fenerbahce (TUR)
PAOK (GRE)
Salzburg (AUT)
Nordsjaelland (DEN)
Grasshoppers (SUI)
Zulte Waregem (BEL)

### UEFA CHAMPIONS LEAGUE THIRD QUALIFYING ROUND – CHAMPIONS ROUTE
Basel (SUI)
APOEL (CYP)
Austria Vienna (AUT)

### UEFA CHAMPIONS LEAGUE SECOND QUALIFYING ROUND
BATE Borisov (BLR)
Celtic (SCO)
Steau Bucharest (ROU)
Viktoria Plzen (CZE)
Dinamo Zagreb (CRO)
Partizan Belgrade (SRB)
Legia Warsaw (POL)
Sheriff (MDA)
Maribor (SVN)
Slovan Bratislava (SVK)
IF Elfsborg (SWE)
Maccabi Tel Aviv (ISR)
Molde (NOR)
HJK Helsinki (FIN)
Ekranas (LTU)
Neftchi (AZE)
Dinamo Tbilisi (GEO)
Zeljeznicar (BIH)
FH Hafnarfjordur (ISL)
Gyori ETO (HUN)
The New Saints (WAL)
Ludogorets Razgrad (BUL)
Sligo Rovers (IRL)
Shakhter Karagandy (KAZ)
Skenderbeu (ALB)
Birkirkara (MLT)
Vardar (MKD)
Cliftonville (NIR)
Daugava Daugavpils (LVA)
Sutjeska (MNE)
Nomme Kalju (EST)
Fola Esch (LUX)

### UEFA CHAMPIONS LEAGUE FIRST QUALIFYING ROUND
EB/Streymur (FRO)
Tre Penne (SMR)
Lusitans (AND)
Shirak (ARM)

# UEFA EUROPA LEAGUE 2013–14

## PARTICIPATING CLUBS
*The list below is provisional and is subject to pending legal proceedings and final confirmation from UEFA.*

### UEFA EUROPA LEAGUE GROUP STAGE
Valencia (ESP)
Bordeaux (FRA)*
Lazio (ITA)*
Anzhi Makhachkala (RUS)
Wigan Ath (ENG)*
Freiburg (GER)
Vitoria SC (POR)*

### UEFA EUROPA LEAGUE PLAY-OFFS
Tottenham H (ENG)
Dynamo Kyiv (UKR)

Braga (POR)
Fiorentina (ITA)
Spartak Moscow (RUS)
AZ Alkmaar (NED)*
Besiktas (TUR)
Genk (BEL)*
Dnipro Dnipropetrovsk (UKR)
Real Betis (ESP)
Eintracht Frankfurt (GER)
Feyenoord (NED)
Nice (FRA)
Atromitos (GRE)
Apollon Limassol (CYP)*
St Gallen (SUI)
Esbjerg (DEN)*
Pasching (AUT)*

**UEFA EUROPA LEAGUE
THIRD QUALIFYING ROUND**
VfB Stuttgart (GER)
Sevilla (ESP)
Udinese (ITA)
Club Brugge (BEL)
Saint Etienne (FRA) †
Zurich (SUI)
Bursaspor (TUR)
Swansea C (ENG)
Rapid Vienna (AUT)
Metalurh Donetsk (UKR)
Estoril (POR)
Vitesse (NED)
Kuban Krasnodar (RUS)
Asteras Tripolis (GRE)
Randers (DEN)
Motherwell (SCO)
Jablonec (CZE)*
Hapoel Ramat Gan (ISR)*

**UEFA EUROPA LEAGUE
SECOND QUALIFYING ROUND**
Rubin Kazan (RUS)
Standard Liege (BEL)
Hapoel Tel Aviv (ISR)
Sparta Prague (CZE)
Lech Poznan (POL)
Trabzonspor (TUR) §
Aalborg (DEN)
Anorthosis Famagusta (CYP)
Utrecht (NED)
Maccabi Haifa (ISR)
Sturm Graz (AUT)
Omonia (CYP)
Chornomorets (UKR) §
Debrecen (HUN)*
Hajduk Split (CRO)*
Red Star Belgrade (SRB)
Slovan Liberec (CZE)
Thun (SUI)
Slask Wroclaw (POL)
Giannina (GRE)
Shakhtyor Soligorsk (BLR)
IFK Gothenburg (SWE)*
Rijeka (CRO)
FU Minsk (BLR)*
Petrolul Ploiesti (ROU)*
Pandurii Targu Jiu (ROU)
Senica (SVK)
Piast Gliwice (POL)
Hacken (SWE)
Hibernian (SCO) §
Lokomotiva Zagreb (CRO)
Stromsgodset (NOR)
Honka (FIN)*
Olimpija (SVN)
St Johnstone (SCO)
Beroe Stara Zagora (BUL)*
Dila Gori (GEO)
Siroki Brijeg (BIH)*
Jagodina (SRB)*
Trencin (SVK)
Hodd (NOR)*
Derry C (IRL)*

**UEFA EUROPA LEAGUE FIRST QUALIFYING ROUND**
Rosenborg (NOR)
Zilina (SVK) §
Levski Sofia (BUL)
CSKA Sofia (BUL)
Videoton (HUN)

Ventspils (LVA)*
Tromso (NOR) ¶
Aktobe (KAZ)
Dinamo Minsk (BLR)
St Patrick's Ath (IRL)
Karabakh (AZE)
Vojvodina (SRB)
Malmo (SWE)
Sarajevo (BIH)
Astra Ploiesti (ROU)
KR Reykjavik (ISL)*
F91 Dudelange (LUX)
Inter Turku (FIN)
Dacia Chisinau (MDA)
Levadia Tallinn (EST)
Linfield (NIR)
Budapest Honved (HUN)
Valletta (MLT)
Differdange 03 (LUX)
Liepajas Metalurgs (LVA)
Gefle (SWE) ¶
Pyunik (ARM)*
Zrinjski (BIH)
Inter Baku (AZE)
Skonto (LVA)
Suduva (LTU)
Vaduz (LIE)*
Flora (EST)*
Xazar Lankaran (AZE) §
HB Torshavn (FRO)
Rudar Pljevlja (MNE)
TPS Turku (FIN)
Breidablik (ISL)
Domzale (SVN)
Glentoran (NIR)*
Metalurg Skopje (MKD)
Milsami (MDA)
Celje (SVN) §
Torpedo Kutaisi (GEO)
Teteks (MKD)*
Irtysh Pavlodar (KAZ)
Jeunesse d'Esch (LUX)*
Crusaders (NIR)
Santa Coloma (AND)
Chikhura Sachkhere (GEO) §
VMFD Zalgiris (LTU)*
Mariehamn (FIN) ¶
Mika (ARM)
IBV Vestmannaeyjar (ISL)
Celik Niksic (MNE)
Sliema Wanderers (MLT)
Hibernians (MLT)*
Tiraspol (MDA)*
Drogheda U (IRL)
Narva Trans (EST)
Gandzasar (ARM)
Kruoja Pakruojis (LTU)
Astana (KAZ)*
Laci (ALB)*
Teuta (ALB)
Vikingur (FRO)*
Mladost Podgorica (MNE)
Turnovo (MKD)
UE Santa Coloma (AND)*
Kukesi (ALB)
IF Fuglafjordur (FRO)
Bala T (WAL)
Airbus UK Broughton (WAL)
Prestatyn T (WAL)*
La Fiorita (SMR)*
Libertas (SMR)

* – cup winners; † – league cup winners; § – losing cup finalists; ¶ – Fair Play winners.

# SUMMARY OF APPEARANCES

## EUROPEAN CUP AND CHAMPIONS LEAGUE (1955–2013)

**ENGLISH CLUBS**
25 Manchester U
20 Liverpool
17 Arsenal
11 Chelsea
4 Leeds U
3 Everton, Manchester C, Newcastle U, Nottingham F
2 Aston Villa, Derby Co, Tottenham H,
Wolverhampton W
1 Blackburn R, Burnley, Ipswich T

**SCOTTISH CLUBS**
30 Rangers
27 Celtic
3 Aberdeen, Hearts
1 Dundee, Dundee U, Hibernian, Kilmarnock,
Motherwell

**WELSH CLUBS**
6 Barry T, The New Saints
2 Rhyl
1 Bangor C, Cwmbran T, Llanelli

**NORTHERN IRELAND CLUBS**
27 Linfield
12 Glentoran
3 Crusaders, Portadown
2 Glenavon
1 Ards, Cliftonville, Coleraine, Derry C, Distillery

**REPUBLIC OF IRELAND CLUBS**
9 Shamrock R
7 Dundalk
6 Bohemians, Shelbourne, Waterford
3 Derry C*, Drumcondra, St Patrick's Ath
2 Athlone T, Cork City, Limerick
1 Celtic, Cork Hibs, Cork Drogheda U, Sligo R
**Winners: Celtic 1966–67; Manchester U 1967–68, 1998–99,
2007–08; Liverpool 1976–77, 1977–78, 1980–81, 1983–84,
2004–05; Nottingham F 1978–79, 1979–80; Aston Villa
1981–82; Chelsea 2011–12**

**Finalists: Celtic 1969–70; Leeds U 1974–75; Liverpool
1984–85, 2006–07; Arsenal 2005–06; Chelsea 2007–08;
Manchester U 2008–09, 2010–11**

## UEFA EUROPA LEAGUE 2010–13

**ENGLISH CLUBS**
3 Liverpool
2 Aston Villa, Fulham, Manchester C, Tottenham H
1 Birmingham C, Chelsea, Everton, Manchester U,
Newcastle U, Stoke C

**SCOTTISH CLUBS**
3 Celtic, Dundee U, Hearts
2 Motherwell, Rangers
1 Aberdeen, Falkirk, Hibernian, St Johnstone

**WELSH CLUBS**
4 Llanelli  3 Bangor C  2 The New Saints
1 Cefn Druids, Neath Ath, Port Talbot

**NORTHERN IRELAND CLUBS**
3 Cliftonville, Crusaders
2 Glentoran, Portadown
1 Linfield, Lisburn Distillery

**REPUBLIC OF IRELAND CLUBS**
3 Sligo R
2 Bohemians, Shamrock R, St Patrick's Ath
1 Derry C*, Dundalk, Sporting Fingal

**Winners: Chelsea 2012–13**

**Finalists: Fulham 2009–10**

## EUROPEAN CUP-WINNERS' CUP (1960–99)

**ENGLISH CLUBS**
6 Tottenham H  5 Chelsea, Liverpool, Manchester U
4 West Ham U  3 Arsenal, Everton  2 Manchester C
1 Ipswich T, Leeds U, Leicester C, Newcastle U,
Southampton, Sunderland, WBA, Wolverhampton W

**SCOTTISH CLUBS**
10 Rangers  8 Aberdeen, Celtic  3 Dundee U, Hearts
2 Dunfermline Ath  1 Airdrieonians, Dundee,
Hibernian, Kilmarnock, Motherwell, St Mirren

**WELSH CLUBS**
14 Cardiff C  8 Wrexham  7 Swansea C  3 Bangor C
1 Barry T, Borough U, Cwmbran T, Llansantffraid,
Merthyr Tydfil, Newport Co

**NORTHERN IRELAND CLUBS**
9 Glentoran  5 Glenavon  4 Ballymena U, Coleraine
3 Crusaders, Linfield  2 Ards, Bangor  1 Derry C,
Distillery, Carrick Rangers, Cliftonville, Portadown

**REPUBLIC OF IRELAND CLUBS**
6 Shamrock R  4 Shelbourne  3 Bohemians, Dundalk,
Limerick, Waterford  2 Cork City, Cork Hibs, Derry C*,
Galway U, Sligo R  1 Bray W, Cork Celtic, Finn Harps,
Home Farm, St Patrick's Ath, University College Dublin

**Winners: Tottenham H 1962–63; West Ham U 1964–65;
Manchester C 1969–70; Chelsea 1970–71, 1997–98;
Rangers 1971–72; Aberdeen 1982–83; Everton 1984–85;
Manchester U 1990–91; Arsenal 1993–94**

**Finalists: Rangers 1960–61, 1966–67; Liverpool 1965–66;
Leeds U 1972–73; West Ham U 1975–76; Arsenal
1979–80, 1994–95**

## EUROPEAN FAIRS CUP & UEFA CUP (1955–2009)

**ENGLISH CLUBS**
13 Leeds U, Liverpool  11 Aston Villa  10 Ipswich T,
Newcastle U  9 Arsenal, Everton, Tottenham H
7 Manchester U  6 Blackburn R, Chelsea, Manchester C,
Southampton  5 Nottingham F  4 Birmingham C, WBA,
Wolverhampton W  3 Sheffield W  2 Bolton W,
Derby Co, Leicester C, Middlesbrough, QPR, Stoke C,
West Ham U  1 Burnley, Coventry C, Fulham, London
Rep XI, Millwall, Norwich C, Portsmouth, Watford

**SCOTTISH CLUBS**
19 Dundee U  17 Rangers  16 Aberdeen, Celtic,
Hibernian  13 Hearts  7 Dunfermline Ath, Kilmarnock
5 Dundee  3 Motherwell, St Mirren  2 Partick T,
St Johnstone  1 Gretna, Livingston, Morton,
Queen of the S, Raith R

**WELSH CLUBS**
5 Bangor C, TNS  3 Cwmbran T, Inter Cardiff (formerly
Inter Cable-Tel), Rhyl  2 Barry T, Carmarthen T,
Newtown  1 Afan Lido, Llanelli, Haverfordwest

**NORTHERN IRELAND CLUBS**
18 Glentoran  9 Coleraine  8 Linfield, Portadown
5 Glenavon  3 Crusaders  1 Ards, Ballymena U,
Bangor, Cliftonville, Dungannon Swifts

**REPUBLIC OF IRELAND CLUBS**
11 Bohemians  7 Shelbourne  6 Dundalk,
St Patrick's Ath  5 Cork City, Shamrock R  4 Derry C*
3 Drogheda U, Finn Harps, Longford T  2 Drumcondra
1 Athlone T, Bray Wanderers, Cork Hibs, Galway U,
Limerick
**Winners: Leeds U 1967–68, 1970–71; Newcastle U 1968–69;
Arsenal 1969–70, 1999–2000; Tottenham H 1971–72,
1983–84; Liverpool 1972–73, 1975–76, 2000–01; Ipswich T
1980–81**

**Finalists: London 1955–58, Birmingham C 1958–60,
1960–61; Leeds U 1966–67; Wolverhampton W 1971–72;
Tottenham H 1973–74; Dundee U 1986–87; Celtic
2002–03; Middlesbrough 2005–06; Rangers 2007–08**

*Now play in League of Ireland*

# FIFA CLUB WORLD CUP 2012

Formerly known as the FIFA Club World Championship, this tournament is played annually between the champion clubs from all 6 continental confederations, although since 2007 the champions of Oceania must play a qualifying play-off against the champion club of the host country.

## FIFA CLUB WORLD CUP 2012
(Finals in Japan)

■ *Denotes player sent off.*

### QUARTER-FINAL PLAY-OFF
Thursday 6 December 2012
**Sanfrecce Hiroshima (0) 1** *(Aoyama 66)*
**Auckland City (0) 0**                                   25,174
*Sanfrecce Hiroshima:* Nishikawa; Moriwaki, Chiba, Aoyama, Mizumoto, Kazuyuki Morisaki, Shimizu (Yamagishi 61), Mikic (Hwang 82), Takahagi, Koji Morisaki (Ishihara 90), Sato.
*Auckland City:* Williams; Milne, Vicelich, Berlanga, Iwata, Bale, Feneridis, Dickinson, Riera, Exposito (Tade 78), Koprivcic (Corrales).

### QUARTER-FINALS
Sunday 9 December 2012
**Ulsan Hyundai (0) 1** *(Lee Keunho 88)*
**CF Monterrey (1) 3** *(Corona 9, Delgado 77, 84)*    20,353
*Ulsan Hyundai:* Kim Youngkwang; Lee Yong, Kwak Taehwi, Kim Youngsam (Lee JaeSung 56), Kim Chigon, Lee Ho, Kim Seung Yong (Ko Changhyun 71), Juan Estiven Velez, Kim Shinwook (Maranhao 78), Lee Keunho, Rafinha.
*CF Monterrey:* Orozco; Meza, Chavez, Basanta, Mier, Perez, Ayovi, Corona (Morales 90), Cardozo (Solis 90), Di Nigris, Delgado (Carreno 90).

**Sanfrecce Hiroshima (1) 1** *(Sato 32)*
**Al-Ahly SC (1) 2** *(Hamdi 15, Aboutrika 57)*          27,314
*Sanfrecce Hiroshima:* Nishikawa (Masuda 8); Koji Morisaki, Aoyama, Chiba, Mizumoto, Sato, Kazuyuki Morisaki, Moriwaki (Hwang 46), Takahagi, Mikic, Shimizu (Yamagishi 82).
*Al-Ahly SC:* Ekramy, Ghaly (Aboutrika 34), Kenawi, Soliman (Barakat 80), Gomaa, Naguib, Said, Elsayed Hamdi (Trezeguet 71), Gedo, Ahmed Fathi, Ashour.

### MATCH FOR FIFTH PLACE
Wednesday 12 December 2012
**Ulsan Hyundai (1) 2** *(Mizumoto 17 (og), Lee Yong 90)*
**Sanfrecce Hiroshima (1) 3** *(Yamagishi 35, Sato 56, 72)*
                                                          17,581
*Ulsan Hyundai:* Kim Youngkwang; Lee Yong, Kwak Taehwi, Lee Ho, Kim Chigon (Lee JaeSung 52), Kim Seung Yong (Maranhao 76), Kim Youngsam, Ko Seulki, Kim Shinwook, Lee Keunho, Rafinha.
*Sanfrecce Hiroshima:* Nishikawa; Koji Morisaki, Aoyama, Hwang, Mizumoto, Yamagishi (Shimizu 75), Shiotani, Kazuyuki Morisaki (Ishihara 79), Takahagi, Sato, Isikawa (Chiba 90).

### SEMI-FINALS
Wednesday 12 December 2012
**Al-Ahly SC (0) 0**
**Corinthians (1) 1** *(Guerrero 30)*                     31,417
*Al-Ahly SC:* Ekramy (Abou Elseoud 65), Rabia, Gomaa, Naguib, Kenawi, Gedo (Meteab 80), Ahmed Fathi, Ashour, Soliman, Elsayed Hamdi, Said (Aboutrika 55).
*Corinthians:* Cassio; Alessandro, Chicao, Fabio Santos, Paulo Andre, Ralf, Paulinho, Douglas (Jorge Henrique 80), Danilo, Guerrero (Guilherme Andrade 92), Emerson (Romarinho 75).

Thursday 13 December 2012
**CF Monterrey (0) 1** *(Di Nigris 90)*
**Chelsea (1) 3** *(Mata 17, Torres 46, Chavez 48 (og))* 36,648
*CF Monterrey:* Orozco; Meza (Solis 83), Chavez, Basanta, Mier, Perez (Osorio 57), Ayovi, Corona, Cardozo, Delgado (Carreno 83), Di Nigris.
*Chelsea:* Cech, Azpilicueta, Ivanovic, Cahill, Cole, Mikel, David Luiz (Lampard 63), Mata (Ferreira 74), Oscar, Hazard, Torres (Moses 79).

### MATCH FOR THIRD PLACE
Sunday 16 December 2012
**Al-Ahly SC (0) 0**
**CF Monterrey (1) 2** *(Corona 3, Delgado 66)*          56,301
*Al-Ahly SC:* Abou Elseoud; Rabia, Gomaa, Naguib, Moawad, Said, Ahmed Fathi (Barakat 62), Ashour, Aboutrika, Emad Meteab (Elsayed Hamdi 53), Soliman (Gedo 77).
*CF Monterrey:* Orozco; Meza, Chavez, Basanta, Mier, Osorio, Ayovi, Corona (Carreno 63), Cardozo (Solis 84), Di Nigris, Delgado (Morales 79).

## FINAL 2012
Sunday 16 December 2012 (attendance 68,275)

**Corinthians (0) 1** *(Guerrero 69)*     **Chelsea (0) 0**

*Corinthians:* Cassio; Alessandro, Chicao, Fabio Santos, Paulo Andre, Ralf, Paulinho, Jorge Henrique, Danilo, Guerrero (Martinez 87), Emerson (Wallace 90).

*Chelsea:* Cech, Ivanovic (Azpilicueta 83), Cahill■, David Luiz, Cole, Moses (Oscar 73), Lampard, Mata, Ramires, Hazard (Marin 87), Torres.

### PREVIOUS FINALS

2000  Corinthians beat Vaso de Gama 4-3 on penalties
      after 0-0 draw
2005  Sao Paulo beat Liverpool 1-0
2006  Internacional beat Barcelona 1-0
2007  AC Milan beat Boca Juniors 4-2

2008  Manchester U beat Liga De Quito 1-0
2009  Barcelona beat Estudiantes 2-1
2010  Internazionale beat TP Mazembe Englebert 3-0
2011  Barcelona beat Santos 4-0
2012  Corinthians beat Chelsea 1-0

# WORLD CLUB CHAMPIONSHIP

Played annually up to 1974 and intermittently since then between the winners of the European Cup and the winners of the South American Champions Cup — known as the Copa Libertadores. In 1980 the winners were decided by one match arranged in Tokyo in February 1981 which remained the venue until 2004, when the match was superseded by the FIFA Club World Championship. AC Milan replaced Marseille who had been stripped of their European Cup title in 1993.

1960 Real Madrid beat Penarol 0-0, 5-1
1961 Penarol beat Benfica 0-1, 5-0, 2-1
1962 Santos beat Benfica 3-2, 5-2
1963 Santos beat AC Milan 2-4, 4-2, 1-0
1964 Inter-Milan beat Independiente 0-1, 2-0, 1-0
1965 Inter-Milan beat Independiente 3-0, 0-0
1966 Penarol beat Real Madrid 2-0, 2-0
1967 Racing Club beat Celtic 0-1, 2-1, 1-0
1968 Estudiantes beat Manchester United 1-0, 1-1
1969 AC Milan beat Estudiantes 3-0, 1-2
1970 Feyenoord beat Estudiantes 2-2, 1-0
1971 Nacional beat Panathinaikos* 1-1, 2-1
1972 Ajax beat Independiente 1-1, 3-0
1973 Independiente beat Juventus* 1-0
1974 Atlético Madrid* beat Independiente 0-1, 2-0
1975 Independiente and Bayern Munich could not agree dates; no matches.
1976 Bayern Munich beat Cruzeiro 2-0, 0-0
1977 Boca Juniors beat Borussia Moenchengladbach* 2-2, 3-0
1978 Not contested
1979 Olimpia beat Malmö* 1-0, 2-1
1980 Nacional beat Nottingham Forest 1-0
1981 Flamengo beat Liverpool 3-0
1982 Penarol beat Aston Villa 2-0
1983 Gremio Porto Alegre beat SV Hamburg 2-1
1984 Independiente beat Liverpool 1-0

1985 Juventus beat Argentinos Juniors 4-2 on penalties after a 2-2 draw
1986 River Plate beat Steaua Bucharest 1-0
1987 FC Porto beat Penarol 2-1 after extra time
1988 Nacional (Uru) beat PSV Eindhoven 7-6 on penalties after 1-1 draw
1989 AC Milan beat Atletico Nacional (Col) 1-0 after extra time
1990 AC Milan beat Olimpia 3-0
1991 Red Star Belgrade beat Colo Colo 3-0
1992 Sao Paulo beat Barcelona 2-1
1993 Sao Paulo beat AC Milan 3-2
1994 Velez Sarsfield beat AC Milan 2-0
1995 Ajax beat Gremio Porto Alegre 4-3 on penalties after 0-0 draw
1996 Juventus beat River Plate 1-0
1997 Borussia Dortmund beat Cruzeiro 2-0
1998 Real Madrid beat Vasco da Gama 2-1
1999 Manchester U beat Palmeiras 1-0
2000 Boca Juniors beat Real Madrid 2-1
2001 Bayern Munich beat Boca Juniors 1-0 after extra time
2002 Real Madrid beat Olimpia 2-0
2003 Boca Juniors beat AC Milan 3-1 on penalties after 1-1 draw
2004 Porto beat Once Caldas 8-7 on penalties after 0-0 draw

*European Cup runners-up; winners declined to take part.

# EUROPEAN SUPER CUP 2012

Played annually between the winners of the European Champions' Cup and the European Cup-Winners' Cup (UEFA Cup from 2000; UEFA Europa League from 2010). AC Milan replaced Marseille in 1993–94.

■ Denotes player sent off.

## EUROPEAN SUPER CUP 2012
Monaco, 31 August 2012, attendance 14,312
**Atletico Madrid (3) 4** *(Falcao 6, 19, 45, Miranda 60)*     **Chelsea (0) 1** *(Cahill 75)*

*Atletico Madrid:* Courtois; Juanfran, Miranda, Godin, Filipe Luis, Mario Suarez, Gabi, Adrian (Rodriguez 56), Koke (Raul Garcia 81), Turan, Falcao (Emre 87).

*Chelsea:* Cech; Ivanovic, Cahill, David Luiz, Cole (Bertrand 89), Mikel, Lampard, Ramires (Oscar 46), Hazard, Mata (Sturridge 81), Torres.

*Referee:* D. Skomina (Slovenia).

**PREVIOUS MATCHES**

1972 Ajax beat Rangers 3-1, 3-2
1973 Ajax beat AC Milan 0-1, 6-0
1974 Not contested
1975 Dynamo Kiev beat Bayern Munich 1-0, 2-0
1976 Anderlecht beat Bayern Munich 4-1, 1-2
1977 Liverpool beat Hamburg 1-1, 6-0
1978 Anderlecht beat Liverpool 3-1, 1-2
1979 Nottingham F beat Barcelona 1-0, 1-1
1980 Valencia beat Nottingham F 1-0, 1-2
1981 Not contested
1982 Aston Villa beat Barcelona 0-1, 3-0
1983 Aberdeen beat Hamburg 0-0, 2-0
1984 Juventus beat Liverpool 2-0
1985 Juventus v Everton not contested due to UEFA ban on English clubs
1986 Steaua Bucharest beat Dynamo Kiev 1-0
1987 FC Porto beat Ajax 2-0, 1-0
1988 KV Mechelen beat PSV Eindhoven 3-0, 0-1
1989 AC Milan beat Barcelona 1-1, 1-0
1990 AC Milan beat Sampdoria 1-1, 2-0
1991 Manchester U beat Red Star Belgrade 1-0

1992 Barcelona beat Werder Bremen 1-1, 2-1
1993 Parma beat AC Milan 0-1, 2-0
1994 AC Milan beat Arsenal 0-0, 2-0
1995 Ajax beat Zaragoza 1-1, 4-0
1996 Juventus beat Paris St Germain 6-1, 3-1
1997 Barcelona beat Borussia Dortmund 2-0, 1-1
1998 Chelsea beat Real Madrid 1-0
1999 Lazio beat Manchester U 1-0
2000 Galatasaray beat Real Madrid 2-1
2001 Liverpool beat Bayern Munich 3-2
2002 Real Madrid beat Feyenoord 3-1
2003 AC Milan beat Porto 1-0
2004 Valencia beat Porto 2-1
2005 Liverpool beat CSKA Moscow 3-1
2006 Sevilla beat Barcelona 3-0
2007 AC Milan beat Sevilla 3-1
2008 Zenit beat Manchester U 2-1
2009 Barcelona beat Shakhtar Donetsk 1-0
2010 Atletico Madrid beat Internazionale 2-0
2011 Barcelona beat Porto 2-0
2012 Atletico Madrid beat Chelsea 4-1

# INTERNATIONAL DIRECTORY

The latest available information has been given regarding numbers of clubs and players registered with FIFA, the world governing body. Where known, official colours are listed. With European countries, League tables show a number of signs: * team relegated, + team not relegated after play-offs, *+ team relegated after play-offs, ++ team promoted.

There are 209 member associations. The four home countries, England, Scotland, Northern Ireland and Wales, are dealt with elsewhere in the Yearbook; but basic details appear in this directory. The following countries are not members of FIFA: Gibraltar, Kosovo, and Northern Cyprus. *N.B. In this edition international results for 2012–13 include matches played from 1 January 2012 to 30 June 2013.*

There are a number of associate members and others who have affiliation to their confederations, but there is only one recent official addition and that is South Sudan. Of the many affiliated countries, they include Northern Mariana Islands, Reunion, Zanzibar, French Guiana, Saint-Martin, Sint Maarten, Kiribati, Niue and Tuvalu.

## EUROPE

### ALBANIA

Football Association of Albania, Rruga e Elbasanit, 1000 Tirana.
*Founded:* 1930; *National Colours:* Red shirts, black shorts, red socks.

**International matches 2012–13**
Georgia (a) 1-2, Qatar (a) 2-1, Iran (h) 1-0, Moldova (h) 0-0, Cyprus (h) 3-1, Switzerland (a) 0-2, Iceland (h) 1-2, Slovenia (h) 1-0, Cameroon (h) 0-0, Norway (a) 1-0, Norway (h) 1-1.

**League Championship wins (1930–37; 1945–2013)**
KF Tirana 24 (formerly SK Tirana; includes 17 Nentori 8); Dinamo Tirana 18; Partizani Tirana 15; Vllaznia 9; Skenderbeu 4; Elbasan 2 (including Labinoti 1); Flamurtari 1; Teuta 1.

**Cup wins (1948–2013)**
Partizani Tirana 15; KF Tirana 15 (formerly SK Tirana; includes 17 Nentori 8); Dinamo Tirana 13; Vllaznia 6; Teuta 3; Flamurtari 3; Elbasan 2 (including Labinoti 1); Besa 2; Apolonia 1; Laci 1.

**Final League Table 2012–13**

| | P | W | D | L | F | A | GD | Pts |
|---|---|---|---|---|---|---|---|---|
| Skenderbeu | 26 | 18 | 4 | 4 | 43 | 14 | 29 | 58 |
| Kukesi | 26 | 15 | 7 | 4 | 49 | 25 | 24 | 52 |
| Teuta | 26 | 14 | 6 | 6 | 32 | 24 | 8 | 48 |
| Flamurtari | 26 | 13 | 7 | 6 | 49 | 33 | 16 | 46 |
| KF Tirana | 26 | 12 | 7 | 7 | 30 | 23 | 7 | 43 |
| Vllaznia | 26 | 11 | 5 | 10 | 30 | 26 | 4 | 38 |
| Laci | 26 | 11 | 5 | 10 | 32 | 31 | 1 | 38 |
| Kastrioti | 26 | 10 | 4 | 12 | 25 | 35 | –10 | 34 |
| Besa | 26 | 8 | 8 | 10 | 23 | 26 | –3 | 32 |
| Bylis (–3) | 26 | 9 | 6 | 11 | 32 | 29 | 3 | 30 |
| Shkumbini* | 26 | 7 | 8 | 11 | 18 | 33 | –15 | 29 |
| Tomori* | 26 | 4 | 7 | 15 | 30 | 50 | –20 | 19 |
| Luftetari* | 26 | 5 | 4 | 17 | 24 | 44 | –20 | 19 |
| Apolonia* | 26 | 1 | 10 | 15 | 16 | 40 | –24 | 13 |

*Top scorer:* Memelli (Flamurtari) 19.
*Cup Final:* Laci 1, Bylis 0.

### ANDORRA

Federacio Andorrana de Futbol, Avda Carlemany 67, 3er Pis, Apartado postal 65, Escaldes-Engordany.
*Founded:* 1994; *National Colours:* All red.

**International matches 2012–13**
Azerbaijan (a) 0-0, Poland (a) 0-4, Liechtenstein (a) 0-1, Hungary (h) 0-5, Romania (a) 0-4, Holland (a) 0-3, Estonia (h) 0-1, Iceland (h) 0-2, Turkey (h) 0-2, Estonia (a) 0-2.

**League Championship wins (1996–2013)**
FC Santa Coloma 6; Principat 3; Encamp 2; Ranger's 2; Sant Julia 2; Lusitanos 2; Constelacio 1.

**Cup wins (1991–2013)**
FC Santa Coloma 9; Principat 6; Sant Julia 3; Constelacio 1; Lusitanos 1; UE Santa Coloma 1.

**Qualifying League Table 2012–13**

| | P | W | D | L | F | A | GD | Pts |
|---|---|---|---|---|---|---|---|---|
| Lusitanos | 14 | 10 | 3 | 1 | 44 | 11 | 33 | 33 |
| UE Santa Coloma | 14 | 9 | 3 | 2 | 39 | 14 | 25 | 30 |
| Sant Julia | 14 | 9 | 3 | 2 | 32 | 9 | 23 | 30 |
| FC Santa Coloma | 14 | 8 | 5 | 1 | 25 | 12 | 13 | 29 |
| Principat | 14 | 3 | 3 | 8 | 17 | 30 | –13 | 12 |
| Encamp | 14 | 3 | 1 | 10 | 14 | 49 | –35 | 10 |
| Engordany | 14 | 2 | 2 | 10 | 14 | 47 | –33 | 8 |
| Inter Club | 14 | 2 | 0 | 12 | 14 | 38 | –24 | 6 |

**Championship Play-Offs**

| | P | W | D | L | F | A | GD | Pts |
|---|---|---|---|---|---|---|---|---|
| Lusitanos | 20 | 13 | 5 | 2 | 64 | 16 | 48 | 44 |
| FC Santa Coloma | 20 | 10 | 9 | 1 | 30 | 15 | 15 | 39 |
| UE Santa Coloma | 20 | 11 | 4 | 5 | 47 | 25 | 22 | 37 |
| Sant Julia | 20 | 10 | 4 | 6 | 38 | 18 | 20 | 34 |

**Relegation Play-Offs**

| | P | W | D | L | F | A | GD | Pts |
|---|---|---|---|---|---|---|---|---|
| Principat | 20 | 6 | 3 | 11 | 23 | 35 | –12 | 21 |
| Inter Club | 20 | 6 | 0 | 14 | 22 | 42 | –20 | 18 |
| Encamp+ | 20 | 5 | 2 | 13 | 18 | 55 | –37 | 17 |
| Engordany* | 20 | 4 | 3 | 13 | 20 | 56 | –36 | 15 |

*Top scorer:* Bruninho (Lusitanos) 17.
*Cup Final:* UE Santa Coloma 3, Sant Julia 2.

### ARMENIA

Football Federation of Armenia, Khanjyan 27, 0010 Yerevan, Armenia.
*Founded:* 1992; *National Colours:* Red shirts, red shorts, red and yellow socks.

**International matches 2012–13**
Serbia (n) 0-2, Canada (n) 3-1, Greece (n) 0-1, Kazakhstan (h) 3-0, Belarus (h) 1-2, Malta (a) 1-0, Bulgaria (a) 0-1, Italy (h) 1-3, Lithuania (h) 4-2, Luxembourg (a) 1-1, Czech Republic (h) 0-3, Malta (h) 0-1, Denmark (a) 4-0.

**League Championship wins (1992–2013)**
Pyunik 13 (including Homenetmen); Shirak 5*; Ararat Yerevan 2*; Araks 2 (including Tsement); FC Yerevan 1; Ulisses 1.
*Includes one unofficial title.

**Cup wins (1992–2013)**
Mika 6; Ararat Yerevan 5; Pyunik 5; Tsement 2; Banants 2; Pyunik (including Homenetmen) 1; Shirak 1.

**Final League Table 2012–13**

| | P | W | D | L | F | A | GD | Pts |
|---|---|---|---|---|---|---|---|---|
| Shirak | 42 | 26 | 10 | 6 | 70 | 38 | 32 | 88 |
| Mika | 42 | 24 | 7 | 11 | 57 | 40 | 17 | 79 |
| Gandzasar | 42 | 18 | 13 | 11 | 48 | 37 | 11 | 67 |
| Pyunik | 42 | 19 | 6 | 17 | 67 | 51 | 16 | 63 |
| Impuls | 42 | 18 | 6 | 18 | 66 | 65 | 1 | 60 |
| Ulisses | 42 | 11 | 12 | 19 | 41 | 50 | –9 | 45 |
| Ararat | 42 | 9 | 6 | 27 | 28 | 69 | –41 | 33 |
| Banants* | 42 | 5 | 16 | 21 | 37 | 64 | –27 | 31 |

*Top scorer:* Gyozalyan (Impuls) 22.
*Cup Final:* Pyunik 1, Shirak 0.

### AUSTRIA

Oesterreichischer Fussball-Bund, Ernst-Happel Stadion – Sektor A/F, Postfach 340, Meierestrasse 7, Wien 1021.
*Founded:* 1904; *National Colours:* White shirts, black shorts, white socks.

**International matches 2012–13**
Finland (h) 3-1, Ukraine (h) 3-2, Romania (h) 0-0, Turkey (h) 2-0, Germany (h) 1-2, Kazakhstan (a) 0-0, Kazakhstan (h) 4-0, Ivory Coast (h) 0-3, Wales (a) 1-2, Faroe Islands (h) 6-0, Republic of Ireland (a) 2-2, Sweden (h) 2-1.

**League Championship wins (1912–2013)**
Rapid Vienna 32; FK Austria Vienna (formerly Amateure) 24; Wacker Innsbruck 10 (incl. Svarowski Tirol 2, Tirol Innsbruck 3); Admira Vienna (now Admira Wacker Modling) 9 (incl. Wacker Vienna 1); Red Bull Salzburg 7 (incl. Austria Salzburg 3); First Vienna 6;

Wiener Sportklub 3; Sturm Graz 3; WAF 1; WAC 1; Florisdorfer 1; Hakoah 1; Linz ASK 1; Voest Linz 1; Graz 1.

**Cup wins (1919–2013)**
FK Austria Vienna (formerly Amateure) 27; Rapid Vienna 14; Wacker Innsbruck 7 (incl. Svarowski Tirol 1, Tirol Innsbruck); Admira Vienna 6 (including Wacker Vienna 1); Graz 4; Sturm Graz 4; First Vienna 3; WAC 2; Ried 2; Linz ASK 1; WAF 1; Wiener Sportklub 1; Kremser 1; Stockerau 1; Karnten 1; Kremser 1; Horn 1; Red Bull Salzburg 1; Pasching 1.

**Final League Table 2012–13**

| | P | W | D | L | F | A | GD | Pts |
|---|---|---|---|---|---|---|---|---|
| FK Austria Vienna | 36 | 25 | 7 | 4 | 84 | 31 | 53 | 82 |
| Red Bull Salzburg | 36 | 22 | 11 | 3 | 91 | 39 | 52 | 77 |
| Rapid Vienna | 36 | 16 | 9 | 11 | 57 | 39 | 18 | 57 |
| Sturm Graz | 36 | 13 | 9 | 14 | 49 | 56 | −7 | 48 |
| Wolfsberger | 36 | 12 | 11 | 13 | 53 | 56 | −3 | 47 |
| Ried | 36 | 13 | 7 | 16 | 60 | 59 | 1 | 46 |
| Wiener Neustadt | 36 | 9 | 9 | 18 | 32 | 60 | −28 | 36 |
| Wacker Innsbruck | 36 | 11 | 3 | 22 | 41 | 75 | −34 | 36 |
| Admira | 36 | 9 | 8 | 19 | 47 | 68 | −21 | 35 |
| SV Mattersburg* | 36 | 9 | 8 | 19 | 36 | 67 | −31 | 35 |

*Top scorer:* Hosiner (FK Austria Vienna) 32 (incl. 5 for Admira Wacker).
*Cup Final:* FK Austria Vienna 0, Pasching 1.

### AZERBAIJAN
Association of Football Federations of Azerbaijan, 2208 Nobel prospekti, 1025 Baku.
*Founded:* 1992; *National Colours:* White shirts, blue shorts, white socks.

**International matches 2012–13**
Singapore (h) 2-2, India (h) 3-0, Japan (h) 0-2, Andorra (h) 0-0, Bahrain (h) 0-3, Israel (a) 1-1, Portugal (a) 3-0, Russia (h) 0-1, Northern Ireland (a) 1-1, Liechtenstein (h) 1-0, Luxembourg (a) 0-0, Portugal (h) 0-2, Qatar (a) 1-1, Luxembourg (h) 1-1.

**League Championship wins (1992–2013)**
Neftchi 8; Kapaz 3; Shamkir 3; FK Baku 2; Inter Baku 2; Karabakh 1; Turan 1; Xazar Lankaran 1.
*Includes one unofficial title for Shamkir in 2002.*

**Cup wins (1992–2013)**
Neftchi 6; Kapaz 4; Karabakh 3; Xazar Lankaran 3; FK Baku 3; Inshatchi 1; Shafa 1.

**Qualifying League Table 2012–13**

| | P | W | D | L | F | A | GD | Pts |
|---|---|---|---|---|---|---|---|---|
| Neftchi | 22 | 14 | 2 | 6 | 47 | 24 | 23 | 44 |
| Inter Baku | 22 | 11 | 8 | 3 | 24 | 12 | 12 | 41 |
| Karabakh | 22 | 10 | 9 | 3 | 30 | 19 | 11 | 39 |
| Simurq | 22 | 9 | 9 | 4 | 25 | 10 | 10 | 36 |
| Gabala | 22 | 9 | 5 | 8 | 26 | 27 | −1 | 32 |
| FK Baku | 22 | 6 | 12 | 4 | 24 | 15 | 9 | 30 |
| AZAL | 22 | 7 | 8 | 7 | 32 | 25 | 7 | 29 |
| Xazar Lankaran | 22 | 7 | 7 | 8 | 32 | 27 | 5 | 28 |
| Turan | 22 | 6 | 5 | 11 | 24 | 35 | −9 | 23 |
| Sumgayit | 22 | 5 | 7 | 10 | 20 | 39 | −19 | 22 |
| Ravan Baku | 22 | 6 | 4 | 12 | 23 | 36 | −13 | 22 |
| Kapaz | 22 | 2 | 4 | 16 | 12 | 45 | −33 | 10 |

*The game between Simurq and Ravan Baku was awarded 3-0 to Simurq.*

**Final League Table 2012–13**

| | P | W | D | L | F | A | GD | Pts |
|---|---|---|---|---|---|---|---|---|
| Neftchi | 32 | 15 | 5 | 8 | 59 | 32 | 27 | 62 |
| Karabakh | 32 | 16 | 11 | 5 | 43 | 26 | 17 | 59 |
| Inter Baku | 32 | 16 | 9 | 7 | 38 | 22 | 16 | 57 |
| Simurq | 32 | 12 | 12 | 8 | 32 | 26 | 6 | 48 |
| FK Baku | 32 | 9 | 14 | 9 | 33 | 27 | 6 | 41 |
| Gabala | 32 | 10 | 8 | 14 | 32 | 40 | −8 | 38 |

**Relegation Table 2012–13**

| | P | W | D | L | F | A | GD | Pts |
|---|---|---|---|---|---|---|---|---|
| AZAL | 32 | 16 | 9 | 7 | 57 | 32 | 25 | 57 |
| Ravan Baku | 32 | 12 | 4 | 16 | 46 | 54 | −8 | 40 |
| Khazar Lankaran | 32 | 10 | 10 | 12 | 40 | 37 | 3 | 40 |
| Sumgayit | 32 | 9 | 8 | 15 | 31 | 49 | −18 | 35 |
| Turan* | 32 | 8 | 6 | 18 | 34 | 59 | −25 | 30 |
| Kapaz* | 32 | 5 | 4 | 23 | 23 | 64 | −41 | 19 |

*Top scorer:* Canales (Neftchi) 26.
*Cup Final:* Neftchi 0, Xazar Lankaran 0.
*Neftchi won 5-3 on penalties.*

### BELARUS
Belarus Football Federation, Prospekt Pobeditelei 20/3, Minsk 220020.
*Founded:* 1992; *National Colours:* All red.

**International matches 2012–13**
Moldova (a) 0-0, Lithuania (h) 1-1, Armenia (a) 2-1, Georgia (a) 0-1, France (a) 1-3, Spain (h) 0-4, Georgia (h) 2-0, Israel (a) 2-1, Hungary (a) 1-1, Jordan (a) 0-1, Canada (a) 2-1, Estonia (a) 2-0, Finland (a) 0-1, Finland (a) 1-1.

**League Championship wins (1992–2012)**
BATE Borisov 9; Dinamo Minsk 7; Slavia Mozyr (formerly MPKC Mozyr) 2; Dnepr Mogilev 1; Belshina Bobruisk 1; Gomel 1; Shakhtyor Soligorsk 1.

**Cup wins (1992–2013)**
Belshina Bobruisk 3; Dinamo Minsk 3; Slavia Mozyr (formerly MPKC Mozyr) 2; MTZ-RIPA 2; BATE Borisov 2; Gomel 2; Naftan 2; Neman 1; Dinamo 93 Minsk 1; Lokomotiv 96 1; Shakhtyor Soligorsk 1; Dinamo Brest 1; FK Minsk 1.

**Final League Table 2012**

| | P | W | D | L | F | A | GD | Pts |
|---|---|---|---|---|---|---|---|---|
| BATE Borisov | 30 | 21 | 5 | 4 | 51 | 16 | 35 | 68 |
| Shakhtyor Soligorsk | 30 | 18 | 7 | 5 | 59 | 24 | 35 | 61 |
| Dinamo Minsk | 30 | 16 | 8 | 6 | 37 | 19 | 18 | 56 |
| Gomel | 30 | 14 | 8 | 8 | 39 | 24 | 15 | 50 |
| Neman Grodno | 30 | 10 | 11 | 9 | 43 | 36 | 7 | 41 |
| FK Minsk | 30 | 11 | 6 | 13 | 36 | 46 | −10 | 39 |
| Belshina Bobruisk | 30 | 7 | 9 | 14 | 26 | 40 | −14 | 30 |
| Dinamo Brest | 30 | 8 | 5 | 17 | 27 | 38 | −11 | 29 |
| Naftan Novopolotsk | 30 | 7 | 8 | 15 | 23 | 40 | −17 | 29 |
| Slavia Mozyr | 30 | 7 | 6 | 17 | 22 | 58 | −36 | 27 |
| Torpedo-BelAZ Zhodino | 30 | 5 | 9 | 16 | 17 | 39 | −22 | 24 |

*Top scorer:* Osipenko (Shakhtyor Soligorsk) 14.
*Cup Final:* Dinamo Minsk 1, FK Minsk 1.
*FK Minsk won 4-1 on penalties.*

### BELGIUM
Union Royale Belge des Societes de Football-Association, 145 Avenue Houba de Strooper, B-1020 Bruxelles.
*Founded:* 1895; *National Colours:* All red.

**International matches 2012–13**
Greece (a) 1-1, Montenegro (h) 2-2, England (a) 0-1, Holland (h) 4-2, Wales (a) 2-0, Croatia (h) 1-1, Serbia (a) 3-0, Scotland (h) 2-0, Romania (a) 1-2, Slovakia (h) 2-1, FYR Macedonia (a) 2-0, FYR Macedonia (h) 1-0, USA (a) 4-2, Serbia (h) 2-1.

**League Championship wins (1896–2013)**
Anderlecht 32; Club Brugge 13; Union St Gilloise 11; Standard Liege 10; Beerschot VAC (became Germinal) 7; RC Brussels 6; FC Liege 5; Daring Brussels 5; Antwerp 4; Mechelen 4; Lierse 4; Cercle Brugge 3; KRC Genk 3; Beveren 2; RWD Molenbeek 1.

**Cup wins (1912–14; 1927; 1935; 1954–2013)**
Club Brugge 11; Anderlecht 9; Standard Liege 6; KRC Genk 4; KAA Gent 3; Beerschot VAC (became Germinal) 2; Waterschei (became Racing Genk) 2; Beveren 2; Antwerp 2; Lierse 2; Union St Gilloise 2; Cercle Brugge 2; Beerschot Antwerpen Club (incl. Germinal Ekeren) 2; Mechelen 1; FC Liege 1; Westerlo 1; La Louviere 1; Zulte-Waregem 1; Daring 1; Tournai 1; Racing 1; Waregem 1; Lokeren 1.

**Qualifying League Table 2012–13**

| | P | W | D | L | F | A | GD | Pts |
|---|---|---|---|---|---|---|---|---|
| Anderlecht | 30 | 20 | 7 | 3 | 69 | 27 | 42 | 67 |
| Zulte-Waregem | 30 | 19 | 6 | 5 | 49 | 29 | 20 | 63 |
| KRC Genk | 30 | 15 | 10 | 5 | 63 | 40 | 23 | 55 |
| Club Brugge | 30 | 15 | 9 | 6 | 66 | 43 | 23 | 54 |
| Lokeren | 30 | 14 | 9 | 7 | 53 | 38 | 15 | 51 |
| Standard Liege | 30 | 15 | 5 | 10 | 54 | 33 | 21 | 50 |
| Mons | 30 | 13 | 5 | 12 | 48 | 53 | −5 | 44 |
| Mechelen | 30 | 12 | 5 | 13 | 44 | 42 | 2 | 41 |
| Kortrijk | 30 | 11 | 6 | 13 | 31 | 30 | 1 | 39 |
| Leuven | 30 | 8 | 12 | 10 | 46 | 51 | −5 | 36 |
| Charleroi | 30 | 10 | 4 | 16 | 30 | 49 | −19 | 34 |
| KAA Gent | 30 | 8 | 10 | 12 | 33 | 40 | −7 | 34 |
| Waasland-Beveren | 30 | 7 | 9 | 14 | 28 | 49 | −21 | 30 |
| Lierse | 30 | 5 | 11 | 14 | 28 | 53 | −25 | 26 |
| Germinal Beerschot | 30 | 6 | 5 | 19 | 31 | 61 | −30 | 23 |
| Cercle Brugge | 30 | 3 | 5 | 22 | 30 | 65 | −35 | 14 |

*NB: Points earned in Qualifying phase are halved and rounded up at start of Championship play-off phase.*

**Championship Play-off**

| | P | W | D | L | F | A | GD | Pts |
|---|---|---|---|---|---|---|---|---|
| Anderlecht | 10 | 4 | 3 | 3 | 16 | 11 | 5 | 49 |
| Zulte-Waregem | 10 | 4 | 3 | 3 | 20 | 20 | 0 | 47 |
| Club Brugge | 10 | 6 | 1 | 3 | 21 | 17 | 4 | 46 |
| Standard Liege | 10 | 5 | 2 | 3 | 22 | 20 | 2 | 42 |
| KRC Genk | 10 | 3 | 3 | 4 | 11 | 13 | -2 | 40 |
| Lokeren | 10 | 1 | 2 | 7 | 15 | 24 | -9 | 31 |

**Europa League Qualifying Table A**

| | P | W | D | L | F | A | GD | Pts |
|---|---|---|---|---|---|---|---|---|
| Gent | 6 | 4 | 2 | 0 | 9 | 3 | 6 | 14 |
| Mons | 6 | 3 | 1 | 2 | 7 | 8 | -1 | 10 |
| Lierse | 6 | 1 | 1 | 4 | 5 | 8 | -3 | 4 |
| Kortrijk | 6 | 1 | 2 | 3 | 4 | 6 | -2 | 2 |

**Europa League Qualifying Table B**

| | P | W | D | L | F | A | GD | Pts |
|---|---|---|---|---|---|---|---|---|
| Leuven | 6 | 3 | 1 | 2 | 9 | 8 | 1 | 10 |
| Mechelen | 6 | 3 | 1 | 2 | 8 | 7 | 1 | 10 |
| Charleroi | 6 | 1 | 4 | 1 | 5 | 3 | 2 | 8 |
| Waasland-Beveren | 6 | 1 | 2 | 3 | 3 | 7 | -4 | 5 |

**Europa League Qualifying Play-off**
Leuven 1, 1, Gent 4, 4

**Europa League Testmatch**
Gent 1, 0, Standard Liege 0, 7

**Relegation Table**

| | P | W | D | L | F | A | GD | Pts |
|---|---|---|---|---|---|---|---|---|
| Cercle Brugge+ | 4 | 3 | 0 | 1 | 3 | 2 | 1 | 9 |
| Germinal Beerschot* | 4 | 1 | 0 | 3 | 2 | 3 | -1 | 6 |

*Top scorer:* Bacca (Club Brugge) 25.
*Cup Final:* Cercle Brugge 0, KRC Genk 2.

### BOSNIA-HERZEGOVINA
Football Federation of Bosnia & Herzegovina, Ferhadija 30, Sarajevo 71000.
*Founded:* 1992; *National Colours:* White shirts, blue shorts, white socks.

**International matches 2012–13**
Poland (a) 0-1*, Brazil (h) 1-2, Republic of Ireland (a) 0-1, Mexico (a) 1-2, Wales (a) 2-0, Liechtenstein (a) 8-1, Latvia (h) 4-1, Greece (a) 0-0, Lithuania (h) 3-0, Algeria (a) 1-0, Slovenia (a) 3-0, Greece (h) 3-1, Latvia (a) 5-0.
* *Played 16.12.2011, result omitted from last edition.*

**League Championship wins (1998; 2000–13)**
Zeljeznicar 6; Siroki Brijeg 2; Sarajevo 2; Zrinjski 2; Brotnjo 1; Leotar 1; Modrica 1; Borac Banja Luka 1.

**Cup wins (1998; 2000–13)**
Zeljeznicar 5; Sarajevo 3; Siroki Brijeg 2; Modrica 1; Orasje 1; Zrinjski 1; Slavija 1; Borac Banja Luka 1.

**Final League Table 2012–13**

| | P | W | D | L | F | A | GD | Pts |
|---|---|---|---|---|---|---|---|---|
| Zeljeznicar | 30 | 20 | 6 | 4 | 48 | 20 | 28 | 66 |
| Sarajevo | 30 | 17 | 9 | 4 | 52 | 19 | 33 | 60 |
| Borac Banja Luka | 30 | 14 | 9 | 7 | 43 | 25 | 18 | 51 |
| Celik | 30 | 14 | 9 | 7 | 44 | 30 | 14 | 51 |
| Olimpik | 30 | 13 | 10 | 7 | 34 | 26 | 8 | 49 |
| Siroki Brijeg | 30 | 13 | 6 | 11 | 48 | 31 | 17 | 45 |
| Slavija | 30 | 12 | 7 | 11 | 29 | 28 | 1 | 43 |
| Leotar | 30 | 10 | 9 | 11 | 28 | 40 | -12 | 39 |
| Zrinjski | 30 | 11 | 6 | 13 | 26 | 42 | -16 | 39 |
| Rudar Prijedor | 30 | 10 | 6 | 14 | 37 | 42 | -5 | 36 |
| Zvijezda | 30 | 10 | 6 | 14 | 38 | 44 | -6 | 36 |
| Radnik | 30 | 8 | 11 | 11 | 27 | 35 | -8 | 35 |
| Velez | 30 | 8 | 10 | 12 | 31 | 34 | -3 | 34 |
| Travnik | 30 | 9 | 7 | 14 | 29 | 45 | -16 | 34 |
| GOSK Gabela* | 30 | 7 | 9 | 14 | 29 | 42 | -13 | 30 |
| Gradina* | 30 | 1 | 6 | 23 | 17 | 57 | -40 | 9 |

*Top scorer:* Hadzic (Sarajevo) 20.
*Cup Final:* Zeljeznicar 1, 1, Siroki Brijeg 1, 1.
*Siroki Brijeg won 5-4 on penalties.*

### BULGARIA
Bulgarian Football Union, 26 Tzar Ivan Assen II Str., 1124 Sofia.
*Founded:* 1923; *National Colours:* White shirts, green shorts, red socks.

**International matches 2012–13**
Hungary (a) 1-1, Holland (a) 2-1, Turkey (h) 0-2, Cyprus (h) 1-0, Italy (h) 2-2, Armenia (h) 1-0, Denmark (h) 1-1, Czech Republic (a) 0-0, Ukraine (h) 0-1, Malta (h) 6-0, Denmark (a) 1-1, Japan (a) 2-0, Kazakhstan (a) 2-1.

**League Championship wins (1925–2013)**
CSKA Sofia 31; Levski Sofia 26; Slavia Sofia 7; Lokomotiv Sofia 4; Litex Lovech 4; Vladislav Varna 3; Botev Plovdiv (includes Trakija) 2 ; Ludogorets Razgrad 2; AC 23 Sofia 1; Sokol (Spartak) Varna 1; Sportklub Sofia 1; Ticha Varna 1; Spartak Plovdiv 1; Beroe Stara Zagora 1; Etar 1; Lokomotiv Plovdiv 1.

**Cup wins (1946–2013)**
Levski Sofia 24; CSKA Sofia 19; Slavia Sofia 7; Lokomotiv Sofia 4; Litex Lovech 4; Botev Plovdiv (includes Trakija) 2; Beroe Stara Zagora 2; Spartak Plovdiv 1; Septemvri Sofia 1; Spartak Sofia 1; Marek Dupnica 1; Sliven 1; Ludogorets Razgrad 1.

**Final League Table 2012–13**

| | P | W | D | L | F | A | GD | Pts |
|---|---|---|---|---|---|---|---|---|
| Ludogorets Razgrad | 30 | 22 | 6 | 2 | 58 | 13 | 45 | 72 |
| Levski Sofia | 30 | 22 | 5 | 3 | 59 | 20 | 39 | 71 |
| CSKA Sofia | 30 | 19 | 6 | 5 | 54 | 20 | 34 | 63 |
| Botev Plovdiv | 30 | 18 | 6 | 6 | 51 | 21 | 30 | 60 |
| Litex Lovech | 30 | 15 | 5 | 10 | 56 | 24 | 32 | 50 |
| Chernomorets Burgas | 30 | 14 | 5 | 11 | 32 | 29 | 3 | 47 |
| Beroe Stara Zagora | 30 | 13 | 6 | 11 | 36 | 38 | -2 | 45 |
| Slavia Sofia | 30 | 12 | 6 | 12 | 40 | 35 | 5 | 42 |
| Lokomotiv Plovdiv | 30 | 10 | 9 | 11 | 37 | 34 | 3 | 39 |
| Cherno More Varna | 30 | 9 | 8 | 13 | 33 | 39 | -6 | 35 |
| Pirin Gotse Delchev | 30 | 10 | 4 | 16 | 27 | 57 | -30 | 34 |
| Lokomotiv Sofia | 30 | 7 | 10 | 13 | 27 | 38 | -11 | 31 |
| Botev Vratsa* | 30 | 8 | 7 | 15 | 23 | 51 | -28 | 31 |
| Minyor Pernik* | 30 | 5 | 5 | 20 | 20 | 49 | -29 | 20 |
| Montana* | 30 | 4 | 4 | 22 | 27 | 57 | -30 | 16 |
| Etar Veliko Tarnovo* (-3) | 30 | 4 | 2 | 22 | 20 | 75 | -55 | 16 |

*Top scorer:* De Carvalho (Levski Sofia) 19.
*Cup Final:* Beroe Stara Zagora 3, Levski Sofia 3.
*Beroe Stara Zagora won 3-1 on penalties.*

### CHANNEL ISLANDS

**Guernsey**

**League Championship wins (1894–2013)**
Northerners 30; Rangers 17; Vale Recreation 15; St Martin's 13; Sylvans 10; Belgrave Wanderers 7; 2nd Bn Manchesters 3; 2nd Bn Royal Irish Regt 2; 2nd Bn Wiltshires 2; 10th Comp W Div Royal Artillery 1; 2nd Bn Leicesters 1; 2nd Bn PA Somerset Light Infantry 1; 2nd Middlesex Regt 1; Athletics 1; Band Comp 2nd Bn Royal Fusiliers 1; G&H Comp Royal Fusiliers 1; Grange 1; Yorkshire Regt (Green Howards) 1.

**Final League Table 2012–13**

| | P | W | D | L | F | A | GD | Pts |
|---|---|---|---|---|---|---|---|---|
| Belgrave Wanderers | 24 | 19 | 4 | 1 | 87 | 21 | 66 | 61 |
| Vale Recreation | 24 | 17 | 3 | 4 | 58 | 28 | 30 | 54 |
| St Martin's | 24 | 13 | 5 | 6 | 74 | 43 | 31 | 44 |
| Northerners | 24 | 11 | 5 | 8 | 62 | 36 | 26 | 38 |
| Sylvans | 24 | 7 | 2 | 15 | 35 | 58 | -23 | 23 |
| Rangers | 24 | 6 | 3 | 15 | 44 | 76 | -32 | 21 |
| Rovers | 24 | 0 | 0 | 24 | 15 | 113 | -98 | 0 |

**Jersey**

**League Championship wins (1894–2013)**
Jersey Wanderers 20; First Tower United 19; St Paul's 14; Jersey Scottish 10; Beeches Old Boys 5; Magpies 4; 2nd Bn King's Own Regt 3; Oaklands 3; St Peter 3; 1st Batt Devon Regt 2; 1st Bn East Surrey Regt 2; Georgetown 2; Mechanics 2; YMCA 2; 2nd Bn East Surrey Regt 1; 20th Comp Royal Garrison Artillery 1; National Rovers 1; Sporting Academics 1; Trinity 1.

**Final League Table 2012–13**

| | P | W | D | L | F | A | GD | Pts |
|---|---|---|---|---|---|---|---|---|
| Jersey Scottish | 16 | 14 | 1 | 1 | 55 | 11 | 44 | 43 |
| St Paul's | 16 | 11 | 3 | 2 | 50 | 17 | 33 | 36 |
| Jersey Wanderers | 16 | 11 | 1 | 4 | 35 | 22 | 13 | 34 |
| St Peter | 16 | 4 | 7 | 5 | 26 | 27 | -1 | 19 |
| St Brelade | 16 | 4 | 6 | 6 | 15 | 19 | -4 | 18 |
| Grouville | 16 | 4 | 4 | 8 | 18 | 36 | -18 | 16 |
| St Ouen (-1) | 16 | 4 | 4 | 8 | 19 | 30 | -11 | 15 |
| Rozel Rovers | 16 | 2 | 3 | 11 | 13 | 31 | -18 | 9 |
| St Lawrence | 16 | 2 | 3 | 11 | 17 | 55 | -38 | 9 |

**Upton Park Trophy 2013 (For Guernsey & Jersey League Champions)**
Jersey Scottish 4, Belgrave Wanderers 0

**Upton Park Trophy wins (1907–2013)**
Northerners 18; First Tower United 12; Jersey Wanderers 11; St Martin's 11; St Paul's 6; Jersey Scottish 6; Rangers

5; Vale Recreation 4; Belgrave Wanderers 4; Sylvans 3; Beeches Old Boys 3; Old St Paul's 3; Magpies 3; St Peter 2; Jersey Mechanics 1; Jersey YMCA 1; National Rovers 1; Sporting Academics 1; Trinity 1.

## CROATIA

Croatian Football Federation, Rusanova 13, 10 3000 Zagreb.
*Founded:* 1912; *National Colours:* Red and white check shirts, white shorts, blue socks.

### International matches 2012–13

Sweden (h) 1-3, Estonia (h) 3-1, Norway (a) 1-1, Republic of Ireland (n) 3-1, Italy (n) 1-1, Spain (n) 0-1, Switzerland (a) 2-4, FYR Macedonia (h) 1-0, Belgium (a) 1-1, FYR Macedonia (h) 2-1, Wales (h) 2-0, South Korea (a) 4-0, Serbia (h) 2-0, Wales (a) 2-1, Scotland (h) 0-1, Portugal (h) 0-1.

### League Championship wins (1941–46; 1992–2013)

Dinamo Zagreb (formerly Croatia Zagreb) 15; Hajduk Split 8; Concordia 1; Gradjanski 1; NK Zagreb 1.

### Cup wins (1992–2013)

Dinamo Zagreb (formerly Croatia Zagreb) 12; Hajduk Split 6; Rijeka 2, Inter Zapresic 1; Osijek 1.

### Final League Table 2012–13

| | P | W | D | L | F | A | GD | Pts |
|---|---|---|---|---|---|---|---|---|
| Dinamo Zagreb | 33 | 24 | 5 | 4 | 68 | 20 | 48 | 77 |
| Lokomotiva Zagreb | 33 | 16 | 9 | 8 | 54 | 38 | 16 | 57 |
| Rijeka | 33 | 15 | 8 | 10 | 46 | 42 | 4 | 53 |
| Hajduk Split | 33 | 14 | 10 | 9 | 45 | 31 | 14 | 52 |
| Split | 33 | 15 | 7 | 11 | 49 | 37 | 12 | 52 |
| Istra 1961 | 33 | 11 | 11 | 11 | 35 | 32 | 3 | 44 |
| Osijek | 33 | 9 | 12 | 12 | 25 | 33 | –8 | 39 |
| Slaven Koprivnica | 33 | 10 | 9 | 14 | 35 | 50 | –15 | 39 |
| Zadar | 33 | 9 | 9 | 15 | 39 | 61 | –22 | 36 |
| Inter Zapresic* | 33 | 8 | 11 | 14 | 36 | 41 | –5 | 35 |
| Cibalia* | 33 | 9 | 5 | 19 | 29 | 44 | –15 | 32 |
| NK Zagreb* | 33 | 7 | 6 | 20 | 28 | 60 | –32 | 27 |

*Top scorer:* Benko (Rijeka) 19.
*Cup Final:* Hajduk Split 2, 3, Lokomotiva 1, 3.

## CYPRUS

Cyprus Football Association, 10 Achaion Street, 2413 Engomi, PO Box 25071, 1306 Nicosia.
*Founded:* 1934; *National Colours:* All blue.

### International matches 2012–13

Serbia (h) 0-0, Bulgaria (a) 0-1, Albania (a) 1-3, Iceland (h) 1-0, Slovenia (a) 1-2, Norway (h) 1-3, Finland (h) 0-3, Serbia (h) 1-3, Switzerland (h) 0-0, Switzerland (a) 0-1.

### League Championship wins (1935–2013)

APOEL 22; Omonia 20; Anorthosis 13; AEL 6; EPA 3; Olympiakos 3; Apollon 3; Pezoporikos 2; Trast 1 ; Cetinkaya 1.

### Cup wins (1935–2013)

APOEL 19; Omonia 14; Anorthosis 10; Apollon 7; AEL 6; EPA 5; Trast 3; Cetinkaya 2; Olympiakos 1; Pezoporikos 1; Nea Salamis 1; AEK 1; APOP 1.

### Qualifying League Table 2012–13

| | P | W | D | L | F | A | GD | Pts |
|---|---|---|---|---|---|---|---|---|
| APOEL | 26 | 21 | 3 | 2 | 56 | 10 | 46 | 66 |
| Anorthosis Famagusta | 26 | 18 | 6 | 2 | 57 | 21 | 36 | 60 |
| AEK Larnaca | 26 | 17 | 4 | 5 | 50 | 21 | 29 | 55 |
| Omonia | 26 | 16 | 5 | 5 | 51 | 22 | 29 | 53 |
| AEL Limassol | 26 | 14 | 9 | 3 | 46 | 26 | 20 | 51 |
| Apollon | 26 | 11 | 7 | 8 | 32 | 24 | 8 | 40 |
| Doxa Katokopia | 26 | 8 | 6 | 12 | 26 | 40 | –14 | 30 |
| Enosis Neon Paralimni | 26 | 6 | 10 | 10 | 23 | 35 | –12 | 28 |
| Alki | 26 | 6 | 7 | 13 | 33 | 46 | –13 | 25 |
| Olympiakos (–3) | 26 | 6 | 9 | 11 | 36 | 44 | –8 | 24 |
| Nea Salamis | 26 | 6 | 5 | 15 | 18 | 36 | –18 | 23 |
| Ethnikos Achnas | 26 | 4 | 10 | 12 | 28 | 40 | –12 | 22 |
| Ayia Napa* | 26 | 2 | 2 | 22 | 15 | 59 | –44 | 8 |
| AEP Paphos* (-9) | 26 | 4 | 3 | 19 | 17 | 64 | –47 | 6 |

### Play-Offs League Tables 2012–13

#### Group A

| | P | W | D | L | F | A | GD | Pts |
|---|---|---|---|---|---|---|---|---|
| APOEL | 32 | 23 | 4 | 5 | 62 | 19 | 43 | 73 |
| Anorthosis | 32 | 20 | 8 | 4 | 60 | 29 | 31 | 68 |
| Omonia | 32 | 20 | 6 | 6 | 66 | 27 | 39 | 66 |
| AEK Larnaca | 32 | 19 | 4 | 9 | 55 | 28 | 27 | 61 |

#### Group B

| | P | W | D | L | F | A | GD | Pts |
|---|---|---|---|---|---|---|---|---|
| AEL Limassol | 32 | 18 | 10 | 4 | 59 | 31 | 28 | 64 |
| Apollon | 32 | 13 | 9 | 10 | 40 | 31 | 9 | 48 |
| Doxa Katokopia | 32 | 10 | 9 | 13 | 33 | 47 | –14 | 39 |
| Enosis | 32 | 7 | 10 | 15 | 28 | 49 | –21 | 31 |

#### Group C

| | P | W | D | L | F | A | GD | Pts |
|---|---|---|---|---|---|---|---|---|
| Ethnikos Achnas | 32 | 7 | 12 | 13 | 41 | 50 | –9 | 33 |
| Alki | 32 | 8 | 8 | 16 | 43 | 58 | –15 | 32 |
| Nea Salamis+ | 32 | 8 | 7 | 17 | 27 | 44 | –17 | 31 |
| Olympiakos Nicosia* (–3) | 32 | 8 | 10 | 14 | 46 | 56 | –10 | 31 |

*Top scorer:* Vasconcelos (Alki) 18.
*Cup Final:* AEL Limassol 1, Apollon 2.

## CZECH REPUBLIC

Fotbalova Asociace Ceske Republiky, Diskarska 2431/4, PO Box 11, Praha 6 16017.
*Founded:* 1901; *National Colours:* All red.

### International matches 2012–13

Republic of Ireland (a) 1-1, Israel (h) 2-1, Hungary (h) 1-2, Russia (n) 1-4, Greece (n) 2-1, Poland (n) 1-0, Portugal (n) 0-1, Ukraine (a) 0-0, Denmark (a) 0-0, Finland (h) 0-1, Malta (h) 3-1, Bulgaria (h) 0-0, Slovakia (h) 3-0, Turkey (a) 2-0, Denmark (h) 0-3, Armenia (a) 3-0, Italy (h) 0-0.

### League Championship wins (1925–93)

Sparta Prague 19; Dukla Prague (prev. UDA, now Marila Pribram) 11; Slavia Prague 9; Slovan Bratislava (formerly NV Bratislava) 8; Spartak Trnava 5; Banik Ostrava 3; Inter-Bratislava 1; Spartak Hradec Kralove 1; Viktoria Zizkov 1; Zbrojovka Brno 1; Bohemians 1; Vitkovice 1.

### Cup wins (1961–93)

Dukla Prague 8; Sparta Prague 8; Slovan Bratislava 5; Spartak Trnava 4; Banik Ostrava 3; Lokomotiva Kosice 2; TJ Gottwaldov 1; Dunajska Streda 1; Kosice 1.
*From 1993–94, there were two separate countries: the Czech Republic and Slovakia.*

### League Championship wins (1994–2013)

Sparta Prague 11; Slavia Prague 3; Slovan Liberec 3; Viktoria Plzen 2; Banik Ostrava 1.

### Cup wins (1994–2013)

Sparta Prague 5; Slavia Prague 3; Viktoria Zizkov 2; Jablonec 2; Teplice 2; Hradec Kralove (formerly Spartak) 1; Slovan Liberec 1; Banik Osrava 1; Viktoria Plzen 1; Mlada Boleslav 1; Sigma Olomouc 1.

### Final League Table 2012–13

| | P | W | D | L | F | A | GD | Pts |
|---|---|---|---|---|---|---|---|---|
| Viktoria Plzen | 30 | 20 | 5 | 5 | 54 | 21 | 33 | 65 |
| Sparta Prague | 30 | 19 | 6 | 5 | 55 | 23 | 32 | 63 |
| Slovan Liberec | 30 | 16 | 6 | 8 | 46 | 34 | 12 | 54 |
| FK Jablonec | 30 | 13 | 10 | 7 | 49 | 41 | 8 | 49 |
| Sigma Olomouc | 30 | 13 | 8 | 9 | 38 | 29 | 9 | 47 |
| Dukla Prague | 30 | 11 | 13 | 6 | 48 | 37 | 11 | 46 |
| Slavia Prague | 30 | 11 | 9 | 10 | 41 | 33 | 8 | 42 |
| Mlada Boleslav | 30 | 10 | 8 | 12 | 34 | 43 | –9 | 38 |
| Slovacko | 30 | 10 | 7 | 13 | 37 | 41 | –4 | 37 |
| Vysocina Jihlava | 30 | 7 | 15 | 8 | 36 | 42 | –6 | 36 |
| Pribram | 30 | 7 | 11 | 12 | 27 | 39 | –12 | 32 |
| Teplice | 30 | 8 | 8 | 14 | 36 | 47 | –11 | 32 |
| Zbrojovka Brno | 30 | 9 | 5 | 16 | 34 | 53 | –19 | 32 |
| Banik Ostrava | 30 | 7 | 9 | 14 | 34 | 44 | –10 | 29 |
| Dynamo Ceske Budejovice* | 30 | 7 | 5 | 18 | 24 | 49 | –25 | 26 |
| Hradec Kralove* | 30 | 5 | 10 | 15 | 27 | 44 | –17 | 25 |

*Top scorer:* Lafata (Sparta Prague) 20.
*Cup Final:* Jablonec 2, Mlada Boleslav 2.
*Jablonec won 5-4 on penalties.*

## DENMARK

Dansk Boldspil-Union, Idraettens Hus, DBU Alle 1, DK-2605, Brondby.
*Founded:* 1889; *National Colours:* Red shirts, white shorts, red socks.

### International matches 2012–13

Russia (h) 0-2, Brazil (h) 1-3, Australia (h) 2-0, Holland (n) 1-0, Portugal (n) 2-3, Germany (n) 1-2, Slovakia (h) 1-3, Czech Republic (h) 0-0, Bulgaria (a) 1-1, Italy (a) 1-3, Turkey (a) 1-1, Canada (a) 4-0, Mexico (a) 1-1, FYR Macedonia (a) 0-3, Czech Republic (a) 3-0, Bulgaria (h) 1-1, Georgia (h) 2-1, Armenia (h) 0-4.

**League Championship wins (1913–2013)**
KB Copenhagen 15; Brondby 10; FC Copenhagen 10; B 93 Copenhagen 9; AB (Akademisk) 9; B 1903 Copenhagen 7; Frem 6; Esbjerg 5; Vejle 5; AGF Aarhus 5; Hvidovre 3; OB Odense 3; AaB Aalborg 3; B 1909 Odense 2; Koge 2; Lyngby 2; Silkeborg 1; Herfolge 1; Nordsjaelland 1.

**Cup wins (1955–2013)**
AGF Aarhus 9; Vejle 6; Brondby 6; OB Odense 5; FC Copenhagen 5; Esbjerg 3; Randers Freja 3; Lyngby 3; B 1909 Odense 2; AaB Aalborg 2; Frem 2; B 1903 Copenhagen 2; Nordsjaelland 2; B 93 Copenhagen 1; KB Copenhagen 1; Vanlose 1; Hvidovre 1; B 1913 Odense 1; AB (Akademisk) 1; Viborg 1; Silkeborg 1.

**Final League Table 2012–13**

|  | P | W | D | L | F | A | GD | Pts |
|---|---|---|---|---|---|---|---|---|
| FC Copenhagen | 33 | 18 | 11 | 4 | 62 | 32 | 30 | 65 |
| Nordsjaelland | 33 | 17 | 9 | 7 | 60 | 37 | 23 | 60 |
| Randers | 33 | 15 | 7 | 11 | 36 | 42 | –6 | 52 |
| Esbjerg | 33 | 13 | 8 | 12 | 38 | 32 | 6 | 47 |
| AaB Aalborg | 33 | 13 | 8 | 12 | 51 | 46 | 5 | 47 |
| Midtjylland | 33 | 12 | 11 | 10 | 51 | 47 | 4 | 47 |
| AGF Aarhus | 33 | 11 | 8 | 14 | 50 | 49 | 1 | 41 |
| SonderjyskE | 33 | 12 | 5 | 16 | 53 | 57 | –4 | 41 |
| Brondby | 33 | 9 | 12 | 12 | 39 | 45 | –6 | 39 |
| Odense BK | 33 | 10 | 8 | 15 | 52 | 59 | –7 | 38 |
| AC Horsens | 33 | 8 | 10 | 15 | 31 | 49 | –18 | 34 |
| Silkeborg | 33 | 8 | 7 | 18 | 38 | 66 | –28 | 31 |

*Top scorer:* Cornelius (FC Copenhagen) 18.
*Cup Final:* Randers 0, Esbjerg 1.

### ENGLAND

The Football Association, Wembley Stadium, PO Box 1966, London SW1P 9EQ.
*Founded:* 1863; *National Colours:* All white.

### ESTONIA

Eesti Jalgpalli Liit, A. Le Coq Arena, Asula 4c, 11312 Tallinn.
*Founded:* 1921; *National Colours:* Blue shirts, black shorts, white socks.

**International matches 2012–13**
El Salvador (a) 2-0, Croatia (a) 1-3, Ukraine (a) 0-4, Finland (h) 1-2, Lithuania (h) 1-0, France (a) 0-4, Poland (h) 1-0, Romania (h) 0-2, Turkey (a) 0-3, Hungary (h) 0-1, Andorra (a) 1-0, Oman (a) 2-1, UAE (a) 1-2, Scotland (a) 0-1, Holland (a) 0-3, Andorra (h) 2-0, Belarus (h) 0-2, Trinidad & Tobago (h) 1-0, Kyrgyzstan (h) 1-1.

**League Championship wins (1921–40; 1992–2012)**
Sport 9; Flora 9; Levadia Tallinn (formerly Levadia Maardu) 7; Estonia 5; Tallinn JK 2; Norma 2; Lantana (formerly Nikol) 2; Sillamae Kalev 2; Olimpia Tartu 1; TVMK Tallinn 1; Nomme Kalju 1.

**Cup wins (1993–2013)**
Levadia Tallinn (formerly Levadia Maardu) 7; Flora 6; Sadam 2; TVMK Tallinn 2; Lantana (formerly Nikol) 1; Norma 1; Trans Narva 1; Levadia Tallinn (pre-2004) 1.

**Final League Table 2012**

|  | P | W | D | L | F | A | GD | Pts |
|---|---|---|---|---|---|---|---|---|
| Nomme Kalju | 36 | 29 | 5 | 2 | 106 | 17 | 89 | 92 |
| Levadia | 36 | 25 | 8 | 3 | 85 | 22 | 63 | 83 |
| Flora | 36 | 26 | 3 | 7 | 87 | 24 | 63 | 81 |
| Trans Narva | 36 | 16 | 7 | 13 | 52 | 44 | 8 | 55 |
| Sillamae Kalev | 36 | 15 | 10 | 11 | 51 | 43 | 8 | 55 |
| Paide Linnameeskond | 36 | 11 | 9 | 16 | 34 | 52 | –18 | 42 |
| Viljandi | 36 | 6 | 8 | 22 | 33 | 88 | –55 | 26 |
| Kuressaare | 36 | 5 | 11 | 20 | 31 | 80 | –49 | 26 |
| Tallinna Kalev+ | 36 | 4 | 9 | 23 | 27 | 87 | –60 | 21 |
| Tammeka* | 36 | 4 | 8 | 24 | 30 | 79 | –49 | 20 |

*Top scorer:* Ivanov (Trans Narva) 23 (incl. 10 for Sillamae Kalev).
*Cup Final:* Nomme Kalju 1, Flora 3.

### FAROE ISLANDS

Faroe Islands Football Association, Gundadalur, PO Box 3028, 110 Torshavn.
*Founded:* 1979; *National Colours:* White shirts, blue shorts, white socks.

**International matches 2012–13**
Iceland (a) 0-2, Germany (a) 0-3, Sweden (h) 1-2, Republic of Ireland (h) 1-4, Austria (a) 0-6, Republic of Ireland (a) 0-3, Sweden (a) 0-2.

**League Championship wins (1942–2012)**
HB Torshavn 21; KI Klaksvik 17; B36 Torshavn 9; TB Tvoroyri 7; GI Gota 6; B68 Toftir 3; EB/Streymur 2; SI Sorvag 1; IF Fuglafjordur 1; B71 Sandur 1; VB Vagur 1; NSI Runavik 1.

**Cup wins (1955–2012)**
HB Torshavn 26; GI Gota 6; KI Klaksvik 5; TB Tvoroyri 5; B36 Torshavn 5; EB/Streymur 4; NSI Runavik 2; Vikingur 2; VB Vagur 1; B71 Sandur 1.

**Final League Table 2012**

|  | P | W | D | L | F | A | GD | Pts |
|---|---|---|---|---|---|---|---|---|
| EB/Streymur | 27 | 17 | 7 | 3 | 50 | 27 | 23 | 58 |
| IF Fuglafjordur | 27 | 16 | 6 | 5 | 55 | 23 | 32 | 54 |
| HB Torshavn | 27 | 13 | 6 | 8 | 56 | 34 | 22 | 45 |
| KI Klaksvík | 27 | 13 | 6 | 8 | 59 | 44 | 15 | 45 |
| Víkingur | 27 | 12 | 9 | 6 | 43 | 35 | 8 | 45 |
| B36 Torshavn | 27 | 10 | 8 | 9 | 42 | 36 | 6 | 38 |
| NSI Runavik | 27 | 9 | 4 | 14 | 38 | 42 | –4 | 31 |
| TB Tvoroyri | 27 | 5 | 9 | 13 | 30 | 50 | –20 | 24 |
| B68 Toftir* | 27 | 6 | 6 | 15 | 23 | 43 | –20 | 24 |
| FC Suduroy* | 27 | 2 | 3 | 22 | 16 | 78 | –62 | 9 |

*Top scorer:* Nascimento (IF Fuglafjordur), Klettskard (KI Klaksvík) 22.
*Cup Final:* EB/Streymur 3, Víkingur 3.
*Víkingur won 5-4 on penalties.*

### FINLAND

Suomen Palloliitto Finlands Bollfoerbund, Urheilukatu 5, PO Box 191, 00251 Helsinki.
*Founded:* 1907; *National Colours:* White shirts, blue shorts, white socks.

**International matches 2012–13**
Trinidid & Tobago (a) 3-2, Austria (a) 1-3, Turkey (h) 3-2, Estonia (n) 2-1, Latvia (n) 1-1 (5-6p), Northern Ireland (a) 3-3, France (h) 0-1, Czech Republic (a) 1-0, Georgia (h) 1-1, Cyprus (a) 3-1, Israel (a) 1-2, Spain (a) 1-1, Luxembourg (a) 3-0, Belarus (h) 1-0, Belarus (a) 1-1.

**League Championship wins (1908–2012)**
HJK Helsinki 25; Haka Valkeakoski 9; HPS Helsinki 9; TPS Turku 8; HIFK Helsinki 7; Tampere United (includes Ilves) 5; KuPS Kuopio 5; Kuusysi Lahti 5; KIF Helsinki 4; AIFK Turku 3; Reipas Lahti 3; VIFK Vaasa 3; Jazz Pori 2; KTP Kotka 2; OPS Oulu 2; VPS Vaasa 2; Unitas Helsinki 1; PUS Helsinki 1; Sudet Viipuri 1; HT Helsinki 1; Pyrkiva Turku 1; KPV Kokkola 1; TPV Tampere 1; MyPa Anjalankoski (renamed MYPA) 1; Inter Turku 1.

**Cup wins (1955–2012)**
Haka Valkeakoski 12; HJK Helsinki 11; Reipas Lahti 7; KTP Kotka 4; MyPa Anjalankoski (renamed MYPA) 3; Tampere United (includes Ilves) 3; TPS Turku 3; KuPS Kuopio 2; Kuusysi Lahti 2; Mikkeli 2; PPojat 1; Drott (renamed Jaro) 1; HPS Helsinki 1; AIFK Turku 1; RoPS Rovaniemi 1; Jokerit (formerly PK-35) 1; Allianssi (formerly Atlantis) 1; Inter Turku1 1; Honka 1.

**Final League Table 2012**

|  | P | W | D | L | F | A | GD | Pts |
|---|---|---|---|---|---|---|---|---|
| HJK Helsinki | 33 | 19 | 7 | 7 | 63 | 33 | 30 | 64 |
| Inter Turku | 33 | 17 | 7 | 9 | 57 | 42 | 15 | 58 |
| TPS Turku | 33 | 16 | 6 | 11 | 55 | 33 | 22 | 54 |
| IFK Mariehamn | 33 | 13 | 12 | 8 | 50 | 43 | 7 | 51 |
| FC Lahti | 33 | 16 | 2 | 15 | 45 | 49 | –4 | 50 |
| MYPA Kouvola | 33 | 13 | 10 | 10 | 39 | 33 | 6 | 49 |
| Honka | 33 | 12 | 7 | 14 | 37 | 38 | –1 | 43 |
| Vaasan PS | 33 | 12 | 7 | 14 | 36 | 38 | –2 | 43 |
| JJK Jyvaskyla | 33 | 12 | 4 | 17 | 54 | 65 | –11 | 40 |
| KuPS Kuopio | 33 | 10 | 6 | 17 | 39 | 53 | –14 | 36 |
| FF Jaro | 33 | 8 | 9 | 16 | 28 | 51 | –23 | 33 |
| Haka Valkeakoski* | 33 | 9 | 5 | 19 | 32 | 57 | –25 | 32 |

*Top scorer:* Sirbiladze (Inter Turku) 17.
*Cup Final:* Honka 1, KuPS 0.

### FRANCE

Federation Francaise de Football, 87 Boulevard de Grenelle, 75738 Paris Cedex 15.
*Founded:* 1919; *National Colours:* Blue shirts, white shorts, red socks.

**International matches 2012–13**
Germany (a) 2-1, Iceland (h) 3-2, Serbia (h) 2-0, Estonia (h) 4-0, England (n) 1-1, Ukraine (n) 2-0, Sweden (n) 0-2, Spain (n) 0-2, Uruguay (h) 0-0, Finland (a) 1-0, Belarus (h) 3-1, Japan (h) 0-1, Spain (a) 1-1, Italy (a) 2-1,

Germany (h) 1-2, Georgia (h) 3-1, Spain (h) 0-1, Uruguay (a) 0-1, Brazil (a) 3-0.

**League Championship wins (1933–2013)**
Saint-Etienne 10; Olympique Marseille 9; Nantes 8; AS Monaco 7; Olympique Lyonnais 7; Stade de Reims 6; Bordeaux 6; OGC Nice 4; Lille OSC (includes Olympique Lillois) 4; Paris Saint-Germain 3; FC Sete 2; Sochaux 2; Racing Club Paris 1; Roubaix-Tourcoing 1; Strasbourg 1; Auxerre 1; Lens 1; Montpellier 1.

**Cup wins (1918–2013)**
Olympique Marseille 10; Paris Saint-Germain 8; Saint-Etienne 6; Lille OSC 6; AS Monaco 5; Racing Club Paris 5; Red Star 5; Olympique Lyonnais 5; Bordeaux 4; Auxerre 4; Strasbourg 3; OGC Nice 3; Nantes 3; CAS Genereaux 2; Montpellier 2; FC Sete 2; Stade de Reims 2; Sedan 2; Stade Rennais 2; Metz 2; Sochaux 2; Olympique de Pantin 1; Lille OSC 1; Club Français 1; AS Cannes 1; Excelsior Roubaix 1; EF Nancy-Lorraine 1; Toulouse 1; Le Havre 1; AS Nancy 1; Bastia 1; Lorient 1; Guingamp 1.

**Final League Table 2012–13**

| | P | W | D | L | F | A | GD | Pts |
|---|---|---|---|---|---|---|---|---|
| Paris Saint-Germain | 38 | 25 | 8 | 5 | 69 | 23 | 46 | 83 |
| Olympique Marseille | 38 | 21 | 8 | 9 | 42 | 36 | 6 | 71 |
| Olympique Lyonnais | 38 | 19 | 10 | 9 | 61 | 38 | 23 | 67 |
| OGC Nice | 38 | 18 | 10 | 10 | 57 | 46 | 11 | 64 |
| Saint-Etienne | 38 | 16 | 15 | 7 | 60 | 32 | 28 | 63 |
| Lille OSC | 38 | 16 | 14 | 8 | 59 | 40 | 19 | 62 |
| Bordeaux | 38 | 13 | 16 | 9 | 40 | 34 | 6 | 55 |
| Lorient | 38 | 14 | 11 | 13 | 57 | 58 | –1 | 53 |
| Montpellier | 38 | 15 | 7 | 16 | 54 | 51 | 3 | 52 |
| Toulouse | 38 | 13 | 12 | 13 | 49 | 47 | 2 | 51 |
| Valenciennes | 38 | 12 | 12 | 14 | 49 | 53 | –4 | 48 |
| Bastia | 38 | 13 | 8 | 17 | 50 | 66 | –16 | 47 |
| Stade Rennais | 38 | 13 | 7 | 18 | 48 | 59 | –11 | 46 |
| Stade de Reims | 38 | 10 | 13 | 15 | 33 | 42 | –9 | 43 |
| Sochaux | 38 | 10 | 11 | 17 | 41 | 57 | –16 | 41 |
| Evian | 38 | 10 | 10 | 18 | 46 | 53 | –7 | 40 |
| Ajaccio (–2) | 38 | 9 | 15 | 14 | 39 | 51 | –12 | 40 |
| AS Nancy* | 38 | 9 | 11 | 18 | 38 | 58 | –20 | 38 |
| Troyes* | 38 | 8 | 13 | 17 | 43 | 61 | –18 | 37 |
| Stade Brest* | 38 | 8 | 5 | 25 | 32 | 62 | –30 | 29 |

*Top scorer:* Ibrahimovic (Paris Saint-Germain) 30.
*Cup Final:* Girondins de Bordeaux 3, Evian 2.

**FYR MACEDONIA**
Football Federation of the Former Yugoslav Republic of Macedonia, VIII-ma Udarna Brigada 31-A, PO Box 84, 1000 Skopje.
*Founded:* 1948; *National Colours:* All red.

**International matches 2012–13**
Luxembourg (a) 1-2, Portugal (a) 0-0, Angola (n) 0-0, Lithuania (h) 1-0, Croatia (a) 0-1, Scotland (a) 1-1, Croatia (h) 1-2, Serbia (h) 1-0, Slovenia (h) 3-2, Poland (a) 1-4, Denmark (h) 3-0, Belgium (h) 0-2, Belgium (a) 0-1, Sweden (a) 0-1, Norway (a) 0-2.

**League Championship wins (1992–2013)**
Vardar 7; Sileks 3; Sloga Jugomagnat 3; Rabotnicki 3; Pobeda 2; Makedonija 1; Renova 1; Skendija 1.

**Cup wins (1992–2013)**
Vardar 5; Sloga Jugomagnat 3; Sileks 2; Rabotnicki 2; Teteks 2; Pelister 1; Pobeda 1; Cementarnica 55 1; Bashkimi 1; Makedonija 1; Metalurg 1; Renova 1.

**Final League Table 2012–13**

| | P | W | D | L | F | A | GD | Pts |
|---|---|---|---|---|---|---|---|---|
| Vardar | 33 | 20 | 8 | 5 | 71 | 21 | 50 | 68 |
| Metalurg | 33 | 18 | 9 | 6 | 48 | 28 | 20 | 63 |
| Turnovo | 33 | 17 | 12 | 4 | 49 | 31 | 18 | 63 |
| Rabotnicki | 33 | 16 | 5 | 12 | 47 | 42 | 5 | 53 |
| Skendija | 33 | 13 | 8 | 12 | 52 | 49 | 3 | 44 |
| Bregalnica Stip | 33 | 12 | 7 | 14 | 37 | 35 | 2 | 43 |
| Napredok | 33 | 12 | 7 | 14 | 29 | 39 | –10 | 43 |
| Renova | 33 | 12 | 7 | 14 | 35 | 46 | –11 | 43 |
| Drita*+ | 33 | 11 | 7 | 15 | 35 | 50 | –15 | 40 |
| Pelister+ | 33 | 9 | 10 | 14 | 27 | 36 | –9 | 37 |
| Teteks* | 33 | 6 | 7 | 20 | 22 | 47 | –25 | 25 |
| Sileks* | 33 | 6 | 5 | 22 | 33 | 61 | –28 | 23 |

Top scorer: Kostovski (Vardar) 22.
*Cup Final:* Skendija 1, Teteks 1.
*Teteks won 6-5 on penalties.*

**GEORGIA**
Georgian Football Federation, 76a Chavchavadze Avenue, 0162 Tbilisi.
*Founded:* 1990; *National Colours:* All white.

**International matches 2012–13**
Albania (h) 2-1, Turkey (h) 1-3, Luxembourg (a) 2-1, Belarus (h) 1-0, Spain (h) 0-1, Finland (a) 0-0, Belarus (a) 0-2, Egypt (h) 0-0, France (a) 1-3, Republic of Ireland (a) 0-4, Denmark (a) 1-2.

**League Championship wins (1990–2013)**
Dinamo Tbilisi 14; Torpedo Kutaisi 3; WIT Georgia 2; Metalurgi Rustavi (formerly Olimpi) 2; Zestafoni 2; Sioni 1.

**Cup wins (1990–2013)**
Dinamo Tbilisi 10; Lokomotivi 3; Torpedo Kutaisi 2; Ameri 2; Guria Lanchkhuti 1; Dinamo Batumi 1; Zestafoni 1; WIT Georgia 1; Gagra 1; Dila Gori 1.

**Qualifying League Table 2012–13**

| | P | W | D | L | F | A | GD | Pts |
|---|---|---|---|---|---|---|---|---|
| Dinamo Tbilisi | 22 | 16 | 4 | 2 | 63 | 19 | 44 | 52 |
| Dila Gori | 22 | 16 | 1 | 5 | 36 | 15 | 21 | 49 |
| Torpedo Kutaisi | 22 | 14 | 3 | 5 | 41 | 18 | 23 | 45 |
| Chikhura Sachkhere | 22 | 13 | 4 | 5 | 35 | 21 | 14 | 43 |
| Zestafoni | 22 | 11 | 4 | 7 | 30 | 20 | 10 | 37 |
| Baia Zugdidi | 22 | 10 | 5 | 7 | 27 | 26 | 1 | 35 |
| Metalurgi Rustavi | 22 | 9 | 4 | 9 | 21 | 26 | –5 | 31 |
| Merani Martvili | 22 | 7 | 2 | 13 | 23 | 36 | –13 | 23 |
| WIT Georgia | 22 | 5 | 7 | 10 | 15 | 29 | –14 | 22 |
| Sioni Bolnisi | 22 | 4 | 6 | 12 | 14 | 38 | –24 | 18 |
| Dinamo Batumi | 22 | 3 | 4 | 15 | 22 | 47 | –25 | 13 |
| Kolkheti Poti | 22 | 0 | 4 | 18 | 11 | 43 | –32 | 4 |

**Championship Table 2012–13**

| | P | W | D | L | F | A | GD | Pts |
|---|---|---|---|---|---|---|---|---|
| Dinamo Tbilisi | 32 | 24 | 6 | 2 | 88 | 23 | 65 | 78 |
| Dila Gori | 32 | 22 | 2 | 8 | 60 | 26 | 34 | 68 |
| Torpedo Kutaisi | 32 | 19 | 7 | 6 | 57 | 30 | 27 | 64 |
| Chikhura Sachkhere | 32 | 17 | 6 | 9 | 49 | 38 | 11 | 57 |
| Zestafoni | 32 | 12 | 6 | 14 | 35 | 38 | –3 | 42 |
| Baia Zugdidi | 32 | 10 | 6 | 16 | 31 | 52 | –21 | 36 |

**Relegation Table 2012–13**

| | P | W | D | L | F | A | GD | Pts |
|---|---|---|---|---|---|---|---|---|
| Metalurgi Rustavi | 32 | 12 | 8 | 12 | 29 | 35 | –6 | 44 |
| Merani Martvili | 32 | 10 | 4 | 18 | 31 | 51 | –20 | 34 |
| WIT Georgia | 32 | 8 | 9 | 15 | 25 | 42 | –17 | 33 |
| Sioni Bolnisi | 32 | 8 | 9 | 15 | 21 | 50 | –20 | 33 |
| Dinamo Batumi* | 32 | 8 | 7 | 17 | 39 | 55 | –16 | 31 |
| Kolkheti Poti* | 32 | 3 | 8 | 21 | 22 | 56 | –34 | 17 |

*Top scorer:* Xisco Munoz (Dinamo Tbilisi) 24.
*Cup Final:* Dinamo Tbilisi 3, Chikhura Sachkhere 1.

**GERMANY**
Deutscher Fussball-Bund, Otto-Fleck-Schneise 6, Postfach 710265, 60492 Frankfurt Am Main.
*Founded:* 1900; *National Colours:* White shirts, black shorts, white socks.

**International matches 2012–13**
France (h) 1-2, Switzerland (a) 3-5, Israel (h) 2-0, Portugal (n) 1-0, Holland (n) 2-1, Denmark (n) 2-1, Greece (n) 4-2, Italy (n) 1-2, Argentina (h) 1-3, Faroe Islands (h) 3-0, Austria (a) 2-1, Republic of Ireland (a) 6-1, Sweden (h) 4-4, Holland (a) 0-0, France (a) 2-1, Kazakhstan (a) 3-0, Kazakhstan (h) 4-1, Ecuador (n) 4-2, USA (a) 4-3.

**League Championship wins (1903–2013)**
Bayern Munich 23; 1.FC Nuremberg 9; Borussia Dortmund 8; Schalke 04 7; Hamburger SV 6; VfB Stuttgart 5; Borussia Moenchengladbach 5; 1.FC Kaiserslautern 4; Werder Bremen 4; VfB Leipzig 3; SpVgg Furth 3; 1.FC Cologne 3; Viktoria Berlin 2; Hertha Berlin 2; Hannover 96 2; Dresden SC 2; Union Berlin 1; Freiburger FC 1; Phoenix Karlsruhe 1; Karlsruher FV 1; Holstein Kiel 1; Fortuna Dusseldorf 1; Rapid Vienna 1; VfR Mannheim 1; Rot-Weiss Essen 1; Eintracht Frankfurt 1; Munich 1860 1; Eintracht Brunswick 1; Wolfsburg 1.

**Cup wins (1935–2013)**
Bayern Munich 16; Werder Bremen 6; 1.FC Cologne 4; Eintracht Frankfurt 4; Schalke 04 5; 1.FC Nuremberg 4; Hamburger SV 3; Borussia Moenchengladbach 3; VfB Stuttgart 3; Borussia Dortmund 3; Dresden SC 2; Fortuna Dusseldorf 2; Karlsruhe SC 2; Munich 1860 2; 1.FC

Kaiserslautern 2; First Vienna 1; VfB Leipzig 1; Kickers
Offenbach 1; Rapid Vienna 1; Rot-Weiss Essen 1; SW
Essen 1; Bayer Uerdingen 1; Hannover 96 1; Leverkusen 1.

**Final League Table 2012–13**

|  | P | W | D | L | F | A | GD | Pts |
|---|---|---|---|---|---|---|---|---|
| Bayern Munich | 34 | 29 | 4 | 1 | 98 | 18 | 80 | 91 |
| Borussia Dortmund | 34 | 19 | 9 | 6 | 81 | 42 | 39 | 66 |
| Leverkusen | 34 | 19 | 8 | 7 | 65 | 39 | 26 | 65 |
| Schalke 04 | 34 | 16 | 7 | 11 | 58 | 50 | 8 | 55 |
| SC Freiburg | 34 | 14 | 9 | 11 | 45 | 40 | 5 | 51 |
| Eintracht Frankfurt | 34 | 14 | 9 | 11 | 49 | 46 | 3 | 51 |
| Hamburger SV | 34 | 14 | 6 | 14 | 42 | 53 | –11 | 48 |
| Borussia Moenchengladbach | 34 | 12 | 11 | 11 | 45 | 49 | –4 | 47 |
| Hannover 96 | 34 | 13 | 6 | 15 | 60 | 62 | –2 | 45 |
| 1. FC Nuremberg | 34 | 11 | 11 | 12 | 39 | 47 | –8 | 44 |
| VfL Wolfsburg | 34 | 10 | 13 | 11 | 47 | 52 | –5 | 43 |
| VfB Stuttgart | 34 | 12 | 7 | 15 | 37 | 55 | –18 | 43 |
| 1. FSV Mainz 05 | 34 | 10 | 12 | 12 | 42 | 44 | –2 | 42 |
| Werder Bremen | 34 | 8 | 10 | 16 | 50 | 66 | –16 | 34 |
| Augsburg | 34 | 8 | 9 | 17 | 33 | 51 | –18 | 33 |
| TSG 1899 Hoffenheim+ | 34 | 8 | 7 | 19 | 42 | 67 | –25 | 31 |
| Fortuna Dusseldorf* | 34 | 7 | 9 | 18 | 39 | 57 | –18 | 30 |
| SpVgg Greuther Fuerth* | 34 | 4 | 9 | 21 | 26 | 60 | –34 | 21 |

*Top scorer:* Kiessling (Bayer Leverkusen) 25.
*Cup Final:* Bayern Munich 3, VfB Stuttgart 2.

### GIBRALTAR

Gibraltar Football Association, 32A Rosia Road, PO
Box 515, Gibraltar.
*Founded:* 1895. *National Colours:* Red shirts with white
trim, red shorts, red socks.

**League Championship wins (1896–2013)**

Prince of Wales 19; Lincoln 18 (incl. Newcastle United 5);
Glacis United 17; Britannia 14; Gibraltar United 11;
Manchester United 7; Europa 6; St Theresas 3; Chief
Construction 2; Jubilee 2; Exiles 2; South United 2;
Gibraltar FC 2; Albion 1; Athletic 1; Royal Sovereign 1;
Commander of the Yard 1; St Joseph's 1.

**Cup wins (1895–2013)**

Lincoln (incl. Newcastle United 4) 13; St Joseph's 9;
Europa 5; Glacis United 5; Britannia 3; Gibraltar United
3; Manchester United 3; Gibraltar FC 1; AARA 1; HMS
Hood 1; 2nd Bn The King's Regt 1; RAF New Camp 1;
4th Bn Royal Scots 1; Prince of Wales 1; Manchester
United Reserves 1; 2nd Bn Royal Green Jackets 1; RAF
Gibraltar 1; Lincoln Reliance 1; St Theresas 1.

**Final League Table 2012–13**

|  | P | W | D | L | F | A | GD | Pts |
|---|---|---|---|---|---|---|---|---|
| Lincoln | 15 | 13 | 2 | 0 | 68 | 13 | 55 | 41 |
| St Joseph's | 15 | 10 | 0 | 5 | 43 | 20 | 23 | 30 |
| Manchester United | 15 | 7 | 2 | 6 | 22 | 31 | –9 | 23 |
| Lynx | 15 | 4 | 2 | 9 | 18 | 42 | –24 | 14 |
| Lions Gibraltar | 15 | 3 | 2 | 10 | 24 | 41 | –17 | 11 |
| Glacis | 15 | 3 | 2 | 10 | 20 | 47 | –27 | 11 |

*Cup Final:* St Joseph's 3, Manchester United 1.

### GOZO

Gozo Football Association. GFA Headquarters, Mgarr
Road, Xewkija, XWK 9014, Malta.
*Founded:* 1936.

**League Championship wins (1938–2013)**

Victoria Hotspurs 11; Nadur Youngsters 11; Sannat Lions
10; Xaghra United 6 (incl. Xaghra Blue Stars 1, Xaghra
Young Stars 1); Salesian Youths 6; Ghajnsielem 6;
Xewkija Tigers 5; Victoria Athletics 4; Victoria Stars 1;
Victoria City 1; Calypcians 1; Victoria United 1; Kercem
Ajax 1; Zebbug Rovers 1.

**Cup wins (1972–2013)**

Sannat Lions 9; Xewkija Tigers 9; Nadur Youngsters 7;
Ghajnsielem 5; Xaghra United 4; Kercem Ajax 2;
Calypcians 1; Calypsians Bosco Youths 1; Victoria
Hotspurs 1; Victoria Wanderers 1; Qala St Joseph 1.

**Final League Table 2012–13**

|  | P | W | D | L | F | A | GD | Pts |
|---|---|---|---|---|---|---|---|---|
| Nadur Youngsters | 18 | 13 | 4 | 1 | 49 | 18 | 31 | 43 |
| Kercem Ajax | 18 | 8 | 8 | 2 | 29 | 19 | 10 | 32 |
| Victoria Wanderers | 18 | 7 | 4 | 7 | 29 | 24 | 5 | 25 |
| Xewkija Tigers | 18 | 6 | 3 | 9 | 40 | 42 | –2 | 21 |
| Victoria Hotspurs | 18 | 6 | 3 | 9 | 27 | 30 | –3 | 21 |
| Xaghra United+ | 18 | 5 | 4 | 9 | 25 | 46 | –21 | 19 |
| Sannat Lions* | 18 | 2 | 6 | 10 | 21 | 41 | –20 | 12 |

*Cup Final:* Kercem Ajax 4, Nadur Youngsters 3.

### GREECE

Hellenic Football Federation, Singrou Avenue 137, 17121
Athens.
*Founded:* 1926; *National Colours:* All white.

**International matches 2012–13**

Belgium (h) 1-1, Slovenia (h) 1-1, Armenia (a) 1-0,
Poland (n) 1-1, Czech Republic (n) 1-2, Russia (n) 1-0,
Germany (n) 2-4, Norway (a) 3-2, Latvia (a) 2-1,
Lithuania (h) 2-0, Bosnia-Herzegovina (h) 0-0, Slovakia
(a) 1-0, Republic of Ireland (a) 1-0, Switzerland (h) 0-0,
Bosnia-Herzegovina (a) 1-3, Lithuania (a) 1-0.

**League Championship wins (1928–2013)**

Olympiakos 40; Panathinaikos 20; AEK Athens 11; Aris
Salonika 3; PAOK Salonika 2; Larissa 1.

**Cup wins (1932–2013)**

Olympiakos 26; Panathinaikos 17; AEK Athens 14;
PAOK Salonika 4; Panionios 2; Larissa 2; Ethnikos 1;
Aris Salonika 1; Iraklis 1; Kastoria 1; OFI Crete 1.

**Final League Table 2012–13**

|  | P | W | D | L | F | A | GD | Pts |
|---|---|---|---|---|---|---|---|---|
| Olympiakos | 30 | 24 | 5 | 1 | 64 | 16 | 48 | 77 |
| PAOK | 30 | 18 | 8 | 4 | 46 | 19 | 27 | 62 |
| Asteras Tripolis | 30 | 17 | 5 | 8 | 41 | 25 | 16 | 56 |
| Atromitos | 30 | 11 | 13 | 6 | 26 | 22 | 4 | 46 |
| PAS Giannina | 30 | 12 | 8 | 10 | 28 | 24 | 4 | 44 |
| Panathinaikos (–2) | 30 | 10 | 12 | 8 | 32 | 30 | 2 | 40 |
| Xanthi | 30 | 10 | 10 | 10 | 28 | 26 | 2 | 40 |
| Panionios GSS | 30 | 11 | 3 | 16 | 35 | 42 | –7 | 36 |
| Platanias | 30 | 10 | 6 | 14 | 29 | 42 | –13 | 36 |
| Panthrakikos | 30 | 10 | 6 | 14 | 30 | 33 | –3 | 36 |
| Levadiakos | 30 | 9 | 7 | 14 | 21 | 35 | –14 | 34 |
| Veria | 30 | 8 | 9 | 13 | 30 | 35 | –5 | 33 |
| Aris | 30 | 7 | 12 | 11 | 32 | 40 | –8 | 33 |
| OFI Crete | 30 | 8 | 8 | 14 | 33 | 46 | –13 | 32 |
| AEK Athens* (–3) | 30 | 8 | 6 | 16 | 21 | 36 | –15 | 27 |
| Kerkyra* | 30 | 4 | 8 | 18 | 16 | 41 | –25 | 20 |

*Top scorer:* Djebbour (Olympiakos) 20.
*Cup Final:* Olympiakos 3, Asteras Tripolis 1.

### HOLLAND

Koninklijke Nederlandse Voetbalbond,
Woudenbergseweg 56–58, Postbus 515, 3700 AM Zeist.
*Founded:* 1889; *National Colours:* All orange.

**International matches 2012–13**

England (a) 3-2, Bulgaria (h) 1-2, Slovakia (h) 2-0,
Northern Ireland (h) 6-0, Denmark (n) 0-1, Germany (n)
1-2, Portugal (n) 2-1, Belgium (a) 2-4, Turkey (h) 2-0,
Hungary (a) 4-1, Andorra (h) 3-0, Romania (a) 4-1,
Germany (h) 0-0, Italy (h) 1-1, Estonia (h) 3-0, Romania
(h) 4-0, Indonesia (a) 3-0, China PR (a) 2-0.

**League Championship wins (1889–2013)**

Ajax Amsterdam 32; PSV Eindhoven 21; Feyenoord 14;
HVV The Hague 8; Sparta Rotterdam 6; RAP
Amsterdam 5; Go Ahead Eagles Deventer 4; HFC
Haarlem 3; HBS Craeyenhout 3; Willem II Tilburg 3;
RCH Heemstede 2; Heracles 2; ADO The Hague 2;
AZ 67 Alkmaar 2; VV Concordia 1; Quick The Hague 1;
Be Quick Groningen 1; NAC Breda 1; SC Enschede 1;
Volewijckers Amsterdam 1; Haarlem 1; BVV Den Bosch
1; Schiedam 1; Limburgia 1; EVV Eindhoven 1; Willem II
Rapid JC Den Heerlen 1; DOS Utrecht 1; DWS
Amsterdam 1; FC Twente 1.

**Cup wins (1899–2013)**

Ajax Amsterdam 18; Feyenoord 11; PSV Eindhoven 9;
Quick The Hague 4; AZ 67 Alkmaar 4; HFC Haarlem 3;
Sparta Rotterdam 3; Twente 3; Utrecht 3; Haarlem 2;
VOC 2; HBS Craeyenhout 2; DFC 2; RCH Haarlem 2;
Wageningen 2; Willem II Tilburg 2; Fortuna 54 2; FC
Den Haag (includes ADO) 2; Roda JC 2; RAP
Amsterdam 1; Velocitas Breda 1; HVV The Hague 1;
Concordia Delft 1; CVV 1; Schoten 1; ZFC Zaandam 1;
Longa 1; VUC 1; Velocitas Groningen 1; Roermond 1;
FC Eindhoven 1; VSV 1; Quick 1888 Nijmegen 1; VVV
Groningen 1; NAC Breda 1; Heerenveen 1.

**Final League Table 2012–13**

|  | P | W | D | L | F | A | GD | Pts |
|---|---|---|---|---|---|---|---|---|
| Ajax | 34 | 22 | 10 | 2 | 83 | 31 | 52 | 76 |
| PSV Eindhoven | 34 | 22 | 3 | 9 | 103 | 43 | 60 | 69 |
| Feyenoord | 34 | 21 | 6 | 7 | 64 | 38 | 26 | 69 |
| Vitesse | 34 | 19 | 7 | 8 | 68 | 42 | 26 | 64 |
| Utrecht | 34 | 19 | 6 | 9 | 55 | 41 | 14 | 63 |

| | P | W | D | L | F | A | GD | Pts |
|---|---|---|---|---|---|---|---|---|
| FC Twente | 34 | 17 | 11 | 6 | 60 | 33 | 27 | 62 |
| FC Groningen | 34 | 12 | 7 | 15 | 36 | 53 | -17 | 43 |
| Heerenveen | 34 | 11 | 9 | 14 | 50 | 63 | -13 | 42 |
| ADO Den Haag | 34 | 9 | 13 | 12 | 49 | 63 | -14 | 40 |
| AZ Alkmaar | 34 | 10 | 9 | 15 | 56 | 54 | 2 | 39 |
| PEC Zwolle | 34 | 10 | 9 | 15 | 42 | 55 | -13 | 39 |
| Heracles Almelo | 34 | 9 | 11 | 14 | 58 | 71 | -13 | 38 |
| NAC Breda | 34 | 10 | 8 | 16 | 40 | 56 | -16 | 38 |
| RKC Waalwijk | 34 | 9 | 10 | 15 | 39 | 48 | -9 | 37 |
| NEC Nijmegen | 34 | 10 | 7 | 17 | 44 | 66 | -22 | 37 |
| Roda JC+ | 34 | 7 | 12 | 15 | 51 | 69 | -18 | 33 |
| VVV-Venlo*+ | 34 | 6 | 10 | 18 | 33 | 62 | -29 | 28 |
| Willem II* | 34 | 5 | 8 | 21 | 33 | 76 | -43 | 23 |

*Top scorer:* Bony (Vitesse) 31.
*Cup Final:* AZ Alkmaar 2, PSV Eindhoven 1.

## HUNGARY

Hungarian Football Federation, Koerberek Tovaros Kanai ut 314/24 hrsz., 1112 Budapest.
*Founded:* 1901; *National Colours:* Red shirts, white shorts, green socks.

### International matches 2012–13
Bulgaria (h) 1-1, Czech Republic (a) 2-1, Republic of Ireland (h) 0-0, Israel (h) 1-1, Andorra (a) 5-0, Holland (h) 1-4, Estonia (a) 1-0, Turkey (h) 3-1, Norway (h) 0-2, Belarus (h) 1-1, Romania (h) 2-2, Turkey (a) 1-1, Kuwait (h) 1-0.

### League Championship wins (1901–2013)
Ferencvaros 28; MTK-Hungaria Budapest 23; Ujpest 20; Budapest Honved 13 (incl. Kispest Honved); Vasas Budapest 6; Debrecen 6; Csepel 4; Gyori ETO 4; BTC 2; Nagyvarad 1; Vac 1; Dunaferr (renamed Dunaujvaros) 1; Zalaegerszeg 1; Videoton 1.

### Cup wins (1910–2013)
Ferencvaros 20; MTK-Hungaria Budapest 12; Ujpest 8; Budapest Honved 7 (inc. Kispest Honved); Debrecen 6; Vasas Budapest 4; Gyori ETO 4; Diosgyor 2; Bocskai 1; III Ker 1; Soroksar 1; Szolnoki MAV 1; Siofoki Banyasz 1; Bekescsaba 1; Pecsi 1; Matav 1; Fehervar (renamed Videoton) 1; Kecskemet 1.
*Cup not regularly held until 1964.*

### Final League Table 2012–13
| | P | W | D | L | F | A | GD | Pts |
|---|---|---|---|---|---|---|---|---|
| Gyori ETO | 30 | 19 | 7 | 4 | 57 | 33 | 24 | 64 |
| Videoton | 30 | 16 | 6 | 8 | 52 | 24 | 28 | 54 |
| Budapest Honved | 30 | 15 | 7 | 8 | 50 | 36 | 14 | 52 |
| MTK Budapest | 30 | 15 | 6 | 9 | 43 | 30 | 13 | 51 |
| Ferencvaros | 30 | 13 | 10 | 7 | 51 | 36 | 15 | 49 |
| Debrecen | 30 | 14 | 4 | 12 | 47 | 36 | 11 | 46 |
| Kecskemet | 30 | 12 | 8 | 10 | 42 | 42 | 0 | 44 |
| Szombathelyi Haladas | 30 | 11 | 11 | 8 | 36 | 27 | 9 | 44 |
| Ujpest | 30 | 11 | 8 | 11 | 40 | 42 | -2 | 41 |
| Diosgyor | 30 | 9 | 11 | 10 | 31 | 39 | -8 | 38 |
| Kaposvari Rakoczi | 30 | 10 | 7 | 13 | 35 | 38 | -3 | 37 |
| Pecs | 30 | 10 | 7 | 13 | 33 | 44 | -11 | 37 |
| Paks | 30 | 8 | 11 | 11 | 40 | 38 | 2 | 35 |
| Lombard-Papa | 30 | 7 | 7 | 16 | 26 | 46 | -20 | 28 |
| BFC Siofok* | 30 | 7 | 4 | 19 | 31 | 61 | -30 | 25 |
| Eger* | 30 | 3 | 6 | 21 | 25 | 67 | -42 | 15 |

*Top scorer:* Coulibaly (Debrecen) 18.
*Cup Final:* Debrecen 2, Gyori ETO 1.

## ICELAND

Knattspyrnusamband Islands, Laugardal, 104 Reykjavik.
*Founded:* 1929; *National Colours:* All blue.

### International matches 2012–13
Japan (a) 1-3, Montenegro (a) 1-2, France (a) 2-3, Sweden (a) 2-3, Faroe Islands (h) 2-0, Norway (h) 2-0, Cyprus (a) 0-1, Albania (a) 2-1, Switzerland (h) 0-2, Andorra (a) 2-0, Russia (h) 0-2, Slovenia (a) 2-1, Slovenia (h) 2-4.

### League Championship wins (1912–2012)
KR Reykjavik 25; Valur 20; Fram 18; IA Akranes 18; FH Hafnarfjordur 6; Vikingur 5; IBK Keflavik 4; IBV Vestmannaeyjar 3; KA Akureyri 1; Breidablik 1.

### Cup wins (1960–2012)
KR Reykjavik 13; Valur 9; IA Akranes 9; Fram 7; IBV Vestmannaeyjar 4; IBK Keflavik 4; Fylkir 2; FH Hafnarfjordur 2; IBA Akureyri 1; Vikingur 1; Breidablik 1.

### Final League Table 2012
| | P | W | D | L | F | A | GD | Pts |
|---|---|---|---|---|---|---|---|---|
| FH Hafnarfjordur | 22 | 15 | 4 | 3 | 51 | 23 | 28 | 49 |
| Breidablik | 22 | 10 | 6 | 6 | 32 | 27 | 5 | 36 |
| IBV Vestmannaeyjar | 22 | 10 | 5 | 7 | 36 | 21 | 15 | 35 |
| KR Reykjavik | 22 | 10 | 5 | 7 | 39 | 32 | 7 | 35 |
| Stjarnan | 22 | 8 | 10 | 4 | 44 | 38 | 6 | 34 |
| IA Akranes | 22 | 9 | 5 | 8 | 32 | 36 | -4 | 32 |
| Fylkir | 22 | 8 | 7 | 7 | 30 | 39 | -9 | 31 |
| Valur | 22 | 9 | 1 | 12 | 34 | 34 | 0 | 28 |
| Keflavík | 22 | 8 | 3 | 11 | 35 | 38 | -3 | 27 |
| Fram | 22 | 8 | 3 | 11 | 31 | 36 | -5 | 27 |
| Selfoss* | 22 | 6 | 3 | 13 | 30 | 44 | -14 | 21 |
| Grindavík* | 22 | 5 | 6 | 14 | 31 | 57 | -26 | 12 |

*Top scorer:* Gudnason (FH Hafnarfjordur) 12.
*Cup Final:* Stjarnan 1, KR Reykjavik 2.

## REPUBLIC OF IRELAND

Football Association of Ireland (Cumann Peile na hEireann), National Sports Campus, Abbotstown, Dublin 15.
*Founded:* 1921; *National Colours:* Green shirts, white shorts, green socks.

### League Championship wins (1922–2012)
Shamrock Rovers 17; Shelbourne 13; Bohemians 10; Dundalk 9; Cork Athletic (formerly Cork United) 7; St Patrick's Athletic 7; Waterford United 6; Drumcondra 5; Sligo Rovers 3; St James's Gate 2; Limerick 2; Athlone Town 2; Derry City 2; Cork City 2; Dolphin 1; Cork Hibernians 1; Cork Celtic 1; Drogheda United 1.

### Cup wins (1922–2012)
Shamrock Rovers 24; Dundalk 9; Bohemians 8; Shelbourne 7; Drumcondra 5; Derry City 5; Cork Athletic (formerly Cork United) 4; Sligo Rovers 4; St James's Gate 2; Waterford United 2; St Patrick's Athletic 2; Limerick 2; Cork Hibernians 2; Bray Wanderers 2; Cork City 2; Longford Town 2; Alton United 1; Athlone Town 1; Fordsons 1; Cork 1; Transport 1; Finn Harps 1; Home Farm 1; UC Dublin 1; Galway United 1; Drogheda United 1; Sporting Fingal 1.

### Final League Table 2012
| | P | W | D | L | F | A | GD | Pts |
|---|---|---|---|---|---|---|---|---|
| Sligo Rovers | 30 | 17 | 10 | 3 | 53 | 23 | 30 | 61 |
| Drogheda United | 30 | 17 | 6 | 7 | 51 | 36 | 15 | 57 |
| St Patrick's Athletic | 30 | 15 | 10 | 5 | 44 | 22 | 22 | 55 |
| Shamrock Rovers | 30 | 14 | 10 | 6 | 56 | 37 | 19 | 52 |
| Derry City | 30 | 11 | 6 | 13 | 36 | 36 | 0 | 39 |
| Cork City | 30 | 8 | 12 | 10 | 38 | 36 | 2 | 36 |
| Bohemians | 30 | 9 | 9 | 12 | 35 | 38 | -3 | 36 |
| Shelbourne | 30 | 9 | 8 | 13 | 35 | 43 | -8 | 35 |
| UC Dublin | 30 | 8 | 7 | 15 | 32 | 48 | -16 | 31 |
| Bray Wanderers | 30 | 5 | 10 | 15 | 33 | 54 | -21 | 25 |
| Dundalk+ | 30 | 4 | 8 | 18 | 23 | 63 | -40 | 20 |

*Monaghan United withdrew after 14 games and their record was expunged.*
*Top scorer:* Twigg (Shamrock Rovers) 22.
*Cup Final:* Derry City 3, St Patrick's Athletic 2.

## ISRAEL

Israel Football Association, Ramat-Gan Stadium, 299 Aba Hilell Street, Ramat-Gan 52134.
*Founded:* 1948; *National Colours:* Blue shirts, white shorts, blue socks.

### International matches 2012–13
Ukraine (h) 2-3, Czech Republic (a) 2-1, Germany (a) 0-2, Hungary (a) 1-1, Azerbaijan (a) 1-1, Russia (h) 0-4, Luxembourg (a) 6-0, Luxembourg (h) 3-0, Belarus (h) 1-2, Finland (h) 2-1, Portugal (h) 3-3, Northern Ireland (a) 2-0, Honduras (n) 2-0.

### League Championship wins (1932–2013)
Maccabi Tel Aviv 19; Hapoel Tel Aviv 13; Maccabi Haifa 12; Hapoel Petah Tikva 6; Beitar Jerusalem 6; Maccabi Netanya 5; Hakoah Ramat Gan 2; Hapoel Beersheba 2; British Police 1; Hapoel Ramat Gan 1; Hapoel Kfar Saba 1; Bnei Yehuda 1; Hapoel Haifa 1; Ironi Kiryat Shmona 1.

### Cup wins (1928–2013)
Maccabi Tel Aviv 22; Hapoel Tel Aviv 15; Beitar Jerusalem 7; Maccabi Haifa 5; Hapoel Haifa 3; Hapoel Kfar Saba 3; Maccabi Petah Tikva 2; Beitar Tel Aviv 2; Hapoel Petah Tikva 2; Bnei Yehuda 2; Hakoah Amidar Ramat Gan 2; Hapoel Ramat Gan 2; Maccabi Hashmonai Jerusalem 1; British Police 1; Hapoel Jerusalem 1; Maccabi Netanya 1; Hapoel Yehud 1; Hapoel Lod 1; Hapoel Beersheba 1; Bnei Sakhnin 1.

**Qualifying League Table 2012–13**

| | P | W | D | L | F | A | GD | Pts |
|---|---|---|---|---|---|---|---|---|
| Maccabi Tel Aviv | 26 | 19 | 2 | 5 | 61 | 20 | 41 | 59 |
| Maccabi Haifa | 26 | 14 | 7 | 5 | 41 | 20 | 21 | 49 |
| Ironi Kiryat Shmona | 26 | 11 | 10 | 5 | 34 | 25 | 9 | 43 |
| Hapoel Tel Aviv | 26 | 12 | 6 | 8 | 33 | 29 | 4 | 42 |
| Bnei Yehuda Tel Aviv | 26 | 11 | 5 | 10 | 35 | 31 | 4 | 38 |
| Ironi Nir Ramat HaSharon | 26 | 11 | 4 | 11 | 28 | 30 | –2 | 37 |
| FC Ashdod | 26 | 10 | 5 | 11 | 30 | 30 | 0 | 35 |
| Beitar Jerusalem | 26 | 8 | 9 | 9 | 36 | 42 | –6 | 33 |
| Hapoel Beer Sheva | 26 | 7 | 9 | 10 | 23 | 35 | –12 | 30 |
| Hapoel Haifa | 26 | 6 | 10 | 10 | 28 | 40 | –12 | 28 |
| Maccabi Netanya | 26 | 6 | 9 | 11 | 32 | 39 | –7 | 27 |
| Bnei Sakhnin | 26 | 6 | 8 | 12 | 25 | 45 | –20 | 26 |
| Hapoel Ramat Gan | 26 | 6 | 7 | 13 | 32 | 39 | –7 | 25 |
| Hapoel Ironi Acre | 26 | 5 | 9 | 12 | 29 | 42 | –13 | 24 |

**Championship Play-Off Table 2012–13**

| | P | W | D | L | F | A | GD | Pts |
|---|---|---|---|---|---|---|---|---|
| Maccabi Tel Aviv | 36 | 25 | 5 | 6 | 78 | 30 | 48 | 80 |
| Maccabi Haifa | 36 | 19 | 10 | 7 | 62 | 33 | 29 | 67 |
| Hapoel Tel Aviv | 36 | 17 | 7 | 12 | 47 | 45 | 2 | 58 |
| Bnei Yehuda Tel Avi | 36 | 16 | 7 | 13 | 50 | 40 | 10 | 55 |
| Ironi Kiryat Shmona | 36 | 14 | 11 | 11 | 45 | 38 | 7 | 53 |
| Ironi Nir Ramat HaSharon | 36 | 12 | 4 | 20 | 31 | 50 | –19 | 40 |

**Relegation Table 2012–13**

| | P | W | D | L | F | A | GD | Pts |
|---|---|---|---|---|---|---|---|---|
| FC Ashdod | 33 | 12 | 7 | 14 | 38 | 40 | –2 | 43 |
| Hapoel Beer Sheva | 33 | 10 | 11 | 12 | 32 | 39 | –7 | 41 |
| Hapoel Haifa | 33 | 9 | 12 | 12 | 36 | 45 | –9 | 39 |
| Beitar Jerusalem | 33 | 9 | 12 | 12 | 44 | 54 | –10 | 39 |
| Hapoel Ironi Acre | 33 | 8 | 13 | 12 | 39 | 48 | –9 | 37 |
| Bnei Sakhnin | 33 | 8 | 13 | 12 | 31 | 49 | –18 | 37 |
| Maccabi Netanya* | 33 | 8 | 11 | 14 | 38 | 50 | –12 | 35 |
| Hapoel Ramat Gan* | 33 | 7 | 9 | 17 | 37 | 47 | –10 | 30 |

*Top scorer:* Atar (Maccabi Tel Aviv) 22.
*Cup Final:* Ironi Kiryat Shmona 1, Hapoel Ramat Gan 1.
*Hapoel Ramat Gan won 4-2 on penalties.*

## ITALY

Federazione Italiana Giuoco Calcio, Via Gregorio Allegri 14, CP 2450, 00198 Roma.
*Founded:* 1898; *National Colours:* Blue shirts, white shorts, blue socks.

**International matches 2012–13**
USA (h) 1-2, Russia (h) 0-3, Spain (n) 1-1, Croatia (n) 1-1, Republic of Ireland (n) 2-0, England (n) 0-0 (4-2p), Germany (n) 2-1, Spain (n) 0-4, England (a) 1-2, Bulgaria (a) 2-2, Malta (h) 2-0, Armenia (a) 3-1, Denmark (h) 3-1, France (h) 1-2, Holland (a) 1-1, Brazil (h) 2-2, Malta (a) 2-0, San Marino (h) 4-0, Czech Republic (a) 0-0, Haiti (h) 2-2, Mexico (n) 2-1, Japan (n) 4-3, Brazil (n) 2-4, Spain (n) 0-0 (6-7p), Uruguay (n) 2-2 (3-2p).

**League Championship wins (1898–2013)**
Juventus 29 (excludes two titles revoked); AC Milan 18; Internazionale 18 (includes one title awarded); Genoa 9; Pro Vercelli 7; Bologna 7; Torino 7 (excludes one title revoked); Roma 3; Fiorentina 2; Lazio 2; Napoli 2; Casale 1; Novese 1; Cagliari 1; Verona 1; Sampdoria 1.

**Cup wins (1928–2013)**
Juventus 9; Roma 9; Internazionale 7; Fiorentina 6; Lazio 6; Torino 5; AC Milan 5; Napoli 4; Sampdoria 4; Parma 3; Bologna 2; Vado 1; Genoa 1; Venezia 1; Atalanta 1; Vicenza 1.

**Final League Table 2012–13**

| | P | W | D | L | F | A | GD | Pts |
|---|---|---|---|---|---|---|---|---|
| Juventus | 38 | 27 | 6 | 5 | 71 | 24 | 47 | 87 |
| Napoli | 38 | 23 | 9 | 6 | 73 | 36 | 37 | 78 |
| AC Milan | 38 | 21 | 9 | 8 | 67 | 39 | 28 | 72 |
| Fiorentina | 38 | 21 | 7 | 10 | 72 | 44 | 28 | 70 |
| Udinese | 38 | 18 | 12 | 8 | 59 | 45 | 14 | 66 |
| Roma | 38 | 18 | 8 | 12 | 71 | 56 | 15 | 62 |
| Lazio | 38 | 18 | 7 | 13 | 51 | 42 | 9 | 61 |
| Catania | 38 | 15 | 11 | 12 | 50 | 46 | 4 | 56 |
| Internazionale | 38 | 16 | 6 | 16 | 55 | 57 | –2 | 54 |
| Parma | 38 | 13 | 10 | 15 | 45 | 46 | –1 | 49 |
| Cagliari | 38 | 12 | 11 | 15 | 43 | 55 | –12 | 47 |
| Chievo | 38 | 12 | 9 | 17 | 37 | 52 | –15 | 45 |
| Bologna | 38 | 11 | 11 | 16 | 46 | 52 | –6 | 44 |
| Sampdoria (–1) | 38 | 11 | 10 | 17 | 43 | 51 | –8 | 42 |
| Atalanta (–2) | 38 | 11 | 9 | 18 | 39 | 56 | –17 | 40 |
| Torino (–1) | 38 | 8 | 16 | 14 | 46 | 55 | –9 | 39 |
| Genoa | 38 | 8 | 14 | 16 | 38 | 52 | –14 | 38 |
| Palermo* | 38 | 6 | 14 | 18 | 34 | 54 | –20 | 32 |

| AC Siena* (–6) | 38 | 9 | 9 | 20 | 36 | 57 | –21 | 30 |
|---|---|---|---|---|---|---|---|---|
| Pescara* | 38 | 6 | 4 | 28 | 27 | 84 | –57 | 22 |

*Top scorer:* Cavani (Napoli) 29.
*Cup Final:* Roma 0, Lazio 1.

## KAZAKHSTAN

Football Federation of Kazakhstan, 29 Syganak Str., 14th floor, 010000 Astana.
*Founded:* 1914; *National Colours:* All blue.

**International matches 2012–13**
Latvia (a) 0-0, Kyrgyzstan (h) 5-2, Armenia (a) 0-3, Republic of Ireland (h) 1-2, Sweden (a) 0-2, Austria (h) 0-0, Austria (a) 0-4, Moldova (a) 3-1, Germany (h) 0-3, Germany (a) 1-4, Bulgaria (h) 1-2.

**League Championship wins (1992–2012)**
Irtysh (includes Ansat) 5; Aktobe 4; Yelimay (renamed Semey) 3; FC Astana-64 (incl. Zhenis) 3; Kairat 2; Shakhter Karagandy 2; Taraz 1; Tobol 1.

**Cup wins (1992–2012)**
Kairat 5; FC Astana-64 (incl. Zhenis) 3; Astana (incl. Lokomotiv) 2; Dostyk 1; Vostok 1; Yelimay (renamed Semey) 1; Irtysh 1; Kaisar 1; Taraz 1; Almaty 1; Tobol 1; Aktobe 1; Atirau 1; Ordabasy 1.

**Final League Table 2012**

| | P | W | D | L | F | A | GD | Pts |
|---|---|---|---|---|---|---|---|---|
| Shakhter Karagandy | 26 | 17 | 2 | 7 | 48 | 15 | 33 | 53 |
| Irtysh | 26 | 15 | 6 | 5 | 46 | 20 | 26 | 51 |
| Aktobe | 26 | 15 | 5 | 6 | 44 | 22 | 22 | 50 |
| Taraz | 26 | 14 | 4 | 8 | 32 | 30 | 2 | 46 |
| Astana | 26 | 13 | 7 | 6 | 34 | 24 | 10 | 46 |
| Tobol | 26 | 13 | 6 | 7 | 42 | 27 | 15 | 45 |
| Ordabasy | 26 | 10 | 9 | 7 | 29 | 24 | 5 | 39 |
| Akzhayik | 26 | 10 | 4 | 12 | 34 | 39 | –5 | 34 |
| Kaisar | 26 | 8 | 6 | 12 | 21 | 33 | –12 | 30 |
| Kairat | 26 | 7 | 8 | 11 | 23 | 34 | –11 | 29 |
| Atyrau | 26 | 7 | 6 | 13 | 16 | 32 | –16 | 27 |
| Zhetysu | 26 | 6 | 5 | 15 | 27 | 45 | –18 | 23 |
| Sunkar* | 26 | 5 | 8 | 13 | 16 | 31 | –15 | 23 |
| Okzhetpes* | 26 | 3 | 2 | 21 | 20 | 56 | –36 | 11 |

*Top scorer:* Bakaev (Irtysh) 14.
*Cup Final:* Astana 2, Irtysh 0.

## KOSOVO

Football Federation of Kosovo, Agim Ramadani 45, Prishtina, Kosovo 10000.
*Founded:* 1948; *National Colours:* Blue shirts, white shorts, blue socks.

**League Championship wins (1945–2013)**
Prishtina 14; Vellaznimi 9; KF Trepca 7; Liria 5; Buduqnosti 4; Rudari 3; Red Star 3; Besa 3; Jedinstvo 2; Kosova Prishtina 2; Slloga 2; Obiliqi 2; Fushe-Kosova 2; Proletari 1; KXEK Kosova 1; Rudniku 1; KNI Ramiz Sadiku 1; Dukagjini 1; Besiana 1; Drita 1; Hysi 1.

**Cup wins (1992–2012)**
Liria 3; Flamurtari 2; Besa 2; Prishtina 2; KF Trepca 1; KF 2 Korriku 1; Gjilani 1; Drita 1; Besiana 1; KEK-u 1; Kosova Prishtina 1; Vellaznimi 1; Hysi 1; Trepca'89 1.

**Final League Table 2012–13**

| | P | W | D | L | F | A | GD | Pts |
|---|---|---|---|---|---|---|---|---|
| Prishtina | 33 | 22 | 7 | 4 | 66 | 26 | 40 | 73 |
| Trepca'89 | 33 | 16 | 10 | 7 | 43 | 25 | 18 | 58 |
| Besa | 33 | 14 | 9 | 10 | 35 | 32 | –7 | 51 |
| Hajvalia | 33 | 12 | 10 | 11 | 43 | 40 | 3 | 46 |
| Feronikeli | 33 | 12 | 10 | 11 | 43 | 45 | –12 | 46 |
| KF Trepca | 33 | 12 | 9 | 12 | 35 | 34 | 1 | 45 |
| Drita | 33 | 11 | 12 | 10 | 44 | 45 | –1 | 45 |
| Drenica | 33 | 10 | 13 | 10 | 37 | 39 | –2 | 43 |
| Kosova | 33 | 10 | 12 | 11 | 41 | 34 | 7 | 42 |
| Hysi | 33 | 11 | 9 | 13 | 35 | 31 | 4 | 42 |
| Vellaznimi* | 33 | 6 | 9 | 18 | 23 | 43 | –20 | 27 |
| Liria* | 33 | 2 | 10 | 21 | 22 | 58 | –36 | 16 |

## LATVIA

Latvijas Futbola Federacija, Olympic Sports Centre, Grostonas Street 6b, 1013 Riga.
*Founded:* 1921; *National Colours:* All carmine red.

**International matches 2012–13**
Kazakhstan (h) 0-0, Poland (a) 0-1, Lithuania (n) 5-0, Finland (n) 1-1 (6-5p), Montenegro (a) 0-2, Greece (h) 1-2, Bosnia-Herzegovina (a) 1-4, Slovakia (a) 1-2, Liechtenstein (h) 2-0, Japan (a) 0-3, Liechtenstein (a) 1-1, Qatar (a) 1-3, Turkey (a) 3-3, Bosnia-Herzegovina (a) 0-5.

**League Championship wins (1922–2012)**
Skonto Riga 15; ASK Riga (incl. AVN 2) 11; RFK Riga 8; Sarkanais Metalurgs Liepaya 8; Olympija Liepaya 7; VEF Riga 6; Energija Riga (incl. ESR Riga 2) 4; Elektrons Riga (incl. Alfa 1) 4; FK Ventspils 4; Torpedo Riga 3; Keisermezhs Riga 2; Khimikis Daugavpils 2; Daugava Liepaya 2; RAF Yelgava 2; Liepajas Metalurgs 2; Dinamo Riga 1; Zhmilyeva Team 1; Darba Rezervi 1; RER Riga 1; Starts Brotseni 1; Venta Ventspils 1; Jumieks Riga 1; Gauja Valmiera 1; Daugava Daugavpils 1.

**Cup wins (1937–2013)**
Skonto Riga 8; Elektrons Riga 7; FK Ventspils 6; Sarkanais Metalurgs Liepaya 5; VEF Riga 3; ASK Riga 3; Tseltnieks Riga 3; RAF Yelgava 3; RFK Riga 2; Daugava Liepaya 2; Starts Brotseni 2; Selmash Liepaya 2; Yurnieks Riga 2; Khimikis Daugavpils 2; Rigas Vilki 1; Dinamo Liepaya 1; Dinamo Riga 1; RER Riga 1; Voulkan Kouldiga 1; Baltika Liepaya 1; Venta Ventspils 1; Pilots Riga 1; Lielupe Yurmala 1; Energija Riga (formerly ESR Riga)1; Torpedo Riga 1; Daugava SKIF Riga 1; Tseltnieks Daugavpils 1; Olympija Riga 1; FK Riga 1; Liepajas Metalurgs 1; Daugava Daugavpils 1; Jelgava 1.

**Final League Table 2012**

| | P | W | D | L | F | A | GD | Pts |
|---|---|---|---|---|---|---|---|---|
| Daugava Daugavpils | 36 | 23 | 9 | 4 | 64 | 25 | 39 | 78 |
| Skonto | 36 | 21 | 11 | 4 | 58 | 22 | 36 | 74 |
| Ventspils | 36 | 23 | 5 | 8 | 63 | 22 | 41 | 74 |
| Liepajas Metalurgs | 36 | 21 | 7 | 8 | 60 | 33 | 27 | 70 |
| Spartaks | 36 | 13 | 10 | 13 | 61 | 56 | 5 | 49 |
| Jurmala | 36 | 10 | 9 | 17 | 47 | 49 | –2 | 39 |
| Jelgava | 36 | 7 | 10 | 19 | 32 | 56 | –24 | 31 |
| Metta/LU | 36 | 7 | 8 | 21 | 39 | 82 | –43 | 29 |
| Daugava Riga+ | 36 | 5 | 12 | 19 | 42 | 79 | –37 | 27 |
| Gulbene* | 36 | 5 | 9 | 22 | 28 | 70 | –42 | 24 |

*Top scorer:* Ghonghadze (Daugava Daugavpils) 18.
*Cup Final:* Liepajas Metalurgs 1, Ventspils 2.

## LIECHTENSTEIN

Liechtensteiner Fussballverband, Landstrasse 149, 9494 Schaan.
*Founded:* 1934; *National Colours:* Blue shirts, red shorts, blue socks.

**International matches 2012–13**
Malta (a) 1-2, Andorra (h) 1-0, Bosnia-Herzegovina (h) 1-8, Slovakia (a) 0-2, Lithuania (h) 0-2, Latvia (a) 0-2, Malta (h) 0-1, Azerbaijan (a) 0-1, Latvia (h) 1-1, Poland (a) 0-2, Slovakia (h) 1-1.
*Liechtenstein has no national league. Teams compete in Swiss regional leagues.*

**Cup wins (1937–2013)**
Vaduz 41; Balzers 11; Triesen 8; USV Eschen/Mauren 5; Schaan 3.
*Cup Final:* Balzers 1, Vaduz 1.
*Vaduz won 3-0 on penalties.*

## LITHUANIA

Lithuanian Football Federation, Stadiono g. 2, 02106 Vilnius.
*Founded:* 1922; *National Colours:* Yellow shirts, green shorts, yellow socks.

**International matches 2012–13**
Russia (h) 0-0, Latvia (n) 0-5, Estonia (a) 0-1, Belarus (a) 1-1, FYR Macedonia (a) 0-1, Slovakia (h) 1-1, Greece (a) 0-2, Liechtenstein (a) 2-0, Bosnia-Herzegovina (a) 0-3, Armenia (a) 2-4, Slovakia (a) 1-1, Greece (h) 0-1.

**League Championship wins (1990–2012)**
FBK Kaunas 8 (including Zalgiris Kaunas 1); Ekranas 7; Zalgiris Vilnius (renamed VMFD Zalgiris) 3; Inkaras Kaunas 2; Kareda 2; Sirijus Klaipeda 1; Mazeikiai 1.

**Cup wins (1990–2013)**
Zalgiris Vilnius (renamed VMFD Zalgiris) 7; Ekranas 4; FBK Kaunas 4; Kareda 2; Atlantas 2; Suduva 2; Sirijus Klaipeda 1; Lietuvos Makabi Vilnius 1; Inkaras Kaunas 1.

**Final League Table 2012**

| | P | W | D | L | F | A | GD | Pts |
|---|---|---|---|---|---|---|---|---|
| Ekranas | 36 | 27 | 7 | 2 | 83 | 25 | +58 | 88 |
| Zalgiris | 36 | 27 | 6 | 3 | 80 | 22 | +58 | 87 |
| Suduva | 36 | 21 | 7 | 8 | 77 | 37 | +40 | 70 |
| Kruoja | 36 | 20 | 5 | 11 | 56 | 31 | +25 | 65 |
| Siauliai | 36 | 17 | 4 | 15 | 79 | 57 | +22 | 55 |
| Banga | 36 | 13 | 8 | 15 | 43 | 41 | +2 | 47 |

| Dainava | 36 | 9 | 5 | 22 | 42 | 71 | –29 | 32 |
|---|---|---|---|---|---|---|---|---|
| Atlantas | 36 | 7 | 6 | 23 | 33 | 92 | –59 | 27 |
| Tauras | 36 | 7 | 2 | 27 | 35 | 97 | –62 | 23 |
| REO* | 36 | 5 | 4 | 27 | 26 | 81 | –55 | 19 |

*Top scorer:* Rimkevicius (Siauliai) 35.
*Cup Final:* VMFD Zalgiris 3, Siauliai 3.
*VMFD Zalgiris won 8-7 on penalties.*

## LUXEMBOURG

Federation Luxembourgeoise de Football, BP 5 Rue de Limpach, 3901 Mondercange.
*Founded:* 1908; *National Colours:* All white.

**International matches 2012–13**
FYR Macedonia (h) 2-1, Malta (h) 0-2, Georgia (h) 1-2, Portugal (h) 1-2, Northern Ireland (a) 1-1, Israel (h) 0-6, Israel (a) 0-3, Scotland (h) 1-2, Armenia (h) 1-1, Azerbaijan (h) 0-0, Finland (h) 0-3, Azerbaijan (a) 1-1.

**League Championship wins (1910–2013)**
Jeunesse Esch 28; Spora Luxembourg 11; Stade Dudelange 10; F91 Dudelange 10; Fola Esch 6; Red Boys Differdange (now Differdange 03) 6; Union Luxembourg 6; Avenir Beggen 6; US Hollerich-Bonnevoie 5; Progres Niedercorn 3; Aris Bonnevoie 3; Sporting Club 2; Racing Club 1; National Schifflange 1; Grevenmacher 1.

**Cup wins (1922–2013)**
Red Boys Differdange (now Differdange 03) 15; Jeunesse Esch 13; Union Luxembourg 10; Spora Luxembourg 8; Avenir Beggen 7; F91 Dudelange 5; Progres Niedercorn 4; Stade Dudelange 4; Grevenmacher 4; Fola Esch 3; Alliance Dudelange 2; US Rumelange 2; Differdange 03 2; Racing Club 1; US Dudelange 1; SC Tetange 1; National Schifflange 1; Aris Bonnevoie 1; Jeunesse Hautcharage 1; Swift Hesperange 1; Etzella Ettelbruck 1; CS Petange 1.

**Final League Table 2012–13**

| | P | W | D | L | F | A | GD | Pts |
|---|---|---|---|---|---|---|---|---|
| Fola Esch | 26 | 18 | 5 | 3 | 67 | 23 | 44 | 59 |
| F91 Dudelange | 26 | 16 | 7 | 3 | 53 | 20 | 33 | 55 |
| Jeunesse Esch | 26 | 16 | 2 | 8 | 53 | 31 | 22 | 50 |
| Differdange 03 | 26 | 14 | 5 | 7 | 54 | 34 | 20 | 47 |
| RM Hamm Benfica | 26 | 13 | 7 | 6 | 53 | 38 | 15 | 46 |
| Grevenmacher | 26 | 11 | 9 | 6 | 43 | 32 | 11 | 42 |
| Jeunesse Canach | 26 | 10 | 7 | 9 | 40 | 35 | 5 | 37 |
| Racing FC Union Letzeburg | 26 | 9 | 6 | 11 | 43 | 44 | –1 | 33 |
| UN Kaerjeng 97 | 26 | 9 | 4 | 13 | 44 | 53 | –9 | 31 |
| Wiltz | 26 | 9 | 3 | 14 | 42 | 66 | –24 | 30 |
| Etzella Ettelbruck | 26 | 6 | 9 | 11 | 41 | 61 | –20 | 27 |
| Progres Niedercorn+ | 26 | 7 | 4 | 15 | 29 | 45 | –16 | 25 |
| Petange* | 26 | 3 | 5 | 18 | 21 | 57 | –36 | 14 |
| Union 05 Kayl-Tetange* | 26 | 3 | 3 | 20 | 29 | 73 | –44 | 12 |

*Top scorer:* Osmanovic (Wiltz) 21.
*Cup Final:* Jeunesse d'Esch 2, Differdange 03 1.

## MALTA

Malta Football Association, Millennium Stand, Floor 2 National Stadium, Ta'Qali ATD4000.
*Founded:* 1900; *National Colours:* Red shirts, white shorts, red socks.

**International matches 2012–13**
Liechtenstein (h) 2-1, Luxembourg (a) 2-0, San Marino (a) 3-2, Armenia (h) 1-0, Italy (a) 0-2, Czech Republic (a) 1-3, Liechtenstein (a) 1-0, Northern Ireland (h) 0-0, Bulgaria (a) 0-6, Italy (h) 0-2, Armenia (a) 1-0.

**League Championship wins (1910–2013)**
Sliema Wanderers 26; Floriana 25; Valletta 21; Hibernians 10; Hamrun Spartans 7; Birkirkara 4; Rabat Ajax 2; St George's 1; KOMR 1; Marsaxlokk 1.

**Cup wins (1935–2013)**
Sliema Wanderers 20; Floriana 19; Valletta 12; Hibernians 10; Hamrun Spartans 6; Birkirkara 4; Melita 1; Gzira United 1; Zurrieq 1; Rabat Ajax 1.

**Qualifying League Table 2012–13**

| | P | W | D | L | F | A | GD | Pts |
|---|---|---|---|---|---|---|---|---|
| Valletta | 22 | 13 | 7 | 2 | 49 | 15 | +34 | 46 |
| Hibernians | 22 | 14 | 3 | 5 | 47 | 24 | +23 | 45 |
| Birkirkara | 22 | 12 | 7 | 3 | 47 | 19 | +28 | 43 |
| Tarxien Rainbows | 22 | 11 | 5 | 6 | 39 | 32 | +7 | 38 |
| Sliema Wanderers | 22 | 11 | 4 | 7 | 34 | 22 | +12 | 37 |
| Mosta | 22 | 11 | 1 | 10 | 39 | 33 | +6 | 34 |
| Qormi | 22 | 9 | 3 | 10 | 32 | 34 | –2 | 30 |
| Balzan Youths | 22 | 8 | 3 | 11 | 34 | 36 | –2 | 27 |
| Floriana (–2) | 22 | 5 | 9 | 8 | 26 | 31 | –5 | 22 |

| | | | | | | | |
|---|---|---|---|---|---|---|---|
| Hamrun Spartans (–1) | 22 | 4 | 4 | 14 | 24 | 58 –34 | 15 |
| Melita | 22 | 3 | 5 | 14 | 18 | 56 –38 | 14 |
| Rabat Ajax | 22 | 1 | 8 | 13 | 16 | 45 –29 | 11 |

*NB: Points earned in Qualifying phase are halved at start of Championship and Relegation phase.*

## Championship Table 2012–13

| | P | W | D | L | F | A GD | Pts |
|---|---|---|---|---|---|---|---|
| Birkirkara | 32 | 19 | 9 | 4 | 62 | 22 40 | 45 |
| Hibernians | 32 | 21 | 4 | 7 | 72 | 34 38 | 45 |
| Valletta | 32 | 17 | 8 | 7 | 70 | 29 41 | 36 |
| Sliema Wanderers | 32 | 16 | 6 | 10 | 48 | 32 16 | 36 |
| Tarxien Rainbows | 32 | 14 | 6 | 12 | 53 | 51 2 | 29 |
| Mosta | 32 | 11 | 2 | 19 | 45 | 72 –27 | 18 |

## Relegation Table 2012–13

| | P | W | D | L | F | A GD | Pts |
|---|---|---|---|---|---|---|---|
| Floriana | 32 | 14 | 10 | 8 | 48 | 38 10 | 38 |
| Qormi | 32 | 15 | 4 | 13 | 61 | 50 11 | 34 |
| Balzan Youths | 32 | 9 | 9 | 14 | 48 | 61 –13 | 23 |
| Rabat Ajax | 32 | 6 | 9 | 17 | 38 | 60 –22 | 22 |
| Hamrun Spartans* | 32 | 6 | 5 | 21 | 39 | 88 –49 | 14 |
| Melita* | 32 | 4 | 8 | 20 | 31 | 78 –47 | 13 |

*Top scorer:* Negrin (Rabat Ajax) 22.
*Cup Final:* Qormi 1, Hibernians 3.

## MOLDOVA

Federatia Moldoveneasca de Fotbal, 39 Tricolorului Str, 2012 Chisinau.
*Founded:* 1990; *National Colours:* All blue.

### International matches 2012–13
Belarus (h) 0-0, Venezuela (a) 0-4, El Salvador (n) 0-2, Albania (a) 0-0, England (h) 0-5, Poland (a) 0-2, Ukraine (h) 0-0, San Marino (a) 2-0, Kazakhstan (h) 1-3, Montenegro (h) 0-1, Ukraine (a) 1-2, Poland (h) 1-1, Kyrgyzstan (h) 2-1.

### League Championship wins (1992–2013)
Sheriff 12; Zimbru Chisinau 8; Constructorul 1; Dacia Chisinau 1.

### Cup wins (1992–2013)
Sheriff 7; Zimbru Chisinau 5; Tiligul 3; Tiraspol 3 (incl. Constructorul 2); Comrat 1; Nistru Otaci 1; Iskra-Stal 1; Milsami (formerly Milsami-Ursidos) 1.

### Final League Table 2012–13

| | P | W | D | L | F | A GD | Pts |
|---|---|---|---|---|---|---|---|
| Sheriff | 33 | 25 | 5 | 3 | 65 | 17 48 | 80 |
| Dacia Chisinau | 33 | 18 | 12 | 3 | 47 | 19 28 | 66 |
| Tiraspol | 33 | 18 | 10 | 5 | 54 | 20 34 | 64 |
| Milsami | 33 | 18 | 4 | 11 | 48 | 30 18 | 58 |
| Rapid Ghidighici | 33 | 15 | 4 | 14 | 36 | 38 –2 | 49 |
| Zimbru Chisinau | 33 | 12 | 10 | 11 | 53 | 38 15 | 46 |
| Academia Chisinau | 33 | 12 | 8 | 13 | 55 | 52 3 | 44 |
| Costuleni | 33 | 9 | 11 | 13 | 38 | 48 –10 | 38 |
| Iskra-Stal*† | 33 | 10 | 8 | 15 | 37 | 55 –18 | 38 |
| Olimpia Balti | 33 | 10 | 5 | 18 | 31 | 50 –19 | 35 |
| Speranta Crihana Veche | 33 | 4 | 7 | 22 | 35 | 70 –35 | 19 |
| Nistru Otaci* | 33 | 2 | 6 | 25 | 21 | 83 –62 | 12 |

†*Iskra-Stal withdrew from competition after round 29; remaining opponents awarded 3-0 wins.*
*Top scorer:* Boghiu (Milsami) 16.
*Cup Final:* Veris Draganesti 2, Tiraspol 2.
*Tiraspol 4-2 won on penalties.*

## MONTENEGRO

Football Association of Montenegro, Ulica 19. Decembra 13, PO Box 275, 81000 Podgorica.
*Founded:* 1931; *National Colours:* Red and gold shirts, red shorts, red socks.

### International matches 2012–13
Iceland (h) 2-1, Belgium (a) 2-2, Latvia (h) 2-0, Poland (h) 2-2, San Marino (a) 6-0, Ukraine (a) 1-0, San Marino (h) 3-0, Moldova (a) 1-0, England (h) 1-1, Ukraine (h) 0-4.

### League Championship wins (2006–13)
Buducnost Podgorica 2; Mogren 2; Zeta 1; Rudar Pljevlja 1; Sutjeska 1.

### Cup wins (2006–13)
Rudar Pljevlja 3; Mogren 1; Petrovac 1; Celik 1; Buducnost Podgorica 1.

### Final League Table 2012–13

| | P | W | D | L | F | A GD | Pts |
|---|---|---|---|---|---|---|---|
| Sutjeska | 33 | 20 | 5 | 8 | 50 | 31 19 | 65 |
| Buducnost Podgorica | 33 | 17 | 9 | 7 | 56 | 39 17 | 60 |
| Celik Niksic | 33 | 15 | 8 | 10 | 41 | 35 6 | 53 |
| Grbalj | 33 | 13 | 12 | 8 | 41 | 21 20 | 51 |
| Rudar Pljevlja | 33 | 15 | 6 | 12 | 42 | 40 2 | 51 |
| Mladost Podgorica | 33 | 9 | 12 | 12 | 39 | 48 –9 | 39 |
| Petrovac | 33 | 8 | 14 | 11 | 36 | 42 –6 | 38 |
| Zeta | 33 | 8 | 13 | 12 | 43 | 45 –2 | 37 |
| Lovcen | 33 | 11 | 4 | 18 | 38 | 51 –13 | 37 |
| Mogren*+ (–1) | 33 | 10 | 7 | 16 | 33 | 42 –9 | 36 |
| Mornar*+ | 33 | 9 | 9 | 15 | 36 | 47 –11 | 36 |
| Jedinstvo Bijelo Polje* | 33 | 9 | 9 | 15 | 31 | 45 –14 | 36 |

*Top scorer:* Adrovic (Buducnost Podgorica), Korac (Zeta) 15.
*Cup Final:* Buducnost Podgorica 1, Celik Niksic 0.

## NORTHERN CYPRUS

Turkish Republic of Northern Cyprus Football Federation. (Not a member of FIFA or UEFA.)
*Founded:* 1955; *National Colours:* Red shirts with white trim, red shorts, red socks.

### League Championship wins (1956–63; 1969–74; 1976–2013)
Cetinkaya 15; Gonyeli 9; Magusa 7; Dogan 6; Yenicami 5; BAF Ulku 4; Kucuk 4; Akincilar 1; Binatli 1.

### Cup wins (1956–2013)
Cetinkaya 17; Gonyeli 8; Kucuk 6; Yenicami 6; Magusa 5; Turk Ocagi 4; Dogan 2; Lefke 1; Genclik 1; Yalova 1; Binatli 1.

### Final League Table 2012–13

| | P | W | D | L | F | A GD | Pts |
|---|---|---|---|---|---|---|---|
| Cetinkaya | 26 | 21 | 4 | 1 | 81 | 20 61 | 67 |
| Kaymaklitsk | 26 | 15 | 4 | 7 | 58 | 26 32 | 49 |
| Bagcil | 26 | 13 | 4 | 9 | 46 | 42 4 | 43 |
| Dogan | 26 | 12 | 5 | 9 | 52 | 45 7 | 41 |
| Lefke | 26 | 10 | 7 | 9 | 36 | 32 4 | 37 |
| Cihangir | 26 | 11 | 4 | 11 | 44 | 38 6 | 37 |
| Hamitkoy | 26 | 9 | 6 | 11 | 34 | 47 –13 | 33 |
| Magusa | 26 | 9 | 6 | 11 | 42 | 40 2 | 33 |
| Genclik | 26 | 10 | 2 | 14 | 41 | 53 –12 | 32 |
| Lapta | 26 | 8 | 6 | 12 | 30 | 41 –11 | 30 |
| Serdarli | 26 | 8 | 3 | 15 | 32 | 55 –23 | 27 |
| Turk Ocagi | 26 | 7 | 2 | 17 | 36 | 65 –29 | 23 |
| Gocmenkoy | 26 | 2 | 1 | 23 | 19 | 77 –58 | 7 |

*Top scorer:* Sonay (Cetinkaya) 26.
*Cup Final:* Yenicami 2, Magusa 0.

## NORTHERN IRELAND

Irish Football Association Ltd, 20 Windsor Avenue, Belfast BT9 6EE.
*Founded:* 1880; *National Colours:* Green shirts, white shorts, green socks.

## NORWAY

Norges Fotballforbund, Ullevaal Stadion, Serviceboks 1, 0840 Oslo.
*Founded:* 1902; *National Colours:* Red shirts, white shorts, red socks.

### International matches 2012–13
Thailand (a) 1-0, Northern Ireland (h) 3-0, England (h) 0-1, Croatia (h) 1-1, Greece (h) 2-3, Iceland (a) 0-2, Slovenia (h) 2-1, Switzerland (a) 1-1, Cyprus (a) 3-1, Hungary (a) 2-0, South Africa (a) 1-0, Ukraine (h) 0-2, Albania (h) 0-1, Albania (a) 1-1, FYR Macedonia (h) 2-0.

### League Championship wins (1938–2012)
Rosenborg 22; Fredrikstad 9; Viking Stavanger 8; Lillestrom 5; Valerenga 5; Larvik Turn 3; Brann 3; Lyn Oslo 2; IK Start 2; Molde 2; Freidig 1; Fram 1; Skeid 1; Stromsgodset 1; Moss 1; Stabaek 1.

### Cup wins (1902–2012)
Odd Grenland 12; Fredrikstad 11; Rosenborg 9; Lyn Oslo 8; Skeid 8; Sarpsborg 6; Brann 6; Viking Stavanger 5; Lillestrom 5; Stromsgodset 5; Orn-Horten 4; Valerenga 4; Frigg 3; Mjondalen 3; Mercantile 2; Tromso 2; Bodo/Glimt 2; Molde 2; Aalesund 2; Grane Nordstrand 1; Kvik Halden 1; Sparta 1; Gjovik/Lyn 1; Moss 1; Bryne 1; Stabaek 1; Hodd 1.
(Known as the Norwegian Championship for HM The King's Trophy.)

### Final League Table 2012

| | P | W | D | L | F | A GD | Pts |
|---|---|---|---|---|---|---|---|
| Molde | 30 | 19 | 5 | 6 | 51 | 31 20 | 62 |
| Stromsgodset | 30 | 17 | 7 | 6 | 62 | 40 22 | 58 |
| Rosenborg | 30 | 15 | 10 | 5 | 53 | 26 27 | 55 |

| | | | | | | | | |
|---|---|---|---|---|---|---|---|---|
| Tromso | 30 | 14 | 7 | 9 | 45 | 32 | 13 | 49 |
| Viking | 30 | 14 | 7 | 9 | 41 | 36 | 5 | 49 |
| Brann | 30 | 13 | 3 | 14 | 57 | 50 | 7 | 42 |
| Haugesund | 30 | 11 | 9 | 10 | 46 | 40 | 6 | 42 |
| Valerenga | 30 | 12 | 5 | 13 | 42 | 44 | -2 | 41 |
| Lillestrom | 30 | 9 | 12 | 9 | 46 | 47 | -1 | 39 |
| Odd Grenland | 30 | 11 | 7 | 12 | 40 | 43 | -3 | 39 |
| Aalesunds | 30 | 9 | 11 | 10 | 40 | 41 | -1 | 38 |
| Sogndal | 30 | 8 | 10 | 12 | 29 | 37 | -8 | 34 |
| Honefoss | 30 | 7 | 12 | 11 | 30 | 42 | -12 | 33 |
| Sandnes Ulf+ | 30 | 8 | 8 | 14 | 44 | 56 | -12 | 32 |
| Fredrikstad* | 30 | 9 | 3 | 18 | 42 | 59 | -17 | 30 |
| Stabaek* | 30 | 5 | 2 | 23 | 25 | 69 | -44 | 17 |

*Top scorer:* Kovacs (Stromsgodset) 14.
*Cup Final:* Tromso 1, Hodd 1.
*Hodd won 4-2 on penalties.*

## POLAND

Polish Football Association, Bitwy Warszawskiej 1920 r.
7, 02-366 Warsaw.
*Founded:* 1919; *National Colours:* White shirts, red shorts, white socks.

### International matches 2012–13
Bosnia-Herzegovina (h) 1-0*, Portugal (h) 0-0, Latvia (h) 1-0, Slovakia (h) 1-0, Andorra (h) 4-0, Greece (n) 1-1, Russia (h) 1-1, Czech Republic (n) 0-1, Estonia (a) 0-1, Montenegro (a) 2-2, Moldova (h) 2-0, South Africa (h) 1-0, England (h) 1-1, Uruguay (h) 1-3, FYR Macedonia (h) 4-1, Republic of Ireland (a) 0-2, Ukraine (h) 1-3, San Marino (h) 5-0, Liechtenstein (h) 2-0, Moldova (a) 1-1.
* *Played 16.12.2011, result omitted from last edition.*

### League Championship wins (1921–2013)
Gornik Zabrze 14; Ruch Chorzow 14; Wisla Krakow 13; Legia Warsaw 9; Lech Poznan 6; Cracovia 5; Pogon Lwow 4; Widzew Lodz 4; Warta Poznan 2; Polonia Warsaw 2; Polonia Bytom 2; LKS Lodz 2; Stal Mielec 2; Zaglebie Lubin 2; Slask Wroclaw 2; Garbarnia Krakow 1; Szombierki Bytom 1.

### Cup wins (1926; 1951–2013)
Legia Warsaw 16; Gornik Zabrze 6; Lech Poznan 5; Wisla Krakow 4; Zaglebie Sosnowiec 4; Ruch Chorzow 3; GKS Katowice 3; Amica Wronki 3; Polonia Warsaw 2; Slask Wroclaw 2; Dyskobolia Grodzisk 2; Gwardia Warsaw 1; LKS Lodz 1; Stal Rzeszow 1; Arka Gdynia 1; Lechia Gdansk 1; Widzew Lodz 1; Miedz Legnica 1; Wisla Plock 1; Jagiellonia Bialystok 1.

### Final League Table 2012–13
| | P | W | D | L | F | A | GD | Pts |
|---|---|---|---|---|---|---|---|---|
| Legia Warsaw | 30 | 20 | 7 | 3 | 59 | 22 | 37 | 67 |
| Lech Poznan | 30 | 19 | 4 | 7 | 46 | 22 | 24 | 61 |
| Slask Wroclaw | 30 | 13 | 8 | 9 | 44 | 42 | 2 | 47 |
| Piast Gliwice | 30 | 13 | 7 | 10 | 41 | 41 | 0 | 46 |
| Gornik Zabrze | 30 | 12 | 7 | 11 | 35 | 31 | 4 | 43 |
| Polonia Warsaw | 30 | 11 | 9 | 10 | 45 | 34 | 11 | 42 |
| Wisla Krakow | 30 | 10 | 8 | 12 | 28 | 35 | -7 | 38 |
| Lechia Gdansk | 30 | 10 | 8 | 12 | 42 | 43 | -1 | 38 |
| Zaglebie Lubin (-3) | 30 | 11 | 7 | 12 | 38 | 37 | 1 | 37 |
| Jagiellonia Bialystok | 30 | 8 | 13 | 9 | 31 | 45 | -14 | 37 |
| Korona Kielce | 30 | 9 | 9 | 12 | 32 | 37 | -5 | 36 |
| Pogon Szczecin | 30 | 10 | 5 | 15 | 29 | 39 | -10 | 35 |
| Widzew Lodz | 30 | 8 | 9 | 13 | 30 | 41 | -11 | 33 |
| Podbeskidzie Bielsko-Biala | 30 | 8 | 8 | 14 | 39 | 43 | -4 | 32 |
| Ruch Chorzow | 30 | 8 | 7 | 15 | 35 | 48 | -13 | 31 |
| GKS Belchatow* | 30 | 7 | 10 | 13 | 24 | 38 | -14 | 31 |

*Top scorer:* Demjan (Podbeskidzie Bielsko-Biala) 14.
*Cup Final:* Slask Wroclaw 0, 1, Legia Warsaw 2, 0.

## PORTUGAL

Federacao Portuguesa de Futebol, Rua Alexandre Herculano No. 58, Apartado postal 24013, Lisboa 1251-977.
*Founded:* 1914; *National Colours:* Red shirts, red shorts, red and green socks.

### International matches 2012–13
Poland (a) 0-0, FYR Macedonia (h) 0-0, Turkey (h) 1-3, Germany (n) 0-1, Denmark (n) 3-2, Holland (n) 2-1, Czech Republic (n) 1-0, Spain (h) 0-0 (2-4p), Panama (h) 2-0, Luxembourg (a) 2-1, Azerbaijan (h) 3-0, Russia (a) 0-1, Northern Ireland (h) 1-1, Gabon (a) 2-2, Ecuador (h) 2-3, Israel (a) 3-3, Azerbaijan (a) 2-0, Russia (h) 1-0, Croatia (a) 1-0.

### League Championship wins (1935–2013)
Benfica 32; FC Porto 27; Sporting Lisbon 18; Belenenses 1; Boavista 1.

### Cup wins (1939–2013)
Benfica 24; FC Porto 16; Sporting Lisbon 15; Boavista 5; Belenenses 3; Vitoria de Setubal 3; Academica de Coimbra 2; Leixoes 1; Braga 1; Estrela da Amadora 1; Beira Mar 1; Vitoria de Guimaraes 1.

### Final League Table 2012–13
| | P | W | D | L | F | A | GD | Pts |
|---|---|---|---|---|---|---|---|---|
| FC Porto | 30 | 24 | 6 | 0 | 70 | 14 | 56 | 78 |
| Benfica | 30 | 24 | 5 | 1 | 77 | 20 | 57 | 77 |
| Pacos de Ferreira | 30 | 14 | 12 | 4 | 42 | 29 | 13 | 54 |
| Braga | 30 | 16 | 4 | 10 | 60 | 44 | 16 | 52 |
| Estoril | 30 | 13 | 6 | 11 | 47 | 37 | 10 | 45 |
| Rio Ave | 30 | 12 | 6 | 12 | 35 | 42 | -7 | 42 |
| Sporting Lisbon | 30 | 11 | 9 | 10 | 36 | 36 | 0 | 42 |
| Nacional | 30 | 11 | 12 | 7 | 45 | 51 | -6 | 40 |
| Vitoria de Guimaraes | 30 | 11 | 7 | 12 | 36 | 47 | -11 | 40 |
| Marítimo | 30 | 9 | 11 | 10 | 34 | 45 | -11 | 38 |
| Academica de Coimbra | 30 | 6 | 10 | 14 | 33 | 45 | -12 | 28 |
| Vitoria de Setubal | 30 | 7 | 5 | 18 | 30 | 55 | -25 | 26 |
| Gil Vicente | 30 | 6 | 7 | 17 | 31 | 54 | -23 | 25 |
| Olhanense | 30 | 5 | 10 | 15 | 26 | 42 | -16 | 25 |
| Moreirense* | 30 | 5 | 9 | 16 | 30 | 51 | -21 | 24 |
| Beira-Mar* | 30 | 5 | 8 | 17 | 35 | 55 | -20 | 23 |

*Top scorer:* Martinez (FC Porto) 26.
*Cup Final:* Benfica 1, Vitoria de Guimaraes 2.

## ROMANIA

Federatia Romana de Fotbal, House of Football, Str. Serg. Serbanica Vasile 12, 22186 Bucuresti.
*Founded:* 1909; *National Colours:* All yellow.

### International matches 2012–13
Turkmenistan (n) 4-0, Uruguay (h) 1-1, Switzerland (a) 1-0, Austria (a) 0-0, Slovenia (a) 3-4, Estonia (a) 2-0, Andorra (h) 4-0, Turkey (a) 1-0, Holland (h) 1-4, Belgium (h) 2-1, Australia (h) 3-2, Hungary (a) 2-2, Holland (a) 0-4, Trinidad & Tobago (h) 4-0.

### League Championship wins (1910–2013)
Steaua Bucharest 24; Dinamo Bucharest 18; Venus Bucharest 8; Chinezul Timisoara 6; UT Arad 6; Universitatea Craiova 5; Ripensia Timisoara 4; Rapid Bucharest 4; Petrolul Ploiesti 3; CFR Cluj 3; Olimpia Bucharest 2; Colentina Bucharest 2; Arges Pitesti 2; United Ploiesti 1; Romano-Americana Bucharest 1; Prahova Ploiesti 1; Coltea Brasov 1; Juventus Bucharest 1; Metalochimia Resita 1; Unirea Tricolor 1; ICO Oradea 1; Unirea Urziceni 1; Otelul Galati 1.

### Cup wins (1934–2013)
Steaua Bucharest 22; Rapid Bucharest 13; Dinamo Bucharest 13; Uni Craiova 6; Petrolul Ploiesti 3; CFR Cluj 3; Ripensia Timisoara 2; UT Arad 2; Politehnica Timisoara 2; CFR Turnu Severin 1; Metalochimia Resita 1; Universitata Cluj (includes Stiinta) 1; Progresul Oradea (formerly ICO) 1; Progresul Bucharest 1; Ariesul Turda 1; Chimia Ramnicu Vilcea 1; Jiul Petrosani 1; Gloria Bistrita 1.

### Final League Table 2012–13
| | P | W | D | L | F | A | GD | Pts |
|---|---|---|---|---|---|---|---|---|
| Steaua Bucharest | 34 | 24 | 7 | 3 | 74 | 29 | 45 | 79 |
| Pandurii Targu Jiu | 34 | 19 | 6 | 9 | 57 | 43 | 14 | 63 |
| Petrolul Ploiesti | 34 | 16 | 14 | 4 | 60 | 34 | 26 | 62 |
| Astra Ploiesti | 34 | 17 | 9 | 8 | 64 | 37 | 27 | 60 |
| Vaslui | 34 | 16 | 10 | 8 | 50 | 34 | 16 | 58 |
| Dinamo Bucharest | 34 | 16 | 8 | 10 | 48 | 40 | 8 | 56 |
| Brasov | 34 | 14 | 9 | 11 | 50 | 51 | -1 | 51 |
| CFR Cluj | 34 | 12 | 13 | 9 | 56 | 39 | 17 | 49 |
| Rapid Bucharest*† | 34 | 13 | 10 | 11 | 35 | 35 | 0 | 49 |
| Gaz Metan Medias | 34 | 12 | 10 | 12 | 42 | 46 | -4 | 46 |
| Otelul Galati (-2) | 34 | 11 | 10 | 13 | 38 | 42 | -4 | 41 |
| Universitatea Cluj*† | 34 | 10 | 8 | 16 | 39 | 55 | -16 | 38 |
| Viitorul Constanta | 34 | 8 | 12 | 14 | 45 | 57 | -12 | 36 |
| Ceahlaul Piatra Neamt | 34 | 9 | 7 | 18 | 41 | 59 | -18 | 34 |
| Concordia Chiajna* | 34 | 7 | 12 | 15 | 29 | 49 | -20 | 33 |
| Turnu Severin*† | 34 | 7 | 11 | 16 | 36 | 47 | -11 | 32 |
| CSMS Iasi* | 34 | 7 | 5 | 22 | 31 | 50 | -19 | 26 |
| Gloria Bistrita* | 34 | 3 | 9 | 22 | 21 | 69 | -48 | 18 |

† *Relegated due to financial difficulties.*
*Top scorer:* Rusescu (Steaua Bucharest) 21.
*Cup Final:* Petrolul Ploiesti 1, CFR Cluj 0.

## RUSSIA

Football Union of Russia, Ulitsa Narodnaya 7, 115 172 Moscow.
*Founded:* 1912; *National Colours:* All brick red.

**International matches 2012–13**
Denmark (a) 2-0, Uruguay (h) 1-1, Lithuania (a) 0-0, Italy (a) 3-0, Czech Republic (n) 4-1, Poland (a) 1-1, Greece (n) 0-1, Ivory Coast (h) 1-1, Northern Ireland (h) 2-0, Israel (a) 4-0, Portugal (h) 1-0, Azerbaijan (h) 1-0, USA (h) 2-2, Iceland (a) 2-0, Brazil (a) 1-1, Portugal (a) 0-1.

**League Championship wins (1936–2013)**
Spartak Moscow 21; Dynamo Kiev 13; Dynamo Moscow 11; CSKA Moscow 11; Zenit St Petersburg (formerly Zenit Leningrad) 4; Torpedo Moscow 3; Dinamo Tbilisi 2; Dnepr Dnepropetrovsk 2; Lokomotiv Moscow 2; Rubin Kazan 2; Saria Voroshilovgrad 1; Ararat Erevan 1; Dynamo Minsk 1; Spartak Vladikavkaz (renamed Alania) 1.

**Cup wins (1936–2013)**
Spartak Moscow 13; CSKA Moscow 12; Dynamo Kiev 9; Torpedo Moscow 7; Dynamo Moscow 7; Lokomotiv Moscow 7; Shakhtar Donetsk 4; Zenit St Petersburg (formerly Zenit Leningrad) 3; Dinamo Tbilisi 2; Ararat Erevan 2; Karpaty Lvov 1; SKA Rostov 1; Metalist Kharkov 1; Dnepr 1; Terek Grozny 1; Rubin Kazan 1.

**First Stage Final League Table 2012–13**

| | P | W | D | L | F | A | GD | Pts |
|---|---|---|---|---|---|---|---|---|
| CSKA Moscow | 30 | 20 | 4 | 6 | 49 | 25 | 24 | 64 |
| Zenit St Petersburg | 30 | 18 | 8 | 4 | 53 | 25 | 28 | 62 |
| Anzhi Makhachkala | 30 | 15 | 8 | 7 | 45 | 34 | 11 | 53 |
| Spartak Moscow | 30 | 15 | 6 | 9 | 51 | 39 | 12 | 51 |
| Kuban Krasnodar | 30 | 14 | 9 | 7 | 48 | 28 | 20 | 51 |
| Rubin Kazan | 30 | 15 | 5 | 10 | 39 | 27 | 12 | 50 |
| Dynamo Moscow | 30 | 14 | 6 | 10 | 41 | 34 | 7 | 48 |
| Terek Grozny | 30 | 14 | 6 | 10 | 38 | 40 | -2 | 48 |
| Lokomotiv Moscow | 30 | 12 | 7 | 11 | 39 | 36 | 3 | 43 |
| Krasnodar | 30 | 12 | 6 | 12 | 45 | 39 | 6 | 42 |
| Amkar Perm | 30 | 7 | 8 | 15 | 34 | 51 | -17 | 29 |
| Volga Nizhny Novgorod | 30 | 7 | 8 | 15 | 28 | 46 | -18 | 29 |
| Rostov+ | 30 | 7 | 8 | 15 | 30 | 41 | -11 | 29 |
| Krylya Sovetov Samara* | 30 | 7 | 7 | 16 | 31 | 52 | -21 | 28 |
| Mordovia Saransk* | 30 | 5 | 5 | 20 | 30 | 57 | -27 | 20 |
| Alania Vladikavkaz* | 30 | 4 | 7 | 19 | 26 | 53 | -27 | 19 |

*Top scorer:* Movsisyan (Spartak Moscow) 13 (incl. 9 for Krasnodar).
*Cup Final:* CSKA Moscow 1, Anzhi Makhachkala 1.
*CSKA Moscow won 4-3 on penalties.*

## SAN MARINO

Federazione Sammarinese Giuoco Calcio, Strada di Montecchio 17, 47890 San Marino.
*Founded:* 1931; *National Colours:* All cobalt blue.

**International matches 2012–13**
Malta (h) 2-3, Montenegro (h) 0-6, England (a) 0-5, Moldova (h) 0-2, Montenegro (a) 0-3, England (h) 0-8, Poland (a) 0-5, Italy (a) 0-4.

**League Championship wins (1986–2013)**
Tre Fiori 7; Domagnano 4; Faetano 3; Folgore/Falciano 3; La Fiorita 2; Tre Penne 2; Montevito 1; Libertas 1; Cosmos 1; Pennarossa 1.

**Cup wins (1937–2013)**
Libertas 10; Domagnano 8; Tre Fiori 6; Juvenes 5; Tre Penne 5; Cosmos 4; La Fiorita 3; Faetano 3; Murata 3; Dogana 2; Pennarossa 2; Juvenes/Dogana 2.

**Qualifying League Table 2012**

**Group A**

| | P | W | D | L | F | A | GD | Pts |
|---|---|---|---|---|---|---|---|---|
| Libertas | 20 | 13 | 6 | 1 | 36 | 13 | 23 | 45 |
| La Fiorita | 20 | 13 | 3 | 4 | 35 | 21 | 14 | 42 |
| Murata | 20 | 11 | 3 | 6 | 31 | 19 | 12 | 36 |
| Cailungo | 20 | 6 | 5 | 9 | 30 | 37 | -7 | 23 |
| Faetano | 20 | 5 | 6 | 9 | 20 | 26 | -6 | 21 |
| Juvenes-Dogana | 20 | 5 | 3 | 12 | 24 | 36 | -12 | 18 |
| Virtus | 20 | 3 | 3 | 14 | 15 | 35 | -20 | 12 |

**Group B**

| | P | W | D | L | F | A | GD | Pts |
|---|---|---|---|---|---|---|---|---|
| Folgore/Falciano | 21 | 10 | 9 | 2 | 25 | 17 | 8 | 39 |
| Tre Penne | 21 | 11 | 2 | 8 | 24 | 18 | 6 | 35 |
| Cosmos | 21 | 9 | 8 | 4 | 27 | 19 | 8 | 35 |
| Fiorentino | 21 | 7 | 8 | 6 | 36 | 25 | 11 | 29 |
| San Giovanni | 21 | 6 | 9 | 6 | 35 | 39 | -4 | 27 |
| Domagnano | 21 | 5 | 8 | 8 | 24 | 30 | -6 | 23 |
| Pennarossa | 21 | 5 | 5 | 11 | 23 | 38 | -15 | 20 |
| Tre Fiori | 21 | 5 | 2 | 14 | 22 | 34 | -12 | 17 |

**Play-offs**
(Double-elimination format; Group winners receive byes in first two rounds.)
Rnd 1: La Fiorita 1, Cosmos 1 (6-5p); Tre Penne 1, Murata 2
Rnd 2: La Fiorita 1, Murata 1 (5-3p); Cosmos 0, Tre Penne 0 (3-4p)
Rnd 3: Libertas 2, Folgore 0; Tre Penne 2, Murata 0
Rnd 4: Libertas 1, La Fiorita 0; Tre Penne 2, Folgore 0
Rnd 5: Tre Penne 1, La Fiorita 0; Final: Libertas 0, Tre Penne 0 (3-5p)
*Top scorer:* Cannini (Tre Fiori), Iencinella (Fiorentino) 17.
*Cup Final:* La Fiorita 1, San Giovanni 0.

## SCOTLAND

The Scottish Football Association Ltd, Hampden Park, Glasgow G42 9AY.
*Founded:* 1873; *National Colours:* Dark blue shirts, white shorts, dark blue socks.

## SERBIA

Football Association of Serbia, Terazije 35, PO Box 263, 11000 Beograd.
*Founded:* 1919; *National Colours:* Red shirts, blue shorts, white socks.

**International matches 2012–13**
Armenia (a) 2-0, Cyprus (a) 0-0, Spain (a) 0-2, France (a) 0-2, Sweden (a) 1-2, Republic of Ireland (h) 0-0, Scotland (a) 0-0, Wales (h) 6-1, Belgium (h) 0-3, FYR Macedonia (a) 0-1, Chile (n) 3-1, Cyprus (a) 3-1, Croatia (a) 0-2, Scotland (h) 2-0, Belgium (a) 1-2.

**League Championship wins (1923–2013)**
Partizan Belgrade 25; Red Star Belgrade 25; Hajduk Split 9; Gradjanski Zagreb 5; BSK Belgrade (renamed OFK) 5; Dinamo Zagreb 4; Jugoslavija Belgrade 2; Concordia Zagreb 2; FC Sarajevo 2; Vojvodina Novi Sad 2; HASK Zagreb 1; Zeljeznicar 1; Obilic 1.

**Cup wins (1947–2013)**
Red Star Belgrade 24; Partizan Belgrade 12; Hajduk Split 9; Dinamo Zagreb 8; BSK Belgrade (incl. OFK 2) 4; Rijeka 2; Velez Mostar 2; Vardar Skopje 1; Borac Banjaluka 1; Sartid 1; Zeleznik 1; Jagodina 1.

**Final League Table 2012–13**

| | P | W | D | L | F | A | GD | Pts |
|---|---|---|---|---|---|---|---|---|
| Partizan Belgrade | 30 | 23 | 4 | 3 | 71 | 16 | 55 | 73 |
| Red Star Belgrade | 30 | 20 | 2 | 8 | 55 | 35 | 20 | 62 |
| Vojvodina | 30 | 17 | 10 | 3 | 40 | 20 | 20 | 61 |
| Jagodina | 30 | 15 | 5 | 10 | 35 | 26 | 9 | 50 |
| Sloboda Uzice | 30 | 11 | 12 | 7 | 39 | 37 | 2 | 45 |
| OFK Beograd | 30 | 13 | 6 | 11 | 34 | 32 | 2 | 45 |
| Rad | 30 | 12 | 8 | 10 | 32 | 30 | 2 | 44 |
| Hajduk Kula | 30 | 10 | 8 | 12 | 36 | 32 | 4 | 38 |
| Spartak Zlatibor Voda† | 30 | 9 | 9 | 12 | 36 | 39 | -3 | 36 |
| Javor | 30 | 9 | 7 | 14 | 38 | 40 | -2 | 34 |
| Donji Srem | 30 | 9 | 7 | 14 | 26 | 34 | -8 | 34 |
| Radnicki Nis | 30 | 9 | 7 | 14 | 30 | 44 | -14 | 34 |
| Radnicki 1923 | 30 | 7 | 10 | 13 | 25 | 35 | -10 | 31 |
| Novi Pazar | 30 | 7 | 9 | 14 | 29 | 40 | -11 | 30 |
| BSK Borca* | 30 | 8 | 6 | 16 | 26 | 57 | -31 | 30 |
| Smederevo* | 30 | 3 | 6 | 21 | 18 | 53 | -35 | 15 |

† *Renamed Spartak Subotica from 2013–14.*
*Top scorer:* Stojanovic (Jagodina) 20.
*Cup Final:* Jagodina 1, Vojvodina 0.

## SLOVAKIA

Slovensky Futbalovy Zvaz, Trnavska cesta 100, 821 01 Bratislava.
*Founded:* 1993; *National Colours:* White shirts with blue trim, white shorts, white socks with blue trim.

**International matches 2012–13**
Turkey (a) 2-1, Poland (a) 0-1, Holland (a) 0-2, Denmark (a) 3-1, Lithuania (a) 1-1, Liechtenstein (h) 2-0, Latvia (h) 2-1, Greece (h) 0-1, Czech Republic (a) 0-3, Belgium (a) 1-2, Lithuania (h) 1-1, Sweden (h) 0-0, Liechtenstein (a) 1-1.

**League Championship wins (1939–44; 1994–2013)**
Slovan Bratislava 11; Zilina 6; Kosice 2; Inter Bratislava 2; Artmedia Petrzalka 2; Bystrica 1; OAP Bratislava 1; Ruzomberok 1.

**Cup wins (1994–2013)**
Slovan Bratislava 6; Inter Bratislava 3; Artmedia Petrzalka 2; Humenne 1; Spartak Trnava 1; Koba Senec 1; Matador Puchov 1; Bystrica 1; Ruzomberok 1; ViOn Zlate Moravce 1; Kosice 1; Zilina 1.

**Final League Table 2012–13**

| | P | W | D | L | F | A | GD | Pts |
|---|---|---|---|---|---|---|---|---|
| Slovan Bratislava | 33 | 16 | 11 | 6 | 56 | 33 | 23 | 59 |
| Senica | 33 | 16 | 7 | 10 | 40 | 34 | 6 | 55 |
| Trencin | 33 | 14 | 11 | 8 | 52 | 34 | 18 | 53 |
| Spartak Myjava | 33 | 13 | 9 | 11 | 43 | 37 | 6 | 48 |
| Kosice | 33 | 12 | 11 | 10 | 38 | 33 | 5 | 47 |
| Ruzomberok | 33 | 12 | 9 | 12 | 36 | 46 | –10 | 45 |
| Zilina | 33 | 9 | 15 | 9 | 37 | 28 | 9 | 42 |
| ViOn Zlate Moravce | 33 | 11 | 8 | 14 | 42 | 43 | –1 | 41 |
| Dukla Banska Bystrica | 33 | 9 | 11 | 13 | 28 | 32 | –4 | 38 |
| Nitra (–3) | 33 | 11 | 6 | 16 | 39 | 54 | –15 | 36 |
| Spartak Trnava | 33 | 8 | 11 | 14 | 34 | 51 | –17 | 35 |
| Tatran Presov* | 33 | 8 | 9 | 16 | 21 | 41 | –20 | 33 |

*Top scorer:* Depetris (Trencin) 16.
*Cup Final:* Zilina 0, Slovan Bratislava 2.

## SLOVENIA

Nogometna Zveza Slovenije, Cerinova 4, PO Box 3986, 1001 Ljubljana.
*Founded:* 1920; *National Colours:* White shirts with blue/green trim, white shorts, white stocking with blue/green trim.

**International matches 2012–13**
Scotland (h) 1-1, Greece (a) 1-1, Romania (h) 4-3, Switzerland (h) 0-2, Norway (a) 1-2, Cyprus (h) 2-1, Albania (a) 0-1, FYR Macedonia (a) 0-0, Bosnia-Herzogovina (h) 0-3, Iceland (h) 1-2, Turkey (a) 2-0, Iceland (a) 4-2.

**League Championship wins (1992–2013)**
Maribor 11; Olimpija Ljubljana (pre-2005) 4; Gorica 4; Domzale 2; Koper 1.

**Cup wins (1992–2013)**
Maribor 8; Olimpija Ljubljana (pre-2005) 4; Gorica 2; Koper 2; Interblock 2; Mura (pre-2004) 1; Rudar Velenje 1; Celje 1; Domzale 1.

**Final League Table 2012–13**

| | P | W | D | L | F | A | GD | Pts |
|---|---|---|---|---|---|---|---|---|
| Maribor | 36 | 24 | 6 | 6 | 80 | 35 | +45 | 78 |
| Olimpija Ljubljana | 36 | 21 | 7 | 8 | 73 | 35 | +38 | 70 |
| Domzale | 36 | 17 | 9 | 10 | 42 | 34 | +8 | 60 |
| Koper | 36 | 14 | 13 | 9 | 52 | 42 | +10 | 55 |
| Celje | 36 | 12 | 13 | 11 | 39 | 39 | 0 | 49 |
| Gorica | 36 | 10 | 11 | 15 | 45 | 60 | –15 | 41 |
| Rudar Velenje | 36 | 11 | 7 | 18 | 42 | 59 | –17 | 40 |
| Triglav | 36 | 9 | 11 | 16 | 35 | 50 | –15 | 38 |
| Mura 05*† | 36 | 9 | 6 | 21 | 43 | 66 | –23 | 33 |
| Aluminij* | 36 | 7 | 9 | 20 | 36 | 67 | –31 | 30 |

† *Mura 05 did not contest relegation play-off after failure to regain licence.*
*Top scorer:* Tavares (Maribor) 17.
*Cup Final:* Maribor 1, Celje 0.

## SPAIN

Real Federacion Espanola de Futbol, Ramon y Cajal s/n, Apartado postale 385, 28230 Las Rozas (Madrid).
*Founded:* 1913; *National Colours:* Red shirts, blue shorts, red socks.

**International matches 2012–13**
Venezuela (h) 5-0, Serbia (n) 2-0, South Korea (n) 4-1, China PR (n) 1-0, Italy (n) 1-1, Republic of Ireland (n) 4-0, Croatia (n) 1-0, France (n) 2-0, Portugal (n) 0-0 (4-2p), Italy (n) 4-0, Puerto Rico (a) 2-1, Saudi Arabia (h) 5-0, Georgia (a) 1-0, Belarus (a) 4-0, France (h) 1-1, Panama (a) 5-1, Uruguay (h) 3-1, Finland (h) 1-1, France (a) 1-0, Haiti (n) 2-1, Republic of Ireland (n) 2-0, Uruguay (n) 2-1, Tahiti (n) 10-0, Nigeria (n) 3-0, Italy (n) 0-0 (7-6p), Brazil (n) 0-3.

**League Championship wins (1929–36; 1940–2013)**
Real Madrid 32; Barcelona 22; Atletico Madrid 9; Athletic Bilbao 8; Valencia 6; Real Sociedad 2; Real Betis 1; Sevilla 1; Deportivo La Coruna 1.

**Cup wins (1903–2013)**
Barcelona 26; Athletic Bilbao (includes Vizcaya Bilbao 1) 23; Real Madrid 18; Atletico Madrid 10; Valencia 7; Real Zaragoza 6; Sevilla 5; Espanyol 4; Real Union de Irun 3; Deportivo La Coruna 2; Real Sociedad (includes Ciclista) 2; Real Betis 2; Arenas 1; Racing de Irun 1; Mallorca 1.

**Final League Table 2012–13**

| | P | W | D | L | F | A | GD | Pts |
|---|---|---|---|---|---|---|---|---|
| Barcelona | 36 | 30 | 4 | 2 | 109 | 39 | 70 | 94 |
| Real Madrid | 36 | 25 | 6 | 5 | 96 | 37 | 59 | 81 |
| Atletico Madrid | 36 | 22 | 6 | 8 | 62 | 30 | 32 | 72 |
| Real Sociedad | 36 | 17 | 11 | 8 | 66 | 46 | 20 | 62 |
| Valencia | 36 | 18 | 8 | 10 | 63 | 50 | 13 | 62 |
| Malaga | 36 | 15 | 9 | 12 | 49 | 45 | 4 | 54 |
| Real Betis | 36 | 15 | 7 | 14 | 52 | 55 | –3 | 52 |
| Rayo Vallecano | 36 | 15 | 4 | 17 | 46 | 63 | –17 | 49 |
| Sevilla | 36 | 13 | 8 | 15 | 53 | 49 | 4 | 47 |
| Getafe | 36 | 13 | 8 | 15 | 42 | 53 | –11 | 47 |
| Espanyol | 36 | 11 | 11 | 14 | 43 | 49 | –6 | 44 |
| Athletic Bilbao | 36 | 12 | 8 | 16 | 42 | 62 | –20 | 44 |
| Real Valladolid | 36 | 11 | 10 | 15 | 47 | 52 | –5 | 43 |
| Levante | 36 | 11 | 9 | 16 | 38 | 56 | –18 | 42 |
| Granada | 36 | 10 | 9 | 17 | 35 | 53 | –18 | 39 |
| Osasuna | 36 | 9 | 9 | 18 | 29 | 45 | –16 | 36 |
| Deportivo La Coruna | 36 | 8 | 11 | 17 | 46 | 66 | –20 | 35 |
| Real Zaragoza* | 36 | 9 | 7 | 20 | 36 | 55 | –19 | 34 |
| Mallorca* | 36 | 8 | 8 | 20 | 39 | 70 | –31 | 32 |
| Celta Vigo* | 36 | 8 | 7 | 21 | 34 | 52 | –18 | 31 |

*Top scorer:* Messi (Barcelona) 46.
*Cup Final:* Real Madrid 1, Atletico Madrid 2.

## SWEDEN

Svenska Fotbollfoerbundet, Evenemangsgatan 31, PO Box 1216, SE-171 23 Solna.
*Founded:* 1904; *National Colours:* Yellow shirts, blue shorts, yellow socks.

**International matches 2012–13**
Bahrain (a) 2-0, Croatia (a) 3-1, Iceland (h) 3-2, Serbia (h) 2-1, Ukraine (n) 1-2, England (n) 2-3, France (n) 2-0, Brazil (h) 0-3, China PR (h) 1-0, Kazakhstan (n) 2-0, Faroe Islands (a) 2-1, Germany (a) 4-4, England (h) 4-2, Argentina (n) 2-3, Republic of Ireland (h) 0-0, Slovakia (a) 0-0, FYR Macedonia (h) 1-0, Austria (a) 1-2, Faroe Islands (h) 2-0.

**League Championship wins (1896–2012)**
IFK Gothenburg 19; Malmo 16; Orgryte 14; IFK Norrkoping 12; Djurgaarden 11; AIK Stockholm 11; Helsingborg 7; GAIS Gothenburg 6; IF Elfsborg 6; Oster Vaxjo 4; Halmstad 4; Atvidaberg 1; IF Gothenburg 1; IFK Eskilstuna 1; Fassbergs 1; IF Gavic Brynas 1; IK Sleipner 1; Hammarby 1; Kalmar 1.

**Cup wins (1941–2013)**
Malmo 14; AIK Stockholm 8; IFK Norrkoping 6; IFK Gothenburg 6; Helsingborg 5; Djurgaarden 4; Kalmar 3; Atvidaberg 2; IF Elfsborg 2; GAIS Gothenburg 1; IF Raa 1; Landskrona 1; Oster Vaxjo 1; Degerfors 1; Halmstad 1; Orgryte 1.

**Final League Table 2012**

| | P | W | D | L | F | A | GD | Pts |
|---|---|---|---|---|---|---|---|---|
| IF Elfsborg | 30 | 18 | 5 | 7 | 48 | 29 | 19 | 59 |
| BK Hacken | 30 | 17 | 6 | 7 | 67 | 36 | 31 | 57 |
| Malmo | 30 | 16 | 8 | 6 | 49 | 33 | 16 | 56 |
| AIK Solna | 30 | 15 | 10 | 5 | 41 | 27 | 14 | 55 |
| IFK Norrkoping | 30 | 15 | 7 | 8 | 50 | 43 | 7 | 52 |
| Helsingborg | 30 | 13 | 11 | 6 | 52 | 33 | 19 | 50 |
| IFK Gothenburg | 30 | 9 | 12 | 9 | 36 | 41 | –5 | 39 |
| Atvidaberg | 30 | 9 | 10 | 11 | 48 | 48 | 0 | 37 |
| Djurgaarden | 30 | 8 | 13 | 9 | 37 | 40 | –3 | 37 |
| Kalmar | 30 | 10 | 7 | 13 | 36 | 45 | –9 | 37 |
| Gefle | 30 | 9 | 9 | 12 | 26 | 37 | –11 | 36 |
| Mjallby | 30 | 8 | 10 | 12 | 33 | 39 | –6 | 34 |
| Syrianska | 30 | 9 | 7 | 14 | 35 | 45 | –10 | 34 |
| GIF Sundsvall*+ | 30 | 6 | 11 | 13 | 35 | 46 | –11 | 29 |
| Orebro SK* | 30 | 5 | 9 | 16 | 32 | 46 | –14 | 24 |
| GAIS Gothenburg* | 30 | 5 | 9 | 20 | 24 | 61 | –37 | 12 |

*Top scorer:* Majeed (BK Hacken) 23.
*Cup Final:* IFK Gothenburg 1, Djurgaarden 1.
*IFK Gothenburg won 3-1 on penalties.*

## SWITZERLAND

Schweizerisher Fussballverband, Worbstrasse 48, Postfach 3000, Berne 15.
*Founded:* 1895; *National Colours:* Red shirts, white shorts, red socks.

**International matches 2012–13**
Argentina (h) 1-3, Germany (h) 5-3, Romania (h) 0-1, Croatia (a) 4-2, Slovenia (a) 2-0, Albania (h) 2-0, Norway (h) 1-1, Iceland (a) 2-0, Tunisia (a) 2-1, Greece (a) 0-0, Cyprus (a) 0-0, Cyprus (h) 1-0.

**League Championship wins (1897–2013)**
Grasshoppers 27; Servette 17; FC Basel 16; FC Zurich 12; Young Boys 11; Lausanne-Sport 7; La Chaux-de-Fonds 3; Lugano 3; Winterthur 3; Aarau 3; Neuchatel Xamax 2; Sion 2; St Gallen 2; Anglo-American Club 1; Brühl 1; Cantonal-Neuchatel 1; Biel-Bienne 1; Bellinzona 1; Etoile La Chaux-de-Fonds 1; Luzern 1.

**Cup wins (1926–2013)**
Grasshoppers 19; Sion 12; FC Basel 11; Lausanne-Sport 9; Servette 7; FC Zurich 7; La Chaux-de-Fonds 6; Young Boys 6; Lugano 3; Luzern 2; FC Grenchen 1; St Gallen 1; Urania Geneva 1; Young Fellows Zurich 1; Aarau 1; Wil 1.

**Final League Table 2012–13**

|               | P  | W  | D  | L  | F  | A  | GD  | Pts |
|---------------|----|----|----|----|----|----|-----|-----|
| FC Basel      | 36 | 21 | 9  | 6  | 61 | 31 | 30  | 72  |
| Grasshoppers  | 36 | 20 | 9  | 7  | 48 | 32 | 16  | 69  |
| St Gallen     | 36 | 17 | 8  | 11 | 54 | 36 | 18  | 59  |
| FC Zurich     | 36 | 16 | 7  | 13 | 62 | 48 | 14  | 55  |
| Thun          | 36 | 13 | 9  | 14 | 44 | 46 | –2  | 48  |
| Sion          | 36 | 13 | 9  | 14 | 40 | 54 | –14 | 48  |
| Young Boys    | 36 | 11 | 10 | 15 | 48 | 50 | –2  | 43  |
| Luzern        | 36 | 10 | 12 | 14 | 41 | 52 | –11 | 42  |
| Lausanne-Sport| 36 | 8  | 9  | 19 | 32 | 51 | –19 | 33  |
| Servette*     | 36 | 6  | 8  | 22 | 32 | 62 | –30 | 26  |

*Top scorer: Scarione (St Gallen) 21.*
*Cup Final: FC Basel 1, Grasshoppers 1.*
*Grasshoppers won 4-3 on penalties.*

## TURKEY

Turkiye Futbol Federasyonu, Mahallesi Darussafaka Caddesi No. 45, Kat. 2–3, 34330 Istinye, Istanbul.
*Founded:* 1923; *National Colours:* All red.

**International matches 2012–13**
Slovakia (h) 1-2, Georgia (a) 3-1, Finland (a) 2-3, Bulgaria (a) 2-0, Portugal (a) 3-1, Ukraine (h) 2-0, Austria (a) 0-2, Holland (a) 0-2, Estonia (h) 3-0, Romania (h) 0-1, Hungary (a) 1-3, Denmark (h) 1-1, Czech Republic (h) 0-2, Andorra (a) 2-0, Hungary (h) 1-1, Latvia (h) 3-3, Slovenia (h) 0-2.

**League Championship wins (1959–2013)**
Galatasaray 19; Fenerbahce 18; Besiktas 11; Trabzonspor 6; Bursa 1.

**Cup wins (1963–2013)**
Galatasaray 14; Besiktas 9; Trabzonspor 8; Fenerbahce 6; Altay Izmir 2; Goztepe Izmir 2; Eskisehirspor 1; Ankaragucu 2; Bursapor 1; Genclerbirligi 2; Sakaryaspor 1; Kocaelispor 1; Kayseri 1.

**Final League Table 2012–13**

|                      | P  | W  | D  | L  | F  | A  | GD  | Pts |
|----------------------|----|----|----|----|----|----|-----|-----|
| Galatasaray          | 34 | 21 | 8  | 5  | 66 | 35 | 31  | 71  |
| Fenerbahce           | 34 | 18 | 7  | 9  | 56 | 39 | 17  | 61  |
| Besiktas             | 34 | 16 | 10 | 8  | 63 | 49 | 14  | 58  |
| Bursaspor            | 34 | 14 | 13 | 7  | 52 | 41 | 11  | 55  |
| Kayserispor          | 34 | 15 | 7  | 12 | 48 | 45 | 3   | 52  |
| Kasimpasa            | 34 | 14 | 8  | 12 | 48 | 37 | 11  | 50  |
| Antalyaspor          | 34 | 14 | 5  | 15 | 50 | 52 | –2  | 47  |
| Eskisehirspor        | 34 | 11 | 13 | 10 | 48 | 40 | 8   | 46  |
| Trabzonspor          | 34 | 13 | 7  | 14 | 39 | 40 | –1  | 46  |
| Gaziantepspor        | 34 | 12 | 10 | 12 | 42 | 49 | –7  | 46  |
| Genclerbirligi       | 34 | 10 | 15 | 9  | 46 | 47 | –1  | 45  |
| Sivasspor            | 34 | 12 | 8  | 14 | 42 | 46 | –4  | 44  |
| Elazigspor           | 34 | 10 | 13 | 11 | 31 | 46 | –15 | 43  |
| Akhisar Belediyespor | 34 | 11 | 9  | 14 | 36 | 44 | –8  | 42  |
| Kardemir Karabukspor | 34 | 11 | 8  | 15 | 46 | 41 | 53 –12 | 40 |
| Istanbul BB*         | 34 | 9  | 9  | 16 | 43 | 50 | –7  | 36  |
| Orduspor*            | 34 | 8  | 11 | 17 | 35 | 51 | –16 | 29  |
| Mersin Idmanyurdu*   | 34 | 4  | 10 | 20 | 31 | 53 | –22 | 22  |

*Top scorer: Yilmaz (Galatasaray) 24.*
*Cup Final: Fenerbahce 1, Trabzonspor 0.*

## UKRAINE

Football Federation of Ukraine, Provulok Laboratornyi 7-A, PO Box 55, 01133 Kiev.
*Founded:* 1991; *National Colours:* Yellow shirts with blue trim, yellow shorts with blue trim, yellow socks.

**International matches 2012–13**
Israel (a) 3-2, Estonia (h) 4-0, Austria (a) 2-3, Turkey (a) 0-2, Sweden (h) 2-1, France (h) 0-2, England (h) 0-1, Czech Republic (h) 0-0, England (a) 1-1, Moldova (a) 0-0, Montenegro (h) 0-1, Bulgaria (a) 1-0, Norway (a) 2-0, Poland (a) 3-1, Moldova (h) 2-1, Cameroon (h) 0-0, Montenegro (a) 4-0.

**League Championship wins (1992–2013)**
Dynamo Kyiv 13; Shakhtar Donetsk 8; Tavriya Simferopol 1.

**Cup wins (1992–2013)**
Dynamo Kyiv 9; Shakhtar Donetsk 9; Chornomorets Odessa 2; Vorskla 1; Tavriya Simferopol 1.

**Final League Table 2012–13**

|                         | P  | W  | D  | L  | F  | A  | GD  | Pts |
|-------------------------|----|----|----|----|----|----|-----|-----|
| Shakhtar Donetsk        | 30 | 25 | 4  | 1  | 82 | 18 | 64  | 79  |
| Metalist Kharkiv        | 30 | 20 | 6  | 4  | 59 | 25 | 34  | 66  |
| Dynamo Kyiv             | 30 | 20 | 2  | 8  | 55 | 23 | 32  | 62  |
| Dnipro Dnipropetrovsk   | 30 | 16 | 8  | 6  | 54 | 27 | 27  | 56  |
| Metalurh Donetsk        | 30 | 14 | 7  | 9  | 45 | 35 | 10  | 49  |
| Chornomorets Odessa     | 30 | 12 | 7  | 11 | 32 | 36 | –4  | 43  |
| Kryvbas Kryvyi Rih      | 30 | 12 | 7  | 11 | 36 | 41 | –5  | 43  |
| Arsenal Kyiv            | 30 | 10 | 9  | 11 | 34 | 41 | –7  | 39  |
| Illychivets Mariupil    | 30 | 10 | 8  | 12 | 30 | 32 | –2  | 38  |
| Zorya Luhansk           | 30 | 10 | 7  | 13 | 32 | 43 | –11 | 37  |
| Tavriya Simferopol (–3) | 30 | 10 | 5  | 15 | 27 | 46 | –19 | 32  |
| Vorskla Poltava         | 30 | 8  | 7  | 15 | 31 | 36 | –5  | 31  |
| Volyn Lutsk             | 30 | 7  | 8  | 15 | 26 | 45 | –19 | 29  |
| Karpaty Lviv            | 30 | 7  | 6  | 17 | 37 | 52 | –15 | 27  |
| Hoverla Uzhhorod        | 30 | 5  | 9  | 16 | 29 | 57 | –28 | 22  |
| Metalurh Zaporizhya     | 30 | 1  | 8  | 21 | 12 | 64 | –52 | 11  |

*No relegation. Kryvbas expelled from 2013–14 season due to financial difficulties.*
*Top scorer: Mkhitaryan (Shakhtar Donetsk) 25.*
*Cup Final: Shakhtar Donetsk 3, Chornomorets Odessa 0.*

## WALES

The Football Association of Wales Limited, 11/12 Neptune Court, Vanguard Way, Cardiff CF24 5PJ.
*Founded:* 1876; *National Colours:* All red.

# SOUTH AMERICA

## ARGENTINA

Asociacion Del Futbol Argentina, Viamonte 1366/76, 1053 Buenos Aires.
*Founded:* 1893; *National Colours:* Light blue and white vertical striped shirts, dark blue shorts, white socks.
*International matches 2012–13*
Switzerland (a) 3-1, Ecuador (h) 4-0, Brazil (n) 4-3, Germany (a) 3-1, Paraguay (h) 3-1, Peru (a) 1-1, Brazil (a) 1-2, Uruguay (h) 3-0, Chile (a) 2-1, Saudi Arabia (a) 0-0, Brazil (h) 2-1 (3-4p), Sweden (a) 3-2, Venezuela (h) 3-0, Bolivia (a) 1-1, Colombia (h) 0-0, Ecuador (a) 1-1, Guatemala (a) 4-0.

## BOLIVIA

Federacion Boliviana De Futbol, Av. Libertador Bolivar No. 1168, Casilla de Correo 484, Cochabamba, Bolivia.
*Founded:* 1925; *National Colours:* Green shirts, white shorts, green socks.
*International matches 2012–13*
Cuba (h) 1-0, Chile (h) 0-2, Paraguay (h) 3-1, Guyana (h) 2-0, Ecuador (a) 0-1, Peru (h) 1-1, Uruguay (h) 1-1, Costa Rica (h) 1-1, Haiti (h) 2-1, Colombia (a) 0-5, Argentina (h) 1-1, Brazil (h) 0-4, Venezuela (h) 1-1, Chile (a) 3-1.

## BRAZIL

Confederacao Brasileira De Futebol, Rua Victor Civita 66, Bloco 1-Edificio 5-5 Andar, Barra da Tijuca, Rio De Janeiro 22775-040.
*Founded:* 1914; *National Colours:* Yellow shirts with green collar and cuffs, blue shorts, white socks with green and yellow border.
*International matches 2012–13*
Bosnia-Herzegovina (n) 2-1, Denmark (a) 3-1, USA (a) 4-1, Mexico (n) 0-2, Argentina (n) 3-4, Sweden (a) 3-0, South Africa (h) 1-0, China PR (h) 8-0, Argentina (h) 2-1, Iraq (h) 6-0, Japan (n) 4-0, Colombia (n) 1-1, Argentina (a) 1-2 (4-3p), England (a) 1-2, Italy (n) 2-2, Russia (n) 1-1,

Bolivia (a) 4-0, Chile (h) 2-2, England (h) 2-2, France (h) 3-0, Japan (n) 3-0, Mexico (n) 2-0, Italy (n) 4-2, Uruguay (n) 2-1, Spain (n) 3-0.

### CHILE

Federacion De Futbol De Chile, Avda. Quillin No. 5635, Casilla postal 3733, Correo Central, Santiago de Chile.
*Founded:* 1895; *National Colours:* Red shirts with blue collar and cuffs, blue shorts, white socks.
*International matches 2012–13*
Paraguay (a) 3-2*, Paraguay (a) 0-2, Ghana (n) 1-1, Peru (h) 3-1, Peru (a) 3-0, Bolivia (a) 2-0, Venezuela (a) 2-0, Ecuador (a) 0-3, Colombia (h) 1-3, Ecuador (a) 1-3, Argentina (h) 1-2, Serbia (n) 1-3, Haiti (h) 3-0, Egypt (n) 2-1, Peru (a) 0-1, Uruguay (h) 2-0, Brazil (a) 2-2, Paraguay (a) 2-1, Bolivia (h) 3-1.
* *Played 22.12.2011, result omitted from last edition.*

### COLOMBIA

Federacion Colombiana De Futbol, Avenida 32, No. 16–22 piso 4o. Apartado Aereo 17602, Santafe de Bogota.
*Founded:* 1924; *National Colours:* Yellow shirts, blue shorts, red socks.
*International matches 2012–13*
Mexico (n) 2-0, Peru (a) 1-0, Ecuador (a) 0-1, Uruguay (h) 4-0, Chile (a) 3-1, Paraguay (h) 2-0, Cameroon (h) 3-0, Brazil (n) 1-1, Guatemala (n) 4-1, Bolivia (h) 5-0, Venezuela (a) 1-0, Argentina (a) 0-0, Peru (h) 2-0.

### ECUADOR

Federacion Ecuatoriana del Futbol, km 4 1/2 via a la Costa (Avda. del Bombero), PO Box 09-01-7447 Guayaquil.
*Founded:* 1925; *National Colours:* Yellow shirts, blue shorts, red socks.
*International matches 2012–13*
Honduras (h) 2-0, Argentina (a) 0-4, Colombia (h) 1-0, Chile (n) 3-0, Bolivia (h) 1-0, Uruguay (a) 1-1, Chile (h) 3-1, Venezuela (h) 1-1, Portugal (a) 3-2, El Salvador (h) 5-0, Paraguay (h) 4-1, Germany (n) 2-4, Peru (a) 0-1, Argentina (h) 1-1.

### PARAGUAY

Asociacion Paraguaya de Futbol, Estadio De Los Defensores del Chaco, Calles Mayor Martinez 1393, Asuncion.
*Founded:* 1906; *National Colours:* Red and white shirts, blue shorts, blue socks.
*International matches 2012–13*
Chile (a) 2-3*, Chile (h) 2-0, Guatemala (h) 2-1, Panama (h) 1-0, Guatemala (a) 1-0, Bolivia (a) 3-1, Guatemala (n) 3-3, Argentina (a) 1-3, Venezuela (h) 0-2, Colombia (a) 0-2, Peru (h) 1-0, Guatemala (h) 1-0, El Salvador (h) 0-0, Uruguay (a) 1-1, Ecuador (a) 1-4, Chile (h) 1-2.
* *Played 22.12.2011, result omitted from last edition.*

### PERU

Federacion Peruana De Futbol, Av. Aviacion 2085, San Luis, Lima 30.
*Founded:* 1922; *National Colours:* White shirts with red stripe, white shorts with red lines, white socks with red line.
*International matches 2012–13*
Tunisia (a) 1-1, Chile (a) 1-3, Chile (h) 0-3, Nigeria (h) 1-0, Colombia (h) 0-1, Uruguay (a) 2-4, Costa Rica (a) 1-0, Venezuela (h) 2-1, Argentina (a) 1-1, Bolivia (h) 1-1, Paraguay (h) 1-0, Honduras (n) 0-0, Chile (h) 1-0, Trinidad & Tobago (h) 3-0, Mexico (n) 0-0, Panama (a) 2-1, Ecuador (h) 1-0, Colombia (a) 0-2.

### URUGUAY

Asociacion Uruguaya De Futbol, Guayabo 1531, 11200 Montevideo.
*Founded:* 1900; *National Colours:* Sky blue shirts with white collar/cuffs, black shorts and socks with sky blue borders.
*International matches 2012–13*
Romania (a) 1-1, Russia (a) 1-1, Venezuela (h) 1-1, Peru (h) 4-2, France (a) 0-0, Colombia (a) 0-4, Ecuador (h) 1-1, Argentina (a) 0-3, Bolivia (a) 1-4, Poland (a) 3-1, Spain (n) 0-3, Paraguay (h) 1-1, Chile (a) 0-2, France (h) 1-0, Venezuela (a) 1-0, Spain (n) 1-2, Nigeria (n) 2-1, Tahiti (n) 8-0, Brazil (n) 1-2, Italy (n) 2-2 (2-3p).

### VENEZUELA

Federacion Venezolana De Futbol, Avda. Santos Erminy Ira, Calle las Delicias Torre Mega II, P.H. Sabana Grande, Caracas 1050.
*Founded:* 1926; *National Colours:* Burgundy shirts, white shorts and socks.
*International matches 2012–13*

USA (n) 0-1, Mexico (n) 1-3, Spain (a) 0-5, Moldova (h) 4-0, Uruguay (a) 1-1, Chile (h) 0-2, Japan (a) 1-1, Peru (a) 1-2, Paraguay (a) 2-0, Ecuador (h) 1-1, Nigeria (n) 1-3, Argentina (a) 0-3, Colombia (h) 1-0, El Salvador (h) 2-1, Bolivia (a) 1-1, Uruguay (h) 0-1.

## ASIA

### AFGHANISTAN

Afghanistan Football Federation, PO Box 128, Kabul.
*Founded:* 1933; *National Colours:* All white with red lines.
*International matches 2012–13*
Sri Lanka (n) 1-0, Mongolia (n) 1-0, Laos (n) 1-1.

### AUSTRALIA

Soccer Australia Ltd, Level 3, East Stand, Stadium Australia, Edwin Flack Avenue, Homebush, NSW 2127.
*Founded:* 1961; *National Colours:* All green with gold trim.
*International matches 2012–13*
Saudi Arabia (h) 4-2, Denmark (a) 0-2, Oman (a) 0-0, Japan (h) 1-1, Scotland (a) 1-3, Lebanon (n) 3-0, Jordan (a) 1-2, Iraq (a) 2-1, South Korea (a) 2-1, Hong Kong (a) 1-0, North Korea (n) 1-1, Guam (n) 9-0, Chinese Taipei (n) 8-0, Romania (n) 2-3, Oman (h) 2-2, Japan (a) 1-1, Jordan (h) 4-0, Iraq (h) 1-0.

### BAHRAIN

Bahrain Football Association, P.O. Box 5464, Manama.
*Founded:* 1957; *National Colours:* All red.
*International matches 2012–13*
Sweden (h) 0-2, Indonesia (h) 10-0, Kuwait (h) 0-1, Azerbaijan (a) 0-3, Philippines (h) 0-0, UAE (a) 2-6, Jordan (h) 3-0, Kuwait (a) 1-1, Palestine (a) 2-0, Iraq (h) 0-0, Yemen (n) 1-0, Iran (n) 0-0, Saudi Arabia (n) 1-0, Syria (n) 1-1 (2-3p), Oman (n) 0-1, Burkina Faso (h) 0-0, Guinea (h) 3-0, Oman (h) 0-0, UAE (h) 1-2, Qatar (h) 1-0, Iraq (h) 1-1 (2-4p), Kuwait (a) 1-6, Singapore (h) 3-1, Yemen (a) 2-0, Lebanon (h) 0-0, Qatar (h) 1-0, Kyrgyzstan (h) 1-3.

### BANGLADESH

Bangladesh Football Federation, Bangabandhu National Stadium-1, Dhaka 1000.
*Founded:* 1972; *National Colours:* Orange shirts, white shorts, green socks.
*International matches 2012–13*
Nepal (a) 1-1, Thailand (a) 0-5, Malaysia (a) 1-1, Palestine (n) 0-1, Nepal (n) 2-0, Northern Mariana Islands (n) 4-0.

### BHUTAN

Bhutan Football Federation, P.O. Box 365, Thimphu.
*National Colours:* All yellow and red.
*International matches 2012–13*
Thailand (a) 5-0.

### BRUNEI DARUSSALAM

Football Association of Brunei Darussalam, PO Box 2010, 1920 Bandar Seri Begawan BS 8674.
*Founded:* 1959; *National Colours:* Yellow shirts, black shorts, black and white socks.
*International matches 2012–13*
Indonesia (h) 0-5, Myanmar (n) 1-0, Cambodia (n) 3-2, Laos (n) 1-3, Timor-Leste (n) 2-1.

### CAMBODIA

Cambodian Football Federation, Chaeng Maeng Village, Rd. Kab Srov, Sangkat Samrong Krom, Khan Dangkor, Phnom-Penh.
*Founded:* 1933; *National Colours:* All blue.
*International matches 2012–13*
Philippines (h) 0-0, Malaysia (a) 1-2, Timor-Leste (n) 1-5, Laos (n) 0-1, Brunei (n) 2-3, Myanmar (n) 0-3, Turkmenistan (n) 0-7, Philippines (n) 0-8.

### CHINA PR

Football Association of The People's Republic of China, Dongjiudasha Mansion, Xizhaosi Street, Dongcheng 100061, Beijing.
*Founded:* 1924; *National Colours:* All white.
*International matches 2012–13*
Kuwait (h) 2-0, Jordan (h) 3-1, Spain (a) 0-1, Vietnam (h) 3-0, Ghana (n) 1-1, Sweden (a) 0-1, Brazil (a) 0-8, New Zealand (h) 1-1, Oman (a) 0-1, Saudi Arabia (a) 1-2, Iraq (h) 1-0, Uzbekistan (h) 1-2, Holland (h) 0-2, Thailand (h) 1-5.

### CHINESE TAIPEI

Chinese Taipei Football Association, Room 210, 2F, 55 Chang Chi Street, Tatung 10363, Taipei.
*Founded:* 1936; *National Colours:* Blue shirts and shorts, white socks.

*International matches 2012–13*
Hong Kong (a) 1-5, Macao (n) 2-2, Guam (n) 2-0, Philippines (n) 1-3, North Korea (n) 1-6, Guam (n) 1-1, Hong Kong (n) 0-2, Australia (n) 0-8, India (n) 1-2, Myanmar (a) 1-1, Guam (h) 0-3.

## GUAM
Guam Football Association, PO Box 5093, 96932 Hagatna, Guam.
*Founded:* 1975; *National Colours:* Blue shirts, white shorts, blue socks.
*International matches 2012–13*
Tuvalu (n) 1-1*, Philippines (h) 0-3, Northern Mariana Islands (h) 3-1, Macau (h) 3-0, Philippines (a) 0-0, Chinese Taipei (n) 0-2, Macao (n) 3-0, Hong Kong (n) 1-2, North Korea (n) 0-5, Chinese Taipei (n) 1-1, Australia (n) 0-9, Myanmar (n) 0-5, India (n) 0-4, Chinese Taipei (n) 3-0.
* *Played 04.09.2011, result omitted from last edition.*

## HONG KONG
Hong Kong Football Association Ltd, 55 Fat Kwong Street, Homantin, Kowloon, Hong Kong.
*Founded:* 1914; *National Colours:* All red.
*International matches 2012–13*
Chinese Taipei (h) 5-1, Singapore (h) 1-0, Vietnam (a) 1-2, Singapore (a) 0-2, Malaysia (h) 0-3, Malaysia (a) 1-1, Guam (n) 2-1, Australia (h) 0-1, Chinese Taipei (h) 2-0, North Korea (h) 0-4, Uzbekistan (a) 0-0, Vietnam (h) 1-0, Philippines (n) 0-1.

## INDIA
All India Football Federation, Football House, Sector 19, Phase 1 Dwarka 110075, New Delhi.
*Founded:* 1937; *National Colours:* Sky blue shirts, navy blue shorts, sky and navy blue socks.
*International matches 2012–13*
Oman (a) 1-5, Azerbaijan (n) 0-3, Tajikistan (n) 0-2, Philippines (n) 0-2, North Korea (n) 0-4, Syria (h) 2-1, Maldives (h) 3-0, Nepal (h) 0-0, Cameroon A (h) 0-1, Cameroon A (h) 2-2 (5-4p), Singapore (h) 0-2, Palestine (h) 2-4, Chinese Taipei (n) 2-1, Guam (n) 4-0, Myanmar (n) 0-1.

## INDONESIA
Football Association of Indonesia, Gelora Bung Karno, Pintu X-XI, Senayan, 10270 Jakarta.
*Founded:* 1930; *National Colours:* Red shirts, white shorts, red socks.
*International matches 2012–13*
Bahrain (a) 0-10, Philippines (a) 2-2, North Korea (h) 0-2, Vietnam (h) 0-0, Brunei (a) 5-0, Vietnam (a) 0-0, Timor-Leste (h) 1-0, Cameroon (h) 0-0, Laos (n) 2-2, Singapore (n) 1-0, Malaysia (a) 0-2, Jordan (a) 0-5, Iraq (n) 0-1, Saudi Arabia (h) 1-2, Holland (a) 0-3.

## IRAN
IR Iran Football Federation, No. 2/2 Third St. Seoul Avenue, 19958-73591 Teheran.
*Founded:* 1920; *National Colours:* All white.
*International matches 2012–13*
Jordan (n) 2-2, Qatar (h) 2-2, Mozambique (h) 3-0, Albania (n) 0-1, Uzbekistan (a) 1-0, Qatar (h) 0-0, Tunisia (n) 2-2, Jordan (a) 0-0, Lebanon (a) 0-1, South Korea (h) 1-0, Tajikistan (h) 6-1, Uzbekistan (h) 0-1, Saudi Arabia (n) 0-0, Bahrain (n) 0-0, Yemen (n) 2-1, Lebanon (n) 5-0, Kuwait (a) 1-1, Oman (a) 1-3, Qatar (a) 1-0, Lebanon (h) 4-0, South Korea (a) 1-0.

## IRAQ
Iraqi Football Association, Olympic Committee Building, Palestine Street, PO Box 484, Baghdad.
*Founded:* 1948; *National Colours:* All black.
*International matches 2012–13*
Lebanon (a) 0-1, Singapore (h) 7-1, Egypt (a) 0-0, Sierra Leone (h) 1-0, Jordan (a) 1-1, Oman (a) 1-1, Japan (h) 0-1, Brazil (a) 0-6, Australia (n) 1-2, Qatar (n) 1-2, Jordan (h) 1-0, Bahrain (a) 0-0, Jordan (h) 1-0, Syria (h) 1-1, Oman (a) 2-0, Syria (h) 0-1, Tunisia (h) 1-2, Saudi Arabia (n) 2-0, Kuwait (n) 1-0, Yemen (n) 2-0, Bahrain (a) 1-1 (4-2p), UAE (n) 1-2, Indonesia (n) 0-0, China PR (a) 0-0, Syria (a) 2-1, Liberia (a) 0-1, Oman (a) 0-1, Japan (n) 0-1, Australia (a) 1-0.

## JAPAN
Japan Football Association, JFA House, 3-10-15, Hongo, Bunkyo-ku, Tokyo 113-0033.
*Founded:* 1921; *National Colours:* Blue shirts, white shorts, blue socks.

*International matches 2012–13*
Iceland (h) 3-1, Uzbekistan (h) 0-1, Azerbaijan (h) 2-0, Oman (h) 3-0, Jordan (h) 6-0, Australia (a) 1-1, Venezuela (h) 1-1, UAE (h) 1-0, Iraq (h) 1-0, France (a) 1-0, Brazil (h) 0-4, Oman (a) 2-1, Latvia (h) 3-0, Canada (n) 2-1, Jordan (a) 1-2, Bulgaria (h) 0-2, Australia (h) 1-1, Iraq (a) 1-0, Brazil (a) 0-3, Italy 3-4 (a) 0-0, Mexico (n) 1-2.

## JORDAN
Jordan Football Association, PO Box 962024 Al-Hussein Sports City, 11196 Amman.
*Founded:* 1949; *National Colours:* All white and red.
*International matches 2012–13*
Iran (n) 2-2, China PR (a) 1-3, Lebanon (a) 2-1, Iraq (h) 1-1, Japan (a) 0-6, Uzbekistan (h) 0-1, Uzbekistan (h) 2-0, Iran (h) 0-0, Australia (h) 2-1, Qatar (h) 1-1, Oman (a) 1-2, Bahrain (a) 0-3, Iraq (n) 0-1, Iraq (n) 0-1, Syria (h) 1-2, Indonesia (h) 5-0, Singapore (h) 4-0, Belarus (h) 1-0, Japan (h) 2-1, Libya (h) 1-0, Australia (a) 0-4, Oman (h) 1-0.

## KOREA, NORTH
Football Association of The Democratic People's Rep. of Korea, Kumsong-dong, Kwangbok Street, Mangyongdae Distr, PO Box 56, Pyongyang FNJ-PRK.
*Founded:* 1945; *National Colours:* All white.
*International matches 2012–13*
Kuwait (h) 1-1, Tajikistan (a) 1-1, Philippines (n) 2-0, Tajikistan (n) 2-0, India (n) 4-0, Palestine (n) 2-0, Turkmenistan (n) 2-1, Indonesia (a) 2-0, Chinese Taipei (n) 6-1, Guam (n) 5-0, Australia (n) 1-1, Hong Kong (n) 4-0, Laos (h) 1-0, Qatar (a) 0-0.

## KOREA, SOUTH
Korea Football Association, 1-131 Sinmunno, 2-ga, Jongno-Gu, Seoul 110-062.
*Founded:* 1928; *National Colours:* Red shirts, blue shorts, red socks.
*International matches 2012–13*
Uzbekistan (h) 4-2, Kuwait (h) 2-0, Spain (n) 1-4, Qatar (n) 4-1, Lebanon (h) 3-0, Zambia (h) 2-1, Uzbekistan (a) 2-2, Iran (a) 0-1, Australia (h) 1-2, Croatia (n) 0-4, Qatar (h) 2-1, Lebanon (a) 1-1, Uzbekistan (h) 1-0, Iran (h) 0-1.

## KUWAIT
Kuwait Football Association, PO Box 2029, Udiliya, Block 4 Al-Ittihad Street, Safat 13021.
*Founded:* 1952; *National Colours:* All blue.
*International matches 2012–13*
Uzbekistan (h) 1-0, North Korea (a) 1-1, China PR (h) 2-0, South Korea (a) 0-2, Bahrain (a) 1-0, Uzbekistan (a) 0-3, UAE (a) 0-3, Syria (h) 1-1, Philippines (h) 2-1, Bahrain (h) 1-1, Palestine (h) 2-1, Oman (h) 0-2, Lebanon (h) 2-1, Yemen (n) 2-0, Iraq (n) 0-1, Saudi Arabia (n) 1-0, UAE (n) 0-1, Bahrain (n) 6-1, Thailand (a) 3-1, Palestine (h) 2-1, Iran (h) 1-1, Hungary (a) 0-1.

## KYRGYZSTAN
Football Federation of Kyrgyz Republic, PO Box 1484, Kurenkeeva Street 195, Bishkek 720040, Kyrgyzstan.
*Founded:* 1992; *National Colours:* Red shirts, white shorts, red socks.
*International matches 2012–13*
Kazakhstan (a) 2-5, Macao (h) 1-0, Pakistan (h) 1-0, Tajikistan (h) 1-0, Bahrain (a) 3-1, Estonia (a) 1-1, Moldova (a) 1-2.

## LAOS
Federation Lao de Football, National Stadium, Kounboulo Street, PO Box 3777, Vientiane 856-21, Laos.
*Founded:* 1951; *National Colours:* All red.
*International matches 2012–13*
Philippines (h) 2-1, Thailand (a) 1-2, Cambodia (n) 1-0, Timor-Leste (n) 1-3, Brunei (h) 3-1, Myanmar (n) 0-0, Vietnam (a) 0-4, Turkmenistan (n) 2-4, Indonesia (n) 2-2, Malaysia (n) 1-4, Singapore (n) 3-4, North Korea (a) 1-0, Mongolia (h) 1-1, Sri Lanka (h) 4-2, Afghanistan (h) 1-1, Singapore (h) 2-5.

## LEBANON
Federation Libanaise De Football-Association, P.O. Box 4732, Verdun Street, Bristol, Radwan Centre Building, Beirut.
*Founded:* 1933; *National Colours:* Red shirts, white shorts, red socks.
*International matches 2012–13*
Iraq (h) 1-0, UAE (a) 2-4, Egypt (h) 1-4, Jordan (h) 1-2, Oman (a) 1-1, Qatar (h) 0-1, Uzbekistan (h) 1-1, South Korea (a) 0-3, Australia (h) 0-3, Iran (h) 1-0, Yemen (h) 2-1, Qatar (a) 0-1, Oman (n) 1-0, Palestine (n) 0-1, Kuwait

(a) 1-2, Gabon (h) 0-0, Qatar (a) 0-1, Iran (a) 0-5, Bahrain (a) 0-0, Thailand (h) 5-2, Uzbekistan (a) 0-1, Oman (a) 1-1, South Korea (h) 1-1, Iran (a) 0-4.

## MACAO
Associacao De Futebol De Macau (AFM), Ave. da Amizade 405, Seng Vo Kok, 13 Andar "A", Macau.
*Founded:* 1939; *National Colours:* All green.
*International matches 2012–13*
Northern Mariana Islands (a) 5-1, Guam (n) 0-3, Chinese Taipei (n) 2-2, Philippines (a) 0-5, Guam (n) 0-3, Kyrgyzstan (a) 0-1, Tajikistan (n) 0-3, Pakistan (n) 0-2.

## MALAYSIA
Football Association of Malaysia, 3rd Floor, Wisma Fam, Jalan, SSA/9, Kelana Jaya Selangor Darul Ehsan 47301.
*Founded:* 1933; *National Colours:* All yellow and black.
*International matches 2012–13*
Philippines (a) 1-1, Sri Lanka (h) 6-0, Philippines (h) 0-0, Singapore (a) 2-2, Singapore (h) 2-0, Vietnam (h) 0-2, Cambodia (h) 2-1, Hong Kong (a) 3-0, Vietnam (a) 0-1, Thailand (a) 0-2, Hong Kong (h) 1-1, Bangladesh (h) 1-1, Singapore (h) 0-3, Laos (h) 4-1, Indonesia (h) 2-0, Thailand (h) 1-1, Thailand (h) 0-2, Qatar (a) 0-2, Yemen (h) 2-1, Palestine (h) 0-2.

## MALDIVES REPUBLIC
Football Association of Maldives, FAM House, Ujaalahingun 20388, Male.
*Founded:* 1982; *National Colours:* Red shirts, Green shorts, white socks.
*International matches 2012–13*
Thailand (a) 0-3, Turkmenistan (n) 1-3, Nepal (n) 1-0, Palestine (n) 0-2, Nepal (n) 2-1, India (a) 0-3, Syria (n) 2-1, Cameroon A (n) 1-3, Pakistan (h) 1-1, Pakistan (h) 3-0.

## MONGOLIA
Mongolia Football Federation, PO Box 259, 210646 Ulan Bator.
*National Colours:* White shirts, red shorts, white socks.
*International matches 2012–13*
Laos (a) 1-1, Afghanistan (n) 0-1, Sri Lanka (a) 0-3.

## MYANMAR
Myanmar Football Federation, Wai Za Yan Tar Road, Thingangyun Township, 11072 Yangon.
*Founded:* 1947; *National Colours:* Red shirts, white shorts, red socks.
*International matches 2012–13*
Singapore (h) 1-1, Brunei (h) 1-0, Timor-Leste (h) 1-2, Cambodia (h) 3-0, Laos (h) 0-0, Vietnam (n) 1-1, Thailand (a) 0-4, Philippines (n) 0-2, Philippines (h) 0-1, Guam (h) 5-0, Chinese Taipei (h) 1-1, India (h) 1-0, Singapore (h) 0-2.

## NEPAL
All-Nepal Football Association, AMFA House, Ward No. 4, Bishalnagar, PO Box 12582, Kathmandu.
*Founded:* 1951; *National Colours:* All red.
*International matches 2012–13*
Palestine (h) 0-2, Maldives (h) 0-1, Turkmenistan (h) 0-3, Maldives (n) 0-1, Cameroon A (n) 0-5, India (a) 0-0, Syria (n) 0-2, Bangladesh (n) 1-1, Pakistan (h) 0-1, Pakistan (h) 0-1, Northern Mariana Islands (n) 6-0, Bangladesh (n) 0-2, Palestine (h) 0-0.

## OMAN
Oman Football Association, PO Box 3462, 112 Ruwi.
*Founded:* 1978; *National Colours:* All white.
*International matches 2012–13*
Saudi Arabia (h) 0-0*, Thailand (a) 0-3*, Australia (a) 0-3*, Qatar (a) 0-1*, Australia (h) 0-3*, Saudi Arabia (a) 0-0*, Congo DR (h) 2-2, India (h) 5-1, Thailand (h) 2-0, Lebanon (h) 1-1, Japan (a) 0-3, Australia (h) 0-0, Iraq (a) 1-1, Egypt (h) 1-1, Republic of Ireland (n) 1-4, Yemen (h) 2-1, Qatar (a) 1-1, Jordan (h) 2-1, Estonia (h) 1-2, Japan (h) 1-2, Lebanon (n) 0-1, Kuwait (a) 2-0, Palestine (n) 2-1, Iraq (n) 0-2, Bahrain (n) 1-0, Togo (h) 0-1, Bahrain (a) 0-0, Qatar (n) 1-2, UAE (n) 0-2, China PR (a) 1-0, Syria (h) 1-0, Haiti (h) 3-0, Australia (a) 2-2, Iran (h) 3-1, Lebanon (h) 1-1, Iraq (h) 1-0, Jordan (a) 0-1.
* *Played in 2011, results omitted from last edition.*

## PAKISTAN
Pakistan Football Federation, 6 National Hockey Stadium, Ferozepur Road, 54600 Lahore.
*Founded:* 1948; *National Colours:* All green and white.
*International matches 2012–13*
Singapore (a) 0-4, Nepal (a) 1-0, Nepal (a) 1-0, Maldives (a) 1-1, Maldives (a) 0-3, Tajikistan (n) 0-1, Kyrgyzstan (a) 0-1, Macao (n) 2-0.

## PALESTINE
Palestinian Football Federation, PO Box 4373, Ramallah, Al Bireh, Palestine.
*Founded:* 1928; *National Colours:* White shirts, black shorts, white socks.
*International matches 2012–13*
UAE (a) 0-3, Nepal (a) 2-0, Turkmenistan (n) 0-0, Maldives (a) 2-0, North Korea (n) 0-2, Philippines (n) 3-4, Yemen (a) 2-1, Syria (h) 1-1, Syria (n) 2-1, Bahrain (n) 0-2, Kuwait (a) 1-2, Lebanon (n) 1-0, Oman (n) 1-2, India (a) 4-2, Bangladesh (n) 1-0, Northern Mariana Islands (n) 9-0, Nepal (a) 0-0, Kuwait (a) 1-2, Malaysia (a) 2-0. Qatar (a) 0-2.

## PHILIPPINES
Philippine Football Federation, Room 405, Building V, Philsports Complex, Meralco Avenue, Pasig City, Metro Manila.
*Founded:* 1907; *National Colours:* All blue.
*International matches 2012–13*
Malaysia (h) 1-1, North Korea (n) 0-2, India (n) 2-0, Tajikistan (n) 2-1, Turkmenistan (n) 1-2, Palestine (n) 4-3, Malaysia (a) 0-0, Indonesia (h) 2-2, Guam (h) 3-0, Cambodia (a) 0-0, Singapore (a) 2-0, Laos (a) 1-2, Guam (h) 1-0, Macao (h) 5-0, Chinese Taipei (h) 3-1, Bahrain (a) 0-0, Kuwait (a) 1-2, Singapore (h) 1-0, Thailand (a) 1-2, Vietnam (n) 1-0, Myanmar (n) 2-0, Singapore (n) 0-0, Singapore (n) 0-1, Myanmar (a) 1-0, Brunei (n) 3-0, Cambodia (h) 8-0, Turkmenistan (e) 1-0, Philippines (n) 1-0.

## QATAR
Qatar Football Association, 7th Floor, QNOC Building, Cornich, PO Box 5333, Doha.
*Founded:* 1960; *National Colours:* All white.
*International matches 2012–13*
Iraq (h) 2-2, Albania (h) 1-2, Palestine (h) 0-0, Lebanon (a) 1-0, South Korea (h) 1-4, Iran (a) 0-0, Tajikistan (h) 1-2, Jordan (h) 1-1, Oman (h) 1-1, Uzbekistan (h) 0-1, Iraq (h) 2-1, Lebanon (h) 1-0, Egypt (h) 2-2, UAE (n) 3-0, Oman (n) 1-1, Bahrain (a) 0-0, Lebanon (a) 1-0, Malaysia (a) 0-0, Egypt (h) 2-2, Bahrain (a) 0-0, South Korea (a) 1-4, Palestine (h) 2-0, Latvia (h) 3-1, Azerbaijan (h) 1-1, Iran (h) 0-1, North Korea (h) 0-0, Uzbekistan (a) 1-5.

## SAUDI ARABIA
Saudi Arabian Football Federation, Al Mather Quarter (Olympic Complex), Prince Faisal Bin Fahad Street, PO Box 5844, 11432 Riyadh.
*Founded:* 1959; *National Colours:* White shirts, green shorts, white socks.
*International matches 2012–13*
Australia (a) 4-2, Spain (a) 5-0, Gabon (n) 0-0, Congo (h) 1-0, Argentina (h) 1-4, Zambia (h) 0-0, Iran (n) 0-0, Yemen (n) 1-0, Bahrain (a) 0-1, Iraq (n) 0-2, Yemen (n) 2-0, Kuwait (a) 0-1, China PR (h) 2-1, Indonesia (a) 2-1.

## SINGAPORE
Football Association of Singapore, Jalan Besar Stadium, 100 Tyrwhitt Road, 207542 Singapore.
*Founded:* 1892; *National Colours:* All red.
*International matches 2012–13*
Azerbaijan (n) 2-2, Iraq (a) 1-7, Hong Kong (a) 0-1, Malaysia (h) 2-2, Malaysia (a) 0-2, Hong Kong (h) 2-0, Philippines (h) 0-2, Myanmar (a) 1-1, India (h) 2-0, Philippines (a) 0-1, Pakistan (h) 4-0, Malaysia (a) 3-0, Indonesia (n) 0-1, Laos (n) 4-3, Philippines (a) 0-0, Philippines (h) 1-0, Thailand (h) 3-1, Thailand (a) 0-1, Bahrain (a) 1-3, Jordan (a) 0-4, Myanmar (a) 2-0, Laos (a) 5-2.

## SRI LANKA
Football Federation of Sri Lanka, 100/9, Independence Avenue, Colombo 07.
*Founded:* 1939; *National Colours:* All white.
*International matches 2012–13*
Malaysia (a) 0-6, Afghanistan (n) 0-1, Laos (a) 2-4, Mongolia (n) 3-0.

## SYRIA
Syrian Football Federation, PO Box 421, Maysaloon Street, Damascus.
*Founded:* 1936; *National Colours:* All red.
*International matches 2012–13*
India (a) 1-2, Cameron A (n) 2-2, Maldives (n) 1-2, Nepal (n) 2-0, Kuwait (a) 1-1, Palestine (n) 1-1, Palestine (n) 1-2, Iraq (n) 1-1, Jordan (n) 2-1, Bahrain (n) 1-1 (3-2p), Iraq (n) 1-0, Oman (a) 0-1, Iraq (a) 1-2.

## TAJIKISTAN

Tajikistan Football Federation, 22 Shotemur Ave., Dushanbe 734 025.
*Founded:* 1991; *National Colours:* All white.
*International matches 2012–13*
North Korea (h) 1-1, India (n) 2-0, North Korea (n) 0-2, Philippines (n) 1-2, Qatar (a) 2-1, Iran (a) 1-6, Pakistan (n) 1-0, Macao (n) 3-0, Kyrgyzstan (a) 0-1, Afghanistan (h) 3-2.

## THAILAND

Football Association of Thailand, Gate 3, Rama I Road, Patumwan, Bangkok 10330.
*Founded:* 1916; *National Colours:* All red.
*International matches 2012–13*
Norway (h) 0-1, Maldives (h) 3-0, Oman (a) 0-2, Laos (h) 2-1, Malaysia (h) 2-0, Bhutan (h) 5-0, Bangladesh (h) 5-0, Philippines (h) 2-1, Myanmar (h) 4-0, Vietnam (h) 3-1, Malaysia (a) 1-1, Malaysia (h) 2-0, Singapore (a) 1-3, Singapore (h) 1-0, Kuwait (h) 1-3, Lebanon (a) 2-5, China PR (a) 5-1.

## TIMOR-LESTE

Federacao Futebol Timor-Leste, Rua 12 de Novembro Str., Cruz, Dili.
*Founded:* 2002; *National Colours:* Red shirts, black shorts, red socks.
*International matches 2012–13*
Cambodia (n) 5-1, Myanmar (a) 1-2, Laos (n) 3-1, Brunei (n) 1-2, Indonesia (a) 0-1.

## TURKMENISTAN

Football Association of Turkmenistan, 32 Belinskiy Street, Stadium Kopetdag, 744 001 Ashgabat.
*Founded:* 1992; *National Colours:* Green shirts, white shorts, green socks.
*International matches 2012–13*
Romania (n) 0-4, Maldives (n) 3-1, Palestine (n) 0-0, Nepal (a) 3-0, Philippines (n) 2-1, North Korea (n) 1-2, Vietnam (a) 1-0, Laos (h) 4-2, Cambodia (n) 7-0, Brunei (n) 3-0, Philippines (a) 0-1.

## UNITED ARAB EMIRATES

United Arab Emirates Football Association, PO Box 961, Abu Dhabi.
*Founded:* 1971; *National Colours:* All white.
*International matches 2012–13*
Uzbekistan (h) 1-0, Palestine (h) 3-0, Lebanon (h) 4-2, Japan (a) 0-1, Kuwait (h) 3-0, Uzbekistan (h) 2-2, Bahrain (h) 6-2, Estonia (h) 2-1, Yemen (h) 2-0, Yemen (h) 3-1, Qatar (n) 3-1, Bahrain (n) 2-1, Oman (n) 2-0, Kuwait (a) 1-0, Iraq (n) 2-1, Vietnam (a) 2-1, Uzbekistan (h) 2-1.

## UZBEKISTAN

Uzbekistan Football Federation, Massiv Almazar Furkat Street 15/1, 700 003 Tashkent.
*Founded:* 1946; *National Colours:* All white.
*International matches 2012–13*
Kuwait (a) 0-1, South Korea (a) 2-4, Japan (a) 1-0, Iran (h) 0-1, Lebanon (a) 1-1, Jordan (a) 1-0, Jordan (a) 0-2, Kuwait (h) 3-0, South Korea (h) 2-2, UAE (a) 2-2, Qatar (a) 1-0, Iran (a) 1-0, Hong Kong (h) 2-0, UAE (a) 1-2, Lebanon (a) 1-0, China PR (h) 2-1, South Korea (a) 0-1, Qatar (h) 5-1.

## VIETNAM

Vietnam Football Federation, 18 Ly van Phuc, Dong Da District, Hanoi 844.
*Founded:* 1962; *National Colours:* All red.
*International matches 2012–13*
China PR (a) 0-3, Hong Kong (a) 2-1, Mozambique (h) 1-0, Malaysia (a) 2-0, Indonesia (a) 0-0, Indonesia (h) 0-0, Turkmenistan (h) 0-1, Laos (h) 4-0, Malaysia (h) 1-0, Myanmar (n) 1-1, Philippines (n) 0-1, Thailand (a) 1-3, UAE (h) 1-2, Hong Kong (a) 0-1.

## YEMEN

Yemen Football Association, Quarter of Sport – Al Jeraf, Behind the Stadium of Ali Muhsen Al-Moreisi in the Sport, Al-Thawra City.
*Founded:* 1962; *National Colours:* All green.
*International matches 2012–13*
Palestine (h) 1-2, Oman (a) 1-2, Lebanon (a) 1-2, Bahrain (a) 0-1, Saudi Arabia (n) 0-1, Iran (n) 1-2, UAE (a) 0-2, UAE (a) 1-3, Kuwait (n) 3-0, Saudi Arabia (n) 0-1, Iraq (n) 0-1, Bahrain (n) 2-1, Malaysia (a) 2-1.

# CONCACAF

## ANGUILLA

Anguilla Football Association, Albert Lake Drive, PO Box 1318, 2640 The Valley, Anguilla, BWI.
*National Colours:* Turquoise, white, orange and blue shirts and shorts, turquoise and orange socks.
*International matches 2012–13*
British Virgin Islands (a) 0-1, St Kitts & Nevis (a) 0-2, French Guiana (n) 1-4, Trinidad & Tobago (n) 0-10.

## ANTIGUA & BARBUDA

The Antigua/Barbuda Football Association, Newgate Street, PO Box 773, St John's.
*Founded:* 1928; *National Colours:* Red, black, yellow and blue shirts, black shorts and socks.
*International matches 2012–13*
Trinidad & Tobago (h) 0-4, St Kitts & Nevis (a) 0-1, St Vincent & The Grenadines (a) 0-1, St Vincent & The Grenadines (a) 2-1, USA (a) 1-3, Jamaica (h) 0-0, Guatemala (a) 1-3, Guatemala (h) 0-1, USA (h) 1-2, Jamaica (a) 1-4, Dominican Republic (h) 1-2, Trinidad & Tobago (h) 2-0, Haiti (h) 0-1.

## ARUBA

Arubaanse Voetbal Bond, Ferguson Street, Z/N PO Box 376, Oranjestad, Aruba.
*Founded:* 1932; *National Colours:* Yellow shirts, blue shorts, yellow and blue socks.
*International matches 2012–13*
Curacao (h) 3-2, Suriname (h) 1-0, Dominican Republic (n) 2-2, Dominica (n) 2-3, Barbados (a) 1-2.

## BAHAMAS

Bahamas Football Association, Plaza on the Way, West Bay Street, PO Box N-8434, Nassau, NP.
*Founded:* 1967; *National Colours:* Yellow shirts, black shorts, yellow socks.
*International matches 2012–13*
None played.

## BARBADOS

Barbados Football Association, Hildor No. 4, 10th Avenue, P.O. Box 1362, Belleville-St. Michael, Barbados.
*Founded:* 1910; *National Colours:* Royal blue and gold shirts, gold shorts, white, gold and blue socks.
*International matches 2012–13*
St Vincent & The Grenadines (a) 0-2, St Vincent & The Grenadines (a) 1-1, Dominica (h) 1-0, Dominican Republic (h) 0-1, Aruba (h) 2-1.

## BELIZE

Belize National Football Association, 26 Hummingbird Highway, Belmopan, P.O. Box 1742, Belize City.
*Founded:* 1980; *National Colours:* Red, white and black shirts, black shorts, red and black socks.
*International matches 2012–13*
Costa Rica (a) 0-1, Guatemala (n) 0-0, Nicaragua (n) 2-1, Honduras (n) 0-1, El Salvador (n) 0-1, Trinidad & Tobago (h) 0-0, Guatemala (a) 0-0.

## BERMUDA

The Bermuda Football Association, 48 Cedar Avenue, Hamilton HM12.
*Founded:* 1928; *National Colours:* All blue.
*International matches 2012–13*
Puerto Rico (n) 1-2, Haiti (a) 1-3, Saint-Martin (n) 8-0.

## BRITISH VIRGIN ISLANDS

British Virgin Islands Football Association, PO Box 29, Road Town, Tortola, BVI.
*National Colours:* Gold and green shirts, green shorts, and socks.
*International matches 2012–13*
Anguilla (h) 1-0, Martinique (a) 0-16, Suriname (n) 0-4, Montserrat (n) 0-7.

## US VIRGIN ISLANDS

USVI Soccer Federation Inc., 54, Castle Coakley, PO Box 2346, Kingshill, St Croix 00851.
*National Colours:* Royal blue and gold shirts, royal blue shorts and socks.
*International matches 2012–13*
None played.

## CANADA

The Canadian Soccer Association, Place Soccer Canada, 237 Metcalfe Street, Ottawa, ONT K2P 1R2.
*Founded:* 1912; *National Colours:* All red.

*International matches 2012–13*
Armenia (n) 1-3, USA (h) 0-0, Cuba (a) 1-0, Honduras (n) 0-0, Trinidad & Tobago (h) 2-0, Panama (n) 1-0, Panama (n) 0-2,Cuba (h) 3-0, Honduras (h) 1-8, Denmark (h) 0-4, USA (a) 0-0, Japan (n) 1-2, Belarus (n) 0-2, Costa Rica (h) 0-1.

## CAYMAN ISLANDS
Cayman Islands Football Association, PO Box 178 GT, Truman Bodden Sports Complex, Olympic Way Off Walkers Rd, George Town, Grand Cayman, Cayman Islands WI.
*Founded:* 1966; *National Colours:* Red and white shirts, blue and white shorts, white and red socks.
*International matches 2012–13*
None played.

## COSTA RICA
Federacion Costarricense De Futbol, Costado Norte Estatua Leon Cortes, San Jose 670-1000.
*Founded:* 1921; *National Colours:* Red shirts, blue shorts, white socks.
*International matches 2012–13*
Wales (a) 1-0, Jamaica (a) 0-0, Honduras (h) 1-1, Guatemala (h) 3-2, Guatemala (a) 0-1, El Salvador (h) 2-2, Guyana (a) 4-0, Peru (h) 0-1, Mexico (h) 0-2, Mexico (a) 0-1, El Salvador (a) 1-0, Guyana (h) 7-0, Bolivia (a) 1-1, Belize (h) 1-0, Nicaragua (h) 2-0, Guatemala (h) 1-1, El Salvador (h) 1-0, Honduras (h) 1-0, Panama (a) 2-2, USA (a) 0-1, Jamaica (h) 2-0, Canada (a) 1-0, Honduras (h) 1-0, Mexico (a) 0-0, Panama (a) 2-0.

## CUBA
Asociacion de Futbol de Cuba, Calle 13 No. 661, Esq. C. Vedado, ZP 4, La Habana.
*Founded:* 1924; *National Colours:* All red, white and blue.
*International matches 2012–13*
Jamaica (a) 0-1, Jamaica (a) 0-3, Bolivia (a) 0-1, Canada (h) 0-1, Panama (a) 0-1, Honduras (h) 0-3, Honduras (a) 0-1, Canada (a) 0-3, Panama (h) 1-1, Suriname (n) 5-0, St Vincent & The Grenadines (n) 1-1, Trinidad & Tobago (a) 0-1, Martinique (n) 0-1, French Guiana (n) 2-1, Jamaica (n) 1-0, Haiti (n) 1-0, Trinidad & Tobago (n) 1-0.

## CURACAO
(Formerly Netherlands Antilles)
Curacao Football Federation, Bonamweg 49, PO Box 341, Willemstad, Curacao.
*Founded:* 1921; *National Colours:* Blue shirts, red shorts and socks.
*International matches 2012–13*
Aruba (a) 2-3, St Lucia (a) 1-5, Guyana (n) 1-2, St Vincent & The Grenadines (n) 0-4.

## DOMINICA
Dominica Football Association, 33 Great Marlborough Street, Roseau.
*Founded:* 1970; *National Colours:* Emerald green shirts, black shorts, green socks.
*International matches 2012–13*
Barbados (a) 0-1, Aruba (n) 3-2, Dominican Republic (n) 1-2.

## DOMINICAN REPUBLIC
Federacion Dominicana De Futbol, Centro Olimpico Juan Pablo Duarte, Ensanche Miraflores, Apartado De Correos No. 1953, Santo Domingo.
*Founded:* 1953; *National Colours:* Navy blue shirts, white shorts, red socks.
*International matches 2012–13*
Aruba (n) 2-2, Barbados (a) 1-0, Dominica (n) 2-1, Guadeloupe (a) 2-0, Martinique (n) 1-1, Puerto Rico (n) 3-1, Antigua & Barbuda (a) 2-1, Haiti (n) 1-2, Trinidad & Tobago (n) 1-2, Haiti (h) 3-1.

## EL SALVADOR
Federacion Salvadorena De Futbol, Primera Calle Poniente No. 2025, San Salvador CA1029.
*Founded:* 1935; *National Colours:* All blue.
*International matches 2012–13*
Estonia (n) 0-2, New Zealand (n) 2-2, Moldova (n) 2-0, Honduras (n) 0-3, Costa Rica (a) 2-2, Mexico (h) 1-2, Guatemala (n) 1-0, Jamaica (h) 2-2, Guyana (h) 2-2, Guyana (a) 3-2, Costa Rica (h) 0-1, Mexico (a) 0-2, Honduras (n) 1-1, Panama (n) 0-0, Costa Rica (a) 0-1, Belize (n) 1-0, Paraguay (a) 0-3, Ecuador (h) 0-5, Venezuela (a) 1-2.

## GRENADA
Grenada Football Association, PO Box 326, National Stadium, Queens Park, St George's, Grenada, W.I.
*Founded:* 1924; *National Colours:* Green and yellow striped shirts, red shorts, yellow socks.
*International matches 2012–13*
Guyana (h) 1-2, French Guiana (h) 1-1, Guyana (h) 2-1, Haiti (h) 0-2, St Lucia (h) 2-1, St Vincent & The Grenadines (a) 1-0.

## GUADELOUPE
Ligue Guadeloupeenne de Football, Rue de la Ville D'Orly, Bergevin, 97110, Pointe-a-Pitre.
Not affiliated to FIFA.
*International matches 2012–13*
Dominican Republic (h) 0-2, Puerto Rico (h) 4-1, Martinique (h) 3-3.

## GUATEMALA
Federacion Nacional de Futbol de Guatemala, 2a Calle 15-57, Zona 15, Boulevard Vista Hermosa, 01009 Guatemala City.
*Founded:* 1946; *National Colours:* Blue shirts, white shorts, blue socks.
*International matches 2012–13*
Paraguay (a) 1-2, Guyana (a) 2-0, Paraguay (h) 0-1, Costa Rica (a) 2-3, Costa Rica (h) 1-0, Jamaica (a) 1-2, USA (h) 1-1, El Salvador (a) 0-1, Paraguay (a) 3-3, Antigua & Barbuda (h) 3-1, Antigua & Barbuda (h) 1-0, Jamaica (h) 2-1, USA (a) 1-3, Paraguay (a) 1-3, Panama (n) 0-3, Panama (a) 0-2, Nicaragua (n) 1-1, Belize (n) 0-0, Costa Rica (a) 1-1, Panama (n) 1-3, Colombia (h) 1-4, Belize (h) 0-0, Argentina (h) 0-4, USA (a) 6-0.

## GUYANA
Guyana Football Federation, 159 Rupununi Street, Bel Air Park, PO Box 10727, Georgetown.
*Founded:* 1902; *National Colours:* Green shirts and shorts, yellow socks.
*International matches 2012–13*
St Vincent & The Grenadines (a) 0-1, Grenada (a) 2-1, Guatemala (h) 0-2, Jamaica (a) 0-1, Mexico (a) 1-3, Costa Rica (h) 0-4, Bolivia (a) 0-2, El Salvador (a) 2-2, El Salvador (h) 2-3, Mexico (h) 0-5, Costa Rica (a) 0-7, St Vincent & The Grenadines (n) 1-2, Curacao (n) 2-1, St Lucia (a) 3-0, Haiti (n) 0-1, Grenada (n) 1-2, French Guiana (n) 4-3.

## HAITI
Federation Haitienne De Football, 128 Avenue Christiophe, PO Box 2258, Port-Au-Prince.
*Founded:* 1904; *National Colours:* Blue shirts, red shorts, blue socks.
*International matches 2012–13*
Saint-Martin (h) 7-0, Bermuda (h) 3-1, Puerto Rico (h) 2-1, Guyana (n) 1-0, French Guiana (n) 0-1, Grenada (a) 2-0, Trinidad & Tobago (n) 0-0, Dominican Republic (n) 2-1, Antigua & Barbuda (a) 1-0, Cuba (n) 0-1, Martinique (n) 1-0, Chile (a) 0-3, Bolivia (a) 1-2, Oman (a) 0-3, Dominican Republic (a) 1-3, Spain (n) 1-2, Italy (n) 2-2.

## HONDURAS
Federacion Nacional Autonoma De Futbol De Honduras, Colonia Florencia Norte, Ave Roble, Edificio Plaza America, Ave. Roble 1 y 2 Nivel, Tegucigalpa, D.C.
*Founded:* 1951; *National Colours:* All white.
*International matches 2012–13*
Ecuador (a) 0-2, Costa Rica (a) 1-1, New Zealand (h) 0-1, El Salvador (a) 3-0, Panama (h) 0-2, Canada (a) 0-0, Cuba (a) 3-0, Cuba (h) 1-0, Panama (a) 0-0, Canada (h) 8-1, Peru (h) 0-1, El Salvador (n) 1-1, Panama (n) 1-1, Belize (n) 1-0, Costa Rica (a) 0-1, USA (h) 2-1, Mexico (h) 2-2, Panama (a) 0-2, Israel (n) 0-2, Costa Rica (a) 0-1, Jamaica (h) 2-0, USA (a) 0-1.

## JAMAICA
Jamaica Football Federation Ltd, 20 St Lucia Crescent, Kingston 5.
*Founded:* 1910; *National Colours:* Gold shirts, black shorts, gold socks.
*International matches 2012–13*
Cuba (h) 1-0, Cuba (h) 3-0, New Zealand (a) 3-2, Costa Rica (h) 0-0, Guyana (h) 1-0, Panama (h) 0-1, Panama (a) 1-2, Guatemala (h) 2-1, Antigua & Barbuda (a) 0-0, El Salvador (a) 2-2, USA (h) 2-1, USA (a) 0-1, Guatemala (a) 1-2, Antigua & Barbuda (h) 4-1, French Guiana (n) 1-2, Martinique (n) 0-0, Cuba (n) 0-1, Mexico (a) 0-0, Panama (h) 1-1, Costa Rica (h) 0-2, Mexico (h) 0-1, USA (h) 1-2, Honduras (a) 0-2.

## MARTINIQUE

2, Rue Saint John Perse, Nome Tartenson, BP 307, 97203 Fort de France.
Not affiliated to FIFA.
*International matches 2012–13*
British Virgin Islands (h) 16-0, Montserrat (h) 5-0, Suriname (h) 2-2, Puerto Rico (n) 2-1, Dominican Republic (n) 1-1, Guadeloupe (a) 3-3, Cuba (n) 1-0, Jamaica (n) 0-0, French Guiana (n) 3-1, Trinidad & Tobago (n) 1-1 (4-5p), Haiti (n) 0-1.

## MEXICO

Federacion Mexicana De Futbol Asociacion, A.C., Colima No. 373, Colonia Roma Mexico DF 06700.
*Founded:* 1927; *National Colours:* Green shirts with white collar, white shorts, red socks.
*International matches 2012–13*
Venezuela (n) 3-1, Colombia (n) 0-2, Wales (n) 2-0, Bosnia-Herzegovina (n) 2-1, Brazil (n) 2-0, Guyana (h) 3-1, El Salvador (a) 2-1, USA (h) 0-1, Costa Rica (a) 2-0, Costa Rica (h) 1-0, Guyana (a) 5-0, El Salvador (h) 2-0, Denmark (n) 1-1, Jamaica (a) 0-0, Honduras (h) 2-2, USA (a) 0-0, Peru (n) 0-0, Nigeria (n) 2-2, Jamaica (h) 1-0, Panama (n) 0-0, Costa Rica (h) 0-0, Italy (n) 1-2, Brazil (a) 0-2, Japan (n) 2-1.

## MONTSERRAT

Montserrat Football Association Inc., P.O. Box 505, Woodlands, Montserrat.
*National Colours:* Green shirts with black and white stripes, green shorts with white stripes, green socks with black and white stripes.
*International matches 2012–13*
Suriname (n) 1-7, Martinique (a) 0-5, British Virgin Islands (n) 7-0.

## NICARAGUA

Federacion Nicaraguense De Futbol, Hospital Pautista 1, Cuadra avajo, 1 cuada al Sur y 1/2, Cuadra Abajo, Managua 976.
*Founded:* 1931; *National Colours:* Blue shirts, white shorts, blue socks.
*International matches 2012–13*
Puerto Rico (h) 1-0, Puerto Rico (h) 4-1, Puerto Rico (a) 1-3, Puerto Rico (a) 1-1, Guatemala (n) 1-1, Costa Rica (a) 0-2, Belize (n) 1-2.

## PANAMA

Federacion Panamena De Futbol, Estadio Rommel Fernandez, Puerta 24, Ave. Jose Agustin Araneo, Apartado Postal 8-391, Zona 8, Panama.
*Founded:* 1937; *National Colours:* All red.
*International matches 2012–13*
USA (h) 0-1, Paraguay (a) 0-1, Jamaica (a) 1-0, Jamaica (h) 2-1, Honduras (a) 2-0, Cuba (h) 1-0, Portugal (a) 0-2, Canada (a) 0-1, Canada (h) 2-0, Honduras (h) 0-0, Cuba (a) 1-1, Spain (h) 1-5, Guatemala (h) 3-0, Guatemala (h) 2-0, El Salvador (a) 0-0, Honduras (h) 1-1, Guatemala (a) 3-1, Costa Rica (h) 2-2, Jamaica (a) 1-1, Honduras (n) 2-0, Peru (h) 1-2, Mexico (h) 0-0, USA (a) 0-2, Costa Rica (a) 0-2.

## PUERTO RICO

Federacion Puertorriquena De Futbol, PO Box 193590, 00919 San Juan.
*Founded:* 1940; *National Colours:* Red, blue and white shirts and shorts, red and blue socks.
*International matches 2012–13*
Nicaragua (a) 0-1, Nicaragua (a) 1-4, Nicaragua (h) 3-1, Nicaragua (h) 1-1, Spain (x) 1-2, Bermuda (n) 2-1, Saint-Martin (n) 9-0, Haiti (a) 1-2, Martinique (n) 1-2, Guadeloupe (a) 1-4, Dominican Republic (n) 1-3.

## ST KITTS & NEVIS

St Kitts & Nevis Football Association, PO Box 465, Warner Park, Basseterre, St Kitts, W.I.
*Founded:* 1932; *National Colours:* Green and yellow shirts, red shorts, yellow socks.
*International matches 2012–13*
Antigua & Barbuda (h) 1-0, Anguilla (h) 2-0, Trinidad & Tobago (h) 0-1, French Guiana (h) 0-3.

## ST LUCIA

St Lucia National Football Association, PO Box 255, Sans Souci, Castries, St Lucia.
*Founded:* 1979; *National Colours:* White shirts and shorts with yellow, blue and black stripes, white, blue and yellow socks.
*International matches 2012–13*
Curacao (h) 5-1, St Vincent & The Grenadines (h) 1-0, Guyana (h) 0-3, St Vincent & The Grenadines (n) 2-0, Grenada (a) 1-2.

## ST VINCENT & THE GRENADINES

St Vincent & The Grenadines Football Federation, Sharpe Street, PO Box 1278, St George.
*Founded:* 1979; *National Colours:* Green shirts with yellow border, blue shorts, yellow socks.
*International matches 2012–13*
Guyana (h) 0-2, Antigua & Barbuda (a) 1-0, Antigua & Barbuda (h) 1-2, Barbados (h) 2-0, Barbados (h) 1-1, Guyana (n) 2-1, St Lucia (a) 1-0, Curacao (n) 4-0, Trinidad & Tobago (a) 1-1, Cuba (n) 1-1, Suriname (n) 0-1, St Lucia (h) 0-2, Grenada (h) 0-1.

## SURINAME

Surinaamse Voetbal Bond, Letitia Vriesde Laan 7, PO Box 1223, Paramaribo.
*Founded:* 1920; *National Colours:* White, green and red shirts, green and white shirts and socks.
*International matches 2012–13*
Aruba (a) 0-1, Montserrat (n) 7-1, British Virgin Islands (n) 4-0, Martinique (a) 2-2, Cuba (n) 0-5, Trinidad & Tobago (a) 0-3, St Vincent & The Grenadines (n) 1-0.

## TRINIDAD & TOBAGO

Trinidad & Tobago Football Federation, 24–26 Dundonald Street, PO Box 400, Port of Spain.
*Founded:* 1908; *National Colours:* Red shirts, black shorts, white socks.
*International matches 2012–13*
Finland (h) 2-3, Antigua & Barbuda (a) 4-0, Canada (a) 0-2, French Guiana (n) 4-1, St Kitts & Nevis (a) 1-0, Anguilla (n) 10-0, St Vincent & The Grenadines (h) 1-1, Suriname (h) 3-0, Cuba (h) 1-0, Haiti (n) 0-0, Antigua & Barbuda (a) 0-2, Dominican Republic (n) 2-1, Martinique (n) 1-1 (5-4p), Cuba (n) 0-1, Belize (a) 0-0, Peru (a) 0-3, Romania (a) 0-4, Estonia (a) 0-1.

## TURKS & CAICOS

Turks & Caicos Islands Football Association, PO Box 626, Tropicana Plaza, Leeward Highway, Providenciales.
*National Colours:* All white.
*International matches 2012–13*
None played.

## USA

US Soccer Federation, US Soccer House, 1801–1811 S. Prairie Avenue, Chicago, Illinois 60616.
*Founded:* 1913; *National Colours:* White shirts, blue shorts, white socks.
*International matches 2012–13*
Venezuela (a) 1-0, Panama (a) 1-0, Italy (a) 1-0, Scotland (h) 5-1, Brazil (h) 1-4, Canada (a) 0-0, Antigua & Barbuda (h) 3-1, Guatemala (a) 1-1, Mexico (a) 1-0, Jamaica (a) 1-2, Jamaica (h) 1-0, Antigua & Barbuda (a) 2-1, Guatemala (h) 3-1, Russia (n) 2-2, Canada (h) 0-0, Costa Rica (h) 1-0, Mexico (a) 0-0, Belgium (h) 2-4, Germany (h) 4-3, Jamaica (a) 2-1, Panama (h) 2-0, Honduras (h) 1-0.

# OCEANIA

## AMERICAN SAMOA

American Samoa Football Association, P.O. Box 282, AS 96799 Pago Pago.
*National Colours:* Navy blue shirts, white shorts, red socks.
*International matches 2012–13*
None played.

## COOK ISLANDS

Cook Islands Football Association, Victoria Road, Tupapa, P.O. Box 29, Avarua, Rarotonga, Cook Islands.
*Founded:* 1971; *National Colours:* Green shirts with white sleeves, green shorts, white socks.
*International matches 2012–13*
None played.

## FIJI

Fiji Football Association, PO Box 2514, Government Buildings, Suva.
*Founded:* 1938; *National Colours:* White shirts, blue shorts and socks.
*International matches 2012–13*
New Zealand (h) 0-1, Solomon Islands (h) 0-0, Papua New Guinea (a) 1-1.

## NEW CALEDONIA

Federation Caledonienne de Football, 7 bis, Rue Suffren Quartien latin, BP 560, 99845 Noumea, New Caledonia.
*Founded:* 1928; *National Colours:* Grey shirts, red shorts, grey socks.

*International matches 2012–13*
Vanuatu (n) 5-2, Tahiti (n) 3-4, Samoa (n) 9-0, New Zealand (n) 2-0, Tahiti (n) 0-1, New Zealand (h) 0-2, Tahiti (a) 4-0, Tahiti (h) 0-1, Solomon Islands (a) 6-2, Solomon Islands (h) 5-0, New Zealand (a) 1-2, Tahiti (h) 1-0.

## NEW ZEALAND
New Zealand Soccer Inc., PO Box 301 043, Albany, Auckland, New Zealand.
*Founded:* 1891; *National Colours:* All white.
*International matches 2012–13*
Jamaica (h) 2-3, El Salvador (a) 2-2, Honduras (a) 1-0, Fiji (n) 1-0, Papua New Guinea (n) 2-1, Solomon Islands (a) 1-1, New Caledonia (n) 0-2, Solomon Islands (a) 4-3, New Caledonia (a) 2-0, Solomon Islands (h) 6-1, Tahiti (a) 2-0, Tahiti (h) 3-0, China PR (a) 1-1, New Caledonia (h) 2-1, Solomon Islands (a) 2-0.

## PAPUA NEW GUINEA
Papua New Guinea Football Association, PO Box 957, Room II Level I, Haus Tisa, Lae.
*Founded:* 1962; *National Colours:* Red and yellow shirts, black shorts, yellow socks.
*International matches 2012–13*
Solomon Islands (a) 0-1, New Zealand (n) 1-2, Fiji (n) 1-1.

## SAMOA
The Samoa Football Soccer Federation, P.O. Box 960, Apia.
*Founded:* 1968; *National Colours:* Blue, white and red shirts, blue and white shorts, red and blue socks.
*International matches 2012–13*
Tahiti (n) 1-10, Vanuatu (n) 0-5, New Caledonia (n) 0-9.

## SOLOMON ISLANDS
Solomon Islands Football Federation, PO Box 854, Honiara, Solomon Islands.
*Founded:* 1978; *National Colours:* Gold and blue shirts, blue and white shorts, white and blue socks.
*International matches 2012–13*
Papua New Guinea (h) 1-0, Fiji (h) 0-0, New Zealand (h) 1-1, Tahiti (h) 0-1, New Zealand (h) 3-4, Tahiti (h) 2-0, New Zealand (a) 1-6, New Caledonia (h) 2-6, New Caledonia (a) 0-5, Tahiti (a) 2-0, New Zealand (h) 0-2.

## TAHITI
Federation Tahitienne de Football, Rue Coppenrath Stade de Fautana, PO Box 50858 Pirae 98716.
*Founded:* 1989; *National Colours:* Red shirts, white shorts, red socks.
*International matches 2012–13*
Samoa (n) 10-1, New Caledonia (n) 4-3, Vanuatu (n) 4-1, Solomon Islands (a) 1-0, New Caledonia (n) 1-0, Solomon Islands (a) 0-2, New Caledonia (h) 0-4, New Caledonia (a) 1-0, New Zealand (h) 0-2, New Zealand (a) 0-3, Solomon Islands (h) 2-0, New Caledonia (a) 0-1, Nigeria (n) 1-6, Spain (n) 0-10, Uruguay (n) 0-8.

## TONGA
Tonga Football Association, Tungi Arcade, Taufa'Ahau Road, P.O. Box 852, Nuku'Alofa, Tonga.
*Founded:* 1965; *National Colours:* Red shirts, white shorts, red socks.
*International matches 2012–13*
None played.

## VANUATU
Vanuatu Football Federation, P.O. Box 266, Port Vila, Vanuatu.
*Founded:* 1934; *National Colours:* Gold and black shirts, black shorts, gold and black socks.
*International matches 2012–13*
New Caledonia (n) 2-5, Samoa (n) 5-0, Tahiti (n) 1-4.

# AFRICA
## ALGERIA
Federation Algerienne De Foot-ball, Chemin Ahmed Ouaked, Boite Postale No. 39, Dely-Ibrahim-Alger.
*Founded:* 1962; *National Colours:* Green shirts, white shorts, green socks.
*International matches 2012–13*
Gambia (a) 2-1, Niger (h) 3-0, Rwanda (h) 4-0, Mali (a) 1-2, Gambia (h) 4-1, Libya (n) 1-0, Libya (h) 2-0, Bosnia-Herzegovina (h) 0-1, South Africa (a) 0-0, Tunisia (n) 0-1, Togo (n) 0-2, Ivory Coast (n) 2-2, Benin (h) 3-1, Mauritania (h) 1-0, Burkina Faso (h) 2-0, Benin (a) 3-1, Rwanda (a) 1-0.

## ANGOLA
Federation Angolaise De Football, Compl. da Cidadela Desportiva, BP 3449, Luanda.
*Founded:* 1979; *National Colours:* Red shirts, black shorts, red socks.
*International matches 2012–13*
Sierra Leone (h) 3-1, Burkina Faso (a) 2-1, Sudan (a) 2-2, Ivory Coast (a) 0-2, Zambia (h) 0-0, Macedonia FYR (n) 0-0, Uganda (h) 1-1, Liberia (a) 0-0, Mozambique (h) 2-0, Zimbabwe (a) 1-3, Zimbabwe (h) 2-0, Congo (h) 1-1, Gambia (h) 1-1, Cameroon (h) 1-0, Rwanda (h) 1-0, Morocco (n) 0-0, South Africa (a) 0-2, Cape Verde Islands (n) 1-2, Senegal (a) 1-1, Senegal (h) 1-1, Uganda (a) 1-2.

## BENIN
Federation Beninoise De Football, Stade Rene Pleven d'Akpakpa, BP 965, Cotonou 01.
*Founded:* 1962; *National Colours:* Green shirts, Yellow shorts, red socks.
*International matches 2012–13*
Ethiopia (a) 0-0, Mali (h) 1-0, Rwanda (a) 1-1, Ethiopia (h) 1-1, Algeria (a) 1-3, Algeria (h) 1-3, Mali (h) 2-2.

## BOTSWANA
Botswana Football Association, PO Box 1396, Gaborone.
*Founded:* 1970; *National Colours:* Blue, white and black striped shirts, blue, white and black shorts and socks.
*International matches 2012–13*
Lesotho (n) 3-0*, Zimbabwe (h) 0-0, Ghana (n) 0-1, Guinea (n) 1-6, Mali (h) 1-2, Lesotho (h) 3-0, Central African Republic (a) 0-2, South Africa (h) 1-1, Kenya (n) 1-3, Tanzania (n) 3-3, Mali (a) 0-3, Mali (h) 1-4, Zimbabwe (a) 1-2, Malawi (h) 1-0, Ethiopia (a) 0-1, Egypt (a) 1-1, Ethiopia (h) 1-2, Central African Republic (h) 3-2.
* *Played 21.12.2011, result omitted from last edition.*

## BURKINA FASO
Federation Burkinabe De Foot-Ball, 01 BP 57, Ouagadougou 01.
*Founded:* 1960; *National Colours:* All green, red and white.
*International matches 2012–13*
Gabon (a) 0-0, Angola (n) 1-2, Ivory Coast (n) 0-2, Sudan (n) 1-2, Morocco (a) 0-2, Congo (h) 0-3, Gabon (a) 0-1, Togo (a) 3-0, Central African Republic (a) 0-1, Central African Republic (h) 3-1, Congo DR (a) 1-0, Bahrain (a) 0-0, Swaziland (h) 3-0, Nigeria (n) 1-1, Ethiopia (a) 0-0, Zambia (n) 0-0, Togo (n) 1-0, Ghana (n) 1-1 (3-2p), Nigeria (n) 0-1, Niger (h) 4-0, Algeria (a) 0-2, Niger (a) 1-0, Congo (a) 1-0.

## BURUNDI
Federation De Football Du Burundi, Bulding Nyogozi, Boulevard de l'Uprona, BP 3426, Bujumbura.
*Founded:* 1948; *National Colours:* Red and white shirts, white and red shorts, green socks.
*International matches 2012–13*
Zimbabwe (h) 2-1, Zimbabwe (a) 0-1, Somalia (n) 5-1, Tanzania (n) 1-0, Sudan (n) 1-0, Zanzibar (n) 0-0 (5-6p), Kenya (a) 0-0.

## CAMEROON
Federation Camerounaise De Football, B.P. 1116, Yaounde.
*Founded:* 1959; *National Colours:* Green shirts, red shorts, yellow socks.
*International matches 2012–13*
Angola (n) 1-1*, Guinea-Bissau (a) 1-0, Egypt (a) 1-2, Guinea (a) 1-2, Congo DR (h) 1-0, Libya (n) 12, Guinea-Bissau (h) 1-0, Cape Verde Islands (a) 0-2, Cape Verde Islands (h) 2-1, Colombia (a) 0-3, Albania (n) 0-0, Indonesia (a) 0-0, Angola (a) 0-1, Tanzania (a) 0-1, Togo (h) 2-1, Ukraine (a) 0-0, Togo (n) 3-0, Congo DR (a) 0-0.
* *Played 14.12.2011, result omitted from last edition.*

## CAPE VERDE ISLANDS
Federacao Cabo-Verdiana De Futebol, Praia Cabo Verde, FCF CX, PO Box 234, Praia.
*Founded:* 1982; *National Colours:* Blue and white shirts and shorts, blue and red socks.
*International matches 2012–13*
Madagascar (a) 4-0, Sierra Leone (a) 1-2, Tunisia (h) 1-2, Madagascar (h) 3-1, Cameroon (h 2-0, Cameroon (a) 1-2, Ghana (n) 0-1, Nigeria (n) 0-0, South Africa (a) 0-0, Morocco (n) 1-1, Angola (n) 2-1, Ghana (n) 0-2, Equatorial Guinea (a) 3-4, Equatorial Guinea (h) 2-1, Sierra Leone (h) 1-0.

## CENTRAL AFRICAN REPUBLIC
Federation Centrafricaine De Football, Immeuble Soca Constructa, BP 344, Bangui.
*Founded:* 1937; *National Colours:* Blue and white shirts, white shorts, blue socks.
*International matches 2012–13*
Botswana (h) 2-0, Ethiopia (a) 0-2, Egypt (a) 3-2, Egypt (h) 1-1, Burkina Faso (h) 1-0, Burkina Faso (a) 1-3, South Africa (a) 0-2, South Africa (h) 0-3, Botswana (a) 2-3.

## CHAD
Federation Tchadienne de Football, BP 886, N'Djamena.
*Founded:* 1962; *National Colours:* Blue shirts, yellow shorts, red socks.
*International matches 2012–13*
Malawi (h) 3-2, Egypt (n) 4-0, Malawi (a) 0-2.

## COMOROS
Comoros FA, BP 798, Moroni.
*Founded:* 1979.
*International matches 2012–13*
None played.

## CONGO
Federation Congolaise De Football, 80 Rue Eugene-Etienne, Centre Ville, PO Box 11, Brazzaville.
*Founded:* 1962; *National Colours:* Green shirts, yellow shorts, red socks.
*International matches 2012–13*
Uganda (n) 3-1, Burkina Faso (a) 3-0, Niger (n) 1-0, Uganda (a) 0-4, Egypt (n) 3-0, Saudi Arabia (a) 2-3, Angola (n) 1-1, Gabon (h) 1-0, Gabon (a) 0-0, Burkina Faso (h) 0-1.

## CONGO DR
Federation Congolaise De Football-Association, Av. de l'Enseignement 210, C/Kasa-Vubu, Kinshasa 1.
*Founded:* 1919; *National Colours:* Blue and yellow shirts, yellow and blue shorts, white and blue socks.
*International matches 2012–13*
Oman (a) 2-2, Tanzania (a) 0-0, Burkina Faso (a) 3-0, Seychelles (a) 4-0, Egypt (n) 0-0, Cameroon (a) 0-1, Togo (h) 2-0, Seychelles (h) 3-0, Equatorial Guinea (h) 4-0, Equatorial Guinea (a) 1-2, Burkina Faso (h) 0-1, Ghana (n) 2-2, Niger (n) 0-0, Mali (n) 1-1, Libya (h) 0-0, Libya (a) 0-0, Cameroon (a) 0-0.

## DJIBOUTI
Federation Djiboutienne de Football, Stade el Haoj Hassan Gouled, BP 2694, Djibouti.
*Founded:* 1977; *National Colours:* Green shirts, white shorts, blue socks.
*International matches 2012–13*
None played.

## EGYPT
Egyptian Football Association, 5 Gabalaya Street, Guezira, El Borg Post Office, Cairo.
*Founded:* 1921; *National Colours:* Red shirts, white shorts, black socks.
*International matches 2012–13*
Kenya (n) 5-0, Niger (n) 1-0, Congo DR (n) 0-0, Uganda (n) 2-1, Chad (n) 4-0, Nigeria (n) 3-2, Mauritania (n) 3-0, Iraq (n) 0-0, Lebanon (a) 4-1, Cameroon (n) 2-1, Togo (n) 3-0, Mozambique (h) 2-0, Guinea (a) 3-2, Central African Republic (h) 2-3, Central African Republic (a) 1-1, Oman (a) 1-1, Congo (n) 3-0, Tunisia (n) 0-1, Georgia (a) 0-0, Qatar (a) 2-0, Ghana (n) 0-3, Ivory Coast (n) 2-4, Chile (n) 1-2, Qatar (a) 1-3, Zimbabwe (h) 2-1, Botswana (h) 1-1, Zimbabwe (a) 4-2, Mozambique (a) 1-0.

## ERITREA
The Eritrean National Football Federation, Sematat Avenue 29–31, PO Box 3665, Asmara.
*National Colours:* Blue shirts, red shorts, green socks.
*International matches 2012–13*
Zanzibar (n) 0-0, Malawi (n) 2-3, Rwanda (n) 0-2.

## ETHIOPIA
Ethiopia Football Federation, Addis Ababa Stadium, PO Box 1080, Addis Ababa.
*Founded:* 1943; *National Colours:* Green shirts, yellow shorts, red socks.
*International matches 2012–13*
Benin (h) 0-0, South Africa (a) 1-1, Central African Republic (h) 2-0, Benin (a) 1-1, Sudan (a) 3-5, Sudan (h) 2-0, South Sudan (n) 1-0, Uganda (a) 0-1, Kenya (n) 1-3, Uganda (a) 0-2, Niger (h) 1-0, Tunisia (n) 1-1, Tanzania (h) 2-1, Zambia (n) 1-1, Burkina Faso (n) 0-4, Nigeria (n) 0-2,

## GABON
Botswana (h) 1-0, Sudan (h) 2-0, Botswana (a) 2-1, South Africa (h) 2-1.

## GABON
Federation Gabonaise De Football, BP 181, Libreville.
*Founded:* 1962; *National Colours:* Green, yellow and blue shirts, blue and yellow shorts, white socks with tricolour trims.
*International matches 2012–13*
Burkina Faso (h) 0-0, Sudan (h) 0-0, Niger (h) 2-0, Morocco (h) 3-2, Tunisia (h) 1-0, Mali (h) 1-1 (4-5p), Niger (a) 0-3, Burkina Faso (h) 1-0, South Africa (a) 0-3, Togo (h) 1-1, Saudi Arabia (n) 1-0, Togo (a) 1-2, Portugal (h) 2-2, Tunisia (n) 1-1, Lebanon (a) 0-0, Congo (a) 0-1, Congo (h) 0-0, Niger (h) 4-1.

## GAMBIA
Gambia Football Association, Independence Stadium, Bakau, PO Box 523, Banjul.
*Founded:* 1952; *National Colours:* All red, blue and white.
*International matches 2012–13*
Algeria (h) 1-2, Morocco (h) 1-1, Tanzania (a) 1-2, Algeria (a) 1-4, Angola (a) 1-1, Mauritania (h) 0-2, Mauritania (h) 0-2, Ivory Coast (a) 0-3, Ivory Coast (h) 0-3, Morocco (a) 0-2.

## GHANA
Ghana Football Association, National Sports Council, PO Box 1272, Accra.
*Founded:* 1957; *National Colours:* All yellow.
*International matches 2012–13*
Botswana (n) 1-0, Mali (n) 2-0, Guinea (n) 1-1, Tunisia (n) 2-1, Zambia (n) 0-1, Mali (n) 0-2, Chile (n) 1-1, Lesotho (n) 7-0, Zambia (a) 0-1, China PR (a) 1-1, Malawi (h) 2-0, Liberia (a) 0-2, Malawi (a) 1-0, Cape Verde Islands (n) 1-0, Egypt (n) 3-0, Tunisia (n) 4-2, Congo DR (n) 2-2, Mali (n) 1-0, Niger (n) 3-0, Cape Verde Islands (n) 2-0, Burkina Faso (n) 1-1 (2-3p), Mali (n) 1-3, Sudan (h) 4-0, Sudan (a) 3-1, Ivory Coast (h) 2-1, Ivory Coast (h) 1-1, Lesotho (a) 2-0.

## GUINEA
Federation Guineenne De Football, PO Box 3645, Conakry.
*Founded:* 1959; *National Colours:* Red shirts, yellow shorts, green socks.
*International matches 2012–13*
Mali (n) 0-1, Botswana (n) 6-1, Ghana (n) 1-1, Ivory Coast (a) 0-0, Cameroon (n) 1-2, Zimbabwe (a) 1-0, Egypt (h) 2-3, Morocco (a) 2-1, Niger (h) 1-0, Niger (a) 0-2, Bahrain (a) 0-3, Senegal (n) 1-1, Mozambique (a) 0-0, Mozambique (h) 6-1, Zimbabwe (h) 1-0.

## GUINEA-BISSAU
Federacao De Football Da Guinea-Bissau, Alto Bandim (Nova Sede), PO Box 375, 1035 Bissau.
*Founded:* 1974; *National Colours:* Red, green and yellow shirts, green and yellow shorts, red, green and yellow socks.
*International matches 2012–13*
Cameroon (h) 0-1, Cameroon (a) 0-1.

## GUINEA, EQUATORIAL
Federacion Ecuatoguineana De Futbol, c/P Patricio Lumumba (Estadio La Paz), 1071 Malabo.
*Founded:* 1986; *National Colours:* All red.
*International matches 2012–13*
South Africa (h) 0-0, Libya (h) 1-0, Senegal (h) 2-1, Zambia (n) 0-1, Ivory Coast (h) 0-3, Tunisia (a) 1-3, Sierra Leone (h) 2-2, Liberia (h) 1-0, Congo DR (a) 0-4, Cape Verde Islands (h) 4-3, Togo (h) 0-1, Cape Verde Islands (a) 1-2, Tunisia (h) 1-1.

## IVORY COAST
Federation Ivorienne De Football, PO Box 1202, Abidjan 01.
*Founded:* 1960; *National Colours:* Orange shirts, black shorts, green socks.
*International matches 2012–13*
Tunisia (n) 2-0, Libya (n) 1-0, Sudan (n) 1-0, Burkina Faso (n) 2-0, Angola (n) 2-0, Equatorial Guinea (a) 3-0, Mali (n) 1-0, Zambia (n) 0-0 (7-8p), Chile (n) 0-0, Tanzania (h) 2-0, Morocco (a) 2-2, Russia (a) 1-1, Senegal (h) 4-2, Senegal (a) 2-0, Austria (a) 3-0, Egypt (n) 4-2, Togo (n) 2-1, Tunisia (n) 2-0, Algeria (n) 0-0, Nigeria (n) 0-0, Gambia (n) 3-0, Gambia (a) 3-0, Ghana (a) 1-2, Ghana (a) 1-1, Tanzania (a) 4-2.

## KENYA
Kenya Football Federation, Nyayo National Stadium, PO Box 40234, Nairobi.
*Founded:* 1960; *National Colours:* All red.
*International matches 2012–13*
Egypt (n) 0-5, Togo (h) 2-1, Malawi (h) 0-0, Namibia (a) 0-1, Togo (a) 0-1, Botswana (h) 3-1, South Africa (h) 1-2, Tanzania (a) 0-1, Uganda (a) 0-1, South Sudan (n) 2-0, Ethiopia (n) 3-1, Malawi (n) 1-0, Zanzibar (n) 2-2 (4-2p), Uganda (a) 1-2, Burundi (h) 0-0, Libya (n) 3-0, Nigeria (a) 1-1, Nigeria (h) 0-1, Malawi (a) 2-2.

## LESOTHO
Lesotho Football Association, PO Box 1879, Maseru-100, Lesotho.
*Founded:* 1932; *National Colours:* Blue shirts, green shorts, white socks.
*International matches 2012–13*
Botswana (n) 0-3*, Sao Tome E Principe (a) 0-1, Sao Tome E Principe (h) 0-0, Botswana (a) 0-3, Ghana (a) 0-7, Sudan (h) 0-0, Swaziland (h) 2-1, Swaziland (h) 0-1, Zambia (h) 1-1, South Africa (h) 0-2, Zambia (a) 0-4, Ghana (h) 0-2.
* *Played 21.12.2011, result omitted from last edition.*

## LIBERIA
Liberia Football Association, Broad and Center Streets, PO Box 10-1066, 1000 Monrovia.
*Founded:* 1936; *National Colours:* Blue shirts, white shorts, red socks.
*International matches 2012–13*
Nigeria (h) 0-2, Namibia (h) 1-0, Angola (h) 0-0, Namibia (a) 0-0, Equatorial Guinea (a) 0-1, Malawi (h) 1-0, Nigeria (h) 2-2, Ghana (h) 2-0, Niger (a) 4-3, Nigeria (a) 1-6, Uganda (h) 2-0, Iraq (a) 1-0, Uganda (a) 0-1, Senegal (a) 0-2.

## LIBYA
Libyan Football Federation, Asayadi Street, Near Janat Al-Areet, PO Box 5137, Tripoli.
*Founded:* 1963; *National Colours:* Green and black shirts, black shorts and socks.
*International matches 2012–13*
Ivory Coast (n) 0-1, Equatorial Guinea (a) 0-1, Zambia (n) 2-2, Senegal (n) 2-1, Rwanda (h) 2-0, Togo (a) 1-1, Cameroon (h) 2-1, Algeria (n) 0-1, Algeria (h) 2-0, Kenya (n) 0-3, Senegal (a) 4-0, Rwanda (a) 1-0, Congo DR (a) 0-0, Mauritania (h) 2-0, Jordan (a) 0-1, Uganda (h) 3-0, Congo DR (h) 0-0, Togo (h) 2-0.

## MADAGASCAR
Federation Malagasy de Football, Immeuble Preservatrice Vie-Lot IBF-9B, Rue Rabearivelo-Antsahavola, PO Box 4409, Antananarivo 101.
*Founded:* 1961; *National Colours:* Red and green shirts, white and green shorts, green and white socks.
*International matches 2012–13*
Cape Verde Islands (h) 0-4, Cape Verde Islands (a) 1-3.

## MALAWI
Football Association of Malawi, Mpira House, Old Chileka Road, PO Box 865, Blantyre.
*Founded:* 1966; *National Colours:* Red shirts, white shorts, red and black socks.
*International matches 2012–13*
Chad (a) 2-3, Tanzania (n) 0-0, Kenya (a) 0-0, Nigeria (h) 1-1, Chad (h) 2-0, Zambia (h) 1-0, Liberia (a) 0-1, Ghana (a) 0-2, Ghana (h) 0-1, Rwanda (n) 0-2, Eritrea (n) 3-2, Zanzibar (n) 2-0, Kenya (n) 0-1, South Africa (n) 1-3, Botswana (a) 0-1, Namibia (a) 1-0, Zimbabwe (h) 1-1, Namibia (h) 0-0, Kenya (h) 2-2.

## MALI
Federation Malienne De Football, Avenue du Mali, Hamdallaye ACI 2000, PO Box 1020, Bamako 12582.
*Founded:* 1960; *National Colours:* Green shirts, yellow shorts, red socks.
*International matches 2012–13*
Guinea (n) 1-0, Ghana (n) 0-2, Botswana (n) 2-1, Gabon (a) 1-1 (5-4p), Ivory Coast (n) 0-1, Ghana (n) 2-0, Benin (a) 0-1, Algeria (h) 2-1, Botswana (h) 3-0, Botswana (a) 4-1, Niger (n) 1-0, Ghana (n) 0-1, Congo DR (n) 1-1, South Africa (a) 1-1 (3-1p), Nigeria (n) 1-0, Ghana (n) 0-1, Morocco (a) 1-2, Rwanda (a) 2-1, Rwanda (h) 1-1, Benin (h) 2-2.

## MAURITANIA
Federation De Foot-Ball De La Rep. Islamique. De Mauritanie, BP 566, Nouakchott.
*Founded:* 1961; *National Colours:* Green and yellow shirts, yellow shorts, green socks.
*International matches 2012–13*
Egypt (n) 0-3, Gambia (a) 2-0, Gambia (a) 2-0, Libya (a) 0-2, Algeria (a) 0-1.

## MAURITIUS
Mauritius Football Association, Chancery House, 2nd Floor Nos. 303–305, 14 Lislet Geoffroy Street, Port Louis.
*Founded:* 1952; *National Colours:* All red.
*International matches 2012–13*
None played.

## MOROCCO
Federation Royale Marocaine De Football, 51 Bis Av. Ibn Sina, PO Box 51, Agdal, 10 000 Rabat.
*Founded:* 1955; *National Colours:* All green white and red.
*International matches 2012–13*
Tunisia (n) 1-2, Gabon (a) 2-3, Niger (n) 1-0, Burkina Faso (h) 2-0, Senegal (h) 0-1, Gambia (a) 1-1, Ivory Coast (h) 2-2, Guinea (h) 1-2, Mozambique (a) 0-2, Mozambique (h) 4-0, Togo (h) 0-1, Niger (h) 3-0, Zambia (n) 0-0, Namibia (n) 2-1, Angola (n) 0-0, Cape Verde Islands (n) 1-1, South Africa (a) 2-2, Mali (h) 2-1, Tanzania (a) 1-3, Tanzania (h) 2-1, Gambia (h) 2-0.

## MOZAMBIQUE
Federacao Mocambicana De Futebol, Av. Samora Machel 11-2, Caixa Postal 1467, Maputo.
*Founded:* 1978; *National Colours:* Red shirts, black shorts, red and black socks.
*International matches 2012–13*
Namibia (a) 0-3, Tanzania (a) 1-1, Iran (a) 0-3, Namibia (n) 0-0, Egypt (h) 0-2, Zimbabwe (h) 0-0, Tanzania (h) 1-1 (8-7p), Vietnam (a) 0-1, Angola (a) 0-2, Morocco (h) 2-0, South Africa (a) 0-2, Morocco (a) 0-4, Guinea (h) 0-0, Guinea (a) 1-6, Egypt (h) 0-1.

## NAMIBIA
Namibia Football Association, Abraham Mashego Street 8521, Katurua Council of Churches in Namibia, PO Box 1345, 9000 Windhoek.
*Founded:* 1990; *National Colours:* All red.
*International matches 2012–13*
Zambia (n) 0-0, Mozambique (h) 3-0, Liberia (a) 0-1, Mozambique (n) 0-0, Nigeria (a) 0-1, Kenya (h) 1-0, Liberia (h) 0-0, Rwanda (h) 0-0, Rwanda (a) 2-2, Morocco (n) 1-2, Malawi (h) 0-1, Zambia (h) 1-0, Malawi (a) 0-0, Nigeria (h) 1-1.

## NIGER
Federation Nigerienne De Football, Rue de la Tapoa, PO Box 10299, Niamey.
*Founded:* 1967; *National Colours:* Orange shirts, white shorts, green socks.
*International matches 2012–13*
Gabon (a) 0-2, Tunisia (n) 1-2, Morocco (n) 0-1, Egypt (n) 0-1, Algeria (a) 0-3, Gabon (h) 3-0, Congo (a) 0-1, Nigeria (h) 0-0, Guinea (a) 0-1, Liberia (h) 4-3, Guinea (h) 2-0, Senegal (h) 1-1, Morocco (a) 0-3, Ethiopia (a) 0-1, Mali (n) 0-1, Congo DR (n) 0-0, Ghana (n) 0-3, Burkina Faso (a) 0-4, Burkina Faso (h) 0-1, Gabon (a) 1-4.

## NIGERIA
Nigeria Football Association, Plot 2033, Olusegun, Obasanjo Way, Zone 7, Wuse Abuja, PO Box 5101 Garki, Abuja.
*Founded:* 1945; *National Colours:* All green and white.
*International matches 2012–13*
Liberia (a) 2-2, Rwanda (a) 0-0, Egypt (n) 2-3, Peru (a) 0-1, Namibia (h) 1-0, Malawi (a) 1-1, Rwanda (h) 2-0, Niger (a) 0-0, Liberia (a) 2-2, Liberia (h) 6-1, Venezuela (n) 3-1, Cape Verde Islands (n) 0-0, Burkina Faso (n) 1-1, Zambia (n) 1-1, Ethiopia (n) 2-0, Ivory Coast (n) 2-1, Mali (n) 4-1, Burkina Faso (h) 1-0, Kenya (h) 1-1, Mexico (n) 2-2, Kenya (a) 1-0, Namibia (a) 1-1, Tahiti (n) 6-1, Uruguay (n) 1-2, Spain (n) 0-3.

## RWANDA
Federation Rwandaise De Football Amateur, BP 2000, Kigali.
*Founded:* 1972; *National Colours:* Red, green and yellow shirts, green shorts, red socks.
*International matches 2012–13*
Nigeria (h) 0-0, Libya (a) 0-2, Tunisia (a) 1-5, Algeria (a) 0-4, Benin (h) 1-1, Nigeria (a) 0-2, Namibia (a) 0-0,

Namibia (h) 2-2, Malawi (n) 2-2, Zanzibar (n) 1-2, Eritrea (n) 2-0, Tanzania (n) 0-2, Angola (a) 0-1, Uganda (h) 2-2, Libya (h) 0-1, Mali (h) 1-2, Mali (a) 1-1, Algeria (h) 0-1.

## SAO TOME E PRINCIPE

Federation Santomense De Futebol, Rua Ex-Joao de Deus No. QXXIII-426/26, PO Box 440, Sao Tome.
*Founded:* 1975; *National Colours:* Green and red shirts, yellow shorts, green socks.
*International matches 2012–13*
Lesotho (h) 1-0, Lesotho (a) 0-0, Sierra Leone (h) 2-1, Sierra Leone (a) 2-4.

## SENEGAL

Federation Senegalaise De Football, Stade Leopold Sedar Senghor, Route De L'Aeroport De Yoff, BP 13021, Dakar.
*Founded:* 1960; *National Colours:* All white and green.
*International matches 2012–13*
Sudan (h) 1-0, Zambia (n) 1-2, Equatorial Guinea (a) 1-2, Libya (n) 1-2, South Africa (a) 0-0, Morocco (a) 1-0, Liberia (h) 3-1, Uganda (a) 1-1, Ivory Coast (a) 2-4, Ivory Coast (h) 0-2, Niger (a) 1-1, Guinea (n) 1-1, Libya (h) 0-4, Angola (h) 1-1, Angola (a) 1-1, Liberia (a) 2-0.

## SEYCHELLES

Seychelles Football Federation, PO Box 843, People's Stadium, Victoria-Mahe.
*Founded:* 1979; *National Colours:* Red and green shirts and shorts, red socks.
*International matches 2012–13*
Swaziland (h) 3-0, Swaziland (a) 3-0, Congo DR (h) 0-4, Congo DR (a) 0-3.

## SIERRA LEONE

Sierra Leone Football Association, 21 Battery Street, Kingtorn, PO Box 672, National Stadium, Brookfields, Freetown.
*Founded:* 1967; *National Colours:* Green and blue shirts, green, blue and white shorts and socks.
*International matches 2012–13*
Angola (a) 1-3, Sao Tome E Principe (a) 1-2, Iraq (a) 0-1, Cape Verde Islands (h) 2-1, Equatorial Guinea (a) 2-2, Sao Tome E Principe (h) 4-2, Tunisia (h) 2-2, Tunisia (a) 0-0, Tunisia (a) 1-2, Tunisia (h) 2-2 Cape Verde Islands (h) 0-1.

## SOMALIA

Somali Football Federation, PO Box 222, Mogadishu BN 03040.
*Founded:* 1951; *National Colours:* Sky blue and white shirts and shorts, white and sky blue socks.
*International matches 2012–13*
Zanzibar (h) 0-3*, Burundi (n) 1-5, Sudan (n) 0-1, Tanzania (n) 0-7.
* *Played 01.12.2011, result omitted from last edition.*

## SOUTH AFRICA

South African Football Association, First National Bank Stadium, PO Box 910, Johannesburg 2000, South Africa.
*Founded:* 1991; *National Colours:* White shirts with yellow striped sleeves, white shorts with yellow stripes, white socks.
*International matches 2012–13*
Equatorial Guinea (a) 0-0, Senegal (h) 0-0, Botswana (a) 1-1, Gabon (h) 3-0, Brazil (a) 0-1, Mozambique (h) 2-0, Poland (a) 1-0, Kenya (a) 2-1, Zambia (h) 0-1, Malawi (h) 3-1, Norway (h) 0-1, Algeria (h) 0-0, Cape Verde Islands (h) 0-0, Angola (h) 2-0, Morocco (h) 2-2, Mali (h) 1-1 (1-3p), Central African Republic (h) 2-0, Lesotho (a) 2-0, Central African Republic (a) 3-0, Ethiopia (a) 1-2.

## SUDAN

Sudan Football Association, Bladia Street, Khartoum.
*Founded:* 1936; *National Colours:* Red shirts, white shorts, black socks.
*International matches 2012–13*
Tunisia (n) 0-3, Senegal (a) 0-1, Gabon (a) 0-0, Ivory Coast (n) 0-1, Angola (n) 2-2, Burkina Faso (n) 2-1, Zambia (n) 0-3, Zambia (h) 0-3, Lesotho (a) 0-0, Ethiopia (h) 5-3, Ethiopia (a) 0-2, Tanzania (a) 0-2, Somalia (n) 1-0, Burundi (n) 0-1, Ghana (a) 0-4, Ethiopia (a) 0-2, Tanzania (n) 0-0, Ghana (h) 1-3, Zambia (a) 1-1.

## SWAZILAND

National Football Association of Swaziland, Sigwaca House, Plot 582, Sheffield Road, PO Box 641, Mbabane H100.
*Founded:* 1968; *National Colours:* Blue shirts, gold shorts, red socks.

*International matches 2012–13*
Seychelles (a) 0-3, Seychelles (h) 0-3, Lesotho (a) 1-2, Lesotho (a) 1-0, Burkina Faso (n) 0-3, Botswana (n) 0-0.

## TANZANIA

Football Association of Tanzania, Uhuru/Shaurimoyo Road, Karume Memorial Stadium, PO Box 1574, Ilala/Dar Es Salaam.
*Founded:* 1930; *National Colours:* Green, yellow and blue shirts, black shorts, green socks with horizontal stripe.
*International matches 2012–13*
Congo DR (h) 0-0, Mozambique (h) 1-1, Malawi (n) 0-0, Ivory Coast (a) 0-2, Gambia (h) 2-1, Mozambique (a) 1-1 (7-8p), Botswana (a) 3-3, Kenya (h) 1-0, Sudan (n) 0-2, Burundi (n) 0-1, Somalia (n) 7-0, Rwanda (n) 2-0, Uganda (a) 0-3, Zanzibar (n) 1-1 (5-6p), Zambia (h) 1-0, Ethiopia (a) 1-2, Cameroon (h) 1-0, Morocco (h) 3-1, Sudan (n) 0-0, Morocco (a) 1-2, Ivory Coast (h) 2-4.

## TOGO

Federation Togolaise De Football, C.P. 5, Lome.
*Founded:* 1960; *National Colours:* White shirts, green shorts, red socks with yellow and green stripes.
*International matches 2012–13*
Kenya (a) 1-2, Egypt (n) 0-3, Libya (h) 1-1, Congo DR (a) 0-2, Kenya (h) 1-0, Burkina Faso (n) 0-3, Gabon (a) 1-1, Gabon (h) 2-1, Morocco (a) 1-0, Oman (a) 1-0, Ivory Coast (n) 1-2, Algeria (n) 2-0, Tunisia (n) 1-1, Burkina Faso (n) 0-1, Cameroon (a) 1-2, Equatorial Guinea (a) 1-0, Cameroon (h) 2-0, Libya (a) 0-2.

## TUNISIA

Federation Tunisienne De Football, Maison des Federations Sportives, Cite Olympique, Tunis 1003.
*Founded:* 1956; *National Colours:* Red shirts, white shorts, red socks.
*International matches 2012–13*
Sudan (n) 3-0, Ivory Coast (n) 0-2, Morocco (n) 2-1, Niger (n) 2-1, Gabon (a) 0-1, Ghana (n) 1-2, Peru (h) 1-1, Rwanda (h) 5-1, Equatorial Guinea (h) 3-1, Cape Verde Islands (a) 2-1, Iran (n) 2-2, Sierra Leone (a) 2-2, Sierra Leone (h) 0-0, Egypt (n) 1-0, Switzerland (h) 1-2, Iraq (a) 2-1, Ethiopia (n) 1-1, Gabon (n) 1-1, Ghana (n) 2-4, Algeria (n) 1-0, Ivory Coast (n) 0-3, Togo (a) 1-1, Sierra Leone (h) 2-1, Sierra Leone (a) 2-2, Equatorial Guinea (h) 1-1.

## UGANDA

Federation of Uganda Football Associations, Plot No. 879, Kyadondo Block 8, Mengo Wakaliga Road, PO Box 22518, Kampala.
*Founded:* 1924; *National Colours:* All yellow, red and white.
*International matches 2012–13*
Congo (a) 1-3, Egypt (n) 1-2, Angola (a) 1-1, Senegal (h) 1-1, Congo (h) 4-0, South Sudan (a) 2-2, Zambia (a) 0-1, Zambia (a) 1-0 (8-9p), Kenya (h) 1-0, Ethiopia (h) 1-0, South Sudan (h) 4-0, Ethiopia (h) 2-0, Tanzania (h) 3-0, Kenya (h) 2-1, Rwanda (a) 2-2, Liberia (a) 0-2, Libya (n) 0-3, Liberia (h) 1-0, Angola (h) 2-1.

## ZAMBIA

Football Association of Zambia, Football House, Alick Nkhata Road, PO Box 34751, Lusaka.
*Founded:* 1929; *National Colours:* White and green shirts, green and white shorts, white and green socks.
*International matches 2012–13*
Namibia (n) 0-0, Senegal (n) 2-1, Libya (n) 2-2, Equatorial Guinea (a) 1-0, Sudan (n) 3-0, Ghana (n) 1-0, Ivory Coast (n) 0-0 (8-7p), Angola (a) 0-0, Sudan (a) 3-0, Ghana (h) 1-0, Malawi (a) 0-1, Zimbabwe (h) 2-1, South Korea (a) 1-2, Uganda (h) 1-0, Uganda (a) 1-0 (9-8p), South Africa (a) 1-0, Saudi Arabia (a) 1-2, Tanzania (a) 0-1, Morocco (n) 0-0, Ethiopia (n) 1-1, Nigeria (n) 1-1, Burkina Faso (n) 0-0, Lesotho (a) 1-1, Zimbabwe (h) 2-0, Namibia (a) 0-1, Lesotho (h) 4-0, Sudan (h) 1-1.

## ZIMBABWE

Zimbabwe Football Association, PO Box CY 114, Causeway, Harare.
*Founded:* 1965; *National Colours:* All green and gold.
*International matches 2012–13*
Botswana (a) 0-0, Burundi (a) 1-2, Guinea (h) 0-1, Mozambique (a) 0-0, Burundi (h) 1-0, Zambia (a) 1-2, Angola (h) 3-1, Angola (a) 0-2, Botswana (h) 2-1, Egypt (a) 1-2, Zambia (a) 0-2, Malawi (a) 1-1, Egypt (h) 2-4, Guinea (a) 0-1

# WORLD CUP 2014 QUALIFYING COMPETITION

## EUROPE

**■** *Denotes player sent off.*

### GROUP A

**Friday, 7 September 2012**

**Croatia (0) 1** *(Jelavic 68)*

**FYR Macedonia (0) 0** 15,150

*Croatia:* (352) Pletikosa; Strinic, Simunic, Corluka (Vida 81); Rakitic (Kranjcar 46), Vukojevic, Modric, Srna, Perisic; Mandzukic, Eduardo (Jelavic 63).
*FYR Macedonia:* (442) Bogatinov; Georgievski, Popov, Noveski, Sikov; Gligorov (Tasevski 83), Demiri, Trickovski (Georgiev 73), Ristic (Ivanovski 80); Pandev, Ibraimi.
*Referee:* Alon Yefet.

**Wales (0) 0**

**Belgium (1) 2** *(Kompany 42, Vertonghen 82)* 20,201

*Wales:* (352) Myhill; Blake, Collins■, Williams A; Gunter, Edwards (King 79), Ramsey, Bale, Matthews; Church (Robson-Kanu 71), Morison (Vokes 71).
*Belgium:* (442) Courtois; Gillet G, Vermaelen, Kompany, Vertonghen; Witsel, Dembele (De Bruyne 64), Hazard, Mertens; Mirallas (Lukaku 46), Fellaini.
*Referee:* Stefan Johannesson.

**Saturday, 8 September 2012**

**Scotland (0) 0**

**Serbia (0) 0** 47,473

*Scotland:* (4141) McGregor; Hutton, Webster, Berra, Dixon; Caldwell; Naismith, Snodgrass (Forrest 69), Adam, Morrison (Mackie 81); Miller (Rhodes 81).
*Serbia:* (4141) Stojkovic; Ivanovic, Bisevac, Nastasic, Kolarov; Mijailovic (Fejsa 46); Tosic, Ninkovic, Ignjovski, Djuricic (Lekic 83); Lazovic (Tadic 58).
*Referee:* Jonas Eriksson.

**Tuesday, 11 September 2012**

**Belgium (1) 1** *(Gillet G 45)*

**Croatia (1) 1** *(Perisic 6)* 43,430

*Belgium:* (442) Courtois; Gillet G, Vermaelen, Kompany, Vertonghen; Defour (Fellaini 67), Witsel, Mertens (Mirallas 81), Hazard; Benteke, Dembele (De Bruyne 72).
*Croatia:* (442) Pletikosa; Strinic, Vida, Simunic, Schildenfeld; Radosevic (Vukojevic 78), Modric, Srna, Perisic; Mandzukic (Kalinic 88), Jelavic (Olic 59).
*Referee:* Alberto Undiano Mallenco.

**Scotland (1) 1** *(Miller 43)*

**FYR Macedonia (1) 1** *(Noveski 11)* 32,324

*Scotland:* (4141) McGregor; Hutton, Webster, Berra, Dixon; Caldwell; Forrest, Maloney, Morrison (Rhodes 66), Mackie (Naismith 77); Miller (Adam 58).
*FYR Macedonia:* (4411) Bogatinov; Georgievski, Sikov, Noveski, Popov; Ibraimi (Tasevski 89), Gligorov (Sumulikoski 70), Demiri, Trickovski (Hasani 37); Pandev; Ivanovski.
*Referee:* Sergei Karasev.

**Serbia (3) 6** *(Kolarov 16, Tosic 24, Djuricic 39, Tadic 55, Ivanovic 80, Sulejmani 90)*

**Wales (1) 1** *(Bale 31)* 11,113

*Serbia:* (4141) Stojkovic; Ivanovic, Bisevac, Nastasic, Kolarov; Ignjovski (Mijailovic 85); Tadic, Fejsa, Djuricic (Lekic 81), Tosic (Sulejmani 71); Markovic.
*Wales:* (442) Myhill; Gunter, Williams A, Blake, Matthews (Ricketts 46); Edwards (Vaughan 46), Allen (King 72), Ramsey, Bale; Morison, Church.
*Referee:* Duarte Gomes.

**Friday, 12 October 2012**

**FYR Macedonia (1) 1** *(Ibraimi 16)*

**Croatia (1) 2** *(Corluka 33, Rakitic 60)* 33,330

*FYR Macedonia:* (442) Bogatinov; Georgievski, Popov (Hasani 82), Noveski, Sikov (Grncarov 77); Sumulikoski (Gligorov 54), Demiri, Trickovski, Ristic; Pandev, Ibraimi.
*Croatia:* (442) Pletikosa; Strinic, Simunic, Corluka, Rakitic; Vukojevic, Modric (Badelj 83), Srna, Perisic; Jelavic (Sammir 64), Mandzukic (Kalinic 72).
*Referee:* Peter Rasmussen.

**Serbia (0) 0**

**Belgium (1) 3** *(Benteke 34, De Bruyne 68, Mirallas 90)* 22,220

*Serbia:* (442) Brkic; Bisevac, Nastasic, Ivanovic, Tosic (Stevanovic 67); Tadic (Lekic 80), Kolarov, Mijailovic, Ignjovski; Djuricic (Scepovic 56), Markovic.
*Belgium:* (442) Courtois; Alderweireld, Vermaelen, Kompany, Vertonghen; Witsel, De Bruyne (Mirallas 87), Dembele, Benteke; Hazard (Mertens 55), Chadli.
*Referee:* Pavel Kralovec.

**Wales (0) 2** *(Bale 81 (pen), 89)*

**Scotland (1) 1** *(Morrison 27)* 23,232

*Wales:* (451) Price; Gunter, Blake, Williams, Davies B; Bale, Allen, Vaughan, Ramsey, Ledley (Robson-Kanu 71); Morison (Davies C 64).
*Scotland:* (451) McGregor; Hutton, Caldwell, Berra, Fox; Maloney, Morrison (Miller 84), Fletcher D, Brown (Adam 46), Commons (Mackie 84); Fletcher S.
*Referee:* Florian Meyer.

**Tuesday, 16 October 2012**

**Belgium (0) 2** *(Benteke 69, Kompany 71)*

**Scotland (0) 0** 44,440

*Belgium:* (442) Courtois; Alderweireld, Vermaelen, Kompany, Vertonghen; De Bruyne, Witsel, Chadli, Mertens (Mirallas 55); Dembele (Hazard 46), Benteke (M'Boyo 86).
*Scotland:* (451) McGregor; Hutton, Berra, Caldwell, Fox; Maloney, Morrison (Phillips 79), Fletcher D, McArthur, Commons (Mackie 46); Fletcher S (Miller 76).
*Referee:* Mauricio Morales.

**Croatia (1) 2** *(Mandzukic 27, Eduardo 58)*

**Wales (0) 0** 18,180

*Croatia:* (442) Pletikosa; Strinic, Simunic, Lovren (Schildenfeld 46), Srna; Badelj, Perisic (Vida 85), Rakitic, Modric; Mandzukic, Eduardo (Kranjcar 78).
*Wales:* (442) Price; Williams, Davies B, Gunter, Blake; King (Vokes 72), Vaughan, Bale, Allen; Ledley (Robson-Kanu 82), Morison (Church 61).
*Referee:* Alexandru Dan Tudor.

**FYR Macedonia (0) 1** *(Ibraimi 61 (pen))*

**Serbia (0) 0** 31,310

*FYR Macedonia:* (433) Pacovski; Lazevski, Grncarov, Georgievski; Gligorov, Demiri (Sumulikoski 86), Tasevski (Trickovski 73); Hasani, Ibraimi, Ivanovski (Ristovski 90).
*Serbia:* (442) Brkic; Tomovic■, Bisevac, Nastasic, Kolarov; Ignjovski, Fejsa, Tosic, Tadic (Ivanovic 68); Markovic (Sulejmani 74), Djuricic (Lekic 63).
*Referee:* Bas Nijhuis.

**Friday, 22 March 2013**

**Croatia (2) 2** *(Mandzukic 23, Olic 37)*

**Serbia (0) 0** 36,360

*Croatia:* (442) Pletikosa; Srna, Simunic, Corluka, Strinic (Lovren 80); Kovacic, Modric, Rakitic, Kranjcar (Vida 63); Mandzukic, Olic (Vukojevic 83).
*Serbia:* (442) Brkic; Ivanovic, Subotic, Nastasic, Kolarov; Radovanovic, Ignjovski (Petrovic 75), Tosic, Stevanovic (Tadic 57); Scepovic (Djordjevic 9), Djuricic.
*Referee:* Cuneyt Cakir.

**FYR Macedonia (0) 0**
**Belgium (1) 2** *(De Bruyne 26, Hazard 62 (pen))*     20,200
*FYR Macedonia:* (442) Pacovski; Todorovski, Noveski, Grncarov, Lazevski; Demiri, Trickovski (Tasevski 81), Jahovic (Ivanovski 57), Pandev; Hasani (Trajkovski 81), Ibraimi.
*Belgium:* (442) Courtois; Alderweireld, Vermaelen, Vertonghen, Van Buyten; Witsel, Fellaini, Hazard, De Bruyne; Dembele, Benteke (Chadli 85).
*Referee:* Deniz Aytekin.

**Scotland (1) 1** *(Hanley 45)*
**Wales (0) 2** *(Ramsey 73 (pen), Robson-Kanu 74)*     39,393
*Scotland:* (4411) McGregor; Hutton, Caldwell, Hanley, Mulgrew; Burke (Rhodes 86), McArthur, Dorrans (Adam 63), Snodgrass■; Maloney; Fletcher S (Miller 4).
*Wales:* (433) Myhill; Gunter, Ricketts, Williams A, Davies B; Collison (King 58), Ramsey■, Ledley (Church 89); Bale (Williams J 46), Robson-Kanu, Bellamy.
*Referee:* Antony Gautier.

**Tuesday, 26 March 2013**
**Belgium (0) 1** *(Hazard 62)*
**FYR Macedonia (0) 0**     45,450
*Belgium:* (442) Courtois; Alderweireld, Kompany, Vermaelen, Vertonghen; Witsel, Dembele (Chadli 55), Mertens (Mirallas 46), De Bruyne; Hazard (Fellaini 90), Benteke.
*FYR Macedonia:* (442) Pacovski; Georgievski, Noveski, Sikov, Ristovski (Todorovski 70); Gligorov, Tasevski (Hasani 46), Ibraimi, Trickovski (Trajkovski 64); Pandev, Ivanovski.
*Referee:* Olegario Benquerenca.

**Serbia (0) 2** *(Djuricic 59, 65)*
**Scotland (0) 0**     10,100
*Serbia:* (442) Stojkovic; Ivanovic, Nastasic, Subotic, Tomovic; Basta, Fejsa (Petrovic 85), Milivojevic, Tosic (Stevanovic 90); Tadic (Djordjevic 69), Djuricic.
*Scotland:* (4411) Marshall; Hutton, Caldwell, Hanley, Whittaker; Boyd, McArthur (Adam 46), Bridcutt, Maloney (Burke 79); Naismith; Rhodes (Miller 80).
*Referee:* Istvan Vad.

**Wales (1) 1** *(Bale 21 (pen))*
**Croatia (0) 2** *(Lovren 77, Eduardo 87)*     12,125
*Wales:* (433) Myhill; Gunter, Williams A, Collins, Davies B; Ledley, Williams J (Church 83), King; Bellamy, Robson-Kanu (Richards 63), Bale.
*Croatia:* (442) Pletikosa; Strinic (Olic 73), Corluka, Lovren, Srna; Rakitic, Modric, Sammir (Kovacic 61), Badelj (Schildenfeld 46); Mandzukic, Eduardo.
*Referee:* Luca Banti.

**Friday, 7 June 2013**
**Belgium (1) 2** *(De Bruyne 13, Fellaini 60)*
**Serbia (0) 1** *(Kolarov 87)*     45,458
*Belgium:* (4141) Courtois; Alderweireld, Kompany, Van Buyten, Vertonghen; Witsel; De Bruyne (Lukaku 82), Fellaini (Dembele 71), Chadli, Mirallas (Hazard 64); Benteke.
*Serbia:* (4231) Stojkovic; Ivanovic, Bisevac, Subotic, Kolarov; Milivojevic (Petrovic 68), Fejsa; Tadic, Basta, Markovic; Mitrovic (Scepovic 69).
*Referee:* Stephane Lannoy.

**Croatia (0) 0**
**Scotland (1) 1** *(Snodgrass 26)*     28,280
*Croatia:* (442) Pletikosa; Strinic (Kalinic 70), Simunic, Schildenfeld, Srna; Rakitic, Kovacic, Perisic (Eduardo 55), Sammir; Mandzukic (Kranjcar 87), Olic.
*Scotland:* (451) McGregor; Hutton, Martin, Hanley, Whittaker; Maloney (Conway 75), Morrison, McArthur, Bannan (Naismith 63), Snodgrass; Griffiths (Rhodes 64).
*Referee:* David Fernandez Borbalan.

| Group A Table | P | W | D | L | F | A | GD | Pts |
|---|---|---|---|---|---|---|---|---|
| Belgium | 7 | 6 | 1 | 0 | 13 | 2 | 11 | 19 |
| Croatia | 7 | 5 | 1 | 1 | 10 | 4 | 6 | 16 |
| Serbia | 7 | 2 | 1 | 4 | 9 | 9 | 0 | 7 |
| Wales | 6 | 2 | 0 | 4 | 6 | 14 | -8 | 6 |
| Scotland | 7 | 1 | 2 | 4 | 4 | 9 | -5 | 5 |
| FYR Macedonia | 6 | 1 | 1 | 4 | 3 | 7 | -4 | 4 |

## GROUP B

**Friday, 7 September 2012**
**Bulgaria (1) 2** *(Manolev 30, Milanov G 66)*
**Italy (2) 2** *(Osvaldo 37, 40)*     25,250
*Bulgaria:* (442) Mihailov; Bodurov, Minev I, Minev V, Ivanov; Manolev, Milanov G, Gadzhev (Sarmov 79), Dyakov; Gargorov (Mitsanski 62), Popov (Tonev 81).
*Italy:* (442) Buffon; Maggio, Ogbonna (Peluso 68), Barzagli, Bonucci; Marchisio, Giaccherini (Diamanti 64), De Rossi, Pirlo; Osvaldo, Giovinco (Destro 73).
*Referee:* Martin Atkinson.

**Malta (0) 0**
**Armenia (0) 1** *(Sarkisov 70)*     4000
*Malta:* (352) Hogg; Muscat A, Borg, Agius A; Dimech, Schembri, Sciberras, Briffa (Bajada 85), Bogdanovic; Mifsud, Cohen (Caruana 74).
*Armenia:* (442) Kasparov; Hovsepyan, Hayrapetyan, Arzumanyan (Aleksanyan 79), Mkoyan; Yedigaryan Artak (Manoyan 52), Mkhitaryan, Mkrtchyan, Ozbiliz; Pizelli (Sarkisov 64), Movsisyan.
*Referee:* Rene Eisner.

**Saturday, 8 September 2012**
**Denmark (0) 0**
**Czech Republic (0) 0**     24,240
*Denmark:* (442) Andersen; Jacobsen, Kjaer, Agger, Wass; Kristensen (Andreasen 58), Kvist Jorgensen, Eriksen, Krohn-Delhi; Rommedahl (Mikkelsen 80), Jorgensen (Cornelius 71).
*Czech Republic:* (442) Cech; Gebre Selassie, Sivok, Suchy, Kadlec M; Hubschman, Plasil (Darida 75), Jiracek, Rezek (Husbauer 89); Pekhart, Vydra (Rajtoral 73).
*Referee:* Wolfgang Stark.

**Tuesday, 11 September 2012**
**Bulgaria (1) 1** *(Manolev 44)*
**Armenia (0) 0**     10,100
*Bulgaria:* (442) Mihailov; Bodurov, Ivanov, Minev V, Minev I; Dyakov■, Manolev, Gadzhev (Sarmov 59), Milanov G; Mitsanski (Rangelov 65), Popov (Gargorov 82).
*Armenia:* (4231) Berezovsky; Arzumanyan, Hayrapetyan (Yedigaryan Artak 45), Hovsepyan, Mkoyan; Mkhitaryan, Ozbiliz (Pizelli■ 54); Mkrtchyan, Yedigaryan Artur (Sarkisov 77), Ghazaryan■; Movsisyan.
*Referee:* Stephan Studer.

**Italy (1) 2** *(Destro 5, Peluso 90)*
**Malta (0) 0**     18,180
*Italy:* (442) Buffon; Peluso, Cassani, Barzagli, Bonucci; Marchisio, Nocerino, Diamanti (Insigne 46), Pirlo; Destro (Giovinco 82), Osvaldo (Pazzini 69).
*Malta:* (442) Hogg; Muscat A (Camilleri 85), Herrera, Agius A, Dimech; Borg, Briffa, Schembri, Sciberras; Bogdanovic (Cohen 69), Mifsud.
*Referee:* Antti Munukka.

**Friday, 12 October 2012**
**Armenia (1) 1** *(Mkhitaryan 27)*
**Italy (1) 3** *(Pirlo 11 (pen), De Rossi 64, Osvaldo 81)*     32,320
*Armenia:* (442) Berezovsky; Aleksanyan, Mkoyan, Arzumanyan, Yedigaryan Artak; Ozbiliz, Mkrtchyan, Yedigaryan Artur (Manucharyan 65), Mkhitaryan; Manoyan (Sarkisov 76), Movsisyan.
*Italy:* (442) Buffon; Maggio, Barzagli, Bonucci, Criscito; De Rossi, Pirlo (Giaccherini 74), Marchisio, Montolivo (Candreva 89); Giovinco (El Shaarawy 61), Osvaldo.
*Referee:* Marijo Strahonja.

**Bulgaria (1) 1** *(Rangelov 7)*
**Denmark (1) 1** *(Bendtner 40)*     30,300
*Bulgaria:* (442) Mihailov; Bodurov, Minev I, Bandalovski■, Ivanov; Manolev, Milanov G, Gadzhev, Iliev (Milanov I 35); Rangelov (Tonev 61), Popov (Bojinov 85).
*Denmark:* (442) Andersen; Kristensen (Cornelius 36), Kjaer, Agger, Wass (Mtiglia 54); Jacobsen, Kvist Jorgensen, Eriksen (Poulsen J 90), Krohn-Delhi; Rommedahl, Bendtner.
*Referee:* Tony Chapron.

**Czech Republic (1) 3** *(Gebre Selassie 34, Pekhart 51, Rezek 67)*
**Malta (1) 1** *(Briffa 38)*      10,103
*Czech Republic:* (442) Cech; Gebre Selassie, Sivok, Kadlec, Limbersky; Rajtoral (Petrzela 61), Hubschman, Plasil, Jiracek (Darida 73); Rezek, Pekhart (Lafata 82).
*Malta:* (451) Hogg; Borg, Dimech, Agius A, Muscat A; Herrera, Sciberras, Bajada (Azzopardi 88), Briffa, Schembri (Fenech P 87); Mifsud.
*Referee:* Anar Salmanov.

Tuesday, 16 October 2012
**Czech Republic (0) 0**
**Bulgaria (0) 0**      16,161
*Czech Republic:* (442) Cech; Gebre Selassie, Kadlec, Sivok, Limbersky; Rajtoral (Darida 58), Rezek (Lafata 80), Plasil, Hubschman; Jiracek, Pekhart (Vydra 58).
*Bulgaria:* (442) Mihailov; Zanev (Milanov I 41), Bodurov, Minev I, Ivanov; Manolev, Milanov G, Gadzhev (Bojinov 61), Dyakov; Iliev, Popov (Tonev 75).
*Referee:* Vladislav Bezborodov.

**Italy (2) 3** *(Montolivo 33, De Rossi 37, Balotelli 54)*
**Denmark (1) 1** *(Kvist Jorgensen 45)*      37,370
*Italy:* (4312) De Sanctis; Balzaretti, Barzagli, Chiellini, Abate; De Rossi, Pirlo, Marchisio (Candreva 74); Montolivo (Giaccherini 85); Osvaldo[■], Balotelli (Destro 89).
*Denmark:* (4231) Andersen; Kjaer, Agger, Jacobsen, Silberbauer (Lorentzen 72); Kvist Jorgensen (Kahlenberg 59), Stokholm; Eriksen, Krohn-Delhi (Poulsen J 83), Rommedahl; Bendtner.
*Referee:* Damir Skomina.

Friday, 22 March 2013
**Bulgaria (2) 6** *(Tonev 6, 38, 68, Popov 47, Gargorov 55, Ivanov 78)*
**Malta (0) 0**      0
*Bulgaria:* (442) Mihailov; Bodurov, Minev V, Ivanov, Minev I (Dimitrov 63); Milanov G, Gadzhev (Sarmov 70), Iliev, Gargorov (Bojinov 56); Popov, Tonev.
*Malta:* (442) Hogg; Caruana, Herrera, Agius A (Camilleri 56), Dimech; Briffa, Failla, Fenech P (Muscat R 70), Mifsud; Schembri, Fenech R.
*Referee:* Eitan Shmuelevitz.

**Czech Republic (0) 0**
**Denmark (0) 3** *(Cornelius 57, Kjaer 67, Zimling 82)* 12,120
*Czech Republic:* (4231) Cech; Gebre Selassie, Sivok, Kadlec, Limbersky; Darida, Plasil (Kozak 74); Jiracek (Rosicky 61), Krejci (Dockal 64), Vydra; Lafata.
*Denmark:* (4231) Andersen; Jacobsen, Kjaer, Agger, Poulsen S; Zimling, Stokholm; Eriksen, Krohn-Delhi, Jorgensen (Rommedahl 66); Cornelius (Makienok 85).
*Referee:* Manuel Ricardo Neves.

Tuesday, 26 March 2013
**Armenia (0) 0**
**Czech Republic (0) 3** *(Vydra 47, 81, Kolar 90)*    15,150
*Armenia:* (433) Berezovsky; Arzumanyan, Voskanyan, Hovhannisyan, Aleksanyan; Pizzelli, Mkhitaryan, Muradyan (Manoyan 78); Ghazaryan (Sarkisov 60), Manucharyan (Ozbiliz 50), Movsisyan.
*Czech Republic:* (433) Cech; Gebre Selassie, Kadlec, Sivok (Suchy 43), Limbersky; Rosicky, Plasil, Hubschman; Darida (Jiracek 84), Lafata (Kolar 74), Vydra.
*Referee:* Pavel Balaj.

**Denmark (0) 1** *(Agger 63 (pen))*
**Bulgaria (0) 1** *(Manolev 52)*      22,221
*Denmark:* (433) Andersen; Jacobsen, Kjaer, Agger, Poulsen S; Zimling (Makienok 85), Stokholm, Eriksen; Krohn-Delhi (Schone 69), Rommedahl (Jorgensen 54), Cornelius.
*Bulgaria:* (442) Mihailov; Bodurov (Dimitrov 23), Minev V, Ivanov, Milanov I; Manolev (Gargorov 87), Milanov G, Gadzhev, Dyakov; Tonev, Popov (Iliev 71).
*Referee:* Firat Aydinus.

**Malta (0) 0**
**Italy (2) 2** *(Balotelli 8 (pen), 45)*      18,180
*Malta:* (451) Haber; Caruana, Muscat A, Dimech, Herrera; Camilleri, Sciberras, Failla (Cohen 82), Briffa, Mifsud (Vella 88); Schembri.
*Italy:* (433) Buffon; De Sciglio, Abate, Barzagli, Bonucci; Marchisio, El Shaarawy (Cerci 75), Montolivo; Pirlo, Giaccherini (Candreva 61), Balotelli (Gilardino 86).
*Referee:* Serdar Gozubuyuk.

Friday, 7 June 2013
**Armenia (0) 0**
**Malta (1) 1** *(Mifsud 7)*      9000
*Armenia:* (442) Berezovsky; Hovhannisyan, Arzumanyan, Voskanyan, Aleksanyan; Ozbiliz, Manoyan (Sarkisov 66), Mkrtchyan, Pizzelli; Mkhitaryan, Manucharyan (Movsisyan 46).
*Malta:* (433) Haber; Caruana, Sciberras (Fenech P 56), Camilleri, Dimech; Briffa (Muscat R 84), Muscat A, Failla; Herrera, Schembri, Mifsud (Vella 90).
*Referee:* Arnold Hunter.

**Czech Republic (0) 0**
**Italy (0) 0**      18,182
*Czech Republic:* (4231) Cech; Gebre Selassie, Sivok, Kadlec M, Limbersky (Suchy 20); Darida (Kadlec V 75), Hubschman; Jiracek (Kolar 86), Rosicky, Plasil; Kozak.
*Italy:* (4312) Buffon; Abate, Bonucci, Barzagli, Chiellini; Marchisio, Pirlo (Aquilani 77), De Rossi; Montolivo; Balotelli[■], El Shaarawy (Giovinco 46).
*Referee:* Svein Oddvar Moen.

Tuesday, 11 June 2013
**Denmark (0) 0**
**Armenia (2) 4** *(Movsisyan 1, 59, Ozbiliz 19, Mkhitaryan 82)*      14,147
*Denmark:* (442) Andersen; Kjaer, Bjelland (Okore 46), Poulsen S, Jacobsen; Zimling (Pedersen 28 (Christiansen 53)), Kvist Jorgensen, Eriksen, Krohn-Delhi; Rommedahl, Cornelius.
*Armenia:* (442) Berezovsky; Arzumanyan, Hovhannisyan, Aleksanyan, Haroyan; Ozbiliz (Aslanyan 90), Yedigaryan Artur (Pizzelli 86), Mkhitaryan, Mkrtchyan; Movsisyan (Sarkisov 84), Ghazaryan.
*Referee:* Aleksei Nikolaev.

**Group B Table**

| | P | W | D | L | F | A | GD | Pts |
|---|---|---|---|---|---|---|---|---|
| Italy | 6 | 4 | 2 | 0 | 12 | 4 | 8 | 14 |
| Bulgaria | 6 | 2 | 4 | 0 | 11 | 4 | 7 | 10 |
| Czech Republic | 6 | 2 | 3 | 1 | 6 | 4 | 2 | 9 |
| Armenia | 6 | 2 | 0 | 4 | 6 | 8 | –2 | 6 |
| Denmark | 6 | 1 | 3 | 2 | 6 | 9 | –3 | 6 |
| Malta | 6 | 1 | 0 | 5 | 2 | 14 | –12 | 3 |

## GROUP C

Friday, 7 September 2012
**Germany (1) 3** *(Gotze 28, Ozil 54, 71)*
**Faroe Islands (0) 0**      32,327
*Germany:* (4141) Neuer; Lahm, Mertesacker, Hummels, Badstuber; Khedira; Muller (Schurrle 68), Ozil, Gotze (Draxler 87), Reus; Klose (Podolski 75).
*Faroe Islands:* (4231) Nielsen; Naes, Faeroe, Baldvinsson, Justinussen; Benjaminsen, Hansson; Samuelsen S (Elttor 64), Holst, Udsen (Olsen S 46); Edmundsson (Olsen K 84).
*Referee:* Bobby Madden.

**Kazakhstan (1) 1** *(Nurdauletov 38)*
**Rep of Ireland (0) 2** *(Keane 89 (pen), Doyle 90)*   9500
*Kazakhstan:* (442) Sidelnikov, Kirov, Kislitsyn, Mukhtarov, Nurdauletov; Konysbayev (Gridin 84), Bogdanov, Ostapenko, Schmidtgal; Nusrbayev (Dzholchiyev 68), Rozhkov.
*Rep of Ireland:* (442) Westwood; O'Shea, St. Ledger, O'Dea, Ward; McGeady, Whelan, McCarthy, Cox (Doyle 57); Keane, Walters (Long 70).
*Referee:* Ionut Avram.

Tuesday, 11 September 2012
**Austria (0) 1** *(Junuzovic 57)*
**Germany (1) 2** *(Reus 44, Ozil 52 (pen))*        50,500
*Austria:* (451) Almer; Garics, Prodl, Pogatetz, Fuchs; Ivanschitz (Jantscher 75), Baumgartlinger (Janko 85), Kavlak, Junuzovic, Harnik (Burgstaller 55); Arnautovic.
*Germany:* (4141) Neuer; Lahm, Schmelzer, Hummels, Badstuber; Khedira; Muller, Kroos, Ozil, Reus (Gotze 46); Klose (Podolski 75).
*Referee:* Bjorn Kuipers.

**Sweden (1) 2** *(Elm 38, Berg 90)*
**Kazakhstan (0) 0**        20,204
*Sweden:* (433) Isaksson; Lustig, Olsson J, Granqvist, Safari; Larsson, Elm (Svensson 64), Wernbloom; Elmander (Berg 85), Ibrahimovic, Toivonen (Bajrami 56).
*Kazakhstan:* (442) Sidelnikov; Kirov, Rozhkov, Nurdauletov, Kislitsyn; Nusrbayev (Gridin 68), Schmidtgal, Shabalin (Islamkhan 84), Dmitrenko; Ostapenko (Shakmetov 46), Bogdanov.
*Referee:* Sergiy Boiko.

Friday, 12 October 2012
**Faroe Islands (0) 1** *(Baldvinsson 57)*
**Sweden (0) 2** *(Kacaniklic 65, Ibrahimovic 75)*        5100
*Faroe Islands:* (4411) Nielsen; Naes, Justinussen, Faeroe, Baldvinsson; Hansson (Olsen S 83), Benjaminsen, Holst (Hansen 71), Samuelsen S; Udsen (Elttor 86); Edmundsson.
*Sweden:* (442) Isaksson; Lustig, Olsson J, Granqvist, Olsson M; Larsson, Kallstrom (Svensson 62), Wernbloom, Wilhelmsson (Kacaniklic 62); Ibrahimovic, Ranegie (Berg 77).
*Referee:* Anastasios Sidiropoulos.

**Kazakhstan (0) 0**
**Austria (0) 0**        10,100
*Kazakhstan:* (442) Sidelnikov; Kirov, Nurdauletov, Dmitrenko, Rozhkov; Korobkin, Konysbayev (Gridin 90), Khairullin M (Mukhtarov 90), Bogdanov; Ostapenko, Nusrbayev (Nurgaliev 86).
*Austria:* (442) Almer; Garics, Pogatetz, Fuchs, Prodl; Ivanschitz (Jantscher 73), Junuzovic, Baumgartlinger (Janko 63), Kavlak; Arnautovic, Harnik (Weimann 84).
*Referee:* Tamas Bognar.

**Rep of Ireland (0) 1** *(Keogh A 90)*
**Germany (2) 6** *(Reus 32, 40, Ozil 55 (pen), Klose 58, Kroos 61, 83)*        51,517
*Rep of Ireland:* (442) Westwood; Coleman, O'Shea, O'Dea, Ward; McGeady (Keogh A 69), McCarthy, Andrews, Fahey (Long 51); Cox (Brady 84), Walters.
*Germany:* (4231) Neuer; Boateng, Mertesacker, Badstuber, Schmelzer; Khedira (Kroos 46), Schweinsteiger; Ozil, Muller, Reus (Podolski 66); Klose (Schurrle 72).
*Referee:* Nicola Rizzoli.

Tuesday, 16 October 2012
**Austria (1) 4** *(Janko 23, 64, Alaba 71, Harnik 90)*
**Kazakhstan (0) 0**        40,400
*Austria:* (442) Almer; Pogatetz, Prodl (Dragovic 59), Fuchs, Harnik; Klein, Kavlak, Alaba (Leitgeb 81), Junuzovic; Arnautovic, Janko (Jantscher 81).
*Kazakhstan:* (442) Sidelnikov; Kirov, Mukhtarov, Nurdauletov, Dmitrenko (Gorman 74); Korobkin, Konysbayev, Nurgaliev (Khairullin M 83), Shakmetov (Islamkhan 70); Bogdanov, Gridin.
*Referee:* Jakob Kehlet.

**Faroe islands (0) 1** *(Hansen 68)*
**Rep of Ireland (0) 4** *(Wilson 46, Walters 53, Justinussen 73 (og), O'Dea 88)*        4400
*Faroe Islands:* (442) Nielsen; Naes, Justinussen, Faeroe (Jacobsen 61), Baldvinsson; Hansson, Benjaminsen, Samuelsen S, Udsen (Hansen 61); Hoist, Edmundsson (Elttor 79).
*Rep of Ireland:* (442) Westwood; Coleman, O'Shea, O'Dea, Wilson; Brady (Cox 46), Andrews (Meyler 90), McCarthy, McGeady; Keane (Long 80), Walters.
*Referee:* Lorenc Jemini.

**Germany (3) 4** *(Klose 8, 15, Mertesacker 39, Ozil 55)*
**Sweden (0) 4** *(Ibrahimovic 62, Lustig 64, Elmander 76, Elm 90)*        70,700
*Germany:* (451) Neuer; Boateng, Mertesacker, Badstuber, Lahm; Schweinsteiger, Kroos, Muller (Gotze 67), Ozil, Reus (Podolski 87); Klose.
*Sweden:* (442) Isaksson; Lustig, Granqvist, Olsson J, Safari; Holmen (Kacaniklic 46), Wernbloom (Kallstrom 47), Larsson (Sana 80), Ibrahimovic; Elm, Elmander.
*Referee:* Pedro Proenca.

Friday, 22 March 2013
**Austria (3) 6** *(Hosiner 8, 20, Ivanschitz 28, Junuzovic 77, Alaba 78, Garics 82)*
**Faroe Islands (0) 0**        24,242
*Austria:* (442) Lindner; Garics, Dragovic, Pogatetz, Fuchs (Suttner 70); Ivanschitz (Weimann 41), Alaba, Junuzovic, Kavlak (Leitgeb 55); Arnautovic, Hosiner.
*Faroe Islands:* (442) Nielsen; Naes, Justinussen, Faeroe, Baldvinsson; Hansson, Benjaminsen, Elttor (Gregersen 86), Holst; Samuelsen S (Jacobsen 70), Edmundsson (Hansen 78).
*Referee:* Oleksandr Derdo.

**Kazakhstan (0) 0**
**Germany (2) 3** *(Muller 20, 74, Gotze 22)*        28,280
*Kazakhstan:* (442) Sidelnikov; Kirov, Logvinenko, Gorman, Nurdauletov; Dmitrenko, Khairullin M (Konysbayev 65); Baizhanov (Korobkin 36), Schmidtgal; Dzholchiev, Ostapenko (Khairullin K 84).
*Germany:* (442) Neuer; Schmelzer, Howedes, Lahm, Mertesacker; Khedira (Gundogan 82), Schweinsteiger, Ozil, Draxler (Podolski 19); Muller (Schurrle 82), Gotze.
*Referee:* Anastassios Kakos

**Sweden (0) 0**
**Rep of Ireland (0) 0**        49,494
*Sweden:* (4231) Isaksson; Lustig (Antonsson 46), Olsson J, Granqvist, Safari; Elm, Larsson (Durmaz 87); Kallstrom, Ibrahimovic, Hysen (Toivonen 72); Kacaniklic.
*Rep of Ireland:* (442) Forde; Coleman, Clark, O'Shea, Wilson; McCarthy, McClean (Keogh A 83), Green, Walters; Keane (Hoolahan 76), Long (Sammon 87).
*Referee:* Alberto Undiano Mallenco.

Tuesday, 26 March 2013
**Germany (3) 4** *(Reus 23, 90, Gotze 28, Gundogan 31)*
**Kazakhstan (0) 1** *(Schmidtgal 47)*        40,400
*Germany:* (4231) Neuer; Schmelzer, Boateng, Mertesacker, Lahm; Khedira, Ozil; Muller, Gundogan, Reus (Jansen 90); Gotze.
*Kazakhstan:* (442) Sidelnikov; Kirov, Korobkin, Mukhtarov, Engel; Gorman, Nurdauletov (Dzholchiev 47); Dmitrenko, Konysbayev (Shomko 78); Schmidtgal, Ostapenko (Kukeev 63).
*Referee:* Halis Ozkahya.

**Rep of Ireland (2) 2** *(Walters 25 (pen), 45)*
**Austria (1) 2** *(Harnik 11, Alaba 90)*        50,500
*Rep of Ireland:* (442) Forde; Coleman, O'Shea, Clark (St. Ledger 72); Wilson; Walters, Whelan, McCarthy, McClean; Sammon, Long (Green 83).
*Austria:* (442) Lindner; Garics, Dragovic, Pogatetz, Fuchs; Kavlak (Weimann 69), Alaba, Harnik, Junuzovic (Baumgartlinger 25); Arnautovic, Hosiner (Janko 62).
*Referee:* Marijo Strahonja.

Friday, 7 June 2013
**Austria (2) 2** *(Alaba 26 (pen), Janko 32)*
**Sweden (0) 1** *(Elmander 82)*        48,485
*Austria:* (433) Almer; Dragovic, Pogatetz (Prodl 29), Fuchs, Garics; Alaba, Junuzovic (Schiemer 75), Baumgartlinger; Arnautovic, Harnik, Janko (Weimann 46).
*Sweden:* (442) Isaksson; Lustig, Olsson J, Granqvist, Wendt; Elm (Svensson 60), Larsson, Kallstrom (Toivonen 76), Kacaniklic; Ibrahimovic, Elmander (Durmaz 84).
*Referee:* Gianluca Rocchi.

**Rep of Ireland (1) 3** *(Keane 5, 55, 81)*
**Faroe Islands (0) 0**                              19,190
*Rep of Ireland:* (442) Forde; Coleman, O'Shea, St.
Ledger, Wilson (Kelly 82); McGeady (McClean 76),
Whelan, Hoolahan, Walters (Sammon 73); Keane, Cox.
*Faroe Islands:* (4231) Nielsen; Frederiksberg, Gregersen,
Baldvinsson, Jonsson; Olsen S, Vatnsdal; Samuelsen S,
Holst (Samuelsen H 84), Justinussen; Klettskaro
(Edmundsson 64).
*Referee:* Mattias Gestranius.

**Tuesday, 11 June 2013**
**Sweden (1) 2** *(Ibrahimovic 35, 82 (pen))*
**Faroe Islands (0) 0**                              32,328
*Sweden:* (442) Hansson; Lustig, Granqvist■, Nilsson P,
Bengtsson P; Larsson (Durmaz 63), Kallstrom (Svensson
57), Ekdal, Kacaniklic; Toivonen (Olsson J 83),
Ibrahimovic.
*Faroe Islands:* (442) Nielsen; Naes, Davidsen V,
Gregersen, Davidsen J; Edmundsson, Justinussen,
Hansson (Klettskaro 86), Benjaminsen; Holst
(Samuelsen S 59), Olsen (Vatnsdal 40).
*Referee:* Nikolay Yordanov.

| Group C Table | P | W | D | L | F | A | GD | Pts |
|---|---|---|---|---|---|---|---|---|
| Germany | 6 | 5 | 1 | 0 | 22 | 7 | 15 | 16 |
| Austria | 6 | 3 | 2 | 1 | 15 | 5 | 10 | 11 |
| Sweden | 6 | 3 | 2 | 1 | 11 | 7 | 4 | 11 |
| Republic of Ireland | 6 | 3 | 2 | 1 | 12 | 10 | 2 | 11 |
| Kazakhstan | 6 | 0 | 1 | 5 | 2 | 15 | –13 | 1 |
| Faroe Islands | 6 | 0 | 0 | 6 | 2 | 20 | –18 | 0 |

## GROUP D

**Friday, 7 September 2012**
**Andorra (0) 0**
**Hungary (2) 5** *(Juhasz 12, Gera 33 (pen), Szalai 54,
Priskin 68, Koman 82)*                              600
*Andorra:* (4231) Gomez J; Garcia E, Lima, Rodrigues,
Vales■; Pujol, Clemente (Lorenzo 72); Vieira, Silva,
Garcia M (Maneiro 80); Moreno (Gomez S 69).
*Hungary:* (442) Bogdan; Vanczak, Juhasz, Liptak,
Laczko; Korcsmar, Koman, Hajnal (Elek 75), Dzsudzsak;
Gera (Priskin 46), Szalai (Nemeth 82).
*Referee:* Emer Aleckovic.

**Estonia (0) 0**
**Romania (0) 2** *(Torje 55, Marica 75)*            7936
*Estonia:* (442) Pareiko; Jaager, Morozov, Klavan,
Teniste; Puri (Kink 77), Dmitrijev, Vunk (Voskoboinikov
61), Vassiljev; Ojamaa (Lindpere 46), Oper.
*Romania:* (442) Lobont; Chiriches, Goian (Gaman 90),
Matel, Rat; Bourceanu, Grozav, Lazar (Pintilii 66),
Tanase; Torje, Marica (Niculae 87).
*Referee:* Milorad Mazic.

**Holland (1) 2** *(van Persie 16, Narsingh 90)*
**Turkey (0) 0**                                     53,530
*Holland:* (442) Krul; Janmaat (Van Rhijn 46), Heitinga
(Vlaar 86), Martins Indi, Willems; Clasie (Fer 50),
Strootman, Sneijder, Narsingh; van Persie, Robben.
*Turkey:* (442) Zengin; Ali Kaldirim, Kaya, Toprak, Emre
(Sahin 60); Altintop, Torun (Erdinc 81), Turan, Topal;
Bulut, Sararer (Yilmaz 70).
*Referee:* Carlos Velasco Carballo.

**Tuesday, 11 September 2012**
**Hungary (1) 1** *(Dzsudzsak 8 (pen))*
**Holland (2) 4** *(Lens 3, Martins Indi 19, Lens 53,
Huntelaar 74)*                                       22,220
*Hungary:* (4231) Bogdan; Liptak, Vanczak, Juhasz,
Korcsmar; Varga, Elek (Gyurcso 61); Dzsudzsak, Gera
(Nemeth 80), Koman (Hajnal 46); Priskin.
*Holland:* (4231) Stekelenburg; Van Rhijn, Vlaar, Martins
Indi (Mathijsen 64), Willems; Clasie, Strootman (Maher
78), Sneijder; Narsingh, van Persie (Huntelaar 46), Lens.
*Referee:* Pedro Proenca.

**Romania (2) 4** *(Torje 29, Lazar 44, Gaman 90, Maxim 90)*
**Andorra (0) 0**                                    25,250
*Romania:* (451) Lobont (Tatarusanu 46); Matel, Rat,
Chiriches, Gaman; Bourceanu, Grozav, Lazar, Tanase
(Maxim 80), Torje; Marica (Rusescu 54).
*Andorra:* (334) Gomez J; Garcia E, Lima, Rodrigues;
Pujol (Peppe 79), Clemente (Moreno 86), Ayala; Gomez
S (Maneiro 70), Lorenzo, Vieira, Garcia M.
*Referee:* Pavle Radovanovic.

**Turkey (1) 3** *(Emre 44, Bulut 60, Inan 75)*
**Estonia (0) 0**                                    48,485
*Turkey:* (433) Zengin; Ali Kaldirim, Kaya, Gonul,
Toprak; Turan, Emre (Sahin 82), Topal; Yilmaz, Bulut
(Inan 68), Sararer (Torun 68).
*Estonia:* (532) Pareiko; Rahn, Kruglov, Klavan, Jaager■,
Teniste; Lindpere (Puri 56), Vunk, Vassiljev; Oper (Purje
56), Kink (Saag 77).
*Referee:* Marcin Borski.

**Friday, 12 October 2012**
**Estonia (0) 0**
**Hungary (0) 1** *(Hajnal 46)*                      3500
*Estonia:* (442) Pareiko; Sisov, Rahn, Morozov, Kruglov;
Puri (Mosnikov 69), Lindpere, Vassiljev, Oper; Kink
(Vunk 86), Ojamaa (Purje 52).
*Hungary:* (442) Bogdan; Korcsmar (Elek 61), Varga,
Kadar, Juhasz; Meszaros, Dzsudzsak, Gera (Szabics 79),
Koltai (Gyurcso 84); Hajnal, Szalai.
*Referee:* Liran Liany.

**Holland (2) 3** *(Van der Vaart 7, Huntelaar 15, Schaken 50)*
**Andorra (0) 0**                                    38,380
*Holland:* (442) Stekelenburg; Janmaat, Heitinga, Vlaar,
Martins Indi; De Jong, Strootman (Emanuelson 74), Van
der Vaart (Afellay 70), Schaken; Huntelaar, Lens (Kuyt
70).
*Andorra:* (442) Gomez J; Rodrigues (San Nicolas 52),
Lima, Vieira, Pujol; Moreira (Bernaus 82), Ayala, Vales,
Gomez S (Moreno 74); Lorenzo, Garcia M.
*Referee:* Aliaksei Kulbakou.

**Turkey (0) 0**
**Romania (1) 1** *(Grozav 45)*                      51,510
*Turkey:* (4231) Demirel; Gonul, Kaya, Toprak, Ali
Kaldirim; Emre (Sahin 81), Topal; Altintop (Erdinc 62),
Turan, Sararer (Colak 68); Bulut.
*Romania:* (442) Tatarusanu; Tamas, Chiriches, Goian,
Rat; Bourceanu, Pintilii, Torje, Grozav (Cocis 49); Stancu
(Mutu 82), Marica (Chipciu 79).
*Referee:* Howard Webb.

**Tuesday, 16 October 2012**
**Andorra (0) 0**
**Estonia (0) 1** *(Oper 57)*                        216
*Andorra:* (442) Gomez; San Nicolas, Lima, Pujol, Vieira;
Vales, Moreira (Clemente 69), Ayala (Riera 77),
Lorenzo; Garcia M, Silva (Garcia E 80).
*Estonia:* (442) Pareiko; Sisov, Rahn, Kruglov, Klavan;
Lindpere (Puri 69), Vassiljev, Purje, Neemelo (Vunk 46);
Oper, Kink (Ojamaa 82).
*Referee:* Dimitar Meckarovski.

**Hungary (1) 3** *(Koman 31, Szalai 50, Gera 58 (pen))*
**Turkey (1) 1** *(Erdinc 22)*                       26,260
*Hungary:* (442) Bogdan; Vanczak, Kadar, Elek (Patkai
46), Varga; Szalai, Gera, Koman (Koltai 73), Meszaros;
Hajnal (Pinter 77), Korcsmar.
*Turkey:* (442) Demirel; Korkmaz, Ali Kaldirim, Emre,
Altintop; Ekici (Sararer 64), Sahin, Torun (Yilmaz 46),
Erdinc; Erkin (Bulut 74), Toprak.
*Referee:* Daniele Orsato.

**Romania (1) 1** *(Marica 40)*
**Holland (3) 4** *(Lens 10, Martins Indi 29,
Van der Vaart 45 (pen), van Persie 86)*              53,533
*Romania:* (4231) Tatarusanu; Rat, Goian, Chiriches,
Tamas; Bourceanu (Lazar 61), Torje (Popa 66); Pintilii,
Marica, Grozav (Mutu 74); Stancu.
*Holland:* (4231) Stekelenburg; Van Rhijn, Heitinga,

Vlaar, Martins Indi; De Jong, Strootman; Van der Vaart (Afellay 76), van Persie, Narsingh; Lens (Elia 89).
*Referee:* Craig Thomson.

**Friday, 22 March 2013**

**Andorra (0) 0**

**Turkey (2) 2** *(Inan 30, Yilmaz 45)*                    700
*Andorra:* (4231) Gomez J; Lima, San Nicolas, Martinez (Clemente 69), Vieira; Vales, Peppe (Garcia E 82); Moreira, Ayala (Andorra 77), Gomez S; Garcia M.
*Turkey:* (4132) Kivrak; Irtegun, Ali Kaldirim, Kaya, Gonul; Inan; Sahin (Frei 90), Turan, Bulut (Sahan 81); Yilmaz, Sararer (Potuk 57).
*Referee:* Nerijus Dunauskas.

**Holland (0) 3** *(Van der Vaart 47, van Persie 72, Schaken 84)*

**Estonia (0) 0**                                        49,490
*Holland:* (442) Vermeer; Janmaat, De Vrij, Martins Indi, Blind; de Guzman (Clasie 85), Strootman, Sneijder (Van der Vaart 36), van Persie; Lens (Schaken 73), Robben.
*Estonia:* (442) Pareiko; Kruglov (Kink 62), Jaager, Morozov, Klavan; Teniste, Puri, Vassiljev, Vunk; Ojamaa (Lindpere 77), Oper (Zenjov 46).
*Referee:* Vitaliy Meshkov.

**Hungary (1) 2** *(Vanczak 16, Dzsudzsak 71 (pen))*

**Romania (0) 2** *(Mutu 68 (pen), Chipciu 90)*           400
*Hungary:* (442) Kiraly; Meszaros, Vanczak, Kadar, Korcsmar; Dzsudzsak (Halmosi 90), Koman, Pinter, Hajnal (Kovacs 80); Szabics (Varga 58), Szalai.
*Romania:* (442) Tatarusanu; Tamas, Goian, Chiriches, Radu; Pintilii (Chipciu 86), Torje (Maxim 66), Bourceanu, Mutu; Grozav (Rusescu 71), Stancu.
*Referee:* Wolfgang Stark.

**Tuesday, 26 March 2013**

**Estonia (1) 2** *(Anier 45, Lindpere 61)*

**Andorra (0) 0**                                        5237
*Estonia:* (433) Pareiko; Morozov, Piiroja, Teniste, Jaager; Vassiljev, Mosnikov, Purje (Zenjov 76); Kink, Ahjupera (Oper 55), Anier (Lindpere 55).
*Andorra:* (442) Gomez J; Lima, Martinez, San Nicolas, Vieira; Vales, Peppe (Garcia E 66), Moreira (Bernaus 79), Ayala; Gomez S (Silva 85), Garcia M.
*Referee:* Jan Valasek.

**Holland (1) 4** *(Van der Vaart 11, van Persie 55, 65 (pen), Lens 90)*

**Romania (0) 0**                                        48,480
*Holland:* (433) Vermeer; Janmaat, De Vrij, Martins Indi, Blind; de Guzman (Maher 73), Strootman, Van der Vaart (Clasie 79); Lens, van Persie (De Jong 86), Robben.
*Romania:* (442) Pantilimon; Rat, Tamas, Gardos, Chiriches; Bourceanu, Popa (Torje 62), Pintilii, Tanase (Chipciu 59); Stancu, Grozav (Mutu 67).
*Referee:* Mark Clattenburg.

**Turkey (0) 1** *(Yilmaz 63)*

**Hungary (0) 1** *(Bode 71)*                            46,460
*Turkey:* (442) Kivrak; Gonul, Irtegun, Ali Kaldirim, Kaya; Potuk (Altintop 70), Inan, Sahin (Frei 90); Turan; Yilmaz, Bulut (Erdinc 80).
*Hungary:* (451) Kiraly; Varga, Meszaros, Korcsmar (Guzmics 46), Vanczak; Kadar, Dzsudzsak, Koman, Pinter, Hajnal (Bode 68); Szalai (Elek 78).
*Referee:* Milorad Mazic.

**Group D Table**

| | P | W | D | L | F | A | GD | Pts |
|---|---|---|---|---|---|---|---|---|
| Holland | 6 | 6 | 0 | 0 | 20 | 2 | 18 | 18 |
| Hungary | 6 | 3 | 2 | 1 | 13 | 8 | 5 | 11 |
| Romania | 6 | 3 | 1 | 2 | 10 | 10 | 0 | 10 |
| Turkey | 6 | 2 | 1 | 3 | 7 | 7 | 0 | 7 |
| Estonia | 6 | 2 | 0 | 4 | 3 | 9 | –6 | 6 |
| Andorra | 6 | 0 | 0 | 6 | 0 | 17 | –17 | 0 |

## GROUP E

**Friday, 7 September 2012**

**Albania (1) 3** *(Sadiku 36, Cani 84, Bogdani 86)*

**Cyprus (1) 1** *(Laban 45)*                            6000
*Albania:* (442) Ujkani; Lila, Dallku, Cana, Sadiku (Hyka 57); Bulku, Vila (Bogdani 71), Mavraj, Salihi (Cani 81); Meha, Kukeli.
*Cyprus:* (442) Georgallides (Mastrou 46); Junior, Charalambous E, Merkis, Aloneftis; Charalambidis (Christofi 55), Konstantinou (Avraam 75), Makridis, Demetriou; Laban, Nicolaou.
*Referee:* Artyom Kuchin.

**Iceland (1) 2** *(Arnason 21, Finnbogason 81)*

**Norway (0) 0**                                         8451
*Iceland:* (442) Halldorsson; Sigurdsson R, Eiriksson, Steinsson, Bjarnason; Sigurdsson G, Gislason (Finnbogason 73), Arnason (Ottesen 50), Danielsson; Gunnarsson, Hallfredsson (Jonsson 90).
*Norway:* (433) Pettersen; Ruud, Waehler, Hangeland, Riise J; Nordtveit, Riise B (Henriksen 90), Eikrem; Braaten (Soderlund 67), Abdellaoui (King 67), Elyounoussi.
*Referee:* Antony Gautier.

**Slovenia (0) 0**

**Switzerland (1) 2** *(Xhaka 20, Inler 51)*            13,132
*Slovenia:* (442) Handanovic J; Brecko, Suler, Cesar, Jokic; Birsa (Ilicic 61), Radosavljevic (Kurtic 80), Bacinovic, Kirm; Dedic (Ljubijankic 55), Matavz.
*Switzerland:* (442) Benaglio; Lichtsteiner, Von Bergen, Barnetta■, Inler; Derdiyok, Xhaka (Fernandes 85), Behrami, Rodriguez; Djourou, Shaqiri (Dzemaili 74).
*Referee:* Paolo Tagliavento.

**Tuesday, 11 September 2012**

**Cyprus (0) 1** *(Makridis 57)*

**Iceland (0) 0**                                        2000
*Cyprus:* (442) Kissas; Merkis, Junior, Charalambous E, Solomou; Nicolaou, Laban, Makridis (Demetriou 90), Dobrasinovic (Sielis 77); Konstantinou (Aloneftis 65), Christofi.
*Iceland:* (442) Halldorsson; Sigurdsson R, Eiriksson (Skulason A 63), Saevarsson, Ottesen■; Bjarnason, Gislason, Sigurdsson G, Danielsson (Gudmundsson 77); Gunnarsson, Hallfredsson (Finnbogason 46).
*Referee:* Sebastien Delferiere.

**Norway (1) 2** *(Henriksen 27, Riise J 90 (pen))*

**Slovenia (1) 1** *(Suler 17)*                         11,111
*Norway:* (442) Jarstein; Waehler, Henriksen, Hangeland, Ruud; Riise J, Nordtveit (Riise B 53), Abdellaoui (King 46), Jenssen; Braaten, Elyounoussi (Soderlund 88).
*Slovenia:* (433) Oblak; Brecko, Suler, Cesar, Jokic; Kurtic, Ilicic, Bacinovic (Matic 60); Ljubijankic (Kelhar 90), Birsa (Pecnik 7), Matavz.
*Referee:* Firat Aydinus.

**Switzerland (1) 2** *(Shaqiri 22, Inler 69 (pen))*

**Albania (0) 0**                                       38,385
*Switzerland:* (442) Benaglio; Lichtsteiner, Von Bergen, Rodriguez, Djourou; Inler, Xhaka (Drmic 90), Stocker (Mehmedi 78), Behrami (Dzemaili 73); Shaqiri, Derdiyok.
*Albania:* (442) Ujkani; Dallku, Mavraj, Lila, Meha; Agolli, Cana, Kukeli (Hyka 73), Vila (Roshi 55); Bulku, Bogdani (Cani 55).
*Referee:* Ovidiu Alin Hategan.

**Friday, 12 October 2012**

**Albania (1) 1** *(Cani 29)*

**Iceland (1) 2** *(Bjarnason 19, Sigurdsson G 81)*      4000
*Albania:* (451) Ujkani; Lila, Dallku, Mavraj, Cana; Bulku, Sadiku, Lika (Salihi 74), Meha (Roshi 46), Kukeli; Cani (Bogdani 85).
*Iceland:* (451) Halldorsson; Steinsson, Arnason, Skulason A, Sigurdsson R; Gunnarsson, Hallfredsson, Gislason (Saevarsson 68), Bjarnason (Gudmundsson 85), Sigurdsson G; Finnbogason (Jonsson 90).
*Referee:* Tony Asumaa.

**Slovenia (1) 2** *(Matavz 38, 61)*
**Cyprus (0) 1** *(Aloneftis 83)*                    7988
*Slovenia:* (442) Handanovic S; Brecko, Suler, Cesar[■], Jokic; Ilicic (Cvijanovic 84), Kirm, Kurtic, Radosavljevic (Maroh 90); Dedic (Kampl 68), Matavz.
*Cyprus:* (442) Kissas; Charalambous E, Sielis, Charalambous A, Christou; Demetriou, Dobrasinovic, Charalambidis (Aloneftis 79), Marangos (Artymatas 46); Christofi, Konstantinou (Efrem 64).
*Referee:* Ivan Kruzliak.

**Switzerland (0) 1** *(Gavranovic 79)*
**Norway (0) 1** *(Hangeland 81)*                    31,315
*Switzerland:* (442) Benaglio; Lichtsteiner, Von Bergen, Rodriguez, Djourou; Barnetta (Gavranovic 70), Inler, Xhaka, Behrami (Dzemaili 90); Shaqiri, Derdiyok.
*Norway:* (442) Jarstein; Hangeland, Riise J, Ruud, Forren; Henriksen, Nordtveit, Jenssen, Soderlund (King 71); Braaten, Elyounoussi (Parr 90).
*Referee:* David Fernandez Borbalan.

**Tuesday, 16 October 2012**
**Albania (1) 1** *(Roshi 37)*
**Slovenia (0) 0**                    10,100
*Albania:* (442) Berisha; Mavraj, Lila, Cana, Agolli; Bulku, Vila (Dallku 84), Sadiku (Salihi 46), Kukeli; Roshi, Cani (Curri 75).
*Slovenia:* (442) Handanovic S; Brecko, Suler, Jokic, Maroh; Kirm, Radosavljevic (Kampl 79), Ilicic (Sisic 73), Mertelj; Matavz, Dedic (Cavusevic 58).
*Referee:* Martin Hansson.

**Cyprus (1) 1** *(Aloneftis 42)*
**Norway (1) 3** *(Hangeland 45, Elyounoussi 81 (pen), King 83)*                    3500
*Cyprus:* (442) Kissas (Georgallides 55); Junior, Charalambous E, Charalambous A (Demetriou 46), Aloneftis (Mitidis 88); Solomou, Nicolaou, Dobrasinovic, Laban; Efrem, Christofi.
*Norway:* (442) Jarstein; Forren, Ruud, Hangeland, Riise J; Eikrem (Gashi 90), Jenssen (Berisha 75), Henriksen, Elyounoussi; Braaten, Soderlund (King 46).
*Referee:* Pawel Gil.

**Iceland (0) 0**
**Switzerland (0) 2** *(Barnetta 65, Gavranovic 79)*    8369
*Iceland:* (451) Halldorsson; Skulason, Steinsson, Arnason, Sigurdsson R; Jonsson (Baldvinsson 82), Bjarnason, Sigurdsson G, Gislason (Gudmundsson 70), Hallfredsson; Finnbogason.
*Switzerland:* (442) Benaglio; Rodriguez, Djourou, Lichtsteiner, Von Bergen; Barnetta (Klose 90), Inler, Xhaka, Behrami; Gavranovic (Mehmedi 83), Shaqiri (Dzemaili 80).
*Referee:* Alan Kelly.

**Friday, 22 March 2013**
**Norway (0) 0**
**Albania (0) 1** *(Salihi 67)*                    11,112
*Norway:* (433) Jarstein; Hogli, Hangeland, Riise J, Forren; Jenssen, Henriksen, Nordtveit; Elyounoussi (King 61), Soderlund (Berisha 73), Abdellaoui.
*Albania:* (433) Berisha; Lila[■], Dallku (Hisaj 78), Mavraj, Cana; Agolli, Bulku, Basha; Cani (Bogdani 73), Salihi (Curri 89), Roshi.
*Referee:* Kevin Blom.

**Slovenia (1) 1** *(Novakovic 34)*
**Iceland (0) 2** *(Sigurdsson G 55, 78)*            5500
*Slovenia:* (442) Handanovic S; Brecko, Cesar, Ilic, Jokic; Krhin (Dedic 80), Kurtic, Radosavljevic, Birsa (Lazarevic 51); Ljubijankic (Matavz 65), Novakovic.
*Iceland:* (442) Halldorsson; Sigurdsson R, Skulason A, Saevarsson, Jonsson; Bjarnason, Sigurdsson G, Gunnarsson, Hallfredsson (Gudhjohnsen 76), Sigthorsson (Danielsson 90), Finnbogason (Gudmundsson 47).
*Referee:* Stavros Tritsonis.

**Saturday, 23 March 2013**
**Cyprus (0) 0**
**Switzerland (0) 0**                    3572
*Cyprus:* (442) Georgallides; Junior, Theophilou, Charalambous E, Solomou (Efrem 53); Charalambidis (Alexandrou 74), Makridis, Dobrasinovic, Laban; Nicolaou, Christofi (Sotiriou 90).
*Switzerland:* (442) Sommer; Von Bergen, Lichtsteiner, Djourou (Senderos 52), Rodriguez; Behrami (Derdiyok 76), Inler, Stocker, Shaqiri; Emeghara (Xhaka 46), Seferovic.
*Referee:* Manuel Graefe.

**Friday, 7 June 2013**
**Albania (1) 1** *(Rama 41)*
**Norway (0) 1** *(Hogli 87)*                    15,150
*Albania:* (442) Berisha E; Teli, Mavraj, Dallku, Agolli; Rama, Bulku (Hisaj 90), Vila (Kace 85), Basha; Cani, Salihi (Osmani 77).
*Norway:* (442) Jarstein; Hogli, Ruud, Reginiussen, Hangeland; Henriksen, Jenssen (Skjelbred 84), Nordtveit, Elyounoussi (Berisha 46); King (Soderlund 71), Braaten.
*Referee:* William Collum.

**Iceland (2) 2** *(Bjarnason 22, Finnbogason 27 (pen))*
**Slovenia (2) 4** *(Kirm 11, Birsa 31 (pen), Cesar 61, Krhin 85)*                    9202
*Iceland:* (442) Halldorsson; Saevarsson (Thorvaldsson 83), Sigurdsson R, Arnason, Skulason A; Bjarnason, Gunnarsson (Gudjohnsen 52), Danielsson, Hallfredsson (Gislason 63); Finnbogason, Sigthorsson.
*Slovenia:* (451) Handanovic S; Brecko, Ilic, Cesar, Jokic; Krhin, Birsa (Struna 90), Kampl (Radosavljevic 72), Kurtic, Kirm; Novakovic (Matavz 86).
*Referee:* Felix Zwayer.

**Saturday, 8 June 2013**
**Switzerland (0) 1** *(Seferovic 90)*
**Cyprus (0) 0**                    16,169
*Switzerland:* (442) Benaglio; Lichtsteiner, Djourou, Rodriguez, Von Bergen; Shaqiri, Inler, Behrami (Dzemaili 67), Stocker (Barnetta 77); Gavranovic, Drmic (Seferovic 73).
*Cyprus:* (442) Georgallides; Theophilou (Dobrasinovic 90), Charalambous E, Merkis, Charalambous A; Aloneftis (Kyriakou 61), Alexandrou, Makridis, Laban; Nicolaou, Sotiriou.
*Referee:* Paolo Mazzoleni.

| Group E Table | P | W | D | L | F | A | GD | Pts |
|---|---|---|---|---|---|---|---|---|
| Switzerland | 6 | 4 | 2 | 0 | 8 | 1 | 7 | 14 |
| Albania | 6 | 3 | 1 | 2 | 7 | 6 | 1 | 10 |
| Iceland | 6 | 3 | 0 | 3 | 8 | 9 | –1 | 9 |
| Norway | 6 | 2 | 2 | 2 | 7 | 7 | 0 | 8 |
| Slovenia | 6 | 2 | 0 | 4 | 8 | 10 | –2 | 6 |
| Cyprus | 6 | 1 | 1 | 4 | 4 | 9 | –5 | 4 |

## GROUP F

**Friday, 7 September 2012**
**Azerbaijan (0) 1** *(Abishov 65)*
**Israel (0) 1** *(Natcho 50)*                    15,150
*Azerbaijan:* (442) Agayev K; Shukurov, Sadygov, Abishov, Medvedev; Allahverdiev, Gokdemir (Ismayilov 59), Chertoganov (Amirquliev 76), Javadov; Subasic, Aliyev (Azkara 58).
*Israel:* (442) Aouate; Spungin, Ziv, Mori, Tibi; Melikson (Hzra 71), Natcho, Alberman, Vermouth; Hemed (Damari 67), Shechter (Benayoun 74).
*Referee:* Matej Jug.

**Luxembourg (1) 1** *(Da Mota Alves 14)*
**Portugal (1) 2** *(Ronaldo 28, Postiga 54)*        9000
*Luxembourg:* (442) Joubert; Blaise, Schnell, Bukvic, Mutsch; Janisch, Payal, Bettmer, Joachim; Krogh Gerson, Da Mota Alves (Deville 79).

*Portugal:* (442) Rui Patricio; Joao Pereira, Bruno Alves, Pepe, Fabio Coentrao; Veloso (Varela 46), Joao Moutinho, Meireles (Custodio 67), Nani (Ruben Micael 81); Ronaldo, Postiga.
*Referee:* Kristo Tohver.

**Russia (1) 2** *(Faitzulin 30, Shirokov 78 (pen))*
**Northern Ireland (0) 0**                     12,120
*Russia:* (433) Akinfeev; Aniukov, Berezutsky V, Ignashevich, Kombarov; Denisov, Shirokov, Faitzulin (Glushakov 85); Dzagoev (Kokorin 58), Kerzhakov, Bystrov.
*Northern Ireland:* (442) Carroll; Hughes, Evans J, McAuley, Cathcart; Evans C (Shiels 84), Davis, Baird, Ward (Little 76); Brunt, Lafferty K.
*Referee:* Antonio Miguel Mateu Lahoz.

Tuesday, 11 September 2012
**Israel (0) 0**
**Russia (2) 4** *(Kerzhakov 6, 64, Kokorin 18, Faitzulin 77)*
                                               30,300
*Israel:* (442) Aouate; Tibi, Ben Haim, Spungin, Ziv; Natcho, Radi, Cohen (Ben Basat 46), Benayoun (Vermouth 73); Shechter (Sahar 46), Hzra.
*Russia:* (442) Akinfeev; Aniukov (Yeschenko 50), Ignashevich, Berezutsky V, Denisov; Glushakov, Shirokov, Bystrov (Samedov 22), Kombarov; Kokorin (Faitzulin 35), Kerzhakov.
*Referee:* Mark Clattenburg.

**Northern Ireland (1) 1** *(Shiels 14)*
**Luxembourg (0) 1** *(Da Mota Alves 86)*      11,114
*Northern Ireland:* (4411) Carroll; Hughes, McGivern, McAuley, Ferguson (Ward 74); Evans J, Baird, Davis, Brunt; Shiels (Norwood 83); Lafferty K.
*Luxembourg:* (451) Joubert; Blaise, Schnell, Janisch, Payal; Bukvic, Mutsch, Bettmer (Hoffmann 90), Krogh Gerson (Philipps 50), Da Mota Alves; Joachim (Deville 46).
*Referee:* Vlado Glodjovic.

**Portugal (0) 3** *(Varela 63, Postiga 85, Bruno Alves 88)*
**Azerbaijan (0) 0**                           29,299
*Portugal:* (442) Rui Patricio; Fabio Coentrao, Joao Pereira, Bruno Alves, Pepe; Veloso (Varela 62), Joao Moutinho, Meireles, Nani (Ruben Amorim 77); Postiga (Eder 87), Ronaldo.
*Azerbaijan:* (442) Agayev K; Levin, Medvedev, Shukurov, Allahverdiev; Sadygov, Abishov, Gokdemir (Chertoganov 89), Huseynov (Ismayilov 59); Amirquliev, Ozkara (Subasic 72).
*Referee:* Szymon Marciniak.

Friday, 12 October 2012
**Luxembourg (0) 0**
**Israel (3) 6** *(Radi 4, Ben Basat 12, Hemed 27, 73, 90, Melikson 60)*                        2631
*Luxembourg:* (442) Joubert; Schnell (Leweck 18), Bukvic, Philipps, Mutsch; Janisch, Bettmer, Payal (Hoffmann 78), Krogh Gerson; Da Mota Alves, Joachim (Deville 61).
*Israel:* (442) Aouate; Shish (Ziv 57), Mori, Tibi (Keinan 55), Spungin; Alberman, Melikson, Radi, Natcho (Biton 77); Ben Basat, Hemed.
*Referee:* Leontios Trattou.

**Russia (1) 1** *(Kerzhakov 6)*
**Portugal (0) 0**                             75,750
*Russia:* (4231) Akinfeev; Aniukov, Ignashevich, Berezutsky V, Kombarov; Denisov, Shirokov, Bystrov (Samedov 83), Faitzulin (Glushakov 46), Kokorin; Kerzhakov (Yeschenko 65).
*Portugal:* (4231) Rui Patricio, Joao Pereira, Bruno Alves, Pepe, Fabio Coentrao (Miguel Lopes 20); Veloso, Joao Moutinho; Nani, Ruben Micael (Varela 66), Ronaldo, Postiga (Eder 75).
*Referee:* Viktor Kassai.

Tuesday, 16 October 2012
**Israel (2) 3** *(Hemed 13, 48, Ben Basat 35)*
**Luxembourg (0) 0**                           15,150
*Israel:* (442) Aouate; Keinan, Mori, Gabai, Ziv; Melikson (Abuhatzira 81), Natcho, Alberman, Radi (Vermouth 56 (Ezra 71)); Ben Basat, Hemed.
*Luxembourg:* (442) Joubert; Mutsch, Blaise, Hoffmann, Peters (Philipps 81); Bettmer, Payal, Jans, Leweck; Da Mota Alves (Laterza 86), Joachim (Deville 46).
*Referee:* Harald Lechner.

**Portugal (0) 1** *(Postiga 79)*
**Northern Ireland (1) 1** *(McGinn 30)*       48,487
*Portugal:* (4231) Rui Patricio; Joao Pereira (Eder 73), Bruno Alves, Pepe, Miguel Lopes (Ruben Amorim 47); Veloso, Ruben Micael (Varela 61); Ronaldo, Joao Moutinho, Nani; Postiga.
*Northern Ireland:* (451) Carroll; McGivern, Cathcart, Evans J, Hughes; Baird, Davis, Evans C, McGinn, Norwood; Lafferty K.
*Referee:* Thorsten Kinhoefer.

**Russia (0) 1** *(Shirokov 84 (pen))*
**Azerbaijan (0) 0**                           15,150
*Russia:* (442) Akinfeev; Yeschenko, Berezutsky V, Ignashevich, Kombarov; Shirokov, Denisov, Faitzulin (Glushakov 46), Samedov (Bystrov 62); Kerzhakov (Dzagoev 78), Kokorin.
*Azerbaijan:* (442) Agayev K; Shukurov, Abishov, Medvedev, Levin; Chertoganov (Aliyev 84), Gokdemir, Javadov, Ozkara; Subasic (Amirquliev 62), Nadirov (Huseynov 46).
*Referee:* Aleksandar Stavrev.

Wednesday, 14 November 2012
**Northern Ireland (0) 1** *(Healy 90)*
**Azerbaijan (1) 1** *(Aliyev 5)*              12,123
*Northern Ireland:* (442) Carroll; Hughes, Cathcart (Healy 81), McAuley, Lafferty D; McGinn (Brunt 66), Davis, Baird, Ferguson; Shiels (McCourt 55), Lafferty K.
*Azerbaijan:* (451) Agayev S; Ramaldanov (Naziri 72), Abishov, Levin, Medvedev; Aliyev, Huseynov, Gokdemir (Guseynov 63), Amirquliev, Nadirov; Ozkara (Javadov 78).
*Referee:* Victor Shvetsov.

Friday, 22 March 2013
**Israel (2) 3** *(Hemed 24, Ben Basat 40, Gershon 70)*
**Portugal (1) 3** *(Bruno Alves 2, Postiga 72, Fabio Coentrao 90)*                      40,400
*Israel:* (442) Aouate; Spungin, Ben Haim, Gershon, Yeini; Tibi, Natcho, Melikson (Refaelov 73), Kayal; Hemed (Atar 63), Ben Basat (Benayoun 81).
*Portugal:* (442) Rui Patricio; Bruno Alves (Almeida 74), Joao Pereira, Pepe, Fabio Coentrao; Veloso (Carlos Martins 61), Joao Moutinho, Meireles, Ronaldo; Varela (Vieirinha 61), Postiga.
*Referee:* Stephane Lannoy.

**Luxembourg (0) 0**
**Azerbaijan (0) 0**                           1324
*Luxembourg:* (4141) Joubert; Hoffmann, Janisch, Schnell, Philipps; Mutsch (Bettmer 90); Jans, Krogh Gerson, Joachim (Deville 90), Da Mota Alves (Laterza 67); Bensi.
*Azerbaijan:* (442) Agayev K; Ramaldanov, Shukurov, Sadygov, Abishov; Medvedev, Ismailov, Sadyqov (Huseynov 67), Fardjad-Azad (Ozkara 71); Aliyev, Javadov (Nadirov 59).
*Referee:* Padraigh Sutton.

Tuesday, 26 March 2013
**Azerbaijan (0) 0**
**Portugal (0) 2** *(Bruno Alves 63, Almeida 79)*  30,300
*Azerbaijan:* (442) Agayev K; Medvedev, Sadygov, Abishov, Ramaldanov; Shukurov, Mammadov E (Fardjad-Azad 69), Ismailov, Huseynov; Nadirov (Levin 62), Aliyev*.
*Portugal:* (442) Rui Patricio; Joao Pereira, Pepe, Bruno Alves, Fabio Coentrao; Joao Moutinho, Meireles (Almeida 58), Veloso, Danny (Varela 73); Vieirinha, Postiga (Custodio 82).
*Referee:* Andre Marriner.

**Northern Ireland (0) 0**

**Israel (0) 2** *(Refaelov 77, Ben Basat 84)*      7300

*Northern Ireland:* (4231) Carroll; Hughes, McAuley, Evans J, Lafferty D; Brunt, Clingan (McCourt 79); McGinn, Davis, Ferguson (Magennis 72); Paterson (Healy 83).

*Israel:* (442) Aouate; Spungin, Tibi, Ben Haim, Gershon; Yeini, Natcho, Radi (Zahavi 60), Melikson (Refaelov 69); Shechter (Benayoun 86), Ben Basat.

*Referee:* Hannes Kaasik.

**Friday, 7 June 2013**

**Azerbaijan (0) 1** *(Abishov 71)*

**Luxembourg (0) 1** *(Bensi 80)*      6000

*Azerbaijan:* (4231) Agayev K; Shukurov, Sadygov, Ramaldanov, Abdullayev E; Amirquliev (Subasic■ 62), Abishov; Abdullayev A (Mammadov E 84), Sadyqov, Javadov; Dadasov.

*Luxembourg:* (433) Joubert; Jans, Chanot, Hoffmann, Martino; Mutsch, Philipps (Payal 46), Krogh Gerson; Deville (Laterza 27 (Da Mota Alves 78)), Joachim, Bensi.

*Referee:* Mihaly Fabian.

**Portugal (1) 1** *(Postiga 9)*

**Russia (0) 0**      55,550

*Portugal:* (433) Rui Patricio; Bruno Alves, Fabio Coentrao, Luis Neto, Joao Pereira; Veloso, Joao Moutinho, Meireles (Ruben Amorim 73); Ronaldo, Vieirinha (Custodio 90), Postiga (Nani 66).

*Russia:* (4141) Akinfeev; Aniukov (Kozlov 31), Berezutsky V, Ignashevich, Zhirkov; Denisov; Shirokov, Bystrov, Faitzulin (Glushakov 21), Kombarov; Kerzhakov (Smolov 67).

*Referee:* Damir Skomina.

**Group F Table**

| | P | W | D | L | F | A | GD | Pts |
|---|---|---|---|---|---|---|---|---|
| Portugal | 7 | 4 | 2 | 1 | 12 | 6 | 6 | 14 |
| Russia | 5 | 4 | 0 | 1 | 8 | 1 | 7 | 12 |
| Israel | 6 | 3 | 2 | 1 | 15 | 8 | 7 | 11 |
| Azerbaijan | 7 | 0 | 4 | 3 | 3 | 9 | –6 | 4 |
| Northern Ireland | 5 | 0 | 3 | 2 | 3 | 7 | –4 | 3 |
| Luxembourg | 6 | 0 | 3 | 3 | 3 | 13 | –10 | 3 |

## GROUP G

**Friday, 7 September 2012**

**Latvia (1) 1** *(Cauna 43 (pen))*

**Greece (0) 2** *(Spyropoulos 57, Gekas 70)*      7956

*Latvia:* (442) Vanins; Klava, Krjauklis, Laizans (Gauracs 89), Ivanovs; Cauna, Visnjakovs (Verpakovskis 75), Lukjanovs, Gorkss; Rudnevs, Fertovs (Rugins 76).

*Greece:* (442) Karnezis; Maniatis, Spyropoulos, Papadopoulos, Tziolis; Mitroglou (Samaras 46 (Ninis 69)), Torosidis, Gekas, Papastathopoulos; Katsouranis, Fortounis (Holebas 86).

*Referee:* Ivan Bebek.

**Liechtenstein (0) 1** *(Christen M 61)*

**Bosnia-Herzegovina (4) 8** *(Misimovic 26, 32, Ibisevic 34, 40, 83, Dzeko 46, 64, 81)*      5900

*Liechtenstein:* (442) Jehle; Oehri, Stocklasa, Quintans, Kaufmann; Polverino, Burgmeier, Flatz (Christen M 46); Erne (Beck 71); Hasler N (Eberle 89), Hasler D.

*Bosnia-Herzegovina:* (442) Begovic; Spahic, Sunjic, Vranjes, Vrsajevic; Pjanic (Vrancic 79), Misimovic (Svraka 78), Zahirovic (Ibricic 78), Salihovic; Ibisevic, Dzeko.

*Referee:* Marco Borg.

**Lithuania (1) 1** *(Zaliukas 18)*

**Slovakia (1) 1** *(Sapara 41)*      3000

*Lithuania:* (442) Karcemarskas; Semberas, Radavicius, Andriuskevicius, Zaliukas; Cesnauskis E (Novikovas 58), Sernas, Mikoliunas (Labukas■ 74), Vicius (Cesnauskis D 67); Klimavicius, Borovskij.

*Slovakia:* (433) Mucha; Pekarik, Skrtel, Zabavnik, Stoch (Breznanik 60); Sapara, Bakos (Jakubko 78), Hubocan; Hamsik (Kucka 86), Pecovsky■, Duris.

*Referee:* Carlos Clos Gomez.

**Tuesday, 11 September 2012**

**Bosnia-Herzegovina (2) 4** *(Misimovic 13 (pen), 54, Pjanic 44, Dzeko 90)*

**Latvia (1) 1** *(Gorkss 5)*      12,120

*Bosnia-Herzegovina:* (442) Begovic; Spahic, Mujdza, Vranjes, Pjanic; Lulic (Vrsajevic 30), Misimovic, Zahirovic, Salihovic (Sunjic 90); Ibisevic (Medunjanin 87), Dzeko.

*Latvia:* (442) Vanins; Klava, Krjauklis, Gorkss, Ivanovs; Rugins, Laizans, Cauna, Visnjakovs (Kamess 61); Lukjanovs (Zjuzins 80), Rudnevs (Verpakovskis 61).

*Referee:* Deniz Aytekin.

**Greece (0) 2** *(Ninis 56, Mitroglou 72)*

**Lithuania (0) 0**      22,220

*Greece:* (442) Karnezis; Torosidis, Spyropoulos, Papastathopoulos, Katsouranis, Tziolis, Maniatis (Mitroglou 46), Ninis; Fortounis (Holebas 68), Gekas (Mavrias 80).

*Lithuania:* (442) Karcemarskas; Zaliukas, Borovskij (Cesnauskis D 46), Semberas, Cesnauskis E; Mikoliunas, Vicius, Klimavicius, Sernas (Rimkevicius 57); Velicka (Novikovas 76), Vaitkunas.

*Referee:* Mark Courtney.

**Slovakia (1) 2** *(Sapara 36, Jakubko 78)*

**Liechtenstein (0) 0**      3500

*Slovakia:* (442) Kuciak; Pekarik, Skrtel, Zabavnik, Salata; Weiss (Breznanik 63), Stoch, Sapara, Hamsik (Kucka 82); Guldan, Bakos (Jakubko 60).

*Liechtenstein:* (442) Jehle; Oehri, Kaufmann, Stocklasa, Burgmeier; Erne, Polverino, Hasler N, Christen M (Flatz 84); Hasler D, Beck (Eberle 70).

*Referee:* Simon Evans.

**Friday, 12 October 2012**

**Greece (0) 0**

**Bosnia-Herzegovina (0) 0**      28,280

*Greece:* (442) Karnezis; Torosidis, Spyropoulos, Malezas (Karagounis 66), Papastathopoulos; Katsouranis, Fortounis, Tziolis, Maniatis (Mitroglou 79); Samaras, Gekas (Salpingidis 57).

*Bosnia-Herzegovina:* (442) Begovic; Spahic, Vranjes, Mujdza, Salihovic; Lulic (Stevanovic 75), Zahirovic, Medunjanin (Ibricic 75), Misimovic; Ibisevic, Dzeko.

*Referee:* Antonio Damato.

**Liechtenstein (0) 0**

**Lithuania (0) 2** *(Cesnauskis E 51, 75)*      700

*Liechtenstein:* (442) Buchel; Oehri, Kaufmann, Quintans, Stocklasa; Burgmeier, Erne (Ospelt 87), Hasler N (Kieber 73), Wieser (Eberle 84); Polverino, Beck.

*Lithuania:* (442) Karcemarskas; Kijanskas, Zaliukas, Klimavicius, Semberas; Radavicius (Stankevicius 90), Cesnauskis D (Sernas 58), Cesnauskis E, Mikoliunas; Danilevicius (Rimkevicius 87), Novikovas.

*Referee:* Slavko Vincic.

**Slovakia (2) 2** *(Hamsik 6 (pen), Sapara 9)*

**Latvia (0) 1** *(Verpakovskis 85 (pen))*      4012

*Slovakia:* (352) Kuciak; Pekarik, Skrtel (Durica 90), Salata; Breznanik, Weiss (Duris 42), Stoch, Sapara, Hamsik; Pecovsky, Bakos (Holosko 61).

*Latvia:* (442) Vanins; Klava, Krjauklis, Gorkss, Ivanovs; Laizans (Rugins 69), Cauna (Verpakovskis 76), Visnjakovs, Fertovs; Lukjanovs (Gauracs 53), Rudnevs.

*Referee:* Danny Makkelie.

**Tuesday, 16 October 2012**

**Bosnia-Herzegovina (3) 3** *(Ibisevic 29, Dzeko 35, Pjanic 41)*

**Lithuania (0) 0**      15,150

*Bosnia-Herzegovina:* (352) Begovic; Spahic, Mujdza (Vrsajevic 59), Vranjes; Pjanic (Stevanovic 67), Misimovic, Zahirovic, Salihovic, Lulic (Zukanovic 75); Ibisevic, Dzeko.

*Lithuania:* (532) Karcemarskas; Kijanskas, Zaliukas, Klimavicius, Borovskij, Stankevicius; Semberas, Radavicius (Sernas 51), Panka (Pilibaitis 85); Labukas (Rimkevicius 66), Novikovas.

*Referee:* Miroslav Zelinka.

**Latvia (1) 2** *(Kamess 29, Gauracs 77)*

**Liechtenstein (0) 0** 4073

*Latvia:* (433) Vanins; Bulvitis, Rugins, Ivanovs, Gorkss; Laizans (Gauracs 66), Fertovs, Cauna; Verpakovskis (Zjuzins 85), Rudnevs, Kamess (Visnjakovs 74).
*Liechtenstein:* (451) Bicer; Oehri, Kaufmann■, Quintans, Stocklasa; Burgmeier, Erne (Kieber 80), Hasler N (Eberle 85), Wieser, Polverino; Christen M.
*Referee:* Istvan Kovacs.

**Slovakia (0) 0**

**Greece (0) 1** *(Salpingidis 63)* 7694

*Slovakia:* (442) Kuciak; Skrtel, Zabavnik, Salata, Breznanik; Stoch (Weiss 69), Sapara, Hamsik, Pecovsky; Kucka (Guede 82), Duris (Holosko 71).
*Greece:* (442) Karnezis; Spyropoulos, Siovas (Fotakis 75), Torosidis, Papastathopoulos; Ninis (Karagounis 66), Tziolis, Katsouranis, Samaras; Salpingidis, Gekas (Mitroglou 59).
*Referee:* William Collum.

Friday, 22 March 2013

**Bosnia-Herzegovina (2) 3** *(Dzeko 30, 54, Ibisevic 36)*

**Greece (0) 1** *(Gekas 90)* 15,150

*Bosnia-Herzegovina:* (442) Begovic; Spahic, Vranjes, Mujdza (Vrsajevic 84), Zukanovic; Lulic, Zahirovic, Medunjanin (Rahimic 78), Misimovic; Dzeko, Ibisevic (Stevanovic 84).
*Greece:* (442) Karnezis; Papadopoulos (Gekas 47), Torosidis (Maniatis 58), Papastathopoulos, Tzavelas; Tziolis, Karagounis (Christodoulopoulos 73), Holebas, Katsouranis; Samaras, Salpingidis.
*Referee:* Bjorn Kuipers.

**Liechtenstein (1) 1** *(Polverino 17)*

**Latvia (1) 1** *(Cauna 30)* 1150

*Liechtenstein:* (442) Jehle; Oehri (Quintans 46), Stocklasa, Burgmeier, Erne (Gur 90); Hasler N, Wieser, Polverino, Hasler D; Frick, Christen M (Beck 72).
*Latvia:* (442) Vanins; Klava, Ivanovs, Gorkss, Rugins; Laizans (Visnjakovs 46), Cauna, Lazdins, Kamess (Zigajevs 56); Verpakovskis (Gauracs 66), Rudnevs.
*Referee:* Kevin Clancy.

**Slovakia (1) 1** *(Durica 40)*

**Lithuania (1) 1** *(Sernas 19)* 4560

*Slovakia:* (451) Kuciak; Skrtel, Durica, Hubocan, Pecovsky (Bakos 70); Sapara, Hamsik, Svento, Kucka, Mak (Duris 64); Jakubko.
*Lithuania:* (442) Karcemarskas (Arlauskis 46); Kijanskas, Mikuckis, Cesnauskis E, Semberas; Mikoliunas, Ivaskevicius, Kalonas (Novikovas 69), Panka; Matulevicius, Sernas (Luksa 90).
*Referee:* Michael Oliver.

Friday, 7 June 2013

**Latvia (0) 0**

**Bosnia-Herzegovina (0) 5** *(Lulic 47, Ibisevic 53, Medunjanin 62, Pjanic 80, Dzeko 81)* 7787

*Latvia:* (442) Vanins; Mihadjuks, Klava, Bulvitis, Ivanovs; Gorkss, Fertovs■, Sinelnikovs, Gauracs (Sabala 81); Kamess (Gabovs 59), Verpakovskis (Lazdins 15).
*Bosnia-Herzegovina:* (442) Begovic; Mujdza, Spahic, Zukanovic, Lulic; Salihovic (Ibricic 79), Medunjanin (Stevanovic 69), Rahimic (Visca 69), Pjanic; Ibisevic, Dzeko.
*Referee:* Mike Dean.

**Liechtenstein (1) 1** *(Buchel 13)*

**Slovakia (0) 1** *(Durica 73)* 1623

*Liechtenstein:* (4411) Jehle; Oehri, Kaufmann, Frick (Vogt 25), Quintans; Buchel, Christen A, Hasler N, Wieser (Gubser 90); Christen M (Beck 90); Hasler D.
*Slovakia:* (4411) Kuciak; Hubocan (Pauschek 46), Cisovsky, Durica, Svento; Lasik (Dubek 24), Stoch, Sapara, Mak; Hamsik; Holosko (Bakos 70).
*Referee:* Martin Strombergsson.

**Lithuania (0) 0**

**Greece (1) 1** *(Christodoulopoulos 20)* 8500

*Lithuania:* (433) Zubas; Kijanskas, Mikuckis, Borovskij, Stankevicius; Matulevicius (Cesnauskis D 86), Kalonas, Mikoliunas (Zulpa 73); Ivaskevicius (Eliosius 86), Panka, Cesnauskis E.
*Greece:* (433) Karnezis; Maniatis, Manolas, Torosidis, Papastathopoulos; Holebas (Tzavelas 46), Karagounis, Katsouranis (Tziolis 84); Samaras, Gekas (Salpingidis 64), Christodoulopoulos.
*Referee:* Olegario Benquerenca.

**Group G Table**

| | P | W | D | L | F | A | GD | Pts |
|---|---|---|---|---|---|---|---|---|
| Bosnia-Herzegovina | 6 | 5 | 1 | 0 | 23 | 3 | 20 | 16 |
| Greece | 6 | 4 | 1 | 1 | 7 | 4 | 3 | 13 |
| Slovakia | 6 | 2 | 3 | 1 | 7 | 5 | 2 | 9 |
| Lithuania | 6 | 1 | 2 | 3 | 4 | 8 | −4 | 5 |
| Latvia | 6 | 1 | 1 | 4 | 6 | 14 | −8 | 4 |
| Liechtenstein | 6 | 0 | 2 | 4 | 3 | 16 | −13 | 2 |

## GROUP H

Friday, 7 September 2012

**Moldova (0) 0**

**England (3) 5** *(Lampard 3 (pen), 29, Defoe 32, Milner 74, Baines 83)* 10,102

*Moldova:* (451) Namasco; Armas, Epureanu, Bulgaru, Golovatenco; Kovalchuk, Gatcan, Onica, Suvorov (Dedov 46), Patras; Picusciac (Sidorenco 76 (Ovseanicov 85)).
*England:* (4411) Hart; Johnson G, Lescott, Terry, Baines; Milner, Lampard, Cleverley, Oxlade-Chamberlain (Walcott 58); Gerrard (Carrick 46); Defoe (Welbeck 68).
*Referee:* Paul van Boekel.

**Montenegro (2) 2** *(Drincic 27, Vucinic 45)*

**Poland (1) 2** *(Blaszczykowski 5 (pen), Mierzejewski 54)* 5000

*Montenegro:* (442) Bozovic M; Pavicevic■, Basa, Jovanovic (Kasalica 65), Volkov; Savic, Vukcevic (Pekovic 71), Zverotic, Drincic (Djudovic 84); Jovetic, Vucinic.
*Poland:* (442) Tyton; Glik, Piszczek, Wasilewski, Wawrzyniak; Polanski, Obraniak■, Blaszczykowski, Grosicki (Mierzejewski 46); Borysiuk (Murawski 69), Lewandowski (Saganowski 90).
*Referee:* Kristinn Jakobsson.

Tuesday, 11 September 2012

**England (0) 1** *(Lampard 87 (pen))*

**Ukraine (0) 1** *(Konoplianka 39)* 68,681

*England:* (4231) Hart; Johnson G, Jagielka, Lescott, Baines (Bertrand 73); Lampard, Gerrard■, Milner, Cleverley (Welbeck 62), Oxlade-Chamberlain (Sturridge 69); Defoe.
*Ukraine:* (4231) Pyatov; Gusev, Khacheridi, Rakitskiy, Selin (Shevchuk 75); Tymoschuk, Rotan (Nazarenko 90); Yarmolenko, Garmash, Konoplianka; Zozulya (Devic 89).
*Referee:* Cuneyt Cakir.

**Poland (1) 2** *(Blaszczykowski 33 (pen), Wawrzyniak 81)*

**Moldova (0) 0** 38,380

*Poland:* (442) Tyton; Glik, Piszczek, Wasilewski, Wawrzyniak; Polanski, Borysiuk (Krychowiak 76), Blaszczykowski, Mierzejewski (Sobiech 71); Saganowski (Sobota 46), Lewandowski.
*Moldova:* (451) Namasco; Armas, Epureanu, Racu, Golovatenco; Kovalchuk, Gatcan, Suvorov (Alexeev 82), Ivanov (Onica 73), Patras (Ovseanicov 46); Picusciac.
*Referee:* Ilias Spathas.

**San Marino (0) 0**

**Montenegro (2) 6** *(Djordjevic 25, Beqiraj 26, 52, Zverotic 69, Delibasic 78, 82)* 1947

*San Marino:* (442) Simoncini A; Brolli (Vannucci 83), Cervellini, Simoncini D, Vitaioli F; Gasperoni, Della Valle, Coppini, Rinaldi; Marani (Cibelli 64), Vitaioli M (Mazza 79).
*Montenegro:* (442) Bozovic M; Basa, Savic, Volkov, Djudovic; Vukcevic (Zverotic 65), Jovetic, Pekovic, Beqiraj (Kasalica 75); Damjanovic, Djordjevic (Delibasic 65).
*Referee:* Neil Doyle.

**Friday, 12 October 2012**

**England (2) 5** *(Rooney 35 (pen), 69, Welbeck 38, Welbeck 71, Oxlade-Chamberlain 77)*

**San Marino (0) 0**     85,856

*England:* (442) Hart; Walker, Cahill, Jagielka, Baines; Walcott (Lennon 10), Carrick (Shelvey 66), Cleverley, Oxlade-Chamberlain; Welbeck, Rooney (Carroll 73).
*San Marino:* (442) Simoncini A; Vitaioli F (Bacciocchi 83), Simoncini D, Brolli, Palazzi; Cibelli, Coppini (Buscarini 75), Rinaldi (Selva 78), Della Valle Alessandro; Gasperoni, Cervellini.
*Referee:* Gediminas Mazeika.

**Moldova (0) 0**

**Ukraine (0) 0**     10,100

*Moldova:* (442) Namasco; Bulgaru, Golovatenco, Racu, Epureanu; Onica, Kovalchuk (Pascenco A 60), Gatcan, Suvorov (Ovseanicov 78); Dedov, Picusciac (Doros 84).
*Ukraine:* (442) Pyatov; Butko, Mykhalyk, Selin, Khacheridi; Tymoschuk, Garmash (Seleznyov 60), Zozulya (Milevskiy 74), Gusev (Devic 79); Yarmolenko, Rotan.
*Referee:* Clement Turpin.

**Tuesday, 16 October 2012**

**San Marino (0) 0**

**Moldova (0) 2** *(Dadu 73 (pen), Epureanu 78)*     736

*San Marino:* (442) Simoncini A; Vitaioli F, Palazzi (Vannucci 46), Bollini, Simoncini D; Della Valle Alessandro, Cervellini, Buscarini, Mazza (Cibelli 60); Marani (Selva 67), Vitaioli M.
*Moldova:* (442) Namasco; Golovatenco, Epureanu, Bulgaru, Bordiyan; Onica, Gatcan, Suvorov (Patras 58), Picusciac (Cebotaru 81); Dedov (Dadu 71), Alexeev.
*Referee:* Marios Panayi.

**Ukraine (0) 0**

**Montenegro (1) 1** *(Damjanovic 45)*     50,505

*Ukraine:* (442) Pyatov; Selin, Kucher, Mykhalyk, Butko (Yarmolenko 62); Tymoschuk, Gusev, Konoplianka, Rotan; Seleznyov (Nazarenko 82), Devic (Zozulya 52).
*Montenegro:* (442) Bozovic M; Basa, Jovanovic, Volkov, Djudovic; Savic, Pekovic, Zverotic (Novakovic 88), Drincic; Jovetic (Vucinic 85), Damjanovic (Vukcevic 72).
*Referee:* Michail Koukoulakis.

**Wednesday, 17 October 2012**

**Poland (0) 1** *(Glik 70)*

**England (1) 1** *(Rooney 31)*     43,430

*Poland:* (4231) Tyton; Piszczek, Wasilewski, Wawrzyniak, Glik; Polanski, Krychowiak; Wszolek (Mierzejewski 63), Grosicki (Milik 82), Obraniak (Borysiuk 90); Lewandowski.
*England:* (442) Hart; Johnson G, Jagielka, Lescott, Cole; Milner, Carrick, Gerrard, Cleverley; Rooney (Oxlade-Chamberlain 73), Defoe (Welbeck 67).
*Referee:* Gianluca Rocchi.

**Wednesday, 14 November 2012**

**Montenegro (2) 3** *(Delibasic 15, 32, Zverotic 69)*

**San Marino (0) 0**     7000

*Montenegro:* (433) Bozovic M; Pavicevic, Basa (Kecojevic 71), Savic (Djordjevic 46), Volkov; Vukcevic, Novakovic, Zverotic; Kasalica (Igumanovic 77), Beqiraj, Delibasic.
*San Marino:* (532) Simoncini; Palazzi, Cervellini, Benedettini (Della Valle Alex 83), Della Valle Alessandro, Bollini G; Vannucci, Cibelli (Gasperoni 89), Coppini; Rinaldi, Vitaioli (Buscarini 73).
*Referee:* Sandor Szabo.

**Friday, 22 March 2013**

**Moldova (0) 0**

**Montenegro (0) 1** *(Vucinic 78)*     9000

*Moldova:* (442) Pascenco S; Golovatenco, Bulgaru, Bordiyan, Epureanu; Gatcan**[a]**, Dedov, Ionita, Gheorghiev (Josan 77); Pascenco A, Sidorenco.
*Montenegro:* (442) Bozovic M; Basa, Savic, Volkov, Pavicevic; Zverotic, Pekovic**[a]**, Bozovic V (Vukcevic 64), Jovetic; Kasalica (Damjanovic 45), Vucinic (Novakovic 80).
*Referee:* Daniele Orsato.

**Poland (1) 1** *(Piszczek 18)*

**Ukraine (3) 3** *(Yarmolenko 2, Gusev 7, Zozulya 45)*     55,550

*Poland:* (451) Boruc; Boenisch, Piszczek, Wasilewski, Glik; Lukasik (Obraniak 59), Krychowiak, Blaszczykowski, Majewski (Teodorczyk 76), Rybus (Kosecki 46); Lewandowski.
*Ukraine:* (451) Pyatov; Fedetskiy, Khacheridi, Kucher, Shevchuk; Gusev (Morozyuk 90), Rotan, Stepanenko (Tymoschuk 60), Yarmolenko, Garmash (Bezus 90); Zozulya.
*Referee:* Pavel Kralovec.

**San Marino (0) 0**

**England (5) 8** *(Della Valle Alessandro 12 (og), Oxlade-Chamberlain 28, Defoe 35, 77, Young 39, Lampard 42, Rooney 54, Sturridge 70)*     4900

*San Marino:* (442) Simoncini A; Vitaioli F, Palazzi, Della Valle Alessandro, Simoncini D; Cervellini, Gasperoni, Cibelli (Buscarini 67), Bollini F (Valentini C 81); Selva (Rinaldi 74), Vitaioli M.
*England:* (442) Hart; Walker, Smalling, Lescott, Baines; Oxlade-Chamberlain, Lampard (Parker 66), Cleverley (Osman 56), Young; Rooney (Sturridge 55), Defoe.
*Referee:* Alain Bieri.

**Tuesday, 26 March 2013**

**Montenegro (0) 1** *(Damjanovic 77)*

**England (1) 1** *(Rooney 6)*     12,120

*Montenegro:* (442) Bozovic M; Basa, Savic, Volkov, Djudovic; Zverotic, Vukcevic (Krkotic 62), Bozovic V (Delibasic 76), Novakovic (Damjanovic 46); Jovetic, Vucinic.
*England:* (4231) Hart; Johnson G, Smalling, Lescott, Cole; Gerrard, Carrick; Milner, Cleverley (Young 78), Welbeck; Rooney.
*Referee:* Jonas Eriksson.

**Poland (2) 5** *(Lewandowski 21 (pen), 50 (pen), Piszczek 28, Teodorczyk 61, Kosecki 90)*

**San Marino (0) 0**     45,450

*Poland:* (442) Boruc; Salamon (Wasilewski 86), Piszczek, Glik (Kosecki 46), Wawrzyniak; Polanski, Krychowiak, Grosicki, Mierzejewski; Milik (Teodorczyk 59), Lewandowski.
*San Marino:* (541) Simoncini; Della Valle Alex (Buscarini 80), Palazzi, Vitaioli F, Della Valle Alessandro, Bollini G (Bacciocchi 57); Vitaioli M, Bollini F, Coppini, Selva (Rinaldi 51); Gasperoni.
*Referee:* Ken Henry Johnsen.

**Ukraine (0) 2** *(Yarmolenko 61, Khacheridi 70)*

**Moldova (0) 1** *(Suvorov 80)*     31,310

*Ukraine:* (442) Pyatov; Shevchuk, Fedetskiy, Khacheridi, Kucher; Stepanenko**[a]**, Tymoschuk, Yarmolenko, Gusev (Grechyshkin 90); Seleznyov (Bezus 62), Zozulya.
*Moldova:* (442) Namasco; Golovatenco, Bulgaru, Bordiyan, Epureanu; Ionita, Dedov (Suvorov 78), Gheorghiev, Pascenco A (Onica 67); Sidorenco, Bugaev (Doros 69).
*Referee:* Kenn Hansen.

**Friday, 7 June 2013**

**Moldova (1) 1** *(Sidorenco 37)*

**Poland (1) 1** *(Blaszczykowski 7)*     10,105

*Moldova:* (442) Namasco; Armas, Golovatenco, Bordiyan (Cebotaru 71), Epureanu; Ionita, Gatcan, Antoniuc (Ovseannicov 81), Dedov; Suvorov (Pascenco A 74), Sidorenco.
*Poland:* (442) Boruc; Jedrzejczyk, Komorowski, Salamon, Wawrzyniak; Krychowiak, Polanski (Sobiech 79), Blaszczykowski, Mierzejewski (Zielinski 62); Rybus (Kosecki 64), Lewandowski.
*Referee:* Fernando Teixeira Vitienes.

**Montenegro (0) 0**
**Ukraine (0) 4** *(Garmash 51, Konoplianka 77,*
*Fedetskiy 84, Bezus 90)* 13,130
*Montenegro:* (442) Bozovic M; Pavicevic■, Basa,
Kecojevic, Bozovic V (Delibasic 62); Volkov■, Zverotic,
Pekovic, Jovetic (Damjanovic 43); Vucinic, Kasalica
(Beqiraj 76).
*Ukraine:* (442) Pyatov; Fedetskiy, Rakitskiy, Tymoschuk,
Yarmolenko (Kovpak 90); Gusev, Konoplianka, Rotan
(Bezus 90), Garmash (Kravchenko 69); Edmar, Zozulya■.
*Referee:* Manuel Graefe.

| Group H Table | P | W | D | L | F | A | GD | Pts |
|---|---|---|---|---|---|---|---|---|
| Montenegro | 7 | 4 | 2 | 1 | 14 | 7 | 7 | 14 |
| England | 6 | 3 | 3 | 0 | 21 | 3 | 18 | 12 |
| Ukraine | 6 | 3 | 2 | 1 | 10 | 4 | 6 | 11 |
| Poland | 6 | 2 | 3 | 1 | 12 | 7 | 5 | 9 |
| Moldova | 7 | 1 | 2 | 4 | 4 | 11 | –7 | 5 |
| San Marino | 6 | 0 | 0 | 6 | 0 | 29 | –29 | 0 |

## GROUP I

Friday, 7 September 2012
**Finland (0) 0**
**France (1) 1** *(Diaby 20)* 35,351
*Finland:* (442) Hradecky; Halsti, Arkivuo, Moisander,
Toivio; Eremenko R, Hetemaj (Eremenko A 64), Sparv,
Ring; Hamalainen (Kuqi 77), Pukki.
*France:* (442) Lloris; Reveillere, Yanga-Mbiwa, Evra,
Sakho; Cabaye (Matuidi 72), Diaby, Mavuba, Ribery
(Gomis 88); Benzema, Menez (Valbuena 62).
*Referee:* Craig Thomson.

**Georgia (0) 1** *(Okriashvili 51)*
**Belarus (0) 0** 10,100
*Georgia:* (442) Loria; Grigalava, Kashia, Amisulashvili,
Khizanishvili; Kankava, Daushvili, Okriashvili
(Sirbiladze 83), Targamadze; Ananidze (Gorgiashvili 74),
Mchedlidze (Kvirkvelia D 56).
*Belarus:* (442) Veremko; Zhavnerchik (Balanovich 34),
Polyakov, Martynovich, Tigorev (Dragun 62);
Verkhovtsov, Bressan, Nekhaychik (Bardachov 30),
Putsila; Kulchy, Kornilenko.
*Referee:* Stanislav Todorov.

Tuesday, 11 September 2012
**France (0) 3** *(Capoue 49, Jallet 68, Ribery 80)*
**Belarus (0) 1** *(Putsila 72)* 55,550
*France:* (433) Lloris; Yanga-Mbiwa, Evra, Sakho, Cabaye
(Matuidi 75); Mavuba, Jallet, Capoue; Ribery (Menez
90), Giroud (Valbuena 61), Benzema.
*Belarus:* (451) Veremko; Martynovich, Polyakov,
Radkov, Verkhovtsov (Balanovich 70); Bardachov,
Dragun, Kisliak, Bressan (Kulchy 46); Putsila; Rodionov
(Kornilenko 62).
*Referee:* Huseyin Gocek.

**Georgia (0) 0**
**Spain (0) 1** *(Soldado 86)* 32,320
*Georgia:* (442) Loria (Kvaskhvadze 73); Lobjanidze,
Kashia, Amisulashvili, Khizanishvili; Kankava,
Kvirkvelia D, Daushvili, Targamadze (Dzalamidze 64);
Okriashvili, Mchedlidze (Sirbiladze 79).
*Spain:* (433) Casillas; Jordi Alba, Arbeloa (Fabregas 80),
Pique, Sergio Ramos; Busquets (Pedro 57), Alonso, Xavi;
Iniesta, Silva (Cazorla 64), Soldado.
*Referee:* Svein Oddvar Moen.

Friday, 12 October 2012
**Belarus (0) 0**
**Spain (2) 4** *(Jordi Alba 12, Pedro 20, 69, 72)* 30,300
*Belarus:* (4231) Veremko; Filipenko, Plaskonny, Shitov,
Martynovich; Bardachov, Dragun (Chukhley 79);
Tigorev, Volodko (Kisliak 46), Hleb; Rodionov (Bressan
65).
*Spain:* (433) Casillas; Arbeloa, Sergio Ramos (Albiol 72),
Busquets, Jordi Alba; Xavi (Villa 75), Alonso, Cazorla;
Pedro, Fabregas, Silva (Iniesta 56).
*Referee:* Serge Gumienny.

**Finland (0) 1** *(Hamalainen 62)*
**Georgia (0) 1** *(Kashia 57)* 12,126
*Finland:* (442) Maenpaa; Moisander, Raitala, Uronen,
Ojala J; Eremenko R, Sparv, Ring, Hamalainen; Pukki
(Hetemaj 62), Eremenko A■.
*Georgia:* (442) Revishvili; Grigalava, Kashia,
Khizanishvili, Amisulashvili; Kobakhidze, Kankava,
Daushvili, Targamadze (Kenia 80); Okriashvili
(Ananidze 67), Mchedlidze (Devdariani 59).
*Referee:* Yevhen Aranovskiy.

Tuesday, 16 October 2012
**Belarus (2) 2** *(Bressan 6, Dragun 28)*
**Georgia (0) 0** 22,220
*Belarus:* (442) Veremko; Verkhovtsov, Bardachov,
Polyakov, Filipenko; Tigorev, Dragun, Pavlov (Kisliak
82), Hleb; Bressan (Volodko 85), Rodionov (Chukhley
90).
*Georgia:* (442) Revishvili; Kashia, Khizanishvili,
Amisulashvili, Grigalava; Kankava, Daushvili,
Kobakhidze, Targamadze (Kenia 74); Okriashvili
(Ananidze 48), Devdariani (Mchedlidze 46).
*Referee:* Robert Schoergenhofer.

**Spain (1) 1** *(Sergio Ramos 25)*
**France (0) 1** *(Giroud 90)* 46,460
*Spain:* (442) Casillas; Sergio Ramos, Arbeloa (Juanfran
51), Jordi Alba, Iniesta (Torres 75); Xavi, Fabregas,
Alonso, Busquets; Silva (Cazorla 13), Pedro.
*France:* (442) Lloris; Koscielny, Debuchy, Evra, Sakho;
Valbuena, Cabaye, Gonalons (Matuidi 57); Ribery;
Benzema (Giroud 87), Menez (Sissoko 68).
*Referee:* Felix Brych.

Friday, 22 March 2013
**France (1) 3** *(Giroud 45, Valbuena 47, Ribery 61)*
**Georgia (0) 1** *(Kobakhidze 70)* 77,770
*France:* (442) Lloris; Varane, Clichy, Jallet, Sakho;
Valbuena (Remy 66), Matuidi (Sissoko 67), Pogba,
Ribery (Menez 78); Benzema, Giroud.
*Georgia:* (442) Loria; Lobjanidze, Kvirkvelia D, Kashia,
Amisulashvili; Khizanishvili, Kobakhidze, Daushvili,
Targamadze (Gelashvili 84); Ananidze (Kenia 46),
Vatsadze (Dvalishvili 74).
*Referee:* Ivan Bebek.

**Spain (0) 1** *(Sergio Ramos 49)*
**Finland (0) 1** *(Pukki 79)* 28,280
*Spain:* (4231) Valdes; Arbeloa, Pique, Sergio Ramos,
Jordi Alba; Fabregas (Mata 76), Busquets; Silva, Cazorla
(Pedro 46), Iniesta; Villa (Negredo 65).
*Finland:* (451) Maenpaa; Moisander, Toivio, Arkivuo,
Raitala; Eremenko R, Hetemaj, Tainio (Sparv 69), Ring,
Hamalainen; Pukki (Halsti 90).
*Referee:* Ovidiu Alin Hategan.

Tuesday, 26 March 2013
**France (0) 0**
**Spain (0) 1** *(Pedro 58)* 80,800
*France:* (451) Lloris; Jallet (Giroud 90), Koscielny,
Varane, Evra; Cabaye (Menez 70), Matuidi, Pogba■,
Valbuena, Ribery; Benzema (Sissoko 82).
*Spain:* (433) Valdes; Arbeloa, Pique, Sergio Ramos,
Monreal; Alonso, Busquets, Xavi; Iniesta (Mata 90),
Villa (Jesus Navas 61), Pedro (Fabregas 76).
*Referee:* Viktor Kassai.

Friday, 7 June 2013
**Finland (0) 1** *(Shitov 58 (og))*
**Belarus (0) 0** 24,249
*Finland:* (442) Maenpaa; Raitala, Pasanen, Arkivuo
(Hurme 53), Halsti; Eremenko R, Hetemaj, Tainio
(Sparv 68), Ring; Hamalainen, Pukki (Forssell 77).
*Belarus:* (442) Veremko; Martynovich, Shitov (Kalachev
78), Filipenko, Bardachov; Dragun (Pavlov 66), Hleb,
Putsila, Kisliak; Balanovich (Nekhaychik■ 17), Rodionov.
*Referee:* Eli Hacmon.

Tuesday, 11 June 2013
**Belarus (0) 1** *(Verkhovtsov 85)*
**Finland (1) 1** *(Pukki 24)* 　　　　　　5000
*Belarus:* (4231) Veremko; Veretilo (Kisliak 46), Martynovich (Sitko 79), Verkhovtsov, Olekhnovich; Trubila, Dragun; Kalachev, Hleb, Putsila (Bressan 64); Rodionov.
*Finland:* (442) Maenpaa; Raitala, Pasanen, Moisander, Hurme; Eremenko R, Hetemaj, Sparv, Ring; Hamalainen (Arajuuri 82), Pukki (Furuholm 75).
*Referee:* Libor Kovarik.

| Group I Table | P | W | D | L | F | A | GD | Pts |
|---|---|---|---|---|---|---|---|---|
| Spain | 5 | 3 | 2 | 0 | 8 | 2 | 6 | 11 |
| France | 5 | 3 | 1 | 1 | 8 | 4 | 4 | 10 |
| Finland | 5 | 1 | 3 | 1 | 4 | 4 | 0 | 6 |
| Georgia | 5 | 1 | 1 | 3 | 3 | 7 | –4 | 4 |
| Belarus | 6 | 1 | 1 | 4 | 4 | 10 | –6 | 4 |

## WORLD CUP 2014 – EUROPE REMAINING FIXTURES

**GROUP A**
06/09/13 Macedonia v Wales
06/09/13 Scotland v Belgium
06/09/13 Serbia v Croatia
10/09/13 Wales v Serbia
10/09/13 Macedonia v Scotland
11/10/13 Croatia v Belgium
11/10/13 Wales v FYR Macedonia
15/10/13 Belgium v Wales
15/10/13 Serbia v Macedonia
15/10/13 Scotland v Croatia

**GROUP B**
06/09/13 Czech Republic v Armenia
06/09/13 Italy v Bulgaria
06/09/13 Malta v Denmark
10/09/13 Italy v Czech Republic
10/09/13 Armenia v Denmark
10/09/13 Malta v Bulgaria
11/10/13 Denmark v Italy
11/10/13 Armenia v Bulgaria
11/10/13 Malta v Czech Republic
15/10/13 Bulgaria v Czech Republic
15/10/13 Denmark v Malta
15/10/13 Italy v Armenia

**GROUP C**
06/09/13 Germany v Austria
06/09/13 Republic of Ireland v Sweden
06/09/13 Kazakhstan v Faroe Islands
10/09/13 Kazakhstan v Sweden
10/09/13 Austria v Republic of Ireland
10/09/13 Faroe Islands v Germany
11/10/13 Sweden v Austria
11/10/13 Faroe Islands v Kazakhstan
11/10/13 Germany v Republic of Ireland
15/10/13 Faroe Islands v Austria
15/10/13 Sweden v Germany
15/10/13 Republic of Ireland v Kazakhstan

**GROUP D**
06/09/13 Romania v Hungary
06/09/13 Estonia v Holland
06/09/13 Turkey v Andorra
10/09/13 Romania v Turkey
10/09/13 Hungary v Estonia
10/09/13 Andorra v Holland
11/10/13 Estonia v Turkey
11/10/13 Andorra v Romania
11/10/13 Holland v Hungary
15/10/13 Turkey v Holland
15/10/13 Romania v Estonia
15/10/13 Hungary v Andorra

**GROUP E**
06/09/13 Norway v Cyprus
06/09/13 Switzerland v Iceland
06/09/13 Slovenia v Albania
10/09/13 Norway v Switzerland
10/09/13 Cyprus v Slovenia
10/09/13 Iceland v Albania
11/10/13 Albania v Switzerland
11/10/13 Slovenia v Norway
11/10/13 Iceland v Cyprus
15/10/13 Norway v Iceland
15/10/13 Cyprus v Albania
15/10/13 Switzerland v Slovenia

**GROUP F**
06/09/13 Northern Ireland v Portugal
06/09/13 Israel v Azerbaijan
06/09/13 Russia v Luxembourg
10/09/13 Russia v Israel
10/09/13 Luxembourg v Northern Ireland
11/10/13 Portugal v Israel
11/10/13 Luxembourg v Russia
11/10/13 Azerbaijan v Northern Ireland
15/10/13 Israel v Northern Ireland
15/10/13 Azerbaijan v Russia
15/10/13 Portugal v Luxembourg

**GROUP G**
06/09/13 Latvia v Lithuania
06/09/13 Bosnia-Herzegovina v Slovakia
06/09/13 Liechtenstein v Greece
10/09/13 Greece v Latvia
10/09/13 Lithuania v Liechtenstein
10/09/13 Slovakia v Bosnia-Herzegovina
11/10/13 Greece v Slovakia
11/10/13 Bosnia-Herzegovina v Liechtenstein
11/10/13 Lithuania v Latvia
15/10/13 Lithuania v Bosnia-Herzegovina
15/10/13 Greece v Liechtenstein
15/10/13 Latvia v Slovakia

**GROUP H**
06/09/13 Ukraine v San Marino
06/09/13 England v Moldova
06/09/13 Poland v Montenegro
10/09/13 Ukraine v England
10/09/13 San Marino v Poland
11/10/13 England v Montenegro
11/10/13 Ukraine v Poland
11/10/13 Moldova v San Marino
15/10/13 San Marino v Ukraine
15/10/13 Montenegro v Moldova
15/10/13 England v Poland

**GROUP I**
06/09/13 Georgia v France
06/09/13 Finland v Spain
10/09/13 Belarus v France
10/09/13 Georgia v Finland
11/10/13 Spain v Belarus
15/10/13 Spain v Georgia
15/10/13 France v Finland

## SOUTH AMERICA

■ *Denotes player sent off.*

**Friday, 7 October 2011**
**Argentina (2) 4** *(Higuain 7, 52, 63, Messi 25)*
**Chile (0) 1** *(Fernandez M 59)*                26,161
*Argentina:* Andujar; Zabaleta, Burdisso, Rojo, Otamendi, Di Maria (Gutierrez 85), Sosa (Salvio 79), Higuain, Messi, Banega (Rinaudo 72), Brana.
*Chile:* Bravo; Ponce, Isla, Carmona, Vidal, Suazo, Valdivia, Pinilla (Gonzalez Marcos 54), Fernandez M (Jorquera 81), Beausejour (Vargas 54), Jara.
*Referee:* Roldan (Colombia).

**Ecuador (2) 2** *(Ayovi J 15, Benitez 28)*
**Venezuela (0) 0**                               32,278
*Ecuador:* Banguera; Erazo, Paredes J, Noboa (Arroyo 76), Ayovi W, Benitez (Mendez 83), Suarez (Bolanos 68), Campos, Valencia, Ayovi J, Saritama.
*Venezuela:* Vega; Granados, Rey■, Velazquez, Flores F (Flores A 57), Di Giorgi, Meza, Maldonado (Feltscher F 72), Seijas, Lucena, Aristeguieta (Moreno 46).
*Referee:* Osses (Chile).

**Peru (0) 2** *(Guerrero 46, 71)*
**Paraguay (0) 0**                                39,600
*Peru:* Fernandez; Rodriguez, Acasiete, Guizasola, Balbin, Vargas, Guerrero P (Advincula 90), Farfan, Pizarro, Cruzado (Lobaton 89), Yotun.
*Paraguay:* Barreto D; Piris, Marecos (Samudio 25), Veron, Barreto E, Santa Cruz R, Estigarribia, Da Silva, Riveros, Pirez (Cardozo O 66), Ramirez (Pittoni 55).
*Referee:* Pezzotta (Argentina).

**Uruguay (3) 4** *(Suarez 3, Lugano 25, 71, Cavani 34)*
**Bolivia (1) 2** *(Cardozo 17, Martins 87 (pen))*   25,500
*Uruguay:* Muslera; Lugano, Godin, Suarez, Forlan, Pereira A (Fucile 56), Pirez, Pereira M, Arevalo, Cavani (Rodriguez C 70), Caceres.
*Bolivia:* Arias; Gutierrez, Rivero, Flores (Chavez 81), Rojas (Vaca 60), Martins, Vargas, Robles, Raldes, Saucedo (Pena 46), Cardozo.
*Referee:* Carrillo (Peru).

**Tuesday, 11 October 2011,**
**Bolivia (0) 1** *(Flores 85)*
**Colombia (0) 2** *(Pabon 48, Falcao 90)*        33,155
*Bolivia:* Vaca; Gutierrez (Campos J 70), Alvarez (Chavez 77), Rivero, Flores, Martins (Andaveris 71), Robles, Raldes, Arce, Escobar, Cardozo.
*Colombia:* Ospina; Rodriguez, Sanchez, Armero, Aguilar, Pabon (Moreno 62), Guarin F (Chara 70), Perea, Zuniga, Gutierrez (Falcao 79), Mosquera.
*Referee:* Amarilla (Paraguay).

**Chile (2) 4** *(Ponce 2, Vargas 18, Medel 47, Suazo 63 (pen))*
**Peru (0) 2** *(Pizarro 49, Farfan 59)*          39,000
*Chile:* Bravo; Ponce, Isla, Gonzalez Marcos, Vidal, Suazo (Paredes 72), Valdivia (Carmona 90), Beausejour, Medel, Jara, Vargas (Fernandez M 84).
*Peru:* Fernandez; Rodriguez, Acasiete (Chiroque 87), Balbin (Guizasola 46), Vargas, Guerrero P, Farfan, Revoredo, Pizarro, Cruzado, Yotun (Lobaton 46).
*Referee:* Orosco (Bolivia).

**Paraguay (0) 1** *(Ortiz 90)*
**Uruguay (0) 1** *(Forlan 67)*                   12,922
*Paraguay:* Barreto D; Veron, Bonet (Perez 79), Cardozo O (Caballero 67), Barreto E, Estigarribia, Da Silva, Caceres (Santa Cruz R 77), Riveros, Valdez, Ortiz.
*Uruguay:* Muslera; Lugano, Godin, Suarez, Forlan (Rodriguez C 83), Pereira A (Gonzalez 64), Perez (Eguren 58), Pereira M, Arevalo, Cavani, Caceres.
*Referee:* Seneme (Brazil).

**Venezuela (0) 1** *(Amorebieta 61)*
**Argentina (0) 0**                               37,000
*Venezuela:* Vega; Vizcarrondo, Amorebieta, Cichero, Fedor (Moreno 89), Rincon, Gonzalez C (Alvarez 83), Lucena, Rosales, Arango, Rondon J (Feltscher F 76).
*Argentina:* Andujar; Demichelis, Zabaleta (Banega 66), Burdisso, Rojo, Otamendi, Di Maria (Pastore 84), Sosa (Palacio 74), Higuain, Messi, Mascherano.
*Referee:* Silvera (Uruguay).

**Friday, 11 November 2011**
**Argentina (0) 1** *(Lavezzi 60)*
**Bolivia (0) 1** *(Martins 56)*                  27,592
*Argentina:* Romero; Burdisso, Demichelis, Zabaleta, Rodriguez C, Mascherano (Sosa 82), Gago, Pastore, Alvarez (Lavezzi 59), Messi, Higuain.
*Bolivia:* Arias; Gutierrez, Mendez, Vargas, Rivero, Flores, Robles, Cardozo, Martins (Andaveris 77), Escobar (Chavez 84), Rojas (Segovia 54).
*Referee:* Vera (Ecuador).

**Uruguay (2) 4** *(Suarez 42, 45, 68, 74)*
**Chile (0) 0**                                   40,500
*Uruguay:* Muslera; Lugano, Caceres, Godin, Pereira A, Perez, Gonzalez (Eguren 70), Arevalo, Ramirez (Abreu 58), Suarez (Rodriguez C 77), Cavani.
*Chile:* Bravo; Gonzalez Marcos, Contreras, Isla, Ponce, Diaz (Mirosevic 61), Fernandez M, Medel, Suazo (Paredes 61), Vargas (Canales 72), Campos.
*Referee:* Baldassi (Argentina).

**Saturday, 12 November 2011**
**Colombia (1) 1** *(Guarin F 11)*
**Venezuela (0) 1** *(Feltscher F 79)*            49,612
*Colombia:* Ospina; Yepes, Perea, Vallejo, Armero, Bolivar, Guarin F, Rodriguez (Moreno 90), Gutierrez (Quintero 85), Martinez J, Pabon (Marrugo 77).
*Venezuela:* Vega; Amorebieta, Vizcarrondo, Rosales, Cichero, Arango, Gonzalez C, Flores A, Rincon (Guerra 84), Moreno (Feltscher F 71), Fedor (Rondon J 58).
*Referee:* Ponce (Ecuador).

**Paraguay (0) 2** *(Riveros 47, Veron 57)*
**Ecuador (0) 1** *(Rojas 90)*                    11,173
*Paraguay:* Barreto D; Da Silva, Veron, Bonet, Riveros, Estigarribia (Samudio 80), Caceres, Ayala, Ortiz, Haedo Valdez (Caballero 74), Barrios (Dos Santos 64).
*Ecuador:* Banguera; Achilier, Erazo, Saritama (Rojas 78), Valencia, Noboa, Ayovi W, Morante, Borja (Mendez 71), Suarez (Montero 59), Ayovi J.
*Referee:* Buitrago (Colombia).

**Tuesday, 15 November 2011**
**Chile (1) 2** *(Contreras 28, Campos 86)*
**Paraguay (0) 0**                                44,726
*Chile:* Bravo; Gonzalez Marcos, Contreras, Isla, Ponce, Fernandez M (Mirosevic 87), Medel, Aranguiz, Sanchez, Suazo (Campos 71), Vargas (Paredes 78).
*Paraguay:* Barreto D; Manzur, Veron, Bonet (Hernan Perez 46), Samudio, Barreto E, Dos Santos (Benitez 62), Riveros, Estigarribia (Cardozo O 75), Aquino, Haedo Valdez.
*Referee:* Lopes (Brazil).

**Colombia (1) 1** *(Pabon 45)*
**Argentina (0) 2** *(Messi 61, Aguero 85)*       49,600
*Colombia:* Ospina; Yepes, Zuniga, Mosquera, Armero, Aguilar (Arias 77), Bolivar, Rodriguez, Ramos, Martinez J (Quintero 77), Pabon (Moreno 62).
*Argentina:* Romero; Burdisso (Desabato 38), Zabaleta, Rodriguez C, Fernandez F, Mascherano, Brana, Guinazu (Aguero 46), Sosa, Messi, Higuain (Gago 86).
*Referee:* Filho (Brazil).

**Ecuador (0) 2** *(Mendez 70, Benitez 89)*
**Peru (0) 0**                                          34,481
*Ecuador:* Banguera; Campos, Erazo (Morante 37),
Castillo, Saritama (Minda 81), Valencia, Ayovi W,
Paredes P, Benitez, Rojas (Mendez 46), Ayovi J.
*Peru:* Fernandez; Acasiete, Vilchez, Revoredo, Ramos,
Vargas, Lobaton (Guevara 46), Retamoso, Guerrero P,
Pizarro (Chiroque 63), Farfan (Advincula 66).
*Referee:* Larrionda (Uruguay).

**Venezuela (1) 1** *(Vizcarrondo 26)*
**Bolivia (0) 0**                                       33,351
*Venezuela:* Vega; Amorebieta, Vizcarrondo, Rosales,
Cichero, Arango, Gonzalez C (Feltscher F 63), Rincon,
Julio Alvarez (Lucena 72), Maldonado (Feltscher R 78),
Rondon J.
*Bolivia:* Arias; Raldes, Gutierrez, Christian Vargas,
Rivero, Robles, Chavez, Cardozo (Andaveris 78),
Marcelo Martins, Escobar (Campos J 59), Segovia (Arce
59).
*Referee:* Buckley (Peru).

**Saturday, 2 June 2012**
**Argentina (3) 4** *(Aguero 19, Higuain 29, Messi 31, Di
Maria 76)*
**Ecuador (0) 0**                                       50,000
*Argentina:* Romero; Garay, Zabaleta, Gago, Di Maria
(Rodriguez M 82), Higuain (Lavezzi 73), Messi,
Mascherano, Rodriguez C, Aguero (Sosa 62), Fernandez F.
*Ecuador:* Dominguez; Guagua, Noboa, Ayovi W, Benitez
(Ibarra 84), Suarez (Montero 46), Quinonez, Valencia,
Saritama (Ayovi J 39), Achilier, Campos.
*Referee:* Rivera (Peru).

**Bolivia (0) 0**
**Chile (1) 2** *(Aranguiz 45, Vidal 83)*               34,389
*Bolivia:* Vaca; Mendez, Gutierrez, Vargas, Rivero,
Flores, Arce, Campos J (Cardozo 56), Chumacero,
Pedriel (Andaveris 70), Escobar (Pena 73).
*Chile:* Bravo; Contreras, Gonzalez O, Sanchez, Vidal,
Suazo (Vargas 78), Rojas, Fernandez M (Figueroa 73),
Mena, Aranguiz (Leal 87), Diaz.
*Referee:* Intriago (Ecuador).

**Uruguay (1) 1** *(Forlan 38)*
**Venezuela (0) 1** *(Rondon J 84)*                     57,000
*Uruguay:* Muslera; Lugano (Coates 78), Godin, Suarez,
Forlan (Abreu 88), Pereira A, Perez (Gonzalez 75),
Pereira M, Arevalo, Cavani, Caceres.
*Venezuela:* Vega; Vizcarrondo, Amorebieta, Cichero,
Rincon, Seijas (Perozo 88), Di Giorgi (Orozco 75),
Rosales, Arango, Feltscher F (Fedor 55), Rondon J.
*Referee:* Arias (Paraguay).

**Sunday, 3 June 2012**
**Peru (0) 0** 35,724
**Colombia (0) 1** *(Rodriguez 51)*                     35,724
*Peru:* Penny; Galliquio, Carrillo (Farfan 85), Guerrero P,
Revoredo (Rui Diaz 68), Ramos, Lobaton (Chiroque 57),
Cruzado, Yotun, Ramirez, Alvarez.
*Colombia:* Ospina; Yepes, Cuadrado (Ramirez 72),
Sanchez, Armero, Falcao, Rodriguez (Martinez J 90),
Pabon, Guarin F (Mejia 86), Perea, Mosquera.
*Referee:* Pitana (Argentina).

**Bolivia (1) 3** *(Pena 10, Escobar 70, 80)*
**Paraguay (0) 1** *(Riveros 83)*                       17,320
*Bolivia:* Galarza; Valverde, Vargas, Jimenez, Flores,
Martins (Andaveris 84), Escobar (Cardozo 85), Pena,
Chumacero, Mojica (Chavez 73), Barba.
*Paraguay:* Villar; Roman, Aranda (Perez 74), Zeballos
Mazacotte, Da Silva, Ramos (Benitez 58), Riveros,
Torres, Valdez, Martinez.
*Referee:* Silvera (Uruguay).

**Saturday, 9 June 2012**
**Venezuela (0) 0**
**Chile (0) 2** *(Fernandez M 85, Aranguiz 90)*         35,000
*Venezuela:* Vega; Vizcarrondo, Chicero, Fedor (Del
Valle 63), Seijas (Orozco 82), Di Giorgi, Rosales,
Arango, Perozo, Rondon J, Alvarez (Guerra 63).

**Chile:** Bravo; Contreras (Figueroa 65), Gonzalez O,
Sanchez, Vidal, Suazo (Pinto 79), Rojas (Gonzalez
Marcos 30), Fernandez M, Mena, Aranguiz, Diaz.
*Referee:* Buitrago (Colombia).

**Sunday, 10 June 2012**
**Ecuador (0) 1** *(Benitez 54)*
**Colombia (0) 0**                                      37,353
*Ecuador:* Dominguez; Erazo, Paredes J, Noboa■, Rojas
(Mendez 72), Montero (Saritama 78), Ayovi W, Benitez
(Minda 90), Castillo, Valencia, Campos.
*Colombia:* Ospina; Yepes, Sanchez, Armero, Falcao,
Rodriguez, Pabon, Guarin F (Cuadrado 66), Perea
(Zuniga 35), Soto (Muriel 73), Mosquera.
*Referee:* Seneme (Brazil).

**Montevideo, 10 June 2012,**
**Uruguay (2) 4** *(Coates 15, Pereira M 30, Rodriguez C 63,
Eguren 90)*
**Peru (1) 2** *(Godin 40 (og), Guerrero P 48)*         55,000
*Uruguay:* Muslera; Godin, Coates, Suarez (Eguren 90),
Forlan (Rodriguez C 60), Pereira A (Ramirez 60), Perez,
Pereira M, Arevalo, Cavani, Caceres.
*Peru:* Penny; Galliquio, Gonzales (Lobaton 46),
Guerrero P, Fernandez (Carrillo 76), Ramos, Advincula
(Cueva 68), Cruzado, Yotun, Ramirez, Alvarez.
*Referee:* Pedro (Brazil).

**Friday, 7 September 2012**
**Colombia (1) 4** *(Falcao 3, Gutierrez 49, 53, Zuniga 90)*
**Uruguay (0) 0**                                       40000
*Colombia:* (442) Ospina, Zuniga, Valdes, Perea, Armero,
Rodriguez (Sanchez Moreno 84), Valencia, Torres,
Aguilar (Ramirez 49), Falcao, Gutierrez (Quintero 80).
*Uruguay:* (442) Muslera, Pereira M (Ramirez 60), Lugano,
Godin, Victorino (Gonzalez 47), Rodriguez C, Pereira,
Perez, Arevalo Rios (Gargano 74), Forlan, Cavani.
*Referee:* Heber Roberto Lopes.

**Ecuador (0) 1** *(Caicedo 75 (pen))*
**Bolivia (0) 0**                                       32,322
*Ecuador:* (442) Dominguez; Paredes J, Campos, Erazo,
Ayovi W; Castillo, Saritama, Valencia, Montero (Arroyo
47); Mina (Quinonez 87), Ayovi J (Caicedo 57).
*Bolivia:* (442) Suarez; Mendez, Raldes, Vargas,
Gutierrez; Barba Paz, Azogue, Chavez (Chumacero 78),
Mojica (Cabrera 85); Saucedo (Pena 47), Martins.
*Referee:* Juan Soto Arevalo.

**Saturday, 8 September 2012**
**Argentina (2) 3** *(Di Maria 3, Higuain 31, Messi 64)*
**Paraguay (1) 1** *(Fabbro 18 (pen))*                  48,480
*Argentina:* (442) Romero; Garay, Fernandez F,
Campagnaro, Rojo; Gago, Di Maria (Guinazu 79), Brana
(Biglia 88), Higuain; Messi, Lavezzi (Palacio 65).
*Paraguay:* (442) Villar; Piris, Alcaraz, Da Silva, Ayala;
Estigarribia (Benitez 73), Caceres, Riveros, Fabbro
(Cardozo O 58); Ortiz, Santa Cruz (Haedo Valdez 59).
*Referee:* Wilson Seneme.

**Peru (0) 2** *(Farfan 47, 60)*
**Venezuela (1) 1** *(Arango 43)*                       39,393
*Peru:* (442) Fernandez; Revoredo (Guizasola 73), Vargas,
Zambrano, Rodriguez; Yotun, Ramirez, Cruzado, Farfan
(Lobaton 80); Pizarro, Guerrero P (Carrillo 49).
*Venezuela:* (442) Vega; Vizcarrondo, Rosales, Cichero■,
Tunez; Feltscher, Flores, Flores F (Gonzalez C 64),
Arango; Seijas (Feltscher A 75), Miku (Rondon J 70).
*Referee:* Martin Vazquez Broquetas.

**Tuesday, 11 September 2012**
**Chile (1) 1** *(Fernandez M 43)*
**Colombia (0) 3** *(Rodriguez 60, Falcao 75, Gutierrez 78)*
                                                        38,380
*Chile:* (442) Bravo; Jara Reyes, Gonzalez Marcos, Isla
(Fernandez J 68), Vidal; Fernandez M, Mena, Medel■,
Diaz; Sanchez (Pinilla 83), Suazo (Pinto 72).
*Colombia:* (442) Ospina; Zuniga, Perea, Yepes
(Cuadrado 47), Armero; Aguilar■, Rodriguez (Sanchez
Moreno 81), Torres (Ramirez 70), Valencia; Gutierrez,
Falcao.
*Referee:* Vitor Hugo Carrillo.

**Uruguay (0) 1** *(Cavani 68)*
**Ecuador (1) 1** *(Caicedo 9 (pen))*                    52,520
*Uruguay:* (433) Muslera; Pereira M, Lugano, Godin, Pereira (Gargano 47); Perez (Rodriguez C 60), Ramirez, Alfaro (Gonzalez 47); Suarez, Forlan, Cavani.
*Ecuador:* (442) Dominguez; Campos, Ayovi W, Erazo, Paredes J; Minda, Castillo, Valencia▪, Saritama (Ibarra 84); Benitez (Achilier 90), Caicedo (Ayovi J 58).
*Referee:* Carlos Amarilla.

Wednesday, 12 September 2012
**Paraguay (0) 0**
**Venezuela (1) 2** *(Rondon J 46, 68)*                    20,200
*Paraguay:* (442) Villar; Alcaraz (Ayala 71), Veron, Bonet, Samudio (Estigarribia 41); Da Silva, Caceres (Dos Santos 65), Riveros, Fabbro; Haedo Valdez, Cardozo O.
*Venezuela:* (4411) Hernandez D; Gonzalez, Vizcarrondo, Tunez, Rosales; Gonzalez A (Perez Greco E 81), Lucena, Seijas (Flores A 87), Arango; Martinez (Blanco 74); Rondon J.
*Referee:* Enrique Osses.

**Peru (1) 1** *(Zambrano 22)*
**Argentina (1) 1** *(Higuain 39)*                    39,393
*Peru:* (442) Fernandez; Zambrano, Rodriguez, Yotun, Advincula; Ramirez (Guerrero P 87), Cruzado, Lobaton (Ballon 47), Farfan; Pizarro, Carrillo (Hurtado 77).
*Argentina:* (433) Romero; Campagnaro, Garay, Fernandez F, Rojo; Gago (Guinazu 61), Mascherano, Di Maria (Rodriguez M 85); Messi, Higuain, Lavezzi (Perez 75).
*Referee:* Wilmar Roldan Perez.

Friday, 12 October 2012
**Bolivia (0) 1** *(Chumacero 52)*
**Peru (1) 1** *(Marino 23)*                    35,350
*Bolivia:* (442) Suarez; Mendez, Raldes, Valverde, Vargas (Segovia 47); Flores, Chumacero, Cardozo, Campos J; Arce (Suarez 75), Pena (Martins 47).
*Peru:* (442) Carvallo; Acasiete, Ramos, Farfan, Sanchez; Herrera, Retamoso, Cominges (Ampuero 60), Marino (Cueva 79); Chiroque, Avila (Aguirre 61).
*Referee:* Carlos Vera.

**Colombia (0) 2** *(Falcao 52, 89)*
**Paraguay (0) 0**                    40,404
*Colombia:* (4312) Ospina; Zuniga, Valdes, Yepes, Armero; Valencia (Soto 84), Ramirez (Cuadrado 47), Torres (Benitez 75); Rodriguez; Falcao, Gutierrez.
*Paraguay:* (442) Barreto D; Piris, Ortiz, Da Silva, Aguilar; Ayala, Caceres, Riveros, Estigarribia (Benitez 67); Nunez (Fabbro 80), Haedo Valdez (Caballero 61).
*Referee:* Sergio Pezzotta.

**Ecuador (1) 3** *(Caicedo 33, 56 (pen), Castillo 90)*
**Chile (1) 1** *(Paredes J 26 (og))*                    33,330
*Ecuador:* (433) Dominguez; Paredes J, Achilier, Erazo, Ayovi; Castillo, Saritama, Ibarra (Montero 78); Rojas (Gonzalez 74), Caicedo (Ayovi 63), Benitez.
*Chile:* (451) Pinto; Contreras▪, Gonzalez O, Jara Reyes, Seymour (Gonzalez Mark 63); Diaz, Isla, Vidal▪, Beausejour (Vargas 78), Fernandez M (Fernandez J 61); Sanchez.
*Referee:* Heber Roberto Lopes.

Saturday, 13 October 2012
**Argentina (0) 3** *(Messi 66, 80, Aguero 75)*
**Uruguay (0) 0**                    42,425
*Argentina:* (433) Romero; Zabaleta, Fernandez F, Garay, Rojo (Campagnaro 68); Mascherano, Gago, Di Maria; Aguero (Guinazu 79), Messi, Higuain (Barcos 84).
*Uruguay:* (433) Muslera; Pereira M, Godin, Lugano (Scotti 65); Caceres; Gonzalez (Rodriguez C 68), Arevalo Rios, Gargano; Suarez, Forlan, Cavani.
*Referee:* Leandro Pedro Vauden.

Tuesday, 16 October 2012
**Bolivia (2) 4** *(Saucedo 6, 50, 55Mojica 27)*
**Uruguay (0) 1** *(Suarez 81)*                    9500
*Bolivia:* (442) Galarza; Zenteno, Raldes, Gutierrez, Bejarano; Cardozo, Azogue (Melean 74), Chumacero, Mojica (Campos J 68); Saucedo, Martins (Arce 57).
*Uruguay:* (442) Muslera; Scotti, Victorino, Pereira M (Cavani 37), Pereira; Gonzalez, Arevalo Rios, Gargano (Lodeiro 37), Rodriguez C; Forlan (Fernandez 66), Suarez.
*Referee:* Victor Hugo Rivera.

**Paraguay (0) 1** *(Aguilar 53)*
**Peru (0) 0**                    13,130
*Paraguay:* (442) Barreto D; Piris, Da Silva, Aguilar, Samudio; Oviedo, Dos Santos, Riveros, Benitez (Fabbro 82); Nunez (Caceres 75), Haedo Valdez (Caballero 47).
*Peru:* (442) Fernandez; Rodriguez (Ramos 16), Zambrano, Yotun (Ruidiaz 82), Vargas; Cruzado, Ramirez, Advincula, Farfan; Pizarro, Guerrero P (Carrillo 67).
*Referee:* Pablo Lunati.

**Venezuela (1) 1** *(Arango 6)*
**Ecuador (1) 1** *(Castillo 25)*                    34,345
*Venezuela:* (442) Hernandez D; Gonzalez A (Cichero 82), Perozo, Amorebieta, Rosales; Hernandez G, Lucena, Perez Greco E (Vargas 57), Arango; Martinez (Miku 68), Rondon J.
*Ecuador:* (442) Dominguez; Paredes J, Achilier, Erazo, Ayovi W; Castillo, Noboa (Montero 80), Valencia, Arroyo (Rojas 87); Ayovi J (Minda 72), Benitez.
*Referee:* Nestor Pitana.

Wednesday, 17 October 2012
**Chile (0) 1** *(Gutierrez 90)*
**Argentina (2) 2** *(Messi 28, Higuain 31)*                    51,510
*Chile:* (442) Pinto; Gonzalez Marcos, Jara Reyes, Isla, Gonzalez Mark (Gutierrez 75); Fernandez M, Beausejour, Medel, Diaz; Pinto (Vargas 56), Sanchez.
*Argentina:* (442) Romero; Zabaleta, Garay, Campagnaro, Fernandez F; Gago, Di Maria (Sosa 78), Mascherano, Messi; Aguero (Barcos 87), Higuain (Guinazu 61).
*Referee:* Antonio Arias.

Friday, 22 March 2013
**Colombia (1) 5** *(Torres 21, Valdes 50, Gutierrez 62, Falcao 87, Armero 90)*
**Bolivia (0) 0**
*Colombia:* (4312) Ospina; Valdes, Yepes, Zuniga, Cuadrado (Armero 79); Valencia, Aguilar, Rodriguez (Guarin F 83); Torres (Ramirez 86); Falcao, Gutierrez.
*Bolivia:* (442) Arias (Galarza 47); Jimenez, Zenteno, Bejarano, Gutierrez; Bejarano, Chumacero, Veizaga, Garcia (Arce 58); Saucedo (Cardozo 47), Martins.
*Referee:* Carlos Vera.

**Uruguay (0) 1** *(Suarez 82)*
**Paraguay (0) 1** *(Benitez 86)*                    30,300
*Uruguay:* (442) Muslera; Maxi Pereira (Ramirez 69), Lugano, Godin, Pereira; Gonzalez, Perez (Arevalo Rios 47), Lodeiro, Rodriguez C (Cavani 47); Suarez, Forlan.
*Paraguay:* (442) Barreto D; Piris, Aguilar, Da Silva, Samudio; Ayala, Oviedo, Riveros, Ortiz (Benitez 66); Haedo Valdez (Fabbro 80), Cardozo O (Caballero 66).
*Referee:* Wilmar Roldan Perez.

Saturday, 23 March 2013
**Argentina (2) 3** *(Higuain 29, 59, Messi 46 (pen))*
**Venezuela (0) 0**                    55,550
*Argentina:* (433) Romero; Zabaleta, Fernandez F, Garay, Rojo; Gago (Ever 62), Mascherano, Montillo; Lavezzi (Rodriguez M 84), Messi, Higuain (Palacio 80).
*Venezuela:* (4231) Hernandez D; Gonzalez A, Vizcarrondo, Tunez, Cichero; Lucena, Rincon; Feltscher F, Arango (Gonzalez C 75); Seijas (Otero 58); Rondon J (Miku 82).
*Referee:* Vitor Hugo Carrillo.

**Peru (0) 1** *(Farfan 87)*
**Chile (0) 0**
*Peru:* (433) Fernandez; Herrera, Ramos (Alvarez 25), Rodriguez, Yotun; Lobaton (Marino 47), Ramirez, Cruzado; Farfan, Pizarro (Reyna 80), Hurtado.
*Chile:* (433) Bravo; Medel, Gonzalez Marcos, Rojas, Mena; Isla, Aranguiz (Silva 54), Carmona; Beausejour (Castillo 71), Sanchez, Vargas (Fernandez J 75).
*Referee:* Diego Abal.

Tuesday, 26 March 2013
**Bolivia (1) 1** *(Martins 25)*
**Argentina (1) 1** *(Ever 45)*                    38,380
*Bolivia:* (532) Galarza; Torrico (Bejarano 46), Raldes, Zenteno, Gutierrez, Bejarano (Arce 66); Veizaga, Chumacero, Cardozo (Mojica 74); Saucedo, Martins.
*Argentina:* (532) Romero; Peruzzi, Dominguez, Rodriguez, Basanta, Campagnaro; Ever (Di Santo 63), Mascherano, Di Maria (Guinazu 91); Messi, Palacio R (Ponzio 87).
*Referee:* Enrique Osses.

**Chile (1) 2** *(Paredes 11, Vargas 79)*
**Uruguay (0) 0**                                  45,450
*Chile:* (343) Bravo; Medel, Rojas, Jara Reyes; Isla (Gonzalez Marcos 85), Aranguiz (Fernandez 59), Diaz, Mena; Vargas, Beausejour (Carmona 69), Paredes.
*Uruguay:* (442) Muslera; Aguirregaray (Silva 47), Lugano, Godin, Pereira; Gonzalez, Arevalo Rios, Lodeiro (Rodriguez C 83), Ramirez (Forlan 70); Suarez, Cavani.
*Referee:* Nestor Pitana.

**Ecuador (1) 4** *(Caicedo 39, Montero 51, 76, Benitez 54)*
**Paraguay (1) 1** *(Caballero 16)*               35,357
*Ecuador:* (442) Dominguez; Achilier, Erazo, Ayovi W, Quinonez (Saritama 72); Noboa, Paredes J, Valencia, Montero (Ibarra 83); Benitez, Caicedo (Rojas 80).
*Paraguay:* (442) Barreto D; Piris (Haedo Valdez 61), Da Silva, Aguilar, Samudio; Oviedo, Riveros, Ayala, Ortiz (Caceres 46); Caballero (Velazquez 78), Benitez.
*Referee:* Ricci Sandro.

Wednesday, 27 March 2013
**Venezuela (1) 1** *(Rondon 14)*
**Colombia (0) 0**                                 40,400
*Venezuela:* (442) Hernandez D; Gonzalez C, Vizcarrondo, Tunez (Flores A 63), Cichero (Feltscher R 84); Gonzalez A, Rincon, Lucena, Arango; Aristeguieta (Miku 68), Rondon J.
*Colombia:* (4231) Ospina; Zuniga, Valdes, Perea, Armero; Valencia, Aguilar, Cuadrado (Gutierrez 66), Rodriguez, Torres (Bacca 75); Falcao.
*Referee:* Antonio Arias.

Friday, 7 June 2013
**Argentina (0) 0**
**Colombia (0) 0**                                 60,600
*Argentina:* (442) Romero; Zabaleta, Fernandez F, Garay, Rojo; Mascherano, Biglia, Montillo (Messi 58), Di Maria; Higuain■, Aguero (Lavezzi 82).
*Colombia:* (442) Ospina; Armero, Yepes, Zapata■, Zuniga, Aguilar (Mejia 62), Sanchez C, Ramirez, Rodriguez (Cuadrado 34); Martinez J (Perea 47), Falcao.
*Referee:* Marlon Escalante.

**Bolivia (0) 1** *(Campos J 87)*
**Venezuela (0) 1** *(Arango 59)*                  14,140
*Bolivia:* (442) Galarza; Raldes (Campos J 73), Zenteno, Eguino, Veizaga; Chumacero, Chavez (Mojica 47), Cardozo, Arce; Saucedo, Martins (Fierro 62).
*Venezuela:* (442) Vega; Rosales, Perozo, Cichero, Rincon; Flores A, Gonzalez C (Gonzalez A 71), Seijas, Arango (Feltscher R 82); Martinez, Blanco (Hernandez E 66).
*Referee:* Patricio Loustau.

Saturday, 8 June 2013
**Paraguay (0) 1** *(Santa Cruz 88)*
**Chile (1) 2** *(Vargas 41, Vidal 57)*           15,150
*Paraguay:* (433) Villar; Caceres, Da Silva, Samudio, Candia; Riveros (Ortiz 57), Oviedo, Dos Santos (Caballero 80); Benitez, Lopez (Santa Cruz 59), Cardozo O.
*Chile:* (343) Bravo; Medel, Gonzalez Marcos, Rojas; Isla, Vidal, Diaz, Mena; Sanchez (Pinto 90), Paredes (Fernandez M 60), Vargas (Gutierrez 86).
*Referee:* Leandro Pedro Vauden.

Saturday, 8 June 2013
**Peru (1) 1** *(Pizarro 11)*
**Ecuador (0) 0**                                  39,393
*Peru:* (442) Fernandez; Rodriguez, Herrera, Zambrano, Vargas (Ampuero 80); Yotun, Farfan (Advincula 88), Retamoso, Ramiez; Guerrero P, Pizarro (Ramos 90).
*Ecuador:* (442) Dominguez; Guagua, Erazo, Ayovi W, Paredes J (Ibarra 74); Castillo, Noboa, Valencia, Montero; Rojas (Caicedo 54), Benitez (de Jesus 86).
*Referee:* Marcelo De Lima.

Tuesday, 11 June 2013
**Colombia (2) 2** *(Falcao 13 (pen), Gutierrez 45)*
**Peru (0) 0**
*Colombia:* (442) Ospina; Perea, Yepes, Armero, Zuniga; Cuadrado (Guarin F 77), Sanchez, Aguilar (Mejia 86), Torres; Gutierrez (Muriel 80), Falcao.
*Peru:* (442) Fernandez; Rodriguez, Herrera (Farfan 33), Zambrano■, Vargas; Yotun (Carrillo 32), Advincula, Retamoso (Lobaton 63), Ballon; Guerrero P, Pizarro.
*Referee:* Sandro Meira Ricci.

**Ecuador (1) 1** *(Castillo 15)*
**Argentina (1) 1** *(Aguero 5 (pen))*            32,320
*Ecuador:* (442) Dominguez; Guagua, Erazo, Ayovi W, Paredes J (Ibarra 72); Castillo, Noboa (Saritama 71), Valencia, Montero; Rojas (Anangono 89), Caicedo.
*Argentina:* (442) Romero; Garay, Rojo, Fernandez F, Peruzzi; Basanta, Di Maria, Mascherano■, Ever (Biglia 78); Palacio R (Brana 90), Aguero (Messi 62).
*Referee:* Enrique Caceres.

Wednesday, 12 June 2013
**Chile (2) 3** *(Vargas 16, Sanchez 18, Vidal 91)*
**Bolivia (1) 1** *(Martins 32)*
*Chile:* (433) Bravo; Medel, Gonzalez Marcos, Rojas, Mena (Beausejour 75); Diaz, Pizarro, Vidal; Sanchez, Paredes (Jara Reyes 55), Vargas.
*Bolivia:* (451) Galarza; Zenteno, Raldes, Gutierrez, Bejarano; Mojica, Veizaga, Chumacero (Rojas 47), Chavez (Cardozo 47), Arze (Campos J 70); Martins.
*Referee:* Dario Ubriaco.

**Venezuela (0) 0**
**Uruguay (1) 1** *(Cavani 28)*
*Venezuela:* (442) Hernandez D; Tunez, Vizcarrondo, Cichero (Seijas 59), Rosales; Rincon■, Gonzalez C (Blanco 78), Lucena, Arango; Feltscher F (Aristeguieta 57), Rondon J.
*Uruguay:* (442) Muslera; Lugano, Godin, Pereira M, Caceres; Gargano, Rodriguez C (Pereira A 86), Perez (Eguren 76), Ramirez (Gonzalez 60); Forlan, Cavani.
*Referee:* Paulo Cesar Oliveira.

### South America

| Group Matches Table | P | W | D | L | F | A | GD | Pts |
|---|---|---|---|---|---|---|---|---|
| Argentina | 13 | 7 | 5 | 1 | 25 | 9 | 16 | 26 |
| Colombia | 12 | 7 | 2 | 3 | 21 | 7 | 14 | 23 |
| Ecuador | 12 | 6 | 3 | 3 | 17 | 12 | 5 | 21 |
| Chile | 13 | 7 | 0 | 6 | 21 | 21 | 0 | 21 |
| Uruguay | 12 | 4 | 4 | 4 | 18 | 21 | –3 | 16 |
| Venezuela | 13 | 4 | 4 | 5 | 10 | 14 | –4 | 16 |
| Peru | 12 | 4 | 2 | 6 | 12 | 17 | –5 | 14 |
| Bolivia | 13 | 2 | 4 | 7 | 15 | 24 | –9 | 10 |
| Paraguay | 12 | 2 | 2 | 8 | 9 | 23 | –14 | 8 |

## WORLD CUP 2014 – SOUTH AMERICA REMAINING FIXTURES

06/09/13  Colombia v Ecuador, Chile v Venezuela, Peru v Uruguay, Paraguay v Bolivia
10/09/13  Paraguay v Argentina, Uruguay v Colombia, Venezuela v Peru, Bolivia v Ecuador
11/10/13  Colombia v Chile, Venezuela v Paraguay, Argentina v Peru, Ecuador v Uruguay
15/10/13  Peru v Bolivia, Paraguay v Colombia, Uruguay v Argentina, Chile v Ecuador

## AFRICA

### ROUND 1 – FIRST LEG

| | |
|---|---|
| St Thomas & Principe v Congo | 0-5 |
| Djibouti v Namibia | 0-4 |
| Comoros v Mozambique | 0-1 |
| Eritrea v Rwanda | 1-1 |
| Swaziland v DR Congo | 1-3 |
| Equatorial Guinea v Madagascar | 2-0 |
| Chad v Tanzania | 1-2 |
| Guinea-Bissau v Togo | 1-1 |
| Seychelles v Kenya | 0-3 |
| Lesotho v Burundi | 1-0 |
| Somalia v Ethiopia | 0-0 |

### ROUND 1 – SECOND LEG

| | |
|---|---|
| Congo v St Thomas & Principe | 1-1 |
| Namibia v Djibouti | 4-0 |
| Mozambique v Comoros | 4-1 |
| Rwanda v Eritrea | 3-1 |
| DR Congo v Swaziland | 5-1 |
| Madagascar v Equatorial Guinea | 2-1 |
| Tanzania v Chad | 0-1 |
| Togo v Guinea-Bissau | 1-0 |
| Kenya v Seychelles | 4-0 |
| Burundi v Lesotho | 2-2 |
| Ethiopia v Somalia | 5-0 |

### ROUND 2

#### GROUP A

| | |
|---|---|
| Ethiopia v Central African Rep | 2-0 |
| Botswana v South Africa | 1-1 |
| South Africa v Ethiopia | 1-1 |
| Central African Rep v Botswana | 2-0 |
| South Africa v Central African Rep | 2-0 |
| Ethiopia v Botswana | 1-0 |
| Botswana v Ethiopia | 1-2 |
| Central African Rep v South Africa | 0-3 |
| Botswana v Central African Rep | 2-1 |
| Ethiopia v South Africa | 3-2 |

| Group A Table | P | W | D | L | F | A | Pts |
|---|---|---|---|---|---|---|---|
| Ethiopia | 5 | 4 | 1 | 0 | 8 | 3 | 13 |
| South Africa | 5 | 2 | 2 | 1 | 8 | 4 | 8 |
| Botswana | 5 | 1 | 1 | 3 | 5 | 8 | 4 |
| Central African Republic | 5 | 1 | 0 | 4 | 4 | 10 | 3 |

#### GROUP B

| | |
|---|---|
| Equatorial Guinea v Sierra Leone | 2-2 |
| Cape Verde Islands v Tunisia | 1-2 |
| Tunisia v Equatorial Guinea | 3-1 |
| Sierra Leone v Cape Verde Islands | 2-1 |
| Tunisia v Sierra Leone | 2-1 |
| Equatorial Guinea v Cape Verde Islands | 4-3 |
| Sierra Leone v Tunisia | 2-2 |
| Cape Verde Islands v Equatorial Guinea | 2-1 |
| Cape Verde Islands v Sierra Leone | 1-0 |
| Equatorial Guinea v Tunisia | 1-1 |

| Group B Table | P | W | D | L | F | A | Pts |
|---|---|---|---|---|---|---|---|
| Tunisia | 5 | 3 | 2 | 0 | 10 | 6 | 11 |
| Cape Verde Islands | 5 | 2 | 0 | 3 | 8 | 9 | 6 |
| Sierra Leone | 5 | 1 | 2 | 2 | 7 | 8 | 5 |
| Equatorial Guinea | 5 | 1 | 2 | 2 | 9 | 11 | 5 |

#### GROUP C

| | |
|---|---|
| Tanzania v Gambia | 2-1 |
| Morocco v Ivory Coast | 2-2 |
| Ivory Coast v Tanzania | 2-0 |
| Gambia v Morocco | 1-1 |
| Ivory Coast v Gambia | 3-0 |
| Tanzania v Morocco | 3-1 |
| Gambia v Ivory Coast | 0-3 |
| Morocco v Tanzania | 2-1 |
| Morocco v Gambia | 2-0 |
| Tanzania v Ivory Coast | 2-4 |

| Group C Table | P | W | D | L | F | A | Pts |
|---|---|---|---|---|---|---|---|
| Ivory Coast | 5 | 4 | 1 | 0 | 14 | 4 | 13 |
| Morocco | 5 | 2 | 2 | 1 | 8 | 7 | 8 |
| Tanzania | 5 | 2 | 0 | 3 | 8 | 10 | 6 |
| Gambia | 5 | 0 | 1 | 4 | 2 | 11 | 1 |

#### GROUP D

| | |
|---|---|
| Lesotho v Sudan | 0-0 |
| Zambia v Ghana | 1-0 |
| Sudan v Zambia | 0-3 |
| *Match awarded 0-3 to Zambia; Sudan fielded an ineligible player. Original result 2-0.* | |
| Ghana v Lesotho | 7-0 |
| Ghana v Sudan | 4-0 |
| Lesotho v Zambia | 1-1 |
| Sudan v Ghana | 1-3 |
| Zambia v Lesotho | 4-0 |
| Zambia v Sudan | 1-1 |
| Lesotho v Ghana | 0-2 |

| Group D Table | P | W | D | L | F | A | Pts |
|---|---|---|---|---|---|---|---|
| Ghana | 5 | 4 | 0 | 1 | 16 | 2 | 12 |
| Zambia | 5 | 3 | 2 | 0 | 10 | 2 | 11 |
| Sudan | 5 | 0 | 2 | 3 | 2 | 11 | 2 |
| Lesotho | 5 | 0 | 2 | 3 | 1 | 14 | 2 |

#### GROUP E

| | |
|---|---|
| Gabon v Burkina Faso | 1-0 |
| Congo v Niger | 1-0 |
| Niger v Gabon | 3-0 |
| *Match awarded 3-0 to Niger; Gabon fielded an ineligible player. Original result 0-0.* | |
| Burkina Faso v Congo | 0-3 |
| *Match awarded 0-3 to Congo; Burkino Faso fielded an ineligible player. Original result 0-0.* | |
| Burkina Faso v Niger | 4-0 |
| Congo v Gabon | 1-0 |
| Niger v Burkina Faso | 0-1 |
| Gabon v Congo | 0-0 |
| Gabon v Niger | 4-1 |
| Congo v Burkina Faso | 0-1 |

| Group E Table | P | W | D | L | F | A | Pts |
|---|---|---|---|---|---|---|---|
| Congo | 5 | 3 | 1 | 1 | 5 | 1 | 10 |
| Burkina Faso | 5 | 3 | 0 | 2 | 6 | 4 | 9 |
| Gabon | 5 | 2 | 1 | 2 | 5 | 5 | 7 |
| Niger | 5 | 1 | 0 | 4 | 4 | 10 | 3 |

#### GROUP F

| | |
|---|---|
| Namibia v Kenya | 1-0 |
| Malawi v Nigeria | 1-1 |
| Nigeria v Namibia | 1-0 |
| Kenya v Malawi | 0-0 |
| Nigeria v Kenya | 1-1 |
| Namibia v Malawi | 0-1 |
| Kenya v Nigeria | 0-1 |
| Malawi v Namibia | 0-0 |
| Namibia v Nigeria | 1-1 |
| Malawi v Kenya | 2-2 |

| Group F Table | P | W | D | L | F | A | Pts |
|---|---|---|---|---|---|---|---|
| Nigeria | 5 | 2 | 3 | 0 | 5 | 3 | 9 |
| Malawi | 5 | 1 | 4 | 0 | 4 | 3 | 7 |
| Namibia | 5 | 1 | 2 | 2 | 3 | 3 | 5 |
| Kenya | 5 | 0 | 3 | 2 | 3 | 5 | 3 |

#### GROUP G

| | |
|---|---|
| Guinea v Egypt | 2-3 |
| Mozambique v Zimbabwe | 0-0 |
| Zimbabwe v Guinea | 0-1 |
| Egypt v Mozambique | 2-0 |
| Egypt v Zimbabwe | 2-1 |
| Mozambique v Guinea | 0-0 |
| Zimbabwe v Egypt | 2-4 |
| Guinea v Mozambique | 6-1 |
| Guinea v Zimbabwe | 2-0 |
| Mozambique v Egypt | 0-1 |

| Group G Table | P | W | D | L | F | A | Pts |
|---|---|---|---|---|---|---|---|
| Egypt | 5 | 5 | 0 | 0 | 12 | 5 | 15 |
| Guinea | 5 | 3 | 1 | 1 | 11 | 4 | 10 |
| Mozambique | 5 | 0 | 2 | 3 | 1 | 9 | 2 |
| Zimbabwe | 5 | 0 | 1 | 4 | 3 | 9 | 1 |

#### GROUP H

| | |
|---|---|
| Mali v Algeria | 2-1 |
| Rwanda v Benin | 1-1 |
| Benin v Mali | 1-0 |
| Algeria v Rwanda | 4-0 |
| Algeria v Benin | 3-1 |

| Rwanda v Mali | 1-2 |
|---|---|
| Benin v Algeria | 1-3 |
| Mali v Rwanda | 1-1 |
| Mali v Benin | 2-2 |
| Rwanda v Algeria | 0-1 |

**Group H Table**

| | P | W | D | L | F | A | Pts |
|---|---|---|---|---|---|---|---|
| Algeria | 5 | 4 | 0 | 1 | 12 | 4 | 12 |
| Mali | 5 | 2 | 2 | 1 | 7 | 6 | 8 |
| Benin | 5 | 1 | 2 | 2 | 6 | 9 | 5 |
| Rwanda | 5 | 0 | 2 | 3 | 3 | 9 | 2 |

**GROUP I**

| Libya v Cameroon | 2-1 |
|---|---|
| Congo DR v Togo | 2-0 |
| Togo v Libya | 1-1 |
| Cameroon v Congo DR | 1-0 |
| Cameroon v Togo | 2-1 |
| Congo DR v Libya | 0-0 |
| Togo v Cameroon | 2-0 |
| Libya v Congo DR | 0-0 |
| Libya v Togo | 0-0 |
| Congo DR v Cameroon | 2-0 |

**Group I Table**

| | P | W | D | L | F | A | Pts |
|---|---|---|---|---|---|---|---|
| Libya | 5 | 2 | 3 | 0 | 5 | 2 | 9 |
| Cameroon | 5 | 2 | 1 | 2 | 4 | 5 | 7 |
| Congo DR | 5 | 1 | 3 | 1 | 2 | 1 | 6 |
| Togo | 5 | 1 | 1 | 3 | 4 | 7 | 4 |

**GROUP J**

| Liberia v Angola | 0-0 |
|---|---|
| Uganda v Senegal | 1-1 |
| Angola v Uganda | 1-1 |
| Senegal v Liberia | 3-1 |
| Senegal v Angola | 1-1 |
| Liberia v Uganda | 2-0 |
| Angola v Senegal | 1-1 |
| Uganda v Liberia | 1-0 |
| Uganda v Angola | 0-2 |
| Liberia v Senegal | 2-1 |

**Group J Table**

| | P | W | D | L | F | A | Pts |
|---|---|---|---|---|---|---|---|
| Senegal | 5 | 2 | 3 | 0 | 8 | 4 | 9 |
| Uganda | 5 | 2 | 2 | 1 | 5 | 5 | 8 |
| Angola | 5 | 0 | 4 | 1 | 4 | 5 | 4 |
| Liberia | 5 | 1 | 1 | 3 | 3 | 6 | 4 |

## WORLD CUP 2014 – AFRICA REMAINING FIXTURES

**GROUP A**

| South Africa v Botswana | 6/9/13 |
|---|---|
| Central African Rep v Ethiopia | 6/9/13 |

**GROUP B**

| Sierra Leone v Equatorial Guinea | 6/9/13 |
|---|---|
| Tunisia v Cape Verde Islands | 6/9/13 |

**GROUP C**

| Gambia v Tanzania | 6/9/13 |
|---|---|
| Ivory Coast v Morocco | 6/9/13 |

**GROUP D**

| Sudan v Lesotho | 6/9/13 |
|---|---|
| Ghana v Zambia | 6/9/13 |

**GROUP E**

| Burkina Faso v Gabon | 6/9/13 |
|---|---|
| Niger v Congo | 6/9/13 |

**GROUP F**

| Nigeria v Malawi | 6/9/13 |
|---|---|
| Kenya v Namibia | 6/9/13 |

**GROUP G**

| Egypt v Guinea | 6/9/13 |
|---|---|
| Zimbabwe v Mozambique | 6/9/13 |

**GROUP H**

| Algeria v Mali | 6/9/13 |
|---|---|
| Benin v Rwanda | 6/9/13 |

**GROUP I**

| Cameroon v Libya | 6/9/13 |
|---|---|
| Togo v Congo DR | 6/9/13 |

**GROUP J**

| Angola v Liberia | 6/9/13 |
|---|---|
| Senegal v Uganda | 6/9/13 |

## OCEANIA

**ROUND 1**

| American Samoa v Tonga | 2-1 |
|---|---|
| Cook Islands v Samoa | 2-3 |
| American Samoa v Cook Islands | 1-1 |
| Samoa v Tonga | 1-1 |
| Samoa v American Samoa | 1-0 |
| Tonga v Cook Islands | 2-1 |

**Round 1 Table**

| | P | W | D | L | F | A | Pts |
|---|---|---|---|---|---|---|---|
| Samoa | 3 | 2 | 1 | 0 | 5 | 3 | 7 |
| Tonga | 3 | 1 | 1 | 1 | 4 | 4 | 4 |
| American Samoa | 3 | 1 | 1 | 1 | 3 | 3 | 4 |
| Cook Islands | 3 | 0 | 1 | 2 | 4 | 6 | 1 |

**ROUND 2**

**GROUP A**

| Tahiti v Vanuatu | 4-1 |
|---|---|
| New Caledonia v Samoa | 9-0 |
| Tahiti v New Caledonia | 4-3 |
| Vanuatu v Samoa | 5-0 |
| Vanuatu v New Caledonia | 2-5 |
| Samoa v Tahiti | 1-10 |

**Group A Table**

| | P | W | D | L | F | A | Pts |
|---|---|---|---|---|---|---|---|
| Tahiti | 3 | 3 | 0 | 0 | 18 | 5 | 9 |
| New Caledonia | 3 | 2 | 0 | 1 | 17 | 6 | 6 |
| Vanuatu | 3 | 1 | 0 | 2 | 8 | 9 | 3 |
| Samoa | 3 | 0 | 0 | 3 | 1 | 24 | 0 |

**GROUP B**

| New Zealand v Solomon Islands | 1-1 |
|---|---|
| Papua New Guinea v Fiji | 1-1 |
| Fiji v Solomon Islands | 0-0 |
| Papua New Guinea v New Zealand | 1-2 |
| Solomon Islands v Papua New Guinea | 1-0 |
| Fiji v New Zealand | 0-1 |

**Group B Table**

| | P | W | D | L | F | A | Pts |
|---|---|---|---|---|---|---|---|
| New Zealand | 3 | 2 | 1 | 0 | 4 | 2 | 7 |
| Solomon Islands | 3 | 1 | 2 | 0 | 2 | 1 | 5 |
| Fiji | 3 | 0 | 2 | 1 | 1 | 2 | 2 |
| Papua New Guinea | 3 | 0 | 1 | 2 | 2 | 4 | 1 |

**ROUND 3**

| New Zealand v Tahiti | 3-0 |
|---|---|
| New Caledonia v Solomon Islands | 5-0 |
| Tahiti v New Zealand | 0-2 |
| Solomon Islands v New Caledonia | 2-6 |
| Tahiti v New Caledonia | 0-4 |
| New Zealand v Solomon Islands | 6-1 |
| New Caledonia v New Zealand | 0-2 |
| Solomon Islands v Tahiti | 2-0 |
| New Zealand v New Caledonia | 2-1 |
| Tahiti v Solomon Islands | 2-0 |
| Solomon Islands v New Zealand | 0-2 |
| New Caledonia v Tahiti | 1-0 |

**Round 3 Table**

| | P | W | D | L | F | A | Pts |
|---|---|---|---|---|---|---|---|
| New Zealand | 6 | 6 | 0 | 0 | 17 | 2 | 18 |
| New Caledonia | 6 | 4 | 0 | 2 | 17 | 6 | 12 |
| Tahiti | 6 | 1 | 0 | 5 | 2 | 12 | 3 |
| Solomon Islands | 6 | 1 | 0 | 5 | 5 | 21 | 3 |

*New Zealand qualify for Intercontinental Play-off.*

**INTERCONTINENTAL PLAY-OFF**

*The Intercontinental Play-off is to be played between the fourth-placed team in Concacaf and the winner of Oceania (New Zealand).*

| Concacaf v New Zealand | 15/11/13 |
|---|---|
| New Zealand v Concacaf | 19/11/13 |

# CONCACAF

## ROUND 2

### GROUP A

| | | |
|---|---|---|
| El Salvador v Suriname | | 4-0 |
| Cayman Islands v Dominican Republic | | 1-1 |
| Suriname v El Salvador | | 1-3 |
| Dominican Republic v Cayman Islands | | 4-0 |
| El Salvador v Cayman Islands | | 4-0 |
| Suriname v Dominican Republic | | 1-3 |
| Cayman Islands v Suriname | | 0-1 |
| Dominican Republic v El Salvador | | 1-2 |
| Cayman Islands v El Salvador | | 1-4 |
| Dominican Republic v Suriname | | 1-1 |
| El Salvador v Dominican Republic | | 3-2 |
| Suriname v Cayman Islands | | 1-0 |

| Group A Table | P | W | D | L | F | A | Pts |
|---|---|---|---|---|---|---|---|
| El Salvador | 6 | 6 | 0 | 0 | 20 | 5 | 18 |
| Dominican Republic | 6 | 2 | 2 | 2 | 12 | 8 | 8 |
| Suriname | 6 | 2 | 1 | 3 | 5 | 11 | 7 |
| Cayman Islands | 6 | 0 | 1 | 5 | 2 | 15 | 1 |

### GROUP B

| | | |
|---|---|---|
| Trinidad & Tobago v Guyana | | 3-0 |

*Match awarded 3-0 to Trinidad & Tobago; Guyana fielded an ineligible player. Original result 2-0.*

| | | |
|---|---|---|
| Barbados v Bermuda | | 1-2 |
| Guyana v Trinidad & Tobago | | 2-1 |
| Bermuda v Barbados | | 2-1 |
| Bermuda v Guyana | | 1-1 |
| Trinidad & Tobago v Barbados | | 4-0 |
| Bermuda v Trinidad & Tobago | | 2-1 |
| Barbados v Guyana | | 0-2 |
| Guyana v Bermuda | | 2-1 |
| Barbados v Trinidad & Tobago | | 0-2 |
| Guyana v Barbados | | 2-0 |
| Trinidad & Tobago v Bermuda | | 1-0 |

| Group B Table | P | W | D | L | F | A | Pts |
|---|---|---|---|---|---|---|---|
| Guyana | 6 | 4 | 1 | 1 | 9 | 6 | 13 |
| Trinidad & Tobago | 6 | 4 | 0 | 2 | 12 | 4 | 12 |
| Bermuda | 6 | 3 | 1 | 2 | 8 | 7 | 10 |
| Barbados | 6 | 0 | 0 | 6 | 2 | 14 | 0 |

### GROUP C

| | | |
|---|---|---|
| Panama v Dominica | | 3-0 |
| Nicaragua v Dominica | | 1-0 |
| Panama v Nicaragua | | 5-1 |
| Dominica v Panama | | 0-5 |
| Nicaragua v Panama | | 1-2 |
| Dominica v Nicaragua | | 0-2 |

*Bahamas withdrew.*

| Group C Table | P | W | D | L | F | A | Pts |
|---|---|---|---|---|---|---|---|
| Panama | 4 | 4 | 0 | 0 | 15 | 2 | 12 |
| Nicaragua | 4 | 2 | 0 | 2 | 5 | 7 | 6 |
| Dominica | 4 | 0 | 0 | 4 | 0 | 11 | 0 |

### GROUP D

| | | |
|---|---|---|
| Canada v St Kitts & Nevis | | 4-0 |
| Puerto Rico v St Lucia | | 3-0 |
| St Kitts & Nevis v Canada | | 0-0 |
| St Lucia v Puerto Rico | | 0-4 |

*Match awarded 0-4 to Puerto Rico. Original result 0-4.*

| | | |
|---|---|---|
| St Kitts & Nevis v St Lucia | | 1-1 |
| Canada v Puerto Rico | | 0-0 |
| Puerto Rico v St Kitts & Nevis | | 1-1 |
| St Lucia v Canada | | 0-7 |

*Match awarded 0-7 to Canada. Original result 0-7.*

| | | |
|---|---|---|
| Puerto Rico v Canada | | 0-3 |
| St Lucia v St Kitts & Nevis | | 2-4 |
| Canada v St Lucia | | 4-1 |
| St Kitts & Nevis v Puerto Rico | | 0-0 |

| Group D Table | P | W | D | L | F | A | Pts |
|---|---|---|---|---|---|---|---|
| Canada | 6 | 4 | 2 | 0 | 18 | 1 | 14 |
| Puerto Rico | 6 | 2 | 3 | 1 | 8 | 4 | 9 |
| St Kitts & Nevis | 6 | 1 | 4 | 1 | 6 | 8 | 7 |
| St Lucia | 6 | 0 | 1 | 5 | 4 | 23 | 1 |

### GROUP E

| | | |
|---|---|---|
| St Vincent & the Grenadines v Belize | | 0-2 |
| Grenada v Guatemala | | 1-4 |
| Guatemala v Grenada | | 3-0 |
| Belize v St Vincent & the Grenadines | | 1-1 |
| Grenada v St Vincent & the Grenadines | | 1-1 |
| Guatemala v Belize | | 3-1 |
| Belize v Grenada | | 1-4 |
| St Vincent & the Grenadines v Guatemala | | 0-3 |
| St Vincent & the Grenadines v Grenada | | 2-1 |
| Belize v Guatemala | | 1-2 |
| Guatemala v St Vincent & the Grenadines | | 4-0 |
| Grenada v Belize | | 0-3 |

| Group E Table | P | W | D | L | F | A | Pts |
|---|---|---|---|---|---|---|---|
| Guatemala | 6 | 6 | 0 | 0 | 19 | 3 | 18 |
| Belize | 6 | 2 | 1 | 3 | 9 | 10 | 7 |
| St Vincent & the Grenadines | 6 | 1 | 2 | 3 | 4 | 12 | 5 |
| Grenada | 6 | 1 | 1 | 4 | 7 | 14 | 4 |

### GROUP F

| | | |
|---|---|---|
| Curacao v US Virgin Islands | | 6-1 |
| Haiti v Antigua & Barbuda | | 2-1 |
| Antigua & Barbuda v Haiti | | 1-0 |
| US Virgin Islands v Curacao | | 0-3 |
| Antigua & Barbuda v US Virgin Islands | | 10-0 |
| Haiti v Curacao | | 2-2 |
| Curacao v Antigua & Barbuda | | 0-3 |

*Match awarded 0-3 to Antigua & Barbuda. Original result 0-1.*

| | | |
|---|---|---|
| US Virgin Islands v Haiti | | 0-7 |
| Curacao v Haiti | | 2-4 |
| US Virgin Islands v Antigua & Barbuda | | 1-8 |
| Antigua & Barbuda v Curacao | | 5-2 |
| Haiti v US Virgin Islands | | 6-0 |

| Group F Table | P | W | D | L | F | A | Pts |
|---|---|---|---|---|---|---|---|
| Antigua & Barbuda | 6 | 5 | 0 | 1 | 28 | 5 | 15 |
| Haiti | 6 | 4 | 1 | 1 | 21 | 6 | 13 |
| Curacao | 6 | 2 | 1 | 3 | 15 | 15 | 7 |
| US Virgin Islands | 6 | 0 | 0 | 6 | 2 | 40 | 0 |

## ROUND 3

### GROUP A

| | | |
|---|---|---|
| USA v Guatemala | | 3-1 |
| Jamaica v Antigua & Barbuda | | 4-1 |
| Guatemala v Jamaica | | 2-1 |
| Antigua & Barbuda v USA | | 1-2 |
| USA v Jamaica | | 1-0 |
| Antigua & Barbuda v Guatemala | | 0-1 |
| Guatemala v Antigua & Barbuda | | 3-1 |
| Jamaica v USA | | 2-1 |
| Guatemala v USA | | 1-1 |
| Antigua & Barbuda v Jamaica | | 0-0 |
| Jamaica v Guatemala | | 2-1 |
| USA v Antigua & Barbuda | | 3-1 |

| Group A Table | P | W | D | L | F | A | Pts |
|---|---|---|---|---|---|---|---|
| USA | 6 | 4 | 1 | 1 | 11 | 6 | 13 |
| Jamaica | 6 | 3 | 1 | 2 | 9 | 6 | 10 |
| Guatemala | 6 | 3 | 1 | 2 | 9 | 8 | 10 |
| Antigua & Barbuda | 6 | 0 | 1 | 5 | 4 | 13 | 1 |

### GROUP B

| | | |
|---|---|---|
| Mexico v El Salvador | | 2-0 |
| Costa Rica v Guyana | | 7-0 |
| Guyana v Mexico | | 0-5 |
| El Salvador v Costa Rica | | 0-1 |
| Mexico v Costa Rica | | 1-0 |
| Guyana v El Salvador | | 2-3 |
| Costa Rica v Mexico | | 0-2 |
| El Salvador v Guyana | | 2-2 |
| Guyana v Costa Rica | | 0-4 |
| El Salvador v Mexico | | 1-2 |
| Costa Rica v El Salvador | | 2-2 |
| Mexico v Guyana | | 3-1 |

| Group B Table | P | W | D | L | F | A | Pts |
|---|---|---|---|---|---|---|---|
| Mexico | 6 | 6 | 0 | 0 | 15 | 2 | 18 |
| Costa Rica | 6 | 3 | 1 | 2 | 14 | 5 | 10 |
| El Salvador | 6 | 1 | 2 | 3 | 8 | 11 | 5 |
| Guyana | 6 | 0 | 1 | 5 | 5 | 24 | 1 |

### GROUP C

| | | |
|---|---|---|
| Cuba v Panama | | 1-1 |
| Honduras v Canada | | 8-1 |
| Panama v Honduras | | 0-0 |
| Canada v Cuba | | 3-0 |
| Panama v Canada | | 2-0 |
| Honduras v Cuba | | 1-0 |
| Canada v Panama | | 1-0 |
| Cuba v Honduras | | 0-3 |

| Panama v Cuba | 1-0 |
|---|---|
| Canada v Honduras | 0-0 |
| Honduras v Panama | 0-2 |
| Cuba v Canada | 0-1 |

| Group C Table | P | W | D | L | F | A | Pts |
|---|---|---|---|---|---|---|---|
| Honduras | 6 | 3 | 2 | 1 | 12 | 3 | 11 |
| Panama | 6 | 3 | 2 | 1 | 6 | 2 | 11 |
| Canada | 6 | 3 | 1 | 2 | 6 | 10 | 10 |
| Cuba | 6 | 0 | 1 | 5 | 1 | 10 | 1 |

## ROUND 4

| Panama v Costa Rica | 2-2 |
|---|---|
| Mexico v Jamaica | 0-0 |
| Honduras v USA | 2-1 |
| Honduras v Mexico | 2-2 |
| USA v Costa Rica | 1-0 |
| Jamaica v Panama | 1-1 |
| Costa Rica v Jamaica | 2-0 |
| Mexico v USA | 0-0 |
| Panama v Honduras | 2-0 |
| Jamaica v Mexico | 0-1 |
| Panama v Mexico | 0-0 |
| Jamaica v USA | 1-2 |
| Costa Rica v Honduras | 1-0 |
| Mexico v Costa Rica | 0-0 |
| USA v Panama | 2-0 |
| Honduras v Jamaica | 2-0 |
| USA v Honduras | 1-0 |
| Costa Rica v Panama | 2-0 |

| Round 4 Table | P | W | D | L | F | A | Pts |
|---|---|---|---|---|---|---|---|
| USA | 6 | 4 | 1 | 1 | 7 | 3 | 13 |
| Costa Rica | 6 | 3 | 2 | 1 | 7 | 3 | 11 |
| Mexico | 6 | 1 | 5 | 0 | 3 | 2 | 8 |
| Honduras | 6 | 2 | 1 | 3 | 6 | 7 | 7 |
| Panama | 6 | 1 | 3 | 2 | 5 | 7 | 6 |
| Jamaica | 6 | 0 | 2 | 4 | 2 | 8 | 2 |

### REMAINING FIXTURES

| Mexico v Honduras | 06/09/13 |
|---|---|
| Costa Rica v USA | 06/09/13 |
| Panama v Jamaica | 06/09/13 |
| USA v Mexico | 10/09/13 |
| Honduras v Panama | 10/09/13 |
| Jamaica v Costa Rica | 10/09/13 |
| Mexico v Panama | 11/10/13 |
| Honduras v Costa Rica | 11/10/13 |
| USA v Jamaica | 11/10/13 |
| Jamaica v Honduras | 15/10/13 |
| Costa Rica v Mexico | 15/10/13 |
| Panama v USA | 15/10/13 |

### INTERCONTINENTAL PLAY-OFF

*The Intercontinental Play-off is to be played between the fourth-placed team in Concacaf and the winner of Oceania (New Zealand).*

| Concacaf v New Zealand | 15/11/13 |
|---|---|
| New Zealand v Concacaf | 19/11/13 |

# ASIA

### ROUND 1 – FIRST LEG

| Cambodia v Laos | 4-2 |
|---|---|
| Nepal v Timor-Leste | 2-1 |
| Afghanistan v Palestine | 0-2 |
| Sri Lanka v Philippines | 1-1 |
| Bangladesh v Pakistan | 3-0 |
| Mongolia v Myanmar | 1-0 |
| Vietnam v Macau | 6-0 |
| Malaysia v Chinese Taipei | 2-1 |

### ROUND 1 – SECOND LEG

| Laos v Cambodia | 6-2 |
|---|---|
| Timor-Leste v Nepal | 0-5 |
| Palestine v Afghanistan | 1-1 |
| Philippines v Sri Lanka | 4-0 |
| Pakistan v Bangladesh | 0-0 |
| Myanmar v Mongolia | 2-0 |
| Macau v Vietnam | 1-7 |
| Chinese Taipei v Malaysia | 3-2 |
| *Malaysia won on away goals rule.* | |

### ROUND 2 – FIRST LEG

| China PR v Laos | 7-2 |
|---|---|
| Lebanon v Bangladesh | 4-0 |
| Thailand v Palestine | 1-0 |
| Turkmenistan v Indonesia | 1-1 |
| Iraq v Yemen | 2-0 |
| Syria v Tajikistan | 0-3 |
| *Match awarded 0-3 to Tajikistan. Syria fielded an ineligible player. Original result 2-1.* | |
| Uzbekistan v Kyrgyzstan | 4-0 |
| Jordan v Nepal | 9-0 |
| Qatar v Vietnam | 3-0 |
| Singapore v Malaysia | 5-3 |
| Kuwait v Philippines | 3-0 |
| Iran v Maldives | 4-0 |
| Oman v Myanmar | 2-0 |
| *Match abandoned, awarded to Oman.* | |
| United Arab Emirates v India | 3-0 |
| Saudi Arabia v Hong Kong | 3-0 |

### ROUND 2 – SECOND LEG

| Laos v China PR | 1-6 |
|---|---|
| Bangladesh v Lebanon | 2-0 |
| Palestine v Thailand | 2-2 |
| Indonesia v Turkmenistan | 4-3 |
| Yemen v Iraq | 0-0 |
| Tajikistan v Syria | 3-0 |
| *Match awarded 3-0 to Tajikistan. Syria fielded an ineligible player. Original result 0-4.* | |
| Kyrgyzstan v Uzbekistan | 0-3 |
| Nepal v Jordan | 1-1 |
| Vietnam v Qatar | 2-1 |
| Malaysia v Singapore | 1-1 |

| Philippines v Kuwait | 1-2 |
|---|---|
| Maldives v Iran | 0-1 |
| Myanmar v Oman | 0-2 |
| India v United Arab Emirates | 2-2 |
| Hong Kong v Saudi Arabia | 0-5 |

### ROUND 3

#### GROUP A

| Iraq v Singapore | 7-1 |
|---|---|
| China PR v Jordan | 3-1 |
| Singapore v China PR | 0-4 |
| Jordan v Iraq | 1-3 |
| Jordan v Singapore | 2-0 |
| Iraq v China PR | 1-0 |
| China PR v Iraq | 0-1 |
| Singapore v Jordan | 0-3 |
| Singapore v Iraq | 0-2 |
| Jordan v China PR | 2-1 |
| China PR v Singapore | 2-1 |
| Iraq v Jordan | 0-2 |

| Group A Table | P | W | D | L | F | A | Pts |
|---|---|---|---|---|---|---|---|
| Iraq | 6 | 5 | 0 | 1 | 14 | 4 | 15 |
| Jordan | 6 | 4 | 0 | 2 | 11 | 7 | 12 |
| China PR | 6 | 3 | 0 | 3 | 10 | 6 | 9 |
| Singapore | 6 | 0 | 0 | 6 | 2 | 20 | 0 |

#### GROUP B

| Korea Republic v Kuwait | 2-0 |
|---|---|
| United Arab Emirates v Lebanon | 4-2 |
| Kuwait v United Arab Emirates | 2-1 |
| Lebanon v Korea Republic | 2-1 |
| Kuwait v Lebanon | 0-1 |
| United Arab Emirates v Korea Republic | 0-2 |
| Korea Republic v United Arab Emirates | 2-1 |
| Lebanon v Kuwait | 2-2 |
| Kuwait v Korea Republic | 1-1 |
| Lebanon v United Arab Emirates | 3-1 |
| Korea Republic v Lebanon | 6-0 |
| United Arab Emirates v Kuwait | 2-3 |

| Group B Table | P | W | D | L | F | A | Pts |
|---|---|---|---|---|---|---|---|
| Korea Republic | 6 | 4 | 1 | 1 | 14 | 4 | 13 |
| Lebanon | 6 | 3 | 1 | 2 | 10 | 14 | 10 |
| Kuwait | 6 | 2 | 2 | 2 | 8 | 9 | 8 |
| United Arab Emirates | 6 | 1 | 0 | 5 | 9 | 14 | 3 |

#### GROUP C

| Japan v Uzbekistan | 0-1 |
|---|---|
| Tajikistan v Korea DPR | 1-1 |
| Uzbekistan v Tajikistan | 3-0 |
| Korea DPR v Japan | 1-0 |
| Uzbekistan v Korea DPR | 1-0 |
| Tajikistan v Japan | 0-4 |

| | |
|---|---|
| Japan v Tajikistan | 8-0 |
| Korea DPR v Uzbekistan | 0-1 |
| Uzbekistan v Japan | 1-1 |
| Korea DPR v Tajikistan | 1-0 |
| Japan v Korea DPR | 1-0 |
| Tajikistan v Uzbekistan | 0-1 |

| Group C Table | P | W | D | L | F | A | Pts |
|---|---|---|---|---|---|---|---|
| Uzbekistan | 6 | 5 | 1 | 0 | 8 | 1 | 16 |
| Japan | 6 | 3 | 1 | 2 | 14 | 3 | 10 |
| Korea DPR | 6 | 2 | 1 | 3 | 3 | 4 | 7 |
| Tajikistan | 6 | 0 | 1 | 5 | 1 | 18 | 1 |

**GROUP D**

| | |
|---|---|
| Australia v Saudi Arabia | 4-2 |
| Oman v Thailand | 2-0 |
| Saudi Arabia v Oman | 0-0 |
| Thailand v Australia | 0-1 |
| Saudi Arabia v Thailand | 3-0 |
| Oman v Australia | 1-0 |
| Australia v Oman | 3-0 |
| Thailand v Saudi Arabia | 0-0 |
| Saudi Arabia v Australia | 1-3 |
| Thailand v Oman | 3-0 |
| Australia v Thailand | 2-1 |
| Oman v Saudi Arabia | 0-0 |

| Group D Table | P | W | D | L | F | A | Pts |
|---|---|---|---|---|---|---|---|
| Australia | 6 | 5 | 0 | 1 | 13 | 5 | 15 |
| Oman | 6 | 2 | 2 | 2 | 3 | 6 | 8 |
| Saudi Arabia | 6 | 1 | 3 | 2 | 6 | 7 | 6 |
| Thailand | 6 | 1 | 1 | 4 | 4 | 8 | 4 |

**GROUP E**

| | |
|---|---|
| Iran v Qatar | 2-2 |
| Bahrain v Indonesia | 10-0 |
| Indonesia v Iran | 1-4 |
| Qatar v Bahrain | 0-0 |
| Qatar v Indonesia | 4-0 |
| Bahrain v Iran | 1-1 |
| Iran v Bahrain | 6-0 |
| Indonesia v Qatar | 2-3 |
| Qatar v Iran | 1-1 |
| Indonesia v Bahrain | 0-2 |
| Bahrain v Qatar | 0-0 |
| Iran v Indonesia | 3-0 |

| Group E Table | P | W | D | L | F | A | Pts |
|---|---|---|---|---|---|---|---|
| Iran | 6 | 3 | 3 | 0 | 17 | 5 | 12 |
| Qatar | 6 | 2 | 4 | 0 | 10 | 5 | 10 |
| Bahrain | 6 | 2 | 3 | 1 | 13 | 7 | 9 |
| Indonesia | 6 | 0 | 0 | 6 | 3 | 26 | 0 |

**ROUND 4**

**GROUP A**

| | |
|---|---|
| Iran v Uzbekistan | 0-1 |
| Qatar v Lebanon | 1-0 |
| Iran v Korea Republic | 1-0 |
| Qatar v Uzbekistan | 0-1 |
| Uzbekistan v Korea Republic | 2-2 |
| Lebanon v Iran | 1-0 |
| Korea Republic v Lebanon | 3-0 |

| | |
|---|---|
| Iran v Qatar | 0-0 |
| Qatar v Korea Republic | 1-4 |
| Lebanon v Uzbekistan | 0-1 |
| Lebanon v Qatar | 0-1 |
| Uzbekistan v Iran | 0-1 |
| Uzbekistan v Lebanon | 1-0 |
| Korea Republic v Qatar | 2-1 |
| Qatar v Iran | 0-1 |
| Lebanon v Korea Republic | 1-1 |
| Iran v Lebanon | 4-0 |
| Korea Republic v Uzbekistan | 1-0 |
| Korea Republic v Iran | 0-1 |
| Uzbekistan v Qatar | 5-1 |

| Group A Table | P | W | D | L | F | A | Pts |
|---|---|---|---|---|---|---|---|
| Iran | 8 | 5 | 1 | 2 | 8 | 2 | 16 |
| Korea Republic | 8 | 4 | 2 | 2 | 13 | 7 | 14 |
| Uzbekistan | 8 | 4 | 2 | 2 | 11 | 6 | 14 |
| Qatar | 8 | 2 | 1 | 5 | 5 | 13 | 7 |
| Lebanon | 8 | 1 | 2 | 5 | 3 | 12 | 5 |

**GROUP B**

| | |
|---|---|
| Iraq v Jordan | 1-0 |
| Oman v Japan | 1-2 |
| Iraq v Australia | 1-2 |
| Oman v Jordan | 2-1 |
| Japan v Iraq | 1-0 |
| Jordan v Australia | 2-1 |
| Australia v Japan | 1-1 |
| Iraq v Oman | 1-1 |
| Japan v Jordan | 6-0 |
| Oman v Australia | 0-0 |
| Japan v Oman | 3-0 |
| Jordan v Iraq | 1-1 |
| Jordan v Japan | 2-1 |
| Australia v Oman | 2-2 |
| Japan v Australia | 1-1 |
| Oman v Iraq | 1-0 |
| Iraq v Japan | 0-1 |
| Australia v Jordan | 4-0 |
| Australia v Iraq | 1-0 |
| Jordan v Oman | 1-0 |

| Group B Table | P | W | D | L | F | A | Pts |
|---|---|---|---|---|---|---|---|
| Japan | 8 | 5 | 2 | 1 | 16 | 5 | 17 |
| Australia | 8 | 3 | 4 | 1 | 12 | 7 | 13 |
| Jordan | 8 | 3 | 1 | 4 | 7 | 16 | 10 |
| Oman | 8 | 2 | 3 | 3 | 7 | 10 | 9 |
| Iraq | 8 | 1 | 2 | 5 | 4 | 8 | 5 |

**ROUND 5 – CONTINENTAL PLAY-OFF**
*The two third-placed teams from Group A and Group B of Round 4 contest the Continental Play-off in September 2013.*

**INTERCONTINENTAL PLAY-OFF**
*The Intercontinental Play-off is to be played between the Round 5 winner from Asia and the fifth-placed team in South America.*

| | |
|---|---|
| Asia v South America | 15/11/13 |
| South America v Asia | 19/11/13 |

# FIFA CONFEDERATIONS CUP – BRAZIL 2013

**GROUP A**

| | | | |
|---|---|---|---|
| Brazil v Japan | 3-0 | Italy v Japan | 4-3 |
| Mexico v Italy | 1-2 | Italy v Brazil | 2-4 |
| Brazil v Mexico | 2-0 | Japan v Mexico | 1-2 |

| Group A Table | P | W | D | L | F | A | Pts |
|---|---|---|---|---|---|---|---|
| Brazil | 3 | 3 | 0 | 0 | 9 | 2 | 9 |
| Italy | 3 | 2 | 0 | 1 | 8 | 6 | 6 |
| Mexico | 3 | 1 | 0 | 2 | 3 | 5 | 3 |
| Japan | 3 | 0 | 0 | 3 | 4 | 9 | 0 |

**GROUP B**

| | | | |
|---|---|---|---|
| Spain v Uruguay | 2-1 | Nigeria v Uruguay | 1-2 |
| Tahiti v Nigeria | 1-6 | Nigeria v Spain | 0-3 |
| Spain v Tahiti | 10-0 | Uruguay v Tahiti | 8-0 |

| Group B Table | P | W | D | L | F | A | Pts |
|---|---|---|---|---|---|---|---|
| Spain | 3 | 3 | 0 | 0 | 15 | 1 | 9 |
| Uruguay | 3 | 2 | 0 | 1 | 3 | 6 | 6 |
| Nigeria | 3 | 1 | 0 | 2 | 7 | 6 | 3 |
| Tahiti | 3 | 0 | 0 | 3 | 1 | 24 | 0 |

**SEMI FINALS**

| | |
|---|---|
| Brazil v Uruguay | 2-1 |
| Spain v Italy | 0-0 |

*aet; Spain won 7-6 on penalties.*

**3RD/4TH PLACE PLAY OFF**

| | |
|---|---|
| Uruguay v Italy | 2-2 |

*aet; Italy won 3-2 on penalties.*

**FINAL**

Sunday, 30 June 2013

**Brazil (2) 3** *(Fred 2, 47, Neymar 44)*

**Spain (0) 0**                                        78,000

*Brazil:* Cesar; Alves, Thiago Silva, Luiz, Marcelo, Paulinho (Hernanes 88), Gustavo, Oscar, Hulk (Jadson 73), Neymar, Fred (Jo 80).
*Spain:* Casillas, Arbeloa (Azpilicueta 46), Pique■, Ramos, Alba, Busquets, Xavi, Iniesta, Pedro, Torres (Villa 59), Mata (Navas 52).

# MEN'S OLYMPIC FOOTBALL 2012

■ *Denotes player sent off.*

## GROUP A

Old Trafford, Thursday 26 July 2012
**United Arab Emirates (1) 1** *(Matar 23)*
**Uruguay (1) 2** *(Ramirez 42, Lodeiro 46)*    51,745
*United Arab Emirates:* Khaseif; Khalil, Al-Kamali, Ahmad, Hussain, Sanqour, Eisa R (Ali 73), Esmaeel, Abdulrahman O, Abdulrahman A, Matar (Al Hammadi 60).
*Uruguay:* Campana; Arias, Coates, Rolin, Aguirregaray (Lodeiro 46), Albin, Arevalo, Ramirez (Urretaviscaya 81), Calzada (Rodriguez 70), Cavani, Suarez.
*Referee:* Peter O'Leary (New Zealand).

Old Trafford, Thursday 26 July 2012
**Great Britain (1) 1** *(Bellamy 20)*
**Senegal (0) 1** *(Konate 82)*    72,176
*Great Britain:* Butland; Richards, Caulker, Taylor, Bertrand, Cleverley, Allen (Ramsey 63), Giggs, Bellamy (Cork 80), Sturridge (Sordell 46), Rose.
*Senegal:* Mane O; Souare (Yero 88), Ciss, Ba, Gueye P, Toure, Konate, Mane S, Diame, Gueye I (Kouyate 42), Balde (Gueye M 65).
*Referee:* Ravshan Irmatov (Uzbekistan).

Wembley, Sunday 29 July 2012
**Senegal (2) 2** *(Konate 10, 37)*
**Uruguay (0) 0**    75,093
*Senegal:* Mane O; Souare, Ciss, Ba■, Gueye P, Toure (Mbodji 66), Konate, Mane S, Diame, Kouyate, Badji (Yero 83).
*Uruguay:* Campana; Arias, Coates, Rolin, Albin (Urretaviscaya 72), Lodeiro (Viudez 75), Gelpi, Ramirez, Calzada (Hernandez 46), Cavani, Suarez.
*Referee:* Felix Brych (Germany).

Wembley, Sunday 29 July 2012
**Great Britain (1) 3** *(Giggs 16, Sinclair 73, Sturridge 76)*
**United Arab Emirates (0) 1** *(Eisa 60)*    85,137
*Great Britain:* Butland; Taylor, Caulker, Tomkins, Richards, Cleverley, Allen, Giggs (Sinclair 72), Ramsey, Sordell (Sturridge 46), Bellamy (Cork 83).
*United Arab Emirates:* Khaseif; Hussain (Surour 51), Ahmad, Khalil, Al-Kamali, Esmaeel (Fardan 79), Abdulrahman O, Sanqour, Abdulrahman A, Eisa R, Matar (Ali 72).
*Referee:* Roberto García (Mexico).

City of Coventry Stadium, Wednesday 1 August 2012
**Senegal (0) 1** *(Konate 49)*
**United Arab Emirates (1) 1** *(Matar 21)*    28,652
*Senegal:* Mane O; Mbodji, Souare, Toure, Gueye P, Badji, Mane S (Yero 83), Kouyate, Diame, Gueye M (Balde 46), Konate (Seck 90).
*United Arab Emirates:* Eisa K; Sanqour, Khalil (Al Hammadi 60), Al-Kamali, Ahmad, Fawzi, Eisa R (Mabkhoot 65), Abdulrahman O, Esmaeel, Abdulrahman A, Matar (Fardan 89).
*Referee:* Svein Oddvar Moen (Norway).

Millennium Stadium, Wednesday 1 August 2012
**Great Britain (1) 1** *(Sturridge 45)*
**Uruguay (0) 0**    70,438
*Great Britain:* Butland; Richards, Taylor, Caulker, Bertrand, Cleverley, Allen, Ramsey, Sinclair (Cork 90), Bellamy (Rose 78), Sturridge (Dawson 90).
*Uruguay:* Campana; Arias, Coates, Rolin, Aguirregaray, Ramirez, Rodriguez, Viudez (Lodeiro 58), Arevalo, Suarez, Cavani.
*Referee:* Yuichi Nishimura (Japan).

| Group A Table | P | W | D | L | F | A | Pts |
|---|---|---|---|---|---|---|---|
| Great Britain | 3 | 2 | 1 | 0 | 5 | 2 | 7 |
| Senegal | 3 | 1 | 2 | 0 | 4 | 2 | 5 |
| Uruguay | 3 | 1 | 0 | 2 | 2 | 4 | 3 |
| United Arab Emirates | 3 | 0 | 1 | 2 | 3 | 6 | 1 |

## GROUP B

St James' Park, Thursday 26 July 2012
**Mexico (0) 0**
**South Korea (0) 0**    15,748
*Mexico:* Corona; Vidrio, Reyes, Chavez, Mier, Salcido, Ponce, Aquino, Herrera (Enriquez 71), Fabian (Jimenez R 85), Peralta (Dos Santos 66).
*South Korea:* Jung S; Kim C, Hwang, Kim Y, Yun, Koo, Nam (Ji 87), Kim B, Ki, Park J, Park C (Baek 76).
*Referee:* Slim Jedidi (Tunisia).

St James' Park, Thursday 26 July 2012
**Gabon (1) 1** *(Aubameyang 45)*
**Switzerland (1) 1** *(Mehmedi 5 (pen))*    15,758
*Gabon:* Ovono; Ndoumbou, Engonga, Ndong H, Dinda, Obiang, Boussoughou, Tandjigora, Madinda, Aubameyang, Nono (Meye 74).
*Switzerland:* Benaglio; Morganella, Schaer, Klose, Rodriguez, Frei, Buff■, Hochstrasser, Zuber (Kasami 68), Mehmedi, Emeghara (Abrashi 84).
*Referee:* Wilmar Roldán (Colombia).

City of Coventry Stadium, Sunday 29 July 2012
**Mexico (0) 2** *(Dos Santos 63, 90 (pen))*
**Gabon (0) 0**    28,171
*Mexico:* Corona; Salcido, Mier, Chavez, Reyes, Vidrio, Herrera (Enriquez 48), Aquino, Ponce (Dos Santos 46), Fabian (Cortes 76), Peralta.
*Gabon:* Ovono; Dinda (Nzambe 85), Ndoumbou (Nono 70), Engonga, Ndong H■, Tandjigora, Boussoughou, Madinda, Obiang (Mbingui 83), Meye, Aubameyang.
*Referee:* Ben Williams (Australia).

City of Coventry Stadium, Sunday 29 July 2012
**South Korea (0) 2** *(Park C 57, Kim B 64)*
**Switzerland (0) 1** *(Emeghara 60)*    30,114
*South Korea:* Jung S; Kim C, Hwang, Kim Y, Yun, Koo, Nam (Baek 61), Kim B, Ki, Park J, Park C (Ji 73).
*Switzerland:* Benaglio; Morganella, Schaer, Klose, Rodriguez, Abrashi, Kasami (Wiss 85), Frei, Zuber (Drmic 71), Mehmedi, Emeghara.
*Referee:* Raúl Orosco (Bolivia).

Millennium Stadium, Wednesday 1 August 2012
**Mexico (0) 1** *(Peralta 69)*
**Switzerland (0) 0**    50,000
*Mexico:* Corona; Vidrio (Jimenez I 46), Reyes, Chavez, Mier, Salcido, Enriquez, Aquino, Dos Santos (Jimenez R 84), Fabian (Ponce 79), Peralta.
*Switzerland:* Benaglio; Daprela, Affolter, Klose, Rodriguez, Abrashi (Wiss 76), Kasami (Hochstrasser 85), Frei, Zuber (Drmic 61), Mehmedi, Emeghara.
*Referee:* Ravshan Irmatov (Uzbekistan).

Wembley, Wednesday 1 August 2012
**South Korea (0) 0**
**Gabon (0) 0**    76,927
*South Korea:* Jung S; Hwang, Yun, Kim Y, Kim C, Kim B (Ji 61), Ki, Baek, Koo, Park J (Nam 46), Park C (Kim H 80).
*Gabon:* Ovono; Dinda, Nzambe, Ndong E, Tandjigora (Ndoumbou 10), Boussoughou, Engonga, Madinda (Mbingui 66), Obiang, Aubameyang, Meye (Nono 76).
*Referee:* Pavel Královec (Czech Republic).

| Group B Table | P | W | D | L | F | A | Pts |
|---|---|---|---|---|---|---|---|
| Mexico | 3 | 2 | 1 | 0 | 3 | 0 | 7 |
| South Korea | 3 | 1 | 2 | 0 | 2 | 1 | 5 |
| Gabon | 3 | 0 | 2 | 1 | 1 | 3 | 2 |
| Switzerland | 3 | 0 | 1 | 2 | 2 | 4 | 1 |

## GROUP C

City of Coventry Stadium, Thursday 26 July 2012

**Belarus (1) 1** *(Baga 45)*

**New Zealand (0) 0**                                    14,457

*Belarus:* Gutor; Gordeichuk, Kuzmenok, Politevich, Polyakov, Baga, Dragun, Kozlov, Solovei (Aleksievich 54), Kornilenko (Zubovich 90), Bardini Bressan (Voronkov 81).
*New Zealand:* O'Keeffe; Thomas (McGeorge 77), Nelsen, Smith, Hogg, McGlinchey, Rojas (Howieson 73), Barbarouses, Payne, Wood, Smeltz.
*Referee:* Bakary Gassama (Gambia).

Millennium Stadium, Thursday 26 July 2012

**Brazil (3) 3** *(Rafael 16, Damiao 26, Neymar 30)*

**Egypt (0) 2** *(Aboutrika 52, Salah 76)*               26,812

*Brazil:* Neto; Marcelo, Rafael, Silva, Juan Jesus, Sandro (Danilo 78), Rômulo, Oscar, Neymar, Damiao (Pato 77), Hulk (Ganso 72).
*Egypt:* El Shenawi; Alaa, Ramadan, Hegazi, Fathi, El Neny (Magdy 89), Aboutrika, Gomaa (Ahmed 74), Hassan, Meteab, Mohsen (Salah 46).
*Referee:* Gianluca Rocchi (Italy).

Old Trafford, Sunday 29 July 2012

**Egypt (1) 1** *(Salah 40)*

**New Zealand (1) 1** *(Wood 17)*                        50,050

*Egypt:* El Shenawi; Alaa, Ramadan, Hegazi, Fathi, El Neny (Magdy 68), Aboutrika (Mohsen 88), Gomaa (Ahmed 88), Hassan, Meteab, Salah.
*New Zealand:* O'Keeffe; Thomas (Feneridis 89), Nelsen, Smith, Hogg (Musa 63), McGlinchey, Rojas (Howieson 84), Barbarouses, Payne, Wood, Smeltz.
*Referee:* Mark Clattenburg (Great Britain).

Old Trafford, Sunday 29 July 2012

**Brazil (1) 3** *(Pato 15, Neymar 65, Oscar 90)*

**Belarus (1) 1** *(Bardini Bressan 8)*                  66,212

*Brazil:* Neto; Marcelo, Rafael, Silva, Juan Jesus, Sandro (Ganso 64), Rômulo, Oscar, Neymar, Pato (Lucas 85), Hulk (Danilo 86).
*Belarus:* Gutor; Gordeichuk, Kuzmenok, Politevich, Polyakov, Baga, Dragun, Kozlov (Gavrilovich 80), Aleksievich (Voronkov 70), Kornilenko (Zubovich 78), Bardini Bressan.
*Referee:* Yuichi Nishimura (Japan).

St James' Park, Wednesday 1 August 2012

**Brazil (2) 3** *(Danilo 23, Damiao 29, Sandro 52)*

**New Zealand (0) 0**                                    25,201

*Brazil:* Gabriel; Rafael, Silva, Juan Jesus, Marcelo, Sandro (Rômulo 82), Neto, Neto, Lucas, Damiao (Oscar 80), Neymar (Pato 76).
*New Zealand:* O'Keeffe; Thomas (Myers 46), Nelsen, Smith, Hogg, Barbarouses (Howieson 46), McGlinchey, Payne, Rojas (Lucas 82), Wood, Smeltz.
*Referee:* Bakary Gassama (Gambia).

Hampden Park, Wednesday 1 August 2012

**Egypt (0) 3** *(Salah 56, Mohsen 73, Aboutrika 79)*

**Belarus (0) 1** *(Voronkov 87)*                        8,732

*Egypt:* El Shenawi; Saad, Ramadan, Hegazi, Fathi (Gaber 90), El Neny, Hassan, Ahmed (Mohsen 46), Aboutrika, Meteab (Gomaa 77), Salah.
*Belarus:* Gutor; Polyakov, Kozlov (Voronkov 69), Politevich, Kuzmenok, Gordeichuk (Solovei 60), Aleksievich, Bardini Bressan (Skavysh 75), Baga, Dragun, Kornilenko.
*Referee:* Roberto García (Mexico).

| Group C Table | P | W | D | L | F | A | Pts |
|---|---|---|---|---|---|---|---|
| Brazil | 3 | 3 | 0 | 0 | 9 | 3 | 9 |
| Egypt | 3 | 1 | 1 | 1 | 6 | 5 | 4 |
| Belarus | 3 | 1 | 0 | 2 | 3 | 6 | 3 |
| New Zealand | 3 | 0 | 1 | 2 | 1 | 5 | 1 |

## GROUP D

Hampden Park, Thursday 26 July 2012

**Honduras (0) 2** *(Bengtson 56, 65 (pen))*

**Morocco (1) 2** *(Barrada 39, Labyad 67)*             23,421

*Honduras:* Mendoza; Leveron, Velasquez, Figueroa, Martinez (Peralta O 88), Lopez, Mejia, Peralta A, Espinoza (Lopez 87), Bengtson (Lozano 79), Najar.
*Morocco:* Amsif; Abarhoun, El Kaoutari, Bergdich■, Jebbour, Kharja, Barrada (Najah 89), Fettouhi, Amrabat (El Kaddouri 70), Bidaoui (Noussir 75), Labyad.
*Referee:* Pavel Královec (Czech Republic).

Hampden Park, Thursday 26 July 2012

**Spain (0) 0**

**Japan (1) 1** *(Otsu 34)*                              37,726

*Spain:* De Gea; Montoya, Alba, Dominguez, Isco (Romeu 63), Koke (Tello 81), Martinez I■, Martinez J, Mata, Moreno, López (Herrera 56).
*Japan:* Gonda; Suzuki, Yoshida, Sakai H (Sakai G 74), Tokunaga, Kiyotake, Yamaguchi, Higashi, Ohgihara (Yamamura 86), Nagai, Otsu (Saito 46).
*Referee:* Mark Geiger (United States).

St James' Park, Sunday 29 July 2012

**Japan (0) 1** *(Nagai 84)*

**Morocco (0) 0**                                        24,936

*Japan:* Gonda; Sakai G, Yoshida, Suzuki, Tokunaga, Kiyotake (Sugimoto 90), Yamaguchi, Ohgihara, Higashi, Otsu (Saito 78), Nagai.
*Morocco:* Amsif; Jebbour, Abarhoun, El Kaoutari, Noussir, Barrada, Fettouhi (El Hassnaoui 88), Kharja, Amrabat (Najah 72), Bidaoui (El Kaddouri 74), Labyad.
*Referee:* Svein Oddvar Moen (Norway).

St James' Park, Sunday 29 July 2012

**Spain (0) 0**

**Honduras (1) 1** *(Bengtson 7)*                        26,523

*Spain:* De Gea; Montoya, Botia, Dominguez, Alba, Isco (Moreno 66), Martinez J (Tello 83), Koke (Herrera 46), Muniain, Mata, López.
*Honduras:* Mendoza; Peralta A, Figueroa, Leveron, Velasquez, Najar (Mejia 57), Martinez, Espinoza (Peralta O 72), Garrido, Crisanto, Bengtson (Lozano 81).
*Referee:* Juan Soto (Venezuela).

City of Coventry Stadium, Wednesday 1 August 2012

**Japan (0) 0**

**Honduras (0) 0**                                       25,862

*Japan:* Gonda; Suzuki, Yoshida, Sakai G, Yamamura, Yamaguchi, Muramatsu, Usami, Saito (Nagai 81), Sugimoto (Kiyotake 67), Otsu (Higashi 87).
*Honduras:* Mendoza; Velasquez, Figueroa, Crisanto, Leveron, Garrido, Najar (Lopez 60), Mejia, Martinez, Lozano (Peralta O 77), Bengtson.
*Referee:* Slim Jedidi (Tunisia).

Old Trafford, Wednesday 1 August 2012

**Spain (0) 0**

**Morocco (0) 0**                                        35,973

*Spain:* De Gea; Botia, Alba, Azpilicueta, Isco (Tello 56), Romeu, Muniain (Koke 66), Martinez I, Martinez J (Herrera 46), Mata, López.
*Morocco:* Amsif; Jebbour, Feddal, Abarhoun, Noussir, Kharja, Barrada, Fettouhi, Bidaoui (El Hassnaoui 70), Amrabat, Labyad.
*Referee:* Ben Williams (Australia).

| Group D Table | P | W | D | L | F | A | Pts |
|---|---|---|---|---|---|---|---|
| Japan | 3 | 2 | 1 | 0 | 2 | 0 | 7 |
| Honduras | 3 | 1 | 2 | 0 | 3 | 2 | 5 |
| Morocco | 3 | 0 | 2 | 1 | 2 | 3 | 2 |
| Spain | 3 | 0 | 1 | 2 | 0 | 2 | 1 |

## QUARTER-FINALS

Millennium Stadium, Saturday 4 August 2012
**Great Britain (1) 1** *(Ramsey 36 (pen))*
**South Korea (1) 1** *(Ji 29)* 70,171
*Great Britain:* Butland; Richards, Taylor, Caulker, Bertrand, Cleverley, Allen, Ramsey, Sinclair (Cork 90), Bellamy (Rose 78), Sturridge (Dawson 90).
*South Korea:* Lee; Yun, Kim Y, Hwang, Kim C (Oh 3), Ki, Ji (Baek 13), Nam, Koo, Park J, Park C.
*aet; South Korea won 5-4 on penalties.*
*Referee:* Wilmar Roldán (Colombia).

St James' Park, Saturday 4 August 2012
**Brazil (1) 3** *(Damiao 38, 60, Neymar 51 (pen))*
**Honduras (1) 2** *(Martinez 12, Espinoza 48)* 42,166
*Brazil:* Gabriel; Rafael, Silva, Juan Jesus, Marcelo, Sandro (Danilo 42), Oscar, Rômulo, Neymar, Damiao (Pato 89), Hulk (Lucas 67).
*Honduras:* Mendoza; Crisanto▪, Figueroa, Velasquez, Leveron, Peralta A, Martinez, Peralta O (Mejia 59), Espinoza▪, Garrido (Lopez 73), Bengtson (Lozano 87).
*Referee:* Felix Brych (Germany).

Wembley, Saturday 4 August 2012
**Mexico (1) 4** *(Enriquez 10, Aquino 62, Dos Santos 98, Herrera 109)*
**Senegal (0) 2** *(Konate 69, Balde 76)* 81,855
*Mexico:* Corona; Jimenez I, Mier, Chavez, Salcido, Enriquez, Fabian (Ponce 100), Reyes, Aquino (Herrera 75), Peralta (Jimenez R 107), Dos Santos.
*Senegal:* Mane O; Ciss (Gueye M 69), Ba, Gueye P, Toure, Diame (Mbodji 90), Kouyate, Souare, Konate, Mane S, Yero (Balde 60).
*aet.*
*Referee:* Mark Clattenburg (Great Britain).

Old Trafford, Saturday 4 August 2012
**Japan (1) 3** *(Nagai 14, Yoshida 78, Otsu 83)*
**Egypt (0) 0** 70,772
*Japan:* Gonda; Suzuki, Yoshida, Sakai H, Tokunaga, Kiyotake (Usami 84), Yamaguchi, Higashi (Sakai G 72), Ohgihara, Nagai (Saito 20), Otsu.
*Egypt:* El Shenawi; Saad▪, Ramadan, Hegazi, Fathi, El Neny, Aboutrika, Ahmed (Alaa 45), Hassan, Meteab (Mohsen 74), Salah (Gaber 58).
*Referee:* Mark Geiger (United States).

## SEMI-FINALS

Old Trafford, Tuesday 7 August 2012
**South Korea (0) 0**
**Brazil (1) 3** *(Romulo 38, Damiao 57, 64)* 69,772
*South Korea:* Lee; Hwang, Kim Y, Oh, Yun, Nam, Koo (Jung W 59), Ki, Kim B, Ji (Baek 77), Kim H (Park C 71).
*Brazil:* Gabriel; Rafael, Silva, Juan Jesus (Uvini 83), Marcelo (Hulk 76), Sandro A, Oscar, Rômulo, Sandro, Neymar, Damiao (Pato 78).
*Referee:* Pavel Královec (Czech Republic).

Wembley, Tuesday 7 August 2012
**Mexico (1) 3** *(Fabian 31, Peralta 65, Cortes 90)*
**Japan (1) 1** *(Otsu 12)* 82,372
*Mexico:* Corona; Jimenez I, Mier, Chavez, Reyes, Salcido, Aquino (Cortes 90), Dos Santos (Jimenez R 46), Enriquez, Fabian, Peralta.
*Japan:* Gonda; Higashi (Sugimoto 71), Ohgihara (Saito 83), Sakai H, Suzuki, Tokunaga, Yoshida, Otsu, Kiyotake (Usami 77), Yamaguchi, Nagai.
*Referee:* Gianluca Rocchi (Italy).

## BRONZE MEDAL MATCH

Millennium Stadium, Friday 10 August 2012
**South Korea (1) 2** *(Park C 38, Koo 57)*
**Japan (0) 0** 56,393
*South Korea:* Jung S; Hwang, Kim Y, Yun, Oh, Koo (Kim K 90), Ji (Nam 69), Kim B, Ki, Park J, Park C (Kim H 86).
*Japan:* Gonda; Suzuki, Yoshida, Sakai H, Tokunaga, Kiyotake, Yamaguchi, Higashi (Sugimoto 62), Ohgihara (Yamamura 59), Nagai (Usami 71), Otsu.
*Referee:* Ravshan Irmatov (Uzbekistan).

## GOLD MEDAL MATCH

Wembley, Saturday 11 August 2012
**Brazil (0) 1** *(Hulk 90)*
**Mexico (1) 2** *(Peralta 1, 75)* 86,162
*Brazil:* Gabriel; Rafael (Lucas 85), Silva, Juan Jesus, Marcelo, Sandro A (Hulk 32), Oscar, Rômulo, Sandro (Pato 71), Neymar, Damiao.
*Mexico:* Corona; Jimenez I (Vidrio 81), Mier, Chavez, Reyes, Salcido, Aquino (Ponce 57), Herrera, Enriquez, Fabian, Peralta (Jimenez R 86).
*Referee:* Mark Clattenburg (Great Britain).

# OLYMPIC FOOTBALL PAST MEDALLISTS

\* No official tournament. \*\* No official tournament but gold medal later awarded by IOC.

**1896 Athens\***
1 Denmark
2 Greece

**1900 Paris\***
1 Great Britain
2 France

**1904 St Louis\*\***
1 Canada
2 USA

**1908 London**
1 Great Britain
2 Denmark
3 Holland

**1912 Stockholm**
1 England
2 Denmark
3 Holland

**1920 Antwerp**
1 Belgium
2 Spain
3 Holland

**1924 Paris**
1 Uruguay
2 Switzerland
3 Sweden

**1928 Amsterdam**
1 Uruguay
2 Argentina
3 Italy

**1932 Los Angeles**
no tournament

**1936 Berlin**
1 Italy
2 Austria
3 Norway

**1948 London**
1 Sweden
2 Yugoslavia
3 Denmark

**1952 Helsinki**
1 Hungary
2 Yugoslavia
3 Sweden

**1956 Melbourne**
1 USSR
2 Yugoslavia
3 Bulgaria

**1960 Rome**
1 Yugoslavia
2 Denmark
3 Hungary

**1964 Tokyo**
1 Hungary
2 Czechoslovakia
3 East Germany

**1968 Mexico City**
1 Hungary
2 Bulgaria
3 Japan

**1972 Munich**
1 Poland
2 Hungary
3 E Germany/USSR

**1976 Montreal**
1 East Germany
2 Poland
3 USSR

**1980 Moscow**
1 Czechoslovakia
2 East Germany
3 USSR

**1984 Los Angeles**
1 France
2 Brazil
3 Yugoslavia

**1988 Seoul**
1 USSR
2 Brazil
3 West Germany

**1992 Barcelona**
1 Spain
2 Poland
3 Ghana

**1996 Atlanta**
1 Nigeria
2 Argentina
3 Brazil

**2000 Sydney**
1 Cameroon
2 Spain
3 Chile

**2004 Athens**
1 Argentina
2 Paraguay
3 Italy

**2008 Beijing**
1 Argentina
2 Nigeria
3 Brazil

**2012 London**
1 Mexico
2 Brazil
3 South Korea

# THE WORLD CUP 1930–2010

| Year | Winners | | Runners-up | | Venue | Attendance | Referee |
|------|---------|---|-----------|---|-------|-----------|---------|
| 1930 | Uruguay | 4 | Argentina | 2 | Montevideo | 90,000 | Langenus (B) |
| 1934 | Italy* | 2 | Czechoslovakia | 1 | Rome | 50,000 | Eklind (Se) |
| 1938 | Italy | 4 | Hungary | 2 | Paris | 45,000 | Capdeville (F) |
| 1950 | Uruguay | 2 | Brazil | 1 | Rio de Janeiro | 199,854 | Reader (E) |
| 1954 | West Germany | 3 | Hungary | 2 | Berne | 60,000 | Ling (E) |
| 1958 | Brazi | 5 | Sweden | 2 | Stockholm | 49,737 | Guigue (F) |
| 1962 | Brazil | 3 | Czechoslovakia | 1 | Santiago | 68,679 | Latychev (USSR) |
| 1966 | England* | 4 | West Germany | 2 | Wembley | 93,802 | Dienst (Sw) |
| 1970 | Brazil | 4 | Italy | 1 | Mexico City | 107,412 | Glockner (EG) |
| 1974 | West Germany | 2 | Holland | 1 | Munich | 77,833 | Taylor (E) |
| 1978 | Argentina* | 3 | Holland | 1 | Buenos Aires | 77,000 | Gonella (I) |
| 1982 | Italy | 3 | West Germany | 1 | Madrid | 90,080 | Coelho (Br) |
| 1986 | Argentina | 3 | West Germany | 2 | Mexico City | 114,580 | Filho (Br) |
| 1990 | West Germany | 1 | Argentina | 0 | Rome | 73,603 | Mendez (Mex) |
| 1994 | Brazil* | 0 | Italy | 0 | Los Angeles | 94,194 | Puhl (H) |
| | (Brazil won 3-2 on penalties) | | | | | | |
| 1998 | France | 3 | Brazil | 0 | St-Denis | 75,000 | Belqola (Mor) |
| 2002 | Brazil | 2 | Germany | 0 | Yokohama | 69,029 | Collina (I) |
| 2006 | Italy* | 1 | France | 1 | Berlin | 69,000 | Elizondo (Arg) |
| | (Italy won 5-3 on penalties) | | | | | | |
| 2010 | Spain | 1 | Holland | 0 | Johannesburg | 84,490 | Webb (E) |
| (*After extra time) | | | | | | | |

## GOALSCORING AND ATTENDANCES IN WORLD CUP FINAL ROUNDS

| Venue | | Matches | Goals (av) | Attendance (av) |
|-------|---|---------|-----------|-----------------|
| 1930 | Uruguay | 18 | 70 (3.9) | 434,500 (24,138) |
| 1934 | Italy | 17 | 70 (4.1) | 395,000 (23,235) |
| 1938 | France | 18 | 84 (4.6) | 483,000 (26,833) |
| 1950 | Brazil | 22 | 88 (4.0) | 1,337,000 (60,772) |
| 1954 | Switzerland | 26 | 140 (5.4) | 943,000 (36,270) |
| 1958 | Sweden | 35 | 126 (3.6) | 868,000 (24,800) |
| 1962 | Chile | 32 | 89 (2.8) | 776,000 (24,250) |
| 1966 | England | 32 | 89 (2.8) | 1,614,677 (50,458) |
| 1970 | Mexico | 32 | 95 (2.9) | 1,673,975 (52,311) |
| 1974 | West Germany | 38 | 97 (2.5) | 1,774,022 (46,684) |
| 1978 | Argentina | 38 | 102 (2.7) | 1,610,215 (42,374) |
| 1982 | Spain | 52 | 146 (2.8) | 2,064,364 (38,816) |
| 1986 | Mexico | 52 | 132 (2.5) | 2,441,731 (46,956) |
| 1990 | Italy | 52 | 115 (2.2) | 2,515,168 (48,368) |
| 1994 | USA | 52 | 141 (2.7) | 3,567,415 (68,604) |
| 1998 | France | 64 | 171 (2.6) | 2,775,400 (43,366) |
| 2002 | Japan/S. Korea | 64 | 161 (2.5) | 2,705,566 (42,274) |
| 2006 | Germany | 64 | 147 (2.3) | 3,354,646 (52,416) |
| 2010 | South Africa | 64 | 145 (2.3) | 3,178,856 (49,670) |

## LEADING GOALSCORERS

| Year | Player | Goals |
|------|--------|-------|
| 1930 | Guillermo Stabile (Argentina) | 8 |
| 1934 | Angelo Schiavio (Italy), Oldrich Nejedly (Czechoslovakia), Edmund Conen (Germany) | 4 |
| 1938 | Leonidas da Silva (Brazil) | 8 |
| 1950 | Ademir (Brazil) | 9 |
| 1954 | Sandor Kocsis (Hungary) | 11 |
| 1958 | Just Fontaine (France) | 13 |
| 1962 | Valentin Ivanov (USSR), Leonel Sanchez (Chile), Garrincha, Vava (both Brazil), Florian Albert (Hungary), Drazen Jerkovic (Yugoslavia) | 4 |
| 1966 | Eusebio (Portugal) | 9 |
| 1970 | Gerd Muller (West Germany) | 10 |
| 1974 | Grzegorz Lato (Poland) | 7 |
| 1978 | Mario Kempes (Argentina) | 6 |
| 1982 | Paolo Rossi (Italy) | 6 |
| 1986 | Gary Lineker (England) | 6 |
| 1990 | Salvatore Schillaci (Italy) | 6 |
| 1994 | Oleg Salenko (Russia), Hristo Stoichkov (Bulgaria) | 6 |
| 1998 | Davor Suker (Croatia) | 6 |
| 2002 | Ronaldo (Brazil) | 8 |
| 2006 | Miroslav Klose (Germany) | 5 |
| 2010 | Thomas Muller (Germany), David Villa (Spain), Wesley Sneijder (Holland), Diego Forlan (Uruguay) | 5 |

# EUROPEAN FOOTBALL CHAMPIONSHIP 1960–2012
## (formerly EUROPEAN NATIONS' CUP)

| Year | Winners | | Runners-up | | Venue | Attendance |
|------|---------|---|-----------|---|-------|-----------|
| 1960 | USSR | 2 | Yugoslavia | 1 | Paris | 17,966 |
| 1964 | Spain | 2 | USSR | 1 | Madrid | 120,000 |
| 1968 | Italy | 2 | Yugoslavia | 0 | Rome | 60,000 |
| | After 1-1 draw | | | | | 75,000 |
| 1972 | West Germany | 3 | USSR | 0 | Brussels | 43,437 |
| 1976 | Czechoslovakia | 2 | West Germany | 2 | Belgrade | 45,000 |
| | (Czechoslovakia won on penalties) | | | | | |
| 1980 | West Germany | 2 | Belgium | 1 | Rome | 47,864 |
| 1984 | France | 2 | Spain | 0 | Paris | 48,000 |
| 1988 | Holland | 2 | USSR | 0 | Munich | 72,308 |
| 1992 | Denmark | 2 | Germany | 0 | Gothenburg | 37,800 |
| 1996 | Germany | 2 | Czech Republic | 1 | Wembley | 73,611 |
| | (Germany won on sudden death) | | | | | |
| 2000 | France | 2 | Italy | 1 | Rotterdam | 50,000 |
| | (France won on sudden death) | | | | | |
| 2004 | Greece | 1 | Portugal | 0 | Lisbon | 62,865 |
| 2008 | Spain | 1 | Germany | 0 | Vienna | 51,428 |
| 2012 | Spain | 4 | Italy | 0 | Kiev | 63,170 |

# BRITISH AND IRISH INTERNATIONAL RESULTS 1872–2013

*Note:* In the results that follow, wc=World Cup, ec=European Championship, ui=Umbro International Trophy. tf = Tournoi de France. nc = Nations Cup. Northern Ireland played as Ireland before 1921. *After extra time.

## ENGLAND v SCOTLAND

*Played: 110; England won 45, Scotland won 41, Drawn 24. Goals: England 192, Scotland 169.*

| Year | Date | Venue | E | S | Year | Date | Venue | E | S |
|---|---|---|---|---|---|---|---|---|---|
| 1872 | 30 Nov | Glasgow | 0 | 0 | 1932 | 9 Apr | Wembley | 3 | 0 |
| 1873 | 8 Mar | Kennington Oval | 4 | 2 | 1933 | 1 Apr | Glasgow | 1 | 2 |
| 1874 | 7 Mar | Glasgow | 1 | 2 | 1934 | 14 Apr | Wembley | 3 | 0 |
| 1875 | 6 Mar | Kennington Oval | 2 | 2 | 1935 | 6 Apr | Glasgow | 0 | 2 |
| 1876 | 4 Mar | Glasgow | 0 | 3 | 1936 | 4 Apr | Wembley | 1 | 1 |
| 1877 | 3 Mar | Kennington Oval | 1 | 3 | 1937 | 17 Apr | Glasgow | 1 | 3 |
| 1878 | 2 Mar | Glasgow | 2 | 7 | 1938 | 9 Apr | Wembley | 0 | 1 |
| 1879 | 5 Apr | Kennington Oval | 5 | 4 | 1939 | 15 Apr | Glasgow | 2 | 1 |
| 1880 | 13 Mar | Glasgow | 4 | 5 | 1947 | 12 Apr | Wembley | 1 | 1 |
| 1881 | 12 Mar | Kennington Oval | 1 | 6 | 1948 | 10 Apr | Glasgow | 2 | 0 |
| 1882 | 11 Mar | Glasgow | 1 | 5 | 1949 | 9 Apr | Wembley | 1 | 3 |
| 1883 | 10 Mar | Sheffield | 2 | 3 | wc1950 | 15 Apr | Glasgow | 1 | 0 |
| 1884 | 15 Mar | Glasgow | 0 | 1 | 1951 | 14 Apr | Wembley | 2 | 3 |
| 1885 | 21 Mar | Kennington Oval | 1 | 1 | 1952 | 5 Apr | Glasgow | 2 | 1 |
| 1886 | 31 Mar | Glasgow | 1 | 1 | 1953 | 18 Apr | Wembley | 2 | 2 |
| 1887 | 19 Mar | Blackburn | 2 | 3 | wc1954 | 3 Apr | Glasgow | 4 | 2 |
| 1888 | 17 Mar | Glasgow | 5 | 0 | 1955 | 2 Apr | Wembley | 7 | 2 |
| 1889 | 13 Apr | Kennington Oval | 2 | 3 | 1956 | 14 Apr | Glasgow | 1 | 1 |
| 1890 | 5 Apr | Glasgow | 1 | 1 | 1957 | 6 Apr | Wembley | 2 | 1 |
| 1891 | 6 Apr | Blackburn | 2 | 1 | 1958 | 19 Apr | Glasgow | 4 | 0 |
| 1892 | 2 Apr | Glasgow | 4 | 1 | 1959 | 11 Apr | Wembley | 1 | 0 |
| 1893 | 1 Apr | Richmond | 5 | 2 | 1960 | 9 Apr | Glasgow | 1 | 1 |
| 1894 | 7 Apr | Glasgow | 2 | 2 | 1961 | 15 Apr | Wembley | 9 | 3 |
| 1895 | 6 Apr | Everton | 3 | 0 | 1962 | 14 Apr | Glasgow | 0 | 2 |
| 1896 | 4 Apr | Glasgow | 1 | 2 | 1963 | 6 Apr | Wembley | 1 | 2 |
| 1897 | 3 Apr | Crystal Palace | 1 | 2 | 1964 | 11 Apr | Glasgow | 0 | 1 |
| 1898 | 2 Apr | Glasgow | 3 | 1 | 1965 | 10 Apr | Wembley | 2 | 2 |
| 1899 | 8 Apr | Birmingham | 2 | 1 | 1966 | 2 Apr | Glasgow | 4 | 3 |
| 1900 | 7 Apr | Glasgow | 1 | 4 | ec1967 | 15 Apr | Wembley | 2 | 3 |
| 1901 | 30 Mar | Crystal Palace | 2 | 2 | ec1968 | 24 Jan | Glasgow | 1 | 1 |
| 1902 | 3 Mar | Birmingham | 2 | 2 | 1969 | 10 May | Wembley | 4 | 1 |
| 1903 | 4 Apr | Sheffield | 1 | 2 | 1970 | 25 Apr | Glasgow | 0 | 0 |
| 1904 | 9 Apr | Glasgow | 1 | 0 | 1971 | 22 May | Wembley | 3 | 1 |
| 1905 | 1 Apr | Crystal Palace | 1 | 0 | 1972 | 27 May | Glasgow | 1 | 0 |
| 1906 | 7 Apr | Glasgow | 1 | 2 | 1973 | 14 Feb | Glasgow | 5 | 0 |
| 1907 | 6 Apr | Newcastle | 1 | 1 | 1973 | 19 May | Wembley | 1 | 0 |
| 1908 | 4 Apr | Glasgow | 1 | 1 | 1974 | 18 May | Glasgow | 0 | 2 |
| 1909 | 3 Apr | Crystal Palace | 2 | 0 | 1975 | 24 May | Wembley | 5 | 1 |
| 1910 | 2 Apr | Glasgow | 0 | 2 | 1976 | 15 May | Glasgow | 1 | 2 |
| 1911 | 1 Apr | Everton | 1 | 1 | 1977 | 4 June | Wembley | 1 | 2 |
| 1912 | 23 Mar | Glasgow | 1 | 1 | 1978 | 20 May | Glasgow | 1 | 0 |
| 1913 | 5 Apr | Chelsea | 1 | 0 | 1979 | 26 May | Wembley | 3 | 1 |
| 1914 | 14 Apr | Glasgow | 1 | 3 | 1980 | 24 May | Glasgow | 2 | 0 |
| 1920 | 10 Apr | Sheffield | 5 | 4 | 1981 | 23 May | Wembley | 0 | 1 |
| 1921 | 9 Apr | Glasgow | 0 | 3 | 1982 | 29 May | Glasgow | 1 | 0 |
| 1922 | 8 Apr | Aston Villa | 0 | 1 | 1983 | 1 June | Wembley | 2 | 0 |
| 1923 | 14 Apr | Glasgow | 2 | 2 | 1984 | 26 May | Glasgow | 1 | 1 |
| 1924 | 12 Apr | Wembley | 1 | 1 | 1985 | 25 May | Glasgow | 0 | 1 |
| 1925 | 4 Apr | Glasgow | 0 | 2 | 1986 | 23 Apr | Wembley | 2 | 1 |
| 1926 | 17 Apr | Manchester | 0 | 1 | 1987 | 23 May | Glasgow | 0 | 0 |
| 1927 | 2 Apr | Glasgow | 2 | 1 | 1988 | 21 May | Wembley | 1 | 0 |
| 1928 | 31 Mar | Wembley | 1 | 5 | 1989 | 27 May | Glasgow | 2 | 0 |
| 1929 | 13 Apr | Glasgow | 0 | 1 | ec1996 | 15 June | Wembley | 2 | 0 |
| 1930 | 5 Apr | Wembley | 5 | 2 | ec1999 | 13 Nov | Glasgow | 2 | 0 |
| 1931 | 28 Mar | Glasgow | 0 | 2 | ec1999 | 17 Nov | Wembley | 0 | 1 |

## ENGLAND v WALES

*Played: 101; England won 66, Wales won 14, Drawn 21. Goals: England 245, Wales 90.*

| Year | Date | Venue | E | W | Year | Date | Venue | E | W |
|---|---|---|---|---|---|---|---|---|---|
| 1879 | 18 Jan | Kennington Oval | 2 | 1 | 1882 | 13 Mar | Wrexham | 3 | 5 |
| 1880 | 15 Mar | Wrexham | 3 | 2 | 1883 | 3 Feb | Kennington Oval | 5 | 0 |
| 1881 | 26 Feb | Blackburn | 0 | 1 | 1884 | 17 Mar | Wrexham | 4 | 0 |

| Year | Date | Venue | E | W |
|------|------|-------|---|---|
| 1885 | 14 Mar | Blackburn | 1 | 1 |
| 1886 | 29 Mar | Wrexham | 3 | 1 |
| 1887 | 26 Feb | Kennington Oval | 4 | 0 |
| 1888 | 4 Feb | Crewe | 5 | 1 |
| 1889 | 23 Feb | Stoke | 4 | 1 |
| 1890 | 15 Mar | Wrexham | 3 | 1 |
| 1891 | 7 May | Sunderland | 4 | 1 |
| 1892 | 5 Mar | Wrexham | 2 | 0 |
| 1893 | 13 Mar | Stoke | 6 | 0 |
| 1894 | 12 Mar | Wrexham | 5 | 1 |
| 1895 | 18 Mar | Queen's Club, Kensington | 1 | 1 |
| 1896 | 16 Mar | Cardiff | 9 | 1 |
| 1897 | 29 Mar | Sheffield | 4 | 0 |
| 1898 | 28 Mar | Wrexham | 3 | 0 |
| 1899 | 20 Mar | Bristol | 4 | 0 |
| 1900 | 26 Mar | Cardiff | 1 | 1 |
| 1901 | 18 Mar | Newcastle | 6 | 0 |
| 1902 | 3 Mar | Wrexham | 0 | 0 |
| 1903 | 2 Mar | Portsmouth | 2 | 1 |
| 1904 | 29 Feb | Wrexham | 2 | 2 |
| 1905 | 27 Mar | Liverpool | 3 | 1 |
| 1906 | 19 Mar | Cardiff | 1 | 0 |
| 1907 | 18 Mar | Fulham | 1 | 1 |
| 1908 | 16 Mar | Wrexham | 7 | 1 |
| 1909 | 15 Mar | Nottingham | 2 | 0 |
| 1910 | 14 Mar | Cardiff | 1 | 0 |
| 1911 | 13 Mar | Millwall | 3 | 0 |
| 1912 | 11 Mar | Wrexham | 2 | 0 |
| 1913 | 17 Mar | Bristol | 4 | 3 |
| 1914 | 16 Mar | Cardiff | 2 | 0 |
| 1920 | 15 Mar | Highbury | 1 | 2 |
| 1921 | 14 Mar | Cardiff | 0 | 0 |
| 1922 | 13 Mar | Liverpool | 1 | 0 |
| 1923 | 5 Mar | Cardiff | 2 | 2 |
| 1924 | 3 Mar | Blackburn | 1 | 2 |
| 1925 | 28 Feb | Swansea | 2 | 1 |
| 1926 | 1 Mar | Crystal Palace | 1 | 3 |
| 1927 | 12 Feb | Wrexham | 3 | 3 |
| 1927 | 28 Nov | Burnley | 1 | 2 |
| 1928 | 17 Nov | Swansea | 3 | 2 |
| 1929 | 20 Nov | Chelsea | 6 | 0 |
| 1930 | 22 Nov | Wrexham | 4 | 0 |
| 1931 | 18 Nov | Liverpool | 3 | 1 |
| 1932 | 16 Nov | Wrexham | 0 | 0 |
| 1933 | 15 Nov | Newcastle | 1 | 2 |
| 1934 | 29 Sept | Cardiff | 4 | 0 |
| 1936 | 5 Feb | Wolverhampton | 1 | 2 |
| 1936 | 17 Oct | Cardiff | 1 | 2 |
| 1937 | 17 Nov | Middlesbrough | 2 | 1 |
| 1938 | 22 Oct | Cardiff | 2 | 4 |
| 1946 | 13 Nov | Manchester | 3 | 0 |
| 1947 | 18 Oct | Cardiff | 3 | 0 |
| 1948 | 10 Nov | Aston Villa | 1 | 0 |
| wc1949 | 15 Oct | Cardiff | 4 | 1 |
| 1950 | 15 Nov | Sunderland | 4 | 2 |
| 1951 | 20 Oct | Cardiff | 1 | 1 |
| 1952 | 12 Nov | Wembley | 5 | 2 |
| wc1953 | 10 Oct | Cardiff | 4 | 1 |
| 1954 | 10 Nov | Wembley | 3 | 2 |
| 1955 | 27 Oct | Cardiff | 1 | 2 |
| 1956 | 14 Nov | Wembley | 3 | 1 |
| 1957 | 19 Oct | Cardiff | 4 | 0 |
| 1958 | 26 Nov | Aston Villa | 2 | 2 |
| 1959 | 17 Oct | Cardiff | 1 | 1 |
| 1960 | 23 Nov | Wembley | 5 | 1 |
| 1961 | 14 Oct | Cardiff | 1 | 1 |
| 1962 | 21 Oct | Wembley | 4 | 0 |
| 1963 | 12 Oct | Cardiff | 4 | 0 |
| 1964 | 18 Nov | Wembley | 2 | 1 |
| 1965 | 2 Oct | Cardiff | 0 | 0 |
| EC1966 | 16 Nov | Wembley | 5 | 1 |
| EC1967 | 21 Oct | Cardiff | 3 | 0 |
| 1969 | 7 May | Wembley | 2 | 1 |
| 1970 | 18 Apr | Cardiff | 1 | 1 |
| 1971 | 19 May | Wembley | 0 | 0 |
| 1972 | 20 May | Cardiff | 3 | 0 |
| wc1972 | 15 Nov | Cardiff | 1 | 0 |
| wc1973 | 24 Jan | Wembley | 1 | 1 |
| 1973 | 15 May | Wembley | 3 | 0 |
| 1974 | 11 May | Cardiff | 2 | 0 |
| 1975 | 21 May | Wembley | 2 | 2 |
| 1976 | 24 Mar | Wrexham | 2 | 1 |
| 1976 | 8 May | Cardiff | 1 | 0 |
| 1977 | 31 May | Wembley | 0 | 1 |
| 1978 | 3 May | Cardiff | 3 | 1 |
| 1979 | 23 May | Wembley | 0 | 0 |
| 1980 | 17 May | Wrexham | 1 | 4 |
| 1981 | 20 May | Wembley | 0 | 0 |
| 1982 | 27 Apr | Cardiff | 1 | 0 |
| 1983 | 23 Feb | Wembley | 2 | 1 |
| 1984 | 2 May | Wrexham | 0 | 1 |
| wc2004 | 9 Oct | Old Trafford | 2 | 0 |
| wc2005 | 3 Sept | Cardiff | 1 | 0 |
| EC2011 | 26 Mar | Cardiff | 2 | 0 |
| EC2011 | 6 Sept | Wembley | 1 | 0 |

## ENGLAND v NORTHERN IRELAND

*Played: 98; England won 75, Northern Ireland won 7, Drawn 16. Goals: England 323, Northern Ireland 81.*

| Year | Date | Venue | E | NI |
|------|------|-------|---|----|
| 1882 | 18 Feb | Belfast | 13 | 0 |
| 1883 | 24 Feb | Liverpool | 7 | 0 |
| 1884 | 23 Feb | Belfast | 8 | 1 |
| 1885 | 28 Feb | Manchester | 4 | 0 |
| 1886 | 13 Mar | Belfast | 6 | 1 |
| 1887 | 5 Feb | Sheffield | 7 | 0 |
| 1888 | 31 Mar | Belfast | 5 | 1 |
| 1889 | 2 Mar | Everton | 6 | 1 |
| 1890 | 15 Mar | Belfast | 9 | 1 |
| 1891 | 7 Mar | Wolverhampton | 6 | 1 |
| 1892 | 5 Mar | Belfast | 2 | 0 |
| 1893 | 25 Feb | Birmingham | 6 | 1 |
| 1894 | 3 Mar | Belfast | 2 | 2 |
| 1895 | 9 Mar | Derby | 9 | 0 |
| 1896 | 7 Mar | Belfast | 2 | 0 |
| 1897 | 20 Feb | Nottingham | 6 | 0 |
| 1898 | 5 Mar | Belfast | 3 | 2 |
| 1899 | 18 Feb | Sunderland | 13 | 2 |
| 1900 | 17 Mar | Dublin | 2 | 0 |
| 1901 | 9 Mar | Southampton | 3 | 0 |
| 1902 | 22 Mar | Belfast | 1 | 0 |
| 1903 | 14 Feb | Wolverhampton | 4 | 0 |
| 1904 | 12 Mar | Belfast | 3 | 1 |
| 1905 | 25 Feb | Middlesbrough | 1 | 1 |
| 1906 | 17 Feb | Belfast | 5 | 0 |
| 1907 | 16 Feb | Everton | 1 | 0 |
| 1908 | 15 Feb | Belfast | 3 | 1 |
| 1909 | 13 Feb | Bradford | 4 | 0 |
| 1910 | 12 Feb | Belfast | 1 | 1 |
| 1911 | 11 Feb | Derby | 2 | 1 |
| 1912 | 10 Feb | Dublin | 6 | 1 |
| 1913 | 15 Feb | Belfast | 1 | 2 |
| 1914 | 14 Feb | Middlesbrough | 0 | 3 |
| 1919 | 25 Oct | Belfast | 1 | 1 |
| 1920 | 23 Oct | Sunderland | 2 | 0 |
| 1921 | 22 Oct | Belfast | 1 | 1 |
| 1922 | 21 Oct | West Bromwich | 2 | 0 |
| 1923 | 20 Oct | Belfast | 1 | 2 |
| 1924 | 22 Oct | Everton | 3 | 1 |
| 1925 | 24 Oct | Belfast | 0 | 0 |
| 1926 | 20 Oct | Liverpool | 3 | 3 |
| 1927 | 22 Oct | Belfast | 0 | 2 |

| | | | E | NI |
|---|---|---|---|---|
| 1928 | 22 Oct | Everton | 2 | 1 |
| 1929 | 19 Oct | Belfast | 3 | 0 |
| 1930 | 20 Oct | Sheffield | 5 | 1 |
| 1931 | 17 Oct | Belfast | 6 | 2 |
| 1932 | 17 Oct | Blackpool | 1 | 0 |
| 1933 | 14 Oct | Belfast | 3 | 0 |
| 1935 | 6 Feb | Everton | 2 | 1 |
| 1935 | 19 Oct | Belfast | 3 | 1 |
| 1936 | 18 Nov | Stoke | 3 | 1 |
| 1937 | 23 Oct | Belfast | 5 | 1 |
| 1938 | 16 Nov | Manchester | 7 | 0 |
| 1946 | 28 Sept | Belfast | 7 | 2 |
| 1947 | 5 Nov | Everton | 2 | 2 |
| 1948 | 9 Oct | Belfast | 6 | 2 |
| wc1949 | 16 Nov | Manchester | 9 | 2 |
| 1950 | 7 Oct | Belfast | 4 | 1 |
| 1951 | 14 Nov | Aston Villa | 2 | 0 |
| 1952 | 4 Oct | Belfast | 2 | 2 |
| wc1953 | 11 Nov | Everton | 3 | 1 |
| 1954 | 2 Oct | Belfast | 2 | 0 |
| 1955 | 2 Nov | Wembley | 3 | 0 |
| 1956 | 10 Oct | Belfast | 1 | 1 |
| 1957 | 6 Nov | Wembley | 2 | 3 |
| 1958 | 4 Oct | Belfast | 3 | 3 |
| 1959 | 18 Nov | Wembley | 2 | 1 |
| 1960 | 8 Oct | Belfast | 5 | 2 |
| 1961 | 22 Nov | Wembley | 1 | 1 |
| 1962 | 20 Oct | Belfast | 3 | 1 |
| 1963 | 20 Nov | Wembley | 8 | 3 |
| 1964 | 3 Oct | Belfast | 4 | 3 |
| 1965 | 10 Nov | Wembley | 2 | 1 |
| EC1966 | 20 Oct | Belfast | 2 | 0 |
| EC1967 | 22 Nov | Wembley | 2 | 0 |
| 1969 | 3 May | Belfast | 3 | 1 |
| 1970 | 21 Apr | Wembley | 3 | 1 |
| 1971 | 15 May | Belfast | 1 | 0 |
| 1972 | 23 May | Wembley | 0 | 1 |
| 1973 | 12 May | Everton | 2 | 1 |
| 1974 | 15 May | Wembley | 1 | 0 |
| 1975 | 17 May | Belfast | 0 | 0 |
| 1976 | 11 May | Wembley | 4 | 0 |
| 1977 | 28 May | Belfast | 2 | 1 |
| 1978 | 16 May | Wembley | 1 | 0 |
| EC1979 | 7 Feb | Wembley | 4 | 0 |
| 1979 | 19 May | Belfast | 2 | 0 |
| EC1979 | 17 Oct | Belfast | 5 | 1 |
| 1980 | 20 May | Wembley | 1 | 1 |
| 1982 | 23 Feb | Wembley | 4 | 0 |
| 1983 | 28 May | Belfast | 0 | 0 |
| 1984 | 24 Apr | Wembley | 1 | 0 |
| wc1985 | 27 Feb | Belfast | 1 | 0 |
| wc1985 | 13 Nov | Wembley | 0 | 0 |
| EC1986 | 15 Oct | Wembley | 3 | 0 |
| EC1987 | 1 Apr | Belfast | 2 | 0 |
| wc2005 | 26 Mar | Old Trafford | 4 | 0 |
| wc2005 | 7 Sept | Belfast | 0 | 1 |

## SCOTLAND v WALES

*Played: 107; Scotland won 61, Wales won 23, Drawn 23. Goals: Scotland 243, Wales 124.*

| | | | S | W |
|---|---|---|---|---|
| 1876 | 25 Mar | Glasgow | 4 | 0 |
| 1877 | 5 Mar | Wrexham | 2 | 0 |
| 1878 | 23 Mar | Glasgow | 9 | 0 |
| 1879 | 7 Apr | Wrexham | 3 | 0 |
| 1880 | 3 Apr | Glasgow | 5 | 1 |
| 1881 | 14 Mar | Wrexham | 5 | 1 |
| 1882 | 25 Mar | Glasgow | 5 | 0 |
| 1883 | 12 Mar | Wrexham | 3 | 0 |
| 1884 | 29 Mar | Glasgow | 4 | 1 |
| 1885 | 23 Mar | Wrexham | 8 | 1 |
| 1886 | 10 Apr | Glasgow | 4 | 1 |
| 1887 | 21 Mar | Wrexham | 2 | 0 |
| 1888 | 10 Mar | Edinburgh | 5 | 1 |
| 1889 | 15 Apr | Wrexham | 0 | 0 |
| 1890 | 22 Mar | Paisley | 5 | 0 |
| 1891 | 21 Mar | Wrexham | 4 | 3 |
| 1892 | 26 Mar | Edinburgh | 6 | 1 |
| 1893 | 18 Mar | Wrexham | 8 | 0 |
| 1894 | 24 Mar | Kilmarnock | 5 | 2 |
| 1895 | 23 Mar | Wrexham | 2 | 2 |
| 1896 | 21 Mar | Dundee | 4 | 0 |
| 1897 | 20 Mar | Wrexham | 2 | 2 |
| 1898 | 19 Mar | Motherwell | 5 | 2 |
| 1899 | 18 Mar | Wrexham | 6 | 0 |
| 1900 | 3 Feb | Aberdeen | 5 | 2 |
| 1901 | 2 Mar | Wrexham | 1 | 1 |
| 1902 | 15 Mar | Greenock | 5 | 1 |
| 1903 | 9 Mar | Cardiff | 1 | 0 |
| 1904 | 12 Mar | Dundee | 1 | 1 |
| 1905 | 6 Mar | Wrexham | 1 | 3 |
| 1906 | 3 Mar | Edinburgh | 0 | 2 |
| 1907 | 4 Mar | Wrexham | 0 | 1 |
| 1908 | 7 Mar | Dundee | 2 | 1 |
| 1909 | 1 Mar | Wrexham | 2 | 3 |
| 1910 | 5 Mar | Kilmarnock | 1 | 0 |
| 1911 | 6 Mar | Cardiff | 2 | 2 |
| 1912 | 2 Mar | Tynecastle | 1 | 0 |
| 1913 | 3 Mar | Wrexham | 0 | 0 |
| 1914 | 28 Feb | Glasgow | 0 | 0 |
| 1920 | 26 Feb | Cardiff | 1 | 1 |
| 1921 | 12 Feb | Aberdeen | 2 | 1 |
| 1922 | 4 Feb | Wrexham | 1 | 2 |
| 1923 | 17 Mar | Paisley | 2 | 0 |
| 1924 | 16 Feb | Cardiff | 0 | 2 |
| 1925 | 14 Feb | Tynecastle | 3 | 1 |
| 1925 | 31 Oct | Cardiff | 3 | 0 |
| 1926 | 30 Oct | Glasgow | 3 | 0 |
| 1927 | 29 Oct | Wrexham | 2 | 2 |
| 1928 | 27 Oct | Glasgow | 4 | 2 |
| 1929 | 26 Oct | Cardiff | 4 | 2 |
| 1930 | 25 Oct | Glasgow | 1 | 1 |
| 1931 | 31 Oct | Wrexham | 3 | 2 |
| 1932 | 26 Oct | Edinburgh | 2 | 5 |
| 1933 | 4 Oct | Cardiff | 2 | 3 |
| 1934 | 21 Nov | Aberdeen | 3 | 2 |
| 1935 | 5 Oct | Cardiff | 1 | 1 |
| 1936 | 2 Dec | Dundee | 1 | 2 |
| 1937 | 30 Oct | Cardiff | 1 | 2 |
| 1938 | 9 Nov | Edinburgh | 3 | 2 |
| 1946 | 19 Oct | Wrexham | 1 | 3 |
| 1947 | 12 Nov | Glasgow | 1 | 2 |
| 1948 | 23 Oct | Cardiff | 3 | 1 |
| wc1949 | 9 Nov | Glasgow | 2 | 0 |
| 1950 | 21 Oct | Cardiff | 3 | 1 |
| 1951 | 14 Nov | Glasgow | 0 | 1 |
| 1952 | 18 Oct | Cardiff | 2 | 1 |
| wc1953 | 4 Nov | Glasgow | 3 | 3 |
| 1954 | 16 Oct | Cardiff | 1 | 0 |
| 1955 | 9 Nov | Glasgow | 2 | 0 |
| 1956 | 20 Oct | Cardiff | 2 | 2 |
| 1957 | 13 Nov | Glasgow | 1 | 1 |
| 1958 | 18 Oct | Cardiff | 3 | 0 |
| 1959 | 4 Nov | Glasgow | 1 | 1 |
| 1960 | 20 Oct | Cardiff | 0 | 2 |
| 1961 | 8 Nov | Glasgow | 2 | 0 |
| 1962 | 20 Oct | Cardiff | 3 | 2 |
| 1963 | 20 Nov | Glasgow | 2 | 1 |
| 1964 | 3 Oct | Cardiff | 2 | 3 |
| EC1965 | 24 Nov | Glasgow | 4 | 1 |
| EC1966 | 22 Oct | Cardiff | 1 | 1 |
| 1967 | 22 Nov | Glasgow | 3 | 2 |
| 1969 | 3 May | Wrexham | 5 | 3 |

| | | | S | W | | | | | S | W |
|---|---|---|---|---|---|---|---|---|---|---|
| 1970 | 22 Apr | Glasgow | 0 | 0 | | 1981 | 16 May | Swansea | 0 | 2 |
| 1971 | 15 May | Cardiff | 0 | 0 | | 1982 | 24 May | Glasgow | 1 | 0 |
| 1972 | 24 May | Glasgow | 1 | 0 | | 1983 | 28 May | Cardiff | 2 | 0 |
| 1973 | 12 May | Wrexham | 2 | 0 | | 1984 | 28 Feb | Glasgow | 2 | 1 |
| 1974 | 14 May | Glasgow | 2 | 0 | | wc1985 | 27 Mar | Glasgow | 0 | 1 |
| 1975 | 17 May | Cardiff | 2 | 2 | | wc1985 | 10 Sept | Cardiff | 1 | 1 |
| 1976 | 6 May | Glasgow | 3 | 1 | | 1997 | 27 May | Kilmarnock | 0 | 1 |
| wc1976 | 17 Nov | Glasgow | 1 | 0 | | 2004 | 18 Feb | Cardiff | 0 | 4 |
| 1977 | 28 May | Wrexham | 0 | 0 | | 2009 | 14 Nov | Cardiff | 0 | 3 |
| wc1977 | 12 Oct | Liverpool | 2 | 0 | | NC2011 | 25 May | Dublin | 3 | 1 |
| 1978 | 17 May | Glasgow | 1 | 1 | | wc2012 | 12 Oct | Cardiff | 1 | 2 |
| 1979 | 19 May | Cardiff | 0 | 3 | | wc2013 | 22 Mar | Glasgow | 1 | 2 |
| 1980 | 21 May | Glasgow | 1 | 0 | | | | | | |

## SCOTLAND v NORTHERN IRELAND

*Played: 95; Scotland won 63, Northern Ireland won 15, Drawn 17. Goals: Scotland 260, Northern Ireland 81.*

| | | | S | NI | | | | | S | NI |
|---|---|---|---|---|---|---|---|---|---|---|
| 1884 | 26 Jan | Belfast | 5 | 0 | | 1934 | 20 Oct | Belfast | 1 | 2 |
| 1885 | 14 Mar | Glasgow | 8 | 2 | | 1935 | 13 Nov | Edinburgh | 2 | 1 |
| 1886 | 20 Mar | Belfast | 7 | 2 | | 1936 | 31 Oct | Belfast | 3 | 1 |
| 1887 | 19 Feb | Glasgow | 4 | 1 | | 1937 | 10 Nov | Aberdeen | 1 | 1 |
| 1888 | 24 Mar | Belfast | 10 | 2 | | 1938 | 8 Oct | Belfast | 2 | 0 |
| 1889 | 9 Mar | Glasgow | 7 | 0 | | 1946 | 27 Nov | Glasgow | 0 | 0 |
| 1890 | 29 Mar | Belfast | 4 | 1 | | 1947 | 4 Oct | Belfast | 0 | 2 |
| 1891 | 28 Mar | Glasgow | 2 | 1 | | 1948 | 17 Nov | Glasgow | 3 | 2 |
| 1892 | 19 Mar | Belfast | 3 | 2 | | 1949 | 1 Oct | Belfast | 8 | 2 |
| 1893 | 25 Mar | Glasgow | 6 | 1 | | 1950 | 1 Nov | Glasgow | 6 | 1 |
| 1894 | 31 Mar | Belfast | 2 | 1 | | 1951 | 6 Oct | Belfast | 3 | 0 |
| 1895 | 30 Mar | Glasgow | 3 | 1 | | 1952 | 5 Nov | Glasgow | 1 | 1 |
| 1896 | 28 Mar | Belfast | 3 | 3 | | 1953 | 3 Oct | Belfast | 3 | 1 |
| 1897 | 27 Mar | Glasgow | 5 | 1 | | 1954 | 3 Nov | Glasgow | 2 | 2 |
| 1898 | 26 Mar | Belfast | 3 | 0 | | 1955 | 8 Oct | Belfast | 1 | 2 |
| 1899 | 25 Mar | Glasgow | 9 | 1 | | 1956 | 7 Nov | Glasgow | 1 | 0 |
| 1900 | 3 Mar | Belfast | 3 | 0 | | 1957 | 5 Oct | Belfast | 1 | 1 |
| 1901 | 23 Feb | Glasgow | 11 | 0 | | 1958 | 5 Nov | Glasgow | 2 | 2 |
| 1902 | 1 Mar | Belfast | 5 | 1 | | 1959 | 3 Oct | Belfast | 4 | 0 |
| 1902 | 9 Aug | Belfast | 3 | 0 | | 1960 | 9 Nov | Glasgow | 5 | 2 |
| 1903 | 21 Mar | Glasgow | 0 | 2 | | 1961 | 7 Oct | Belfast | 6 | 1 |
| 1904 | 26 Mar | Dublin | 1 | 1 | | 1962 | 7 Nov | Glasgow | 5 | 1 |
| 1905 | 18 Mar | Glasgow | 4 | 0 | | 1963 | 12 Oct | Belfast | 1 | 2 |
| 1906 | 17 Mar | Dublin | 1 | 0 | | 1964 | 25 Nov | Glasgow | 3 | 2 |
| 1907 | 16 Mar | Glasgow | 3 | 0 | | 1965 | 2 Oct | Belfast | 2 | 3 |
| 1908 | 14 Mar | Dublin | 5 | 0 | | 1966 | 16 Nov | Glasgow | 2 | 1 |
| 1909 | 15 Mar | Glasgow | 5 | 0 | | 1967 | 21 Oct | Belfast | 0 | 1 |
| 1910 | 19 Mar | Belfast | 0 | 1 | | 1969 | 6 May | Glasgow | 1 | 1 |
| 1911 | 18 Mar | Glasgow | 2 | 0 | | 1970 | 18 Apr | Belfast | 1 | 0 |
| 1912 | 16 Mar | Belfast | 4 | 1 | | 1971 | 18 May | Glasgow | 0 | 1 |
| 1913 | 15 Mar | Dublin | 2 | 1 | | 1972 | 20 May | Glasgow | 2 | 0 |
| 1914 | 14 Mar | Belfast | 1 | 1 | | 1973 | 16 May | Glasgow | 1 | 2 |
| 1920 | 13 Mar | Glasgow | 3 | 0 | | 1974 | 11 May | Glasgow | 0 | 1 |
| 1921 | 26 Feb | Belfast | 2 | 0 | | 1975 | 20 May | Glasgow | 3 | 0 |
| 1922 | 4 Mar | Glasgow | 2 | 1 | | 1976 | 8 May | Glasgow | 3 | 0 |
| 1923 | 3 Mar | Belfast | 1 | 0 | | 1977 | 1 June | Glasgow | 3 | 0 |
| 1924 | 1 Mar | Glasgow | 2 | 0 | | 1978 | 13 May | Glasgow | 1 | 1 |
| 1925 | 28 Feb | Belfast | 3 | 0 | | 1979 | 22 May | Glasgow | 1 | 0 |
| 1926 | 27 Feb | Glasgow | 4 | 0 | | 1980 | 17 May | Belfast | 0 | 1 |
| 1927 | 26 Feb | Belfast | 2 | 0 | | wc1981 | 25 Mar | Glasgow | 1 | 1 |
| 1928 | 25 Feb | Glasgow | 0 | 1 | | 1981 | 19 May | Glasgow | 2 | 0 |
| 1929 | 23 Feb | Belfast | 7 | 3 | | wc1981 | 14 Oct | Belfast | 0 | 0 |
| 1930 | 22 Feb | Glasgow | 3 | 1 | | 1982 | 28 Apr | Belfast | 1 | 1 |
| 1931 | 21 Feb | Belfast | 0 | 0 | | 1983 | 24 May | Glasgow | 0 | 0 |
| 1931 | 19 Sept | Glasgow | 3 | 1 | | 1983 | 13 Dec | Belfast | 0 | 2 |
| 1932 | 12 Sept | Belfast | 4 | 0 | | 1992 | 19 Feb | Glasgow | 1 | 0 |
| 1933 | 16 Sept | Glasgow | 1 | 2 | | 2008 | 20 Aug | Glasgow | 0 | 0 |
| | | | | | | NC2011 | 9 Feb | Dublin | 3 | 0 |

## WALES v NORTHERN IRELAND

*Played: 94; Wales won 44, Northern Ireland won 27, Drawn 23. Goals: Wales 189, Northern Ireland 131.*

| | | | W | NI | | | | | W | NI |
|---|---|---|---|---|---|---|---|---|---|---|
| 1882 | 25 Feb | Wrexham | 7 | 1 | | 1886 | 27 Feb | Wrexham | 5 | 0 |
| 1883 | 17 Mar | Belfast | 1 | 1 | | 1887 | 12 Mar | Belfast | 1 | 4 |
| 1884 | 9 Feb | Wrexham | 6 | 0 | | 1888 | 3 Mar | Wrexham | 11 | 0 |
| 1885 | 11 Apr | Belfast | 8 | 2 | | 1889 | 27 Apr | Belfast | 3 | 1 |

| | | | W | NI | | | | | W | NI |
|---|---|---|---|---|---|---|---|---|---|---|
| 1890 | 8 Feb | Shrewsbury | 5 | 2 | | 1938 | 16 Mar | Belfast | 0 | 1 |
| 1891 | 7 Feb | Belfast | 2 | 7 | | 1939 | 15 Mar | Wrexham | 3 | 1 |
| 1892 | 27 Feb | Bangor | 1 | 1 | | 1947 | 16 Apr | Belfast | 1 | 2 |
| 1893 | 8 Apr | Belfast | 3 | 4 | | 1948 | 10 Mar | Wrexham | 2 | 0 |
| 1894 | 24 Feb | Swansea | 4 | 1 | | 1949 | 9 Mar | Belfast | 2 | 0 |
| 1895 | 16 Mar | Belfast | 2 | 2 | wc1950 | 8 Mar | Wrexham | 0 | 0 |
| 1896 | 29 Feb | Wrexham | 6 | 1 | | 1951 | 7 Mar | Belfast | 2 | 1 |
| 1897 | 6 Mar | Belfast | 3 | 4 | | 1952 | 19 Mar | Swansea | 3 | 0 |
| 1898 | 19 Feb | Llandudno | 0 | 1 | | 1953 | 15 Apr | Belfast | 3 | 2 |
| 1899 | 4 Mar | Belfast | 0 | 1 | wc1954 | 31 Mar | Wrexham | 1 | 2 |
| 1900 | 24 Feb | Llandudno | 2 | 0 | | 1955 | 20 Apr | Belfast | 3 | 2 |
| 1901 | 23 Mar | Belfast | 1 | 0 | | 1956 | 11 Apr | Cardiff | 1 | 1 |
| 1902 | 22 Mar | Cardiff | 0 | 3 | | 1957 | 10 Apr | Belfast | 0 | 0 |
| 1903 | 28 Mar | Belfast | 0 | 2 | | 1958 | 16 Apr | Cardiff | 1 | 1 |
| 1904 | 21 Mar | Bangor | 0 | 1 | | 1959 | 22 Apr | Belfast | 1 | 4 |
| 1905 | 18 Apr | Belfast | 2 | 2 | | 1960 | 6 Apr | Wrexham | 3 | 2 |
| 1906 | 2 Apr | Wrexham | 4 | 4 | | 1961 | 12 Apr | Belfast | 5 | 1 |
| 1907 | 23 Feb | Belfast | 3 | 2 | | 1962 | 11 Apr | Cardiff | 4 | 0 |
| 1908 | 11 Apr | Aberdare | 0 | 1 | | 1963 | 3 Apr | Belfast | 4 | 1 |
| 1909 | 20 Mar | Belfast | 3 | 2 | | 1964 | 15 Apr | Swansea | 2 | 3 |
| 1910 | 11 Apr | Wrexham | 4 | 1 | | 1965 | 31 Mar | Belfast | 5 | 0 |
| 1911 | 28 Jan | Belfast | 2 | 1 | | 1966 | 30 Mar | Cardiff | 1 | 4 |
| 1912 | 13 Apr | Cardiff | 2 | 3 | EC1967 | 12 Apr | Belfast | 0 | 0 |
| 1913 | 18 Jan | Belfast | 1 | 0 | EC1968 | 28 Feb | Wrexham | 2 | 0 |
| 1914 | 19 Jan | Wrexham | 1 | 2 | | 1969 | 10 May | Belfast | 0 | 0 |
| 1920 | 14 Feb | Belfast | 2 | 2 | | 1970 | 25 Apr | Swansea | 1 | 0 |
| 1921 | 9 Apr | Swansea | 2 | 1 | | 1971 | 22 May | Belfast | 0 | 1 |
| 1922 | 4 Apr | Belfast | 1 | 1 | | 1972 | 27 May | Wrexham | 0 | 0 |
| 1923 | 14 Apr | Wrexham | 0 | 3 | | 1973 | 19 May | Everton | 0 | 1 |
| 1924 | 15 Mar | Belfast | 1 | 0 | | 1974 | 18 May | Wrexham | 1 | 0 |
| 1925 | 18 Apr | Wrexham | 0 | 0 | | 1975 | 23 May | Belfast | 0 | 1 |
| 1926 | 13 Feb | Belfast | 0 | 3 | | 1976 | 14 May | Swansea | 1 | 0 |
| 1927 | 9 Apr | Cardiff | 2 | 2 | | 1977 | 3 June | Belfast | 1 | 1 |
| 1928 | 4 Feb | Belfast | 2 | 1 | | 1978 | 19 May | Wrexham | 1 | 0 |
| 1929 | 2 Feb | Wrexham | 2 | 2 | | 1979 | 25 May | Belfast | 1 | 1 |
| 1930 | 1 Feb | Belfast | 0 | 7 | | 1980 | 23 May | Cardiff | 0 | 1 |
| 1931 | 22 Apr | Wrexham | 3 | 2 | | 1982 | 27 May | Wrexham | 3 | 0 |
| 1931 | 5 Dec | Belfast | 0 | 4 | | 1983 | 31 May | Belfast | 1 | 0 |
| 1932 | 7 Dec | Wrexham | 4 | 1 | | 1984 | 22 May | Swansea | 1 | 1 |
| 1933 | 4 Nov | Belfast | 1 | 1 | wc2004 | 8 Sept | Cardiff | 2 | 2 |
| 1935 | 27 Mar | Wrexham | 3 | 1 | wc2005 | 8 Oct | Belfast | 3 | 2 |
| 1936 | 11 Mar | Belfast | 2 | 3 | | 2007 | 6 Feb | Belfast | 0 | 0 |
| 1937 | 17 Mar | Wrexham | 4 | 1 | NC2011 | 27 May | Dublin | 2 | 0 |

## OTHER BRITISH INTERNATIONAL RESULTS 1908–2013

### ENGLAND

| | | v ALBANIA | E | A | | | | v AUSTRALIA | E | A |
|---|---|---|---|---|---|---|---|---|---|---|
| wc1989 | 8 Mar | Tirana | 2 | 0 | | 1980 | 31 May | Sydney | 2 | 1 |
| wc1989 | 26 Apr | Wembley | 5 | 0 | | 1983 | 11 June | Sydney | 0 | 0 |
| wc2001 | 28 Mar | Tirana | 3 | 1 | | 1983 | 15 June | Brisbane | 1 | 0 |
| wc2001 | 5 Sept | Newcastle | 2 | 0 | | 1983 | 18 June | Melbourne | 1 | 1 |
| | | | | | | 1991 | 1 June | Sydney | 1 | 0 |
| | | v ALGERIA | E | A | | 2003 | 12 Feb | West Ham | 1 | 3 |
| wc2010 | 18 June | Cape Town | 0 | 0 | | | | | | |
| | | | | | | | | v AUSTRIA | E | A |
| | | v ANDORRA | E | A | | 1908 | 6 June | Vienna | 6 | 1 |
| EC2006 | 2 Sept | Old Trafford | 5 | 0 | | 1908 | 8 June | Vienna | 11 | 1 |
| EC2007 | 28 Mar | Barcelona | 3 | 0 | | 1909 | 1 June | Vienna | 8 | 1 |
| wc2008 | 6 Sept | Barcelona | 2 | 0 | | 1930 | 14 May | Vienna | 0 | 0 |
| wc2009 | 10 June | Wembley | 6 | 0 | | 1932 | 7 Dec | Chelsea | 4 | 3 |
| | | | | | | 1936 | 6 May | Vienna | 1 | 2 |
| | | v ARGENTINA | E | A | | 1951 | 28 Nov | Wembley | 2 | 2 |
| 1951 | 9 May | Wembley | 2 | 1 | | 1952 | 25 May | Vienna | 3 | 2 |
| 1953 | 17 May | Buenos Aires | 0 | 0 | wc1958 | 15 June | Boras | 2 | 2 |
| *(abandoned after 21 mins)* | | | | | | 1961 | 27 May | Vienna | 1 | 3 |
| wc1962 | 2 June | Rancagua | 3 | 1 | | 1962 | 4 Apr | Wembley | 3 | 1 |
| 1964 | 6 June | Rio de Janeiro | 0 | 1 | | 1965 | 20 Oct | Wembley | 2 | 3 |
| wc1966 | 23 July | Wembley | 1 | 0 | | 1967 | 27 May | Vienna | 1 | 0 |
| 1974 | 22 May | Wembley | 2 | 2 | | 1973 | 26 Sept | Wembley | 7 | 0 |
| 1977 | 12 June | Buenos Aires | 1 | 1 | | 1979 | 13 June | Vienna | 3 | 4 |
| 1980 | 13 May | Wembley | 3 | 1 | wc2004 | 4 Sept | Vienna | 2 | 2 |
| wc1986 | 22 June | Mexico City | 1 | 2 | wc2005 | 8 Oct | Old Trafford | 1 | 0 |
| 1991 | 25 May | Wembley | 2 | 2 | | 2007 | 16 Nov | Vienna | 1 | 0 |
| wc1998 | 30 June | St Etienne | 2 | 2 | | | | | | |
| 2000 | 23 Feb | Wembley | 0 | 0 | | | | v AZERBAIJAN | E | A |
| wc2002 | 7 June | Sapporo | 1 | 0 | wc2004 | 13 Oct | Baku | 1 | 0 |
| 2005 | 12 Nov | Geneva | 3 | 2 | wc2005 | 30 Mar | Newcastle | 2 | 0 |

**v BELARUS** — E B

| | | | E | B |
|---|---|---|---|---|
| wc2008 | 15 Oct | Minsk | 3 | 1 |
| wc2009 | 14 Oct | Wembley | 3 | 0 |

**v BELGIUM** — E B

| | | | E | B |
|---|---|---|---|---|
| 1921 | 21 May | Brussels | 2 | 0 |
| 1923 | 19 Mar | Highbury | 6 | 1 |
| 1923 | 1 Nov | Antwerp | 2 | 2 |
| 1924 | 8 Dec | West Bromwich | 4 | 0 |
| 1926 | 24 May | Antwerp | 5 | 3 |
| 1927 | 11 May | Brussels | 9 | 1 |
| 1928 | 19 May | Antwerp | 3 | 1 |
| 1929 | 11 May | Brussels | 5 | 1 |
| 1931 | 16 May | Brussels | 4 | 1 |
| 1936 | 9 May | Brussels | 2 | 3 |
| 1947 | 21 Sept | Brussels | 5 | 2 |
| 1950 | 18 May | Brussels | 4 | 1 |
| 1952 | 26 Nov | Wembley | 5 | 0 |
| wc1954 | 17 June | Basle | 4 | 4* |
| 1964 | 21 Oct | Wembley | 2 | 2 |
| 1970 | 25 Feb | Brussels | 3 | 1 |
| EC1980 | 12 June | Turin | 1 | 1 |
| wc1990 | 27 June | Bologna | 1 | 0* |
| 1998 | 29 May | Casablanca | 0 | 0 |
| 1999 | 10 Oct | Sunderland | 2 | 1 |
| 2012 | 2 June | Wembley | 1 | 0 |

**v BOHEMIA** — E B

| | | | E | B |
|---|---|---|---|---|
| 1908 | 13 June | Prague | 4 | 0 |

**v BRAZIL** — E B

| | | | E | B |
|---|---|---|---|---|
| 1956 | 9 May | Wembley | 4 | 2 |
| wc1958 | 11 June | Gothenburg | 0 | 0 |
| 1959 | 13 May | Rio de Janeiro | 0 | 2 |
| wc1962 | 10 June | Vina del Mar | 1 | 3 |
| 1963 | 8 May | Wembley | 1 | 1 |
| 1964 | 30 May | Rio de Janeiro | 1 | 5 |
| 1969 | 12 June | Rio de Janeiro | 1 | 2 |
| wc1970 | 7 June | Guadalajara | 0 | 1 |
| 1976 | 23 May | Los Angeles | 0 | 1 |
| 1977 | 8 June | Rio de Janeiro | 0 | 0 |
| 1978 | 19 Apr | Wembley | 1 | 1 |
| 1981 | 12 May | Wembley | 0 | 1 |
| 1984 | 10 June | Rio de Janeiro | 2 | 0 |
| 1987 | 19 May | Wembley | 1 | 1 |
| 1990 | 28 Mar | Wembley | 1 | 0 |
| 1992 | 17 May | Wembley | 1 | 1 |
| 1993 | 13 June | Washington | 1 | 1 |
| U11995 | 11 June | Wembley | 1 | 3 |
| TF1997 | 10 June | Paris | 0 | 1 |
| 2000 | 27 May | Wembley | 1 | 1 |
| wc2002 | 21 June | Shizuoka | 1 | 2 |
| 2007 | 1 June | Wembley | 1 | 1 |
| 2009 | 14 Nov | Doha | 0 | 1 |
| 2013 | 6 Feb | Wembley | 2 | 1 |
| 2013 | 2 June | Rio de Janeiro | 2 | 2 |

**v BULGARIA** — E B

| | | | E | B |
|---|---|---|---|---|
| wc1962 | 7 June | Rancagua | 0 | 0 |
| 1968 | 11 Dec | Wembley | 1 | 1 |
| 1974 | 1 June | Sofia | 1 | 0 |
| EC1979 | 6 June | Sofia | 3 | 0 |
| EC1979 | 22 Nov | Wembley | 2 | 0 |
| 1996 | 27 Mar | Wembley | 1 | 0 |
| EC1998 | 10 Oct | Wembley | 0 | 0 |
| EC1999 | 9 June | Sofia | 1 | 1 |
| EC2010 | 3 Sept | Wembley | 4 | 0 |
| EC2011 | 2 Sept | Sofia | 3 | 0 |

**v CAMEROON** — E C

| | | | E | C |
|---|---|---|---|---|
| wc1990 | 1 July | Naples | 3 | 2* |
| 1991 | 6 Feb | Wembley | 2 | 0 |
| 1997 | 15 Nov | Wembley | 2 | 0 |
| 2002 | 26 May | Kobe | 2 | 2 |

**v CANADA** — E C

| | | | E | C |
|---|---|---|---|---|
| 1986 | 24 May | Burnaby | 1 | 0 |

**v CHILE** — E C

| | | | E | C |
|---|---|---|---|---|
| wc1950 | 25 June | Rio de Janeiro | 2 | 0 |
| 1953 | 24 May | Santiago | 2 | 1 |
| 1984 | 17 June | Santiago | 0 | 0 |
| 1989 | 23 May | Wembley | 0 | 0 |
| 1998 | 11 Feb | Wembley | 0 | 2 |

**v CHINA** — E C

| | | | E | C |
|---|---|---|---|---|
| 1996 | 23 May | Beijing | 3 | 0 |

**v CIS** — E C

| | | | E | C |
|---|---|---|---|---|
| 1992 | 29 Apr | Moscow | 2 | 2 |

**v COLOMBIA** — E C

| | | | E | C |
|---|---|---|---|---|
| 1970 | 20 May | Bogota | 4 | 0 |
| 1988 | 24 May | Wembley | 1 | 1 |
| 1995 | 6 Sept | Wembley | 0 | 0 |
| wc1998 | 26 June | Lens | 2 | 0 |
| 2005 | 31 May | New Jersey | 3 | 2 |

**v CROATIA** — E C

| | | | E | C |
|---|---|---|---|---|
| 1996 | 24 Apr | Wembley | 0 | 0 |
| 2003 | 20 Aug | Ipswich | 3 | 1 |
| EC2004 | 21 June | Lisbon | 4 | 2 |
| EC2006 | 11 Oct | Zagreb | 0 | 2 |
| EC2007 | 21 Nov | Wembley | 2 | 3 |
| wc2008 | 10 Sept | Zagreb | 4 | 1 |
| wc2009 | 9 Sept | Wembley | 5 | 1 |

**v CYPRUS** — E C

| | | | E | C |
|---|---|---|---|---|
| EC1975 | 16 Apr | Wembley | 5 | 0 |
| EC1975 | 11 May | Limassol | 1 | 0 |

**v CZECHOSLOVAKIA** — E C

| | | | E | C |
|---|---|---|---|---|
| 1934 | 16 May | Prague | 1 | 2 |
| 1937 | 1 Dec | Tottenham | 5 | 4 |
| 1963 | 29 May | Bratislava | 4 | 2 |
| 1966 | 2 Nov | Wembley | 0 | 0 |
| wc1970 | 11 June | Guadalajara | 1 | 0 |
| 1973 | 27 May | Prague | 1 | 1 |
| EC1974 | 30 Oct | Wembley | 3 | 0 |
| EC1975 | 30 Oct | Bratislava | 1 | 2 |
| 1978 | 29 Nov | Wembley | 1 | 0 |
| wc1982 | 20 June | Bilbao | 2 | 0 |
| 1990 | 25 Apr | Wembley | 4 | 2 |
| 1992 | 25 Mar | Prague | 2 | 2 |

**v CZECH REPUBLIC** — E C

| | | | E | C |
|---|---|---|---|---|
| 1998 | 18 Nov | Wembley | 2 | 0 |
| 2008 | 20 Aug | Wembley | 2 | 2 |

**v DENMARK** — E D

| | | | E | D |
|---|---|---|---|---|
| 1948 | 26 Sept | Copenhagen | 0 | 0 |
| 1955 | 2 Oct | Copenhagen | 5 | 1 |
| wc1956 | 5 Dec | Wolverhampton | 5 | 2 |
| wc1957 | 15 May | Copenhagen | 4 | 1 |
| 1966 | 3 July | Copenhagen | 2 | 0 |
| EC1978 | 20 Sept | Copenhagen | 4 | 3 |
| EC1979 | 12 Sept | Wembley | 1 | 0 |
| EC1982 | 22 Sept | Copenhagen | 2 | 2 |
| EC1983 | 21 Sept | Wembley | 0 | 1 |
| 1988 | 14 Sept | Wembley | 1 | 0 |
| 1989 | 7 June | Copenhagen | 1 | 1 |
| 1990 | 15 May | Wembley | 1 | 0 |
| EC1992 | 11 June | Malmo | 0 | 0 |
| 1994 | 9 Mar | Wembley | 1 | 0 |
| wc2002 | 15 June | Niigata | 3 | 0 |
| 2003 | 16 Nov | Old Trafford | 2 | 3 |
| 2005 | 17 Aug | Copenhagen | 1 | 4 |
| 2011 | 9 Feb | Copenhagen | 2 | 1 |

**v ECUADOR** — E Ec

| | | | E | Ec |
|---|---|---|---|---|
| 1970 | 24 May | Quito | 2 | 0 |
| wc2006 | 25 June | Stuttgart | 1 | 0 |

**v EGYPT** — E Eg

| | | | E | Eg |
|---|---|---|---|---|
| 1986 | 29 Jan | Cairo | 4 | 0 |
| wc1990 | 21 June | Cagliari | 1 | 0 |
| 2010 | 3 Mar | Wembley | 3 | 1 |

| | | | E | Es |
|---|---|---|---|---|
| | | **v ESTONIA** | | |
| EC2007 | 6 June | Tallinn | 3 | 0 |
| EC2007 | 13 Oct | Wembley | 3 | 0 |

| | | | E | FIFA |
|---|---|---|---|---|
| | | **v FIFA** | | |
| 1938 | 26 Oct | Highbury | 3 | 0 |
| 1953 | 21 Oct | Wembley | 4 | 4 |
| 1963 | 23 Oct | Wembley | 2 | 1 |

| | | | E | F |
|---|---|---|---|---|
| | | **v FINLAND** | | |
| 1937 | 20 May | Helsinki | 8 | 0 |
| 1956 | 20 May | Helsinki | 5 | 1 |
| 1966 | 26 June | Helsinki | 3 | 0 |
| wc1976 | 13 June | Helsinki | 4 | 1 |
| wc1976 | 13 Oct | Wembley | 2 | 1 |
| 1982 | 3 June | Helsinki | 4 | 1 |
| wc1984 | 17 Oct | Wembley | 5 | 0 |
| wc1985 | 22 May | Helsinki | 1 | 1 |
| 1992 | 3 June | Helsinki | 2 | 1 |
| wc2000 | 11 Oct | Helsinki | 0 | 0 |
| wc2001 | 24 Mar | Liverpool | 2 | 1 |

| | | | E | F |
|---|---|---|---|---|
| | | **v FRANCE** | | |
| 1923 | 10 May | Paris | 4 | 1 |
| 1924 | 17 May | Paris | 3 | 1 |
| 1925 | 21 May | Paris | 3 | 2 |
| 1927 | 26 May | Paris | 6 | 0 |
| 1928 | 17 May | Paris | 5 | 1 |
| 1929 | 9 May | Paris | 4 | 1 |
| 1931 | 14 May | Paris | 2 | 5 |
| 1933 | 6 Dec | Tottenham | 4 | 1 |
| 1938 | 26 May | Paris | 4 | 2 |
| 1947 | 3 May | Highbury | 3 | 0 |
| 1949 | 22 May | Paris | 3 | 1 |
| 1951 | 3 Oct | Highbury | 2 | 2 |
| 1955 | 15 May | Paris | 0 | 1 |
| 1957 | 27 Nov | Wembley | 4 | 0 |
| EC1962 | 3 Oct | Sheffield | 1 | 1 |
| EC1963 | 27 Feb | Paris | 2 | 5 |
| wc1966 | 20 July | Wembley | 2 | 0 |
| 1969 | 12 Mar | Wembley | 5 | 0 |
| wc1982 | 16 June | Bilbao | 3 | 1 |
| 1984 | 29 Feb | Paris | 0 | 2 |
| 1992 | 19 Feb | Wembley | 2 | 0 |
| EC1992 | 14 June | Malmo | 0 | 0 |
| TF1997 | 7 June | Montpellier | 1 | 0 |
| 1999 | 10 Feb | Wembley | 0 | 2 |
| 2000 | 2 Sept | Paris | 1 | 1 |
| EC2004 | 13 June | Lisbon | 1 | 2 |
| 2008 | 26 Mar | Paris | 0 | 1 |
| 2010 | 17 Nov | Wembley | 1 | 2 |
| EC2012 | 11 June | Donetsk | 1 | 1 |

| | | | E | G |
|---|---|---|---|---|
| | | **v GEORGIA** | | |
| wc1996 | 9 Nov | Tbilisi | 2 | 0 |
| wc1997 | 30 Apr | Wembley | 2 | 0 |

| | | | E | G |
|---|---|---|---|---|
| | | **v GERMANY** | | |
| 1930 | 10 May | Berlin | 3 | 3 |
| 1935 | 4 Dec | Tottenham | 3 | 0 |
| 1938 | 14 May | Berlin | 6 | 3 |
| 1991 | 11 Sept | Wembley | 0 | 1 |
| 1993 | 19 June | Detroit | 1 | 2 |
| EC1996 | 26 June | Wembley | 1 | 1* |
| EC2000 | 17 June | Charleroi | 1 | 0 |
| wc2000 | 7 Oct | Wembley | 0 | 1 |
| wc2001 | 1 Sept | Munich | 5 | 1 |
| 2007 | 22 Aug | Wembley | 1 | 2 |
| 2008 | 19 Nov | Berlin | 2 | 1 |
| wc2010 | 27 June | Bloemfontein | 1 | 4 |

| | | | E | EG |
|---|---|---|---|---|
| | | **v EAST GERMANY** | | |
| 1963 | 2 June | Leipzig | 2 | 1 |
| 1970 | 25 Nov | Wembley | 3 | 1 |
| 1974 | 29 May | Leipzig | 1 | 1 |
| 1984 | 12 Sept | Wembley | 1 | 0 |

| | | | E | WG |
|---|---|---|---|---|
| | | **v WEST GERMANY** | | |
| 1954 | 1 Dec | Wembley | 3 | 1 |
| 1956 | 26 May | Berlin | 3 | 1 |
| 1965 | 12 May | Nuremberg | 1 | 0 |
| 1966 | 23 Feb | Wembley | 1 | 0 |
| wc1966 | 30 July | Wembley | 4 | 2* |
| 1968 | 1 June | Hanover | 0 | 1 |
| wc1970 | 14 June | Leon | 2 | 3* |
| EC1972 | 29 Apr | Wembley | 1 | 3 |
| EC1972 | 13 May | Berlin | 0 | 0 |
| 1975 | 12 Mar | Wembley | 2 | 0 |
| 1978 | 22 Feb | Munich | 1 | 2 |
| wc1982 | 29 June | Madrid | 0 | 0 |
| 1982 | 13 Oct | Wembley | 1 | 2 |
| 1985 | 12 June | Mexico City | 3 | 0 |
| 1987 | 9 Sept | Dusseldorf | 1 | 3 |
| wc1990 | 4 July | Turin | 1 | 1* |

| | | | E | G |
|---|---|---|---|---|
| | | **v GHANA** | | |
| 2011 | 29 Mar | Wembley | 1 | 1 |

| | | | E | G |
|---|---|---|---|---|
| | | **v GREECE** | | |
| EC1971 | 21 Apr | Wembley | 3 | 0 |
| EC1971 | 1 Dec | Piraeus | 2 | 0 |
| EC1982 | 17 Nov | Salonika | 3 | 0 |
| EC1983 | 30 Mar | Wembley | 0 | 0 |
| 1989 | 8 Feb | Athens | 2 | 1 |
| 1994 | 17 May | Wembley | 5 | 0 |
| wc2001 | 6 June | Athens | 2 | 0 |
| wc2001 | 6 Oct | Old Trafford | 2 | 2 |
| 2006 | 16 Aug | Old Trafford | 4 | 0 |

| | | | E | H |
|---|---|---|---|---|
| | | **v HOLLAND** | | |
| 1935 | 18 May | Amsterdam | 1 | 0 |
| 1946 | 27 Nov | Huddersfield | 8 | 2 |
| 1964 | 9 Dec | Amsterdam | 1 | 1 |
| 1969 | 5 Nov | Amsterdam | 1 | 0 |
| 1970 | 14 Jun | Wembley | 0 | 0 |
| 1977 | 9 Feb | Wembley | 0 | 2 |
| 1982 | 25 May | Wembley | 2 | 0 |
| 1988 | 23 Mar | Wembley | 2 | 2 |
| EC1988 | 15 June | Dusseldorf | 1 | 3 |
| wc1990 | 16 June | Cagliari | 0 | 0 |
| 2005 | 9 Feb | Villa Park | 0 | 0 |
| wc1993 | 28 Apr | Wembley | 2 | 2 |
| wc1993 | 13 Oct | Rotterdam | 0 | 2 |
| EC1996 | 18 June | Wembley | 4 | 1 |
| 2001 | 15 Aug | Tottenham | 0 | 2 |
| 2002 | 13 Feb | Amsterdam | 1 | 1 |
| 2006 | 15 Nov | Amsterdam | 1 | 1 |
| 2009 | 12 Aug | Amsterdam | 2 | 2 |
| 2012 | 29 Feb | Wembley | 2 | 3 |

| | | | E | H |
|---|---|---|---|---|
| | | **v HUNGARY** | | |
| 1908 | 10 June | Budapest | 7 | 0 |
| 1909 | 29 May | Budapest | 4 | 2 |
| 1909 | 31 May | Budapest | 8 | 2 |
| 1934 | 10 May | Budapest | 1 | 2 |
| 1936 | 2 Dec | Highbury | 6 | 2 |
| 1953 | 25 Nov | Wembley | 3 | 6 |
| 1954 | 23 May | Budapest | 1 | 7 |
| 1960 | 22 May | Budapest | 0 | 2 |
| wc1962 | 31 May | Rancagua | 1 | 2 |
| 1965 | 5 May | Wembley | 1 | 0 |
| 1978 | 24 May | Wembley | 4 | 1 |
| wc1981 | 6 June | Budapest | 3 | 1 |
| wc1982 | 18 Nov | Wembley | 1 | 0 |
| EC1983 | 27 Apr | Wembley | 2 | 0 |
| EC1983 | 12 Oct | Budapest | 3 | 0 |
| 1988 | 27 Apr | Budapest | 0 | 0 |
| 1990 | 12 Sept | Wembley | 1 | 0 |
| 1992 | 12 May | Budapest | 1 | 0 |
| 1996 | 18 May | Wembley | 3 | 0 |
| 1999 | 28 Apr | Budapest | 1 | 1 |
| 2006 | 30 May | Old Trafford | 3 | 1 |
| 2010 | 11 Aug | Wembley | 2 | 1 |

| | | | E | I |
|---|---|---|---|---|
| | | **v ICELAND** | | |
| 1982 | 2 June | Reykjavik | 1 | 1 |
| 2004 | 5 June | City of Manchester | 6 | 1 |
| EC2007 | 24 Mar | Tel Aviv | 0 | 0 |

| v REPUBLIC OF IRELAND | | E | RI |
|---|---|---|---|
| 1946 | 30 Sept | Dublin | 1 | 0 |
| 1949 | 21 Sept | Everton | 0 | 2 |
| wc1957 | 8 May | Wembley | 5 | 1 |
| wc1957 | 19 May | Dublin | 1 | 1 |
| 1964 | 24 May | Dublin | 3 | 1 |
| 1976 | 8 Sept | Wembley | 1 | 1 |
| EC1978 | 25 Oct | Dublin | 1 | 1 |
| EC1980 | 6 Feb | Wembley | 2 | 0 |
| 1985 | 26 Mar | Wembley | 2 | 1 |
| EC1988 | 12 June | Stuttgart | 0 | 1 |
| wc1990 | 11 June | Cagliari | 1 | 1 |
| EC1990 | 14 Nov | Dublin | 1 | 1 |
| EC1991 | 27 Mar | Wembley | 1 | 1 |
| 1995 | 15 Feb | Dublin | 0 | 1 |
| | *(abandoned after 27 mins)* | | | |
| 2013 | 29 May | Wembley | 1 | 1 |

| v ISRAEL | | E | I |
|---|---|---|---|
| 1986 | 26 Feb | Ramat Gan | 2 | 1 |
| 1988 | 17 Feb | Tel Aviv | 0 | 0 |
| EC2007 | 24 Mar | Tel Aviv | 0 | 0 |
| EC2007 | 8 Sept | Wembley | 3 | 0 |

| v ITALY | | E | I |
|---|---|---|---|
| 1933 | 13 May | Rome | 1 | 1 |
| 1934 | 14 Nov | Highbury | 3 | 2 |
| 1939 | 13 May | Milan | 2 | 2 |
| 1948 | 16 May | Turin | 4 | 0 |
| 1949 | 30 Nov | Tottenham | 2 | 0 |
| 1952 | 18 May | Florence | 1 | 1 |
| 1959 | 6 May | Wembley | 2 | 2 |
| 1961 | 24 May | Rome | 3 | 2 |
| 1973 | 14 June | Turin | 0 | 2 |
| 1973 | 14 Nov | Wembley | 0 | 1 |
| 1976 | 28 May | New York | 3 | 2 |
| wc1976 | 17 Nov | Rome | 0 | 2 |
| wc1977 | 16 Nov | Wembley | 2 | 0 |
| EC1980 | 15 June | Turin | 0 | 1 |
| 1985 | 6 June | Mexico City | 1 | 2 |
| 1989 | 15 Nov | Wembley | 0 | 0 |
| wc1990 | 7 July | Bari | 1 | 2 |
| wc1997 | 12 Feb | Wembley | 0 | 1 |
| TF1997 | 4 June | Nantes | 2 | 0 |
| wc1997 | 11 Oct | Rome | 0 | 0 |
| 2000 | 15 Nov | Turin | 0 | 1 |
| 2002 | 27 Mar | Leeds | 1 | 2 |
| EC2012 | 24 June | Kiev | 0 | 0 |
| 2012 | 15 Aug | Berne | 2 | 1 |

| v JAMAICA | | E | J |
|---|---|---|---|
| 2006 | 3 June | Old Trafford | 6 | 0 |

| v JAPAN | | E | J |
|---|---|---|---|
| UI1995 | 3 June | Wembley | 2 | 1 |
| 2004 | 1 June | City of Manchester | 1 | 1 |
| 2010 | 30 May | Graz | 2 | 1 |

| v KAZAKHSTAN | | E | K |
|---|---|---|---|
| wc2008 | 11 Oct | Wembley | 5 | 1 |
| wc2009 | 6 June | Almaty | 4 | 0 |

| v KUWAIT | | E | K |
|---|---|---|---|
| wc1982 | 25 June | Bilbao | 1 | 0 |

| v LIECHTENSTEIN | | E | L |
|---|---|---|---|
| EC2003 | 29 Mar | Vaduz | 2 | 0 |
| EC2003 | 10 Sept | Old Trafford | 2 | 0 |

| v LUXEMBOURG | | E | L |
|---|---|---|---|
| 1927 | 21 May | Esch-sur-Alzette | 5 | 2 |
| wc1960 | 19 Oct | Luxembourg | 9 | 0 |
| wc1961 | 28 Sept | Highbury | 4 | 1 |
| wc1977 | 30 Mar | Wembley | 5 | 0 |
| wc1977 | 12 Oct | Luxembourg | 2 | 0 |
| EC1982 | 15 Dec | Wembley | 9 | 0 |
| EC1983 | 16 Nov | Luxembourg | 4 | 0 |
| EC1998 | 14 Oct | Luxembourg | 3 | 0 |
| EC1999 | 4 Sept | Wembley | 6 | 0 |

| v MACEDONIA | | E | M |
|---|---|---|---|
| EC2002 | 16 Oct | Southampton | 2 | 2 |
| EC2003 | 6 Sept | Skopje | 2 | 1 |
| EC2006 | 6 Sept | Skopje | 1 | 0 |
| EC2006 | 7 Oct | Old Trafford | 0 | 0 |

| v MALAYSIA | | E | M |
|---|---|---|---|
| 1991 | 12 June | Kuala Lumpur | 4 | 2 |

| v MALTA | | E | M |
|---|---|---|---|
| EC1971 | 3 Feb | Valletta | 1 | 0 |
| EC1971 | 12 May | Wembley | 5 | 0 |
| 2000 | 3 June | Valletta | 2 | 1 |

| v MEXICO | | E | M |
|---|---|---|---|
| 1959 | 24 May | Mexico City | 1 | 2 |
| 1961 | 10 May | Wembley | 8 | 0 |
| wc1966 | 16 July | Wembley | 2 | 0 |
| 1969 | 1 June | Mexico City | 0 | 0 |
| 1985 | 9 June | Mexico City | 0 | 1 |
| 1986 | 17 May | Los Angeles | 3 | 0 |
| 1997 | 29 Mar | Wembley | 2 | 0 |
| 2001 | 25 May | Derby | 4 | 0 |
| 2010 | 24 May | Wembley | 3 | 1 |

| v MOLDOVA | | E | M |
|---|---|---|---|
| wc1996 | 1 Sept | Chisinau | 3 | 0 |
| wc1997 | 10 Sept | Wembley | 4 | 0 |
| wc2012 | 7 Sept | Chisinau | 5 | 0 |

| v MONTENEGRO | | E | M |
|---|---|---|---|
| EC1989 | 8 Mar | Tirana | 2 | 0 |
| 2010 | 12 Oct | Wembley | 0 | 0 |
| EC2011 | 7 Oct | Podgorica | 2 | 2 |
| wc2013 | 26 Mar | Podgorica | 1 | 1 |

| v MOROCCO | | E | M |
|---|---|---|---|
| wc1986 | 6 June | Monterrey | 0 | 0 |
| 1998 | 27 May | Casablanca | 1 | 0 |

| v NEW ZEALAND | | E | NZ |
|---|---|---|---|
| 1991 | 3 June | Auckland | 1 | 0 |
| 1991 | 8 June | Wellington | 2 | 0 |

| v NIGERIA | | E | N |
|---|---|---|---|
| 1994 | 16 Nov | Wembley | 1 | 0 |
| wc2002 | 12 June | Osaka | 0 | 0 |

| v NORWAY | | E | N |
|---|---|---|---|
| 1937 | 14 May | Oslo | 6 | 0 |
| 1938 | 9 Nov | Newcastle | 4 | 0 |
| 1949 | 18 May | Oslo | 4 | 1 |
| 1966 | 29 June | Oslo | 6 | 1 |
| wc1980 | 10 Sept | Wembley | 4 | 0 |
| wc1981 | 9 Sept | Oslo | 1 | 2 |
| wc1992 | 14 Oct | Wembley | 1 | 1 |
| wc1993 | 2 June | Oslo | 0 | 2 |
| 1994 | 22 May | Wembley | 0 | 0 |
| 1995 | 11 Oct | Oslo | 0 | 0 |
| 2012 | 26 May | Oslo | 1 | 0 |

| v PARAGUAY | | E | P |
|---|---|---|---|
| wc1986 | 18 June | Mexico City | 3 | 0 |
| 2002 | 17 Apr | Liverpool | 4 | 0 |
| wc2006 | 10 June | Frankfurt | 1 | 0 |

| v PERU | | E | P |
|---|---|---|---|
| 1959 | 17 May | Lima | 1 | 4 |
| 1962 | 20 May | Lima | 4 | 0 |

| v POLAND | | E | P |
|---|---|---|---|
| 1966 | 5 Jan | Everton | 1 | 1 |
| 1966 | 5 July | Chorzow | 1 | 0 |
| wc1973 | 6 June | Chorzow | 0 | 2 |
| wc1973 | 17 Oct | Wembley | 1 | 1 |
| wc1986 | 11 June | Monterrey | 3 | 0 |
| wc1989 | 3 June | Wembley | 3 | 0 |
| wc1989 | 11 Oct | Katowice | 0 | 0 |
| EC1990 | 17 Oct | Wembley | 2 | 0 |
| EC1991 | 13 Nov | Poznan | 1 | 1 |
| wc1993 | 29 May | Katowice | 1 | 1 |
| wc1993 | 8 Sept | Wembley | 3 | 0 |
| wc1996 | 9 Oct | Wembley | 2 | 1 |

| | | | E | P |
|---|---|---|---|---|
| wc1997 | 31 May | Katowice | 2 | 0 |
| EC1999 | 27 Mar | Wembley | 3 | 1 |
| EC1999 | 8 Sept | Warsaw | 0 | 0 |
| wc2004 | 8 Sept | Katowice | 2 | 1 |
| wc2005 | 12 Oct | Old Trafford | 2 | 1 |
| wc2012 | 17 Oct | Warsaw | 1 | 1 |

**v PORTUGAL**

| | | | E | P |
|---|---|---|---|---|
| 1947 | 25 May | Lisbon | 10 | 0 |
| 1950 | 14 May | Lisbon | 5 | 3 |
| 1951 | 19 May | Everton | 5 | 2 |
| 1955 | 22 May | Oporto | 1 | 3 |
| 1958 | 7 May | Wembley | 2 | 1 |
| wc1961 | 21 May | Lisbon | 1 | 1 |
| wc1961 | 25 Oct | Wembley | 2 | 0 |
| 1964 | 17 May | Lisbon | 4 | 3 |
| 1964 | 4 June | São Paulo | 1 | 1 |
| wc1966 | 26 July | Wembley | 2 | 1 |
| 1969 | 10 Dec | Wembley | 1 | 0 |
| 1974 | 3 Apr | Lisbon | 0 | 0 |
| EC1974 | 20 Nov | Wembley | 0 | 0 |
| EC1975 | 19 Nov | Lisbon | 1 | 1 |
| wc1986 | 3 June | Monterrey | 0 | 1 |
| 1995 | 12 Dec | Wembley | 1 | 1 |
| 1998 | 22 Apr | Wembley | 3 | 0 |
| EC2000 | 12 June | Eindhoven | 2 | 3 |
| 2002 | 7 Sept | Villa Park | 1 | 1 |
| 2004 | 18 Feb | Faro | 1 | 1 |
| EC2004 | 24 June | Lisbon | 2 | 2* |
| wc2006 | 1 July | Gelsenkirchen | 0 | 0 |

**v ROMANIA**

| | | | E | R |
|---|---|---|---|---|
| 1939 | 24 May | Bucharest | 2 | 0 |
| 1968 | 6 Nov | Bucharest | 0 | 0 |
| 1969 | 15 Jan | Wembley | 1 | 1 |
| wc1970 | 2 June | Guadalajara | 1 | 0 |
| wc1980 | 15 Oct | Bucharest | 1 | 2 |
| wc1981 | 29 April | Wembley | 0 | 0 |
| wc1985 | 1 May | Bucharest | 0 | 0 |
| wc1985 | 11 Sept | Wembley | 1 | 1 |
| 1994 | 12 Oct | Wembley | 1 | 1 |
| wc1998 | 22 June | Toulouse | 1 | 2 |
| EC2000 | 20 June | Charleroi | 2 | 3 |

**v RUSSIA**

| | | | E | R |
|---|---|---|---|---|
| EC2007 | 12 Sept | Wembley | 3 | 0 |
| EC2007 | 17 Oct | Moscow | 1 | 2 |

**v SAN MARINO**

| | | | E | SM |
|---|---|---|---|---|
| wc1992 | 17 Feb | Wembley | 6 | 0 |
| wc1993 | 17 Nov | Bologna | 7 | 1 |
| wc2012 | 12 Oct | Wembley | 5 | 0 |
| wc2013 | 22 Mar | Serravalle | 8 | 0 |

**v SAUDI ARABIA**

| | | | E | SA |
|---|---|---|---|---|
| 1988 | 16 Nov | Riyadh | 1 | 1 |
| 1998 | 23 May | Wembley | 0 | 0 |

**v SERBIA-MONTENEGRO**

| | | | E | S-M |
|---|---|---|---|---|
| 2003 | 3 June | Leicester | 2 | 1 |

**v SLOVAKIA**

| | | | E | S |
|---|---|---|---|---|
| EC2002 | 12 Oct | Bratislava | 2 | 1 |
| EC2003 | 11 June | Middlesbrough | 2 | 1 |
| 2009 | 28 Mar | Wembley | 4 | 0 |

**v SLOVENIA**

| | | | E | S |
|---|---|---|---|---|
| 2009 | 5 Sept | Wembley | 2 | 1 |
| wc2010 | 23 June | Port Elizabeth | 1 | 0 |

**v SOUTH AFRICA**

| | | | E | SA |
|---|---|---|---|---|
| 1997 | 24 May | Old Trafford | 2 | 1 |
| 2003 | 22 May | Durban | 2 | 1 |

**v SOUTH KOREA**

| | | | E | SK |
|---|---|---|---|---|
| 2002 | 21 May | Seoguipo | 1 | 1 |

**v SPAIN**

| | | | E | S |
|---|---|---|---|---|
| 1929 | 15 May | Madrid | 3 | 4 |
| 1931 | 9 Dec | Highbury | 7 | 1 |
| wc1950 | 2 July | Rio de Janeiro | 0 | 1 |

| | | | E | S |
|---|---|---|---|---|
| 1955 | 18 May | Madrid | 1 | 1 |
| 1955 | 30 Nov | Wembley | 4 | 1 |
| 1960 | 15 May | Madrid | 0 | 3 |
| 1960 | 26 Oct | Wembley | 4 | 2 |
| 1965 | 8 Dec | Madrid | 2 | 0 |
| 1967 | 24 May | Wembley | 2 | 0 |
| EC1968 | 3 Apr | Wembley | 1 | 0 |
| EC1968 | 8 May | Madrid | 2 | 1 |
| 1980 | 26 Mar | Barcelona | 2 | 0 |
| EC1980 | 18 June | Naples | 2 | 1 |
| 1981 | 25 Mar | Wembley | 1 | 2 |
| wc1982 | 5 July | Madrid | 0 | 0 |
| 1987 | 18 Feb | Madrid | 4 | 2 |
| 1992 | 9 Sept | Santander | 0 | 1 |
| EC 1996 | 22 June | Wembley | 0 | 0 |
| 2001 | 28 Feb | Villa Park | 3 | 0 |
| 2004 | 17 Nov | Madrid | 0 | 1 |
| 2007 | 7 Feb | Old Trafford | 0 | 1 |
| 2009 | 11 Feb | Seville | 0 | 2 |
| 2011 | 12 Nov | Wembley | 1 | 0 |

**v SWEDEN**

| | | | E | S |
|---|---|---|---|---|
| 1923 | 21 May | Stockholm | 4 | 2 |
| 1923 | 24 May | Stockholm | 3 | 1 |
| 1937 | 17 May | Stockholm | 4 | 0 |
| 1947 | 19 Nov | Highbury | 4 | 2 |
| 1949 | 13 May | Stockholm | 1 | 3 |
| 1956 | 16 May | Stockholm | 0 | 0 |
| 1959 | 28 Oct | Wembley | 2 | 3 |
| 1965 | 16 May | Gothenburg | 2 | 1 |
| 1968 | 22 May | Wembley | 3 | 1 |
| 1979 | 10 June | Stockholm | 0 | 0 |
| 1986 | 10 Sept | Stockholm | 0 | 1 |
| wc1988 | 19 Oct | Wembley | 0 | 0 |
| wc1989 | 6 Sept | Stockholm | 0 | 0 |
| EC1992 | 17 June | Stockholm | 1 | 2 |
| UI1995 | 8 June | Leeds | 3 | 3 |
| EC1998 | 5 Sept | Stockholm | 1 | 2 |
| EC1999 | 5 June | Wembley | 0 | 0 |
| 2001 | 10 Nov | Old Trafford | 1 | 1 |
| wc2002 | 2 June | Saitama | 1 | 1 |
| 2004 | 31 Mar | Gothenburg | 0 | 1 |
| wc2006 | 20 June | Cologne | 2 | 2 |
| 2011 | 15 Nov | Wembley | 1 | 0 |
| EC2012 | 15 June | Kiev | 3 | 2 |
| 2012 | 14 Nov | Stockholm | 2 | 4 |

**v SWITZERLAND**

| | | | E | S |
|---|---|---|---|---|
| 1933 | 20 May | Berne | 4 | 0 |
| 1938 | 21 May | Zurich | 1 | 2 |
| 1947 | 18 May | Zurich | 0 | 1 |
| 1948 | 2 Dec | Highbury | 6 | 0 |
| 1952 | 28 May | Zurich | 3 | 0 |
| wc1954 | 20 June | Berne | 2 | 0 |
| 1962 | 9 May | Wembley | 3 | 1 |
| 1963 | 5 June | Basle | 8 | 1 |
| EC1971 | 13 Oct | Basle | 3 | 2 |
| EC1971 | 10 Nov | Wembley | 1 | 1 |
| 1975 | 3 Sept | Basle | 2 | 1 |
| 1977 | 7 Sept | Wembley | 0 | 0 |
| wc1980 | 19 Nov | Wembley | 2 | 1 |
| wc1981 | 30 May | Basle | 1 | 2 |
| 1988 | 28 May | Lausanne | 1 | 0 |
| 1995 | 15 Nov | Wembley | 3 | 1 |
| EC1996 | 8 June | Wembley | 1 | 1 |
| 1998 | 25 Mar | Berne | 1 | 1 |
| EC2004 | 17 June | Coimbra | 3 | 0 |
| 2008 | 6 Feb | Wembley | 2 | 1 |
| EC1989 | 8 Mar | Tirana | 2 | 0 |
| EC2010 | 7 Sept | Basle | 3 | 1 |
| EC2011 | 4 June | Wembley | 2 | 2 |

**v TRINIDAD & TOBAGO**

| | | | E | TT |
|---|---|---|---|---|
| wc2006 | 15 June | Nuremberg | 2 | 0 |
| 2008 | 2 June | Port of Spain | 3 | 0 |

| v TUNISIA | | E | T |
|---|---|---|---|
| 1990 | 2 June | Tunis | 1 | 1 |
| wc1998 | 15 June | Marseilles | 2 | 0 |

| v TURKEY | | E | T |
|---|---|---|---|
| wc1984 | 14 Nov | Istanbul | 8 | 0 |
| wc1985 | 16 Oct | Wembley | 5 | 0 |
| EC1987 | 29 Apr | Izmir | 0 | 0 |
| EC1987 | 14 Oct | Wembley | 8 | 0 |
| EC1991 | 1 May | Izmir | 1 | 0 |
| EC1991 | 16 Oct | Wembley | 1 | 0 |
| wc1992 | 18 Nov | Wembley | 4 | 0 |
| wc1993 | 31 Mar | Izmir | 2 | 0 |
| EC2003 | 2 Apr | Sunderland | 2 | 0 |
| EC2003 | 11 Oct | Istanbul | 0 | 0 |

| v UKRAINE | | E | U |
|---|---|---|---|
| 2000 | 31 May | Wembley | 2 | 0 |
| 2004 | 18 Aug | Newcastle | 3 | 0 |
| wc2009 | 1 Apr | Wembley | 2 | 1 |
| wc2009 | 10 Oct | Dnepr | 0 | 1 |
| EC2012 | 19 June | Donetsk | 1 | 0 |
| wc2012 | 11 Sept | Wembley | 1 | 1 |

| v URUGUAY | | E | U |
|---|---|---|---|
| 1953 | 31 May | Montevideo | 1 | 2 |
| wc1954 | 26 June | Basle | 2 | 4 |
| 1964 | 6 May | Wembley | 2 | 1 |
| wc1966 | 11 July | Wembley | 0 | 0 |
| 1969 | 8 June | Montevideo | 2 | 1 |
| 1977 | 15 June | Montevideo | 0 | 0 |
| 1984 | 13 June | Montevideo | 0 | 2 |
| 1990 | 22 May | Wembley | 1 | 2 |
| 1995 | 29 Mar | Wembley | 0 | 0 |
| 2006 | 1 Mar | Liverpool | 2 | 1 |

| v USA | | E | USA |
|---|---|---|---|
| wc1950 | 29 June | Belo Horizonte | 0 | 1 |
| 1953 | 8 June | New York | 6 | 3 |
| 1959 | 28 May | Los Angeles | 8 | 1 |
| 1964 | 27 May | New York | 10 | 0 |
| 1985 | 16 June | Los Angeles | 5 | 0 |
| 1993 | 9 June | Foxboro | 0 | 2 |
| 1994 | 7 Sept | Wembley | 2 | 0 |
| 2005 | 28 May | Chicago | 2 | 1 |
| 2008 | 28 May | Wembley | 2 | 0 |
| wc2010 | 12 June | Rustenburg | 1 | 1 |

| v USSR | | E | USSR |
|---|---|---|---|
| 1958 | 18 May | Moscow | 1 | 1 |
| wc1958 | 8 June | Gothenburg | 2 | 2 |
| wc1958 | 17 June | Gothenburg | 0 | 1 |
| 1958 | 22 Oct | Wembley | 5 | 0 |
| 1967 | 6 Dec | Wembley | 2 | 2 |
| EC1968 | 8 June | Rome | 2 | 0 |
| 1973 | 10 June | Moscow | 2 | 1 |
| 1984 | 2 June | Wembley | 0 | 2 |
| 1986 | 26 Mar | Tbilisi | 1 | 0 |
| EC1988 | 18 June | Frankfurt | 1 | 3 |
| 1991 | 21 May | Wembley | 3 | 1 |

| v YUGOSLAVIA | | E | Y |
|---|---|---|---|
| 1939 | 18 May | Belgrade | 1 | 2 |
| 1950 | 22 Nov | Highbury | 2 | 2 |
| 1954 | 16 May | Belgrade | 0 | 1 |
| 1956 | 28 Nov | Wembley | 3 | 0 |
| 1958 | 11 May | Belgrade | 0 | 5 |
| 1960 | 11 May | Wembley | 3 | 3 |
| 1965 | 9 May | Belgrade | 1 | 1 |
| 1966 | 4 May | Wembley | 2 | 0 |
| EC1968 | 5 June | Florence | 0 | 1 |
| 1972 | 11 Oct | Wembley | 1 | 1 |
| 1974 | 5 June | Belgrade | 2 | 2 |
| EC1986 | 12 Nov | Wembley | 2 | 0 |
| EC1987 | 11 Nov | Belgrade | 4 | 1 |
| 1989 | 13 Dec | Wembley | 2 | 1 |

## SCOTLAND

| v ARGENTINA | | S | A |
|---|---|---|---|
| 1977 | 18 June | Buenos Aires | 1 | 1 |
| 1979 | 2 June | Glasgow | 1 | 3 |
| 1990 | 28 Mar | Glasgow | 1 | 0 |
| 2008 | 19 Nov | Glasgow | 0 | 1 |

| v AUSTRALIA | | S | A |
|---|---|---|---|
| wc1985 | 20 Nov | Glasgow | 2 | 0 |
| wc1985 | 4 Dec | Melbourne | 0 | 0 |
| 1996 | 27 Mar | Glasgow | 1 | 0 |
| 2000 | 15 Nov | Glasgow | 0 | 2 |
| 2012 | 15 Aug | Edinburgh | 3 | 1 |

| v AUSTRIA | | S | A |
|---|---|---|---|
| 1931 | 16 May | Vienna | 0 | 5 |
| 1933 | 29 Nov | Glasgow | 2 | 2 |
| 1937 | 9 May | Vienna | 1 | 1 |
| 1950 | 13 Dec | Glasgow | 0 | 1 |
| 1951 | 27 May | Vienna | 0 | 4 |
| wc1954 | 16 June | Zurich | 0 | 1 |
| 1955 | 19 May | Vienna | 4 | 1 |
| 1956 | 2 May | Glasgow | 1 | 1 |
| 1960 | 29 May | Vienna | 1 | 4 |
| 1963 | 8 May | Glasgow | 4 | 1 |
| *(abandoned after 79 mins)* | | | |
| 1968 | 6 Nov | Glasgow | 2 | 1 |
| wc1969 | 5 Nov | Vienna | 0 | 2 |
| EC1978 | 20 Sept | Vienna | 2 | 3 |
| EC1979 | 17 Oct | Glasgow | 1 | 1 |
| 1994 | 20 Apr | Vienna | 2 | 1 |
| wc1996 | 31 Aug | Vienna | 0 | 0 |
| wc1997 | 2 Apr | Celtic Park | 2 | 0 |
| 2003 | 30 Apr | Glasgow | 0 | 2 |
| 2005 | 17 Aug | Graz | 2 | 2 |
| 2007 | 30 May | Vienna | 1 | 0 |

| v BELARUS | | S | B |
|---|---|---|---|
| wc1997 | 8 June | Minsk | 1 | 0 |
| wc1997 | 7 Sept | Aberdeen | 4 | 1 |
| wc2005 | 8 June | Minsk | 0 | 0 |
| wc2005 | 8 Oct | Glasgow | 0 | 1 |

| v BELGIUM | | S | B |
|---|---|---|---|
| 1947 | 18 May | Brussels | 1 | 2 |
| 1948 | 28 Apr | Glasgow | 2 | 0 |
| 1951 | 20 May | Brussels | 5 | 0 |
| EC1971 | 3 Feb | Liege | 0 | 3 |
| EC1971 | 10 Nov | Aberdeen | 1 | 0 |
| 1974 | 2 June | Brussels | 1 | 2 |
| EC1979 | 21 Nov | Brussels | 0 | 2 |
| EC1979 | 19 Dec | Glasgow | 1 | 3 |
| EC1982 | 15 Dec | Brussels | 2 | 3 |
| EC1983 | 12 Oct | Glasgow | 1 | 1 |
| EC1987 | 1 Apr | Brussels | 1 | 4 |
| EC1987 | 14 Oct | Glasgow | 2 | 0 |
| wc2001 | 24 Mar | Glasgow | 2 | 2 |
| wc2001 | 5 Sept | Brussels | 0 | 2 |
| wc2012 | 16 Oct | Brussels | 0 | 2 |

| v BOSNIA | | S | B |
|---|---|---|---|
| EC1999 | 4 Sept | Sarajevo | 2 | 1 |
| EC1999 | 5 Oct | Glasgow | 1 | 0 |

| v BRAZIL | | S | B |
|---|---|---|---|
| 1966 | 25 June | Glasgow | 1 | 1 |
| 1972 | 5 July | Rio de Janeiro | 0 | 1 |
| 1973 | 30 June | Glasgow | 0 | 1 |
| wc1974 | 18 June | Frankfurt | 0 | 0 |
| 1977 | 23 June | Rio de Janeiro | 0 | 2 |
| wc1982 | 18 June | Seville | 1 | 4 |
| 1987 | 26 May | Glasgow | 0 | 2 |
| wc1990 | 20 June | Turin | 0 | 1 |

|  |  |  | S | B |
|---|---|---|---|---|
| wc1998 | 10 June | Saint-Denis | 1 | 2 |
| 2011 | 27 Mar | Emirates | 0 | 2 |

| **v BULGARIA** |  |  | S | B |
|---|---|---|---|---|
| 1978 | 22 Feb | Glasgow | 2 | 1 |
| EC1986 | 10 Sept | Glasgow | 0 | 0 |
| EC1987 | 11 Nov | Sofia | 1 | 0 |
| EC1990 | 14 Nov | Sofia | 1 | 1 |
| EC1991 | 27 Mar | Glasgow | 1 | 1 |
| 2006 | 11 May | Kobe | 5 | 1 |

| **v CANADA** |  |  | S | C |
|---|---|---|---|---|
| 1983 | 12 June | Vancouver | 2 | 0 |
| 1983 | 16 June | Edmonton | 3 | 0 |
| 1983 | 20 June | Toronto | 2 | 0 |
| 1992 | 21 May | Toronto | 3 | 1 |
| 2002 | 15 Oct | Easter Road | 3 | 1 |

| **v CHILE** |  |  | S | C |
|---|---|---|---|---|
| 1977 | 15 June | Santiago | 4 | 2 |
| 1989 | 30 May | Glasgow | 2 | 0 |

| **v CIS** |  |  | S | C |
|---|---|---|---|---|
| EC1992 | 18 June | Norrkoping | 3 | 0 |

| **v COLOMBIA** |  |  | S | C |
|---|---|---|---|---|
| 1988 | 17 May | Glasgow | 0 | 0 |
| 1996 | 30 May | Miami | 0 | 1 |
| 1998 | 23 May | New York | 2 | 2 |

| **v COSTA RICA** |  |  | S | CR |
|---|---|---|---|---|
| wc1990 | 11 June | Genoa | 0 | 1 |

| **v CROATIA** |  |  | S | C |
|---|---|---|---|---|
| wc2000 | 11 Oct | Zagreb | 1 | 1 |
| wc2001 | 1 Sept | Glasgow | 0 | 0 |
| 2008 | 26 Mar | Glasgow | 1 | 1 |
| wc2013 | 7 June | Zagreb | 1 | 0 |

| **v CYPRUS** |  |  | S | C |
|---|---|---|---|---|
| wc1968 | 17 Dec | Nicosia | 5 | 0 |
| wc1969 | 11 May | Glasgow | 8 | 0 |
| wc1989 | 8 Feb | Limassol | 3 | 2 |
| wc1989 | 26 Apr | Glasgow | 2 | 1 |
| 2011 | 11 Nov | Larnaca | 2 | 1 |

| **v CZECHOSLOVAKIA** |  |  | S | C |
|---|---|---|---|---|
| 1937 | 22 May | Prague | 3 | 1 |
| 1937 | 8 Dec | Glasgow | 5 | 0 |
| wc1961 | 14 May | Bratislava | 0 | 4 |
| wc1961 | 26 Sept | Glasgow | 3 | 2 |
| wc1961 | 29 Nov | Brussels | 2 | 4* |
| 1972 | 2 July | Porto Alegre | 0 | 0 |
| wc1973 | 26 Sept | Glasgow | 2 | 1 |
| wc1973 | 17 Oct | Prague | 0 | 1 |
| wc1976 | 13 Oct | Prague | 0 | 2 |
| wc1977 | 21 Sept | Glasgow | 3 | 1 |

| **v CZECH REPUBLIC** |  |  | S | C |
|---|---|---|---|---|
| EC1999 | 31 Mar | Glasgow | 1 | 2 |
| EC1999 | 9 June | Prague | 2 | 3 |
| 2008 | 30 May | Prague | 1 | 3 |
| 2010 | 3 Mar | Glasgow | 1 | 0 |
| EC2010 | 8 Oct | Prague | 0 | 1 |
| EC2011 | 3 Sept | Glasgow | 2 | 2 |

| **v DENMARK** |  |  | S | D |
|---|---|---|---|---|
| 1951 | 12 May | Glasgow | 3 | 1 |
| 1952 | 25 May | Copenhagen | 2 | 1 |
| 1968 | 16 Oct | Copenhagen | 1 | 0 |
| EC1970 | 11 Nov | Glasgow | 1 | 0 |
| EC1971 | 9 June | Copenhagen | 0 | 1 |
| wc1972 | 18 Oct | Copenhagen | 4 | 1 |
| wc1972 | 15 Nov | Glasgow | 2 | 0 |
| EC1975 | 3 Sept | Copenhagen | 1 | 0 |
| EC1975 | 29 Oct | Glasgow | 3 | 1 |
| wc1986 | 4 June | Nezahualcayotl | 0 | 1 |
| 1996 | 24 Apr | Copenhagen | 0 | 2 |
| 1998 | 25 Mar | Glasgow | 0 | 1 |
| 2002 | 21 Aug | Glasgow | 0 | 1 |

|  |  |  | S | D |
|---|---|---|---|---|
| 2004 | 28 Apr | Copenhagen | 0 | 1 |
| 2011 | 10 Aug | Glasgow | 2 | 1 |

| **v ECUADOR** |  |  | S | E |
|---|---|---|---|---|
| 1995 | 24 May | Toyama | 2 | 1 |

| **v EGYPT** |  |  | S | E |
|---|---|---|---|---|
| 1990 | 16 May | Aberdeen | 1 | 3 |

| **v ESTONIA** |  |  | S | E |
|---|---|---|---|---|
| wc1993 | 19 May | Tallinn | 3 | 0 |
| wc1993 | 2 June | Aberdeen | 3 | 1 |
| wc1997 | 11 Feb | Monaco | 0 | 0 |
| wc1997 | 29 Mar | Kilmarnock | 2 | 0 |
| EC1998 | 10 Oct | Edinburgh | 3 | 2 |
| EC1999 | 8 Sept | Tallinn | 0 | 0 |
| 2004 | 27 May | Tallinn | 1 | 0 |
| 2013 | 6 Feb | Aberdeen | 1 | 0 |

| **v FAROE ISLANDS** |  |  | S | F |
|---|---|---|---|---|
| EC1994 | 12 Oct | Glasgow | 5 | 1 |
| EC1995 | 7 June | Toftir | 2 | 0 |
| EC1998 | 14 Oct | Aberdeen | 2 | 1 |
| EC1999 | 5 June | Toftir | 1 | 1 |
| EC2002 | 7 Sept | Toftir | 2 | 2 |
| EC2003 | 6 Sept | Glasgow | 3 | 1 |
| EC2006 | 2 Sept | Celtic Park | 6 | 0 |
| EC2007 | 6 June | Toftir | 2 | 0 |
| 2010 | 16 Nov | Aberdeen | 3 | 0 |

| **v FINLAND** |  |  | S | F |
|---|---|---|---|---|
| 1954 | 25 May | Helsinki | 2 | 1 |
| wc1964 | 21 Oct | Glasgow | 3 | 1 |
| wc1965 | 27 May | Helsinki | 2 | 1 |
| 1976 | 8 Sept | Glasgow | 6 | 0 |
| 1992 | 25 Mar | Glasgow | 1 | 1 |
| EC1994 | 7 Sept | Helsinki | 2 | 0 |
| EC1995 | 6 Sept | Glasgow | 1 | 0 |
| 1998 | 22 Apr | Edinburgh | 1 | 1 |

| **v FRANCE** |  |  | S | F |
|---|---|---|---|---|
| 1930 | 18 May | Paris | 2 | 0 |
| 1932 | 8 May | Paris | 3 | 1 |
| 1948 | 23 May | Paris | 0 | 3 |
| 1949 | 27 Apr | Glasgow | 2 | 0 |
| 1950 | 27 May | Paris | 1 | 0 |
| 1951 | 16 May | Glasgow | 1 | 0 |
| wc1958 | 15 June | Orebro | 1 | 2 |
| 1984 | 1 June | Marseilles | 0 | 2 |
| wc1989 | 8 Mar | Glasgow | 2 | 0 |
| wc1989 | 11 Oct | Paris | 0 | 3 |
| 1997 | 12 Nov | St Etienne | 1 | 2 |
| 2000 | 29 Mar | Glasgow | 0 | 2 |
| 2002 | 27 Mar | Paris | 0 | 5 |
| EC2006 | 7 Oct | Glasgow | 1 | 0 |
| EC2007 | 12 Sept | Paris | 1 | 0 |

| **v GEORGIA** |  |  | S | G |
|---|---|---|---|---|
| EC2007 | 24 Mar | Glasgow | 2 | 1 |
| EC2007 | 17 Oct | Tblisi | 0 | 2 |

| **v GERMANY** |  |  | S | G |
|---|---|---|---|---|
| 1929 | 1 June | Berlin | 1 | 1 |
| 1936 | 14 Oct | Glasgow | 2 | 0 |
| EC1992 | 15 June | Norrkoping | 0 | 2 |
| 1993 | 24 Mar | Glasgow | 0 | 1 |
| 1998 | 28 Apr | Bremen | 1 | 0 |
| EC2003 | 7 June | Glasgow | 1 | 1 |
| EC2003 | 10 Sept | Dortmund | 1 | 2 |

| **v EAST GERMANY** |  |  | S | EG |
|---|---|---|---|---|
| 1974 | 30 Oct | Glasgow | 3 | 0 |
| 1977 | 7 Sept | East Berlin | 0 | 1 |
| EC1982 | 13 Oct | Glasgow | 2 | 0 |
| EC1983 | 16 Nov | Halle | 1 | 2 |
| 1985 | 16 Oct | Glasgow | 0 | 0 |
| 1990 | 25 Apr | Glasgow | 0 | 1 |

| **v WEST GERMANY** |  |  | S | WG |
|---|---|---|---|---|
| 1957 | 22 May | Stuttgart | 3 | 1 |
| 1959 | 6 May | Glasgow | 3 | 2 |

| | | | S | WG |
|---|---|---|---|---|
| 1964 | 12 May | Hanover | 2 | 2 |
| wc1969 | 16 Apr | Glasgow | 1 | 1 |
| wc1969 | 22 Oct | Hamburg | 2 | 3 |
| 1973 | 14 Nov | Glasgow | 1 | 1 |
| 1974 | 27 Mar | Frankfurt | 1 | 2 |
| wc1986 | 8 June | Queretaro | 1 | 2 |

| | | **v GREECE** | S | G |
|---|---|---|---|---|
| EC1994 | 18 Dec | Athens | 0 | 1 |
| EC1995 | 16 Aug | Glasgow | 1 | 0 |

| | | **v HOLLAND** | S | H |
|---|---|---|---|---|
| 1929 | 4 June | Amsterdam | 2 | 0 |
| 1938 | 21 May | Amsterdam | 3 | 1 |
| 1959 | 27 May | Amsterdam | 2 | 1 |
| 1966 | 11 May | Glasgow | 0 | 3 |
| 1968 | 30 May | Amsterdam | 0 | 0 |
| 1971 | 1 Dec | Rotterdam | 1 | 2 |
| wc1978 | 11 June | Mendoza | 3 | 2 |
| 1982 | 23 Mar | Glasgow | 2 | 1 |
| 1986 | 29 Apr | Eindhoven | 0 | 0 |
| EC1992 | 12 June | Gothenburg | 0 | 1 |
| 1994 | 23 Mar | Glasgow | 0 | 1 |
| 1994 | 27 May | Utrecht | 1 | 3 |
| EC1996 | 10 June | Birmingham | 0 | 0 |
| 2000 | 26 Apr | Arnhem | 0 | 0 |
| EC2003 | 15 Nov | Glasgow | 1 | 0 |
| EC2003 | 19 Nov | Amsterdam | 0 | 6 |
| wc2009 | 28 Mar | Amsterdam | 0 | 3 |
| wc2009 | 9 Sept | Glasgow | 0 | 1 |

| | | **v HONG KONG XI** | S | HK |
|---|---|---|---|---|
| †2002 | 23 May | Hong Kong | 4 | 0 |

†*match not recognised by FIFA*

| | | **v HUNGARY** | S | H |
|---|---|---|---|---|
| 1938 | 7 Dec | Glasgow | 3 | 1 |
| 1954 | 8 Dec | Glasgow | 2 | 4 |
| 1955 | 29 May | Budapest | 1 | 3 |
| 1958 | 7 May | Glasgow | 1 | 1 |
| 1960 | 5 June | Budapest | 3 | 3 |
| 1980 | 31 May | Budapest | 1 | 3 |
| 1987 | 9 Sept | Glasgow | 2 | 0 |
| 2004 | 18 Aug | Glasgow | 0 | 3 |

| | | **v ICELAND** | S | I |
|---|---|---|---|---|
| wc1984 | 17 Oct | Glasgow | 3 | 0 |
| wc1985 | 28 May | Reykjavik | 1 | 0 |
| EC2002 | 12 Oct | Reykjavik | 2 | 0 |
| EC2003 | 29 Mar | Glasgow | 2 | 1 |
| wc2008 | 10 Sept | Reykjavik | 2 | 1 |
| wc2009 | 1 Apr | Glasgow | 2 | 1 |

| | | **v IRAN** | S | I |
|---|---|---|---|---|
| wc1978 | 7 June | Cordoba | 1 | 1 |

| | | **v REPUBLIC OF IRELAND** | S | RI |
|---|---|---|---|---|
| wc1961 | 3 May | Glasgow | 4 | 1 |
| wc1961 | 7 May | Dublin | 3 | 0 |
| 1963 | 9 June | Dublin | 0 | 1 |
| 1969 | 21 Sept | Dublin | 1 | 1 |
| EC1986 | 15 Oct | Dublin | 0 | 0 |
| EC1987 | 18 Feb | Glasgow | 0 | 1 |
| 2000 | 30 May | Dublin | 2 | 1 |
| 2003 | 12 Feb | Glasgow | 0 | 2 |
| NC2011 | 29 May | Dublin | 0 | 1 |

| | | **v ISRAEL** | S | I |
|---|---|---|---|---|
| wc1981 | 25 Feb | Tel Aviv | 1 | 0 |
| wc1981 | 28 Apr | Glasgow | 3 | 1 |
| 1986 | 28 Jan | Tel Aviv | 1 | 0 |

| | | **v ITALY** | S | I |
|---|---|---|---|---|
| 1931 | 20 May | Rome | 0 | 3 |
| wc1965 | 9 Nov | Glasgow | 1 | 0 |
| wc1965 | 7 Dec | Naples | 0 | 3 |
| 1988 | 22 Dec | Perugia | 0 | 2 |
| wc1992 | 18 Nov | Glasgow | 0 | 0 |
| wc1993 | 13 Oct | Rome | 1 | 3 |
| wc2005 | 26 Mar | Milan | 0 | 2 |

| | | | S | I |
|---|---|---|---|---|
| wc2005 | 3 Sept | Glasgow | 1 | 1 |
| EC2007 | 28 Mar | Bari | 0 | 2 |
| EC2007 | 17 Nov | Glasgow | 3 | 1 |

| | | **v JAPAN** | S | J |
|---|---|---|---|---|
| 1995 | 21 May | Hiroshima | 0 | 0 |
| 2006 | 13 May | Saitama | 0 | 0 |
| 2009 | 10 Oct | Yokohama | 0 | 2 |

| | | **v LATVIA** | S | L |
|---|---|---|---|---|
| wc1996 | 5 Oct | Riga | 2 | 0 |
| wc1997 | 11 Oct | Glasgow | 2 | 0 |
| wc2000 | 2 Sept | Riga | 1 | 0 |
| wc2001 | 6 Oct | Glasgow | 2 | 1 |

| | | **v LIECHTENSTEIN** | S | L |
|---|---|---|---|---|
| EC2010 | 7 Sept | Glasgow | 2 | 1 |
| EC2011 | 8 Oct | Vaduz | 1 | 0 |

| | | **v LITHUANIA** | S | L |
|---|---|---|---|---|
| EC1998 | 5 Sept | Vilnius | 0 | 0 |
| EC1999 | 9 Oct | Glasgow | 3 | 0 |
| EC2003 | 2 Apr | Kaunas | 0 | 1 |
| EC2003 | 11 Oct | Glasgow | 1 | 0 |
| EC2006 | 6 Sept | Kaunas | 2 | 1 |
| EC2007 | 8 Sept | Glasgow | 3 | 1 |
| EC2010 | 3 Sept | Kaunas | 0 | 0 |
| EC2011 | 6 Sept | Glasgow | 1 | 0 |

| | | **v LUXEMBOURG** | S | L |
|---|---|---|---|---|
| 1947 | 24 May | Luxembourg | 6 | 0 |
| EC1986 | 12 Nov | Glasgow | 3 | 0 |
| EC1987 | 2 Dec | Esch | 0 | 0 |
| 2012 | 14 Nov | Luxembourg | 2 | 1 |

| | | **v MACEDONIA** | S | M |
|---|---|---|---|---|
| wc2008 | 6 Sept | Skopje | 0 | 1 |
| wc2009 | 5 Sept | Glasgow | 2 | 0 |
| wc2012 | 11 Sept | Glasgow | 1 | 1 |

| | | **v MALTA** | S | M |
|---|---|---|---|---|
| 1988 | 22 Mar | Valletta | 1 | 1 |
| 1990 | 28 May | Valletta | 2 | 1 |
| wc1993 | 17 Feb | Valletta | 3 | 0 |
| wc1993 | 17 Nov | Valletta | 2 | 0 |
| 1997 | 1 June | Valletta | 3 | 2 |

| | | **v MOLDOVA** | S | M |
|---|---|---|---|---|
| EC2004 | 13 Oct | Chisinau | 1 | 1 |
| EC2005 | 4 June | Glasgow | 2 | 0 |

| | | **v MOROCCO** | S | M |
|---|---|---|---|---|
| wc1998 | 23 June | St Etienne | 0 | 3 |

| | | **v NEW ZEALAND** | S | NZ |
|---|---|---|---|---|
| wc1982 | 15 June | Malaga | 5 | 2 |
| 2003 | 27 May | Tynecastle | 1 | 1 |

| | | **v NIGERIA** | S | N |
|---|---|---|---|---|
| 2002 | 17 Apr | Aberdeen | 1 | 2 |

| | | **v NORWAY** | S | N |
|---|---|---|---|---|
| 1929 | 28 May | Oslo | 7 | 3 |
| 1954 | 5 May | Glasgow | 1 | 0 |
| 1954 | 19 May | Oslo | 1 | 1 |
| 1963 | 4 June | Bergen | 3 | 4 |
| 1963 | 7 Nov | Glasgow | 6 | 1 |
| 1974 | 6 June | Oslo | 2 | 1 |
| EC1978 | 25 Oct | Glasgow | 3 | 2 |
| EC1979 | 7 June | Oslo | 4 | 0 |
| wc1988 | 14 Sept | Oslo | 2 | 1 |
| wc1989 | 15 Nov | Glasgow | 1 | 1 |
| 1992 | 3 June | Oslo | 0 | 0 |
| wc1998 | 16 June | Bordeaux | 1 | 1 |
| 2003 | 20 Aug | Oslo | 0 | 0 |
| wc2004 | 9 Oct | Glasgow | 0 | 1 |
| wc2005 | 7 Sept | Oslo | 2 | 1 |
| wc2008 | 11 Oct | Glasgow | 0 | 0 |
| wc2009 | 12 Aug | Oslo | 0 | 4 |

| | | **v PARAGUAY** | S | P |
|---|---|---|---|---|
| wc1958 | 11 June | Norrkoping | 2 | 3 |

### v PERU

| | | | S | P |
|---|---|---|---|---|
| 1972 | 26 Apr | Glasgow | 2 | 0 |
| wc1978 | 3 June | Cordoba | 1 | 3 |
| 1979 | 12 Sept | Glasgow | 1 | 1 |

### v POLAND

| | | | S | P |
|---|---|---|---|---|
| 1958 | 1 June | Warsaw | 2 | 1 |
| 1960 | 4 June | Glasgow | 2 | 3 |
| wc1965 | 23 May | Chorzow | 1 | 1 |
| wc1965 | 13 Oct | Glasgow | 1 | 2 |
| 1980 | 28 May | Poznan | 0 | 1 |
| 1990 | 19 May | Glasgow | 1 | 1 |
| 2001 | 25 Apr | Bydgoszcz | 1 | 1 |

### v PORTUGAL

| | | | S | P |
|---|---|---|---|---|
| 1950 | 21 May | Lisbon | 2 | 2 |
| 1955 | 4 May | Glasgow | 3 | 0 |
| 1959 | 3 June | Lisbon | 0 | 1 |
| 1966 | 18 June | Glasgow | 0 | 1 |
| EC1971 | 21 Apr | Lisbon | 0 | 2 |
| EC1971 | 13 Oct | Glasgow | 2 | 1 |
| 1975 | 13 May | Glasgow | 1 | 0 |
| EC1978 | 29 Nov | Lisbon | 0 | 1 |
| EC1980 | 26 Mar | Glasgow | 4 | 1 |
| wc1980 | 15 Oct | Glasgow | 0 | 0 |
| wc1981 | 18 Nov | Lisbon | 1 | 2 |
| wc1992 | 14 Oct | Glasgow | 0 | 0 |
| wc1993 | 28 Apr | Lisbon | 0 | 5 |
| 2002 | 20 Nov | Braga | 0 | 2 |

### v ROMANIA

| | | | S | R |
|---|---|---|---|---|
| EC1975 | 1 June | Bucharest | 1 | 1 |
| EC1975 | 17 Dec | Glasgow | 1 | 1 |
| 1986 | 26 Mar | Glasgow | 3 | 0 |
| EC1990 | 12 Sept | Glasgow | 2 | 1 |
| EC1991 | 16 Oct | Bucharest | 0 | 1 |
| 2004 | 31 Mar | Glasgow | 1 | 2 |

### v RUSSIA

| | | | S | R |
|---|---|---|---|---|
| EC1994 | 16 Nov | Glasgow | 1 | 1 |
| EC1995 | 29 Mar | Moscow | 0 | 0 |

### v SAN MARINO

| | | | S | SM |
|---|---|---|---|---|
| EC1991 | 1 May | Serravalle | 2 | 0 |
| EC1991 | 13 Nov | Glasgow | 4 | 0 |
| EC1995 | 26 Apr | Serravalle | 2 | 0 |
| EC1995 | 15 Nov | Glasgow | 5 | 0 |
| wc2000 | 7 Oct | Serravalle | 2 | 0 |
| wc2001 | 28 Mar | Glasgow | 4 | 0 |

### v SAUDI ARABIA

| | | | S | SA |
|---|---|---|---|---|
| 1988 | 17 Feb | Riyadh | 2 | 2 |

### v SERBIA

| | | | S | Se |
|---|---|---|---|---|
| wc2012 | 8 Sept | Glasgow | 0 | 0 |
| wc2013 | 26 Mar | Novi Sad | 0 | 2 |

### v SLOVENIA

| | | | S | Sl |
|---|---|---|---|---|
| wc2004 | 8 Sept | Glasgow | 0 | 0 |
| wc2005 | 12 Oct | Celje | 3 | 0 |
| 2012 | 29 Feb | Koper | 1 | 1 |

### v SOUTH AFRICA

| | | | S | SA |
|---|---|---|---|---|
| 2002 | 20 May | Hong Kong | 0 | 2 |
| 2007 | 22 Aug | Aberdeen | 1 | 0 |

### v SOUTH KOREA

| | | | S | SK |
|---|---|---|---|---|
| 2002 | 16 May | Busan | 1 | 4 |

### v SPAIN

| | | | S | Sp |
|---|---|---|---|---|
| wc1957 | 8 May | Glasgow | 4 | 2 |
| wc1957 | 26 May | Madrid | 1 | 4 |
| 1963 | 13 June | Madrid | 6 | 2 |
| 1965 | 8 May | Glasgow | 0 | 0 |
| EC1974 | 20 Nov | Glasgow | 1 | 2 |
| EC1975 | 5 Feb | Valencia | 1 | 1 |
| 1982 | 24 Feb | Valencia | 0 | 3 |
| wc1984 | 14 Nov | Glasgow | 3 | 1 |
| wc1985 | 27 Feb | Seville | 0 | 1 |
| 1988 | 27 Apr | Madrid | 0 | 0 |
| 2004 | 3 Sept | Valencia | 1 | 1 |

*Match abandoned afer 60 minutes; floodlight failure.*

| | | | S | Sp |
|---|---|---|---|---|
| EC2010 | 12 Oct | Glasgow | 2 | 3 |
| EC2011 | 11 Oct | Alicante | 1 | 3 |

### v SWEDEN

| | | | S | Sw |
|---|---|---|---|---|
| 1952 | 30 May | Stockholm | 1 | 3 |
| 1953 | 6 May | Glasgow | 1 | 2 |
| 1975 | 16 Apr | Gothenburg | 1 | 1 |
| 1977 | 27 Apr | Glasgow | 3 | 1 |
| wc1980 | 10 Sept | Stockholm | 1 | 0 |
| wc1981 | 9 Sept | Glasgow | 2 | 0 |
| wc1990 | 16 June | Genoa | 2 | 1 |
| 1995 | 11 Oct | Stockholm | 0 | 2 |
| wc1996 | 10 Nov | Glasgow | 1 | 0 |
| wc1997 | 30 Apr | Gothenburg | 1 | 2 |
| 2004 | 17 Nov | Edinburgh | 1 | 4 |
| 2010 | 11 Aug | Stockholm | 0 | 3 |

### v SWITZERLAND

| | | | S | Sw |
|---|---|---|---|---|
| 1931 | 24 May | Geneva | 3 | 2 |
| 1948 | 17 May | Berne | 1 | 2 |
| 1950 | 26 Apr | Berne | 3 | 1 |
| wc1957 | 19 May | Basle | 2 | 1 |
| wc1957 | 6 Nov | Glasgow | 3 | 2 |
| 1973 | 22 June | Berne | 0 | 1 |
| 1976 | 7 Apr | Glasgow | 1 | 0 |
| EC1982 | 17 Nov | Berne | 0 | 2 |
| EC1983 | 30 May | Glasgow | 2 | 2 |
| EC1990 | 17 Oct | Glasgow | 2 | 1 |
| EC1991 | 11 Sept | Berne | 2 | 2 |
| wc1992 | 9 Sept | Berne | 1 | 3 |
| wc1993 | 8 Sept | Aberdeen | 1 | 1 |
| wc1996 | 18 June | Birmingham | 1 | 0 |
| 2006 | 1 Mar | Glasgow | 1 | 3 |

### v TRINIDAD & TOBAGO

| | | | S | TT |
|---|---|---|---|---|
| 2004 | 30 May | Edinburgh | 4 | 1 |

### v TURKEY

| | | | S | T |
|---|---|---|---|---|
| 1960 | 8 June | Ankara | 2 | 4 |

### v UKRAINE

| | | | S | U |
|---|---|---|---|---|
| EC2006 | 11 Oct | Kiev | 0 | 2 |
| EC2007 | 13 Oct | Glasgow | 3 | 1 |

### v URUGUAY

| | | | S | U |
|---|---|---|---|---|
| wc1954 | 19 June | Basle | 0 | 7 |
| 1962 | 2 May | Glasgow | 2 | 3 |
| 1983 | 21 Sept | Glasgow | 2 | 0 |
| wc1986 | 13 June | Nezahualcoyotl | 0 | 0 |

### v USA

| | | | S | USA |
|---|---|---|---|---|
| 1952 | 30 Apr | Glasgow | 6 | 0 |
| 1992 | 17 May | Denver | 1 | 0 |
| 1996 | 26 May | New Britain | 1 | 2 |
| 1998 | 30 May | Washington | 0 | 0 |
| 2005 | 11 Nov | Glasgow | 1 | 1 |
| 2012 | 26 May | Jacksonville | 1 | 5 |

### v USSR

| | | | S | USSR |
|---|---|---|---|---|
| 1967 | 10 May | Glasgow | 0 | 2 |
| 1971 | 14 June | Moscow | 0 | 1 |
| wc1982 | 22 June | Malaga | 2 | 2 |
| 1991 | 6 Feb | Glasgow | 0 | 1 |

### v YUGOSLAVIA

| | | | S | Y |
|---|---|---|---|---|
| 1955 | 15 May | Belgrade | 2 | 2 |
| 1956 | 21 Nov | Glasgow | 2 | 0 |
| wc1958 | 8 June | Vasteras | 1 | 1 |
| 1972 | 29 June | Belo Horizonte | 2 | 2 |
| wc1974 | 22 June | Frankfurt | 1 | 1 |
| 1984 | 12 Sept | Glasgow | 6 | 1 |
| wc1988 | 19 Oct | Glasgow | 1 | 1 |
| wc1989 | 6 Sept | Zagreb | 1 | 3 |

### v ZAIRE

| | | | S | Z |
|---|---|---|---|---|
| wc1974 | 14 June | Dortmund | 2 | 0 |

# WALES

| v ALBANIA | | | W | A |
|---|---|---|---|---|
| EC1994 | 7 Sept | Cardiff | 2 | 0 |
| EC1995 | 15 Nov | Tirana | 1 | 1 |

| v ARGENTINA | | | W | A |
|---|---|---|---|---|
| 1992 | 3 June | Tokyo | 0 | 1 |
| 2002 | 13 Feb | Cardiff | 1 | 1 |

| v ARMENIA | | | W | A |
|---|---|---|---|---|
| wc2001 | 24 Mar | Erevan | 2 | 2 |
| wc2001 | 1 Sept | Cardiff | 0 | 0 |

| v AUSTRALIA | | | W | A |
|---|---|---|---|---|
| 2011 | 10 Aug | Cardiff | 1 | 2 |

| v AUSTRIA | | | W | A |
|---|---|---|---|---|
| 1954 | 9 May | Vienna | 0 | 2 |
| 1955 | 23 Nov | Wrexham | 1 | 2 |
| EC1974 | 4 Sept | Vienna | 1 | 2 |
| 1975 | 19 Nov | Wrexham | 1 | 0 |
| 1992 | 29 Apr | Vienna | 1 | 1 |
| EC2005 | 26 Mar | Cardiff | 0 | 2 |
| EC2005 | 30 Mar | Vienna | 0 | 1 |
| 2013 | 6 Feb | Swansea | 2 | 1 |

| v AZERBAIJAN | | | W | A |
|---|---|---|---|---|
| EC2002 | 20 Nov | Baku | 2 | 0 |
| EC2003 | 29 Mar | Cardiff | 4 | 0 |
| wc2004 | 4 Sept | Baku | 1 | 1 |
| wc2005 | 12 Oct | Cardiff | 2 | 0 |
| wc2008 | 6 Sept | Cardiff | 1 | 0 |
| wc2009 | 6 June | Baku | 1 | 0 |

| v BELARUS | | | W | B |
|---|---|---|---|---|
| EC1998 | 14 Oct | Cardiff | 3 | 2 |
| EC1999 | 4 Sept | Minsk | 2 | 1 |
| wc2000 | 2 Sept | Minsk | 1 | 2 |
| wc2001 | 6 Oct | Cardiff | 1 | 0 |

| v BELGIUM | | | W | B |
|---|---|---|---|---|
| 1949 | 22 May | Liege | 1 | 3 |
| 1949 | 23 Nov | Cardiff | 5 | 1 |
| EC1990 | 17 Oct | Cardiff | 3 | 1 |
| EC1991 | 27 Mar | Brussels | 1 | 1 |
| wc1992 | 18 Nov | Brussels | 0 | 2 |
| wc1993 | 31 Mar | Cardiff | 2 | 0 |
| wc1997 | 29 Mar | Cardiff | 1 | 2 |
| wc1997 | 11 Oct | Brussels | 2 | 3 |
| wc2012 | 7 Sept | Cardiff | 0 | 2 |

| v BOSNIA | | | W | B |
|---|---|---|---|---|
| 2003 | 12 Feb | Cardiff | 2 | 2 |
| 2012 | 15 Aug | Llanelli | 0 | 2 |

| v BRAZIL | | | W | B |
|---|---|---|---|---|
| wc1958 | 19 June | Gothenburg | 0 | 1 |
| 1962 | 12 May | Rio de Janeiro | 1 | 3 |
| 1962 | 16 May | São Paulo | 1 | 3 |
| 1966 | 14 May | Rio de Janeiro | 1 | 3 |
| 1966 | 18 May | Belo Horizonte | 0 | 1 |
| 1983 | 12 June | Cardiff | 1 | 1 |
| 1991 | 11 Sept | Cardiff | 1 | 0 |
| 1997 | 12 Nov | Brasilia | 0 | 3 |
| 2000 | 23 May | Cardiff | 0 | 3 |
| 2006 | 5 Sept | Cardiff | 0 | 2 |

| v BULGARIA | | | W | B |
|---|---|---|---|---|
| EC1983 | 27 Apr | Wrexham | 1 | 0 |
| EC1983 | 16 Nov | Sofia | 0 | 1 |
| EC1994 | 14 Dec | Cardiff | 0 | 3 |
| EC1995 | 29 Mar | Sofia | 1 | 3 |
| 2006 | 15 Aug | Swansea | 0 | 0 |
| 2007 | 22 Aug | Burgas | 1 | 0 |
| EC2010 | 8 Oct | Cardiff | 0 | 1 |
| EC2011 | 12 Oct | Sofia | 1 | 0 |

| v CANADA | | | W | C |
|---|---|---|---|---|
| 1986 | 10 May | Toronto | 0 | 2 |
| 1986 | 20 May | Vancouver | 3 | 0 |
| 2004 | 30 May | Wrexham | 1 | 0 |

| v CHILE | | | W | C |
|---|---|---|---|---|
| 1966 | 22 May | Santiago | 0 | 2 |

| v COSTA RICA | | | W | CR |
|---|---|---|---|---|
| 1990 | 20 May | Cardiff | 1 | 0 |
| 2012 | 29 Feb | Cardiff | 0 | 1 |

| v CROATIA | | | W | C |
|---|---|---|---|---|
| 2002 | 21 Aug | Varazdin | 1 | 1 |
| 2010 | 23 May | Osijek | 0 | 2 |
| wc2012 | 16 Oct | Osijek | 0 | 2 |
| wc2013 | 26 Mar | Swansea | 1 | 2 |

| v CYPRUS | | | W | C |
|---|---|---|---|---|
| wc1992 | 14 Oct | Limassol | 1 | 0 |
| wc1993 | 13 Oct | Cardiff | 2 | 0 |
| 2005 | 16 Nov | Limassol | 0 | 1 |
| EC2006 | 11 Oct | Cardiff | 3 | 1 |
| EC2007 | 13 Oct | Nicosia | 1 | 3 |

| v CZECHOSLOVAKIA | | | W | C |
|---|---|---|---|---|
| wc1957 | 1 May | Cardiff | 1 | 0 |
| wc1957 | 26 May | Prague | 0 | 2 |
| EC1971 | 21 Apr | Swansea | 1 | 3 |
| EC1971 | 27 Oct | Prague | 0 | 1 |
| wc1977 | 30 Mar | Wrexham | 3 | 0 |
| wc1977 | 16 Nov | Prague | 0 | 1 |
| wc1980 | 19 Nov | Cardiff | 1 | 0 |
| wc1981 | 9 Sept | Prague | 0 | 2 |
| EC1987 | 29 Apr | Wrexham | 1 | 1 |
| EC1987 | 11 Nov | Prague | 0 | 2 |
| wc1993 | 28 Apr | Ostrava† | 1 | 1 |
| wc1993 | 8 Sept | Cardiff† | 2 | 2 |

†*Czechoslovakia played as RCS (Republic of Czechs and Slovaks).*

| v CZECH REPUBLIC | | | W | CR |
|---|---|---|---|---|
| 2002 | 27 Mar | Cardiff | 0 | 0 |
| EC2006 | 2 Sept | Teplice | 1 | 2 |
| EC2007 | 2 June | Cardiff | 0 | 0 |

| v DENMARK | | | W | D |
|---|---|---|---|---|
| wc1964 | 21 Oct | Copenhagen | 0 | 1 |
| wc1965 | 1 Dec | Wrexham | 4 | 2 |
| EC1987 | 9 Sept | Cardiff | 1 | 0 |
| EC1987 | 14 Oct | Copenhagen | 0 | 1 |
| 1990 | 11 Sept | Copenhagen | 0 | 1 |
| EC1998 | 10 Oct | Copenhagen | 2 | 1 |
| EC1999 | 9 June | Liverpool | 0 | 2 |
| 2008 | 19 Nov | Brondby | 1 | 0 |

| v ESTONIA | | | W | E |
|---|---|---|---|---|
| 1994 | 23 May | Tallinn | 2 | 1 |
| 2009 | 29 May | Llanelli | 1 | 0 |

| v FINLAND | | | W | F |
|---|---|---|---|---|
| EC1971 | 26 May | Helsinki | 1 | 0 |
| EC1971 | 13 Oct | Swansea | 3 | 0 |
| EC1987 | 10 Sept | Helsinki | 1 | 1 |
| EC1987 | 1 Apr | Wrexham | 4 | 0 |
| wc1988 | 19 Oct | Swansea | 2 | 2 |
| wc1989 | 6 Sept | Helsinki | 0 | 1 |
| 2000 | 29 Mar | Cardiff | 1 | 2 |
| EC2002 | 7 Sept | Helsinki | 2 | 0 |
| EC2003 | 10 Sept | Cardiff | 1 | 1 |
| wc2009 | 28 Mar | Cardiff | 0 | 2 |
| wc2009 | 10 Oct | Helsinki | 1 | 2 |

| v FAROE ISLANDS | | | W | F |
|---|---|---|---|---|
| wc1992 | 9 Sept | Cardiff | 6 | 0 |
| wc1993 | 6 June | Toftir | 3 | 0 |

| v FRANCE | | W | F |
|---|---|---|---|
| 1933 | 25 May Paris | 1 | 1 |
| 1939 | 20 May Paris | 1 | 2 |
| 1953 | 14 May Paris | 1 | 6 |
| 1982 | 2 June Toulouse | 1 | 0 |

| v GEORGIA | | W | G |
|---|---|---|---|
| EC1994 | 16 Nov Tbilisi | 0 | 5 |
| EC1995 | 7 June Cardiff | 0 | 1 |
| 2008 | 20 Aug Swansea | 1 | 2 |

| v GERMANY | | W | G |
|---|---|---|---|
| EC1995 | 26 Apr Dusseldorf | 1 | 1 |
| EC1995 | 11 Oct Cardiff | 1 | 2 |
| 2002 | 14 May Cardiff | 1 | 0 |
| EC2007 | 8 Sept Cardiff | 0 | 2 |
| EC2007 | 21 Nov Frankfurt | 0 | 0 |
| wc2008 | 15 Oct Moenchengladbach | 0 | 1 |
| wc2009 | 1 Apr Cardiff | 0 | 2 |

| v EAST GERMANY | | W | EG |
|---|---|---|---|
| wc1957 | 19 May Leipzig | 1 | 2 |
| wc1957 | 25 Sept Cardiff | 4 | 1 |
| wc1969 | 16 Apr Dresden | 1 | 2 |
| wc1969 | 22 Oct Cardiff | 1 | 3 |

| v WEST GERMANY | | W | WG |
|---|---|---|---|
| 1968 | 8 May Cardiff | 1 | 1 |
| 1969 | 26 Mar Frankfurt | 1 | 1 |
| 1976 | 6 Oct Cardiff | 0 | 2 |
| 1977 | 14 Dec Dortmund | 1 | 1 |
| EC1979 | 2 May Wrexham | 0 | 2 |
| EC1979 | 17 Oct Cologne | 1 | 5 |
| wc1989 | 31 May Cardiff | 0 | 0 |
| wc1989 | 15 Nov Cologne | 1 | 2 |
| EC1991 | 5 June Cardiff | 1 | 0 |
| EC1991 | 16 Oct Nuremberg | 1 | 4 |

| v GREECE | | W | G |
|---|---|---|---|
| wc1964 | 9 Dec Athens | 0 | 2 |
| wc1965 | 17 Mar Cardiff | 4 | 1 |

| v HOLLAND | | W | H |
|---|---|---|---|
| wc1988 | 14 Sept Amsterdam | 0 | 1 |
| wc1989 | 11 Oct Wrexham | 1 | 2 |
| 1992 | 30 May Utrecht | 0 | 4 |
| wc1996 | 5 Oct Cardiff | 1 | 3 |
| wc1996 | 9 Nov Eindhoven | 1 | 7 |
| 2008 | 1 June Rotterdam | 0 | 2 |

| v HUNGARY | | W | H |
|---|---|---|---|
| wc1958 | 8 June Sanviken | 1 | 1 |
| wc1958 | 17 June Stockholm | 2 | 1 |
| 1961 | 28 May Budapest | 2 | 3 |
| EC1962 | 7 Nov Budapest | 1 | 3 |
| EC1963 | 20 Mar Cardiff | 1 | 1 |
| EC1974 | 30 Oct Cardiff | 2 | 0 |
| EC1975 | 16 Apr Budapest | 2 | 1 |
| 1985 | 16 Oct Cardiff | 0 | 3 |
| 2004 | 31 Mar Budapest | 2 | 1 |
| 2005 | 9 Feb Cardiff | 2 | 0 |

| v ICELAND | | W | I |
|---|---|---|---|
| wc1980 | 2 June Reykjavik | 4 | 0 |
| wc1981 | 14 Oct Swansea | 2 | 2 |
| wc1984 | 12 Sept Reykjavik | 0 | 1 |
| wc1984 | 14 Nov Cardiff | 2 | 1 |
| 1991 | 1 May Cardiff | 1 | 0 |
| 2008 | 28 May Reykjavik | 1 | 0 |

| v IRAN | | W | I |
|---|---|---|---|
| 1978 | 18 Apr Teheran | 1 | 0 |

| v REPUBLIC OF IRELAND | | W | RI |
|---|---|---|---|
| 1960 | 28 Sept Dublin | 3 | 2 |
| 1979 | 11 Sept Swansea | 2 | 1 |
| 1981 | 24 Feb Dublin | 3 | 1 |
| 1986 | 26 Mar Dublin | 1 | 0 |
| 1990 | 28 Mar Dublin | 0 | 1 |
| 1991 | 6 Feb Wrexham | 0 | 3 |
| 1992 | 19 Feb Dublin | 1 | 0 |

| | | W | RI |
|---|---|---|---|
| 1993 | 17 Feb Dublin | 1 | 2 |
| 1997 | 11 Feb Cardiff | 0 | 0 |
| EC2007 | 24 Mar Dublin | 0 | 1 |
| EC2007 | 17 Nov Cardiff | 2 | 2 |
| NC2011 | 8 Feb Dublin | 0 | 3 |

| v ISRAEL | | W | I |
|---|---|---|---|
| wc1958 | 15 Jan Tel Aviv | 2 | 0 |
| wc1958 | 5 Feb Cardiff | 2 | 0 |
| 1984 | 10 June Tel Aviv | 0 | 0 |
| 1989 | 8 Feb Tel Aviv | 3 | 3 |

| v ITALY | | W | I |
|---|---|---|---|
| 1965 | 1 May Florence | 1 | 4 |
| wc1968 | 23 Oct Cardiff | 0 | 1 |
| wc1969 | 4 Nov Rome | 1 | 4 |
| 1988 | 4 June Brescia | 1 | 0 |
| 1996 | 24 Jan Terni | 0 | 3 |
| EC1998 | 5 Sept Liverpool | 0 | 2 |
| EC1999 | 5 June Bologna | 0 | 4 |
| EC2002 | 16 Oct Cardiff | 2 | 1 |
| EC2003 | 6 Sept Milan | 0 | 4 |

| v JAMAICA | | W | J |
|---|---|---|---|
| 1998 | 25 Mar Cardiff | 0 | 0 |

| v JAPAN | | W | J |
|---|---|---|---|
| 1992 | 7 June Matsuyama | 1 | 0 |

| v KUWAIT | | W | K |
|---|---|---|---|
| 1977 | 6 Sept Wrexham | 0 | 0 |
| 1977 | 20 Sept Kuwait | 0 | 0 |

| v LATVIA | | W | L |
|---|---|---|---|
| 2004 | 18 Aug Riga | 2 | 0 |

| v LIECHTENSTEIN | | W | L |
|---|---|---|---|
| 2006 | 14 Nov Swansea | 4 | 0 |
| wc2008 | 11 Oct Cardiff | 2 | 0 |
| wc2009 | 14 Oct Vaduz | 2 | 0 |

| v LUXEMBOURG | | W | L |
|---|---|---|---|
| EC1974 | 20 Nov Swansea | 5 | 0 |
| EC1975 | 1 May Luxembourg | 3 | 1 |
| EC1990 | 14 Nov Luxembourg | 1 | 0 |
| EC1991 | 13 Nov Cardiff | 1 | 0 |
| 2008 | 26 Mar Luxembourg | 2 | 0 |
| 2010 | 11 Aug Llanelli | 5 | 1 |

| v MALTA | | W | M |
|---|---|---|---|
| EC1978 | 25 Oct Wrexham | 7 | 0 |
| EC1979 | 2 June Valletta | 2 | 0 |
| 1988 | 1 June Valletta | 3 | 2 |
| 1998 | 3 June Valletta | 3 | 0 |

| v MEXICO | | W | M |
|---|---|---|---|
| wc1958 | 11 June Stockholm | 1 | 1 |
| 1962 | 22 May Mexico City | 1 | 2 |
| 2012 | 27 May New Jersey | 0 | 2 |

| v MOLDOVA | | W | M |
|---|---|---|---|
| EC1994 | 12 Oct Kishinev | 2 | 3 |
| EC1995 | 6 Sept Cardiff | 1 | 0 |

| v MONTENEGRO | | W | M |
|---|---|---|---|
| 2009 | 12 Aug Podgorica | 1 | 2 |
| EC2010 | 3 Sept Podgorica | 0 | 1 |
| EC2011 | 2 Sept Cardiff | 2 | 1 |

| v NEW ZEALAND | | W | NZ |
|---|---|---|---|
| 2007 | 26 May Wrexham | 2 | 2 |

| v NORWAY | | W | N |
|---|---|---|---|
| EC1982 | 22 Sept Swansea | 1 | 0 |
| EC1983 | 21 Sept Oslo | 0 | 0 |
| 1984 | 6 June Trondheim | 0 | 1 |
| 1985 | 26 Feb Wrexham | 1 | 1 |
| 1985 | 5 June Bergen | 2 | 4 |
| 1994 | 9 Mar Cardiff | 1 | 3 |
| wc2000 | 7 Oct Cardiff | 1 | 1 |

| | | | W | N |
|---|---|---|---|---|
| wc2001 | 5 Sept | Oslo | 2 | 3 |
| 2004 | 27 May | Oslo | 0 | 0 |
| 2008 | 6 Feb | Wrexham | 3 | 0 |
| 2011 | 12 Nov | Cardiff | 4 | 1 |

| **v PARAGUAY** | | | W | P |
|---|---|---|---|---|
| 2006 | 1 Mar | Cardiff | 0 | 0 |

| **v POLAND** | | | W | P |
|---|---|---|---|---|
| wc1973 | 28 Mar | Cardiff | 2 | 0 |
| wc1973 | 26 Sept | Katowice | 0 | 3 |
| 1991 | 29 May | Radom | 0 | 0 |
| wc2000 | 11 Oct | Warsaw | 0 | 0 |
| wc2001 | 2 June | Cardiff | 1 | 2 |
| wc2004 | 13 Oct | Cardiff | 2 | 3 |
| wc2005 | 7 Sept | Warsaw | 0 | 1 |
| 2009 | 11 Feb | Vila Real | 0 | 1 |

| **v PORTUGAL** | | | W | P |
|---|---|---|---|---|
| 1949 | 15 May | Lisbon | 2 | 3 |
| 1951 | 12 May | Cardiff | 2 | 1 |
| 2000 | 2 June | Chaves | 0 | 3 |

| **v QATAR** | | | W | Q |
|---|---|---|---|---|
| 2000 | 23 Feb | Doha | 1 | 0 |

| **v ROMANIA** | | | W | R |
|---|---|---|---|---|
| EC1970 | 11 Nov | Cardiff | 0 | 0 |
| EC1971 | 24 Nov | Bucharest | 0 | 2 |
| 1983 | 12 Oct | Wrexham | 5 | 0 |
| wc1992 | 20 May | Bucharest | 1 | 5 |
| wc1993 | 17 Nov | Cardiff | 1 | 2 |

| **v RUSSIA** | | | W | R |
|---|---|---|---|---|
| EC2003 | 15 Nov | Moscow | 0 | 0 |
| EC2003 | 19 Nov | Cardiff | 0 | 1 |
| wc2008 | 10 Sept | Moscow | 1 | 2 |
| wc2009 | 9 Sept | Cardiff | 1 | 3 |

| **v SAN MARINO** | | | W | SM |
|---|---|---|---|---|
| wc1996 | 2 June | Serravalle | 5 | 0 |
| wc1996 | 31 Aug | Cardiff | 6 | 0 |
| EC2007 | 28 Mar | Cardiff | 3 | 0 |
| EC2007 | 17 Oct | Serravalle | 2 | 1 |

| **v SAUDI ARABIA** | | | W | SA |
|---|---|---|---|---|
| 1986 | 25 Feb | Dahran | 2 | 1 |

| **v SERBIA** | | | W | S |
|---|---|---|---|---|
| wc2012 | 11 Sept | Novi Sad | 1 | 6 |

| **v SERBIA-MONTENEGRO** | | | W | SM |
|---|---|---|---|---|
| EC2003 | 20 Aug | Belgrade | 0 | 1 |
| EC2003 | 11 Oct | Cardiff | 2 | 3 |

| **v SLOVAKIA** | | | W | S |
|---|---|---|---|---|
| EC2006 | 7 Oct | Cardiff | 1 | 5 |
| EC2007 | 12 Sept | Trnava | 5 | 2 |

| **v SLOVENIA** | | | W | Sl |
|---|---|---|---|---|
| 2005 | 17 Aug | Swansea | 0 | 0 |

| **v SPAIN** | | | W | S |
|---|---|---|---|---|
| wc1961 | 19 Apr | Cardiff | 1 | 2 |
| wc1961 | 18 May | Madrid | 1 | 1 |
| 1982 | 24 Mar | Valencia | 1 | 1 |

| | | | W | S |
|---|---|---|---|---|
| wc1984 | 17 Oct | Seville | 0 | 3 |
| wc1985 | 30 Apr | Wrexham | 3 | 0 |

| **v SWEDEN** | | | W | S |
|---|---|---|---|---|
| wc1958 | 15 June | Stockholm | 0 | 0 |
| 1988 | 27 Apr | Stockholm | 1 | 4 |
| 1989 | 26 Apr | Wrexham | 0 | 2 |
| 1990 | 25 Apr | Stockholm | 2 | 4 |
| 1994 | 20 Apr | Wrexham | 0 | 2 |
| 2010 | 3 Mar | Swansea | 0 | 1 |

| **v SWITZERLAND** | | | W | S |
|---|---|---|---|---|
| 1949 | 26 May | Berne | 0 | 4 |
| 1951 | 16 May | Wrexham | 3 | 2 |
| 1996 | 24 Apr | Lugano | 0 | 2 |
| EC1999 | 31 Mar | Zurich | 0 | 2 |
| EC1999 | 9 Oct | Wrexham | 0 | 2 |
| EC2010 | 12 Oct | Basle | 1 | 4 |
| EC2011 | 8 Oct | Swansea | 2 | 0 |

| **v TRINIDAD & TOBAGO** | | | W | TT |
|---|---|---|---|---|
| 2006 | 27 May | Graz | 2 | 1 |

| **v TUNISIA** | | | W | T |
|---|---|---|---|---|
| 1998 | 6 June | Tunis | 0 | 4 |

| **v TURKEY** | | | W | T |
|---|---|---|---|---|
| EC1978 | 29 Nov | Wrexham | 1 | 0 |
| EC1979 | 21 Nov | Izmir | 0 | 1 |
| wc1980 | 15 Oct | Cardiff | 4 | 0 |
| wc1981 | 25 Mar | Ankara | 1 | 0 |
| wc1996 | 14 Dec | Cardiff | 0 | 0 |
| wc1997 | 20 Aug | Istanbul | 4 | 6 |

| **v REST OF UNITED KINGDOM** | | | W | UK |
|---|---|---|---|---|
| 1951 | 5 Dec | Cardiff | 3 | 2 |
| 1969 | 28 July | Cardiff | 0 | 1 |

| **v UKRAINE** | | | W | U |
|---|---|---|---|---|
| wc2001 | 28 Mar | Cardiff | 1 | 1 |
| wc2001 | 6 June | Kiev | 1 | 1 |

| **v URUGUAY** | | | W | U |
|---|---|---|---|---|
| 1986 | 21 Apr | Wrexham | 0 | 0 |

| **v USA** | | | W | USA |
|---|---|---|---|---|
| 2003 | 27 May | San Jose | 0 | 2 |

| **v USSR** | | | W | USSR |
|---|---|---|---|---|
| wc1965 | 30 May | Moscow | 1 | 2 |
| wc1965 | 27 Oct | Cardiff | 2 | 1 |
| wc1981 | 30 May | Wrexham | 0 | 0 |
| wc1981 | 18 Nov | Tbilisi | 0 | 3 |
| 1987 | 18 Feb | Swansea | 0 | 0 |

| **v YUGOSLAVIA** | | | W | Y |
|---|---|---|---|---|
| 1953 | 21 May | Belgrade | 2 | 5 |
| 1954 | 22 Nov | Cardiff | 1 | 3 |
| EC1976 | 24 Apr | Zagreb | 0 | 2 |
| EC1976 | 22 May | Cardiff | 1 | 1 |
| EC1982 | 15 Dec | Titograd | 4 | 4 |
| EC1983 | 14 Dec | Cardiff | 1 | 1 |
| 1988 | 23 Mar | Swansea | 1 | 2 |

# NORTHERN IRELAND

| **v ALBANIA** | | | NI | A |
|---|---|---|---|---|
| wc1965 | 7 May | Belfast | 4 | 1 |
| wc1965 | 24 Nov | Tirana | 1 | 1 |
| EC1982 | 15 Dec | Tirana | 0 | 0 |
| EC1983 | 27 Apr | Belfast | 1 | 0 |
| wc1992 | 9 Sept | Belfast | 3 | 0 |
| wc1993 | 17 Feb | Tirana | 2 | 1 |
| wc1996 | 14 Dec | Belfast | 2 | 0 |
| wc1997 | 10 Sept | Zurich | 0 | 1 |
| 2010 | 3 Mar | Tirana | 0 | 1 |

| **v ALGERIA** | | | NI | A |
|---|---|---|---|---|
| wc1986 | 3 June | Guadalajara | 1 | 1 |

| **v ARGENTINA** | | | NI | A |
|---|---|---|---|---|
| wc1958 | 11 June | Halmstad | 1 | 3 |

| **v ARMENIA** | | | NI | A |
|---|---|---|---|---|
| wc1996 | 5 Oct | Belfast | 1 | 1 |
| wc1997 | 30 Apr | Erevan | 0 | 0 |
| EC2003 | 29 Mar | Erevan | 0 | 1 |
| EC2003 | 10 Sept | Belfast | 0 | 1 |

| | | v AUSTRALIA | NI | A |
|---|---|---|---|---|
| 1980 | 11 June | Sydney | 2 | 1 |
| 1980 | 15 June | Melbourne | 1 | 1 |
| 1980 | 18 June | Adelaide | 2 | 1 |

| | | v AUSTRIA | NI | A |
|---|---|---|---|---|
| wc1982 | 1 July | Madrid | 2 | 2 |
| EC1982 | 13 Oct | Vienna | 0 | 2 |
| EC1983 | 21 Sept | Belfast | 3 | 1 |
| EC1990 | 14 Nov | Vienna | 0 | 0 |
| EC1991 | 16 Oct | Belfast | 2 | 1 |
| EC1994 | 12 Oct | Vienna | 2 | 1 |
| EC1995 | 15 Nov | Belfast | 5 | 3 |
| wc2004 | 13 Oct | Belfast | 3 | 3 |
| wc2005 | 12 Oct | Vienna | 0 | 2 |

| | | v AZERBAIJAN | NI | A |
|---|---|---|---|---|
| wc2004 | 9 Oct | Baku | 0 | 0 |
| wc2005 | 3 Sept | Belfast | 2 | 0 |
| wc2012 | 14 Nov | Belfast | 1 | 1 |

| | | v BARBADOS | NI | B |
|---|---|---|---|---|
| 2004 | 30 May | Waterford | 1 | 1 |

| | | v BELGIUM | NI | B |
|---|---|---|---|---|
| wc1976 | 10 Nov | Liege | 0 | 2 |
| wc1977 | 16 Nov | Belfast | 3 | 0 |
| 1997 | 11 Feb | Belfast | 3 | 0 |

| | | v BRAZIL | NI | B |
|---|---|---|---|---|
| wc1986 | 12 June | Guadalajara | 0 | 3 |

| | | v BULGARIA | NI | B |
|---|---|---|---|---|
| wc1972 | 18 Oct | Sofia | 0 | 3 |
| wc1973 | 26 Sept | Sheffield | 0 | 0 |
| EC1978 | 29 Nov | Sofia | 2 | 0 |
| EC1979 | 2 May | Belfast | 2 | 0 |
| wc2001 | 28 Mar | Sofia | 3 | 4 |
| wc2001 | 2 June | Belfast | 0 | 1 |
| 2008 | 6 Feb | Belfast | 0 | 1 |

| | | v CANADA | NI | C |
|---|---|---|---|---|
| 1995 | 22 May | Edmonton | 0 | 2 |
| 1999 | 27 Apr | Belfast | 1 | 1 |
| 2005 | 9 Feb | Belfast | 0 | 1 |

| | | v CHILE | NI | C |
|---|---|---|---|---|
| 1989 | 26 May | Belfast | 0 | 1 |
| 1995 | 25 May | Edmonton | 1 | 2 |
| 2010 | 30 May | Chillan | 0 | 1 |

| | | v COLOMBIA | NI | C |
|---|---|---|---|---|
| 1994 | 4 June | Boston | 0 | 2 |

| | | v CYPRUS | NI | C |
|---|---|---|---|---|
| EC1971 | 3 Feb | Nicosia | 3 | 0 |
| EC1971 | 21 Apr | Belfast | 5 | 0 |
| wc1973 | 14 Feb | Nicosia | 0 | 1 |
| wc1973 | 8 May | London | 3 | 0 |
| 2002 | 21 Aug | Belfast | 0 | 0 |

| | | v CZECHOSLOVAKIA | NI | C |
|---|---|---|---|---|
| wc1958 | 8 June | Halmstad | 1 | 0 |
| wc1958 | 17 June | Malmo | 2 | 1* |

*After extra time

| | | v CZECH REPUBLIC | NI | C |
|---|---|---|---|---|
| wc2001 | 24 Mar | Belfast | 0 | 1 |
| wc2001 | 6 June | Teplice | 1 | 3 |
| wc2008 | 10 Sept | Belfast | 0 | 0 |
| wc2009 | 14 Oct | Prague | 0 | 0 |

| | | v DENMARK | NI | D |
|---|---|---|---|---|
| EC1978 | 25 Oct | Belfast | 2 | 1 |
| EC1979 | 6 June | Copenhagen | 0 | 4 |
| 1986 | 26 Mar | Belfast | 1 | 1 |
| EC1990 | 17 Oct | Belfast | 1 | 1 |
| EC1991 | 13 Nov | Odense | 1 | 2 |
| wc1992 | 18 Nov | Belfast | 0 | 1 |
| wc1993 | 13 Oct | Copenhagen | 0 | 1 |
| wc2000 | 7 Oct | Belfast | 1 | 1 |
| wc2001 | 1 Sept | Copenhagen | 1 | 1 |

| | | | NI | D |
|---|---|---|---|---|
| EC2006 | 7 Oct | Copenhagen | 0 | 0 |
| EC2007 | 17 Nov | Belfast | 2 | 1 |

| | | v ESTONIA | NI | E |
|---|---|---|---|---|
| 2004 | 31 Mar | Tallinn | 1 | 0 |
| 2006 | 1 Mar | Belfast | 1 | 0 |
| EC2011 | 6 Sept | Tallinn | 1 | 4 |
| EC2011 | 7 Oct | Belfast | 1 | 2 |

| | | v FAROE ISLANDS | NI | F |
|---|---|---|---|---|
| EC1991 | 1 May | Belfast | 1 | 1 |
| EC1991 | 11 Sept | Landskrona | 5 | 0 |
| EC2010 | 12 Oct | Toftir | 1 | 1 |
| EC2011 | 10 Aug | Belfast | 4 | 0 |

| | | v FINLAND | NI | F |
|---|---|---|---|---|
| wc1984 | 27 May | Pori | 0 | 1 |
| wc1984 | 14 Nov | Belfast | 2 | 1 |
| EC1998 | 10 Oct | Belfast | 1 | 0 |
| EC1998 | 9 Oct | Helsinki | 1 | 4 |
| 2003 | 12 Feb | Belfast | 0 | 1 |
| 2006 | 16 Aug | Helsinki | 2 | 1 |
| 2012 | 15 Aug | Belfast | 3 | 3 |

| | | v FRANCE | NI | F |
|---|---|---|---|---|
| 1928 | 21 Feb | Paris | 0 | 4 |
| 1951 | 12 May | Belfast | 2 | 2 |
| 1952 | 11 Nov | Paris | 1 | 3 |
| wc1958 | 19 June | Norrkoping | 0 | 4 |
| 1982 | 24 Mar | Paris | 0 | 4 |
| wc1982 | 4 July | Madrid | 1 | 4 |
| 1986 | 26 Feb | Paris | 0 | 0 |
| 1988 | 27 Apr | Belfast | 0 | 0 |
| 1999 | 18 Aug | Belfast | 0 | 1 |

| | | v GEORGIA | NI | G |
|---|---|---|---|---|
| 2008 | 26 Mar | Belfast | 4 | 1 |

| | | v GERMANY | NI | G |
|---|---|---|---|---|
| 1992 | 2 June | Bremen | 1 | 1 |
| 1996 | 29 May | Belfast | 1 | 1 |
| wc1996 | 9 Nov | Nuremberg | 1 | 1 |
| wc1997 | 20 Aug | Belfast | 1 | 3 |
| EC1999 | 27 Mar | Belfast | 0 | 3 |
| EC1999 | 8 Sept | Dortmund | 0 | 4 |
| 2005 | 4 June | Belfast | 1 | 4 |

| | | v WEST GERMANY | NI | WG |
|---|---|---|---|---|
| wc1958 | 15 June | Malmo | 2 | 2 |
| wc1960 | 26 Oct | Belfast | 3 | 4 |
| wc1961 | 10 May | Hamburg | 1 | 2 |
| 1966 | 7 May | Belfast | 0 | 2 |
| 1977 | 27 Apr | Cologne | 0 | 5 |
| EC1982 | 17 Nov | Belfast | 1 | 0 |
| EC1983 | 16 Nov | Hamburg | 1 | 0 |

| | | v GREECE | NI | G |
|---|---|---|---|---|
| wc1961 | 3 May | Athens | 1 | 2 |
| wc1961 | 17 Oct | Belfast | 2 | 0 |
| 1988 | 17 Feb | Athens | 2 | 3 |
| EC2003 | 2 Apr | Belfast | 0 | 2 |
| EC2003 | 11 Oct | Athens | 0 | 1 |

| | | v HOLLAND | NI | H |
|---|---|---|---|---|
| 1962 | 9 May | Rotterdam | 0 | 4 |
| wc1965 | 17 Mar | Belfast | 2 | 1 |
| wc1965 | 7 Apr | Rotterdam | 0 | 0 |
| wc1976 | 13 Oct | Rotterdam | 2 | 2 |
| wc1977 | 12 Oct | Belfast | 0 | 1 |
| 2012 | 2 June | Amsterdam | 0 | 6 |

| | | v HONDURAS | NI | H |
|---|---|---|---|---|
| wc1982 | 21 June | Zaragoza | 1 | 1 |

| | | v HUNGARY | NI | H |
|---|---|---|---|---|
| wc1988 | 19 Oct | Budapest | 0 | 1 |
| wc1989 | 6 Sept | Belfast | 1 | 2 |
| 2000 | 26 Apr | Belfast | 0 | 1 |
| 2008 | 19 Nov | Belfast | 0 | 2 |

### v ICELAND

| | | | NI | I |
|---|---|---|---|---|
| wc1977 | 11 June | Reykjavik | 0 | 1 |
| wc1977 | 21 Sept | Belfast | 2 | 0 |
| wc2000 | 11 Oct | Reykjavik | 0 | 1 |
| wc2001 | 5 Sept | Belfast | 3 | 0 |
| EC2006 | 2 Sept | Belfast | 0 | 3 |
| EC2007 | 12 Sept | Reykjavik | 1 | 2 |

### v REPUBLIC OF IRELAND

| | | | NI | RI |
|---|---|---|---|---|
| EC1978 | 20 Sept | Dublin | 0 | 0 |
| EC1979 | 21 Nov | Belfast | 1 | 0 |
| wc1988 | 14 Sept | Belfast | 0 | 0 |
| wc1989 | 11 Oct | Dublin | 0 | 3 |
| wc1993 | 31 Mar | Dublin | 0 | 3 |
| wc1993 | 17 Nov | Belfast | 1 | 1 |
| EC1994 | 16 Nov | Belfast | 0 | 4 |
| EC1995 | 29 Mar | Dublin | 1 | 1 |
| 1999 | 29 May | Dublin | 1 | 0 |
| NC2011 | 24 May | Dublin | 0 | 5 |

### v ISRAEL

| | | | NI | I |
|---|---|---|---|---|
| 1968 | 10 Sept | Jaffa | 3 | 2 |
| 1976 | 3 Mar | Tel Aviv | 1 | 1 |
| wc1980 | 26 Mar | Tel Aviv | 0 | 0 |
| wc1981 | 18 Nov | Belfast | 1 | 0 |
| 1984 | 16 Oct | Belfast | 3 | 0 |
| 1987 | 18 Feb | Tel Aviv | 1 | 1 |
| 2009 | 12 Aug | Belfast | 1 | 1 |
| wc2013 | 26 Mar | Belfast | 0 | 2 |

### v ITALY

| | | | NI | I |
|---|---|---|---|---|
| wc1957 | 25 Apr | Rome | 0 | 1 |
| 1957 | 4 Dec | Belfast | 2 | 2 |
| wc1958 | 15 Jan | Belfast | 2 | 1 |
| 1961 | 25 Apr | Bologna | 2 | 3 |
| 1997 | 22 Jan | Palermo | 0 | 2 |
| 2003 | 3 June | Campobasso | 0 | 2 |
| 2009 | 6 June | Pisa | 0 | 3 |
| EC2010 | 8 Oct | Belfast | 0 | 0 |
| EC2011 | 11 Oct | Pescara | 0 | 3 |

### v LATVIA

| | | | NI | L |
|---|---|---|---|---|
| wc1993 | 2 June | Riga | 2 | 1 |
| wc1993 | 8 Sept | Belfast | 2 | 0 |
| EC1995 | 26 Apr | Riga | 1 | 0 |
| EC1995 | 7 June | Belfast | 1 | 2 |
| EC2006 | 11 Oct | Belfast | 1 | 0 |
| EC2007 | 8 Sept | Riga | 0 | 1 |

### v LIECHTENSTEIN

| | | | NI | L |
|---|---|---|---|---|
| EC1994 | 20 Apr | Belfast | 4 | 1 |
| EC1995 | 11 Oct | Eschen | 4 | 0 |
| 2002 | 27 Mar | Vaduz | 0 | 0 |
| EC2007 | 24 Mar | Vaduz | 4 | 1 |
| EC2007 | 22 Aug | Belfast | 3 | 1 |

### v LITHUANIA

| | | | NI | L |
|---|---|---|---|---|
| wc1992 | 28 Apr | Belfast | 2 | 2 |
| wc1993 | 25 May | Vilnius | 1 | 0 |

### v LUXEMBOURG

| | | | NI | L |
|---|---|---|---|---|
| 2000 | 23 Feb | Luxembourg | 3 | 1 |
| wc2012 | 11 Sept | Belfast | 1 | 1 |

### v MALTA

| | | | NI | M |
|---|---|---|---|---|
| wc1988 | 21 May | Belfast | 3 | 0 |
| wc1989 | 26 Apr | Valletta | 2 | 0 |
| 2000 | 28 Mar | Valletta | 3 | 0 |
| wc2000 | 2 Sept | Belfast | 1 | 0 |
| wc2001 | 6 Oct | Valletta | 1 | 0 |
| 2005 | 17 Aug | Ta'Qali | 1 | 1 |
| 2013 | 6 Feb | Ta'Qali | 0 | 0 |

### v MEXICO

| | | | NI | M |
|---|---|---|---|---|
| 1966 | 22 June | Belfast | 4 | 1 |
| 1994 | 11 June | Miami | 0 | 3 |

### v MOLDOVA

| | | | NI | M |
|---|---|---|---|---|
| EC1998 | 18 Nov | Belfast | 2 | 2 |
| EC1999 | 31 Mar | Chisinau | 0 | 0 |

### v MONTENEGRO

| | | | NI | M |
|---|---|---|---|---|
| 2010 | 11 Aug | Podgorica | 0 | 2 |

### v MOROCCO

| | | | NI | M |
|---|---|---|---|---|
| 1986 | 23 Apr | Belfast | 2 | 1 |
| 2010 | 17 Nov | Belfast | 1 | 1 |

### v NORWAY

| | | | NI | N |
|---|---|---|---|---|
| 1922 | 25 May | Bergen | 1 | 2 |
| EC1974 | 4 Sept | Oslo | 1 | 2 |
| EC1975 | 29 Oct | Belfast | 3 | 0 |
| 1990 | 27 Mar | Belfast | 2 | 3 |
| 1996 | 27 Mar | Belfast | 0 | 2 |
| 2001 | 28 Feb | Belfast | 0 | 4 |
| 2004 | 18 Feb | Belfast | 1 | 4 |
| 2012 | 29 Feb | Belfast | 0 | 3 |

### v POLAND

| | | | NI | P |
|---|---|---|---|---|
| EC1962 | 10 Oct | Katowice | 2 | 0 |
| EC1962 | 28 Nov | Belfast | 2 | 0 |
| 1988 | 23 Mar | Belfast | 1 | 1 |
| 1991 | 5 Feb | Belfast | 3 | 1 |
| 2002 | 13 Feb | Limassol | 1 | 4 |
| EC2004 | 4 Sept | Belfast | 0 | 3 |
| EC2005 | 30 Mar | Warsaw | 0 | 1 |
| wc2009 | 28 Mar | Belfast | 3 | 2 |
| wc2009 | 5 Sept | Chorzow | 1 | 1 |

### v PORTUGAL

| | | | NI | P |
|---|---|---|---|---|
| wc1957 | 16 Jan | Lisbon | 1 | 1 |
| wc1957 | 1 May | Belfast | 3 | 0 |
| wc1973 | 28 Mar | Coventry | 1 | 1 |
| wc1973 | 14 Nov | Lisbon | 1 | 1 |
| wc1980 | 19 Nov | Lisbon | 0 | 1 |
| wc1981 | 29 Apr | Belfast | 1 | 0 |
| EC1994 | 7 Sept | Belfast | 1 | 2 |
| EC1995 | 3 Sept | Lisbon | 1 | 1 |
| wc1997 | 29 Mar | Belfast | 0 | 0 |
| wc1997 | 11 Oct | Lisbon | 0 | 1 |
| 2005 | 15 Nov | Belfast | 1 | 1 |
| wc2012 | 16 Oct | Porto | 1 | 1 |

### v ROMANIA

| | | | NI | R |
|---|---|---|---|---|
| wc1984 | 12 Sept | Belfast | 3 | 2 |
| wc1985 | 16 Oct | Bucharest | 1 | 0 |
| 1994 | 23 Mar | Belfast | 2 | 0 |
| 2006 | 27 May | Chicago | 0 | 2 |

### v RUSSIA

| | | | NI | R |
|---|---|---|---|---|
| wc2012 | 7 Sept | Moscow | 0 | 2 |

### v SAN MARINO

| | | | NI | SM |
|---|---|---|---|---|
| wc2008 | 15 Oct | Belfast | 4 | 0 |
| wc2009 | 11 Feb | Serravalle | 3 | 0 |

### v ST KITTS & NEVIS

| | | | NI | SK |
|---|---|---|---|---|
| 2004 | 2 June | Basseterre | 2 | 0 |

### v SERBIA

| | | | NI | S |
|---|---|---|---|---|
| 2009 | 14 Nov | Belfast | 0 | 1 |
| EC2011 | 25 Mar | Belgrade | 1 | 2 |
| EC2011 | 2 Sept | Belfast | 0 | 1 |

### v SERBIA-MONTENEGRO

| | | | NI | SM |
|---|---|---|---|---|
| 2004 | 28 Apr | Belfast | 1 | 1 |

### v SLOVAKIA

| | | | NI | S |
|---|---|---|---|---|
| 1998 | 25 Mar | Belfast | 1 | 0 |
| wc2008 | 6 Sept | Bratislava | 1 | 2 |
| wc2009 | 9 Sept | Belfast | 0 | 2 |

### v SLOVENIA

| | | | NI | S |
|---|---|---|---|---|
| wc2008 | 11 Oct | Maribor | 0 | 2 |
| wc2009 | 1 Apr | Belfast | 1 | 0 |
| EC2010 | 3 Sept | Maribor | 1 | 0 |
| EC2011 | 29 Mar | Belfast | 0 | 0 |

### v SOUTH AFRICA

| | | | NI | SA |
|---|---|---|---|---|
| 1924 | 24 Sept | Belfast | 1 | 2 |

### v SPAIN

| | | | NI | S |
|---|---|---|---|---|
| 1958 | 15 Oct | Madrid | 2 | 6 |
| 1963 | 30 May | Bilbao | 1 | 1 |

| | | | NI | S |
|---|---|---|---|---|
| 1963 | 30 Oct | Belfast | 0 | 1 |
| EC1970 | 11 Nov | Seville | 0 | 3 |
| EC1972 | 16 Feb | Hull | 1 | 1 |
| wc1982 | 25 June | Valencia | 1 | 0 |
| 1985 | 27 Mar | Palma | 0 | 0 |
| wc1986 | 7 June | Guadalajara | 1 | 2 |
| wc1988 | 21 Dec | Seville | 0 | 4 |
| wc1989 | 8 Feb | Belfast | 0 | 2 |
| wc1992 | 14 Oct | Belfast | 0 | 0 |
| wc1993 | 28 Apr | Seville | 1 | 3 |
| 1998 | 2 June | Santander | 1 | 4 |
| 2002 | 17 Apr | Belfast | 0 | 5 |
| EC2002 | 12 Oct | Albacete | 0 | 3 |
| EC2003 | 11 June | Belfast | 0 | 0 |
| EC2006 | 6 Sept | Belfast | 3 | 2 |
| EC2007 | 21 Nov | Las Palmas | 0 | 1 |

| | **v SWEDEN** | | NI | S |
|---|---|---|---|---|
| EC1974 | 30 Oct | Solna | 2 | 0 |
| EC1975 | 3 Sept | Belfast | 1 | 2 |
| wc1980 | 15 Oct | Belfast | 3 | 0 |
| wc1981 | 3 June | Solna | 0 | 1 |
| 1996 | 24 Apr | Belfast | 1 | 2 |
| EC2007 | 28 Mar | Belfast | 2 | 1 |
| EC2007 | 17 Oct | Stockholm | 1 | 1 |

| | **v SWITZERLAND** | | NI | S |
|---|---|---|---|---|
| wc1964 | 14 Oct | Belfast | 1 | 0 |
| wc1964 | 14 Nov | Lausanne | 1 | 2 |
| 1998 | 22 Apr | Belfast | 1 | 0 |
| 2004 | 18 Aug | Zurich | 0 | 0 |

| | **v THAILAND** | | NI | T |
|---|---|---|---|---|
| 1997 | 21 May | Bangkok | 0 | 0 |

| | **v TRINIDAD & TOBAGO** | | NI | TT |
|---|---|---|---|---|
| 2004 | 6 June | Bacolet | 3 | 0 |

| | **v TURKEY** | | NI | T |
|---|---|---|---|---|
| wc1968 | 23 Oct | Belfast | 4 | 1 |
| wc1968 | 11 Dec | Istanbul | 3 | 0 |

| | | | NI | T |
|---|---|---|---|---|
| EC1983 | 30 Mar | Belfast | 2 | 1 |
| EC1983 | 12 Oct | Ankara | 0 | 1 |
| wc1985 | 1 May | Belfast | 2 | 0 |
| wc1985 | 11 Sept | Izmir | 0 | 0 |
| EC1986 | 12 Nov | Izmir | 0 | 0 |
| EC1987 | 11 Nov | Belfast | 1 | 0 |
| EC1998 | 5 Sept | Istanbul | 0 | 3 |
| EC1999 | 4 Sept | Belfast | 0 | 3 |
| 2010 | 26 May | New Britain | 0 | 2 |

| | **v UKRAINE** | | NI | U |
|---|---|---|---|---|
| wc1996 | 31 Aug | Belfast | 0 | 1 |
| wc1997 | 2 Apr | Kiev | 1 | 2 |
| EC2002 | 16 Oct | Belfast | 0 | 0 |
| EC2003 | 6 Sept | Donetsk | 0 | 0 |

| | **v URUGUAY** | | NI | U |
|---|---|---|---|---|
| 1964 | 29 Apr | Belfast | 3 | 0 |
| 1990 | 18 May | Belfast | 1 | 0 |
| 2006 | 21 May | New Jersey | 0 | 1 |

| | **v USSR** | | NI | USSR |
|---|---|---|---|---|
| wc1969 | 19 Sept | Belfast | 0 | 0 |
| wc1969 | 22 Oct | Moscow | 0 | 2 |
| EC1971 | 22 Sept | Moscow | 0 | 1 |
| EC1971 | 13 Oct | Belfast | 1 | 1 |

| | **v YUGOSLAVIA** | | NI | Y |
|---|---|---|---|---|
| EC1975 | 16 Mar | Belfast | 1 | 0 |
| EC1975 | 19 Nov | Belgrade | 0 | 1 |
| wc1982 | 17 June | Zaragoza | 0 | 0 |
| EC1987 | 29 Apr | Belfast | 1 | 2 |
| EC1987 | 14 Oct | Sarajevo | 0 | 3 |
| EC1990 | 12 Sept | Belfast | 0 | 2 |
| EC1991 | 27 Mar | Belgrade | 1 | 4 |
| 2000 | 16 Aug | Belfast | 1 | 2 |

# REPUBLIC OF IRELAND

| | **v ALBANIA** | | RI | A |
|---|---|---|---|---|
| wc1992 | 26 May | Dublin | 2 | 0 |
| wc1993 | 26 May | Tirana | 2 | 1 |
| EC2003 | 2 Apr | Tirana | 0 | 0 |
| EC2003 | 7 June | Dublin | 2 | 1 |

| | **v ALGERIA** | | RI | A |
|---|---|---|---|---|
| 1982 | 28 Apr | Algiers | 0 | 2 |
| 2010 | 28 May | Dublin | 3 | 0 |

| | **v ANDORRA** | | RI | A |
|---|---|---|---|---|
| wc2001 | 28 Mar | Barcelona | 3 | 0 |
| wc2001 | 25 Apr | Dublin | 3 | 1 |
| EC2010 | 7 Sept | Dublin | 3 | 1 |
| EC2011 | 7 Oct | Andorra La Vella | 2 | 0 |

| | **v ARGENTINA** | | RI | A |
|---|---|---|---|---|
| 1951 | 13 May | Dublin | 0 | 1 |
| †1979 | 29 May | Dublin | 0 | 0 |
| 1980 | 16 May | Dublin | 0 | 1 |
| 1998 | 22 Apr | Dublin | 0 | 2 |
| 2010 | 11 Aug | Dublin | 0 | 1 |

†*Not considered a full international.*

| | **v ARMENIA** | | RI | A |
|---|---|---|---|---|
| EC2010 | 3 Sept | Erevan | 1 | 0 |
| EC2011 | 11 Oct | Dublin | 2 | 1 |

| | **v AUSTRALIA** | | RI | A |
|---|---|---|---|---|
| 2003 | 19 Aug | Dublin | 2 | 1 |
| 2009 | 12 Aug | Limerick | 0 | 3 |

| | **v AUSTRIA** | | RI | A |
|---|---|---|---|---|
| 1952 | 7 May | Vienna | 0 | 6 |
| 1953 | 25 Mar | Dublin | 4 | 0 |
| 1958 | 14 Mar | Vienna | 1 | 3 |

| | | | RI | A |
|---|---|---|---|---|
| 1962 | 8 Apr | Dublin | 2 | 3 |
| EC1963 | 25 Sept | Vienna | 0 | 0 |
| EC1963 | 13 Oct | Dublin | 3 | 2 |
| 1966 | 22 May | Vienna | 0 | 1 |
| 1968 | 10 Nov | Dublin | 2 | 2 |
| EC1971 | 30 May | Dublin | 1 | 4 |
| EC1971 | 10 Oct | Linz | 0 | 6 |
| EC1995 | 11 June | Dublin | 1 | 3 |
| EC1995 | 6 Sept | Vienna | 1 | 3 |
| wc2013 | 26 Mar | Dublin | 2 | 2 |

| | **v BELGIUM** | | RI | B |
|---|---|---|---|---|
| 1928 | 12 Feb | Liege | 4 | 2 |
| 1929 | 30 Apr | Dublin | 4 | 0 |
| 1930 | 11 May | Brussels | 3 | 1 |
| wc1934 | 25 Feb | Dublin | 4 | 4 |
| 1949 | 24 Apr | Dublin | 0 | 2 |
| 1950 | 10 May | Brussels | 1 | 5 |
| 1965 | 24 Mar | Dublin | 0 | 2 |
| 1966 | 25 May | Liege | 3 | 2 |
| wc1980 | 15 Oct | Dublin | 1 | 1 |
| wc1981 | 25 Mar | Brussels | 0 | 1 |
| EC1986 | 10 Sept | Brussels | 2 | 2 |
| EC1987 | 29 Apr | Dublin | 0 | 0 |
| wc1997 | 29 Oct | Dublin | 1 | 1 |
| wc1997 | 16 Nov | Brussels | 1 | 2 |

| | **v BOLIVIA** | | RI | B |
|---|---|---|---|---|
| 1994 | 24 May | Dublin | 1 | 0 |
| 1996 | 15 June | New Jersey | 3 | 0 |
| 2007 | 26 May | Boston | 1 | 1 |

| | **v BOSNIA** | | RI | B |
|---|---|---|---|---|
| 2012 | 26 May | Dublin | 1 | 0 |

| | | v BRAZIL | RI | B |
|---|---|---|---|---|
| 1974 | 5 May | Rio de Janeiro | 1 | 2 |
| 1982 | 27 May | Uberlandia | 0 | 7 |
| 1987 | 23 May | Dublin | 1 | 0 |
| 2004 | 18 Feb | Dublin | 0 | 0 |
| 2008 | 6 Feb | Dublin | 0 | 1 |
| 2010 | 2 Mar | Emirates | 0 | 2 |

| | | v BULGARIA | RI | B |
|---|---|---|---|---|
| wc1977 | 1 June | Sofia | 1 | 2 |
| wc1977 | 12 Oct | Dublin | 0 | 0 |
| EC1979 | 19 May | Sofia | 0 | 1 |
| EC1979 | 17 Oct | Dublin | 3 | 0 |
| wc1987 | 1 Apr | Sofia | 1 | 2 |
| wc1987 | 14 Oct | Dublin | 2 | 0 |
| 2004 | 18 Aug | Dublin | 1 | 1 |
| wc2009 | 28 Mar | Dublin | 1 | 1 |
| wc2009 | 6 June | Sofia | 1 | 1 |

| | | v CAMEROON | RI | C |
|---|---|---|---|---|
| wc2002 | 1 June | Niigata | 1 | 1 |

| | | v CANADA | RI | C |
|---|---|---|---|---|
| 2003 | 18 Nov | Dublin | 3 | 0 |

| | | v CHILE | RI | C |
|---|---|---|---|---|
| 1960 | 30 Mar | Dublin | 2 | 0 |
| 1972 | 21 June | Recife | 1 | 2 |
| 1974 | 12 May | Santiago | 2 | 1 |
| 1982 | 22 May | Santiago | 0 | 1 |
| 1991 | 22 May | Dublin | 1 | 1 |
| 2006 | 24 May | Dublin | 0 | 1 |

| | | v CHINA | RI | C |
|---|---|---|---|---|
| 1984 | 3 June | Sapporo | 1 | 0 |
| 2005 | 29 Mar | Dublin | 1 | 0 |

| | | v COLOMBIA | RI | C |
|---|---|---|---|---|
| 2008 | 29 May | Fulham | 1 | 0 |

| | | v CROATIA | RI | C |
|---|---|---|---|---|
| 1996 | 2 June | Dublin | 2 | 2 |
| EC1998 | 5 Sept | Dublin | 2 | 0 |
| EC1999 | 4 Sept | Zagreb | 0 | 1 |
| 2001 | 15 Aug | Dublin | 2 | 2 |
| 2004 | 16 Nov | Dublin | 1 | 0 |
| 2011 | 10 Aug | Dublin | 0 | 0 |
| EC2012 | 10 June | Poznan | 1 | 3 |

| | | v CYPRUS | RI | C |
|---|---|---|---|---|
| wc1980 | 26 Mar | Nicosia | 3 | 2 |
| wc1980 | 19 Nov | Dublin | 6 | 0 |
| wc2001 | 24 Mar | Nicosia | 4 | 0 |
| wc2001 | 6 Oct | Dublin | 4 | 0 |
| wc2004 | 4 Sept | Dublin | 3 | 0 |
| wc2005 | 8 Oct | Nicosia | 1 | 0 |
| EC2006 | 7 Oct | Nicosia | 2 | 5 |
| EC2007 | 17 Oct | Dublin | 1 | 1 |
| 2008 | 15 Oct | Dublin | 1 | 0 |
| wc2009 | 5 Sept | Nicosia | 2 | 1 |

| | | v CZECHOSLOVAKIA | RI | C |
|---|---|---|---|---|
| 1938 | 18 May | Prague | 2 | 2 |
| EC1959 | 5 Apr | Dublin | 2 | 0 |
| EC1959 | 10 May | Bratislava | 0 | 4 |
| wc1961 | 8 Oct | Dublin | 1 | 3 |
| wc1961 | 29 Oct | Prague | 1 | 7 |
| EC1967 | 21 May | Dublin | 0 | 2 |
| EC1967 | 22 Nov | Prague | 2 | 1 |
| wc1969 | 4 May | Dublin | 1 | 2 |
| wc1969 | 7 Oct | Prague | 0 | 3 |
| 1979 | 26 Sept | Prague | 1 | 4 |
| 1981 | 29 Apr | Dublin | 3 | 1 |
| 1986 | 27 May | Reykjavik | 1 | 0 |

| | | v CZECH REPUBLIC | RI | C |
|---|---|---|---|---|
| 1994 | 5 June | Dublin | 1 | 3 |
| 1996 | 24 Apr | Prague | 0 | 2 |
| 1998 | 25 Mar | Olomouc | 1 | 2 |
| 2000 | 23 Feb | Dublin | 3 | 2 |
| 2004 | 31 Mar | Dublin | 2 | 1 |
| EC2006 | 11 Oct | Dublin | 1 | 1 |
| EC2007 | 12 Sept | Prague | 0 | 1 |
| 2012 | 29 Feb | Dublin | 1 | 1 |

| | | v DENMARK | RI | D |
|---|---|---|---|---|
| wc1956 | 3 Oct | Dublin | 2 | 1 |
| wc1957 | 2 Oct | Copenhagen | 2 | 0 |
| wc1968 | 4 Dec | Dublin | 1 | 1 |
| *(abandoned after 51 mins)* | | | | |
| wc1969 | 27 May | Copenhagen | 0 | 2 |
| wc1969 | 15 Oct | Dublin | 1 | 1 |
| EC1978 | 24 May | Copenhagen | 3 | 3 |
| EC1979 | 2 May | Dublin | 2 | 0 |
| wc1984 | 14 Nov | Copenhagen | 0 | 3 |
| wc1985 | 13 Nov | Dublin | 1 | 4 |
| wc1992 | 14 Oct | Copenhagen | 0 | 0 |
| wc1993 | 28 Apr | Dublin | 1 | 1 |
| 2002 | 27 Mar | Dublin | 3 | 0 |
| 2007 | 22 Aug | Copenhagen | 4 | 0 |

| | | v ECUADOR | RI | E |
|---|---|---|---|---|
| 1972 | 19 June | Natal | 3 | 2 |
| 2007 | 23 May | New Jersey | 1 | 1 |

| | | v EGYPT | RI | E |
|---|---|---|---|---|
| wc1990 | 17 June | Palermo | 0 | 0 |

| | | v ENGLAND | RI | E |
|---|---|---|---|---|
| 1946 | 30 Sept | Dublin | 0 | 1 |
| 1949 | 21 Sept | Everton | 2 | 0 |
| wc1957 | 8 May | Wembley | 1 | 5 |
| wc1957 | 19 May | Dublin | 1 | 1 |
| 1964 | 24 May | Dublin | 1 | 3 |
| 1976 | 8 Sept | Wembley | 1 | 1 |
| EC1978 | 25 Oct | Dublin | 1 | 1 |
| EC1980 | 6 Feb | Wembley | 0 | 2 |
| 1985 | 26 Mar | Wembley | 1 | 2 |
| EC1988 | 12 June | Stuttgart | 1 | 0 |
| wc1990 | 11 June | Cagliari | 1 | 1 |
| EC1990 | 14 Nov | Dublin | 1 | 1 |
| EC1991 | 27 Mar | Wembley | 1 | 1 |
| 1995 | 15 Feb | Dublin | 1 | 0 |
| *(abandoned after 27 mins)* | | | | |
| 2013 | 29 May | Wembley | 1 | 1 |

| | | v ESTONIA | RI | E |
|---|---|---|---|---|
| wc2000 | 11 Oct | Dublin | 2 | 0 |
| wc2001 | 6 June | Tallinn | 2 | 0 |
| EC2011 | 11 Nov | Tallinn | 4 | 0 |
| EC2011 | 15 Nov | Dublin | 1 | 1 |

| | | v FAROE ISLANDS | RI | F |
|---|---|---|---|---|
| EC2004 | 13 Oct | Dublin | 2 | 0 |
| EC2005 | 8 June | Toftir | 2 | 0 |
| wc2012 | 16 Oct | Torshavn | 4 | 1 |
| wc2013 | 7 June | Dublin | 3 | 0 |

| | | v FINLAND | RI | F |
|---|---|---|---|---|
| wc1949 | 8 Sept | Dublin | 3 | 0 |
| wc1949 | 9 Oct | Helsinki | 1 | 1 |
| 1990 | 16 May | Dublin | 1 | 1 |
| 2000 | 15 Nov | Dublin | 3 | 0 |
| 2002 | 21 Aug | Helsinki | 3 | 0 |

| | | v FRANCE | RI | F |
|---|---|---|---|---|
| 1937 | 23 May | Paris | 2 | 0 |
| 1952 | 16 Nov | Dublin | 1 | 1 |
| wc1953 | 4 Oct | Dublin | 3 | 5 |
| wc1953 | 25 Nov | Paris | 0 | 1 |
| wc1972 | 15 Nov | Dublin | 2 | 1 |
| wc1973 | 19 May | Paris | 1 | 1 |
| wc1976 | 17 Nov | Paris | 0 | 2 |
| wc1977 | 30 Mar | Dublin | 1 | 0 |
| wc1980 | 28 Oct | Paris | 0 | 2 |
| wc1981 | 14 Oct | Dublin | 3 | 2 |
| 1989 | 7 Feb | Dublin | 0 | 0 |
| wc2004 | 9 Oct | Paris | 0 | 0 |
| wc2005 | 7 Sept | Dublin | 0 | 1 |
| wc2009 | 14 Nov | Dublin | 0 | 1 |
| wc2009 | 18 Nov | Paris | 1 | 1 |

### v GEORGIA

| | | | RI | G |
|---|---|---|---|---|
| EC2003 | 29 Mar | Tbilisi | 2 | 1 |
| EC2003 | 11 June | Dublin | 2 | 0 |
| wc2008 | 6 Sept | Mainz | 2 | 1 |
| wc2009 | 11 Feb | Dublin | 2 | 1 |
| 2013 | 2 June | Dublin | 3 | 0 |

### v GERMANY

| | | | RI | G |
|---|---|---|---|---|
| 1935 | 8 May | Dortmund | 1 | 3 |
| 1936 | 17 Oct | Dublin | 5 | 2 |
| 1939 | 23 May | Bremen | 1 | 1 |
| 1994 | 29 May | Hanover | 2 | 0 |
| wc2002 | 5 June | Ibaraki | 1 | 1 |
| EC2006 | 2 Sept | Stuttgart | 0 | 1 |
| EC2007 | 13 Oct | Dublin | 0 | 0 |
| wc2012 | 12 Oct | Dublin | 1 | 6 |

### v WEST GERMANY

| | | | RI | WG |
|---|---|---|---|---|
| 1951 | 17 Oct | Dublin | 3 | 2 |
| 1952 | 4 May | Cologne | 0 | 3 |
| 1955 | 28 May | Hamburg | 1 | 2 |
| 1956 | 25 Nov | Dublin | 3 | 0 |
| 1960 | 11 May | Dusseldorf | 1 | 0 |
| 1966 | 4 May | Dublin | 0 | 4 |
| 1970 | 9 May | Berlin | 1 | 2 |
| 1975 | 1 Mar | Dublin | 1 | 0† |
| 1979 | 22 May | Dublin | 1 | 3 |
| 1981 | 21 May | Bremen | 0 | 3† |
| 1989 | 6 Sept | Dublin | 1 | 1 |

†v West Germany 'B'

### v GREECE

| | | | RI | G |
|---|---|---|---|---|
| 2000 | 26 Apr | Dublin | 0 | 1 |
| 2002 | 20 Nov | Athens | 0 | 0 |
| 2012 | 14 Nov | Dublin | 0 | 1 |

### v HOLLAND

| | | | RI | N |
|---|---|---|---|---|
| 1932 | 8 May | Amsterdam | 2 | 0 |
| 1934 | 8 Apr | Amsterdam | 2 | 5 |
| 1935 | 8 Dec | Dublin | 3 | 5 |
| 1955 | 1 May | Dublin | 1 | 0 |
| 1956 | 10 May | Rotterdam | 4 | 1 |
| wc1980 | 10 Sept | Dublin | 2 | 1 |
| wc1981 | 9 Sept | Rotterdam | 2 | 2 |
| EC1982 | 22 Sept | Rotterdam | 1 | 2 |
| EC1983 | 12 Oct | Dublin | 2 | 3 |
| EC1988 | 18 June | Gelsenkirchen | 0 | 1 |
| wc1990 | 21 June | Palermo | 1 | 1 |
| 1994 | 20 Apr | Tilburg | 1 | 0 |
| wc1994 | 4 July | Orlando | 0 | 2 |
| EC1995 | 13 Dec | Liverpool | 0 | 2 |
| 1996 | 4 June | Rotterdam | 1 | 3 |
| wc2000 | 2 Sept | Amsterdam | 2 | 2 |
| wc2001 | 1 Sept | Dublin | 1 | 0 |
| 2004 | 5 June | Amsterdam | 1 | 0 |
| 2006 | 16 Aug | Dublin | 0 | 4 |

### v HUNGARY

| | | | RI | H |
|---|---|---|---|---|
| 1934 | 15 Dec | Dublin | 2 | 4 |
| 1936 | 3 May | Budapest | 3 | 3 |
| 1936 | 6 Dec | Dublin | 2 | 3 |
| 1939 | 19 Mar | Cork | 2 | 2 |
| 1939 | 18 May | Budapest | 2 | 2 |
| wc1969 | 8 June | Dublin | 1 | 2 |
| wc1969 | 5 Nov | Budapest | 0 | 4 |
| wc1989 | 8 Mar | Budapest | 0 | 0 |
| wc1989 | 4 June | Dublin | 2 | 0 |
| 1991 | 11 Sept | Gyor | 2 | 1 |
| 2012 | 4 June | Budapest | 0 | 0 |

### v ICELAND

| | | | RI | I |
|---|---|---|---|---|
| EC1962 | 12 Aug | Dublin | 4 | 2 |
| EC1962 | 2 Sept | Reykjavik | 1 | 1 |
| EC1982 | 13 Oct | Dublin | 2 | 0 |
| EC1983 | 21 Sept | Reykjavik | 3 | 0 |
| 1986 | 25 May | Reykjavik | 2 | 1 |
| wc1996 | 10 Nov | Dublin | 0 | 0 |
| wc1997 | 6 Sept | Reykjavik | 4 | 2 |

### v IRAN

| | | | RI | I |
|---|---|---|---|---|
| 1972 | 18 June | Recife | 2 | 1 |
| wc2001 | 10 Nov | Dublin | 2 | 0 |
| wc2001 | 15 Nov | Tehran | 0 | 1 |

### v N. IRELAND

| | | | RI | NI |
|---|---|---|---|---|
| EC1978 | 20 Sept | Dublin | 0 | 0 |
| EC1979 | 21 Nov | Belfast | 0 | 1 |
| wc1988 | 14 Sept | Belfast | 0 | 0 |
| wc1989 | 11 Oct | Dublin | 3 | 0 |
| wc1993 | 31 Mar | Dublin | 3 | 0 |
| wc1993 | 17 Nov | Belfast | 1 | 1 |
| EC1994 | 16 Nov | Belfast | 4 | 0 |
| EC1995 | 29 Mar | Dublin | 1 | 1 |
| 1999 | 29 May | Dublin | 0 | 1 |
| NC2011 | 24 May | Dublin | 5 | 0 |

### v ISRAEL

| | | | RI | I |
|---|---|---|---|---|
| 1984 | 4 Apr | Tel Aviv | 0 | 3 |
| 1985 | 27 May | Tel Aviv | 0 | 0 |
| 1987 | 10 Nov | Dublin | 5 | 0 |
| EC2005 | 26 Mar | Tel Aviv | 1 | 1 |
| EC2005 | 4 June | Dublin | 2 | 2 |

### v ITALY

| | | | RI | I |
|---|---|---|---|---|
| 1926 | 21 Mar | Turin | 0 | 3 |
| 1927 | 23 Apr | Dublin | 1 | 2 |
| EC1970 | 8 Dec | Rome | 0 | 3 |
| EC1971 | 10 May | Dublin | 1 | 2 |
| 1985 | 5 Feb | Dublin | 1 | 2 |
| wc1990 | 30 June | Rome | 0 | 1 |
| 1992 | 4 June | Foxboro | 0 | 2 |
| wc1994 | 18 June | New York | 1 | 0 |
| 2005 | 17 Aug | Dublin | 1 | 2 |
| wc2009 | 1 Apr | Bari | 1 | 1 |
| wc2009 | 10 Oct | Dublin | 2 | 2 |
| 2011 | 7 June | Liege | 2 | 0 |
| EC2012 | 18 June | Poznan | 0 | 2 |

### v JAMAICA

| | | | RI | J |
|---|---|---|---|---|
| 2004 | 2 June | Charlton | 1 | 0 |

### v KAZAKHSTAN

| | | | RI | K |
|---|---|---|---|---|
| wc2012 | 7 Sept | Astana | 2 | 1 |

### v LATVIA

| | | | RI | L |
|---|---|---|---|---|
| wc1992 | 9 Sept | Dublin | 4 | 0 |
| wc1993 | 2 June | Riga | 2 | 1 |
| EC1994 | 7 Sept | Riga | 3 | 0 |
| EC1995 | 11 Oct | Dublin | 2 | 1 |

### v LIECHTENSTEIN

| | | | RI | L |
|---|---|---|---|---|
| EC1994 | 12 Oct | Dublin | 4 | 0 |
| EC1995 | 3 June | Eschen | 0 | 0 |
| wc1996 | 31 Aug | Eschen | 5 | 0 |
| wc1997 | 21 May | Dublin | 5 | 0 |

### v LITHUANIA

| | | | RI | L |
|---|---|---|---|---|
| wc1993 | 16 June | Vilnius | 1 | 0 |
| wc1993 | 8 Sept | Dublin | 2 | 0 |
| wc1997 | 20 Aug | Dublin | 0 | 0 |
| wc1997 | 10 Sept | Vilnius | 2 | 1 |

### v LUXEMBOURG

| | | | RI | L |
|---|---|---|---|---|
| 1936 | 9 May | Luxembourg | 5 | 1 |
| wc1953 | 28 Oct | Dublin | 4 | 0 |
| wc1954 | 7 Mar | Luxembourg | 1 | 0 |
| EC1987 | 28 May | Luxembourg | 2 | 0 |
| EC1987 | 9 Sept | Dublin | 2 | 1 |

### v MACEDONIA

| | | | RI | M |
|---|---|---|---|---|
| wc1996 | 9 Oct | Dublin | 3 | 0 |
| wc1997 | 2 Apr | Skopje | 2 | 3 |
| EC1999 | 9 June | Dublin | 1 | 0 |
| EC1999 | 9 Oct | Skopje | 1 | 1 |
| EC2011 | 26 Mar | Dublin | 2 | 1 |
| EC2011 | 4 June | Podgorica | 2 | 0 |

### v MALTA

| | | | RI | M |
|---|---|---|---|---|
| EC1983 | 30 Mar | Valletta | 1 | 0 |
| EC1983 | 16 Nov | Dublin | 8 | 0 |
| wc1989 | 28 May | Dublin | 2 | 0 |
| wc1989 | 15 Nov | Valletta | 2 | 0 |
| 1990 | 2 June | Valletta | 3 | 0 |
| EC1998 | 14 Oct | Dublin | 5 | 0 |
| EC1999 | 8 Sept | Valletta | 3 | 2 |

### v MEXICO

| | | | RI | M |
|---|---|---|---|---|
| 1984 | 8 Aug | Dublin | 0 | 0 |
| wc1994 | 24 June | Orlando | 1 | 2 |
| 1996 | 13 June | New Jersey | 2 | 2 |
| 1998 | 23 May | Dublin | 0 | 0 |
| 2000 | 4 June | Chicago | 2 | 2 |

### v MONTENEGRO

| | | | RI | M |
|---|---|---|---|---|
| wc2008 | 10 Sept | Podgorica | 0 | 0 |
| wc2009 | 14 Oct | Dublin | 0 | 0 |

### v MOROCCO

| | | | RI | M |
|---|---|---|---|---|
| 1990 | 12 Sept | Dublin | 1 | 0 |

### v NIGERIA

| | | | RI | N |
|---|---|---|---|---|
| 2002 | 16 May | Dublin | 1 | 2 |
| 2004 | 29 May | Charlton | 0 | 3 |
| 2009 | 29 May | Fulham | 1 | 1 |

### v NORWAY

| | | | RI | N |
|---|---|---|---|---|
| wc1937 | 10 Oct | Oslo | 2 | 3 |
| wc1937 | 7 Nov | Dublin | 3 | 3 |
| 1950 | 26 Nov | Dublin | 2 | 2 |
| 1951 | 30 May | Oslo | 3 | 2 |
| 1954 | 8 Nov | Dublin | 2 | 1 |
| 1955 | 25 May | Oslo | 3 | 1 |
| 1960 | 6 Nov | Dublin | 3 | 1 |
| 1964 | 13 May | Oslo | 4 | 1 |
| 1973 | 6 June | Oslo | 1 | 1 |
| 1976 | 24 Mar | Dublin | 3 | 0 |
| 1978 | 21 May | Oslo | 0 | 0 |
| wc1984 | 17 Oct | Oslo | 0 | 1 |
| wc1985 | 1 May | Dublin | 0 | 0 |
| 1988 | 1 June | Oslo | 0 | 0 |
| wc1994 | 28 June | New York | 0 | 0 |
| 2003 | 30 Apr | Dublin | 1 | 0 |
| 2008 | 20 Aug | Oslo | 1 | 1 |
| 2010 | 17 Nov | Dublin | 1 | 2 |

### v OMAN

| | | | RI | O |
|---|---|---|---|---|
| 2012 | 11 Sept | London | 4 | 1 |

### v PARAGUAY

| | | | RI | P |
|---|---|---|---|---|
| 1999 | 10 Feb | Dublin | 2 | 0 |
| 2010 | 25 May | Dublin | 2 | 1 |

### v POLAND

| | | | RI | P |
|---|---|---|---|---|
| 1938 | 22 May | Warsaw | 0 | 6 |
| 1938 | 13 Nov | Dublin | 3 | 2 |
| 1958 | 11 May | Katowice | 2 | 2 |
| 1958 | 5 Oct | Dublin | 2 | 2 |
| 1964 | 10 May | Kracow | 1 | 3 |
| 1964 | 25 Oct | Dublin | 3 | 2 |
| 1968 | 15 May | Dublin | 2 | 2 |
| 1968 | 30 Oct | Katowice | 0 | 1 |
| 1970 | 6 May | Dublin | 1 | 2 |
| 1970 | 23 Sept | Dublin | 0 | 2 |
| 1973 | 16 May | Wroclaw | 0 | 2 |
| 1973 | 21 Oct | Dublin | 1 | 0 |
| 1976 | 26 May | Poznan | 2 | 0 |
| 1977 | 24 Apr | Dublin | 0 | 0 |
| 1978 | 12 Apr | Lodz | 0 | 3 |
| 1981 | 23 May | Bydgoszcz | 0 | 3 |
| 1984 | 23 May | Dublin | 0 | 0 |
| 1986 | 12 Nov | Warsaw | 0 | 1 |
| 1988 | 22 May | Dublin | 3 | 1 |
| EC1991 | 1 May | Dublin | 0 | 0 |
| EC1991 | 16 Oct | Poznan | 3 | 3 |
| 2004 | 28 Apr | Bydgoszcz | 0 | 0 |

| | | | RI | P |
|---|---|---|---|---|
| 2008 | 19 Nov | Dublin | 2 | 3 |
| 2013 | 6 Feb | Dublin | 2 | 0 |

### v PORTUGAL

| | | | RI | P |
|---|---|---|---|---|
| 1946 | 16 June | Lisbon | 1 | 3 |
| 1947 | 4 May | Dublin | 0 | 2 |
| 1948 | 23 May | Lisbon | 0 | 2 |
| 1949 | 22 May | Dublin | 1 | 0 |
| 1972 | 25 June | Recife | 1 | 2 |
| 1992 | 7 June | Boston | 2 | 0 |
| EC1995 | 26 Apr | Dublin | 1 | 0 |
| EC1995 | 15 Nov | Lisbon | 0 | 3 |
| 1996 | 29 May | Dublin | 0 | 1 |
| wc2000 | 7 Oct | Lisbon | 1 | 1 |
| wc2001 | 2 June | Dublin | 1 | 1 |
| 2005 | 9 Feb | Dublin | 1 | 0 |

### v ROMANIA

| | | | RI | R |
|---|---|---|---|---|
| 1988 | 23 Mar | Dublin | 2 | 0 |
| wc1990 | 25 June | Genoa | 0 | 0* |
| wc1997 | 30 Apr | Bucharest | 0 | 1 |
| wc1997 | 11 Oct | Dublin | 1 | 1 |
| 2004 | 27 May | Dublin | 1 | 0 |

### v RUSSIA

| | | | RI | R |
|---|---|---|---|---|
| 1994 | 23 Mar | Dublin | 0 | 0 |
| 1996 | 27 Mar | Dublin | 0 | 2 |
| 2002 | 13 Feb | Dublin | 2 | 0 |
| EC2002 | 7 Sept | Moscow | 2 | 4 |
| EC2003 | 6 Sept | Dublin | 1 | 1 |
| EC2010 | 8 Oct | Dublin | 2 | 3 |
| EC2011 | 6 Sept | Moscow | 0 | 0 |

### v SAN MARINO

| | | | RI | SM |
|---|---|---|---|---|
| EC2006 | 15 Nov | Dublin | 5 | 0 |
| EC2007 | 7 Feb | Serravalle | 2 | 1 |

### v SAUDI ARABIA

| | | | RI | SA |
|---|---|---|---|---|
| wc2002 | 11 June | Yokohama | 3 | 0 |

### v SERBIA

| | | | RI | S |
|---|---|---|---|---|
| 2008 | 24 May | Dublin | 1 | 1 |
| 2012 | 15 Aug | Belgrade | 0 | 0 |

### v SCOTLAND

| | | | RI | S |
|---|---|---|---|---|
| wc1961 | 3 May | Glasgow | 1 | 4 |
| wc1961 | 7 May | Dublin | 0 | 3 |
| 1963 | 9 June | Dublin | 1 | 0 |
| 1969 | 21 Sept | Dublin | 1 | 1 |
| EC1986 | 15 Oct | Dublin | 0 | 0 |
| EC1987 | 18 Feb | Glasgow | 1 | 0 |
| 2000 | 30 May | Dublin | 1 | 2 |
| 2003 | 12 Feb | Glasgow | 2 | 0 |
| NC2011 | 29 May | Dublin | 1 | 0 |

### v SLOVAKIA

| | | | RI | S |
|---|---|---|---|---|
| EC2007 | 28 Mar | Dublin | 1 | 0 |
| EC2007 | 8 Sept | Bratislava | 2 | 2 |
| EC2010 | 12 Oct | Zilina | 1 | 1 |
| EC2011 | 2 Sept | Dublin | 0 | 0 |

### v SOUTH AFRICA

| | | | RI | SA |
|---|---|---|---|---|
| 2000 | 11 June | New Jersey | 2 | 1 |
| 2009 | 8 Sept | Limerick | 1 | 0 |

### v SPAIN

| | | | RI | S |
|---|---|---|---|---|
| 1931 | 26 Apr | Barcelona | 1 | 1 |
| 1931 | 13 Dec | Dublin | 0 | 5 |
| 1946 | 23 June | Madrid | 1 | 0 |
| 1947 | 2 Mar | Dublin | 3 | 2 |
| 1948 | 30 May | Barcelona | 1 | 2 |
| 1949 | 12 June | Dublin | 1 | 4 |
| 1952 | 1 June | Madrid | 0 | 6 |
| 1955 | 27 Nov | Dublin | 2 | 2 |
| EC1964 | 11 Mar | Seville | 1 | 5 |
| EC1964 | 8 Apr | Dublin | 0 | 2 |
| wc1965 | 5 May | Dublin | 1 | 0 |
| wc1965 | 27 Oct | Seville | 1 | 4 |
| wc1965 | 10 Nov | Paris | 0 | 1 |

### v SPAIN

| | | | RI | S |
|---|---|---|---|---|
| EC1966 | 23 Oct | Dublin | 0 | 0 |
| EC1966 | 7 Dec | Valencia | 0 | 2 |
| 1977 | 9 Feb | Dublin | 0 | 1 |
| EC1982 | 17 Nov | Dublin | 3 | 3 |
| EC1983 | 27 Apr | Zaragoza | 0 | 2 |
| 1985 | 26 May | Cork | 0 | 0 |
| WC1988 | 16 Nov | Seville | 0 | 2 |
| WC1989 | 26 Apr | Dublin | 1 | 0 |
| WC1992 | 18 Nov | Seville | 0 | 0 |
| WC1993 | 13 Oct | Dublin | 1 | 3 |
| WC2002 | 16 June | Suwon | 1 | 1 |
| EC2012 | 14 June | Gdansk | 0 | 4 |
| 2013 | 11 June | New York | 0 | 2 |

### v SWEDEN

| | | | RI | S |
|---|---|---|---|---|
| WC1949 | 2 June | Stockholm | 1 | 3 |
| WC1949 | 13 Nov | Dublin | 1 | 3 |
| 1959 | 1 Nov | Dublin | 3 | 2 |
| 1960 | 18 May | Malmo | 1 | 4 |
| EC1970 | 14 Oct | Dublin | 1 | 1 |
| EC1970 | 28 Oct | Malmo | 0 | 1 |
| 1999 | 28 Apr | Dublin | 2 | 0 |
| 2006 | 1 Mar | Dublin | 3 | 0 |
| WC2013 | 22 Mar | Stockholm | 0 | 0 |

### v SWITZERLAND

| | | | RI | S |
|---|---|---|---|---|
| 1935 | 5 May | Basle | 0 | 1 |
| 1936 | 17 Mar | Dublin | 1 | 0 |
| 1937 | 17 May | Berne | 1 | 0 |
| 1938 | 18 Sept | Dublin | 4 | 0 |
| 1948 | 5 Dec | Dublin | 0 | 1 |
| EC1975 | 11 May | Dublin | 2 | 1 |
| EC1975 | 21 May | Berne | 0 | 1 |
| 1980 | 30 Apr | Dublin | 2 | 0 |
| WC1985 | 2 June | Dublin | 3 | 0 |
| WC1985 | 11 Sept | Berne | 0 | 0 |
| 1992 | 25 Mar | Dublin | 2 | 1 |
| EC2002 | 16 Oct | Dublin | 1 | 2 |
| EC2003 | 11 Oct | Basle | 0 | 2 |
| WC2004 | 8 Sept | Basle | 1 | 1 |
| WC2005 | 12 Oct | Dublin | 0 | 0 |

### v TRINIDAD & TOBAGO

| | | | RI | TT |
|---|---|---|---|---|
| 1982 | 30 May | Port of Spain | 1 | 2 |

### v TUNISIA

| | | | RI | T |
|---|---|---|---|---|
| 1988 | 19 Oct | Dublin | 4 | 0 |

### v TURKEY

| | | | RI | T |
|---|---|---|---|---|
| EC1966 | 16 Nov | Dublin | 2 | 1 |
| EC1967 | 22 Feb | Ankara | 1 | 2 |
| EC1974 | 20 Nov | Izmir | 1 | 1 |
| EC1975 | 29 Oct | Dublin | 4 | 0 |

| | | | RI | T |
|---|---|---|---|---|
| 1976 | 13 Oct | Ankara | 3 | 3 |
| 1978 | 5 Apr | Dublin | 4 | 2 |
| 1990 | 26 May | Izmir | 0 | 0 |
| EC1990 | 17 Oct | Dublin | 5 | 0 |
| EC1991 | 13 Nov | Istanbul | 3 | 1 |
| EC2000 | 13 Nov | Dublin | 1 | 1 |
| EC2000 | 17 Nov | Bursa | 0 | 0 |
| 2003 | 9 Sept | Dublin | 2 | 2 |

### v URUGUAY

| | | | RI | U |
|---|---|---|---|---|
| 1974 | 8 May | Montevideo | 0 | 2 |
| 1986 | 23 Apr | Dublin | 1 | 1 |
| 2011 | 29 Mar | Dublin | 2 | 3 |

### v USA

| | | | RI | USA |
|---|---|---|---|---|
| 1979 | 29 Oct | Dublin | 3 | 2 |
| 1991 | 1 June | Boston | 1 | 1 |
| 1992 | 29 Apr | Dublin | 4 | 1 |
| 1992 | 30 May | Washington | 1 | 3 |
| 1996 | 9 June | Boston | 1 | 2 |
| 2000 | 6 June | Boston | 1 | 1 |
| 2002 | 17 Apr | Dublin | 2 | 1 |

### v USSR

| | | | RI | USSR |
|---|---|---|---|---|
| WC1972 | 18 Oct | Dublin | 1 | 2 |
| WC1973 | 13 May | Moscow | 0 | 1 |
| EC1974 | 30 Oct | Dublin | 3 | 0 |
| EC1975 | 18 May | Kiev | 1 | 2 |
| WC1984 | 12 Sept | Dublin | 1 | 0 |
| WC1985 | 16 Oct | Moscow | 0 | 2 |
| EC1988 | 15 June | Hanover | 1 | 1 |
| 1990 | 25 Apr | Dublin | 1 | 0 |

### v WALES

| | | | RI | W |
|---|---|---|---|---|
| 1960 | 28 Sept | Dublin | 2 | 3 |
| 1979 | 11 Sept | Swansea | 1 | 2 |
| 1981 | 24 Feb | Dublin | 1 | 3 |
| 1986 | 26 Mar | Dublin | 0 | 1 |
| 1990 | 28 Mar | Dublin | 1 | 0 |
| 1991 | 6 Feb | Wrexham | 3 | 0 |
| 1992 | 19 Feb | Dublin | 0 | 1 |
| 1993 | 17 Feb | Dublin | 2 | 1 |
| 1997 | 11 Feb | Cardiff | 0 | 0 |
| EC2007 | 24 Mar | Dublin | 1 | 0 |
| EC2007 | 17 Nov | Cardiff | 2 | 2 |
| NC2011 | 8 Feb | Dublin | 3 | 0 |

### v YUGOSLAVIA

| | | | RI | Y |
|---|---|---|---|---|
| 1955 | 19 Sept | Dublin | 1 | 4 |
| 1988 | 27 Apr | Dublin | 2 | 0 |
| EC1998 | 18 Nov | Belgrade | 0 | 1 |
| EC1999 | 1 Sept | Dublin | 2 | 1 |

# OTHER BRITISH AND IRISH INTERNATIONAL MATCHES 2012–13

## FRIENDLIES

■ *Denotes player sent off.*

### ENGLAND

**Wednesday, 15 August 2012**

**England (1) 2** *(Jagielka 27, Defoe 79)*

**Italy (1) 1** *(De Rossi 15)* 15,000

*England:* (4231) Butland (Ruddy 46); Walker, Cahill, Jagielka (Lescott 61), Baines (Bertrand 78); Carrick, Lampard (Livermore 69); Johnson, Cleverley, Young (Milner 62); Carroll (Defoe 46).
*Italy:* (433) Sirigu; Ogbonna, Abate (Schelotto 86), Balzaretti (Peluso 46), Astori; Aquilani (Poli 68), De Rossi, Nocerino; Destro (Fabbrini 84), Diamanti (Verratti 59), El Shaarawy (Gabbiadini 58).
*Referee:* Sascha Kever.

**Wednesday, 14 November 2012**

**Sweden (1) 4** *(Ibrahimovic 20, 77, 84, 90)*

**England (2) 2** *(Welbeck 35, Caulker 38)* 49,967

*Sweden:* (4231) Isaksson; Lustig (Sana 73), Granqvist (Antonsson 73), Olsson J, Olsson M (Safari 46); Larsson (Jansson 85), Elm; Kallstrom (Svensson 61), Kacaniklic, Ibrahimovic; Ranegie (Wernbloom 89).
*England:* (4411) Hart; Johnson G (Jenkinson 74), Caulker (Shawcross 74), Cahill, Baines; Cleverley (Wilshere 61), Gerrard (Huddlestone 74), Osman, Young (Sturridge 61); Sterling (Zaha 85); Welbeck.
*Referee:* Svein Oddvar Moen.

**Wednesday, 6 February 2013**

**England (1) 2** *(Rooney 27, Lampard 60)*

**Brazil (0) 1** *(Fred 48)* 87,453

*England:* (433) Hart; Johnson, Cahill, Smalling, Cole (Baines 46); Cleverley (Lampard 46), Gerrard, Wilshere; Walcott (Lennon 75), Rooney, Welbeck (Milner 61).
*Brazil:* (433) Julio Cesar; Dani Alves, Luiz (Miranda 78), Dante, Adriano (Filipe Luis 69); Paulinho (Jean 62), Ramires (Arouca 46), Ronaldinho (Lucas Moura 46); Neymar, Luis Fabiano (Fred 46), Oscar.
*Referee:* Pedro Proenca.

**Wednesday, 29 May 2013**

**England (1) 1** *(Lampard 23)*

**Republic of Ireland (1) 1** *(Long 14)* 80,126

*England:* (442) Hart (Foster 45); Johnson G (Jones 45), Cahill, Jagielka, Cole (Baines 53); Walcott, Lampard, Carrick, Oxlade-Chamberlain (Milner 87); Rooney, Sturridge (Defoe 33).
*Republic of Ireland:* (442) Forde; Coleman, O'Shea, St. Ledger, Kelly; Walters (Sammon 81), McCarthy, Whelan (Hendrick 73), McGeady (McClean 68); Long, Keane (Cox 65).
*Referee:* William Collum.

**Sunday, 2 June 2013**

**Brazil (0) 2** *(Fred 57, Paulinho 82)*

**England (0) 2** *(Oxlade-Chamberlain 67, Rooney 79)* 66,015

*Brazil:* (4231) Julio Cesar; Dani Alves, Thiago Silva, Luiz, Filipe Luis (Marcelo 46); Gustavo (Hernanes 46), Paulinho (Bernard 83); Hulk (Fernando 72), Oscar (Lucas Moura 56), Neymar; Fred (Leandro Damiao 80).
*England:* (433) Hart; Johnson G (Oxlade-Chamberlain 61), Jagielka, Cahill, Baines (Cole 31); Jones, Carrick, Lampard; Walcott (Rodwell 83), Rooney, Milner.
*Referee:* Wilmar Roldan Perez.

### SCOTLAND

**Wednesday, 15 August 2012**

**Scotland (1) 3** *(Rhodes 29, Davidson 63 (og), McCormack 76)*

**Australia (1) 1** *(Bresciano 19)* 11,110

*Scotland:* (352) McGregor (Gilks 22); Webster, Caldwell (Black 87), Berra; Hutton (Martin 67), Snodgrass, Adam, Morrison (Maloney 77), Fox (Mulgrew 69); Naismith, Rhodes (McCormack 67).
*Australia:* (442) Schwarzer (Federici 46); Williams, Ognenovski (McGowan 79), Neill, Carney (Davidson 60); Kruse, Valeri, Bresciano (Jedinak 46), Wilkshire; Holman (McDonald 46), Brosque (Thompson 84).
*Referee:* Tom Harald Hagen.

Sir Bobby Charlton shakes hands with Steven Gerrard at Wembley in February as the Liverpool midfielder receives an award for achieving 100 caps for his country.
(Action Images)

Before England's friendly with Ireland, Ashley Cole is congratulated on winning his 100th international cap by manager Roy Hodgson at Wembley at the end of May.
(Action Images)

Wednesday, 14 November 2012
**Luxembourg (0) 1** *(Krogh Gerson 47)*
**Scotland (2) 2** *(Rhodes 11, 24)* 2521
*Luxembourg:* (442) Joubert; Mutsch, Bukvic, Deville (Bensi 63), Schnell; Janisch (Da Mota Alves 52), Blaise, Krogh Gerson, Payal (Peters 46); Bettmer (Turpel 70), Leweck (Laterza 76).
*Scotland:* (442) Gilks; Whittaker, Dixon, Berra, Hanley; Mulgrew (Kelly 46), Fletcher, Shinnie (Griffiths 69), Naismith; Rhodes (Davidson 90), Miller.
*Referee:* Cyrill Zimmermann.

Wednesday, 6 February 2013
**Scotland (1) 1** *(Mulgrew 39)*
**Estonia (0) 0** 16,102
*Scotland:* (442) McGregor; Hutton, Webster, Berra, Mulgrew; Maloney (Rhodes 45), Brown (Morrison 62), Adam (McArthur 61), Burke (Snodgrass 45); Naismith (Commons 75), Fletcher (Miller 67).
*Estonia:* (442) Pareiko; Jaager, Morozov, Klavan, Teniste; Puri (Purje 58), Mosnikov, Vassiljev, Oper (Ahjupera 45); Kink (Luts 58), Ojamaa (Kams 73).
*Referee:* Clement Turpin.

## WALES

Wednesday, 15 August 2012
**Wales (0) 0**
**Bosnia & Herzegovina (1) 2** *(Ibisevic 21, Stevanovic 54)* 6253
*Wales:* (442) Myhill; Gunter (Ricketts 69), Blake (Lynch 78), Williams A, Taylor; Bale (Robson-Kanu 62), Ramsey, Allen, Crofts (Earnshaw 88); Church (Bellamy 62), Vokes (Morison 69).
*Bosnia & Herzegovina:* (352) Begovic; Pandza (Sunjic 71), Spahic, Mujdza (Vranjes 86); Salihovic, Pjanic (Sesar 82), Zahirovic (Vrancic 86), Stevanovic, Lulic (Besic 63); Ibisevic (Svraka 74), Dzeko.
*Referee:* Marco Borg.

Wednesday, 6 February 2013
**Wales (1) 2** *(Bale 21, Vokes 52)*
**Austria (0) 1** *(Janko 75)*
*Wales:* (442) Myhill; Matthews (Gunter 72), Ricketts, Williams A, Davies B; Ledley, Allen, Vaughan (King 46); Bale (Robson-Kanu 60); Bellamy (Vokes 46), Collison (Church 84).
*Austria:* (4231) Almer; Pogatetz, Suttner (Schiemer 87), Prodl, Klein; Alaba, Kavlak (Leitgeb 75); Ivanschitz (Junuzovic 61), Arnautovic, Weimann (Jantscher 62); Janko.
*Referee:* Menashe Masiah.

## NORTHERN IRELAND

Wednesday, 15 August 2012
**Northern Ireland (2) 3** *(Ferguson 7, Lafferty K 19, Paterson 84 (pen))*
**Finland (2) 3** *(Sparv 22, Pukki 24, Hetemaj 78)* 9575
*Northern Ireland:* (442) Carroll (Camp 46); Hodson (Norwood 84), Cathcart, McAuley, McGivern; Brunt (Ward 46), Baird, Davis, Ferguson (Carson 84); Shiels, Lafferty K (Paterson 63).
*Finland:* (433) Maenpaa; Uronen, Toivio, Arkivuo, Moisander; Eremenko R, Hamalainen (Kolehmainen 69), Sparv; Eremenko A (Hetemaj 69), Pukki (Riski 46), Kuqi (Sjolund 84).
*Referee:* Richard Liesveld.

Wednesday, 6 February 2013
**Malta (0) 0**
**Northern Ireland (0) 0** 1000
*Malta:* (4141) Hogg; Muscat A, Agius A (Camilleri 46), Dimech, Herrera; Sciberras; Failla, Fenech P, Cohen, Schembri (Bajada 90); Mifsud (Vella 89).
*Northern Ireland:* (4411) Mannus; Hughes, McAuley, Evans J (Cathcart 46), Lafferty; Brunt, McGinn, Bruce (McCourt 72), Ferguson (McKay 63); Davis; Grigg (Magennis 86).
*Referee:* Nikolay Yordanov.

## REPUBLIC OF IRELAND

Wednesday, 15 August 2012
**Serbia (0) 0**
**Republic of Ireland (0) 0** 7800
*Serbia:* (451) Stojkovic; Ivanovic, Bisevac (Maksimovic 46), Nastasic, Kolarov; Mijailovic (Ninkovic 63), Kuzmanovic (Basta 81), Ignjovski, Tadic (Djuricic 63), Tosic (Tomic 81); Lekic (Markovic 46).
*Republic of Ireland:* (442) Westwood; McShane, O'Shea, O'Dea, Kelly; McGeady (Coleman 78), McCarthy, Whelan (Green 60), McClean (Keogh A 69); Cox, Walters (O'Brien 78).
*Referee:* Alexandru Dan Tudor.

Tuesday, 11 September 2012
**Republic of Ireland (3) 4** *(Long 7, Brady 23, Doyle 36, Pearce 85)*
**Oman (0) 1** *(Al Farsi 72)* 6420
*Republic of Ireland:* (442) Forde (Randolph 46); Kelly, St. Ledger, Meyler, Wilson (Pearce 46); Coleman, Keogh, McCarthy (Cox 65), Brady (McGeady 70); Doyle (McClean 61), Long (O'Brien 73).
*Oman:* (442) Al Habsi; Al Musalami, Muhaiyri (Al Jabri 77), Ghailani, Al Mukhaini S; Al Balushi (Al Mukhaini A 78), Saleh (Al Hadhri 69), Al Farsi, Al Maashari; Al Muqbali (Bashir 70), Al Hosni.
*Referee:* Andre Marriner.

Wednesday, 14 November 2012
**Republic of Ireland (0) 0**
**Greece (1) 1** *(Holebas 29)* 16,256
*Republic of Ireland:* (442) Forde; Coleman, O'Shea, Clark, Ward; Brady (Hoolahan 46), McCarthy (Meyler 70), Whelan (Andrews 34), McClean; Cox (Keogh A 61), Long (Doyle 46).
*Greece:* (442) Karnezis; Torosidis (Maniatis 60), Papastathopoulos, Papadopoulos, Holebas (Fortounis 46); Stafylidis (Spyropoulos 82), Tziolis, Tachtsidis, Ninis (Vyntra 60); Mitroglou (Salpingidis 46), Samaras (Athanasiadis 46).
*Referee:* Eitan Shmuelevitz.

Wednesday, 6 February 2013
**Republic of Ireland (1) 2** *(Clark 35, Hoolahan 76)*
**Poland (0) 0** 43,112
*Republic of Ireland:* (442) Forde; McShane, O'Shea, Clark (Keogh R 84), Cunningham; Brady (Walters 71), McCarthy (Hendrick 71), Whelan (Green 46), McClean (Cox 81); Long (Hoolahan 62), Sammon.
*Poland:* (451) Boruc (Szczesny 46); Perquis, Glik, Boenisch (Wasilewski 46), Wawrzyniak; Lukasik (Mierzejewski 77), Krychowiak, Blaszczykowski, Obraniak (Milik 60), Pawlowski (Grosicki 46); Lewandowski.
*Referee:* Sebastien Delferiere.

Sunday, 2 June 2013
**Republic of Ireland (1) 4** *(Keogh R 42, Cox 48, Keane 77, 88)*
**Georgia (0) 0** 20,100
*Republic of Ireland:* (442) Westwood; Delaney, McShane, Keogh R, Wilson (Dunne 65); Keogh A (Keane 46), McCarthy (Sammon 71), Hoolahan (Quinn 75), McClean (McGeady 65); Cox, Long (Hendrick 71).
*Georgia:* (442) Loria[a]; Lobjanidze (Targamadze 46), Khubutia, Khizanishvili, Kvirkvelia D (Popkhadze 69); Kashia, Daushvili (Dzaria 54), Kankava, Ananidze (Migineishvili 22); Kobakhidze (Gorgiashvili 90), Gelashvili (Maisuradze 61).
*Referee:* Serbastain Coltescu.

Wednesday, 12 June 2013
**Spain (0) 2** *(Soldado 69, Mata 88)*
**Republic of Ireland (0) 0** 39,368
*Spain:* (442) Valdes (Casillas 58); Pique, Sergio Ramos, Arbeloa, Jordi Alba; Iniesta (Fabregas 59), Xavi (Mata 69), Busquets, Silva (Jesus Navas 46); Pedro (Cazorla 80), Villa (Soldado 59).
*Republic of Ireland:* (442) Forde (Randolph 73); St. Ledger, Coleman, Kelly (Delaney 90), O'Dea; McShane, McCarthy, Hendrick (Quinn 46), Sammon (Cox 57); Keogh A (McClean 74).
*Referee:* Jair Marrufo.

# BRITISH AND IRISH INTERNATIONAL APPEARANCES 1872–2013

This is a list of full international appearances by Englishmen, Irishmen, Scotsmen and Welshmen in matches against the Home Countries and against foreign nations. It does not include unofficial matches against Commonwealth and Empire countries. The year indicated refers to the player's international debut season; i.e. 2013 is the 2012–13 season. **Bold** type indicates players who have made an international appearance in season 2012–13.

*As at July 2013.*

## ENGLAND

| | |
|---|---|
| Abbott, W. 1902 (Everton) | 1 |
| A'Court, A. 1958 (Liverpool) | 5 |
| Adams, T. A. 1987 (Arsenal) | 66 |
| Adcock, H. 1929 (Leicester C) | 5 |
| Agbonlahor, G. 2009 (Aston Villa) | 3 |
| Alcock, C. W. 1875 (Wanderers) | 1 |
| Alderson, J. T. 1923 (Crystal Palace) | 1 |
| Aldridge, A. 1888 (WBA, Walsall Town Swifts) | 2 |
| Allen, A. 1888 (Aston Villa) | 1 |
| Allen, A. 1960 (Stoke C) | 3 |
| Allen, C. 1984 (QPR, Tottenham H) | 5 |
| Allen, H. 1888 (Wolverhampton W) | 5 |
| Allen, J. P. 1934 (Portsmouth) | 2 |
| Allen, R. 1952 (WBA) | 5 |
| Alsford, W. J. 1935 (Tottenham H) | 1 |
| Amos, A. 1885 (Old Carthusians) | 2 |
| Anderson, R. D. 1879 (Old Etonians) | 1 |
| Anderson, S. 1962 (Sunderland) | 2 |
| Anderson, V. A. 1979 (Nottingham F, Arsenal, Manchester U) | 30 |
| Anderton, D. R. 1994 (Tottenham H) | 30 |
| Angus, J. 1961 (Burnley) | 1 |
| Armfield, J. C. 1959 (Blackpool) | 43 |
| Armitage, G. H. 1926 (Charlton Ath) | 1 |
| Armstrong, D. 1980 (Middlesbrough, Southampton) | 3 |
| Armstrong, K. 1955 (Chelsea) | 1 |
| Arnold, J. 1933 (Fulham) | 1 |
| Arthur, J. W. H. 1885 (Blackburn R) | 7 |
| Ashcroft, J. 1906 (Woolwich Arsenal) | 3 |
| Ashmore, G. S. 1926 (WBA) | 1 |
| Ashton, C. T. 1926 (Corinthians) | 1 |
| Ashton, D. 2008 (West Ham U) | 1 |
| Ashurst, W. 1923 (Notts Co) | 5 |
| Astall, G. 1956 (Birmingham C) | 2 |
| Astle, J. 1969 (WBA) | 5 |
| Aston, J. 1949 (Manchester U) | 17 |
| Athersmith, W. C. 1892 (Aston Villa) | 12 |
| Atyeo, P. J. W. 1956 (Bristol C) | 6 |
| Austin, S. W. 1926 (Manchester C) | 1 |
| | |
| Bach, P. 1899 (Sunderland) | 1 |
| Bache, J. W. 1903 (Aston Villa) | 7 |
| Baddeley, T. 1903 (Wolverhampton W) | 5 |
| Bagshaw, J. J. 1920 (Derby Co) | 1 |
| Bailey, G. R. 1985 (Manchester U) | 2 |
| Bailey, H. P. 1908 (Leicester Fosse) | 5 |
| Bailey, M. A. 1964 (Charlton Ath) | 2 |
| Bailey, N. C. 1878 (Clapham R) | 19 |
| Baily, E. F. 1950 (Tottenham H) | 9 |
| Bain, J. 1877 (Oxford University) | 1 |
| **Baines, L. J. 2010 (Everton)** | **17** |
| Baker, A. 1928 (Arsenal) | 1 |
| Baker, B. H. 1921 (Everton, Chelsea) | 2 |
| Baker, J. H. 1960 (Hibernian, Arsenal) | 8 |
| Ball, A. J. 1965 (Blackpool, Everton, Arsenal) | 72 |
| Ball, J. 1928 (Bury) | 1 |
| Ball, M. J. 2001 (Everton) | 1 |
| Balmer, W. 1905 (Everton) | 1 |
| Bamber, J. 1921 (Liverpool) | 1 |
| Bambridge, A. L. 1881 (Swifts) | 3 |
| Bambridge, E. C. 1879 (Swifts) | 18 |
| Bambridge, E. H. 1876 (Swifts) | 1 |
| Banks, G. 1963 (Leicester C, Stoke C) | 73 |
| Banks, H. E. 1901 (Millwall) | 1 |
| Banks, T. 1958 (Bolton W) | 6 |
| Bannister, W. 1901 (Burnley, Bolton W) | 2 |
| Barclay, R. 1932 (Sheffield U) | 3 |
| Bardsley, D. J. 1993 (QPR) | 2 |
| Barham, M. 1983 (Norwich C) | 2 |

| | |
|---|---|
| Barkas, S. 1936 (Manchester C) | 5 |
| Barker, J. 1935 (Derby Co) | 11 |
| Barker, R. 1872 (Herts Rangers) | 1 |
| Barker, R. R. 1895 (Casuals) | 1 |
| Barlow, R. J. 1955 (WBA) | 1 |
| Barmby, N. J. 1995 (Tottenham H, Middlesbrough, Everton, Liverpool) | 23 |
| Barnes, J. 1983 (Watford, Liverpool) | 79 |
| Barnes, P. S. 1978 (Manchester C, WBA, Leeds U) | 22 |
| Barnet, H. H. 1882 (Royal Engineers) | 1 |
| Barrass, M. W. 1952 (Bolton W) | 3 |
| Barrett, A. F. 1930 (Fulham) | 1 |
| Barrett, E. D. 1991 (Oldham Ath, Aston Villa) | 3 |
| Barrett, J. W. 1929 (West Ham U) | 1 |
| Barry, G. 2000 (Aston Villa, Manchester C) | 53 |
| Barry, L. 1928 (Leicester C) | 5 |
| Barson, F. 1920 (Aston Villa) | 1 |
| Barton, J. 1890 (Blackburn R) | 1 |
| Barton, J. 2007 (Manchester C) | 1 |
| Barton, P. H. 1921 (Birmingham) | 7 |
| Barton, W. D. 1995 (Wimbledon, Newcastle U) | 3 |
| Bassett, W. I. 1888 (WBA) | 16 |
| Bastard, S. R. 1880 (Upton Park) | 1 |
| Bastin, C. S. 1932 (Arsenal) | 21 |
| Batty, D. 1991 (Leeds U, Blackburn R, Newcastle U, Leeds U) | 42 |
| Baugh, R. 1886 (Stafford Road, Wolverhampton W) | 2 |
| Bayliss, A. E. J. M. 1891 (WBA) | 1 |
| Baynham, R. L. 1956 (Luton T) | 3 |
| Beardsley, P. A. 1986 (Newcastle U, Liverpool, Newcastle U) | 59 |
| Beasant, D. J. 1990 (Chelsea) | 2 |
| Beasley, A. 1939 (Huddersfield T) | 1 |
| Beats, W. E. 1901 (Wolverhampton W) | 2 |
| Beattie, J. S. 2003 (Southampton) | 5 |
| Beattie, T. K. 1975 (Ipswich T) | 9 |
| Beckham, D. R. J. 1997 (Manchester U, Real Madrid, LA Galaxy) | 115 |
| Becton, F. 1895 (Preston NE, Liverpool) | 2 |
| Bedford, H. 1923 (Blackpool) | 2 |
| Bell, C. 1968 (Manchester C) | 48 |
| Bennett, W. 1901 (Sheffield U) | 2 |
| Benson, R. W. 1913 (Sheffield U) | 1 |
| Bent, D. A. 2006 (Charlton Ath, Tottenham H, Sunderland, Aston Villa) | 13 |
| Bentley, D. M. 2008 (Blackburn R, Tottenham H) | 7 |
| Bentley, R. T. F. 1949 (Chelsea) | 12 |
| Beresford, J. 1934 (Aston Villa) | 1 |
| Berry, A. 1909 (Oxford University) | 1 |
| Berry, J. J. 1953 (Manchester U) | 4 |
| **Bertrand, R. 2013 (Chelsea)** | **2** |
| Bestall, J. G. 1935 (Grimsby T) | 1 |
| Betmead, H. A. 1937 (Grimsby T) | 1 |
| Betts, M. P. 1877 (Old Harrovians) | 1 |
| Betts, W. 1889 (Sheffield W) | 1 |
| Beverley, J. 1884 (Blackburn R) | 3 |
| Birkett, R. H. 1879 (Clapham R) | 1 |
| Birkett, R. J. E. 1936 (Middlesbrough) | 1 |
| Birley, F. H. 1874 (Oxford University, Wanderers) | 2 |
| Birtles, G. 1980 (Nottingham F) | 3 |
| Bishop, S. M. 1927 (Leicester C) | 4 |
| Blackburn, F. 1901 (Blackburn R) | 3 |
| Blackburn, G. F. 1924 (Aston Villa) | 1 |
| Blenkinsop, E. 1928 (Sheffield W) | 26 |
| Bliss, H. 1921 (Tottenham H) | 1 |
| Blissett, L. L. 1983 (Watford, AC Milan) | 14 |
| Blockley, J. P. 1973 (Arsenal) | 1 |
| Bloomer, S. 1895 (Derby Co, Middlesbrough) | 23 |
| Blunstone, F. 1955 (Chelsea) | 5 |

| | |
|---|---|
| Bond, R. 1905 (Preston NE, Bradford C) | 8 |
| Bonetti, P. P. 1966 (Chelsea) | 7 |
| Bonsor, A. G. 1873 (Wanderers) | 2 |
| Booth, F. 1905 (Manchester C) | 1 |
| Booth, T. 1898 (Blackburn R, Everton) | 2 |
| Bothroyd, J. 2011 (Cardiff C) | 1 |
| Bould, S. A. 1994 (Arsenal) | 2 |
| Bowden, E. R. 1935 (Arsenal) | 6 |
| Bower, A. G. 1924 (Corinthians) | 5 |
| Bowers, J. W. 1934 (Derby Co) | 3 |
| Bowles, S. 1974 (QPR) | 5 |
| Bowser, S. 1920 (WBA) | 1 |
| Bowyer, L. D. 2003 (Leeds U) | 1 |
| Boyer, P. J. 1976 (Norwich C) | 1 |
| Boyes, W. 1935 (WBA, Everton) | 3 |
| Boyle, T. W. 1913 (Burnley) | 1 |
| Brabrook, P. 1958 (Chelsea) | 3 |
| Bracewell, P. W. 1985 (Everton) | 3 |
| Bradford, G. R. W. 1956 (Bristol R) | 1 |
| Bradford, J. 1924 (Birmingham) | 12 |
| Bradley, W. 1959 (Manchester U) | 3 |
| Bradshaw, F. 1908 (Sheffield W) | 1 |
| Bradshaw, T. H. 1897 (Liverpool) | 1 |
| Bradshaw, W. 1910 (Blackburn R) | 4 |
| Brann, G. 1886 (Swifts) | 3 |
| Brawn, W. F. 1904 (Aston Villa) | 2 |
| Bray, J. 1935 (Manchester C) | 6 |
| Brayshaw, E. 1887 (Sheffield W) | 1 |
| Bridge W. M. 2002 (Southampton, Chelsea, Manchester C) | 36 |
| Bridges, B. J. 1965 (Chelsea) | 4 |
| Bridgett, A. 1905 (Sunderland) | 11 |
| Brindle, T. 1880 (Darwen) | 2 |
| Brittleton, J. T. 1912 (Sheffield W) | 5 |
| Britton, C. S. 1935 (Everton) | 9 |
| Broadbent, P. F. 1958 (Wolverhampton W) | 7 |
| Broadis, I. A. 1952 (Manchester C, Newcastle U) | 14 |
| Brockbank, J. 1872 (Cambridge University) | 1 |
| Brodie, J. B. 1889 (Wolverhampton W) | 3 |
| Bromilow, T. G. 1921 (Liverpool) | 5 |
| Bromley-Davenport, W. E. 1884 (Oxford University) | 2 |
| Brook, E. F. 1930 (Manchester C) | 18 |
| Brooking, T. D. 1974 (West Ham U) | 47 |
| Brooks, J. 1957 (Tottenham H) | 3 |
| Broome, F. H. 1938 (Aston Villa) | 7 |
| Brown, A. 1882 (Aston Villa) | 3 |
| Brown, A. 1971 (WBA) | 1 |
| Brown, A. S. 1904 (Sheffield U) | 2 |
| Brown, G. 1927 (Huddersfield T, Aston Villa) | 9 |
| Brown, J. 1881 (Blackburn R) | 5 |
| Brown, J. H. 1927 (Sheffield W) | 6 |
| Brown, K. 1960 (West Ham U) | 1 |
| Brown, W. 1924 (West Ham U) | 1 |
| Brown, W. M. 1999 (Manchester U) | 23 |
| Bruton, J. 1928 (Burnley) | 3 |
| Bryant, W. I. 1925 (Clapton) | 1 |
| Buchan, C. M. 1913 (Sunderland) | 6 |
| Buchanan, W. S. 1876 (Clapham R) | 1 |
| Buckley, F. C. 1914 (Derby Co) | 1 |
| Bull, S. G. 1989 (Wolverhampton W) | 13 |
| Bullock, F. E. 1921 (Huddersfield T) | 1 |
| Bullock, N. 1923 (Bury) | 3 |
| Burgess, H. 1904 (Manchester C) | 4 |
| Burgess, H. 1931 (Sheffield W) | 4 |
| Burnup, C. J. 1896 (Cambridge University) | 1 |
| Burrows, H. 1934 (Sheffield W) | 3 |
| Burton, F. E. 1889 (Nottingham F) | 1 |
| Bury, L. 1877 (Cambridge University, Old Etonians) | 2 |
| Butcher, T. 1980 (Ipswich T, Rangers) | 77 |
| **Butland, J. 2013 (Birmingham C)** | **1** |
| Butler, J. D. 1925 (Arsenal) | 1 |
| Butler, W. 1924 (Bolton W) | 1 |
| Butt, N. 1997 (Manchester U, Newcastle U) | 39 |
| Byrne, G. 1963 (Liverpool) | 2 |
| Byrne, J. J. 1962 (Crystal Palace, West Ham U) | 11 |
| Byrne, R. W. 1954 (Manchester U) | 33 |
| | |
| **Cahill, G. J. 2011 (Bolton W, Chelsea)** | **15** |
| Callaghan, I. R. 1966 (Liverpool) | 4 |
| Calvey, J. 1902 (Nottingham F) | 1 |
| Campbell, A. F. 1929 (Blackburn R, Huddersfield T) | 8 |
| Campbell, F. L. 2012 (Sunderland) | 1 |

| | |
|---|---|
| Campbell, S. 1996 (Tottenham H, Arsenal, Portsmouth) | |
| | 73 |
| Camsell, G. H. 1929 (Middlesbrough) | 9 |
| Capes, A. J. 1903 (Stoke) | 1 |
| Carr, J. 1905 (Newcastle U) | 2 |
| Carr, J. 1920 (Middlesbrough) | 2 |
| Carr, W. H. 1875 (Owlerton, Sheffield) | 1 |
| Carragher, J. L. 1999 (Liverpool) | 38 |
| **Carrick, M. 2001 (West Ham U, Tottenham H, Manchester U)** | **29** |
| **Carroll, A. T. 2011 (Newcastle U, Liverpool)** | **9** |
| Carson, S. P. 2008 (Liverpool, WBA) | 4 |
| Carter, H. S. 1934 (Sunderland, Derby Co) | 13 |
| Carter, J. H. 1926 (WBA) | 3 |
| Catlin, A. E. 1937 (Sheffield W) | 5 |
| **Caulker, S. A. 2013 (Tottenham H)** | **1** |
| Chadwick, A. 1900 (Southampton) | 2 |
| Chadwick, E. 1891 (Everton) | 7 |
| Chamberlain, M. 1983 (Stoke C) | 8 |
| Chambers, H. 1921 (Liverpool) | 8 |
| Channon, M. R. 1973 (Southampton, Manchester C) | 46 |
| Charles, G. A. 1991 (Nottingham F) | 2 |
| Charlton, J. 1965 (Leeds U) | 35 |
| Charlton, R. 1958 (Manchester U) | 106 |
| Charnley, R. O. 1963 (Blackpool) | 1 |
| Charsley, C. C. 1893 (Small Heath) | 1 |
| Chedgzoy, S. 1920 (Everton) | 8 |
| Chenery, C. J. 1872 (Crystal Palace) | 3 |
| Cherry, T. J. 1976 (Leeds U) | 27 |
| Chilton, A. 1951 (Manchester U) | 2 |
| Chippendale, H. 1894 (Blackburn R) | 1 |
| Chivers, M. 1971 (Tottenham H) | 24 |
| Christian, E. 1879 (Old Etonians) | 1 |
| Clamp, E. 1958 (Wolverhampton W) | 4 |
| Clapton, D. R. 1959 (Arsenal) | 1 |
| Clare, T. 1889 (Stoke) | 4 |
| Clarke, A. J. 1970 (Leeds U) | 19 |
| Clarke, H. A. 1954 (Tottenham H) | 1 |
| Clay, T. 1920 (Tottenham H) | 4 |
| Clayton, R. 1956 (Blackburn R) | 35 |
| Clegg, J. C. 1872 (Sheffield W) | 1 |
| Clegg, W. E. 1873 (Sheffield W, Sheffield Alb) | 2 |
| Clemence, R. N. 1973 (Liverpool, Tottenham H) | 61 |
| Clement, D. T. 1976 (QPR) | 5 |
| **Cleverley, T. W. 2013 (Manchester U)** | **9** |
| Clough, B. H. 1960 (Middlesbrough) | 2 |
| Clough, N. H. 1989 (Nottingham F) | 14 |
| Coates, R. 1970 (Burnley, Tottenham H) | 4 |
| Cobbold, W. N. 1883 (Cambridge University, Old Carthusians) | 9 |
| Cock, J. G. 1920 (Huddersfield T, Chelsea) | 2 |
| Cockburn, H. 1947 (Manchester U) | 13 |
| Cohen, G. R. 1964 (Fulham) | 37 |
| **Cole, A. 2001 (Arsenal, Chelsea)** | **103** |
| Cole, A. A. 1995 (Manchester U) | 15 |
| Cole, C. 2009 (West Ham U) | 7 |
| Cole, J. J. 2001 (West Ham U, Chelsea) | 56 |
| Colclough, H. 1914 (Crystal Palace) | 1 |
| Coleman, E. H. 1921 (Dulwich Hamlet) | 1 |
| Coleman, J. 1907 (Woolwich Arsenal) | 1 |
| Collymore, S. V. 1995 (Nottingham F, Aston Villa) | 3 |
| Common, A. 1904 (Sheffield U, Middlesbrough) | 3 |
| Compton, L. H. 1951 (Arsenal) | 2 |
| Conlin, J. 1906 (Bradford C) | 1 |
| Connelly, J. M. 1960 (Burnley, Manchester U) | 20 |
| Cook, T. E. R. 1925 (Brighton) | 1 |
| Cooper, C. T. 1995 (Nottingham F) | 2 |
| Cooper, N. C. 1893 (Cambridge University) | 1 |
| Cooper, T. 1928 (Derby Co) | 15 |
| Cooper, T. 1969 (Leeds U) | 20 |
| Coppell, S. J. 1978 (Manchester U) | 42 |
| Copping, W. 1933 (Leeds U, Arsenal, Leeds U) | 20 |
| Corbett, B. O. 1901 (Corinthians) | 1 |
| Corbett, R. 1903 (Old Malvernians) | 1 |
| Corbett, W. S. 1908 (Birmingham) | 3 |
| Corrigan, J. T. 1976 (Manchester C) | 9 |
| Cottee, A. R. 1987 (West Ham U, Everton) | 7 |
| Cotterill, G. H. 1891 (Cambridge University, Old Brightonians) | 4 |
| Cottle, J. R. 1909 (Bristol C) | 1 |
| Cowan, S. 1926 (Manchester C) | 3 |
| Cowans, G. S. 1983 (Aston Villa, Bari, Aston Villa) | 10 |

| | |
|---|---|
| Cowell, A. 1910 (Blackburn R) | 1 |
| Cox, J. 1901 (Liverpool) | 3 |
| Cox, J. D. 1892 (Derby Co) | 1 |
| Crabtree, J. W. 1894 (Burnley, Aston Villa) | 14 |
| Crawford, J. F. 1931 (Chelsea) | 1 |
| Crawford, R. 1962 (Ipswich T) | 2 |
| Crawshaw, T. H. 1895 (Sheffield W) | 10 |
| Crayston, W. J. 1936 (Arsenal) | 8 |
| Creek, F. N. S. 1923 (Corinthians) | 1 |
| Cresswell, W. 1921 (South Shields, Sunderland, Everton) | |
| | 7 |
| Crompton, R. 1902 (Blackburn R) | 41 |
| Crooks, S. D. 1930 (Derby Co) | 26 |
| Crouch, P. J. 2005 (Southampton, Liverpool, | |
| Portsmouth, Tottenham H) | 42 |
| Crowe, C. 1963 (Wolverhampton W) | 1 |
| Cuggy, F. 1913 (Sunderland) | 2 |
| Cullis, S. 1938 (Wolverhampton W) | 12 |
| Cunliffe, A. 1933 (Blackburn R) | 2 |
| Cunliffe, D. 1900 (Portsmouth) | 1 |
| Cunliffe, J. N. 1936 (Everton) | 1 |
| Cunningham, L. 1979 (WBA, Real Madrid) | 6 |
| Curle, K. 1992 (Manchester C) | 3 |
| Currey, E. S. 1890 (Oxford University) | 2 |
| Currie, A. W. 1972 (Sheffield U, Leeds U) | 17 |
| Cursham, A. W. 1876 (Notts Co) | 6 |
| Cursham, H. A. 1880 (Notts Co) | 8 |
| | |
| Daft, H. B. 1889 (Notts Co) | 5 |
| Daley, A. M. 1992 (Aston Villa) | 7 |
| Danks, T. 1885 (Nottingham F) | 1 |
| Davenport, P. 1985 (Nottingham F) | 1 |
| Davenport, J. K. 1885 (Bolton W) | 2 |
| Davies, K. C. 2011 (Bolton W) | 1 |
| Davis, G. 1904 (Derby Co) | 2 |
| Davis, H. 1903 (Sheffield W) | 3 |
| Davison, J. E. 1922 (Sheffield W) | 1 |
| Dawson, J. 1922 (Burnley) | 2 |
| Dawson, M. R. 2011 (Tottenham H) | 4 |
| Day, S. H. 1906 (Old Malvernians) | 3 |
| Dean, W. R. 1927 (Everton) | 16 |
| Deane, B. C. 1991 (Sheffield U) | 3 |
| Deeley, N. V. 1959 (Wolverhampton W) | 2 |
| **Defoe, J. C. 2004 (Tottenham H, Portsmouth,** | |
| **Tottenham H)** | **54** |
| Devey, J. H. G. 1892 (Aston Villa) | 2 |
| Devonshire, A. 1980 (West Ham U) | 8 |
| Dewhurst, F. 1886 (Preston NE) | 9 |
| Dewhurst, G. P. 1895 (Liverpool Ramblers) | 1 |
| Dickinson, J. W. 1949 (Portsmouth) | 48 |
| Dimmock, J. H. 1921 (Tottenham H) | 3 |
| Ditchburn, E. G. 1949 (Tottenham H) | 6 |
| Dix, R. W. 1939 (Derby Co) | 1 |
| Dixon, J. A. 1885 (Notts Co) | 1 |
| Dixon, K. M. 1985 (Chelsea) | 8 |
| Dixon, L. M. 1990 (Arsenal) | 22 |
| Dobson, A. T. C. 1882 (Notts Co) | 4 |
| Dobson, C. F. 1886 (Notts Co) | 1 |
| Dobson, J. M. 1974 (Burnley, Everton) | 5 |
| Doggart, A. G. 1924 (Corinthians) | 1 |
| Dorigo, A. R. 1990 (Chelsea, Leeds U) | 15 |
| Dorrell, A. R. 1925 (Aston Villa) | 4 |
| Douglas, B. 1958 (Blackburn R) | 36 |
| Downing, S. 2005 (Middlesbrough, Aston Villa, | |
| Liverpool) | 34 |
| Downs, R. W. 1921 (Everton) | 1 |
| Doyle, M. 1976 (Manchester C) | 5 |
| Drake, E. J. 1935 (Arsenal) | 5 |
| Dublin, D. 1998 (Coventry C, Aston Villa) | 4 |
| Ducat, A. 1910 (Woolwich Arsenal, Aston Villa) | 6 |
| Dunn, A. T. B. 1883 (Cambridge University, | |
| Old Etonians) | 4 |
| Dunn, D. J. I. 2003 (Blackburn R) | 1 |
| Duxbury, M. 1984 (Manchester U) | 10 |
| Dyer, K. C. 2000 (Newcastle U, West Ham U) | 33 |
| | |
| Earle, S. G. J. 1924 (Clapton, West Ham U) | 2 |
| Eastham, G. 1963 (Arsenal) | 19 |
| Eastham, G. R. 1935 (Bolton W) | 1 |
| Eckersley, W. 1950 (Blackburn R) | 17 |
| Edwards, D. 1955 (Manchester U) | 18 |
| Edwards, J. H. 1874 (Shropshire Wanderers) | 1 |

| | |
|---|---|
| Edwards, W. 1926 (Leeds U) | 16 |
| Ehiogu, U. 1996 (Aston Villa, Middlesbrough) | 4 |
| Ellerington, W. 1949 (Southampton) | 2 |
| Elliott, G. W. 1913 (Middlesbrough) | 3 |
| Elliott, W. H. 1952 (Burnley) | 5 |
| Evans, R. E. 1911 (Sheffield U) | 4 |
| Ewer, F. H. 1924 (Casuals) | 2 |
| | |
| Fairclough, P. 1878 (Old Foresters) | 1 |
| Fairhurst, D. 1934 (Newcastle U) | 1 |
| Fantham, J. 1962 (Sheffield W) | 1 |
| Fashanu, J. 1989 (Wimbledon) | 2 |
| Felton, W. 1925 (Sheffield W) | 1 |
| Fenton, M. 1938 (Middlesbrough) | 1 |
| Fenwick, T. W. 1984 (QPR, Tottenham H) | 20 |
| Ferdinand, L. 1993 (QPR, Newcastle U, Tottenham H) | 17 |
| Ferdinand, R. G. 1998 (West Ham U, Leeds U, | |
| Manchester U) | 81 |
| Field, E. 1876 (Clapham R) | 2 |
| Finney, T. 1947 (Preston NE) | 76 |
| Fleming, H. J. 1909 (Swindon T) | 11 |
| Fletcher, A. 1889 (Wolverhampton W) | 2 |
| Flowers, R. 1955 (Wolverhampton W) | 49 |
| Flowers, T. D. 1993 (Southampton, Blackburn R) | 11 |
| Forman, Frank 1898 (Nottingham F | 9 |
| Forman, F. R. 1899 (Nottingham F) | 3 |
| Forrest, J. H. 1884 (Blackburn R) | 11 |
| Fort, J. 1921 (Millwall) | 1 |
| **Foster, B. 2007 (Manchester U, Birmingham C, WBA)** | **6** |
| Foster, R. E. 1900 (Oxford University, Corinthians) | 5 |
| Foster, S. 1982 (Brighton & HA) | 3 |
| Foulke, W. J. 1897 (Sheffield U) | 1 |
| Foulkes, W. A. 1955 (Manchester U) | 1 |
| Fowler, R. B. 1996 (Liverpool, Leeds U) | 26 |
| Fox, F. S. 1925 (Millwall) | 1 |
| Francis, G. C. J. 1975 (QPR) | 12 |
| Francis, T. 1977 (Birmingham C, Nottingham F, | |
| Manchester C, Sampdoria) | 52 |
| Franklin, C. F. 1947 (Stoke C) | 27 |
| Freeman, B. C. 1909 (Everton, Burnley) | 5 |
| Froggatt, J. 1950 (Portsmouth) | 13 |
| Froggatt, R. 1953 (Sheffield W) | 4 |
| Fry, C. B. 1901 (Corinthians) | 1 |
| Furness, W. I. 1933 (Leeds U) | 1 |
| | |
| Galley, T. 1937 (Wolverhampton W) | 1 |
| Gardner, A. 2004 (Tottenham H) | 1 |
| Gardner, T. 1934 (Aston Villa) | 2 |
| Garfield, B. 1898 (WBA) | 1 |
| Garraty, W. 1903 (Aston Villa) | 1 |
| Garrett, T. 1952 (Blackpool) | 3 |
| Gascoigne, P. J. 1989 (Tottenham H, Lazio, Rangers, | |
| Middlesbrough) | 57 |
| Gates, E. 1981 (Ipswich T) | 2 |
| Gay, L. H. 1893 (Cambridge University, | |
| Old Brightonians) | 3 |
| Geary, F. 1890 (Everton) | 2 |
| Geaves, R. L. 1875 (Clapham R) | 1 |
| Gee, C. W. 1932 (Everton) | 3 |
| Geldard, A. 1933 (Everton) | 4 |
| George, C. 1977 (Derby Co) | 1 |
| George, W. 1902 (Aston Villa) | 3 |
| **Gerrard, S. G. 2000 (Liverpool)** | **102** |
| Gibbins, W. V. T. 1924 (Clapton) | 2 |
| Gibbs, K. J. R. 2011 (Arsenal) | 2 |
| Gidman, J. 1977 (Aston Villa) | 1 |
| Gillard, I. T. 1975 (QPR) | 3 |
| Gilliat, W. E. 1893 (Old Carthusians) | 1 |
| Goddard, P. 1982 (West Ham U) | 1 |
| Goodall, F. R. 1926 (Huddersfield T) | 25 |
| Goodall, J. 1888 (Preston NE, Derby Co) | 14 |
| Goodhart, H. C. 1883 (Old Etonians) | 3 |
| Goodwyn, A. G. 1873 (Royal Engineers) | 1 |
| Goodyer, A. C. 1879 (Nottingham F) | 1 |
| Gosling, R. C. 1892 (Old Etonians) | 5 |
| Gosnell, A. A. 1906 (Newcastle U) | 1 |
| Gough, H. C. 1921 (Sheffield U) | 1 |
| Goulden, L. A. 1937 (West Ham U) | 14 |
| Graham, L. 1925 (Millwall) | 2 |
| Graham, T. 1931 (Nottingham F) | 2 |
| Grainger, C. 1956 (Sheffield U, Sunderland) | 7 |
| Gray, A. A. 1992 (Crystal Palace) | 1 |

Gray, M. 1999 (Sunderland) — 3
Greaves, J. 1959 (Chelsea, Tottenham H) — 57
Green, F. T. 1876 (Wanderers) — 1
Green, G. H. 1925 (Sheffield U) — 8
Green, R. P. 2005 (Norwich C, West Ham U) — 12
Greenhalgh, E. H. 1872 (Notts Co) — 2
Greenhoff, B. 1976 (Manchester U, Leeds U) — 18
Greenwood, D. H. 1882 (Blackburn R) — 2
Gregory, J. 1983 (QPR) — 6
Grimsdell, A. 1920 (Tottenham H) — 6
Grosvenor, A. T. 1934 (Birmingham) — 3
Gunn, W. 1884 (Notts Co) — 2
Guppy, S. 2000 (Leicester C) — 1
Gurney, R. 1935 (Sunderland) — 1

Hacking, J. 1929 (Oldham Ath) — 3
Hadley, H. 1903 (WBA) — 1
Hagan, J. 1949 (Sheffield U) — 1
Haines, J. T. W. 1949 (WBA) — 1
Hall, A. E. 1910 (Aston Villa) — 1
Hall, G. W. 1934 (Tottenham H) — 10
Hall, J. 1956 (Birmingham C) — 17
Halse, H. J. 1909 (Manchester U) — 1
Hammond, H. E. D. 1889 (Oxford University) — 1
Hampson, J. 1931 (Blackpool) — 3
Hampton, H. 1913 (Aston Villa) — 4
Hancocks, J. 1949 (Wolverhampton W) — 3
Hapgood, E. 1933 (Arsenal) — 30
Hardinge, H. T. W. 1910 (Sheffield U) — 1
Hardman, H. P. 1905 (Everton) — 4
Hardwick, G. F. M. 1947 (Middlesbrough) — 13
Hardy, H. 1925 (Stockport Co) — 1
Hardy, S. 1907 (Liverpool, Aston Villa) — 21
Harford, M. G. 1988 (Luton T) — 2
Hargreaves, F. W. 1880 (Blackburn R) — 3
Hargreaves, J. 1881 (Blackburn R) — 2
Hargreaves, O. 2002 (Bayern Munich, Manchester U) — 42
Harper, E. C. 1926 (Blackburn R) — 1
Harris, G. 1966 (Burnley) — 1
Harris, P. P. 1950 (Portsmouth) — 2
Harris, S. S. 1904 (Cambridge University, Old Westminsters) — 6
Harrison, A. H. 1893 (Old Westminsters) — 2
Harrison, G. 1921 (Everton) — 2
Harrow, J. H. 1923 (Chelsea) — 2
**Hart, C. J. J. 2008 (Manchester C)** — **32**
Hart, E. 1929 (Leeds U) — 8
Hartley, F. 1923 (Oxford C) — 1
Harvey, A. 1881 (Wednesbury Strollers) — 1
Harvey, J. C. 1971 (Everton) — 1
Hassall, H. W. 1951 (Huddersfield T, Bolton W) — 5
Hateley, M. 1984 (Portsmouth, AC Milan, Monaco, Rangers) — 32
Hawkes, R. M. 1907 (Luton T) — 5
Haworth, G. 1887 (Accrington) — 5
Hawtrey, J. P. 1881 (Old Etonians) —
Haygarth, E. B. 1875 (Swifts) — 1
Haynes, J. N. 1955 (Fulham) — 56
Healless, H. 1925 (Blackburn R) — 2
Hector, K. J. 1974 (Derby Co) — 2
Hedley, G. A. 1901 (Sheffield U) — 1
Hegan, K. E. 1923 (Corinthians) — 4
Hellawell, M. S. 1963 (Birmingham C) — 2
Henderson, J. B. 2011 (Sunderland, Liverpool) — 5
Hendrie, L. A. 1999 (Aston Villa) — 1
Henfrey, A. G. 1891 (Cambridge University, Corinthians) — 5
Henry, R. P. 1963 (Tottenham H) — 1
Heron, F. 1876 (Wanderers) — 1
Heron, G. H. H. 1873 (Uxbridge, Wanderers) — 5
Heskey, E. W. I. 1999 (Leicester C, Liverpool, Birmingham C, Wigan Ath, Aston Villa) — 62
Hibbert, W. 1910 (Bury) — 1
Hibbs, H. E. 1930 (Birmingham) — 25
Hill, F. 1963 (Bolton W) — 2
Hill, G. A. 1976 (Manchester U) — 6
Hill, J. H. 1925 (Burnley, Newcastle U) — 11
Hill, R. 1983 (Luton T) — 3
Hill, R. H. 1926 (Millwall) — 1
Hillman, J. 1899 (Burnley) — 1
Hills, A. F. 1879 (Old Harrovians) — 1
Hilsdon, G. R. 1907 (Chelsea) — 8

Hinchcliffe, A. G. 1997 (Everton, Sheffield W) — 7
Hine, E. W. 1929 (Leicester C) — 6
Hinton, A. T. 1963 (Wolverhampton W, Nottingham F) — 3
Hirst, D. E. 1991 (Sheffield W) — 3
Hitchens, G. A. 1961 (Aston Villa, Internazionale) — 7
Hobbis, H. H. F. 1936 (Charlton Ath) — 2
Hoddle, G. 1980 (Tottenham H, Monaco) — 53
Hodge, S. B. 1986 (Aston Villa, Tottenham H, Nottingham F) — 24
Hodgetts, D. 1888 (Aston Villa) — 6
Hodgkinson, A. 1957 (Sheffield U) — 5
Hodgson, G. 1931 (Liverpool) — 3
Hodkinson, J. 1913 (Blackburn R) — 3
Hogg, W. 1902 (Sunderland) — 3
Holdcroft, G. H. 1937 (Preston NE) — 2
Holden, A. D. 1959 (Bolton W) — 5
Holden, G. H. 1881 (Wednesbury OA) — 4
Holden-White, C. 1888 (Corinthians) — 2
Holford, T. 1903 (Stoke) — 1
Holley, G. H. 1909 (Sunderland) — 10
Holliday, E. 1960 (Middlesbrough) — 3
Hollins, J. W. 1967 (Chelsea) — 1
Holmes, R. 1888 (Preston NE) — 7
Holt, J. 1890 (Everton, Reading) — 10
Hopkinson, E. 1958 (Bolton W) — 14
Hossack, A. H. 1892 (Corinthians) — 2
Houghton, W. E. 1931 (Aston Villa) — 7
Houlker, A. E. 1902 (Blackburn R, Portsmouth, Southampton) — 5
Howarth, R. H. 1887 (Preston NE, Everton) — 5
Howe, D. 1958 (WBA) — 23
Howe, J. R. 1948 (Derby Co) — 3
Howell, L. S. 1873 (Wanderers) — 1
Howell, R. 1895 (Sheffield U, Liverpool) — 2
Howey, S. N. 1995 (Newcastle U) — 4
**Huddlestone, T. A. 2010 (Tottenham H)** — **4**
Hudson, A. A. 1975 (Stoke C) — 2
Hudson, J. 1883 (Sheffield) — 1
Hudspeth, F. C. 1926 (Newcastle U) — 1
Hufton, A. E. 1924 (West Ham U) — 6
Hughes, E. W. 1970 (Liverpool, Wolverhampton W) — 62
Hughes, L. 1950 (Liverpool) — 3
Hulme, J. H. A. 1927 (Arsenal) — 9
Humphreys, P. 1903 (Notts Co) — 1
Hunt, G. S. 1933 (Tottenham H) — 3
Hunt, Rev. K. R. G. 1911 (Leyton) — 2
Hunt, R. 1962 (Liverpool) — 34
Hunt, S. 1984 (WBA) — 2
Hunter, J. 1878 (Sheffield Heeley) — 7
Hunter, N. 1966 (Leeds U) — 28
Hurst, G. C. 1966 (West Ham U) — 49

Ince, P. E. C. 1993 (Manchester U, Internazionale, Liverpool, Middlesbrough) — 53
Iremonger, J. 1901 (Nottingham F) — 2

Jack, D. N. B. 1924 (Bolton W, Arsenal) — 9
Jackson, E. 1891 (Oxford University) — 1
**Jagielka, P. N. 2008 (Everton)** — **18**
James, D. B. 1997 (Liverpool, Aston Villa, West Ham U, Manchester C, Portsmouth) — 53
Jarrett, B. G. 1876 (Cambridge University) — 3
Jarvis, M. T. 2011 (Wolverhampton W) — 1
Jefferis, F. 1912 (Everton) — 2
Jeffers, F. 2003 (Arsenal) — 1
Jenas, J. A. 2003 (Newcastle U, Tottenham H) — 21
**Jenkinson, C. D. 2013 (Arsenal)** — **1**
Jezzard, B. A. G. 1954 (Fulham) — 2
Johnson, A. 2005 (Crystal Palace, Everton) — 8
**Johnson, A. 2010 (Manchester C)** — **12**
Johnson, D. E. 1975 (Ipswich T, Liverpool) — 8
Johnson, E. 1880 (Saltley College, Stoke) — 2
**Johnson, G. M. C. 2004 (Chelsea, Portsmouth, Liverpool)** — **48**
Johnson, J. A. 1937 (Stoke C) — 5
Johnson, S. A. M. 2001 (Derby Co) — 1
Johnson, T. C. F. 1926 (Manchester C, Everton) — 5
Johnson, W. H. 1900 (Sheffield U) — 6
Johnston, H. 1947 (Blackpool) — 10
Jones, A. 1882 (Walsall Swifts, Great Lever) — 3
Jones, H. 1923 (Nottingham F) — 1
Jones, H. 1927 (Blackburn R) — 6

| | |
|---|---|
| Jones, M. D. 1965 (Sheffield U, Leeds U) | 3 |
| **Jones, P. A. 2012 (Manchester U)** | **7** |
| Jones, R. 1992 (Liverpool) | 8 |
| Jones, W. 1901 (Bristol C) | 1 |
| Jones, W. H. 1950 (Liverpool) | 2 |
| Joy, B. 1936 (Casuals) | 1 |
| | |
| Kail, E. I. L. 1929 (Dulwich Hamlet) | 3 |
| Kay, A. H. 1963 (Everton) | 1 |
| Kean, F. W. 1923 (Sheffield W, Bolton W) | 9 |
| Keegan, J. K. 1973 (Liverpool, SV Hamburg, Southampton) | 63 |
| Keen, E. R. L. 1933 (Derby Co) | 4 |
| Kelly, M. R. 2012 (Liverpool) | 1 |
| Kelly, R. 1920 (Burnley, Sunderland, Huddersfield T) | 14 |
| Kennedy, A. 1984 (Liverpool) | 2 |
| Kennedy, R. 1976 (Liverpool) | 17 |
| Kenyon-Slaney, W. S. 1873 (Wanderers) | 1 |
| Keown, M. R. 1992 (Everton, Arsenal) | 43 |
| Kevan, D. T. 1957 (WBA) | 14 |
| Kidd, B. 1970 (Manchester U) | 2 |
| King, L. B. 2002 (Tottenham H) | 21 |
| King, R. S. 1882 (Oxford University) | 1 |
| Kingsford, R. K. 1874 (Wanderers) | 1 |
| Kingsley, M. 1901 (Newcastle U) | 1 |
| Kinsey, G. 1892 (Wolverhampton W, Derby Co) | 4 |
| Kirchen, A. J. 1937 (Arsenal) | 3 |
| Kirkland, C. E. 2007 (Liverpool) | 1 |
| Kirton, W. J. 1922 (Aston Villa) | 1 |
| Knight, A. E. 1920 (Portsmouth) | 1 |
| Knight, Z. 2005 (Fulham) | 2 |
| Knowles, C. 1968 (Tottenham H) | 4 |
| Konchesky, P. M. 2003 (Charlton Ath, West Ham U) | 2 |
| | |
| Labone, B. L. 1963 (Everton) | 26 |
| **Lampard, F. J. 2000 (West Ham U, Chelsea)** | **97** |
| Lampard, F. R. G. 1973 (West Ham U) | 2 |
| Langley, E. J. 1958 (Fulham) | 3 |
| Langton, R. 1947 (Blackburn R, Preston NE, Bolton W) | 11 |
| Latchford, R. D. 1978 (Everton) | 12 |
| Latheron, E. G. 1913 (Blackburn R) | 2 |
| Lawler, C. 1971 (Liverpool) | 4 |
| Lawton, T. 1939 (Everton, Chelsea, Notts Co) | 23 |
| Leach, T. 1931 (Sheffield W) | 2 |
| Leake, A. 1904 (Aston Villa) | 5 |
| Lee, E. A. 1904 (Southampton) | 1 |
| Lee, F. H. 1969 (Manchester C) | 27 |
| Lee, J. 1951 (Derby Co) | 1 |
| Lee, R. M. 1995 (Newcastle U) | 21 |
| Lee, S. 1983 (Liverpool) | 14 |
| Leighton, J. E. 1886 (Nottingham F) | 1 |
| **Lennon, A. J. 2006 (Tottenham H)** | **21** |
| **Lescott, J. P. 2008 (Everton, Manchester C)** | **26** |
| Le Saux, G. P. 1994 (Blackburn R, Chelsea) | 36 |
| Le Tissier, M. P. 1994 (Southampton) | 8 |
| Lilley, H. E. 1892 (Sheffield U) | 1 |
| Linacre, H. J. 1905 (Nottingham F) | 2 |
| Lindley, T. 1886 (Cambridge University, Nottingham F) | 13 |
| Lindsay, A. 1974 (Liverpool) | 4 |
| Lindsay, W. 1877 (Wanderers) | 1 |
| Lineker, G. 1984 (Leicester C, Everton, Barcelona, Tottenham H) | 80 |
| Lintott, E. H. 1908 (QPR, Bradford C) | 7 |
| Lipsham, H. B. 1902 (Sheffield U) | 1 |
| Little, B. 1975 (Aston Villa) | 1 |
| **Livermore, J. C. 2013 (Tottenham H)** | **1** |
| Lloyd, L. V. 1971 (Liverpool, Nottingham F) | 4 |
| Lockett, A. 1903 (Stoke) | 1 |
| Lodge, L. V. 1894 (Cambridge University, Corinthians) | 5 |
| Lofthouse, J. M. 1885 (Blackburn R, Accrington, Blackburn R) | 7 |
| Lofthouse, N. 1951 (Bolton W) | 33 |
| Longworth, E. 1920 (Liverpool) | 5 |
| Lowder, A. 1889 (Wolverhampton W) | 1 |
| Lowe, E. 1947 (Aston Villa) | 3 |
| Lucas, T. 1922 (Liverpool) | 3 |
| Luntley, E. 1880 (Nottingham F) | 2 |
| Lyttelton, Hon. A. 1877 (Cambridge University) | 1 |
| Lyttelton, Hon. E. 1878 (Cambridge University) | 1 |

| | |
|---|---|
| Mabbutt, G. 1983 (Tottenham H) | 16 |
| Macaulay, R. H. 1881 (Cambridge University) | 1 |
| McCall, J. 1913 (Preston NE) | 5 |
| McCann, G. P. 2001 (Sunderland) | 1 |
| McDermott, T. 1978 (Liverpool) | 25 |
| McDonald, C. A. 1958 (Burnley) | 8 |
| Macdonald, M. 1972 (Newcastle U) | 14 |
| McFarland, R. L. 1971 (Derby Co) | 28 |
| McGarry, W. H. 1954 (Huddersfield T) | 4 |
| McGuinness, W. 1959 (Manchester U) | 2 |
| McInroy, A. 1927 (Sunderland) | 1 |
| McMahon, S. 1988 (Liverpool) | 17 |
| McManaman, S. 1995 (Liverpool, Real Madrid) | 37 |
| McNab, R. 1969 (Arsenal) | 4 |
| McNeal, R. 1914 (WBA) | 2 |
| McNeil, M. 1961 (Middlesbrough) | 9 |
| Macrae, S. 1883 (Notts Co) | 5 |
| Maddison, F. B. 1872 (Oxford University) | 1 |
| Madeley, P. E. 1971 (Leeds U) | 24 |
| Magee, T. P. 1923 (WBA) | 5 |
| Makepeace, H. 1906 (Everton) | 4 |
| Male, C. G. 1935 (Arsenal) | 19 |
| Mannion, W. J. 1947 (Middlesbrough) | 26 |
| Mariner, P. 1977 (Ipswich T, Arsenal) | 35 |
| Marsden, J. T. 1891 (Darwen) | 1 |
| Marsden, W. 1930 (Sheffield W) | 3 |
| Marsh, R. W. 1972 (QPR, Manchester C) | 9 |
| Marshall, T. 1880 (Darwen) | 2 |
| Martin, A. 1981 (West Ham U) | 17 |
| Martin, H. 1914 (Sunderland) | 1 |
| Martyn, A. N. 1992 (Crystal Palace, Leeds U) | 23 |
| Marwood, B. 1989 (Arsenal) | 1 |
| Maskrey, H. M. 1908 (Derby Co) | 1 |
| Mason, C. 1887 (Wolverhampton W) | 3 |
| Matthews, R. D. 1956 (Coventry C) | 5 |
| Matthews, S. 1935 (Stoke C, Blackpool) | 54 |
| Matthews, V. 1928 (Sheffield U) | 2 |
| Maynard, W. J. 1872 (1st Surrey Rifles) | 2 |
| Meadows, J. 1955 (Manchester C) | 1 |
| Medley, L. D. 1951 (Tottenham H) | 6 |
| Meehan, T. 1924 (Chelsea) | 1 |
| Melia, J. 1963 (Liverpool) | 2 |
| Mercer, D. W. 1923 (Sheffield U) | 2 |
| Mercer, J. 1939 (Everton) | 5 |
| Merrick, G. H. 1952 (Birmingham C) | 23 |
| Merson, P. C. 1992 (Arsenal, Middlesbrough, Aston Villa) | 21 |
| Metcalfe, V. 1951 (Huddersfield T) | 2 |
| Mew, J. W. 1921 (Manchester U) | 1 |
| Middleditch, B. 1897 (Corinthians) | 1 |
| Milburn, J. E. T. 1949 (Newcastle U) | 13 |
| Miller, B. G. 1961 (Burnley) | 1 |
| Miller, H. S. 1923 (Charlton Ath) | 1 |
| Mills, D. J. 2001 (Leeds U) | 19 |
| Mills, G. R. 1938 (Chelsea) | 3 |
| Mills, M. D. 1973 (Ipswich T) | 42 |
| Milne, G. 1963 (Liverpool) | 14 |
| **Milner, J. P. 2010 (Aston Villa, Manchester C)** | **38** |
| Milton, C. A. 1952 (Arsenal) | 1 |
| Milward, A. 1891 (Everton) | 4 |
| Mitchell, C. 1880 (Upton Park) | 5 |
| Mitchell, J. F. 1925 (Manchester C) | 1 |
| Moffat, H. 1913 (Oldham Ath) | 1 |
| Molyneux, G. 1902 (Southampton) | 4 |
| Moon, W. R. 1888 (Old Westminsters) | 7 |
| Moore, H. T. 1883 (Notts Co) | 2 |
| Moore, J. 1923 (Derby Co) | 1 |
| Moore, R. F. 1962 (West Ham U) | 108 |
| Moore, W. G. B. 1923 (West Ham U) | 1 |
| Mordue, J. 1912 (Sunderland) | 2 |
| Morice, C. J. 1872 (Barnes) | 1 |
| Morley, A. 1982 (Aston Villa) | 6 |
| Morley, H. 1910 (Notts Co) | 1 |
| Morren, T. 1898 (Sheffield U) | 1 |
| Morris, F. 1920 (WBA) | 2 |
| Morris, J. 1949 (Derby Co) | 3 |
| Morris, W. W. 1939 (Wolverhampton W) | 3 |
| Morse, H. 1879 (Notts Co) | 1 |
| Mort, T. 1924 (Aston Villa) | 3 |
| Morten, A. 1873 (Crystal Palace) | 1 |
| Mortensen, S. H. 1947 (Blackpool) | 25 |
| Morton, J. R. 1938 (West Ham U) | 1 |

Mosforth, W. 1877 (Sheffield W, Sheffield Alb, Sheffield W) 9
Moss, F. 1922 (Aston Villa) 5
Moss, F. 1934 (Arsenal) 4
Mosscrop, E. 1914 (Burnley) 2
Mozley, B. 1950 (Derby Co) 3
Mullen, J. 1947 (Wolverhampton W) 12
Mullery, A. P. 1965 (Tottenham H) 35
Murphy, D. B. 2002 (Liverpool) 9

Neal, P. G. 1976 (Liverpool) 50
Needham, E. 1894 (Sheffield U) 16
Neville, G. A. 1995 (Manchester U) 85
Neville, P. J. 1996 (Manchester U, Everton) 59
Newton, K. R. 1966 (Blackburn R, Everton) 27
Nicholls, J. 1954 (WBA) 2
Nicholson, W. E. 1951 (Tottenham H) 1
Nish, D. J. 1973 (Derby Co) 5
Norman, M. 1962 (Tottenham H) 23
Nugent, D. J. 2007 (Preston NE) 1
Nuttall, H. 1928 (Bolton W) 3

Oakley, W. J. 1895 (Oxford University, Corinthians) 16
O'Dowd, J. P. 1932 (Chelsea) 3
O'Grady, M. 1963 (Huddersfield T, Leeds U) 2
Ogilvie, R. A. M. M. 1874 (Clapham R) 1
Oliver, L. F. 1929 (Fulham) 1
Olney, B. A. 1928 (Aston Villa) 2
Osborne, F. R. 1923 (Fulham, Tottenham H) 4
Osborne, R. 1928 (Leicester C) 1
Osgood, P. L. 1970 (Chelsea) 4
**Osman, L. 2013 (Everton)** 2
Osman, R. 1980 (Ipswich T) 11
Ottaway, C. J. 1872 (Oxford University) 2
Owen, J. R. B. 1874 (Sheffield) 1
Owen, M. J. 1998 (Liverpool, Real Madrid, NewcastleU) 89
Owen, S. W. 1936 (Luton T) 3
**Oxlade-Chamberlain, A. M. D. 2012 (Arsenal)** 12

Page, L. A. 1927 (Burnley) 7
Paine, T. L. 1963 (Southampton) 19
Pallister, G. A. 1988 (Middlesbrough, Manchester U) 22
Palmer, C. L. 1992 (Sheffield W) 18
Pantling, H. H. 1924 (Sheffield U) 1
Paravicini, P. J. de 1883 (Cambridge University) 3
Parker, P. A. 1989 (QPR, Manchester U) 19
**Parker, S. M. 2004 (Charlton Ath, Chelsea, Newcastle U, West Ham U, Tottenham H)** 18
Parker, T. R. 1925 (Southampton) 1
Parkes, P. B. 1974 (QPR) 1
Parkinson, J. 1910 (Liverpool) 2
Parlour, R. 1999 (Arsenal) 10
Parr, P. C. 1882 (Oxford University) 1
Parry, E. H. 1879 (Old Carthusians) 3
Parry, R. A. 1960 (Bolton W) 2
Patchitt, B. C. A. 1923 (Corinthians) 2
Pawson, F. W. 1883 (Cambridge University, Swifts) 2
Payne, J. 1937 (Luton T) 1
Peacock, A. 1962 (Middlesbrough, Leeds U) 6
Peacock, J. 1929 (Middlesbrough) 3
Pearce, S. 1987 (Nottingham F, West Ham U) 78
Pearson, H. F. 1932 (WBA) 1
Pearson, J. H. 1892 (Crewe Alex) 1
Pearson, J. S. 1976 (Manchester U) 15
Pearson, S. C. 1948 (Manchester U) 8
Pease, W. H. 1927 (Middlesbrough) 1
Pegg, D. 1957 (Manchester U) 1
Pejic, M. 1974 (Stoke C) 4
Pelly, F. R. 1893 (Old Foresters) 3
Pennington, J. 1907 (WBA) 25
Pentland, F. B. 1909 (Middlesbrough) 5
Perry, C. 1890 (WBA) 3
Perry, T. 1898 (WBA) 1
Perry, W. 1956 (Blackpool) 3
Perryman, S. 1982 (Tottenham H) 1
Peters, M. 1966 (West Ham U, Tottenham H) 67
Phelan, M. C. 1990 (Manchester U) 1
Phillips, K. 1999 (Sunderland) 8
Phillips, L. H. 1952 (Portsmouth) 3
Pickering, F. 1964 (Everton) 3
Pickering, J. 1933 (Sheffield U) 1

Pickering, N. 1983 (Sunderland) 1
Pike, T. M. 1886 (Cambridge University) 1
Pilkington, B. 1955 (Burnley) 1
Plant, J. 1900 (Bury) 1
Platt, D. 1990 (Aston Villa, Bari, Juventus, Sampdoria, Arsenal) 62
Plum, S. L. 1923 (Charlton Ath) 1
Pointer, R. 1962 (Burnley) 3
Porteous, T. S. 1891 (Sunderland) 1
Powell, C. G. 2001 (Charlton Ath) 5
Priest, A. E. 1900 (Sheffield U) 1
Prinsep, J. F. M. 1879 (Clapham R) 1
Puddefoot, S. C. 1926 (Blackburn R) 2
Pye, J. 1950 (Wolverhampton W) 1
Pym, R. H. 1925 (Bolton W) 3

Quantrill, A. 1920 (Derby Co) 4
Quixall, A. 1954 (Sheffield W) 5

Radford, J. 1969 (Arsenal) 2
Raikes, G. B. 1895 (Oxford University) 4
Ramsey, A. E. 1949 (Southampton, Tottenham H) 32
Rawlings, A. 1921 (Preston NE) 1
Rawlings, W. E. 1922 (Southampton) 2
Rawlinson, J. F. P. 1882 (Cambridge University) 1
Rawson, H. E. 1875 (Royal Engineers) 1
Rawson, W. S. 1875 (Oxford University) 2
Read, A. 1921 (Tufnell Park) 1
Reader, J. 1894 (WBA) 1
Reaney, P. 1969 (Leeds U) 3
Redknapp, J. F. 1996 (Liverpool) 17
Reeves, K. P. 1980 (Norwich C, Manchester C) 2
Regis, C. 1982 (WBA, Coventry C) 5
Reid, P. 1985 (Everton) 13
Revie, D. G. 1955 (Manchester C) 6
Reynolds, J. 1892 (WBA, Aston Villa) 8
Richards, C. H. 1898 (Nottingham F) 1
Richards, G. H. 1909 (Derby Co) 1
Richards, J. P. 1973 (Wolverhampton W) 1
Richards, M. 2007 (Manchester C) 13
Richardson, J. R. 1933 (Newcastle U) 2
Richardson, K. 1994 (Aston Villa) 1
Richardson, K. E. 2005 (Manchester U) 8
Richardson, W. G. 1935 (WBA) 1
Rickaby, S. 1954 (WBA) 1
Ricketts, M. B. 2002 (Bolton W) 1
Rigby, A. 1927 (Blackburn R) 5
Rimmer, E. J. 1930 (Sheffield W) 4
Rimmer, J. J. 1976 (Arsenal) 1
Ripley, S. E. 1994 (Blackburn R) 2
Rix, G. 1981 (Arsenal) 17
Robb, G. 1954 (Tottenham H) 1
Roberts, C. 1905 (Manchester U) 3
Roberts, F. 1925 (Manchester C) 4
Roberts, G. 1983 (Tottenham H) 6
Roberts, H. 1931 (Arsenal) 1
Roberts, H. 1931 (Millwall) 1
Roberts, R. 1887 (WBA) 3
Roberts, W. T. 1924 (Preston NE) 2
Robinson, J. 1937 (Sheffield W) 4
Robinson, J. W. 1897 (Derby Co, New Brighton Tower, Southampton) 11
Robinson, P. W. 2003 (Leeds U, Tottenham H, Blackburn R) 41
Robson, B. 1980 (WBA, Manchester U) 90
Robson, R. 1958 (WBA) 20
Rocastle, D. 1989 (Arsenal) 14
**Rodwell, J. 2012 (Everton)** 3
**Rooney, W. 2003 (Everton, Manchester U)** 83
Rose, W. C. 1884 (Swifts, Preston NE, Wolverhampton W) 5
Rostron, T. 1881 (Darwen) 2
Rowe, A. 1934 (Tottenham H) 1
Rowley, J. F. 1949 (Manchester U) 6
Rowley, W. 1889 (Stoke) 2
Royle, J. 1971 (Everton, Manchester C) 6
Ruddlesdin, H. 1904 (Sheffield W) 3
Ruddock, N. 1995 (Liverpool) 1
**Ruddy, J. T. G. 2013 (Norwich C)** 1
Ruffell, J. W. 1926 (West Ham U) 6
Russell, B. B. 1883 (Royal Engineers) 1
Rutherford, J. 1904 (Newcastle U) 11

## NORTHERN IRELAND

| | |
|---|---|
| Addis, D. J. 1922 (Cliftonville) | 1 |
| Aherne, T. 1947 (Belfast Celtic, Luton T) | 4 |
| Alexander, T. E. 1895 (Cliftonville) | 1 |
| Allan, C. 1936 (Cliftonville) | 1 |
| Allen, J. 1887 (Limavady) | 1 |
| Anderson, J. 1925 (Distillery) | 1 |
| Anderson, T. 1973 (Manchester U, Swindon T, Peterborough U) | 22 |
| Anderson, W. 1898 (Linfield, Cliftonville) | 4 |
| Andrews, W. 1908 (Glentoran, Grimsby T) | 3 |
| Armstrong, G. J. 1977 (Tottenham H, Watford, Real Mallorca, WBA, Chesterfield) | 63 |
| | |
| **Baird, C. P. 2003 (Southampton, Fulham)** | **61** |
| Baird, G. 1896 (Distillery) | 3 |
| Baird, H. C. 1939 (Huddersfield T) | 1 |
| Balfe, J. 1909 (Shelbourne) | 2 |
| Bambrick, J. 1929 (Linfield, Chelsea) | 11 |
| Banks, S. J. 1937 (Cliftonville) | 1 |
| Barr, H. H. 1962 (Linfield, Coventry C) | 3 |
| Barron, J. H. 1894 (Cliftonville) | 7 |
| Barry, J. 1888 (Cliftonville) | 3 |
| Barry, J. 1900 (Bohemians) | 1 |
| Barton, A. J. 2011 (Preston NE) | 1 |
| Baxter, R. A. 1887 (Distillery) | 1 |
| Baxter, S. N. 1887 (Cliftonville) | 1 |
| Bennett, L. V. 1889 (Dublin University) | 1 |
| Best, G. 1964 (Manchester U, Fulham) | 37 |
| Bingham, W. L. 1951 (Sunderland, Luton T, Everton, Port Vale) | 56 |
| Black, K. T. 1988 (Luton T, Nottingham F) | 30 |
| Black, T. 1901 (Glentoran) | 1 |
| Blair, H. 1928 (Portadown, Swansea T) | 4 |
| Blair, J. 1907 (Cliftonville) | 5 |
| Blair, R. V. 1975 (Oldham Ath) | 5 |
| Blanchflower, J. 1954 (Manchester U) | 12 |
| Blanchflower, R. D. 1950 (Barnsley, Aston Villa, Tottenham H) | 56 |
| Blayney, A. 2006 (Doncaster R, Linfield) | 5 |
| Bookman, L. J. O. 1914 (Bradford C, Luton T) | 4 |
| Bothwell, A. W. 1926 (Ards) | 5 |
| Bowler, G. C. 1950 (Hull C) | 3 |
| Boyce, L. 2011 (Werder Bremen) | 4 |
| Boyle, P. 1901 (Sheffield U) | 5 |
| Braithwaite, R. M. 1962 (Linfield, Middlesbrough) | 10 |
| Braniff, K. R. 2010 (Portadown) | 2 |
| Breen, T. 1935 (Belfast Celtic, Manchester U) | 9 |
| Brennan, B. 1912 (Bohemians) | 1 |
| Brennan, R. A. 1949 (Luton T, Birmingham C, Fulham) | 5 |
| Briggs, W. R. 1962 (Manchester U, Swansea T) | 2 |
| Brisby, D. 1891 (Distillery) | 1 |
| Brolly, T. H. 1937 (Millwall) | 4 |
| Brookes, E. A. 1920 (Shelbourne) | 1 |
| Brotherston, N. 1980 (Blackburn R) | 27 |
| Brown, J. 1921 (Glenavon, Tranmere R) | 3 |
| Brown, J. 1935 (Wolverhampton W, Coventry C, Birmingham C) | 10 |
| Brown, N. M. 1887 (Limavady) | 1 |
| Brown, W. G. 1926 (Glenavon) | 1 |
| Browne, F. 1887 (Cliftonville) | 5 |
| Browne, R. J. 1936 (Leeds U) | 6 |
| Bruce, A. 1925 (Belfast Celtic) | 1 |
| **Bruce, A. S. 2013 (Hull C)** | **1** |
| Bruce, W. 1961 (Glentoran) | 2 |
| **Brunt, C. 2005 (Sheffield W, WBA)** | **42** |
| Bryan, M. A. 2010 (Watford) | 2 |
| Buckle, H. R. 1903 (Cliftonville, Sunderland, Bristol R) | 3 |
| Buckle, J. 1882 (Cliftonville) | 1 |
| Burnett, J. 1894 (Distillery, Glentoran) | 5 |
| Burnison, J. 1901 (Distillery) | 1 |
| Burnison, S. 1908 (Distillery, Bradford, Distillery) | 8 |
| Burns, J. 1923 (Glenavon) | 1 |
| Burns, W. 1925 (Glentoran) | 1 |
| Butler, M. P. 1939 (Blackpool) | 1 |
| | |
| ~~Camp, L. M. J. 2011 (Nottingham F)~~ | 9 |
| Campbell, A. C. 1963 (Crusaders) | 2 |
| Campbell, D. A. 1986 (Nottingham F, Charlton Ath) | 10 |
| Campbell, James 1897 (Cliftonville) | 14 |
| Campbell, John 1896 (Cliftonville) | 1 |
| Campbell, J. P. 1951 (Fulham) | 2 |

| | |
|---|---|
| Campbell, R. M. 1982 (Bradford C) | 2 |
| Campbell, W. G. 1968 (Dundee) | 6 |
| Capaldi, A. C. 2004 (Plymouth Arg, Cardiff C) | 22 |
| Carey, J. J. 1947 (Manchester U) | 7 |
| Carroll, E. 1925 (Glenavon) | 1 |
| **Carroll, R. E. 1997 (Wigan Ath, Manchester U, West Ham U, Olympiakos)** | **26** |
| **Carson, J. G. 2011 (Ipswich T)** | **4** |
| Carson, S. 2009 (Coleraine) | 1 |
| Casement, C. 2009 (Ipswich T) | 1 |
| Casey, T. 1955 (Newcastle U, Portsmouth) | 12 |
| Caskey, W. 1979 (Derby Co, Tulsa Roughnecks) | 8 |
| Cassidy, T. 1971 (Newcastle U, Burnley) | 24 |
| **Cathcart, C. G. 2011 (Blackpool)** | **14** |
| Caughey, M. 1986 (Linfield) | 2 |
| Chambers, R. J. 1921 (Distillery, Bury, Nottingham F) | 12 |
| Chatton, H. A. 1925 (Partick Th) | 3 |
| Christian, J. 1889 (Linfield) | 1 |
| Clarke, C. J. 1986 (Bournemouth, Southampton, QPR, Portsmouth) | 38 |
| Clarke, R. 1901 (Belfast Celtic) | 2 |
| Cleary, J. 1982 (Glentoran) | 5 |
| Clements, D. 1965 (Coventry C, Sheffield W, Everton, New York Cosmos) | 48 |
| **Clingan, S. G. 2006 (Nottingham F, Norwich C, Coventry C, Kilmarnock)** | **34** |
| Clugston, J. 1888 (Cliftonville) | 14 |
| Clyde, M. G. 2005 (Wolverhampton W) | 3 |
| Coates, C. 2009 (Crusaders) | 6 |
| Cochrane, D. 1939 (Leeds U) | 12 |
| Cochrane, G. 1903 (Cliftonville) | 1 |
| Cochrane, G. T. 1976 (Coleraine, Burnley, Middlesbrough, Gillingham) | 26 |
| Cochrane, M. 1898 (Distillery, Leicester Fosse) | 8 |
| Collins, F. 1922 (Celtic) | 1 |
| Collins, R. 1922 (Cliftonville) | 1 |
| Condy, J. 1882 (Distillery) | 3 |
| Connell, T. E. 1978 (Coleraine) | 1 |
| Connor, J. 1901 (Glentoran, Belfast Celtic) | 13 |
| Connor, M. J. 1903 (Brentford, Fulham) | 3 |
| Cook, W. 1933 (Celtic, Everton) | 15 |
| Cooke, S. 1889 (Belfast YMCA, Cliftonville) | 3 |
| Coote, A. 1999 (Norwich C) | 6 |
| Coulter, J. 1934 (Belfast Celtic, Everton, Grimsby T, Chelmsford C) | 11 |
| Cowan, J. 1970 (Newcastle U) | 1 |
| Cowan, T. S. 1925 (Queen's Island) | 1 |
| Coyle, F. 1956 (Coleraine, Nottingham F) | 4 |
| Coyle, L. 1989 (Derry C) | 1 |
| Coyle, R. I. 1973 (Sheffield W) | 5 |
| Craig, A. B. 1908 (Rangers, Morton) | 9 |
| Craig, D. J. 1967 (Newcastle U) | 25 |
| Craigan, S. J. 2003 (Partick Th, Motherwell) | 54 |
| Crawford, A. 1889 (Distillery, Cliftonville) | 7 |
| Croft, T. 1922 (Queen's Island) | 3 |
| Crone, R. 1889 (Distillery) | 4 |
| Crone, W. 1882 (Distillery) | 12 |
| Crooks, W. J. 1922 (Manchester U) | 1 |
| Crossan, E. 1950 (Blackburn R) | 3 |
| Crossan, J. A. 1960 (Sparta-Rotterdam, Sunderland, Manchester C, Middlesbrough) | 24 |
| Crothers, C. 1907 (Distillery) | 1 |
| Cumming, L. 1929 (Huddersfield T, Oldham Ath) | 3 |
| Cunningham, W. 1892 (Ulster) | 4 |
| Cunningham, W. E. 1951 (St Mirren, Leicester C, Dunfermline Ath) | 30 |
| Curran, S. 1926 (Belfast Celtic) | 4 |
| Curran, J. J. 1922 (Glenavon, Pontypridd, Glenavon) | 5 |
| Cush, W. W. 1951 (Glenavon, Leeds U, Portadown) | 26 |
| | |
| Dallas, S. 2011 (Crusaders) | 1 |
| Dalrymple, J. 1922 (Distillery) | 1 |
| Dalton, W. 1888 (YMCA, Linfield) | 11 |
| D'Arcy, S. D. 1952 (Chelsea, Brentford) | 5 |
| Darling, J. 1897 (Linfield) | 22 |
| Davey, H. H. 1926 (Reading, Portsmouth) | 5 |
| **Davis, S. 2005 (Aston Villa, Fulham, Rangers, Southampton)** | **59** |
| Davis, T. L. 1937 (Oldham Ath) | 1 |
| Davison, A. J. 1996 (Bolton W, Bradford C, Grimsby T) | 3 |
| Davison, J. R. 1882 (Cliftonville) | 8 |

Dennison, R. 1988 (Wolverhampton W) — 18
Devine, A. O. 1886 (Limavady) — 4
Devine, J. 1990 (Glentoran) — 1
Dickson, D. 1970 (Coleraine) — 4
Dickson, T. A. 1957 (Linfield) — 1
Dickson, W. 1951 (Chelsea, Arsenal) — 12
Diffin, W. J. 1931 (Belfast Celtic) — 1
Dill, A. H. 1882 (Knock, Down Ath, Cliftonville) — 9
Doherty, I. 1901 (Belfast Celtic) — 1
Doherty, J. 1928 (Portadown) — 1
Doherty, J. 1933 (Cliftonville) — 2
Doherty, L. 1985 (Linfield) — 2
Doherty, M. 1938 (Derry C) — 1
Doherty, P. D. 1935 (Blackpool, Manchester C, Derby
Co, Huddersfield T, Doncaster R) — 16
Doherty, T. E. 2003 (Bristol C) — 9
Donaghey, B. 1903 (Belfast Celtic) — 1
Donaghy, M. M. 1980 (Luton T, Manchester U, Chelsea) — 91
Donnelly, L. 1913 (Distillery) — 1
Donnelly, M. 2009 (Crusaders) — 1
Doran, J. F. 1921 (Brighton) — 3
Dougan, A. D. 1958 (Portsmouth, Blackburn R,
Aston Villa, Leicester C, Wolverhampton W) — 43
Douglas, J. P. 1947 (Belfast Celtic) — 1
Dowd, H. O. 1974 (Glenavon, Sheffield W) — 3
Dowie, I. 1990 (Luton T, West Ham U, Southampton,
C Palace, West Ham U, QPR) — 59
Duff, M. J. 2002 (Cheltenham T, Burnley) — 24
Duggan, H. A. 1930 (Leeds U) — 8
Dunlop, G. 1985 (Linfield) — 4
Dunne, J. 1928 (Sheffield U) — 7

Eames, W. L. E. 1885 (Dublin University) — 3
Eglington, T. J. 1947 (Everton) — 6
Elder, A. R. 1960 (Burnley, Stoke C) — 40
Elleman, A. R. 1889 (Cliftonville) — 1
Elliott, S. 2001 (Motherwell, Hull C) — 39
Elwood, J. H. 1929 (Bradford) — 2
Emerson, W. 1920 (Glentoran, Burnley) — 11
English, S. 1933 (Rangers) — 2
Enright, J. 1912 (Leeds C) — 1
**Evans, C. J. 2009 (Manchester U, Hull C)** — **18**
**Evans, J. G. 2007 (Manchester U)** — **34**

Falloon, E. 1931 (Aberdeen) — 2
Farquharson, T. G. 1923 (Cardiff C) — 7
Farrell, P. 1901 (Distillery) — 2
Farrell, P. 1938 (Hibernian) — 1
Farrell, P. D. 1947 (Everton) — 7
Feeney, J. M. 1947 (Linfield, Swansea T) — 2
Feeney, W. 1976 (Glentoran) — 1
Feeney, W. J. 2002 (Bournemouth, Luton T, Cardiff C,
Oldham Ath, Plymouth Arg) — 46
Ferguson, G. 1999 (Linfield) — 5
**Ferguson, S. 2009 (Newcastle U)** — **8**
Ferguson, W. 1966 (Linfield) — 2
Ferris, J. 1920 (Belfast Celtic, Chelsea, Belfast Celtic) — 6
Ferris, R. O. 1950 (Birmingham C) — 3
Fettis, A. W. 1992 (Hull C, Nottingham F, Blackburn R) — 25
Finney, T. 1975 (Sunderland, Cambridge U) — 14
Fitzpatrick, J. C. 1896 (Bohemians) — 2
Flack, H. 1929 (Burnley) — 1
Fleming, J. G. 1987 (Nottingham F, Manchester C,
Barnsley) — 31
Forbes, G. 1888 (Limavady, Distillery) — 3
Forde, J. T. 1959 (Ards) — 4
Foreman, T. A. 1899 (Cliftonville) — 1
Forsythe, J. 1888 (YMCA) — 2
Fox, W. T. 1887 (Ulster) — 2
Frame, T. 1925 (Linfield) — 1
Fulton, R. P. 1928 (Larne, Belfast Celtic) — 21

Gaffikin, G. 1890 (Linfield Ath) — 15
Galbraith, W. 1890 (Distillery) — 1
Gallagher, P. 1920 (Celtic, Falkirk) — 11
Gallogly, C. 1951 (Huddersfield T) — 2
Gara, A. 1902 (Preston NE) — 3
Gardiner, A. 1930 (Cliftonville) — 5
Garrett, J. 1925 (Distillery) — 1
Garrett, R. 2009 (Linfield) — 5

Gaston, R. 1969 (Oxford U) — 1
Gaukrodger, G. 1895 (Linfield) — 1
Gault, M. 2008 (Linfield) — 1
Gaussen, A. D. 1884 (Moyola Park, Magherafelt) — 6
Geary, J. 1931 (Glentoran) — 2
Gibb, J. T. 1884 (Wellington Park, Cliftonville) — 10
Gibb, T. J. 1936 (Cliftonville) — 1
Gibson W. K. 1894 (Cliftonville) — 14
Gillespie, K. R. 1995 (Manchester U, Newcastle U,
Blackburn R, Leicester C, Sheffield U) — 86
Gillespie, S. 1886 (Hertford) — 6
Gillespie, W. 1889 (West Down) — 1
Gillespie, W. 1913 (Sheffield U) — 25
Goodall, A. L. 1899 (Derby Co, Glossop) — 10
Goodbody, M. F. 1889 (Dublin University) — 2
Gordon, H. 1895 (Linfield) — 3
Gordon R. W. 1891 (Linfield) — 7
Gordon, T. 1884 (Linfield) — 2
Gorman, R. J. 2010 (Wolverhampton W) — 9
Gorman, W. C. 1947 (Brentford) — 4
Gough, J. 1925 (Queen's Island) — 1
Gowdy, J. 1920 (Glentoran, Queen's Island, Falkirk) — 6
Gowdy, W. A. 1932 (Hull C, Sheffield W, Linfield,
Hibernian) — 6
Graham, W. G. L. 1951 (Doncaster R) — 14
Gray, P. 1993 (Luton T, Sunderland, Nancy, Luton T,
Burnley, Oxford U) — 26
Greer, W. 1909 (QPR) — 3
Gregg, H. 1954 (Doncaster R, Manchester U) — 25
Griffin, D. J. 1996 (St Johnstone, Dundee U,
Stockport Co) — 29
**Grigg, W. D. 2012 (Walsall)** — **2**

Hall, G. 1897 (Distillery) — 1
Halligan, W. 1911 (Derby Co, Wolverhampton W) — 2
Hamill, M. 1912 (Manchester U, Belfast Celtic,
Manchester C) — 7
Hamill, R. 1999 (Glentoran) — 1
Hamilton, B. 1969 (Linfield, Ipswich T, Everton,
Millwall, Swindon T) — 50
Hamilton, G. 2003 (Portadown) — 5
Hamilton, J. 1882 (Knock) — 2
Hamilton, R. 1928 (Rangers) — 5
Hamilton, W. D. 1885 (Dublin Association) — 1
Hamilton, W. J. 1885 (Dublin Association) — 1
Hamilton, W. J. 1908 (Distillery) — 1
Hamilton, W. R. 1978 (QPR, Burnley, Oxford U) — 41
Hampton, H. 1911 (Bradford C) — 9
Hanna, J. 1912 (Nottingham F) — 2
Hanna, J. D. 1899 (Royal Artillery, Portsmouth) — 1
Hannon, D. J. 1908 (Bohemians) — 6
Harkin, J. T. 1968 (Southport, Shrewsbury T) — 5
Harland, A. I. 1922 (Linfield) — 2
Harris, J. 1921 (Cliftonville, Glenavon) — 2
Harris, V. 1906 (Shelbourne, Everton) — 20
Harvey, M. 1961 (Sunderland) — 34
Hastings, J. 1882 (Knock, Ulster) — 7
Hatton, S. 1963 (Linfield) — 2
Hayes, W. E. 1938 (Huddersfield T) — 4
**Healy, D. J. 2000 (Manchester U, Preston NE, Leeds U,
Fulham, Sunderland, Rangers, Bury)** — **95**
Healy, P. J. 1982 (Coleraine, Glentoran) — 4
Hegan, D. 1970 (WBA, Wolverhampton W) — 7
Henderson, J. 1885 (Ulster) — 3
Hewison, G. 1885 (Moyola Park) — 2
Hill, C. F. 1990 (Sheffield U, Leicester C, Trelleborg,
Northampton T) — 27
Hill, M. J. 1959 (Norwich C, Everton) — 7
Hinton, E. 1947 (Fulham, Millwall) — 7
**Hodson, L. J. S. 2011 (Watford)** — **9**
Holmes, S. P. 2002 (Wrexham) — 1
Hopkins, J. 1926 (Brighton) — 1
Horlock, K. 1995 (Swindon T, Manchester C) — 32
Houston, J. 1912 (Linfield, Everton) — 6
Houston, W. 1933 (Linfield) — 1
Houston, W. J. 1885 (Moyola Park) — 2
**Hughes, A. W. 1998 (Newcastle U, Aston Villa, Fulham)** — **86**
Hughes, J. 2006 (Lincoln C) — 2
Hughes, M.A. 2006 (Oldham Ath) — 2
Hughes, M. E. 1992 (Manchester C, Strasbourg,
West Ham U, Wimbledon, Crystal Palace) — 71

Hughes, P. A. 1987 (Bury) 3
Hughes, W. 1951 (Bolton W) 1
Humphries, W. M. 1962 (Ards, Coventry C, Swansea T) 14
Hunter, A. 1905 (Distillery, Belfast Celtic) 8
Hunter, A. 1970 (Blackburn R, Ipswich T) 53
Hunter, B. V. 1995 (Wrexham, Reading) 15
Hunter, R. J. 1884 (Cliftonville) 3
Hunter, V. 1962 (Coleraine) 2

Ingham, M. G. 2005 (Sunderland, Wrexham) 3
Irvine, R. J. 1962 (Linfield, Stoke C) 8
Irvine, R. W. 1922 (Everton, Portsmouth, Connah's Quay, Derry C) 15
Irvine, W. J. 1963 (Burnley, Preston NE, Brighton & HA) 23
Irving, S. J. 1923 (Dundee, Cardiff C, Chelsea) 18

Jackson, T. A. 1969 (Everton, Nottingham F, Manchester U) 35
Jamison, J. 1976 (Glentoran) 1
Jenkins, I. 1997 (Chester C, Dundee U) 6
Jennings, P. A. 1964 (Watford, Tottenham H, Arsenal, Tottenham H) 119
Johnson, D. M. 1999 (Blackburn R, Birmingham C) 56
Johnston, H. 1927 (Portadown) 1
Johnston, R. S. 1882 (Distillery) 5
Johnston, R. S. 1905 (Distillery) 1
Johnston, S. 1890 (Linfield) 4
Johnston, W. 1885 (Oldpark) 2
Johnston, W. C. 1962 (Glenavon, Oldham Ath) 2
Jones, J. 1930 (Linfield, Hibernian, Glenavon) 23
Jones, J. 1956 (Glenavon) 3
Jones, J. 1934 (Distillery, Blackpool) 2
Jones, S. G. 2003 (Crewe Alex, Burnley) 29
Jordan, T. 1895 (Linfield) 2

Kavanagh, P. J. 1930 (Celtic) 1
Keane, T. R. 1949 (Swansea T) 1
Kearns, A. 1900 (Distillery) 6
Kee, P. V. 1990 (Oxford U, Ards) 9
Keith, R. M. 1958 (Newcastle U) 23
Kelly, H. R. 1950 (Fulham, Southampton) 4
Kelly, J. 1896 (Glentoran) 1
Kelly, J. 1932 (Derry C) 11
Kelly, P. J. 1921 (Manchester C) 1
Kelly, P. M. 1950 (Barnsley) 1
Kennedy, A. L. 1923 (Arsenal) 2
Kennedy, P. H. 1999 (Watford, Wigan Ath) 20
Kernaghan, N. 1936 (Belfast Celtic) 3
Kirk, A. R. 2000 (Hearts, Boston U, Northampton T, Dunfermline Ath) 11
Kirkwood, H. 1904 (Cliftonville) 1
Kirwan, J. 1900 (Tottenham H, Chelsea, Clyde) 17

Lacey, W. 1909 (Everton, Liverpool, New Brighton) 23
**Lafferty, D. P. 2012 (Burnley)** 4
**Lafferty, K. 2006 (Burnley, Rangers, FC Sion)** 35
Lawrie, J. 2009 (Port Vale) 3
Lawther, R. 1888 (Glentoran) 2
Lawther, W. I. 1960 (Sunderland, Blackburn R) 4
Leatham, J. 1939 (Belfast Celtic) 1
Ledwidge, J. J. 1906 (Shelbourne) 2
Lemon, J. 1886 (Glentoran, Belfast YMCA) 1
Lennon, N. F. 1994 (Crewe Alex, Leicester C, Celtic) 40
Leslie, W. 1887 (YMCA) 1
Lewis, J. 1899 (Glentoran, Distillery) 4
**Little, A. 2009 (Rangers)** 9
Lockhart, H. 1884 (Rossall School) 1
Lockhart, N. H. 1947 (Linfield, Coventry C, Aston Villa) 8
Lomas, S. M. 1994 (Manchester C, West Ham U) 45
Loyal, J. 1891 (Clarence) 1
Lutton, R. J. 1970 (Wolverhampton W, West Ham U) 6
Lynas, R. 1925 (Cliftonville) 1
Lyner, D. R. 1920 (Glentoran, Manchester U, Kilmarnock) 6
Lytle, J. 1898 (Glentoran) 1

McAdams, W. J. 1954 (Manchester C, Bolton W, Leeds U) 15
McAlery, J. M. 1882 (Cliftonville) 2

McAlinden, J. 1938 (Belfast Celtic, Portsmouth, Southend U) 4
McAllen, J. 1898 (Linfield) 9
McAlpine, S. 1901 (Cliftonville) 1
McArdle, R. A. 2010 (Rochdale, Aberdeen) 5
McArthur, A. 1886 (Distillery) 1
**McAuley, G. 2005 (Lincoln C, Leicester C, Ipswich T, WBA)** 42
McAuley, J. L. 1911 (Huddersfield T) 6
McAuley, P. 1900 (Belfast Celtic) 1
McBride, S. D. 1991 (Glenavon) 4
McCabe, J. J. 1949 (Leeds U) 6
McCabe, W. 1891 (Ulster) 1
McCambridge, J. 1930 (Ballymena, Cardiff C) 4
McCandless, J. 1912 (Bradford) 5
McCandless, W. 1920 (Linfield, Rangers) 9
McCann, G. S. 2002 (West Ham U, Cheltenham T, Barnsley, Scunthorpe U, Peterborough U) 39
McCann, P. 1910 (Belfast Celtic, Glentoran) 7
McCarthy, J. D. 1996 (Port Vale, Birmingham C) 18
McCartney, A. 1903 (Ulster, Linfield, Everton, Belfast Celtic, Glentoran) 15
McCartney, G. 2002 (Sunderland, West Ham U, Sunderland) 34
McCashin, J. W. 1896 (Cliftonville) 5
McCavana, W. T. 1955 (Coleraine) 3
McCaw, J. H. 1927 (Linfield) 6
McClatchey, J. 1886 (Distillery) 3
McClatchey, J. 1895 (Distillery) 1
McCleary, J. W. 1955 (Cliftonville) 1
McCleery, W. 1922 (Cliftonville, Linfield) 10
McClelland, J. 1980 (Mansfield T, Rangers, Watford, Leeds U) 53
McClelland, J. T. 1961 (Arsenal, Fulham) 6
McCluggage, A. 1922 (Cliftonville, Bradford, Burnley) 13
McClure, G. 1907 (Cliftonville, Distillery) 4
McConnell, E. 1904 (Cliftonville, Glentoran, Sunderland, Sheffield W) 12
McConnell, P. 1928 (Doncaster R, Southport) 2
McConnell, W. G. 1912 (Bohemians) 6
McConnell, W. H. 1925 (Reading) 8
McCourt, F. J. 1952 (Manchester C) 6
**McCourt, P. J. 2002 (Rochdale, Celtic)** 13
McCoy, R. K. 1987 (Coleraine) 1
McCoy, S. 1896 (Distillery) 1
McCracken, E. 1928 (Barking) 1
McCracken, R. 1921 (Crystal Palace) 4
McCracken, R. 1922 (Linfield) 1
McCracken, W. R. 1902 (Distillery, Newcastle U, Hull C) 16
McCreery, D. 1976 (Manchester U, QPR, Tulsa Roughnecks, Newcastle U, Hearts) 67
McCrory, S. 1958 (Southend U) 1
McCullough, K. 1935 (Belfast Celtic, Manchester C) 5
McCullough, W. J. 1961 (Arsenal, Millwall) 10
McCurdy, C. 1980 (Linfield) 1
McDonald, A. 1986 (QPR) 52
McDonald, R. 1930 (Rangers) 2
McDonnell, J. 1911 (Bohemians) 4
McElhinney, G. M. A. 1984 (Bolton W) 6
McEvilly, L. R. 2002 (Rochdale) 1
McFaul, W. S. 1967 (Linfield, Newcastle U) 6
McGarry, J. K. 1951 (Cliftonville) 3
McGaughey, M. 1985 (Linfield) 1
McGibbon, P. C. G. 1995 (Manchester U, Wigan Ath) 7
**McGinn, N. 2009 (Celtic, Aberdeen)** 22
**McGivern, R. 2009 (Manchester C)** 19
McGovern, M. 2010 (Ross Co) 1
McGrath, R. C. 1974 (Tottenham H, Manchester U) 21
McGregor, S. 1921 (Glentoran) 1
McGrillen, J. 1924 (Clyde, Belfast Celtic) 2
McGuire, E. 1907 (Distillery) 1
McGuire, J. 1928 (Linfield) 1
McIlroy, H. 1906 (Cliftonville) 1
McIlroy, J. 1952 (Burnley, Stoke C) 55
McIlroy, S. B. 1972 (Manchester U, Stoke C, Manchester C) 88
McIlvenny, P. 1924 (Distillery) 1
McIlvenny, R. 1890 (Distillery, Ulster) 2
**McKay, W. R. 2013 (Inverness CT)** 1
McKeag, W. 1968 (Glentoran) 2
McKeague, T. 1925 (Glentoran) 1

McKee, F. W. 1906 (Cliftonville, Belfast Celtic) 5
McKelvey, H. 1901 (Glentoran) 2
McKenna, J. 1950 (Huddersfield T) 7
McKenzie, H. 1922 (Distillery) 2
McKenzie, R. 1967 (Airdrieonians) 1
McKeown, N. 1892 (Linfield) 7
McKie, H. 1895 (Cliftonville) 3
Mackie, J. A. 1923 (Arsenal, Portsmouth) 3
McKinney, D. 1921 (Hull C, Bradford C) 2
McKinney, V. J. 1966 (Falkirk) 1
McKnight, A. D. 1988 (Celtic, West Ham U) 10
McKnight, J. 1912 (Preston NE, Glentoran) 2
McLaughlin, C. G. 2012 (Preston NE) 1
McLaughlin, J. C. 1962 (Shrewsbury T, Swansea T) 12
McLean, B. S. 2006 (Rangers) 1
McLean, T. 1885 (Limavady) 1
McMahon, G. J. 1995 (Tottenham H, Stoke C) 17
McMahon, J. 1934 (Bohemians) 1
McMaster, G. 1897 (Glentoran) 3
McMichael, A. 1950 (Newcastle U) 40
McMillan, G. 1903 (Distillery) 2
McMillan, S. T. 1963 (Manchester U) 2
McMillen, W. S. 1934 (Manchester U, Chesterfield) 7
McMordie, A. S. 1969 (Middlesbrough) 21
McMorran, E. J. 1947 (Belfast Celtic, Barnsley,
　Doncaster R) 15
McMullan, D. 1926 (Liverpool) 3
McNally, B. A. 1986 (Shrewsbury T) 5
McNinch, J. 1931 (Ballymena) 3
McPake, J. 2012 (Coventry C) 1
McParland, P. J. 1954 (Aston Villa, Wolverhampton W)
　34
McQuoid, J. J. B. 2011 (Millwall) 5
McShane, J. 1899 (Cliftonville) 4
McVeigh, P. M. 1999 (Tottenham H, Norwich C) 20
McVicker, J. 1888 (Linfield, Glentoran) 2
McWha, W. B. R. 1882 (Knock, Cliftonville) 7
Madden, O. 1938 (Norwich C) 1
Magee, G. 1885 (Wellington Park) 3
**Magennis, J. B. D. 2010 (Cardiff C, Aberdeen)** **5**
Magill, E. J. 1962 (Arsenal, Brighton & HA) 26
Magilton, J. 1991 (Oxford U, Southampton, Sheffield W,
　Ipswich T) 52
Maginnis, H. 1900 (Linfield) 8
Mahood, J. 1926 (Belfast Celtic, Ballymena) 9
**Mannus, A. 2004 (Linfield, St Johnstone)** **5**
Manderson, R. 1920 (Rangers) 3
Mansfield, J. 1901 (Dublin Freebooters) 1
Martin, C. 1882 (Cliftonville) 1
Martin, C. 1925 (Bo'ness) 1
Martin, C. J. 1947 (Glentoran, Leeds U, Aston Villa) 6
Martin, D. K. 1934 (Belfast Celtic, Wolverhampton W,
　Nottingham F) 10
Mathieson, A. 1921 (Luton T) 1
Maxwell, J. 1902 (Linfield, Glentoran, Belfast Celtic) 7
Meek, H. L. 1925 (Glentoran) 1
Mehaffy, J. A. C. 1922 (Queen's Island) 1
Meldon, P. A. 1899 (Dublin Freebooters) 2
Mercer, H. V. A. 1908 (Linfield) 1
Mercer, J. T. 1898 (Distillery, Linfield, Distillery,
　Derby Co) 12
Millar, W. 1932 (Barrow) 2
Miller, J. 1929 (Middlesbrough) 3
Milligan, D. 1939 (Chesterfield) 1
Milne, R. G. 1894 (Linfield) 28
Mitchell, E. J. 1933 (Cliftonville, Glentoran) 2
Mitchell, W. 1932 (Distillery, Chelsea) 15
Molyneux, T. B. 1883 (Ligoniel, Cliftonville) 11
Montgomery, F. J. 1955 (Coleraine) 1
Moore, C. 1949 (Glentoran) 1
Moore, P. 1933 (Aberdeen) 1
Moore, R. 1891 (Linfield Ath) 1
Moore, R. L. 1887 (Ulster) 2
Moore, W. 1923 (Falkirk) 1
Moorhead, F. W. 1885 (Dublin University) 1
Moorhead, G. 1923 (Linfield) 4
Moran, J. 1912 (Leeds C) 1
Moreland, V. 1979 (Derby Co) 6
Morgan, G. F. 1922 (Linfield, Nottingham F) 8
Morgan, S. 1972 (Port Vale, Aston Villa, Brighton & HA,
　Sparta Rotterdam) 18
Morrison, R. 1891 (Linfield Ath) 2

Morrison, T. 1895 (Glentoran, Burnley) 7
Morrogh, D. 1896 (Bohemians) 1
Morrow, S. J. 1990 (Arsenal, QPR) 39
Morrow, W. J. 1883 (Moyola Park) 3
Muir, R. 1885 (Oldpark) 2
Mulgrew, J. 2008 (Linfield) 2
Mulholland, T. S. 1906 (Belfast Celtic) 2
Mullan, G. 1983 (Glentoran) 4
Mulligan, J. 1921 (Manchester C) 1
Mulryne, P. P. 1997 (Manchester U, Norwich C,
　Cardiff C) 27
Murdock, C. J. 2000 (Preston NE, Hibernian,
　Crewe Alex, Rotherham U) 34
Murphy, J. 1910 (Bradford C) 3
Murphy, N. 1905 (QPR) 3
Murray, J. M. 1910 (Motherwell, Sheffield W) 3

Napier, R. J. 1966 (Bolton W) 1
Neill, W. J. T. 1961 (Arsenal, Hull C) 59
Nelis, P. 1923 (Nottingham F) 1
Nelson, S. 1970 (Arsenal, Brighton & HA) 51
Nicholl, C. J. 1975 (Aston Villa, Southampton,
　Grimsby T) 51
Nicholl, H. 1902 (Belfast Celtic) 3
Nicholl, J. M. 1976 (Manchester U, Toronto Blizzard,
　Sunderland, Toronto Blizzard, Rangers,
　Toronto Blizzard, WBA) 73
Nicholson, J. J. 1961 (Manchester U, Huddersfield T) 41
Nixon, R. 1914 (Linfield) 3
Nolan, I. R. 1997 (Sheffield W, Bradford C, Wigan Ath)
　18
Nolan-Whelan, J. V. 1901 (Dublin Freebooters) 5
**Norwood, O. J. 2011 (Manchester U, Huddersfield T)** **9**

O'Boyle, G. 1994 (Dunfermline Ath, St Johnstone) 13
O'Brien, M. T. 1921 (QPR, Leicester C, Hull C,
　Derby Co) 10
O'Connell, P. 1912 (Sheffield W, Hull C) 5
O'Connor, M. J. 2008 (Crewe Alex, Scunthorpe U) 10
O'Doherty, A. 1970 (Coleraine) 2
O'Driscoll, J. F. 1949 (Swansea T) 3
O'Hagan, C. 1905 (Tottenham H, Aberdeen) 11
O'Hagan, W. 1920 (St Mirren) 2
O'Hehir, J. C. 1910 (Bohemians) 1
O'Kane, W. J. 1970 (Nottingham F) 20
O'Mahoney, M. T. 1939 (Bristol R) 1
O'Neill, C. 1989 (Motherwell) 3
O'Neill, J. 1962 (Sunderland) 1
O'Neill, J. P. 1980 (Leicester C) 39
O'Neill, M. A. M. 1988 (Newcastle U, Dundee U,
　Hibernian, Coventry C) 31
O'Neill, M. H. M. 1972 (Distillery, Nottingham F,
　Norwich C, Manchester C, Norwich C, Notts Co) 64
O'Reilly, H. 1901 (Dublin Freebooters) 3
Owens, J. 2011 (Crusaders) 1

Parke, J. 1964 (Linfield, Hibernian, Sunderland) 14
**Paterson, M. A. 2008 (Scunthorpe U, Burnley)** **15**
Paterson, D. J. 1994 (Crystal Palace, Luton T,
　Dundee U) 17
Patterson, R. 2010 (Coleraine, Plymouth Arg) 5
Peacock, R. 1952 (Celtic, Coleraine) 31
Peden, J. 1887 (Linfield, Distillery) 24
Penney, S. 1985 (Brighton & HA) 17
Percy, J. C. 1889 (Belfast YMCA) 1
Platt, J. A. 1976 (Middlesbrough, Ballymena U,
　Coleraine) 23
Pollock, W. 1928 (Belfast Celtic) 1
Ponsonby, J. 1895 (Distillery) 9
Potts, R. M. C. 1883 (Cliftonville) 2
Priestley, T. J. M. 1933 (Coleraine, Chelsea) 2
Pyper, Jas. 1897 (Cliftonville) 7
Pyper, John 1897 (Cliftonville) 9
Pyper, M. 1932 (Linfield) 1

Quinn, J. M. 1985 (Blackburn R, Swindon T, Leicester C,
　Bradford C, West Ham U, Bournemouth, Reading) 46
Quinn, S. J. 1996 (Blackpool, WBA, Willem II,
　Sheffield W, Peterborough U, Northampton T) 50

Rafferty, P. 1980 (Linfield) 1
Ramsey, P. C. 1984 (Leicester C) 14

Rankine, J. 1883 (Alexander) — 2
Rattray, D. 1882 (Avoniel) — 3
Rea, R. 1901 (Glentoran) — 1
Redmond, R. 1884 (Cliftonville) — 1
Reid, G. H. 1923 (Cardiff C) — 1
Reid, J. 1883 (Ulster) — 6
Reid, S. E. 1934 (Derby Co) — 3
Reid, W. 1931 (Hearts) — 1
Reilly, M. M. 1900 (Portsmouth) — 2
Renneville, W. T. J. 1910 (Leyton, Aston Villa) — 4
Reynolds, J. 1890 (Distillery, Ulster) — 5
Reynolds, R. 1905 (Bohemians) — 1
Rice, P. J. 1969 (Arsenal) — 49
Roberts, F. C. 1931 (Glentoran) — 1
Robinson, P. 1920 (Distillery, Blackburn R) — 2
Robinson, S. 1997 (Bournemouth, Luton T) — 7
Rogan, A. 1988 (Celtic, Sunderland, Millwall) — 18
Rollo, D. 1912 (Linfield, Blackburn R) — 16
Roper, E. O. 1886 (Dublin University) — 1
Rosbotham, A. 1887 (Cliftonville) — 7
Ross, W. E. 1969 (Newcastle U) — 1
Rowland, K. 1994 (West Ham U, QPR) — 19
Rowley, R. W. M. 1929 (Southampton, Tottenham H) — 6
Rushe, F. 1925 (Distillery) — 1
Russell, A. 1947 (Linfield) — 1
Russell, S. R. 1930 (Bradford C, Derry C) — 3
Ryan, R. A. 1950 (WBA) — 1

Sanchez, L. P. 1987 (Wimbledon) — 3
Scott, E. 1920 (Liverpool, Belfast Celtic) — 31
Scott, J. 1958 (Grimsby) — 2
Scott, J. E. 1901 (Cliftonville) — 1
Scott, L. J. 1895 (Dublin University) — 2
Scott, P. W. 1975 (Everton, York C, Aldershot) — 10
Scott, T. 1894 (Cliftonville) — 13
Scott, W. 1903 (Linfield, Everton, Leeds C) — 25
Scraggs, M. J. 1921 (Glentoran) — 2
Seymour, H. C. 1914 (Bohemians) — 1
Seymour, J. 1907 (Cliftonville) — 2
Shanks, T. 1903 (Woolwich Arsenal, Brentford) — 3
Sharkey, P. G. 1976 (Ipswich T) — 1
Sheehan, Dr G. 1899 (Bohemians) — 3
Sheridan, J. 1903 (Everton, Stoke C) — 6
Sherrard, J. 1885 (Limavady) — 3
Sherrard, W. C. 1895 (Cliftonville) — 3
Sherry, J. J. 1906 (Bohemians) — 2
Shields, R. J. 1957 (Southampton) — 1
**Shiels, D. 2006 (Hibernian, Doncaster R, Kilmarnock) 14**
Silo, M. 1888 (Belfast YMCA) — 1
Simpson, W. J. 1951 (Rangers) — 12
Sinclair, J. 1882 (Knock) — 2
Slemin, J. C. 1909 (Bohemians) — 1
Sloan, A. S. 1925 (London Caledonians) — 1
Sloan, D. 1969 (Oxford U) — 2
Sloan, H. A. de B. 1903 (Bohemians) — 8
Sloan, J. W. 1947 (Arsenal) — 1
Sloan, T. 1926 (Cardiff C, Linfield) — 11
Sloan, T. 1979 (Manchester U) — 3
Small, J. M. 1887 (Clarence, Cliftonville) — 4
Smith, A. W. 2003 (Glentoran, Preston NE) — 18
Smith, E. E. 1921 (Cardiff C) — 4
Smith, J. E. 1901 (Distillery) — 2
Smyth, R. H. 1886 (Dublin University) — 1
Smyth, S. 1948 (Wolverhampton W, Stoke C) — 9
Smyth, W. 1949 (Distillery) — 4
Snape, A. 1920 (Airdrieonians) — 1
Sonner, D. J. 1998 (Ipswich T, Sheffield W,
Birmingham C, Nottingham F, Peterborough U) — 13
Spence, D. W. 1975 (Bury, Blackpool, Southend U) — 29
Spencer, S. 1890 (Distillery) — 6
Spiller, E. A. 1883 (Cliftonville) — 5
Sproule, I. 2006 (Hibernian, Bristol C) — 11
Stanfield, O. M. 1887 (Distillery) — 30
Steele, A. 1926 (Charlton Ath, Fulham) — 4
Stevenson, A. E. 1934 (Rangers, Everton) — 17
Stewart, A. 1967 (Glentoran, Derby Co) — 7
Stewart, D. C. 1978 (Hull C) — 1
Stewart, I. 1982 (QPR, Newcastle U) — 31
Stewart, R. K. 1890 (St Columb's Court, Cliftonville) — 11

Stewart, T. C. 1961 (Linfield) — 1
Swan, S. 1899 (Linfield) — 1

Taggart, G. P. 1990 (Barnsley, Bolton W, Leicester C) — 51
Taggart, J. 1899 (Walsall) — 1
Taylor, M. S. 1999 (Fulham, Birmingham C, unattached) — 88
Thompson, A. L. 2011 (Watford) — 2
Thompson, F. W. 1910 (Cliftonville, Linfield, Bradford
C, Clyde) — 12
Thompson, J. 1897 (Distillery) — 1
Thompson, P. 2006 (Linfield, Stockport Co) — 8
Thompson, R. 1928 (Queen's Island) — 1
Thompson, W. 1889 (Belfast Ath) — 1
Thunder, P. J. 1911 (Bohemians) — 1
Todd, S. J. 1966 (Burnley, Sheffield W) — 11
Toner, C. 2003 (Leyton Orient) — 2
Toner, J. 1922 (Arsenal, St Johnstone) — 8
Torrans, R. 1893 (Linfield) — 1
Torrans, S. 1889 (Linfield) — 26
Trainor, D. 1967 (Crusaders) — 1
Tuffey, J. 2009 (Partick T, Inverness CT) — 8
Tully, C. P. 1949 (Celtic) — 10
Turner, A. 1896 (Cliftonville) — 1
Turner, E. 1896 (Cliftonville) — 1
Turner, W. 1886 (Cliftonville) — 3
Twomey, J. F. 1938 (Leeds U) — 2

Uprichard, W. N. M. C. 1952 (Swindon T, Portsmouth) — 18

Vernon, J. 1947 (Belfast Celtic, WBA) — 17

Waddell, T. M. R. 1906 (Cliftonville) — 1
Walker, J. 1955 (Doncaster R) — 1
Walker, T. 1911 (Bury) — 1
Walsh, D. J. 1947 (WBA) — 9
Walsh, W. 1948 (Manchester C) — 5
**Ward, J. J. 2012 (Derby Co)** — **4**
Waring, J. 1899 (Cliftonville) — 1
Warren, P. 1913 (Shelbourne) — 2
Watson, J. 1883 (Ulster) — 9
Watson, P. 1971 (Distillery) — 1
Watson, T. 1926 (Cardiff C) — 1
Wattie, J. 1899 (Distillery) — 1
Webb, C. G. 1909 (Brighton & HA) — 3
Webb, S. M. 2006 (Ross Co) — 4
Weir, E. 1939 (Clyde) — 1
Welsh, E. 1966 (Carlisle U) — 4
Whiteside, N. 1982 (Manchester U, Everton) — 38
Whiteside, T. 1891 (Distillery) — 1
Whitfield, E. R. 1886 (Dublin University) — 1
Whitley, Jeff 1997 (Manchester C, Sunderland, Cardiff C) — 20
Whitley, Jim 1998 (Manchester C) — 3
Williams, J. R. 1886 (Ulster) — 2
Williams, M. S. 1999 (Chesterfield, Watford, Wimbledon,
Stoke C, Wimbledon, Milton Keynes D) — 36
Williams, P. A. 1991 (WBA) — 1
Williamson, J. 1890 (Cliftonville) — 3
Willighan, T. 1933 (Burnley) — 2
Willis, G. 1906 (Linfield) — 4
Wilson, D. J. 1987 (Brighton & HA, Luton T,
Sheffield W) — 24
Wilson, H. 1925 (Linfield) — 2
Wilson, K. J. 1987 (Ipswich T, Chelsea, Notts Co,
Walsall) — 42
Wilson, M. 1884 (Distillery) — 3
Wilson, R. 1888 (Cliftonville) — 1
Wilson, S. J. 1962 (Glenavon, Falkirk, Dundee) — 12
Wilton, J. M. 1888 (St Columb's Court, Cliftonville, St
Columb's Court) — 7
Winchester, C. 2011 (Oldham Ath) — 1
Wood, T. J. 1996 (Walsall) — 1
Worthington, N. 1984 (Sheffield W, Leeds U, Stoke C) — 66
Wright, J. 1906 (Cliftonville) — 6
Wright, T. J. 1989 (Newcastle U, Nottingham F,
Manchester C) — 31

Young, S. 1907 (Linfield, Airdrieonians, Linfield) — 9

## SCOTLAND

| | |
|---|---|
| **Adam, C. G. 2007 (Rangers, Blackpool, Liverpool, Stoke C)** | **23** |
| Adams, J. 1889 (Hearts) | 3 |
| Agnew, W. B. 1907 (Kilmarnock) | 3 |
| Aird, J. 1954 (Burnley) | 4 |
| Aitken, A. 1901 (Newcastle U, Middlesbrough, Leicester Fosse) | 14 |
| Aitken, G. G. 1949 (East Fife, Sunderland) | 8 |
| Aitken, R. 1886 (Dumbarton) | 2 |
| Aitken, R. 1980 (Celtic, Newcastle U, St Mirren) | 57 |
| Aitkenhead, W. A. C. 1912 (Blackburn R) | 1 |
| Albiston, A. 1982 (Manchester U) | 14 |
| Alexander, D. 1894 (East Stirlingshire) | 2 |
| Alexander, G. 2002 (Preston NE, Burnley) | 40 |
| Alexander, N. 2006 (Cardiff C) | 3 |
| Allan, D. S. 1885 (Queen's Park) | 3 |
| Allan, G. 1897 (Liverpool) | 1 |
| Allan, H. 1902 (Hearts) | 1 |
| Allan, J. 1887 (Queen's Park) | 2 |
| Allan, T. 1974 (Dundee) | 2 |
| Ancell, R. F. D. 1937 (Newcastle U) | 2 |
| Anderson, A. 1933 (Hearts) | 23 |
| Anderson, F. 1874 (Clydesdale) | 1 |
| Anderson, G. 1901 (Kilmarnock) | 1 |
| Anderson, H. A. 1914 (Raith R) | 1 |
| Anderson, J. 1954 (Leicester C) | 1 |
| Anderson, K. 1896 (Queen's Park) | 3 |
| Anderson, R. 2003 (Aberdeen, Sunderland) | 11 |
| Anderson, W. 1882 (Queen's Park) | 6 |
| Andrews, P. 1875 (Eastern) | 1 |
| Archibald, A. 1921 (Rangers) | 8 |
| Archibald, S. 1980 (Aberdeen, Tottenham H, Barcelona) | 27 |
| Armstrong, M. W. 1936 (Aberdeen) | 3 |
| Arnott, W. 1883 (Queen's Park) | 14 |
| Auld, J. R. 1887 (Third Lanark) | 3 |
| Auld, R. 1959 (Celtic) | 3 |
| Baird, A. 1892 (Queen's Park) | 2 |
| Baird, D. 1890 (Hearts) | 3 |
| Baird, H. 1956 (Airdrieonians) | 1 |
| Baird, J. C. 1876 (Vale of Leven) | 3 |
| Baird, S. 1957 (Rangers) | 7 |
| Baird, W. U. 1897 (St Bernard) | 1 |
| **Bannan, B. 2011 (Aston Villa)** | **12** |
| Bannon, E. J. 1980 (Dundee U) | 11 |
| Barbour, A. 1885 (Renton) | 1 |
| Bardsley, P. A. 2011 (Sunderland) | 12 |
| Barker, J. B. 1893 (Rangers) | 2 |
| Barr, D. 2009 (Falkirk) | 1 |
| Barrett, F. 1894 (Dundee) | 2 |
| Battles, B. 1901 (Celtic) | 3 |
| Battles, B. jun. 1931 (Hearts) | 1 |
| Bauld, W. 1950 (Hearts) | 3 |
| Baxter, J. C. 1961 (Rangers, Sunderland) | 34 |
| Baxter, R. D. 1939 (Middlesbrough) | 3 |
| Beattie, A. 1937 (Preston NE) | 7 |
| Beattie, C. 2006 (Celtic, WBA) | 7 |
| Beattie, R. 1939 (Preston NE) | 1 |
| Begbie, I. 1890 (Hearts) | 4 |
| Bell, A. 1912 (Manchester U) | 1 |
| Bell, C. 2011 (Kilmarnock) | 1 |
| Bell, J. 1890 (Dumbarton, Everton, Celtic) | 10 |
| Bell, M. 1901 (Hearts) | 1 |
| Bell, W. J. 1966 (Leeds U) | 2 |
| Bennett, A. 1904 (Celtic, Rangers) | 11 |
| Bennie, R. 1925 (Airdrieonians) | 3 |
| Bernard, P. R. J. 1995 (Oldham Ath) | 2 |
| **Berra, C. 2008 (Hearts, Wolverhampton W)** | **27** |
| Berry, D. 1894 (Queen's Park) | 3 |
| Berry, W. H. 1888 (Queen's Park) | 4 |
| Bett, J. 1982 (Rangers, Lokeren, Aberdeen) | 25 |
| Beveridge, W. W. 1879 (Glasgow University) | 3 |
| Black, A. 1938 (Hearts) | 3 |
| Black, D. 1889 (Hurlford) | 1 |
| Black, E. 1988 (Metz) | 2 |
| **Black, I. 2013 (Rangers)** | **1** |
| Black, I. H. 1948 (Southampton) | 1 |
| Blackburn, J. E. 1873 (Royal Engineers) | 1 |
| Blacklaw, A. S. 1963 (Burnley) | 3 |

| | |
|---|---|
| Blackley, J. 1974 (Hibernian) | 7 |
| Blair, D. 1929 (Clyde, Aston Villa) | 8 |
| Blair, J. 1920 (Sheffield W, Cardiff C) | 8 |
| Blair, J. 1934 (Motherwell) | 1 |
| Blair, J. A. 1947 (Blackpool) | 1 |
| Blair, W. 1896 (Third Lanark) | 1 |
| Blessington, J. 1894 (Celtic) | 4 |
| Blyth, J. A. 1978 (Coventry C) | 2 |
| Bone, J. 1972 (Norwich C) | 2 |
| Booth, S. 1993 (Aberdeen, Borussia Dortmund, Twente) | 21 |
| Bowie, J. 1920 (Rangers) | 2 |
| Bowie, W. 1891 (Linthouse) | 1 |
| Bowman, D. 1992 (Dundee U) | 6 |
| Bowman, G. A. 1892 (Montrose) | 1 |
| **Boyd, G. I. 2013 (Peterborough U)** | **1** |
| Boyd, J. M. 1934 (Newcastle U) | 1 |
| Boyd, K. 2006 (Rangers, Middlesbrough) | 18 |
| Boyd, R. 1889 (Mossend Swifts) | 2 |
| Boyd, T. 1991 (Motherwell, Chelsea, Celtic) | 72 |
| Boyd, W. G. 1931 (Clyde) | 2 |
| Bradshaw, T. 1928 (Bury) | 1 |
| Brand, R. 1961 (Rangers) | 8 |
| Brandon, T. 1896 (Blackburn R) | 1 |
| Brazil, A. 1980 (Ipswich T, Tottenham H) | 13 |
| Breckenridge, T. 1888 (Hearts) | 1 |
| Bremner, D. 1976 (Hibernian) | 1 |
| Bremner, W. J. 1965 (Leeds U) | 54 |
| Brennan, F. 1947 (Newcastle U) | 7 |
| Breslin, B. 1897 (Hibernian) | 1 |
| Brewster, G. 1921 (Everton) | 1 |
| **Bridcutt, L. 2013 (Brighton & HA** | **1** |
| Broadfoot, K. 2009 (Rangers) | 4 |
| Brogan, J. 1971 (Celtic) | 4 |
| Brown, A. 1890 (St Mirren) | 2 |
| Brown, A. 1904 (Middlesbrough) | 1 |
| Brown, A. D. 1950 (East Fife, Blackpool) | 14 |
| Brown, G. C. P. 1931 (Rangers) | 19 |
| Brown, H. 1947 (Partick Th) | 3 |
| Brown, J. B. 1939 (Clyde) | 1 |
| Brown, J. G. 1975 (Sheffield U) | 1 |
| Brown, R. 1884 (Dumbarton) | 2 |
| Brown, R. 1890 (Cambuslang) | 1 |
| Brown, R. 1947 (Rangers) | 3 |
| Brown, R. jun. 1885 (Dumbarton) | 1 |
| **Brown, S. 2006 (Hibernian, Celtic)** | **30** |
| Brown, W. D. F. 1958 (Dundee, Tottenham H) | 28 |
| Browning, J. 1914 (Celtic) | 1 |
| Brownlie, J. 1909 (Third Lanark) | 16 |
| Brownlie, J. 1971 (Hibernian) | 7 |
| Bruce, D. 1890 (Vale of Leven) | 1 |
| Bruce, R. F. 1934 (Middlesbrough) | 1 |
| Bryson, C. 2011 (Kilmarnock) | 1 |
| Buchan, M. M. 1972 (Aberdeen, Manchester U) | 34 |
| Buchanan, J. 1889 (Cambuslang) | 1 |
| Buchanan, J. 1929 (Rangers) | 2 |
| Buchanan, P. S. 1938 (Chelsea) | 1 |
| Buchanan, R. 1891 (Abercorn) | 1 |
| Buckley, P. 1954 (Aberdeen) | 3 |
| Buick, A. 1902 (Hearts) | 2 |
| Burchill, M. J. 2000 (Celtic) | 6 |
| **Burke, C. 2006 (Rangers, Birmingham C)** | **5** |
| Burley, C. W. 1995 (Chelsea, Celtic, Derby Co) | 46 |
| Burley, G. E. 1979 (Ipswich T) | 11 |
| Burns, F. 1970 (Manchester U) | 1 |
| Burns, K. 1974 (Birmingham C, Nottingham F) | 20 |
| Burns, T. 1981 (Celtic) | 8 |
| Busby, M. W. 1934 (Manchester C) | 1 |
| Cairns, T. 1920 (Rangers) | 8 |
| Calderhead, D. 1889 (Q of S Wanderers) | 1 |
| Calderwood, C. 1995 (Tottenham H) | 36 |
| Calderwood, R. 1885 (Cartvale) | 3 |
| Caldow, E. 1957 (Rangers) | 40 |
| **Caldwell, G. 2002 (Newcastle U, Hibernian, Celtic, Wigan Ath)** | **55** |
| Caldwell, S. 2001 (Newcastle U, Sunderland, Burnley, Wigan Ath) | 12 |
| Callaghan, P. 1900 (Hibernian) | 1 |
| Callaghan, W. 1970 (Dunfermline Ath) | 2 |

| | |
|---|---|
| Ferguson, D. 1988 (Rangers) | 2 |
| Ferguson, D. 1992 (Dundee U, Everton) | 7 |
| Ferguson, I. 1989 (Rangers) | 9 |
| Ferguson, J. 1874 (Vale of Leven) | 6 |
| Ferguson, R. 1966 (Kilmarnock) | 7 |
| Fernie, W. 1954 (Celtic) | 12 |
| Findlay, R. 1898 (Kilmarnock) | 1 |
| Fitchie, T. T. 1905 (Woolwich Arsenal, Queen's Park) | 4 |
| Flavell, R. 1947 (Airdrieonians) | 2 |
| Fleck, R. 1990 (Norwich C) | 4 |
| Fleming, C. 1954 (East Fife) | 1 |
| Fleming, J. W. 1929 (Rangers) | 3 |
| Fleming, R. 1886 (Morton) | 1 |
| **Fletcher, D. B. 2004 (Manchester U)** | **61** |
| **Fletcher, S. 2008 (Hibernian, Burnley, Wolverhampton W, Sunderland)** | **12** |
| Forbes, A. R. 1947 (Sheffield U, Arsenal) | 14 |
| Forbes, J. 1884 (Vale of Leven) | 5 |
| Ford, D. 1974 (Hearts) | 3 |
| Forrest, J. 1958 (Motherwell) | 1 |
| Forrest, J. 1966 (Rangers, Aberdeen) | 5 |
| **Forrest, J. 2011 (Celtic)** | **7** |
| Forsyth, A. 1972 (Partick Th, Manchester U) | 10 |
| Forsyth, C. 1964 (Kilmarnock) | 4 |
| Forsyth, T. 1971 (Motherwell, Rangers) | 22 |
| **Fox, D. J. 2010 (Burnley, Southampton)** | **4** |
| Foyers, R. 1893 (St Bernards) | 2 |
| Fraser, D. M. 1968 (WBA) | 2 |
| Fraser, J. 1891 (Moffat) | 1 |
| Fraser, M. J. E. 1880 (Queen's Park) | 5 |
| Fraser, J. 1907 (Dundee) | 1 |
| Fraser, W. 1955 (Sunderland) | 2 |
| Freedman, D. A. 2002 (Crystal Palace) | 2 |
| Fulton, W. 1884 (Abercorn) | 1 |
| Fyfe, J. H. 1895 (Third Lanark) | 1 |
| | |
| Gabriel, J. 1961 (Everton) | 2 |
| Gallacher, H. K. 1924 (Airdrieonians, Newcastle U, Chelsea, Derby Co) | 20 |
| Gallacher, K. W. 1988 (Dundee U, Coventry C, Blackburn R, Newcastle U) | 53 |
| Gallacher, P. 1935 (Sunderland) | 1 |
| Gallacher, P. 2002 (Dundee U) | 8 |
| Gallagher, P. 2004 (Blackburn R) | 1 |
| Galloway, M. 1992 (Celtic) | 1 |
| Galt, J. H. 1908 (Rangers) | 2 |
| Gardiner, I. 1958 (Motherwell) | 1 |
| Gardner, D. R. 1897 (Third Lanark) | 1 |
| Gardner, R. 1872 (Queen's Park, Clydesdale) | 5 |
| Gemmell, T. 1955 (St Mirren) | 2 |
| Gemmell, T. 1966 (Celtic) | 18 |
| Gemmill, A. 1971 (Derby Co, Nottingham F, Birmingham C) | 43 |
| Gemmill, S. 1995 (Nottingham F, Everton) | 26 |
| Gibb, W. 1873 (Clydesdale) | 1 |
| Gibson, D. W. 1963 (Leicester C) | 7 |
| Gibson, J. D. 1926 (Partick Th, Aston Villa) | 8 |
| Gibson, N. 1895 (Rangers, Partick Th) | 14 |
| Gilchrist, J. E. 1922 (Celtic) | 1 |
| Gilhooley, M. 1922 (Hull C) | 1 |
| **Gilks, M. 2013 (Blackpool)** | **2** |
| Gillespie, G. 1880 (Rangers, Queen's Park) | 7 |
| Gillespie, G. T. 1988 (Liverpool) | 13 |
| Gillespie, Jas 1898 (Third Lanark) | 1 |
| Gillespie, John 1896 (Queen's Park) | 1 |
| Gillespie, R. 1927 (Queen's Park) | 4 |
| Gillick, T. 1937 (Everton) | 5 |
| Gilmour, J. 1931 (Dundee) | 1 |
| Gilzean, A. J. 1964 (Dundee, Tottenham H) | 22 |
| Glass, S. 1999 (Newcastle U) | 1 |
| Glavin, R. 1977 (Celtic) | 1 |
| Glen, A. 1956 (Aberdeen) | 2 |
| Glen, R. 1895 (Renton, Hibernian) | 3 |
| Goodwillie, D. 2011 (Dundee U, Blackburn R) | 3 |
| Goram, A. L. 1986 (Oldham Ath, Hibernian, Rangers) | 43 |
| Gordon, C. S. 2004 (Hearts, Sunderland) | 40 |
| Gordon, J. E. 1912 (Rangers) | 10 |
| Gossland, J. 1884 (Rangers) | 1 |
| Goudie, J. 1884 (Abercorn) | 1 |
| Gough, C. R. 1983 (Dundee U, Tottenham H, Rangers) | 61 |
| Gould, J. 2000 (Celtic) | 2 |

| | |
|---|---|
| Gourlay, J. 1886 (Cambuslang) | 2 |
| Govan, J. 1948 (Hibernian) | 6 |
| Gow, D. R. 1888 (Rangers) | 1 |
| Gow, J. J. 1885 (Queen's Park) | 1 |
| Gow, J. R. 1888 (Rangers) | 1 |
| Graham, A. 1978 (Leeds U) | 11 |
| Graham, G. 1972 (Arsenal, Manchester U) | 12 |
| Graham, J. 1884 (Annbank) | 1 |
| Graham, J. A. 1921 (Arsenal) | 1 |
| Grant, J. 1959 (Hibernian) | 2 |
| Grant, P. 1989 (Celtic) | 2 |
| Gray, A. 1903 (Hibernian) | 1 |
| Gray, A. D. 2003 (Bradford C) | 2 |
| Gray, A. M. 1976 (Aston Villa, Wolverhampton W, Everton) | 20 |
| Gray, D. 1929 (Rangers) | 10 |
| Gray, E. 1969 (Leeds U) | 12 |
| Gray, F. T. 1976 (Leeds U, Nottingham F, Leeds U) | 32 |
| Gray, W. 1886 (Pollokshields Ath) | 1 |
| Green, A. 1971 (Blackpool, Newcastle U) | 6 |
| Greig, J. 1964 (Rangers) | 44 |
| **Griffiths, L. 2013 (Hibernian)** | **2** |
| Groves, W. 1888 (Hibernian, Celtic) | 3 |
| Gulliland, W. 1891 (Queen's Park) | 4 |
| Gunn, B. 1990 (Norwich C) | 6 |
| | |
| Haddock, H. 1955 (Clyde) | 6 |
| Haddow, D. 1894 (Rangers) | 1 |
| Haffey, F. 1960 (Celtic) | 2 |
| Hamilton, A. 1885 (Queen's Park) | 4 |
| Hamilton, A. W. 1962 (Dundee) | 24 |
| Hamilton, G. 1906 (Port Glasgow Ath) | 1 |
| Hamilton, G. 1947 (Aberdeen) | 5 |
| Hamilton, J. 1892 (Queen's Park) | 3 |
| Hamilton, J. 1924 (St Mirren) | 1 |
| Hamilton, R. C. 1899 (Rangers, Dundee) | 11 |
| Hamilton, T. 1891 (Hurlford) | 1 |
| Hamilton, T. 1932 (Rangers) | 1 |
| Hamilton, W. M. 1965 (Hibernian) | 1 |
| Hammell, S. 2005 (Motherwell) | 1 |
| **Hanley, G. 2011 (Blackburn R)** | **7** |
| Hannah, A. B. 1888 (Renton) | 1 |
| Hannah, J. 1889 (Third Lanark) | 1 |
| Hansen, A. D. 1979 (Liverpool) | 26 |
| Hansen, J. 1972 (Partick Th) | 2 |
| Harkness, J. D. 1927 (Queen's Park, Hearts) | 12 |
| Harper, J. M. 1973 (Aberdeen, Hibernian, Aberdeen) | 4 |
| Harper, W. 1923 (Hibernian, Arsenal) | 11 |
| Harris, J. 1921 (Partick Th) | 2 |
| Harris, N. 1924 (Newcastle U) | 1 |
| Harrower, W. 1882 (Queen's Park) | 3 |
| Hartford, R. A. 1972 (WBA, Manchester C, Everton, Manchester C) | 50 |
| Hartley, P. J. 2005 (Hearts, Celtic, Bristol C) | 25 |
| Harvey, D. 1973 (Leeds U) | 16 |
| Hastings, A. C. 1936 (Sunderland) | 2 |
| Haughney, M. 1954 (Celtic) | 1 |
| Hay, D. 1970 (Celtic) | 27 |
| Hay, J. 1905 (Celtic, Newcastle U) | 11 |
| Hegarty, P. 1979 (Dundee U) | 8 |
| Heggie, C. 1886 (Rangers) | 1 |
| Henderson, G. H. 1904 (Rangers) | 1 |
| Henderson, J. G. 1953 (Portsmouth, Arsenal) | 7 |
| Henderson, W. 1963 (Rangers) | 29 |
| Hendry, E. C. J. 1993 (Blackburn R, Rangers, Coventry C, Bolton W) | 51 |
| Hepburn, J. 1891 (Alloa Ath) | 1 |
| Hepburn, R. 1932 (Ayr U) | 1 |
| Herd, A. C. 1935 (Hearts) | 1 |
| Herd, D. G. 1959 (Arsenal) | 5 |
| Herd, G. 1958 (Clyde) | 5 |
| Herriot, J. 1969 (Birmingham C) | 8 |
| Hewie, J. D. 1956 (Charlton Ath) | 19 |
| Higgins, A. 1885 (Kilmarnock) | 1 |
| Higgins, A. 1910 (Newcastle U) | 4 |
| Highet, T. C. 1875 (Queen's Park) | 4 |
| Hill, D. 1881 (Rangers) | 3 |
| Hill, D. A. 1906 (Third Lanark) | 1 |
| Hill, F. R. 1930 (Aberdeen) | 3 |
| Hill, J. 1891 (Hearts) | 2 |
| Hogg, G. 1896 (Hearts) | 2 |
| Hogg, J. 1922 (Ayr U) | 1 |

| | |
|---|---|
| Hogg, R. M. 1937 (Celtic) | 1 |
| Holm, A. H. 1882 (Queen's Park) | 3 |
| Holt, D. D. 1963 (Hearts) | 5 |
| Holt, G. J. 2001 (Kilmarnock, Norwich C) | 10 |
| Holton, J. A. 1973 (Manchester U) | 15 |
| Hope, R. 1968 (WBA) | 2 |
| Hopkin, D. 1997 (Crystal Palace, Leeds U) | 7 |
| Houliston, W. 1949 (Queen of the South) | 3 |
| Houston, S. M. 1976 (Manchester U) | 1 |
| Howden, W. 1905 (Partick Th) | 1 |
| Howe, R. 1929 (Hamilton A) | 2 |
| Howie, H. 1949 (Hibernian) | 1 |
| Howie, J. 1905 (Newcastle U) | 3 |
| Howieson, J. 1927 (St Mirren) | 1 |
| Hughes, J. 1965 (Celtic) | 8 |
| Hughes, R. D. 2004 (Portsmouth) | 5 |
| Hughes, S. R. 2010 (Norwich C) | 1 |
| Hughes, W. 1975 (Sunderland) | 1 |
| Humphries, W. 1952 (Motherwell) | 1 |
| Hunter, A. 1972 (Kilmarnock, Celtic) | 4 |
| Hunter, J. 1909 (Dundee) | 1 |
| Hunter, J. 1874 (Third Lanark, Eastern, Third Lanark) | 4 |
| Hunter, J. 1960 (Motherwell) | 3 |
| Hunter, R. 1890 (St Mirren) | 1 |
| Husband, J. 1947 (Partick Th) | 1 |
| Hutchison, D. 1999 (Everton, Sunderland, West Ham U) | |
| | 26 |
| Hutchison, T. 1974 (Coventry C) | 17 |
| **Hutton, A. 2007 (Rangers, Tottenham H, Aston Villa) 32** | |
| Hutton, J. 1887 (St Bernards) | 1 |
| Hutton, J. 1923 (Aberdeen, Blackburn R) | 10 |
| Hyslop, T. 1896 (Stoke, Rangers) | 2 |
| | |
| Imlach, J. J. S. 1958 (Nottingham F) | 4 |
| Imrie, W. N. 1929 (St Johnstone) | 2 |
| Inglis, J. 1883 (Rangers) | 2 |
| Inglis, J. 1884 (Kilmarnock Ath) | 1 |
| Irons, J. H. 1900 (Queen's Park) | 1 |
| Irvine, B. 1991 (Aberdeen) | 9 |
| Iwelumo, C.R. 2009 (Wolverhampton W, Burnley) | 4 |
| | |
| Jackson, A. 1886 (Cambuslang) | 2 |
| Jackson, A. 1925 (Aberdeen, Huddersfield T) | 17 |
| Jackson, C. 1975 (Rangers) | 8 |
| Jackson, D. 1995 (Hibernian, Celtic) | 28 |
| Jackson, J. 1931 (Partick Th, Chelsea) | 8 |
| Jackson, T. A. 1904 (St Mirren) | 6 |
| James, A. W. 1926 (Preston NE, Arsenal) | 8 |
| Jardine, A. 1971 (Rangers) | 38 |
| Jarvie, A. 1971 (Airdrieonians) | 3 |
| Jenkinson, T. 1887 (Hearts) | 1 |
| Jess, E. 1993 (Aberdeen, Coventry C, Aberdeen) | 18 |
| Johnston, A. 1999 (Sunderland, Rangers, Middlesbrough) | 18 |
| Johnston, L. H. 1948 (Clyde) | 2 |
| Johnston, M. 1984 (Watford, Celtic, Nantes, Rangers) | 38 |
| Johnston, R. 1938 (Sunderland) | 1 |
| Johnston, W. 1966 (Rangers, WBA) | 22 |
| Johnstone, D. 1973 (Rangers) | 14 |
| Johnstone, J. 1888 (Abercorn) | 1 |
| Johnstone, J. 1965 (Celtic) | 23 |
| Johnstone, Jas 1894 (Kilmarnock) | 1 |
| Johnstone, J. A. 1930 (Hearts) | 3 |
| Johnstone, R. 1951 (Hibernian, Manchester C) | 17 |
| Johnstone, W. 1887 (Third Lanark) | 3 |
| Jordan, J. 1973 (Leeds U, Manchester U, AC Milan) | 52 |
| | |
| Kay, J. L. 1880 (Queen's Park) | 6 |
| Keillor, A. 1891 (Montrose, Dundee) | 6 |
| Keir, L. 1885 (Dumbarton) | 5 |
| Kelly, H. T. 1952 (Blackpool) | 1 |
| Kelly, J. 1888 (Renton, Celtic) | 8 |
| Kelly, J. C. 1949 (Barnsley) | 2 |
| **Kelly, L. M. 2013 (Kilmarnock)** | **1** |
| Kelso, R. 1885 (Renton, Dundee) | 7 |
| Kelso, T. 1914 (Dundee) | 1 |
| Kennaway, J. 1934 (Celtic) | 1 |
| Kennedy, A. 1875 (Eastern, Third Lanark) | 6 |
| Kennedy, J. 1897 (Hibernian) | 1 |
| Kennedy, J. 1964 (Celtic) | 6 |
| Kennedy, J. 2004 (Celtic) | 1 |
| Kennedy, S. 1905 (Partick Th) | 1 |

| | |
|---|---|
| Kennedy, S. 1975 (Rangers) | 5 |
| Kennedy, S. 1978 (Aberdeen) | 8 |
| Kenneth, G. 2011 (Dundee U) | 2 |
| Ker, G. 1880 (Queen's Park) | 5 |
| Ker, W. 1872 (Queen's Park) | 2 |
| Kerr, A. 1955 (Partick Th) | 2 |
| Kerr, B. 2003 (Newcastle U) | 3 |
| Kerr, P. 1924 (Hibernian) | 1 |
| Key, G. 1902 (Hearts) | 1 |
| Key, W. 1907 (Queen's Park) | 1 |
| King, A. 1896 (Hearts, Celtic) | 6 |
| King, J. 1933 (Hamilton A) | 2 |
| King, W. S. 1929 (Queen's Park) | 1 |
| Kinloch, J. D. 1922 (Partick Th) | 1 |
| Kinnaird, A. F. 1873 (Wanderers) | 1 |
| Kinnear, D. 1938 (Rangers) | 1 |
| Kyle, K. 2002 (Sunderland, Kilmarnock) | 10 |
| | |
| Lambert, P. 1995 (Motherwell, Borussia Dortmund, Celtic) | 40 |
| Lambie, J. A. 1886 (Queen's Park) | 3 |
| Lambie, W. A. 1892 (Queen's Park) | 9 |
| Lamont, W. 1885 (Pilgrims) | 1 |
| Lang, A. 1880 (Dumbarton) | 1 |
| Lang, J. J. 1876 (Clydesdale, Third Lanark) | 2 |
| Latta, A. 1888 (Dumbarton) | 2 |
| Law, D. 1959 (Huddersfield T, Manchester C, Torino, Manchester U, Manchester C) | 55 |
| Law, G. 1910 (Rangers) | 3 |
| Law, T. 1928 (Chelsea) | 2 |
| Lawrence, J. 1911 (Newcastle U) | 1 |
| Lawrence, T. 1963 (Liverpool) | 3 |
| Lawson, D. 1923 (St Mirren) | 1 |
| Leckie, R. 1872 (Queen's Park) | 1 |
| Leggat, G. 1956 (Aberdeen, Fulham) | 18 |
| Leighton, J. 1983 (Aberdeen, Manchester U, Hibernian, Aberdeen) | 91 |
| Lennie, W. 1908 (Aberdeen) | 2 |
| Lennox, R. 1967 (Celtic) | 10 |
| Leslie, L. G. 1961 (Airdrieonians) | 5 |
| Levein, C. 1990 (Hearts) | 16 |
| Liddell, W. 1947 (Liverpool) | 28 |
| Liddle, D. 1931 (East Fife) | 3 |
| Lindsay, D. 1903 (St Mirren) | 1 |
| Lindsay, J. 1880 (Dumbarton) | 8 |
| Lindsay, J. 1888 (Renton) | 3 |
| Linwood, A. B. 1950 (Clyde) | 1 |
| Little, R. J. 1953 (Rangers) | 1 |
| Livingstone, G. T. 1906 (Manchester C, Rangers) | 2 |
| Lochhead, A. 1889 (Third Lanark) | 1 |
| Logan, J. 1891 (Ayr) | 1 |
| Logan, T. 1913 (Falkirk) | 1 |
| Logie, J. T. 1953 (Arsenal) | 1 |
| Loney, W. 1910 (Celtic) | 2 |
| Long, H. 1947 (Clyde) | 1 |
| Longair, W. 1894 (Dundee) | 1 |
| Lorimer, P. 1970 (Leeds U) | 21 |
| Love, A. 1931 (Aberdeen) | 3 |
| Low, A. 1934 (Falkirk) | 1 |
| Low, J. 1891 (Cambuslang) | 1 |
| Low, T. P. 1897 (Rangers) | 1 |
| Low, W. L. 1911 (Newcastle U) | 5 |
| Lowe, J. 1887 (St Bernards) | 1 |
| Lundie, J. 1886 (Hibernian) | 1 |
| Lyall, J. 1905 (Sheffield W) | 1 |
| | |
| McAdam, J. 1880 (Third Lanark) | 1 |
| McAllister, B. 1997 (Wimbledon) | 3 |
| McAllister, G. 1990 (Leicester C, Leeds U, Coventry C) | 57 |
| McAllister, J. R. 2004 (Livingston) | 1 |
| Macari, L. 1972 (Celtic, Manchester U) | 24 |
| McArthur, D. 1895 (Celtic) | 3 |
| **McArthur, J. 2011 (Wigan Ath)** | **12** |
| McAtee, A. 1913 (Celtic) | 1 |
| McAulay, J. 1884 (Arthurlie) | 1 |
| McAulay, J. D. 1882 (Dumbarton) | 9 |
| McAulay, R. 1932 (Rangers) | 2 |
| Macauley, A. R. 1947 (Brentford, Arsenal) | 7 |
| McAvennie, F. 1986 (West Ham U, Celtic) | 5 |
| McBain, E. 1894 (St Mirren) | 1 |
| McBain, N. 1922 (Manchester U, Everton) | 3 |

| | |
|---|---|
| McBride, J. 1967 (Celtic) | 2 |
| McBride, P. 1904 (Preston NE) | 6 |
| McCall, A. 1888 (Renton) | 1 |
| McCall, A. S. M. 1990 (Everton, Rangers) | 40 |
| McCall, J. 1886 (Renton) | 5 |
| McCalliog, J. 1967 (Sheffield W, Wolverhampton W) | 5 |
| McCallum, N. 1888 (Renton) | 1 |
| McCann, N. 1999 (Hearts, Rangers, Southampton) | 26 |
| McCann, R. J. 1959 (Motherwell) | 5 |
| McCartney, W. 1902 (Hibernian) | 1 |
| McClair, B. 1987 (Celtic, Manchester U) | 30 |
| McClory, A. 1927 (Motherwell) | 3 |
| McCloy, P. 1924 (Ayr U) | 2 |
| McCloy, P. 1973 (Rangers) | 4 |
| McCoist, A. 1986 (Rangers, Kilmarnock) | 61 |
| McColl, I. M. 1950 (Rangers) | 14 |
| McColl, R. S. 1896 (Queen's Park, Newcastle U, Queen's Park) | 13 |
| McColl, W. 1895 (Renton) | 1 |
| McCombie, A. 1903 (Sunderland, Newcastle U) | 4 |
| McCorkindale, J. 1891 (Partick Th) | 1 |
| McCormack, R. 2008 (Motherwell, Cardiff C, Leeds U) | 8 |
| McCormick, R. 1886 (Abercorn) | 1 |
| McCrae, D. 1929 (St Mirren) | 2 |
| McCreadie, A. 1893 (Rangers) | 2 |
| McCreadie, E. G. 1965 (Chelsea) | 23 |
| McCulloch, D. 1935 (Hearts, Brentford, Derby Co) | 7 |
| McCulloch, L. 2005 (Wigan Ath, Rangers) | 18 |
| MacDonald, A. 1976 (Rangers) | 1 |
| McDonald, J. 1886 (Edinburgh University) | 1 |
| McDonald, J. 1956 (Sunderland) | 2 |
| MacDougall, E. J. 1975 (Norwich C) | 7 |
| McDougall, J. 1877 (Vale of Leven) | 5 |
| McDougall, J. 1926 (Airdrieonians) | 1 |
| McDougall, J. 1931 (Liverpool) | 2 |
| McEveley, J. 2008 (Derby Co) | 3 |
| McFadden, J. 2002 (Motherwell, Everton, Birmingham C) | 48 |
| McFadyen, W. 1934 (Motherwell) | 2 |
| Macfarlane, A. 1904 (Dundee) | 5 |
| Macfarlane, W. 1947 (Hearts) | 1 |
| McFarlane, R. 1896 (Greenock Morton) | 1 |
| McGarr, E. 1970 (Aberdeen) | 2 |
| McGarvey, F. P. 1979 (Liverpool, Celtic) | 7 |
| McGeoch, A. 1876 (Dumbreck) | 4 |
| McGhee, J. 1886 (Hibernian) | 1 |
| McGhee, M. 1983 (Aberdeen) | 4 |
| McGinlay, J. 1994 (Bolton W) | 13 |
| McGonagle, W. 1933 (Celtic) | 6 |
| McGrain, D. 1973 (Celtic) | 62 |
| **McGregor, A. 2007 (Rangers, Besiktas)** | **29** |
| McGregor, J. C. 1877 (Vale of Leven) | 4 |
| McGrory, J. 1928 (Celtic) | 7 |
| McGrory, J. E. 1965 (Kilmarnock) | 3 |
| McGuire, W. 1881 (Beith) | 2 |
| McGurk, F. 1934 (Birmingham) | 1 |
| McHardy, H. 1885 (Rangers) | 1 |
| McInally, A. 1989 (Aston Villa, Bayern Munich) | 8 |
| McInally, J. 1987 (Dundee U) | 10 |
| McInally, T. B. 1926 (Celtic) | 2 |
| McInnes, D. 2003 (WBA) | 2 |
| McInnes, T. 1889 (Cowlairs) | 1 |
| McIntosh, W. 1905 (Third Lanark) | 1 |
| McIntyre, A. 1878 (Vale of Leven) | 2 |
| McIntyre, H. 1880 (Rangers) | 1 |
| McIntyre, J. 1884 (Rangers) | 1 |
| MacKay, D. 1959 (Celtic) | 14 |
| Mackay, D. C. 1957 (Hearts, Tottenham H) | 22 |
| Mackay, G. 1988 (Hearts) | 4 |
| Mackay, M. 2004 (Norwich C) | 5 |
| McKay, J. 1924 (Blackburn R) | 1 |
| McKay, R. 1928 (Newcastle U) | 1 |
| McKean, R. 1976 (Rangers) | 1 |
| McKenzie, D. 1938 (Brentford) | 1 |
| Mackenzie, J. A. 1954 (Partick Th) | 9 |
| McKeown, M. 1889 (Celtic) | 2 |
| McKie, J. 1898 (East Stirling) | 1 |
| McKillop, T. R. 1938 (Rangers) | 1 |
| McKimmie, S. 1989 (Aberdeen) | 40 |
| McKinlay, D. 1922 (Liverpool) | 2 |
| McKinlay, T. 1996 (Celtic) | 22 |
| McKinlay, W. 1994 (Dundee U, Blackburn R) | 29 |

| | |
|---|---|
| McKinnon, A. 1874 (Queen's Park) | 1 |
| McKinnon, R. 1966 (Rangers) | 28 |
| McKinnon, R. 1994 (Motherwell) | 3 |
| MacKinnon, W. 1883 (Dumbarton) | 4 |
| MacKinnon, W. W. 1872 (Queen's Park) | 9 |
| McLaren, A. 1929 (St Johnstone) | 5 |
| McLaren, A. 1947 (Preston NE) | 4 |
| McLaren, A. 1992 (Hearts, Rangers) | 24 |
| McLaren, A. 2001 (Kilmarnock) | 1 |
| McLaren, J. 1888 (Hibernian, Celtic) | 3 |
| McLean, A. 1926 (Celtic) | 4 |
| McLean, D. 1896 (St Bernards) | 2 |
| McLean, D. 1912 (Sheffield W) | 1 |
| McLean, G. 1968 (Dundee) | 1 |
| McLean, T. 1969 (Kilmarnock) | 6 |
| McLeish, A. 1980 (Aberdeen) | 77 |
| McLeod, D. 1905 (Celtic) | 4 |
| McLeod, J. 1888 (Dumbarton) | 5 |
| MacLeod, J. M. 1961 (Hibernian) | 4 |
| MacLeod, M. 1985 (Celtic, Borussia Dortmund, Hibernian) | 20 |
| McLeod, W. 1886 (Cowlairs) | 1 |
| McLintock, A. 1875 (Vale of Leven) | 3 |
| McLintock, F. 1963 (Leicester C, Arsenal) | 9 |
| McLuckie, J. S. 1934 (Manchester C) | 1 |
| McMahon, A. 1892 (Celtic) | 6 |
| McManus, S. 2007 (Celtic, Middlesbrough) | 26 |
| McMenemy, J. 1905 (Celtic) | 12 |
| McMenemy, J. 1934 (Motherwell) | 1 |
| McMillan, I. L. 1952 (Airdrieonians, Rangers) | 6 |
| McMillan, J. 1897 (St Bernards) | 1 |
| McMillan, T. 1887 (Dumbarton) | 1 |
| McMullan, J. 1920 (Partick Th, Manchester C) | 16 |
| McNab, A. 1921 (Morton) | 2 |
| McNab, A. 1937 (Sunderland, WBA) | 2 |
| McNab, C. D. 1931 (Dundee) | 6 |
| McNab, J. S. 1923 (Liverpool) | 1 |
| McNair, A. 1906 (Celtic) | 15 |
| McNamara, J. 1997 (Celtic, Wolverhampton W) | 33 |
| McNamee, D. 2004 (Livingston) | 4 |
| McNaught, W. 1951 (Raith R) | 5 |
| McNaughton, K. 2002 (Aberdeen, Cardiff C) | 4 |
| McNeill, W. 1961 (Celtic) | 29 |
| McNiel, H. 1874 (Queen's Park) | 10 |
| McNiel, M. 1876 (Rangers) | 2 |
| McPhail, J. 1950 (Celtic) | 5 |
| McPhail, R. 1927 (Airdrieonians, Rangers) | 17 |
| McPherson, D. 1892 (Kilmarnock) | 1 |
| McPherson, D. 1989 (Hearts, Rangers) | 27 |
| McPherson, J. 1875 (Clydesdale) | 1 |
| McPherson, J. 1879 (Vale of Leven) | 8 |
| McPherson, J. 1888 (Kilmarnock, Cowlairs, Rangers) | 9 |
| McPherson, J. 1891 (Hearts) | 1 |
| McPherson, R. 1882 (Arthurlie) | 1 |
| McQueen, G. 1974 (Leeds U, Manchester U) | 30 |
| McQueen, M. 1890 (Leith Ath) | 2 |
| McRorie, D. M. 1931 (Morton) | 1 |
| McSpadyen, A. 1939 (Partick Th) | 2 |
| McStay, P. 1984 (Celtic) | 76 |
| McStay, W. 1921 (Celtic) | 13 |
| McSwegan, G. 2000 (Hearts) | 2 |
| McTavish, J. 1910 (Falkirk) | 1 |
| McWattie, G. C. 1901 (Queen's Park) | 2 |
| McWilliam, P. 1905 (Newcastle U) | 8 |
| Mackail-Smith, C. 2011 (Peterborough U, Brighton & HA) | 7 |
| **Mackie, J. C. 2011 (QPR)** | **9** |
| Madden, J. 1893 (Celtic) | 2 |
| Maguire, C. 2011 (Aberdeen) | 2 |
| Main, F. R. 1938 (Rangers) | 1 |
| Main, J. 1909 (Hibernian) | 1 |
| Maley, W. 1893 (Celtic) | 2 |
| **Maloney, S. R. 2006 (Celtic, Aston Villa, Celtic, Wigan Ath)** | **28** |
| Malpas, M. 1984 (Dundee U) | 55 |
| **Marshall, D. J. 2005 (Celtic, Cardiff C)** | **6** |
| Marshall, G. 1992 (Celtic) | 1 |
| Marshall, H. 1899 (Celtic) | 2 |
| Marshall, J. 1885 (Third Lanark) | 4 |
| Marshall, J. 1921 (Middlesbrough, Llanelly) | 7 |
| Marshall, J. 1932 (Rangers) | 3 |
| Marshall, R. W. 1892 (Rangers) | 2 |

| | |
|---|---|
| Martin, B. 1995 (Motherwell) | 2 |
| Martin, F. 1954 (Aberdeen) | 6 |
| Martin, N. 1965 (Hibernian, Sunderland) | 3 |
| **Martin, R. K. A. 2011 (Norwich C)** | **5** |
| Martis, J. 1961 (Motherwell) | 1 |
| Mason, J. 1949 (Third Lanark) | 7 |
| Massie, A. 1932 (Hearts, Aston Villa) | 18 |
| Masson, D. S. 1976 (QPR, Derby Co) | 17 |
| Mathers, D. 1954 (Partick Th) | 1 |
| Matteo, D. 2001 (Leeds U) | 6 |
| Maxwell, W. S. 1898 (Stoke C) | 1 |
| May, J. 1906 (Rangers) | 5 |
| Meechan, P. 1896 (Celtic) | 1 |
| Meiklejohn, D. D. 1922 (Rangers) | 15 |
| Menzies, A. 1906 (Hearts) | 3 |
| Mercer, R. 1912 (Hearts) | 2 |
| Middleton, R. 1930 (Cowdenbeath) | 1 |
| Millar, J. 1897 (Rangers) | 3 |
| Millar, J. 1963 (Rangers) | 2 |
| Miller, A. 1939 (Hearts) | 1 |
| Miller, C. 2001 (Dundee U) | 1 |
| Miller, J. 1931 (St Mirren) | 5 |
| **Miller, K. 2001 (Rangers, Wolverhampton W, Celtic, Derby Co, Rangers, Bursa, Cardiff C, Vancouver Whitecaps)** | **67** |
| Miller, L. 2006 (Dundee U, Aberdeen) | 3 |
| Miller, P. 1882 (Dumbarton) | 3 |
| Miller, T. 1920 (Liverpool, Manchester U) | 3 |
| Miller, W. 1876 (Third Lanark) | 1 |
| Miller, W. 1947 (Celtic) | 6 |
| Miller, W. 1975 (Aberdeen) | 65 |
| Mills, W. 1936 (Aberdeen) | 3 |
| Milne, J. V. 1938 (Middlesbrough) | 2 |
| Mitchell, D. 1890 (Rangers) | 5 |
| Mitchell, J. 1908 (Kilmarnock) | 3 |
| Mitchell, R. C. 1951 (Newcastle U) | 2 |
| Mochan, N. 1954 (Celtic) | 3 |
| Moir, W. 1950 (Bolton W) | 1 |
| Moncur, R. 1968 (Newcastle U) | 16 |
| Morgan, H. 1898 (St Mirren, Liverpool) | 2 |
| Morgan, W. 1968 (Burnley, Manchester U) | 21 |
| Morris, D. 1923 (Raith R) | 6 |
| Morris, H. 1950 (East Fife) | 1 |
| **Morrison, J. C. 2008 (WBA)** | **27** |
| Morrison, T. 1927 (St Mirren) | 1 |
| Morton, A. L. 1920 (Queen's Park, Rangers) | 31 |
| Morton, H. A. 1929 (Kilmarnock) | 2 |
| Mudie, J. K. 1957 (Blackpool) | 17 |
| Muir, W. 1907 (Dundee) | 1 |
| Muirhead, T. A. 1922 (Rangers) | 8 |
| **Mulgrew, C. 2012 (Celtic)** | **6** |
| Mulhall, G. 1960 (Aberdeen, Sunderland) | 3 |
| Munro, A. D. 1937 (Hearts, Blackpool) | 3 |
| Munro, F. M. 1971 (Wolverhampton W) | 9 |
| Munro, I. 1979 (St Mirren) | 7 |
| Munro, N. 1888 (Abercorn) | 2 |
| Murdoch, J. 1931 (Motherwell) | 1 |
| Murdoch, R. 1966 (Celtic) | 12 |
| Murphy, F. 1938 (Celtic) | 1 |
| Murray, I. 2003 (Hibernian, Rangers) | 6 |
| Murray, J. 1895 (Renton) | 1 |
| Murray, J. 1958 (Hearts) | 5 |
| Murray, J. W. 1890 (Vale of Leven) | 1 |
| Murray, P. 1896 (Hibernian) | 2 |
| Murray, S. 1972 (Aberdeen) | 1 |
| Murty, G. S. 2004 (Reading) | 4 |
| Mutch, G. 1938 (Preston NE) | 1 |
| | |
| **Naismith, S. J. 2007 (Kilmarnock, Rangers, Everton)** | **22** |
| Napier, C. E. 1932 (Celtic, Derby Co) | 5 |
| Narey, D. 1977 (Dundee U) | 35 |
| Naysmith, G. A. 2000 (Hearts, Everton, Sheffield U) | 46 |
| Neil, R. G. 1896 (Hibernian, Rangers) | 2 |
| Neill, R. W. 1876 (Queen's Park) | 5 |
| Neilson, R. 2007 (Hearts) | 1 |
| Nellies, P. 1913 (Hearts) | 2 |
| Nelson, J. 1925 (Cardiff C) | 4 |
| Nevin, P. K. F. 1986 (Chelsea, Everton, Tranmere R) | 28 |
| Niblo, T. D. 1904 (Aston Villa) | 1 |
| Nibloe, J. 1929 (Kilmarnock) | 11 |
| Nicholas, C. 1983 (Celtic, Arsenal, Aberdeen) | 20 |
| Nicholson, B. 2001 (Dunfermline Ath) | 3 |

| | |
|---|---|
| Nicol, S. 1985 (Liverpool) | 27 |
| Nisbet, J. 1929 (Ayr U) | 3 |
| Niven, J. B. 1885 (Moffat) | 1 |
| | |
| O'Connor, G. 2002 (Hibernian, Lokomotiv Moscow, Birmingham C) | 16 |
| O'Donnell, F. 1937 (Preston NE, Blackpool) | 6 |
| O'Donnell, P. 1994 (Motherwell) | 1 |
| Ogilvie, D. H. 1934 (Motherwell) | 1 |
| O'Hare, J. 1970 (Derby Co) | 13 |
| O'Neil, B. 1996 (Celtic, Wolfsburg, Derby Co, Preston NE) | 7 |
| O'Neil, J. 2001 (Hibernian) | 1 |
| Ormond, W. E. 1954 (Hibernian) | 6 |
| O'Rourke, F. 1907 (Airdrieonians) | 1 |
| Orr, J. 1892 (Kilmarnock) | 1 |
| Orr, R. 1902 (Newcastle U) | 2 |
| Orr, T. 1952 (Morton) | 2 |
| Orr, W. 1900 (Celtic) | 3 |
| Orrock, R. 1913 (Falkirk) | 1 |
| Oswald, J. 1889 (Third Lanark, St Bernards, Rangers) | 3 |
| | |
| Parker, A. H. 1955 (Falkirk, Everton) | 15 |
| Parlane, D. 1973 (Rangers) | 12 |
| Parlane, R. 1878 (Vale of Leven) | 3 |
| Paterson, G. D. 1939 (Celtic) | 1 |
| Paterson, J. 1920 (Leicester C) | 1 |
| Paterson, J. 1931 (Cowdenbeath) | 3 |
| Paton, A. 1952 (Motherwell) | 2 |
| Paton, D. 1896 (St Bernards) | 1 |
| Paton, M. 1883 (Dumbarton) | 5 |
| Paton, R. 1879 (Vale of Leven) | 2 |
| Patrick, J. 1897 (St Mirren) | 2 |
| Paul, H. McD. 1909 (Queen's Park) | 3 |
| Paul, W. 1888 (Partick Th) | 3 |
| Paul, W. 1891 (Dykebar) | 1 |
| Pearson, S. P. 2004 (Motherwell, Celtic, Derby Co) | 10 |
| Pearson, T. 1947 (Newcastle U) | 2 |
| Penman, A. 1966 (Dundee) | 1 |
| Pettigrew, W. 1976 (Motherwell) | 5 |
| Phillips, J. 1877 (Queen's Park) | 3 |
| **Phillips, M. 2012 (Blackpool)** | **2** |
| Plenderleith, J. B. 1961 (Manchester C) | 1 |
| Porteous, W. 1903 (Hearts) | 1 |
| Pressley, S. J. 2000 (Hearts) | 32 |
| Pringle, C. 1921 (St Mirren) | 1 |
| Provan, D. 1964 (Rangers) | 5 |
| Provan, D. 1980 (Celtic) | 10 |
| Pursell, P. 1914 (Queen's Park) | 1 |
| | |
| Quashie, N. F. 2004 (Portsmouth, Southampton, WBA) | 14 |
| Quinn, J. 1905 (Celtic) | 11 |
| Quinn, P. 1961 (Motherwell) | 4 |
| | |
| Rae, G. 2001 (Dundee, Rangers, Cardiff C) | 14 |
| Rae, J. 1889 (Third Lanark) | 2 |
| Raeside, J. S. 1906 (Third Lanark) | 1 |
| Raisbeck, A. G. 1900 (Liverpool) | 8 |
| Rankin, G. 1890 (Vale of Leven) | 2 |
| Rankin, R. 1929 (St Mirren) | 3 |
| Redpath, W. 1949 (Motherwell) | 9 |
| Reid, J. G. 1914 (Airdrieonians) | 3 |
| Reid, R. 1938 (Brentford) | 2 |
| Reid, W. 1911 (Rangers) | 9 |
| Reilly, L. 1949 (Hibernian) | 38 |
| Rennie, H. G. 1900 (Hearts, Hibernian) | 13 |
| Renny-Tailyour, H. W. 1873 (Royal Engineers) | 1 |
| Rhind, A. 1872 (Queen's Park) | 1 |
| **Rhodes, J. L. 2012 (Huddersfield T, Blackburn R)** | **9** |
| Richmond, A. 1906 (Queen's Park) | 1 |
| Richmond, J. T. 1877 (Clydesdale, Queen's Park) | 3 |
| Ring, T. 1953 (Clyde) | 12 |
| Rioch, B. D. 1975 (Derby Co, Everton, Derby Co) | 24 |
| Riordan, D. G. 2006 (Hibernian) | 3 |
| Ritchie, A. 1891 (East Stirlingshire) | 1 |
| Ritchie, H. 1923 (Hibernian) | 2 |
| Ritchie, J. 1897 (Queen's Park) | 1 |
| Ritchie, P. S. 1999 (Hearts, Bolton W, Walsall) | 7 |
| Ritchie, W. 1962 (Rangers) | 1 |
| Robb, D. T. 1971 (Aberdeen) | 5 |
| Robb, W. 1926 (Rangers, Hibernian) | 2 |

| | |
|---|---|
| Robertson, A. 1955 (Clyde) | 5 |
| Robertson, D. 1992 (Rangers) | 3 |
| Robertson, G. 1910 (Motherwell, Sheffield W) | 4 |
| Robertson, G. 1938 (Kilmarnock) | 1 |
| Robertson, H. 1962 (Dundee) | 1 |
| Robertson, J. 1931 (Dundee) | 2 |
| Robertson, J. 1991 (Hearts) | 16 |
| Robertson, J. N. 1978 (Nottingham F, Derby Co) | 28 |
| Robertson, J. G. 1965 (Tottenham H) | 1 |
| Robertson, J. T. 1898 (Everton, Southampton, Rangers) | |
| | 16 |
| Robertson, P. 1903 (Dundee) | 1 |
| Robertson, S. 2009 (Dundee U) | 2 |
| Robertson, T. 1889 (Queen's Park) | 4 |
| Robertson, T. 1898 (Hearts) | 1 |
| Robertson, W. 1887 (Dumbarton) | 2 |
| Robinson, R. 1974 (Dundee) | 4 |
| Robson, B. G. G. 2008 (Dundee U, Celtic, Middlesbrough) | 17 |
| Ross, M. 2002 (Rangers) | 13 |
| Rough, A. 1976 (Partick Th, Hibernian) | 53 |
| Rougvie, D. 1984 (Aberdeen) | 1 |
| Rowan, A. 1880 (Caledonian, Queen's Park) | 2 |
| Russell, D. 1895 (Hearts, Celtic) | 6 |
| Russell, J. 1890 (Cambuslang) | 1 |
| Russell, W. F. 1924 (Airdrieonians) | 2 |
| Rutherford, E. 1948 (Rangers) | 1 |
| | |
| St John, I. 1959 (Motherwell, Liverpool) | 21 |
| Saunders, S. 2011 (Motherwell) | 1 |
| Sawers, W. 1895 (Dundee) | 1 |
| Scarff, P. 1931 (Celtic) | 1 |
| Schaedler, E. 1974 (Hibernian) | 1 |
| Scott, A. S. 1957 (Rangers, Everton) | 16 |
| Scott, J. 1966 (Hibernian) | 1 |
| Scott, J. 1971 (Dundee) | 2 |
| Scott, M. 1898 (Airdrieonians) | 1 |
| Scott, R. 1894 (Airdrieonians) | 1 |
| Scoular, J. 1951 (Portsmouth) | 9 |
| Sellar, W. 1885 (Battlefield, Queen's Park) | 9 |
| Semple, W. 1886 (Cambuslang) | 1 |
| Severin, S. D. 2002 (Hearts, Aberdeen) | 15 |
| Shankly, W. 1938 (Preston NE) | 5 |
| Sharp, G. M. 1985 (Everton) | 12 |
| Sharp, J. 1904 (Dundee, Woolwich Arsenal, Fulham) | 5 |
| Shaw, D. 1947 (Hibernian) | 8 |
| Shaw, F. W. 1884 (Pollokshields Ath) | 2 |
| Shaw, J. 1947 (Rangers) | 4 |
| Shearer, D. 1994 (Aberdeen) | 7 |
| Shearer, R. 1961 (Rangers) | 4 |
| **Shinnie, A. M. 2013 (Inverness CT)** | **1** |
| Sillars, D. C. 1891 (Queen's Park) | 5 |
| Simpson, J. 1895 (Third Lanark) | 3 |
| Simpson, J. 1935 (Rangers) | 14 |
| Simpson, N. 1983 (Aberdeen) | 5 |
| Simpson, R. C. 1967 (Celtic) | 5 |
| Sinclair, G. L. 1910 (Hearts) | 3 |
| Sinclair, J. W. E. 1966 (Leicester C) | 1 |
| Skene, L. H. 1904 (Queen's Park) | 1 |
| Sloan, T. 1904 (Third Lanark) | 1 |
| Smellie, R. 1887 (Queen's Park) | 6 |
| Smith, A. 1898 (Rangers) | 20 |
| Smith, D. 1966 (Aberdeen, Rangers) | 2 |
| Smith, G. 1947 (Hibernian) | 18 |
| Smith, H. G. 1988 (Hearts) | 3 |
| Smith, J. 1924 (Ayr U) | 1 |
| Smith, J. 1935 (Rangers) | 2 |
| Smith, J. 1968 (Aberdeen, Newcastle U) | 4 |
| Smith, J. 2003 (Celtic) | 2 |
| Smith, J. E. 1959 (Celtic) | 2 |
| Smith, Jas 1872 (Queen's Park) | 1 |
| Smith, John 1877 (Mauchline, Edinburgh University, Queen's Park) | 10 |
| Smith, N. 1897 (Rangers) | 12 |
| Smith, R. 1872 (Queen's Park) | 2 |
| Smith, T. M. 1934 (Kilmarnock, Preston NE) | 2 |
| **Snodgrass, R. 2011 (Leeds U, Norwich C)** | **10** |
| Somers, P. 1905 (Celtic) | 4 |
| Somers, W. S. 1879 (Third Lanark, Queen's Park) | 3 |
| Somerville, G. 1886 (Queen's Park) | 1 |
| Souness, G. J. 1975 (Middlesbrough, Liverpool, Sampdoria) | 54 |

| | |
|---|---|
| Speedie, D. R. 1985 (Chelsea, Coventry C) | 10 |
| Speedie, F. 1903 (Rangers) | 3 |
| Speirs, J. H. 1908 (Rangers) | 1 |
| Spencer, J. 1995 (Chelsea, QPR) | 14 |
| Stanton, P. 1966 (Hibernian) | 16 |
| Stark, J. 1909 (Rangers) | 2 |
| Steel, W. 1947 (Morton, Derby Co, Dundee) | 30 |
| Steele, D. M. 1923 (Huddersfield) | 3 |
| Stein, C. 1969 (Rangers, Coventry C) | 21 |
| Stephen, J. F. 1947 (Bradford) | 2 |
| Stevenson, G. 1928 (Motherwell) | 12 |
| Stewart, A. 1888 (Queen's Park) | 2 |
| Stewart, A. 1894 (Third Lanark) | 1 |
| Stewart, D. 1888 (Dumbarton) | 1 |
| Stewart, D. 1893 (Queen's Park) | 3 |
| Stewart, D. S. 1978 (Leeds U) | 1 |
| Stewart, G. 1906 (Hibernian, Manchester C) | 4 |
| Stewart, J. 1977 (Kilmarnock, Middlesbrough) | 2 |
| Stewart, M. J. 2002 (Manchester U, Hearts) | 4 |
| Stewart, R. 1981 (West Ham U) | 10 |
| Stewart, W. G. 1898 (Queen's Park) | 2 |
| Stockdale, R. K. 2002 (Middlesbrough) | 5 |
| Storrier, D. 1899 (Celtic) | 3 |
| Strachan, G. D. 1980 (Aberdeen, Manchester U, Leeds U) | 50 |
| Sturrock, P. 1981 (Dundee U) | 20 |
| Sullivan, N. 1997 (Wimbledon, Tottenham H) | 28 |
| Summers, W. 1926 (St Mirren) | 1 |
| Symon, J. S. 1939 (Rangers) | 1 |
| | |
| Tait, T. S. 1911 (Sunderland) | 1 |
| Taylor, J. 1872 (Queen's Park) | 6 |
| Taylor, J. D. 1892 (Dumbarton, St Mirren) | 4 |
| Taylor, W. 1892 (Hearts) | 1 |
| Teale, G. 2006 (Wigan Ath, Derby Co) | 13 |
| Telfer, P. N. 2000 (Coventry C) | 1 |
| Telfer, W. 1933 (Motherwell) | 2 |
| Telfer, W. D. 1954 (St Mirren) | 1 |
| Templeton, R. 1902 (Aston Villa, Newcastle U, Woolwich Arsenal, Kilmarnock) | 11 |
| Thompson, S. 2002 (Dundee U, Rangers) | 16 |
| Thomson, A. 1886 (Arthurlie) | 1 |
| Thomson, A. 1889 (Third Lanark) | 1 |
| Thomson, A. 1909 (Airdrieonians) | 1 |
| Thomson, A. 1926 (Celtic) | 3 |
| Thomson, C. 1904 (Hearts, Sunderland) | 21 |
| Thomson, C. 1937 (Sunderland) | 1 |
| Thomson, D. 1920 (Dundee) | 1 |
| Thomson, J. 1930 (Celtic) | 4 |
| Thomson, J. J. 1872 (Queen's Park) | 3 |
| Thomson, J. R. 1933 (Everton) | 1 |
| Thomson, K. 2009 (Rangers, Middlesbrough) | 3 |
| Thomson, R. 1932 (Celtic) | 1 |
| Thomson, R. W. 1927 (Falkirk) | 1 |
| Thomson, S. 1884 (Rangers) | 2 |
| Thomson, W. 1892 (Dumbarton) | 4 |
| Thomson, W. 1896 (Dundee) | 1 |
| Thomson, W. 1980 (St Mirren) | 7 |
| Thornton, W. 1947 (Rangers) | 7 |
| Toner, W. 1959 (Kilmarnock) | 2 |
| Townsley, T. 1926 (Falkirk) | 1 |
| Troup, A. 1920 (Dundee, Everton) | 5 |
| Turnbull, E. 1948 (Hibernian) | 8 |
| Turner, T. 1884 (Arthurlie) | 1 |
| Turner, W. 1885 (Pollokshields Ath) | 2 |
| | |
| Ure, J. F. 1962 (Dundee, Arsenal) | 11 |
| Urquhart, D. 1934 (Hibernian) | 1 |
| | |
| Vallance, T. 1877 (Rangers) | 7 |
| Venters, A. 1934 (Cowdenbeath, Rangers) | 3 |
| | |
| Waddell, T. S. 1891 (Queen's Park) | 6 |
| Waddell, W. 1947 (Rangers) | 17 |
| Wales, H. M. 1933 (Motherwell) | 1 |
| Walker, A. 1988 (Celtic) | 3 |
| Walker, F. 1922 (Third Lanark) | 1 |
| Walker, G. 1930 (St Mirren) | 4 |
| Walker, J. 1895 (Hearts, Rangers) | 5 |
| Walker, J. 1911 (Swindon T) | 9 |
| Walker, J. N. 1993 (Hearts, Partick Th) | 2 |
| Walker, R. 1900 (Hearts) | 29 |

## WALES

Keenor, F. C. 1920 (Cardiff C, Crewe Alex) 32
Kelly, F. C. 1899 (Wrexham, Druids) 3
Kelsey, A. J. 1954 (Arsenal) 41
Kenrick, S. L. 1876 (Druids, Oswestry,
Shropshire Wanderers) 5
Ketley, C. F. 1882 (Druids) 1
**King, A. 2009 (Leicester C)** **18**
King, J. 1955 (Swansea T) 1
Kinsey, N. 1951 (Norwich C, Birmingham C) 7
Knill, A. R. 1989 (Swansea C) 1
Koumas, J. 2001 (Tranmere R, WBA, Wigan Ath) 34
Krzywicki, R. L. 1970 (WBA, Huddersfield T) 8

Lambert, R. 1947 (Liverpool) 5
Latham, G. 1905 (Liverpool, Southport Central,
Cardiff C) 10
Law, B. J. 1990 (QPR) 1
Lawrence, E. 1930 (Clapton Orient, Notts Co) 3
Lawrence, S. 1932 (Swansea T) 8
Lea, A. 1889 (Wrexham) 4
Lea, C. 1965 (Ipswich T) 2
Leary, P. 1889 (Bangor) 1
**Ledley, J. C. 2006 (Cardiff C, Celtic)** **46**
Leek, K. 1961 (Leicester C, Newcastle U, Birmingham C,
Northampton T) 13
Legg, A. 1996 (Birmingham C, Cardiff C) 6
Lever, A. R. 1953 (Leicester C) 1
Lewis, B. 1891 (Chester, Wrexham, Middlesbrough,
Wrexham) 10
Lewis, D. 1927 (Arsenal) 3
Lewis, D. 1983 (Swansea C) 1
Lewis, D. J. 1933 (Swansea T) 2
Lewis, D. M. 1890 (Bangor) 2
Lewis, J. 1906 (Bristol R) 1
Lewis, J. 1926 (Cardiff C) 1
Lewis, T. 1881 (Wrexham) 2
Lewis, W. 1885 (Bangor, Crewe Alex, Chester,
Manchester C, Chester) 27
Lewis, W. L. 1927 (Swansea T, Huddersfield T) 6
Llewellyn, C. M. 1998 (Norwich C, Wrexham) 6
Lloyd, B. W. 1976 (Wrexham) 3
Lloyd, J. W. 1879 (Wrexham, Newtown) 2
Lloyd, R. A. 1891 (Ruthin) 2
Lockley, A. 1898 (Chirk) 1
Lovell, S. 1982 (Crystal Palace, Millwall) 6
Lowndes, S. R. 1983 (Newport Co, Millwall, Barnsley) 10
Lowrie, G. 1948 (Coventry C, Newcastle U) 4
Lucas, P. M. 1962 (Leyton Orient) 4
Lucas, W. H. 1949 (Swansea T) 7
Lumberg, A. 1929 (Wrexham, Wolverhampton W) 4
**Lynch, J. J. 2013 (Huddersfield T)** **1**

MacDonald, S. B. 2011 (Swansea C) 1
McCarthy, T. P. 1889 (Wrexham) 1
McMillan, R. 1881 (Shrewsbury Engineers) 2
Maguire, G. T. 1990 (Portsmouth) 7
Mahoney, J. F. 1968 (Stoke C, Middlesbrough,
Swansea C) 51
Mardon, P. J. 1996 (WBA) 1
Margetson, M. W. 2004 (Cardiff C) 1
Marriott, A. 1996 (Wrexham) 5
Martin, T. J. 1930 (Newport Co) 1
Marustik, C. 1982 (Swansea C) 6
Mates, J. 1891 (Chirk) 3
**Matthews, A. J. 2011 (Cardiff C, Celtic)** **10**
Matthews, R. W. 1921 (Liverpool, Bristol C,
Bradford) 3
Matthews, W. 1905 (Chester) 2
Matthias, J. S. 1896 (Brymbo, Shrewsbury T,
Wolverhampton W) 5
Matthias, J. T. 1914 (Wrexham) 12
Mays, A. W. 1929 (Wrexham) 1
Medwin, T. C. 1953 (Swansea T, Tottenham H) 30
Melville, A. K. 1990 (Swansea C, Oxford U, Sunderland,
Fulham, West Ham U) 65
Meredith, S. 1900 (Chirk, Stoke, Leyton) 3
Meredith, W. H. 1895 (Manchester C, Manchester U) 48
Mielczarek, R. 1971 (Rotherham U) 1
Millership, H. 1920 (Rotherham Co) 6
Millington, A. H. 1963 (WBA, Crystal Palace,
Peterborough U, Swansea C) 21
Mills, T. J. 1934 (Clapton Orient, Leicester C) 4

Mills-Roberts, R. H. 1885 (St Thomas' Hospital,
Preston NE, Llanberis) 8
Moore, G. 1960 (Cardiff C, Chelsea, Manchester U,
Northampton T, Charlton Ath) 21
Morgan, C. 2007 (Milton Keynes D, Peterborough U,
Preston NE) 23
Morgan, J. R. 1877 (Cambridge University,
Derby School Staff) 10
Morgan, J. T. 1905 (Wrexham) 1
Morgan-Owen, H. 1902 (Oxford University, Corinthians)
4
Morgan-Owen, M. M. 1897 (Oxford University,
Corinthians) 13
**Morison, S. W. 2011 (Millwall, Norwich C)** **20**
Morley, E. J. 1925 (Swansea T, Clapton Orient) 4
Morris, A. G. 1896 (Aberystwyth, Swindon T,
Nottingham F) 21
Morris, C. 1900 (Chirk, Derby Co, Huddersfield T) 27
Morris, E. 1893 (Chirk) 3
Morris, H. 1894 (Sheffield U, Manchester C, Grimsby T)
3
Morris, J. 1887 (Oswestry) 1
Morris, J. 1898 (Chirk) 1
Morris, R. 1900 (Chirk, Shrewsbury T) 6
Morris, R. 1902 (Newtown, Druids, Liverpool, Leeds C,
Grimsby T, Plymouth Arg) 11
Morris, S. 1937 (Birmingham) 5
Morris, W. 1947 (Burnley) 5
Moulsdale, J. R. B. 1925 (Corinthians) 1
Murphy, J. P. 1933 (WBA) 15
**Myhill, G. O. 2008 (Hull C, WBA)** **16**

Nardiello, D. 1978 (Coventry C) 2
Nardiello, D. A. 2007 (Barnsley, QPR) 3
Neal, J. E. 1931 (Colwyn Bay) 2
Neilson, A. B. 1992 (Newcastle U, Southampton) 5
Newnes, J. 1926 (Nelson) 1
Newton, L. F. 1912 (Cardiff Corinthians) 1
Nicholas, D. S. 1923 (Stoke, Swansea T) 3
Nicholas, P. 1979 (Crystal Palace, Arsenal, Crystal Palace,
Luton T, Aberdeen, Chelsea, Watford) 73
Nicholls, J. 1924 (Newport Co, Cardiff C) 4
Niedzwiecki, E. A. 1985 (Chelsea) 2
Nock, W. 1897 (Newtown) 1
Nogan, L. M. 1992 (Watford, Reading) 2
Norman, A. J. 1986 (Hull C) 5
Nurse, M. T. G. 1960 (Swansea T, Middlesbrough) 12
Nyatanga, L. J. 2006 (Derby Co, Bristol C) 34

O'Callaghan, E. 1929 (Tottenham H) 11
Oliver, A. 1905 (Bangor, Blackburn R) 2
Oster, J. M. 1998 (Everton, Sunderland) 13
O'Sullivan, P. A. 1973 (Brighton & HA) 3
Owen, D. 1879 (Oswestry) 1
Owen, E. 1884 (Ruthin Grammar School) 3
Owen, G. 1888 (Chirk, Newton Heath, Chirk) 4
Owen, J. 1892 (Newton Heath) 2
Owen, T. 1879 (Oswestry) 1
Owen, Trevor 1899 (Crewe Alex) 2
Owen, W. 1884 (Chirk) 16
Owen, W. P. 1880 (Ruthin) 12
Owens, J. 1902 (Wrexham) 1

Page, M. E. 1971 (Birmingham C) 28
Page, R. J. 1997 (Watford, Sheffield U, Cardiff C,
Coventry C) 41
Palmer, D. 1957 (Swansea T) 3
Parris, J. E. 1932 (Bradford) 1
Parry, B. J. 1951 (Swansea T) 1
Parry, C. 1891 (Everton, Newtown) 13
Parry, E. 1922 (Liverpool) 5
Parry, M. 1901 (Liverpool) 16
Parry, P. I. 2004 (Cardiff C) 12
Parry, T. D. 1900 (Oswestry) 7
Parry, W. 1895 (Newtown) 1
Partridge, D. W. 2005 (Motherwell, Bristol C) 7
Pascoe, C. 1984 (Swansea C, Sunderland) 10
Paul, R. 1949 (Swansea T, Manchester C) 33
Peake, E. 1908 (Aberystwyth, Liverpool) 11
Peers, E. J. 1914 (Wolverhampton W, Port Vale) 12
Pembridge, M. A. 1992 (Luton T, Derby Co, Sheffield
W, Benfica, Everton, Fulham) 54

Perry, E. 1938 (Doncaster R) 3
Perry, J. 1994 (Cardiff C) 1
Phennah, E. 1878 (Civil Service) 1
Phillips, C. 1931 (Wolverhampton W, Aston Villa) 13
Phillips, D. 1984 (Plymouth Arg, Manchester C,
  Coventry C, Norwich C, Nottingham F) 62
Phillips, L. 1971 (Cardiff C, Aston Villa, Swansea C,
  Charlton Ath) 58
Phillips, T. J. S. 1973 (Chelsea) 4
Phoenix, H. 1882 (Wrexham) 1
Pipe, D. R. 2003 (Coventry C) 1
Poland, G. 1939 (Wrexham) 2
Pontin, K. 1980 (Cardiff C) 2
Powell, A. 1947 (Leeds U, Everton, Birmingham C) 8
Powell, D. 1968 (Wrexham, Sheffield U) 11
Powell, I. V. 1947 (QPR, Aston Villa) 8
Powell, J. 1878 (Druids, Bolton W, Newton Heath) 15
Powell, Seth 1885 (Oswestry, WBA) 7
Price, H. 1907 (Aston Villa, Burton U, Wrexham) 5
Price, J. 1877 (Wrexham) 12
**Price, L. P. 2006 (Ipswich T, Derby Co,**
  **Crystal Palace)** **11**
Price, P. 1980 (Luton T, Tottenham H) 25
Pring, K. D. 1966 (Rotherham U) 3
Pritchard, H. K. 1985 (Bristol C) 1
Pryce-Jones, A. W. 1895 (Newtown) 1
Pryce-Jones, W. E. 1887 (Cambridge University) 5
Pugh, A. 1889 (Rhostyllen) 1
Pugh, D. H. 1896 (Wrexham, Lincoln C) 7
Pugsley, J. 1930 (Charlton Ath) 1
Pullen, W. J. 1926 (Plymouth Arg) 1

**Ramsey, A. 2009 (Arsenal)** **26**
Rankmore, F. E. J. 1966 (Peterborough U) 1
Ratcliffe, K. 1981 (Everton, Cardiff C) 59
Rea, J. C. 1894 (Aberystwyth) 9
Ready, K. 1997 (QPR) 5
Reece, G. I. 1966 (Sheffield U, Cardiff C) 29
Reed, W. G. 1955 (Ipswich T) 2
Rees, A. 1984 (Birmingham C) 1
Rees, J. M. 1992 (Luton T) 1
Rees, R. R. 1965 (Coventry C, WBA, Nottingham F) 39
Rees, W. 1949 (Cardiff C, Tottenham H) 4
Ribeiro, C. M. 2010 (Bristol C) 2
Richards, A. 1932 (Barnsley) 1
**Richards, A. D. J. 2012 (Swansea C)** **2**
Richards, D. 1931 (Wolverhampton W, Brentford,
  Birmingham) 21
Richards, G. 1899 (Druids, Oswestry, Shrewsbury T) 6
Richards, R. W. 1920 (Wolverhampton W, West Ham U,
  Mold) 9
Richards, S. V. 1947 (Cardiff C) 1
Richards, W. E. 1933 (Fulham) 1
**Ricketts, S. D. 2005 (Swansea C, Hull C, Bolton W)** **48**
Roach, J. 1885 (Oswestry) 1
Robbins, W. W. 1931 (Cardiff C, WBA) 11
Roberts, A. M. 1993 (QPR) 2
Roberts, D. F. 1973 (Oxford U, Hull C) 17
Roberts, G. W. 2000 (Tranmere R) 9
Roberts, I. W. 1990 (Watford, Huddersfield T,
  Leicester C, Norwich C) 15
Roberts, Jas 1913 (Wrexham) 2
Roberts, J. 1879 (Corwen, Berwyn R) 7
Roberts, J. 1881 (Ruthin) 2
Roberts, J. 1906 (Bradford C) 2
Roberts, J. G. 1971 (Arsenal, Birmingham C) 22
Roberts, J. H. 1949 (Bolton W) 1
Roberts, N. W. 2000 (Wrexham, Wigan Ath) 4
Roberts, P. S. 1974 (Portsmouth) 4
Roberts, R. 1884 (Druids, Bolton W, Preston NE) 9
Roberts, R. 1886 (Wrexham) 3
Roberts, R. 1891 (Rhos, Crewe Alex) 2
Roberts, R. L. 1890 (Chester) 1
Roberts, S. W. 2005 (Wrexham) 1
Roberts, W. 1879 (Llangollen, Berwyn R) 6
Roberts, W. 1883 (Rhyl) 1
Roberts, W. 1886 (Wrexham) 4
Roberts, W. H. 1882 (Ruthin, Rhyl) 6
Robinson, C. P. 2000 (Wolverhampton W, Portsmouth,
  Sunderland, Norwich C, Toronto Lynx) 52
Robinson, J. R. C. 1996 (Charlton Ath) 30
**Robson-Kanu, T. H. 2010 (Reading)** **14**

Rodrigues, P. J. 1965 (Cardiff C, Leicester C,
  Sheffield W) 40
Rogers, J. P. 1896 (Wrexham) 3
Rogers, W. 1931 (Wrexham) 2
Roose, L. R. 1900 (Aberystwyth, London Welsh, Stoke,
  Everton, Stoke, Sunderland) 24
Rouse, R. V. 1959 (Crystal Palace) 1
Rowlands, A. C. 1914 (Tranmere R) 1
Rowley, T. 1959 (Tranmere R) 1
Rush, I. 1980 (Liverpool, Juventus, Liverpool) 73
Russell, M. R. 1912 (Merthyr T, Plymouth Arg) 23

Sabine, H. W. 1887 (Oswestry) 1
Saunders, D. 1986 (Brighton & HA, Oxford U,
  Derby Co, Liverpool, Aston Villa, Galatasaray,
  Nottingham F, Sheffield U, Benfica, Bradford C) 75
Savage, R. W. 1996 (Crewe Alex, Leicester C,
  Birmingham C) 39
Savin, G. 1878 (Oswestry) 1
Sayer, P. A. 1977 (Cardiff C) 7
Scrine, F. H. 1950 (Swansea T) 2
Sear, C. R. 1963 (Manchester C) 1
Shaw, E. G. 1882 (Oswestry) 3
Sherwood, A. T. 1947 (Cardiff C, Newport Co) 41
Shone, W. W. 1879 (Oswestry) 1
Shortt, W. W. 1947 (Plymouth Arg) 12
Showers, D. 1975 (Cardiff C) 2
Sidlow, C. 1947 (Liverpool) 7
Sisson, H. 1885 (Wrexham Olympic) 3
Slatter, N. 1983 (Bristol R, Oxford U) 22
Smallman, D. P. 1974 (Wrexham, Everton) 7
Southall, N. 1982 (Everton) 92
Speed, G. A. 1990 (Leeds U, Everton, Newcastle U,
  Bolton W) 85
Sprake, G. 1964 (Leeds U, Birmingham C) 37
Stansfield, F. 1949 (Cardiff C) 1
Stevenson, B. 1978 (Leeds U, Birmingham C) 15
Stevenson, N. 1982 (Swansea C) 4
Stitfall, R. F. 1953 (Cardiff C) 2
Stock, B. B. 2010 (Doncaster R) 3
Sullivan, D. 1953 (Cardiff C) 17
Symons, C. J. 1992 (Portsmouth, Manchester C, Fulham,
  Crystal Palace) 37

Tapscott, D. R. 1954 (Arsenal, Cardiff C) 14
Taylor, G. K. 1996 (Crystal Palace, Sheffield U, Burnley,
  Nottingham F) 15
Taylor, J. 1898 (Wrexham) 1
**Taylor, N. J. 2010 (Wrexham, Swansea C)** **10**
Taylor, O. D. S. 1893 (Newtown) 4
Thatcher, B. D. 2004 (Leicester C, Manchester C) 7
Thomas, C. 1899 (Druids) 2
Thomas, D. A. 1957 (Swansea T) 2
Thomas, D. S. 1948 (Fulham) 4
Thomas, E. 1925 (Cardiff Corinthians) 1
Thomas, G. 1885 (Wrexham) 2
Thomas, H. 1927 (Manchester U) 1
Thomas, Martin R. 1987 (Newcastle U) 1
Thomas, Mickey 1977 (Wrexham, Manchester U,
  Everton, Brighton & HA, Stoke C, Chelsea, WBA) 51
Thomas, R. J. 1967 (Swindon T, Derby Co, Cardiff C) 50
Thomas, T. 1898 (Bangor) 2
Thomas, W. R. 1931 (Newport Co) 2
Thomson, D. 1876 (Druids) 1
Thomson, G. F. 1876 (Druids) 2
Toshack, J. B. 1969 (Cardiff C, Liverpool, Swansea C) 40
Townsend, W. 1887 (Newtown) 2
Trainer, H. 1895 (Wrexham) 3
Trainer, J. 1887 (Bolton W, Preston NE) 20
Trollope, P. J. 1997 (Derby Co, Fulham, Coventry C,
  Northampton T) 9
Tudur-Jones, O. 2008 (Swansea C, Norwich C) 6
Turner, H. G. 1937 (Charlton Ath) 8
Turner, J. 1892 (Wrexham) 1
Turner, R. E. 1891 (Wrexham) 2
Turner, W. H. 1887 (Wrexham) 5

Van Den Hauwe, P. W. R. 1985 (Everton) 13
**Vaughan, D. O. 2003 (Crewe Alex, Real Sociedad,**
  **Blackpool, Sunderland)** **33**
Vaughan, Jas 1893 (Druids) 4
Vaughan, John 1879 (Oswestry, Druids, Bolton W) 11

Vaughan, J. O. 1885 (Rhyl) 4
Vaughan, N. 1983 (Newport Co, Cardiff C) 10
Vaughan, T. 1885 (Rhyl) 1
Vearncombe, G. 1958 (Cardiff C) 2
Vernon, T. R. 1957 (Blackburn R, Everton, Stoke C) 32
Villars, A. K. 1974 (Cardiff C) 3
Vizard, E. T. 1911 (Bolton W) 22
**Vokes, S. M. 2008 (Bournemouth, Wolverhampton W, Burnley) 25**

Walley, J. T. 1971 (Watford) 1
Walsh, I. P. 1980 (Crystal Palace, Swansea C) 18
Ward, D. 1959 (Bristol R, Cardiff C) 2
Ward, D. 2000 (Notts Co, Nottingham F) 5
Warner, J. 1937 (Swansea T, Manchester U) 2
Warren, F. W. 1929 (Cardiff C, Middlesbrough, Hearts) 6
Watkins, A. E. 1898 (Leicester Fosse, Aston Villa, Millwall) 5
Watkins, W. M. 1902 (Stoke, Aston Villa, Sunderland, Stoke) 10
Webster, C. 1957 (Manchester U) 4
Weston, R. D. 2000 (Arsenal, Cardiff C) 7
Whatley, W. J. 1939 (Tottenham H) 2
White, P. F. 1896 (London Welsh) 1
Wilcock, A. R. 1890 (Oswestry) 1
Wilding, J. 1885 (Wrexham Olympians, Bootle, Wrexham) 9
Williams, A. 1994 (Reading, Wolverhampton W, Reading) 13
**Williams, A. E. 2008 (Stockport Co, Swansea C) 41**
Williams, A. L. 1931 (Wrexham) 1
Williams, A. P. 1998 (Southampton) 2
Williams, B. 1930 (Bristol C) 1
Williams, B. 1928 (Swansea T, Everton) 10
Williams, D. G. 1988 (Derby Co, Ipswich T) 13

Williams, D. M. 1986 (Norwich C) 5
Williams, D. R. 1921 (Merthyr T, Sheffield W, Manchester U) 8
Williams, E. 1893 (Crewe Alex) 2
Williams, E. 1901 (Druids) 5
Williams, G. 1893 (Chirk) 6
Williams, G. E. 1960 (WBA) 26
Williams, G. G. 1961 (Swansea T) 5
Williams, G. J. 2006 (West Ham U, Ipswich T) 2
Williams, G. J. J. 1951 (Cardiff C) 1
Williams, G. O. 1907 (Wrexham) 1
Williams, H. J. 1965 (Swansea T) 3
Williams, H. T. 1949 (Newport Co, Leeds U) 4
Williams, J. H. 1884 (Oswestry) 1
Williams, J. J. 1939 (Wrexham) 1
Williams, J. T. 1925 (Middlesbrough) 1
**Williams, J. P. 2013 (Crystal Palace) 2**
Williams, J. W. 1912 (Crystal Palace) 2
Williams, R. 1935 (Newcastle U) 2
Williams, R. P. 1886 (Caernarvon) 1
Williams, S. G. 1954 (WBA, Southampton) 43
Williams, W. 1876 (Druids, Oswestry, Druids) 11
Williams, W. 1925 (Northampton T) 1
Witcomb, D. F. 1947 (WBA, Sheffield W) 3
Woosnam, A. P. 1959 (Leyton Orient, West Ham U, Aston Villa) 17
Woosnam, G. 1879 (Newtown Excelsior) 1
Worthington, T. 1894 (Newtown) 1
Wynn, G. A. 1909 (Wrexham, Manchester C) 11
Wynn, W. 1903 (Chirk) 1

Yorath, T. C. 1970 (Leeds U, Coventry C, Tottenham H, Vancouver Whitecaps) 59
Young, E. 1990 (Wimbledon, Crystal Palace, Wolverhampton W) 21

## REPUBLIC OF IRELAND

Aherne, T. 1946 (Belfast Celtic, Luton T) 16
Aldridge, J. W. 1986 (Oxford U, Liverpool, Real Sociedad, Tranmere R) 69
Ambrose, P. 1955 (Shamrock R) 5
Anderson, J. 1980 (Preston NE, Newcastle U) 16
**Andrews, K. J. 2009 (Blackburn R, WBA) 35**
Andrews, P. 1936 (Bohemians) 1
Arrigan, T. 1938 (Waterford) 1

Babb, P. A. 1994 (Coventry C, Liverpool, Sunderland) 35
Bailham, E. 1964 (Shamrock R) 1
Barber, E. 1966 (Shelbourne, Birmingham C) 2
Barrett, G. 2003 (Arsenal, Coventry C) 6
Barry, P. 1928 (Fordsons) 2
Beglin, J. 1984 (Liverpool) 15
Bennett, A. J. 2007 (Reading) 2
Bermingham, J. 1929 (Bohemians) 1
Bermingham, P. 1935 (St James' Gate) 1
Best, L. J. B. 2009 (Coventry C, Newcastle U) 7
Bonner, P. 1981 (Celtic) 80
**Brady, R. 2013 (Hull C) 5**
Braddish, S. 1978 (Dundalk) 2
Bradshaw, P. 1939 (St James' Gate) 5
Brady, F. 1926 (Fordsons) 1
Brady, T. R. 1964 (QPR) 6
Brady, W. L. 1975 (Arsenal, Juventus, Sampdoria, Internazionale, Ascoli, West Ham U) 72
Branagan, K. G. 1997 (Bolton W) 1
Breen, G. 1996 (Birmingham C, Coventry C, West Ham U, Sunderland) 63
Breen, T. 1937 (Manchester U, Shamrock R) 5
Brennan, F. 1965 (Drumcondra) 1
Brennan, S. A. 1965 (Manchester U, Waterford) 19
Brown, J. 1937 (Coventry C) 1
Browne, W. 1964 (Bohemians) 3
Bruce, A. S. 2007 (Ipswich T) 2
Buckley, L. 1984 (Shamrock R, Waregem) 2
Burke, F. 1952 (Cork Ath) 1
Burke, J. 1929 (Shamrock R) 1
Burke, J. 1934 (Cork) 1
Butler, P. J. 2000 (Sunderland) 1
Butler, T. 2003 (Sunderland) 2

Byrne, A. B. 1970 (Southampton) 14
Byrne, D. 1929 (Shelbourne, Shamrock R, Coleraine) 3
Byrne, J. 1928 (Bray Unknowns) 1
Byrne, J. 1985 (QPR, Le Havre, Brighton & HA, Sunderland, Millwall) 23
Byrne, J. 2004 (Shelbourne) 2
Byrne, P. 1931 (Dolphin, Shelbourne, Drumcondra) 3
Byrne, P. 1984 (Shamrock R) 8
Byrne, S. 1931 (Bohemians) 1

Campbell, A. 1985 (Santander) 3
Campbell, N. 1971 (St Patrick's Ath, Fortuna Cologne) 11
Cannon, H. 1926 (Bohemians) 2
Cantwell, N. 1954 (West Ham U, Manchester U) 36
Carey, B. P. 1992 (Manchester U, Leicester C) 3
Carey, J. J. 1938 (Manchester U) 29
Carolan, J. 1960 (Manchester U) 2
Carr, S. 1999 (Tottenham H, Newcastle U) 44
Carroll, B. 1949 (Shelbourne) 2
Carroll, T. R. 1968 (Ipswich T, Birmingham C) 17
Carsley, L. K. 1998 (Derby Co, Blackburn R, Coventry C, Everton) 39
Cascarino, A. G. 1986 (Gillingham, Millwall, Aston Villa, Celtic, Chelsea, Marseille, Nancy) 88
Chandler, J. 1980 (Leeds U) 2
Chatton, H. A. 1931 (Shelbourne, Dumbarton, Cork) 3
**Clark, C. 2011 (Aston Villa) 6**
Clarke, C. R. 2004 (Stoke C) 2
Clarke, J. 1978 (Drogheda U) 1
Clarke, K. 1948 (Drumcondra) 1
Clarke, M. 1950 (Shamrock R) 1
Clinton, T. J. 1951 (Everton) 3
Coad, P. 1947 (Shamrock R) 11
Coffey, T. 1950 (Drumcondra) 1
**Coleman, S. 2011 (Everton) 14**
Colfer, M. D. 1950 (Shelbourne) 2
Colgan, N. 2002 (Hibernian, Barnsley) 9
Collins, F. 1927 (Jacobs) 1
Conmy, O. M. 1965 (Peterborough U) 5
Connolly, D. J. 1996 (Watford, Feyenoord, Wolverhampton W, Excelsior, Feyenoord, Wimbledon, West Ham U, Wigan Ath) 41

Connolly, H. 1937 (Cork) 1
Connolly, J. 1926 (Fordsons) 1
Conroy, G. A. 1970 (Stoke C) 27
Conway, J. P. 1967 (Fulham, Manchester C) 20
Corr, P. J. 1949 (Everton) 4
Courtney, E. 1946 (Cork U) 1
**Cox, S. R. 2011 (WBA, Nottingham F) 26**
Coyle, O. C. 1994 (Bolton W) 1
Coyne, T. 1992 (Celtic, Tranmere R, Motherwell) 22
Crowe, G. 2003 (Bohemians) 2
Cummins, G. P. 1954 (Luton T) 19
Cuneen, T. 1951 (Limerick) 1
**Cunningham, G. R. 2010 (Manchester C, Bristol C) 4**
Cunningham, K. 1996 (Wimbledon, Birmingham C) 72
Curtis, D. P. 1957 (Shelbourne, Bristol C, Ipswich T, Exeter C) 17
Cusack, S. 1953 (Limerick) 1

Daish, L. S. 1992 (Cambridge U, Coventry C) 5
Daly, G. A. 1973 (Manchester U, Derby Co, Coventry C, Birmingham C, Shrewsbury T) 48
Daly, J. 1932 (Shamrock R) 2
Daly, M. 1978 (Wolverhampton W) 2
Daly, P. 1950 (Shamrock R) 1
Davis, T. L. 1937 (Oldham Ath, Tranmere R) 4
Deacy, E. 1982 (Aston Villa) 4
**Delaney, D. F. 2008 (QPR, Ipswich T, Crystal Palace) 7**
Delap, R. J. 1998 (Derby Co, Southampton) 11
De Mange, K. J. P. P. 1987 (Liverpool, Hull C) 2
Dempsey, J. T. 1967 (Fulham, Chelsea) 19
Dennehy, J. 1972 (Cork Hibernians, Nottingham F, Walsall) 11
Desmond, P. 1950 (Middlesbrough) 4
Devine, J. 1980 (Arsenal, Norwich C) 13
Doherty, G. M. T. 2000 (Luton T, Tottenham H, Norwich C) 34
Donnelly, J. 1935 (Dundalk) 10
Donnelly, T. 1938 (Drumcondra, Shamrock R) 2
Donovan, D. C. 1955 (Everton) 5
Donovan, T. 1980 (Aston Villa) 2
Douglas, J. 2004 (Blackburn R, Leeds U) 8
Dowdall, C. 1928 (Fordsons, Barnsley, Cork) 3
Doyle, C. 1959 (Shelbourne) 1
Doyle, Colin 2007 (Birmingham C) 1
Doyle, D. 1926 (Shamrock R) 1
**Doyle, K. E. 2006 (Reading, Wolverhampton W) 53**
Doyle, L. 1932 (Dolphin) 1
Doyle, M. P. 2004 (Coventry C) 1
Duff, D. A. 1998 (Blackburn R, Chelsea, Newcastle U, Fulham) 100
Duffy, B. 1950 (Shamrock R) 1
Duggan, H. A. 1927 (Leeds U, Newport Co) 5
Dunne, A. P. 1962 (Manchester U, Bolton W) 33
Dunne, J. 1930 (Sheffield U, Arsenal, Southampton, Shamrock R) 15
Dunne, J. C. 1971 (Fulham) 1
Dunne, L. 1935 (Manchester C) 2
Dunne, P. A. J. 1965 (Manchester U) 5
**Dunne, R. P. 2000 (Everton, Manchester C, Aston Villa) 77**
Dunne, S. 1953 (Luton T) 15
Dunne, T. 1956 (St Patrick's Ath) 3
Dunning, P. 1971 (Shelbourne) 2
Dunphy, E. M. 1966 (York C, Millwall) 23
Dwyer, N. M. 1960 (West Ham U, Swansea T) 14

Eccles, P. 1986 (Shamrock R) 1
Egan, R. 1929 (Dundalk) 1
Eglington, T. J. 1946 (Shamrock R, Everton) 24
Elliott, S. W. 2005 (Sunderland) 9
Ellis, P. 1935 (Bohemians) 7
Evans, M. J. 1998 (Southampton) 1

Fagan, E. 1973 (Shamrock R) 1
Fagan, F. 1955 (Manchester C, Derby Co) 8
Fagan, J. 1926 (Shamrock R) 1
**Fahey, K. D. 2010 (Birmingham C) 16**
Fairclough, M. 1982 (Dundalk) 2
Fallon, S. 1951 (Celtic) 8

Fallon, W. J. 1935 (Notts Co, Sheffield W) 9
Farquharson, T. G. 1929 (Cardiff C) 4
Farrell, P. 1937 (Hibernian) 2
Farrell, P. D. 1946 (Shamrock R, Everton) 28
Farrelly, G. 1996 (Aston Villa, Everton, Bolton W) 6
Feenan, J. J. 1937 (Sunderland) 2
Finnan, S. 2000 (Fulham, Liverpool, Espanyol) 53
Finucane, A. 1967 (Limerick) 11
Fitzgerald, F. J. 1955 (Waterford) 2
Fitzgerald, P. J. 1961 (Leeds U, Chester) 5
Fitzpatrick, K. 1970 (Limerick) 1
Fitzsimons, A. G. 1950 (Middlesbrough, Lincoln C) 26
Fleming, C. 1996 (Middlesbrough) 10
Flood, J. J. 1926 (Shamrock R) 5
Fogarty, A. 1960 (Sunderland, Hartlepools U) 11
Folan, C. C. 2009 (Hull C) 7
Foley, D. J. 2000 (Watford) 6
Foley, J. 1934 (Cork, Celtic) 7
Foley, K. P. 2009 (Wolverhampton W) 8
Foley, M. 1926 (Shelbourne) 1
Foley, T. C. 1964 (Northampton T) 9
**Forde, D. 2011 (Millwall) 10**
Foy, T. 1938 (Shamrock R) 2
Fullam, J. 1961 (Preston NE, Shamrock R) 11
Fullam, R. 1926 (Shamrock R) 2

Gallagher, C. 1967 (Celtic) 2
Gallagher, M. 1954 (Hibernian) 1
Gallagher, P. 1932 (Falkirk) 1
Galvin, A. 1983 (Tottenham H, Sheffield W, Swindon T) 29
Gamble, J. 2007 (Cork C) 2
Gannon, E. 1949 (Notts Co, Sheffield W, Shelbourne) 14
Gannon, M. 1972 (Shelbourne) 1
Gaskins, J. 1934 (Shamrock R, St James' Gate) 7
Gavin, J. T. 1950 (Norwich C, Tottenham H, Norwich C) 7
Geoghegan, M. 1937 (St James' Gate) 2
Gibbons, A. 1952 (St Patrick's Ath) 4
Gibson, D. T. D. 2008 (Manchester U, Everton) 19
Gilbert, R. 1966 (Shamrock R) 1
Giles, C. 1951 (Doncaster R) 1
Giles, M. J. 1960 (Manchester U, Leeds U, WBA, Shamrock R) 59
Given, S. J. J. 1996 (Blackburn R, Newcastle U, Manchester C, Aston Villa) 125
Givens, D. J. 1969 (Manchester U, Luton T, QPR, Birmingham C, Neuchatel X) 56
Gleeson, S. M. 2007 (Wolverhampton W) 2
Glen, W. 1927 (Shamrock R) 8
Glynn, D. 1952 (Drumcondra) 2
Godwin, T. F. 1949 (Shamrock R, Leicester C, Bournemouth) 13
Golding, J. 1928 (Shamrock R) 2
Goodman, J. 1997 (Wimbledon) 4
Goodwin, J. 2003 (Stockport Co) 1
Gorman, W. C. 1936 (Bury, Brentford) 13
Grace, J. 1926 (Drumcondra) 1
Grealish, A. 1976 (Orient, Luton T, Brighton & HA, WBA) 45
**Green, P. J. 2010 (Derby Co, Leeds U) 16**
Gregg, E. 1978 (Bohemians) 8
Griffith, R. 1935 (Walsall) 1
Grimes, A. A. 1978 (Manchester U, Coventry C, Luton T) 18
Hale, A. 1962 (Aston Villa, Doncaster R, Waterford) 14
Hamilton, T. 1959 (Shamrock R) 2
Hand, E. K. 1969 (Portsmouth) 20
Harrington, W. 1936 (Cork) 5
Harte, I. P. 1996 (Leeds U, Levante) 64
Hartnett, J. B. 1949 (Middlesbrough) 2
Haverty, J. 1956 (Arsenal, Blackburn R, Millwall, Celtic, Bristol R, Shelbourne) 32
Hayes, A. W. P. 1979 (Southampton) 1
Hayes, W. E. 1947 (Huddersfield T) 2
Hayes, W. J. 1949 (Limerick) 1
Healey, R. 1977 (Cardiff C) 2
Healy, C. 2002 (Celtic, Sunderland) 13

Heighway, S. D. 1971 (Liverpool, Minnesota K)     34
Henderson, B. 1948 (Drumcondra)     2
Henderson, W. C. P. 2006 (Brighton & HA, Preston NE)     6
**Hendrick, J. P. 2013 (Derby Co)**     **4**
Hennessy, J. 1965 (Shelbourne, St Patrick's Ath)     5
Herrick, J. 1972 (Cork Hibernians, Shamrock R)     3
Higgins, J. 1951 (Birmingham C)     1
Holland, M. R. 2000 (Ipswich T, Charlton Ath)     49
Holmes, J. 1971 (Coventry C, Tottenham H, Vancouver Whitecaps)     30
**Hoolahan, W. 2008 (Blackpool, Norwich C)**     **6**
Horlacher, A. F. 1930 (Bohemians)     7
Houghton, R. J. 1986 (Oxford U, Liverpool, Aston Villa, Crystal Palace, Reading)     73
Howlett, G. 1984 (Brighton & HA)     1
Hoy, M. 1938 (Dundalk)     6
Hughton, C. 1980 (Tottenham H, West Ham U)     53
Hunt, N. 2009 (Reading)     3
Hunt, S. P. 2007 (Reading, Hull C, Wolverhampton W)     39
Hurley, C. J. 1957 (Millwall, Sunderland, Bolton W)     40
Hutchinson, F. 1935 (Drumcondra)     2

Ireland S .J. 2006 (Manchester C)     6
Irwin, D. J. 1991 (Manchester U)     56

Jordan, D. 1937 (Wolverhampton W)     2
Jordan, W. 1934 (Bohemians)     2

Kavanagh, G. A. 1998 (Stoke C, Cardiff C, Wigan Ath)     16
Kavanagh, P. J. 1931 (Celtic)     1
**Keane, R. D. 1998 (Wolverhampton W, Coventry C, Internazionale, Leeds U, Tottenham H, Liverpool, Tottenham H, LA Galaxy)**     **127**
Keane, R. M. 1991 (Nottingham F, Manchester U)     67
Keane, T. R. 1949 (Swansea T)     4
Kearin, M. 1972 (Shamrock R)     1
Kearns, F. T. 1954 (West Ham U)     1
Kearns, M. 1971 (Oxford U, Walsall, Wolverhampton W)     18
Kelly, A. T. 1993 (Sheffield U, Blackburn R)     34
Kelly, D. T. 1988 (Walsall, West Ham U, Leicester C, Newcastle U, Wolverhampton W, Sunderland, Tranmere R)     26
Kelly, G. 1994 (Leeds U)     52
Kelly, J. 1932 (Derry C)     4
Kelly, J. A. 1957 (Drumcondra, Preston NE)     47
Kelly, J. P. V. 1961 (Wolverhampton W)     5
Kelly, M. J. 1988 (Portsmouth)     4
Kelly, N. 1954 (Nottingham F)     1
**Kelly, S. M. 2006 (Tottenham H, Birmingham C, Fulham)**     **34**
Kendrick, J. 1927 (Everton, Dolphin)     4
Kenna, J. J. 1995 (Blackburn R)     27
Kennedy, M. F. 1986 (Portsmouth)     2
Kennedy, M. J. 1996 (Liverpool, Wimbledon, Manchester C, Wolverhampton W)     34
Kennedy, W. 1932 (St James' Gate)     3
Kenny, P. 2004 (Sheffield U)     7
**Keogh, A. D. 2007 (Wolverhampton W)**     **29**
Keogh, J. 1966 (Shamrock R)     1
**Keogh, R. J. 2013 (Derby Co)**     **2**
Keogh, S. 1959 (Shamrock R)     1
Kernaghan, A. N. 1993 (Middlesbrough, Manchester C)     22
Kiely, D. L. 2000 (Charlton Ath, WBA)     11
Kiernan, F. W. 1951 (Shamrock R, Southampton)     5
Kilbane, K. D. 1998 (WBA, Sunderland, Everton, Wigan Ath, Hull C)     110
Kinnear, J. P. 1967 (Tottenham H, Brighton & HA)     26
Kinsella, J. 1928 (Shelbourne)     1
Kinsella, M. A. 1998 (Charlton Ath, Aston Villa, WBA)     48
Kinsella, O. 1932 (Shamrock R)     2
Kirkland, A. 1927 (Shamrock R)     1

Lacey, W. 1927 (Shelbourne)     3

Langan, D. 1978 (Derby Co, Birmingham C, Oxford U)     26
Lapira, J. 2007 (Notre Dame)     1
Lawler, J. F. 1953 (Fulham)     8
Lawlor, J. C. 1949 (Drumcondra, Doncaster R)     3
Lawlor, M. 1971 (Shamrock R)     5
Lawrence, L. 2009 (Stoke C, Portsmouth)     15
Lawrenson, M. 1977 (Preston NE, Brighton & HA, Liverpool)     39
Lee, A. D. 2003 (Rotherham U, Cardiff C, Ipswich T)     10
Leech, M. 1969 (Shamrock R)     8
Lennon, C. 1935 (St James' Gate)     3
Lennox, G. 1931 (Dolphin)     2
**Long, S. P. 2007 (Reading, WBA)**     **37**
Lowry, D. 1962 (St Patrick's Ath)     1
Lunn, R. 1939 (Dundalk)     2
Lynch, J. 1934 (Cork Bohemians)     1

McAlinden, J. 1946 (Portsmouth)     2
McAteer, J. W. 1994 (Bolton W, Liverpool, Blackburn R, Sunderland)     52
McCann, J. 1957 (Shamrock R)     1
McCarthy, J. 1926 (Bohemians)     3
**McCarthy, J. 2010 (Wigan Ath)**     **15**
McCarthy, M. 1932 (Shamrock R)     1
McCarthy, M. 1984 (Manchester C, Celtic, Lyon, Millwall)     57
**McClean, J. 2012 (Sunderland)**     **13**
McConville, T. 1972 (Dundalk, Waterford)     6
McDonagh, Jacko 1984 (Shamrock R)     3
McDonagh, J. 1981 (Everton, Bolton W, Notts Co, Wichita Wings)     25
McEvoy, M. A. 1961 (Blackburn R)     17
**McGeady, A. 2004 (Celtic, Spartak Moscow)**     **60**
McGee, P. 1978 (QPR, Preston NE)     15
McGoldrick, E. J. 1992 (Crystal Palace, Arsenal)     15
McGowan, D. 1949 (West Ham U)     3
McGowan, J. 1947 (Cork U)     1
McGrath, M. 1958 (Blackburn R, Bradford)     22
McGrath, P. 1985 (Manchester U, Aston Villa, Derby Co)     83
McGuire, W. 1936 (Bohemians)     1
Macken, A. 1977 (Derby Co)     1
Macken J. P. 2005 (Manchester C)     1
McKenzie, G. 1938 (Southend U)     9
Mackey, G. 1957 (Shamrock R)     3
McLoughlin, A. F. 1990 (Swindon T, Southampton, Portsmouth)     42
McLoughlin, F. 1930 (Fordsons, Cork)     2
McMillan, W. 1946 (Belfast Celtic)     2
McNally, J. B. 1959 (Luton T)     3
McPhail, S. 2000 (Leeds U)     10
**McShane, P. D. 2007 (WBA, Sunderland, Hull C)**     **31**
Madden, O. 1936 (Cork)     1
Maguire, J. 1929 (Shamrock R)     1
Mahon, A. J. 2000 (Tranmere R)     2
Malone, G. 1949 (Shelbourne)     1
Mancini, T. J. 1974 (QPR, Arsenal)     5
Martin, C. 1927 (Bo'ness)     1
Martin, C. J. 1946 (Glentoran, Leeds U, Aston Villa)     30
Martin, M. P. 1972 (Bohemians, Manchester U, WBA, Newcastle U)     52
Maybury, A. 1998 (Leeds U, Hearts, Leicester C)     10
Meagan, M. K. 1961 (Everton, Huddersfield T, Drogheda)     17
Meehan, P. 1934 (Drumcondra)     1
**Meyler, D. 2013 (Sunderland, Hull C)**     **4**
Miller, L. W. P. 2004 (Celtic, Manchester U, Sunderland, Hibernian)     21
Milligan, M. J. 1992 (Oldham Ath)     1
Monahan, P. 1935 (Sligo R)     2
Mooney, J. 1965 (Shamrock R)     2
Moore, A. 1996 (Middlesbrough)     8
Moore, P. 1931 (Shamrock R, Aberdeen, Shamrock R)     9
Moran, K. 1980 (Manchester U, Sporting Gijon, Blackburn R)     71
Moroney, T. 1948 (West Ham U, Evergreen U)     12
Morris, C. B. 1988 (Celtic, Middlesbrough)     35

Morrison, C. H. 2002 (Crystal Palace, Birmingham C,
   Crystal Palace) — 36
Moulson, C. 1936 (Lincoln C, Notts Co) — 5
Moulson, G. B. 1948 (Lincoln C) — 3
Muckian, C. 1978 (Drogheda U) — 1
Muldoon, T. 1927 (Aston Villa) — 1
Mulligan, P. M. 1969 (Shamrock R, Chelsea,
   Crystal Palace, WBA, Shamrock R) — 50
Munroe, L. 1954 (Shamrock R) — 1
Murphy, A. 1956 (Clyde) — 1
Murphy, B. 1986 (Bohemians) — 1
Murphy, D. 2007 (Sunderland) — 9
Murphy, J. 1980 (Crystal Palace) — 3
Murphy, J. 2004 (WBA, Scunthorpe U) — 2
Murphy, P. M. 2007 (Carlisle U) — 1
Murray, T. 1950 (Dundalk) — 1

Newman, W. 1969 (Shelbourne) — 1
Nolan. E. W. 2009 (Preston NE) — 3
Nolan, R. 1957 (Shamrock R) — 10

O'Brien, A. 2007 (Newcastle U) — 5
O'Brien, A. J. 2001 (Newcastle U, Portsmouth) — 26
O'Brien, F. 1980 (Philadelphia F) — 3
**O'Brien J. M. 2006 (Bolton W, West Ham U)** — **5**
O'Brien, L. 1986 (Shamrock R, Manchester U,
   Newcastle U, Tranmere R) — 16
O'Brien, M. T. 1927 (Derby Co, Walsall, Norwich C,
   Watford) — 4
O'Brien, R. 1976 (Notts Co) — 5
O'Byrne, L. B. 1949 (Shamrock R) — 1
O'Callaghan, B. R. 1979 (Stoke C) — 6
O'Callaghan, K. 1981 (Ipswich T, Portsmouth) — 21
O'Cearuill, J. 2007 (Arsenal) — 2
O'Connell, A. 1967 (Dundalk, Bohemians) — 2
O'Connor, T. 1950 (Shamrock R) — 4
O'Connor, T. 1968 (Fulham, Dundalk, Bohemians) — 7
**O'Dea, D. 2010 (Celtic, Toronto)** — **19**
O'Driscoll, J. F. 1949 (Swansea T) — 3
O'Driscoll, S. 1982 (Fulham) — 3
O'Farrell, F. 1952 (West Ham U, Preston NE) — 9
O'Flanagan, K. P. 1938 (Bohemians, Arsenal) — 10
O'Flanagan, M. 1947 (Bohemians) — 1
O'Halloran, S. E. 2007 (Aston Villa) — 2
O'Hanlon, K. G. 1988 (Rotherham U) — 1
O'Kane, P. 1935 (Bohemians) — 3
O'Keefe, E. 1981 (Everton, Port Vale) — 5
O'Keefe, T. 1934 (Cork, Waterford) — 3
O'Leary, D. 1977 (Arsenal) — 68
O'Leary, P. 1980 (Shamrock R) — 7
O'Mahoney, M. T. 1938 (Bristol R) — 6
O'Neill, F. S. 1962 (Shamrock R) — 20
O'Neill, J. 1952 (Everton) — 17
O'Neill, J. 1961 (Preston NE) — 1
O'Neill, K. P. 1996 (Norwich C, Middlesbrough) — 13
O'Neill, W. 1936 (Dundalk) — 11
O'Regan, K. 1984 (Brighton & HA) — 4
O'Reilly, J. 1932 (Brideville, Aberdeen, Brideville,
   St James' Gate) — 20
O'Reilly, J. 1946 (Cork U) — 2
**O'Shea, J. F. 2002 (Manchester U, Sunderland)** — **89**

**Pearce, A. J. 2013 (Reading)** — **1**
Peyton, G. 1977 (Fulham, Bournemouth, Everton) — 33
Peyton, N. 1957 (Shamrock R, Leeds U) — 6
Phelan, T. 1992 (Wimbledon, Manchester C, Chelsea,
   Everton, Fulham) — 42
Potter, D. M. 2007 (Wolverhampton W) — 5

Quinn, A. 2003 (Sheffield W, Sheffield U) — 8
Quinn, B. S. 2000 (Coventry C) — 4
Quinn, N. J. 1986 (Arsenal, Manchester C, Sunderland)
    — 91
**Quinn, S. 2013 (Hull C)** — **2**

**Randolf, D. E. 2013 (Motherwell)** — **2**
Reid, A. M. 2004 (Nottingham F, Tottenham H,
   Charlton Ath, Sunderland) — 27

Reid, C. 1931 (Brideville) — 1
Reid, S. J. 2002 (Millwall, Blackburn R) — 23
Richardson, D. J. 1972 (Shamrock R, Gillingham) — 3
Rigby, A. 1935 (St James' Gate) — 3
Ringstead, A. 1951 (Sheffield U) — 20
Robinson, J. 1928 (Bohemians, Dolphin) — 2
Robinson, M. 1981 (Brighton & HA, Liverpool, QPR) — 24
Roche, P. J. 1972 (Shelbourne, Manchester U) — 8
Rogers, E. 1968 (Blackburn R, Charlton Ath) — 19
Rowlands, M. C. 2004 (QPR) — 5
Ryan, G. 1978 (Derby Co, Brighton & HA) — 18
Ryan, R. A. 1950 (WBA, Derby Co) — 16

Sadlier, R. T. 2002 (Millwall) — 1
**Sammon, C. 2013 (Derby Co)** — **7**
Savage, D. P. T. 1996 (Millwall) — 5
Saward, P. 1954 (Millwall, Aston Villa, Huddersfield T)
    — 18
Scannell, T. 1954 (Southend U) — 1
Scully, P. J. 1989 (Arsenal) — 1
Sheedy, K. 1984 (Everton, Newcastle U) — 46
Sheridan, C. 2010 (Celtic, CSKA Sofia) — 3
Sheridan, J. J. 1988 (Leeds U, Sheffield W) — 34
Slaven, B. 1990 (Middlesbrough) — 7
Sloan, J. W. 1946 (Arsenal) — 2
Smyth, M. 1969 (Shamrock R) — 1
Squires, J. 1934 (Shelbourne) — 1
Stapleton, F. 1977 (Arsenal, Manchester U, Ajax,
   Le Havre, Blackburn R) — 71
Staunton, S. 1989 (Liverpool, Aston Villa, Liverpool,
   Aston Villa) — 102
**St Ledger-Hall, S. P. 2009 (Preston NE, Leicester C)** — **36**
Stevenson, A. E. 1932 (Dolphin, Everton) — 7
Stokes, A. 2007 (Sunderland, Celtic) — 4
Strahan, F. 1964 (Shelbourne) — 5
Sullivan, J. 1928 (Fordsons) — 1
Swan, M. M. G. 1960 (Drumcondra) — 1
Synnott, N. 1978 (Shamrock R) — 3

Taylor, T. 1959 (Waterford) — 1
Thomas, P. 1974 (Waterford) — 2
Thompson, J. 2004 (Nottingham F) — 1
Townsend, A. D. 1989 (Norwich C, Chelsea, Aston Villa,
   Middlesbrough) — 70
Traynor, T. J. 1954 (Southampton) — 8
Treacy, K. 2011 (Preston NE, Burnley) — 6
Treacy, R. C. P. 1966 (WBA, Charlton Ath, Swindon T,
   Preston NE, WBA, Shamrock R) — 42
Tuohy, L. 1956 (Shamrock R, Newcastle U, Shamrock
   R) — 8
Turner, C. J. 1936 (Southend U, West Ham U) — 10
Turner, P. 1963 (Celtic) — 2

Vernon, J. 1946 (Belfast Celtic) — 2

Waddock, G. 1980 (QPR, Millwall) — 21
Walsh, D. J. 1946 (Linfield, WBA, Aston Villa) — 20
Walsh, J. 1982 (Limerick) — 1
Walsh, M. 1976 (Blackpool, Everton, QPR, Porto) — 21
Walsh, M. 1982 (Everton) — 4
Walsh, W. 1947 (Manchester C) — 9
**Walters, J. R. 2011 (Stoke C)** — **19**
**Ward, S. R. 2011 (Wolverhampton W)** — **18**
Waters, J. 1977 (Grimsby T) — 2
Watters, F. 1926 (Shelbourne) — 1
Weir, E. 1939 (Clyde) — 3
**Westwood, K. 2009 (Coventry C, Sunderland)** — **15**
**Whelan, G. D. 2008 (Stoke C)** — **49**
Whelan, R. 1964 (St Patrick's Ath) — 2
Whelan, R. 1981 (Liverpool, Southend U) — 53
Whelan, W. 1956 (Manchester U) — 4
White, J. J. 1928 (Bohemians) — 1
Whittaker, R. 1959 (Chelsea) — 1
Williams, J. 1938 (Shamrock R) — 1
**Wilson, M. D. 2011 (Stoke C)** — **7**

# BRITISH AND IRISH INTERNATIONAL GOALSCORERS 1872–2013

Where two players with the same surname and initials have appeared for the same country, and one or both have scored, they have been distinguished by reference to the club which appears *first* against their name in the international appearances section.

**Bold** type indicates players who have scored international goals in season 2012–13.

**ENGLAND**

|  | |
|---|---|
| A'Court, A. | 1 |
| Adams, T. A. | 5 |
| Adcock, H. | 1 |
| Alcock, C. W. | 1 |
| Allen, A. | 3 |
| Allen, R. | 2 |
| Amos, A. | 1 |
| Anderson, V. | 2 |
| Anderton, D. R. | 7 |
| Astall, G. | 1 |
| Athersmith, W. C. | 3 |
| Atyeo, P. J. W. | 5 |
| Bache, J. W. | 4 |
| Bailey, N. C. | 2 |
| Baily, E. F. | 5 |
| **Baines, L. J.** | **1** |
| Baker, J. H. | 3 |
| Ball, A. J. | 8 |
| Bambridge, A. L. | 1 |
| Bambridge, E. C. | 11 |
| Barclay, R. | 2 |
| Barmby, N. J. | 4 |
| Barnes, J. | 11 |
| Barnes, P. S. | 4 |
| Barry, G. | 3 |
| Barton, J. | 1 |
| Bassett, W. I. | 8 |
| Bastin, C. S. | 12 |
| Beardsley, P. A. | 9 |
| Beasley, A. | 1 |
| Beattie, T. K. | 1 |
| Beckham, D. R. J. | 17 |
| Becton, F. | 2 |
| Bedford, H. | 1 |
| Bell, C. | 9 |
| Bent, D. A. | 4 |
| Bentley, R. T. F. | 9 |
| Bishop, S. M. | 1 |
| Blackburn, F. | 1 |
| Blissett, L. | 3 |
| Bloomer, S. | 28 |
| Bond, R. | 2 |
| Bonsor, A. G. | 1 |
| Bowden, E. R. | 1 |
| Bowers, J. W. | 2 |
| Bowles, S. | 1 |
| Bradford, G. R. W. | 1 |
| Bradford, J. | 7 |
| Bradley, W. | 2 |
| Bradshaw, F. | 3 |
| Brann, G. | 1 |
| Bridge, W. M. | 1 |
| Bridges, B. J. | 1 |
| Bridgett, A. | 3 |
| Brindle, T. | 1 |
| Britton, C. S. | 1 |
| Broadbent, P. F. | 2 |
| Broadis, I. A. | 8 |
| Brodie, J. B. | 1 |
| Bromley-Davenport, W. | 2 |
| Brook, E. F. | 10 |
| Brooking, T. D. | 5 |
| Brooks, J. | 2 |
| Broome, F. H. | 3 |
| Brown, A. | 4 |
| Brown, A. S. | 1 |
| Brown, G. | 5 |
| Brown, J. | 3 |
| Brown, W. | 1 |
| Brown, W. M. | 1 |
| Buchan, C. M. | 4 |
| Bull, S. G. | 4 |
| Bullock, N. | 2 |
| Burgess, H. | 4 |
| Butcher, T. | 3 |
| Byrne, J. J. | 8 |
| Cahill, G. | 2 |
| Campbell, S. J. | 1 |
| Camsell, G. H. | 18 |
| Carroll, A. T. | 2 |
| Carter, H. S. | 7 |
| Carter, J. H. | 4 |
| **Caulker, S. A.** | **1** |
| Chadwick, E. | 3 |
| Chamberlain, M. | 1 |
| Chambers, H. | 5 |
| Channon, M. R. | 21 |
| Charlton, J. | 6 |
| Charlton, R. | 49 |
| Chenery, C. J. | 1 |
| Chivers, M. | 13 |
| Clarke, A. J. | 10 |
| Cobbold, W. N. | 6 |
| Cock, J. G. | 2 |
| Cole, A. | 1 |
| Cole, J. J. | 10 |
| Common, A. | 2 |
| Connelly, J. M. | 7 |
| Coppell, S. J. | 7 |
| Cotterill, G. H. | 2 |
| Cowans, G. | 2 |
| Crawford, R. | 1 |
| Crawshaw, T. H. | 1 |
| Crayston, W. J. | 1 |
| Creek, F. N. S. | 1 |
| Crooks, S. D. | 7 |
| Crouch, P. J. | 22 |
| Currey, E. S. | 2 |
| Currie, A. W. | 3 |
| Cursham, A. W. | 2 |
| Cursham, H. A. | 5 |
| Daft, H. B. | 3 |
| Davenport, J. K. | 2 |
| Davis, G. | 1 |
| Davis, H. | 1 |
| Day, S. H. | 2 |
| Dean, W. R. | 18 |
| **Defoe, J. C.** | **19** |
| Devey, J. H. G. | 1 |
| Dewhurst, F. | 11 |
| Dix, W. R. | 1 |
| Dixon, K. M. | 4 |
| Dixon, L. M. | 1 |
| Dorrell, A. R. | 1 |
| Douglas, B. | 11 |
| Drake, E. J. | 6 |
| Ducat, A. | 1 |
| Dunn, A. T. B. | 2 |
| Eastham, G. | 2 |
| Edwards, D. | 5 |
| Ehiogu, U. | 1 |
| Elliott, W. H. | 3 |
| Evans, R. E. | 1 |
| Ferdinand, L. | 5 |
| Ferdinand, R. G. | 3 |
| Finney, T. | 30 |
| Fleming, H. J. | 9 |
| Flowers, R. | 10 |
| Forman, Frank | 1 |
| Forman, Fred | 3 |
| Foster, R. E. | 3 |
| Fowler, R. B. | 7 |
| Francis, G. C. J. | 3 |
| Francis, T. | 12 |
| Freeman, B. C. | 3 |
| Froggatt, J. | 2 |
| Froggatt, R. | 2 |
| Galley, T. | 1 |
| Gascoigne, P. J. | 10 |
| Geary, F. | 3 |
| Gerrard, S. G. | 19 |
| Gibbins, W. V. T. | 3 |
| Gilliatt, W. E. | 3 |
| Goddard, P. | 1 |
| Goodall, J. | 12 |
| Goodyer, A. C. | 1 |
| Gosling, R. C. | 2 |
| Goulden, L. A. | 4 |
| Grainger, C. | 3 |
| Greaves, J. | 44 |
| Grosvenor, A. T. | 2 |
| Gunn, W. | 1 |
| Haines, J. T. W. | 2 |
| Hall, G. W. | 9 |
| Halse, H. J. | 2 |
| Hampson, J. | 5 |
| Hampton, H. | 2 |
| Hancocks, J. | 2 |
| Hardman, H. P. | 1 |
| Harris, S. S. | 2 |
| Hassall, H. W. | 4 |
| Hateley, M. | 9 |
| Haynes, J. N. | 18 |
| Hegan, K. E. | 4 |
| Henfrey, A. G. | 2 |
| Heskey, E. W. | 7 |
| Hilsdon, G. R. | 14 |
| Hine, E. W. | 4 |
| Hinton, A. T. | 1 |
| Hirst, D. E. | 1 |
| Hitchens, G. A. | 5 |
| Hobbis, H. H. F. | 1 |
| Hoddle, G. | 8 |
| Hodgetts, D. | 1 |
| Hodgson, G. | 1 |
| Holley, G. H. | 8 |
| Houghton, W. E. | 5 |
| Howell, R. | 1 |
| Hughes, E. W. | 1 |
| Hulme, J. H. A. | 4 |
| Hunt, G. S. | 1 |
| Hunt, R. | 18 |
| Hunter, N. | 2 |
| Hurst, G. C. | 24 |
| Ince, P. E. C. | 2 |
| Jack, D. N. B. | 3 |
| **Jagielka, P. N.** | **1** |
| Jeffers, F. | 1 |
| Jenas, J. A. | 1 |
| Johnson, A. | 2 |
| Johnson, D. E. | 6 |
| Johnson, E. | 2 |
| Johnson, G. M. C. | 1 |
| Johnson, J. A. | 2 |
| Johnson, T. C. F. | 5 |
| Johnson, W. H. | 1 |
| Kail, E. I. L. | 2 |
| Kay, A. H. | 1 |
| Keegan, J. K. | 21 |
| Kelly, R. | 8 |
| Kennedy, R. | 3 |
| Kenyon-Slaney, W. S. | 2 |
| Keown, M. R. | 2 |
| Kevan, D. T. | 8 |
| Kidd, B. | 1 |
| King, L. B. | 2 |
| Kingsford, R. K. | 1 |
| Kirchen, A. J. | 2 |
| Kirton, W. J. | 1 |
| **Lampard, F. J.** | **29** |
| Langton, R. | 1 |
| Latchford, R. D. | 5 |
| Latheron, E. G. | 1 |
| Lawler, C. | 1 |
| Lawton, T. | 22 |
| Lee, F. | 10 |
| Lee, J. | 1 |
| Lee, R. M. | 2 |
| Lee, S. | 2 |
| Lescott, J. | 1 |
| Le Saux, G. P. | 1 |
| Lindley, T. | 14 |
| Lineker, G. | 48 |
| Lofthouse, J. M. | 3 |
| Lofthouse, N. | 30 |
| Hon. A. Lyttelton | 1 |
| Mabbutt, G. | 1 |
| Macdonald, M. | 6 |
| Mannion, W. J. | 11 |
| Mariner, P. | 13 |
| Marsh, R. W. | 1 |
| Matthews, S. | 11 |
| Matthews, V. | 1 |
| McCall, J. | 1 |
| McDermott, T. | 3 |
| McManaman, S. | 3 |
| Medley, L. D. | 1 |
| Melia, J. | 1 |
| Mercer, D. W. | 1 |
| Merson, P. C. | 3 |
| Milburn, J. E. T. | 10 |
| Miller, H. S. | 1 |
| Mills, G. R. | 3 |
| **Milner, J. P.** | **1** |
| Milward, A. | 3 |
| Mitchell, C. | 5 |
| Moore, J. | 1 |
| Moore, R. F. | 2 |
| Moore, W. G. B. | 2 |
| Morren, T. | 1 |
| Morris, F. | 1 |
| Morris, J. | 3 |
| Mortensen, S. H. | 23 |
| Morton, J. R. | 1 |
| Mosforth, W. | 3 |
| Mullen, J. | 6 |
| Mullery, A. P. | 1 |
| Murphy, D. B | 1 |
| Neal, P. G. | 5 |
| Needham, E. | 3 |
| Nicholls, J. | 1 |

|  | |
|---|---|
| Nicholson, W. E. | 1 |
| Nugent, D. J. | 1 |
| O'Grady, M. | 3 |
| Osborne, F. R. | 3 |
| Owen, M. J. | 40 |
| **Own goals** | **32** |
| **Oxlade-Chamberlain, A. M. D.** | **3** |
| Page, L. A. | 1 |
| Paine, T. L. | 7 |
| Palmer, C. L. | 1 |
| Parry, E. H. | 1 |
| Parry, R. A. | 1 |
| Pawson, F. W. | 1 |
| Payne, J. | 2 |
| Peacock, A. | 3 |
| Pearce, S. | 5 |
| Pearson, J. S. | 5 |
| Pearson, S. C. | 5 |
| Perry, W. | 2 |
| Peters, M. | 20 |
| Pickering, F. | 5 |
| Platt, D. | 27 |
| Pointer, R. | 2 |
| Quantrill, A. | 1 |
| Ramsay, A. E. | 3 |
| Revie, D. G. | 4 |
| Redknapp, J. F. | 1 |
| Reynolds, J. | |
| Richards, M. | 1 |
| Richardson, K. E. | 2 |
| Richardson, J. R. | 2 |
| Rigby, A. | 3 |
| Rimmer, E. J. | 1 |
| Roberts, F. | 2 |
| Roberts, H. | 1 |
| Roberts, W. T. | 2 |
| Robinson, J. | 3 |
| Robson, B. | 26 |
| Robson, R. | 4 |
| **Rooney, W.** | **36** |
| Rowley, J. F. | 6 |
| Royle, J. | 2 |
| Rutherford, J. | 3 |
| Sagar, C. | 1 |
| Sandilands, R. R. | 3 |
| Sansom, K. | 1 |
| Schofield, J. | 1 |
| Scholes, P. | 14 |
| Seed, J. M. | 1 |
| Settle, J. | 6 |
| Sewell, J. | 3 |
| Shackleton, L. F. | 1 |
| Sharp, J. | 1 |
| Shearer, A. | 30 |
| Shelton, A. | 1 |
| Shepherd, A. | 2 |
| Sheringham, E. P. | 11 |
| Simpson, J. | 1 |
| Smith, A. | 1 |
| Smith, A. M. | 2 |
| Smith, G. O. | 11 |
| Smith, Joe | 1 |
| Smith, J. R. | 2 |
| Smith, J. W. | 4 |
| Smith, R. | 13 |
| Smith, S. | 1 |
| Sorby, T. H. | 1 |
| Southgate, G. | 2 |
| Southworth, J. | 3 |
| Sparks, F. J. | 3 |
| Spence, J. W. | 1 |
| Spiksley, F. | 5 |
| Spilsbury, B. W. | 3 |
| Steele, F. C. | 8 |
| Stephenson, G. T. | 2 |
| Steven, T. M. | 1 |
| Stewart, J. | 2 |
| Stiles, N. P. | 1 |

|  | |
|---|---|
| Storer, H. | 1 |
| Stone, S. B. | 2 |
| **Sturridge, D.** | **1** |
| Summerbee, M. G. | 1 |
| Tambling, R. V. | 1 |
| Taylor, P. J. | 2 |
| Taylor, T. | 16 |
| Terry, J. G. | 6 |
| Thompson, P. B. | 1 |
| Thornewell, G. | 1 |
| Tilson, S. F. | 6 |
| Townley, W. J. | 2 |
| Tueart, D. | 2 |
| Upson, M. J. | 2 |
| Vassell, D. | 6 |
| Vaughton, O. H. | 6 |
| Veitch, J. G. | 3 |
| Viollet, D. S. | 1 |
| Waddle, C. R. | 6 |
| Walcott, T. J. | 4 |
| Walker, W. H. | 9 |
| Wall, G. | 2 |
| Wallace, D. | 1 |
| Walsh, P. | 1 |
| Waring, T. | 4 |
| Warren, B. | 2 |
| Watson, D. V. | 4 |
| Watson, V. M. | 4 |
| Webb, G. W. | 1 |
| Webb, N. | 4 |
| Wedlock, W. J. | 2 |
| **Welbeck, D.** | **5** |
| Weller, K. | 1 |
| Welsh, D. | 1 |
| Whateley, O. | 2 |
| Wheldon, G. F. | 6 |
| Whitfield, H. | 1 |
| Wignall, F. | 2 |
| Wilkes, A. | 1 |
| Wilkins, R. G. | 3 |
| Willingham, C. K. | 1 |
| Wilshaw, D. J. | 10 |
| Wilson, G. P. | 1 |
| Winckworth, W. N. | 1 |
| Windridge, J. E. | 7 |
| Wise, D. F. | 1 |
| Withe, P. | 1 |
| Wollaston, C. H. R. | 1 |
| Wood, H. | 1 |
| Woodcock, T. | 16 |
| Woodhall, G. | 1 |
| Woodward, V. J. | 29 |
| Worrall, F. | 1 |
| Worthington, F. S. | 2 |
| Wright, I. E. | 9 |
| Wright, M. | 1 |
| Wright, W. A. | 3 |
| Wright-Phillips, S. C. | 6 |
| Wylie, J. G. | 1 |
| Yates, J. | 3 |
| **Young, A. S.** | **7** |

**NORTHERN IRELAND**

|  | |
|---|---|
| Anderson, T. | 4 |
| Armstrong, G. | 12 |
| Bambrick, J. | 12 |
| Barr, H. H. | 1 |
| Barron, H. | 3 |
| Best, G. | 9 |
| Bingham, W. L. | 10 |
| Black, K. | 1 |
| Blanchflower, D. | 2 |
| Blanchflower, J. | 1 |
| Brennan, B. | 1 |
| Brennan, R. A. | 1 |
| Brotherston, N. | 3 |
| Brown, J. | 1 |

|  | |
|---|---|
| Browne, F. | 2 |
| Brunt, C. | 1 |
| Campbell, J. | 1 |
| Campbell, W. G. | 1 |
| Casey, T. | 2 |
| Caskey, W. | 1 |
| Cassidy, T. | 1 |
| Chambers, J. | 3 |
| Clarke, C. J. | 13 |
| Clements, D. | 2 |
| Cochrane, T. | 1 |
| Condy, J. | 1 |
| Connor, M. J. | 1 |
| Coulter, J. | 1 |
| Croft, T. | 1 |
| Crone, W. | 1 |
| Crossan, E. | 1 |
| Crossan, J. A. | 10 |
| Curran, S. | 2 |
| Cush, W. W. | 5 |
| Dalton, W. | 4 |
| D'Arcy, S. D. | 1 |
| Darling, L. | 1 |
| Davey, H. H. | 1 |
| Davis, S. | 4 |
| Davis, T. L. | 1 |
| Dill, A. H. | 1 |
| Doherty, L. | 1 |
| Doherty, P. D. | 3 |
| Dougan, A. D. | 8 |
| Dowie, I. | 12 |
| Dunne, J. | 4 |
| Elder, A. R. | 1 |
| Elliott, S. | 4 |
| Emerson, W. | 1 |
| English, S. | 1 |
| Evans, C. | 1 |
| Evans, J. G. | 1 |
| Feeney, W. | 1 |
| Feeney, W. J. | 5 |
| **Ferguson, S.** | **1** |
| Ferguson, W. | 1 |
| Ferris, J. | 1 |
| Ferris, R. O. | 1 |
| Finney, T. | 2 |
| Gaffkin, W. | 4 |
| Gara, A. | 3 |
| Gaukrodger, G. | 1 |
| Gibb, J. T. | 2 |
| Gibb, T. J. | 1 |
| Gibson, W. | 1 |
| Gillespie, K. R. | 2 |
| Gillespie, W. | 13 |
| Goodall, A. L. | 2 |
| Griffin, D. J. | 1 |
| Gray, P. | 6 |
| Halligan, W. | 1 |
| Hamill, M. | 1 |
| Hamilton, B. | 4 |
| Hamilton, W. R. | 5 |
| Hannon, D. J. | 1 |
| Harkin, J. T. | 2 |
| Harvey, M. | 3 |
| **Healy, D. J.** | **36** |
| Hill, C. F. | 1 |
| Hughes, A. | 1 |
| Hughes, M. E. | 5 |
| Humphries, W. | 1 |
| Hunter, A. *(Distillery)* | 1 |
| Hunter, A. *(Blackburn R)* | 1 |
| Hunter, B. V. | 1 |
| Irvine, R. W. | 3 |
| Irvine, W. J. | 8 |
| Johnston, H. | 2 |
| Johnston, S. | 2 |
| Johnston, W. C. | 1 |

|  | |
|---|---|
| Jones, S. *(Distillery)* | 1 |
| Jones, S. *(Crewe Alex)* | 1 |
| Jones, J. | 1 |
| Kelly, J. | 4 |
| Kernaghan, N. | 2 |
| Kirwan, J. | 2 |
| Lacey, W. | 3 |
| **Lafferty, K.** | **9** |
| Lemon, J. | 2 |
| Lennon, N. F. | 1 |
| Lockhart, N. | 3 |
| Lomas, S. M. | 3 |
| Magilton, J. | 5 |
| Mahood, J. | 2 |
| Martin, D. K. | 3 |
| Maxwell, J. | 2 |
| McAdams, W. J. | 7 |
| McAllen, J. | 1 |
| McAuley, G. | 2 |
| Mcauley, J. L. | 1 |
| McCann, G. S. | 4 |
| McCartney, G. | 1 |
| McCandless, J. | 2 |
| McCandless, W. | 1 |
| McCaw, J. H. | 1 |
| McClelland, J. | 1 |
| McCluggage, A. | 2 |
| McCourt, P. | 2 |
| McCracken, W. | 1 |
| McCrory, S. | 1 |
| McCurdy, C. | 1 |
| McDonald, A. | 3 |
| McGarry, J. K. | 1 |
| McGrath, R. C. | 4 |
| **McGinn, N.** | **1** |
| McIlroy, J. | 10 |
| McIlroy, S. B. | 5 |
| McKenzie, H | 1 |
| McKnight, J. | 2 |
| McLaughlin, J. C. | 6 |
| McMahon, G. J. | 2 |
| McMordie, A. S. | 3 |
| McMorran, E. J. | 4 |
| McParland, P. J. | 10 |
| McWha, W. B. R. | 1 |
| Meldon, P. A. | 1 |
| Mercer, J. T. | 1 |
| Millar, W. | 1 |
| Milligan, D. | 1 |
| Milne, R. G. | 2 |
| Molyneux, T. B. | 1 |
| Moreland, V. | 1 |
| Morgan, S. | 3 |
| Morrow, S. J. | 1 |
| Morrow, W. J. | 1 |
| Mulryne, P. P. | 3 |
| Murdock, C. J. | 1 |
| Murphy, N. | 1 |
| Neill, W. J. T. | 2 |
| Nelson, S. | 1 |
| Nicholl, C. J. | 3 |
| Nicholl, J. M. | 1 |
| Nicholson, J. J. | 6 |
| O'Boyle, G. | 1 |
| O'Hagan, C. | 2 |
| O'Kane, W. J. | 1 |
| O'Neill, J. | 2 |
| O'Neill, M. A. | 4 |
| O'Neill, M. H. | 8 |
| Own goals | 10 |
| **Paterson, M. A.** | **1** |
| Paterson, D. J. | 1 |
| Patterson, R. | 1 |
| Peacock, R. | 2 |
| Peden, J. | 7 |
| Penney, S. | 2 |
| Pyper, James | 2 |
| Pyper, John | 1 |

| Player | Goals |
|---|---|
| Quinn, J. M. | 12 |
| Quinn, S. J. | 4 |
| Reynolds, J. | 1 |
| Rowland, K. | 1 |
| Rowley, R. W. M. | 2 |
| Rushe, F. | 1 |
| Sheridan, J. | 2 |
| Sherrard, J. | 1 |
| Sherrard, W. C. | 2 |
| **Shields, D.** | **1** |
| Simpson, W. J. | 5 |
| Sloan, H. A. de B. | 4 |
| Smyth, S. | 5 |
| Spence, D. W. | 3 |
| Sproule, I. | 1 |
| Stanfield, O. M. | 11 |
| Stevenson, A. E. | 5 |
| Stewart, I. | 2 |
| Taggart, G. P. | 7 |
| Thompson, F. W. | 2 |
| Torrans, S. | 1 |
| Tully, C. P. | 3 |
| Turner, A. | 1 |
| Walker, J. | 1 |
| Walsh, D. J. | 5 |
| Welsh, E. | 1 |
| Whiteside, N. | 9 |
| Whiteside, T. | 1 |
| Whitley, Jeff | 2 |
| Williams, J. R. | 1 |
| Williams, M. S. | 1 |
| Williamson, J. | 1 |
| Wilson, D. J. | 1 |
| Wilson, K. J. | 6 |
| Wilson, S. J. | 7 |
| Wilton, J. M. | 2 |
| Young, S. | 1 |

*N.B. In 1914 Young goal should be credited to Gillespie W v Wales*

## SCOTLAND

| Player | Goals |
|---|---|
| Aitken, R. *(Celtic)* | 1 |
| Aitken, R. *(Dumbarton)* | 1 |
| Aitkenhead, W. A. C. | 2 |
| Alexander, D. | 1 |
| Allan, D. S. | 4 |
| Allan, J. | 2 |
| Anderson, F. | 1 |
| Anderson, W. | 1 |
| Andrews, P. | 1 |
| Archibald, A. | 4 |
| Archibald, S. | 4 |
| Baird, D. | 2 |
| Baird, J. C. | 2 |
| Baird, S. | 2 |
| Bannon, E. | 1 |
| Barbour, A. | 1 |
| Barker, J. B. | 4 |
| Battles, B. Jr | 1 |
| Bauld, W. | 2 |
| Baxter, J. C. | 3 |
| Beattie, C. | 1 |
| Bell, J. | 5 |
| Bennett, A. | 2 |
| Berra, C. | 2 |
| Berry, D. | 1 |
| Bett, J. | 1 |
| Beveridge, W. W. | 1 |
| Black, A. | 3 |
| Black, D. | 1 |
| Bone, J. | 1 |
| Booth, S. | 6 |
| Boyd, K | 7 |
| Boyd, R. | 2 |
| Boyd, T. | 1 |
| Boyd, W. G. | 1 |
| Brackenridge, T. | 1 |
| Brand, R. | 8 |
| Brazil, A. | 1 |
| Bremner, W. J. | 3 |
| Broadfoot, K. | 1 |
| Brown, A. D. | 6 |
| Brown, S. | 2 |
| Buchanan, P. S. | 1 |
| Buchanan, R. | 1 |
| Buckley, P. | 1 |
| Buick, A. | 2 |
| Burke, C. | 2 |
| Burley, C. W. | 3 |
| Burns, K. | 1 |
| Cairns, T. | 1 |
| Caldwell, G. | 2 |
| Calderwood, C. | 1 |
| Calderwood, R. | 2 |
| Caldow, E. | 4 |
| Cameron, C. | 2 |
| Campbell, C. | 1 |
| Campbell, John *(Celtic)* | 5 |
| Campbell, John *(Rangers)* | 4 |
| Campbell, J. (South Western) | 1 |
| Campbell, P. | 2 |
| Campbell, R. | 1 |
| Cassidy, J. | 1 |
| Chalmers, S. | 3 |
| Chambers, T. | 1 |
| Cheyne, A. G. | 4 |
| Christie, A. J. | 1 |
| Clarkson, D. | 1 |
| Clunas, W. L. | 1 |
| Collins, J. | 12 |
| Collins, R. Y. | 10 |
| Combe, J. R. | 1 |
| Commons, K. | 2 |
| Conn, A. | 1 |
| Cooper, D. | 6 |
| Craig, J. | 1 |
| Craig, T. | 1 |
| Crawford, S. | 4 |
| Cunningham, A. N. | 5 |
| Curran, H. P. | 1 |
| Dailly, C. | 6 |
| Dalglish, K. | 30 |
| Davidson, D. | 1 |
| Davidson, J. A. | 1 |
| Delaney, J. | 3 |
| Devine, A. | 1 |
| Dewar, G. | 1 |
| Dewar, N. | 4 |
| Dickov, P. | 1 |
| Dickson, W. | 4 |
| Divers, J. | 1 |
| Dobie, R. S. | 1 |
| Docherty, T. H. | 1 |
| Dodds, D. | 1 |
| Dodds, W. | 7 |
| Donaldson, A. | 1 |
| Donnachie, J. | 1 |
| Dougall, J. | 1 |
| Drummond, J. | 2 |
| Dunbar, M. | 1 |
| Duncan, D. | 7 |
| Duncan, D. M. | 1 |
| Duncan, J. | 1 |
| Dunn, J. | 2 |
| Durie, G. S. | 7 |
| Easson, J. F. | 1 |
| Elliott, M. S. | 1 |
| Ellis, J. | 1 |
| Ferguson, B. | 3 |
| Ferguson, J. | 6 |
| Fernie, W. | 1 |
| Fitchie, T. T. | 1 |
| Flavell, R. | 2 |
| Fleming, C. | 2 |
| Fleming, J. W. | 3 |
| Fletcher, D. | 5 |
| Fletcher, S. | 1 |
| Fraser, M. J. E. | 3 |
| Freedman, D. A. | 1 |
| Gallacher, H. K. | 23 |
| Gallacher, K. W. | 9 |
| Gallacher, P. | 1 |
| Galt, J. H. | 1 |
| Gemmell, T. *(St Mirren)* | 1 |
| Gemmell, T. *(Celtic)* | 1 |
| Gemmill, A. | 8 |
| Gemmill, S. | 1 |
| Gibb, W. | 1 |
| Gibson, D. W. | 3 |
| Gibson, J. D. | 1 |
| Gibson, N. | 1 |
| Gillespie, Jas. | 3 |
| Gillick, T. | 3 |
| Gilzean, A. J. | 12 |
| Goodwillie, D. | 1 |
| Gossland, J. | 2 |
| Goudie, J. | 1 |
| Gough, C. R. | 6 |
| Gourlay, J. | 1 |
| Graham, A. | 2 |
| Graham, G. | 3 |
| Gray, A. | 7 |
| Gray, E. | 3 |
| Gray, F. | 1 |
| Greig, J. | 3 |
| Groves, W. | 4 |
| Hamilton, G. | 4 |
| Hamilton, G. (Queen's Park) | 3 |
| Hamilton, R. C. | 15 |
| **Hanley, G.** | **1** |
| Harper, J. M. | 2 |
| Hartley, P. J. | 1 |
| Harrower, W. | 5 |
| Hartford, R. A. | 4 |
| Heggie, C. W | 4 |
| Henderson, J. G. | 1 |
| Henderson, W. | 5 |
| Hendry, E. C. J. | 3 |
| Herd, D. G. | 3 |
| Herd, G. | 1 |
| Hewie, J. D. | 2 |
| Higgins, A. *(Newcastle U)* | 1 |
| Higgins, A. *(Kilmarnock)* | 4 |
| Highet, T. C. | 1 |
| Holt, G.J. | 1 |
| Holton, J. A. | 2 |
| Hopkin, D. | 2 |
| Houliston, W. | 2 |
| Howie, H. | 1 |
| Howie, J. | 2 |
| Hughes, J. | 1 |
| Hunter, W. | 1 |
| Hutchison, D. | 6 |
| Hutchison, T. | 1 |
| Hutton, J. | 1 |
| Hyslop, T. | 1 |
| Imrie, W. N. | 1 |
| Jackson, A. | 8 |
| Jackson, C. | 1 |
| Jackson, D. | 4 |
| James, A. W. | 4 |
| Jardine, A. | 1 |
| Jenkinson, T. | 1 |
| Jess, E. | 2 |
| Johnston, A. | 2 |
| Johnston, L. H. | 1 |
| Johnston, M. | 14 |
| Johnstone, D. | 2 |
| Johnstone, J. | 4 |
| Johnstone, Jas. | 1 |
| Johnstone, R. | 10 |
| Johnstone, W. | 1 |
| Jordan, J. | 11 |
| Kay, J. L. | 5 |
| Keillor, A. | 3 |
| Kelly, J. | 1 |
| Kelso, R. | 1 |
| Ker, G. | 10 |
| King, A. | 1 |
| King, J. | 1 |
| Kinnear, D. | 1 |
| Kyle, K. | 1 |
| Lambert, P. | 1 |
| Lambie, J. | 1 |
| Lambie, W. A. | 5 |
| Lang, J. J. | 2 |
| Latta, A. | 2 |
| Law, D. | 30 |
| Leggat, G. | 8 |
| Lennie, W. | 1 |
| Lennox, R. | 3 |
| Liddell, W. | 6 |
| Lindsay, J. | 6 |
| Linwood, A. B. | 1 |
| Logan, J. | 1 |
| Lorimer, P. | 4 |
| Love, A. | 1 |
| Low, J. *(Cambuslang)* | 1 |
| Lowe, J. *(St Bernards)* | 1 |
| Macari, L. | 5 |
| MacDougall, E. J. | 3 |
| MacFarlane, A. | 1 |
| MacLeod, M. | 1 |
| Mackay, D. C. | 4 |
| Mackay, G. | 1 |
| MacKenzie, J. A. | 1 |
| Mackail-Smith, C. | 1 |
| Mackie, J. C. | 2 |
| MacKinnon, W. W. | 5 |
| Madden, J. | 1 |
| Maloney, S. | 1 |
| Marshall, H. | 1 |
| Marshall, J. | 1 |
| Mason, J. | 4 |
| Massie, A. | 1 |
| Masson, D. S. | 5 |
| McAdam, J. | 1 |
| McAllister, G. | 5 |
| McArthur, J. | 1 |
| McAulay, J. D. | 1 |
| McAvennie, F. | 1 |
| McCall, J. | 1 |
| McCall, S. M. | 1 |
| McCalliog, J. | 1 |
| McCallum, N. | 1 |
| McCann, N. | 3 |
| McClair, B. J. | 2 |
| McCoist, A. | 19 |
| McColl, R. S. | 13 |
| **McCormack, R.** | **2** |
| McCulloch, D. | 3 |
| McCulloch, L. | 1 |
| McDougall, J. | 4 |
| McFadden, J. | 15* |
| McFadyen, W. | 2 |
| McGhee, M. | 2 |
| McGinlay, J. | 4 |
| McGregor, J. | 1 |
| McGrory, J. | 6 |
| McGuire, W. | 1 |
| McInally, A. | 3 |
| McInnes, T. | 2 |
| McKie, J. | 2 |
| McKimmie, S. | 1 |
| McKinlay, W. | 4 |
| McKinnon, A. | 1 |
| McKinnon, R. | 1 |

|  | |
|---|---|
| McLaren, A. | 4 |
| McLaren, J. | 1 |
| McLean, A. | 1 |
| McLean, T. | 1 |
| McLintock, F. | 1 |
| McMahon, A. | 6 |
| McManus, S. | 2 |
| McMenemy, J. | 5 |
| McMillan, I. L. | 2 |
| McNeill, W. | 3 |
| McNiel, H. | 5 |
| McPhail, J. | 3 |
| McPhail, R. | 7 |
| McPherson, J. *(Kilmarnock)* | 7 |
| McPherson, J. *(Vale of Leven)* | 1 |
| McPherson, R. | 1 |
| McQueen, G. | 5 |
| McStay, P. | 9 |
| McSwegan, G. | 1 |
| Meiklejohn, D. D. | 3 |
| Millar, J. | 2 |
| **Miller, K.** | **17** |
| Miller, T. | 2 |
| Miller, W. | 1 |
| Mitchell, R. C. | 1 |
| Morgan, W. | 1 |
| Morris, D. | 1 |
| Morris, H. | 3 |
| **Morrison, J. C.** | **2** |
| Morton, A. L. | 5 |
| Mudie, J. K. | 9 |
| **Mulgrew, C.** | **1** |
| Mulhall, G. | 1 |
| Munro, A. D. | 1 |
| Munro, N. | 2 |
| Murdoch, R. | 5 |
| Murphy, F. | 1 |
| Murray, J. | 1 |
| Napier, C. E. | 3 |
| Narey, D. | 1 |
| Naismith, S. | 2 |
| Naysmith, G. A. | 1 |
| Neil, R. G. | 2 |
| Nevin, P. K. F. | 5 |
| Nicholas, C. | 5 |
| Nisbet, J. | 2 |
| O'Connor, G. | 4 |
| O'Donnell, F. | 2 |
| O'Hare, J. | 5 |
| Ormond, W. E. | 2 |
| O'Rourke, F. | 1 |
| Orr, R. | 1 |
| Orr, T. | 1 |
| Oswald, J. | 1 |
| **Own goals** | **20** |
| Parlane, D. | 1 |
| Paul, H. McD. | 2 |
| Paul, W. | 5 |
| Pettigrew, W. | 2 |
| Provan, D. | 1 |
| Quashie, N. F. | 1 |
| Quinn, J. | 7 |
| Quinn, P. | 1 |
| Rankin, G. | 2 |
| Rankin, R. | 2 |
| Reid, W. | 4 |
| Reilly, L. | 22 |
| Renny-Tailyour, H. W. | 1 |
| **Rhodes, J. L.** | **3** |
| Richmond, J. T. | 1 |
| Ring, T. | 2 |
| Rioch, B. D. | 6 |
| Ritchie, J. | 1 |
| Ritchie, P. S. | 1 |
| Robertson, A. | 2 |
| Robertson, J. | 3 |
| Robertson, J. N. | 8 |

|  | |
|---|---|
| Robertson, J. T. | 2 |
| Robertson, T. | 1 |
| Robertson, W. | 1 |
| Russell, D. | 1 |
| Scott, A. S. | 5 |
| Sellar, W. | 4 |
| Sharp, G. | 1 |
| Shaw, F. W. | 1 |
| Shearer, D. | 2 |
| Simpson, J. | 1 |
| Smith, A. | 5 |
| Smith, G. | 4 |
| Smith, J. | 1 |
| Smith, John | 13 |
| **Snodgrass, R.** | **2** |
| Somerville, G. | 1 |
| Souness, G. J. | 4 |
| Speedie, F. | 2 |
| St John, I. | 9 |
| Steel, W. | 12 |
| Stein, C. | 10 |
| Stevenson, G. | 4 |
| Stewart, A. | 1 |
| Stewart, R. | 1 |
| Stewart, W. E. | 1 |
| Strachan, G. | 5 |
| Sturrock, P. | 3 |
| Taylor, J. D. | 1 |
| Templeton, R. | 1 |
| Thompson, S. | 3 |
| Thomson, A. | 1 |
| Thomson, C. | 4 |
| Thomson, R. | 1 |
| Thomson, W. | 1 |
| Thornton, W. | 1 |
| Waddell, T. S. | 1 |
| Waddell, W. | 6 |
| Walker, J. | 2 |
| Walker, R. | 7 |
| Walker, J. | 9 |
| Wallace, I. A. | 1 |
| Wark, J. | 7 |
| Watson, J. A. K. | 1 |
| Watt, F. | 2 |
| Watt, W. W. | 1 |
| Webster, A. | 1 |
| Weir, A. | 1 |
| Weir, D. | 1 |
| Weir, J. B. | 2 |
| White, J. A. | 3 |
| Wilkie, L. | 1 |
| Wilson, A. *(Sheffield W)* | 2 |
| Wilson, A. N. *(Dunfermline Ath)* | 13 |
| Wilson, D. *(Liverpool)* | 1 |
| Wilson, D. *(Queen's Park)* | 2 |
| Wilson, D. *(Rangers)* | 9 |
| Wilson, H. | 1 |
| Wylie, T. G. | 1 |
| Young, A. | 5 |

**WALES**

|  | |
|---|---|
| Allchurch, I. J. | 23 |
| Allen, M. | 3 |
| Astley, D. J. | 12 |
| Atherton, R. W. | 2 |
| **Bale, G.** | **11** |
| Bamford, T. | 1 |
| Barnes, W. | 1 |
| Bellamy, C. D. | 19 |
| Blackmore, C. G. | 1 |
| Blake, D. | 1 |
| Blake, N. A. | 4 |
| Bodin, P. J. | 3 |
| Boulter, L. M. | 1 |
| Bowdler, J. C. H. | 3 |
| Bowen, D. L. | 1 |
| Bowen, M. | 3 |

|  | |
|---|---|
| Boyle, T. | 1 |
| Bryan, T. | 1 |
| Burgess, W. A. R. | 1 |
| Burke, T. | 1 |
| Butler, W. T. | 1 |
| Chapman, T. | 2 |
| Charles, J. | 1 |
| Charles, M. | 6 |
| Charles, W. J. | 15 |
| Church, S. R. | 1 |
| Clarke, R. J. | 5 |
| Coleman, C. | 4 |
| Collier, D. J. | 1 |
| Collins, J. | 2 |
| Cotterill, D. | 1 |
| Crosse, K. | 1 |
| Cumner, R. H. | 1 |
| Curtis, A. | 6 |
| Curtis, E. R. | 3 |
| Davies, D. W. | 1 |
| Davies, E. Lloyd | 1 |
| Davies, G. | 2 |
| Davies, L. S. | 6 |
| Davies, R. T. | 9 |
| Davies, R. W. | 6 |
| Davies, Simon | 6 |
| Davies, Stanley | 5 |
| Davies, W. | 6 |
| Davies, W. H. | 1 |
| Davies, William | 5 |
| Davis, W. O. | 1 |
| Deacy, N. | 4 |
| Doughty, J. | 6 |
| Doughty, R. | 2 |
| Durban, A. | 2 |
| Dwyer, P. | 2 |
| Earnshaw, R. | 16 |
| Eastwood, F. | 4 |
| Edwards, D. | 3 |
| Edwards, G. | 2 |
| Edwards, R. I. | 4 |
| England, H. M. | 4 |
| Evans, C. | 2 |
| Evans, I. | 1 |
| Evans, J. | 1 |
| Evans, R. E. | 2 |
| Evans, W. | 1 |
| Eyton-Jones, J. A. | 1 |
| Fletcher, C. | 1 |
| Flynn, B. | 7 |
| Ford, T. | 23 |
| Foulkes, W. I. | 1 |
| Fowler, J. | 3 |
| Giles, D. | 2 |
| Giggs, R. J. | 12 |
| Glover, E. M. | 7 |
| Godfrey, B. C. | 2 |
| Green, A. W. | 3 |
| Griffiths, A. T. | 6 |
| Griffiths, M. W. | 2 |
| Griffiths, T. P. | 3 |
| Harris, C. S. | 1 |
| Hartson, J. | 14 |
| Hersee, R. | 1 |
| Hewitt, R. | 1 |
| Hockey, T. | 1 |
| Hodges, G. | 2 |
| Hole, W. J. | 1 |
| Hopkins, I. J. | 2 |
| Horne, B. | 2 |
| Howell, E. G. | 3 |
| Hughes, L. M. | 16 |
| James, E. | 2 |
| James, L. | 10 |
| James, R. | 7 |
| Jarrett, R. H. | 3 |
| Jenkyns, C. A. | 1 |

|  | |
|---|---|
| Jones, A. | 1 |
| Jones, Bryn | 6 |
| Jones, B. S. | 2 |
| Jones, Cliff | 16 |
| Jones, C. W. | 1 |
| Jones, D. E. | 1 |
| Jones, Evan | 1 |
| Jones, H. | 1 |
| Jones, I. | 1 |
| Jones, J. L. | 1 |
| Jones, J. O. | 1 |
| Jones, J. P. | 1 |
| Jones, Leslie J. | 1 |
| Jones, R. A. | 2 |
| Jones, W. L. | 6 |
| Keenor, F. C. | 2 |
| King, A. | 1 |
| Koumas, J. | 10 |
| Krzywicki, R. L. | 1 |
| Ledley, J. | 3 |
| Leek, K. | 5 |
| Lewis, B. | 4 |
| Lewis, D. M. | 2 |
| Lewis, W. | 8 |
| Lewis, W. L. | 3 |
| Llewelyn, C. M | 1 |
| Lovell, S. | 1 |
| Lowrie, G. | 2 |
| Mahoney, J. F. | 1 |
| Mays, A. W. | 1 |
| Medwin, T. C. | 6 |
| Melville, A. K. | 3 |
| Meredith, W. H. | 11 |
| Mills, T. J. | 1 |
| Moore, G. | 1 |
| Morgan, J. R. | 2 |
| Morgan-Owen, H. | 1 |
| Morgan-Owen, M. M. | 2 |
| Morison, S. | 1 |
| Morris, A. G. | 9 |
| Morris, H. | 2 |
| Morris, R. | 1 |
| Morris, S. | 2 |
| Nicholas, P. | 2 |
| O'Callaghan, E. | 3 |
| O'Sullivan, P. A. | 1 |
| Owen, G. | 2 |
| Owen, W. | 4 |
| Owen, W. P. | 6 |
| Own goals | 14 |
| Palmer, D. | 3 |
| Parry, P. I. | 1 |
| Parry, T. D. | 3 |
| Paul, R. | 1 |
| Peake, E. | 1 |
| Pembridge, M. | 6 |
| Perry, E. | 1 |
| Phillips, C. | 5 |
| Phillips, D. | 2 |
| Powell, A. | 1 |
| Powell, D. | 1 |
| Price, J. | 4 |
| Price, P. | 1 |
| Pryce-Jones, W. E. | 3 |
| Pugh, D. H. | 2 |
| **Ramsay, A.** | **6** |
| Reece, G. I. | 2 |
| Rees, R. R. | 3 |
| Richards, R. W. | 1 |
| Roach, J. | 2 |
| Robbins, W. W. | 4 |
| Roberts, J. *(Corwen)* | 1 |
| Roberts, Jas. | 1 |
| Roberts, P. S. | 1 |
| Roberts, R. *(Druids)* | 1 |
| Roberts, W. *(Llangollen)* | 2 |

# BRITISH AND IRISH INTERNATIONAL MANAGERS

**England**
Walter Winterbottom 1946–1962 (after period as coach); Alf Ramsey 1963–1974; Joe Mercer (caretaker) 1974; Don Revie 1974–1977; Ron Greenwood 1977–1982; Bobby Robson 1982–1990; Graham Taylor 1990–1993; Terry Venables (coach) 1994–1996; Glenn Hoddle 1996–1999; Kevin Keegan 1999–2000; Sven-Goran Eriksson 2001–2006; Steve McClaren 2006–2007; Fabio Capello 2008–2012; Roy Hodgson from May 2012.

**Northern Ireland**
Peter Doherty 1951–1952; Bertie Peacock 1962–1967; Billy Bingham 1967–1971; Terry Neill 1971–1975; Dave Clements (player-manager) 1975–1976; Danny Blanchflower 1976–1979; Billy Bingham 1980–1994; Bryan Hamilton 1994–1998; Lawrie McMenemy 1998–1999; Sammy McIlroy 2000–2003; Lawrie Sanchez 2004–2007; Nigel Worthington 2007–2011; Michael O'Neill from December 2011.

**Scotland (since 1967)**
Bobby Brown 1967–1971; Tommy Docherty 1971–1972; Willie Ormond 1973–1977; Ally MacLeod 1977–1978; Jock Stein 1978–1985; Alex Ferguson (caretaker) 1985–1986 Andy Roxburgh (coach) 1986–1993; Craig Brown 1993–2001; Berti Vogts 2002–2004; Walter Smith 2004–2007; Alex McLeish 2007; George Burley 2008–2009; Craig Levein 2009–2012; Gordon Strachan from February 2013.

**Wales (since 1974)**
Mike Smith 1974–1979; Mike England 1980–1988; David Williams (caretaker) 1988; Terry Yorath 1988–1993; John Toshack 1994 for one match; Mike Smith 1994–1995; Bobby Gould 1995–1999; Mark Hughes 1999–2004; John Toshack 2004–2010; Gary Speed 2010–2011; Chris Coleman from January 2012.

**Republic of Ireland**
Liam Tuohy 1971–1972; Johnny Giles 1973–1980 (after period as player-manager); Eoin Hand 1980–1985; Jack Charlton 1986–1996; Mick McCarthy 1996–2002; Brian Kerr 2003–2006; Steve Staunton 2006–2007; Giovanni Trapattoni from February 2008.

Gordon Strachan is announced as the new manager of Scotland at Hampden Park in January. (Action Images)

# SOUTH AMERICA

## COPA SUDAMERICANA 2012

**FIRST ROUND – FIRST LEG**

| | |
|---|---|
| Danubio v Olimpia Asuncion | 0-0 |
| Tacuary v CD Cobreloa | 0-1 |
| Liverpool v Universitario Sucre | 3-0 |
| Deportivo Tachira v Barcelona SC | 0-0 |
| Guarani v Oriente Petrolero | 0-1 |
| Club Aurora v Cerro Largo | 2-1 |
| O'Higgins v Cerro Porteno | 3-3 |
| CD Union Comercio v Envigado | 0-0 |
| Deportes Iquique v Nacional | 2-0 |
| CS Emelec v Universidad San Martin | 1-0 |
| Deportes Tolima v CD Lara | 3-1 |
| Deportivo Quito v Leon de Huanuco | 1-0 |
| Inti Gas v Millonarios | 0-0 |
| La Equidad v Mineros de Guayana | 0-1 |
| Club Blooming v Universidad Catolica | 1-1 |
| Monagas v LDU Loja | 0-2 |

**FIRST ROUND – SECOND LEG** (agg)

| | |
|---|---|
| Olimpia Asuncion v Danubio | 2-1 (2-1) |
| CD Cobreloa v Tacuary | 2-2 (3-2) |
| Universitario Sucre v Liverpool | 1-2 (1-5) |
| Barcelona SC v Deportivo Tachira | 5-1 (5-1) |
| Oriente Petrolero v Guarani | 1-2 (2-2) |
| *Guarani won on away goals rule.* | |
| Cerro Largo v Club Aurora | 0-0 (1-2) |
| Cerro Porteno v O'Higgins | 4-0 (7-3) |
| Envigado v CD Union Comercio | 2-0 (2-0) |
| Nacional v Deportes Iquique | 4-0 (4-2) |
| Universidad San Martin v CS Emelec | 1-1 (1-2) |
| CD Lara v Deportes Tolima | 0-0 (1-3) |
| Leon de Huanuco v Deportivo Quito | 2-3 (2-4) |
| Millonarios v Inti Gas | 3-0 (3-0) |
| Mineros de Guayana v La Equidad | 2-1 (3-1) |
| Universidad Catolica v Club Blooming | 3-0 (4-1) |
| LDU Loja v Monagas | 4-2 (6-2) |

**SECOND ROUND – FIRST LEG**

| | |
|---|---|
| Gremio Porto Alegre v Coritiba | 1-0 |
| Atletico GO v Figueirense | 1-1 |
| EC Bahia v Sao Paulo | 0-2 |
| SE Palmeiras v Botafogo RJ | 2-0 |
| Argentinos Juniors v Tigre | 1-2 |
| Boca Juniors v Independiente | 3-3 |
| CA Colon v Racing Club | 3-1 |
| CD Cobreloa v Barcelona SC | 0-0 |
| Envigado v Liverpool | 1-1 |
| Olimpia Asuncion v CS Emelec | 0-1 |
| LDU Loja v Nacional | 0-1 |
| Mineros de Guayana v Cerro Porteno | 2-2 |
| Universidad Catolica v Deportes Tolima | 2-0 |
| Deportivo Quito v Club Aurora | 2-1 |
| Guarani v Millonarios | 2-4 |

**SECOND ROUND – SECOND LEG** (agg)

| | |
|---|---|
| Coritiba v Gremio Porto Alegre | 3-2 (3-3) |
| *Gremio Porto Alegre won on away goals rule.* | |
| Figueirense v Atletico GO | 1-1 (2-2) |
| *aet; Figueirense won 4-2 on penalties.* | |
| Sao Paulo v EC Bahia | 2-0 (4-0) |
| Botafogo RJ v SE Palmeiras | 3-1 (3-3) |
| *SE Palmeiras won on away goals rule.* | |
| Tigre v Argentinos Juniors | 4-1 (6-2) |
| Independiente v Boca Juniors | 0-0 (3-3) |
| *Independiente won on away goals rule.* | |

| | |
|---|---|
| Racing Club v CA Colon | 1-2 (2-5) |
| Barcelona SC v CD Cobreloa | 4-3 (4-3) |
| Liverpool v Envigado | 1-0 (2-1) |
| CS Emelec v Olimpia Asuncion | 0-0 (1-0) |
| Nacional v LDU Loja | 1-2 (2-2) |
| *LDU Loja won on away goals rule.* | |
| Cerro Porteno v Mineros de Guayana | 4-0 (6-2) |
| Deportes Tolima v Universidad Catolica | 3-1 (3-3) |
| *Deportes Tolima won on away goals rule.* | |
| Club Aurora v Deportivo Quito | 1-3 (2-5) |
| Millonarios v Guarani | 1-1 (5-3) |

**ROUND OF 16 – FIRST LEG**

| | |
|---|---|
| Deportivo Quito v Tigre | 2-0 |
| Independiente v Liverpool | 2-1 |
| LDU Loja v Sao Paulo | 1-1 |
| Barcelona SC v Gremio Porto Alegre | 0-1 |
| CA Colon v Cerro Porteno | 1-2 |
| Universidad de Chile v CS Emelec | 2-2 |
| SE Palmeiras v Millonarios | 3-1 |
| Universidad Catolica v Atletico GO | 2-0 |

**ROUND OF 16 – SECOND LEG** (agg)

| | |
|---|---|
| Tigre v Deportivo Quito | 4-0 (4-2) |
| Liverpool v Independiente | 1-2 (2-4) |
| Sao Paulo v LDU Loja | 0-0 (1-1) |
| *Sao Paulo won on away goals rule.* | |
| Gremio Porto Alegre v Barcelona SC | 2-1 (3-1) |
| Cerro Porteno v CA Colon | 2-1 (4-2) |
| CS Emelec v Universidad de Chile | 0-1 (2-3) |
| Millonarios v SE Palmeiras | 3-0 (4-3) |
| Atletico GO v Universidad Catolica | 3-1 (3-3) |
| *Universidad Catolica won on away goals rule.* | |

**QUARTER-FINALS – FIRST LEG**

| | |
|---|---|
| Gremio Porto Alegre v Millonarios | 1-0 |
| Universidad de Chile v Sao Paulo | 0-2 |
| Cerro Porteno v Tigre | 1-0 |
| Independiente v Universidad Catolica | 2-2 |

**QUARTER-FINALS – SECOND LEG** (agg)

| | |
|---|---|
| Millonarios v Gremio Porto Alegre | 3-1 (3-2) |
| Sao Paulo v Universidad de Chile | 5-0 (7-0) |
| Tigre v Cerro Porteno | 4-2 (4-3) |
| Universidad Catolica v Independiente | 2-1 (4-3) |

**SEMI-FINALS – FIRST LEG**

| | |
|---|---|
| Universidad Catolica v Sao Paulo | 1-1 |
| Tigre v Millonarios | 0-0 |

**SEMI-FINALS – SECOND LEG** (agg)

| | |
|---|---|
| Sao Paulo v Universidad Catolica | 0-0 (1-1) |
| *Sao Paulo won on away goals rule.* | |
| Millonarios v Tigre | 1-1 (1-1) |
| *Tigre won on away goals rule* | |

**FINAL – FIRST LEG**

| | |
|---|---|
| Tigre v Sao Paulo | 0-0 |

**FINAL – SECOND LEG** (agg)

| | |
|---|---|
| Sao Paulo v Tigre | 2-0 (2-0) |

*Match abandoned at half time – tie awarded to Sao Paulo.*

## COPA SANTANDER LIBERTADORES 2013

**FIRST ROUND – FIRST LEG**

| | |
|---|---|
| Tigre v Deportivo Anzoategui | 2-1 |
| Club Leon v Deportes Iquique | 1-1 |
| LDU Quito v Gremio Porto Alegre | 1-0 |
| Sao Paulo v Club Bolívar | 5-0 |
| Defensor Sporting v Olimpia Asuncion | 0-0 |
| Deportes Tolima v Universidad Cesar Vallejo | 1-0 |

**FIRST ROUND – SECOND LEG** (agg)

| | |
|---|---|
| Deportivo Anzoategui v Tigre | 0-3 (1-5) |
| Deportes Iquique v Club Leon | 1-1 (2-2) |
| *Deportes Iquique won 4-2 on penalties.* | |
| Gremio Porto Alegre v LDU Quito | 1-0 (1-1) |
| *Gremio Porto Alegre won 5-4 on penalties.* | |
| Club Bolívar v Sao Paulo | 4-3 (4-8) |

| | |
|---|---|
| Olimpia Asuncion v Defensor Sporting | 2-0 (2-0) |
| Universidad Cesar Vallejo v Deportes Tolima | 1-1 (1-2) |

**SECOND ROUND**

**GROUP 1**

| | |
|---|---|
| Nacional v Barcelona SC | 2-2 |
| Boca Juniors v Deportivo Toluca | 1-2 |
| Deportivo Toluca v Nacional | 2-3 |
| Barcelona SC v Boca Juniors | 1-2 |
| Deportivo Toluca v Barcelona SC | 1-1 |
| Boca Juniors v Nacional | 0-1 |
| Barcelona SC v Deportivo Toluca | 0-0 |
| Nacional v Boca Juniors | 0-1 |
| Boca Juniors v Barcelona SC | 1-0 |

| | |
|---|---|
| Nacional v Deportivo Toluca | 4-0 |
| Barcelona SC v Nacional | 1-0 |
| Deportivo Toluca v Boca Juniors | 3-2 |

**Group 1 Table**

| | P | W | D | L | F | A | GD | Pts |
|---|---|---|---|---|---|---|---|---|
| Nacional | 6 | 3 | 1 | 2 | 10 | 6 | 4 | 10 |
| Boca Juniors | 6 | 3 | 0 | 3 | 7 | 7 | 0 | 9 |
| Deportivo Toluca | 6 | 2 | 2 | 2 | 8 | 11 | -3 | 8 |
| Barcelona SC | 6 | 1 | 3 | 2 | 5 | 6 | -1 | 6 |

## GROUP 2

| | |
|---|---|
| SE Palmeiras v Sporting Cristal | 2-1 |
| Tigre v Libertad | 0-2 |
| Sporting Cristal v Tigre | 2-0 |
| Libertad v SE Palmeiras | 2-0 |
| Libertad v Sporting Cristal | 2-2 |
| Tigre v SE Palmeiras | 1-0 |
| Sporting Cristal v Libertad | 2-2 |
| SE Palmeiras v Tigre | 2-0 |
| Tigre v Sporting Cristal | 3-1 |
| SE Palmeiras v Libertad | 1-0 |
| Sporting Cristal v SE Palmeiras | 1-0 |
| Libertad v Tigre | 3-5 |

**Group 2 Table**

| | P | W | D | L | F | A | GD | Pts |
|---|---|---|---|---|---|---|---|---|
| SE Palmeiras | 6 | 3 | 0 | 3 | 5 | 5 | 0 | 9 |
| Tigre | 6 | 3 | 0 | 3 | 9 | 10 | -1 | 9 |
| Libertad | 6 | 2 | 2 | 2 | 10 | 9 | 1 | 8 |
| Sporting Cristal | 6 | 2 | 2 | 2 | 8 | 8 | 0 | 8 |

## GROUP 3

| | |
|---|---|
| Atletico Mineiro v Sao Paulo | 2-1 |
| The Strongest v Arsenal | 2-1 |
| Arsenal v Atletico Mineiro | 2-5 |
| Sao Paulo v The Strongest | 2-1 |
| Sao Paulo v Arsenal | 1-1 |
| Atletico Mineiro v The Strongest | 2-1 |
| The Strongest v Atletico Mineiro | 1-2 |
| Arsenal v Sao Paulo | 2-1 |
| Atletico Mineiro v Arsenal | 5-2 |
| The Strongest v Sao Paulo | 2-1 |
| Arsenal v The Strongest | 2-1 |
| Sao Paulo v Atletico Mineiro | 2-0 |

**Group 3 Table**

| | P | W | D | L | F | A | GD | Pts |
|---|---|---|---|---|---|---|---|---|
| Atletico Mineiro | 6 | 5 | 0 | 1 | 16 | 9 | 7 | 15 |
| Sao Paulo | 6 | 2 | 1 | 3 | 8 | 8 | 0 | 7 |
| Arsenal | 6 | 2 | 1 | 3 | 10 | 15 | -5 | 7 |
| The Strongest | 6 | 2 | 0 | 4 | 8 | 10 | -2 | 6 |

## GROUP 4

| | |
|---|---|
| CS Emelec v Velez Sarsfield | 1-0 |
| Deportes Iquique v CA Penarol | 1-2 |
| CA Penarol v CS Emelec | 1-0 |
| Velez Sarsfield v Deportes Iquique | 3-0 |
| CA Penarol v Velez Sarsfield | 0-1 |
| Deportes Iquique v CS Emelec | 2-0 |
| CS Emelec v Deportes Iquique | 2-1 |
| Velez Sarsfield v CA Penarol | 3-1 |
| CS Emelec v CA Penarol | 2-0 |
| Deportes Iquique v Velez Sarsfield | 1-3 |
| CA Penarol v Deportes Iquique | 3-0 |
| Velez Sarsfield v CS Emelec | 0-0 |

**Group 4 Table**

| | P | W | D | L | F | A | GD | Pts |
|---|---|---|---|---|---|---|---|---|
| Velez Sarsfield | 6 | 4 | 1 | 1 | 10 | 3 | 7 | 13 |
| CS Emelec | 6 | 3 | 1 | 2 | 5 | 4 | 1 | 10 |
| CA Penarol | 6 | 3 | 0 | 3 | 7 | 7 | 0 | 9 |
| Deportes Iquique | 6 | 1 | 0 | 5 | 5 | 13 | -8 | 3 |

## GROUP 5

| | |
|---|---|
| Millonarios v Club Tijuana | 0-1 |
| Club San Jose v Corinthians SP | 1-1 |
| Club Tijuana v Club San Jose | 4-0 |
| Corinthians SP v Millonarios | 2-0 |
| Millonarios v Club San Jose | 2-1 |
| Club Tijuana v Corinthians SP | 1-0 |
| Corinthians SP v Club Tijuana | 3-0 |
| Club San Jose v Millonarios | 2-0 |
| Club San Jose v Club Tijuana | 1-1 |
| Millonarios v Corinthians SP | 0-1 |
| Corinthians SP v Club San Jose | 3-0 |
| Club Tijuana v Millonarios | 1-0 |

**Group 5 Table**

| | P | W | D | L | F | A | GD | Pts |
|---|---|---|---|---|---|---|---|---|
| Corinthians SP | 6 | 4 | 1 | 1 | 10 | 2 | 8 | 13 |
| Club Tijuana | 6 | 4 | 1 | 1 | 8 | 4 | 4 | 13 |
| Club San Jose | 6 | 1 | 2 | 3 | 5 | 11 | -6 | 5 |
| Millonarios | 6 | 1 | 0 | 5 | 2 | 8 | -6 | 3 |

## GROUP 6

| | |
|---|---|
| Real Garcilaso v Santa Fe | 1-1 |
| Deportes Tolima v Cerro Porteno | 2-1 |
| Cerro Porteno v Real Garcilaso | 0-1 |
| Santa Fe v Deportes Tolima | 1-1 |
| Deportes Tolima v Real Garcilaso | 0-1 |
| Cerro Porteno v Santa Fe | 1-2 |
| Santa Fe v Cerro Porteno | 1-0 |
| Real Garcilaso v Deportes Tolima | 0-3 |
| Deportes Tolima v Santa Fe | 1-2 |
| Real Garcilaso v Cerro Porteno | 5-1 |
| Santa Fe v Real Garcilaso | 2-0 |
| Cerro Porteno v Deportes Tolima | 0-0 |

**Group 6 Table**

| | P | W | D | L | F | A | GD | Pts |
|---|---|---|---|---|---|---|---|---|
| Santa Fe | 6 | 4 | 2 | 0 | 9 | 4 | 5 | 14 |
| Real Garcilaso | 6 | 3 | 1 | 2 | 8 | 7 | 1 | 10 |
| Deportes Tolima | 6 | 2 | 2 | 2 | 7 | 5 | 2 | 8 |
| Cerro Porteno | 6 | 0 | 1 | 5 | 3 | 11 | -8 | 1 |

## GROUP 7

| | |
|---|---|
| Universidad de Chile v CD Lara | 2-0 |
| Newell's Old Boys v Olimpia Asuncion | 3-1 |
| Olimpia Asuncion v Universidad de Chile | 3-0 |
| CD Lara v Newell's Old Boys | 2-1 |
| Olimpia Asuncion v CD Lara | 2-2 |
| Newell's Old Boys v Universidad de Chile | 1-2 |
| Universidad de Chile v Newell's Old Boys | 0-2 |
| CD Lara v Olimpia Asuncion | 1-5 |
| Universidad de Chile v Olimpia Asuncion | 0-1 |
| Newell's Old Boys v CD Lara | 3-1 |
| CD Lara v Universidad de Chile | 2-4 |
| Olimpia Asuncion v Newell's Old Boys | 4-1 |

**Group 7 Table**

| | P | W | D | L | F | A | GD | Pts |
|---|---|---|---|---|---|---|---|---|
| Olimpia Asuncion | 6 | 4 | 1 | 1 | 16 | 7 | 9 | 13 |
| Newell's Old Boys | 6 | 3 | 0 | 3 | 11 | 10 | 1 | 9 |
| Universidad de Chile | 6 | 3 | 0 | 3 | 7 | 9 | -2 | 9 |
| CD Lara | 6 | 1 | 1 | 4 | 8 | 16 | -8 | 4 |

## GROUP 8

| | |
|---|---|
| Caracas v Fluminense RJ | 0-1 |
| Gremio Porto Alegre v CD Huachipato | 1-2 |
| CD Huachipato v Caracas | 1-3 |
| Fluminense RJ v Gremio Porto Alegre | 0-3 |
| CD Huachipato v Fluminense RJ | 1-2 |
| Gremio Porto Alegre v Caracas | 4-1 |
| Fluminense RJ v CD Huachipato | 1-1 |
| Caracas v Gremio Porto Alegre | 2-1 |
| Caracas v CD Huachipato | 0-4 |
| Gremio Porto Alegre v Fluminense RJ | 0-0 |
| Fluminense RJ v Caracas | 1-0 |
| CD Huachipato v Gremio Porto Alegre | 1-1 |

**Group 8 Table**

| | P | W | D | L | F | A | GD | Pts |
|---|---|---|---|---|---|---|---|---|
| Fluminense RJ | 6 | 3 | 2 | 1 | 5 | 5 | 0 | 11 |
| Gremio Porto Alegre | 6 | 2 | 2 | 2 | 10 | 6 | 4 | 8 |
| CD Huachipato | 6 | 2 | 2 | 2 | 10 | 8 | 2 | 8 |
| Caracas | 6 | 2 | 0 | 4 | 6 | 12 | -6 | 6 |

## THIRD ROUND – FIRST LEG

| | |
|---|---|
| Newell's Old Boys v Velez Sarsfield | 0-1 |
| Real Garcilaso v Nacional | 1-0 |
| Tigre v Olimpia Asuncion | 2-1 |
| Club Tijuana v SE Palmeiras | 0-0 |
| Gremio Porto Alegre v Santa Fe | 2-1 |
| Boca Juniors v Corinthians SP | 1-0 |
| Sao Paulo v Atletico Mineiro | 1-2 |
| CS Emelec v Fluminense RJ | 2-1 |

## THIRD ROUND – SECOND LEG

| | |
|---|---|
| Velez Sarsfield v Newell's Old Boys | 1-2 |
| Nacional v Real Garcilaso | 1-0 |
| *aet; Real Garcilaso won 4-1 on penalties.* | |
| Olimpia Asuncion v Tigre | 2-0 |
| SE Palmeiras v Club Tijuana | 1-2 |
| Santa Fe v Gremio Porto Alegre | 1-0 |
| Corinthians SP v Boca Juniors | 1-1 |
| Atletico Mineiro v Sao Paulo | 4-1 |
| Fluminense RJ v CS Emelec | 2-0 |

## QUARTER-FINALS – FIRST LEG

| | |
|---|---|
| Real Garcilaso v Santa Fe | 1-3 |
| Fluminense RJ v Olimpia Asuncion | 0-0 |
| Club Tijuana v Atletico Mineiro | 2-2 |
| Boca Juniors v Newell's Old Boys | 0-0 |

## QUARTER-FINALS – SECOND LEG

| | |
|---|---|
| Santa Fe v Real Garcilaso | 2-0 |
| Olimpia Asuncion v Fluminense RJ | 2-1 |
| Atletico Mineiro v Club Tijuana | 1-1 |
| Newell's Old Boys v Boca Juniors | 0-0 |
| *Newell's Old Boys won 10-9 on penalties.* | |

*Competition still being played.*

# AFRICA

## AFRICA CUP OF NATIONS 2013

### GROUP A
| South Africa v Cape Verde | 0-0 |
| Angola v Morocco | 0-0 |
| South Africa v Angola | 2-0 |
| Morocco v Cape Verde | 1-1 |
| Morocco v South Africa | 2-2 |
| Cape Verde v Angola | 2-1 |

| Group A Table | P | W | D | L | F | A | Pts |
|---|---|---|---|---|---|---|---|
| South Africa | 3 | 1 | 2 | 0 | 4 | 2 | 5 |
| Cape Verde | 3 | 1 | 2 | 0 | 3 | 2 | 5 |
| Morocco | 3 | 0 | 3 | 0 | 3 | 3 | 3 |
| Angola | 3 | 0 | 1 | 1 | 1 | 4 | 1 |

### GROUP B
| Ghana v DR Congo | 2-2 |
| Mali v Niger | 1-0 |
| Ghana v Mali | 1-0 |
| Niger v DR Congo | 0-0 |
| Niger v Ghana | 0-3 |
| DR Congo v Mali | 1-1 |

| Group B Table | P | W | D | L | F | A | Pts |
|---|---|---|---|---|---|---|---|
| Ghana | 3 | 2 | 1 | 0 | 6 | 2 | 7 |
| Mali | 3 | 1 | 1 | 1 | 2 | 2 | 4 |
| DR Congo | 3 | 0 | 3 | 0 | 3 | 3 | 3 |
| Niger | 3 | 0 | 1 | 2 | 0 | 4 | 1 |

### GROUP C
| Zambia v Ethiopia | 1-1 |
| Nigeria v Burkina Faso | 1-1 |
| Zambia v Nigeria | 1-1 |
| Burkina Faso v Ethiopia | 4-0 |
| Burkina Faso v Zambia | 0-0 |
| Ethiopia v Nigeria | 0-2 |

| Group C Table | P | W | D | L | F | A | Pts |
|---|---|---|---|---|---|---|---|
| Burkina Faso | 3 | 1 | 2 | 0 | 5 | 1 | 5 |
| Nigeria | 3 | 1 | 2 | 0 | 4 | 2 | 5 |
| Zambia | 3 | 0 | 3 | 0 | 2 | 2 | 3 |
| Ethiopia | 3 | 0 | 1 | 2 | 1 | 7 | 1 |

### GROUP D
| Ivory Coast v Togo | 2-1 |
| Tunisia v Algeria | 1-0 |
| Ivory Coast v Tunisia | 3-0 |
| Algeria v Togo | 0-2 |
| Algeria v Ivory Coast | 2-2 |
| Togo v Tunisia | 1-1 |

| Group D Table | P | W | D | L | F | A | Pts |
|---|---|---|---|---|---|---|---|
| Ivory Coast | 3 | 2 | 1 | 0 | 7 | 3 | 7 |
| Togo | 3 | 1 | 1 | 1 | 4 | 3 | 4 |
| Tunisia | 3 | 1 | 1 | 1 | 2 | 4 | 4 |
| Algeria | 3 | 0 | 1 | 2 | 2 | 5 | 1 |

### QUARTER-FINALS
| Ghana v Cape Verde | 2-0 |
| South Africa v Mali | 1-1 |
| *aet; Mali won 3-1 on penalties.* | |
| Ivory Coast v Nigeria | 1-2 |
| Burkina Faso v Togo | 1-0 |
| *aet.* | |

### SEMI-FINALS
| Mali v Nigeria | 1-4 |
| Burkina Faso v Ghana | 1-1 |
| *Burkina Faso won 3-2 on penalties.* | |

### FINAL
Johannesburg, 10 February 2013

**Nigeria (1) 1** *(Mba 40)*

**Burkina Faso (0) 0**    85,000

*Nigeria:* Enyeama; Echiejile (Oshaniwa 67), Omeruo, Oboabona, Ambrose; Onanzi, Mikel, Mba (Yobo 89), Moses; Ideye, Uche (Musa 54).
*Burkina Faso:* Diakite; B Kone, Koffi, Koulibaly (Dagano 84), Panandetiguiri; D Kone (Traore 90), Kabore, Rouamba (Sanou 65), Nakoulma, Pitroipa; Bance.
*Referee:* Djamel Haimoudi (Algeria).

# NORTH AMERICA

## MAJOR LEAGUE SOCCER 2012

| EASTERN CONFERENCE | P | W | D | L | F | A | GD | Pts |
|---|---|---|---|---|---|---|---|---|
| Sporting Kansas City | 34 | 18 | 9 | 7 | 42 | 27 | 15 | 63 |
| D.C. United | 34 | 17 | 7 | 10 | 53 | 43 | 10 | 58 |
| New York Red Bulls | 34 | 16 | 9 | 9 | 57 | 46 | 11 | 57 |
| Chicago Fire | 34 | 17 | 6 | 11 | 46 | 41 | 5 | 57 |
| Houston Dynamo | 34 | 14 | 11 | 9 | 48 | 41 | 7 | 53 |
| Columbus Crew | 34 | 15 | 7 | 12 | 44 | 44 | 0 | 52 |
| Montreal Impact | 34 | 12 | 6 | 16 | 45 | 51 | -6 | 42 |
| Philadelphia Union | 34 | 10 | 6 | 18 | 37 | 45 | -8 | 36 |
| New England Revolution | 34 | 9 | 8 | 17 | 39 | 44 | -5 | 35 |
| Toronto | 34 | 5 | 8 | 21 | 36 | 62 | -26 | 23 |

| WESTERN CONFERENCE | P | W | D | L | F | A | GD | Pts |
|---|---|---|---|---|---|---|---|---|
| San Jose Earthquakes | 34 | 19 | 9 | 6 | 72 | 43 | 29 | 66 |
| Real Salt Lake | 34 | 17 | 6 | 11 | 46 | 35 | 11 | 57 |
| Seattle Sounders | 34 | 15 | 11 | 8 | 51 | 33 | 18 | 56 |
| LA Galaxy | 34 | 16 | 6 | 12 | 59 | 47 | 12 | 54 |
| Vancouver Whitecaps | 34 | 11 | 10 | 13 | 35 | 41 | -6 | 43 |
| FC Dallas | 34 | 9 | 12 | 13 | 42 | 47 | -5 | 39 |
| Colorado Rapids | 34 | 11 | 4 | 19 | 44 | 50 | -6 | 37 |
| Portland Timbers | 34 | 8 | 10 | 16 | 34 | 56 | -22 | 34 |
| Chivas USA | 34 | 7 | 9 | 18 | 24 | 58 | -34 | 30 |

### KNOCKOUT ROUND
| Chicago Fire v Houston Dynamo | 1-2 |
| LA Galaxy v Vancouver Whitecaps | 2-1 |

### SEMI-FINALS – EASTERN FIRST LEG
| Houston Dynamo v Sporting Kansas City | 2-0 |
| D.C. United v New York Red Bulls | 1-1 |

### SEMI-FINALS – EASTERN SECOND LEG
| Sporting Kansas City v Houston Dynamo | 0-1 |
| New York Red Bulls v D.C. United | 0-1 |

### SEMI-FINALS – WESTERN FIRST LEG
| LA Galaxy v San Jose Earthquakes | 0-1 |
| Seattle Sounders v Real Salt Lake | 0-0 |

### SEMI-FINALS – WESTERN SECOND LEG
| San Jose Earthquakes v LA Galaxy | 1-3 |
| Real Salt Lake v Seattle Sounders | 0-1 |

### CHAMPIONSHIP – EASTERN FIRST LEG
| Houston Dynamo v D.C. United | 3-1 |

### CHAMPIONSHIP – EASTERN SECOND LEG
| D.C. United v Houston Dynamo | 1-1 |

### CHAMPIONSHIP – WESTERN FIRST LEG
| LA Galaxy v Seattle Sounders | 3-0 |

### CHAMPIONSHIP – WESTERN SECOND LEG
| Seattle Sounders v LA Galaxy | 2-1 |

### MLS CUP FINAL
1 December 2012

**LA Galaxy (0) 3** *(Gonzalez 60, Donovan 65 (pen), Keane 90 (pen))*

**Houston Dynamo (1) 1** *(Carr 44)*    30,510

*LA Galaxy:* Saunders; Franklin, Gonzalez, Meyer, Dunivant, Wilhelmsson (Buddle 74), Beckham (Sarvas 90), Juninho (Stephens 76), Magee, Keane, Donovan.
*Houston Dynamo:* Hall; Sarkodie (Ching 77), Boswell, Taylor, Ashe, Gacia, Moffat (Barnes 71), Clark, Davis, Bruin, Carr (Kandji 59).

# UEFA UNDER-21 CHAMPIONSHIP 2011–13

## QUALIFYING ROUND

### GROUP 1

| | |
|---|---|
| Cyprus v San Marino | 6-0 |
| San Marino v Bosnia & Herzegovina | 0-3 |
| Germany v Cyprus | 4-1 |
| Greece v Belarus | 2-3 |
| Germany v San Marino | 7-0 |
| Belarus v Bosnia & Herzegovina | 1-1 |
| Cyprus v Greece | 0-2 |
| Belarus v Germany | 0-1 |
| Greece v San Marino | 2-0 |
| Germany v Bosnia & Herzegovina | 3-0 |
| Cyprus v Belarus | 1-3 |
| San Marino v Germany | 0-8 |
| Bosnia & Herzegovina v Cyprus | 5-1 |
| Belarus v Greece | 1-3 |
| Greece v Germany | 4-5 |
| San Marino v Belarus | 0-2 |
| Cyprus v Bosnia & Herzegovina | 2-1 |
| Greece v Bosnia & Herzegovina | 0-1 |
| Cyprus v Germany | 0-3 |
| Germany v Greece | 1-0 |
| San Marino v Cyprus | 1-2 |
| Bosnia & Herzegovina v Belarus | 3-0 |
| San Marino v Greece | 0-0 |
| Bosnia & Herzegovina v San Marino | 3-1 |
| Belarus v Cyprus | 0-3 |
| Bosnia & Herzegovina v Greece | 4-0 |
| Germany v Belarus | 3-0 |
| Greece v Cyprus | 1-0 |
| Bosnia & Herzegovina v Germany | 4-4 |
| Cyprus v San Marino | 6-0 |

| Group 1 Table | P | W | D | L | F | A | GD | Pts |
|---|---|---|---|---|---|---|---|---|
| Germany | 10 | 9 | 1 | 0 | 39 | 9 | 30 | 28 |
| Bosnia & Herzegovina | 10 | 6 | 2 | 2 | 25 | 12 | 13 | 20 |
| Greece | 10 | 4 | 1 | 5 | 14 | 15 | –1 | 13 |
| Belarus | 10 | 4 | 1 | 5 | 11 | 17 | –6 | 13 |
| Cyprus | 10 | 4 | 0 | 6 | 16 | 20 | –4 | 12 |
| San Marino | 10 | 0 | 1 | 9 | 2 | 34 | –32 | 1 |

### GROUP 2

| | | | | |
|---|---|---|---|---|
| Lithuania v Slovenia | 0-1 | Ukraine v Lithuania | 2-0 |
| Finland v Malta | 0-0 | Malta v Sweden | 0-1 |
| Lithuania v Malta | 1-2 | Ukraine v Sweden | 6-0 |
| Finland v Slovenia | 1-0 | Slovenia v Malta | 2-1 |
| Lithuania v Sweden | 0-1 | Lithuania v Ukraine | 1-0 |
| Malta v Slovenia | 1-4 | Slovenia v Finland | 1-1 |
| Sweden v Lithuania | 4-0 | Sweden v Malta | 4-0 |
| Malta v Finland | 1-2 | Finland v Ukraine | 1-2 |
| Slovenia v Ukraine | 2-0 | Sweden v Finland | 3-0 |
| Sweden v Slovenia | 1-1 | Finland v Lithuania | 3-4 |
| Malta v Ukraine | 2-2 | Ukraine v Slovenia | 2-0 |
| Finland v Sweden | 0-1 | Ukraine v Malta | 5-1 |
| Malta v Lithuania | 0-2 | Slovenia v Sweden | 2-1 |
| Slovenia v Lithuania | 2-0 | Lithuania v Finland | 1-3 |
| Ukraine v Finland | 1-1 | Sweden v Ukraine | 2-1 |

| Group 2 Table | P | W | D | L | F | A | GD | Pts |
|---|---|---|---|---|---|---|---|---|
| Sweden | 10 | 7 | 1 | 2 | 18 | 10 | 8 | 22 |
| Slovenia | 10 | 6 | 2 | 2 | 15 | 8 | 7 | 20 |
| Ukraine | 10 | 5 | 2 | 3 | 21 | 10 | 11 | 17 |
| Finland | 10 | 3 | 3 | 4 | 12 | 14 | –2 | 12 |
| Lithuania | 10 | 3 | 0 | 7 | 9 | 18 | –9 | 9 |
| Malta | 10 | 1 | 2 | 7 | 8 | 23 | –15 | 5 |

### GROUP 3

| | |
|---|---|
| Andorra v Wales | 0-1 |
| Andorra v Montenegro | 0-5 |
| Armenia v Montenegro | 4-1 |
| Czech Republic v Andorra | 8-0 |
| Andorra v Armenia | 0-1 |
| Czech Republic v Armenia | 1-1 |
| Montenegro v Wales | 3-1 |
| Wales v Montenegro | 1-0 |
| Wales v Czech Republic | 0-1 |
| Montenegro v Andorra | 4-0 |
| Armenia v Czech Republic | 0-2 |
| Armenia v Wales | 0-0 |
| Wales v Andorra | 4-0 |
| Czech Republic v Montenegro | 2-1 |
| Andorra v Czech Republic | 1-5 |

| | |
|---|---|
| Armenia v Andorra | 4-1 |
| Wales v Armenia | 0-1 |
| Montenegro v Czech Republic | 0-0 |
| Czech Republic v Wales | 5-0 |
| Montenegro v Armenia | 0-0 |

| Group 3 Table | P | W | D | L | F | A | GD | Pts |
|---|---|---|---|---|---|---|---|---|
| Czech Republic | 8 | 6 | 2 | 0 | 24 | 3 | 21 | 20 |
| Armenia | 8 | 4 | 3 | 1 | 11 | 5 | 6 | 15 |
| Montenegro | 8 | 3 | 2 | 3 | 14 | 8 | 6 | 11 |
| Wales | 8 | 3 | 1 | 4 | 7 | 10 | –3 | 10 |
| Andorra | 8 | 0 | 0 | 8 | 2 | 32 | –30 | 0 |

### GROUP 4

| | |
|---|---|
| Faroe Islands v Northern Ireland | 0-0 |
| Northern Ireland v Faroe Islands | 4-0 |
| Serbia v Northern Ireland | 1-0 |
| Northern Ireland v Denmark | 0-3 |
| Serbia v Faroe Islands | 5-1 |
| Macedonia v Serbia | 1-1 |
| Denmark v Faroe Islands | 4-0 |
| Serbia v Denmark | 0-0 |
| Macedonia v Faroe Islands | 1-0 |
| Macedonia v Denmark | 1-1 |
| Northern Ireland v Serbia | 0-2 |
| Macedonia v Northern Ireland | 1-0 |
| Faroe Islands v Macedonia | 1-1 |
| Denmark v Macedonia | 6-5 |
| Faroe Islands v Serbia | 0-2 |
| Faroe Islands v Denmark | 1-1 |
| Denmark v Serbia | 1-1 |
| Northern Ireland v Macedonia | 1-3 |
| Denmark v Northern Ireland | 3-0 |
| Serbia v Macedonia | 0-0 |

| Group 4 Table | P | W | D | L | F | A | GD | Pts |
|---|---|---|---|---|---|---|---|---|
| Serbia | 8 | 5 | 3 | 0 | 17 | 4 | 13 | 18 |
| Denmark | 8 | 4 | 4 | 0 | 19 | 8 | 11 | 16 |
| Macedonia | 8 | 3 | 3 | 2 | 14 | 15 | –1 | 12 |
| Northern Ireland | 8 | 1 | 1 | 6 | 5 | 13 | –8 | 4 |
| Faroe Islands | 8 | 0 | 3 | 5 | 3 | 18 | –15 | 3 |

### GROUP 5

| | |
|---|---|
| Croatia v Georgia | 0-1 |
| Estonia v Switzerland | 0-0 |
| Georgia v Spain | 2-7 |
| Switzerland v Croatia | 4-0 |
| Spain v Georgia | 2-0 |
| Croatia v Spain | 0-2 |
| Georgia v Switzerland | 0-1 |
| Estonia v Croatia | 0-1 |
| Switzerland v Georgia | 5-0 |
| Spain v Estonia | 6-0 |
| Croatia v Estonia | 4-0 |
| Spain v Switzerland | 3-0 |
| Estonia v Spain | 0-1 |
| Croatia v Switzerland | 1-2 |
| Estonia v Georgia | 1-2 |
| Georgia v Croatia | 1-1 |
| Georgia v Estonia | 2-1 |
| Switzerland v Spain | 0-0 |
| Spain v Croatia | 6-0 |
| Switzerland v Estonia | 3-0 |

| Group 5 Table | P | W | D | L | F | A | GD | Pts |
|---|---|---|---|---|---|---|---|---|
| Spain | 8 | 7 | 1 | 0 | 27 | 2 | 25 | 22 |
| Switzerland | 8 | 5 | 2 | 1 | 15 | 4 | 11 | 17 |
| Georgia | 8 | 3 | 1 | 4 | 8 | 18 | –10 | 10 |
| Croatia | 8 | 2 | 1 | 5 | 7 | 16 | –9 | 7 |
| Estonia | 8 | 0 | 1 | 7 | 2 | 19 | –17 | 1 |

### GROUP 6

| | | | | |
|---|---|---|---|---|
| Moldova v Portugal | 0-2 | Poland v Moldova | 0-1 |
| Albania v Poland | 0-3 | Albania v Portugal | 2-2 |
| Albania v Moldova | 4-3 | Moldova v Poland | 2-4 |
| Poland v Russia | 0-2 | Portugal v Russia | 1-0 |
| Portugal v Poland | 1-1 | Portugal v Albania | 3-1 |
| Moldova v Russia | 0-6 | Russia v Albania | 0-0 |
| Poland v Albania | 4-3 | Russia v Poland | 4-1 |
| Russia v Portugal | 2-1 | Moldova v Albania | 2-1 |
| Albania v Russia | 0-1 | Russia v Moldova | 2-2 |
| Portugal v Moldova | 5-0 | Poland v Portugal | 0-0 |

**Group 6 Table**

| | P | W | D | L | F | A | GD | Pts |
|---|---|---|---|---|---|---|---|---|
| Russia | 8 | 5 | 2 | 1 | 17 | 5 | 12 | 17 |
| Portugal | 8 | 4 | 3 | 1 | 15 | 6 | 9 | 15 |
| Poland | 8 | 3 | 2 | 3 | 13 | 13 | 0 | 11 |
| Moldova | 8 | 2 | 1 | 5 | 10 | 24 | –14 | 7 |
| Albania | 8 | 1 | 2 | 5 | 11 | 18 | –7 | 5 |

## GROUP 7

| | |
|---|---|
| Turkey v Liechtenstein | 6-1 |
| Republic of Ireland v Hungary | 2-1 |
| Liechtenstein v Turkey | 0-3 |
| Hungary v Italy | 0-3 |
| Turkey v Republic of Ireland | 1-0 |
| Liechtenstein v Italy | 2-7 |
| Turkey v Hungary | 2-1 |
| Italy v Turkey | 2-0 |
| Liechtenstein v Republic of Ireland | 1-4 |
| Turkey v Italy | 0-2 |
| Republic of Ireland v Liechtenstein | 2-0 |
| Italy v Hungary | 2-0 |
| Hungary v Turkey | 1-0 |
| Republic of Ireland v Italy | 2-2 |
| Liechtenstein v Hungary | 0-4 |
| Republic of Ireland v Turkey | 0-1 |
| Italy v Liechtenstein | 7-0 |
| Hungary v Republic of Ireland | 2-1 |
| Hungary v Liechtenstein | 2-0 |
| Italy v Republic of Ireland | 2-4 |

**Group 7 Table**

| | P | W | D | L | F | A | GD | Pts |
|---|---|---|---|---|---|---|---|---|
| Italy | 8 | 6 | 1 | 1 | 27 | 8 | 19 | 19 |
| Turkey | 8 | 5 | 0 | 3 | 13 | 7 | 6 | 15 |
| Republic of Ireland | 8 | 4 | 1 | 3 | 15 | 10 | 5 | 13 |
| Hungary | 8 | 4 | 0 | 4 | 11 | 10 | 1 | 12 |
| Liechtenstein | 8 | 0 | 0 | 8 | 4 | 35 | –31 | 0 |

## GROUP 8

| | | | |
|---|---|---|---|
| Iceland v Belgium | 2-1 | Belgium v England | 2-1 |
| England v Azerbaijan | 6-0 | Azerbaijan v Iceland | 1-0 |
| Belgium v Azerbaijan | 4-1 | England v Belgium | 4-0 |
| Iceland v Norway | 0-2 | Norway v Azerbaijan | 1-0 |
| Azerbaijan v Norway | 0-2 | Iceland v Azerbaijan | 1-2 |
| Iceland v England | 0-3 | Norway v Iceland | 2-1 |
| Azerbaijan v Belgium | 2-2 | Azerbaijan v England | 0-2 |
| Norway v England | 1-2 | Belgium v Norway | 1-3 |
| Norway v Belgium | 2-2 | England v Norway | 1-0 |
| England v Iceland | 5-0 | Belgium v Iceland | 5-0 |

**Group 8 Table**

| | P | W | D | L | F | A | GD | Pts |
|---|---|---|---|---|---|---|---|---|
| England | 8 | 7 | 0 | 1 | 24 | 3 | 21 | 21 |
| Norway | 8 | 5 | 1 | 2 | 13 | 7 | 6 | 16 |
| Belgium | 8 | 3 | 2 | 3 | 17 | 15 | 2 | 11 |
| Azerbaijan | 8 | 2 | 1 | 5 | 6 | 18 | –12 | 7 |
| Iceland | 8 | 1 | 0 | 7 | 4 | 21 | –17 | 3 |

## GROUP 9

| | | | |
|---|---|---|---|
| Romania v Kazakhstan | 0-0 | France v Slovakia | 2-0 |
| Slovakia v Latvia | 2-0 | Slovakia v Romania | 0-2 |
| Kazakhstan v Romania | 1-1 | France v Latvia | 3-0 |
| Latvia v France | 0-3 | Romania v Slovakia | 2-0 |
| Kazakhstan v Slovakia | 0-1 | Kazakhstan v France | 0-3 |
| Romania v Latvia | 2-0 | Kazakhstan v Latvia | 0-0 |
| France v Kazakhstan | 2-0 | Latvia v Kazakhstan | 1-1 |
| Latvia v Slovakia | 0-6 | Slovakia v France | 2-1 |
| Romania v France | 0-2 | Latvia v Romania | 0-4 |
| France v Romania | 3-0 | Slovakia v Kazakhstan | 6-0 |

**Group 9 Table**

| | P | W | D | L | F | A | GD | Pts |
|---|---|---|---|---|---|---|---|---|
| France | 8 | 7 | 0 | 1 | 19 | 2 | 17 | 21 |
| Slovakia | 8 | 5 | 0 | 3 | 17 | 7 | 10 | 15 |
| Romania | 8 | 4 | 2 | 2 | 11 | 6 | 5 | 14 |
| Kazakhstan | 8 | 0 | 4 | 4 | 2 | 14 | –12 | 4 |
| Latvia | 8 | 0 | 2 | 6 | 1 | 21 | –20 | 2 |

## GROUP 10

| | |
|---|---|
| Luxembourg v Austria | 1-4 |
| Bulgaria v Holland | 0-1 |
| Scotland v Bulgaria | 0-0 |
| Holland v Luxembourg | 4-0 |
| Austria v Holland | 0-1 |
| Luxembourg v Scotland | 1-5 |
| Scotland v Austria | 2-2 |
| Bulgaria v Luxembourg | 3-2 |
| Austria v Bulgaria | 0-2 |
| Holland v Scotland | 1-2 |
| Bulgaria v Austria | 1-1 |
| Scotland v Holland | 0-0 |
| Bulgaria v Scotland | 2-2 |
| Luxembourg v Holland | 0-5 |
| Austria v Luxembourg | 4-1 |
| Holland v Bulgaria | 5-0 |
| Scotland v Luxembourg | 3-0 |
| Holland v Austria | 4-1 |
| Austria v Scotland | 3-2 |
| Luxembourg v Bulgaria | 1-3 |

**Group 10 Table**

| | P | W | D | L | F | A | GD | Pts |
|---|---|---|---|---|---|---|---|---|
| Holland | 8 | 6 | 1 | 1 | 21 | 3 | 18 | 19 |
| Scotland | 8 | 3 | 4 | 1 | 16 | 9 | 7 | 13 |
| Bulgaria | 8 | 3 | 3 | 2 | 11 | 12 | –1 | 12 |
| Austria | 8 | 3 | 2 | 3 | 15 | 14 | 1 | 11 |
| Luxembourg | 8 | 0 | 0 | 8 | 6 | 31 | –25 | 0 |

## PLAY-OFFS – FIRST LEG

| | |
|---|---|
| Slovakia v Netherlands | 0-2 |
| Spain v Denmark | 5-0 |
| Czech Republic v Russia | 0-2 |
| Germany v Switzerland | 1-1 |
| France v Norway | 1-0 |
| England v Serbia | 1-0 |
| Italy v Sweden | 1-0 |

## PLAY-OFFS – SECOND LEG

| | (agg) |
|---|---|
| Netherlands v Slovakia | 2-0 (4-0) |
| Russia v Czech Republic | 2-2 (4-2) |
| Switzerland v Germany | 1-3 (2-4) |
| Serbia v England | 0-1 (0-2) |
| Norway v France | 5-3 (5-4) |
| Sweden v Italy | 2-3 (2-4) |
| Denmark v Spain | 1-3 (1-8) |

## FINAL TOURNAMENT IN ISRAEL

### GROUP A

| | |
|---|---|
| Israel v Norway | 2-2 |
| England v Italy | 0-1 |
| England v Norway | 1-3 |
| Italy v Israel | 4-0 |
| Israel v England | 1-0 |
| Norway v Italy | 1-1 |

**Group A Table**

| | P | W | D | L | F | A | GD | Pts |
|---|---|---|---|---|---|---|---|---|
| Italy | 3 | 2 | 1 | 0 | 6 | 1 | 5 | 7 |
| Norway | 3 | 1 | 2 | 0 | 6 | 4 | 2 | 5 |
| Israel | 3 | 1 | 1 | 1 | 3 | 6 | –3 | 4 |
| England | 3 | 0 | 0 | 3 | 1 | 5 | –4 | 0 |

### GROUP B

| | |
|---|---|
| Spain v Russia | 1-0 |
| Holland v Germany | 3-2 |
| Holland v Russia | 5-1 |
| Germany v Spain | 0-1 |
| Spain v Holland | 3-0 |
| Russia v Germany | 1-2 |

**Group B Table**

| | P | W | D | L | F | A | GD | Pts |
|---|---|---|---|---|---|---|---|---|
| Spain | 3 | 3 | 0 | 0 | 5 | 0 | 5 | 9 |
| Holland | 3 | 2 | 0 | 1 | 8 | 6 | 2 | 6 |
| Germany | 3 | 1 | 0 | 2 | 4 | 5 | –1 | 3 |
| Russia | 3 | 0 | 0 | 3 | 2 | 8 | –6 | 0 |

### SEMI-FINALS

| | |
|---|---|
| Spain v Norway | 3-0 |
| Italy v Holland | 1-0 |

### FINAL (at Jerusalem)

Tuesday 18 June 2013

**Spain (3) 4** *(Thiago 6, 31, 38 (pen), Isco 66 (pen))*

**Italy (1) 2** *(Immobile 10, Borini 79)*     28,000

*Spain:* (433) De Gea; Montoya, Bartra, Inigo Martinez; Moreno; Koke (Camacho 86), Illarramendi, Thiago; Tello (Muniain 70), Morata (Rodrigo 80), Isco.

*Italy:* (442) Bardi; Donati, Bianchetti, Caldirola, Regini; Florenzi (Sapanara 58), Rossi, Verratti (Crimi 76), Insigne; Borini, Immobile (Gabbiadini 58).

*Referee:* Matej Jug (Slovenia).

# NEXTGEN SERIES TROPHY 2012–13

## GROUP 1

| | |
|---|---|
| Tottenham H v Anderlecht | 0-2 |
| Wolfsburg v Anderlecht | 2-3 |
| Barcelona v Wolfsburg | 3-1 |
| Barcelona v Tottenham H | 1-4 |
| Anderlecht v Tottenham H | 1-1 |
| Tottenham H v Wolfsburg | 2-2 |
| Anderlecht v Barcelona | 0-0 |
| Wolfsburg v Barcelona | 0-5 |
| Tottenham H v Barcelona | 0-2 |
| Anderlecht v Wolfsburg | 1-2 |
| Wolfsburg v Tottenham H | 2-3 |
| Barcelona v Anderlecht | 1-1 |

| Group 1 Table | P | W | D | L | F | A | GD | Pts |
|---|---|---|---|---|---|---|---|---|
| Barcelona | 6 | 3 | 2 | 1 | 12 | 6 | 6 | 11 |
| Anderlecht | 6 | 2 | 3 | 1 | 8 | 6 | 2 | 9 |
| Tottenham H | 6 | 2 | 2 | 2 | 10 | 10 | 0 | 8 |
| Wolfsburg | 6 | 1 | 1 | 4 | 9 | 17 | –8 | 4 |

## GROUP 2

| | |
|---|---|
| Paris St Germain v Juventus | 2-2 |
| Fenerbahce v Juventus | 1-2 |
| Paris St Germain v Manchester C | 2-1 |
| Manchester C v Juventus | 2-3 |
| Paris St Germain v Fenerbahce | 2-0 |
| Juventus v Manchester C | 1-1 |
| Fenerbahce v Paris St Germain | 0-2 |
| Fenerbahce v Manchester C | 1-1 |
| Juventus v Paris St Germain | 2-0 |
| Manchester C v Fenerbahce | 3-1 |
| Manchester C v Paris St Germain | 0-2 |
| Juventus v Fenerbahce | 3-3 |

| Group 2 Table | P | W | D | L | F | A | GD | Pts |
|---|---|---|---|---|---|---|---|---|
| Paris St Germain | 6 | 4 | 1 | 1 | 10 | 5 | 5 | 13 |
| Juventus | 6 | 3 | 3 | 0 | 13 | 9 | 4 | 12 |
| Manchester C | 6 | 1 | 2 | 3 | 9 | 8 | 1 | 5 |
| Fenerbahce | 6 | 0 | 2 | 4 | 6 | 13 | –7 | 2 |

## GROUP 3

| | |
|---|---|
| Ajax v Chelsea | 3-3 |
| Chelsea v Ajax | 0-0 |
| Chelsea v Molde | 6-0 |
| Ajax v CSKA Moscow | 2-1 |
| Molde v Chelsea | 1-1 |
| CSKA Moscow v Ajax | 2-0 |
| CSKA Moscow v Chelsea | 0-1 |
| Molde v Ajax | 0-5 |
| Molde v CSKA Moscow | 0-1 |
| Chelsea v CSKA Moscow | 1-2 |
| CSKA Moscow v Molde | 2-1 |

| Group 3 Table | P | W | D | L | F | A | GD | Pts |
|---|---|---|---|---|---|---|---|---|
| CSKA Moscow | 6 | 4 | 0 | 2 | 8 | 5 | 3 | 12 |
| Ajax | 6 | 3 | 2 | 1 | 15 | 6 | 9 | 11 |
| Chelsea | 6 | 2 | 3 | 1 | 12 | 6 | 6 | 9 |
| Molde | 6 | 0 | 1 | 5 | 2 | 20 | –18 | 1 |

## GROUP 4

| | |
|---|---|
| Sporting Lisbon v Aston Villa | 1-5 |
| PSV Eindhoven v Celtic | 1-0 |
| Sporting Lisbon v Celtic | 2-1 |
| Aston Villa v PSV Eindhoven | 2-0 |
| Sporting Lisbon v PSV Eindhoven | 4-2 |
| Celtic v Aston Villa | 2-2 |
| Ajax v Molde | 5-0 |
| Celtic v PSV Eindhoven | 3-1 |
| PSV Eindhoven v Sporting Lisbon | 1-0 |
| Aston Villa v Celtic | 2-1 |
| Celtic v Sporting Lisbon | 1-2 |
| PSV Eindhoven v Aston Villa | 1-0 |
| Aston Villa v Sporting Lisbon | 1-3 |

| Group 4 Table | P | W | D | L | F | A | GD | Pts |
|---|---|---|---|---|---|---|---|---|
| Sporting Lisbon | 6 | 4 | 0 | 2 | 12 | 11 | 1 | 12 |
| Aston Villa | 6 | 3 | 1 | 2 | 12 | 8 | 4 | 10 |
| PSV Eindhoven | 6 | 3 | 0 | 3 | 6 | 9 | –3 | 9 |
| Celtic | 6 | 1 | 1 | 4 | 8 | 10 | –2 | 4 |

## GROUP 5

| | |
|---|---|
| Liverpool v Inter Milan | 4-1 |
| Inter Milan v Rosenborg | 3-1 |
| Liverpool v Borussia Dortmund | 3-0 |
| Borussia Dortmund v Rosenborg | 2-2 |
| Liverpool v Rosenborg | 4-1 |
| Rosenborg v Liverpool | 3-0 |
| Borussia Dortmund v Inter Milan | 1-1 |
| Borussia Dortmund v Liverpool | 2-1 |
| Rosenborg v Inter Milan | 2-1 |
| Rosenborg v Borussia Dortmund | 1-0 |
| Inter Milan v Borussia Dortmund | 1-0 |
| Inter Milan v Liverpool | 3-2 |

| Group 5 Table | P | W | D | L | F | A | GD | Pts |
|---|---|---|---|---|---|---|---|---|
| Inter Milan | 6 | 3 | 1 | 2 | 10 | 10 | 0 | 10 |
| Rosenborg | 6 | 3 | 1 | 2 | 10 | 10 | 0 | 10 |
| Liverpool | 6 | 3 | 0 | 3 | 14 | 10 | 4 | 9 |
| Borussia Dortmund | 6 | 1 | 2 | 3 | 5 | 9 | –4 | 5 |

## GROUP 6

| | |
|---|---|
| Olympiacos v Athletic Bilbao | 1-0 |
| Arsenal v Athletic Bilbao | 4-2 |
| Athletic Bilbao v Marseille | 5-0 |
| Athletic Bilbao v Arsenal | 0-0 |
| Olympiacos v Marseille | 1-1 |
| Marseille v Arsenal | 1-0 |
| Arsenal v Olympiacos | 0-0 |
| Marseille v Olympiacos | 0-0 |
| Marseille v Athletic Bilbao | 2-1 |
| Olympiacos v Arsenal | 2-0 |
| Arsenal v Marseille | 3-0 |
| Athletic Bilbao v Olympiacos | 4-0 |

| Group 6 Table | P | W | D | L | F | A | GD | Pts |
|---|---|---|---|---|---|---|---|---|
| Olympiacos | 6 | 2 | 3 | 1 | 4 | 5 | –1 | 9 |
| Arsenal | 6 | 2 | 2 | 2 | 7 | 5 | 2 | 8 |
| Marseille | 6 | 2 | 2 | 2 | 4 | 10 | –6 | 8 |
| Athletic Bilbao | 6 | 2 | 1 | 3 | 12 | 7 | 5 | 7 |

## ROUND OF 16

| | |
|---|---|
| Juventus v Rosenborg | 1-0 |
| Inter Milan v Arsenal | 0-1 |
| Olympiacos v Anderlecht | 2-1 |
| CSKA Moscow v PSV Eindhoven | 3-0 |
| Sporting Lisbon v Liverpool | 4-0 |
| Barcelona v Chelsea | 0-2 |
| Paris St Germain v Tottenham H | 1-1 |
| *Tottenham H won 4-3 on penalties.* | |
| Ajax v Aston Villa | 1-2 |

## QUARTER-FINALS

| | |
|---|---|
| Arsenal v CSKA Moscow | 1-0 |
| Aston Villa v Olympiacos | 1-0 |
| Tottenham H v Sporting Lisbon | 3-5 |
| *aet.* | |
| Chelsea v Juventus | 4-1 |

## SEMI-FINAL

| | |
|---|---|
| Aston Villa v Sporting Lisbon | 3-1 |
| Chelsea v Arsenal | 4-3 |

## 3RD & 4TH PLACE FINAL

| | |
|---|---|
| Arsenal v Sporting Lisbon | 1-3 |

## FINAL (at Giuseppe Sinigaglia, Como)

**Monday 1 April 2013**

**Aston Villa (0) 2** *(Burke 49 (pen), 90 (pen))*

**Chelsea (0) 0**                                               392

*Aston Villa:* Watkins; Webb, Kinsella, Calder, Donacien,
Lewis, Barton, Carruthers, Robinson, Burke, Grealish
*Chelsea:* Beeney; Christiensen, Davey (Colkett 75),
Pappoe, Wright, Ake, Kiwomya[a], Loftus-Cheek (Hunte
70), Feruz, Baker, Boga

# FIFA UNDER-20 WORLD CUP 2013

## FINALS IN TURKEY

### GROUP A

| France v Ghana | 3-1 | Spain v Ghana | 1-0 |
| USA v Spain | 1-4 | Spain v France | 2-1 |
| France v USA | 1-1 | Ghana v USA | 4-1 |

| Group A Table | P | W | D | L | F | A | Pts |
|---|---|---|---|---|---|---|---|
| Spain | 3 | 3 | 0 | 0 | 7 | 2 | 9 |
| France | 3 | 1 | 1 | 1 | 5 | 4 | 4 |
| Ghana | 3 | 1 | 0 | 2 | 5 | 5 | 3 |
| USA | 3 | 0 | 1 | 2 | 3 | 9 | 1 |

### GROUP B

| Cuba v South Korea | 1-2 | Portugal v South Korea | 2-2 |
| Nigeria v Portugal | 2-3 | South Korea v Nigeria | 0-1 |
| Cuba v Nigeria | 0-3 | Portugal v Cuba | 5-0 |

| Group B Table | P | W | D | L | F | A | Pts |
|---|---|---|---|---|---|---|---|
| Portugal | 3 | 2 | 1 | 0 | 10 | 4 | 7 |
| Nigeria | 3 | 2 | 0 | 1 | 6 | 3 | 6 |
| South Korea | 3 | 1 | 1 | 1 | 4 | 4 | 4 |
| Cuba | 3 | 0 | 0 | 3 | 1 | 10 | 0 |

### GROUP C

| Colombia v Australia | 1-1 | Turkey v Colombia | 0-1 |
| Turkey v El Salvador | 3-0 | Australia v Turkey | 1-2 |
| Australia v El Salvador | 1-2 | El Salvador v Colombia | 0-3 |

| Group C Table | P | W | D | L | F | A | Pts |
|---|---|---|---|---|---|---|---|
| Colombia | 3 | 2 | 1 | 0 | 5 | 1 | 7 |
| Turkey | 3 | 2 | 0 | 1 | 5 | 2 | 6 |
| El Salvador | 3 | 1 | 0 | 2 | 2 | 7 | 3 |
| Australia | 3 | 0 | 1 | 2 | 3 | 5 | 1 |

### GROUP D

| Mexico v Greece | 1-2 | Mali v Greece | 0-0 |
| Paraguay v Mali | 1-1 | Greece v Paraguay | 1-1 |
| Mexico v Paraguay | 0-1 | Mali v Mexico | 1-4 |

| Group D Table | P | W | D | L | F | A | Pts |
|---|---|---|---|---|---|---|---|
| Greece | 3 | 1 | 2 | 0 | 3 | 2 | 5 |
| Paraguay | 3 | 1 | 2 | 0 | 3 | 2 | 5 |
| Mexico | 3 | 1 | 0 | 2 | 5 | 4 | 3 |
| Mali | 3 | 0 | 2 | 1 | 2 | 5 | 2 |

### GROUP E

| Chile v Egypt | 2-1 | Iraq v Egypt | 2-1 |
| England v Iraq | 2-2 | Iraq v Chile | 2-1 |
| Chile v England | 1-1 | Egypt v England | 2-0 |

| Group E Table | P | W | D | L | F | A | Pts |
|---|---|---|---|---|---|---|---|
| Iraq | 3 | 2 | 1 | 0 | 6 | 4 | 7 |
| Chile | 3 | 1 | 1 | 1 | 4 | 4 | 4 |
| Egypt | 3 | 1 | 0 | 2 | 4 | 4 | 3 |
| England | 3 | 0 | 2 | 1 | 3 | 5 | 2 |

### GROUP F

| New Zealand v Uzbekistan | | 0-3 |
| Uruguay v Croatia | | 0-1 |
| New Zealand v Uruguay | | 0-2 |
| Croatia v Uzbekistan | | 1-1 |
| Uzbekistan v Uruguay | | 0-4 |
| Croatia v New Zealand | | 2-1 |

| Group F Table | P | W | D | L | F | A | Pts |
|---|---|---|---|---|---|---|---|
| Croatia | 3 | 2 | 1 | 0 | 4 | 2 | 7 |
| Uruguay | 3 | 2 | 0 | 1 | 6 | 1 | 6 |
| Uzbekistan | 3 | 1 | 1 | 1 | 4 | 5 | 4 |
| New Zealand | 3 | 0 | 0 | 3 | 1 | 7 | 0 |

### ROUND OF 16

| Spain v Mexico | 2-1 |
| Greece v Uzbekistan | 1-3 |
| Nigeria v Uruguay | 1-2 |
| France v Turkey | 4-1 |
| Portugal v Ghana | 2-3 |
| Croatia v Chile | 0-2 |
| Colombia v South Korea | 1-1 |
| *South Korea won 8-7 on penalties* | |
| Iraq v Paraguay | 1-0 |
| *aet.* | |

### QUARTER-FINALS

| France v Uzbekistan | 4-0 |
| Uruguay v Spain | 1-0 |
| *aet.* | |
| Iraq v South Korea | 3-3 |
| *aet; Iraq won 4-4 on penalties.* | |
| Ghana v Chile | 4-3 |
| *aet.* | |
| *Competition still being played.* | |

# UEFA UNDER-19 CHAMPIONSHIP 2012–13

## QUALIFYING ROUND

### GROUP 1 (HUNGARY)

| Austria v Andorra | 9-0 | Andorra v Hungary | 0-3 |
| Hungary v Bulgaria | 1-1 | Austria v Bulgaria | 2-1 |
| Hungary v Austria | 1-2 | Bulgaria v Andorra | 7-0 |

| Group 1 Table | P | W | D | L | F | A | GD | Pts |
|---|---|---|---|---|---|---|---|---|
| Austria | 3 | 3 | 0 | 0 | 13 | 2 | 11 | 9 |
| Bulgaria | 3 | 1 | 1 | 1 | 9 | 3 | 6 | 4 |
| Hungary | 3 | 1 | 1 | 1 | 5 | 3 | 2 | 4 |
| Andorra | 3 | 0 | 0 | 3 | 0 | 19 | –19 | 0 |

### GROUP 2 (CYPRUS)

| Finland v Montenegro | 2-0 | Montenegro v Denmark | 2-3 |
| Denmark v Cyprus | 3-1 | Denmark v Finland | 3-0 |
| Finland v Cyprus | 0-1 | Cyprus v Montenegro | 1-1 |

| Group 2 Table | P | W | D | L | F | A | GD | Pts |
|---|---|---|---|---|---|---|---|---|
| Denmark | 3 | 3 | 0 | 0 | 9 | 3 | 6 | 9 |
| Cyprus | 3 | 1 | 1 | 1 | 3 | 4 | –1 | 4 |
| Finland | 3 | 1 | 0 | 2 | 2 | 4 | –2 | 3 |
| Montenegro | 3 | 0 | 1 | 2 | 3 | 6 | –3 | 1 |

### GROUP 3 (POLAND)

| Poland v San Marino | 2-0 | Poland v Malta | 5-0 |
| Holland v Malta | 5-0 | Holland v Poland | 3-1 |
| San Marino v Holland | 0-4 | Malta v San Marino | 4-0 |

| Group 3 Table | P | W | D | L | F | A | GD | Pts |
|---|---|---|---|---|---|---|---|---|
| Holland | 3 | 3 | 0 | 0 | 12 | 1 | 11 | 9 |
| Poland | 3 | 2 | 0 | 1 | 8 | 3 | 5 | 6 |
| Malta | 3 | 1 | 0 | 2 | 4 | 10 | –6 | 3 |
| San Marino | 3 | 0 | 0 | 3 | 0 | 10 | –10 | 0 |

### GROUP 4 (NORTHERN IRELAND)

| Greece v Moldova | | 0-0 |
| Czech Republic v Northern Ireland | | 1-1 |
| Czech Republic v Moldova | | 2-0 |
| Northern Ireland v Greece | | 0-2 |
| Greece v Czech Republic | | 1-2 |
| Moldova v Northern Ireland | | 1-8 |

| Group 4 Table | P | W | D | L | F | A | GD | Pts |
|---|---|---|---|---|---|---|---|---|
| Czech Republic | 3 | 2 | 1 | 0 | 5 | 2 | 3 | 7 |
| Greece | 3 | 1 | 1 | 1 | 3 | 1 | 2 | 4 |
| Northern Ireland | 3 | 1 | 1 | 1 | 9 | 4 | 5 | 4 |
| Moldova | 3 | 0 | 1 | 2 | 1 | 10 | –9 | 1 |

### GROUP 5 (LUXEMBOURG)

| Germany v Macedonia | | 5-0 |
| Republic of Ireland v Luxembourg | | 5-2 |
| Germany v Luxembourg | | 5-0 |
| Macedonia v Republic of Ireland | | 0-1 |
| Republic of Ireland v Germany | | 2-2 |
| Luxembourg v Macedonia | | 0-1 |

| Group 5 Table | P | W | D | L | F | A | GD | Pts |
|---|---|---|---|---|---|---|---|---|
| Germany | 3 | 2 | 1 | 0 | 12 | 2 | 10 | 7 |
| Republic of Ireland | 3 | 2 | 1 | 0 | 8 | 4 | 4 | 7 |
| Macedonia | 3 | 1 | 0 | 2 | 1 | 6 | –5 | 3 |
| Luxembourg | 3 | 0 | 0 | 3 | 2 | 11 | –9 | 0 |

### GROUP 6 (PORTUGAL)

| France v Israel | | 2-1 |
| Portugal v Latvia | | 2-0 |
| France v Latvia | | 6-0 |
| Israel v Portugal | | 0-5 |
| Portugal v France | | 2-2 |
| Latvia v Israel | | 3-5 |

| Group 6 Table | P | W | D | L | F | A | GD | Pts |
|---|---|---|---|---|---|---|---|---|
| France | 3 | 2 | 1 | 0 | 10 | 3 | 7 | 7 |
| Portugal | 3 | 2 | 1 | 0 | 9 | 2 | 7 | 7 |
| Israel | 3 | 1 | 0 | 2 | 6 | 10 | –4 | 3 |
| Latvia | 3 | 0 | 0 | 3 | 3 | 13 | –10 | 0 |

### GROUP 7 (ALBANIA)

| | | | |
|---|---|---|---|
| Belgium v Belarus | 1-0 | Belgium v Albania | 1-3 |
| Italy v Albania | 3-0 | Italy v Belgium | 1-2 |
| Belarus v Italy | 1-1 | Albania v Belarus | 0-2 |

| Group 7 Table | P | W | D | L | F | A | GD | Pts |
|---|---|---|---|---|---|---|---|---|
| Belgium | 3 | 2 | 0 | 1 | 4 | 4 | 0 | 6 |
| Italy | 3 | 1 | 1 | 1 | 5 | 3 | 2 | 4 |
| Belarus | 3 | 1 | 1 | 1 | 3 | 2 | 1 | 4 |
| Albania | 3 | 1 | 0 | 2 | 3 | 6 | –3 | 3 |

### Group 8 (Bosnia & Herzegovina)

| | |
|---|---|
| Slovakia v Kazakhstan | 5-0 |
| Norway v Bosnia & Herzegovina | 3-1 |
| Slovakia v Bosnia & Herzegovina | 0-4 |
| Kazakhstan v Norway | 2-6 |
| Norway v Slovakia | 1-2 |
| Bosnia & Herzegovina v Kazakhstan | 4-2 |

| Group 8 Table | P | W | D | L | F | A | GD | Pts |
|---|---|---|---|---|---|---|---|---|
| Bosnia & Herzegovina | 3 | 2 | 0 | 1 | 9 | 5 | 4 | 6 |
| Norway | 3 | 2 | 0 | 1 | 10 | 5 | 5 | 6 |
| Slovakia | 3 | 2 | 0 | 1 | 7 | 5 | 2 | 6 |
| Kazakhstan | 3 | 0 | 0 | 3 | 4 | 15 | –11 | 0 |

### GROUP 9 (SCOTLAND)

| | | | |
|---|---|---|---|
| Scotland v Armenia | 4-0 | Armenia v Switzerland | 0-4 |
| Switzerland v Romania | 1-1 | Switzerland v Scotland | 3-4 |
| Scotland v Romania | 1-0 | Romania v Armenia | 1-0 |

| Group 9 Table | P | W | D | L | F | A | GD | Pts |
|---|---|---|---|---|---|---|---|---|
| Scotland | 3 | 3 | 0 | 0 | 9 | 3 | 6 | 9 |
| Switzerland | 3 | 1 | 1 | 1 | 8 | 5 | 3 | 4 |
| Romania | 3 | 1 | 1 | 1 | 2 | 2 | 0 | 4 |
| Armenia | 3 | 0 | 0 | 3 | 0 | 9 | –9 | 0 |

# ELITE ROUND

## GROUP 1 (AUSTRIA)

| | |
|---|---|
| France v Sweden | 3-0 |
| Austria v Bosnia & Herzegovina | 6-0 |
| Bosnia & Herzegovina v France | 0-1 |
| Austria v Sweden | 3-0 |
| France v Austria | 1-0 |
| Sweden v Bosnia & Herzegovina | 3-2 |

| Group 1 Table | P | W | D | L | F | A | GD | Pts |
|---|---|---|---|---|---|---|---|---|
| France | 3 | 3 | 0 | 0 | 5 | 0 | 5 | 9 |
| Austria | 3 | 2 | 0 | 1 | 9 | 1 | 8 | 6 |
| Sweden | 3 | 1 | 0 | 2 | 3 | 8 | –5 | 3 |
| Bosnia & Herzegovina | 3 | 0 | 0 | 3 | 2 | 10 | –8 | 0 |

## GROUP 2 (SERBIA)

| | |
|---|---|
| Serbia v Slovakia | 4-0 |
| Republic of Ireland v Switzerland | 2-2 |
| Serbia v Switzerland | 0-1 |
| Slovakia v Republic of Ireland | 2-2 |
| Republic of Ireland v Serbia | 0-0 |
| Switzerland v Slovakia | 0-2 |

| GROUP 2 Table | P | W | D | L | F | A | GD | Pts |
|---|---|---|---|---|---|---|---|---|
| Serbia | 3 | 1 | 1 | 1 | 4 | 1 | 3 | 4 |
| Switzerland | 3 | 1 | 1 | 1 | 3 | 4 | –1 | 4 |
| Slovakia | 3 | 1 | 1 | 1 | 4 | 6 | –2 | 4 |
| Republic of Ireland | 3 | 0 | 3 | 0 | 4 | 4 | 0 | 3 |

## GROUP 3 (PORTUGAL)

| | |
|---|---|
| Denmark v Czech Republic | 5-0 |
| Portugal v Bulgaria | 7-0 |
| Denmark v Bulgaria | 5-0 |
| Czech Republic v Portugal | 1-4 |
| Portugal v Denmark | 1-0 |
| Bulgaria v Czech Republic | 1-2 |

| GROUP 3 Table | P | W | D | L | F | A | GD | Pts |
|---|---|---|---|---|---|---|---|---|
| Portugal | 3 | 3 | 0 | 0 | 12 | 1 | 11 | 9 |
| Denmark | 3 | 2 | 0 | 1 | 10 | 1 | 9 | 6 |
| Czech Republic | 3 | 1 | 0 | 2 | 3 | 10 | –7 | 3 |
| Bulgaria | 3 | 0 | 0 | 3 | 1 | 14 | –13 | 0 |

### GROUP 10 (SLOVENIA)

| | | | |
|---|---|---|---|
| Wales v Sweden | 1-3 | Sweden v Russia | 1-3 |
| Russia v Slovenia | 0-0 | Russia v Wales | 2-1 |
| Wales v Slovenia | 2-1 | Slovenia v Sweden | 1-1 |

| Group 10 Table | P | W | D | L | F | A | GD | Pts |
|---|---|---|---|---|---|---|---|---|
| Russia | 3 | 2 | 1 | 0 | 5 | 2 | 3 | 7 |
| Sweden | 3 | 1 | 1 | 1 | 5 | 5 | 0 | 4 |
| Wales | 3 | 1 | 0 | 2 | 4 | 6 | –2 | 3 |
| Slovenia | 3 | 0 | 2 | 1 | 2 | 3 | –1 | 2 |

### GROUP 11 (CROATIA)

| | | | |
|---|---|---|---|
| Croatia v Georgia | 2-0 | Georgia v Azerbaijan | 1-1 |
| Azerbaijan v Iceland | 1-2 | Azerbaijan v Croatia | 1-7 |
| Croatia v Iceland | 2-2 | Iceland v Georgia | 0-2 |

| Group 11 Table | P | W | D | L | F | A | GD | Pts |
|---|---|---|---|---|---|---|---|---|
| Croatia | 3 | 2 | 1 | 0 | 11 | 3 | 8 | 7 |
| Georgia | 3 | 1 | 1 | 1 | 3 | 3 | 0 | 4 |
| Iceland | 3 | 1 | 1 | 1 | 4 | 5 | –1 | 4 |
| Azerbaijan | 3 | 0 | 1 | 2 | 3 | 10 | –7 | 1 |

### GROUP 12 (ESTONIA)

| | | | |
|---|---|---|---|
| Ukraine v Faroe Islands | 6-0 | Ukraine v Estonia | 2-0 |
| England v Estonia | 3-0 | England v Ukraine | |
| Faroe Islands v England | 0-6 | Estonia v Faroe Islands | 2-1 |

| Group 12 Table | P | W | D | L | F | A | GD | Pts |
|---|---|---|---|---|---|---|---|---|
| England | 3 | 2 | 1 | 0 | 10 | 1 | 9 | 7 |
| Ukraine | 3 | 2 | 1 | 0 | 9 | 1 | 8 | 7 |
| Estonia | 3 | 1 | 0 | 2 | 2 | 6 | –4 | 3 |
| Faroe Islands | 3 | 0 | 0 | 3 | 1 | 14 | –13 | 0 |

### GROUP 4 (POLAND)

| | | | |
|---|---|---|---|
| Croatia v Greece | 1-1 | Poland v Croatia | 0-2 |
| Spain v Poland | 1-0 | Croatia v Spain | 1-1 |
| Spain v Greece | 2-0 | Greece v Poland | 1-1 |

| GROUP 4 Table | P | W | D | L | F | A | GD | Pts |
|---|---|---|---|---|---|---|---|---|
| Spain | 3 | 2 | 1 | 0 | 4 | 1 | 3 | 7 |
| Croatia | 3 | 1 | 2 | 0 | 4 | 2 | 2 | 5 |
| Greece | 3 | 0 | 2 | 1 | 2 | 4 | –2 | 2 |
| Poland | 3 | 0 | 1 | 2 | 1 | 4 | –3 | 1 |

### GROUP 5 (NORWAY)

| | | | |
|---|---|---|---|
| Germany v Cyprus | 3-1 | Norway v Germany | 3-1 |
| Holland v Norway | 2-1 | Germany v Holland | 0-1 |
| Holland v Cyprus | 0-1 | Cyprus v Norway | 0-3 |

| GROUP 5 Table | P | W | D | L | F | A | GD | Pts |
|---|---|---|---|---|---|---|---|---|
| Holland | 3 | 2 | 0 | 1 | 3 | 2 | 1 | 6 |
| Norway | 3 | 2 | 0 | 1 | 7 | 3 | 4 | 6 |
| Germany | 3 | 1 | 0 | 2 | 4 | 5 | –1 | 3 |
| Cyprus | 3 | 1 | 0 | 2 | 2 | 6 | –4 | 3 |

### GROUP 6 (BELGIUM)

| | | | |
|---|---|---|---|
| Scotland v Belgium | 2-2 | Belgium v England | 1-1 |
| England v Georgia | 1-1 | England v Scotland | 3-0 |
| Scotland v Georgia | 1-3 | Georgia v Belgium | 2-0 |

| GROUP 6 Table | P | W | D | L | F | A | GD | Pts |
|---|---|---|---|---|---|---|---|---|
| Georgia | 3 | 2 | 1 | 0 | 6 | 2 | 4 | 7 |
| England | 3 | 1 | 2 | 0 | 5 | 2 | 3 | 5 |
| Belgium | 3 | 0 | 2 | 1 | 3 | 5 | –2 | 2 |
| Scotland | 3 | 0 | 1 | 2 | 3 | 8 | –5 | 1 |

### GROUP 7 (RUSSIA)

| | | | |
|---|---|---|---|
| Ukraine v Italy | 0-1 | Russia v Ukraine | 1-2 |
| Turkey v Russia | 2-1 | Ukraine v Turkey | 0-2 |
| Turkey v Italy | 5-1 | Italy v Russia | 3-3 |

| GROUP 7 Table | P | W | D | L | F | A | GD | Pts |
|---|---|---|---|---|---|---|---|---|
| Turkey | 3 | 3 | 0 | 0 | 9 | 2 | 7 | 9 |
| Italy | 3 | 1 | 1 | 1 | 5 | 8 | –3 | 4 |
| Ukraine | 3 | 1 | 0 | 2 | 2 | 4 | –2 | 3 |
| Russia | 3 | 0 | 1 | 2 | 5 | 7 | –2 | 1 |

*Finals in Lithuania 20 July–1 August 2013.*

# UEFA UNDER-17 CHAMPIONSHIP 2012–13

## QUALIFYING ROUND

### GROUP 1 (SERBIA)

| | |
|---|---|
| Belarus v Moldova | 1-0 |
| Serbia v Armenia | 5-0 |
| Belarus v Armenia | 5-0 |
| Moldova v Serbia | 0-4 |
| Serbia v Belarus | 7-0 |
| Armenia v Moldova | 0-3 |

| Group 1 Table | P | W | D | L | F | A | GD | Pts |
|---|---|---|---|---|---|---|---|---|
| Serbia | 3 | 3 | 0 | 0 | 16 | 0 | 16 | 9 |
| Belarus | 3 | 2 | 0 | 1 | 6 | 7 | –1 | 6 |
| Moldova | 3 | 1 | 0 | 2 | 3 | 5 | –2 | 3 |
| Armenia | 3 | 0 | 0 | 3 | 0 | 13 | –13 | 0 |

### GROUP 2 (FINLAND)

| | |
|---|---|
| Germany v San Marino | 5-0 |
| Finland v Andorra | 3-0 |
| Andorra v Germany | 1-10 |
| Finland v San Marino | 5-0 |
| Germany v Finland | 8-1 |
| San Marino v Andorra | 1-1 |

| Group 2 Table | P | W | D | L | F | A | GD | Pts |
|---|---|---|---|---|---|---|---|---|
| Germany | 3 | 3 | 0 | 0 | 23 | 2 | 21 | 9 |
| Finland | 3 | 2 | 0 | 1 | 9 | 8 | 1 | 6 |
| San Marino | 3 | 0 | 1 | 2 | 1 | 11 | –10 | 1 |
| Andorra | 3 | 0 | 1 | 2 | 2 | 14 | –12 | 1 |

### GROUP 3 (BELGIUM)

| | |
|---|---|
| Holland v Latvia | 2-1 |
| Belgium v Lithuania | 2-0 |
| Lithuania v Holland | 0-0 |
| Belgium v Latvia | 5-0 |
| Holland v Belgium | 2-1 |
| Latvia v Lithuania | 1-0 |

| Group 3 Table | P | W | D | L | F | A | GD | Pts |
|---|---|---|---|---|---|---|---|---|
| Holland | 3 | 2 | 1 | 0 | 4 | 2 | 2 | 7 |
| Belgium | 3 | 2 | 0 | 1 | 8 | 2 | 6 | 6 |
| Latvia | 3 | 1 | 0 | 2 | 2 | 7 | –5 | 3 |
| Lithuania | 3 | 0 | 1 | 2 | 0 | 3 | –3 | 1 |

### GROUP 4 (BULGARIA)

| | |
|---|---|
| Poland v Bulgaria | 2-1 |
| Spain v Azerbaijan | 2-0 |
| Azerbaijan v Poland | 0-1 |
| Spain v Bulgaria | 0-1 |
| Poland v Spain | 0-1 |
| Bulgaria v Azerbaijan | 4-1 |

| Group 4 Table | P | W | D | L | F | A | GD | Pts |
|---|---|---|---|---|---|---|---|---|
| Bulgaria | 3 | 2 | 0 | 1 | 6 | 3 | 3 | 6 |
| Poland | 3 | 2 | 0 | 1 | 3 | 2 | 1 | 6 |
| Spain | 3 | 2 | 0 | 1 | 3 | 1 | 2 | 6 |
| Azerbaijan | 3 | 0 | 0 | 3 | 1 | 7 | –6 | 0 |

### GROUP 5 (BOSNIA & HERZEGOVINA)

| | |
|---|---|
| Greece v Slovenia | 0-0 |
| France v Bosnia & Herzegovina | 3-1 |
| Greece v Bosnia & Herzegovina | 1-2 |
| Slovenia v France | 1-0 |
| France v Greece | 2-2 |
| Bosnia & Herzegovina v Slovenia | 0-1 |

| Group 5 Table | P | W | D | L | F | A | GD | Pts |
|---|---|---|---|---|---|---|---|---|
| Slovenia | 3 | 2 | 1 | 0 | 2 | 0 | 2 | 7 |
| France | 3 | 1 | 1 | 1 | 5 | 4 | 1 | 4 |
| Bosnia & Herzegovina | 3 | 1 | 0 | 2 | 3 | 5 | –2 | 3 |
| Greece | 3 | 0 | 2 | 1 | 3 | 4 | –1 | 2 |

### GROUP 6 (AUSTRIA)

| | |
|---|---|
| Switzerland v Faroe Islands | 3-0 |
| Austria v Cyprus | 0-0 |
| Cyprus v Switzerland | 1-5 |
| Austria v Faroe Islands | 6-0 |
| Switzerland v Austria | 1-1 |
| Faroe Islands v Cyprus | 1-1 |

| Group 6 Table | P | W | D | L | F | A | GD | Pts |
|---|---|---|---|---|---|---|---|---|
| Switzerland | 3 | 2 | 1 | 0 | 9 | 2 | 7 | 7 |
| Austria | 3 | 1 | 2 | 0 | 7 | 1 | 6 | 5 |
| Cyprus | 3 | 0 | 2 | 1 | 2 | 6 | –4 | 2 |
| Faroe Islands | 3 | 0 | 1 | 2 | 1 | 10 | –9 | 1 |

### GROUP 7 (ESTONIA)

| | |
|---|---|
| Northern Ireland v Wales | 4-0 |
| England v Estonia | 2-0 |
| England v Wales | 1-0 |
| Estonia v Northern Ireland | 1-1 |
| Northern Ireland v England | 2-3 |
| Wales v Estonia | 1-3 |

| Group 7 Table | P | W | D | L | F | A | GD | Pts |
|---|---|---|---|---|---|---|---|---|
| England | 3 | 3 | 0 | 0 | 6 | 2 | 4 | 9 |
| Northern Ireland | 3 | 1 | 1 | 1 | 7 | 4 | 3 | 4 |
| Estonia | 3 | 1 | 1 | 1 | 4 | 4 | 0 | 4 |
| Wales | 3 | 0 | 0 | 3 | 1 | 8 | –7 | 0 |

### GROUP 8 (HUNGARY)

| | |
|---|---|
| Italy v Albania | 1-0 |
| Hungary v Liechtenstein | 5-0 |
| Italy v Liechtenstein | 4-0 |
| Albania v Hungary | 0-1 |
| Hungary v Italy | 3-2 |
| Liechtenstein v Albania | 0-6 |

| Group 8 Table | P | W | D | L | F | A | GD | Pts |
|---|---|---|---|---|---|---|---|---|
| Hungary | 3 | 3 | 0 | 0 | 9 | 2 | 7 | 9 |
| Italy | 3 | 2 | 0 | 1 | 7 | 3 | 4 | 6 |
| Albania | 3 | 1 | 0 | 2 | 6 | 2 | 4 | 3 |
| Liechtenstein | 3 | 0 | 0 | 3 | 0 | 15 | –15 | 0 |

### GROUP 9 (MALTA)

| | |
|---|---|
| Norway v Malta | 2-1 |
| Portugal v Iceland | 4-2 |
| Norway v Iceland | 2-0 |
| Malta v Portugal | 1-2 |
| Portugal v Norway | 0-1 |
| Iceland v Malta | 2-0 |

| Group 9 Table | P | W | D | L | F | A | GD | Pts |
|---|---|---|---|---|---|---|---|---|
| Norway | 3 | 3 | 0 | 0 | 5 | 1 | 4 | 9 |
| Portugal | 3 | 2 | 0 | 1 | 6 | 4 | 2 | 6 |
| Iceland | 3 | 1 | 0 | 2 | 4 | 6 | –2 | 3 |
| Malta | 3 | 0 | 0 | 3 | 2 | 6 | –4 | 0 |

### GROUP 10 (MACEDONIA)

| | |
|---|---|
| Republic of Ireland v Sweden | 1-1 |
| Romania v Macedonia | 1-1 |
| Republic of Ireland v Macedonia | 4-1 |
| Sweden v Romania | 2-1 |
| Romania v Republic of Ireland | 0-2 |
| Macedonia v Sweden | 0-4 |

| Group 10 Table | P | W | D | L | F | A | GD | Pts |
|---|---|---|---|---|---|---|---|---|
| Republic of Ireland | 3 | 2 | 1 | 0 | 7 | 2 | 5 | 7 |
| Sweden | 3 | 2 | 1 | 0 | 7 | 2 | 5 | 7 |
| Romania | 3 | 0 | 1 | 2 | 2 | 5 | –3 | 1 |
| Macedonia | 3 | 0 | 1 | 2 | 2 | 9 | –7 | 1 |

### GROUP 11 (CZECH REPUBLIC)

| | |
|---|---|
| Czech Republic v Russia | 3-0 |
| Denmark v Montenegro | 3-0 |
| Montenegro v Czech Republic | 0-2 |
| Denmark v Russia | 1-2 |
| Czech Republic v Denmark | 3-0 |
| Russia v Montenegro | 3-0 |

| Group 11 Table | P | W | D | L | F | A | GD | Pts |
|---|---|---|---|---|---|---|---|---|
| Czech Republic | 3 | 3 | 0 | 0 | 8 | 0 | 8 | 9 |
| Russia | 3 | 2 | 0 | 1 | 5 | 4 | 1 | 6 |
| Denmark | 3 | 1 | 0 | 2 | 4 | 5 | –1 | 3 |
| Montenegro | 3 | 0 | 0 | 3 | 0 | 8 | –8 | 0 |

### GROUP 12 (CROATIA)

| | |
|---|---|
| Turkey v Kazakhstan | 3-0 |
| Croatia v Israel | 4-2 |
| Turkey v Israel | 2-4 |
| Kazakhstan v Croatia | 0-2 |
| Croatia v Turkey | 4-3 |
| Israel v Kazakhstan | 6-2 |

| Group 12 Table | P | W | D | L | F | A | GD | Pts |
|---|---|---|---|---|---|---|---|---|
| Croatia | 3 | 3 | 0 | 0 | 10 | 5 | 5 | 9 |
| Israel | 3 | 2 | 0 | 1 | 12 | 8 | 4 | 6 |
| Turkey | 3 | 1 | 0 | 2 | 8 | 8 | 0 | 3 |
| Kazakhstan | 3 | 0 | 0 | 3 | 2 | 11 | –9 | 0 |

## GROUP 13 (GEORGIA)

| | |
|---|---|
| Scotland v Luxembourg | 5-2 |
| Georgia v Ukraine | 1-3 |
| Scotland v Ukraine | 0-0 |
| Luxembourg v Georgia | 1-3 |
| Georgia v Scotland | 3-0 |
| Ukraine v Luxembourg | 6-0 |

| Group 13 Table | P | W | D | L | F | A | GD | Pts |
|---|---|---|---|---|---|---|---|---|
| Ukraine | 3 | 2 | 1 | 0 | 9 | 1 | 8 | 7 |
| Georgia | 3 | 2 | 0 | 1 | 7 | 4 | 3 | 6 |
| Scotland | 3 | 1 | 1 | 1 | 5 | 5 | 0 | 4 |
| Luxembourg | 3 | 0 | 0 | 3 | 3 | 14 | −11 | 0 |

# ELITE ROUND

## GROUP 1 (CROATIA)

| | |
|---|---|
| Croatia v Spain | 3-2 |
| Belgium v France | 1-4 |
| Croatia v France | 1-0 |
| Spain v Belgium | 2-1 |
| Belgium v Croatia | 1-1 |
| France v Spain | 3-2 |

| Group 1 Table | P | W | D | L | F | A | GD | Pts |
|---|---|---|---|---|---|---|---|---|
| Croatia | 3 | 2 | 1 | 0 | 5 | 3 | 2 | 7 |
| France | 3 | 2 | 0 | 1 | 7 | 4 | 3 | 6 |
| Spain | 3 | 1 | 0 | 2 | 6 | 7 | −1 | 3 |
| Belgium | 3 | 0 | 1 | 2 | 3 | 7 | −4 | 1 |

## GROUP 2 (AUSTRIA)

| | |
|---|---|
| Serbia v Georgia | 2-0 |
| Republic of Ireland v Austria | 1-0 |
| Georgia v Republic of Ireland | 3-0 |
| Serbia v Austria | 0-1 |
| Republic of Ireland v Serbia | 1-1 |
| Austria v Georgia | 2-1 |

| Group 2 Table | P | W | D | L | F | A | GD | Pts |
|---|---|---|---|---|---|---|---|---|
| Austria | 3 | 2 | 0 | 1 | 3 | 2 | 1 | 6 |
| Serbia | 3 | 1 | 1 | 1 | 3 | 2 | 1 | 4 |
| Republic of Ireland | 3 | 1 | 1 | 1 | 2 | 4 | −2 | 4 |
| Georgia | 3 | 1 | 0 | 2 | 4 | 4 | 0 | 3 |

## GROUP 3 (HUNGARY)

| | |
|---|---|
| Hungary v Finland | 3-2 |
| Sweden v Belarus | 4-1 |
| Hungary v Belarus | 3-0 |
| Finland v Sweden | 0-5 |
| Sweden v Hungary | 1-1 |
| Belarus v Finland | P-P |
| *Match cancelled.* | |

| Group 3 Table | P | W | D | L | F | A | GD | Pts |
|---|---|---|---|---|---|---|---|---|
| Sweden | 3 | 2 | 1 | 0 | 10 | 2 | 8 | 7 |
| Hungary | 3 | 2 | 1 | 0 | 7 | 3 | 4 | 7 |
| Finland | 2 | 0 | 0 | 2 | 2 | 8 | −6 | 0 |
| Belarus | 2 | 0 | 0 | 2 | 1 | 7 | −6 | 0 |

## GROUP 4 (GERMANY)

| | |
|---|---|
| Ukraine v Estonia | 5-1 |
| Germany v Bulgaria | 5-2 |
| Germany v Estonia | 6-0 |
| Bulgaria v Ukraine | 0-0 |
| Ukraine v Germany | 1-0 |
| Estonia v Bulgaria | 1-4 |

| Group 4 Table | P | W | D | L | F | A | GD | Pts |
|---|---|---|---|---|---|---|---|---|
| Ukraine | 3 | 2 | 1 | 0 | 6 | 1 | 5 | 7 |
| Germany | 3 | 2 | 0 | 1 | 11 | 3 | 8 | 6 |
| Bulgaria | 3 | 1 | 1 | 1 | 6 | 6 | 0 | 4 |
| Estonia | 3 | 0 | 0 | 3 | 2 | 15 | −13 | 0 |

## GROUP 5 (SWITZERLAND)

| | |
|---|---|
| Czech Republic v Israel | 1-1 |
| Switzerland v Poland | 0-0 |
| Israel v Switzerland | 1-2 |
| Czech Republic v Poland | 1-1 |
| Switzerland v Czech Republic | 1-0 |
| Poland v Israel | 2-1 |

| Group 5 Table | P | W | D | L | F | A | GD | Pts |
|---|---|---|---|---|---|---|---|---|
| Switzerland | 3 | 2 | 1 | 0 | 3 | 1 | 2 | 7 |
| Poland | 3 | 1 | 2 | 0 | 3 | 2 | 1 | 5 |
| Czech Republic | 3 | 0 | 2 | 1 | 2 | 3 | −1 | 2 |
| Israel | 3 | 0 | 1 | 2 | 3 | 5 | −2 | 1 |

## GROUP 6 (ENGLAND)

| | |
|---|---|
| Slovenia v Russia | 1-2 |
| England v Portugal | 1-0 |
| Portugal v Slovenia | 3-1 |
| England v Russia | 1-2 |
| Slovenia v England | 1-2 |
| Russia v Portugal | 0-1 |

| Group 6 Table | P | W | D | L | F | A | GD | Pts |
|---|---|---|---|---|---|---|---|---|
| Russia | 3 | 2 | 0 | 1 | 4 | 3 | 1 | 6 |
| England | 3 | 2 | 0 | 1 | 4 | 3 | 1 | 6 |
| Portugal | 3 | 2 | 0 | 1 | 4 | 2 | 2 | 6 |
| Slovenia | 3 | 0 | 0 | 3 | 3 | 7 | −4 | 0 |

## GROUP 7 (HOLLAND)

| | |
|---|---|
| Norway v Italy | 0-1 |
| Holland v Northern Ireland | 2-2 |
| Norway v Northern Ireland | 2-1 |
| Italy v Holland | 1-0 |
| Holland v Norway | 1-1 |
| Northern Ireland v Italy | 0-0 |

| Group 7 Table | P | W | D | L | F | A | GD | Pts |
|---|---|---|---|---|---|---|---|---|
| Italy | 3 | 2 | 1 | 0 | 2 | 0 | 2 | 7 |
| Norway | 3 | 1 | 1 | 1 | 3 | 3 | 0 | 4 |
| Holland | 3 | 0 | 2 | 1 | 3 | 4 | −1 | 2 |
| Northern Ireland | 3 | 0 | 2 | 1 | 3 | 4 | −1 | 2 |

# FINAL TOURNAMENT (SLOVAKIA) GROUP STAGE

## GROUP A

| | |
|---|---|
| Slovakia v Austria | 1-0 |
| Switzerland v Sweden | 0-1 |
| Austria v Sweden | 1-1 |
| Slovakia v Switzerland | 2-2 |
| Sweden v Slovakia | 0-0 |
| Austria v Switzerland | 2-1 |

| Group A Table | P | W | D | L | F | A | GD | Pts |
|---|---|---|---|---|---|---|---|---|
| Slovakia | 3 | 1 | 2 | 0 | 3 | 2 | 1 | 5 |
| Sweden | 3 | 1 | 2 | 0 | 2 | 1 | 1 | 5 |
| Austria | 3 | 1 | 1 | 1 | 3 | 3 | 0 | 4 |
| Switzerland | 3 | 0 | 1 | 2 | 5 | 5 | −1 | 1 |

## GROUP B

| | |
|---|---|
| Russia v Ukraine | 3-0 |
| Croatia v Italy | 0-0 |
| Russia v Croatia | 0-0 |
| Ukraine v Italy | 1-2 |
| Italy v Russia | 1-1 |
| Ukraine v Croatia | 1-2 |

| Group B Table | P | W | D | L | F | A | GD | Pts |
|---|---|---|---|---|---|---|---|---|
| Russia | 3 | 1 | 2 | 0 | 4 | 1 | 3 | 5 |
| Italy | 3 | 1 | 2 | 0 | 3 | 2 | 1 | 5 |
| Croatia | 3 | 1 | 2 | 0 | 2 | 1 | 1 | 5 |
| Ukraine | 3 | 0 | 0 | 3 | 2 | 7 | −5 | 0 |

## SEMI-FINALS

| | |
|---|---|
| Slovakia v Italy | 0-2 |
| Russia v Sweden | 0-0 |
| *Russia won 10-9 on penalties.* | |

## FINAL

| | |
|---|---|
| Italy v Russia | 0-0 |
| *Russia won 5-4 on penalties.* | |

# UEFA REGIONS' CUP 2012–13

## PRELIMINARY ROUND

### GROUP A (TURKEY)

| | |
|---|---|
| Karmiel Tzfat v Prahova Muntenia | 0-0 |
| Merkuriy v Istanbul | 0-5 |
| Merkuriy v Karmiel Tzfat | 1-7 |
| Prahova Muntenia v Istanbul | 2-1 |
| Prahova Muntenia v Merkuriy | 9-1 |
| Istanbul v Karmiel Tzfat | 3-2 |

| Group A Table | P | W | D | L | F | A | GD | Pts |
|---|---|---|---|---|---|---|---|---|
| Prahova Muntenia | 3 | 2 | 1 | 0 | 11 | 2 | 9 | 7 |
| Istanbul | 3 | 2 | 0 | 1 | 9 | 4 | 5 | 6 |
| Karmiel Tzfat | 3 | 1 | 1 | 1 | 9 | 4 | 5 | 4 |
| Merkuriy | 3 | 0 | 0 | 3 | 2 | 21 | –19 | 0 |

### GROUP B (MACEDONIA)

| | |
|---|---|
| SE Macedonia v North Wales | 1-0 |
| Hestrafors v Eastern Region (N Ireland) | 0-2 |
| SE Macedonia v Hestrafors | 7-0 |
| Eastern Region (N Ireland) v North Wales | 2-1 |
| Eastern Region (N Ireland) v SE Macedonia | 0-0 |
| North Wales v Hestrafors | 1-1 |

| Group B Table | P | W | D | L | F | A | GD | Pts |
|---|---|---|---|---|---|---|---|---|
| SE Macedonia | 3 | 2 | 1 | 0 | 8 | 0 | 8 | 7 |
| Eastern Region (N Ireland) | 3 | 2 | 1 | 0 | 4 | 1 | 3 | 7 |
| North Wales | 3 | 0 | 1 | 2 | 2 | 4 | –2 | 1 |
| Hestrafors | 3 | 0 | 1 | 2 | 1 | 10 | –9 | 1 |

## INTERMEDIARY ROUND

### GROUP 1 (BELARUS)

| | |
|---|---|
| Isloch v Paris Ile de France | 2-0 |
| Savez Tuzlanskog v Central Slovakia | 2-3 |
| Isloch v Savez Tuzlanskog | 2-1 |
| Central Slovakia v Paris Ile de France | 0-2 |
| Central Slovakia v Isloch | 0-1 |
| Paris Ile de France v Savez Tuzlanskog | 2-2 |

| Group 1 Table | P | W | D | L | F | A | GD | Pts |
|---|---|---|---|---|---|---|---|---|
| Isloch | 3 | 3 | 0 | 0 | 5 | 1 | 4 | 9 |
| Paris Ile de France | 3 | 1 | 1 | 1 | 4 | 4 | 0 | 4 |
| Central Slovakia | 3 | 1 | 0 | 2 | 3 | 5 | –2 | 3 |
| Savez Tuzlanskog | 3 | 0 | 1 | 2 | 5 | 7 | –2 | 1 |

### GROUP 2 (BULGARIA)

| | |
|---|---|
| Yugoiztochen Region v Prahova Muntenia | 3-0 |
| Geneve v Rijeka | 1-1 |
| Yugoiztochen Region v Geneve | 2-0 |
| Rijeka v Prahova Muntenia | 0-0 |
| Rijeka v Yugoiztochen Region | 5-0 |
| Prahova Muntenia v Geneve | 1-0 |

| Group 2 Table | P | W | D | L | F | A | GD | Pts |
|---|---|---|---|---|---|---|---|---|
| Yugoiztochen Region | 3 | 2 | 0 | 1 | 5 | 5 | 0 | 6 |
| Rijeka | 3 | 1 | 2 | 0 | 6 | 1 | 5 | 5 |
| Prahova Muntenia | 3 | 1 | 1 | 1 | 3 | –2 | 4 |
| Geneve | 3 | 0 | 1 | 2 | 1 | 4 | –3 | 1 |

### GROUP 3 (CZECH REPUBLIC)

| | |
|---|---|
| Zlin v Keleti Regio | 1-2 |
| Wurttemberg v West Central Scotland | 6-1 |
| Zlin v Wurttemberg | 0-4 |
| West Central Scotland v Keleti Regio | 2-4 |
| West Central Scotland v Zlin | 2-6 |
| Keleti Regio v Wurttemberg | 6-1 |

| Group 3 Table | P | W | D | L | F | A | GD | Pts |
|---|---|---|---|---|---|---|---|---|
| Keleti Regio | 3 | 3 | 0 | 0 | 12 | 4 | 8 | 9 |
| Wurttemberg | 3 | 2 | 0 | 1 | 11 | 7 | 4 | 6 |
| Zlin | 3 | 1 | 0 | 2 | 7 | 8 | –1 | 3 |
| West Central Scotland | 3 | 0 | 0 | 3 | 5 | 16 | –11 | 0 |

### GROUP 4 (LITHUANIA)

| | |
|---|---|
| Belgrade v SE Macedonia | 1-2 |
| Lietava v Qarachala | 0-3 |
| SE Macedonia v Qarachala | 0-2 |
| Lietava v Belgrade | 0-5 |
| SE Macedonia v Lietava | 3-0 |
| Qarachala v Belgrade | 2-1 |

| Group 4 Table | P | W | D | L | F | A | GD | Pts |
|---|---|---|---|---|---|---|---|---|
| Qarachala | 3 | 3 | 0 | 0 | 7 | 1 | 6 | 9 |
| SE Macedonia | 3 | 2 | 0 | 1 | 5 | 3 | 2 | 6 |
| Belgrade | 3 | 1 | 0 | 2 | 7 | 4 | 3 | 3 |
| Lietava | 3 | 0 | 0 | 3 | 0 | 11 | –11 | 0 |

### GROUP 5 (MALTA)

| | |
|---|---|
| Gozo v Rinuzi/Strong | 3-2 |
| Olimp v Ialoveni | 4-0 |
| Gozo v Olimp | 0-6 |
| Ialoveni v Rinuzi/Strong | 2-2 |
| Ialoveni v Gozo | 2-2 |
| Rinuzi/Strong v Olimp | 0-4 |

| Group 5 Table | P | W | D | L | F | A | GD | Pts |
|---|---|---|---|---|---|---|---|---|
| Olimp | 3 | 3 | 0 | 0 | 14 | 0 | 14 | 9 |
| Gozo | 3 | 1 | 1 | 1 | 5 | 10 | –5 | 4 |
| Ialoveni | 3 | 0 | 2 | 1 | 4 | 8 | –4 | 2 |
| Rinuzi/Strong | 3 | 0 | 1 | 2 | 4 | 9 | –5 | 1 |

### GROUP 6 (SAN MARINO)

| | |
|---|---|
| Leinster & Munster v Jersey | 1-2 |
| San Marino v Eastern Region (N Ireland) | 0-1 |
| San Marino v Leinster & Munster | 0-0 |
| Jersey v Eastern Region (N Ireland) | 1-2 |
| Jersey v San Marino | 1-0 |
| Eastern Region (N Ireland) v Leinster & Munster | 0-2 |

| Group 6 Table | P | W | D | L | F | A | GD | Pts |
|---|---|---|---|---|---|---|---|---|
| Eastern Region (N Ireland) | 3 | 2 | 0 | 1 | 3 | 3 | 0 | 6 |
| Jersey | 3 | 2 | 0 | 1 | 4 | 3 | 1 | 6 |
| Leinster & Munster | 3 | 1 | 1 | 1 | 3 | 2 | 1 | 4 |
| San Marino | 3 | 0 | 1 | 2 | 0 | 2 | –2 | 1 |

### GROUP 7 (UKRAINE)

| | |
|---|---|
| Nove Zhytya v Ljubljana | 3-0 |
| Ardennes v Seleccion Catalana | 1-2 |
| Nove Zhytya v Ardennes | 0-1 |
| Seleccion Catalana v Ljubljana | 2-0 |
| Seleccion Catalana v Nove Zhytya | 4-1 |
| Ljubljana v Ardennes | 3-4 |

| Group 7 Table | P | W | D | L | F | A | GD | Pts |
|---|---|---|---|---|---|---|---|---|
| Seleccion Catalana | 3 | 3 | 0 | 0 | 8 | 2 | 6 | 9 |
| Ardennes | 3 | 2 | 0 | 1 | 6 | 5 | 1 | 6 |
| Nove Zhytya | 3 | 1 | 0 | 2 | 4 | 5 | –1 | 3 |
| Ljubljana | 3 | 0 | 0 | 3 | 3 | 9 | –6 | 0 |

### GROUP 8 (ITALY)

| | |
|---|---|
| Western Estonia v Kujawsko-Pomorski | 0-3 |
| Veneto v Eastern Finland | 6-0 |
| Western Estonia v Veneto | 0-7 |
| Eastern Finland v Kujawsko-Pomorski | 0-3 |
| Eastern Finland v Western Estonia | 5-1 |
| Kujawsko-Pomorski v Veneto | 0-1 |

| Group 8 Table | P | W | D | L | F | A | GD | Pts |
|---|---|---|---|---|---|---|---|---|
| Veneto | 3 | 3 | 0 | 0 | 14 | 0 | 14 | 9 |
| Kujawsko-Pomorski | 3 | 2 | 0 | 1 | 6 | 1 | 5 | 6 |
| Eastern Finland | 3 | 1 | 0 | 2 | 5 | 10 | –5 | 3 |
| Western Estonia | 3 | 0 | 0 | 3 | 1 | 15 | –14 | 0 |

*Final Tournament in Veneto, Italy. Results in next edition.*

# ENGLAND UNDER-21 RESULTS 1976–2013

EC *UEFA Competition for Under-21 Teams*

| Year | Date | | Venue | | |
|------|------|----|-------|---|---|
| | | | **v ALBANIA** | *Eng* | *Alb* |
| EC1989 | Mar | 7 | Shkroda | 2 | 1 |
| EC1989 | April | 25 | Ipswich | 2 | 0 |
| EC2001 | Mar | 27 | Tirana | 1 | 0 |
| EC2001 | Sept | 4 | Middlesbrough | 5 | 0 |
| | | | **v ANGOLA** | *Eng* | *Ang* |
| 1995 | June | 10 | Toulon | 1 | 0 |
| 1996 | May | 28 | Toulon | 0 | 2 |
| | | | **v ARGENTINA** | *Eng* | *Arg* |
| 1998 | May | 18 | Toulon | 0 | 2 |
| 2000 | Feb | 22 | Fulham | 1 | 0 |
| | | | **v AUSTRIA** | *Eng* | *Aus* |
| 1994 | Oct | 11 | Kapfenberg | 3 | 1 |
| 1995 | Nov | 14 | Middlesbrough | 2 | 1 |
| EC2004 | Sept | 3 | Krems | 2 | 0 |
| EC2005 | Oct | 7 | Leeds | 1 | 2 |
| 2013 | June | 26 | Brighton | 4 | 0 |
| | | | **v AZERBAIJAN** | *Eng* | *Az* |
| EC2004 | Oct | 12 | Baku | 0 | 0 |
| EC2005 | Mar | 29 | Middlesbrough | 2 | 0 |
| 2009 | June | 8 | Milton Keynes | 7 | 0 |
| EC2011 | Sept | 1 | Watford | 6 | 0 |
| EC2012 | Sept | 6 | Baku | 2 | 0 |
| | | | **v BELGIUM** | *Eng* | *Bel* |
| 1994 | June | 5 | Marseille | 2 | 1 |
| 1996 | May | 24 | Toulon | 1 | 0 |
| EC2011 | Nov | 14 | Mons | 1 | 2 |
| EC2012 | Feb | 29 | Middlesbrough | 4 | 0 |
| | | | **v BRAZIL** | *Eng* | *B* |
| 1993 | June | 11 | Toulon | 0 | 0 |
| 1995 | June | 6 | Toulon | 0 | 2 |
| 1996 | June | 1 | Toulon | 1 | 2 |
| | | | **v BULGARIA** | *Eng* | *Bul* |
| EC1979 | June | 5 | Pernik | 3 | 1 |
| EC1979 | Nov | 20 | Leicester | 5 | 0 |
| 1989 | June | 5 | Toulon | 2 | 3 |
| EC1998 | Oct | 9 | West Ham | 1 | 0 |
| EC1999 | June | 8 | Vratsa | 1 | 0 |
| EC2007 | Sept | 11 | Sofia | 2 | 0 |
| EC2007 | Nov | 16 | Milton Keynes | 2 | 0 |
| | | | **v CROATIA** | *Eng* | *Cro* |
| 1996 | Apr | 23 | Sunderland | 0 | 1 |
| 2003 | Aug | 19 | West Ham | 0 | 3 |
| | | | **v CZECHOSLOVAKIA** | *Eng* | *Cz* |
| 1990 | May | 28 | Toulon | 2 | 1 |
| 1992 | May | 26 | Toulon | 1 | 2 |
| 1993 | June | 9 | Toulon | 1 | 1 |
| | | | **v CZECH REPUBLIC** | *Eng* | *CzR* |
| 1998 | Nov | 17 | Ipswich | 0 | 1 |
| EC2007 | June | 11 | Arnhem | 0 | 0 |
| 2008 | Nov | 18 | Bramall Lane | 2 | 0 |
| EC2011 | June | 19 | Viborg | 1 | 2 |
| | | | **v DENMARK** | *Eng* | *Den* |
| EC1978 | Sept | 19 | Hvidovre | 2 | 1 |
| EC1979 | Sept | 11 | Watford | 1 | 0 |
| EC1982 | Sept | 21 | Hvidovre | 4 | 1 |
| EC1983 | Sept | 20 | Norwich | 4 | 1 |
| EC1986 | Mar | 12 | Copenhagen | 1 | 0 |
| EC1986 | Mar | 26 | Manchester | 1 | 1 |
| 1988 | Sept | 13 | Watford | 0 | 0 |
| 1994 | Mar | 8 | Brentford | 1 | 0 |
| 1999 | Oct | 8 | Bradford | 4 | 1 |
| 2005 | Aug | 16 | Herning | 1 | 0 |
| 2011 | Mar | 24 | Viborg | 4 | 0 |
| | | | **v EQUADOR** | *Eng* | *E* |
| 2009 | Feb | 10 | Malaga | 2 | 3 |

| Year | Date | | Venue | | |
|------|------|----|-------|---|---|
| | | | **v FINLAND** | *Eng* | *Fin* |
| EC1977 | May | 26 | Helsinki | 1 | 0 |
| EC1977 | Oct | 12 | Hull | 8 | 1 |
| EC1984 | Oct | 16 | Southampton | 2 | 0 |
| EC1985 | May | 21 | Mikkeli | 1 | 3 |
| EC2000 | Oct | 10 | Valkeakoski | 2 | 2 |
| EC2001 | Mar | 23 | Barnsley | 4 | 0 |
| EC2009 | June | 15 | Halmstad | 2 | 1 |
| | | | **v FRANCE** | *Eng* | *Fra* |
| EC1984 | Feb | 28 | Sheffield | 6 | 1 |
| EC1984 | Mar | 28 | Rouen | 1 | 0 |
| 1987 | June | 11 | Toulon | 0 | 2 |
| EC1988 | April | 13 | Besancon | 2 | 4 |
| EC1988 | April | 27 | Highbury | 2 | 2 |
| 1988 | June | 12 | Toulon | 2 | 4 |
| 1990 | May | 23 | Toulon | 7 | 3 |
| 1991 | June | 3 | Toulon | 1 | 0 |
| 1992 | May | 28 | Toulon | 0 | 0 |
| 1993 | June | 15 | Toulon | 1 | 0 |
| 1994 | May | 31 | Aubagne | 0 | 3 |
| 1995 | June | 10 | Toulon | 0 | 2 |
| 1998 | May | 14 | Toulon | 1 | 1 |
| 1999 | Feb | 9 | Derby | 2 | 1 |
| EC2005 | Nov | 11 | Tottenham | 1 | 1 |
| EC2005 | Nov | 15 | Nancy | 1 | 2 |
| 2009 | Mar | 31 | Nottingham | 0 | 2 |
| | | | **v GEORGIA** | *Eng* | *Geo* |
| EC1996 | Nov | 8 | Batumi | 1 | 0 |
| EC1997 | April | 29 | Charlton | 0 | 0 |
| 2000 | Aug | 31 | Middlesbrough | 6 | 1 |
| | | | **v GERMANY** | *Eng* | *Ger* |
| 1991 | Sept | 10 | Scunthorpe | 2 | 1 |
| EC2000 | Oct | 6 | Derby | 1 | 1 |
| EC2001 | Aug | 31 | Frieburg | 2 | 1 |
| 2005 | Mar | 25 | Hull | 2 | 2 |
| 2005 | Sept | 6 | Mainz | 1 | 1 |
| EC2006 | Oct | 6 | Coventry | 1 | 0 |
| EC2006 | Oct | 10 | Leverkusen | 2 | 0 |
| EC2009 | June | 22 | Halmstad | 1 | 1 |
| EC2009 | June | 29 | Malmo | 0 | 4 |
| 2010 | Nov | 16 | Wiesbaden | 0 | 2 |
| | | | **v EAST GERMANY** | *Eng* | *EG* |
| EC1980 | April | 16 | Sheffield | 1 | 2 |
| EC1980 | April | 23 | Jena | 0 | 1 |
| | | | **v WEST GERMANY** | *Eng* | *WG* |
| EC1982 | Sept | 21 | Sheffield | 3 | 1 |
| EC1982 | Oct | 12 | Bremen | 2 | 3 |
| 1987 | Sept | 8 | Ludenscheid | 0 | 2 |
| | | | **v GREECE** | *Eng* | *Gre* |
| EC1982 | Nov | 16 | Piraeus | 0 | 1 |
| EC1983 | Mar | 29 | Portsmouth | 2 | 1 |
| 1989 | Feb | 7 | Patras | 0 | 1 |
| EC1997 | Nov | 13 | Heraklion | 0 | 2 |
| EC1997 | Dec | 17 | Norwich | 4 | 2 |
| EC2001 | June | 5 | Athens | 1 | 3 |
| EC2001 | Oct | 5 | Ewood Park | 2 | 1 |
| EC2009 | Sept | 8 | Tripoli | 1 | 1 |
| EC2010 | Mar | 3 | Doncaster | 1 | 2 |
| | | | **v HOLLAND** | *Eng* | *H* |
| EC1993 | April | 27 | Portsmouth | 3 | 0 |
| EC1993 | Oct | 12 | Utrecht | 1 | 1 |
| 2001 | Aug | 14 | Reading | 4 | 0 |
| EC2001 | Nov | 9 | Utrecht | 2 | 2 |
| EC2001 | Nov | 13 | Derby | 1 | 0 |
| 2004 | Feb | 17 | Hull | 3 | 2 |
| 2005 | Feb | 8 | Derby | 1 | 2 |

| | | | | Eng | H |
|---|---|---|---|---|---|
| 2006 | Nov | 14 | Alkmaar | 1 | 0 |
| EC2007 | June | 20 | Heerenveen | 1 | 1 |
| 2009 | Aug | 11 | Groningen | 0 | 0 |

| | | | v HUNGARY | Eng | Hun |
|---|---|---|---|---|---|
| EC1981 | June | 5 | Keszthely | 2 | 1 |
| EC1981 | Nov | 17 | Nottingham | 2 | 0 |
| EC1983 | April | 26 | Newcastle | 1 | 0 |
| EC1983 | Oct | 11 | Nyiregyhaza | 2 | 0 |
| 1990 | Sept | 11 | Southampton | 3 | 1 |
| 1992 | May | 12 | Budapest | 2 | 2 |
| 1999 | April | 27 | Budapest | 2 | 2 |

| | | | v ICELAND | Eng | Ice |
|---|---|---|---|---|---|
| 2011 | Mar | 28 | Preston | 1 | 2 |
| EC2011 | Oct | 6 | Reykjavik | 3 | 0 |
| EC2011 | Nov | 10 | Colchester | 5 | 0 |

| | | | v REPUBLIC OF IRELAND | Eng | RoI |
|---|---|---|---|---|---|
| 1981 | Feb | 25 | Liverpool | 1 | 0 |
| 1985 | Mar | 25 | Portsmouth | 3 | 2 |
| 1989 | June | 9 | Toulon | 0 | 0 |
| EC1990 | Nov | 13 | Cork | 3 | 0 |
| EC1991 | Mar | 26 | Brentford | 3 | 0 |
| 1994 | Nov | 15 | Newcastle | 1 | 0 |
| 1995 | Mar | 27 | Dublin | 2 | 0 |
| EC2007 | Oct | 16 | Cork | 3 | 0 |
| EC2008 | Feb | 5 | Southampton | 3 | 0 |

| | | | v ISRAEL | Eng | Isr |
|---|---|---|---|---|---|
| 1985 | Feb | 27 | Tel Aviv | 2 | 1 |
| 2011 | Sept | 5 | Barnsley | 4 | 1 |
| EC2013 | June | 11 | Jerusalem | 0 | 1 |

| | | | v ITALY | Eng | Italy |
|---|---|---|---|---|---|
| EC1978 | Mar | 8 | Manchester | 2 | 1 |
| EC1978 | April | 5 | Rome | 0 | 0 |
| EC1984 | April | 18 | Manchester | 3 | 1 |
| EC1984 | May | 2 | Florence | 0 | 1 |
| EC1986 | April | 9 | Pisa | 0 | 2 |
| EC1986 | April | 23 | Swindon | 1 | 1 |
| EC1997 | Feb | 12 | Bristol | 1 | 0 |
| EC1997 | Oct | 10 | Rieti | 1 | 0 |
| EC2000 | May | 27 | Bratislava | 0 | 2 |
| 2000 | Nov | 14 | Monza* | 0 | 0 |
| 2002 | Mar | 26 | Valley Parade | 1 | 1 |
| EC2002 | May | 20 | Basle | 1 | 2 |
| 2003 | Feb | 11 | Pisa | 0 | 1 |
| 2007 | Mar | 24 | Wembley | 3 | 3 |
| EC2007 | June | 14 | Arnhem | 2 | 2 |
| 2011 | Feb | 8 | Empoli | 0 | 1 |
| EC2013 | June | 5 | Tel Aviv | 0 | 1 |

*Abandoned 11 mins; fog.

| | | | v LATVIA | Eng | Lat |
|---|---|---|---|---|---|
| 1995 | April | 25 | Riga | 1 | 0 |
| 1995 | June | 7 | Burnley | 4 | 0 |

| | | | v LITHUANIA | Eng | Lith |
|---|---|---|---|---|---|
| EC2009 | Nov | 17 | Vilnius | 0 | 0 |
| EC2010 | Sept | 7 | Colchester | 3 | 0 |

| | | | v LUXEMBOURG | Eng | Lux |
|---|---|---|---|---|---|
| EC1998 | Oct | 13 | Greven Macher | 5 | 0 |
| EC1999 | Sept | 3 | Reading | 5 | 0 |

| | | | v MACEDONIA | Eng | M |
|---|---|---|---|---|---|
| EC2002 | Oct | 15 | Reading | 3 | 1 |
| EC2003 | Sept | 5 | Skopje | 1 | 1 |
| EC2009 | Sept | 4 | Prilep | 2 | 1 |
| EC2009 | Oct | 9 | Coventry | 6 | 3 |

| | | | v MALAYSIA | Eng | Mal |
|---|---|---|---|---|---|
| 1995 | June | 8 | Toulon | 2 | 0 |

| | | | v MEXICO | Eng | Mex |
|---|---|---|---|---|---|
| 1988 | June | | Toulon | 2 | 1 |
| 1991 | May | 29 | Toulon | 6 | 0 |
| 1992 | May | 25 | Toulon | 1 | 1 |
| 2001 | May | 24 | Leicester | 3 | 0 |

| | | | v MOLDOVA | Eng | Mol |
|---|---|---|---|---|---|
| EC1996 | Aug | 31 | Chisinau | 2 | 0 |
| EC1997 | Sept | 9 | Wycombe | 1 | 0 |
| EC2006 | Aug | 15 | Ipswich | 2 | 2 |

| | | | v MONTENEGRO | Eng | M |
|---|---|---|---|---|---|
| EC2007 | Sept | 7 | Podgorica | 3 | 0 |
| EC2007 | Oct | 12 | Leicester | 1 | 0 |

| | | | v MOROCCO | Eng | Mor |
|---|---|---|---|---|---|
| 1987 | June | 7 | Toulon | 2 | 0 |
| 1988 | June | 9 | Toulon | 1 | 0 |

| | | | v NORTHERN IRELAND | Eng | NI |
|---|---|---|---|---|---|
| 2012 | Nov | 13 | Blackpool | 2 | 0 |

| | | | v NORWAY | Eng | Nor |
|---|---|---|---|---|---|
| EC1977 | June | 1 | Bergen | 2 | 1 |
| EC1977 | Sept | 6 | Brighton | 6 | 0 |
| 1980 | Sept | 9 | Southampton | 3 | 0 |
| 1981 | Sept | 8 | Drammen | 0 | 0 |
| EC1992 | Oct | 13 | Peterborough | 0 | 2 |
| EC1993 | June | 1 | Stavanger | 1 | 1 |
| 1995 | Oct | 10 | Stavanger | 2 | 2 |
| 2006 | Feb | 28 | Reading | 3 | 1 |
| 2009 | Mar | 27 | Sandefjord | 5 | 0 |
| 2011 | June | 5 | Southampton | 2 | 0 |
| EC2011 | Oct | 10 | Drammen | 2 | 1 |
| EC2012 | Sept | 10 | Chesterfield | 1 | 0 |
| EC2013 | June | 8 | Petah Tikva | 1 | 3 |

| | | | v POLAND | Eng | Pol |
|---|---|---|---|---|---|
| EC1982 | Mar | 17 | Warsaw | 2 | 1 |
| EC1982 | April | 7 | West Ham | 2 | 2 |
| EC1989 | June | 2 | Plymouth | 2 | 1 |
| EC1989 | Oct | 10 | Jastrzebie | 3 | 1 |
| EC1990 | Oct | 16 | Tottenham | 0 | 1 |
| EC1991 | Nov | 12 | Pila | 1 | 2 |
| EC1993 | May | 28 | Zdroj | 4 | 1 |
| EC1993 | Sept | 7 | Millwall | 1 | 2 |
| EC1996 | Oct | 8 | Wolverhampton | 0 | 0 |
| EC1997 | May | 30 | Katowice | 1 | 1 |
| EC1999 | Mar | 26 | Southampton | 5 | 0 |
| EC1999 | Sept | 7 | Plock | 1 | 3 |
| EC2004 | Sept | 7 | Rybnik | 3 | 1 |
| EC2005 | Oct | 11 | Hillsborough | 4 | 1 |
| 2008 | Mar | 25 | Wolverhampton | 0 | 0 |

| | | | v PORTUGAL | Eng | Por |
|---|---|---|---|---|---|
| 1987 | June | 13 | Toulon | 0 | 0 |
| 1990 | May | 21 | Toulon | 0 | 1 |
| 1993 | June | 7 | Toulon | 2 | 0 |
| 1994 | June | 7 | Toulon | 2 | 0 |
| EC1994 | Sept | 6 | Leicester | 0 | 0 |
| 1995 | Sept | 2 | Lisbon | 0 | 2 |
| 1996 | May | 30 | Toulon | 1 | 3 |
| 2000 | Apr | 16 | Stoke | 0 | 1 |
| EC2002 | May | 22 | Zurich | 1 | 3 |
| EC2003 | Mar | 28 | Rio Major | 2 | 4 |
| EC2003 | Sept | 9 | Everton | 1 | 2 |
| EC2008 | Nov | 20 | Agueda | 1 | 1 |
| 2008 | Sept | 5 | Wembley | 2 | 0 |
| EC2009 | Nov | 14 | Wembley | 1 | 0 |
| EC2010 | Sept | 3 | Barcelos | 1 | 0 |

| | | | v ROMANIA | Eng | Rom |
|---|---|---|---|---|---|
| EC1980 | Oct | 14 | Ploesti | 0 | 4 |
| EC1981 | April | 28 | Swindon | 3 | 0 |
| EC1985 | April | 30 | Brasov | 0 | 0 |
| EC1985 | Sept | 10 | Ipswich | 3 | 0 |
| 2007 | Aug | 21 | Bristol | 1 | 1 |
| EC2010 | Oct | 8 | Norwich | 2 | 1 |
| EC2010 | Oct | 12 | Botosani | 0 | 0 |
| 2013 | Mar | 21 | Wycombe | 3 | 0 |

| | | | v RUSSIA | Eng | Rus |
|---|---|---|---|---|---|
| 1994 | May | 30 | Bandol | 2 | 0 |

| | | | v SAN MARINO | Eng | SM |
|---|---|---|---|---|---|
| EC1993 | Feb | 16 | Luton | 6 | 0 |
| EC1993 | Nov | 17 | San Marino | 4 | 0 |

| v SCOTLAND | | | Eng | Sco |
|---|---|---|---|---|
| 1977 | April | 27 | Sheffield | 1 | 0 |
| EC1980 | Feb | 12 | Coventry | 2 | 1 |
| EC1980 | Mar | 4 | Aberdeen | 0 | 0 |
| EC1982 | April | 19 | Glasgow | 1 | 0 |
| EC1982 | April | 28 | Manchester | 1 | 1 |
| EC1988 | Feb | 16 | Aberdeen | 1 | 0 |
| EC1988 | Mar | 22 | Nottingham | 1 | 0 |
| 1993 | June | 13 | Toulon | 1 | 0 |

| v SENEGAL | | | Eng | Sen |
|---|---|---|---|---|
| 1989 | June | 7 | Toulon | 6 | 1 |
| 1991 | May | 27 | Toulon | 2 | 1 |

| v SERBIA | | | Eng | Ser |
|---|---|---|---|---|
| EC2007 | June | 17 | Nijmegen | 2 | 0 |
| EC2012 | Oct | 12 | Norwich | 1 | 0 |
| EC2012 | Oct | 16 | Krusevac | 1 | 0 |

| v SERBIA-MONTENEGRO | | | Eng | S-M |
|---|---|---|---|---|
| 2003 | June | 2 | Hull | 3 | 2 |

| v SLOVAKIA | | | Eng | Slo |
|---|---|---|---|---|
| EC2002 | June | 1 | Bratislava | 0 | 2 |
| EC2002 | Oct | 11 | Trnava | 4 | 0 |
| EC2003 | June | 10 | Sunderland | 2 | 0 |
| 2007 | June | 5 | Norwich | 5 | 0 |

| v SLOVENIA | | | Eng | Slo |
|---|---|---|---|---|
| 2000 | Feb | 12 | Nova Gorica | 1 | 0 |
| 2008 | Aug | 19 | Hull | 2 | 1 |

| v SOUTH AFRICA | | | Eng | SA |
|---|---|---|---|---|
| 1998 | May | 16 | Toulon | 3 | 1 |

| v SPAIN | | | Eng | Spa |
|---|---|---|---|---|
| EC1984 | May | 17 | Seville | 1 | 0 |
| EC1984 | May | 24 | Sheffield | 2 | 0 |
| 1987 | Feb | 18 | Burgos | 2 | 1 |
| 1992 | Sept | 8 | Burgos | 1 | 0 |
| 2001 | Feb | 27 | Birmingham | 0 | 4 |
| 2004 | Nov | 16 | Alcala | 0 | 1 |
| 2007 | Feb | 6 | Derby | 2 | 2 |
| EC2009 | June | 18 | Gothenburg | 2 | 0 |
| EC2011 | June | 12 | Herning | 1 | 1 |

| v SWEDEN | | | Eng | Swe |
|---|---|---|---|---|
| 1979 | June | 9 | Vasteras | 2 | 1 |
| 1986 | Sept | 9 | Ostersund | 1 | 1 |
| EC1988 | Oct | 18 | Coventry | 1 | 1 |
| EC1989 | Sept | 5 | Uppsala | 0 | 1 |
| EC1998 | Sept | 4 | Sundvall | 2 | 0 |
| EC1999 | June | 4 | Huddersfield | 3 | 0 |
| 2004 | Mar | 30 | Kristiansund | 2 | 2 |
| EC2009 | June | 26 | Gothenburg | 3 | 3 |
| 2013 | Feb | 5 | Walsall | 4 | 0 |

| v SWITZERLAND | | | Eng | Swit |
|---|---|---|---|---|
| EC1980 | Nov | 18 | Ipswich | 5 | 0 |
| EC1981 | May | 31 | Neuenburg | 0 | 0 |
| 1988 | May | 28 | Lausanne | 1 | 1 |
| 1996 | April | 1 | Swindon | 0 | 0 |
| 1998 | Mar | 24 | Brugglifeld | 0 | 2 |
| EC2002 | May | 17 | Zurich | 2 | 1 |
| EC2006 | Sept | 6 | Lucerne | 3 | 2 |

| v TURKEY | | | Eng | Tur |
|---|---|---|---|---|
| EC1984 | Nov | 13 | Bursa | 0 | 0 |
| EC1985 | Oct | 15 | Bristol | 3 | 0 |
| EC1987 | April | 28 | Izmir | 0 | 0 |
| EC1987 | Oct | 13 | Sheffield | 1 | 1 |
| EC1991 | April | 30 | Izmir | 2 | 2 |
| 1991 | Oct | 15 | Reading | 2 | 0 |
| EC1992 | Nov | 17 | Orient | 0 | 1 |
| EC1993 | Mar | 30 | Izmir | 0 | 0 |
| EC2000 | May | 29 | Bratislava | 6 | 0 |
| EC2003 | April | 1 | Newcastle | 1 | 1 |
| EC2003 | Oct | 10 | Istanbul | 0 | 1 |

| v UKRAINE | | | Eng | Uk |
|---|---|---|---|---|
| 2004 | Aug | 17 | Middlesbrough | 3 | 1 |
| EC2011 | June | 15 | Herning | 0 | 0 |

| v USA | | | Eng | USA |
|---|---|---|---|---|
| 1989 | June | 11 | Toulon | 0 | 2 |
| 1994 | June | 2 | Toulon | 3 | 0 |

| v UZBEKISTAN | | | Eng | Uzb |
|---|---|---|---|---|
| 2010 | Aug | 10 | Bristol | 2 | 0 |

| v USSR | | | Eng | USSR |
|---|---|---|---|---|
| 1987 | June | 9 | Toulon | 0 | 0 |
| 1988 | June | 7 | Toulon | 1 | 0 |
| 1990 | May | 25 | Toulon | 2 | 1 |
| 1991 | May | 31 | Toulon | 2 | 1 |

| v WALES | | | Eng | Wales |
|---|---|---|---|---|
| 1976 | Dec | 15 | Wolverhampton | 0 | 0 |
| 1979 | Feb | 6 | Swansea | 1 | 0 |
| 1990 | Dec | 5 | Tranmere | 0 | 0 |
| EC2004 | Oct | 8 | Blackburn | 2 | 0 |
| EC2005 | Sept | 2 | Wrexham | 4 | 0 |
| 2008 | May | 5 | Wrexham | 2 | 0 |
| EC2008 | Oct | 10 | Cardiff | 3 | 2 |
| EC2008 | Oct | 14 | Villa Park | 2 | 2 |

| v YUGOSLAVIA | | | Eng | Yugo |
|---|---|---|---|---|
| EC1978 | April | 19 | Novi Sad | 1 | 2 |
| EC1978 | May | 2 | Manchester | 1 | 0 |
| EC1986 | Nov | 11 | Peterborough | 1 | 1 |
| EC1987 | Nov | 10 | Zemun | 5 | 1 |
| EC2000 | Mar | 29 | Barcelona | 3 | 0 |
| 2002 | Sept | 6 | Bolton | 1 | 1 |

# ENGLAND C 2012–13

## INTERNATIONAL CHALLENGE TROPHY

Zaventem, 12 September 2012

**Belgium (1) 1** *(Naudts 38)*
**England (1) 2** *(Spencer 14 (pen), Gray 76)*
*England:* Edwards; Turley, Thomas, Oshodi, Forbes (Watkins 45), Ainge, Gilles (Taylor 90), Vincent, Spencer (Wilson 87), Brogan (Gray 46), Meikle.

Dartford, 5 February 2013

~~England (0) 0~~

**Turkey (1) 1** *(Yilmaz 87)* 3212
*England:* Edwards; Turley, Thomas, Ainge (Jackson 88), Wedgbury, Oshodi, Gillies, Forbes, Gray (Spencer 82), Davis (Jolley 90), Meikle.

## FRIENDLY

Durres, 16 October 2012

**Albania v England** – *postponed due to waterlogged pitch*
*England:* Edwards; Turley, Thomas, Ainge, Oshodi, Vincent, Gilles, Watkins, Gray, Forbes, Meikle.
*Substitutes:* McAuley, Farman, Taylor, Wilson, Spencer.

National Sports Centre, Bermuda, 4 June 2013

**Bermuda (1) 1** *(Nusum 40)*
**England (2) 6** *(Sarcevic 5, Jackson 21 (pen), Norwood 53, 70, 80 (pen), Gray 87))*
*England:* Edwards (Walker 46), Jackson, Franks, Acheampong, Demetriou (Stokes 46), Beautyman, Hunt, Sarcevic (Bradley 46), Clucas, Jackson (Norwood 46), Cook (Gray 46).

# BRITISH AND IRISH UNDER-21 TEAMS 2012–13

■ *Denotes player sent off.*

## ENGLAND

### FRIENDLIES

**Tuesday, 13 November 2012**

**England (1) 2** *(Wickham 45, Afobe 77 (pen))*

**N Ireland (0) 0**                                          8040

*England:* (442) Amos (Steele 46); Smith (Clyne 60), Wisdom (Maguire 60), Lees, Robinson (Moore 84); McEachran (Hughes 66), Ince (Waghorn 77), Henderson J (Chalobah 77), Townsend (Afobe 60); Powell, Wickham.

**Tuesday, 5 February 2013**

**England (3) 4** *(Ince 10, 42, Shelvey 30, Wickham 77)*

**Sweden (0) 0**                                          9758

*England:* (4231) Steele; Smith (Lees 75), Wisdom, Dawson, Robinson; Henderson J (Hughes 47), McEachran (Chalobah 67); Ince, Shelvey (Lansbury 46), Afobe (Wickham 46); Zaha (Lowe 59).

**Thursday, 21 March 2013**

**England (1) 3** *(Zaha 34, Robinson 61, Delfouneso 88)*

**Romania (0) 0**                                          6354

*England:* (451) Butland (Steele 87); Clyne (Smith 74), Wisdom, Dawson, Rose (Robinson 46); Sterling (Sordell 64), Chalobah (Carroll 74), Shelvey, Henderson J (Lowe 75), Lansbury (Delfouneso 7); Zaha (Wickham 88).

**Monday, 25 March 2013**

**England (1) 4** *(Shelvey 40, McEachran 49 (pen), Sordell 66, Wickham 74)*

**Austria (0) 0**                                          20,003

*England:* (4411) Steele; Wisdom (Keane 78), Lees (Clyne 75), Dawson (Smith 46), Rose (Robinson 46); Townsend, Lowe, Chalobah (McEachran 46), Sterling (Henderson J 61); Shelvey (Sordell 61); Wickham (Delfouneso 77).

### UEFA UNDER-21 CHAMPIONSHIP QUALIFYING

**Thursday, 6 September 2012**

**Azerbaijan (0) 0**

**England (1) 2** *(Caulker 28, Shelvey 83)*               214

*England:* (442) Amos; Kelly, Caulker, Dawson, Rose; Lowe, Henderson, Shelvey, Ince (Delfouneso 86); Zaha (Marshall 61), Sordell (Wickham 69).

**Monday, 10 September 2012**

**England (1) 1** *(Wickham 43)*

**Norway (0) 0**                                          9947

*England:* (442) Steele; Kelly (Clyne 46), Caulker, Bennett, Rose; Marshall, Shelvey, Henderson J, Ince; Wickham (Lees 77), Waghorn (Zaha 77).

**Friday, 12 October 2012**

**England (0) 1** *(Dawson 65 (pen))*

**Serbia (0) 0**                                          17,266

*England:* (442) Butland; Smith, Caulker, Dawson, Rose; Sterling (Townsend 66), Henderson J, Rodwell (Lowe 46), Ince; Zaha, Sordell (Wickham 78).

**Tuesday, 16 October 2012**

**Serbia (0) 0**

**England (0) 1** *(Wickham 90)*                          10,000

*England:* (442) Butland; Smith, Dawson, Caulker, Rose■; Zaha (Sterling 76), Lowe, Henderson, Ince; Sordell (Lees 62), Delfouneso (Wickham 89).

### UEFA UNDER-21 CHAMPIONSHIP FINALS

**Wednesday, 5 June 2013**

**England (0) 0**

**Italy (0) 1** *(Insigne 79)*                            14,000

*England:* (4231) Butland; Clyne, Dawson, Caulker, Robinson; Henderson J, Lowe; Redmond, Shelvey (McEachran 75), Sordell (Chalobah 65); Wickham (Delfouneso 82).

**Saturday, 8 June 2013**

**England (0) 1** *(Dawson 57 (pen))*

**Norway (2) 3** *(Semb Berge 15, Berget 34, Eikrem 51)* 6500

*England:* (433) Butland; Smith, Caulker, Dawson (Wisdom 85), Rose; Chalobah, Henderson J, Lowe (Wickham 46); Ince, Zaha, Redmond (Shelvey 67).

**Tuesday, 11 June 2013**

**Israel (0) 1** *(Kriaf 80)*

**England (0) 0**                                          15,000

*England:* (4231) Steele; Clyne, Wisdom, Lees, Rose; Chalobah (Sordell 78), McEachran (Redmond 71); Zaha, Shelvey, Ince (Henderson J 46); Wickham.

## NORTHERN IRELAND

### FRIENDLIES

**Wednesday, 15 August 2012**

**Hungary (1) 3**

**N Ireland (1) 2** *(McEleney 41, Gray 91 (pen))*        2500

*N Ireland:* (442) Devlin; Thompson, McKeown, Jones, Hegarty; McEleney, Ball, Mitchell, Dallas; Gray, McAlinden.

### UEFA UNDER-21 CHAMPIONSHIP QUALIFYING

**Friday, 7 September 2012**

**N Ireland (1) 1** *(Magennis 11)*

**FYR Macedonia (0) 3** *(Spirovski 49, Timov 73, Stankov 91)*

*N Ireland:* (442) Devlin; Magennis, McKeown, Clucas, Thompson; McLaughlin■, Winchester, Mitchell (Lund 61), Kee (Gray 70); McLaughlin (Ball 79), McAlinden.

**Monday, 10 September 2012**

**Denmark (3) 3** *(Larsen 9, Albaek 28 (pen), Laudrup 46)*

**N Ireland (0) 0**                                        3689

*N Ireland:* (442) Glendinning; Magennis, McKeown, Clucas, Thompson; Hegarty, Winchester (Millar 56), Ball (Kee 82), Gray (McClure 65); McLaughlin, Kane.

**Thursday, 30 May 2013**

**Cyprus (1) 3** *(Roushias 20, Theodorou 60, Sotiriou 70)*

**N Ireland (0) 0**                                        500

*N Ireland:* (451) Glendinning; Robinson, McKeown, McNally, Sendles-White; Mitchell, Tempest (Reid 62), Lester, Brobbell, Winchester (Shields 61); Gray (Ball 71).

# SCOTLAND

**FRIENDLIES**

**Tuesday, 14 August 2012**
**Scotland (0) 0**
**Belgium (0) 1** *(Badibanga 56)*     1594
*Scotland:* (4141) Ridgers (Archer 42); Jack (Toshney 60), Wilson, Wallace, Hanlon (Shinnie 60); Kelly (McLean 60); Pawlett (Wotherspoon 79), Armstrong, Allan (Ness 46), Wylde (Park 67); O'Halloran (Watt 68).

**Friday, 12 October 2012**
**USA U20 (2) 2** *(Villarreal 22, 32)*
**Scotland (0) 0**     250
*Scotland:* (451) Archer; Jack (Duffie 56), Robertson, Kerr, Wallace; Fyvie, McGeouch, McLean (Smith 74), Armstrong (Holt 66), Scougall; Watt.

**Monday, 15 October 2012**
**Canada U20 (0) 0**
**Scotland (1) 2** *(Armstrong 11, Watt 91)*     200
*Scotland:* (442) Kettings; Duffie, McHattie, Kerr, Wallace (Robertson 47); Fyvie (McLean 70), McGeouch, Holt, Carrick (Watt 63); Armstrong, Smith.

**Wednesday, 14 November 2012**
**Portugal (0) 3** *(Paulo Oliveira 54, Aldair 58, Sergio Oliveira 70 (pen))*
**Scotland (2) 2** *(Feruz 13, 22)*     7500
*Scotland:* (433) Archer; Duffie (Fraser 83), McHattie (Macleod 78), Toshney, Robertson; McLean (Findlay 78), Fyvie, Holt (Herron 78); Paterson (Kennedy 68), Feruz, Smith.

**Wednesday, 6 February 2013**
**Greece (1) 1** *(Karelis 14)*
**Scotland (0) 1** *(Watt 59 (pen))*
*Scotland:* (451) Kettings; Duffie, McHattie, Kerr, Robertson; Tapping, McGeouch, McCabe, Armstrong, Bannigan; Watt.

**UEFA UNDER-21 CHAMPIONSHIP QUALIFYING**

**Thursday, 6 September 2012**
**Scotland (0) 3** *(Armstrong 63, Griffiths 68, Watt 83 (pen))*
**Luxembourg (0) 0**     2004
*Scotland:* (4411) Archer; Jack, Wilson, Perry (McLean 85), Hanlon; Armstrong, Kelly (Pawlett 64), Allan, McCabe; Russell; Griffiths (Watt 79).

**Monday, 10 September 2012**
**Austria (1) 3** *(Gregoritsch 9, Weimann 76, Holzhauser 91)*
**Scotland (0) 2** *(Watt 55, Russell 76)*     800
*Scotland:* (442) Archer; Jack, Hanlon, Wilson, Perry; Kelly, Armstrong (Wylde 84), Allan (Pawlett 61), Wotherspoon; Watt, Russell.

**Monday, 25 March 2013**
**Scotland (1) 3** *(Walker 45, Watt 66, Toshney L 84)*
**Luxembourg (0) 0**     1541
*Scotland:* (433) Archer; Jack, Toshney L, Robertson, McHattie; Fyvie, Armstrong, Bannigan (Feruz 68); McGeouch, Watt (McLean 76), Walker (Fraser 59).

# WALES

**FRIENDLY**

**Wednesday, 6 February 2013**
**Wales (0) 3** *(Burns 79, Williams 81, Ogleby 90)*
**Iceland (0) 0**
*Wales:* (451) Ward; Hewitt, Freeman, Walsh, Tancock; Lucas, Bodin, Huws, Lawrence, Williams; Cassidy.

**UEFA UNDER-21 CHAMPIONSHIP QUALIFYING**

**Wednesday, 15 August 2012**
**Wales (0) 0**
**Armenia (1) 1** *(Hambardzumyan 8 (pen))*     2000
*Wales:* (442) Maxwell; Henley, Freeman, Richards, Alfei, Stephens■, Bodin, Lucas, Cassidy; Taylor (Brown 11), Howells (Pritchard 79).

**Monday, 10 September 2012**
**Czech Rep (1) 5** *(Novak 18, Wagner 61, Vanek 69, Tecl 74 (pen), 80)*
**Wales (0) 0**     2138
*Wales:* (442) Cornell; Henley (Meades 78), Freeman, Huws (Doughty 78), Taylor; Alfei, Bodin, Lucas, Taylor; Cassidy, Edwards (Bradshaw 61).

**Friday, 22 March 2013**
**Wales (1) 1** *(Lawrence 11)*
**Moldova (0) 0**
*Wales:* (442) Ward; Tancock, Walsh, Freeman, Meades; Lucas, Huws, Lawrence, Bodin; Burns, Cassidy.

# REPUBLIC OF IRELAND

**FRIENDLY**

**Wednesday, 6 February 2013**
**Rep of Ireland (2) 3** *(O'Brien 11, 38, Forde 58 (pen))*
**Holland (0) 0**
*Rep of Ireland:* (451) McCarey (McDermott 46); Doherty M, McGinty (McHugh 46), Williams (O'Connor 46), Duffy; Reilly (Bolger 65), Ferdinand (O'Sullivan 37), Carruthers (Sutherland 46), Murray, Forde; O'Brien (Forrester 57).

**Monday, 25 March 2013**
**Rep of Ireland (0) 1** *(Doherty M 72)*
**Portugal (1) 2** *(Junior 15, O'Brien 58 (og))*
*Rep of Ireland:* (442) McDermott (McCarey 47); Doherty M (Bolger 73), McGinty (McHugh 47), O'Connor, Duffy (Shaughnessy 47); Ferdinand (Forrester 47), Carruthers (O'Sullivan 47), Reilly, Murray (Burke 73); Sutherland (Forde 47), O'Brien.

**Friday, 31 May 2013**
**Denmark (0) 0**     **Rep of Ireland (0) 0**
*Rep of Ireland:* (442) McCarey; Shaughnessy, Duffy, O'Connor, McGinty■; Doherty, O'Sullivan, Carruthers, Murray; Forde, O'Brien.

**UEFA UNDER-21 CHAMPIONSHIP QUALIFYING**

**Tuesday, 14 August 2012**
**Rep of Ireland (0) 0**
**Turkey (0) 1** *(Ozyakup 85)*
*Rep of Ireland:* (442) McLoughlin; Egan, Cunningham, Duffy, Canavan; Towell, White, Henderson (Scannell 83), Collins; O'Kane, Brady.

**Thursday, 6 September 2012**
**Hungary (2) 2** *(Futacs 16, Kovacs 28)*
**Rep of Ireland (1) 1** *(Brady 40)*     178
*Rep of Ireland:* (442) McLoughlin; Egan, Cunningham, Kiernan, Duffy; White (Forde 90), Henderson, Hendrick, O'Kane (Barton 71); Murphy (Doran 71), Brady.

**Monday, 10 September 2012**
**Italy (1) 2** *(Caldirola 36, El Shaarawy 90)*
**Rep of Ireland (1) 4** *(Murray 24, Doran 58, 81, Henderson 59)*     6000
*Rep of Ireland:* (442) McCarey; Doherty, White, Egan, Williams■; Henderson, Forde■, Carruthers, Doran; Murray, O'Kane.

# BRITISH UNDER-21 APPEARANCES 1976–2013

**Bold type** indicates players who made an international appearance in season 2011–12.

## ENGLAND

| | | | |
|---|---|---|---|
| Ablett, G. 1988 (Liverpool) | 1 | Briggs, M. 2012 (Fulham) | 2 |
| Adams, N. 1987 (Everton) | 1 | Brightwell, I. 1989 (Manchester C) | 4 |
| Adams, T. A. 1985 (Arsenal) | 5 | Briscoe, L. S. 1996 (Sheffield W) | 5 |
| Addison, M. 2010 (Derby Co) | 1 | Brock, K. 1984 (Oxford U) | 4 |
| **Afobe, B. T. 2012 (Arsenal)** | **2** | Broomes, M. C. 1997 (Blackburn R) | 2 |
| Agbonlahor, G. 2007 (Aston Villa) | 16 | Brown, M. R. 1996 (Manchester C) | 4 |
| Albrighton, M. K. 2011 (Aston Villa) | 8 | Brown, W. M. 1999 (Manchester U) | 8 |
| Allen, B. 1992 (QPR) | 8 | Bull, S. G. 1989 (Wolverhampton W) | 5 |
| Allen, C. 1980 (QPR, Crystal Palace) | 3 | Bullock, M. J. 1998 (Barnsley) | 1 |
| Allen, C. A. 1995 (Oxford U) | 2 | Burrows, D. 1989 (WBA, Liverpool) | 7 |
| Allen, M. 1987 (QPR) | 2 | Butcher, T. I. 1979 (Ipswich T) | 7 |
| Allen, P. 1985 (West Ham U, Tottenham H) | 3 | **Butland, J. 2012 (Birmingham C, Stoke C)** | **11** |
| Allen, R. W. 1998 (Tottenham H) | 3 | Butt, N. 1995 (Manchester U) | 7 |
| Alnwick, B. R. 2008 (Tottenham H) | 1 | Butters, G. 1988 (Tottenham H) | 3 |
| Ambrose, D. P. F. 2003 (Ipswich T, Newcastle U, | | Butterworth, I. 1985 (Coventry C, Nottingham F) | 8 |
| Charlton Ath) | 10 | Bywater, S. 2001 (West Ham U) | 6 |
| Ameobi, F. 2001 (Newcastle U) | 19 | | |
| Ameobi, S. 2012 (Newcastle U) | 2 | Cadamarteri, D. L. 1999 (Everton) | 3 |
| **Amos, B. P. 2012 (Manchester U)** | **3** | Caesar, G. 1987 (Arsenal) | 3 |
| Anderson, V. A. 1978 (Nottingham F) | 1 | Cahill, G. J. 2007 (Aston Villa) | 3 |
| Anderton, D. R. 1993 (Tottenham H) | 12 | Callaghan, N. 1983 (Watford) | 9 |
| Andrews, I. 1987 (Leicester C) | 1 | Camp, L. M. J. 2005 (Derby Co) | 5 |
| Ardley, N. C. 1993 (Wimbledon) | 10 | Campbell, A. P. 2000 (Middlesbrough) | 4 |
| Ashcroft, L. 1992 (Preston NE) | 1 | Campbell, F. L. 2008 (Manchester U) | 14 |
| Ashton, D. 2004 (Crewe Alex, Norwich C) | 9 | Campbell, K. J. 1991 (Arsenal) | 4 |
| Atherton, P. 1992 (Coventry C) | 1 | Campbell, S. 1994 (Tottenham) | 11 |
| Atkinson, B. 1991 (Sunderland) | 6 | Carbon, M. P. 1996 (Derby Co) | 4 |
| Awford, A. T. 1993 (Portsmouth) | 9 | Carr, C. 1985 (Fulham) | 1 |
| | | Carr, F. 1987 (Nottingham F) | 9 |
| Bailey, G. R. 1979 (Manchester U) | 14 | Carragher, J. L. 1997 (Liverpool) | 27 |
| Baines, L. J. 2005 (Wigan Ath) | 16 | Carroll, A. T. 2010 (Newcastle U) | 5 |
| Baker, G. E. 1981 (Southampton) | 2 | **Carroll, T. J. 2013 (Tottenham H)** | **1** |
| Baker, N. L. 2011 (Aston Villa) | 3 | Carlisle, C. J. 2001 (QPR) | 3 |
| Ball, M. J. 1999 (Everton) | 7 | Carrick, M. 2001 (West Ham U) | 14 |
| Bannister, G. 1982 (Sheffield W) | 1 | Carson, S. P. 2004 (Leeds U, Liverpool) | 29 |
| Barker, S. 1985 (Blackburn R) | 4 | Casper, C. M. 1995 (Manchester U) | 1 |
| Barkley, R. 2012 (Everton) | 4 | Caton, T. 1982 (Manchester C) | 14 |
| Barmby, N. J. 1994 (Tottenham H, Everton) | 4 | Cattermole, L. B. 2008 (Middlesbrough, Wigan Ath, | |
| Barnes, J. 1983 (Watford) | 2 | Sunderland) | 16 |
| Barnes, P. S. 1977 (Manchester C) | 9 | **Caulker, S. R. 2011 (Tottenham H)** | **10** |
| Barrett, E. D. 1990 (Oldham Ath) | 4 | Chadwick, L. H. 2000 (Manchester U) | 13 |
| Barry, G. 1999 (Aston Villa) | 27 | Challis, T. M. 1996 (QPR) | 2 |
| Barton, J. 2004 (Manchester C) | 2 | **Chalobah, N. N. 2012 (Chelsea)** | **7** |
| Bart-Williams, C. G. 1993 (Sheffield W) | 16 | Chamberlain, M. 1983 (Stoke C) | 4 |
| Batty, D. 1988 (Leeds U) | 7 | Chaplow, R. D. 2004 (Burnley) | 1 |
| Bazeley, D. S. 1992 (Watford) | 1 | Chapman, L. 1981 (Stoke C) | 1 |
| Beagrie, P. 1988 (Sheffield U) | 2 | Charles, G. A. 1991 (Nottingham F) | 4 |
| Beardsmore, R. 1989 (Manchester U) | 5 | Chettle, S. 1988 (Nottingham F) | 12 |
| Beattie, J. S. 1999 (Southampton) | 5 | Chopra, R. M. 2004 (Newcastle U) | 1 |
| Beckham, D. R. J. 1995 (Manchester U) | 9 | Clark, L. R. 1992 (Newcastle U) | 11 |
| Bennett, J. 2011 (Middlesbrough) | 3 | Clarke, P. M. 2003 (Everton) | 8 |
| **Bennett, R. 2012 (Norwich C)** | **2** | Christie, M. N. 2001 (Derby Co) | 11 |
| Bent, D. A. 2003 (Ipswich T, Charlton Ath) | 14 | Clegg, M. J. 1998 (Manchester U) | 2 |
| Bent, M. N. 1998 (Crystal Palace) | 2 | Clemence, S. N. 1999 (Tottenham H) | 1 |
| Bentley, D. M. 2004 (Arsenal, Blackburn R) | 8 | Cleverley, T. W. 2010 (Manchester U) | 16 |
| Beeston, C 1988 (Stoke C) | 1 | Clough, N. H. 1986 (Nottingham F) | 15 |
| Benjamin, T. J. 2001 (Leicester C) | 1 | **Clyne, N. E. 2012 (Crystal Palace)** | **8** |
| Bertrand, R. 2009 (Chelsea) | 16 | Cole, A. 2001 (Arsenal) | 4 |
| Bertschin, K. E. 1977 (Birmingham C) | 3 | Cole, A. A. 1992 (Arsenal, Bristol C, Newcastle U) | 8 |
| Birtles, G. 1980 (Nottingham F) | 2 | Cole, C. 2003 (Chelsea) | 19 |
| Blackstock, D. A. 2008 (QPR) | 2 | Cole, J. J. 2000 (West Ham U) | 8 |
| Blackwell, D. R. 1991 (Wimbledon) | 6 | Coney, D. 1985 (Fulham) | 4 |
| Blake, M. A. 1990 (Aston Villa) | 8 | Connor, T. 1987 (Brighton & HA) | 1 |
| Blissett, L. L. 1979 (Watford) | 4 | Cooke, R. 1986 (Tottenham H) | 1 |
| Booth, A. D. 1995 (Huddersfield T) | 3 | Cooke, T. J. 1996 (Manchester U) | 4 |
| Bothroyd, J. 2001 (Coventry C) | 1 | Cooper, C. T. 1988 (Middlesbrough) | 8 |
| Bowyer, L. D. 1996 (Charlton Ath, Leeds U) | 13 | Cork, J. F. P. 2009 (Chelsea) | 13 |
| Bracewell, P. 1983 (Stoke C) | 13 | Corrigan, J. T. 1978 (Manchester C) | 3 |
| Bradbury, L. M. 1997 (Portsmouth, Manchester C) | 3 | Cort, C. E. R. 1999 (Wimbledon) | 12 |
| Bramble, T. M. 2001 (Ipswich T, Newcastle U) | 10 | Cottee, A. R. 1985 (West Ham U) | 8 |
| Branch, P. M. 1997 (Everton) | 1 | Couzens, A. J. 1995 (Leeds U) | 3 |
| Bradshaw, P. W. 1977 (Wolverhampton W) | 4 | Cowans, G. S. 1979 (Aston Villa) | 5 |
| Breacker, T. 1986 (Luton T) | 2 | Cox, N. J. 1993 (Aston Villa) | 6 |
| Brennan, M. 1987 (Ipswich T) | 5 | Cranie, M. J. 2008 (Portsmouth) | 16 |
| Bridge, W. M. 1999 (Southampton) | 8 | Cranson, I. 1985 (Ipswich T) | 5 |
| Bridges, M. 1997 (Sunderland, Leeds U) | 3 | | |

Cresswell, R. P. W. 1999 (York C, Sheffield W) 4
Croft, G. 1995 (Grimsby T) 4
Crooks, G. 1980 (Stoke C) 4
Crossley, M. G. 1990 (Nottingham F) 3
Crouch, P. J. 2002 (Portsmouth, Aston Villa) 5
Cundy, J. V. 1991 (Chelsea) 3
Cunningham, L. 1977 (WBA) 6
Curbishley, L. C. 1981 (Birmingham C) 1
Curtis, J. C. K. 1998 (Manchester U) 16

Daniel, P. W. 1977 (Hull C) 7
Dann, S. 2008 (Coventry C) 2
Davenport, C. R. P. 2005 (Tottenham H) 8
Davies, A. J. 2004 (Middlesbrough) 1
Davies, C. E. 2006 (WBA) 3
Davies, K. C. 1998 (Southampton, Blackburn R,
  Southampton) 3
Davis, K. G. 1995 (Luton T) 3
Davis, P. 1982 (Arsenal) 11
Davis, S. 2001 (Fulham) 11
**Dawson, C. 2012 (WBA)** 15
Dawson, M. R. 2003 (Nottingham F, Tottenham H) 13
Day, C. N. 1996 (Tottenham H, Crystal Palace) 6
D'Avray, M. 1984 (Ipswich T) 2
Deehan, J. M. 1977 (Aston Villa) 7
Defoe, J. C. 2001 (West Ham U) 23
**Delfouneso, N. 2010 (Aston Villa)** 17
Delph, F. 2009 (Leeds U, Aston Villa) 4
Dennis, M. E. 1980 (Birmingham C) 3
Derbyshire, M. A. 2007 (Blackburn R) 14
Dichio, D. S. E. 1996 (QPR) 1
Dickens, A. 1985 (West Ham U) 1
Dicks, J. 1988 (West Ham U) 4
Digby, F. 1987 (Swindon T) 5
Dillon, K. P. 1981 (Birmingham C) 1
Dixon, K. M. 1985 (Chelsea) 1
Dobson, A. 1989 (Coventry C) 4
Dodd, J. R. 1991 (Southampton) 8
Donowa, L. 1985 (Norwich C) 3
Dorigo, A. R. 1987 (Aston Villa) 11
Downing, S. 2004 (Middlesbrough) 8
Dozzell, J. 1987 (Ipswich T) 9
Draper, M. A. 1991 (Notts Co) 3
Driver, A. 2009 (Hearts) 1
Duberry, M. W. 1997 (Chelsea) 5
Dunn, D. J. I. 1999 (Blackburn R) 20
Duxbury, M. 1981 (Manchester U) 7
Dyer, B. A. 1994 (Crystal Palace) 10
Dyer, K. C. 1998 (Ipswich T, Newcastle U) 11
Dyson, P. I. 1981 (Coventry C) 4

Eadie, D. M. 1994 (Norwich C) 7
Ebanks-Blake, S. 2009 (Wolverhampton W) 1
Ebbrell, J. 1989 (Everton) 14
Edghill, R. A. 1994 (Manchester C) 3
Ehiogu, U. 1992 (Aston Villa) 15
Elliott, P. 1985 (Luton T) 3
Elliott, R. J. 1996 (Newcastle U) 2
Elliott, S. W. 1998 (Derby Co) 3
Etherington, N, 2002 (Tottenham H) 3
Euell, J. J. 1998 (Wimbledon) 6
Evans, R. 2003 (Chelsea) 2

Fairclough, C. 1985 (Nottingham F, Tottenham H) 7
Fairclough, D. 1977 (Liverpool) 1
Fashanu, J. 1980 (Norwich C, Nottingham F) 11
Fear, P. 1994 (Wimbledon) 3
Fenton, G. A. 1995 (Aston Villa) 1
Fenwick, T. W. 1981 (Crystal Palace, QPR) 11
Ferdinand, A. J. 2005 (West Ham U) 17
Ferdinand, R. G. 1997 (West Ham U) 5
Fereday, W. 1985 (QPR) 5
Fielding, F. D. 2009 (Blackburn R) 12
Flanagan, J. 2012 (Liverpool) 3
Flitcroft, G. W. 1993 (Manchester C) 10
Flowers, T. D. 1987 (Southampton) 3
Ford, M. 1996 (Leeds U) 2
Forster, N. M. 1995 (Brentford) 4
Forsyth, M. 1988 (Derby Co) 1
Foster, S. 1980 (Brighton & HA) 1
Fowler, R. B. 1994 (Liverpool) 8
Fox, D. J. 2008 (Coventry C) 1

Froggatt, S. J. 1993 (Aston Villa) 2
Futcher, P. 1977 (Luton T, Manchester C) 11

Gabbiadini, M. 1989 (Sunderland) 2
Gale, A. 1982 (Fulham) 1
Gallen, K. A. 1995 (QPR) 4
Gardner, A. 2002 (Tottenham H) 1
Gardner, C. 2008 (Aston Villa) 14
Gardner, G. 2012 (Aston Villa) 5
Gascoigne, P. J. 1987 (Newcastle U) 13
Gayle, H. 1984 (Birmingham C) 3
Gernon, T. 1983 (Ipswich T) 1
Gerrard, P. W. 1993 (Oldham Ath) 18
Gerrard, S. G. 2000 (Liverpool) 4
Gibbs, K. J. R. 2009 (Arsenal) 15
Gibbs, N. 1987 (Watford) 5
Gibson, C. 1982 (Aston Villa) 1
Gilbert, W. A. 1979 (Crystal Palace) 11
Goddard, P. 1981 (West Ham U) 8
Gordon, D. 1987 (Norwich C) 4
Gordon, D. D. 1994 (Crystal Palace) 10
Gosling, D. 2010 (Everton, Newcastle U) 3
Grant, A. J. 1996 (Everton) 1
Grant, L. A. 2003 (Derby Co) 4
Granville, D. P. 1997 (Chelsea) 3
Gray, A. 1988 (Aston Villa) 2
Greening, J. 1999 (Manchester U, Middlesbrough) 18
Griffin, A. 1999 (Newcastle U) 3
Guppy, S. A. 1998 (Leicester C) 1

Haigh, P. 1977 (Hull C) 1
Hall, M. T. J. 1997 (Coventry C) 8
Hall, R. A. 1992 (Southampton) 11
Hamilton, D. V. 1997 (Newcastle U) 1
Hammill, A. 2010 (Wolverhampton W) 1
Harding, D. A. 2005 (Brighton & HA) 4
Hardyman, P. 1985 (Portsmouth) 2
Hargreaves, O. 2001 (Bayern Munich) 3
Harley, J. 2000 (Chelsea) 3
Hart, C. 2007 (Manchester C) 21
Hateley, M. 1982 (Coventry C, Portsmouth) 10
Hayes, M. 1987 (Arsenal) 3
Hazell, R. J. 1979 (Wolverhampton W) 1
Heaney, N. A. 1992 (Arsenal) 6
Heath, A. 1981 (Stoke C, Everton) 8
Heaton, T. D. 2008 (Manchester U) 3
**Henderson, J. B. 2011 (Sunderland, Liverpool)** 27
Hendon, I. M. 1992 (Tottenham H) 7
Hendrie, L. A. 1996 (Aston Villa) 13
Hesford, I. 1981 (Blackpool) 7
Heskey, E. W. I. 1997 (Leicester C, Liverpool) 16
Hilaire, V. 1980 (Crystal Palace) 9
Hill, D. R. L. 1995 (Tottenham H) 4
Hillier, D. 1991 (Arsenal) 1
Hinchcliffe, A. 1989 (Manchester C) 1
Hines, Z. 2010 (West Ham U) 2
Hinshelwood, P. A. 1978 (Crystal Palace) 3
Hirst, D. E. 1988 (Sheffield W) 7
Hislop, N. S. 1998 (Newcastle U) 1
Hoddle, G. 1977 (Tottenham H) 12
Hodge, S. B. 1983 (Nottingham F, Aston Villa) 8
Hodgson, D. J. 1981 (Middlesbrough) 6
Holdsworth, D. 1989 (Watford) 1
Holland, C. J. 1995 (Newcastle U) 10
Holland, P. 1995 (Mansfield T) 4
Holloway, D. 1998 (Sunderland) 1
Horne, B. 1989 (Millwall) 5
Howe, E. J. F. 1998 (Bournemouth) 2
Howson, D. M. 2011 (Leeds U) 1
Hoyte, J. R. 2004 (Arsenal) 18
Hucker, P. 1984 (QPR) 2
Huckerby, D. 1997 (Coventry C) 4
Huddlestone, T. A. 2005 (Derby Co,
  Tottenham H) 33
Hughes, S. J. 1997 (Arsenal) 8
**Hughes, W. J. 2012 (Derby Co)** 2
Humphreys, R. J. 1997 (Sheffield W) 3
Hunt, N. B. 2004 (Bolton W) 10

Impey, A. R. 1993 (QPR) 1
Ince, P. E. C. 1989 (West Ham U) 2
**Ince, T. C. 2012 (Blackpool)** 8

Jackson, M. A. 1992 (Everton) 10
Jagielka, P. N. 2003 (Sheffield U) 6
James, D. B. 1991 (Watford) 10
James, J. C. 1990 (Luton T) 2
Jansen, M. B. 1999 (Crystal Palace, Blackburn R) 6
Jeffers, F. 2000 (Everton, Arsenal) 16
Jemson, N. B. 1991 (Nottingham F) 1
Jenas, J. A. 2002 (Newcastle U) 9
Jerome, C. 2006 (Cardiff C, Birmingham C) 10
Joachim, J. K. 1994 (Leicester C) 9
Johnson, A. 2008 (Middlesbrough) 19
Johnson, G. M. C. 2003 (West Ham U, Chelsea) 14
Johnson, M. 2008 (Manchester C) 2
Johnson, S. A. M. 1999 (Crewe Alex, Derby Co,
 Leeds U) 15
Johnson, T. 1991 (Notts Co, Derby Co) 7
Johnston, C. P. 1981 (Middlesbrough) 2
Jones, D. R. 1977 (Everton) 1
Jones, C. H. 1978 (Tottenham H) 1
Jones, D. F. L. 2004 (Manchester U) 1
Jones, P. A. 2011 (Blackburn R) 9
Jones, R. 1993 (Liverpool) 2

**Keane, M. V. 2013 (Manchester U)** **1**
Keane, W. D. 2012 (Manchester U) 3
Keegan, G. A. 1977 (Manchester C) 1
**Kelly, M. R. 2011 (Liverpool)** **8**
Kenny, W. 1993 (Everton) 1
Keown, M. R. 1987 (Aston Villa) 8
Kerslake, D. 1986 (QPR) 1
Kightly, M. J. 2008 (Wolverhampton W) 7
Kilcline, B. 1983 (Notts C) 2
Kilgallon, M. 2004 (Leeds U) 5
King, A. E. 1977 (Everton) 2
King, L. B. 2000 (Tottenham H) 12
Kirkland, C. E. 2001 (Coventry C, Liverpool) 9
Kitson, P. 1991 (Leicester C, Derby Co) 7
Knight, A. 1983 (Portsmouth) 2
Knight, I. 1987 (Sheffield W) 2
Knight, Z. 2002 (Fulham) 4
Konchesky, P. M. 2002 (Charlton Ath) 15
Kozluk, R. 1998 (Derby Co) 2

Lake, P. 1989 (Manchester C) 5
Lallana, A. D. 2009 (Southampton) 1
Lampard, F. J. 1998 (West Ham U) 19
Langley, T. W. 1978 (Chelsea) 1
**Lansbury, H. G. 2010 (Arsenal, Nottingham F)** **16**
Leadbitter, G. 2008 (Sunderland) 3
Lee, D. J. 1990 (Chelsea) 10
Lee, R. M. 1986 (Charlton Ath) 2
Lee, S. 1981 (Liverpool) 6
**Lees, T. J. 2012 (Leeds U)** **6**
Lennon, A. J. 2006 (Tottenham H) 5
Le Saux, G. P. 1990 (Chelsea) 4
Lescott, J. P. 2003 (Wolverhampton W) 2
Lewis, J. P. 2008 (Peterborough U) 5
Lita, L. H. 2005 (Bristol C, Reading) 9
Loach, S. J. 2009 (Watford) 14
Lowe, D. 1988 (Ipswich T) 2
**Lowe, J. J. 2012 (Blackburn R)** **11**
Lukic, J. 1981 (Leeds U) 7
Lund, G. 1985 (Grimsby T) 3

McCall, S. H. 1981 (Ipswich T) 6
McCarthy, A. S. 2011 (Reading) 3
McDonald, N. 1987 (Newcastle U) 5
**McEachran, J. M. 2011 (Chelsea)** **13**
McEveley, J. 2003 (Blackburn R) 1
McGrath, L. 1986 (Coventry C) 1
MacKenzie, S. 1982 (WBA) 3
McLeary, A. 1988 (Millwall) 1
McLeod, I. M. 2006 (Milton Keynes D) 1
McMahon, S. 1981 (Everton, Aston Villa) 6
McManaman, S. 1991 (Liverpool) 7
Mabbutt, G. 1982 (Bristol R, Tottenham H) 7
**Maguire, J. H. 2012 (Sheffield U)** **1**
Makin, C. 1994 (Oldham Ath) 5
Mancienne, M. I. 2008 (Chelsea) 30
Marney, D. E. 2005 (Tottenham H) 1
Marriott, A. 1992 (Nottingham F) 1
Marsh, S. T. 1998 (Oxford U) 1

Marshall, A. J. 1995 (Norwich C) 4
**Marshall, B. 2012 (Leicester C)** **2**
Marshall, L. K. 1999 (Norwich C) 1
Martin, L. 1989 (Manchester U) 2
Martyn, A. N. 1988 (Bristol R) 11
Matteo, D. 1994 (Liverpool) 4
Mattock, J. W. 2008 (Leicester C) 5
Matthew, D. 1990 (Chelsea) 2
May, A. 1986 (Manchester C) 1
Mee, B. 2011 (Manchester C) 2
Merson, P. C. 1989 (Arsenal) 4
Middleton, J. 1977 (Nottingham F, Derby Co) 3
Miller, A. 1988 (Arsenal) 4
Mills, D. J. 1999 (Charlton Ath, Leeds U) 14
Mills, G. R. 1981 (Nottingham F) 2
Milner, J. P. 2004 (Leeds U, Newcastle U, Aston Villa) 46
Mimms, R. 1985 (Rotherham U, Everton) 3
Minto, S. C. 1991 (Charlton Ath) 6
Moore, I. 1996 (Tranmere R, Nottingham F) 7
**Moore, L. 2012 (Leicester C)** **1**
Moore, L. I. 2006 (Aston Villa) 5
Moran, S. 1982 (Southampton) 2
Morgan, S. 1987 (Leicester C) 2
Morris, J. 1997 (Chelsea) 7
Mortimer, P. 1989 (Charlton Ath) 2
Moses, A. P. 1997 (Barnsley) 2
Moses, R. M. 1981 (WBA, Manchester U) 8
Moses, V. 2011 (Wigan Ath) 1
Mountfield, D. 1984 (Everton) 1
Muamba, F. N. 2008 (Birmingham C, Bolton W) 33
Muggleton, C. D. 1990 (Leicester C) 1
Mullins, H. I. 1999 (Crystal Palace) 3
Murphy, D. B. 1998 (Liverpool) 4
Murray, P. 1997 (QPR) 4
Murray, M. W. 2003 (Wolverhampton W) 5
Mutch, A. 1989 (Wolverhampton W) 1
Mutch, J. J. E. S. 2011 (Birmingham C) 1
Myers, A. 1995 (Chelsea) 4

Naughton, K. 2009 (Sheffield U, Tottenham H) 9
Naylor, L. M. 2000 (Wolverhampton W) 3
Nethercott, S. H. 1994 (Tottenham H) 8
Neville, P. J. 1995 (Manchester U) 7
Newell, M. 1986 (Luton T) 4
Newton, A. L. 2001 (West Ham U) 1
Newton, E. J. I. 1993 (Chelsea) 2
Newton, S. O. 1997 (Charlton Ath) 3
Nicholls, A. 1994 (Plymouth Arg) 1
Noble, M. J. 2007 (West Ham U) 20
Nolan, K. A. J. 2003 (Bolton W) 1
Nugent, D. J. 2006 (Preston NE) 14

Oakes, M. C. 1994 (Aston Villa) 6
Oakes, S. J. 1993 (Luton T) 1
Oakley, M. 1997 (Southampton) 4
O'Brien, A. J. 1999 (Bradford C) 1
O'Connor, J. 1996 (Everton) 3
O'Hara, J. D. 2008 (Tottenham H) 7
Oldfield, D. 1989 (Luton T) 1
Olney, I. A. 1990 (Aston Villa) 10
O'Neil, G. P. 2005 (Portsmouth) 9
Onuoha, C. 2006 (Manchester C) 21
Ord, R. J. 1991 (Sunderland) 3
Osman, R. C. 1979 (Ipswich T) 7
Owen, G. A. 1977 (Manchester C, WBA) 22
Owen, M. J. 1998 (Liverpool) 1
Oxlade-Chamberlain, A. M. D. 2011 (Southampton,
 Arsenal) 8

Painter, I. 1986 (Stoke C) 1
Palmer, C. L. 1989 (Sheffield W) 4
Parker, G. 1986 (Hull C, Nottingham F) 6
Parker, P. A. 1985 (Fulham) 8
Parker, S. M. 2001 (Charlton Ath) 12
Parkes, P. B. F. 1979 (QPR) 1
Parkin, S. 1987 (Stoke C) 5
Parlour, R. 1992 (Arsenal) 12
Parnaby, S. 2003 (Middlesbrough) 4
Peach, D. S. 1977 (Southampton) 6
Peake, A. 1982 (Leicester C) 1
Pearce, I. A. 1995 (Blackburn R) 3
Pearce, S. 1987 (Nottingham F) 1

| | |
|---|---|
| Pennant, J. 2001 (Arsenal) | 24 |
| Pickering N. 1983 (Sunderland, Coventry C) | 15 |
| Platt, D. 1988 (Aston Villa) | 3 |
| Plummer, C. S. 1996 (QPR) | 5 |
| Pollock, J. 1995 (Middlesbrough) | 3 |
| Porter, G. 1987 (Watford) | 12 |
| Potter, G. S. 1997 (Southampton) | 1 |
| **Powell, N. E. 2012 (Manchester U)** | **1** |
| Pressman, K. 1989 (Sheffield W) | 1 |
| Proctor, M. 1981 (Middlesbrough, Nottingham F) | 4 |
| Prutton, D. T. 2001 (Nottingham F, Southampton) | 25 |
| Purse, D. J. 1998 (Birmingham C) | 2 |
| | |
| Quashie, N. F. 1997 (QPR) | 4 |
| Quinn, W. R. 1998 (Sheffield U) | 2 |
| | |
| Ramage, C. D. 1991 (Derby Co) | 3 |
| Ranson, R. 1980 (Manchester C) | 10 |
| Redknapp, J. F. 1993 (Liverpool) | 19 |
| **Redmond, N. D. J. 2013 (Birmingham C)** | **3** |
| Redmond, S. 1988 (Manchester C) | 14 |
| Reeves, K. P. 1978 (Norwich C, Manchester C) | 10 |
| Regis, C. 1979 (WBA) | 6 |
| Reid, N. S. 1981 (Manchester C) | 6 |
| Reid, P. 1977 (Bolton W) | 6 |
| Reo-Coker, N. S. A. 2004 (Wimbledon, West Ham U) | 23 |
| Richards, D. I. 1995 (Wolverhampton W) | 4 |
| Richards, J. P. 1977 (Wolverhampton W) | 2 |
| Richards, M. 2007 (Manchester C) | 15 |
| Richards, M. L. 2005 (Ipswich T) | 1 |
| Richardson, K. E. 2005 (Manchester U) | |
| Rideout, P. 1985 (Aston Villa, Bari) | 5 |
| Ridgewell, L. M. 2004 (Aston Villa) | 8 |
| Riggott, C. M. 2001 (Derby Co) | 8 |
| Ripley, S. E. 1988 (Middlesbrough) | 8 |
| Ritchie, A. 1982 (Brighton & HA) | 1 |
| Rix, G. 1978 (Arsenal) | 7 |
| Roberts, A. J. 1995 (Millwall, Crystal Palace) | 5 |
| Roberts, B. J. 1997 (Middlesbrough) | 1 |
| Robins, M. G. 1990 (Manchester U) | 6 |
| **Robinson, J. 2012 (Liverpool)** | **5** |
| Robinson, P. P. 1999 (Watford) | 3 |
| Robinson, P. W. 2000 (Leeds U) | 11 |
| Robson, B. 1979 (WBA) | 7 |
| Robson, S. 1984 (Arsenal, West Ham U) | 8 |
| Rocastle, D. 1987 (Arsenal) | 14 |
| Roche, L. P. 2001 (Manchester U) | 1 |
| Rodger, G. 1987 (Coventry C) | 4 |
| Rodriguez, J. E. 2011 (Burnley) | 1 |
| **Rodwell, J. 2009 (Everton)** | **21** |
| Rogers, A. 1998 (Nottingham F) | 4 |
| Rosario, R. 1987 (Norwich C) | 4 |
| **Rose, D. L. 2009 (Tottenham H)** | **29** |
| Rose, M. 1997 (Arsenal) | 2 |
| Rosenior, L. J. 2005 (Fulham) | 7 |
| Routledge, W. 2005 (Crystal Palace, Tottenham H) | 12 |
| Rowell, G. 1977 (Sunderland) | 1 |
| **Rudd, D. T. 2013 (Norwich C)** | **1** |
| Ruddock, N. 1989 (Southampton) | 4 |
| Rufus, R. R. 1996 (Charlton Ath) | 6 |
| Ryan, J. 1983 (Oldham Ath) | 1 |
| Ryder, S. H. 1995 (Walsall) | 3 |
| | |
| Samuel, J. 2002 (Aston Villa) | 7 |
| Samways, V. 1988 (Tottenham H) | 5 |
| Sansom, K. G. 1979 (Crystal Palace) | 8 |
| Scimeca, R. 1996 (Aston Villa) | 9 |
| Scowcroft, J. B. 1997 (Ipswich T) | 5 |
| Seaman, D. A. 1985 (Birmingham C) | 10 |
| Sears, F. D. 2010 (West Ham U) | 3 |
| Sedgley, S. 1987 (Coventry C, Tottenham H) | 11 |
| Sellars, S. 1988 (Blackburn R) | 3 |
| Selley, I. 1994 (Arsenal) | 3 |
| Serrant, C. 1998 (Oldham Ath) | 2 |
| Sharpe, L. S. 1989 (Manchester U) | 8 |
| Shaw, G. R. 1981 (Aston Villa) | 7 |
| Shawcross, R. J. 2008 (Stoke C) | 2 |
| Shearer, A. 1991 (Southampton) | 11 |
| Shelton, G. 1985 (Sheffield W) | 1 |
| **Shelvey, J. 2012 (Liverpool)** | **12** |
| Sheringham, E. P. 1988 (Millwall) | 1 |
| Sheron, M. N. 1992 (Manchester C) | 16 |

| | |
|---|---|
| Sherwood, T. A. 1990 (Norwich C) | 4 |
| Shipperley, N. J. 1994 (Chelsea, Southampton) | 7 |
| Sidwell, S. J. 2003 (Reading) | 5 |
| Simonsen, S. P. A. 1998 (Tranmere R, Everton) | 4 |
| Simpson, P. 1986 (Manchester C) | 5 |
| Sims, S. 1977 (Leicester C) | 10 |
| Sinclair, S. A. 2011 (Swansea C) | 7 |
| Sinclair, T. 1994 (QPR, West Ham U) | 5 |
| Sinnott, L. 1985 (Watford) | 1 |
| Slade, S. A. 1996 (Tottenham H) | 4 |
| Slater, S. I. 1990 (West Ham U) | 3 |
| Small, B. 1993 (Aston Villa) | 12 |
| Smalling, C. L. 2010 (Fulham, Manchester U) | 14 |
| Smith, A. 2000 (Leeds U) | 10 |
| **Smith, A. J. 2012 (Tottenham H)** | **11** |
| Smith, D. 1988 (Coventry C) | 10 |
| Smith, M. 1981 (Sheffield W) | 5 |
| Smith, M. 1995 (Sunderland) | 1 |
| Smith, T. W. 2001 (Watford) | 1 |
| Snodin, I. 1985 (Doncaster R) | 4 |
| Soares, T. J. 2006 (Crystal Palace) | 4 |
| **Sordell, M. A. 2012 (Watford, Bolton W)** | **14** |
| Spence, J. 2011 (West Ham U) | 1 |
| Stanislaus, F. J. 2010 (West Ham U) | 2 |
| Statham, B. 1988 (Tottenham H) | 3 |
| Statham, D. J. 1978 (WBA) | 6 |
| Stead, J. G. 2004 (Blackburn R, Sunderland) | 11 |
| Stearman, R. J. 2009 (Wolverhampton W) | 4 |
| **Steele, J. 2011 (Middlesbrough)** | **7** |
| Stein, B. 1984 (Luton T) | 3 |
| Sterland, M. 1984 (Sheffield W) | 7 |
| **Sterling, R. S. 2012 (Liverpool)** | **4** |
| Steven, T. M. 1985 (Everton) | 2 |
| Stevens, G. A. 1983 (Brighton & HA, Tottenham H) | 8 |
| Stewart, J. 2003 (Leicester C) | 1 |
| Stewart, P. 1988 (Manchester C) | 1 |
| Stockdale, R. K. 2001 (Middlesbrough) | 1 |
| Stuart, G. C. 1990 (Chelsea) | 5 |
| Stuart, J. C. 1996 (Charlton Ath) | 4 |
| Sturridge, D. A. 2010 (Chelsea) | 15 |
| Suckling, P. 1986 (Coventry C, Manchester C, Crystal Palace) | 10 |
| Summerbee, N. J. 1993 (Swindon T) | 3 |
| Sunderland, A. 1977 (Wolverhampton W) | 1 |
| Surman, A. R. E. 2008 (Southampton) | 4 |
| Sutch, D. 1992 (Norwich C) | 1 |
| Sutton, C. R. 1993 (Norwich C) | 13 |
| Swindlehurst, D. 1977 (Crystal Palace) | 1 |
| | |
| Talbot, B. 1977 (Ipswich T) | 1 |
| Taylor, A. D. 2007 (Middlesbrough) | 13 |
| Taylor, M. 2001 (Blackburn R) | 4 |
| Taylor, M. S. 2003 (Portsmouth) | 3 |
| Taylor, R. A. 2006 (Wigan Ath) | 4 |
| Taylor, S. J. 2002 (Arsenal) | 3 |
| Taylor, S. V. 2004 (Newcastle U) | 29 |
| Terry, J. G. 2001 (Chelsea) | 9 |
| Thatcher, B. D. 1996 (Millwall, Wimbledon) | 4 |
| Thelwall, A. A. 2001 (Tottenham H) | 1 |
| Thirlwell, P. 2001 (Sunderland) | 1 |
| Thomas, D. 1981 (Coventry C, Tottenham H) | 7 |
| Thomas, J. W. 2006 (Charlton Ath) | 2 |
| Thomas, M. 1986 (Luton T) | 3 |
| Thomas, M. L. 1988 (Arsenal) | 12 |
| Thomas, R. E. 1990 (Watford) | 1 |
| Thompson, A. 1995 (Bolton W) | 2 |
| Thompson, D. A. 1997 (Liverpool) | 7 |
| Thompson, G. L. 1981 (Coventry C) | 6 |
| Thorn, A. 1988 (Wimbledon) | 5 |
| Thornley, B. L. 1996 (Manchester U) | 3 |
| Tiler, C. 1990 (Barnsley, Nottingham F) | 13 |
| Tomkins, J. O. C. 2009 (West Ham U) | 10 |
| Tonge, M. W. E. 2004 (Sheffield U) | 2 |
| **Townsend, A. D. 2012 (Tottenham H)** | **3** |
| Trippier, K. J. 2011 (Manchester C) | 2 |
| | |
| Unsworth, D. G. 1995 (Everton) | 6 |
| Upson, M. J. 1999 (Arsenal) | 11 |
| | |
| Vassell, D. 1999 (Aston Villa) | 11 |
| Vaughan, J. O. 2007 (Everton) | 4 |
| Venison, B. 1983 (Sunderland) | 10 |

Vernazza, P. A. P. 2001 (Arsenal, Watford) 2
Vinnicombe, C. 1991 (Rangers) 12

Waddle, C. R. 1985 (Newcastle U) 1
**Waghorn, M. T. 2012 (Leicester C)** 5
Walcott, T. J. 2007 (Arsenal) 21
Wallace, D. L. 1983 (Southampton) 14
Wallace, Ray 1989 (Southampton) 4
Wallace, Rod 1989 (Southampton) 11
Walker, D. 1985 (Nottingham F) 7
Walker, I. M. 1991 (Tottenham H) 9
Walker, K. 2010 (Tottenham H) 7
Walsh, G. 1988 (Manchester U) 2
Walsh, P. A. 1983 (Luton T) 4
Walters, K. 1984 (Aston Villa) 9
Ward, P. 1978 (Brighton & HA) 2
Warhurst, P. 1991 (Oldham Ath, Sheffield W) 8
Watson, B. 2007 (Crystal Palace) 1
Watson, D. 1984 (Norwich C) 7
Watson, D. N. 1994 (Barnsley) 5
Watson, G. 1991 (Sheffield W) 2
Watson, S. C. 1993 (Newcastle U) 12
Weaver, N. J. 2000 (Manchester C) 10
Webb, N. J. 1985 (Portsmouth, Nottingham F) 3
Welbeck, D. 2009 (Manchester U) 14
Welsh, J. J. 2004 (Liverpool, Hull C) 8
Wheater, D. J. 2008 (Middlesbrough) 11
Whelan, P. J. 1993 (Ipswich T) 3
Whelan, N. 1995 (Leeds U) 2
Whittingham, P. 2004 (Aston Villa, Cardiff C) 17
White, D. 1988 (Manchester C) 6

Whyte, C. 1982 (Arsenal) 4
**Wickham, C. N. R. 2011 (Ipswich T, Sunderland)** 16
Wicks, S. 1982 (QPR) 1
Wilkins, R. C. 1977 (Chelsea) 1
Wilkinson, P. 1985 (Grimsby T, Everton) 4
Williams, D. 1998 (Sunderland) 2
Williams, P. 1989 (Charlton Ath) 4
Williams, P. D. 1991 (Derby Co) 6
Williams, S. C. 1977 (Southampton) 14
Wilshere, J. A. 2010 (Arsenal) 7
Wilson, M. A. 2001 (Manchester U, Middlesbrough) 6
Winterburn, N. 1986 (Wimbledon) 1
**Wisdom, A. 2012 (Liverpool)** 7
Wise, D. F. 1988 (Wimbledon) 1
Woodcook, A. S. 1978 (Nottingham F) 2
Woodgate, J. S. 2000 (Leeds U) 1
Woodhouse, C. 1999 (Sheffield U) 4
Woods, C. C. E. 1979 (Nottingham F, QPR, Norwich C) 6
Wright, A. G. 1993 (Blackburn R) 2
Wright, M. 1983 (Southampton) 4
Wright, R. I. 1997 (Ipswich T) 15
Wright, S. J. 2001 (Liverpool) 10
Wright, W. 1979 (Everton) 6
Wright-Phillips, S. C. 2002 (Manchester C) 6

Yates, D. 1989 (Notts Co) 5
Young, A. S. 2007 (Watford, Aston Villa) 10
Young, L. P. 1999 (Tottenham H, Charlton Ath) 12

**Zaha, D. W. A. 2012 (Crystal Palace, Manchester U)** 9
Zamora, R. L. 2002 (Brighton & HA) 6

## NORTHERN IRELAND

Allen, C. 2009 (Lisburn Distillery) 1
Armstrong, D. T. 2007 (Hearts) 1

Bagnall, L. 2011 (Sunderland) 1
Bailie, N. 1990 (Linfield) 2
Baird, C. P. 2002 (Southampton) 6
**Ball, D. 2013 (Tottenham H)** 1
**Ball, M. 2011 (Norwich C)** 5
Beatty, S. 1990 (Chelsea, Linfield) 2
Black, J. 2003 (Tottenham H) 1
Black, K. T. 1990 (Luton T) 1
Black, R. Z. 2002 (Morecambe) 1
Blackledge, G. 1978 (Portadown) 1
Blake, R. G. 2011 (Brentford) 2
Blayney, A. 2003 (Southampton) 4
**Boyce, L. 2010 (Cliftonville, Werder Bremen)** 8
Boyle, W. S. 1998 (Leeds U) 7
Braniff, K. R. 2002 (Millwall) 11
Breeze, J. 2011 (Wigan Ath) 4
**Brobbel, R. 2013 (Middlesbrough)** 1
Brotherston, N. 1978 (Blackburn R) 1
Browne, G. 2003 (Manchester C) 5
Brunt, C. 2005 (Sheffield W) 2
Bryan, M. A. 2010 (Watford) 4
Buchanan, D. T. H. 2006 (Bury) 15
Buchanan, W. B. 2002 (Bolton W, Lisburn Distillery) 5
Burns, L. 1998 (Port Vale) 13

Callaghan, A. 2006 (Limavady U, Ballymena U,
    Derry C) 15
Campbell, S. 2003 (Ballymena U) 1
Capaldi, A. C. 2002 (Birmingham C, Plymouth Arg) 14
Carlisle, W. T. 2000 (Crystal Palace) 9
Carroll, R. E. 1998 (Wigan Ath) 11
**Carson, J. G. 2011 (Ipswich T)** 7
Carson, S. 2000 (Rangers, Dundee U) 2
Carson, T. 2007 (Sunderland) 15
Carvill, M. D. 2008 (Wrexham, Linfield) 8
Casement, C. 2007 (Ipswich T, Dundee) 18
Cathcart, C. 2007 (Manchester U) 15
Catney, R. 2007 (Lisburn Distillery) 1
Chapman, A. 2008 (Sheffield U, Oxford U) 7
Clarke, L. 2003 (Peterborough U) 4
Clarke, R. 2006 (Newry C) 7
Clarke, R. D. J. 1999 (Portadown) 5
Clingan, S. G. 2003 (Wolverhampton W, Nottingham F) 11
Close, B. 2002 (Middlesbrough) 10

**Clucas, M. S. 2011 (Preston NE, Bristol R)** 9
Clyde, M. G. 2002 (Wolverhampton W) 5
Colligan, L. 2009 (Ballymena U) 1
Connell, T. E. 1978 (Coleraine) 1
Coote, A. 1998 (Norwich C) 12
Convery, J. 2000 (Celtic) 4

**Dallas, S. 2012 (Crusaders, Brentford)** 2
Davey, H. 2004 (UCD) 3
Davis, S. 2004 (Aston Villa) 3
Devine, D. 1994 (Omagh T) 1
Devine, D. G. 2011 (Preston NE) 2
Devine, J. 1990 (Glentoran) 1
**Devlin, C. 2011 (Manchester U, unattached,
    Cliftonville)** 11
Dickson, M. 2002 (Wigan Ath) 1
Doherty, M. 2007 (Hearts) 1
Dolan, J. 2000 (Millwall) 6
Donaghy, M. M. 1978 (Larne) 1
**Donnelly, L. 2012 (Fulham)** 1
Donnelly, M. 2007 (Sheffield U, Crusaders) 5
Dowie, I. 1990 (Luton T) 1
Drummond, W. 2011 (Rangers) 2
Dudgeon, J. P. 2010 (Manchester U) 4
Duff, S. 2003 (Cheltenham T) 1
Duffy, S. P. M. 2010 (Everton) 3

Elliott, S. 1999 (Glentoran) 3
Ervin, J. 2005 (Linfield) 2
Evans, C. J. 2009 (Manchester U) 10
Evans, J. 2006 (Manchester U) 3

Feeney, L. 1998 (Linfield, Rangers) 8
Feeney, W. 2002 (Bournemouth) 8
Ferguson, M. 2000 (Glentoran) 2
Ferguson, S. 2009 (Newcastle U) 11
Fitzgerald, D. 1998 (Rangers) 4
**Flanagan, T. M. 2012 (Milton Keynes D)** 1
Flynn, J. J. 2009 (Blackburn R, Ross Co) 11
Fordyce, D. T. 2007 (Portsmouth, Glentoran) 12
Friars, E. C. 2005 (Notts Co) 7
Friars, S. M. 1998 (Liverpool, Ipswich T) 21

Garrett, R. 2007 (Stoke C, Linfield) 14
Gault, M. 2005 (Linfield) 2
Gibb, S. 2009 (Falkirk, Drogheda U) 2
Gilfillan, B. J. 2005 (Gretna, Peterhead) 9

| | | | |
|---|---|---|---|
| Teggart, N. 2005 (Sunderland) | 2 | Ward, S. 2005 (Glentoran) | 10 |
| **Tempest, G. 2013 (Notts Co)** | 1 | Waterman, D. G. 1998 (Portsmouth) | 14 |
| **Thompson, A. L. 2011 (Watford)** | 8 | Waterworth, A. 2008 (Lisburn Distillery, Hamilton A) | 7 |
| Thompson, P. 2006 (Linfield) | 4 | Webb, S. M. 2004 (Ross Co, St Johnstone, Ross Co) | 6 |
| Toner, C. 2000 (Tottenham H, Leyton Orient) | 17 | Weir, R. J. 2009 (Sunderland) | 8 |
| Tuffey, J. 2007 (Partick Th) | 13 | Wells, D. P. 1999 (Barry T) | 1 |
| Turner, C. 2007 (Sligo R, Bohemians) | 12 | Whitley, J. 1998 (Manchester C) | 17 |
| | | Willis, P. 2006 (Liverpool) | 1 |
| Ward, J. J. 2006 (Aston Villa, Chesterfield) | 7 | **Winchester, C. 2011 (Oldham Ath)** | 7 |
| Ward, M. 2006 (Dungannon Swifts) | 1 | **Winchester, J. 2013 (Kilmarnock)** | 1 |

## SCOTLAND

| | | | |
|---|---|---|---|
| Adam, C. G. 2006 (Rangers) | 5 | Cameron, G. 2008 (Dundee U) | 3 |
| Adam, G. 2011 (Rangers) | 6 | Campbell, R. 2008 (Hibernian) | 6 |
| Adams, J. 2007 (Kilmarnock) | 1 | Campbell, S. 1989 (Dundee) | 3 |
| Aitken, R. 1977 (Celtic) | 16 | Campbell, S. P. 1998 (Leicester C) | 15 |
| Albiston, A. 1977 (Manchester U) | 5 | Canero, P. 2000 (Kilmarnock) | 17 |
| Alexander, N. 1997 (Stenhousemuir, Livingston) | 10 | Carey, L. A. 1998 (Bristol C) | 1 |
| **Allan, S. 2012 (WBA)** | 10 | **Carrick, D. 2012 (Hearts)** | 1 |
| Anderson, I. 1997 (Dundee, Toulouse) | 15 | Casey, J. 1978 (Celtic) | 1 |
| Anderson, R. 1997 (Aberdeen) | 15 | Christie, M. 1992 (Dundee) | 3 |
| Andrews, M. 2011 (East Stirling) | 1 | Clark, R. B. 1977 (Aberdeen) | 3 |
| Anthony, M. 1997 (Celtic) | 3 | Clarke, S. 1984 (St Mirren) | 8 |
| Archdeacon, O. 1987 (Celtic) | 1 | Clarkson, D. 2004 (Motherwell) | 13 |
| **Archer, J. G. 2012 (Tottenham H)** | 6 | Cleland, A. 1990 (Dundee U) | 11 |
| Archibald, A. 1998 (Partick Th) | 5 | Cole, D. 2011 (Rangers) | 2 |
| Archibald, S. 1980 (Aberdeen, Tottenham H) | 5 | Collins, J. 1988 (Hibernian) | 8 |
| Arfield, S. 2008 (Falkirk, Huddersfield T) | 17 | Collins, N. 2005 (Sunderland) | 7 |
| **Armstrong, S. 2011 (Dundee U)** | 13 | Connolly, P. 1991 (Dundee U) | 3 |
| | | Connor, R. 1981 (Ayr U) | 2 |
| Bagen, D. 1997 (Kilmarnock) | 4 | Conroy, R. 2007 (Celtic) | 4 |
| Bain, K. 1993 (Dundee) | 4 | Considine, A. 2007 (Aberdeen) | 5 |
| Baker, M. 1993 (St Mirren) | 10 | Cooper, D. 1977 (Clydebank, Rangers) | 6 |
| Baltacha, S. S. 2000 (St Mirren) | 3 | Cooper, N. 1982 (Aberdeen) | 13 |
| Bannan, B. 2009 (Aston Villa) | 10 | Coutts, P. A. 2009 (Peterborough U, Preston NE) | 7 |
| **Bannigan, S. 2013 (Partick Th)** | 2 | Crabbe, S. 1990 (Hearts) | 2 |
| Bannon, E. J. 1979 (Hearts, Chelsea, Dundee U) | 7 | Craig, M. 1998 (Aberdeen) | 2 |
| Barclay, J. 2011 (Falkirk) | 1 | Craig, T. 1977 (Newcastle U) | 1 |
| Beattie, C. 2004 (Celtic) | 7 | Crainey, S. D. 2000 (Celtic) | 14 |
| Beattie, J. 1992 (St Mirren) | 4 | Crainie, D. 1983 (Celtic) | 1 |
| Beaumont, D. 1985 (Dundee U) | 1 | Crawford, S. 1994 (Raith R) | 19 |
| Bell, D. 1981 (Aberdeen) | 2 | Creaney, G. 1991 (Celtic) | 11 |
| Bernard, P. R. J. 1992 (Oldham Ath) | 15 | Cummings, W. 2000 (Chelsea) | 8 |
| Berra, C. 2005 (Hearts) | 6 | Cuthbert, S. 2007 (Celtic, St Mirren) | 13 |
| Bett, J. 1981 (Rangers) | 7 | | |
| Black, E. 1983 (Aberdeen) | 8 | Dailly, C. 1991 (Dundee U) | 34 |
| Blair, A. 1980 (Coventry C, Aston Villa) | 5 | Dalglish, P. 1999 (Newcastle U, Norwich C) | 6 |
| Bollan, G. 1992 (Dundee U, Rangers) | 17 | Dargo, C. 1998 (Raith R) | 10 |
| Bonar, P. 1997 (Raith R) | 4 | Davidson, C. I. 1997 (St Johnstone) | 2 |
| Booth, C. 2011 (Hibernian) | 4 | Davidson, H. N. 2000 (Dundee U) | 3 |
| Booth, S. 1991 (Aberdeen) | 14 | Davidson, M. 2011 (St Johnstone) | 1 |
| Bowes, M. J. 1992 (Dunfermline Ath) | 1 | Dawson, A. 1979 (Rangers) | 8 |
| Bowman, D. 1985 (Hearts) | 1 | Deas, P. A. 1992 (St Johnstone) | 2 |
| Boyack, S. 1997 (Rangers) | 1 | Dempster, J. 2004 (Rushden & D) | 1 |
| Boyd, K. 2003 (Kilmarnock) | 8 | Dennis, S. 1992 (Raith R) | 1 |
| Boyd, T. 1987 (Motherwell) | 5 | Diamond, A. 2004 (Aberdeen) | 12 |
| Brazil, A. 1978 (Hibernian) | 1 | Dickov, P. 1992 (Arsenal) | 4 |
| Brazil, A. 1979 (Ipswich T) | 8 | Dixon, P. 2008 (Dundee) | 2 |
| Brebner, G. I. 1997 (Manchester U, Reading, Hibernian) | | Dodds, D. 1978 (Dundee U) | 1 |
| | 18 | Dods, D. 1997 (Hibernian) | 5 |
| Brighton, T. 2005 (Rangers, Clyde) | 7 | Doig, C. R. 2000 (Nottingham F) | 13 |
| Broadfoot, K. 2005 (St Mirren) | 5 | Donald, G. S. 1992 (Hibernian) | 3 |
| Brough, J. 1981 (Hearts) | 1 | Donnelly, S. 1994 (Celtic) | 11 |
| Brown, A. H. 2004 (Hibernian) | 1 | Dorrans, G. 2007 (Livingston) | 6 |
| Brown, S. 2005 (Hibernian) | 10 | Dow, A. 1993 (Dundee, Chelsea) | 3 |
| Browne, P. 1997 (Raith R) | 1 | Dowie, A. J. 2003 (Rangers, Partick Th) | 14 |
| Bryson, C. 2006 (Clyde) | 1 | Duff, J. 2009 (Inverness CT) | 1 |
| Buchan, J. 1997 (Aberdeen) | 13 | Duff, S. 2003 (Dundee U) | 9 |
| Burchill, M. J. 1998 (Celtic) | 15 | **Duffie, K. 2011 (Falkirk)** | 5 |
| Burke, A. 1997 (Kilmarnock) | 4 | Duffy, D. A. 2005 (Falkirk, Hull C) | 8 |
| Burke, C. 2004 (Rangers) | 3 | Duffy, J. 1987 (Dundee) | 1 |
| Burley, C. W. 1992 (Chelsea) | 7 | Durie, G. S. 1987 (Chelsea) | 4 |
| Burley, G. E. 1977 (Ipswich T) | 5 | Durrant, I. 1987 (Rangers) | 4 |
| Burns, H. 1985 (Rangers) | 2 | Doyle, J. 1981 (Partick Th) | 2 |
| Burns, T. 1977 (Celtic) | 5 | | |
| | | Easton, B. 2009 (Hamilton A) | 3 |
| Caddis, P. 2008 (Celtic, Dundee U, Celtic, Swindon T) | 13 | Easton, C. 1997 (Dundee U) | 21 |
| Cairney, T. 2011 (Hull C) | 6 | Edwards, M. 2012 (Rochdale) | 1 |
| Caldwell, G. 2000 (Newcastle U) | 19 | Elliot, B. 1998 (Celtic) | 2 |
| Caldwell, S. 2001 (Newcastle U) | 4 | Elliot, C. 2006 (Hearts) | 9 |

Esson, R. 2000 (Aberdeen) 7

Fagan, S. M. 2005 (Motherwell) 1
Ferguson, B. 1997 (Rangers) 12
Ferguson, D. 1987 (Rangers) 5
Ferguson, D. 1992 (Dundee U) 7
Ferguson, D. 1992 (Manchester U) 5
Ferguson, I. 1983 (Dundee) 4
Ferguson, I. 1987 (Clyde, St Mirren, Rangers) 6
Ferguson, R. 1977 (Hamilton A) 1
**Feruz, I. 2012 (Chelsea)** 3
**Findlay, S. 2012 (Celtic)** 1
Findlay, W. 1991 (Hibernian) 5
Fitzpatrick, A. 1977 (St Mirren) 5
Fitzpatrick, M. 2007 (Motherwell) 4
Flannigan, C. 1993 (Clydebank) 1
Fleck, J. 2009 (Rangers) 4
Fleck, R. 1987 (Rangers, Norwich C) 6
Fleming, G. 2008 (Gretna) 1
Fletcher, D. B. 2003 (Manchester U) 2
Fletcher, S. 2007 (Hibernian) 7
Forrest, J. 2011 (Celtic) 4
Foster, R. M. 2005 (Aberdeen) 5
Fotheringham, M. M. 2004 (Dundee) 3
Fowler, J. 2002 (Kilmarnock) 3
Foy, R. A. 2004 (Liverpool) 5
**Fraser, M. 2012 (Celtic)** 1
**Fraser, R. 2013 (Bournemouth)** 1
Fraser, S. T. 2000 (Luton T) 4
Freedman, D. A. 1995 (Barnet, Crystal Palace) 8
Fridge, L. 1989 (St Mirren) 2
Fullarton, J. 1993 (St Mirren) 17
Fulton, M. 1980 (St Mirren) 5
Fulton, S. 1991 (Celtic) 7
**Fyvie, F. 2012 (Wigan Ath)** 4

Gallacher, K. W. 1987 (Dundee U) 7
Gallacher, P. 1999 (Dundee U) 7
Gallacher, S. 2009 (Rangers) 2
Gallagher, P. 2003 (Blackburn R) 11
Galloway, M. 1989 (Hearts, Celtic) 2
Gardiner, J. 1993 (Hibernian) 1
Geddes, R. 1982 (Dundee) 5
Gemmill, S. 1992 (Nottingham F) 4
Germaine, G. 1997 (WBA) 1
Gilles, R. 1997 (St Mirren) 7
Gillespie, G. T. 1979 (Coventry C) 8
Glass, S. 1995 (Aberdeen) 11
Glover, L. 1988 (Nottingham F) 3
Goodwillie, D. 2009 (Dundee U) 9
Goram, A. L. 1987 (Oldham Ath) 1
Gordon, C. S. 2003 (Hearts) 5
Gough, C. R. 1983 (Dundee U) 5
Graham, D. 1998 (Rangers) 8
Grant, P. 1985 (Celtic) 10
Gray, D. P. 2009 (Manchester U) 2
Gray, S. 1987 (Aberdeen) 1
Gray S. 1995 (Celtic) 7
**Griffiths, L. 2010 (Dundee, Wolverhampton W)** 11
Gunn, B. 1984 (Aberdeen) 9

Hagen, D. 1992 (Rangers) 8
Hamill, J. 2008 (Kilmarnock) 11
Hamilton, B. 1989 (St Mirren) 4
Hamilton, J. 1995 (Dundee, Hearts) 14
Hammell, S. 2001 (Motherwell) 11
Handyside, P. 1993 (Grimsby T) 7
Hanley, G. 2011 (Blackburn R) 1
**Hanlon, P. 2009 (Hibernian)** 23
Hannah, D. 1993 (Dundee U) 16
Harper, K. 1995 (Hibernian) 7
Hartford, R. A. 1977 (Manchester C) 1
Hartley, P. J. 1997 (Millwall) 1
Hegarty, P. 1987 (Dundee U) 6
Hendry, J. 1992 (Tottenham H) 1
**Herron, J. 2012 (Celtic)** 1
Hetherston, B. 1997 (St Mirren) 1
Hewitt, J. 1982 (Aberdeen) 6
Hogg, G. 1984 (Manchester U) 4
**Holt, J. 2012 (Hearts)** 3
Hood, G. 1993 (Ayr U) 3
Horn, R. 1997 (Hearts) 6

Howie, S. 1993 (Cowdenbeath) 5
Hughes, R. D. 1999 (Bournemouth) 9
Hughes, S. 2002 (Rangers) 12
Hunter, G. 1987 (Hibernian) 3
Hunter, P. 1989 (East Fife) 3
Hutton, A. 2004 (Rangers) 7
Hutton, K. 2011 (Rangers) 1

Inman, B. 2011 (Newcastle U) 2
Irvine, G. 2006 (Celtic) 2

**Jack, R. 2012 (Aberdeen)** 12
James, K. F. 1997 (Falkirk) 1
Jardine, I. 1979 (Kilmarnock) 1
Jess, E. 1990 (Aberdeen) 14
Johnson, G. I. 1992 (Dundee U) 6
Johnston, A. 1994 (Hearts) 3
Johnston, F. 1993 (Falkirk) 1
Johnston, M. 1984 (Partick Th, Watford) 3
Jordan, A. J. 2000 (Bristol C) 3
Jupp, D. A. 1995 (Fulham) 9

**Kelly, L. 2012 (Kilmarnock)** 9
Kennedy, J. 2003 (Celtic) 15
**Kennedy, M. 2012 (Kilmarnock)** 1
Kenneth, G. 2008 (Dundee U) 8
Kerr, B. 2003 (Newcastle U) 14
**Kerr, F. 2012 (Birmingham C)** 3
Kerr, M. 2001 (Kilmarnock) 1
Kerr, S. 1993 (Celtic) 10
**Kettings, C. D. 2012 (Blackpool)** 2
Kinninburgh, W. D. 2004 (Motherwell) 3
Kirkwood, D. 1990 (Hearts) 1
Kyle, K. 2001 (Sunderland) 12

Lambert, P. 1991 (St Mirren) 11
Langfield, J. 2000 (Dundee) 2
Lappin, S. 2004 (St Mirren) 10
Lauchlan, J. 1998 (Kilmarnock) 11
Lavety, B. 1993 (St Mirren) 9
Lavin, G. 1993 (Watford) 7
Lawson, P. 2004 (Celtic) 10
Leighton, J. 1982 (Aberdeen) 1
Lennon, S. 2008 (Rangers) 6
Levein, C. 1985 (Hearts) 2
Leven, P. 2005 (Kilmarnock) 2
Liddell, A. M. 1994 (Barnsley) 12
Lindsey, J. 1979 (Motherwell) 1
Locke, G. 1994 (Hearts) 10
Love, G. 1995 (Hibernian) 1
Loy, R. 2009 (Dunfermline Ath, Rangers) 5
Lynch, S. 2003 (Celtic, Preston NE) 13

McAllister, G. 1990 (Leicester C) 1
McAllister, R. 2008 (Inverness CT) 2
McAlpine, H. 1983 (Dundee U) 5
McAnespie, K. 1998 (St Johnstone) 4
McArthur, J. 2008 (Hamilton A) 2
McAuley, S. 1993 (St Johnstone) 1
McAvennie, F. 1982 (St Mirren) 5
McBride, J. 1981 (Everton) 1
McBride, J. P. 1998 (Celtic) 2
**McCabe, R. 2012 (Rangers, Sheffield W)** 3
McCall, A. S. M. 1988 (Bradford C, Everton) 2
McCann, K. 2008 (Hibernian) 4
McCann, N. 1994 (Dundee) 9
McClair, B. 1984 (Celtic) 8
McCluskey, G. 1979 (Celtic) 6
McCluskey, S. 1997 (St Johnstone) 14
McCoist, A. 1984 (Rangers) 1
McConnell, I. 1997 (Clyde) 1
McCormack, D. 2008 (Hibernian) 1
McCormack, R. 2006 (Rangers, Motherwell, Cardiff C) 13
McCracken, D. 2002 (Dundee U) 5
McCulloch, A. 1981 (Kilmarnock) 5
McCulloch, I. 1982 (Notts Co) 2
McCulloch, L. 1997 (Motherwell) 14
McCunnie, J. 2001 (Dundee U, Ross Co, Dunfermline Ath) 20
MacDonald, A. 2011 (Burnley) 6
MacDonald, J. 1980 (Rangers) 8
MacDonald, J. 2007 (Hearts) 11

McDonald, C. 1995 (Falkirk) 5
McDonald, K. 2008 (Dundee, Burnley) 14
McEwan, C. 1997 (Clyde, Raith R) 17
McEwan, D. 2003 (Livingston) 2
McFadden, J. 2003 (Motherwell) 7
McFarlane, D. 1997 (Hamilton A) 3
McGarry, S. 1997 (St Mirren) 3
McGarvey, F. P. 1977 (St Mirren, Celtic) 3
McGarvey, S. 1982 (Manchester U) 4
**McGeough, D. 2012 (Celtic)** **5**
McGhee, M. 1981 (Aberdeen) 1
McGinn, S. 2009 (St Mirren, Watford) 8
McGinnis, G. 1985 (Dundee U) 1
McGlinchey, M. R. 2007 (Celtic) 1
McGregor, A. 2003 (Rangers) 6
McGrillen, P. 1994 (Motherwell) 2
McGuire, D. 2002 (Aberdeen) 2
**McHattie, K. 2012 (Hearts)** **4**
McInally, J. 1989 (Dundee U) 1
**McKay, B. 2012 (Rangers)** **1**
McKean, K. 2011 (St Mirren) 1
**McKenzie, R. 2013 (Kilmarnock)** **1**
McKenzie, R. 1997 (Hearts) 2
McKimmie, S. 1985 (Aberdeen) 3
McKinlay, T. 1984 (Dundee) 6
McKinlay, W. 1989 (Dundee U) 6
McKinnon, R. 1991 (Dundee U) 1
McLaren, A, 1989 (Hearts) 11
McLaren, A. 1993 (Dundee U) 4
McLaughlin, B. 1995 (Celtic) 8
McLaughlin, J. 1981 (Morton) 10
McLean, E. 2008 (Dundee U, St Johnstone) 2
McLean, S. 2003 (Rangers) 4
McLeish, A. 1978 (Aberdeen) 6
MacLeod, A. 1979 (Hibernian) 3
**McLean, K. 2012 (St Mirren)** **8**
McLeod, J. 1989 (Dundee U) 2
**MacLeod, L. 2012 (Rangers)** **1**
MacLeod, M. 1979 (Dumbarton, Celtic) 5
McManus, T. 2001 (Hibernian) 14
McMillan, S. 1997 (Motherwell) 4
McNab, N. 1978 (Tottenham H) 1
McNally, M. 1991 (Celtic) 2
McNamara, J. 1994 (Dunfermline Ath, Celtic) 12
McNaughton, K. 2002 (Aberdeen) 1
McNeil, A. 2007 (Hibernian) 1
McNichol, J. 1979 (Brentford) 1
McNiven, D. 1977 (Leeds U) 3
McNiven, S. A. 1996 (Oldham Ath) 1
McParland, A. 2003 (Celtic) 1
McPhee, S. 2002 (Port Vale) 1
McPherson, D. 1984 (Rangers, Hearts) 4
McQuilken, J. 1993 (Celtic) 2
McStay, P. 1983 (Celtic) 5
McWhirter, N. 1991 (St Mirren) 1
Mackay-Steven, G. 2012 (Dundee U) 3
Maguire, C. 2009 (Aberdeen) 12
Main, A. 1988 (Dundee U) 3
Malcolm, R. 2001 (Rangers) 1
Maloney, S. 2002 (Celtic) 21
Malpas, M. 1983 (Dundee U) 8
Marr, B. 2011 (Ross Co) 1
Marshall, D. J. 2004 (Celtic) 10
Marshall, S. R. 1995 (Arsenal) 5
Martin, A. 2009 (Leeds U, Ayr U) 12
Mason, G. R. 1999 (Manchester C, Dunfermline Ath) 2
Mathieson, D. 1997 (Queen of the South) 3
May, E. 1989 (Hibernian) 2
Meldrum, C. 1996 (Kilmarnock) 6
Melrose, J. 1977 (Partick Th) 8
Millar, M, 2009 (Celtic) 1
Miller, C. 1995 (Rangers) 8
Miller, J. 1987 (Aberdeen, Celtic) 7
Miller, K. 2000 (Hibernian, Rangers) 7
Miller, W. 1991 (Hibernian) 7
Miller, W. F. 1978 (Aberdeen) 1
Milne, K. 2000 (Hearts) 1
Milne, R. 1982 (Dundee U) 3
Mitchell, C. 2008 (Falkirk) 7
Money, I. C. 1987 (St Mirren) 3
Montgomery, N. A. 2003 (Sheffield U) 2
Morrison, S. A. 2004 (Aberdeen, Dunfermline Ath) 12

Muir, L. 1977 (Hibernian) 1
Mulgrew, C. P. 2006 (Celtic, Wolverhampton W, Aberdeen) 14
Murphy J. 2009 (Motherwell) 13
Murray, H. 2000 (St Mirren) 3
Murray, I. 2001 (Hibernian) 15
Murray, N. 1993 (Rangers) 16
Murray, R. 1993 (Bournemouth) 1
Murray, S. 2004 (Kilmarnock) 2

Narey, D. 1977 (Dundee U) 4
Naismith, S. J. 2006 (Kilmarnock, Rangers) 15
Naysmith, G. A. 1997 (Hearts) 22
Neilson, R. 2000 (Hearts) 1
**Ness, J, 2011 (Rangers)** **2**
Nevin, P. 1985 (Chelsea) 5
Nicholas, C. 1981 (Celtic, Arsenal) 6
Nicholson, B. 1999 (Rangers) 7
Nicol, S. 1981 (Ayr U, Liverpool) 14
Nisbet, S. 1989 (Rangers) 5
Noble, D. J. 2003 (West Ham U) 2
Notman, A. M. 1999 (Manchester U) 10

O'Brien, B. 1999 (Blackburn R, Livingston) 6
O'Connor, G. 2003 (Hibernian) 8
O'Donnell, P. 1992 (Motherwell) 8
**O'Donnell, S. 2013 (Partick Th)** **1**
**O'Halloran, M. 2012 (Bolton W)** **2**
O'Leary, R. 2008 (Kilmarnock) 2
O'Neil, B. 1992 (Celtic) 7
O'Neil, J. 1991 (Dundee U) 1
O'Neill, M. 1995 (Clyde) 6
Orr, N. 1978 (Morton) 7

Palmer, L. J. 2011 (Sheffield W) 8
**Park, C. 2012 (Middlesbrough)** **1**
Parker, K. 2001 (St Johnstone) 1
Parlane, D. 1977 (Rangers) 1
Paterson, C. 1981 (Hibernian) 2
**Paterson, C. 2012 (Hearts)** **1**
Paterson, J. 1997 (Dundee U) 9
**Pawlett, P. 2012 (Aberdeen)** **7**
Payne, G. 1978 (Dundee U) 3
Peacock, L. A. 1997 (Carlisle U) 1
Pearce, A. J. 2008 (Reading) 2
Pearson, S. P. 2003 (Motherwell) 8
**Perry, R. 2010 (Rangers, Falkirk, Rangers)** **16**
Pressley, S. J. 1993 (Rangers, Coventry C, Dundee U) 26
Provan, D. 1977 (Kilmarnock) 1
Prunty, B. 2004 (Aberdeen) 6

Quinn, P. C. 2004 (Motherwell) 3
Quinn, R. 2006 (Celtic) 9

Rae, A. 1991 (Millwall) 8
Rae, G. 1999 (Dundee) 6
Redford, I. 1981 (Rangers) 6
Reid, B. 1991 (Rangers) 4
Reid, C. 1993 (Hibernian) 3
Reid, M. 1982 (Celtic) 2
Reid, R. 1977 (St Mirren) 3
Reilly, A. 2004 (Wycombe W) 1
Renicks, S. 1997 (Hamilton A) 1
Reynolds, M. 2007 (Motherwell) 9
Rhodes, J. L. 2011 (Huddersfield T) 8
Rice, B. 1985 (Hibernian) 1
Richardson, L. 1980 (St Mirren) 2
**Ridgers, M. 2012 (Hearts)** **5**
Riordan, D. G. 2004 (Hibernian) 5
Ritchie, A. 1980 (Morton) 1
Ritchie, P. S. 1996 (Hearts) 7
Robertson, A. 1991 (Rangers) 1
Robertson, C. 1977 (Rangers) 1
**Robertson, C. (Aberdeen)** **5**
Robertson, D. 1987 (Aberdeen) 7
Robertson, D. 2007 (Dundee U) 4
Robertson, G. A. 2004 (Nottingham F, Rotherham U) 15
Robertson, H. 1994 (Aberdeen) 2
Robertson, J. 1985 (Hearts) 2
Robertson, L. 1993 (Rangers) 3
Robertson, S. 1998 (St Johnstone) 2
Roddie, A. 1992 (Aberdeen) 5

| | |
|---|---|
| Ross, G. 2007 (Dunfermline Ath) | 1 |
| Ross, N. 2011 (Inverness CT) | 2 |
| Ross, T. W. 1977 (Arsenal) | 1 |
| Rowson, D. 1997 (Aberdeen) | 5 |
| **Russell, J. 2011 (Dundee U)** | **11** |
| Russell, R. 1978 (Rangers) | 3 |
| | |
| Salton, D. B. 1992 (Luton T) | 6 |
| Samson, C. I. 2004 (Kilmarnock) | 6 |
| Saunders, S. 2011 (Motherwell) | 2 |
| Scobbie, T. 2008 (Falkirk) | 12 |
| Scott, M. 2006 (Livingston) | 1 |
| Scott, P. 1994 (St Johnstone) | 4 |
| **Scougall, S. 2012 (Livingston)** | **1** |
| Scrimgour, D. 1997 (St Mirren) | 3 |
| Seaton, A. 1998 (Falkirk) | 1 |
| Severin, S. D. 2000 (Hearts) | 10 |
| Shannon, R. 1987 (Dundee) | 7 |
| Sharp, G. M. 1982 (Everton) | 1 |
| Sharp, R. 1990 (Dunfermline Ath) | 4 |
| Sheerin, P. 1996 (Southampton) | 1 |
| Shields, G. 1997 (Rangers) | 2 |
| Shinnie, A. 2009 (Dundee, Rangers) | 3 |
| **Shinnie, G. 2012 (Inverness CT)** | **2** |
| Simmons, S. 2003 (Hearts) | 1 |
| Simpson, N. 1982 (Aberdeen) | 11 |
| Sinclair, G. 1977 (Dumbarton) | 1 |
| Skilling, M. 1993 (Kilmarnock) | 2 |
| Smith, B. M. 1992 (Celtic) | 5 |
| Smith, C. 2008 (St Mirren) | 2 |
| **Smith, D. 2012 (Hearts)** | **3** |
| Smith, D. L. 2006 (Motherwell) | 2 |
| Smith, G. 1978 (Rangers) | 1 |
| Smith, G. 2004 (Rangers) | 8 |
| Smith, H. G. 1987 (Hearts) | 2 |
| Smith, S. 2007 (Rangers) | 1 |
| Sneddon, A. 1979 (Celtic) | 1 |
| Snodgrass, R. 2008 (Livingston) | 2 |
| Soutar, D. 2003 (Dundee) | 11 |
| Speedie, D. R. 1985 (Chelsea) | 1 |
| Spencer, J. 1991 (Rangers) | 3 |
| Stanton, P. 1977 (Hibernian) | 1 |
| Stark, W. 1985 (Aberdeen) | 1 |
| Stephen, R. 1983 (Dundee) | 1 |
| Stevens, G. 1977 (Motherwell) | 1 |
| Stevenson, L. 2008 (Hibernian) | 8 |
| Stewart, C. 2002 (Kilmarnock) | 1 |
| Stewart, J. 1978 (Kilmarnock, Middlesbrough) | 3 |
| Stewart, M. J. 2000 (Manchester U) | 17 |
| Stewart, R. 1979 (Dundee U, West Ham U) | 12 |
| Stillie, D. 1995 (Aberdeen) | 14 |
| Strachan, G. D. 1998 (Coventry C) | 7 |
| Sturrock, P. 1979 (Dundee U) | 9 |
| Sweeney, P. H. 2004 (Millwall) | 8 |

| | |
|---|---|
| Sweeney, S. 1991 (Clydebank) | 7 |
| | |
| **Tapping, C. 2013 (Hearts)** | **1** |
| Tarrant, N. K. 1999 (Aston Villa) | 5 |
| Teale, G. 1997 (Clydebank, Ayr U) | 6 |
| Telfer, P. N. 1993 (Luton T) | 3 |
| Templeton, D. 2011 (Hearts) | 2 |
| Thomas, K. 1993 (Hearts) | 8 |
| Thompson, S. 1997 (Dundee U) | 12 |
| Thomson, C. 2011 (Hearts) | 2 |
| Thomson, K. 2005 (Hibernian) | 6 |
| Thomson, W. 1977 (Partick Th, St Mirren) | 10 |
| Tolmie, J. 1980 (Morton) | 1 |
| Tortolano, J. 1987 (Hibernian) | 2 |
| **Toshney, L. 2012 (Celtic)** | **5** |
| Turner, I. 2005 (Everton) | 6 |
| Tweed, S. 1993 (Hibernian) | 3 |
| | |
| Wales, G. 2000 (Hearts) | 1 |
| Walker, A. 1988 (Celtic) | 1 |
| **Walker, J. 2013 (Hearts)** | **1** |
| Wallace, I. A. 1978 (Coventry C) | 1 |
| Wallace, L. 2007 (Hearts) | 10 |
| **Wallace, M. 2012 (Huddersfield T)** | **4** |
| Wallace, R. 2004 (Celtic, Sunderland) | 4 |
| Walsh, C. 1984 (Nottingham F) | 5 |
| Wark, J. 1977 (Ipswich T) | 8 |
| Watson, A. 1981 (Aberdeen) | 4 |
| Watson, K. 1977 (Rangers) | 2 |
| **Watt, A. 2012 (Celtic)** | **7** |
| Watt, M. 1991 (Aberdeen) | 12 |
| Watt. S. M. 2005 (Chelsea) | 5 |
| Webster, A. 2003 (Hearts) | 2 |
| Whiteford, A. 1997 (St Johnstone) | 1 |
| Whittaker, S. G. 2005 (Hibernian) | 18 |
| Whyte, D. 1987 (Celtic) | 9 |
| Wilkie, L. 2000 (Dundee) | 6 |
| Will, J. A. 1992 (Arsenal) | 3 |
| Williams, G. 2002 (Nottingham F) | 9 |
| **Wilson, D. 2011 (Liverpool, Hearts)** | **13** |
| Wilson, M. 2004 (Dundee U, Celtic) | 19 |
| Wilson, S. 1999 (Rangers) | 7 |
| Wilson, T. 1983 (St Mirren) | 1 |
| Wilson, T. 1988 (Nottingham F) | 4 |
| Winnie, D. 1988 (St Mirren) | 1 |
| Woods, M. 2006 (Sunderland) | 2 |
| **Wotherspoon, D. 2011 (Hibernian)** | **16** |
| Wright, P. 1989 (Aberdeen, QPR) | 2 |
| Wright, S. 1991 (Aberdeen) | 14 |
| Wright, T. 1987 (Oldham Ath) | 1 |
| **Wylde, G. 2011 (Rangers)** | **7** |
| | |
| Young, Darren 1997 (Aberdeen) | 8 |
| Young, Derek 2000 (Aberdeen) | 5 |

# WALES

| | |
|---|---|
| Adams, N. W. 2008 (Bury, Leicester C) | 5 |
| **Alfei, D. M. 2010 (Swansea C)** | **12** |
| Aizlewood, M. 1979 (Luton T) | 2 |
| Allen, J. M. 2008 (Swansea U) | 13 |
| Anthony, B. 2005 (Cardiff C) | 8 |
| | |
| Baddeley, L. M. 1996 (Cardiff C) | 2 |
| Balcombe, S. 1982 (Leeds U) | 1 |
| Bale, G. 2006 (Southampton, Tottenham H) | 4 |
| Barnhouse, D. J. 1995 (Swansea C) | 3 |
| Basey, G. W. 2009 (Charlton Ath) | 1 |
| Bater, P. T. 1977 (Bristol R) | 2 |
| Beevers, L. J. 2005 (Boston U, Lincoln C) | 7 |
| Bellamy, C. D. 1996 (Norwich C) | 8 |
| Bender, T. J. 2011 (Colchester U) | 4 |
| Birchall, A. S. 2003 (Arsenal, Mansfield T) | 12 |
| Bird, A. 1993 (Cardiff C) | 6 |
| Blackmore, C. 1984 (Manchester U) | 3 |
| Blake, D. J. 2007 (Cardiff C) | 14 |
| Blake, N. A. 1991 (Cardiff C) | 5 |
| Blaney, S. D. 1997 (West Ham U) | 3 |
| Bloom, J. 2011 (Falkirk) | 1 |
| **Bodin, B. P. 2010 (Swindon T)** | **16** |
| Bodin, P. J. 1983 (Cardiff C) | 1 |
| Bond, J. H. 2011 (Watford) | 1 |

| | |
|---|---|
| Bowen, J. P. 1993 (Swansea C) | 5 |
| Bowen, M. R. 1983 (Tottenham H) | 3 |
| Boyle, T. 1982 (Crystal Palace) | 1 |
| Brace, D. P. 1995 (Wrexham) | 6 |
| Bradley, M. S. 2007 (Walsall) | 17 |
| **Bradshaw, T. 2012 (Shrewsbury T)** | **6** |
| Brough, M. 2003 (Notts Co) | 3 |
| Brown, J. D. 2008 (Cardiff C) | 6 |
| Brown, J. R. 2003 (Gillingham) | 7 |
| **Brown, T. A. F. 2011 (Ipswich T, Rotherham U, Aldershot T)** | **10** |
| **Burns, W. 2013 (Bristol C)** | **2** |
| Byrne, M. T. 2003 (Bolton W) | 1 |
| Calliste, R. T. 2005 (Manchester U, Liverpool) | 15 |
| Carpenter, R. E. 2005 (Burnley) | 1 |
| **Cassidy, J. A. 2011 (Wolverhampton W)** | **6** |
| Cegielski, W. 1977 (Wrexham) | 2 |
| Chamberlain, E. C. 2010 (Leicester C) | 9 |
| Chapple, S. R. 1992 (Swansea C) | 8 |
| Charles, J. M. 1979 (Swansea C) | 2 |
| Church, S. R. 2008 (Reading) | 15 |
| Clark, J. 1978 (Manchester U, Derby Co) | 2 |
| Coates, J. S. 1996 (Swansea C) | 5 |
| Coleman, C. 1990 (Swansea C) | 3 |
| Collins, J. M. 2003 (Cardiff C) | 7 |

Collins, M. J. 2007 (Fulham, Swansea C) 2
Collison, J. D. 2008 (West Ham U) 7
**Cornell, D. J. 2010 (Swansea C)** **4**
Cotterill, D. R. G. B. 2005 (Bristol C, Wigan Ath) 11
Coyne, D. 1992 (Tranmere R) 7
Craig, N. L. 2009 (Everton) 4
Critchell, K. A. R. 2005 (Southampton) 3
Crofts, A. L. 2005 (Gillingham) 10
Crowell, M. T. 2004 (Wrexham) 7
Curtis, A. T. 1977 (Swansea C) 1

Davies, A. 1982 (Manchester U) 6
Davies, A. G. 2006 (Cambridge U) 6
Davies, A. R. 2005 (Southampton, Yeovil T) 14
Davies, C. M. 2005 (Oxford U, Verona, Oldham Ath) 9
Davies, D. 1999 (Barry T) 1
Davies, G. M. 1993 (Hereford U, Crystal Palace) 7
Davies, I. C. 1978 (Norwich C) 1
Davies, L. 2005 (Bangor C) 1
Davies, R. J. 2006 (WBA) 4
Davies, S. 1999 (Peterborough U, Tottenham H) 10
**Dawson, C. 2013 (Leeds U)** **1**
Day, R. 2000 (Manchester C, Mansfield T) 11
Deacy, N. 1977 (PSV Eindhoven) 1
De-Vulgt, L. S. 2002 (Swansea C) 2
Dibble, A. 1983 (Cardiff C) 3
Doble, R. A. 2010 (Southampton) 10
**Doughty, M. E. 2012 (QPR)** **1**
Doyle, S. C. 1979 (Preston NE, Huddersfield T) 2
Duffy, R. M. 2005 (Portsmouth) 7
Dummett, P. 2011 (Newcastle U) 3
Dwyer, P. J. 1979 (Cardiff C) 1

Eardley, N. 2007 (Oldham Ath, Blackpool) 11
Earnshaw, R. 1999 (Cardiff C) 10
Easter, D. J. 2006 (Cardiff C) 1
Ebdon, M. 1990 (Everton) 2
Edwards, C. N. H. 1996 (Swansea C) 7
Edwards, D. A. 2006 (Shrewsbury T, Luton T,
  Wolverhampton W) 9
**Edwards, G. D. R. 2012 (Swansea C)** **1**
Edwards, R. I. 1977 (Chester) 2
Edwards, R. W. 1991 (Bristol C) 13
Evans, A. 1977 (Bristol R) 1
Evans, C. 2007 (Manchester C, Sheffield U) 13
Evans, K. 1999 (Leeds U, Cardiff C) 4
Evans, P. S. 1996 (Shrewsbury T) 1
Evans, S. J. 2001 (Crystal Palace) 2
Evans, T. 1995 (Cardiff C) 3

Fish, N. 2005 (Cardiff C) 2
Fleetwood, S. 2005 (Cardiff C) 5
Flynn, C. P. 2007 (Crewe Alex) 1
Folland, R. W. 2000 (Oxford U) 1
Foster, M. G. 1993 (Tranmere R) 1
Fowler, L. A. 2003 (Coventry C, Huddersfield T) 9
**Freeman, K. 2012 (Nottingham F)** **10**
Freestone, R. 1990 (Chelsea) 1

Gabbidon, D. L. 1999 (WBA, Cardiff C) 17
Gale, D. 1983 (Swansea C) 2
Gall, K. A. 2002 (Bristol R, Yeovil T) 8
Gibson, N. D. 1999 (Tranmere R, Sheffield W) 11
Giggs, R. J. 1991 (Manchester U) 1
Gilbert, P. 2005 (Plymouth Arg) 12
Giles, D. C. 1977 (Cardiff C, Swansea C,
  Crystal Palace) 4
Giles, P. 1982 (Cardiff C) 3
Graham, D. 1991 (Manchester U) 1
Green, R. M. 1998 (Wolverhampton W) 16
Griffith, C. 1990 (Cardiff C) 1
Griffiths, C. 1991 (Shrewsbury T) 1
Grubb, D. 2007 (Bristol C) 1
Gunter, C. 2006 (Cardiff C, Tottenham H) 8

Haldane, L. O. 2007 (Bristol R) 1
Hall, G. D. 1990 (Chelsea) 1
Hartson, J. 1994 (Luton T, Arsenal) 9
Haworth, S. O. 1997 (Cardiff C, Coventry C, Wigan Ath)
  12
**Henley, A. 2012 (Blackburn R)** **3**
Hennessey, W. R. 2006 (Wolverhampton W) 6

**Hewitt, E. J. 2012 (Macclesfield T, Ipswich T)** **6**
Hillier, I. M. 2001 (Tottenham H, Luton T) 5
Hodges, G. 1983 (Wimbledon) 5
Holden, A. 1984 (Chester C) 1
Holloway, C. D. 1999 (Exeter C) 2
Hopkins, J. 1982 (Fulham) 5
Hopkins, S. A. 1999 (Wrexham) 1
**Howells, J. 2012 (Luton T)** **5**
Huggins, D. S. 1996 (Bristol C) 1
Hughes, D. 2005 (Kaiserslautern, Regensburg) 2
Hughes, D. R. 1994 (Southampton) 1
Hughes, I. 1992 (Bury) 11
Hughes, L. M. 1983 (Manchester U) 5
Hughes, R. D. 1996 (Aston Villa, Shrewsbury T) 13
Hughes, W. 1977 (WBA) 3
**Huws, E. W. 2012 (Manchester C)** **3**

**Isgrove, L. J. 2013 (Southampton)** **1**

Jackett, K. 1981 (Watford) 2
Jacobson, J. M. 2006 (Cardiff C, Bristol R) 15
James, L. R. S. 2006 (Southampton) 10
James, R. M. 1977 (Swansea C) 3
Jarman, L. 1996 (Cardiff C) 10
Jeanne, L. C. 1999 (QPR) 8
Jelleyman, G. A. 1999 (Peterborough U) 1
Jenkins, L. D. 1998 (Swansea C) 9
Jenkins, S. R. 1993 (Swansea C) 2
Jones, C. T. 2007 (Swansea C) 1
Jones, E. P. 2000 (Blackpool) 1
Jones, F. 1981 (Wrexham) 1
Jones, J. A. 2001 (Swansea C) 3
Jones, L. 1982 (Cardiff C) 3
Jones, M. A. 2004 (Wrexham) 4
Jones, M. G. 1998 (Leeds U) 7
Jones, P. L. 1992 (Liverpool) 12
Jones, R. 2011 (AFC Wimbledon) 1
Jones, R. A. 1994 (Sheffield W) 3
Jones, S. J. 2005 (Swansea C) 1
Jones, V. 1979 (Bristol R) 2

Kendall, L. M. 2001 (Crystal Palace) 2
Kendall, M. 1978 (Tottenham H) 1
Kenworthy, J. R. 1994 (Tranmere R) 3
King, A. 2008 (Leicester C) 11
Knott, G. R. 1996 (Tottenham H) 1

Law, B. J. 1990 (QPR) 2
Lawless, A. 2006 (Torquay U) 1
**Lawrence, T. 2013 (Manchester U)** **2**
Ledley, J. C. 2005 (Cardiff C) 5
Letheran, G. 1977 (Leeds U) 2
Letheran, K. C. 2006 (Swansea C) 1
Lewis, D. 1982 (Swansea C) 9
Lewis, J. 1983 (Cardiff C) 1
Llewellyn, C. M. 1998 (Norwich C) 14
Loveridge, J. 1982 (Swansea C) 3
Low, J. D. 1999 (Bristol R, Cardiff C) 1
Lowndes, S. R. 1979 (Newport Co, Millwall) 4
**Lucas, L. P. 2011 (Swansea C)** **13**

MacDonald, S. B. 2006 (Swansea C) 25
McCarthy, A. J. 1994 (QPR) 3
McDonald, C. 2006 (Cardiff C) 3
Mackin, L. 2006 (Wrexham) 1
Maddy, P. 1982 (Cardiff C) 2
Margetson, M. W. 1992 (Manchester C) 7
Martin, A. P. 1999 (Crystal Palace) 1
Martin, D. A. 2006 (Notts Co) 1
Marustik, C. 1982 (Swansea C) 7
Matthews, A. J. 2010 (Cardiff C) 5
**Maxwell, C. 2009 (Wrexham)** **16**
Maxwell, L. J. 1999 (Liverpool, Cardiff C) 14
**Meades, J. 2012 (Cardiff C)** **4**
Meaker, M. J. 1994 (QPR) 2
Melville, A. K. 1990 (Swansea C, Oxford U) 2
Micallef, C. 1982 (Cardiff C) 3
Morgan, A. M. 1995 (Tranmere R) 4
Morgan, C. 2004 (Wrexham, Milton Keynes D) 12
Morris, A. J. 2009 (Cardiff C, Aldershot T) 8
Moss, D. M. 2003 (Shrewsbury T) 6
Mountain, P. D. 1997 (Cardiff C) 2

| | |
|---|---|
| Mumford, A. O. 2003 (Swansea C) | 4 |
| Nardiello, D. 1978 (Coventry C) | 1 |
| Neilson, A. B. 1993 (Newcastle U) | 7 |
| Nicholas, P. 1978 (Crystal Palace, Arsenal) | 3 |
| Nogan, K. 1990 (Luton T) | 2 |
| Nogan, L. M. 1991 (Oxford U) | 1 |
| Nyatanga, L. J. 2005 (Derby Co) | 10 |
| | |
| **Oakley, A. 2013 (Swindon T)** | **1** |
| **Ogleby, R. 2011 (Hearts, Wrexham)** | **8** |
| Oster, J. M. 1997 (Grimsby T, Everton) | 9 |
| Owen, G. 1991 (Wrexham) | 8 |
| | |
| Page, R. J. 1995 (Watford) | 4 |
| Parslow, D. 2005 (Cardiff C) | 4 |
| Partington, J. M. 2009 (Bournemouth) | 8 |
| Partridge, D. W. 1997 (West Ham U) | 1 |
| Pascoe, C. 1983 (Swansea C) | 4 |
| Pearce, S. 2006 (Bristol C) | 3 |
| Pejic, S. M. 2003 (Wrexham) | 6 |
| Pembridge, M. A. 1991 (Luton T) | 1 |
| Peniket, R. 2012 (Fulham) | 1 |
| Perry, J. 1990 (Cardiff C) | 3 |
| Peters, M. 1992 (Manchester C, Norwich C) | 3 |
| Phillips, D. 1984 (Plymouth Arg) | 3 |
| Phillips, G. R. 2001 (Swansea C) | 3 |
| Phillips, L. 1979 (Swansea C, Charlton Ath) | 2 |
| Pipe, D. R. 2003 (Coventry C, Notts Co) | 12 |
| Pontin, K. 1978 (Cardiff C) | 1 |
| Powell, L. 1991 (Southampton) | 4 |
| Powell, L. 2004 (Leicester C) | 3 |
| Powell, R. 2006 (Bolton W) | 1 |
| Price, J. J. 1998 (Swansea C) | 7 |
| Price, L. P. 2005 (Ipswich T) | 10 |
| Price, M. D. 2001 (Everton, Hull C, Scarborough) | 13 |
| Price, P. 1981 (Luton T) | 1 |
| Pritchard, M. O. 2006 (Swansea C) | 4 |
| Pugh, D. 1982 (Doncaster R) | 2 |
| Pugh, S. 1993 (Wrexham) | 2 |
| Pulis, A. J. 2006 (Stoke C) | 5 |
| | |
| Ramasut, M. W. T. 1997 (Bristol R) | 4 |
| Ramsey, A. J. 2008, (Cardiff C, Arsenal) | 12 |
| Ratcliffe, K. 1981 (Everton) | 2 |
| Ready, K. 1992 (QPR) | 5 |
| Rees, A. 1984 (Birmingham C) | 1 |
| Rees, J. M. 1990 (Luton T) | 3 |
| Rees, M. R. 2003 (Millwall) | 4 |
| Ribeiro, C. M. 2008 (Bristol C) | 8 |
| **Richards, A. D. J. 2010 (Swansea C)** | **16** |
| **Richards, E. A. 2012 (Bristol R)** | **1** |
| Roberts, A. M. 1991 (QPR) | 2 |
| **Roberts, C. 2013 (Cheltenham T)** | **1** |
| Roberts, C. J. 1999 (Cardiff C) | 1 |
| Roberts, G. 1983 (Hull C) | 1 |
| Roberts, G. W. 1997 (Liverpool, Panionios, Tranmere R) | 11 |
| Roberts, J. G. 1977 (Wrexham) | 1 |
| Roberts, N. W. 1999 (Wrexham) | 3 |
| Roberts, P. 1997 (Porthmadog) | 1 |
| Roberts, S. I. 1999 (Swansea C) | 13 |
| Roberts, S. W. 2000 (Wrexham) | 3 |
| Robinson, C. P. 1996 (Wolverhampton W) | 6 |
| Robinson, J. R. C. 1992 (Brighton & HA, Charlton Ath) | 5 |
| Robson-Kanu, K. H. 2010 (Reading) | 4 |
| Rowlands, A. J. R. 1996 (Manchester C) | 5 |
| Rush, I. 1981 (Liverpool) | 2 |
| | |
| Savage, R. W. 1995 (Crewe Alex) | 3 |

| | |
|---|---|
| Sayer, P. A. 1977 (Cardiff C) | 2 |
| Searle, D. 1991 (Cardiff C) | 6 |
| Slatter, D. 2000 (Chelsea) | 6 |
| Slatter, N. 1983 (Bristol R) | 6 |
| Somner, M. J. 2004 (Brentford) | 2 |
| Speed, G. A. 1990 (Leeds U) | 3 |
| Spender, S. 2005 (Wrexham) | 6 |
| **Stephens, D. 2011 (Hibernian)** | **7** |
| Stevenson, N. 1982 (Swansea C) | 2 |
| Stevenson, W. B. 1977 (Leeds U) | 3 |
| Stock, B. B. 2003 (Bournemouth) | 4 |
| Symons, C. J. 1991 (Portsmouth) | 2 |
| | |
| **Tancock, S. 2013 (Swansea C)** | **2** |
| **Taylor, A. J. 2012 (Tranmere R)** | **3** |
| Taylor, G. K. 1995 (Bristol R) | 4 |
| **Taylor, J. W. T. 2010 (Reading)** | **12** |
| Taylor, N. J. 2008 (Wrexham, Swansea C) | 13 |
| Taylor, R. F. 2008 (Chelsea) | 5 |
| Thomas, C. E. 2010 (Swansea C) | 3 |
| Thomas, D. G. 1977 (Leeds U) | 3 |
| Thomas, D. J. 1998 (Watford) | 2 |
| Thomas, J. A. 1996 (Blackburn R) | 21 |
| Thomas, Martin R. 1979 (Bristol R) | 2 |
| Thomas, Mickey R. 1977 (Wrexham) | 2 |
| Thomas, S. 2001 (Wrexham) | 5 |
| Tibbott, L. 1977 (Ipswich T) | 1 |
| Tipton, M. J. 1998 (Oldham Ath) | 6 |
| Tolley, J. C. 2001 (Shrewsbury T) | 12 |
| Tudur-Jones, O. 2006 (Swansea C) | 3 |
| Twiddy, C. 1995 (Plymouth Arg) | 3 |
| | |
| Valentine, R. D. 2001 (Everton, Darlington) | 8 |
| Vaughan, D. O. 2003 (Crewe Alex) | 8 |
| Vaughan, N. 1982 (Newport Co) | 2 |
| Vokes, S. M. 2007 (Bournemouth, Wolverhampton W) | 14 |
| | |
| Walsh, D. 2000 (Wrexham) | 8 |
| Walsh, I. P. 1979 (Crystal Palace, Swansea C) | 2 |
| **Walsh, J. 2012 (Swansea C)** | **4** |
| Walton, M. 1991 (Norwich C.) | 1 |
| Ward, D. 1996 (Notts Co) | 2 |
| **Ward, D. 2013 (Liverpool)** | **2** |
| Warlow, O. J. 2007 (Lincoln C) | 2 |
| Weston, R. D. 2001 (Arsenal, Cardiff C) | 4 |
| Whitfield, P. M. 2003 (Wrexham) | 1 |
| Wiggins, R. 2006 (Crystal Palace) | 9 |
| Williams, A. P. 1998 (Southampton) | 9 |
| Williams, A. S. 1996 (Blackburn R) | 16 |
| Williams, D. 1983 (Bristol R) | 1 |
| Williams, D. I. L. 1998 (Liverpool, Wrexham) | 9 |
| Williams, D. T. 2006 (Yeovil T) | 1 |
| Williams, E. 1997 (Caernarfon T) | 2 |
| Williams, G. 1983 (Bristol R) | 2 |
| Williams, G. A. 2003 (Crystal Palace) | 5 |
| **Williams, J. P. 2011 (Crystal Palace)** | **8** |
| Williams, M. 2001 (Manchester U) | 10 |
| Williams, M. P. 2006 (Wrexham) | 14 |
| Williams, M. R. 2006 (Wrexham) | 6 |
| Williams, O. fon 2007 (Crewe Alex, Stockport Co) | 11 |
| Williams, R. 2007 (Middlesbrough) | 10 |
| Williams, S. J. 1995 (Wrexham) | 4 |
| Wilmot, R. 1982 (Arsenal) | 6 |
| Wilson, J. S. 2009 (Bristol C) | 3 |
| Worgan, L. J. 2005 (Milton Keynes D, Rushden & D) | 5 |
| Wright, A. A. 1998 (Oxford U) | 3 |
| | |
| Young, S. 1996 (Cardiff C) | 5 |

# FA SCHOOLS AND YOUTH GAMES 2012–13

## ENGLAND UNDER-16

### SKY SPORTS VICTORY SHIELD

Dungannon, 27 September 2012

**Northern Ireland (0) 0**

**England (3) 5** *(Brewitt 21, Mitchell 30, Rossiter 40, Cook 47, 58)*                660

*Northern Ireland:* Long; Foster, Edgar, Quigley, Byers, Law, Fallon, Kennedy, Smith (Mallon 55), Hoey (Barton 79), Thompson (Doherty 61).
*England:* Woodman; Moore (Kenny 53), Lowe (Cooke 41), Dowell (Borthwick-Jackson 41), Brewitt, Maghoma, Brown (Roberts 53), Rossiter, Armstrong, Amos (Rashford 53), Mitchell.

Port Talbot, 1 November 2012

**Wales (0) 0**

**England (0) 1** *(Solanke 54)*

*Wales:* Pilling; Smith, Harries, Evans, Graham, Menayese, James, Humphries, Penny (Lemonheigh-Evans 41), Morrell (Bellamy 77), Byrnes (Edge 60).
*England:* Henderson; Kenny, Suliman (Ali 41), Ledson, Gomez, Borthwick-Jackson, Onomah, Cooke (Cameron 41), Boadu (Nabay 63), Rashford (Walsh 58), Solanke (King 58).

Burton, 29 November 2012

**England (0) 1** *(Rasulo 80)*

**Scotland (0) 0**                2,126

*England:* Huddart; Egbo, Dasilva, Ledson (Pybus 67), Gomez (Adarabioyo 41), Brewitt, Roberts (Rasulo 41), Rossiter, Onomah, Ali (Fox 65), Mitchell (Cooke 58).
*Scotland:* McCrorie; Wardrop, Hodge, Breslin, Kelly, Caird, Miller (Thomson 72), Petrie, Lafferty (Nesbitt 63), Boyd (Hardie 63), Kiltie (Spence 41).

Cologne, 13 February 2013

**Germany (1) 4** *(Ochs 27, Besuschkow 48, Heinrichs 70, 74)*

**England (1) 3** *(Brown 22, Mitchell 43, Armstrong 61)*   1,600

*England:* Woodman (Ward 41); Moore, Cameron (Adarabioyo 41), Borthwick, Brewitt (Kenny 56), Mitchell (Scott 50), Ledson, Roberts, Lowe (Solanke 56), Onomah (Cooke 50), Brown (Armstrong 50).

### MONTAIGU TOURNAMENT

Beauvoir sur Mer, 26 March 2013

**Holland (1) 1** *(Schuurman 35)*

**England (0) 1** *(Edwards 42)*

*England:* Ward; Moore, Edwards (Roberts 57), Ledson, Brewitt, Cameron, Solanke (Egbo 57), Lowe, Armstrong, Onomah (Rasulo 75), Mitchell (Cook 70).

Beauvoir sur Mer, 28 March 2013

**Chile (0) 1** *(Reyes 52)*

**England (3) 3** *(Rasulo 5, 12, Roberts 6)*

*England:* Howes; Moore (Edwards 52), Ledson (Lowe 52), Brewitt (Cameron 14), Armstrong (Mitchell 52), Adarabioyo, Christie-Davies, Roberts (Solanke 65), Rasulo, Egbo, Cook.

La Roche-sur-Yon, 30 March 2013

**England (1) 1** *(Onomah 7)*

**Germany (1) 1** *(Aydogan 14)*

*England:* Howes; Ledson, Cameron, Lowe (Edwards 41), Onomah (Moore 66), Mitchell (Armstrong 63), Adarabioyo, Christie-Davies (Rasulo 41), Roberts (Solanke 55), Egbo, Cook.

### MONTAIGU TOURNAMENT FINAL

Beauvoir sur Mer, 1 April 2013

**Turkey (2) 2** *(Unal, Ersoy)*

**England (1) 2** *(Armstrong 33, Mitchell 73)*

*Turkey won 4-2 on penalties.*

*England:* Ward; Edwards (Adarabioyo 63), Ledson, Cameron, Solanke, Armstrong, Onomah, Christie-Davies (Roberts 50), Rasulo (Moore 41), Egbo (Mitchell 41), Cook.

## ENGLAND UNDER-17

### NORDIC TOURNAMENT – GROUP STAGES

Klaksvik, 6 August 2012

**Faroe Islands (0) 0**

**England (0) 2** *(Fewster 71 (pen), O'Brien 78)*

*England:* Woodman; Griffiths, Ogilvie, Calder, Winks, Cook (Regis 41), Alli (Brown 59), Wright (Jones 41), Fewster, Oduwa (Galloway 71), Bailey (O'Brien 41).

Torshavn, 7 August 2012

**Finland (1) 2** *(Lehtinen 17, Kose 55 (pen))*

**England (1) 4** *(O'Brien 2, Regis 60, Fewster 72, 79)*

*England:* Burton; Griffiths, Ogilvie (Calder 41), Jones, Winks, O'Hanlon, Galloway (Bailey 61), O'Brien (Alli 41), Brown, Regis, Oduwa (Fewster 61).

Torshavn, 9 August 2012

**Norway (0) 0**

**England (0) 0**

*England:* Woodman; Cook (Calder 55), Jones, Ogilvie, Regis (Oduwa 55), Fewster, Alli (Winks 75), Wright (Griffiths 79), Bailey, O'Hanlon, O'Brien (Galloway 55).

| | P | W | D | L | F | A | GD | Pts |
|---|---|---|---|---|---|---|---|---|
| England | 3 | 2 | 1 | 0 | 6 | 2 | 4 | 7 |
| Norway | 3 | 1 | 2 | 0 | 3 | 2 | 1 | 5 |
| Finland | 3 | 0 | 2 | 1 | 4 | 6 | –2 | 2 |
| Faroe Islands | 3 | 0 | 1 | 2 | 0 | 3 | –3 | 1 |

### NORDIC TOURNAMENT – FINAL

Torshavn, 11 August 2012

**Sweden (1) 2** *(Engvall 13, Ssewankambo 65)*

**England (0) 0**

*England:* Burton; Griffiths (O'Hanlon 56), Calder, Jones, Ogilvie, Brown (Regis 66), Winks, Oduwa, Fewster (Bailey 72), Alli (O'Brien 66), Galloway (Cook 28).

### ST GEORGE'S PARK INTERNATIONAL TOURNAMENT

Burton, 29 August 2012

**England (2) 2** *(Bennett 20, Colkett 26)*

**Italy (1) 3** *(Tutino 39, Cerri 54, 63)*

*England:* Atkinson; Aina, Smith-Brown, Morris, Clark (Bryan 66), Jones, Kiwomya (Oduwa 59), Colkett (Crowley 59), Sinclair (Ojo 74), Hunte, Bennett.

Northampton, 31 August 2012

**England (1) 4** *(Sinclair 22, Brown 49, Bryan 51, Ogilvie 57)*

**Turkey (0) 1** *(Ceylan)*

*England:* Burton; Aina (Jones 55); Smith-Brown (Clark 65), Morris, Sinclair (Kiwomya 55), Ogilvie, Brown, Crowley (Colkett 65), Ojo, Bryan, Oduwa (Hunte 70).

Burton, 2 September 2012

**England (0) 0**

**Portugal (0) 1** *(Guedes 46)*

*England:* Atkinson (Burton 41); Smith-Brown (Clark 50), Morris, Jones (Aina 73), Kiwomya (Sinclair 50), Colkett (Brown 60), Bennett, Ogilvie, Crowley (Hunte 60), Ojo (Oduwa 73), Bryan.

|          | P | W | D | L | F | A | GD | Pts |
|----------|---|---|---|---|---|---|----|-----|
| Portugal | 3 | 2 | 1 | 0 | 3 | 1 | 2  | 7   |
| Italy    | 3 | 2 | 0 | 1 | 6 | 4 | 2  | 6   |
| England  | 3 | 1 | 0 | 2 | 6 | 5 | 1  | 3   |
| Turkey   | 3 | 0 | 1 | 2 | 3 | 8 | -5 | 1   |

## UEFA EUROPEAN UNDER-17 CHAMPIONSHIP – QUALIFYING ROUND, GROUP 7

Tallinn, 21 October 2012

**England (0) 2** *(Green 54, Allassani 72)*

**Estonia (0) 0**

*England:* Woodman; Aina, Morris, Ogilvie, Smith-Brown, Bryan, Kiwomya (Gilliead 68), Loftus-Cheek (Colkett 60), Brown, Green, Sinclair (Allassani 50).

Tallinn, 23 October 2012

**England (1) 1** *(Bryan 35)*

**Wales (0) 0**

*England:* Woodman; Aina, Morris, Ogilvie, Bryan, Jones, Colkett (Smith-Brown 63), Gilliead, Brown (Loftus-Cheek 56), Green (Ojo 74), Allassani.
*Wales:* Owen; Tattum, Llewellyn, Burridge, Atyeo, Copp, Charles, Noor, Davies, Francis (Menayese 72), Jones (Wisdom 74).

Tallinn, 26 October 2012

**Northern Ireland (1) 2** *(McDonagh 18, 71)*

**England (1) 3** *(Loftus-Cheek 39, Morris 55 (pen), 66)*

*Northern Ireland:* Mitchell; Dummigan, Doherty (Doran 73), Harney, Donnelly, McDonagh, McCawl, Lavery, McCallister, Bradley (Gorman 80), McDaid (Kennedy 67).
*England:* Burton; Smith-Brown, Jones, Morris, Kiwomya (Gilliead 76), Loftus-Cheek (Brown 71), Sinclair (Green 55), Ogilvie, Ojo, Griffiths, Allassani.

| GROUP 7          | P | W | D | L | F | A | GD | Pts |
|------------------|---|---|---|---|---|---|----|-----|
| England          | 3 | 3 | 0 | 0 | 6 | 2 | 4  | 9   |
| Northern Ireland | 3 | 1 | 1 | 1 | 7 | 4 | 3  | 4   |
| Estonia          | 3 | 1 | 1 | 1 | 4 | 4 | 0  | 4   |
| Wales            | 3 | 0 | 0 | 3 | 1 | 8 | -7 | 0   |

## UEFA EUROPEAN UNDER-17 CHAMPIONSHIP – ELITE ROUND, GROUP 6

Burton, 23 March 2013

**England (0) 1** *(Kiwomya 50)*

**Portugal (0) 0**

*England:* Gunn; Aina, O'Hanlon, Bryan, Gomez, Morris, Kiwomya (Gilliead 61), Loftus-Cheek, Fewster (Alli 56), Crowley, Bennett!.

Burton, 25 March 2013

**England (1) 1** *(Chernov 6 (og))*

**Russia (1) 2** *(Guliev 32, Sheydaev 51)*

*England:* Gunn; Aina, O'Hanlon, Bryan (Alli 57), Gomez, Morris, Kiwomya (Gilliead 62), Loftus-Cheek, Fewster, Crowley, Colkett (Allassani 69).

Burton, 28 March 2013

**England (2) 2** *(Colkett 13, Morris 28)*

**Slovenia (0) 1** *(Krivicic 68)*

*England:* Woodman; Aina (Griffiths 41), Ogilvie, O'Hanlon, Allassani (Gomez 62), Alli, Colkett (Kiwomya 69), Morris, Crowley■, Fewster, Gilliead.

| GROUP 6  | P | W | D | L | F | A | GD | Pts |
|----------|---|---|---|---|---|---|----|-----|
| Russia   | 3 | 2 | 0 | 1 | 4 | 3 | 1  | 6   |
| England  | 3 | 2 | 0 | 1 | 4 | 3 | 1  | 6   |
| Portugal | 3 | 2 | 0 | 1 | 4 | 2 | 2  | 6   |
| France   | 3 | 0 | 0 | 3 | 3 | 7 | -4 | 0   |

## THE ALGARVE TOURNAMENT

Lagos, 8 February 2013

**England (1) 1** *(Green 11)*

**Germany (1) 2** *(Avdijaj 36, Werner 51)*

*England:* Gunn; Aina (Gomez 77), O'Hanlon, Morris, Ogilvie, Loftus-Cheek, Bennett (Iwobi 70), Crowley, Green, Jones (Palmer 70), Winks.

Parchal, 10 February 2013

**Portugal (0) 2** *(Lima 49, Martins 56)*

**England (1) 1** *(Allassani 5)*

*England:* Atkinson; Aina (Jones 41), Morris (Loftus-Cheek 60), Gomez, Ogilvie (O'Hanlon 41), Allassani (Crowley 71), Palmer, Alli, Gilliead, Seagar (Bennett 60), Iwobi (Green 71).

Lagos, 12 February 2013

**Holland (0) 1** *(van Bruggen 16 (pen))*

**England (0) 0**

*England:* Gunn; O'Hanlon, Morris (Iwobi 51), Allassani, Loftus-Cheek (Aina 41), Crowley (Palmer 51), Green (Seagar 41), Jones (Ogilvie 41), Alli, Gilliead (Bennett 41), Winks.

## ENGLAND UNDER-18

Mansfield, 24 October 2012

**England (1) 2** *(Long 3, Cole 68)*

**Italy (0) 0**

*England:* Coddington (Dawson 46); Grimshaw, Webster, Swift, Coulson (Gordon 53), Chambers, Hayden (Weir 61), Ibe (Josh Murphy 69), Cole (Jacob Murphy 69), Long, Grant (Woodland 61).

La Louviere, 5 March 2013

**Belgium (0) 1** *(Sallaets 69)*

**England (0) 0**

*England:* Dawson (Coddington 60); Grimshaw (Holmes-Dennis 60), Toffolo (Williams 46), Pearson, Webb, Cooper (Iorfa 46), Weir (Fosu-Henry 68), Starkey (Tshibola 60), Sho-Silva, Long, Ibe (Dadoo 60).

# ENGLAND UNDER-19

## UEFA EUROPEAN UNDER-19 CHAMPIONSHIP – ESTONIA 2012

Tallinn, 3 July 2012

**England (0) 1** *(Chalobah 60)*
**Croatia (0) 1** *(Pavicic 56)*
*England:* Johnstone; Dier, Coady (Robinson 64), Keane, Thorpe, Barkley (Redmond 84), Chalobah, Kane (Hall 77), Thorne, Garbutt, Afobe.

Rakvere, 6 July 2012

**Serbia (0) 1** *(Ninkovic 70)*
**England (1) 2** *(Afobe 6, Redmond 63)*
*England:* Johnstone; Robinson, Coady, Thorpe, Barkley (Lundstram 63), Chalobah, Kane (Hope 79), Redmond, Thorne, Garbutt, Afobe (Berahino 71).

Tallinn, 9 July 2012

**France (1) 1** *(Veretout 31)*
**England (2) 2** *(Lundstram 16, Kane 39)*
*England:* Johnstone; Dier, Robinson, Thorpe, Chalobah, Berahino, Kane (Coady 84), Redmond (Hope 77), Hall (Garbutt 69), Thorne, Lundstram.

### SEMI-FINAL

Tallinn, 12 July 2012

**England (0) 1** *(Afobe 57)*
**Greece (0) 2** *(Bougaidis 38, Lykogiannis 108)*
*England:* Johnstone; Dier (Garbutt 57), Robinson, Keane, Thorpe, Barkley, Chalobah, Berahino (Redmond 77), Hall, Afobe, Lundstram (Thorne 91).
*aet.*

## UEFA EUROPEAN UNDER-19 CHAMPIONSHIP – QUALIFYING ROUND, GROUP 12

Tallinn, 26 September 2012

**England (1) 3** *(Hiwyka-Mayifuila 23, Turgott 56, Akpom 83)*
**Estonia (0) 0**
*England:* Pickford; Chambers, Lundstram, O'Connell, Turgott, Hiwula-Mayifuila, Hope (Swift 83), Hanley (Osborn 46), Stephens, Fenton, Barmby (Akpom 46).

Tallinn, 28 September 2012

**Faroe Islands (0) 0**
**England (3) 6** *(Turgott 12, 82, Akpom 23, 45, Hope 72, Chambers 84)*
*England:* Willis G; Smith (Hope 66), Lundstram, Turgott, Akpom, Azeez (Barmby 59), Osborn, Stephens (Chambers 46), Fenton, Swift, Magri.

Tallinn, 1 October 2012

**England (0) 1** *(Hope 90)*
**Ukraine (0) 1** *(Pavlenko 88)*
*England:* Pickford; Chambers, Smith (Azeez 68), Lundstram, O'Connell, Turgott, Hiwula-Mayifuila, Hope, Hanley (Fenton 57), Stephens, Barmby (Osborn 76).

## UEFA EUROPEAN UNDER-19 CHAMPIONSHIP – ELITE ROUND, GROUP 6

Bornem, 24 May 2013

**England (1) 1** *(Clayton 38)*
**Georgia (1) 1** *(Pantsulaia 8)*
*England:* Pickford■; Chambers, Leigh, Turnbull, Browning, O'Connell, Clayton (Campbell 73), Baker, Akpom, Harriott (Webster 86), Pearson (Dawson 8).

Geel, 26 May 2013

**Belgium (1) 1** *(Foket 27)*
**England (0) 1** *(Baker 90)*
*England:* Chambers; Leigh (Swift 46), Turnbull, Browning, O'Connell, Clayton (Coulthirst 62), Baker, Akpom, Harriott (Campbell 46), Dawson, Pearson.

Oosterzonen, 29 May 2013

**England (2) 3** *(Coulthirst 17, Baker 33 (pen), Akpom 74))*
**Scotland (0) 0**
*England:* Pickford; Browning, O'Connell, Baker, Akpom, Campbell, Coulthirst (Harriott 75), Murphy (Chambers 61), Webster, Wallace (Pearson 53), Swift.
*Scotland:* O'Hara; Grimmer, McManus (Beck 56), Heron, Fraser, Henley, Davey, Souttar, McGinn (Lindsay 70), Gauld (Kennedy 70), King.

## FRIENDLIES

Hamburg, 6 September 2012

**Germany (1) 3** *(Yesil 2, 47, Kerk 58)*
**England (1) 1** *(Powell 31)*
*England:* Pickford (Sutherland 75); Stones, Blackett, Chalobah, Dier, Jackson (Evans 61), Sterling (Redmond 65), Powell, Morgan (Turgott 75), Clayton (Akpom 61), Ward-Prowse (Barmby 75).

Telford, 13 November 2012

**England (0) 1** *(Lundstram 90 (pen))*
**Finland (0) 0**                                            2910
*England:* Pickford (Garratt 46); Stones (Chambers 46); Potts D, Potts B (Hanley 46), Stephens (Webster 46), O'Connell, Ward-Prowse (Josh Murphy 69), Lundstram, Storey (Azeez 62), Turgott, Jacob Murphy (Weir 62).

Doncaster, 5 February 2013

**England (2) 3** *(Akpom 18, 27, Samuel 66)*
**Denmark (0) 1** *(Amankwaa 52)*
*England:* Pickford (Snedker 85); Stones (Chambers 67), Leigh, Ward-Prowse, Dier (Willis 79), O'Connell, Blackett (Baker 67), Lundstram, Akpom (Jacob Murphy 57), Turgott (Josh Murphy 58), Redmond (Samuel 57).

Telford, 21 March 2013

**England (1) 1** *(Chambers 31)*
**Turkey (0) 0**
*England:* Pickford (Dawson 75); Chambers (Pennington 65), Webster (Leigh 71), Potts, Browning, O'Connell, Baker (Hope 65), Ward-Prowse, Powell, Clayton (Josh, Murphy 55), Redmond (Campbell 55).

# ENGLAND UNDER-20

## FIFA WORLD CUP – TURKEY 2013

Antalya, 23 June 2013

**England (1) 2** *(Coady 41, Williams 52)*
**Iraq (0) 2** *(Faez 75 (pen), Adnan 90)*                3148
*England:* Johnstone; Potts, Flanagan, Dier, Coady, Ward-Prowse, Kane, Lascelles, Williams (Long 69), Lundstram (Reach 69), Barkley (Bigirimana 89).

Antalya, 26 June 2013

**Chile (1) 1** *(Castillo 32 (pen))*     **England (0) 1** *(Kane 64)*
*England:* Johnstone; Potts, Dier, Coady, Ward-Prowse, Kane, Reach (Cole 75), Stones, Thorpe, Williams (Pritchard 62), Barkley.

Bursa, 29 June 2013

**Egypt (0) 2** *(Trezeget 79, Ahmed Hassan 90)*
**England (0) 0**
*England:* Johnstone; Dier, Coady, Ward-Prowse (Reach 62), Cole, Kane, Stones, Thorpe, Williams (Pritchard 46), Garbutt, Barkley.

# SCHOOLS FOOTBALL 2012–13

## BOODLES INDEPENDENT SCHOOLS FA CUP 2012–13

### 1ST ROUND

| | |
|---|---|
| Ackworth v Gresham's | 5-0 |
| ACS Cobham v Solihull | 2-0 |
| Ardingly v Haberdashers' Aske's | 1-2 |
| Aldenham v Queen Ethelburga's College | 11-1 |
| Alleyn's v Winchester | 3-0 |
| Bede's v City of London | 2-0 |
| Bedford Modern v Oswestry | 9-0 |
| Bolton v Cheadle Hulme | 1-0 |
| Box Hill v KES Witley | 4-4 |
| *aet; KES Witley won 4-2 on penalties.* | |
| Bradfield v John Lyon | 3-0 |
| Charterhouse v St. Bede's College | 2-1 |
| *aet.* | |
| Claremont Fan Court v Dover College | 3-8 |
| Dulwich College v Kimbolton | 3-1 |
| Forest v Bedales | 2-0 |
| Frensham Heights v St. Columba's College | 0-1 |
| Grange v Eton | 1-6 |
| Hampton v Malvern | 3-0 |
| Harrodian v Hurstpierpoint | 2-3 |
| King's School, Chester v University College School | 2-1 |
| Lancing v Haileybury | 2-1 |
| Latymer Upper v Westminster | 3-1 |
| Licensed Victuallers v Bury GS | 1-4 |
| Manchester GS v Ibstock Place | 4-3 |
| Millfield v Repton | 2-0 |
| Oldham Hulme GS v Colfe's | 1-4 |
| RGS Newcastle v Birkdale | 3-1 |
| Royal Russell v Norwich | 3-0 |
| QEGS Blackburn v Grammar School at Leeds | 3-4 |
| Shrewsbury v Highgate | 1-0 |
| Tonbridge v Brentwood | 1-2 |
| Wolverhampton GS v Chigwell | 2-1 |

### SECOND ROUND

| | |
|---|---|
| ACS Cobham v Hampton | 1-2 |
| Aldenham v Latymer Upper | 0-2 |
| Alleyn's v Brentwood | 3-0 |
| Bedford Modern v Millfield | 1-2 |
| Bolton v RGS Newcastle | 4-3 |
| Bury GS v Dulwich College | 3-5 |
| Colfe's v St. Columba's College | 0-1 |
| Dover College v Bradfield | 1-13 |
| Eton v Ackworth | 11-0 |
| Haberdashers' Aske's v King's School, Chester | 1-2 |
| Hurstpierpoint v Charterhouse | 0-4 |
| KES Witley v Bede's | 1-5 |
| Manchester GS v Lancing | 2-2 |
| *aet; MGS won 10-9 on penalties.* | |
| Shrewsbury v Royal Russell | 4-0 |
| St. Edmund's, Canterbury v Forest | 1-8 |
| Wolverhampton GS v Grammar School at Leeds | 1-6 |

### THIRD ROUND

| | |
|---|---|
| Alleyn's v King's School, Chester | 3-2 |
| *aet.* | |
| Bede's v Dulwich College | 5-3 |
| Bolton v Bradfield | 3-1 |
| Grammar School at Leeds v Charterhouse | 2-1 |
| Latymer Upper v Shrewsbury | 2-2 |
| *aet; Shrewsbury won 3-1 on penalties.* | |
| Manchester GS v Forest | 0-2 |
| Millfield v Eton | 7-4 |
| St. Columba's College v Hampton | 1-5 |

### FOURTH ROUND

| | |
|---|---|
| Alleyn's v Grammar School at Leeds | 2-1 |
| Forest v Bede's | 2-1 |
| Hampton v Millfield | 0-4 |
| Shrewsbury v Bolton | 4-2 |

### SEMI-FINALS

| | |
|---|---|
| Shrewsbury v Millfield | 0-5 |
| Alleyn's v Forest | 4-0 |

### FINAL

**Millfield 2**

**Alleyn's 0**

*at Milton Keynes Dons FC*

*Millfield:* W. Godmon, K. McConnachie, D. Webb, H. Turner, M. Vittroti, T. Whelan, A. Gibbs, H. Mennem, B. Downing, M. Golby, J. Gallagher.
*Substitutes:* E. Duffy, H. Farmer.

*Alleyn's:* J. Savage, F. Charnock, C. Leslie, S. Redmayne, T. Sealy, N. Jeyarajah, L. Fox, M. Caseby, J. Kelly, S. Barclay, T. Derry.
*Substitutes:* J. Robins, C. Williams, C. Haldecott.

*Referee:* Mr. M. Atkinson (Yorkshire).

### INVESTEC ISFA U15 CUP FINAL

| | |
|---|---|
| Whitgift v Brentwood | 3-1 |
| *(at Burton Albion FC)* | |

### INVESTEC ISFA U13 CUP FINAL

| | |
|---|---|
| Whitgift v Priory | 5-0 |
| *(at Burton Albion FC)* | |

# UNIVERSITY FOOTBALL 2013

## 129th UNIVERSITY MATCH

(Saturday 30 March, at Crystal Palace's Selhurst Park)

**Oxford (2) 2     Cambridge (1) 3**

*Oxford:* Thomas Haigh; Michael Moneke, Daniel Bassett, Mark Jamison, Adam Fellows, Anthony Bedows, Ezra Rubenstein (Edward Grimer 78), Luke Devereux (Adam Healy 85), Sam Donald (c), Julian Austin, Peder Beck-Friis (Sam Firman 70).
*Scorers:* Julian Austin 28, Ezra Rubenstein 42.
*Substitutes:* Casey O'Brien, Benjamin Szreter.

*Cambridge:* Fergus Kent; Simon Court, James Day, Jamie Rutt, Solomon Elliott, Anthony Childs, Ross Broadway (c), Richard Totten, Ben Tsuda (Patrick Grigg 70), Daniel Forde, Haitham Sherif.
*Scorers:* Richard Totten 34, 60, 67.
*Substitutes:* Alex Coburn, George Hill, Michael Smith, Chris Hutton.

*Referee:* Lee Probert.

*Oxford have won 50 games, Cambridge 49 and 30 drawn.     Oxford have scored 205 goals, Cambridge 204 goals.*

# WOMEN'S FOOTBALL 2012–13

## WOMEN'S SUPER LEAGUE 2012

| | | P | Home W | D | L | F | A | Away W | D | L | F | A | Total W | D | L | F | A | GD | Pts |
|---|---|---|---|---|---|---|---|---|---|---|---|---|---|---|---|---|---|---|---|
| 1 | Arsenal Ladies | 14 | 6 | 1 | 0 | 20 | 10 | 4 | 3 | 0 | 19 | 8 | 10 | 4 | 0 | 39 | 18 | 21 | 34 |
| 2 | Birmingham City Ladies | 14 | 4 | 2 | 1 | 17 | 8 | 3 | 3 | 1 | 14 | 10 | 7 | 5 | 2 | 31 | 18 | 13 | 26 |
| 3 | Everton Ladies | 14 | 4 | 3 | 0 | 9 | 4 | 3 | 1 | 3 | 11 | 12 | 7 | 4 | 3 | 20 | 16 | 4 | 25 |
| 4 | Bristol Academy Women | 14 | 2 | 2 | 3 | 7 | 10 | 2 | 4 | 1 | 10 | 6 | 4 | 6 | 4 | 17 | 16 | 1 | 18 |
| 5 | Lincoln Ladies | 14 | 2 | 3 | 2 | 14 | 14 | 3 | 0 | 4 | 10 | 12 | 5 | 3 | 6 | 24 | 26 | −2 | 18 |
| 6 | Chelsea Ladies | 14 | 2 | 2 | 3 | 12 | 12 | 3 | 0 | 4 | 8 | 11 | 5 | 2 | 7 | 20 | 23 | −3 | 17 |
| 7 | Doncaster Rovers Belles | 14 | 1 | 1 | 5 | 4 | 13 | 2 | 1 | 4 | 10 | 15 | 3 | 2 | 9 | 14 | 28 | −14 | 11 |
| 8 | Liverpool Ladies | 14 | 0 | 0 | 7 | 6 | 20 | 1 | 2 | 4 | 9 | 15 | 1 | 2 | 11 | 15 | 35 | −20 | 5 |

## FA WOMEN'S PREMIER LEAGUE NATIONAL DIVISION 2012–13

| | | P | Home W | D | L | F | A | Away W | D | L | F | A | Total W | D | L | F | A | GD | Pts |
|---|---|---|---|---|---|---|---|---|---|---|---|---|---|---|---|---|---|---|---|
| 1 | Sunderland | 18 | 8 | 1 | 0 | 31 | 7 | 6 | 2 | 1 | 23 | 9 | 14 | 3 | 1 | 54 | 16 | 38 | 45 |
| 2 | Watford | 18 | 6 | 2 | 1 | 19 | 7 | 5 | 3 | 1 | 13 | 10 | 11 | 5 | 2 | 32 | 17 | 15 | 38 |
| 3 | Leeds U | 18 | 6 | 1 | 2 | 16 | 6 | 6 | 1 | 2 | 16 | 13 | 12 | 2 | 4 | 32 | 19 | 13 | 38 |
| 4 | Manchester C | 18 | 4 | 2 | 3 | 16 | 12 | 3 | 2 | 4 | 16 | 13 | 7 | 4 | 7 | 32 | 25 | 7 | 25 |
| 5 | Coventry C | 18 | 3 | 1 | 5 | 12 | 19 | 5 | 0 | 4 | 13 | 8 | 8 | 1 | 9 | 25 | 27 | −2 | 25 |
| 6 | Aston Villa | 18 | 4 | 1 | 4 | 11 | 15 | 3 | 2 | 4 | 10 | 14 | 7 | 3 | 8 | 21 | 29 | −8 | 24 |
| 7 | Charlton Ath | 18 | 3 | 3 | 3 | 18 | 17 | 3 | 1 | 5 | 7 | 14 | 6 | 4 | 8 | 25 | 31 | −6 | 22 |
| 8 | Cardiff C | 18 | 2 | 2 | 5 | 7 | 13 | 3 | 2 | 4 | 16 | 13 | 5 | 4 | 9 | 23 | 26 | −3 | 19 |
| 9 | Portsmouth | 18 | 2 | 2 | 5 | 12 | 15 | 1 | 2 | 6 | 10 | 29 | 3 | 4 | 11 | 22 | 44 | −22 | 13 |
| 10 | Barnet | 18 | 0 | 2 | 7 | 3 | 17 | 0 | 2 | 7 | 4 | 22 | 0 | 4 | 14 | 7 | 39 | −32 | 4 |

## FA WOMEN'S PREMIER LEAGUE NORTHERN DIVISION 2012–13

| | | P | Home W | D | L | F | A | Away W | D | L | F | A | Total W | D | L | F | A | GD | Pts |
|---|---|---|---|---|---|---|---|---|---|---|---|---|---|---|---|---|---|---|---|
| 1 | Sheffield | 16 | 7 | 1 | 0 | 24 | 7 | 6 | 1 | 1 | 22 | 9 | 13 | 2 | 1 | 46 | 16 | 30 | 41 |
| 2 | Nottingham F | 16 | 5 | 1 | 2 | 17 | 13 | 5 | 1 | 2 | 18 | 9 | 10 | 2 | 4 | 35 | 22 | 13 | 32 |
| 3 | Blackburn R | 16 | 5 | 1 | 2 | 18 | 10 | 4 | 2 | 2 | 17 | 15 | 9 | 3 | 4 | 35 | 25 | 10 | 30 |
| 4 | Sporting Club Alb | 16 | 3 | 2 | 3 | 19 | 12 | 5 | 1 | 2 | 21 | 12 | 8 | 3 | 5 | 40 | 24 | 16 | 27 |
| 5 | Preston NE | 16 | 4 | 4 | 0 | 20 | 14 | 3 | 0 | 5 | 9 | 13 | 7 | 4 | 5 | 29 | 27 | 2 | 25 |
| 6 | Newcastle U | 16 | 3 | 0 | 5 | 17 | 19 | 3 | 2 | 3 | 14 | 20 | 6 | 2 | 8 | 31 | 39 | −8 | 20 |
| 7 | Wolverhampton W | 16 | 3 | 0 | 5 | 10 | 18 | 2 | 1 | 5 | 10 | 22 | 5 | 1 | 10 | 20 | 40 | −20 | 16 |
| 8 | Derby Co | 16 | 2 | 0 | 6 | 12 | 20 | 2 | 0 | 6 | 16 | 23 | 4 | 0 | 12 | 28 | 43 | −15 | 12 |
| 9 | Leicester C | 16 | 0 | 0 | 8 | 4 | 24 | 1 | 1 | 6 | 10 | 18 | 1 | 1 | 14 | 14 | 42 | −28 | 4 |

## FA WOMEN'S PREMIER LEAGUE SOUTHERN DIVISION 2012–13

| | | P | Home W | D | L | F | A | Away W | D | L | F | A | Total W | D | L | F | A | GD | Pts |
|---|---|---|---|---|---|---|---|---|---|---|---|---|---|---|---|---|---|---|---|
| 1 | Reading | 18 | 9 | 0 | 0 | 39 | 5 | 6 | 0 | 3 | 18 | 11 | 15 | 0 | 3 | 57 | 16 | 41 | 45 |
| 2 | Millwall Lionesses | 18 | 6 | 0 | 3 | 15 | 13 | 6 | 1 | 2 | 10 | 5 | 12 | 1 | 5 | 25 | 18 | 7 | 37 |
| 3 | Yeovil T | 18 | 6 | 1 | 2 | 18 | 9 | 3 | 2 | 4 | 11 | 8 | 9 | 3 | 6 | 29 | 17 | 12 | 30 |
| 4 | Brighton & HA | 18 | 5 | 2 | 2 | 20 | 17 | 3 | 2 | 4 | 12 | 13 | 8 | 4 | 6 | 32 | 30 | 2 | 28 |
| 5 | Lewes | 18 | 6 | 1 | 2 | 17 | 8 | 1 | 1 | 7 | 6 | 16 | 7 | 2 | 9 | 23 | 24 | −1 | 23 |
| 6 | West Ham U | 17 | 3 | 4 | 2 | 11 | 7 | 3 | 0 | 5 | 9 | 11 | 6 | 4 | 7 | 20 | 18 | 2 | 22 |
| 7 | Gillingham | 18 | 3 | 2 | 4 | 6 | 9 | 2 | 2 | 5 | 13 | 20 | 5 | 4 | 9 | 19 | 29 | −10 | 19 |
| 8 | Tottenham H | 17 | 3 | 2 | 4 | 11 | 13 | 1 | 2 | 5 | 11 | 20 | 4 | 4 | 9 | 22 | 33 | −11 | 16 |
| 9 | Colchester U | 16 | 3 | 3 | 1 | 6 | 5 | 0 | 4 | 5 | 11 | 25 | 3 | 7 | 6 | 17 | 30 | −13 | 16 |
| 10 | QPR | 18 | 1 | 2 | 6 | 7 | 22 | 1 | 3 | 5 | 7 | 21 | 2 | 5 | 11 | 14 | 43 | −29 | 11 |

*Colchester U v West Ham U postponed; Colchester U v Tottenham H postponed.*

## WOMEN'S PREMIER LEAGUE CUP FINAL

Sunday 5 May 2013
(at York City)

**Leeds U (0) 0     Aston Villa (0) 0**
*aet; Aston Villa won 5-4 on penalties.*

*Leeds U:* Draycott; Emmonds, Huegett, Lee A (Bass 45), Lee R, Lipman, Rich (Thackray 81), Sharp, Sheen, Staneff (Coates 90), Sykes.

*Aston Villa:* Clarke; Cusak (Davies 100), Follis (Ferguson 75), Jones, Mannion, Merritt, Moran (McCue 55), Petrovic, Richards, Vaughan, Walsh.

*Referee:* Helen Byrne.

# THE FA WOMEN'S CUP 2012–13

**FIRST ROUND QUALIFYING**

| | |
|---|---|
| Crown Newlaithes v Jarrow Ladies | 1-5 |
| Workington Reds v Whitley Bay | 0-5 |
| St Nicholas v Launceston | 3-2 |
| Lichfield Diamonds v Crusaders | 0-2 |
| Chester-Le-Street T v York C | 6-1 |
| Consett v Peterlee St Francis | 1-12 |
| Forest Hall Women's YPC v Durham Wildcats | 0-10 |
| Redcar Ath v Kendal T | 3-3 |
| *Kendal T won 3-2 on penalties.* | |
| Lowick U v Norton & Stockton Ancients | 3-5 |
| North Shields v Birtley T | 5-2 |
| Whickham Fellside v California | 5-0 |
| Keighley Oaks v Steel C Wanderers | 0-2 |
| Appleby Frodingham v Rothwell | 0-12 |
| Barnsley v Kirklees | 3-0 |
| Bradford Park Avenue v Brighouse | 5-1 |
| Handsworth v Guiseley AFC Ladies | 0-3 |
| Wetherby Ath v Ossett Alb | 1-4 |
| Accrington Girls & Ladies v Tranmere R | 3-5 |
| Crewe Alex v Irlam | 3-1 |
| Warrington T v Blackpool Ladies | 1-11 |
| Padiham v Preston NE | 2-3 |
| Middleton Ath v City of Manchester | 3-5 |
| Morecambe v Blackpool Wren R | 4-1 |
| Long Eaton U v Nettleham | 1-2 |
| Sandiacre T v Retford U | 4-2 |
| Oadby & Wigston Dynamo v Dronfield T | 2-1 |
| West Bridgford v Mansfield T | 1-6 |
| Ruddington Village v Rise Park | 3-4 |
| Arnold T v Lutterworth Ath | 2-6 |
| Birmingham & West Midlands Police v AFC Telford U Ladies | 7-1 |
| Cottage Farm Rangers v Coventry Sphinx | 0-9 |
| Coventry Ladies Development v Walsall | 2-3 |
| Pegasus Juniors v Malvern T | 2-1 |
| Bradwell Belles v FC Reedswood Ladies | 0-8 |
| Allscott v Lightwood | 2-1 |
| TNS v Bilbrook | 4-1 |
| Lye T v Kenilworth T KH | 1-7 |
| Shenstone v Ellistown | 1-2 |
| Peterborough Sports Parkway v Raunds T | 10-0 |
| AFC Trinity v Gt Shelford | 6-5 |
| Roade w.o. v Outwell Swifts withdrawn | |
| Netherton U v Stewarts & Lloyds Corby | 3-1 |
| Huntingdon T v Brackley Sports | 4-3 |
| AFC Sudbury Ladies v Colchester T | 5-2 |
| Chelmsford C w.o. v Fakenham T withdrawn | |
| Hutton v Haverhill R | 2-3 |
| Hockering v Wymondham T | 1-3 |
| West Billericay v Assandun Vikings | 5-0 |
| Hethersett Ath v Lowestoft T | 4-2 |
| Leighton U Vixens v Leverstock Green | 2-1 |
| Barking v Stevenage Borough | 4-2 |
| Standon & Puckeridge v Sandy | 4-1 |
| MSA v Sawbridgeworth T | 3-1 |
| Kikk U v Haringey Borough | 3-1 |
| Royston T v St Albans C | 0-1 |
| Old Actonians v Launton | 1-3 |
| Maidenhead U v Banbury U | 5-1 |
| Tring Ath v City Belles | 2-4 |
| Headington v Denham U | 0-3 |
| Oxford C v Ascot U | 5-0 |
| Reading v Colne Valley | 1-2 |
| Marlow v Bracknell T | 4-6 |
| Hemel Hempstead T v Newbury | 6-3 |
| Abbey Rangers v Meridian | 2-1 |
| Rusthall v Maidstone U Rascals | 1-4 |
| Ashford Girls v South Park | 4-1 |
| AFC Wimbledon Ladies w.o. v East Preston removed | |
| Ramsgate v Crawley Wasps | 2-5 |
| Milford & Witley v Eastbourne | 0-6 |
| Eastbourne T v Claygate Royals | 8-1 |
| Parkwood Rangers v Anchorians | 3-3 |
| *Parkwood Rangers won 5-4 on penalties.* | |
| Haywards Heath T v London Corinthians | 3-4 |
| Long Lane v Bexhill U | 3-2 |
| Prince of Wales v Knaphill | 2-3 |
| Regents Park Rangers v Battersea Ironsides | 2-2 |
| *Battersea Ironsides won 7-6 on penalties.* | |
| Victoire withdrawn v Maidstone T w.o. | |
| Dartford YMCA v Westfield | 1-4 |
| Rottingdean Village v New Forest | 3-1 |

| | |
|---|---|
| Weymouth v Aldershot T | 3-3 |
| *Aldershot T won 3-2 on penalties.* | |
| Parley v Shanklin | 1-5 |
| Fleet T v Poole T | 0-5 |
| Swindon Spitfires v Gosport Borough | 2-1 |
| Wootton Bassett T v Southampton Women's | 2-6 |
| Andover New Street v Christchurch | 3-1 |
| Cheltenham Civil Service v Brislington | 0-6 |
| Quedgeley Wanderers v Bristol Ladies Union | 2-7 |
| Forest Of Dean v Heavitree Social | 1-0 |
| Larkhall Ath v Bude T | 5-1 |
| Ilminster T v Street | 6-0 |
| Pen Mill v Bitton | 3-5 |
| Falmouth T v Cheltenham T | 8-2 |
| Downend Flyers v AEK Boco | 9-1 |

**SECOND ROUND QUALIFYING**

| | |
|---|---|
| City of Manchester v Blackpool Ladies | 1-2 |
| Jarrow Ladies v Whitley Bay | 2-1 |
| Peterlee St Francis v Whickham Fellside | 7-1 |
| Kendal T v Chester-Le-Street T | 1-5 |
| Abbeytown v North Shields | 3-1 |
| Prudhoe T v Penrith | 2-5 |
| Norton & Stockton Ancients v Durham Wildcats | 2-8 |
| Guiseley AFC Ladies v Barnsley | 1-3 |
| Ossett Alb v Hull C | 2-6 |
| Steel C Wanderers v Bradford Park Avenue | 6-2 |
| Rothwell v Westella & Willerby | 4-2 |
| Morecambe v Birkenhead | 7-0 |
| Tranmere R v Preston NE | 3-0 |
| Crewe Alex v Chester C | 1-0 |
| Rise Park v Nettleham | 2-1 |
| Mansfield T v Oadby & Wigston Dynamo | 4-1 |
| Sandiacre T v Lutterworth Ath | 3-4 |
| Pegasus Juniors v Ellistown | 3-4 |
| Kenilworth T KH v TNS | 1-4 |
| FC Reedswood Ladies v Crusaders | 6-2 |
| Walsall v Coventry Sphinx | 2-3 |
| Birmingham & West Midlands Police v Allscott | 2-1 |
| Huntingdon T v Roade | 2-5 |
| Peterborough Northern Star v Hampton | 7-3 |
| Peterborough Sports Parkway v Netherton U | 10-1 |
| AFC Trinity v Moulton | 6-2 |
| West Billericay v Haverhill R | 4-0 |
| Hethersett Ath v Billericay T | 0-2 |
| AFC Sudbury Ladies v Wymondham T | 3-1 |
| Chelmsford C v C&K Basildon | 2-3 |
| Kikk U v Leighton U Vixens | 9-3 |
| MSA v Standon & Puckeridge | 3-1 |
| Barking v St Albans C | 6-1 |
| Oxford C v C Belles | 3-0 |
| Colne Valley v Bracknell T | 4-1 |
| Launton v Denham U | 0-4 |
| Maidenhead U v Hemel Hempstead T | 4-1 |
| Panthers v Long Lane | 4-2 |
| Ashford Girls v Battersea Ironsides | 3-5 |
| London Corinthians v Maidstone U Rascals | 14-0 |
| Maidstone T v Rottingdean Village | 9-1 |
| Knaphill v Eastbourne T | 1-4 |
| Eastbourne v Westfield | 0-7 |
| AFC Wimbledon Ladies v Abbey Rangers | 6-0 |
| Parkwood Rangers v Crawley Wasps | 2-1 |
| Southampton Women's v Aldershot T | 0-3 |
| Swindon Spitfires v Poole T | 3-4 |
| Shanklin v Andover New Street | 2-0 |
| Forest Of Dean v Stoke Lane | 3-1 |
| Downend Flyers v Bitton | 4-2 |
| Larkhall Ath v Falmouth T | 5-1 |
| St Nicholas v Bristol Ladies Union | 1-3 |
| Brislington v Ilminster T | 4-2 |

**THIRD ROUND QUALIFYING**

| | |
|---|---|
| Cambridge Women's v Kikk U | 3-1 |
| Middlesbrough v Curzon Ashton | 6-4 |
| Chester-Le-Street T v Stockport Co | 1-7 |
| Bradford C v Rothwell | 4-0 |
| Crewe Alex v Tranmere R | 3-1 |
| Rise Park v Coventry Sphinx | 2-1 |
| Leamington Lions v MK Dons | 0-3 |
| Leafield Ath v Birmingham & West Midlands Police | 5-4 |
| Oxford C v Ipswich T | 0-7 |
| Chichester C v Denham U | 1-0 |
| Larkhall Ath v Bristol Ladies Union | 2-0 |
| Steel C Wanderers v Blackpool Ladies | 0-2 |

| | |
|---|---|
| Abbeytown v Leeds C Vixens | 0-4 |
| Sheffield U Community v Jarrow Ladies | 1-0 |
| Chorley v Rotherham U | 4-1 |
| Cheadle Heath Nomads v Huddersfield T | 0-4 |
| Peterlee St Francis v Hull C | |
| *Tie awarded to Peterlee St Francis - Hull C failed to fulfil fixture.* | |
| Durham Wildcats v Wakefield Ladies | 10-0 |
| Mossley Hill v South Durham & Cestria | 2-1 |
| Penrith v Morecambe | 2-6 |
| Barnsley v Liverpool Feds | 1-2 |
| Ellistown v Stoke C | 0-4 |
| Loughborough Foxes v Daventry T | 5-0 |
| Loughborough Students v Copsewood Coventry | 0-3 |
| Lutterworth Ath v Mansfield T | 4-1 |
| Leicester C v FC Reedswood Ladies | 4-3 |
| Radcliffe Olympic v TNS | 2-0 |
| MSA v AFC Trinity | 2-1 |
| Billericay T v Brentwood T | 2-4 |
| Arlesey T v Peterborough Northern Star | 2-0 |
| Norwich C v Luton T Ladies | 2-4 |
| Peterborough Sports Parkway v C&K Basildon | 3-4 |
| Chesham U v Roade | 15-0 |
| Barking v Enfield T | 0-4 |
| AFC Sudbury Ladies v West Billericay | 5-1 |
| AFC Wimbledon Ladies v Aldershot T | 1-0 |
| London Corinthians v Panthers | 7-1 |
| Oxford U v Battersea Ironsides | 5-0 |
| Eastbourne T v Southampton Saints | 0-1 |
| Maidenhead U v Colne Valley | 2-3 |
| Maidstone T v University Of Portsmouth | 1-3 |
| Westfield v Ebbsfleet U | 3-2 |
| Crystal Palace v Parkwood Rangers | 1-4 |
| Shanklin v Brislington | 1-3 |
| Forest Of Dean v Exeter C | 3-9 |
| Forest Green R v Downend Flyers | 7-3 |
| Plymouth Arg v Keynsham T Development | 4-2 |
| Poole T v Swindon T | 1-9 |
| Gloucester C v Keynsham T | 0-5 |

**FIRST ROUND**

| | |
|---|---|
| Leeds C Vixens v Huddersfield T | 3-3 |
| *Huddersfield T won 5-4 on penalties.* | |
| Middlesbrough v Peterlee St Francis | 5-2 |
| Cambridge Women's v Brentwood T | 4-0 |
| Enfield T v Chesham U | 1-3 |
| Keynsham T v University Of Portsmouth | 8-0 |
| Chichester C v Swindon T | 1-4 |
| Chorley v Morecambe | 2-4 |
| Bradford C v Stockport Co | 3-1 |
| Durham Wildcats v Blackpool Ladies | 4-0 |
| Sheffield U Community v Mossley Hill | 2-1 |
| Liverpool Feds v Crewe Alex | 1-0 |
| Loughborough Foxes v Leicester C | 1-0 |
| Stoke C v Leafield Ath | 2-3 |
| MK Dons v Luton T Ladies | 2-1 |
| Rise Park v Copsewood Coventry | 1-3 |
| Radcliffe Olympic v Lutterworth Ath | 6-1 |
| Arlesey T v C&K Basildon | 1-3 |
| AFC Sudbury Ladies v London Corinthians | 0-5 |
| Parkwood Rangers v Colne Valley | 1-4 |
| Ipswich T v AFC Wimbledon Ladies | 5-1 |
| Westfield v MSA | 2-1 |
| Forest Green R v Plymouth Arg | 2-3 |
| Southampton Saints v Larkhall Ath | 0-2 |
| Oxford U v Newquay | 2-1 |
| Exeter C v Brislington | 7-0 |

**SECOND ROUND**

| | |
|---|---|
| Nottingham F v Bradford C | 6-3 |
| Gillingham v MK Dons | 6-1 |

| | |
|---|---|
| Leafield Ath v C&K Basildon | 6-0 |
| Larkhall Ath v Plymouth Arg | 0-2 |
| Middlesbrough v Huddersfield T | 4-1 |
| Leicester C v Preston NE | 0-2 |
| Newcastle U v Radcliffe Olympic | 2-0 |
| Sheffield U Community v Durham Wildcats | 4-2 |
| Sheffield Ladies v Blackburn R | 2-1 |
| Loughborough Foxes v Derby Co | 0-2 |
| Morecambe v Liverpool Feds | 6-3 |
| Millwall Lionesses v Wolverhampton Wanderers | 3-1 |
| London Corinthians v West Ham U | 0-3 |
| Ipswich T v Cambridge Women's | 1-0 |
| Chesham U v QPR | 1-2 |
| Colchester U v Sporting Club Alb | 1-5 |
| Tottenham H v Copsewood Coventry | 2-0 |
| Westfield v Brighton & HA | 2-9 |
| Oxford U v Keynsham T | 6-1 |
| Lewes v Reading Women | 1-2 |
| Exeter C v Swindon T | 2-3 |
| Colne Valley v Yeovil T | 0-8 |

**THIRD ROUND**

| | |
|---|---|
| Sheffield U Community v Nottingham F | 1-5 |
| Middlesbrough v Sunderland | 1-6 |
| Charlton Ath v Oxford U | 1-2 |
| Tottenham H v Cardiff C | 0-4 |
| Reading Women v Brighton & HA | 4-2 |
| Portsmouth v QPR | 5-0 |
| Ipswich T v Aston Villa | 0-2 |
| Barnet Ladies v Yeovil T | 0-3 |
| Preston NE v Millwall Lionesses | 3-2 |
| Leeds U v West Ham U | 3-2 |
| Manchester C v Sheffield Ladies | 3-2 |
| Derby Co v Watford | 0-4 |
| Coventry C v Morecambe | 2-1 |
| Swindon T v Gillingham | 0-1 |
| Newcastle U v Plymouth Arg | 2-1 |
| Leafield Ath v Sporting Club Alb | 2-3 |

**FOURTH ROUND**

| | |
|---|---|
| Yeovil T v Portsmouth | 3-0 |
| Gillingham v Nottingham F | 2-3 |
| Coventry C v Manchester C | 0-1 |
| Watford v Leeds U | 0-2 |
| Cardiff C v Reading Women | 2-1 |
| Aston Villa v Preston NE | 3-0 |
| Oxford U v Newcastle U | 2-1 |
| Sporting Club Alb v Sunderland | 1-2 |

**FIFTH ROUND**

| | |
|---|---|
| Sunderland v Manchester C | 4-0 |
| Aston Villa v Liverpool | 0-5 |
| Doncaster R Belles v Bristol Academy | 0-2 |
| Cardiff C v Birmingham C | 1-3 |
| Nottingham F v Arsenal | 0-7 |
| Lincoln v Chelsea | 1-0 |
| Leeds U v Yeovil T | 4-0 |
| Oxford U v Everton | 0-7 |

**SIXTH ROUND**

| | |
|---|---|
| Sunderland v Liverpool | 1-2 |
| Lincoln v Leeds U | 4-0 |
| Arsenal v Birmingham C | 6-0 |
| Bristol Academy v Everton | 3-2 |

**SEMI-FINAL**

| | |
|---|---|
| Liverpool v Arsenal | 1-2 |
| Bristol Academy v Lincoln | 2-0 |

# WOMEN'S FA CUP FINAL

### Sunday 26 May 2013

(at Doncaster R, attendance 4988)

**Arsenal (1) 3          Bristol Academy (0) 0**

*Arsenal:* Byrne; Houghton, Flaherty, Grant (Tracy 90), Nobbs, White, Yankey (Carter 85), Davison, Beattie (Bailey 90), Little, Scott.
*Scorers:* Houghton 2, Nobbs 72, White 90.

*Bristol Academy:* Chamberlain; Dykes (Del Rio 74), Yorston, Matthews, Pablos Sanchon, Windell (James 46), Heatherson, Watts, Rose, Harding, Staniforth (McCatty 66).

*Referee:* Jane Simms.

# UEFA WOMEN'S CHAMPIONS LEAGUE 2012–13

## QUALIFYING ROUND

### GROUP 1 – SLOVENIA

| | |
|---|---|
| Zurich v Pomurje | 2-0 |
| Gintra v Atasehir | 2-3 |
| Zurich v Atasehir | 4-0 |
| Pomurje v Gintra | 9-1 |
| Gintra v Zurich | 0-8 |
| Atasehir v Pomurje | 2-4 |

| Group 1 Table | P | W | D | L | F | A | GD | Pts |
|---|---|---|---|---|---|---|---|---|
| Zurich | 3 | 3 | 0 | 0 | 14 | 0 | 14 | 9 |
| Pomurje | 3 | 2 | 0 | 1 | 13 | 5 | 8 | 6 |
| Atasehir | 3 | 1 | 0 | 2 | 5 | 10 | –5 | 3 |
| Gintra | 3 | 0 | 0 | 3 | 3 | 20 | –17 | 0 |

### GROUP – SERBIA

| | |
|---|---|
| BIIK v Parnu | 3-0 |
| NSA Sofia v Spartak Subotica | 0-7 |
| NSA Sofia v Parnu | 2-0 |
| Spartak Subotica v BIIK | 0-2 |
| BIIK v NSA Sofia | 4-0 |
| Parnu v Spartak Subotica | 0-1 |

| Group 2 Table | P | W | D | L | F | A | GD | Pts |
|---|---|---|---|---|---|---|---|---|
| BIIK | 3 | 3 | 0 | 0 | 9 | 0 | 9 | 9 |
| Spartak Subotica | 3 | 2 | 0 | 1 | 8 | 2 | 6 | 6 |
| NSA Sofia | 3 | 1 | 0 | 2 | 2 | 11 | –9 | 3 |
| Parnu | 3 | 0 | 0 | 3 | 0 | 6 | –6 | 0 |

### GROUP 3 – MALTA

| | |
|---|---|
| 1st Dezembro v Glentoran | 4-0 |
| Olimpia Cluj v Birkirkara | 8-0 |
| 1st Dezembro v Birkirkara | 1-0 |
| Glentoran v Olimpia Cluj | 2-4 |
| Olimpia Cluj v 1st Dezembro | 4-1 |
| Birkirkara v Glentoran | 1-3 |

| Group 3 Table | P | W | D | L | F | A | GD | Pts |
|---|---|---|---|---|---|---|---|---|
| Olimpia Cluj | 3 | 3 | 0 | 0 | 16 | 3 | 13 | 9 |
| 1st Dezembro | 3 | 2 | 0 | 1 | 6 | 4 | 2 | 6 |
| Glentoran | 3 | 1 | 0 | 2 | 5 | 9 | –4 | 3 |
| Birkirkara | 3 | 0 | 0 | 3 | 1 | 12 | –11 | 0 |

### GROUP 4 – SLOVAKIA

| | |
|---|---|
| Unia Raciborz v Slovan Bratislava | 5-0 |
| Bobruichanka v Ekonomist | 5-1 |
| Unia Raciborz v Ekonomist | 7-1 |
| Slovan Bratislava v Bobruichanka | 3-2 |
| Bobruichanka v Unia Raciborz | 0-5 |
| Ekonomist v Slovan Bratislava | 0-8 |

| Group 4 Table | P | W | D | L | F | A | GD | Pts |
|---|---|---|---|---|---|---|---|---|
| Unia Raciborz | 3 | 3 | 0 | 0 | 17 | 1 | 16 | 9 |
| Slovan Bratislava | 3 | 2 | 0 | 1 | 11 | 7 | 4 | 6 |
| Bobruichanka | 3 | 1 | 0 | 2 | 7 | 9 | –2 | 3 |
| Ekonomist | 3 | 0 | 0 | 3 | 2 | 20 | –18 | 0 |

### GROUP 5 – BOSNIA & HERZEGOVINA

| | |
|---|---|
| Sarajevo v Peamount United | 4-0 |
| ASA Tel-Aviv v UWIC | 5-0 |
| Peamount United v ASA Tel-Aviv | 5-0 |
| Sarajevo v UWIC | 1-0 |
| ASA Tel-Aviv v Sarajevo | 1-1 |
| UWIC v Peamount United | 0-4 |

| Group 5 Table | P | W | D | L | F | A | GD | Pts |
|---|---|---|---|---|---|---|---|---|
| Sarajevo | 3 | 2 | 1 | 0 | 6 | 1 | 5 | 7 |
| Peamount United | 3 | 2 | 0 | 1 | 9 | 4 | 5 | 6 |
| ASA Tel-Aviv | 3 | 1 | 1 | 1 | 6 | 6 | 0 | 4 |
| UWIC | 3 | 0 | 0 | 3 | 0 | 10 | –10 | 0 |

### GROUP 6 – CYPRUS

| | |
|---|---|
| Apollon Limassol v Klaksvik | 7-0 |
| Kharkiv v Ada Velipoje | 14-1 |
| Klaksvik v Kharkiv | 1-2 |
| Apollon Limassol v Ada Velipoje | 21-0 |
| Kharkiv v Apollon Limassol | 0-3 |
| Ada Velipoje v Klaksvik | 1-11 |

| Group 6 Table | P | W | D | L | F | A | GD | Pts |
|---|---|---|---|---|---|---|---|---|
| Apollon Limassol | 3 | 3 | 0 | 0 | 31 | 0 | 31 | 9 |
| Kharkiv | 3 | 2 | 0 | 1 | 16 | 5 | 11 | 6 |
| Klaksvik | 3 | 1 | 0 | 2 | 12 | 10 | 2 | 3 |
| Ada Velipoje | 3 | 0 | 0 | 3 | 2 | 46 | –44 | 0 |

### GROUP 7 – MACEDONIA

| | |
|---|---|
| PAOK Thessaloniki v Nase Taksi | 1-0 |
| MTK Hungaria v Skonto | 5-0 |
| PAOK Thessaloniki v Skonto | 8-0 |
| Nase Taksi v MTK Hungaria | 0-7 |
| MTK Hungaria v PAOK Thessaloniki | 2-0 |
| Skonto v Nase Taksi | 2-5 |

| Group 7 Table | P | W | D | L | F | A | GD | Pts |
|---|---|---|---|---|---|---|---|---|
| MTK Hungaria | 3 | 3 | 0 | 0 | 14 | 0 | 14 | 9 |
| PAOK Thessaloniki | 3 | 2 | 0 | 1 | 9 | 2 | 7 | 6 |
| Nase Taksi | 3 | 1 | 0 | 2 | 5 | 10 | –5 | 3 |
| Skonto | 3 | 0 | 0 | 3 | 2 | 18 | –16 | 0 |

### GROUP 8 – FINLAND

| | |
|---|---|
| PK-35 Vantaa v Noroc Nimoreni | 6-0 |
| Glasgow City v Osijek | 3-2 |
| Glasgow City v Noroc Nimoreni | 11-0 |
| Osijek v PK-35 Vantaa | 1-3 |
| PK-35 Vantaa v Glasgow City | 1-1 |
| Noroc Nimoreni v Osijek | 1-11 |

| Group 8 Table | P | W | D | L | F | A | GD | Pts |
|---|---|---|---|---|---|---|---|---|
| Glasgow City | 3 | 2 | 1 | 0 | 15 | 3 | 12 | 7 |
| PK-35 Vantaa | 3 | 2 | 0 | 1 | 10 | 2 | 8 | 7 |
| Osijek | 3 | 1 | 0 | 2 | 14 | 7 | 7 | 3 |
| Noroc Nimoreni | 3 | 0 | 0 | 3 | 1 | 28 | –27 | 0 |

## ROUND OF 32 FIRST LEG

| | |
|---|---|
| Zurich v Juvisy | 1-1 |
| BIIK v Roa | 0-4 |
| Birmingham v Verona | 2-0 |
| Spartak Subotica v Gothenburg | 0-1 |
| Apollon Limassol v Torres | 2-3 |
| PK-35 Vantaa v Lyon | 0-7 |
| Olimpia Cluj v Neulengbach | 1-1 |
| Barcelona v Arsenal | 0-3 |
| Stabaek v Brondby | 2-0 |
| Standard v Potsdam | 1-3 |
| Glasgow City v Fortuna Hjorring | 1-2 |
| Stjarnan v Zorkiy | 0-0 |
| Unia Raciborz v Wolfsburg | 1-5 |
| Sarajevo v Sparta Prague | 0-3 |
| MTK Hungaria v Malmo | 0-4 |
| Den Haag v Rossiyanka | 1-4 |

## ROUND OF 32 SECOND LEG

| | |
|---|---|
| Potsdam v Standard | 5-0 |
| Brondby v Stabaek | 3-3 |
| Lyon v PK-35 Vantaa | 5-0 |
| Malmo v MTK Hungaria | 6-1 |
| Gothenburg v Spartak Subotica | 3-0 |
| Neulengbach v Olimpia Cluj | 2-2 |
| *Olimpia Cluj won on away goals.* | |
| Torres v Apollon Limassol | 3-1 |
| Fortuna Hjorring v Glasgow City | 0-0 |
| Bardolino Verona v Birmingham | 3-0 |
| *aet.* | |
| Zorkiy v Stjarnan | 3-1 |
| Rossiyanka v Den Haag | 1-2 |
| Arsenal v Barcelona | 4-0 |
| Roa v BIIK | 4-0 |
| Wolfsburg v Unia Raciborz | 6-1 |
| Juvisy v Zurich | 1-0 |
| Sparta Prague v Sarajevo | 3-0 |

## ROUND OF 16 FIRST LEG

| | |
|---|---|
| Zorkiy v Lyon | 0-9 |
| Stabaek v Juvisy | 0-0 |
| Fortuna Hjorring v Gothenburg | 1-1 |
| Malmo v Verona | 1-0 |
| Torres v Olimpia Cluj | 4-1 |
| Sparta Prague v Rossiyanka | 0-1 |
| Arsenal v Potsdam | 2-1 |
| Wolfsburg v Roa | 4-1 |

**ROUND OF 16 SECOND LEG**

| | |
|---|---|
| Roa v Wolfsburg | 1-1 |
| Lyon v Zorkiy | 2-0 |
| Potsdam v Arsenal | 3-4 |
| Gothenburg v Fortuna Hjorring | 3-2 |
| Bardolino Verona v Malmo | 0-2 |
| Rossiyanka v Sparta Prague | 2-2 |
| Olimpia Cluj v Torres | 0-3 |
| Juvisy v Stabaek | 2-1 |

**QUARTER-FINALS FIRST LEG**

| | |
|---|---|
| Arsenal v Torres | 3-1 |
| Wolfsburg v Rossiyanka | 2-1 |
| Lyon v Malmo | 5-0 |
| Juvisy v Gothenburg | 1-0 |

**QUARTER-FINALS SECOND LEG**

| | |
|---|---|
| Torres v Arsenal | 0-1 |
| Rossiyanka v Wolfsburg | 0-2 |
| Malmo v Lyon | 0-3 |
| Gothenburg v Juvisy | 1-3 |

**SEMI-FINALS FIRST LEG**

| | |
|---|---|
| Lyon v Juvisy | 3-0 |
| Arsenal v Wolfsburg | 0-2 |

**SEMI-FINALS SECOND LEG**

| | |
|---|---|
| Juvisy v Lyon | 1-6 |
| Wolfsburg v Arsenal | 2-1 |

**FINAL**

**Thursday 23 May 2013**

**(at Stamford Bridge)**

**Wolfsburg (0) 1** *(Müller 73 (pen))*
**Lyon (0) 0** 19,278

*Wolfsburg:* Vetterlein; Wensing, Jakabfi (Magull 78), Blässe, Popp, Kessler, Hartmann, Müller, Pohlers (Omilade 82), Henning, Goessling.

*Lyon:* Bouhaddi; Renard, Georges, Henry, Rapinoe (Dickenmann 46 (Majri 89)), Schelin, Necib, Thomis, Franco, Bompastor, Abily (Le Sommer 67).

*Referee:* Teodora Albon (Romania).

# WOMEN'S WORLD CUP CANADA 2015

## EUROPEAN QUALIFICATION

**GROUP A – MALTA**

| | |
|---|---|
| Albania v Malta | 1-1 |
| Luxembourg v Latvia | 0-0 |
| Albania v Latvia | 2-0 |
| Malta v Luxembourg | 6-0 |
| Luxembourg v Albania | 1-2 |
| Latvia v Malta | 0-2 |

| Group A Table | P | W | D | L | F | A | GD | Pts |
|---|---|---|---|---|---|---|---|---|
| Malta | 3 | 2 | 1 | 0 | 9 | 1 | 8 | 7 |
| Albania | 3 | 2 | 1 | 0 | 5 | 2 | 3 | 7 |
| Latvia | 3 | 0 | 1 | 2 | 0 | 4 | -4 | 1 |
| Luxembourg | 3 | 0 | 1 | 2 | 1 | 8 | -7 | 1 |

**GROUP B – LITHUANIA**

| | |
|---|---|
| Faroe Islands v Montenegro | 3-3 |
| Georgia v Lithuania | 4-3 |
| Georgia v Montenegro | 0-2 |
| Lithuania v Faroe Islands | 0-1 |
| Faroe Islands v Georgia | 2-1 |
| Montenegro v Lithuania | 1-1 |

| Group B Table | P | W | D | L | F | A | GD | Pts |
|---|---|---|---|---|---|---|---|---|
| Faroe Islands | 3 | 2 | 1 | 0 | 6 | 4 | 2 | 7 |
| Montenegro | 3 | 1 | 2 | 0 | 6 | 4 | 2 | 5 |
| Georgia | 3 | 1 | 0 | 2 | 5 | 7 | -2 | 3 |
| Lithuania | 3 | 0 | 1 | 2 | 4 | 6 | -2 | 1 |

**QUALIFYING GROUP STAGE**

The qualifying group matches will be played between 20 September 2013 and 17 September 2014. The seven group winners and four runners-up with the best records will qualify from Europe for the finals in Canada.

**GROUP 1**
Germany
Russia
Republic of Ireland
Slovakia
Sovenia
Croatia

**GROUP 2**
Italy
Spain
Czech Republic
Romania
Estonia
Macedonia

**GROUP 3**
Denmark
Iceland
Switzerland
Serbia
Israel
Malta

**GROUP 4**
Sweden
Scotland
Poland
Northern Ireland
Bosnia & Herzegovina
Faroe Islands

**GROUP 5**
Norway
Holland
Belgium
Portugal
Greece
Albania

**GROUP 6**
England
Ukraine
Belarus
Wales
Turkey
Montenegro

**GROUP 7**
France
Finland
Austria
Hungary
Bulgaria
Kazakhstan

# WOMEN'S EUROPEAN CHAMPIONSHIP 2011–13

## PRELIMINARY ROUND

### GROUP 1

| | |
|---|---|
| Lithuania v Macedonia | 1-1 |
| Luxembourg v Latvia | 2-0 |
| Luxembourg v Macedonia | 1-5 |
| Latvia v Lithuania | 1-0 |
| Lithuania v Luxembourg | 4-1 |
| Macedonia v Latvia | 1-0 |

| Group 1 Table | P | W | D | L | F | A | GD | Pts |
|---|---|---|---|---|---|---|---|---|
| Macedonia | 3 | 2 | 1 | 0 | 7 | 2 | 5 | 7 |
| Lithuania | 3 | 1 | 1 | 1 | 5 | 3 | 2 | 4 |
| Luxembourg | 3 | 1 | 0 | 2 | 4 | 9 | –5 | 3 |
| Latvia | 3 | 1 | 0 | 2 | 1 | 3 | –2 | 3 |

### GROUP 2

| | |
|---|---|
| Georgia v Malta | 0-1 |
| Faroe Islands v Armenia | 0-1 |
| Armenia v Georgia | 0-0 |
| Faroe Islands v Malta | 2-0 |
| Malta v Armenia | 1-1 |
| Georgia v Faroe Islands | 1-0 |

| Group 2 Table | P | W | D | L | F | A | GD | Pts |
|---|---|---|---|---|---|---|---|---|
| Armenia | 3 | 1 | 2 | 0 | 2 | 1 | 1 | 5 |
| Malta | 3 | 1 | 1 | 1 | 2 | 3 | –1 | 4 |
| Georgia | 3 | 1 | 1 | 1 | 1 | 1 | 0 | 4 |
| Faroe Islands | 3 | 1 | 0 | 2 | 2 | 2 | 0 | 3 |

## QUALIFYING GROUP STAGE

### GROUP 1

| | |
|---|---|
| Bosnia & Herzegovina v Italy | 0-1 |
| Poland v Russia | 0-2 |
| *Russia awarded 3-0 victory by default.* | |
| Russia v Bosnia & Herzegovina | 4-1 |
| Macedonia v Italy | 0-9 |
| Poland v Greece | 2-0 |
| Macedonia v Greece | 1-1 |
| Italy v Russia | 2-0 |
| Poland v Bosnia & Herzegovina | 4-0 |
| Macedonia v Bosnia & Herzegovina | 2-6 |
| Greece v Russia | 0-4 |
| Poland v Italy | 0-5 |
| Macedonia v Poland | 0-3 |
| Italy v Greece | 2-0 |
| Greece v Bosnia & Herzegovina | 2-3 |
| Russia v Macedonia | 8-0 |
| Greece v Poland | 1-1 |
| Italy v Bosnia & Herzegovina | 4-0 |
| Russia v Italy | 0-2 |
| Greece v Macedonia | 2-2 |
| Italy v Macedonia | 9-0 |
| Russia v Greece | 4-0 |
| Bosnia & Herzegovina v Poland | 0-2 |
| Poland v Macedonia | 4-0 |
| Bosnia & Herzegovina v Russia | 0-1 |
| Macedonia v Russia | 0-6 |
| Bosnia & Herzegovina v Greece | 1-1 |
| Italy v Poland | 1-0 |
| Greece v Italy | 0-0 |
| Bosnia & Herzegovina v Macedonia | 1-0 |
| Russia v Poland | 1-0 |

| Group 1 Table | P | W | D | L | F | A | GD | Pts |
|---|---|---|---|---|---|---|---|---|
| Italy | 10 | 9 | 1 | 0 | 35 | 0 | 35 | 28 |
| Russia | 10 | 7 | 1 | 2 | 31 | 6 | 25 | 22 |
| Poland | 10 | 5 | 2 | 3 | 17 | 11 | 6 | 17 |
| Bosnia & Herzegovina | 10 | 3 | 1 | 6 | 12 | 21 | –9 | 10 |
| Greece | 10 | 0 | 5 | 5 | 7 | 20 | –13 | 5 |
| Macedonia | 10 | 0 | 2 | 8 | 5 | 49 | –44 | 2 |

### GROUP 2

| | |
|---|---|
| Kazakhstan v Romania | 0-3 |
| Germany v Switzerland | 4-1 |
| Turkey v Spain | 1-10 |
| Switzerland v Romania | 4-1 |
| Kazakhstan v Turkey | 2-0 |
| Turkey v Kazakhstan | 0-0 |
| Romania v Germany | 0-3 |
| Spain v Switzerland | 3-2 |
| Kazakhstan v Spain | 0-4 |
| Romania v Turkey | 7-1 |
| Germany v Kazakhstan | 17-0 |
| Romania v Spain | 0-4 |
| Turkey v Romania | 1-2 |
| Switzerland v Kazakhstan | 8-1 |
| Spain v Germany | 2-2 |
| Turkey v Germany | 0-5 |
| Romania v Kazakhstan | 3-0 |
| Germany v Spain | 5-0 |
| Switzerland v Turkey | 5-0 |
| Spain v Kazakhstan | 13-0 |
| Switzerland v Germany | 0-6 |
| Germany v Romania | 5-0 |
| Switzerland v Spain | 4-3 |
| Spain v Turkey | 4-0 |
| Romania v Switzerland | 4-2 |
| Kazakhstan v Germany | 0-7 |
| Turkey v Switzerland | 1-3 |
| Kazakhstan v Switzerland | 1-0 |
| Germany v Turkey | 10-0 |
| Spain v Romania | 0-0 |

| Group 2 Table | P | W | D | L | F | A | GD | Pts |
|---|---|---|---|---|---|---|---|---|
| Germany | 10 | 9 | 1 | 0 | 64 | 3 | 61 | 28 |
| Spain | 10 | 6 | 2 | 2 | 43 | 14 | 29 | 20 |
| Romania | 10 | 5 | 1 | 4 | 20 | 20 | 0 | 16 |
| Switzerland | 10 | 5 | 0 | 5 | 29 | 24 | 5 | 15 |
| Kazakhstan | 10 | 2 | 1 | 7 | 4 | 55 | –51 | 7 |
| Turkey | 10 | 0 | 1 | 9 | 4 | 48 | –44 | 1 |

### GROUP 3

| | |
|---|---|
| Iceland v Bulgaria | 6-0 |
| Belgium v Hungary | 2-1 |
| Iceland v Norway | 3-1 |
| Norway v Hungary | 6-0 |
| Iceland v Belgium | 0-0 |
| Hungary v Iceland | 0-1 |
| Bulgaria v Northern Ireland | 0-6 |
| Belgium v Norway | 1-1 |
| Northern Ireland v Iceland | 0-2 |
| Bulgaria v Hungary | 0-4 |
| Belgium v Bulgaria | 5-0 |
| Northern Ireland v Norway | 3-1 |
| Bulgaria v Belgium | 0-1 |
| Hungary v Northern Ireland | 2-2 |
| Belgium v Northern Ireland | 2-2 |
| Bulgaria v Norway | 0-3 |
| Hungary v Norway | 0-5 |
| Belgium v Iceland | 1-0 |
| Northern Ireland v Hungary | 0-1 |
| Northern Ireland v Bulgaria | 4-1 |
| Norway v Bulgaria | 11-0 |
| Iceland v Hungary | 3-0 |
| Hungary v Belgium | 1-3 |
| Norway v Northern Ireland | 2-0 |
| Bulgaria v Iceland | 0-10 |
| Norway v Belgium | 3-2 |
| Iceland v Northern Ireland | 2-0 |
| Hungary v Bulgaria | 9-0 |
| Northern Ireland v Belgium | 0-2 |
| Norway v Iceland | 2-1 |

| Group 3 Table | P | W | D | L | F | A | GD | Pts |
|---|---|---|---|---|---|---|---|---|
| Norway | 10 | 8 | 0 | 2 | 35 | 9 | 26 | 24 |
| Iceland | 10 | 7 | 1 | 2 | 28 | 4 | 24 | 22 |
| Belgium | 10 | 6 | 2 | 2 | 18 | 8 | 10 | 20 |
| Northern Ireland | 10 | 3 | 2 | 5 | 12 | 15 | –3 | 11 |
| Hungary | 10 | 3 | 1 | 6 | 18 | 22 | –4 | 10 |
| Bulgaria | 10 | 0 | 0 | 10 | 1 | 54 | –53 | 0 |

### GROUP 4

| | |
|---|---|
| Israel v France | 0-5 |
| Wales v Republic of Ireland | 0-2 |
| Republic of Ireland v France | 1-3 |
| Israel v Scotland | 1-6 |
| Republic of Ireland v Israel | 2-0 |
| Wales v France | 1-4 |
| France v Israel | 5-0 |
| Scotland v Wales | 2-2 |
| Israel v Wales | 0-2 |
| France v Scotland | 2-0 |
| France v Wales | 4-0 |
| Scotland v Republic of Ireland | 2-1 |
| Scotland v Israel | 8-0 |
| Republic of Ireland v Wales | 0-1 |
| Wales v Israel | 5-0 |
| Republic of Ireland v Scotland | 0-1 |
| Wales v Scotland | 1-2 |

| France v Republic of Ireland | 4-0 |
| Israel v Republic of Ireland | 0-2 |
| Scotland v France | 0-5 |

| Group 4 Table | P | W | D | L | F | A | GD | Pts |
|---|---|---|---|---|---|---|---|---|
| France | 8 | 8 | 0 | 0 | 32 | 2 | 30 | 24 |
| Scotland | 8 | 5 | 1 | 2 | 21 | 9 | 16 | 16 |
| Wales | 8 | 3 | 1 | 4 | 12 | 14 | –2 | 10 |
| Republic of Ireland | 8 | 3 | 0 | 5 | 8 | 11 | –3 | 9 |
| Israel | 8 | 0 | 0 | 8 | 1 | 35 | –34 | 0 |

## GROUP 5

| Belarus v Estonia | 2-1 |
| Estonia v Ukraine | 1-4 |
| Ukraine v Slovakia | 0-0 |
| Finland v Estonia | 6-0 |
| Slovakia v Estonia | 3-1 |
| Belarus v Finland | 2-2 |
| Slovakia v Belarus | 3-0 |
| Ukraine v Belarus | 0-1 |
| Slovakia v Finland | 0-1 |
| Ukraine v Estonia | 5-0 |
| Finland v Slovakia | 2-0 |
| Estonia v Belarus | 2-4 |
| Ukraine v Finland | 1-2 |
| Finland v Belarus | 4-0 |
| Slovakia v Ukraine | 0-2 |
| Estonia v Slovakia | 0-2 |
| Estonia v Finland | 0-5 |
| Belarus v Ukraine | 0-5 |
| Belarus v Slovakia | 1-0 |
| Finland v Ukraine | 0-1 |

| Group 5 Table | P | W | D | L | F | A | GD | Pts |
|---|---|---|---|---|---|---|---|---|
| Finland | 8 | 6 | 1 | 1 | 22 | 4 | 18 | 19 |
| Ukraine | 8 | 5 | 1 | 2 | 18 | 4 | 14 | 16 |
| Belarus | 8 | 4 | 1 | 3 | 10 | 17 | –7 | 13 |
| Slovakia | 8 | 3 | 1 | 4 | 8 | 7 | 1 | 10 |
| Estonia | 8 | 0 | 0 | 8 | 5 | 31 | –26 | 0 |

## GROUP 6

| Serbia v England | 2-2 |
| Holland v Serbia | 6-0 |
| England v Slovenia | 4-0 |
| Croatia v Holland | 0-3 |
| Slovenia v Serbia | 1-2 |
| Croatia v Slovenia | 3-3 |
| Holland v England | 0-0 |
| Serbia v Croatia | 4-2 |
| Slovenia v Holland | 0-2 |
| England v Serbia | 2-0 |
| Holland v Croatia | 2-0 |
| Croatia v England | 0-6 |
| Holland v Slovenia | 3-1 |
| Croatia v Serbia | 1-4 |

| England v Holland | 1-0 |
| Serbia v Holland | 0-4 |
| Slovenia v England | 0-4 |
| Slovenia v Croatia | 1-0 |
| Serbia v Slovenia | 3-0 |
| England v Croatia | 3-0 |

| Group 6 Table | P | W | D | L | F | A | GD | Pts |
|---|---|---|---|---|---|---|---|---|
| England | 8 | 6 | 2 | 0 | 22 | 2 | 20 | 20 |
| Holland | 8 | 6 | 1 | 1 | 20 | 2 | 18 | 19 |
| Serbia | 8 | 4 | 1 | 3 | 15 | 18 | –3 | 13 |
| Slovenia | 8 | 1 | 1 | 6 | 6 | 21 | –15 | 4 |
| Croatia | 8 | 0 | 1 | 7 | 6 | 26 | –20 | 1 |

## GROUP 7

| Armenia v Portugal | 0-8 |
| Austria v Czech Republic | 1-1 |
| Armenia v Denmark | 0-5 |
| Czech Republic v Portugal | 1-0 |
| Denmark v Austria | 3-0 |
| Austria v Armenia | 3-0 |
| Portugal v Denmark | 0-3 |
| Portugal v Austria | 0-1 |
| Czech Republic v Armenia | 5-0 |
| Denmark v Armenia | 11-0 |
| Portugal v Armenia | 6-0 |
| Portugal v Czech Republic | 2-5 |
| Armenia v Austria | 2-4 |
| Czech Republic v Denmark | 0-2 |
| Austria v Portugal | 1-0 |
| Czech Republic v Austria | 2-3 |
| Denmark v Czech Republic | 1-0 |
| Austria v Denmark | 3-1 |
| Armenia v Czech Republic | 0-2 |
| Denmark v Portugal | 2-0 |

| Group 7 Table | P | W | D | L | F | A | GD | Pts |
|---|---|---|---|---|---|---|---|---|
| Denmark | 8 | 7 | 0 | 1 | 28 | 3 | 25 | 21 |
| Austria | 8 | 6 | 1 | 1 | 16 | 9 | 7 | 19 |
| Czech Republic | 8 | 4 | 1 | 3 | 16 | 9 | 7 | 13 |
| Portugal | 8 | 2 | 0 | 6 | 16 | 13 | 3 | 6 |
| Armenia | 8 | 0 | 0 | 8 | 2 | 44 | –42 | 0 |

## PLAY-OFFS FIRST LEG

| Scotland v Spain | 1-1 |
| Ukraine v Iceland | 2-3 |
| Austria v Russia | 0-2 |

## PLAY-OFFS SECOND LEG

| Spain v Scotland | 3-2 |
| *aet.* | |
| Iceland v Ukraine | 3-2 |
| Russia v Austria | 1-1 |

*Final tournament to be played in Sweden July 2013.*

# WOMEN'S OLYMPIC FOOTBALL 2012

## GROUP E

| Great Britain v New Zealand | 1-0 |
| Cameroon v Brazil | 0-5 |
| New Zealand v Brazil | 0-1 |
| Great Britain v Cameroon | 3-0 |
| New Zealand v Cameroon | 3-1 |
| Great Britain v Brazil | 1-0 |

| Group E Table | P | W | D | L | F | A | Pts |
|---|---|---|---|---|---|---|---|
| Great Britain | 3 | 3 | 0 | 0 | 5 | 0 | 9 |
| Brazil | 3 | 2 | 0 | 1 | 6 | 1 | 6 |
| New Zealand | 3 | 1 | 0 | 2 | 3 | 3 | 3 |
| Cameroon | 3 | 0 | 0 | 3 | 1 | 11 | 0 |

## GROUP F

| Japan v Canada | 2-1 |
| Sweden v South Africa | 4-1 |
| Japan v Sweden | 0-0 |
| Canada v South Africa | 3-0 |
| Japan v South Africa | 0-0 |
| Canada v Sweden | 2-2 |

| Group F Table | P | W | D | L | F | A | Pts |
|---|---|---|---|---|---|---|---|
| Sweden | 3 | 1 | 2 | 0 | 6 | 3 | 5 |
| Japan | 3 | 1 | 2 | 0 | 2 | 1 | 5 |
| Canada | 3 | 1 | 1 | 1 | 6 | 4 | 4 |
| South Africa | 3 | 0 | 1 | 2 | 1 | 7 | 1 |

## GROUP G

| United States v France | 4-2 |

| Colombia v North Korea | 0-2 |
| United States v Colombia | 3-0 |
| France v North Korea | 5-0 |
| United States v North Korea | 1-0 |
| France v Colombia | 1-0 |

| Group G Table | P | W | D | L | F | A | Pts |
|---|---|---|---|---|---|---|---|
| United States | 3 | 3 | 0 | 0 | 8 | 2 | 9 |
| France | 3 | 2 | 0 | 1 | 8 | 4 | 6 |
| DPR Korea | 3 | 1 | 0 | 2 | 2 | 6 | 3 |
| Colombia | 3 | 0 | 0 | 3 | 0 | 6 | 0 |

## QUARTER-FINALS

| Sweden v France | 1-2 |
| United States v New Zealand | 2-0 |
| Brazil v Japan | 0-2 |
| Great Britain v Canada | 0-2 |

## SEMI-FINALS

| France v Japan | 1-2 |
| Canada v United States | 3-4 |
| *aet.* | |

## BRONZE MEDAL MATCH

| Canada v France | 1-0 |

## GOLD MEDAL MATCH

| United States v Japan | 2-1 |

# ENGLAND WOMEN'S INTERNATIONALS 2012–13

## EUROPEAN CHAMPIONSHIP QUALIFYING
Walsall, 19 September 2012
**England (1) 3** *(Scott J 21, Aluko 47, Stoney 80)*
**Croatia (0) 0**                                                5821
*England:* Bardsley; Scott A, Houghton, Scott J, Bradley, Stoney (Rafferty 87), Carney, Asante, Aluko, Williams F, Yankey (Duggan 79).

## EUROPEAN CHAMPIONSHIP FINALS (SWEDEN)
*Competition between 10 July and 28 July 2013*

**GROUP A** – Denmark, Finland, Italy, Sweden.

**GROUP B** – Germany, Iceland, Holland, Norway.

**GROUP C** – England, France, Russia, Spain.

## FRIENDLIES
Paris, 20 October 2012
**France (0) 2** *(Delie 59, 82)*
**England (2) 2** *(Houghton 34, Scott J 39)*
*England:* Bardsley (Chamberlain 70); Scott A, Houghton, Scott J, Bradley (Bassett 79), Stoney, Aluko (Williams F 46), Asante, White E (Susi 79), Carney, Yankey (Duggan 46).

Rotherham, 7 April 2013
**England (0) 1** *(White E 90)*
**Canada (0) 0**
*England:* Bardsley (Brown 60); Scott A, Houghton, Asante (Nobbs 60), Bradley, Stoney, Aluko (Duggan 70), Scott J, White E, Williams F, Yankey (Clarke 83).

Burton, 26 June 2013
**England (1) 1** *(Aluko 41)*
**Japan (0) 1** *(Kawasumi 76)*
*England:* Bardsley; Susi (Moore 66), Scott A, Scott J (Clarke 82), Bradley, Bassett (Bronze 66), Aluko (Duggan 82), Asante, White (Nobbs 82), Williams F, Yankey.

## THE CYPRUS CUP
Nicosia, 6 March 2013
**England (3) 4** *(Nobbs 7, Houghton 29, Clarke 33, White E 83)*
**Italy (2) 2** *(Camporese 17, 27)*
*England:* Bardsley; Scott A, Houghton, Bradley (Williams F 46), Asante, Aluko (Duggan 68), Smith K (Scott J 79), Yankey (White E 46), Clarke (Carney 80), Nobbs, Bassett.
*Italy:*

Nicosia, 8 March 2013
**Scotland (1) 4** *(Evans 18, Ross J 48, Little 53, Mitchell 82)*
**England (2) 4** *(White E 40, Duggan 45, Williams R 73, Smith K 77)*
*Scotland:* Fay; Jones, McSorley (Ross L 69), Love (Mitchell 74), Little, Sneddon, Beattie, Ross J, Crichton, Evans, Brown.
*England:* Brown; Houghton, Scott J, Stoney (Asante 28), Carney (Smith K 46), Williams F, White E, Susi, Unitt, Duggan (Aluko 78), Williams R.

Nicosia, 11 March 2013
**England (0) 3** *(White E 71, Aluko 73, Duggan 90)*
**New Zealand (1) 1** *(Hearn 7)*
*England:* Chamberlain; Scott A, Houghton (Asante 46), Scott J, Bradley (Bassett 66), Stoney (Williams F 46), Carney (Unitt 46), Aluko, Yankey (Duggan 79), Clarke (White E 69), Nobbs.

## THE CYPRUS CUP FINAL
Nicosia, 13 March 2013
**England (0) 1** *(Yankey 70)*
**Canada (0) 0**
*England:* Bardsley; Scott A, Houghton (Carney 46 (Clarke 59)), Scott J, Bradley (Susi 46), Stoney (Bassett 69), Asante, Aluko (Nobbs 46), Yankey, Williams F, White E (Williams R 71).

Shelley Kerr and Steph Houghton of Arsenal lift the FA Women's Cup following their 3-0 win over Bristol Academy at Doncaster's Keepmoat Stadium. (PA)

# NON-LEAGUE TABLES 2012–13

## EVO-STIK NORTHERN PREMIER LEAGUE 2012–13

| | | Total | | | | | Home | | | | | Away | | | | | | |
|---|---|---|---|---|---|---|---|---|---|---|---|---|---|---|---|---|---|---|
| | | P | W | D | L | F | A | W | D | L | F | A | W | D | L | F | A | GD | Pts |
| 1 | North Ferriby U | 42 | 28 | 9 | 5 | 96 | 43 | 12 | 7 | 2 | 45 | 20 | 16 | 2 | 3 | 51 | 23 | 53 | 93 |
| 2 | Hednesford T¶ | 42 | 28 | 9 | 5 | 91 | 47 | 15 | 2 | 4 | 49 | 25 | 13 | 7 | 1 | 42 | 22 | 44 | 93 |
| 3 | FC United of Manchester | 42 | 25 | 8 | 9 | 86 | 48 | 13 | 2 | 6 | 42 | 20 | 12 | 6 | 3 | 44 | 28 | 38 | 83 |
| 4 | Witton Alb | 42 | 24 | 8 | 10 | 85 | 57 | 11 | 4 | 6 | 43 | 30 | 13 | 4 | 4 | 42 | 27 | 28 | 80 |
| 5 | AFC Fylde | 42 | 23 | 6 | 13 | 93 | 51 | 13 | 1 | 7 | 52 | 29 | 10 | 5 | 6 | 41 | 22 | 42 | 75 |
| 6 | Rushall Olympic | 42 | 20 | 10 | 12 | 69 | 55 | 8 | 6 | 7 | 26 | 27 | 12 | 4 | 5 | 43 | 28 | 14 | 70 |
| 7 | Buxton | 42 | 18 | 13 | 11 | 72 | 56 | 12 | 4 | 5 | 41 | 24 | 6 | 9 | 6 | 31 | 32 | 16 | 67 |
| 8 | Chorley | 42 | 20 | 7 | 15 | 63 | 52 | 10 | 4 | 7 | 35 | 29 | 10 | 3 | 8 | 28 | 23 | 11 | 67 |
| 9 | Worksop T | 42 | 20 | 6 | 16 | 91 | 68 | 11 | 3 | 7 | 48 | 32 | 9 | 3 | 9 | 43 | 36 | 23 | 66 |
| 10 | Ashton U | 42 | 15 | 14 | 13 | 71 | 66 | 7 | 6 | 8 | 39 | 35 | 8 | 8 | 5 | 32 | 31 | 5 | 59 |
| 11 | Marine | 42 | 16 | 11 | 15 | 61 | 61 | 9 | 6 | 6 | 34 | 31 | 7 | 5 | 9 | 27 | 30 | 0 | 59 |
| 12 | Ilkeston | 42 | 15 | 13 | 14 | 67 | 55 | 10 | 6 | 5 | 35 | 27 | 5 | 7 | 9 | 32 | 28 | 12 | 58 |
| 13 | Whitby T | 42 | 16 | 9 | 17 | 68 | 72 | 7 | 4 | 10 | 27 | 35 | 9 | 5 | 7 | 41 | 37 | −4 | 57 |
| 14 | Nantwich T | 42 | 15 | 8 | 19 | 63 | 76 | 7 | 4 | 10 | 26 | 38 | 8 | 4 | 9 | 37 | 38 | −13 | 53 |
| 15 | Stafford Rangers | 42 | 12 | 15 | 15 | 54 | 60 | 8 | 7 | 6 | 30 | 23 | 4 | 8 | 9 | 24 | 37 | −6 | 51 |
| 16 | Blyth Spartans (R) | 42 | 15 | 6 | 21 | 70 | 87 | 9 | 5 | 7 | 37 | 36 | 6 | 1 | 14 | 33 | 51 | −17 | 51 |
| 17 | Matlock T | 42 | 12 | 9 | 21 | 54 | 80 | 6 | 6 | 9 | 27 | 38 | 6 | 3 | 12 | 27 | 42 | −26 | 45 |
| 18 | Frickley Ath | 42 | 10 | 9 | 23 | 58 | 88 | 8 | 6 | 7 | 31 | 31 | 2 | 3 | 16 | 27 | 57 | −30 | 39 |
| 19 | Grantham T | 42 | 9 | 9 | 24 | 56 | 75 | 5 | 5 | 11 | 35 | 41 | 4 | 4 | 13 | 21 | 34 | −19 | 36 |
| 20 | Stocksbridge PS | 42 | 9 | 9 | 24 | 67 | 106 | 5 | 5 | 11 | 40 | 52 | 4 | 4 | 13 | 27 | 54 | −39 | 36 |
| 21 | Kendal T | 42 | 9 | 6 | 27 | 65 | 112 | 5 | 3 | 13 | 35 | 51 | 4 | 3 | 14 | 30 | 61 | −47 | 33 |
| 22 | Eastwood T (R) | 42 | 3 | 6 | 33 | 36 | 121 | 1 | 4 | 16 | 23 | 62 | 2 | 2 | 17 | 13 | 59 | −85 | 15 |

¶Hednesford U promoted via play-offs.

## EVO-STIK SOUTHERN PREMIER LEAGUE 2012–13

| | | Total | | | | | Home | | | | | Away | | | | | | |
|---|---|---|---|---|---|---|---|---|---|---|---|---|---|---|---|---|---|---|
| | | P | W | D | L | F | A | W | D | L | F | A | W | D | L | F | A | GD | Pts |
| 1 | Leamington | 42 | 30 | 5 | 7 | 85 | 46 | 16 | 2 | 3 | 47 | 24 | 14 | 3 | 4 | 38 | 22 | 39 | 95 |
| 2 | Stourbridge | 42 | 25 | 8 | 9 | 94 | 42 | 13 | 3 | 5 | 53 | 18 | 12 | 5 | 4 | 41 | 24 | 52 | 83 |
| 3 | Chesham U | 42 | 21 | 12 | 9 | 69 | 48 | 10 | 9 | 2 | 34 | 18 | 11 | 3 | 7 | 35 | 30 | 21 | 75 |
| 4 | Hemel Hempstead T | 42 | 22 | 6 | 14 | 95 | 72 | 11 | 3 | 7 | 54 | 36 | 11 | 3 | 7 | 41 | 36 | 23 | 72 |
| 5 | Gosport Borough¶ | 42 | 19 | 13 | 10 | 78 | 43 | 9 | 5 | 7 | 35 | 21 | 10 | 8 | 3 | 43 | 22 | 35 | 70 |
| 6 | Arlesey T | 42 | 21 | 6 | 15 | 70 | 51 | 12 | 2 | 7 | 43 | 25 | 9 | 4 | 8 | 27 | 26 | 19 | 69 |
| 7 | Barwell | 42 | 19 | 12 | 11 | 67 | 50 | 8 | 6 | 7 | 26 | 24 | 11 | 6 | 4 | 41 | 26 | 17 | 69 |
| 8 | Cambridge C | 42 | 20 | 6 | 16 | 63 | 57 | 10 | 4 | 7 | 26 | 28 | 10 | 2 | 9 | 37 | 29 | 6 | 66 |
| 9 | Weymouth | 42 | 18 | 8 | 16 | 59 | 71 | 10 | 4 | 7 | 29 | 35 | 8 | 4 | 9 | 30 | 36 | −12 | 62 |
| 10 | Bedford T | 42 | 18 | 7 | 17 | 61 | 56 | 10 | 4 | 7 | 30 | 22 | 8 | 3 | 10 | 31 | 34 | 5 | 61 |
| 11 | St Albans C | 42 | 18 | 6 | 18 | 81 | 71 | 10 | 4 | 7 | 46 | 38 | 8 | 2 | 11 | 35 | 33 | 10 | 60 |
| 12 | St Neots T | 42 | 15 | 7 | 20 | 77 | 77 | 8 | 3 | 10 | 45 | 42 | 7 | 4 | 10 | 32 | 35 | 0 | 52 |
| 13 | Hitchin T | 42 | 15 | 7 | 20 | 62 | 68 | 9 | 2 | 10 | 30 | 28 | 6 | 5 | 10 | 32 | 40 | −6 | 52 |
| 14 | AFC Totton | 42 | 15 | 7 | 20 | 62 | 84 | 13 | 3 | 5 | 45 | 33 | 2 | 4 | 15 | 17 | 51 | −22 | 52 |
| 15 | Chippenham T | 42 | 13 | 12 | 17 | 63 | 67 | 6 | 7 | 8 | 35 | 39 | 7 | 5 | 9 | 28 | 28 | −4 | 51 |
| 16 | Banbury U | 42 | 14 | 9 | 19 | 60 | 75 | 7 | 7 | 7 | 32 | 31 | 7 | 2 | 12 | 28 | 44 | −15 | 51 |
| 17 | Bashley | 42 | 13 | 10 | 19 | 47 | 63 | 9 | 3 | 9 | 22 | 30 | 4 | 7 | 10 | 25 | 33 | −16 | 49 |
| 18 | Frome T | 42 | 11 | 12 | 19 | 40 | 55 | 6 | 4 | 11 | 22 | 20 | 5 | 8 | 8 | 18 | 25 | −15 | 45 |
| 19 | Redditch U | 42 | 12 | 7 | 23 | 32 | 65 | 6 | 4 | 11 | 16 | 33 | 6 | 3 | 12 | 16 | 32 | −33 | 43 |
| 20 | Bideford | 42 | 11 | 9 | 22 | 58 | 73 | 9 | 6 | 6 | 30 | 25 | 2 | 3 | 16 | 28 | 48 | −15 | 42 |
| 21 | Bedworth U | 42 | 11 | 9 | 22 | 39 | 73 | 7 | 5 | 9 | 20 | 31 | 4 | 4 | 13 | 19 | 42 | −34 | 42 |
| 22 | Kettering T (R) | 42 | 8 | 8 | 26 | 47 | 102 | 5 | 3 | 13 | 28 | 50 | 3 | 5 | 13 | 19 | 52 | −55 | 22 |

*Kettering T deducted 10 points. ¶Gosport Borough promoted via play-offs.

## RYMAN ISTHMIAN PREMIER LEAGUE 2012–13

| | | Total | | | | | Home | | | | | Away | | | | | | |
|---|---|---|---|---|---|---|---|---|---|---|---|---|---|---|---|---|---|---|
| | | P | W | D | L | F | A | W | D | L | F | A | W | D | L | F | A | GD | Pts |
| 1 | Whitehawk | 42 | 25 | 13 | 4 | 88 | 42 | 12 | 8 | 1 | 46 | 18 | 13 | 5 | 3 | 42 | 24 | 46 | 88 |
| 2 | Lowestoft T | 42 | 23 | 11 | 8 | 71 | 38 | 13 | 4 | 4 | 37 | 16 | 10 | 7 | 4 | 34 | 22 | 33 | 80 |
| 3 | Wealdstone | 42 | 22 | 13 | 7 | 70 | 38 | 15 | 4 | 2 | 48 | 18 | 7 | 9 | 5 | 22 | 20 | 32 | 79 |
| 4 | Concord Rangers¶ | 42 | 22 | 10 | 10 | 80 | 54 | 9 | 6 | 6 | 46 | 37 | 13 | 4 | 4 | 34 | 17 | 26 | 76 |
| 5 | East Thurrock U | 42 | 18 | 16 | 8 | 65 | 45 | 10 | 7 | 4 | 33 | 21 | 8 | 9 | 4 | 32 | 24 | 20 | 70 |
| 6 | Metropolitan Police | 42 | 20 | 10 | 12 | 65 | 56 | 10 | 4 | 7 | 35 | 31 | 10 | 6 | 5 | 30 | 25 | 9 | 70 |
| 7 | Bury T | 42 | 19 | 9 | 14 | 66 | 64 | 8 | 5 | 8 | 26 | 29 | 11 | 4 | 6 | 40 | 35 | 2 | 66 |
| 8 | Canvey Island | 42 | 18 | 10 | 14 | 60 | 55 | 10 | 4 | 7 | 32 | 26 | 8 | 6 | 7 | 28 | 29 | 5 | 64 |
| 9 | Margate | 42 | 17 | 11 | 14 | 61 | 49 | 11 | 4 | 6 | 34 | 22 | 6 | 7 | 8 | 27 | 27 | 12 | 62 |
| 10 | Hendon | 42 | 16 | 12 | 14 | 48 | 50 | 6 | 9 | 6 | 22 | 23 | 10 | 3 | 8 | 26 | 27 | −2 | 60 |
| 11 | Kingstonian | 42 | 18 | 5 | 19 | 63 | 62 | 10 | 2 | 9 | 35 | 27 | 8 | 3 | 10 | 28 | 35 | 1 | 59 |
| 12 | Leiston | 42 | 13 | 17 | 12 | 55 | 57 | 7 | 9 | 5 | 28 | 26 | 6 | 8 | 7 | 27 | 31 | −2 | 56 |
| 13 | Hampton & Richmond (R) | 42 | 13 | 14 | 15 | 58 | 56 | 7 | 7 | 7 | 28 | 29 | 6 | 7 | 8 | 30 | 27 | 2 | 53 |
| 14 | Bognor Regis T | 42 | 15 | 8 | 19 | 48 | 58 | 8 | 4 | 9 | 21 | 27 | 7 | 4 | 10 | 27 | 31 | −10 | 53 |
| 15 | Harrow Borough | 42 | 12 | 9 | 21 | 53 | 71 | 8 | 4 | 9 | 38 | 38 | 4 | 5 | 12 | 15 | 33 | −18 | 45 |
| 16 | Enfield T | 42 | 13 | 5 | 24 | 60 | 83 | 7 | 2 | 12 | 30 | 35 | 6 | 3 | 12 | 30 | 48 | −23 | 44 |
| 17 | Cray W | 42 | 10 | 13 | 19 | 60 | 85 | 3 | 6 | 12 | 23 | 44 | 7 | 7 | 7 | 37 | 41 | −25 | 43 |
| 18 | Wingate & Finchley | 42 | 12 | 6 | 24 | 56 | 82 | 5 | 5 | 11 | 27 | 37 | 7 | 1 | 13 | 29 | 45 | −26 | 42 |
| 19 | Thurrock (R) | 42 | 11 | 8 | 23 | 40 | 62 | 5 | 4 | 12 | 22 | 31 | 6 | 4 | 11 | 18 | 31 | −22 | 41 |
| 20 | Lewes | 42 | 9 | 13 | 20 | 59 | 75 | 6 | 5 | 10 | 27 | 31 | 3 | 8 | 10 | 32 | 44 | −16 | 40 |
| 21 | Carshalton Ath | 42 | 12 | 4 | 26 | 55 | 76 | 7 | 3 | 11 | 29 | 32 | 5 | 1 | 15 | 26 | 44 | −21 | 40 |
| 22 | Hastings U | 42 | 8 | 15 | 19 | 49 | 72 | 4 | 10 | 7 | 24 | 31 | 4 | 5 | 12 | 15 | 31 | −23 | 39 |

¶Concord Rangers promoted via play-offs.

# THE FA TROPHY 2012–13

## IN PARTNERSHIP WITH CARLSBERG

**PRELIMINARY ROUND**

| | |
|---|---|
| Slough T v Hungerford T | 2-1 |
| New Mills v Ossett Alb | 1-0 |
| Lancaster C v Wakefield | 1-2 |
| Northwich Vic v Clitheroe | 1-1, 3-0 |
| Harrogate Railway Ath v Bamber Bridge | 2-1 |
| Warrington T v Leek T | 1-2 |
| Farsley AFC v Radcliffe Bor | 1-1, 0-1 |
| Brigg T v Ramsbottom U | 0-1 |
| Garforth T v Burscough | 1-2 |
| Trafford v Sheffield | 2-0 |
| Goole AFC v Curzon Ashton | 1-1, 3-3 |
| *Curzon Ashton won 4-3 on penalties.* | |
| Skelmersdale U v Salford C | 4-2 |
| Loughborough Dyn v Belper T | 3-4 |
| Carlton T v Newcastle T | 0-2 |
| Sutton Coldfield T v Gresley | 0-1 |
| Stamford v Evesham U | 1-0 |
| Mickleover Sports v Romulus | 0-3 |
| Rainworth MW v Leighton T | 3-0 |
| Biggleswade T v Halesowen T | 2-2, 1-4 |
| Hucknall T v Market Drayton T | 2-1 |
| Kidsgrove Ath v Daventry T | 4-1 |
| Brentwood T v Harlow T | 0-0, 4-0 |
| Grays Ath v Aylesbury | 2-1 |
| Walton & Hersham v Maldon & Tiptree | 3-2 |
| Hythe T v Ware | 4-0 |
| Thamesmead T v Burgess Hill T | 1-1, 2-0 |
| Royston T v Aveley | 5-1 |
| Wroxham v AFC Hayes | 3-1 |
| Corinthian Cas v Potters Bar T | 1-2 |
| Romford v Dulwich Hamlet | 3-1 |
| Folkestone Invicta v Merstham | 0-0, 0-2 |
| Northwood v Leatherhead | 0-4 |
| Needham Market v Maidstone U | 3-4 |
| Heybridge Swifts v Worthing | 4-1 |
| Cheshunt v Waltham Forest | 1-3 |
| Sittingbourne v Horsham | 4-0 |
| Chipstead v Waltham Abbey | 0-1 |
| Walton Casuals v Ashford T (Middlesex) | 1-5 |
| Chertsey T v Tilbury | 4-1 |
| Faversham T v AFC Sudbury | 1-0 |
| Herne Bay v Chatham T | 0-2 |
| Crawley Down Gatwick v Witham T | 2-1 |
| North Greenford U v Tooting & Mitcham U | 1-3 |
| Clevedon U v Wimborne T | 2-2, 0-3 |
| Merthyr T v Fleet T | 1-1, 4-0 |
| Winchester C v Sholing | 1-2 |
| Thatcham T v Tiverton T | 0-1 |
| Godalming T v North Leigh | 0-1 |
| Abingdon U v Bridgwater T | 2-4 |
| Cirencester T v Guildford C | 2-3 |
| Didcot T v Paulton R | 0-0, 3-2 |
| Beaconsfield SYCOB v Poole T | 0-0, 1-3 |
| Swindon Supermarine v Yate T | 0-0, 3-0 |
| Mangotsfield U v Shortwood U | 0-0, 0-0 |
| *Shortwood U won 5-4 on penalties.* | |

**FIRST ROUND QUALIFYING**

| | |
|---|---|
| Lewes v Lowestoft T | 1-0 |
| Witton Alb v Blyth Spartans | 4-1 |
| AFC Fylde v Marine | 1-0 |
| Cammell Laird v Kendal T | 1-1, 2-0 |
| Ramsbottom U v Northwich Vic | 4-2 |
| Leek T v Radcliffe Bor | 2-1 |
| Frickley Ath v North Ferriby U | 1-4 |
| Burscough v Wakefield | 3-2 |
| FC United of Manchester v Mossley AFC | 3-3, 3-1 |
| Chorley v Whitby T | 1-3 |
| Prescot Cables v Skelmersdale U | 0-3 |
| Harrogate Railway Ath v Trafford | 2-4 |
| Lincoln U v Buxton | 0-4 |
| Curzon Ashton v Worksop T | 2-3 |
| Ossett T v Ashton U | 1-0 |

| | |
|---|---|
| New Mills v Stocksbridge PS | 3-2 |
| Stourbridge v Ilkeston | 0-1 |
| Grantham T v Bedford T | 0-2 |
| King's Lynn T v Barwell | 1-0 |
| Halesowen T v Gresley | 3-0 |
| Romulus v Rainworth MW | 2-0 |
| Hednesford T v Bedworth U | 3-1 |
| Hucknall T v Newcastle T | 2-1 |
| Rushall Olympic v Woodford U | 3-0 |
| Nantwich T v Redditch U | 2-1 |
| Barton R v Coalville T | 0-5 |
| Stamford v Kidsgrove Ath | 3-1 |
| Eastwood T v Matlock T | 1-2 |
| Chasetown v St Neots T | 3-2 |
| Rugby T v Stafford Rangers | 1-1, 0-1 |
| Belper T v Leamington | 2-2, 2-2 |
| *Belper T won 4-3 on penalties.* | |
| Soham T Rangers v Tooting & Mitcham U | 2-0 |
| Enfield T v Cambridge C | 4-1 |
| Crawley Down Gatwick v Three Bridges | 1-2 |
| Canvey Island v Wroxham | 0-0, 2-1 |
| Chatham T v Merstham | 2-4 |
| Faversham T v Leatherhead | 0-2 |
| Ramsgate v Waltham Forest | 4-0 |
| Whitstable T v Harrow Bor | 2-0 |
| Wealdstone v Chertsey T | 3-1 |
| East Thurrock U v Hastings U | 4-0 |
| Kettering T v Concord Rangers | 0-3 |
| Burnham v Waltham Abbey | 4-3 |
| Thamesmead T v Cray W | 0-1 |
| Grays Ath v Ashford T (Middlesex) | 1-1, 2-1 |
| Wingate & Finchley v Potters Bar T | 2-1 |
| Margate v Maidstone U | 1-2 |
| Kingstonian v Eastbourne T | 2-1 |
| Romford v Thurrock | 1-3 |
| Uxbridge v Royston T | 2-2, 3-1 |
| Bury T v Whitehawk | 0-0, 0-1 |
| Redbridge v Metropolitan Police | 0-5 |
| Carshalton Ath v Heybridge Swifts | 3-0 |
| St Albans C v Arlesey T | 1-2 |
| Walton & Hersham v Brentwood T | 1-2 |
| Bognor Regis T v Ilford | 4-1 |
| Hampton & Richmond Bor v Hythe T | 1-1, 4-0 |
| Hitchin T v Sittingbourne | 3-1 |
| Leiston v Hendon | 2-1 |
| Banbury U v Wimborne T | 1-1, 3-3 |
| *Wimborne T won 6-5 on penalties.* | |
| Didcot T v Cinderford T | 3-1 |
| Chippenham T v Swindon Supermarine | 4-0 |
| Shortwood U v Guildford C | 4-0 |
| Bridgwater T v Hemel Hempstead T | 2-2, 3-1 |
| Weymouth v Tiverton T | 3-0 |
| AFC Totton v Bideford | 2-0 |
| Merthyr T v Chalfont St Peter | 1-0 |
| Bishop's Cleeve v Chesham U | 1-2 |
| Slough T v Gosport Bor | 0-4 |
| Poole T v Bashley | 1-1, 4-0 |
| Frome T v Taunton T | 0-1 |
| North Leigh v Sholing | 2-2, 3-4 |

**SECOND ROUND QUALIFYING**

| | |
|---|---|
| Cray W v Arlesey T | 0-0, 3-2 |
| Kingstonian v Burnham | 2-1 |
| Matlock T v Leek T | 0-0, 3-1 |
| Witton Alb v Skelmersdale U | 2-3 |
| Romulus v Hucknall T | 1-0 |
| Burscough v Ossett T | 0-1 |
| Belper T v Cammell Laird | 0-2 |
| AFC Fylde v Nantwich T | 0-0, 2-2 |
| *AFC Fylde won 3-1 on penalties.* | |
| Buxton v North Ferriby U | 2-1 |
| Chasetown v Rushall Olympic | 1-3 |
| Trafford v Hednesford T | 0-2 |
| New Mills v Coalville T | 5-2 |

| | |
|---|---|
| Stafford Rangers v Ramsbottom U | 3-0 |
| Stamford v FC United of Manchester | 2-1 |
| Whitby T v Ilkeston | 4-2 |
| Halesowen T v Worksop T | 0-1 |
| Soham T Rangers v Ramsgate | 1-2 |
| Leiston v Metropolitan Police | 1-1, 4-3 |
| Uxbridge v Canvey Island | 3-3, 2-4 |
| Whitstable T v Leatherhead | 0-1 |
| Merstham v Wealdstone | 2-6 |
| Wingate & Finchley v Hitchin T | 2-2, 0-3 |
| East Thurrock U v Thurrock | 1-1, 3-4 |
| Hampton & Richmond Bor v Three Bridges | 1-0 |
| Bedford T v Maidstone U | 2-3 |
| Concord Rangers v Enfield T | 0-2 |
| King's Lynn T v Carshalton Ath | 6-1 |
| Whitehawk v Grays Ath | 1-1, 1-0 |
| Brentwood T v Lewes | 3-3, 3-0 |
| Bognor Regis T v Bridgwater T | 3-0 |
| Poole T v Didcot T | 1-1, 0-2 |
| Chesham U v Taunton T | 5-1 |
| Wimborne T v Merthyr T | 1-5 |
| AFC Totton v Gosport Bor | 3-2 |
| Chippenham T v Sholing | 1-2 |
| Weymouth v Shortwood U | 1-2 |

## THIRD ROUND QUALIFYING

| | |
|---|---|
| Cray W v Welling U | 0-1 |
| Gloucester C v Maidenhead U | 0-1 |
| Romulus v Hednesford T | 1-2 |
| Matlock T v Stalybridge Celtic | 2-1 |
| Guiseley v Whitby T | 7-0 |
| Cammell Laird v FC Halifax T | 0-1 |
| Gainsborough Trinity v Hinckley U | 1-1, 4-1 |
| Worcester C v Altrincham | 0-3 |
| Vauxhall Motors v Harrogate T | 1-3 |
| Stamford v Buxton | 0-2 |
| Chester v Worksop T | 2-2, 0-2 |
| Skelmersdale U v New Mills | 3-1 |
| Stafford Rangers v Bradford PA | 3-1 |
| Solihull Moors v AFC Fylde | 2-1 |
| Droylsden v Rushall Olympic | 1-2 |
| Boston U v Colwyn Bay | 3-1 |
| Ossett T v Workington | 2-1 |
| Thurrock v Brackley T | 0-2 |
| King's Lynn T v Eastbourne Bor | 3-0 |
| Histon v Boreham Wood | 1-2 |
| Sutton U v Ramsgate | 3-0 |
| Canvey Island v Chesham U | 1-1, 1-2 |
| Bromley v Staines T | 1-1, 2-0 |
| Kingstonian v Brentwood T | 2-2, 4-1 |
| Maidstone U v Whitehawk | 3-2 |
| AFC Hornchurch v Bishop's Stortford | 2-3 |
| Wealdstone v Corby T | 1-1, 2-3 |
| Tonbridge Angels v Hitchin T | 2-1 |
| Billericay v Enfield T | 3-2 |
| Chelmsford C v Dover Ath | 1-1, 4-2 |
| Leiston v Hampton & Richmond Bor | 1-1, 2-3 |
| Sholing v Oxford C | 0-1 |
| AFC Totton v Basingstoke T | 3-0 |
| Didcot T v Dorchester T | 1-2 |
| Eastleigh v Hayes & Yeading U | 1-4 |
| Farnborough v Truro C | 3-2 |
| Leatherhead v Bath C | 4-4, 0-2 |
| Shortwood U v Merthyr T | 1-1, 1-2 |
| Bognor Regis T v Havant & Waterlooville | 1-4 |
| Salisbury C v Weston Super Mare | 3-0 |

## FIRST ROUND

| | |
|---|---|
| Oxford C v Bishop's Stortford | 1-0 |
| Braintree T v Havant & Waterlooville | 1-2 |
| Maidenhead U v Sutton U | 0-1 |
| Dorchester T v Luton T | 2-2, 1-3 |
| Merthyr T v Tonbridge Angels | 1-2 |
| Alfreton T v Kidderminster H | 1-3 |
| Hednesford T v Solihull Moors | 1-2 |
| Gainsborough Trinity v Harrogate T | 2-0 |
| Wrexham v Rushall Olympic | 5-0 |
| Tamworth v Lincoln C | 3-1 |
| Boston U v Skelmersdale U | 1-1, 1-2 |
| FC Halifax T v Altrincham | 5-2 |

| | |
|---|---|
| Mansfield T v Matlock T | 1-1, 1-2 |
| Stafford Rangers v Southport | 0-4 |
| Guiseley v Brackley T | 3-1 |
| Worksop T v King's Lynn T | 0-1 |
| AFC Telford U v Nuneaton T | 1-0 |
| Hyde v Barrow | 1-1, 0-1 |
| Stockport Co v Ossett T | 6-0 |
| Grimsby T v Buxton | 0-0, 1-0 |
| Woking v Farnborough | 7-0 |
| Kingstonian v Dartford | 0-4 |
| Welling U v Newport Co | 2-0 |
| Ebbsfleet U v Hereford U | 0-1 |
| Chesham U v Bath C | 2-1 |
| Corby T v Hayes & Yeading U | 3-2 |
| Bromley v Boreham Wood | 1-1, 2-0 |
| Billericay T v Cambridge U | 0-3 |
| Forest Green R v AFC Totton | 2-1 |
| Maidstone U v Salisbury C | 2-0 |
| Hampton & Richmond Bor v Chelmsford C | 1-1, 2-3 |
| Gateshead v Macclesfield T | 2-0 |

## SECOND ROUND

| | |
|---|---|
| FC Halifax T v Maidstone U | 2-1 |
| Dartford v Tonbridge Angels | 3-0 |
| Stockport Co v Southport | 1-1, 1-3 |
| Sutton U v Oxford C | 1-0 |
| King's Lynn T v AFC Telford U | 3-1 |
| Bromley v Kidderminster H | 1-0 |
| Forest Green R v Gainsborough Trinity | 1-2 |
| Tamworth v Corby T | 1-1, 4-2 |
| Cambridge U v Gateshead | 0-1 |
| Woking v Welling U | 0-1 |
| Wrexham v Solihull Moors | 3-2 |
| Chesham U v Barrow | 1-5 |
| Hereford U v Chelmsford C | 0-3 |
| Grimsby T v Havant & Waterlooville | 4-0 |
| Skelmersdale U v Guiseley | 2-0 |
| Matlock T v Luton T | 1-2 |

## THIRD ROUND

| | |
|---|---|
| King's Lynn T v Southport | 0-2 |
| Sutton U v Wrexham | 0-5 |
| Dartford v Bromley | 4-2 |
| Welling U v Grimsby T | 1-2 |
| FC Halifax T v Chelmsford C | 3-0 |
| Gainsborough Trinity v Tamworth | 2-1 |
| Luton T v Skelmersdale U | 2-0 |
| Gateshead v Barrow | 2-3 |

## FOURTH ROUND

| | |
|---|---|
| Gainsborough Trinity v Barrow | 2-0 |
| FC Halifax T v Dartford | 1-1, 2-3 |
| Grimsby T v Luton T | 3-0 |
| Southport v Wrexham | 1-3 |

## SEMI-FINALS – FIRST LEG

| | |
|---|---|
| Gainsborough Trinity v Wrexham | 2-1 |
| Dartford v Grimsby T | 0-0 |

## SEMI-FINALS – SECOND LEG

| | |
|---|---|
| Grimsby T v Dartford | 3-0 |
| Wrexham v Gainsborough Trinity | 3-1 |

## FINAL (at Wembley)

Sunday 24 March 2013

**Grimsby T (0) 1** *(Cook 70)*

**Wrexham (0) 1** *(Thornton 82 (pen))*      35,266

*Wrexham won 4-1 on penalties.*

*Grimsby T:* McKeown, Hatton; Thomas, Pearson S, Miller, Colbeck, Disley, Artus, Cook, Hannah (Thanoj 55), Marshall (Brodie 87).

*Wrexham:* Maxwell; Wright S, Riley, Harris, Wright D, Ormerod (Ogleby 77), Morrell (Cieslewicz 61), Keates, Hunt, Westwood, Thornton (Clarke 87).

*Referee:* Jonathan Moss.

# THE FA VASE 2012–13

## IN PARTNERSHIP WITH CARLSBERG

**FIRST QUALIFYING ROUND**

| | |
|---|---|
| Tow Law T v Penrith | 0-1 |
| Continental Star v Ellesmere Rangers | 1-1, 4-3 |
| Harold Hill v Walsham-le-Willows | 0-3 |
| Bush Hill Rangers v Cranfield U | 2-2, 1-4 |
| Canterbury C v Greenwich Bor | 5-1 |
| Cobham v Oakwood | 3-2 |
| Esh Winning v Tadcaster Alb | 3-2 |
| Guisborough T v Crook T | 2-1 |
| Darlington Railway Ath v Eccleshill U | 2-1 |
| Billingham T v Pickering T | 1-3 |
| Thornaby v Stokesley SC | 0-3 |
| Seaham Red Star v Willington | 1-2 |
| Celtic Nation v Birtley T | 4-0 |
| Marske U v Morpeth T | 0-0, 1-1 |
| *Morpeth T won 4-3 on penalties.* | |
| West Allotment Celtic v Thackley | 1-5 |
| Holker OB v Hebburn T | 1-2 |
| Liversedge v North Shields | 2-1 |
| Jarrow Roofing Boldon CA v Brandon U | 7-4 |
| Consett v Alnwick T | 5-0 |
| Hemsworth MW v Nostell MW | 1-3 |
| Atherton Coll v Ashton T | 2-4 |
| Rochdale T v Dinnington T | 1-0 |
| Wigan Robin Park v Oldham Boro | 2-1 |
| Bottesford T v Hallam | 2-0 |
| Winsford U v Abbey Hey | 2-1 |
| West Didsbury & Chorlton AFC v Cheadle T | 1-3 |
| AFC Liverpool v Bacup Bor | 0-0, 1-0 |
| Worsbrough Bridge Ath v Parkgate | 0-1 |
| Formby v Padiham | 5-1 |
| Atherton LR v Kinsley Boys | 1-4 |
| Northwich Villa v Daisy Hill | 0-1 |
| Ashton Ath v Runcorn Linnets | 0-2 |
| Glossop NE v Barton T OB | 2-1 |
| Nelson v Appleby Frodingham | 3-2 |
| Irlam v Maltby Main | 2-3 |
| Congleton T v Rossington Main | 3-0 |
| Pinxton v Ollerton T | 4-3 |
| Boston T v Loughborough Univ | 4-3 |
| Ibstock U v Stapenhill | 3-2 |
| Grimsby Bor v St Andrews | 0-1 |
| Bardon Hill Sports v Dunkirk | 1-2 |
| Arnold T v Thurnby Nirvana | 5-3 |
| Teversal v Radcliffe Olympic | 4-2 |
| Holwell Sports v Kirby Muxloe | 5-6 |
| Holbrook Sports v Birstall U | 7-2 |
| Long Eaton U v Lincoln Moorlands R | 3-0 |
| Harborough T v Barrow T | 3-1 |
| Glapwell v Radford | 0-1 |
| Malvern T v Bromyard T | 3-5 |
| AFC Wombourne U v Shifnal T | 0-3 |
| Pilkington XXX v Wellington | 2-1 |
| Pegasus Juniors v Coventry Copsewood | 4-3 |
| Earlswood T v Alvechurch | 2-5 |
| Pelsall Villa v AFC Wulfrunians | 0-4 |
| Dudley T v Causeway U | 2-4 |
| Heath Hayes v Boldmere St M | 0-3 |
| Sporting Khalsa v Rocester | 1-2 |
| Tipton T v Bolehall Swifts | 2-1 |
| Coleshill T v Stafford T | 2-3 |
| Cradley T v Studley | 4-1 |
| Wednesfield v Bridgnorth T | 0-3 |
| Atherstone T v Gornal Ath | 2-5 |
| Pershore T v Wolverhampton Cas | 3-0 |
| Brocton v Shawbury U | 2-3 |
| Highgate U v Warstones W | 3-2 |
| Stone Dominoes v Bilston T | 0-2 |
| Bloxwich U v Dudley Sports | 4-1 |
| Cambridge Reg Coll v Fakenham T | 0-1 |
| March T U v Thrapston T | 1-2 |

| | |
|---|---|
| Godmanchester R v Rothwell Corinthians | 2-1 |
| Wellingborough T v Bugbrooke St M | 0-3 |
| Cornard U v Haverhill R | 0-11 |
| Ipswich W v Eton Manor | 2-0 |
| Stowmarket T v Stansted | 0-2 |
| Long Melford v Bowers & Pitsea | 3-2 |
| Great Yarmouth T v Gorleston | 1-4 |
| Newmarket T v Mildenhall T | 3-2 |
| Halstead T v Basildon U | 2-0 |
| Stanway R v Debenham LC | 3-1 |
| Felixstowe & Walton U v Kirkley & Pakefield | 2-1 |
| Welwyn Garden C v London Lions | 0-3 |
| AFC Kempston R v Stotfold | 3-2 |
| Barking v Barkingside | 3-1 |
| Haringey Bor v Staines Lammas | 3-1 |
| Kings Langley v Biggleswade U | 1-3 |
| Sawbridgeworth T v London APSA | 1-0 |
| Kentish T v Langford | 0-1 |
| FC Romania v Tring Ath | 3-1 |
| Bedfont Sports v Leverstock Green | 4-1 |
| Codicote v Wodson Park | 1-0 |
| Harefield U v Colney Heath | 0-5 |
| Ascot U v Slimbridge | 1-0 |
| Henley T v Amersham T | 0-5 |
| Cheltenham Saracens v Abingdon T | 5-1 |
| Hartley Wintney v Shrivenham | 0-3 |
| Thame U v Clanfield 85 | 3-2 |
| Westfield v Holmesdale | 2-3 |
| Shoreham v Ringmer | 1-7 |
| Worthing T v Horsham YMCA | 3-3, 0-4 |
| Ash U v Knaphill | 2-1 |
| Mole Valley SCR v Sidley U | 2-0 |
| Crowborough Ath v Guernsey | 2-3 |
| AFC Croydon Ath v Southwick | 3-1 |
| Beckenham T v Corinthian | 3-2 |
| Warlingham v Lordswood | 0-3 |
| Epsom Ath v Camberley T | 3-4 |
| Colliers Wood U v Badshot Lea | 3-1 |
| Steyning T v Pagham | 2-3 |
| Dorking W v Eastbourne U | 1-0 |
| Dorking v Peacehaven & Telscombe | 2-4 |
| Frimley Green v Selsey | 4-0 |
| Hailsham T v Arundel | 1-3 |
| Farnham T v Kent Football U | 3-2 |
| St Francis Rangers v Epsom & Ewell | 2-1 |
| Newhaven v Littlehampton T | 1-4 |
| Saltdean U v Banstead Ath | 1-7 |
| Redhill v Horley T | 1-3 |
| Cray Valley (PM) v Lingfield | 1-2 |
| AFC Uckfield v Molesey | 2-1 |
| East Grinstead T v Raynes Park Vale | 0-0, 1-2 |
| Blackfield & Langley v Pewsey Vale | 4-1 |
| Verwood T v Hayling U | 1-1, 0-3 |
| Almondsbury UWE v Bristol Academy | 1-2 |
| Melksham T v East Cowes Vic Ath | 3-0 |
| Totton & Eling v Petersfield T | 1-3 |
| GE Hamble v Wootton Bassett T | 6-0 |
| Highworth T v Calne T | 0-0, 2-4 |
| Downton v Oldland Abbotonians | 5-3 |
| Swanage T & Herston v Andover New Street | 3-0 |
| AFC Portchester v Hythe & Dibden | 4-1 |
| Team Solent v Whitchurch U | 0-2 |
| Shrewton U v Cadbury Heath | 0-4 |
| Cowes Sports v Brockenhurst | 3-0 |
| Fleet Spurs v Devizes T | 4-1 |
| Warminster T v Ringwood T | 2-0 |
| Laverstock & Ford v Roman Glass St George | 0-1 |
| New Milton T v Tadley Calleva | 1-0 |
| Fareham T v Amesbury T | 6-0 |
| Corsham T v Longwell Green Sports | 1-2 |
| Plymouth Parkway v Gillingham T | 1-2 |

| | |
|---|---|
| Ilfracombe T v Brislington | 0-1 |
| Keynsham T v Sherborne T | 1-2 |
| Tavistock v Bridport | 0-2 |
| Radstock T v Shepton Mallet | 2-1 |
| St Blazey v Wadebridge T | 4-1 |
| Elmore v Exmouth T | 0-2 |
| Buckland Ath v Portishead T | 5-1 |
| Chard T v Odd Down | 0-1 |
| Crediton U v Bishop Sutton | 0-2 |
| Huntingdon T v Desborough T | 1-5 |
| Worksop Parramore v Glasshoughton Wel | 1-2 |
| Willenhall T v Lye T | 0-3 |
| Haringey & Waltham Dev v St Margaretsbury | 1-1, 0-2 |

## SECOND QUALIFYING ROUND

| | |
|---|---|
| Shildon v Liversedge | 3-2 |
| Esh Winning v Albion Sports | 4-2 |
| Silsden v Northallerton T | 2-3 |
| Chester-le-Street T v Norton & Stockton Ancients | 1-2 |
| Morpeth T v Whitehaven | 2-0 |
| Willington v Newton Aycliffe | 0-1 |
| Ryton & Crawcrook Alb v Bishop Auckland | 0-2 |
| Stokesley SC v Guisborough T | 0-5 |
| Penrith v Horden CW | 6-0 |
| Pickering T v Team Northumbria | 3-1 |
| Thackley v Celtic Nation | 2-0 |
| Washington v Jarrow Roofing Boldon CA | 0-2 |
| Yorkshire Amateur v South Shields | 0-2 |
| Bedlington Terriers v Darlington Railway Ath | 7-0 |
| Consett v Hebburn T | 1-0 |
| Kinsley Boys v Rochdale T | 0-3 |
| Glossop NE v Winsford U | 1-1, 1-4 |
| Pontefract Coll v Cheadle T | 1-3 |
| Ashton T v Parkgate | 0-2 |
| Nostell MW v AFC Blackpool | 2-1 |
| Alsager T v Runcorn Linnets | 0-1 |
| Maine Road v Glasshoughton Wel | 4-0 |
| Selby T v Formby | 1-5 |
| Maltby Main v AFC Emley | 0-1 |
| Askern Villa v AFC Liverpool | 1-3 |
| Hall Road Rangers v Chadderton | 2-1 |
| Daisy Hill v St Helens T | 0-5 |
| Colne v Bottesford T | 1-2 |
| Congleton T v Winterton Rangers | 3-0 |
| Nelson v Wigan Robin Park | 2-3 |
| Armthorpe Wel v Squires Gate | 3-1 |
| Harborough T v Boston T | 0-2 |
| Heanor T v Arnold T | 4-2 |
| Greenwood Meadows v Teversal | 3-2 |
| Blackstones v Holbrook Sports | 1-3 |
| Pinxton v Heather St Johns | 1-2 |
| Ellistown v Shirebrook T | 0-3 |
| Blidworth Wel v Ibstock U | 1-2 |
| *Tie awarded to Blidworth Wel – Ibstock U removed.* | |
| Radford v Long Eaton U | 0-2 |
| Anstey Nomads v Sutton T | 1-2 |
| Gedling MW v Kirby Muxloe | 2-3 |
| Lutterworth Ath v Spalding U | 0-2 |
| South Normanton Ath v Graham St Prims | 0-4 |
| Louth T v Dunkirk | 1-3 |
| Blaby & Whetstone Ath v Sleaford T | 0-1 |
| Borrowash Vic v St Andrews | 3-0 |
| Basford U v Holbeach U | 1-0 |
| Leek CSOB v Bewdley T | 0-3 |
| Stafford T v Tipton T | 0-3 |
| Bartley Green v Pilkington XXX | 4-2 |
| Nuneaton Griff v Gornal Ath | 0-2 |
| Bridgnorth T v Racing Club Warwick | 5-1 |
| Pershore T v AFC Wulfrunians | 2-5 |
| Bustleholme v Bilston T | 0-4 |
| Bloxwich U v Shifnal T | 1-3 |
| Pegasus Juniors v Wolverhampton SC | 3-0 |
| Alvechurch v Walsall Wood | 2-3 |
| Causeway U v Highgate U | 3-2 |
| Lye T v Cradley T | 4-2 |

| | |
|---|---|
| Rocester v Castle Vale JKS | 4-0 |
| Shawbury U v Bromyard T | 8-3 |
| Stratford T v Eccleshall | 1-3 |
| Boldmere St M v Black Country Rangers | 0-4 |
| Rushden & Higham U v Eynesbury R | 0-3 |
| Cambridge Univ Press v Thrapston T | 3-0 |
| Stewarts & Lloyds Corby v Raunds T | 3-1 |
| Swaffham T v Wellingborough Whitworths | 2-1 |
| Rushden & D v Fakenham T | 4-1 |
| Thetford T v Godmanchester R | 0-3 |
| Bugbrooke St M v Yaxley | 1-2 |
| Downham T v Northampton Spencer | 0-2 |
| Dereham T v Cogenhoe U | 2-1 |
| Desborough T v Irchester U | 2-0 |
| Wivenhoe T v Hullbridge Sports | 1-1, 0-2 |
| Walsham-le-Willows v Stansted | 5-0 |
| Whitton U v FC Clacton | 3-2 |
| Norwich U v Haverhill Sports Association | 0-1 |
| Haverhill R v Saffron Walden T | 4-2 |
| Gorleston v Newmarket T | 2-0 |
| Woodbridge T v Long Melford | 2-3 |
| Diss T v Halstead T | 3-1 |
| Stanway R v Hadleigh U | 1-4 |
| Felixstowe & Walton U v Ipswich W | 0-1 |
| Hoddesdon T v FC Romania | 7-0 |
| Feltham v Hanwell T | 2-6 |
| Hillingdon Bor v Clapton | 1-2 |
| Potton U v Hatfield T | 1-2 |
| Biggleswade U v Colney Heath | 1-3 |
| Haringey Bor v Hadley | 0-4 |
| Hertford T v Crawley Green | 2-2, 3-2 |
| St Margaretsbury v London Lions | 0-3 |
| Cranfield U v Berkhamsted | 1-2 |
| Barking v London Tigers | 1-0 |
| Sawbridgeworth T v Sporting Bengal U | 4-5 |
| Oxhey Jets v Bedfont Sports | 5-2 |
| Wembley v London Colney | 4-1 |
| Cockfosters v AFC Kempston R | 3-2 |
| Codicote v Langford | 2-0 |
| Holyport v Winslow U | 3-0 |
| Fairford T v Hook Norton | 2-2, 3-0 |
| Amersham T v Carterton | 4-2 |
| Kidlington v Bracknell T | 3-2 |
| Holmer Green v Witney T | 0-6 |
| Sandhurst T v Milton U | 6-1 |
| Newbury v Lydney T | 6-0 |
| Highmoor Ibis v Wokingham & Emmbrook | 1-3 |
| Cove v Wantage T | 1-6 |
| Shrivenham v Cheltenham Saracens | 0-4 |
| Chinnor v Ascot U | 0-1 |
| Thame U v Buckingham Ath | 3-2 |
| Fisher v Canterbury C | 1-2 |
| Pagham v Chichester C | 3-1 |
| Peacehaven & Telscombe v AFC Uckfield | 5-2 |
| Beckenham T v Wick | 3-0 |
| Ash U v Banstead Ath | 4-1 |
| Lingfield v Dorking W | 3-2 |
| Cobham v AFC Croydon Ath | 0-1 |
| Ringmer v Littlehampton T | 1-2 |
| Horley T v Seaford T | 4-1 |
| Camberley T v Colliers Wood U | 1-4 |
| Arundel v Deal T | 1-2 |
| Horsham YMCA v Holmesdale | 4-2 |
| East Preston v Croydon | 0-1 |
| St Francis Rangers v Ashford U | 2-0 |
| Guernsey v Farnham T | 2-0 |
| Sevenoaks T v Chessington & Hook U | 3-2 |
| Lordswood v Raynes Park Vale | 2-1 |
| Whitchurch U v Bristol Academy | 3-3 |
| *Bristol Academy won 4-2 on penalties.* | |
| Fleet Spurs v Calne T | 0-3 |
| Bradford T v Downton | 1-2 |
| Hayling U v AFC Portchester | 5-2 |
| Blackfield & Langley v Bristol Manor Farm | 3-2 |
| Longwell Green Sports v Cowes Sports | 2-0 |
| Horndean v Melksham T | 4-3 |

| | |
|---|---|
| Westbury U v Romsey T | 4-1 |
| New Milton T v Lymington T | 3-1 |
| U Services Portsmouth v Swanage T & Herston | 0-3 |
| Hamworthy U v Fawley | 1-5 |
| Cadbury Heath v Roman Glass St George | 2-1 |
| Winterbourne U v GE Hamble | 0-3 |
| Fareham T v Alton T | 3-6 |
| Warminster T v Petersfield T | 0-4 |
| Newport (IW) v Alresford T | 2-1 |
| Odd Down v Cullompton Rangers | 8-1 |
| Barnstaple T v Wellington AFC | 2-1 |
| Brislington v Hengrove Ath | 1-0 |
| Wells C v Exmouth T | 0-1 |
| Bovey Tracey v Welton R | 3-0 |
| St Blazey v Bishop Sutton | 3-1 |
| AFC St Austell v Ashton & Backwell U | 1-0 |
| Buckland Ath v Porthleven | 7-1 |
| Minehead v Bodmin T | 0-4 |
| Bridport v Sherborne T | 0-3 |
| Street v Gillingham T | 5-0 |
| Radstock T v Saltash U | 1-2 |
| Southam U v Continental Star | 4-3 |
| Team Bury v Brightlingsea Regent | 2-3 |
| Mole Valley SCR v Frimley Green | 0-1 |

**FIRST ROUND**

| | |
|---|---|
| South Shields v Shildon | 2-3 |
| Barnoldswick T v Maine Road | 4-2 |
| Jarrow Roofing Boldon CA v Norton & Stockton A | 1-0 |
| Causeway U v Stourport Swifts | 2-0 |
| Haverhill Sports Association v Ipswich W | 3-2 |
| Wokingham & Emmbrook v Marlow | 0-1 |
| Aylesbury U v Kidlington | 0-2 |
| London Lions v Codicote | 2-1 |
| Oxford C Nomads v Windsor | 2-1 |
| Hadley v Berkhamsted | 4-4, 0-2 |
| Sunderland RCA v Bishop Auckland | 1-0 |
| Newton Aycliffe v Esh Winning | 1-2 |
| Bridlington T v Spennymoor T | 1-5 |
| Thackley v Scarborough Ath | 3-2 |
| Morpeth T v Guisborough T | 1-0 |
| Pickering T v Durham C | 4-1 |
| Penrith v Bedlington Terriers | 1-2 |
| Northallerton T v Consett | 1-1, 2-3 |
| Runcorn Linnets v Winsford U | 1-3 |
| Bootle v Stockport Sports | 3-2 |
| Hall Road Rangers v Brighouse T | 2-5 |
| Bottesford T v Rochdale T | 2-1 |
| St Helens T v Parkgate | 2-4 |
| Nostell MW v Formby | 1-2 |
| AFC Liverpool v Armthorpe Wel | 1-3 |
| AFC Emley v Congleton T | 1-0 |
| Cheadle T v Wigan Robin Park | 1-3 |
| Shepshed Dyn v Blidworth Wel | 2-0 |
| Shirebrook T v Heanor T | 0-0, 4-2 |
| Deeping Rangers v Quorn | 2-1 |
| Spalding U v Retford U | 3-2 |
| Dunkirk v Boston T | 1-2 |
| Graham St Prims v Holbrook Sports | 2-3 |
| Heather St Johns v Long Eaton U | 0-1 |
| Kirby Muxloe v Basford U | 1-4 |
| Sutton T v Sleaford T | 3-1 |
| Greenwood Meadows v Borrowash Vic | 2-2, 2-5 |
| Coventry Sphinx v Bilston T | 5-4 |
| AFC Wulfrunians v Tipton T | 3-0 |
| Westfields v Black Country Rangers | 1-4 |
| Rocester v Bewdley T | 4-0 |
| Lye T v Gornal Ath | 1-3 |
| Bridgnorth T v Shifnal T | 3-1 |
| Walsall Wood v Eccleshall | 2-0 |
| Pegasus Juniors v Southam U | 1-2 |
| Bartley Green v Shawbury U | 0-5 |
| Long Buckby v Northampton Spencer | 0-0, 0-1 |
| Yaxley v Rushden & D | 1-2 |
| Godmanchester R v Cambridge Univ Press | 1-3 |

| | |
|---|---|
| Ely C v Eynesbury R | 2-0 |
| Swaffham T v Desborough T | 0-6 |
| Dereham T v Stewarts & Lloyds Corby | 4-1 |
| Whitton U v Brightlingsea Regent | 0-1 |
| Hullbridge Sports v Diss T | 0-2 |
| Hadleigh U v Walsham-le-Willows | 0-0, 2-0 |
| Long Melford v Brantham Ath | 0-8 |
| Takeley v Great Wakering R | 3-2 |
| Burnham Ramblers v Gorleston | 3-1 |
| Haverhill R v Southend Manor | 0-2 |
| Colney Heath v Sporting Bengal U | 3-2 |
| Oxhey Jets v Hanwell T | 1-1, 1-0 |
| AFC Dunstable v Hatfield T | 1-3 |
| Clapton v Cockfosters | 0-3 |
| Barking v Dunstable T | 0-3 |
| Hanworth Villa v Wembley | 2-0 |
| Hoddesdon T v Hertford T | 3-5 |
| Witney T v Ascot U | 0-2 |
| Thame U v Fairford T | 3-2 |
| Sandhurst T v Wantage T | 1-8 |
| Amersham T v Flackwell Heath | 4-3 |
| Cheltenham Saracens v Ardley U | 1-2 |
| Holyport v Newbury | 1-4 |
| Pagham v Horsham YMCA | 0-0, 0-1 |
| VCD Ath v Erith & Belvedere | 0-0, 2-3 |
| Sevenoaks T v Ash U | 2-4 |
| Littlehampton T v Beckenham T | 2-1 |
| Erith T v AFC Croydon Ath | 3-2 |
| Egham T v Lordswood | 2-3 |
| Lingfield v Colliers Wood U | 1-2 |
| Lancing v Peacehaven & Telscombe | 0-5 |
| St Francis Rangers v Croydon | 0-2 |
| Rye U v Horley T | 3-2 |
| Deal T v Hassocks | 2-0 |
| Frimley Green v Canterbury C | 2-1 |
| Christchurch v Horndean | 1-3 |
| Longwell Green Sports v Calne T | 2-0 |
| Moneyfields v Hallen | 6-0 |
| Fawley v Bemerton Heath Harlequins | 1-2 |
| GE Hamble v Bristol Academy | 3-1 |
| Cadbury Heath v Hayling U | 3-2 |
| Blackfield & Langley v Westbury U | 5-1 |
| Swanage T & Herston v Newport (IW) | 0-2 |
| New Milton T v Alton T | 2-1 |
| Downton v Petersfield T | 2-1 |
| Saltash U v Buckland Ath | 0-1 |
| AFC St Austell v Bovey Tracey | 4-3 |
| St Blazey v Barnstaple T | 2-1 |
| Street v Odd Down | 0-1 |
| Exmouth T v Sherborne T | 1-2 |
| Bodmin T v Brislington | 3-2 |
| Whyteleafe v Guernsey | 2-3 |

**SECOND ROUND**

| | |
|---|---|
| Southam U v Long Eaton U | 0-1 |
| Bootle v Thackley | 1-3 |
| London Lions v Brightlingsea Regent | 2-3 |
| Erith & Belvedere v Frimley Green | 5-1 |
| AFC Emley v Bottesford T | 3-2 |
| Bedlington Terriers v Wigan Robin Park | 1-2 |
| Pickering T v Billingham Synthonia | 2-3 |
| Dunston UTS v West Auckland T | 5-0 |
| Ashington v Sunderland RCA | 2-1 |
| Staveley MW v Brighouse T | 1-3 |
| Barnoldswick T v Armthorpe Wel | 5-2 |
| Consett v Shildon | 2-3 |
| Winsford U v Morpeth T | 1-0 |
| Whitley Bay v Jarrow Roofing Boldon CA | 2-1 |
| Runcorn T v Formby | 2-1 |
| Spennymoor T v Newcastle Benfield | 5-1 |
| Parkgate v Esh Winning | 4-2 |
| Sutton T v Tividale | 2-1 |
| Bridgnorth T v Boston T | 2-3 |
| Rushden & D v Basford U | 5-3 |
| Oadby T v Spalding U | 2-3 |

| | |
|---|---|
| Shirebrook T v Walsall Wood | 2-2, 0-3 |
| AFC Wulfrunians v Shawbury U | 5-3 |
| Causeway U v Desborough T | 2-1 |
| Shepshed Dyn v Rocester | 1-3 |
| Black Country Rangers v Holbrook Sports | 2-3 |
| Coventry Sphinx v Gornal Ath | 1-8 |
| Deeping Rangers v Norton U | 0-1 |
| Borrowash Vic v Northampton Spencer | 1-0 |
| Ampthill T v Diss T | 1-0 |
| Colney Heath v Hadleigh U | 1-2 |
| Oxhey Jets v Cockfosters | 4-0 |
| Peterborough Northern Star v Dunstable T | 1-3 |
| Hatfield T v Ely C | 3-7 |
| Berkhamsted v Southend Manor | 1-2 |
| Haverhill Sports Association v Dereham T | 2-1 |
| Takeley v Hertford T | 0-1 |
| St Ives T v Wisbech T | 0-0, 1-2 |
| Newport Pagnell T v Enfield 1893 | 1-2 |
| Burnham Ramblers v Bethnal Green U | 1-2 |
| Brantham Ath v Cambridge Univ Press | 3-2 |
| Tunbridge Wells v Wantage T | 2-0 |
| Amersham T v Rye U | 1-0 |
| *Tie awarded to Rye U – Amersham T removed.* | |
| Marlow v Kidlington | 2-4 |
| Ascot U v Reading T | 3-0 |
| Croydon v Newbury | 9-2 |
| Oxford C Nomads v Peacehaven & Telscombe | 0-3 |
| Deal T v Binfield | 2-5 |
| Ash U v South Park | 0-2 |
| Littlehampton T v Hanworth Villa | 1-1, 1-2 |
| Horsham YMCA v Ardley U | 0-1 |
| Thame U v Lordswood | 2-3 |
| Colliers Wood U w.o. v Old Woodstock T removed | |
| Horndean v Willand R | 4-3 |
| Buckland Ath v Downton | 2-5 |
| Sherborne T v St Blazey | 1-4 |
| Newport (IW) v Cadbury Heath | 1-0 |
| AFC St Austell v Bemerton Heath Harlequins | 2-3 |
| Larkhall Ath v Longwell Green Sports | 0-0, 2-1 |
| Bodmin T v Odd Down | 5-1 |
| Blackfield & Langley v Bournemouth | 1-0 |
| Moneyfields v GE Hamble | 0-1 |
| New Milton T v Bitton AFC | 1-2 |
| Erith T v Guernsey | 3-4 |

---

### THIRD ROUND

| | |
|---|---|
| Walsall Wood v Wigan Robin Park | 4-1 |
| Rye U v South Park | 1-0 |
| Shildon v Parkgate | 3-1 |
| Spennymoor T v Billingham Synthonia | 2-0 |
| Sutton T v Spalding U | 1-5 |
| Bethnal Green U v Ely C | 1-3 |
| Guernsey v Erith & Belvedere | 4-0 |
| Thackley v Wisbech T | 2-4 |
| Ashington v Rushden & D | 2-1 |
| Rocester v Long Eaton U | 2-1 |
| Brighouse T v Holbrook Sports | 4-1 |
| AFC Wulfrunians v Borrowash Vic | 2-3 |
| Winsford U v Runcorn T | 1-3 |
| Whitley Bay v Causeway U | 6-0 |
| Norton U v Dunston UTS | 0-2 |
| Barnoldswick T v AFC Emley | 1-3 |
| Gornal Ath v Boston T | 1-0 |
| Brightlingsea Regent v Brantham Ath | 2-3 |
| Lordswood v Southend Manor | 3-0 |
| Croydon v Hanworth Villa | 0-2 |
| Haverhill Sports Association v Peacehaven & Telscombe | 3-4 |
| Enfield 1893 v Dunstable T | 1-0 |

| | |
|---|---|
| Hadleigh U v Oxhey Jets | 2-0 |
| Binfield v Tunbridge Wells | 1-2 |
| Ampthill T v Hertford T | 1-0 |
| Colliers Wood U v Ascot U | 2-3 |
| Larkhall Ath v Kidlington | 3-2 |
| St Blazey v Bitton AFC | 0-3 |
| GE Hamble v Blackfield & Langley | 0-2 |
| Bodmin T v Downton | 2-0 |
| Ardley U v Newport (IW) | 1-4 |
| Horndean v Bemerton Heath Harlequins | 0-5 |

---

### FOURTH ROUND

| | |
|---|---|
| Bodmin T v Ashington | 3-2 |
| Rye U v Guernsey | 5-6 |
| Bitton AFC v Shildon | 0-2 |
| Larkhall Ath v Peacehaven & Telscombe | 2-1 |
| Brantham Ath v Whitley Bay | 1-0 |
| Newport (IW) v Brighouse T | 2-1 |
| Bemerton Heath Harlequins v Blackfield & Langley | 3-2 |
| Ely C v Spalding U | 1-2 |
| Gornal Ath v Wisbech T | 4-2 |
| AFC Emley v Hadleigh U | 0-1 |
| Tunbridge Wells v Dunston UTS | 1-0 |
| Ampthill T v Enfield 1893 | 3-0 |
| Spennymoor T v Lordswood | 3-1 |
| Rocester v Runcorn T | 1-2 |
| Borrowash Vic v Ascot U | 0-3 |
| Walsall Wood v Hanworth Villa | 3-2 |

---

### FIFTH ROUND

| | |
|---|---|
| Runcorn T v Walsall Wood | 1-2 |
| Larkhall Ath v Tunbridge Wells | 3-4 |
| Newport (IW) v Ascot U | 2-2, 1-2 |
| Spennymoor T v Bemerton Heath Harlequins | 4-2 |
| Spalding U v Guernsey | 1-3 |
| Brantham Ath v Shildon | 1-4 |
| Ampthill T v Hadleigh U | 1-2 |
| Bodmin T v Gornal Ath | 0-1 |

---

### SIXTH ROUND

| | |
|---|---|
| Walsall Wood v Guernsey | 0-0, 1-3 |
| Shildon v Ascot U | 1-1, 4-1 |
| Spennymoor T v Gornal Ath | 3-1 |
| Tunbridge Wells v Hadleigh U | 2-0 |

---

### SEMI-FINAL FIRST LEG

| | |
|---|---|
| Guernsey v Spennymoor T | 1-3 |
| Tunbridge Wells v Shildon | 2-0 |

---

### SEMI-FINAL SECOND LEG

| | |
|---|---|
| Spennymoor T v Guernsey | 1-0 |
| Shildon v Tunbridge Wells | 3-2 |

---

### FINAL (at Wembley)

Saturday 4 May 2013

**Spennymoor T (1) 2** *(Cogdon 18, Graydon 81)*
**Tunbridge Wells (0) 1** *(Stanford 78)*　　16,751

*Spennymoor T:* Dean; Griffiths, Mason, Dodds, Ryan, Capper, Walton (Stephenson 73), Graydon, Davison (Rae 75), Cogdon, Phillips (Peacock 65).
*Tunbridge Wells:* Oladogba; Bourne, Mingle, Fuller (Davey 57), Whibley, Spackman, Pilbeam (Sinden 85), McMath, Irvine, Cornell (Harris 57), Stanford.
*Referee:* Michael Naylor.

# THE FA YOUTH CUP 2012–13

## PRELIMINARY ROUND

| | |
|---|---|
| Altrincham v Macclesfield T | 1-2 |
| Thurrock v Witham T | 1-0 |
| Salisbury C v Moneyfields | 5-0 |
| Chelmsford C v Waltham Abbey | 3-0 |
| Potters Bar v St Margaretsbury | 2-0 |
| Dartford v Welling U | 1-2 |
| Hatfield T v Royston T | 0-5 |
| Salford C v Vauxhall Motors | 2-3 |
| Stratford T v Newcastle T | 2-3 |
| Cornard U v Norwich U | 3-0 |
| AFC Kempston R v AFC Dunstable | 2-1 |
| Peterborough Northern Star v Rushden & Higham U | 3-1 |
| Bowers & Pitsea v Boreham Wood | 1-6 |
| AFC Hornchurch v Brentwood T | 0-6 |
| Northwood v Harefield U | 1-1 |
| *Northwood won 8-7 on penalties.* | |
| Colliers Wood U v St Francis Rangers | 3-1 |
| Eastbourne Bor v Sittingbourne | 2-1 |
| Shoreham v Leatherhead | 0-6 |
| Horsham v Burgess Hill T | 1-4 |
| Chesham U v Windsor | 0-1 |
| Fleet T v Thame U | 1-1 |
| *Thame U won 3-0 on penalties.* | |
| Elmore v Tiverton T | 0-3 |
| Weston Super M v Gloucester C | 4-1 |
| Frome T v Odd Down | 1-5 |
| Earlswood T v Solihull Moors | 1-2 |
| Clapton w.o. v Stansted withdrawn | |
| Hanworth Villa v North Greenford U | 3-1 |
| Thamesmead T v Margate | 2-2 |
| *Thamesmead T won 6-5 on penalties.* | |
| Corinthian v Chipstead | 2-1 |
| Aylesbury v Binfield | 5-2 |
| Flackwell Heath v Thatcham T | 2-5 |
| Sholing v Dorchester T | 2-0 |
| Nantwich T v Runcorn Linnets | 3-9 |
| North Leigh v Didcot T | 2-4 |
| Harrogate T v Ossett Alb | 5-2 |
| Buxton v Ibstock U | 2-1 |
| Retford U v Holwell Sports | 1-2 |
| Teversal v Blaby & Whetstone Ath | 2-4 |
| Walsall Wood v Lye T | 2-1 |
| Hednesford T v Hereford U | 1-2 |
| Cradley T v Atherstone T | 2-4 |
| Highgate U v Chasetown | 1-4 |
| Halesowen T v Rugby T | 2-5 |
| Nuneaton Griff v Racing Club Warwick | 4-0 |
| Eccleshall v Gornal Ath | 1-4 |
| Pegasus Juniors v Stone Dominoes | 4-0 |
| Stowmarket T v Cambridge U | 0-13 |
| Needham Market v Fakenham T | 5-1 |
| Bedford T v Stewarts & Lloyds Corby | 2-1 |
| Southend Manor v Kings Langley | 4-1 |
| Halstead T v Hoddesdon T | 1-3 |
| Cheshunt v Barking | 0-0 |
| *Cheshunt won 6-5 on penalties.* | |
| Hitchin T v Tilbury | 2-4 |
| St Albans C v Romford | 4-2 |
| Sawbridgeworth T v Leverstock Green | 4-1 |
| Bishop's Stortford v Ware | 2-0 |
| Hampton & Richmond Bor v Uxbridge | 1-4 |
| Maidstone U v Redhill | 13-0 |
| Erith & Belvedere v Saltdean U | 2-0 |
| Horley T v Folkestone Invicta | 2-5 |
| Ebbsfleet U v Fisher | 6-7 |
| Molesey v Three Bridges | 2-1 |
| Ashford U v Cray W | 0-4 |
| Farnham T v Lancing | 5-2 |
| Dorking v Crawley Down Gatwick | 2-1 |
| Farnborough v Hartley Wintney | 2-1 |
| Maidenhead U v Fleet Spurs | 2-0 |
| Burnham v Ascot U | 4-7 |
| Marlow v Banbury U | 1-3 |
| Forest Green R v Bishop's Cleeve | 3-1 |

| | |
|---|---|
| Marine v Stalybridge Celtic | 2-4 |
| Ashton T v Southport | 1-0 |
| Grimsby T v Pontefract Coll | 9-1 |
| Spalding U v Oadby T | 0-10 |
| Oxhey Jets v Hullbridge Sports | 7-0 |
| East Thurrock U v Billericay T | 0-2 |
| Colney Heath v FC Clacton | 2-1 |
| Dulwich Hamlet v Metropolitan Police | 6-0 |
| Westfield v Erith T | 0-3 |
| Bournemouth v AFC Portchester | 2-1 |
| Cirencester T v Hengrove Ath | 3-2 |
| North Ferriby v Hall Road Rangers | 1-2 |
| Glossop NE v Mansfield T | 0-3 |
| Concord Rangers v Redbridge | 2-5 |
| Bristol Academy v Bishop Sutton | 1-0 |
| Wingate & Finchley v Bedfont Sports | 12-1 |
| Sevenoaks T v Dover Ath | 4-3 |
| Reading T v Sandhurst T | 8-0 |
| Chard T v Taunton T | 3-0 |
| Radstock T v Bristol Manor Farm | 1-3 |
| Bury T v Swaffham T | 9-0 |
| Wivenhoe T v Heybridge Swifts | 0-3 |
| Tonbridge Angels v South Park | 1-2 |
| Tooting & Mitcham U v Ramsgate | 1-0 |
| Faversham T v Bromley | 5-2 |
| Hastings U v Sutton U | 1-5 |
| Carshalton Ath v Lewes | 5-4 |
| Eastbourne T v VCD Ath | 2-6 |
| Kingstonian v Crowborough Ath | 1-7 |
| Cove v Oxford C | 3-11 |
| Chippenham T v Gillingham T | 1-0 |
| Larkhall Ath v Wells C | 2-3 |
| Boldmere St M w.o. v Coventry Copsewood withdrawn | |
| Godalming T v Walton & Hersham | 3-1 |
| Cheltenham Saracens v Bath C | 1-2 |
| Lydney T v Mangotsfield U | 1-2 |
| Pickering T v Gateshead | 1-5 |
| Lutterworth Ath v Lincoln C | 0-9 |
| Ilford removed v Canvey Island w.o. | |
| Burnham Ramblers withdrawn v Berkhamsted w.o. | |
| Witney T withdrawn v Newport Pagnell T w.o. | |
| Barnstaple T withdrawn v Paulton R w.o. | |

## FIRST QUALIFYING ROUND

| | |
|---|---|
| Alton T v Ardley U | 6-4 |
| Lancaster C v Stalybridge Celtic | 2-0 |
| Ashton & Backwell U v Cirencester T | 0-4 |
| Mansfield T v Gresley | 6-0 |
| Worksop T v FC Halifax T | 2-4 |
| Rugby T v Ellesmere Rangers | 2-0 |
| Gornal Ath v Coleshill T | 0-9 |
| Coventry Sphinx v Walsall Wood | 1-5 |
| Diss T v Woodbridge T | 1-7 |
| Daventry T v Bedford T | 1-5 |
| St Ives T v Barton R | 3-3 |
| *Barton R won 4-2 on penalties.* | |
| Thrapston T v St Neots T | 1-10 |
| Yaxley v Corby T | 4-3 |
| Stotfold v Woodford U | 2-0 |
| Cogenhoe U v Peterborough Northern Star | 0-3 |
| Langford v Brackley T | 2-0 |
| Kettering T v Leighton T | 1-1 |
| *Leighton T won 3-1 on penalties.* | |
| Northwood v Hanworth Villa | 4-0 |
| Enfield 1893 v Enfield T | 2-1 |
| Cray W v Whitstable T | 1-0 |
| VCD Ath v Folkestone Invicta | 10-0 |
| Colliers Wood U v Eastbourne Bor | 4-1 |
| Camberley T v Leatherhead | 1-0 |
| Pagham v Burgess Hill T | 1-8 |
| Didcot T v Chalfont St Peter | 11-0 |
| Aylesbury v Ascot U | 3-1 |
| Petersfield T v Eastleigh | 1-7 |
| Poole T v Bournemouth | 3-0 |
| AFC Totton v Hamworthy U | 10-2 |

| | |
|---|---|
| Hemel Hempstead T v Redbridge | 2-3 |
| Oxhey Jets v Billericay T | 1-1 |
| *Billericay T won 6-5 on penalties.* | |
| South Park v Lordswood | 4-3 |
| Ashton T v Ashton Ath | 1-3 |
| Lingfield v Erith & Belvedere | 5-4 |
| Burscough v Chester | 1-2 |
| Silsden v Stocksbridge PS | 2-1 |
| Sheffield v Yorkshire Amateur | 1-2 |
| Lincoln U v Boston U | 0-6 |
| New Mills v Holwell Sports | 2-0 |
| St Andrews v Matlock T | 0-1 |
| Redditch U v Newcastle T | 0-1 |
| Chasetown v Malvern T | 6-0 |
| Ipswich W v Needham Market | 2-3 |
| Lowestoft T v Walsham-le-Willows | 2-1 |
| Newmarket T v AFC Sudbury | 2-3 |
| Brantham Ath v Haverhill R | 0-4 |
| Hadleigh U v Bury T | 1-12 |
| Cambridge U v Dereham T | 3-0 |
| Leiston v Soham T Rangers | 1-3 |
| Canvey Island v Royston T | 4-0 |
| Thurrock v Potters Bar T | 2-1 |
| Cheshunt v St Albans C | 3-1 |
| Uxbridge v Wingate & Finchley | 2-1 |
| Dulwich Hamlet v Molesey | 6-1 |
| Bognor Regis T v Whyteleafe | 5-4 |
| Thatcham T v Farnborough | 2-5 |
| Basingstoke T v Reading T | 2-1 |
| Banbury U v Kidlington | 2-1 |
| Bracknell T v Newport Pagnell T | 2-5 |
| Christchurch v Wimborne T | 5-3 |
| Chester-le-Street T v Bedlington Terriers | 0-1 |
| Newton Aycliffe v Whitley Bay | 4-1 |
| Skelmersdale U v AFC Blackpool | 0-1 |
| Runcorn Linnets v Northwich Vic | 3-1 |
| Blaby & Whetstone Ath v Lincoln C | 1-6 |
| Dunkirk v Oadby T | 2-1 |
| Stourbridge v Nuneaton Griff | 4-2 |
| Solihull Moors v Pegasus Juniors | 1-3 |
| Bishop's Stortford v Heybridge Swifts | 5-2 |
| Chelmsford C v Hoddesdon T | 0-1 |
| Clapton v Colney Heath | 4-4 |
| *Colney Heath won 5-3 on penalties.* | |
| Guildford C v Arundel | 0-1 |
| Windsor v Thame U | 6-0 |
| Chippenham T v Sherborne T | 2-1 |
| Yate T v Chard T | 0-7 |
| Bristol Manor Farm v Bitton | 3-2 |
| Almondsbury UWE v Weston Super M | 2-5 |
| Warrington U v Wrexham | 2-4 |
| Gateshead v Ryton & Crawcrook Alb | 8-1 |
| Bootle v Macclesfield T | 1-4 |
| Ilkeston v Hinckley U | 1-0 |
| Havant & Waterlooville v Salisbury C | 4-2 |
| Liversedge v Thackley | 1-3 |
| Romulus v Hereford U | 0-6 |
| AFC Kempston R v Luton T | 0-4 |
| Southend Manor v Grays Ath | 3-2 |
| Tilbury v Boreham Wood | 0-6 |
| Brentwood T v Stanway R | 6-0 |
| Welling U v Sutton U | 3-3 |
| *Welling U won 5-4 on penalties.* | |
| Shrivenham v Oxford C | 3-4 |
| Slough T v Maidenhead U | 0-6 |
| Birtley T v Scarborough Ath | 3-0 |
| Hall Road Rangers v Kinsley Boys | 4-1 |
| Berkhamsted v Sawbridgeworth T | 5-2 |
| Sevenoaks T v Crowborough Ath | 2-0 |
| Woking v Dorking | 7-0 |
| Weymouth v Bemerton Heath Harlequins | 1-4 |
| Bath C v Odd Down | 3-0 |
| Brislington v Mangotsfield U | 1-2 |
| Tiverton T v Paulton R | 7-0 |
| Goole v Grimsby T | 0-4 |
| Forest Green R v Newport Co | 3-1 |
| Prescot Cables v Curzon Ashton | 0-1 |
| Staveley MW v Bottesford T | 2-4 |
| Farsley v Harrogate T | 1-6 |

| | |
|---|---|
| Arnold T v Buxton | 2-2 |
| *Buxton won 4-2 on penalties.* | |
| Southam U v Kidderminster H | 1-6 |
| Histon v Felixstowe & Walton U | 7-1 |
| Rothwell Corinthians v Wellingborough Whitworths | 5-2 |
| Hanwell T v Wealdstone | 0-4 |
| Staines T v Cockfosters | 3-0 |
| Tooting & Mitcham U v Faversham T | 1-3 |
| Carshalton Ath v Thamesmead T | 6-0 |
| Fisher v Maidstone U | 2-4 |
| Worthing v Chichester C | 3-1 |
| AFC Fylde v Padiham | 0-3 |
| Wroxham v Cornard U | 4-1 |
| Hayes & Yeading U v Ashford T (Middlesex) | 0-1 |
| Godalming T v Cobham | 0-3 |
| Bristol Academy v Wells C | 2-0 |
| Stockport Sports withdrawn v Vauxhall Motors w.o. | |
| Dinnington T withdrawn v Brighouse T w.o. | |
| Boldmere St M v Atherstone T | 0-2 |
| Erith T v Corinthian | 2-3 |
| Horsham YMCA withdrawn v Farnham T w.o. | |
| Ringwood T withdrawn v Sholing w.o. | |
| Bridgwater T v Merthyr T | 1-2 |
| Guiseley v Hallam | 5-3 |

## SECOND QUALIFYING ROUND

| | |
|---|---|
| New Mills v Ilkeston | 1-5 |
| Farnborough v Alton T | 3-2 |
| Buxton v Matlock T | 1-2 |
| Runcorn Linnets v Lancaster C | 0-0 |
| *Runcorn Linnets won 5-4 on penalties.* | |
| Bottesford T v Thackley | 5-1 |
| Barton R v Rothwell Corinthians | 7-2 |
| Hall Road Rangers v Harrogate T | 2-0 |
| Chester v Ashton Ath | 5-2 |
| Newcastle T v Chasetown | 0-4 |
| Yaxley v St Neots T | 3-2 |
| Brentwood T v Bishop's Stortford | 2-0 |
| Northwood v Ashford T (Middlesex) | 0-1 |
| South Park v Faversham T | 4-4 |
| *Faversham T won 5-4 on penalties.* | |
| Aylesbury v Newport Pagnell T | 4-2 |
| Didcot T v Basingstoke T | 6-0 |
| Sholing v Christchurch | 2-0 |
| Vauxhall Motors v Curzon Ashton | 3-2 |
| Padiham v AFC Blackpool | 2-3 |
| Atherstone T v Walsall Wood | 3-0 |
| Colliers Wood U v Welling U | 2-6 |
| Woking v Arundel | 3-0 |
| Bath C v Merthyr T | 2-0 |
| Boston U v Dunkirk | 2-3 |
| Rugby T v Kidderminster H | 0-2 |
| Coleshill T v Stourbridge | 0-1 |
| Cambridge U v Bury T | 1-3 |
| Needham Market v Woodbridge T | 4-2 |
| Bedford T v Stotfold | 1-2 |
| Hoddesdon T v Colney Heath | 4-2 |
| Cheshunt v Berkhamsted | 2-0 |
| Thurrock v Boreham Wood | 0-2 |
| Maidenhead U v Windsor | 4-0 |
| Eastleigh v Havant & Waterlooville | 4-4 |
| *Havant & Waterlooville won 4-3 on penalties.* | |
| Poole T v Chippenham T | 0-3 |
| Bedlington Terriers v Birtley T | 1-0 |
| Grimsby T v Yorkshire Amateur | 6-0 |
| Luton T v Peterborough Northern Star | 6-0 |
| Canvey Island v Redbridge | 3-2 |
| Dulwich Hamlet v Corinthian | 5-3 |
| Bristol Manor Farm v Mangotsfield U | 1-6 |
| Macclesfield T v Wrexham | 1-4 |
| FC Halifax T v Silsden | 0-0 |
| *FC Halifax T won 7-6 on penalties.* | |
| Cirencester T v Bristol Academy | 4-0 |
| Southend Manor v Billericay T | 1-4 |
| Maidstone U v VCD Ath | 2-3 |
| Sevenoaks T v Lingfield | 4-1 |
| AFC Totton v Bemerton Heath Harlequins | 4-2 |
| Chard T v Forest Green R | 1-3 |
| Gateshead v Newton Aycliffe | 5-2 |

| | |
|---|---|
| Tiverton T v Weston Super M | 3-0 |
| Lincoln C v Mansfield T | 8-1 |
| Wroxham v Lowestoft T | 6-0 |
| Haverhill R v AFC Sudbury | 0-3 |
| Soham T Rangers v Histon | 0-7 |
| Leighton T v Langford | 1-3 |
| Staines T v Uxbridge | 4-2 |
| Wealdstone v Enfield 1893 | 0-2 |
| Cray W v Carshalton Ath | 0-4 |
| Worthing v Farnham T | 3-0 |
| Camberley v Cobham | 4-1 |
| Oxford C v Banbury U | 4-1 |
| Hereford U v Pegasus Juniors | 3-1 |
| Burgess Hill T v Bognor Regis T | 2-7 |
| Guiseley v Brighouse T | 0-2 |

### THIRD QUALIFYING ROUND

| | |
|---|---|
| Mangotsfield U v Oxford C | 3-2 |
| Gateshead v Wrexham | 3-1 |
| Cirencester T v Tiverton T | 7-1 |
| Welling U v Sevenoaks T | 2-3 |
| FC Halifax T v Bedlington Terriers | 1-0 |
| Matlock T v Kidderminster H | 0-4 |
| Wroxham v Needham Market | 2-0 |
| Enfield 1893 v Bury T | 0-1 |
| Dulwich Hamlet v Camberley T | 0-2 |
| Didcot T v Havant & Waterlooville | 3-0 |
| Runcorn Linnets v Chester | 0-3 |
| Vauxhall Motors v Grimsby T | 0-4 |
| Brighouse T v Hall Road Rangers | 4-1 |
| Aylesbury v Woking | 0-2 |
| Sholing v Chippenham T | 2-0 |
| Dunkirk v Yaxley | 5-0 |
| Chasetown v Stourbridge | 1-2 |
| Cheshunt v Histon | 0-2 |
| Hoddesdon T v Langford | 1-0 |
| Stotfold v Billericay T | 2-1 |
| Farnborough v VCD Ath | 4-3 |
| Luton T v Barton R | 3-1 |
| Canvey Island v Boreham Wood | 2-1 |
| Ilkeston v Lincoln C | 1-4 |
| AFC Blackpool v Bottesford T | 0-4 |
| Brentwood v AFC Sudbury | 2-0 |
| Carshalton Ath v Worthing | 4-2 |
| Hereford U v Atherstone T | 3-0 |
| AFC Totton v Bath C | 2-1 |
| Faversham T v Bognor Regis T | 4-2 |
| Staines T v Ashford T (Middlesex) | 3-1 |
| Maidenhead U v Forest Green R | 2-1 |

### FIRST ROUND

| | |
|---|---|
| Stotfold v Leyton Orient | 1-7 |
| Staines T v Wroxham | 4-2 |
| Colchester U v Camberley T | 13-1 |
| Faversham T v Sevenoaks T | 4-2 |
| Didcot T v Aldershot T | 0-6 |
| Cirencester T v Mangotsfield U | 5-2 |
| Bury T v Histon | 1-4 |
| AFC Wimbledon v Farnborough | 2-0 |
| Hoddesdon T v Canvey Island | 0-3 |
| Brentwood T v Gillingham | 2-0 |
| Oxford U v Yeovil T | 4-2 |
| Swindon T v Sholing | 6-1 |
| Gateshead v Preston North End | 1-1 |
| *Gateshead won 4-1 on penalties.* | |
| Chester v York C | 0-3 |
| Doncaster R v Morecambe | 1-0 |
| FC Halifax T v Scunthorpe U | 1-4 |
| Crewe Alex v Carlisle U | 2-1 |
| Bristol R v Torquay U | 2-1 |
| Bottesford T v Brighouse T | 1-0 |
| Dunkirk v Stourbridge | 1-4 |
| Cheltenham T v Maidenhead U | 8-0 |
| Hereford U v Milton Keynes D | 0-5 |
| AFC Bournemouth v AFC Totton | 1-1 |
| *AFC Totton won 11-10 on penalties.* | |
| Tranmere R v Bury | 0-2 |
| Stevenage v Luton T | 3-0 |
| Burton Alb v Kidderminster H | 2-1 |

| | |
|---|---|
| Crawley T v Dagenham & Redbridge | 3-2 |
| Carshalton Ath v Woking | 1-3 |
| Port Vale v Walsall | 1-0 |
| Oldham Ath v Accrington S | 2-0 |
| Portsmouth v Southend U | 2-1 |
| Bradford C v Grimsby T | 2-0 |
| Hartlepool U v Fleetwood T | 1-1 |
| *Hartlepool U won 5-3 on penalties.* | |
| Lincoln C v Notts Co | 3-2 |
| Coventry C v Shrewsbury T | 4-3 |
| Chesterfield v Northampton T | 0-3 |
| Plymouth Argyle v Exeter C | 3-0 |
| Brentford v Barnet | 5-1 |
| Rochdale v Rotherham U | 2-1 |

### SECOND ROUND

| | |
|---|---|
| AFC Wimbledon v Cheltenham T | 2-5 |
| Oldham Ath v Coventry C | 0-2 |
| Milton Keynes D v Stevenage | 2-6 |
| Leyton Orient v Aldershot T | 2-3 |
| AFC Totton v Canvey Island | 1-2 |
| Stourbridge v Bradford C | 2-2 |
| *Bradford C won 5-3 on penalties.* | |
| Oxford U v Plymouth Argyle | 3-2 |
| Rochdale v Sheffield U | 2-1 |
| Lincoln C v Hartlepool U | 1-3 |
| Northampton T v York C | 5-0 |
| Bristol R v Staines T | 3-0 |
| Portsmouth v Woking | 2-1 |
| Crewe Alex v Scunthorpe U | 5-3 |
| Bury v Port Vale | 1-2 |
| Swindon T v Cirencester T | 6-1 |
| Crawley T v Histon | 2-4 |
| Colchester U v Faversham T | 8-1 |
| Burton Alb v Bottesford T | 5-0 |
| Brentford v Brentwood T | 3-2 |
| Doncaster R v Gateshead | 1-2 |

### THIRD ROUND

| | |
|---|---|
| Oxford U v Barnsley | 1-3 |
| Bradford C v Histon | 2-2 |
| *Histon won 4-2 on penalties.* | |
| Peterborough U v Aston Villa | 4-0 |
| Hull C v Swansea C | 3-2 |
| Cheltenham T v Tottenham H | 0-1 |
| Rochdale v Crewe Alex | 3-2 |
| Coventry C v Bristol R | 0-1 |
| Fulham v Middlesbrough | 6-4 |
| Crystal Palace v Port Vale | 0-2 |
| Northampton T v Canvey Island | 2-1 |
| Brentford v Reading | 1-5 |
| Wolverhampton W v Charlton Ath | 0-1 |
| Manchester C v Sunderland | 3-1 |
| Nottingham F v Cardiff C | 2-1 |
| Derby Co v Gateshead | 4-0 |
| Brighton & HA v Stoke C | 0-4 |
| Hartlepool U v Huddersfield T | 0-3 |
| Blackburn R v Leicester C | 1-3 |
| Birmingham C v WBA | 3-1 |
| Southampton v Everton | 0-2 |
| Aldershot T v West Ham U | 1-3 |
| Bolton W v Portsmouth | 2-1 |
| Manchester U v Burnley | 3-4 |
| Norwich C v QPR | 1-0 |
| Swindon T v Liverpool | 0-5 |
| Millwall v Blackpool | 4-3 |
| Bristol C v Ipswich T | 0-1 |
| Burton Alb v Sheffield W | 2-1 |
| Stevenage v Wigan Ath | 2-1 |
| Colchester U v Chelsea | 2-3 |
| Watford v Leeds U | 0-4 |
| Arsenal v Newcastle U | 3-0 |

### FOURTH ROUND

| | |
|---|---|
| Histon v Liverpool | 0-4 |
| Port Vale v Everton | 2-3 |
| Barnsley v Stevenage | 4-3 |
| Norwich C v Millwall | 2-1 |
| Birmingham C v Bristol R | 1-0 |

| | |
|---|---|
| Northampton T v Hull C | 0-1 |
| Arsenal v Fulham | 2-1 |
| Derby Co v Ipswich T | 3-2 |
| Leicester C v Peterborough U | 4-1 |
| West Ham U v Tottenham H | 2-5 |
| Reading v Bolton W | 0-2 |
| Stoke C v Huddersfield T | 2-3 |
| Charlton Ath v Chelsea | 2-3 |
| Leeds U v Burton Alb | 6-1 |
| Nottingham F v Rochdale | 2-1 |
| Manchester C v Burnley | 2-0 |

**FIFTH ROUND**

| | |
|---|---|
| Liverpool v Leeds U | 3-1 |
| Hull C v Leicester C | 3-1 |
| Derby Co v Manchester C | 2-0 |
| Norwich C v Birmingham C | 2-1 |
| Arsenal v Everton | 2-4 |
| Chelsea v Barnsley | 3-0 |
| Tottenham H v Bolton W | 4-8 |
| Nottingham F v Huddersfield T | 3-2 |

**SIXTH ROUND**

| | |
|---|---|
| Everton v Norwich C | 2-4 |
| Hull C v Liverpool | 0-3 |
| Derby Co v Chelsea | 1-2 |
| Nottingham F v Bolton W | 3-2 |

**SEMI-FINALS FIRST LEG**

| | |
|---|---|
| Liverpool v Chelsea | 0-2 |
| Nottingham F v Norwich C | 0-1 |

**SEMI-FINALS SECOND LEG**

| | |
|---|---|
| Chelsea v Liverpool | 2-1 |

*Chelsea won 4-1 on aggregate.*

| | |
|---|---|
| Norwich C v Nottingham F | 0-1 |

*1-1 on aggregate, Norwich C won 5-4 on penalties.*

**FINAL – First Leg**

Monday 29 April 2013

**Norwich C (0) 1** *(McGeehan 90 (pen))*

| | |
|---|---|
| **Chelsea (0) 0** | 21,595 |

*Norwich C:* Britt; Norman, McFadden, Toffolo, Wyatt, McGeehan, Murphy Jacob, Randall, King (Young 75), Murphy Joshua, Morris.
*Chelsea:* Beeney; Aina, Davey, Ake, Wright, Baker, Kiwomya, Loftus-Cheek, Colkett (Swift 60), Boga, Feruz (Musonda 73).
*Referee:* Neil Swarbrick.

**FINAL – Second Leg**

Monday 13 May 2013

**Chelsea (1) 2** *(Boga 15, 87)*

**Norwich C (2) 3** *(Nditi 21 (og), McGeehan 36 (pen),*
| *Murphy Joshua 76)* | 17,626 |

*Chelsea:* Beeney; Aina (Musonda 72), Davey, Christensen, Nditi (Wright 70), Baker, Swift (Colkett 63), Loftus-Cheek, Feruz, Boga, Kiwomya.
*Norwich C:* Norman; Wyatt, McGeehan, McFadden, Toffolo, Murphy Jacob, Randall (Hodd 90), Morris, King (Young, 81), Murphy Joshua.
*Referee:* Neil Swarbrick.

# THE FA COUNTY YOUTH CUP 2012–13

**FIRST ROUND**

| | |
|---|---|
| Sussex v Middlesex | 2-2 |

*Sussex won 5-4 on penalties.*

| | |
|---|---|
| Worcestershire v Bedfordshire | 0-4 |
| Guernsey v Oxfordshire | 1-4 |
| Northumberland v Westmorland | 7-1 |
| Kent v Cornwall | 3-1 |
| Sheffield & Hallamshire v Nottinghamshire | 3-2 |
| North Riding v Cumberland | 2-2 |

*Cumberland won 4-3 on penalties.*

| | |
|---|---|
| Suffolk v Gloucestershire | 7-2 |
| Leicestershire & Rutland v Birmingham | 4-2 |
| Shropshire v Cheshire | 2-4 |
| Devon v Norfolk | 0-5 |
| Cambridgeshire v Jersey | 4-0 |

**SECOND ROUND**

| | |
|---|---|
| Liverpool v Lancashire | 3-2 |
| Northumberland v Durham | 5-5 |

*Northumberland won 5-3 on penalties.*

| | |
|---|---|
| Essex v Oxfordshire | 4-1 |
| Norfolk v Suffolk | 4-1 |
| Herefordshire v Huntingdonshire | 5-2 |
| Isle Of Man v Staffordshire | 1-4 |
| Bedfordshire v Northamptonshire | 5-1 |
| Somerset v Sussex | 3-5 |
| East Riding v Lincolnshire | 2-4 |
| Leicestershire & Rutland v Cheshire | 2-1 |
| West Riding v Cumberland | 4-1 |
| Berks & Bucks v Wiltshire | 1-3 |
| Hertfordshire v Dorset | 6-3 |
| Kent v Amateur Football Alliance | 0-1 |
| London v Cambridgeshire | 5-2 |
| Manchester v Sheffield & Hallamshire | 4-1 |

**THIRD ROUND**

| | |
|---|---|
| Leicestershire & Rutland v Northumberland | 5-0 |
| Lincolnshire v Manchester | 0-3 |
| Hertfordshire v Staffordshire | 1-2 |
| Essex v Wiltshire | 1-2 |
| Norfolk v Amateur Football Alliance | 5-0 |
| Bedfordshire v Herefordshire | 7-1 |
| London v West Riding | 0-4 |
| Sussex v Liverpool | 0-3 |

**FOURTH ROUND**

| | |
|---|---|
| West Riding v Manchester | 1-2 |
| Leicestershire & Rutland v Liverpool | 1-2 |
| Norfolk v Bedfordshire | 2-3 |
| Wiltshire v Staffordshire | 2-1 |

**SEMI-FINALS**

| | |
|---|---|
| Liverpool v Manchester | 0-1 |
| Wiltshire v Bedfordshire | 1-3 |

**FINAL (at Rochdale)**

Saturday 20 April 2013

**Manchester (0) 4** *(Bezzina 47 (pen), 53, 114 (pen),*
*Smethurst 59)*

**Bedfordshire (0) 4** *(Terry 63, 90, Johnson 85,*
| *Stevens 112)* | 558 |

*aet; Bedfordshire won 4-2 on penalties.*

*Manchester:* Green; Allen, Wallwork (James 82), Callacher (Rattigan 69), Rathbone, Rutter (Smethurst 58), Goodwin, Gregory, Bezzina, Taylor, Poizer.
*Bedfordshire:* Fulton; Terry, Reinsford, Sweeney (Gosling 73), Collins, Norman, Stevens, O'Neill (Brasier 55), Lannon (Danobrega), Caglar, Johnson.
*Referee:* Seb Stockbridge.

# THE FA SUNDAY CUP 2012–13

**PRELIMINARY ROUND**

| | |
|---|---|
| FC Labour v Sportsmans | 0-6 |
| JOB v Queens Park | 4-3 |
| Alder v Lobster | 2-0 |
| FC Houghton Centre v AC Sportsman | 2-4 |
| Enfield Rangers v London Maccabi Lions | 2-1 |

**FIRST ROUND**

| | |
|---|---|
| Windmill (Yarmouth) v Enfield Rangers | 5-0 |
| Britannia U v Highfield Social Club | 6-0 |
| Sungate v El Sol | 0-1 |
| Dee Road Rangers v Hammer | 0-2 |
| Worthing Park Vale v Barnes Alb | 0-2 |
| Sporting Bristol v Kings Tamerton CA | 5-1 |
| Upshire v Torrun U | 6-1 |
| Kelloe WMC v Stockton Rosegale N&SA | 3-1 |
| Hartlepool R Quoit v Burradon & New Fordley | 0-1 |
| Club Victoria Ath v Northallerton Police | 0-9 |
| Thornton U v Hessle Rangers | 4-0 |
| Kirkdale v Nicosia | 2-4 |
| Garston v Alder | 2-3 |
| Mariners v HT Sports | 0-1 |
| St John Fisher OB v Oak Tree Pub | 3-0 |
| Home & Bargain v Larkspur | 3-0 |
| Suttonfields v BRNESC | 4-0 |
| Pineapple v Poulton Royal | 1-1 |
| *Poulton Royal won 7-6 on penalties.* | |
| Eden Vale v St Sebastians | 5-7 |
| *Tie awarded to Eden Vale – St Sebastians removed.* | |
| West Bowling AFC v Thirly | 1-1 |
| *Thirly won 5-4 on penalties.* | |
| Bolton Woods v Drum | 2-1 |
| Salisbury Ath v St Johns | 3-2 |
| Chapeltown Fforde Grene v JOB | 0-2 |
| Paddock v AFC Blackburn Leisure | 7-0 |
| Derby Lane Gym v Oyster Martyrs | 0-7 |
| Liverpool North withdrawn v Allerton w.o. | |
| Bilsthorpe Celtic v Premier Works | 4-1 |
| RHP Sports & Social v Birstall Stamford | 4-2 |
| Whitwick Compass v Sileby Ath | 4-1 |
| Plough Barfly's withdrawn v Loughborough Saints w.o. | |
| Magnet Tavern v T8's | 2-5 |
| Clumber v Sparta Moshdock | 3-2 |
| Wymeswold v Pattesons | 3-2 |
| Travellers v Sporting Khalsa (Sunday) | 3-6 |
| Seven Allstars w.o. v Pelsall Bush 2012 withdrawn | |
| Advance Couriers v Albion AFC | 2-0 |
| Duke Of Rutland v Hundred Acre | 2-4 |
| Punchbowl v Bartley Green Sunday | 2-1 |
| AC Sportsman v Co-op Sports | 4-3 |
| Cube OB v AC Cadoza | 0-2 |
| Crawley Green (Sunday) v Club Lewsey | 1-5 |
| Wycombe T withdrawn v Stanbridge & Tilsworth w.o. | |
| New Salamis v Manor House | 1-2 |
| Bedfont Sunday v Broadfields U | 5-2 |
| Comets Sports Club v North Wembley | 5-1 |
| NLO v CB Hounslow U (Sunday) | 1-3 |
| AFC Donsville v Belstone (Sunday) | 3-3 |
| *Belstone won 5-0 on penalties.* | |
| Rosehill Ath withdrawn v Marquis Rangers w.o. | |
| FC Camberley v Putney T | 5-2 |
| AFC Kumazi Strikers v Ajax LA | 2-0 |
| Knighton Arms v Windmill | 4-0 |
| The Railway Inn v Cutters Friday | 7-3 |
| All Saints v Queens Park (Hampshire) | 2-0 |
| Navy Inn v Lebeqs Tavern Courage | 1-6 |
| Lambeth All Stars v Artois U | 5-0 |
| Coxhoe WMC v Cleator Moor | 2-1 |
| Gadeside Rangers v Rayners Lane (Sunday) | 3-5 |
| Humbledon Plains Farm Nissan v Witton Park Rose & Crown | 10-2 |
| RCA Grangetown Florists v Sportsmans | 2-1 |
| Herrington CW v South Bank (2006) | 2-4 |
| Newton Aycliffe WMC v Winlaton Commercial | 3-1 |
| Dawdon CW v Hartlepool Ath R | 4-1 |

**SECOND ROUND**

| | |
|---|---|
| RCA Grangetown Florists v Eden Vale | 3-0 |
| Hetton Lyons CC v JOB | 5-0 |
| South Bank (2006) v Bolton Woods | 8-2 |
| El Sol v Upshire | 0-1 |
| Sporting Bristol v All Saints | 4-0 |
| Thornton U v Punchbowl | 3-7 |

| | |
|---|---|
| Coxhoe WMC v HT Sports | 0-5 |
| Canada v Kelloe WMC | 2-3 |
| Humbledon Plains Farm Nissan v Newton Aycliffe WMC | 2-0 |
| Salisbury Ath v Nicosia | 4-1 |
| Stanbridge & Tilsworth v Britannia U | 3-4 |
| Rayners Lane (Sunday) v Belstone (Sunday) | 4-1 |
| Bedfont Sunday v Manor House | 4-1 |
| Comets Sports Club v Windmill (Yarmouth) | 3-2 |
| Barnes Alb v Knighton Arms | 3-1 |
| Oyster Martyrs v St John Fisher OB | 5-0 |
| Home & Bargain v Dawdon CW | 3-0 |
| Suttonfields v Alder | 1-4 |
| Poulton Royal v Northallerton Police | 0-3 |
| Allerton v Paddock | 2-0 |
| Loughborough Saints v Wymeswold | 1-0 |
| Clumber v Hundred Acre | 1-4 |
| Sporting Khalsa (Sunday) v Bilsthorpe Celtic | 3-2 |
| RHP Sports & Social v Whitwick Compass | 2-0 |
| Club Lewsey v AC Sportsman | 2-0 |
| AC Cadoza v Seven Allstars | 2-1 |
| FC Camberley v AFC Kumazi Strikers | 0-5 |
| Marquis Rangers v Lambeth All Stars | 2-4 |
| Lebeqs Tavern Courage v The Railway Inn | 4-3 |
| Thirly v Burradon & New Fordley | 1-3 |
| Advance Couriers v T8's | 1-2 |
| CB Hounslow U (Sunday) v Hammer | 3-1 |

**THIRD ROUND**

| | |
|---|---|
| Upshire v CB Hounslow U (Sunday) | 2-0 |
| T8's v RCA Grangetown Florists | 0-1 |
| Oyster Martyrs v Burradon & New Fordley | 3-1 |
| Allerton v Home & Bargain | 5-3 |
| Hetton Lyons CC v Northallerton Police | 3-0 |
| Kelloe WMC v South Bank (2006) | 3-3 |
| *South Bank won 5-4 on penalties.* | |
| Punchbowl v Britannia U | 4-1 |
| RHP Sports & Social v Club Lewsey | 2-5 |
| Bedfont Sunday v Loughborough Saints | 4-2 |
| AFC Kumazi Strikers v Barnes Alb | 2-5 |
| Alder v Humbledon Plains Farm Nissan | 3-1 |
| HT Sports v Salisbury Ath | 3-1 |
| Hundred Acre v Comets Sports Club | 2-3 |
| Sporting Khalsa (Sunday) v AC Cadoza | 6-3 |
| Rayners Lane (Sunday) v Lambeth All Stars | 2-1 |
| Lebeqs Tavern Courage v Sporting Bristol | 2-0 |

**FOURTH ROUND**

| | |
|---|---|
| Barnes Alb v Bedfont Sunday | 0-0 |
| *Barnes Alb won 7-6 on penalties.* | |
| South Bank (2006) v Punchbowl | 3-0 |
| HT Sports v RCA Grangetown Florists | 2-0 |
| Hetton Lyons CC v Allerton | 3-2 |
| Oyster Martyrs v Alder | 4-3 |
| Upshire v Rayners Lane (Sunday) | 2-1 |
| Club Lewsey v Lebeqs Tavern Courage | 3-4 |
| Sporting Khalsa (Sunday) v Comets Sports Club | 2-3 |

**FIFTH ROUND**

| | |
|---|---|
| Barnes Alb v Hetton Lyons CC | 2-1 |
| Lebeqs Tavern Courage v Oyster Martyrs | 2-3 |
| South Bank (2006) v HT Sports | 1-3 |
| Upshire v Comets Sports Club | 3-2 |

**SEMI-FINAL**

| | |
|---|---|
| Barnes Alb v Upshire | 4-3 |
| HT Sports v Oyster Martyrs | 2-3 |

**FINAL (at Burton Alb)**

Sunday 21 April 2013

**Barnes Alb (1) 3** *(Willis A 39 (pen), Gallagher 50, Willis L 54)*

**Oyster Martyrs (2) 4** *(McGivern 21, 45, 69, Astbury 64)*

392

*Barnes Alb:* Priest; Willis J, Crane, Morris, Martin, Dyatt, Willis A, Olufemi (Nicholls 84), Buckle (Gough 67), Gallagher (Mendy 63), Willis L.
*Oyster Martyrs:* Mano; Jones, Agger, McDonaghue, Latham, Astbury, Moores, Porter (Smith G 57), Rooney, McGivern, Rimmer (Forshaw 76).
*Referee:* Graham Scott.

# FA PREMIER UNDER-21 LEAGUE 2012–13

## PHASE 1

### NATIONAL GROUP 1

| | P | W | D | L | F | A | GD | Pts |
|---|---|---|---|---|---|---|---|---|
| 1 West Ham U | 14 | 9 | 1 | 4 | 23 | 14 | 9 | 28 |
| 2 Arsenal | 14 | 7 | 3 | 4 | 25 | 17 | 8 | 24 |
| 3 WBA | 14 | 6 | 3 | 5 | 21 | 21 | 0 | 21 |
| 4 Everton | 14 | 6 | 2 | 6 | 20 | 22 | –2 | 20 |
| 5 Blackburn R | 14 | 5 | 4 | 5 | 16 | 17 | –1 | 19 |
| 6 Norwich C | 14 | 6 | 1 | 7 | 17 | 26 | –9 | 19 |
| 7 Reading | 14 | 4 | 6 | 4 | 26 | 20 | 6 | 18 |
| 8 Bolton W | 14 | 1 | 4 | 9 | 11 | 22 | –11 | 7 |

### NATIONAL GROUP 2

| | P | W | D | L | F | A | GD | Pts |
|---|---|---|---|---|---|---|---|---|
| 1 Tottenham H | 12 | 7 | 2 | 3 | 43 | 22 | 21 | 23 |
| 2 Manchester U | 12 | 5 | 5 | 2 | 20 | 16 | 4 | 20 |
| 3 Southampton | 12 | 5 | 4 | 3 | 24 | 22 | 2 | 19 |
| 4 Aston Villa | 12 | 5 | 3 | 4 | 21 | 22 | –1 | 18 |
| 5 Sunderland | 12 | 4 | 5 | 3 | 20 | 16 | 4 | 17 |
| 6 Newcastle U | 12 | 4 | 2 | 6 | 28 | 32 | –4 | 14 |
| 7 Stoke C | 12 | 1 | 1 | 10 | 11 | 37 | –26 | 4 |

### NATIONAL GROUP 3

| | P | W | D | L | F | A | GD | Pts |
|---|---|---|---|---|---|---|---|---|
| 1 Liverpool | 12 | 9 | 3 | 0 | 31 | 12 | 19 | 30 |
| 2 Wolverhampton W | 12 | 5 | 4 | 3 | 19 | 21 | –2 | 19 |
| 3 Chelsea | 12 | 5 | 3 | 4 | 28 | 23 | 5 | 18 |
| 4 Middlesbrough | 12 | 4 | 3 | 5 | 17 | 18 | –1 | 15 |
| 5 Fulham | 12 | 3 | 2 | 7 | 10 | 20 | –10 | 11 |
| 6 Manchester C | 12 | 1 | 7 | 4 | 15 | 16 | –1 | 10 |
| 7 Crystal Palace | 12 | 2 | 4 | 6 | 15 | 25 | –10 | 10 |

## PHASE 2

### ELITE GROUP

| | P | W | D | L | F | A | GD | Pts |
|---|---|---|---|---|---|---|---|---|
| 1 Tottenham H | 14 | 9 | 3 | 2 | 34 | 15 | 19 | 30 |
| 2 Manchester U | 14 | 7 | 4 | 3 | 16 | 10 | 6 | 25 |
| 3 Liverpool | 14 | 6 | 4 | 4 | 21 | 19 | 2 | 22 |
| 4 Southampton | 14 | 5 | 5 | 4 | 21 | 18 | 3 | 20 |
| 5 Arsenal | 14 | 4 | 5 | 5 | 21 | 23 | –2 | 17 |
| 6 West Ham U | 14 | 4 | 4 | 6 | 19 | 22 | –3 | 16 |
| 7 Wolverhampton W | 14 | 3 | 3 | 8 | 19 | 28 | –9 | 12 |
| 8 WBA | 14 | 2 | 4 | 8 | 10 | 26 | –16 | 1 |

### GROUP 1

| | P | W | D | L | F | A | GD | Pts |
|---|---|---|---|---|---|---|---|---|
| 1 Everton | 12 | 6 | 6 | 0 | 17 | 8 | 9 | 24 |
| 2 Aston Villa | 12 | 5 | 4 | 3 | 17 | 12 | 5 | 19 |
| 3 Fulham | 12 | 5 | 4 | 3 | 16 | 12 | 4 | 19 |
| 4 Chelsea | 12 | 5 | 2 | 5 | 11 | 11 | 0 | 17 |
| 5 Middlesbrough | 12 | 4 | 4 | 4 | 15 | 13 | 2 | 16 |
| 6 Blackburn R | 12 | 4 | 0 | 8 | 11 | 20 | –9 | 12 |
| 7 Sunderland | 12 | 0 | 6 | 6 | 9 | 20 | –11 | 6 |

### GROUP 2

| | P | W | D | L | F | A | GD | Pts |
|---|---|---|---|---|---|---|---|---|
| 1 Newcastle U | 12 | 6 | 4 | 2 | 21 | 13 | 8 | 22 |
| 2 Bolton W | 12 | 6 | 4 | 2 | 18 | 14 | 4 | 22 |
| 3 Reading | 12 | 6 | 2 | 4 | 15 | 11 | 4 | 20 |
| 4 Norwich C | 12 | 5 | 2 | 5 | 18 | 14 | 4 | 17 |
| 5 Manchester C | 12 | 4 | 4 | 4 | 24 | 22 | 2 | 16 |
| 6 Crystal Palace | 12 | 2 | 5 | 5 | 21 | 29 | –8 | 11 |
| 7 Stoke C | 12 | 2 | 1 | 9 | 14 | 28 | –14 | 7 |

## PHASE 3

### PLAY-OFF

| | |
|---|---|
| Everton v Newcastle U | 3-3 |

*aet; Everton won 5-3 on penalties.*

### SEMI-FINALS

| | |
|---|---|
| Manchester U v Liverpool | 3-0 |
| Tottenham H v Everton | 3-2 |

### FINAL

| | |
|---|---|
| Manchester U v Tottenham H | 3-2 |

# FA ACADEMY UNDER-18 LEAGUE 2012–13

## PHASE 1

### NATIONAL GROUP 1

| | P | W | D | L | F | A | GD | Pts |
|---|---|---|---|---|---|---|---|---|
| 1 Reading | 14 | 11 | 2 | 1 | 40 | 13 | 27 | 35 |
| 2 Bolton W | 14 | 10 | 3 | 1 | 38 | 17 | 21 | 33 |
| 3 Everton | 14 | 5 | 4 | 5 | 24 | 20 | 4 | 19 |
| 4 WBA | 14 | 5 | 2 | 7 | 20 | 27 | –7 | 17 |
| 5 West Ham U | 14 | 5 | 2 | 7 | 20 | 27 | –7 | 17 |
| 6 Blackburn R | 14 | 5 | 1 | 8 | 20 | 33 | –13 | 16 |
| 7 Arsenal | 14 | 4 | 3 | 7 | 23 | 32 | –9 | 15 |
| 8 Norwich C | 14 | 2 | 1 | 11 | 21 | 37 | –16 | 7 |

### NATIONAL GROUP 2

| | P | W | D | L | F | A | GD | Pts |
|---|---|---|---|---|---|---|---|---|
| 1 Southampton | 12 | 9 | 1 | 2 | 33 | 22 | 11 | 28 |
| 2 Manchester U | 12 | 9 | 0 | 3 | 32 | 13 | 19 | 27 |
| 3 Tottenham H | 12 | 5 | 1 | 6 | 31 | 26 | 5 | 16 |
| 4 Sunderland | 12 | 5 | 0 | 7 | 25 | 30 | –5 | 15 |
| 5 Stoke C | 12 | 5 | 0 | 7 | 16 | 21 | –5 | 15 |
| 6 Aston Villa | 12 | 4 | 1 | 7 | 20 | 22 | –2 | 13 |
| 7 Newcastle U | 12 | 3 | 1 | 8 | 14 | 37 | –23 | 10 |

### NATIONAL GROUP 3

| | P | W | D | L | F | A | GD | Pts |
|---|---|---|---|---|---|---|---|---|
| 1 Chelsea | 12 | 9 | 2 | 1 | 30 | 14 | 16 | 29 |
| 2 Fulham | 12 | 8 | 1 | 3 | 38 | 19 | 19 | 25 |
| 3 Crystal Palace | 12 | 5 | 3 | 4 | 32 | 26 | 6 | 18 |
| 4 Liverpool | 12 | 4 | 2 | 6 | 25 | 25 | 0 | 14 |
| 5 Wolverhampton W | 12 | 3 | 4 | 5 | 21 | 27 | –6 | 13 |
| 6 Manchester C | 12 | 4 | 1 | 7 | 13 | 26 | –13 | 13 |
| 7 Middlesbrough | 12 | 1 | 3 | 8 | 10 | 32 | –22 | 6 |

## PHASE 2

### ELITE GROUP

| | P | W | D | L | F | A | GD | Pts |
|---|---|---|---|---|---|---|---|---|
| 1 Fulham | 14 | 10 | 1 | 3 | 36 | 17 | 19 | 31 |
| 2 Reading | 14 | 10 | 1 | 3 | 30 | 15 | 15 | 31 |
| 3 Everton | 14 | 7 | 3 | 4 | 28 | 21 | 7 | 24 |
| 4 Manchester U | 14 | 7 | 3 | 4 | 20 | 17 | 3 | 24 |
| 5 Southampton | 14 | 6 | 3 | 5 | 28 | 25 | 3 | 21 |
| 6 Chelsea | 14 | 4 | 2 | 8 | 15 | 25 | –10 | 14 |
| 7 Bolton W | 14 | 3 | 1 | 10 | 15 | 31 | –16 | 10 |
| 8 Crystal Palace | 14 | 1 | 2 | 11 | 21 | 42 | –21 | 5 |

### GROUP 1

| | P | W | D | L | F | A | GD | Pts |
|---|---|---|---|---|---|---|---|---|
| 1 Sunderland | 12 | 7 | 2 | 3 | 27 | 23 | 4 | 23 |
| 2 Tottenham H | 12 | 6 | 3 | 3 | 28 | 14 | 14 | 21 |
| 3 West Ham U | 12 | 5 | 2 | 5 | 16 | 16 | 0 | 17 |
| 4 Stoke C | 12 | 4 | 3 | 5 | 17 | 16 | 1 | 15 |
| 5 Liverpool | 12 | 4 | 3 | 5 | 17 | 19 | –2 | 15 |
| 6 Wolverhampton W | 12 | 4 | 2 | 6 | 16 | 25 | –9 | 14 |
| 7 WBA | 12 | 3 | 3 | 6 | 11 | 19 | –8 | 12 |

### GROUP 2

| | P | W | D | L | F | A | GD | Pts |
|---|---|---|---|---|---|---|---|---|
| 1 Aston Villa | 12 | 6 | 2 | 4 | 37 | 22 | 15 | 20 |
| 2 Newcastle U | 12 | 6 | 1 | 5 | 25 | 23 | 2 | 19 |
| 3 Manchester C | 12 | 5 | 3 | 4 | 26 | 24 | 2 | 18 |
| 4 Arsenal | 12 | 5 | 3 | 4 | 16 | 21 | –5 | 18 |
| 5 Blackburn R | 12 | 5 | 2 | 5 | 19 | 21 | –2 | 17 |
| 6 Middlesbrough | 12 | 3 | 4 | 5 | 23 | 16 | 7 | 13 |
| 7 Norwich C | 12 | 3 | 3 | 6 | 12 | 31 | –19 | 12 |

## PHASE 3

### PLAY-OFF

| | |
|---|---|
| Sunderland v Aston Villa | 1-1 |

*aet; Sunderland won 4-2 on penalties.*

### SEMI-FINALS

| | |
|---|---|
| Reading v Everton | 4-0 |
| Fulham v Sunderland | 4-3 |

### FINAL

| | |
|---|---|
| Fulham v Reading | 3-0 |

# THE CENTRAL LEAGUE 2012–13

## DIVISIONAL SECTION DIVISION 1

| | | P | W | D | L | F | A | GD | Pts |
|---|---|---|---|---|---|---|---|---|---|
| 1 | Shrewsbury T | 8 | 5 | 1 | 2 | 18 | 6 | 12 | 16 |
| 2 | Chesterfield | 8 | 5 | 1 | 2 | 21 | 12 | 9 | 16 |
| 3 | Hull C | 8 | 5 | 1 | 2 | 14 | 8 | 6 | 16 |
| 4 | Rotherham U | 8 | 3 | 2 | 3 | 17 | 13 | 4 | 11 |
| 5 | Hartlepool U | 8 | 3 | 2 | 3 | 10 | 9 | 1 | 11 |
| 6 | Walsall | 8 | 2 | 4 | 2 | 12 | 10 | 2 | 10 |
| 7 | Tranmere R | 8 | 3 | 1 | 4 | 15 | 16 | –1 | 10 |
| 8 | Oldham Ath | 8 | 2 | 2 | 4 | 10 | 16 | –6 | 8 |
| 9 | Bury | 8 | 0 | 2 | 6 | 5 | 32 | –27 | 2 |

## DIVISIONAL SECTION DIVISION 2

| | | P | W | D | L | F | A | GD | Pts |
|---|---|---|---|---|---|---|---|---|---|
| 1 | Port Vale | 7 | 5 | 0 | 2 | 13 | 4 | 9 | 15 |
| 2 | Gateshead | 7 | 4 | 2 | 1 | 12 | 3 | 9 | 14 |
| 3 | Mansfield T | 7 | 4 | 1 | 2 | 23 | 6 | 17 | 13 |
| 4 | Morecambe | 7 | 4 | 1 | 2 | 12 | 18 | –6 | 13 |
| 5 | Bradford C | 7 | 2 | 2 | 3 | 12 | 18 | –6 | 8 |
| 6 | Burton Alb | 7 | 2 | 1 | 4 | 11 | 15 | –4 | 7 |
| 7 | Wrexham | 7 | 1 | 2 | 4 | 9 | 17 | –8 | 5 |
| 8 | Grimsby T | 7 | 1 | 1 | 5 | 6 | 17 | –11 | 4 |

## REGIONAL SECTION EAST DIVISION

| | | P | W | D | L | F | A | GD | Pts |
|---|---|---|---|---|---|---|---|---|---|
| 1 | Hull C | 7 | 7 | 0 | 0 | 21 | 5 | 16 | 21 |
| 2 | Gateshead | 7 | 3 | 3 | 1 | 11 | 7 | 4 | 12 |
| 3 | Mansfield T | 7 | 3 | 1 | 3 | 14 | 9 | 5 | 10 |
| 4 | Rotherham U | 7 | 2 | 2 | 3 | 9 | 8 | 1 | 8 |
| 5 | Chesterfield | 7 | 2 | 2 | 3 | 14 | 14 | 0 | 8 |
| 6 | Bradford C | 7 | 2 | 2 | 3 | 11 | 13 | –2 | 8 |
| 7 | Hartlepool U | 7 | 2 | 2 | 3 | 9 | 16 | –7 | 8 |
| 8 | Grimsby T | 7 | 0 | 2 | 5 | 5 | 22 | –17 | 2 |

## REGIONAL SECTION WEST DIVISION

| | | P | W | D | L | F | A | GD | Pts |
|---|---|---|---|---|---|---|---|---|---|
| 1 | Walsall | 8 | 4 | 3 | 1 | 18 | 7 | 11 | 15 |
| 2 | Port Vale | 8 | 4 | 2 | 2 | 10 | 13 | –3 | 14 |
| 3 | Shrewsbury T | 8 | 4 | 1 | 3 | 17 | 10 | 7 | 13 |
| 4 | Burton Alb | 8 | 3 | 4 | 1 | 16 | 12 | 4 | 13 |
| 5 | Bury | 8 | 4 | 1 | 3 | 14 | 13 | 1 | 13 |
| 6 | Oldham Ath | 8 | 3 | 1 | 4 | 15 | 15 | 0 | 10 |
| 7 | Morecambe | 8 | 2 | 2 | 4 | 14 | 17 | –3 | 8 |
| 8 | Tranmere R | 8 | 2 | 1 | 5 | 12 | 15 | –3 | 7 |
| 9 | Wrexham | 8 | 1 | 3 | 4 | 12 | 26 | –14 | 6 |

## CENTRAL LEAGUE CUP

### GROUP A

| | | P | W | D | L | F | A | GD | Pts |
|---|---|---|---|---|---|---|---|---|---|
| 1 | Tranmere R | 3 | 3 | 0 | 0 | 10 | 1 | 9 | 9 |
| 2 | Rotherham U | 4 | 3 | 0 | 1 | 13 | 8 | 5 | 9 |
| 3 | Fleetwood T | 4 | 2 | 0 | 2 | 8 | 9 | –1 | 6 |
| 4 | Stoke C | 3 | 1 | 0 | 2 | 4 | 8 | –4 | 3 |
| 5 | Morecambe | 4 | 0 | 0 | 4 | 3 | 12 | –9 | 0 |

*Note* – Stoke C v Tranmere R was not completed.

### GROUP B

| | | P | W | D | L | F | A | GD | Pts |
|---|---|---|---|---|---|---|---|---|---|
| 1 | Gateshead | 3 | 2 | 0 | 1 | 3 | 2 | 1 | 6 |
| 2 | Mansfield T | 3 | 1 | 1 | 1 | 3 | 0 | 4 | 4 |
| 3 | Hull C | 3 | 1 | 1 | 1 | 1 | 1 | 0 | 4 |
| 4 | Hartlepool U | 3 | 1 | 0 | 2 | 4 | 5 | –1 | 3 |

### SEMI FINALS

| | |
|---|---|
| Gateshead v Rotherham U | 1-0 |
| Mansfield T v Tranmere R | 5-0 |

### FINAL

| | |
|---|---|
| Mansfield T v Gateshead | 1-2 |

# FOOTBALL LEAGUE YOUTH ALLIANCE 2012–13

## NORTH WEST CONFERENCE

| | | P | W | D | L | F | A | GD | Pts |
|---|---|---|---|---|---|---|---|---|---|
| 1 | Wrexham | 22 | 14 | 5 | 3 | 43 | 16 | 27 | 47 |
| 2 | Preston NE | 22 | 14 | 3 | 5 | 59 | 27 | 32 | 45 |
| 3 | Rochdale | 22 | 12 | 8 | 2 | 57 | 21 | 36 | 44 |
| 4 | Walsall | 22 | 12 | 6 | 4 | 50 | 24 | 26 | 42 |
| 5 | Burnley | 22 | 13 | 1 | 8 | 51 | 34 | 17 | 40 |
| 6 | Bury | 22 | 12 | 2 | 8 | 42 | 44 | –2 | 38 |
| 7 | Carlisle U | 22 | 11 | 4 | 7 | 50 | 36 | 14 | 37 |
| 8 | Oldham Ath | 22 | 10 | 3 | 9 | 34 | 29 | 5 | 33 |
| 9 | Port Vale | 22 | 8 | 6 | 8 | 27 | 25 | 2 | 30 |
| 10 | Macclesfield T | 22 | 7 | 6 | 9 | 28 | 28 | 0 | 27 |
| 11 | Shrewsbury T | 22 | 8 | 0 | 14 | 29 | 40 | –11 | 24 |
| 12 | Blackpool | 22 | 7 | 3 | 12 | 37 | 67 | –30 | 24 |
| 13 | Tranmere R | 22 | 5 | 5 | 12 | 30 | 39 | –9 | 20 |
| 14 | Fleetwood T | 22 | 4 | 5 | 13 | 26 | 44 | –18 | 17 |
| 15 | Morecambe | 22 | 4 | 3 | 15 | 30 | 71 | –41 | 15 |
| 16 | Accrington S | 22 | 3 | 4 | 15 | 25 | 73 | –48 | 13 |

## NORTH EAST CONFERENCE

| | | P | W | D | L | F | A | GD | Pts |
|---|---|---|---|---|---|---|---|---|---|
| 1 | Hull C | 22 | 15 | 6 | 1 | 58 | 15 | 43 | 51 |
| 2 | Doncaster R | 22 | 15 | 4 | 3 | 39 | 14 | 25 | 49 |
| 3 | Scunthorpe U | 22 | 12 | 4 | 6 | 50 | 36 | 14 | 40 |
| 4 | York C | 22 | 10 | 4 | 8 | 32 | 34 | –2 | 34 |
| 5 | Burton Alb | 22 | 9 | 5 | 8 | 42 | 36 | 6 | 32 |
| 6 | Rotherham U | 22 | 9 | 2 | 11 | 37 | 45 | –8 | 29 |
| 7 | Notts Co | 22 | 8 | 4 | 10 | 43 | 40 | 3 | 28 |
| 8 | Bradford C | 22 | 7 | 5 | 10 | 36 | 38 | –2 | 26 |
| 9 | Chesterfield | 22 | 6 | 5 | 11 | 31 | 40 | –9 | 23 |
| 10 | Grimsby T | 22 | 5 | 6 | 11 | 26 | 43 | –17 | 21 |
| 11 | Lincoln C | 22 | 3 | 10 | 9 | 26 | 49 | –23 | 19 |
| 12 | Hartlepool U | 22 | 4 | 3 | 15 | 28 | 58 | –30 | 15 |

## SOUTH WEST CONFERENCE

| | | P | W | D | L | F | A | GD | Pts |
|---|---|---|---|---|---|---|---|---|---|
| 1 | Bristol R | 16 | 13 | 2 | 1 | 31 | 10 | 21 | 41 |
| 2 | Oxford U | 16 | 13 | 1 | 2 | 43 | 21 | 22 | 40 |
| 3 | Plymouth Arg | 16 | 10 | 1 | 5 | 33 | 20 | 13 | 31 |
| 4 | Exeter C | 16 | 7 | 3 | 6 | 31 | 22 | 9 | 24 |
| 5 | Cheltenham T | 16 | 5 | 3 | 8 | 36 | 36 | 0 | 18 |
| 6 | Torquay U | 16 | 6 | 0 | 10 | 28 | 31 | –3 | 18 |
| 7 | Swindon T | 16 | 4 | 3 | 9 | 30 | 33 | –3 | 15 |
| 8 | Hereford U | 16 | 3 | 3 | 10 | 17 | 44 | –27 | 12 |
| 9 | Yeovil T | 16 | 1 | 4 | 11 | 14 | 46 | –32 | 7 |

## SOUTH EAST CONFERENCE

| | | P | W | D | L | F | A | GD | Pts |
|---|---|---|---|---|---|---|---|---|---|
| 1 | Leyton Orient | 21 | 10 | 6 | 5 | 52 | 38 | 14 | 36 |
| 2 | Luton T | 21 | 10 | 6 | 5 | 39 | 29 | 10 | 36 |
| 3 | Watford | 21 | 10 | 5 | 6 | 48 | 34 | 14 | 35 |
| 4 | Portsmouth | 20 | 10 | 5 | 5 | 44 | 32 | 12 | 35 |
| 5 | Peterborough U | 21 | 10 | 3 | 8 | 42 | 38 | 4 | 33 |
| 6 | Milton Keynes D | 21 | 10 | 2 | 9 | 56 | 56 | 0 | 32 |
| 7 | Dagenham & R | 21 | 8 | 6 | 7 | 31 | 32 | –1 | 30 |
| 8 | Gillingham | 20 | 7 | 8 | 5 | 42 | 40 | 2 | 29 |
| 9 | Southend U | 20 | 7 | 6 | 7 | 33 | 38 | –5 | 27 |
| 10 | Aldershot T | 20 | 8 | 3 | 9 | 31 | 37 | –6 | 27 |
| 11 | Bournemouth | 20 | 6 | 7 | 7 | 29 | 33 | –4 | 25 |
| 12 | Stevenage | 21 | 6 | 5 | 10 | 33 | 48 | –15 | 23 |
| 13 | AFC Wimbledon | 20 | 5 | 7 | 8 | 33 | 39 | –6 | 22 |
| 14 | Northampton T | 21 | 5 | 3 | 13 | 27 | 36 | –9 | 18 |
| 15 | Crawley T | 20 | 4 | 4 | 12 | 35 | 45 | –10 | 16 |

*Because some teams played more than others, the championship was decided on a points per game basis. Portsmouth were crowned champions, see table below.*

## SOUTH EAST CONFERENCE (points per game)

| | | P | W | D | L | F | A | GD | Pts |
|---|---|---|---|---|---|---|---|---|---|
| 1 | Portsmouth | 20 | 10 | 5 | 5 | 44 | 32 | 12 | 1.75 |
| 2 | Leyton Orient | 21 | 10 | 6 | 5 | 52 | 38 | 14 | 1.71 |
| 3 | Luton T | 21 | 10 | 6 | 5 | 39 | 29 | 10 | 1.71 |
| 4 | Watford | 21 | 10 | 5 | 6 | 48 | 34 | 14 | 1.67 |
| 5 | Peterborough U | 21 | 10 | 3 | 8 | 42 | 38 | 4 | 1.57 |
| 6 | Milton Keynes D | 21 | 10 | 2 | 9 | 56 | 56 | 0 | 1.52 |
| 7 | Gillingham | 20 | 7 | 8 | 5 | 42 | 40 | 2 | 1.45 |
| 8 | Dagenham & R | 21 | 8 | 6 | 7 | 31 | 32 | –1 | 1.43 |
| 9 | Southend U | 20 | 7 | 6 | 7 | 33 | 38 | –5 | 1.35 |
| 10 | Aldershot T | 20 | 7 | 3 | 9 | 31 | 37 | –6 | 1.35 |
| 11 | Bournemouth | 20 | 6 | 7 | 7 | 29 | 33 | –4 | 1.25 |
| 12 | AFC Wimbledon | 20 | 5 | 7 | 8 | 33 | 39 | –6 | 1.10 |
| 13 | Stevenage | 21 | 6 | 5 | 10 | 33 | 48 | –15 | 1.10 |
| 14 | Northampton T | 21 | 5 | 3 | 13 | 27 | 36 | –9 | 0.86 |
| 15 | Crawley T | 20 | 4 | 4 | 12 | 35 | 45 | –10 | 0.80 |

# IMPORTANT ADDRESSES

**The Football Association:** Wembley Stadium, P.O. Box 1966, London SW1P 9EQ. *0844 980 8200*

**Scotland:** Hampden Park, Glasgow G42 9AY. *0141 616 6000*

**Northern Ireland** (Irish FA): Chief Executive, 20 Windsor Avenue, Belfast BT9 6EG. *028 9066 9458*

**Wales:** 11/12 Neptune Court, Vanguard Way, Cardiff CF24 5PJ. *029 2043 5830*

**Republic of Ireland** National Sports Campus, Abbotstown, Dublin 15. *00 353 1 8999 500*

**International Federation** (FIFA): Strasse 20, P.O. Box 8044, Zurich, Switzerland. *00 41 43 222 7777. Fax: 00 41 222 7878*

**Union of European Football Associations:** Secretary, Route de Geneve 46, P.O. Box 1260, Nyon 2, Switzerland. *Fax: 00 41 848 00 2727*

## THE LEAGUES

**The Premier League:** M. Foster, 30 Gloucester Place, London W1U 8PL. *0207 864 9000*

**The Football League:** Andy Williamson, Unit 5, Edward VII Quay, Navigation Way, Preston, Lancashire PR2 2YF. *0844 463 1888. Fax 0870 442 0 1188*

**Scottish Premier League:** Hampden Park, Somerville Drive, Glasgow G42 9OE. *0141 620 4140*

**The Scottish League:** Hampden Park, Glasgow G42 9EB. *0141 620 4160*

**Football League of Ireland:** D. Crowther, 80 Merrion Square, Dublin 2. *00353 16765120*

**Football Conference:** D. Strudwick, 3rd Floor, Wellington House, 31–34 Waterloo Street, Birmingham B2 5TJ. *0121 214 1950*

**Southern League:** J. Mills, Sansome Lodge, 4–6 Sansome Walk, Worcester WR1 1LH. *01905 330 444*

**Northern Premier League:** Ms A. Firth, 23 High Lane, Norton Tower, Halifax, W. Yorkshire HX2 0NW. *01422 410 691*

**Isthmian League:** Ms K. Discipline, The Base, Dartford Business Park, Victoria Park, Dartford, Kent DA1 5FS. *01322 314 999*

**Eastern Counties League:** N. Spurling, 16 Thanet Road, Ipswich, Suffolk IP4 5LB. *07855 279062*

**Essex Senior League:** Secretary: K. Wilmot, 35 Cecil Road, Walthamstow, London E17 5DH. *07540 441 829*

**Hellenic League:** B. King, 7 Stoneleigh Drive, Carterton, Oxon OX18 1EE. *0845 260 6644*

**Kent League:** A.R. Vinter, 4 Staple Court, Chilham Castle Estate, Chilham, Canterbury CT4 8DB. *01277 730457*

**Midland Alliance:** J. Shaw, 176 Springthorpe Road, Erdington, Birmingham B24 0SN. *0121 350 5869*

**North West Counties League:** J. Deal, 24 The Pastures, Crossens, Southport PR9 8RH. *07713 622210*

**Northern Counties East:** B. Gould, 42 Thirlmere Drive, Dronfield, Derbyshire S18 2HW. *07773 653 238*

**Northern League:** T. Golightly, 85 Park Road North, Chester-le-Street, Co. Durham DH3 3SA. *0191 388 2056*

**Spartan South Midlands League:** M. Mitchell, 26 Leighton Court, Dunstable, Beds LU6 1EW. *07710 455 409*

**Sussex County League:** P. Beard, 2 Van Gogh Place, North Bersted, Bognor Regis, West Sussex PO22 9BG. *07831 497 913*

**United Counties League:** N. Haycox, 12 Glenfield Drive, Great Doddington, Wellingborough NN29 7TE. *07879 036235*

**Wessex League:** J. Gorman, 6 Overton House, London Road, Overton, Hants RG25 3TP. *01256 770059*

**Western League:** K.A. Clarke, 32 Westmead Lane, Chippenham, Wilts SN15 3HZ. *07790 002279*

**Combined Counties League:** M.J. Bidmead, 55 Grange Road, Chessington, Surrey KT9 1EZ. *0208 397 4834*

**Midland Combination:** N. Wood, 30 Glalsdale Road, Hall Green, Birmingham B28 8PX. *07967 440007*

**West Midlands League:** N.R. Juggins, 14 Badger Way, Blackwell, Bromsgrove, Worcs B60 1EX. *07977 422 362.*

**South West Peninsula League:** P. Hiscox, 45a Serge Court, The Quay, Exeter, Devon EX2 4EB. *07788 897706*

## OTHER USEFUL ADDRESSES

**Amateur Football Alliance:** M. Brown, Unit 3, 7 Wenlock Road, London N1 7SL. *0208 733 2613*

**English Schools FA:** J. Read, 4 Parker Court, Staffordshire Technology Park, Stafford ST18 0WP. *01785 785 970*

**British Universities Sports Association:** G. Gregory-Jones, Chief Executive: BUSA, 20–24 King's Bench Street, London SE1 0QX. *0207 633 5050*

**The Football Supporters Federation:** The Fans Stadium, Kingsmeadow, Jack Goodchild Way, 422a Kingston Road, Kingston-upon-Thames KT1 3PB. *0208 547 3577*

**National Playing Fields Association:** 57B, 25 Ovington Square, London SW3 1LQ. *0207 584 6445*

**Professional Footballers' Association:** G. Taylor, 2 Oxford Court, Bishopsgate, Off Lower Moseley Street, Manchester M2 3WQ. *0161 236 0575*

**Referees' Association:** A.W.S. Smith, 1 Westhill Road, Coundon, Coventry CV6 2AD. *0247 6601 701*

**Women's Football Alliance:** Miss K. Doyle, The Football Association, 25 Soho Square, London W1D 4FA. *020 7745 4545*

**Women's Football Conference:** Mike Appleby, Wembley Stadium, PO Box 1966, London SW1P 9EQ. *0844 980 8200*

**League Managers Association:** St George's Park, Newborough, Needwood, Burton on Trent DE13 9PD. *0128 357 6350*

**Institute of Football Management and Administration:** St George's Park, Newborough, Needwood, Burton on Trent DE13 9PD. *0128 357 6350*

**World Cup (1966) Association:** Hon. Secretary, David Duncan, 96 Glenlea Road, Eltham, London SE9 1DZ.

**The Ninety-Two Club:** Mr M. Kimberley, The Ninety-Two Club, 153 Hayes Lane, Kenley, Surrey CR8 5HP.

**Association of Provincial Football Supporters Clubs in London:** Tina A. Robertson, 45 Durham Avenue, Heston, Middlesex TW5 0HG. *0208 843 9854*

**World Association of Friends of English Football:** Carlisle Hill, Gluck, Habichthof 2, D24939 Flensburg, Germany. *0049 461 4700222*

**Football Postcard Collectors Club:** PRO: Bryan Horsnell, 275 Overdown Road, Tilehurst, Reading RG31 6NX. *0118 942 4448 (and fax)*

**UK Programme Collectors Club:** PM Publications, 38 Lowther Road, Norwich NR4 6QW. *01603 449 237*

**Programme Monthly & Football Collectable Magazine:** 11 Tannington Terrace, London N5 1LE.

**Scottish Football Historians Association:** John Lister, 46 Milton Road, Kirkcaldy, Fife KY1 1TL. *01592 268718*

**Phil Gould** (Licensed Football Agent), c/o Whoppit Management Ltd, P.O. Box 27204, London N11 2WS. *07071 732 468. Fax: 07070 732 469*

**The Scandinavian Union of Supporters of British Football:** Postboks, 15 Stovner, N-0913 Oslo, Norway.

**Programme Promotions:** 21 Roughwood Close, Watford WD17 3HN. *01923 861 468*
Web: www.footballprogrammes.com

**Football Safety Officers Association:** Chris Patzelt, P.O. Box 7482, Alfreton, Derbyshire. *0114 288 3366.*

**Football Foundation:** Whittinghton House, 19–30 Alfred Place, London WC1E 7EA. *0845 345 4555*

**Football Licensing Authority:** 27 Harcourt House, 19 Cavendish Square, London W1G 0PL. *0207 491 7191*

**Sport England:** 16 Upper Woburn Place, London WC1H 0QP. *0207 388 1277*

**Association of Football Badge Collectors:** K. Wilkinson, 18 Hinton St, Fairfield, Liverpool L6 3AR.

**Soccer Nostalgia:** G. Wallis, Albion Chambers, 1 Albion Road, Birchington, Kent CT7 9DN. *01303 275 432.*

**Sir Norman Chester Centre for Football Research:** Department of Sociology, University of Leicester, University Road LE1 7RH. *0116 252 2741/5.*

**Sports Turf Research Institute:** Bingley, West Yorkshire BD16 1AU. *01274 565 131*

# FOOTBALL CLUB CHAPLAINCY

'Hey Rev, what's so special about a football chaplain?' The question is a fair one which demands a response.

The chaplain will be a church minister or leader who believes that God has called him to this particular work. He is often a supporter of the club in question, but that is not essential. What is absolutely necessary is that he can relate well to everyone within the community of the club in question, from the gatemen and programme sellers to the chairman and his wife.

It is also vital that the chaplain should be able to retain any confidence which has been entrusted to him. But perhaps the most 'special' thing about a chaplain is that he represents something or someone amongst those he seeks to serve.

THE REV

## OFFICIAL CHAPLAINS TO FA PREMIERSHIP AND FOOTBALL LEAGUE CLUBS

Aldershot T – Co-Chaplains Rev George Newton and Rev Mike Pusey
Aston Villa – Rev Ken Baker
Barnsley – Rev Peter Amos
Blackburn R – Rev Ken Howles
Blackpool – Rev Michael Ward
Bolton W – Mr Phil Mason
Bournemouth – Rev Andy Rimmer
Bristol C – Rev Derek Cleave
Bristol R – Rev David Jeal
Burnley – Rev Mark Hirst
Bury – Rev David Ottley
Cardiff C – Rev Dr John Weaver
Carlisle U – Rev Alun Jones
Charlton Ath / Pastoral Supp. Direc. – Rev Matt Baker
Cheltenham T – Rev Malcolm Allen
Chesterfield – Rev Jim McGlade
Crystal Palace – Rev Chris Roe
Derby Co – Rev Tony Luke
Doncaster R – Rev Jim Magee
Everton – Co-Chaplains Rev Henry Corbett and Rev Harry Ross
Fulham – Rev Gary Piper
Gillingham – Rev Richard Hayton
Hull C – Rev Allen Bagshawe
Ipswich T – Rev Kevan McCormack
Leeds U – Rev Paul Welch
Leicester C – Rev Andrew Hulley
Leyton Orient – Rev Alan Comfort
Liverpool – Rev Bill Bygroves
Manchester C – Rev Peter Horlock
Manchester U – Rev John Boyers
Millwall – Rev Canon Owen Beament

MK Dons – Rev Ron Smith
Newcastle U Academy – Rev Glyn Evans
Norwich C – Co-Chaplains Rev Arthur Bowles and Rev Albert Cadmore
Nottingham F – Rev Steve Silvester
Notts Co – Rev Liam O'Boyle
Oldham Ath – Rev John Simmons
Peterborough U – Rev Richard Longfoot
Plymouth Arg – Rev Arthur Goode
Port Vale – Rev John Hibberts
Portsmouth – Co-Chaplains Mr Mick Mellows and Rev Jonathan Jeffrey
Preston NE – Rev Chris Nelson
QPR – Co-Chaplains Rev Cameron Collington and Rev Bob Mayo
Reading – Rev Steven Prince
Scunthorpe U – Rev Alan Wright
Sheffield U – Rev Nigel Manges
Sheffield W – Rev Peter Allen
Shrewsbury T – Rev Christopher Deakin
Southampton – Rev Andy Bowerman
Sunderland – Father Marc Lyden-Smith
Swansea C – Rev Kevin Johns
Swansea C Academy – Rev Eirian Wyn
Swindon T – Rev Simon Stevenette
Torquay U – Rev Tim Smith
Walsall – Rev Peter Hart
Watford – Rev Clive Ross
West Ham U – Rev Alan Bolding
Wolverhampton W – Co-Chaplains Rev David Wright and Mr Steve Davies
Wycombe W – Rev John Roberts
Yeovil T. – Rev Jim Pearce

*The chaplains hope that those who read this page will see the value and benefit of chaplaincy work in football and will take appropriate steps to spread the word where this is possible. They would also like to thank the editors of the Football Yearbook for their continued support for this specialist and growing area of work.*

*For further information, please contact: Sports Chaplaincy UK, PO Box 123, Sale, Cheshire M33 4ZA. Telephone: 0161 962 6068 or email: admin@sportschaplaincy.org.uk. Website: www.sportschaplaincy.org.uk*

# OBITUARIES

**Charlie Adam** (Born Dundee, 5 April 1962. Died Dundee, 18 December 2012.) Charlie Adam was a midfield player who began his senior career with St Johnstone. He went on to make over 250 Scottish League appearances between 1985 and 1994 in a career that also saw him turn out for Brechin City, Dundee United, Partick Thistle, Forfar Athletic and Arbroath. Charlie was the father of Scotland international player Charlie Adam and also of Grant Adam (St Mirren).

**Chris Adams** (Born Hornchurch, Essex, 6 September 1927. Died Brentwood, Essex, 24 June 2012.) Chris Adams was a pacy winger who was on the books of Tottenham Hotspur between 1947 and 1952. Although mostly with the reserves and juniors, he made six first-team appearances during his time at White Hart Lane. After moving on to Norwich in December 1952 he signed for Watford, making 81 senior appearances for the Hornets before switching to Southern League football.

**Milija Aleksic** (Born Newcastle-under-Lyme, Staffs, 14 April 1951. Died Johannesburg, South Africa, 17 October 2012.) Milija Aleksic was on Port Vale's books as a youngster, and after a spell in non-league football he returned to the senior game with Plymouth Argyle in February 1973. A brave 'keeper with fine reflexes, he moved on to Luton Town where he was a near ever-present for two years before earning a transfer to Tottenham. The high point of his career came at White Hart Lane where he featured in both FA Cup final ties with Manchester City in May 1981 as Spurs went on to secure the trophy.

**Jimmy Andrews** (Born Invergordon, 1 February 1927. Died 12 September 2012.) Jimmy Andrews was a skilful inside forward or winger who started out with Dundee, making his debut towards the end of the 1944–45 season. After completing his National Service he showed sufficient promise to earn a move to West Ham United in November 1951 and he went on to play more than 100 games for the Hammers. After spells with Leyton Orient and Queens Park Rangers he joined the coaching staff at Loftus Road, later serving a number of clubs in this capacity, while also having a four-year spell as manager of Cardiff City.

**Brian Arblaster** (Born Kensington, London, 6 June 1943. Died Killamarsh, Derbyshire, 24 January 2013.) Goalkeeper Brian Arblaster was a youngster with Sheffield United but was unable to break into the first team at Bramall Lane and it was with Chesterfield that he came to prominence. A solid and consistent 'keeper, he then had a short spell with Scunthorpe United before switching to Barnsley where he spent five seasons, making over 100 appearances. He later moved to non-league Boston United.

**Peter Armit** (Born Edinburgh, 1926. Died Newby, North Yorkshire, 20 April 2013.) Peter Armit was a winger who made 70 first-team appearances for St Johnstone in the early 1950s. After brief spells with Gloucester City and Stenhousemuir he joined Hamilton Academical in 1954 where he was a regular over the next three years before injury ended his career prematurely.

**Alan Arnell** (Born Chichester, Sussex, 25 November 1933. Died 5 May 2013.) Alan Arnell was a tall, powerful centre forward who signed for Liverpool from amateur club Worthing towards the end of the 1953–54 season. Although mostly second choice to the likes of Billy Liddell and Louis Bimpson he scored at a rate of nearly a goal every other game for the Reds and was equally prolific in a two-year stay at Tranmere Rovers before concluding his career at Halifax.

**Eric Bell** (Born Clayton, Manchester, 27 November 1929. Died Wythenshawe, Manchester, 22 July 2012.) Eric Bell was a wing half who was on Manchester United's books as a youngster, but having failed to make the grade at Old Trafford he spent his entire senior career with Bolton Wanderers. The high point in his career came when he scored his side's third goal against Blackpool in the 1953 FA Cup final, only to see the Seasiders take the trophy with a last-gasp finish. He made over 100 appearances during his time at Burnden Park before retiring through injury. Eric was capped for England B and the Football League representative team.

**Alf Bellis** (Born Liverpool, 8 October 1920. Died 28 April 2013.) Alf Bellis was a winger who signed for Port Vale in March 1938, making his Football League debut shortly afterwards. He spent 10 years at Vale Park, interrupted by military service during the war, before going on to play for Bury, Swansea Town and Chesterfield, making over 200 appearances in peacetime football.

**Willie Benvie** (Born Kirkcaldy, Fife, 27 October 1931. Died Kirkcaldy, Fife, 31 December 2012.) Willie Benvie was an inside forward who developed in Scottish Junior football with Lochore Welfare before joining Stirling Albion in January 1957. He was a regular in the team that won the Division Two title in 1957–58 and made over 100 appearances during his stay at Annfield. He went on to play for Dunfermline Athletic, Raith Rovers, Cowdenbeath and Berwick Rangers then returned to Raith where he spent 12 years on the coaching staff before retiring.

**Reg Beresford** (Born Pilsley, Derbyshire, 29 June 1925. Died Nottingham, October 2012.) Reg Beresford was a regular on the right wing for Notts County during the 1945–46 season and remained with the club when peacetime football resumed, adding a further nine Football League appearances. A part-time player who also worked for the NCB, he later played for Central Alliance club Creswell Colliery for many years.

**Ivan Beswick** (Born Manchester, 2 January 1936. Died St Martin's, Guernsey, 4 June 2012.) Full back Ivan Beswick was a member of the Manchester United team that won the FA Youth Cup in 1953–54 but was unable to make the first team during his stay at Old Trafford. In August 1958 he signed for Oldham Athletic and he spent three seasons with the Latics, making almost 50 appearances.

**Dave Bewley** (Born Bournemouth, 22 September 1920. Died Luton, 6 March 2013.) Dave Bewley was a reliable wing half whose career was delayed by the war and it was not until he was in his mid-20s that he made his senior debut. He had two spells at Fulham with eight months at Reading sandwiched in between. However, it was not until joining Watford in the summer of 1953 that he experienced regular first-team football and he went on to make over 100 appearances for the Hornets.

**Ian Black** (Born Aberdeen, 27 March 1924. Died London, 13 December 2012.) Ian Black was a goalkeeper who joined Aberdeen as a youngster during the war. He guested for Chelsea when they won the Football League South Cup in 1944–45 and eventually returned south permanently in December 1947, when he signed for Southampton. After winning a solitary cap for Scotland, he moved to Fulham in the summer of 1950 and went on to make over 250 appearances during his stay at Craven Cottage.

**John Bond** (Born Dedham, Essex, 17 December 1932. Died Manchester, 25 September 2012.) John Bond was a full back who signed for West Ham United in March 1950, establishing himself in the first team in 1954–55. A regular in the side that won promotion from the Second Division in 1957–58, he went on to make over 400 appearances for the Hammers gaining an FA Cup winners' medal in 1964. He later had a spell with Torquay United before becoming a successful manager. At Norwich he won promotion and a place in the Football League Cup final in 1974–75 while he also led Manchester City to the 1981 FA Cup final.

**Peter Boyle** (Born 24 March 1951. Died Australia, January 2013.) Peter Boyle developed as a striker with Clyde in the 1970s, leading the club's scoring charts in 1972–73 when the Second Division title was won. He emigrated to Australia in 1977 where he turned out for the West Adelaide club, winning a single cap for his adopted country against Czechoslovakia in January 1980.

**Colin Brittan** (Born Bristol, 2 June 1927. Died Bristol, 4 April 2013.) Colin Brittan joined Tottenham Hotspur in October 1948 and spent 10 years on the books at White Hart Lane, principally appearing for the reserve and 'A' teams. During that time he made 45 senior appearances, mostly at wing half. He later switched to the Southern League where he played for Bedford Town and Tunbridge Wells United.

**Nick Broad** (Born Plymouth, 1974. Died Paris, France, 18 January 2013.) Nick Broad was employed by Blackburn Rovers and Birmingham City as a sports nutritionist, before moving on to Chelsea where he was Head of Sports Science. He subsequently followed Carlo Ancelotti to Paris Saint-Germain where he held a similar post at the time of his death.

**Dr Malcolm Brodie, MBE** (Born Glasgow, 27 September 1926. Died 29 January 2013.) Malcolm Brodie was perhaps the best known of all sports journalists in Northern Ireland in the post-war period. He was sports editor for the *Belfast Telegraph* from 1950 to 1991 and had the distinction of covering 14 World Cup tournaments. The author of several books on Irish soccer, he was President of the Northern Ireland Football Writers' Association and received a Jules Rimet Award from FIFA in 2004.

**Eddie Brown** (Born Preston, 28 February 1926. Died Preston, 12 July 2012.) Eddie Brown began his career with his home town club, Preston North End, before going on to develop a reputation as an all-action centre forward with an excellent scoring ratio. He netted a total of 190 goals in 399 Football League games during a career that saw him also play for Southampton, Coventry City, Birmingham City and Leyton Orient. One of the highlights of his career came in the 1955–56 season when his goals helped fire Birmingham to an FA Cup final tie with Manchester City where they went down by a 3-1 margin.

**Ray Bumstead** (Born Ringwood, Hants, 27 January 1936. Died Bournemouth, 17 March 2013.) Ray Bumstead was a winger who signed for Bournemouth from Hampshire League club Ringwood Town in May 1958. A skilful player on the right flank, he was effective in a traditional wing role, cutting inside to set up chances for his colleagues. He went on to establish a then club record total of 414 Football League appearances before retiring in 1969.

**Eric Burgin** (Born Sheffield, 4 January 1924. Died Sheffield, 16 November 2012.) Eric Burgin was a centre half who was on the books of York City for two seasons from the summer of 1949. He made 23 appearances during his stay at Bootham Crescent before injury led to his retirement. Eric was also a medium pace bowler for Yorkshire, appearing in 12 County Championship games in 1952 and 1953.

**Angus Carmichael** (Born Fort Rosebery, Northern Rhodesia, 12 June 1925. Died Horncastle, Lincolnshire, 21 March 2013.) Angus Carmichael was a full back who played for Queen's Park in the immediate post-war period. He made 42 Scottish League appearances and was selected as a member of the Great Britain squad for the 1948 Olympic Games where he played in the bronze medal play-off tie against Denmark.

**Steve Carney** (Born Wallsend, Northumberland, 22 September 1957. Died 6 May 2013.) Steve Carney was a centre half who starred with the Blyth Spartans team that reached the FA Cup fifth round in 1977–78. He went on to sign for Newcastle United and make almost 150 senior appearances during his stay, helping the Magpies win promotion from Division Two in 1983–84. He later played for Darlington and Hartlepool United.

**Stan Charlton** (Born Exeter, 28 June 1929. Died Dorchester, 20 December 2012.) Stan Charlton came to prominence with Bromley, for whom he won England Amateur international honours before joining Leyton Orient at the start of the 1952–53 season. He immediately established himself as a regular for the O's and three years later he was sold to Arsenal where he made over 100 first-team appearances before returning to Brisbane Road. He skippered Orient to promotion to the First Division in 1961–62 before leaving to become manager of Weymouth.

**Arnold Coates** (Born Crook, Co Durham, 24 July 1936. Died Nelson, Lancashire, 25 February 2013.) Arnold Coates was an all-action centre forward who played amateur football with Crook Town and Evenwood Town, He was a member of the Crook team that won the FA Amateur Cup in 1959 and 1962, winning three caps for England Amateurs. He was also a member of the Great Britain squad for the 1960 Olympic Games. Arnold spent two seasons with Scottish League club Queen of the South and later played for Scarborough.

**Mitchell Cole** (Born Luton, 6 October 1985. Died 1 December 2012.) Mitchell Cole was a skilful left-sided midfield player who spent two seasons on the books of Southend United between 2005 and 2007 helping the Shrimpers win promotion from League One in 2005–06. He then switched to non-league football, representing the England C team and assisting Stevenage Borough to promotion to the Football League in 2009–10.

**John Connelly** (Born St Helens, Lancashire, 18 July 1938. Died Barrowford, Lancashire, 25 October 2012.) John Connelly signed for Burnley in November 1956 and went on to make a significant contribution to the team that won the Football League title in 1959–60, finishing as the side's leading scorer. A powerful right winger with tremendous pace and a useful shot, he played over 250 games before leaving Turf Moor for Manchester United in April 1964. John spent two years at Old Trafford, gaining a further Football League champions' medal in the 1964–65 season. He also played for Blackburn and Bury. John won 20 England caps and was included in the squad for the 1966 World Cup finals, featuring in the opening match against Uruguay.

**Tibor Csernai** (Born Pilis, Hungary, 3 December 1938. Died Tatabánya, Hungary, 11 September 2012.) Tibor Csernai was an attacking midfield player with the Hungary team that won the gold medal at the 1964 Tokyo Olympic Games. He scored six goals during the tournament and was a member of the side that defeated Czechoslovakia 2-1 to win the final. He played his club football for the Tatabánya club.

**Glyn Davies** (Born Swansea, 31 May 1932. Died 7 February 2013.) Glyn Davies was a tough tackling defender who made his debut for Derby County in December 1953. He went on to make 200 Football League appearances for the Rams and he was a member of the team that won the Division Three North title in 1956–57. He later had a couple of seasons at Swansea Town then went to Yeovil Town as player-manager before returning to the Vetch Field as manager from June 1965 to October 1966.

**Malcolm Davies** (Born Aberdare, 26 June 1931. Died 31 July 2012.) Malcolm Davies was a pacy wing man who could appear on either flank. He joined Plymouth Argyle as a teenager towards the end of the 1948–49 season but he had to wait almost three years before breaking into the first team at Home Park. He went on to play in 87 League and Cup games before moving on to Weymouth and then Llanelly.

**Ron Davies** (Born Holywell, Flintshire, 25 May 1942. Died Albuquerque, New Mexico, United States, 24 May 2013.) Ron Davies was a powerful centre forward who was one of the best headers of a ball in the game in the late 1960s when he topped the First Division scoring charts two years in a row. His career started with Chester, where he made his debut as a teenager in the 1959–60 season and established himself as a regular scorer. Spells with Luton and Norwich followed before a move to Southampton in the summer of 1966. Saints had just been promoted to the top flight and Ron's 37 goals that season ensured they retained their place. Ron went on to net 153 goals during his stay at The Dell, later turning out for Portsmouth and Manchester United before playing in the United States. He won 29 caps for Wales, scoring nine goals.

**Eric Day** (Born Dartford, 6 November 1921 Died Broughton Gifford, Wiltshire, 10 November 2012.) Eric Day joined Southampton in April 1945 after wartime service in the RAF and went on to become the first player to make over 400 post-war appearances for Saints. A versatile player who could feature both on the wing or at centre forward, he scored 158 senior goals before moving on to Gravesend & Northfleet in the summer of 1957.

**Wattie Dick** (Born Newmains, Lanarkshire, 20 August 1927. Died December 2012.) Wattie Dick was a wing half or inside forward who made over 400 senior appearances in a career that spanned the late 1940s to the early '60s. After making his name with Third Lanark, he became one of many Scottish players to sign for Accrington Stanley in the mid-'50s before concluding his career at Bradford Park Avenue.

**Henry Dove** (Born Stepney, London, 11 March 1932. Died Hemel Hempstead, Hertfordshire, 22 July 2012.) Defender Henry Dove spent eight years on the books of Arsenal without making the first team. In April 1958 he signed for Millwall and he went on to make eight senior appearances for the Lions during his season at the Den.

**Johnny Downie** (Born Lanark, 19 July 1925. Died Tynemouth, Tyne & Wear, 19 February 2013.) Johnny Downie was a goalscoring inside forward who developed with Bradford Park Avenue in the early post-war

years before joining Manchester United in March 1949. A member of the United team that won the Football League title in 1951–52, he moved on to Luton for the 1953–54 season and went on to play for Hull City, Mansfield Town, Wisbech and Darlington before leaving the senior game.

**Ray Drake** (Born Stockport, 24 October 1934. Died 31 March 2013.) Ray Drake was a centre forward with Stockport County in the late 1950s who overcame a hearing impairment and diabetes to play in the Football League. He scored 19 goals from 22 appearances in the 1956–57 season including the Hatters' quickest-ever goal, after 7 seconds against Accrington Stanley on Christmas Day 1956. He later played for Altrincham and Hyde United.

**Frank Dudley** (Born Southend, 9 May 1925. Died Southend, 14 September 2012.) Frank Dudley was a strong, pacy forward who joined Southend United after wartime service in the RAF. He led the Shrimpers' scoring charts in 1948–49 and at the end of the season was sold to Leeds United. He continued to find the net regularly during spells with Leeds, Southampton and Brentford in between which there was a very brief stay at Cardiff City. He later returned to Southend as a member of the coaching staff.

**Charlie Dyke** (Born Llanbradach, Monmouthshire, 23 September 1926. Died Penarth, South Glamorgan, 4 January 2013.) Charlie Dyke was an outside right who was a member of the Troedyrhiw team that won the Welsh Amateur Cup in 1947. He went on to spend three seasons with Chelsea where he made 24 Football League appearances, before returning to Wales to sign for Barry Town. A high point in his career came when he netted a late winner in the Welsh Cup final replay against Chester in 1955 to secure the trophy for the Southern League club for the first time in their history.

**George Falconer** (Born 23 November 1946. Died Dundee, 3 January 2013.) George Falconer was a striker who was a regular scorer with Montrose and Raith Rovers in the late 1960s. He moved on to Dundee for the 1970–71 campaign only to suffer a broken leg which left him on the sidelines for some time before he eventually resumed his career with Elgin City and Forfar Athletic.

**Sean Fallon** (Born Sligo, Irish Free State, 31 July 1922. Died Glasgow, 18 January 2013.) Sean Fallon was principally a left back who played for Sligo Rovers and Glentoran before joining Celtic in March 1950. He went on to make over 250 appearances and win eight caps for the Republic of Ireland before an injury suffered in March 1958 ended his playing career. He later spent several years on the backroom staff at Parkhead and also had a spell as manager of Dumbarton.

**Harry Fearnley** (Born Penistone, Yorkshire, 16 June 1935. Died Poole, Dorset, 12 January 2013.) Harry Fearnley was a goalkeeper who joined Huddersfield Town from local club Penistone Church in 1951 but it was not until the 1955–56 season that he made his debut in senior football. He went on to make over 200 Football League appearances, gaining promotions with Oxford United in 1963–64 and Doncaster Rovers in 1965–66 before turning to coaching with Emley. Harry was also a talented cricketer who captained the Huddersfield League representative side.

**Felix** (Born São Paulo, Brazil, 24 December 1937. Died São Paulo, Brazil, 24 August 2012.) Felix was the goalkeeper for the Brazil team that defeated Italy to win the 1970 World Cup final in Mexico. He won a total of 38 caps for his country between 1965 and 1972. Felix principally played his club football with Portuguesa and Fluminense, winning five Rio de Janeiro state championships with the latter.

**Alwyn Fielden** (Born Denshaw, Oldham, 12 May 1920. Died St Austell, Cornwall, 15 June 2012.) Alwyn Fielden was an amateur centre forward whose only Football League appearance came playing for Oldham Athletic against Rochdale at the end of 1938, when he scored his team's goal in a 1-1 draw. He also played for a number of non-league clubs in the North West including Hurst, Witton Albion and Droylesden.

**Steve Fox** (Born Tamworth, Staffs, 17 February 1958. Died 1 December 2012.) Steve Fox was a hard working winger who began his career as an apprentice with Birmingham City. He moved on to a four-year spell with Wrexham, where he made over 150 competitive appearances helping the club reach the FA Cup quarter-finals on two occasions. Following this he had spells with Port Vale, where he was a member of the 1982–83 promotion team, and Chester before switching to non-league football.

**Archie Gibson** (Born Dailly, Ayrshire, 30 December 1933. Died 23 July 2012.) Archie Gibson was a wing half who signed for Leeds United as a 17-year-old from Scottish juvenile football in May 1951. It was five years before he became a regular first-team player but he went on to make 174 first-team appearances. In the summer of 1960 he moved on to Scunthorpe United, then members of the old Second Division, and here too he was a fixture in the side for three-and-a-half seasons, captaining the side.

**Bobby Gilfillan** (Born Cowdenbeath, 29 June 1938. Died 8 November 2012.) Centre forward Bobby Gilfillan established himself as a regular scorer with Cowdenbeath in the late 1950s to earn a move to Newcastle United, but he struggled to win a place in the Magpies' line-up. After returning to Scotland he played for St Johnstone and Raith Rovers, then had a spell with Southend United. He is perhaps best known for his time at Doncaster Rovers between 1965 and 1971 where he scored 33 goals in 186 Football League games and was a member of two Division Four title winning sides.

**Malcolm Glazzard** (Born Bebington, Cheshire, 1 July 1931. Died Providence, Rhode Island, United States, 26 June 2012.) Malcolm Glazzard was an amateur on the books at Liverpool before joining Macclesfield, then members of the Cheshire League, where he proved to be a prolific goalscorer over several seasons. He

later emigrated to the United States where he played for Los Angeles Scottish. His only Football League appearance came when he played as a triallist for Accrington Stanley at Mansfield in August 1951.

**Dick Graham** (Born Corby, Northamptonshire, 6 May 1922. Died Colchester, 7 March 2013.) Dick Graham was the regular goalkeeper for Crystal Palace in the seasons after the war until injury ended his career. Later he returned to Selhurst Park as manager, leading the club to promotion from Division Three in 1963–64. He also managed Orient, Walsall and Colchester United with his finest hour coming when he led the U's to a shock FA Cup victory over Leeds United in February 1971.

**Tony Grealish** (Born Paddington, London, 21 September 1956. Died Ilfracombe, Devon, 23 April 2013.) Tony Grealish was a powerful, all-action midfield player who was an apprentice with Leyton Orient before progressing to a professional contract. He went on to make over 200 competitive appearances for the O's, helping them reach the FA Cup semi-finals in 1977–78. After a spell with Luton he joined Brighton, where he was captain of the team that lost out to Manchester United in the 1981 FA Cup final. He went on to turn out for West Bromwich Albion, Manchester City, Rotherham and Walsall, playing more than 550 Football League games. Tony won 44 caps for the Republic of Ireland.

**Brian Green** (Born Droylesden, Lancs, 5 June 1935. Died Rochdale, 14 August 2012.) Brian Green was a versatile attacking player who made 80 Football League appearances in the 1950s and early '60s with a number of lower division clubs, notably Rochdale and Southport. He subsequently moved into coaching and management with some success, taking charge of the Australia national team in 1975–76, managing Rochdale (June 1976 to September 1977) and coaching with a number of clubs including Leeds United.

**Les Green** (Born Atherstone, Warwickshire, 17 October 1941. Died Leicester, 30 July 2012.) Les Green was an agile goalkeeper who was on the books of Hull City before dropping into non-league football with Nuneaton Borough and then Burton Albion. He linked up with legendary manager Brian Clough at Hartlepool and then Derby where he was an ever-present in the Rams' team that won the Division Two title in 1968–69. He later spent time in South Africa where he played for Durban City.

**Brian Greenhoff** (Born Barnsley, 28 April 1953. Died Norden, Rochdale, 22 May 2013.) Brian Greenhoff was a versatile and athletic player who was perhaps best used as a central defender. After graduating through the ranks with Manchester United he went on to make over 250 first-team appearances, gaining a Division Two winners' medal in 1974–75 and helping the Reds defeat Liverpool to win the 1977 FA Cup final. He subsequently had spells with Leeds United and, briefly, Rochdale, before leaving the senior game. Brian won 18 full caps for England between 1976 and 1980.

**Tony Gubba** (Born Manchester, 23 September 1943. Died 11 March 2013.) Tony Gubba was a sports broadcaster who commentated on football and other sports for BBC Television for some 40 years, covering every World Cup tournament from 1976 to 2004. He also presented both *Sportsnight* and *Grandstand* programmes during his career.

**Bill Guttridge** (Born Darlaston, Staffordshire, 4 March 1931. Died Walsall, 6 April 2013.) Defender Bill Guttridge spent seven years on the books of Wolverhampton Wanderers, but managed just six first-team appearances during his stay at Molineux. A hard tackling full back, he moved on to Walsall in November 1954 where he enjoyed better fortune, making over 200 appearances and captaining the side before injury ended his career in 1962.

**Helmut Haller** (Born Augsburg, Germany, 21 July 1939. Died Augsburg, Germany, 11 October 2012.) Helmut Haller was an attacking midfield player who won 33 caps for West Germany between 1958 and 1970. A member of his country's squad for three World Cup tournaments, he played in the team defeated by England in the 1966 final at Wembley, scoring the opening goal of the game. He began his career with BC Augsburg, but spent the best years of his career playing in Italy, firstly for Bologna and then Juventus.

**Ron Hansell** (Born Norwich, 3 October 1930. Died Caister-on-Sea, Norfolk, 8 February 2013.) Ron Hansell was an inside forward who signed for Norwich City from local football in the summer of 1950. Although he spent six years on the books at Carrow Road he was mostly a reserve, with his highlights coming in the FA Cup campaign of 1953–54 when he scored twice to eliminate Hastings United and then played in the team that defeated Arsenal in the fourth round. He later had a season at Chester before joining Lowestoft Town.

**Dave Harper** (Born Peckham, London, 29 September 1938. Died Eastbourne, Sussex, 24 January 2013.) Dave Harper was a hardworking midfield player who began his career with Millwall, winning England youth international honours and making over 150 League appearances. He moved to Ipswich Town in March 1965, later becoming the first-ever substitute to be used by the Portman Road club. After a brief spell with Swindon Town he finished his career at Orient, helping the O's win promotion in 1969–70.

**Hughie Hay** (Born October 1931. Died Laurencekirk, 23 October 2012.) Hughie Hay was a skilful inside forward who spent seven years on the books of Aberdeen in the 1950s scoring 26 goals from 58 appearances in a career interrupted by National Service and injury. He went on to play for Dundee United and Arbroath before moving into the Highland League with Deveronvale.

**George Hazlett** (Born Glasgow, 10 March 1923. Died 21 December 2012.) George Hazlett was a tricky winger who achieved the unusual feat of playing professional football in each of the four Home Nations. On the books of Celtic as the war ended, he made 23 peacetime appearances during his stay at Parkhead

before signing for Belfast Celtic. He played in the notorious game against Linfield in December 1948 which led to the club withdrawing from the Irish League and went on to enjoy spells with Bury, Cardiff City and Millwall where he made over 100 Football League appearances.

**Tommy Henderson** (Born Burnley, 1 October 1927. Died 31 May 2013.) Tommy Henderson was a pacy winger who made three appearances for Burnley in the 1944–45 season, but was mostly a reserve during his time with the Clarets, helping the club win the Central League title in 1948–49. He made two first-team appearances the following season before eventually leaving the club in the summer of 1951, later playing for Rossendale United and Nelson.

**Tommy Higginson** (Born Newtongrange, Midlothian, 6 January 1937. Died 22 July 2012.) Tommy Higginson was an inside forward with Kilmarnock as a youngster but failed to break into the first team at Rugby Park, moving south to sign for Brentford in the summer of 1959. He went on to become one of the stalwarts of the Bees' team during the 1960s, making some 435 senior appearances before eventually leaving to sign for Hillingdon Borough in 1970.

**Raymond Hogg** (Born Lowick, Northumberland, 11 December 1929. Died 10 March 2013.) Raymond Hogg was a full back who joined Berwick Rangers from local team Lowick Rovers for the start of the 1951–52 season, featuring in the Shielfield club's first-ever Scottish League game. He was a near ever-present from then onwards, featuring in the team that defeated Dundee to reach the Scottish Cup quarter-finals in 1953–54. He was sold to Aston Villa 12 months later but was never a regular at Villa Park, and later played for Mansfield Town and Peterborough United.

**Graham Horn** (Born Westminster, London, 23 August 1954. Died 29 June 2012.) Graham Horn was a goalkeeper who began his career with Arsenal, making his League debut whilst on loan to Portsmouth. He enjoyed useful spells with both Luton Town and Torquay United while he also spent two seasons with Aldershot, principally as a reserve. He later played for Barnstaple Town.

**Roy Horobin** (Born Brownhills, Staffs, 10 March 1935. Died 30 August 2012.) Roy Horobin was a creative attacking player who joined West Bromwich Albion on leaving school. He moved on to Notts County in November 1958, where he was a member of the team that won promotion to Division Three in 1959–60 and scored the only hat-trick of his career. After two further seasons as a regular with Peterborough United he finished off with a handful of games for Crystal Palace.

**Gary Ingham** (Born Rotherham, 9 October 1964. Died Rotherham, 20 November 2012.) Gary Ingham was a goalkeeper who started out as a youngster with Rotherham United and went on to make 11 League appearances for Doncaster Rovers, mostly in a run of games towards the end of the 1997–98 season. He also played for a number of non-league clubs including Gainsborough Trinity, Stalybridge Celtic and Frickley Athletic.

**Norman Ireland** (Born Circa 1922. Died May 2013.) Norman Ireland was a forward who played Junior football in the Dundee area during the war, occasionally guesting in the North Eastern League. He spent the 1945–46 season with St Johnstone before moving on to play for Brechin City who were then members of Division C.

**Jimmy Jackson** (Born Glasgow, 26 March 1931. Died York, 2 March 2013.) Jimmy Jackson was a centre forward who signed for Notts County in March 1949 after serving in the RAF. He led the Magpies' scoring charts in 1954–55 and 1955–56 before eventually leaving to sign for Southern League club Headington United in 1957.

**Iain Jamieson** (Born Dumbarton, 14 October 1928. Died Kirkcudbright, 19 October 2012.) Iain Jamieson was an attacking wing half or inside forward who was on the fringes of the Aberdeen squad when he signed for Coventry City in January 1949. He went on to make more than 150 appearances during his time at Highfield Road when he was captain of the side for a while. Later he returned to the club as a director and then chairman from 1983 to 1984.

**Reg Jenkins** (Born Millbrook, Cornwall, 7 October 1938. Died Tenerife, Spain, 29 January 2013.) Reg Jenkins was a powerful centre forward who made his debut for Plymouth Argyle as a youngster before moving on to Exeter and then Torquay. He signed for Rochdale in the summer of 1964 and proved to be a revelation for the Spotland club over the next nine seasons, establishing an all-time club record of 119 Football League goals. He led the club scoring charts on six occasions and helped fire Dale to their first-ever promotion in 1968–69.

**Hans Jeppson** (Born Kungsbacka, Sweden, 10 May 1925. Died Rome, Italy, 21 February 2013.) Hans Jeppson developed as a prolific scorer in Sweden with Djurgårdens IF before joining Charlton Athletic in January 1951. In a three-month spell at The Valley he netted nine goals in 11 games to help the Addicks avoid relegation before moving to Italy where he became a star in Serie A with Atalanta, Napoli and Torino. He won 12 caps for Sweden, featuring in the 1950 World Cup finals in Brazil.

**Dennis John** (Born Swansea, 27 January 1935. Died Cardiff, 9 April 2013.) Dennis John was a defender who signed for Plymouth Argyle as a teenager. However, he made little impact at first-team level in six seasons at Home Park, nor in a 12-month spell with Swansea. He signed for Scunthorpe United in the summer of 1959 and established himself in the team at full back before concluding his career with Millwall

where he was a member of the team that was unbeaten at home for almost three years from August 1964, although he left The Den at the end of the 1965–66 season.

**Ralph Johnson** (Born Hethersett, Norfolk, 15 April 1922. Died 23 April 2013.) Ralph Johnson was a prolific scorer for Norwich City in wartime, but found his opportunities in peacetime football restricted. He created a club record for the Canaries when he scored after just 10 seconds of the game against Leyton Orient in October 1946 and made a move to the O's the following April. He was mostly a reserve during his time at Brisbane Road, returning to East Anglia to sign for Lowestoft Town in 1950.

**Freddie Jones** (Born Gelligaer, Glamorgan, 11 January 1938. Died Derby, 22 March 2013.) Freddie Jones was a flying winger who starred with Southern League club Hereford United before being sold to Arsenal in January 1958. He failed to break into the first team at Highbury but subsequently built a solid career with Brighton, Swindon, Grimsby and Reading making 175 League appearances. He won two caps for Wales at U23 level.

**Ken Jones** (Born Aberdare, 2 January 1936. Died Stoke-on-Trent, 18 January 2013.) Ken Jones was a goalkeeper who was capped for Wales Schoolboys before joining Cardiff City. After waiting four years he made his debut for the Bluebirds, but it was when he moved to Scunthorpe United in December 1958 that he began to shine. A regular in the side from the second half of the 1959–60 campaign, he went on to make 186 appearances for the Iron, then had spells with Charlton Athletic and Exeter City before moving into non-league football with Yeovil Town.

**Ken Jones** (Born Havercroft, Wakefield, 26 June 1944. Died 27 December 2012.) Ken Jones signed for Bradford Park Avenue from local club Monckton Colliery as a 17-year-old. He became a regular in the line-up from March 1963, playing at various times in both full-back positions. In the summer of 1965 he was sold to Southampton where he played eight times in the club's promotion campaign to the First Division and went on to gain experience of European football. He finished his career with a spell at Cardiff City.

**Tommy Keane** (Born Dublin, 16 September 1968. Died Galway, Republic of Ireland, 28 December 2012.) Tommy Keane was a midfield player who made a total of 19 Football League appearances, nine from the bench, in spells with Bournemouth and Colchester United in the late 1980s. He subsequently returned home and turned out for several League of Ireland clubs including Galway United, Sligo Rovers, Finn Harps and Athlone Town.

**Frank Keating** (Born 4 October 1937. Died Hereford, 25 January 2013.) Frank Keating was well known for his work as a journalist for the *Guardian* newspaper, for whom he produced some of the best modern writing on a range of sports including football. He continued to write a column for the *Observer* until shortly before his death. Earlier in his career he had worked for ITV, covering two World Cups, also reporting on the 1970 tournament for *The Times*.

**Stan Keery** (Born Derby, 9 September 1931. Died Crewe, 7 March 2013.) Stan Keery had a brief spell of first-team football with Shrewsbury Town before being signed by Newcastle United in November 1952. A tenacious wing half, he was mostly a reserve at St James' Park before moving on to Mansfield. His best years were spent at Crewe Alexandra, where he made over 250 first-team appearances and was a member of the team that won promotion from the Fourth Division in 1962–63.

**Phil Kelly** (Born Dublin, 10 July 1939. Died 16 August 2012.) Full back Phil Kelly signed for Wolverhampton Wanderers in September 1957 but managed just a handful of appearances during a five-year stay at Molineux. He fared much better during a spell with Norwich City, making over 100 first-team appearances before injury led to his retirement from the full-time game in the summer of 1967. He also won five caps for the Republic of Ireland while with Wolves.

**Trevor Kemp** (Died Ashington, Northumberland, 15 October 2012.) Trevor Kemp made 31 appearances for Berwick Rangers between 1961 and 1963, later spending time in Australia where he played for Melbourne Hungaria. He eventually returned to play in local football in the Berwick area.

**Derek Kevan** (Born Ripon, Yorkshire, 6 March 1935. Died Birmingham, 4 January 2013.) Derek Kevan was a big, powerful centre forward who signed for West Bromwich Albion in the summer of 1953 after a brief period of first-team football for Bradford Park Avenue. He went on to become one of the Baggies' post-war greats, netting over 150 League goals during a decade at The Hawthorns. Derek was joint top scorer in the First Division in 1961–62 before moving on for a brief spell at Chelsea and then Manchester City, then dropping into the lower divisions. He won 14 caps for England and was a member of the squad at the 1958 World Cup finals.

**John Kilford** (Born Derby, 8 November 1938. Died 8 October 2012.) John Kilford was a full back who joined Notts County as an amateur from Derby Corinthians, signing professional terms in the summer of 1957. He had a run of games at right back the following season before moving on to Leeds United in February 1959. In four seasons at Elland Road he was mostly a reserve before joining Southern League club Tonbridge.

**Jimmy Knox** (Born Brechin, 26 November 1935. Died 24 December 2012.) Jimmy Knox signed for Coventry City in the summer of 1957 and made two Football League appearances before moving on to Rugby Town in November 1958. He became something of a legendary figure in football in Rugby, firstly as

a player with the Southern League club and then as manager of VS Rugby, leading them to success in the FA Vase in 1983.

**Rudolf Kreitlein** (Born Fürth, Germany, 14 November 1919. Died Stuttgart, Germany, 31 July 2012.) Rudolf Kreitlein was a West German referee who took charge of the World Cup quarter-final tie between England and Argentina in 1966 when he dismissed the Argentine captain Antonio Rattin during the first half of the game. Earlier that year he had refereed the European Cup final between Real Madrid and Partizan Belgrade.

**Peter Laverick** (Born Cleethorpes, 29 January 1939. Died Scartho, North East Lincs, 29 March 2013.) Peter Laverick spent five years on the books of Grimsby Town where he mostly turned out for the reserves, making four senior appearances at inside and outside left. He later spent a season with Bristol City without breaking into the first team, before returning to the Grimsby area to play for Lincolnshire League outfit Ross Group.

**Brian Leach** (Born Reading, 20 July 1932. Died Caversham, Reading, March 2013.) Brian Leach was a creative attacking player who made over 100 appearances for Reading in the 1950s. He later switched to Southern League football with Headington, Tunbridge Wells and Clacton before becoming something of a legendary figure for Henley Town for many years.

**Derek Leaver** (Born Blackburn, 13 November 1930. Died 24 March 2013.) Derek Leaver was an inside forward who made over 70 Football League appearances for Blackburn Rovers, Bournemouth and Crewe Alexandra in the 1950s before injury ended his senior career. He later played in non-league football in the North West for Macclesfield and Mossley.

**Bert Linnecor** (Born Birmingham, 30 November 1933. Died Lincoln, 25 November 2012.) Bert Linnecor was a wing half who started out with Birmingham City before joining Lincoln City in April 1957 as part of the deal that saw Dick Neal move in the opposite direction. He went on to make over 250 appearances for the Imps before leaving in 1964 to play for Boston FC, later turning out for Grantham Town.

**Ian Lister** (Born Kirkcaldy, 5 September 1946. Died Inverness, 8 February 2013.) Ian Lister was a winger who made his debut for Aberdeen as a teenager and went on to play over 200 senior games in a career that saw him also turn out for Raith Rovers, St Mirren, Dunfermline Athletic and Berwick Rangers. A highlight of his career came when he played and scored for the Pars in their 3-1 Scottish Cup final victory over Hearts at Hampden in April 1968.

**Joe McBride** (Born Glasgow, 10 June 1938. Died Glasgow, 11 July 2012.) Joe McBride was a powerful, stocky centre forward who started out with Kilmarnock. He went on to enjoy a prolific career, netting some 223 goals from just over 300 League games. Much travelled, his many clubs included Luton Town, Motherwell, Partick Thistle and Hibernian. He did well for most of a three-year spell with Celtic, finishing as the Scottish League's leading scorer in 1965–66 but missing out on a place in the 1967 European Cup final team through injury. Joe won two full caps for Scotland.

**Willie McCulloch** (Born Tarbolton, Ayrshire, 24 May 1927. Died Prestwick, Ayrshire, 7 March 2013.) Willie McCulloch was an outside left who struggled to make an impact at Kilmarnock in the late 1940s and returned to the Juniors with Cumnock. In 1950 he signed for Airdrieonians where he stayed eight seasons, making over 170 Scottish League appearances, before winding down his career with spells at St Mirren and Morton. He won representative honours for Scotland Juniors and Scotland B.

**Jimmy McGill** (Born Kilsyth, 10 March 1926. Died 21 April 2013.) Jimmy McGill was an inside forward who played for Bury and Derby County in the immediate post-war period without establishing himself as a first-team player. He struggled too at Kilmarnock, but after joining Berwick Rangers on their entry to Scottish League football in 1951 he flourished. A transfer to Queen of the South followed and he made over 100 appearances for the Doonhamers before concluding his career with Cowdenbeath.

**Ian MacLeod** (Born East Kilbride, 19 November 1959. Died 6 May 2013.) Ian MacLeod was a defender who made over 200 appearances for Motherwell between 1979 and 1986 where he was part of two First Division championship sides. Later he spent time with Falkirk, Raith Rovers and Meadowbank Thistle, adding a further 200-odd appearances and winning a third First Division title with Raith in 1992–93.

**Harry McShane** (Born Holytown, Lanarkshire, 8 April 1920. Died Manchester, 7 November 2012.) Harry McShane was a winger who made his debut for Blackburn Rovers as a teenager during the 1937–38 season before losing some of the best years of his career to the war. He played plenty of football during the hostilities, guesting for a number of clubs including Hamilton Academical. When peace returned he moved on to Huddersfield Town and then Bolton Wanderers where he made close to 100 League appearances. He subsequently spent almost four seasons at Manchester United, contributing to their League title campaign of 1951–52, before finishing off with a spell at Oldham Athletic.

**Tony McShane** (Born Belfast, 28 February 1927. Died Derriford, Plymouth, 24 December 2012.) Tony McShane was a combative wing half who developed in Irish League football before signing for Plymouth Argyle in December 1948. He made 90 competitive appearances for the Pilgrims then spent a couple of seasons at Swindon. Later he was player-manager of Goole Town, then served both Scunthorpe United (1958–59) and Chesterfield (1962–1967) as manager.

**Stan Machent** (Born Chesterfield, 23 March 1921. Died Chesterfield, 17 December 2012.) Stan Machent was an inside forward who signed for Sheffield United during the 1938–39 season but he had to wait until after the war to make his full debut. He later had a couple of seasons with Chesterfield before injuries brought his time at Saltergate to an end and he moved into non-league football, firstly with Buxton and then Hereford United.

**Ernie Machin** (Born Swinton, Lancashire, 26 April 1944. Died 22 July 2012.) Ernie Machin enjoyed a 10-year spell with Coventry City from March 1962. A busy attacking player, he helped the club rise from the Third Division to reach the top flight, making close on 300 first-team appearances. He moved on to Plymouth in December 1972 and enjoyed a successful 18 months with the Pilgrims, helping them reach a Football League Cup semi-final place in 1973–74. Ernie concluded his career with two seasons at Brighton where he was club captain and came close to helping them win promotion to the old First Division.

**Con Martin** (Born Dublin, 20 March 1923. Died 24 April 2013.) Con Martin played Gaelic football representing Dublin as a youngster before going on to build a career in the association game. A player who was versatile enough to turn out in goal and as an outfield player, he progressed from Drumcondra and Glentoran to Leeds United at the beginning of 1947. Eighteen months later he moved on to Aston Villa where he was to make over 200 League and Cup appearances, mostly at centre half and full back although he had a short run in the side as goalkeeper. Con was a dual international, winning 6 caps for Northern Ireland and 30 for the Republic of Ireland.

**Barry Mealand** (Born Carshalton, Surrey, 24 January 1943. Died Tunbridge Wells, 2 April 2013.) Barry Mealand was a full back who signed professional terms for Fulham in October 1961, but he was mainly a reserve to the likes of George Cohen during a seven-year stay at Craven Cottage. He was more of a regular in two seasons with Rotherham United which concluded his senior career, after which he signed for Northern Premier League club Goole Town.

**Kevin Moore** (Born Grimsby, 29 April 1958. Died Hedge End, Hampshire, 29 April 2013.) Kevin Moore was a strong and powerful central defender who went on to make over 400 League and Cup appearances for Grimsby Town, featuring in the team that rose from the Fourth Division to the Second with successive promotions in 1978–79 and 1979–80. He left the Mariners for Oldham Athletic but stayed only briefly before entering the top flight with Southampton. Kevin played 180 times for Saints before concluding his career with Fulham.

**Kenny Morgans** (Born Swansea, 16 March 1939. Died Swansea, 18 November 2012.) Kenny Morgans was a winger who was capped by Wales schoolboys before joining the groundstaff at Manchester United. He made his first-team debut in December 1957, but within a matter of months he had the misfortune to be on the plane that crashed whilst departing from Munich, killing many of his colleagues Although he was soon back playing, Kenny found it difficult to recover his form and after returning to south Wales in March 1961 he completed his career with spells at Swansea Town and Newport County. He was capped on two occasions for Wales U23s.

**Jackie Myles** (Born 18 December 1960. Died Edinburgh, 28 January 2013.) Jackie Myles was an inside forward who had brief spells of action in senior football with Raith Rovers and Falkirk but is much better known as one of the most important figures in Junior football from the 1980s onwards as a player and then manager. He was capped 13 times by Scotland Juniors and assisted a string of clubs in the Edinburgh and Lothians region, notably Bonnyrigg Rose.

**Dick Neal** (Born Dinnington, Yorkshire, 1 October 1933. Died 21 February 2013.) Dick Neal was a powerful and combative wing half who developed with the Wolves nursery team Wath Wanderers but although he went on to sign a professional contract he failed to make the grade at Molineux and moved on to Lincoln City. He became the Imps' star man and won England U23 honours earning a move to Birmingham City where he went on to captain the team and play in the 1960 Inter Cities Fairs Cup final with Barcelona when Blues went down 4-1 over the two legs. After a spell with Middlesbrough he concluded his senior career back at Lincoln.

**Jacky Neilson** (Born Newtongrange, Midlothian, 1 April 1929. Died Edinburgh, 22 June 2012.) Jacky Neilson joined St Mirren from Newtongrange Star in 1949 and went on to stay with the Paisley club for 12 seasons, making over 300 competitive appearances before injury brought his career to a close. He was a member of the team that defeated Aberdeen to win the Scottish Cup final in 1959 and also won a League Cup runners-up prize in 1955–56. Jacky was capped for Scotland B.

**Bobby Nicol** (Born Edinburgh, 11 May 1936. Died Newmarket, Ontario, Canada, 11 July 2012.) Bobby Nicol was a wing half who joined Hibernian from Edinburgh City in 1952 and stayed at Easter Road for a decade, making almost 50 first-team appearances. He moved south to play for Barnsley, then had a season with Berwick Rangers before emigrating to Canada where he played for Toronto City.

**Seamus O'Connell** (Born Carlisle, 1 January 1930. Died Spain, 24 February 2013.) Seamus O'Connell was one of the best of the amateur centre forwards of the 1950s. He spent much of that time on the books of Bishop Auckland, winning two FA Amateur Cup winners' medals and once scoring eight goals in a match. He made occasional Football League appearances, turning out for Middlesbrough, Chelsea and Carlisle United. Seamus is best known for his time at Stamford Bridge where he hit a hat-trick on his debut and

scored 8 goals from 11 appearances in the 1954–55 Football League championship season. He also played for Crook Town (where he won a third Amateur Cup winners' medal) and Penrith as well as winning England Amateur caps.

**Alan O'Meara** (Born Grantham, Lincs, 15 December 1958. Died Leicester, 18 January 2013.) Goalkeeper Alan O'Meara made 41 League appearances for Scunthorpe United in the 1975–76 and 1976–77 seasons before moving into non-league football. He later turned out for several non-league clubs in the South Lincolnshire area and was still playing veterans' football until shortly before his death.

**John O'Neill** (Born Dublin, 9 September 1935. Died Blackpool, 23 September 2012.) John O'Neill was a defender who joined Preston North End from League of Ireland club Drumcondra in April 1958 but it took him more than two years to establish himself in the first team. He went on to make over 50 appearances during his time at Deepdale then had 12 months with Barrow before spending several years in Australia where he played for the Hakoah club. He was capped once for the Republic of Ireland.

**Emilio Pacione** (Born Dundee, 20 March 1920. Died 25 August 2012.) Emilio Pacione was a small but speedy winger who joined Dundee United from Lochee Harp in November 1945. He stayed at Tannadice until the end of the 1949–50 season, finishing as top scorer in 1945–46 and making a total of 89 Scottish League appearances. He moved on for a brief spell at Coleraine and then spent time with Division C club Brechin City.

**Harry Parfitt** (Born Cardiff, 26 September 1929. Died 17 October 2012.) Full back Harry Parfitt made a solitary top flight appearance for Cardiff City, but played almost 60 times in an 18-month loan spell at Torquay. He left Ninian Park in the summer of 1955 and then spent two seasons with Southern League club Worcester City before moving on to Abergavenny.

**Jim Patterson** (Born Luncarty, Perthshire, 17 August 1928. Died Dumfries, 15 December 2012.) Jim Patterson was a big, powerful centre forward who joined Queen of the South from Luncarty Juniors in April 1949. A one-club man, he remained at Palmerston Park until the 1962–63 season, establishing an all-time club record of 251 competitive goals.

**Tony Pawson, OBE** (Born Chertsey, Surrey, 22 August 1921. Died 12 October 2012.) Tony Pawson was a fine all-round sportsman who played cricket for Kent, won the world individual fly fishing title in 1984 and played first class football. An Oxford University Blue in 1947–48, he was a member of the Pegasus team that won the FA Amateur Cup in 1951, was capped by England Amateurs and featured in the Great Britain squad for the 1952 Olympic Games. A talented right winger, he also played two senior games for Charlton Athletic in the early 1950s.

**Jimmy Payne** (Born Bootle, Liverpool, 10 March 1926. Died Kendal, Cumbria, 22 January 2013.) Jimmy Payne was a skilful right winger who made over 200 first-team appearances for Liverpool in the early post-war period. Signed by the Reds from local football during the war years, he had to wait until the 1948–49 season for his first-team debut. He gained an FA Cup runners-up medal in 1950 and also won England B international honours before ending his career with a spell at Merseyside rivals Everton.

**George Petherbridge** (Born Devenport, Plymouth, 19 May 1927. Died 4 March 2013.) George Petherbridge was a traditional winger who signed for Bristol Rovers towards the end of the war and remained with the club through to the summer of 1962, amassing more than 450 Football League appearances during his stay. Highlights of his career included two runs to the FA Cup quarter-finals and a Division Three South title in 1952–53. After leaving Eastville he signed for Western League club Salisbury.

**Reg Pickett** (Born Bareilly, Uttar Pradesh, India, 6 January 1927. Died Rowland's Castle, Hampshire, 4 November 2012.) Reg Pickett was a versatile wing half who signed for Portsmouth in March 1949 and went on to play 14 times in the team that won the First Division title in 1949–50. In total he made 127 appearances for Pompey before moving on to Ipswich Town in the 1957 close season. He had three seasons of regular first-team football at Portman Road before eventually leaving to sign for Stevenage Town.

**Ivor Powell, MBE** (Born Gilfach, nr. Bargoed, Glamorgan, 5 July 1916. Died 6 November 2012.) Ivor Powell was a hard working defensive wing half who made his debut in senior football in the final season before war broke out and remained active in the game for over 70 years as player, manager and coach. He was a near ever-present in the Queens Park Rangers team that won the Division Three South title in 1947–48. Later he spent three seasons in the top flight with Aston Villa, before spells as player-manager of Port Vale and Bradford City. Thereafter he mostly worked as a coach, most recently with Team Bath, retiring at the age of 93, by which time he had become known as the world's oldest coach. He won 8 peacetime caps for Wales.

**Ernie Price** (Born Easington, Co Durham, 12 May 1926. Died Taunton, Somerset, 25 February 2013.) Ernie Price was a wing half or inside forward who signed for Sunderland towards the end of the war. He was unable to break into the Wearsiders' first team, but enjoyed fairly regular football during a two-and-a-half-year stay at Darlington and added further appearances for Crystal Palace. He then moved to the West Country where he played for Weymouth and Bideford before becoming player-manager of Taunton Town.

**Jack Price** (Born Shotton, Co Durham, 29 August 1918. Died Horden, Co Durham, 18 April 2013.) Jack Price was a winger who had spells with both Portsmouth and Wolves without breaking into the first team. He joined Hartlepools for the final season of pre-war football, when he featured regularly in the side and

remained on the club's books through to December 1948. He later had a brief spell with York City before signing for Horden CW.

**Willie Purvis** (Born Berwick-upon-Tweed, 14 December 1938. Died Cleethorpes, 30 July 2012.) Forward Willie Purvis joined Berwick Rangers from Alnwick Town and played two seasons for the Scottish League club before moving south to sign for Grimsby Town in the summer of 1961. However, he was mostly a reserve at Blundell Park and also at Doncaster Rovers before leaving the full-time game.

**Len Quested** (Born Folkestone, Kent, 9 January 1925. Died Buderim, Queensland, Australia, 20 August 2012.) Len Quested was an energetic wing half who signed for Fulham during the war and went on to make almost 200 peacetime appearances for the Cottagers, winning international honours for England B and featuring in the side that won the Second Division title in 1948–49. In November 1951 he was transferred to Huddersfield Town where he gained a further Second Division title in 1952–53, turning out at left half in what was famously an unchanged defence. In 1957 he emigrated to Australia where he continued to play for several years.

**Keith Ripley** (Born Normanton, Yorkshire, 29 March 1935. Died Normanton, Yorkshire, 5 November 2012.) Keith Ripley was a wing half who began his career with Leeds United where he was often a stand-in for regular players. After spells with Norwich City and Mansfield Town he joined Peterborough United for their inaugural Football League campaign and was a near ever-present as they won the Fourth Division title. Keith finished off at Doncaster Rovers where he added further appearances to take his career total to beyond the 300-mark.

**Don Roby** (Born Wigan, 15 November 1933. Died Nottingham, 10 June 2013.) Don Roby was a quick, tricky winger who spent a decade on the books of Notts County, making a total of 226 Football League appearances and featuring in the team that won promotion from Division Four in 1959–60. He signed for Derby County in the summer of 1961 where he spent three more seasons before injury ended his senior career and he joined Burton Albion.

**Albie Roles** (Born Southampton, 29 September 1921. Died Southampton, 3 October 2012.) Albie Roles was a full back who played in 188 wartime games for Southampton, but managed just one appearance in peacetime football. He left The Dell in the summer of 1949, spending the 1949–50 campaign as a regular with Gloucester City before taking over as player-manager of Cowes.

**Jim Rollo** (Born Helmsdale, Sutherland, 16 November 1937. Died Perth, 13 October 2012.) Jim Rollo joined Hibernian from Jeanfield Swifts in 1955 but made only two senior appearances at Easter Road before joining non-league club Poole Town. He subsequently returned to senior football with Oldham and went on to play for Southport and Bradford City, featuring regularly in goal for all three clubs during his time.

**Bill Roost** (Born Bristol, 22 March 1924. Died Bristol, 10 February 2013.) Bill Roost was a centre or inside forward who signed for Bristol Rovers from non-league club Stonehouse in 1948. He scored twice on his debut against Reading and was Rovers' leading scorer in 1949–50, going on to make 177 Football League appearances for the club. He later spent a couple of seasons with Swindon Town before moving into non-league football with Minehead.

**Charlie Rutter** (Born Bromley, Kent, 22 December 1927. Died 19 October 2012.) Charlie Rutter joined Cardiff City from Taunton Town in September 1949 and established himself as a first-team regular in 1952–53 when the Bluebirds won promotion to the top flight. Thereafter he was in competition with Ron Stitfall for the right-back slot at Ninian Park before eventually moving on in the summer of 1958.

**Harry Searson** (Born Mansfield, 3 June 1924. Died Corby, Northamptonshire, 5 January 2013.) Harry Searson was a goalkeeper who joined Sheffield Wednesday during the war, but after failing to make an impact at Hillsborough he moved on to Mansfield Town in time for the 1946–47 season. A brave and solid 'keeper, he went on to make over 200 Football League appearances in a career that also saw him play for Leeds United and York City. He later played in non-league football for Corby and Kettering Town.

**Dave Sexton, OBE** (Born Islington, London, 6 April 1930. Died 25 November 2012.) Dave Sexton was something of a journeyman inside forward throughout his career save for a spell at West Ham United in the mid-1950s where he was a member of the group known as 'The Academy' who would meet in a local cafe to discuss football matters. He made over 180 Football League appearances in a career that also took in spells with Luton Town, Leyton Orient, Brighton and Crystal Palace. Dave went on to become one of the most highly regarded coaches and managers in the English game, taking charge of Chelsea, Queens Park Rangers, Manchester United and Coventry City. He achieved great success during his time at Stamford Bridge with the Blues winning the FA Cup for the first time in 1971 and following this up by defeating Real Madrid 12 months later to take the European Cup Winners' Cup.

**George Showell** (Born Bilston, Staffordshire, 9 February 1934. Died Wrexham, 18 December 2012.) George Showell was a defender who made 200 first-team appearances for Wolverhampton Wanderers, having been on the club's books for some 14 years. An FA Cup winner in 1960 when the Wolves beat Blackburn Rovers 3–0, he had previously been generally regarded as a reserve but was a more regular performer in the 1960s. He moved on for a short spell with Bristol City and then to Wrexham where he stayed almost 25 years, serving the club as player, trainer and physiotherapist during his time at the Racecourse Ground.

**Jimmy Silcock** (Died Larbert, Stirlingshire, 30 October 2012.) Jimmy Silcock was a goalscoring inside forward who was a stalwart figure for Stenhousemuir in the 1950s scoring 82 goals from 190 Scottish League appearances in two separate spells with the club. He also played senior football for Falkirk, Stirling Albion and Berwick Rangers. After retiring as a player Jimmy returned to Falkirk for a 12-year spell as groundsman at Brockville.

**Ken Simcoe** (Born Nottingham, 14 February 1937. Died Sherwood, Nottingham, 16 September 2012.) Versatile forward Ken Simcoe spent four-and-a-half seasons in senior football but managed just 12 Football League appearances in total in a career that saw him play for Nottingham Forest, Coventry City and Notts County. He later played in the Midland League with Heanor, Loughborough and Ilkeston, retiring though injury at the beginning of 1967.

**Roy Sinclair** (Born Liverpool, 10 December 1944. Died Allerton, Liverpool, 12 January 2013.) Roy Sinclair was a stylish, hard working midfield player who made over a century of appearances for Tranmere Rovers before moving to Watford in March 1969. He went on to score a memorable goal for the Hornets against Plymouth later that season to gain the club promotion to the old Second Division for the first time in their history. Roy later returned to Tranmere before spending several years playing in the United States.

**Doug Smith** (Born Aberdeen, 18 November 1937. Died Dundee, 5 December 2012.) Doug Smith enjoyed an association of almost 40 years with Dundee United as a player, director and finally club chairman. A centre half, he made his first appearance for the Tannadice club in the 1958–59 season and stayed until 1975–76 making more than 600 appearances in competitive matches and gaining a Scottish Cup runners-up medal in 1974. He returned as a director in 1983, having a spell as chairman from 2000 and also serving as Scottish League President in 1997–98.

**Mike Smith** (Born Quarndon, Derbyshire, 22 September 1935. Died 22 April 2013.) Mike Smith was a centre half who spent nine seasons on the books of Derby County, mostly playing for the reserves in the Central League. He signed for Bradford City in the 1961 close season and had three seasons as a regular at Valley Parade, eventually returning to the Derby area in 1966 when he signed for Central Alliance club Crewton Sports, later moving on to Lockheed Leamington.

**Stan Smith** (Born Coventry, 24 February 1925. Died 6 October 2012.) Stan Smith was a wing half who signed for Coventry City during the war and stayed until the summer of 1950, although he managed only 29 Football League appearances. Following this he had a brief association with Swansea Town, where he did not break into the first team, before returning to the Midlands with Stafford Rangers and Nuneaton Borough.

**Bill Souter** (Born Dundee, 3 May 1931. Died Chester, 24 August 2012.) Bill Souter was a full back who spent six years as a reserve with Burnley before making his Football League debut following his move to join Chester in the summer of 1957. He went on to make over 50 appearances for Chester but left in 1960 to join Bangor City. Bill was a member of the Bangor team that won the Welsh Cup in 1961–62 and the following season played in the non-league club's epic tie against Napoli in the European Cup Winners' Cup which saw the teams level over two legs before Bangor went out in a replay.

**Alan Steen** (Born Crewe, 26 June 1922. Died 26 August 2012.) Alan Steen was Wolverhampton Wanderers' youngest-ever Football League goalscorer finding the net when he made his first-team debut as a 16-year-old outside right in a 3-0 win over Manchester United in March 1939. His career was interrupted by the Second World War and in 1943 he was in an aircraft which was shot down resulting in him being a prisoner of war until the end of the conflict. Alan subsequently had spells with Luton Town, Aldershot, Rochdale and Carlisle United.

**Jimmy Stephen** (Born Johnshaven, Kincardineshire, 23 August 1922. Died Plymouth, 5 November 2012.) Jimmy Stephen was Scotland's oldest surviving international player when he died at the age of 90. Jimmy joined Bradford Park Avenue as a 16-year-old making his senior debut a year later in the opening weeks of the 1939–40 season. He made almost 200 war-time appearances for Avenue and guested for Halifax Town, Huddersfield Town and Middlesbrough as well as appearing for Scotland in unofficial war-time internationals. Jimmy resumed playing with Avenue after the war and in October 1946 earned his first official Scotland cap when he skippered the team against Wales at Wrexham. He played one further game for his country and went on to join Portsmouth in November 1949 for whom he made 100 Football League appearances.

**Denis Stevens** (Born Dudley, Worcestershire, 30 November 1933. Died 20 December 2012.) Denis Stevens was an industrious inside forward or wing half who made his name with Bolton Wanderers in the 1950s. He gained an FA Cup winners' medal as a member of the team that defeated Manchester United to win the 1958 final at Wembley and in the same season he was capped for the Football League against the Irish League. In March 1962 he moved on to Everton and he helped the Toffees to the Football League title in 1962–63 when he was an ever-present in the side. Denis concluded his career with spells at Oldham and Tranmere, taking his total of Football League appearances beyond the 450-mark.

**Doug Stockdale** (Born Sunderland, 3 September 1926. Died 23 December 2012.) Doug Stockdale was a forward who made his senior debut for Raith Rovers in 1948–49. He remained with the Kirkcaldy club until March 1951 when he signed for Ayr United and later played for Forfar Athletic and Cowdenbeath before finishing his career at Montrose.

**Geoff Strong** (Born Kirkheaton, Northumberland, 19 September 1937. Died Southport, 17 June 2013.) Geoff Strong signed for Arsenal in 1958 making his first-team debut two years later. He went on to form a prolific scoring partnership with Joe Baker before being sold to Liverpool in November 1964. Geoff was initially used as a wing half by the Reds but later played at inside forward and outside left before ending his time at Anfield at left back. He won an FA Cup winners' medal in 1965 and a Football League championship medal the following season. Geoff moved on to join Coventry City in 1970, finishing his senior career with the Sky Blues.

**Jeff Suddards** (Born Bradford, 17 January 1929. Died Fakenham, Norfolk, 28 August 2012.) Jeff Suddards was a full back who signed for Bradford Park Avenue in March 1949 making his senior debut against Leeds United a year later. Jeff went on to complete 327 Football League appearances for Avenue before leaving in the summer of 1959 to join Southern League club Cambridge City.

**Jimmy Tansey** (Born Liverpool, 29 January 1929. Died Liverpool, 7 July 2012.) Jimmy Tansey was a solid and reliable left back who made 133 Football League appearances for Everton after joining the Toffees as a teenager. Jimmy lost his first-team place in the 1958–59 season but stayed at Goodison Park until the summer of 1960 when he signed for Crewe Alexandra. He made occasional appearances for the Gresty Road club before retiring from full-time football.

**Jack Taylor, OBE** (Born Wolverhampton, 21 April 1930. Died Lower Upton, Shifnal, Shropshire, 27 July 2012.) Jack Taylor was a renowned referee who made history when he awarded the first-ever penalty in a World Cup final. Jack, a butcher by trade, took charge of over 1,000 matches during a 33-year career with the highlight being that 1974 final between West Germany and Holland. He refereed the 1966 FA Cup final and the 1971 European Cup final, and in 1975 was awarded the OBE for services to football. Jack gained the distinction of being inducted into the FIFA Hall of Fame in 1999.

**Phil Taylor** (Born Bristol, 18 September 1917. Died 1 December 2012.) Phil Taylor broke into the Bristol Rovers line-up in September 1935 and after establishing himself he was sold to Liverpool the following March. He went straight in the Reds' team, scoring a late goal on his debut against Derby County and going on to play over 300 games for the club in peacetime football. Initially an inside or centre forward, he dropped back to wing half, gaining a Football League champions' medal in 1946–47 and captained the side that lost to Arsenal in the 1950 FA Cup final. After retiring as a player he turned to coaching at Anfield and served the club as manager between May 1956 and November 1959. He won three full caps for England and also played for the Football League representative team.

**Geoff Thomas** (Born Swansea, 18 February 1948. Died 13 January 2013.) Geoff Thomas captained the Swansea Schools team before becoming an apprentice with his home town club. He went on to become an influential midfield player for the Swans, making more than 350 first-team appearances and helping the team win promotion from the Fourth Division in 1969–70. Geoff won three U23 caps for Wales.

**Harry Thomson** (Born Loanhead, Midlothian, 25 August 1940. Died 14 March 2013.) Harry Thomson joined Burnley from Bo'ness United at the start of the 1959–60 season, but it took him until March 1965 to make it into the first team at Turf Moor. He made over 100 appearances in goal for the Clarets, then had a couple of seasons with Blackpool, helping them back to the top flight in 1968–69, before concluding his career with Barrow in 1971–72.

**Jimmy Thomson** (Born 10 April 1937. Died 4 August 2012.) Jimmy Thomson was a solid and consistent right half who progressed from Valleyfield Juniors to St Mirren as a teenager. Released by the Paisley club at the end of the 1960–61 season he signed for Dunfermline Athletic and went on to become one of the stars of the Pars' successful team of the 1960s, making over 300 competitive appearances and gaining a Scottish Cup runners-up medal in 1965. He later spent a decade as a coach at East End Park and also had spells as manager of Alloa Athletic and Berwick Rangers.

**Ron Tindall** (Born Streatham, London, 23 September 1935. Died Perth, Australia, 9 September 2012.) Ron Tindall was a forward who appeared for Chelsea between 1955 and 1961 forming a strike partnership with Jimmy Greaves. Ron scored 67 goals in 160 appearances for the Stamford Bridge club before joining West Ham United. He later appeared for Reading and Portsmouth before managing Pompey between 1970 and 1973. Ron emigrated to Australia where he was involved in coaching and in the country's 2008 honours list he was awarded the Order of Australia Medal for services to sport.

**Peter Wakeham** (Born Kingsbridge, Devon, 14 March 1936. Died 2013) Peter Wakeham was a goalkeeper who developed at Torquay United before he was sold to Sunderland in September 1958. He went on to make 134 Football League appearances for the Black Cats before moving to Charlton Athletic. Peter finished his senior career after spending the 1965–66 season with Lincoln City.

**George Walker** (Born Sunderland, 30 May 1934. Died Carlisle, 8 August 2012.) George Walker was a forward who began his senior career with Bristol City before joining Carlisle United in March 1959. He scored twice on his debut and found the net regularly during his time at Brunton Park. George was leading scorer in 1961–62 when Carlisle won promotion for the first time in their history and when injury forced his retirement the following season he had scored 53 goals in 164 Football League appearances for the club.

**Jack Walls** (Born Seaham, Co Durham, 8 May 1932. Died 2 February 2013.) Jack Walls was a goalkeeper who signed for Barnsley as a teenager making his senior debut for the club in 1953. He later joined Peterborough United, then in the Midland League, and spent six seasons at London Road. Jack was an ever-present in the club's first Football League season in 1960–61 assisting them to the Fourth Division title.

**Don Walton** (Born 1928. Died Exmouth, Devon, 16 December 2012.) Don Walton was an outside left who played for Finchley and also represented the London and Middlesex associations. He won two caps for England Amateurs in the mid-1950s.

**Paul Ware** (Born Congleton, Cheshire, 7 November 1970. Died 17 April 2013.) Paul Ware was a tireless and committed midfield player who began his career as a trainee with Stoke City, going on to play more than 100 games for the Potters. He moved on to Stockport County in September 1994, and later spent time with Macclesfield Town and Rochdale before leaving the senior game at the end of the 2001–02 season.

**Jackie Watters** (Born Waterside, Ayrshire, 5 September 1919. Died 12 August 2012.) Jackie Watters was a forward who made his debut for Celtic in 1938. He made further appearances before enlisting for military service. Jackie briefly guested for Newcastle United during the war and later became a physiotherapist working in that capacity for Sunderland for almost 30 years.

**Len Weare** (Born Monmouthshire, 23 July 1934. Died Newport, Monmouthshire 21 September 2012.) Len Weare was a goalkeeper who held Newport County's all-time appearance record, playing over 500 Football League games for the Welsh club. Len made his debut in the 1955–56 season in Division Three South and was first choice goalkeeper over the next 15 years, eventually retiring in May 1970.

**Ian Wells** (Born Wolverhampton, 27 October 1964. Died Zakynthos, Greece, 19 January 2013.) Ian Wells was a tall, powerfully built striker who joined Hereford United in the summer of 1985. He scored on his Football League debut for the Bulls and made regular appearances in his two seasons at Edgar Street before switching back to non-league football.

**David Wilkie** (Born Paisley, 6 August 1923. Died Surrey, 3 March 2013.) David Wilkie was a forward who played for Queen's Park in war-time football while studying at Glasgow University. David, who was capped for Scotland Schools, later also appeared for Albion Rovers. He was a distinguished scientist who went on to become a Professor at University College, London.

**Brian Williamson** (Born Blyth, Northumberland, 6 October 1939. Died Sydney, Australia, 13 May 2013.) Brian Williamson was a goalkeeper who began his senior career with Gateshead in 1958. He made over 50 appearances during the club's final two seasons in the Football League before signing for Crewe Alexandra. Brian later had spells at Leeds United and Nottingham Forest before finishing his career at Fulham.

**Jim Williamson** (Died East Kilbride, 22 April 2013.) Jim Williamson was a goalkeeper who made his debut for Arbroath in the 1965–66 season after signing from Penicuik Athletic. Jim was first choice 'keeper in 1967–68 when the club won promotion to the Scottish First Division but left at the end of the following season.

**Ernie Winchester** (Born Aberdeen, 18 May 1944. Died Watford, 8 May 2013.) Ernie Winchester was a bustling forward who made his Scottish League debut for Aberdeen as a 17-year-old in April 1962. He scored regularly during his time at Pittodrie finishing with 72 League goals in 121 starts before departing to play in the NASL. Ernie, who was capped by Scotland Schools, returned to his home country in 1968 signing for Heart of Midlothian before ending his senior career with Arbroath.

**Brian Woolnough** (Born Walton on Thames, Surrey, 30 September 1948. Died Weybridge, Surrey, 18 September 2012.) Brian Woolnough was a respected sports journalist who began working for *The Sun* in 1974 progressing to become the newspaper's chief football writer. Brian spent 27 years with the newspaper before switching to the *Daily Star* where he was appointed chief sports writer. He presented Sky Sports' *Sunday Supplement* from 2007 and also wrote a number of books including biographies of Glenn Hoddle and Rodney Marsh.

**Peter Wright** (Born Colchester, 26 January 1934. Died Colchester, 24 October 2012.) Peter Wright was a goalscoring winger who signed for his home town club of Colchester United in 1951. He went on to play over 400 Football League games for the U's scoring 90 goals in a 13-year career at Layer Road and was the U's fourth highest appearance maker. In 2000 Peter was voted Colchester's Player of the Century and in later life he was chairman of the club's Former Players' Association. His son Steve also played for Colchester.

**Ian Nannestad www.soccer-history.co.uk**

# THE FOOTBALL RECORDS

## BRITISH FOOTBALL RECORDS

### ALL-TIME PREMIER LEAGUE CHAMPIONSHIP SEASONS ON POINTS AVERAGE

| | Team | Season | P | W | D | L | F | A | Pts | Pts Av |
|---|---|---|---|---|---|---|---|---|---|---|
| 1 | Chelsea | 2004–05 | 38 | 29 | 8 | 1 | 72 | 15 | 95 | 2.50 |
| 2 | Manchester U | 1999–2000 | 38 | 28 | 7 | 3 | 97 | 45 | 91 | 2.39 |
| 3 | Chelsea | 2005–06 | 38 | 29 | 4 | 5 | 72 | 22 | 91 | 2.39 |
| 4 | Arsenal | 2003–04 | 38 | 26 | 12 | 0 | 73 | 26 | 90 | 2.36 |
| | Manchester U | 2008–09 | 38 | 28 | 6 | 4 | 68 | 24 | 90 | 2.36 |
| 6 | Manchester C | 2011–12 | 38 | 28 | 5 | 5 | 93 | 29 | 89 | 2.34 |
| | Manchester U | 2006–07 | 38 | 28 | 5 | 5 | 83 | 27 | 89 | 2.34 |
| | Manchester U | 2012–13 | 38 | 28 | 5 | 5 | 86 | 43 | 89 | 2.34 |
| 9 | Arsenal | 2001–02 | 38 | 26 | 9 | 3 | 79 | 36 | 87 | 2.28 |
| | Manchester U | 2007–08 | 38 | 27 | 6 | 5 | 80 | 22 | 87 | 2.28 |
| 11 | Chelsea | 2009–10 | 38 | 27 | 5 | 6 | 103 | 32 | 86 | 2.26 |
| 12 | Manchester U | 1993–94 | 42 | 27 | 11 | 4 | 80 | 38 | 92 | 2.19 |
| 13 | Manchester U | 2002–03 | 38 | 25 | 8 | 5 | 74 | 34 | 83 | 2.18 |
| 14 | Manchester U | 1995–96 | 38 | 25 | 7 | 6 | 73 | 35 | 82 | 2.15 |
| 15 | Blackburn R | 1994–95 | 42 | 27 | 8 | 7 | 80 | 39 | 89 | 2.11 |
| 16 | Manchester U | 2000–01 | 38 | 24 | 8 | 6 | 79 | 31 | 80 | 2.10 |
| | Manchester U | 2010–11 | 38 | 23 | 11 | 4 | 78 | 37 | 80 | 2.10 |
| 18 | Manchester U | 1998–99 | 38 | 22 | 13 | 3 | 80 | 37 | 79 | 2.07 |
| 19 | Arsenal | 1997–98 | 38 | 23 | 9 | 6 | 68 | 33 | 78 | 2.05 |
| 20 | Manchester U | 1992–93 | 42 | 24 | 12 | 6 | 67 | 31 | 84 | 2.00 |
| 21 | Manchester U | 1996–97 | 38 | 21 | 12 | 5 | 76 | 44 | 75 | 1.97 |

### PREMIER LEAGUE EVER-PRESENT CLUBS

| | P | W | D | L | F | A | Pts |
|---|---|---|---|---|---|---|---|
| Manchester U | 810 | 528 | 168 | 114 | 1627 | 704 | 1752 |
| Arsenal | 810 | 436 | 214 | 160 | 1417 | 755 | 1522 |
| Chelsea | 810 | 423 | 208 | 179 | 1357 | 782 | 1477 |
| Liverpool | 810 | 396 | 207 | 207 | 1307 | 796 | 1395 |
| Tottenham H | 810 | 315 | 213 | 282 | 1138 | 1066 | 1158 |
| Aston Villa | 810 | 293 | 251 | 266 | 1020 | 992 | 1130 |
| Everton | 810 | 288 | 233 | 289 | 1029 | 1019 | 1097 |

### TOP TEN PREMIERSHIP APPEARANCES

| | | | | | | |
|---|---|---|---|---|---|---|
| 1 | Giggs, Ryan | 620 | 6 | Carragher, Jamie | 508 |
| 2 | James, David | 572 | 7 | Neville, Phil | 505 |
| 3 | Lampard, Frank | 550 | 8 | Schwarzer, Mark | 504 |
| 4 | Speed, Gary | 534 | 9 | Campbell, Sol | 503 |
| 5 | Heskey, Emile | 517 | 10 | Scholes, Paul | 499 |

### TOP TEN PREMIERSHIP GOALSCORERS

| | | | | | | |
|---|---|---|---|---|---|---|
| 1 | Shearer, Alan | 260 | 6 | Rooney, Wayne | 156 |
| 2 | Cole, Andy | 187 | 7 | Owen, Michael | 150 |
| 3 | Henry, Thierry | 175 | 8 | Ferdinand, Les | 149 |
| 4 | Lampard, Frank | 165 | 9 | Sheringham, Teddy | 146 |
| 5 | Fowler, Robbie | 163 | 10 | Hasselbaink, Jimmy Floyd | 127 |

### SCOTTISH PREMIER LEAGUE SINCE 1998–99

| | P | W | D | L | F | A | Pts |
|---|---|---|---|---|---|---|---|
| Celtic | 566 | 412 | 82 | 72 | 1304 | 453 | 1318 |
| Rangers | 528 | 364 | 93 | 71 | 1123 | 418 | 1175 |
| Hearts | 566 | 229 | 139 | 198 | 733 | 670 | 826 |
| Motherwell | 566 | 195 | 132 | 239 | 708 | 839 | 717 |
| Kilmarnock | 566 | 189 | 145 | 232 | 685 | 811 | 712 |
| Aberdeen | 566 | 188 | 143 | 235 | 651 | 785 | 707 |
| Hibernian | 530 | 183 | 134 | 213 | 712 | 761 | 683 |
| Dundee U | 566 | 173 | 162 | 231 | 674 | 845 | 681 |

## DOMESTIC LANDMARKS

**August 2012**
15   Jack Butland of Birmingham C became England's youngest ever goalkeeper when making his debut in the 2-1 win over Italy in Berne at the age of 19 years and 158 days. Four other players made their England debuts in the match: Ryan Bertrand, Tom Cleverley, Jake Livermore and John Ruddy.

**September 2012**
2   Manchester U beat Southampton 3-2 at St Mary's with a Robin van Persie hat-trick to mark Sir Alex Ferguson's 1,000th English League game as manager.
15   Paul Scholes made his 700th career appearance for Manchester U. Scholes scored in the 4-0 home win against Wigan Ath. In the same game Ryan Giggs made his 600th Premier League appearance and Rio Ferdinand made his 400th career appearance for United.
17   Newcastle U became the sixth team in Premier League history to reach 1,000 goals when Demba Ba scored against Everton at Goodison Park. The goal came in the 49th minute of the 2-2 draw.
29   Luis Suarez scored the 250th hat-trick in Premier League history in Liverpool's 5-2 victory at Norwich C.

**October 2012**
7   The Tottenham H goalkeeper Brad Friedel's record run of 310 consecutive Premier League games came to a halt when he was substitute for the home 2-0 win over Aston Villa.

**November 2012**
14   Steven Gerrard became the sixth player to reach 100 caps for England in the friendly international against Sweden in Stockholm. Gerrard played 74 minutes and was substituted by Tom Huddlestone. The match was to celebrate the opening of the new Friends Arena Stadium and Sweden won 4-2 with all four of their goals scored by Zlatan Ibrahimovic. Ibrahimovic became the first player to score four goals against England.

**December 2012**
3   Gael Bigirimana, a half-time substitute, became the first player from Burundi to score in the Premier League in the 3-0 win by Newcastle U at home to Wigan Ath.
5   Chelsea became the first Champions League holders to be eliminated at the Group stages.
8   QPR, having failed to win any of their opening 16 Premier League games, surpassed the record of 15 set by Swindon T in the 1993–94 season.
    Wayne Rooney scores his 150th Premier League goal becoming the sixth player and the youngest to achieve the feat. Rooney scored in the 16th and 29th minute of the 3-2 win at rivals Manchester C.

**January 2013**
12   Frank Lampard became the second highest scorer in Chelsea history, scoring his 194th goal in a 4-0 defeat of Stoke C. Lampard moved one ahead of Kerry Dixon and remains eight behind Bobby Tambling. The goal came in the 65th minute from the penalty spot.
16   Michael Owen scores his 150th Premier League goal. It came for Stoke C in the 90th minute of the 3-1 defeat at Swansea. Owen became the seventh player to reach 150 goals in the Premiership.
22   Bradford C became the first team from the fourth division of the English League pyramid to reach a major domestic cup final after beating Aston Villa 4-3 on aggregate in the Capital One Cup.
26   Luton T became the first non-league club to defeat a Premier League club in the FA Cup when they beat Norwich C 1-0 at Carrow Road. Scott Rendell scored the only goal in the 80th minute.

**February 2013**
6   Ashley Cole became the seventh player to reach 100 caps for England in the friendly international against Brazil at Wembley. England won 2-1 with goals from Wayne Rooney and Frank Lampard.
    Gordon Strachan took charge of the Scottish national side for the first time against Estonia in the friendly international at Aberdeen. Scotland won 1-0 with a first-half goal from Charlie Mulgrew.
10   Ryan Giggs' goal in Manchester U's 2-0 home win against Everton means that he has scored a league goal in every one of the 21 Premier League seasons.
21   Jamie Carragher made his 150th European appearance for Liverpool in the 3-1 win over Zenit St Petersburg in the 2nd leg of the round of 32 of the Europa League at Anfield. Unfortunately Liverpool lost the tie on away goals.
24   Swansea C won the Capital One Cup, their first major domestic honour. Their 5-0 victory over Bradford C was a record score in a League Cup final, beating Manchester U's 4-0 defeat of Wigan Ath in 2006.

**March 2013**
5   Ryan Giggs played his 1,000th professional career match in the European Champions League round of 16 second leg against Real Madrid at Old Trafford. Real Madrid won the match 2-1 and the tie 3-2 on aggregate with Giggs' former United colleage Cristiano Ronaldo scoring the winner.
10   The Ryman Premier League match between Wingate & Finchley and Thurrock was abandoned after 85 minutes with the score at 0-1 when Wingate & Finchley had a fifth man sent off.
16   Celtic's Kris Commons scored the quickest goal in the Scottish Premier League history after 12 seconds of the 4-3 home victory over Aberdeen.
17   Shola Ameobi of Newcastle U made his 122nd Premier League substitute appearance, the most substitute appearances in Premier League history.
    St Mirren came from behind to win the Scottish League Cup for the first time in their history.

**April 2013**
27   Jordan Allan became the youngest player ever to play in Scottish league football. He made his debut, coming on as a substitute for Airdrie U against Livingston aged 14 years and 189 days.

**May 2013**
8   Sir Alex Ferguson announced his retirement as Manchester U manager.
9   David Moyes announced as Sir Alex Ferguson's successor.
11   Wigan Ath won the FA Cup for the first time in their history with a 1-0 victory over Manchester C at Wembley. They became the 43rd different club to win the cup.
12   Stoke C celebrated their 150th anniversary with a 2-1 home defeat by Tottenham H.
    Steven Nzonzi scored the 1,000th Premier League goal of the season.
12   Frank Lampard became Chelsea's all-time record goalscorer. His two goals against Aston Villa at Villa Park took him past Bobby Tambling's record of 202 to 203 goals.
15   Chelsea became the first team to hold both major European club trophies at the same time when they defeated Benfica 2-1 in the Europa League final in Amsterdam. They were already holders of the Champions League after last season's penalty shoot-out win over Bayern Munich.

**June 2013**
7   Robbie Keane celebrated his record breaking 126th appearance for the Republic of Ireland by scoring a hat-trick in the World Cup Qualifying match against Faroe Islands in Dublin. His total of 59 goals for the Republic means that he now holds both appearance and goalscoring records.

## EUROPEAN CUP AND CHAMPIONS LEAGUE RECORDS

**MOST WINS BY CLUB**

| | | |
|---|---|---|
| Real Madrid | 9 | 1956, 1957, 1958, 1959, 1960, 1966, 1998, 2000, 2002. |
| AC Milan | 7 | 1963, 1969, 1989, 1990, 1994, 2003, 2007. |
| Bayern Munich | 5 | 1974, 1975, 1976, 2001, 2013. |
| Liverpool | 5 | 1977, 1978, 1981, 1984, 2005. |

**MOST APPEARANCES IN FINAL**
Real Madrid 12; AC Milan 11, Bayern Munich 10.

**MOST FINAL APPEARANCES PER COUNTRY**
Italy 26 (12 wins, 14 defeats).
Spain 22 (13 wins, 9 defeats)
England 19 (12 wins, 7 defeats)
Germany 17 (7 wins, 10 defeats).

**MOST CHAMPIONS LEAGUE/EUROPEAN CUP APPEARANCES**
144 Raul (Real Madrid, Schalke)
144 Ryan Giggs (Manchester U)
139 Paolo Maldini (AC Milan)
137 Xavi (Barcelona)
130 Clarence Seedorf (Ajax, Real Madrid, Internazionale, AC Milan)
130 Paul Scholes (Manchester U)
129 Iker Casillas (Real Madrid)
128 Roberto Carlos (Internazionale, Real Madrid, Fenerbahce)
119 Carles Puyol (Barcelona)
116 Andriy Shevchenko (Dynamo Kiev, AC Milan, Chelsea)

**MOST WINS WITH DIFFERENT CLUBS**
Clarence Seedorf (Ajax) 1995; (Real Madrid) 1998; (AC Milan) 2003, 2007.

**MOST WINNERS MEDALS**
6 Francisco Gento (Real Madrid) 1956, 1957, 1958, 1959, 1960, 1966.
5 Alfredo Di Stefano (Real Madrid) 1956, 1957, 1958, 1959, 1960.
5 Jose Maria Zarraga (Real Madrid) 1956, 1957, 1958, 1959, 1960.
5 Paolo Maldini (AC Milan) 1989, 1990, 1994, 2003, 2007.
4 Jose-Hector Rial (Real Madrid) 1956, 1957, 1958, 1959.
4 Marquitos (Real Madrid) 1956, 1957, 1959, 1960.
4 Phil Neal (Liverpool) 1977, 1978, 1981, 1984.
4 Clarence Seedorf (Ajax) 1995; (Real Madrid) 1998; (AC Milan) 2003, 2007.

**CHAMPIONS LEAGUE BIGGEST WINS**
HJK Helsinki 10, Bangor C 0 19.7.2011.
Liverpool 8 Besiktas 0 6.11.2007
Juventus 7, Olympiakos 0 10.12.2003
Marseille 6, CKSA Moscow 0 17.3.93

**MOST SUCCESSIVE CHAMPIONS LEAGUE APPEARANCES**
Manchester U (England) 17: 1996–97 to 2012–13.

**MOST SUCCESSIVE EUROPEAN CUP APPEARANCES**
Real Madrid (Spain) 15: 1955–56 to 1969–70.

**MOST SUCCESSIVE WINS IN THE CHAMPIONS LEAGUE**
Barcelona (Spain) 11: 2002–03.

**LONGEST UNBEATEN RUN IN THE CHAMPIONS LEAGUE**
Manchester U (England) 25: 2007–08 to 2009 (Final).

**MOST GOALS OVERALL**
71 Raul (Real Madrid, Schalke).
60 Ruud van Nistelrooy (PSV Eindhoven, Manchester U, Real Madrid).
59 Lionel Messi (Barcelona).
58 Andriy Shevchenko (Dynamo Kiev, AC Milan, Chelsea, Dynamo Kiev).
51 Thierry Henry (Monaco, Arsenal, Barcelona). Cristiano Ronaldo (Manchester U, Real Madrid).
50 Filippo Inzaghi (Juventus, AC Milan).

49 Alfredo Di Stefano (Real Madrid).
47 Eusebio (Benfica).
44 Alessandro Del Piero (Juventus).
40 Didier Drogba (Marseille, Chelsea).
39 Fernando Morientes (Real Madrid, Monaco, Liverpool, Valencia).

**MOST GOALS IN CHAMPIONS LEAGUE MATCH**
5 Lionel Messi, Barcelona v Leverkusen (25, 42, 49, 58, 84 mins) 7-1, 7.3.2012.
4 Marco van Basten, AC Milan v IFK Gothenburg (33, 53 (pen), 61, 62 mins) 4-0, 25.11.1992.
4 Simone Inzaghi, Lazio v Marseille (17, 37, 38, 71 mins) 5-1, 14.3.2000.
4 Ruud van Nistelrooy, Manchester U v Sparta Prague (14, 25 (pen), 60, 90 mins) 4-1, 3.11.2004.
4 Dado Prso, Monaco v La Coruna (26, 30, 45, 49, 23 mins) 8-3, 5.11.2003.
4 Andriy Shevchenko, AC Milan at Fenerbahce (16, 52, 70, 76 mins) 4-0, 23.11.2005.
4 Robert Lewandowski, Borussia Dortmund v Real Madrid (8, 50, 55, 66 (pen) mins) 4-1, 24.4.13.

**MOST GOALS IN ONE SEASON**
14 Jose Altafini 1962–63
14 Ruud van Nistelrooy 2002–03
14 Lionel Messi 2011–12

**MOST GOALS SCORED IN FINALS**
7 Alfredo Di Stefano (Real Madrid), 1956 (1), 1957 (1 pen), 1958 (1), 1959 (1), 1960 (3).
7 Ferenc Puskas (Real Madrid), 1960 (4), 1962 (3).

**HIGHEST SCORE IN A EUROPEAN CUP MATCH**
Feyenoord (Holland) 12, KR Reykjavik (Iceland) 0
*(First Round First Leg 1969–70)*

**HIGHEST AGGREGATE IN A EUROPEAN CUP MATCH**
Benfica (Portugal) 18, Dudelange (Luxembourg) 0
*(Preliminary Round 1965–66)*

**FASTEST GOALS SCORED IN CHAMPIONS LEAGUE**

| | |
|---|---|
| 10.2 sec | Roy Makaay for Bayern Munich v Real Madrid 7 March 2007. |
| 20.07 sec | Gilberto Silva for Arsenal at PSV Eindhoven 25 September 2002. |
| 20.12 sec | Alessandro Del Piero for Juventus at Manchester United 1 October 1997. |

**YOUNGEST CHAMPIONS LEAGUE GOALSCORER**
Peter Ofori-Quaye for Olympiakos v Rosenborg at 17 years 195 days in 1997–98.

**FASTEST HAT-TRICK SCORED IN CHAMPIONS LEAGUE**
Bafétimbi Gomis, 8 mins for Lyon in Dinamo Zagreb v Lyon (1-7) 7.12.2001.

**HIGHEST AGGREGATE OF GOALS**
11: Monaco 8, La Coruna 3 5.11.2003

**FIRST TEAM TO SCORE SEVEN GOALS**
Paris St Germain 7, Rosenborg 2 24.10.2000

**MOST GOALS BY A GOALKEEPER**
Hans-Jorg Butt (for three different clubs)
Hamburg 13.9.2000, Leverkusen 12.5.2002, Bayern Munich 8.12.2009 – all achieved against Juventus.

**LANDMARK GOALS CHAMPIONS LEAGUE**
1st Daniel Amokachi, Club Brugge v CSKA Moscow 17 minutes 25.11.1992
1,000th Dmitri Khokhlov, PSV Eindhoven v Benfica 41 minutes 9.12.1998
5,000th Luisao, Benfica v Hapoel Tel Aviv 21 minutes 14.9.2010.

**HIGHEST SCORING DRAW**
Hamburg 4, Juventus 4 13.9.2000
Chelsea 4, Liverpool 4 14.4.2009

## EUROPEAN CUP AND CHAMPIONS LEAGUE RECORDS – continued

**MOST CLEAN SHEETS**
10: Arsenal 2005–06 (995 minutes with two goalkeepers Manuel Almunia 347 minutes and Jens Lehmann 648 minutes).

**CHAMPIONS LEAGUE ATTENDANCES AND GOALS FROM GROUP STAGES ONWARDS**

| Season | Attendances | Average | Goals | Games |
|---|---|---|---|---|
| 1992–93 | 873,251 | 34,930 | 56 | 25 |
| 1993–94 | 1,202,289 | 44,529 | 71 | 27 |
| 1994–95 | 2,328,515 | 38,172 | 140 | 61 |
| 1995–96 | 1,874,316 | 30,726 | 159 | 61 |
| 1996–97 | 2,093,228 | 34,315 | 161 | 61 |
| 1997–98 | 2,868,271 | 33,744 | 239 | 85 |
| 1998–99 | 3,608,331 | 42,451 | 238 | 85 |
| 1999–2000 | 5,490,709 | 34,973 | 442 | 157 |
| 2000–01 | 5,773,486 | 36,774 | 449 | 157 |
| 2001–02 | 5,417,716 | 34,508 | 393 | 157 |
| 2002–03 | 6,461,112 | 41,154 | 431 | 157 |
| 2003–04 | 4,611,214 | 36,890 | 309 | 125 |
| 2004–05 | 4,946,820 | 39,575 | 331 | 125 |
| 2005–06 | 5,291,187 | 42,330 | 285 | 125 |
| 2006–07 | 5,591,463 | 44,732 | 309 | 125 |
| 2007–08 | 5,454,718 | 43,638 | 330 | 125 |
| 2008–09 | 5,003,754 | 40,030 | 329 | 125 |
| 2009–10 | 5,295,708 | 42,366 | 320 | 125 |
| 2010–11 | 5,474,654 | 43,797 | 355 | 125 |
| 2011–12 | 5,225,363 | 41,803 | 345 | 125 |
| 2012–13 | 5,773,366 | 46,187 | 368 | 125 |

**HIGHEST AVERAGE ATTENDANCE IN ONE EUROPEAN CUP SEASON**
1959–60  50,545 from a total attendance of 2,780,000.

**GREATEST COMEBACKS**
Werder Bremen beat Anderlecht 5-3 after being three goals down in 33 minutes on 8.12.1993. They scored five goals in 23 second-half minutes.
Deportivo La Coruna beat Paris St Germain 4-3 after being three goals down in 55 minutes on 7.3.2001. They scored four goals in 27 second-half minutes.
Liverpool after being three goals down in the first half on 25.5.2005 in the Champions League Final. They scored three goals in five second-half minutes and won the penalty shoot-out after extra time 3-2.
Liverpool three goals down to Basle in 29 minutes on 12.11.2002. They scored three second half goals in 24 minutes to draw 3-3.

**MOST SUCCESSFUL MANAGER**
Bob Paisley (Liverpool) 1977, 1978, 1981.

**REINSTATED WINNERS EXCLUDED FROM NEXT COMPETITION**
1993 Marseille originally stripped of title. This was rescinded but they were not allowed to compete the following season.

## FOREIGN LANDMARKS 2012–13

**August 2012**
23   David Beckham scored direct from a corner for Los Angeles Galaxy to register the 1,000th goal in Concacaf Champions League history. It was the third goal in a 5-2 victory over Isidro Metapan from Salvador.
27   The fastest ever hat-trick in Denmark's Superliga was scored by AGF Aarhus striker Aron Johannsson. His three goals came in 3 minutes and 50 seconds in the 4-1 victory over Horsens. Johannsson also scored the fourth goal.

**September 2012**
6   Fulham's Mark Schwarzer played his 100th international for Australia in the 3-0 World Cup Qualifying win over Lebanon.
7   Fernando Torres of Chelsea reaches 100th international caps for Spain in a 3-1 win over Uruguay in friendly match.

**October 2012**
12   Rafael van der Vart of the Netherlands played his 100th international match in the 3-0 World Cup Qualifying match at home to Andorra.
16   Kostas Katsouranis made his 100th international appearance for Greece in the World Cup Qualifier in Slovakia. Greece won 1-0.

**December 2012**
10   Lionel Messi of Barcelona equalled and then surpassed Gerd Muller's goalscoring record of 85 goals in a calendar year. The goals came in a 2-1 win at Real Betis.
22   Lionel Messi scored his 91st goal in the calendar year, scoring in Barcelona's 3-1 victory at Real Valladolid.

**January 2013**
7   Lionel Messi won a record fourth successive Ballon d'Or. The Barcelona player beat Cristiano Ronaldo from Real Madrid and his team-mate Andres Iniesta.

**February 2013**
6   Carles Puyol made his 100th international appearance for Spain in a 3-1 win over Uruguay in friendly match.
6   Three Croatian players made their 100th international appearance in the friendly match with South Korea at Fulham's Craven Cottage. Josip Simunic, Stipe Pletikosa and Darijo Srna all became centurions in the 4-0 victory.
27   Lionel Messi became the youngest player in La Liga history to score 200 goals. He scored four goals in Barcelona's 5-1 victory of Osasuna.

**March 2013**
22   Sergio Ramos of Real Madrid became the youngest European player to reach 100 international caps at 26 year and 358 days. He reached his century in Spain's World Cup Qualifying 1-1 draw against Finland. He marked the occasion with a 49th minute goal.
26   Petr Cech of Chelsea and Czech Republic reached 100 caps for his country in the 1-0 win over Armenia.
30   Lionel Messi scored for a record 19th successive La Liga match. He became the first player in La Liga history to score against every other club in the league in consecutive matches.

**April 2013**
27   Bayern Munich's 1-0 victory over Freiburg gave them a new Bundesliga points record of 84 and still with three games to play. They eventually ended the season with 91 points.

**May 2013**
25   First ever all-German final of the Champions League ends in a 2-1 victory for Bayern Much over Borussia Dortmund at Wembley. Former Chelsea player Arjen Robben scored the winner in the 89th minute.

**June 2013**
1   Bayern Munich beat Stuttgart 3-2 in the German Cup final to become the first German team to win the Champions League, Bundesliga and the German Cup in the same season.

## TOP TEN PREMIER LEAGUE AVERAGE ATTENDANCES 2012–13

| | | |
|---|---|---|
| 1 | Manchester U | 75,530 |
| 2 | Arsenal | 60,079 |
| 3 | Newcastle U | 50,517 |
| 4 | Manchester C | 46,974 |
| 5 | Liverpool | 44,749 |
| 6 | Chelsea | 41,462 |
| 7 | Sunderland | 40,544 |
| 8 | Everton | 36,356 |
| 9 | Tottenham H | 36,030 |
| 10 | Aston Villa | 35,060 |

## TOP TEN FOOTBALL LEAGUE AVERAGE ATTENDANCES 2012–13

| | | |
|---|---|---|
| 1 | Brighton & HA | 26,236 |
| 2 | Sheffield W | 24,078 |
| 3 | Derby Co | 23,228 |
| 4 | Nottingham F | 23,082 |
| 5 | Cardiff C | 22,999 |
| 6 | Leicester C | 22,054 |
| 7 | Wolverhampton W | 21,789 |
| 8 | Leeds U | 21,572 |
| 9 | Sheffield U | 18,612 |
| 10 | Charlton Ath | 18,500 |

## TOP TEN AVERAGE ATTENDANCES

| | | | |
|---|---|---|---|
| 1 | Manchester U | 2006–07 | 75,826 |
| 2 | Manchester U | 2007–08 | 75,691 |
| 3 | Manchester U | 2012–13 | 75,530 |
| 4 | Manchester U | 2011–12 | 75,387 |
| 5 | Manchester U | 2008–09 | 75,308 |
| 6 | Manchester U | 2010–11 | 75,109 |
| 7 | Manchester U | 2009–10 | 74,863 |
| 8 | Manchester U | 2005–06 | 68,765 |
| 9 | Manchester U | 2004–05 | 67,871 |
| 10 | Manchester U | 2003–04 | 67,641 |

## TOP TEN AVERAGE WORLD CUP FINAL CROWDS

| | | | |
|---|---|---|---|
| 1 | In USA | 1994 | 68,604 |
| 2 | In Brazil | 1950 | 60,772 |
| 3 | In Germany | 2006 | 52,416 |
| 4 | In Mexico | 1970 | 52,311 |
| 5 | In England | 1966 | 50,458 |
| 6 | In South Africa | 2010 | 49,670 |
| 7 | In Italy | 1990 | 48,368 |
| 8 | In Mexico | 1986 | 46,956 |
| 9 | In West Germany | 1974 | 46,684 |
| 10 | In France | 1998 | 43,366 |

## TOP TEN ALL-TIME ENGLAND CAPS

| | | |
|---|---|---|
| 1 | Peter Shilton | 125 |
| 2 | David Beckham | 115 |
| 3 | Bobby Moore | 108 |
| 4 | Bobby Charlton | 106 |
| 5 | Billy Wright | 105 |
| 6 | Ashley Cole | 103 |
| 7 | Steven Gerrard | 102 |
| 8 | Frank Lampard | 97 |
| 9 | Bryan Robson | 90 |
| 10 | Michael Owen | 89 |

## TOP TEN ALL-TIME ENGLAND GOALSCORERS

| | | |
|---|---|---|
| 1 | Bobby Charlton | 49 |
| 2 | Gary Lineker | 48 |
| 3 | Jimmy Greaves | 44 |
| 4 | Michael Owen | 40 |
| 5 | Wayne Rooney | 36 |
| | Tom Finney | 30 |
| 6 | Nat Lofthouse | 30 |
| | Alan Shearer | 30 |
| 9 | Vivian Woodward | 29 |
| | Frank Lampard | 29 |

## GOALKEEPING RECORDS
### *(without conceding a goal)*

**BRITISH RECORD (all competitive games)**
Chris Woods (Rangers) in 1,196 minutes from 26 November 1986 to 31 January 1987.

**FA PREMIER LEAGUE**
Edwin van der Sar (Manchester U) in 1,311 minutes during the 2008–09 season.

**FOOTBALL LEAGUE**
Steve Death (Reading) 1,103 minutes from 24 March to 18 August 1979.

## MOST CLEAN SHEETS IN A SEASON
Petr Cech (Chelsea) 24 2004–05

## MOST CLEAN SHEETS OVERALL IN PREMIER LEAGUE
David James (Liverpool, Aston Villa, West Ham U, Manchester C, Portsmouth and Bristol C) 173 games.

## MOST GOALS FOR IN A SEASON

| FA PREMIER LEAGUE | | Goals | Games |
|---|---|---|---|
| 2009–10 | Chelsea | 103 | 38 |
| **FOOTBALL LEAGUE** | | | |
| **Division 4** | | | |
| 1960–61 | Peterborough U | 134 | 46 |
| **SCOTTISH PREMIER LEAGUE** | | | |
| 2003–04 | Celtic | 105 | 38 |
| **SCOTTISH LEAGUE** | | | |
| **Division 2** | | | |
| 1937–38 | Raith R | 142 | 34 |

## MOST GOALS AGAINST IN A SEASON

| FA PREMIER LEAGUE | | Goals | Games |
|---|---|---|---|
| 1993–94 | Swindon T | 100 | 42 |
| **FOOTBALL LEAGUE** | | | |
| **Division 2** | | | |
| 1898–99 | Darwen | 141 | 34 |
| **SCOTTISH PREMIER LEAGUE** | | | |
| 1999–2000 | Aberdeen | 83 | 36 |
| **SCOTTISH LEAGUE** | | | |
| **Division 2** | | | |
| 1931–32 | Edinburgh C | 146 | 38 |

## MOST LEAGUE GOALS IN A SEASON

| FA PREMIER LEAGUE | | Goals | Games |
|---|---|---|---|
| 1993–94 | Andy Cole (Newcastle U) | 34 | 40 |
| 1994–95 | Alan Shearer (Blackburn R) | 34 | 42 |
| **FOOTBALL LEAGUE** | | | |
| **Division 1** | | | |
| 1927–28 | Dixie Dean (Everton) | 60 | 39 |
| **Division 2** | | | |
| 1926–27 | George Camsell (Middlesbrough) | 59 | 37 |
| **Division 3(S)** | | | |
| 1936–37 | Joe Payne (Luton T) | 55 | 39 |
| **Division 3(N)** | | | |
| 1936–37 | Ted Harston (Mansfield T) | 55 | 41 |
| **Division 3** | | | |
| 1959–60 | Derek Reeves (Southampton) | 39 | 46 |
| **Division 4** | | | |
| 1960–61 | Terry Bly (Peterborough U) | 52 | 46 |
| **FA CUP** | | | |
| 1887–88 | Jimmy Ross (Preston NE) | 20 | 8 |
| **LEAGUE CUP** | | | |
| 1986–87 | Clive Allen (Tottenham H) | 12 | 9 |
| **SCOTTISH PREMIER LEAGUE** | | | |
| 2000–01 | Henrik Larsson (Celtic) | 35 | 37 |
| **SCOTTISH LEAGUE** | | | |
| **Division 1** | | | |
| 1931–32 | William McFadyen (Motherwell) | 52 | 34 |
| **Division 2** | | | |
| 1927–28 | Jim Smith (Ayr U) | 66 | 38 |

## MOST FA CUP FINAL GOALS

Ian Rush (Liverpool) 5: 1986(2), 1989(2), 1992(1)

## SCORED IN EVERY PREMIERSHIP GAME

Arsenal 2001–02: 38 matches

## FEWEST GOALS FOR IN A SEASON

| FA PREMIER LEAGUE | | Goals | Games |
|---|---|---|---|
| 2007–08 | Derby Co | 20 | 38 |
| **FOOTBALL LEAGUE** | | | |
| **Division 2** | | | |
| 1899–1900 | Loughborough T | 18 | 34 |
| **SCOTTISH PREMIER LEAGUE** | | | |
| 2010–11 | St Johnstone | 23 | 38 |
| **SCOTTISH LEAGUE** | | | |
| **New Division 1** | | | |
| 1980–81 | Stirling Alb | 18 | 39 |

## FEWEST GOALS AGAINST IN A SEASON

| FA PREMIER LEAGUE | | Goals | Games |
|---|---|---|---|
| 2004–05 | Chelsea | 15 | 38 |
| **FOOTBALL LEAGUE** | | | |
| **Division 1** | | | |
| 1978–79 | Liverpool | 16 | 42 |
| **SCOTTISH PREMIER LEAGUE** | | | |
| 2001–02 | Celtic | 18 | 38 |
| **SCOTTISH LEAGUE** | | | |
| **Division 1** | | | |
| 1913–14 | Celtic | 14 | 38 |

## MOST LEAGUE GOALS IN A CAREER

| FOOTBALL LEAGUE | | | |
|---|---|---|---|
| **Arthur Rowley** | Goals | Games | Season |
| WBA | 4 | 24 | 1946–48 |
| Fulham | 27 | 56 | 1948–50 |
| Leicester C | 251 | 303 | 1950–58 |
| Shrewsbury T | 152 | 236 | 1958–65 |
| | 434 | 619 | |
| **SCOTTISH LEAGUE** | | | |
| **Jimmy McGrory** | | | |
| Celtic | 1 | 3 | 1922–23 |
| Clydebank | 13 | 30 | 1923–24 |
| Celtic | 396 | 375 | 1924–38 |
| | 410 | 408 | |

## MOST HAT-TRICKS

**Career**
37: Dixie Dean (Tranmere R, Everton, Notts Co, England)

**Division 1 (one season post-war)**
6: Jimmy Greaves (Chelsea), 1960–61

**Three for one team in one match**
West, Spouncer, Hooper, Nottingham F v Leicester Fosse, Division 1, 21 April 1909
Loasby, Smith, Wells, Northampton T v Walsall, Division 3S, 5 Nov 1927
Bowater, Hoyland, Readman, Mansfield T v Rotherham U, Division 3N, 27 Dec 1932
Barnes, Ambler, Davies, Wrexham v Hartlepools U, Division 4, 3 March 1962
Adcock, Stewart, White, Manchester C v Huddersfield T, Division 2, 7 Nov 1987

## MOST CUP GOALS IN A CAREER

**FA CUP (pre-Second World War)**
Henry Cursham  48  (Notts Co)

**FA CUP (post-war)**
Ian Rush  43  (Chester, Liverpool)

**LEAGUE CUP**
Geoff Hurst  49  (West Ham U, Stoke C)
Ian Rush  49  (Chester, Liverpool, Newcastle U)

## GOALS PER GAME (Football League to 1991–92)

| Goals per game | Division 1 Games | Division 1 Goals | Division 2 Games | Division 2 Goals | Division 3 Games | Division 3 Goals | Division 4 Games | Division 4 Goals | Division 3(S) Games | Division 3(S) Goals | Division 3(N) Games | Division 3(N) Goals |
|---|---|---|---|---|---|---|---|---|---|---|---|---|
| 0 | 2465 | 0 | 2665 | 0 | 1446 | 0 | 1438 | 0 | 997 | 0 | 803 | 0 |
| 1 | 5606 | 5606 | 5836 | 5836 | 3225 | 3225 | 3106 | 3106 | 2073 | 2073 | 1914 | 1914 |
| 2 | 8275 | 16550 | 8609 | 17218 | 4569 | 9138 | 4441 | 8882 | 3314 | 6628 | 2939 | 5878 |
| 3 | 7731 | 23193 | 7842 | 23526 | 3784 | 11352 | 4041 | 12123 | 2996 | 8988 | 2922 | 8766 |
| 4 | 6229 | 24920 | 5897 | 23588 | 2837 | 11348 | 2784 | 11136 | 2445 | 9780 | 2410 | 9640 |
| 5 | 3752 | 18755 | 3634 | 18170 | 1566 | 7830 | 1506 | 7530 | 1554 | 7770 | 1599 | 7995 |
| 6 | 2137 | 12822 | 2007 | 12042 | 769 | 4614 | 786 | 4716 | 870 | 5220 | 930 | 5580 |
| 7 | 1092 | 7644 | 1001 | 7007 | 357 | 2499 | 336 | 2352 | 451 | 3157 | 461 | 3227 |
| 8 | 542 | 4336 | 376 | 3008 | 135 | 1080 | 143 | 1144 | 209 | 1672 | 221 | 1768 |
| 9 | 197 | 1773 | 164 | 1476 | 64 | 576 | 35 | 315 | 76 | 684 | 102 | 918 |
| 10 | 83 | 830 | 68 | 680 | 13 | 130 | 8 | 80 | 33 | 330 | 45 | 450 |
| 11 | 37 | 407 | 19 | 209 | 2 | 22 | 7 | 77 | 15 | 165 | 15 | 165 |
| 12 | 12 | 144 | 17 | 204 | 1 | 12 | 0 | 0 | 7 | 84 | 8 | 96 |
| 13 | 4 | 52 | 4 | 52 | 0 | 0 | 0 | 0 | 2 | 26 | 4 | 52 |
| 14 | 2 | 28 | 1 | 14 | 0 | 0 | 0 | 0 | 0 | 0 | 0 | 0 |
| 17 | 0 | 0 | 0 | 0 | 0 | 0 | 0 | 0 | 0 | 0 | 1 | 17 |
| | **38164** | **117061** | **38140** | **113030** | **18768** | **51826** | **18631** | **51461** | **15042** | **46577** | **14374** | **46466** |

| New Overall Totals (since 1992) | | Totals (up to 1991–92) | | Complete Overall Totals (since 1888–89) | |
|---|---|---|---|---|---|
| Games | 42732 | Games | 143119 | Games | 185851 |
| Goals | 110644 | Goals | 426421 | Goals | 537065 |

*Extensive research by statisticians has unearthed seven results from early years of the Football League which differ from the original scores. These are 26 January 1889 Wolverhampton W 5 Everton 0 (not 4-0), 16 March 1889 Notts Co 3 Derby Co 5 (not 2-5), 4 January 1896 Arsenal 5 Loughborough 0 (not 6-0), 28 November 1896 Leicester Fosse 4 Walsall 2 (not 4-1), 21 April 1900 Burslem Port Vale 2 Lincoln City 1 (not 2-0), 25 December 1902 Glossop NE 3 Stockport Co 0 (not 3-1), 26 April 1913 Hull C 2 Leicester C 0 (not 2-1).*

## GOALS PER GAME (from 1992–93)

| Goals per game | Premier Games | Premier Goals | Championship/Div 1 Games | Championship/Div 1 Goals | League One/Div 2 Games | League One/Div 2 Goals | League Two/Div 3 Games | League Two/Div 3 Goals |
|---|---|---|---|---|---|---|---|---|
| 0 | 711 | 0 | 954 | 0 | 906 | 0 | 918 | 0 |
| 1 | 1501 | 1501 | 2161 | 2161 | 2166 | 2166 | 2189 | 2189 |
| 2 | 2016 | 4032 | 2951 | 5902 | 2968 | 5936 | 2877 | 5754 |
| 3 | 1731 | 5193 | 2478 | 7434 | 2527 | 7581 | 2481 | 7443 |
| 4 | 1190 | 4760 | 1604 | 6416 | 1626 | 6504 | 1528 | 6112 |
| 5 | 589 | 2945 | 879 | 4395 | 846 | 4230 | 774 | 3870 |
| 6 | 291 | 1746 | 382 | 2292 | 347 | 2082 | 347 | 2082 |
| 7 | 124 | 868 | 131 | 917 | 144 | 1008 | 139 | 973 |
| 8 | 57 | 456 | 38 | 304 | 43 | 344 | 44 | 352 |
| 9 | 10 | 90 | 7 | 63 | 16 | 144 | 17 | 153 |
| 10 | 5 | 50 | 5 | 50 | 3 | 30 | 5 | 50 |
| 11 | 1 | 11 | 2 | 22 | 0 | 0 | 3 | 33 |
| | **8226** | **21652** | **11592** | **29956** | **11592** | **30025** | **11322** | **29011** |

## A CENTURY OF LEAGUE AND CUP GOALS IN CONSECUTIVE SEASONS

| George Camsell | League | Cup | Season |
|---|---|---|---|
| Middlesbrough | 59 | 5 | 1926–27 |
| (101 goals) | 33 | 4 | 1927–28 |

(*Camsell's cup goals were all scored in the FA Cup.*)

| Steve Bull | | | |
|---|---|---|---|
| Wolverhampton W | 34 | 18 | 1987–88 |
| (102 goals) | 37 | 13 | 1988–89 |

(*Bull had 12 in the Sherpa Van Trophy, 3 Littlewoods Cup, 3 FA Cup in 1987–88; 11 Sherpa Van Trophy, 2 Littlewoods Cup in 1988–89.*)

## PENALTIES

**Most in a Season (individual)**

| Division 1 | Goals | Season |
|---|---|---|
| Francis Lee (Manchester C) | 13 | 1971–72 |

**Most awarded in one game**

Five    Crystal Palace (4 – 1 scored, 3 missed)
        v Brighton & HA (1 scored), Div 2    1988–89

**Most saved in a Season**

Division 1
Paul Cooper (Ipswich T)    8 (of 10)    1979–80

## MOST GOALS IN A GAME

**FA PREMIER LEAGUE**
| | |
|---|---|
| 19 Sept 1999 | Alan Shearer (Newcastle U) 5 goals v Sheffield W |
| 4 Mar 1995 | Andy Cole (Manchester U) 5 goals v Ipswich T |
| 22 Nov 2009 | Jermain Defoe (Tottenham H) 5 goals v Wigan Ath |
| 27 Nov 2010 | Dimitar Berbatov (Manchester U) 5 goals v Blackburn R |

**FOOTBALL LEAGUE**
**Division 1**
| | |
|---|---|
| 14 Dec 1935 | Ted Drake (Arsenal) 7 goals v Aston V |

**Division 2**
| | |
|---|---|
| 5 Feb 1955 | Tommy Briggs (Blackburn R) 7 goals v Bristol R |
| 23 Feb 1957 | Neville Coleman (Stoke C) 7 goals v Lincoln C |

**Division 3(S)**
| | |
|---|---|
| 13 April 1936 | Joe Payne (Luton T) 10 goals v Bristol R |

**Division 3(N)**
| | |
|---|---|
| 26 Dec 1935 | Bunny Bell (Tranmere R) 9 goals v Oldham Ath |

**Division 3**
| | |
|---|---|
| 16 Sept 1969 | Steve Earle (Fulham) 5 goals v Halifax T |
| 24 April 1965 | Barrie Thomas (Scunthorpe U) 5 goals v Luton T |
| 20 Nov 1965 | Keith East (Swindon T) 5 goals v Mansfield T |
| 2 Oct 1971 | Alf Wood (Shrewsbury T) 5 goals v Blackburn R |
| 10 Sept 1983 | Tony Caldwell (Bolton W) 5 goals v Walsall |
| 4 May 1987 | Andy Jones (Port Vale) 5 goals v Newport Co |
| 3 April 1990 | Steve Wilkinson (Mansfield T) 5 goals v Birmingham C |
| 5 Sept 1998 | Giuliano Grazioli (Peterborough U) 5 goals v Barnet |
| 6 April 2002 | Lee Jones (Wrexham) 5 goals v Cambridge U |

**Division 4**
| | |
|---|---|
| 26 Dec 1962 | Bert Lister (Oldham Ath) 6 goals v Southport |

**FA CUP**
| | |
|---|---|
| 20 Nov 1971 | Ted MacDougall (Bournemouth) 9 goals v Margate (*1st Round*) |

**LEAGUE CUP**
| | |
|---|---|
| 25 Oct 1989 | Frankie Bunn (Oldham Ath) 6 goals v Scarborough |

**SCOTTISH LEAGUE**
**Premier Division**
| | |
|---|---|
| 17 Nov 1984 | Paul Sturrock (Dundee U) 5 goals v Morton |

**Premier League**
| | |
|---|---|
| 23 Aug 1996 | Marco Negri (Rangers) 5 goals v Dundee U |
| 4 Nov 2000 | Kenny Miller (Rangers) 5 goals v St Mirren |
| 25 Sept 2004 | Kris Boyd (Kilmarnock) 5 goals v Dundee U |
| 30 Dec 2009 | Kris Boyd (Rangers) 5 goals v Dundee U |
| 13 May 2012 | Gary Hooper (Celtic) 5 goals v Hearts |

**Division 1**
| | |
|---|---|
| 14 Sept 1928 | Jimmy McGrory (Celtic) 8 goals v Dunfermline Ath |

**Division 2**
| | |
|---|---|
| 1 Oct 1927 | Owen McNally (Arthurlie) 8 goals v Armadale |
| 2 Jan 1930 | Jim Dyet (King's Park) 8 goals v Forfar Ath |
| 18 April 1936 | John Calder (Morton) 8 goals v Raith R |
| 20 Aug 1937 | Norman Hayward (Raith R) 8 goals v Brechin C |

**SCOTTISH CUP**
| | |
|---|---|
| 12 Sept 1885 | John Petrie (Arbroath) 13 goals v Bon Accord (*1st Round*) |

## LONGEST SEQUENCE OF CONSECUTIVE DEFEATS

| **FOOTBALL LEAGUE** **Division 2** | *Team* | *Games* |
|---|---|---|
| 1898–99 | Darwen | 18 |

## LONGEST UNBEATEN SEQUENCE

| **FA PREMIER LEAGUE** | *Team* | *Games* |
|---|---|---|
| May 2003–October 2004 | Arsenal | 49 |
| **FOOTBALL LEAGUE – League 1** | | |
| Jan 2011–Nov 2011 | Huddersfield T | 43 |

## LONGEST UNBEATEN CUP SEQUENCE

| Liverpool | 25 rounds | League/Milk Cup | 1980–84 |
|---|---|---|---|

## LONGEST UNBEATEN SEQUENCE IN A SEASON

| **FA PREMIER LEAGUE** | *Team* | *Games* |
|---|---|---|
| 2003–04 | Arsenal | 38 |
| **FOOTBALL LEAGUE – Division 1** | | |
| 1920–21 | Burnley | 30 |
| **SCOTTISH PREMIER LEAGUE** | | |
| 2003–04 | Celtic | 32 |

## LONGEST UNBEATEN START TO A SEASON

| **FA PREMIER LEAGUE** | *Team* | *Games* |
|---|---|---|
| 2003–04 | Arsenal | 38 |
| **FOOTBALL LEAGUE – Division 1** | | |
| 1973–74 | Leeds U | 29 |
| 1987–88 | Liverpool | 29 |

## LONGEST SEQUENCE WITHOUT A WIN IN A SEASON

| **FA PREMIER LEAGUE** | *Team* | *Games* |
|---|---|---|
| 2007–08 | Derby Co | 32 |
| **FOOTBALL LEAGUE** **Division 2** | *Team* | *Games* |
| 1983–84 | Cambridge U | 31 |

## LONGEST SEQUENCE WITHOUT A WIN FROM SEASON'S START

| **FOOTBALL LEAGUE** **Division 4** | *Team* | *Games* |
|---|---|---|
| 1970–71 | Newport Co | 25 |

## LONGEST SEQUENCE OF CONSECUTIVE SCORING (individual)

| **FA PREMIER LEAGUE** Ruud van Nistelrooy (Manchester U) | 15 in 10 games | 2003–04 |
|---|---|---|
| **FOOTBALL LEAGUE RECORD** Tom Phillipson (Wolverhampton W) | 23 in 13 games | 1926–27 |

## LONGEST WINNING SEQUENCE

| **FA PREMIER LEAGUE** | *Team* | *Games* |
|---|---|---|
| 2001–02 and 2002–03 | Arsenal | 14 |
| **FOOTBALL LEAGUE – Division 2** | | |
| 1904–05 | Manchester U | 14 |
| 1905–06 | Bristol C | 14 |
| 1950–51 | Preston NE | 14 |
| **FROM SEASON'S START – Division 3** | | |
| 1985–86 | Reading | 13 |
| **SCOTTISH PREMIER LEAGUE** | | |
| 2003–04 | Celtic | 25 |

## HIGHEST WINS

**Highest win in a First-Class Match**
*(Scottish Cup 1st Round)*
Arbroath       36 Bon Accord     0   12 Sept 1885

**Highest win in an International Match**
England       13 Ireland       0   18 Feb 1882

**Highest win in an FA Cup Match**
Preston NE     26 Hyde U       0   15 Oct 1887
*(1st Round)*

**Highest win in a League Cup Match**
West Ham U    10 Bury         0   25 Oct 1983
*(2nd Round, 2nd Leg)*
Liverpool      10 Fulham       0   23 Sept 1986
*(2nd Round, 1st Leg)*

**Highest win in an FA Premier League Match**
Manchester U    9 Ipswich T     0   4 Mar 1995
Tottenham H     9 Wigan Ath    1   22 Nov 2009

**Highest win in a Football League Match**
**Division 2 – highest home win**
Newcastle U    13 Newport Co    0   5 Oct 1946
**Division 3(N) – highest home win**
Stockport Co    13 Halifax T      0   6 Jan 1934
**Division 2 – highest away win**
Burslem Port Vale 0 Sheffield U    10   10 Dec 1892

**Highest wins in a Scottish League Match**
**Scottish Premier League – highest home win**
Celtic         9 Aberdeen      0   6 Nov 2010
**Scottish Division 2 – highest home win**
Airdrieonians    15 Dundee Wanderers 1   1 Dec 1894
**Scottish Premier League – away win**
Hamilton A      0 Celtic         8   5 Nov 1988

## MOST HOME WINS IN A SEASON

Brentford won all 21 games in Division 3(S), 1929–30

## RECORD AWAY WINS IN A SEASON

Doncaster R won 18 of 21 games in Division 3(N), 1946–47

## CONSECUTIVE AWAY WINS

**FA PREMIER LEAGUE**
Chelsea 9 games 2004–05

**FOOTBALL LEAGUE**
**Division 1**
Tottenham H 10 games (1959–60 (2), 1960–61 (8))

## MOST WINS IN A SEASON

| FA PREMIER LEAGUE | | Wins | Games |
|---|---|---|---|
| 2004–05 | Chelsea | 29 | 38 |
| 2005–06 | Chelsea | 29 | 38 |
| **FOOTBALL LEAGUE** | | | |
| **Division 3(N)** | | | |
| 1946–47 | Doncaster R | 33 | 42 |
| **SCOTTISH PREMIER LEAGUE** | | | |
| 2001–02 | Celtic | 33 | 38 |
| **SCOTTISH LEAGUE** | | | |
| **Division 1** | | | |
| 1920–21 | Rangers | 35 | 42 |

## MOST POINTS IN A SEASON

*(under old system of two points for a win)*

| FOOTBALL LEAGUE | | Points | Games |
|---|---|---|---|
| **Division 4** | | | |
| 1975–76 | Lincoln C | 74 | 46 |
| **SCOTTISH LEAGUE** | | | |
| **Division 1** | | | |
| 1920–21 | Rangers | 76 | 42 |

## FEWEST WINS IN A SEASON

| FA PREMIER LEAGUE | | Wins | Games |
|---|---|---|---|
| 2007–08 | Derby Co | 1 | 38 |
| **FOOTBALL LEAGUE** | | | |
| **Division 2** | | | |
| 1899–1900 | Loughborough T | 1 | 34 |
| **SCOTTISH PREMIER LEAGUE** | | | |
| 1998–99 | Dunfermline Ath | 4 | 36 |
| **SCOTTISH LEAGUE** | | | |
| **Division 1** | | | |
| 1891–92 | Vale of Leven | 0 | 22 |

## UNDEFEATED AT HOME OVERALL

Liverpool 85 games (63 League, 9 League Cup,
7 European, 6 FA Cup), Jan 1978–Jan 1981

## UNDEFEATED AT HOME LEAGUE

Chelsea 86 games, March 2004–October 2008

## UNDEFEATED AWAY

Arsenal 19 games, FA Premier League 2001–02 and
2003–04 (only Preston NE with 11 in 1888–89 had
previously remained unbeaten away) in the top flight.

## HIGHEST AGGREGATE SCORES

| FA PREMIER LEAGUE | | | |
|---|---|---|---|
| Portsmouth | 7 Reading | 4 | 29 Sept 2007 |
| **Highest Aggregate Score England** | | | |
| **Division 3(N)** | | | |
| Tranmere R | 13 Oldham Ath | 4 | 26 Dec 1935 |
| **Highest Aggregate Score Scotland** | | | |
| **Division 2** | | | |
| Airdrieonians | 15 Dundee Wanderers 1 | | 1 Dec 1894 |

## MOST POINTS IN A SEASON

*(three points for a win)*

| FA PREMIER LEAGUE | | Points | Games |
|---|---|---|---|
| 2004–05 | Chelsea | 95 | 38 |
| **FOOTBALL LEAGUE** | | | |
| **Championship** | | | |
| 2005–06 | Reading | 106 | 46 |
| **SCOTTISH PREMIER LEAGUE** | | | |
| 2001–02 | Celtic | 103 | 38 |
| **SCOTTISH LEAGUE** | | | |
| **New Division 3** | | | |
| 2004–05 | Gretna | 98 | 36 |

## FEWEST POINTS IN A SEASON

| FA PREMIER LEAGUE | | Points | Games |
|---|---|---|---|
| 2007–08 | Derby Co | 11 | 38 |
| **FOOTBALL LEAGUE** | | | |
| **Division 2** | | | |
| 1904–05 | Doncaster R | 8 | 34 |
| 1899–1900 | Loughborough T | 8 | 34 |
| **SCOTTISH PREMIER LEAGUE** | | | |
| 2007–08 | Gretna | 13 | 38 |
| **SCOTTISH LEAGUE** | | | |
| **Division 1** | | | |
| 1954–55 | Stirling Alb | 6 | 30 |

## NO DEFEATS IN A SEASON

**FA PREMIER LEAGUE**
2003–04    Arsenal    won 26, drew 12

**FOOTBALL LEAGUE**
**Division 1**
1888–89    Preston NE    won 18, drew 4
**Division 2**
1893–94    Liverpool    won 22, drew 6

**SCOTTISH LEAGUE DIVISION 1**
1898–99    Rangers    won 18

## ONE DEFEAT IN A SEASON

| **FA PREMIER LEAGUE** | *Defeats* | *Games* |
|---|---|---|
| 2004–05    Chelsea | 1 | 38 |

| **FOOTBALL LEAGUE** | | |
|---|---|---|
| **Division 1** | | |
| 1990–91    Arsenal | 1 | 38 |

| **SCOTTISH PREMIER LEAGUE** | | |
|---|---|---|
| 2001–02    Celtic | 1 | 38 |

| **SCOTTISH LEAGUE** | | |
|---|---|---|
| **Premier Division** | | |
| **Division 1** | | |
| 1920–21    Rangers | 1 | 42 |
| **Division 2** | | |
| 1956–57    Clyde | 1 | 36 |
| 1962–63    Morton | 1 | 36 |
| 1967–68    St Mirren | 1 | 36 |
| **New Division 1** | | |
| 2011–12    Ross Co | 1 | 36 |
| **New Division 2** | | |
| 1975–76    Raith R | 1 | 26 |

## MOST DEFEATS IN A SEASON

| **FA PREMIER LEAGUE** | *Defeats* | *Games* |
|---|---|---|
| 1994–95    Ipswich T | 29 | 42 |
| 2005–06    Sunderland | 29 | 38 |
| 2007–08    Derby Co | 29 | 38 |

| **FOOTBALL LEAGUE** | | |
|---|---|---|
| **Division 3** | | |
| 1997–98    Doncaster R | 34 | 46 |

| **SCOTTISH PREMIER LEAGUE** | | |
|---|---|---|
| 2005–06    Livingston | 28 | 38 |

| **SCOTTISH LEAGUE** | | |
|---|---|---|
| **New Division 1** | | |
| 1992–93    Cowdenbeath | 34 | 44 |

## SENDINGS-OFF

**SEASON**
451 (League alone)                                    2003–04
*(Before rescinded cards taken into account)*

**DAY**
19 (League)                                    13 Dec 2003

**FA CUP FINAL**
Kevin Moran, Manchester U v Everton          1985
Jose Antonio Reyes, Arsenal v Manchester U   2005

**QUICKEST**
**FA Premier League**
Andreas Johansson, Wigan Ath v Arsenal 7 May 2006
and Keith Gillespie, Sheffield U v Reading 20 January
2007 both in 10 seconds
**Football League**
Walter Boyd, Swansea C v Darlington Div 3 as
substitute in zero seconds                23 Nov 1999

**MOST IN ONE GAME**
Five: Chesterfield (2) v Plymouth Arg (3) 22 Feb 1997
Five: Wigan Ath (1) v Bristol R (4)        2 Dec 1997
Five: Exeter C (3) v Cambridge U (2)      23 Nov 2002

**MOST IN ONE TEAM**
Wigan Ath (1) v Bristol R (4)              2 Dec 1997
Hereford U (4) v Northampton T (0)        6 Sept 1992

## MOST DRAWN GAMES IN A SEASON

| **FA PREMIER LEAGUE** | *Draws* | *Games* |
|---|---|---|
| 1993–94    Manchester C | 18 | 42 |
| 1993–94    Sheffield U | 18 | 42 |
| 1994–95    Southampton | 18 | 42 |

| **FOOTBALL LEAGUE** | | |
|---|---|---|
| **Division 1** | | |
| 1978–79    Norwich C | 23 | 42 |
| **Division 3** | | |
| 1997–98    Cardiff C | 23 | 46 |
| 1997–98    Hartlepool U | 23 | 46 |
| **Division 4** | | |
| 1986–87    Exeter C | 23 | 46 |

| **SCOTTISH PREMIER LEAGUE** | | |
|---|---|---|
| 1998–99    Dunfermline Ath | 16 | 38 |

| **SCOTTISH LEAGUE** | | |
|---|---|---|
| **Premier Division** | | |
| 1993–94    Aberdeen | 21 | 44 |
| **New Division 1** | | |
| 1986–87    East Fife | 21 | 44 |

## MOST SUCCESSFUL MANAGERS

**Sir Alex Ferguson** CBE
**Manchester U**
1986–2013, 25 major trophies:
13 Premier League, 5 FA Cup, 4 League Cup,
2 Champions League, 1 Cup-Winners' Cup.

**Aberdeen**
1976–86, 9 major trophies:
3 League, 4 Scottish Cup, 1 League Cup, 1 Cup-
Winners' Cup.

**Bob Paisley – Liverpool**
1974–83, 13 major trophies:
6 League, 3 European Cup, 3 League Cup, 1 UEFA
Cup.

**Bill Struth – Rangers**
1920–54, 30 major trophies:
18 League, 10 Scottish Cup, 2 League Cup

## LEAGUE CHAMPIONSHIP HAT-TRICKS

| **Huddersfield T** | 1923–24 to 1925–26 |
|---|---|
| **Arsenal** | 1932–33 to 1934–35 |
| **Liverpool** | 1981–82 to 1983–84 |
| **Manchester U** | 1998–99 to 2000–01 |
| **Manchester U** | 2006–07 to 2008–09 |

## MOST FA CUP MEDALS

Ashley Cole 7 (Arsenal 2002, 2003, 2005, Chelsea
2007, 2009, 2010, 2012)

## MOST LEAGUE MEDALS

Ryan Giggs (Manchester U) 13: 1993, 1994, 1996, 1997,
1999, 2000, 2001, 2003, 2007, 2008, 2009, 2011 and 2013.

## MOST SENIOR MATCHES

1,390 Peter Shilton (1,005 League, 86 FA Cup, 102
League Cup, 125 Internationals, 13 Under-23, 4
Football League XI, 20 European Cup, 7 Texaco Cup,
5 Simod Cup, 4 European Super Cup, 4 UEFA Cup, 3
Screen Sport Super Cup, 3 Zenith Data Systems Cup,
2 Autoglass Trophy, 2 Charity Shield, 2 Full Members
Cup, 1 Anglo-Italian Cup, 1 Football League play-offs,
1 World Club Championship)

## MOST LEAGUE APPEARANCES
### (750+ matches)

1,005　Peter Shilton (286 Leicester C, 110 Stoke C, 202 Nottingham F, 188 Southampton, 175 Derby Co, 34 Plymouth Arg, 1 Bolton W, 9 Leyton Orient) 1966–97

931　Tony Ford (355 Grimsby T, 9 Sunderland (loan), 112 Stoke C, 114 WBA, 68 Grimsby T, 5 Bradford C (loan), 76 Scunthorpe U, 103 Mansfield T, 89 Rochdale) 1975–2002

909　Graeme Armstrong (204 Stirling A, 83 Berwick R, 353 Meadowbank Th, 268 Stenhousemuir, 1 Alloa Ath) 1975–2001

863　Tommy Hutchison (165 Blackpool, 314 Coventry C, 46 Manchester C, 92 Burnley, 178 Swansea C, 68 Alloa Ath) 1965–91

833　Graham Alexander (159 Scunthorpe U, 150 Luton T, 370 Preston NE, 154 Burnley) 1990–2012

824　Terry Paine (713 Southampton, 111 Hereford U) 1957–77

790　Neil Redfearn (35 Bolton W, 10 Lincoln C (loan), 90 Lincoln C, 46 Doncaster R, 57 Crystal Palace, 24 Watford, 62 Oldham Ath, 292 Barnsley, 30 Charlton Ath, 17 Bradford C, 22 Wigan Ath, 42 Halifax T, 54 Boston U, 9 Rochdale) 1982–2004

788　David James (89 Watford, 214 Liverpool, 67 Aston Villa, 91 West Ham U, 93 Manchester C, 134 Portsmouth, 81 Bristol C, 19 Bournemouth) 1988–2013

782　Robbie James (484 Swansea C, 48 Stoke C, 87 QPR, 23 Leicester C, 89 Bradford C, 51 Cardiff C) 1973–94

777　Alan Oakes (565 Manchester C, 211 Chester C, 1 Port Vale) 1959–84

774　Dave Beasant (340 Wimbledon, 20 Newcastle U, 133 Chelsea, 6 Grimsby T (loan), 4 Wolverhampton W (loan), 88 Southampton, 139 Nottingham F, 27 Portsmouth, 1 Tottenham H (loan), 16 Brighton & HA) 1979–2003

771　John Burridge (27 Workington, 134 Blackpool, 65 Aston Villa, 6 Southend U (loan), 88 Crystal Palace, 39 QPR, 74 Wolverhampton W, 6 Derby Co (loan), 109 Sheffield U, 62 Southampton, 67 Newcastle U, 65 Hibernian, 3 Scarborough, 4 Lincoln C, 3 Aberdeen, 3 Dumbarton, 3 Falkirk, 4 Manchester C, 3 Darlington, 6 Queen of the S) 1968–96

770　John Trollope (all for Swindon T) 1960–80†

764　Jimmy Dickinson (all for Portsmouth) 1946–65

763　Stuart McCall (395 Bradford C, 103 Everton, 194 Rangers, 71 Sheffield U) 1982–2004

761　Roy Sproson (all for Port Vale) 1950–72

760　Mick Tait (64 Oxford U, 106 Carlisle U, 33 Hull C, 240 Portsmouth, 99 Reading, 79 Darlington, 139 Hartlepool U) 1975–97

758　Ray Clemence (48 Scunthorpe U, 470 Liverpool, 240 Tottenham H) 1966–87

758　Billy Bonds (95 Charlton Ath, 663 West Ham U) 1964–88

757　Pat Jennings (48 Watford, 472 Tottenham H, 237 Arsenal) 1963–86

757　Frank Worthington (171 Huddersfield T, 210 Leicester C, 84 Bolton W, 75 Birmingham C, 32 Leeds U, 19 Sunderland, 34 Southampton, 31 Brighton & HA, 59 Tranmere R, 23 Preston NE, 19 Stockport Co) 1966–88

752　Wayne Allison (84 Halifax T, 7 Watford, 195 Bristol C, 101 Swindon T, 74 Huddersfield T, 103 Tranmere R, 73 Sheffield U, 115 Chesterfield) 1987–2008

† record for one club

### CONSECUTIVE
401　Harold Bell (401 Tranmere R; 459 in all games) 1946–55

## YOUNGEST PLAYERS

**FA Premier League appearance**
Matthew Briggs, 16 years 65 days, Fulham v Middlesbrough, 13.5.2007

**FA Premier League scorer**
James Vaughan, 16 years 271 days, Everton v Crystal Palace 10.4.2005

**Football League appearance**
Reuben Noble-Lazarus 15 years 45 days, Barnsley v Ipswich T, FL Championship 30.9.2008

**Football League scorer**
Ronnie Dix, 15 years 180 days, Bristol Rovers v Norwich C, Division 3S, 3.3.1928

**Division 1 appearance**
Derek Forster, 15 years 185 days, Sunderland v Leicester C, 22.8.1964

**Division 1 scorer**
Jason Dozzell, 16 years 57 days as substitute Ipswich T v Coventry C, 4.2.1984

**Division 1 hat-tricks**
Alan Shearer, 17 years 240 days, Southampton v Arsenal, 9.4.88
Jimmy Greaves, 17 years 10 months, Chelsea v Portsmouth, 25.12.1957

**FA Cup appearance (any round)**
Andy Awford, 15 years 88 days as substitute Worcester City v Boreham Wood, 3rd Qual. rd, 10.10.1987

**FA Cup competition proper appearance**
Brendon Galloway, 15 years 240 days, MK Dons v Nantwich T

**FA Cup Final appearance**
Curtis Weston, 17 years 119 days, Millwall v Manchester U, 2004

**FA Cup Final scorer**
Norman Whiteside, 18 years 18 days, Manchester United v Brighton & HA, 1983

**FA Cup Final captain**
David Nish, 21 years 212 days, Leicester C v Manchester C, 1969

**League Cup appearance**
Chris Coward, 16 years 30 days, Stockport Co v Sheffield W, 2005

**League Cup Final scorer**
Norman Whiteside, 17 years 324 days, Manchester U v Liverpool, 1983

**League Cup Final captain**
Barry Venison, 20 years 7 months 8 days, Sunderland v Norwich C, 1985

**Scottish Premier League appearance**
Scott Robinson, 16 years 45 days, Hearts v Inverness CT, 26.4.2008

**Scottish Football League appearance**
Jordan Allan, 14 years 189 days, Airdrie U v Livingston, 26.4.2013

**Scottish Premier League scorer**
Fraser Fyvie, 16 years 306 days, Aberdeen v Hearts, 27.1.2010

## OLDEST PLAYERS

**FA Premier League appearance**
John Burridge, 43 years 5 months, Manchester C v QPR, 14.5.1995

**Football League appearance**
Neil McBain, 52 years 4 months, New Brighton v Hartlepools United, Div 3N, 15.3.47 (McBain was New Brighton's manager and had to play in an emergency)

**Division 1 appearance**
Stanley Matthews, 50 years 5 days, Stoke City v Fulham, 6.2.65

# INTERNATIONAL RECORDS

## MOST GOALS IN AN INTERNATIONAL

| | | |
|---|---|---|
| Record/World Cup | Archie Thompson (Australia) 13 goals v American Samoa | 11.4.2001 |
| England | Malcolm Macdonald (Newcastle U) 5 goals v Cyprus, at Wembley | 16.4.1975 |
| | Willie Hall (Tottenham H) 5 goals v Ireland, at Old Trafford | 16.11.1938 |
| | Steve Bloomer (Derby Co) 5 goals v Wales, at Cardiff | 16.3.1896 |
| | Howard Vaughton (Aston Villa) 5 goals v Ireland, at Belfast | 18.2.1882 |
| Northern Ireland | Joe Bambrick (Linfield) 6 goals v Wales, at Belfast | 1.2.1930 |
| Wales | John Price (Wrexham) 4 goals v Ireland, at Wrexham | 25.2.1882 |
| | Mel Charles (Cardiff C) 4 goals v Ireland, at Cardiff | 11.4.1962 |
| | Ian Edwards (Chester) 4 goals v Malta, at Wrexham | 25.10.1978 |
| Scotland | Alexander Higgins (Kilmarnock) 4 goals v Ireland, at Hampden Park | 14.3.1885 |
| | Charles Heggie (Rangers) 4 goals v Ireland, at Belfast | 20.3.1886 |
| | William Dickson (Dundee Strathmore) 4 goals v Ireland, at Belfast | 24.3.1888 |
| | William Paul (Partick Th) 4 goals v Wales, at Paisley | 22.3.1890 |
| | Jake Madden (Celtic) 4 goals v Wales, at Wrexham | 18.3.1893 |
| | Duke McMahon (Celtic) 4 goals v Ireland, at Celtic Park | 23.2.1901 |
| | Bob Hamilton (Rangers) 4 goals v Ireland, at Celtic Park | 23.2.1901 |
| | Jimmy Quinn (Celtic) 4 goals v Ireland, at Dublin | 14.3.1908 |
| | Hughie Gallacher (Newcastle U) 4 goals v Ireland, at Belfast | 23.2.1929 |
| | Billy Steel (Dundee) 4 goals v N. Ireland, at Hampden Park | 1.11.1950 |
| | Denis Law (Manchester U) 4 goals v N. Ireland, at Hampden Park | 7.11.1962 |
| | Denis Law (Manchester U) 4 goals v Norway, at Hampden Park | 7.11.1963 |
| | Colin Stein (Rangers) 4 goals v Cyprus, at Hampden Park | 17.5.1969 |

## MOST GOALS IN AN INTERNATIONAL CAREER

| | | Goals | Games |
|---|---|---|---|
| England | Bobby Charlton (Manchester U) | 49 | 106 |
| Scotland | Denis Law (Huddersfield T, Manchester C, Torino, Manchester U) | 30 | 55 |
| | Kenny Dalglish (Celtic, Liverpool) | 30 | 102 |
| Northern Ireland | David Healy (Manchester U, Preston NE, Leeds U, Fulham, Sunderland, Rangers) | 35 | 93 |
| Wales | Ian Rush (Liverpool, Juventus) | 28 | 73 |
| Republic of Ireland | Robbie Keane (Wolverhampton W, Coventry C, Internazionale, Leeds U, Tottenham H, Liverpool, Tottenham H, LA Galaxy) | 59 | 127 |

## HIGHEST SCORES

| | | | | | |
|---|---|---|---|---|---|
| Record/World Cup Match | Australia | 31 | American Samoa | 0 | 2001 |
| European Championship | San Marino | 0 | Germany | 13 | 2006 |
| Olympic Games | Denmark | 17 | France | 1 | 1908 |
| | Germany | 16 | USSR | 0 | 1912 |
| Other International Match | Libya | 21 | Oman | 0 | 1966 |
| European Cup | Feyenoord | 12 | KR Reykjavik | 2 | 1969 |
| European Cup-Winners' Cup | Sporting Lisbon | 16 | Apoel Nicosia | 1 | 1963 |
| Fairs & UEFA Cups | Ajax | 14 | Red Boys | 0 | 1984 |

## GOALSCORING RECORDS

| | | |
|---|---|---|
| World Cup Final | Geoff Hurst (England) 3 goals v West Germany | 1966 |
| World Cup Final tournament | Just Fontaine (France) 13 goals | 1958 |
| Career | Artur Friedenreich (Brazil) 1,329 goals | 1910–30 |
| | Pele (Brazil) 1,281 goals | *1956–78 |
| | Franz 'Bimbo' Binder (Austria, Germany) 1,006 goals | 1930–50 |
| World Cup Finals fastest | Hakan Sukur (Turkey) 10.8 secs v South Korea | 2002 |

*Pele subsequently scored two goals in Testimonial matches making his total 1,283.*

## MOST CAPPED INTERNATIONALS IN THE BRITISH ISLES

| | | | |
|---|---|---|---|
| England | Peter Shilton | 125 appearances | 1970–90 |
| Northern Ireland | Pat Jennings | 119 appearances | 1964–86 |
| Scotland | Kenny Dalglish | 102 appearances | 1971–86 |
| Wales | Neville Southall | 92 appearances | 1982–97 |
| Republic of Ireland | Robbie Keane | 127 appearances | 1998–2013 |

# THE FA BARCLAYS PREMIER LEAGUE AND FOOTBALL LEAGUE FIXTURES 2013–14

*Sky Sports*    *All fixtures subject to change.*

**Friday, 2 August 2013**
**Football League One**
Sheffield U v Notts Co* (7.45)

**Saturday, 3 August 2013**
**Football League Championship**
Barnsley v Wigan Ath
Birmingham C v Watford
Bournemouth v Charlton Ath
Burnley v Bolton W* (12.15)
Doncaster R v Blackpool
Leeds U v Brighton & HA
Middlesbrough v Leicester C
Millwall v Yeovil T
Nottingham F v Huddersfield T
QPR v Sheffield W
Reading v Ipswich T

**Football League One**
Bristol C v Bradford C
Carlisle U v Leyton Orient
Crawley T v Coventry C
Crewe Alex v Rotherham U
Gillingham v Colchester U
Peterborough U v Swindon T
Port Vale v Brentford
Preston NE v Wolverhampton W
Shrewsbury T v Milton Keynes D
Stevenage v Oldham Ath
Walsall v Tranmere R

**Football League Two**
Bury v Chesterfield
Cheltenham T v Burton Alb
Exeter C v Bristol R
Fleetwood T v Dagenham & R
Newport Co v Accrington S
Portsmouth v Oxford U
Rochdale v Hartlepool U
Scunthorpe U v Mansfield T
Southend U v Plymouth Arg
Torquay U v AFC Wimbledon
Wycombe W v Morecambe
York C v Northampton T

**Sunday, 4 August 2013**
**Football League Championship**
Derby Co v Blackburn R* (4.00)

**Saturday, 10 August 2013**
**Football League Championship**
Blackburn R v Nottingham F
Blackpool v Barnsley
Bolton W v Reading
Brighton & HA v Derby Co
Charlton Ath v Middlesbrough
Huddersfield T v QPR
Ipswich T v Millwall
Sheffield W v Burnley
Watford v Bournemouth
Yeovil T v Birmingham C

**Football League One**
Bradford C v Carlisle U
Brentford v Sheffield U
Colchester U v Port Vale
Coventry C v Bristol C
Leyton Orient v Shrewsbury T
Milton Keynes D v Crewe Alex
Notts Co v Peterborough U
Oldham Ath v Walsall
Rotherham U v Preston NE
Swindon T v Stevenage

Tranmere R v Crawley T
Wolverhampton W v Gillingham

**Football League Two**
AFC Wimbledon v Wycombe W
Accrington S v Portsmouth* (12.15)
Bristol R v Scunthorpe U
Burton Alb v Rochdale
Chesterfield v Cheltenham T
Dagenham & R v York C
Hartlepool U v Southend U
Mansfield T v Exeter C
Morecambe v Torquay U
Northampton T v Newport Co
Oxford U v Bury
Plymouth Arg v Fleetwood T

**Sunday, 11 August 2013**
**Football League Championship**
Leicester C v Leeds U* (4.30)

**Saturday, 17 August 2013**
**Barclays Premier League**
Arsenal v Aston Villa
Liverpool v Stoke C
Norwich C v Everton
Sunderland v Fulham
Swansea C v Manchester U* (5.30)
WBA v Southampton
West Ham U v Cardiff C

**Football League Championship**
Barnsley v Charlton Ath
Birmingham C v Brighton & HA
Bournemouth v Wigan Ath
Burnley v Yeovil T
Derby Co v Leicester C
Doncaster R v Blackburn R
Leeds U v Sheffield W* (12.15)
Middlesbrough v Blackpool
Millwall v Huddersfield T
Nottingham F v Bolton W
QPR v Ipswich T
Reading v Watford

**Football League One**
Bristol C v Wolverhampton W
Carlisle U v Coventry C
Crawley T v Rotherham U
Crewe Alex v Tranmere R
Gillingham v Brentford
Peterborough U v Oldham Ath
Port Vale v Bradford C
Preston NE v Milton Keynes D
Sheffield U v Colchester U
Shrewsbury T v Swindon T
Stevenage v Leyton Orient
Walsall v Notts Co

**Football League Two**
Bury v Accrington S
Cheltenham T v Plymouth Arg
Exeter C v AFC Wimbledon
Fleetwood T v Burton Alb
Newport Co v Bristol R
Portsmouth v Morecambe
Rochdale v Chesterfield
Scunthorpe U v Dagenham & R
Southend U v Northampton T
Torquay U v Oxford U
Wycombe W v Mansfield T
York C v Hartlepool U

**Sunday, 18 August 2013**
**Barclays Premier League**
Crystal Palace v Tottenham H* (1.30)
Chelsea v Hull C* (4.00)

**Monday, 19 August 2013**
**Barclays Premier League**
Manchester C v Newcastle U* (8.00)

**Tuesday, 20 August 2013**
**Football League Championship**
Wigan Ath v Doncaster R

**Friday, 23 August 2013**
**Football League Championship**
Wolverhampton W v Crawley T* (7.30)

**Saturday, 24 August 2013**
**Barclays Premier League**
Aston Villa v Liverpool* (5.30)
Everton v WBA
Fulham v Arsenal
Hull C v Norwich C
Newcastle U v West Ham U
Southampton v Sunderland
Stoke C v Crystal Palace
Tottenham H v Swansea C

**Football League Championship**
Blackburn R v Barnsley
Blackpool v Reading
Bolton W v QPR* (12.15)
Brighton & HA v Burnley
Charlton Ath v Doncaster R
Huddersfield T v Bournemouth
Ipswich T v Leeds U
Leicester C v Birmingham C
Sheffield W v Millwall
Watford v Nottingham F
Wigan Ath v Middlesbrough
Yeovil T v Derby Co

**Football League One**
Bradford C v Sheffield U
Brentford v Walsall
Colchester U v Carlisle U
Coventry C v Preston NE
Leyton Orient v Crewe Alex
Milton Keynes D v Bristol C
Notts Co v Stevenage
Oldham Ath v Port Vale
Rotherham U v Shrewsbury T
Swindon T v Gillingham
Tranmere R v Peterborough U

**Football League Two**
AFC Wimbledon v Scunthorpe U
Accrington S v Cheltenham T
Bristol R v York C
Burton Alb v Bury
Chesterfield v Southend U
Dagenham & R v Newport Co
Hartlepool U v Fleetwood T
Mansfield T v Portsmouth
Morecambe v Exeter C
Northampton T v Torquay U
Oxford U v Wycombe W
Plymouth Arg v Rochdale

**Sunday, 25 August 2013**
**Barclays Premier League**
Cardiff C v Manchester C* (4.00)

**Monday, 26 August 2013**
**Barclays Premier League**
Manchester U v Chelsea* (8.00)

**Saturday, 31 August 2013**
**Barclays Premier League**
Cardiff C v Everton
Chelsea v Aston Villa
Crystal Palace v Sunderland* (5.30)
Manchester C v Hull C
Newcastle U v Fulham
Norwich C v Southampton
WBA v Swansea C
West Ham U v Stoke C

**Football League Championship**
Barnsley v Huddersfield T
Birmingham C v Ipswich T
Blackburn R v Bolton W
Blackpool v Watford
Brighton & HA v Millwall
Charlton Ath v Leicester C
Derby Co v Burnley
Doncaster R v Bournemouth
Leeds U v QPR* (12.15)
Middlesbrough v Sheffield W
Wigan Ath v Nottingham F
Yeovil T v Reading

**Football League One**
Brentford v Carlisle U
Colchester U v Leyton Orient
Gillingham v Bristol C
Notts Co v Rotherham U
Oldham Ath v Tranmere R
Peterborough U v Crawley T
Port Vale v Wolverhampton W
Sheffield U v Milton Keynes D
Shrewsbury T v Coventry C
Stevenage v Bradford C
Swindon T v Crewe Alex
Walsall v Preston NE

**Football League Two**
AFC Wimbledon v Fleetwood T
Accrington S v Burton Alb
Bristol R v Northampton T
Bury v Cheltenham T
Exeter C v York C
Mansfield T v Dagenham & R
Morecambe v Plymouth Arg
Oxford U v Rochdale
Portsmouth v Chesterfield
Scunthorpe U v Newport Co
Torquay U v Hartlepool U
Wycombe W v Southend U

**Sunday, 1 September 2013**
**Barclays Premier League**
Liverpool v Manchester U* (1.30)
Arsenal v Tottenham H* (4.00)

**Saturday, 7 September 2013**
**Football League One**
Bradford C v Brentford
Bristol C v Shrewsbury T
Carlisle U v Port Vale
Coventry C v Colchester U
Crawley T v Gillingham
Crewe Alex v Peterborough U
Leyton Orient v Notts Co
Milton Keynes D v Swindon T* (12.00)
Rotherham U v Sheffield U
Tranmere R v Stevenage
Wolverhampton W v Walsall

**Football League Two**
Burton Alb v Oxford U
Cheltenham T v Portsmouth
Chesterfield v Accrington S
Dagenham & R v Exeter C
Fleetwood T v Torquay U
Hartlepool U v Wycombe W
Newport Co v Mansfield T
Northampton T v Scunthorpe U

Plymouth Arg v Bristol R
Rochdale v Bury
Southend U v Morecambe
York C v AFC Wimbledon

**Monday, 9 September 2013**
**Football League Championship**
Preston NE v Oldham Ath* (7.45)

**Saturday, 14 September 2013**
**Barclays Premier League**
Aston Villa v Newcastle U
Everton v Chelsea* (5.30)
Fulham v WBA
Hull C v Cardiff C
Manchester U v Crystal Palace
Stoke C v Manchester C
Sunderland v Arsenal
Tottenham H v Norwich C

**Football League Championship**
Bolton W v Leeds U
Bournemouth v Blackpool
Burnley v Blackburn R* (12.15)
Huddersfield T v Doncaster R
Ipswich T v Middlesbrough
Leicester C v Wigan Ath
Millwall v Derby Co
Nottingham F v Barnsley
QPR v Birmingham C
Reading v Brighton & HA
Sheffield W v Yeovil T
Watford v Charlton Ath

**Football League One**
Bradford C v Colchester U
Bristol C v Peterborough U
Carlisle U v Sheffield U
Coventry C v Gillingham
Crawley T v Shrewsbury T
Crewe Alex v Walsall
Leyton Orient v Port Vale
Milton Keynes D v Notts Co
Preston NE v Stevenage
Rotherham U v Oldham Ath
Tranmere R v Brentford
Wolverhampton W v Swindon T

**Football League Two**
Burton Alb v Portsmouth
Cheltenham T v Oxford U
Chesterfield v AFC Wimbledon
Dagenham & R v Bristol R
Fleetwood T v Bury
Hartlepool U v Accrington S
Newport Co v Morecambe
Northampton T v Exeter C
Plymouth Arg v Wycombe W
Rochdale v Torquay U
Southend U v Scunthorpe U
York C v Mansfield T

**Sunday, 15 September 2013**
**Barclays Premier League**
Southampton v West Ham U* (4.00)

**Monday, 16 September 2013**
**Barclays Premier League**
Swansea C v Liverpool* (8.00)

**Tuesday, 17 September 2013**
**Football League Championship**
Bolton W v Derby Co
Bournemouth v Barnsley
Burnley v Birmingham C
Huddersfield T v Charlton Ath
Ipswich T v Yeovil T
Leicester C v Blackburn R
Millwall v Blackpool
Nottingham F v Middlesbrough
QPR v Brighton & HA
Reading v Leeds U
Sheffield W v Wigan Ath
Watford v Doncaster R

**Saturday, 21 September 2013**
**Barclays Premier League**
Cardiff C v Tottenham H
Chelsea v Fulham* (5.30)
Crystal Palace v Swansea C
Liverpool v Southampton
Newcastle U v Hull C
Norwich C v Aston Villa
WBA v Sunderland
West Ham U v Everton

**Football League Championship**
Barnsley v Watford
Birmingham C v Sheffield W
Blackburn R v Huddersfield T
Blackpool v Leicester C
Brighton & HA v Bolton W
Charlton Ath v Millwall* (12.15)
Derby Co v Reading
Doncaster R v Nottingham F
Leeds U v Burnley
Middlesbrough v Bournemouth
Wigan Ath v Ipswich T
Yeovil T v QPR

**Football League One**
Brentford v Leyton Orient
Colchester U v Crawley T
Gillingham v Bradford C
Notts Co v Tranmere R
Oldham Ath v Crewe Alex
Peterborough U v Milton Keynes D
Port Vale v Coventry C
Sheffield U v Preston NE
Shrewsbury T v Wolverhampton W
Stevenage v Carlisle U
Swindon T v Bristol C
Walsall v Rotherham U

**Football League Two**
AFC Wimbledon v Burton Alb
Accrington S v Rochdale
Bristol R v Hartlepool U
Bury v Southend U
Exeter C v Newport Co
Mansfield T v Northampton T
Morecambe v Dagenham & R
Oxford U v Chesterfield
Portsmouth v Fleetwood T
Scunthorpe U v Plymouth Arg
Torquay U v Cheltenham T
Wycombe W v York C

**Sunday, 22 September 2013**
**Barclays Premier League**
Arsenal v Stoke C* (1.30)
Manchester C v Manchester U* (4.00)

**Saturday, 28 September 2013**
**Barclays Premier League**
Aston Villa v Manchester C
Fulham v Cardiff C
Hull C v West Ham U
Manchester U v WBA
Southampton v Crystal Palace
Swansea C v Arsenal* (5.30)
Tottenham H v Chelsea

**Football League Championship**
Bolton W v Yeovil T
Bournemouth v Blackburn R
Burnley v Charlton Ath
Huddersfield T v Blackpool
Ipswich T v Brighton & HA
Leicester C v Barnsley
Millwall v Leeds U
Nottingham F v Derby Co* (12.15)
QPR v Middlesbrough
Reading v Birmingham C
Sheffield W v Doncaster R
Watford v Wigan Ath

**Football League One**
Bradford C v Shrewsbury T
Bristol C v Colchester U
Carlisle U v Notts Co

Coventry C v Brentford
Crawley T v Oldham Ath
Crewe Alex v Gillingham
Leyton Orient v Walsall
Milton Keynes D v Stevenage
Preston NE v Swindon T
Rotherham U v Peterborough U
Tranmere R v Port Vale
Wolverhampton W v Sheffield U

**Football League Two**
Burton Alb v Scunthorpe U
Cheltenham T v AFC Wimbledon
Chesterfield v Mansfield T
Dagenham & R v Bury
Fleetwood T v Exeter C
Hartlepool U v Oxford U
Newport Co v Torquay U
Northampton T v Morecambe
Plymouth Arg v Accrington S
Rochdale v Wycombe W
Southend U v Bristol R
York C v Portsmouth

**Sunday, 29 September 2013**
**Barclays Premier League**
Stoke C v Norwich C* (1.30)
Sunderland v Liverpool* (4.00)

**Monday, 30 September 2013**
**Barclays Premier League**
Everton v Newcastle U* (8.00)

**Tuesday, 1 October 2013**
**Football League Championship**
Barnsley v Reading
Birmingham C v Millwall
Blackburn R v Watford
Blackpool v Bolton W
Brighton & HA v Sheffield W
Charlton Ath v Nottingham F
Derby Co v Ipswich T
Doncaster R v Burnley
Leeds U v Bournemouth
Middlesbrough v Huddersfield T
Wigan Ath v QPR
Yeovil T v Leicester C

**Saturday, 5 October 2013**
**Barclays Premier League**
Cardiff C v Newcastle U
Fulham v Stoke C
Hull C v Aston Villa
Liverpool v Crystal Palace
Manchester C v Everton
Southampton v Swansea C
Sunderland v Manchester U* (5.30)
Tottenham H v West Ham U

**Football League Championship**
Birmingham C v Bolton W
Bournemouth v Millwall
Brighton & HA v Nottingham F
Burnley v Reading
Charlton Ath v Blackpool
Derby Co v Leeds U
Doncaster R v Leicester C
Huddersfield T v Watford
Middlesbrough v Yeovil T
QPR v Barnsley
Sheffield W v Ipswich T
Wigan Ath v Blackburn R

**Football League One**
Brentford v Rotherham U
Colchester U v Wolverhampton W
Gillingham v Milton Keynes D
Notts Co v Crewe Alex
Oldham Ath v Leyton Orient
Peterborough U v Preston NE
Port Vale v Bristol C
Sheffield U v Crawley T
Shrewsbury T v Carlisle U
Stevenage v Coventry C

Swindon T v Tranmere R
Walsall v Bradford C

**Football League Two**
AFC Wimbledon v Northampton T
Accrington S v Dagenham & R
Bristol R v Fleetwood T
Bury v Newport Co
Exeter C v Plymouth Arg
Mansfield T v Hartlepool U
Morecambe v Chesterfield
Oxford U v Southend U
Portsmouth v Rochdale
Scunthorpe U v Cheltenham T
Torquay U v York C
Wycombe W v Burton Alb

**Sunday, 6 October 2013**
**Barclays Premier League**
Norwich C v Chelsea* (1.30)
WBA v Arsenal* (4.00)

**Saturday, 12 October 2013**
**Football League One**
Bradford C v Tranmere R
Bristol C v Crawley T
Carlisle U v Wolverhampton W
Colchester U v Walsall
Coventry C v Sheffield U
Leyton Orient v Milton Keynes D
Notts Co v Oldham Ath
Port Vale v Peterborough U
Preston NE v Crewe Alex
Rotherham U v Swindon T
Shrewsbury T v Gillingham
Stevenage v Brentford

**Football League Two**
AFC Wimbledon v Accrington S
Burton Alb v Southend U
Bury v Morecambe
Dagenham & R v Cheltenham T
Exeter C v Hartlepool U
Fleetwood T v Chesterfield
Mansfield T v Bristol R
Oxford U v Northampton T
Plymouth Arg v Portsmouth* (12.15)
Rochdale v Newport Co
Wycombe W v Torquay U
York C v Scunthorpe U

**Saturday, 19 October 2013**
**Barclays Premier League**
Arsenal v Norwich C
Chelsea v Cardiff C
Everton v Hull C
Manchester U v Southampton
Newcastle U v Liverpool
Stoke C v WBA
Swansea C v Sunderland
West Ham U v Manchester C* (5.30)

**Football League Championship**
Barnsley v Middlesbrough
Blackburn R v Charlton Ath
Blackpool v Wigan Ath
Bolton W v Sheffield W
Ipswich T v Burnley
Leeds U v Birmingham C
Leicester C v Huddersfield T
Millwall v QPR
Nottingham F v Bournemouth
Reading v Doncaster R
Watford v Derby Co
Yeovil T v Brighton & HA

**Football League One**
Brentford v Colchester U
Crawley T v Bradford C
Crewe Alex v Bristol C
Gillingham v Preston NE
Milton Keynes D v Rotherham U
Oldham Ath v Carlisle U
Peterborough U v Shrewsbury T
Sheffield U v Port Vale
Swindon T v Notts Co
Tranmere R v Leyton Orient

Walsall v Stevenage
Wolverhampton W v Coventry C

**Football League Two**
Accrington S v Oxford U
Bristol R v Wycombe W
Cheltenham T v Rochdale
Chesterfield v Burton Alb
Hartlepool U v Plymouth Arg
Morecambe v AFC Wimbledon
Newport Co v York C
Northampton T v Dagenham & R
Portsmouth v Bury
Scunthorpe U v Exeter C
Southend U v Fleetwood T
Torquay U v Mansfield T

**Sunday, 20 October 2013**
**Barclays Premier League**
Aston Villa v Tottenham H* (4.00)

**Monday, 21 October 2013**
**Barclays Premier League**
Crystal Palace v Fulham* (8.00)

**Tuesday, 22 October 2013**
**Football League One**
Bristol C v Brentford
Coventry C v Leyton Orient
Crawley T v Port Vale
Crewe Alex v Stevenage
Gillingham v Notts Co
Milton Keynes D v Carlisle U
Peterborough U v Sheffield U
Preston NE v Bradford C
Rotherham U v Tranmere R
Shrewsbury T v Colchester U
Swindon T v Walsall
Wolverhampton W v Oldham Ath

**Football League Two**
Accrington S v Bristol R
Burton Alb v Torquay U
Bury v Mansfield T
Cheltenham T v Morecambe
Chesterfield v York C
Fleetwood T v Scunthorpe U
Hartlepool U v AFC Wimbledon
Oxford U v Exeter C
Plymouth Arg v Newport Co
Portsmouth v Wycombe W
Rochdale v Northampton T
Southend U v Dagenham & R

**Saturday, 26 October 2013**
**Barclays Premier League**
Aston Villa v Everton
Crystal Palace v Arsenal
Liverpool v WBA
Manchester U v Stoke C
Norwich C v Cardiff C
Southampton v Fulham* (5.30)
Swansea C v West Ham U
Tottenham H v Hull C

**Football League Championship**
Barnsley v Sheffield W* (12.00)
Blackpool v Blackburn R
Bolton W v Ipswich T
Brighton & HA v Watford
Burnley v QPR
Charlton Ath v Wigan Ath
Derby Co v Birmingham C
Huddersfield T v Leeds U
Leicester C v Bournemouth
Middlesbrough v Doncaster R
Reading v Millwall
Yeovil T v Nottingham F

**Football League One**
Bradford C v Wolverhampton W
Brentford v Shrewsbury T
Carlisle U v Bristol C
Colchester U v Peterborough U
Leyton Orient v Rotherham U
Notts Co v Preston NE
Oldham Ath v Swindon T
Port Vale v Gillingham

Sheffield U v Crewe Alex
Stevenage v Crawley T
Tranmere R v Milton Keynes D
Walsall v Coventry C

**Football League Two**
AFC Wimbledon v Oxford U
Bristol R v Chesterfield
Dagenham & R v Rochdale
Exeter C v Burton Alb
Mansfield T v Plymouth Arg
Morecambe v Accrington S
Newport Co v Southend U
Northampton T v Cheltenham T
Scunthorpe U v Hartlepool U
Torquay U v Portsmouth
Wycombe W v Bury
York C v Fleetwood T

**Sunday, 27 October 2013**
**Barclays Premier League**
Chelsea v Manchester C* (1.30)
Sunderland v Newcastle U* (4.00)

**Saturday, 2 November 2013**
**Barclays Premier League**
Arsenal v Liverpool* (5.30)
Fulham v Manchester U
Hull C v Sunderland
Manchester C v Norwich C
Newcastle U v Chelsea
Stoke C v Southampton
WBA v Crystal Palace
West Ham U v Aston Villa

**Football League Championship**
Birmingham C v Charlton Ath
Blackburn R v Middlesbrough
Bournemouth v Bolton W
Doncaster R v Brighton & HA
Ipswich T v Barnsley
Leeds U v Yeovil T
Millwall v Burnley
Nottingham F v Blackpool
QPR v Derby Co
Sheffield W v Reading
Watford v Leicester C* (12.15)
Wigan Ath v Huddersfield T

**Football League One**
Bristol C v Oldham Ath
Coventry C v Notts Co
Crawley T v Brentford
Crewe Alex v Bradford C
Gillingham v Carlisle U
Milton Keynes D v Walsall
Peterborough U v Leyton Orient
Preston NE v Tranmere R
Rotherham U v Colchester U
Shrewsbury T v Sheffield U
Swindon T v Port Vale
Wolverhampton W v Stevenage

**Football League Two**
Accrington S v Wycombe W
Burton Alb v Morecambe
Bury v Torquay U
Cheltenham T v York C
Chesterfield v Scunthorpe U
Fleetwood T v Newport Co
Hartlepool U v Dagenham & R
Oxford U v Bristol R
Plymouth Arg v Northampton T
Portsmouth v Exeter C
Rochdale v AFC Wimbledon
Southend U v Mansfield T

**Sunday, 3 November 2013**
**Barclays Premier League**
Everton v Tottenham H* (1.30)
Cardiff C v Swansea C* (4.00)

**Saturday, 9 November 2013**
**Barclays Premier League**
Aston Villa v Cardiff C
Chelsea v WBA

Crystal Palace v Everton
Liverpool v Fulham
Norwich C v West Ham U* (5.30)
Southampton v Hull C
Swansea C v Stoke C

**Football League Championship**
Barnsley v Doncaster R
Blackpool v Ipswich T
Bolton W v Millwall
Brighton & HA v Blackburn R
Burnley v Bournemouth
Charlton Ath v Leeds U
Derby Co v Sheffield W
Huddersfield T v Birmingham C
Leicester C v Nottingham F
Middlesbrough v Watford
Reading v QPR* (12.15)
Yeovil T v Wigan Ath

**Sunday, 10 November 2013**
**Barclays Premier League**
Tottenham H v Newcastle U* (12.00)
Sunderland v Manchester C* (2.05)
Manchester U v Arsenal* (4.10)

**Saturday, 16 November 2013**
**Football League One**
Bradford C v Coventry C
Brentford v Crewe Alex
Carlisle U v Crawley T
Colchester U v Swindon T
Leyton Orient v Preston NE
Notts Co v Wolverhampton W
Oldham Ath v Milton Keynes D
Port Vale v Shrewsbury T
Sheffield U v Gillingham
Stevenage v Rotherham U
Tranmere R v Bristol C
Walsall v Peterborough U

**Football League Two**
AFC Wimbledon v Portsmouth
Bristol R v Bury
Dagenham & R v Burton Alb
Exeter C v Southend U
Mansfield T v Oxford U
Morecambe v Rochdale
Newport Co v Hartlepool U
Northampton T v Fleetwood T
Scunthorpe U v Accrington S
Torquay U v Chesterfield
Wycombe W v Cheltenham T
York C v Plymouth Arg

**Saturday, 23 November 2013**
**Barclays Premier League**
Arsenal v Southampton
Everton v Liverpool
Fulham v Swansea C
Hull C v Crystal Palace
Manchester C v Tottenham H* (5.30)
Newcastle U v Norwich C
Stoke C v Sunderland

**Football League Championship**
Birmingham C v Blackpool
Blackburn R v Reading
Bournemouth v Derby Co
Doncaster R v Yeovil T
Ipswich T v Leicester C
Leeds U v Middlesbrough
Millwall v Barnsley
Nottingham F v Burnley
QPR v Charlton Ath
Sheffield W v Huddersfield T* (12.15)
Watford v Bolton W
Wigan Ath v Brighton & HA

**Football League One**
Bristol C v Sheffield U
Coventry C v Tranmere R
Crawley T v Walsall
Crewe Alex v Port Vale
Gillingham v Oldham Ath
Milton Keynes D v Bradford C

Peterborough U v Stevenage
Preston NE v Colchester U
Rotherham U v Carlisle U
Shrewsbury T v Notts Co
Swindon T v Leyton Orient
Wolverhampton W v Brentford

**Football League Two**
Accrington S v Torquay U
Burton Alb v Bristol R
Bury v AFC Wimbledon
Cheltenham T v Newport Co
Chesterfield v Wycombe W
Fleetwood T v Mansfield T
Hartlepool U v Northampton T
Oxford U v Morecambe
Plymouth Arg v Dagenham & R
Portsmouth v Scunthorpe U
Rochdale v Exeter C
Southend U v York C

**Sunday, 24 November 2013**
**Barclays Premier League**
West Ham U v Chelsea* (1.30)
Cardiff C v Manchester U* (4.00)

**Monday, 25 November 2013**
**Barclays Premier League**
WBA v Aston Villa* (8.00)

**Tuesday, 26 November 2013**
**Football League One**
Bradford C v Notts Co
Brentford v Peterborough U
Bristol C v Leyton Orient
Carlisle U v Crewe Alex
Colchester U v Milton Keynes D
Coventry C v Rotherham U
Crawley T v Swindon T
Gillingham v Stevenage
Port Vale v Preston NE
Sheffield U v Walsall
Shrewsbury T v Oldham Ath
Wolverhampton W v Tranmere R

**Football League Two**
AFC Wimbledon v Dagenham & R
Accrington S v Fleetwood T
Burton Alb v Mansfield T
Bury v Hartlepool U
Cheltenham T v Bristol R
Chesterfield v Northampton T
Morecambe v York C
Oxford U v Newport Co
Portsmouth v Southend U
Rochdale v Scunthorpe U
Torquay U v Plymouth Arg
Wycombe W v Exeter C

**Saturday, 30 November 2013**
**Barclays Premier League**
Aston Villa v Sunderland
Cardiff C v Arsenal
Everton v Stoke C
Manchester C v Swansea C
Newcastle U v WBA* (5.30)
Norwich C v Crystal Palace
Tottenham H v Manchester U
West Ham U v Fulham

**Football League Championship**
Barnsley v Birmingham C
Blackburn R v Leeds U
Blackpool v Sheffield W
Bournemouth v Brighton & HA* (12.15)
Charlton Ath v Ipswich T
Doncaster R v QPR
Huddersfield T v Burnley
Leicester C v Millwall
Middlesbrough v Bolton W
Nottingham F v Reading
Watford v Yeovil T
Wigan Ath v Derby Co

**Football League One**
Crewe Alex v Crawley T
Leyton Orient v Sheffield U
Milton Keynes D v Coventry C
Notts Co v Brentford
Oldham Ath v Bradford C
Peterborough U v Wolverhampton W
Preston NE v Bristol C
Rotherham U v Gillingham
Stevenage v Shrewsbury T
Swindon T v Carlisle U
Tranmere R v Colchester U
Walsall v Port Vale

**Football League Two**
Bristol R v AFC Wimbledon
Dagenham & R v Wycombe W
Exeter C v Bury
Fleetwood T v Oxford U
Hartlepool U v Portsmouth
Mansfield T v Morecambe
Newport Co v Chesterfield
Northampton T v Accrington S
Plymouth Arg v Burton Alb
Scunthorpe U v Torquay U
Southend U v Cheltenham T
York C v Rochdale

**Sunday, 1 December 2013**
**Barclays Premier League**
Hull C v Liverpool* (1.30)
Chelsea v Southampton* (4.00)

**Tuesday, 3 December 2013**
**Barclays Premier League**
Arsenal v Hull C
Crystal Palace v West Ham U
Liverpool v Norwich C
Manchester U v Everton
Southampton v Aston Villa
Stoke C v Cardiff C
Sunderland v Chelsea
Swansea C v Newcastle U
WBA v Manchester C

**Football League Championship**
Birmingham C v Doncaster R
Bolton W v Huddersfield T
Brighton & HA v Barnsley
Burnley v Watford
Derby Co v Middlesbrough
Ipswich T v Blackburn R
Leeds U v Wigan Ath
Millwall v Nottingham F
QPR v Bournemouth
Reading v Charlton Ath
Sheffield W v Leicester C
Yeovil T v Blackpool

**Wednesday, 4 December 2013**
**Barclays Premier League**
Fulham v Tottenham H

**Saturday, 7 December 2013**
**Barclays Premier League**
Arsenal v Everton
Crystal Palace v Cardiff C
Fulham v Aston Villa
Liverpool v West Ham U
Manchester U v Newcastle U
Southampton v Manchester C
Stoke C v Chelsea
Sunderland v Tottenham H
Swansea C v Hull C
WBA v Norwich C

**Football League Championship**
Birmingham C v Middlesbrough
Bolton W v Doncaster R
Brighton & HA v Leicester C
Burnley v Barnsley
Derby Co v Blackpool
Ipswich T v Huddersfield T
Leeds U v Watford
Millwall v Wigan Ath

QPR v Blackburn R
Reading v Bournemouth
Sheffield W v Nottingham F
Yeovil T v Charlton Ath

**Saturday, 14 December 2013**
**Barclays Premier League**
Aston Villa v Manchester U
Cardiff C v WBA
Chelsea v Crystal Palace
Everton v Fulham
Hull C v Stoke C
Manchester C v Arsenal
Newcastle U v Southampton
Norwich C v Swansea C
Tottenham H v Liverpool
West Ham U v Sunderland

**Football League Championship**
Barnsley v Yeovil T
Blackburn R v Millwall
Blackpool v QPR
Bournemouth v Birmingham C
Charlton Ath v Derby Co
Doncaster R v Leeds U
Huddersfield T v Reading
Leicester C v Burnley
Middlesbrough v Brighton & HA
Nottingham F v Ipswich T
Watford v Sheffield W
Wigan Ath v Bolton W

**Football League One**
Bradford C v Leyton Orient
Brentford v Oldham Ath
Bristol C v Rotherham U
Carlisle U v Tranmere R
Colchester U v Notts Co
Coventry C v Crewe Alex
Crawley T v Preston NE
Gillingham v Peterborough U
Port Vale v Stevenage
Sheffield U v Swindon T
Shrewsbury T v Walsall
Wolverhampton W v Milton Keynes D

**Football League Two**
AFC Wimbledon v Mansfield T
Accrington S v Exeter C
Burton Alb v York C
Bury v Northampton T
Cheltenham T v Hartlepool U
Chesterfield v Plymouth Arg
Morecambe v Bristol R
Oxford U v Dagenham & R
Portsmouth v Newport Co
Rochdale v Fleetwood T
Torquay U v Southend U
Wycombe W v Scunthorpe U

**Saturday, 21 December 2013**
**Barclays Premier League**
Arsenal v Chelsea
Crystal Palace v Newcastle U
Fulham v Manchester C
Liverpool v Cardiff C
Manchester U v West Ham U
Southampton v Tottenham H
Stoke C v Aston Villa
Sunderland v Norwich C
Swansea C v Everton
WBA v Hull C

**Football League Championship**
Birmingham C v Nottingham F
Bolton W v Charlton Ath
Brighton & HA v Huddersfield T
Burnley v Blackpool
Derby Co v Doncaster R
Ipswich T v Watford
Leeds U v Barnsley
Millwall v Middlesbrough
QPR v Leicester C
Reading v Wigan Ath

Sheffield W v Bournemouth
Yeovil T v Blackburn R

**Football League One**
Crewe Alex v Shrewsbury T
Leyton Orient v Crawley T
Milton Keynes D v Port Vale
Notts Co v Bristol C
Oldham Ath v Colchester U
Peterborough U v Bradford C
Preston NE v Brentford
Rotherham U v Wolverhampton W
Stevenage v Sheffield U
Swindon T v Coventry C
Tranmere R v Gillingham
Walsall v Carlisle U

**Football League Two**
Bristol R v Portsmouth
Dagenham & R v Torquay U
Exeter C v Chesterfield
Fleetwood T v Cheltenham T
Hartlepool U v Burton Alb
Mansfield T v Accrington S
Newport Co v AFC Wimbledon
Northampton T v Wycombe W
Plymouth Arg v Bury
Scunthorpe U v Morecambe
Southend U v Rochdale
York C v Oxford U

**Thursday, 26 December 2013**
**Barclays Premier League**
Aston Villa v Crystal Palace
Cardiff C v Southampton
Chelsea v Swansea C
Everton v Sunderland
Hull C v Manchester U
Manchester C v Liverpool
Newcastle U v Stoke C
Norwich C v Fulham
Tottenham H v WBA
West Ham U v Arsenal

**Football League Championship**
Barnsley v Bolton W
Blackburn R v Sheffield W
Blackpool v Leeds U
Bournemouth v Yeovil T
Charlton Ath v Brighton & HA
Doncaster R v Ipswich T
Huddersfield T v Derby Co
Leicester C v Reading
Middlesbrough v Burnley
Nottingham F v QPR
Watford v Millwall
Wigan Ath v Birmingham C

**Football League One**
Bradford C v Rotherham U
Brentford v Swindon T
Bristol C v Walsall
Carlisle U v Preston NE
Colchester U v Stevenage
Coventry C v Peterborough U
Crawley T v Milton Keynes D
Gillingham v Leyton Orient
Port Vale v Notts Co
Sheffield U v Oldham Ath
Shrewsbury T v Tranmere R
Wolverhampton W v Crewe Alex

**Football League Two**
AFC Wimbledon v Southend U
Accrington S v York C
Burton Alb v Northampton T
Bury v Scunthorpe U
Cheltenham T v Exeter C
Chesterfield v Hartlepool U
Morecambe v Fleetwood T
Oxford U v Plymouth Arg
Portsmouth v Dagenham & R
Rochdale v Mansfield T
Torquay U v Bristol R
Wycombe W v Newport Co

**Saturday, 28 December 2013**
**Barclays Premier League**
Aston Villa v Swansea C
Cardiff C v Sunderland
Chelsea v Liverpool
Everton v Southampton
Hull C v Fulham
Manchester C v Crystal Palace
Newcastle U v Arsenal
Norwich C v Manchester U
Tottenham H v Stoke C
West Ham U v WBA

**Sunday, 29 December 2013**
**Football League Championship**
Barnsley v Derby Co
Blackburn R v Birmingham C
Blackpool v Brighton & HA
Bournemouth v Ipswich T
Charlton Ath v Sheffield W
Doncaster R v Millwall
Huddersfield T v Yeovil T
Leicester C v Bolton W
Middlesbrough v Reading
Nottingham F v Leeds U
Watford v QPR
Wigan Ath v Burnley

**Football League One**
Bradford C v Swindon T
Brentford v Milton Keynes D
Bristol C v Stevenage
Carlisle U v Peterborough U
Colchester U v Crewe Alex
Coventry C v Oldham Ath
Crawley T v Notts Co
Gillingham v Walsall
Port Vale v Rotherham U
Sheffield U v Tranmere R
Shrewsbury T v Preston NE
Wolverhampton W v Leyton Orient

**Football League Two**
AFC Wimbledon v Plymouth Arg
Accrington S v Southend U
Burton Alb v Newport Co
Bury v York C
Cheltenham T v Mansfield T
Chesterfield v Dagenham & R
Morecambe v Hartlepool U
Oxford U v Scunthorpe U
Portsmouth v Northampton T
Rochdale v Bristol R
Torquay U v Exeter C
Wycombe W v Fleetwood T

**Wednesday, 1 January 2014**
**Barclays Premier League**
Arsenal v Cardiff C
Crystal Palace v Norwich C
Fulham v West Ham U
Liverpool v Hull C
Manchester U v Tottenham H
Southampton v Chelsea
Stoke C v Everton
Sunderland v Aston Villa
Swansea C v Manchester C
WBA v Newcastle U

**Football League Championship**
Birmingham C v Barnsley
Bolton W v Middlesbrough
Brighton & HA v Bournemouth
Burnley v Huddersfield T
Derby Co v Wigan Ath
Ipswich T v Charlton Ath
Leeds U v Blackburn R
Millwall v Leicester C
QPR v Doncaster R
Reading v Nottingham F
Sheffield W v Blackpool
Yeovil T v Watford

**Football League One**
Crewe Alex v Carlisle U
Leyton Orient v Bristol C
Milton Keynes D v Colchester U
Notts Co v Bradford C
Oldham Ath v Shrewsbury T
Peterborough U v Brentford
Preston NE v Port Vale
Rotherham U v Coventry C
Stevenage v Gillingham
Swindon T v Crawley T
Tranmere R v Wolverhampton W
Walsall v Sheffield U

**Football League Two**
Bristol R v Cheltenham T
Dagenham & R v AFC Wimbledon
Exeter C v Wycombe W
Fleetwood T v Accrington S
Hartlepool U v Bury
Mansfield T v Burton Alb
Newport Co v Oxford U
Northampton T v Chesterfield
Plymouth Arg v Torquay U
Scunthorpe U v Rochdale
Southend U v Portsmouth
York C v Morecambe

**Saturday, 4 January 2014**
**Football League One**
Bristol C v Coventry C
Carlisle U v Bradford C
Crawley T v Tranmere R
Crewe Alex v Milton Keynes D
Gillingham v Wolverhampton W
Peterborough U v Notts Co
Port Vale v Colchester U
Preston NE v Rotherham U
Sheffield U v Brentford
Shrewsbury T v Leyton Orient
Stevenage v Swindon T
Walsall v Oldham Ath

**Football League Two**
Bury v Oxford U
Cheltenham T v Chesterfield
Exeter C v Mansfield T
Fleetwood T v Plymouth Arg
Newport Co v Northampton T
Portsmouth v Accrington S
Rochdale v Burton Alb
Scunthorpe U v Bristol R
Southend U v Hartlepool U
Torquay U v Morecambe
Wycombe W v AFC Wimbledon
York C v Dagenham & R

**Saturday, 11 January 2014**
**Barclays Premier League**
Aston Villa v Arsenal
Cardiff C v West Ham U
Everton v Norwich C
Fulham v Sunderland
Hull C v Chelsea
Manchester U v Swansea C
Newcastle U v Manchester C
Southampton v WBA
Stoke C v Liverpool
Tottenham H v Crystal Palace

**Football League Championship**
Blackburn R v Doncaster R
Blackpool v Middlesbrough
Bolton W v Nottingham F
Brighton & HA v Birmingham C
Charlton Ath v Barnsley
Huddersfield T v Millwall
Ipswich T v QPR
Leicester C v Derby Co
Sheffield W v Leeds U
Watford v Reading
Wigan Ath v Bournemouth
Yeovil T v Burnley

**Football League One**
Bradford C v Bristol C
Brentford v Port Vale
Colchester U v Gillingham
Coventry C v Crawley T
Leyton Orient v Carlisle U
Milton Keynes D v Shrewsbury T
Notts Co v Sheffield U
Oldham Ath v Stevenage
Rotherham U v Crewe Alex
Swindon T v Peterborough U
Tranmere R v Walsall
Wolverhampton W v Preston NE

**Football League Two**
AFC Wimbledon v Torquay U
Accrington S v Newport Co
Bristol R v Exeter C
Burton Alb v Cheltenham T
Chesterfield v Bury
Dagenham & R v Fleetwood T
Hartlepool U v Rochdale
Mansfield T v Scunthorpe U
Morecambe v Wycombe W
Northampton T v York C
Oxford U v Portsmouth
Plymouth Arg v Southend U

**Saturday, 18 January 2014**
**Barclays Premier League**
Arsenal v Fulham
Chelsea v Manchester U
Crystal Palace v Stoke C
Liverpool v Aston Villa
Manchester C v Cardiff C
Norwich C v Hull C
Sunderland v Southampton
Swansea C v Tottenham H
WBA v Everton
West Ham U v Newcastle U

**Football League Championship**
Barnsley v Blackpool
Birmingham C v Yeovil T
Bournemouth v Watford
Burnley v Sheffield W
Derby Co v Brighton & HA
Doncaster R v Wigan Ath
Leeds U v Leicester C
Middlesbrough v Charlton Ath
Millwall v Ipswich T
Nottingham F v Blackburn R
QPR v Huddersfield T
Reading v Bolton W

**Football League One**
Bristol C v Milton Keynes D
Carlisle U v Colchester U
Crawley T v Wolverhampton W
Crewe Alex v Leyton Orient
Gillingham v Swindon T
Peterborough U v Tranmere R
Port Vale v Oldham Ath
Preston NE v Coventry C
Sheffield U v Bradford C
Shrewsbury T v Rotherham U
Stevenage v Notts Co
Walsall v Brentford

**Football League Two**
Bury v Burton Alb
Cheltenham T v Accrington S
Exeter C v Morecambe
Fleetwood T v Hartlepool U
Newport Co v Dagenham & R
Portsmouth v Mansfield T
Rochdale v Plymouth Arg
Scunthorpe U v AFC Wimbledon
Southend U v Chesterfield
Torquay U v Northampton T
Wycombe W v Oxford U
York C v Bristol R

**Saturday, 25 January 2014**
**Football League Championship**
Blackburn R v Derby Co
Blackpool v Doncaster R
Bolton W v Burnley
Brighton & HA v Leeds U
Charlton Ath v Bournemouth
Huddersfield T v Nottingham F
Ipswich T v Reading
Leicester C v Middlesbrough
Sheffield W v QPR
Watford v Birmingham C
Wigan Ath v Barnsley
Yeovil T v Millwall

**Football League One**
Bradford C v Port Vale
Brentford v Gillingham
Colchester U v Sheffield U
Coventry C v Carlisle U
Leyton Orient v Stevenage
Milton Keynes D v Preston NE
Notts Co v Walsall
Oldham Ath v Peterborough U
Rotherham U v Crawley T
Swindon T v Shrewsbury T
Tranmere R v Crewe Alex
Wolverhampton W v Bristol C

**Football League Two**
AFC Wimbledon v Exeter C
Accrington S v Bury
Bristol R v Newport Co
Burton Alb v Fleetwood T
Chesterfield v Rochdale
Dagenham & R v Scunthorpe U
Hartlepool U v York C
Mansfield T v Wycombe W
Morecambe v Portsmouth
Northampton T v Southend U
Oxford U v Torquay U
Plymouth Arg v Cheltenham T

**Tuesday, 28 January 2014**
**Barclays Premier League**
Aston Villa v WBA
Crystal Palace v Hull C
Liverpool v Everton
Manchester U v Cardiff C
Norwich C v Newcastle U
Southampton v Arsenal
Sunderland v Stoke C
Swansea C v Fulham

**Football League Championship**
Barnsley v Blackburn R
Birmingham C v Leicester C
Bournemouth v Huddersfield T
Burnley v Brighton & HA
Derby Co v Yeovil T
Doncaster R v Charlton Ath
Leeds U v Ipswich T
Middlesbrough v Wigan Ath
Millwall v Sheffield W
Nottingham F v Watford
QPR v Bolton W
Reading v Blackpool

**Football League One**
Bradford C v Preston NE
Brentford v Bristol C
Carlisle U v Milton Keynes D
Colchester U v Shrewsbury T
Leyton Orient v Coventry C
Notts Co v Gillingham
Oldham Ath v Wolverhampton W
Port Vale v Crawley T
Sheffield U v Peterborough U
Stevenage v Crewe Alex
Tranmere R v Rotherham U
Walsall v Swindon T

**Football League Two**
AFC Wimbledon v Hartlepool U
Bristol R v Accrington S
Dagenham & R v Southend U
Exeter C v Oxford U

Mansfield T v Bury
Morecambe v Cheltenham T
Newport Co v Plymouth Arg
Northampton T v Rochdale
Scunthorpe U v Fleetwood T
Torquay U v Burton Alb
Wycombe W v Portsmouth
York C v Chesterfield

**Wednesday, 29 January 2014**
**Barclays Premier League**
Chelsea v West Ham U
Tottenham H v Manchester C

**Saturday, 1 February 2014**
**Barclays Premier League**
Arsenal v Crystal Palace
Cardiff C v Norwich C
Everton v Aston Villa
Fulham v Southampton
Hull C v Tottenham H
Manchester C v Chelsea
Newcastle U v Sunderland
Stoke C v Manchester U
WBA v Liverpool
West Ham U v Swansea C

**Football League Championship**
Birmingham C v Derby Co
Blackburn R v Blackpool
Bournemouth v Leicester C
Doncaster R v Middlesbrough
Ipswich T v Bolton W
Leeds U v Huddersfield T
Millwall v Reading
Nottingham F v Yeovil T
QPR v Burnley
Sheffield W v Barnsley
Watford v Brighton & HA
Wigan Ath v Charlton Ath

**Football League One**
Bristol C v Carlisle U
Coventry C v Walsall
Crawley T v Stevenage
Crewe Alex v Sheffield U
Gillingham v Port Vale
Milton Keynes D v Tranmere R
Peterborough U v Colchester U
Preston NE v Notts Co
Rotherham U v Leyton Orient
Shrewsbury T v Brentford
Swindon T v Oldham Ath
Wolverhampton W v Bradford C

**Football League Two**
Accrington S v Morecambe
Burton Alb v Exeter C
Bury v Wycombe W
Cheltenham T v Northampton T
Chesterfield v Bristol R
Fleetwood T v York C
Hartlepool U v Scunthorpe U
Oxford U v AFC Wimbledon
Plymouth Arg v Mansfield T
Portsmouth v Torquay U
Rochdale v Dagenham & R
Southend U v Newport Co

**Saturday, 8 February 2014**
**Barclays Premier League**
Aston Villa v West Ham U
Chelsea v Newcastle U
Crystal Palace v WBA
Liverpool v Arsenal
Manchester U v Fulham
Norwich C v Manchester C
Southampton v Stoke C
Sunderland v Hull C
Swansea C v Cardiff C
Tottenham H v Everton

**Football League Championship**
Barnsley v Ipswich T
Blackpool v Nottingham F
Bolton W v Bournemouth
Brighton & HA v Doncaster R

Burnley v Millwall
Charlton Ath v Birmingham C
Derby Co v QPR
Huddersfield T v Wigan Ath
Leicester C v Watford
Middlesbrough v Blackburn R
Reading v Sheffield W
Yeovil T v Leeds U

**Football League One**
Bradford C v Crewe Alex
Brentford v Crawley T
Carlisle U v Gillingham
Colchester U v Rotherham U
Leyton Orient v Peterborough U
Notts Co v Coventry C
Oldham Ath v Bristol C
Port Vale v Swindon T
Sheffield U v Shrewsbury T
Stevenage v Wolverhampton W
Tranmere R v Preston NE
Walsall v Milton Keynes D

**Football League Two**
AFC Wimbledon v Rochdale
Bristol R v Oxford U
Dagenham & R v Hartlepool U
Exeter C v Portsmouth
Mansfield T v Southend U
Morecambe v Burton Alb
Newport Co v Fleetwood T
Northampton T v Plymouth Arg
Scunthorpe U v Chesterfield
Torquay U v Bury
Wycombe W v Accrington S
York C v Cheltenham T

**Tuesday, 11 February 2014**
**Barclays Premier League**
Arsenal v Manchester U
Cardiff C v Aston Villa
Hull C v Southampton
Stoke C v Swansea C
WBA v Chelsea
West Ham U v Norwich C

**Wednesday, 12 February 2014**
**Barclays Premier League**
Everton v Crystal Palace
Fulham v Liverpool
Manchester C v Sunderland
Newcastle U v Tottenham H

**Saturday, 15 February 2014**
**Football League Championship**
Birmingham C v Huddersfield T
Blackburn R v Brighton & HA
Bournemouth v Burnley
Doncaster R v Barnsley
Ipswich T v Blackpool
Leeds U v Charlton Ath
Millwall v Bolton W
Nottingham F v Leicester C
QPR v Reading
Sheffield W v Derby Co
Watford v Middlesbrough
Wigan Ath v Yeovil T

**Football League One**
Bristol C v Tranmere R
Coventry C v Bradford C
Crawley T v Carlisle U
Crewe Alex v Brentford
Gillingham v Sheffield U
Milton Keynes D v Oldham Ath
Peterborough U v Walsall
Preston NE v Leyton Orient
Rotherham U v Stevenage
Shrewsbury T v Port Vale
Swindon T v Colchester U
Wolverhampton W v Notts Co

**Football League Two**
Accrington S v Scunthorpe U
Burton Alb v Dagenham & R
Bury v Bristol R
Cheltenham T v Wycombe W

Chesterfield v Torquay U
Fleetwood T v Northampton T
Hartlepool U v Newport Co
Oxford U v Mansfield T
Plymouth Arg v York C
Portsmouth v AFC Wimbledon
Rochdale v Morecambe
Southend U v Exeter C

**Saturday, 22 February 2014**
**Barclays Premier League**
Arsenal v Sunderland
Cardiff C v Hull C
Chelsea v Everton
Crystal Palace v Manchester U
Liverpool v Swansea C
Manchester C v Stoke C
Newcastle U v Aston Villa
Norwich C v Tottenham H
WBA v Fulham
West Ham U v Southampton

**Football League Championship**
Barnsley v Millwall
Blackpool v Birmingham C
Bolton W v Watford
Brighton & HA v Wigan Ath
Burnley v Nottingham F
Charlton Ath v QPR
Derby Co v Bournemouth
Huddersfield T v Sheffield W
Leicester C v Ipswich T
Middlesbrough v Leeds U
Reading v Blackburn R
Yeovil T v Doncaster R

**Football League One**
Bradford C v Milton Keynes D
Brentford v Wolverhampton W
Carlisle U v Rotherham U
Colchester U v Preston NE
Leyton Orient v Swindon T
Notts Co v Shrewsbury T
Oldham Ath v Gillingham
Port Vale v Crewe Alex
Sheffield U v Bristol C
Stevenage v Peterborough U
Tranmere R v Coventry C
Walsall v Crawley T

**Football League Two**
AFC Wimbledon v Bury
Bristol R v Burton Alb
Dagenham & R v Plymouth Arg
Exeter C v Rochdale
Mansfield T v Fleetwood T
Morecambe v Oxford U
Newport Co v Cheltenham T
Northampton T v Hartlepool U
Scunthorpe U v Portsmouth
Torquay U v Accrington S
Wycombe W v Chesterfield
York C v Southend U

**Saturday, 1 March 2014**
**Barclays Premier League**
Aston Villa v Norwich C
Everton v West Ham U
Fulham v Chelsea
Hull C v Newcastle U
Manchester U v Manchester C
Southampton v Liverpool
Stoke C v Arsenal
Sunderland v WBA
Swansea C v Crystal Palace
Tottenham H v Cardiff C

**Football League Championship**
Bolton W v Blackburn R
Bournemouth v Doncaster R
Burnley v Derby Co
Huddersfield T v Barnsley
Ipswich T v Birmingham C
Leicester C v Charlton Ath
Millwall v Brighton & HA
Nottingham F v Wigan Ath
QPR v Leeds U

Reading v Yeovil T
Sheffield W v Middlesbrough
Watford v Blackpool

**Football League One**
Bradford C v Stevenage
Bristol C v Gillingham
Carlisle U v Brentford
Coventry C v Shrewsbury T
Crawley T v Peterborough U
Crewe Alex v Swindon T
Leyton Orient v Colchester U
Milton Keynes D v Sheffield U
Preston NE v Walsall
Rotherham U v Notts Co
Tranmere R v Oldham Ath
Wolverhampton W v Port Vale

**Football League Two**
Burton Alb v Accrington S
Cheltenham T v Bury
Chesterfield v Portsmouth
Dagenham & R v Mansfield T
Fleetwood T v AFC Wimbledon
Hartlepool U v Torquay U
Newport Co v Scunthorpe U
Northampton T v Bristol R
Plymouth Arg v Morecambe
Rochdale v Oxford U
Southend U v Wycombe W
York C v Exeter C

**Saturday, 8 March 2014**
**Barclays Premier League**
Arsenal v Swansea C
Cardiff C v Fulham
Chelsea v Tottenham H
Crystal Palace v Southampton
Liverpool v Sunderland
Manchester C v Aston Villa
Newcastle U v Everton
Norwich C v Stoke C
WBA v Manchester U
West Ham U v Hull C

**Football League Championship**
Barnsley v Nottingham F
Birmingham C v QPR
Blackburn R v Burnley
Blackpool v Bournemouth
Brighton & HA v Reading
Charlton Ath v Watford
Derby Co v Millwall
Doncaster R v Huddersfield T
Leeds U v Bolton W
Middlesbrough v Ipswich T
Wigan Ath v Leicester C
Yeovil T v Sheffield W

**Football League One**
Brentford v Bradford C
Colchester U v Coventry C
Gillingham v Crawley T
Notts Co v Leyton Orient
Oldham Ath v Preston NE
Peterborough U v Crewe Alex
Port Vale v Carlisle U
Sheffield U v Rotherham U
Shrewsbury T v Bristol C
Stevenage v Tranmere R
Swindon T v Milton Keynes D
Walsall v Wolverhampton W

**Football League Two**
AFC Wimbledon v York C
Accrington S v Chesterfield
Bristol R v Plymouth Arg
Bury v Rochdale
Exeter C v Dagenham & R
Mansfield T v Newport Co
Morecambe v Southend U
Oxford U v Burton Alb
Portsmouth v Cheltenham T
Scunthorpe U v Northampton T
Torquay U v Fleetwood T
Wycombe W v Hartlepool U

**Tuesday, 11 March 2014**
**Football League Championship**
Barnsley v Leicester C
Birmingham C v Burnley
Blackburn R v Bournemouth
Blackpool v Millwall
Brighton & HA v QPR
Charlton Ath v Huddersfield T
Derby Co v Bolton W
Doncaster R v Watford
Leeds U v Reading
Middlesbrough v Nottingham F
Wigan Ath v Sheffield W
Yeovil T v Ipswich T

**Football League One**
Brentford v Tranmere R
Colchester U v Bradford C
Gillingham v Coventry C
Notts Co v Milton Keynes D
Oldham Ath v Rotherham U
Peterborough U v Bristol C
Port Vale v Leyton Orient
Sheffield U v Carlisle U
Shrewsbury T v Crawley T
Stevenage v Preston NE
Swindon T v Wolverhampton W
Walsall v Crewe Alex

**Football League Two**
AFC Wimbledon v Chesterfield
Accrington S v Hartlepool U
Bristol R v Dagenham & R
Bury v Fleetwood T
Exeter C v Northampton T
Mansfield T v York C
Morecambe v Newport Co
Oxford U v Cheltenham T
Portsmouth v Burton Alb
Scunthorpe U v Southend U
Torquay U v Rochdale
Wycombe W v Plymouth Arg

**Saturday, 15 March 2014**
**Barclays Premier League**
Aston Villa v Chelsea
Everton v Cardiff C
Fulham v Newcastle U
Hull C v Manchester C
Manchester U v Liverpool
Southampton v Norwich C
Stoke C v West Ham U
Sunderland v Crystal Palace
Swansea C v WBA
Tottenham H v Arsenal

**Football League Championship**
Bolton W v Brighton & HA
Bournemouth v Middlesbrough
Burnley v Leeds U
Huddersfield T v Blackburn R
Ipswich T v Wigan Ath
Leicester C v Blackpool
Millwall v Charlton Ath
Nottingham F v Doncaster R
QPR v Yeovil T
Reading v Derby Co
Sheffield W v Birmingham C
Watford v Barnsley

**Football League One**
Bradford C v Gillingham
Bristol C v Swindon T
Carlisle U v Stevenage
Coventry C v Port Vale
Crawley T v Colchester U
Crewe Alex v Oldham Ath
Leyton Orient v Brentford
Milton Keynes D v Peterborough U
Preston NE v Sheffield U
Rotherham U v Walsall
Tranmere R v Notts Co
Wolverhampton W v Shrewsbury T

**Football League Two**
Burton Alb v AFC Wimbledon
Cheltenham T v Torquay U
Chesterfield v Oxford U
Dagenham & R v Morecambe
Fleetwood T v Portsmouth
Hartlepool U v Bristol R
Newport Co v Exeter C
Northampton T v Mansfield T
Plymouth Arg v Scunthorpe U
Rochdale v Accrington S
Southend U v Bury
York C v Wycombe W

**Saturday, 22 March 2014**
**Barclays Premier League**
Aston Villa v Stoke C
Cardiff C v Liverpool
Chelsea v Arsenal
Everton v Swansea C
Hull C v WBA
Manchester C v Fulham
Newcastle U v Crystal Palace
Norwich C v Sunderland
Tottenham H v Southampton
West Ham U v Manchester U

**Football League Championship**
Barnsley v Bournemouth
Birmingham C v Reading
Blackburn R v Leicester C
Blackpool v Huddersfield T
Brighton & HA v Ipswich T
Charlton Ath v Burnley
Derby Co v Nottingham F
Doncaster R v Sheffield W
Leeds U v Millwall
Middlesbrough v QPR
Wigan Ath v Watford
Yeovil T v Bolton W

**Football League One**
Brentford v Coventry C
Colchester U v Bristol C
Gillingham v Crewe Alex
Notts Co v Carlisle U
Oldham Ath v Crawley T
Peterborough U v Rotherham U
Port Vale v Tranmere R
Sheffield U v Wolverhampton W
Shrewsbury T v Bradford C
Stevenage v Milton Keynes D
Swindon T v Preston NE
Walsall v Leyton Orient

**Football League Two**
AFC Wimbledon v Cheltenham T
Accrington S v Plymouth Arg
Bristol R v Southend U
Bury v Dagenham & R
Exeter C v Fleetwood T
Mansfield T v Chesterfield
Morecambe v Northampton T
Oxford U v Hartlepool U
Portsmouth v York C
Scunthorpe U v Burton Alb
Torquay U v Newport Co
Wycombe W v Rochdale

**Tuesday, 25 March 2014**
**Football League Championship**
Bolton W v Blackpool
Bournemouth v Leeds U
Burnley v Doncaster R
Huddersfield T v Middlesbrough
Ipswich T v Derby Co
Leicester C v Yeovil T
Millwall v Birmingham C
Nottingham F v Charlton Ath
QPR v Wigan Ath
Reading v Barnsley
Sheffield W v Brighton & HA
Watford v Blackburn R

**Football League One**
Bradford C v Walsall
Bristol C v Port Vale

Carlisle U v Shrewsbury T
Coventry C v Stevenage
Crawley T v Sheffield U
Crewe Alex v Notts Co
Leyton Orient v Oldham Ath
Milton Keynes D v Gillingham
Preston NE v Peterborough U
Rotherham U v Brentford
Tranmere R v Swindon T
Wolverhampton W v Colchester U

**Football League Two**
Burton Alb v Wycombe W
Cheltenham T v Scunthorpe U
Chesterfield v Morecambe
Dagenham & R v Accrington S
Fleetwood T v Bristol R
Hartlepool U v Mansfield T
Newport Co v Bury
Northampton T v AFC Wimbledon
Plymouth Arg v Exeter C
Rochdale v Portsmouth
Southend U v Oxford U
York C v Torquay U

**Saturday, 29 March 2014**
**Barclays Premier League**
Arsenal v Manchester C
Crystal Palace v Chelsea
Fulham v Everton
Liverpool v Tottenham H
Manchester U v Aston Villa
Southampton v Newcastle U
Stoke C v Hull C
Sunderland v West Ham U
Swansea C v Norwich C
WBA v Cardiff C

**Football League Championship**
Birmingham C v Bournemouth
Bolton W v Wigan Ath
Brighton & HA v Middlesbrough
Burnley v Leicester C
Derby Co v Charlton Ath
Ipswich T v Nottingham F
Leeds U v Doncaster R
Millwall v Blackburn R
QPR v Blackpool
Reading v Huddersfield T
Sheffield W v Watford
Yeovil T v Barnsley

**Football League One**
Crewe Alex v Coventry C
Leyton Orient v Bradford C
Milton Keynes D v Wolverhampton W
Notts Co v Colchester U
Oldham Ath v Brentford
Peterborough U v Gillingham
Preston NE v Crawley T
Rotherham U v Bristol C
Stevenage v Port Vale
Swindon T v Sheffield U
Tranmere R v Carlisle U
Walsall v Shrewsbury T

**Football League Two**
Bristol R v Morecambe
Dagenham & R v Oxford U
Exeter C v Accrington S
Fleetwood T v Rochdale
Hartlepool U v Cheltenham T
Mansfield T v AFC Wimbledon
Newport Co v Portsmouth
Northampton T v Bury
Plymouth Arg v Chesterfield
Scunthorpe U v Wycombe W
Southend U v Torquay U
York C v Burton Alb

**Saturday, 5 April 2014**
**Barclays Premier League**
Aston Villa v Fulham
Cardiff C v Crystal Palace
Chelsea v Stoke C
Everton v Arsenal
Hull C v Swansea C

Manchester C v Southampton
Newcastle U v Manchester U
Norwich C v WBA
Tottenham H v Sunderland
West Ham U v Liverpool

**Football League Championship**
Barnsley v Brighton & HA
Blackburn R v Ipswich T
Blackpool v Yeovil T
Bournemouth v QPR
Charlton Ath v Reading
Doncaster R v Birmingham C
Huddersfield T v Bolton W
Leicester C v Sheffield W
Middlesbrough v Derby Co
Nottingham F v Millwall
Watford v Burnley
Wigan Ath v Leeds U

**Football League One**
Bradford C v Oldham Ath
Brentford v Notts Co
Bristol C v Preston NE
Carlisle U v Swindon T
Colchester U v Tranmere R
Coventry C v Milton Keynes D
Crawley T v Crewe Alex
Gillingham v Rotherham U
Port Vale v Walsall
Sheffield U v Leyton Orient
Shrewsbury T v Stevenage
Wolverhampton W v Peterborough U

**Football League Two**
AFC Wimbledon v Bristol R
Accrington S v Northampton T
Burton Alb v Plymouth Arg
Bury v Exeter C
Cheltenham T v Southend U
Chesterfield v Newport Co
Morecambe v Mansfield T
Oxford U v Fleetwood T
Portsmouth v Hartlepool U
Rochdale v York C
Torquay U v Scunthorpe U
Wycombe W v Dagenham & R

**Tuesday, 8 April 2014**
**Football League Championship**
Barnsley v Burnley
Blackburn R v QPR
Blackpool v Derby Co
Bournemouth v Reading
Charlton Ath v Yeovil T
Doncaster R v Bolton W
Huddersfield T v Ipswich T
Leicester C v Brighton & HA
Middlesbrough v Birmingham C
Nottingham F v Sheffield W
Watford v Leeds U
Wigan Ath v Millwall

**Saturday, 12 April 2014**
**Barclays Premier League**
Arsenal v West Ham U
Crystal Palace v Aston Villa
Fulham v Norwich C
Liverpool v Manchester C
Manchester U v Hull C
Southampton v Cardiff C
Stoke C v Newcastle U
Sunderland v Everton
Swansea C v Chelsea
WBA v Tottenham H

**Football League Championship**
Birmingham C v Wigan Ath
Bolton W v Barnsley
Brighton & HA v Charlton Ath
Burnley v Middlesbrough
Derby Co v Huddersfield T
Ipswich T v Doncaster R
Leeds U v Blackpool
Millwall v Watford
QPR v Nottingham F
Reading v Leicester C

Sheffield W v Blackburn R
Yeovil T v Bournemouth

**Football League One**
Crewe Alex v Wolverhampton W
Leyton Orient v Gillingham
Milton Keynes D v Crawley T
Notts Co v Port Vale
Oldham Ath v Sheffield U
Peterborough U v Coventry C
Preston NE v Carlisle U
Rotherham U v Bradford C
Stevenage v Colchester U
Swindon T v Brentford
Tranmere R v Shrewsbury T
Walsall v Bristol C

**Football League Two**
Bristol R v Torquay U
Dagenham & R v Portsmouth
Exeter C v Cheltenham T
Fleetwood T v Morecambe
Hartlepool U v Chesterfield
Mansfield T v Rochdale
Newport Co v Wycombe W
Northampton T v Burton Alb
Plymouth Arg v Oxford U
Scunthorpe U v Bury
Southend U v AFC Wimbledon
York C v Accrington S

**Saturday, 19 April 2014**
**Barclays Premier League**
Aston Villa v Southampton
Cardiff C v Stoke C
Chelsea v Sunderland
Everton v Manchester U
Hull C v Arsenal
Manchester C v WBA
Newcastle U v Swansea C
Norwich C v Liverpool
Tottenham H v Fulham
West Ham U v Crystal Palace

**Football League Championship**
Barnsley v Leeds U
Blackburn R v Yeovil T
Blackpool v Burnley
Bournemouth v Sheffield W
Charlton Ath v Bolton W
Doncaster R v Derby Co
Huddersfield T v Brighton & HA
Leicester C v QPR
Middlesbrough v Millwall
Nottingham F v Birmingham C
Watford v Ipswich T
Wigan Ath v Reading

**Football League One**
Bradford C v Peterborough U
Brentford v Preston NE
Bristol C v Notts Co
Carlisle U v Walsall
Colchester U v Oldham Ath
Coventry C v Swindon T
Crawley T v Leyton Orient
Gillingham v Tranmere R
Port Vale v Milton Keynes D
Sheffield U v Stevenage
Shrewsbury T v Crewe Alex
Wolverhampton W v Rotherham U

**Football League Two**
AFC Wimbledon v Newport Co
Accrington S v Mansfield T
Burton Alb v Hartlepool U
Bury v Plymouth Arg
Cheltenham T v Fleetwood T
Chesterfield v Exeter C
Morecambe v Scunthorpe U
Oxford U v York C
Portsmouth v Bristol R
Rochdale v Southend U
Torquay U v Dagenham & R
Wycombe W v Northampton T

**Monday, 21 April 2014**
**Football League Championship**
Birmingham C v Blackburn R
Bolton W v Leicester C
Brighton & HA v Blackpool
Burnley v Wigan Ath
Derby Co v Barnsley
Ipswich T v Bournemouth
Leeds U v Nottingham F
Millwall v Doncaster R
QPR v Watford
Reading v Middlesbrough
Sheffield W v Charlton Ath
Yeovil T v Huddersfield T

**Football League One**
Crewe Alex v Colchester U
Leyton Orient v Wolverhampton W
Milton Keynes D v Brentford
Notts Co v Crawley T
Oldham Ath v Coventry C
Peterborough U v Carlisle U
Preston NE v Shrewsbury T
Rotherham U v Port Vale
Stevenage v Bristol C
Swindon T v Bradford C
Tranmere R v Sheffield U
Walsall v Gillingham

**Football League Two**
Bristol R v Rochdale
Dagenham & R v Chesterfield
Exeter C v Torquay U
Fleetwood T v Wycombe W
Hartlepool U v Morecambe
Mansfield T v Cheltenham T
Newport Co v Burton Alb
Northampton T v Portsmouth
Plymouth Arg v AFC Wimbledon
Scunthorpe U v Oxford U
Southend U v Accrington S
York C v Bury

**Saturday, 26 April 2014**
**Barclays Premier League**
Arsenal v Newcastle U
Crystal Palace v Manchester C
Fulham v Hull C
Liverpool v Chelsea
Manchester U v Norwich C
Southampton v Everton
Stoke C v Tottenham H
Sunderland v Cardiff C
Swansea C v Aston Villa
WBA v West Ham U

**Football League Championship**
Birmingham C v Leeds U
Bournemouth v Nottingham F
Brighton & HA v Yeovil T
Burnley v Ipswich T
Charlton Ath v Blackburn R
Derby Co v Watford
Doncaster R v Reading
Huddersfield T v Leicester C
Middlesbrough v Barnsley
QPR v Millwall
Sheffield W v Bolton W
Wigan Ath v Blackpool

**Football League One**
Bradford C v Crawley T
Bristol C v Crewe Alex
Carlisle U v Oldham Ath
Colchester U v Brentford
Coventry C v Wolverhampton W
Leyton Orient v Tranmere R
Notts Co v Swindon T
Port Vale v Sheffield U
Preston NE v Gillingham
Rotherham U v Milton Keynes D
Shrewsbury T v Peterborough U
Stevenage v Walsall

**Football League Two**
AFC Wimbledon v Morecambe
Burton Alb v Chesterfield
Bury v Portsmouth
Dagenham & R v Northampton T
Exeter C v Scunthorpe U
Fleetwood T v Southend U
Mansfield T v Torquay U
Oxford U v Accrington S
Plymouth Arg v Hartlepool U
Rochdale v Cheltenham T
Wycombe W v Bristol R
York C v Newport Co

**Saturday, 3 May 2014**
**Barclays Premier League**
Arsenal v WBA
Aston Villa v Hull C
Chelsea v Norwich C
Crystal Palace v Liverpool
Everton v Manchester C
Manchester U v Sunderland
Newcastle U v Cardiff C
Stoke C v Fulham
Swansea C v Southampton
West Ham U v Tottenham H

**Football League Championship**
Barnsley v QPR
Blackburn R v Wigan Ath
Blackpool v Charlton Ath
Bolton W v Birmingham C
Ipswich T v Sheffield W
Leeds U v Derby Co
Leicester C v Doncaster R
Millwall v Bournemouth
Nottingham F v Brighton & HA
Reading v Burnley
Watford v Huddersfield T
Yeovil T v Middlesbrough

**Football League One**
Brentford v Stevenage
Crawley T v Bristol C
Crewe Alex v Preston NE
Gillingham v Shrewsbury T
Milton Keynes D v Leyton Orient
Oldham Ath v Notts Co
Peterborough U v Port Vale
Sheffield U v Coventry C
Swindon T v Rotherham U
Tranmere R v Bradford C
Walsall v Colchester U
Wolverhampton W v Carlisle U

**Football League Two**
Accrington S v AFC Wimbledon
Bristol R v Mansfield T
Cheltenham T v Dagenham & R
Chesterfield v Fleetwood T
Hartlepool U v Exeter C
Morecambe v Bury
Newport Co v Rochdale
Northampton T v Oxford U
Portsmouth v Plymouth Arg
Scunthorpe U v York C
Southend U v Burton Alb
Torquay U v Wycombe W

**Sunday, 11 May 2014**
**Barclays Premier League**
Cardiff C v Chelsea
Fulham v Crystal Palace
Hull C v Everton
Liverpool v Newcastle U
Manchester C v West Ham U
Norwich C v Arsenal
Southampton v Manchester U
Sunderland v Swansea C
Tottenham H v Aston Villa
WBA v Stoke C

# FOOTBALL CONFERENCE FIXTURES 2013–14

**Saturday, 10 August 2013**
Barnet v Chester
Cambridge U v FC Halifax T
Dartford v Alfreton T
Forest Green R v Hyde U
Grimsby T v Aldershot T
Hereford U v Braintree T
Kidderminster H v Gateshead
Macclesfield T v Nuneaton T
Salisbury C v Tamworth
Southport v Luton T
Woking v Lincoln C
Wrexham v Welling U

**Tuesday, 13 August 2013**
Aldershot T v Dartford
Alfreton T v Kidderminster H
Braintree T v Woking
Chester v Hereford U
FC Halifax T v Wrexham
Gateshead v Grimsby T
Hyde U v Southport
Lincoln C v Macclesfield T
Luton T v Salisbury C
Nuneaton T v Forest Green R
Tamworth v Barnet
Welling U v Cambridge U

**Saturday, 17 August 2013**
Aldershot T v Cambridge U
Alfreton T v Salisbury C
Braintree T v Kidderminster H
Chester v Woking
FC Halifax T v Dartford
Gateshead v Barnet
Hyde U v Hereford U
Lincoln C v Forest Green R
Luton T v Macclesfield T
Nuneaton T v Southport
Tamworth v Wrexham
Welling U v Grimsby T

**Saturday, 24 August 2013**
Barnet v Nuneaton T
Cambridge U v Lincoln C
Dartford v Braintree T
Forest Green R v Luton T
Grimsby T v Alfreton T
Hereford U v Tamworth
Kidderminster H v Chester
Macclesfield T v FC Halifax T
Salisbury C v Aldershot T
Southport v Gateshead
Woking v Welling U
Wrexham v Hyde U

**Monday, 26 August 2013**
Aldershot T v Woking
Alfreton T v Hereford U
Braintree T v Barnet
Chester v Forest Green R
FC Halifax T v Southport
Gateshead v Macclesfield T
Hyde U v Grimsby T
Lincoln C v Wrexham
Luton T v Cambridge U
Nuneaton T v Kidderminster H
Tamworth v Dartford
Welling U v Salisbury C

**Saturday, 31 August 2013**
Barnet v Hyde U
Cambridge U v Tamworth

Dartford v Lincoln C
Forest Green R v Alfreton T
Grimsby T v Nuneaton T
Hereford U v Welling U
Kidderminster H v Luton T
Macclesfield T v Braintree T
Salisbury C v FC Halifax T
Southport v Aldershot T
Woking v Gateshead
Wrexham v Chester

**Saturday, 7 September 2013**
Aldershot T v Macclesfield T
Alfreton T v Woking
Braintree T v Forest Green R
Chester v Dartford
FC Halifax T v Barnet
Gateshead v Hereford U
Hyde U v Cambridge U
Lincoln C v Salisbury C
Luton T v Grimsby T
Nuneaton T v Wrexham
Tamworth v Southport
Welling U v Kidderminster H

**Saturday, 14 September 2013**
Barnet v Lincoln C
Cambridge U v Gateshead
Dartford v Nuneaton T
Forest Green R v FC Halifax T
Grimsby T v Braintree T
Hereford U v Aldershot T
Kidderminster H v Hyde U
Macclesfield T v Alfreton T
Salisbury C v Chester
Southport v Welling U
Woking v Tamworth
Wrexham v Luton T

**Tuesday, 17 September 2013**
Aldershot T v Barnet
Alfreton T v Cambridge U
Chester v Macclesfield T
FC Halifax T v Grimsby T
Gateshead v Wrexham
Hyde U v Woking
Lincoln C v Southport
Luton T v Dartford
Nuneaton T v Hereford U
Salisbury C v Braintree T
Tamworth v Kidderminster H
Welling U v Forest Green R

**Saturday, 21 September 2013**
Aldershot T v Wrexham
Alfreton T v Barnet
Braintree T v Southport
Cambridge U v Forest Green R
Chester v Grimsby T
Dartford v Kidderminster H
FC Halifax T v Hereford U
Hyde U v Welling U
Luton T v Lincoln C
Macclesfield T v Woking
Nuneaton T v Salisbury C
Tamworth v Gateshead

**Tuesday, 24 September 2013**
Barnet v Macclesfield T
Cambridge U v Nuneaton T
Forest Green R v Tamworth
Gateshead v Chester
Grimsby T v Dartford

Hereford U v Lincoln C
Kidderminster H v FC Halifax T
Salisbury C v Hyde U
Southport v Alfreton T
Welling U v Aldershot T
Woking v Luton T
Wrexham v Braintree T

**Saturday, 28 September 2013**
Barnet v Salisbury C
Braintree T v Alfreton T
Dartford v Southport
FC Halifax T v Chester
Forest Green R v Gateshead
Grimsby T v Tamworth
Hereford U v Luton T
Kidderminster H v Aldershot T
Lincoln C v Hyde U
Macclesfield T v Welling U
Woking v Nuneaton T
Wrexham v Cambridge U

**Saturday, 5 October 2013**
Aldershot T v Grimsby T
Alfreton T v Forest Green R
Cambridge U v Hereford U
Chester v Kidderminster H
Gateshead v Dartford
Hyde U v Braintree T
Luton T v FC Halifax T
Nuneaton T v Lincoln C
Salisbury C v Wrexham
Southport v Woking
Tamworth v Macclesfield T
Welling U v Barnet

**Tuesday, 8 October 2013**
Aldershot T v Luton T
Alfreton T v Chester
Braintree T v Welling U
Dartford v Salisbury C
FC Halifax T v Nuneaton T
Grimsby T v Cambridge U
Hyde U v Gateshead
Kidderminster H v Forest Green R
Lincoln C v Tamworth
Macclesfield T v Hereford U
Woking v Barnet
Wrexham v Southport

**Saturday, 12 October 2013**
Barnet v Wrexham
Chester v Cambridge U
Forest Green R v Macclesfield T
Gateshead v Alfreton T
Hereford U v Dartford
Lincoln C v Aldershot T
Luton T v Hyde U
Nuneaton T v Braintree T
Salisbury C v Grimsby T
Southport v Kidderminster H
Welling U v Tamworth
Woking v FC Halifax T

**Saturday, 19 October 2013**
Aldershot T v Alfreton T
Braintree T v Chester
Cambridge U v Salisbury C
Dartford v Hyde U
FC Halifax T v Welling U
Grimsby T v Forest Green R
Hereford U v Barnet
Kidderminster H v Lincoln C

Macclesfield T v Southport
Nuneaton T v Gateshead
Tamworth v Luton T
Wrexham v Woking

**Saturday, 2 November 2013**
Alfreton T v FC Halifax T
Barnet v Kidderminster H
Chester v Aldershot T
Forest Green R v Dartford
Gateshead v Luton T
Hyde U v Nuneaton T
Macclesfield T v Wrexham
Salisbury C v Hereford U
Southport v Cambridge U
Tamworth v Braintree T
Welling U v Lincoln C
Woking v Grimsby T

**Saturday, 9 November 2013**
Aldershot T v Braintree T
Cambridge U v Macclesfield T
Dartford v Barnet
Grimsby T v Welling U
Hereford U v FC Halifax T
Hyde U v Chester
Kidderminster H v Woking
Lincoln C v Gateshead
Luton T v Southport
Nuneaton T v Alfreton T
Salisbury C v Forest Green R
Wrexham v Tamworth

**Tuesday, 12 November 2013**
Barnet v Welling U
Braintree T v Luton T
Cambridge U v Aldershot T
FC Halifax T v Hyde U
Forest Green R v Nuneaton T
Hereford U v Chester
Macclesfield T v Kidderminster H
Southport v Lincoln C
Tamworth v Alfreton T
Woking v Dartford
Wrexham v Gateshead

**Saturday, 16 November 2013**
Alfreton T v Braintree T
Barnet v Cambridge U
Chester v Luton T
FC Halifax T v Aldershot T
Forest Green R v Lincoln C
Gateshead v Salisbury C
Kidderminster H v Wrexham
Macclesfield T v Dartford
Southport v Hereford U
Tamworth v Grimsby T
Welling U v Nuneaton T
Woking v Hyde U

**Tuesday, 19 November 2013**
Dartford v Wrexham
Lincoln C v Alfreton T

**Saturday, 23 November 2013**
Aldershot T v Southport
Braintree T v FC Halifax T
Cambridge U v Woking
Dartford v Gateshead
Grimsby T v Barnet
Hyde U v Alfreton T
Kidderminster H v Tamworth
Lincoln C v Hereford U
Luton T v Welling U
Nuneaton T v Chester
Salisbury C v Macclesfield T
Wrexham v Forest Green R

**Saturday, 7 December 2013**
Alfreton T v Luton T
Barnet v Dartford
Chester v Braintree T
FC Halifax T v Salisbury C
Forest Green R v Grimsby T
Gateshead v Aldershot T
Hereford U v Nuneaton T
Macclesfield T v Lincoln C
Southport v Wrexham
Tamworth v Cambridge U
Welling U v Hyde U
Woking v Kidderminster H

**Saturday, 14 December 2013**
Barnet v Aldershot T
Cambridge U v Luton T
Dartford v FC Halifax T
Forest Green R v Braintree T
Gateshead v Welling U
Kidderminster H v Alfreton T
Lincoln C v Nuneaton T
Macclesfield T v Salisbury C
Southport v Grimsby T
Tamworth v Hyde U
Woking v Chester
Wrexham v Hereford U

**Saturday, 21 December 2013**
Aldershot T v Tamworth
Alfreton T v Dartford
Braintree T v Macclesfield T
Chester v Lincoln C
FC Halifax T v Forest Green R
Grimsby T v Kidderminster H
Hereford U v Cambridge U
Hyde U v Barnet
Luton T v Gateshead
Nuneaton T v Woking
Salisbury C v Southport
Welling U v Wrexham

**Thursday, 26 December 2013**
Barnet v Luton T
Cambridge U v Braintree T
Dartford v Welling U
Forest Green R v Aldershot T
Gateshead v FC Halifax T
Kidderminster H v Hereford U
Lincoln C v Grimsby T
Macclesfield T v Hyde U
Southport v Chester
Tamworth v Nuneaton T
Woking v Salisbury C
Wrexham v Alfreton T

**Saturday, 28 December 2013**
Aldershot T v Welling U
Alfreton T v Southport
Braintree T v Tamworth
Chester v Gateshead
Dartford v Woking
FC Halifax T v Lincoln C
Grimsby T v Macclesfield T
Hereford U v Forest Green R
Hyde U v Wrexham
Luton T v Kidderminster H
Nuneaton T v Cambridge U
Salisbury C v Barnet

**Wednesday, 1 January 2014**
Aldershot T v Forest Green R
Alfreton T v Wrexham
Braintree T v Cambridge U
Chester v Southport
FC Halifax T v Gateshead

Grimsby T v Lincoln C
Hereford U v Kidderminster H
Hyde U v Macclesfield T
Luton T v Barnet
Nuneaton T v Tamworth
Salisbury C v Woking
Welling U v Dartford

**Saturday, 4 January 2014**
Barnet v Alfreton T
Cambridge U v Grimsby T
Forest Green R v Salisbury C
Gateshead v Hyde U
Kidderminster H v Dartford
Lincoln C v Luton T
Macclesfield T v Chester
Southport v Nuneaton T
Tamworth v FC Halifax T
Welling U v Braintree T
Woking v Hereford U
Wrexham v Aldershot T

**Saturday, 11 January 2014**
Barnet v Grimsby T
Cambridge U v Alfreton T
Dartford v Aldershot T
Forest Green R v Hereford U
Gateshead v Nuneaton T
Kidderminster H v Salisbury C
Lincoln C v Welling U
Macclesfield T v Luton T
Southport v Hyde U
Tamworth v Chester
Woking v Braintree T
Wrexham v FC Halifax T

**Saturday, 18 January 2014**
Aldershot T v Kidderminster H
Alfreton T v Tamworth
Braintree T v Lincoln C
Chester v Barnet
FC Halifax T v Cambridge U
Grimsby T v Gateshead
Hereford U v Southport
Hyde U v Forest Green R
Luton T v Wrexham
Nuneaton T v Macclesfield T
Salisbury C v Dartford
Welling U v Woking

**Saturday, 25 January 2014**
Aldershot T v FC Halifax T
Barnet v Southport
Braintree T v Gateshead
Dartford v Cambridge U
Forest Green R v Chester
Hereford U v Salisbury C
Hyde U v Tamworth
Kidderminster H v Macclesfield T
Lincoln C v Woking
Luton T v Nuneaton T
Welling U v Alfreton T
Wrexham v Grimsby T

**Tuesday, 28 January 2014**
Salisbury C v Nuneaton T

**Saturday, 1 February 2014**
Alfreton T v Hyde U
Cambridge U v Wrexham
Chester v Welling U
Dartford v Luton T
Gateshead v Kidderminster H
Grimsby T v Hereford U
Lincoln C v FC Halifax T
Macclesfield T v Barnet
Nuneaton T v Aldershot T

Southport v Braintree T
Tamworth v Salisbury C
Woking v Forest Green R

**Saturday, 8 February 2014**
Aldershot T v Chester
Braintree T v Nuneaton T
FC Halifax T v Woking
Forest Green R v Barnet
Grimsby T v Southport
Hereford U v Macclesfield T
Hyde U v Lincoln C
Kidderminster H v Cambridge U
Luton T v Tamworth
Salisbury C v Alfreton T
Welling U v Gateshead
Wrexham v Dartford

**Saturday, 15 February 2014**
Alfreton T v Aldershot T
Barnet v Tamworth
Braintree T v Wrexham
Cambridge U v Welling U
Chester v FC Halifax T
Dartford v Grimsby T
Gateshead v Woking
Lincoln C v Kidderminster H
Luton T v Hereford U
Macclesfield T v Forest Green R
Nuneaton T v Hyde U
Southport v Salisbury C

**Tuesday, 18 February 2014**
FC Halifax T v Braintree T

**Saturday, 22 February 2014**
Alfreton T v Gateshead
Dartford v Hereford U
Forest Green R v Southport
Grimsby T v FC Halifax T
Hyde U v Aldershot T
Kidderminster H v Braintree T
Lincoln C v Chester
Nuneaton T v Luton T
Salisbury C v Cambridge U
Tamworth v Welling U
Woking v Macclesfield T
Wrexham v Barnet

**Saturday, 1 March 2014**
Aldershot T v Lincoln C
Barnet v Woking
Braintree T v Hyde U
Cambridge U v Kidderminster H
Chester v Nuneaton T
FC Halifax T v Tamworth
Gateshead v Forest Green R
Grimsby T v Salisbury C
Hereford U v Wrexham
Luton T v Alfreton T
Southport v Dartford
Welling U v Macclesfield T

**Saturday, 8 March 2014**
Alfreton T v Lincoln C
Barnet v Gateshead
Braintree T v Hereford U
Dartford v Chester

Forest Green R v Cambridge U
Hyde U v FC Halifax T
Macclesfield T v Grimsby T
Nuneaton T v Welling U
Salisbury C v Luton T
Tamworth v Aldershot T
Woking v Southport
Wrexham v Kidderminster H

**Saturday, 15 March 2014**
Aldershot T v Nuneaton T
Cambridge U v Dartford
Chester v Alfreton T
Grimsby T v Wrexham
Hereford U v Hyde U
Kidderminster H v Barnet
Lincoln C v Braintree T
Luton T v Woking
Salisbury C v Gateshead
Southport v Macclesfield T
Tamworth v Forest Green R
Welling U v FC Halifax T

**Saturday, 22 March 2014**
Barnet v Hereford U
Braintree T v Aldershot T
FC Halifax T v Alfreton T
Forest Green R v Welling U
Gateshead v Lincoln C
Hyde U v Dartford
Kidderminster H v Southport
Luton T v Chester
Macclesfield T v Tamworth
Nuneaton T v Grimsby T
Woking v Cambridge U
Wrexham v Salisbury C

**Tuesday, 25 March 2014**
Aldershot T v Gateshead
Chester v Tamworth
Grimsby T v Luton T

**Saturday, 29 March 2014**
Aldershot T v Hyde U
Alfreton T v Nuneaton T
Cambridge U v Barnet
Dartford v Macclesfield T
FC Halifax T v Luton T
Gateshead v Braintree T
Hereford U v Grimsby T
Salisbury C v Kidderminster H
Southport v Forest Green R
Tamworth v Lincoln C
Welling U v Chester
Woking v Wrexham

**Tuesday, 1 April 2014**
Macclesfield T v Cambridge U

**Saturday, 5 April 2014**
Alfreton T v Welling U
Barnet v Forest Green R
Braintree T v Salisbury C
Cambridge U v Southport
Chester v Hyde U
Gateshead v Tamworth
Hereford U v Woking
Kidderminster H v Grimsby T

Lincoln C v Dartford
Luton T v Aldershot T
Nuneaton T v FC Halifax T
Wrexham v Macclesfield T

**Tuesday, 8 April 2014**
Forest Green R v Kidderminster H
Grimsby T v Woking
Hyde U v Salisbury C
Southport v Barnet
Welling U v Hereford U

**Saturday, 12 April 2014**
Barnet v FC Halifax T
Cambridge U v Hyde U
Dartford v Forest Green R
Grimsby T v Chester
Hereford U v Gateshead
Kidderminster H v Welling U
Luton T v Braintree T
Macclesfield T v Aldershot T
Salisbury C v Lincoln C
Southport v Tamworth
Woking v Alfreton T
Wrexham v Nuneaton T

**Saturday, 19 April 2014**
Aldershot T v Salisbury C
Alfreton T v Grimsby T
Braintree T v Dartford
Chester v Wrexham
FC Halifax T v Macclesfield T
Forest Green R v Woking
Gateshead v Southport
Hyde U v Kidderminster H
Lincoln C v Cambridge U
Nuneaton T v Barnet
Tamworth v Hereford U
Welling U v Luton T

**Monday, 21 April 2014**
Barnet v Braintree T
Cambridge U v Chester
Dartford v Tamworth
Grimsby T v Hyde U
Hereford U v Alfreton T
Kidderminster H v Nuneaton T
Luton T v Forest Green R
Macclesfield T v Gateshead
Salisbury C v Welling U
Southport v FC Halifax T
Woking v Aldershot T
Wrexham v Lincoln C

**Saturday, 26 April 2014**
Aldershot T v Hereford U
Alfreton T v Macclesfield T
Braintree T v Grimsby T
Chester v Salisbury C
FC Halifax T v Kidderminster H
Forest Green R v Wrexham
Gateshead v Cambridge U
Hyde U v Luton T
Lincoln C v Barnet
Nuneaton T v Dartford
Tamworth v Woking
Welling U v Southport

# THE SCOTTISH PREMIER LEAGUE AND SCOTTISH LEAGUE FIXTURES 2013–14

*Sky Sports*   *All fixtures subject to change.*

**Saturday, 3 August 2013**
**Scottish Premier League**
Aberdeen v Kilmarnock
Celtic v Ross Co* (5.15)
Inverness CT v St Mirren
Partick Th v Dundee U
St Johnstone v Hearts

**Sunday, 4 August 2013**
**Scottish Premier League**
Hibernian v Motherwell* (1.15)

**Saturday, 10 August 2013**
**Scottish Premier League**
Celtic v St Mirren
Dundee U v Inverness CT
Kilmarnock v St Johnstone
Ross Co v Partick Th

**Scottish Football League**
**First Division**
Alloa Ath v Livingston
Dumbarton v Falkirk
Greenock Morton v Cowdenbeath
Queen of the S v Dundee
Raith R v Hamilton A

**Scottish Football League**
**Second Division**
Arbroath v Ayr U
East Fife v Dunfermline Ath
Forfar Ath v Airdrie U
Rangers v Brechin C
Stenhousemuir v Stranraer

**Scottish Football League**
**Third Division**
Clyde v Berwick R
Elgin C v Albion R
Montrose v Stirling Alb
Peterhead v Annan Ath
Queen's Park v East Stirlingshire

**Sunday, 11 August 2013**
**Scottish Premier League**
Hearts v Hibernian* (12.05)
Motherwell v Aberdeen

**Saturday, 17 August 2013**
**Scottish Premier League**
Aberdeen v Celtic
Hibernian v Dundee U
Inverness CT v Motherwell
Partick Th v Hearts
St Johnstone v Ross Co
St Mirren v Kilmarnock

**Scottish Football League**
**First Division**
Cowdenbeath v Raith R
Dundee v Alloa Ath
Falkirk v Greenock Morton
Hamilton A v Dumbarton
Livingston v Queen of the S

**Scottish Football League**
**Second Division**
Airdrie U v Stenhousemuir
Ayr U v Forfar Ath
Brechin C v East Fife
Dunfermline Ath v Arbroath
Stranraer v Rangers

**Scottish Football League**
**Third Division**
Albion R v Clyde
Annan Ath v Montrose
Berwick R v Queen's Park
East Stirlingshire v Elgin C
Stirling Alb v Peterhead

**Saturday, 24 August 2013**
**Scottish Premier League**
Celtic v Inverness CT
Dundee U v St Johnstone
Hearts v Aberdeen
Kilmarnock v Hibernian
Motherwell v Partick Th
Ross Co v St Mirren

**Scottish Football League**
**First Division**
Alloa Ath v Cowdenbeath
Dumbarton v Greenock Morton
Hamilton A v Queen of the S
Livingston v Falkirk
Raith R v Dundee

**Scottish Football League**
**Second Division**
Airdrie U v Rangers
Brechin C v Forfar Ath
East Fife v Arbroath
Stenhousemuir v Dunfermline Ath
Stranraer v Ayr U

**Scottish Football League**
**Third Division**
Annan Ath v Albion R
Clyde v Queen's Park
Montrose v Berwick R
Peterhead v Elgin C
Stirling Alb v East Stirlingshire

**Saturday, 31 August 2013**
**Scottish Premier League**
Aberdeen v St Johnstone
Dundee U v Celtic* (12.45)
Hibernian v Ross Co
Inverness CT v Hearts
Motherwell v Kilmarnock
St Mirren v Partick Th

**Scottish Football League**
**First Division**
Cowdenbeath v Dumbarton
Dundee v Livingston
Falkirk v Hamilton A
Greenock Morton v Raith R
Queen of the S v Alloa Ath

**Scottish Football League**
**Second Division**
Arbroath v Brechin C
Ayr U v Airdrie U
Dunfermline Ath v Stranraer
Forfar Ath v Stenhousemuir
Rangers v East Fife

**Scottish Football League**
**Third Division**
Albion R v Montrose
Berwick R v Annan Ath
East Stirlingshire v Peterhead
Elgin C v Clyde
Queen's Park v Stirling Alb

**Saturday, 14 September 2013**
**Scottish Premier League**
Hearts v Celtic
Kilmarnock v Inverness CT
Partick Th v Aberdeen
Ross Co v Dundee U
St Johnstone v Hibernian
St Mirren v Motherwell

**Scottish Football League**
**First Division**
Alloa Ath v Dumbarton
Cowdenbeath v Falkirk
Dundee v Hamilton A
Livingston v Greenock Morton
Queen of the S v Raith R

**Scottish Football League**
**Second Division**
Airdrie U v Stranraer
Brechin C v Dunfermline Ath
East Fife v Forfar Ath
Rangers v Arbroath
Stenhousemuir v Ayr U

**Scottish Football League**
**Third Division**
Albion R v Berwick R
Clyde v East Stirlingshire
Elgin C v Montrose
Peterhead v Queen's Park
Stirling Alb v Annan Ath

**Saturday, 21 September 2013**
**Scottish Premier League**
Aberdeen v Inverness CT
Celtic v St Johnstone
Dundee U v Motherwell
Hibernian v St Mirren
Partick Th v Kilmarnock
Ross Co v Hearts

**Scottish Football League**
**First Division**
Dumbarton v Livingston
Falkirk v Dundee
Hamilton A v Cowdenbeath
Greenock Morton v Queen of the S
Raith R v Alloa Ath

**Scottish Football League**
**Second Division**
Arbroath v Stenhousemuir
Ayr U v Brechin C
Dunfermline Ath v Airdrie U
Forfar Ath v Rangers
Stranraer v East Fife

**Scottish Football League**
**Third Division**
Annan Ath v Clyde
Berwick R v Stirling Alb
East Stirlingshire v Albion R
Montrose v Peterhead
Queen's Park v Elgin C

**Saturday, 28 September 2013**
**Scottish Premier League**
Hearts v Dundee U
Inverness CT v Hibernian
Kilmarnock v Celtic
Motherwell v Ross Co
St Johnstone v Partick Th
St Mirren v Aberdeen

**Scottish Football League
First Division**
Alloa Ath v Hamilton A
Dundee v Greenock Morton
Livingston v Cowdenbeath
Queen of the S v Dumbarton
Raith R v Falkirk

**Scottish Football League
Second Division**
Arbroath v Forfar Ath
Brechin C v Stranraer
Dunfermline Ath v Ayr U
East Fife v Airdrie U
Rangers v Stenhousemuir

**Scottish Football League
Third Division**
Albion R v Peterhead
Clyde v Montrose
East Stirlingshire v Berwick R
Elgin C v Stirling Alb
Queen's Park v Annan Ath

**Saturday, 5 October 2013**
**Scottish Premier League**
Celtic v Motherwell
Dundee U v Kilmarnock
Hearts v St Mirren
Partick Th v Hibernian
Ross Co v Aberdeen
St Johnstone v Inverness CT

**Scottish Football League
First Division**
Cowdenbeath v Dundee
Dumbarton v Raith R
Falkirk v Queen of the S
Hamilton A v Livingston
Greenock Morton v Alloa Ath

**Scottish Football League
Second Division**
Airdrie U v Brechin C
Ayr U v Rangers
Forfar Ath v Dunfermline Ath
Stenhousemuir v East Fife
Stranraer v Arbroath

**Saturday, 12 October 2013**
**Scottish Football League
First Division**
Alloa Ath v Falkirk
Dumbarton v Dundee
Greenock Morton v Hamilton A
Queen of the S v Cowdenbeath
Raith R v Livingston

**Scottish Football League
Second Division**
Arbroath v Airdrie U
East Fife v Ayr U
Forfar Ath v Stranraer
Rangers v Dunfermline Ath
Stenhousemuir v Brechin C

**Scottish Football League
Third Division**
Annan Ath v East Stirlingshire
Berwick R v Elgin C
Montrose v Queen's Park
Peterhead v Clyde
Stirling Alb v Albion R

**Saturday, 19 October 2013**
**Scottish Premier League**
Aberdeen v Dundee U
Hibernian v Celtic
Inverness CT v Partick Th
Kilmarnock v Ross Co
Motherwell v Hearts

St Mirren v St Johnstone

**Scottish Football League
First Division**
Cowdenbeath v Greenock Morton
Dundee v Queen of the S
Falkirk v Dumbarton
Hamilton A v Raith R
Livingston v Alloa Ath

**Scottish Football League
Second Division**
Airdrie U v Forfar Ath
Ayr U v Arbroath
Brechin C v Rangers
Dunfermline Ath v East Fife
Stranraer v Stenhousemuir

**Scottish Football League
Third Division**
Albion R v Elgin C
Annan Ath v Peterhead
Berwick R v Clyde
East Stirlingshire v Queen's Park
Stirling Alb v Montrose

**Saturday, 26 October 2013**
**Scottish Premier League**
Dundee U v St Mirren
Hibernian v Aberdeen
Kilmarnock v Hearts
Partick Th v Celtic
Ross Co v Inverness CT
St Johnstone v Motherwell

**Scottish Football League
First Division**
Alloa Ath v Queen of the S
Dumbarton v Cowdenbeath
Hamilton A v Falkirk
Livingston v Dundee
Raith R v Greenock Morton

**Scottish Football League
Second Division**
Airdrie U v Ayr U
Brechin C v Arbroath
East Fife v Rangers
Stenhousemuir v Forfar Ath
Stranraer v Dunfermline Ath

**Scottish Football League
Third Division**
Clyde v Stirling Alb
Elgin C v Annan Ath
Montrose v East Stirlingshire
Peterhead v Berwick R
Queen's Park v Albion R

**Saturday, 2 November 2013**
**Scottish Premier League**
Aberdeen v Partick Th
Celtic v Dundee U
Hearts v St Johnstone
Inverness CT v Kilmarnock
Motherwell v Hibernian
St Mirren v Ross Co

**Saturday, 9 November 2013**
**Scottish Premier League**
Aberdeen v Hearts
Hibernian v Inverness CT
Motherwell v Dundee U
Partick Th v St Mirren
Ross Co v Celtic
St Johnstone v Kilmarnock

**Scottish Football League
First Division**
Cowdenbeath v Alloa Ath
Dundee v Raith R

Falkirk v Livingston
Greenock Morton v Dumbarton
Queen of the S v Hamilton A

**Scottish Football League
Second Division**
Arbroath v East Fife
Ayr U v Stranraer
Dunfermline Ath v Stenhousemuir
Forfar Ath v Brechin C
Rangers v Airdrie U

**Scottish Football League
Third Division**
Albion R v Annan Ath
Berwick R v Montrose
East Stirlingshire v Stirling Alb
Elgin C v Peterhead
Queen's Park v Clyde

**Saturday, 16 November 2013**
**Scottish Football League
First Division**
Alloa Ath v Raith R
Cowdenbeath v Hamilton A
Dundee v Falkirk
Livingston v Dumbarton
Queen of the S v Greenock Morton

**Scottish Football League
Second Division**
Airdrie U v Dunfermline Ath
Brechin C v Ayr U
East Fife v Stranraer
Rangers v Forfar Ath
Stenhousemuir v Arbroath

**Scottish Football League
Third Division**
Annan Ath v Berwick R
Clyde v Elgin C
Montrose v Albion R
Peterhead v East Stirlingshire
Stirling Alb v Queen's Park

**Saturday, 23 November 2013**
**Scottish Premier League**
Celtic v Aberdeen
Dundee U v Partick Th
Hearts v Ross Co
Inverness CT v St Johnstone
Kilmarnock v Motherwell
St Mirren v Hibernian

**Scottish Football League
First Division**
Dumbarton v Alloa Ath
Falkirk v Cowdenbeath
Hamilton A v Dundee
Greenock Morton v Livingston
Raith R v Queen of the S

**Scottish Football League
Second Division**
Arbroath v Rangers
Ayr U v Stenhousemuir
Dunfermline Ath v Brechin C
Forfar Ath v East Fife
Stranraer v Airdrie U

**Scottish Football League
Third Division**
Annan Ath v Stirling Alb
Berwick R v Albion R
East Stirlingshire v Clyde
Montrose v Elgin C
Queen's Park v Peterhead

**Saturday, 30 November 2013**
**Scottish Football League**
**Third Division**
Albion R v East Stirlingshire
Clyde v Annan Ath
Elgin C v Queen's Park
Peterhead v Montrose
Stirling Alb v Berwick R

**Saturday, 7 December 2013**
**Scottish Premier League**
Dundee U v Hearts
Hibernian v Partick Th
Motherwell v Celtic
Ross Co v Kilmarnock
St Johnstone v Aberdeen
St Mirren v Inverness CT

**Scottish Football League**
**First Division**
Cowdenbeath v Livingston
Dumbarton v Queen of the S
Falkirk v Raith R
Hamilton A v Alloa Ath
Greenock Morton v Dundee

**Scottish Football League**
**Second Division**
Arbroath v Stranraer
Brechin C v Airdrie U
Dunfermline Ath v Forfar Ath
East Fife v Stenhousemuir
Rangers v Ayr U

**Scottish Football League**
**Third Division**
Albion R v Stirling Alb
Clyde v Peterhead
East Stirlingshire v Annan Ath
Elgin C v Berwick R
Queen's Park v Montrose

**Saturday, 14 December 2013**
**Scottish Premier League**
Aberdeen v St Mirren
Celtic v Hibernian
Hearts v Inverness CT
Kilmarnock v Dundee U
Partick Th v St Johnstone
Ross Co v Motherwell

**Scottish Football League**
**First Division**
Alloa Ath v Greenock Morton
Dundee v Cowdenbeath
Livingston v Hamilton A
Queen of the S v Falkirk
Raith R v Dumbarton

**Scottish Football League**
**Second Division**
Airdrie U v East Fife
Ayr U v Dunfermline Ath
Forfar Ath v Arbroath
Stenhousemuir v Rangers
Stranraer v Brechin C

**Scottish Football League**
**Third Division**
Annan Ath v Queen's Park
Berwick R v East Stirlingshire
Montrose v Clyde
Peterhead v Albion R
Stirling Alb v Elgin C

**Saturday, 21 December 2013**
**Scottish Premier League**
Celtic v Hearts
Dundee U v Ross Co
Hibernian v St Johnstone
Inverness CT v Aberdeen

Kilmarnock v Partick Th
Motherwell v St Mirren

**Thursday, 26 December 2013**
**Scottish Premier League**
Aberdeen v Motherwell
Hearts v Kilmarnock
Partick Th v Inverness CT
Ross Co v Hibernian
St Johnstone v Celtic
St Mirren v Dundee U

**Scottish Football League**
**First Division**
Alloa Ath v Dundee
Dumbarton v Hamilton A
Greenock Morton v Falkirk
Queen of the S v Livingston
Raith R v Cowdenbeath

**Scottish Football League**
**Second Division**
Arbroath v Dunfermline Ath
East Fife v Brechin C
Forfar Ath v Ayr U
Rangers v Stranraer
Stenhousemuir v Airdrie U

**Scottish Football League**
**Third Division**
Clyde v Albion R
Elgin C v East Stirlingshire
Montrose v Annan Ath
Peterhead v Stirling Alb
Queen's Park v Berwick R

**Saturday, 28 December 2013**
**Scottish Football League**
**First Division**
Cowdenbeath v Queen of the S
Dundee v Dumbarton
Falkirk v Alloa Ath
Hamilton A v Greenock Morton
Livingston v Raith R

**Scottish Football League**
**Second Division**
Airdrie U v Arbroath
Ayr U v East Fife
Brechin C v Stenhousemuir
Dunfermline Ath v Rangers
Stranraer v Forfar Ath

**Scottish Football League**
**Third Division**
Albion R v Queen's Park
Annan Ath v Elgin C
Berwick R v Peterhead
East Stirlingshire v Montrose
Stirling Alb v Clyde

**Sunday, 29 December 2013**
**Scottish Premier League**
Aberdeen v Ross Co
Hibernian v Kilmarnock
Inverness CT v Celtic
Partick Th v Motherwell
St Johnstone v Dundee U
St Mirren v Hearts

**Wednesday, 1 January 2014**
**Scottish Premier League**
Celtic v Partick Th
Dundee U v Aberdeen
Hibernian v Hearts
Inverness CT v Ross Co
Kilmarnock v St Mirren
Motherwell v St Johnstone

**Thursday, 2 January 2014**
**Scottish Football League**
**First Division**
Alloa Ath v Cowdenbeath
Dumbarton v Greenock Morton
Hamilton A v Queen of the S
Livingston v Falkirk
Raith R v Dundee

**Scottish Football League**
**Second Division**
Airdrie U v Rangers
Brechin C v Forfar Ath
East Fife v Arbroath
Stenhousemuir v Dunfermline Ath
Stranraer v Ayr U

**Scottish Football League**
**Third Division**
Annan Ath v Albion R
Clyde v Queen's Park
Montrose v Berwick R
Peterhead v Elgin C
Stirling Alb v East Stirlingshire

**Saturday, 4 January 2014**
**Scottish Premier League**
Dundee U v Hibernian
Hearts v Partick Th
Kilmarnock v Aberdeen
Motherwell v Inverness CT
Ross Co v St Johnstone
St Mirren v Celtic

**Saturday, 11 January 2014**
**Scottish Premier League**
Aberdeen v Hibernian
Celtic v Kilmarnock
Hearts v Motherwell
Inverness CT v Dundee U
Partick Th v Ross Co
St Johnstone v St Mirren

**Scottish Football League**
**First Division**
Cowdenbeath v Dumbarton
Dundee v Livingston
Falkirk v Hamilton A
Greenock Morton v Raith R
Queen of the S v Alloa Ath

**Scottish Football League**
**Second Division**
Arbroath v Brechin C
Ayr U v Airdrie U
Dunfermline Ath v Stranraer
Forfar Ath v Stenhousemuir
Rangers v East Fife

**Scottish Football League**
**Third Division**
Albion R v Montrose
Berwick R v Annan Ath
East Stirlingshire v Peterhead
Elgin C v Clyde
Queen's Park v Stirling Alb

**Saturday, 18 January 2014**
**Scottish Premier League**
Aberdeen v Inverness CT
Celtic v Motherwell
Hibernian v St Mirren
Partick Th v Kilmarnock
Ross Co v Dundee U
St Johnstone v Hearts

**Scottish Football League**
**First Division**
Alloa Ath v Dumbarton
Cowdenbeath v Falkirk
Dundee v Hamilton A

Livingston v Greenock Morton
Queen of the S v Raith R

**Scottish Football League**
**Second Division**
Arbroath v Stenhousemuir
Ayr U v Brechin C
Dunfermline Ath v Airdrie U
Forfar Ath v Rangers
Stranraer v East Fife

**Scottish Football League**
**Third Division**
Annan Ath v Clyde
Berwick R v Stirling Alb
East Stirlingshire v Albion R
Montrose v Peterhead
Queen's Park v Elgin C

**Saturday, 25 January 2014**
**Scottish Premier League**
Dundee U v St Johnstone
Hibernian v Celtic
Kilmarnock v Inverness CT
Motherwell v Aberdeen
Ross Co v Hearts
St Mirren v Partick Th

**Scottish Football League**
**First Division**
Dumbarton v Livingston
Falkirk v Dundee
Hamilton A v Cowdenbeath
Greenock Morton v Queen of the S
Raith R v Alloa Ath

**Scottish Football League**
**Second Division**
Airdrie U v Stranraer
Brechin C v Dunfermline Ath
East Fife v Forfar Ath
Rangers v Arbroath
Stenhousemuir v Ayr U

**Scottish Football League**
**Third Division**
Albion R v Berwick R
Clyde v East Stirlingshire
Elgin C v Montrose
Peterhead v Queen's Park
Stirling Alb v Annan Ath

**Saturday, 1 February 2014**
**Scottish Premier League**
Aberdeen v Celtic
Hearts v St Mirren
Inverness CT v Hibernian
Kilmarnock v Ross Co
Partick Th v Dundee U
St Johnstone v Motherwell

**Scottish Football League**
**First Division**
Cowdenbeath v Raith R
Dundee v Alloa Ath
Falkirk v Greenock Morton
Hamilton A v Dumbarton
Livingston v Queen of the S

**Scottish Football League**
**Second Division**
Arbroath v Ayr U
East Fife v Dunfermline Ath
Forfar Ath v Airdrie U
Rangers v Brechin C
Stenhousemuir v Stranraer

**Scottish Football League**
**Third Division**
Clyde v Berwick R
Elgin C v Albion R

Montrose v Stirling Alb
Peterhead v Annan Ath
Queen's Park v East Stirlingshire

**Saturday, 8 February 2014**
**Scottish Football League**
**Second Division**
Airdrie U v Stenhousemuir
Ayr U v Forfar Ath
Brechin C v East Fife
Dunfermline Ath v Arbroath
Stranraer v Rangers

**Scottish Football League**
**Third Division**
Albion R v Clyde
Annan Ath v Montrose
Berwick R v Queen's Park
East Stirlingshire v Elgin C
Stirling Alb v Peterhead

**Saturday, 15 February 2014**
**Scottish Premier League**
Celtic v St Johnstone
Dundee U v Kilmarnock
Hibernian v Ross Co
Inverness CT v Hearts
Motherwell v Partick Th
St Mirren v Aberdeen

**Scottish Football League**
**First Division**
Alloa Ath v Livingston
Dumbarton v Falkirk
Greenock Morton v Cowdenbeath
Queen of the S v Dundee
Raith R v Hamilton A

**Scottish Football League**
**Second Division**
Airdrie U v Brechin C
Ayr U v Rangers
Forfar Ath v Dunfermline Ath
Stenhousemuir v East Fife
Stranraer v Arbroath

**Scottish Football League**
**Third Division**
Annan Ath v East Stirlingshire
Berwick R v Elgin C
Montrose v Queen's Park
Peterhead v Clyde
Stirling Alb v Albion R

**Saturday, 22 February 2014**
**Scottish Premier League**
Dundee U v Motherwell
Hearts v Celtic
Kilmarnock v Hibernian
Partick Th v Aberdeen
Ross Co v St Mirren
St Johnstone v Inverness CT

**Scottish Football League**
**First Division**
Cowdenbeath v Dundee
Dumbarton v Raith R
Falkirk v Queen of the S
Hamilton A v Livingston
Greenock Morton v Alloa Ath

**Scottish Football League**
**Second Division**
Arbroath v Forfar Ath
Brechin C v Stranraer
Dunfermline Ath v Ayr U
East Fife v Airdrie U
Rangers v Stenhousemuir

**Scottish Football League**
**Third Division**
Albion R v Peterhead
Clyde v Montrose
East Stirlingshire v Berwick R
Elgin C v Stirling Alb
Queen's Park v Annan Ath

**Saturday, 1 March 2014**
**Scottish Premier League**
Aberdeen v St Johnstone
Celtic v Inverness CT
Hibernian v Dundee U
Motherwell v Hearts
Ross Co v Partick Th
St Mirren v Kilmarnock

**Scottish Football League**
**First Division**
Alloa Ath v Hamilton A
Dundee v Greenock Morton
Livingston v Cowdenbeath
Queen of the S v Dumbarton
Raith R v Falkirk

**Scottish Football League**
**Second Division**
Airdrie U v Ayr U
Brechin C v Arbroath
East Fife v Rangers
Stenhousemuir v Forfar Ath
Stranraer v Dunfermline Ath

**Scottish Football League**
**Third Division**
Annan Ath v Berwick R
Clyde v Elgin C
Montrose v Albion R
Peterhead v East Stirlingshire
Stirling Alb v Queen's Park

**Saturday, 8 March 2014**
**Scottish Football League**
**First Division**
Cowdenbeath v Alloa Ath
Dundee v Raith R
Falkirk v Livingston
Greenock Morton v Dumbarton
Queen of the S v Hamilton A

**Scottish Football League**
**Second Division**
Arbroath v East Fife
Ayr U v Stranraer
Dunfermline Ath v Stenhousemuir
Forfar Ath v Brechin C
Rangers v Airdrie U

**Scottish Football League**
**Third Division**
Albion R v Annan Ath
Berwick R v Montrose
East Stirlingshire v Stirling Alb
Elgin C v Peterhead
Queen's Park v Clyde

**Saturday, 15 March 2014**
**Scottish Premier League**
Dundee U v St Mirren
Hearts v Aberdeen
Inverness CT v Motherwell
Kilmarnock v Celtic
Partick Th v Hibernian
St Johnstone v Ross Co

**Scottish Football League**
**First Division**
Alloa Ath v Queen of the S
Dumbarton v Cowdenbeath
Hamilton A v Falkirk

Livingston v Dundee
Raith R v Greenock Morton

**Scottish Football League**
**Second Division**
Arbroath v Airdrie U
East Fife v Ayr U
Forfar Ath v Stranraer
Rangers v Dunfermline Ath
Stenhousemuir v Brechin C

**Scottish Football League**
**Third Division**
Clyde v Stirling Alb
Elgin C v Annan Ath
Montrose v East Stirlingshire
Peterhead v Berwick R
Queen's Park v Albion R

**Saturday, 22 March 2014**
**Scottish Premier League**
Aberdeen v Kilmarnock
Celtic v St Mirren
Hearts v Dundee U
Inverness CT v Partick Th
Motherwell v Ross Co
St Johnstone v Hibernian

**Scottish Football League**
**First Division**
Alloa Ath v Falkirk
Dumbarton v Dundee
Greenock Morton v Hamilton A
Queen of the S v Cowdenbeath
Raith R v Livingston

**Scottish Football League**
**Second Division**
Airdrie U v Forfar Ath
Ayr U v Arbroath
Brechin C v Rangers
Dunfermline Ath v East Fife
Stranraer v Stenhousemuir

**Scottish Football League**
**Third Division**
Albion R v Elgin C
Annan Ath v Peterhead
Berwick R v Clyde
East Stirlingshire v Queen's Park
Stirling Alb v Montrose

**Tuesday, 25 March 2014**
**Scottish Football League**
**First Division**
Cowdenbeath v Greenock Morton
Dundee v Queen of the S
Falkirk v Dumbarton
Hamilton A v Raith R
Livingston v Alloa Ath

**Wednesday, 26 March 2014**
**Scottish Premier League**
Dundee U v Inverness CT
Hibernian v Motherwell
Kilmarnock v Hearts
Partick Th v Celtic
Ross Co v Aberdeen
St Mirren v St Johnstone

**Saturday, 29 March 2014**
**Scottish Premier League**
Aberdeen v Dundee U
Celtic v Ross Co
Hearts v Hibernian
Inverness CT v St Mirren
Motherwell v Kilmarnock
St Johnstone v Partick Th

**Scottish Football League**
**First Division**
Alloa Ath v Raith R
Cowdenbeath v Hamilton A
Dundee v Falkirk
Livingston v Dumbarton
Queen of the S v Greenock Morton

**Scottish Football League**
**Second Division**
Arbroath v Rangers
Ayr U v Stenhousemuir
Dunfermline Ath v Brechin C
Forfar Ath v East Fife
Stranraer v Airdrie U

**Scottish Football League**
**Third Division**
Annan Ath v Stirling Alb
Berwick R v Albion R
East Stirlingshire v Clyde
Montrose v Elgin C
Queen's Park v Peterhead

**Saturday, 5 April 2014**
**Scottish Premier League**
Dundee U v Celtic
Hibernian v Aberdeen
Kilmarnock v St Johnstone
Partick Th v Hearts
Ross Co v Inverness CT
St Mirren v Motherwell

**Scottish Football League**
**First Division**
Dumbarton v Alloa Ath
Falkirk v Cowdenbeath
Hamilton A v Dundee
Greenock Morton v Livingston
Raith R v Queen of the S

**Scottish Football League**
**Second Division**
Airdrie U v Dunfermline Ath
Brechin C v Ayr U
East Fife v Stranraer
Rangers v Forfar Ath
Stenhousemuir v Arbroath

**Scottish Football League**
**Third Division**
Albion R v East Stirlingshire
Clyde v Annan Ath
Elgin C v Queen's Park
Peterhead v Montrose
Stirling Alb v Berwick R

**Saturday, 12 April 2014**
**Scottish Football League**
**First Division**
Alloa Ath v Greenock Morton
Dundee v Cowdenbeath
Livingston v Hamilton A
Queen of the S v Falkirk
Raith R v Dumbarton

**Scottish Football League**
**Second Division**
Arbroath v Stranraer
Brechin C v Airdrie U
Dunfermline Ath v Forfar Ath
East Fife v Stenhousemuir
Rangers v Ayr U

**Scottish Football League**
**Third Division**
Albion R v Stirling Alb
Clyde v Peterhead
East Stirlingshire v Annan Ath
Elgin C v Berwick R
Queen's Park v Montrose

**Saturday, 19 April 2014**
**Scottish Football League**
**First Division**
Cowdenbeath v Livingston
Dumbarton v Queen of the S
Falkirk v Raith R
Hamilton A v Alloa Ath
Greenock Morton v Dundee

**Scottish Football League**
**Second Division**
Airdrie U v East Fife
Ayr U v Dunfermline Ath
Forfar Ath v Arbroath
Stenhousemuir v Rangers
Stranraer v Brechin C

**Scottish Football League**
**Third Division**
Annan Ath v Queen's Park
Berwick R v East Stirlingshire
Montrose v Clyde
Peterhead v Albion R
Stirling Alb v Elgin C

**Saturday, 26 April 2014**
**Scottish Football League**
**First Division**
Alloa Ath v Dundee
Dumbarton v Hamilton A
Greenock Morton v Falkirk
Queen of the S v Livingston
Raith R v Cowdenbeath

**Scottish Football League**
**Second Division**
Arbroath v Dunfermline Ath
East Fife v Brechin C
Forfar Ath v Ayr U
Rangers v Stranraer
Stenhousemuir v Airdrie U

**Scottish Football League**
**Third Division**
Clyde v Albion R
Elgin C v East Stirlingshire
Montrose v Annan Ath
Peterhead v Stirling Alb
Queen's Park v Berwick R

**Saturday, 3 May 2014**
**Scottish Football League**
**First Division**
Cowdenbeath v Queen of the S
Dundee v Dumbarton
Falkirk v Alloa Ath
Hamilton A v Greenock Morton
Livingston v Raith R

**Scottish Football League**
**Second Division**
Airdrie U v Arbroath
Ayr U v East Fife
Brechin C v Stenhousemuir
Dunfermline Ath v Rangers
Stranraer v Forfar Ath

**Scottish Football League**
**Third Division**
Albion R v Queen's Park
Annan Ath v Elgin C
Berwick R v Peterhead
East Stirlingshire v Montrose
Stirling Alb v Clyde

# OTHER FIXTURES 2013–14

**July 2013**

| | |
|---|---|
| 2 Tuesday | UEFA Champions League 1Q(1) |
| 3 Wednesday | UEFA Champions League 1Q(1) |
| 4 Thursday | UEFA Europa League 1Q(1) |
| 9 Tuesday | UEFA Champions League 1Q(2) |
| 10 Wednesday | UEFA Champions League 1Q(2) |
| 11 Thursday | UEFA Europa League 1Q(2) |
| 16 Tuesday | UEFA Champions League 2Q(1) |
| 17 Wednesday | UEFA Champions League 2Q(1) |
| 18 Thursday | UEFA Europa League 2Q(1) |
| 23 Tuesday | UEFA Champions League 2Q(2) |
| 24 Wednesday | UEFA Champions League 2Q(2) |
| 25 Thursday | UEFA Europa League 2Q(2) |
| 30 Tuesday | UEFA Champions League 3Q(1) |
| 31 Wednesday | UEFA Champions League 3Q(1) |

**August 2013**

| | |
|---|---|
| 1 Thursday | UEFA Europa League 3Q(1) |
| 3 Saturday | FL Championship, League 1&2 commences |
| 6 Tuesday | UEFA Champions League 3Q(2) |
| 7 Wednesday | UEFA Champions League 3Q(2) |
| | Football League Cup 1 |
| 8 Thursday | UEFA Europa League 3Q(2) |
| 11 Sunday | FA Community Shield |
| 14 Wednesday | England v Scotland – Friendly |
| 17 Saturday | FA Cup with Budweiser EP |
| | Premier League commences |
| 20 Tuesday | UEFA Champions League Qualifying Play-Off (1) |
| 21 Wednesday | UEFA Champions League Qualifying Play-Off (1) |
| 22 Thursday | UEFA Europa League Qualifying Play-Off (1) |
| 27 Tuesday | UEFA Champions League Qualifying Play-Off (2) |
| 28 Wednesday | UEFA Champions League Qualifying Play-Off (2) |
| | Football League Cup 2 |
| 29 Thursday | UEFA Europa League Qualifying Play-Off (2) |
| 31 Saturday | FA Cup with Budweiser P |

**September 2013**

| | |
|---|---|
| 4 Wednesday | Football League Trophy 1 |
| 6 Friday | England v Moldova – FIFA World Cup |
| 7 Saturday | FA Carlsberg Trophy P |
| | FA Carlsberg Vase 1Q |
| 9 Monday | FA Youth Cup P+ |
| 10 Tuesday | Ukraine v England – FIFA World Cup |
| | England C |
| 14 Saturday | FA Cup with Budweiser 1Q |
| 17 Tuesday | UEFA Champions League MD1 |
| 18 Wednesday | UEFA Champions League MD1 |
| 19 Thursday | UEFA Europa League MD1 |
| 21 Saturday | FA Carlsberg Vase 2Q |
| | England v Belarus – Women's FIFA World Cup |

| | |
|---|---|
| 22 Sunday | FA Women's Cup 1Q |
| 23 Monday | FA Youth Cup 1Q+ |
| 25 Wednesday | Football League Cup 3 |
| 26 Thursday | England v Turkey – Women's FIFA World Cup |
| 28 Saturday | FA Cup with Budweiser 2Q |

**October 2013**

| | |
|---|---|
| 1 Tuesday | UEFA Champions League MD2 |
| 2 Wednesday | UEFA Champions League MD2 |
| 3 Thursday | UEFA Europa League MD2 |
| 5 Saturday | FA Carlsberg Trophy 1Q |
| 6 Sunday | FA Women's Cup 2Q |
| 7 Monday | FA Youth Cup 2Q+ |
| 9 Wednesday | Football League Trophy 2 |
| 11 Friday | England v Montenegro – FIFA World Cup |
| 12 Saturday | FA Cup with Budweiser 3Q |
| | FA County Youth Cup 1* |
| 15 Tuesday | England v Poland – FIFA World Cup |
| 19 Saturday | FA Carlsberg Trophy 2Q |
| | FA Carlsberg Vase 1P |
| 20 Sunday | FA Carlsberg Sunday Cup 1 |
| 21 Monday | FA Youth Cup 3Q+ |
| 22 Tuesday | UEFA Champions League MD3 |
| 23 Wed | UEFA Champions League MD3 |
| 24 Thursday | UEFA Europa League MD3 |
| 26 Saturday | FA Cup with Budweiser 4Q |
| | England v Wales – Women's FIFA World Cup |
| 30 Wednesday | Football League Cup 4 |
| 31 Thursday | Turkey v England – Women's FIFA World Cup |

**November 2013**

| | |
|---|---|
| 2 Saturday | FA Carlsberg Trophy 3Q |
| 3 Sunday | FA Women's Cup 3Q |
| 5 Tuesday | UEFA Champions League MD4 |
| 6 Wednesday | UEFA Champions League MD4 |
| 7 Thursday | UEFA Europa League MD4 |
| 9 Saturday | FA Cup with Budweiser 1P |
| | FA Youth Cup 1P* |
| | FA County Youth Cup 2* |
| 13 Wednesday | Football League Trophy QF |
| 15 Friday | International (Qualifying Play-Off) |
| 16 Saturday | FA Carlsberg Vase 2 |
| 17 Sunday | FA Carlsberg Sunday Cup 2 |
| 19 Tuesday | International (Qualifying Play-Off) |
| | England C |
| 23 Saturday | FA Carlsberg Trophy 1P |
| | FA Youth Cup 2P* |
| 26 Tuesday | UEFA Champions League MD5 |
| 27 Wednesday | UEFA Champions League MD5 |
| 28 Thursday | UEFA Europa League MD5 |

**December 2013**

| | |
|---|---|
| 1 Sunday | FA Women's Cup 1P |
| 7 Saturday | FA Cup with Budweiser 2P |
| | FA Carlsberg Vase 3P |

| | |
|---|---|
| 10 Tuesday | UEFA Champions League MD6 |
| 11 Wednesday | UEFA Champions League MD6 |
| | Football League Trophy SF |
| 12 Thursday | UEFA Europa League MD6 |
| 14 Saturday | FA Carlsberg Trophy 2P |
| | FA County Youth Cup 3* |
| 15 Sunday | FA Carlsberg Sunday Cup 3 |
| 18 Wednesday | Football League Cup 5 |
| 21 Saturday | FA Youth Cup 3P* |

**January 2014**

| | |
|---|---|
| 4 Saturday | FA Cup with Budweiser 3P |
| 8 Wednesday | Football League Cup SF1 |
| 11 Saturday | FA Carlsberg Trophy 3P |
| 18 Saturday | FA Carlsberg Vase 4P |
| 19 Sunday | FA Women's Cup 2P |
| | FA Carlsberg Sunday Cup 4 |
| 22 Wednesday | Football League Cup SF2 |
| 25 Saturday | FA Cup with Budweiser 4P |
| | FA Youth Cup 4P* |
| | FA County Youth Cup 4* |

**February 2014**

| | |
|---|---|
| 1 Saturday | FA Carlsberg Trophy 4P |
| 5 Wednesday | Football League Trophy AF1 |
| 15 Saturday | FA Cup with Budweiser 5P |
| | FA Carlsberg Trophy SF1 |
| | FA Carlsberg Vase 5P |
| | FA Youth Cup 5P* |
| 16 Sunday | FA Carlsberg Sunday Cup 5 |
| | FA Women's Cup 3P |
| 18 Tuesday | UEFA Champions League 16(1) |
| 19 Wednesday | UEFA Champions League 16(1) |
| | Football League Trophy AF2 |
| 20 Thursday | UEFA Europa League 32(1) |
| 22 Saturday | FA Carlsberg Trophy SF2 |
| 25 Tuesday | UEFA Champions League 16(1) |
| 26 Wednesday | UEFA Champions League 16(1) |
| 27 Thursday | UEFA Europa League 32(2) |

**March 2014**

| | |
|---|---|
| 1 Saturday | FA County Youth Cup SF* |
| 2 Sunday | Football League Cup Final |
| 4 Tuesday | England C |
| 5 Wednesday | International Friendly |
| 8 Saturday | FA Cup with Budweiser 6P |
| | FA Carlsberg Vase 6P |
| | FA Youth Cup 6P* |
| 11 Tuesday | UEFA Champions League 16(2) |
| 12 Wednesday | UEFA Champions League 16(2) |
| 13 Thursday | UEFA Europa League 16(1) |
| 16 Sunday | FA Carlsberg Sunday Cup SF |
| | FA Women's Cup 4P |
| 18 Tuesday | UEFA Champions League 16(2) |
| 19 Wednesday | UEFA Champions League 16(2) |
| 20 Thursday | UEFA Europa League 16(2) |

| | |
|---|---|
| 22 Saturday | FA Youth Cup SF1* |
| 23 Sunday | FA Carlsberg Trophy Final |
| 29 Saturday | FA Carlsberg Vase SF1 |
| 30 Sunday | Football League Trophy Final |

**April 2014**

| | |
|---|---|
| 1 Tuesday | UEFA Champions League QF(1) |
| 2 Wednesday | UEFA Champions League QF(1) |
| 3 Thursday | UEFA Europa League QF(1) |
| 5 Saturday | FA Carlsberg Vase SF2 |
| | FA Youth Cup SF2* |
| | England v Montenegro – |
| | Women's FIFA World Cup |
| 8 Tuesday | UEFA Champions League QF(2) |
| 9 Wednesday | UEFA Champions League QF(2) |
| 10 Thursday | UEFA Europa League QF(2) |
| 12 Saturday | FA Cup with Budweiser SF |
| 13 Sunday | FA Cup with Budweiser SF |
| | FA Women's Cup 5P |
| 22 Tuesday | UEFA Champions League SF(1) |
| 23 Wednesday | UEFA Champions League SF(1) |
| 24 Thursday | UEFA Europa League SF(1) |
| 26 Saturday | FA County Youth Cup Final (Prov) |
| 27 Sunday | FA Carlsberg Sunday Cup Final (Prov) |
| | FA Women's Cup 6P |
| 29 Tuesday | UEFA Champions League SF(2) |
| 30 Wednesday | UEFA Champions League SF(2) |

**May 2014**

| | |
|---|---|
| 1 Thursday | UEFA Europa League SF(2) |
| 3 Saturday | FL Championship & FL League1&2 Ends |
| 8 Thursday | England v Ukraine – Women's FIFA World Cup |
| 10 Saturday | FA Carlsberg Vase Final |
| 11 Sunday | Premier League Ends |
| | FA Women's Cup SF |
| 14 Wednesday | UEFA Europa League Final |
| 17 Saturday | FA Cup with Budweiser Final |
| 18 Sunday | Football Conference PO Final |
| 24 Saturday | UEFA Champions League Final |
| | FL Championship PO Final |
| 25 Sunday | FL League 1 PO Final |
| 26 Monday | FL League 2 PO Final |

**June 2014**

| | |
|---|---|
| 1 Sunday | FA Women's Cup Final (Prov) |
| 12 Wednesday | FIFA World Cup in Brazil commences |
| 14 Saturday | Belarus v England – Women's FIFA World Cup |
| 19 Thursday | Ukraine v England – Women's FIFA World Cup |

**July 2014**

| | |
|---|---|
| 13 Sunday | FIFA World Cup Final |

*Football League Play-off Semi Finals for all Divisions will be dated during the period 8–17 May 2014.*
*FA Youth Cup Final 2 Legs dates to be confirmed*
*\* closing date of round*
*+ week commencing*

Now you can buy any of these other bestselling sports titles from your bookshop or *direct from the publisher.*

### FREE P&P AND UK DELIVERY
(Overseas and Ireland £3.50 per book)

| | | |
|---|---|---|
| The Secret Player | Anonymous | £13.99 |
| The Gaffer | Neil Warnock | £16.99 |
| The Didi Man | Dietmar Hamann | £8.99 |
| Champions League Dreams | Rafa Benitez | £8.99 |
| Jeffanory | Jeff Stelling | £7.99 |
| Manchester United Ruined My Life | Colin Shindler | £8.99 |
| Manchester City Ruined My Life | Colin Shindler | £8.99 |
| My Story | Sven-Göran Eriksson | £20.00 |
| Mourinho on Football | Jose Mourinho | £20.00 |
| Tuffers' Cricket Tales | Phil Tufnell | £8.99 |
| Tuffers' Alternative Guide to the Ashes | Phil Tufnell | £16.99 |
| Lions Tales | Matt Dawson | £20.00 |

## TO ORDER SIMPLY CALL THIS NUMBER

### 01235 400 414

or visit our website:
www.headline.co.uk

Prices and availability subject to change without notice.